NEW SCHOLASTIC DICTIONARY OF AMERICAN ENGLISH

(Original title:
Holt School Dictionary of American English)

SCHOLASTIC INC.
New York Toronto London Auckland Sydney

The following distinguished linguists and educators were consulted in the preparation of the *Holt Intermediate Dictionary of American English* on which the *Holt School Dictionary of American English* is based:

Editorial Policy Committee

Samuel I. Hayakawa, San Francisco State College; Hans Kurath, University of Michigan; Helen F. Olson, Seattle Public Schools; James Sledd, University of Texas

Special Consultants and Contributors

Beryl Loftman Bailey, Yeshiva University (Grammar and Linguistics); Richard Bratset, San Francisco State College (Usage Notes); Jean Kerns, Staten Island Community College of the City University of New York (Etymologies); William Labov, Columbia University (Pronunciations); Eugene D. Nichols, The Florida State University (Mathematics); Frederick E. Trinklein, Long Island High School (Science)

Many people in all parts of the United States volunteered suggestions for new words and advised on local pronunciations and usage.

ISBN 0-590-40415-6

12 11 10 9 8 7 6 5 4 3 2 1 8 6 7 8 9/8 0 1/9

Printed in the U.S.A. 24

TABLE OF CONTENTS

SAMPLE COLUMN

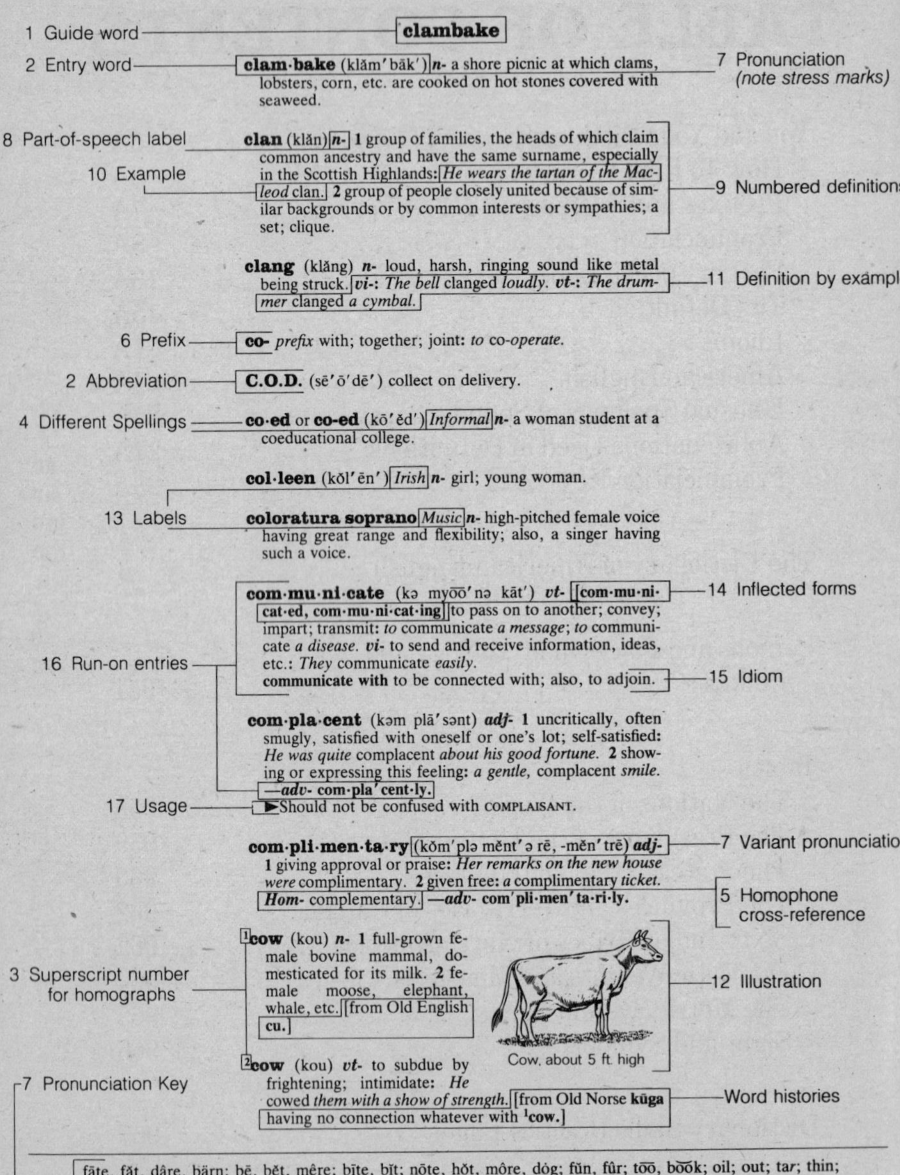

clambake

clam·bake (klăm′ bāk′) *n-* a shore picnic at which clams, lobsters, corn, etc. are cooked on hot stones covered with seaweed.

clan (klăn) *n-* **1** group of families, the heads of which claim common ancestry and have the same surname, especially in the Scottish Highlands: *He wears the tartan of the Macleod* clan. **2** group of people closely united because of similar backgrounds or by common interests or sympathies; a set; clique.

clang (klăng) *n-* loud, harsh, ringing sound like metal being struck. *vi-*: *The bell* clanged *loudly.* *vt-*: *The drummer* clanged *a cymbal.*

co- *prefix* with; together; joint: *to co-operate.*

C.O.D. (sē′ ō′ dē′) collect on delivery.

co·ed or **co-ed** (kō′ ĕd′) *Informal* *n-* a woman student at a coeducational college.

col·leen (kŏl′ ēn′) *Irish* *n-* girl; young woman.

coloratura soprano *Music* *n-* high-pitched female voice having great range and flexibility; also, a singer having such a voice.

com·mu·ni·cate (kə myōō′ nə kāt′) *vt-* [**com·mu·ni·cat·ed, com·mu·ni·cat·ing**] to pass on to another; convey; impart; transmit: *to* communicate *a message*; *to* communicate *a disease.* *vi-* to send and receive information, ideas, etc.: *They* communicate *easily.*
communicate with to be connected with; also, to adjoin.

com·pla·cent (kəm plā′ sənt) *adj-* **1** uncritically, often smugly, satisfied with oneself or one's lot; self-satisfied: *He was quite* complacent *about his good fortune.* **2** showing or expressing this feeling: *a gentle,* complacent *smile.* —*adv-* **com·pla′ cent·ly.**
►Should not be confused with COMPLAISANT.

com·pli·men·ta·ry (kŏm′ plə mĕnt′ ə rē, -mĕn′ trē) *adj-* **1** giving approval or praise: *Her remarks on the new house were* complimentary. **2** given free: *a* complimentary *ticket.* *Hom-* complementary. —*adv-* **com′ pli·men′ ta·ri·ly.**

[1]**cow** (kou) *n-* **1** full-grown female bovine mammal, domesticated for its milk. **2** female moose, elephant, whale, etc. [from Old English **cu.**]

Cow, about 5 ft. high

[2]**cow** (kou) *vt-* to subdue by frightening; intimidate: *He* cowed *them with a show of strength.* [from Old Norse **kūga** having no connection whatever with [1]**cow.**]

fāte, făt, dâre, bärn; bē, bĕt, mêre; bīte, bĭt; nōte, hŏt, môre, dóg; fŭn, fûr; tōō, bŏŏk; oil; out; tar; thin; then; hw for wh as in *wh*at; zh for s as in u*s*ual; ə for a, e, i, o, u, as in *a*go, lin*e*n, per*i*l, at*o*m, min*u*s

YOU AND YOUR DICTIONARY

HOW TO FIND WORDS

This dictionary contains a wealth of useful information about words—how they are spelled and pronounced, what they mean, in what circumstances they are used, and many other facts about them. To avail yourself of this information, you must know how to find it. Simply knowing that words are entered in a dictionary alphabetically is some help, but with only this to go on you will waste a great deal of time in flipping pages back and forth and scanning dictionary columns. To find the information you want quickly and easily requires a little strategy.

Your first object will be to open your dictionary at a place close to the word you are hunting. You can find **eccentric** eventually if you open your book to the **m's** or **s's;** you will not have to flip as many pages, however, if you open to the **e's** or **f's.** With a little practice you can train your thumb to find the right spot if you think of your dictionary as consisting of four large, roughly equal parts. Think of the first fourth as containing all the entries that begin with **a** through **d,** the second fourth, all those beginning with **e** through **l,** and the third, all those beginning with **m** through **r.** The last fourth will contain all the rest of the entries—those beginning with **s** through **z.** Grouped this way, the alphabet looks like this:

abcd efghijkl mnopqr stuvwxyz

Division of your dictionary into fourths reveals an important fact about English: the words of our language are not evenly distributed among the twenty-six letters. Notice, for example, that words beginning with the four letters **a, b, c,** and **d** occupy as much space as those beginning with the last nine letters of the alphabet.

Some important features of this dictionary are illustrated in the sample column on page 4A. These sample entries do not actually appear together in your dictionary. They have been put together to show in one place all of the main kinds of information this dictionary gives about words. The key numbers at the left of the entries correspond to numbered explanations in the pages that follow.

1. GUIDE WORDS

Once you have opened to the right fourth of your dictionary, your next step is to find the right page. To help you find it quickly, guide words have been printed in boldface (very black) type at the top of each page after page 1. For example:

(page 21)	**al fresco**	**all-American**
(page 145)	**cloudburst**	**c.o.**

The guide word at the left of the page tells you the first entry that begins on that page. The one at the right tells you the last entry that begins on that page. Thus, the guide words for page 21 tell you that all entries that fall alphabetically between **al fresco** and **all-American** will appear on that page. You will expect to find **algebra** and **alive** on page 21, but not **agate,** which must be on an earlier page, or **ambition** which must come later.

To make use of these guide words, you must of course use the other letters that follow the first. In this dictionary, there are nearly 90 pages beginning with **c,** and of these nearly 17 pages are devoted to words beginning with **ca.** To find the particular word beginning with **ca** that you want, you may have to use the first four, five, six or even more letters of the word.

2. THE ENTRY WORD

The word to be defined (the *entry word*) is printed in large boldface type a little to the left of the rest of the type. In addition to identifying the entry, the entry word gives the spelling and syllable division of the word. If the word is capitalized or hyphenated, the entry word shows this also. (See **C.O.D.** and **co-ed** on page 4A.)

Although it is usually a good idea to avoid dividing a word at the end of a line in your compositions, you will sometimes find it necessary to do so. When you divide a word, you must divide it between two of its syllables. This dictionary indicates the syllables of a word by placing a centered period (·) between them. One-syllable words should never be divided at the end of a line.

Most of the words defined in this dictionary are single words like **dog, intricate,** and **provide.** Some entries, however, consist of more than one word. These may be written as separate words **(dining room, blank verse)** or hyphenated **(mother-of-pearl, daddy-longlegs).** Whether written as two or more separate words or with its parts joined by a hyphen, such an entry is alphabetized as though it were written as one word.

3. DIFFERENT WORDS WITH THE SAME SPELLING

In English there are a number of words that are spelled the same but have quite different meanings. Such words are called *homographs.* For example, the word "arm" meaning a part of the body is of Old English origin, but the word that is spelled the same way and means "weapon" comes to our language from Latin. To distinguish different words that are identical in spelling, your dictionary provides separate entries marked with small numbers called superscript numbers:

[1]**baste** (bāst) ***vt-*** **[bast·ed, bast·ing]** to sew temporarily with long stitches. [from Old French **bastir,** "to sew loosely," originally from an Old High German word meaning "to sew up with a bast."]
[2]**baste** (bāst) ***vt-*** **[bast·ed, bast·ing]** to moisten with fat, gravy, or other liquid while roasting: *She* basted *the turkey with melted butter.* [from Old French **basser,** "to soak," altered from **bassiner,** from **bassin** "basin."]
[3]**baste** (bāst) *Informal* ***vt-*** **[bast·ed, bast·ing]** to beat or thrash; cudgel. [from Old Norse **beysta.**]

Superscript numbers are also used for words that have different pronunciations for different parts of speech:

[1]**af·fix** (ə fĭks′) ***vt-*** to attach or add: *I* affixed *my signature to the letter.*
[2]**af·fix** (ăf′ ĭks′) ***n-*** something attached or added, especially a prefix or suffix added to a root word.

When you see a small number to the left of the entry you are looking for, be sure to look for the other numbered entries. You cannot be certain you have the meaning you want until you have checked the other possibilities.

4. DIFFERENT SPELLINGS OF THE SAME WORD

Although most English words have only one correct spelling, some words can be spelled correctly in more than one way. If two spellings are both in common use, your dictionary gives both. When one spelling is more common than the other, it is given first.

co·ny (kō′ nē) ***n-*** [*pl.* **co·nies**] **1** rabbit, especially the European rabbit. **2** any of several rabbitlike animals of Asia, Africa, and North America, especially the Old World hyrax. **3** rabbit fur. Also **coney.**

5. WORDS THAT SOUND ALIKE

In English there are a number of words like **by/buy** and **rain/reign/rein** that are pronounced the same but are spelled differently and have different meanings. Such words are called *homophones.* When you encounter a homophone in your reading, the spelling will guide you to the right entry. But when you hear such a word for the first time, you may have difficulty. This dictionary solves that problem for you. You simply look up the spelling you know. If there are other sound-alike words, they will be listed at the end of the entry.

com·pli·men·ta·ry (kŏm′ plə mĕnt′ ə rē, -mĕn′ trē) ***adj-*** **1** giving approval or praise: *Her remarks on the new house were* complimentary. **2** given free: *a* complimentary *ticket.* ***Hom-*** complementary. ***—adv-*** **com′ pli·men′ ta·ri·ly.**

6. PREFIXES AND SUFFIXES

Occasionally, you will find that a word you are looking up does not appear in this dictionary as an entry word. The reason may be that the word you are looking for is formed from another shorter word called a *base word.*

In English many new words can be formed by adding certain syllables to the beginning or to the end of the base word. Additions made to the beginning of the base word are called *prefixes;* those made to the end are called *suffixes.* Let us take some examples. Starting with the base word "help," we can add the suffix "-ful" or the suffix "-less" to produce the new words "helpful" and "helpless."

The common prefixes and suffixes in English are entered and labeled in this dictionary. In the examples that follow, notice the short dash that is placed after the prefix and before the suffix as a reminder that these forms combine with base words:

dis- *prefix* **1** not; the opposite of: *a* dis*obedient child*; *sharp* dis*agreement*. **2** fail to; cease to; refuse to: *to* dis*satisfy*; *to* dis*agree*; *to* dis*obey*. **3** do the reverse of: *to* dis*entangle*. **4** lack of: *a* dis*union*. [from Latin **dis-** meaning "apart; away; opposite."]

-ability or **-ibility** *suffix* (used to form nouns from adjectives by substitution for the adjective suffixes -able or -ible) state or condition of being. "*Approach*ability" is the condition of being "*approach*able."

Although prefixes and suffixes do not have the specific meanings that base words have, they often have general meanings that help to unlock the meaning of new words. For example, the prefix "dis-" usually means "not" or "the opposite of," as in "dislike," "disobey," and "distrust." The suffix "-ful" usually has the meaning "full of" or "possessing the quality of," as in "helpful," "powerful," and "thoughtful." A few common prefixes and suffixes, their general meanings, and sample words are listed below:

bi-	twice	biannual, biweekly
mid-	in or near the middle of	midnight, midstream
-able	fit to be, inclined or suited to	eatable, peaceable

Many common prefixes and suffixes like these are entered in this dictionary and their general meanings are given. Knowing these general meanings for prefixes and suffixes will sometimes, though not always, help you to figure out the meanings of new words.

Although the meaning of many prefixes and suffixes varies somewhat from word to word, there are several prefixes that have a constant meaning—the prefixes "non-," "re-," and "un-." After the entry for these prefixes, this dictionary gives a list of common words made with this prefix. See, for example, the entries for **non-**.

For help in finding words with unusual spellings, see the chart on pages 26A-27A.

7. PRONUNCIATION

The pronunciation of a word is shown by means of *accent marks, diacritical marks,* and *phonetic respelling.* Pronunciation information is enclosed in parentheses immediately following the boldface entry word, and wherever else it is needed for inflected forms and special cases.

Why do we need to look in a dictionary for the pronunciation of a word? Most of us can get along in ordinary conversation with words that we could pronounce before we learned to read. We learned their pronunciations by listening. Yet there are several good reasons for using a dictionary often for pronunciations. Here are some of them:

1. Years of schooling are required before a person can recognize in print all the words that he already knows how to use and pronounce. A word that looks unfamiliar in print is often easily recognized when we can hear it pronounced or pronounce it ourselves. By looking at the pronunciation of a word in the dictionary and carefully pronouncing it ourselves, we often recognize it as a word we know and use all the time. One such word is "colonel," which is difficult to recognize because it is not spelled the

way it sounds.

2. As we read more and more, we learn the meaning of many words by context clues, without ever knowing how to pronounce them. However, when we want to use them in conversation, we have to ask how they are pronounced or look them up in the dictionary.

3. Because English vowel letters, and some consonant letters, stand for several different sounds, we quickly forget how to pronounce many words unless we use them often. The dictionary refreshes our memory.

4. Many English words have two or more pronunciations that are used frequently by educated people. We often need to consult the dictionary to be sure that our own pronunciation is a correct one after hearing another pronunciation in conversation or on television.

The dictionary maker faces some special problems in representing pronunciations. We must indicate about forty different sounds, but there are only twenty-six letters in the English alphabet. Moreover, these forty sounds are represented in conventional spelling in more than two hundred different ways. Obviously, if we are going to distinguish the different sounds of English accurately, the dictionary maker must use a special alphabet or use the alphabet in a special way.

The dictionary maker's other big problem is that people in different parts of the country pronounce many words differently. These differences are not the result of a particular speaker's not knowing better. How does the dictionary maker solve these problems? When more than one pronunciation is given, all are considered to be equally acceptable. In a few cases, however, a second or additional pronunciation is preceded by the word *"also,"* which means that this pronunciation is used by relatively few people or by a special group.

The system chosen by the editors of this dictionary is to use symbols to which the speakers of the different regions can fit their own speech sounds. For example, this dictionary uses the letters /ou/ to represent the vowel sound in "house." This sound is made by people in New England and most of the northern states by combining the sounds /ä/ and /o͞o/, while in a large part of the South it is made by combining the vowel sound /ă/ with /o͞o/. The symbol /ou/ does not stand for one of these sounds or the other. It stands for both because the people of New England and the northern United States read it one way, and the people of the South read it another way.

The point to remember is that a pronunciation symbol will be interpreted differently. To find out what any symbol stands for in your area, you can look at the pronunciation key at the bottom of each right-hand page. Here you will find the symbol in a common word you already know how to pronounce. By using the same sound in any other word where that pronunciation symbol occurs, you will have the right sound for your region. When the same symbol cannot represent both sounds (as in the case of **greasy,** which has an /s/ sound some places and a /z/ sound other places), both possibilities are shown.

With the problems of describing the sounds of words in writing clearly in mind, let us take a closer look at the pronunciation system of this dictionary.

Accent marks. In English words of two or more syllables, one syllable is usually pronounced with more emphasis than the others. This syllable is said to be accented, or stressed, and it is marked in the pronunciation with a heavy accent mark /′/:

mas′ter

Words with three or more syllables often have both a syllable that receives heavy stress and another syllable that receives a weaker stress. This weaker stress is marked with a light accent mark /′/:

mas′ter piece′

For most words these two accent marks serve very well. There are some cases, however, in which it is impossible to say that a certain syllable is always accented more than the others. Words, like "forthcoming," are accented differently according to their position in sentences. For example:

a forth′coming book

a book that is forthcom′ing

To indicate accent in these special cases, this dictionary uses two heavy accent marks:

forth·com·ing (fôrth′ kŭm′ ĭng) ***adj*- 1** about to appear or happen; approaching: *We put notices of* forthcoming

Diacritical marks indicate the sound of vowels. Six single letters in English represent many different vowel sounds (a, e, i, o, u, y). The letter "a," for example, stands for such different vowel sounds as the one in "fat," the one in "hate," and the first one in "father." To show the sound of a vowel in a particular word, this dictionary uses a different combination of letter and diacritical mark for each vowel sound. You will find a short key showing the value of the various pronunciation symbols at the bottom of every right-hand page in your dictionary.

Symbols for sounds. A good pronunciation system requires one symbol for each different sound in the language. The symbol may consist of several letters, as in the case of /sh/ for the first sound in "sharp," but then the combination must stand for that one sound and that sound only. Since our writing system does not provide a single letter or combination of letters that consistently represents each different sound, the dictionary maker must modify the alphabet. Below is a complete pronunciation key followed by explanations of the vowel and consonant symbols used.

PRONUNCIATION KEY

ā	as in fate, age
ă	as in fat, map
â	as in dare, air
ä	as in father, pa, barn
ē	as in be, equal
ĕ	as in bet, ebb
ê	as in mere, near
ī	as in bite, ice, ride
ĭ	as in bit, if
ō	as in note, boat, low
ŏ	as in hot, box
ȯ	as in dog, law, fought
ô	as in more, roar, door, four
oi	as in oil, boy
ou	as in out, loud
o͞o	as in too, rule
o͝o	as in book, put
ŭ	as in fun, up
û	as in fur, term

ə stands for the sound of: "a" in ago, Senate; "e" in open, hopeless, fairness; "i" in peril, trellis; "o" in lemon; "u" in minus, argument; "ou" in famous; "ai" in mountain; "oi" in tortoise.

b	as in bed (bĕd), tub (tŭb)
ch	as in chill (chĭl), batch (băch)
d	as in deed (dēd)
f	as in fate (fāt), huff (hŭf)
g	as in get (gĕt), leg (lĕg)
h	as in hop (hŏp)
hw	for "wh" as in what (hwŏt), wheel (hwēl)
j	as in jam (jăm), job (jŏb); and for "g" in gentle (jĕn′təl) and range (rānj)
k	as in kin (kĭn), smoke (smōk); for "c" in coal (kōl); and for "ck" in rack (răk)
l	as in let (lĕt), bell (bĕl)
m	as in men (mĕn), him (hĭm)
n	as in not (nŏt), ran (răn)
ng	as in song (sȯng); and for "n" in think (thĭngk)
p	as in pup (pŭp)
r	as in ride (rīd), very (vĕr′ē)
r	as in fur (fû*r*), tar (tä*r*) (This *r* is not pronounced in some sections of the country.)
s	as in sod (sŏd), must (mŭst) and for "c" as in cent (sĕnt), price (prīs)
sh	as in she (shē), rush (rŭsh)
t	as in tea (tē), hot (hŏt)
th	as in thin (thĭn), bath (băth), breath (brĕth)
ŧħ	as in then (ŧħĕn), bathe (bāŧħ), breathe (brēŧħ)
v	as in vat (văt), dove (dŭv); and for "f" in of (ŏv)
w	as in we (wē)
y	as in yet (yĕt)
z	as in zero (zêr′ō), buzz (bŭz); and for "s" in wise (wīz)
zh	for "s" as in usual (yo͞o′zho͞o əl), vision (vĭzh′ən); also for some "g's" as in mirage (mə räzh′)

Vowels. The fact that most of the symbols in the table above are modified with some kind of mark indicates the problem of distinguishing vowel sounds. In general, these modifying marks, called *diacritical marks,* are of three kinds: The macron /¯/ is used to indicate the "long" sound of a vowel—the sound used in naming the vowels. The breve /˘/ indicates the "short" sound of vowels:

- ă the sound spelled a in fat
- ĕ the sound spelled e in bet
- ĭ the sound spelled i in bit
- ŏ the sound spelled o in hot
- ŭ the sound spelled u in fun

The circumflex /ˆ/ indicates the distinctive sound a vowel sometimes has before an r: dare, mere, more, fur.

The vowels â, ê, and ô are pronounced differently in different parts of the country. If you always pronounce /â/ as in "dare," the /ê/ as in "mere," and the /ô/ as in "more," you will be pronouncing them correctly for your region.

Two other vowel markings need some study, the /ä/ and the /ȯ/. The /ä/ is the so-called "broad a" in "far" and "father." For some people, "father" rhymes with "bother," and the "a" is like the short o /ŏ/. For others, the "a" sound in "father" is almost like the "a" sound in "gather." Therefore a dictionary needs a special symbol for the sound in words like "father" and "far."

Many people pronounce "caught" and a large group of other words, such as "law," with a kind of "o" sound that is neither /ô/ nor /ŏ/ but somewhere in between. So a dictionary needs another vowel symbol for the vowel sound between four (fô*r*) and cot (kŏt). This in-between sound is close to the vowel sound in "dog," and this dictionary gives it as /ȯ/. And all you have to remember is to pronounce the sound of /ȯ/ like the "o" in "dog." In addition to these modified single letters, certain vowel sounds are represented by combinations of letters:

oi	as in oil, boy
ou	as in out, loud
o͞o	as in too, rule
o͝o	as in took, put
yo͞o	as in fuse, use
yo͝o	as in cure, pure

The Schwa. In addition to the vowel sounds that can be conveniently represented by a modification of the letters a, e, i, o, and u, there is a sound, sometimes represented by each of these letters in ordinary spelling, which cannot consistently be represented by any of them. This is the sound spelled:

a	in ago
e	in open
i	in peril, trellis
o	in lemon
u	in minus, argument
ou	in famous
ai	in mountain
oi	in tortoise

To represent these similar, though not identical, sounds, this dictionary uses the symbol /ə/, called a *schwa.* As you can see, the schwa is simply a printed e turned upside down. It represents the blurred "uh" sound that vowels usually have in unaccented syllables.

Consonants. As you can see, the consonants of English can mainly be represented by the letters of the alphabet usually associated with them. Only three English letters, c, q, and x do not appear in this key. This is because c can be pronounced like either /k/ or /s/ (cat, cent), q is simply another way of writing the sound /k/ (quick, Iraq), and x can be pronounced like /ks/, /gz/, or /z/ (explain, exact, xylophone). The rule of one symbol for one sound rules out all three letters in pronunciations.

Notice the special symbol /t͟h/ which is used to distinguish the initial sound of "this" or "bathe" from the initial sound of "thin" or the final sound of "bath." There are two other combinations which you ought to look at carefully: /zh/ and /hw/. /zh/ has the same relationship to /sh/ as /z/ has to /s/ ("treasure" and "fresher"). /hw/ represents the actual order in which we make the sounds in the word "what," and thirteen hundred years ago, the word "what" was spelled "hwæt," and the word "whale" was spelled "hwæl." Today, in American English, we often drop the /h/ sound entirely.

You have probably seen /t͟h/, /zh/, and /hw/ before; they occur in most dictionaries. However, in this table of consonant sounds you will see something you haven't seen before: two r's. One is a regular /r/. The other is an italic, slanting /*r*/. How do you pronounce "career"? Do you pronounce the two r's the same or differently? Many people pronounce the two r's the same. Many others, however, do not pronounce the second r at all. Still others pronounce it as a vowel sound like the last syllable of "area." Therefore, this dictionary uses an italic /*r*/ to show that all Americans do not pronounce the r at the end of English words the same way. Likewise, some Americans pronounce the r in "guard," but many English-speaking people pronounce "guard" to rhyme with "god." Therefore, this dictionary uses the italic /*r*/ for r's that come before another consonant or a syllable beginning with a consonant. Some people pronounce both r's in "farther." Others pronounce neither, and make the word sound like "fä′ thə." So this dictionary shows the pronunciation of "farther" as (fä*r*′ thə*r*). Many people who drop their r's except between vowels, as in "very," often add r at the end of a word when the following word begins with a vowel. For "law and order," these people will say lȯ′ rən ȯ′ də. How do you say it?

Foreign sounds. In your reading you will encounter some foreign words that English-speaking people attempt to pronounce more or less as they are pronounced in the original language. To pronounce such words properly, you must have some acquaintance with the language they come from. A dictionary like this one can only give you a general idea. To do this, the following special symbols are used:

ø — as in the French words "feu," "peu," "lieu" and the German word "schön." This sound can be made by rounding the lips for /ō/ and trying to pronounce /ā/.

Y — as in the French word "lune" and the German word "für." This sound can be made by rounding the lips for /o͞o/ and trying to pronounce /ē/.

KH — as in German "ach" and Scottish "loch." Pronounce a strong /h/ with your mouth in position to make the /k/ sound in cook.

ⁿ — This symbol means that the preceding vowel has a nasal quality as in "salon" [să lōⁿ]. The symbol does *not* indicate that word ends with /n/ sounded as a consonant, as in the English word "can." You can pronounce this sound by starting to pronounce an /n/ but not letting your tongue touch the roof of your mouth. Try it with "salon."

8. PART-OF-SPEECH LABEL

Immediately after the pronunciation, the part of speech of a word is given in abbreviated form. The following abbreviations are used:

n-	noun	*the tall* man, New York City
vi-	intransitive verb	*Birds* sing. *The moon* rises.
vt-	transitive verb	*Cats* chase *mice. Dogs* bury *bones.*
adj-	adjective	pretty, small, beautiful
adv-	adverb	slowly, very, gracefully

conj-	conjunction	and, but, for, or, if, although, because
pron-	pronoun	I, you, he, me, it, they, everyone, somebody
prep-	preposition	by, at, in, to, under
interj-	interjection	oh, ouch, wow.

Many words can be used as two or more different parts of speech. For example, "run" can be a verb (*Horses* run *fast.*) or a noun (*We lost by one* run.). "Run" can be a transitive verb (***vt-***) or an intransitive verb (***vi-***) as these examples illustrate: *The tracks* run *through the city* (***vi-***). *The favorite* ran *a poor race* (***vt-***). In such cases, an additional label appears in the appropriate place in the definition. (See **communicate,** in the sample column on page 4A.)

Some prepositions seem to be adverbs when their object is omitted. We might say, "*Gulls hovered* above *us*." Here, "above" is a preposition, and "us" is its object. Or we might say, "*Gulls hovered* above." Here, "above" seems to be an adverb because it has no object, and most people will consider it an adverb. However, we really don't know whether "above" means "above us," "above the sea," or "above the ship," unless something seen or previously said tells us. This dictionary identifies prepositions that are often used without their understood object, by the following note in parentheses: (considered an adverb when the object is implied but not expressed).

In addition to the parts of speech listed above, which are probably familiar to you from your work in English, this dictionary uses the label *definite article* for "the" and *indefinite article* for "a" and "an." It also uses two additional labels that do not fall readily into any of the parts of speech listed above. They are *determiner* and *modifier.*

Determiners. Traditional grammar usually labels words like "any," "both," "several," and "some" adjectives when they occur before nouns in sentences: I haven't any jackets. However, these words do not behave much like other adjectives. They cannot be compared like "strong" or "beautiful." In addition, they do not normally appear after a verb like "is" or "seems" in simple sentences:

The man { is / seems } strong. but not

The jacket { is / seems } any.

Also, these words always come before adjectives or nouns, if any, that modify the main noun in a phrase. We can say, "Any strong man can do it," but we cannot say, "Strong any man can do it." We can say, "Young men are strong," or "Both young men are strong," but we cannot say "Young both men are strong." For these reasons, many modern grammarians are reluctant to call such words "adjectives" but give them the name *determiner* to distinguish them from regular adjectives. Many determiners can stand alone like pronouns in place of the noun phrase previously stated. They occur in sentences such as the second of the following:

Do you want both sweaters? (noun phrase)
Yes, I think I'll take both. (determiner)

Modifiers. Adjectives are often called *modifiers* because they modify nouns. Nouns can also modify other nouns, as in the following expressions:

the barn *door*
a cattle *ranch*
a petroleum *geologist.*

These nouns used as modifiers function much like adjectives, but differ from adjectives in three important ways. They cannot be compared. They usually come after any other modifier in a noun phrase. "A white barn door" makes sense, but "a barn white door" doesn't. Finally, a noun modifier cannot appear in the second of the two positions occupied by adjectives:

First position:
the red *door* (adjective modifier)
the barn *door* (noun modifier)
Second position:
The door seems red. (adjective modifier after "seems")
The door seems barn. (noun modifier does not make sense here)

This dictionary identifies nouns that are frequently used as modifiers by the label *as* ***modifier,*** followed by an example of a common phrase in which the noun is so used.

bal·let (băl′ ā, bă lā′) ***n*-** **1** story or idea acted out in dance form; also, the music for it. **2** a group that performs such dances. *as* ***modifier*:** *a* ballet *dancer.*

Intensifiers. In a few of the definitions in this dictionary you will find one other word you may not be familiar with. For example, in the entry **blooming** you will find two slang senses that are not defined except by the words in parentheses (intensifier only).

bloom·ing (blōō′ mĭng) ***adj*-** **1** blossoming; in flower. **2** full of youthful freshness and health; flourishing: *his* blooming *enthusiasm.* **3** *Slang* (intensifier only): *a* blooming *idiot.* ***adv*-** *Slang* (intensifier only): *He'd* blooming *well better do it!*

A number of perfectly proper words are used to convey strong feeling or to emphasize the following word or expression. Otherwise, these words have no meaning at all and cannot be defined except, perhaps, by another such meaningless word. This dictionary, therefore, simply gives examples of their use in such situations.

9. THE DEFINITION

The main function of a dictionary is to give the meaning of words, and most of the space in each entry is devoted to this purpose. There are several different ways in which a word's meaning can be given—by expressing the same meaning in other words, by showing the object that the word stands for, by giving a *synonym* (another word of similar meaning), or by using the word in a phrase or sentence that gives a clue to its meaning. This dictionary uses all of these methods, sometimes separately and sometimes in combination.

Since most English words have several different meanings, the typical dictionary entry must contain not just one but several definitions. When these definitions are distinctly different, they are distinguished by boldface numbers, as in the following example:

clear·ance (klêr′əns) ***n-*** **1** the space or amount of space between a moving vehicle, ship, etc., and another object: *a* clearance *of 25 feet between the ship and the dock.* **2** permission granted a ship, plane, passenger, etc., to enter or leave a place: *The plane received* clearance *from the control tower.* **3** the exchanging of checks and other notes from banks and the settling of accounts at a clearinghouse. **4** official approval given to a person to handle restricted material or information.

Differences between related meanings —especially those that have to do with the same field of knowledge—are indicated by means of lighter numbers in parentheses:

ar·my (är′mē) ***n-*** [*pl.* **ar·mies**] **1** the branch of a nation's military force that is responsible for warfare on land. **2** large number of persons or things; multitude: *an* army *of insects.* **3 Army** (1) the military land forces of the United States. (2) in the U.S. Army, the largest military unit, consisting of two or more corps: *the Third* Army. (3) *Informal* the U.S. Military Academy at West Point, New York.

The different meanings of a word are generally given in order of their frequency of use—the most common meaning first and the least common last.

There are, however, certain cases in which it is convenient for the reader not to have the most common meaning first. With common words that have a scientific meaning, for example, the scientific meaning is usually given first because it is this meaning that most students will be looking up.

force (fôrs) ***n-*** **1** a push or pull that can produce a change in the motion of something; that which causes or tends to cause an object to accelerate or decelerate. **2** strength; power; vigor: *the* force *of the wind*; *the* force *of a blow*; *the* force *of his character.* **3** the use of physical strength, superior power, or compulsion: *to arrest someone by* force. **4** (often **forces**) particular group of persons, especially one organized in a military fashion: *the police* force; *the labor* force *of a factory*; *the armed* forces. **5** power to convince or persuade: *the* force *of the evidence.* **6** powerful influence: *a* force *for social improvement.* ***vt-*** [**forced, forc·ing**] **1** to compel: *to* force *a person to do something against his will.* **2** to

There is another situation in which it is useful to have a certain meaning given first, even if it is not the most common one. Take "watchdog," for example. One meaning of this word is, of course, "a dog that guards a house or other property." These days, however, we are more likely to encounter the word "watchdog" in such a sentence as this: "*The 'Herald' is the* watchdog *of the people.*" In this sentence "watchdog" does not refer to a real dog that is guarding something, but to a newspaper. The implication is that the newspaper is looking out for the interests of its readers and others in much the same way that a watchdog looks out for the interest of its master. A meaning like this one, which derives from an earlier specific meaning, is called a *figurative meaning.* Even though the figurative meaning may be more common than the original or *literal meaning,* you can see why it is important to begin with the definition of the literal meaning.

bush leaguer *Slang* ***n-*** **1** baseball player in a bush league. **2** incompetent or mediocre person.

blunt (blŭnt) ***adj-*** [**blunt·er, blunt·est**] **1** without a sharp edge or point; not sharp; dull: *a* blunt *knife.* **2** frank and plain-spoken; abrupt: *a* blunt *answer.* ***vt-*** to make less sharp or keen: *He* blunted *his knife on a stone. Fatigue* blunts *one's wits.* ***—adv-*** **blunt′ly.** ***n-*** **blunt′ness.**

Sometimes the figurative sense is introduced by the word "hence":

bête noire (bĕt nwär′) *French* ***n-*** black beast; hence, something that is especially disliked; bugbear.

Sometimes the word "also" is used to add an additional sense that is not different enough to be a separate numbered definition:

bean (bēn) ***n-*** **1** the seed or the seed pod, or both, of various plants of the pea family, such as the kidney bean, soybean, and string bean; also, the plants themselves. **2** any of various seeds of a similar shape, such as cacao beans and coffee beans.

[2]**bail** (bāl) ***n-*** container used as a dipper for removing water from a boat; also, a small pump used for the same purpose. ***vt-*** to remove water from a boat with any such device: *to* bail *water with a bucket*; *to* bail *a boat.* ***vi-***: *We* bailed *desperately for two hours until rescued.* [from Old French **baille** meaning "bucket or scoop for dipping," from Late Latin **bāiula** meaning "(thing) carrying."] ***Homs-*** bale, Baal.

The word "especially" is similarly used when the word has a general meaning, but is used more often in some particular meaning:

ag·ri·cul·tur·ist (ăg′ rə kŭl′ chər ĭst′) ***n-*** **1** an expert in agriculture. **2** a farmer, especially one who practices the more modern or scientific methods of farming. Also **ag′ ri·cul′ tur·al·ist.**

When a number of different meanings are given in an entry, the problem of finding the right one arises. To help you make sure you have found the meaning you want, this dictionary, whenever possible, provides a definition that can actually be substituted in a sentence for the word being defined. Suppose for example you want to know the meaning of the word "compile" in the following sentence:

> *The Senator had been urged to* compile *his campaign speeches for publication.*

On page 157, this meaning of compile is defined this way:

> to put together (facts, articles, etc.) in a collection

This definition can be substituted for "compile" in the original sentence:

> *The Senator had been urged to* put together in a collection *campaign speeches for publication.*

As you can see, the wording of the definition itself provides a handy way of testing whether or not you have found the appropriate meaning. Apply this test whenever you have trouble selecting one of a number of closely related meanings.

10. EXAMPLES

In addition to giving substituting definitions, this dictionary provides thousands of examples to show how words are used. These examples are especially useful in distinguishing between similar meanings of the same word. Notice how the examples illustrating the different meanings of "away" help you to understand the definitions themselves:

a·way (ə wā′) ***adv-*** **1** from a place; off: *to go* away. **2** aside: *to look* away. **3** at a distance; distant: *ten miles* away. **4** absent: *to be* away *from home.* **5** out of one's possession: *to give money* away. **6** out of existence: *The echo died* away. **7** on and on; without stopping: *to work* away *at a job.*
►For usage note see WAY.

11. DEFINITION BY EXAMPLE

In addition to helping distinguish similar meanings of a word, examples are used in a special way in this dictionary. From early in its history, English has made use of words that are normally one part of speech to do the work of another part of speech, and the practice of using nouns as verbs or as adjectives and of shifting a word from one part of speech to another is especially common in American English. To define some words that have been shifted in this way, this dictionary gives an illustrative example, when the meaning of the additional part of speech can be clearly understood from the preceding definitions. Study the following entries to see how examples are used to make clear the use of a word in an additional part of speech:

beige (bāzh) ***n-*** the pale-tan color of unbleached wool. ***adj-*:** *a* beige *spaniel.*

bi·week·ly (bī′ wēk′ lē) ***adj-*** occurring or appearing every two weeks: *a* biweekly *trip to the city.* ***adv-*:** *She reports* biweekly *on the progress of the book.* ***n-*** [*pl.* **bi·week·lies**] periodical issued once every two weeks.

12. ILLUSTRATIONS

Your dictionary sometimes uses pictures, as well as definitions and examples, to show the meanings of words. Notice how the illustration contributes to your understanding of the meaning of "gyroscope":

gy·ro·scope (jī′ rə skōp′) ***n-*** device consisting of a heavy wheel mounted on gimbals. When the wheel is spinning rapidly, its axis tends to point in the same direction, no matter how the mounting is titled. Gyroscopes are used in navigational instruments, rocket guidance systems, and as toys, etc.

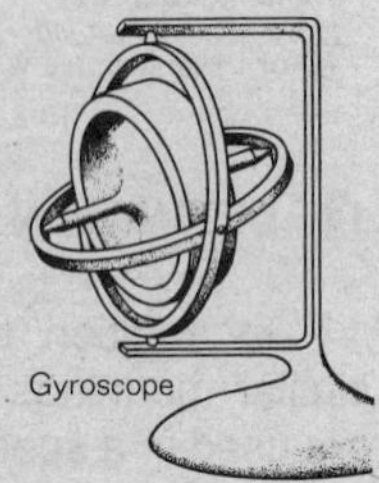

Gyroscope

13. LABELS

Most of the words entered in this dictionary belong to the general vocabulary of English. We encounter them in coversation, hear them on television, and read them in books and newspapers in a wide variety of contexts. However, some words and certain meanings of otherwise standard words need special treatment. These special cases are given labels to distinguish them from words and meanings of general usefulness. Three main kinds of labels are used in this dictionary: *field labels,* which indicate that a word has a special meaning in a certain field of knowledge; *local labels,* which show that a word has a meaning in a particular part of the English-speaking world that it does not have in the United States; and *usage labels,* which indicate the circumstances under which a word may be suitable or not suitable. The following entries illustrate the three kinds of labels:

chlo·rate (klôr′ āt′) ***n-*** *Chemistry* a salt of a metal and the chemical radical containing one chlorine and three oxygen atoms: *potassium* chlorate ($KClO_3$).

cat·a·pult (kăt′ ə pŭlt′) ***n-*** **1** in ancient and medieval times, a military device for hurling stones, arrows, or the like. **2** in modern times, a device for launching an airplane from the deck of a ship. **3** *Brit.* slingshot. ***vt-*** to hurl (something) from or as from such a device: *to* catapult *a plane from a ship's deck.* ***vi-*:** *The acrobat* catapulted *from a cannon into a net.*

Catapult

clob·ber (klŏb′ ər) *Slang* ***vt-*** **1** to pound or beat severely; to maul. **2** to defeat completely.

Field labels and local labels are easy enough to understand and use, but usage labels may need some further explanation.

You use language in such a variety of situations every day that it is impossible for a dictionary to anticipate just what would be appropriate in each one. A slang expression that would be appropriate when talking with friends might not be acceptable in one of your compositions. Furthermore, words keep entering and dropping out of the language—especially slang words.

Words that begin as slang often become wholly respectable members of the English vocabulary. The word "jazz," for example, was once considered to be slang. It has now become a respectable word in our language. Some words, on the other hand, have been in the language for centuries and are still considered slang. The word "clink," meaning jail, is an example.

It is the responsibility of a dictionary like this one to give you as much guidance as possible in fitting the right word to the occasion. This is done in several ways.

The first indication about appropriateness is given in the usage label. The label *Informal* is used for words that would be acceptable in casual conversation on all occasions. Informal words and expressions are understood by the majority of Americans, but they sometimes have a breezy quality that makes them not quite right for formal writing and speaking.

The label *Slang* is used for words that are generally newer to the language and of more limited appropriateness than those labeled *Informal*.

slang (slăng) ***n-*** special words or phrases (or special meanings of standard expressions) which are in common use in one or more particular groups such as musicians, soldiers, sailors, or the underworld, but are not accepted as standard spoken English by most educated people. Some slang spreads beyond its original groups, but remains slang as long as it is consciously used by outsiders only for humorous, folksy, satirical, socially defiant, or contemptuous expression. ***adj-***: *a* slang *word.*

Many words labeled *Slang* in this dictionary may become informal words before long; others will drop out of the language altogether.

The label *Archaic* indicates that a word or meaning is no longer in common use. Many give a definite feeling of some period of the past. A writer will use an archaic word like "canst" or "forsooth" only when he wishes to give such a feeling or to be amusing.

In addition to usage labels, this dictionary gives helpful advice about words in the form of parenthetical comments within a definition and in longer notes following the definition. For example:

an·cient (ān′ shənt) ***adj-*** **1** belonging to times long past, especially to the times of the Greeks and the Romans: *an* ancient *coin bearing the profile of Alexander.* **2** very old: *an* ancient *tree.* **3** (as a humorous term) old-fashioned; out-of-date: *Where did you get that* ancient *hat?* ***n-*** **1** very old person. **2 the ancients** (1) the civilized peoples of old, especially of Greece and Rome. (2) the classical writers of Greece and Rome. **—*adv-* an′ cient·ly.**

ag·gra·vate (ăg′ rə vāt′) ***vt-*** **[ag·gra·vat·ed, ag·gra·vat·ing]** **1** to make worse: *Scratching a mosquito bite* aggravates *it.* **2** *Informal* to irritate: *He* aggravated *his parents by staying out late at night.*

al·lude (ə lo͞od′) ***vi-*** **[al·lud·ed, al·lud·ing]** to refer to indirectly or in passing.
►Should not be confused with ELUDE.

14. INFLECTED FORMS

Most English words change in form according to their use in a particular sentence. Most nouns add either "-s" or "-es" (representing the sounds /s/ or /z/ or /ĭz/) to form plurals: book/book*s*, boy/boy*s*, dress/dress*es*. Many adjectives and adverbs have a change in form to show degree of comparison: cold/cold*er*/cold*est*. All but a few verbs have forms to indicate the various tenses: walk/walk*ed*, drive/drove. These changes in the form of words give important grammatical signals. The forms that result from such changes are called *inflected forms*.

Plurals of nouns. The vast majority of nouns in English form their plurals by adding the letter "-s" (representing the sound of /s/ in "cakes" or the sound of /z/ in "dogs") or the letters "-es" when the singular ends in ss, sh, ch, or z (losses, marshes, riches, matches, topazes). Nouns that form their plurals by adding a simple "-s" or "-es" are said to have *regular plurals.* To save space this dictionary does not show the plural forms for nouns with regular plurals. Words that form their plurals in any other way have their plurals given:

a·lum·na (ə lŭm′ nə) ***n-*** [*pl.* **a·lum·nae** (-nē)] woman graduated from a school, college, or university.

ber·ry (bĕr′ ē) ***n-*** [*pl.* **ber·ries**] **1** any small juicy and stoneless fruit, such as a strawberry. **2** *Biology* a fleshy,

bi·son (bī′ sən) ***n-*** [*pl.* **bi·son**] any of several large, shaggy-maned, wild grazing animals of the ox family, extinct

In addition, plural forms are given for all words ending in "-o" because some of them add only "-s" while others add "-es":

Comparative and superlative forms of adjectives. When you wish to compare the extent to which two or more people or things possess a particular quality, you can usually do it by choosing the appropriate comparative or superlative form of an adjective:

Jerry is brighter *than Alice.* (comparative)

He is the brightest *student in the class.* (superlative)

This winter is colder *than last winter.* (comparative)

It is the coldest *winter in the state's history.* (superlative)

As the examples indicate, comparatives are used mainly for making comparisons involving two people or things, and superlatives are used for comparisons involving more than two.

There are two systems for comparing adjectives in English. One of them, illustrated by the two examples just given, adds the endings "-er" and "-est" onto the regular form of the adjective (cold/colder/coldest). Most adjectives and adverbs of one syllable, and some longer ones, form their comparative and superlative degrees in this way:

late	later	latest
short	shorter	shortest
merry	merrier	merriest

In this dictionary, all adjectives and adverbs that can be compared by adding "-er," "-est" have these forms given in the entry. For example:

bald (bòld) ***adj-*** [**bald·er, bald·est**] **1** bare of hair. **2** without the natural or usual covering of hair, feathers, fur,

A few adjectives in English form their comparatives and superlatives by changing the base word. This dictionary shows these forms in the entry. For example:

bad (băd) ***adj-*** [**worse, worst**] **1** immoral; wicked: *Theft is* bad. **2** unfavorable to one's purposes, health, taste, etc.:

The other method for comparing adjectives and adverbs adds "more" or "most" before the adjective or adverb:

beautiful more beautiful most beautiful

If you do not find the comparative and superlative forms given for a particular adjective, you know that it can be compared only by adding "more" or "most."

Principal parts of verbs. Most verbs in English form their past tense and past participle by adding "-ed" to the infinitive to represent the sound of /d/ or /t/. They form the present participle by adding "-ing":

walk	walked	walking

Verbs that form the past tense, past participle, and present participle in this way are so common that to give these forms for each of them would be a great waste of space. They are not given in this dictionary. But for verbs that form their past tense, past participle, and present participle in any other way, these forms are given. Therefore, if you find no indication of these forms in the entry for a verb, you can assume that you need only add "-ed" to form the past tense and past participle, and "-ing" to form the present participle.

If the inflected forms present any kind of spelling problem, they are given. For example, principal parts are given for verbs that double the final consonant (omit/omitted), verbs that drop the final "e" before "-ed" and "-ing" (race/raced/racing), verbs that change "y" to "i" (hurry/hurried/hurrying), as well as verbs that are very irregular (drive/drove/driven/driving). In the last example (drive), the past tense and past participle are different. When this is the case, the past tense is always given before the past participle.

The following entries show how this information is presented in this dictionary:

care (kâr) ***n-*** **1** troubled state of mind caused by fear, doubt, etc.; anxiety; trouble; concern. **2** a cause of this: *The* cares *of the war years weighed heavily on the President.* **3** close and serious attention; heed; watchfulness: *work done with* care. **4** supervision; protection; charge: *under a doctor's* care. ***vi-*** **[cared, car·ing]** **1** to be worried or troubled; be concerned: *Would you* care

car·ry (kăr′ ē) ***vt-*** **[car·ried, car·ry·ing]** **1** to transport or convey, especially as the load of a vehicle, person, or

15. IDIOMS

An idiom is a group of words having a special meaning that would be difficult or impossible to guess from the meanings of the separate words. For example, "hold up" literally means "to keep in a raised position"; "hold up" is also an idiom meaning "to rob."

In this dictionary, idioms are entered after the definition for the key word in the idiom. The key word is always the one that has a meaning in the idiom that would be hardest to guess. For example, "pinch" is the key word in the idiom "in a pinch." If there are two possible key words, as in the idiom "a pig in a poke," look under the first one.

com·pare (kəm pâr) ***vt-*** **[com·pared, com·par·ing]** **1** to examine in order to find out, or show, likeness or difference in: *Before buying, she* compared *the two watches.* **2** to describe as similar; liken: *The writer* compared *the sound of guns to thunder.* **3** *Grammar* to give the positive, comparative, and superlative of (an adjective or adverb). ***vi-*** to be capable or worthy of comparison: *His cooking* compares *with mine.*
beyond compare above comparison; incomparable: *Her beauty was* beyond compare.

Idioms that begin with a verb are given at the end of the entry. If there are more than one, the idioms are listed in alphabetical order according to the word that follows the verb.

Note: We give only the idiomatic senses, not the literal sense, of an idiom.

[1]**burn** (bûrn) ***vt-*** **[burned** or **burnt, burn·ing]** **1** to cause to be consumed or destroyed by fire: *They* burned *the*
. . .
burn down to destroy or be destroyed by fire.
burn out **1** to stop burning. **2** to clean or remove by burning: *to* burn out *a nest of wasps.*
burn up **1** to destroy or be completely destroyed by fire. **2** *Slang* to be or make angry or enraged.

All idioms that do not begin with a verb are given before idioms beginning with a verb.

16. RUN-ON ENTRIES

Many English words have companion forms whose meanings are apparent. Such related words are formed by adding a suffix such as "-ly" or "-ness" to the base form of the word. These words are listed after the definition for the base form and are separated from it by a heavy dash:

[2]**arch** (ärch) ***adj-*** mischievous; playful; roguish; coy: *her* arch *look.* [from **arch-**. The meaning "mischievous" perhaps arose from words like "arch-knave" and "arch-rogue."] ***—adv-*** **arch′ ly.** ***n-*** **arch′ ness.**

Some suffixes change an adjective to a noun. Others change adjectives to adverbs or nouns to adjectives.

The following table lists the suffixes used in the run-on entries of this dictionary. The table gives an illustration of how each suffix is added to a main entry and tells the general meaning of the suffix. This meaning can be added to the meaning of the main word to get the meaning of the run-on entry. A fuller definition of each suffix is given at the main entry for the suffix.

NOUN SUFFIXES

Suffix	Main Entry and Run-on Entry	Definition of Suffix
—an	Africa African	(added to nouns) "person of a certain group" or "native of."
—ance or —ancy	dominant dominance relevant relevance or relevancy	(corresponds to the adjective suffix —ant) "state, condition, or quality of being."
—ation	confiscate confiscation	(corresponding to the verb suffix —ate) "the act of" or "result of."
—ence or —ency	abhorrent abhorrence truculent truculence or truculency	(corresponds to the adjective suffix —ent) "state, condition, or quality of being."
—er	forecast forecaster	(added to verbs) "person or thing that (does something)," or "specialist in."
—ess	arbiter arbitress	(forms a special feminine of certain nouns)
—ian	Abyssinia Abyssinian	(added to nouns) "person of a certain group" or "native of."
—ing	housebreak housebreaking	(suffix of the present participle) "the act of doing."
—ist	canoe canoeist altruism altruist	(added to nouns, or replacing the noun suffix —ism) "person who practices, specializes in, or believes in."
—ity	amicable amicability bestial bestiality	(added to certain adjectives, and having the same meaning as the suffix —ness) "state, condition, or quality of being."
—ment	aggrandize aggrandizement	(added to verbs) "the act of" or "result of."
—ness	drowsy drowsiness awesome awesomeness	(added to certain adjectives, and having the same meaning as the suffix —ity) "state, condition, or quality of being."

Suffix	Main Entry and Run-on Entry	Definition of Suffix
—or	donate donator devastate devastator	(added to verbs) "person or thing that (does something)."
—trix	executor executrix	(forms a special feminine of certain nouns ending in the suffix —tor).

ADJECTIVE SUFFIXES

Suffix	Main Entry and Run-on Entry	Definition of Suffix
—able or —ible	fix fixable detect detectable or detectible	(added to verbs) "fit to be; inclined or suited to."
—an	Alabama Alabaman	(added to nouns) "having to do with a person of a certain group."
—ed	bobtail bobtailed	(added to nouns) "having (a bobtail)."
—ian	Brazil Brazilian	(added to nouns) "having to do with a person of a certain group."
—ic or —ical	anemia anemic satire satiric or satirical	(added to nouns or noun stems) "having the nature of" or "having to do with."
—ish	pink pinkish coquette coquettish	(added to nouns and adjectives) "somewhat" or "somewhat like a."
—less	dust dustless date dateless	(added to nouns) "without (any)."
—like	dog doglike	(added to nouns) "resembling a."
—ous	cancer cancerous	(added to nouns) "full of" or "having."
—y	syrup syrupy	(added to nouns) "full of" or "resembling."

ADVERB SUFFIXES

Suffix	Main Entry and Run-on Entry	Definition of Suffix
—ly	beautiful beautifully accurate accurately	(added to adjectives) "in a given manner."

17. USAGE NOTES

Some words and expressions bring up points of style, correctness, and special use that have little to do with their meanings, but must be understood by careful writers and speakers.

beg·gar (bĕg′ər) ***n*-** **1** person who lives by asking for food, money, etc. **2** any very poor person; pauper. **3** *Informal* a fellow; a rascal (often used playfully): *a kind-hearted little* beggar.

A large number of such words and expressions have been treated in separate paragraphs following the entire definition; these are preceded by a distinctive black pointer (►):

ain't (ānt) **1** am not; are not. **2** have not; has not.
►Do not use AIN'T unless you are trying to show informality, or poor education, or folksiness: *The old gray mare, she* ain't *what she used to be.*

AMERICAN ENGLISH

The history of a language, like the history of a form of government, is the record of changes made by one generation after another. The people of each generation learn their language from their parents and pass it on to their children. When they pass it on, it is somewhat changed from the language they learned when they were little. The changes that occur reflect the experiences of the people using the language—the things they are particularly interested in, the way they occupy their time, the things that happen to them. A language is always changing.

One of the historical events to have an important effect upon the development of English was the settlement of the American colonies. Settlers came from all parts of Britain bringing their dialects with them, and they founded separate communities which often had little contact with each other. Each of these communities developed its own way of speaking, different from that of the others and different from the varieties of English spoken in Britain. Later, people from these communities moved on to settle most of the rest of the United States. It is from their original dialects of English that American English developed.

Even though you may never have traveled to England, your exposure to English people on television or in the movies tells you that the English they speak is somewhat different from the same language as spoken in America. The main differences are in pronunciation and vocabulary.

Although the differences in pronunciation between American and British English are obvious, there are not as many of them as some people think.

Speakers of British English use a vowel sound in words like *clock* and *got* that is different from that used by most Americans. The British, as well as some Americans living in the East, round their lips to produce this sound. Other features of British English are the long /ē/ (of "Eve") at the beginning of such words as *epoch* and *evolution* and the pronunciation of words ending with *-ile* to rhyme with *file: agile, fragile, mobile,* etc. Americans pronounce some *-ile* words that way *(juvenile, textile),* but not so many as the British do.

A difference that is easy to hear but not so easy to describe is the difference in the *intonation* patterns of British and American English. Intonation refers to the rise and fall of speech without special attention to the words themselves. British English is characterized by more rises and falls and stronger accents than are found in American English.

Vocabulary. As you might expect, vocabulary differences between American and British English reflect the different experiences of the two peoples. For example, the American colonists needed names for the plants and animals they encountered in the New World and borrowed from the Indian languages such words as *hickory, squash,* and *skunk.* Most of the borrowings from the Indian languages were place names: *Mackinaw, Cheyenne,* and *Chicago.* In most cases, these borrowed words were shortened or otherwise adapted to English.

Like earlier speakers of English, Americans have borrowed freely from the other languages they encountered. Through early contacts with the French settlers, a number of new borrowings from French came into American English. In the nineteenth century, increasing contacts with the Spanish civilization of Mexico and Central America added new Spanish words: *chaps, poncho, ranch, adobe, filibuster,* and *tornado.* Immigrations from all parts of Europe from the seventeenth century to today have contributed still other words to American English. A few examples: *pretzel, delicatessen, ouch,* and *hamburger* from German; *spaghetti* and *pizza* from Italian; *waffle, boss,* and *spook* from Dutch.

Another special feature of American English is the creation of a number of new words and expressions not found in British English. Some of these new words have to do with areas of technology developed since the settlement of the New World: *railroad* (British *railway*), *freight train* (British *goods train*), *windshield* (British *windscreen*), *fender* (British *wing*), *street car* (British *tram*), *flashlight* (British *torch*), and many others.

In some cases, American English has given new meanings to existing words in British English or has kept older meanings that the British no longer use. For example, American English has kept the word *druggist* while British English now uses the word *chemist.* The word *cabin* now refers only to part of a ship in British English, but used to have the meaning "cottage or small house," a meaning still common in American English. In England, the word *pie* originally meant a kind of pastry filled with meat, while in America *pie* usually refers to pastry filled with fruit or something sweet.

The few examples given here are only a small sample of the new words and meanings in American English. As with English in general, free borrowing and adaptation of early forms has produced a rich and cosmopolitan vocabulary.

Spelling. Most of you have read books printed in Great Britain. You have probably noticed that they write "honour" where we write "honor," and "analyse" where we write "analyze."

In addition, it is more common in Britain to double the final consonant when adding word endings, as in "travel" to write "travelled." In the United States, it is more common to write "traveled."

British spelling differs from American spelling in most words having such endings. Since this is a dictionary of American English, British spellings are given in only a few cases and not as a rule.

UNUSUAL SPELLINGS OF SOUNDS

You often hear the word "psychology," and you probably know its general meaning and how to spell it. But when you first heard it, you didn't think to look for it among the p's in your dictionary. You might have had the same trouble with "chord" and "phrase." If you try to find the word "account" and look for only one "c," you will be two pages away from where "account" is actually listed.

Everyone who uses a dictionary sometimes has trouble in finding a word he or she doesn't know how to spell. Including homophone references, as in this dictionary, often helps. But for unusual spellings that are not homophones, we just have to try various spellings for the same sound. The following table will help you do this. You should consult it when you need it.

COMMON SPELLINGS FOR THE SOUNDS OF AMERICAN ENGLISH

Sound		Spellings	Examples
b	as in bed	b, bb	tub, lobby
ch	as in chill	ch, tch, te, ti, tu	church, catch, righteous, bastion, naturally
d	as in deed	d, dd, ed, ld	dog, fodder, moved, could
f	as in fate	f, ff, gh, ph, lf	frog, huff, rough, physical, calf
g	as in get	g, gg, gh, gu, gue	leg, egg, ghost, guarantee, rogue
h	as in hop	h, wh	hat, whole
hw	as the "wh" in what	wh	what, wheel
j	as in jam	j, g, gg, dj, di, du, dge, dg	job, gentle, exaggeration, adjoin, soldier, gradual, badge, judgment
k	as in kin, quill [kw]	k, lk, c, cc, ch, ck, cqu, cq, qu, que, cu, q	smoke, yolk, canary, accordion, chorus, sack, lacquer, acquire, liquor, antique, biscuit, antiquity
l	as in let	l, ll, sl	lot, bell, islet
m	as in men	m, mm, mb, mn, lm, gm	him, mommy, dumb, hymn, salmon, paradigm
n	as in not	n, nn, gn, kn, pn, mn	ran, running, gnu, knight, pneumonia, mnemonic
ng	as in song	ng, ngue, n	song, tongue, think
p	as in pup	p, pp	pink, pepper
r	as in ride	r, rr, rh, wr	very, merry, rhinoceros, wrist
r	as in fur	r, rps	tar, liar, marble, order, corps
sh	as in she	sh, s, ss, sch, sci, si, ssi, ce, ch, ci, ti, se, chsi	rush, sugar, fissure, schwa, conscience, mansion, fission, ocean, machine, racial, ration, nauseous, fuchsia
s	as in sod	s, ss, sci, c, ps, sch, ce, sse	sat, miss, science, cent, psalm, schism, price, finesse
t	as in tea	t, th, tt, ed, phth, pt	hot, Theresa, matter, camped, phthisic, pterodactyl
th	as in thin	th	bath, width
~~th~~	as in then	th, the	that, bathe
v	as in vat	v, lve, f, ph, vv	dove, salve, of, Stephen, flivver
w	as in we	w, o, u	we, choir, acquire
y	as in yet	y, i, j, gn	you, onion, hallelujah, chignon
z	as in zero	z, zz, se, ss, s, x	zero, buzz, wise, scissors, dogs, xylophone
zh	as the "s" in usual or the "g" in mirage	z, g, s, si, zi	azure, loge, leisure, division, glazier

Sound		Spellings	Examples
ā	as in fate	a, ai, au, ay, ea, ei, eigh, ey, uet, et	age, maid, gauge, bay, break, veil, weight, hey, bouquet, buffet
ă	as in fat	a, ai, au	map, plaid, laugh
â	as in dare	a, ai, ay, e, ea, ei, ae	fare, air, prayer, where, wear, their, aerogram
ä	as in father	a, ea, au, e	art, heart, laugh, sergeant
ē	as in be	e, ee, ea, ei, eo, ey, i, ie, ae, oe, ay	equal, free, beam, perceive, people, key, machine, belief, caesium, phoebe, quay
ĕ	as in bet	e, ea, eo, a, ae, ie, ai, ay, u, ei	ebb, ferry, heavy, jeopardy, anyway, aesthetic, friend, said, says, bury, heifer
ê	as in mere	e, ea, ie, ee	mere, near, pier, peer
ī	as in bite	i, igh, ye, ie, uy, y ai, eye, aye	ice, nigh, rye, die, buy, by, Kaiser, eye, aye
ĭ	as bit	i, e, ee, ie, o, y, ui, u, a	if, enclose, been, sieve, women, hymn, build, busy, courage
ō	as in note	o, oa, au, oe, oh, eau, ew, eo, oo, ou, ough, au, ow	low, boat, hauteur, toe, oh, beau, sewing, yeoman, brooch, soul, though, gauche, grow
ŏ	as in hot	o, a	box, watt
ȯ	as in dog	o, aw, au, augh, a, o, ah, ough, oa	bog, law, laud, caught, ball, order, Utah, ought, broad
ô	as in more	o, oa, oo, ou	sore, roar, door, four
oi	as in oil	oi, oy	oil, boy
ou	as in out	ou, ow, ough	out, loud, plow, bough
o͞o	as in too	oo, u, ew, eu, oe, ough, ou, ue, ui, ooh, ioux	too, rule, brew, pneumatic, canoe, through, croup, blue, suit, pooh, Sioux
o͝o	as in book	oo, u, ou, o	look, put, could, wolf
ŭ	as in fun	u, o, oo, oe, ou	fun, ton, blood, does, trouble
û	as in fur	u, e, i, ea, ou, o, y	fur, term, sir, learn, journey, worm, myrrh
ə	as in above, opinion		The schwa sound may be spelled by any vowel letter or almost any combination of vowel letters, but at the beginning of words it is most often spelled "a" or "o."

ABBREVIATIONS USED IN DEFINITIONS

Abbr.	abbreviation
A.D.	Anno Domini (after Christ)
adj—	adjective
adv—	adverb
At. No.	atomic number
At. Wt.	atomic weight
B.C.	before Christ
Brit.	British
C.	Celsius (Centigrade)
CCD	Confraternity of Christian Doctrine
compar.	comparative of adjective
conj—	conjunction
etc.	et cetera
F.	Fahrenheit
fem.	feminine
Fr.	French
ft.	foot, feet
Hom—	homophone
in.	inch, inches
interj.	interjection
m.	mile, miles
n—	noun
NE	northeastern
NW	northwestern
pl.	plural
p.p.	past participle
prep.	preposition
pres. p.	present participle
pron—	pronoun
p.t.	past tense
SE	southeastern
sing.	singular
Span.	Spanish
S.S.R.	Soviet Socialist Republic (constituent republic)
St.	Saint
superl.	superlative of adjective
SW	southwestern
U.S.	United States
U.S.S.R.	Union of Soviet Socialist Republics
vi—	intransitive verb
vt—	transitive verb

PRONUNCIATION KEY

ā	as in fate, age
ă	as in fat, map
â	as in dare, air
ä	as in father, pa, barn
ē	as in be, equal
ĕ	as in bet, ebb
ê	as in mere, near
ī	as in bite, ice, ride
ĭ	as in bit, if
ō	as in note, boat, low
ŏ	as in hot, box
ȯ	as in dog, law, fought
ô	as in more, roar, door, four
oi	as in oil, boy
ou	as in out, loud
o͞o	as in too, rule
o͝o	as in book, put
ŭ	as in fun, up
û	as in fur, term

ə stands for the sound of: "a" in ago, Senate; "e" in open, hopeless, fairness; "i" in peril, trellis; "o" in lemon; "u" in minus, argument; "ou" in famous; "ai" in mountain; "oi" in tortoise.

b	as in bed (bĕd), tub (tŭb)
ch	as in chill (chĭl), batch (băch)
d	as in deed (dēd)
f	as in fate (fāt), huff (hŭf)
g	as in get (gĕt), leg (lĕg)
h	as in hop (hŏp)
hw	for "wh" as in what (hwŏt), wheel (hwēl)
j	as in jam (jăm), job (jŏb); and for "g" in gentle (jĕn′təl) and range (rānj)
k	as in kin (kĭn), smoke (smōk); for "c" in coal (kōl); and for "ck" in rack (răk)
l	as in let (lĕt), bell (bĕl)
m	as in men (mĕn), him (hĭm)
n	as in not (nŏt), ran (răn)
ng	as in song (sȯng); and for "n" in think (thĭngk)
p	as in pup (pŭp)
r	as in ride (rīd), very (vĕr′ē)
r	as in fur (fû*r*), tar (tä*r*) (This *r* is not pronounced in some sections of the country.)
s	as in sod (sŏd), must (mŭst) and for "c" as in cent (sĕnt), price (prīs)
sh	as in she (shē), rush (rŭsh)
t	as in tea (tē), hot (hŏt)
th	as in thin (thĭn), bath (băth), breath (brĕth)
t̶h̶	as in then (t̶h̶ĕn), bathe (bāt̶h̶), breathe (brēt̶h̶)
v	as in vat (văt), dove (dŭv); and for "f" in of (ŏv)
w	as in we (wē)
y	as in yet (yĕt)
z	as in zero (zêr′ō), buzz (bŭz); and for "s" in wise (wīz)
zh	for "s" as in usual (yo͞o′zho͞o əl), vision (vĭzh′ən); also for some "g's" as in mirage (mə räzh′)

FOREIGN SOUNDS

ø	as in the French words "feu," "peu," "lieu" and the German word "schön." This sound can be made by rounding the lips for /ō/ and trying to pronounce /ā/.
Y	as in the French word "lune" and the German word "für." This sound can be made by rounding the lips for /o͞o/ and trying to pronounce /ē/.
KH	as in German "ach" and Scottish "loch." Pronounce a strong /h/ with your mouth in position to make the /k/ sound in cook.
^{n}	This symbol means that the preceding vowel has a nasal quality as in "salon" [să lō^{n}].

ACCENT MARKS

In English words of two or more syllables, one syllable is usually pronounced with more emphasis than the others. This syllable is said to be accented, or stressed, and it is marked in the pronunciation with a heavy accent mark /**′**/:

mas′ter

Words with three or more syllables often have both a syllable that receives heavy stress and another syllable that receives a weaker stress. This weaker stress is marked with a light accent mark /′/:

mas′ter piece′

A

A, a (ā) ***n-*** [*pl.* **A's, a's**] **1** the first letter of the English alphabet. **2** A (1) *Music* the sixth note of the C-major scale. (2) a rating of first in order or class.

a or **an** (ə or ən when unstressed; ā or ăn when stressed) ***indefinite article*** (**a** is used before words beginning with consonant sounds: *quite* a *man*, a *youth*, a *unit*, a *horse*; **an** is used before words beginning with vowel sounds: *just* an *ounce*, an *uncle*, an *hour*.) **1** one (of an indefinite number): *He entered* a *room. I need* a *dollar for lunch.* **2** any: *I think* a *good horse can win it.* **3** (often considered a preposition) each; for every: *twice* a *year*; *two dollars* an *hour*. [from Old English **ān** meaning "one."]

a- *prefix* not; lacking; away from: *an* a*septic bandage*; *an* a*typical plant*. Also **an-** before vowels: *chronic* an*emia* (lacking blood). [from Greek **a-, an-** meaning "not; without."]

A.A.A. Automobile Association of America.

aard·vark (ärd′ värk′) ***n-*** a burrowing nocturnal animal of southern and central Africa, with a long snout, sharp claws, and a very long sticky tongue used to catch ants and termites, its only food.

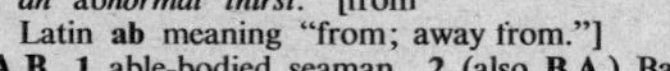

Aardvark, 4—6 ft. from snout to tail

Aar·on (ăr′ ən, âr′ -) ***n-*** brother of Moses; first high priest of the Hebrews.

ab- *prefix* from; away from: *an* ab*normal thirst*. [from Latin **ab** meaning "from; away from."]

A.B. 1 able-bodied seaman. **2** (also **B.A.**) Bachelor of Arts.

a·ba·cá (ăb′ ə kä′) ***n-*** **1** the leaf fiber of a banana plant of the Philippines; Manila hemp. **2** the plant that yields this fiber.

a·back (ə băk′) **take aback** to surprise or upset: *I was* taken aback *by his rudeness.*

ab·a·cus (ăb′ ə kəs) ***n-*** [*pl.* **ab·a·ci** (-sī) or **ab·a·cus·es**] a frame with beads sliding on rods, used in America and Europe for teaching arithmetic and in the Far East for calculating.

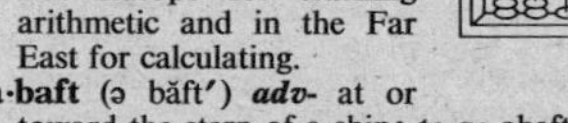

Abacus

a·baft (ə băft′) ***adv-*** at or toward the stern of a ship: *to go* abaft. ***prep-*** behind: *The sailor stood* abaft *the bridge.*

ab·a·lo·ne (ăb′ ə lō′ nē) ***n-*** a large oysterlike Pacific shellfish, valued both for food and for its single saucer-like shell lined with mother-of-pearl. [American word from American Spanish **abulón,** from American Indian **aulun.**]

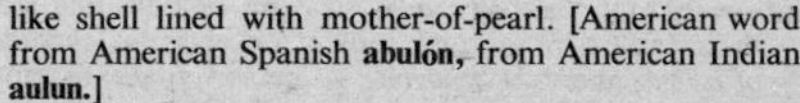

a·ban·don (ə băn′ dən) ***vt-*** **1** to give up completely: *to* abandon *all hope.* **2** to leave (a place) for good: *They* abandoned *ship.* **3** to desert; to leave in a heartless way: *to* abandon *one's family.* ***n-*** a letting oneself go: *She danced with* abandon. —***n-*** **a·ban′ don·ment.**

abandon (oneself) to to give oneself over to: *He* abandoned himself to *despair.*

a·base (ə bās′) ***vt-*** [**a·based, a·bas·ing**] to lower (a person or persons) in dignity, character, reputation, etc.; degrade: *He* abased *himself by his cowardly behavior.* —***n-*** **a·base′ ment.**

a·bash (ə băsh′) ***vt-*** to embarrass; shame; disconcert: *The rebuke* abashed *him.*

a·bate (ə bāt′) ***vi-*** [**a·bat·ed, a·bat·ing**] to become less: *After the storm, the wind* abated. ***vt-*** **1** to lessen; reduce: *The City administration* abated *local taxes.* **2** in law, to put an end to: *to* abate *a nuisance.*

a·bate·ment (ə bāt′ mənt) ***n-*** a lessening or diminishing; reduction: *an* abatement *of a storm*; *an* abatement *of a debt.*

ab·at·toir (ăb′ ə twär′) ***n-*** slaughterhouse.

ab·bé (ăb′ ā′) ***n-*** in France, a title of respect for a priest or another man wearing religious dress.

ab·bess (ăb′ əs) ***n-*** head of a religious community of women.

ab·bey (ăb′ ē) ***n-*** **1** one or more buildings used as a monastery or convent, governed by an abbot or abbess. **2** church that is or was once part of a monastery.

ab·bot (ăb′ ət) ***n-*** head of a religious community of men.

ab·bre·vi·ate (ə brē′ vē āt′) ***vt-*** [**ab·bre·vi·at·ed, ab·bre·vi·at·ing**] to make shorter by omitting letters or words: *to* abbreviate *"Mister" to "Mr."*; *to* abbreviate *a speech.*

ab·bre·vi·a·tion (ə brē′ vē ā′ shən) ***n-*** a shortened form: *The accepted* abbreviation *for "inch" is "in."*

Ab·di·a (ăb dī′ ə) ***n-*** the CCD Bible name for Obadiah.

ab·di·cate (ăb′ də kāt′) ***vt-*** [**ab·di·cat·ed, ab·di·cat·ing**] to give up (a position of power, a throne, or a serious responsibility); renounce; resign: *to* abdicate *a throne.* ***vi-***: *The King* abdicated. —***n-*** **ab′ di·ca′ tion.**

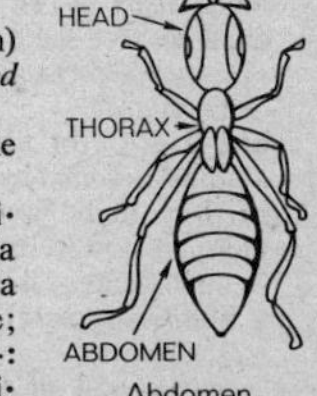

Abdomen

ab·do·men (ăb′ də mən, ăb dō′-) ***n-*** **1** the part of the human body containing the stomach, intestines, etc.; belly. **2** the rear section of the body of an insect.

---

fāte, făt, dâre, bärn; bē, bĕt, mêre; bīte, bĭt; nōte, hŏt, môre, dòg; fŭn, fûr; tōō, bŏŏk; oil; out; tar; thin; then; hw for wh as in *wh*at; zh for s as in u*s*ual; ə for a, e, i, o, u, as in *a*go, lin*e*n, per*i*l, at*o*m, min*u*s

ab·dom·i·nal (əb dŏm′ə nəl, ăb-) ***adj-*** having to do with the abdomen: *an* abdominal *pain*; *an* abdominal *operation.* ***—adv-*** **ab·dom′i·nal·ly.**

ab·duct (əb dŭkt′, ăb-) ***vt-*** to kidnap. ***—n-*** **ab·duc′tion.**

ab·duc·tor (əb dŭk′ tər) ***n-*** kidnaper.

a·beam (ə bēm′) ***adv-*** beside, or straight across, a ship.

a·bed (ə bĕd′) ***adv-*** in bed: *to lie* abed.

A·bel (ā′ bəl) ***n-*** in the Bible, the second son of Adam. He was slain by his brother Cain. ***Hom-*** able.

Ab·er·deen An·gus (ăb′ ər dēn′ ăng′ əs) ***n-*** a breed of black hornless beef cattle first raised in Scotland and bred for their high-grade meat.

ab·er·rance (ə bĕr′ əns) or **ab·er·ran·cy** (ə bĕr′ ən sē) ***n-*** [*pl.* **ab·er·ran·ces** or **ab·er·ran·cies**] a straying or deviation from what is expected.

ab·er·rant (ə bĕr′ ənt) ***adj-*** straying or deviating from the standard or normal course: *an* aberrant *curvature of a line*; aberrant *behavior.* ***n-*** person, thing, or group that deviates from the normal or usual.

ab·er·ra·tion (ăb′ ə rā′ shən) ***n-*** **1** a straying or deviation from the normal or usual: *His speech was full of* aberrations *from his main theme.* **2** degree of mental illness not serious enough to be considered insanity. **3** apparent change in the position of a celestial body because of change in the position of the observer as the earth moves through space. **4** in optics, a condition in which a lens or mirror does not focus light sharply but produces a blurred image **(spherical aberration)**, or breaks up light so that the image is fringed with color **(chromatic aberration)**.

a·bet (ə bĕt′) ***vt-*** [**a·bet·ted, a·bet·ting**] **1** to encourage or aid: *Foreign countries* abetted *both parties in the Civil War.* **2** to assist; incite; connive at, especially in a crime: *By handling stolen goods they* abetted *thieves.*
aid and abet in law, to help someone willfully in committing a crime.

a·bet·tor (ə bĕt′ ər) ***n-*** person who abets.

a·bey·ance (ə bā′ əns) ***n-*** **1** temporary inactivity or disuse: *His interest in stamps has been in* abeyance *for weeks.* **2** suspension or postponement: *The President held in* abeyance *his decision to name a running mate.*

ab·hor (əb hŏr′, əb hôr′, ăb-) ***vt-*** [**ab·horred, ab·hor·ring**] to shrink from with disgust; detest; loathe.

ab·hor·rent (əb hŏr′ ənt, əb hŏr′ ənt, ăb-) ***adj-*** hateful; detestable; loathesome: *Treachery is* abhorrent. ***—n-*** **ab·hor′rence:** *his* abhorrence *of treachery.*

a·bide (ə bīd′) ***vi-*** [**a·bid·ed, a·bid·ing**] **1** to remain; last; endure: *Even after disappointment, hope still* abides. **2** to dwell; live. ***vt-*** **1** to await: *Who will* abide *the day of His coming?* **2** to put up with; tolerate: *She can't* abide *his rudeness.*
abide by to adhere to; act according to: *to* abide by *the umpire's decision*; *to* abide by *the terms of the contract we signed.*

a·bid·ing (ə bī′ dĭng) ***adj-*** never-ending; lasting: *an* abiding *devotion to his country*; abiding *faith.*

a·bil·i·ty (ə bĭl′ ə tē) ***n-*** [*pl.* **a·bil·i·ties**] **1** mental or physical power to do something: *the* ability *to reason.* **2** intelligence; skill; talent: *his* ability *as a plumber.* **3 abilities** general mental powers or gifts: *a man of many* abilities.
to the best of (one's) ability as well as (one) can: *I'll do the job* to the best of my ability.

-ability or **-ibility** *suffix* (used to form nouns from adjectives by substitution for the adjective suffixes -able or -ible) state or condition of being. "*Approach*ability" is the condition of being "*approach*able."

ab·ject (ăb′ jĕkt′) ***adj-*** fallen as far as one could; mean and low; wretched; miserable: *an* abject *liar*; *in* abject *poverty*; *in* abject *submission.* ***—adv-*** **ab′ject′ly.** ***n-*** **ab′ject′ness.**

ab·jure (əb jŏŏr′, ăb-) ***vt-*** [**ab·jured, ab·jur·ing**] to promise solemnly to give up; renounce: *to* abjure *one's religion.* ***—n-*** **ab′ju·ra′tion.** ***n-*** **ab·jur′er.**

ab·la·tive (ăb′ lə tĭv) ***adj-*** in the grammar of certain languages, such as Latin, pertaining to a case which expresses "from" or "by" used with or without the preposition.

a·blaze (ə blāz′) ***adj-*** **1** on fire; burning: *logs* ablaze *in the fireplace.* **2** shining brightly; flashing: *a house* ablaze *with lights*; *a face* ablaze *with anger.*

a·ble (ā′ bəl) ***adj-*** [**a·bler, a·blest**] **1** capable through power, skill, or money; with the ability or means (to): *When I'm not tired, I'm* able *to work faster. The President is* able *to declare war.* **2** talented; skillful: *an* able *speaker.* **3** showing skill: *an* able *speech.* ***Hom-*** Abel. ***—adv-*** **a′bly:** *He spoke* ably *in defense of his plan.*

-able *suffix* **1** (used to form adjectives from verbs) fit to be, or is worthy to be: *endur*able; *lov*able; *print*able. **2** (used to make adjectives from nouns) (1) inclined toward or suited to: *peace*able; *fashion*able; *season*able. (2) able to; apt to: *dur*able; *perish*able. Also **-ible,** especially in some words originally from Latin: *horr*ible; *resist*ible. [from Latin **-abilis, -ibilis** meaning "able to; worthy of," often by way of French **-able.**]

a·ble-bod·ied (ā′ bəl bŏd′ ēd) ***adj-*** in good physical condition; sound of body.

able-bodied seaman ***n-*** experienced seaman who has passed an examination on his ability. Also called **able seaman.** *Abbr.* A.B.

ab·lu·tion (ə blōō′ shən, ăb lōō′-) ***n-*** **1** a washing, especially the ceremonial cleansing of the hands or other parts of the body as a purifying rite in the Mass, baptism, etc. **2 ablutions** washing of the body or any part of it.

Ab·na·ki (ăb nä′ kē) ***n-*** [*pl.* **Ab·na·kis,** also **Ab·na·ki**] one of a tribe of Algonquian Indians who lived in southern Maine and Quebec. ***adj-***: *an* Abnaki *village.* Also **Ab′e·na′ki.**

ab·ne·ga·tion (ăb′ nə gā′ shən) ***n-*** **1** the act of denying oneself something; self-denial. **2** self-sacrifice.

ab·nor·mal (ăb nŏr′ məl, ăb nôr′-) ***adj-*** not normal; different from the ordinary or the average; unusual: *an* abnormal *situation.* ***—adv-*** **ab·nor′mal·ly.**

ab·nor·mal·i·ty (ăb′ nŏr măl′ ə tē) ***n-*** [*pl.* **ab·nor·mal·i·ties**] **1** abnormal thing; irregularity: *a speech* abnormality. **2** abnormal condition or quality.

a·board (ə bôrd′) ***adv-*** into or on a ship, bus, train, or airplane. ***prep-*** on board.
all aboard! Get on! The bus (or train, etc.) is about to leave.

[1]**a·bode** (ə bōd′) *Archaic p.t. & p.p.* of **abide.** [from Middle English **ābōd,** from Old English **ābād,** past tense of **ābīdan** meaning "to abide; wait for."]

[2]**a·bode** (ə bōd′) ***n-*** home or dwelling, especially a fixed and permanent residence. [from Middle English **ābōd** meaning "a stay; a delay," related to Old English **ābīdan** and to **abide.**]

a·bol·ish (ə bŏl′ ĭsh) ***vt-*** to do away with; put an end to.

ab·o·li·tion (ăb ə lĭsh′ ən) ***n-*** a doing away with or a putting an end to; an abolishing: *the* abolition *of poverty*; *the* abolition *of slavery.*

ab·o·li·tion·ist (ăb′ ə lĭsh′ ə nĭst) ***n-*** person in favor of abolishing something; especially, one who strongly favored an immediate end to Negro slavery.

ab·o·ma·sum (ăb′ ō mā′ səm) ***n-*** fourth and last pouch of the stomach of a cud-chewing animal, in which true digestion takes place.

A-bomb (ā′ bŏm′) ***n-*** atom bomb.

a·bom·i·na·ble (ə bŏm′ ə nə bəl) ***adj-*** **1** very hateful: *the* abominable *cruelties of Nero.* **2** very bad or unpleasant: *an* abominable *winter.* ***—adv-*** **a·bom′ i·na·bly.**

abominable snowman ***n-*** mysterious, hairy, apelike or bearlike creature said to live in the Himalayas. Its existence has never been proved.

a·bom·i·nate (ə bŏm′ ə nāt′) ***vt-*** **[a·bom·i·nat·ed, a·bom·i·nat·ing]** to hate; detest; loathe: *He* abominates *militarism.*

a·bom·i·na·tion (ə bŏm′ ə nā′ shən) ***n-*** **1** anything vile, hateful, or wicked; a shameful vice: *The man's cruelty is an* abomination. **2** a feeling of disgust or loathing: *an* abomination *for cruelty to animals.*

ab·o·rig·i·nal (ăb′ ə rĭj′ ə nəl) ***adj-*** of living things, belonging to a place from the beginning: *an* aboriginal *plant.* ***n-***: *Maize is an American* aboriginal.

ab·o·rig·i·ne (ăb′ ə rĭj′ ə nē) ***n-*** **1** person whose people have inhabited a region from their beginnings. **2 aborigines** the original plant and animal life of a region.

a·bort (ə bȯrt′, -bôrt′) ***vi-*** **1** to give birth to a fetus that has not developed enough to live. **2** *Biology* to fail to develop completely or properly, as an embryo. **3** to come to nothing; go wrong; fail: *The attack* aborted *because of a breakdown in communications.*

a·bor·tion (ə bȯr′ shən, ə bôr′-) ***n-*** **1** the birth of a fetus that has not developed fully enough to live; miscarriage. **2** *Biology* incomplete or improper development, as of an embryo. **3** an idea, plan, project, etc., that has failed to be completed or perfected.

a·bor·tive (ə bȯr′ tĭv, ə bôr′-) ***adj-*** **1** coming to nothing; fruitless: *an* abortive *plan.* **2** *Medicine* (1) producing the abortion of a fetus. (2) of a disease, short and mild, not developing all the usual symptoms: *an* abortive *case of measles.* ***—adv-*** **a·bor′ tive·ly.** ***n-*** **a·bor′ tive·ness.**

a·bound (ə bound′) ***vi-*** to be plentiful; be in abundance: *Trout* abound *here.*

abound in (or **with**) to be rich in; teem with: *The poem* abounds in *imagery. The lakes* abound with *fish.*

a·bout (ə bout′) ***adv-*** **1** near; nearby, especially on every side: *Are there any wild animals* about? **2** here and there; around, also moving around: *They drove* about *in search of antiques. He is up and* about. **3** in a turn or to a reversed direction or position: *He whirled his partner* about. *Let's change* about *for the next game.* **4** approximately: *I found* about *a hundred people there.* **5** nearly; almost: *He is* about *dead from hunger.* ***prep-*** **1** near and on all sides of; around: *scattered trees* about *the house.* **2** concerning; in regard to: *a story* about *a bear; something wrong* about *the plan.* **3** on the person of: *I haven't a cent* about *me.*

about to going to immediately; on the point of: *He is* about to *leave.*

a·bout-face (ə bout′ fās′) ***vi-*** **[a·bout-faced, a·bout-fac·ing]** to do an about face.

about face ***n-*** **1** *Military* a turning about from facing in one direction to facing in the opposite direction while standing; also, the command to perform this. **2** any turning from one direction, opinion, feeling, etc., to its opposite.

a·bove (ə bŭv′) ***adv-*** **1** overhead; directly overhead: *the sky* above. **2** farther up; in a higher place: *a deer on the hill* above. **3** higher on the page or on a page before this one: *See the picture* above. ***prep-*** **1** over; higher than: *one brick* above *another;* above *the clouds.* **2** uphill from; also upstream from: *We walked* above *the tree line. The factories* above *the town are polluting the stream.* **3** superior to in rank, authority, quality, morality, etc.: *A captain is* above *a corporal. Her workmanship is* above *imitation. He was far* above *envy.* **4** in excess of: *We paid* above *a thousand dollars.*

a·bove·board (ə bŭv′ bôrd′) ***adv-*** openly; without trickery: *He acted* aboveboard. ***adj-*** honest: *His actions were* aboveboard.

ab·ra·ca·dab·ra (ăb′ rə kə dăb′ rə) ***n-*** **1** an expression once used as a charm against disease, now used as a conjuring word in magic. **2** any meaningless or foolish talk; gibberish; nonsense.

a·brade (ə brād′) ***vt-*** **[a·brad·ed, a·brad·ing]** **1** to rub or scrape off; chafe: *John* abraded *the skin of his elbow when he fell.* **2** to wear away or wear down: *A moving glacier* abrades *the rocks along its path.*

A·bra·ham (ā′ brə hăm′) ***n-*** in the Bible, the first great patriarch of the Hebrews.

a·bra·sion (ə brā′ zhən) ***n-*** **1** a wearing away: *the* abrasion *of a cliff by wind.* **2** an injury to the skin from scraping or rubbing: *cuts and* abrasions.

a·bra·sive (ə brā′ sĭv, -zĭv) ***adj-*** capable of scraping, rubbing, or wearing away: *Some cleansing powders are* abrasive. ***n-*** a substance, such as pumice, emery, etc., used for polishing and grinding.

a·breast (ə brĕst′) ***adv-*** side by side: *The soldiers marched three* abreast.

keep abreast of to keep up with: *to* keep abreast of *the times.*

a·bridge (ə brĭj′) ***vt-*** **[a·bridged, a·bridg·ing]** **1** to lessen, reduce, or deprive of: *to* abridge *one's liberties.* **2** to shorten or cut (a book, speech, etc.) while keeping the sense; condense.

a·bridg·ment (ə brĭj′ mənt) ***n-*** **1** a shortened version of a book, speech, etc.; condensation. **2** the act of abridging: *the* abridgment *of one's liberties.* Also **a·bridge′ ment.**

a·broad (ə brȯd′) ***adv-*** **1** in or to a foreign country: *to live* abroad; *to travel* abroad. **2** widely: *Spread the news* abroad. **3** outside the house: *to be* abroad *early.*

ab·ro·gate (ăb′ rə gāt′) ***vt-*** **[ab·ro·gat·ed, ab·ro·gat·ing]** to repeal or cancel (a law or privilege). ***—n-*** **ab′ ro·ga′ tion.**

a·brupt (ə brŭpt′) ***adj-*** **1** sudden; unexpected: *an* abrupt *stop.* **2** steep: *an* abrupt *incline.* **3** curt in speech; short and blunt. ***—adv-*** **a·brupt′ ly.**

Ab·sal·om (ăb′ sə lŏm′) ***n-*** in the Bible, David's favorite son, slain in rebellion against his father.

ab·scess (ăb′ sĕs′) ***n-*** mass of pus at an infected point in the body; a boil; carbuncle. ***—adj-*** **ab′ scessed′**: *an* abscessed *tooth.*

ab·scis·sa (ăb sĭs′ ə) ***n-*** [*pl.* **ab·scis·sae** (-sē) or **ab·scis·sas**] **1** in Cartesian coordinates, the distance of a point from the y axis, measured parallel to the x axis. **2** the number, term, or line segment that represents this distance.

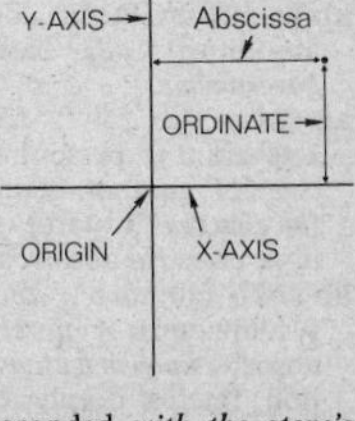

ab·scond (əb skŏnd′, ăb-) ***vi-*** to flee suddenly and secretly and go into hiding to avoid arrest; decamp: *The clerk* absconded *with the store's money.*

ab·sence (ăb′ səns) ***n-*** **1** a being away: *His* absence *was noted.* **2** a being without; lack: *an* absence *of humor.*

---

fāte, făt, dâre, bärn; bē, bĕt, mêre; bīte, bĭt; nōte, hŏt, môre, dȯg; fŭn, fûr; to͞o, bo͝ok; oil; out; tar; thin; then; hw for wh as in what; zh for s as in usual; ə for a, e, i, o, u, as in ago, linen, peril, atom, minus

[1]**ab·sent** (ăb′sənt) ***adj-*** **1** not present; away; missing. **2** lost in thought; not paying attention: *She was day-dreaming, and answered in an* absent *manner.*

[2]**ab·sent** (əb sĕnt′, ăb-) ***vt-*** to take or keep (oneself) away: *to* absent *oneself from class.*

ab·sen·tee (ăb′ sən tē′) ***n-*** **1** one who is absent, especially from work or school. **2** an absentee landlord.

absentee ballot ***n-*** ballot sent in by an absentee voter.

ab·sen·tee·ism (ăb′ sən tē′ĭz əm) ***n-*** **1** the frequent or habitual absence of an employee or group of employees. **2** the practice of an absentee landlord.

absentee landlord ***n-*** **1** formerly, a landlord who did not live on the land from which he received his income. **2** now, a landlord who transfers the handling of his property to an agent.

absentee voter ***n-*** voter who is not able to go to the polls but has qualified legally to vote by mail.

ab·sent·ly (ăb′sənt lē) ***adv-*** in an absent-minded way: *She* absently *nodded in response to the question.*

ab·sent-mind·ed (ăb′sənt mīn′dəd) ***adj-*** lost in thought; hence, inattentive; forgetful. ***—adv-*** **ab′sent-mind′ed·ly.** ***n-*** **ab′sent-mind′ed·ness.**

ab·sinthe (ăb′sĭnth′) ***n-*** a bitter, green alcoholic liquor containing wormwood, now generally outlawed. Also **ab′sinth′.**

ab·so·lute (ăb′sə lo͞ot′) ***adj-*** **1** complete; perfect: *the* absolute *truth.* **2** not limited or restricted in any way: *Very few rulers nowadays have* absolute *power.* **3** certain; positive: *to have* absolute *proof.*

absolute ceiling ***n-*** the maximum altitude a particular type of airplane can maintain under normal conditions.

absolute humidity ***n-*** the weight of the water vapor in a given volume of air.

ab·so·lute·ly (ăb′sə lo͞ot′lē) ***adv-*** **1** wholly; completely: *You're* absolutely *right.* **2** certainly; positively: *He* absolutely *refuses to go.*

absolute value *Mathematics* ***n-*** the distance of a number on a number line in either direction, from zero to the point representing the number.

absolute zero ***n-*** theoretically, the lowest temperature matter can have; the temperature point at which molecules have no motion and, hence, no heat. It is the zero of the Kelvin temperature scale and is equal to −273.16° C. (−459.72° F.).

ab·so·lu·tion (ăb′sə lo͞o′shən) ***n-*** **1** a formal forgiveness of sins: *The priest pronounced* absolution. **2** a release from any obligation, charge, or penalty.

ab·so·lut·ism (ăb′sə lo͞o′tĭz′əm) ***n-*** the principles and practices of government by a ruler with unlimited power or authority; autocracy; despotism.

ab·so·lut·ist (ăb′sə lo͞o′tĭst) ***n-*** person who advocates absolutism. ***adj-*** based on absolutism: *an* absolutist *government.*

ab·solve (əb zŏlv′, -sŏlv′) ***vt-*** **[ab·solved, ab·solv·ing] 1** to grant (a person) a formal forgiveness of sins. **2** to clear of guilt or blame: *The jury* absolved *him of all the charges.* **3** to free (someone) from a promise, obligation, etc.: *He* absolved *me from the promise I made.*

ab·sorb (əb sȯrb′, -zȯrb′) ***vt-*** **1** to take in; soak up; swallow up: *A towel* absorbs *water. A bright child* absorbs *knowledge easily.* **2** to occupy all one's attention; interest deeply; engross: *Stamp collecting* absorbs *John now.* **3** to make part of a greater whole; assimilate: *The city* absorbed *its suburbs.* **4** of a business, to meet (increased costs) without raising prices. **5** to receive (light, heat, or sound) without reflection or echo, as do sound-proofing materials. See also *adsorb.*

absorbed in completely interested in or occupied with; engrossed in: *He was* absorbed in *his studies.*

ab·sorb·ent (əb sȯr′bənt, əb zȯr′-) ***adj-*** capable of taking up moisture: *an* absorbent *cotton.* ***n-*** substance that absorbs: *Cotton is an* absorbent.

ab·sorb·ing (əb sȯr′bĭng, əb zȯr′-) ***adj-*** taking up all one's attention; very interesting: *an* absorbing *tale.* ***—adv-*** **ab·sorb′ing·ly.**

ab·sorp·tion (əb sȯrp′shən, əb zȯrp′-) ***n-*** **1** the act of absorbing something: *the* absorption *of knowledge; the* absorption *of water.* **2** the passing of substances from one part of the body into another, as from the blood into the cells, or from the digestive system into the blood and body fluids.

absorption spectrum ***n-*** spectrum in which dark lines appear where certain wavelengths have been absorbed by a gas or vapor through which the light or other electromagnetic radiation has passed.

ab·sorp·tive (əb sȯrp′tĭv, əb zȯrp′-) ***adj-*** able to absorb; absorbent.

ab·stain (əb stān′, ăb-) ***vi-*** to hold oneself back (from an action); refrain: *Vegetarians* abstain *from eating meat. Five persons voted for the measure, two voted against, and one* abstained.

ab·ste·mi·ous (əb stē′mē əs, ăb-) ***adj-*** moderate and sparing in the use of food and drink; temperate: *an* abstemious *use of tobacco; an* abstemious *man.* ***—adv-*** **ab·ste′mi·ous·ly.** ***n-*** **ab·ste′mi·ous·ness.**

ab·sten·tion (əb stĕn′shən, ăb-) ***n-*** an abstaining or refraining; also, an act of abstaining, often officially recorded as a kind of vote: *his* abstention *from alcohol; three votes in favor, two against, and three* abstentions.

►To ABSTAIN from something means not to do it. ABSTINENCE is the practice or habit of abstaining, often because of a vow or promise, while ABSTENTION usually refers to an act of abstaining.

ab·sti·nence (ăb′stĭ nəns) ***n-*** a refraining from something; a giving up of certain foods, alcoholic drinks, etc. ***—adj-*** **ab′sti·nent.**

[1]**ab·stract** (ăb′străkt′, əb străkt′) ***adj-*** **1** concerned with or based on theory more than facts or real situations: *to speak of* abstract *justice; an* abstract *subject; an* abstract *thinker.* **2** *Grammar* describing a noun that expresses a quality or characteristic but does not name the person or thing possessing it: *"Strength" is an* abstract *noun.* **3** in art, describing a style that, either wholly or in part, avoids representing natural objects: *an* abstract *painting.* **4** difficult to understand; abstruse. ***n-*** (ăb′străkt′ *only*) short account of the main points in a book, speech, etc.: *He published the full speech as well as an* abstract *of it.* ***—adv-*** **ab′stract′ly.** ***n-*** **ab′stract′ness.**

[2]**ab·stract** (əb străkt′, ăb-) ***vt-*** **1** to separate: *to* abstract *gold from ore.* **2** to make a summary of: *to* abstract *a book.* **3** to take out or away, often dishonestly: *George slyly* abstracted *a dollar from his sister's purse when she wasn't looking.*

ab·stract·ed (əb străk′təd, ăb-) ***adj-*** absent-minded; lost in thought. ***—adv-*** **ab·stract′ed·ly,**

ab·strac·tion (ăb străk′shən, əb-) ***n-*** **1** a drawing out or taking away: *the* abstraction *of metal from ore.* **2** an abstract idea: *the* abstractions *of philosophy.* **3** state of being lost in thought; absent-mindedness: *In a moment of* abstraction *he grabbed the wrong hat.*

ab·strac·tion·ism (ăb străk′shən ĭz′əm) ***n-*** a style of art that stresses the importance of form and color and avoids realistic objects or selects only certain qualities from them.

ab·struse (əb stro͞os′, ăb-) ***adj-*** hard to understand; obscure in meaning: *an* abstruse *remark.* ***—adv-*** **ab·struse′ly.** ***n-*** **ab·struse′ness.**

ab·surd (əb sûrd′, -zûrd′) ***adj-*** ridiculous; silly; contrary to reason or sense. ***—adv-*** **ab·surd′ly.**

ab·surd·i·ty (əb sûr′də tē, əb zûr′-) ***n-*** [*pl.* **ab·surd·i·ties**] **1** foolishness, as of dress, speech, or conduct; *the* absurdity *of the hat.* **2** something contrary to reason or sense; something absurd: *His remark was a gross* absurdity.

a·bun·dance (əbŭn′dəns) ***n-*** quantity that is more than enough; overflowing supply; great plenty: *an* abundance *of food.*

live in abundance to have plenty of the things that make life enjoyable.

a·bun·dant (ə bŭn′dənt) ***adj-*** plenty of; more than enough: *The settlers found* abundant *game in the forests.* ***—adv-*** **a·bun′dant·ly.**

[1]**a·buse** (ə byo͞oz′) ***vt-*** [**a·bused, a·bus·ing**] **1** to treat badly or harshly: *to* abuse *one's eyes by reading in dim light.* **2** to make improper use of; misuse: *The manager* abused *his authority. He* abused *his host's hospitality.* **3** to use insulting language to or about: *The candidates* abused *each other during the campaign.*

[2]**a·buse** (ə byo͞os′) ***n-*** **1** wrong or harsh treatment. **2** wrong use; misuse: *the* abuse *of power.* **3** corrupt custom or practice: *Such* abuses *as bribery or graft are punishable by law.* **4** insulting language.

a·bus·ive (ə byo͞o′sĭv) ***adj-*** **1** given to cruel treatment or harsh language. **2** of behavior, harsh or insulting. ***—adv-*** **a·bus′ive·ly.**

a·but (ə bŭt′) ***vi-*** [**a·but·ted, a·but·ting**] **1** to border (on, upon, or against): *The house* abuts *on the hill.* **2** to be in contact: *The two houses* abut.

a·but·ment (ə bŭt′mənt) ***n-*** the supporting structure at either end of an arch or bridge, or a wedge-shaped piece on the upstream side of a bridge pier to resist pressure from water or ice.

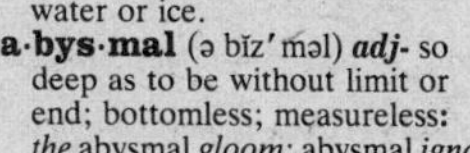
Abutments of an arched bridge

a·bys·mal (ə bĭz′məl) ***adj-*** so deep as to be without limit or end; bottomless; measureless: *the* abysmal *gloom*; abysmal *ignorance.* ***—adv-*** **a·bys′mal·ly.**

a·byss (ə bĭs′) ***n-*** **1** deep natural cut in the earth; gorge; chasm. **2** anything of limitless depth: *the* abyss *of space*; *the* abyss *of misery.*

a.c. or **A.C.** or **AC** alternating current.

a·ca·cia (ə kā′shə) ***n-*** **1** any of a group of thorny trees and shrubs growing in warm regions and having fernlike leaves and clusters of yellow or white flowers. **2** gum arabic.

ac·a·dem·ic (ăk′ə dĕm′ĭk) ***adj-*** **1** of an academy, school, or college: *an* academic *degree*; academic *studies.* **2** having to do with theory rather than practice; without practical effect; idle: *Whether or not to have a monarchy in this country is now an* academic *question.*

ac·ad·e·mi·cian (ăk′ə də mĭsh′ən) ***n-*** **1** member of a society for promoting literature, art, or science. **2** one who insists on the forms or methods of tradition in literature, art, etc.

ac·a·dem·i·cism (ăk′ə dĕm′ə sĭz′əm) ***n-*** an insistence on rules, convention, and tradition in literature, art, etc.

a·cad·e·my (ə kăd′ə mē) ***n-*** [*pl.* **a·cad·e·mies**] **1** private high school. **2** school for special study: *a military* academy. **3** a society of learned people organized to encourage arts, letters, or sciences.

a·can·thus (ə kăn′thəs) ***n-*** **1** any of a group of Mediterranean shrubs with beautiful, deeply cleft leaves. **2** in art and architecture, a design resembling such leaves. Acanthus leaves are used on Corinthian capitals.

a cap·pel·la (ä′kə pĕl′ə) *Music* ***adv-*** without instrumental accompaniment: *to sing* a cappella. ***adj-***: *the* a cappella *choir.*

ac·cede (ăk sēd′) ***vi-*** [**ac·ced·ed, ac·ced·ing**] **1** to agree or yield (to): *He* acceded *to my request.* **2** to succeed or attain (to a position, throne, etc.): *She* acceded *to the presidency.*

ac·cel·er·an·do (ăk sĕl′ə rän′dō) *Music* ***adj- & adv-*** gradually increasing in tempo.

ac·cel·e·rate (ăk sĕl′ə rāt′) ***vt-*** [**ac·cel·e·rat·ed, ac·cel·e·rat·ing**] **1** to increase the speed of: *to* accelerate *the motor by stepping on the pedal.* **2** to bring about sooner; hasten: *The dictator's harsh measures* accelerated *his fall.* ***vi-*** to pick up speed; move more swiftly: *The sled* accelerated *as it swept down the hill.*

ac·cel·e·ra·tion (ăk sĕl′ə rā′shən) ***n-*** **1** increase of speed; a hastening: *an* acceleration *in the pulse rate of a runner.* **2** *Physics* rate at which the speed of an object changes for each unit of time. Gravity subjects a body to an acceleration of 32 feet per second per second. See also *deceleration.*

ac·cel·er·a·tor (ăk sĕl′ə rā′tər) ***n-*** **1** device to increase speed; especially, in an automobile, the pedal which regulates the flow of gasoline and, thus, controls the speed. **2** any of several electromagnetic machines, such as a cyclotron or synchrotron, used to accelerate atomic particles, especially protons or electrons; atom smasher. **3** substance that increases the speed of a chemical reaction.

ac·cel·e·rom·e·ter (ăk sĕl′ə rŏm′ə tər) ***n-*** instrument used to measure acceleration, especially in aircraft and spacecraft.

[1]**ac·cent** (ăk′sĕnt′) ***n-*** **1** special or regional way of pronouncing: *a foreign* accent; *a Southern* accent. **2** stress on a syllable in a word or a note of music. **3** accent mark.

[2]**ac·cent** (ăk′sĕnt′, ăk sĕnt′) ***vt-*** **1** to pronounce with special stress or emphasis, as with the second syllable of the word "relation." **2** to indicate by an accent mark. **3** to emphasize or stress; accentuate: *The scarf* accented *the color of the coat.*

accent mark ***n-*** **1** mark used in writing and printing to indicate which syllable of a word is to be stressed (accented). **2** in some foreign languages, a mark used to show the pronunciation of a letter in a word. For example, in the French word "paté" the accent mark indicates that the "e" is pronounced /ā/.

ac·cen·tu·ate (ăk sĕn′cho͞o āt′) ***vt-*** [**ac·cen·tu·at·ed, ac·cen·tu·at·ing**] **1** to emphasize or stress in speech, writing, or music. **2** to heighten; make prominent: *That event* accentuated *my happiness.*

ac·cept (ăk sĕpt′) ***vt-*** (in senses 1, 2, and 3 considered intransitive when the direct object is implied but not expressed) **1** to take (what is offered): *to* accept *a gift.* **2** to answer yes to: *to* accept *an invitation.* **3** to agree to: *to* accept *a proposal.* **4** to recognize as true: *The jury* accepted *his story.* **5** to receive into a group; include: *The children immediately* accepted *their new classmate.*

►ACCEPT means "to take or approve." EXCEPT means "to single out." I ACCEPT your invitation means "I will come." I EXCEPT your invitation means "I will accept the other invitations, but not yours (or vice versa)."

---

fāte, făt, dâre, bärn; bē, bĕt, mêre; bīte, bĭt; nōte, hŏt, môre, dôg; fŭn, fûr; to͞o, bo͝ok; oil; out; tar; thin; then; hw for wh as in what; zh for s as in usual; ə for a, e, i, o, u, as in ago, linen, peril, atom, minus

ac·cept·a·ble (ăk sĕp′ tə bəl) ***adj-*** **1** worth accepting; welcome: *The plan was* acceptable *to everyone.* **2** fitting or satisfactory: *quite* acceptable *behavior.* ***—adv-*** **ac·cept′ a·bly.**

ac·cept·ance (ăk sĕp′ təns) ***n-*** **1** a taking or willingness to receive something offered or given: *the* acceptance *of responsibilities*; *the* acceptance *of a gift.* **2** approval: *The invention found widespread* acceptance.

ac·cept·ed (ăk sĕp′ təd) ***adj-*** approved or believed by nearly everyone: *Once it was an* accepted *belief that the world is flat.*

ac·cess (ăk′ sĕs′) ***n-*** **1** entrance or approach: *They gained* access *through a back window.* **2** way or right of admittance or approach: *The avalanche cut off* access *to the mountain village. He had* access *to the records.* **3** an attack; fit: *an* access *of coughing.*

ac·ces·si·ble (ăk sĕs′ ə bəl) ***adj-*** easy to get at, reach, obtain, talk to, etc.: *an* accessible *mountain village*; accessible *public documents*; *an* accessible *man.* ***—adv-*** **ac·ces′ si·bly.**

ac·ces·sion (ăk sĕsh′ ən) ***n-*** **1** the act of coming to an office, dignity, or a throne: *the* accession *of a king.* **2** increase, as of wealth; addition: *the zoo's* accession *of a black leopard.*

ac·ces·so·ry (ăk sĕs′ ə rē) ***adj-*** aiding in a secondary way; contributory; additional: *an* accessory *fund*; *an* accessory *act.* ***n-*** [*pl.* **ac·ces·so·ries**] **1** something which is not essential but adds to the usefulness or appearance of machines, dress, etc.: *automobile* accessories. **2** (also spelled **accessary**) in law, a person who is not at the scene of a crime but who contributes to its commission, called an **accessory before the fact,** or one who knowingly conceals the crime or helps the criminal escape, called an **accessory after the fact.**

ac·ci·dent (ăk′ sə dənt) ***n-*** **1** something unexpected or unplanned: *Meeting him yesterday was a lucky* accident. **2** unintentional happening resulting in loss, injury, or death: *The road* accident *took several lives. The bridge was completed without* accident.

by accident by chance or coincidence: *I found it* by accident.

ac·ci·den·tal (ăk′ sə dĕn′ təl) ***adj-*** happening unintentionally or by chance: *an* accidental *discovery of oil.* ***n-*** *Music* a sharp, flat, or natural sign showing that a note is to be raised or lowered by a half tone; also, the note itself. ***—adv-*** **ac′ ci·den′ tal·ly.**

accident insurance ***n-*** insurance that pays for personal injuries or death due to accidents.

ac·claim (ə klām′) ***vt-*** to praise; shout approval; pay tribute to: *All the newspapers* acclaimed *the explorers for their bravery.* ***n-*** applause; show of approval or praise: *They greeted the winner with loud* acclaim.

ac·cla·ma·tion (ăk′ lə mā′ shən) ***n-*** a shout or other demonstration of approval. ***Hom-*** acclimation.

by acclamation by loud shouts and without taking a vote: *elected* by acclamation.

ac·cli·mate (ăk′ lə māt′, ə klī′ mət) ***vi-*** [**ac·cli·mat·ed, ac·cli·mat·ing**] to become accustomed (to) or physically able to live in an unfamiliar place, climate, etc.; adapt (to): *The dogs* acclimated *quickly to the colder country.* ***vt-***: *Tom* acclimated *himself readily to the new town. The botanists* acclimated *the wheat to the drier region.*

ac·cli·ma·tion (ăk′ lə mā′ shən) ***n-*** an acclimating; adapting or accustoming to a certain place or set of conditions. ***Hom-*** acclamation.

ac·cli·ma·tize (ə klī′ mə tīz′) ***vi-*** [**ac·cli·ma·tized, ac·cli·ma·tiz·ing**] to become acclimated. ***vt-***: *They* acclimatized *the plants to the dry region.* ***—n-*** **ac·cli′ ma·ti·za′ tion.**

ac·co·lade (ăk′ ə lād′) ***n-*** **1** something that shows praise, recognition, or respect; an honor; award: *The highest* accolade *in the American movies is the Oscar.* **2** the ceremony for admitting to knighthood, formerly an embrace or a kiss, now a light tap on the shoulder with the flat of a sword.

ac·com·mo·date (ə kŏm′ ə dāt′) ***vt-*** [**ac·com·mo·dat·ed, ac·com·mo·dat·ing**] **1** to have room for: *The hotel room will* accommodate *two guests.* **2** to oblige; help out: *He will* accommodate *me with the use of his car.* **3** to adjust (oneself to): *He* accommodated *himself to his circumstances.* ***vi-*** to become adjusted: *The eye* accommodates *to light.*

ac·com·mo·dat·ing (ə kŏm′ ə dā′ tĭng) ***adj-*** obliging; courteous: *An* accommodating *host sees to the needs of his guests.* ***—adv-*** **ac·com′ mo·dat′ ing·ly.**

ac·com·mo·da·tion (ə kŏm′ ə dā′ shən) ***n-*** **1** convenience: *The hotel has a restaurant for the* accommodation *of its guests.* **2** a fitting or adjusting of one thing to another: *the* accommodation *of the eye to distances*; *the* accommodation *of one's plans to those of another.* **3** something done or given in order to oblige: *That $10.00 loan was an* accommodation. **4** (usually **accommodations**) lodging, or food and lodging: *They finally found* accommodations *at a motel.*

ac·com·pa·ni·ment (ə kŭm′ pə nĭ mənt) ***n-*** **1** something that naturally goes with something else: *Fever is an* accompaniment *of most diseases.* **2** music to support instruments, voice, or dance: *a drum* accompaniment *to a dance.*

ac·com·pa·nist (ə kŭm′ pə nĭst) ***n-*** musician who supplies an accompaniment.

ac·com·pa·ny (ə kŭm′ pə nē) ***vt-*** [**ac·com·pa·nied, ac·com·pa·ny·ing**] **1** to go along with; escort: *Father will* accompany *us to the concert.* **2** to be or to happen together with: *Wind* accompanied *the rain.* **3** to play or sing accompaniment to another: *Ted* accompanied *the singer on the guitar.*

ac·com·plice (ə kŏm′ plĭs) ***n-*** person who aids another in a crime or wrongdoing.

ac·com·plish (ə kŏm′ plĭsh) ***vt-*** to carry out; complete; finish: *to* accomplish *a task.*

ac·com·plished (ə kŏm′ plĭsht) ***adj-*** **1** completed; carried out: *an* accomplished *task.* **2** perfected by training; expert: *He is an* accomplished *musician.*

ac·com·plish·ment (ə kŏm′ plĭsh mənt) ***n-*** **1** a carrying into effect or completion; doing: *the* accomplishment *of a purpose.* **2** a skill or excellence, especially one acquired by training: *Singing and dancing were among the many* accomplishments *of the actress.* **3** achievement; something carried out with skill and knowledge: *Columbus's first voyage was a remarkable* accomplishment.

ac·cord (ə kòrd′, -kôrd′) ***vi-*** to agree or be in harmony (with): *He gets along with them because his ideas* accord *with theirs.* ***vt-*** to grant: *We* accord *praise to those who deserve it.* ***n-*** agreement showing harmony of ideas, especially between nations: *France and England reached an* accord *over certain tariffs.*

in accord in agreement or harmony: *His statement is not* in accord *with the facts.* **of (one's) own accord** without being asked.

ac·cord·ance (ə kòr′ dəns, ə kôr′ -) ***n-*** agreement: *carried out in* accordance *with instructions.*

ac·cord·ing (ə kòr′ dĭng, ə kôr′ -) ***adj*** agreeing; harmonizing: *The three judges delivered* according *decisions.*

according to 1 in agreement with: *The game was played* according to *the rules.* **2** in proportion to: *Give* according to *your ability.* **3** on the authority of; as indicated by: *We turn right,* according to *the map.*

ac·cord·ing·ly (ə kŏr′dĭng lē, ə kôr′-) *adv-* 1 in agreement with what is expected; correspondingly: *Observe the situation carefully and act* accordingly. 2 therefore; so: *He felt unwell and,* accordingly, *left.*

ac·cor·di·on (ə kŏr′dē ən, ə kôr′-) *n-* portable musical instrument having a keyboard, bellows, and metal reeds. The bellows are stretched and squeezed to force air through reeds selected by pressing the right keys. *adj-* folded or pleated like the bellows of an accordion: *a skirt's* accordion *pleats.*

Accordion

ac·cost (ə kŏst′) *vt-* to speak to first; address: *A beggar* accosted *me.*

ac·count (ə kount′) *n-* 1 a written or oral report (or an event, person, etc.), especially a factual and objective report; record; narrative: *an* account *of the accident*; *an* account *of animal life in Africa.* 2 a reason or cause for an event, etc.; explanation: *Give me an* account *for your behavior.* 3 financial record, such as of money paid out or received, owed, etc.: *the* accounts *of a business*; *a bank* account; *a charge* account. 4 customer; client: *The company lost three* accounts *last year. vt-* to consider; think; judge; deem: *Einstein is often* accounted *the greatest modern scientist.*

by all accounts from all that has been said or written: *It seems,* by all accounts, *Wallace was a close rival of Darwin.* **call (someone) to account** to ask (someone) to explain the reasons for his behavior. **give a good account of (oneself)** to perform in a satisfactory manner: *He* gave a good account of himself *under fire.* **of no account** having little or no use; worthless: *His advice was* of no account. **on account** of a purchase, charged to one's account; not paid for in cash: *Jim bought his furniture* on account. **on account of** because of: *We could not work in the fields* on account of *the rain.* **take into account** or **take account of** 1 to consider; pay attention to; notice: *Let us* take into account *their heroism.* 2 to allow for; make allowance for: *Before building his house, Mr. Frank* took into account *the increased cost of materials.* **turn to good account** to make useful or profitable: *He* turned *even his unhappy experiences* to good account.

account for 1 to explain; give satisfactory reasons for: *We must* account for *every dollar spent. How do you* account for *your lateness?* 2 to be the cause of: *A dry spell* accounted for *the poor crops.* 3 to be responsible for killing, wounding, capturing, or destroying: *The bombers* accounted for *two factories in the raid.*

ac·count·a·ble (ə kount′ə bəl) *adj-* responsible; answerable (often in the phrase **hold accountable**): *He was held* accountable *for the accident.* —*n-* **ac·count′a·bil′i·ty.**

ac·count·ant (ə kount′ənt) *n-* 1 person who is employed to keep or examine financial records for a business or in a public office. 2 certified public accountant.

ac·count·ing (ə kount′ĭng) *n-* the work or profession of an accountant. *Barbara says that* accounting *is very interesting work.*

ac·cou·ter (ə ko͞o′tər) *vt-* to supply with dress and equipment, especially for military service; equip; outfit: *The regiment was* accoutered *for battle. Also* **ac·cou′tre.**

ac·cou·ter·ments (ə ko͞o′tər mənts) or **ac·cou·tre·ments** (ə ko͞o′trə mənts) *n- pl.* 1 accessory items of clothing or equipment, such as a handbag, umbrella, etc. 2 the equipment of a soldier other than clothes and weapons.

ac·cred·it (ə krĕd′ət) *vt-* 1 to send with letters of authority: *to* accredit *an ambassador to Spain.* 2 to accept or approve as true, up to standard, etc.: *to* accredit *a report*; *to* accredit *a college.*

ac·cre·tion (ə krē′shən) *n-* 1 increase in size by outside additions or natural growth; enlargement. 2 something added to another; addition: *an* accretion *of dirt.*

ac·crue (ə kro͞o′) *vi-* [**ac·crued, ac·cru·ing**] 1 to come or happen as a result of something: *Benefits* accrue *to society from better education.* 2 to increase in amount; accumulate: *Interest will* accrue *on my savings account.*

ac·cu·mu·late (ə kyo͞o′myə lāt′) *vt-* [**ac·cu·mu·lat·ed, ac·cu·mu·lat·ing**] to pile up; collect; gather: *Children* accumulate *many things in their pockets. vi-* to become greater in amount; increase: *Dust* accumulated *in every corner of the room.*

ac·cu·mu·la·tion (ə kyo͞o′myə lā′shən) *n-* 1 a growing by repeated additions: *the steady* accumulation *of interest.* 2 a collected mass: *an* accumulation *of odds and ends in the attic.*

ac·cu·mu·la·tive (ə kyo͞om′yə lā′tĭv) *adj-* tending to accumulate; resulting from accumulation; cumulative. —*adv-* **ac·cu′mu·la′tive·ly.** *n-* **ac·cu′mu·la′tive·ness.**

ac·cu·mu·la·tor (ə kyo͞om′yə lā′tər) *n-* 1 someone or something that collects, stores, or piles something up.

ac·cu·ra·cy (ăk′yə rə sē′) *n-* [*pl.* **ac·cu·ra·cies**] freedom from error or mistake; exactness: *I trust the* accuracy *of his story.*

ac·cu·rate (ăk′yə rət) *adj-* correct; exact: *an* accurate *report.* —*adv-* **ac′cu·rate·ly.**

ac·curs·ed (ə kûr′səd) or **ac·curst** (ə kûrst′) *adj-* 1 under a curse; ill-fated; doomed: *The poor man felt himself* accursed. 2 miserable; wretched; hateful: *his* accursed *poverty.*

ac·cu·sa·tion (ăk′yə zā′shən) *n-* a charge of wrongdoing: *The man denied the* accusation *that he was a thief.*

ac·cu·sa·tive (ə kyo͞o′zə tĭv′) *Grammar n-* 1 the objective case. 2 word in this case. *adj-*: *the* accusative *case.*

ac·cuse (ə kyo͞oz′) *vt-* [**ac·cused, ac·cus·ing**] to blame for wrongdoing or crime; bring a charge against.

ac·cused, the (ə kyo͞ozd′) *n-* the defendant or defendants in a criminal case.

ac·cus·tom (ə kŭs′təm) *vt-* to habituate (someone); make (someone) accept something as ordinary and routine (followed by "to"): *The job* accustomed *him to meeting many new people.*

ac·cus·tomed (ə kŭs′təmd) *adj-* habitual; usual: *People prefer to keep to their* accustomed *ways.*

accustomed to used to: *to be* accustomed to *cold.*

ace (ās) *n-* 1 card with a single mark indicating the suit; also the side of one of a pair of dice having a single spot. 2 flyer in an air force who has brought down at least five enemy planes. 3 an expert. 4 in tennis and some other sports, a point made on an unreturned serve. *adj-* first-class: *an* ace *athlete.*

Ace

a·cer·bi·ty (ə sûr′bə tē) *n-* 1 sharpness of speech, manner, temper, etc.; bitterness; harshness: *the* acerbity *of his remarks.* 2 acid taste; sourness.

ac·e·tate (ăs′ə tāt′) *n-* 1 *Chemistry* a salt or ester of acetic acid: *sodium* acetate. 2 cellulose acetate or any of its products, including acetate rayon and cellophane.

a·ce·tic (ə sē′tĭk) *adj-* sour; biting.

acetic acid ***n-*** colorless, sharp-smelling acid, compound of carbon, oxygen, and hydrogen (CH_3COOH). It is the acid in vinegar.

ac·e·tone (ăs′ə tōn) ***n-*** colorless, highly volatile, and flammable organic liquid used to remove paint, varnish, and nail polish, and as an industrial solvent.

a·cet·y·lene (ə sĕt′ə lēn′) ***n-*** colorless, flammable gas (C_2H_2) produced when calcium carbide is mixed with water. It is mixed with oxygen to make the fuel in oxyacetylene torches.

a·ce·tyl·sal·i·cyl·ic acid (ə sē′ təl săl′ə sĭl′ĭk) ***n-*** chemical name of aspirin.

A·chae·an (ə kē′ ən) ***adj-*** of or pertaining to Achaea or its people and culture. ***n-*** a native or inhabitant of Achaea. Also **A·cha′ian** (ə kā′ ən).

A·cha·tes (ə kā′ tēz) ***n-*** in Roman legend, the faithful friend of Aeneas.

ache (āk) ***n-*** steady pain. ***vi-*** **[ached, ach·ing] 1** to be in pain; suffer pain: *His back* ached *all day.* **2** *Informal* to wish very strongly; yearn; long: *He* ached *for his freedom.*

a·chieve (ə chēv′) ***vt-*** **[a·chieved, a·chiev·ing] 1** to accomplish; complete; carry out; do: *He* achieved *much in a short time.* **2** to attain; win; gain: *to* achieve *success.*

a·chieve·ment (ə chēv′ mənt) ***n-*** **1** something accomplished, especially by great effort or superior ability; feat: *The Hoover Dam is an engineering* achievement. **2** an attaining: *The* achievement *of skill takes practice.*

A·chil·les (ə kĭl′ ēz) ***n-*** in the "Iliad," the foremost Greek hero of the Trojan War.

Achilles tendon ***n-*** the strong tendon at the back of the ankle connecting the calf muscle with the heel.

ach·ro·mat·ic lens (ăk′rə măt′ĭk) ***n-*** compound lens made of two lenses of different glass, one of which corrects the chromatic aberration of the other so that, together, they produce an image nearly free from fringes of color.

ac·id (ăs′ əd) ***n-*** *Chemistry* sour substance that reacts with bases to form water and a salt, and turns blue litmus paper red. ***adj-*** **1** sour: *the* acid *taste of vinegar.* **2** biting; sarcastic: *an* acid *comment.*

►Should not be confused with ACRID.

a·cid·ic (ə sĭd′ĭk) ***adj-*** containing or forming acid.

a·cid·i·fy (ə sĭd′ə fī′) ***vi-*** **[a·cid·i·fied, a·cid·i·fy·ing]** to become acid. ***vt-*** **1** to change or convert (something) into an acid. **2** to make acid.

a·cid·i·ty (ə sĭd′ə tē) ***n-*** **1** sourness. **2** amount of acid in something.

a·cid·ly (ăs′ əd lē) ***adv-*** in a sour, sharp, or cutting manner: *to speak* acidly.

ac·i·do·sis (ăs′ə dō′ səs) ***n-*** condition in which the blood is more than normally acidic.

acid test ***n-*** a final or crucial test to determine worth, quality, genuineness, etc.: *The race was her* acid test.

ac·knowl·edge (ĭk nŏl′əj, ăk-) ***vt-*** **[ac·knowl·edged, ac·knowl·edg·ing] 1** to admit or recognize as being true, genuine, legal, etc.: *I* acknowledge *my faults. The court* acknowledged *his claim to the property.* **2** to recognize and honor (a person) publicly: *The nation* acknowledged *him their leader.* **3** to make known the receipt or appreciation of: *Fred* acknowledged *the letter yesterday. The speaker* acknowledged *the applause with a grin.*

ac·knowl·edg·ment or **ac·knowl·edge·ment** (ăk nŏl′əj mənt) ***n-*** **1** an admitting or recognizing that something is true, real, legal, etc.: *an* acknowledgment *of guilt.* **2** recognition: *The company gave Mr. Jones a medal in* acknowledgment *of his long service.* **3** thing or sign showing receipt or appreciation of something.

ac·me (ăk′ mē) ***n-*** the highest point; perfection: *His dancing was the* acme *of grace.*

ac·ne (ăk′ nē) ***n-*** pimples caused by swollen and infected oil glands under the skin.

ac·o·lyte (ăk′ə līt′) ***n-*** **1** one who assists a minister or priest in a church service; altar boy. **2** in the Roman Catholic Church, a member of an order next below a subdeacon.

ac·o·nite (ăk′ ə nīt′) ***n-*** **1** the plant monkshood. **2** poisonous drug from this plant used in medicine.

a·corn (ā′ kôrn′, -kôrn′) ***n-*** the fruit of the oak, a nut with its base set in a woody cup.

Acorn

a·cous·ti·cal (ə ko͞o′ stĭ kəl) ***adj-*** **1** relating to sound. **2** having special qualities for transmitting or absorbing sound: *an* acoustical *panel.* Also **a·cous′tic.** ***—adv-*** **a·cous′ti·cal·ly.**

a·cous·tics (ə ko͞o′ stĭks) ***n-*** **1** (takes singular verb) the science of sound. **2** (takes plural verb) the properties of auditoriums, concert halls, etc., that determine how well sound is heard in them.

ac·quaint (ə kwānt′) ***vt-*** to make familiar: *I* acquainted *the new clerk with his duties.*

ac·quaint·ance (ə kwān′ təns) ***n-*** **1** person known slightly: *He is an* acquaintance, *not a close friend.* **2** knowledge from experience or contact: *I have a close* acquaintance *with the facts.*

ac·quaint·ed (ə kwān′ təd) ***adj-*** known to one another: *We have been* acquainted *for many years.*

be acquainted with to have personal knowledge of; be familiar with: *I* am acquainted with *the work.*

ac·qui·esce (ăk′wē ĕs′) ***vi-*** **[ac·qui·esced, ac·qui·esc·ing]** to give consent by remaining silent: *He* acquiesced *in our plans.* ***—n-*** **ac′qui·es′cence.** ***adj-*** **ac′qui·es′cent.** ***adv-*** **ac′qui·es′cent·ly.**

ac·quire (ə kwīər′) ***vt-*** **[ac·quired, ac·quir·ing]** to get; gain; come by: *to* acquire *land; to* acquire *skill in running; to* acquire *good taste.*

ac·quire·ment (ə kwīər′ ment) ***n-*** **1** a receiving or gaining, especially of nonmaterial possessions: *the* acquirement *of knowledge.* **2** that which is gained, as a skill, taste, reputation, etc.: *One of her recent* acquirements *is a knowledge of French.*

ac·qui·si·tion (ăk′wə zĭsh′ ən) ***n-*** **1** a receiving or gaining, especially of material possessions: *the* acquisition *of wealth.* **2** that which is received or gained, as money, land, etc.: *This land is a recent* acquisition.

ac·quis·i·tive (ə kwĭz′ ə tĭv′) ***adj-*** having a strong desire or tendency to collect and to own, especially material things: *a greedy,* acquisitive *person.* ***—adv-*** **ac·quis′i·tive′ly.** ***n-*** **ac·quis′i·tive′ness.**

ac·quit (ə kwĭt′) ***vt-*** **[ac·quit·ted, ac·quit·ting] 1** to set free from a charge of crime; declare (someone) not guilty: *The jury* acquitted *the man.* **2** to behave or conduct (oneself); to do one's part: *The new player* acquitted *herself well in the soccer game.*

ac·quit·tal (ə kwĭt′əl) ***n-*** in law, a setting free of a defendant by a court.

a·cre (ā′ kər) ***n-*** unit used in measuring land. An acre is about the area of a square field 208 feet on each side.

a·cre·age (ā′ kər ĭj) ***n-*** land measured in acres.

ac·rid (ăk′ rĭd) ***adj-*** sharp, bitter, or biting in taste, smell, tone, manner, etc.: *the* acrid *smell of wood smoke; the* acrid *tone of the debate.* ***—adv-*** **ac′rid·ly.**

►Should not be confused with ACID.

ac·ri·mo·ni·ous (ăk′rə mō′ nē əs) ***adj-*** sharp and biting; stinging; cutting: *the speaker's* acrimonious *words.* ***—adv-*** **ac′ri·mo′ni·ous·ly.** ***n-*** **ac′ri·mo′ni·ous·ness.**

ac·ri·mo·ny (ăk′ rə mō′nē) ***n-*** bitterness or sharpness, as of temper or speech.

ac·ro·bat (ăk′rə băt) ***n-*** person who does daring and skillful exercises or stunts requiring great physical agility, such as walking a tightrope.

ac·ro·bat·ic (ăk′rə băt′ĭk) ***adj-*** of or suggesting an acrobat. **—*adv-* ac′ro·bat′i·cal·ly.**

ac·ro·bat·ics (ăk′rə băt′ĭks) ***n-*** **1** (takes singular verb) the feats or tricks of an acrobat. **2** (takes plural verb) any difficult or tricky performances: *mental* acrobatics.

ac·ro·nym (ăk′rə nĭm′) ***n-*** word formed from the initial letters or syllables of other words. "Radar" is an acronym of *ra*dio *d*etection *a*nd *r*anging.

a·cro·po·lis (ə krŏp′ə lĭs) ***n-*** **1** highest part of an old Greek city, used as a fortress; citadel. **2 the Acropolis** the citadel of Athens.

a·cross (ə krŏs′) ***prep-*** (in sense 1 considered an adverb when the object is clearly implied but not expressed) **1** from one side to the other side of: *We walked* across *the park.* **2** lying along the short dimension of; crosswise on: *A tree was* across *the path.* **3** over or on top of, so as to cross: *Put the red wire* across *the blue wire.* **4** on the other side of; beyond: *They live* across *the ocean.*

come (or **run**) **across** to meet with or find unexpectedly: *I* came across *an interesting book yesterday.*
put (or **get**) **across** to make understandable or acceptable: *Did you* put *your point* across?

a·cros·tic (ə krŏs′tĭk) ***n-*** **1** an arrangement of words in which initial or other letters, when taken in order, form words or phrases. **2** an arrangement of letters that form the same words when read horizontally or vertically.

act (ăkt) ***n-*** **1** a thing done; deed; action: *an* act *of kindness*; *an* act *of mercy.* **2** one of the main divisions of a play or opera: *the third* act *of "Othello."* **3** one of the segments of a variety show, circus, etc.: *a dog* act. **4** a show of false behavior; pretense: *He isn't really friendly; it's all an* act. *He put on an* act *to get out of work.* **5 Act** a law; decree; edict: *an* Act *of Congress.* **6 Acts** or **Acts of the Apostles** the fifth book of the New Testament. ***vt-*** **1** to perform (a role in a play, movie, etc.); play: *to* act *the king in "Hamlet."* **2** to behave in a manner befitting: *Please* act *your age. Don't* act *the fool.* ***vi-*** **1** to do something; carry out a function: *He* acted *quickly to save the child. This drug takes time to* act. **2** to behave; conduct oneself: *He knows how to* act *at a party.* **3** to pretend; feign: *He wasn't sick; he was just* acting. **4** to perform on stage; play a role: *He* acted *well in "Hamlet."*

act as to do the work of; serve as: *He* acted as *interpreter. The drug* acts as *a stimulant.*
act for to represent someone; to do service in someone's behalf: *My lawyer* acts for *me in my absence.*
act on (or **upon**) **1** to follow; obey: *They* acted on *my suggestion.* **2** to have an effect on: *The acid* acted on *the metal.*
act up *Informal* to behave mischievously or playfully: *The children* acted up *as soon as we left.*

ACTH (ā′sē′tē′āch′) ***n-*** hormone secreted by the pituitary gland. It stimulates the secretion of cortisone by the adrenal glands.

act·ing (ăk′tĭng) ***n-*** **1** the art of performing on the stage or screen. **2** a pretending or feigning; pretense: *His* acting *fooled nobody.* ***adj-*** performing the duties of another; temporary: *the* acting *chairman.*

ac·tin·ic rays (ăk tĭn′ĭk) ***n-*** those portions of the sun's rays, including blue, green, violet, and ultraviolet rays, which are especially capable of producing chemical changes in many substances.

ac·tin·ism (ăk′tə nĭz′əm) ***n-*** the ability of visible and ultraviolet light to cause chemical changes.

ac·tin·i·um (ăk tĭn′ē əm) ***n-*** rare, radioactive metal element found in pitchblende and other uranium ores. Symbol Ac, At. No. 89, At. Wt. 227.

ac·ti·no·zo·an (ăk′tə nō zō′ən) ***n-*** any of a class **(Actinozoa)** of sea animals including the sea anemones and corals.

ac·tion (ăk′shən) ***n-*** **1** the doing of something; a deed: *a kind* action. **2** energetic motion or activity: *The adventure story was packed with* action. **3** the effect of one body or substance upon another: *the* action *of sunlight on plants.* **4** lawsuit. **5** the effective or acting part of a mechanism: *the* action *of a rifle.* **6** the progress of events, as in a play. **7** battle: *injured in* action.

ac·ti·vate (ăk′tə vāt′) ***vt-*** **[ac·ti·vat·ed, ac·ti·vat·ing]** **1** to start an action or process. **2** to make something ready for an action or process: *to* activate *a reserve army unit.* **3** *Chemistry* to cause a reaction to start or to make a substance reactive, more reactive, or adsorptive. **—*n-* ac′ti·va′tion.**

ac·tive (ăk′tĭv) ***adj-*** **1** lively; vigorous: *an* active *mind.* **2** energetic; moving about a good deal: *Children are more* active *in the morning than at night.* **3** capable of action; not dormant: *an* active *chemical*; *an* active *volcano.* **4** in present use: *an* active *file.* **5** taking full part in: *an* active *member of an organization.* **6** *Grammar* of a verb, in the active voice (see *active voice*). **—*adv-* ac′tive·ly. *n-* ac′tive·ness.**

active sun ***n-*** the sun during a period of time when the number of sunspots, solar flares, etc., is observed to be at a maximum. See also *quiet sun.*

active voice *Grammar* ***n-*** form of a transitive verb or verb phrase which shows that the subject of the sentence is performing the action. Examples: *The teacher* scolded *the boy for his insolence. John* has lost *his hat.* See also *passive voice.*

ac·tiv·ist (ăk′tə vĭst′) ***n-*** one who very vigorously promotes and works for a cause, especially a political one. ***adj-***: *the* activist *attitudes of many college students.*

ac·tiv·i·ty (ăk tĭv′ə tē) ***n-*** [*pl.* **ac·tiv·i·ties**] **1** movement; action: *physical and mental* activity. **2** liveliness: *There is much* activity *at the zoo at feeding time.* **3** (usually **activities**) things done regularly by a club, group, etc.: *classroom* activities; *church* activities.

act of God ***n-*** in law, an event that could not possibly have been foreseen, prevented, or controlled by a human being: *The flood was termed an* act of God.

ac·tor (ăk′tər) ***n-*** person who performs or takes the part of a character in a stage play, motion picture, or broadcast. **—*n-* *fem.* ac′tress.**

ac·tu·al (ăk′chōō əl) ***adj-*** real; not imaginary: *Davy Crockett was an* actual *person.*

ac·tu·al·i·ty (ăk′chōō ăl′ə tē) ***n-*** [*pl.* **ac·tu·al·i·ties**] **1** real existence; reality; fact: *In* actuality, *the battle never took place.* **2** a real thing or condition: *The plan never became an* actuality.

ac·tu·al·ly (ăk′chōō ə lē) ***adv-*** really; in fact: *Did you* actually *build this beautiful table?*

ac·tu·ar·y (ăk′chōō ĕr′ē) ***n-*** [*pl.* **ac·tu·ar·ies**] person who calculates risks and premiums for an insurance company.

ac·tu·ate (ăk′chōō āt′) ***vt-*** **[ac·tu·at·ed, ac·tu·at·ing]** **1** to put into motion or action; to start: *to* actuate *a mechanism.* **2** to influence or incite; motivate; impel: *He was* actuated *by ambition.*

---

a·cu·men (ə kyōō′ mən) ***n-*** keenness of understanding or insight; mental sharpness: *His business* acumen *made him rich.*

ac·u·punc·ture (ăk′ yōō pŭngk′chər) ***n-*** originally a Chinese practice of inserting needles into certain parts of the body to relieve pain and treat diseases.

a·cute (ə kyōōt′) ***adj-*** **1** keen; alert: *an* acute *sense of hearing; an* acute *observer of facts.* **2** sharp and intense: *an* acute *pang of hunger; an* acute *sense of pleasure.* **3** of a disease, coming on suddenly and reaching a crisis quickly: *an attack of* acute *appendicitis.* **4** very important; critical; crucial: *an* acute *stage of an illness; an* acute *shortage.* ***—adv-*** **a·cute′ly.** ***n-*** **a·cute′ness.**

acute accent ***n-*** accent mark [′] that is placed over a vowel to indicate its sound, as in French "café."

acute angle ***n-*** angle whose measure is less than 90° and greater than 0°. For picture, see *angle.*

ad (ăd) ***n-*** advertisement. ***Hom-*** add.

ad- *prefix* to; toward: *to* ad*join; to* ad*mix.* Also **a-** before "sc," "sp," or "st"; **ab-** before "b"; **ac-** before "c" or "q"; **af-** before "f"; **ag-** before "g"; **al-** before "l"; **an-** before "n"; **ap-** before "p"; **ar-** before "r"; **as-** before "s"; **at-** before "t". [from Latin **ad** meaning "toward" or "near."]

A.D. in the year of our Lord; after the birth of Christ [from Latin **anno Domini**].

ad·age (ăd′ ĭj) ***n-*** a pointed and well-known saying; a proverb. "Waste not, want not" is an adage.

a·da·gio (ə dä′ zhō, -jē ō) *Music* ***adj- & adv-*** slow; faster than lento but slower than andante.

Ad·am (ăd′ əm) ***n-*** the first man in the Bible story of the Creation.

ad·a·mant (ăd′ ə mənt, -mănt′) ***n-*** mythical rock as hard as the diamond and assumed to be magnetic. ***adj-*** hard; unyielding: *Once he had made his decision, he was* adamant. ***—adv-*** **ad′a·mant·ly.**

ad·a·man·tine (ăd′ə măn′tēn, -tīn) ***adj-*** **1** extremely hard and unyielding: *his* adamantine *resistance to political pressures.* **2** like a diamond in hardness or luster: *an* adamantine *mineral.*

Adam's apple ***n-*** a cartilage forming the forepart of the human voice box, or larynx, noticeable, especially in men, as an enlargement in the front of the throat.

a·dapt (ə dăpt′) ***vt-*** to change (a person or thing) so as to fit new conditions or uses; make suitable; adjust: *to* adapt *oneself to new circumstances; to* adapt *a novel to the movies.* ***vi-*** of living things, to undergo a change in physical structure or habit in adjustment to a change in the environment: *Cats* adapt *to hot weather by shedding.*
►Should not be confused with ADOPT.

a·dapt·a·ble (ə dăp′tə bəl) ***adj-*** **1** easily changed to fit new situations: *an* adaptable *schedule.* **2** capable of changing easily to meet new situations; flexible: *an* adaptable *person.* ***—n-*** **a·dapt′a·bil′i·ty** or **a·dapt′a·ble·ness.**

ad·ap·ta·tion (ăd′əp tā′shən) ***n-*** **1** a changing to fit different conditions: *He found* adaptation *to the hot climate difficult.* **2** something produced by a process of changing and arranging: *The play was a successful* adaptation *of the novel.* **3** *Biology* permanent change in the bodies or the habits of living things which helps them to survive and reproduce in a different environment; also, the result of such a change: *The webbed foot of a duck is an* adaptation *for swimming.*

a·dap·ted (ə dăp′təd) ***adj-*** suitable, fitted.

a·dapt·er (ə dăp′tər) ***n-*** **1** person who adapts something: *an* adapter *of stories for TV.* **2** any device used to make something suitable for another use, or to connect different-sized things such as pipes of different diameters.

add (ăd) ***vt-*** **1** to sum up (numbers). **2** to join or unite (to): *to* add *water to flour; to* add *books to a library; to* add *insult to injury.* **3** to say or write further: *"And don't go swimming alone," she* added. ***vi-*** **1** in arithmetic, to sum up numbers; total: *He* adds *correctly, but he cannot divide.* **2** to be or make an addition (to): *His father's illness* added *to his troubles.* ***Hom-*** ad.

add up **1** to make the total expected: *These numbers don't* add up. **2** *Informal* to make sense; be sound or reasonable: *His remarks just don't* add up.

ad·dend (ăd′ĕnd′, ə dĕnd′) ***n-*** number added to another number. In the example 2 + 5 = 7, both 2 and 5 are addends.

ad·der (ăd′ər) ***n-*** any of various snakes of different parts of the world, including the common European adder and the puff adder of Africa, both poisonous, and several harmless American snakes.

ad·dict (ăd′ ĭkt) ***n-*** person completely given over to a habit: *a drug* addict.

ad·dict·ed (ə dĭk′ təd) ***adj-*** given over (to a habit or activity); habituated (to): *to be* addicted *to drugs;* addicted *to gossip.*

ad·dic·tion (ə dĭk′shən) ***n-*** **1** state of being a slave to a habit. **2** compulsive physical need for a habit-forming drug such as heroin. ***—adj-*** **ad·dic′tive.**

Ad·di·son's disease (ăd′ə sənz) ***n-*** a darkening of the skin and wasting of the muscles due to damage to the cortex of the adrenal glands.

ad·di·tion (ə dĭsh′ ən) ***n-*** **1** process involving two or more numbers which produces their sum. Examples: 5 + 7 = 12; 3 + 3 + 6 = 12; 24 + 35 + 53 = 112. **2** the adding or joining of one thing to another: *the* addition *of a gymnasium to the school.* **3** something that is added or joined: *an* addition *to a house.*

in addition to as well as; besides: *He works* in addition to *going to school.*

ad·di·tion·al (ə dĭsh′ən əl) ***adj-*** extra; more: *to need* additional *income.* ***—adv-*** **ad·di′tion·al·ly.**

ad·di·tive (ăd′ə tĭv′) ***n-*** chemical substance added in small quantities to something for a special purpose: *Most gasoline contains* additives *to prevent engine knocking.*

ad·dle (ăd′ əl) ***vt-*** **[ad·dled, ad·dling]** **1** to confuse (one's mind); muddle. **2** to spoil (an egg). ***vi-:*** *His mind* addles *whenever he faces that subject. Those eggs have* addled.

¹ad·dress (ăd′drĕs′) ***n-*** place in which a person or group lives, works, etc.; also, the name and destination written on a letter or package.

²ad·dress (ə drĕs′) ***vt-*** **1** to speak or write to: *They* addressed *the man politely.* **2** to place the destination on (a letter, package, etc.). ***n-*** **1** a speech, especially a formal one: *The President delivered an* address *to Congress.* **2** manner and bearing; deportment: *Franklin D. Roosevelt was a man of remarkable* address. **3** skill and tact: *He managed the difficult affair with admirable* address.

address (oneself) to to apply (oneself) to: *He* addressed himself to *the task with great energy.*

ad·dress·ee (ăd′rĕs′ē′) ***n-*** one to whom a letter or a package is directed.

ad·duce (ə dōōs′, -dyōōs′) ***vt-*** **[ad·duced, ad·duc·ing]** to present or offer as a reason, proof, or evidence; cite as an example: *To prove his point, the lawyer* adduced *a previous decision.*
►Should not be confused with EDUCE.

ad·e·noids (ăd′ ə noidz′) ***n-*** *pl.* an abnormal swelling of the spongy glandular tissue (**adenoid tissue**) in the passage leading from the nose to the throat. Adenoids often make breathing difficult.

Adenoids

[1]**a·dept** (ə dĕpt′) ***adj-*** highly skilled; expert: *John is* adept *at repairing things about the house.* **—*adv-*** **a·dept′ ly.** ***n-*** **a·dept′ ness.**

[2]**a·dept** (ăd′ ĕpt′) ***n-*** one who is fully proficient or skilled in an art; an expert: *He is an* adept *at swimming and diving.*

ad·e·qua·cy (ăd′ ə kwə sē) ***n-*** the condition of being sufficient or suitable for what is needed: *We doubt the* adequacy *of his training.*

ad·e·quate (ăd′ ə kwət) ***adj-*** sufficient; suitable; fit: *The lawyer presented* adequate *proof of his client's innocence.* **—*adv-*** **ad′ e·quate·ly.** ***n-*** **ad′ e·quate·ness.**

ad·here (əd hêr′, ăd-) ***vi-*** **[ad·hered, ad·her·ing] 1** to stick fast, as if glued: *Gum* adheres *to your fingers.* **2** to be attached or devoted (to); give steady support (to): *to* adhere *to a political party*; *to* adhere *to a religious creed.* **3** to follow closely; hold firmly (to): *to* adhere *to the blueprints.*

ad·her·ence (əd hêr′ əns, ăd-) ***n-*** a sticking fast (to); close following or attachment (to): *He declared again his* adherence *to the cause of freedom.*

ad·her·ent (əd hêr′ ənt, ăd-) ***n-*** a follower or supporter, as of a party, leader, cult, etc. ***adj-*** sticking fast: *We scraped the hull to remove the* adherent *barnacles.*

ad·he·sion (əd hē′ zhən, ăd-) ***n-*** **1** the condition of sticking fast to something. **2** *Medicine* an abnormal joining together in the body of tissues that are normally separate.

ad·he·sive (əd hē′ sĭv, ăd-) ***adj-*** sticking fast or causing to stick: *an* adhesive *tape.* ***n-*** sticky substance used to hold things together: *Paste, glue, and sealing wax are* adhesives.

adhesive tape ***n-*** white tape having a sticky coating on one side and used to hold dressings on wounds, bind injured parts, etc. Also **adhesive plaster.**

ad hoc (ăd′ hŏk′) *Latin* for a specific or particular thing, purpose, etc.; not general; special: *an* ad hoc *committee.*

a·di·a·bat·ic (ăd′ ē ə băt′ ĭk) ***adj-*** without gain or loss in the total amount of heat possessed: *Some chemical reactions are* adiabatic.

a·dieu (ə dyōō′, ə dōō′) ***interj-*** farewell; good-by. ***n-*** [*pl.* **a·dieus, a·dieux** (ə dyōōz′)]: *He made his* adieus *and left.* [from French **adieu.**] ***Hom-*** ado.

ad in·fi·ni·tum (ăd′ ĭn′ fə nī′ təm) *Latin* without limit; endlessly.

a·di·os (ä′ dē ōs′) ***interj-*** good-by. [American word from Spanish **adiós,** from earlier **a Dios** meaning "(I entrust you) to God."]

ad·i·pose (ăd′ ə pōs′) ***adj-*** fatty; having to do with fat.

adj. adjective.

Adj. Adjutant.

ad·ja·cent (ə jā′ sənt) ***adj-*** **1** lying close (to); next (to); near; adjoining: *a house* adjacent *to the church.* **2** *Mathematics* designating either or both of two angles with a common vertex and a common side between. **—*adv-*** **ad·ja′ cent·ly.**

ad·jec·tiv·al (ăj′ ək tī′ vəl) ***adj-*** **1** of or relating to adjectives. **2** modifying a noun: *an* adjectival *phrase.* ***n-*** phrase or clause which can modify a noun. Examples: *The picture* on the wall *was a great work* of art. *The dog* that he had on the leash *was a collie* with very long hair. **—*adv-*** **ad′ jec·ti′ val·ly.**

ad·jec·tive (ăj′ ək tĭv′) *Grammar* ***n-*** **1** a word that can modify a noun and may be used in the blank spaces in both the following patterns:

The book seems__________.

I want the__________book.

The words "red," "heavy," "easy," "beautiful," "exciting," etc., can be used in both spaces. They are adjectives. **2** one of a special group of words beginning with "a-," such as "asleep," "ajar," "akin," "afloat," or "askew."

Most adjectives can be used to compare, either by adding the "-er" or "-est" ending or the words "more" or "most" in front of them.

That's a dull *play.*

I never saw a duller *play.*

That's the dullest *play I've ever seen.*

It's a beautiful (exciting, etc.) *painting.*

This painting is more beautiful (exciting, etc.) *than that one.*

That's the most beautiful (exciting, etc.) *painting I've ever seen.*

ad·join (ə join′) ***vt-*** to be so near as to touch; be next to: *Canada* adjoins *the United States.* ***vi-***: *Canada and the United States* adjoin.

ad·journ (ə jûrn′) ***vt-*** **1** to put off or suspend (a meeting, session, decision, etc.) to a later time or to another place: *The judge* adjourned *the court until the following day. The chairman* adjourned *the meeting to the large conference room.* **2** to end (a meeting or session) officially. ***vi-***: *The court* adjourned *for three days. The meeting* adjourned *at 10 o'clock.*

ad·journ·ment (ə jûrn′ mənt) ***n-*** **1** a putting off or suspension of a meeting, session, decision, etc., to a later time or another place. **2** the time or period during which this is in effect.

ad·judge (ə jŭj′) ***vt-*** **[ad·judged, ad·judg·ing] 1** to decide (a dispute) according to law; hence, to declare or sentence by law: *The defendant was* adjudged *insane.* **2** to award or grant by law: *The estate was* adjudged *to him.*

ad·junct (ăj′ ŭngkt′) ***n-*** something added to another thing, but not a necessary part of it: *A lean-to is an* adjunct *of a house.*

ad·jure (ə jŏŏr′) ***vt-*** **[ad·jured, ad·jur·ing]** to charge solemnly, as if under oath; entreat earnestly: *I* adjure *you to tell the truth.* **—*n-*** **ad′ ju·ra′ tion.**

ad·just (ə jŭst′) ***vt-*** **1** to make mechanical changes so that parts fit or work together properly; regulate: *The mechanic* adjusted *the fuel pump in the engine.* **2** to make or become suitable; fit: *to* adjust *the length of a coat.* **3** to adapt: *to* adjust *oneself to new circumstances.* **4** to settle: *to* adjust *differences in a quarrel*; *to* adjust *a claim.* ***vi-***: *After moving she found it hard to* adjust. **—*adj-*** **ad·just′ a·ble:** *an* adjustable *wrench.* ***n-*** **ad·just′ er** or **ad·jus′ tor.**

ad·just·ment (ə jŭst′ mənt) ***n-*** **1** an adjusting. **2** arrangement; settlement: *the* adjustment *of my insurance claim.*

ad·ju·tant (ăj′ ə tənt) ***n-*** an assistant; especially, in the army, a regimental staff officer who assists the commanding officer.

ad-lib (ăd′ lĭb′) ***vt-*** **[ad-libbed, ad-lib·bing]** to improvise (remarks, songs, etc.): *He* ad-libbed *a clever dance.*

vi-: *He* ad-libbed *for ten minutes.* *adj*-: *an* ad-lib *comment.*

ad lib (ăd′ lĭb′) *n*- a remark, joke, song, etc., that is unplanned and unexpected. *adv*- in a free, inventive manner; extemporaneously: *He talked* ad lib.

ad lib. or **ad libit.** ad libitum.

ad lib·i·tum (ăd′ lĭb′ ə təm) *Latin* freely; as you wish, used chiefly as a direction in music.

Adm. admiral.

ad·min·is·ter (əd mĭn′ əs tər, ăd-) *vt*- **1** to manage; look after; direct: *Mr. Perez* administers *the accounting department.* **2** to put (a law) into effect; execute. **3** to give, supply, or dispense in a formal or official way: *to* administer *an oath*; *to* administer *a drug*; *to* administer *the last rites.*

ad·min·is·tra·tion (əd mĭn′ ə strā′ shən, ăd-) *n*- **1** act of administering. **2** direction; management: *His* administration *of the government was honest.* **3** that part of the government which directs the business of a nation, state, or city. **4** the term of office of one Administration. **5 Administration** the President of the United States, the members of his cabinet, and the departments they run.

ad·min·is·tra·tive (əd mĭn′ ə strā′ tĭv, ăd-) *adj*- pertaining to the management of affairs, as of the government; executive.

ad·min·is·tra·tor (əd mĭn′ əs trā′ tər, ăd-) *n*- **1** one who manages, directs, or governs affairs. **2** one appointed legally to administer an estate; an executor.

ad·mi·ra·ble (ăd′ mər ə bəl) *adj*- worthy of wonder and approval; excellent: *His behavior during the emergency was* admirable. —*adv*- **ad′ mi·ra·bly.** *n*- **ad′ mi·ra·ble·ness.**

ad·mi·ral (ăd′ mər əl) *n*- **1** in the U.S. Navy and Coast Guard, a commissioned officer ranking next below an Admiral of the Fleet and next above a vice admiral. **2** a shortened form of address for a rear admiral, vice admiral, and Admiral of the Fleet.

Admiral of the Fleet *n*- in the U.S. Navy, the highest rank; also, a commissioned officer holding this rank.

ad·mi·ral·ty (ăd′ mə rəl tē) *n*- [*pl.* **ad·mi·ral·ties**] **1** in Great Britain, the department of government in charge of the Navy. **2** court having jurisdiction over laws of shipping.

ad·mi·ra·tion (ăd′ mə rā′ shən) *n*- **1** a feeling of wonder, delight, and approval: *our* admiration *for a great violinist.* **2** person or thing that is the object of such feelings: *He was the* admiration *of many young violinists.*

ad·mire (əd mīər′, ăd-) *vt*- [**ad·mired, ad·mir·ing**] **1** to look at with pleasure and wonder: *to* admire *a fine painting.* **2** to have a high opinion of; esteem: *to* admire *someone's good sense.*

ad·mir·er (əd mīər′ ər, ăd-) *n*- person who regards (someone or something) with approval, delight, or affection: *She has many* admirers.

ad·mis·si·ble (əd mĭs′ ə bəl, ăd-) *adj*- **1** worthy of being permitted to enter. **2** allowable; permissible: *This form of argument is not* admissible. —*adv*- **ad·mis′ si·bly.** *n*- **ad·mis′ si·bil′ i·ty.**

ad·mis·sion (əd mĭsh′ ən, ăd-) *n*- **1** permission to enter: *Free* admission *is limited to certain days.* **2** price paid in order to enter. **3** acceptance or appointment to a profession, group, etc.: *his* admission *to the bar.* **4** a saying that something is true; acknowledgment; confession: *an* admission *of his guilt.*

ad·mit (əd mĭt′) *vt*- [**ad·mit·ted, ad·mit·ting**] **1** to allow to enter; grant entrance to; let in: *The guard* admitted *Tom to the vault.* *The club* admitted *Bob last week.* **2** to accept as true, valid, genuine, etc; acknowledge; concede: *He* admitted *his guilt.* *I* admit *his right to differ.* **3** to allow; permit: *This plan* admits *no delays.* *vi*- to allow entrance: *This door* admits *to the main auditorium.*

admit of to permit; allow; afford the possibility of.

admit to to state as true; confess to: *He would not* admit to *having stolen the money.*

ad·mit·tance (əd mĭt′ əns, ăd-) *n*- **1** an entering or letting in; entrance: *They gained* admittance *through a back window.* **2** right or permission to enter: *Tom was denied* admittance *to the meeting.*

ad·mit·ted·ly (əd mĭt′ əd lē, ăd-) *adv*- by general consent; confessedly: *He was,* admittedly, *the thief.*

ad·mix (ăd mĭks′) *vt*- to mix into or with; blend.

ad·mix·ture (ăd mĭks′ chər) *n*- **1** the act of mixing; mingling. **2** something added to a mixture: *an* admixture *of common sense in a confused situation.*

ad·mon·ish (əd mŏn′ ĭsh, ăd-) *vt*- **1** to take to task; to reprove mildly: *The boys were* admonished *for their misbehavior.* **2** to warn; caution: *Ben* admonished *us not to sail far.*

ad·mo·ni·tion (ăd′ mə nĭsh′ ən) *n*- an admonishing; warning.

ad·mon·i·to·ry (əd mŏn′ ə tôr′ ē, ăd-) *adj*- expressing gentle or friendly warning or reproof: *John's father stopped him with an* admonitory *word.*

a·do (ə do͞o′) *n*- fuss; bustle; stir: *There was much* ado *over the new baby.* ***Hom***- adieu.

a·do·be (ə dō′ bē) *n*- **1** unburnt brick dried in the sun, used in southwestern United States and Mexico. **2** structure made of such brick. *as **modifier***: *an* adobe *hut.*

Adobe house

ad·o·les·cence (ăd′ ə lĕs′ əns) *n*- the change from childhood to manhood or womanhood; also, the period of years when this happens; youth.

ad·o·les·cent (ăd′ ə lĕs′ ənt) *n*- person in the process of changing from a child into an adult. *adj*-: *his* adolescent *years.*

A·don·is (ə dŏn′ əs, -dō′ nəs) *n*- in Greek mythology, a beautiful youth beloved by Aphrodite; hence, any very handsome man.

a·dopt (ə dŏpt′) *vt*- **1** to take by choice as one's own: *to* adopt *a child*; *to* adopt *a name.* **2** to approve; accept: *The committee* adopted *the chairman's plan.*
►Should not be confused with ADAPT.

a·dop·tion (ə dŏp′ shən) *n*- **1** a taking as one's own: *the* adoption *of the child.* **2** approval; acceptance: *the* adoption *of a law.*

a·dor·a·ble (ə dôr′ ə bəl) *adj*- **1** worthy of deep love or worship. **2** lovely; charming: *an* adorable *baby.* —*adv*- **a·dor′ a·bly.**

ad·o·ra·tion (ăd′ ə rā′ shən) *n*- **1** worship of God or of a person or thing regarded as holy. **2** devoted love.

a·dore (ə dôr′) *vt*- [**a·dored, a·dor·ing**] **1** to love and worship. **2** to regard with deep affection and respect: *She* adored *her family.* **3** *Informal* to like very much: *I* adore *swimming.*

a·dorn (ə dôrn′, -dôrn′) *vt*- to add beauty to; decorate: *to* adorn *a hat with flowers.*

a·dorn·ment (ə dôrn′ mənt, ə dôrn′-) *n*- **1** something that adds beauty; decoration: *A jeweled pin was the only* adornment *on the dress.* **2** a decorating: *to be busy with the* adornment *of the room the day before the party.*

ad·re·nal (ə drē′ nəl) *adj*- **1** located in the area near the kidneys. **2** having to do with the adrenal glands or their secretions.

adrenal glands *n-* two small glands, one on top of each kidney, which secrete cortisone, adrenaline, and other vital hormones. Also **adrenals.**

ad·ren·al·ine or **ad·ren·al·in** (ə drĕn′ə lən) *n-* hormone secreted by the adrenal glands to brace the body for danger and stress, as for flight or violence.

a·drift (ə drĭft′) *adj-* floating about at random; without moorings or means of propulsion: *The small sailboat was* adrift.

a·droit (ə droit′) *adj-* clever; skillful: *We admired the lawyer's* adroit *questioning of the witness.* **—*adv-*** **a·droit′ly.** ***n-*** **a·droit′ness.**

ad·sorb (ăd sŏrb′, -zŏrb′) *vt-* to take up a gas, liquid, or solid by the process of adsorption. See also *absorb.*

ad·sorp·tion (ăd sŏrp′shən, ăd zŏrp′-) *n-* process by which a thin film of gas, liquid, or solid adheres to the surface of another substance: *Charcoal takes up large volumes of gases by* adsorption.

ad·u·la·tion (ăj′ə lā′shən) *n-* uncritical and excessive praise; flattery: *The movie star inspired* adulation *among her followers.* ***adj-*** **ad′u·la·tor′y** (ăj′ə lə tôr′ē): *an* adulatory *speech about a leader.*

a·dult (ə dŭlt′, ăd′ŭlt′) *n-* **1** full-grown plant, animal, or person. **2** mature person; man or woman. *adj-* **1** grown to full size. **2** made by or for a mature person: *an* adult *decision*; *an* adult *drama.*

a·dul·ter·ant (ə dŭl′tər ənt) *n-* any substance used to adulterate another substance.

a·dul·ter·ate (ə dŭl′tə rāt′) *vt-* [**a·dul·ter·at·ed, a·dul·ter·at·ing**] to make poorer or thinner by mixing in some other substance: *to* adulterate *milk with water.*

a·dul·ter·at·ed (ə dŭl′tə rā′təd) *adj-* made impure by the addition of something inferior or less valuable: *a tank of* adulterated *gasoline.*

a·dul·ter·a·tion (ə dŭl′tə rā′shən) *n-* **1** the adding of something inferior to a substance or mixture. **2** the product so adulterated, such as milk thinned with water.

a·dul·ter·er (ə dŭl′tər ər) *n-* a person who has committed adultery.

a·dul·ter·y (ə dŭl′tə rē) *n-* [*pl.* **a·dul·ter·ies**] the act of breaking the marriage vow of sexual fidelity. **—*adj-*** **a·dul′ter·ous.**

a·dult·hood (ăd′ŭlt′ho͝od′, ə dŭlt′-) *n-* the time or period of full physical development and maturity.

adv. adverb.

ad va·lor·em (ăd′və lôr′əm) *Latin* according to value.

ad·vance (əd văns′) *vt-* [**ad·vanced, ad·vanc·ing**] **1** to move (persons or things) forward or upward: *to* advance *a cause*; *to* advance *a person to a higher position*; *to* advance *prices or costs*; *to* advance *a meeting to a later date.* **2** to offer; propose: *to* advance *a plan.* **3** to lend or pay (money) beforehand: *The bank* advanced *$1000 to Ms. Smith.* ***vi-*** to go forward or upward: *The hot lava* advanced *down the slope. Prices have* advanced *over the past two years.* ***n-*** **1** a going forward or upward: *an enemy* advance; *a sudden* advance *in prices*; *the rapid* advance *of science.* **2** loan or prepayment. *as* ***modifier***: *to receive* advance *information*; *an* advance *guard.*

in advance before; beforehand: *If you decide to come with us, let me know* in advance.

ad·vanced (əd vănst′) *adj-* ahead of others in position, time, progress, etc.: *an* advanced *observation post*; *a person of* advanced *years*; *a seminar in* advanced *chemistry.*

ad·vance·ment (əd văns′mənt, ăd-) *n-* **1** a moving forward. **2** promotion in rank or standing: *to have hopes of* advancement.

ad·van·tage (əd văn′tĭj, ăd-) *n-* thing or condition that gives one help, superiority, benefit, etc.: *Her early training was clearly an* advantage. *Jack's talent gave him the* advantage *over the other candidate.*

take advantage of **1** to make the best use of: *He* took advantage of *the lull in the activity to rest.* **2** to impose upon or treat (someone) unfairly: *Don't let him* take advantage of *you.* **to (one's) advantage** to (one's) benefit or gain: *It is* to *your* advantage *to study.*

ad·van·ta·geous (ăd′vən tā′jəs) *adj-* favorable; useful; profitable: *an* advantageous *position.* **—*adv-*** **ad′van·ta′geous·ly.** ***n-*** **ad′van·ta′geous·ness.**

ad·vent (ăd′vĕnt′) *n-* **1** a coming into place or being; arrival: *the* advent *of spring.* **2 Advent** the coming of Jesus Christ into the world; also, the season (including four Sundays) of preparation for Christmas.

Ad·vent·ist (əd vĕn′tĭst, ăd′vĕnt′ĭst) *n-* one who believes that the second coming of Christ and the end of the world are near at hand.

ad·ven·ti·tious (ăd′vən tĭsh′əs) *adj-* **1** coming from the outside, and, hence, unexpected: *an* adventitious *development in the trial.* **2** *Biology* growing in an unusual location in a plant or animal: *An* adventitious *bud appeared on the plant's leaf.* **—*adv-*** **ad′ven·ti′tious·ly.** ***n-*** **ad′ven·ti′tious·ness.**

ad·ven·ture (əd vĕn′chər) *n-* **1** bold and difficult undertaking in which risks are run: *Climbing any high mountain is an* adventure. **2** an exciting or unexpected experience: *Exploring the old castle was a pleasant* adventure. **3** activity filled with danger, excitement, etc.: *the love of* adventure; *the spirit of* adventure.

ad·ven·tur·er (əd vĕn′chər ər) *n-* **1** person who seeks or has adventures. **2** person who lives by questionable schemes; schemer. **—*n-*** *fem.* **ad·ven′tur·ess.**

ad·ven·tur·ous (əd vĕn′chər əs) *adj-* **1** inclined to seek exciting experiences. **2** risky and requiring courage: *an* adventurous *undertaking.* **—*adv-*** **ad·ven′tur·ous·ly.**

ad·verb (ăd′vûrb′) *Grammar* *n-* a modifier that is not an adjective, a determiner, or a noun. Adverbs usually modify with respect to time, place, manner, or degree, and may be found in various positions in sentences:

He will arrive soon. (time)
She has just *returned.* (time)
My sister has gone abroad. (place)
He suddenly *left.* (manner)
Lily plays the violin well. (manner)

Many adverbs, like adjectives, can be compared:

John plays the violin well.
Gloria plays it better.
Joe plays best *when he is rested.*
Edith runs fast.
Edith can run faster *than I can.*
Edith runs fastest *in the morning.*

ad·verb·i·al (ăd vûr′bē əl) *adj-* **1** of or relating to adverbs. **2** modifying as an adverb does: *an* adverbial *phrase.* ***n-*** phrase or clause which modifies as an adverb does. Examples: *We were told to come* whenever we could. *His face was* red as a beet. **—*adv-*** **ad·verb′i·al·ly.**

ad·ver·sar·y (ăd′vər sĕr′ē) *n-* [*pl.* **ad·ver·sar·ies**] **1** enemy. **2** opponent; rival.

ad·verse (ăd′vûrs, ăd vûrs′) *adj-* **1** unfavorable: *The judge gave an* adverse *decision. He struggled against* adverse *circumstances.* **2** in a contrary direction; opposing, and often unfriendly: *An* adverse *wind delayed the boat.* ***—adv-*** **ad·verse′ly.** ***n-*** **ad·verse′ness.**

ad·ver·si·ty (əd vûr′sə tē, ăd-) ***n-*** [*pl.* **ad·ver·si·ties**] great trouble or trial; misfortune; hardship: *He knew many days of* adversity.

ad·ver·tise (ăd′vər tīz′) ***vt-*** [**ad·ver·tised, ad·ver·tis·ing**] **1** to give public notice of: *to* advertise *the hour of the town meeting.* **2** to call attention to in the newspapers, over the radio, on television, etc., in order to arouse a desire to buy: *to* advertise *a sale of shoes.* ***vi-*** to give public notice of things for sale: *That company doesn't* advertise *on television.* ***—n-*** **ad′ver·tis′er.**

advertise for to ask for by public notice: *to* advertise for *a lost article.*

ad·ver·tise·ment (ăd′vər tīz′mənt, əd vûr′təz mənt) ***n-*** public notice about things that are sold, needed, lost, or found.

ad·ver·tis·ing (ăd′vər tīz′ĭng) ***n-*** **1** the use of announcements in newspapers, on television, etc., to tell people about a product, service, or a personal need. **2** the business of writing, designing, and circulating advertisements: *Joan found a career in* advertising *as an illustrator.* **3** advertisements or their character. *as* ***modifier:*** *the* advertising *industry.*

ad·vice (əd vīs′, ăd-) ***n-*** opinion about what ought to be done; counsel; guidance.

ad·vis·a·ble (əd vī′zə bəl) ***adj-*** worth taking as good advice; sensible; wise: *It is* advisable *to cross streets only at corners.* ***—n-*** **ad·vis′a·bil′i·ty.** ***adv-*** **ad·vis′a·bly.**

ad·vise (əd vīz′, ăd-) ***vt-*** [**ad·vised, ad·vis·ing**] **1** to give advice to: *He* advised *me to go.* **2** to notify: *He* advised *me of my promotion.* ***vi-*** to seek counsel; consult: *He* advised *with me about his trip.* ***—n-*** **ad·vis′er** or **ad·vi′sor.**

ad·vised (əd vīzd′, ăd-) ***adj-*** informed; notified: *He was kept* advised *of the latest developments.*

ad·vis·ed·ly (əd vī′zəd lē, ăd-) ***adv-*** after careful consideration; deliberately: *He used the word* advisedly.

ad·vise·ment (əd vīz′mənt, ăd-) ***n-*** consideration; deliberation: *Keep the matter under* advisement.

ad·vi·so·ry (əd vī′zə rē, ăd-) ***adj-*** having power to suggest or to give advice: *an* advisory *board.*

ad·vo·ca·cy (ăd′və kə sē) ***n-*** an urging or supporting: *his* advocacy *of a strong navy.*

[1]**ad·vo·cate** (ăd′və kāt′) ***vt-*** [**ad·vo·cat·ed, ad·vo·cat·ing**] to recommend publicly; favor; urge: *The senator* advocates *careful spending of our country's money.*

[2]**ad·vo·cate** (ăd′və kət) ***n-*** **1** person who speaks in favor of any cause; defender; supporter: *Mahatma Gandhi was an* advocate *of passive resistance.* **2** *Brit.* one who pleads a person's cause in a law court.

adz or **adze** (ădz) ***n-*** cutting tool for shaping and finishing timber.

a·e·des (ā ē′dēz) ***n-*** a tropical and subtropical mosquito, carrier of yellow fever, dengue, and some other diseases.

ae·gis (ē′jəs) ***n-*** **1** (also **egis**) protecting power or influence; support; backing: *He acted under the* aegis *of the federal government.* **2** in Greek mythology, the shield of Zeus or the breastplate of Athena.

Ae·ne·as (ə nē′əs) ***n-*** in classical legend, son of Venus and a mortal. The wanderings of Aeneas and his companions after the sack of Troy are the subject of Virgil's **"Aeneid"** (ə nē′ĭd).

ae·o·li·an harp (ē ō′lē ən) ***n-*** a boxlike instrument, the strings of which make musical sounds when the wind blows through them.

ae·on (ē′ŏn′) ***n-*** eon.

aer·ate (âr′āt′) ***vt-*** [**aer·at·ed, aer·at·ing**] **1** to expose to the action of air: *Water is purified by* aerating *it in a fine spray.* **2** to dissolve or mix air or another gas in a liquid under pressure. **3** to supply (the blood) with oxygen: *Blood is* aerated *in the lungs.* ***—n-*** **aer′a′tion.**

aer·i·al (âr′ē əl) ***adj-*** **1** having to do with, or taking place in the air: *an* aerial *photograph.* **2** high; lofty: *the city's* aerial *towers.* **3** lacking substance; imaginary: *an* aerial *flight of fancy.* **4** growing in air without roots in the ground as does Spanish moss. ***Hom-*** Ariel. ***—adv-*** **aer′i·al·ly.**

aer·i·al·ist (âr′ē əl ĭst′) ***n-*** one who performs on a trapeze or highwire.

aer·ie (âr′ē, êr′ē) ***n-*** the nest of an eagle or other bird of prey that builds high among the rocks. Also **eyrie** or **eyry.** ***Hom-*** airy or eerie.

aero- *combining form* air: *an* aero*duct;* aero*dynamics.* [from Greek **aero-** meaning "air."]

aer·obe (âr′ōb′) ***n-*** any plant or animal that requires oxygen to live and grow, especially most bacteria.

aer·o·bic (âr ō′bĭk) ***adj-*** **1** requiring oxygen to live and grow. **2** having to do with exercise that increases the body's consumption of oxygen.

aer·o·bics (âr ō′bĭks) ***n-*** system of aerobic exercises.

aer·o·duct (âr′ō dŭkt′) ***n-*** ramjet engine in an airplane or spacecraft that uses ions and electrons collected from space to generate thrust.

aer·o·dy·nam·ics (âr′ō dī năm′ĭks) ***n-*** the science that deals with the flow of air and its effects, especially on aircraft.

aer·ol·o·gy (âr ŏl′ə jē) ***n-*** **1** branch of meteorology that deals only with the atmosphere. **2** meteorology.

aer·o·naut (âr′ə nȯt′) ***n-*** one who operates or rides in an aircraft.

aer·o·nau·tics (âr′ə nȯ′tĭks) ***n-*** (takes singular verb) the science of aviation, or of operating aircraft. ***—adj-*** **aer′o·nau′tic** or **aer′o·nau′ti·cal.**

aer·o·pause (âr′ō pȯz′) ***n-*** region of the atmosphere where the conditions of temperature, pressure, etc., gradually become more and more similar to those of outer space.

aer·o·sol (âr′ə sŏl′, -sȯl′) ***n-*** suspension of fine particles of a solid or liquid in a gas, as mist, smoke, or fog.

aer·o·space (âr′ō spās′) ***n-*** **1** region consisting of the earth's atmosphere and outer space. **2** the study of this region, especially in connection with rockets and other spacecraft.

Aes·cu·la·pi·us (ĕs′kə lā′pē əs) ***n-*** in Roman mythology, the god of medicine and healing. He is identified with the Greek **As·cle·pi·us** (ə sklē′pē əs).

aes·thete (ĕs′thēt′) ***n-*** esthete.

aes·thet·ic (ĕs thĕt′ĭk) ***adj-*** esthetic. ***—adj-*** **aes·thet′i·cal.** ***adv-*** **aes·thet′i·cal·ly.**

aes·thet·ics (ĕs thĕt′ĭks) ***n-*** esthetics.

aes·ti·vate (ĕs′tə vāt′) ***vi-*** [**aes·ti·vat·ed, aes·ti·vat·ing**] estivate.

a·far (ə fär′) ***adv-*** far away; far off; from a distance.

af·fa·ble (ăf′ə bəl) ***adj-*** courteous in speech and manner; friendly. ***—n-*** **af′fa·bil′i·ty.** ***adv-*** **af′fa·bly.**

af·fair (ə fâr′) ***n-*** **1** any matter of interest, concern, or duty; business; job: *an* affair *of state; a difficult* affair *to handle.* **2** *Informal* an object; thing: *The hut was a crude* affair. **3** *Informal* social gathering or celebration. **4** a romance, usually a temporary one. **5 affairs** business of any sort: *He put his* affairs *in order before he left.*

affair of honor ***n-*** a duel [from French **affaire d'honneur** (ă fâr′dȯ nûr′), meaning "duel"].

[1]**af·fect** (ə fĕkt′) ***vt-*** **1** to influence; have an effect on: *Edison's inventions have greatly* affected *modern civilization.* **2** to move the feelings of; stir the emotions of: *The story of his escape and wanderings* affected *me deeply.* [from Latin **affectus** meaning "an influence."]

►AFFECT and EFFECT are often confused in writing because they sound alike and have closely related meanings. EFFECT is commonly used both as a verb and as a noun, while AFFECT is common only as a verb. EFFECT as a noun means "result": *The* effect *of his mother's death was to make him cry.* EFFECT as a verb means "to cause (a specified result)": *His mother's death* effected *a change in his way of life.* AFFECT, on the other hand, means "to act on or influence (something)" without requiring that the influence be stated: *Her death* affected *him strongly.* Studying this dictionary will EFFECT (cause) an improvement in your language. The amount you study will AFFECT (influence) the rate at which you improve.

[2]**af·fect** (ə fĕkt′) ***vt-*** **1** to pretend to do or to have: *He* affected *a sorrow he did not feel.* **2** to like to use: *He* affects *loud neckties.* [from French **affecter,** from Latin **affectare** meaning "to influence."]

af·fec·ta·tion (ăf′ĕk tā′shən) ***n-*** the assuming of a manner merely to create an impression; also, an instance of this: *His* affectations *of speech made us laugh.*

af·fect·ed (ə fĕk′təd) ***adj-*** **1** not natural; assumed: *her* affected *manners; an* affected *accent.* **2** moved; stirred: *He seemed much* affected *by the news.*

af·fect·ing (ə fĕk′tĭng) ***adj-*** having power to excite the emotions; pathetic: *Her grief was most* affecting.

af·fec·tion (ə fĕk′shən) ***n-*** **1** fondness; love: *Although he teased her sometimes, he had a great* affection *for his sister.* **2** disease or complaint: *an* affection *of the lung.*

af·fec·tion·ate (ə fĕk′shən ət) ***adj-*** having or expressing affection; loving; tender: *She has an* affectionate *nature.* ***—adv-*** **af·fec′tion·ate·ly.** ***n-*** **af·fec′tion·ate·ness.**

af·fi·ance (ə fī′əns) ***vt-*** **[af·fi·anced, af·fi·anc·ing]** to promise (oneself or another) in marriage.

af·fi·da·vit (ăf′ə dā′vət) ***n-*** a sworn statement in writing, especially one made before a court or a notary public.

[1]**af·fil·i·ate** (ə fĭl′ē āt′) ***vi-*** **[af·fil·i·at·ed, af·fil·i·at·ing]** to join or become associated (with): *The local refused to* affiliate *with the new union.* ***vt-*** to associate (oneself with). ***—n-*** **af·fil′i·a′tion.**

[2]**af·fil·i·ate** (ə fĭl′ē ət) ***n-*** person or company associated with another organization.

af·fin·i·ty (ə fĭn′ə tē) ***n-*** [*pl.* **af·fin·i·ties**] **1** a close relationship: *an* affinity *between two tribes; an* affinity *between two languages.* **2** mutual understanding and attraction, based on similarity of temperament. **3** *Chemistry* the force of attraction by which the atoms of different elements enter into and remain in combination.

af·firm (ə fûrm′) ***vt-*** **1** to assert strongly; declare positively: *He* affirmed *his innocence.* **2** to give formal approval to; confirm; ratify: *to* affirm *the decision of a lower court.*

af·firm·a·tion (ăf′ər mā′shən) ***n-*** an affirming.

af·firm·a·tive (ə fûr′mə tĭv) ***adj-*** declaring assent or agreement; saying yes; affirming: *Some* affirmative *expressions are "OK," "all right," "certainly." Fred was on the* affirmative *side in the debate.* ***n-*** **1** word or expression indicating assent or agreement. Examples: "Yes," "I shall." **2** in a debate, the side arguing for the truth of a statement or proposition. ***—adv-*** **af·firm′a·tive·ly.**

in the affirmative in favor of the proposition being voted on.

[1]**af·fix** (ə fĭks′) ***vt-*** to attach or add: *I* affixed *my signature to the letter.*

[2]**af·fix** (ăf′ĭks′) ***n-*** something attached or added, especially a prefix or suffix added to a root word.

af·flict (ə flĭkt′) ***vt-*** to cause great pain or trouble to; make miserable; distress: *War has long* afflicted *mankind.*

af·flic·tion (ə flĭk′shən) ***n-*** **1** a state of pain or distress: *She was brave in her* affliction. **2** anything that causes suffering or grief: *Some diseases are terrible* afflictions.

af·flu·ence (ăf′lo͞o əns) ***n-*** abundant supply, as of riches, words, ideas, etc.; especially, material wealth.

af·flu·ent (ăf′lo͞o ənt) ***adj-*** having abundance; wealthy: *an* affluent *man*; affluent *times.* ***—adv-*** **af′flu·ent·ly.**

af·ford (ə fôrd′) ***vt-*** **1** to give; furnish: *Swimming* affords *enjoyment and muscular training.* **2** to have the resources to pay for, compensate for, or expend: *Is he able to* afford *a new car? I can't. Can you* afford *such carelessness? Can you* afford *the time?*

af·for·es·ta·tion (ă′fòr′ə stā′shən, ă′fŏr′-) ***n-*** the creation of new forests by planting of selected trees.

af·fray (ə frā′) ***n-*** noisy quarrel; brawl.

af·fright (ə frīt′) *Archaic* ***vt-*** to frighten; terrify.

af·front (ə frŭnt′) ***vt-*** to insult openly and on purpose: *He* affronted *me by walking out in the middle of my speech.* ***n-*** open insult: *The speech is an* affront *to us.*

af·ghan (ăf′gən) ***n-*** a crocheted or knitted wool blanket or shawl.

Afghan hound ***n-*** one of a breed of hunting dogs having a long narrow head and thick, silky hair.

a·fi·ci·o·na·do (ə fĭs′ē ə nä′dō, ə fĭsh′-) ***n-*** [*pl.* **a·fi·ci·o·na·dos**] an enthusiastic follower; devotee; fan. [from Spanish **aficionado** meaning "a lover of; one fond of," from **afición,** "affection."]

a·field (ə fēld′) ***adv-*** **1** in or to the field. **2** to, or at, a distance; away: *The traveler wandered far* afield. **3** away from the subject: *To discuss that topic takes us too far* afield.

a·fire (ə fīər′) ***adj-*** on fire: *A spark set the forest* afire. *The house is* afire.

a·flame (ə flām′) ***adj-*** **1** on fire; flaming. **2** as if on fire: *to be* aflame *with anger.*

AFL-CIO or **A.F.L.-C.I.O.** ***n-*** an organization of labor unions formed in 1955 when the American Federation of Labor (A.F.L.) merged with the Congress of Industrial Organizations (C.I.O.).

a·float (ə flōt′) ***adj-*** **1** carried on water; floating: *The logs are* afloat. **2** on board ship: *The company has tons of cargo* afloat. **3** flooded: *The ship's deck was* afloat *during the storm.* **4** in circulation: *There were many rumors* afloat.

a·flut·ter (ə flŭt′ər) ***adj-*** fluttering; agitated; excited: *She was* aflutter *with anticipation.*

a·foot (ə fo͝ot′) ***adj-*** **1** on foot; walking. **2** taking place; on the move; astir: *Trouble was* afoot.

a·fore·men·tioned (ə fôr′mĕn′shənd) ***adj-*** mentioned earlier: *The* aforementioned *students are excused.*

a·fore·said (ə fôr′sĕd′) ***adj-*** mentioned before: *the* aforesaid *person.*

a·fore·thought (ə fôr′thòt′) ***adj-*** planned beforehand: *malice* aforethought.

a·foul (ə foul′) ***adj-*** in a tangle; snarled: *The lines of our sailboat are* afoul.

run afoul of to get into trouble or difficulty with: *He* ran afoul of *the tax collector.*

Afr. **1** Africa. **2** African.

a·fraid (ə frād′) ***adj-*** full of fear; frightened.

a·fresh (ə frĕsh′) ***adv-*** again; anew: *He had to start* afresh *because of his mistakes.*

Af·ri·can (ăf′rĭ kən) ***adj-*** of or pertaining to Africa, or its people. ***n-*** **1** person born in Africa. **2** citizen of a country in Africa.

African violet ***n-*** a small house plant, native to Africa, with fuzzy oval leaves and white, pink, blue, or violet-colored flowers.

Af·ri·kaans (ăf′rĭ känz′, -käns′) ***n-*** South African language developed from 17th century Dutch.

Af·ri·ka·ner (ăf′rĭ kä′nər) ***n-*** a South African of Dutch ancestry, who speaks Afrikaans.

Afro- *combining form* **1** Africa. **2** African.

Af·ro (ăf′rō) ***n-*** [*pl.* **Af·ros**] a bushy hairdo similar to that worn in parts of Africa.

Af·ro-A·mer·i·can (ăf′rō ə mĕr′ə kən) ***adj-*** of or pertain to Americans of African descent.

aft (aft) ***adv-*** toward the stern of a ship: *The sailor went* aft. ***adj-***: *the* aft *funnel.*

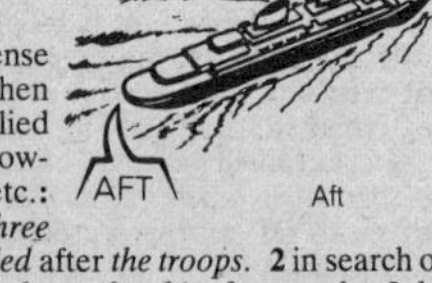

Aft

af·ter (ăf′tər) ***prep-*** (in sense 1 becomes an adverb when the object is clearly implied but not expressed) **1** following in time, place, rank, etc.: *Please come* after *three o'clock. The supplies trailed* after *the troops.* **2** in search or pursuit of: *The police have been* after *him for months. John ran* after *his dog.* **3** in spite of; notwithstanding: *He was still tired, even* after *a long rest.* **4** concerning; about: *to ask* after *one's health.* **5** for: *She is named* after *her aunt.* **6** in the manner or style of; imitated or copied from: *a painting* after *Rembrandt.* ***conj-*** following the time that: *We left* after *we ate.* ***adj-*** **1** later: *in* after *years.* **2** toward the rear or stern of a ship: *an* after *compartment.*

look after to take care of: *Please* look after *him while I'm gone.* **take after** to be or look like: *He* takes after *his grandfather.*

af·ter·birth (ăf′tər bûrth′) ***n-*** mass of tissues, including the placenta and fetal membrane, expelled immediately after giving birth.

af·ter·burn·er (ăf′tər bûr′nər) ***n-*** device in the tail pipe of a jet engine which, by spraying additional fuel into the exhaust gases, causes a second combustion or "afterburning" that greatly increases the thrust of the engine.

af·ter·deck (ăf′tər dĕk′) ***n-*** the deck toward the rear or stern of the ship.

af·ter·ef·fect (ăf′tər ə fĕkt′) ***n-*** delayed effect of something: *Many drugs have undesirable* aftereffects.

af·ter·glow (ăf′tər glō′) ***n-*** **1** any glow lingering where there was a light, especially a purplish glow in the western sky after sundown. **2** warm, pleasant feeling remaining from a past event.

aft·er·math (ăf′tər măth′) ***n-*** **1** that which follows; result: *Misery is an* aftermath *of war.* **2** a second mowing in a season.

af·ter·noon (ăf′tər nōōn′) ***n-*** the time from noon until evening. *as* ***modifier***: *an* afternoon *nap.*

aft·er·thought (ăf′tər thôt′) ***n-*** second or later thought about something, especially, one that comes too late: *The idea came to me as an* afterthought.

af·ter·ward (ăf′tər wərd′) or **af·ter·wards** (ăf′tər wərdz′) ***adv-*** at a later time.

a·gain (ə gĕn′) ***adv-*** **1** a second time; once more: *Do it* again. **2** (used for emphasis): *Give the book back* again. **3** further; on the other hand: *I believe the train arrives at noon.* Again, *I am not absolutely certain.*

a·gainst (ə gĕnst′) ***prep-*** **1** in an opposite direction to: *They tried to row* against *the tide.* **2** upon; in contact with; touching: *He leaned* against *the fence.* **3** in contrast with: *black* against *gold.* **4** in opposition to: *There were twenty votes* against *the increase in club dues.* **5** in preparation for: *to save money* against *a rainy day.*

Ag·a·mem·non (ăg′ə mĕm′nŏn) ***n-*** in Greek legend, king of Mycenae and leader of the Greeks in the Trojan War. He was the brother of Menelaus.

a·gape (ə găp′) ***adj-*** having the mouth wide open, as in wonder.

a·gar (ä′gər, ăg′ər) or **a·gar-a·gar** ***n-*** a gelatinous material obtained from certain red seaweeds, used commercially to thicken soups, ice cream, etc., and also as a medium in which bacteria are grown.

ag·ate (ăg′ət) ***n-*** **1** a kind of quartz with colored bands or cloudy spots, used in jewelry. **2** child's playing marble made to look like this.

Agate

a·ga·ve (ə gä′vē) ***n-*** any of several tropical American plants of the amaryllis family, including the century plant or maguey, having fleshy, spiny-edged leaves, and yielding commercial fiber.

age (āj) ***n-*** **1** length of life or existence: *the* age *of a man; the* age *of a star.* **2** point of time in life or existence: *the* age *of ten.* **3** period in life or history: *the* age *of childhood; the* age *of space travel; the* age *of reptiles.* **4** *Informal* (also **ages**) a long time. ***vi-*** **[aged, ag·ing]** **1** to become old, usually prematurely: *After the shock he* aged *overnight.* **2** to mature by standing for a time: *This wine* ages *well.* ***vt-*** **1** to make old prematurely: *Fear and worry have* aged *him.* **2** to give time to mature: *to* age *cheese or wine.*

of age 21 years old: *He will inherit his grandfather's estate when he is* of age.

-age *suffix* (used to form nouns) **1** collection; aggregate; sum: *the* mileage; *some* baggage. **2** place; dwelling: *an* anchorage; *a* parsonage. **3** act, process, or result: *unnecessary* spoilage; *a* pilgrimage. **4** fee or charge: *to pay* cartage; *cheap* postage. **5** condition: *in* bondage.

[1]aged (ājd) ***adj-*** **1** of the age of: *a boy* aged *five.* **2** matured; ripened: *an* aged *wine.*

[2]ag·ed (ā′jəd) ***adj-*** old: *an* aged *horse.*

age·ism (ā′jĭz′əm) ***n-*** discrimination or prejudice against a certain age group, especially the elderly.

age·less (āj′ləs) ***adj-*** **1** not appearing to grow old: *her* ageless *features.* **2** eternal; everlasting: *the* ageless *beauty of marble.*

a·gen·cy (ā′jən sē) ***n-*** [*pl.* **a·gen·cies**] **1** business or office of a person or company that acts for another: *an employment* agency; *advertising* agency. **2** an administrative, often regulatory, department of the government, such as the FTC (Federal Trade Commission). **3** means; operation; action: *the* agency *of friends; the* agency *of Providence.*

a·gen·da (ə jĕn′də) ***n-*** *pl.* [*sing* **a·gen·dum**] list or outline of things to be done or discussed; schedule: *The secretary read the* agenda *of the meeting.*

a·gent (ā′jənt) ***n-*** **1** person or company that acts for another: *a real estate* agent; *a press* agent. **2** official or representative of a government, company, etc.: *an* agent *of the FBI.* **3** substance or power that produces a result, reaction, change, etc.: *Water and wind are natural* agents *of erosion.*

a·ger·a·tum (ăj′ər ā′təm) ***n-*** any of a group of plants of the aster family, especially a popular garden variety with small blue or sometimes white flowers.

[1]**ag·glom·er·ate** (ə glŏm′ ə rāt′) ***vt-*** **[ag·glom·er·at·ed, ag·glom·er·at·ing]** to gather into a pile or ball.

[2]**ag·glom·er·ate** (ə glŏm′ ə rət) ***n-*** **1** a piled or heaped collection of things; an agglomeration. **2** in geology, a kind of rock made up of volcanic fragments fused together without order. ***adj-*** **1** heaped up, mixed up, or clustered. **2** of a flower, composite.

ag·glom·er·a·tion (ə glŏm′ ə rā′ shən) ***n-*** **1** act of piling or gathering things together, especially things of different sizes and shapes. **2** heap or collection of things so formed.

ag·glu·ti·na·tion (ə glo͞o′ tə nā′ shən) ***n-*** **1** a uniting or sticking together; adhesion. **2** *Biology* process in which bacteria or living cells collect or clump together, usually because of the presence of an antibody.

a·ggran·dize (ə grăn′ dīz′, ăg′ grən dīz′) ***vt-*** **[ag·gran·dized, ag·gran·diz·ing]** to enlarge or increase (a thing); also, to increase the power, rank, or wealth of (a person or state): *He* aggrandized *himself at the expense of others.* **—*n-*** **ag·gran′dize·ment** (ə grăn′ dəz mənt). ***n-*** **ag′gran·diz′er.**

ag·gra·vate (ăg′ rə vāt′) ***vt-*** **[ag·gra·vat·ed, ag·gra·vat·ing]** **1** to make worse: *Scratching a mosquito bite* aggravates *it.* **2** *Informal* to irritate: *He* aggravated *his parents by staying out late at night.*

►AGGRAVATE means "to make worse," in writing and careful speech. It is used informally and casually to mean "to annoy or trouble." Either IRRITATE or the stronger word EXASPERATE is preferable if you mean "annoy" or "trouble." Use AGGRAVATE, IRRITATE, or the very formal word EXACERBATE if you mean "make worse": *The salt water* aggravated (*or* irritated *or* exacerbated) *George's wound, and this* exasperated (*not* aggravated) *him.*

ag·gra·va·tion (ăg′ rə vā′ shən) ***n-*** **1** a making worse: *the* aggravation *of a cold by neglect.* **2** *Informal* irritation; exasperation; also the cause of this: *Her son's stubbornness caused her much* aggravation.

[1]**ag·gre·gate** (ăg′ rə gāt′) ***vt-*** **[ag·gre·gat·ed, ag·gre·gat·ing]** **1** to bring into a whole mass; collect: *He* aggregated *his holdings into one company.* **2** to add up to: *The year's sales* aggregated *$100,000.*

[2]**ag·gre·gate** (ăg′ rə gət) ***n-*** **1** the total; entire number: *The* aggregate *of all his debts was $1,000.* **2** the rocky material such as sand, pebbles, etc., added to cement to make concrete. *as **modifier**: the* aggregate *amount.*

in the aggregate taken all together.

ag·gre·ga·tion (ăg′ rə gā′ shən) ***n-*** a collection of people or things; mass; whole; group: *an* aggregation *of visiting delegates; an* aggregation *of boulders in a riverbed.*

ag·gres·sion (ə grĕsh′ ən) ***n-*** **1** unprovoked attack or assault, especially by one nation against another. **2** in psychology, a feeling of intense hostility.

ag·gres·sive (ə grĕs′ ĭv) ***adj-*** **1** first to attack; quick to pick a quarrel: *an* aggressive *boy.* **2** energetic; enterprising: *an* aggressive *salesman.* **—*adv-*** **ag·gres′sive·ly.** ***n-*** **ag·gres′sive·ness.**

ag·gres·sor (ə grĕs′ ər) ***n-*** one who attacks another; one who begins a quarrel.

ag·grieved (ə grēvd′) ***adj-*** **1** having a grievance; wronged; hurt in one's feeling: *He felt* aggrieved *when his pay was cut.* **2** wronged by having been deprived of legal rights.

a·ghast (ə găst′) ***adj-*** struck with sudden surprise, horror, or terror: *He was* aghast *at the damage he had caused.*

ag·ile (ăj′ əl) ***adj-*** quick, light, and nimble in movement or thought: *an* agile *dancer; an* agile *mind.* **—*adv-*** **ag′ile·ly.** ***n-*** **a·gil′i·ty** (ə jĭl′ ə tē): *a dancer's* agility.

ag·i·tate (ăj′ ə tāt′) ***vt-*** **[ag·i·tat·ed, ag·i·tat·ing]** **1** to disturb; excite: *The bad news* agitated *him.* **2** to stir up violently: *The wind* agitated *the lake.* ***vi-*** to stir up public opinion: *The paper* agitated *for better housing.*

ag·i·ta·tion (ăj′ ə tā′ shən) ***n-*** **1** anxiety; worry: *to show* agitation *over a friend's safety.* **2** excited discussion; energetic activity to promote a cause: *There was general* agitation *for lower taxes.* **3** a moving to and fro: *an* agitation *of air.*

ag·i·ta·tor (ăj′ ə tā′ tər) ***n-*** **1** one who makes a political or industrial disturbance. **2** an implement for stirring.

a·gleam (ə glēm′) ***adj-*** gleaming; bright.

a·glit·ter (ə glĭt′ ər) ***adj-*** glittering.

a·glow (ə glō′) ***adj-*** bright; flushed: *cheeks* aglow *with pleasure.*

ag·nos·tic (ăg nŏs′ tĭk) ***n-*** one who, without denying the existence of God, believes that there is no evidence in man's experience to prove that God exists. ***adj-*** relating to such a belief.

ag·nos·ti·cism (ăg nŏs′ tə sĭz′ əm) ***n-*** the belief or doctrine that it is impossible to know certainly about the existence of God and the origin and real nature of things.

Ag·nus De·i (ăg′ nəs dā′ ē) *Latin* ***n-*** **1** a representation of Christ the Savior as a lamb, often shown bearing a banner marked with a cross. **2** a prayer in the Mass beginning with these words; also, any music for this prayer.

a·go (ə gō′) ***adj-*** past; back; gone by: *two days* ago. ***adv-*** in the past: *It happened long* ago.

a·gog (ə gŏg′) ***adj-*** aroused; alive with interest; excited; eager: *We are* agog *with curiosity.*

a·gon·ic line (ə gŏn′ ĭk, ā′-) ***n-*** imaginary line on the earth along which a magnetic compass points to true north without declination.

ag·o·nize (ăg′ ə nīz′) ***vi-*** **[ag·o·nized, ag·o·niz·ing]** to suffer extreme pain or grief: *Even though he was right, he* agonized *over his decision for weeks.* ***vt-*** to torment or torture: *His decision* agonized *him for weeks.*

ag·o·niz·ing (ăg′ ə nīz′ ĭng) ***adj-*** causing great suffering of mind or body: *an* agonizing *experience.* **—*adv-*** **ag′o·niz′ing·ly:** *The day dragged on* agonizingly *while we waited for news.*

ag·o·ny (ăg′ ə nē) ***n-*** [*pl.* **ag·o·nies**] **1** intense suffering of body or mind: *An earache is* agony. *She suffered* agonies *of remorse for her carelessness.* **2** the last struggle of a dying person or animal.

a·gou·ti (ə go͞o′ tē) ***n-*** any of several rabbitlike rodents of tropical American forests. Also **a·gou′ty.**

Agouti, 16 1/2—25 1/2 in.

a·grar·i·an (ə grâr′ ē ən) ***adj-*** relating to land, or to the right or manner of holding land: *our* agrarian *laws.* ***n-*** one who is in favor of a redistribution of land.

a·gree (ə grē′) ***vi-*** **[a·greed, a·gree·ing]** **1** to consent (to): *They* agreed *to buy it.* **2** to be of the same mind or opinion; concur; also, to harmonize or correspond.

agree on (or **upon**) to decide or settle on: *We* agreed *on a price.*

agree with **1** to be in accord or harmony with: *His story of the collision* agrees with *mine.* **2** to be good for (one's health): *Rich foods don't* agree with *me.* **3** *Grammar* to correspond with: *The verb* agrees with *its subject in person and number.*

fāte, făt, dâre, bärn; bē, bĕt, mêre; bīte, bĭt; nōte, hŏt, môre, dȯg; fŭn, fûr; to͞o, bo͝ok; oil; out; tar; thin; then; hw for wh as in *wh*at; zh for s as in u*s*ual; ə for a, e, i, o, u, as in *a*go, lin*e*n, per*i*l, at*o*m, min*u*s

a·gree·a·ble (ə grē′ ə bəl) ***adj-*** **1** pleasant: *A good dinner and* agreeable *talk go together.* **2** willing to agree: *Are you* agreeable *to this plan?* ***—adv-*** **a·gree′ a·bly.**

a·gree·ment (ə grē′ mənt) ***n-*** **1** a being of the same opinion; an understanding: *The two countries came to* agreement *on the terms of the treaty.* **2** harmony; accord: *There was complete* agreement *between the stories of the two witnesses.* **3** a contract; an understanding: *an* agreement *to buy.* **4** *Grammar* the correspondence of one word with another in gender, number, case, or person.

ag·ri·cul·tur·al (ăg′ rə kŭl′ chər əl) ***adj-*** of or having to do with agriculture: *modern* agricultural *methods.* ***—adv-*** **ag′ ri·cul′ tur·al·ly:** *That land is not* agriculturally *productive.*

ag·ri·cul·ture (ăg′ rə kŭl′ chər) ***n-*** **1** the cultivation of land and the breeding and raising of farm animals; farming. **2** the art or science of farming.

ag·ri·cul·tur·ist (ăg′ rə kŭl′ chər ĭst′) ***n-*** **1** an expert in agriculture. **2** a farmer, especially one who practices the more modern or scientific methods of farming. Also **ag′ ri·cul′ tur·al·ist.**

a·gron·o·my (ə grŏn′ ə mē) ***n-*** farming by scientific methods. ***—n-*** **a·gron′ o·mist.**

a·ground (ə ground′) ***adj-*** stranded on the bottom in shallow water, on a beach, reef, etc.

agt. agent.

a·gue (ā′ gyōō′) ***n-*** disease marked by regularly recurring chills and fever.

ah ***interj-*** exclamation of pity, surprise, joy, etc.

a·ha (ä′ hä′, ə hä′) ***interj-*** an exclamation of surprise, triumph, mockery, etc.: *She cried,* "Aha, *so this is it!*"

A·hab (ā′ hăb′) ***n-*** **1** in the Bible, a ninth-century B.C. king of Israel. **2** a sea captain in Melville's "Moby Dick."

a·head (ə hĕd′) ***adv-*** (sometimes considered an adjective when used after a form of the verb "to be") **1** beyond or in advance of something or someone else; in or to the front: *The red car raced* ahead. *We started together, but she is now far* ahead. **2** to or toward a more advanced place, position, or time; forward: *The men marched straight* ahead. *Think* ahead, *and plan your vacation now. There are rough seas* ahead.

ahead of 1 in front of: *She sat three rows* ahead of *us.* **2** in advance of: *His scientific discoveries were far* ahead of *the times.* **get ahead** to be successful: *to* get ahead *in business.*

a·hem (ə hĕm′) ***interj-*** exclamation, made by a clearing of the throat or similar sound, used to attract attention, express doubt, etc.

a·hoy (ə hoi′) ***interj-*** call used by sailors to hail a ship: *Ship,* ahoy!

aid (ād) ***vt-*** (considered intransitive when the direct object is implied but not expressed) to help or assist. ***n-*** **1** person or thing that helps or assists: *Books are an* aid *to learning.* **2** help: *with the* aid *of a doctor.* ***Hom-*** aide.

aide (ād) ***n-*** **1** helper or assistant: *a nurse's* aide; *a diplomatic* aide; *a military* aide. **2** aide-de-camp. ***Hom-*** aid.

aide-de-camp (ād′ də kămp′) ***n-*** [*pl.* **aides-de-camp**] military officer who acts as a personal assistant to a superior; aide. [from French, meaning literally "aide or assistant for the camp."]

ai·grette (ā′ grĕt′, ā grĕt′) ***n-*** **1** the egret, a kind of heron. **2** plume of feathers from this heron, worn as a head ornament; also, any similar ornament, such as a spray of gems, worn as a headdress.

ail (āl) ***vt-*** to cause pain or discomfort to; be the matter with; trouble: *What* ails *the man?* ***Hom-*** ale.

ai·lan·thus (ā lăn′ thəs) ***n-*** large, hardy, fast-growing tree with long feathery leaves, small greenish flowers, and winged seeds, often planted in cities.

ai·ler·on (ā′ lə rŏn′) ***n-*** hinged part on the rear edge of each wing of an airplane to steady it in flight. For picture, see *airplane.*

ail·ing (ā′ lĭng) ***adj-*** ill or always in ill health: *He has an* ailing *mother. The children are* ailing *today.*

ail·ment (āl′ mənt) ***n-*** sickness; illness.

aim (ām) ***vi-*** **1** to point or sight a weapon, or direct a blow, remark, etc.: *to* aim *at a target*; *to* aim *for an opponent's chin.* **2** to have in mind or intend: *He* aims *to become an engineer.* ***vt-:*** *to* aim *a rifle at a target*; *to* aim *insults at enemies.* ***n-*** **1** the pointing or directing of a weapon, blow, remark, etc. **2** the direction in which a weapon is pointed to hit a target; line of sighting: *His* aim *was off.* **3** purpose; goal; end: *What is your* aim *in life?*

aim·less (ām′ ləs) ***adj-*** having no particular goal or purpose: *an* aimless *life*; *his* aimless *wanderings.* ***—adv-*** **aim′ less·ly.** ***n-*** **aim′ less·ness:** *the* aimlessness *of his life.*

ain't (ānt) **1** am not; are not. **2** have not; has not.

►Do not use AIN'T unless you are trying to show informality, or poor education, or folksiness: *The old gray mare, she* ain't *what she used to be.*

air (âr) ***n-*** **1** mixture of gases, mostly nitrogen and oxygen, surrounding the earth and making up the earth's atmosphere. **2** tune or melody: *an old English* air. **3** general appearance or manner; look or feeling of a person or thing: *The old gentleman maintained an* air *of dignity. The hotel had an* air *of luxury.* **4 airs** manners or appearance put on to impress people; affected attitudes: *Jane's city* airs *annoyed her friends at home.* ***vt-*** **1** to expose to the air so as to cool or freshen: *to* air *a stuffy room.* **2** to make public: *to* air *one's grievances.* *as* ***modifier****: an* air *duct*; *an* air *drill*; *an* air *conditioner*; air *mail*; air *speed*; *an* air *base*; *an* air *lane.* ***Homs-*** [2]are, e'er, ere, heir.

clear the air to get rid of or resolve bad feelings, misunderstandings, etc., by discussion. **give (oneself) airs** to be haughty or conceited. **in the air 1** in circulation; current: *Rumors of war were* in the air. **2** not settled; undecided. **on (or off) the air** being (or not being) broadcast by radio or television. **put on airs** to assume a superior manner. **up in the air** not settled; undecided: *We don't know if we will take the trip; our plans are still* up in the air. **walk on air** to feel very happy or joyous.

air base ***n-*** landing field and buildings where military aircraft are kept and repaired.

air bladder ***n-*** air-filled sac in many kinds of fishes which helps to regulate their buoyancy.

air brake ***n-*** brake operated by compressed air, of the type found on trailer trucks.

air·brush (âr′ brŭsh′) ***n-*** a small, pencil-shaped spray gun used for drawing and for painting. *as* ***modifier****: an* airbrush *portrait.* ***vt-:*** *to* airbrush *a drawing.*

air castle ***n-*** visionary and impractical plan, idea, etc.

air coach ***n-*** low-priced accommodations on a passenger airplane.

air-con·di·tion (âr′ kən dĭsh′ ən) ***vt-*** to equip with air-conditioning machinery or to supply with air treated by such machinery. ***—adj-*** **air′-con·di′ tioned.**

air conditioner ***n-*** machine for air conditioning.

air conditioning ***n-*** treatment of air to regulate its temperature, humidity, cleanliness, and circulation. *as* ***modifier*** **(air-con·ditioning):** *an* air-conditioning *unit.*

air-cool (âr′ kōōl′) ***vt-*** to cool with air, especially to cool an internal-combustion engine by passing air directly around its cylinders.

air·craft (âr′krăft′) ***n-*** [*pl.* **air·craft**] any flying machine, such as an airplane, airship, glider, or balloon, designed to operate in the atmosphere.

aircraft carrier ***n-*** warship with a large, level deck, designed to carry and launch aircraft.

air division ***n-*** in the U.S. Air Force, a unit composed of two to five smaller units called wings.

air·drome (âr′drōm′) ***n-*** airport.

air·drop (âr′drŏp′) ***n-*** a parachuting of supplies or troops.

Aire·dale (âr′dāl′) ***n-*** large black-and-tan terrier with a rough coat.

air·field (âr′fēld′) ***n-*** level field with runways where airplanes may take off and land.

air·foil (âr′foil′) ***n-*** anything with a surface or shape designed to produce a special effect when it moves through air, especially an airplane wing.

air force ***n-*** **1** the branch of a nation's military defense that uses aircraft as its primary weapon. **2 Air Force** (1) the air force of the United States, established as a separate unit in 1947. (2) the U.S. Air Force Academy at Colorado Springs, Colorado.

air·glow (âr′glō′) ***n-*** steady light or glow seen in the night sky and caused by chemical changes produced in the upper atmosphere by radiation from the sun.

air gun ***n-*** **1** rifle, pistol, or gun which uses compressed air or gas to shoot a projectile. **2** airbrush.

air hole ***n-*** **1** opening or vent through which air passes, such as a hole in ice through which seals can breathe. **2** hollow space filled with air, such as a bubble in cast metal, a loaf of bread, etc.

air·i·ly (âr′ə lē) ***adv-*** in an airy manner; light-heartedly.

air·i·ness (âr′ē nəs) ***n-*** **1** openness to the air. **2** delicacy; lightness. **3** sprightliness.

air·ing (âr′ĭng) ***n-*** **1** an exposure to the air, for freshening, drying, etc. **2** a walk or ride in the outdoors. **3** a public display or discussion (of ideas, opinions, etc.): *an* airing *of the grievances.*

air lane ***n-*** route regularly used by aircraft in flight.

air·less (âr′ləs) ***adj-*** **1** without air or fresh air; stuffy: *The* airless *room made him ill.* **2** without moving air; calm: *a still,* airless *evening.*

air letter ***n-*** a letter sent by air mail.

air·lift (âr′lĭft′) ***n-*** a transporting of supplies and personnel by aircraft to a blockaded area; especially the **Berlin airlift** of 1948, during which American military airplanes overcame the Soviet land blockade of Berlin. ***vt-:*** *They* airlifted *supplies into the besieged area.*

air·line (âr′līn′) ***n-*** company that owns and operates airplanes to carry passengers and freight.

air·lin·er (âr′lī′nər) ***n-*** large commercial passenger airplane.

air·lock (âr′lŏk) ***n-*** an air space or airtight compartment in which air pressure can be adjusted to allow people to move between places that have different air pressures.

air mail ***n-*** **1** mail carried by aircraft. **2** system for carrying mail by aircraft.

air·man (âr′mən) ***n-*** [*pl.* **air·men**] **1** in the Air Force, a person who ranks next below a sergeant and next above a recruit. **2** any crew member of an airplane.

air mass ***n-*** widespread body of air all of which has the same general temperature, humidity, and other weather conditions.

air·plane (âr′plān′) ***n-*** flying machine heavier than air, driven by engines and having fixed wings.

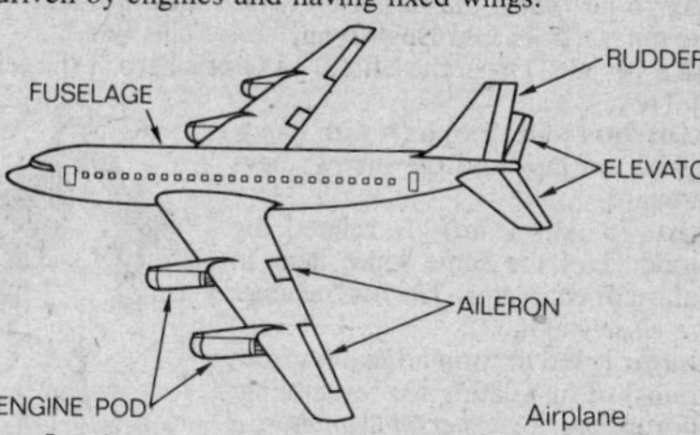

Airplane

air plant ***n-*** rootless plant that clings to trees or to other plants instead of growing on the ground.

air pocket ***n-*** downdraft or other atmospheric condition in an airplane's path that causes it to drop suddenly.

air police ***n-*** group that performs police duties in an air force unit.

air pollution ***n-*** the contamination of air by waste and chemicals from industry and fuel exhaust.

air·port (âr′pôrt′) ***n-*** a place for the taking off, landing, loading, fueling, or repairing of aircraft.

air pressure ***n-*** **1** the pressure a given body of air exerts in all directions. **2** atmospheric pressure.

air pump ***n-*** pump used to compress, draw out, or drive air.

air raid ***n-*** military attack by aircraft.

air rifle ***n-*** rifle that uses compressed air or gas.

air sacs ***n-*** air-filled spaces in the bodies and bones of birds, actually extensions of their lungs.

air shaft ***n-*** shaft or passage for ventilating a building, mine, etc.

air·ship (âr′shĭp′) ***n-*** lighter-than-air aircraft driven by one or more engines; a dirigible balloon.

air·sick (âr′sĭk′) ***adj-*** sick from the motions of a plane in flight. **—*n-* air′sick′ness.**

air sleeve ***n-*** cone, usually cloth, supported at the larger end and above the ground to show wind direction.

air speed ***n-*** speed of an airplane in relation to the air. A plane that flies 300 miles in an hour against a headwind of 50 mph has an air speed of 350 mph.

air·strip (âr′strĭp′) ***n-*** runway for the take-off and landing of airplanes.

air·tight (âr′tīt′) ***n-*** **1** closed or sealed so that no air can get in or out. **2** without a flaw or weakness: *an* airtight *legal case*; *an* airtight *alibi.*

air·waves (âr′wāvz) ***n-*** (takes plural verb) the medium of radio or television broadcasting. *This program comes to you over the* airwaves.

air·way (âr′wā′) ***n-*** **1** air lane. **2** air shaft. **3** radio channel of a specific radio frequency.

air·y (âr′ē) ***adj-*** **[air·i·er, air·i·est]** **1** in or of the air: high up: *the* airy *flight of the monarch butterfly.* **2** with air moving freely; breezy: *an* airy *room.* **3** light-hearted; graceful; gay: airy *laughter.* **4** unreal; imaginary; visionary: airy *schemes.* ***Hom-*** aerie. **—*adv-* air′i·ly.**

aisle (īl) ***n-*** **1** passageway between seats, as in a church, theater, or courtroom. **2** passageway between counters in a store. ***Homs-*** I'll, isle.

[1]a·jar (ə jär′) ***adj-*** slightly open, as a door. [from Middle English **on char,** from Old English **on cyrr** meaning "on the turn."]

²a·jar (ə jär′) ***adj-*** out of harmony: *His ideas are* ajar *with the times.* [from Old English **an,** "on," plus **¹jar.**]

A·jax (ā′ jăks′) ***n-*** in the "Iliad," a Greek hero at the seige of Troy.

a·kim·bo (ə kĭm′ bō) ***adj-*** with hands resting on hips and the elbows bent outward.

Akimbo

a·kin (ə kĭn′) ***adj-*** **1** related by blood. **2** of the same kind; near in nature or character: *The two schemes are closely* akin.

¹-al *suffix* (used to form adjectives from nouns) of or relating to; resembling; appropriate to: *a person*al *matter*; *a post*al *clerk.*

²-al *suffix* (used to form nouns from verbs) action or result: *a dismiss*al; *a portray*al; *an arriv*al.

Ala. Alabama.

à la (ä′ lə, ä′ lä′, ă′ lă′) *French* in the manner of; according to: *to dress* à la *mode*; *to order dinner* à la *carte.*

al·a·bas·ter (ăl′ ə băs′ tər) ***n-*** stone of fine texture, usually white and translucent, often carved into vases or other ornaments. ***adj-***: *an* alabaster *lamp.*

à la carte (äl′ ə kärt′) ***adj-*** & ***adv-*** listed separately on the menu and charged for separately, in contrast to *table d'hôte.* [French for "according to the bill of fare."]

a·lack (ə lăk′) *Archaic* ***interj-*** an exclamation expressing sorrow, surprise, or regret.

a·lac·ri·ty (ə lăk′ rə tē) ***n-*** eager readiness to do something: *They accepted the invitation with* alacrity.

A·lad·din (ə lăd′ ən) ***n-*** in the "Arabian Nights," a boy who by rubbing his magic lamp could summon a jinni to do his bidding.

Al·a·mo (ăl′ ə mō′) ***n-*** mission house in San Antonio, Texas, scene of a historic siege in 1836.

à la mode (ä′ lä′ mōd′, ə lə-) ***adj-*** & ***adv-*** **1** in fashion: *a style no longer* à la mode. **2** served with ice cream: *pie* à la mode. **3** prepared with vegetables: *beef* à la mode. [French for "according to fashion."]

a·larm (ə lärm′) ***n-*** **1** a warning of danger: *She gave the* alarm. **2** device to warn or awaken persons: *a fire* alarm. **3** the fear of danger: *As the waves increased,* alarm *seized the passengers.* **4** *Archaic* a call to arms. ***vt-*** to arouse to a sense of danger; startle: *The smell of smoke* alarmed *the campers.*

alarm clock ***n-*** clock which can be set to ring at any desired time.

a·larm·ing (ə lär′ mĭng) ***adj-*** causing a fear of danger; terrifying. **—*adv-* a·larm′ing·ly:** *The fire is* alarmingly *close.*

a·larm·ist (ə lär′ mĭst) ***n-*** one who exaggerates bad news or foretells calamities.

a·las (ə lăs′) ***interj-*** exclamation showing sorrow, pity, or regret.

a·late (ā′ lāt) ***adj-*** having wings or winglike parts.

alb (ălb) ***n-*** long, white, linen robe worn by a priest celebrating the Mass.

al·ba·core (ăl′ bə kôr′) ***n-*** **1** the long-finned tuna. **2** any of several fishes related to it.

al·ba·tross (ăl′ bə trŏs′) ***n-*** very large web-footed sea bird of southern waters, capable of remarkably long flights from land.

al·be·it (ôl′ bē′ ət) ***conj-*** although; even though.

al·bi·no (ăl bī′ nō) ***n-*** [*pl.* **al·bi·nos**] person or animal with unusually light skin, pink eyes, and nearly white hair, all due to partial or complete lack of natural pigment.

Al·bi·on (ăl′ bē ən) ***n-*** poetic name for England.

al·bum (ăl′ bəm) ***n-*** **1** book with blank pages in which to keep photographs, stamps, autographs, etc. **2** holder, in the form of a book, for phonograph records. **3** set of one or more phonograph records sold as a unit.

al·bu·men (ăl byo͞o′ mən) ***n-*** **1** white of an egg. **2** albumin.

al·bu·min (ăl byo͞o′ mən) ***n-*** any of a large group of simple, water-soluble proteins found in all living matter.

al·bu·mi·nous (ăl byo͞o′ mə nəs) ***adj-*** having to do with or rich in albumin or albumen.

al·che·mist (ăl′ kə mĭst) ***n-*** one who studied or practiced alchemy.

al·che·my (ăl′ kə mē) ***n-*** the chemistry of the Middle Ages, the chief purposes of which were to turn common metals into gold and to find a method of prolonging life.

al·co·hol (ăl′ kə hôl′) ***n-*** **1** colorless, volatile, flammable liquid (C_2H_5OH) produced in the fermentation of fruit, grain, or other sugary or starchy substances; ethanol; ethyl alcohol; grain alcohol; spirits. **2** wood alcohol. **3** *Chemistry* any hydrocarbon whose molecules include one or more hydroxyl groups (OH−).

al·co·hol·ic (ăl′ kə hôl′ ĭk, -hŏl′ ĭk) ***adj-*** **1** containing alcohol: *Whiskey is an* alcoholic *drink.* **2** of alcohol: *an* alcoholic *vapor.* ***n-*** person addicted to the use of liquor.

al·co·hol·ism (ăl′ kə hô′ lĭz əm) ***n-*** **1** uncontrollable addiction to alcohol. **2** the poisoning and deterioration of the body caused by such addiction.

al·cove (ăl′ kōv′) ***n-*** small room opening out of a larger room; nook.

Alcove

Al·deb·a·ran (ăl dĕb′ ə rən) ***n-*** a red star, the brightest star in the constellation Taurus.

al·der (ôl′ dər) ***n-*** any of several trees and shrubs related to the birches, often growing thickly in moist or swampy places. The bark is used in tanning and dyeing.

al·der·man (ôl′ dər mən) ***n-*** [*pl.* **al·der·men**] member of the governing body of a ward, district, or city, or of a church.

ale (āl) ***n-*** a fermented drink similar to beer, made from malt and hops. ***Hom-*** ail.

a·lee (ə lē′) ***adv-*** at or toward the lee.

a·lert (ə lûrt′) ***adj-*** **1** mentally quick in perception and action: *an* alert *mind.* **2** attentive; wide-awake; watchful; bright: *an* alert *student.* ***vt-*** to warn of coming danger: *The commander* alerted *the troops before the enemy attack.* ***n-*** a warning of coming danger: *an air* alert. **—*adv-* a·lert′ly.** ***n-*** **a·lert′ness.**

on the alert on the lookout; watchful.

A·leut (ə lo͞ot′) ***n-*** **1** a native of the Aleutian Islands and the western part of Alaska. **2** the language spoken by these people. **—*adj-* A·leu′tian** (ə lo͞o′ shən): *the* Aleutian *dialect.*

ale·wife (āl′ wīf′) ***n-*** [*pl.* **ale·wives**] small North American fish related to the herring and found mainly along the Atlantic coast.

Al·ex·an·drine (ăl′ ĭg zăn′ drən) ***n-*** line of poetry consisting of six iambic feet with a slight pause after the third. Example: "Our sweet′/est songs′/are those′//which tell′/of sad′/est thought′"/.

Alfalfa

al·fal·fa (ăl făl′ fə) ***n-*** plant resembling clover and having purple flowers and very deep roots. It is grown for hay, often yielding several cuttings a year.

al fresco (ăl' frĕs' kō) ***adv-*** in the open air; outdoors: *to eat* al fresco. ***adj-***: *We had an* al fresco *dinner.* Also **al·fres' co.**

al·gae (ăl' jē) ***n-*** *pl.* [*sing.* **al·ga** (-gə)] a large group of primitive plants having chlorophyll but lacking true roots, flowers, stems, and leaves. Algae are the chief marine and fresh-water plants, ranging in size from pond scum to kelp.

al·ge·bra (ăl' jə brə) ***n-*** branch of mathematics which represents quantities and relations between them by the use of letters, numerals, and other symbols. ***adj-*** **al' ge·bra' ic** (ăl' jə brā' ĭk) or **al' ge·bra' i·cal.** ***adv-*** **al' ge·bra' i·cal·ly.**

Al·gon·qui·an (ăl gŏng' kwē ən, -kē ən) ***n-*** [*pl.* **Al·gon·qui·ans,** also **Al·gon·qui·an**] **1** a widespread family of Indian languages spoken from Labrador to the Carolinas and westward to the Great Plains. **2** member of an Indian tribe speaking any one of these languages. ***adj-***: *an* Algonquian *word.*

Al·gon·quin or **Al·gon·kin** (ăl' gŏng' kən, -kwən) ***n-*** [*pl.* **Al·gon·quins,** also **Al·gon·quin**] **1** member of an Algonquian Indian tribe that lived in the forests of the Ottawa River valley. **2** the language spoken by these Indians. ***adj-***: *an* Algonquin *legend.*

al·go·rithm (ăl' gər ith' əm) *Mathematics* ***n-*** any process that is regularly used to perform a mathematical computation.

Al·ham·bra (ăl hăm' brə) ***n-*** palace of the Moorish kings in Granada, Spain, built in the thirteenth and fourteenth centuries.

a·li·as (ā' lē əs) ***n-*** [*pl.* **a·li·as·es**] an assumed name: *The forger had two* aliases. ***adv-*** otherwise called: *Max,* alias *Slinky Sam.*

A·li Ba·ba (ăl' ē bä' bə, ä' lē-) ***n-*** in the "Arabian Nights," a poor woodcutter who became rich by outwitting a band of forty thieves.

a·li·bi (ăl' ə bī) ***n-*** **1** claim made by a person accused of a crime or wrongdoing that he was somewhere else when the crime was committed. **2** *Informal* an excuse for failure: *Tom has a ready* alibi *each time he's late with his work.*

al·i·en (ā' lī ən or āl' yən) ***n-*** foreigner; person who is not a citizen of the country in which he is living. ***adj-*** foreign: *an* alien *people*; *an* alien *land.*

alien to strange to; not characteristic of: *Dishonesty is* alien to *his nature.*

al·i·en·ate (ā' lē ə nāt') ***vt-*** [**al·i·en·at·ed, al·i·en·at·ing**] to cause (a person) to withdraw his affections, trust, etc.; make hostile or indifferent: *His selfish habits soon* alienated *his friends.* **—*n-*** **al' i·en·a' tion.**

al·i·en·ist (ā' lē ə nist) ***n-*** psychiatrist, especially one dealing with the legal aspects of insanity.

[1]**a·light** (ə līt') ***adj-*** **1** kindled or burning: *The fire is* alight *on the hearth.* **2** bright: *His face was* alight *with excitement.* [from a combination of Old English **an,** "on," and **lēoht** meaning "light."]

[2]**a·light** (ə līt') ***vi-*** **1** to get down from a train, airplane, etc.; step down (from): *They* alighted *and went into the terminal.* **2** to land or settle on the earth: *The plane* alighted. [from Old English **alīhtan** meaning "make light; take weight off," from Old English **līht** meaning "light (in weight)."]

a·lign (ə līn') ***vt-*** **1** to bring (the parts of a machine or electronic device) into proper relationship with each other. **2** to make (the front wheels of a car) parallel. **3** to set in a line: *We* aligned *the chairs along the wall.* **4** to ally (oneself) with one side of an argument or cause: *The three nations* aligned *themselves against the common enemy.* ***vi-*** to be adjusted or in line: *This wheel* aligns *with the other.* Also **aline. —*n-*** **a·lign' ment** or **a·line' ment.**

a·like (ə līk') ***adj-*** similar: *The two brothers are* alike *in their interests.* ***adv-*** similarly; in the same way: *The twins dress* alike, *walk* alike, *talk* alike *and sometimes think* alike.

al·i·men·ta·ry (ăl' ə mĕn' tə rē) ***adj-*** pertaining to food and nutrition.

alimentary canal ***n-*** the whole digestive tract, including the esophagus, stomach, and intestines.

al·i·mo·ny (ăl' ə mō' nē) ***n-*** an allowance for support paid by one's former spouse by court order, after a divorce.

a·line (ə līn') ***vi- & vt-*** [**a·lined, a·lin·ing**] to align.

a·live (ə līv') ***adj-*** **1** having life. **2** lively; animated: *Jane is one of the most* alive *girls we know.* **3** attentive; sensitive: *She is* alive *to the opportunities.* **4** full of living things; swarming: *The stream is* alive *with fish.*

a·liz·a·rin (ə līz' ə rən) ***n-*** red dye formerly obtained from the madder plant and now made from coal tar.

al·ka·li (ăl' kə lī') ***n-*** [*pl.* **al·ka·lis** or **al·kal·ies**] **1** a mixture of soluble salts, such as sodium carbonate or sodium sulfate, often occurring in the soil and water of deserts. **2** *Chemistry* a strong base that dissolves in water, such as sodium or potassium hydroxide.

al·ka·line (ăl' kə lən, -līn') ***adj-*** **1** containing alkali. **2** able to combine with an acid to form a salt.

al·ka·loid (ăl' kə loid') ***n-*** one of a group of bitter, alkaline compounds including caffeine, cocaine, quinine, and strychnine. They are often very poisonous but are valuable in medicine in small amounts.

all (ȯl) ***determiner*** (traditionally called adjective or pronoun) **1** the whole of: *in* all *the world.* **2** each and every one of: *to* all *people.* **3** as much as possible: *with* all *speed.* **4** nothing but: *This is* all *work and no play.* **5** everyone: All *agreed.* ***n-*** **1** the whole number or quantity: *They asked* all *of us to the party.* **2** one's full resources, material or moral: *He would give* all *to win. They gave their* all. ***adv-*** wholly: *He's* all *wrong.* ***Hom-*** awl.

above all before everyone or everything; most of all: *You,* above all, *should know better.* **after all** everything considered: *It appears the best plan* after all. **all but** on the brink of; almost: *He* all but *collapsed.* **all in** *Informal* completely exhausted: *After running a mile, he was* all in. **all in all** (or **in all,** or **all told**) as a whole; on the whole; altogether: All in all, *it was good training.* **all over** **1** finished: *The concert is* all over. **2** in every part of; everywhere: *She went* all over *town.* **3** *Informal* typically; characteristically: *That's Fred* all over. **all over with** ruined; undone: *Once the police discovered his identity, it was* all over with *him.* **at all** in any way: *We didn't care for him* at all. **for all** **1** in spite of; despite: *The doctor is very modest,* for all *her knowledge.* **2** as far as; to the extent that: *You can go alone to the pool,* for all *I care.*

►ALL OF is used before definite articles in conversation, whereas ALL is preferred in writing. We might say: All of *the countries signed the treaty.* However, we should write: All *the countries signed the treaty.* ALL OF is used before pronouns in both writing and speaking: *Are* all of *them here?*

Al·lah (ăl' ə or äl' ə) ***n-*** Muslim name for God.

all-A·mer·i·can (ȯl' ə mĕr' ə kən) ***adj-*** **1** representative or typical of the entire United States: *an* all-American *boy.* **2** representing the best in a certain activity or group in the United States: *an* all-American *football player.* **3** made up exclusively of Americans: *an* all-American *chess tournament.* ***n***- football, lacrosse, or other player who has received the highest national recognition in a particular year.

all-a·round (ȯl'ə round') ***adj***- all-round.

al·lay (ə lā') ***vt***- to quiet; calm; make less or reduce: *The doctor* allayed *his fears.*

all clear ***n***- signal indicating that an air raid or air-raid drill is over.

al·le·ga·tion (ăl'ə gā'shən) ***n***- assertion, whether or not supported by proof.

al·lege (ə lĕj') ***vt***- [**al·leged, al·leg·ing**] **1** to offer as an argument, plea, or excuse: *He* alleged *illness as the reason for his failure to come.* **2** to assert: *They* allege *their innocence.*

al·leged (ə lĕjd') ***adj***- declared without proof: *The* alleged *thief proved to be innocent after investigation.* **—*adv*- al·leg'ed·ly.**

al·le·giance (ə lē'jəns) ***n***- loyalty and devotion, especially to one's country.

al·le·gor·y (ăl'ə gôr'ē) ***n***- [*pl.* **al·le·gor·ies**] story in which the characters and happenings stand for ideas or qualities, such as truth, loyalty, virtue, etc. Examples: the parables of the Bible; "Aesop's Fables." **—*adj*- al'le·gor'i·cal:** *an* allegorical *tale.* ***adv***- **al'le·gor'i·cal·ly.**

al·le·gret·to (ăl'ə grĕt'ō) *Music* ***adj***- ***& adv***- somewhat fast; slower than allegro but faster than moderato.

al·le·gro (ə lĕg'rō, ə lā'grō) *Music* ***adj***- ***& adv***- fast; lively; slower than presto but faster than allegretto.

al·le·lu·ia (ăl'ə lo͞o'yə) hallelujah.

al·ler·gen (ăl'ər jən) ***n***- any substance to which one has an allergy.

al·ler·gist (ăl'ər jĭst) ***n***- doctor who treats allergies.

al·ler·gy (ăl'ər jē) ***n***- [*pl.* **al·ler·gies**] sensitivity of the body to certain foods, chemicals, pollens, insect bites, etc. **—*adj*- al·ler'gic** (ə lûr'jĭk): *He is* allergic *to strawberries.*

al·le·vi·ate (ə lē'vē āt') ***vt***- [**al·le·vi·at·ed, al·le·vi·at·ing**] to lighten; lessen; make easier: *a medicine to* alleviate *pain.* **—*n*- al·le'vi·a'tion:** *the* alleviation *of severe pain.*

[1]**al·ley** (ăl'ē) ***n***- [*pl.* **al·leys**] **1** narrow street or passage, especially one at the rear of buildings. **2** formal pathway in a garden, usually lined with trees. **3** bowling alley. **4** a strip on each side of a tennis court that is part of the playing area when four persons play but not when two persons play (for picture, see *tennis court*). [from Old French **alee** meaning "passage," from **aller,** "to go."]

[2]**al·ley** (ăl'ē) ***n***- [*pl.* **al·leys**] in marbles, a large marble used to hit the others; a taw. [short for **alabaster.**]

al·ley·way (ăl'ē wā') ***n***- narrow passageway between buildings.

All Fools' Day ***n***- the first of April; April Fools' Day.

All·hal·lows (ŏl'hăl'ōz) ***n***- All Saints' Day, celebrated on November 1 in honor of all the saints.

al·li·ance (ə lī'əns) ***n***- union or joining together by agreement of two or more persons, families, groups, or nations: *an* alliance *by marriage*; *an* alliance *for war*; *an international* alliance.

al·lied (ăl'īd'or ə līd') ***adj***- **1** united or joined, especially by treaty or other agreement: *the* allied *powers.* **2** related or similar: *some* allied *chemical compounds*; allied *industries.*

Al·lies, the (al'īz') ***n***- ***pl.*** **1** the countries that fought against Germany and Austria in World War I. **2** the countries that fought against Germany, Italy, and Japan in World War II.

al·li·ga·tor (ăl'ə gā'tər) ***n***- **1** large, lizardlike, flesh-eating animal related to the crocodile, with a short, broad head and blunt snout. One kind, growing to about twelve feet, lives in the fresh waters of southern United States. **2** leather made from the skin of this animal. *as* ***modifier***: *an* alligator *den.* [from Spanish **el lagarto** meaning "the lizard."]

Alligator 10 to 12 ft. long

al·lit·er·a·tion (ə lĭt ə rā'shən) ***n***- use of the same consonant sound at the beginning of words throughout a line or passage. Example: "In a *s*ummer *s*eason when *s*oft was the *s*un . . ." **—*adj*- al·lit'er·a'tive:** *an* alliterative *expression.* ***adv***- **al·lit'er·a'tive·ly.**

al·lo·cate (ăl'ə kāt') ***vt***- [**al·lo·cat·ed, al·lo·cat·ing**] to set aside or distribute for a special purpose; assign; allot: *He* allocated *part of his income for a vacation trip.* ***n***- **al'lo·ca'tion:** *the* allocation *of materials for a project.*

al·lot (ə lŏt') ***vt***- [**al·lot·ted, al·lot·ting**] to distribute (amounts or shares); assign: *to* allot *an hour.*

al·lot·ment (ə lŏt'mənt) ***n***- **1** distribution in parts or shares: *An* allotment *of preferred stock is to be made.* **2** a share or part distributed.

all-out (ȯl'out') ***adj***- complete; total: *an* all-out *effort.*

all·o·ver (ȯl'ō'vər) ***adj***- covering the whole of anything.

al·low (ə lou') ***vt***- **1** to permit; let: *The doctor* allowed *the patient to sit up.* **2** to permit the presence of: *This hotel does not* allow *dogs.* **3** to acknowledge as right or valid: *The court* allowed *his claim to the property.*

allow for to make provision or concession for; make allowance for: *to* allow for *a hem*; allow for *his youth.*

allow of to permit; admit of: *This story* allows of *two completely different interpretations.*

al·low·a·ble (ə lou'ə bəl) ***adj***- permissible; proper.

al·low·ance (ə lou'əns) ***n***- **1** an accepting or admitting; concession: *the judge's* allowance *of a claim.* **2** definite amount or quantity, especially of money, given for a particular purpose: *a travel* allowance. **3** amount added to or subtracted from a price: *a $200 trade-in* allowance.

make allowance(s) for to take into consideration or account: *We made* allowance *for Jack's inexperience.*

[1]**al·loy** (ăl'oi) ***n***- **1** a metal usually made by the fusion of two or more metallic elements: *Bronze is an* alloy *of tin and copper.* **2** something that takes away from the perfection or full enjoyment of another thing: *pleasure without* alloy.

[2]**al·loy** (ə loi', *also* ăl'oi) ***vt***- **1** to combine (two or more metals). **2** to lessen (perfection, enjoyment, etc.): *His hope was* alloyed *by fear.*

all right ***adj***- **1** satisfactory; OK: *His work is* all right. **2** healthy; not sick or injured; safe and sound: *Do you feel* all right? ***adv***- **1** yes: *He said,* "All right, *I'll do it.*" **2** without fail; certainly: *I'll be there,* all right. **3** *Informal* satisfactorily.

►Careful writers avoid the spelling ALRIGHT.

all-round (ȯl′round′) ***adj-*** able to do many things; versatile; not limited; all-around: *an* all-round *baseball player; an* all-round *education.*

All Saints' Day ***n-*** November 1, celebrated in honor of all the saints.

All Souls' Day ***n-*** in the Roman Catholic Church, the day (November 2) on which special prayers are said for the souls in purgatory.

all·spice (ȯl′spīs′) ***n-*** **1** berry of the West Indian pimento tree. **2** spice made from it, suggesting the combined flavors of cinnamon, nutmeg, and clover.

all-star (ȯl′stär′) ***adj-*** made up entirely of outstanding players or entertainers: *an* all-star *team; an* all-star *cast.*

al·lude (ə lo͞od′) ***vi-*** [**al·lud·ed, al·lud·ing**] to refer to indirectly or in passing.
►Should not be confused with ELUDE.

al·lure (ə lo͝or′) ***n-*** the power to attract; enticement: *the* allure *of mountain climbing.* ***vt-*** [**al·lured, al·lur·ing**] to attract; entice: *The sea* allured *him.*

al·lure·ment (ə lo͝or′mənt) ***n-*** **1** the power to allure: *the* allurement *of her wealth.* **2** something that allures: *The higher salary was a strong* allurement.

al·lu·sion (ə lo͞o′zhən) ***n-*** **1** a passing reference: *Do not make any* allusion *to his loss.* **2** a reference to something generally familiar, used by way of illustration: *a literary* allusion. ***adj-*** **al·lu′sive:** *an* allusive *remark.*
►Should not be confused with ELUSION or ILLUSION.

al·lu·vi·al (ə lo͞o′vē əl) ***adj-*** composed of mud, sand, and gravel deposited by flowing water: *the rich* alluvial *soil of deltas.*

Alluvial fan

alluvial fan ***n-*** a fan-shaped delta of sediments deposited where a swift river comes onto flat land.

al·lu·vi·um (ə lo͞o′vē əm) ***n-*** [*pl.* **al·lu·vi·a** (-vē ə)] materials, such as clay, sand, and gravel, carried and deposited by running water; also, any one of these materials.

[1]**al·ly** (ăl′ī′) ***n-*** [*pl.* **al·lies**] person or group of persons, especially a nation, united with another for a common purpose: *They were natural* allies *and agreed perfectly.*

[2]**al·ly** (ə lī′) ***vt-*** [**al·lied, al·ly·ing**] to join (oneself, a nation, etc.) with or to another for a special purpose: *The United States* allied *itself with England and France during the World Wars.*

Al·ma Ma·ter (äl′mə mä′tər, ăl′mə mā′tər) ***n-*** one's school, college, or university. Also **alma mater.**

al·ma·nac (ȯl′mə năk′) ***n-*** **1** a book arranged according to the days, weeks, and months of the year, giving information about the weather, time of sunrise and sunset, tides, etc. **2** a book compiled annually, giving useful facts and statistics.

al·might·y (ȯl′mī′tē) ***adj-*** all-powerful. ***n-*** **the Almighty** God.

al·mond (ä′mənd, ă′-, äl′-) ***n-*** **1** nut of a small tree somewhat like the peach tree. **2** the tree itself.

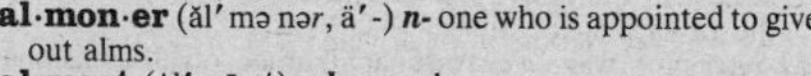
Almond, shell and kernel

al·mond-eyed (ä′mənd īd′, ă′-, äl′-) ***adj-*** having eyes shaped somewhat like an almond.

al·mon·er (ăl′mə nər, ä′-) ***n-*** one who is appointed to give out alms.

al·most (ȯl′mōst′) ***adv-*** nearly.
►For usage note see MOST.

alms (ämz) ***n-*** [*pl.* **alms**] money given to the poor; charity: *to give* alms *to a beggar.*

alms·house (ämz′hous′) ***n-*** free home for the poor, supported by public funds.

al·oe (ăl′ō) ***n-*** **1** garden plant whose thick, fleshy leaves have spiny edges and grow in a cluster from the base of the plant. **2** (usually **aloes**) a bitter drug made from the juice of its leaves. **3** the century plant or **American aloe. 4** the fragrant wood or resin of an East Indian tree.

a·loft (ə lȯft′) ***adj-*** above the earth; high up: *The planes were* aloft *at the time of the air raid.* ***adv-*** high above the deck of a ship in the upper rigging: *The sailor nimbly climbed* aloft.

a·lo·ha (ä lō′hä) ***interj-*** **1** hello; you are welcome. **2** goodby; farewell. [from Hawaiian, meaning literally "love."]

a·lone (ə lōn′) ***adj-*** **1** without anyone or anything else; solitary: *He was* alone *with his thoughts.* **2** and no other; only: *Mr. Jones* alone *has the solution to the problem.* ***adv-*** with no assistance; singly: *She can do it* alone.
leave alone to allow to remain undisturbed: Leave *it* alone. **leave** (or **let**) **well enough alone** to be content with things as they are. **let alone 1** to allow (something) to be without trying to change it: *If you approve of the plan,* let *it* alone. **2** not to mention; not to speak of: *He doesn't have the money,* let alone *the time.* **stand alone** to be without equal; be unique: *He* stands alone *among Shakespearean actors.*

a·long (ə lȯng′) ***prep-*** **1** over the length of: *to walk* along *the beach.* **2** at the edge of: *the trees* along *the path.* ***adv-*** **1** onward: *to move* along. **2** with someone: *They brought him* along.
all along all the while: *We knew it* all along. **along with** together with. **get along 1** to move onward. **2** to manage; get by: *Their family* gets along *on very little.* **3** to progress: *How are you* getting along *in your science course?* **4** to be friendly or agree: *They* got along *well together.* **go along with** to cooperate with or support: *to* go along with *his decision.*

a·long·side (ə lȯng′sīd′) ***prep-*** (considered an adverb when the object is clearly implied but not expressed) by the side of; next to: *He parked his car* alongside *the building. They brought the boat* alongside.
alongside of close by the side of; side by side with: *This tree will grow* alongside of *the birch and maple.*

a·loof (ə lo͞of′) ***adj-*** distant in position, manner, or feeling (often used with "stand," "keep," or "hold"): *Their leader stood* aloof *throughout the crisis.* **—*n-* a·loof′ness.**

a·loud (ə loud′) ***adv-*** **1** in a voice one can hear; not in a whisper: *He read the story* aloud *to the class.* **2** loudly: *She sang* aloud *for joy.*

alp (ălp) ***n-*** rugged mountain peak.

al·pac·a (ăl păk′ə) ***n-*** **1** domesticated grazing animal of South America, related to the llama and vicuña, and valued for its long silky wool. **2** yarn or cloth of this wool. **3** thin, wiry silk cloth with a fine texture. ***as modifier:*** *an* alpaca *coat.*

al·pen·horn (ăl′pən hȯrn′, -hôrn′) ***n-*** long, wooden horn, used by herdsmen in the Alps. Also **alp′horn.**

al·pen·stock (ăl′pən stŏk′) ***n-*** strong staff with a pointed metal tip on one end, used by mountain climbers.

al·pha (ăl′fə) ***n-*** first letter of the Greek alphabet, equivalent to English "a"; hence, the beginning of anything.
alpha and omega the beginning and the end.

al·pha·bet (ăl′ fə bĕt′) ***n-*** the system of letters or characters used in writing the words or indicating the sounds of a language, arranged in order, such as A, B, C, etc.

al·pha·bet·i·cal (ăl′ fə bĕt′ ĭ kəl) ***adj-*** in the order of the letters of the alphabet: *The words in a dictionary are arranged in* alphabetical *order.* **—*adv-*** **al′ pha·bet′ i·cal·ly.**

al·pha·bet·ize (ăl′ fə bə tīz′) ***vt-*** [**al·pha·bet·ized, al·pha·bet·iz·ing**] to arrange in the order of the letters of the alphabet: *Please* alphabetize *this list of names for me.*

alpha particle ***n-*** small, positively charged particle, identical to a helium nucleus, given off by radioactive elements.

alpha ray ***n-*** stream of alpha particles.

al·pine (ăl′ pīn′) ***adj-*** **1** belonging to high mountains: *fine* alpine *snow*; alpine *flowers.* **2 Alpine** belonging to the Alps.

al·read·y (ôl′ rĕd′ ē) ***adv-*** **1** some time before now; by this (or that) time: *He has* already *left.* **2** (*often* ôl′ rĕd′ ē) so soon: *Are you here* already?

►ALREADY is an adverb. *Are you here* already? The two words ALL and READY might occur in the sentence *Are you* all ready? meaning "Are all of you ready?" In the second example, ALL is a pronoun, and READY is an adjective.

al·so (ôl′ sō) ***adv-*** in addition; as well; too.

not only . . . but also both . . . and: *He was* not only *a good student,* but also *an outstanding athlete.*

al·so-ran (ôl′ sō răn′) ***n-*** **1** in a race, a contestant that fails to finish among the first three. **2** any unsuccessful contestant.

Alta. Alberta.

al·tar (ôl′ tər) ***n-*** **1** raised place or structure on which religious sacrifices are offered, or at which religious ceremonies are performed. **2** in many Christian churches, the communion table. ***Hom-*** alter.

altar boy ***n-*** man or boy who assists a minister or priest in religious services; acolyte.

al·ter (ôl′ tər) ***vt-*** **1** to change; make or become different: *to* alter *a suit; to* alter *plans; to* alter *one's views.* **2** to castrate or spay (an animal). ***Hom-*** altar.

al·ter·a·tion (ôl′ tə rā′ shən) ***n-*** **1** a change: *a necessary* alteration *in design.* **2** the act of changing or modifying anything: *I had to pay for the* alteration *of this dress.*

al·ter·ca·tion (ôl′ tər kā′ shən) ***n-*** a quarrel or dispute; wrangle: *The conference ended in a stormy* altercation *between the two chief delegates.*

al·ter ego (ôl′ tər) ***n-*** another self; an intimate friend sharing one's tastes, ideals, thoughts, etc.

[1]**al·ter·nate** (ôl′ tər nət, ăl′-) ***adj-*** **1** every other of a series: *The boys and girls used the gymnasium on* alternate *days of the week.* **2** first one and then the other; by turns: *the child's* alternate *tears and laughter.* ***n-*** a substitute: *When the juror fell ill, an* alternate *took his place.* **—*adv-*** **al′ ter·nate·ly.**

[2]**al·ter·nate** (ôl′ tər nāt′, ăl′-) ***vi-*** [**al·ter·nat·ed, al·ter·nat·ing**] **1** to take turns: *The workmen* alternate *in running the machine.* **2** to take place or appear by turns: *White tiles* alternated *with black.* ***vt-*** to cause to take place or appear by turns: *The farmer* alternated *corn and soybeans.*

alternating current ***n-*** electric current that flows first in one direction and then in the other. The alternating current used in the home usually reverses direction 120 times per second. *Abbr.* A.C. See also *direct current.*

al·ter·na·tion (ôl′ tər nā′ shən, ăl′-) ***n-*** a following in succession, one after the other: *the* alternation *of day and night.*

al·ter·na·tive (ôl tər′ nə tĭv′, ăl′-) ***n-*** **1** one of two or more things to choose from: *Our choice is between slavery or resistance, and we choose the second* alternative. **2** *Informal* a choice between two or more things. ***adj-*** **1** offering a choice between two or more things: *He was presented with* alternative *plans.* **2** substitute: *an* alternative *menu.* **—*adv-*** **al·ter′ na·tive′ ly.**

►Traditionally ALTERNATIVE meant one of only two things or courses to be chosen: *Our* alternatives *are the movies or the ball game.* Today, however, ALTERNATIVE is used to mean one of several courses; the movies, the ball game, and the dance. Also, ALTERNATIVE is now widely used to mean "a choice," although precise speakers still prefer to speak of a CHOICE between or among ALTERNATIVES.

al·ter·na·tor (ôl′ tər nā′ tər, ăl′-) ***n-*** electric generator that produces alternating current.

al·though (ôl thō′) ***conj-*** even though; in spite of the fact that: *I don't know him well,* although *he lives next door.* Also **al·tho′.**

al·tim·e·ter (ăl tĭm′ ə tər, ăl′ tə mē′ tər) ***n-*** radio or barometric instrument used to measure altitude; especially, a barometric device used in airplanes.

al·ti·tude (ăl′ tə tōōd′, -tyōōd′) ***n-*** **1** vertical distance above the earth, especially above sea level; height. **2** in geometry, the perpendicular distance from the base of a figure or solid to its highest point.

al·to (ăl′ tō) *Music* ***n-*** [*pl.* **al·tos**] musical range of the lowest female or boy's singing voice; contralto; also, a singer having this range, or a part composed for it, especially in four-part choral works. ***adj-*** having this or a similar range: *an* alto *voice*; *an* alto *flute.*

al·to·cu·mu·lus (ăl′ tō kyōōm′ yə ləs) ***n-*** [*pl.* **al·to·cum·u·lus·es** or **al·to·cum·u·li** (-lī)] gray or white fleecy cloud having a rounded formation and often occurring in patches. For picture, see *cloud.*

al·to·geth·er (ôl′ tə gĕth′ ər) ***adv-*** **1** entirely; wholly; completely: *He missed the target* altogether. *Her composition was not* altogether *bad.* **2** all told: *There were five pieces of luggage* altogether.

al·to·stra·tus (ăl′ tō strā′ təs, -străt′ əs) ***n-*** [*pl.* **al·to·stra·tus·es** of **al·to·stra·ti** (-tī)] low-lying gray or bluish cloud, often seen in compact, streaked layers.

al·tru·ism (ăl′ trōō ĭz əm) ***n-*** unselfish regard for the interests of others. **—*n-*** **al′ tru·ist.**

al·tru·is·tic (ăl′ trōō ĭs′ tĭk) ***adj-*** unselfishly concerned with the welfare of others. **—*adv-*** **al′ tru·is′ ti·cal·ly.**

al·um (ăl′ əm) ***n-*** transparent, whitish mineral salt, used as a medicine either externally to stop bleeding or internally to cause vomiting. It is also used in dyeing and in the purification of water.

a·lu·mi·nize (ə lōō′ mə nīz′) ***vt-*** [**a·lu·mi·nized, a·lu·mi·niz·ing**] to coat or otherwise treat with aluminum.

a·lu·mi·num (ə lōō′ mə nəm) ***n-*** very lightweight silver-white metallic element that does not corrode in air. Symbol Al, At. No. 13, At. Wt. 26.9815.

a·lum·na (ə lŭm′ nə) ***n-*** [*pl.* **a·lum·nae** (-nē)] woman graduated from a school, college, or university.

a·lum·nus (ə lŭm′ nəs) ***n-*** [*pl.* **a·lum·ni** (-nī)] man or woman graduated from a school, college, or university.

al·ve·o·lus (ăl vē′ ə ləs) ***n-*** [*pl.* **al·ve·o·li** (-ə lī)] small hollow in the body, especially a tooth socket or one of the air sacs in the lungs.

al·ways (ôl′ wāz, -wēz) ***adv-*** at all times; on all occasions; without exception: *My father is* always *generous.*

am (ăm) form of **be** used with "I" in the present tense.

AM amplitude modulation.

Am. **1** America. **2** American.

a.m. or **A.M.** before noon [from Latin **ante meridiem**].

A.M. Master of Arts. Also **M.A.**

a·mah (ä′ mə, ä′ mä′) ***n-*** in Asia, a female servant or nurse, especially a wet nurse.

a·mal·gam (ə măl′ gəm) ***n-*** **1** an alloy consisting of any metal dissolved in mercury, especially the alloy of silver and mercury that is used to fill dental cavities. **2** any mixture or combination: *In our Southwest we find an* amalgam *of American and Mexican cultures.*

a·mal·ga·mate (ə măl′ gə māt′) ***vt-*** **[a·mal·ga·mat·ed, a·mal·ga·mat·ing] 1** to dissolve (a metal) in mercury. **2** to unite, combine, or merge: *to* amalgamate *two publishing companies.* ***vi-*** to mix and blend completely; to become one (with): *In the past, one culture has often* amalgamated *with another.*

a·mal·ga·ma·tion (ə măl′ gə mā′ shən) ***n-*** **1** combination or union; merger: *an* amalgamation *of small corporations.* **2** a dissolving of a metal in mercury. **3** process used to extract gold and silver from their ores by dissolving them out with mercury.

am·a·ni·ta (ăm′ə nī′ tə, -nē′ tə) ***n-*** any of a large group of mushrooms and toadstools, most of them deadly poisonous; especially, the death cup and the **fly amanita,** a large yellow to red variety with white gills.

Amanita (death cup)

a·man·u·en·sis (ə măn′ yo͞o ĕn′ səs) ***n-*** [*pl.* **a·man·u·en·ses** (-sēz′)] one who writes for another, either from dictation or from copy; a secretary.

am·a·ranth (ăm′ ə rănth′) ***n-*** any of several plants cultivated for their brilliant green, purple, or crimson flowers.

am·a·ryl·lis (ăm′ ə rĭl′ əs) ***n-*** any of a family of lilylike, bulbous plants, especially one grown for its large, bright-colored blossoms; also, the blossom.

a·mass (ə măs′) ***vt-*** to collect into a heap; gather; accumulate: *He* amassed *great wealth.*

am·a·teur (ăm′ ə chər, -cho͝or′, -tər) ***n-*** **1** one who engages in any art, study, or sport for pleasure, and not for money: *a golf* amateur. **2** one whose work lacks professional finish. ***adj-*** nonprofessional: *a play suitable for* amateur *dramatics.*

am·a·teur·ish (ăm′ ə cho͝or′ ĭsh, -to͝or′ ĭsh) ***adj-*** lacking in professional finish; inexpert. ***—adv-*** **am′ a·teur′ ish·ly.** ***n-*** **am′ a·teur′ ish·ness:** *Their enthusiasm almost made up for the* amateurishness *of their performance.*

am·a·tor·y (ăm′ ə tôr′ ē) ***adj-*** relating to, or expressive of, love: *Robert Burns wrote much* amatory *poetry.*

a·maze (ə māz′) ***vt-*** **[a·mazed, a·maz·ing]** to surprise greatly; overwhelm with astonishment: *The magician* amazed *the children when he lifted a rabbit out of his hat.*

a·maze·ment (ə māz′ mənt) ***n-*** bewilderment arising from sudden surprise; astonishment.

a·maz·ing (ə mā′ zĭng) ***adj-*** causing amazement; astonishing; very surprising. ***—adv-*** **a·maz′ ing·ly.**

Am·a·zon (ăm′ ə zŏn′) ***n-*** **1** in Greek legend, one of a group of female warriors who aided the Trojans in the Trojan War. **2 amazon** any large, powerful, aggressive woman.

Am·a·zo·ni·an (ăm′ ə zō′ nē ən) ***adj-*** **1** of or relating to the Amazon River or the region it drains. **2** (also **amazonian**) pertaining to an Amazon; of women, warlike or masculine. ***n-*** a native of the Amazon region.

am·bas·sa·dor (ăm băs′ ə dər, əm-) ***n-*** **1** government agent of highest rank representing his country's interests at a foreign capital. **2** any representative or agent charged with a special mission.

am·ber (ăm′ bər) ***n-*** **1** a hard, yellow or yellow-brown gum that can be polished and made into jewelry and pipe stems. Amber is actually fossil resin. **2** a yellow or yellowish-brown color. ***adj-:*** *a string of* amber *beads; the* amber *glow of a lamp.*

am·ber·gris (ăm′ bər grĭs′, -grēs′) ***n-*** a valuable waxy material secreted by the intestines of the sperm whale and used in making perfume.

am·bi·dex·trous (ăm′ bə dĕk′ strəs) ***adj-*** able to use both hands with equal skill. ***—adv-*** **am′ bi·dex′ trous·ly.**

am·bi·ent (ăm′ bē ənt) ***adj-*** completely encircling; surrounding.

am·bi·gu·i·ty (ăm′ bə gyo͞o′ ə tē) ***n-*** [*pl.* **am·bi·gu·i·ties**] **1** vagueness or uncertainty of meaning; doubtfulness: *a statement full of* ambiguity. **2** something that has more than one meaning or is otherwise ambiguous: *His "no" is an* ambiguity, *since it also means "yes."*

am·big·u·ous (ăm′ bĭg′ yo͞o əs) ***adj-*** doubtful; having two or more possible meanings: *the speaker's* ambiguous *words; his* ambiguous *actions.* ***—adv-*** **am·big′ u·ous·ly.** ***n-*** **am·big′ u·ous·ness:** *The* ambiguousness *of his remarks puzzled me.*

am·bi·tion (ăm bĭsh′ ən) ***n-*** **1** an eager desire or strong drive to gain or do something: *an* ambition *to be an explorer; a man of* ambition. **2** the thing desired: *It is her* ambition *to be the first woman President.*

am·bi·tious (ăm bĭsh′ əs) ***adj-*** **1** full of ambition; determined to succeed. **2** eager; aspiring: *a student* ambitious *for knowledge.* **3** requiring great skill or effort for success: *an* ambitious *plan.* ***—adv-*** **am·bi′ tious·ly.**

am·biv·a·lence (ăm bĭv′ ə ləns) ***n-*** **1** presence of two opposing emotions or impulses at the same time. **2** *Chemistry* the possession of both a positive and a negative valence by an element. ***—adj-*** **am·biv′ a·lent:** *an* ambivalent *attitude.* ***adv-*** **am·biv′ a·lent·ly.**

am·ble (ăm′ bəl) ***vi-*** **[am·bled, am·bling] 1** of horses, to pace, or go at a gait in which the animal lifts the two feet on the same side together. **2** to walk at an easy pace. ***n-*** **1** the ambling gait of a horse. **2** any easy gait. ***—n-*** **am′ bler.**

am·bro·si·a (ăm′ brō′ zhə, -zhē ə) ***n-*** **1** in mythology, the food of the gods. **2** anything extremely pleasing to taste or smell. ***—adj-*** **am·bro′ si·al:** *an* ambrosial *fragrance.*

am·bu·lance (ăm′ byə ləns) ***n-*** enclosed vehicle for carrying the sick and wounded.

ambulance chaser *Slang* ***n-*** lawyer who tries to persuade people injured in accidents to sue for damages as his clients.

am·bu·la·to·ry (ăm′ byə lə tôr′ ē) ***adj-*** **1** able to walk: *an* ambulatory *patient.* **2** of or pertaining to walking: *an* ambulatory *exercise.*

am·bus·cade (ăm′ bə skād′) ***n-*** **1** an ambush; place where troops hide for sudden attack. **2** troops so hidden. ***vt-*** **[am·bus·cad·ed, am·bus·cad·ing]** to ambush.

am·bush (ăm′ bo͝osh′) ***n-*** **1** a surprise attack from a concealed place; also, the attackers. **2** the concealed place itself. ***vt-*** to waylay; attack from a concealed place: *to* ambush *troops.*

a·me·ba (ə mē′ bə) ***n-*** microscopic water animal having only one cell and no definite shape. It represents one of the simplest forms of life. Also **amoeba.**

Ameba, magnified 100 times

fāte, făt, dâre, bärn; bē, bĕt, mêre; bīte, bĭt; nōte, hŏt, môre, dȯg; fŭn, fûr; to͞o, bo͝ok; oil; out; tar; thin; then; hw for wh as in *wh*at; zh for s as in u*s*ual; ə for a, e, i, o, u, as in *a*go, lin*e*n, per*i*l, at*o*m, min*u*s

a·me·bic (ə mē′bĭk) ***adj-*** of, related to, or caused by amebas: *a case of* amebic *dysentery.* Also **ame′ban.**

amebic dysentery ***n-*** type of dysentery caused by a one-celled parasitic organism such as the ameba.

a·mel·io·rate (ə mēl′yə rāt′, ə mēl′ē ə rāt′) ***vt-*** [**a·mel·io·rat·ed, a·me·lio·rat·ing**] to make better; cause to improve: *laws to* ameliorate *living conditions.* ***vi-***: *Our living conditions will* ameliorate *soon.* **—*n-*** **a·mel′io·ra′tion.** ***adj-*** **a·mel′io·ra′tive.**

a·men (ā′mĕn′, ä′mĕn′) ***interj-*** **1** may it be so; may God will it so (used at the end of prayers). **2** I agree; you are right: *When I said it was cold, he said* "Amen." ***n-*** an uttering of this word: *They all shouted an* amen.

a·me·na·ble (ə mē′nə bəl, ə mĕn′-) ***adj-*** **1** open or disposed to; readily accepting or yielding; responsive: *He is not* amenable *to the change.* **2** liable; answerable: *We are all* amenable *to the law.* **—*n-*** **a·me′na·bil′i·ty** or **a·me′na·ble·ness.** ***adv-*** **a·me′na·bly.**

a·mend (ə mĕnd′) ***vt-*** **1** to change formally: *to* amend *a law.* **2** to change for the better; correct.

►Both AMEND and EMEND mean "to change for the better," but AMEND means to change by adding to as well as subtracting from, whereas EMEND usually means to correct a particular error, such as a misprint.

a·mend·ment (ə mĕnd′mənt) ***n-*** **1** formal change, as in a legal document: *an* amendment *to the Constitution.* **2** a change (of one's ways) for the better.

a·mends (ə mĕndz′) **make amends** to make up for harm or injury: *His letter* made amends *for his rudeness.*

a·men·i·ty (ə mĕn′ə tē) ***n-*** [*pl.* **a·men·i·ties**] **1** pleasantness; agreeableness. **2 amenities** agreeable or polite actions or manners: *the* amenities *of life.*

Amer. 1 America. **2** American.

A·mer·i·ca (ə mĕr′ə kə) ***n-*** **1** United States of America. **2** (also **the Americas**) North, South, and Middle America.

A·mer·i·can (ə mĕr′ə kən) ***adj-*** **1** of or pertaining to the United States, its people, government, or history. **2** pertaining to the lands and people of the Americas. ***n-*** **1** citizen or inhabitant of the United States. **2** inhabitant of the Americas. **3** American English.

American eagle ***n-*** the bald eagle, adopted as the national emblem of the United States.

American English ***n-*** the English language as spoken and written in the United States.

American Indian ***n-*** one of the people who have been living in America since before the first European settlement there. ***adj-*** of or relating to these people, their language or culture.

A·mer·i·can·ism (ə mĕr′ə kə nĭz′əm) ***n-*** **1** word, phrase, or usage found chiefly in American English. **2** custom or tradition characteristic of Americans. **3** loyalty to the institutions of the United States; also, a strong preference for things typical of American life.

A·mer·i·can·ize (ə mĕr′ĭ kə nīz′) ***vt-*** [**A·mer·i·can·ized, Amer·i·can·iz·ing**] **1** to cause to adopt American customs, institutions, styles, speech, etc.: *Our films* Americanize *people.* **2** to adopt American ways in. ***vi-***: *He* Americanized *quickly.* **—*n-*** **A·mer′i·can·i·za′tion.**

American plan ***n-*** in hotels, the inclusion of meals in the fixed rate for a stated period. See also *European plan.*

American Revolution ***n-*** war from 1775–1783 in which the American colonies won their independence from Great Britain.

American Spanish ***n-*** the Spanish language as generally spoken in Latin America, especially the vocabulary.

am·er·ic·i·um (ăm′ə rĭsh′ē əm) ***n-*** a radioactive, synthesized element. Symbol Am, At. No. 95.

am·e·thyst (ăm′ə thəst, -thĭst′) ***n-*** **1** kind of purple or violet quartz used as a gem. **2** a deep purple color. ***adj-***: *an* amethyst *ring; an* amethyst *velvet.*

a·mi·a·ble (ā′mē ə bəl) ***adj-*** friendly; pleasant; good-natured: *She is too* amiable *to lose her temper.* **—*n-*** **a′mi·a·bil′i·ty** also **a′mi·a·ble·ness.** ***adv-*** **a′mi·a·bly.**

am·i·ca·ble (ăm′ə kə bəl) ***adj-*** friendly; peaceable. **—*n-*** **am′i·ca·bil′i·ty.** ***adv-*** **am′i·ca·bly.**

a·mid (ə mĭd′) ***prep-*** in the middle of; among.

a·mid·ships (ə mĭd′shĭps′) ***adv-*** in or toward the middle of a ship.

a·midst (ə mĭdst′) ***prep-*** amid.

a·mi·no acid (ə mē′nō) ***n-*** one of a group of compounds of which proteins, present in all living tissues, are composed.

a·mir (ə mêr′) emir.

A·mish (ā′mĭsh′) ***n-*** *pl.* a sect of Mennonites. ***adj-***: *the* Amish *settlers.*

a·miss (ə mĭs′) ***adj-*** wrong; out of order: *The doctor examined him and found nothing* amiss.

take amiss to have one's feelings hurt: *Don't take it* amiss *if I criticize your work.*

am·i·ty (ăm′ə tē) ***n-*** [*pl,* **am·i·ties**] friendship; peaceful relations: *The United States and Canada have lived in* amity *for many years.*

am·me·ter (ăm′mē′tər) ***n-*** instrument that measures, in amperes, the amount of electric current flowing through a circuit.

am·mo·ni·a (ə mōn′yə) ***n-*** **1** a colorless gas with a sharp, irritating odor. **2** (also **ammonia water** or **household ammonia**) a water solution of this gas used in cleaning.

am·mo·ni·um (ə mō′nē əm) ***n-*** *Chemistry* group of bonded atoms, made up of one nitrogen and four hydrogen atoms (NH_4), found only in combination with other elements. It combines with negative ions to form salts.

am·mu·ni·tion (ăm′yə nĭsh′ən) ***n-*** **1** cartridges, shells, etc., used to load weapons for fighting or hunting. **2** anything usable as a weapon: *The discovery gave him* ammunition *in his campaign.*

am·ne·si·a (ăm nē′zhə) ***n-*** loss of memory caused by brain injury or emotional shock.

am·nes·ty (ăm′nəs tē) ***n-*** [*pl.* **am·nes·ties**] general pardon for offenses against the government.

am·ni·o·cen·te·sis (ăm′nē ō sĕn tē′sĭs) ***n-*** medical procedure involving withdrawal of a small amount of amniotic fluid from a pregnant woman for the purpose of diagnosing the health of the fetus.

am·ni·on (ăm′nē ŏn′) ***n-*** innermost of two layers of the fluid-filled sac in which the embryos of birds, reptiles, and mammals develop. **—*adj-*** **am′ni·ot′ic.**

a·moe·ba (ə mē′bə) ***n-*** [*pl.* **a·moe·bas** or **a·moe·bae** (-bē)] ameba. **—*adj-*** **a·moe′ban** or **a·moe′bic.**

a·mok (ə mŭk′, -mŏk′) amuck.

a·mong (ə mŭng′) ***prep-*** **1** in the midst of; surrounded by: *You are* among *friends.* **2** in the number or group of: *Tom was listed* among *the graduates.* **3** between (more than two): *They discussed the matter* among *themselves.* **4** in shares; to each of: *The land was divided equally* among *the heirs.*

►BETWEEN should be restricted to two parties or things, whereas AMONG should be used with three or more: *He divided the cake* between *John and Jim. He divided the cake* among *Steve, Beth, and Joan.*

a·mor·al (ā′môr′əl) ***adj-*** not caring or concerned about right and wrong; not applying or admitting of moral distinctions or judgments; neither moral nor immoral.

am·o·rous (ăm′ər əs) ***adj-*** inclined to love; having to do with love: *an* amorous *nature*; amorous *letters.* **—*adv-*** **am′o·rous·ly.** ***n-*** **am′o·rous·ness.**

a·morph·ous (ə môr′ fəs, ə môr′ -) ***adj-*** **1** without definite form, shape, or character: *On the potter's wheel, the wet,* amorphous *clay became a vase.* **2** *Chemistry* of a solid, lacking a definite crystalline structure, as glass or tar. ***—adv-*** **a·morph′ ous·ly.** ***n-*** **a·morph′ ous·ness.**

am·or·tize (ăm′ ər tīz′) ***vt-*** **[am·or·tized, am·or·tiz·ing]** to pay off gradually (a debt, mortgage, charge, etc.) in installments. ***—n-*** **am′ or·ti·za′ tion** (-tə zā′ shən).

A·mos (ā′ məs) ***n-*** **1** in the Bible, a Hebrew prophet of the eighth century B.C. **2** a book of the Old Testament containing his prophecies.

a·mount (ə mount′) ***n-*** quantity or sum: *an* amount *of money*; *a small* amount *of sand.*

amount to 1 to add up to: *The whole bill* amounts to *$10. That* amounts to *a complaint.* **2** *Informal* to have merit or value as a person: *He'll* amount to *much.*

a·mour (ə mo͝or′) ***n-*** secret love affair.

am·per·age (ăm′ pər ĭj) ***n-*** the strength of an electric current, measured in amperes.

am·pere (ăm′ pêr′) ***n-*** unit for measuring the rate at which electricity flows. One ampere equals a flow of one coulomb of electricity per second.

am·phib·i·an (ăm fĭb′ ē ən) ***n-*** **1** animal of a class (**Amphibia**) including frogs, toads, and salamanders, which as larvae have gills and live in water and as adults have lungs and live on land. **2** airplane that can take off and alight on water or land. **3** an amphibious vehicle. ***adj-*** of or relating to the class of Amphibia or to aircraft that operate both on land and water.

am·phib·i·ous (ăm fĭb′ ē əs) ***adj-*** **1** able to live on land or in water: *an* amphibious *animal*; *an* amphibious *plant.* **2** able to operate on land or water: *an* amphibious *vehicle.* **3** carried out by the use of land, sea, and air military forces: *an* amphibious *attack.*

am·phi·the·a·ter or **am·phi·the·a·tre** (ăm′ fĭ thē′ ə tər) ***n-*** **1** any round or oval theater with a central stage or arena around which rows of seats slope upward. **2** classroom or surgical operating room of this form. **3** a clearing closely surrounded by hills; a natural arena.

am·ple (ăm′ pəl) ***adj-*** **1** of large size or amount: *The* ample *rooms held all of the furniture.* **2** enough: *He has* ample *money on which to live comfortably.* **3** abundant; more than enough: *We have* ample *food for the trip and can easily share it with you.* ***—adv-*** **am′ ply.**

am·pli·fi·ca·tion (ăm′ plə fə kā′ shən) ***n-*** **1** an enlarging, extending, or supplementing: *an* amplification *of a report.* **2** the material or details so added. **3** in electronics, an increasing of the strength of an electric signal or current.

am·pli·fi·er (ăm′ plə fī′ ər) ***n-*** **1** in electronics, an electrical circuit that magnifies an electrical impulse. **2** a component, as in a sound reproduction system, that contains such a circuit.

am·pli·fy (ăm′ plə fī′) ***vt-*** **[am·pli·fied, am·pli·fy·ing]** **1** to increase the strength of (sound or an electric current). **2** to add fuller details to; enlarge on: *Will you please* amplify *that statement?*

am·pli·tude (ăm′ plə to͞od′, -tyo͞od′) ***n-*** **1** fullness and richness; abundance: *the* amplitude *of his generosity.* **2** *Physics* the perpendicular distance from the highest or lowest point in a wave to its center line; also, a similar distance from the highest to the lowest point in the swing of a pendulum.

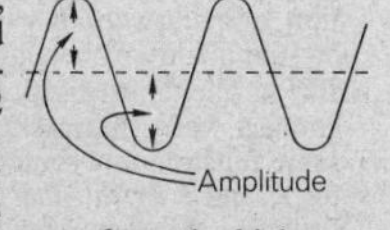

amplitude modulation ***n-*** way of radio broadcasting in which the amplitude of the radio wave is changed according to the sound being broadcast. *Abbr.* AM See also *frequency modulation.*

am·pu·tate (ăm′ pyə tāt′) ***vt-*** **[am·pu·tat·ed, am·pu·tat·ing]** to cut off; especially, to remove (an arm, leg, etc.) surgically. ***—n-*** **am′ pu·ta′ tion.**

am·pu·tee (ămp′ yə tē′) ***n-*** person who has lost a limb or limbs by amputation.

amt. amount.

a.m.u. atomic mass unit.

a·muck (ə mŭk′, -mŏk′) **run amuck** to rush about wildly, especially with intent to kill or destroy. Also **amok.**

am·u·let (ăm′ yə lət) ***n-*** charm or token worn as a protection against evil or harm.

a·muse (ə myo͞oz′) ***vt-*** **[a·mused, a·mus·ing]** to cause (a person or persons) to laugh and feel pleasure; entertain.

a·mused (ə myo͞ozd′) ***adj-*** **1** pleasantly occupied; entertained; diverted: *an* amused *spectator.* **2** expressing enjoyment: *an* amused *smile.* ***—adv-*** **a·mus′ ed·ly.**

a·muse·ment (ə myo͞oz′ mənt) ***n-*** **1** enjoyment; pleasure; diversion: *He plays the violin for his own* amusement. **2** something that amuses or entertains, as a carnival ride, sport, etc. *as* ***modifier***: *an* amusement *park.*

to (one's) amusement arousing pleasure, laughter, etc.: *Much* to our amusement, *the clowns waltzed.*

a·mus·ing (ə myo͞o′ zĭng) ***adj-*** causing enjoyment or laughter: *an* amusing *situation.* ***—adv-*** **a·mus′ ing·ly:** *The story was* amusingly *illustrated.*

an (ən, ăn) ***indefinite article-*** used before vowel sounds. See *a.*

an- *prefix* See *a-*.

-an or **-ian** or **-ean** *suffix* **1** (used to form adjectives) of or relating to; resembling; appropriate to: *a re*publican *principle*; *a reptil*ian *form*; *a Mozart*ean *melody.* **2** (used to form nouns) (1) person or animal of a certain group: *an Americ*an; *a Paris*ian; *a crustac*ean. (2) practicer of, or specialist in: *a music*ian; *politic*ian.

a·nab·o·lism (ə năb′ ə lĭz′ əm) ***n-*** a stage of metabolism in which the complex materials in living matter are built from simpler substances taken from food.

a·nach·ro·nism (ə năk′ rə nĭz′ əm) ***n-*** **1** the placing of an object in a period to which it does not belong, either because it was not yet known, or because it was no longer used; a chronological error. **2** the object so misplaced: *A horse and buggy is an* anachronism *in the era of cars.* ***—adj-*** **a·nach′ ro·nis′ tic:** *an* anachronistic *detail in a book.* ***adv-*** **a·nach′ ro·nis′ ti·cal·ly.**

an·a·con·da (ăn′ ə kŏn′ də) ***n-*** very large tropical South American snake, sometimes 40 feet long, which crushes and kills its prey in its coils before swallowing it.

a·nae·mi·a (ə nē′ mē ə) anemia. ***—adj-*** **a·nae′ mic.**

an·aer·obes (ăn′ ə rōbz′, ăn âr′ ōbz) ***n-*** anaerobic organisms, especially bacteria.

an·aer·o·bic (ăn′ ər ō′ bĭk, ăn âr′-) ***adj-*** of certain bacteria, not needing oxygen to live and grow.

an·aes·the·sia (ăn′ əs thē′ zhə, -zē ə) anesthesia.

an·aes·thet·ic (ăn′ əs thĕt′ ĭk) anesthetic.

an·aes·the·tize (ă nĕs′ thə tīz′, ə-) anesthetize.

an·a·gram (ăn′ ə grăm′) ***n-*** **1** word or phrase obtained by changing the order of the letters of another word or phrase. Example: "Live" is an anagram of "evil." **2 anagrams** game in which the players strive to form the largest number of words from any given letters.

fāte, făt, dâre, bärn; bē, bĕt mêre; bīte, bĭt; nōte, hŏt, môre, dȯg; fŭn, fûr; to͞o, bo͝ok; oil; out; ta*r*; thin; *th*en; hw for wh as in *wh*at; zh for s as in u*s*ual; ə for a, e, i, o, u, as in *a*go, lin*e*n, per*i*l, at*o*m, min*u*s

a·nal (ā′ nəl) ***adj-*** pertaining to the anus.

an·al·ge·sia (ăn′əl jē′ zē ə, -zhə) ***n-*** absence of pain, produced by a drug without loss of consciousness.
►Should not be confused with ANESTHESIA.

an·al·ge·sic (ăn′əl jē′ zĭk) ***adj-*** dulling or removing pain: *the* analgesic *effect of aspirin.* ***n-*** drug that does this: *Aspirin is an* analgesic.

an·a·log computer (ăn′ə lŏg′) ***n-*** computing machine which uses electrical or other physical quantities, such as voltages, resistances, etc., to represent numbers. Also **analogue computer.**

a·nal·o·gous (ə năl′ə gəs) ***adj-*** having resemblance; corresponding in certain ways: *A bird's wing and a human arm are* analogous. **—*adv-* a·nal′o·gous·ly.**

a·nal·o·gy (ə năl′ə jē′) ***n-*** [*pl.* **a·nal·o·gies**] partial agreement or likeness between two different things: *the* analogy *between an eye and a camera.*

an·a·lyse (ăn′ə līz′) analyze.

a·nal·y·sis (ə năl′ə səs) ***n-*** [*pl.* **a·nal·y·ses** (-sēz)] **1** the division of anything into its parts to study it carefully: *An* analysis *of the plan proved that it was impractical.* **2** the testing of anything by laboratory methods to learn its nature or composition: *an* analysis *of drinking water*; *an* analysis *of a poison.* **3** psychoanalysis.

an·a·lyst (ăn′ə lĭst) ***n-*** **1** one who makes a careful examination. **2** psychoanalyst. ***Hom-*** annalist.

an·a·lyt·ic (ăn′ə lĭt′ĭk) or **an·a·lyt·i·cal** (-ĭ kəl) ***adj-*** using or related to analysis: *an* analytic *mind*; *a course in* analytical *chemistry.* **—*adv-* an·a·lyt′i·cal·ly.**

analytic geometry ***n-*** kind of geometry in which lines, curves, figures, etc., are described in terms of algebra and plotted in space by the co-ordinates of their points.

an·a·lyze (ăn′ə līz′) ***vt-*** [**an·a·lyzed, an·a·lyz·ing**] **1** to separate into parts or elements: *to* analyze *a chemical compound.* **2** to examine critically: *to* analyze *evidence*; *to* analyze *someone's character.* Also **an′a·lyse′.**

an·a·pest (ăn′ə pĕst′) ***n-*** **1** measure or foot of poetry made up of two unaccented syllables followed by one accented syllable. **2** line of poetry made up of such measures. Example: "I am mon′/arch of all′/I sur vey′." Also **an′a·paest′.** **—*adj-* an′a·pes′tic.**

an·arch·ism (ăn′ər kĭz′əm) ***n-*** political belief that all government is unnecessary and therefore an evil.

an·arch·ist (ăn′ər kĭst) ***n-*** **1** one who regards all government as evil and believes, as a political ideal, in living without any government. **2** any person who stirs up violent revolt against established rule. **—*adj-* an′ar·chis′tic.** ***adv-*** **an′ar·chis′ti·cal·ly.**

an·ar·chy (ăn′ər kē) ***n-*** **1** absence of law and government. **2** confusion; disorder: *complete* anarchy *in the hall.* **—*adj-* an·ar′chic** (ăn är′kĭk) or **an·ar′chi·cal:** *the* anarchic *life of the forty-niners.* ***adv-*** **an·ar′chi·cal·ly.**

a·nath·e·ma (ə năth′ə mə) ***n-*** **1** solemn curse of the church, accompanied by expulsion from the church. **2** any strong denunciation or curse. **3** person or thing regarded with extreme dislike or loathing.

a·nath·e·ma·tize (ə năth′ə mə tīz′) ***vt-*** [**a·nath·e·ma·tized, a·nath·e·ma·tiz·ing**] to pronounce a curse against.

an·a·tom·i·cal (ăn′ə tŏm′ĭ kəl) or **an·a·tom·ic** (-tŏm′ĭk) ***adj-*** relating to anatomy. **—*adv-* an′a·tom′i·cal·ly.**

a·nat·o·mize (ə năt′ə mīz′) ***vt-*** [**a·nat·o·mized, a·nat·o·miz·ing**] **1** to cut (an animal or plant) apart in order to study the structure. **2** to analyze anything in detail.

a·nat·o·my (ə năt′ə mē) ***n-*** [*pl.* **a·nat·o·mies**] **1** the physical structure of living things. **2** the science dealing with the physical structure of living things, especially involving the dissection of animals and plants to determine the location and relation of their various organs. **3** a detailed examination; analysis: *the* anatomy *of a crime.* ***n-*** **a·nat′o·mist** one skilled in anatomy.

-ance or **-ence** *suffix* (used to form nouns) **1** process or action: *continu*ance; *emerg*ence. **2** state, condition, or quality: *eleg*ance; *differ*ence.

an·ces·tor (ăn′sĕs tər) ***n-*** person from whom one is directly descended and who is usually of a generation before that of one's grandparents; forefather; forebear.

an·ces·tral (ăn sĕs′trəl) ***adj-*** belonging to, or inherited from, ancestors: *an* ancestral *home.*

an·ces·try (ăn′sĕs′trē) ***n-*** [*pl.* **an·ces·tries**] line of one's descent traced back through parents, grandparents, etc.; also, one's ancestors.

an·chor (ăng′kər) ***n-*** **1** any of various devices attached by a line to a ship, boat, buoy, float, etc., and lowered to the bottom to prevent drifting or other movement. **2** any device for holding or fastening something in place: *a balloon* anchor; *an* anchor *for holding a bolt in a cement floor.* **3** anything that makes one feel safe, stable, or secure: *His faith was his* anchor *in a hostile world.* ***vt-*** to hold (something or someone) fast or in place by means of such a device: *They* anchored *the boat. The climbers* anchored *themselves firmly.* ***vi-*** of a ship, to lower an anchor, especially on arrival in port: *The ocean liner* anchored *at noon.*

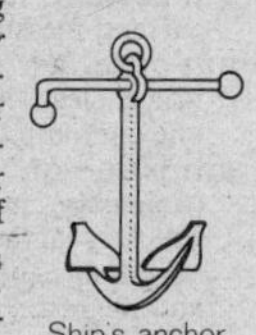
Ship's anchor

at anchor held fast by an anchor. **drag anchor** to drift because the anchor is not gripping the bottom. **drop** (or **cast**) **anchor** to lower an anchor. **ride at anchor** to be held fast by an anchor. **weigh anchor** to raise a ship's anchor in order to depart.

an·chor·age (ăng′kər ĭj) ***n-*** **1** place where ships are anchored. **2** firm grip, such as the hold of an anchor on sea bottom.

an·cho·rite (ăng′kə rīt′) ***n-*** one who forsakes the world and lives alone for study, etc.; recluse; hermit.

anchor person ***n-*** news broadcaster on radio or television who coordinates the reports from correspondents in different places.

an·cho·vy (ăn′chō′vē) ***n-*** [*pl.* **an·cho·vies**] very small Mediterranean herring, used in sauces, salads, and as an appetizer.

an·cient (ān′shənt) ***adj-*** **1** belonging to times long past, especially to the times of the Greeks and the Romans: *an* ancient *coin.* **2** very old: *an* ancient *tree.* **3** (as a humorous term) old-fashioned; out-of-date: *Where did you get that* ancient *hat?* ***n-*** **1** very old person. **2 the ancients** (1) the civilized peoples of old, especially of Greece and Rome. (2) the classical writers of Greece and Rome. **—*adv-* an′cient·ly.**

an·cil·lar·y (ăn′sə lĕr′ē) ***adj-*** **1** dependent; subsidiary. **2** assisting; supplementary: *an* ancillary *motor on a cruise ship.* [from Latin **ancilla** meaning "female servant."]

-ancy or **-ency** *suffix* (used to form nouns) state, condition, or quality: *tru*ancy (condition of being truant); *de*cency (the quality of being decent).

and (ən when unstressed; ănd when stressed) ***conj-*** (used to connect words, phrases, or clauses that have exactly the same function in a sentence or other construction): *I said once,* and *I repeat, that I will not go. They had made a promise,* and *they intended to keep it.* The word usually suggests one or more of the meanings "plus," "also," "as well as," "in addition to a": *Two* and *two make four. I want to stay here,* and *I want to rest. She is kind* and *brave. I want a bat* and *ball.*

an·dan·te (ăn′ dän′ tā) *Music* ***adj- & adv-*** moderately slow; slower than moderato but faster than adagio.

and·i·ron (ănd′ ī′ ərn) ***n-*** one of two metal supports for holding logs in a fireplace; firedog.

Andirons

An·drew (ăn′ drōō′) ***n-*** in the New Testament, one of the twelve apostles of Jesus. Also **St. Andrew.**

An·dro·cles (ăn′ drə klēz′) ***n-*** in Roman legend, a slave whose life was spared by a lion from whose foot he had once drawn a thorn. Also **An′ dro·clus′** (-kləs).

an·dro·gen (ăn′ drə jən) ***n-*** any of the hormones responsible for masculine body characteristics.

An·drom·a·che (ăn drŏm′ ə kē) ***n-*** in the legend of Troy, the wife of Hector.

An·drom·e·da (ăn drŏm′ ə də) ***n-* 1** in Greek mythology, the daughter of Cassiopeia and wife of Perseus, who rescued her from a sea monster. **2** a northern constellation.

an·ec·dote (ăn′ ək dōt′) ***n-*** brief story intended to amuse or instruct, often told about a famous person.

a·ne·mi·a (ə nē′ mē ə) ***n-*** physical condition in which there are too few red blood cells in the blood, caused by disease, diet deficiency, or bleeding. Also **anaemia.** ***—adj-*** **a·ne′ mic:** *She has been slightly* anemic *since her operation.*

an·e·mom·e·ter (ăn′ ə mŏm′ ə tər) ***n-*** instrument for measuring the speed of the wind.

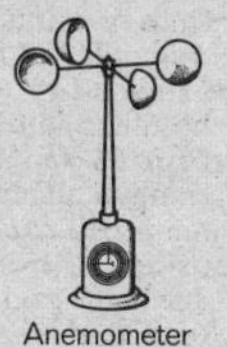
Anemometer

a·nem·o·ne (ə nĕm′ ə nē′) ***n-* 1** any of several North American woodland flowers, especially the windflower, or wood anemone, which bears delicate white flowers. Other common anemones have pink or purple flowers. **2** sea anemone.

a·nent (ə nĕnt′) *Archaic* ***prep-*** in regard to; concerning.

an·e·roid barometer (ăn′ ə roid′) ***n-*** barometer made up of an airtight box containing a partial vacuum and having a flexible top to which a pointer is attached. Changes in atmospheric pressure cause the top to bend in or out, moving the pointer.

an·es·the·si·a (ăn′ əs thē′ zhə) ***n-*** partial or complete loss of feeling in the body or a part of it, caused by injury, disease, or an anesthetic; numbness. Also **an′ aes·the′ si·a.**
►Should not be confused with ANALGESIA.

an·es·the·si·o·lo·gist (ăn′ əs thē′ zē ŏl′ ə jĭst) ***n-*** physician who is a specialist in anesthesiology.

an·es·the·si·o·lo·gy (ăn′ əs thē′ zē ŏl′ ə jē) ***n-*** study of anesthesia and anesthetics.

an·es·thet·ic (ăn′ əs thĕt′ ĭk) ***n-*** a drug that produces anesthesia. ***adj-****: an* anesthetic *gas.*

an·es·the·tist (ə nĕs′ thə tĭst′) ***n-*** person who gives anesthetics to patients before and during surgery.

an·es·the·tize (ə nĕs′ thə tīz′) ***vt-*** **[an·es·the·tized, an·es·the·tiz·ing]** to make incapable of feeling pain, usually by means of drugs, in preparation for surgery. Also **anaesthetize.**

a·new (ə nōō′, -nyōō′) ***adv-*** a second time; over again: *She had to learn to walk* anew *after the accident.*

an·gel (ān′ jəl) ***n-* 1** spiritual being that is an attendant or messenger of God. **2** person thought of as very kind, good, or beautiful. **3** *Informal* person who provides the money to produce a play; financial backer.

an·gel·fish (ān′ jəl fĭsh′) ***n-*** any of several colorful South American fishes, especially a graceful disk-shaped aquarium fish with a black-striped silvery body, long arched fins, and slender feelers.

Angelfish

an·gel·ic (ăn jĕl′ ĭk) ***adj-*** relating to, or like, the angels; hence, pure or saintly: *an* angelic *face; an* angelic *disposition.*

An·ge·lus (ăn′ jə ləs) ***n-*** in the Roman Catholic Church, a prayer commemorating the Incarnation, said at morning, noon, and sunset at the ringing of a bell called the Angelus.

an·ger (ăng′ gər) ***n-*** strong, hostile feeling stirred up by wrong or injury to oneself or to others; emotion that makes a person want to quarrel or fight; rage; wrath. ***vt-*** to make angry: *The nasty remark* angered *her.*

an·gi·na (ăn jī′ nə) ***n-*** choking spasms of pain, especially of the throat or chest; also, the disease that causes this.

angina pec·to·ris (pĕk′ tə rəs) ***n-*** a very painful, suffocating spasm of the chest muscles caused by a heart condition.

an·gi·o·sperm (ăn′ jē ə spûrm′) ***n-*** any plant that has its seed enclosed in a fruit, shell, or other protective covering. Angiosperms include all flowering plants. See also *gymnosperm.*

¹an·gle (ăng′ gəl) ***vi-*** **[an·gled, an·gling] 1** to fish with hook and line. **2** to use tricks in obtaining something: *to* angle *for compliments.* [from Old English **angul** meaning "fishhook."]

ACUTE RIGHT OBTUSE
Angles

²an·gle (ăng′ gəl) ***n-* 1** *Mathematics* geometric figure formed by two rays that have a common endpoint. Its size is measured in degrees. **2** corner; sharp edge. **3** *Informal* point of view. [from French **angle** of the same meaning, from Latin **angulus.**]

An·gle (ăng′ gəl) ***n-*** member of a Germanic people who, together with the Jutes and Saxons, invaded and occupied England in the fifth century A.D.

angle of incidence ***n-*** in optics, the angle between a ray of light striking a surface and a line perpendicular to the surface at the same point.

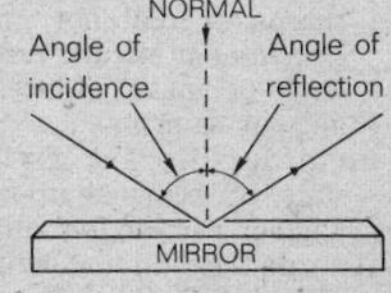

angle of reflection ***n-*** in optics, the angle between a reflected ray of light and a line perpendicular to the reflecting surface at the same point.

angle of refraction ***n-*** in optics, the angle formed by a ray of light passing through a substance and a line perpendicular to the surface of the substance at the point where the ray entered.

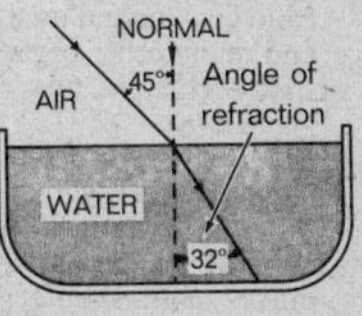

an·gler (ăng′ glər) ***n-* 1** fisherman, especially one who fishes for pleasure. **2** salt-water fish with a large, broad head, on which are projections that lure smaller fish within reach of its huge mouth; devilfish.

an·gle·worm (ăng′ gəl wûrm′) ***n-*** earthworm, often used by anglers as bait.

An·gli·can (ăng′ glĭ kən) ***adj-*** of or pertaining to the established Church of England or to its member churches in other countries: *the* Anglican *service.* ***n-*** member of such a church.

An·gli·can·ism (ăng′ glĭ kə nĭz′ əm) ***n-*** beliefs and practices of the Anglican churches.

an·gli·cize (ăng′ glə sīz′) ***vt-*** **[an·gli·cized, an·gli·ciz·ing]** to make (a word, phrase, pronunciation, etc.) seem natural or at home in the English language: *English has* anglicized *the French "chauffeur."*

an·gling (ăng′ glĭng) ***n-*** fishing with hook and line, especially for recreation.

Anglo- *combining form* **1** England. **2** English.

An·glo-Sax·on (ăng′ glō săk′ sən) ***adj-*** of or relating to the mingled Germanic tribes that settled in England in the fifth century and generally dominated England until the Norman Conquest. ***n-*** **1** member of these tribes. **2** their language, often called Old English. **3** any descendant of these people.

an·go·ra (ăng gôr′ ə) ***n-*** **1** soft, fluffy wool of the Angora goat; mohair. **2** yarn or cloth made from the hair of the Angora rabbit.

Angora cat ***n-*** domestic cat with long, fluffy hair.

Angora goat ***n-*** domestic goat with long, silky hair.

Angora rabbit ***n-*** rabbit with long, fine hair, usually white.

an·gry (ăng′ grē) ***adj-*** **[an·gri·er, an·gri·est]** **1** feeling or showing rage or resentment: *an* angry *beast; an* angry *look.* **2** inflamed; red: *an* angry *wound.* ***—adv-*** **an′ gri·ly.**

ang·strom (ăng′ strəm) *Physics* ***n-*** unit for measuring very small distances such as wavelengths of light and equal to one one-hundred millionth of a centimeter. *Abbr.* A or Å. Also **angstrom unit.**

an·guish (ăng′ gwĭsh′) ***n-*** extreme suffering, especially of mind: *a mother's* anguish *over the death of her child.*

an·guished (ăng′ gwĭsht′) ***adj-*** having or showing intense mental or bodily pain; agonized: *an* anguished *man; an* anguished *look.*

an·gu·lar (ăng′ gyə lər) ***adj-*** **1** having angles or points; sharp-cornered; not smooth or rounded: *an* angular *structure; an* angular *face.* **2** of or relating to a geometric angle or angles. **3** measured by a geometric angle: *an* angular *motion.*

an·gu·lar·i·ty (ăng′ gyə lăr′ ə tē) ***n-*** [*pl.* **an·gu·lar·i·ties**] state of being sharp-cornered or pointed; also, an angular part or formation: *the* angularities *of a figure.*

An·gus (ăng′ əs) ***n-*** Aberdeen Angus.

an·hy·drous (ăn hī′ drəs) ***adj-*** not containing water, especially water of crystallization.

a·ni·line or **an·i·lin** (ăn′ ə lən) ***n-*** colorless, oily, liquid compound of carbon, nitrogen, and hydrogen derived from coal tar and used in the synthesis of dyes, medicines, and many other organic chemicals.

aniline dye ***n-*** any dye prepared from aniline. Also **anilin dye.**

an·i·mad·ver·sion (ăn′ ə măd vûr′ zhən) ***n-*** unfavorable comment; derogatory statement; criticism; censure: *He softened his* animadversions *on his rival's character.*

an·i·mal (ăn′ ə məl) ***n-*** **1** living being that can feel and move about spontaneously, as a man, dog, sparrow, fish, snake, fly, or the like. **2** any mammal other than man, such as a dog, monkey, or horse. ***adj-*** **1** relating to animals: *the* animal *kingdom.* **2** like or characteristic of an animal: *the child's* animal *spirits.*

animal husbandry ***n-*** science of breeding and raising domestic animals.

an·i·mal·ism (ăn′ ə mə lĭz′ əm) ***n-*** **1** concern only for sensual instincts or appetities; sensuality. **2** the theory that man is an animal having no spirit or soul.
►Should not be confused with ANIMISM.

an·i·mal·i·ty (ăn′ ə măl′ ə tē) ***n-*** animal nature as distinct from spiritual nature.

[1]**an·i·mate** (ăn′ ə māt′) ***vt-*** **[an·i·mat·ed, an·i·mat·ing]** to give life to; inspire with energy or activity; enliven: *Joy* animates *his face.*

[2]**an·i·mate** (ăn′ ə mət) ***adj-*** alive: *Biology deals with* animate *beings.*

an·i·mat·ed (ăn′ ə mā′ təd) ***adj-*** **1** full of life; lively; vivacious. **2** made to seem alive and moving: *an* animated *doll.* ***—adv-*** **an′ i·mat′ ed·ly.**

animated cartoon ***n-*** a series of drawings, each representing a small enough change of position to give the impression of continuous motion when photographed and run through a motion-picture projector.

animate nature (ăn′ ə mət) ***n-*** all living things.

an·i·ma·tion (ăn′ ə mā′ shən) ***n-*** **1** liveliness; spirit; life. **2** the process of preparing drawings to be filmed as animated cartoons.

a·ni·ma·to (ăn′ ə mä′ tō) *Music* ***adj-*** & ***adv-*** animated; lively and gay.

an·i·mism (ăn′ ə mĭz′ əm) ***n-*** the theory that the universe and natural objects, such as trees, clouds, etc., contain souls or spirits.
►Should not be confused with ANIMALISM.

an·i·mos·i·ty (ăn′ ə mŏs′ ə tē) ***n-*** [*pl.* **an·i·mos·i·ties**] hostility; hatred; enmity.

an·i·mus (ăn′ ə məs) ***n-*** feeling of dislike; ill will; enmity; animosity: *He displayed considerable* animus *toward his rival.*

an·i·on (ăn′ ī′ ən) ***n-*** ion with a negative electrical charge due to the gain of one or more electrons.

an·ise (ăn′ əs) ***n-*** **1** plant cultivated for its spicy seeds, which are used in medicine and as flavoring. **2** (also **an′ i·seed**) the seed of this plant.

an·kle (ăng′ kəl) ***n-*** **1** the joint connecting the foot with the leg. **2** slender part of the leg just above this joint.

an·klet (ăng′ klət) ***n-*** **1** a sock which reaches just above the ankle. **2** bracelet worn around the ankle.

an·nal·ist (ăn′ ə lĭst) ***n-*** person who records events as they occur year by year. ***Hom-*** analyst.

an·nals (ăn′ əlz) ***n-*** *pl.* **1** an account or history of events as they happen, written or issued year by year: *The* annals *of the academy are published regularly.* **2** records; history: *the* annals *of ancient Rome.*

an·neal (ə nēl′) ***vt-*** **1** to heat and then cool slowly, so as to make less brittle: *to* anneal *glass; to* anneal *steel.* **2** to toughen or temper: *to* anneal *the mind against hardships.*

an·ne·lid (ăn′ ə lĭd′) ***n-*** any of a group of worms and wormlike animals (**Annelida**) whose bodies are made up of a series of segments, or rings. Examples are earthworms, sandworms, and leeches.

[1]**an·nex** (ə nĕks′) ***vt-*** to unite, as a smaller thing to a greater: *to* annex *a province to a kingdom.*

[2]**an·nex** (ăn′ ĕks) ***n-*** an extra building, or addition to a building, that is used for a related purpose: *the* annex *of a library.*

an·nex·a·tion (ăn′ ĭk sā′ shən) ***n-*** act of adding or attaching; addition: *the* annexation *of Gaul to the Roman Empire.*

an·ni·hi·late (ə nī′ ə lāt′) ***vt-*** **[an·ni·hi·lat·ed, an·ni·hi·lat·ing]** to destroy completely; wipe out: *to* annihilate *an army.* ***—n-*** **an·ni′ hi·la′ tion.**

an·ni·ver·sa·ry (ăn'ə vûr'sə rē) ***n-*** [*pl.* **an·ni·ver·sa·ries**] yearly occurrence of the date on which something happened in some previous year, especially a marriage. *as* ***modifier****: an* anniversary *gift.*

an·no Dom·in·i (ăn'ō dō'mə nē) *Latin* in the year of the Lord; in a (specified) year within the Christian era; A.D.

an·no·tate (ăn'ə tāt', ăn'ō-) ***vt-*** [**an·no·tat·ed, an·no·tat·ing**] to make notes upon, by way of comment or criticism: *to* annotate *a book.*

an·no·ta·tion (ăn'ə tā'shən, ăn'ō-) ***n-*** the writing of notes in explanation or criticism of a text; also, a note so written.

an·nounce (ə nouns') ***vt-*** [**an·nounced, an·nounc·ing**] **1** to give formal notice of; make known: *to* announce *an engagement*; *to* announce *a guest.* **2** on radio and television, to act as an announcer for (a program, commercial, etc.): *She* announces *ball games.* ***vi-*** to be a radio or television announcer.

an·nounce·ment (ə nouns'mənt) ***n-*** **1** act of announcing or declaring. **2** public notice or advertisement: *an* announcement *in a newspaper.*

an·nounc·er (ə noun'sər) ***n-*** one who announces, especially news, commercials, etc., on radio or television.

an·noy (ə noi') ***vt-*** to vex or bother; irritate.

an·noy·ance (ə noi'əns) ***n-*** **1** feeling of being bothered or vexed: *to express* annoyance *because of noise.* **2** thing that annoys: *The buzzing of the mosquito is an* annoyance. **3** act of bothering or vexing: *The* annoyance *of mosquitoes kept me awake.*

an·nu·al (ăn'yōō əl) ***adj-*** **1** done, happening, etc., once a year; yearly: *an* annual *banquet*; *an* annual *bulletin.* **2** in or for the year: *an* annual *wage*; *an average* annual *rainfall of 20 inches.* **3** taking a year to complete: *the* annual *course of the sun.* **4** in botany, of a plant that lives only one season or one year. ***n-*** **1** magazine, pamphlet, etc., appearing once a year. **2** in botany, a plant living only one season or year. **—*adv-*** **an'nu·al·ly.**

annual ring ***n-*** any of the rings seen in the cross section of a tree trunk. Each represents a year's growth.

an·nu·i·ty (ə nōō'ə tē, ə nyōō'-) ***n-*** [*pl.* **an·nu·i·ties**] money paid out periodically to a person for life or for a certain number of years.

an·nul (ə nŭl') ***vt-*** [**an·nulled, an·nul·ling**] to abolish or do away with (a law, decree, or compact): *to* annul *a marriage.* **—*n-*** **an·nul'ment:** *the* annulment *of a contract.*

an·nu·lar (ăn'yə lər) ***adj-*** made of rings or shaped like a ring.

annular eclipse ***n-*** solar eclipse in which all of the sun is blocked out except for its corona, which appears as a ring of light surrounding the disk of the moon.

An·nun·ci·a·tion, the (ə nŭn'sē ā'shən) ***n-*** **1** announcement to Mary by the angel Gabriel that she was to be the mother of Jesus. **2** the feast day, March 25, celebrating this event. **3** a picture of this scene.

an·nun·ci·a·tor (ə nŭn'sē ā' tər) ***n-*** electrically controlled indicator used in hotels, elevators, etc., to show where service is required.

an·ode (ăn'ōd') ***n-*** **1** in electronics, the positive electrode, or pole, of batteries and other electrical devices. **2** in radio, X-ray, and other electron tubes, the positively charged electrode, or plate, to which electrons jump from the cathode.

an·o·dyne (ăn'ə dīn') ***n-*** **1** a drug that relieves pain. **2** something that calms or soothes: *Her calm voice was an* anodyne *to the frightened child.*

a·noint (ə noint') ***vt-*** **1** to cover with oil or an oily substance: *to* anoint *one's body with suntan lotion.* **2** to apply oil to, especially as a sacred rite: *to* anoint *a king*; *to* anoint *a sick man.* **—*n-*** **a·noint'ment.**

a·nom·a·ly (ə nŏm'ə lē) ***n-*** [*pl.* **a·nom·a·lies**] anything differing from the usual or normal; irregularity; abnormality: *A winter thunderstorm is an* anomaly. **—*adj-*** **a·nom'a·lous:** *She has* anomalous *tastes.*

a·non (ə nŏn') ***adv-*** **1** soon; in a little while. **2** at another time; again: *About that, more* anon.

anon. anonymous.

an·o·nym·i·ty (ăn'ə nĭm'ə tē) ***n-*** condition of being anonymous: *the* anonymity *of many kindly deeds.*

a·non·y·mous (ə nŏn'ə məs) ***adj-*** **1** not known by name: *an* anonymous *author.* **2** without the doer's name; of unknown origin: *an* anonymous *poem*; *an* anonymous *phone call.* **3** lacking individuality; not identifiable with an individual: *rows of* anonymous *houses.* **—*adv-*** **a·non'y·mous·ly.** ***n-*** **a·non'y·mous·ness.**

a·noph·e·les (ə nŏf'ə lēz') ***n-*** [*pl.* **a·noph·e·les**] mosquito that is the carrier of malaria.

an·oth·er (ə nŭth'ər) ***determiner*** (traditionally called adjective or pronoun) **1** one more; an additional: *He took* another *sip.* **2** a different: *I don't want that book, I want* another *(book).* **3** similar in character, achievements, etc., to: *He's* another *Nero.* ***n-*** one more; one other: *This is* another *of the possible answers.*

one another each person to the others: *They hurled insults at* one another.

ans. answer.

an·swer (ăn'sər) ***n-*** **1** response or reply: *I'll give him my* answer *tomorrow.* **2** solution to any problem: *an* answer *in subtraction*; *an* answer *to a person's dilemma.* ***vt-*** **1** to speak, write, or act in reply to: *to* answer *a question*; *to* answer *a telephone*; *to* answer *a threat.* **2** to be suitable for; fulfill: *This tool* answers *the purpose.* ***vi-****: He refused to* answer *when asked his name.*

answer back to reply rudely; talk back.

answer for to be held responsible or accountable for.

answer to to correspond to: *He* answers to *the description.*

an·swer·a·ble (ăn'sər ə bəl) ***adj-*** **1** accountable; responsible: *People should be* answerable *for their conduct.* **2** such as can be answered or disproved: *an* answerable *argument.*

ant (ănt) ***n-*** any of a group of small winged or wingless insects that live in organized communities in underground tunnels, decayed logs, or nests.

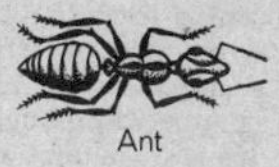
Ant

-ant or **-ent** *suffix* **1** (used to form nouns) one who or that which does a certain thing: *defend*ant; *assist*ant; *correspond*ent. **2** (used to form adjectives) doing a certain thing: *defi*ant (defying); *dependent on.*

ant·ac·id (ănt'ăs'əd) ***n-*** remedy for an acid stomach.

an·tag·o·nism (ăn tăg'ə nĭz əm) ***n-*** **1** strong feeling of dislike expressed in some way. **2** active opposition.

an·tag·o·nist (ăn tăg'ə nĭst) ***n-*** one who fights or competes with another for the same object, in sports, politics, battle, etc.; an opponent; adversary.

an·tag·o·nis·tic (ăn tăg'ə nĭs'tĭk) ***adj-*** contending; opposed; hostile: *their* antagonistic *views*; *his* antagonistic *feelings.* **—*adv-*** **an·tag'o·nis'ti·cal·ly.**

an·tag·o·nize (ăn tăg'ə nīz') ***vt-*** [**an·tag·o·nized, an·tag·o·niz·ing**] to make unfriendly or hostile: *Their rudeness* antagonizes *everyone they meet.*

---

fāte, făt, dâre, bärn; bē, bĕt, mêre; bīte, bĭt; nōte, hŏt, môre, dóg; fŭn, fûr; tōō, bŏŏk; oil; out; tar; thin; then; hw for wh as in *wh*at; zh for s as in u*s*ual; ə for a, e, i, o, u, as in *a*go, lin*e*n, per*i*l, at*o*m, min*u*s

ant·arc·tic (ănt′ är′ tĭk, -ärk′ tĭk) ***adj-* 1** opposite to the north polar, or arctic, regions. **2** located in, or relating to, the south polar regions.

Antarctic Circle ***n-*** imaginary boundary of the south polar region. On maps and globes, it is shown as a line parallel to the equator at 23 degrees and 30 minutes (23° 30′) north of the South Pole.

ant bear ***n-*** the giant gray anteater of Central and South American forests.

ante- *prefix* before; in front of: *an* ante*diluvian monster* (before the Flood); *the* ante*room.*

ant·eat·er (ănt′ ēt′ ər) ***n-* 1** any of several toothless Central and South American mammals with long slender snouts and very long sticky tongues used to feed on ants and termites. **2** any ant-eating animal.

an·te-bel·lum (ăn′ tĭ bĕl′ əm) ***adj-*** before the war, especially before the Civil War in the United States: *the* ante-bellum *South.*

an·te·ced·ent (ăn′ tə sē′ dənt) ***n-* 1** someone or something that goes before or precedes: *the* antecedents *of war.* **2** *Grammar* a noun, pronoun, etc., later referred to by a pronoun. In the sentence, "James played football until he hurt his leg," "James" is the antecedent of "he." **3 antecedents** the previous events or influences in a person's life; also, ancestry: *The man's* antecedents *accounted for his interest in the arts.* ***adj-*** going before; preceding: *the events* antecedent *to the meeting.*

an·te·cham·ber (ăn′ tĭ chām′ bər) ***n-*** room leading into a principal room or apartment; waiting room.

an·te·date (ăn′ tə dāt′) ***vt-*** **[an·te·dat·ed, an·te·dat·ing] 1** to occur at an earlier time than: *Sailing ships* antedated *steamships.* **2** to mark with an earlier date than the correct one: *to* antedate *a check.*

an·te·di·lu·vi·an (ăn′ tə dĭ lōō′ vē ən) ***adj-*** belonging to or having to do with the time before the Flood; hence, ancient; antiquated: *an* antediluvian *idea.* ***n-*** old or old-fashioned person.

Antelope, about 2 1/2 ft high at shoulder

an·te·lope (ăn′ tə lōp′) ***n-* 1** any of a group of deerlike animals of Africa and Asia, including the gazelle, impala, kudu, and eland. **2** pronghorn of western North America, though not a true antelope.

an·ten·na (ăn tĕn′ ə) ***n-* 1** [*pl.* **an·ten·nae** (-tĕn′ ē)] one of the pair of long, fragile, sensitive feelers on the heads of insects and crustaceans. **2** [*pl.* **an·ten·nas**] a metallic device, such as a coil of wire or a metal framework, for transmitting or receiving radio, television, or radar signals.

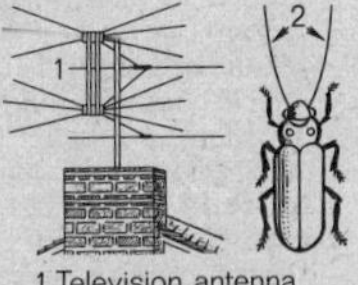

1 Television antenna
2 Antennae of insect

an·te·pe·nult (ăn′tĭ pē′nŭlt′) ***n-*** the syllable before the penult; the third syllable from the end of a word. In the word "al ter a tion," the antepenult is "ter."

an·te·ri·or (ăn′ têr′ ē ər) ***adj-* 1** fore; toward the front: *an* anterior *lobe of the brain.* **2** prior; occurring earlier: *The American Revolution was* anterior *to the French Revolution.*

an·te·room (ăn′ tĭ rōōm′) ***n-*** a room leading into another; antechamber.

an·them (ăn′ thəm) ***n-* 1** piece of sacred music, usually a passage from the Bible set to music. **2** song of praise or triumph: *a national* anthem.

an·ther (ăn′ thər) ***n-*** in a flower, the part of the stamen which produces the pollen.

ANTHER
STAMEN
FILAMENT
Anther

ant hill ***n-*** mound of earth piled up by ants at the entrances to their tunnels.

an·thol·o·gist (ăn thŏl′ ə jĭst) ***n-*** one who gathers the material for an anthology.

an·thol·o·gy (ăn thŏl′ ə jē) ***n-*** [*pl.* **an·thol·o·gies**] collection of poems or prose passages from various authors.

an·thra·cite (ăn′ thrə sīt′) ***n-*** a very hard coal that burns with little smoke or flame; hard coal.

an·thrax (ăn′ thrăks′) ***n-*** a highly infectious, usually fatal, disease of cattle and sheep, in which boils form on their skin and lungs. It may also infect people who have worked with diseased animals or their hides.

an·thro·poid (ăn′ thrə poid′) ***adj-*** manlike; resembling man: *The chimpanzee is an* anthropoid *ape.* ***n-*** one of the higher apes resembling man, such as the gorilla.

an·thro·pol·o·gist (ăn′ thrə pŏl′ ə jĭst) ***n-*** person trained in anthropology and usually engaged in it as a profession.

an·thro·pol·o·gy (ăn′ thrə pŏl′ ə jē) ***n-*** the science that deals with man, his origin, physical and cultural development, ways of living, language, customs, beliefs, etc. ***—adj-*** **an′ thro·po·log′ ic** (-pə lŏj′ ĭk) or **an′ thro·po·log′ ical.** ***adv-*** **an′ thro·po·log′ i·cal·ly.**

an·ti (ăn′ tī′, -tē′) *Informal* ***n-*** [*pl.* **an·tis**] person who is opposed to a policy, movement, law, etc.

anti- *prefix-* against; opposed to: *an* anti-*American demonstration*; anti*slavery*; anti*trust.* [from Greek.]

an·ti-air·craft (ăn′ tē âr′ krăft′, ăn′ tī-) ***adj-*** used in defense against attack by enemy aircraft: *an* antiaircraft *gun.*

an·ti-A·mer·i·can (ăn′ tē ə mĕr′ ə kən, ăn′ tī-) ***adj-*** opposed to the United States government, people, way of life, etc.

an·ti·bi·ot·ic (ăn′ tĭ bī ŏt′ ĭk) ***n-*** any of a group of drugs, such as penicillin, streptomycin, and terramycin, which are extracted from microscopic funguses, molds, and bacteria. They are used to cure many diseases by killing or stopping the growth of bacteria.

an·ti·bod·y (ăn′ tĭ bŏd′ ē) ***n-*** [*pl.* **an·ti·bod·ies**] any protein produced by the body in reaction to toxins, bacteria, or foreign blood cells. The antibody neutralizes, destroys, or removes these from the blood.

an·tic (ăn′ tĭk) ***adj-*** odd and comical; fantastic: *an* antic *disposition.* ***n-*** (usually **antics**) comical trick; prank; caper: *the* antics *of a puppy.*

an·tic·i·pate (ăn tĭs′ ə pāt′) ***vt-*** **[an·tic·i·pat·ed, an·tic·i·pat·ing] 1** to look forward to: *We* anticipate *a good time at the picnic.* **2** to foresee (a desire, question, etc.) and act or be ready to act: *I had* anticipated *the questions and was ready for them.* **3** to be ahead of (someone in some attempt): *The Vikings* anticipated *Columbus in the discovery of America.*

an·tic·i·pa·tion (ăn tĭs′ ə pā′ shən) ***n-*** expectation; a looking forward with pleasure: *The children waited with eager* anticipation *for vacation.*

an·tic·i·pa·to·ry (ăn′ tĭs′ ə pə tŏr′ ē) ***adj-* 1** filled with or showing anticipation; anticipating: *The hungry boy cast an* anticipatory *glance at the food.* **2** giving a hint of something coming later: *an* anticipatory *phrase in music.*

an·ti·cler·i·cal (ăn′ tĭ klĕr′ ə kəl, ăn′ tī-) ***adj-*** opposed to the influence of any church in government and education.

an·ti·cli·max (ăn′ tĭ klī′ măks′) *n-* an abrupt falling from the important or dignified to the trivial or absurd; a sudden letdown after a point of high interest or excitement: *The villain's reform in the last scene of the play was an* anticlimax. *—adj-* **an′ ti·cli·mac′ tic:** *an* anticlimactic *last scene.*

an·ti·cline (ăn′ tə klīn′) *n-* folded layers of rock that are arched upward. See also *syncline.*

an·ti·cy·clone (ăn′ tĭ sī′ klōn′) *n-* **1** circular wind motion around a region of high barometric pressure, clockwise in the Northern Hemisphere and counterclockwise in the Southern Hemisphere. **2** the high pressure region itself.

an·ti·dote (ăn′ tə dōt′) *n-* **1** medicine which counteracts a poison. **2** any remedy: *Work is an* antidote *to trouble.*

an·ti·freeze (ăn′ tə frēz′) *n-* substance that keeps water or other liquids from freezing at given temperatures by lowering the freezing point, as alcohol or ethylene glycol do to the water in car radiators.

an·ti·gen (ăn′ tĭ jən) *n-* anything, such as bacteria, toxins, or foreign blood cells, that causes the body to produce antibodies.

An·tig·o·ne (ăn tĭg′ ə nē) *n-* in Greek legend, a daughter of Oedipus. Antigone was sentenced to death by her uncle, Creon, for illegally burying her brother, Polynices.

an·ti·his·ta·mine (ăn′ tĭ hĭs′ tə mēn′) *n-* drug that relieves allergy by blocking the action of histamine.

an·ti·knock (ăn′ tĭ nŏk′) *n-* substance added to gasoline to prevent it from knocking in engines.

an·ti·ma·cas·sar (ăn′ tə mə kăs′ ər) *n-* small ornamental cloth put over the backs and arms of chairs and sofas to prevent them from being soiled.

an·ti·mat·ter (ăn′ tĭ măt′ ər, ăn′ tĭ′-) *n-* a kind of matter made up of particles, called antiparticles, that exactly correspond to the basic particles making up ordinary matter except that they have electric charges of opposite sign (negative or positive) and, or, reverse magnetic properties. Corresponding particles of antimatter and matter, such as a proton and an antiproton, destroy each other on contact, releasing great energy.

an·ti·mo·ny (ăn′ tə mō′nē) *n-* dense, brittle, silvery-white metallic element used in alloys, especially in printers' type metal and in pewter. Symbol Sb, At. No. 51, At. Wt. 121.75.

an·ti·neu·tron (ăn′ tĭ nōō′ trŏn) *n-* antiparticle corresponding to the neutron and resembling it in mass and lack of electric charge, but having different magnetic properties.

an·ti·par·ti·cle (ăn′ tĭ pär′ tĭ kəl) *n-* particle of antimatter.

an·ti·pas·to (ăn′ tĭ păs′ tō) *n-* [*pl.* **an·ti·pas·tos**] an appetizer of bits of fish, meat, and vegetables, seasoned with oil and vinegar. [Italian for "before the meal."]

an·tip·a·thy (ăn′ tĭp′ ə thē) *n-* [*pl.* **an·tip·a·thies**] strong feeling of hatred or dislike; aversion: *an* antipathy *to violence.* *—adj-* **an·tip′ a·thet′ ic** (-thĕt′ ĭk). *adv-* **an·tip′ a·thet′ i·cal·ly.**

an·tiph·o·ny (ăn tĭf′ ə nē) *n-* [*pl.* **an·tiph·o·nies**] **1** the singing or chanting of a psalm, hymn, etc., by the alternation of two choirs. **2** psalm, hymn, etc., sung this way. *—adj-* **an·tiph′ o·nal:** *the* antiphonal *singing of the choir.*

an·tip·o·des (ăn′ tĭp′ ə dēz′) *n- pl.* **1** places on exactly opposite sides of the earth: *The north and the south poles are* antipodes. **2** two exactly opposite things: *Love and hate are* antipodes. *—adj-* **an·tip′ o·dal:** *two* antipodal *points on the globe.*

an·ti·pro·ton (ăn′ tĭ prō′ tŏn) *n-* antiparticle corresponding to the proton and having the same mass but an opposite (negative) electric charge.

an·ti·quar·i·an (ăn′ tə kwâr′ ē ən) *adj-* relating to ancient times or to the relics and ruins of past peoples: *an* antiquarian *study.* *n-* an antiquary.

an·ti·quar·y (ăn′ tə kwĕr′ ē) *n-* [*pl.* **an·ti·quar·ies**] one who collects ancient relics, or who studies the customs, events, and records of peoples of the past.

an·ti·quat·ed (ăn′ tə kwā′ təd) *adj-* old-fashioned; out-of-date: *the woman's* antiquated *clothes*; antiquated *ideas.*

an·tique (ăn tēk′) *adj-* belonging to an earlier period: *an* antique *vase*; *an* antique *car.* *n-* art object or piece of furniture of a former period; especially, in the United States, something made before 1830. *vt-* [**an·tiqued, an·ti·quing**] to give the appearance of being old: *to* antique *a chair.*

an·tiq·ui·ty (ăn′ tĭk′ wə tē) *n-* [*pl.* **an·tiq·ui·ties**] **1** the early ages, especially before the Middle Ages: *The pyramids are a relic of* antiquity. **2** great age: *the* antiquity *of the castle.* **3 antiquities** relics that throw light upon ancient times: *Chinese* antiquities *in a museum.*

an·ti·scor·bu·tic (ăn′ tĭ skôr′ byōō′ tĭk) *n-* remedy for scurvy. *adj-* relieving or curing scurvy: *Vitamin C is the* antiscorbutic *vitamin.*

an·ti-Sem·i·tism (ăn′ tĭ sĕm′ ə tĭz′ əm) *n-* prejudice or discrimination against the Jews or Jewish culture. *—adj-* **an′ ti-Se·mit′ ic** (-sə mĭt′ ĭk): *an* anti-Semitic *book.*

an·ti·sep·tic (ăn′ tə sĕp′ tĭk) *n-* substance or preparation used to destroy harmful germs; disinfectant. *adj-* **1** having the power to destroy harmful germs. **2** free of harmful germs; sterile. *—adv-* **an′ ti·sep′ ti·cal·ly.**

an·ti·slav·er·y (ăn′ tĭ slā′ və rē, ăn′ tĭ′-) *adj-* opposed to slavery.

an·ti·so·cial (ăn′ tĭ sō′ shəl, ăn′ tĭ′-) *adj-* **1** opposed to the good of society: *Robbery is an* antisocial *act.* **2** unwilling or unable to get along with one's fellows; not sociable: *He's a good citizen, but somewhat* antisocial.

an·ti·tank (ăn′ tĭ tăngk′) *adj-* designed to destroy or cripple armored vehicles: *an* antitank *rocket.*

an·tith·e·sis (ăn tĭth′ ə sĭs) *n-* [*pl.* **an·tith·e·ses** (-sēz′)] **1** exact opposite: *Hope is the* antithesis *of despair.* **2** opposition; contrast: *an* antithesis *of ideas.* **3** expression that emphasizes contrast. Example: "Give me liberty, or give me death."

an·ti·tox·in (ăn′ tĭ tŏk′ sĭn) *n-* substance produced by the body to neutralize a poison (toxin) from a disease germ; also, a serum made from the blood of animals that have been injected with germ poison.

an·ti·trades (ăn′ tĭ trādz′) *n- pl.* tropical winds blowing steadily above the trade winds, and in an opposite direction; also, prevailing westerly winds of the middle latitudes.

an·ti·trust (ăn′ tĭ trŭst′, ăn′ tĭ-) *adj-* aimed at preventing the formation or activities of unfair business combinations or monopolies that interfere with normal business practices: *an* antitrust *law.*

an·ti·ve·nin (ăn′ tĭ vĕn′ ən, ăn′ tĭ′-) *n-* serum that neutralizes snake venom.

ant·ler (ănt′ lər) *n-* **1** one of the two solid branching horns of an animal of the deer family, shed and replaced yearly. **2** one of the branches of these horns.

---

fāte, făt, dâre, bärn; bē, bĕt, mêre; bīte, bĭt; nōte, hŏt, môre, dòg; fŭn, fûr; tōō, bŏŏk; oil; out; tar; thin; then; hw for wh as in *wh*at; zh for s as in u*s*ual; ə for a, e, i, o, u, as in *a*go, lin*e*n, per*i*l, at*o*m, min*u*s

an·to·nym (ăn'tə nĭm') ***n-*** word that means the opposite of another word. The antonym of "hard" is "soft."

a·nus (ā'nəs) ***n-*** opening at the lower end of the large intestine, through which waste passes from the body.

an·vil (ăn'vĭl) ***n-*** **1** block of iron on which metals are hammered and shaped. **2** the middle one of three tiny, sound-transmitting bones in the middle ear (for picture, see [1]*ear*).

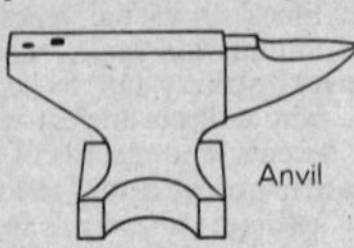
Anvil

anx·i·e·ty (ăng zī'ə tē) ***n-*** [*pl.* **anx·i·e·ties**] **1** feeling of uncertainty or uneasiness about the future; worry: *The* anxiety *of the sailors increased as the wind rose.* **2** something that causes this: *His illness is one of my* anxieties. **3** eager desire tinged with fear: *his* anxiety *to play music well.* **4** in psychology, an abnormal fear or worry, usually without foundation.

anx·ious (ăngk'shəs, ăng'shəs) ***adj-*** **1** worried; deeply troubled: *to be* anxious *about money.* **2** eager; wishing very strongly. **—*adv-*** **anx'ious·ly.** ***n-*** **anx'ious·ness.**

►EAGER has a positive force. *She was* eager *to go,* means that she wanted very much to go. ANXIOUS implies worry or anxiety—something negative—although in ordinary speech it often has the force of EAGER.

an·y (ĕn'ē) ***determiner*** (traditionally called adjective or sometimes pronoun) **1** one of several, but no matter which: *You may have* any *book here.* **2** some (used with a negative or in a question): *I haven't* any *time. Do you have* any *ginger ale? No, I haven't* any. **3** *every*: *I did what* any *person would do.* ***n-*** one of a group, but no particular one: *Give him* any *of the extra glasses.* ***adv-*** (used with a comparative) even the least bit; at all: *Don't go* any *farther.*

at any rate at least. **in any case** whatever happens.

an·y·bod·y (ĕn'ē bŏd'ē, -bŭd'ē) ***pron-*** any person; anyone: *Is* anybody *home?* ***n-*** an important person: *Everyone who was* anybody *attended the ball.*

an·y·how (ĕn'ē hou') ***adv-*** **1** in any way; hence, carelessly; in a haphazard way: *She just does her work* anyhow. **2** at any rate: *Well,* anyhow, *you are here now.*

an·y·more (ĕn'ē môr) ***adv-*** at the present time; currently: *We don't go there* anymore.

an·y·one (ĕn'ē wŭn') ***pron-*** any person; anybody.

an·y·place (ĕn'ē plās') *Informal* ***adv-*** anywhere.

an·y·thing (ĕn'ē thĭng') ***pron-*** a thing of any sort. ***adv-*** in any way; at all: *Is this* anything *like yours?*

anything but *Informal* certainly not.

an·y·way (ĕn'ē wā') ***adv-*** nevertheless; in any case: *I know I shouldn't spend that money, but I'll do it* anyway.

►ANYWAYS is characteristic of some regional speech patterns for ANYWAY. ANYWAY should be used unless it is desired to show regional speech or lack of education.

an·y·where (ĕn'ē hwâr') ***adv-*** **1** in or at any place: *Put the book* anywhere. **2** in or to any degree: *I haven't* anywhere *near a hundred dollars.* ***n-*** any place: *tourists from* anywhere *and everywhere.*

►ANYWHERES *is characteristic of some regional speech patterns for* ANYWHERE. ANYWHERE *should be used unless it is desired to show regional speech or lack of education.*

A-one (ā'wŭn') *Informal* ***adj-*** excellent; first-rate; topflight: *It's in* A-one *shape.* Also **A-1** or **A number 1.**

a·or·ta (ā ôr'tə) **n-** main artery of man and other mammals. It arches backward from the top of the heart to the lower body, carrying blood everywhere except to the lungs. For picture, see *heart.*

a·pace (ə pās') ***adv-*** at a good pace; rapidly; speedily: *Time passed, and the work went on* apace.

a·pache (ə păsh') *French* ***n-*** roughneck; hooligan; tough of the Paris streets. [a French borrowing from American Indian **Apache.**]

A·pach·e (ə păch'ē) ***n-*** [*pl.* **A·pach·es,** also **A·pach·e**] **1** member of a tribe of Plains Indians who formerly roamed over most of southwestern United States. **2** their language. ***adj-***: *an* Apache *chief.*

a·part (ə pärt') ***adv-*** **1** separately in time or place: *They live* apart. **2** in or into pieces: *It fell* apart.

apart from 1 separated from: *She lives* apart from *her parents.* **2** not considering; except for; leaving out of account: *The book interested me,* apart from the *the plot.* **tell apart** to distinguish one from the other: *It was difficult to* tell *the twins* apart.

a·part·heid (ə pärt'hāt, -hīt) ***n-*** official policy of racial segregation practiced in the Union of South Africa.

a·part·ment (ə pärt'mənt) ***n-*** room or group of rooms for a single household and, generally, located in a large building.

apartment house ***n-*** a building divided into apartments.

ap·a·thet·ic (ăp'ə thĕt'ĭk) ***adj-*** without interest; indifferent: *The child was* apathetic *toward all attempts to amuse her.* **—*adv-*** **ap'a·thet'i·cal·ly.**

ap·a·thy (ăp'ə thē) ***n-*** [*pl.* **ap·a·thies**] lack of feeling or interest; indifference: *to arouse a person from* apathy.

ape (āp) ***n-*** **1** long-armed tailless monkey such as the chimpanzee, gibbon, gorilla, or orang-utan. **2** person who mimics or imitates. ***vt-*** **[aped, ap·ing]** to mimic or imitate: *The boys* aped *the circus clown's actions.* **—*adj-*** **ape'like'.**

ap·er·ture (ăp'ər chər) ***n-*** **1** hole; gap: *an* aperture *in the stone wall.* **2** opening through which light passes into a camera or other optical instrument.

a·pex (ā'pĕks') ***n-*** [**a·pex·es** or **a·pi·ces (ā'pə sēz')**] peak or summit: *the* apex *of a triangle; the* apex *of his career.*

a·pha·si·a (ə fā'zhə, -zē ə) ***n-*** loss of the ability to speak, read, write, or to understand, usually caused by brain injury.

a·phe·lion (ă fēl'yən, -ē ən) ***n-*** the farthest point from the sun in the orbit of a planet or planetoid.

a·phid (ā'fĭd, ăf'ĭd) ***n-*** tiny green insect that infests plants and sucks their sap; plant louse. Also called **a'phis** [*pl.* **a·phid·es** (ā'fə dēz')].

Aphid on edge of elm leaf

a·phor·ism (ăf'ə rĭz'əm) ***n-*** short, concise statement expressing a truth; proverb; maxim; adage. Example: A penny saved is a penny earned.

Aph·ro·di·te (ăf rə dī'tē) ***n-*** in Greek mythology, the goddess of love and beauty, identified with the Roman Venus and with the Phoenician Astarte.

a·pi·ar·y (ā'pē ĕr'ē) ***n-*** [*pl.* **a·pi·ar·ies**] place where bees are kept; also, a collection of beehives.

a·piece (ə pēs') ***adv-*** for each one; each: *The pencils cost five cents* apiece. *Give them an orange* apiece.

ap·ish (ā'pĭsh) ***adj-*** **1** similar to an ape in shape, habits, etc.: *an* apish *walk.* **2** foolishly imitative: *the* apish *tricks of a little boy.* **—*adv-*** **ap'ish·ly.**

a·plomb (ə plŏm', -plŭm') ***n-*** assurance; self-confidence; poise: *He faced the crisis with his usual* aplomb.

a·poc·a·lypse (ə pŏk'ə lĭps') ***n-*** **1** any disclosure or revelation of the future; prophecy. **2 Apocalypse** the last book of the New Testament; Revelation. **—*adj-*** **a·poc'a·lyp'tic:** *an* apocalyptic *vision.*

a·poc·ry·pha (ə pŏk'rə fə) ***n-*** (takes a singular verb) **1** writings or statements of doubtful authorship or authority. **2 Apocrypha** (1) certain Biblical books included in the Septuagint and Vulgate but not authorized for the Jewish or Protestant Old Testament. (2) early Christian writings not included in the New Testament.

a·poc·ry·phal (ə pŏk′ rə fəl) ***adj-*** **1** having to do with the Apocrypha: *the* apocryphal *books of the Bible.* **2** of doubtful genuineness: *an* apocryphal *story.*

ap·o·gee (ăp′ ə jē′) ***n-*** farthest point from the earth in the orbit of a satellite.

apogee rocket ***n-*** rocket designed to fire when the satellite or spacecraft to which it is attached reaches its farthest point from the earth. This added thrust causes the vehicle to move into a different orbit.

A·pol·lo (ə pŏl′ ō) ***n-*** in Greek and Roman mythology, the god of music, poetry, prophecy, and medicine.

a·pol·o·get·ic (ə pŏl′ ə jĕt′ ĭk) or **a·pol·o·get·i·cal** (-jĕt′ ĭ kəl) ***adj-*** expressing regret for a fault or failure: *the* apologetic *remarks of the latecomers.* ***—adv-*** **a·pol′ o·get′ i·cal·ly.**

a·pol·o·gist (ə pŏl′ e jĭst′) ***n-*** one who speaks or writes in defense of a cause, institution, or person: *The senator is an* apologist *for increased foreign aid.*

a·pol·o·gize (ə pŏl′ ə jīz′) ***vi-*** **[a·pol·o·gized, a·pol·o·giz·ing]** **1** to express regret for something; say one is sorry: *I* apologize *for troubling you.* **2** to offer an excuse: *There's no need to* apologize *for a hearty appetite.*

a·pol·o·gy (ə pŏl′ ə jē) ***n-*** [*pl.* **a·pol·o·gies**] **1** an excuse or expression of regret for something one has said or done: *He made an* apology *for being noisy.* **2** something spoken, written, or offered in defense: *an* apology *for communism.* **3** poor substitute; makeshift: *This drawing is only an* apology *for a map.*

ap·o·plec·tic (ăp′ ə plĕk′ tĭk) ***adj-*** afflicted or threatened with apoplexy. ***—adv-*** **ap′ o·plec′ ti·cal·ly.**

ap·o·plex·y (ăp′ ə plĕk′ sē) ***n-*** sudden loss of consciousness and the power to feel or move caused by the breaking of a blood vessel in the brain; a stroke.

a·port (ə pôrt) ***adv-*** on or toward the left: *to see rocks* aport; *to steer hard* aport.

a·pos·ta·sy (ə pŏs′ tə sē) ***n-*** [*pl.* **a·pos·ta·sies**] the giving up of a religious faith, political creed, loyalty, etc.

a·pos·tate (ə pŏs′ tāt′) ***n-*** one who has forsaken his faith or party: *a Republican* apostate.

a·pos·tle (ə pŏs′ əl) ***n-*** **1** one of the twelve men chosen by Jesus to teach his gospel to the world. **2** leader of any movement: *an* apostle *of nonviolence.*

Apostles' Creed ***n-*** a fundamental statement of Christian faith, beginning "I believe in God the Father Almighty." It was formerly thought to have been written by the twelve apostles, but is now generally believed to have been written in the fourth or fifth century A.D.

ap·os·tol·ic (ăp′ ə stŏl′ ĭk) ***adj-*** **1** relating to the twelve apostles of Christ, or their times, doctrine, or practice. **2** coming from the Pope; papal: *an* apostolic *blessing.*

[1]**a·pos·tro·phe** (ə pŏs′ trə fē′) ***n-*** punctuation mark (') used to show: (1) contraction of two words. Example: I'll for I will. (2) omission of one or more letters from a word. Example: e'er for ever; '49 for 1849. (3) the possessive case of nouns. Example: cat's fur; Ulysses' shield. (4) the plural of letters and figures. Example: x's and y's; two 7's. [from French, from Latin **apostrophus,** from Greek **apostrephein,** "to turn away."]

[2]**a·pos·tro·phe** (ə pŏs′ trə fē′) ***n-*** a breaking off in a speech to address a person, usually absent or dead, or an abstract idea or imaginary object; also, the address inserted. [from Latin, from Greek **apostrophē.**]

a·pos·tro·phize (ə pŏs′ trə fīz′) ***vt-*** **[a·pos·tro·phized, a·pos·tro·phiz·ing]** to address an apostrophe to: *The mayor* apostrophized *freedom in his Fourth of July speech.* ***vi-***: *He* apostrophized *for forty minutes.*

apothecaries' weight ***n-*** system of weights used to weigh drugs.

a·poth·e·car·y (ə pŏth′ə kĕr′ ē) ***n-*** [*pl.* **a·poth·e·car·ies**] one who prepares and sells medicines and drugs; pharmacist; druggist.

ap·o·thegm (ăp′ ə thĕm′) ***n-*** short, pointed saying or proverb; aphorism; maxim. Example: Haste makes waste.

a·poth·e·o·sis (ə pŏth′ ē ō′ səs, ăp′ ə thē′ ə səs) ***n-*** [*pl.* **a·poth·e·o·ses** (-sēz′)] **1** the elevation to divine status, as with a deceased emperor in ancient Rome; deification. **2** a glorified ideal; the ideal example: *To her husband she was the* apotheosis *of womanhood.*

a·poth·e·o·size (ăp′ ə thē′ ə sīz′) ***vt-*** **[a·poth·e·o·sized, a·poth·e·o·siz·ing]** to deify.

ap·pall or **ap·pal** (ə pọl′) ***vt-*** **[ap·palled, ap·pal·ing]** to frighten; shock; dismay: *The danger of war* appalled *us.*

ap·pal·ling (ə pọl′ ĭng) ***adj-*** causing, or filling with, terror and dismay; terrifying; shocking: *an* appalling *number of victims.* ***—adv-*** **ap·pal′ ing·ly.**

ap·pa·nage (ăp′ ə nĭj) ***n-*** **1** in feudal times, land or office given by a king to his younger sons; later, any public provision made for the support of a member of a royal family. **2** natural accompaniment or endowment: *Responsibility is the* appanage *of high office.*

ap·pa·ra·tus (ăp′ ə răt′ əs, ăp′ ə rā′ təs) ***n-*** [*pl.* **ap·pa·ra·tus** or **ap·pa·ra·tus·es**] **1** equipment, instruments, etc., put together for a special purpose: *laboratory* apparatus; *gymnasium* apparatus. **2** group of bodily organs: *our digestive* apparatus.

ap·par·el (ə păr′ əl) ***n-*** clothing; dress: *boys'* apparel. ***vt-*** to clothe; fit out.

ap·par·ent (ə păr′ ənt, ə pâr′ ənt) ***adj-*** **1** easily understood; evident; obvious: *It is quite* apparent *that he is sick.* **2** appearing or seeming rather than true or real: *His* apparent *remorse fooled us.* ***—adv-*** **ap·par′ ent·ly.**

ap·pa·ri·tion (ăp′ ə rĭsh′ ən) ***n-*** **1** ghost or phantom: *He does not believe in* apparitions. **2** something startling or unusual that suddenly appears: *the* apparition *of the black ship as the fog lifted.*

ap·peal (ə pēl′) ***vi-*** **1** to make a plea (for); request: *The committee* appealed *for funds.* **2** to be interesting or attractive (to): *Both classical music and jazz* appeal *to me.* ***vt-*** to transfer or refer to a superior court or judge: *to* appeal *a case.* ***n-*** **1** a call for aid or sympathy: *An* appeal *went out from the flooded town.* **2** interest; attraction: *The picture has a wide* appeal *because of its soft colors.* **3** a request to have a case tried again before a higher court or judge. ***—adj-*** **ap·peal′ ing.**

ap·pear (ə pêr′) ***vi-*** **1** to come into sight: *The first flowers* appeared *above the snow.* **2** to seem: *The book* appears *to have been used many times.* **3** to come before the public: *That actor* appeared *in a new play.*

ap·pear·ance (ə pêr′ əns) ***n-*** **1** a coming into view; appearing: *A bear made a sudden* appearance. **2** outward aspect; look; bearing: *He has the* appearance *of a good runner.* **3** outward show; semblance: *to keep up an* appearance *of wealth*; *an* appearance *of modesty.* **4** a coming before the people: *the* appearance *of an actor in a play.* **5 appearances** general indications: *To all* appearances *he will win the election.*

put in an appearance to appear briefly.

---

fāte, făt, dâre, bärn; bē, bĕt, mêre; bīte, bĭt; nōte, hŏt, môre, dọg; fŭn, fûr; tōō, bŏŏk; oil; out; tar; thin; then; hw for wh as in *wh*at; zh for s as in u*s*ual; ə for a, e, i, o, u, as in *a*go, lin*e*n, per*i*l, at*o*m, min*u*s

ap·pease (ə pēz′) *vt-* [**ap·peased, ap·peas·ing**] **1** to make calm or peaceful; quiet: *His gentle words* appeased *the angry crowd.* **2** to satisfy: *to* appease *hunger; to* appease *curiosity.* **3** to pacify with concessions, usually contrary to one's principles: *Before World War II, many nations attempted to* appease *Nazi Germany.* **—n- ap·pease′ ment:** *Churchill opposed British* appeasement *of Hitler.*

ap·pel·lant (ə pĕl′ ənt) *n-* one who appeals from a lower to a higher court.

ap·pel·late (ə pĕl′ ət) *adj-* dealing with appeals from lower court decisions: *an* appellate *court.*

ap·pel·la·tion (ăp′ə lā′ shən) *n-* name or title by which a person or thing is described or known: *One* appellation *of Pennsylvania is the "Keystone State."*

ap·pend (ə pĕnd′) *vt-* to add to; attach: *to* append *a signature; to* append *a seal.*

ap·pend·age (ə pĕn′dĭj) *n-* **1** something added or attached to, hanging from, or accompanying a greater or more important thing. **2** *Biology* a limb, tail, horn, or other secondary part attached to the head or body of an animal.

ap·pen·dec·to·my (ăp′ən dĕk′tə mē) *n-* [*pl.* **ap·pen·dec·to·mies**] surgical operation in which the appendix is removed.

ap·pen·di·ci·tis (ə pĕn′də sī′ təs) *n-* inflammation of the vermiform appendix.

ap·pen·dix (ə pĕn′dĭks) *n-* [*pl.* **ap·pen·dix·es** or **ap·pen·dic·es** (-də sēz′)] **1** section of additional related information at the end of a book or other writing. **2** appendage. **3** a slim sac projecting from the large intestine, about 3 to 6 inches long, located near the junction of the small and large intestines in the lower right abdomen; vermiform appendix (for picture, see *intestine*).

ap·per·tain (ăp′ər tān′) *vi-* **1** to belong by right, nature, or custom: *These lands* appertain *to the abbey. The right to vote* appertains *to all citizens.* **2** to relate (to): *These experiments* appertain *to biochemistry.*

ap·pe·tite (ăp′ə tīt′) *n-* **1** desire for food. **2** strong and active liking or desire: *an* appetite *for reading.*

ap·pe·tiz·er (ăp′ə tī′zər) *n-* **1** food or drink served before a meal to stimulate the desire for food. **2** anything that arouses interest in things to follow.

ap·pe·tiz·ing (ăp′ə tī′zĭng) *adj-* exciting or pleasing the appetite: *a buffet of* appetizing *dishes.*

Ap·pi·an Way (ăp′ē ən) *n-* most famous of ancient Roman roads, begun 312 B.C. and running 336 miles southeast from Rome to Brundisium. Parts of it still exist.

ap·plaud (ə plȯd′) *vt-* **1** to express approval or enjoyment of, especially by clapping the hands: *The audience* applauded *the pianist's performance.* **2** to admire: *I* applaud *your courage.* ***vi-***: *Everyone* applauded.

ap·plause (ə plȯz′) *n-* **1** a clapping of the hands to show approval or appreciation. **2** admiration: *courage worthy of* applause.

ap·ple (ăp′ əl) *n-* **1** the rounded fleshy fruit of a tree common throughout the middle latitudes. **2** the tree itself. **3** (also **ap′ple·wood′**) the wood of this tree.

apple of (someone's) eye person or thing that is especially loved or cherished: *Fred was the* apple of his mother's eye.

Apple

apple butter *n-* thick, brown, spiced applesauce used as a spread for bread.

ap·ple·jack (ăp′əl jăk′) *n-* brandy made from apple cider.

ap·ple·sauce (ăp′əl sȯs′) *n-* **1** apples stewed to a pulp.

ap·pli·ance (ə plī′əns) *n-* article or device for some special use or purpose, such as an electric iron or a washing machine.

ap·pli·ca·ble (ăp′lĭ kə bəl, *also* ə plĭk′-) *adj-* of a nature that permits using or applying: relevant; appropriate: *That rule is not* applicable *in this case.* **—n- ap′pli·ca·bil′i·ty.**

ap·pli·cant (ăp′lə kənt) *n-* one who asks or applies for something; candidate: *an* applicant *for a position.*

ap·pli·ca·tion (ăp′lə kā′shən) *n-* **1** request made personally or in writing: *an* application *for a job; a letter of* application. **2** a putting something to use: *the* application *of astronomy to navigation.* **3** connection; relationship (to); relevance (to): *The preceding witness's testimony has no* application *to the case.* **4** a putting on: *The* application *of bandages will protect his wound.* **5** things put on or applied: *This* application *will relieve the itching.* **6** close attention or effort: *The student's* application *to his studies should result in higher grades.*

ap·pli·ca·tor (ăp′lə kāt′ər) *n-* a device for applying a substance such a polish, medicine, etc.

ap·plied (ə plīd′) *adj-* **1** put to practical use; utilitarian as distinct from theoretical or abstract: *a textbook of* applied *mathematics*; applied *religion.* **2** having been put on or over: *a newly* applied *coat of paint.*

applied science science as used for practical problems, such as building a supersonic jet plane or purifying sea water economically. Engineering is an applied science.

ap·pli·qué (ăp′lə kā′) *n-* an ornamentation, as for clothes or fancywork, made by cutting figures out of one material and applying them upon another. *vt-* [**ap·pli·quéd, ap·pli·qué·ing**]: *to* appliqué *flowers on an apron.*

ap·ply (ə plī′) *vt-* [**ap·plied, ap·ply·ing**] **1** to cover with; put on: *to* apply *a bandage.* **2** to put into use or practice: *to* apply *one's training to a task.* **3** to devote (oneself) to a particular purpose: *You should* apply *yourself to your studies.* ***vi-*** **1** to make a request: *to* apply *for a job*; *to* apply *for a loan.* **2** to have reference; be suitable or fit: *The new law does not* apply *to this case.*

ap·point (ə point′) *vt-* **1** to name or choose for an office or position: *The basketball team* appointed *her captain.* **2** to fix by agreement; decide on: *The judge* appointed *Tuesday as the day of the trial.*

ap·point·ee (ə poin′tē′, ă′-) *n-* person named to an office: *a political* appointee.

ap·poin·tive (ə poin′tĭv) *adj-* filled by appointment, not by election: *an* appointive *position at the White House.*

ap·point·ment (ə point′mənt) *n-* **1** a naming or appointing to an office; a choosing: *The* appointment *of a city manager was delayed.* **2** the office or position itself: *He held a key* appointment *in the government.* **3** agreement to be at a certain place or to meet someone; engagement: *an* appointment *with the dentist at 5 o'clock.* **4 appointments** the furnishings of a room, house, building, etc.

ap·por·tion (ə pôr′shən) *vt-* to divide and distribute; allot: *to* apportion *the profits among the partners.*

ap·por·tion·ment (ə pôr′shən mənt) *n-* distribution; allotment: *the* apportionment *of representatives by population.*

ap·po·site (ăp′ə sət) *adj-* suitable; to the point: *an* apposite *remark.*

►Should not be confused with OPPOSITE.

ap·po·si·tion (ăp′ə zĭsh′ən) *n-* **1** the act of placing together; also, the condition of being in close contact. **2** *Grammar* the relation of a noun or noun phrase to another noun or moun phrase near which it is placed, as an explanatory equivalent. In the expression "Crusoe spoke to Friday, his servant," "his servant" is in apposition to "Friday."

ap·pos·i·tive (ə pŏz′ ə tĭv′) ***adj-*** in apposition; explanatory. ***n-*** word or phrase in apposition. ***—adv-*** **ap·pos′ i·tive·ly.**

ap·prais·al (ə prā′ zəl) ***n-*** **1** the setting of a value or price. **2** the value assigned; valuation: *The* appraisal *of the painting was too high.*

ap·praise (ə prāz′) ***vt-*** **[ap·praised, ap·prais·ing]** to estimate or fix the value or price of: *to* appraise *a man's worth*; *to* appraise *land for taxation.* ***—n-*** **ap·prais′ er.** ►Should not be confused with APPRISE (APPRIZE).

ap·pre·cia·ble (ə prē′ shə bəl) ***adj-*** large or important enough to be seen or felt; noticeable: *an* appreciable *improvement.* ***—adv-*** **ap·pre′ cia·bly.**

ap·pre·ci·ate (ə prē′ shē āt′) ***vt-*** **[ap·pre·ci·at·ed, ap·pre·ci·at·ing]** **1** to realize the worth of; hold in high regard; value; enjoy: *I really* appreciate *a hot drink on a cold night.* **2** to be grateful for: *We* appreciate *your help.* **3** to judge the worth of; enjoy intelligently: *to* appreciate *music or poetry.* **4** to be aware of; be fully sensitive to: *to* appreciate *the full horror of war.* ***vi-*** to rise in value: *The stocks have* appreciated *twofold over the last year.*

ap·pre·ci·a·tion (ə prē′ shē ā′ shən) ***n-*** **1** understanding and approval: *the* appreciation *of music.* **2** an increasing, especially of money value: *the* appreciation *of his government bonds.* **3** a critical judgement; critique: *We asked the expert for an* appreciation *of our work.*

ap·pre·ci·a·tive (ə prē′ shə tĭv, ə prē′ shē ā′ -) ***adj-*** showing appreciation or gratitude.

ap·pre·hend (ăp′ rĭ hĕnd′) ***vt-*** **1** to arrest; seize. **2** to grasp with the mind; understand thoroughly: *He fully* apprehended *what he read.* **3** to forsee with fear: *Mother* apprehended *the danger of driving on icy roads.*

ap·pre·hen·sion (ăp′ rĭ hĕn′ shən) ***n-*** **1** process of understanding or perceiving; also, the power or ability to understand: *This part of the test deals with* apprehension. **2** fear of what may happen: *a mother's* apprehension *for her son's welfare.* **3** arrest or capture: *the* apprehension *of a thief.*

ap·pre·hen·sive (ăp′ rĭ hĕn′ sĭv) ***adj-*** fearful; worried; uneasy about an outcome, a person's safety, etc.: *Jerry was* apprehensive *about his test marks.* ***—adv-*** **ap′ pre·hen′ sive·ly.** ***n-*** **ap′pre·hen′ sive·ness:** *The* apprehensiveness *of a wild animal.*

ap·pren·tice (ə prĕn′ təs) ***n-*** **1** person who is learning a trade or craft by practical experience under a skilled worker. **2** formerly, one bound by an agreement to work for a definite length of time in return for his training. **3** novice, or one slightly versed in anything. ***vt-*** **[ap·pren·ticed, ap·pren·tic·ing]** to put under a master for training in a trade.

ap·pren·tice·ship (ə prĕn′ təs shĭp′) ***n-*** **1** condition of being an apprentice. **2** time during which one serves as an apprentice.

ap·prise (ə prīz′) ***vt-*** **[ap·prised, ap·pris·ing]** to give notice to; warn; inform: *I* apprised *him of danger.* Also **ap·prize′.**
►Should not be confused with APPRAISE.

ap·proach (ə prōch′) ***vi-*** to come or draw near: *Winter is* approaching. ***vt-*** **1** to come near to; to move toward: *We are* approaching *the city.* **2** to come close to but never reach; approximate: *to* approach *perfection.* **3** to deal with or treat. **4** to make proposals to: *When is the best time to* approach *him?* ***n-*** **1** a coming near; a moving toward: *They fled at our* approach. *We started for home at the* approach *of night.* **2** the way or road by which a place is reached: *the* approaches *to the city.* **3** way of dealing with or treating: *a new* approach *to the study of language.* **4** in golf, a shot intended to place the ball on the green.

ap·proach·a·ble (ə prō′ chə bəl) ***adj-*** **1** located so that it can be approached; accessible: *a mountain peak* approachable *from the north side.* **2** easy to approach: *a friendly,* approachable *man.* ***—n-*** **ap·proach′ a·bil′ i·ty.**

ap·pro·ba·tion (ăp′ rə bā′ shən) ***n-*** the expressing of a favorable opinion; approval: *She found it difficult to earn her aunt's* approbation.

[1]**ap·pro·pri·ate** (ə prō′ prē ət) ***adj-*** fitting; suitable: *That dress is hardly* appropriate *for a formal dance.* ***—adv-*** **ap·pro′ pri·ate·ly.** ***n-*** **ap·pro′ pri·ate·ness:** *Its* appropriateness *is highly questionable.*

[2]**ap·pro·pri·ate** (ə prō′ prē āt′) ***vt-*** **[ap·pro·pri·at·ed, ap·pro·pri·at·ing]** **1** to set aside for a particular use: *The government* appropriated *money for road improvement.* **2** to take and use for onself: *The escaped convicts* appropriated *the farmer's car.*

ap·pro·pri·a·tion (ə prō′ prē ā′ shən) ***n-*** **1** money set aside for a particular purpose: *The* appropriation *was for the improvement of the subway system.* **2** the taking over of something as one's own or for use by a governmental body: *the* appropriation *of land for a school.*

ap·prov·al (ə prōō′ vəl) ***n-*** **1** favorable acceptance or agreement: *News of the extra holiday was hailed with* approval. **2** official consent: *The governor gave his* approval *to the bill.*
on approval on trial: *We bought the machine* on approval *and got our money back when it proved unsatisfactory.* **meet with approval** to be acceptable or agreeable to someone: *His plan* meets with *my full* approval.

ap·prove (ə prōōv′) ***vi-*** **[ap·proved, ap·prov·ing]** to speak or think well (of): *I cannot* approve *of his new friends.* ***vt-*** to agree or give official consent to: *Congress* approved *the bill after heated debate.*

[1]**ap·prox·i·mate** (ə prŏk′ sə mət) ***adj-*** not exact but nearly so; almost correct: *The* approximate *weight of a pint of milk is one pound.* ***—adv-*** **ap·prox′ i·mate·ly.**

[2]**ap·prox·i·mate** (ə prŏk′ sə māt′) ***vt-*** **[ap·prox·i·mat·ed, ap·prox·i·mat·ing]** to come near to; approach: *The translation* approximates *the original.*

ap·prox·i·ma·tion (ə prŏk′ sə mā′ shən) ***n-*** something more or less exact or true: *an* approximation *of the true story.*

ap·pur·te·nance (ə pûr′ tə nəns) ***n-*** **1** in law, a right, privilege, or property that belongs to a principal property and passes along with it when sold. **2 appurtenances** all of the things associated with an activity; apparatus; gear: *a rubber suit and other* appurtenances *of skin diving.*

Apr. April.

a·pri·cot (ăp′ rə kŏt′, ā′ prə-) ***n-*** **1** small, round, orange-colored fruit with downy skin somewhat like a peach. **2** tree which bears this fruit. **3** a pale yellow-orange color. ***adj-:*** *an* apricot *pie*; *an* apricot *silk.*

A·pril (ā′ prəl) ***n-*** the fourth month of the year, having 30 days.

April Fool ***n-*** victim of a prank on April Fools' day.

April Fools' Day ***n-*** April 1, a day marked by practical jokes, tricks, etc.

a pri·o·ri (ā′ prī′ ôr′ ī′, ä′ prē′ ôr′ ē) ***adj-*** **1** proceeding from cause to effect or from general principle to particular instance. **2** based on theory rather than observation or experience. ***adv-:*** *to reason* a priori.

a·pron (ā'prən) ***n-*** **1** piece of wearing apparel worn over the front of the body to protect clothing. **2** the area that lies in front: *the* apron *of the stage.*

ap·ro·pos (ă'prə pō') ***adj-*** appropriate; fitting: *an* apropos *remark.*

apropos of with reference to: *My question is* apropos of *his remark.*

apse (ăps) ***n-*** semicircular recess covered with a half dome, especially at the pulpit end of a church, beyond the choir as viewed from the nave.

apt (ăpt) ***adj-*** **1** suitable; appropriate: *The "space age" is an* apt *name for the period we are living in.* **2** quick to learn: *She is an* apt *student of arithmetic.* **3** likely: *When in a hurry, anyone is* apt *to be careless.* **—*adv-* apt'ly. *n-* apt'ness:** *the* aptness *of a name.*

apt. apartment.

ap·ti·tude (ăp'tə to͞od', -tyo͞od') ***n-*** **1** talent; flair: *an* aptitude *for painting.* **2** natural ability, skill, or quickness to learn: *an* aptitude *for mathematics.*

aptitude test ***n-*** test to determine a person's ability to acquire certain skills, as in music, languages, etc.; also, any test to determine a person's fitness for an activity, job, etc.

aq·ua (ăk'wə, äk'-) ***n-*** **1** *Latin* water. **2** pale blue-green color; aquamarine.

aq·ua·cade (ăk'wə kād') ***n-*** show consisting of swimming, diving, water ballet, etc., accompanied by music.

Aq·ua-Lung (ăk'wə lŭng') ***n-*** trade name for a type of scuba gear. Also **aq'ua·lung'.**

aq·ua·ma·rine (ăk'wə mə rēn') ***n-*** **1** transparent semiprecious stone of a pale blue, green, or blue-green color. **2** a pale blue-green color. ***adj-*** of this color.

a·qua·naut (ăk'wə nôt') ***n-*** person who explores underwater.

aq·ua·plane (ăk'wə plān') ***n-*** board ridden for sport, attached by ropes to the stern of a motorboat and ridden by a person standing on it. ***vi-*** **[aq·ua·planed, aq·ua·plan·ing]** *We* aquaplaned *two hours yesterday.*

aqua re·gia (rē'jə) ***n-*** mixture of concentrated nitric and hydrochloric acids, used to disslove such metals as gold and platinum.

a·quar·i·um (ə kwâr'ē əm) ***n-*** [*pl.* **a·quar·i·ums** or **a·quar·i·a**] **1** tank, bowl, or artificial pond in which living water plants and water animals are kept. **2** place devoted to the care and exhibition of large collections of water plants and animals.

A·quar·i·us (ə kwâr'ē əs) ***n-*** constellation of stars thought to outline the figure of a water carrier.

a·quat·ic (ə kwăt'ĭk) ***adj-*** **1** in or on water: *Swimming is an* aquatic *sport.* **2** living in water: *The porpoise is an* aquatic *animal.* ***n-*** **1** anything that lives in water, especially a plant. **2 aquatics** water sports.

aq·ua·tint (ăk'wə tĭnt') ***n-*** **1** engraving process in which the surface of a copper plate is etched with an acid and used to make a print like an ink drawing or water color. **2** a print made by this process. ***vt-*** to engrave by this process.

aq·ue·duct (ăk'wə dŭkt') ***n-*** **1** large pipe or other artificial channel for conducting water. **2** bridgelike structure that supports such a pipe or channel.

Aqueduct

a·que·ous (ā'kwē əs, ăk'-) ***adj-*** diluted with or resembling water; watery: *an* aqueous *solution.*

aqueous humor ***n-*** clear, watery liquid filling the space between the cornea and the lens of the eye.

aq·ui·fer (ăk'wə fər) ***n-*** underground layer of sand, gravel, porous rock, etc., that holds ground water.

aq·ui·line (ăk'wə līn', -lən) ***adj-*** curved like an eagle's beak.

a·quiv·er (ə kwĭv'ər) ***adj-*** quivering; trembling: *He was* aquiver *with excitement.*

-ar *suffix* **1** (used to form adjectives) belonging to; characteristic of: *pol*ar; *consul*ar; *column*ar. **2** (used to form nouns) doer or agent: *registr*ar (one in charge of registration).

Ar·ab (ăr'əb) ***n-*** **1** native of Arabia, a peninsula of southwest Asia. **2** member of Semitic people now scattered over the African and Syrian deserts. **3** horse of intelligent breed noted for its speed and fiery spirit. ***adj-***: *an* Arab *steed*; *an* Arab *headdress.*

ar·a·besque (ăr'ə bĕsk') ***n-*** **1** decoration in low relief or color, representing fruits, flowers, etc., fancifully combined. **2** ballet position in which a dancer extends one leg straight back, one arm forward, and one arm back.

A·ra·bi·an Nights, the (ə rā'bē ən) ***n-*** a collection of folk stories from India, Arabia, Persia, etc., dating from the 10th century A.D. Also called **The Thousand and One Nights.**

Ar·a·bic (ăr'ə bĭk) ***adj-*** of or pertaining to Arabia, the Arabs, their language and culture. ***n-*** the Semitic language now widely spoken in many Muslim countries of the Middle East and Africa.

Arabic numerals ***n-*** the figures, 1, 2, 3, 4, 5, 6, 7, 8, 9, and 0, used to write numbers, borrowed from the Arabs.

1234567890

Arabic Numerals

ar·a·ble (ăr'ə bəl) ***adj-*** of land, suitable for cultivation.

a·rach·nid (ə răk'nĭd) ***n-*** any of a large group of insectlike animals including spiders, scorpions, mites, and ticks. Arachnids differ from insects in having four pairs of legs and lacking wings and antennae.

A·rap·a·ho (ə răp'ə hō') ***n-*** [*pl.* **A·rap·a·hoes,** also **A·rap·a·ho**] member of a tribe of Plains Indian who formerly lived in Colorado and Wyoming and now are on reservations in Oklahoma and Wyoming. ***adj-***: *the* Arapaho *reservation.*

Ar·au·ca·ni·an (ăr'ô kā'nē ən) ***n-*** [*pl.* **Ar·au·ca·ni·ans**] member of a tribe of South American Indians of Argentina and northern Chile. ***adj-***: *an* Araucanian *spear.*

A·ra·wak (ăr'ə wäk) ***n-*** [*pl.* **A·ra·waks,** also **A·ra·wak**] **1** member of a tribe of South American Indians now living chiefly along the coast of British Guiana. **2** the language of these Indians. ***adj-***: *an* Arawak *canoe.*

ar·bi·ter (är'bə tər) ***n-*** **1** person chosen or appointed to settle a dispute; umpire **2** one who has full power to make decisions: *I am the* arbiter *of my own life.*

ar·bi·trar·y (är'bə trĕr ē) ***adj-*** **1** ruled only by one's own wishes or ideas in making decisions; despotic: *He is an intelligent, but* arbitrary, *ruler.* **2** based on one's own opinions and wishes, not on any rule or law: *an* arbitrary *decision.* **—*adv-* ar'bi·trar'i·ly.**

ar·bi·trate (är'bə trāt) ***vt-*** **[ar·bi·trat·ed, ar·bi·trat·ing]** **1** to hear as a judge, and decide: *The mother* arbitrated *the family differences.* **2** to refer (a dispute) to others for settlement: *We decided to* arbitrate *the issue.* ***vi-*** to act as arbiter or judge.

ar·bi·tra·tion (är'bə trā'shən) ***n-*** way of settling a dispute in which the two sides submit their arguments to a third person or group for decision.

ar·bi·tra·tor (är′ bə trā′ tər) ***n-*** **1** person chosen to settle or to assist in settling a dispute between parties. **2** one who has legal authority to make decisions.

ar·bor (är′ bər) ***n-*** **1** bower formed by vines trained over a lattice: *a grape* arbor. **2** shaded nook or walk.

Arbor Day ***n-*** a day generally observed in the United States for planting trees and shrubs.

ar·bor·e·al (är′ bôr′ ē əl) ***adj-*** **1** of, relating to, or resembling trees: *an* arboreal *region*; *an* arboreal *shape*. **2** living in trees, as do monkeys and squirrels.

ar·bo·re·tum (är′ bə rē′ təm) ***n-*** [*pl.* **ar·bo·re·tums** or **ar·bo·re·ta**] garden in which shrubs and trees, especially rare trees, are cultivated and exhibited.

ar·bor·vi·tae (är′ bər vī′ tē) ***n-*** evergreen tree or shrub with fanlike branches, cultivated for gardens and hedges.

Arcs

ar·bu·tus (är′ byōō′ təs) ***n-*** **1** any of several evergreen shrubs having scarlet or red berries. **2** a creeping plant which has fragrant pink or white flowers in the early spring.

arc (ärk) ***n-*** **1** in geometry, a part of a circle. **2** in electronics, a band of light, often arched, produced by the flow of electricity across a gap separating two electrodes. ***Hom-*** ark.

ar·cade (är kād′) ***n-*** **1** row of arches supported by pillars. **2** arched gallery or passageway, frequently between buildings, especially one lined with shops.

Arcade

Ar·ca·di·a (är kā′ dē ə) ***n-*** region in ancient Greece where simple, pastoral people lived; hence, any place of quiet contentment and peace. **—*adj-*** **Ar·ca′ di·an.**

[1]**arch** (ärch) ***n-*** **1** curved structure used in buildings, bridges, etc., for supporting a load over an open space by transferring the downward thrust of the load to the sides. **2** monument consisting of such a structure, and usually erected to celebrate a victory. **3** anything resembling such a structure: *the* arch *of the foot*; *the* arch *of a cat's back.* **4** archway. ***vt-*** **1** to cover or span with such a structure: *to* arch *a gate in stone*; *to* arch *a river with a bridge.* **2** to curve (something) so that it resembles such a structure: *The cat* arched *its back.* ***vi-***: *The great bridge* arched *over the river.* [from Old French **arche,** from Late Latin plural **arca,** from Latin **arcus** meaning "bow; arc."]

Arches

[2]**arch** (ärch) ***adj-*** mischievous; playful; roguish; coy: *her* arch *look.* [from **arch-.** The meaning "mischievous" perhaps arose from words like "arch-knave" and "arch-rogue."] **—*adv-*** **arch′ ly.** ***n-*** **arch′ ness.**

arch- *combining form* principal; chief; first: *an* arch*bishop*; arch*enemy.* [from Greek and Latin **arch-** meaning "leading."]

ar·chae·ol·o·gy (är′ kē ŏl′ ə jē) archeology.

ar·cha·ic (är kā′ ĭk) ***adj-*** **1** of language, no longer in use, except for a special purpose. Examples: methinks, thou, in sooth. **2** of ancient times: *He studied* archaic *Roman customs.*

ar·cha·ism (är′ kē ĭz əm, âr′ kā′ -) ***n-*** a word or expression no longer in common use. Also **ar·cha′ i·cism′** (är kā′ ə sĭz′ əm).

arch·an·gel (ärk′ ān′ jəl) ***n-*** chief angel.

arch·bish·op (ärch′ bĭsh′ əp) ***n-*** bishop at the head of church province.

arch·dea·con (ärch′ dē′ kən) ***n-*** in some Christian churches, the chief deacon, immediately below a bishop in rank.

arch·di·o·cese (ärch′ dī′ ə səs, -sēs) ***n-*** an area or district under the ecclesiastical jurisdiction of an archbishop.

arch·duch·y (ärch′ dŭch′ ē) ***n-*** [*pl.* **arch·duch·ies**] the territory governed by an archduke or archduchess.

arch·duke (ärch′ dōōk′, -dyōōk′) ***n-*** prince of the imperial house of Austria. **—*n-*** *fem.* **arch′ duch′ ess.**

arch·en·e·my (ärch′ ĕn′ ə mē) ***n-*** [*pl.* **arch·en·e·mies**] **1** a chief enemy. **2** Satan.

ar·che·o·log·i·cal (är′ kē ə lŏj′ ə kəl) ***adj-*** connected with archeology: *books on* archeological *expeditions.* Also **ar′ chae·o·log′ i·cal.** **—*adv-*** **ar′ che·o·log′ i·cal·ly.**

ar·che·ol·o·gist (är′ kē ŏl′ ə jĭst′) ***n-*** person trained in archeology and, usually, engaged in it as a profession. Also **ar′ chae·ol′ o·gist.**

ar·che·ol·o·gy (är′ kē ŏl′ ə jē) ***n-*** scientific study of the life of earlier peoples, based on the remains of their towns or villages, and on relics, such as weapons, utensils, or ornaments, found in these remains. Also **ar′ chae·ol′ o·gy.**

Ar·che·o·zo·ic (är kē ə zō′ ĭk) ***n-*** era of geologic time which lasted from the cooling of the earth's crust about 2 billion years ago to about 1 billion years ago, during which the first forms of life probably appeared. ***adj-***: *the* Archeozoic *era.*

arch·er (är′ chər) ***n-*** person who shoots with the bow and arrow.

Archer

arch·er·y (är′ chə rē) ***n-*** use of bow and arrows, especially as a sport.

ar·che·type (är′ kə tīp′) ***n-*** **1** the original model or pattern from which later things are made or developed; first form; prototype: *The Wright brothers' plane is the* archetype *of today's great airliners.* **2** a perfect or typical example: *an* archetype *of the successful salesman.*

arch-Fiend (ärch′ fēnd′) ***n-*** Satan.

ar·chi·pel·a·go (är′ kə pĕl′ ə gō′, är′ chə-) ***n-*** [*pl.* **ar·chi·pel·a·gos** or **ar·chi·pel·a·goes**] **1** sea with many islands. **2** group of islands in a sea.

ar·chi·tect (är′ kə tĕkt′) ***n-*** person who plans and directs the construction of houses, churches, bridges, etc.

ar·chi·tec·tur·al (är′ kə tĕk′ chər əl) ***adj-*** of or relating to architecture or to the art of building: *an* architectural *design.* **—*adv-*** **ar′ chi·tec′ tur·al·ly.**

ar·chi·tec·ture (är′ kə tĕk′ chər) ***n-*** **1** the art and work of designing buildings and supervising their construction. **2** manner or style of building: *modern* architecture; *Greek* architecture. **3** a building, or buildings collectively: *The city tried to save its museum and other fine* architecture. **4** manner of putting parts together; construction: *the* architecture *of our foreign policy.*

ar·chi·trave (är′ kə trāv′) ***n-*** in architecture, a horizontal part which rests on the columns of a building.

ar·chive (är′ kīv′) ***n-*** **1** record preserved as evidence. **2 archives** (1) the place in which public records or documents of historical value are kept. (2) these documents or records.

---

arch·way (ärch'wā') ***n-*** **1** passageway under an arch or curved roof. **2** entrance with an arch above it.

arc lamp ***n-*** electric lamp that emits intense light from an electric arc between two electrodes, usually made of carbon. Also called **arc light.**

arc·tic (är'tĭk, ärk'tĭk) ***adj-*** having to do with the north polar regions: *white* arctic *animals*; *cold* arctic *winds.* ***n-*** **1** a high, warmly lined, waterproof overshoe. **2 Arctic** the north polar region.

Arctic Circle ***n-*** imaginary boundary of the north polar region. On maps and globes it is shown as a line parallel to the equator at 23 degrees and 30 minutes (23° 30') south of the North Pole.

Arc·tu·rus (ärk'tŏŏr'əs, -tyŏŏr'əs) ***n-*** large, bright, orange-tinted star in the constellation Boötes.

ar·dent (är'dənt) ***adj-*** eager; enthusiastic; warm: *an* ardent *lover of music.* ***—adv-*** **ar'dent·ly.**

ar·dor (är'dər) ***n-*** great eagerness; passion; intensity of feeling: *an* ardor *for knowledge.*

ar·du·ous (är'jōō əs) ***adj-*** difficult; hard to do, strenuous: *an* arduous *task.* ***—adv-*** **ar'du·ous·ly.** ***n-*** **ar'du·ous·ness.**

[1]**are** (är) form of **be** used with "you," "we," "they," or plural noun subjects in the present tense. ***Hom-*** our

[2]**are** (âr, är) ***n-*** in the metric system, a measure of surface, especially of land, equal to 100 square meters or 119.6 square yards. [from French **are,** from Latin **area** "flat place; area."] ***Homs-*** air, e'er, ere, heir or our.

ar·e·a (âr'ē ə) ***n-*** **1** any surface, of land, a floor, etc. **2** measure of the surface of a piece of land or of a geometric figure or solid: *the* area *of the United States*; *the* area *of a sphere.* **3** region or district: *a mountainous* area; *an industrial* area. **4** range or scope of a subject, activity, etc.: *Tom's major* area *of study is physics.*

area code ***n-*** three-digit numeral used to designate telephone service areas in the United States and Canada.

ar·e·a·way (âr'ē ə wā') ***n-*** **1** a sunken yard or court leading to the cellar or basement of a building. **2** passageway between buildings.

a·re·na (ə rē'nə) ***n-*** **1** the enclosed space of a Roman amphitheater, in which fights between gladiators took place. **2** any scene or field where men compete: *the* arena *of politics.*

are·n't (ärnt, är'ənt) are not.

ar·gon (är'gŏn') ***n-*** colorless, odorless, inert gas that is one of the elements found in the air, used chiefly for filling electric light bulbs and vacuum tubes. Symbol Ar, At. No. 18, At. Wt. 39.948.

Ar·go·naut (är'gə nòt') ***n-*** in Greek legend, any of the men who sailed with Jason to find the Golden Fleece.

ar·go·sy (är'gə sē) ***n-*** [*pl.* **ar·go·sies**] **1** large merchant ship. **2** fleet of ships.

ar·got (är'gŏt', är'gō') ***n-*** the special slang of any group, especially in the underworld. [from French **argot,** the dialect of the Parisian underworld.]

ar·gue (är'gyōō) ***vi-*** [**ar·gued, ar·gu·ing**] **1** to give reasons for or against something: *I* argued *for disarmament, and he* argued *against it.* **2** to dispute: *He and his brother always* argued *over politics.* ***vt-*** to persuade by giving reasons: *You've* argued *me into going.*

ar·gu·ment (är'gyə mənt) ***n-*** **1** discussion in which reasons are given for or against something; debate: *an* argument *over whether movies should be censored or not.* **2** a dispute; verbal quarrel: *an* argument *about money.* **3** a reason: *The best* argument *for this plan is that it will save money.*

ar·gu·men·ta·tion (är'gyə mən tā'shən) ***n-*** **1** the process of giving reasons and drawing conclusions from them; reasoning. **2** any discussion or debate.

ar·gu·men·ta·tive (är'gyə mĕn'tə tiv') ***adj-*** fond of arguing or discussing; quarrelsome; contentious. ***—adv-*** **ar'gu·men'ta·tive'ly.** ***n-*** **ar'gu·men'ta·tive'ness.**

Ar·gus (är'gəs) ***n-*** in Greek mythology, a monster with a hundred eyes, whom Hermes lulled to sleep and killed, and whose eyes were then placed in the peacock's tail.

Ar·gus-eyed (är'gəs īd') ***adj-*** like Argus in Greek mythology, able to see in all directions; sharp-sighted; observant; watchful: *an* Argus-eyed *sentry.*

a·ri·a (är'ē ə) ***n-*** solo part in an opera, oratorio, or the like.

Ar·i·ad·ne (ăr'ē ăd'nē) ***n-*** in Greek mythology, daughter of Minos, King of Crete. Ariadne gave Theseus a ball of thread to guide him out of the Labyrinth.

ar·id (ăr'ĭd) ***adj-*** **1** dry; parched; having little or no rain: *the* arid *regions in the western United States.* **2** uninteresting: *an* arid *subject*; *an* arid *personality.* ***—adv-*** **ar'id·ly.**

a·rid·i·ty (ə rĭd'ə tē) ***n-*** dryness.

Ar·i·el (âr'ē ĕl') ***n-*** in Shakespeare's "Tempest," a prankish spirit who helped Prospero. ***Hom-*** aerial.

A·ries (âr'ēz) ***n-*** constellation of stars thought to outline the figure of a ram.

a·right (ə rīt') ***adv-*** correctly; rightly.

A·ri·ka·ra (ə rĭk'ə rə) ***n-*** [*pl.* **A·ri·ka·ras,** also **A·ri·ka·ra**] member of a tribe of Plains Indians who formerly lived in the Dakotas. ***adj-***: *the* Arikara *hair style.*

a·rise (ə rīz') ***vi-*** [**a·rose** (ə rōz'), **a·ris·en** (ə rĭz'ən), **a·ris·ing**] **1** to rise; get up: *The spectators* arose *when the judge entered the courtroom.* **2** to move upward; ascend: *Clouds of smoke* arose *above the forest fire.* **3** to begin; start up: *If an argument should* arise, *keep your temper.*

ar·is·toc·ra·cy (ăr'ə stŏk'rə sē) ***n-*** [*pl.* **ar·is·toc·ra·cies**] **1** class of persons of high rank or noble birth; the nobility. **2** class of persons superior in ability, culture, or wealth. **3** government in which the nobles rule. **4** a state so governed.

a·ris·to·crat (ə rĭs'tə krăt') ***n-*** **1** person of high rank, birth, or title. **2** person superior in ability, intellect, or culture.

a·ris·to·crat·ic (ə rĭs'tə krăt'ĭk) ***adj-*** **1** belonging to a person of high rank or noble birth: *an* aristocratic *name*; aristocratic *manners.* **2** of or like an aristocrat. ***—adv-*** **a·ris'to·crat'i·cal·ly.**

[1]**a·rith·me·tic** (ə rĭth'mə tĭk') ***n-*** branch of mathematics dealing with the properties and relationships of numbers and the computations with them; the art of using numbers to add, subtract, multiply, divide, etc.

[2]**ar·ith·met·ic** (ăr'ĭth mĕt'ĭk) or **ar·ith·met·i·cal** (-ĭ kəl) ***adj-*** having to do with or calculated by real numbers. ***—adv-*** **ar'ith·met'i·cal·ly.**

arithmetical progression ***n-*** series of numbers in which each number is larger than the last by a fixed amount. Example: 1, 3, 5, 7, 9.

a·rith·me·ti·cian (ə rĭth'mə tĭsh'ən) ***n-*** person skilled in arithmetic.

ar·ith·met·ic mean (ăr'ĭth mĕt'ĭk) ***n-*** average.

Ariz. Arizona.

ark (ärk) ***n-*** **1** the oblong box containing the Covenant, or tables of the Law, in the Jewish Tabernacle. **2** the ship in which Noah and his family remained during the Flood. ***Hom-*** arc.

Ark. Arkansas.

[1]**arm** (ärm) ***n-*** **1** in men, apes, and monkeys, one of the two upper limbs; especially, that part between shoulder and hand. **2** forelimb of any animal having a backbone. **3** any part extending from a main body: *the* arms *of a chair*; *an* arm *of the sea*; *an* arm *(ray) of a starfish.*

4 branch or department exercising power: *The F.B.I. is an* arm *of the Justice Department.* [from Old English **earm.**]

arm in arm with arms linked: *The friends walked* arm in arm. **hold** (or **keep) someone at arm's length** to avoid becoming friendly with someone. **with open arms** with great friendliness and cordiality.

²**arm** (ärm) ***vt-*** **1** to equip with weapons: *In wartime the navy* arms *all cargo ships.* **2** to set (a fuse, detonator, etc.) to explode under certain conditions: *Pull this pin to* arm *the grenade.* ***vi-*** to prepare for war or other conflict: *The nation* armed *overnight.* ***n-*** branch of a military service: *the air* arm *of the navy.* [from **arms,** "weapons," from Old French **armes,** from Latin **arma.**]

ar·ma·da (är mä′ də) ***n-*** **1** fleet of armed ships. **2** large force of military aircraft, tanks, etc. **3 the Armada** Spanish Armada.

Armadillo, 2 ft. long, including tail

ar·ma·dil·lo (är′ mə dĭl′ ō) ***n-*** [*pl.* **ar·ma·dil·los**] any of several burrowing animals of the Americas, having the head and body protected by an armor of bony plates. [American word from Spanish **armadillo** meaning, literally, "little armored one," from Latin **armatus,** "armed; armored."]

Ar·ma·ged·don (är′ mə gĕd′ ən) ***n-*** **1** in the Bible, the scene of the final battle between the forces of good and evil, to take place at the end of the world. **2** any great or decisive battle.

ar·ma·ment (är′ mə mənt) ***n-*** **1** a nation's entire war equipment or military strength. **2** equipment in guns and ammunition.

ar·ma·ture (är′ mə chər, -chŏŏr) ***n-*** **1** armor: *the battleship's* armature. **2** armorlike covering of living things, such as a turtle's shell. **3** in electronics, a rotating iron cylinder in an electric motor or generator which often serves as the core for coils of insulated wire. **4** an internal supporting framework used in the making of a piece of sculpture.

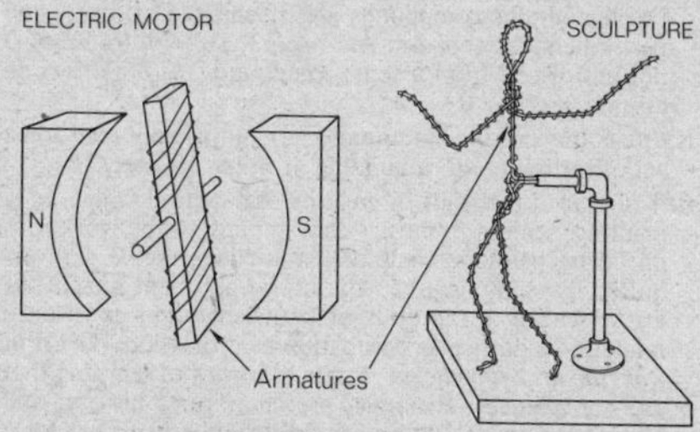

arm·band (ärm′ bănd′) ***n-*** a band worn around the upper part of the arm, indicating military rank, mourning, etc.; brassard.

arm·chair (ärm′ châr′) ***n-*** chair with arms.

¹**armed** (ärmd) ***adj-*** **1** having an arm or arms. **2** having an arm or arms of a stated kind, number, etc.: *a* long-armed *tennis player*; *an* eight-armed *idol.* [from ¹**arm.**]

²**armed** (ärmd) ***adj-*** **1** having a weapon or weapons: *an* armed *trawler.* **2** having a weapon or weapons of a stated kind: *a poorly* armed *cargo vessel.* **3** prepared for conflict: *He came in* armed *for a quarrel.* **4** set to explode under certain conditions: *an* armed *bomb.* [from ²**arm.**]

armed forces ***n-*** the entire military force of a nation, including the army, navy, marines, etc.

arm·ful (ärm′ fŏŏl) ***n-*** [*pl.* **arm·fuls**] as much as one arm, or both, can hold.

arm·hole (ärm′ hōl′) ***n-*** in a garment, a hole or opening through which the arm passes or at which the sleeve is attached.

ar·mi·stice (är′ mə stĭs′) ***n-*** agreement between two opposing armies to suspend fighting; truce.

Armistice Day ***n-*** November 11, 1918, the day on which the World War I armistice was declared. The anniversary of it is now called Veterans Day.

Chain and plate armor

ar·mor (är′ mər) ***n-*** **1** a covering to protect the body while fighting: *Battle* armor *used to be made of metal or leather.* **2** the steel plating of a warship. **3** any protective covering: *the* armor *of a turtle.* **4** military tank forces. ***vt-*** to provide with a protective covering: *The king* armored *them with shields and helmets. Faith* armors *him against fear.*

ar·mored (är′ mərd) ***adj-*** **1** covered or protected by armor plate: *an* armored *car.* **2** equipped with tanks, armored cars, and other armored vehicles: *an* armored *division.*

ar·mor·er (är′ mər ər) ***n-*** in the Middle Ages, a maker of armor.

ar·mor·i·al (är môr′ ē əl) ***adj-*** relating to armor or to coats of arms.

armor plate ***n-*** a covering of steel plate used to protect warships, planes, tanks, etc., from enemy fire.

ar·mor·y (är′ mə rē) ***n-*** [*pl.* **ar·mor·ies**] **1** place where arms are stored. **2** large building containing drill halls and offices where soldiers assemble. **3** place where arms are manufactured.

arm·pit (ärm′ pĭt′) ***n-*** the hollow beneath the arm where it joins the shoulder.

arms (ärmz) ***n-*** *pl.* **1** weapons, especially those that are carried, such as rifles and pistols: *to carry* arms. **2** coat of arms.

take up arms to prepare to fight. **under arms** equipped and ready for war. **up in arms** aroused to fight; hostile; indignant.

ar·my (är′ mē) ***n-*** [*pl.* **ar·mies**] **1** the branch of a nation's military force that is responsible for warfare on land. **2** large number of persons or things; multitude: *an* army *of insects.* **3 Army** (1) the military land forces of the United States. (2) in the U.S. Army, the largest military unit, consisting of two or more corps: *the Third* Army. (3) *Informal* the U.S. Military Academy at West Point, New York.

ar·ni·ca (är′ nĭ kə) ***n-*** **1** plant related to the aster, from which a healing lotion for bruises is made. **2** the lotion made from this plant.

a·ro·ma (ə rō′ mə) ***n-*** pleasant odor; fragrance.

ar·o·mat·ic (ăr′ ə măt′ ĭk) ***adj-*** spicy; fragrant. ***n-*** plant or herb with a fragrant smell, such as ginger or cinnamon.

a·rose (ə rōz′) *p.t.* of **arise.**

a·round (ə round′) ***prep-*** (in senses 1, 2, 3, and 4, considered an adverb when the object is clearly implied but not expressed) **1** in a circle about: *They walked* around *the tree.* **2** on every side of; surrounding: *The police were stationed* around *the house.* **3** about (from one place to another: *They traveled* around *the country.* **4** near a place: *He stayed* around *the house.* **5** approximately; about: *She arrived* around *noon. He had* around *$100.* ***adv-*** **1** in circumference: *The earth measures 25,000 miles* around. **2** in the opposite direction: *Turn* around *and you'll see.*

around the clock all day and night: *The factory works around the clock.* **come around 1** to regain consciousness; revive. **2** *Informal* to give in or yield (to): *He* came around *to our demands.* **3** drop by; visit: *Please* come around *at six.* **get around 1** to move about: *He* gets around *by car.* **2** to come to public notice; circulate widely: *Bad news* gets around *quickly.* **3** to evade: *He* got around *your objections with clever arguments.* **4** to influence or outwit by flattery, cajolery, etc.: *He easily* got around *his sister, and she lent him the money.* **5** *Slang* possessing worldly knowledge.

a·rouse (ə rouz′) ***vt-*** [**a·roused, a·rous·ing**] **1** to awaken: *The singing of the birds* aroused *her early this morning.* **2** to stir up; excite: *His troubles* aroused *our sympathy.*

ar·peg·gio (är pĕj′ē ō) *Music* ***n-*** [*pl.* **ar·peg·gios**] **1** the playing of the notes of a chord in rapid succession. **2** chord played this way.

ar·raign (ə rān′) ***vt-*** to summon (a prisoner) into court to answer a charge; accuse.

ar·raign·ment (ə rān′mənt) ***n-*** summoning to answer a charge in court; also, an instance of this.

ar·range (ə rānj′) ***vt-*** [**ar·ranged, ar·ranged, ar·rang·ing**] **1** to put in order: *The librarian* arranged *the books on the shelf.* **2** to come to an agreement about: *I am sure we can* arrange *a compromise.* **3** *Music* to write out or adapt (a tune, song, etc.) in a form or style different from the original, and often for performance by a particular artist or group. ***vi-*** to make plans and preparations: *I have* arranged *for the use of the hall.*

ar·range·ment (ə rānj′mənt) ***n-*** **1** a putting in order: *an* arrangement *of books by subject.* **2** order in which things are put: *We changed the* arrangement *of furniture in the room.* **3** an agreement. **4** *Music* adaptation: *a jazz* arrangement *of an old tune.* **5 arrangements** plans and preparations: *The* arrangements *for the picnic were made by the committee.*

ar·rant (ăr′ənt) ***adj-*** notorious; out-and-out; utter: *an* arrant *coward.*

ar·ras (ăr′əs) ***n-*** tapestry; hangings of tapestry.

ar·ray (ə rā′) ***n-*** **1** orderly or formal arrangement: *troops in battle* array. **2** fine or imposing collection or display: *an* array *of silver; an* array *of talent.* **3** clothing, especially fine clothing: *The crowds were in holiday* array. ***vt-*** **1** to place or dispose in order; to marshal: *to* array *troops in battle formation.* **2** to deck or dress: *The guests* arrayed *themselves magnificently for the banquet.*

ar·rears (ə rêrz′) ***n-*** *pl.* that which should be done or paid, but remains undone or unpaid: *the* arrears *of a debt.* **—*n-*** **ar·rear′age.**

in arrears behindhand (with obligations or duties): *He is* in arrears *with his rent.*

ar·rest (ə rĕst′) ***vt-*** to sieze or hold a person by authority of the law: *The sheriff* arrested *him for stealing horses.* **2** to stop; bring to a stop: *to* arrest *a flow of water.* ***n-*** **1** seizure or holding of a person by authority of the law. **2** the act of checking or stopping: *the* arrest *of decay.* ***adj-*** [**ə·rĕs′tĭng**] attracting attention; striking: *an* arresting *sight.* **—*adv-*** **ar·rest′ing·ly.**

ar·riv·al (ə rī′vəl) ***n-*** **1** a coming to a place; a reaching a destination: *a car's* arrival. **2** a reaching of a goal, conclusion, etc. **3** person or thing coming to a place.

ar·rive (ə rīv′) ***vi-*** [**ar·rived, ar·riv·ing**] to reach or come to a place or condition: *to* arrive *in a city; to* arrive *at a conclusion.*

ar·ro·gance (ăr′ə gəns) ***n-*** show of too great confidence in oneself or one's abilities, accompanied by disrespect for others; haughtiness.

ar·ro·gant (ăr′ə gənt) ***adj-*** overestimating one's importance or ability; haughty and overbearing. **—*adv-*** **ar′ro·gant·ly.**

ar·ro·gate (ăr′ə gāt′) ***vt-*** [**ar·ro·gat·ed, ar·ro·gat·ing**] to take unjustly; claim presumptuously as one's own: *The governor* arrogated *to himself the authority of the legislators.* **—*n-*** **ar′ro·ga′tion:** *his illegal* arrogation *of authority.*

ar·row (ăr′ō) ***n-*** **1** slender stick or shaft made to be shot from a bow, usually pointed at one end and having feathers at the other end to guide it. **2** a mark with a similar shape, either straight or curved, used to indicate directions or position.

Arrow

ar·row·head (ăr′ō hĕd′) ***n-*** piercing end of an arrow or a tip for this end, often barbed.

ar·row·root (ăr′ō ro͞ot′) ***n-*** **1** an easily digested, starchy flour made from the roots of any of several tropical plants. **2** one of these plants, especially a West Indian variety. *as* ***modifier:*** *an* arrowroot *biscuit; an* arrowroot *leaf.* [from an American Indian word **araruta** with the same meanings.]

ar·roy·o (ə roi′ō, -ə) ***n-*** [*pl.* **ar·roy·os**] small stream, or the dry bed of a creek or brook. [American word from Spanish **arroyo,** from Latin **arrugia** meaning "mine shaft."]

ar·se·nal (är′sə nəl) ***n-*** **1** a building for storing, making, or repairing military equipment of all kinds. **2** any collection of weapons intended for use.

ar·se·nate of lead (är′sə nāt′, -nət) ***n-*** very poisonous white powder, a compound of arsenic and lead, used to kill insects and weeds. Also called **lead arsenate.**

ar·se·nic (är′sə nĭk′) ***n-*** **1** poisonous, brittle, gray metallic element. Its compounds are much used as insect and pest killers. Symbol As, At. No. 33, At. Wt. 74.9216. **2** poison formed from arsenic compounds. *as* ***modifier:*** *an* arsenic *mine.*

ar·son (är′sən) ***n-*** the intentional, and usually malicious, act of setting fire to a building or other property.

[1]art (ärt) ***n-*** **1** the study or creation of beautiful things, as in painting, sculpture, music, etc.; fine art. **2** the work produced by painters, sculptors, musicians, etc. **3** skill acquired by study or practice; natural aptitude; knack: *the* art *of sewing.* **4** the body of knowledge and experience related to a particular occupation or profession: *the* art *of war; the* art *of medicine.* **5 arts** branches of learning that are not sciences. Examples are: literature, history, and philosophy. [from Old French **art,** from Latin **artis,** a form of **ars** meaning "art; craft; skill."]

[2]art (ärt) *Archaic* form of **be** used only with "thou" in the present tense.

Ar·te·mis (är′tə məs) ***n-*** in Greek mythology, goddess of the moon and of the hunt, and twin sister of Apollo. She is identified with the Roman Diana.

ar·te·ri·al (är′têr′ē əl) ***adj-*** **1** having to do with an artery. **2** of blood, bright red and rich in oxygen. **3** planned and used as a major route: *an* arterial *highway.*

ar·te·ri·ole (är têr′ē ōl′) ***n-*** any of the small blood vessels that carry blood from the arteries to the capillaries.

ar·te·ri·o·scle·ro·sis (är têr′ ē ō sklə rō′ səs) ***n-*** disease in which the walls of the arteries harden and thicken, often interfering with circulation.

ar·te·ry (är′ tə rē) ***n-*** [*pl.* **ar·te·ries**] **1** any of the tubes in the body that carry blood from the heart to any part of the body. **2** any main road or important channel: *The new highway is the main* artery *of travel across the state.*

ar·te·sian well (är tē′ zhən) ***n-*** a well drilled through hard rock to porous rock containing water under pressure. The pressure forces the water to gush to the surface without being pumped.

art·ful (ärt′ fəl) ***adj-*** **1** cunning; tricky: *an* artful *excuse to avoid work.* **2** skillful; clever: *an* artful *arrangement of flowers.* **—*adv-* art′ ful·ly.**

ar·thri·tis (är thrī′ təs) ***n-*** a disease in which the joints of the body become inflamed and painful. **—*adj-* ar·thrit′ ic** (är thrĭt′ ĭk).

ar·thro·pod (är′ thrə pŏd′) ***n-*** member of the largest phylum in the animal world **(Arthropoda),** which includes spiders, crabs, and insects. Arthropods have a hard outside skin or shell, and jointed legs.

Ar·thur (är′ thər) ***n-*** legendary sixth-century king of the Britons; hero of the Round Table. **—*adj-* Ar·thu′ ri·an** (är thŏŏr′ ē ən): *an* Arthurian *legend of chivalry.*

ar·ti·choke (är′ tə chōk′) ***n-*** **1** tall plant, the flowering head of which is used as a vegetable. **2** the vegetable itself.

Artichoke

ar·ti·cle (är′ tə kəl) ***n-*** **1** prose composition, complete in itself, in a newspaper, magazine, etc. **2** thing belonging to a particular class of things: *an* article *of clothing.* **3** single section of a written document, as a clause of a contract, treaty, creed, or the like. **4** *Grammar* any of the three determiners, "a," "an," or "the," which cannot replace the noun phrases they introduce. *Abbr.* art or art.

Articles of Confederation ***n-*** the constitution of the thirteen original American colonies, adopted in 1781 and replaced in 1788 by the present Constitution.

[1]**ar·tic·u·late** (är tĭk′ yə lāt′) ***vt-*** **[ar·tic·u·lat·ed, ar·tic·u·lat·ing]** **1** to utter in distinct syllables; pronounce distinctly: *Do not mumble;* articulate *your words.* **2** to unite by means of joints. **3** to make movable by providing with a joint. ***vi-*** **1** to utter distinct sounds; enunciate. **2** to move by means of a joint: *The bones* articulated *well in spite of the injury.* **—*n-* ar·tic′ u·la′ tor.**

[2]**ar·tic·u·late** (är tĭk′ yə lət) ***adj-*** **1** spoken with distinctness: *an* articulate *sentence.* **2** able to express oneself clearly: *an* articulate *person.* **3** jointed. **—*adv-* ar·tic′ u·late·ly. *n-* ar·tic′ u·late·ness.**

ar·tic·u·la·tion (är tĭk′ yə lā′ shən) ***n-*** **1** act or process of articulating. **2** condition of being articulated. **3** a bone joint.

ar·ti·fact (är′ tə făkt′) ***n-*** product of human skill or workmanship, especially a simple product of primitive art.

ar·ti·fice (är′ tə fəs) ***n-*** ruse or stratagem used with skill: *the* artifice *of flattery.*

ar·ti·fic·er (är′ tə fəs ər) ***n-*** skilled or artistic worker; craftsman.

ar·ti·fi·cial (är′ tə fĭsh′ əl) ***adj-*** **1** made by man; not occurring naturally: *a bouquet of* artificial *flowers;* artificial *pearls.* **2** not natural; affected: *an* artificial *way of speaking.* **—*adv-* ar′ ti·fi′ cial·ly.**

artificial respiration ***n-*** a life-saving action in which air is forced into and out of the lungs of a person whose breathing has stopped or is failing.

ar·til·ler·y (är tĭl′ ə rē) ***n-*** **1** mounted guns, together with their ammunition. **2** the branch of an army using these guns. **—*n-* ar·til′ ler·y·man.**

ar·ti·san (är′ tə zən) ***n-*** man specially trained to work with his hands, such as a bricklayer or carpenter.

art·ist (är′ tĭst) ***n-*** **1** person who practices one of the fine arts, especially a painter or sculptor. **2** in any field, a person who shows creative power in his work: *Your cook is an* artist.

ar·tiste (är tēst′) ***n-*** **1** a theatrical performer, especially a dancer or singer. **2** a humorous or contemptuous term for artist.

ar·tis·tic (är tĭs′ tĭk) ***adj-*** **1** having to do with art or artists: *an* artistic *gathering.* **2** appreciative of beauty: *an* artistic *nature.* **3** showing skill: *an* artistic *design.* **—*adv-* ar·tis′ ti·cal·ly.**

art·ist·ry (är′ təs trē) ***n-*** **1** beauty of workmanship or effect. **2** artistic talent and skill.

art·less (ärt′ ləs) ***adj-*** **1** without guile; natural; sincere: *the* artless *grace of her movements.* **2** lacking skill or art; clumsy: *That painting is an* artless *daub!* **—*adv-* art′ less·ly. *n-* art′ less·ness.**

art·y (är′ tē) ***adj-*** **[ar·ti·er, ar·ti·est]** **1** pretentiously or self-consciously artistic in speech, manner, etc.: *an* arty *neighbor.* **2** imitating art in a showy manner: *an* arty *movie.*

ar·um (âr′ əm, âr-′) ***n-*** any of a large group of plants, including the skunk cabbage and jack-in-the-pulpit, having a spike of tiny flowers growing from the base of a white or colored leaf which looks like a large flower.

-ary *suffix* **1** (used to form nouns) (1) person belonging to, connected with, or working at or in: *mission*ary; *function*ary. (2) thing belonging to or connected with, especially a place for: *sanctu*ary (place of safety); *libr*ary (place for books). **2** (used to form adjectives) having to do with: *budget*ary; *legend*ary; *second*ary.

Ar·y·an (âr′ ē ən) ***adj-*** **1** former term for Indo-European. **2** in Nazi ideology, belonging or related to a supposedly pure and superior Nordic race. ***n-***: *The Nazis called themselves* Aryans.

as (ăz) ***adv-*** **1** to the same degree or extent; equally: *This paper is* as *good.* **2** for example; typically: *Some birds, such* as *chickadees and crows, do not fly south for the winter.* ***conj-*** **1** in the way or manner that: *Try to act* as *a brave man would.* **2** at the time that; while; when: *They ran* as *we approached.* **3** though: *Dark* as *it was, we could still see the sign.* **4** for the reason that; since: As *he had inherited his father's fortune, he was now very rich.* ***prep-*** in the role or function of: *He acted* as *umpire. She used her spoon* as *a shovel.* ***pron-*** (relative pronoun) that; which: *Send me such equipment* as *you have.*

as . . . as word combination used in sentences to make a comparison, or to show manner, degree, extent, etc.: *He is* as *lazy* as *I am. I am* as *hungry* as *a starving lion. Do it* as *well* as *you can. This train goes* as *far* as *Chicago.* **as for** or **as to** in regard to; concerning: *And* as for *his mistakes, we'll ignore them.* **as if** or **as though** in a manner similar to the way it would be if: *He ran* as if *a bear were chasing him. She looks* as though *she might fall asleep.*

►AS can mean either "while" or "because." To avoid confusion, write BECAUSE if that is what is meant.

as·bes·tos (ăs bĕs′ təs, ăz-) ***n-*** a fibrous, unburnable mineral, used in making fireproof materials.

as·cend (ə sĕnd′) ***vt-*** to climb or go up: *They* ascended *a hill.* ***vi-***: *They* ascended *slowly.*

ascend the throne to become king or queen.

as·cend·an·cy or **as·cend·en·cy** (ə sĕn′ dən sē) ***n-*** domination; control: *to gain* ascendancy *over fear.*

as·cend·ant or **as·cend·ent** (ə sĕn′ dənt) ***adj-*** **1** moving upward; rising in power, position, etc.: *an* ascendant *nation.* **2** *Astronomy* above the eastern horizon.

in the ascendant rising to a position of power, fame, etc.

as·cen·sion (ə sĕn′ shən) ***n-*** **1** a moving upward; a rising. **2 the Ascension** Christ's ascent to heaven after his resurrection.

as·cent (ə sĕnt′) ***n-*** **1** act of climbing: *our* ascent *of the mountain.* **2** a going up; a rising: *the* ascent *of a balloon.* **3** an upward slope. ***Hom-*** assent.

as·cer·tain (ăs′ ər tān′) ***vt-*** to find out definitely: *to* ascertain *the truth.* ***—adj-*** **as′ cer·tain′ a·ble:** *The truth is not easily* ascertainable.

as·cet·ic (ə sĕt′ ĭk) ***n-*** person who renounces the comforts and pleasures of life and devotes himself to religious duties; also, any person who practices self-denial. ***adj-*** self-denying: *The monks lived* ascetic *lives.* ***—adv-*** **as·cet′ i·cal·ly.**

as·cet·i·cism (ə sĕt′ ə sĭz′ əm) ***n-*** self-denial, usually as a religious duty.

as·cor·bic acid (ə skôr′ bĭk, ə skôr′-) ***n-*** chemical name of vitamin C.

as·cot (ăs′ kət, -kŏt′) ***n-*** necktie or scarf with broad ends which, when knotted, are laid flat, one over the other.

Ascot

as·cribe (ə skrīb′) ***vt-*** **[as·cribed, as·crib·ing]** to regard (something) as caused by or belonging (to); attribute (to): *She* ascribed *her success to hard work.*

as·crip·tion (ə skrĭp′ shən) ***n-*** **1** an ascribing: *the* ascription *of the letter to him.* **2** statement that ascribes something.

a·sep·tic (ā sĕp′ tĭk, ə-) ***adj-*** free from disease germs; surgically clean: *an* aseptic *bandage.*

a·sex·u·al (ā sĕk′ shōō əl) *Biology* ***adj-*** **1** having no sex. **2** of reproduction of living things, without sexual action: *The reproduction of an ameba is* asexual.

[1]**ash** (ăsh) ***n-*** **1** widely distributed tree of the middle latitudes, valued for its shade and for its tough, elastic wood. **2** the wood of this tree. [from Old English **æsc,** the name of this tree.]

[2]**ash** (ăsh) ***n-*** **1** what remains of a substance that has been burned: *wood* ash; *volcanic* ash. **2** a whitish or brownish gray. **3 ashes** (1) the remains of a human body after it has been cremated or reduced to dust by natural decay. (2) remnants of burning used as a sign of grief or repentance: *She cast* ashes *upon her head.* [from Old English **æsce,** of the same meaning.]

a·shamed (ə shāmd′) ***adj-*** **1** feeling shame, guilt, embarrassment, etc.: *He didn't speak because he was* ashamed. **2** fearing or reluctant to do something that may bring about such feelings: *He was* ashamed *to wear his worn clothes.*

ashamed of feeling shame and guilt over: *There is no reason to be* ashamed of *your conduct.*

[1]**ash·en** (ăsh′ ən) ***adj-*** made of the wood of the ash tree [from [1]**ash.**]

[2]**ash·en** (ăsh′ ən) ***adj-*** of the color of ashes; pale. [from [2]**ash.**]

a·shore (ə shôr′) ***adv-*** on the shore; to the shore: *to go* ashore *at Naples.*

ash tray ***n-*** dish or other receptacle for tobacco ashes, and cigar and cigarette butts.

Ash Wednesday ***n-*** the first day of Lent, so called because blessed ashes are then placed on the foreheads of the faithful.

ash·y (ăsh′ ē) ***adj-*** **[ash·i·er, ash·i·est] 1** containing or having the texture of ashes: *an* ashy *soil.* **2** of the color of ashes; ashen; pale: *an* ashy *complexion.*

A·sian (ā′ zhən) ***adj-*** of or relating to Asia or its people: *an* Asian *country.* ***n-*** a native or inhabitant of Asia.

A·si·at·ic (ā′ zhē ăt′ ĭk) ***adj-*** of or pertaining to Asia or its culture: *an* Asiatic *beetle.* ***n-*** Asian.

►Asians do not like to be called Asiatics.

a·side (ə sīd′) ***adv-*** **1** to one side: *Pull the curtain* aside. *Step* aside. **2** out of mind or consideration: *to put* aside *worries; all joking* aside. **3** in reserve: *Please set these books* aside *for me.* ***n-*** on the stage, a remark to the audience which other players are not supposed to hear.

aside from apart from; except for; besides: *There is nothing left to do,* aside from *packing.*

as·i·nine (ăs′ ə nīn′) ***adj-*** stupid; silly: *an* asinine *remark.* ***—adv-*** **as′ i·nine′ ly.** ***n-*** **as′ i·nin′ i·ty** (ăs′ ə-nĭn′ ə tē).

ask (ăsk) ***vt-*** **1** to seek an answer to; also, to put a question to: *He* asked *a question. The doctor* asked *her how old she was.* **2** to beg or request: *to* ask *a favor.* **3** to inquire about: *to* ask *the way.* **4** to invite: *I was* asked *to the party.* **5** to claim; demand: *What price do you* ask? ***vi-*** **1** to make a request: *to* ask *for money.* **2** to inquire: *to* ask *for the chief.* ***—n-*** **ask′ er.**

a·skance (ə skăns′) ***adv-*** sidelong; to one side.

look askance (at) to look at with disapproval, distrust, or suspicion.

a·skew (ə skyōō′) ***adj-*** out of line; crooked: *Her hat is* askew.

a·slant (ə slănt′) ***prep-*** on a slant across: *The rays of the sun fell* aslant *the barn.* ***adv-*** in a slanting direction.

a·sleep (ə slēp′) ***adj-*** **1** sleeping: *He was* asleep *by nine o'clock.* **2** without feeling; numb: *His foot was* asleep.

fall asleep to go to sleep.

asp (ăsp) ***n-*** any of several poisonous Old World snakes, especially the Egyptian cobra, the horned viper of Egypt and Arabia, and the common European viper.

as·par·a·gus (ə spăr′ ə gəs) ***n-*** **1** the tender shoots of a garden plant of the lily family, eaten as a vegetable. **2** the plant itself. **3** any of a group of related plants used in gardens and landscaping for their attractive feathery leaves.

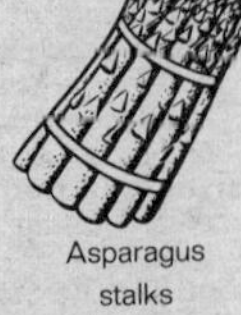

Asparagus stalks

as·pect (ăs′ pĕkt′) ***n-*** **1** side or element of a situation, plan, etc.: *Look at all* aspects *of a problem before trying to solve it.* **2** appearance; look: *the stranger's fierce* aspect. **3** a view: *a home with a southern* aspect.

as·pen (ăs′ pən) ***n-*** any of several poplar trees, whose silvery leaves quiver in the slightest breeze. ***adj-***: *an* aspen *leaf.*

as·per·i·ty (ă spĕr′ ə tē) ***n-*** harshness or sharpness of temper: *He answered his critics with* asperity.

as·perse (ə spûrs′) ***vt-*** **[as·persed, as·pers·ing]** to slander; malign; revile. ***—adj-*** **as·pers′ ive:** *I resent your* aspersive *remarks.*

as·per·sion (ə spûr′ zhən) ***n-*** **1** a damaging or untrue remark about a person: *They cast* aspersions *on us.* **2** a sprinkling with holy water, in a religious service.

as·phalt (ăs′fŏlt′) ***n***- a sticky, black, petroleum tar used for making roofs waterproof and, mixed with crushed rock or gravel, for making road surfaces.

as·pho·del (ăs′fə dĕl′) ***n***- **1** a European plant of the lily family with white or yellow flowers. **2** in poetry, the daffodil. **3** in Greek mythology, the immortal flower of the Elysian fields.

as·phyx·i·a (ăs fĭk′sē ə) ***n***- loss of consciousness due to a lack of oxygen and too much carbon dioxide in the blood, as in drowning or suffocation.

as·phyx·i·ate (ăs fĭk′sē āt′) ***vt***- [**as·phyx·i·at·ed, as·phyx·i·at·ing**] to kill or make unconscious by cutting off the supply of air, replacing air with a harmful substance, or the like; suffocate: *The gas* asphyxiated *them.* ***vi***-: *He* asphyxiated *in the locked closet.*

as·pic (ăs′pĭk) ***n***- clear meat or fish jelly, served cold as a garnish or as a mold of meat, fish, or vegetables.

as·pir·ant (ăs′pə rənt, ə spī′rənt) ***n***- person ambitious for high honor or position: *Some students were* aspirants *for the honor roll.*

[1]**as·pi·rate** (ăs′pə rāt′) ***vt***- [**as·pi·rat·ed, as·pi·rat·ing**] **1** to pronounce with the sound of the letter "h": *We* aspirate *the "h" in "horse" but not in "honor."* **2** to draw (blood, fluids, or gases) from a body cavity by suction with an aspirator.

[2]**as·pi·rate** (ăs′pə rət) ***n***- **1** the sound of the letter "h" as in "horse." **2** a consonant, such as "h," or "k," at the end of a syllable, that is pronounced with such a sound.

as·pi·ra·tion (ăs′pə rā′shən) ***n***- **1** strong desire; ambition: *She has* aspirations *to be a doctor.* **2** act of breathing; also, a breath. **3** pronunciation of the letter "h," as in "horse."

as·pi·ra·tor (ăs′pə rā′tər) ***n***- **1** suction pump whose action is due to the pull of a stream of flowing water in a pipe. **2** *Medicine* small suction pump for drawing fluids from body cavities.

as·pire (ə spiər′) ***vi***- [**as·pired, as·pir·ing**] to desire eagerly; be filled with ambition for a particular thing: *Many politicians* aspire *to be president.*

as·pi·rin (ăs′pə rĭn) ***n***- a medicine for easing the pain of colds, headaches, etc.

ass (ăs) ***n***- **1** donkey. **2** dull, stupid, or foolish person; dolt.

as·sa·gai (ăs′ə gī′) ***n***- lightweight iron-tipped spear used by various peoples in southern Africa.

as·sail (ə sāl′) ***vt***- to attack violently by force of arms or with words: *The enemy* assailed *the castle. They* assailed *him with jeers.*

as·sail·ant (ə sāl′ənt) ***n***- person who makes an attack or assault.

as·sas·sin (ə săs′ĭn) ***n***- person who commits a sudden and treacherous murder, usually for political reasons.

as·sas·si·nate (ə săs′ə nāt′) ***vt***- [**as·sas·si·nat·ed, as·sas·si·nat·ing**] to murder or destroy by a sudden and treacherous attack, usually for political reasons. **—*n*- as·sas′si·na′tion.**

as·sault (ə sŏlt′) ***n***- violent attack, by physical force or by force of words: *an* assault *on the enemy's camp*; *an* assault *on the character of an opponent.* ***vt***- to attack violently; assail.

assault and battery ***n***- in law, a threatening of a person followed by an actual attack.

[1]**as·say** (ăs′ā′) ***n***- **1** act or process of analyzing a metallic compound, ore, or alloy; especially the testing of gold or silver coin or bullion to see if it is of standard purity. **2** the substance tested.

[2]**as·say** (ə sā′, ăs′ā′) ***vt***- **1** to make a chemical analysis of. **2** to attempt: *to* assay *a hard task.* **—*n*- as·say′er.**

as·sem·blage (ə sĕm′blĭj) ***n***- **1** a collection of persons or things: *an* assemblage *of important people.* **2** the act of gathering together: *He was responsible for the* assemblage *of facts.*

as·sem·ble (ə sĕm′bəl) ***vt***- [**as·sem·bled, as·sem·bling**] **1** to bring together: *to* assemble *members of the party.* **2** to put together the parts of: *to* assemble *a motor.* ***vi***- to come together; meet: *The students* assembled.

as·sem·bly (ə sĕm′blē) ***n***- [*pl.* **as·sem·blies**] **1** company or people gathered together for a common purpose: *a student* assembly. **2** a legislative body: *the United Nations* Assembly. **3** a putting together of parts: *the* assembly *of a model airplane.* **4** collection of parts that make up a part of a machine: *a wheel* assembly.

assembly line ***n***- a line or other arrangement of machines and workers for assembling machines. A product passes along it while one specialized worker after another attaches a part until the product is completed.

as·sem·bly·man (ə sĕm′blē mən) ***n***- [*pl.* **as·sem·bly·men**] **1** member of an assembly. **2 Assemblyman** in certain States, a member of the lower body of the legislature. **—*n*- *fem.* as·sem′bly·wom′an.**

as·sent (ə sĕnt′) ***n***- agreement; an accepting: *The governor's* assent *is needed before the bill becomes law.* ***vi***- to agree; consent: *She* assented *to my request.* ***Hom***- ascent.

as·sert (ə sûrt′) ***vt***- **1** to declare; state positively: *The lawyer* asserted *that his client was innocent of the crime.* **2** to insist upon: *By revolting, the colonies* asserted *their right to govern themselves.* **3** to put in force; enforce: *The tyrant* asserted *his authority over most of Europe.* **assert (oneself)** to insist on one's rights.

as·ser·tion (ə sûr′shən) ***n***- **1** act of declaring positively. **2** positive declaration or statement.

as·ser·tive (ə sûr′tĭv) ***adj***- inclined to make very positive statements: *In all our meetings she has been very* assertive. **—*adv*- as·ser′tive·ly. *n*- as·ser′tive·ness.**

as·sess (ə sĕs′) ***vt***- **1** to fix or determine the amount of: *to* assess *the damages.* **2** to fix or set (a tax), as on property; also to hold (someone) responsible for such a tax. **3** to value officially for the purpose of taxation: *The property was* assessed *at $500.* **—*adj*- as·sess′a·ble:** *The damage is not* assessable *at the moment.*

as·sess·ment (ə sĕs′mənt) ***n***- **1** act of determining an amount to be paid. **2** official valuation for the purpose of taxation. **3** tax paid on property. **4** any fixed tax; a share of joint expenses: *The* assessment *on each member was a dollar.*

as·ses·sor (ə sĕs′ər) ***n***- one appointed to estimate the value of property.

as·set (ăs′ĕt) ***n***- **1** anything of value that belongs to a person, business, etc.: *A good reputation is an* asset. **2 assets** all the property of a person, business, or estate that may be changed into cash.

as·sev·er·ate (ə sĕv′ə rāt′) ***vt***- [**as·sev·er·at·ed, as·sev·er·at·ing**] to declare positively or solemnly: *The man* asseverated *his innocence.* **—*n*- as·sev′er·a′tion.**

as·si·du·i·ty (ăs′ə dyōō′ə tē) [*pl.* **as·si·du·i·ties**] close and constant attention; persistent endeavor.

as·sid·u·ous (ə sĭj′ōō əs) ***adj***- persistent and hardworking: *John was an* assiduous *worker for peace.* **—*adv*- as·sid′u·ous·ly. *n*- as·sid′u·ous·ness:** *Her* assiduousness *at school is commendable.*

as·sign (ə sīn′) ***vt-*** **1** to allot; give out. **2** to appoint, as to a duty. **3** to settle definitely: *to* assign *a time for meeting.* **4** to transfer (property) to another. **—*n-* as·sign′ er** or **as·sign′ or.**

as·sign·ee (ə sī′ nē′, ăs′ ə nē′) ***n-*** person to whom anything is assigned.

as·sign·ment (ə sīn′ mənt) ***n-*** **1** a setting apart for some particular person or use; allotment. **2** thing given out or alloted, as a lesson. **3** a legal transfer, as of property.

as·sim·i·late (ə sĭm′ ə lāt′) ***vt-*** **[as·sim·i·lat·ed, as·sim·i·lat·ing]** to take in and make a part of oneself; absorb: *Plants* assimilate *nourishment through their roots. He* assimilated *the customs of his new country.*

as·sim·i·la·tion (ə sĭm′ ə lā′ shən) ***n-*** **1** a becoming or being made part of a larger thing; incorporation. **2** *Biology* process in which digested food materials are converted into energy and protoplasm. **3** the adoption of the language, customs, ways of life, etc., of one people by another.

As·sin·i·boin (ə sĭn′ ə boin′) ***n-*** [*pl.* **As·sin·i·boins,** also **As·sin·i·boin**] one of a tribe of North American Indians who were a branch of the Dakotas and belonged to the Sioux nation. They lived between the upper Missouri and the Saskatchewan rivers. ***adj-***: *an* Assiniboin *moccasin.*

as·sist (ə sĭst′) ***vt-*** to help; to aid: *Our government* assisted *them by sending a team of doctors.* ***vi-*** **1** to give help or aid. **2** to be present: *to* assist *at a birth.*

as·sist·ance (ə sĭs′ təns) ***n-*** help; aid.

as·sist·ant (ə sĭs′ tənt) ***n-*** helper: *She had three* assistants *working on the costumes.* ***adj-*** acting under another person: *an* assistant *editor.*

as·size (ə sīz′) ***n-*** (usually **assizes**) in England, sessions of court held periodically in each county for jury trial of criminal and civil cases.

assn. association.

[1]**as·so·ci·ate** (ə sō′ sē āt′, -shē āt′) ***vt-*** **[as·so·ci·at·ed, as·so·ci·at·ing]** **1** to connect or combine, especially in one's mind: *I* associate *green with grass.* **2** to join or ally (oneself) with a group, cause, etc.: *I do not care to* associate *myself with criminals.* ***vi-*** to be in company (with); have to do (with): *I don't* associate *with criminals.*

[2]**as·so·ci·ate** (ə sō′ sē ət, ə sō′ shət) ***n-*** **1** person joined with another in some undertaking; colleague; partner: *a business* associate. **2** member of a society or institution: *an* associate *of an academy of fine arts.* ***adj-*** of a member or membership, not having all rights and privileges.

as·so·ci·a·tion (ə sō′ sē ā′ shən) ***n-*** **1** group of persons organized for a common purpose: *a trade* association. **2** a joining together; an associating: *an* association *of ideas.* **3** an idea connected with another idea: *What are the* associations *of the word "good"?* **4** companionship.

as·so·ci·a·tive law (ə sō′ sē ə tĭv′) ***n-*** *Mathematics* the law stating that the sum or product of several quantities is the same no matter how they are grouped. Example: (a + b) + c = a + (b + c).

as·so·nance (ăs′ ə nəns) ***n-*** **1** repetition of the same vowel sounds through a line or passage. Example: He leads fearlessly before. **2** kind of rhyme in which the final stressed vowel sounds of the rhyme words are alike, but the consonants following them differ. Examples: take and mate, mother and button.

as·sort (ə sôrt′, -sôrt′) ***vt-*** to separate into classes; sort; classify. ***vi-*** to agree (with): *His actions* assort *well with his character.*

as·sort·ed (ə sôr′ təd, ə sôr′-) ***adj-*** of different kinds; various: *a box of* assorted *crackers.*

as·sort·ment (ə sôrt′ mənt, ə sôrt′-) ***n-*** a collection of different kinds: *an* assortment *of candy.*

asst. assistant.

as·suage (ə swāj′) ***vt-*** **[as·suaged, as·suag·ing]** to make easier; relieve; to make less painful; calm.

as·sume (ə so͞om′, -syo͞om′) ***vt-*** **[as·sumed, as·sum·ing]** **1** to take for granted: *We* assume *that you will be home for dinner.* **2** to take on as a task or duty; become responsible for; undertake: *Mr. Wilkins* assumed *the president's duties during his absence.* **3** to adopt as a pretense: *He* assumed *an air of friendship.*

as·sump·tion (ə sŭmp′ shən) ***n-*** **1** an assuming or taking on: *the* assumption *of one's duties*; *the* assumption *of power.* **2** idea, opinion, or fact, either stated or not stated, that is a basis for further reasoning or statements; axiom: *What are the* assumptions *of your argument?* **3 the Assumption** the taking up into heaven of the Virgin Mary; also, the church festival, August 15, commemorating this.

as·sur·ance (ə sho͞or′ əns) ***n-*** **1** statement to inspire confidence or certainty: *We had his* assurance *that he would take care of the matter.* **2** certainty; confidence: *We had every* assurance *our team would win.* **3** self-confidence: *The actor played the part with* assurance.

as·sure (ə sho͞or′) ***vt-*** **[as·sured, as·sur·ing]** **1** to say positively: *They* assured *us that there would be no delay.* **2** to make certain: *Practice can* assure *better playing.*

as·sured (ə sho͞ord′) ***adj-*** confident: *the speaker's* assured *manner.* ***n-*** person whose life or property is insured.

as·sur·ed·ly (ə sho͞or′ əd lē) ***adv-*** **1** certainly; surely; unquestionably. **2** with confidence; with assurance.

As·tar·te (ə stär′ tē) ***n-*** in Phoenician mythology, the goddess of love, identified with the Greek Aphrodite.

as·ta·tine (ăs′ tə tēn′) ***n-*** short-lived, radioactive element that is one of the halogens. Symbol At, At. No. 85, At. Wt. 210.

as·ter (ăs′ tər) ***n-*** **1** plant related to the daisy, with white, pink, blue, or purple flower heads. **2** its flower. Some asters have large, many-flowered heads that look like chrysanthemums.

Aster

as·ter·isk (ăs′ tə rĭsk′) ***n-*** figure of a star [*], used in printing or writing as a reference mark, or to show an omission. ***vt-*** to mark with such a star.

a·stern (ə stûrn′) ***adv-*** **1** toward the rear end of a ship. **2** behind a ship: *A shark dived close* astern.

as·ter·oid (ăs′ tə roid) ***n-*** one of numerous tiny planets orbiting the sun, chiefly between Mars and Jupiter; planetoid.

asth·ma (ăz′ mə) ***n-*** disease marked by wheezing, coughing, and short breath.

asth·mat·ic (ăz măt′ ĭk) ***adj-*** **1** having to do with asthma. **2** having asthma. ***n-*** person with asthma.

a·stig·ma·tism (ə stĭg′ mə tĭz′ əm) ***n-*** defect in the shape of the eye, causing blurred vision.

a·stir (ə stûr′) ***adj-*** in a state of activity; about: *The campers were* astir *before dawn.*

as·ton·ish (ə stŏn′ ĭsh) ***vt-*** to surprise greatly; amaze: *His boldness* astonished *us.*

as·ton·ish·ing (ə stŏn′ ĭsh ĭng) ***adj-*** very surprising; amazing: *an* astonishing *feat.* **—*adv-* as·ton′ ish·ing·ly.**

as·ton·ish·ment (ə stŏn′ ĭsh mənt) ***n-*** extreme surprise; amazement: *He expressed* astonishment *at the invention.*

as·tound (ə stound′) ***vt-*** to strike with amazement; astonish greatly: *Achievements of science* astound *us.*

a·strad·dle (ə străd′ əl) ***prep-*** astride.

as·tra·khan or **as·tra·chan** (ăs′ trə kən, -kăn′) ***n-*** **1** closely curled fur of young lambs native to Astrakhan in southeast Russia. **2** cloth that imitates this fur.

as·tral (ăs′trəl) *adj-* having to do with, or coming from the stars: *the* astral *rays.*

a·stray (ə strā′) *adv-* in the wrong direction; to the wrong place: *The letter went* astray. *adj-* wandering; confused: *His thoughts are* astray.

a·stride (ə strīd′) *prep-* with one leg on each side of; straddling: *He sat* astride *the log.*

as·trin·gent (ə strĭn′jent) *adj-* sharply contracting and tightening the skin, leaving a feeling of freshness. *n-* substance, such as alum, that shrinks or contracts body tissues. *—adv-* **as·trin′gent·ly,** *n-* **as·trin′gen·cy:** *the* astringency *of a lotion.*

astro- *combining form* outer space; stars, planets, and other objects in outer space: *an* astro*naut* (voyager in outer space); astro*physics.* [from Greek **astro-,** from **astron** meaning "star."]

as·trol·o·gy (ə strŏl′ə jē) *n-* the practice which claims to predict events by the position and mysterious influence on human affairs of the sun, moon, and planets. *—adj-* **as′tro·log′i·cal** (ăs′trə lŏj′ə kəl). *n-* **as·trol′o·ger.**

as·tro·naut (ăs′trə nȯt′) *n-* one of the crew of a spaceship.

as·tro·naut·ics (ăs′trə nȯ′tĭks) *n-* (takes singular verb) science of space flight.

as·tron·o·mer (ə strŏn′ə mər) *n-* person who makes a scientific study of the sun, moon, planets, and stars.

as·tro·nom·i·cal (ăs′trə nŏm′ĭ kəl) *adj-* **1** having to do with astronomy. **2** immensely or unimaginably large: *an* astronomical *price.* *—adv-* **as′tro·nom′i·cal·ly.**

astronomical unit *n-* unit used to express distances in astronomy, equal to the distance between the earth and sun.

astronomical year *n-* tropical year.

as·tron·o·my (ə strŏn′ə mē) *n-* the scientific study of the sun, moon, planets, stars, and other heavenly bodies.

as·tro·phys·ics (ăs′trō fĭz′ĭks) *n-* branch of astronomy dealing with the chemical and physical nature of heavenly bodies. *—adj-* **as′tro·phys′i·cal.**

as·tute (ə stōōt′, -styōōt′) *adj-* **1** keen of mind: *an* astute *man.* **2** showing keenness of mind; shrewd: *an* astute *appraisal of foreign policy.* *—adv-* **as·tute′ly.** *n-* **as·tute′ness.**

a·sun·der (ə sŭn′dər) *adv-* in or into two or more parts; apart: *The tree was split* asunder *by lightning. They were driven* asunder *by the war.*

a·sy·lum (ə sī′ləm) *n-* **1** institution or hospital for the care of the helpless or the insane. **2** refuge: *The rebel found* asylum *in a neighboring country.*

a·sym·met·ric (ā sə mĕ′trĭk) or **a·sym·met·ri·cal** (-trĭ kəl) *adj-* not symmetrical. *—adv-* **a·sym·met′ri·cal·ly.** *n-* **a·sym′me·try.**

at (ăt) *prep-* **1** in the place, time, or condition of: *Tom is waiting* at *home. The plant operates* at *night. Please come* at *your convenience. The nation was* at *peace.* **2** in the manner of: *The horse came toward us* at *a trot.* **3** directly toward: *Aim* at *the target.* **4** with a rate of: *The plane flew* at *500 miles per hour. His apples sell* at *a very high price.* **5** as a result of: *to shudder* at *the thought.*

At·a·brine (ăt′ə brēn′, -brən) *n-* trademark name for a chemical drug used in the treatment of malaria. Also **at′a·brine.**

at·a·vism (ăt′ə vĭz′əm) *Biology n-* reappearance of an inherited trait that was absent for several generations. *—adj-* **at′a·vis′tic.**

a·tax·i·a (ə tăk′sē ə) *Medicine n-* lack of ability to coordinate muscular movements.

ate (āt) *p.t.* of **eat.** *Hom-* eight.

a·the·ism (ā′thē ĭz′əm) *n-* the belief that there is no God. *—adj-* **a′the·is′tic:** *an* atheistic *article in a magazine.*

a·the·ist (ā′thē ĭst) *n-* one who believes that there is no God.

A·the·na (ə thē′nə) *n-* in Greek mythology, the goddess of wisdom and of women's arts and crafts. She is identified with Roman Minerva. Also **A·the′ne** (-nē).

ath·e·ne·um (ăth′ə nē′əm) *n-* **1** club or academy for the promotion of literature, art, or science. **2** library or reading room. Also **ath′ae·ne′um.**

A·the·ni·an (ə thē′nē ən) *adj-* of or relating to Athens, its culture, or its art. *n-* a native of ancient or modern Athens.

a·thirst (ə thûrst′) *adj-* **1** thirsty. **2** having a keen desire: *to be* athirst *for knowledge.*

ath·lete (ăth′lēt′) *n-* person good at sports and exercises requiring strength, speed, skill, and endurance.

ath·let·ic (ăth let′ĭk) *adj-* **1** active and strong. **2** of or like an athlete: *an* athletic *build.* **3** of or for athletics: *to buy* athletic *equipment.*

ath·let·ics (ăth lĕt′ĭks) *n-* (take singular or plural verb) games and sports requiring strenth, agility, and stamina.

a·thwart (ə thwȯrt′) *prep-* (in sense 2 considered an adverb when the object is clearly implied but not expressed) **1** across the course or direction of. **2** from side to side of: *beams set* athwart *the ship.*

-ation *suffix* (used to form nouns from verbs, often in substitution for the verb suffix "-ate") **1** the act or process of: *cre*ation (act of creating); *flirt*ation. **2** the condition or quality: *starv*ation; *emaci*ation. **3** the result of: *plant*ation. (Many words ending in -ation can have two or all three of these meanings. Examples: reservation; deformation; discoloration.)

-ative *suffix* (used to form adjectives) **1** having to do with: *compar*ative; *authorit*ative. **2** likely to: *cur*ative; *restor*ative; *talk*ative.

At·lan·tic (ăt lăn′tĭk) *adj-* of or pertaining to the Atlantic Ocean. *n-* the Atlantic Ocean.

at·las (ăt′ləs) *n-* bound volume of maps or charts.

At·las (ăt′ləs) *n-* in Greek mythology, a Titan forced to bear the heavens on his shoulders.

at·mos·phere (ăt′məs fêr′) *n-* **1** the air that surrounds the earth. **2** air in a particular place: *the damp* atmosphere *of the cellar.* **3** surrounding influence: *the quiet* atmosphere *of the library.*

at·mos·pher·ic (ăt′məs fêr′ĭk, -fĕr′ĭk) *adj-* having to do with the atmosphere: *poor* atmospheric *conditions.*

atmospheric pressure *n-* pressure caused by the weight of the atmosphere (about 15 pounds per square inch at sea level).

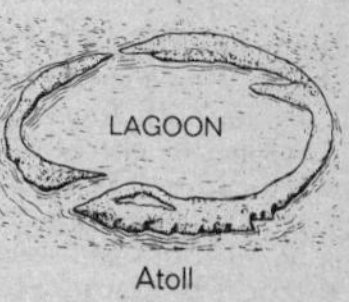

Atoll

At. No. atomic number.

at·oll (ă′tȯl′, -tōl′) *n-* a ring-shaped island or string of islands formed by a coral reef and enclosing a lagoon.

at·om (ăt′əm) *n-* **1** the smallest particle of an element that can take part in a chemical change without being permanently changed itself. Atoms contain protons, electrons, and (except for ordinary hydrogen) neutrons. **2** a tiny bit: *not an* atom *of sense.*

atom bomb *n-* bomb that gets its enormous power from the splitting of atoms; fission bomb. Also **atomic bomb.**

a·tom·ic (ə tŏm′ĭk) *adj-* having to do with atoms or run by energy from the splitting of atoms: *an* atomic *submarine.*

atomic age *n-* the modern period in history that began with the first controlled nuclear reaction.

atomic clock *n-* extremely accurate clock regulated by the vibrations of the atoms of certain elements.

atomic energy *n-* the energy released by nuclear fission or nuclear fusion.

atomic fission *n-* nuclear fission.

atomic furnace *n-* atomic reactor; nuclear reactor.

atomic fusion *n-* nuclear fusion.

atomic mass *n-* the mass of an atom, usually given in atomic mass units.

atomic mass number *n-* the sum of protons and neutrons in one atom of an element; mass number. It is written after the name of the element or as a superscript after the symbol; thus, an atom of cobalt 60 has 27 protons and 33 neutrons.

atomic mass unit *n-* unit of mass equal to the mass of a proton or a neutron and officially defined as 1/12 of the mass of the most abundant kind of carbon atom. *Abbr.* a.m.u.

atomic number *n-* the number of protons in an atom of an element. *Abbr.* At. No.

atomic pile *n-* nuclear reactor.

atomic power *n-* atomic energy or electricity developed from it.

atomic reactor *n-* nuclear reactor.

atomic weight *n-* a number that shows the weight of an atom in comparison to the weight of the most abundant kind of carbon atom, which is set at 12. Most hydrogen atoms, because they weigh only 1/12 as much as a carbon atom, are assigned an atomic weight of 1. *Abbr.* At. Wt.

at·om·ize (ăt′ə mīz′) *vt-* **[at·om·ized, at·om·iz·ing] 1** to break up into atoms. **2** to spray (a liquid) as a very fine mist. **—*n-* at′om·i·za′tion.**

at·om·iz·er (ăt′ə mī′zər) *n-* device for changing a liquid to a fine spray.

atom smasher *Informal n-* electromagnetic accelerator.

a·ton·al (ā′ tō′ nəl, ă′-) *Music adj-* without key.

a·tone (ə tōn′) *vi-* **[a·toned, a·ton·ing]** to make amends (for): *to* atone *for one's sins; to* atone *for one's rudeness.*

a·tone·ment (ə tōn′ mənt) *n-* a making amends for a wrong, crime, sin, etc.

the Atonement the sufferings and death of Jesus Christ to save mankind from sin. **Day of Atonement** Yom Kippur.

a·top (ə tŏp′) *prep-* on top of.

ATP *n-* an enzyme, **adenosine triphosphate** (ə dĕn′ ə sēn′ trī′ fŏs′ fāt), found in all cells. Its chemical reactions release the energy to do work.

a·tro·cious (ə trō′ shəs) *adj-* **1** extremely cruel or wicked: *an* atrocious *crime.* **2** ridiculously ugly or poorly made: *an* atrocious *hat.* **—*adv-* a·tro′cious·ly.**

a·troc·i·ty (ə trŏs′ ə tē) *n-* [*pl.* **a·troc·i·ties**] **1** wicked or cruel act or thing: *wartime* atrocities. **2** something ridiculously ugly or poorly made: *Her hat is an* atrocity.

at·ro·phy (ă′ trə fē′) *Biology n-* a wasting and shrinking, or an arrest in development: *Poliomyelitis can cause* atrophy *in muscles. vt-* **[at·ro·phied, at·ro·phy·ing]** to cause this condition: *Lack of sunlight* atrophies *green plants. vi-: The muscle* atrophied.

at·ro·pine (ă′ trə pēn′, -pən) *n-* poisonous drug from the belladonna plant, used in medicine.

At·si·na (ăt sē′ nə) *n-* Gros Ventre.

at·tach (ə tăch′) *vt-* **1** to fasten to or upon; join: *He* attached *the label to the suitcase.* **2** to assign to a military company: *Please* attach *Corporal Smith to Company G.* **3** to affix or append (a signature, comment, etc.). **4** to attribute to: *He* attaches *great importance to his new work.* **5** to take (property) by a court order: *His creditors* attached *his salary. vi-* to adhere or belong (to): *Certain duties* attach *to this position.*

attached to to be bound to by affection or love.

at·ta·ché (ăt′ə shā′, ă′ tă′ shā′) *n-* member of a staff, especially a subordinate attached to the staff of a foreign minister or ambassador.

attaché case *n-* rigid, thin briefcase.

at·tach·ment (ə tăch′ mənt) *n-* **1** something to be attached to something else for a particular purpose: *Several* attachments *came with the vacuum cleaner.* **2** something which ties or fastens one thing to another. **3** affection or regard: *The two had a strong* attachment *for each other.*

at·tack (ə tăk′) *vt-* **1** to set upon forcefully; assault: *The enemy* attacked *us from the rear. The enemy* attacked *the hill.* **2** to criticize sharply: *The newspapers* attacked *the senator's speech.* **3** to have a harmful effect upon: *Some insects* attack *our garden plants.* **4** to begin on: *to* attack *a job with vigor. vi-: The enemy* attacked *at dawn. n-* **1** an assaulting; onset: *an enemy* attack; *an* attack *of flu.* **2** way of approaching or solving: *This problem calls for a different* attack. **3** way of playing a note or passage in music: *a staccato* attack.

at·tain (ə tān′) *vt-* **1** to achieve or gain by effort: *He* attained *his goal by hard work.* **2** to reach; arrive at: *Grandfather* attained *the age of ninety.*

at·tain·der (ə tān′ dər) *n-* the taking away from a person of all civil or legal rights upon sentence for a serious crime.

at·tain·ment (ə tān′ mənt) *n-* **1** an achieving; a gaining: *His chief goal was* attainment *of the prize.* **2** accomplishment; skill: *His* attainments *included skill in painting.*

at·taint (ə tānt′) *vt-* to deprive (a condemned person) of all rights.

at·tar (ăt′ər) *n-* fragrant oil extracted from the petals of flowers, chiefly roses.

at·tempt (ə tĕmpt′) *vt-* to try; make an effort at: *The pilot* attempted *a landing in the fog. n-* effort; trial: *His second* attempt *at skating was more successful.*

at·tend (ə tĕnd′) *vt-* **1** to be present at: *to* attend *school; to* attend *church.* **2** to accompany; escort: *A company of nobles* attended *the king.* **3** to serve or wait upon: *The maid* attends *her mistress. vi-* **1** to give heed (to): *The child* attended *to his mother's warning.* **2** to be in waiting: *Two bridesmaids* attended *at the wedding.* **3** to look after something: *to* attend *to business.*

at·tend·ance (ə tĕn′ dəns) *n-* **1** fact of being present, as at school. **2** state of looking after or waiting upon some person or thing: *The nurse is in* attendance. **3** the number of persons present; also, the record of this number: *to take the* attendance *at school.*

at·tend·ant (ə tĕn′ dənt) *n-* **1** person who is with another for service or company. **2** employee who serves customers: *a gas-station* attendant. *adj-* **1** serving or helping another: *an* attendant *nurse.* **2** going along with; accompanying: *certain* attendant *circumstances.*

at·ten·tion (ə tĕn′ shən) *n-* **1** a looking, listening, or thinking carefully and steadily: *The students gave their full* attention *to the experiment.* **2** care; consideration: *Give* attention *to this request.* **3** position of a soldier in which he stands straight with eyes front and arms down at the sides (often used as a command). **4 attentions**

polite, ingratiating, or kind acts: *The patient thanked his friends for their many* attentions.

at·ten·tive (ə tĕn′tĭv) ***adj-*** **1** observant; heedful: *The* attentive *student learns his lessons well.* **2** eager to offer service; courteous: *a waiter* attentive *to patrons.* ***—adv-*** **at·ten′tive·ly** ***n-*** **at·ten′tive·ness.**

at·ten·u·ate (ə tĕn′yōō āt′) ***vt-*** **[at·ten·u·at·ed, at·ten·u·at·ing]** **1** to make thin or slender: *His body was* attenuated *by disease. Stretching* attenuates *a rubber band.* **2** *Biology* to weaken (disease germs or other organisms); to make less harmful: *to* attenuate *a polio virus with formaldehyde.*

at·test (ə tĕst′) ***vt-*** **1** to bear witness to; affirm the truth of, especially by signing one's name or by oath. **2** to give proof of: *Your work* attests *your ability.* ***vi-*** to bear witness (to): *to* attest *to a truth.*

at·tic (ăt′ĭk) ***n-*** space in a house directly under the roof; garret. *as* ***modifier***: *an* attic *studio.*

At·tic (ăt′ĭk) ***adj-*** **1** of or pertaining to Athens, the Athenians, or their culture and art. **2** simple, graceful, and refined.

at·tire (ə tiər′) ***vt-*** **[at·tired, at·tir·ing]** to dress or adorn, especially for formal occasions: *They were* attired *in red gowns.* ***n-*** clothes or apparel: *formal* attire.

at·ti·tude (ăt′ə tōōd′, -tyōōd′) ***n-*** **1** way of thinking, feeling, or acting: *What accounts for his hostile* attitude *toward us?* **2** position of the body to show feeling, mood, or purpose: *He jumped to his feet in a startled* attitude. **3** *Space* the inclination of a vehicle in space toward the earth, horizon, or some other point of reference.

at·tor·ney (ə tûr′nē) ***n-*** [*pl.* **at·tor·neys**] lawyer; one legally appointed by another to act for him or her in any legal matter. Also called **attorney at law.**

attorney general ***n-*** [*pl.* **at·tor·neys gen·er·al** or **at·tor·ney gen·er·als**] chief law officer of a state or nation.

at·tract (ə trăkt′) ***vt-*** to draw to oneself or itself: *A magnet* attracts *iron. He shouted to* attract *attention.*

at·trac·tion (ə trăk′shən) ***n-*** **1** a drawing toward; attracting: *the* attraction *of gravity.* **2** power of attracting: *Adventure stories have great* attraction *for me.* **3** thing that attracts: *The clowns were the main* attraction *at the circus.*

at·trac·tive (ə trăk′tĭv) ***adj-*** **1** appealing; charming; pleasing. **2** having the power to attract: *the* attractive *force of a magnet.* ***—adv-*** **at·trac′tive·ly.**

at·trac·tive·ness (ə trăk′tĭv nəs) ***n-*** power to please and delight; charm: *the* attractiveness *of the scenery.*

¹at·trib·ute (ə trĭb′yōōt) ***vt-*** **[at·trib·ut·ed, at·trib·ut·ing]** **1** to consider as belonging to: *This play is* attributed *by some to Shakespeare.* **2** to consider (a thing) as caused by: *He* attributes *his success to hard work.* ***—adj-*** **at·trib′ut·a·ble:** *Success is* attributable *to hard work.*

²at·trib·ute (ă′trə byōōt′) ***n-*** **1** a quality or trait considered as belonging to a person or thing; characteristic: *Her chief* attributes *are honesty and courage.* **2** mark or object regarded as a symbol: *The crown is an* attribute *of royalty.*

at·tri·bu·tion (ă′trə byōō′shən) ***n-*** an attributing; an assigning of cause, authorship, etc.

at·trib·u·tive (ə trĭb′yə tĭv′) *Grammar* ***n-*** an adjective or noun that modifies a noun. Attributives always occur immediately before the chief noun of a noun phrase or another attributive. In the phrase, "a long business conference," both "business," a noun, and "long," an adjective, are attributives. ***adj-*** *the* attributive *position in a phrase.* ***—adv-*** **at·trib′u·tive′ly.**

at·tri·tion (ə trĭsh′ən) ***n-*** **1** a wearing away by rubbing, scraping, etc. **2** a wearing down or weakening by constant harassment, attack, etc.: *a war of* attrition.

at·tune (ə tōōn′, -tyōōn′) ***vt-*** **[at·tuned, at·tun·ing]** **1** to put in tune. **2** to bring into harmony: *His spirit was* attuned *to nature.*

atty. attorney.

At. Wt. atomic weight.

a·typ·i·cal (ā′tĭp′ə kəl) ***adj-*** not typical or regular; irregular; abnormal: *Cancerous cells display* atypical *growth.* ***—adv-*** **a′typ′i·cal·ly.**

Au Symbol for gold.

au·burn (ȯ′bûrn′) ***adj-*** reddish brown.

auc·tion (ȯk′shən) ***n-*** public sale at which property or goods are sold to the highest bidder. ***vt-*** to sell to the highest bidder.

auc·tion·eer (ȯk′shə nêr′) ***n-*** person who conducts an auction.

au·da·cious (ȯ dā′shəs) ***adj-*** **1** bold; daring: *an* audacious *rescue attempt.* **2** intolerant or impatient of custom, restraint, etc.; impudent: *The* audacious *remark surprised everyone.* ***—adv-*** **au·da′cious·ly.** ***n-*** **au·da′cious·ness.**

au·dac·i·ty (ȯ dăs′ə tē) ***n-*** [*pl.* **au·dac·i·ties**] **1** reckless daring; boldness. **2** insolent boldness; impudence: *He had the* audacity *to ask me to do his work.*

au·di·ble (ȯ′də bəl) ***adj-*** loud enough to be heard: *a barely* audible *whisper.* ***—adv-*** **au′di·bly.**

au·di·ence (ȯ′dē əns) ***n-*** **1** group of people gathered to hear or see something. **2** people within hearing range; listeners: *a television* audience. **3** interview with a person of high rank: *an* audience *with the king.*

au·di·o (ȯ′dē ō) ***adj-*** of or dealing with hearing or sound reproduction, especially with high-fidelity equipment. ***n-*** reproduction of sound.

audio- *combining form* hearing: audio*visual* (having to do with hearing and seeing). [from Latin **audire** meaning "to hear."]

audio frequency ***n-*** the maximum range of sound a human ear can hear, about 20 to 20,000 cycles per second.

au·di·om·e·ter (ȯ′dē ŏm′ə tər) ***n-*** an instrument that measures how well a person hears.

au·di·o·vis·u·al (ȯ′dē ō vĭzh′ōō əl) ***adj-*** of or related to those aids or methods in classroom teaching other than books, such as films, recordings, diagrams, etc.

au·dit (ȯ′dət) ***vt-*** **1** to examine or adjust (a business record, claim, etc.) **2** to attend (a college course) as a listener without getting credit. ***n-*** official examination or adjustment of an account or claim.

au·di·tion (ȯ dĭsh′ən) ***n-*** trial or test at which a musician, actor, dancer, etc., gives a sample performance in hope of being hired or accepted. ***vi-*** to perform in such a trial: *She* auditioned *for the new play.* ***vt-***: *They* auditioned *five singers today.*

au·di·tor (ȯ′də tər) ***n-*** **1** a listener. **2** person who examines accounts, records, and claims.

au·di·tor·i·um (ȯ′də tôr′ē əm) ***n-*** **1** building or large room used for public gatherings. **2** the part of a church, theater, etc., where the audience sits.

au·di·tor·y (ȯ′də tôr′ē) ***adj-*** having to do with hearing.

auditory nerve ***n-*** one of the two nerves of hearing.

auf Wie·der·seh·en (ouf vē′dər zān′) *German* until we see each other again; farewell.

Aug. August.
Au·ge·an stables (ȯ jē′ ən) *n-* in Greek mythology, the stables of King Augeas in which 3,000 oxen were kept. Uncleaned for 30 years, the stables were cleaned in one day when Hercules turned two rivers through them.
au·ger (ȯ′ gər) *n-* tool for boring holes. ***Hom-*** augur.

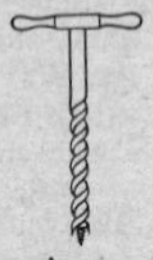

Auger

[1]**aught** (ȯt) *n-* any part; anything: *for* aught *I know.* [from Old English **aht,** contraction of **a-wiht** meaning "ever a thing; a whit."] ***Hom-*** ought.
[2]**aught** (ȯt) *n-* in arithmetic, a cipher; a naught; nothing. [from **a naught** mistaken as **an aught,** from Old English **nā wiht** meaning "no thing; no whit."] ***Hom-*** ought.
aug·ment (ȯg mĕnt′) *vt-* to make larger; increase: *He* augmented *his income by taking an additional job.*
au gra·tin (ō grä′ tən, -grăt′ ən) *adj-* baked with a crust of bread crumbs and, often, grated cheese: *a dish of* au gratin *potatoes.*
au·gur (ȯ′ gər) *n-* in Roman times, a religious official who foretold events by signs or omens, such as the flight of birds, thunder, etc.; soothsayer; prophet. *vi-* to foretell events from signs. *vt-* to predict; give promise of: *Everything* augurs *success.* ***Hom-*** auger.
augur well (or **ill**) to give reason to expect a good (or bad) outcome: *His general weakness* augurs ill *for his recovery.*
au·gu·ry (ȯ′ gə rē) *n-* [*pl.* **au·gu·ries**] **1** art or practice of foretelling events by signs or omens. **2** omen; prediction.
au·gust (ȯ gŭst′) *adj-* **1** having great dignity; majestic. **2** inspiring great respect: *an* august *personage.*
Au·gust (ȯ′ gəst) *n-* the eighth month of the year, having 31 days.
Au·gus·tan (ȯ gŭs′ tən) *adj-* **1** of or relating to Augustus Caesar or his age. **2** in England, of or relating to the period of Queen Anne.
au jus (ō zhōōs′, *Fr.* ō zhʏ′) *adj-* served in its natural juice or gravy: *beef* au jus.
auk (ȯk) *n-* any of several arctic sea birds related to gulls and having heavy bodies, short wings, and webbed feet.

Auk, 16 in. long

auld (ȯld) *Scottish adj-* old.
auld lang syne (ȯld′ lăng′ sīn′) *Scottish n-* the days of long ago, especially those that seem happy and full of sweet memories.
aunt (ănt, änt) *n-* **1** sister of one's father or mother. **2** wife of one's uncle. ***Hom-*** ant.
au·ra (ȯr′ ə) *n-* character which a person or thing has in the mind or feelings of a beholder: *an* aura *of calm.*
au·ral (ȯr′ əl, ŏr′-) *adj-* having to do with the ear or hearing. ***Hom-*** oral.
au·re·ole (ȯr′ ē ōl′) *n-* **1** halo or ring of light, as around the sun in a total eclipse. **2** in Christian art, a halo around the head of a martyr, saint, or other sacred person.
Au·re·o·my·cin (ȯr′ ē ō mī′ sən) *n-* trademark name of an antibiotic drug, produced by a mold that grows in soil. It is used against many bacteria and some viruses.
au re·voir (ō rə vwär′) *French* good-by; until I see you again.
au·ri·cle (ȯr′ ə kəl, ŏr′-) *n-* **1** the part of the ear outside the head; the outer ear. **2** either of the two upper chambers of the heart, which receive the blood from the veins and transmit it to the ventricles (for picture, see *heart*). ***Hom-*** oracle.
au·ric·u·lar (ȯ rĭk′ yə lər) *adj-* **1** relating to the ear or to the sense of hearing. **2** told in private, as to a priest in the confessional. **3** ear-shaped. **4** pertaining to the auricles of the heart.
au·rif·er·ous (ȯ rĭf′ ər əs) *adj-* containing or yielding gold: *an* auriferous *ore.*
Au·ri·ga (ȯ rī′ gə) *n-* star constellation in the sky of the Northern Hemisphere. It is also called the Charioteer or the Wagoner.
au·rochs (ȯr′ ŏks′, our′-) *n-* [*pl.* **au·rochs**] **1** the bison of Europe. **2** extinct wild ox of Europe.
au·ror·a (ȯ rôr′ ə) *n-* glowing, flickering bands and streamers of colored light seen at night in the sky in middle and high latitudes, and caused by the bombardment of energetic particles ejected from the sun during solar flares.
Au·ro·ra (ȯ rôr′ ə) *n-* Roman goddess of the dawn.
aurora aus·tra·lis (ȯ strā′ ləs) *n-* the aurora seen in the Southern Hemisphere; southern lights.
aurora bor·e·al·is (bôr′ ē ăl′ əs) *n-* the aurora seen in the Northern Hemisphere; northern lights.
aus·pic·es (ȯ′ spə səz) *n- pl.* **1** a sponsoring; patronage: *He traveled abroad under government* auspices. **2** omens or signs: *The ancient Romans studied the flights of birds for* auspices *to guide their actions.*
aus·pi·cious (ȯ spĭsh′ əs) *adj-* favorable; promising success: *Our team made an* auspicious *beginning by winning the first game.* ***—adv-*** **aus·pi′ cious·ly.** *n-* **aus·pi′ cious·ness:** *the* auspiciousness *of the circumstances.*
aus·tere (ȯ stêr′) *adj-* **1** severe and stern in manner or appearance: *the* austere *look on the old judge's face.* **2** strict and severely simple in manner of living or behaving: *the* austere *life of the first pioneers.* **3** plain; without ornament: *The castle hall looked dark and* austere. ***—adv-*** **aus·tere′ ly.**
aus·ter·i·ty (ȯ stĕr′ ə tē) *n-* [*pl.* **aus·ter·i·ties**] **1** severity, sternness, or coldness of manner or behavior. **2** harsh or severely simple living conditions: *wartime* austerity. **3** extreme simplicity or bareness: *a cell's* austerity.
Australian ballot *n-* ballot having the names of all the candidates and marked by the voter privately to ensure secrecy; the secret ballot used in the United States.
au·then·tic (ȯ thĕn′ tĭk) *adj-* **1** genuine; not falsified: *an* authentic *signature.* **2** true; trustworthy: *Is this an* authentic *account of what happened?* ***—adv-*** **au·then′ ti·cal·ly.** *n-* **au′ then·tic′ i·ty** (ȯ′ thĕn tĭs′ ə tē): *The* authenticity *of this signature is beyond question.*
au·then·ti·cate (ȯ thĕn′ tə kāt′) *vt-* [**au·then·ti·cat·ed, au·then·ti·cat·ing**] **1** to determine the truth, genuineness, legality, etc., of; verify: *to* authenticate *a painting.* **2** to declare genuine or valid: *The court* authenticated *his claim to the property.* ***—n-*** **au·then′ ti·ca′ tion.**
author (ȯ′ thər) *n-* **1** person who writes a book, story, article, etc. **2** person who begins or originates anything.
au·thor·i·tar·i·an (ə thȯr′ ə târ′ ē ən, ə thŏr-′) *adj-* requiring or favoring strict obedience to authority and opposed to individual freedom: *the* authoritarian *methods of dictators.* *n-*: *an* authoritarian *in matters of discipline.*
au·thor·i·tar·i·an·ism (ə thȯr′ ə târ′ ē ən ĭz′ əm, ə thŏr′-) *n-* the principle of strict obedience to authority, as distinct from that of individual freedom.
au·thor·i·ta·tive (ə thȯr′ ə tā′ tĭv, ə thŏr′-) *adj-* **1** having the weight of authority; worthy of belief: *The news came from an* authoritative *source.* **2** commanding: *The officer spoke to the crew in an* authoritative *tone.* ***—adv-*** **au·thor′ i·ta′ tive·ly.** *n-* **au·thor′ i·ta′ tive·ness.**
au·thor·i·ty (ə thȯr′ ə tē, ə thŏr′-) *n-* [*pl.* **au·thor·i·ties**] **1** power or right (to command, direct, or act): *The general had* authority *to start the attack.* **2** accepted source of

expert information or advice, such as a writing or a person: *He is an* authority *on plants.* **3 authorities** government officials: *The* authorities *stopped all traffic.*

au·thor·i·za·tion (ô'thər ə zā'shən) ***n-*** **1** an authorizing: *We need* authorization *before we can act.* **2** power or right: *He had no* authorization *to sign my name.*

au·thor·ize (ô'thə rīz') ***vt-*** [**au·thor·ized, au·thor·iz·ing**] **1** to give the right or power to do something; empower: *He was* authorized *to buy supplies for the office.* **2** to allow by law; approve: *The legislature* authorized *funds for roads.* **3** to justify; give sanction for: *Halloween pranks are* authorized *by tradition.*

Authorized Version ***n-*** a revision of the English Bible, issued in 1611 under James I, and commonly used by English-speaking Protestants.

au·thor·ship (ô'thər shĭp') ***n-*** identity of a writer or writers: *The* authorship *of this book is uncertain.*

au·tis·tic (ô tĭs'tĭk) *Psychology* ***adj-*** possessing a mental condition characterized by emotional withdrawal and mechanical behavior. **—*n-* au'tism.**

au·to (ô'tō) ***n-*** [*pl.* **au·tos**] automobile.

auto- *combining form* self; oneself; itself: auto*biography;* auto*mobile.* [from Greek **auto-**, from **autos,** meaning "self."]

Au·to·bahn (ou'tō bän') *German* ***n-*** superhighway with two or more traffic lanes in each direction.

au·to·bi·o·graph·ic (ô'tō bī'ə grăf'ĭk) or **au·to·bi·o·graph·i·cal** (-ĭ kəl) ***adj-*** of or related to one's own life: *an* autobiographic *novel.* **—*adv-* au'to·bi'o·graph'i·cal·ly.**

au·to·bi·og·ra·phy (ô'tō bī ŏg'rə fē) ***n-*** [*pl.* **au·to·bi·og·ra·phies**] life history of a person, written by that person. **—*n-* au'to·bi·og'ra·pher.**

au·toc·ra·cy (ô tŏk'rə sē) ***n-*** [*pl.* **au·toc·ra·cies**] government by a person whose will is law; absolute monarchy.

au·to·crat (ô'tō krăt') ***n-*** **1** ruler with unlimited power. **2** person who demands complete obedience from others: *The scientist was an* autocrat *when working.* **—*adj-* au'to·crat'ic:** *an* autocratic *government; an* autocratic *personality.* ***adv-*** **au'to·crat'i·cal·ly.**

au·to·gi·ro (ô'tō jī'rō) ***n-*** [*pl.* **au·to·gi·ros**] airplane with windmill-like mechanism above, which allows the craft to take off or to land in a small space. Also **au·to·gy'ro.**

au·to·graph (ôt'ə grăf') ***n-*** person's own signature or handwriting. ***vt-*** write one's name on or in: *to* autograph *one's picture.*

au·to·mate (ôt'ə māt') ***vt-*** [**au·to·mat·ed, au·to·mat·ing**] to equip with, operate, or control by automation: *to* automate *machinery; to* automate *a factory.*

au·to·mat·ic (ôt'ə măt'ĭk) ***adj-*** **1** self-operating; self-acting; capable of being run or worked without an operator: *an* automatic *elevator; an* automatic *washing machine.* **2** done unconsciously or from habit: *Breathing is* automatic. ***n-*** firearm that continues to fire so long as the trigger is held and the ammunition lasts. **—*adv-* au'to·mat'i·cal·ly.**

au·to·ma·tion (ôt'ə mā'shən) ***n-*** large-scale use of automatic machinery, often controlled by electronic computers, for manufacturing, bookkeeping, etc.

au·tom·a·ton (ô tŏm'ə tŏn', -tən) ***n-*** [*pl.* **au·tom·a·ta** (-tä) or **au·tom·a·tons**] **1** a self-acting mechanism, as a robot. **2** human being whose actions are mechanical.

au·to·mo·bile (ôt'ə mō bēl') ***n-*** four-wheeled passenger vehicle having an engine by which it is propelled; motorcar. *as* ***modifier:*** *an* automobile *engine.*

au·to·mo·tive (ôt'ə mō'tĭv) ***adj-*** **1** moving under its own power. **2** relating to self-propelling vehicles or mechanisms.

au·to·no·mic (ôt'ə nŏm'ĭk) ***adj-*** **1** belonging to, affecting, or dealing with the autonomic nervous system. **2** in botany, relating to plant movement due only to internal causes, such as a slow spiraling movement made by a growing plant stem, caused by faster growth on first one side and then the other.

autonomic nervous system ***n-*** division of the nervous system that controls the involuntary actions of the body, such as the beating of the heart, the movement of food through the intestines, reflexes, etc.

au·ton·o·mous (ô tŏn'ə məs) ***adj-*** self-governing; independent: *an* autonomous *nation; an* autonomous *position in a government.* **—*adv-* au·ton'o·mous·ly.**

au·ton·o·my (ô tŏn'ə mē) ***n-*** [*pl.* **au·ton·o·mies**] **1** right to be autonomous; self-government: *They did not respect the* autonomy *of neutral states.* **2** autonomous condition.

au·top·sy (ô'tŏp'sē) ***n-*** [*pl.* **au·top·sies**] examination and dissection of a dead body to find the cause of death or the effects of a disease or injury. See also *biopsy.*

au·to·sug·ges·tion (ôt'ō səg jĕs'chən) ***n-*** the unconscious suggestion of an idea or action to a person by his own mind rather than by an outside influence.

au·tumn (ôt'əm) ***n-*** the season of the year between summer and winter, in the Northern Hemisphere usually from September 22 to December 21; fall. *as* ***modifier:*** *the* autumn *leaves.*

au·tum·nal (ô tŭm'nəl) ***adj-*** belonging to or peculiar to autumn: *the beauty of* autumnal *foliage.*

aux·il·ia·ry (ôg zĭl'yə rē, -lə rē) ***adj-*** helping; assisting: *The fire department called out* auxiliary *forces.* ***n-*** [*pl.* **aux·il·ia·ries**] **1** helper; ally; aid of any kind. **2** an auxiliary verb. **3 auxiliaries** foreign troops in the service of a nation at war.

auxiliary verb *Grammar* ***n-*** any of a group of verbs that can precede the chief verb in a verb phrase; helping verb. Examples: *They* have *come. I* will *go.* May *I leave? He* should *arrive soon.*

A.V. Authorized Version (of the Bible).

a·vail (ə vāl') ***vt-*** **1** to help or profit: *The money did not* avail *him.* **2** to give: *Her fame* availed *her little happiness.* ***vi-*** to be of use or value; help: *Nothing can* avail.

of (or **to**) **no avail** of no use or help; without effect: *His protests were* of no avail.

avail (oneself) of to take advantage of: *She* availed *herself* of *the first opportunity.*

a·vail·a·ble (ə vā'lə bəl) ***adj-*** **1** at hand and ready for use or service: *My assistants are* available *if you need them.* **2** obtainable by hire, purchase, etc.: *Is this* available *in blue?* **—*n-* a·vail'a·bil'i·ty *adv-* a·vail'a·bly.**

av·a·lanche (ăv'ə lănch') ***n-*** **1** large mass of snow, ice, or earth suddenly sliding or falling down a mountain. **2** anything that overwhelms by speed and volume: *an* avalanche *of words.*

avant-garde (ă'vänt'gärd') ***n-*** people, usually in the arts or in fashion, who create or adopt new ideas, means of expression, designs, etc., considered extreme or daring by others. ***adj-:*** *an* avant-garde *play; a very* avant-garde *design.* [from French, meaning literally "advance guard."]

av·a·rice (ăv'ə rəs) ***n-*** greed for money.

av·a·ri·cious (ăv'ə rĭsh'əs) ***adj-*** greedy; stingy; worshipping money. **—*adv-* av·a·ri'cious·ly.** ***n-*** **av·a·ri'cious·ness:** *His* avariciousness *hurts his friends.*

a·vast (ə văst′) ***interj-*** sailor's term meaning "Stop!"
a·vaunt (ə vȯnt′) *Archaic* ***interj-*** away! depart! begone!
Ave. avenue.
A·ve Ma·ri·a (ä′ vā′ mə rē′ ə) *Latin* Hail Mary! a prayer to the Virgin Mary, often set to music.
a·venge (ə vĕnj′) ***vt-*** [**a·venged, a·veng·ing**] to inflict punishment in return for or in behalf of: *to* avenge *an insult*; *to* avenge *one's brother.* **—*n-* a·veng′ er.**
avenge (oneself) on to get even by inflicting punishment on: *He* avenged himself on *his captors.*
av·e·nue (ăv′ ə no͞o′, -nyo͞o′) ***n-*** **1** wide street. **2** road with trees on each side. **3** way of reaching; approach: *Hard work is a sure* avenue *to success.*
a·ver (ə vûr′) ***vt-*** [**a·verred, a·ver·ring**] to state positively; assert: *The man* averred *that he had not slept.*
av·er·age (ăv′ ər ĭj) ***n-*** **1** the number that is the result of dividing the sum of several addends by the number of addends; arithmetic mean. Example: The average of 5, 8, and 14 is 27/3, or 9. See also *mean* and *median.* **2** something of a usual character, midway between extremes; between too much and too little, very good and very bad, etc.: *ability above the* average. ***vt-*** [**av·er·aged, av·er·ag·ing**] to find the arithmetic mean of (a set of quantities). ***vi-*** to do, perform, or get as a mean rate, sum, amount, etc.: *The car* averaged *20 miles per hour.* ***adj-*** **1** arrived at by calculating the mean value of (age, height, etc.): *the* average *height of the boys.* **2** ordinary: *an* average *kind of mind.*
a·verse (ə vûrs′) ***adj-*** opposed; not inclined: *Tom Sawyer was* averse *to hard work.* **—*adv-* a·verse′ ly.** ***n-*** **a·verse′ ness:** *His* averseness *to hard work is well known.*
a·ver·sion (ə vûr′ zhən) ***n-*** **1** dislike; disgust: *She has an* aversion *to snakes.* **2** thing or person disliked: *One of her pet* aversions *was mosquitoes.*
a·vert (ə vûrt′) ***vt-*** **1** to turn away: *He* averted *his eyes from the sight of the accident.* **2** to avoid: *to* avert *danger by quick thinking.* **3** to prevent: *to* avert *a strike.*
a·vi·ar·y (ā′ vē ĕr′ ē) ***n-*** [*pl.* **a·vi·ar·ies**] large cage or other pen for birds.
a·vi·a·tion (ā′ vē ā′ shən) ***n-*** the science and practice of flying aircraft.
a·vi·a·tor (ā′ vē ā′ tər) ***n-*** person who flies an airplane; airplane pilot.
av·id (ăv′ ĭd) ***adj-*** **1** eager: *an* avid *reader.* **2** desirous of; greedy for: *to be* avid *of praise*; *to be* avid *for food.* **—*adv-* av′ id·ly.** ***n-*** **a·vid′ i·ty** or **av′ id·ness.**
av·o·ca·do (ăv′ ə kä′ dō, äv′-) ***n-*** [*pl* **av·o·ca·dos**] **1** pear-shaped tropical American fruit, green to black in color, with a very large, hard pit; alligator pear. **2** the tree that it grows on.

Avocado

av·o·ca·tion (ăv′ ō kā′ shən) ***n-*** an interest or occupation outside one's regular work: *The lawyer's* avocation *was painting.*
a·void (ə void′) ***vt-*** to keep away from; shun.
a·void·a·ble (ə voi′ də bəl) ***adj-*** such as can be kept away or avoided: *an* avoidable *accident.*
a·void·ance (ə void′ əns) ***n-*** a keeping away from: *The surest way of keeping slim is* avoidance *of fattening food.*
av·oir·du·pois (ăv′ ər də poiz′) ***n-*** **1** common system of weighing, based on 16 ounces to the pound. **2** *Informal* a person's weight; heaviness.
a·vouch (ə vouch′) ***vt-*** to declare positively; maintain; affirm: *The spectators* avouched *the man was injured.*
a·vow (ə vou′) ***vt-*** to admit; confess; declare directly and openly: *He* avowed *his faults.*
a·vow·al (ə vou′ əl) ***n-*** free and open statement, declaration, or admission: *an open* avowal *of one's intentions.*
a·vowed (ə voud′) ***adj-*** openly declared: *His* avowed *intention was to rob the bank.* **—*adv-* a·vow′ ed·ly.**
a·wait (ə wāt′) ***vt-*** **1** to wait for: *to* await *a visitor.* **2** to be ready for; be in store for: *A welcome* awaits *you.*
a·wake (ə wāk′) ***vt-*** [**a·woke** or **a·waked, a·waked, a·wak·ing**] **1** to rouse from sleep. **2** to rouse from inactivity; stimulate: *to* awake *interest.* ***vi-*** **1** to cease to sleep. **2** to rouse oneself; become alert: *He* awoke *suddenly to his danger.* ***adj-*** not asleep.
awake to aware of: *He was* awake to *danger.*
a·wak·en (ə wā′ kən) ***vt-*** to wake up; rouse from sleep. ***vi-*** to awake.
a·wak·en·ing (ə wā′ kən ĭng) ***n-*** **1** a waking up. **2** sudden awareness: *an* awakening *to danger.*
a·ward (ə wȯrd′) ***vt-*** **1** to give or assign, as does a judge or an umpire, after careful consideration. **2** to bestow, as a prize. ***n-*** **1** a careful and deliberate decision. **2** that which is given or bestowed.
a·ware (ə wâr′) ***adj-*** realizing; knowing; being conscious of: *to be* aware *of danger.* **—*n-* a·ware′ ness.**
a·wash (ə wŏsh′, -wŏsh′) ***adj-*** covered with water: *The street was* awash *after the sudden downpour.*
a·way (ə wā′) ***adv-*** **1** from a place; off: *to go* away. **2** aside: *to look* away. **3** at a distance; distant: *ten miles* away. **4** absent: *to be* away *from home.* **5** out of one's possession: *to give money* away. **6** out of existence: *The echo died* away. **7** on and on; without stopping: *to work* away *at a job.*
►For usage note see WAY.
awe (ȯ) ***n-*** feeling of great wonder combined with fear or reverence: *He stood in* awe *of the judge.* ***vt-*** [**awed, aw·ing**] to fill with such a feeling: *to be* awed *by thunder.*
a·wea·ry (ə wêr′ ē) ***adj-*** weary.
awe·some (ȯ′ səm) ***adj-*** associated with wonder and fear; majestic and terrifying: *Seeing a volcanic eruption is an* awesome *experience.* **—*n-* awe′ some·ness:** *The* awesomeness *of the volcano.*
awe-struck (ȯ′ strŭk′) ***adj-*** filled with awe, dread, or wonder: *He was* awe-struck *at the size of the skyscraper.* Also **awe′-strick′ en.**
aw·ful (ȯ′ fəl) ***adj-*** **1** dreadful; inspiring awe: *the* awful *power of a lightning bolt.* **2** *Informal* very bad; very ugly: *His handwriting is* awful. ***Hom-*** offal. **—*n-* aw′ ful·ness:** *the* awfulness *of the hurricane.*
►AWFUL as an adverb in the sense of VERY is illiterate. But even the correct adverb, AWFULLY, is to be avoided in writing, as in the sentence: *The speaker was* awfully *good.* Write VERY instead of AWFULLY.
aw·ful·ly (ȯf′ lē) ***adv-*** **1** terribly; frightfully. **2** *Informal* very: *It's* awfully *hot today.*
a·while (ə hwīl′) ***adv-*** for a short time.
awk·ward (ȯk′ wərd) ***adj-*** **1** ungainly in action or bearing; clumsy: *an* awkward *carpenter*; *an* awkward *child.* **2** difficult to handle: *an* awkward *situation*; *an* awkward *turn in the road.* **—*adv-* awk′ ward·ly.** ***n-*** **awk′ ward·ness.**
awl (ȯl) ***n-*** pointed tool for making small holes in leather or wood. ***Hom-*** all.

Awl

awn·ing (ȯn′ ĭng) ***n-*** rooflike covering that overhangs a door or window as a protection from sun or rain.
a·woke (ə wōk′) *p.t.* of **awake.**
a·wry (ə rī′) ***adj-*** to one side; askew: *The wind blew her hat* awry.
go awry to go wrong; go amiss: *Our plans went* awry.

Ax

ax or **axe** (ăks) ***n-*** a chopping tool now chiefly used for felling and trimming trees and chopping wood.

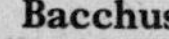

[1]**ax·es** (ăk′ səz′) ***n-*** *pl.* of **ax** or **axe.**
[2]**ax·es** (ăk′ sēz′) ***n-*** *pl.* of **axis.**
ax·il (ăk′ səl, -sĭl′) ***n-*** **1** in anatomy, the armpit. **2** in botany, the angle formed by the upper side of a leaf or its stem and the stem or branch it grows from. ***Hom-*** axle.
ax·il·la·ry (ăk′ sə lĕr′ ē) ***adj-*** **1** in anatomy, having to do with the armpit. **2** in botany, in or near an axil of a plant: *an* axillary *bud between a leaf and a branch.*
ax·i·om (ăk′ sē əm) ***n-*** statement or principle that is accepted without proof, often because it seems obvious. Example: The whole is greater than any of its parts.
ax·i·o·mat·ic (ăk′ sē ə măt′ ĭk) ***adj-*** like an axiom; self-evident; accepted as true without proof.
ax·is (ăk′ sĭs) ***n-*** [*pl.* **ax·es** (ăk′ sēz′)] **1** straight line about which a body or figure rotates: *The earth's* axis *runs from the North Pole to the South Pole.* **2** (also **axis of symmetry**) similar line which divides a body, figure, or object into symmetrical parts. **3** *Mathematics* vertical or horizontal scale or number line used in a graph. **4 Axis** alliance of Germany, Japan, and Italy during World War II.

ax·le (ăk′ səl) ***n-*** **1** shaft on which a wheel turns. **2** shaft that connects two opposite wheels of a vehicle and turns with them. **3** axletree. ***Hom-*** axil.

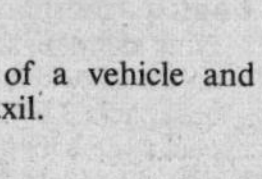

ax·le·tree (ăk′ səl trē′) ***n-*** bar connecting two opposite wheels of a vehicle and forming the axle of both.
ax·on (ăk′ sŏn′) ***n-*** the threadlike extension of a nerve cell that carries impulses away from the cell body. For picture, see *neuron.*
[1]**ay** or **aye** (ā) ***adv-*** always; ever: *forever and* ay. [from Old Norse **ei** meaning "ever; always."]
[2]**ay** or **aye** (ī) ***adv-*** yes. ***n-*** a vote in favor of something: *The* ayes *have it.* [of unknown origin.] ***Homs-*** eye, I.
aye-aye (ī′ ī′) ***n-*** small lemur of Madagascar, with large eyes and ears and a bushy tail.
Ay·ma·ra (ī′ mə rä′) ***n-*** [*pl.* **Ay·ma·ras,** also **Ay·ma·ra**] **1** member of South American Indian tribe of Bolivia and Peru. **2** the language of these Indians, still spoken. ***adj-*:** *the* Aymara *territory.*
Ayr·shire (âr′ shər) ***n-*** a breed of dairy cattle first raised in Ayr, a county in southwest Scotland.
a·zal·ea (ə zāl′ yə) ***n-*** **1** any of a group of shrubs of the rhododendron family. **2** trumpet-shaped flower of this shrub, growing in clusters.
az·i·muth (ăz′ ə məth) ***n-*** angle between a line (such as the centerline of a road or a line of sight toward an object) and north or any other fixed direction.

Az·tec (ăz′ tĕk′) ***n-*** member of a highly civilized Indian tribe of central Mexico, destroyed at its height by Cortes (1519). ***adj-*:** *the* Aztec *calendar.* **—*adj-* Az·tec′ an.**
az·ure (ăzh′ ər) ***n-*** the blue color of the clear sky in daytime. ***adj-*:** *an* azure *silk.*

B

B, b (bē) ***n-*** [*pl.* **B's, b's**] **1** the second letter of the alphabet. **2** *Music* the seventh note of the C-major scale.
B.A. or **A.B.** bachelor of arts.
baa (bă, bä) ***vi-*** to bleat or cry as does a sheep or lamb. ***n-*** the bleat of a sheep or lamb.
Baal (bāl, bā′ əl) ***n-*** any of several ancient Phoenician gods of fertility. ***Homs-*** bail, bale.
Babbitt metal ***n-*** any of several tin alloys used between moving parts of machinery in order to reduce friction.
bab·ble (băb′ əl) ***vi-*** [**bab·bled, bab·bling**] **1** to make indistinct or meaningless sounds, like a baby; prattle. **2** to talk idly, foolishly, or excessively; chatter. **3** to make a low, murmuring sound, like moving water. ***n-*:** *a* babble *of voices*; *the* babble *of a brook.* ***Hom-*** Babel.
Bab·cock test (băb′ kŏk′) ***n-*** test that shows the amount of butterfat in milk.
babe (bāb) ***n-*** very young child or baby.
Ba·bel (bā′ bəl, băb′ əl) ***n-*** **1** in the Bible, the city and tower where the confusion of languages took place. **2 babel** tumult; confusion, as of many persons talking at once. ***Hom-*** babble.
ba·by's- breath (bā′ bēz brĕth′) ***n-*** **1** any of several common plants bearing tiny fragrant white or pink flowers. **2** the flower.
ba·boon (bă bōōn′) ***n-*** type of monkey that has a dog-like face and a short tail and lives on the ground. Baboons are very intelligent, have fierce tempers, and live together in highly organized herds.

Baboon, body 2 ft. long, tail 18 in.

ba·bush·ka (bă bŏŏsh′ kə) ***n-*** a women's kerchief folded in a triangle and worn over the head.
ba·by (bā′ bē) ***n-*** [*pl.* **ba·bies**] **1** young child or infant. **2** youngest member of a family. ***vt-*** [**ba·bied, ba·by·ing**] to treat (someone) as a baby.
ba·by·hood (bā′ bē hŏŏd′) ***n-*** condition of being a baby; also, the time during which one is a baby.
Bab·y·lo·ni·an (băb′ ə lō′ nē ən) ***n-*** **1** a native or inhabitant of ancient Babylon. **2** the Semitic language of ancient Babylon. ***adj-*** **1** of or relating to Babylon. **2 babylonian** luxurious or wicked.
ba·by-sit (bā′ bē sĭt′) ***vi-*** [**ba·by-sat, ba·by-sit·ting**] to care for a young child, usually in the evening, while the parents are away. **—*n-* baby sitter.**
bac·ca·lau·re·ate (băk′ ə lôr′ ē ət) ***n-*** **1** the bachelor's degree given by colleges and universities. **2** sermon given to a graduating class at commencement.
bac·cha·nal (băk′ ə năl′, -näl′) ***n-*** **1** follower of Bacchus. **2** dance or song in honor of Bacchus. **3** drunken reveler. **4** wild drinking party; orgy.
Bac·cha·na·li·a (băk′ ə nāl′ ē ə) ***n-*** **1** ancient Roman festival in honor of Bacchus. **2 bacchanalia** wild drinking party; orgy. **—*adj-* bac′cha·na′li·an:** *The party turned into a noisy,* bacchanalian *affair.*
Bac·chus (băk′ əs) ***n-*** in classical mythology, the god of wine, identified with the Greek Dionysus.

bach·e·lor (băch′ə lər) ***n-*** **1** man who has never married. **2** one who has taken the first degree at a college or university: *a* bachelor *of arts or of science.*

bach·e·lor's-but·ton (băch′ə lərz bŭt′ən) ***n-*** cornflower.

ba·cil·lus (bə sĭl′əs) ***n-*** [*pl.* **ba·cil·li** (-sĭl′ī)] **1** rod-shaped bacterium, especially one of the spore-forming family **Bacillaceae. 2** any bacterium.

back (băk) ***n-*** **1** in humans and other animals having a spine, the rear or upper part of the body from the neck to the end of the spine; in other animals, the upper part of the body. **2** the part opposite the front or part normally used: *the* back *of the house*; *the* back *of his head*; *the* back *of the hand.* **3** the part of a chair or bench against which one leans. **4** of a book, the spine. **5** in football, one of the four offensive players whose position is behind the line of scrimmage. ***adj-*** **1** in the rear: *the* back *seat of a car.* **2** not settled or civilized; frontier: *the* back *country.* **3** left over from the past: *his* back *pay*; back *files.* ***adv-*** **1** to or toward the rear: *"Move* back!" *shouted the bus driver.* **2** away: *The police held the crowd* back *from the fire.* **3** to or toward a former place, time, or condition ***vt-*** **1** cause to move backwards: *to* back *a car to the wall.* **2** to support or uphold (a plan, candidate, etc.). ***vi-*** **1** to move backwards: *he* backed *up.* **2** of the wind, to shift in a counterclockwise direction. **—*adj-* back′less.**

back and forth first in one direction and then in another; to and fro. **behind (someone's) back** secretly, with the intention of keeping (someone) in ignorance. **break (one's) back** to work or cause to work very hard. **get back at** to revenge oneself on. **get (one's) back up** to become angry or stubborn; bristle. **go back on** to refuse to keep (a promise or commitment). **put (one's) back into** to work very hard at a (task, etc.). **take a back seat (to)** to assume a secondary position (to). **turn (one's) back on** to ignore or refuse to help (someone in need of help). **with (one's) back to the wall** in such a desperate position so as to have to fight; cornered.

back and fill **1** to adjust the sails of a boat so that it moves along with the current in midstream. **2** *Informal* to be always changing one's mind; vacillate.

back down to give up or abandon a claim, opinion, attitude, etc.: *he claimed he could fix the engine, but* backed down *when asked to do it.*

back off to retreat or withdraw from contact; shy away (from): *to* back off *from a task.*

back out (of) to withdraw from an undertaking, agreement, etc.

back·ache (băk′āk′) ***n-*** pain or ache in the spine or back.

back·bit·er (băk′bī′tər) ***n-*** one who speaks evil of a person who is absent. **—*n-* back′bit′ing:** Backbiting *and hypocrisy earn few friends.*

back·bone (băk′bōn′) ***n-*** **1** the spine. **2** courage; firmness: *It took* backbone *to accept the challenge.*

back·drop (băk′drŏp′) ***n-*** large cloth sheet, often with a scene painted on it, hung at the rear of a stage to form the back of the setting.

back·er (băk′ər) ***n-*** one who supports a person or undertaking with money or influence.

back·field (băk′fēld′) ***n-*** in football, the players behind the line in the offensive line-up.

back·fire (băk′fīər′) ***n-*** **1** in a gasoline engine, a noisy explosion of gas that occurs at the wrong time. **2** a controllable fire started to check a prairie fire by burning a space in its path. ***vi-*** **[back·fired, back·fir·ing]** **1** to have an explosion in a gasoline engine at the wrong time. **2** to have a result opposite to the intended result: *The scheme* backfired.

back·gam·mon (băk′găm′ən) ***n-*** game played with dice by two persons with fifteen pieces each, on a specially marked board.

back·ground (băk′ground′) ***n-*** **1** parts of a view, picture, etc., that lie farthest from the eye of the viewer: *There were mountains in the* background *of the picture.* **2** surface on which patterns or designs are placed: *The stars of the flag are sewn on a blue* background. **3** past education, experience, etc.: *His* background *includes courses in French and German.*

in the background out of sight or notice.

back·hand (băk′hănd′) ***n-*** **1** backward-slanting handwriting. **2** stroke in tennis, badminton, etc., with the arm drawn across the body and the back of the hand moving toward the net. *as* ***modifier:*** *She hit the ball with a powerful* backhand *stroke.*

back·hand·ed (băk′hăn′dəd) ***adj-*** not straightforward; lefthanded: *a* backhanded *compliment.*

back·ing (băk′ĭng) ***n-*** **1** support or help: *The show had strong financial* backing. **2** something used to support, form, or strengthen the back of a garment, chair, etc.

back·log (băk′lȯg′, -lŏg′) ***n-*** **1** log at the back of the fireplace. **2** reserve supply: *a* backlog *of funds.* **3** mass of unfinished work: *a* backlog *of untried cases in the courts.*

back number ***n-*** **1** an out-of-date issue of a magazine or newspaper. **2** *Informal* person or thing that is old-fashioned.

back·pack (băk′păk′) ***n-*** a satchel, especially one for carrying camping supplies, worn on the back: *Put the food in the* backpack. ***vi-*** to travel, especially to hike, wearing a backpack: *They* backpacked *all day.* ***vt-*** to carry in a backpack: *We* backpacked *the supplies.*

back seat ***n-*** *Informal* a secondary or inferior position (used chiefly in the phrase **take a back seat to**).

back-seat driver *Informal* ***n-*** anyone who gives unwanted advice on what is not his responsibility, such as a car passenger to the driver.

back·side (băk′sīd′) ***n-*** person's rump.

back·slap·per (băk′slăp′ər) ***n-*** person who makes a great, often insincere, display of friendliness and goodwill.

back·slide (băk′slīd′) ***vi-*** **[back·slid, back·slid** or **back·slid·den, back·slid·ing]** to slip back, especially from a condition of religious faith, virtue, etc. ***n-*** **back′slid′er.**

back·stop (băk′stŏp′) ***n-*** **1** in baseball, tennis, etc., a screen or net to keep a ball from getting too far away. **2** *Slang* a baseball catcher.

back stretch ***n-*** the part of an oval racetrack that is opposite to the starting and finish lines. See also *homestretch.*

back·stroke (băk′strōk′) ***n-*** style of swimming in which the swimmer moves through the water on his back.

back talk ***n-*** impudent or argumentative talk to a parent, teacher, superior, etc.

back·track (băk′trăk′) ***vi-*** **1** to return over the same route or path; retrace one's steps. **2** to retreat from a position or policy: *When I needed more money than I expected, Ernest* backtracked *on his offer of support.*

back·ward (băk′wərd) ***adj-*** **1** toward the rear: *a* backward *stroke with the hand.* **2** lacking average intelligence or growth; retarded: *a* backward *young man*; *a* backward *region.* ***adv-*** (also **back′wards**) **1** in the opposite or reverse direction: *to spell* backward; *to run a machine* backward. **2** to the back or rear: *to glance* backward. **3** with the back first: *to walk* backward. **4** toward the past: *They looked* backward *to happier times.* **—*adv-* back′ward·ly.** ***n-*** **back′ward·ness.**

back·wash (băk′wȯsh′, -wŏsh′) ***n-*** **1** a backward current of water from a boat's oars or screws. **2** a backward current of air from an airplane's propellers or jets. **3** the result of an event or condition; aftermath: *Some communities still show the* backwash *of last year's earthquake.*

back·wa·ter (băk′wŏ′tər, -wŏt′ər) ***n-*** water held back by a dam, or a current turned backwards by an obstruction: *The boat was caught in the* backwater *of the mill pond.* ***as modifier***: *Oldville is a* backwater *town where nothing changes.*

back woods (băk′wŏŏdz′) ***n-*** (takes singular or plural verb) **1** uncleared or partly cleared forest land on the frontier. **2** country area that is backward or behind the times. ***as modifier***: *a* backwoods *settlement*; *a* backwoods *newspaper.*

back·yard (băk yärd′) ***n-*** yard at the back of a house or other building.

ba·con (bā′kən) ***n-*** salted and smoked meat from the back and sides of a hog.

bring home the bacon *Informal* **1** to provide, as for a family; to earn a salary. **2** to succeed in what one has set out to do.

bac·te·ri·a (băk têr′ē ə) ***n-*** *pl.* [*sing.* **bac·te·ri·um**] large class of microscopic, one-celled organisms considered to be plants, but also having animal characteristics. Their action is the cause of a number of diseases and of many processes, including decay, fermentation, and soil enrichment. ***—adj-*** **bac·te′ri·al:** *a* bacterial *disease.*

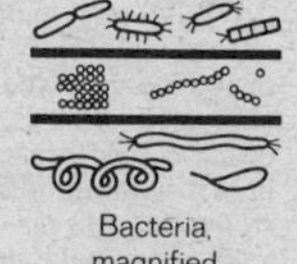
Bacteria, magnified 1,000 times

bac·te·ri·ol·o·gy (băk′têr′ē ŏl′ə jē) ***n-*** study of bacteria and their effects.

Bac·tri·an camel (băk′trē ən) See *camel.*

bad (băd) ***adj-*** [**worse, worst**] **1** immoral; wicked: *Theft is* bad. **2** unfavorable to one's purposes, health, taste, etc.: *a* bad *time to call*; *a weekend of* bad *weather*; *a* bad *odor*; *a* bad *movie.* **3** below a certain standard; incorrect; faulty: bad *grammar*; bad *table manners.* **4** not working properly; defective: *a* bad *watch.* **5** lacking skill or talent: *a* bad *painter.* **6** spoiled; rotten: *a* bad *apple.* **7** in poor health; sick: *I have felt* bad *for a week.* **8** sorry; regretful: *I feel* bad *about your loss.* **9** severe: *A* bad *storm is brewing.* ***n-*** evil. ***Hom-*** bade.

be in bad *Informal* to be in trouble or disfavor. **go bad 1** to become rotten or spoiled. **2** (also **go to the bad**) to become wicked or corrupt. **not bad** or **not so bad** or **not half bad** fairly good.

►BAD and BADLY may be used interchangeably with the verb "to feel": *He felt* bad. *He felt* badly.

bad blood ***n-*** a strong feeling of hatred and hostility; enmity: *There was* bad blood *between the clans.*

bade (băd) *p.t.* of **bid. *Hom-*** bad.

badge (băj) ***n-*** a mark, token, or something worn to show membership, authority, or achievement: *a policeman's* badge; *a* badge *for perfect attendance.*

badg·er (băj′ər) ***n-*** **1** hairy burrowing animal, about two feet long. **2** its fur. ***vt-*** to tease; worry; pester (from the former practice of baiting badgers for sport): *The child* badgered *his mother all day with questions.*

Badger, about 2 ft. long

bad·ly (băd′lē) ***adv-*** **1** in an imperfect way; not well; poorly: *The house is* badly *heated. The project turned out* badly. **2** in a way causing pain, danger, or harm: *The prisoners were* badly *treated.* **3** very much: *The car was* badly *damaged.*

bad·min·ton (băd′mĭn tən) ***n-*** a game, similar to tennis, played by hitting a round, feathered cork, called a shuttlecock, with a light racket over a net five feet high.

bad-tem·pered (băd′tĕm′pərd) ***adj-*** often in a bad humor; quarrelsome and disagreeable. ***—adv-*** **bad′tem′pered·ly.**

baf·fle (băf′əl) ***vt-*** [**baf·fled, baf·fling**] **1** to confuse or puzzle very much: *The fox* baffled *the hounds. This algebra problem* baffles *me.* **2** to slow up or change the flow of liquids or gases with a grid, vane, or other obstruction, or to deflect or absorb sound by the use of a partition, as in loud-speaker enclosures. ***n-*** grid, vane, or partition so used.

bag (băg) ***n-*** **1** sack for holding anything; container made of paper, cloth, etc., that can be closed at the top. **2** purse; handbag. **3** suitcase; valise. **4** game taken on a hunting trip: *The day's* bag *was eight ducks.* ***vi-*** [**bagged, bag·ging**] **1** to put into a sack. **2** to capture or kill while hunting: *The hunter* bagged *two deer.* ***vi-*** to bulge; hang loosely: *The jacket* bagged *at the elbow.*

left holding the bag *Informal* left to take the blame, responsibility, etc.

ba·gasse (bə găs′) ***n-*** the crushed pulp of sugar cane remaining after the juice has been extracted for making sugar. [American word from French, from Provençal **bagasso** meaning "refuse of wine-making."]

bag·a·telle (băg′ə tĕl′) ***n-*** **1** trifle; matter of no importance. **2** a game something like pool.

ba·gel (bā′gəl) ***n-*** doughnut-shaped roll made of unsalted yeast dough. The bagel is simmered in water before it is baked.

bag·gage (băg′ĭj) ***n-*** **1** bags, trunks, suitcases, and boxes a person takes on a trip; luggage. **2** movable army equipment.

bag·gy (băg′ē) ***adj-*** [**bag·gi·er, bag·gi·est**] having a loose or flabby appearance.

bag·pipe (băg′pīp′) ***n-*** shrill musical instrument consisting of a leather bag from which air is forced by the player's arm into pipes. ***—n-*** **bag′pip′er.**

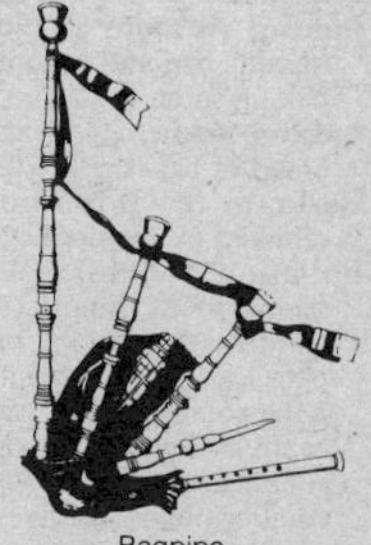
Bagpipe

¹bail (bāl) ***n-*** **1** temporary release of an arrested person on the payment of money to the court as a guarantee that he will appear in court when summoned: *In certain serious crimes a judge may not allow* bail. **2** sum given as a guarantee: *The accused was released on $5,000* bail. **3** person providing the money. ***vt-*** to obtain the temporary release of (an arrested person) by providing a guarantee (usually followed by "out"). [from Old French **bail** meaning "custody," from Old French **baillier** meaning "to deliver up," from Latin **bajulārē** meaning "to bear; carry."] ***Homs-*** bale, Baal.

go bail to provide bail: *His lawyer will* go *his* bail.

²bail (bāl) ***n-*** container used as a dipper for removing water from a boat; also, a small pump used for the same purpose. *vt-* to remove water from a boat with any such device: *to* bail *water with a bucket*; *to* bail *a boat.* *vi-*: *We* bailed *desperately for two hours until rescued.* [from Old French **baille** meaning "bucket or scoop for dipping," from Late Latin **bāiula** meaning "(thing) carrying."] ***Homs-*** bale, Baal.

bail out to jump from an airplane with a parachute.

[3]**bail** (bāl) ***n-*** curved handle of a kettle or bucket. [from Middle English **beil,** probably from Old Norse **beygla** meaning "hoop; bow."] ***Homs-*** bale, Baal.

bail·iff (bā′ lĭf) ***n-*** **1** officer who guards prisoners and watches over jurors in a courtroom. **2** *chiefly Brit.* the deputy of a sheriff.

bai·li·wick (bā′ lē wĭk′, bā′ lĭ-) ***n-*** **1** the district or the jurisdiction of a bailiff. **2** the field in which a person has special or superior skills, interest, or authority: *The entertainment committee is his* bailiwick, *not mine.*

bairn (bârn) *Scottish* ***n-*** young child.

bait (bāt) ***n-*** **1** food, real or sham, used to attract or catch fish or other animals. **2** anything that attracts or tempts; allurement; enticement; especially in the phrase **fall for the bait.** ***vt-*** **1** to put food or other objects on a fishhook or in a trap to catch animals: *He* baited *his hook with minnows.* **2** to torment or worry a chained animal with dogs: *It was once thought a sport to* bait *bears.* **3** to torment or worry (a defenseless person) with jeers, insults, etc.; badger; harass. ***Hom-*** bate.

baize (bāz) ***n-*** thick cotton or wool cloth similar to felt and usually green, used on billiard tables, doors, etc.

bake (bāk) ***vt-*** **[baked, bak·ing] 1** to cook by dry heat in an oven or on heated stones, etc.: *to* bake *bread.* **2** to dry or harden by heat; to heat through: *The sun* baked *the countryside.* ***vi-***: *Bread* bakes *slowly.*

bak·er (bā′ kər) ***n-*** one who makes bread, cakes, etc.

baker's dozen ***n-*** thirteen. Bakers once added an extra roll to the dozen sold, probably to avoid a penalty for accidentally giving too few.

bak·er·y (bā′ kə rē) ***n-*** [*pl.* **bak·er·ies**] place where bread, cakes, and pastries are made or sold.

bak·ing (bā′ kĭng) ***n-*** **1** act of cooking in an oven. **2** amount baked at one time.

baking powder ***n-*** powder used to make cake or biscuits rise and become light. Baking powder contains baking soda.

baking soda ***n-*** bicarbonate of soda, used to make bread or cakes rise.

Ba·laam (bā′ ləm) ***n-*** in the Bible, a prophet who was rebuked by the donkey he rode.

bal·ance (băl′ əns) ***n-*** **1** an apparatus for weighing, consisting in its simplest form of a beam pivoted at its middle, with hooks, platforms, or pans suspended from the ends. **2** the condition of a scale when the beam is about horizontal; hence, equality of any opposing forces; equilibrium or steadiness. **3** general good sense; sanity. **4** an equality between the two sides of an account; also, the excess shown on either side. **5** in a watch, the wheel which regulates the rate of running. ***vt-*** **[bal·anced, bal·anc·ing]. 1** to support in a state of equilibrium: *to* balance *a book on one's head.* **2** to compare as if weighing: *to* balance *the merits of the two schools.* **3** to compensate for in weight, amount, etc.; counterbalance: *This month's gains* balance *last month's losses.* **4** to adjust in order to bring about proportion, symmetry, etc.: *to* balance *a menu*; *to* balance *paintings on a wall.* **5** to find out the difference between the debits and credits (of an account); also, to make them equal. **6** to adjust (a scale) to weigh correctly. ***vi-*** **1** to be of the same weight, force, amount, etc.: *The merits of the two schools* balance. **2** to keep one's equilibrium: *The seal* balanced *on a large ball.*

Balance

balance of power ***n-*** a division of power among nations so no one nation or group of nations becomes so powerful as to be dangerous.

bal·bo·a (băl bō′ ə) ***n-*** monetary unit of Panama.

bal·brig·gan (băl brĭg′ ən) ***n-*** knitted cotton fabric for underwear, pajamas, etc.

bal·co·ny (băl′ kə nē) ***n-*** **[bal·co·nies]** platform, with a railing, built out from the wall of a building.

Balcony

bald (bȯld) ***adj-*** **[bald·er, bald·est] 1** bare of hair. **2** without the natural or usual covering of hair, feathers, fur, or foliage upon the head, top, or summit: *a* bald *mountaintop.* **3** of birds, having a white head: *a* bald *eagle.* **4** unadorned; bare; without disguise: *a* bald *statement of the facts.* ***—adv-*** **bald′ ly.** ***n-*** **bald′ ness.**

bald eagle ***n-*** large dark-brown eagle of North America, having, when mature, a white head, neck, and tail; American eagle, symbol of the United States.

bal·der·dash (bȯl′ dər dăsh′) ***n-*** meaningless talk or writing; nonsense. ***interj-*** nonsense!

bald·pate (bȯld′ pāt′) ***n-*** person having a bald head.

bal·dric (bȯl′ drĭk) ***n-*** broad belt, often richly decorated, worn over a shoulder to support a bugle or sword.

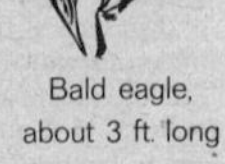

Bald eagle, about 3 ft. long

bale (bāl) ***n-*** large and closely pressed package of merchandise, prepared for storage or transportation: *a* bale *of cotton.* ***vt-*** **[baled, bal·ing]**: *Modern farm machines* bale *hay.* ***Homs-*** bail, Baal.

ba·leen (bə lēn′) ***n-*** whalebone.

bale·ful (bāl′ fəl) ***adj-*** full of spite and ill will; sinister; evil: *the witch's* baleful *look.* ***—adv-*** **bale′ ful·ly.**

balk (bȯk) ***vi-*** **1** to stop short and refuse to go on: *The horse* balked *at the high jump.* **2** in baseball, of a pitcher, to make an illegal motion, especially to fail to complete a throw he has started. ***vt-*** to hinder or check; thwart: *The tackle* balked *the play.* ***n-***: *The pitcher made a* balk.

balk·y (bȯ′ kē) ***adj-*** **[balk·i·er, balk·i·est]** unwilling to budge; stubbornly refusing to move: *a* balky *mule.*

[1]**ball** (bȯl) ***n-*** **1** any round body; sphere: *the flaming* ball *of the sun.* **2** round, or nearly round, object used in a game: *a golf* ball; *a croquet* ball; *a tennis* ball. **3** game using such an object, especially baseball: *to play* ball. **4** in baseball, a pitch of a ball too high, or too low, or not over the home plate, and not struck at by the batter; not a strike. **5** solid bullet or shot for a firearm: *musket* ball. **6** rounded part at the base of the thumb or great toe. [from Old Norse **böllr.**] ***Hom-*** bawl.

[2]**ball** (bȯl) ***n-*** **1** large formal dance: *Cinderella rode to the* ball *in a pumpkin coach.* **2** *Slang* a wonderful time. [from French **bal,** from Old French **baller** meaning "to dance," from Latin **ballare.**] ***Hom-*** bawl.

bal·lad (băl′əd) ***n-*** **1** simple song, especially one with several verses sung to the same melody. **2** poem that tells a story, written in four-line stanzas.

bal·lade (bə läd′) ***n-*** poem of three stanzas and l'envoi, all built on the same rhyme scheme.

ball-and-sock·et joint (bȯl′ən sŏk′ət) ***n-*** a joint which allows rotary motion. The moving part of the joint has a ball-shaped end that fits into a socket in the fixed part.

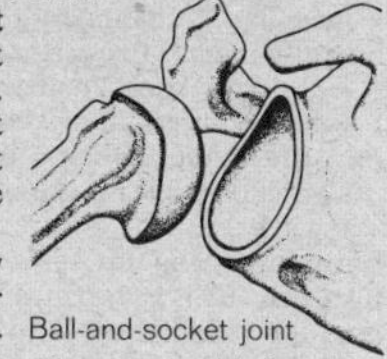
Ball-and-socket joint (human shoulder)

bal·last (băl′əst) ***n-*** **1** weighty material, such as sand or rock, carried in a ship's bottom to steady it, and by balloons from which it is dropped to make the balloon rise higher. **2** stones used for the roadbed of a railway. **3** something that stabilizes a person emotionally: *His wife's good sense was* ballast *for him.* ***vt-*** **1** to steady with a weight. **2** to fill in (the roadbed of a railway).

ball bearing ***n-*** **1** grooved ring holding small metal balls on which some moving part of a machine turns. **2** any metal ball of a bearing. For picture, see *bearing.*

bal·le·ri·na (băl′ə rē′nə) ***n-*** female ballet dancer.

bal·let (băl′ā, bă lā′) ***n-*** **1** story or idea acted out in dance form; also, the music for it. **2** a group that performs such dances. *as* ***modifier***: *a* ballet *dancer.*

bal·lis·tic (bə lĭs′tĭk) ***adj-*** of or relating to ballistics: *a* ballistic *calculation.* ***—adv-*** **bal·lis′ti·cal·ly.**

ballistic missile ***n-*** self-propelled projectile, such as a rocket, aimed before firing and not guided in flight.

bal·lis·tics (bə lĭs′tĭks) ***n-*** (takes singular verb) **1** study of the flight of projectiles. **2** study of the firing process inside guns, especially the motion of the bullet or shell in the gun and the force of the exploding gunpowder. **3** study of the impact and penetration of projectiles.

bal·loon (bə lo͞on′) ***n-*** **1** an airtight bag filled with a gas that is lighter than air, used to lift passengers or scientific instruments into the air. **2** a child's toy, which consists of a rubber bag that can be blown up. ***vi-*** to swell up.

Balloon

bal·lot (băl′ət) ***n-*** **1** system of secret voting in which the choice of candidates is shown on a paper form or a voting machine. **2** written or printed form used in secret voting. **3** total number of votes cast. **4** the right to vote: *Women won the* ballot *in 1920.* ***vi-*** to vote.

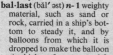

ballot box ***n-*** a closed box in which a voter places his ballot.

ball park ***n-*** stadium or other grounds used for baseball or football.

ball·play·er (bȯl′plā′ər) ***n-*** baseball player.

ball-point pen (bȯl′point′) ***n-*** pen having for a point a small ball bearing that rolls the ink from a cartridge onto the writing surface.

ball·room (bȯl′ro͞om′) ***n-*** a large room or hall for social dancing.

bal·ly·hoo (băl′ē ho͞o′) *Informal* ***n-*** a sensational attempt to attract customers, sell a product, or further a cause; loud or exaggerated advertising or propaganda: *There was a great deal of* ballyhoo *surrounding the new drug.* ***vt-***: *They* ballyhooed *their candidate.*

balm (bäm, bälm) ***n-*** **1** an oily or gummy substance from certain plants and trees, used as a healing salve; balsam. **2** anything that heals or soothes: *His kind words were a* balm *to her hurt feelings.*

balm·y (bä′mē, bäl′mē) ***adj-*** **[balm·i·er, balm·i·est]** **1** soft and gentle; soothing: *the* balmy *weather.* **2** sweet-smelling; fragrant. ***—adv-*** **balm′i·ly.** ***n-*** **balm′i·ness.**

ba·lo·ney (bə lō′nē) ***n-*** **1** bologna. **2** *Slang* nonsense. Also **ba·lo′ny.**

bal·sa (bȯl′sə, bŏl′-) ***n-*** **1** tropical American tree with strong wood lighter than cork. **2** the wood of this tree, used in making life preservers, life rafts, etc. **3** very light boat made of thousands of reeds tied together.

bal·sam (bȯl′səm) ***n-*** **1** an oily, fragrant substance obtained from certain shrubs and trees and used in medicine and perfumes; balm. **2** shrub or tree of the fir family from which this substance is taken. **3** flowering plant, with flowers like those of the lady's-slipper.

bal·us·ter (băl′ə stər) ***n-*** one of a set of small pillars that support the handrail of a parapet or balustrade.

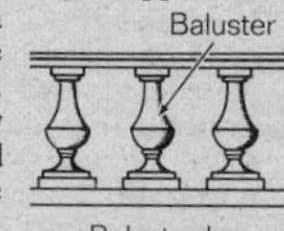

Balustrade

bal·us·trade (băl′ə strād′) ***n-*** row of small pillars, or balusters, topped by a protective rail, such as those along the edge of a bridge, balcony, or staircase.

bam·bi·no (băm bē′nō) ***n-*** [*pl.* **bam·bi·ni** (-nē) or **bam·bi·nos**] **1** little child or baby. **2** image of the infant Jesus. [from Italian.]

bam·boo (băm′ bo͞o′) ***n-*** [*pl.* **bam·boos**] **1** treelike, tropical plant related to the grasses. **2** its hollow, jointed stems, used in building in tropical climates, and in making furniture, fishing poles, canes, etc. *as* ***modifier***: *a* bamboo *screen.*

Bamboo

bam·boo·zle (băm bo͞o′zəl) *Informal* ***vt-*** **[bam·boo·zled, bam·boo·zling]** to trick or cheat by misleading or confusing completely: *He* bamboozled *us with his fast talk.*

ban (băn) ***n-*** **1** the formal forbidding of an act, as by law: *a* ban *on lotteries.* **2** condemnation, as by public opinion. **3** decree of excommunication by the church. ***vt-*** **[banned, ban·ning]** **1** to curse; call evil down upon. **2** to prohibit; forbid: *Noise is* banned *in the library.*

ba·nal (bə năl′, bā′nəl) ***adj-*** commonplace; trivial; hackneyed; trite: *She made the* banal *remark, "It isn't the heat, it's the humidity."* ***—adv-*** **ba′nal·ly** (bā′nə lē).

ba·nal·i·ty (bə năl′ə tē, bā-) ***n-*** [*pl.* **ba·nal·i·ties**] a commonplace remark: *His conversation is full of* banalities.

ba·nan·a (bə năn′ə) ***n-*** **1** long and slightly curved fruit with soft, sweet, starchy flesh and a thick yellow or red skin. **2** (also **banana plant**) the large treelike tropical plant that bears this fruit.

Banana plant

fāte, făt, dâre, bärn; bē, bĕt, mêre; bīte, bĭt; nōte, hŏt, môre, dȯg; fŭn, fûr; to͞o, bo͝ok; oil; out; tar; thin; then; hw for wh as in what; zh for s as in usual; ə for a, e, i, o, u, as in ago, linen, peril, atom, minus

[1]**band** (bănd) ***n-*** **1** thin, flat, flexible strip used for binding, supporting, trimming, etc. **2** bar or stripe: *a* band *of white around a pole.* **3** in radio, a particular range of wavelengths. ***vt-***: *to* band *the leg of a pigeon with a metal marker.* [partly from Scandinavian **band,** partly from Old French **bande**, "a strip; ribbon," related to [2]**band.**]

[2]**band** (bănd) ***n-*** **1** group of persons or animals: *a* band *of robbers*; *a* band *of sheep.* **2** company of musicians, especially one having chiefly wind and percussion instruments: *a military* band; *a jazz* band. *as* ***modifier***: *The tuba is a* band *instrument.* ***vi-*** (often followed by "themselves," "ourselves," etc.) to unite in a group: *The states* banded *into a union. They* banded *themselves together.* [from French **bande** meaning "a sign; token," from early Germanic **banner** meaning "a mark."]

band·age (băn′ dĭj) ***n-*** strip of cloth used in dressing and binding wounds, sprains, etc. ***vt-*** **[band·aged, band·ag·ing]** to dress, cover, or bind an injury with a strip of any soft material.

ban·dan·na or **ban·dan·a** (băn dăn′ ə) ***n-*** large colored handkerchief.

band·box (bănd′bŏks′) ***n-*** box made of light wood or pasteboard, used to hold hats, collars, etc.

ban·deau (băn′dō′) ***n-*** [*pl.* **ban·deaux** (-dōz′) or **ban·deaus**] **1** band worn by women about the hair to keep it in place. **2** a light, narrow brassiere.

ban·di·coot (băn′ dĭ ko͞ot′) ***n-*** **1** very large rat of India. **2** small rabbitlike animal of Australia, related to the kangaroo.

ban·dit (băn′ dĭt) ***n-*** outlaw or robber.

ban·dit·ry (băn′ dĭ trē) ***n-*** a roving and raiding for plunder: *Where there is no law,* banditry *is common.*

band·mas·ter (bănd′ măs′ tər) ***n-*** leader or conductor of a band.

ban·do·leer or **ban·do·lier** (băn′ də lêr′) ***n-*** broad leather or cloth belt having pockets or loops for carrying bullets. It is worn over the shoulder.

band saw ***n-*** saw consisting of an endless saw-toothed metal band running over two wheels.

band·stand (bănd′ stănd′) ***n-*** platform, often with a roof, for outdoor band concerts.

band·wag·on (bănd′ wăg′ ən) ***n-*** **1** a large wagon for carrying a band in a parade. **2** great and noisy enthusiasm for a person or cause.

climb (or **get**) **on the bandwagon** *Informal* to shift support to a person or cause that seems sure of success.

ban·dy (băn′ dē) ***vt*** **[ban·died, ban·dy·ing] 1** to throw or knock to and fro: *They* bandied *the tennis ball about the court.* **2** to give and take; exchange: *to* bandy *words about.*

ban·dy-leg·ged (băn′ dē lĕg′ əd) ***adj-*** having legs bent outward at the knees; bowlegged.

bane (bān) ***n-*** **1** originally, poison; still used in names of plants: *hen*bane. **2** a cause of ruin or destruction; curse: *Drink is the* bane *of his life.*

bane·ber·ry (bān′ bĕr′ ē) ***n-*** [*pl.* **bane·ber·ries**] **1** small plant which has a short, thick stalk of white flowers that turn into poisonous red or white berries. **2** the poisonous berry of this plant.

bane·ful (bān′ fəl) ***adj-*** **1** harmful; destructive: *the* baneful *effects of his greed.* **2** expressive of harm; threatening; ominous: *their* baneful *anger.* —***adv-*** **bane′ ful·ly.** ***n-*** **bane′ ful·ness**: *the* banefulness *of his appearance.*

[1]**bang** (băng) ***n-*** **1** heavy, noisy blow; whack: *I gave the pan a* bang. **2** loud, sudden noise; an explosive sound. **3** *Informal* sudden burst of energy: *The game started with a* bang. **4** *Slang* sudden pleasure; thrill. ***vt-*** to strike noisily; thump; slam: *to* bang *a door*; *to* bang *an elbow on a table.* ***vi-*** **1** to beat (on) noisily: *to* bang *on a table.* **2** to bump suddenly or violently: *to* bang *into a door*; *to* bang *against a chair.* ***adv-*** *Informal* directly; exactly: *He drove* bang *into the pole.* [perhaps an imitation of a noise, or from Old Norse **banga** meaning "to hammer."]

[2]**bang** (băng) ***vt-*** to cut (the hair) short across the forehead. ***n-*** (usually **bangs**) hair worn in this manner. [American word of uncertain origin.]

ban·gle (băng′ gəl) ***n-*** **1** ornamental bracelet worn upon a wrist or ankle. **2** one of several slender bracelets worn together.

bang-up (băng′ ŭp′) *Slang* ***adj-*** excellent; first-rate.

ban·ian (băn′ yən) banyan.

ban·ish (băn′ ĭsh) ***vt-*** **1** to condemn to leave; send from a country by legal decree; expel: *The former dictator was* banished *from the country.* **2** to drive out; send away: *The doctor's talk* banished *his fears of illness.*

ban·ish·ment (băn′ ĭsh mənt) ***n-*** expulsion from a country; exile.

ban·is·ter (băn′ ə stər) ***n-*** handrail and upright supports along the edge of a staircase, bridge, balcony, etc.; balustrade. Also **ban′ is·ters.**

ban·jo (băn′ jō) ***n-*** [*pl.* **ban·jos**] stringed musical instrument played with the fingers or with a small piece of wood or metal.

Banjo

[1]**bank** (băngk) ***n-*** **1** long pile or heap: *a* bank *of sand*; banks *of clouds.* **2** steep slope. **3** ridge of earth bordering a river, stream, etc. **4** submerged mass of earth in the sea or at the mouth of a river over which the water is shallow; shoal: *the* banks *off Newfoundland.* **5** the crosswise tilt of a road or airplane. ***vt-*** **1** to pile or heap: *to* bank *earth along a wall.* **2** to cover (a fire) with ashes or fuel to make it burn slowly. **3** to incline or tilt (a road or airplane) in making a turn so that the inner edge or wing is lower than the outside one. ***vi-*** **1** to form in long piles: *The clouds* banked *low across the horizon.* **2** to incline: *The pilot* banked *too steeply and almost crashed.* [from Middle English **banke,** from Old Norse **banki** meaning "a bench," related to [2]**bank** and **bench.**]

[2]**bank** (băngk) ***n-*** **1** a row or tier, especially of keys on a typewriter, organ, etc. **2** bench for rowers in a galley. ***vt-*** to arrange or form in a tier. [from Old French **banc** meaning "bench."]

[3]**bank** (băngk) ***n-*** **1** place of business which takes care of money for its depositors, lends money at interest, and often helps in the transfer of money. **2** any reserve supply: *a blood* bank; *soil* bank. *as* ***modifier***: *a* bank *employee.* ***vt-*** to put (money) in such a place. ***vi-*** to have a checking or savings account (at): *We* bank *at the local branch.* [from French **banque,** from Italian **banca** meaning "money changer's counter," from Old High German **bank** meaning "bench."]

bank on to rely on; count upon: *I'm* banking *on a raise before Christmas.*

bank account ***n-*** money deposited in a bank, which can be withdrawn by the depositor.

bank·er (băng′ kər) ***n-*** person who manages or works for a bank.

bank·ing (băng′ kĭng) ***n-*** the business of investing, lending, and guarding money.

bank note ***n-*** piece of paper resembling government paper money and used as money, but actually issued by a bank.

bank·rupt (băngk′rŭpt′) ***adj-*** unable to pay one's debts. ***n-*** person who is legally declared insolvent or unable to pay his debts, and whose property is divided among his creditors. ***vt-***: *Careless spending* bankrupted *him.*
bankrupt of completely lacking in: *Some people are* bankrupt of *common sense.*

bank·rupt·cy (băngk′rŭp′sē) ***n-*** [*pl.* **bank·rupt·cies**] state of being bankrupt or financially ruined.

ban·ner (băn′ər) ***n-*** **1** flag. **2** piece of cloth with a design, picture, or writing on it. ***adj-*** outstanding; exceptional: *a* banner *year.*

ban·nock (băn′ək) ***n-*** thick homemade cake or loaf, usually made without yeast; baked on a hot stone or griddle. The bannock is popular in Scotland.

Ban·nock (băn′ək) ***n-*** [*pl.* **Ban·nocks,** also **Ban·nock**] **1** one of a tribe of American Indians who lived in southern Utah. **2** the language of these Indians. ***adj-***: *a* Bannock *settlement.*

banns (bănz) ***n-*** (takes plural verb) notice, given in church, of a proposed marriage: *The* banns *were read for Joyce and Bill last Sunday.*

ban·quet (băng′kwət) ***n-*** elaborate, often formal, dinner for many people. ***vt-*** to treat (a person) to such a dinner: *The townspeople* banqueted *the returning hero.* ***vi-***: *They* banqueted *at the hotel.*

Ban·quo (băng′kwō′) ***n-*** in Shakespeare's "Macbeth," a nobleman who haunts his slayer, Macbeth.

ban·shee (băn′shē′) ***n-*** in the folklore of Ireland and Scotland, a spirit whose wailing was believed to foretell death.

ban·tam (băn′təm) ***n-*** **1** (also **Bantam**) kind of very small domestic fowl. **2** small, often scrappy, person. ***adj-*** small: *a* bantam *athlete.*

ban·tam·weight (băn′təm wāt′) ***n-*** boxer who weighs between 113 and 118 pounds.

ban·ter (băn′tər) ***n-*** good-natured teasing. ***vt-*** to tease in a friendly, joking way; make fun of. ***vi-*** to exchange joking remarks.

Ban·tu (băn′to͞o′) ***n-*** **1** any of a large group of southern and central African tribes. **2** family of languages spoken by these people and in this region.

ban·yan (băn′yən) ***n-*** an East Indian tree the branches of which send roots down to the ground so as to form new trunks. Also **ban′ian.**

ban·zai (bän′zī′) *Japanese* ***interj-*** "May you live a thousand years," used as a greeting, cheer, or battle cry.

banzai attack ***n-*** a reckless or suicidal attack by Japanese troops in World War II. Also **banzai charge.**

ba·o·bab (bā′ō băb′) ***n-*** African tree with an enormously thick trunk and an edible fruit resembling a gourd.

Baobab

bap·tism (băp′tĭz′əm) ***n-*** **1** practice of pouring or sprinkling water on a person or dipping him in water, as a sign of admission into a Christian church. **2** first experience; initiation; trial: *The recruit had her* baptism *in wilderness survival.*

bap·tis·mal (băp tĭz′məl) ***adj-*** having to do with baptism: *the* baptismal *water.*

Bap·tist (băp′tĭst) ***n-*** member of a Protestant denomination believing that baptism, usually by immersion, should be given to a person only after he reaches the age of reason.

bap·tis·ter·y or **bap·tis·try** (băp′tə strē) ***n-*** [*pl.* **bap·tis·ter·ies, bap·tis·tries**] that part of a church building in which baptism is performed.

bap·tize (băp′tīz′, băp tīz′) ***vt-*** [**bap·tized, bap·tiz·ing**] **1** to pour or sprinkle water on (a person) or dip (a person) in water, as a sign of admission into a Christian church. **2** to give a name to at the time of baptism; christen: *They* baptized *their son Joseph.*

bar (bär) ***n-*** **1** piece of wood, metal, etc., that is longer than it is wide or thick. **2** any barrier or obstacle; obstruction: *a* bar *to one's success.* **3** band or stripe: *a* bar *of red across the painting.* **4** place in court where defendants stand trial or await sentence. **5** lawyers as a class; also, the profession of law: *to admit someone to the* bar. **6** counter in a barroom, over which liquor is served; also, the barroom itself. **7** *Music* one of the upright lines dividing a staff into equal measures of time; also a measure of the music between two such lines. ***prep-*** except; but: *He won the support of his neighbors,* bar *none.* ***vt-*** [**barred, bar·ring**] **1** to fasten or obstruct: *I locked and* barred *the door. The guards* barred *our way.* **2** to cover or protect with metal strips, rods, etc.: *to* bar *a window.*

Bar of music

Ba·rab·bas (bə răb′əs, băr′ə bəs) ***n-*** in the New Testament, a thief released in place of Jesus at the demand of the crowd.

barb (bärb) ***n-*** sharp hook or point extending backward, as on the tip of a fishhook, arrow, etc. ***vt-*** to furnish with one or more such points.

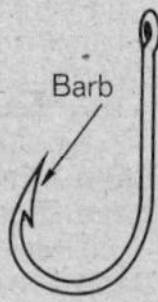

bar·bar·i·an (bär băr′ē ən) ***n-*** **1** in ancient history, a foreigner; one not a Greek or a Roman, and therefore regarded as uncivilized. **2** person of uncultivated taste. ***adj-*** rude; uncivilized; savage: *a* barbarian *custom.*

bar·bar·ic (bär băr′ĭk, bär bâr′-) ***adj-*** **1** uncivilized; primitive: *The music was* barbaric *and wild.* **2** savage: *their* barbaric *cruelty.*

bar·ba·rism (bär′bə rĭz əm) ***n-*** **1** stage of development between savagery and civilization. **2** act or custom characteristic of a barbarous condition: *He feels that capital punishment is a* barbarism. **3** word or expression not in accepted use; also, anything contrary to what is judged sound or in good taste.

bar·bar·i·ty (bär băr′ə tē, bär bâr′-) ***n-*** [*pl.* **bar·bar·i·ties**] brutal or inhuman conduct.

bar·ba·rous (bär′bə rəs) ***adj-*** **1** uncivilized; crude; outlandish: *his* barbarous *manners.* **2** cruel; inhuman. —***adv-*** **bar′ba·rous·ly** ***n-*** **bar′bar·ous·ness.**

bar·be·cue (bär′bə kyo͞o′) ***n-*** **1** outdoor party at which meat, originally a whole carcass, is roasted over an open fire. **2** the roasted meat. **3** the pit, grill, or spit used for roasting the meat. ***vt-*** [**bar·be·cued, bar·be·cu·ing**] **1** to roast (meat) over an open fire: *to* barbecue *a chicken.* **2** to cook (meat) with a highly seasoned sauce.

barbed (bärbd) ***adj-*** **1** having sharp points as some fence wires, or barbs as some fishhooks. **2** sharp; cutting; biting: *a* barbed *remark.*

barbed wire *n-* twisted wire with sharp points that are spaced at intervals along its length.

bar·bel (bär′ bəl) *n-* **1** a long threadlike growth on the lips or nostrils of fishes such as the catfish. For picture, see *catfish.* **2** large freshwater fish of Europe having such growths.

Barbed wire

bar·ber (bär′ bər) *n-* person who makes a business of cutting hair and shaving or trimming beards.

bar·ber·ry (bär′ bĕr′ē, *also* -bə rē) *n-* [*pl.* **bar·ber·ries**] **1** prickly shrub bearing berries that turn red in the fall. **2** the berry.

bar·ber·shop (bär′ bər shŏp′) *n-* a barber's place of business.

barbershop quartet *n-* quartet that sings mainly sentimental songs in close harmony.

bar·bi·can (bär′ bĭ kən) *n-* fortified tower, gatehouse, or other outpost guarding the entrance to a bridge or castle.

bar·bi·tu·rate (bär bĭch′ ə rət, -rāt′) *n-* any of a group of chemicals that are powerful, sleep-producing drugs.

bar·ca·role (bär′ kə rōl′) *n-* **1** Venetian gondolier's song. **2** kind of music imitating this song. Also **bar′ca·rolle.**

bar·chan (bär′ kän′) *n-* crescent-shaped, moving sand dune.

bard (bärd) *n-* **1** poet or singer in olden times. **2** any poet. *Hom-* barred.

[1]**bare** (bâr) *adj-* [**bar·er, bar·est**] **1** not covered, especially, not covered with clothing: *a* bare *hillside; the child's* bare *arms.* **2** unadorned; simple; plainly or scantily furnished: *the* bare *truth;* bare *lodgings.* **3** scanty; mere: *He earned a* bare *living. vt-* [**bared, bar·ing**] to uncover; expose: *Upon entering the church, he* bared *his head. Hom- bear. —n-* **bare′ness.** [from Old English **bær.**]

lay bare to expose; reveal; disclose.

bare·back (bâr′ băk′) *adv-* without a saddle.

bare·faced (bâr′ fāst′) *adj-* unconcealed; bold; impudent: *a* barefaced *fraud.*

bare·foot (bâr′ fo͝ot′) *adj-* with bare feet: *the* barefoot *boy. Also* **bare′foot′ed.**

bare·hand·ed (bâr′ hăn′ dəd) *adj-* without a weapon or tool: *She built a shelter* barehanded.

catch barehanded *Informal* to catch in the act, usually of a crime.

bare·head·ed (bâr′ hĕd′ əd) *adj-* with nothing on the head; without a hat.

bare·ly (bâr′ lē) *adv-* **1** hardly; scarcely: *We* barely *had time to escape the flood.* **2** in a bare way; poorly; scantily: *a* barely *furnished room.*

bar·gain (bär′ gən) *n-* **1** agreement on the terms of a deal: *He made a* bargain *to deliver the coal weekly.* **2** something bought cheap or offered for sale at a low price. *vi-* to argue over a price; haggle: *I* bargained *with the rug dealer for an hour, and got him down to half his asking price.*

drive a hard bargain to insist on terms good for oneself and hard for the other: *When it comes to money matters, she* drives a hard bargain. **strike a bargain** to make an agreement; come to terms.

bargain for to be prepared for; expect: *His staying all night was more than we* bargained for.

Barge

barge (bärj) *n-* **1** boat with a flat bottom, used in inland and coastal waters for carrying freight. **2** a pleasure boat, often elegantly furnished. *vt-* [**barged, barg·ing**] to transport freight by flatbottomed boat. *vi-* **1** to move in a clumsy manner; also, to bump (into): *As he* barged *out of the room, he* barged *into his host.* **2** to force oneself (into) rudely or heedlessly: *to* barge *into a party.*

bar graph *n-* graph using rectangles whose lengths correspond proportionately to the quantities they represent.

bar·i·tone (băr′ ə tōn′) *Music n-* musical range of the male voice between tenor and bass; also, a singer having this range, or a musical part written for it. *adj-* having this or a similar range: *a* baritone *voice.*

bar·i·um (băr′ ē əm) *n-* soft, silver-white, heavy metallic element used in alloys, luminous paints, etc. Symbol Ba; At. No. 56; At. Wt. 137.34.

barium sulfate *n-* insoluble white salt of barium found naturally as the mineral, **barite,** and much used in making white paint. Also **barium sulphate.**

[1]**bark** (bärk) *n-* outer covering of trees and other woody plants. *vt-* to damage the surface of by abrasion; abrade: *to* bark *a shin on a chair; to* bark *a shoe on a rock.* [from Scandinavian **börkr.**] *Hom-* barque.

[2]**bark** (bärk) *n-* **1** sharp, explosive sound made by a dog, fox, seal, etc. **2** any similar sound. *vi-* to make such a sound: *The watchdog* barked *at the stranger. vt-* to speak in a sharp or gruff way: *The captain* barked *his orders.* [from Old English **beorcan.**] *Hom-* barque.

bark up the wrong tree to pursue the wrong possibility.

[3]**bark** (bärk) *n-* three-masted sailing ship, with the foremast and mainmast square-rigged, and the mizzenmast fore-and-aft rigged. [from Italian **barca** meaning "vessel," from Late Latin **barca.**]

Bark

bar·keep·er (bär′ kē′ pər) *n-* person who owns or manages a bar; bartender. Also **bar′keep.**

bark·en·tine (bär′ kən tēn′) *n-* three-masted sailing ship with the foremast square-rigged and the other two fore-and-aft rigged.

bark·er (bär′ kər) *n-* person who stands at the entrance of a show, urging people to go inside.

bar·ley (bär′ lē) *n-* **1** grasslike cereal plant. **2** its grain, used as a food and in the manufacture of malt.

bar·ley·corn (bär′ lē kôrn′, -kôrn′) *n-* grain of barley.

bar·maid (bar′ mād′) *n-* woman who serves drinks at a bar.

bar·man (bär′ mən) *n-* [*pl.* **bar·men**] barkeeper or bartender.

bar mitz·vah (bär′ mĭts′ və) *n-* **1** ceremony held for a Jewish boy at his thirteenth year to mark his adulthood in his religion. **2** boy for whom this ceremony has been held. *—n-fem.* **bat′mitz′vah** (bät-).

barn (bärn) *n-* farm building used for storing grain, hay, etc., and for housing livestock. *as* ***modifier:*** *a* barn *door.*

bar·na·cle (bär′ nə kəl) *n-* small sea animal with a thin shell. It attaches itself to the bottoms of ships and to rocks, wharves, etc.

barn dance *n-* social gathering with square dances or other folk dances, usually danced to the directions of a caller.

barn·storm (bärn′ stôrm′, -stôrm′) *vi-* **1** to tour rural areas, as a stunt flyer, member of a theatrical company, etc. **2** to tour the rural areas as a candidate for political office: *The presidential candidate* barnstormed *through the Middle West. vt-*: *We* barnstormed *the Middle West. —n-* **barn′storm′er.**

barn swallow *n-* swallow that has a sharply forked tail and often builds its nest in the eaves or rafters of barns.

barn·yard (bärn′ yärd′) *n-* yard around a barn.

bar·o·graph (băr′ō grăf′) ***n-*** barometer that automatically traces pressure readings on a graph.

ba·rom·e·ter (bə rŏm′ə tər) ***n-*** an instrument for measuring atmospheric pressure, used in showing height above sea level and in forecasting weather. ***—adj-*** **bar′o·met′ric** (băr′ə mĕ′trĭk) or **bar′o·met′ri·cal.**

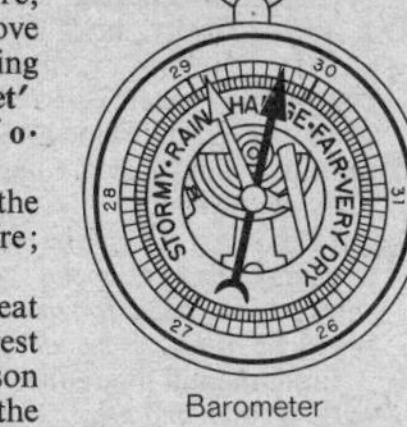

Barometer

barometric pressure ***n-*** the pressure of the atmosphere; atmospheric pressure.

bar·on (băr′ən) ***n-*** **1** in Great Britain, the title of the lowest rank of nobility. **2** person holding this title. **3** in the Middle Ages, a person who held an estate directly from the king. **4** *Informal* man of great power or influence in business; tycoon: *an oil* baron. ***Hom-*** barren. ***—n-*** *fem.* **bar′on·ess.**

bar·on·et (băr′ə nĕt′) ***n-*** **1** in Great Britain, the title of a hereditary rank below that of a baron and made up of commoners. **2** person holding this title. *Abbr.* Bart.

ba·ro·ni·al (bə rō′nē əl) ***adj-*** **1** having to do with a baron or a barony. **2** suitable for a baron: *an imposing* baronial *mansion.*

bar·o·ny (băr′ə nē) ***n-*** [*pl.* **bar·o·nies**] the rank or landed property of a baron.

ba·roque (bə rōk′) ***adj-*** **1** of or resembling the ornate art and architecture popular in Europe in the 17th century. **2** of or resembling an ornate style of music written between 1600 and 1750. **3** of pearls, irregular in shape.

ba·rouche (bə ro͞osh′) ***n-*** carriage with a driver's seat, two other seats facing each other, and a folding top.

barque (bärk) ***n-*** 3bark.

bar·rack (băr′ək) ***vt-*** to house in barracks. ***vi-*** to live in barracks.

bar·racks (băr′əks) ***n-*** *pl.* large building or group of buildings for lodging soldiers.

bar·ra·cu·da (băr′ə ko͞o′də) ***n-*** [*pl.* **bar·ra·cu·da; bar·ra·cu·das** (kinds of barracuda)] very voracious fish of warm seas, having a long body, powerful jaws, and sharp teeth.

bar·rage (bə räzh′, -räj′) ***n-*** **1** volley of bursting shells, fired so as to fall just in front of advancing troops, in order to screen and protect them. **2** an overwhelming number of anything sent or received: *a* barrage *of letters; a* barrage *of phone calls.*

barred (bärd) ***adj-*** **1** having bars: *The* barred *gate clanked behind him.* **2** having stripes or bands; striped: *a* barred *feather.* ***Hom-*** bard.

bar·rel (băr′əl) ***n-*** **1** round, usually bulging cask greater in length than in width, usually of wood, with flat ends. **2** quantity which such a cask contains; especially, a standard U.S. measure, such as 31.5 gallons for oil. **3** part or case of something in the shape of a tube: *a gun* barrel. ***vt-*** to put or pack in a cask.

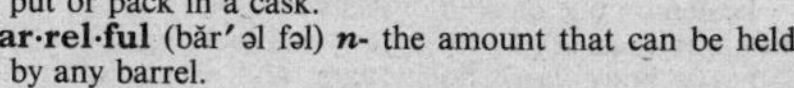
Barrel

bar·rel·ful (băr′əl fəl) ***n-*** the amount that can be held by any barrel.

bar·rel·house (băr′əl hous′) ***n-*** **1** a low, cheap drinking place. **2** kind of jazz played in such a place. ***adj-***: *He plays* barrelhouse *blues.*

barrel organ ***n-*** hand organ.

bar·ren (băr′ən) ***adj-*** **1** not fertile or productive: *a stretch of* barren *land.* **2** not bearing young or fruit: *a* barren *mare; a* barren *pear tree.* **3** without profit; empty: *a* barren *victory;* barren *labor.* **4 barrens** stretch of land, usually flat, with sparse or stunted vegetation. ***Hom-*** baron. ***—n-*** **bar′ren·ness.**

bar·rette (bă rĕt′, bə-) ***n-*** clasp or bar for keeping a woman's hair in place.

bar·ri·cade (băr′ə kād′) ***n-*** crude wall or barrier, especially one hastily put in place to keep back an enemy. ***vt-*** [**bar·ri·cad·ed, bar·ri·cad·ing**] to block with a makeshift wall or barrier: *They* barricaded *the road to the fort with logs.*

bar·ri·er (băr′ē ər) ***n-*** **1** something built to bar or prevent passage: *The Great Wall of China was a* barrier *against invasion.* **2** anything that prevents progress or creates difficulty: *a language* barrier; *a* barrier *to trade; a* barrier *to success.*

barrier reef ***n-*** offshore coral reef parallel to the coastline.

bar·ring (bär′ĭng) ***prep-*** except for: *I shall arrive on Tuesday,* barring *delay.*

bar·ris·ter (băr′ə stər) *Brit.* ***n-*** lawyer who argues cases in court.

bar·room (bär′ro͞om′) ***n-*** room in a tavern, hotel, club, etc., in which liquor is sold by the drink over a counter.

1bar·row (băr′ō) ***n-*** **1** wheelbarrow. **2** (also **hand′bar′row**) flat wooden frame with handles at the ends, on which things may be carried. [from Old English **bearwe,** from **beran** meaning "to bear."]

2bar·row (băr′ō) ***n-*** ancient artificial mound of earth or stones over a grave. [from Old English **beorg.**]

bar sinister ***n-*** on a coat of arms, a diagonal band from lower left to upper right, indicating illegitimate birth of a person or of one of his ancestors.

Bart. Baronet.

bar·tend·er (bär′tĕn′dər) ***n-*** man who serves alcoholic drinks at a bar.

bar·ter (bär′tər) ***vt-*** to exchange or trade (one thing for another) without the use of money: *Indians used to* barter *furs for guns.* ***vi-***: *Eskimos* barter *at the trading post every spring.* ***n-*** the trade or exchange of one thing for another without the use of money.

Bar·thol·o·mew (bär thŏl′ə myo͞o′) ***n-*** in the New Testament, one of the twelve apostles. Also **St. Bartholomew.**

Bar·uch (bâr′ək) ***n-*** **1** the scribe and friend of Jeremiah. **2** a book in the Old Testament Apocrypha attributed to Baruch.

bas·al (bā′səl) ***adj-*** **1** having to do with a foundation; used as a base: *the* basal *parts of a column.* **2** fundamental; basic. ***Hom-*** basil.

basal metabolism ***n-*** rate at which the body uses up energy while at rest, indicating the general metabolism of the body.

ba·salt (bə sȯlt′, bā′sȯlt′) ***n-*** hard, heavy, fine-grained, greenish-black rock of volcanic origin. *as* ***modifier***: *a* basalt *cliff.*

1base (bās) ***n-*** **1** lowest part of something, on which it stands or rests: *a lamp* base. **2** the main part of a mixture; foundation: *Beef stock is the* base *of many soups.* **3** starting place for an operation; headquarters: *the* base *of an exploring party; a naval* base. **4** a station or goal in some games, such as baseball. **5** *Chemistry* substance which will combine with an acid to form a salt and which turns litmus paper blue. **6** *Mathematics* (1) of a numeration system, the number by which the value of a digit is multiplied when it is moved one place to the left. Example: 10 is the base of the decimal system, so that $10^1 = 10$, $10^2 = 100$, $10^3 = 1000$, and so forth. (2) in exponential notation, the number that is used as a factor. Example: In 2^3, 2 is the base. (3) in geometry, the side on which a figure or solid rests. ***vt-*** [**based, bas·ing**] to establish or support firmly: *to* base *a story on facts*; *to* base *a statue on concrete.* [from the same Greek word **basis** that gives us the word "basis."] ***Hom-*** 2bass.

2base (bās) ***adj-*** [**bas·er, bas·est**] **1** of metals, not precious. **2** inferior in quality; made of inferior metal: *a* base *coin.* **3** morally bad or low; mean-spirited; vile: *Taking credit for someone else's work is a* base *act.* **4** coarse; not refined: *a* base *expression.* [from Old French **bas,** from Late Latin **bassus** meaning "short; low."] ***Hom-*** 2bass.

base·ball (bās′ bol′) ***n-*** **1** game played with a ball and bat by teams of nine players on a side. The game is played on a field with four bases at the corners of a square called a diamond. **2** ball used in this game. ***as modifier***: *a* baseball *bat.*

base·board (bās′ bôrd′) ***n-*** wide molding running around the lower part of the wall of a room, against the floor.

base·born (bās′ bôrn′) *Archaic* ***adj-*** **1** of humble birth. **2** born out of wedlock.

base hit ***n-*** in baseball, a ball so struck that the batter can reach base safely.

base·less (bās′ ləs) ***adj-*** without a basis in fact; groundless; unfounded: *a* baseless *accusation.*

base line ***n-*** in baseball, the white line between bases, along which a base runner moves.

base·man (bās′ mən) ***n-*** [*pl.* **base·men**] in baseball, any of the three infielders at first, second, or third base (used only in the compounds **first baseman, second baseman,** and **third baseman**).

base·ment (bās′ mənt) ***n-*** bottom story of a building, partly or completely underground.

ba·sen·ji (bə sĕn′ jē) ***n-*** small short-haired dog of central Africa that cannot bark.

base pay ***n-*** person's regular salary, before any additions or deductions.

base runner ***n-*** in baseball, a member of the team at bat who is on base.

1bas·es (bā′ səz) ***n-*** *pl.* of **1base.**

2ba·ses (bā′ sēz′) ***n-*** *pl.* of **basis.**

bash (băsh) *Informal* ***vi-*** to strike with a smashing blow; smash (in): *He* bashed *in the man's skull.* ***n-***: *a* bash *over the head.*

bash·ful (băsh′ fəl) ***adj-*** very shy and easily embarrassed. —***adv-*** **bash′ ful·ly.** ***n-*** **bash′ ful·ness.**

ba·sic (bā′ sĭk) ***adj-*** **1** chief or main; essential; fundamental: *He cited his* basic *reasons for the decision.* **2** *Chemistry* being a base or having its properties.

ba·si·cal·ly (bā′ sĭk lē) ***adv-*** in the main part; primarily; fundamentally: *The house is* basically *sound. He is* basically *honest.*

bas·il (băz′ əl, bā′ səl) ***n-*** plant related to mint, having spicy leaves used for seasoning food. ***Hom-*** basal.

Basilica

ba·sil·i·ca (bə sĭl′ ə kə) ***n-*** **1** in ancient Rome, an oblong hall with columns along the two sides and a semicircular recess, or apse, at one end. **2** church built on such a plan.

bas·i·lisk (băs′ ə lĭsk′) ***n-*** fabled lizard of the African desert, whose breath and look were supposed to be fatal.

ba·sin (bā′ sən) ***n-*** **1** wide, shallow vessel, usually round or oval, for holding water or other liquids; a bowl. **2** the quantity held by such a vessel. **3** hollow or enclosed area containing water: *a yacht* basin. **4** all the land drained by a river and its tributaries: *the* basin *of the Columbia River.*

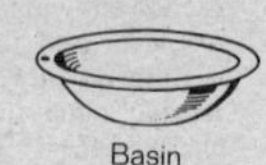
Basin

ba·sis (bā′ sĭs) ***n-*** [*pl.* **ba·ses** (bā′ sēz′)] **1** part on which anything rests or depends; foundation: *Common interests form a good* basis *for friendship.* **2** fundamental facts or reasons: *What* basis *do you have for that statement?* **3** fundamental ingredient or mixture: *The* basis *of a cake is flour and eggs.*

bask (băsk) ***vi-*** to lie in comfortable warmth; warm oneself pleasantly: *to* bask *in the sun.* ***Hom-*** basque.

bas·ket (băs′ kət) ***n-*** **1** container made of thin strips of wood, straw, twigs, reeds, etc., woven together: *Easter* basket; *clothes* basket. **2** (also **bas′ ket·ful′**) amount such a container will hold. **3** hoop with a bottomless net through which a basketball player must toss the ball to score points. **4** a toss of the ball through this hoop, counted as a score.

bas·ket·ball (băs′ kət bol′) ***n-*** **1** game in which the opposing teams score points by tossing a ball through baskets at either end of the court. **2** ball used in this game.

Basket Maker ***n-*** member of an early American Indian culture in the Southwest, characterized by its basket-making and lack of pottery.

bas·ket·ry (băs′ kə trē) ***n-*** **1** baskets. **2** the craft or art of making baskets. Also **bas′ ket·work′** (băs′ kət wûrk′).

basque (băsk) ***n-*** tight-fitting upper garment worn by women. ***Hom-*** bask.

Basque (băsk) ***n-*** **1** one of a people of unknown origin, living in the western Pyrenees of Spain and France. **2** the language of these people, also of unknown origin. ***adj-***: *the* Basque *provinces.* ***Hom-*** bask.

bas-re·lief (bä′ rĭ lēf′, băs′-) ***n-*** form of sculpture in which figures stand out slightly from a background.

1bass (băs) ***n-*** [*pl.* **bass** (of the same variety), **bass·es** (of different varieties)] any of various fresh-water and ocean food and game fishes. [a changed form of the dialect word **barse,** from Old English **bears.**]

2bass (bās) *Music* ***n-*** **1** tones of low pitch: *Turn up the* bass *and lower the treble on the phonograph.* **2** musical range of the lowest male singing voice; also, a singer having this range, or a musical part written for it. **3** double bass; bass viol. ***adj-*** low in pitch: *a* bass *voice*; *a* bass *tuba.* [from **2base,** plus Italian **basso.**] ***Hom-*** base.

3bass (băs) ***n-*** **1** basswood. **2** bast. [from **bast,** from Old English **bæst.**]

bass clef (bās) *Music* ***n-*** symbol, originally a letter F, centered on the fourth line of a musical staff to indicate the position of F below middle C; F clef.

Bass clef

bass drum (bās) ***n-*** a large drum with a low pitch, beaten on one or both of its two heads.

bas·set (băs′ ət) ***n-*** long, low, sad-looking dog with a heavy body, large floppy ears, and usually a spotted white, black, and tan coat.

bas·si·net (băs′ ə nĕt′) ***n-*** basket used as an infant's crib, with legs and, usually, a hood over one end.

bas·so (băs′ ō) ***n-*** [*pl.* **bas·sos**] **1** male singer having the lowest, or bass, voice; a bass. **2** the lowest male voice or voice part.

bas·soon (bə so͞on′) *n-* musical wind instrument of deep tone, having a long, curved mouthpiece with a double reed, and a wooden tube.

bass viol (bās) *n-* **1** (also **bass fiddle**) the double bass. **2** the bass of the viol family of instruments.

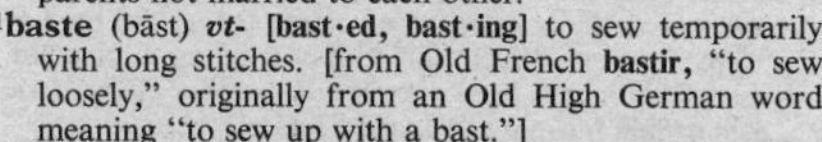

Man playing bassoon

bass·wood (băs′wo͝od′) *n-* **1** the American linden tree. **2** the wood of this tree.

bast (băst) *n-* the tough, inner fibrous bark of various trees, such as the linden, used in making rope or matting.

bas·tard (băs′tərd) *n-* child born of parents not married to each other.

[1]**baste** (bāst) *vt-* **[bast·ed, bast·ing]** to sew temporarily with long stitches. [from Old French **bastir,** "to sew loosely," originally from an Old High German word meaning "to sew up with a bast."]

[2]**baste** (bāst) *vt-* **[bast·ed, bast·ing]** to moisten with fat, gravy, or other liquid while roasting: *She* basted *the turkey with melted butter.* [from Old French **basser,** "to soak," altered from **bassiner,** from **bassin** "basin."]

[3]**baste** (bāst) *Informal vt-* **[bast·ed, bast·ing]** to beat or thrash; cudgel. [from Old Norse **beysta.**]

bas·tille (băs tēl′) *n-* **1** (also **bas·tile′**) a prison. **2 the Bastille** an old prison in Paris, destroyed by the people during the French Revolution in 1789.

Bastille Day *n-* July 14, the national holiday of France, similar to our Independence Day, commemorating the fall of the Bastille.

[1]**bast·ing** (bās′tĭng) *n-* temporary set of long stitches. Also called **bast′ ings.** [from [1]**baste.**]

[2]**bast·ing** (bās′tĭng) *n-* drippings or sauce used to baste meat. [from [2]**baste.**]

[3]**bast·ing** (bās′tĭng) *Informal n-* a severe beating. [from [3]**baste.**]

bas·tion (băs′chən, -tē ən) *n-* **1** part projecting out from the main body of a fortification. **2** anything strongly fortified or firmly established: *a* bastion *of faith.*

[1]**bat** (băt) *n-* wooden stick or club, especially one used in baseball or cricket. *vt-* **[bat·ted, bat·ting]** to strike with such a stick or club: *to* bat *a ball. vi-*: *John* bats *next.* [from Old English **batt.**]

at bat in the hitter's position: *Who's* at bat? **go to bat for** to come to the defense of; defend; champion: *At the first sign of trouble they* went to bat for *him.* **right off the bat** at once; immediately.

[2]**bat** (băt) *n-* small, flying, nocturnal mammal with a furry body like that of a mouse and large wings of thin, hairless skin. [greatly changed form of a Middle English word **bakke** from Old Norse.]

have bats in (one's) belfry *Slang* to be crazy.

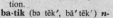

Brown bat, about 3 1/2 in. long

bat·boy (băt′boi′) *n-* in baseball, a boy who takes care of a team's bats and other equipment.

batch (băch) *n-* **1** amount baked at one time; a baking: *a* batch *of cookies.* **2** quantity of material to be used or made at one time: *a* batch *of cement.* **3** group of similar things: *a* batch *of letters.*

bate (bāt) *Archaic vi- & vt-* abate. ***Hom-*** bait.

with bated breath with fear, anticipation, etc.: *We watched* with bated breath *as he made his ascent.*

ba·teau (bă tō′) *n-* [*pl.* **ba·teaux** (bă tōz′)] **1** a light, flat-bottomed boat used chiefly on rivers in Canada and the United States. **2** pontoon for a floating bridge.

bath (băth) *n-* **1** a cleansing or washing of all the body. **2** water for bathing: *He drew a* bath. **3** room equipped for bathing; bathroom: *There are two* baths *on the second floor.* **4** (usually **baths**) building for bathing or steam bathing: *the public* baths *of Rome.* **5** heated liquid or a chemical solution in which objects are immersed for controlled heating or for chemical treatment. **6** *Informal* a drenching with any liquid.

bathe (bāth) *vt-* **[bathed, bath·ing]** **1** to immerse in water to clean or refresh; give a bath to: *to* bathe *a child; to* bathe *sore feet.* **2** to wash with water or other liquid: *to* bathe *a wound.* **3** to make wet: *Tears* bathed *his face.* **4** to cover or surround as water does: *Light* bathed *the stage. vi-* **1** to take a bath: *I like to* bathe *before dinner.* **2** to go into the sea, a lake, pool, etc. for enjoyment.

bath·house (băth′hous′) *n-* **1** a building with showers or pools for bathing. **2** a building in which swimmers can change clothes.

ba·thos (bā′thŏs′) *n-* **1** in speech and writing, a sudden and ridiculous descent from the lofty to the commonplace; anticlimax. Example: To be a good lawyer a person needs intelligence, integrity, and a loud voice. **2** false or insincere pathos; sentimentality: *the* bathos *of a popular song.*

bath·robe (băth′rōb′) *n-* long, loose garment, opening in front, worn to and from the bath and as a robe.

bath·room (băth′ro͞om′) *n-* room with a bathtub and basin, and usually a toilet.

bath·tub (băth′tŭb′) *n-* tub, now usually equipped with faucets and drain, used for taking a bath.

bathy- *combining form* deep; deep-sea: *a* bathy*sphere.* [from Greek **bathy-,** from **bathys** meaning "deep."]

bath·y·scaphe (băth′ə skăf′, -skāf′) *n-* a self-propelled diving craft consisting of a gasoline-filled tank carrying a bathysphere attached to its bottom. It is able to dive to the deepest parts of the ocean.

bath·y·sphere (băth′ə sfêr′) *n-* very strong steel diving sphere for deep-sea exploration.

Bathyscaphe

ba·tik (bə tēk′, bă′tēk′) *n-* **1** an Indonesian hand method of dyeing a design on fabric, in which the parts not to be dyed are covered with wax. **2** fabric dyed by this process. *adj-*: *a* batik *dress.*

ba·tiste (bə tēst′) *n-* sheer, very fine, lightweight fabric of cotton, silk, or other fiber.

bat·man (băt′mən) *n-* [*pl.* **bat·men**] servant to a British army officer.

ba·ton (bă tŏn′) *n-* **1** stick used by the leader of a band or orchestra for beating time. **2** staff used as a badge of office or symbol of authority.

ba·tra·chi·an (bə trā′kē ən) *n-* an amphibian animal.

bat·tal·ion (bə tăl′yən) *n-* an army unit of two of more companies that forms part of a regiment.

bat·ten (băt′ən) *n-* a light strip of wood used for covering joints between boards or for fastening canvas over a ship's hatch. *vt-* to fasten or strengthen with such strips.

batten down the hatches **1** to fasten canvas over a ship's hatches in preparation for a storm. **2** to prepare for any difficult situation, crisis, etc.: *Let's* batten down the hatches, *boys, the colonel's in a rage.*

[1]**bat·ter** (băt′ ər) ***vt-*** **1** to strike with heavy, repeated blows: *The sea* battered *the wall.* **2** to damage; bruise; subject to rough usage: *The champion* battered *his opponent.* ***vi-***: *The stranger* battered *at the door.* [partly from [1]**bat**, partly from French **battre** meaning "to beat."]

[2]**bat·ter** (băt′ ər) ***n-*** thin mixture of flour, liquid, and other ingredients: *pancake* batter. [from Old French **bature**, from **battre**, "to beat," from Latin **battuere.**]

[3]**bat·ter** (băt′ ər) ***n-*** player who is batting or whose turn it is to bat. [from [1]**bat.**]

bat·tered (băt′ ərd) ***adj-*** damaged by pounding, use, or misuse: *a* battered *old ship*; *the* battered *sofa.*

bat·ter·ing-ram (băt′ ər ĭng răm′) ***n-*** large, iron-headed beam, used before the invention of the cannon to beat down the walls of besieged places.

bat·ter·y (băt′ ə rē) ***n-*** [*pl.* **bat·ter·ies**] **1** a device that uses chemicals to produce or store electricity; also, two or more electric cells connected together: *a flashlight* battery; *a storage* battery. **2** number of like things used as a unit: *a* battery *of lights.* **3** two or more cannons placed together under a single command: *a field* battery. **4** in baseball, the combination of pitcher and catcher. **5** *Law* an unlawful attack, with or without a weapon, upon a person. See also *assault and battery.* ***as modifier***: *a* battery *terminal*; *a* battery *commander.*

bat·ting (băt′ ĭng) ***n-*** wool or other fiber matted in sheets, used in quilts, quilted garments, etc.

bat·tle (băt′ əl) ***n-*** **1** fight between opposing armies, fleets, or air forces. **2** any fight or struggle: *a* battle *between the two gangs*; *a* battle *against the jungle.* ***vt-*** [**bat·tled, bat·tling**] to fight; struggle: *to* battle *a hurricane.* ***vi-***: *to* battle *for freedom*; *to* battle *against wind and rain.*

bat·tle-ax or **bat·tle-axe** (băt′ əl ăks′) ***n-*** **1** broad-faced ax formerly used as a weapon in battle. **2** *Slang* aggressive and quarrelsome woman.

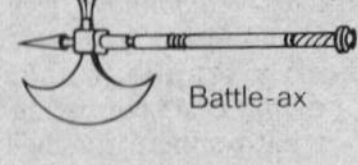
Battle-ax

battle cruiser ***n-*** large, fast warship having the heavy guns of a battleship but less armor.

battle cry ***n-*** **1** a shout or yell used by soldiers in combat. **2** slogan or motto of a party, movement, etc.; watchword: *Our* battle cry *is "more jobs."*

bat·tle·dore (băt′ əl dôr′) ***n-*** kind of light, paddle-shaped racket used in the game badminton.

battle fatigue ***n-*** combat fatigue.

bat·tle·field (băt′ əl fēld′) or **bat·tle·ground** (băt′ əl ground′) ***n-*** place where a battle is, or has been, fought.

bat·tle·ment (băt′ əl mənt) ***n-*** wall at the top of a building or tower, constructed with a series of gaps or openings through which, formerly, men shot at their enemies.

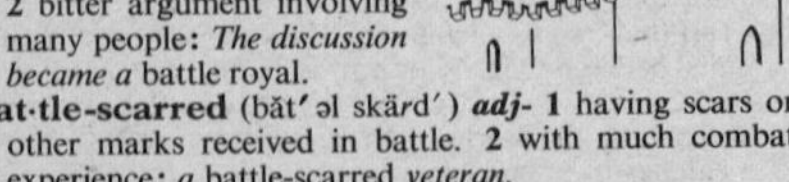

battle royal ***n-*** **1** a wild, confused fight involving many people; melee; riot. **2** bitter argument involving many people: *The discussion became a* battle royal.

bat·tle-scarred (băt′ əl skärd′) ***adj-*** **1** having scars or other marks received in battle. **2** with much combat experience: *a* battle-scarred *veteran.*

bat·tle·ship (băt′ əl shĭp′) ***n-*** large warship with heavy armor and very powerful guns.

bat·ty (băt′ ē) *Slang* ***adj-*** [**bat·ti·er, bat·ti·est**] crazy.

bau·ble (bò′ bəl) ***n-*** cheap ornament; a thing that is showy, but of little value: *This bracelet is just a* bauble.

baux·ite (bòk′ sīt′) ***n-*** a claylike mineral, the chief ore of aluminum.

bawd (bòd) ***n-*** woman who runs a house of prostitution.

bawd·y (bò′ dē) ***adj-*** [**bawd·i·er, bawd·i·est**] immodest; obscene; immoral; indecent: *their* bawdy *talk.* **—*n-*** **bawd′ i·ness.**

bawl (bòl) ***vi-*** to cry or wail loudly: *The child is* bawling *with rage.* ***vt-*** to utter by shouting: *The sergeant* bawled *his orders.* ***n-***: *a* bawl *of rage.* ***Hom-*** ball.

bawl out *Informal* to scold; reprimand.

[1]**bay** (bā) ***n-*** body of water partly surrounded by land, formed by a recess in the shoreline. [from Old French **baie,** from Spanish **bahia,** from Latin **baia.**] ***Hom-*** bey.

[2]**bay** (bā) ***n-*** **1** part of a room extending beyond the main outside wall, often having several windows in it. **2** compartment in the body of an airplane. **3** forward part of a ship between decks, sometimes used as a hospital. [from Old French **baee** meaning "opening," from Late Latin **badāre** meaning "to gape."] ***Hom-*** bey.

[3]**bay** (bā) ***n-*** **1** the laurel. **2** any of several shrubs related to or resembling the laurel, such as the mountain laurel and the bayberry. [from Old French **baie,** from Latin **bāca** meaning "berry."] ***Hom-*** bey.

[4]**bay** (bā) ***n-*** the deep-toned prolonged cry of a dog, especially of a pursuing hound. ***vi-*** to bark with such a cry: *The hounds* bayed *at the moon.* [from Old French **abaier** meaning "to bark," from Late Latin **badāre** meaning "to gape (open)."] ***Hom-*** bey.

at bay 1 in a position ready to fight off pursuers: *a stag* at bay. **2** in a position from which attack or escape is impossible: *The guard held the robbers* at bay.

[5]**bay** (bā) ***adj-*** having a reddish brown color: *a* bay *horse.* ***n-*** a horse with a reddish-brown coat and black mane and tail. [from Old French **bai**, from Latin **badius** meaning "chestnut brown."] ***Hom-*** bey.

bay·ber·ry (bā′ bĕr′ ē) ***n-*** [*pl.* **bay·ber·ries**] **1** shrub of the coast of eastern North America which bears clusters of gray berries that yield a wax used to make candles; bay; also, the waxy berry. **2** a fragrant West Indian tree whose leaves are used to perfume bay rum.

bay leaf ***n-*** dried leaf of the European laurel, used as an herb in cooking.

bay·o·net (bā′ ə nĕt′) ***n-*** dagger that can be attached to the muzzle of a rifle and used for stabbing or slashing. ***vt-*** **1** to stab with such an instrument. **2** to impale on something long and sharp.

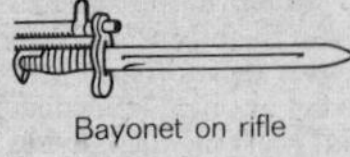
Bayonet on rifle

bay·ou (bī′ ō′, -o͞o′) ***n-*** [*pl.* **bay·ous**] sluggish stream flowing through marshy land, into or out of a river, lake, etc., especially in Louisiana. [American word from Louisiana French, from American Indian **bayuk** meaning "small stream."]

bay rum ***n-*** liquid perfumed with the leaves of a species of bayberry and used as a scent and a lotion.

bay window ***n-*** **1** window which projects outward from the line of the building. **2** *Slang* big belly.

ba·zaar (bə zär′) ***n-*** **1** sale of various kinds of articles for some special purpose: *a charity* bazaar. **2** place for the sale of a variety of goods. **3** in Oriental countries, a marketplace or street lined with shops. Also **bazar.** ***Hom-*** bizarre.

ba·zoo·ka (bə zo͞o′ kə) ***n-*** portable antitank rocket gun usually operated by two men.

bbl. barrel.

B.C. 1 before Christ. **2** British Columbia.

be (bē) ***vi-*** [*pres. tense*: **I am,** he (she, it) **is,** you, (we, they) **are**; *p.t.*: I (he, she, it) **was,** you (we, they) **were**; *p.p.*: **been**; *pres. p.*: **be·ing**] **1** to exist: *There* is *a strong feeling* *against war.* **2** to occupy a position, condition, etc.: *He* is *on the chair. She has* been *on the critical list for two weeks.* **3** to happen; occur; take place: *The party will* be *on Saturday.* **4** to equal; stand for; coincide with: *That girl* is *my sister. Let x* be *ten.* **5** to belong to the class of: *He* is *tired. She* is *an author.* **6** auxiliary used with: (1) a present participle to indicate an action continuing at a particular time or at a future time: *They* are *building a bridge.* (2) past participle to form the passive voice: *She* was *called on to speak.* (3) infinitive to indicate duty or intention: *We* are *to leave at 10 P.M.* ***Hom-*** bee.

be- *prefix* **1** to cause to be; make: *to* be*foul; to* be*dim.* **2** all over; thoroughly; completely: *to* be*smear.* [from Old English **bi-**, a form of **bi**, the preposition "by."]

beach (bēch) ***n-*** sandy or pebbly shore of the ocean washed by waves; also, a similar place on a lake or river. ***vt-*** to bring or drive onto a shore. ***Hom-*** beech.

beach buggy ***n-*** car or truck with oversize balloon tires for traveling over sand.

beach·comb·er (bēch′kō′mər) ***n-*** person who lives on the wreckage or refuse found along beaches; loafer.

beach·head (bēch′hĕd′) ***n-*** part of an enemy shore first captured by an invading army and used as a base for further operations.

beach wagon ***n-*** station wagon.

bea·con (bē′kən) ***n-*** fire, light, or radio signal used for guiding or warning, especially in the navigation of ships and airplanes; also, the structure bearing this signal.

bead (bēd) ***n-*** **1** small ball or piece of wood, glass, stone, or the like, pierced through to be strung together with others. **2** any small, round body: *a* bead *of dew; skin glistening with* beads *of sweat.* **3** small metal knob at the muzzle end of a gun barrel, used in taking aim. **4 beads** a rosary. ***vt-*** to decorate with small balls or bits of wood, stone, glass, etc., or with beading.

tell (one's) beads to pray in a sequence according to the beads on a rosary.

bead·ing (bēd′ĭng) ***n-*** **1** ornamental work made of beads, as on a dress. **2** band or molding with elevations like beads. **3** kind of openwork trimming through which ribbon may be run.

bea·gle (bē′gəl) ***n-*** small, short-legged hound with drooping ears, used in hunting rabbits.

beak (bēk) ***n-*** **1** the bill of a bird. **2** anything pointed or shaped like the bill of a bird, such as the lip of a pitcher or the prow of an ancient warship.

Beak

beak·er (bē′kər) ***n-*** **1** cup or glass with a pouring lip, used in laboratories. **2** large drinking cup or vessel with a wide mouth.

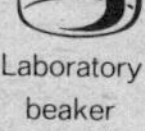

Laboratory beaker

beam (bēm) ***n-*** **1** long, heavy piece of wood or metal, used as a horizontal support in a building, ship, etc. **2** any supporting bar: *the* beam *of a plow; the* beam *of a balance.* **3** widest part of a ship. **4** waves of light, sound, radio, etc., traveling along a narrow path in the same direction; ray. **5** something suggestive of a ray of light in the darkness: *a* beam *of hope.* ***vt-*** to direct or transmit (a signal, broadcast, etc.) in a particular direction: *to* beam *a program to Europe.* ***vi-*** **1** to shine: *The sun* beamed *down.* **2** to radiate warmth and joy: *She* beamed *with happiness.*

on the beam 1 of an airplane, following the direction of a guiding radio signal. **2** *Informal* on the right track; just right: *His remarks make sense; I think he's* on the beam.

beam·ing (bē′mĭng) ***adj-*** shining; glowing; radiant: *a* beaming *smile; a* beaming *face.* ***—adv-*** **beam′ing·ly.**

bean (bēn) ***n-*** **1** the seed or the seed pod, or both, of various plants of the pea family, such as the kidney bean, soybean, and string bean; also, the plants themselves. **2** any of various seeds of a similar shape, such as cacao beans and coffee beans.

bean·bag (bēn′băg′) ***n-*** small cloth bag filled with beans and used in games.

bean·ball (bēn′bȯl′) *Slang* ***n-*** in baseball, a pitch deliberately thrown at a batter's head.

bean·pole (bēn′pōl′) ***n-*** **1** tall, narrow pole for a growing bean plant to climb on. **2** *Slang* tall, thin person.

bean·stalk (bēn′stȯk′) ***n-*** the stem of a bean plant.

[1]**bear** (bâr) ***n-*** **1** large animal with long shaggy hair and a very short tail. **2** rough surly person. **3** on the stock exchange, one who tries to lower prices for his own advantage (see also *bull*). [from Old English **bera.**] ***Hom-*** bare. ***—adj-*** **bear′like′.**

Black bear, about 5 ft. long

[2]**bear** (bâr) ***vt-*** [**bore, borne, bear·ing**] **1** to support; hold up; sustain: *The pillars* bear *the weight of the roof.* **2** to carry or convey; transport: *The letter* bears *good news.* **3** to stand up under; endure; abide: *He has* borne *much pain. That will not* bear *scrutiny.* **4** to have on one's person, or mind, or feelings: *to* bear *a scar; to* bear *a grudge.* **5** to bring forth; produce: *to* bear *young; to* bear *fruit.* ***vi-*** **1** to produce or be able to produce fruit, young, etc.: *This tree* bore *heavily last year.* **2** to move toward or be situated on a certain point of the compass: *We were* bearing *due north.* [from Old English **beran.**] ***Hom-*** bare.

bear away to change (a ship's course) away from the wind.

bear down to make a strong effort in trying to win: *He* bore down *in the last lap of the race.*

bear down (on or **upon)** to approach rapidly: *The care* bore down on *him.*

bear on 1 to press or weigh down on: *He* bore *too hard* on *the tool and broke it. Her sorrow* bears *heavily* on *her.* **2** to have to do with; be relevant to: *The policeman's testimony* bears on *the crime.*

bear out to confirm; support: *The facts* bear out *my story.*

bear up to keep up one's spirits in the face of misfortune; not lose heart: *They* bore up *well during the crisis.*

bear watching, investigating, etc. to require watching, etc.: *His behavior will* bear watching *in the future.*

bear with to be patient or tolerant toward; put up with.

bear·a·ble (bâr′ə bəl) ***adj-*** of a nature that allows being endured or borne; tolerable: *a* bearable *ache.*

bear·bait·ing (bâr′bā′tĭng) ***n-*** in former times, the sport of setting dogs on a captive bear.

beard (bêrd) ***n-*** **1** growth of hair on the cheeks, chin, and throat. **2** any similar appendage of fishes or birds. **3** hairlike tuft on the heads of some grains, such as wheat or barley. ***vt-*** to confront with daring; defy: *to* beard *the lion in his den.* ***—n-*** **beard′less:** *a* beardless *youth.*

beard·ed (bêrd′əd) ***adj-*** **1** having a beard: *a* bearded *soldier.* **2** having a beard of a stated kind or color: *a red-*bearded *sailor.*

bear·er (bâr′ər) *n-* **1** person or thing that carries, supports, or gives birth. **2** one who presents a check or other order for the payment of money.

BALL BEARING
ROLLER BEARING
Bearings

bear·ing (bâr′ĭng) *n-* **1** way of carrying oneself, standing, walking, etc.; manner: *The leader had a proud* bearing. **2** a part of a machine in or on which another part moves: *A bicycle wheel turns on ball* bearings. **3** meaning; relation: *The question has no* bearing *on the subject.* **4** act or power of producing: *a fruit tree past* bearing. **5 bearings** direction or position in relation to other things: *The boy lost his* bearings *in the forest.*

bear·ish (bâr′ĭsh) *adj-* **1** rude; surly: *his* bearish *behavior.* **2** of the stock market, showing fears or signs of failing (see also *bullish*). *—adv-* **bear′ish·ly.** *n-* **bear′ish·ness.**

bear·skin (bâr′skĭn′) *n-* **1** the skin or fur of a bear. **2** a coat, robe, or rug made of this skin. **3** a high, black fur hat worn by some soldiers and drum majors.

beast (bēst) *n-* **1** any four-footed animal, especially a large or ferocious animal. **2** a coarse or brutal person.

beast·ly (bēst′ lē) *adj-* [**beast·li·er, beast·li·est**] **1** savage; brutal; disgusting: *a* beastly *crime*; beastly *manners.* **2** unpleasant; annoying: *a* beastly *nuisance.* *—n-* **beast′li·ness:** *The* beastliness *of the crime revolts me.*

beast of burden *n-* an animal used to carry loads.

beat (bēt) *vt-* [**beat, beat·en, beat·ing**] **1** to strike or hit repeatedly: *to* beat *a drum*; *to* beat *a donkey.* **2** to flap repeatedly: *A bird* beats *its wings.* **3** to stir vigorously: *to* beat *eggs.* **4** to defeat; conquer: *We can* beat *their team if the field isn't muddy.* **5** *Music* to measure (time) by tapping, waving a baton, etc. *vi-* **1** to throb: *The heart* beats. **2** to strike repeatedly upon or against: *The waves* beat *upon the rocks.* **3** to sail against the wind by tacking: *The boat* beat *along the shore.* *n-* **1** sound or stroke made again and again: *the* beat *of marching feet.* **2** a round or course which is frequently gone over: *the policeman's* beat. **3** *Music* the rise and fall of the stroke marking the divisions of time; also, any such stroke: *three* beats *to a measure.* *adj- Informal* very tired; fatigued. *Hom-* beet. *—n-* **beat′er.**

beat back (or **off**) to force or drive back.

beat down to cause (a price) to be lowered; also, to force (a seller) to lower his price.

beat it! *Slang* go away! scram!

beat up to thrash or whip soundly; give a beating to.

beat·en (bē′tən) *adj-* **1** hammered; shaped by hammering: *a bowl made of* beaten *brass.* **2** worn by many footsteps: *a* beaten *path.* **3** conquered; overcome.

be·a·tif·ic (bē′ə tĭf′ĭk) *adj-* blissfully happy.

be·at·i·fy (bē ăt′ə fī′) *vt-* [**be·at·i·fied, be·at·i·fy·ing**] **1** to make happy. **2** in the Roman Catholic Church, to declare (a worthy person who has died) to have attained the rank of "blessed" and the right to public veneration. *—n-* **be·at′i·fi·ca′tion.**

beat·ing (bē′tĭng) *n-* **1** a pulsating; throbbing: *the* beating *of the heart.* **2** whipping, as punishment. **3** severe defeat: *The team took a* beating.

be·at·i·tude (bē ăt′ə to͞od′, -tyo͞od′) *n-* **1** supreme happiness. **2 the Beatitudes** eight declarations made in the Sermon on the Mount, each beginning "Blessed are . . ."

beat·nik (bēt′nĭk) *Informal n-* after World War II, person who withdraws from conventional society and adopts odd behavior and dress. [American word from a slang past participle of **beat,** plus Yiddish **-nik** meaning "person or thing which (is)."]

beau (bō) *n-* [*pl.* **beaux** or **beaus** (bōz)] **1** a man who escorts a lady; admirer; preferred suitor. **2** dude; dandy. *Hom-* [1]bow.

Beau Brum·mell (brŭm′əl) *n-* dandy or fop; so called after George "Beau" Brummell (1778-1840), English clotheshorse.

Beau·fort scale (bō′fərt) *n-* number scale for wind speeds ranging from zero for calm air to twelve for hurricane winds.

beau geste (bō′ zhĕst′) *French n-* [*pl.* **beaux gestes** (bō′-zhĕst′)] fine or gracious gesture.

beau ideal (bō′ ī dē′əl) *n-* perfect model of beauty or excellence.

beau·te·ous (byo͞o′ tē əs) *adj-* beautiful.

beau·ti·ful (byo͞o′ tə fəl) *adj-* delighting the ear, eye, or mind; lovely. *— adv-* **beau′ti·ful·ly.**

beau·ti·fy (byo͞o′ tə fī′) *vt-* [**beau·ti·fied, beau·ti·fy·ing**] to make beautiful; adorn: *to* beautify *a yard with flowers.*

beau·ty (byo͞o′ tē) *n-* [*pl.* **beau·ties**] **1** quality or combination of qualities that pleases or gratifies the eye, ear, or mind. **2** beautiful person or thing, especially a lovely woman.

beauty parlor *n-* place in which women have their hair cared for, nails manicured, etc. Also called **beauty salon, beauty shop.**

beaux (bōz) *pl.* of **beau.**

beaux arts (bō zär′) *French n-pl.* the fine arts, especially painting, drawing, sculpture, and architecture. *as* ***modifier*** **(beaux-arts):** *Many artists attend the annual* beaux-arts *ball.*

Beaver, about 2 ft. long

[1]**bea·ver** (bē′vər) *n-* **1** small fur-bearing animal that lives both in water and on land, having a broad, flat, powerful tail, strong teeth shaped for gnawing, and webbed hind feet. It is remarkable for the way in which it fells trees and dams streams. **2** the fur of this animal. **3** a man's high hat, formerly made of beaver fur. [from Old English **beofor.**]

[2]**bea·ver** (bē′ vər) *n-* movable part of a knight's metal helmet that protected the mouth and chin. [from Old French **baviere** originally meaning "a bib to catch saliva."]

be·bop (bē′bŏp′) *Slang n-* a style of jazz music with extreme variations in the rhythm and changes in the key.

be·calmed (bĭ kämd′, -kälmd′) *adj-* of a sailing ship, motionless because of a lack of wind: *The galleon was* becalmed *off the Azores.*

be·came (bĭ kām′) *p.t.* of **become.**

be·cause (bĭ kòz′, -kŭz′) *conj-* for the reason that; since; for: *We didn't stay outside long* because *it was too cold.*

because of on account of: *I couldn't sleep* because of *the heat.*

beck (bĕk) *n-* nod or gesture as a signal of summoning or command.

at (one's) beck and call at one's service.

beck·on (bĕk′ən) *vt-* to signal (someone) to approach with a movement of the head or hand. *vi-* to attract or call: *The sea* beckoned.

be·cloud (bĭ kloud′, bē-) *vt-* to darken; obscure: *His talk* beclouds *the truth.*

be·come (bĭ kŭm′, bē-) ***vi-*** **[be·came, be·come, be·com·ing]** to come or grow to be: *A lamb* becomes *a sheep.* ***vt-*** to suit; be suitable to; look well on: *That new pink dress* becomes *her. Childish behavior does not* become *you.*
become of to be the fate of; happen to: *What will* become of *Jim after graduation?*

be·com·ing (bĭ kŭm′ĭng) ***adj-*** going well with the appearance or character; suitable; appropriate: *a* becoming *dress; conduct not* becoming *to a lady.* —***adv-*** **be·com′ing·ly.**

Bec·que·rel rays (bĕ krĕl′, bĕk′ə rəl) ***n-*** former name for rays given off by radioactive substances.

bed (bĕd) ***n-*** **1** anything used for resting or sleeping, especially an article of furniture consisting of a frame and mattress. **2** plot of ground in which things are grown: *a* bed *of tulips*; *a* bed *of oysters.* **3** bottom or base: *the* bed *of a lake*; *a* bed *of gravel under a road.* **4** horizontal layer of rock, coal, etc.; stratum. ***vt-*** **[bed·ded, bed·ding] 1** to provide with sleeping quarters: *to* bed *horses in a barn.* **2** to set or plant in the ground: *to* bed *roses.*
put (or go) to bed of a newspaper, etc., to make ready for printing.
bed down 1 to provide (cattle, horses, etc.) with food and sleeping quarters. **2** to go to sleep, usually out-of-doors.

be·daub (bĭ dòb′, bē-) ***vt-*** to smear with something oily or dirty.

be·daz·zle (bĭ dăz′əl, bē-) ***vt-*** **[be·daz·zled, be·daz·zling]** to bewilder or confuse; dazzle: *He* bedazzled *the audience with his sleight of hand.*

bed·bug (bĕd′bŭg′) ***n-*** small bloodsucking insect with an unpleasant odor, sometimes found in bedding, upholstered furniture, etc.

bed·cham·ber (bĕd′chām′bər) ***n-*** bedroom.

bed·clothes (bĕd′klōz′, bĕd′klōthz′) ***n-*** *pl.* sheets, blankets, etc., used on a bed.

bed·ding (bĕd′ĭng) ***n-*** **1** bedclothes. **2** materials for a bed: *Straw is used as* bedding *for horses.*

be·deck (bĭ dĕk′, bē-) ***vt-*** to adorn; decorate.

be·dev·il (bĭ dĕv′əl, bē-) ***vt-*** **1** to trouble or worry; harass; bother: *A lack of money constantly* bedeviled *him.* **2** to gain power over by magic; bewitch. —***n-*** **be·dev′il·ment.**

be·dew (bĭ dōō′, -dyōō′, bē-) ***vt-*** to moisten with dew or as if with dew: *Tears* bedewed *her cheeks.*

bed·fast (bĕd′făst′) ***adj-*** confined to bed by age or illness; bedridden.

bed·fel·low (bĕd′fĕl′ō) ***n-*** one who shares a bed with another.

be·dim (bĭ dĭm′, bē-) ***vt-*** **[be·dimmed, be·dim·ming]** to darken; cloud; dim: *A haze* bedimmed *the horizon.*

be·diz·en (bĭ dī′zən, -dĭz′ən) ***vt-*** to dress or adorn, especially with gaudy finery: *She* bedizened *herself with cheap jewelry.*

bed·lam (bĕd′ləm) ***n-*** **1** scene of confusion and noisy disorder: *The street was a* bedlam *during the riot.* **2** *Archaic* an insane asylum. **3 Bedlam** the London Hospital of St. Mary of Bethlehem used since 1547 as an insane asylum.

Bed·ou·in (bĕd′ōō ən) ***n-*** **1** a wandering Arab or tent dweller of northern Africa, Syria, and Arabia. **2** any nomad or wanderer. ***adj-***: *a* Bedouin *headdress.*

bed·pan (bĕd′păn′) ***n-*** open, shallow receptacle used as a toilet by a person confined to bed.

be·drag·gled (bĭ drăg′əld) ***adj-*** wet, limp, and dirty: *My dress was* bedraggled *when I came in from the rain.*

bed·rid·den (bĕd′rĭd′ən) or **bed·rid** (bĕd′rĭd′) ***adj-*** confined to bed by illness.

bed·rock (bĕd′rŏk′) ***n-*** **1** the solid rock underlying the looser upper crust of the earth. **2** the lowest state or bottom of a thing: *My savings account has reached* bedrock.

bed·roll (bĕd′rōl′) ***n-*** a sleeping bag or blankets, rolled up for carrying.

bed·room (bĕd′rōōm′) ***n-*** a room with a bed in it; a sleeping room.

bed·side (bĕd′sīd′) ***n-*** the space beside a bed: *The doctor sat at the patient's* bedside. *as* ***modifier***: *a* bedside *lamp*; *the doctor's* bedside *manner.*

bed·sore (bĕd′sôr′) ***n-*** sore caused by a person's being confined to bed too long.

bed·spread (bĕd′sprĕd′) ***n-*** covering, often decorative, spread over a bed during the day.

bed·stead (bĕd′stĕd′) ***n-*** the wood or metal framework of a bed that holds the springs and mattress.

bed·time (bĕd′tīm′) ***n-*** the time when a person usually goes or should go to bed.

bee (bē) ***n-*** **1** small insect that sucks nectar and gathers pollen from flowers; especially, the honeybee, a kind that stores honey and lives in the strictly ordered society of a beehive. **2** social gathering for work, competition, or amusement: *a quilting* bee; *a spelling* bee. ***Hom-*** be.

bee·bread (bē′brĕd′) ***n-*** bitter substance made of pollen and stored by bees, who mix it with honey to feed their larvae.

beech (bēch) ***n-*** **1** spreading hardwood tree with smooth gray bark and dark green leaves. Its nuts, called **beech′nuts,** are edible. **2** (also **beech′wood**) the wood of this tree. ***Hom-*** beach.

beef (bēf) ***n-*** [*pl.* **beeves** (bēvz)] **1** flesh of an ox, cow, or steer used for food. **2** a fully-grown ox, bull, steer, or cow that is raised for its meat. **3** *Slang* [*pl.* **beefs**] complaint.
beef up *Informal* to add strength or vigor to; reinforce: *to* beef up *one's defenses.*

beef·steak (bēf′stāk′) ***n-*** slice of meat from a steer, cow, or bull, suitable for broiling or frying.

beef·y (bē′fē) ***adj-*** **[beef·i·er, beef·i·est]** brawny or fleshy; also, fat.

bee·hive (bē′hīv′) ***n-*** box (or other shelter) made to house a swarm of bees and to store their honey.

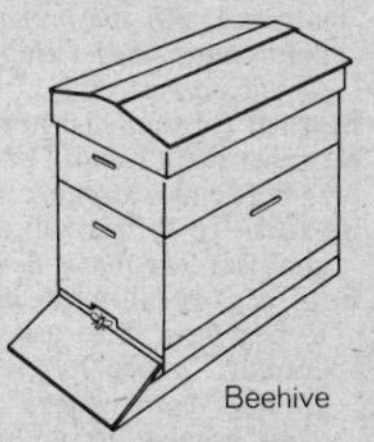
Beehive

bee·keep·er (bē′kē′pər) ***n-*** one whose occupation is raising bees.

bee·line (bē′līn′) ***n-*** **1** the straight course of a bee returning to the hive with honey or pollen. **2** the most direct way from one point to another: *I made a* beeline *for home.*

Be·el·ze·bub (bē ĕl′zə bŭb′, bĕl′zə-) ***n-*** in the Bible, the prince of devils.

been (bĭn) *p.p.* of **be.** ***Hom-*** bin.

beer (bêr) ***n-*** **1** an alcoholic beverage usually made from malted barley and flavored with hops. **2** drink made from roots or plants: *root* beer. ***Hom-*** bier.

beer and skittles *Informal* ***n-*** carefree pleasure or enjoyment, especially from drink and play.

---

fāte, făt, dâre, bärn; bē, bĕt, mêre; bīte, bĭt; nōte, hŏt, môre, dòg; fŭn, fûr; tōō, bŏŏk; oil; out; tar; thin; thĕn; hw for wh as in *wh*at; zh for s as in u*s*ual; ə for a, e, i, o, u, as in *a*go, lin*e*n, per*i*l, at*o*m, min*u*s

bees·wax (bēz′ wăks′) ***n-*** tough, yellowish-brown wax that bees make and use for honeycomb. It is used to stiffen thread, to make candles, etc.

beet (bēt) ***n-*** plant with a thick, fleshy root. The root and leaves of one variety, the red beet, are eaten as vegetables. The white root of the sugar beet is an important source of sugar. ***Hom-*** beat.

[1]**bee·tle** (bē′ təl) ***n-*** any of an order of horny-skinned insects with a pair of tough, brittle wings that fold over their delicate inner wings. [from Old English **bitela,** from **bitan** meaning "to bite."]

Beetle

[2]**bee·tle** (bē′ təl) ***n-*** heavy wooden mallet for hammering, leveling, or crushing. [from Old English **bētel,** from **bēatan** meaning "to beat."]

bee·tle·browed (bē′ təl broud′) ***adj-*** **1** having large, projecting eyebrows. **2** scowling; gloomy: *a* beetle-browed *glance.*

bee·tling (bēt′ lĭng) ***adj-*** jutting out; prominent; overhanging: *bare and* beetling *cliffs.*

beeves (bēvz) ***n-*** *pl.* cattle intended for beef.

be·fall (bĭ fòl′) ***vt-*** [**be·fell, be·fall·en, be·fall·ing**] to happen to: *Whatever* befalls *them, they are ready to meet it.*

be·fit (bĭ fĭt′) ***vt-*** [**be·fit·ted, be·fit·ting**] to be suited to; be suitable or appropriate for: *a dress to* befit *the occasion.* **—*adv-*** **be·fit′ ting·ly:** *Zoe was* befittingly *respectful to her aunt.*

be·fog (bē fŏg′, -fòg′) ***vt-*** [**be·fogged, be·fog·ging**] **1** to envelop in a fog or mist. **2** to confuse: *to* befog *an issue.*

be·fore (bĭ fôr′) ***prep-*** (in senses 1 through 4 considered an adverb when the object is clearly implied but not expressed) **1** in front of: *She stopped* before *the gate. A new life lay* before *us.* **2** at the head of; in advance of: *He rode* before *his troops.* **3** earlier or sooner than: *They arrived* before *dinner.* **4** preceding in serial order: *X comes* before *Y.* **5** of concern to; occupying: *The question* before *us is very delicate.* ***conj-*** **1** previous to the time of: *I must leave now;* before *I do, I want to thank you all.* **2** rather or sooner than: *I'd die* before *I'd submit to that sort of treatment.*

be·fore·hand (bĭ fôr′ hănd′) ***adv-*** ahead of time; in advance: *All the preparations for the party were made* beforehand. ***adj-:*** *He was* beforehand *in his preparation for the party.*

be·foul (bĭ foul′, bē-) ***vt-*** to make dirty; pollute.

be·friend (bĭ frĕnd′) ***vt-*** to act as a friend toward; help: *to* befriend *a stranger in town.*

be·fud·dle (bĭ fŭd′ əl) ***vt-*** [**be·fud·dled, be·fud·dling**] to confuse: *The liquor he drank* befuddled *him.*

beg (bĕg) ***vt-*** [**begged, beg·ging**] **1** to ask for as charity: *to* beg *food.* **2** to ask for humbly; ask for as a favor; entreat: *to* beg *forgiveness; to* beg *one's pardon.* ***vi-:*** *He* begs *on the streets. She* begged *for a part in the play.*

go begging to go unwanted or unclaimed: *If this leftover party food is* going begging, *I'll take some home.*

beg off to ask to be excused (from), especially by entreaty; decline: *He* begged off *from the bridge game.*

beg the question *Informal* to avoid giving a direct answer; sidestep.

be·gan (bĭ găn′) *p.t.* of **begin.**

be·gat (bĭ găt′) *Archaic p.t.* of **beget.**

be·get (bĭ gĕt′) ***vt-*** [**be·got, be·got** or **be·got·ten, be·get·ting**] **1** to become the father of. **2** to produce; cause: *Idleness* begets *discontent.* **—*n-*** **be·get′ ter.**

beg·gar (bĕg′ ər) ***n-*** **1** person who lives by asking for food, money, etc. **2** any very poor person; pauper. **3** *Informal* a fellow; a rascal (often used playfully): *a kind-hearted little* beggar. ***vt-*** **1** to reduce to poverty: *Unwise investments* beggared *him.* **2** to outstrip the resources of; outdo: *The size of the universe* beggars *the imagination.*

beg·gar·ly (bĕg′ ər lē) ***adj-*** poor; contemptible; mean: *clad in* beggarly *rags.*

beg·gar-ticks (bĕg′ ər tĭks′) ***n-*** [*pl.* **beg·gar-ticks**] plant related to the sunflower, with barbed seeds that stick to clothing, the fur of animals, etc.; also, the seeds of this plant. Also **beg′ gar's-ticks′.**

beg·gar·y (bĕg′ ə rē) ***n-*** extreme poverty.

be·gin (bĭ gĭn′) ***vi-*** [**be·gan, be·gun, be·gin·ning**] **1** to come into existence; arise; commence: *Life* began *many million years ago. The stream* begins *up in the hills. The story* begins *on page 30.* **2** to take the first step or do the first act; start: *I'll* begin *tomorrow. Work* began *yesterday.* ***vt-:*** *to* begin *a fad; to* begin *rehearsals.*

be·gin·ner (bĭ gĭn′ ər) ***n-*** one who is just starting in; one who has had no training or experience; novice.

be·gin·ning (bĭ gĭn′ ĭng) ***n-*** **1** a start: *the* beginning *of a race.* **2** time or place of origin; source: *a river's* beginning *in the mountains.* **3** first part: *the* beginning *of a tale.*

be·gone (bē gòn′, -gŏn′) ***interj-*** go away!

be·gon·ia (bĭ gōn′ yə) ***n-*** any of various related plants grown for their decorative leaves and variously colored, often very showy flowers.

be·got (bĭ gŏt′) *p.t. & p.p.* of **beget.**

be·got·ten *p.p.* of **beget.**

be·grime (bĭ grīm′, bē-) ***vt-*** [**be·grimed, be·grim·ing**] to soil; make grimy.

be·grudge (bĭ grŭj′) ***vt-*** [**be·grudged, be·grudg·ing**] **1** to envy (a person) the possession of something: *I don't* begrudge *him the honor.* **2** to give reluctantly: *I* begrudge *the money it cost me.* **3** to regard with displeasure; disapprove of: *He* begrudged *the pleasures of others.* **—*adv-*** **be·grudg′ ing·ly:** *He spoke* begrudgingly *of his opponent's victory.*

be·guile (bĭ gīl′) ***vt-*** [**be·guiled, be·guil·ing**] **1** to deceive: *They* beguiled *the enemy into an ambush.* **2** to amuse; charm; delight: *He* beguiled *us with stories.* **3** to pass pleasantly: *to* beguile *the time.*

be·guine (bĭ gēn′) ***n-*** **1** a lively dance of the West Indies, similar to the rhumba. **2** music for this dance.

be·gum (bē′ gəm) ***n-*** princess or other high-ranking lady among Muslims.

be·gun (bĭ gŭn′) *p.p.* of **begin.**

be·half (bĭ hăf′) ***n-*** interest; support; favor.

in (or **on**) **behalf of** for; in the interest of: *He spoke* in behalf of *the plan.*

be·have (bĭ hāv′) ***vi-*** [**be·haved, be·hav·ing**] **1** to act; conduct oneself: *He* behaved *like a fool.* **2** to act properly; do what is right (often with "oneself," "himself," etc.): *Please let me go and I'll* behave *myself.*

be·hav·ior (bĭ hāv′ yər) ***n-*** way of acting; conduct; actions: *good* behavior. **—*adj-*** **be·hav′ ior·al.**

behavioral sciences ***n-*** *pl.* branches of study having to do with human behavior; especially, the fields of anthropology, psychology, and sociology.

be·head (bĭ hĕd, bē-) ***vt-*** to cut off the head of: *Charles I of England was* beheaded *in 1649.*

be·held (bĭ hĕld′) *p.t. & p.p.* of **behold.**

be·he·moth or **Be·he·moth** (bē′ ə mòth′, bĭ hē′ məth) ***n-*** **1** in the Bible, an enormous animal, perhaps a hippopotamus. **2** anything huge or oppressive.

be·hest (bĭ hĕst′) ***n-*** urging; prompting: *At the* behest *of friends he decided to take a rest.*

be·hind (bĭ hīnd′) ***prep-*** (in senses 3, 4, and 5 considered an adverb when the object is clearly implied but not expressed) 1 in or at the rear of; at the back: *The children are* behind *the house.* 2 to or on the other side of; beyond: *They hid* behind *some rocks. The army disappeared* behind *the hill.* 3 following: *He trailed along* behind *the marching column.* 4 remaining after: *He left much unfinished work* behind *him when he died.* 5 inferior to; below the level of: *Tom was* behind *the others in his studies.* 6 later than or after: *The train is* behind *schedule.* 7 in support of; backing up: *Congress was* behind *the President on the foreign aid bill.* 8 hidden by; not revealed by: *There's something* behind *her words.* ***adv-*** in arrears; not up to date: *She has fallen* behind *in her payments.*

be·hind·hand (bĭ hīnd′ hănd′) ***adj-*** behind; slow.

be·hold (bĭ hōld′) ***vt-*** **[be·held, be·hold·ing]** to look at; gaze upon; see: *At last they* beheld *the Promised Land.* **—*n-* be·hold′ er.**

be·hoove (bĭ ho͞ov′) ***vt-*** **[be·hooved, be·hoov·ing]** to be necessary or proper or fitting for: *It* behooves *you to apologize.* Also **be·hove** (bĭ hōv′).

beige (bāzh) ***n-*** the pale-tan color of unbleached wool. ***adj-***: *a* beige *spaniel.*

be·ing (bē′ ĭng) ***n-*** 1 living creature: *a human* being. 2 existence: *The airplane did not come into* being *until gasoline engines were invented.* 3 that which makes a thing or person what it is; essence: *His very* being *rebelled at the suggestion.* 4 **the Supreme Being** God.

be·jew·el (bĭ jo͞o′ əl, bē-) ***vt-*** to adorn or deck with jewels.

be·lab·or (bĭ lā′ bər) ***vt-*** 1 to beat with hard blows: *The farmer* belabored *his mule.* 2 to keep after; assail: *They* belabored *the candidate with questions.* 3 to work on or discuss (something) to an absurd length: *We understand your position; let's not* belabor *the question any longer.*

be·lat·ed (bĭ lā′ təd) ***adj-*** delayed: *a* belated *birthday greeting*; *a* belated *arrival.* **—*adv-* be·lat′ ed·ly. *n-* be·lat′ ed·ness.**

be·lay (bĭ lā′) ***vt-*** in sailors' language, to make fast, as a running rope, by winding around a pin, cleat, or the like. ***interj-*** stop!

belaying pin ***n-*** adjustable pin to which ropes are made fast.

belch (bĕlch) ***vi-*** 1 to discharge gas noisily from the stomach through the mouth. 2 to throw out its contents violently: *The volcano rumbled and* belched. ***vt-*** to throw out with force: *The volcano* belched *molten rock and ashes.* ***n-***: *He stifled a* belch *with his hand.*

bel·dam or **bel·dame** (bĕl′ dəm) ***n-*** ugly old woman; hag; witch.

be·lea·guer (bĭ lē′ gər) ***vt-*** to besiege; surround: *The enemy* beleaguered *the city.*

bel·fry (bĕl′ frē) ***n-*** [*pl.* **bel·fries**] bell tower; the part of a tower or cupola where a bell is hung.

Belfry

Belgian hare ***n-*** breed of unusually large, red-brown, domestic rabbits.

Be·li·al (bē′ lē əl) ***n-*** 1 in the Bible, Satan. 2 in Milton's "Paradise Lost," one of the fallen angels.

be·lie (bĭ lī′) ***vt-*** **[be·lied, be·ly·ing]** 1 to give a false notion of: *his appearance* belies *his feelings.* 2 to fail to come up to or to accord with: *His acts* belie *his words.*

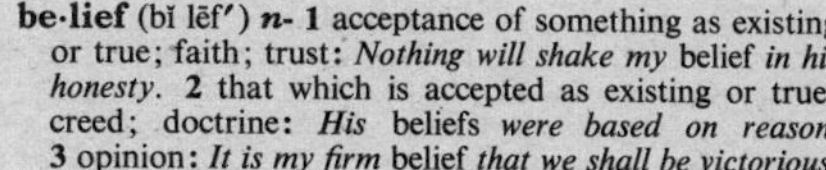

be·lief (bĭ lēf′) ***n-*** 1 acceptance of something as existing or true; faith; trust: *Nothing will shake my* belief *in his honesty.* 2 that which is accepted as existing or true; creed; doctrine: *His* beliefs *were based on reason.* 3 opinion: *It is my firm* belief *that we shall be victorious.*

be·lieve (bĭ lēv′) ***vt-*** **[be·lieved, be·liev·ing]** 1 to accept as true: *We* believe *her story.* 2 to trust the word of; have confidence in: *I* believe *him.* 3 to have the opinion that: *Do you* believe *it will rain tomorrow?* ***vi-*** to have faith, trust, or confidence (in): *to* believe *in God*; *to* believe *in our ability to win.* **—*adj-* be·liev′ able.**

make believe to pretend; imagine; fancy: *Children often* make believe *they are famous heroes.*

be·liev·er (bĭ lē′ vər) ***n-*** 1 one who believes: *a* believer *of gossip.* 2 one who has faith in a religious doctrine.

be·lit·tle (bĭ lĭt′ əl, bē-) ***vt-*** **[be·lit·tled, be·lit·tling]** to make little of; speak scornfully of: *He* belittles *our city in his book.* **—*n-* be·lit′ tle·ment:** *His* belittlement *of everything is annoying.*

[1]**bell** (bĕl) ***n-*** 1 hollow metal instrument, usually cup-shaped, which makes a ringing sound when struck with a clapper or hammer. 2 anything shaped like a bell: *the* bell *of a horn*; *a diving* bell. 3 stroke sounded on a ship's chimes, each stroke meaning a half hour of time. ***vt-*** to put a bell on: *The mice decided to* bell *the cat.* [from Old English **belle.**] ***Hom-*** belle.

Bells

[2]**bell** (bĕl) ***vi-*** to cry, as a stag or a hound. ***n-***: *the* bell *of the hounds.* [from Old English **bellan,** related to **bellow.**] ***Hom-*** belle.

bel·la·don·na (bĕl′ ə dŏn′ ə) ***n-*** 1 poisonous Old World plant from which the drug atropine is obtained; deadly nightshade. 2 the drug itself.

bell·bird (bĕl′ bûrd′) ***n-*** any of various birds of the Southern Hemisphere whose songs sound like ringing bells.

bell·boy (bĕl′ boi′) ***n-*** boy or man who carries suitcases, runs errands, etc., in a hotel.

bell buoy ***n-*** a warning buoy having a bell that rings because of the movement of the waves.

belle (bĕl) ***n-*** 1 beautiful woman or girl. 2 the most popular girl or woman: *the* belle *of the ball.* ***Hom-*** bell.

belles-let·tres (bĕl′ lĕt′ rə) ***n-*** *pl.* types of literature having largely an artistic rather than an informational value or appeal, including novels, drama, poetry, etc.

bell·flow·er (bĕl′ flou′ ər) ***n-*** any of many plants that bear blue or violet bell-shaped flowers.

bell·hop (bĕl′ hŏp′) ***n-*** *Informal* bellboy.

bel·li·cose (bĕl′ ə kōs′) ***adj-*** inclined to fight; quarrelsome: *a* bellicose *disposition*; *a* bellicose *nation.*

bel·lig·er·ence (bə lĭj′ er əns) ***n-*** 1 tendency or eagerness to fight: *I can't understand Harry's* belligerence *about such a trivial matter.* 2 belligerency.

bel·lig·er·en·cy (bə lĭj′ ər ən sē) ***n-*** 1 of a nation, the condition of being at war, formally recognized by other nations. 2 belligerence.

bel·lig·er·ent (bə lĭj′ ər ənt) ***adj-*** 1 waging war: *a* belligerent *nation.* 2 quarrelsome; warlike: *the speaker's* belligerent *words*; *a* belligerent *person.* ***n-*** nation or person at war. **—*adv-* bel·lig′ er·ent·ly.**

bell jar ***n-*** bell-shaped glass cover used in laboratories for protecting instruments, creating vacuums, etc.

fāte, făt, dâre, bärn; bē, bĕt, mêre; bīte, bĭt; nōte, hŏt, môre, dȯg; fŭn, fûr; to͞o, bo͝ok; oil; out; tar; thin; then; hw for wh as in *wh*at; zh for s as in u*s*ual; ə for a, e, i, o, u, as in *a*go, lin*e*n, per*i*l, at*o*m, min*u*s

bell·man (bĕl′ mən) ***n-*** [*pl.* **bell·men**] town crier.

bel·low (bĕl′ ō) ***n-* 1** the loud, deep roar of a bull. **2** any loud, deep cry. ***vi-* 1** to make a loud, roaring cry: *The bulls* bellowed *when they saw each other.* **2** to cry out in a loud, deep voice; roar; bawl: *The movie director* bellowed *at the cameraman.* ***vt-***: *The bulls* bellowed *defiance at each other. The captain* bellowed *his orders.*

bel·lows (bĕl′ ōz) ***n-*** instrument for blowing air into a fire, the pipes of an organ, etc.

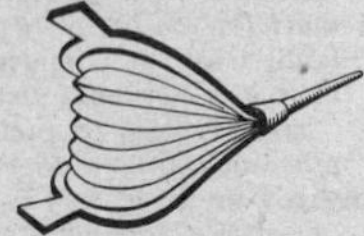

Bellows for fire

bell·weth·er (bĕl′ wĕth′ ər) ***n-*** a male sheep, or wether, wearing a bell and leading the flock.

bel·ly (bĕl′ē) ***n-*** [*pl.* **bel·lies**] **1** front part of the body of man between the chest and the thighs, containing the stomach and bowels; the abdomen; also, the similar underside of the body of an animal. **2** the inside or underside of anything, such as a ship or plane. **3** the bulging part of anything, such as a laboratory flask. ***vi-*** [**bel·lied, bel·ly·ing**] to swell out; bulge: *The sails* bellied *in the wind.* ***vt-***: *The wind* bellied *the sails.*

bel·ly·ache (bĕl′ ē āk′) ***n-*** a stomach ache. ***vi-*** *Slang* [**bel·ly·ached, bel·ly·ach·ing**] to complain loudly or for a long time.

be·long (bĭ lòng′) ***vi-*** to have a proper, suitable, or rightful place: *This tool* belongs *in the drawer. Small children* belong *in bed after dinner.*

belong to 1 to be the property of: *This book* belongs to *the library.* **2** to be a member or part of: *He* belongs to *the club. The spoon* belongs to *that set.*

be·long·ings (bĭ lòng′ ĭngz) ***n-*** *pl.* personal property; possessions, especially those that can be moved, such as clothes, furniture, etc.

be·lov·ed (bĭ lŭv′ əd, -lŭvd′) ***adj-*** greatly loved. ***n-*** person who is greatly loved.

be·low (bĭ lō′) ***prep-*** (in senses 1 and 2 considered an adverb when the object is clearly implied but not expressed) **1** lower than, in place, rank, excellence, price, etc.; underneath: *He has the locker* below *mine. They live in the apartment* below. *Write your signature* below. **2** under or down from (the upper parts of a ship): *Go* below *decks. Stow the gear* below. *The sailors* below *were sleeping.* **3** undeserving or unworthy of; beneath: *The play is so bad that it is* below *criticism.*

Bel·shaz·zar (bĕl shăz′ ər) ***n-*** in the Old Testament, the son of Nebuchadnezzar and last ruler of Babylon.

belt (bĕlt) ***n-* 1** band of leather, cloth, or other material worn around the waist as an ornament or as a support for a garment or weapon. **2** a wide strip or band: *a* belt *of trees around a town.* **3** a region having certain distinctive characteristics: *the Cotton* Belt. **4** a band running around two or more wheels or pulleys to pass motion from one to the other. ***vt-* 1** to encircle with, or as with, a band: *The equator* belts *the earth.* **2** to fasten (on) with a waist strap: *The knight* belted *on his sword.* **3** to beat with a strap. **4** *Informal* to hit. **5** *Slang* to sing loudly and with force.

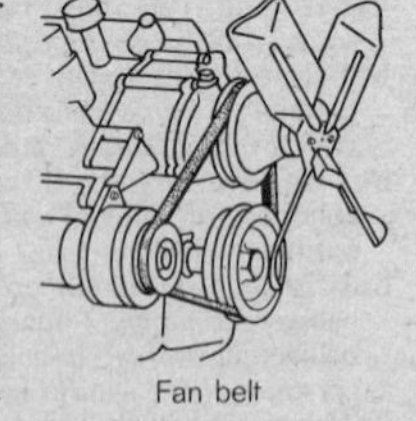

Fan belt

hit below the belt to fight unfairly. **tighten (one's) belt** to spend less; become thrifty and frugal.

belt·ing (bĕl′ tĭng) ***n-* 1** material used for belts. **2** belts. **3** *Informal* a severe beating.

be·lu·ga (bə lo͞o′ gə) ***n-* 1** large, white, Arctic dolphin, often called the white whale. **2** large, white sturgeon of the Black and Caspian seas, whose roe is used for caviar.

be·moan (bĭ mōn′, bē-) ***vt-*** to grieve for; bewail: *to* bemoan *one's misfortunes.*

be·mused (bĭ myo͞ozd′, bē-) ***adj-* 1** bewildered; confused. **2** lost in thought; absent-minded.

bench (bĕnch) ***n-* 1** a long seat. **2** the seat judges sit on in court. **3** position of judge: *He was chosen for the* bench *by the President.* **4** judges as a group. **5** a strong work table at which craftsmen work. ***vt-*** in sports, to keep (a player) out of a game.

bench mark ***n-*** in surveying, a mark made on a rock, wall, etc., having a known position and elevation, and used as a reference point to determine elevations of other places.

bench warrant ***n-*** in law, a warrant issued by a judge in court for the arrest of a person.

bend (bĕnd) ***vt-*** [**bent, bend·ing**] **1** to make curved or crooked: *This machine* bends *metal rods. The wind* bent *the poplar.* **2** to turn (one's attention, thoughts, steps, etc.) in a certain direction: *Let's* bend *our energies to finishing the task. He* bent *his steps toward home.* **3** to force to submit or yield: *The tyrant* bent *the people to his will.* ***vi-* 1** to become curved or crooked: *The beam* bent *under the heavy weight.* **2** to turn: *The road* bends *to the left.* **3** to submit or yield: *I* bend *to your wishes.* ***n-* 1** a turn or curve: *a* bend *in the road.* **2** knot which fastens one rope to another rope or to something else.

bend·ed (bĕn′ dəd) ***adj-*** *Archaic* bent.

on bended knee in a humble or imploring manner: *He asked* on bended knee *for the release of his daughter.*

bends (bĕnz) ***n-*** *pl.* caisson disease.

be·neath (bĭ nēth′) ***prep-*** (in sense 1 considered an adverb when the object is clearly implied but not expressed) **1** under: *The great fish lurked* beneath *the rock.* **2** under the power or weight of: *to sink* beneath *troubles.* **3** lower than: *a rank* beneath *captain.* **5** undeserving or unworthy of: *The letter was* beneath *his notice. The work was* beneath *him.*

ben·e·dic·i·te (bĕn′ ə dĭs′ ə tē) ***n-* 1** the asking of a blessing; also, the blessing. **2 Benedicite** Latin hymn of praise in the Book of Common Prayer, beginning with this word.

Ben·e·dic·tine (bĕn′ ə dĭk′ tēn, -tən) ***n-* 1** monk or nun of the order founded by St. Benedict in Italy about 530 A.D. **2** trademark name of a liqueur originally made by the monks of this order. ***adj-***: *a* Benedictine *monastery.*

ben·e·dic·tion (bĕn′ ə dĭk′ shən) ***n-*** a blessing, such as the one pronounced at the end of a church service.

ben·e·fac·tion (bĕn′ ə făk′ shən) ***n-*** charitable gift.

ben·e·fac·tor (bĕn′ ə făk′ tər) ***n-*** person who helps another, either with service or with money; patron.

ben·e·fice (bĕn′ ə fəs) ***n-*** an endowed office or position in the Church of England.

be·nef·i·cence (bə nĕf′ ə səns, bə nĭf′-) ***n-*** active kindness; charitable gift: *His* beneficence *relieved the poor.*

be·nef·i·cent (bə nĕf′ ə sənt, bə nĭf′-) ***adj-*** doing or causing good. ***—adv-*** **be·nef′ i·cent·ly.**

ben·e·fi·cial (bĕn′ ə fĭsh′ əl) ***adj-*** helpful; producing good results: *Food and sleep are* beneficial *to health.* ***—adv-*** **ben·e·fi′ cial·ly.**

ben·e·fi·ci·ar·y (bĕn′ ə fĭsh′ ə rē, -fĭsh′ ē ĕr′ ē) ***n-*** [*pl.* **ben·e·fi·ci·ar·ies**] one who receives anything as a gift or benefit; especially, the person named on an insurance policy to receive part or all of the insurance.

ben·e·fit (bĕn′ ə fĭt′) *n-* **1** anything that is of help; advantage. **2** act of kindness. **3** public entertainment to raise money for a worthy cause. *vt-* to do good to; help: *The rest* benefited *his health.* *vi-* to get good (from); receive help; profit: *He* benefited *from his past experience.*

Ben·e·lux (bĕn′ ə lŭks′) *n-* the economic union of Belgium, the Netherlands, and Luxemburg.

be·nev·o·lence (bə nĕv′ ə ləns) *n-* **1** desire to do good for others; good will: *His* benevolence *led him to work for charitable organizations.* **2** an act of kindness.

be·nev·o·lent (bə nĕv′ ə lənt) *adj-* wanting and promoting good for others; kind and helpful. *—adv-* **be·nev′ o·lent·ly.**

be·night·ed (bĭ nī′ təd) *adj-* **1** in moral or intellectual darkness; ignorant: *a* benighted *savage.* **2** *Archaic* overtaken by the darkness of night.

be·nign (bĭ nīn′) *adj-* **1** of a kind or gentle disposition. **2** favorable; healthful: *a* benign *sea breeze.* **3** *Medicine* not malignant; harmless. *—adv-* **be·nign′ ly.**

be·nig·nant (bə nĭg′ nənt) *adj-* benign. *—n-* **be·nig′ nan·cy.**

be·nig·ni·ty (bĭ nĭg′ nə tē) *n-* [*pl.* **be·nig·ni·ties**] kindliness of nature; graciousness.

ben·i·son (bĕn′ ə sən) *n-* blessing; benediction.

Ben·ja·min (bĕn′ jə mən) *n-* in the Old Testament, the youngest son of Jacob; founder of one of the twelve tribes of Israel.

bent (bĕnt) *p.t. & p.p.* of **bend.** *adj-* **1** curved; crooked: *a* bent *twig.* **2** determined; set: *He is* bent *on becoming a doctor.* *n-* a natural ability or inclination: *He has a* bent *for painting.*

be·numb (bĭ nŭm′, bē-) *vt-* to make numb; deprive of feeling or ability to act: *The cold* benumbed *our fingers. Fear* benumbed *his mind.*

Ben·ze·drine (bĕn′ zə drēn′) *n-* trademark name for a powerful, stimulant drug. Also **ben′ ze·drine′.**

ben·zene (bĕn′ zēn, bĕn zēn′) *n-* colorless, flammable liquid (C_6H_6); benzol. It is distilled from coal tar and used chiefly to make organic chemicals and as an industrial solvent. It is sometimes confused with benzine.

ben·zine (bĕn′ zēn, bĕn zēn′) *n-* colorless flammable liquid, a mixture of several compounds distilled from petroleum, used as a motor fuel and industrial solvent. It is sometimes confused with benzene.

ben·zo·ate of soda (bĕn′ zō āt′) *n-* sodium benzoate.

ben·zo·ic acid (bĕn zō′ ĭk) *n-* white, crystalline, organic acid (C_6H_5COOH) found in certain berries and made synthetically for manufacturing other organic chemicals.

ben·zo·in (bĕn′ zō ən) *n-* fragrant yellowish resin of a tree of Southeast Asia, used in medicine, perfumes, and incense; also, the tree itself, the spicebush.

ben·zol (bĕn′ zòl′, -zōl′) *n-* benzene, especially an impure industrial grade.

Be·o·wulf (bā′ ə wo͝olf′) *n-* **1** hero of an Anglo-Saxon epic poem of the eighth century, who killed the monsters Grendel and Grendel's mother. **2** the poem itself.

be·queath (bĭ kwēth′, bĭ kwēth′) *vt-* **1** to give or leave by will: *He* bequeathed *his money to his sons.* **2** to hand down: *Our forefathers* bequeathed *us a love of liberty.*

be·quest (bĭ kwĕst′) *n-* something given or left by will; a legacy: *Small* bequests *went to the grandchildren.*

be·rate (bĭ rāt′) *vt-* [**be·rat·ed, be·rat·ing**] to scold; upbraid: *The mother* berated *him for losing his skates.*

Ber·ber (bûr′ bər) *n-* **1** member of a group of northern African Muslims. **2** the language of these people. *adj-*: *a* Berber *tribesman.*

be·reave (bĭ rēv′) *vt-* [**be·reaved, be·reav·ing**] to deprive (a person) of a loved one, usually by death: *The accident* bereaved *him of his entire family.*

be·reave·ment (bĭ rēv′ mənt) *n-* **1** the condition of being left desolate. **2** the loss of a relative or friend by death.

be·reft (bĭ rĕft′) *adj-* stripped (of): *He was* bereft *of happiness. She is* bereft *of good sense.*

be·ret (bə rā′) *n-* round, close-fitting cap of wool or other soft material, without a brim.

Man wearing beret

berg (bûrg) *n-* iceberg.

be·rib·boned (bĭ rĭb′ ənd) *adj-* covered or adorned with many ribbons: *a* beribboned *general.*

ber·i·ber·i (bĕ′ rē bĕ′ rē) *n-* disease of the nervous system, caused by lack of vitamin B_1.

berke·li·um (bûr′ klē əm, bûr′ kē′ lē əm) *n-* man-made radioactive metallic element. Symbol Bk, At. No. 97.

Ber·noul·li's principle (bûr no͞o′ lēz) *n-* principle of physics which states that the faster a horizontally moving fluid flows, the less pressure it exerts. The principle helps to explain how an airplane wing provides lift.

ber·ry (bĕr′ ē) *n-* [*pl.* **ber·ries**] **1** any small juicy and stoneless fruit, such as a strawberry. **2** *Biology* a fleshy, many-seeded fruit such as the tomato, currant, or cranberry. **3** the dry seed or kernel of some grains: *wheat* berry. **4** fruit of the coffee tree; coffee berry. ***Hom-*** bury. *—adj-* **ber′ ry·like′.**

ber·ry·ing (bĕr′ ē ĭng) *n-* picking or gathering berries: *We went* berrying *in July.*

ber·serk (bər sûrk′, -zûrk′, bûr′ sûrk′) *adj-* in a violent or destructive rage; frenzied; frantic.

go (or **run**) **berserk** to go into an uncontrollable, often violent, rage.

ber·serk·er (bûr′ sûr′ kər) *n-* in Norse legend, a warrior who became frenzied in battle.

berth (bûrth) *n-* **1** bed, in a train, ship, or plane, which is built like a large shelf; a bunk. **2** place where a ship ties up or lies at anchor. **3** a position or job: *He has a good* berth *with the government.* ***Hom-*** birth.

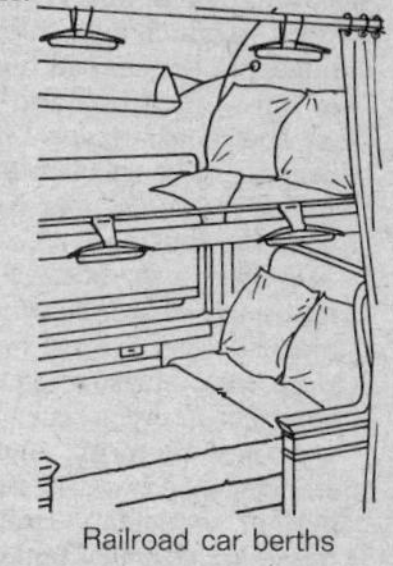

Railroad car berths

Ber·til·lon system (bûr′ tə lŏn′, bĕr tē ōn′) *n-* system for identifying persons, based on body measurements, scars, hair and eye color, etc., now replaced by fingerprint identification.

ber·yl (bĕr′ əl) *n-* semi-precious or precious stone of varying colors, commonly green or greenish blue. The aquamarine and the emerald are beryls.

be·ryl·li·um (bə rĭl′ ē əm) *n-* very light, whitish-gray, strong, brittle metal element. Symbol Be, At. No. 4, At. Wt. 9.1022.

be·seech (bĭ sēch′) *vt-* [**be·sought, be·seech·ing**] **1** to implore; entreat: *We* beseech *you, O King, to hear our plea.* **2** to beg for; plead strongly for: *We* beseech *your mercy.*

be·seem (bĭ sēm′) *vt-* to be suitable or becoming to; befit: *It hardly* beseems *you to bully your sister.*

be·set (bĭ sĕt′) ***vt-*** [**be·set, be·set·ting**] **1** to attack from all sides; assail: *Many doubts* beset *him.* **2** to surround; hem in: *Danger* beset *his path.*

be·set·ting (bĭ sĕt′ĭng) ***adj-*** constantly attacking; habitually tempting: *Greed is the miser's* besetting *sin.*

be·shrew (bĭ shrōō′, bē-) *Archaic* ***vt-*** to curse; plague.

be·side (bĭ sīd′) ***prep-*** **1** at or by the side of; nearby: *He stood* beside *me.* **2** in comparison with: *My foot is small* beside *yours.* **3** away from: *a case* beside *the point.*

beside (oneself) very excited; out of one's senses, as from anger, fear, etc.: *He was* beside himself *with rage.*

be·sides (bĭ sīdz′) ***adv-*** in addition; also; as well: *There will be hunting, fishing, and hiking, and swimming* besides. ***prep-*** in addition to; over and above: *The book club is giving a record album* besides *its book dividend.*

be·siege (bĭ sēj′) ***vt-*** [**be·sieged, be·sieg·ing**] **1** to lay siege to; to surround in order to capture: *For nine weeks the enemy* besieged *the castle.* **2** to pester or harass: *They* besieged *the actor for autographs.*

be·smear (bĭ smêr′, bē-) ***vt-*** to smear or daub with something greasy or sticky.

be·smirch (bĭ smûrch′) ***vt-*** to soil or sully, especially to sully someone's reputation, honor, etc.

be·sot·ted (bĭ sŏt′əd) ***adj-*** **1** stupefied, especially with drink. **2** infatuated: *a person* besotted *with his own self-importance.*

be·sought (bĭ sȯt′) *p.t. & p.p.* of **beseech.**

be·span·gle (bĭ spăng′gəl, bē-) ***vt-*** [**be·span·gled, be·span·gling**] to sprinkle or adorn with, or as if with, spangles.

be·spat·ter (bĭ spăt′ər, bē-) ***vt-*** to soil by splashing with wet mud, paint, or the like.

be·speak (bĭ spēk′, bē-) ***vt-*** [**be·spoke, be·spo·ken** or **be·spoke, be·speak·ing**] to give evidence of; show: *His good manners* bespeak *a fine upbringing.*

be·spec·ta·cled (bĭ spĕk′tə kəld, bē-) ***adj-*** wearing eyeglasses: *the small,* bespectacled *professor.*

Bes·se·mer process (bĕs′ə mər) ***n-*** process for making steel, in which air is blown through molten pig iron in a huge, pitcher-shaped furnace called a **Bessemer converter** to burn off carbon and impurities.

best (bĕst) ***adj-*** (*superl.* of **good**) **1** good in the highest degree; most excellent; finest: *Jane's work is good, but Ralph's is better, and Stan's is* best. **2** largest: *The job took the* best *part of a week to finish.* ***n-*** **1** the finest: *You deserve the* best. **2** height of excellence: *I am at my* best *early in the morning.* ***adv-*** (*superl.* of [2]**well**) in the most successful way: *I can write* best *after a good night's sleep.* ***vt-*** surpass; get the better of: *He* bested *his opponent in every race.*

at best at most; under the most favorable circumstances: *The book,* at best, *may sell 1000 copies.* **get the best of** to defeat. **make the best of** to do as well as possible: *We must* make the best of *a bad bargain.*

bes·tial (bĕs′chəl, bēs′-) ***adj-*** like the beasts; brutish; savage: *The fighting was carried on with* bestial *cruelty.* **—*n-*** **bes′ti·al′i·ty** (bĕs′chē ăl′ə tē). ***adv-*** **bes′tial·ly.**

be·stir (bĭ stûr′) ***vt-*** [**be·stirred, be·stir·ring**] to rouse; exert: *He* bestirred *himself to answer the telephone.*

best man ***n-*** bridegroom's chief attendant at a wedding.

be·stow (bĭ stō′) ***vt-*** to give or confer: *to* bestow *a medal on a hero.*

be·stow·al (bĭ stō′əl) ***n-*** act of giving or bestowing: *the* bestowal *of many favors.*

be·strew (bĭ strōō′) ***vt-*** [**be·strewed, be·strewed** or **be·strewn, be·strew·ing**] **1** to cover (a surface) with things scattered: *to* bestrew *a table with papers.* **2** to scatter (things) about. **3** to lie scattered over: *Stars* bestrewed *the sky.*

be·stride (bĭ strīd′) ***vt-*** [**be·strode, be·strid·den, be·strid·ing**] to mount, sit on, or stand over with one leg on each side; straddle: *to* bestride *a horse.*

best seller ***n-*** book that has a very large sale. ***as modifier*** **(best-seller):** *The* best-seller *list.*

bet (bĕt) ***vt-*** [**bet** or **bet·ted, bet·ting**] to stake, risk, or wager (money or the like) that something will or will not happen, or on the victory of a chosen competitor: *I* bet *a dollar that it will rain today. I* bet *ten dollars on the home team.* ***vi-*** **1** to lay a wager: *to* bet *on a horse.* **2** to guess with some conviction: *I'll* bet *Danny was there yesterday.* ***n-*** **1** a wager: *to make a* bet. **2** the amount staked or wagered: *My* bet *was ten dollars.* **3** something on which a wager is laid: *This horse is a safe* bet.

be·ta (bā′tə) ***n-*** second letter in the Greek alphabet (β), corresponding to the English "B."

be·take (bĭ tāk′, bē-) ***vt-*** [**be·took, be·tak·en, be·tak·ing**] to take (oneself): *They* betook *themselves to a place of safety.*

beta particle ***n-*** electron given off by an atom of a radioactive element and moving at nearly the speed of light.

beta ray ***n-*** stream of beta particles.

be·ta·tron (bā′tə trŏn′) ***n-*** atomic particle accelerator that drives electrons to nearly the speed of light for bombarding atoms.

be·tel (bē′təl) ***n-*** **1** Asian palm tree that produces the **betel nut.** **2** an Asian vine of the pepper family from which **betel leaves** are obtained. **3** a chewing wad made up of a piece of betel nut rolled up in a lime-covered betel leaf. It is chewed for physical stimulation. ***Hom-*** beetle.

Be·tel·geuse (bĕt′əl jōōz′) ***n-*** very bright reddish star in the constellation Orion.

bête noire (bĕt nwär′) *French* ***n-*** black beast; hence, something that is especially disliked; bugbear.

beth·el (bĕth′əl) ***n-*** **1** holy place. **2** chapel; especially, a seamen's chapel.

be·think (bĭ thĭngk′) ***vt-*** [**be·thought, be·think·ing**] to remember (often used with "myself," "himself," etc.): *I* bethought *myself of an errand.*

be·tide (bĭ tīd′, bē tīd′) *Informal* ***vt-*** [**be·tid·ed, be·tid·ing**] to happen to; befall: *What will* betide *us, none can tell.* ***vi-*** to come to pass.

be·times (bĭ tīmz′) ***adv-*** early; promptly.

be·to·ken (bĭ tō′kən) ***vt-*** to be a token or sign of; foreshadow: *A red sunset is said to* betoken *hot weather.*

be·took (bĭ tōōk′, bē-) *p.t.* of **betake.**

be·tray (bĭ trā′) ***vt-*** **1** to give into the hands of an enemy by deceit: *A disloyal soldier* betrayed *the army.* **2** to be disloyal to: *Would you* betray *a friend?* **3** to reveal (something intended to be hidden): *to* betray *a secret; to* betray *one's nervousness by stammering.* **—*n-*** **be·tray′al:** *a dastardly* betrayal *of my confidence.* ***n-*** **be·tray′er.**

be·troth (bĭ trŏth′, -trōth′) ***vt-*** to promise to give (a daughter) in marriage.

be·troth·al (bĭ trŏth′əl, -trōth′əl) ***n-*** a promise to marry; engagement: *Her* betrothal *was announced in the newspaper.*

be·trothed (bĭ trōthd′, -trŏtht′) ***n-*** the person to whom one is engaged to be married.

bet·ter (bĕt′ər) ***adj-*** (*compar.* of **good**) **1** more excellent; of higher quality: *Apples are* better *in the fall. My work is* better *now. His swimming stroke is* better *than mine.* **2** larger; greater: *The walk takes the* better *part of an hour.* **3** improved in health: *The patient is* better *today.* ***adv-*** (*compar.* of [2]**well**) **1** in a finer way: *He swims* better *than I do.* **2** to a larger degree: *I like her* better *than I* *used to.* **3** *Informal* more: *It is* better *than an hour since he telephoned.* ***vt-*** to improve: *She took some courses to* better *herself.* ***n-*** of two, the one of higher quality: *She bought the* better *of the two coats.* ***Hom-*** bettor.

better off in better conditions or circumstances. **(one's) betters** those who exceed one in rank, ability, wealth, wisdom, etc. **get the better of** to win an advantage over: *He* got the better of *his opponent.* **had better** would be safer to or wiser to; ought to: *You* had better *go before it rains. Yes, he* had better *start looking for another job.* **think better of** to reconsider in favor of a wiser course: *I wanted to go, but* thought better of *it when it began to snow.*

bet·ter·ment (bět′ ər mənt) ***n-*** a bringing to a better condition, improvement.

bet·tor (bět′ər) ***n-*** person who bets; gambler. Also **bet·ter.**

be·tween (bĭ twēn′) ***prep-*** (in senses 1-5 and 7, considered an adverb when the object is clearly implied but not expressed) **1** in the space which separates two objects or things: *There is a narrow lane* between *the two houses.* **2** in the time which separates one thing from another: *The accident happened* between *dusk and dark.* **3** more than one thing and less than another: *It is* between *5 and 6 feet long.* **4** from one to another of: *Not a word passed* between *them.* **5** connecting: *There is a bridge* between *the two cities.* **6** by joint action of: *We shall finish this job* between *us.* **7** one or the other of: *Choose* between *the two vases.*

between you and me or **between ourselves** in confidence: *Keep what we found out* between you and me. **in between 1** between. **2** not definitely one or the other; undecided; intermediate; betwixt and between: *Ed and George have made up their minds, but I'm somewhat* in between.

►For usage note see AMONG.

be·twixt (bĭ twĭkst′) ***prep-*** between: *That dream came* betwixt *waking and sleeping.*

betwixt and between in a middle position; neither the one nor the other.

bev or **BEV** billion electron volts.

bev·a·tron (bĕv′ ə trŏn′) ***n-*** very powerful cyclotron capable of accelerating protons to speeds above a billion electron volts.

bev·el (bĕv′əl) ***n-*** **1** slanted face or faces cut along the edge of a table, mirror, piece of crystal, etc.; also, the slanted edge of a cutting tool, such as a chisel. **2** the acute angle of such slanted edges. **3** an instrument used to draw the angles for cutting such an edge. *as modifier*: *a* bevel *edge.* ***vt-*** to cut such an edge (on something): *to* bevel *the edge of a table.*

Bevel

bev·er·age (bĕv′ər ĭj) ***n-*** any kind of drink, as coffee, lemonade, wine, etc.

bev·y (bĕv′ē) ***n-*** [*pl.* **bev·ies**] **1** large group or collection. **2** flock of birds, especially of quail.

be·wail (bĭ wāl′) ***vt-*** to lament; mourn for: *They* bewailed *the death of their leader.*

be·ware (bĭ wâr′, bē-) ***vt-*** (now used only as an imperative or infinitive) to be on guard against: Beware *the dog!* ***vi-*** to be on guard against the hazards (of): Beware *of the dangerous crossing.*

be·wil·der (bĭ wĭl′dər) ***vt-*** to confuse and perplex, especially by too many figures, ideas, directions, etc. ***—n-*** **be′wil′der·ment:** *His* bewilderment *was obvious, so I spoke more slowly.*

be·witch (bĭ wĭch′) ***vt-*** **1** to cast a magic spell over: *The magician* bewitched *the subject.* **2** to fascinate or delight; charm: *The actor* bewitched *the audience.*

be·witch·ing (bĭ wĭch′ĭng) ***adj-*** fascinating; enchanting: *a* bewitching *smile.* ***—adv-*** **be·witch′ing·ly:** *The child smiled* bewitchingly.

bey (bā) ***n-*** **1** governor of a province or district in Turkey. **2** title of the former ruler of the Kingdom of Tunis. ***Hom-*** bay.

be·yond (bĭ yŏnd′) ***prep-*** (in senses 1 and 2 considered an adverb when the object is clearly implied but not expressed) **1** on the farther side of: *My house is* beyond *the hill.* **2** farther than; past: *He dashed well* beyond *the finish line. We talked till well* beyond *five o'clock.* **3** out of the reach of: *She is* beyond *medical help.* ***n-*** **the beyond** (also **the great beyond**) life after death.

bez·el (bĕz′ əl) ***n-*** **1** sloping edge of a cutting tool. **2** any of the sloping faces of a cut gem. For picture, see *gem.* **3** rim or flange on a ring for holding a gem.

bi- *prefix* **1** every two: *a* bi*monthly; a* bi*weekly.* **2** two: *a* bi*cameral legislature* (consisting of two chambers). **3** twice; doubly: *a* bi*convex lens.* [from Latin **bi-**, from **bis** meaning "twice."]

►BI- most often means two, and should not be confused with SEMI-, which means one-half. They are sometimes mixed up in referring to time periods. For example, BIMONTHLY is often used to mean twice a month, although SEMIMONTHLY is preferable. BIANNUAL, however, does mean twice a year (SEMIANNUAL) and not every two years (BIENNIAL).

bi·an·nu·al (bī ăn′yo͞o əl) ***adj-*** occurring twice a year. ***—adv-*** **bi·an′nu·al·ly.**

bi·as (bī′əs) ***n-*** **1** slanting line; the diagonal direction of a cut, seam, or stitching made to slant across the threads of material: *to cut a skirt on the* bias. **2** prejudice: *That article shows a strong* bias *against labor unions.* ***adj-*** slanting; diagonal: *a* bias *seam or joint.* ***vt-*** [**bi·ased, bi·as·ing**] to make a person feel or think a certain way; to prejudice: *The three misstatements in his speech* bias *me against him.*

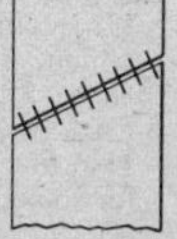
Bias joint on belt

bi·ased (bī əst) ***adj-*** willing to see only one side; prejudiced: *a* biased *editorial; a* biased *speaker.*

bib (bĭb) ***n-*** **1** cloth like a small apron worn under the chin to protect clothes from food. **2** the upper part of an apron or a pair of overalls.

Bib. **1** Bible. **2** Biblical.

Bi·ble (bī′ bəl) ***n-*** **1** sacred writings of the Old and the New Testaments. **2** sacred writings of any religion. **3 bible** *Informal* book on which one relies for accurate information.

bib·li·cal (bĭb′ lĭ kəl) ***adj-*** having to do with the Bible or with times, persons, and events connected with the Bible: *the* biblical *wars;* biblical *scholars;* biblical *geography.*

biblio- *combining form* book: *a* biblio*phile* (one who loves books). [from Greek **biblio-**, from **biblion** meaning "little book."]

bib·li·og·ra·pher (bĭb′lē ŏg′ re fər) ***n-*** maker of bibliographies.

bib·li·og·ra·phy (bĭb′lē ŏg′ rə fē) ***n-*** [*pl.* **bib·li·og·ra·phies**] **1** the study of books, authors, style of printing, dates, editions, and the like. **2** list of books relating to a given subject or author. ***—adj-*** **bib′li·o·graph′i·cal** (bĭb′lē ə grăf′ ĭ kəl). ***adv-*** **bib′li·o·graph′i·cal·ly.**

bib·li·o·phile (bĭb′ lē ə fīl′) ***n-*** book lover.
bib·u·lous (bĭb′yə ləs) ***adj-*** overly fond of alcoholic drink.
bi·cam·er·al (bī′ kăm′ ər əl) ***adj-*** consisting of two legislative chambers or branches. The U.S. Congress is bicameral.
bi·car·bon·ate (bī kär′ bə nət) ***n-*** a chemical compound containing the hydrogen carbonate radical (HCO_3—); a salt of carbonic acid.
bicarbonate of soda ***n-*** sodium bicarbonate.
bi·cen·ten·ni·al (bī′ sĕn tĕn′ ē əl) ***adj-*** occurring every 200 years. ***n-*** a 200th anniversary or its celebration.
bi·ceps (bī′ sĕps′) ***n-*** [*pl.* **bi·ceps**] **1** the large muscle on the front of the upper arm. **2** a similar leg muscle that flexes the knee.
bi·chlor·ide (bī klôr′ īd) ***n-*** **1** mercuric chloride. **2** any salt whose molecules contain two chlorine atoms each.
bichloride of mercury ***n-*** mercuric chloride.
bick·er (bĭk′ ər) ***vi-*** to quarrel; squabble: *The girls* bickered *over which TV program to turn on.* ***n-*** angry or petty dispute: *to get into a* bicker.
bi·con·cave (bī′ kŏn′ kāv′) ***adj-*** of surfaces and lenses, concave on both sides.
bi·con·vex (bī′ kŏn′ vĕks′) ***adj-*** of surfaces and lenses, convex on both sides.
bi·cus·pid (bī kŭs′ pĭd) ***n-*** one of the eight teeth having two points. For picture, see *teeth.*
bi·cy·cle (bī′ sĭ kəl) ***n-*** light vehicle with two wheels, one behind the other, a saddlelike seat, foot pedals for propelling it, and handlebars for steering. ***vi-*** **[bi·cy·cled, bi·cy·cling]**: *Let's* bicycle *over to the park.* **—*n-*** **bi′ cy·cler** or **bi′ cy·clist.**
bid (bĭd) ***vt-*** **[bade** (băd) or **bid, bid·den** or **bid, bid·ding]** **1** to command; order; request: *The captain* bade *us to halt.* **2** to invite: *The host* bade *us make ourselves at home.* **3** to say as a greeting or farewell: *Let's* bid *them good-by.* **4** to offer as a price, especially in an auction; *I* bid *five dollars for the bicycle.* ***n-*** **1** the amount offered for something: *The* bid *was five dollars.* **2** an attempt to get: *a* bid *for fame.* **3** in card games, a statement of what a player intends to do for the privilege of naming trumps: *My* bid *was two hearts.*
bid defiance to challenge; express readiness to fight: *He* bade defiance *to his enemies.*
bid fair to to seem likely to: *He* bids fair to *win.*
bid·da·ble (bĭd′ ə bəl) ***adj-*** worth bidding on: *a* biddable *bridge hand*; *a* biddable *suit.*
bid·der (bĭd′ ər) ***n-*** one who bids at an auction, in a card game, or in competing for a business contract.
bid·ding (bĭd′ ĭng) ***n-*** **1** an offering of prices on something: *The* bidding *at the auction was brisk.* **2** request; command; order: *He came and went at his master's* bidding.
bid·dy (bĭd′ ē) ***n-*** [*pl.* **bid·dies**] **1** a chicken, especially a hen. **2** *Slang* a prying and interfering old lady.
bide (bīd) ***vt-*** **[bode** or **bid·ed, bid·ing]** to wait.
bide one's time to wait for the right time.
bi·en·ni·al (bī ĕn′ ē əl) ***adj-*** **1** happening every two years: *a* biennial *election.* **2** lasting two years: *a* biennial *plant.* ***n-*** **1** event that occurs once in two years. **2** a plant which produces roots and leaves in the first year, and flowers, fruit, and seed in the second, and then dies: *Carrots and beets are* biennials. **—*adv-*** **bi·en′ ni·al·ly:** *We elect our congressmen* biennially.
bier (bêr) ***n-*** frame on which a dead person or a coffin is placed or carried. ***Hom-*** beer.
bi·fo·cal (bī fō′ kəl, bī′-) ***adj-*** having two focal points, as a lens. ***n-*** **1** lens ground to form a combination of two lenses, one for near and the other for distant objects. **2 bifocals** eyeglasses with this type of lens.

[1]**bi·fur·cate** (bī′ fər kāt′, bī fûr′ kāt′) ***vi-*** **[bi·fur·cat·ed, bi·fur·cat·ing]** to branch or fork into two parts, as a road or a tree limb.
[2]**bi·fur·cate** (bī′ fər kāt′, bī fûr′ kət) ***adj-*** branched or forked in two.
big (bĭg) ***adj-*** **[big·ger, big·gest]** **1** great in size, amount, extent, or volume, etc.: *a* big *city*; *a* big *sum*; *a* big *ranch*; *a* big *voice.* **2** full grown; tall; mature: *Her children are* big *now.* **3** full of; bursting (with): *Her eyes were* big *with tears.* **4** important: *a* big *businessman*; *the* big *issue of the campaign.* **—*n-*** **big′ ness.**
talk big *Informal* to boast; brag: *He* talked big *about his small triumphs.*
big·a·mist (bĭg′ ə mĭst) ***n-*** man who has two wives, or woman who has two husbands, at the same time.
big·a·my (bĭg′ ə mē) ***n-*** act of marrying a person while married to another.
Big Ben ***n-*** the clock or its big bell in the tower of the British Parliament in London.

Big Dipper

Big Dipper ***n-*** group of seven stars of the northern sky that outlines a long-handled dipper.
big game ***n-*** **1** large animals, such as elephants, tigers, etc., hunted for sport. **2** any important person or thing sought after.
big·heart·ed (bĭg′ härt′ əd) ***adj-*** generous; open; kind: *He was* bighearted *about giving to charity.*
big·horn (bĭg′ hôrn′, -hŏrn′) ***n-*** wild sheep of the Rocky Mountains.
big·ot (bĭg′ ət) ***n-*** person who is unreasonably and obstinately attached to his beliefs and opinions on such subjects as religion, morals, politics, etc.
big·ot·ed (bĭg′ ət əd) ***adj-*** obstinately attached to one's own beliefs and opinions; intolerant.
big·ot·ry (bĭg′ ə trē) ***n-*** [*pl.* **big·ot·ries**] obstinate and unreasonable attachment to one's beliefs and opinions on religion, morals, politics, or the like; intolerance.
big shot *Slang* ***n-*** a very important person. Also **big wheel, big′ wig.**
big top ***n-*** **1** the main tent of a circus. **2** the circus.
big tree ***n-*** the giant sequoia of California; also, popularly, the redwood.
bi·jou (bē′ zho͞o′) ***n-*** [*pl.* **bi·joux** (bē′ zho͞oz′)] trinket; jewel.
bike (bīk) *Informal* ***n-*** bicycle. ***vi-*** **[biked, bik·ing]:** *Let's* bike *into town.*
bi·ki·ni (bə kē′ nē) ***n-*** very scanty two-piece woman's bathing suit.
bi·la·bi·al (bī lā′ bē əl) ***adj-*** pronounced with both lips. In our pronunciation key *b, p, m,* and *w* signify bilabial sounds. ***n-*** a sound formed by both lips.
bi·lat·er·al (bī lăt′ ər əl) ***adj-*** **1** participated in by two sides or parties: *a* bilateral *contract.* **2** *Biology* affecting the right and left sides of an animal, organ, etc. **—*adv-*** **bi·lat′ er·al·ly.**
bilateral symmetry ***n-*** symmetry of two halves of something, as of the human body on either side of the spine, or of the leaves of many trees.
bile (bīl) ***n-*** **1** bitter, yellow or greenish fluid produced by the liver to aid in digestion. **2** ill-humor; resentment.
bilge (bĭlj) ***n-*** **1** bulging part of a cask. **2** the bottom of a ship up to the point where the sides become vertical. **3** bilge water. ***vi-*** **[bilged, bilg·ing]** **1** to spring a leak through a break in the bilge. **2** to bulge. ***vt-*** to stave in the bottom of (a ship).
bilge water ***n-*** **1** stale water which collects in the bottom of a ship. **2** *Slang* stale or stupid talk or writing.

bi·lin·e·ar (bī lĭn′ ē ər) *Mathematics* ***adj-*** of or having to do with two straight lines.

bi·lin·gual (bī lĭng′ gwəl) ***adj-*** **1** expressed in two languages: *a* bilingual *inscription.* **2** speaking in two languages.

bil·ious (bĭl′ yəs) ***adj-*** **1** having to do with bile. **2** caused by a disorder of the liver, especially from too much bile: *a* bilious *attack.* **3** bad-tempered; peevish: *Cheevers takes a* bilious *view of life.* **4** of a sickly, yellowish-green color: *a* bilious *complexion.* ***—adv-*** **bil′ious·ly.** ***n-*** **bil′ious·ness.**

bilk (bĭlk) ***vt-*** to deceive or defraud; swindle; cheat: *He* bilked *his creditors of a small fortune.*

[1]**bill** (bĭl) ***n-*** **1** statement of charges for goods or services: *a garage* bill; *a restaurant* bill. **2** printed advertisement or notice; poster; placard: "*Post no* bills." **3** any paper listing items or events, such as a playbill, bill of fare, etc. **4** plan or draft of a law. **5** in law, formal complaint or accusation; petition. **6** piece of paper money: *a ten-dollar* bill. ***vt-*** **1** to send a statement of charges to: *Please* bill *me without delay.* **2** to enter (a purchase) as a charge: Bill *the repairs to my father.* **3** to advertise; announce: *The producer* billed *him as the star.*. [from Medieval Latin **billa** meaning "seal; document," from earlier Latin **bulla** meaning "a blob; bubble (of wax or lead used to seal documents)."]

[2]**bill** (bĭl) ***n-*** **1** beak of a bird. **2** similar beak in other animals, such as some turtles. ***vi-*** to join beaks; show affection: *Doves* bill *and coo.* [from Old English **bile.**]

Bill of hummingbird

[3]**bill** (bĭl) ***n-*** **1** in former times, a spear with a broad hook-shaped blade. **2** billhook. [from Old English **bil** or **bill** meaning "broadsword."]

bill·board (bĭl′ bôrd′) ***n-*** large panel, usually set up outdoors to display public notices or advertising.

[1]**bil·let** (bĭl′ ət) ***n-*** **1** place where a soldier is lodged. **2** the paper that orders such lodgings. **3** situation; appointment: *He has a comfortable* billet *in Washington.* ***vt-*** to quarter or lodge: *I* billeted *my men in the town.* ***vi-***: *Men, we'll* billet *in the town.* [from Old French **billette,** from **bille** meaning "[1]bill; writing."]

[2]**bil·let** (bĭl′ ət) ***n-*** thick piece of wood, cut for fuel. [from Old French **billette** from **bille** meaning "log."]

bil·let-doux (bĭ′ lā dōō′) ***n-*** [*pl.* **bil·lets-doux** (bĭ′ lā-dōōz)] love letter. [from French **billet doux** (bē′ yā′ dōō′) meaning "sweet letter."]

bill·fold (bĭl′ fōld′) ***n-*** a folding wallet.

bill·hook (bĭl′ hŏŏk′) ***n-*** tool with a hook-shaped blade, used by farmers for pruning trees and cutting brush.

bil·liards (bĭl′ yərdz) ***n-*** indoor game played by two or more players, on an oblong **billiard table** having raised, cushioned sides. A player has a long stick, called a **billiard cue,** which he uses to drive one **billiard ball** against others.

bil·lings·gate (bĭl′ ĭngz gāt′) ***n-*** coarse or abusive language.

bil·lion (bĭl′ yən) ***n-*** in the United States, a thousand million (1,000,000,000); in Great Britain, a million million (1,000,000,000,000).

bil·lion·aire (bĭl′ yən âr′) ***n-*** person who has a billion dollars, francs, pounds, etc.

bil·lionth (bĭl′ yənth) ***adj-*** **1** last in a series of a billion. **2** the ordinal of 1,000,000,000. ***n-*** **1** the last in a series of a billion. **2** one of a billion equal parts of a whole or group. **3** the last term in the name of a common fraction having a denominator of 1,000,000,000, or of the corresponding decimal fraction, .000000001.

bill of exchange ***n-*** written order for the payment of money to a person; draft.

bill of fare ***n-*** list of the various dishes which may be ordered in a restaurant; menu.

bill of health ***n-*** an official certificate given to a ship's captain at time of sailing. It records the state of health of the crew and passengers, and health conditions at the port of departure. It must be shown to the authorities at the next port.

a clean bill of health a statement that a ship's company and passengers are free of disease; hence, a statement, after examination of the facts, that a condition is satisfactory: *The union got* a clean bill of health.

bill of lading ***n-*** receipt for goods shipped, issued to the shipper by a railroad or other carrier.

Bill of Rights ***n-*** **1** the first ten amendments to the Constitution of the United States stating the fundamental rights and freedoms of Americans. **2** a declaration of the fundamental rights of Englishmen, enacted by Parliament in 1689. **3 bill of rights** any formal declaration of the fundamental rights of a nation's people.

bill of sale ***n-*** formal paper transferring to a buyer the title to personal property.

bil·low (bĭl′ ō) ***n-*** great wave of the sea. ***vi-*** **1** to rise and roll in large waves. **2** to swell out; bulge: *The sails* billow *in the breeze.* ***vt-***: *The wind* billowed *the sails.*

bil·low·y (bĭl′ ō ē) ***adj-*** surging; swelling: *the* billowy *ocean*; *the* billowy *sails.*

bill·post·er (bĭl′ pōs′ tər) ***n-*** person who sticks advertisements or notices on billboards, fences, etc.

bil·ly (bĭl′ ē) ***n-*** [*pl.* **bil·lies**] club, especially one a policeman carries.

billy goat ***n-*** a male goat.

bi·me·tal·lic (bī′ mə tăl′ ĭk) ***adj-*** **1** having or using two metals: *a* bimetallic *compound.* **2** based on the monetary system of bimetallism: *a* bimetallic *nation.*

bi·met·al·lism (bī mĕt′ əl ĭz′ əm) ***n-*** use of two metals jointly, usually gold and silver, as a standard of value in a monetary system.

bi·month·ly (bī mŭnth′ lē) ***adj-*** occurring once every two months: *a* bimonthly *club meeting.* ***adv-***: *The magazine appeared* bimonthly. ***n-*** a publication issued every two months.

bin (bĭn) ***n-*** box or enclosed place used for storing things: *a coal* bin; *a* grain *bin.* ***Hom-*** been.

bi·na·ry (bī′ nə rē) ***adj-*** made up of, or dealing with, two parts.

binary compound *Chemistry* ***n-*** compound of two elements.

binary fission ***n-*** division of a living cell into two equal cells.

binary number system ***n-*** numeration system in which the number 2 is the base and all numbers are named with only the two symbols, 1 and 0. Example: The binary numeral 1101 names the number 13.

binary star ***n-*** pair of stars held together by mutual gravitation and revolving around the common center of gravity between them; double star.

bin·au·ral (bī nôr′ əl) ***adj-*** **1** of, or designed for, hearing with both ears at once: *The radio had* binaural *earphones.* **2** having two ears. **3** stereophonic.

bind (bīnd) ***vt-*** **[bound, bind·ing] 1** to tie together or fasten with a cord, strap, etc.; make fast; tie up: *to*

---

fāte, făt, dâre, bärn; bē, bĕt, mêre; bīte, bĭt; nōte, hŏt, môre, dòg; fŭn, fûr; tōō, bŏŏk; oil; out; tar; thin; then; hw for wh as in *wh*at; zh for s as in u*s*ual; ə for a, e, i, o, u, as in *a*go, lin*e*n, per*i*l, at*o*m, min*u*s

bind *a captive's arms and legs.* **2** to wrap around: *to* bind *one's waist with a girdle*; *to* bind *a wound with gauze.* **3** to cause to stick together: *to* bind *loose soil with grass*; *to* bind *one's life to another.* **4** to finish or protect (a seam, edge, etc.) with a band or border. **5** to hold or oblige by a promise, oath, legal contract, etc.: *The contract* binds *him for five years.* **6** to fasten together and attach a cover to the pages of (a book).

bind·er (bīn′ dər) ***n-*** **1** person who binds. **2** machine that cuts and binds grain into bundles. **3** anything that binds, such as tar on roads, or a stiff cover for holding loose sheets of paper.

bind·er·y (bīn′ də rē) ***n-*** [*pl.* **bind·er·ies**] place where books are bound.

bind·ing (bīn′ dĭng) ***n-*** **1** something that covers or binds. **2** the covers of a book. **3** a strip used to strengthen and finish the seams and edges of dresses, etc. ***adj-*** having the force to hold one to an agreement, promise, etc.: *An unsigned contract is not* binding. ***—adv-*** **bind′ing·ly.**

binding energy *Physics* ***n-*** amount of energy needed to break a molecule, atom, or atomic nucleus into the parts they are made of.

bind·weed (bīnd′ wēd′) ***n-*** plant such as the morning glory or various closely related plants that twine around other plants or objects.

bin·go (bĭng′ gō) ***n-*** game played by covering numbers on a card as they are called out. The winner is the first person to cover all the numbers in a row.

bin·na·cle (bĭn′ ə kəl) ***n-*** case or stand near the steering wheel of a ship and containing the ship's compass.

bin·oc·u·lar (bə nŏk′ yə lər, bī-) ***adj-*** for use by both eyes at once: *a* binocular *microscope.* ***n-*** **binoculars** pair of telescopes of low power and broad field, joined together parallel to one another; especially, prism binoculars.

Binoculars

bi·no·mi·al (bī nō′ mē əl) ***n-*** in algebra, an expression having two terms. Examples: *a* + *b*; 3*x*/2 − *y*. ***adj-*** consisting of two terms: *a* − *b is a* binomial *expression.* ***—adv-*** **bi·no′ mi·al·ly.**

bio- *combining form* life: bio*logy* (study of life); bio*chemistry* (the chemistry of life processes). [from Greek **bio-**, from **bios,** meaning "life."]

bi·o·chem·i·cal (bī′ō kĕm′ ĭ kəl) ***adj-*** dealing with or belonging to biochemistry. ***—adv-*** **bi′o·chem′ i·cal·ly.**

bi·o·chem·ist (bī′ō kĕm′ ĭst) ***n-*** person trained in biochemistry and, usually, engaged in it as a profession.

bi·o·chem·ist·ry (bī′ō kĕm′ əs trē) ***n-*** science dealing with the chemistry of living things.

bi·o·de·grad·a·ble (bī′ō dĭ grā′ də bəl) ***adj-*** able to be decomposed by natural processes, especially by bacteria and fungi: *a* biodegradable *detergent.* ***—vi-*** **bi′·o·de·grade′** [**bi·o·de·grad·ed, bi·o·de·grad·ing**].

bi·o·gen·e·sis (bī′ō jĕn′ ə sĭs) See *germ theory.*

bi·og·ra·pher (bī ŏg′ rə fər) ***n-*** one who writes the history of a person's life.

bi·o·graph·ic (bī ə grăf′ ĭk) or **bi·o·graph·i·cal** (-ĭ kəl) ***adj-*** having to do with a person's life story: *a* biographical *novel.* ***—adv-*** **bi′o·graph′ ic·al·ly.**

bi·og·ra·phy (bī ŏg′ rə fē) ***n-*** [*pl.* **bi·og·ra·phies**] **1** the story of a person's life. **2** the branch of literature dealing with the lives of people.

bi·o·log·i·cal (bī′ ə lŏj′ ĭ kəl) ***adj-*** relating to biology: *a* biological *process.* ***—adv-*** **bi′o·log′ i·cal·ly.**

biological sciences ***n-*** the group of sciences, including zoology and botany, devoted to study of living things.

biological warfare ***n-*** use of disease germs as military weapons.

bi·ol·o·gist (bī ŏl′ ə jĭst) ***n-*** person trained in biology and, usually, engaged in it as a profession.

bi·ol·o·gy (bī ŏl′ ə jē) ***n-*** science of living things and life processes, including such branches as botany, zoology, ecology, etc.

bi·o·lu·mi·nes·cence (bī′ō lo͞o′ mə nĕs′ əns) ***n-*** emission of light by living things such as fireflies and certain fishes. ***—adj-*** **bi′o·lu′mi·nes′ cent.**

bi·om·e·try (bī ŏm′ ə trē) or **bi·o·met·rics** (bī′ə mĕt′ rĭks) ***n-*** the use of statistics for analyzing biological information.

bi·on·ic (bī ŏn′ ik) ***adj-*** created by technology to replace a part of a living creature: *a* bionic *hip.*

bi·on·ics (bī ŏn′ ĭks) ***n-*** study and practice of making bionic parts.

bi·o·phys·ics (bī′ō fĭz′ ĭks) ***n-*** the application of physics to the study of structure and behavior of living organisms, such as the dolphin's use of sound to navigate.

bi·op·sy (bī′ ŏp′ sē) *Medicine* ***n-*** [*pl.* **bi·op·sies**] the taking of a specimen of tissue from a living person or animal; also, the examination of this tissue for signs of disease. See also *autopsy.*

bi·o·sphere (bī′ ə sfêr′) ***n-*** all the land, water, and air inhabited by life.

bi·o·tin (bī′ ə tən) ***n-*** powerful growth-promoting vitamin of the group called the vitamin B complex.

bi·par·ti·san (bī pär′ tə zən, -sən) ***adj-*** favored by or made up of members of two political parties: *a* bipartisan *foreign-aid bill*; *a* bipartisan *committee.*

bi·par·tite (bī′ pär′ tīt′) ***adj-*** **1** made by two parties, such as nations: *a* bipartite *agreement.* **2** *Biology* divided into two parts almost to the base: *a* bipartite *leaf.*

bi·ped (bī′ pĕd′) ***n-*** animal with two feet. Humans and birds are bipeds.

bi·plane (bī′ plān′) ***n-*** airplane with two sets of wings, one above the other.

Biplane

birch (bûrch) ***n-*** **1** any of several trees with smooth outer bark which in some varieties may be removed in thin, papery sheets. **2** wood of these trees. **3** whip made of a branch from one of these trees. ***vt-*** to punish with such a whip; flog; whip.

birch bark ***n-*** the smooth outer bark of the birch, especially of the **white** or **paper birch.** *as modifier* **(birch-bark):** *They purchased a* birch-bark *canoe.*

bird (bûrd) ***n-*** **1** any member of a class of warm-blooded, feathered, winged, egg-laying animals. **2** any small game bird, as distinguished from a waterfowl. **3** shuttlecock. **4** *Slang* fellow, chap: *He is an odd* bird. **5** *Slang* an insulting or taunting sound; jeer; hiss; especially in the phrases **give (someone) the bird** or **get the bird.**

bird·bath (bûrd′ băth′) ***n-*** wide, shallow basin for birds to bathe in and drink from.

bird·call (bûrd′ kôl′) ***n-*** **1** the sound or call of a bird. **2** an instrument imitating a bird's voice.

bird·house (bûrd′ hous′) **n-** small box, often shaped like a house, for birds to nest in.

bird·ie (bûr′ dē) ***n-*** **1** in golf, a score of one stroke less than par for a hole. **2** *Informal* a small bird.

bird of paradise ***n-*** **1** any of a group of birds found chiefly in New Guinea and noted for their colorful and beautiful feathers. **2** a showy orange flower.

bird of passage ***n-*** **1** migratory bird. **2** any wandering person.

bird of prey ***n-*** any bird, such as a hawk or eagle, that hunts other animals.

bird·seed (bûrd′ sēd′) ***n-*** small seed fed chiefly to caged birds.

bird's-eye (bŭrd′ zī′) ***adj-*** **1** seen from above, as if by a flying bird: *a* bird's-eye *view of the city.* **2** general; sweeping; not detailed: *a* bird's-eye *view of the labor problem.* **3** marked with spots resembling a bird's eye: *a table of* bird's-eye *maple.*

bi·ret·ta (bə rĕt′ ə) ***n-*** stiff black, red, or purple cap, square at the top with three or four projections, worn by the Roman Catholic clergy.

birth (bûrth) ***n-*** **1** a coming into the world from the body of the mother. **2** beginning: *The* birth *of a nation.* **3** descent; ancestry: *of French* birth. ***Hom-*** berth.

give birth to to bring forth: *to* give birth to *an idea.*

birth control ***n-*** control of birth rate by preventing or lessening the frequency of conception. *as* ***modifier:*** *a* birth control *device.* **—*adj-* birth control.**

birth·day (bûrth′ dā′) ***n-*** **1** day on which a person is born. **2** yearly celebration of that day. *as* ***modifier:*** *a* birthday *present.*

birth·mark (bûrth′ märk′) ***n-*** mark or blemish existing on the skin from birth.

birth·place (bûrth′ plās′) ***n-*** **1** place where a person is born. **2** place of beginning or origin: *Philadelphia was the* birthplace *of the Constitution of the United States.*

birth rate (bûrth′ rāt′) ***n-*** the number of live births within a particular group in a given time, usually stated as so many births per thousand inhabitants.

birth·right (bûrth′ rīt′) ***n-*** **1** any right, privilege, or possession to which a person is entitled by birth. **2** the right of the oldest son to inherit; also, the inheritance.

birth·stone (bûrth′ stōn′) ***n-*** gem associated with a month of the year, supposed to bring good luck to a person whose birthday falls in that month.

bis·cuit (bĭs′ kət) ***n-*** **1** kind of bread baked in small, flat cakes. **2** cracker or cooky.

bi·sect (bī′ sĕkt′) ***vt-*** to cut or divide into two equal parts. **—*n-* bi·sec′ tion.**

bi·sec·tor (bī sĕk′ tər) ***n-*** **1** that which bisects. **2** *Mathematics* line or plane that bisects an angle, line, or figure.

bi·sex·u·al (bī sĕk′ sho͞o əl) ***adj-*** **1** *Biology* having both male and female organs of reproduction, as earthworms; hermaphrodite. **2** in psychology, attracted by both sexes. **—*adv-* bi·sex′ u·al·ly.**

bish·op (bĭsh′ əp) ***n-*** **1** clergyman of high rank, the head of a diocese or church district. **2** piece used in chess.

bish·op·ric (bĭsh′ əp rĭk′) ***n-*** **1** the office of bishop. **2** diocese or church district.

bis·muth (bĭz′ məth) ***n-*** hard, brittle, silvery white metallic element used in alloys. Its salts are used in medicines and cosmetics. Symbol Bi, At. No. 83, At. Wt. 208.98.

bi·son (bī′ sən) ***n-*** [*pl.* **bi·son**] any of several large, shaggy-maned, wild grazing animals of the ox family, extinct except for two kinds, the North American buffalo and European aurochs, which exist in protected herds.

Bison, 5½–6 ft. high at shoulder

[1]**bisque** (bĭsk) ***n-*** **1** thick, rich, cream soup made from meat, fish, or tomatoes. **2** a kind of ice cream containing finely chopped nuts or macaroons. [from French.]

[2]**bisque** (bĭsk) ***n-*** pottery after the first baking and before glazing. [apparently shortened from **biscuit.**]

bis·tro (bĭs′ trō) *Informal* ***n-*** [*pl.* **bis·tros**] a small nightclub or bar.

[1]**bit** (bĭt) ***n-*** **1** small piece of anything: *a* bit *of bread.* **2** a little while: *Please wait a* bit. **3** single unit of basic computer information. **4** in western United States, a money value of 12½ cents, used only in the expressions **two bits, four bits, six bits.** [from Old English **bita,** from **bītan** meaning "to bite."] ***Hom-*** bitt.

a bit slightly: *It's* a bit *small.* **not a bit** not at all; none at all.

[2]**bit** (bĭt) ***n-*** **1** a replaceable tool for drilling, boring, driving screws, etc., that is gripped and turned by another tool such as a brace or electric drill. **2** the cutting part of a tool. **3** the metal mouthpiece of a bridle. **4** the part of a key that enters and works a lock. [from Old English **bite** meaning "a bite," from **bītan,** "to bite."] ***Hom-*** bitt.

Carpenter's bit

Bit for horse

bitch (bĭch) ***n-*** the female of the dog, wolf, etc.

bite (bīt) ***vi-*** [**bit, bit·ten** or **bit, bit·ing**] **1** to cut into or cut off with the teeth. **2** to pierce the skin for food as do certain blood-sucking insects: *A mosquito* bites. **3** to take the bait: *Fish are* biting *today.* ***vt-*** **1** to seize or grasp with the teeth; wound with the teeth: *The police dog* bit *the thief.* **2** to cause pain to: *The icy wind was* biting *my face.* ***n-*** **1** a piece bitten off; morsel: *Have a* bite *to eat.* **2** wound made by biting: *a flea* bite; *a snake* bite; *a dog* bite.

bit·ing (bī′ tĭng) ***adj-*** **1** sharp: *the* biting *taste of vinegar.* **2** sarcastic; sneering: *to give a* biting *answer.* **3** stinging; sharp; bitter: *a* biting *wind.* **—*adv-* bit′ ing·ly.**

bit·ter (bĭt′ ər) ***adj-*** [**bit·ter·er, bit·ter·est**] **1** sharp and unpleasant to the taste. **2** sharp; painful; stinging: *the* bitter *cold.* **3** hard to bear or receive: *a* bitter *lesson.* **4** severe; harsh: *the exchange of* bitter *words.* **5** unforgiving; unyielding: *to remain* bitter *enemies*; *out of* bitter *hatred.* **—*adv-* bit′ ter·ly.** ***n-*** **bit′ ter·ness.**

bit·tern (bĭt′ ərn) ***n-*** any of several marsh birds related to the heron and having a booming cry.

bit·ter·root (bĭt′ ər ro͞ot′) ***n-*** a plant of the Rocky Mountains, with fleshy roots and pink flowers. The bitterroot is the State flower of Montana.

bit·ters (bĭt′ ərz) ***n-*** *pl.* a liquid flavoring, containing bitter herbs.

bit·ter·sweet (bĭt′ ər swēt′) ***n-*** **1** an American twining shrub showing, in the fall, scarlet seeds in open, orange pods. **2** vine of the nightshade family. ***adj-*** both bitter and sweet, or painful and pleasant.

bi·tu·men (bĭ to͞o′ mən, bĭ tyo͞o′ -) ***n-*** any of several tarry substances, such as asphalt, found in petroleum or occurring separately in natural deposits. **—*adj-* bi·tu′ min·ous:** *a* bituminous *deposit.*

bituminous coal ***n-*** grade of coal containing a large proportion of bituminous matter; soft coal.

bi·va·lent (bī′ vā′ lənt) *Chemistry* ***adj-*** having a valence of two. **—*n-* bi′ val′ ence.**

bi·valve (bī′ vălv′) ***n-*** a shellfish, such as the oyster or clam, with a shell consisting of two valves hinged at one side. ***adj-:*** *a* bivalve *mollusk.*

biv·ou·ac (bĭv'ə wăk') ***n-*** temporary camp in the open air. ***vt-*** **[biv·ou·acked, biv·ou·ack·ing]** to encamp, as for the night, in the open air.

bi·week·ly (bī'wēk'lē) ***adj-*** occurring or appearing every two weeks: *a* biweekly *trip to the city.* ***adv-***: *She reports* biweekly *on the progress of the book.* ***n-*** [*pl.* **bi·week·lies**] periodical issued once every two weeks.

bi·zarre (bə zär') ***adj-*** odd in manner or appearance, fantastic; grotesque: *Their Halloween costumes were* bizarre. ***Hom-*** bazaar.

blab (blăb) ***vt-*** **[blabbed, blab·bing]** to tell thoughtlessly. ***vi-*** to tell tales; talk too much and unwisely. ***n-*** **1** one who lets out secrets, or tells tales. **2** silly chatter.

blab·ber·mouth (blăb'ər mouth') *Informal* ***n-*** person who talks too much and unwisely; tattletale.

black (blăk) ***n-*** **1** the darkest of all colors, that of materials like coal, soot, and tar that reflect no light whatever. It is not strictly a color, but the total absence or absorption of color or light. **2** a dye of this color. **3** clothes of this color; mourning. **4 Black** a Negro. ***adj-*** **[black·er, black·est] 1** having the color of coal, soot, tar, etc.: *a* black *cat.* **2** almost without light; very dark: *a* black *cellar.* **3** gloomy; threatening: *a* black *outlook.* **4** without moral goodness; evil: *a* black *deed.* **5** indicating disgrace: *a* black *mark for conduct.* **6** having a dark skin; Negro. ***vt-*** to blacken: *to* black *shoes.*

black out 1 to turn off or hide lights in: *to* black out *a stage.* **2** to lose consciousness.

black-and-blue (blăk'ən blōō') ***adj-*** of skin, discolored from a pinch or bruise.

black art ***n-*** the art that witches and conjurers claim to practice; black magic.

black·ball (blăk'bȯl') ***vt-*** **1** to exclude from a club by adverse votes, formerly recorded by the placing of black balls in a ballot box. **2** to exclude from society in general; ostracize. ***n-*** an adverse vote.

black bass (băs) ***n-*** either of two fresh-water game fishes of eastern North America, the **large-mouthed black bass** or the **small-mouthed black bass.**

black bear ***n-*** the common bear of North America. Its coat varies from a glossy black to a rich brown.

black·ber·ry (blăk'bĕr'ē) ***n-*** [*pl.* **black·ber·ries**] a bramble bearing seedy berries which turn bluish black when ripe; also, the berry. *as* ***modifier:*** *some* blackberry *jam.*

Blackberry leaves and fruit

black·bird (blăk'bûrd') ***n-*** **1** any of several American birds, including the **red-winged blackbird,** and the **yellow-headed blackbird,** the males of which are nearly all black. **2** an English thrush.

black·board (blăk'bôrd') ***n-*** dark, smooth surface, often of slate, for writing or drawing on with chalk.

black book ***n-*** a blacklist.

be in (someone's) black book to be in disfavor.

black·cap (blăk'kăp') ***n-*** **1** popular name for any of several birds that have black crowns, such as the chickadee. **2** the black raspberry.

black damp ***n-*** a suffocating gas, mostly carbon dioxide, that accumulates in mines; choke damp.

Black Death ***n-*** in the 14th century, the bubonic plague, which spread throughout Europe killing more than half the population.

black·en (blăk'ən) ***vt-*** **1** to make black; darken: *Soot* blackens *kettles.* **2** to sully by speech or acts: *to* blacken *a person's reputation.* ***vi-*** to grow dark or threatening: *The sky* blackened.

black eye ***n-*** **1** a dark bruise around the eye, usually caused by a blow. **2** *Informal* discredit or shame; a blot: *Litter is a* black eye *on the landscape.*

black-eyed pea ***n-*** cowpea seed.

black-eyed Su·san (sōō'zən) ***n-*** flower with yellow to orange petals surrounding a dark brown cone-shaped center.

black·fish (blăk'fĭsh') ***n-*** **1** kind of small black whale. **2** any of several black or dark fishes, such as the tautog or the black sea bass. **3** small, dark, fresh-water food fish of Alaska and Siberia.

black flag ***n-*** the pirate flag, usually with a white skull and crossbones on a black field; the Jolly Roger.

Black·foot (blăk'fŏŏt') ***n-*** [*pl.* **Black·feet,** also **Black·foot**] **1** a member of a tribe of Algonquian Indians, living in Alberta, Saskatchewan, and Montana. **2** the language of these Indians. ***adj-***: *a* Blackfoot *custom.*

black·guard (blăg'ärd', -ərd) ***n-*** shameless villain; scoundrel. ***vt-*** to revile.

black·guard·ly (blăg'ərd lē) ***adj-*** mean; vile; base: *a* blackguardly *villain.*

Black Hand ***n-*** a secret criminal society, first organized in Sicily.

black·head (blăk'hĕd') ***n-*** **1** a tiny, black-tipped piece of fatty matter in the pore of the skin, especially of the face. **2** disease of turkeys. **3** any of various birds having a black head.

black hole ***n-*** region in space formed by a collapsed star where the force of gravity is strong enough to prevent the escape of light.

black·ing (blăk'ĭng) ***n-*** black paste, cream, or liquid for polishing shoes or other articles.

black·jack (blăk'jăk') ***n-*** **1** small club with a weighted head and a flexible handle. **2** small, scrubby oak tree with black bark, common in southern United States. **3** a card game; twenty-one. ***vt-*** to strike with a small heavy club.

black·leg (blăk'lĕg') ***n-*** **1** an infectious, often fatal disease of cattle and sheep. **2** disease of cabbage or potatoes. **3** *Brit.* a strikebreaker; scab.

black·list (blăk'lĭst') ***n-*** list of persons or organizations to be punished, denied approval, refused work, etc.; black book. ***vt:*** *to* blacklist *an actor.*

black magic ***n-*** magic used for evil ends; witchcraft.

black·mail (blăk'māl') ***n-*** **1** an attempt to get money from a person by threatening to say something bad about him. **2** the money thus collected. ***vt-*** to make, or try to make, a person pay in this way. **—*n-* black'mail'er.**

Black Ma·ri·a (mə rī'ə) *Informal* ***n-*** patrol wagon.

black mark ***n-*** mark or cause of disapproval or censure: *a* black mark *on one's record.*

black market ***n-*** **1** illegal sale of goods, especially in violation of official prices and amounts. **2** everywhere this is done. **—*n-* black mar'ket·eer'** (mär'kə têr').

black·ness (blăk'nəs) ***n-*** dark or black color; darkness.

black·out (blăk'out') ***n-*** **1** a turning off or hiding of lights visible to an enemy. **2** a turning off of stage lights to mark the end of an act or scene. **3** sudden loss of sight or consciousness.

black sheep ***n-*** person of a good family, but looked upon as worthless or disgraceful.

black·smith (blăk'smĭth') ***n-*** person who works iron by heating it in fire and then hammering it into shape; person who shoes horses.

black snake or **black·snake** (blăk'snāk') ***n-*** **1** any of several dark, harmless snakes. **2** long cowhide whip.

black·thorn (blăk′thôrn′, -thôrn′) ***n-*** low, thorny, Old World bush with black bark, white flowers, and small dark-blue berries.

black tie ***n-*** semiformal dress for men, with which a black bow tie is worn; tuxedo.

black·top (blăk′tŏp′) ***n-*** **1** asphalt or any similar black material used for paving roads. **2** road paved with such material.

black walnut ***n-*** **1** kind of walnut tree of eastern North America, with heavy dark brown wood, valuable for furniture. **2** the edible nut or the wood of this tree.

black widow ***n-*** kind of small spider that looks like a small black bead. The female is poisonous and has a red hourglass-shaped mark on the underside of its abdomen.

Black widow, about 1 1/2 in. long underside view

blad·der (blăd′ər) ***n-*** **1** a small bag or sac in the body which receives and temporarily holds urine from the kidneys. **2** any similar inside bag or sac: *a football* bladder; *the air* bladder *of a fish.* **—*adj-*** **blad′der·like′.**

blad·der·wort (blăd′ər wôrt) ***n-*** any of a group of insect-eating water plants with stringy, bladderlike sacs that open suddenly to trap tiny insects in an inrush of water.

blade (blād) ***n-*** **1** cutting part of a knife, sword, tool, instrument, or machine. **2** flat, narrow leaf: *a* blade *of grass*; *a* blade *of wheat.* **3** broad flat object or part: *shoulder* blade; blade *of an oar.* For picture, see [1]*paddle.* **4** sword or knife.

blam·a·ble (blām′ə bəl) ***adj-*** deserving of blame or censure; censurable.

blame (blām) ***vt-*** **[blamed, blam·ing] 1** to hold responsible (for); attribute guilt to: *The truck driver* blamed *the bus driver for the accident.* **2** to find fault with: *I don't* blame *you.* ***n-*** responsibility for some fault, wrong, or failure: *She has the* blame *for her son's bad manners.*

be to blame to be at fault; deserve the blame: *Who* is to blame *for the mistake?*

blame·less (blām′ləs) ***adj-*** free from fault or guilt. **—*adv-*** **blame′less·ly.** ***n-*** **blame′less·ness.**

blame·wor·thy (blām′wûr′thē) ***adj-*** deserving blame or reproof.

blanch (blănch) ***vt-*** **1** to whiten by taking out color. **2** to put in boiling water and then into cold water to remove skins: *to* blanch *almonds.* ***vi-*** to turn pale from shame or fear.

blanc·mange (blə mänj′, *Fr.* blä^n′mä^{n}zh′) ***n-*** custardlike dessert of some starchy substance, such as cornstarch, combined with milk, sweetened, and flavored.

bland (blănd) ***adj-*** **[bland·er, bland·est] 1** mild and soft; not irritating: *a* bland *food*; *a* bland *manner.* **2** lacking character or emphasis; flat; undistinguished: *a* bland *speech.* **—*adv-*** **bland′ly.** ***n-*** **bland′ness.**

blan·dish (blăn′dĭsh) ***vt-*** to flatter; coax; wheedle.

blan·dish·ment (blăn′dĭsh mənt) ***n-*** **1** flattery; cajolery. **2** flattering act or expression: *He could not resist her gentle* blandishments.

blank (blăngk) ***adj-*** **[blank·er, blank·est]** having nothing on or in it; lacking or empty of marks, decorations, feelings, ideas, etc.: *a* blank *sheet of paper*; *a* blank *look*; *a* blank *mind.* ***n-*** **1** empty space or condition: *He left* blanks *for the unanswered questions. His mind was a complete* blank. **2** printed form containing empty spaces to be filled in: *an order* blank. **3** cartridge containing powder but no bullet. **—*adv-*** **blank′ly.** ***n-*** **blank′ness.**

blan·ket (blăng′kət) ***n-*** **1** covering of soft cloth, such as wool, cotton, etc., used to keep people or animals warm. **2** any thick covering: *a* blanket *of fog.* ***vt-***: *Snow* blanketed *the earth.*

blank verse ***n-*** unrhymed verse; especially, in English literature, verse written in unrhymed iambic pentameter.

blare (blâr) ***n-*** loud sound like that of a trumpet. ***vi-*** **[blared, blar·ing]** to give forth a loud, brassy sound like that of a trumpet. ***vt-***: *He* blared *his instructions over the public-address system.*

blar·ney (blär′nē) ***n-*** skillful flattery. ***vt-***: *Don't* blarney *me!*

Blarney Stone ***n-*** a stone in the wall of Blarney Castle, in Ireland, said to confer skill in flattery upon those who kiss it.

blas·pheme (blăs′fēm′, blăs′fēm′) ***vt-*** **[blas·phemed, blas·phem·ing]** to speak profanely or impiously of (God or sacred things). ***vi-*** to talk irreverently. **—*n-*** **blas′phem′er.**

blas·phe·my (blăs′fə mē) ***n-*** [*pl.* **blas·phe·mies**] words that show contempt for God or sacred things. **—*adj-*** **blas′phe·mous:** *a* blasphemous *remark.* ***adv-*** **blas′phe·mous·ly.**

blast (blăst) ***n-*** **1** strong gust of wind. **2** forcible stream of air or gas from an opening: *a* blast *of heat from a furnace.* **3** a sudden sound, as from a wind instrument. **4** sudden harmful influence upon plants or animals; a blight. **5** explosion, as of dynamite, used in blowing up rocks; also, the charge so used. ***vi-*** to use explosives: *They're* blasting *now.* ***vt-*** **1** to cause to fade or wither; destroy: *A late frost* blasted *the crops.* **2** to break or shatter by an explosive.

full blast at maximum operation or speed: *The furnace was going* full blast. *The ship steamed ahead* full blast.

blast off of rockets, guided missiles, etc., to take off; leave the launching pad.

blast furnace ***n-*** furnace for separating a metal from its ore. The great heat needed is built up by a blast of hot air forced in at the bottom of the furnace.

blast-off (blăst′ôf′) ***n-*** the firing of a space rocket.

blas·tu·la (blăs′chə lə) ***n-*** [*pl.* **blas·tu·las** or **blas·tu·lae** (-lē)] an embryo in an early stage of development, consisting of a hollow sphere enclosed by a single layer of cells.

blat (blăt) ***vi-*** **[blat·ted, blat·ting]** to make a cry like a calf or sheep; bleat. ***vt-*** *Slang* to blurt out.

bla·tan·cy (blā′tən sē) ***n-*** [*pl.* **bla·tan·cies**] vulgarly conspicuous quality: *The* blatancy *of his remarks offended his audience.*

bla·tant (blā′tənt) ***adj-*** **1** conspicuous or obvious, often in a vulgar way: *a* blatant *display of wealth.* **2** noisy. **—*adv-*** **bla′tant·ly.**

[1]**blaze** (blāz) ***n-*** **1** bright flame; fire. **2** strong direct light: *the* blaze *of noon.* **3** brilliant display: *a* blaze *of color from the sunset.* **4** sudden outburst: *He reached the finish line in a* blaze *of energy.* ***vi-*** **[blazed, blaz·ing] 1** to burn with a bright flame. **2** to burst into flame; flare up: *The signal fires suddenly* blazed *along the hills.* **3** to glow or shine like a flame: *Lights* blazed *from the windows.* [from Old English **blæse** meaning "torch."]

[2]**blaze** (blāz) ***n-*** **1** white spot on the face of an animal. **2** mark made on a tree by removing a piece of the bark. ***vt-*** **[blazed, blaz·ing] 1** to mark (a tree) by chipping

off bark. **2** to indicate (a trail) by marking trees in this way. [from early German **bläse.**]

[3]**blaze** (blāz) ***vt-*** **[blazed, blaz·ing]** to spread abroad (news); make public. [from early Dutch **blasen.**]

blaz·er (blāz′ ər) ***n-*** brightly colored jacket with straight lines used for sport wear.

bla·zon (blā′ zən) ***n-*** coat of arms. ***vt-*** **1** to decorate in color, as a shield; inscribe. **2** to proclaim: *His face* blazons *his evil deeds.*

bla·zon·ry (blā′ zən rē) ***n-*** **1** coat of arms. **2** art of describing or representing a coat of arms. **3** a bright display.

bldg. building.

bleach (blēch) ***vt-*** to remove color from or to whiten, by exposure to the sun or by a chemical process. ***vi-*** to lose color. ***n-*** substance that whitens or removes color.

bleach·ers (blē′ chərz) ***n-*** *pl.* plank seats built in tiers for spectators at an outdoor sports event. *as* ***modifier*** **(bleach′ er):** *a* bleacher *ticket.*

bleaching powder ***n-*** chlorinated lime.

bleak (blēk) ***adj-*** **[bleak·er, bleak·est] 1** unsheltered; exposed to wind and cold. **2** dismal; cold: *The weather was* bleak. **3** cheerless; gloomy: *a* bleak *outlook on life.* ***—adv-*** **bleak′ ly.** ***n-*** **bleak′ ness.**

blear (blêr) ***vt-*** **1** to make (the eyes) sore or watery. **2** to blur or make dim, especially with water. ***adj-*** bleary.

blear·y (blêr′ ē) ***adj-*** **[blear·i·er, blear·i·est] 1** of the eyes, sore or watery. **2** dim; blurred.

bleat (blēt) ***n-*** the cry of a sheep, goat, or calf; also, any similar cry. ***vi-*** to utter any such cry.

bleed (blēd) ***vi-*** **[bled** (blĕd), **bleed·ing] 1** to lose or shed blood. **2** of a plant, to lose sap or juice from a cut surface: *The tree* bled *where the branch was trimmed.* **3** of wet dyes, to run. **4** to suffer wounds or die, especially (for) one's country or cause: *They fought and* bled *for freedom.* **5** to feel grief or pity (for): *One's heart* bleeds *for these valiant dead.* ***vt-*** **1** formerly, to take blood from as a medical treatment. **2** to draw a fluid from: *The mechanic* bled *the brake cylinder.* **3** *Informal* to extort money from: *Mortimer* bled *his grandaunt of all her money.*

bleed white to exhaust one's resources over a long time: *The nation was being* bled white *by the long war.*

bleed·er (blē′ dər) ***n-*** person who bleeds because his blood does not clot normally; hemophiliac.

blem·ish (blĕm′ ĭsh) ***n-*** a mark that spoils the appearance; a flaw. ***vt-*** to put a bad mark on; mar; stain: *One bad mistake can* blemish *a man's reputation.*

[1]**blench** (blĕnch) ***vi-*** to start or shrink back; quail; flinch: *to* blench *at gunfire.* [probably from Old English **blencan** meaning "to deceive; steal away."]

[2]**blench** (blĕnch) blanch. [varied form of **blanch.**]

blend (blĕnd) ***vt-*** to mix so thoroughly that the ingredients can no longer be separated or told apart. ***vi-*** to shade into each other: *The colors in the sunset* blend *well.* ***n-*** mixture of colors or flavors: *a* blend *of blue and gray*; *a* blend *of coffee.*

blend·er (blĕn′ dər) ***n-*** **1** person who blends paint, tobacco, coffee, or the like. **2** tool or machine for blending food, paint, or the like.

bless (blĕs) ***vt-*** **[blessed** or **blest, bless·ing] 1** to make holy: *to* bless *an altar.* **2** to call down the favor of God upon (a person, thing, or event). **3** to favor (with a blessing, happiness, success, etc.): *Fortune* blessed *him with a good disposition.* **4** to praise; honor: *to* bless *the Lord.*

bless·ed (blĕs′ əd) ***adj-*** **1** holy: *the* blessed *saints.* **2** extremely happy: *What a* blessed *bit of news!* **3** (intensifier only): *I haven't a* blessed *cent.* ***—adv-*** **bless′ ed·ly.** ***n-*** **bless′ ed·ness.**

Bless·ed Virgin (blĕs′ əd) ***n-*** the Virgin Mary.

bless·ing (blĕs′ ing) ***n-*** **1** prayer asking for the favor of God: *The pastor gave the travelers his* blessing. **2** prayer of thanks at a meal; a grace. **3** something that makes for happiness, health, or good fortune: *Peace of mind is a great* blessing.

blew (bloo͞) *p.t.* of **blow.** ***Hom-*** blue.

blight (blīt) ***n-*** **1** a disease that withers and kills plants or trees, especially over large areas; also, the fungus, bacterium, or virus that causes the disease. **2** anything that ruins or destroys: *War is the* blight *of mankind.* ***vt-*** to destroy or ruin; decay: *Slums* blight *the city.*

blimp (blĭmp) ***n-*** small, nonrigid airship.

blind (blīnd) ***adj-*** **[blind·er, blind·est] 1** unable to see; sightless. **2** unable or unwilling to understand: *He was* blind *to his own weaknesses.* **3** unthinking; heedless; rash; without reason: *in* blind *haste*; *a* blind *panic.* **4** hidden: *a* blind *curve.* **5** with no outlet: *a* blind *alley.* ***n-*** **1** something to obstruct vision or keep out light: *a window* blind. **2** something meant to mislead: *His fishing trips were a* blind *for smuggling operations.* **3** place or means of concealment, as in hunting. ***vt-*** **1** to take away the power to see: *The sun* blinded *me for a moment.* **2** to deprive of judgment: *Anger* blinded *him.* ***—adv-*** **blind′ ly.** ***n-*** **blind′ ness.**

blind alley ***n-*** alley or other passageway closed off at one end.

up a blind alley defeated in one's search; in a hopeless situation: *John's research led him* up a blind alley.

blind·er (blīn′ dər) ***n-*** a panel on a horse's bridle which prevents him from seeing objects beside him; blinker.

blind flying ***n-*** flying an aircraft entirely by instruments, as in fog or clouds.

blind·fold (blīnd′ fōld′) ***vt-*** to cover the eyes of, as with a bandage. ***n-*** the bandage or covering over the eyes. ***adj-*** with the eyes covered and unable to see.

blind·man's buff (blīnd′ manz′ bŭf′) ***n-*** game in which a blindfolded player tries to catch and identify one of several other players.

blind spot ***n-*** **1** small area on the retina, where the optic nerve enters it, that is not sensitive to light. **2** part of a person's field of vision blocked by an external object. **3** subject about which a person is ignorant or prejudiced without realizing it: *One of his few* blind spots *is modern jazz.* **4** place where radio or television reception is poorer than in the surrounding area.

blink (blĭngk) ***vi-*** **1** to wink quickly. **2** of a light, to twinkle; also, to go on and off rapidly. ***vt-*** **1** to wink (the eyes) rapidly. **2** to turn (lights) off and on rapidly. **3** to close the mind to. ***n-*** **1** a rapid winking. **2** a sudden gleam of light.

blink at to close the mind to; ignore.

blink·er (blĭng′ kər) ***n-*** **1** (usually **blinkers**) leather flap placed one on each side of a horse's bridle to prevent him from seeing objects beside him. **2** a blinking light used as a warning signal, as at a crossing.

blin·tze (blĭnt′ sə) ***n-*** thin pancake folded around cottage cheese or other filling, fried, and often eaten with sour cream. Also **blintz** (blĭnts).

blip (blĭp) ***n-*** spot of light on a radar screen that indicates the presence of an object that reflects radar.

bliss (blĭs) ***n-*** great happiness; perfect joy; ecstasy.

bliss·ful (blĭs′ fəl) ***adj-*** very happy; joyful. ***—adv-*** **bliss′ ful·ly.** ***n-*** **bliss′ ful·ness.**

blis·ter (blĭs′ tər) ***n-*** **1** a little swollen pocket of watery liquid under the surface of the skin, caused by a burn or other injury. **2** bubble formed beneath the surface of a layer of paint or within a slab of glass. ***vt-***: *The sunburn* blistered *my back.* ***vi-***: *My back* blistered.

blithe (blīth, blīth) ***adj-*** **[blith·er, blith·est]** gay; glad; cheerful: *a* blithe *tune.* **—*adv-* blithe′ ly.** ***n-*** **blithe′ ness.**

blitz (blĭts) *Slang* ***n-*** blitzkrieg; hence, any fast-moving, concentrated attack. ***vt-*** to make a fast attack on.

blitz·krieg (blĭts′ krēg′) ***n-*** war waged with great speed, especially with motorized and armored troops. [from German **blitz**, meaning "lightning," plus **krieg**, "war."]

bliz·zard (blĭz′ ərd) ***n-*** a storm with snow, strong winds, and bitter cold.

bloat (blōt) ***vt-*** to cause to swell; puff up: *All that food has really* bloated *me!* ***vi-***: *The cow* bloated.

bloat·er (blō′ tər) ***n-*** large herring, salted, smoked, and half dried.

blob (blŏb) ***n-*** soft, shapeless mass of anything, especially of a thick liquid: *a* blob *of paint.*

bloc (blŏk) ***n-*** political group, often of different parties, who unite for a time in order to promote some common interest: *the farm* bloc. ***Hom-*** block.

block (blŏk) ***n-* 1** solid piece of wood, stone, metal, etc. **2** form for molding or shaping articles, such as hats. **3** stand on which articles are put up for sale by an auctioneer. **4** grooved pulley in a frame. **5** connected row of houses or shops; also, a large building divided into separate houses or shops. **6** part of a city bounded by four streets; square; also, the length of one side of such an area. **7** number or section of things taken as a unit: *a* block *of theater seats.* **8** obstacle; hindrance; hence, standstill: *a traffic* block. ***vt-* 1** to obstruct; hinder: *He* blocked *my way.* **2** to mold on a form: *to* block *hats.* **3** in football or basketball, to check the progress of, or interfere with (an opponent or his play). **4** to secure or hold up, as by square wooden supports. ***vi-***: *A football guard must* block *well.* ***Hom-*** bloc.

Block of a pulley

block in (or **out**) to plan or outline roughly: *He* blocked in *the drawing before adding any details.*

block·ade (blŏ kād′) ***n-* 1** the shutting off of a place, especially a port, by ships or troops to keep anything or anybody from coming in or going out. **2** any barrier or obstruction: *The barrels piled at the entrance made an effective* blockade. ***vt-*** **[block·ad·ed, block·ad·ing]**: *to* blockade *the enemy's ports.*

run a blockade to penetrate a blockade by speed or stealth.

block·ade-run·ner (blŏ kād′ rŭn′ ər) ***n-*** person or ship that tries to slip through an enemy blockade.

block and tackle ***n-*** set of pulleys (blocks) and ropes (tackle) used to lift heavy objects.

block·bust·er (blŏk′ bŭs′ tər) ***n-* 1** in World War II, powerful aerial bomb capable of destroying a large area, like an entire city block. **2** *Slang* any very large, impressive, or successful event or object.

block·head (blŏk′ hĕd′) ***n-*** stupid person; dunce.

block·house (blŏk′ hous′) ***n-* 1** fortified building, usually of concrete and steel, with loopholes in the walls for shooting at the enemy. **2** similar building that is the control center for a rocket launching. **3** fort built of logs or heavy timber, with a projecting upper story.

Blockhouse

block·ish (blŏk′ ĭsh) ***adj-*** dull; stupid: *a* blockish *oaf.*

block mountains ***n-*** mountains formed by the uplift of huge blocks of earth from the earth's crust.

block system ***n-*** automatic system for the safe passage of railway trains, by which the line of track is divided into short sections called blocks. The entrance to each block is regulated by automatic signals called **block signals**, and no train is allowed to leave a block until the next block is signaled clear.

block·y (blŏk′ ē) ***adj-*** **[block·i·er, block·i·est] 1** having uneven blocks or patches of light and shade, as some photographs. **2** short and stocky; chunky.

bloke (blōk) *Brit. Slang* ***n-*** fellow; guy.

blond (blŏnd) ***adj-*** **[blond·er, blond·est] 1** having light skin and hair: *Many Swedish people are* blond. **2** light in color: *They bought* blond *furniture.* ***n-*** person with skin and hair of light color. **—*n-* blond′ ness.**

blonde (blŏnd) ***n-*** *fem.* girl or woman with skin and hair of light color.

blood (blŭd) ***n-* 1** a red fluid which circulates through the bodies of men and animals. It carries food, oxygen, and hormones to all parts of the body and removes waste. **2** kinship: *related by* blood. **3** descent; especially, noble or royal lineage: *a prince of the* blood. **4** man of spirit: *a young* blood. **5** temper; passion: *His* blood *was up.*

bad blood hatred; dislike: *There is* bad blood *between the feuding families.* **in cold blood** cruelly; ruthlessly.

blood bank ***n-* 1** a supply of different types of blood for blood transfusions. **2** the place where such a supply is kept.

blood bath ***n-*** great slaughter; massacre.

blood cell See *red blood cell* and *white blood cell.*

blood count ***n-*** health test in which the number of red blood cells and white blood cells in a measured sample of a person's blood are counted.

blood·curd·ling (blŭd′ kûrd′ lĭng) ***adj-*** terrifying; frightening; horrible: *a* bloodcurdling *shriek.*

blood·ed (blŭd′ əd) ***adj-*** of good stock or breed; thoroughbred: *The farmer buys only* blooded *cattle.*

blood group ***n-*** one of four main types (A, AB, B, or O) into which human blood is classified, depending on the presence or absence of certain substances; blood type.

blood·hound (blŭd′ hound′) ***n-* 1** large black and tan dog with a wrinkled face and drooping ears, whose sharp sense of smell makes him useful in tracking criminals or lost persons. **2** *Informal* a detective.

blood·less (blŭd′ ləs) ***adj-* 1** without shedding blood: *a* bloodless *victory.* **2** very pale: *her* bloodless *cheeks.* **3** lacking emotion or spirit; cold-hearted; unfeeling. **—*adv-* blood′ less·ly.**

blood·line (blŭd′ līn′) ***n-*** line of descent, especially of an animal; pedigree.

blood·mo·bile (blŭd′ mō bēl′) ***n-*** a medical truck specially equipped to collect blood from donors.

blood money ***n-*** money got at the cost of a life, as money received by a murderer for killing someone, or money received for betraying the whereabouts of a fugitive from justice or assisting in his arrest and conviction.

blood poisoning ***n-*** diseased condition of the blood due to poisons or germs.

blood pressure ***n-*** pressure of the blood against the walls of the arteries.

blood·root (blŭd′ ro͞ot′) ***n-*** plant of the poppy family with a red root and red sap, bearing a white flower which blooms in early spring.

blood serum ***n-*** clear fluid remaining after the blood cells and clotting materials in the blood have been removed.
blood·shed (blŭd′ shĕd′) ***n-*** destruction of life; spilling of blood: *The city was captured without* bloodshed.
blood·shot (blŭd′ shŏt′) ***adj-*** red and inflamed: *tired,* bloodshot *eyes.*
blood·stain (blŭd′ stān′) ***n-*** a stain caused by blood. ***—adj-*** **blood′ stained′** : *a* bloodstained *knife.*
blood·stone (blŭd′ stōn′) ***n-*** opaque green stone flecked with red, often used in jewelry.
blood·stream (blŭd′ strēm′) ***n-*** the circulating blood in a living body.
blood·suck·er (blŭd′ sŭk′ ər) ***n-*** **1** an animal that sucks blood; especially, a leech. **2** *Informal* one who extorts money from others.
blood sugar ***n-*** glucose.
blood test ***n-*** any of various medical tests of the blood.
blood·thirst·y (blŭd′ thûrs′ tē) ***adj-*** eager to shed blood; brutal; intent upon killing. ***—adv-*** **blood′ thirst′ i·ly.** ***n-*** **blood′ thirst′ i·ness.**
blood type ***n-*** blood group.
blood vessel ***n-*** an artery, vein, or capillary.
blood·y (blŭd′ ē) ***adj-*** **[blood·i·er, blood·i·est] 1** stained with blood: *The bandage has become* bloody. **2** bleeding: *a* bloody *nose*; *a* bloody *wound.* **3** with much shedding of blood: *a* bloody *war.* ***—adv-*** **blood′ i·ly.**
bloom (blōōm) ***n-*** **1** the flower of a plant: *The violet has a delicate* bloom. **2** a time of flowering. **3** time when one is at the peak of health, beauty, etc.; prime: *the* bloom *of youth.* **4** a fine white coating, as on some fruit or leaves: *the* bloom *on a grape.* ***vi-*** **1** to produce blossoms; flower. **2** to glow with youth and freshness; flourish.
bloom·ers (blōō′ mərz) ***n-*** (takes plural verb) loose, wide trousers gathered and ending at the knees, once worn by women in athletic sports; also, an undergarment of similar design.
bloom·ing (blōō′ mĭng) ***adj-*** **1** blossoming; in flower. **2** full of youthful freshness and health; flourishing: *his* blooming *enthusiasm.* **3** *Slang* (intensifier only): *a* blooming *idiot.* ***adv-*** *Slang* (intensifier only): *He'd* blooming *well better do it!*
blos·som (blŏs′ əm) ***n-*** **1** the flower of a plant, especially a plant which bears fruit: *apple* blossom; *peach* blossom. **2** stage of bearing flowers: *The trees are in* blossom. ***vi-*** to bloom: *The cherry trees are about to* blossom.
blot (blŏt) ***n-*** **1** a spot or stain: *The ink left a* blot *on the paper.* **2** something against a person's reputation or character: *His bad marks left a* blot *on his record.* ***vt-*** **[blot·ted, blot·ting] 1** to make a spot or stain on. **2** to dry or soak up with a blotter.
blot out 1 to hide completely; obscure: *The eclipse* blotted out *the sun.* **2** to destroy wholly: *The eruption of a volcano can* blot out *a town.*
blotch (blŏch) ***n-*** **1** a large irregular spot: *There is a big* blotch *of ink on the curtain.* **2** an ugly, often inflamed spot or mark on the skin: *He had a large* blotch *on his neck from poison ivy.* ***vt-*** to mark with stains. ***—adj-*** **blotch′ y [blotch·i·er, blotch·i·est]**: *a* blotchy *skin.*
blot·ter (blŏt′ ər) ***n-*** a piece of blotting paper.
blotting paper ***n-*** porous, absorbent paper, specially made to absorb and dry wet ink.
blouse (blous) ***n-*** **1** a kind of loose outer garment or shirt extending to the waist or below, worn by women and children; shirtwaist. **2** in parts of Europe, a loose smock worn by workmen and farmers to protect their clothes. **3** coat or jacket of military uniforms.
[1]**blow** (blō) ***vi-*** **[blew, blown, blow·ing] 1** of wind or air, to be in motion: *The wind* blew *all afternoon.* **2** to be moved or carried along by the wind: *The papers* blew *all over the room.* **3** to make a sound by having air or steam forced through: *The whistle* blew *and the workers went to lunch.* **4** to direct a current of air from the mouth: *to* blow *on a burned finger*; *to* blow *into a trumpet.* **5** of whales, to spout air from their blowholes: *"Thar she* blows," *is the cry of whalers sighting a whale.* ***vt-*** **1** to move or drive by the motion of the air: *The wind had* blown *the leaves about.* **2** to make or shape by forcing air on or into something: *to* blow *bubbles*; *to* blow *glass.* **3** to cause (a musical instrument, whistle, etc.) to sound by forcing air into it. **4** to break or damage: *to* blow *a tire*; *to* blow *a gasket.* **5** to clean or empty (a tube, one's nose, etc.) by forcing air through it. **6** to melt or burn out (a fuse). **7** *Slang* to spend (money) quickly and foolishly. ***n-*** strong wind; gale. [from Old English **blāwan** of the same meaning.]
blow hot and cold to change one's mind too often; be uncertain; vacillate.
blow into *Slang* to arrive in (a town, etc.)
blow off 1 to release (steam or air) from boiler, valve, etc. **2** *Informal* to release (pent-up emotions, anger, ideas, etc.) by talking; especially in the phrase **blow off steam.**
blow out 1 to extinguish or be extinguished by a gust of air: *to* blow out *a candle.* **2** to burst. **3** to melt or burn out (a fuse).
blow over to pass away; cease; subside: *The storm* blew over *and went out to sea. After the scandal* blew over, *he returned to town.*
blow up 1 to inflate; expand: *to* blow up *a balloon*; *to* blow up *a tire.* **2** to explode: *The boiler* blew up *because of too much steam pressure.* **3** to enlarge (a photograph). **4** to begin; come up: *A bad storm* blew up *over the mountain.* **5** *Informal* to lose one's temper.
[2]**blow** (blō) ***n-*** **1** a hard stroke from a hand, fist, stick, or weapon. **2** sudden shock or upset: *The bad news was quite a* blow. [from Middle English **blaw.** It is probably related to [1]**blow.**]
at a (or **one**) **blow** suddenly; at one effort; by one single action: *The entire southern province fell to the enemy* at one blow. **come to blows** to begin to fight: *One word led to another, and they soon* came to blows.
blow·er (blō′ ər) ***n-*** **1** a device for forcing air through a building, furnace, machine, mine, etc. **2** one who blows: *a glass* blower.
blow·fish (blō′ fĭsh′) ***n-*** **1** any of several fish of warm seas which inflate themselves into a spiny balloon when in danger; globefish. **2** in southern United States, the walleyed pike.
blow·fly (blō′ flī′) ***n-*** [*pl.* **blow·flies**] any of several kinds of shiny blue or green flies whose eggs and larvae (maggots) develop in dead or living flesh; bluebottle.
blow·gun (blō′ gŭn′) ***n-*** tube through which a poisoned dart or other missile may be blown by a person's breath. It is used as weapon in certain parts of Asia and South America.
blow·hole (blō′ hōl′) ***n-*** **1** the nostril of a whale, located on the top of its head. **2** hole in ice through which sea mammals such as seals, whales, etc., breathe. **3** in mines and tunnels, a vent for the escape of gases. **4** an air bubble in metal or glass.
blown (blōn) *p.p.* of [1]**blow.**
blow·out (blō′ out′) ***n-*** explosive escape of air from a punctured automobile tire or any other inflated object.
blow·pipe (blō′ pīp′) ***n-*** **1** small tube for blowing air into a flame to direct it properly, and to increase its heat. **2** primitive gun of cane, from which a dart is blown by the breath; blowgun. **3** long metal tube used

by glassmakers to blow and spin molten glass into the intended shape.

blow·torch (blō′tórch′, -tôrch′) ***n-*** portable pressure torch that produces an intensely hot flame from a jet of vaporized gasoline or other fuel mixed with air.

blow·up (blō′ŭp′) ***n-*** **1** an explosion. **2** *Informal* an angry outburst. **3** an enlargement of a photograph.

blow·zy (blou′zē) ***adj-*** [**blowz·i·er, blowz·i·est**] **1** red-faced; having a coarse complexion. **2** frowzy; unkempt. Also **blow′sy.**

blub·ber (blŭb′ər) ***vi-*** to weep noisily; sob. ***vt-*** to utter with chokes and sobs: *He* blubbers *his miseries to everyone.* ***n-*** **1** noisy sob. **2** layer of fat under the skin of whales, seals, and walruses, used as a source of oil. ***adj-*** swollen: *teary eyes and* blubber *lips.* **—*n-*** **blub′ber·er:** *What a* blubberer *that child is!* ***adj-*** **blub′ber·y:** *a* blubbery, *tear-stained face; the* blubbery *decks of the whaler.*

bludg·eon (blŭj′ən) ***n-*** short, heavy-headed stick used as a weapon. ***vt-*** to strike with, or as with, a club.

blue (blōō) ***n-*** **1** the color of the clear daytime sky, cornflowers, and forget-me-nots. Blue is between green and indigo on the spectrum. **2** pigment of this color. **3 the blue** (1) the sea. (2) the sky. ***adj-*** [**blu·er, blu·est**] **1** having the color between green and indigo. **2** of a bluish tinge: *My nose is* blue *with the cold.* **3** sad; gloomy; dismal: *He was lonely and* blue. ***vt.*** [**blued, blu·ing** or **blue·ing**] **1** to treat with bluing: *to* blue *linens.* **2** to paint or dye this color. ***Hom-*** blew. See also *blues.* **—*adv-*** **blue′ly.** ***n-*** **blue′ness.**

out of the blue as if from nowhere; at a completely unexpected time: *He attacked me* out of the blue.

blue baby ***n-*** child with bluish skin color, usually resulting from a heart defect.

blue·bell (blōō′bĕl′) ***n-*** any of several plants bearing blue bell-shaped flowers, such as the harebell.

blue·ber·ry (blōō′bĕr′ē) ***n-*** [*pl.* **blue·ber·ries**] **1** round, edible blue berry that grows on a shrub or tall bush. **2** the bush or shrub it grows on. *as **modifier**: a* blueberry *pie.*

blue·bird (blōō′bûrd′) ***n-*** songbird related to the robin and thrush, having a blue back and a reddish breast.

blue blood ***n-*** **1** noble or royal ancestry. **2** member of a noble or prominent family; aristocrat. **—*adj-*** **blue′blood′ed.**

blue·bon·net (blōō′bŏn′ət) ***n-*** **1** a plant with blue, white, pink, or purple flowers. The bluebonnet is the state flower of Texas. **2** the cornflower. **3** a broad, flat cap made of blue wool, worn in Scotland.

blue book ***n-*** **1** *Informal* a list of socially prominent people; social register. **2** booklet, usually having blue paper covers, used for writing answers in college tests. **3** in Great Britain, any official government publication, especially one issued by Parliament.

blue·bot·tle (blōō′bŏt′əl) ***n-*** **1** any various large blowflies that have iridescent blue bodies and fly with a loud buzzing sound. **2** the cornflower.

blue·coat (blōō′kōt′) *Informal* ***n-*** uniformed policeman.

blue·fish (blōō′fish′) ***n-*** [**blue·fish; blue·fish·es** (kinds of bluefish)] blue and silver food and game fish of the Atlantic and Indian oceans.

blue·grass (blō′grăs) ***n-*** **1** a pasture grass with bluish green stems. **2** country music played on unamplified, stringed instruments.

blue·ing (blōō′ing) bluing.

blue·jack·et (blōō′jăk′ət) ***n-*** a sailor in the Navy.

blue·jay (blōō′jā′) ***n-*** crested bird of eastern North America with a gray-white underside and throat and blue wings and tail handsomely marked with black and white bands.

blue jeans ***n-*** (takes plural verb) pants, usually made of blue denim.

Bluejay, about 11 in. long

blue law ***n-*** **1** any of the strict laws concerning personal behavior passed by the early American colonists, especially the Connecticut Puritans. **2** a law prohibiting certain activities on Sunday.

blue note ***n-*** in jazz music, a note lowered a half-tone from the major tone, especially either the 3rd of 7th note of the scale.

blue·print (blōō′prĭnt′) ***n-*** **1** a photographic print, white on blue paper, used as a plan in building operations, etc. **2** a precise plan of action: *a* blueprint *for success.*

blue racer ***n-*** a bluish-green black snake.

blue ribbon ***n-*** a blue-colored ribbon awarded to the winner of the first prize; also the first prize itself.

blue-ribbon jury ***n-*** jury that has been selected from a list of specially qualified jurors for an unusually difficult or complicated case.

blues (blōōz) ***n-*** (takes singular or plural verb) **1** a kind of music having a slow jazz rhythm and a sad, mournful quality obtained by frequent use of blue notes; also, a song of this type. **2** melancholy; depression. Also **the blues.** *as **modifier**: a* blues *singer.*

blue whale ***n-*** whale with blue-gray dorsal coloration, narrow ridges along its throat, and yellowish underside. It is considered the largest living animal.

¹bluff (blŭf) ***n-*** bold, flat headland (as opposed to a sharp, overhanging cliff). ***adj-*** **1** rising steeply: *the* bluff *headlands that rose along the shore.* **2** rough but hearty and full of good humor: *a* bluff *greeting.* [from early German **blaf** meaning "flat."] **—*adv-*** **bluff′ly.** ***n-*** **bluff′ness:** *the* bluffness *of his manner.*

²bluff (blŭf) ***vt-*** **1** to mislead or overawe by assuming a bold or pretentious manner or speech: *He* bluffed *the guard into admitting him.* **2** to try to get by (something) by pretense: *to* bluff *a test.* ***vi:*** *He* bluffed *all through the interview.* ***n-*** **1** show of pretended confidence, knowledge, etc. **2** (also **bluf′fer**) person who bluffs. [probably from Dutch **verbluffen** meaning "to baffle; mislead."]

call (someone's) bluff to demand a showdown.

blu·ing or **blue·ing** (blōō′ĭng) ***n-*** blue coloring substance used in laundering white clothes.

blun·der (blŭn′dər) ***n-*** stupid or careless mistake. ***vi-*** **1** to make a mistake from stupidity, ignorance, or lack of attention. **2** to move clumsily; stumble: *The boy* blundered *around in the dark room.* **—*n-*** **blun′der·er.**

blunder upon to find or discover by accident.

blun·der·buss (blŭn′dər bŭs′) ***n-*** old-time gun with a bell-shaped muzzle that spreads a quantity of shot at close range.

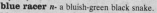

Blunderbuss

blunt (blŭnt) ***adj-*** [**blunt·er, blunt·est**] **1** without a sharp edge or point; not sharp;

fāte, făt, dâre, bärn; bē, bĕt, mêre; bīte, bĭt; nōte, hŏt, môre, dóg; fŭn, fûr; tōō, bŏŏk; oil; out; tar; thin; then; hw for wh as in what; zh for s as in usual; ə for a, e, i, o, u, as in ago, linen, peril, atom, minus

dull: *a* blunt *knife.* **2** frank and plain-spoken; abrupt: *a* blunt *answer.* ***vt-*** to make less sharp or keen: *He* blunted *his knife on a stone. Fatigue* blunts *one's wits.* **—*adv-* blunt′ ly. *n-* blunt′ ness.**

blur (blûr) ***vt-*** **[blurred, blur·ring]** to make indistinct or obscure; dim: *The fog* blurred *the outlines of the buildings. Time had* blurred *her memory.* ***vi-***: *His eyes* blurred *with tears.* ***n-*** indistinct shape or appearance: *The road ahead was one big* blur *to him.* **—*adj-* blur′ ry [blur·ri·er, blur·ri·est].**

blurb (blûrb) *Informal* ***n-*** a brief notice or advertisement praising a book or its author and usually appearing on the book jacket. [American word coined by Gelett Burgess.]

blurt (blûrt) ***vt-*** to speak suddenly and without thinking: *He rushed in and* blurted *out the bad news.*

blush (blŭsh) ***vi-*** **1** to become red in the face from shame or embarrassment. **2** to feel shame or embarrassment: *I* blush *for your mistake.* ***n-*** **1** a reddening of the face from shame or embarrassment. **2** rosy color: *the first* blush *of dawn.*

blus·ter (blŭs′ tər) ***vi-*** **1** to blow gustily, as wind; to be rough and windy, as a storm. **2** to talk in a noisy, threatening style. ***n-*** **1** the noise and violence of a storm, or of a high wind. **2** noisy talk; empty threats. **—*n-* blus′ ter·er. *adj-* blus′ ter·y**: *a cold,* blustery *day.*

blvd. boulevard.

bo·a (bō′ ə) ***n-*** **1** any of a large group of nonpoisonous snakes, ranging from 2 to 25 feet in length. Various kinds are found in North and South America, southern Asia, and northern Africa. Boas are constrictors, killing their prey by squeezing it in their coils before swallowing it. **2** a woman's long scarf of feathers or fur.

boa constrictor ***n-*** large boa of tropical America, growing to about 11 feet in length.

boar (bôr) ***n-*** **1** male pig or hog. **2** wild hog. ***Hom-*** bore.

Wild boar, about 4 ft. long

board (bôrd) ***n-*** **1** flat piece of sawed timber, longer or wider than it is thick. **2** flat piece of wood or other material prepared for a definite use: *a cutting* board. **3** group of persons with power to advise, manage, or direct: *a* board *of health.* **4** table ready for serving food: *the festive* board. **5** meals provided regularly for pay: *She pays for room and* board *by the week.* **6** blackboard or similar panel for posting notices, such as airplane arrivals. **7** flat panel used for checkers, card games, etc. ***vt-*** **1** to cover (up) with pieces of sawed timber: *to* board *up windows.* **2** to provide with meals, and sometimes lodging: *to* board *students.* **3** to go on (a ship, train, or plane). ***vi-*** to eat or live at a house where paying guests are accepted.

on board on a ship, train, etc.

board·er (bôr′ dər) ***n-*** person who regularly gets meals, or meals and lodging, at a fixed charge. ***Hom-*** border.

board foot ***n-*** **[*pl.* board feet]** unit for measuring quantity of lumber, equal to the volume of an unplaned board one foot square and one inch thick, or 144 cubic inches.

board·ing (bôr′ dĭng) ***n-*** **1** boards. **2** something made of boards.

boarding house ***n-*** house, usually a person's home, where people get regular meals for a weekly rate.

boarding school ***n-*** school where students live and get room and board during the school year.

board·walk (bôrd′ wŏk′) ***n-*** wide walk or promenade along a beach, usually made of boards.

boast (bōst) ***vi-*** to brag; praise loudly and rashly oneself and one's belongings or actions. ***vt-*** to pride oneself on: *The city* boasted *a fifteen-story hotel.* ***n-*** **1** bragging statement: *His* boasts *about his own cleverness bored everyone.* **2** something to be proud of: *The new hospital was the* boast *of the town.* **—*n-* boast′ er**: *What a* boaster *he is!*

boast·ful (bōst′ fəl) ***adj-*** speaking too highly about oneself; full of self-praise: *Alec was* boastful *of his strength.* **—*adv-* boast′ ful·ly. *n-* boast′ ful·ness.**

boat (bōt) ***n-*** **1** any kind of small open watercraft, named according to the power by which it moves, such as *row*boat, *sail*boat; *motor*boat; also, a ship. **2** long, narrow dish. ***vi-*** to go in a small open vessel; row; sail. ***vt-*** to bring into a rowboat or other craft: *We* boated *three sailfish before noon.* ***as modifier***: *a* boat *whistle.* **—*n-* boat′ ing.**

boat hook ***n-*** long pole with a metal point and hook at one end, used to hold a boat to a ship's side or dock, or to push it away.

boat·house (bōt′ hous′) ***n-*** house or shed at the water's edge for storing boats.

boat·man (bōt′ mən) ***n-*** **[*pl.* boat·men]** man who manages or works around boats.

boat·swain (bō′ sən) ***n-*** an under officer of a ship in charge of the crew and of the rigging and anchors.

[1]bob (bŏb) ***n-*** **1** quick jerking movement up and down or to and fro. **2** weight attached to the end of a line: *a pendulum* bob. **3** a float on a fish line. **4** short haircut for girls or women. ***vt-*** **[bobbed, bob·bing]** to cut (a girl's or woman's hair) short. ***vi-*** to move rapidly or jerkily up and down or to and fro: *The little boat* bobbed *on the rough sea.* [from Middle English **bobbe** meaning "bunch," of uncertain origin.]

[2]bob (bŏb) *Brit. slang* ***n-*** **[*pl.* bob]** shilling. [perhaps from **Bob**, short for **Robert.**]

bob·bin (bŏb′ ən) ***n-*** spool or reel for thread, used in making fabrics or in sewing machines.

bob·ble (bŏb′ əl) *Informal* ***n-*** **1** in baseball or football, a dropping or juggling of a ball; fumble. **2** bobbing motion, as of a cork. ***vt-*** **[bob·bled, bob·bling]**: *The shortstop* bobbled *the ball.*

bob·by (bŏb′ ē) *Brit. slang* ***n-*** **[*pl.* bob·bies]** policeman.

bobby pin ***n-*** hairpin with two springy closed prongs for holding the hair tightly.

bob·by·socks (bŏb′ ē sŏks′) ***n-*** (takes plural verb) thick, white, ankle-high socks worn by girls.

bob·by·sox·er (bŏb′ ē sŏk′ sər) *Informal* ***n-*** a young girl who follows the latest teen-age fashions and fads.

bob·cat (bŏb′ kăt′) ***n-*** small North American lynx having a reddish-brown, spotted coat and a short tail; wildcat.

bob·o·link (bŏb ə lĭngk′) ***n-*** common songbird of the New World related to the oriole and the blackbird and named for its call; ricebird; reedbird.

bob·sled (bŏb′ slĕd′) ***n-*** **1** long racing sled having two pairs of runners, a steering wheel, and brakes. **2** long sled made by joining two shorter sleds; also, either of the two sleds so joined. ***vi-*** **[bob·sled·ded, bob·sled·ding]**: *The children* bobsledded *all morning.*

bob·tail (bŏb′ tāl′) ***n-*** **1** a short tail or a tail cut short. **2** an animal with such a tail. ***adj-*** (also **bob′ tailed′**): *a* bobtail *cat.*

bob·white (bŏb′ hwīt′) ***n-*** small, brownish American quail with a whistling call that sounds like its name.

[1]bode (bōd) ***vt-*** **[bod·ed, bod·ing]** to be a sign of; foretell: *The frequent mishaps* boded *disaster.* [from Old English **bodian**, from **boda** meaning "a messenger."]

bode ill (or **well**) to be a good (or bad) sign or omen: *This* bodes well *for his political success.*

bode (bōd) *p.t.* of **bide.** 2

bod·ice (bŏd′əs) ***n-*** **1** the part of a woman's dress above the waist. **2** wide belt or girdle, laced and tight-fitting.

bod·i·less (bŏd′ē ləs) ***adj-*** having no body or material form: *the* bodiless *souls.*

bod·i·ly (bŏd′ə lē) ***adj-*** having to do with the body: *a* bodily *ill.* ***adv-*** **1** physically; also, by physical force: *He was dragged away* bodily. **2** as one mass or body; entirely; altogether: *The wind lifted the roof* bodily *from the house.*

bod·kin (bŏd′kin) ***n-*** **1** pointed instrument used to pierce holes for embroidery. **2** blunt needle with a large eye for drawing tape or ribbon through loops or hems. **3** small dagger.

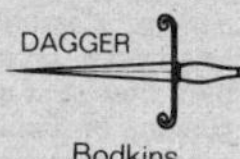

Bodkins

bod·y (bŏd′ē) ***n-*** [*pl.* **bod·ies**] **1** whole physical form of a living thing: *His* body *ached.* **2** dead person or animal: *The* body *was taken home for burial.* **3** main or central part of anything: *the* body *of a car; the* body *of a book.* **4** group of persons or things; collection: *a* body *of facts; a legislative* body. **5** distinct mass of matter: *a heavenly* body; *a* body *of water.* **5** thickness or substance; consistency: *This soup has no* body *to it.*

bod·y·guard (bŏd′ē gärd′) ***n-*** a protective escort made up of one or more people who are usually armed and often trained in martial arts.

body politic ***n-*** the people of a nation, state, or community, especially when acting as a political unit.

Boer (bôr, bŏŏr) ***n-*** South African colonist or farmer of Dutch descent. ***adj-***: *the* Boer *territory.*

bog (bŏg) ***n-*** wet, spongy ground made up of partly decayed plants; marsh; swamp; quagmire. ***vi-*** [**bogged, bog·ging**] to sink and stick fast in wet ground: *The wagon* bogged *down in the mud.* ***vt-***: *He* bogged *the car in the mud.*

bo·gey (bō′gē) ***n-*** [*pl.* **bo·geys**] **1** in golf, one stroke over par on a hole. **2** bogie. **3** bogy.

bo·gey·man (bŏŏg′ē mən, bŏŏg′ər-, bō′gē-, bŏŏ′gē-) ***n-*** [*pl.* **bo·gey·men**] a monstrous spirit, especially one described to children to frighten or threaten them.

bog·gle (bôg′əl) ***vi-*** [**bog·gled, bog·gling**] **1** to jump or shy away with fear: *The horse* boggled *at the swift stream.* **2** to hesitate; waver; shrink: *The diver* boggled *at the risk involved.* **3** to be clumsy; bungle; fumble: *He* boggled *along through the work.*

bog·gy (bŏg′ē) ***adj-*** [**bog·gi·er, bog·gi·est**] full of wet, muddy places; marshy.

bo·gie (bō′gē) ***n-*** **1** the frame of four wheels supporting either side of a railroad car. **2** one of the wheels supporting the tread of a tank or tractor. **3** bogey. **4** bogy.

bo·gus (bō′gəs) ***adj-*** fake; counterfeit; not genuine: *to pass* bogus *money.*

bo·gy (bŏŏg′ē, bō′gē, bŏŏg′ər) ***n-*** [*pl.* **bo·gies**] **1** an evil spirit; hobgoblin. **2** person or thing that causes trouble or annoyance; bugbear. **3** *Slang* an attacking enemy fighter plane. **4** bogey. **5** bogie.

Bo·he·mi·an (bō hē′mē ən) ***n-*** **1** a native of Bohemia. **2** **bohemian** someone with artistic or literary leanings who is indifferent to the conventions of social life. ***adj-***: *a* Bohemian *costume; their* bohemian *manners.*

[1]**boil** (boil) ***vi-*** **1** of a liquid, to give off vapor so fast that the surface bubbles. **2** to be stirred up as if boiling: *The water* boiled *through the canyon.* **3** to be very angry: *He* boiled *with rage.* ***vt-*** **1** to cause (a liquid) to boil by heating it: *to* boil *milk.* **2** to cook by boiling: *to* boil *an egg.* ***n-*** the boiling point: *Bring the syrup to a* boil. [from Old French **boillir**, from Latin **bullire** meaning "to form bubbles."]

boil down **1** to reduce the amount (of something) by boiling it to evaporate some of the liquid in it. **2** to shorten (a report, etc.) by leaving out unnecessary details.

boil over **1** to overflow because of rapid boiling. **2** to lose one's temper.

[2]**boil** (boil) ***n-*** a painful, pus-filled swelling in the skin, caused by infection in a hair follicle or a skin gland. [from Old English **bȳle.**]

boil·er (boi′lər) ***n-*** **1** large metal vessel in which steam is produced for heating buildings and driving engines. **2** tank for storing hot water. **3** vessel in which things are boiled: *a wash* boiler. *as* ***modifier***: *a* boiler *factory.*

boiling point ***n-*** **1** lowest temperature at which a liquid boils. **2** *Physics* lowest temperature at which a pure liquid boils at standard pressure.

bois·ter·ous (boi′stər əs) ***adj-*** **1** stormy; rough: *a* boisterous *sea.* **2** noisily cheerful: *a burst of* boisterous *laughter.* ***—adv-*** **bois′ter·ous·ly.** ***n-*** **bois′ter·ous·ness.**

bo·la (bō′lə) ***n-*** device used in South America, consisting of two or more stone or metal balls fastened to long cords. It is thrown at cattle or game in order to entangle and capture them. Also **bo′las** (bō′ləs).

Gaucho using a bola

bold (bōld) ***adj-*** [**bold·er, bold·est**] **1** showing or demanding courage: *a* bold *fighter for freedom.* **2** daring; audacious: *a* bold *remark.* **3** strongly, sharply marked: *a* bold *signature.* **4** boldface. ***—adv-*** **bold′ly.** ***n-*** **bold′ness.**

make bold to to have the courage to; to venture to.

bold·face (bōld′fās′) ***n-*** type cut with thick lines so as to be heavy and conspicuous. **This is printed in boldface.** ***adj-***: *a* boldface *type; a* boldface *heading in a book.*

bole (bōl) ***n-*** trunk of a tree. ***Homs-*** boll, bowl.

bo·le·ro (bō lâr′ō) ***n-*** [*pl.* **bo·le·ros**] **1** a lively Spanish dance in 3/4 measure; also, a musical piece for this dance. **2** a short, open jacket ending at or above the waist.

bol·i·var (bŏl′ə vər, bō lē′vär) ***n-*** monetary unit of Venezuela, a silver coin.

bo·li·via·no (bə lĭv′ē ăn′ō) ***n-*** [*pl.* **bo·li·via·nos**] former monetary unit of Bolivia, a silver coin.

boll (bōl) ***n-*** the seed pod of a plant such as cotton or flax. ***Homs-*** bole, bowl.

boll weevil ***n-*** grayish beetle, about one quarter of an inch long, which lays its eggs in cotton bolls. The larvae cause serious damage to the cotton crop.

Boll weevil, 1/4 in. long

boll worm ***n-*** **1** pink wormlike larva of a small brown moth. It is a serious cotton pest. **2** corn earworm.

bo·lo (bō′lō) ***n-*** [*pl.* **bo·los**] large, heavy, swordlike knife used in the Philippines.

bo·lo·gna (bə lō′nē, -nə) ***n-*** a large sausage filled with a mixture of smoked meats. Also **baloney.**

Bol·she·vik or **bol·she·vik** (bōl′shə vĭk′, bŏl′-) ***n-*** [*pl.* **Bol·she·viks** or **Bol·she·vi·ki** (-vĭk′ē)] **1** member of the dominant radical wing of the Russian Social Democratic Party which seized power in November, 1917, during the Russian Revolution and, in 1918, became the Communist Party; Communist. **2** loosely, any person thought to have extreme or revolutionary views; radical. ***adj-***: *the* Bolshevik *theory of revolution.* Also **Bol′she·vist** or **bol′she·vist.**

Bol·she·vism or **bol·she·vism** (bōl′shə vĭz′əm, bŏl′-) ***n-*** **1** the theories and practices of the Bolsheviks; revolutionary socialism. **2** loosely, any radical political theory or movement. ***—adj-*** **Bol′she·vis′tic** or **bol′she·vis′tic.**

bol·ster (bōl′stər) ***n-*** **1** long pillow that extends across a bed. **2** cushioned pad or support. ***vt-*** to support; brace: *The song* bolstered *our courage.*

[1]**bolt** (bōlt) ***n-*** **1** short, heavy-headed arrow for a crossbow; dart. **2** anything coming dartingly or suddenly: *a* bolt *of lightning.* **3** metal pin or rod for fastening together parts of machinery, furniture, etc., threaded to hold a nut. **4** sliding catch for a door or gate; also, that part of a lock which is shot or drawn back by the key. **5** roll of cloth, usually containing about 40 yards. **6** a sudden dashing or darting away.

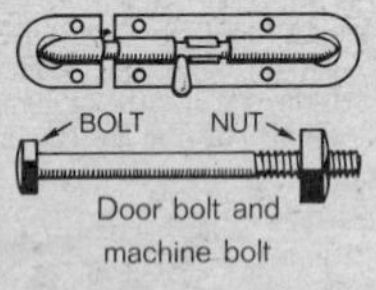

Door bolt and machine bolt

vt- **1** to fasten with a sliding catch: *He* bolted *the door.* **2** to attach with threaded fastenings: *to* bolt *a handle on an oven door.* **3** to swallow (food) very rapidly, or without chewing. **4** in politics, to break away from (one's party). ***vi-*** to dash away suddenly. [from Old English **bolt** meaning "shaft used in a crossbow."]

bolt upright directly up or upward: *He sat* bolt upright *at the news.*

[2]**bolt** (bōlt) ***vt-*** to sift, as flour. [from Old French **buleter,** from Old High German **būtil,** "sieve."]

bolt·er (bōl′tər) ***n-*** machine for separating flour from bran.

bomb (bŏm) ***n-*** **1** war weapon, usually a metal casing containing explosives or incendiary materials, dropped from aircraft to explode upon impact or at a certain altitude over its target. **2** any package of explosive materials equipped with a fuse or detonating mechanism: *a time* bomb; *a gasoline* bomb. ***vt-*** to attack with bombs; drop bombs on.

bom·bard (bŏm bärd′) ***vt-*** **1** to attack with bombs or artillery: *The city was* bombarded *from land and sea.* **2** to assail or beset; to shower: *The audience* bombarded *him with questions.* **3** to subject an element to a stream of high-speed atomic particles. ***—n-*** **bom·bard′ment:** *The* bombardment *destroyed many buildings.*

bom·bar·dier (bŏm′bər dêr′) ***n-*** **1** the member of a bomber crew who works the bombsight and releases the bombs. **2** in the British army, a noncommissioned officer in the artillery.

bom·bast (bŏm′băst′) ***n-*** high-sounding or pompous language. ***—adj-*** **bom·bas′tic:** *a* bombastic *speech.* ***adv-*** **bom·bas′ti·cal·ly.**

bomb bay ***n-*** the section of a bomber in which the bombs are carried until dropped.

bomb·er (bŏm′ər) ***n-*** airplane from which bombs may be dropped.

bomb·shell (bŏm′shĕl′) ***n-*** **1** bomb. **2** something sudden and overwhelming.

bomb·sight (bŏm′sīt′) ***n-*** instrument in a bomber for aiming bombs at targets below.

bo·na fi·de (bō′nə fīd′, bŏn′ə-, -fī′dē) ***adj-*** in good faith; genuine: *a* bona fide *offer*; *a* bona fide *antique.*

bo·nan·za (bə năn′zə) ***n-*** **1** rich vein of ore in a gold or silver mine. **2** anything which brings great wealth. [from Spanish **bonanza** meaning "prosperity; good weather," from Latin **bonus,** "good."]

bon·bon (bŏn′bŏn′) ***n-*** a candy made from a thick, creamy sugar paste.

bond (bŏnd) ***n-*** **1** anything that fastens or connects; band; tie: *The prisoner broke his* bonds *and escaped. The treaty strengthened the* bond *between the two nations.* **2** certificate issued by a government or business to a lender, promising to pay back the money borrowed plus interest at a specified time. **3** in law, bail; also, the person, or bondsman, who provides it. **4** policy or contract covering losses to an employer through the negligence, theft, etc., of an employee. **5** storage of goods in a warehouse under government supervision until taxes or duties are paid. **6** *Chemistry* linkage that holds together the atoms of the elements in molecules, produced by the transfer or sharing of electrons. **7** watermarked stationery of good quality. ***vt-*** **1** to insure an employer against losses caused by (an employee). **2** to place (goods) in a warehouse until taxes on them are paid.

bond·age (bŏn′dĭj) ***n-*** slavery; servitude: *The Jews were held in* bondage *in Egypt.*

bond·ed (bŏn′dəd) ***adj-*** **1** of goods, stored in a bonded warehouse. **2** of an employee, insured against loss to the employer.

bonded warehouse ***n-*** warehouse in which goods are stored under government supervision until taxes or duties are paid.

bond·hold·er (bŏnd′hōl′dər) ***n-*** person who owns a bond.

bond·man (bŏnd′mən) ***n-*** [*pl.* **bond·men**] a male slave or serf. ***—n-*** *fem.* **bond′wom·an, bond′maid.**

bond·ser·vant (bŏnd′sûr′vənt) ***n-*** slave or serf.

bonds·man (bŏndz′mən) ***n-*** [*pl.* **bonds·men**] **1** bondman. **2** person who makes himself responsible for another's debt, appearance in court, etc., by furnishing a bond; surety. ***—n-*** *fem.* **bonds′wom·an.**

bone (bōn) ***n-*** **1** the hard, white, calcified material forming the internal skeleton. **2** any similar substance, such as the tusks of an elephant or walrus, the horns of a deer, whalebone, etc. **3** any one of the separate parts of the internal skeleton. **4 bones** (1) mortal remains: *The* bones *of the poet lie in Westminster Abbey.* (2) *Slang* dice. ***vt-*** **[boned, bon·ing] 1** to remove parts of the skeleton from (a chicken, etc.). **2** to stiffen (corsets, etc.) with whalebone or other stays.

feel in (one's) bones to be very sure of something without knowing the reason. **have a bone to pick (with someone)** to have cause for complaint or disagreement. **make no bones about** to be very direct or blunt about; make no effort to conceal: *She* made no bones about *her dislike of the lawyer.*

bone up on *Informal* to become well informed on or to review (a subject) by hard study.

bone black ***n-*** a black powdery ash produced by roasting animal bones in air-tight containers. It is mostly pure carbon and calcium phosphate and is used in refining sugar and as a pigment. Also **bone′black.**

bone·head (bōn′hĕd′) ***n-*** *Slang* a stupid person; boob; dolt; numbskull.

bone meal ***n-*** powdered bone, used as fertilizer or animal feed.

bon·er (bō′nər) *Slang* ***n-*** silly, stupid error; goof.

bon·fire (bŏn′fīər′) ***n-*** outdoor fire for a celebration or for burning rubbish, leaves, etc.

bon·go (bŏng′ gō) ***n-*** [*pl.* **bon·gos**] a drum, usually one of a pair, held between the knees and played with the hands.

bo·ni·to (bə nē′tō) ***n-*** [*pl.* **bo·ni·to**; **bo·ni·tos** (kinds of bonito)] small food fish related to the tuna, with a silvery belly and blue-striped back.

bon·net (bŏn′ət) ***n-*** **1** head covering for women and children, with ribbons or strings which tie under the chin. **2** cap worn by men and boys in Scotland. **3** ceremonial headdress of feathers worn by some American Indians. **4** protective cover for a machine or one of its parts.

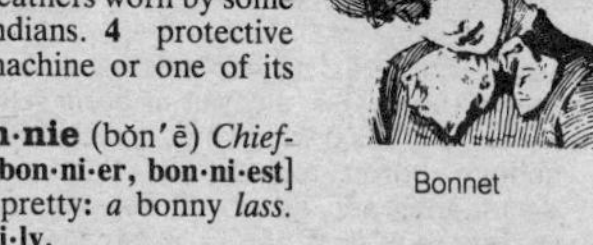
Bonnet

bon·ny or **bon·nie** (bŏn′ ē) *Chiefly Scot.* ***adj-*** [**bon·ni·er, bon·ni·est**] handsome or pretty: *a* bonny *lass.* **—*adv-* bon′ ni·ly.**

bon·sai (bŏn′ sī′) ***n-*** [*pl.* **bon·sai**] *Japanese* **1** a potted plant that has been dwarfed but kept healthy by special gardening methods. **2** the practice or art of dwarfing plants.

bo·nus (bō′ nəs) ***n-*** something extra; a sum paid in addition to what is usual or due: *a Christmas* bonus.

bon vi·vant (bō^{n} vē vä^{n}′) ***n-*** *French* [*pl.* **bons vi·vants** (bō^{n} vē vä^{n}′)] person who enjoys good food, entertainment, and other luxuries of life.

bon vo·yage (bō^{n}′vwä yäzh′) ***n-*** *French* a pleasant, safe journey. *as* ***modifier***: a bon voyage *party.*

bon·y (bō′ nē) ***adj-*** [**bon·i·er, bon·i·est**] **1** made of bone or like bone. **2** full of bones: *a* bony *fish.* **3** having prominent bones: *long,* bony *fingers.*

boo (bo͞o) ***interj-*** **1** exclamation of dislike, disapproval, or contempt. **2** a sound uttered suddenly to startle someone. ***vt-*** to jeer at in disapproval: *to* boo *a speaker.* ***vi-***: *The crowd* booed. ***n-*** a hoot.

boob (bo͞ob) *Slang* ***n-*** stupid person; dunce.

boo·by (bo͞o′ bē) ***n-*** [*pl.* **boo·bies**] **1** stupid person. **2** in a game, the player ending with the poorest score. **3** tropical sea bird, related to gannets and pelicans.

booby prize ***n-*** any prize, usually a ridiculous one, given for the poorest score in a game.

booby trap ***n-*** **1** hidden bomb that explodes when a harmless-looking object attached to it is touched. **2** any device for taking someone by surprise.

boog·ie-woog·ie (bo͝og′ ē wo͝og′ ē) ***n-*** style of jazz music played on the piano, characterized by a steady, rhythmic bass melody, popular in the late 1930's.

book (bo͝ok) ***n-*** **1** a work of prose, poetry, pictures, etc., printed on sheets of paper that are bound together between covers. **2** bound set of blank or ruled sheets, used for taking notes, keeping financial records, etc.: *an account* book. **3** bound set of stamps, tickets, matches, etc. **4** section of a literary work: *Genesis is the first* book *of the Bible. Homer's "Iliad" is divided into 24* books. **5** the words or text of an opera or musical comedy, as distinct from the music or score; libretto. ***vt-*** **1** to arrange for; reserve; engage: *to* book *a seat on an airplane*; *to* book *a theatrical act.* **2** to enter (an order, a person's name, etc.) on a record.

book·case (bo͝ok′ kās′) ***n-*** cabinet or set of shelves to hold books.

book club ***n-*** **1** business organization that sells books at reduced prices to members who have agreed to buy a certain number of books each year. **2** a club for discussing books.

book end ***n-*** movable support placed at the end of a row of books to hold them upright.

book·ish (bo͝ok′ ĭsh) ***adj-*** **1** fond of study. **2** thoroughly acquainted with books; learned. **3** making a display of learning: *the student's* bookish *talk.* **—*adv-* book′ ish·ly.** ***n-*** **book′ ish·ness.**

book·keep·er (bo͝ok′ kē′pər) ***n-*** person who keeps business accounts.

book·keep·ing (bo͝ok′ kē′pĭng) ***n-*** the work of keeping business accounts.

book·let (bo͝ok′ lət) ***n-*** small book, often with a paper binding; pamphlet.

book·mark (bo͝ok′ märk′) ***n-*** loose, flat object put in a book to mark a page.

book·mo·bile (bo͝ok′ mə bēl′) ***n-*** truck equipped to carry and lend books, serving as a traveling library.

Book of Common Prayer ***n-*** the official book of services and prayers of the Anglican churches.

book·plate (bo͝ok′ plāt′) ***n-*** label pasted inside a book to tell the name of the owner.

book·stall (bo͝ok′ stȯl′) ***n-*** outdoor booth or stand where books, usually secondhand ones, are sold.

book·store (bo͝ok′ stôr′) ***n-*** store where books are sold. Also **book′ shop′**.

book·worm (bo͝ok′ wûrm′) ***n-*** **1** person who is very fond, sometimes too fond, of reading and studying books. **2** insect larva that eats book bindings and pages.

[1]boom (bo͞om) ***n-*** deep, rumbling sound: *the* boom *of a cannon.* ***vi-*** to make or utter such a sound: *His voice* boomed *out in the empty room.* [from a Dutch word which was probably the imitation of a sound.]

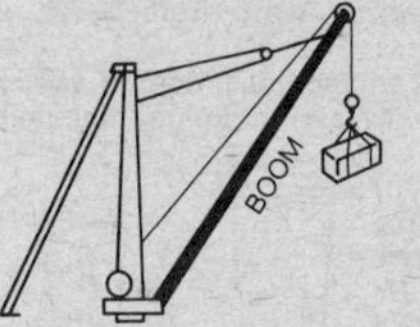

Boom of a derrick and of a boat

[2]boom (bo͞om) ***n-*** **1** long pole or beam attached to a ship's mast to hold out the bottom edge of a sail. **2** the lifting arm of a derrick. **3** a chain of connected floating timbers used to keep logs from drifting away or to obstruct the mouth of a harbor in wartime. [from a Dutch word meaning "tree; pole."]

[3]boom (bo͞om) ***vi-*** to increase or develop swiftly: *Business* boomed. ***n-*** a great increase: *the business* boom. [apparently an American use of **[1]boom.**]

boom·e·rang (bo͞o′ mə răng′) ***n-*** **1** bent, flat piece of wood used as a throwing weapon by the original inhabitants of Australia. Some boomerangs can be thrown so that they return to the thrower. **2** any aggressive remark or act that recoils to harm its author. ***vi-***: *His campaign charges* boomeranged; *people resented them and voted against him.*

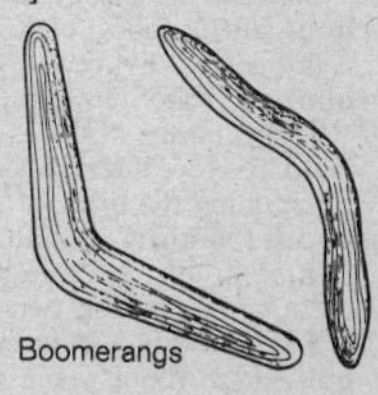
Boomerangs

boom town ***n-*** town that is fast-growing because of sudden prosperity, as from a discovery of gold or oil.

fāte, făt, dâre, bärn; bē, bĕt, mêre; bīte, bĭt; nōte, hŏt, môre, dȯg; fŭn, fûr; to͞o, bo͝ok; oil; out; tar; thin; then; hw for wh as in *wh*at; zh for s as in u*s*ual; ə for a, e, i, o, u, as in *a*go, lin*e*n, per*i*l, at*o*m, min*u*s

[1]**boon** (bo͞on) ***n-*** a favor, gift, or blessing: *Grant me a* boon, *O King.* [from Old Norse **bōn** meaning "wish; petition."]

[2]**boon** (bo͞on) ***adj-*** cheerful and congenial; jovial: *a* boon *companion.* [from Old French **bon,** from Latin **bonus** meaning "good."]

boon·dock·ers (bo͞on′ dŏk′ ərz) *Slang* ***n-*** *pl.* heavy and sturdy boots for hiking in rough country.

boon·docks (bo͞on′ dŏks′) *Slang* ***n-*** the backwoods; rough and remote country. [from Philippine **bundok** meaning "mountain," brought back by U.S. servicemen stationed in the Philippines.]

boon·dog·gle (bo͞on′ dŏg′ əl) ***vi-*** **[boon·dog·gled, boon·dog·gling]** to engage in useless or trivial work at public expense. ***n-*** the work itself. ***—n-*** **boon′ dog′ gler:** *The congressman had three* boondogglers *on his staff.*

boor (bo͝or) ***n-*** crude person with bad manners.

boor·ish (bo͝or′ ĭsh) ***adj-*** ill-mannered; clumsy; rude: *His* boorish *table manners angered the host.* ***—adv-*** **boor′ ish·ly.** ***n-*** **boor′ ish·ness.**

boost (bo͞ost) ***vt-*** **1** to lift by pushing up from underneath: *If you* boost *me I can climb that tree.* **2** in electricity, to increase the voltage of (an electric circuit). ***n-*** **1** a push or shove that helps someone or something to rise or advance. **2** increase: *a* boost *in pay.*

boost·er (bo͞os′ tər) ***n-*** **1** enthusiastic supporter or promoter of an idea, thing, or person. **2** device that increases power, as a fresh car battery connected to a weak one to help start a car. **3** first-stage engine of a multistage rocket vehicle providing the thrust for take-off; an additional rocket used to provide extra take-off power for rocket vehicles and airplanes. *as* ***modifier:*** *a* booster *rocket.* [American word from **boost,** of uncertain origin.]

booster shot *Medicine* ***n-*** an additional dose of vaccine or other serum given to increase or prolong immunity to a disease.

[1]**boot** (bo͞ot) ***n-*** rubber or leather footwear extending above the ankle, often above the calf. ***vt-*** to kick: *He* booted *the ball.* [from Old French **bote,** from an early Germanic language.]

have (one's) heart in (one's) boots to have a severe sensation of fear or anxiety. **lick the boots of (someone)** to act like a slave toward; fawn on.

Rubber boot and hunting boot

[2]**boot** (bo͞ot) *Archaic* ***vt-*** to benefit; profit: *It* boots *me nothing.* [from Old English **bot** meaning "a bettering."]

to boot in addition; into the bargain: *She gave her time and her money* to boot.

boot·black (bo͞ot′ blăk′) ***n-*** one who polishes shoes and boots for a living.

boot·ee (bo͞o′ tē, bo͞o tē′) ***n-*** a baby's knitted shoe. ***Hom-*** booty.

Bo·ö·tes (bō ō′ tēz) ***n-*** star constellation of northern skies including the brilliant star, Arcturus.

booth (bo͞oth) ***n-*** **1** small compartment: *a telephone* booth; *a toll* booth; *a voting* booth. **2** restaurant compartment containing facing benches with a table between them. **3** stall at a fair or bazaar, or in a market.

boot·jack (bo͞ot′ jăk′) ***n-*** device to hold the heel of a boot while one pulls one's foot out of it.

boot·leg (bo͞ot′ lĕg′) *Informal* ***vt-*** **[boot·legged, boot·leg·ging]** to make, sell, transport, or communicate (liquor, cameras, information, etc.) illegally. ***n-*** liquor, etc., made, sold, or transported illegally. ***adj-:*** *He had a bottle of* bootleg *whiskey.* ***—n-*** **boot′ leg′ ger.**

boot·less (bo͞ot′ ləs) ***adj-*** useless: *a* bootless *effort.*

boot·lick (bo͞ot′ lĭk′) ***vt-*** to seek favor with (someone) by flattery, cringing, etc.; to toady to. ***vi-:*** *He* bootlicked *all his career.* ***—n-*** **boot′ lick′ er.**

boo·ty (bo͞o′ tē) ***n-*** [*pl.* **boo·ties**] **1** plunder taken by robbers, bandits, pirates, etc. **2** supplies, arms, or treasure taken from an enemy in time of war; loot. **3** rich prize or gain. ***Hom-*** bootee.

booze (bo͞oz) *Informal* ***n-*** drink; liquor. ***vi-*** **[boozed, booz·ing]** to drink and keep on drinking; guzzle; tipple.

bop (bŏp) *Slang* ***n-*** bebop.

bor. borough.

bo·rac·ic (bə răs′ ĭk) ***adj-*** relating to boric acid.

bor·ate (bôr′ āt) ***n-*** any salt of boric acid.

bor·ax (bôr′ ăks) ***n-*** white, crystalline compound of sodium, boron, and oxygen. It is used as a cleaning agent, antiseptic, water softener, or the like.

bor·der (bòr′ dər, bôr′-) ***n-*** **1** edge: *reeds along the* border *of a stream.* **2** narrow strip along or around something: *a* border *of flowers along a walk.* **3** frontier of a country; boundary: *to patrol the* border. ***vt-*** **1** to make a narrow strip along or around: *to* border *a path with flowers.* **2** to be next to; adjoin; touch: *His land* borders *mine.* ***Hom-*** boarder.

border on 1 to have a common border with: *Mexico* borders on *the United States.* **2** to come near to being: *His excuse* bordered on *the ridiculous.*

bor·der·land (bòr′ dər lănd′, bôr′-) ***n-*** **1** land on or near a frontier. **2** an intermediate state or stage between two distinct states or stages and not belonging entirely to either: *Twilight is the* borderland *between day and night.*

bor·der·line (bòr′ dər līn′, bôr′-) ***n-*** boundary line. ***adj-*** at or near any boundary; doubtful; uncertain: *a* borderline *skirmish*; *a* borderline *case of pneumonia.*

[1]**bore** (bôr) ***vt-*** **[bored, bor·ing] 1** to make a circular hole in by twisting a screwlike tool with a cutting edge: *The drill* bores *the ground.* **2** to make (a tunnel, hole, etc.) by, or as by, drilling: *They plan to* bore *a tunnel through a mountain.* ***vi-*** **1** to make a hole; pierce: *They* bored *all day.* **2** to be drilled by an instrument: *This wood* bores *easily.* ***n-*** **1** the distance across the inside of a hollow tube such as a pipe or gun barrel. **2** the hole inside a gun barrel, pipe, etc. [from Old English **borian.**] ***Hom-*** boar.

[2]**bore** (bôr) ***vt-*** **[bored, bor·ing]** to make weary: *His old jokes* bore *us.* ***n-*** tiresome person or thing: *That tune is a* bore. [probably [1]**bore** in a later and different meaning.] ***Hom-*** boar. ***—adv-*** **bor′ ing·ly.**

[3]**bore** (bôr) *p.t.* of [2]**bear.** ***Hom-*** boar.

[4]**bore** (bôr) ***n-*** sudden violent rush of a flood tide into the mouth of a river. [from Old Norse **bāra** meaning "wave; billow."] ***Hom-*** boar.

bore·dom (bôr′ dəm) ***n-*** mental weariness brought about by uninteresting people, situations, etc.

bor·er (bôr′ ər) ***n-*** **1** person or tool that drills. **2** an insect or worm that drills holes in wood or plants.

bo·ric acid (bôr′ ĭk) ***n-*** white powder (H_3BO_3), used as a mild antiseptic.

born (bòrn, bôrn) *p.p.* of [2]**bear,** used only for the passive meaning "brought into life": *John was* born *in May.* ***adj-*** natural; so disposed from birth: *a* born *writer.*

be born to to be brought into life by: *Twins* were born *to the Smiths.*

borne (bôrn) *p.p.* of [2]**bear,** used in all meanings except the passive meaning "brought into life."

bo·ron (bôr′ ŏn′) ***n-*** a yellowish-brown solid element used in steels and heat-resistant glass. Symbol B, At. No. 5, At. Wt. 10.811.

bor·ough (bûr′ ō) ***n-*** **1** in some U.S. states, an incorporated town that is smaller than a city. **2** one of the five political divisions of New York City. **3** in England, an incorporated town; also, a town that elects one or more representatives to Parliament. ***Homs-*** burrow, burro.

bor·row (bòr′ ō, bŏr′-) ***vt-*** (considered intransitive when the direct object is implied but not expressed) **1** to get something to use for a while with the understanding that it must be returned: *to* borrow *a book from the library.* **2** to copy; adopt: *Many English words were* borrowed *from the French.* **—*n-* bor′ row·er.**

borscht (bòrsht) ***n-*** a Russian beet soup, served hot, or cold with sour cream. Also **borsch** (bòrsh).

bosh (bŏsh) *Informal* ***n-*** absurd or empty talk; utter nonsense. ***interj-*** nonsense!

bo's'n (bō′ sən) ***n-*** boatswain.

bos·om (bo͝oz′ əm, bo͞o′ zəm) ***n-*** **1** the breast of a human being. **2** the part of a garment which covers the breast. **3** the breast as the seat of affections, passions, emotions, or desires; the heart: *My* bosom *swells with pride.* **4** intimacy; privacy: *in the* bosom *of the family.* **5** anything resembling the breast: *the* bosom *of the sea.* ***adj-*** intimate: *a* bosom *friend.*

[1]boss (bòs) ***n-*** **1** person in charge, especially of workmen; foreman; employer. **2** politician who controls a large number of votes. ***vt-*** to manage; give orders to: *He* bosses *the crew.* [American word from Dutch **baas.**]

[2]boss (bòs, bŏs) ***n-*** knob which stands out from a flat surface, as of a shield. ***vt-*** to ornament with knobs; to emboss. [from Old French **boce,** possibly from an early Germanic word related to **beat.**]

boss·y (bòs′ sē) *Informal* ***adj-*** **[boss·i·er, boss·i·est]** fond of bossing other people; domineering.

Bos·ton terrier (bòs′ tən) ***n-*** small, stout-bodied dog usually having a dark smooth coat with white markings and somewhat resembling the bulldog. Also **Boston bull, Boston bull terrier, Boston bulldog.**

bot (bŏt) ***n-*** wormlike larva (maggot) of the botfly. Also **bott.**

bo·tan·i·cal (bə tăn′ ĭ kəl) or **bo·tan·ic** (-tăn′ ĭk) ***adj-*** of or having to do with plants or botany: *a* botanical *association.* **—*adv-* bo·tan′ i·cal·ly.**

bot·a·nist (bŏt′ ə nĭst) ***n-*** person trained in botany and, usually, engaged in it as a profession.

bot·a·ny (bŏt′ ə nē) ***n-*** the scientific study of plant life.

botch (bŏch) ***vt-*** to spoil by poor work; bungle: *He* botched *the letter and had to write it over.* ***n-*** a bungled or poor piece of work; clumsy job. **—*adj-* botch·y [botch·i·er, botch·i·est]:** *a* botchy *piece of carpentry.*

bot·fly (bŏt′ flī′) ***n-*** [*pl.* **bot·flies**] any of several flies which lay their eggs under the skin of animals, where they hatch into larvae (bots) that feed on the animals' flesh.

both (bōth) ***determiner*** (traditionally called adjective or pronoun) the two; one and the other (of): *I know* both *girls. Are* both *here?* ***n-:*** Both *of his automobiles are red and white.* ***conj-*** (used with "and" to signal that two are to be mentioned and to add emphasis): *The class includes* both *boys and girls. He was* both *abusive and crude. She* both *wept and laughed.*

►BOTH is often transferred to the end of the clause for further emphasis: *She wept and laughed* both.

both·er (bŏth′ ər) ***vt-*** to give trouble to; worry; pester: *The ringing telephone* bothers *the busy doctor.* ***vi-*** to take trouble: *Don't* bother *to do that now.* ***n-*** source of worry; nuisance: *This broken zipper is a* bother.

both·er·some (bŏth′ ər səm) ***adj-*** annoying; troublesome: *a* bothersome *cold.*

bot·tle (bŏt′ əl) ***n-*** **1** hollow container with a narrow neck or mouth, usually made of glass. **2** contents of such a container: *a* bottle *of milk.* ***vt-*** **[bot·tled, bot·tling]** to put into bottles: *Milk is* bottled *by machines.*

bottle up to shut in or hold back: *to* bottle up *feelings; to* bottle up *an enemy fleet in port.*

Bottle

bot·tle·neck (bŏt′ əl nĕk′) ***n-*** **1** narrow or crowded route or passageway. **2** anything that obstructs or slows progress.

bot·tle·nose (bŏt′ əl nōz′) ***n-*** any of various small, toothed whales with snouts that taper like the neck of a bottle. Also **bottle-nosed dolphin.**

bot·tom (bŏt′ əm) ***n-*** **1** lowest part of anything: *the* bottom *of a hill.* **2** underside: *the* bottom *of a plate.* **3** the ground under water: *the* bottom *of the lake.* **4** the part of a ship below the water line; also, the ship. **5** important part; foundation: *Let's get to the* bottom *of the matter.* **6** seat; buttocks. **7** lowland bordering a stream: *the Mississippi River* bottoms. *as* ***modifier:*** *the* bottom *shelves.* ***vi-*** to sink to or touch the ground under water.

at bottom basically; fundamentally: *He's a good sort* at bottom. **be at the bottom of** to be the underlying cause of: *He* was at the bottom of *the scheme.*

bot·tom·less (bŏt′ əm ləs) ***adj-*** **1** without a bottom. **2** extremely deep: *in the* bottomless *pit of a volcano.*

bot·u·lism (bŏt′ yə lĭz′ əm) ***n-*** a type of food poisoning often causing death by respiratory paralysis. It is caused by a toxin, **botulin** (bŏt′ yə lən), produced by an anaerobic bacterium, **botulinus** (bŏt′ yə lī′ nəs), which sometimes occurs in sausages and improperly sterilized canned or packaged foods.

bou·clé (bo͞o clā′) ***n-*** a woven or knitted fabric with a rough, knobby surface; also, the yarn used to make this fabric. ***adj-:*** *a* bouclé *blouse.*

bou·doir (bo͞o′ dwär′) ***n-*** a lady's private sitting room or bedroom. *as* ***modifier:*** *a* boudoir *chair.*

bouf·fant (bo͞o′ fänt′, *Fr.* bo͞o fäⁿ′) ***adj-*** puffed out: *a* bouffant *hairdo; a* bouffant *sleeve.*

bou·gain·vil·le·a (bo͞o′ gən vĭl′ yə, bō-) ***n-*** any of a group of tall tropical American shrubs and vines with many small flowers that are surrounded by showy red, orange, or purple petallike leaves.

bough (bou) ***n-*** limb or branch of a tree. ***Homs-*** [2]bow, [3]bow.

bought (bòt, bŏt) *p.t. & p.p.* of **buy.** ***Hom-*** bot.

bouil·la·baisse (bo͞ol′ yə bās′, bo͞o′ yə, bo͞o′ lə-) ***n-*** a thick soup or stew usually made with several kinds of fish and vegetables.

bouil·lon (bo͞ol′ yŏn′, -yən *Fr.* bo͞oyoⁿ′) ***n-*** a clear soup or broth usually made from beef. ***Hom-*** bullion.

boul·der (bōl′ dər) ***n-*** large piece of loose rock rounded or worn smooth by water, weather, or moving ice. ***Hom-*** bolder.

boul·e·vard (bo͞ol′ ə värd′, bo͞o′ lĕ-) ***n-*** a broad avenue, often landscaped.

bounce (bouns) ***vi-*** **[bounced, bounc·ing]** **1** to spring back when thrown against something; rebound: *How far did the ball* bounce? **2** to leap up suddenly; bound: *He* bounced *out of his chair.* **3** *Informal* of a check, to be returned to the writer because his bank account is too small to pay for it. ***vt-*** **1** to throw so as to cause to spring back: *to* bounce *a ball against the wall.* **2** *Slang* to throw (a person) out by force; also, to fire from a job.

---

fāte, făt, dâre, bärn; bē, bĕt, mêre; bīte, bĭt; nōte, hŏt, môre, dòg; fŭn, fûr; to͞o, bo͝ok; oil; out; tar; thin; then; hw for wh as in *wh*at; zh for s as in u*s*ual; ə for a, e, i, o, u, as in *a*go, lin*e*n, per*i*l, at*o*m, min*u*s

n- **1** a springing back; rebound: *He caught the ball on the first* bounce. **2** ability to spring back; springiness: *The ball has no* bounce.

bounce back to recover quickly from a blow, defeat, etc.

bounc·er (boun′ sər) *Slang n-* person hired by a saloon to throw out disorderly customers.

bounc·ing (boun′ sĭng) *adj-* large; active; healthy.

bouncing Bet (bĕt) *n-* common roadside plant with clusters of pink or white flowers and leaves that produce a soapy lather when crushed in water.

[1]**bound** (bound) *vi-* **1** to leap or spring; jump: *The dancer* bounded *onto the stage. Her heart* bounded *with joy.* **2** to rebound. *n-* a leap or jump: *With one* bound *he made the distance from boat to shore.* [from French **bondir** meaning "rebound."]

[2]**bound** (bound) *p.t.* & *p.p.* of **bind.** *adj-* **1** morally or legally obliged (to): *You are* bound *to obey.* **2** certain (to); sure (to): *You're* bound *to be tired if you hike all day.* **3** *Informal* determined; resolved: *He is* bound *to have his way.* [from Old English **band,** a form of **bind.**]

bound up in (or **with**) closely connected with; dependent on: *lives* bound up in *one another.*

[3]**bound** (bound) *n-* (usually **bounds**) **1** anything that outlines or encloses a region or area; boundary: *the* bounds *of a ranch.* **2** area within a boundary or limit: *the* bounds *of propriety*; *the outermost* bounds *of the kingdom.* *vt-* **1** to form a boundary of: *A highway* bounds *the farm on the west.* **2** to name the boundaries of: *Can you* bound *Texas?* [from Old French **bodne, bonde** of the same meaning.]

out of bounds beyond a permitted area; off limits.

bound on to lie adjacent to: *Our land* bounds on *theirs.*

[4]**bound** (bound) *adj-* ready to start (for); on the way: *The plane is* bound *for New York. We are homeward* bound. [from Middle English **boun** meaning "ready," from Old Norse **būinn.**]

bound·a·ry (boun′ də rē) *n-* [*pl.* **bound·a·ries**] **1** anything that limits or marks a limit: *The Rio Grande is part of the* boundary *of Texas.* **2** a dividing line: *The United States-Canada* boundary *was fixed by treaties.*

bound·en duty (boun′ dən) *n-* a duty imposed as an obligation.

bound·less (bound′ ləs) *adj-* unlimited; vast: *the* boundless *ocean*; *a man of* boundless *energy.* —*adv-* **bound′ less·ly.** *n-* **bound′ less·ness.**

boun·te·ous (boun′ tē əs) *adj-* **1** giving freely; generous: *a* bounteous *nature.* **2** plentiful: *a* bounteous *harvest.* —*adv-* **boun′ te·ous·ly.** *n-* **boun′ te·ous·ness.**

boun·ti·ful (boun′ tĭ fəl) *adj-* **1** liberal; generous: *a* bountiful *giver.* **2** plentiful; yielding abundantly: *the* bountiful *acres.* —*adv-* **boun′ ti·ful·ly.** *n-* **boun′ ti·ful·ness.**

boun·ty (boun′ tē) *n-* [*pl.* **boun·ties**] **1** generosity in giving; also, generous gifts: *This hospital is supported by the* bounty *of one man.* **2** money offered or paid by a government as a reward for killing harmful animals.

bou·quet (bo͞o kā′) *n-* **1** (*also* bō kā′) bunch of flowers. **2** pleasant odor; aroma.

Bour·bon (bo͞or′ bən, *Fr.* bo͞or bō^n′) *n-* **1** ancient royal family that ruled in France, Spain, and Naples during the eighteenth and nineteenth centuries. **2** someone stubborn or conservative in politics. **3 bourbon** (bûr′- bən) a whiskey made mainly from corn and produced originally in Bourbon County, Kentucky.

bour·geois (bo͞orzh′ wä′) *n-* [*pl.* **bour·geois** (-wä, -wäz)] member of the middle class of society. *adj-* belonging to the middle class; having the characteristics and outlook of the middle class. [from French.]

bour·geois·ie (bo͞orzh′ wä′ zē′) *n-* the middle class. [from French.]

bourn (bôrn, bo͞orn) *Archaic n-* **1** a boundary; limit. **2** a destination; goal. Also **bourne.**

bout (bout) *n-* **1** a contest; test of strength or skill: *a wrestling* bout; *a* boxing *bout.* **2** period of time; spell: *a long* bout *of fever.*

bou·tique (bo͞o tēk′) *n-* shop, especially a small one, selling trinkets, fine ladies' wear, etc.

bou·ton·niere or **bou·ton·nière** (bo͞o′ tən yĕr′, -êr) *n-* flower worn in the buttonhole of a lapel.

bo·vine (bō′ vīn′) *adj-* **1** relating to, or like, the ox or cow. **2** sluggish; stolid.

[1]**bow** (bō) *n-* **1** anything curved, as a rainbow. **2** weapon for shooting arrows. It is usually a strip of wood bent by a cord tightly stretched between its two ends. **3** slender stick strung with horsehairs for playing the violin or other stringed instruments. **4** a knot with loops: *a* bow *of ribbon.* [from Old English **boga,** related to [2]**bow.**] ***Hom-*** beau.

[2]**bow** (bou) *n-* a bending of the head, body, or knee expressing greeting, farewell, thanks, or respect. *vi-* **1** to make this motion: *The singer* bowed *in response to the applause.* **2** to give in; yield: *I* bow *to your wishes.* [from Old English **būgan** meaning "bend."] ***Hom-*** bough.

make one's bow to make one's first formal appearance in society.

bow and scrape to act in a servile manner; fawn.

bow out to withdraw; resign.

[3]**bow** (bou) *n-* front end of a boat, ship, or aircraft. [of uncertain origin.] ***Hom-*** bough.

bow·el (bou′ əl, boul) *n-* **1** intestine. **2 bowels** innermost, hidden part of anything: *the* bowels *of the earth.*

bow·er (bou′ ər) *n-* shelter of tree branches or vines; arbor.

Bow·er·y (bou′ rē) *n-* **1** street in lower New York City, once famous for its amusements. **2 bowery** a colonial Dutch plantation or farm.

bow·ie knife (bo͞o′ ē, *also* bō′ ē) *n-* strong, single-edged hunting knife, about a foot long, with a curved point. [American word from Col. J. Bowie, an adventurer who popularized it.]

Bowie knife

[1]**bowl** (bōl) *n-* **1** hollow, rounded dish. **2** contents of such a dish; bowlful: *She ate a* bowl *of rice.* **3** rounded, hollow part of something: *the* bowl *of a spoon*; *the* bowl *of a pipe.* **4** round or oval stadium. [from Old English **bolla.**] ***Homs-*** bole, boll.

Bowls

[2]**bowl** (bōl) *n-* round ball used in some games. *vi-* **1** to play the game of bowling. **2** to move rapidly and smoothly as if rolling: *The huge truck* bowled *down the mountain road.* [from French word **boule,** from Latin **bulla,** "bubble."] ***Homs-*** bole, boll. —*n-* **bowl′ er.**

bowl over 1 to knock over: *He was* bowled over *by a motorcycle rounding the corner.* **2** to confuse; stagger: *He was* bowled over *by the bad news.*

bow·leg (bō′ lĕg′) *n-* leg with an outward curve at the knee. —*adj-* **bow′ leg′ ged:** *a* bowlegged *horse.*

bowl·er (bō′ lər) *Brit.* ***n-*** a derby.
bowl·ful (bōl′ fəl) ***n-*** the amount held by a bowl.
bow·line (bō′ lĭn, *also* -līn′) ***n-*** a kind of loop knot that will not slip. For picture, see *knot.*
bowl·ing (bō′ lĭng) ***n-*** **1** game in which a heavy ball is rolled over a smooth floor at ten bottle-shaped pins, with the object of knocking them down; also, a game in which a ball is rolled over turf at a stationary ball. **2** the act of playing this game.
bowling alley ***n-*** a long narrow, strip of wooden floor used in the game of bowling; also, the building containing it.
bowling green ***n-*** a level lawn for the game of bowls.
bowls (bōlz) ***n-*** (takes singular verb) **1** outdoor game played by rolling a slightly flattened or weighted ball (the **bowl**) as close as possible to a stationary ball (the **jack**). **2** the game of ninepins, tenpins, or skittles.

Bowman

bow·man (bō′ mən) ***n-*** [*pl.* **bow·men**] person who shoots with a bow and arrow; archer.
bow·shot (bō′ shŏt′) ***n-*** distance an arrow is shot.
bow·sprit (bou′ sprĭt′) ***n-*** long spar jutting forward from the bow of a ship.
bow·string (bō′ strĭng′) ***n-*** **1** cord stretched between the two ends of a bow. **2** a type of girder, truss, or bridge in which a steel arch is strengthened by connecting its ends with a beam. For picture, see *bridge.*

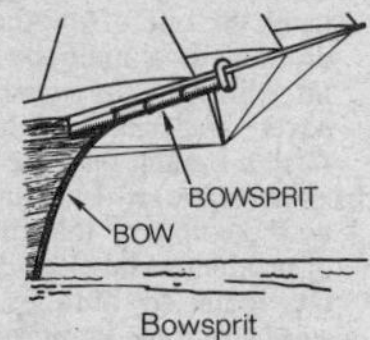

Bowsprit

bow tie ***n-*** a necktie worn tied in a bow.
[1]**box** (bŏks) ***vt-*** to fight (another) with fists as a sport, usually with gloves. ***vi-***: *The champions* boxed *for five rounds.* ***n-*** light slap or cuff. [of unknown origin.]
box (someone's) ears to slap or cuff about the head.
[2]**box** (bŏks) ***n-*** **1** case or container, usually rectangular and furnished with a lid. **2** contents of a box: *a* box *of crackers.* **3** enclosure for one or more persons: *a jury* box; *a theater* box; *a sentry* box. **4** in baseball, the place where the batter or pitcher stands. ***vt-*** to put in a rectangular container: *She* boxed *the candy attractively.* [from Old English **box,** from Latin **buxus** meaning both [2]**box** and [3]**box.**] ***—adj-*** **box′ like′.**
box in to surround, or block the movement of.
box the compass to name all 32 points of the compass in a clockwise direction, starting from North.
[3]**box** (bŏks) ***n-*** any of various small evergreen shrubs or trees with glossy, dark-green leaves. [from [2]**box,** because boxes were first made from the wood of this tree.]
box·car (bŏks′ kär′) ***n-*** enclosed freight car.
box elder ***n-*** fast-growing kind of maple tree with leaves like those of the ash; often planted to provide shade.
box·er (bŏk′ sər) ***n-*** **1** stocky, muscular dog of medium size, usually having a tan or brindle coat with white markings. It is named for the playful way it strikes out with its front paws. **2** person who fights with his fists as a sport, usually wearing padded gloves; prizefighter.
Box·er (bŏk′ sər) ***n-*** a member of a Chinese secret society that led an unsuccessful uprising, the **Boxer Rebellion,** (1900), to rid China of all foreigners by massacre.

boxing gloves ***n-*** heavily padded gloves used for boxing.
box office ***n-*** **1** office or booth where tickets for a play, movie, etc., are sold. **2** *Informal* income from sale of such tickets; also, whatever contributes to the income: *Westerns are good* box office.
box score ***n-*** a summary of a baseball game, listing the players and their hits, runs, errors, etc.
box seat ***n-*** seat in a box at a theater, stadium, etc.
box·wood (bŏks′ wŏŏd′) ***n-*** hard, close-grained wood of the box. See [3]*box.*
boy (boi) ***n-*** **1** male child from the time he is a baby until he is a young man. **2** lad who does errands: *messenger* boy. **3** *Informal* fellow. ***Hom-*** buoy.
boy·cott (boi′ kŏt′) ***vt-*** **1** to refuse, in agreement with others, to buy from, sell to, or have dealings with (a person, firm, nation, etc.). **2** to refuse as a group to use or purchase (a thing). ***n-*** an organized refusal to have any dealings with a person, firm, or nation, in an effort to force the adoption of a certain course of action. [from **Captain Boycott,** English land agent so treated by his neighbors in Ireland in 1880.]
boy·hood (boi′ hŏŏd′) ***n-*** time of being a boy.
boy·ish (boi′ ĭsh) ***adj-*** like a boy; suitable for a boy; youthful: *a* boyish *trick.* ***—adv-*** **boy′ ish·ly.** ***n-*** **boy′ ish·ness.**
Boyle's law (boilz) *Physics* ***n-*** a law first stated by Robert Boyle: at a constant temperature, the volume of a gas decreases uniformly as the pressure increases, and increases as the pressure decreases.
Boy Scouts ***n-*** **1** organization for training boys in physical fitness, good citizenship, and helpfulness to others. **2 boy scout** member of the Boy Scouts, or one who observes the aims of Boy Scouts.
boy·sen·ber·ry (boi′ zən bĕr′ ē) ***n-*** [*pl.* **boy·sen·ber·ries**] **1** large, deep red berry related to the blackberry and raspberry. **2** the prickly bush on which it grows.
Bp. Bishop.
bra (brä) *Informal* ***n-*** brassiere.

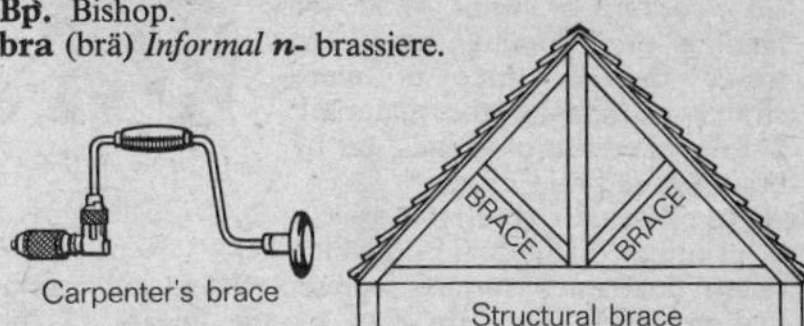

Carpenter's brace
Structural brace

brace (brās) ***n-*** **1** something that holds parts together or in place; something that supports or steadies, as in the framework of a building or machine, or a device to support or straighten a part of the body. **2** a pair: *a* brace *of ducks.* **3** a curved line [{] or [}] connecting two or more lines of print, staffs of music, or the like. **4** a frame for turning and holding a boring tool. **5 braces** (1) suspenders. (2) *Mathematics* symbols [{ }] used to enclose the elements in a set. ***vt-*** **[braced, brac·ing] 1** to steady or support: *We* braced *the wall to withstand the wind. Sit down and* brace *yourself for a shock.* **2** to strengthen; invigorate: *The mountain air* braced *our exhausted spirits.*
brace and bit ***n-*** carpenter's boring tool having a crank (brace) which holds and turns an augur, drill, or other cutting tool (bit).
brace·let (brā′ slət) ***n-*** ornamental band for the wrist or arm.

brac·er (brā′ sər) ***n-*** a support or prop; brace.
brack·en (brăk′ ən) ***n-*** a large, coarse fern; brake.
brack·et (brăk′ ət) ***n-* 1** triangular or L-shaped support attached to a wall to hold up a shelf, etc. **2** similar support for a machine part. For picture, see *collar.* **3** one of a pair of punctuation marks [ ] used to enclose a part of a text. **4** classification or grouping, usually of wage earners or taxpayers: *an income* bracket. ***vt-* 1** to enclose in such punctuation marks [ ]: *to* bracket *an error in spelling.* **2** to classify or group together: *to* bracket *income groups.*

Brackets supporting a shelf

brack·ish (brăk′ ĭsh) ***adj-*** slightly salty: *a pond of* brackish *water.*
bract (brăkt) ***n-*** special kind of leaf at the base of a flower, sometimes large and brightly colored and resembling a petal, as in the poinsettia.
brad (brăd) ***n-*** small, thin nail.
brae (brā) *Scottish* ***n-*** a hillside.
brag (brăg) ***vi-*** **[bragged, brag·ging]** to boast. ***n-*** boastful talk.
brag·ga·do·ci·o (brăg′ ə dō′ shē ō, -sē ō) ***n-*** empty boasting; bragging.
brag·gart (brăg′ ərt) ***n-*** person given to bragging; a boaster. ***adj-*** boastful: *his* braggart *manner.*
Brah·ma (brä′ mə) ***n-*** in Hindu religion, the creator of the world.
Brah·man (brä′ mən) ***n-*** [*pl.* **Brah·mans**] a Hindu of the sacred or priestly caste. Also **Brahmin.**
Brah·man·ism (brä′ mən ĭz′ əm) ***n-*** the religious and social system of the Brahmans.
braid (brād) ***n-* 1** a woven length of three or more strands of hair. **2** a flat band made of machine-plaited silk, cotton, or wool, used for binding or trimming. ***vt-* 1** to weave together three or more strands of (hair or other material). **2** to make out of braids or by braiding: *to* braid *a rug.*

Braid in mat making

braille or **Braille** (brāl) ***n-* 1** system of printing for the blind, in which raised dots on a surface represent letters and punctuation. These dots are read by the fingers. **2** the raised dots used in this system.
brain (brān) ***n-* 1** the soft mass of gray nerve tissue in the skull; the center of thought, emotion, and sensation. **2** mind; intelligence: *You have a good* brain*; use it.* **3 brains** intelligence.
beat (cudgel or **rack) one's brains** to think hard. **pick (someone's) brains** to draw out a person on a subject in order to use his ideas for oneself.
brain·child (brān′ chīld′) *Informal* ***n-*** an original idea, invention, method, etc.
brain·less (brān′ ləs) ***adj-*** without brains; stupid. **—*n-* brain′ less·ness. *adv-* brain′ less·ly.**
brain·storm (brān′ stŏrm′, -stôrm′) *Informal* ***n-*** a sudden inspiration or idea.
brain trust ***n-*** a group of expert advisers to an executive or political leader, especially to President Franklin D. Roosevelt during his first term in office. **—*n-* brain truster.**
brain·wash (brān′ wŏsh′, -wŏsh′) ***vt-*** to change the political beliefs and habits of (a person) by intense, mandatory, often hypnotic indoctrination. **—*n-* brain′ wash′ ing.**
brain wave ***n-* 1** weak electrical currents in the brain that have definite rhythms and may be recorded by delicate instruments. **2** *Informal* a sudden idea.
brain·y (brā′ nē) *Informal* ***adj-*** **[brain·i·er, brain·i·est]** intelligent; bright.
braise (brāz) ***vt-*** **[braised, brais·ing]** to brown (meat or vegetables) lightly in a little fat and then simmer slowly with a little moisture in a covered pot.
[1]**brake** (brāk) ***n-*** device for slowing or stopping the motion of a wheel, vehicle, etc. ***vt-*** **[braked, brak·ing]**: *He* braked *the car to a stop.* ***vi-***: *Always* brake *before a curve.* [probably from early Dutch **braeke** meaning "a rakelike device."] ***Hom-*** break.
[2]**brake** (brāk) ***n-*** place overgrown with bushes, shrubs, etc.; thicket. [probably of Germanic origin, for example, Dutch **brāke.**] ***Hom-*** break.
[3]**brake** (brāk) ***n-*** a kind of large, coarse fern. [probably of Scandinavian origin.] ***Hom-*** break.
brake·man (brāk′ mən) ***n-*** [*pl.* **brake·men**] on a railroad, a trainman who operates the brakes and assists the conductor.
bram·ble (brăm′ bəl) ***n-*** a rough, prickly shrub.
bram·bly (brăm′ blē) ***adj-* 1** full of brambles: *the* brambly *woods.* **2** prickly; thorny: *a* brambly *bush.*
bran (brăn) ***n-*** outer coat or husk of ground grain.
branch (brănch) ***n-* 1** limb of a tree that grows out of the trunk or out of another limb. **2** any limb; a part or division of a main body: *a* branch *of the family; the three* branches *of government.* ***vi-*** to divide into separate parts: *The road* branches *in three directions.* ***as modifier***: *a* branch *line; the* branch *offices of a business.*
brand (brănd) ***n-* 1** a mark, name, or label given a product by the company that makes it; trade name. **2** the make of product so labeled. **3** any identifying mark, especially one made by burning the skin with a hot iron: *The rancher put his* brand *on the cattle.* **4** a bad reputation; stigma: *He wears the* brand *of a traitor.* **5** a piece of burning or charred wood. ***vt-* 1** to mark by burning the skin. **2** to point out (a person) as deserving disgrace; to label: *They* branded *him as a spy.*
bran·died (brăn′ dēd) ***adj-*** flavored or preserved with brandy: *He likes* brandied *cherries.*
bran·dish (brăn′ dĭsh) ***vt-*** to wave about or shake as a threat: *The guards* brandished *their rifles.*
brand-new (brănd′ no͞o′) ***adj-*** very new; unused.
bran·dy (brăn′ dē) ***n-*** [*pl.* **bran·dies**] a strong alcoholic beverage distilled from wine or other fermented fruit juice.
brant (brănt) ***n-*** small, dark, wild goose.
brash (brăsh) ***adj-*** **[brash·er, brash·est] 1** rudely bold; impudent; insolent: *His* brash *manners offend us.* **2** recklessly quick; impetuous; rash: *a* brash *cavalry officer.* **—*adv-* brash′ ly. *n-* brash′ ness:** *He apologized for his* brashness.
brass (brăs) ***n-* 1** yellow alloy made by melting copper and zinc together. **2** musical instrument made of this alloy, such as the trumpet or horn; also, the section of an orchestra or band made up of these instruments. **3** *Informal* bold impudence: *He had the* brass *to tell me he wouldn't pay.* **4 the brass** high-ranking military officers; also, any important person. ***as modifier***: *a* brass *knob.*
brass hat *Slang* ***n-*** member of the brass.
brass·ie (brăs′ ē) ***n-*** a golf club with a wooden head, weighted with brass or other metal, used for long shots off the fairway. Also **brass′ ey** or **brassy.**
bras·siere (brə zêr′) ***n-*** an undergarment for supporting or covering the breasts.
brass tacks ***n-*** fundamental facts; serious and important matters, used especially in the phrase **get** (or **come**) **down to brass tacks.**

brass·y (brăs′ ē) ***adj-*** **[brass·i·er, brass·i·est] 1** made of brass. **2** like brass in color or sheen. **3** like the sound made by a brass instrument: *a* brassy *voice.* **4** *Informal* impudent: *a* brassy *remark.* ***n-*** brassie.

brat (brăt) ***n-*** spoiled or naughty child.

bra·va·do (brə vä′ dō, *also* -vā′ dō) ***n-*** [*pl.* **bra·va·does** or **bra·va·dos**] pretense of courage or indifference; boastful defiance: *He assumed an air of* bravado.

brave (brāv) ***adj-*** **[brav·er, brav·est]** having or showing courage: *The* brave *soldiers attacked.* ***n-*** North American Indian warrior. ***vt-*** **[braved, brav·ing]** to meet or face with courage: *to* brave *the storm.* **—*adv-*** **brave′ ly.**

brav·er·y (brā′ və rē) ***n-*** courage; fearlessness.

[1]**bra·vo** (brä′ vō, -vō′) ***interj-*** well done! ***n-*** [*pl.* **bra·vos**] a shout of applause. [from Italian **bravo** meaning literally "brave; good."]

[2]**bra·vo** (brä′ vō) ***n-*** [*pl.* **bra·vos** or **bra·voes**] bandit; hired assassin; desperado. [from Italian **bravo** meaning literally "a brave or wild one."]

bra·vu·ra (brə vo͝or′ ə, -vyo͝or′ ə) ***n-*** **1** a bold and dashing display of courage; dash. **2** in music, dance, etc., passage or piece requiring great skill and brilliance in the performer; also, a brilliant performing style.

brawl (brȯl) ***n-*** noisy quarrel or fight. ***vi-***: *The rowdies* brawled *in the street.*

brawn (brȯn) ***n-*** **1** firm, strong muscles. **2** muscular strength: *The boxer had more* brawn *than skill.*

brawn·y (brȯ′ nē) ***adj-*** **[brawn·i·er, brawn·i·est]** muscular; strong: *his* brawny *arms.*

bray (brā) ***n-*** **1** a harsh, loud cry made by a donkey. **2** any sound like it. ***vi-*** to utter a loud, harsh sound.

braze (brāz) ***vt-*** **[brazed, braz·ing]** to weld with a solder that melts only at high temperatures.

bra·zen (brā′ zən) ***adj-*** **1** made of brass; like brass. **2** bold and shameless: *a* brazen *lie.* **—*adv-*** **bra′ zen·ly.** ***n-*** **bra′ zen·ness**: *The* brazenness *of the girl, lying about her age!*

brazen out to put on a bold and shameless front to get out of a bad situation: *When he was caught stealing, he tried to* brazen *it* out.

bra·zen-faced (brā′ zən fāst′) ***adj-*** offensively bold; impudent; shameless: *a* brazen-faced *liar.*

[1]**bra·zier** (brā′ zhər) ***n-*** open pan for holding burning charcoal or live coals. [from French **brasier,** from **braise** meaning "live coals."]

[2]**bra·zier** (brā′ zhər) ***n-*** a worker in brass. [from **braze,** from Old English **brasian,** from **bræs,** "brass."]

brazil nut ***n-*** **1** edible nut of a large Brazilian tree. Its oily white meat is enclosed by a very hard, three-sided, brown shell. **2** the tree that bears this nut.

bra·zil·wood (brə zĭl′ wo͝od′) ***n-*** wood of several trees of tropical America and the East Indies, used as a base for purple or crimson dyes and as a fine red wood for making violins and furniture. Also **bra·zil′.**

breach (brēch) ***n-*** **1** an opening made by breaking through; a gap: *a* breach *in a wall.* **2** the action of breaking (a law, a promise, etc.); violation: *a* breach *of contract*; *a* breach *of duty*; *a* breach *of friendship.* ***vt-*** to make a break, opening, or gap in: *to* breach *the enemy's defenses.* ***Hom-*** breech.

breach of promise ***n-*** in law, failure to keep a promise, especially a promise to marry someone.

breach of the peace ***n-*** in law, an unlawful public disturbance, such as keeping neighbors awake at night.

bread (brĕd) ***n-*** **1** article of food made from flour or meal which is moistened, raised, kneaded, and baked. **2** livelihood: *He earns his* bread *by hard work.* ***vt-*** to cover with bread crumbs. ***Hom-*** bred.

bread-and-butter (brĕd′ ən bŭt′ ər) ***adj-*** **1** related to earning a living: *a* bread-and-butter *education.* **2** yielding a steady source of income; financially dependable: *a* bread-and-butter *product.*

bread and butter *Informal* ***n-*** one's means of earning a living; livelihood: *Acting is his* bread and butter.

bread-and-butter note ***n-*** note thanking a host.

bread·board (brĕd′ bôrd′) ***n-*** board on which bread is sliced.

bread·fruit (brĕd′ fro͞ot′) ***n-*** **1** a large, round fruit which grows on a tree in the islands of the South Pacific. When roasted, it resembles bread. **2** the tree this fruit grows on.

Breadfruit

bread line ***n-*** line of needy persons waiting for free food.

bread·stuff (brĕd′ stŭf′) ***n-*** **1** the grain, flour, or meal used in making bread. **2** bread.

breadth (brĕdth) ***n-*** **1** the measure of a thing from side to side; width; also, spaciousness. **2** a piece of fabric of a certain width: *a* breadth *of carpet.* **3** freedom from narrowness; liberality: *his* breadth *of mind.*

breadth·ways (brĕdth′ wāz′) or **breadth·wise** (-wīz′) ***adv-*** in the direction of the breadth or width.

bread·win·ner (brĕd′ wĭn′ ər) ***n-*** the family wage earner.

break (brāk) ***vt-*** **[broke, brok·en, break·ing] 1** to knock apart by a blow or strain; fracture; burst: *to* break *a dish*; *to* break *a bone*; *to* break *the skin.* **2** to put out of working order; damage; ruin: *to* break *a watch.* **3** to stop the course, order, or regularity of; interrupt: *to* break *the monotony*; *to* break *formation*; *to* break *an electrical circuit.* **4** to fail to keep; violate: *to* break *the law*; *to* break *a promise.* **5** to weaken the force of; lessen; diminish: *The tree* broke *his fall.* **6** to tame; curb; discipline: *to* break *a bronco*; *to* break *one's will.* **7** to go beyond; surpass: *to* break *a swimming record.* **8** *Informal* to make bankrupt: *That shopping spree nearly* broke *me.* **9** to make known; disclose; reveal: *to* break *the good news.* **10** to stop (a bad habit); also, to cause (a person) to stop a bad habit, especially in the phrase **break (someone) of a habit. 11** to divide (money) into smaller units: *He* broke *a ten-dollar bill.* **12** to lower in rank; demote: *The commander* broke *Sgt. Jones to a private.* ***vi-*** **1** to become smashed, cracked, etc.: *The glass* broke *under hot water. The bone* broke *in several places.* **2** to become useless or damaged: *His watch has* broken. **3** to scatter or dissolve; disperse: *The crowd* broke *and ran. The clouds* broke, *and the sun came out.* **4** to happen, appear, or become known: *Day* broke. *The news story* broke. **5** to move or get away quickly and suddenly: *He* broke *and ran.* **6** of a voice, to fall away suddenly from normal pitch, etc. ***n-*** **1** a crack; fracture; a new opening: *a* break *in a water main*; *a* break *in the clouds.* **2** a start: *at the* break *of day.* **3** any abrupt change or interruption: *a* break *in the conversation*; *a* break *in the circuit.* **4** *Informal* brief rest or pause from work. **5** *Informal* a chance or opportunity: *a lucky* break. ***Hom-*** brake.

break away 1 to escape; run away. **2** to start too soon, as a horse in a race.

break down 1 to fail; cease to work properly: *My car* broke down *this morning.* **2** to give way under pressure: *The prisoner* broke down *and told the truth.* 3 to cause to give way by blows or pressure: *to* break down *a door*; *to* break down *the enemy's resistance.* 4 to analyze: *to* break down *a chemical compound.*

break even to have the same amount of money at the end of an enterprise as one had at the beginning.

break in 1 to train; get ready for work or use: *The sergeant* broke in *the recruits.* 2 to enter by forcing.

break in on 1 to interrupt: *to* break in on *a conversation.* 2 to intrude on.

break into 1 to begin suddenly: *The horse* broke into *a gallop.* 2 to enter forcibly.

break off 1 to put an end to; discontinue: *to* break off *relations with another country.* 2 to stop suddenly; cease abruptly: *He* broke off *in the middle of his speech.*

break out 1 to force a way out: *to* break out *of prison.* 2 to get a rash: *to* break out *with measles.* 3 to start suddenly: *A fire* broke out *during the night.*

break up 1 to stop: *to* break up *a fight.* 2 to separate; scatter: *The crowd* broke up.

break with to stop being friendly with; stop relations with: *They* broke with *each other.*

break·a·ble (brā′ kə bəl) ***adj-*** of a nature such that it can be easily broken; fragile: *a* breakable *dish.*

break·age (brā′ kĭj) ***n-* 1** the act of breaking. **2** things broken. **3** loss or damage caused by breaking, or an equivalent in money for such loss or damage.

break·down (brāk′ doun′) ***n-* 1** mental or physical collapse. **2** a sudden failure to work properly: *A* breakdown *of machinery stopped production.*

break·er (brā′ kər) ***n-* 1** wave which hits the rocks or the shore and breaks into foam. **2** person or thing that breaks.

break·fast (brĕk′ fəst) ***n-*** first meal of the day. ***vi-***: *We* breakfast *at eight.*

break·neck (brāk′ nĕk′) ***adj-*** reckless; rash; dangerous: *Wallace rode his bicycle at* breakneck *speed.*

break·through (brāk′ thro͞o′) ***n-*** movement or advance through and beyond a barrier, especially in warfare or scientific research.

break·up (brāk′ ŭp′) ***n-* 1** a falling apart or scattering; disintegration: *the* breakup *of a ship in a stormy sea*; *the* breakup *of ice in spring.* **2** an end; finish: *the* breakup *of a friendship.*

Breakwater

break·wa·ter (brāk′ wòt′ ər, -wŏt′ ər) ***n-*** wall or barrier built to break the force of waves.

bream (brēm) ***n-*** [*pl.* **bream**] **1** a fresh-water European fish of the carp family. **2** an American fresh-water sunfish.

breast (brĕst) ***n-* 1** upper front part of the body between the neck and the abdomen; chest. **2** either of the milk glands of a woman. **3** the heart; feelings. ***vt-*** to oppose; struggle with: *to* breast *waves.*

make a clean breast of to confess fully.

breast·bone (brĕst′ bōn′) ***n-*** sternum.

breast·plate (brĕst′ plāt′) ***n-*** a piece of armor to protect the chest.

Breastplate

breast stroke ***n-*** a swimming stroke in which a swimmer, lying face down with arms forward, brings his arms sideways to a right angle with his body and then thrusts them in and forward as he gives a frog kick.

breast·work (brĕst′ wûrk′) ***n-*** hastily constructed wall for defense, usually chest high.

breath (brĕth) ***n-* 1** air drawn into and forced out of the lungs. **2** a drawing in or a forcing out of air: *Take a deep* breath. **3** the power to breathe easily: *Wait until I get my* breath. **4** slight stirring (of air): *There's not a* breath *of air.* **5** a whisper: *a* breath *of scandal.*

under (one's) breath in a whisper: *to mutter* under one's breath.

breathe (brēth) ***vi-*** **[breathed, breath·ing] 1** to draw air into the lungs and force it out. **2** to stop to rest after action or strain: *The worst is over; we can* breathe *again.* ***vt-* 1** to whisper: *Don't* breathe *a word of this.* **2** to inspire: *The pitcher* breathed *new life into the team.*

breath·er (brē′ thər) ***n-* 1** one who breathes (in a certain way): *a shallow* breather. **2** *Informal* a short rest period.

breathing space ***n-*** a pause to rest or think. Also **breathing spell.**

breath·less (brĕth′ ləs) ***adj-* 1** out of breath: *The climb left him* breathless. **2** holding the breath; tense: *The spectators were* breathless *with excitement.* ***—adv-*** **breath′ less·ly.** ***n-*** **breath′ less·ness.**

breath·tak·ing (brĕth′ tā′ kĭng) ***adj-*** exciting; thrilling: *a* breathtaking *adventure.* ***—adv-*** **breath′ tak′ ing·ly.**

bred (brĕd) *p.t. & p.p.* of **breed.** ***Hom-*** bread.

breech (brēch) ***n-* 1** the hinder part of anything, especially of firearms. **2** buttocks; rump. ***Hom-*** breach.

breech·cloth (brēch′ klŏth′, -klòth′) ***n-*** cloth worn about one's loins; loincloth. Also **breech′ clout′** (brēch′- klout′).

breech·es (brē′ chəz) ***n-*** *pl.* **1** short trousers fastened below the knee. **2** *Informal* trousers.

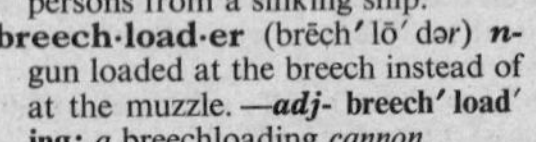

breeches buoy ***n-*** life-saving device of ships. It consists of a pair of short-legged canvas trousers hung on a life preserver, which moves along a tight line to carry persons from a sinking ship.

breech·load·er (brēch′ lō′ dər) ***n-*** gun loaded at the breech instead of at the muzzle. ***—adj-*** **breech′ load′ ing:** *a* breechloading *cannon.*

Breeches buoy

breed (brēd) ***vt-*** **[bred, breed·ing] 1** to give birth to: *The cat has* bred *four litters.* **2** to mate or raise, in order to maintain or improve the stock: *The ranch owner* breeds *cattle for beef.* **3** to train; rear: *The prince was* bred *to be a king.* **4** to be a fertile place for; give rise to: *Swamps* breed *mosquitoes. Slums* breed *crime.* ***vi-* 1** to bear young. **2** to develop; thrive: *Crime* breeds *in slums.* ***n-*** a variety or strain (of a species of plant or animal): *The Holstein is a fine* breed *of cattle.*

breed·er (brē′ dər) ***n-*** person who raises and breeds animals or plants.

breeder reactor ***n-*** type of nuclear reactor that produces more fissionable material from uranium 238 than the uranium 235 it consumes. Also **breeder pile.**

breed·ing (brē′ dĭng) ***n-* 1** the training or bringing up of young; especially, the results of training; good manners: *a man of* breeding. **2** a producing of plants and animals to get better kinds: *the* breeding *of livestock.*

breeze (brēz) ***n-*** a gentle wind.

breeze·way (brēz′ wā′) ***n-*** an open, roofed passageway between two buildings, usually between a home and a garage.

breez·y (brē′ zē) ***adj-*** **[breez·i·er, breez·i·est] 1** fanned by light winds: *a large,* breezy *porch.* **2** lively; jolly; gay and cheerful: *a* breezy *manner.* ***—adv-*** **breez′ i·ly.** ***n-*** **breez′ i·ness.**

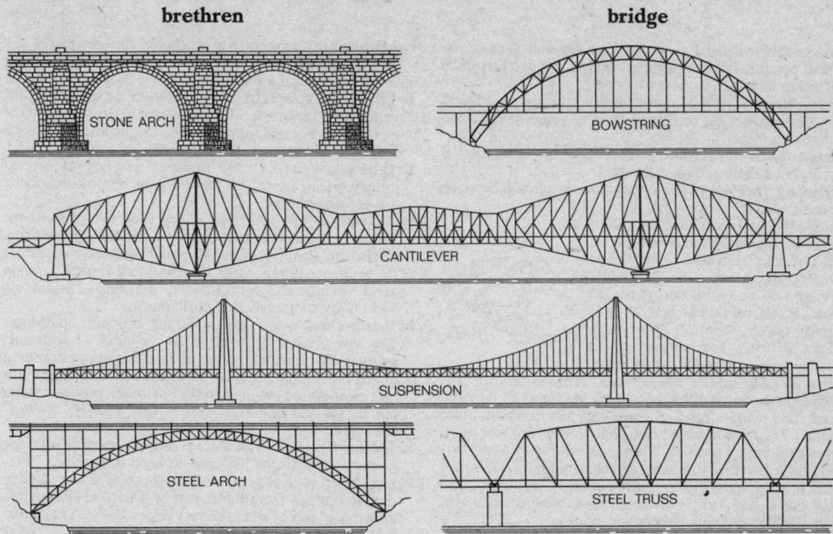

Typical bridges

breth·ren (brĕth′ rən) ***n-*** *pl.* brothers (used in serious speech to address fellow members of a community, church, etc.).

Bret·on (brĕt′ ən) ***n-*** **1** a native of Brittany. **2** the language of the people of Brittany. **3** a woman's hat with a wide turned-up brim. ***adj-*** of or relating to Brittany, its people, language, and customs.

breve (brĕv, brēv) ***n-*** a mark [˘] used to indicate a short vowel or syllable, as in "băt."

bre·vi·ar·y (brē′ vyə rē, -vē ĕr′ ē) ***n-*** [*pl.* **bre·vi·ar·ies**] a book containing the daily prayers and readings of priests of the Roman Catholic and Anglican churches.

brev·i·ty (brĕv′ ə tē) ***n-*** shortness; briefness.

brew (broo͞) ***vt-*** **1** to ferment with yeast: *Beer is* brewed. **2** to make by boiling or steeping one or more ingredients: *to* brew *tea; to* brew *a potion from herbs.* **3** to plan; plot; concoct: *to* brew *mischief.* ***vi-*** to grow in force; gather: *A storm* brewed. ***n-*** a drink made by boiling or steeping.

brew·er (broo͞′ ər) ***n-*** person whose business is making beer, ale, or the like.

brew·er·y (broo͞′ ə rē) ***n-*** [*pl.* **brew·er·ies**] a place where beer and other malt liquors are made.

brew·ing (broo͞′ ĭng) ***n-*** **1** the making of beer and other malt liquors. **2** the quantity of such made at one time.

[1]**bri·ar** (brī′ ər) [1]brier.

[2]**bri·ar** (brī′ ər) [2]brier.

bri·ar·wood (brī′ ər wo͝od′) ***n-*** brierroot.

bribe (brīb) ***n-*** gift made or promised to a person to influence him to decide or act dishonestly: *The man tried to give the policeman a* bribe *to let him go.* ***vt-*** **[bribed, brib·ing]**: *The man tried to* bribe *the policeman.*

brib·er·y (brī′ bə rē) ***n-*** [*pl.* **brib·er·ies**] the giving or taking of bribes; also, an instance of this.

bric-a-brac (brĭk′ ə brăk′) ***n-*** small articles of artistic or sentimental value put on display; knicknacks.

brick (brĭk) ***n-*** **1** oblong block of clay hardened by baking in the sun or in an oven; also, such blocks used as building material: *a pile of* bricks; *a house of* brick. **2** something shaped like such a block. **3** *Informal* a good fellow. *as* ***modifier***: *a* brick *wall.*

brick in, over, or **up** to enclose, cover, or fill with bricks.

brick·bat (brĭk′ băt′) ***n-*** a piece of brick, or anything similar, thrown in a fight.

brick·lay·er (brĭk′ lā′ ər) ***n-*** one whose occupation is to lay bricks.

brick red ***n-*** any of several shades of dull, orange-red like the color of building bricks.

brick·work (brĭk′ wûrk′) ***n-*** **1** work done by a bricklayer. **2** walls, towers, houses, etc., made of brick.

brick·yard (brĭk′ yärd′) ***n-*** place where bricks are made.

bri·dal (brī′ dəl) ***adj-*** having to do with a bride or a wedding: *a* bridal *bouquet.* ***Hom-*** bridle.

bride (brīd) ***n-*** woman newly married or about to be married.

bride·groom (brīd′ groo͞m′) ***n-*** man newly married or about to be married.

brides·maid (brīdz′ mād′) ***n-*** one of the women who attend a bride at her wedding.

[1]**bridge** (brĭj) ***n-*** **1** structure built across a river, valley, etc., to allow passage for men or vehicles. **2** raised platform on a ship, from which the ship is navigated and controlled. **3** the upper, bony part of the nose. **4** the arched support for the strings on a violin, cello, etc. **5** one or more false teeth with a mounting for holding in place. ***vt-*** **[bridged, bridg·ing] 1** to build a passageway over: *to* bridge *a river.* **2** to get over; overcome: *to* bridge *a difficulty; to* bridge *the gap between different peoples.* [from Old English **brycg.**] **—*adj-* bridge′like′.**

burn (one's) bridges or **burn (one's) bridges behind (one)** to cut off any and all ways of going back.

---

[2]**bridge** (brĭj) ***n-*** card game for four players. One of the most common types is **contract bridge.** [apparently from Russian **biritch,** an old card game.]

bridge·head (brĭj' hĕd') ***n-*** military position established on an enemy coast or riverbank in advance of the main attacking force.

bridge·work (brĭj' wûrk') ***n-*** **1** one or more dental bridges. **2** the building of bridges.

bridg·ing (brĭj' ĭng) ***n-*** wooden braces placed between beams to keep them apart.

bri·dle (brī' dəl) ***n-*** **1** head harness of a horse, including the bit and reins. **2** a check; restraint: *a* bridle *on one's tongue.* ***vt-*** **[bri·dled, bri·dling] 1** to put a bit and reins on: *Saddle and* bridle *the horses.* **2** to hold; check; control: *You must learn to* bridle *your temper.* ***vi-*** to throw back the head, as in anger or pride: *She* bridled *at his words.* ***Hom-*** bridal.

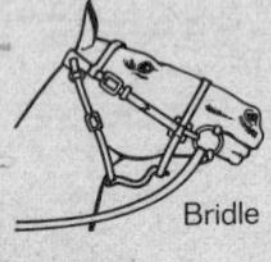
Bridle

bridle path ***n-*** path for horseback riding.

brief (brēf) ***adj-*** **[brief·er, brief·est]** not long in time; short: *The train made a* brief *stop. The speech was* brief. ***n-*** a summary, especially a lawyer's outline of a case. ***vt-*** to give a detailed summary of instructions to: *The captain* briefed *his officers.* ***—adv-*** **brief' ly.** ***n-*** **brief' ness.**

brief·case (brēf' kās') ***n-*** leather or plastic case with handles, for carrying papers and books.

[1]**bri·er** or **bri·ar** (brī' ər) ***n-*** **1** a thorny shrub, such as one of the rose family. **2** a thorn, as of a rose. **3** a patch of thorny shrubs. [from Old English **brēr.**] ***—adj-*** **bri' e·ry** or **bri' a·ry.**

[2]**bri·er** or **bri·ar** (brī' ər) ***n-*** **1** the European white heath. **2** a tobacco pipe made from its root. [from French **bruyere** meaning "thorny heath tree," from Celtic.]

bri·er·root or **bri·ar·root** (brī' ər ro͞ot', ro͞ot') ***n-*** the wood of the root of the brier, much used to make smoking pipes. Also **briarwood, brierwood.**

bri·er·wood (brī' ər wo͝od') ***n-*** brierroot.

[1]**brig** (brĭg) ***n-*** prison cell on a warship. [a special use of [2]**brig,** probably an American word.]

[2]**brig** (brĭg) ***n-*** a two-masted square-rigged vessel. [short for **brigantine,** from French **brigantine,** from Italian **brigantino,** "fighting ship."]

Brig

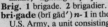

Brig. 1 brigade. **2** brigadier.

bri·gade (brĭ gād') ***n-*** **1** in the U.S. Army, a unit consisting of two or more regiments, usually under the command of a brigadier general. **2** group of men organized for a particular purpose: *a fire* brigade.

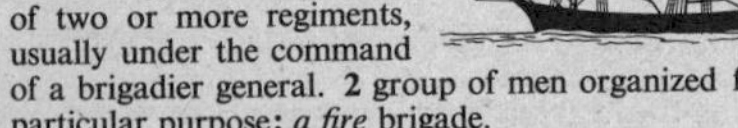

brig·a·dier general (brĭg' ə dêr') ***n-*** in the Army, Air Force, and Marine Corps, a commissioned officer who ranks next below a major general and next above a colonel. Also **brigadier.**

brig·and (brĭg' ənd) ***n-*** member of a gang of robbers; bandit.

brig·and·age (brĭg' ən dĭj) ***n-*** the practices of brigands; plundering.

brig·an·tine (brĭg' ən tēn') ***n-*** a kind of two-masted sailing vessel.

bright (brīt) ***adj-*** **[bright·er, bright·est] 1** giving or reflecting light; shining: *Rub the silver to a* bright *polish.* **2** vivid; intense: *to wear* bright *colors.* **3** cheerful; happy: *They tried to be* bright *and gay.* **4** clever: *a* bright *idea; a* bright *student.* **5** favorable; hopeful: *The future looks* bright. ***—adv-*** **bright' ly.** ***n-*** **bright' ness.**

bright·en (brī' tən) ***vi-*** to grow clearer or lighter: *The day* brightens. ***vt-*** to make more pleasant or cheerful: *Flowers* brighten *a room.*

bright-line spectrum ***n-*** spectrum given off by incandescent vapors, in which only particular wave lengths of light are emitted, appearing as bright lines on a dark background.

Bright's disease (brīts) *Medicine* ***n-*** any of several kidney diseases in which these organs become inflamed; a type of nephritis.

brill (brĭl) ***n-*** [*pl.* **brill**] flat-bodied food fish of northern European waters related to and resembling the flounder.

bril·liance (brĭl' yəns) ***n-*** **1** great brightness; splendor: *the* brilliance *of the stars.* **2** outstanding ability: *Einstein was a scientist of great* brilliance. **3** in music, brightness and clarity of sound. Also **bril' lian·cy.**

bril·liant (brĭl' yənt) ***adj-*** **1** shining brightly; sparkling: *The lake looked* brilliant *in the sunlight.* **2** splendid; magnificent: *a* brilliant *celebration.* **3** having outstanding ability: *a* brilliant *scholar.* **4** in music, having a bright and clear sound. ***n-*** a diamond or other precious stone cut to sparkle brightly. ***—adv-*** **bril' liant·ly.** ***n-*** **bril' liant·ness.**

bril·lian·tine (brĭl' yən tēn') ***n-*** an oily mixture used for giving a gloss to the hair and to keep it in place.

brim (brĭm) ***n-*** **1** edge or rim: *the* brim *of a cup.* **2** edge that stands out from the crown of a hat. ***vi-*** **[brimmed, brim·ming]** to be full to the very edge: *Her eyes* brimmed *with tears.* ***—adj-*** **brim' less.**

brim·ful (brĭm' fo͝ol') ***adj-*** full to the edge; completely filled: *a* brimful *cup of coffee.*

brimmed (brĭmd) ***adj-*** having a brim.

brim·stone (brĭm' stōn') ***n-*** sulfur.

brin·dle (brĭn' dəl) ***n-*** **1** a brown or grayish color, with dark spots or streaks. **2** an animal of this color. ***adj-*** (also **brin' dled**): *a* brindle *cow; a* brindled *cow.*

brine (brīn) ***n-*** **1** strong salt solution. **2** the ocean or its water.

bring (brĭng) ***vt-*** **[brought, bring·ing] 1** to cause (a person or thing) to come along with one by leading, carrying, driving, etc.: *to* bring *home a friend; to* bring *lunch to school; to* bring *horses to the corral.* **2** to be accompanied by; result in: *Springtime* brings *flowers.* **3** sell for: *Your jewelry will* bring *a good price.* **4** to persuade; induce: *I cannot* bring *myself to tell him.* **5** to start (a legal action) against someone: *to* bring *suit.*

► BRING means to carry to the person to whom one is speaking or to the place presently occupied by the speaker. TAKE means to carry away from the place presently occupied by the speaker or to carry from one entirely separate place to another. Mother asks, "Will someone please BRING me the scissors?" Ella calls back, "I'll BRING them right away." Ella says to Jo, "Excuse me while I TAKE the scissors to Mother." Ella says to Mother, "I've BROUGHT you the scissors." Mother says to Ella, "Thank you. While you are downstairs, please TAKE the coffee off the stove."

bring about 1 to cause to happen. **2** to reverse the course of (a ship or boat).

bring around to persuade; convince.

bring down to make fall: *to* bring down *a tyrant; to* bring down *a price.*

bring forth to produce (fruit); give birth to (young).

bring forward to present (arguments or proof).

bring in 1 to produce (profit, income, etc.): *Auto sales* bring in *millions of dollars.* **2** to give (a verdict).

bring off to accomplish in spite of difficulties.

bring on to lead to; cause to begin or appear: *to* bring on *sickness.*

bring out 1 to reveal; make clear: *to* bring out *the facts.* **2** to publish or produce: *to* bring out *a book.*

bring to 1 to revive (an unconscious person). **2** to cause (a ship or boat) to turn into the wind and stop.

bring up 1 to rear; educate. **2** to mention; broach: *May I* bring up *one question?* **3** to vomit; cast up: *The cat* brought up *a hairball.*

bring·ing-up (brĭng′ ĭng ŭp′) ***n-*** the rearing and education of a child; upbringing.

brink (brĭngk) ***n-*** **1** edge or margin of a steep place: *the* brink *of a pit.* **2** verge: *the* brink *of disaster.*

brin·y (brī′ nē) ***adj-*** **[brin·i·er, brin·i·est]** very salty.

bri·quette or **bri·quet** (brĭ kĕt′) ***n-*** a pressed brick of coal dust or other fuel.

brisk (brĭsk) ***adj-*** **1** active; lively; swift; nimble: *a* brisk *walker.* **2** keen; bracing: *a* brisk *wind.* **—*adv-* brisk′ly.** ***n-*** **brisk′ness.**

bris·ket (brĭs′ kət) ***n-*** the breast or lower chest of an animal used for food.

bris·tle (brĭs′ əl) ***n-*** a short, stiff, coarse hair. ***vi-*** **[bris·tled, bris·tling] 1** to stand up in a stiff, prickly way: *The cat's hair* bristled *when the dog barked.* **2** to show signs of anger or defiance: *The witness* bristled *at the rude question.* **—*adj-* bris′tly [bris·tli·er, bris·tli·est]:** *a short* bristly *beard; a* bristly, *quarrelsome woman.*

bristle with to be thick with or as if with bristles: *The battlefield* bristled with *bayonets. The subject* bristles with *difficulties.*

bris·tle·tail (brĭs′ əl tāl′) ***n-*** any of several primitive wingless insects that have two or three long appendages like bristles. The silverfish, a common pest, is a bristletail.

Bris·tol board (brĭs′ təl) ***n-*** hard cardboard with a smooth finish.

Brit. 1 Britain. **2** British.

Bri·tan·nic (brĭ tăn′ ĭk) ***adj-*** of or relating to Britain or the British people.

britch·es (brĭch′ ez) ***n-*** *pl.* breeches.

too big for (one's) britches to sure of oneself; cocky or arrogant.

Brit·i·cism (brĭt′ ə sĭz′ əm) ***n-*** word, phrase, or idiom used especially in the British Isles but rarely in the United States. Examples: lorry (truck), lift (elevator), and petrol (gasoline).

Brit·ish (brĭt′ ĭsh) ***adj-*** of or relating to the people of Great Britain, the United Kingdom, or the British Empire. ***n-*** **1** the language of the ancient Britons. **2 the British** the people of Great Britain.

British thermal unit ***n-*** unit for measuring heat, equal to the amount needed to increase the temperature of one pound of water one degree Fahrenheit. *Abbr.* BTU.

Brit·on (brĭt′ ən) ***n-*** **1** member of one of the Celtic tribes that occupied ancient Britain before the Roman and Anglo-Saxon invasions. **2** a native or inhabitant of Great Britain.

brit·tle (brĭt′ əl) ***adj-*** **[brit·tler, brit·tlest]** easily broken; apt to break: *a* brittle *glass.* **—*n-* brit′tle·ness.**

Bro. [*pl.* **Bros.**] brother.

broach (brōch) ***vt-*** **1** to begin to talk about; introduce: *How do you* broach *an unpleasant subject?* **2** to pierce or tap: *to* broach *a keg of cider.* ***n-*** **1** a spit for roasting meat. **2** a tool for boring or reaming, especially one used to tap a cask. ***Hom-*** brooch.

broad (brȯd) ***adj-*** **[broad·er, broad·est] 1** wide from side to side. **2** spacious; large. **3** tolerant; liberal; without prejudice: *a* broad *view; a* broad *outlook.* **4** clear: *in* broad *daylight.* **5** plain; obvious; evident: *a* broad *hint.* **—*adv-* broad′ly.** ***n-*** **broad′ness.**

broad·ax or **broad·axe** (brȯd′ ăks′) ***n-*** **1** broad-bladed ax for cutting timber. **2** ancient weapon with a wide blade.

broad·brim (brȯd′ brĭm′) ***adj-*** (also **broad′brimmed′**) of a hat, having a wide brim. ***n-*** **Broadbrim** *Informal* a Quaker.

broad·cast (brȯd′ kăst′) ***vt-*** **[broad·cast** or **broad·cast·ed, broad·cast·ing] 1** to send out over radio or television. **2** to spread around: *Don't* broadcast *the secret I just told you.* **3** to scatter: *The seed was* broadcast *rather than sown in rows.* ***adv-*** so as to scatter widely: *to sow* broadcast. ***n-*** act of sending a radio or television program.

broad·cast·ing (brȯd′ kăs′ tĭng) ***n-*** the transmitting of shows, news, music, etc., over radio and television. *as* ***modifier:*** *the* broadcasting *industry.*

broad·cloth (brȯd′ klȯth′, klŏth′) ***n-*** **1** a fine grade of cotton or silk cloth used for shirts, skirts, dresses, blouses, etc. **2** fine woolen cloth with a smooth surface.

broad·en (brȯd′ ən) ***vi-*** to grow wider: *The river* broadens *at this point.* ***vt-*** to make broader or more tolerant.

broad jump ***n-*** in athletics, a jump made for distance, either from a standing position or from a running start.

broad·leaf (brȯd′ lēf′) ***adj-*** having flat, broad leaves, as distinguished from needles on pines, firs, etc. Also **broad-leaved** (-lēvd).

broad·loom (brod′ lo͞om′) ***n-*** carpet woven on a wide loom, usually in widths of more than six feet.

broad-mind·ed (brȯd′ mīn′ dəd) ***adj-*** liberal in opinions; tolerant.

broad·side (brȯd′ sīd′) ***n-*** **1** entire side of a ship that shows above the water. **2** a firing of all the guns on one side of a ship. **3** *Informal* a printed or verbal attack on some person. ***adv-*** with the widest side turned toward an object: *The barge bore down* broadside *upon the tug.*

broad·sword (brȯd′ sôrd′) ***n-*** sword with a broad, flat blade.

Broad·way (brȯd′ wā′) ***n-*** **1** street in New York City, noted for the brilliantly lighted theatrical and entertainment area along part of it. **2** U.S. center of legitimate theater, situated in New York City.

bro·cade (brō kād′) ***n-*** cloth woven with gold and silver threads or ornamented with raised designs of flowers, etc. ***vt-*** **[bro·cad·ed, bro·cad·ing]** to weave with a raised pattern.

broc·co·li (brŏk′ ə lē) ***n-*** plant related to the cauliflower, having stalks and tight clusters of green buds, eaten as a vegetable.

Broccoli

bro·chure (brō sho͞or′) ***n-*** printed booklet or pamphlet.

bro·gan (brō′ gən) ***n-*** heavy, coarse work shoe, usually having a hobnailed sole, formerly worn in Ireland and Scotland.

[1]**brogue** (brōg) ***n-*** **1** oxford shoe decorated with stitching, pinking, and perforations. **2** brogan. [from Gaelic **brōg** meaning "shoe."]

[2]**brogue** (brōg) ***n-*** a pronunciation characteristic of a dialect of English, especially Irish or Scottish. [of uncertain origin.]

---

broil (broil) ***vt-*** **1** to cook by exposing to radiant heat, as in an oven broiler or on a grid over coals: *to* broil *a steak.* **2** to subject to great heat; make very hot: *The sun* broiled *the men on the raft.* ***vi-***: *The steak* broiled *in no time. The sailors* broiled *under the blazing sun.*

broil·er (broil′ ər) ***n-*** **1** rack, pan, or part of a stove for broiling; also, a separate electrical unit for broiling. **2** young chicken suitable for broiling.

broke (brōk) *p.t.* of **break.**

bro·ken (brō′ kən) *p.p.* of **break.** ***adj-*** **1** having breaks or gaps; discontinuous: *a* broken *line.* **2** having a rough surface; uneven: *a stretch of* broken *ground.* **3** lacking parts; incomplete: *a* broken *set of chessmen.* **4** of a language, imperfectly spoken: *He speaks* broken *English.* **5** weakened; damaged; imperfect: *in* broken *health.* **6** crushed by harsh treatment, misfortune, etc.: *a* broken *spirit.* ***—adv-*** **bro′ ken·ly.**

bro·ken-down (brō′ kən doun′) ***adj-*** in poor condition because of old age or neglect: *a* broken-down *horse.*

bro·ken·heart·ed (brō′ kən här′ təd) ***adj-*** crushed in spirit by grief or despair.

bro·ker (brō′ kər) ***n-*** person who buys or sells for another person as his agent: *a cotton* broker; *a real estate* broker.

bro·ker·age (brō′ kər ĭj) ***n-*** the business of a broker; also, his fee or commission.

bro·mide (brō′ mīd′, -mĭd) ***n-*** compound in which bromine is combined with another element or a radical, especially such a compound used as a sedative drug.

bro·mine (brō′ mēn′, -mĭn) ***n-*** reddish-brown liquid chemical element with irritating fumes. Symbol Br, At. No. 35, At. Wt. 79.91.

bronc (brŏngk) ***n-*** *Informal* bronco.

bron·chi·a (brŏng′ kē ə) ***n-*** *pl.* the larger tubes into which each of the bronchi divides.

bron·chi·al tubes (brŏng′ kē əl) ***n-*** the larger air tubes of the lungs, including the bronchi and bronchia.

bron·chi·tic (brŏng kĭt′ ĭk) ***adj-*** having to do with or caused by bronchitis: *a* bronchitic *cough.*

bron·chi·tis (brŏng kī′ tĭs) ***n-*** inflammation of the bronchial tubes.

bron·cho·scope (brŏng′ kō skōp′) ***n-*** tube which is inserted into the windpipe to see the bronchi.

bron·chus (brŏng′ kəs) ***n-*** [*pl.* **bron·chi** (-kē, -kī)] one of the two main tubes into which the windpipe divides.

bron·co or **bron·cho** (brŏng′ kō) ***n-*** [*pl.* **bron·cos** or **bron·chos**] small wild or half-tamed horse of western North America. [American word from Spanish **bronco** meaning literally "rough; rude."]

bron·co·bust·er or **bron·cho·bust·er** (brŏng′ kō bŭs′ tər) *Slang* ***n-*** person who tames broncos for riding. Also **bronc′ bust′ er.**

bron·to·saur·us (brŏn′ tō sôr′ əs) ***n-*** large vegetarian dinosaur that lived 100,000,000 years ago and grew to as much as 100 feet in length. For picture, see *dinosaur.* Also **bron′ to·saur.**

bronze (brŏnz) ***n-*** **1** hard and durable alloy of copper and tin, sometimes containing small amounts of other metals. **2** work of art cast or wrought in this alloy. **3** a paint that looks like this alloy. **4** a metallic golden-brown color. ***adj-***: *a* bronze *statue*; bronze *skin.* ***vt-*** [**bronzed, bronz·ing**] **1** to give the appearance of this alloy to: *to* bronze *a lead paperweight.* **2** to brown: *The sun* bronzed *his face.*

Bronze Age ***n-*** in the early civilizations of some peoples, the period between the Stone Age and the Iron Age, marked by the use of bronze tools, weapons, etc.

Brooch

brooch (brōch, brōōch) ***n-*** ornamental pin fastened with a clasp. ***Hom-*** broach.

brood (brōōd) ***n-*** **1** all the young hatched by a bird at one time: *a* brood *of chickens.* **2** all the children of one mother: *a* brood *of ten children.* ***vi-*** **1** to sit on eggs: *The hen* brooded. **2** to think long and moodily. ***vt-*** to sit on (eggs) to hatch them.

brood on (or **over**) to think about something long and moodily; worry over: *to* brood over *one's misfortunes.*

brood·er (brōō′ dər) ***n-*** **1** a bird that hatches eggs. **2** a person lost in moody thought. **3** artificially heated box for raising young chicks.

brood·y (brōō′ dē) ***adj-*** [**brood·i·er, brood·i·est**] **1** seriously thinking; pondering. **2** of hens, inclined to sit on eggs. ***—adv-*** **brood′ i·ly.** ***n-*** **brood′ i·ness.**

[1]**brook** (brŏŏk) ***n-*** small, natural stream of water; creek. [from Old English **brōc,** related to **break.**]

[2]**brook** (brŏŏk) ***vt-*** to bear; tolerate: *I will* brook *no interference with my plans.* [from Old English **brūcan** meaning "to enjoy."]

brook·let (brŏŏk′ lət) ***n-*** little brook.

brook trout ***n-*** kind of trout with pink to red dots on its sides, common in the cold streams and lakes of eastern North America; speckled trout.

broom (brōōm, brŏŏm) ***n-*** **1** long-handled brush used for sweeping. **2** shrub related to the clover, with stiff, slender branches and yellow flowers. ***Hom-*** brougham.

broom·corn (brōōm′ kôrn′, brŏŏm′-) ***n-*** tall grass with stiff, branching flower stalks used in making brooms.

broom·stick (brōōm′ stĭk′, brŏŏm′-) ***n-*** the long handle of a broom.

broth (brôth, brŏth) ***n-*** thin soup made by boiling meat in water.

broth·er (brŭth′ ər) ***n-*** [*pl.* **bro·thers** or **breth·ren**] **1** boy or man having the same parents as another person. **2** male fellow member of a race, nation, profession, lodge, union, or other group. **3** member of a male religious order who is not a priest; friar. *as **modifier***: *a* brother *officer*; *my* brother *men.*

broth·er·hood (brŭth′ ər hŏŏd′) **1** group of men with common interests; fraternal organization. **2** fellowship; kinship: *the* brotherhood *of man.*

broth·er-in-law (brŭth′ ər ĭn lō′) ***n-*** [*pl.* **broth·ers-in-law**] **1** husband of one's sister. **2** brother of one's husband or wife.

broth·er·ly (brŭth′ ər lē) ***adj-*** **1** of or like a brother; kindly. **2** friendly: *There was a* brotherly *feeling among the boys in the class.* ***—n-*** **broth′ er·li·ness.**

brougham (brōōm, brōō′ əm, brō′ əm) ***n-*** a closed automobile or light carriage with the driver's seat outside. ***Hom-*** broom.

brought (brōt) *p.t.* & *p.p.* of **bring.**

brow (brou) ***n-*** **1** the forehead. **2** arch of hair over an eye; eyebrow. **3** the edge of a steep place: *the* brow *of a hill.*

brow·beat (brou′ bēt′) ***vt-*** [**brow·beat, brow·beat·en, brow·beat·ing**] to frighten by stern looks or words; bully.

brown (broun) ***n-*** the color of chocolate, coffee, and most tree trunks. ***adj-*** [**brown·er, brown·est**] of this color: *the* brown *autumn leaves.* ***vt-*** to cause to have this color by cooking, roasting, etc.: *to* brown *a chicken in the oven.* ***vi-***: *The chicken* browned *in the oven.* ***—n-*** **brown′ ness.**

brown bear ***n-*** **1** medium-size bear of Europe and northern Asia, having a brown coat. **2** very large bear of Alaska, the **Alaskan brown bear,** or a closely related bear of Kodiak Island, the **Kodiak bear,** both of which have brown coats and are the largest of all bears.

brown coal ***n-*** lignite.

Brown·i·an movement (brou′ nē ən) ***n-*** rapid, jerky movement of tiny particles suspended in a liquid, due to the jostling of them by the liquid's molecules.

brown·ie (brou′ nē) ***n-*** **1** in stories, a good elf or fairy who does useful household tasks by night. **2** a small, flat, sweet, rich chocolate cake containing nuts. **3** **Brownie** member of the junior division of the Girl Scouts.
brown·ish (brou′ nĭsh) ***adj-*** somewhat brown.
brown·stone (broun′ stōn′) ***n-*** **1** reddish-brown sandstone used for building. **2** house with a facing of such stone or a similar material.
brown study ***n-*** condition of absent-mindedness caused by deep, serious thought; reverie.
brown sugar ***n-*** sugar whose crystals are colored brown by a film of molasses.
brown thrasher ***n-*** large, reddish-brown songbird of eastern North America, whose song resembles that of the mockingbird, also called **brown thrush.**
browse (brouz) ***vi-*** **[browsed, brows·ing]** **1** to nibble on grass or young shoots; graze: *The cattle* browsed *in the fields.* **2** to look over various objects idly and at random.
bru·in (brōō′ ən) ***n-*** a bear.
bruise (brōōz) ***n-*** **1** an injury, caused by a blow or fall, which does not break the skin but discolors it. **2** an injury to the outside of a fruit, vegetable, or plant. ***vt-*** **[bruised, bruis·ing]** **1** to injure and produce a black-and-blue mark: *I fell and* bruised *my leg.* **2** to hurt (someone's feelings). ***vi-*** to become bruised: *Tomatoes* bruise *easily.*
bruis·er (brōō′ zər) ***n-*** **1** *Informal* a strong, tough fellow. **2** *Slang* a prize fighter.
bruit (brōōt) ***vt-*** to report; spread abroad: *The story was* bruited *about.* ***Hom-*** brute.
brunch (brŭnch) ***n-*** combination breakfast and lunch.
bru·net (brōō nĕt′) ***adj-*** having dark hair and eyes. ***n-*** person with dark hair and eyes. ***—n-*** *fem.* **bru·nette′.**
Brün·hil·de (brōōn hĭl′ də, *Ger.* brʏn-) ***n-*** **1** in Wagner's "Ring of the Nibelung," the Valkyrie whom Siegfried releases from a spell. **2** in Teutonic myth, a queen of Iceland.
brunt (brŭnt) ***n-*** heaviest part of a shock or strain.
[1]**brush** (brŭsh) ***n-*** **1** implement made of bristles, hairs, or wire, set in a stiff back or fastened to a handle, and used for scrubbing, cleaning, painting, smoothing, etc. **2** electrical conductor, often a spring-loaded carbon block, that delivers current to the commutator of an electric motor or takes it from that of a generator. **3** short, quick fight or skirmish: *The troops had a* brush *with the enemy.* **4** a slight touching or grazing: *It was no collision, only a* brush. **5** bushy tail of an animal, especially of a fox. ***vt-*** (in sense 3 considered intransitive when the direct object is implied but not expressed) **1** to smooth or clean (something) with a bristly tool, the hand, etc. **2** to apply or remove with a bristly tool: *to* brush *paint on.* **3** to touch or graze in passing: *The two speeding cars* brushed *fenders.* [from Old French **brosse** meaning originally "brushwood; [2]brush," perhaps from an Old High German form of **brusta** "bristle."]
brush aside or **brush off** to give only slight attention to.
brush up (on) to review (something) previously studied.
[2]**brush** (brŭsh) ***n-*** **1** brushwood. **2** land covered with small, dense trees and shrubs. [from Old French **brosse** meaning "brushwood," as in [1]**brush.**]
brush-off (brŭsh′ ôf′) *Slang* ***n-*** sudden, rude dismissal.
brush·wood (brŭsh′ wŏŏd′) ***n-*** **1** branches broken or cut from trees. **2** dense thicket of shrubs and small trees.
[1]**brush·y** (brŭsh′ ē) ***adj-*** **[brush·i·er, brush·i·est]** like a brush; rough; bristly: *a* brushy *tail.* [from [1]**brush.**]
[2]**brush·y** (brŭsh′ ē) ***adj-*** **[brush·i·er, brush·i·est]** covered with dense growth of bushes and shrubs. [from [2]**brush.**]
brusque (brŭsk) ***adj-*** **[brusqu·er, brusqu·est]** rough or abrupt in speech or manner: *Bruce gave a* brusque *reply.* ***—adv-*** **brusque′ ly.** ***n-*** **brusque′ ness.**
brus·sels sprouts (brŭs′ əlz) ***n-*** *pl.* [*sing.* **brus·sels sprout**] **1** plant which bears on its stalk closely rolled heads (leaf balls) that look like little cabbages. **2** these heads used as food.
bru·tal (brōō′ təl) ***adj-*** cruel; savage. ***—adv-*** **bru′ tal·ly.**
bru·tal·i·ty (brōō tăl′ ə tē) ***n-*** [*pl.* **bru·tal·i·ties**] **1** violent and inhuman cruelty. **2** inhuman act.
bru·tal·ize (brōō′ təl īz′) ***vt-*** **[bru·tal·ized, bru·tal·iz·ing]** to make cruel or inhuman: *War tends to* brutalize *men.*
brute (brōōt) ***n-*** **1** beast; animal without reasoning power. **2** a cruel, inhuman person. *as* ***modifier:*** *His* brute *strength enabled him to go on. Hurricanes and floods show nature's* brute *forces.* ***Hom-*** bruit.
brut·ish (brōō′ tĭsh) ***adj-*** uncultured; stupid. ***—n-*** **brut′ ish·ness.** ***adv-*** **brut′ ish·ly.**
bry·o·phyte (brī′ ə fīt′) ***n-*** one of a very large group of plants that includes the mosses and liverworts.
BTU British thermal unit. Also **B.T.U., btu,** or **b.t.u.**
bu. bushel.
bub·ble (bŭb′ əl) ***n-*** **1** a thin, globelike film of liquid filled with air or gas: *a soap* bubble. **2** a small, globelike ball of air or gas rising to the surface of water or liquid, or held within a solid such as ice or glass. **3** plan or scheme that seems promising but collapses for lack of substance or practicality. ***vi-*** **[bub·bled, bub·bling]** **1** to rise in bubbles; also, to form bubbles, as does soda water. **2** to make a gurgling sound, as does a stream. **3** to express animated enthusiasm. ***—adj-*** **bub′ bly.**
bubble chamber ***n-*** vessel containing a transparent, superheated liquid, used to study atomic particles. A string of bubbles forms along the path of a particle as it moves through the liquid.
bu·bo (byōō′ bō, bōō′-) ***n-*** [*pl.* **bu·boes**] an inflammation of a lymph gland, especially one in the groin or armpit, as in bubonic plague and other diseases.
bu·bon·ic (byōō bŏn′ ĭk, bōō-) ***adj-*** having to do with or causing buboes, as bubonic plague.
bubonic plague ***n-*** a deadly contagious disease, marked by chills, fever, and buboes in the glands of neck, armpit, and groin. It is spread chiefly by the bites of fleas which have fed on infected rats.
buc·ca·neer (bŭk′ ə nêr) ***n-*** pirate; sea robber.
buck (bŭk) ***n-*** **1** the male of certain animals, especially the deer, antelope, and rabbit. The female is called a doe. **2** young man, especially a jaunty, dapper fellow. **3** a sudden jump upward, as of an untamed or unruly horse. **4** *Slang* a dollar. ***vi-*** to jump upward with the back arched, as a horse does to throw off a rider. ***vt-*** **1** to charge or push one's way through: *The quarterback* bucked *the line of the opposing team.* **2** to struggle against; oppose: *to* buck *the crowds during the rush hour.*

Bucking horse

pass the buck *Informal* to shift responsibility.
buck up *Informal* to make or become more cheerful.
buck·a·roo (bŭk′ ə rōō′) ***n-*** cowboy. [American word from Spanish **vaquero,** from **vaca** "cow."]

buck·board (bŭk′ bôrd′) ***n-*** light wagon with the seat set on a long, flexible board without springs.

Buckboard

buck·et (bŭk′ ət) ***n-*** **1** container to hold or carry water, milk, etc.; a pail. **2** bucketful.

buck·et·ful (bŭk′ ət fo͝ol′) ***n-*** the amount held by any bucket.

bucket seat ***n-*** a deep, padded, single seat used chiefly in sports cars and racing cars.

buck·eye (bŭk′ ī′) ***n-*** **1** any of several trees related to the horse chestnut tree. **2** the nut of such a tree.

Buck·ing·ham Palace (bŭk′ ĭng əm) ***n-*** the official London residence of British sovereigns since 1837.

[1]**buck·le** (bŭk′ əl) ***n-*** **1** a clasp for holding together the ends of a strap or belt. **2** a clasplike ornament for shoes, etc. ***vt-*** [**buck·led, buck·ling**] to fasten with such a clasp: *to* buckle *a seat belt.* [from Old French **boucle.**]

buckle down to apply oneself with energy: *to* buckle down *to the job.*

[2]**buck·le** (bŭk′ əl) ***vi-*** [**buck·led, buck·ling**] to bend or twist from heat or strain: *The bridge* buckled *as the armored tanks crossed it.* ***vt-***: *The weight* buckled *the bridge.* ***n-*** a bend or kink in a piece of metal. [from [1]**buckle**, probably because of the bend in the metal.]

buck·ler (bŭk′ lər) ***n-*** small, round shield.

buck private *Slang* ***n-*** in the U.S. Army, the lowest grade of enlisted man; recruit.

buck·ram (bŭk′ rəm) ***n-*** coarse cloth of linen, cotton, or hemp stiffened with glue, used in making hat frames, binding books, etc. *as* ***modifier***: *a* buckram *lining.*

buck·saw (bŭk′ sô′) ***n-*** narrow saw set in a deep, H-shaped frame, used with both hands for sawing wood.

Bucksaw

buck·shot (bŭk′ shŏt′) ***n-*** heavy lead shot used in a shotgun.

buck·skin (bŭk′ skĭn′) ***n-*** **1** soft yellowish or grayish leather made of the skin of a deer or sheep. **2 buckskins** clothing made of this leather. *as* ***modifier***: *a* buckskin *jacket.*

buck·thorn (bŭk′ thôrn′) ***n-*** **1** any of a group of shrubs and small trees, often thorny, with long oval leaves and clusters of small black berries. **2** (also called **southern buckthorn**) small tree of the sapodilla family growing in southern United States.

buck·tooth (bŭk′ to͞oth′) ***n-*** [*pl.* **buck·teeth**] a projecting upper front tooth.

buck·toothed (bŭk′ to͞otht′) ***adj-*** having buckteeth.

buck·wheat (bŭk′ hwēt′) ***n-*** **1** cereal plant with black, triangular seeds used for flour. **2** the flour itself.

buckwheat cake ***n-*** pancake made of buckwheat flour.

bu·col·ic (byo͞o kŏl′ ĭk) ***adj-*** pastoral; rustic.

bud (bŭd) ***n-*** **1** a flower or leaf that is not yet open, such as a lily bud; also, anything in an early stage of development. **2** an undeveloped shoot on the stem of a plant, seen as a small bulge or swelling. **3** in primitive animals, a small outgrowth that develops into a new animal. ***vi-*** [**bud·ded, bud·ding**] **1** to put forth new shoots; sprout. **2** to begin to emerge or develop.

in bud in the first stage of growth of a branch, leaf, or flower. **nip in the bud** to stop in the first or earliest stage.

Bud·dha (bo͞od′ ə) ***n-*** "The Enlightened One," title of Gautama, holy man of India (563? to 483? B.C.) who founded Buddhism, regarded by his followers as the last of a series of deified religious teachers.

Bud·dhism (bo͞od′ ĭz əm) ***n-*** great Asiatic religion founded by Gautama Buddha in the sixth century, B.C. It teaches the "Eightfold Path" of "right belief, right resolve, right word, right act, right life, right effort, right thinking, and right meditation."

Bud·dhist (bo͞od′ ĭst) ***n-*** a believer in Buddhism. ***adj-***: *a* Buddhist *monk.*

bud·dy (bŭd′ ē) *Informal* ***n-*** [*pl.* **bud·dies**] a close friend; pal.

budge (bŭj) ***vt-*** [**budged, budg·ing**] (usually in a negative sentence) to move slightly: *The box was so heavy that no one could* budge *it.* ***vi-***: *The mule wouldn't* budge.

bud·ger·i·gar (bŭj′ rē gär′) ***n-*** Australian parakeet, usually green with a blue tail and yellow face, popular as a pet. Also called **budg′ ie.**

bud·get (bŭj′ ət) ***n-*** a listing or plan that shows how much money is available and how it is to be divided up and spent for various purposes: *a family* budget; *a government* budget. ***vt-*** to plan how to spend (money, time, etc.) by making a plan; allot: *to* budget *time.*

bud·get·ar·y (bŭj′ ə tĕr′ ē) ***adj-*** of or relating to a budget.

[1]**buff** (bŭf) ***n-*** **1** pale yellowish-tan color. **2** soft, yellowish leather formerly made from the skin of a buffalo and now from that of an ox. **3** wheel or other tool covered with this leather, used for polishing. ***vt-*** to polish with such a tool. ***adj-***: *a* buff *wall*; *a* buff *jacket.* [from earlier **buffle** from French, from Italian **bufalo** meaning "buffalo."]

[2]**buff** (bŭf) *Informal* ***n-*** a fan; enthusiast; amateur expert: *a racing* buff. [American word of uncertain origin.]

buf·fa·lo (bŭf′ ə lō′) ***n-*** [*pl.* **buf·fa·loes, buf·fa·los,** or **buf·fa·lo**] **1** any of several kinds of oxen, such as the water buffalo of Eastern Asia or the Cape buffalo of South Africa. **2** the bison of North America.

Cape buffalo, about 5 ft. high at shoulder

buffalo grass ***n-*** **1** low-growing pasture grass of the plains east of the Rocky Mountains. **2** any of several similar pasture grasses.

[1]**buff·er** (bŭf′ ər) ***n-*** **1** anything that absorbs or cushions the shock of a blow, tension, strain, etc. **2** chemical that keeps the pH of a solution at a constant level by reacting with excess acid or base. [from archaic English **buff** meaning "a blow."]

[2]**buff·er** (bŭf′ ər) ***n-*** **1** worker who polishes. **2** a polishing tool or machine: *We have a* buffer *for our silver.* [from [1]**buff**, from the use of hide in polishing.]

buffer state ***n-*** small neutral nation located between larger rival powers, serving as a military barrier and helping to reduce friction.

[1]**buf·fet** (bŭf′ ət) ***n-*** **1** a blow struck by the hand or fist. **2** a knock or stroke. ***vt-*** **1** to strike with the hand or fist. **2** to beat; knock about: *The waves* buffeted *the boat.* [from an Old French word **buffe** meaning "a blow."]

[2]**buf·fet** (bə fā′, bo͞o fā′) ***n-*** **1** sideboard or low cabinet for dishes, silver, and table linen. **2** refreshment counter, or restaurant with such a counter. **3** a meal put out on a sideboard or table, at which guests help themselves. [from French **buffet,** of uncertain origin.]

buf·foon (bə fo͞on′) ***n-*** one who amuses others by jokes, antics, etc.; a clown.

buf·foon·er·y (bə fo͞o′ nə rē) ***n-*** [*pl.* **buf·foon·er·ies**] the pranks or jokes of a clown or low comedian; also, vulgar jesting.

bug (bŭg) ***n-*** **1** any crawling insect. **2** a flattened insect with a sucking mouth, with or without wings: *a water* bug. **3** *Informal* a disease germ. **4** *Informal* person who is overly enthusiastic about a subject, hobby, etc.

5 *Informal* defect in a machine or plan. 6 *Informal* a concealed microphone or a telephone tap. ***vt-*** **[bugged, bug·ging]** *Informal* to conceal a microphone or any voice-recording device in; also, to tap (a phone).

bug·a·boo (bŭg′ ə bo͞o) ***n-*** [*pl.* **bug·a·boos**] **1** an imaginary monster used to frighten children into obedience. **2** anything real or imaginary that causes fear.

Buggy

bug·bear (bŭg′ bâr′) ***n-*** something feared without reason; bugaboo.

bug·gy (bŭg′ ē) ***n-*** [*pl.* **bug·gies**] a light carriage with a single seat and a removable top.

bu·gle (byo͞o′ gəl) ***n-*** a trumpetlike, brass wind instrument for sounding military calls.

bu·gler (byo͞o′ glər) ***n-*** person who plays a bugle.

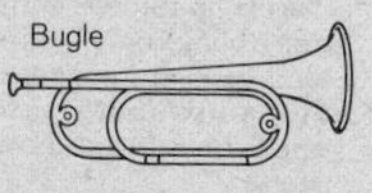
Bugle

build (bĭld) ***vt-*** **[built, build·ing]** to make by putting materials or parts together; construct: *Men* build *houses and ships. Birds* build *nests.* ***n-*** way, form, or shape in which the body is put together: *a heavy* build.

build up to make steadily larger or better: *to* build up *a business*; *to* build up *your health.*

build·er (bĭl′ dər) ***n-*** **1** person whose business is the construction of buildings. **2** person who makes or develops something: *the* builders *of a new nation.*

build·ing (bĭl′ dĭng) ***n-*** **1** the constructing of houses, churches, factories, bridges, ships, etc. **2** thing constructed; a structure, such as a house, school, barn, factory, etc.: *the Empire State* Building.

build-up (bĭld′ ŭp′) ***n-*** an increasing or strengthening: *a* build-up *of troops along the border.*

built (bĭlt) *p.t.* & *p.p.* of **build.**

built-in (bĭlt′ ĭn′) ***adj-*** **1** permanently attached to a room or building: *a* built-in *bookcase.* **2** *Informal* inherited or natural: *a* built-in *love of hard work.*

bulb (bŭlb) ***n-*** **1** rounded underground bud of some plants, such as the lily, onion, tulip, and narcissus, from which the plant grows. **2** anything shaped like such a bud: *the* bulb *of a thermometer.* **3** small glass globe containing a fine wire that gives off light when electricity passes through it: *light* bulb. **—*adj-*** **bulb′ like′.**

Electric bulb
Onion bulb

bul·bar (bŭl′ bər, -bär′) *Medicine* ***adj-*** affecting, or having to do with a bulb-shaped organ, especially the medulla oblongata.

bul·bous (bŭl′ bəs) ***adj-*** **1** in botany, growing from and producing bulbs, as tulips. **2** like a bulb; somewhat round; swollen: *The clown had a* bulbous *red nose.*

bulge (bŭlj) ***n-*** a rounded swelling which stands out; a protuberance. ***vi-*** **[bulged, bulg·ing]** to swell outward: *His schoolbag* bulged *with books.* ***vt-***: *The books* bulged *his schoolbag.* **—*adj-*** **bulg′ y [bulg·i·er, bulg·i·est]**: *his* bulgy *pockets.*

bulk (bŭlk, bo͝olk) ***n-*** size; mass; great size: *In spite of its* bulk, *the elephant can move quickly.*

the bulk of the greater part of: *I've paid* the bulk of *the debt. Oceans form* the bulk of *the earth's surface.*

bulk·head (bŭlk′ hĕd′, bo͝olk′ -) ***n-*** **1** an upright partition in a ship, separating watertight compartments. **2** any structure built to resist the pressure of water, air, or earth, such as a sea wall.

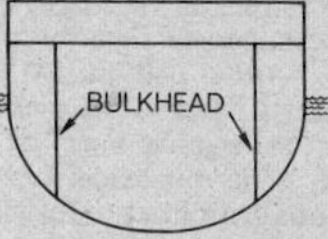

Bulkhead of a ship

bulk·y (bŭl′ kē, bo͝olk′-) ***adj-*** **[bulk·i·er, bulk·i·est]** massive; big; broad; of large volume. **—*adv-*** **bulk′ i·ly.** ***n-*** **bulk′ i·ness:** *the* bulkiness *of a mohair sweater.*

[1]**bull** (bo͝ol) ***n-*** **1** the male of any animal of the ox family. **2** any of several other large male animals, such as the whale or elephant. **3** on the stock exchange, a person who tries to raise prices for his own advantage (see also [1]*bear*). **4** *Slang* policeman. ***vi-*** to push or force ahead: *to* bull *through a crowd.* ***vt-***: *He* bulled *his way to the head of the line.* [from Old English **bula.**]

bull in a china shop person who is clumsy in circumstances demanding great care. **take the bull by the horns** **1** to deal boldly with difficulties. **2** to take the initiative.

[2]**bull** (bo͝ol) ***n-*** an official document, edict, or decree, especially of the Pope. [from Latin **bulla,** "bubble of sealing wax," as in [1]**bill.**]

bull·dog (bo͝ol′ dŏg′) ***n-*** breed of short-haired medium-sized dog with a heavy head and projecting lower jaw, remarkable for its courage and its strong grip. ***as modifier:*** *their* bulldog *tenacity.* ***vt-*** to throw a steer off its feet by grabbing its horns and twisting its neck.

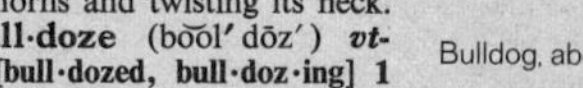
Bulldog, about 15 in. high

bull·doze (bo͝ol′ dōz′) ***vt-*** **[bull·dozed, bull·doz·ing]** **1** to level or clear land with bulldozers. **2** *Informal* to bully.

bull·doz·er (bo͝ol′ dō′ zər) ***n-*** **1** powerful tractor with a scraping blade for moving earth and clearing land. **2** *Informal* one who bullies another into doing things.

bul·let (bo͝ol′ ət) ***n-*** small piece of metal shaped to be fired from a rifle, pistol, machine gun, etc.

Bulldozer

bul·le·tin (bo͝ol′ ə tən) ***n-*** **1** a brief report on some matter of public interest: *The doctor released a* bulletin *on his famous patient's condition.* **2** a notice. **3** magazine published regularly, containing the reports of a club, society, business organization, etc.

bul·let·proof (bo͝ol′ ət pro͞of′) ***adj-*** designed to stop bullets: *a* bulletproof *window*; *a* bulletproof *vest*; *a* bulletproof *car.*

bull·fight (bo͝ol′ fīt′) ***n-*** the traditional sport of Spain and Latin America, involving a struggle between men and a bull in an open arena, the **bull ring.** **—*n-*** **bull′ fight′ er.** ***n-*** **bull′ fight′ ing.**

bull·finch (bo͝ol′ fĭnch′) ***n-*** a European finch with a rose-colored breast, prized as a songbird.

bull·frog (bo͝ol′ frŏg′, -frôg′) ***n-*** the largest North American frog. It has a very deep croaking voice.

bull·head (bo͝ol′ hĕd′) ***n-*** **1** any of several small to medium U.S. catfishes. **2** any of various sculpins.

bull·head·ed (bo͝ol′ hĕd′ əd) ***adj-*** unreasonably stubborn; obstinate. **—*n-*** **bull′ head′ ed·ness.**

---

fāte, făt, dâre, bärn; bē, bĕt, mêre; bīte, bĭt; nōte, hŏt, môre, dôg; fŭn, fûr; to͞o, bo͝ok; oil; out; tar; thin; then; hw for wh as in *wh*at; zh for s as in u*s*ual; ə for a, e, i, o, u, as in *a*go, lin*e*n, per*i*l, at*o*m, min*u*s

bul·lion (bo͝ol′ yən) ***n-*** uncoined gold or silver in a mass, lumps, or bars. ***Hom-*** bouillon.
bull·ish (bo͝ol′ ĭsh) ***adj-*** **1** like a bull in appearance, strength, or character. **2** of the stock market, showing hopes or signs of rising; optimistic (see also *bearish*). **—*adv-*** **bull′ ish·ly.** ***n-*** **bull′ ish·ness.**
Bull Moose ***n-*** member of a political party, called the Progressive Party or Bull Moose Party, formed in 1912 under the leadership of Theodore Roosevelt.
bull·necked (bo͝ol′ nĕkt′) ***adj-*** **1** having a short, thick neck like a bull's. **2** *Informal* stubborn.
bull·ock (bo͝ol′ ək) ***n-*** ox; steer.
bull's-eye (bo͝ol′ zī′) ***n-*** **1** center point of a target, or a shot that hits it; hence, anything especially successful. **2** a bulging lens used to focus the light from a lantern upon a small spot; also, a lantern having such a lens. **3** round piece of thick glass in a floor or deck to transmit light. **4** a hard, round candy which looks like a marble.
bull terrier ***n-*** strong, quick, and alert medium-sized dog originally bred by crossing the bulldog and the terrier, usually white or brindled with white markings.
bul·ly (bo͝ol′ ē) ***n-*** [*pl.* **bul·lies**] quarrelsome person who teases, threatens, or torments a smaller or weaker person. ***vt-*** [**bul·lied, bul·ly·ing**]: *He is always* bullying *his employees.* ***adj-*** *Informal* excellent.
bul·rush (bo͝ol′ rush′) ***n-*** tall plant with slender stalks that grows in wet places.
bul·wark (bo͝ol′ wərk) ***n-*** **1** a barrier or wall built for defense or protection. Earthworks, ramparts, and breakwaters are bulwarks. **2** anything that protects: *The Bill of Rights is a* bulwark *of our freedom.* **3** the solid part of a ship's side above the level of the deck.

Bulwark of a ship

bum (bŭm) *Slang* ***vi-*** [**bummed, bum·ming**] to idle or loaf. ***vt-*** to get (something) by imposing on somebody: *He always* bums *rides.* ***n-*** a loafer. ***adj-*** [**bum·mer, bum·mest**] of very bad quality; worthless.
bum·ble·bee (bŭm′ bəl bē′) ***n-*** a large, hairy bee that hums loudly.

Bumblebee, about life size

bump (bŭmp) ***n-*** **1** a heavy blow or knock; a jolt: *The plane landed with a* bump. **2** a swelling due to a blow or knock; a lump. **3** a small place raised above the level of the area around it: *a* bump *in a road.* ***vt-*** **1** to hit or strike against something with a jolt; knock against or with: *The baby* bumped *his head when he fell.* **2** to knock together: *We* bumped *our heads.* ***vi-*** **1** to move with jolts: *The wagon* bumped *along.* **2** to collide into or against.
[1]**bump·er** (bŭm′ pər) ***n-*** something that protects against shock or collision; especially, one of the thick metal strips in the front or rear of a car. [from **bump.**]
[2]**bump·er** (bŭm′ pər) ***n-*** an overflowing cup; especially one used in drinking a toast. ***adj-*** very large: *a* bumper *crop.* [perhaps from **bump** but influenced by French **bombarde** meaning "a large cup or glass."]
bump·kin (bŭmp′ kĭn) ***n-*** a clumsy fellow.
bump·tious (bŭmp′ shəs) ***adj-*** conceited; self-assertive. **—*n-*** **bump′ tious·ness.** ***adv-*** **bump′ tious·ly.**
bump·y (bŭm′ pē) ***adj-*** [**bump·i·er, bump·i·est**] **1** having bumps: *a* bumpy *road.* **2** jolting; jarring: *a* bumpy *ride.* **—*adv-*** **bump′ i·ly.** ***n-*** **bump′ i·ness.**
bun (bŭn) ***n-*** **1** a raised rounded roll of bread or cake. **2** knot of hair usually worn at the nape of the neck.
bu·na (byo͞o′ nə, bo͞o′-) ***n-*** any of several synthetic rubbers made from butadiene and one or more other compounds, such as styrene.
bunch (bŭnch) ***n-*** **1** a number of things growing together; a cluster: *a* bunch *of grapes.* **2** a collection of similar things fastened or grouped together: *a* bunch *of flowers; a* bunch *of keys.* ***vt-*** to gather or consider together. ***vi-***: *The dress* bunches *at the waist.*
bunch·y (bŭnch′ ē) ***adj-*** [**bunch·i·er, bunch·i·est**] gathering into a bunch. **—*n-*** **bunch′ i·ness.**
bun·co (bŭng′ kō) bunko.
bun·combe (bŭng′ kəm) bunkum.
bun·dle (bŭn′ dəl) ***n-*** **1** a number of things bound or tied together: *a* bundle *of rags.* **2** a package. ***vt-*** [**bun·dled, bun·dling**] to tie or wrap: *Will you please* bundle *these shirts together?*
bundle off to send away in a hurry.
bundle up to dress warmly.
bung (bŭng) ***n-*** **1** stopper of wood or cork for the hole of a cask. **2** bunghole.
bun·ga·low (bŭng′ gə lō′) ***n-*** small house, usually of one story.

Bungalow

bung·hole (bŭng′ hōl′) ***n-*** the small, round hole in the side of a cask; bung.
bun·gle (bŭng′ gəl) ***vt-*** [**bun·gled, bun·gling**] to do or handle in a clumsy or unskillful way; botch: *The fullback* bungled *the play.* ***vi-***: *to* bungle *through a game.* ***n-*** clumsy performance.
bun·ion (bŭn′ yən) ***n-*** an inflamed swelling on the foot, usually on the first joint of the great toe.
[1]**bunk** (bŭngk) ***n-*** **1** a bed built as a shelf on a wall or built into a recess in a wall. **2** a narrow bed or cot. ***vi-*** to sleep in a makeshift bed: *You can* bunk *on the sofa.* [perhaps short for **bunker,** "a ship's bin," itself of uncertain origin.]
[2]**bunk** (bŭngk) *Slang* ***n-*** empty talk; exaggeration; lies; nonsense. [short for **bunkum.**]
bunk·er (bŭng′ kər) ***n-*** **1** large bin, usually for coal on a ship. **2** natural obstacle on a golf course, such as a sandy hollow or mound of earth. **3** strong defensive fortification, such as a deep trench protected by logs or an underground chamber built of reinforced concrete and steel.
bunk·house (bŭngk′ hous′) ***n-*** building on a ranch, near a mine, etc., with cots or bunks for workers.
bun·ko (bŭng′ kō) *Informal* ***n-*** [*pl.* **bun·kos**] a swindling game or scheme. ***vt-*** to swindle or cheat. Also **bunco.**
bun·kum or **bun·combe** (bŭng′ kəm) *Informal* ***n-*** anything said or done for mere show or effect. [American word from Buncombe County, N.C.]
bun·ny (bŭn′ ē) ***n-*** [*pl.* **bun·nies**] in children's language, a rabbit.
Bun·sen burner (bŭn′ sən) ***n-*** laboratory gas burner which mixes air with gas, forming a mixture that burns with a very hot blue flame.
bunt (bŭnt) ***vt-*** **1** to butt. **2** in baseball, to tap (the ball) a short distance within the infield by meeting it with a loosely held bat. ***vi-***: *The third man at bat* bunted *and was thrown out at first.* ***n-*** **1** a push, as with horns. **2** in baseball, a lightly tapped ball.
[1]**bun·ting** (bŭn′ tĭng) ***n-*** a kind of small, thick-billed bird about the size of a sparrow. [from an earlier word **bountyng.**]
[2]**bun·ting** (bŭn′ tĭng) ***n-*** **1** coarse cotton material used for flags. **2** long pieces of this material with flaglike patterns, used for decoration on holidays. [of uncertain origin.]
Bun·yan, Paul (bŭn′ yən), See *Paul Bunyan.*

buoy (bo͞o′ ē, *also* boi) ***n-*** **1** a float carrying a whistle, light, bell, or marker, anchored to show the position of rocks, shoals, or a channel or anchorage. **2** device to keep a person afloat: *a life* buoy. ***vt-*** to support or raise in the water or as if in water (usually followed by "up"): *to* buoy *up a swimmer*; *to* buoy *one's spirits.*

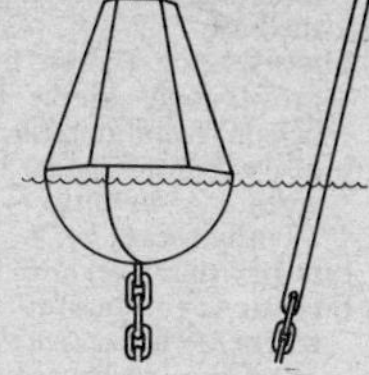
Conical and spar buoys

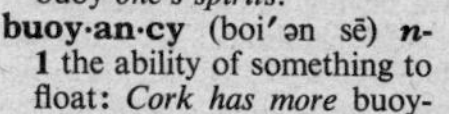

buoy·an·cy (boi′ ən sē) ***n-*** **1** the ability of something to float: *Cork has more* buoyancy *than iron.* **2** the upward force a liquid exerts on an object partly or entirely submerged in the liquid. **3** the process of floating. **4** cheerfulness.

buoy·ant (boi′ ənt) ***adj-*** **1** able to float. **2** capable of keeping an object afloat. **3** light-hearted; gay: *in* buoyant *spirits.* **4** springy; light: *a* buoyant *stride.* ***—adv-*** **buoy′ ant·ly.**

bur or **burr** (bûr) ***n-*** prickly, clinging seedcase, or a plant bearing such seedcases.

bur·ble (bûr′ bəl) ***vi-*** **[bur·bled, bur·bling]** to make a sound of bubbling; gurgle.

[1]**bur·den** (bûr′ dən) ***n-*** **1** something carried; a load. **2** weight or load on the mind or spirit: *a* burden *of grief, sorrow, or care.* ***vt-*** to weary; put too much upon. [from Old English **brythan,** related to [2]**bear.**]

[2]**bur·den** (bûr′ dən) ***n-*** **1** refrain or chorus of a song. **2** main theme of a poem, story, or the like. [from Old French **bourdon,** probably influenced by [1]**burden.**]

burden of proof ***n-*** the responsibility of proving something, as in a lawsuit.

bur·den·some (bûr′ dən səm) ***adj-*** hard to bear; weighty; troublesome: *a* burdensome *chore.*

bur·dock (bûr′ dŏk′) ***n-*** coarse weed with broad leaves and prickly burs that stick to clothing and animals.

bu·reau (byo͝or′ ō) ***n-*** [*pl.* **bu·reaus** or **bu·reaux** (-ōz)] **1** chest of drawers for holding clothing. **2** office for special business: *a travel* bureau. **3** government office or department: *Federal* Bureau *of Investigation.*

bu·reauc·ra·cy (byo͝or′ ŏk′ rə sē) ***n-*** [*pl.* **bu·reauc·ra·cies**] **1** government by an organized system of bureaus or departments. **2** officials of such a government, spoken of as a group.

bu·reau·crat (byo͝or′ ə krăt′) ***n-*** **1** an official in a bureaucracy, especially one who loves and insists on rigid rules. ***—adj-*** **bu′ reau·crat′ ic:** *He is too* bureaucratic *to listen to new ideas in government.* ***adv-*** **bu′ reau·crat′ ic·al·ly:** *He runs his office* bureaucratically.

burg (bûrg) *Slang* ***n-*** a town or city.

bur·geon (bûr′ jən) ***vi-*** **1** to bud or sprout with new growth: *Plants* burgeon *in the spring.* **2** to grow and prosper; expand; flourish; boom: *The town* burgeoned *overnight.*

bur·gess (bûr′ jəs) ***n-*** **1** in England, a citizen of a borough. **2** in some American localities, a town official. **3** in colonial Virginia and Maryland, a member of the lower house (**House of Burgesses**) of the legislature.

burgh·er (bûr′ gər) ***n-*** in former times, a citizen of a borough or town.

bur·glar (bûr′ glər) ***n-*** person who breaks into a building to steal.

bur·glar·ize (bûr′ glə rīz′) ***vt-*** **[bur·glar·ized, bur·glar·iz·ing]** to commit a burglary in (a house, office, etc.).

bur·glar·proof (bûr′ glər pro͞of′) ***adj-*** designed to be safe from burglary: *a* burglarproof *vault.*

bur·glar·y (bûr′ glə rē) ***n-*** [*pl.* **bur·glar·ies**] crime of breaking into a building to steal.

bur·go·mas·ter (bûr′ gə măs′ tər) ***n-*** the mayor of a town in Germany, Austria, Holland, or Belgium.

Bur·gun·dy (bûr′ gən dē) ***n-*** red or white wine from the province of Burgundy; also, any similar wine.

bur·i·al (bĕr′ ē əl) ***n-*** the placing of a body in a grave. *as* ***modifier:*** *a* burial *ground.*

bur·lap (bûr′ lap′) ***n-*** coarse cloth of hemp or other fiber, used mostly in making bags and wrappings.

bur·lesque (bûr′ lĕsk′) ***n-*** **1** a ridiculous imitation; a parody. **2** composition or play in which a trifling subject is treated with mock dignity, or a dignified subject with irreverence. ***adj-:*** *a* burlesque *poem.* ***vt-*** **[bur·lesqued, bur·les·quing]** to ridicule by exaggeration.

bur·ley or **Bur·ley** (bûr′ lē) [*pl.* **bur·leys**] ***n-*** a fine, light-colored tobacco grown chiefly in Kentucky.

bur·ly (bûr′ lē) ***adj-*** **[bur·li·er, bur·li·est]** big and strong; muscular. ***—n-*** **bur′ li·ness.**

Bur·mese (bŭr mēz′) ***adj-*** [*pl.* **Bur·mese**] of or pertaining to Burma, its people, or their language. Also **Bur·man** (bûr′ mən). ***n-*** **1** a native or inhabitant of Burma. **2** the language of Burma.

[1]**burn** (bûrn) ***vt-*** **[burned** or **burnt, burn·ing] 1** to cause to be consumed or destroyed by fire: *They* burned *the secret papers.* **2** to injure or damage by fire, heat, chemicals, steam, etc.: *The match* burned *my finger.* **3** to use as fuel: *The furnace* burns *gas.* **4** to cause by fire, heat, chemicals, etc.: *The acid* burned *a hole in his coat.* **5** *Chemistry* to cause (something) to undergo combustion. ***vi-*** **1** to be on fire: *A log* burned *in the fireplace.* **2** to be damaged or spoiled by heat: *The roast* burned. **3** to give light; glow: *The lights* burned *all night.* **4** to seethe; be consumed with: *to* burn *with anger*; *to* burn *with love.* ***n-*** injury or damage caused by fire, heat, chemicals, etc.: *a bad* burn *on the hand.* [from Old English **bærnan,** a form of **brinnan.**] ***—adj-*** **burn′ a·ble.**

burn down to destroy or be destroyed by fire.

burn out 1 to stop burning. **2** to clean or remove by burning: *to* burn out *a nest of wasps.*

burn up 1 to destroy or be completely destroyed by fire. **2** *Slang* to be or make angry or enraged.

[2]**burn** (bûrn) ***n-*** in Scotland, a brook. [from Old English **brunne,** later **burna,** meaning "a spring-fed stream."]

burn·er (bûr′ nər) ***n-*** part of a lamp, stove, or furnace from which the flame or heat comes.

burning glass ***n-*** convex lens used to focus the sun's rays for heating or igniting substances.

bur·nish (bûr′ nĭsh) ***vt-*** to polish by rubbing; give a shiny finish to: *Mother* burnished *the copper pots.*

bur·noose or **bur·nous** (bər no͞os′ or bûr′ no͞os′) ***n-*** cloak with a hood, worn by Arabs.

Burnoose

burn·out (bûrn′ out′) ***n-*** time when the fuel in a rocket is burned out.

burnt (bûrnt) *pt. & p.p.* of **burn.**

burp (bûrp) *Informal* ***vi-*** to belch. ***vt-*** to cause (a baby) to belch. ***n-*** a belch.

burr (bûr) ***n-*** **1** thin ridge or roughness left by a tool in cutting or shaping metal. **2** rough, round bit for a dentist's drill. **3** rough, guttural pronunciation of "r." **4** bur. ***vt-*** to pronounce with a rough or guttural sound: *to* burr *one's r's.*

bur·ro (bûr′ ō or bo͝or′ ō) ***n-*** [*pl.* **bur·ros**] in Mexico and southwestern United States, a small donkey used as a pack animal. [from Spanish **burro,** from an earlier word **burrico** meaning "little horse."] ***Homs-*** borough, burrow.

Burro, 3—3 1/2 ft. high at shoulder

bur·row (bŭr′ ō) ***n-*** **1** hole in the ground, such as is dug by a fox, rabbit, or other animal as a refuge or nest. **2** a secluded dwelling place or place of retreat. ***vi-*** **1** to dig a hole in the earth, as for shelter. **2** to lodge in a burrow. **3** to dig or search: *He was* burrowing *in an old trunk.* ***Homs-*** borough, burro. **—*n-* bur′ row·er.**

bur·sa (bûr′ sə) ***n-*** in anatomy, a small sac or pouch in the body, especially one located at a joint of the body and filled with lubricating fluid.

bur·sar (bûr′ sər) ***n-*** treasurer; purser.

bur·si·tis (bûr′ sī′ təs) ***n-*** painfully inflamed bursa.

burst (bûrst) ***vi-*** [**burst, burst·ing**] **1** to break open violently; explode: *Bombs* burst *in the air.* **2** to come, go, begin, or do something suddenly: *The boy* burst *into the room. The storm* burst. **3** to start or break out (into) some action or expression of feeling: *The birds* burst *into song. She* burst *into tears.* **4** to be full to overflowing: *The paper bag was* bursting *with apples.* ***vt-*** to cause to break open violently: *He* burst *the balloon with a pin.* ***n-*** **1** outbreak: *a* burst *of laughter.* **2** a spurt; rush: *a* burst *of energy.*

bur·y (bĕr′ ē) ***vt-*** [**bur·ied, bur·y·ing**] **1** to put in a grave; inter. **2** to cover, especially with earth. **3** to sink; embed: *He* buried *his sword in the boar.* **4** to put nearly out of reach: *They've* buried *themselves in the coutry.* **5** to absorb; engross: *He* buried *himself in his work to forget his troubles.* ***Hom-*** berry.

bus (bŭs) ***n-*** [*pl.* **bus·es** or **bus·ses**] large automobile with several rows of seats; omnibus. ***vt-*** [**bused** or **bussed, bus·ing** or **bus·sing**] to convey by bus: *The children were* bused *to school.* ***vi-***: *to* bus *to school.* ***Hom-*** buss.

bus·boy (bŭs′ boi′) ***n-*** man or boy who helps a waiter in a restaurant by removing dishes, filling glasses, etc.

bush (bo͝osh) ***n-*** **1** any low shrub with many branches. **2** (also **bush country**) land that is not cleared; especially, a region covered with brushwood, shrubs, and trees in Australia and Africa. ***vt-*** *Slang* to tire out.

beat around the bush to talk around the subject.

bush·el (bo͝osh′ əl) ***n-*** measure used for grains, fruits, vegetables, or other dry products. A bushel is equal to four pecks or eight gallons. *as* ***modifier***: *a* bushel *basket.*

hide (one's) light under a bushel to be modest about one's talents or good qualities.

bush·ing (bo͝osh′ ĭng) ***n-*** **1** in machinery, a hollow metal cylinder used as a replaceable bearing around a rotating shaft or axle. **2** liner placed around an electrical connection to insulate it or to protect it from abrasion.

bush league *Slang* ***n-*** in baseball, an unimportant minor league.

bush leaguer *Slang* ***n-*** **1** baseball player in a bush league. **2** incompetent or mediocre person.

Bush·man (bo͝osh′ mən) ***n-*** [*pl.* **Bush·men**] **1** member of a small, nomadic, primitive hunting people of South Africa. **2** the language of these people.

bush·mas·ter (bo͝osh′ măs′ tər) ***n-*** very large and dangerous pit viper of tropical America.

bush pilot ***n-*** person who flies a small commercial plane out of small airports in sparsely settled country.

bush·rang·er (bo͝osh′ rān′ jər) ***n-*** **1** frontiersman; mountain man. **2** in Australia, a robber who lives in the bush.

bush·whack (bo͝osh′ hwăk′) *Informal* ***vi-*** to live in or prowl about in the bush country. ***vt-*** to attack (a person) from ambush; ambush. **—*n-* bush′ whack′ er.**

bush·y (bo͝osh′ ē) ***adj-*** [**bush·i·er, bush·i·est**] **1** thick and spreading: *his* bushy *eyebrows.* **2** overgrown with shrubs: *a* bushy *vacant lot.*

bus·i·ly (bĭz′ ə lē) ***adv-*** in a busy, active manner.

busi·ness (bĭz′ nəs) ***n-*** **1** a buying and selling of goods; trade: *My father is in the clothing* business. **2** commercial enterprise, such as a factory, store, etc.: *Their small* business *has been handed down from father to son.* **3** work; occupation: *My* business *takes up all my free time.* **4** something of interest or duty; concern; responsibility: *Why don't you mind your own* business? **5** happening; matter; affair: *The trial was an unpleasant* business. *as* ***modifier***: *a* business *agreement.*

busi·ness·like (bĭz′ nəs līk′) ***adj-*** orderly; efficient.

busi·ness·man (bĭz′ nəs măn′) ***n-*** [*pl.* **busi·ness·men**] **1** man who owns or manages a business. **2** anyone concerned with matters of profit and loss: *Johnny's handling of the club's money showed him to be a good* businessman. **—*n-* *fem.* busi′ ness·wom′ an.**

bus·kin (bŭs′ kĭn) ***n-*** **1** high, laced boot. **2** thick-soled boot worn in ancient times by tragic actors and used as a symbol of tragedy.

Buskins

bus·man (bŭs′ mən) ***n-*** [*pl.* **bus·men**] man who drives a bus.

busman's holiday ***n-*** holiday passed in doing something similar to one's regular job, as a postman taking a long walk.

buss (bŭs) *Archaic* ***n-*** a hearty kiss. ***vt-***: *He* bussed *her on the cheek.* ***Hom-*** bus.

[1]**bust** (bŭst) ***n-*** **1** the chest or breast; bosom. **2** a sculpture of a person's head and shoulders. [from French **buste,** from Italian **busto,** from Latin **bustum** meaning "a bust-length sculpture."]

[2]**bust** (bŭst) *Slang* ***n-*** **1** blow; punch. **2** a failure. ***vt-*** **1** to hit; punch. **2** to burst or break. **3** to ruin financially. **4** to reduce in rank; demote. [variant form of **burst.**]

bus·tard (bŭs′tərd) ***n-*** large, swift-running game bird of the Old World, related to the cranes and plovers.

[1]**bus·tle** (bŭs′ əl) ***vi-*** [**bus·tled, bus·tling**] to hurry in a noisy or fussy way: *He* bustled *about the room.* ***n-*** noisy flurry of activity. [of uncertain origin.]

[2]**bus·tle** (bŭs′ əl) ***n-*** pad or framework of wire, formerly worn by women under the skirt at the back, to shape the dress. [perhaps a special use of [1]**bustle.**]

bus·y (bĭz′ ē) ***adj-*** [**bus·i·er, bus·i·est**] **1** at work; not idle; active. **2** crowded with activity: *a* busy *day; a* busy *street.* **3** of a telephone line, in use. **4** cluttered with detail: *a* busy *print or design.* ***vt-*** [**bus·ied, bus·y·ing**] to make or keep (oneself) occupied: *Tim* busied *himself with the puzzle until dinner.* **—*n-* bus′ y·ness.**

bus·y·bod·y (bĭz′ ē bŏd′ ē) ***n-*** [*pl.* **bus·y·bod·ies**] a meddling person who interferes in other people's affairs.

but (bŭt) ***conj-*** **1** in comparison or contrast; on the contrary; *He is young,* but *I am old.* **2** contrary to expectation; yet: *I planted the seed,* but *it didn't grow.* **3** (often after a negative statement) that: *I do not doubt* but *he will go.* ***prep-*** except; save: *He invited everyone* but *me.* ***adv-*** only: *There is* but *one way.* ***Hom-*** butt.

bu·ta·di·ene (byo͞o′ tə dī′ ēn) ***n-*** colorless flammable gas, a compound of carbon and hydrogen (C_4H_6) produced from petroleum and used in making synthetic rubber.

bu·tane (byōō′ tān′) ***n-*** colorless flammable gas, a compound of carbon and hydrogen (C_4H_{10}).
butch·er (bŏŏch′ ər) ***n-*** **1** person whose job is killing animals and preparing their meat for food. **2** person who cuts and sells meat. **3** person who kills men or animals needlessly. ***vt-*** **1** to slaughter. **2** to spoil; ruin.
butch·er·bird (bŏŏch′ ər bûrd′) ***n-*** any of several shrikes that impale their prey on thorns while eating it.
butch·er·y (bŏŏch′ ər ē) ***n-*** [*pl.* **butch·er·ies**] brutal killing; unnecessary slaughter; also, an instance of this.
but·ler (bŭt′ lər) ***n-*** the chief male servant of a household.
[1]**butt** (bŭt) ***vt-*** to strike with the lowered head: *A goat* butts *people who annoy him.* ***n-***: *The calf gave a playful* butt. [from Old French **buter,** "to thrust against," and from Germanic, related to [2]**butt.**] ***Hom-*** but.
[2]**butt** (bŭt) ***n-*** **1** the thicker or heavier end of something: *the* butt *of a rifle stock.* **2** an unused end of something; remaining part; stub: *a* cigarette *butt.* [partly from Middle English **bott,** from **buttock,** and partly from Old French **bout** meaning "end of a log."] ***Hom-*** but.
[3]**butt** (bŭt) ***n-*** target; especially, a person who is the target for ridicule, jokes, criticism, etc. [from French **but** meaning "goal," related to [2]**butt.**] ***Hom-*** but.
[4]**butt** (bŭt) ***n-*** large cask or barrel, as for wine, ale, or beer. [from Old French **botte,** from Late Latin **butta,** from Greek **bytinē** meaning "flask."] ***Hom-*** but.
butte (byōōt) ***n-*** steep, flat-topped hill standing alone. [American word from French **butte.**]

Butte

but·ter (bŭt′ ər) ***n-*** **1** soft, pale-yellow food fat obtained from cream by churning. **2** any of various food spreads: *apple* butter. ***vt-*** **1** to cover with a food spread. **2** *Informal* (also **butter up**) to flatter: *Let's* butter *him* up. **—*adj-*** **but′ ter·like′.**
but·ter·cup (bŭt′ ər cŭp′) ***n-*** **1** common meadow plant with glossy, cup-shaped, yellow flowers. **2** the flower.
but·ter·fat (bŭt′ ər făt′) ***n-*** the natural fat in milk.
but·ter·fin·gers (bŭt′ ər fĭng′ gərz) *Informal* ***n-*** **1** person who drops things easily. **2** a tendency to drop things easily. **—*adj-*** **but′ ter·fin′ gered.**
but·ter·fish (bŭt′ ər fĭsh′) ***n-*** any of several small marine food fishes having very slippery skins.
but·ter·fly (bŭt′ ər flī′) ***n-*** [*pl.* **but·ter·flies**] **1** day-flying insect with a long sucking beak, two long, knobbed antennae, and four wings, usually brightly colored. **2** a racing stroke in swimming.

Butterfly

butterfly weed ***n-*** kind of milkweed with bright orange flowers that attract butterflies.
but·ter·milk (bŭt′ ər mĭlk′) ***n-*** liquid left after butter has been removed from churned milk.
but·ter·nut (bŭt′ ər nŭt′) ***n-*** **1** the oily nut of the American white walnut tree. For picture, see *husk.* **2** the tree that bears this nut.
but·ter·scotch (bŭt′ ər skŏch′) ***n-*** candy or flavoring made with brown sugar, corn syrup, butter, etc. ***adj-***: *a* butterscotch *pudding.*
but·ter·y (bŭt′ ə rē) ***adj-*** **1** like butter: *a* buttery *mixture.* **2** containing or smeared with butter: *a* buttery *sauce.* **3** *Informal* overly flattering: *a* buttery *speech.*
but·tock (bŭt′ ək) ***n-*** either of the two rounded fleshy hind parts of the body that together form the rump.
but·ton (bŭt′ ən) ***n-*** **1** small, usually disk-shaped piece of plastic, shell, bone, metal, etc., sewn to one side of a garment and slipped through a buttonhole or loop on an opposite side to hold the garment closed. Buttons are also often used for decoration. **2** disk that is pushed to operate a switch: *elevator* button. ***vt-*** to fasten (something) with a button: *He* buttoned *his coat.* ***vi-***: *This coat does not* button.
but·ton·hole (bŭt′ ən hōl′) ***n-*** a stitched slit for a button to pass through. ***vt-*** [**but·ton·holed, but·ton·hol·ing**] **1** to make such openings in. **2** to force (a person) to listen as if by taking hold of him by the buttonhole.

Buttonhole stitch

but·ton·wood (bŭt′ ən wŏŏd′) ***n-*** sycamore.
but·tress (bŭ′ trəs) ***n-*** a supporting structure built against a wall or building to brace it. ***vt-*** to support or strengthen; to brace: *to* buttress *a wall*; *to* buttress *an argument with facts.*

Buttress

bux·om (bŭk′ səm) ***adj-*** of women, plump and healthy; also, full-bosomed. **—*n-*** **bux′ om·ness.**
buy (bī) ***vt-*** [**bought** (bŏt, bŏt), **buy·ing**] **1** to get by paying a price; purchase: *We'll* buy *a new chair. Money cannot* buy *happiness.* **2** *Informal* to bribe. ***vi-***: *I cannot* buy *without money.* ***n-*** *Informal* a bargain: *We got a good* buy *on the furniture.* ***Homs-*** by, bye.
buy·er (bī′ ər) ***n-*** **1** person who buys. **2** person whose work is buying for a store.
buzz (bŭz) ***n-*** a steady humming sound; a prolonged sound of "z": *the* buzz *of flies*; *a* buzz *of conversation.* ***vi-*** to make this sound. ***vt-*** **1** to signal someone with a buzzer: *The editor* buzzed *his secretary.* **2** to fly a plane very low over: *The pilot* buzzed *the signal tower.*

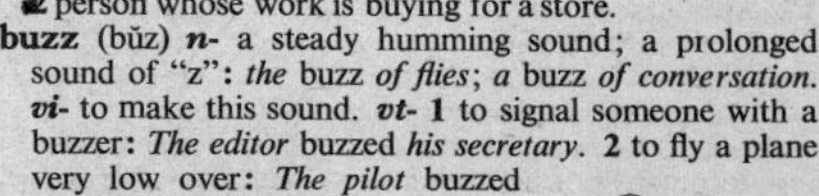

buz·zard (bŭz′ ərd) ***n-*** any of various hawks and vultures; in the United States especially, the turkey buzzard.
buzz bomb ***n-*** jet-propelled guided missile used by Germany in World War II; robot bomb; V-1.
buz·zer (bŭz′ ər) ***n-*** an electrical device for signaling with a buzz.
buzz saw ***n-*** circular saw.

Turkey buzzard, about 30 in. long

by (bī) ***prep-*** (in senses 1, 2, and 3, becomes an adverb when the object is clearly implied but not expressed) **1** close to; near; beside: *The lamp is* by *the bed.* **2** past; beyond: *to drive* by *a friend's house*; *to watch the trains go* by. **3** in or at: *Drop* by *our house soon.* **4** through the means or use of: *to travel* by *bus*; *to enter* by *a side door.* **5** according to: *to play* by *the rules*; *to judge* by *appearances.* **6** through the action or agency of: *a painting* by *a famous artist.* **7** with regard to: *They have done well* by *us.* **8** during: *to travel* by *night.* **9** not any later than: *We'll finish* by *noon.* **10** in the number of: *younger* by *three years.* **11** in the measure or amount of: *to sell eggs* by *the dozen.* **12** in succession after; following: *He grew taller year* by *year.* **13** *Mathematics* (1) in division, into groups of:

fāte, făt, dâre, bärn; bē, bĕt, mêre; bīte, bĭt; nōte, hŏt, môre, dòg; fŭn, fûr; tōō, bŏŏk; oil; out; tar; thin; then; hw for wh as in *wh*at; zh for s as in u*s*ual; ə for a, e, i, o, u, as in *a*go, lin*e*n, per*i*l, at*o*m, min*u*s

to divide 35 by *5.* (2) in multiplication, times: *to multiply 7* by *5.* (3) in measurement, with another dimension of: *a rug measuring 9 feet* by *12 feet.* ***adv-*** in reserve; aside: *to put money* by *for an emergency.* ***Homs-*** buy, bye.

by and by after a while; before long. **by and large** on the whole; in general. **by the by** or **by the bye** incidentally.

by- *prefix* meaning **1** not the main; out of the way: by*path,* by*road.* **2** near: by*stander.* **3** past: by*gone.*

by-and-by (bī′ ən bī′) ***n-*** time still to come; the future.

bye (bī) ***n-*** in certain sports, the condition of a contestant, team, etc., who is not paired with an opponent but is moved ahead to the next round of a series of competitions. ***Homs-*** by, buy.

by·gone (bī′ gón′, -gŏn′) ***adj-*** past; gone by: *in* bygone *days.* ***n-*** thing of the past: *Let* bygones *be* bygones.

by·law (bī′ ló′) ***n-*** rule or law made by an organization to govern its own activities.

by·line (bī′ līn′) ***n-*** a line at the head of a newspaper or magazine article giving the writer's name.

by·pass (bī′ păs′) ***n-*** road, path, or channel that can be used as a substitute or alternate for the main route, especially, a time-saving route around a city. ***vt-*** to go around: *We* bypassed *Pittsburgh this trip.*

by·path (bī′ păth′) ***n-*** a side path.

by·play (bī′ plā′) ***n-*** action, often in pantomime, not directly connected with the main situation, especially on the stage.

by·prod·uct (bī′ prŏd′ əkt) ***n-*** product that is not the main product of a manufacturing process, but has a value.

by·road (bī′ rōd′) ***n-*** side road.

by·stand·er (bī′ stăn′ dər) ***n-*** person who looks on, but does not take part.

by·way (bī′ wā′) ***n-*** road that is not much used.

by·word (bī′ wûrd′) ***n-*** **1** familiar saying or proverb. **2** person or thing that becomes widely known in an unfavorable way; object of scorn or mocking.

Byz·an·tine (bĭz′ ən tēn′, -tīn′, bə zăn′ tən) ***adj-*** **1** of or relating to the Byzantine Empire, its people, and civilization. **2** relating to the style of art and architecture developed there in the fifth and sixth centuries A.D., characterized by large domes, mosaics, and rich color. ***n-*** a native of the Byzantine Empire.

C

C, c (sē) ***n-*** [*pl.* **C's c's**] **1** the third letter of the English alphabet. **2** Roman numeral for 100. **3** *Music* the first and eighth notes of the C-major scale.

C symbol for carbon.

C. 1 centigrade or Celsius. **2** cape.

C_{14} symbol for carbon 14.

Ca symbol for calcium.

cab (kăb) ***n-*** **1** taxicab. **2** one-horse carriage for hire with a driver. **3** the compartment of a locomotive, truck, crane, etc., where the operator sits. *as* ***modifier:*** *a* cab *driver.*

Hansom cab

ca·bal (kə băl′) ***n-*** **1** secret scheme. **2** a few people closely united in some secret scheme or plot: *A* cabal *of five generals formed to overthrow the government.* **—*adj-*** **ca′ba·lis′tic′**: *a* cabalistic *society.*

ca·bal·le·ro (kăb′ ə lâr′ ō, -yâr′ ō, *Spanish* käb′ äl yâr′ ō) ***n-*** [*pl.* **ca·bal·le·ros**] **1** gentleman; cavalier. **2** especially in the Southwest, a horseman. [American word from Spanish **caballero,** from Late Latin **caballarius** meaning "horseman."]

ca·ba·ña (kə băn′ yə) ***n-*** **1** beach shelter, often a tent, with an open, canopied side facing the water. **2** small building of light construction, used for recreation. Also **ca·ba′na** (kə băn′ ə). [American word from Spanish **cabaña,** from Late Latin **capanna** meaning "hut."]

cab·a·ret (kăb′ ə rā′) ***n-*** **1** restaurant in which guests are entertained with dancing and vaudeville acts. **2** the entertainment itself.

cab·bage (kăb′ ĭj) ***n-*** plant having broad, thick leaves that curl together to form a hard, round head eaten as a vegetable.

Cabbage

cabbage butterfly ***n-*** any of several white butterflies whose green wormlike larvae feed on cabbage.

cab·in (kăb′ ən) ***n-*** **1** small hut or house. **2** room on a ship, used as quarters for officers or passengers. **3** enclosed part of an airplane occupied by the passengers.

cabin boy ***n-*** boy or man employed to wait on passengers and officers of a ship.

cabin class ***n-*** class of accommodations on a passenger ship next below first class and above tourist class.

Cabin

cab·i·net (kăb′ ə nət) ***n-*** **1** piece of furniture with shelves or drawers in which articles are stored or displayed: *a medicine* cabinet; *a kitchen* cabinet. **2** group of advisers chosen by the head of a nation to help manage the country's affairs. *as* ***modifier:*** *a* cabinet *door; a* cabinet *meeting.*

cab·i·net·mak·er (kăb′ ə nət mā′ kər) ***n-*** a maker of fine woodwork, especially of fine household furniture.

cab·i·net·work (kăb′ ə nət wûrk′) ***n-*** fine woodwork.

ca·ble (kā′ bəl) ***n-*** **1** thick, heavy rope of hemp or wire, used for supporting suspension bridges, towing automobiles, mooring ships, etc. **2** insulated, waterproof rope of wires used to carry electric current. **3** message sent by telegraph wires laid under the sea. ***vt-*** [**ca·bled, ca·bling**] to send a cablegram to: *Please* cable *the message.* ***vi-***: *I'll* cable *for money.*

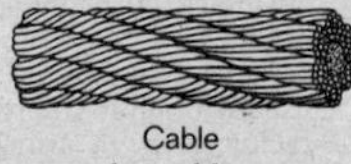

Cable

cable car ***n-*** car pulled along an overhead cable or on tracks by a moving cable.

cable·gram (kā′ bəl grăm) ***n-*** message sent by underwater cables.

cable's length ***n-*** nautical measure of length, in U.S. use 720 feet (120 fathoms), and in British use 608 feet (about 100 fathoms). Also **cable length.**

cable TV ***n-*** a system of television distribution that uses transmission over wires instead of transmission through air.

ca·boose (kə bōōs′) ***n-*** small car, usually at the end of a train, in which railroad workers can rest or sleep.

cab·ri·o·let (kăb′ rē ə lā′) ***n-*** **1** enclosed automobile with a folding top. **2** covered, two-seated carriage drawn by one horse.

ca·ca·o (kə kou′, kə kā′ ō) ***n-*** [*pl.* **ca·ca·os**] **1** seeds of a small, evergreen tree of tropical America, from which cocoa and chocolate are made. **2** the tree itself.

Cacao, leaf, pod, and beans

cach·a·lot (kăsh′ ə lŏt′, -lō′) ***n-*** sperm whale.

cache (kăsh) ***n-*** **1** hiding place for treasure or supplies. **2** something hidden in such a place: *a* cache *of food.* ***vt-*** [**cached, cach·ing**] to hide: *He* cached *the treasure at the back of the cave.* ***Hom-*** cash.

ca·cique (kə sēk′) ***n-*** **1** in Latin America, an Indian chief. **2** any of many orioles of tropical America.

cack·le (kăk′ əl) ***n-*** sharp, broken sound that a hen or goose makes after laying an egg. ***vi-*** [**cack·led, cack·ling**] to make such a sound; also, to chatter or laugh.

ca·coph·o·ny (kă kŏf′ ə nē) ***n-*** [*pl.* **ca·coph·o·nies**] harsh, disagreeable sound; dissonance: *the* cacophony *of an unrehearsed orchestra.* ***—adj-*** **ca·coph′ o·nous:** *the* cacophonous *street noises.* ***adv-*** **ca·coph′ o·nous·ly.**

cac·tus (kăk′ təs) ***n-*** [*pl.* **cac·tus·es** or **cac·ti** (-tī)] leafless, desert plant with sharp spines or prickles along a fleshy stem and branches.

Fishhook cactus

cad (kăd) ***n-*** a dishonorable, ungentlemanly man.

ca·dav·er (kə dăv′ ər) ***n-*** dead body, especially of a human being.

ca·dav·er·ous (kə dăv′ ər əs) ***adj-*** corpselike; pale; gaunt.

cad·die or **cad·dy** (kăd′ ē) ***n-*** [*pl.* **cad·dies**] **1** person hired by a golf player to carry his clubs. **2** (also **caddie cart**) small two-wheeled cart for carrying things, especially for golf bag and clubs. ***vi-*** [**cad·died, cad·dy·ing**]: *The student* caddies *on weekends.*

cad·dis fly (kăd′ əs) ***n-*** any of an order of slender insects with two pairs of membranous, fuzzy wings. Its larva, the **caddis worm,** lives in a silk tube covered with tiny stones, bits of leaves, roots etc., and is used for fish bait.

cad·dish (kăd′ ĭsh) ***adj-*** ungentlemanly; ill-bred. ***—adv-*** **cad′ dish·ly.** ***n-*** **cad′ dish·ness.**

Cad·do (kăd′ ō) ***n-*** [*pl.* **Cad·does,** also **Cad·do**] member of a group of American Indians originally from Arkansas, Louisiana, and Texas. ***—adj-*** **Cad′ do·an.**

cad·dy (kăd′ ē) ***n-*** [*pl.* **cad·dies**] small box, can, or chest with very small drawers: *a tea* caddy; *a spice* caddy.

ca·dence (kā′ dəns) ***n-*** **1** rhythm; beat: *the steady* cadence *of my heart.* **2** rhythmic rise and fall of a sound, especially of a voice: *the* cadences *of her speech.* **3** notes forming the conclusion of a musical passage.

ca·det (kə dĕt′) ***n-*** student in a naval or military academy.

Ca·dette (kə dĕt′) ***n-*** Girl Scout from twelve through fourteen years of age.

cadge (kăj) *Informal* ***vt-*** [**cadged, cadg·ing**] to get by begging: *to* cadge *a dime from a passer-by.* ***vi-***: *to* cadge *for a meal.* ***—n-*** **cadg′ er.**

cad·mi·um (kăd′ mē əm) ***n-*** soft, metallic element that looks like tin. It is used to coat iron and steel to prevent corrosion, and to make alloys with low melting points. Symbol Cd, At. No. 48, At. Wt. 112.41.

cad·re (kăd′ rē) ***n-*** group of trained persons capable of recruiting and training others: *military* cadres; *the* cadres *of the revolutionary party.* *as* ***modifier***: *the* cadre *barracks.*

ca·du·ce·us (kə do͞o′ sē əs, kə dyo͞o′-) ***n-*** [*pl.* **ca·du·ce·i** (-sē ī)] winged, serpent-twined staff of the god Mercury; also, a picture or insignia of this used as a symbol of the medical profession.

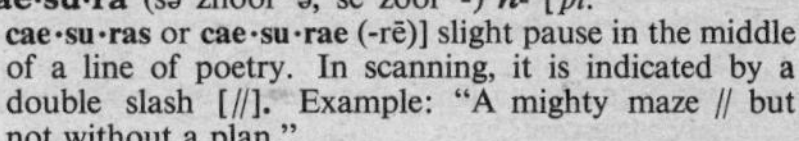
Caduceus

Cae·sar (sē′ zər) ***n-*** **1** title assumed by Roman emperors. **2** any dictator or tyrant.

cae·si·um (sē′ zē əm) cesium.

cae·su·ra (sə zho͝or′ ə, se zo͝or′-) ***n-*** [*pl.* **cae·su·ras** or **cae·su·rae** (-rē)] slight pause in the middle of a line of poetry. In scanning, it is indicated by a double slash [//]. Example: "A mighty maze // but not without a plan."

ca·fé (kə fā′) ***n-*** restaurant.

caf·e·te·ri·a (kăf′ ə têr′ ē ə) ***n-*** restaurant in which people carry their own food from a counter to tables. [American word from Mexican Spanish **cafetería** meaning "coffee shop."]

caf·feine or **caf·fein** (kă′ fēn′) ***n-*** the stimulant drug in coffee or tea.

caf·tan (kăf′ tăn′) ***n-*** loose, ankle-length robe with long sleeves and a sash, worn in the Near East.

cage (kāj) ***n-*** **1** boxlike container, usually made of wires or bars, for keeping birds or other animals. **2** any similar container or car: *an elevator* cage. **3** in basketball, the basket through which the ball is thrown. **4** in hockey, the net-covered structure behind the goal line. ***vt-*** [**caged, cag·ing**] to confine; shut up; also, to imprison: *to* cage *a bird.*

cage·y (kā′ jē) ***adj-*** [**cag·i·er, cag·i·est**] shrewd and careful; wary: *a* cagey *fox.* Also **cag′ y.** ***—adv-*** **cag′ i·ly.** ***n-*** **cag′ i·ness.**

Cai·a·phas (kī′ ə fəs, kā′-) ***n-*** in the Bible, the Jewish high priest who presided at the trial condemning Jesus to death.

cai·man (kā′ mən, kā măn′) ***n-*** any of several tropical American crocodilians resembling and closely related to alligators. Also **cay′ man.**

Cain (kān) ***n-*** in the Bible, the eldest son of Adam and killer of Abel, his own brother. ***Hom-*** cane.

raise Cain *Slang* to make a disturbance; be boisterous.

cairn (kârn) ***n-*** heap of stones set up as a tombstone, memorial, or landmark.

cais·son (kā′ sən, -sŏn′) ***n-*** **1** ammunition wagon. **2** watertight chamber in which men work underwater when building bridges, dams, tunnels, etc. **3** watertight float used to raise sunken vessels.

caisson disease ***n-*** condition marked by paralysis, pain, and unconsciousness, caused by the formation of nitrogen bubbles in body tissues when air pressure on the body is reduced too quickly, as in a rapid ascent from a caisson or deep underwater dive; bends.

cai·tiff (kā′ tĭf) *Archaic* ***n-*** mean, cowardly person; wretch. ***adj-*** vile; cowardly.

ca·jole (kə jōl′) ***vt-*** [**ca·joled, ca·jol·ing**] to coax or deceive by flattery or promises; wheedle: *He* cajoled *me into signing the note.*

ca·jol·er·y (kə jōl′ ə rē) ***n-*** [*pl.* **ca·jol·er·ies**] the use of flattery, promises, etc., to get one's way; wheedling: *Jimmy tried* cajolery *to get his father to lend him the car.*

Ca·jun (kā′ jən) ***n-*** a descendant of the French-speaking Acadians who settled in Louisiana in the 18th century.

cake (kāk) ***n-*** **1** mixture of flour, milk, sugar, eggs, etc., usually baked as a loaf or in layers, often covered with frosting. **2** small, shaped mass of cooked batter, ground meat, fish, potatoes, etc. **3** any small, solid mass that is shaped or flattened: *a* cake *of soap.* ***vi-*** **[caked, cak·ing]** to form into a hard mass; harden: *The mud* caked *on his shoes.*

cal. small calorie. See *calorie.*

Cal. large calorie. See *calorie.*

cal·a·bash (kăl′ ə băsh′) ***n-*** **1** tropical American tree with a hard-shelled fruit. **2** fruit of this tree; also, a pipe, bowl, dipper, etc., made from the dried shell; gourd.

cal·a·mine (kăl′ ə mīn′, -mən) ***n-*** pink powdery mixture of zinc and ferric oxides, used in lotions and ointments for skin irritations.

ca·lam·i·tous (kə lăm′ ə təs) ***adj-*** causing affliction or misery; disastrous.

ca·lam·i·ty (kə lăm′ ə tē) ***n-*** *[pl.* **ca·lam·i·ties]** **1** event causing widespread destruction and misery; disaster. **2** severe personal misfortune.

cal·car·e·ous (kăl kăr′ ē əs) ***adj-*** made up of, containing, or resembling limestone or calcium carbonate; chalky.

cal·ci·fi·ca·tion (kăl′sə fə kā′shən) ***n-*** **1** process of changing into lime, as in rocks and fossils. **2** *Medicine* the depositing of calcium salts in living tissues; also, a hard, stony growth resulting from this.

cal·ci·fy (kăl′ sə fī′) ***vi-*** **[cal·ci·fied, cal·ci·fy·ing]** to undergo calcification. ***vt-*** to produce calcification in.

cal·ci·mine (kăl′ sə mīn′) ***n-*** a white or tinted powder that is mixed with water and used for washing or decorating walls or ceilings. ***vt-*** **[cal·ci·mined, cal·ci·min·ing]** to cover with such a wash. Also **kal′ so·mine.**

cal·cine (kăl′ sīn′) ***vt-*** **[cal·cined, cal·cin·ing]** the roasting of rocks, ores, or chemicals to pulverize or change them chemically: *to* calcine *limestone into lime.* ***vi-***: *Limestone* calcines *into lime.* **—*n-* cal′ ci·na′ tion.**

cal·cite (kăl′ sīt′) ***n-*** pure crystalline calcium carbonate; Iceland spar. In large crystals it produces double refraction, and is therefore useful in optical instruments.

cal·ci·um (kăl′ sē əm) ***n-*** very active, silver-white, metallic chemical element common in limestone, marble, sea shells, and bones and teeth. Symbol Ca, At. No. 20, At. Wt. 40.08.

calcium carbide ***n-*** grayish black, lumpy solid compound (CaC_2), made by heating limestone with coke. It reacts with water to form acetylene gas.

calcium carbonate ***n-*** a white or colorless compound ($CaCO_3$) found in marble and limestone, and in bones, shells, teeth, and plant ashes.

calcium chloride ***n-*** white crystalline compound ($CaCl_2$) produced when hydrochloric acid acts on calcium carbonate.

calcium hydroxide ***n-*** compound of calcium, hydrogen, and oxygen ($Ca(OH)_2)_2$; slaked lime.

cal·cu·la·ble (kăl′ kyə lə bəl) ***adj-*** measurable by calculation: *a* calculable *loss.* **—*adv-* cal′ cu·la·bly.**

cal·cu·late (kăl′kyə lāt′) ***vt-*** **[cal·cu·lat·ed, cal·cu·lat·ing]** **1** to determine or figure out by mathematics; compute; *to* calculate *the speed of light.* **2** to estimate by various methods of judgment: *to* calculate *the benefits of atomic energy.*

calculated to planned or intended to: *Her book was* calculated to *appeal to adults.*

calculate on to rely or depend on: *He* calculated on *the books being popular.*

cal·cu·lat·ing (kăl′ kyə lā′ tĭng) ***adj-*** **1** used for computing: *a* calculating *machine.* **2** shrewd and cautious, especially for selfish purposes, scheming.

cal·cu·la·tion (kăl′ kyə lā′shən) ***n-*** **1** the use of mathematics in solving a problem; also, the results of this: *The engineer's* calculations *show the rocket to be off course.* **2** forethought, especially of a shrewd or sly sort.

cal·cu·la·tor (kăl′ kyə lā′ tər) ***n-*** person or machine that makes a calculation.

cal·cu·lus (kăl′ kyə ləs) ***n-*** *[pl.* **cal·cu·li** (-lī) or **cal·cu·lus·es]** **1** branch of mathematics that uses special methods to deal with problems involving rates of change, the area under a given curve, etc. **2** a hard stonelike mass, such as a kidney stone or gallstone, formed in an organ of the body.

cal·dron (kôl′ drən) cauldron.

JUNE
SUN MON TUE WED THU FRI SAT
1 2 3 4
5 6 7 8 9 10 11
12 13 14 15 16 17 18
19 20 21 22 23 24 25
26 27 28 29 30

Calendar

cal·en·dar (kăl′ ən dər) ***n-*** **1** way of reckoning time by days, weeks, months, and years. See also *Gregorian calendar, Julian calendar.* **2** table showing the arrangement of days, weeks, and months of a year. **3** list or schedule of things to be done or that happen at certain times: a *church* calendar *of festivals.* ***Hom-*** calender.

cal·en·der (kăl′ ən dər) ***n-*** machine with a series of rollers between which paper or cloth is passed to give it a smooth, hard, or glossy surface. ***vt-***: *That factory* calenders *paper.* ***Hom-*** calendar.

cal·ends (kăl′ əndz) ***n-*** first day of the month in the ancient Roman calendar.

ca·len·du·la (kə lĕn′ jə lə) ***n-*** any of a group of plants resembling the common marigold, especially a cultivated plant with bright orange flowers.

[1]calf (kăf) ***n-*** *[pl.* **calves** (kăvs)] **1** the young of the domestic cow. **2** the young of certain other large mammals, such as the whale, elephant, or moose. **3** calfskin, the leather. [from Old English **cealf** of the same meaning.]

[2]calf (kăf) ***n-*** *[pl.* **calves** (kăvz)] muscular back part of the leg between the knee and ankle. [probably from Old Norse **kālfi.**]

Calf

calf·skin (kăf′ skin) ***n-*** leather made of the skin of a calf; also, the skin or hide itself.

Cal·i·ban (kăl′ ə băn′) ***n-*** in Shakespeare's "Tempest," a deformed, savage slave.

cal·i·ber or **cal·i·bre** (kăl′ ə bər) ***n-*** **1** diameter of the bore of a gun, or of a bullet or shell: *a* .22-caliber *pistol.* **2** degree of merit or importance; capability: *a commission of high* caliber.

cal·i·brate (kăl′ ə brāt′) ***vt-*** **[cal·i·brat·ed, cal·i·brat·ing]** **1** to graduate or mark off the scale of (a measuring instrument) into appropriate units. **2** to correct or check (a measuring scale). **3** to determine the caliber of (a tube, bore, etc.). **—*n-* cal′ i·bra′ tion.**

cal·i·co (kăl′ ə kō′) ***n-*** *[pl.* **cal·i·coes** or **cal·i·cos]** cheap cotton cloth printed with small flowers or other colored designs. ***adj-*** **1** made of this cloth: *a* calico *dress.* **2** dappled or spotted like some of this cloth: *a* calico *cat.*

Calif. California.

cal·i·for·ni·um (kăl′ə fôr′ nē əm, -fôr′ nē əm) ***n-*** manmade radioactive metallic element which is heavier than uranium. Symbol Cf, At. No. 98.

Calipers
OUTSIDE
INSIDE

cal·i·per rule (kăl′ ə pər) ***n-*** rule graduated to show distance between a fixed and a sliding jaw. Also **caliper.**

cal·i·pers or **cal·li·pers** (kăl′ ə pərz) ***n-*** **1** (takes plural verb) instrument with two adjustable curved legs, used to measure an inside or outside diameter, thickness, etc. **2** caliper rule.

ca·liph or **ca·lif** (kā′ lĭf, kăl′ ĭf) ***n-*** formerly, the political and spiritual head of a Muslim state.

cal·iph·ate (kăl′ ə fāt′, -fət) ***n-*** formerly, the office, reign, or country of a caliph.

cal·is·then·ics or **cal·lis·then·ics** (kăl′ əs thĕn′ ĭks) ***n-pl.*** simple gymnastic exercises. **—*adj-* cal′ is·then′ ic** or **cal′ lis·then′ ic:** *a* calisthenic *exercise.*

[1]**calk** (kȯk) caulk. [from French **calquer,** from Latin **calcāre** "press in; tread," from **calx,** "heel."]

[2]**calk** (kȯk) ***n-*** piece of metal projecting downward from a shoe or boot, or from a horseshoe, to prevent slipping. ***vt-:*** *The shoemaker* calked *my hiking boots.* [from Latin **calx** meaning "heel."]

calk·ing (kȯ′ kĭng) ***n-*** substance, such as hemp fiber, used to caulk joints or cracks.

call (kȯl) ***vt-* 1** to summon; send for: *to* call *a policeman.* **2** to telephone: *I* called *him, but the line was busy.* **3** to give a name to; name; specify: *They* called *him "Deerslayer." He who pays the piper* calls *the tune.* **4** to utter or announce in a loud voice: *to* call *the roll.* **5** to bring about or initiate by declaration: *to* call *a meeting*; *to* call *a strike.* **6** to appeal to; invoke: *to* call *God to witness.* **7** to awaken: *Please* call *me at seven o'clock.* **8** to say (a person or thing) is something specified: *Would you* call *him a great man?* **9** to halt or postpone (an outdoor sports event) because of darkness, poor weather, etc. **10** in poker, to require (a player) to show the cards he is betting on. ***vi-* 1** to cry out; appeal loudly; shout: *She* called *for help.* **2** to make a visit: *We* called, *but he wasn't home.* **3** to telephone: *We* called *from New York.* ***n-* 1** loud cry; shout: *a* call *for help.* **2** summons; request: *a* call *to dinner*; *a* call *for volunteers.* **3** characteristic cry or sound of a bird or animal: *the* call *of a bluejay.* **4** appeal; lure; fascination: *the* call *of the sea.* **5** demand; claim: *We have first* call *on his services.* **6** *Informal* need; reason; justification: *He had no* call *to talk that way.* **7** a visit. **8** a contact or conversation by telephone. **9** in sports, the decision of an official: *the umpire's* call.

close call a narrow escape. **on call 1** available when summoned; ready: *The doctor was* on call *all night.* **2** of loans, payable on demand. **pay (or make) a call** to visit. **port of call** seaport at which one makes regular stops.

call back 1 to ask or command to return: *The president* called *him* back *from Asia.* **2** to return a phone call.

call down 1 to rebuke sharply; scold. **2** to invoke from above: *He* called down *a curse on his enemy.*

call for 1 to go and get: *We will* call for *you at 2 P.M.* **2** to require; demand: *Boxing* calls for *quick footwork.*

call forth to bring into use or play; evoke: *Danger* called forth *all his energy.*

call in 1 to request or invite for advice: *We* called in *an expert.* **2** to demand payment of (a debt, etc.). **3** to withdraw or retire (money) from circulation.

call into question to raise a doubt about.

call off 1 to make go away: *Please* call off *your dogs.* **2** to read or speak aloud (names, items, etc.) in some sequence. **3** to cancel: *to* call off *a game.*

call on 1 to pay a visit to: *to* call on *friends.* **2** to appeal to: *You can* call on *me for help.*

call (one's) bluff to challenge what is believed to be an empty threat.

call out 1 to utter in a loud voice: *to* call out *answers.* **2** to summon into action: *to* call out *the Army.*

call (someone) names to attack with insulting language.

call to mind to remind one of.

call up 1 to telephone (someone). **2** to summon into service or action. **3** to bring to mind.

cal·la (kăl′ ə) or **calla lily** ***n-*** any of several related plants having a spike of tiny flowers enclosed in a showy, petallike white or yellow spathe.

call·boy (kȯl′ boi′) ***n-*** boy who summons actors when it is time for them to appear on stage.

call·er (kŏl′ ər) ***n-* 1** one who pays a brief visit. **2** one who announces train arrivals and departures. **3** one who calls the figures or steps for a square dance.

cal·lig·ra·phy (kə lĭg′ rə fē′) ***n-*** [*pl.* **cal·lig·ra·phies**] handwriting; especially, beautiful and artistic handwriting. **—*adj-* cal′ li·graph′ ic** (kăl′ ə grăf′ ĭk).

call·ing (kȯl′ ĭng) ***n-* 1** profession; occupation; vocation: *It is important to find the right* calling. **2** strong inner feeling or impulse to undertake a particular duty or follow a certain way of life.

Cal·li·o·pe (kə lī′ ə pē′) ***n-* 1** in Greek mythology, the Muse of eloquence and heroic poetry. **2 calliope** a mechanical organ in which the tones are produced by a series of steam whistles.

cal·li·pers (kăl′ ə pərz) calipers.

cal·los·i·ty (kə lŏs′ ə tē, kăl′ ŏs′-) ***n-*** [*pl.* **cal·los·i·ties**] **1** lack of sensitive feelings; callousness. **2** hardened, thickened place on the skin or on bark.

cal·lous (kăl′ əs) ***adj-*** lacking sympathy and affection; unfeeling; insensitive: *a* callous *disregard for the welfare of others.* ***vt-* 1** to form calluses on: *Rough work will* callous *your hands.* **2** to make insensitive or unfeeling: *His hard life* calloused *his heart.* ***Hom-*** callus. **—*adv-* cal′ lous·ly.** ***n-*** **cal′ lous·ness.**

cal·low (kăl′ ō) ***adj-* 1** young and inexperienced: *a* callow *youth.* **2** of a bird, not yet feathered; unfledged. **—*adv-* cal′ low·ly.** ***n-*** **cal′ low·ness.**

cal·lus (kăl′ əs) ***n-*** hardened skin. ***Hom-*** callous.

calm (käm, kälm) ***adj-*** [**calm·er, calm·est**] quiet and peaceful. ***n-*** condition or period of quiet and peacefulness: *The sea was motionless during the* calm. ***vt-*** to quiet (often with "down"): *to* calm *a crying child.* ***vi-:*** *The sea* calmed. **—*n-* calm′ ness.** ***adv-*** **calm′ ly.**

cal·o·mel (kăl′ ə məl, -mĕl′) ***n-*** mercurous chloride.

ca·lor·ic (kə lôr′ ĭk) ***adj-*** of or having to do with heat or calories; calorific.

cal·or·ie (kăl′ ə rē) ***n-* 1** (also **small calorie, gram calorie**) unit of energy equal to the amount of heat needed to raise the temperature of one gram of water one degree centigrade. *Abbr.* cal. **2** (also **large calorie, great calorie, kilocalorie**) energy unit, equal to 1000 small calories, used to measure the amount of energy the body gets from food. One egg has about 75 calories. *Abbr.* Cal. Also **cal′ or·y.**

cal·o·rif·ic (kăl′ ə rĭf′ ĭk) ***adj-* 1** producing heat. **2** caloric.

cal·o·rim·e·ter (kăl′ ə rĭm′ ə tər) ***n-*** apparatus for measuring how much heat is absorbed or given off.

cal·u·met (kăl′ yə mĕt′) ***n-*** tobacco pipe smoked by North American Indians in various ceremonies as a symbol of peace and friendship; peace pipe.

ca·lum·ni·ate (kə lŭm′ nē āt′) ***vt-*** [**ca·lum·ni·at·ed, ca·lum·ni·at·ing**] to make false and harmful statements about (a person); slander. **—*n-* ca·lum′ ni·a′ tor.**

ca·lum·ni·ous (kə lŭm′ nē əs) ***adj-*** containing calumny; slanderous. **—*adv-* ca·lum′ ni·ous·ly.**

cal·um·ny (kăl′ əm nē) ***n-*** [*pl.* **cal·um·nies**] the making of a false statement harmful to someone's character or reputation; also, the statement itself; slander.

---

fāte, făt, dâre, bärn; bē, bĕt, mêre; bīte, bĭt; nōte, hŏt, môre, dȯg; fŭn, fûr; to͞o, bo͝ok; oil; out; t*a*r; thin; t͟hen; hw for wh as in *wh*at; zh for s as in u*s*ual; ə for a, e, i, o, u, as in *a*go, lin*e*n, per*i*l, at*o*m, min*u*s

Cal·va·ry (kăl′ və rē) ***n-*** place where Christ was crucified, near the site of ancient Jerusalem; Golgotha.

calve (kăv) ***vi-*** [**calved, calv·ing**] to bring forth young, said of cows, whales and elephants.

calves (kăvz) *pl.* of [1]**calf** or [2]**calf.**

Ca·lyp·so (kə lĭp′ sō) ***n-*** **1** in Greek legend, a sea nymph who detained Odysseus (Ulysses) on her island for seven years. **2 calypso** [*pl.* **ca·lyp·sos**] a type of improvised song originally from Trinidad, usually about love or current events.

ca·lyx (kā′ lĭks, kăl′ ĭks) ***n-*** [*pl.* **ca·lyx·es** or **ca·ly·ces** (kā′ lĭ sēz′)] outermost part of a flower, usually consisting of sepals that enclose the bud and remain at the base of the opened flower.

cam (kăm) ***n-*** movable machine part, usually an irregularly shaped wheel or shaft, that gives back-and-forth motion to another part resting against it.

ca·ma·ra·de·rie (kä′mə rä′ də rē, kăm′ ə răd′-) ***n-*** friendly fellowship, comradeship.

cam·ass or **cam·as** (kăm′ əs) ***n-*** any of several plants related to the lilies and hyacinths, especially the **common camass,** whose bulbs are edible, and the **death camass** which is poisonous.

cam·ber (kăm′ bər) ***n-*** **1** the setting of the wheels of an automobile so that they are closer together at the bottom than at the top. **2** any slight arch of a girder, road surface, deck, etc. ***vt-*** to shape with a slight arch.

cam·bi·um (kăm′ bē əm) ***n-*** layer of growing tissue between the bark and sapwood of trees and woody plants, which forms both new bark and the annual rings of new wood.

Cam·bri·an (kăm′ brē ən, kăm′-) ***n-*** the first of the six periods of the Paleozoic era, the earliest time in which the existence of invertebrate animals is known. ***adj-:*** *the* Cambrian *period.*

cam·bric (kām′ brĭk) ***n-*** fine, thin linen fabric or a similar cotton material. ***adj-:*** *a* cambric *handkerchief.*

cambric tea ***n-*** a drink made from hot water, sugar, milk, and sometimes a little tea.

came (kām) *p.t.* of **come.**

cam·el (kăm′ əl) ***n-*** large, cud-chewing mammal well suited to desert life. The swift, single-humped **Arabian camel,** or dromedary, of Africa and the Middle East is used for riding and as a beast of burden. (For picture, see *dromedary.*) The double-humped **Bactrian camel** of Central Asia is chiefly a beast of burden.

Camel, 7 1/2 ft. high

cam·el·li·a (kə mēl′ yə) ***n-*** small tree or shrub of warm climates, cultivated for its large and showy red, pink, or white flowers; also, the flower itself.

ca·mel·o·pard (kə mĕl′ ə pärd′) ***n-*** **1** *Archaic* giraffe. **2 Camelopard** a northern constellation between Cassiopeia and Ursa Major.

Cam·e·lot (kăm′ ə lŏt′) ***n-*** legendary seat of King Arthur's court, in England.

camel's hair ***n-*** **1** warm, yellowish-tan cloth woven from the hair of the camel. **2** fine, soft hairs, sometimes of the camel but now usually from the tail of the squirrel, used to make small paintbrushes. ***—adj-*** **(camel's-hair):** *a* camel's-hair *coat; a* camel's-hair *brush.*

cam·e·o (kăm′ ē ō) ***n-*** [*pl.* **cam·e·os**] gem or ornament with a raised design, carved from agate, shell, etc. Usually the design color contrasts with the background.

cam·er·a (kăm′ rə, -ər ə) ***n-*** **1** lightproof box with a lens that focuses light on a film or plate to make photographs or motion pictures. **2** piece of electronic equipment that changes visual images into electrical impulses for television broadcasting.

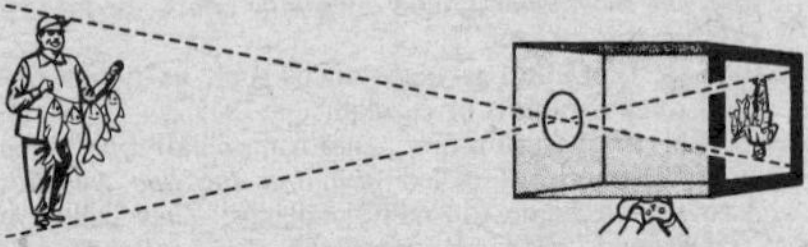
Camera, showing upside-down image on film

cam·er·a·man (kăm rə mən, -măn′) ***n-*** [*pl.* **cam·er·a·men**] person who operates a camera, especially in motion pictures or television broadcasting ***—n-*** *fem.* **cam′er·a·wom′an.**

cam·i·sole (kăm′ ə sōl′) ***n-*** girl's or woman's undergarment, often with wide, decorative shoulder straps, worn under a sheer blouse or dress.

cam·o·mile or **cham·o·mile** (kăm′ ə mīl′) ***n-*** plant related to the daisy, with strong-smelling flowers and leaves that are sometimes dried and steeped in hot water to make **camomile tea,** a medicine.

cam·ou·flage (kăm′ ə fläzh′) ***n-*** disguise or concealment, especially by means of colors, patterns, or materials that blend with the background or surroundings. ***vt-*** [**cam·ou·flaged, cam·ou·flag·ing**] to conceal or disguise by a deceptive appearance or manner: *to* camouflage *guns with green paint; to* camouflage *uneasiness.*

camp (kămp) ***n-*** **1** place where people live temporarily in tents, cabins, or other informal shelters: *a summer* camp; *a military* camp; *a hunter's* camp. **2** side or faction: *He abandoned his old beliefs and joined the opposing* camp. ***vi-*** **1** to set up or stay in temporary living quarters: *We* camped *at night in the woods.* **2** to settle oneself; remain: *to* camp *on a sofa all day.*

cam·paign (kăm pān′) ***n-*** **1** series of military operations carried on for a particular purpose: *The general planned a* campaign *to capture the city.* **2** organized activity for a particular purpose: *a political* campaign. ***vi-:*** *to* campaign *for a candidate's election.* ***—n-*** **cam·paign′er.**

cam·pa·ni·le (kăm′pə nē′ lē) ***n-*** [*pl.* **cam·pa·ni·les** or **cam·pa·ni·li** (-lē)] tower, usually a separate building, that contains a bell or set of bells.

camp·er (kăm′ pər′) ***n-*** person who stays at a camp for recreation.

camp·fire (kămp′ fīər′) ***n-*** outdoor open fire used for cooking, warmth, or as a center for social gatherings.

Camp-Fire, Inc. ***n-*** **1** organization aiming to prepare girls and boys for useful, healthy lives through supervised outdoor activities. **2 campfire girl** or **boy** member of this organization.

camp·ground (kămp′ ground′) ***n-*** area used for camping or holding a camp meeting.

cam·phor (kăm′ fər) ***n-*** whitish, crystalline substance with a strong odor, obtained chiefly from the **camphor tree** of eastern Asia, used in medicines, mothballs, etc.

cam·pho·ra·ted (kăm′fə rā′ təd) ***adj-*** treated with or containing camphor: *a bottle of* camphorated *oil.*

camp meeting ***n-*** outdoor religious gathering, usually lasting for several days.

camp·site (kămp′ sīt′) *n-* area used for camping, usually by an individual party of hikers, vacationers, etc.

camp·stool (kămp′ stōōl′) *n-* light, backless folding chair.

cam·pus (kăm′ pəs) *n-* grounds of a large school or college. [American word from Latin **campus** meaning "field; plain."]

[1]**can** (kăn) ***auxiliary verb*** [*p.t.* **could**] **1** am, is, or are physically or mentally able to. **2** may possibly; might; could: *Do you think that* can *be the way it happened?* **3** *Informal* am, is, or are permitted to: *You* can *go now.* [from Old English **can(n)**, "he knows (how)," part of the verb **cunnan** meaning "to know."]

►CAN should be used in writing to indicate ability; MAY should be used to indicate permission or possibility: *You* may *swim across the lake as far as I am concerned, but I don't know if you* can *swim that far.*

[2]**can** (kăn) *n-* **1** metal container, usually with straight sides and a cover or sealed top: *a coffee* can; *a garbage* can. **2** amount such a container holds: *We ate two* cans *of beets for dinner.* ***vt-*** [**canned, can·ning**] to preserve (food) in sealed metal or glass containers. [from Old English word **canne** meaning "cup."]

Can. 1 Canada. **2** Canadian.

Canada goose *n-* large wild goose of North America, mostly grayish brown with a black head and neck.

Ca·na·di·an (kə nā′ dē ən) *n-* a native or citizen of Canada. ***adj-*** of or pertaining to Canada or to the Canadians: *a* Canadian *airline.*

Canadian French *n-* the French language as spoken and written by French Canadians.

ca·nal (kə năl′) *n-* **1** man-made water channel used for navigation, irrigation, or drainage. **2** tubelike part of the body, such as the alimentary canal.

ca·nal·ize (kăn′ ə līz′) ***vt-*** [**ca·nal·ized, ca·nal·iz·ing**] **1** to make into a canal or canals: *They* canalized *the two creeks and the small lake.* **2** to furnish with canals: *The Dutch* canalized *their country centuries ago.* **3** to concentrate or direct into a certain channel or channels: *War* canalizes *our efforts and feelings.*

can·a·pe (kăn′ ə pā′, -pē′) *n-* cracker or small piece of toast or bread topped with a tasty spread, bit of fish or cheese, etc., and served as an appetizer.

ca·nard (kə närd′) *n-* false and absurd story or rumor to deceive the public; hoax.

ca·na·ry (kə nâr′ ē) *n-* [*pl.* **ca·nar·ies**] **1** small, usually yellow, bird popular as a caged pet because of its song. **2** (also **canary yellow**) a light, bright yellow.

ca·nas·ta (kə năs′ tə) *n-* card game resembling rummy, played with two decks of cards.

can·can (kăn′ kăn′) *n-* dance performed chiefly as entertainment, in which the legs are kicked very high.

can·cel (kăn′ səl) ***vt-*** **1** to call off; abolish; annul: *to* cancel *a magazine subscription*; *to* cancel *a debt*; *to* cancel *an appointment.* **2** to mark, cross out, etc., especially so as to prevent use or reuse: *to* cancel *a stamp*; *to* cancel *a numeral.* **3** to offset; balance: *My vote* canceled *hers, and the result was a tie.*

can·cel·la·tion (kăn′ sə lā′ shən) *n-* **1** a canceling or annulling: *the* cancellation *of a privilege, debt, engagement, etc.* **2** mark used to cancel, as on a postage stamp.

can·cer (kăn′ sər) *n-* **1** any of several diseases caused by abnormal growth of cells in the body. **2** dangerous and abnormal mass of growing cells; malignant tumor. **3** rapidly spreading source of harm or evil: *Crime is a* cancer *that must be checked.* **—*adj-*** **can′ cer·ous.**

Can·cer (kăn′ sər) *n-* constellation thought to outline the figure of a crab. See also *Tropic of Cancer.*

can·de·la·bra (kăn′ də lä′ brə, -lăb′ rə) *n-* a candelabrum.

can·de·la·brum (kăn′ də lä′ brəm, -lăb′ rəm) *n-* [*pl.* **can·de·la·bra** (-brə) or **can·de·la·brums**] candlestick with several branches for holding candles.

can·did (kăn′ dĭd) ***adj-*** **1** honest and frank; sincere: *a* candid *opinion.* **2** of photographs, informal and unposed. **—*adv-*** **can′ did·ly.**

can·di·da·cy (kăn′ də də sē) *n-* [*pl.* **can·di·da·cies**] condition or fact of being a candidate: *his* candidacy *for office.* Also, *chiefly Brit.*, **can′ di·da·ture** (kăn′ də də chər).

can·di·date (kăn′ də dāt′) *n-* person who is a contestant for an office or honor.

can·died (kăn′ dēd) ***adj-*** cooked with sugar or covered with a glaze of sugar: *a* candied *apple.*

can·dle (kăn′ dəl) *n-* **1** stick of wax or tallow with a wick inside it, burned to give light. **2** *Physics* unit of strength or intensity of a light source. One candle is the intensity of light emitted through a 1/60 sq. cm. opening in the side of a hollow sphere having an interior temperature of 1773° C. ***vt-*** [**can·dled, can·dling**] to examine (eggs) for quality by holding between the eye and a small light.

hold a candle to (usually in a negative statement) to deserve comparison with: *As a cook, she can't* hold a candle to *her mother.* **not worth the candle** not worth the expense or trouble.

can·dle·light (kăn′ dəl līt′) *n-* **1** light given off by a candle. **2** time when candles are lighted; twilight.

Can·dle·mas (kăn′ dəl məs) *n-* a Christian feast commemorating the purification of the Virgin Mary (February 2).

can·dle·pow·er (kăn′ dəl pou′ ər) *n-* brightness or intensity of a light source, measured in candles.

can·dle·stick (kăn′ dəl stĭk′) *n-* holder for a candle.

can·dle·wick (kăn′ dəl wĭk′) *n-* **1** wick of a candle. **2** (also **can′ dle·wick′ ing**) thick cotton thread used to make embroidered or tufted designs on bedspreads, curtains, etc. ***adj-***: *a* candlewick *bedspread.*

can·dor (kăn′ dər) *n-* outspoken honesty; frankness: *her embarrassing* candor.

Candlestick

can·dy (kăn′ dē) *n-* [*pl.* **can·dies**] sweet food, usually in the form of small pieces, made chiefly from sugar or sugar syrup to which flavoring, fruits, nuts, etc., are often added; also, a single piece of such food. ***vt-*** [**can·died, can·dy·ing**] to cook, coat, or preserve with sugar: *to* candy *fruit.* ***vi-*** to turn into sugar: *to cook syrup until it* candies.

can·dy·tuft (kăn′ dē tŭft′) *n-* garden plant with flat clusters of small white, pink, or lavender flowers.

cane (kān) *n-* **1** stick used as an aid in walking; walking stick. **2** any of various plants having jointed, hollow, woody stems, such as the bamboo and sugar cane; also, the stem of such a plant. **3** narrow strips of rattan, wicker, etc., used in making furniture. ***vt-*** [**caned, can·ing**] **1** to beat with a walking stick or similar rod. **2** to equip or repair with strips of interwoven wicker: *to* cane *a chair seat.* ***Hom-*** Cain.

cane·brake (kān′ brāk′) *n-* section of land densely covered with cane or similar plants.

cane sugar *n-* sugar made from sugar cane, as distinguished from sugar made from beets.

---

fāte, făt, dâre, bärn; bē, bĕt, mêre; bīte, bĭt; nōte, hŏt, môre, dôg; fŭn, fûr; tōō, bŏŏk; oil; out; tar; thin; then; hw for wh as in *wh*at; zh for s as in u*s*ual; ə for a, e, i, o, u, as in *a*go, lin*e*n, per*i*l, at*o*m, min*u*s

ca·nine (kā′nīn′) ***adj-*** of, like, or characteristic of a dog. ***n-*** 1 any of a family of animals including the dog, wolf, etc. 2 (also **canine tooth**) one of the sharp, pointed teeth located next to the outer incisors in the upper and lower jaw; cuspid (for picture, see *tooth*).

can·is·ter (kăn′ə stər) ***n-*** box or small container, usually metal, with a tightly fitting lid, for flour, coffee, etc.

can·ker (kăng′kər) ***n-*** 1 open sore inside the mouth, related to cold sores. 2 disease which destroys the hooves of horses. 3 disease of the lining of a dog's or cat's ear. 4 anything that causes evil or corruption. ***—adj-*** **can′ker·ous.**

can·ker·worm (kăng′kər wûrm′) ***n-*** any of several caterpillars especially destructive to fruit and shade trees.

can·na (kăn′ə) ***n-*** garden plant with large red or yellow flowers, and broad, sometimes purplish leaves.

canned (kănd) ***adj-*** 1 preserved and sealed in airtight tins or glass jars, as are vegetables, fruit, etc. 2 *Informal* recorded: *a program of* canned *music.*

can·nel coal (kăn′əl) ***n-*** kind of soft coal that yields oils and gases.

can·ner·y (kăn′ə rē) ***n-*** [*pl.* **can·ner·ies**] factory where food is canned.

can·ni·bal (kăn′ə bəl) ***n-*** 1 human being who eats human flesh. 2 any animal that eats its own kind. *as* ***modifier:*** *a* cannibal *ant.*

can·ni·bal·ism (kăn′ə bəl ĭz′əm) ***n-*** act or habit of eating one's own kind: *Among some fish, such as guppies,* cannibalism *is common.* ***—adj-*** **can′ni·bal·is′tic.**

can·ni·bal·ize (kăn′ə bəl īz′) ***vt-*** [**can·ni·bal·ized, can·ni·bal·iz·ing**] to take parts from (machines, equipment, etc.) to make repairs in others.

can·non (kăn′ən) ***n-*** [*pl.* **can·nons** or **can·non**] large gun mounted on wheels or a fixed base; artillery piece. ***Hom-*** canon.

Cannon

can·non·ade (kăn′ən ād′) ***n-*** a continuous firing of cannon. ***vt-*** [**can·non·ad·ed, can·non·ad·ing**] to attack with cannon; bombard: *The enemy* cannonaded *the fort.*

can·non·ball (kăn′ən bȯl′) ***n-*** 1 in earlier times, a large spherical piece of shot fired from a cannon. 2 *Slang* a fast express train.

can·non·eer (kăn′ə nêr′) ***n-*** soldier who fires or tends a cannon; artilleryman.

can·not (kăn′ŏt, kă nŏt′) am, is, or are unable to.

can·ny (kăn′ē) ***adj-*** [**can·ni·er, can·ni·est**] shrewd and cautious. ***—adv-*** **can′ni·ly.** ***n-*** **can′ni·ness.**

ca·noe (kə nōō′) ***n-*** light, narrow boat moved through the water by people using paddles. ***vi-*** [**ca·noed, ca·noe·ing**] to travel in or paddle such a boat.

Canoe

can·oe·ist (kə nōō′ĭst) ***n-*** person who paddles a canoe.

[1]**can·on** (kăn′ən) ***n-*** 1 official rule or code of a church, especially the Roman Catholic Church. 2 principle or standard by which things are judged: *the* canons *of good conduct.* 3 in various religions, the books of scripture that are accepted. 4 (often **Canon**) the most important part of the Mass. 5 musical piece in which one voice after another starts and continues the same melody. 6 works of an author that are accepted by experts as genuine: *the Shakespeare* canon. [from Latin **canon,** from Greek **kanōn** meaning "a rule."] ***Hom-*** cannon.

[2]**can·on** (kăn′ən) ***n-*** clergyman with duties in a cathedral. [from Old French **canoine,** from Latin **canonicus** meaning "belonging to a rule."] ***Hom-*** cannon.

ca·ñon (kăn′yən) ***n-*** canyon.

ca·non·i·cal (kə nŏn′ə kəl) ***adj-*** 1 of, conforming to, or established by church law or rule. 2 considered genuine or authoritative. ***—adv-*** **can·on′i·cal·ly.**

canonical hour ***n-*** in some churches, one of the fixed periods of the day set aside for specific prayers and services.

can·on·ize (kăn′ə nīz′) ***vt-*** [**can·on·ized, can·on·iz·ing**] to give the official status of a saint to: *Joan of Arc was* canonized *long after her death.* ***—n-*** **can′on·i·za′tion.**

canon law ***n-*** the official system of laws of a Christian church.

ca·no·pic jar (kə nō′pĭk) ***n-*** in ancient Egypt, a vase or urn used to hold the entrails of an embalmed body.

can·o·py (kăn′ə pē) ***n-*** [*pl.* **can·o·pies**] 1 covering of cloth or other material fixed above a bed or a throne, held up on poles above an important personage, or erected at the entrance to a building. 2 anything similar to this: *a* canopy *of leafy branches.* 3 transparent, sliding enclosure of an airplane's cockpit. ***vt-*** [**can·o·pied, can·o·py·ing**]: *A great flock of birds* canopied *the sky.*

Canopy

canst (kănst) *Archaic* form of **can** used with "thou."

[1]**cant** (kănt) ***n-*** 1 specialized language of a group or profession; jargon: *thieves'* cant; *legal* cant. 2 insincere expression of religious or moral truths; hypocritical talk. *as* ***modifier:*** *a* cant *phrase; a* cant *exhortation.* [from Latin **cantus** meaning "song."]

[2]**cant** (kănt) ***n-*** 1 a slant or tilt; slope: *the* cant *of a roof.* 2 sudden, forceful push that moves something to a diagonal position. ***vt-*** 1 to tilt or slant; slope. 2 to push or pitch sideways: *The wind* canted *the sailboat.* ***vi-:*** *The boat* canted *around the buoy.* [from early Dutch or Old French, from Latin **cantus** meaning "corner."]

can't (kănt) cannot.

can·ta·loupe or **can·ta·loup** (kăn′tə lōp′) ***n-*** melon with a hard, rough rind and sweet, juicy, orange-colored flesh.

can·tan·ker·ous (kăn tăng′kər əs) ***adj-*** hard to get along with; fault-finding; cranky: *a* cantankerous *movie director.* ***—adv-*** **can·tan′ker·ous·ly.** ***n-*** **can·tan′ker·ous·ness.**

can·ta·ta (kən tä′ tə) *Music* ***n-*** short musical drama intended to be sung but not acted.

can·teen (kăn tēn′) ***n-*** 1 metal or plastic bottle for carrying drinking water. 2 shop in a camp, factory, etc., selling refreshments and tobacco. 3 place where recreation and refreshments are provided for members of the armed services.

can·ter (kăn′tər) ***n-*** slow, easy gallop. ***vi-*** to ride or run at such a gallop: *He* cantered *across the field.* ***vt-:*** *He* cantered *his horse for half a mile.*

Can·ter·bur·y bell (kăn′tər bĕr′ē) ***n-*** a kind of bellflower, with showy blue, pink, or white flowers.

cant·hook (kănt′hŏŏk′) ***n-*** wooden lever with an adjustable hook at one end, used for handling logs; peavey.

can·ti·cle (kăn′tə kəl) ***n-*** any of several hymns used in church services. The words of canticles are usually taken directly from the Bible.

Canticle of Canticles ***n-*** in the CCD Bible, the name given to the Song of Solomon.

can·ti·le·ver (kăn′tə lĕv′ər, -lē′vər) ***n-*** 1 bracket or block projecting from the wall of a house to support a balcony, cornice, etc. **2** projecting beam supported only at one end. ***adj-***: *a* cantilever *house*.

cantilever bridge ***n-*** bridge made up of two rigid sections or cantilevers, anchored on piers at each end and connected by a central span. For picture, see *bridge*.

can·tle (kăn′ təl) ***n-*** raised part at the rear of a saddle.

can·to (kăn′ tō) ***n-*** [*pl.* **can·tos**] part or section of a long poem.

can·ton (kăn′ tŏn) ***n-*** small political division of a country or territory, especially Switzerland.

Can·ton·ese (kăn′ tə nēz′) ***n-*** [*pl.* **Can·ton·ese**] **1** a native of Canton, China. **2** Chinese dialect spoken in and around Canton. ***adj-***: *good* Cantonese *cooking*.

can·ton·ment (kăn tŏn′ mənt, -tōn′ mənt) ***n-*** camping place or quarters assigned to a body of troops.

can·tor (kăn′ tər) ***n-*** **1** choir leader in a church. **2** soloist in the Jewish religious service.

can·vas (kăn′ vəs) ***n-*** **1** coarse heavy cloth of cotton, hemp, or flax, used for tents, sails, awnings, tennis shoes, etc., and as a material on which to paint pictures. **2** oil painting: *a* canvas *by Rembrandt*. ***Hom-*** canvass.

can·vas·back (kăn′ vəs băk′) ***n-*** a North American wild duck.

can·vass (kăn′ vəs) ***vt-*** **1** to visit (a district, house, or person) in order to get information, votes, or contributions, or to make sales. **2** to discuss in detail: *We* canvassed *the topic of skiing*. ***vi-***: *They* canvassed *all morning for the Heart Fund*. ***n-*** **1** a soliciting for information, contributions, etc. **2** thorough discussion. ***Hom-*** canvas. **—*n-* can′ vas·ser.**

can·yon (kăn′ yən) ***n-*** deep valley with steep sides, usually with a stream flowing through it; a gorge. [American word from Spanish **cañon** meaning literally "tube," from Late Latin **canna** meaning "reed; cane."]

caou·tchouc (kou′ cho͝ok′) ***n-*** natural rubber, especially crude rubber; India rubber.

cap (kăp) ***n-*** **1** a small covering for the head: *a baseball* cap; *a nurse's* cap. **2** anything circular suggesting or used as a cover: *a mushroom* cap; *a bottle* cap. **3** small explosive charge in a wrapper, such as one used in toy pistols or one used as a primer to set off a larger amount of explosive. **4** writing paper of various large sizes: *fools*cap; *legal* cap. **5** the feathering around the top of a bird's head. **6** *Informal* a capital letter. ***vt-*** **[capped, cap·ping] 1** to put a cover on the top of; also, to cover: *I forgot to* cap *the bottle. Snow* capped *the mountains.* **2** to match and do better than: *Can you* cap *this story*?

set (one's) cap for to try to get (a man) to propose marriage.

ca·pa·bil·i·ty (kā′ pə bĭl′ ə tē) ***n-*** [*pl.* **ca·pa·bil·i·ties**] **1** ability; competence. **2** quality that can be developed; potentiality. **3** *Military* maximum strength or power available at a particular time: *nuclear* capability.

ca·pa·ble (kā′ pə bəl) ***adj-*** gifted or skillful; able; competent: *a* capable *surgeon*. **—*adv-* ca′ pa·bly.**

capable of 1 having the ability or skill to do something: *He's* capable of *great things*. **2** susceptible to; open to: *a novel* capable of *many interpretations*.

ca·pa·cious (kə pā′ shəs) ***adj-*** able to hold much; roomy: *a* capacious *handbag*. **—*adv-* ca·pa′ cious·ly**: *a man* capaciously *endowed with courage*. ***n-* ca·pa′ cious·ness**: *the* capaciousness *of his understanding*.

ca·pac·i·tance (cə păs′ ə təns) ***n-*** the ability of an object or a circuit to store up a charge of electricity, equal to the ratio of charge to voltage and measured in farads and subdivisions of farads.

ca·pac·i·tor (kə păs′ ə tər) ***n-*** device made of two conducting surfaces separated by insulation, used to store up a charge of electricity in radios, television sets, and other electrical systems; condenser.

ca·pac·i·ty (kə păs′ ə tē) ***n-*** [*pl.* **ca·pac·i·ties**] **1** ability or capability: *his* capacity *for learning*; *to work to full* capacity. **2** maximum or indicated limit to what can be received or held: *a seating* capacity *of twenty*; *a percolator of six-cup* capacity; *a bridge with a ten-ton* capacity. **3** position; role; relationship: *He spoke in his* capacity *as mayor*. **4** capacitance. *as* ***modifier***: *A* capacity *audience crowded the theater*.

cap and bells ***n-*** a cap trimmed with little bells, worn by medieval court jesters or fools.

cap and gown ***n-*** traditional academic dress of mortarboard and long robe, worn at ceremonies.

ca·par·i·son (kə păr′ ə sən) ***n-*** ornamental covering or harness for a horse; hence; gay or rich clothing. ***vt-***: *to* caparison *a horse*.

[1]**cape** (kāp) ***n-*** loose outer garment without sleeves, worn over the shoulders. [from Spanish **capa** meaning "hood," from Late Latin **cappa,** from Latin **caput** "head."]

Policeman wearing cape

[2]**cape** (kāp) ***n-*** point of land jutting out into a body of water; headland. [from French **cap,** from Spanish **cabo,** from Latin **caput** meaning "head."]

Cape buffalo ***n-*** large, black, wild ox found in swampy areas in South Africa and having two curved horns that nearly join at their base. For picture, see *buffalo*.

[1]**ca·per** (kā′ pər) ***vi-*** to skip or leap about playfully: *Clowns* capered *about the circus ring*. ***n-*** **1** playful leap or jump. **2** a prank; antic. [from French **capriole,** "a leap," from Latin **capreolus** meaning "a young goat."]

cut a caper to caper.

[2]**ca·per** (kā′ pər) ***n-*** **1** one of the green flower buds or berries of a Mediterranean shrub, pickled and used as a relish. **2** the shrub itself. [from Latin **capparis,** from Greek **kapparis,** from Persian **kabar.**]

cap·il·lar·i·ty (kăp′ ə lăr′ ə tē) ***n-*** **1** the condition of being capillary. **2** capillary attraction or repulsion.

cap·il·lar·y (kăp′ ə lĕr′ ē) ***n-*** [*pl.* **cap·il·lar·ies**] a very minute blood vessel. ***adj-*** **1** fine as a hair; slender; having a tiny bore. **2** relating to the minute blood vessels of the body.

capillary attraction ***n-*** the attraction between the molecules of a liquid and a solid, which causes the surface of the liquid to rise where it touches the solid.

capillary tube ***n-*** tube of small enough bore to conduct liquids by capillary attraction.

cap·i·tal (kăp′ ə təl) ***n-*** **1** city which is the seat of government of a country or State: *Washington, D.C. is the* capital *of the United States*. **2** capital letter. **3** wealth and property that can be used in business and industry to make more money. **4** broad, ornamental top part of a column. For pictures, see *Corinthian, Doric,* and *Ionic*. ***adj-*** **1** first in importance; chief: *the* capital *points in a discussion*. **2** first-rate; excellent: *a* capital *idea*. **3** punishable by death: *a* capital *crime*. ***Hom-*** capitol.

cap·i·tal·ism (kăp′ ə tə lĭz′ əm) ***n-*** economic system based on private ownership of the means of production and distribution, and characterized by profit, a free market, and open competition.

cap·i·tal·ist (kăp′ ə tə lĭst′) ***n-*** **1** person whose wealth is invested in business enterprises. **2** supporter of capitalism. ***—adj-:*** *a* capitalist *point of view.*

cap·i·tal·is·tic (kăp′ ə təl ĭs′ tĭk) ***adj-*** identified with or relating to capitalism or capitalists.

cap·i·tal·i·za·tion (kăp′ ə təl ə zā′ shən) ***n-*** **1** the act of writing or printing a letter or letters as a capital or capitals. **2** the money invested in a business: *This firm has a* capitalization *of $60,000,000.*

cap·i·tal·ize (kăp′ ə tə līz′) ***vt-*** **[cap·i·tal·ized, cap·i·tal·iz·ing] 1** to put (a word or the first letter of a word) in capital letters. **2** to furnish (a business, project, etc.) with capital. *They* capitalized *the firm at $100,000.*
capitalize on to make profitable use of.

capital letter ***n-*** large or upper-case letter, such as A, B, or C, used to begin a sentence, a proper name, etc.

cap·i·tal·ly (kăp′ ə tə lē) ***adv-*** excellently; admirably.

capital punishment ***n-*** punishment by death.

capital ship ***n-*** first-class warship, such as a battleship or aircraft carrier.

capital sins ***n-*** deadly sins.

cap·i·ta·tion (kăp′ ə tā′ shən) ***n-*** a tax of the same amount from each person, such as a poll tax.

Cap·i·tol (kăp′ ə təl) ***n-*** **1** building in Washington, D.C., in which Congress meets. **2** temple of Jupiter in ancient Rome that stood on **Capitoline Hill** (kăp′ ə tə lĭn′). **3** (also **capitol**) building in which a State legislature meets. ***Hom-*** capital.

ca·pit·u·late (kə pĭch′ ə lāt′) ***vi-*** **[ca·pit·u·lat·ed, ca·pit·u·lat·ing]** to surrender to an enemy, usually on certain conditions: *The town* capitulated *to the enemy.*

ca·pit·u·la·tion (kə pĭch′ ə lā′ shən) ***n-*** **1** surrender, usually on certain conditions. **2** statement giving the main points of a topic; summary.

ca·pon (kā′ pŏn) ***n-*** a castrated rooster, especially raised and fattened for eating.

ca·price (kə prēs′) ***n-*** **1** sudden, unreasoning change of mind or conduct; whim: *Her refusal to go is a mere* caprice. **2** tendency to change suddenly and unpredictably: *the* caprice *of fortune.*

ca·pri·cious (kə prĭsh′ əs) ***adj-*** changing suddenly without reason; given to whim; unpredictable: *That girl is so* capricious *that you never know what she'll do next.* ***—adv-*** **ca·pri′ cious·ly.** ***n-*** **ca·pri′ cious·ness.**

Cap·ri·corn (kă′ prə kŏrn, -kôrn) ***n-*** constellation thought to outline the figure of a goat. See also *Tropic of Capricorn.*

cap·si·cum (kăp′ sə kəm) ***n-*** tropical plant bearing variously shaped, very spicy berries from which cayenne pepper is prepared.

cap·size (kăp′ sīz′) ***vt-*** **[cap·sized, cap·siz·ing]** to overturn (a boat): *A sudden squall* capsized *the yacht.* ***vi-:*** *The yacht* capsized.

Capstan

cap·stan (kăp′ stən) ***n-*** large, spool-shaped machine to raise or lower heavy weights, such as ships' anchors, as the cable around it is wound or unwound.

capstan bar ***n-*** strong rod used as a lever to turn a capstan.

cap·su·lar (kăp′ sə lər) ***adj-*** shaped like or enclosed in a capsule.

cap·sule (kăp′ səl) ***n-*** **1** small gelatin case containing a dose of medicine. **2** protective enclosure for astronauts, instruments, etc., that is a separable part of a space craft. **3** seed pod. **4** skinlike sac enclosing an organ or part of the body.

SEED
MEDICAL
Capsules

Capt. captain.

cap·tain (kăp′ tən) ***n-*** **1** in the Army, Air Force, and Marine Corps, a commissioned officer who ranks next below a major and next above a first lieutenant. **2** in the Navy and Coast Guard, a commissioned officer who ranks next below a rear admiral and next above a commander. **3** master of any ship. **4** person in authority over others in a group; leader: *the* captain *of a baseball team.* ***vt-:*** *Mike* captained *the team for two years.*

cap·tain·cy (kăp′ tən sē) ***n-*** [*pl.* **cap·tain·cies**] rank or authority of a captain. Also **cap′ tain·ship′.**

cap·tion (kăp′ shən) ***n-*** **1** title or explanation of a picture. **2** brief title for an article, chapter, etc., set above it in large type; heading.

cap·tious (kăp′ shəs) ***adj-*** **1** inclined to find fault; faultfinding: *a* captious *critic.* **2** designed to confuse or perplex: *a* captious *question.* ***—adv-*** **cap′ tious·ly.** ***n-*** **cap′ tious·ness.**

cap·ti·vate (kăp′ tə vāt′) ***vt-*** **[cap·ti·vat·ed, cap·ti·vat·ing]** to charm by beauty, intelligence, etc.; fascinate: *She* captivated *us with her songs.* ***—n-*** **cap′ ti·va′ tion.**

cap·tive (kăp′ tĭv) ***adj-*** not free; captured: *a* captive *nation*; *a* captive *deer.* ***n-*** person or animal taken into captivity; prisoner.

cap·tiv·i·ty (kăp tĭv′ ə tē) ***n-*** a condition of being held captive; forcible restraint: *Some birds cannot live in* captivity.

cap·tor (kăp′ tər) ***n-*** person who captures another person or an animal.

cap·ture (kăp′ chər) ***vt-*** **[cap·tured, cap·tur·ing]** to take, seize, or win by force, skill, surprise, trickery, charm or other means: *to* capture *a thief*; *to* capture *attention.* ***n-*** **1** person or thing seized: *Our first* capture *was a lion.* **2** a seizing or being seized: *the* capture *of a criminal.*

cap·u·chin (kăp′ yə shən, kə pyōō′-) ***n-*** **1** South American monkey with a hoodlike growth of hair on its head. **2** woman's hooded cloak, similar to that of the Capuchin friar's.

Cap·u·chin (kăp′ ə shən, kə pyōō′-) ***n-*** member of a branch of the Franciscan order instituted about 1525, who wear a distinctive pointed hood **(capuchin).** Also called **Capuchin friar.**

car (kär) ***n-*** **1** automobile. **2** vehicle running on rails: *a trolley* car; *a railway* car. **3** the cage of an elevator. **4** the part of an airship or balloon which carries people and freight.

ca·ra·ba·o (kär′ ə bou′, kär′-) ***n-*** [*pl.* **ca·ra·ba·os**] water buffalo of the Philippine Islands.

car·a·bin·eer or **car·a·bin·ier** (kăr′ ə bə nêr′) ***n-*** soldier armed with a carbine.

ca·ra·cul (kăr′ ə kəl) karakul.

ca·rafe (kə răf′) ***n-*** a bottle resembling a chemist's flask and used to hold water, coffee, etc.; decanter.

Carabao, about 5 ft high at shoulder

car·a·mel (kăr′ ə məl, kär-) ***n-*** **1** sugar, slowly melted and browned, used for coloring and flavoring. **2** soft chewy candy cut in small cubes and flavored with this sugar, and vanilla or chocolate.

car·a·pace (kăr′ ə pās′, -pəs) ***n-*** the hard upper shell of a turtle, lobster, crab, armadillo, etc.

car·at (kăr′ ət) ***n-*** unit of weight for precious stones, equal to 200 milligrams. ***Homs-*** caret, carrot, karat.

car·a·van (kăr′ ə văn′) ***n-*** **1** company of merchants, pilgrims, etc., traveling together for safety, as across a desert or through dangerous country. **2** a train of pack animals or vehicles. **3** *Brit.* wagon equipped for living.

car·a·van·sa·ry (kăr′ ə văn′ sə rē) ***n-*** [*pl.* **car·a·van·sa·ries**] **1** in Eastern countries, a large, walled-in court and shelter where caravans can rest at night. **2** inn. Also **car′ a·van′ se·rai′** (-rī′).

car·a·vel (kăr′ ə vĕl′, -vəl) ***n-*** a small, fast sailing vessel of the 15th and 16th centuries, such as was used by Columbus. It had a high stern and three masts. Also **car′ vel.**

Caravel

car·a·way (kăr′ ə wā′) ***n-*** plant related to the carrot and parsley, with small, spicy, crescent-shaped seeds used as a flavoring in cooking and baking.

car·bide (kär′ bīd′) ***n-*** **1** compound of carbon and a metal. **2** calcium carbide.

car·bine (kär′ bīn′) ***n-*** a short, light rifle.

car·bo·hy·drate (kär′ bō hī′ drāt′) ***n-*** any of a class of compounds of carbon, hydrogen, and oxygen, such as sugars, starches, and cellulose, which are manufactured by plants and are the ultimate source of animal food.

car·bo·lat·ed (kär bə lā′ təd) ***adj-*** treated with, or containing, carbolic acid.

car·bol·ic acid (kär bŏl′ ĭk) ***n-*** poisonous acid made from coal tar and used in water solution as an antiseptic and disinfectant.

car·bon (kär′ bən) ***n-*** chemical element which is the main element in coal and is found pure in two distinct forms, diamond and graphite. It is the basic element of all living matter. Symbol C, At. No. 6, At. Wt. 12.

carbon 14 ***n-*** radioactive isotope of carbon. At. Wt. 14; radiocarbon. Half-life: 5,570 years.

car·bon·a·ceous (kär′ bə nā′ shəs) ***adj-*** of or containing carbon; rich in carbon.

car·bon·ate (kär′ bə nāt′) ***n-*** a salt of carbonic acid. ***vt-*** [**car·bon·at·ed, car·bon·at·ing**] to dissolve carbon dioxide in a liquid to make it effervescent. For example, water is carbonated to make soda water.

car·bon·a·tion (kär′ bə nā′ shən) ***n-*** the carbonating of water or another liquid.

carbon cycle ***n-*** **1** chain of nuclear fusion reactions of carbon and hydrogen by which hydrogen atoms are fused into helium atoms, releasing the vast amounts of energy of the sun and stars. **2** carbon dioxide cycle.

carbon di·ox·ide (dī ŏk′ sīd) ***n-*** heavy colorless and odorless gas (CO_2), found in the atmosphere and produced naturally in the burning of organic matter and in breathing and fermentation.

carbon dioxide cycle ***n-*** cycle in which atmospheric carbon dioxide is used by plants to build their tissues, then changed to animal matter by animals which feed on plants, and eventually returned to the air through respiration or decomposition.

car·bon·ic (kär bŏn′ ĭk) ***adj-*** of, formed from, or having to do with carbon.

carbonic acid ***n-*** weak acid (H_2CO_3), formed when carbon dioxide dissolves in water.

car·bon·if·er·ous (kär′ bə nĭf′ ər əs) ***adj-*** containing or producing carbon.

Car·bon·if·er·ous (kär′ bə nĭf′ ər əs) ***n-*** the fifth of the six periods of the Paleozoic era. Much of the world's coal was formed during the Carboniferous. ***adj-***: *the* Carboniferous *period.*

car·bon·i·za·tion (kär′ bə nə zā′ shən) ***n-*** the changing of organic matter so as to leave coal or charcoal.

car·bon·ize (kär′ bə nīz′) ***vt-*** [**car·bon·ized, car·bon·iz·ing**] **1** to char with heat or acid, leaving a residue of carbon. **2** to coat or combine with carbon.

carbon monoxide ***n-*** a colorless, odorless, poisonous gas, produced by the incomplete burning of carbon, and found in the exhaust gases from automobiles.

carbon paper ***n-*** thin paper which is coated with coloring matter, used to reproduce on a lower sheet any marks made by pressure on an upper sheet.

carbon tet·ra·chlo·ride (tĕ′ trə klôr′ īd) ***n-*** colorless liquid compound (CCl_4) with a heavy, poisonous, nonflammable vapor.

Car·bo·run·dum (kär′ bə rŭn′ dəm) ***n-*** trademark name for certain very hard compounds used in grinding and polishing, especially silicon carbide.

car·bun·cle (kär′ bŭng′ kəl) ***n-*** **1** painful, inflamed swelling of the skin, more serious than a boil. **2** a deep-red garnet.

car·bu·ret·or or **car·bu·ret·tor** (kär′ bə rā′ tər) ***n-*** apparatus used to mix air with gasoline in the engine of an automobile.

car·cass (kär′ kəs) ***n-*** **1** dead body of an animal. **2** contemptuously, the living or dead body of a human being.

car·cin·o·gen (kär sĭn′ ə jən) ***n-*** substance that causes cancer.

car·ci·no·ma (kär′ sə nō′ mə) ***n-*** kind of malignant tumor. Carcinoma is the most common type of cancer.

[1]**card** (kärd) ***n-*** **1** piece of thin, stiff paper or pasteboard. **2** playing card. **3** in sports, a list of events. **4 cards** any game played with playing cards. [from Old French **carte,** ultimately from Greek **chartēs,** "layer of papyrus."]
have a card up (one's) sleeve to have some further resource, such as a secret plan. **in the cards** very likely to happen. **put** (or **lay**) **(one's) cards on the table** to lay bare one's intentions.

[2]**card** (kärd) ***n-*** toothed device for combing wool, flax, cotton, or the like, to prepare it for spinning. ***vt-*** to comb (wool, flax, etc.) with such an instrument. [from Middle English **carde,** from Latin **carduus,** "thistle."]

car·da·mom (kär′ də məm) ***n-*** fruit and seed of any of several plants of the ginger family, used as seasoning and in medicine. Also **car′ da·mon, car′ da·mum.**

card·board (kärd′ bôrd′) ***n-*** thin, stiff pasteboard, used in making posters, boxes, etc.

cardi- or **cardio-** *combining form* heart: *a* cardio*vascular disease.* [from Greek **kardia** meaning "heart."]

car·di·ac (kär′ dē ăk′) ***adj-*** relating to, or situated in or near, the heart: *a* cardiac *patient*; *the* cardiac *muscle.*

car·di·gan (kär′ də gən) ***n-*** collarless sweater or jacket that opens down the front.

car·di·nal (kär′ də nəl) ***adj-*** **1** of first importance; principal; chief: *Honesty is his* cardinal *quality.* **2** of a rich red color. ***n-*** **1** in the Roman Catholic Church, one of a group of officials, the **College of Cardinals,** whose rank is next below that of the Pope. **2** (also **cardinal bird, cardinal grosbeak**) a finch of eastern United States the males of which are bright red and the females brown with streaks of red; redbird.

Cardinal, about 10 in. long

cardinal flower ***n-*** plant that has long clusters of bright red flowers and grows along streams and in swampy ground.

cardinal number ***n-*** any one of the numbers zero, one, two, three, four, etc., used to tell how many.

cardinal point *n-* one of the main directions of the compass; north, east, south, or west.

cardinal virtues *n-* justice, prudence, temperance, and fortitude, considered by ancient philosophers to be the essentials of moral excellence.

card·ing (kär′ dĭng) *n-* the process of combing wool, flax, cotton, etc., to prepare it for spinning. *as* ***modifier***: *a* carding *machine.*

car·dio·gram (kär′ dē ə grăm′) *n-* electrocardiogram.

car·dio·graph (kär′ dē ə grăf′) *n-* electrocardiograph.

car·di·o·vas·cu·lar (kär′ dē ō văs′ kyə lər) *adj-* of or having to do with the heart and blood vessels.

care (kâr) *n-* **1** troubled state of mind caused by fear, doubt, etc.; anxiety; trouble; concern. **2** a cause of this: *The* cares *of the war years weighed heavily on the President.* **3** close and serious attention; heed; watchfulness: *work done with* care. **4** supervision; protection; charge: *under a doctor's* care. *vi-* **[cared, car·ing] 1** to be worried or troubled; be concerned: *Would you* care *if I go?* **2** to want or desire (to): *I don't* care *to leave.*
take care or **have a care** to take heed; be careful.
take care of to look after; attend to.
care for 1 to like. **2** to look after; provide for.

ca·reen (kə rēn′) *vt-* to tilt (a ship) in order to clean or repair its bottom. *vi-* to lurch or sway while moving: *The car hit the pole and* careened *across the road.*
►Should not be confused with CAREER.

ca·reer (kə rêr′) *n-* **1** course or progress of one's life: *He had a checkered* career. **2** occupation or calling: *a scientific* career. **3** rushing course; full speed: *a horse in full* career. *vi-* to move with a rush; dash along: *The truck* careered *down the road.*
►Should not be confused with CAREEN.

care·free (kâr′ frē′) *adj-* without worry; lighthearted.

care·ful (kâr′ fəl) *adj-* **1** watchful; cautious: *Be* careful *to stay on the sidewalk.* **2** done or made with care: *a* careful *piece of work.* **3** mindful: *to be* careful *of the rights of others.* —*adv-* **care′ ful·ly.** *n-* **care′ ful·ness.**

care·less (kâr′ ləs) *adj-* **1** not paying enough attention; heedless; inattentive: *to be* careless *in crossing the street.* **2** inaccurate; inexact: *messy,* careless *work.* —*adv-* **care′ less·ly.** *n-* **care′ less·ness.**

ca·ress (kə rĕs′) *n-* affectionate or gentle touch or stroke. *vt-*: *The little girl* caressed *her kitten.*

car·et (kăr′ ət) *n-* mark [‸], used in writing or correcting to indicate an insertion. ***Homs-*** carat, carrot, karat.

care·tak·er (kâr′ tā′ kər) *n-* person who takes care of a place or property: *the* caretaker *of a cemetery.*

care·worn (kâr′ wôrn′) *adj-* showing signs of having undergone care and anxiety: *a* careworn *face.*

car·fare (kär′ fâr′) *n-* streetcar or local bus fare.

car·go (kär′ gō) *n-* [*pl.* **car·goes** or **car·gos**] goods carried by a ship; freight. *as* ***modifier***: *a* cargo *ship.*

car·hop (kär′ hŏp′) *n-* waiter or waitress who serves customers in their cars at a drive-in restaurant.

Car·ib (kăr′ əb) *n-* [*pl.* **Car·ibs,** also **Car·ib**] **1** one of a tribe of Indians formerly living in the Caribbean area. **2** the language of these Indians. *adj-*: *a* Carib *custom.* —*adj-* **Car′ ib·be′ an.**

Mountain caribou, 4 ft. high at shoulder

car·i·bou (kăr′ ə bo͞o′) *n-* [*pl.* **car·i·bou**] a wild reindeer of northern North America. [from Canadian French **caribou,** from Algonquian **xalibu** meaning "one who paws."]

car·i·ca·ture (kăr′ ĭ kə chər, -cho͞or′) *n-* picture or description of a person or thing, in which the defects or peculiarities are so exaggerated as to appear ridiculous. *vt-* **[car·i·ca·tured, car·i·ca·tur·ing]**: *The cartoonist* caricatured *the actor.*

car·i·ca·tur·ist (kăr′ ĭ kə chər ĭst′, -cho͞or′ ĭst) *n-* one who caricatures others.

car·ies (kăr′ ēz, kâr′-) *n-* [*pl.* **car·ies**] **1** gradual decay of tooth or bone. **2** dental cavity.

car·il·lon (kăr′ ə lŏn′, kə rĭl′ yən) *n-* **1** set of tuned bells on which music may be played. **2** melody played on such bells.

car·i·o·ca (kăr′ ē ō′ kə) *n-* **1** person from Rio de Janeiro. **2** a dance also known as the samba.

car·load (kär′ lōd′) *n-* amount that a car, especially a railroad freight car, can carry.

Car·mel·ite (kär′ mə līt′) *n-* monk or nun of the Order of Our Lady of Mt. Carmel, founded in Syria (1156). *adj-*: *a group of* Carmelite *nuns.*

car·mine (kär′ mīn′, -mən) *n-* **1** pigment made from cochineal. **2** the intense red or purplish-red color of this pigment.

car·nage (kär′ nĭj) *n-* great slaughter, especially in a battle.

car·nal (kär′ nəl) *adj-* fleshly; sensual: *man's* carnal *interests.*

car·na·tion (kär nā′ shən) *n-* a cultivated pink with large red, pink, or white flowers.

Carnation

car·nau·ba wax (kär nô′ bə) *n-* hard, brittle, high-grade wax from the **carnauba palm** of Brazil, used in polishes.

car·nel·ian (kär nēl′ yən) *n-* flesh-colored, deep-red, or reddish-white, semi-precious stone, used for jewelry and seals.

car·ni·val (kär′ nə vəl) *n-* **1** a public amusement show, often with booths, Ferris wheel, merry-go-round, games, side shows, etc. **2** season just before Lent, devoted to merrymaking. *adj-*: *the* carnival *atmosphere.*

Car·niv·o·ra (kär′ nə vôr′ ə) *n-* an order of mammals that feed chiefly on flesh, including the cat, dog, bear, and other families.

car·ni·vore (kär′ nə vôr′) *n-* **1** an animal that feeds on flesh. **2** an insect-eating plant.

car·niv·o·rous (kär nĭv′ ə rəs) *adj-* flesh-eating: *Dogs and cats are* carnivorous *animals.* —*adv-* **car·niv′ o·rous·ly.** *n-* **car·niv′ o·rous·ness.**

car·no·tite (kär′ nə tīt′) *n-* yellow mineral, a chief ore of uranium and vanadium.

car·ol (kăr′ əl) *n-* song of joy or praise, especially a Christmas song. *vt-* to sing joyfully: *We* caroled *hymns. vi-*: *We* caroled *in the snow.* —*n-* **car′ ol·er.**

car·om (kăr′ əm) *n-* in billiards, a shot in which the cue ball hits two or more balls, one after the other. *vi-* to strike and rebound (off): *The handball* caromed *off the wall.*

car·o·tene (kăr′ ə tēn′) *n-* any of three yellow to orange hydrocarbons found in plants and converted to vitamin A by the liver.

ca·rot·id (kə rŏt′ əd, *also* kăr′ ə tĭd′) *adj-* of or having to do with either or both of the chief arteries, one on each side of the neck, that carry blood to the head. *n-* one of these arteries.

ca·rous·al (kə rou′ zəl) *n-* a carouse.

ca·rouse (kə rouz′) *n-* wild, noisy drinking party. *vi-* **[ca·roused, ca·rous·ing]**: *They'll* carouse *all night long.* —*n-* **ca·rous′ er.**

car·ou·sel (kăr′ə sĕl′, -zĕl′) ***n-*** carrousel.

[1]**carp** (kärp) ***vi-*** to find fault; complain: *You're always* carping *about my work.* [probably from Old Norse **karpa** meaning "to boast," plus Lating **carpere** meaning "to pluck."] **—*n-* carp′er.**

[2]**carp** (kärp) ***n-*** [*pl.* **carp**; rarely, **carps**] bony freshwater fish that lives in ponds [from Old French **carp(e),** from Late Latin **carpa.**]

Carp

car·pal (kär′pəl) ***adj-*** in anatomy, of or having to do with the carpus. ***n-*** one of the wrist bones. ***Hom-*** carpel.

car·pel (kär′pəl) ***n-*** the part of a plant which bears seeds; one of the parts of a compound ovary. ***Hom-*** carpal.

car·pen·ter (kär′pən tər) ***n-*** person who builds or repairs the woodwork of houses, ships, cabinets, etc.

car·pen·try (kär′pən trē) ***n-*** work of a carpenter.

car·pet (kär′pət) ***n-*** **1** large piece of heavy fabric for covering floors. **2** any continuous covering on the floor or ground: *a* carpet *of pine needles.* ***vt-***: *to* carpet *a room.*

car·pet·bag (kär′pət băg′) ***n-*** a traveling bag, originally made of carpeting, common in the 19th century.

car·pet·bag·ger (kär′pət băg′ər) ***n-*** one of the Northern adventurers who went to the South after the Civil War to exploit the unsettled political and social conditions.

car pool ***n-*** **1** arrangement made by two or more people to take turns driving on a regular basis to and from a place: *The parents formed a* car pool *to take the children swimming.* **2** group of such people: *Our* car pool *has four people in it.* ***vi-***: *Kathy* car pools *with me on holidays.*

car·port (kär′pôrt′) ***n-*** shelter for an automobile, usually under an extension of the roof of a house.

car·pus (kär′pəs) ***n-*** [*pl.* **car·pi** (-pē, -pī′)] in anatomy, the wrist or the group of bones that make it up.

car·riage (kăr′ĭj) ***n-*** **1** wheeled vehicle for carrying people, usually drawn by horses. **2** light, often folding, vehicle for a baby, pushed by a person on foot. **3** a carrying or transporting of goods; also, the charge for this. **4** moving part of a machine which supports another part: *a typewriter* carriage. **5** wheeled support for a heavy load: *the* carriage *for a cannon.* **6** manner of holding one's body: *The soldier has an erect* carriage.

Carriages: baby carriage, Concord buggy

car·rick bend (kăr′ĭk) ***n-*** kind of knot used to join two large ropes or cables. For picture, see *knot.*

car·ri·er (kăr′ē ər) ***n-*** **1** person or vehicle who carries something, especially a person who carries and delivers mail. **2** person or firm whose business it is to transport goods or people. **3** person, animal, or thing that carries disease germs and may pass them on to others: *a typhoid* carrier. **4** a device or part in a machine for carrying, driving, or guiding something. **5** aircraft carrier. **6** radio wave regulated to transmit a signal.

carrier pigeon ***n-*** **1** pigeon trained to fly home and used to carry messages; homing pigeon. **2** large, slender show pigeon having fleshy growths on its beak and around its eyes.

carrier wave ***n-*** electromagnetic wave that is made to vary in patterns that represent sound and light waves so as to transmit sound or pictures.

car·ri·on (kăr′ē ən) ***n-*** dead and decaying flesh.

car·rot (kăr′ət) ***n-*** cultivated plant related to the parsley, with an edible, orange-yellow tapering root. ***Homs-*** carat, caret, karat. **—*adj-* car′rot·y.**

car·rou·sel or **car·ou·sel** (kăr′ə sĕl′, -zĕl′) ***n-*** merry-go-round.

car·ry (kăr′ē) ***vt-*** [**car·ried, car·ry·ing**] **1** to transport or convey, especially as the load of a vehicle, person, or animal; bear: *I* carried *the box upstairs.* **2** to have on one's person: *I always* carry *my driver's license.* **3** to transfer or add (a number, bookkeeping entry, etc.) to the next column. **4** to hold up; bear; sustain: *Steel posts* carry *the weight of the upper floors.* **5** to extend; continue with: *to* carry *the war into enemy territory.* **6** to have as a usual or necessary accompaniment: *The motor* carries *a full guarantee.* **7** to hold and move (oneself): *She* carries *herself in a distinguished manner.* **8** to keep on hand for sale: *The store* carries *tobacco.* **9** to win most of the votes of: *to* carry *Wisconsin.* ***vi-*** **1** to perform the act of bearing or conveying: *Some watched and some* carried. **2** to reach or travel to a distance: *The ball* carried *all the way to the fence.* ***n-*** [*pl.* **car·ries**] **1** distance over which a gun will send a bullet. **2** a portage. **3** in golf, the distance from the place where the ball is struck to the place where it lands.

carry all before (one) to be completely successful; defeat all.

carry away 1 to enchant; move to ecstasy: *The music* carried *me away.* **2** to be broken off and washed away at sea: *The mast* carried away *in the storm.*

carry off 1 to win: *The team* carried off *every honor.* **2** to cause the death of: *The plague* carried off *millions.*

carry on 1 to keep on; continue: *She* carried on *her father's work.* **2** to manage; conduct: *to* carry on *a correspondence.* **3** to behave wildly or frivolously.

carry out 1 to obey; follow: *They* carried out *the orders.* **2** to finish; accomplish: *to* carry out *a task.*

[1]**car·ry·all** (kăr′ē ȯl′) ***n-*** light, one-horse carriage. [an alteration of French **carriole** of the same meaning.]

[2]**car·ry·all** (kăr′ē ȯl′) ***n-*** large bag or basket [from **carry** plus **all.**]

carrying charge ***n-*** interest on the money owed for goods bought on the installment plan.

car·ry-ov·er (kăr′ē ō′vər) ***n-*** **1** something that persists; remnant: *Throwing rice at the bride and groom is a* carry-over *from a bygone era.* **2** in bookkeeping, a sum carried forward to the next column or page.

car-sick (kär′sĭk′) ***adj-*** nauseated from the motion of a car. **—*n-* car′-sick′ness.**

cart (kärt) ***n-*** **1** two-wheeled vehicle for carrying heavy loads: *a farm* cart. **2** light delivery wagon, often moved by hand. **3** light two-wheeled carriage. ***vi-*** **1** to transport by wagon: *Please* cart *my baggage out to the plane.* **2** *Informal* to take away: *They* carted *him off to jail.*

cart·age (kär′tĭj) ***n-*** a transporting of goods by cart or truck; also, the charge for this.

carte blanche (kärt′blänch′, *Fr.* -blä^{n}sh′) ***n-*** absolute freedom of action or judgment; unrestricted authority. [from French.]

car·tel (kär tĕl′) ***n-*** combination of industrial groups, usually international, formed to fix prices, regulate output, control a market, etc.
cart·er (kär′ tər) ***n-*** person who drives a cart or truck.
Car·te·sian coordinates (kär tē′ zhən) ***n-*** system of coordinates that locates a point in a plane by its distances from two perpendicular axes (usually labeled the x axis and the y axis). The distance from one axis is measured parallel to the other axis. For picture, see *abscissa.*
Car·tha·gin·i·an (kär′ thə jĭn′ ē ən) ***adj-*** of or pertaining to the ancient city-state of Carthage.
Car·thu·sian (kär thōō′ zhən) ***n-*** a monk of an order founded in France at Chartreuse (1084). ***adj-***: *a small* Carthusian *hermitage.*
car·ti·lage (kär′ tə lĭj) ***n-*** tough, rubbery tissue that forms much of the skeleton of young animals and infants and usually develops into bone; gristle.
car·ti·lag·i·nous (kär′ tə lăj′ ə nəs) ***adj-*** **1** like cartilage. **2** of animals, having a skeleton made mostly of cartilage, as a shark does.
car·tog·ra·pher (kär′ tŏg′ rə fər) ***n-*** mapmaker.
car·tog·ra·phy (kär′ tŏg′ rə fē) ***n-*** the making of maps and charts. ***—adj-*** **car′to·graph′ic** (kär′ tə grăf′ ĭk).
car·ton (kär′ tən) ***n-*** **1** pasteboard or cardboard box. **2** amount held by such a box: *a* carton *of tea.*
car·toon (kär tōōn′) ***n-*** **1** a drawing, especially in a newspaper or magazine, that deals with well-known people or public events in a humorous or critical way. **2** animated cartoon. **3** comic strip. **4** the original design for a painting or tapestry.
car·toon·ist (kär tōō′ nĭst) ***n-*** artist who draws cartoons.
car·tridge (kär′ trĭj) ***n-*** **1** case made of metal or cardboard, containing powder and usually a bullet or shot for a firearm. **2** container of material for use, to be fitted into another device: *a camera loaded with a film* cartridge.

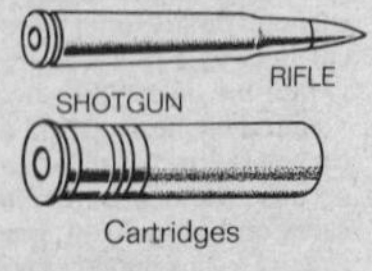

Cartridges

cart·wheel or **cart wheel** (kärt′ hwēl′) ***n-*** **1** wheel of a cart. **2** sidewise handspring.
carve (kärv) ***vt-*** **[carved, carv·ing] 1** to make or design by cutting: *to* carve *a statue out of marble*; *to* carve *a panel with floral patterns.* **2** to cut into parts or slices: *to* carve *a turkey.* ***vi-***: *My father always* carves.
carv·er (kär′ vər) ***n-*** **1** person who carves. **2** knife used for carving meat.
carv·ing (kär′ vĭng) ***n-*** **1** design or figure made by cutting: *an ivory* carving *of an elephant.* **2** work or art of one who carves.
carving knife ***n-*** knife for cutting meat. For picture, see *knife.*
car·y·at·id (kăr′ ē ăt′ ĭd) ***n-*** [*pl.* **car·y·at·ids** or **car·y·at·i·des** (-ə dēs)] supporting column carved in the form of a woman.
ca·sa·ba (kə sä′ bə) ***n-*** a sweet winter muskmelon with a yellow rind. Also **cassaba.**
cas·cade (kăs kād′) ***n-*** **1** small waterfall, or a series of small waterfalls. **2** anything that resembles a waterfall: *a* cascade *of ruffles.* ***vi-*** **[cas·cad·ed, cas·cad·ing]** to fall in torrents: *The rain* cascaded *from the eaves.*

Cascade

cas·car·a (kăs kăr′ ə) ***n-*** **1** buckthorn of the Pacific Coast. **2** its dried bark or a mild laxative made from it. [American word from Spanish **cáscara** meaning "bark."]

[1]**case** (kās) ***n-*** **1** state of affairs; set of circumstances: *If that's the* case, *you must pay.* **2** matter or problem for investigation or solution: *The police finally closed the* case *of the missing heiress.* **3** specific instance or occurrence, especially of a disease or injury: *a* case *of mumps.* **4** lawsuit or question decided or to be decided in court: *The* case *of Brown vs. the United States.* **5** evidence or arguments for or against something: *The lawyer stated his* case *briefly. He presented the* case *against capital punishment.* **6** *Grammar* the form of a noun, pronoun, or adjective which shows its relationship to some other word or words in a sentence. English nouns have a **common case,** as "farmer" in "*I saw the* farmer" or "*The* farmer *has* a cart," and a **possessive case,** as "farmer's" in "*I saw the* farmer's *cart.*" The personal pronouns have three cases: a **subjective case,** as in *"He gave Mary three apples"*; an **objective case,** as in *"Mary saw* him *eating apples"*; and a possessive case, as in "*John gave Mary* his *apples.*" Adjectives in some languages, such as Latin, also have cases. [from Old French **cas,** from Latin **cāsus** meaning "a happening."]
[2]**case** (kās) ***n-*** **1** container for shipping; also, the amount it holds when full: *a* case *of canned milk.* **2** container to hold things; receptacle: *a jewelry* case; *a typewriter* case. **3** in printing, a tray for holding unset type. **4** a frame or casing, as of a window. ***vt-*** **[cased, cas·ing]** to cover or enclose in a container; encase: *to* case *oranges for shipping.* [from Old French **casse,** from Latin **capsa,** "chest," from **capere** meaning "to hold."]
case·hard·en (cās′ här′ dən) ***vt-*** **1** to harden the surface of (steel or glass). **2** to harden a person against emotion; make insensitive or callous: *Prison life* casehardened *him.*
case history ***n-*** a record of facts about the past of an individual, family, or group, made by doctors, social workers, etc.
ca·sein (kā′ sēn′) ***n-*** chief protein in milk and the main ingredient in cheese. Casein is used in making plastics, adhesives, and paints.
case knife ***n-*** **1** knife kept in a sheath. **2** table knife.
case·mate (kās′ māt′) ***n-*** an armored enclosure in a fort or on a warship with openings through which guns may be fired.
case·ment (kās′ mənt) ***n-*** window built to open on hinges like a door.

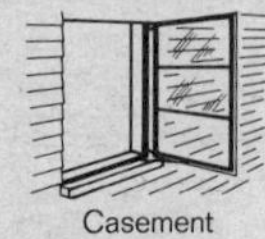
Casement

case·work·er (kās′ wûr′ kər) ***n-*** social worker assigned to gather information about, and advise, a person or family that is in difficulty and needs assistance.
cash (kăsh) ***n-*** **1** money in the form of coins or bills. **2** money paid at the time something is bought: *He paid* cash *for the rug, but bought the car on credit.* **3** bank deposits, certain notes, etc., easily exchangeable for coins and bills. ***vt-*** to exchange for coins or bills: *to* cash *a check*; *to* cash *a bond.* ***Hom-*** cache.
cash·book (kăsh′ bŏŏk′) ***n-*** book in which an account is kept of money received and paid out.
cash·ew (kăsh′ ōō) ***n-*** **1** the kidney-shaped nut of a tropical evergreen. **2** the tree itself.
[1]**cash·ier** (kă shêr′) ***n-*** person in charge of receiving and paying out money in a business. [from French **caissier** meaning "treasurer," from **caisse** meaning "cash box; record case," from Latin **capsa.**]
[2]**cash·ier** (kă shêr′) ***vt-*** to dismiss in disgrace from a position of trust or from military service. [from Dutch **casseren,** from Latin **quassare** "to quash; shatter."]
cashier's check ***n-*** check drawn by a bank on its own funds and signed by a cashier.

cash·mere (kăsh′mêr′, kăzh′-) ***n-*** soft, fine fabric or yarn made from the wool of the **Cashmere goat** of India and Tibet. ***adj-***: *a* cashmere *sweater.*

cash register ***n-*** device, usually with a money drawer, that records and shows the amount of a sale.

cas·ing (cā′sĭng) ***n-*** **1** something that covers or encloses, such as a membrane into which sausage is packed, or a pipe lining an oil well. **2** frame of a window or door.

ca·si·no (kə sē′nō) ***n-*** [*pl.* **ca·si·nos**] **1** room or building for dancing, gambling, etc. **2** in Italy, a summer house. **3** (also **cassino**) card game for two to four people.

cask (kăsk) ***n-*** barrel-shaped wooden container for liquids; large keg; also, the amount this holds when full.

Cask

cask·et (kăs′kət) ***n-*** **1** small chest or box, such as one used for jewels. **2** coffin.

cas·sa·ba (kə sä′bə) casaba.

Cas·san·dra (kə săn′drə) ***n-*** in Greek legend, a daughter of King Priam of Troy. She had the gift of prophecy, but was never believed.

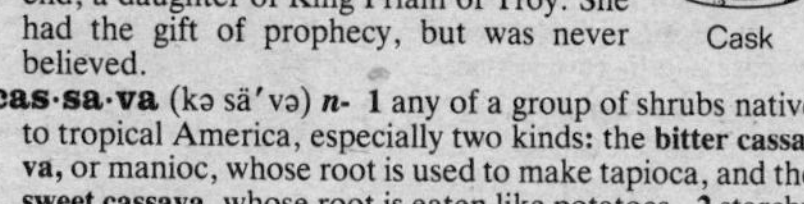

cas·sa·va (kə sä′və) ***n-*** **1** any of a group of shrubs native to tropical America, especially two kinds: the **bitter cassava,** or manioc, whose root is used to make tapioca, and the **sweet cassava,** whose root is eaten like potatoes. **2** starchy roots of this plant.

cas·se·role (kăs′ə rōl′) ***n-*** **1** deep glass or earthenware dish in which food is baked and served. **2** food cooked and served in such a dish.

cas·sette (kă sĕt′, kə-) ***n-*** a closed case which holds magnetic recording tape that can be played forward and wound in reverse.

cas·si·a (kăsh′ə) ***n-*** **1** any of several related plants, from some of which the medicine senna is obtained. **2** spice similar to cinnamon.

cas·si·no (kə sē′nō) ***n-*** casino, the card game.

Cas·si·o·pe·ia (kăs′ē ō pē′ə) ***n-*** **1** in Greek mythology, the mother of Andromeda. **2** constellation of the northern sky.

cas·sock (kăs′ək) ***n-*** long, close-fitting, usually black gown worn by clergymen, choir singers, etc.

cas·so·war·y (kăs′ə wĕr′ē) ***n-*** [*pl.* **cas·so·war·ies**] flightless, swift-footed bird of Australia and New Guinea, about five feet tall and resembling the ostrich.

cast (kăst) ***vt-*** [**cast, cast·ing**] **1** to throw: *to* cast *a fishing lure; to* cast *stones; to* cast *a glance; to* cast *a shadow.* **2** to make (a part, statue, etc.) by pouring liquid material into a mold; also, to make molded objects of: *That foundry* casts *bronze.* **3** to assign a role to; also, to assign all the roles of: *He* cast *Mr. Ogden as Hamlet. The director will* cast *the new play next week.* **4** to register: *to* cast *one's vote.* **5** to put off; shed: *The snake* cast *its skin.* ***vi-*** **1** to throw fishing bait at the end of a line: *He usually* casts *towards the weeds.* **2** to be shaped in a mold: *Iron* casts *easily.* ***n-*** **1** the act or manner of throwing; also, the distance something is thrown. **2** the actors and actresses in a play, motion picture, etc. **3** a copy formed by molding: *a* cast *of his footprint.* **4** hard, molded covering applied to keep a broken bone motionless while healing: *He had a plaster* cast *on his leg.* **5** form, quality, or shape: *a gloomy* cast *of mind*; *the* cast *of his features.* **6** tinge or hue: *a grayish* cast. **7** squint: *a* cast *in one eye.* ***Hom-*** caste.

cast down dejected; depressed; downcast.

cast about for to try to find: *He* cast about for *a new job.*

cast off **1** to untie from and leave a dock, mooring, etc., in a boat or ship. **2** to discard; rid oneself of.

cast (one's) lot with to choose to share the fate of: *Washington* cast his lot with *the revolutionaries.*

cast up **1** to compute by arithmetic: *to* cast up *a customer's bill.* **2** to throw or direct upwards.

cas·ta·nets (kăs′tə nĕts′) ***n-*** *pl.* pair of spoon-shaped shells of hard wood or ivory, clicked with the fingers to beat time to music, especially in Spanish dances.

Castanets

cast·a·way (kăs′tə wā′) ***n-*** **1** person shipwrecked or set adrift at sea. **2** social outcast. ***adj-*** thrown away; castoff; *a pair of* castaway *shoes.*

caste (kăst) ***n-*** **1** any of the rigid, hereditary social classes of the Hindus. **2** any system of social divisions based on birth, wealth, and rank. ***Hom-*** cast.

lose caste to lose one's standing or good name.

cas·tel·lat·ed (kăs′tə lā′təd) ***adj-*** built with battlements and turrets, like a castle.

cast·er or **cas·tor** (kăs′tər) ***n-*** **1** small roller or wheel on a swivel, used under furniture or other heavy articles to permit easy moving. **2** a cruet; also, a stand for a number of cruets. **3** (**caster** only) person or thing that casts.

cas·ti·gate (kăs′tə gāt′) ***vt-*** [**cas·ti·gat·ed, cas·ti·gat·ing**] to criticize severely; rebuke: *He was* castigated *by the newspapers.*

cas·ti·ga·tion (kăs′tə gā′shən) ***n-*** **1** severe criticism or rebuke. **2** a severe reproof.

Cas·tile soap (kăs′tēl′) ***n-*** fine soap made from pure olive oil and originally manufactured in Castile, Spain.

Cas·til·i·an (kăs tĭl′yən) ***n-*** **1** the standard form of Spanish as spoken in most of Spain; originally a dialect of Castile. **2** a native of Castile. ***adj-*** *the* Castilian *pronunciation.*

cast·ing (kăs′tĭng) ***n-*** object that has been cast in a mold.

cast iron ***n-*** hard and rigid kind of iron that contains much carbon and is shaped by casting in molds. ***adj-***: *a* cast-iron *stove.*

Castle

cas·tle (kăs′əl) ***n-*** **1** building or group of buildings fortified for defense, especially the feudal fortress. **2** any large, imposing house of a person of wealth or title. **3** a piece used in chess; rook.

castles in Spain or **castles in the air** very impractical schemes; daydreams.

cast-off (kăst′ŏf′) ***adj-*** discarded as worthless; thrown away: *a* castoff *pair of shoes.* ***n-***: *He sold the* castoffs *at a yard sale.*

[1]**cas·tor** (kăs′tər) caster. [alteration of **caster.**]

[2]**cas·tor** (kăs′tər) ***n-*** **1** substance obtained from beavers and used in perfumery and medicine. **2** hat, especially of beaver fur. [from Latin, from Greek **kastor** meaning "beaver."]

Cas·tor and Pol·lux (kăs′tər ənd pŏl′əks) ***n-*** **1** in Greek mythology, twin sons of Leda and Zeus. **2** the two brightest stars in the constellation Gemini.

castor bean ***n-*** the seed of the castor-oil plant, from which castor oil is made.

castor oil ***n-*** thick, yellowish oil from the castor bean, used as a laxative and a machine lubricant. *as* ***modifier*** (**castor-oil**): *a* castor-oil *mixture.*

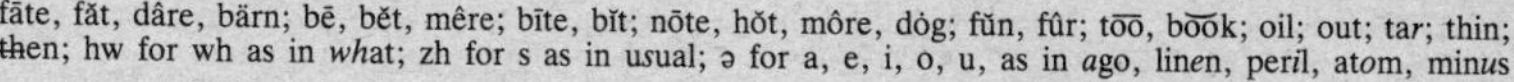

castor-oil plant *n-* small treelike plant native to Africa and widely cultivated for its seeds, castor beans.

cas·trate (kăs′trāt′) *vt-* [**cas·trat·ed, cas·trat·ing**] to remove the sex glands of (an animal, especially a male). *—n-* **cas·tra′tion.**

cas·u·al (kăzh′o͞o əl) *adj-* **1** happening by chance; accidental: *a* casual *meeting on the street.* **2** happening irregularly or occasionally: *a* casual *profit.* **3** unconcerned; offhand: *a* casual *remark.* **4** informal: casual *clothes.* *—adv-* **cas′u·al·ly.** *n-* **cas′ual·ness.**

cas·u·al·ty (kăzh′o͞o əl tē) *n-* [*pl.* **cas·u·al·ties**] someone or something hurt or destroyed by a misfortune, especially someone killed, wounded, or lost in war.

cas·u·is·try (kăzh′o͞o ĭs trē) *n-* false, deceptive, overly clever reasoning; sophistry.

cat (kăt) *n-* **1** small fur-covered animal often kept as a household pet or to catch rats and mice. **2** any of a family of animals including lions, tigers, leopards, pumas, etc.; feline. *as modifier*: *the* cat *family;* cat *fur.* *—adj-* **cat′like′.**

Siamese and Persian cats

let the cat out of the bag to give away a secret. **rain cats and dogs** to rain very hard.

ca·tab·o·lism (kə tăb′ə lĭz′əm) *n-* stage of metabolism in which complex food matter is broken down into simpler substances by living cells, with a release of energy needed for the cell's activities.

cat·a·clysm (kăt′ə klĭz′əm) *n-* **1** natural upheaval, such as an earthquake or a great flood. **2** violent political upheaval, such as a revolution or war. *—adj-* **cat′a·clys′mal** or **cat′a·clys′mic.**

cat·a·combs (kăt′ə kōmz′) *n- pl.* underground cemeteries with long passageways lined with burial niches, such as those of the early Christians in Rome.

cat·a·falque (kăt′ə fălk′, -fȯlk′) *n-* raised support on which the coffin rests during a funeral.

Cat·a·lan (kăt′ə lăn′) *n-* **1** a native or inhabitant of Catalonia. **2** the Romance language spoken in Catalonia, Valencia, and the Balearic Islands.

cat·a·lo (kăt′ə lō′) *n-* [*pl.* **cat·a·los**] a hybrid of a North American bison and a cow. Also **cat′ta·lo.**

cat·a·log or **cat·a·logue** (kăt′ə lȯg′, -lŏg′) *n-* list of names, books, things, places, etc., often arranged alphabetically: *the* catalog *of a library.* *vt-* [**cat·a·loged** or **cat·a·logued, cat·a·log·ing** or **cat·a·logu·ing**]: *to* catalog *books in a library.*

ca·tal·pa (kə tăl′pə) *n-* tree with large heart-shaped leaves, clusters of showy white, pink, or yellow flowers, and long, narrow seed pods. [American word from American Indian **kutuhlpa.**]

ca·tal·y·sis (kə tăl′ə səs) *n-* the action of a catalyst in a chemical reaction. *—adj-* **cat′a·lyt′ic.**

cat·a·lyst (kăt′əl ĭst) *n-* chemical substance that increases or decreases the rate of a chemical reaction or causes the reaction to occur, without being chemically changed itself. Also **cat′a·lyz′er.**

Modern catamaran

catalytic converter *n-* pollution-control device in the exhaust system of an automobile or other motor vehicle that contains a chemical catalyst which changes carbon monoxide and hydrocarbons to carbon dioxide and water vapor.

cat·a·ma·ran (kăt′ə mə răn′) *n-* **1** vessel with two hulls side by side. **2** a raft made of logs and moved by paddles, sails, or an engine.

cat·a·mount (kăt′ə mount′) **1** cougar. **2** lynx.

cat·a·pult (kăt′ə pŭlt′) *n-* **1** in ancient and medieval times, a military device for hurling stones, arrows, or the like. **2** in modern times, a device for launching an airplane from the deck of a ship. **3** *Brit.* slingshot, *vt-* to hurl (something) from or as from such a device: *to* catapult *a plane from a ship's deck.* *vi-*: *The acrobat* catapulted *from a cannon into a net.*

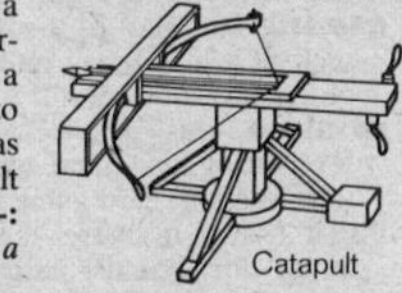

Catapult

cat·a·ract (kăt′ə răkt′) *n-* **1** large waterfall. **2** series of steep rapids. **3** disease of the eye.

Cataract

ca·tarrh (kə tär′) *n-* inflammation of the mucous membranes of the nose and throat, producing a discharge of mucus. *—adj-* **ca·tarrh′al.**

ca·tas·tro·phe (kə tăs′trə fē) *n-* a sudden calamity or widespread disaster, such as an earthquake or a great fire. *—adj-* **cat′a·stroph′ic** (kăt′ ə strŏf′ ĭk). *adv-* **cat′a·stroph′i·cal·ly.**

Ca·taw·ba (kə tȯ′bə) *n-* [*pl.* **Ca·taw·bas,** also **Ca·taw·ba**] **1** member of a tribe of Siouan Indians who formerly lived in the forests of North and South Carolina. **2** a red grape first cultivated in the Carolinas; also the light, dry, white wine made from it. *adj-*: *the* Catawba *villages.*

cat·bird (kăt′bûrd′) *n-* slate-colored American songbird related to the mockingbird.

cat·boat (kăt′bōt′) *n-* small sailboat with one mast in the bow and one large sail.

cat·call (kăt′kȯl′) *n-* loud, shrill cry of disapproval or scorn, as from the audience in a theater.

catch (kăch, kĕch) *vt-* [**caught, catch·ing**] **1** to get hold of (a thing in motion); grasp and stop; grab: *to* catch *a ball and run.* **2** to capture (a person, thing, idea, etc.): *to* catch *a thief*; *to* catch *a trout*; *to* catch *one's meaning*; *to* catch *one's eye.* **3** to hook accidentally: *He* caught *his jacket on a nail.* **4** to discover; surprise: *We* caught *him trying to sneak out of the room.* **5** to reach or overtake: *Did you* catch *her before she left*? **6** to board (a train, plane, etc.): *We* caught *the train in Chicago.* **7** to become infected with; contract: *to* catch *a cold*; *to* catch *the spirit of the crowd.* **8** to strike; hit: *He* caught *me a blow to the head.* **9** *Informal* to see (a show, television program, etc.). *vi-* **1** to become entangled or hooked: *Her sleeve* caught *in the door.* **2** to take and hold: *The lock finally* caught. **3** to play as a baseball catcher: *He* catches *for the home team.* *n-* **1** a taking and holding, especially of a ball: *The left fielder made a good* catch. **2** something taken and held, especially a load of fish. **3** a device for holding or fastening, such as a hook, snap, latch, etc. **4** *Informal* trick or trap in a business deal, contract, etc.; pitfall: *The price seems too low*; *there's a* catch *in it somewhere.* **5** small part; scrap; fragment: *She played* catches *of songs from the show.* **6** a break in the voice; also a choking sensation in the throat because of emotion. **7** *Music* a round, usually for humorous effect. **8** informal game of throwing and catching a ball. **9** *Informal* man or woman regarded as desirable for marriage.

catch sight (or **a glimpse**) **of** to see for a moment.
catch up to come from behind so as to overtake.
catch up with (or **up to**) to overtake.

catch·all (kăch′ ȯl′) ***n-*** **1** basket, drawer, etc., used to hold odds and ends. **2** word, phrase, etc., used to cover a variety of situations: *The word freedom is often used as a* catchall.

catch·er (kăch′ ər, kĕch′-) ***n-*** **1** person or thing that catches or seizes. **2** player on a baseball team who stands behind home plate to catch the ball thrown by the pitcher.

catch·ing (kăch′ ĭng, kech′-) ***adj-*** likely to be carried from one person to another; contagious; infectious: *Measles is a* catching *disease. Her laughter is* catching.

catch·up (kĕch′ əp, kăch′-) ***n-*** ketchup.

catch·word (kăch′ wûrd′) ***n-*** word or phrase that is repeated over and over to impress or arouse people; slogan.

catch·y (kăch′ ē) ***adj-*** **[catch·i·er, catch·i·est]** quick to win popular fancy: *a* catchy *tune.*

cat·dom (kăt′ dəm) ***n-*** all cats together.

cat·e·chet·i·cal (kăt′ ə kĕt′ ĭ kəl) ***adj-*** of or like catechism: *the* catechetical *method of teaching.* Also **cat′ e·chet′ ic.**

cat·e·chism (kăt′ ə kĭz′ əm) ***n-*** **1** small book of instruction in the Christian religion in the form of questions and answers. **2** any method of teaching by questions and answers. **3** set of questions to be answered.

cat·e·chize (kăt′ ə kīz′) ***vt-*** **[cat·e·chized, cat·e·chiz·ing] 1** to instruct by questions and answers, especially in the Christian religion. **2** to question closely. Also **cat′ e·chise′. —*n-* cat′ e·chiz′ er.**

cat·e·gor·i·cal (kăt′ ə gôr′ ĭ kəl) ***adj-*** without qualifications; absolute; unconditional: *a* categorical *reply.*

cat·e·go·ry (kăt′ ə gôr′ ē) ***n-*** [*pl.* **cat·e·gor·ies**] any broad class or division.

ca·ter (kā′ tər) ***vi-*** **1** to supply someone or something with what is wanted: *This novel* caters *to popular tastes.* **2** to supply and serve food, as for a party or banquet. ***vt-:*** *to* cater *a banquet.*

cat·er-cor·ner (kăt′ ē kȯr′ nər) catty-corner. Also **kitty-corner.**

ca·ter·er (kā′ tər ər) ***n-*** one whose business is to supply and serve food for banquets, weddings, etc.

cat·er·pil·lar (kăt′ ər pĭl′ ər) ***n-*** the wormlike larva that hatches from the eggs of such insects as the moth or butterfly.

Caterpillar

Caterpillar tractor ***n-*** trademark name for a tractor that moves on a pair of endless metal belts.

cat·er·waul (kăt′ ər wȯl′) ***vi-*** to cry, as cats at night; yowl. ***n-*** such a cry.

cat·fish (kăt′ fĭsh′) ***n-*** [*pl.* **cat·fish; cat·fish·es** (kinds of catfish)] any of several fish, usually scaleless, with long, whiskerlike feelers around the mouth.

cat·gut (kăt′ gŭt′) ***n-*** dried and twisted cord made from intestines of sheep or other animals, used for strings of tennis rackets, musical instruments, etc.

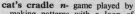

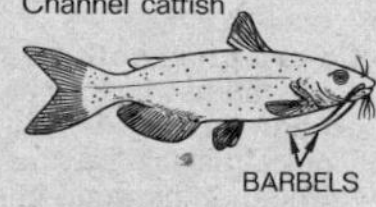

Channel catfish

Cath. Catholic.

ca·thar·tic (kə thär′ tĭk) ***adj-*** causing the bowels to empty; laxative: *the* cathartic *effect of some herbs.* ***n-*** a medicine that has this effect; laxative; physic.

Ca·thay (kă thā′) *Archaic* ***n-*** China.

cat·head (kăt′ hĕd′) ***n-*** projecting beam on the bow of a ship, to which the anchor is hoisted and fastened.

ca·the·dral (kə thē′ drəl) ***n-*** **1** resident church of a bishop, and chief church of a diocese. **2** any large and important church. ***as modifier:*** *a* cathedral *town.*

Cathedral

cath·ode (kăth′ ōd′) ***n-*** in an electron tube or an electrolytic cell, the negative electrode; in a storage battery, the positive electrode or pole.

cathode rays ***n-*** invisible streams of high-speed electrons given off by the cathode (filament) of a vacuum tube.

cath·o·lic (kăth′ ə lĭk) ***adj-*** of taste, interests, etc., all-inclusive; not narrow; broad: *a* catholic *appreciation for different styles of art.* **—*n-* cath′ o·lic′ i·ty** (kăth′ ə lĭs′ ə tē): *the* catholicity *of one's taste in reading.*

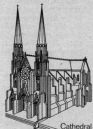

Cath·o·lic (kăth′ ə lĭk) ***adj-*** **1** of or pertaining to a universal church. **2** relating to the ancient, undivided Christian church, or to a church claiming historical continuity from it. ***n-*** a member of any of these churches, especially of the Roman Catholic Church.

Ca·thol·i·cism (kə thŏl′ ə sĭz′ əm) ***n-*** the faith, doctrine, and organization of the Roman Catholic Church.

cat·i·on (kăt′ ī′ ən) ***n-*** an ion bearing a positive charge.

cat·kin (kăt′ kĭn) ***n-*** slender, hanging cluster of tiny, scalelike flowers, such as those of the willow or birch.

Catkin of birch

cat·nap (kăt′ năp′) ***n-*** short nap.

cat·nip (kăt′ nĭp) ***n-*** plant of the mint family, with strong-smelling leaves that cats like.

cat-o′-nine-tails (kăt′ ə nīn′ tālz′) ***n-*** a whip with nine lashes of knotted cord, formerly used for flogging offenders.

cat's cradle ***n-*** game played by making patterns with a loop of string as one enlaces it on his fingers from someone else's fingers.

cat's-paw (kăts′ pȯ′) ***n-*** **1** person who is deceived and made use of by another; dupe. **2** light breeze that ruffles calm water. **3** kind of hitch or knot. For picture, see *knot.*

cat·sup (kăt′ səp, kĕch′ əp) ***n-*** ketchup.

cat·tail (kăt′ tāl′) ***n-*** tall marsh plant with long narrow leaves and candle-shaped spikes made of tiny brown flowers.

cat·tle (kăt′ əl) ***n-*** *pl.* livestock, especially cows, bulls, and steers kept on a farm or ranch.

cat·tle·man (kăt′ əl mən) ***n-*** [*pl.* **cat·tle·men**] man who raises or deals in cattle.

cat·ty (kăt′ ē) ***adj-*** **[cat·ti·er, cat·ti·est]** sly and malicious; spiteful.

cat·ty-cor·ner (kăt′ ē kȯr′ nər) or **cat·ty-cor·nered** (kăt′ ē kȯr′ nərd) ***adv-*** diagonally: *He placed the chair* catty-corner. Also **cater-corner.**

cat·walk (kăt′ wȯk′) ***n-*** narrow walk for workmen or crew on a bridge, around an engine room, etc.

Cau·ca·si·an (kȯ kā′ zhən) ***adj-*** **1** of or pertaining to the Caucasus, the people living there, or to their language. **2** of or pertaining to a major division of the human species that includes people of Europe, northern Africa, and southwestern Asia. ***n-*** **1** member of this division of the human species. **2** a native of the Caucasus. **3** a family of languages spoken in the region of the Caucasus.

cau·cus (kô′ kəs) ***n-*** a meeting of political party leaders to discuss party policies or choose party candidates. ***vi-***: *The delegates will* caucus *to decide on their choice for minority leader.* [American word from the **Caucus Club,** an early political group which took its name from Late Greek **kaukos** meaning "a drinking vessel."]

cau·dal (kô′ dəl) ***adj-*** relating to the tail: *the* caudal *fin of a fish.*

caught (kôt, kŏt) *p.t. & p.p.* of **catch.** ***Hom-*** cot.

caul·dron (kôl′ drən) ***n-*** large kettle or boiler.

cau·li·flow·er (kô′ lĭ flou′ ər, kŏl′ĭ-) ***n-*** plant related to the cabbage, having a head of tiny, tightly-packed, whitish flowers eaten as a vegetable.

Cauliflower

caulk or **calk** (kôk) ***vt-*** to fill (seams, joints, or cracks in a ship, building, etc.) with any of various substances called **caulking** or **calking** so as to make watertight. **—*n-* caulk′ er** or **calk′ er.**

caus·al (kô′ zəl) ***adj-*** indicating or acting as a cause; causative: *the* causal *relationship between germs and disease.* **—*adv-* caus′ al·ly:** *two* causally *related events.*

caus·al·i·ty (kô zăl′ ə tē) ***n-*** **1** the relation between cause and effect, or between causes and effects: *Finding that certain bacteria always occurred with the signs of a certain disease, they suspected* causality. **2** the fact of causing; ability or power to cause: *We now accept the bacterial* causality *of some diseases.*

cause (kôz) ***n-*** **1** person or thing that makes something happen or brings about a result: *The sudden storm was the* cause *of the shipwreck.* **2** subject which arouses interest and emotions, and to which people give support: *the* cause *of freedom.* **3** reason or motive for doing something, especially good or sufficient reason: *You have no* cause *to complain.* ***vt-*** **[caused, caus·ing]** to make happen; bring about; produce: *Speeding* causes *accidents.* **—*adj-* cause′ less.**

cause·way (kôz′ wā′) ***n-*** raised path or road over low or marshy ground.

caus·tic (kôs′ tĭk) ***adj-*** **1** able to eat away or destroy by chemical action; corrosive: *Lye is* caustic. **2** sarcastic; biting: *a* caustic *remark.* ***n-*** substance which by chemical action burns or eats away animal tissues. **—*adv-* caus′ ti·cal·ly.**

caustic soda ***n-*** sodium hydroxide.

cau·ter·ize (kô′ tər īz′) ***vt-*** **[cau·ter·ized, cau·ter·iz·ing]** to sear with a hot iron or caustic, especially to prevent infection or stop bleeding: *to* cauterize *a wound.* **—*n-* cau′ ter·i·za′ tion.**

cau·tion (kô′ shən) ***n-*** **1** act, word, etc., that warns, as against danger; warning: *He heeded my brother's numerous* cautions *to drive carefully.* **2** heedfulness; care in avoiding danger: *Handle chemicals with* caution. ***vt-***: *He* cautioned *me about the icy roads.*

cau·tion·ary (kô′ shən ĕr′ ē) ***adj-*** giving a warning: *a* cautionary *sign.*

cau·tious (kô′ shəs) ***adj-*** careful to avoid danger or trouble: *a* cautious *driver*; *a* cautious *suggestion.* **—*adv-* cau′ tious·ly.** ***n-*** **cau′ tious·ness:** *His* cautiousness *on every matter delayed the meeting.*

cav·al·cade (kăv′ əl kād′) ***n-*** procession or parade, especially of people on horseback or in autos.

cav·a·lier (kăv′ ə lêr′) ***n-*** **1** horseman; knight. **2** courteous, chivalrous man. **3 Cavalier** in 17th-century England, a supporter of King Charles I in his struggle with Parliament. ***adj-*** free and easy, and often haughty; offhand: *the* cavalier *manner with which he treated my objection.* **—*adv-* cav′ a·lier′ ly.**

cav·al·ry (kăv′ əl rē) ***n-*** [*pl.* **cav·al·ries**] soldiers who fight on horseback; mounted troops. **—*n-* cav′ al·ry·man.**

cave (kāv) ***n-*** natural hollow beneath the earth. ***vi-*** **[caved, cav·ing]** to fall in; collapse: *Look out, the wall is* caving!

cave in to fall or cause to fall in; collapse.

ca·ve·at emp·tor (kăv′ ē ăt′ ĕmp′ tôr, kā′-) *Latin* let the buyer beware.

cave-in (kāv′ ĭn′) ***n-*** a falling in of the walls of a mine, tunnel, etc.; also, the place where it happens.

cave·man (kāv′ măn′) ***n-*** [*pl.* **cave·men**] **1** a man of the Stone Age. **2** humorously, any man who is rough or overbearing, especially toward women.

cav·ern (kăv′ ərn) ***n-*** large cave.

cav·ern·ous (kăv′ ər nəs) ***adj-*** **1** hollow and deep like a cavern. **2** containing caverns: *a* cavernous *mountain.*

cav·i·ar (kăv′ ē är′) ***n-*** the eggs of certain large fishes, especially the sturgeon, prepared as an appetizer. Also **cav′ i·are′.**

cav·il (kăv′ əl) ***vi-*** to find fault without good reason; raise foolish or frivolous objections; carp: *to* cavil *at a proposed plan.* ***n-*** petty objection. **—*n-* cav′ il·er.**

cav·i·ty (kăv′ ə tē) ***n-*** [*pl.* **cav·i·ties**] hollow place; hole: *a* cavity *in a tooth.*

ca·vort (kə vôrt′, -vôrt′) ***vi-*** to prance or leap about playfully: *The colts* cavorted *in the meadow.*

caw (kô) ***n-*** cry of a crow or raven. ***vi-*** to make this sound.

cay (kē) ***n-*** small offshore island or exposed reef; key.

cay·enne pepper (kī′ ĕn′) ***n-*** a hot, biting, red seasoning powder prepared from the fruit or seeds of certain pepper plants; red pepper.

cay·man (kā′ mən, kā măn′) ***n-*** caiman.

Ca·yu·ga (kā yōō′ gə, kī-) ***n-*** [*pl.* **Ca·yu·gas,** also **Ca·yu·ga**] one of a tribe of Iroquois Indians who belonged to the Five Nations. ***adj-***: *a* Cayuga *council.*

Cay·use (kī yōōs′) ***n-*** [*pl.* **Cay·us·es,** also **Cay·use**] **1** member of a tribe of American Indians who formerly inhabited the forests of Oregon. **2 cayuse** an Indian pony or range horse of the western United States.

Cb symbol for columbium.

c.c. cubic centimeter.

CCD Bible ***n-*** Roman Catholic revision of the Old and New Testaments in English, made in the mid-20th century by the *C*onfraternity of *C*hristian *D*octrine.

C clef *Music* ***n-*** sign on the staff indicating the position of middle C.

cease (sēs) ***vi-*** **[ceased, ceas·ing]** to come to an end: *The rain* ceased. ***vt-***: *They* ceased *firing.*

cease·less (sēs′ ləs) ***adj-*** without end or pause: *the brook's* ceaseless *murmur.* **—*adv-* cease′ less·ly.** ***n-*** **cease′ less·ness.**

Ce·cro·pi·a moth (sə krō′ pē ə) ***n-*** large North American moth, whose larva spins a cocoon of silk.

ce·dar (sē′ dər) ***n-*** **1** any of various trees related to the pines, having flattened leaves and durable, aromatic wood. **2** the wood of these trees. ***adj-***: *a* cedar *chest.*

ce·dar·bird (sē′ dər bûrd′) ***n-*** crested American bird with red patches on its wings. Also called **cedar waxwing.**

cede (sēd) ***vt-*** **[ced·ed, ced·ing]** to give up; surrender to another: *to* cede *land*; *to* cede *a point.* ***Hom-*** seed.

ce·dil·la (sə dĭl′ ə) ***n-*** an accent mark placed under the letter **c** to show that it has the sound of /s/, as in the French word "façade."

ceil·ing (sē′ lĭng) ***n-*** **1** inner overhead covering of a room. **2** the greatest altitude at which an airplane can operate under certain conditions. **3** distance of the lowest clouds from the earth. **4** upper limit; maximum: *a price* ceiling.

cel·an·dine (sĕl′ ən dīn′, -dēn′) ***n-*** a biennial herb of the poppy family, with small yellow flowers and acrid yellow juice. It is used in medicine as a purgative.

cel·e·brant (sĕl′ ə brənt) ***n-*** one who performs a religious ceremony, especially the priest who officiates at Mass.

cel·e·brate (sĕl′ ə brāt′) ***vt-*** [**cel·e·brat·ed, cel·e·brat·ing**] **1** to perform publicly with suitable ceremonies, such as a Mass. **2** to make known with praise; honor: *We* celebrate *the names of great men.* **3** to observe suitably, as with a holiday and ceremonies: *to* celebrate *Christmas.* ***vi-*** to make merry: *Let's* celebrate.

cel·e·brat·ed (sĕl′ ə brā′ təd) ***adj-*** famous; well-known: *Mark Twain is a* celebrated *author.*

cel·e·bra·tion (sĕl′ ə brā′ shən) ***n-*** **1** a performing of a public religious ceremony. **2** ceremonies or festivities on a special occasion, such as Christmas, a birthday, etc.

ce·leb·ri·ty (sə lĕb′ rə tē) ***n-*** [*pl.* **ce·leb·ri·ties**] renowned or famous person.

ce·ler·i·ty (sə lĕr′ ə tē) ***n-*** swiftness; speed.

cel·er·y (sĕl′ ə rē) ***n-*** [*pl.* **cel·er·ies**] garden plant with crisp stalks that are good to eat either raw or cooked.

ce·les·ta (sə lĕs′ tə) ***n-*** musical instrument that looks like a small piano and produces sweet, bell-like tones from steel plates struck by small hammers.

ce·les·ti·al (sə lĕs′ chəl) ***adj-*** **1** of or related to the heavens: *The stars are* celestial *bodies.* **2** heavenly; divine: *a* celestial *joy.* **—*adv-*** **ce·les′ ti·al·ly.**

celestial equator ***n-*** the great circle traced on the celestial sphere by the plane of the earth's equator.

celestial pole ***n-*** either of the two points on the celestial sphere that are directly above the poles of the earth.

celestial sphere ***n-*** imaginary sphere of the sky, on which the stars, planets, etc., seem to move.

cel·i·ba·cy (sĕl′ ə bə sē) ***n-*** the state of being unmarried; single life, especially in accordance with religious vows.

cel·i·bate (sĕl′ ə bət) ***n-*** one bound by a religious vow not to marry. ***adj-***: *a* celibate *life.*

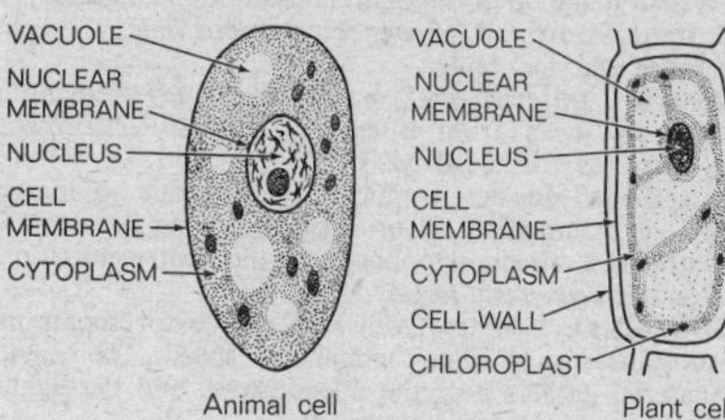

Animal cell Plant cell

cell (sĕl) ***n-*** **1** tiny living body, the smallest unit of an animal or plant able to carry on the basic functions of life, such as growing and reproducing. **2** small room in a prison, monastery, or convent. **3** small, enclosed space: *a honeycomb* cell. **4** device for generating electricity. It consists of a container with two electrodes and chemicals that release an electric current when they react. ***Hom-*** sell.

cel·lar (sĕl′ ər) ***n-*** underground room or group of rooms, generally under a building and often used for storage. ***Hom-*** seller.

cel·list or **'cel·list** (chĕl′ ĭst) ***n-*** person who plays the cello.

cel·lo or **'cel·lo** (chĕl′ ō) ***n-*** [*pl.* **cel·los**] stringed musical instrument, deeper and larger in tone than a viola or violin; violoncello.

Man playing cello

cel·lo·phane (sĕl′ ə fān′) ***n-*** transparent, waterproof plastic made in thin sheets for wrapping food and other goods.

cel·lu·lar (sĕl′ yə lər) ***adj-*** related to or consisting of cells: *a* cellular *mass.*

Cel·lu·loid (sĕl′ yə loid′) ***n-*** **1** trademark name for a highly flammable plastic made from cellulose. It is used to make photographic film and is colored to imitate amber, tortoise, or ivory for combs, brushes, etc. **2 celluloid** *Informal* motion picture film.

cel·lu·lose (sĕl′ yə lōs′) ***n-*** fibrous substance that forms the woody parts of trees and plants, used to make paper, plastics, etc. Cotton is nearly pure cellulose.

cellulose acetate ***n-*** a tough plastic material made by treating cellulose with acetic acid. It is used to make acetate rayon, plastic wrapping materials, and lacquers.

cellulose nitrate ***n-*** nitrocellulose.

Cel·si·us scale (sĕl′ sē əs) ***n-*** now the official name of the centigrade thermometer scale which sets the freezing point of water at 0° and the boiling point at 100°.

Celt (sĕlt) ***n-*** a member of any Celtic-speaking people, including the ancient Gauls and Britons, as well as the modern Irish, Welsh, Highland Scots, and Bretons.

Celt·ic (sĕl′ tĭk) ***n-*** a group of languages spoken in parts of Britain, Ireland, and northwestern France. ***adj-*** of or pertaining to the Celts, their languages, or cultures.

ce·ment (sĭ mĕnt′) ***n-*** **1** fine gray powder made from limestone, clay, gypsum, and iron oxide which, when mixed with water, dries to the hardness of rock. It is mixed with sand or gravel to make concrete. **2** any similar substance that binds or sticks things together, as glue or paste. **3** *Informal* concrete. **4** material for filling teeth. *as* ***modifier***: *a* cement *mixer.* ***vt-*** **1** to join together as with mortar: *to* cement *bricks.* **2** to cover or pave with concrete: *to* cement *a walk.*

cem·e·ter·y (sĕm′ ə tĕr′ ē) ***n-*** [*pl.* **cem·e·ter·ies**] burial ground; graveyard.

Cen. Am. Central America.

cen·o·taph (sĕn′ ə tăf′) ***n-*** monument in memory of a person whose body is buried in another place.

Ce·no·zo·ic (sĕn′ ə zō′ ĭk) ***n-*** era of geologic time lasting from about 60 million years ago to the present, marked by the rise of mammals, birds, and, more recently, man. ***adj-***: *the* Cenozoic *era.*

cen·ser (sĕn′ sər) ***n-*** container in which incense is burned, especially one carried and swung on chains. ***Hom-*** censor.

cen·sor (sĕn′ sər) ***n-*** **1** official who examines books, motion pictures, etc., to keep out anything that is thought wrong or undesirable. **2** official who, in time of war, examines letters and printed matter to keep out anything that might help the enemy. **3** in ancient Rome, one of the two magistrates who took the census and regulated morals. ***vt-***: *to* censor *a movie.* ***Hom-*** censer.

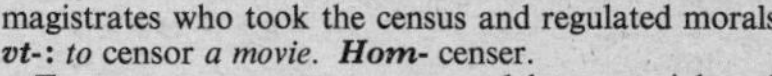
Censer

►To CENSOR means to repress or delete material, such as passages in a book or scenes in a movie, for political

fāte, făt, dâre, bärn; bē, bĕt, mêre; bīte, bĭt; nōte, hŏt, môre, dȯg; fŭn, fûr; to͞o, bo͝ok; oil; out; tar; thin; then; hw for wh as in *wh*at; zh for s as in u*s*ual; ə for a, e, i, o, u, as in *a*go, lin*e*n, per*i*l, at*o*m, min*u*s

or moral reasons. To CENSURE means to blame or find fault for any reason. A CENSORIOUS person is one who CENSURES others habitually, but is not necessarily one who CENSORS.

cen·sor·i·ous (sĕn sôr′ ē əs) ***adj-*** given to or containing censure; faultfinding: *a* censorious *report.* ***—adv-*** **cen·sor′ i·ous·ly.** ***n-*** **cen·sor′ i·ous·ness.**

cen·sor·ship (sĕn′ sər shĭp′) ***n-*** act or practice of censoring; control over what is said or written: *to exercise* censorship *over books.*

cen·sur·a·ble (sĕn′ shər ə bəl) ***adj-*** deserving censure or blame: *a* censurable *act.*

cen·sure (sĕn′ shər) ***n-*** expression of disapproval or condemnation: *A man in public office often receives* censure *from all sides.* ***vt-*** **[cen·sured, cen·sur·ing]:** *The Senate* censured *Mr. Doe for slandering people.*
►For usage note see CENSOR.

cen·sus (sĕn′ səs) ***n-*** official count of the population, including information about age, sex, employment, etc.

cent (sĕnt) ***n-*** **1** the hundredth part of a dollar. **2** coin of this value; penny. ***Homs-*** scent, sent.

cent. 1 century. **2** centigrade. **3** central.

cen·taur (sĕn′ tôr′) ***n-*** in Greek myths, a creature that is half man and half horse.

Centaur

cen·ta·vo (sĕn tä′ vō) ***n-*** [*pl.* **cen·ta·vos**] a small coin of some Spanish-speaking countries, equal to the hundredth part of a peso.

cen·te·nar·i·an (sĕn′ tə nâr′ ē ən) ***n-*** person who is one hundred years old or over.

cen·te·nar·y (sĕn tĕn′ ə rē, sĕn′ tə-nĕr′ ē) ***n-*** [*pl.* **cen·te·nar·ies**] **1** a period of 100 years. **2** celebration of a 100th anniversary; centennial.

cen·ten·ni·al (sĕn tĕn′ ē əl) ***n-*** the 100th anniversary of an event; also, the celebration of this anniversary. *as* ***modifier:*** *a* centennial *celebration.* ***—adv-*** **cen·ten′ ni·al·ly.**

cen·ter (sĕn′ tər) ***n-*** **1** middle point of a circle or sphere. **2** point about which something turns: *the* center *of a wheel.* **3** place where people gather for a particular purpose: *a shopping* center. **4** principal object: *She is the* center *of attention.* **5** the middle: *the* center *of the road.* **6** group holding moderate political views. **7** in games such as basketball, football, and hockey, a player whose base position is in the center of the playing field. ***vt-*** **1** to place in a middle or central position: *We* centered *the picture over the sofa.* **2** to concentrate; centralize: *The new laws* center *all power in the president.* **3** in football, to pass (the ball) from the line of scrimmage to a back. Also, *chiefly Brit.,* **centre.**
center around *Informal* to center on.
center on (or **upon**) to concentrate or focus on: *The crowd's attention* centered on *the man on the roof.*

cen·ter·board (sĕn′ tər bôrd′) ***n-*** fin-shaped board that can be lowered through a slot in the floor of a flat-bottomed sailboat to prevent sideways drifting.

center field ***n-*** in baseball, the section of the outfield behind second base; also, the position of the player who covers this section. ***—n-*** **center fielder.**

center of gravity or **center of mass** ***n-*** the point in an object around which its mass is equally distributed.

cen·ter·piece (sĕn′ tər pēs′) ***n-*** ornament of silver, glass, etc., or a bowl of flowers, placed in the center of a dining table.

cen·tes·i·mal (sĕn tĕs′ ə məl) ***adj-*** divided into 100 parts: *a* centesimal *scale.* ***—adv-*** **cen·tes′ i·mal·ly.**

centi- *combining form* **1** hundred: *a* centi*pede.* **2** one-hundredth: *a* centi*meter.* [from Latin **centi-,** from **centum** meaning "hundred."]

cen·ti·grade (sĕn′ tə grād′) ***adj-*** having 100 equal divisions called degrees. For picture, see *thermometer.*

centigrade thermometer ***n-*** a thermometer on which the distance between the freezing point of water, marked at 0°, and the boiling point, marked at 100°, is divided into 100 equal degrees.

cen·ti·gram (sĕn′ tə grăm′) ***n-*** in the metric system, 1/100 of a gram or 0.15432 grain troy. *Abbr.* cg. Also, *chiefly Brit.,* **cen′ ti·gramme′.**

cen·time (sän′ tēm′) ***n-*** small French coin, equal in value to 1/100 of a franc.

cen·ti·me·ter (sĕn′ tə mē′ tər) ***n-*** in the metric system, 1/100 of a meter, or 0.3937 inch. Also, *Brit.* **cen′ ti·me′ tre.** *Abbr.* cm.

cen·ti·pede (sĕn′ tə pēd′) ***n-*** any of a group of small wormlike animals with a long, flattened body made up of many segments, each bearing a pair of legs. The foremost pair of legs is a set of claws for grasping prey and injecting venom.

Centipede

cen·tral (sĕn′ trəl) ***adj-*** **1** in, at, or near the middle: *the* central *part of the city.* **2** main; leading: *the* central *idea of the book.* ***n-*** **1** telephone exchange. **2** telephone operator. ***—adv-*** **cen′ tral·ly.**

central angle ***n-*** an angle whose sides are radii of a circle and whose vertex is the circle's center.

cen·tral·i·za·tion (sĕn′ trə lə zā′ shən) ***n-*** a centralizing; a bringing to a central point or under one control, as in government.

cen·tral·ize (sĕn′ trə līz′) ***vt-*** **[cen·tral·ized, cen·tral·iz·ing]** to bring together or concentrate (activities, authority, devices, etc., that had been separated): *The new plan* centralizes *the control of purchases.*

central nervous system ***n-*** the part of the nervous system made up of the brain and the spinal cord.

Central Standard Time See *standard time.*

cen·tre (sĕn′ tər) center.

cen·trif·u·gal (sĕn trĭf′ yə gəl, -ə gəl) ***adj-*** moving or pressing away from a center. See also *centripetal.* ***—adv-*** **cen·trif′ u·gal·ly.**

centrifugal force ***n-*** outward force, due to inertia, that is assumed to act on a mass moving in a curved path, in a direction opposite to the centripetal force. See also *centripetal force.*

cen·tri·fuge (sĕn′ trə fyo͞oj′) ***n-*** device for separating substances by whirling them at high speed. The heavier material gathers near the outside wall, and the lighter remains near the center.

cen·trip·e·tal (sĕn trĭp′ ə təl) ***adj-*** moving or pulling toward a center. See also *centrifugal.* ***—adv-*** **cen·trip′ e·tal·ly.**

centripetal force ***n-*** the real inward pull exerted on a mass rotating around a point to keep the mass from flying off in a straight line. Example: the gravitational pull of the earth on a satellite that keeps the satellite in orbit. See also *centrifugal force.*

cen·tro·some (sĕn′ trə sōm′) ***n-*** tiny body in living cells thought to control cell division.

cen·tu·ri·on (sĕn to͝or′ ē ən) ***n-*** in ancient Rome, an officer commanding a unit of about 100 soldiers.

cen·tu·ry (sĕn′ chə rē) ***n-*** [*pl.* **cen·tu·ries**] **1** a period of 100 years. **2** each group of 100 years before or after some fixed date, such as the birth of Christ: *the 20th* century *A.D.*

century plant ***n-*** an agave which requires from five to fifty years to bloom; maguey; American aloe.

ce·phal·ic (sə făl′ĭk) ***adj-*** of or having to do with the head.

ceph·a·lo·pod (sĕf′ ə lə pŏd′) ***n-*** any of a class of marine mollusks, **Cephalopoda** (sĕf′-ə lä′ pə də), such as octopuses, squid, and cuttlefish, having long, fleshy tentacles around their mouths.

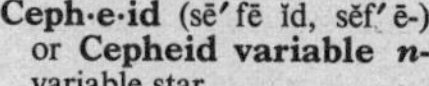

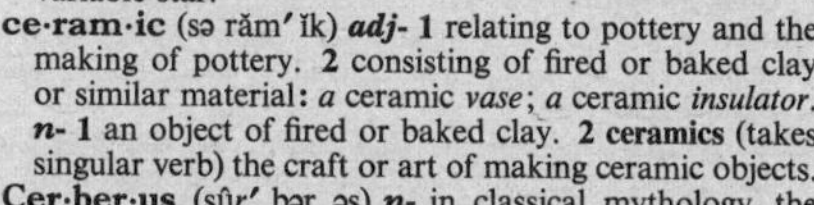

Century plant

Ceph·e·id (sē′fē ĭd, sĕf′ ē-) or **Cepheid variable** ***n-*** variable star.

ce·ram·ic (sə răm′ ĭk) ***adj-*** **1** relating to pottery and the making of pottery. **2** consisting of fired or baked clay or similar material: *a* ceramic *vase*; *a* ceramic *insulator.* ***n-*** **1** an object of fired or baked clay. **2 ceramics** (takes singular verb) the craft or art of making ceramic objects.

Cer·ber·us (sûr′ bər əs) ***n-*** in classical mythology, the three-headed dog guarding the gates of Hades.

ce·re·al (sêr′ ē əl) ***n-*** **1** any grass that yields a grain or seed used for food, such as rice, wheat, oats, or the like. **2** any of these grains, in a natural state or as put on the market. **3** a prepared food, especially a breakfast food, made from any of these grains. *as* ***modifier:*** *a* cereal *grass.* ***Hom-*** serial.

cer·e·bel·lum (sĕr′ ə bĕl′ əm) ***n-*** the smaller of the two main parts of the brain. It is located in the back of the skull and co-ordinates muscle movements.

cer·e·bral (sə rē′ brəl, sĕr′ə brəl) ***adj-*** of, or having to do with the brain, especially the cerebrum: *a* cerebral *hemorrhage.*

cerebral hemorrhage ***n-*** bleeding within the brain from a break in one of its blood vessels.

cerebral palsy ***n-*** paralysis or lack of control over muscle movement as the result of brain damage at birth or a brain defect.

ce·re·bro·spi·nal (sə rē′ brō spī′ nəl) ***adj-*** of or affecting the brain and the spinal cord: *Meningitis is a* cerebrospinal *disease.*

cer·e·brum (sĕr′ə brəm, sə rē′-) ***n-*** the larger of the two main parts of the brain. It fills most of the skull and is the seat of conscious thought.

cer·e·ment (sĕr′ ə mənt) ***n-*** shroud for a dead body.

cer·e·mo·ni·al (sĕr′ ə mō′ nē əl) ***adj-*** **1** formal; with ceremony: *a* ceremonial *dinner.* **2** used in a ceremony: *a* ceremonial *robe.* ***n-*** system of rites or formalities observed on a particular occasion: *the* ceremonial *of graduation.* ***—adv-*** **cer′ e·mo′ nial·ly.**

cer·e·mo·ni·ous (sĕr′ ə mō′ nē əs) ***adj-*** **1** formally polite; courtly: *a* ceremonious *bow.* **2** with rites or formalities; formal: *a* ceremonious *reception.* ***—adv-*** **cer′ e·mo′ ni·ous·ly.** ***n-*** **cer′ e·mo′ ni·ous·ness.**

cer·e·mo·ny (sĕr′ ə mō′ nē) ***n-*** [*pl.* **cer·e·mo·nies**] **1** formal rite or observance: *a wedding* ceremony; *the inauguration* ceremony. **2** very formal behavior; formality: *The chief insisted on* ceremony.

stand on ceremony to insist on very formal or polite behavior.

Ce·res (sêr′ ēz) ***n-*** in Roman mythology, the goddess of vegetation and harvests, identified with the Greek Demeter.

ce·rise (sə rēs′) ***n-*** bright, light-red color like that of certain cherries. ***—adj-:*** *a* cerise *blouse.*

ce·ri·um (sêr′ ē əm) ***n-*** very active, rare, silver-gray, metallic element. Symbol Ce, At. No. 58, At. Wt. 140.13.

cer·tain (sûr′ tən) ***adj-*** **1** beyond doubt or question; indisputable; sure: *We have* certain *proof of his guilt.* **2** positive; confident; sure: *I am* certain *of victory.* **3** sure to happen; inevitable: *You are going to* certain *death.* **4** definite but not named or specified; particular: *Our plans didn't please* certain *people.*

cer·tain·ly (sûr′ tən lē) ***adv-*** definitely; without doubt: *They will* certainly *come.* Certainly, *you may come on the trip!*

cer·tain·ty (sûr′ tən tē) ***n-*** [*pl.* **cer·tain·ties**] **1** freedom from doubt; clear and definite truth or knowledge: *a feeling of* certainty. **2** something that is sure: *It is a* certainty *that the sun will rise tomorrow.*

cer·ti·fi·a·ble (sûr′ tə fī′ ə bəl) ***adj-*** of a kind or nature that can be certified as such: *his* certifiable *honesty.* ***—adv-*** **cer′ ti·fi′ a·bly.**

cer·tif·i·cate (sûr tĭf′ ĭ kət) ***n-*** **1** official document stating the truth of some fact, fitness for some work, etc.: *a* birth *certificate*; *a* health *certificate*; *a teacher's* certificate. **2** any solemn signed statement, often sworn to under oath.

cer·ti·fi·ca·tion (sûr′ tə fə kā′ shən) ***n-*** **1** a certifying or being certified. **2** certificate.

certified milk ***n-*** milk produced according to the official health regulations of a medical milk commission.

certified public accountant ***n-*** accountant who has received a certificate after meeting certain requirements set by his State. *Abbr.* CPA

cer·ti·fy (sûr′ tə fī′) ***vt-*** [**cer·ti·fied, cer·ti·fy·ing**] **1** to state, confirm, or verify by a signed statement or official document: *to* certify *the date of one's birth.* **2** to guarantee: *to* certify *a check.* ***—n-*** **cer′ ti·fi′ er.**

cer·ti·tude (sûr′ tə tōōd′, -tyōōd′) ***n-*** strong feeling of being certain; assurance.

ce·ru·le·an (sə rōōl′ ē ən) ***adj-*** sky-blue.

cer·vi·cal (sûr′ vĭ kəl) ***adj-*** of or relating to the neck or to a cervix.

cer·vix (sûr′ vĭks′) ***n-*** [*pl.* **cer·vi·ces** (sûr′ və sēz′)] **1** the neck, especially the back of the neck. **2** narrow neck-shaped part of a body organ such as the uterus.

ce·sar·e·an or **ce·sar·i·an** (sĭ zăr′ ē ən, sĭ zâr′-) *Medicine* ***n-*** surgical opening of a woman's abdomen and uterus for the delivery of a child. Also called **cesarean section, cesarean operation.** [from **Julius Caesar,** who was born this way.]

ce·si·um (sē′ zē əm) ***n-*** an extremely active, very soft, silver-white metallic element used in photoelectric cells and in radio and electron tubes. Symbol Cs, At. No. 55, At. Wt. 132.91. Also **cae′ si·um.**

ces·sa·tion (sĕ sā′ shən) ***n-*** a ceasing or halting; stopping: *a* cessation *of pain*; *the* cessation *of hostilities.*

ces·sion (sĕsh′ ən) ***n-*** a ceding; formal giving up to another; surrender: *a* cession *of territory.* ***Hom-*** session.

cess·pool (sĕs′ pōōl′) ***n-*** deep pit or well for sewage.

ce·ta·cean (sə tā′ shən) ***n-*** one of an order of mammals, **Cetacea** (sə tā′ sē ə), that look like fish and live entirely in water, such as whales, dolphins, and porpoises. ***—adj-*** **ce·ta′ ceous** (-shəs).

cf. compare [from Latin **confer**].

cg. or **cg** centigram or centigrams.

ch. chapter.

cha-cha (chä′ chä′) ***n-*** modern ballroom dance of Latin-American origin.

chac·ma (chăk′ mə) ***n-*** dark-colored baboon, the largest known, found in southernmost Africa.

chafe (chāf) ***vt-*** [**chafed, chaf·ing**] **1** to restore warmth or sensation to by rubbing: *to* chafe *numb hands.* **2** to wear away or irritate by rubbing: *A starched collar may* chafe *the neck. The pulley* chafed *the rope.* ***vi-*** **1** to rub: *to* chafe *against the deck.* **2** to be irritated and impatient: *to* chafe *at the least delay.*

[1]**chaff** (chăf) ***n-*** **1** the husks of grain, separated by threshing and winnowing. **2** anything worthless: *to separate the wheat from the* chaff. [from Old English word **ceaf.**]

[2]**chaff** (chăf) ***n-*** good-natured teasing; banter. ***vt-*** to tease or ridicule good-naturedly: *Joe* chaffed *Tony about his new suit.* ***vi-***: *They* chaff *at one another.* [of unknown origin, perhaps from **chaffer** meaning "to bargain."]

chaf·fer (chăf′ ər) ***vi-*** to bargain, especially to haggle and dispute about a purchase. ***—n-*** **chaf′fer·er.**

chaf·finch (chăf′ ĭnch′, chăf′ fĭnch′) ***n-*** a common European songbird that picks its food from chaff.

chafing dish ***n-*** metal dish with a heating apparatus beneath it, to cook or keep food warm at the table.

cha·grin (shə grĭn′) ***n-*** feeling of annoyance because of disappointment, failure, or humiliation; mortification; embarrassment. ***vt-***: *It* chagrined *him that he lost.*

chain (chān) ***n-*** **1** series of links or rings, usually metal, joined one after another. **2** anything that binds or restrains. **3** connected series or succession: *a* chain *of events.* **4** set of hotels, stores, banks, etc., under one management. **5** measure used in land surveying, equal to 100 links or 66 feet. **6 chains** imprisonment or bondage: *The Hebrews broke their* chains *and departed from Egypt.* ***vt-*** **1** to fasten or secure with a series of strong links. **2** to fetter; restrain.

Chain

chain gang ***n-*** a number of convicts chained together while working outside prison walls.

chain letter ***n-*** letter sent to several people asking each to send a copy to a specific number of persons.

chain reaction ***n-*** **1** *Physics* continuous atomic fission in which neutrons released by the splitting of nuclei go on to bombard and split other nuclei. **2** any series of events in which each is caused by the one before.

chain store ***n-*** one of a number of stores having the same name and controlled by a single company.

chair (châr) ***n-*** **1** a movable single seat, usually with four legs and a back. **2** office or position, especially of a professor: *the* chair *of history at the university.* **3** chairman: *to address the* chair. **4** *Informal* the electric chair. ***vt-*** to act as chairman at: *to* chair *a meeting.*

take the chair to become a chairman.

chair·man (châr′ mən) ***n-*** [*pl.* **chair·men**] person who presides over a meeting, committee, organization, etc.; presiding officer. ***—n-*** *fem.* **chair′ wom′an.**

chair·man·ship (châr′ mən shĭp′) ***n-*** the office or work of a chairman.

chair·per·son (châr′ pûr′sən) ***n-*** person who presides over a meeting, committee, organization, etc.; presiding officer.

chaise (shāz) ***n-*** a light, one-horse carriage with a folding top, usually with two wheels and for two persons.

chaise longue (shāz′lòng′) ***n-*** [*pl.* **chaises longues** (shāz′lòng′)] chair with a long seat on which a person can sit with his or her legs stretched out. Also **chaise.**

cha·lah or **chal·lah** (KHä′ lə) ***n-*** white bread, usually baked in a braided loaf, traditionally eaten by Jews on the Sabbath. Also **hal′lah.**

chal·ced·o·ny (kăl sĕd′ ə nē) ***n-*** **1** type of quartz that has a waxy luster. **2** a pale-gray or pale-blue variety of this quartz, used as a gem stone.

cha·let (shă lā′) ***n-*** **1** frame house of the Swiss mountains, having a sloping roof and a very wide overhang; also, any house of this style. **2** herdsman's hut in the Alps.

chal·ice (chăl′ əs) ***n-*** **1** a goblet. **2** the cup used in celebrating the Eucharist, or Lord's Supper. **3** cup-shaped flower, such as a tulip.

chalk (chòk) ***n-*** **1** soft, powdery limestone made mostly of tiny seashells. **2** white or colored marker or crayon made of this limestone or a similar material: *tailor's* chalk. ***vt-*** **1** to mark, draw, or write with such a crayon: *She* chalked *the score on the blackboard.* **2** to rub or treat with this substance: *to* chalk *the tip of a billiard cue.* ***adj-***: *a* chalk *drawing.* ***—adj-*** **chalk′ like′.**

chalk up *Informal* to score: *to* chalk up *points.*

chalk·y (chò′ kē) ***adj-*** [**chalk·i·er, chalk·i·est**] of or like chalk: *The medicine had a* chalky *consistency.* ***—n-*** **chalk′ i·ness.**

chal·lenge (chăl′ ənj) ***vt-*** [**chal·lenged, chal·leng·ing**] **1** to dare (a person, group, team, etc.) to fight or compete: *I* challenge *anyone to race me.* **2** to call forth or excite the energies, interests, or talents of; arouse: *Science* challenges *today's young people.* **3** to question or dispute (a statement, claim, idea, etc.); take exception to: *to* challenge *a hasty remark.* **4** to demand identification from: *The guard* challenged *the visitor at the gate.* **5** in law, to question the qualifications or legality of (a juror, voter, or vote). ***n-*** **1** a summons or invitation to fight or compete. **2** a sentry's demand for identification. **3** something that calls forth one's utmost energies, talents, etc.: *The job offers many* challenges *to an intelligent person.* **4** in law, formal objection to a juror, voter, or vote. ***—n-*** **chal′ leng·er.**

chal·lis (shăl′ ē) ***n-*** soft, lightweight fabric of wool, rayon, or cotton, usually with a small, floral print. Also **chal′ lie.**

cham·ber (chām′ bər) ***n-*** **1** a room, especially a bedroom. **2** a room for official occasions: *the judge's* chamber; *the Senate* chamber; *the* chamber *where the Pope meets his guests.* **3** division or house of a legislature: *The Senate is the upper* chamber *of Congress.* **4** enclosed space or cavity: *the* chamber *of a gun*; *a* chamber *in a cave.* ***—adj-*** **cham′ bered:** *a many-*chambered *house.*

cham·ber·lain (chām′ bər lən) ***n-*** **1** person in charge of the household of a king or nobleman. **2** treasurer.

cham·ber·maid (chām′ bər mād′) ***n-*** a servant who cleans bedrooms and makes beds.

chamber music ***n-*** music composed for only a few instruments, and ideally performed in a small hall.

chamber of commerce ***n-*** [*pl.* **chambers of commerce**] an association of merchants, businesspersons, etc., to regulate and promote their business activities.

cham·bray (shăm′ brā′) ***n-*** fine cotton gingham fabric made in a plain weave with a colored warp and a white filling which gives it a frosted appearance.

cha·me·le·on (kə mēl′ ē ən) ***n-*** **1** any of a group of small Old World lizards that change color according to variations in light, temperature, and other factors. **2** any of several smaller American lizards that also change color. **3** a person of quickly changeable disposition and views.

Chameleon, 6 or 7 in. long

cham·fer (chăm′ fər) ***vt-*** **1** to cut away a sharp or square edge or corner of (a board, etc.); bevel. **2** to cut a groove; flute. ***n-*** beveled edge or corner; bevel.

cham·ois (shăm′ ē) ***n-*** [*pl.* **cham·ois**] **1** small mountain antelope of Europe and Asia. **2** (also **cham′ my**) soft, napped leather, originally from this animal but now also from goats and deer, and used especially to make washing and polishing cloths. **3** the color of this leather, a light tannish yellow.

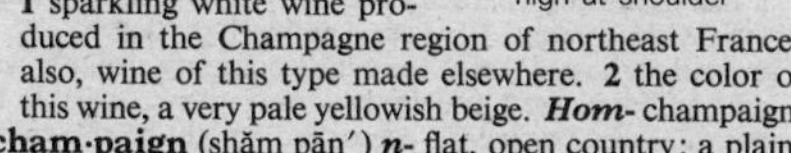
Chamois, 30 in. high at shoulder

cham·o·mile (kăm′ ə mīl′) camomile.
champ (chămp) ***vt-*** to chew or bite on noisily or restlessly: *The horse* champed *its bit.* ***vi-***: *The horse* champed *noisily.*
champ at the bit to be impatient for action or departure.
cham·pagne (shăm pān′) ***n-*** **1** sparkling white wine produced in the Champagne region of northeast France; also, wine of this type made elsewhere. **2** the color of this wine, a very pale yellowish beige. ***Hom-*** champaign.
cham·paign (shăm pān′) ***n-*** flat, open country; a plain. ***Hom-*** champagne.
cham·pi·on (chăm′ pē ən) ***n-*** **1** winner of first place in a competition: *a tennis* champion; *a heavyweight boxing* champion. **2** person who defends another person or a cause: *a* champion *of liberty.* *as* ***modifier***: *the* champion *player.* ***vt-***: *He* championed *freedom of the press.*
cham·pi·on·ship (chăm′ pē ən shĭp′) ***n-*** **1** position of first place in a competition. **2** defense or support (of a person or cause): *his* championship *of a four-day week.*
chance (chăns) ***n-*** **1** opportunity; suitable occasion: *I'll go when I get a* chance. **2** luck; fortune; accident: *We met by* chance. *It was* chance, *not skill, that decided the winner.* **3** a risk; gamble; hazard: *You are taking a* chance *to drive in this weather.* **4** likelihood; probability: *What is the* chance *that it will rain*? **5** fair possibility of winning, surviving, etc.: *The challenger didn't have a* chance. **6** lottery ticket: *She bought five* chances *for the turkey raffle.* ***adj-*** unforeseen; accidental: *a* chance *meeting.* ***vt-*** [**chanced, chanc·ing**] to risk; hazard: *Don't* chance *it with that old car.* ***vi-*** to happen accidentally: *We* chanced *to meet.*
chance on or **chance upon** to meet, find, or come upon accidentally: *He* chanced on *the very book he wanted.*
chan·cel (chăn′ səl) ***n-*** the space surrounding the altar of a church, reserved for the clergy and the choir.
chan·cel·ler·y (chăn′ səl rē) ***n-*** [*pl.* **chan·cel·ler·ies**] **1** the position or department of a chancellor. **2** place where a chancellor has his office. **3** office of an embassy or consulate. Also **chan′ cel·lor·y.**
chan·cel·lor (chăn′ sə lər, chăn′ slər) ***n-*** **1** presiding judge of a court of equity. **2** at some universities, the president. **3** in some European countries, the chief minister of state. **4** in England, the chief secretary of an embassy. **5 Lord Chancellor** in Great Britain, the highest judge of the realm. **6 Chancellor of the Exchequer** in Great Britain, the minister of finance.
chan·cel·lor·ship (chăn′ slər shĭp′) ***n-*** position or office of a chancellor.
chan·cer·y (chăn′ sər ē) ***n-*** [*pl.* **chan·cer·ies**] **1** a court of equity. **2** in England, the court of the Lord Chancellor. **3** the office in which the business of a diocese is transacted.
chan·cre (shăng′ kər) ***n-*** an ulcerated sore, one type of which is the first symptom of syphilis.
chan·cy (chăn′ sə) ***adj-*** [**chanc·i·er, chanc·i·est**] *Informal* having a strong element of chance; risky.
chan·de·lier (shăn′ də lêr′) ***n-*** fixture that hangs from the ceiling, with branches for holding lights.

Chandelier

chan·dler (chănd′ lər) ***n-*** **1** person who makes or sells candles. **2** dealer in ship's supplies.
change (chānj) ***vt-*** [**changed, chang·ing**] (in senses **2** and **3** considered intransitive when the direct object is implied but not expressed) **1** to make different; alter; modify; transform: *to* change *one's habits*; *to* change *color*; *to* change *a dull story into an interesting one.* **2** to take and use (something) in place of something similar; switch: *to* change *one's coat*; *to* change *one's name*; *to* change *one's partner.* **3** to exchange (things) one for another; switch: *to* change *trains*; *to* change *clothes.* **4** of money, to give or get the same amount in smaller denominations for: *to* change *a quarter.* ***vi-*** to become different; alter: *The leaves* change *in the fall. He is* changing *every day.* ***n-*** **1** a making or becoming different; alteration; modification; transformation: *a* change *of scene*; *a* change *in his feelings*; change *that happens all the time.* **2** something different from one's ordinary routine, giving variety or novelty: *It would be a nice* change *to eat at a restaurant tonight.* **3** coins or bills equal in value to a coin or bill of higher denomination: *Do you have* change *for a dollar*? **4** money equal to the difference between the cost of something bought and the money given as payment: *He gave the clerk $10 and got $3.50* change. **5** coins as distinguished from bills.
for a change as a break from one's ordinary routine.
change a baby to put a clean diaper on a baby.
change a bed to put clean sheets on a bed.
change hands to shift from one owner to another.
change (one's) mind to alter one's intentions or ideas.
change (one's) tune *Informal* to alter one's behavior or attitude; speak quite differently than before.
change·a·ble (chān′ jə bəl) ***adj-*** likely to change, or to keep changing from moment to moment; variable: *a* changeable *mood.* **—*n-* change′ a·ble·ness** or **change′ a·bil′ i·ty.** ***adv-*** **change′ a·bly.**
change·ful (chānj′ fəl) ***adj-*** full of change; variable. **—*adv-* change′ ful·ly.** ***n-*** **change′ ful·ness.**
change·less (chānj′ ləs) ***adj-*** unchanging; constant. **—*adv-* change′ less·ly.** ***n-*** **change′ less·ness.**
change·ling (chānj′ lĭng) ***n-*** **1** in folklore, an elf child left by fairies in exchange for a human infant. **2** any child secretly substituted for another.
change-over (chānj′ ō′ vər) ***n-*** shift or change from one method, activity, etc., to another.
channel (chăn′ əl) ***n-*** **1** the course through which a stream, river, or brook passes; also, a tubular passage for liquids. **2** way or course for anything: *the* channels *of communication.* **3** course of thought or action: *He directed his energies into other* channels. **4** deepest part of a river, bay, etc., affording passage for ships. **5** groove or furrow: *the deep* channels *of grief in his face.* **6 channels** official ways or methods of communicating information or requests: *The general forwarded his orders through* channels. ***vt-*** **1** to cut or wear (a course, way, groove, etc.): *The river* channeled *its way over the plain.* **2** to direct or guide in a chosen course: *to* channel *a stream into another field*: *to* channel *one's talents.*

---

fāte, făt, dâre, bärn; bē, bĕt, mêre; bīte, bĭt; nōte, hŏt, môre, dȯg; fŭn, fûr; to͞o, bo͝ok; oil; out; tar; thin; *th*en; hw for wh as in *wh*at; zh for s as in u*s*ual; ə for a, e, i, o, u, as in *a*go, lin*e*n, per*i*l, at*o*m, min*u*s

chan·son (shä^n sō^n′) *French* ***n-*** song.
chant (chănt) ***n-*** **1** a song, especially a solemn, measured song. **2** any measured and repetitious singing or shouting. ***vt-*** **1** to sing; especially, to intone: *to* chant *the litany.* **2** to recite or shout in this way: *The crowd* chanted *"We want a touchdown!"* ***vi-***: *The choir* chanted *softly.*
chant·ey (shăn′tē, chăn′-) ***n-*** [*pl.* **chant·eys**] a song sailors sing in rhythm with their work. Also **chant′y.** ***Hom-*** shanty.
chan·ti·cleer (chăn′tə klêr′) ***n-*** a name for a rooster, used chiefly in medieval fables.
Cha·nu·kah (KHän′ə kə) Hanukkah.
cha·os (kā′ŏs) ***n-*** **1** great confusion; utter disorder: *The city was in* chaos *after the hurricane.* **2** (also **Chaos**) in some mythologies, the formless and disordered condition of matter from which the universe evolved.
cha·ot·ic (kā ŏt′ĭk) ***adj-*** extremely confused; without order: *a room in a* chaotic *condition*; *a* chaotic *rush of ideas.* **—*adv-*** **cha·ot′i·cal·ly.**
1**chap** (chăp) ***vt-*** [**chapped, chap·ping**] to cause to crack or become rough: *Cold* chaps *the skin.* ***vi-***: *My hands* chap *quickly.* ***n-*** a roughened spot or crack in the skin. [from earlier English **chappen,** related to 1**chop** and **chip.**]
2**chap** (chăp) *Informal* ***n-*** fellow; man or boy; guy. [once meaning "one who buys," it is a short form of the older English **chapman,** "one who buys or sells," and is related to **cheap.**]
chap. chapter.
cha·peau (shă pō′) *Informal* ***n-*** [*pl.* **cha·peaux** or **cha·peaus** (-pō′, -pōz′)] hat. [from French.]
chap·el (chăp′əl) ***n-*** **1** small church; also, an enclosed part or recess of a church with its own altar for small or special services. **2** place for religious services in a school, funeral home, etc. **3** religious services performed at a school: *Tom was late for* chapel.
chap·er·on or **chap·er·one** (shăp′ə rōn′) ***n-*** older woman who accompanies an unmarried girl in public; also, anyone who supervises the social activities of young people to maintain proper behavior. ***vt-*** [**chap·er·oned, chap·er·on·ing**]: *Her parents* chaperoned *the dance.*
chap·lain (chăp′lən) ***n-*** **1** clergyman attached to a military unit, a legislative body, a school, etc. **2** clergyman in charge of a chapel.
chap·let (chăp′lət) ***n-*** **1** garland for the head. **2** string of beads; especially, a part of a rosary.
chap·man (chăp′mən) *Brit.* ***n-*** [*pl.* **chap·men**] a peddler; hawker.
chaps (shăps, chăps) ***n-*** *pl.* protective leg coverings, usually leather, worn by cowboys. [American word, short for **chaparajos** from Mexican Spanish.]

Chaps

chap·ter (chăp′tər) ***n-*** **1** one of the main divisions of a book. **2** group forming a branch of a larger organization: *a local* chapter *of a fraternity.*
char (chär) ***vt-*** [**charred, char·ring**] **1** to blacken by partial burning: *to* char *meat by cooking it too close to a flame.* **2** to change (wood) into charcoal by partial burning.
char·ac·ter (kăr′ĭk tər) ***n-*** **1** combination of qualities typical of a thing; individual nature: *the dry and barren* character *of the desert.* **2** personal qualities by which others judge one; moral nature: *a man of heroic* character; *the weak* character *of a coward.* **3** moral excellence: *The President must be a man of* character. **4** person in a story, play, etc. **5** *Informal* odd or amusing person: *My uncle is quite a* character. **6** a mark, such as a letter of the alphabet, used as a symbol. **7** role; function: *He serves in two* characters, *that of president and that of treasurer.* **8** physical trait carried by a gene or genes.
in character conforming to typical or expected behavior: *He is always* in character. **out of character** not typical of or consistent with one's usual behavior; unexpected: *His burst of anger was* out of character.
char·ac·ter·is·tic (kär′ĭk tər ĭs′tĭk) ***adj-*** showing the distinctive qualities or traits of a person or thing; typical: *her* characteristic *kindness.* ***n-*** distinguishing mark or quality: *the* characteristics *of a scholar.* **—*adv-*** **char′ac·ter·is′ti·cal·ly:** *his* characteristically *rude behavior.*
char·ac·ter·ize (kăr′ĭk tə rīz′) ***vt-*** [**char·ac·ter·ized, char·ac·ter·iz·ing**] **1** to describe or depict; portray: *The author* characterizes *his hero as a bold man.* **2** to be a distinguishing characteristic of: *Stubbornness* characterizes *the donkey.* **—*n-*** **char′ac·ter·i·za′tion.**
cha·rade (shə rād′) ***n-*** **1** the acting out of a word, phrase, etc., to be guessed, usually by showing each syllable in pantomime. The word "persuaded" might be shown by acting out "purr," "sway," and "dead." **2 charades** game played in this way.
char·coal (chär′kōl′) ***n-*** soft, black substance consisting chiefly of carbon, produced by the partial burning of wood. It is used as fuel, for drawing, and for filtering smoke and liquids.
charge (chärj) ***vt-*** [**charged, charg·ing**] (in senses 1 and 3 considered intransitive when the direct object is implied but not expressed) **1** to require as payment: *He* charged *a dime for a candy bar. How much did they* charge *you for that hat? Do you* charge *for this service?* **2** to record the transfer of (merchandise) for which the buyer intends to pay later: *Please* charge *these groceries.* **3** to rush toward in an attack: *The troops* charged *the enemy fort.* **4** to load or fill: *to* charge *a cartridge*; *to* charge *a battery.* **5** to urge or order to do something: *The judge* charged *the jury to consider all the evidence.* **6** to make or consider responsible; indict: *The umpire* charged *the shortstop with the error.* **7** to place or lay the blame for: *The police* charged *the accident to careless driving.* ***vi-*** to go rapidly and energetically; rush: *He* charged *through the door.* ***n-*** **1** required payment: *The* charge *for parking is a dollar.* **2** a rushing attack: *The enemy* charge *was repulsed.* **3** supervisory care: *The nurse has* charge *of the children.* **4** person or thing entrusted to one's care: *the baby sitter's mischievous* charges. **5** formal or legal accusation: *The* charge *was murder.* **6** an order or instruction giving responsibility: *the judge's* charge *to the jury.* **7** material with which an apparatus, such as a cartridge, firecracker, blast furnace, etc., is loaded. **8** quantity of electrical energy possessed by an object. **9** electrical property of a particle by which it attracts or repels other particles. See also *positive charge* and *negative charge.*
in charge in the position of responsibility or authority; in command: *Who's* in charge *here?* **in charge of** in control of; responsible for: *He is* in charge of *books.*
charge·a·ble (chär′jə bəl) ***adj-*** **1** of a nature that permits charging as an expense, responsibility, etc.: *These debts are* chargeable *to him.* **2** open to a charge or accusation; liable: *He is* chargeable *with the crime.*
charge account ***n-*** business arrangement with a merchant, enabling a customer to buy goods or services and to pay for them at a later time.
char·gé d'af·faires (shär′zhā də fâr′) ***n-*** [*pl.* **char·gés d'af·faires** (shär′zhā də fâr′)] **1** diplomat who substitutes for an ambassador or minister who is absent.

2 diplomatic representative of one government sent to the minister of foreign affairs of another. [from French]

[1]**charg·er** (chär′ jər) ***n-*** **1** horse ridden into battle; war-horse. **2** something that charges, especially a device for charging storage batteries. [from **charge.**]

[2]**charg·er** (chär′ jər) *Archaic* ***n-*** large platter. [from an assumed Old French **chargeoir,** from **charger** meaning "to load (as a cart)," from Latin **carrus,** "cart."]

char·i·ly (chăr′ ə lē, châr′-) ***adv-*** in a chary manner; cautiously; sparingly.

char·i·ness (chăr′ ē nəs, châr′-) ***n-*** the quality of being chary; caution; sparingness.

char·i·ot (chăr′ ē ət) ***n-*** vehicle with two wheels, drawn by horses, used in ancient times for war, racing, etc.

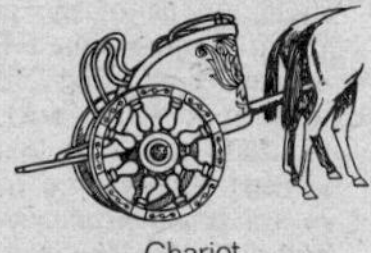
Chariot

char·i·ot·eer (chăr′ ē ə têr′) ***n-*** driver of a chariot.

char·is·ma (kə rĭz′ mə) ***n-*** **1** rare personal power that attracts the allegiance and devotion of great numbers of people. **2** in theology, spiritual gift granted to individuals to be used for the good of others, such as the power to lead. **—*adj-*** **char′ is·mat′ ic** (kăr′ əs măt′ ĭk).

char·i·ta·ble (chăr′ ə tə bəl) ***adj-*** **1** generous in helping people who are in need. **2** providing assistance for the poor: *a* charitable *institution.* **3** kindly and forgiving, especially in judging others: *It was* charitable *of you to overlook my mistakes.* **—*n-*** **char′ i·ta·ble·ness.** ***adv-*** **char′ i·ta·bly.**

char·i·ty (chăr′ ə tē) ***n-*** [*pl.* **char·i·ties**] **1** love of one's fellow men; good will, especially in judging the faults of others: *"With malice toward none, with* charity *for all . . ."* **2** assistance given voluntarily to the poor, the sick, and other needy people. **3** organization that assists the needy: *Give to your favorite* charity.

char·la·tan (shär′ lə tən) ***n-*** person who deceives others by claiming to have special skill or knowledge that he does not possess; quack.

char·la·tan·ism (shär′ lə tən ĭz′ əm) ***n-*** deceitful practices or trickery of a charlatan. Also **char′ la·tan·ry** (shär′ lə tən rē) [*pl.* **char′ la·tan·ries**].

Charles·ton (chärl′ stən) ***n-*** lively ballroom dance that first became popular in the 1920's.

char·ley horse (chär′ lē hôrs′) *Informal* ***n-*** muscular soreness and stiffness in an arm or leg, caused by strain.

char·lotte russe (shär′ lət rōōs′) ***n-*** dessert usually consisting of sponge cake topped by whipped cream.

charm (chärm) ***n-*** **1** power to attract and please; fascination: *Paris has great* charm *for tourists.* **2** trait that attracts and pleases: *Her friendly smile is her chief* charm. **3** word, verse, object, etc., supposed to have magic power or to bring good luck. **4** trinket worn on a bracelet, chain, etc. ***vt-*** **1** to attract and please: *His friendliness* charmed *the audience.* **2** to act on by, or as if by, magic: *Her sympathy* charmed *his fears away.* **—*n-*** **charm′ er.**

charm·ing (chär′ mĭng) ***adj-*** pleasing and attractive, delightful; fascinating. **—*adv-*** **charm′ ing·ly.**

char·nel house (chär′ nəl) ***n-*** vault, room, etc., in which the bodies or bones of the dead are placed.

Char·on (kâr′ ən) ***n-*** in Greek mythology, the boatman who ferried the souls of the dead over the river Styx to Hades.

chart (chärt) ***n-*** map, especially one for use by mariners, showing depths of water, rocks and islands, currents, etc. **2** sheet of paper giving information in the form of graphs, diagrams, or other illustrations: *a weather* chart; *an anatomy* chart. ***vt-*** to mark (a flight, voyage, or other journey) on a map; hence, to plan: *to* chart *one's future.*

char·ter (chär′ tər) ***n-*** **1** official document giving certain rights and privileges: *The king granted William Penn a* charter *to form the colony of Pennsylvania.* **2** declaration giving the aims or principles of a group or organization: *the* charter *of the United Nations.* **3** a leasing or renting of (a plane, bus, boat, etc.) for private use: *Captain Smith has made his boat available for* charter. *as* ***modifier:*** *a* charter *colony; a* charter *flight; a* charter *pilot.* ***vt-*** **1** to grant or give a charter to: *to* charter *a new organization.* **2** to hire or lease temporarily for private use: *to* charter *a bus.*

char·treuse (shär trōōz′, -trōōs′) ***n-*** **1** liqueur, usually pale green or yellow, originally made by French Carthusian monks. **2** a light, bright, yellowish green. ***adj-***: *a* chartreuse *scarf.*

char·wom·an (chär′ wŏŏ′ mən) *chiefly Brit.* ***n-*** [*pl.* **char·wom·en**] woman hired by the day to do household chores or to clean offices in a large building.

char·y (châr′ ē) ***adj-*** [**char·i·er, char·i·est**] **1** careful; cautious; wary: *She is* chary *of talking to strangers.* **2** not free or extravagant; sparing: *to be* chary *in giving.*

Cha·ryb·dis (kə rĭb′ dĭs) See *Scylla.*

[1]**chase** (chās) ***vt-*** [**chased, chas·ing**] **1** to go after and try to catch; pursue: *to* chase *a rabbit.* **2** to get rid of by or as if by driving away: *to* chase *chickens out of the garden; to* chase *a child's fears away.* ***vi-*** *Informal* to rush about: *I've* chased *all over town looking for you.* ***n-*** **1** energetic pursuit: *After a long* chase, *they caught the thief.* **2 the chase** hunting as a sport. [from Old French **chacier,** from Late Latin **captiāre** meaning "seek to catch."]

give chase to follow in pursuit.

[2]**chase** (chās) ***vt-*** [**chased, chas·ing**] to decorate (metal) by embossing or engraving: *to* chase *silver.* [from earlier **enchase.**]

chasm (kăz′ əm) ***n-*** deep opening in the earth; gorge.

chas·sis (shăs′ ē, chăs′-) ***n-*** [*pl.* **chas·sis** (-ēz)] **1** steel frame, engine, springs, wheels, etc., on which the body of a motor vehicle is mounted. **2** metal framework which holds the tubes and other electrical components of a radio or television set. **3** main landing gear of an airplane; also, the plane's body framework.

chaste (chāst) ***adj-*** **1** pure and virtuous. **2** simple and restrained in style or taste. **—*adv-*** **chaste′ ly.** ***n-*** **chaste′ ness.**

chas·ten (chā′ sən) ***vt-*** **1** to punish for the purpose of correcting; discipline. **2** to curb; tame; subdue: *Experience may* chasten *his reckless spirit.*

chas·tise (chăs′ tīz′) ***vt-*** [**chas·tised, chas·tis·ing**] to punish or discipline severely.

chas·tise·ment (chăs tīz′ mənt, chăs′ təz-) ***n-*** severe punishment or discipline.

chas·ti·ty (chăs′ tə tē) ***n-*** **1** moral purity; virtue; innocence. **2** simplicity in design or style.

cha·su·ble (chăz′ ə bəl, chăs′-) ***n-*** sleeveless outer garment worn by a priest celebrating Mass or the Eucharist.

chat (chăt) ***vi-*** [**chat·ted, chat·ting**] to converse in an easy, friendly way. ***n-*** **1** an informal, friendly talk or conversation. **2** any of various songbirds, especially a North American warbler, the **yellow-breasted chat.**

châ·teau (shă tō′) *French* ***n-*** [*pl.* **châ·teaux** (-tō′)] 1 castle. 2 large country house in France, or a house built in a similar style.

chat·e·laine (shăt′ ə lān′) ***n-*** 1 the lady of a château or castle. 2 chain or clasp worn at a woman's waist, to which a purse, keys, or trinkets may be attached.

chat·tel (chăt′ əl) ***n-*** article of personal property that is not a house or piece of land; movable possession, such as a piece of furniture.

chat·ter (chăt′ ər) ***vi-*** 1 to make short, rapid sounds, as some monkeys and birds do. 2 to talk fast and foolishly; jabber. 3 to make a rattling or clacking sound: *My teeth* chattered *from the cold.* ***n-*** 1 foolish or pointless talk; gabble. 2 short, sharp, repeated sounds. ***—n-*** **chat′ ter·er.**

chat·ter·box (chăt′ ər bŏks′) ***n-*** person who talks all the time.

chat·ty (chăt′ ē) ***adj-*** [**chat·ti·er, chat·ti·est**] given to or full of friendly informal talk, news, etc.: *a* chatty *person*; *a* chatty *newspaper column.* ***—adv-*** **chat′ ti·ly.** ***n-*** **chat′ ti·ness.**

chauf·feur (shō′ fər, shō fûr′) ***n-*** person whose work is driving an automobile, especially a limousine. ***vt-*** to have the job of driving: *He* chauffeured *his aunt around town.* ***vi-***: *He* chauffeurs *for a living.*

Chau·tau·qua or **chau·tau·qua** (shə tô′ kwə) ***n-*** 1 popular summer educational course for adults offered at Chautauqua, New York. 2 similar program conducted by traveling lecturers and performing artists.

chau·vin·ism (shō′ və nĭz′ əm) ***n-*** blind, exaggerated, and uncritical pride in one's own group or nation, associated with militarism and, often, racism. ***—n-*** **chau′ vin·ist.** ***adj-*** **chau′ vin·is′ tic.**

cheap (chēp) ***adj-*** [**cheap·er, cheap·est**] 1 low in cost: *a* cheap *car*; *a* cheap *victory.* 2 of poor quality; in bad taste; mean and low: *a* cheap *novel*; *his* cheap *remarks.* 3 charging low prices or rates: *a* cheap *department store.* 4 selfish about spending money; ungenerous; stingy. ***Hom-*** cheep. ***—adv-*** **cheap′ ly.** ***n-*** **cheap′ ness.**

cheap·en (chē′ pən) ***vt-*** to make cheap; lower the price or value of. ***vi-*** to become cheap.

cheap·skate (chēp′ skāt′) *Informal* ***n-*** stingy person.

cheat (chēt) ***vi-*** to act dishonestly or use trickery to gain an advantage: *to* cheat *on a test.* ***vt-*** to deceive, trick, or swindle: *to* cheat *a customer.* ***n-*** (also **cheat′ er**) person who acts dishonestly or deceitfully.

check (chĕk) ***n-*** 1 person or thing that controls or limits: *Contour plowing acts as a* check *on soil erosion.* 2 test or investigation; verification: *a* check *on his figures*; *a* check *on the pupil's progress*; *a loyalty* check. 3 mark (√) used to show that something has been examined or verified. 4 written order to a bank to pay a specified amount from the account of the signer to the person or place named on the order; draft. 5 a bill in a restaurant. 6 ticket, tag, or disk given to reclaim clothes or luggage left for temporary safekeeping. 7 pattern of squares; also, one of the squares in the pattern. ***vt-*** 1 to stop or control; restrain; curb: *to* check *the spread of disease.* 2 to test or examine for accuracy, efficiency, etc.; verify: *to* check *a gauge every hour*; *to* check *a person's qualifications.* 3 to mark with a check (√). 4 to leave (clothes or luggage) for temporary safekeeping: *to* check *a coat.* ***vi-*** to correspond accurately; agree; be in harmony: *Our figures* check *with his.* ***interj-*** in chess, a warning to one's opponent that his king may be captured. ***Hom-*** Czech.

in check 1 under control; in restraint: *He kept his temper* in check. 2 of a king in chess, in a position of exposure to being captured.

check in to register as a guest at a hotel, inn, etc.

check on or **check up on** to investigate; inquire into: *to* check *on a story.*

check out 1 to pay one's bill and leave a hotel, inn, etc. 2 *Informal* to be correct, accurate, etc.

check·book (chĕk′ bŏŏk′) ***n-*** book containing bank check forms.

[1]**check·er** (chĕk′ ər) ***n-*** person who checks, especially an employee whose duty it is to check items for price, safekeeping, delivery, etc: *a package* checker. [from **check.**]

[2]**check·er** (chĕk′ ər) ***n-*** 1 one of the squares of a pattern marked in squares of alternating colors. 2 the pattern itself. 3 one of the pieces used in playing checkers. [from **checkers,** used for the game, from Old French **eschequier** meaning "chessboard."]

check·ered (chĕk′ ərd) ***adj-*** 1 marked with squares of alternate colors or textures, or seeming to be so patterned: *a* checkered *tablecloth*; *a landscape* checkered *by woods and meadows.* 2 marked by changes of fortune, especially for the worse; full of ups and downs: *a* checkered *career.*

check·ers (chĕk′ ərz) ***n-*** (takes singular verb) game for two people, each playing with twelve disks called checkers, which are moved across a **check′ er·board′** of 64 squares.

Checkerboard

checking account ***n-*** bank account from which the depositor may withdraw money by check at any time.

check·mate (chĕk′ māt′) ***n-*** 1 in chess, the putting an opponent's king in such a position that he cannot escape. 2 any complete obstruction or defeat. ***vt-*** [**check·mat·ed, check·mat·ing**] to obstruct or defeat utterly: *to* checkmate *a plan.*

check·rein (chĕk′ rān′) ***n-*** 1 short rein reaching from the bit to the saddle of the harness and used to keep the horse's head up. 2 either of two cross reins between the driving rein of one horse and the bit of the other in a team.

check·room (chĕk′ rōōm′) ***n-*** room where people may leave coats, packages, etc. for a short time.

check·up (chĕk′ ŭp′) ***n-*** thorough examination to determine the condition of something: *a routine physical* checkup; *a government* checkup *of housing.*

Ched·dar (chĕd′ ər) ***n-*** any of several kinds of firm, crumbly, yellow cheeses originally made in Cheddar, England.

cheek (chēk) ***n-*** 1 either side of the face below the eyes and above the level of the mouth. 2 impudence; insolence: *He had the* cheek *to disobey orders.*

cheek by jowl 1 close together; touching or almost touching. 2 intimate; familiar.

cheek·y (chē′ kē) *Informal* ***adj-*** [**cheek·i·er, cheek·i·est**] impudent; insolent. ***—adv-*** **cheek′ i·ly.** ***n-*** **cheek′ i·ness.**

cheep (chēp) ***n-*** shrill, weak note, such as that of a young bird; peep. ***vi-*** to peep. ***Hom-*** cheap.

cheer (chêr) ***n-*** 1 shout of joy, approval, or encouragement: *a* cheer *for our team.* 2 encouragement; comfort: *The doctor's report gave us some* cheer. 3 high spirits; gaiety: especially in the phrase **be of good cheer.** ***vt-***: *The crowd* cheered *the winning runner. The words of praise* cheered *him.* ***vi-***: *The delegates* cheered *wildly.*

cheer on to urge on; incite: *to* cheer on *the team.*

cheer up to make or become hopeful or glad.

cheer·ful (chêr′ fəl) ***adj-*** **1** in good spirits; gay: *a* cheerful *person.* **2** bringing cheer: *a* cheerful *fire.* **3** willing; eager: *a* cheerful *worker.* ***—adv-*** **cheer′ ful·ly.** ***n-*** **cheer′ ful·ness.**

cheer·lead·er (chêr′ lē′ dər) ***n-*** person who leads the cheering at certain sports events.

cheer·less (chêr′ ləs) ***adj-*** gloomy; forlorn; dismal. ***—adv-*** **cheer′ less·ly.** ***n-*** **cheer′ less·ness.**

cheer·y (chêr′ ē) ***adj-*** [**cheer·i·er, cheer·i·est**] lively and merry, gay and bright: *a* cheery *smile*; *a room painted in* cheery *colors.* ***—adv-*** **cheer′ i·ly.** ***n-*** **cheer′ i·ness.**

cheese (chēz) ***n-*** food made of the pressed curd of milk.

cheese·burg·er (chēz′ bûr′ gər) ***n-*** hamburger topped with melted cheese.

cheese·cloth (chēz′ klòth′) ***n-*** thin, loosely woven cotton cloth.

chees·y (chē′ zē) ***adj-*** [**chees·i·er, chees·i·est**] **1** having the taste, smell, or consistency of cheese. **2** *Slang* cheap; inferior; poorly made.

chee·tah (chē′ tə) ***n-*** swift leopardlike cat found in parts of Africa and, formerly, Persia and India. It is often trained to hunt.

Cheetah, about 3 ft. high at shoulder

chef (shĕf) ***n-*** **1** head cook of a hotel or restaurant. **2** any male cook.

chef d'oeu·vre (shā dûv′ rə) *French* [*pl.* **chefs d'oeu·vre**] masterpiece.

che·lo·ni·an (kə lō′ nē ən) ***n-*** any of the order of reptiles consisting of the tortoises or turtles. ***adj-***: *a* chelonian *skeleton.*

chem. **1** chemical. **2** chemist. **3** chemistry.

chem·i·cal (kĕm′ ĭ kəl) ***adj-*** **1** pertaining to chemistry: *a* chemical *experiment.* **2** produced by, or used in the operations of chemistry: *a* chemical *compound.* ***n-*** a substance such as alcohol, hydrogen, soda, or the like, produced by or used in a chemical process. ***—adv-*** **chem′ i·cal·ly.**

chemical engineering ***n-*** the applied science that deals with the design of chemical plants and processes.

che·mise (shə mēz′) ***n-*** **1** woman's sleeveless undergarment, usually knee length. **2** a straight dress fitting closely and having no marked waistline.

chem·ist (kĕm′ ĭst) ***n-*** **1** person trained in chemistry and, usually, engaged in it as a profession. **2** *Brit.* druggist.

chem·is·try (kĕm′ ə strē′) ***n-*** **1** the science that deals with the characteristics and composition of substances, how they are formed, how they change, and how they react. **2** chemical composition, properties, and reactions of substances: *the* chemistry *of rubber.* **3** chemical processes, especially of living things: *body* chemistry.

chem·o·ther·a·py (kĕm′ ō thĕr′ ə pē) ***n-*** treatment and control of diseases by the use of chemical drugs.

chem·ur·gy (kĕm′ ûr′ jē) ***n-*** branch of chemistry that finds new uses for agricultural products, especially as raw materials for chemical manufacturing.

che·nille (shə nēl′) ***n-*** **1** yarn with a long, velvety pile used in tufting and fringing: *a pillow edged with* chenille. **2** fabric made with such yarn. ***adj-***: *a* chenille *spread.*

cheque (chĕk) *Brit.* ***n-*** a check or draft on a bank.

cher·ish (chĕr′ ĭsh) ***vt-*** **1** to love; care for tenderly: *She* cherishes *her children.* **2** to hold dear; keep in mind; treasure: *Grandmother* cherished *her childhood memories.* **3** to cling to: *He* cherished *the hope of being famous.*

Cher·o·kee (chĕr′ ə kē) ***n-*** [*pl.* **Cher·o·kees,** also **Cher·o·kee**] **1** member of a tribe of American Indians related to the Iroquois. The Cherokees formerly lived in southeastern Georgia and the Carolinas, and now live in Oklahoma. **2** the language of this tribe. ***adj-***: *the* Cherokee *alphabet.*

Cherokee rose ***n-*** a white rose grown in the southern United States, originally from China.

che·root (chə ro͞ot′, shə-) ***n-*** cigar with both ends square.

cher·ry (chĕr′ ē) ***n-*** [*pl.* **cher·ries**] **1** tree related to the plum, bearing a small, smooth, fleshy fruit with a stone in the center. **2** the fruit or the wood of this tree. **3** a bright red like that of a red variety of this fruit. ***adj-***: *The fabric is* cherry *in color.*

chert (chûrt) ***n-*** gray to brownish-black kind of flint found in limestones.

cher·ub (chĕr′ əb) ***n-*** **1** [*pl.* **cher·u·bim** (-ə bĭm′)] an angel of the second rank of the nine orders, often represented in art as a beautiful winged child or head of a child. **2** [*pl.* **cher·ubs**] a lovely, sweet child.

cher·vil (chûr′ vəl) ***n-*** any of several European herbs related to parsley, especially two kinds used in salads and soups.

Chesh·ire cat (chĕsh′ ər) ***n-*** the grinning cat in "Alice in Wonderland," who gradually faded away until only its grin remained.

chess (chĕs) ***n-*** a game played by two persons, each having 16 pieces called **chess′ men,** which are moved about on a **chess′ board** of 64 squares.

Chessboard

chest (chĕst) ***n-*** **1** upper front part of a human body, enclosed by the ribs and containing the heart and lungs. **2** large box with a lid, used for storage or shipping; also, the amount contained in it: *a* chest *for linen*; *a* chest *of tea.* **3** (also **chest of drawers**) piece of furniture with drawers for storing clothes.

ches·ter·field (chĕs′ tər fēld′) ***n-*** **1** slightly fitted cloth topcoat with a velvet collar, for men or women. **2** davenport with straight arms. *as **modifier***: *a* chesterfield *coat*; *a* chesterfield *sofa.*

chest·nut (chĕs′ nŭt′) ***n-*** **1** tree of the beech family bearing nuts in a prickly bur. **2** nut or the wood of this tree. **3** a reddish-brown color. **4** horse with a reddish-brown coat, mane, and tail. **5** *Slang* an old or stale joke. ***adj-***: *a* chestnut *log*; *a* chestnut *horse.*

Chestnut bur and nuts

chev·a·lier (shĕv′ ə lêr′, *Fr.* shə văl yā′) ***n-*** **1** knight. **2** in France, a member of an order of merit: *a* chevalier *of the Legion of Honor.*

chev·i·ot (shĕv′ ē ət) ***n-*** **1** heavy wool fabric with a rough twill weave. **2** any fabric with this weave.

chev·ron (shĕv′ rən) ***n-*** mark or emblem showing rank or length of service made of stripes meeting at an angle and worn on the sleeve of a noncommissioned officer, policeman, etc.

Chevrons

fāte, făt, dâre, bärn; bē, bĕt, mêre; bīte, bĭt; nōte, hŏt, môre, dòg; fŭn, fûr; to͞o, bo͝ok; oil; out; tar; thin; then; hw for wh as in *wh*at; zh for s as in u*s*ual; ə for a, e, i, o, u, as in *a*go, lin*e*n, per*i*l, at*o*m, min*u*s

chew (cho͞o) ***vt-*** to crush and grind (food, gum, etc.) with the teeth; masticate. ***n-*** piece of gum, tobacco, or the like, held in the mouth and chewed.

chewing gum ***n-*** sweetened flavored chicle for chewing.

che·wink (chĭ wingk′) ***n-*** towhee.

chew·y (cho͞o′ē) ***adj-*** **[chew·i·er, chew·i·est]** soft but very sticky or viscous and needing much chewing to eat. **—*n-* chew′i·ness.**

Chey·enne (shī ăn′, -ĕn′) ***n-*** [*pl.* **Chey·ennes,** also **Chey·enne**] member of a tribe of Algonquian Indians who formerly ranged over the Dakota plains and now live in Montana and Oklahoma. ***adj-*** *a* Cheyenne *village.*

Chib·cha (chĭb′chə) ***n-*** [*pl.* **Chib·chas,** also **Chib·cha**] member of an extinct, culturally advanced South American Indian tribe of Colombia. **—*adj-* Chib′chan.**

chic (shēk) ***adj-*** stylish; fashionable; smart: *a* chic *black dress.* ***Hom-*** sheik.

chi·can·er·y (chĭ kā′nə rē) ***n-*** the use of trickery and deception for one's own advantage; sophistry: *The lawyer's courtroom* chicanery *was obvious to the judge.*

Chi·ca·no (chē kä′nō) ***n-*** [*pl.* **Chi·ca·nos**] American of Mexican descent. **—*n-*** *fem.* **Chi·ca′na** (-nä). ***adj-*** *the* Chicano *culture.*

chick (chĭk) ***n-*** **1** baby chicken. **2** baby bird. **3** young child.

chick·a·dee (chĭk′ə dē′) ***n-*** small bird having a grayish body with black, brown, and white markings, and a black cap.

Chick·a·saw (chĭk′ə sò′) ***n-*** [*pl.* **Chick·a·saws,** also **Chick·a·saw**] member of a tribe of American Indians of Mississippi and Alabama. ***adj-***: *the* Chickasaw *dialect.*

chick·en (chĭk′ən) ***n-*** **1** hen or rooster, especially a young one. **2** any young bird. **3** the flesh of hen or rooster, used as food.

chick·en·coop (chĭk′ən ko͞op′) ***n-*** a cage or pen in which chickens are kept.

chick·en·heart·ed (chĭk′ən här′təd) ***adj-*** cowardly; fearful.

chicken pox ***n-*** mild contagious disease, causing red spots on the skin.

chick·weed (chĭk′wēd′) ***n-*** a common white-flowering weed, the seeds and young leaves of which are eaten by birds.

chic·le (chĭk′əl) ***n-*** a gum obtained from certain Central American trees, used in making chewing gum.

chic·o·ry (chĭk′ə rē) ***n-*** **1** plant related to lettuce, and having showy blue flowers. **2** the broad, curly leaves of this plant, eaten as salad; curly endive. **3** the root of this plant, often roasted and added to coffee.

chide (chīd) ***vt-*** [**chid·ed** or **chid** (chĭd), **chid·ed** or **chid** or **chid·den** (chĭd′ən), **chid·ing**] to scold; rebuke: *The teacher* chided *him for being rude.*

chief (chēf) ***n-*** the head or leader of a group, organization, department, etc.: *an Indian* chief; *a* chief *of police.* ***adj-*** **1** highest in rank or authority; head: *the* chief *clerk.* **2** most important; leading; principal: *the* chief *crop.*

Chief Executive ***n-*** the President of the United States.

chief justice ***n-*** **1** the presiding judge of a court composed of several judges. **2 Chief Justice** the presiding judge of the U.S. Supreme Court.

chief·ly (chēf′lē) ***adv-*** principally; for the most part: *Candy is made* chiefly *of sugar.*

chief of staff ***n-*** **1** in the armed forces, the highest-ranking staff officer in a division or higher, and chief adviser to the commanding officer. **2 Chief of Staff** senior officer of the Army or Air Force.

chief·tain (chēf′tən) ***n-*** leader of a tribe, clan, etc.; chief: *a Seneca* chieftain.

chief·tain·cy (chēf′tən sē) ***n-*** [*pl.* **chief·tain·cies**] **1** position or rank of a chieftain. **2** government headed by a chieftain. Also **chief′tain·ship.**

chif·fon (shĭ fŏn′, shĭf′ŏn′) ***n-*** soft, thin, transparent fabric. ***adj-*** **1** made of this fabric: *a* chiffon *dress.* **2** very light and fluffy: *a* chiffon *pie.*

chif·fo·nier (shĭf′ə nêr′) ***n-*** a high chest of drawers, sometimes with a mirror.

chig·ger (chĭg′ər) ***n-*** tiny, reddish, wormlike larva of a kind of mite. It sucks the blood of human beings, causing an itchy rash.

chi·hua·hua (chē wä′wä′, -wə) ***n-*** tiny dog with a slender body and large, pointed ears, native to Mexico.

chil·blain (chĭl′blān′) ***n-*** an itching, inflamed swelling, usually on the foot or hand, caused by exposure to cold.

child (chīld) ***n-*** [*pl.* **child·ren** (chĭl′drən)] **1** baby. **2** young boy or girl. **3** son or daughter. **4** offspring.

child·birth (chīld′bûrth′) ***n-*** the act of giving birth to a child.

child·hood (chīld′ho͝od′) ***n-*** the time of being a child.

child·ish (chīl′dish) ***adj-*** **1** like a child. **2** foolish; immature: *a* childish *impulse.* **—*adj-* child′ish·ly.** ***n-*** **child′ish·ness.**

►Should not be confused with CHILDLIKE.

child labor ***n-*** the employment of children by a factory, business, etc., now limited by state or federal law.

child·less (chīld′ləs) ***adj-*** having no children; without offspring. **—*n-* child′less·ness.**

child·like (chīld′līk′) ***adj-*** like a child, especially having the pleasant qualities of a child, such as frankness, eagerness, etc.

►Should not be confused with CHILDISH.

chil·dren (chĭl′drən) *pl.* of **child.**

chil·i (chĭl′ē) ***n-*** [*pl.* **chil·lies**] **1** the ripe, red pods of a tropical pepper plant, or a powdered seasoning made from them. **2** dish of meat and beans flavored with this seasoning. ***Hom-*** chilly.

chili sauce ***n-*** condiment made by cooking together tomatoes, chopped onions, celery, chili, etc.

chill (chĭl) ***n-*** **1** coldness: *an autumn* chill *in the air.* **2** sudden cold feeling in the body, accompanied by shivering. **3** a check upon enthusiasm: *She put a* chill *on the party.* ***adj-*** **1** very cool: *In the evening a* chill *breeze blew across the lake.* **2** not warm or friendly; discouraging: *He met with a* chill *response to his offer of help.* ***vt-*** to make cold: *Please* chill *the fruit.* ***vi-*** to become or feel cold.

chill·y (chĭl′ē) ***adj-*** [**chill·i·er, chill·i·est**] **1** very cool; rather cold: *a* chilly *day.* **2** without warmth; unfriendly: *a* chilly *reception.* ***Hom-*** chili. **—*adv-* chill′i·ly.** ***n-*** **chill′i·ness.**

chime (chīm) ***n-*** **1** set of bells tuned to a musical scale. **2** the sound of such bells. ***vi-*** **[chimed, chim·ing]** to ring: *The bells* chimed *at noon.* ***vt-*** to indicate or announce (the hour) by ringing.

chime in to join in (a conversation, singing, etc.).

chi·me·ra (kī mêr′ə, kə-) ***n-*** **1** in Greek mythology, a fire-belching she-monster, with a lion's head, a goat's body, and a serpent's tail. **2** a frightful creature of the imagination. **3** a wild or fanciful idea. Also **chi·mae′ra.**

chi·mer·i·cal (kə mĕr′ĭ kəl) or **chi·mer·ic** (-mĕr′ĭk) ***adj-*** **1** fantastic; imaginary; visionary: *a* chimerical *plan to redistribute the earth's population.* **2** given to fanciful thinking; full of wild dreams; visionary.

chim·ney (chĭm′nē) ***n-*** **1** an outlet for smoke from a fireplace, furnace, etc., especially the part extending above the roof of a house. **2** the glass tube shielding the flame of a lamp or lantern.

chimney pot ***n-*** earthenware or metal pipe placed on the top of a chimney to improve the draft.

chimney sweep ***n-*** person whose work is to clean chimneys.

chimney swift ***n-*** small, short-tailed, sooty-colored American swift that nests in chimneys. Also called **chimney swallow.**

chim·pan·zee (chĭm′ păn′ zē′, chĭm păn′ zē) ***n-*** highly intelligent ape of equatorial Africa, somewhat smaller than the gorilla.

Chimpanzee, 4 1/2 to 5 ft. tall

chin (chĭn) ***n-*** the part of the face below the mouth. ***vt-*** **[chinned, chin·ning]** to pull (oneself) up by the hands on a horizontal bar until the level of the chin is just above the bar.

chi·na (chī′ nə) ***n-*** **1** fine porcelain with a white background, made of clay baked in a special way, originally produced in China. **2** dishes made of china or other porcelain: *a set of* china. ***adj-***: *a* china *teapot.*

chi·na·ber·ry (chī′ nə bĕr′ ē) ***n-*** [*pl.* **chi·na·ber·ries**] small to medium-sized shade tree of the southern United States with clusters of purple flowers and yellow berries. Also **China tree.**

chi·na·ware (chī′ nə wâr′) ***n-*** dishes, plates, cups, etc., made of china or other porcelain; china.

chinch (chĭnch) ***n-*** **1** bedbug. **2** chinch bug. [American word from Spanish **chinche,** from Latin **cimex** meaning "bedbug."]

chinch bug ***n-*** small, white-winged, black insect that is very destructive to cereal grasses.

chin·chil·la (chĭn chĭl′ ə) ***n-*** **1** a small gnawing animal of the Andes with a soft, fine, pearl-gray fur. **2** the fur of this animal. **3** a heavy woolen cloth.

chine (chīn) ***n-*** **1** backbone; spine. **2** cut of meat with the backbone in it.

Chi·nese (chī nēz′) ***n-*** [*pl.* **Chi·nese**] **1** a native of China or one of his descendants. **2** a citizen of the Republic of China or of the People's Republic of China. **3** a group of related languages spoken in China, especially the standard language, Mandarin. ***adj-*** of or pertaining to China, its people, or their culture.

Chinese lantern ***n-*** collapsible paper lantern made in bright colors and of ornamental shape.

Chinese puzzle ***n-*** **1** intricate puzzle invented by the Chinese. **2** something very complicated and hard to solve: *How to handle big city traffic is becoming a* Chinese puzzle.

Chinese Wall ***n-*** wall about 1400 miles long built by the Chinese for defense against the Mongols during the third century B.C.

Chinese white ***n-*** artists' name for pure ground zinc oxide, or a paint made from it; zinc white.

[1]**chink** (chĭngk) ***n-*** a narrow crack or opening. ***vt-*** to fill the cracks of: *The walls of the log cabin were* chinked *with earth.* [probably from Old English **cinu** also meaning "a crack."]

[2]**chink** (chĭngk) ***n-*** ringing or tinkling sound like that made by small pieces of metal or glass striking together. [probably from the imitation of a sound.]

chi·nook (chī nŏŏk′) ***n-*** **1** warm, moist sea wind blowing onto the coasts of Oregon and Washington. **2** warm dry wind blowing down the eastern slopes of the Rocky Mountains. [American word from the name of the Indian tribe.]

Chi·nook (chī nŏŏk′) ***n-*** [*pl.* **Chi·nooks,** also **Chi·nook**] **1** member of a tribe of American Indians who formerly lived in Oregon along the north shore of the Columbia River. **2** the language of these Indians. ***—adj-*** **Chi·nook′ an.**

Chinook jargon ***n-*** the blend of Chinook, English, and French used by early traders and settlers in the Northwest and the Pacific Coast areas.

chin·qua·pin (chĭng′ kə pĭn′) ***n-*** **1** any of several chestnut trees, especially the common or dwarf chinquapin. **2** a related chestnut of the Pacific Coast. **3** the sweet nut of any of these trees. [American word from Algonquian.]

chintz (chĭntz) ***n-*** cotton cloth with a smooth, glossy finish, often printed in bold colorful patterns.

chip (chĭp) ***n-*** **1** small bit or piece cut or broken off wood, stone, metal, or china. **2** gap left when a small piece is broken from something. **3** small, thin slice of a food: *a potato* chip. **4** round, flat counter used in games of chance. ***vt-*** **[chipped, chip·ping]** to cut or break small bits or pieces from: *to* chip *ice.* ***vi-***: *The dish* chipped *when I dropped it.* ***—n-*** **chip′ per.**

chip·munk (chĭp′ mŭngk′) ***n-*** small, striped, burrowing animal related to squirrels and gophers. [American word from American Indian **atchitamon** meaning "(he who descends from trees) head first."]

Chipmunk, about 10 in. long

chipped beef ***n-*** dried smoked beef cut in very thin slices. Also called **dried beef.**

chip·per (chĭp′ ər) *Informal* ***adj-*** lively and cheerful; spruce; sprightly: *He looks* chipper *for an old man.*

Chip·pe·wa (chĭp′ ə wô′, -wä′) ***n-*** [*pl.* **Chip·pe·was,** also **Chip·pe·wa**] member of a tribe of Algonquian Indians who formerly lived in the regions around Lake Superior and Lake Huron. ***adj-***: *the ruffled* Chippewa *moccasin.*

chipping sparrow (chĭp′ ĭng) ***n-*** small sparrow, reddish brown on the top of the head, very common in eastern North America.

Chi·ron (kī′ rŏn′) ***n-*** in Greek mythology, a wise centaur, teacher of Achilles and other Greek heroes.

chi·rop·o·dist (kə rŏp′ ə dĭst′) ***n-*** podiatrist.

chi·rop·o·dy (kə rŏp′ ə dē′) ***n-*** podiatry.

chi·ro·prac·tic (kī′ rō prăk′ tĭk) ***n-*** a system of treating bodily disorders by manipulating the joints, especially of the spine, without the use of drugs or surgery. ***as modifier***: *a* chiropractic *school.*

chi·ro·prac·tor (kī′ rō prăk′ tər) ***n-*** one who treats bodily diseases by manipulating the joints, especially of the spine.

chi·rop·ter (kī rŏp′ tər) ***n-*** any member of the order of winged mammals **(Chiroptera)**, made up only of the bats; bat. Also **chi·rop′ te·ran.**

chirp (chûrp) ***n-*** short, sharp sound made by birds and insects. ***vi-*** to make such a sound.

chirr (chûr) ***n-*** vibrant, trilling sound, short and usually repeated, made by some insects such as grasshoppers and crickets. ***vi-***: *A cricket* chirred. ***Hom-*** churr.

chir·rup (chĭr′ əp) ***n-*** sound of chirping repeatedly. ***vi-*** to chirp repeatedly.

---

fāte, făt, dâre, bärn; bē, bĕt, mêre; bīte, bĭt; nōte, hŏt, môre, dôg; fŭn, fûr; tōō, bŏŏk; oil; out; tar; thin; then; hw for wh as in *wh*at; zh for s as in u*s*ual; ə for a, e, i, o, u, as in *a*go, lin*e*n, per*i*l, at*o*m, min*u*s

chis·el (chĭz′ əl) ***n-*** tool with a sharp steel edge for cutting, shaping, or engraving. ***vi-* 1** to cut or shape with such a tool. **2** *Slang* to cheat; to get something by shrewd, deceitful means: *He* chisels *from his friends.* ***vt-***: *to* chisel *a statue out of marble.* **—*n-* chis′ el·er.**

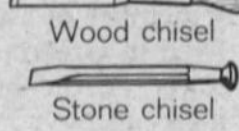
Wood chisel
Stone chisel

chis·eled (chĭz′ əld) ***adj-* 1** cut or shaped by a chisel. **2** having clearly defined features, as if cut by a chisel: *a* chiseled *profile.* Also **chis′ elled.**

Chisholm Trail (chĭz′ əm) ***n-*** popular route for driving cattle northward, extending from San Antonio, Texas, to Abilene, Kansas and used chiefly from 1867 to 1885.

1**chit** (chĭt) ***n-* 1** child. **2** person compared with a child, especially a pert, forward girl or young woman: *a* chit *of a girl.* [apparently a use of the dialect word **chit** meaning "kitten; puss."]

2**chit** (chĭt) ***n-*** short note written for any social or business purpose, such as an invitation, an acknowledgment of a debt, etc., used especially in the Orient. [short for **chitty,** from Hindi **citthi** of the same meaning.]

chit-chat (chĭt′ chăt′) ***n-*** small talk; prattle; gossip. ***vi-*** **[chit-chat·ted, chit-chat·ting]**: *We don't mind the interruption; we are just* chit-chatting.

chi·tin (kī′ tən) ***n-*** tough, horny substance, the main material in the shells and skins of insects and crustaceans. **—*adj-* chi′ tin·ous.**

chit·ter·lings (chĭt′ lənz) ***n-*** the small intestines of pigs, calves, etc., especially as prepared for food. Also **chit′ lings** or **chit′ lins.**

chiv·al·ric (shə văl′ rĭk) ***adj-*** relating to medieval chivalry.

chiv·al·rous (shĭv′ əl rəs) ***adj-* 1** relating to chivalry. **2** gallant; considerate (used especially of a gentleman in reference to his manner toward a lady). **—*adv-* chiv′ al·rous·ly. *n-* chiv′ al·rous·ness.**

chiv·al·ry (shĭv′ əl rē) ***n-* 1** the ideal qualities of a knight, such as courage, honor, and courtesy. **2** the system of knighthood. **3** a body of knights; hence, a company of gallant gentlemen.

chive (chīv) ***n-*** (often **chives**) plant related to the onion, with slender, grasslike leaves used to flavor foods. *as **modifier**: some* chive *cheese.*

chlor·al (klôr′ əl) ***n-* 1** colorless oily liquid compound used in making DDT. **2** chloral hydrate.

chloral hydrate ***n-*** powerful sedative drug, a white powder with a slightly bitter, biting taste. In an alcoholic drink, it is dangerous and quickly produces unconsciousness.

chlo·rate (klôr′ āt′) ***n-*** *Chemistry* a salt of a metal and the chemical radical containing one chlorine and three oxygen atoms: *potassium* chlorate ($KClO_3$).

chlor·dane (klôr′ dān, klôr′-) ***n-*** powerful liquid insecticide used especially against roaches and aphids.

chlo·rel·la (klə rĕl′ ə) ***n-*** kind of nutritious one-celled green algae, a potential source of food.

chlo·ride (klôr′ īd′) ***n-*** salt of chlorine and another element or chemical radical: *sodium* chloride (NaCl); *ammonium* chloride (NH_4Cl).

chloride of lime ***n-*** white powder with a strong odor, made by treating slaked lime with chlorine and used for bleaching and disinfecting.

chlo·rin·ate (klôr′ ə nāt′) ***vt-*** **[chlo·rin·ated, chlo·rin·at·ing]** to add chlorine to, especially to water to make it safe to drink or bathe in. **—*n-* chlo′ rin·a′ tion.**

chlo·rine (klô′ rēn′) ***n-*** greenish-yellow, irritating gas with a strong odor, used for bleaching and in purifying water. Chemical element, symbol Cl, At. No. 17, At. Wt. 35.46.

chlo·ro·form (klôr′ ə fôrm′, -fôrm′) ***n-*** colorless, heavy, fast-evaporating liquid with a characteristic sweet odor. Its vapor produces unconsciousness when inhaled and is used as an anesthetic. ***vt-*** to make unconscious by giving chloroform.

Chlo·ro·my·ce·tin (klôr′ ō mī′ sē′ tən) ***n-*** trademark name for an antibiotic used against typhoid, pneumonia, and several other diseases.

chlo·ro·phyll or **chlo·ro·phyl** (klôr′ ə fĭl) ***n-*** the green coloring matter of plants that uses light to combine carbon dioxide and water into the food needed by the plants.

chlo·ro·plast (klôr′ ə plăst′) ***n-*** one of the tiny bodies that contain the chlorophyll of a plant cell. For picture, see *cell.*

chock (chŏk) ***n-* 1** block or wedge to fill in a space so as to prevent motion: *to put a* chock *under the wheel of a cart.* **2** on a ship, a metal casting or wooden part for ropes or cables to run through. ***vt-***: *to* chock *wheels.*

Chock

chock-a-block (chŏk′ ə blŏk′) ***adj-* 1** of a ship's tackle, drawn close with the blocks touching. **2** crowded: *a room* chock-a-block *with knick-knacks.*

chock-full (chŏk′ fo͝ol′) ***adj-*** full to capacity; crammed; chuck-full: *a briefcase* chock-full *of papers.*

choc·o·late (chŏk′ lət, chŏk′-) ***n-* 1** food substance made by roasting and grinding cacao beans. **2** a candy made from this substance. **3 hot chocolate** drink made of chocolate and milk or water. ***adj-***: *a* chocolate *pie.*

Choc·taw (chŏk′ tô′) ***n-*** [*pl.* **Choc·taws,** also **Choc·taw**] **1** member of a tribe of American Indians who formerly lived in the forests of Alabama and Mississippi and now are divided between Mississippi and Oklahoma. **2** the language of the Choctaw and Chickasaw peoples. ***adj-***: *the* Choctaw *woodsmen.*

choice (chois) ***n-* 1** act of choosing: *I will leave the* choice *of a movie to you.* **2** power to choose: *We had a* choice *between the mountains and the seashore for vacation.* **3** the thing or person chosen: *My* choice *in flavors is peppermint.* **4** large selection from which to choose: *a wide* choice *of colors.* ***adj-*** **[choic·er, choic·est] 1** of fine quality: *a* choice *cut of beef.* **2** carefully chosen; appropriate: *a* choice *remark.*

►For usage note see ALTERNATIVE.

choir (kwī′ ər) ***n-* 1** a group of trained singers, usually in a church. **2** the part of a church in which the choir sings. ***Hom-*** quire.

choir·boy (kwī′ ər boi′) ***n-*** boy who sings in a choir, especially in a church service.

choir·mas·ter (kwī′ ər măs′ tər) ***n-*** director of a choir.

choke (chōk) ***vt-*** **[choked, chok·ing] 1** to stop or almost stop the breath or speech by blocking, pressing, or irritating the windpipe; stifle: *A bone* choked *the dog. Smoke* choked *the firemen.* **2** to block or check by clogging or crowding: *Leaves* choked *the drain. Weeds* choked *the flowers.* **3** to fill beyond the reasonable capacity; cram: *The wastebasket was* choked *with newspapers.* ***vi-*** to be suddenly unable to breathe or speak: *The dog* choked *on a bone. The boy* choked *with laughter.* ***n-* 1** constriction in the throat caused by emotion, irritation, etc.: *a* choke *in her voice.* **2** valve in an automobile engine, to regulate the air intake.

choke back to hold back or suppress (anger or other emotion).

choke off to check or stop quickly: *The demonstration was* choked off *by the arrival of police.*

choke up to be unable to speak: *He* choked up *when he said good-by.*

choke·cher·ry (chōk′chĕr′rē) ***n-*** **1** [*pl.* **choke·cher·ries**] any of several small, wild, North American cherry trees with very tart or bitter fruit. **2** the fruit itself.

chok·er (chō′kər) ***n-*** **1** person or thing that chokes. **2** anything worn close around the neck, such as a small fur piece, a short necklace, or a high collar.

chok·y or **chok·ey** (chō′kē) ***adj-*** [**chok·i·er, chok·i·est**] tending to choke or smother: *dry,* choky *bread.*

chol·er (kŏl′ər) ***n-*** anger; irritability. ***Hom-*** collar. ***—adj-*** **chol′er·ic:** *a* choleric *disposition.*

chol·er·a (kŏl′ər ə) ***n-*** an inflammatory disease of the intestines, causing pain and diarrhea. A highly contagious and often fatal type is called **Asiatic cholera.**

chol·er·ic (kŏl′ər ĭk) ***adj-*** easily made angry; hot tempered.

cho·les·ter·ol (kə lĕs′tə rol′) ***n-*** fatty substance in animal tissues. It forms gallstones and may be deposited in the walls of the arteries.

chol·la (choi′ə) ***n-*** the prickly pear cactus.

choose (cho͞oz) ***vt-*** [**chose** (chōz), **chos·en** (chō′zən), **choos·ing**] **1** to select from among others; pick out: *to* choose *a heavier bat.* **2** to decide; see fit: *He* chose *to leave.*

[1]chop (chŏp) ***vt-*** [**chopped, chop·ping**] **1** to cut by blows with an ax or similar tool. **2** to cut into small pieces: *to* chop *vegetables.* **3** to cut short, as one's speech. ***n-*** **1** short, cutting blow: *the* chop *of the woodman's axe.* **2** small cut of meat containing a rib or section of bone. **3** short, rough movement of waves. [from earlier English **choppen** of the same meaning.]

[2]chop (chŏp) ***vi-*** [**chopped, chop·ping**] to veer; shift suddenly, as the wind. [from **[1]chop.**]

chop·house (chŏp′hous′) ***n-*** restaurant which specializes in chops, steaks, etc.

chop·per (chŏp′ər) ***n-*** **1** person or tool that chops. **2** *slang* helicopter.

[1]chop·py (chŏp′ē) ***adj-*** [**chop·pi·er, chop·pi·est**] full of short, rough waves: *a* choppy *sea.* [from **[1]chop**]

[2]chop·py (chŏp′ē) ***adj-*** [**chop·pi·er, chop·pi·est**] changeable: *a* choppy *wind.* [from earlier **chappen** meaning "to bargain", related to **[1]chap.**]

chops (chŏps) ***n-*** *pl.* **1** the jaws or the flesh covering them; jowls: *The dog licked his* chops. **2** mouth.

chop·sticks (chŏp′stĭks′) ***n-*** two small sticks of wood or ivory used by the Chinese and Japanese to lift food to the mouth.

Chopsticks in use

chop su·ey (chŏp′so͞o′ē) ***n-*** a Chinese-American dish of diced meat or fish, mushrooms, celery, bamboo shoots, and bean sprouts, cooked together and served hot over rice.

chor·al (kôr′əl) ***adj-*** **1** pertaining to a choir or chorus: choral *singing.* **2** sung by a choir: *a* choral *service.* ***n-*** **chorale.**

cho·rale (kə răl′) ***n-*** hymn tune or a composition based on a hymn tune. ***Hom-*** corral.

[1]chord (kȯrd, kôrd) ***n-*** **1** straight line segment joining any two points on a circle or an arc. For picture, see *circle..* **2** (also **cord**) stringlike part of the body, such as one of the vocal chords. **3** emotion; feeling: a *sympathetic* chord. [from Latin **chorda** meaning "string," from Greek **chordē** meaning "gut; string of a musical instrument," related to "cord."] ***Hom-*** cord.

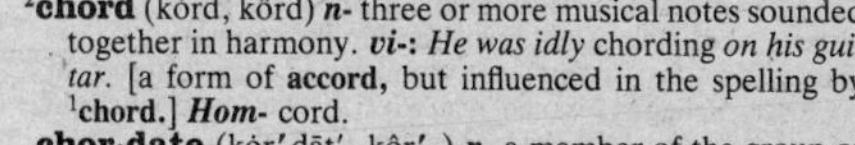

[2]chord (kȯrd, kôrd) ***n-*** three or more musical notes sounded together in harmony. ***vi-:*** *He was idly* chording *on his guitar.* [a form of **accord,** but influenced in the spelling by **[1]chord.**] ***Hom-*** cord.

chor·date (kôr′dāt′, kôr′-) ***n-*** a member of the group of animals (**Chordata**) that have backbones.

chore (chôr) ***n-*** **1** routine job, especially a daily task around the house or farm. **2** an odd job, especially an irksome or disagreeable one.

cho·re·a (kə rē′ə) ***n-*** disease of the nervous system that chiefly affects children, causing muscular twitching and jerking; St. Vitus's dance.

cho·re·og·ra·pher (kôr′ē ŏg′rə fər) ***n-*** person who creates or directs dances for the stage.

cho·re·og·ra·phy (kôr′ē ŏg′rə fē) ***n-*** art of composing or performing dances for ballet, opera, TV shows, etc. ***adj-*** **cho′re·o·graph′ic** (-ē ə grăf′ĭk).

chor·is·ter (kôr′əs tər) ***n-*** **1** member of a choir; especially, a boy singer. **2** choir leader who sets the pitch.

chor·tle (chôr′təl, chôr′-) ***vi-*** [**chor·tled, chor·tling**] to laugh with chuckling sounds or in a snorting fashion.

cho·rus (kôr′əs) ***n-*** [*pl.* **cho·rus·es**] **1** group of people organized to sing or recite together. **2** group of singers and dancers in a musical show. **3** piece of music arranged for a number of voices. **4** part of a song that is repeated at the end of each verse; a refrain. **5** something called out by a number of people at one time: *a* chorus *of "ayes."* ***vt-*** to sing or say together.

chose (chōz) *p.t.* of **choose.**

cho·sen (chō′zən) *p.p.* of **choose.**

chow (chou) ***n-*** a medium-sized, muscular dog of a breed originating in China. It has a black tongue, thick black or red-brown coat, and a short tail curved over the back.

chow·der (chou′dər) ***n-*** thick soup made of clams or fish and vegetables.

chow mein (chou′mān′) ***n-*** Chinese-American dish of onions, diced meat, mushrooms, celery, bamboo shoots, and bean sprouts, stewed together in a thick sauce and served over fried noodles. [American word from Chinese **ch'ao mien** meaning "fried flour."]

Christ (krīst) ***n-*** the Anointed; the Messiah; Jesus of Nazareth, regarded by Christians as being the Son of God foretold by the Hebrew prophets; founder of the Christian religion; Jesus Christ.

christ·en (krĭs′ən) ***vt-*** **1** to baptize. **2** to give a name to at baptism: *The baby was* christened *"John."* **3** to name (a ship, etc.), often at a formal ceremony. **4** *Informal* to use for the first time, especially with ceremony.

Chris·ten·dom (krĭs′ən dəm) ***n-*** **1** Christian people, collectively. **2** the part of the world where Christianity predominates.

chris·ten·ing (krĭs′ən ing) ***n-*** **1** ceremony at which a person is christened. **2** an occasion at which some new thing is named, dedicated, or used for the first time.

Chris·tian (krĭs′chən) ***n-*** person who believes in the teachings of Jesus Christ. ***adj-*** **1** believing in or belonging to the religion of Christ: *all* Christian *nations.* **2** having to do with Christ or the religion that bears His name. **3** showing the qualities taught by Christ, such as gentleness, patience, generosity, and humility.

Chris·ti·an·i·ty (krĭs′chē ăn′ə tē) ***n-*** **1** the system of religion of Christ and his apostles. **2** Christendom.

Chris·tian·ize (krĭs′chə nīz′) ***vt-*** [**Chris·tian·ized, Chris·tian·iz·ing**] **1** to convert to Christianity. **2** to make (something) conform to Christian principles: *to* Christianize *the law.* ***—n-*** **Chris′tian·i·za′tion.**

Christian name ***n-*** the name a person is given at baptism, as distinguished from the family name.

Christian Scientist ***n-*** member of the **Church of Christ, Scientist,** which teaches a mental and spiritual approach to health and disease.

Christ·like (krīst′ līk′) ***adj-*** resembling Christ in patience, gentleness, forgiveness, etc.

Christ·mas (krĭs′ məs) ***n-*** yearly celebration (December 25) of the birth of Christ. Also **Christmas Day.**

Christ·mas·tide (krĭs′ məs tīd′) ***n-*** the Christmas season, from Christmas Eve through Epiphany, January 6.

Christmas tree ***n-*** an evergreen or artificial tree customarily decorated at Christmas time.

chro·mate (krō′ māt′) ***n-*** a salt containing a chemical radical composed of one chromium and four oxygen atoms: *potassium* chromate (K_2CrO_4).

chro·mat·ic (krə măt′ ĭk) ***adj-*** **1** pertaining to color. **2** relating to or based on the chromatic scale. ***—adv-*** **chro·mat′ i·cal·ly.**

chromatic scale *Music* ***n-*** a scale in which the intervals are half steps, played by striking all the keys, white and black, in order, from any key on a piano to the key an octave above.

chro·ma·tin (krō′ mə tən) ***n-*** the substance in a cell's nucleus that contains the genes.

chrome (krōm) ***n-*** chromium.

chrome steel ***n-*** very hard steel made with chromium.

chro·mic (krō′ mĭk) ***adj-*** of, combined with, or containing chromium.

chrom·i·um (krō′ mē əm) ***n-*** shiny, silver-colored metal element used for plating other metals and in alloys; chrome. Symbol Cr, At. No. 24, At. Wt. 52.01.

chromium steel ***n-*** chrome steel.

chro·mo·some (krō′ mə sōm′) ***n-*** threadlike structure formed by the chromatin in the nucleus of a plant or animal cell just before the cell divides.

chro·mo·sphere (krō′ mə sfêr′) ***n-*** brilliant red sphere of incandescent gases that surrounds the sun. It is seen within the corona during a total eclipse.

chron·ic (krŏn′ ĭk) ***adj-*** **1** lasting over a long period of time: *He has a* chronic *cough.* **2** habitual: *She is a* chronic *complainer.* ***—adv-*** **chron′ i·cal·ly.**

chron·i·cle (krŏn′ ĭ kəl) ***n-*** record of events in the order in which they happened; a history. ***vt-*** **[chron·i·cled, chron·i·cling]** to record. ***—n-*** **chron′ i·cler.**

Chron·i·cles (krŏn′ ĭ kəlz) ***n-*** in the Old Testament, either of two historical books, "I and II Chronicles"; in the CCD Bible called "I and II Paralipomenon."

chron·o·graph (krō′ nə grăf′) ***n-*** **1** time-keeping instrument made up of a revolving drum driven by a clock and a pen that marks off time intervals on a graph carried by the drum. **2** stopwatch.

chron·o·log·i·cal (krŏn′ ə lŏj′ ĭ kəl) ***adj-*** arranged in the order of time: *a* chronological *list of the year's events.* ***—adv-*** **chron′ o·log′ i·cal·ly.**

chro·nol·o·gy (krə nŏl′ ə jē) ***n-*** [*pl.* **chro·nol·o·gies**] **1** the science that deals with events and arranges their dates in proper order. **2** table of events given in order of occurrence: *a* chronology *of the war.*

chro·nom·e·ter (krə nŏm′ ə tər) ***n-*** very accurate clock, used chiefly in navigation.

chron·o·scope (krō′ nə skōp′) ***n-*** electronic instrument for measuring extremely small time intervals.

Butterfly chrysalis

chrys·a·lis (krĭs′ ə ləs) ***n-*** **1** the hard case which encloses the pupa of a butterfly. **2** the case and the pupa inside it, together. *as* ***modifier:*** *the* chrysalis *state of a butterfly.* Also **chrys′ a·lid.**

chry·san·the·mum (krĭ săn′ thə məm) ***n-*** any of several plants, many of which are cultivated for their showy flowers; also, the flower itself.

Chrysanthemum

chub (chŭb) ***n-*** any of several common fresh-water fish of Europe and North America, related to the dace.

chub·by (chŭb′ ē) ***adj-*** **[chub·bi·er, chub·bi·est]** plump and round: *a baby's* chubby *fists.* ***—n-*** **chub′ bi·ness.**

[1]**chuck** (chŭk) ***n-*** light stroke; tap: *a* chuck *under the chin.* ***vt-*** **1** to stroke or tap: *to* chuck *a baby under the chin.* **2** to toss; throw away; discard: *He* chucked *the letter into the wastebasket.* [probably imitative.]

[2]**chuck** (chŭk) ***n-*** **1** cut of beef including most of the neck and the shoulder blade. **2** clamp for holding a tool or piece of work in a lathe or drill. [apparently from French **choque** meaning "log."]

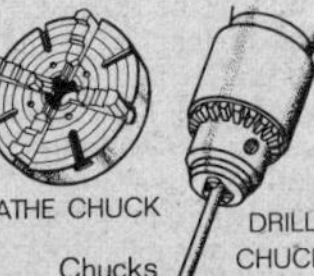

Chucks

chuck-full (chŭk′ fo͝ol′) chock-full.

chuck·hole (chŭk′ hōl′) ***n-*** hole or rut in a road.

chuck·le (chŭk′ əl) ***vi-*** **[chuck·led, chuck·ling]** to laugh quietly to oneself, expressing satisfaction. ***n-*** low, quiet laugh.

chuck·le·head (chŭk′ əl hĕd′) *Informal* ***n-*** head like a block; hence, a stupid person; dolt. ***—adj-*** **chuck′ le·head′ ed.**

chuck wagon ***n-*** wagon carrying cooking equipment and food for ranch hands, lumberers, etc.

chuck·wal·la (chŭk′ wä′ lə) ***n-*** rust-colored desert lizard of southwestern United States, about a foot long.

chug (chŭg) ***n-*** a muffled, explosive sound made by an engine exhaust. ***vi-*** **[chugged, chug·ging]** to make or move with such sounds: *The car* chugged *along.*

chum (chŭm) ***n-*** friend; pal. ***vi-*** **[chummed, chum·ming]** to be very close friends (with).

chum with to be very friendly with; go around with: *Beth* chums with *Barbara and Helen.*

chum together to be close friends; go around together; consort: *George, Fred, and Bill* chum together.

chum·my (chŭm′ ē) ***adj-*** **[chum·mi·er, chum·mi·est]** very friendly and sociable: *He's* chummy *with us.*

chump (chŭmp) *Slang* ***n-*** one who is easily taken in; one who always gets the worst of a bargain; dupe.

chunk (chŭngk) ***n-*** thick piece or mass: *a* chunk *of meat.*

chunk·y (chŭng′ kē) ***adj-*** **[chunk·i·er, chunk·i·est]** **1** stocky; solidly and compactly built: *a* chunky *lad.* **2** thick and solid: *meat cut in* chunky *pieces.*

church (chûrch) ***n-*** **1** building for religious worship, especially Christian worship. **2** Christian worship; services: *He accompanied her to* church. **3** organized group of Christians having the same beliefs and practices; sect; denomination: *the Methodist* Church. **4** the clergy as a profession: *to enter the* church. **5 the Church** all Christians. *as* ***modifier:*** *soft* church *music*; church *art.*

church·go·er (chûrch′ gō′ ər) ***n-*** person who goes to church regularly.

church·ly (chûrch′ lē) ***adj-*** **1** related or suitable to the church: *a* churchly *custom.* **2** devoted to or believing strongly in the church: *The Puritans were a* churchly *people.*

church·man (chûrch′ mən) ***n-*** [*pl.* **church·men**] **1** member of the clergy; clergyman. **2** man who is an active supporter of his church ***—n-*** *fem.* **church′ wo·man.**

Church of England ***n-*** the national church of England, established in the 16th century and having the monarch as its head.

Church of Jesus Christ of Latter-Day Saints ***n-*** a Christian sect founded by Joseph Smith in 1830 at Fayette, New York; Mormon Church.

church·ward·en (chûrch′ wòr′ dən) ***n-*** in the Episcopal church, a parish officer who looks after church property, finances, etc.

church·yard (chûrch′ yärd′) ***n-*** ground around a church, sometimes used in part as a graveyard.

churl (chûrl) ***n-*** **1** formerly, a person of low birth. **2** surly person; boor.

churl·ish (chûr′ lĭsh) ***adj-*** rude; boorish. ***—adv-*** **churl′ ish·ly.** ***n-*** **churl′ ish·ness.**

churn (chûrn) ***n-*** vessel or machine in which cream is shaken or beaten to make butter. ***vt-*** **1** to shake or beat (cream) in such a vessel to make butter. **2** to stir up violently: *The injured whale* churned *the water.* ***vi-*** to foam; seethe; wash to and fro: *The water* churned *around the rocks.*

Churn

churr (chûr) ***n-*** whirring sound made by some birds, such as a partridge, and by some insects. ***vi-***: *In the thicket a partridge* churred *softly.* ***Hom-*** chirr.

chute (sho͞ot) ***n-*** **1** slanting slide or shaft: *a coal* chute; *a laundry* chute; *a letter* chute. **2** waterfall or rapid in a river. **3** parachute. **4** toboggan slide. ***Hom-*** shoot.

chut·ney (chŭt′ nē) ***n-*** [*pl.* **chut·neys**] highly spiced condiment or relish of East Indian origin, made of fruits, herbs, and spices.

chyle (kīl) ***n-*** milky fluid composed of lymph and food fats absorbed from the small intestine.

chyme (kīm) ***n-*** partly digested food in the small intestine.

ci·bor·i·um (sə bôr′ ē əm) ***n-*** [*pl.* **ci·bo·ri·a**] **1** cup with a dome-shaped cover, used to hold consecrated wafers of the Eucharist. **2** canopy or arch above an altar.

ci·ca·da (sə kā′ də) ***n-*** large insect with transparent wings, the male of which makes a long, shrill, trilling sound.

cic·a·trix (sĭk′ ə trĭks′) ***n-*** [*pl.* **cic·a·tri·ces** (-trī sēz′)] a scar on a plant or animal. Also **cic′ a·trice** (-trĭs′).

ci·ce·ro·ne (sĭs′ ə rō′ nē, *Ital.* chĕ′- chā rō′ nā) ***n-*** [*pl.* **ci·ce·ro·ni** (-nē)] guide who explains particular points of interest.

-cide *combining form* killer or killing of: *a regi*cide (killer or killing of a king); *a sui*cide (killer or killing of oneself). [from Latin **-cidium** meaning "a killing," and **-cida** meaning "a killer."]

Cicada, 1 1/4 in. long

ci·der (sī′ dər) ***n-*** **1** (also **sweet cider**) partially fermented juice of apples. **2** (also **hard cider**) fully fermented apple juice.

ci·gar (sĭ gär′) ***n-*** roll of tobacco leaves for smoking.

cig·a·rette (sĭg′ ə rĕt′) ***n-*** shredded tobacco rolled in a thin paper for smoking. [from French **cigarette** meaning "little cigar."]

cil·i·a (sĭl′ ē ə) ***n-*** *pl.* **1** eyelashes. **2** hairlike structures found on plant leaves, insect wings, etc.

cil·i·ar·y (sĭl′ ē ĕr′ ē) ***adj-*** **1** hairlike. **2** of or relating to the muscle in the eye that controls the shape of the lens, and to the nerves and blood vessels associated with this muscle.

cil·i·ate (sĭl′ ē ət) ***n-*** any of a class of one-celled animals that have cilia. ***adj-*** having cilia.

cinch (sĭnch) ***n-*** **1** strap for holding a saddle or a pack on a horse; girth. **2** *Slang* a sure or easy thing. ***vt-*** **1** to tighten the girth of (a horse). **2** *Informal* to get a tight grasp on; tie up tightly; clinch: *That* cinches *the deal.* [American word from Spanish **cincha,** from Latin **cincta** meaning "girdle; anything which binds."]

cin·cho·na (sĭng kō′ nə, sĭn chō′-) ***n-*** an evergreen tree of South America, the dried bark of which is a source of quinine.

Cinch on a saddle

cinc·ture (sĭngk′ chər) ***n-*** belt worn round the waist.

cin·der (sĭn′ dər) ***n-*** **1** small piece of partly burned coal or wood that has ceased to flame but is not yet ash. **2** a piece of ash.

cinder block ***n-*** **1** rectangular, hollow concrete block, made with coal cinders and used for building purposes. **2** a block which closes the front of a blast furnace.

Cin·der·el·la (sĭn′də rĕl′ ə) ***n-*** in an old fairy tale, a maiden treated as a drudge by her stepmother until, aided by her fairy godmother, she marries a prince.

cin·e·ma (sĭn′ ə mə) ***n-*** *chiefly Brit.* **1** motion pictures. **2** business or art of making movies.

cin·er·ar·i·um (sĭn′ ər âr′ ē əm) ***n-*** [*pl.* **cin·er·ar·i·a** (âr′ ē ə)] place to receive the ashes of cremated bodies. ***—adj-*** **cin′ er·ar′ y:** *a* cinerary *urn.*

cin·na·bar (sĭn′ ə bär) ***n-*** **1** bright-red ore of mercury; mercuric sulfide. **2** a red pigment made of artificial mercuric sulfide; vermilion.

cin·na·mon (sĭn′ ə mən) ***n-*** **1** spice that comes from the inner bark of an East Indian tree. **2** the tree itself. **3** a reddish-brown color. ***adj-*** **1** flavored with this spice: *a* cinnamon *bun.* **2** reddish-brown.

cinque·foil (sĭngk′ foil′) ***n-*** **1** any of several related plants having yellow flowers and small leaves that are divided into five small leaflets. **2** in architecture, a decoration consisting of five connected semicircles or lobes.

CIO or **C.I.O.** Congress of Industrial Organizations.

ci·pher (sī′ fər) ***n-*** **1** zero; the cardinal number zero. **2** secret writing. ***vi-*** (no longer in general use) to do arithmetic. Also **cy′ pher.**

cir·ca (sûr′ kə) ***prep-*** about; around, used in giving a date: *a French clock made* circa *1850.*

Cir·ce (sûr′ sē) ***n-*** in the "Odyssey," an enchantress who changed the companions of Odysseus (Ulysses) into swine by means of a magic drink.

cir·cle (sûr′ kəl) ***n-*** **1** *Mathematics* a closed plane curve, every point of which is the same distance from the center. **2** disk. **3** a ring: *They made a* circle *for the folk dance.* **4** group of people held together by common interests: *a* circle *of friends;*

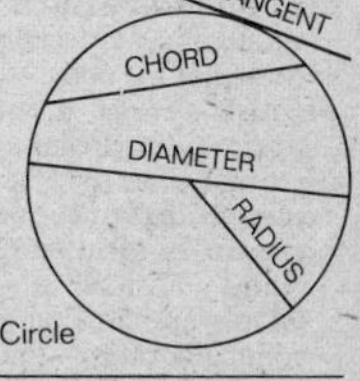

Circle

fāte, făt, dâre, bärn; bē, bĕt, mêre; bīte, bĭt; nōte, hŏt, môre, dòg; fŭn, fûr; to͞o, bo͝ok; oil; out; tar; thin; then; hw for wh as in *wh*at; zh for s as in u*s*ual; ə for a, e, i, o, u, as in *a*go, lin*e*n, per*i*l, at*o*m, min*u*s

family circle. ***vt-*** **[cir·cled, cir·cling]** **1** to move in a curve around: *The airplane* circled *the field.* **2** to surround: *Guards* circled *the prison.* **3** to draw a closed curve around.

cir·clet (sûrk′ lət) ***n-*** **1** a small circle. **2** a circular ornament for the head, arm, neck, or finger.

cir·cuit (sûr′ kət) ***n-*** **1** a going around; revolution: *Every year the earth completes its* circuit *of the sun.* **2** route regularly traveled by a judge who holds court in different towns, or by a preacher who serves a number of widely scattered churches. **3** boundary line around an area. **4** distance around any space or area; circumference. **5** group of theaters under one management, showing plays or movies simultaneously or in turn. **6** complete path of an electric current.

circuit breaker ***n-*** an electric switch that interrupts the flow of current in an overloaded circuit without causing an electric arc, especially an automatic one commonly used in place of fuses.

circuit court ***n-*** general trial court that sits in several places within a judicial district.

cir·cu·i·tous (sər kyōō′ ə təs) ***adj-*** roundabout; not direct: *We took a* circuitous *route to town to avoid the flood waters.* **—*adv-*** **cir·cu′ i·tous·ly.** ***n-*** **cir·cu′ i·tous·ness.**

circuit rider ***n-*** preacher who holds services in several places within a district, especially a Methodist traveling preacher of frontier times.

cir·cu·lar (sûr′ kyə lər) ***adj-*** **1** round: *a* circular *table.* **2** moving in a circle; revolving: *The turning of a phonograph record is a* circular *motion.* ***n-*** printed letter or notice for circulation among the public. **—*n-*** **cir′ cu·lar′ i·ty.** ***adv-*** **cir′ cu·lar·ly.**

cir·cu·lar·ize (sûr′ kyə lə rīz′) ***vt-*** **[cir·cu·lar·ized, cir·cu·lar·iz·ing]** to send letters or circulars to, for information or advertising.

circular saw ***n-*** a disk-shaped saw with large teeth. It is rotated at high speed by a motor, and used chiefly for cutting logs and planks; buzz saw. For picture, see [1]*saw.*

cir·cu·late (sûr′ kyə lāt′) ***vi-*** **[cir·cu·lat·ed, cir·cu·lat·ing]** **1** to move round in a course leading back to the starting place: *Hot water* circulates *in a heating system. Blood* circulates *in the body.* **2** to go or send from place to place or person to person: *Money* circulates. ***vt-***: *He* circulated *the postcards around the classroom.*

circulating library ***n-*** library from which members may borrow or rent books; lending library.

cir·cu·la·tion (sûr′ kyə lā′ shən) ***n-*** **1** passage of anything from place to place, person to person, etc.: *the* circulation *of news.* **2** a moving in a circle or in a course that leads back to the starting place: *the* circulation *of the blood.* **3** the number of copies distributed of each issue of a magazine or newspaper.

cir·cu·la·tor (sûr′ kyə lā′ tər) ***n-*** machine that circulates heat, water, etc.

cir·cu·la·to·ry (sûr′ kyə lə tôr′ ē) ***adj-*** having to do with circulation, especially of the blood: *the* circulatory *system of the body.*

circum- *prefix* around; roundabout: circum*navigate.* [from Latin **circum-**, from Latin **circus** "circle."]

cir·cum·cise (sûr′ kəm sīz′) ***vt-*** **[cir·cum·cised, cir·cum·cis·ing]** to cut off the foreskin.

cir·cum·ci·sion (sûr′ kəm sĭzh′ ən) ***n-*** **1** act of circumcising. **2** ritual of several religions in which male infants are circumcised. **3 Circumcision** church festival commemorating the circumcision of Jesus Christ, observed on January 1.

cir·cum·fer·ence (sər kŭm′ fər əns) ***n-*** the measure of the line that bounds a circle or any curved plane figure.

cir·cum·flex (sûr′ kəm flĕks′) ***n-*** accent mark [^] placed over a vowel to show length or quality of sound. ***adj-*** pronounced or marked with such an accent.

cir·cum·lo·cu·tion (sûr′ kəm lō kyōō′ shən) ***n-*** a roundabout or indirect way of speaking; use of too many words; also, the words used.

cir·cum·nav·i·gate (sûr′ kəm năv′ ə gāt′) ***vt-*** **[cir·cum·nav·i·gat·ed, cir·cum·nav·i·gat·ing]** to sail completely around (the earth, an island, etc.). **—*n-*** **cir′ cum·nav′ i·ga′ tion.**

cir·cum·po·lar (sûr′ kəm pō′ lər) ***adj-*** surrounding, or moving around a pole, especially one of the earth's poles or one of the celestial poles: *a* circumpolar *land mass*; *a* circumpolar *star.*

cir·cum·scribe (sûr′ kəm skrīb′) ***vt-*** **[cir·cum·scribed, cir·cum·scrib·ing]** **1** in geometry, to draw a figure, especially a circle, around a polygon so that every corner of the polygon or other figure touches the circle. **2** to restrict, limit: *to* circumscribe *the powers of a king.*

cir·cum·scrip·tion (sûr′ kəm skrĭp′ shən) ***n-*** a bounding, limitation, or restriction: *the* circumscription *of federal and state rights.*

cir·cum·spect (sûr′ kəm spĕkt′) ***adj-*** cautious; considering all sides of a problem before acting; prudent. **—*n-*** **cir′ cum·spec′ tion.** ***adv-*** **cir′ cum·spect′ ly.**

cir·cum·stance (sûr′ kəm stăns′) ***n-*** **1** condition, fact, or event surrounding and usually affecting another fact or event: *Good weather and other* circumstances *favored the polar expedition.* **2** full and particular detail: *Darwin wrote with* circumstance *about the expedition.* **3** pomp; ceremony. **4 circumstances** state of affairs; conditions generally, especially financial conditions: *In our present* circumstances *we can't afford a car.*

cir·cum·stan·tial (sûr′ kəm stăn′ shəl) ***adj-*** **1** affected by or depending on circumstances: *the* circumstantial *developments of his campaign.* **2** incidental; unimportant; secondary: *matters too* circumstantial *to worry about.* **3** detailed: *His account of the crime was so* circumstantial *we had to believe him.* **—*adv-*** **cir′ cum·stan′ tial·ly.**

circumstantial evidence ***n-*** evidence that deals with the circumstances surrounding an act rather than with the act itself. Proof that a defendant was at the scene of a crime when it was committed is circumstantial evidence. See also *direct evidence.*

cir·cum·stan·ti·ate (sûr′ kəm stăn′ shē āt′) ***vt-*** **[cir·cum·stan·ti·at·ed, cir·cum·stan·ti·at·ing]** to present facts to support (a statement, report, etc.): *The records* circumstantiated *his claims.*

cir·cum·vent (sûr′ kəm vĕnt′) ***vt-*** to block or hinder by better strategy; outwit: *The colonel* circumvented *the plan of the enemy to blow up the bridge.*

cir·cus (sûr′ kəs) ***n-*** **1** a traveling show of acrobats, clowns, horses, wild animals, etc.; also, the performance. **2** large level space surrounded by tiers of seats, usually within a tent, for putting on such shows. **3** in ancient Rome, a large oval space enclosed on three sides by tiers of seats, and used for chariot races, games, etc. **4** in England, a circular space at an intersection of streets: *Piccadilly* Circus.

cirque (sûrk) ***n-*** a steep, bowl-shaped hollow left in a mountainside by a glacier.

cir·rho·sis (sə rō′ səs) ***n-*** a diseased condition in which the liver shrinks and hardens, and scar tissue forms on it.

cir·ro·cu·mu·lus (sĭr′ ō kyōōm′ yə ləs) ***n-*** white puffy cloud found at high altitudes. For picture, see *cloud.*

cir·ro·stra·tus (sĭr′ ō strā′ təs, -străt′ əs) ***n-*** layer of cloud like a milky sheet or veil, found at high altitudes. For picture, see *cloud.*

cir·rus (sĭr′əs) *n-* [*pl.* **cir·ri** (sĭr′ī′)] a cloud formation in which the clouds spread in filmy wisps at a great height. For picture, see *cloud.*

Cis·ter·cian (sĭs tûr′shən) *n-* monk or nun belonging to a branch of the Benedictine Order, founded at Citeaux, France, in 1098. *adj-*: *a* Cistercian *monastery.*

cis·tern (sĭs′tərn) *n-* tank or man-made reservoir for storing water, often underground.

cit·a·del (sĭt′ə dəl) *n-* 1 fortress from which a city is dominated, and which also serves for defense and refuge during a siege. 2 any stronghold or place of refuge.

ci·ta·tion (sī tā′shən) *n-* 1 direct reference or quotation: *A* citation *from Scripture is usual in sermons.* 2 honorable mention of a soldier or military unit for bravery. 3 a summons to appear at a court of law.

cite (sīt) *vt-* [**cit·ed, cit·ing**] 1 to quote or refer to as an example, proof, or authority: *He* cited *a poem as an illustration. The lawyer* cited *the evidence.* 2 to summon to appear in court. 3 to give honorable mention to: *The soldier was* cited *for bravery.* ***Hom-*** site, sight.

cith·a·ra (sĭth′ər ə) *n-* an ancient Greek lyre. Also **kithara.**

cit·i·zen (sĭt′ə zən) *n-* 1 member of a state or nation who has political rights and privileges, and gives in return his allegiance to the government. 2 permanent resident of a town or city; also, a native of a town or city: *the* citizens *of Chicago.* 3 a civilian, as distinguished from a soldier, police officer, etc.

cit·i·zen·ry (sĭt′ə zən rē) *n-* the body of citizens, especially as distinguished from officials or soldiers.

citizens band *n-* one of the radio frequency bands in the United States used for radio communication by the public; CB. *as* ***modifier***: citizens band *radio.*

cit·i·zen·ship (sĭt′ə zən ship′) *n-* 1 the status of a citizen of a nation. 2 behavior as a citizen of a nation or some smaller community. *as* ***modifier***: a citizenship *award.*

cit·rate (sĭ′trāt′) *n-* a salt of citric acid: *sodium* citrate.

cit·ric (sĭ′trĭk) *adj-* having to do with or obtained from citrus fruits: *a* citric *flavor.*

citric acid *n-* fruit acid found especially in citrus fruits and widely used in soft drinks and medicines.

cit·ron (sĭ′trən) *n-* 1 small tree or shrub of oriental origin. 2 its fruit, like the lemon, but larger and not so acid. 3 the thick rind of this fruit, used in cooking.

cit·ro·nel·la (sĭ′trə nĕl′ə) *n-* 1 a fragrant grass grown in Ceylon, Java, etc. 2 the aromatic oil of this grass, which was formerly much used as a mosquito repellent. Also **oil of citronella.**

cit·rus (sĭ′trəs) *adj-* of or relating to a group of trees which includes the orange, lemon, lime, and citron.

citrus fruit *n-* a lemon, lime, orange, grapefruit, or citron.

cit·y (sĭt′ē) *n-* [*pl.* **cit·ies**] 1 a large or important town having local self-government. 2 all the people of such a town.

city editor *n-* newspaper editor in charge of local news and reporters.

city hall *n-* 1 the administration building of a city government. 2 *Informal* the city government itself.

city manager *n-* official appointed by an elected city council to manage a city.

cit·y-state (sĭ′tē stāt′) *n-* completely self-governing state consisting of a city and the dependent area around it, such as ancient Athens.

civ·et (sĭv′ət) *n-* thick yellowish substance with a musky odor, secreted by the civet cat, used in making perfume.

civet cat *n-* long, short-legged, weasellike animal of tropical Africa and Asia.

civ·ic (sĭv′ĭk) *adj-* having to do with a city, a citizen, or citizenship: *a concern for* civic *beauty; one's* civic *duties.*

civ·ics (sĭv′ ĭks) *n-* (takes singular verb) the study or science of community government and of the rights and duties of a citizen.

civil (sĭv′əl) *adj-* 1 having to do with citizens or the state: *our* civil *rights; a* civil *war.* 2 not connected with the church or military: *a* civil *marriage ceremony.* 3 polite; courteous but showing no warmth: *Her manner was* civil *but not friendly.* 4 showing the stamp of civilization; not barbarous: *a* civil *society.*

civil defense *n-* program under civilian authority for safeguarding civilians and maintaining vital services in the event of a hostile attack. It is also available for emergencies such as hurricanes and earthquakes.

civil disobedience *n-* refusal to obey a law in order to protest against the law or a condition felt to require legal remedy; passive resistance.

civil engineer *n-* an engineer employed in the designing and construction of roads, bridges, dams, harbors, and similar projects. ***—n-*** **civil engineering.**

ci·vil·ian (sə vĭl′yən) *n-* any person not a member of the armed services or of the police force.

ci·vil·i·ty (sə vĭl′ə tē) *n-* [*pl.* **ci·vil·i·ties**] courtesy; also, an act or expression of politeness.

civ·i·li·za·tion (sĭv′ə lə zā′shən) *n-* 1 condition of people who have advanced far beyond a primitive level in government, arts, religion, sciences, etc. 2 a particular stage or level of this; also, a particular culture: *the Babylonian* civilization. 3 process of making or becoming civilized: Civilization *is a long, hard struggle.* 4 all civilized countries and people.

civ·i·lize (sĭv′ə līz′) *vt-* [**civ·i·lized, civ·i·liz·ing**] to bring out of a primitive or barbarous way of life; educate in the arts, sciences, government, etc.

civ·i·lized (sĭv′ə līzd′) *adj-* 1 advanced far beyond a primitive or barbarous level of life: *a* civilized *nation.* 2 refined and enlightened in behavior and ideas: *a* civilized *person.*

civil law *n-* 1 system of rules regulating conduct between persons in such matters as property rights, auto accidents, business relations, etc., as distinguished from military or criminal law. 2 community, state, or national law as distinguished from church law.

civil liberty *n-* the Constitutional right to enjoy freedom of religion, speech, ownership of property, etc., without undue interference by the government.

civ·il·ly (sĭv′ə lē) *adv-* in a well-bred manner; politely: *He replied* civilly *to the insulting question.*

civil rights *n-* a citizen's rights in the areas of employment, housing, education, suffrage, etc., established by the thirteenth and fourteenth Constitutional amendments and reinforced by a series of other laws.

civil service *n-* government public service handling matters which are not military, judicial, or legislative. Civil servants are appointed from a list of applicants who have proved their merit, often by competitive tests.

civil war *n-* a war between opposing groups of the same nation.

Civil War *n-* 1 in United States' history, the war between the North and the South, from 1861 to 1865; War Between the States. 2 in English history, the war fought from 1642 to 1649 between supporters of Parliament (mostly Puritans) and supporters of the King.

Cl symbol for chlorine.
clab·ber (klăb′ər) *n-* soured, curdled milk. *vt-* to curdle. *vi-*: *The milk* clabbered *in the warm room.*
clack (klăk) *n-* sudden sharp sound or succession of sounds: *the* clack *of a typewriter.* *vi-*: *Her heels* clacked *on the pavement.* *Hom-* claque.
clad (klăd) *adj-* covered, sheathed, clothed, or plated (often used in compound adjectives: *tin*-clad, *copper*-clad. *vt-* [**clad, clad·ding**] to cover, sheath, or plate (a metal) with a layer of another metal: *to* clad *copper with tin.*
claim (klām) *vt-* **1** to demand or assert as one's own or one's due: *to* claim *an inheritance.* **2** to call for; deserve: *This matter* claims *our attention.* **3** to state as a fact; assert: *I* claim *this to be true.* *n-* **1** a demand for something as due: *a* claim *for damages.* **2** an assertion of a right or title to do something: *I have a* claim *to the property.* **3** the assertion of something as a fact: *the* claims *of a company about its product.* **4** the thing demanded; especially, land which a miner marks out.
have a claim on to have a right to demand something from. **lay claim** to assert one's right to obtain. **put in a claim** to try to establish a right to obtain.
claim·ant (klā′mənt) *n-* person who makes a claim; one who demands something as his or her due.
clair·voy·ance (klâr voi′əns) *n-* **1** the power, claimed by some people, of seeing objects and events beyond the natural range of vision, or before they happen. **2** unusual insight or perception; clear-sightedness.
clair·voy·ant (klâr voi′ənt) *adj-* **1** having the power to see things beyond the natural range of vision. **2** unusually perceptive or discerning. *n-* **1** person claiming the supernatural power of clairvoyance. **2** person who is unusually perceptive.—*adv-* **clair·voy′ant·ly.**
clam (klăm) *n-* mollusk with a hinged double shell, living partly or wholly buried in sand or mud, and used as food. *vi-* [**clammed, clam·ming**] to gather or dig for clams.
clam up *Slang* to become close-mouthed, like a clam.

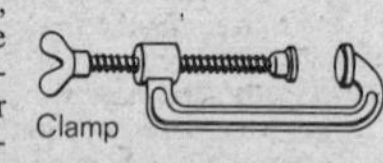
Clam

clam·bake (klăm′bāk′) *n-* a shore picnic at which clams, lobsters, corn, etc., are cooked on hot stones covered with seaweed.
clam·ber (klăm′bər) *vi-* to climb using both hands and feet; climb with difficulty: *to* clamber *up rocks.*
clam·my (klăm′ē) *adj-* [**clam·mi·er, clam·mi·est**] cold, moist, and sticky: *a* clammy *hand.* —*n-* **clam′mi·ness.**
clamor (klăm′ər) *n-* loud and continued outcry or demand; uproar. *vi-*: *The people* clamored *for more.*
clam·or·ous (klăm′ər əs) *adj-* loud and noisy: *the* clamorous *applause.* —*adv-* ***clam′or·ous·ly.*** *n-* **clam′or·ous·ness:** *the* clamorousness *of a heckler.*
clamp (klămp) *n-* a brace, band, clasp, or other device for holding things tightly together; cramp. *vt-* to fasten or strengthen with such a device.

Clamp

clamp down to impose greater restrictions; to become more strict: *The police* clamped down *on speeders.*
clan (klăn) *n-* **1** group of families, the heads of which claim common ancestry and have the same surname, especially in the Scottish Highlands: *He wears the tartan of the Macleod* clan. **2** group of people closely united because of similar backgrounds or by common interests or sympathies; a set; clique.
clan·des·tine (klăn dĕs′tən) *adj-* secret; private, usually for an underhand purpose: *a* clandestine *meeting.* —*adv-* **clan·des′tine·ly.**
clang (klăng) *n-* loud, harsh, ringing sound like metal being struck. *vi-*: *The bell* clanged *loudly.* *vt-*: *The drummer* clanged *a cymbal.*
clan·gor (klăng′ər) *n-* a loud metallic sound, or a medley of such sounds: *the* clangor *of many bells.* —*adj-* **clan′gor·ous.**
clank (klăngk) *n-* sharp, harsh, brief metallic sound: *the* clank *of a loose chain.* *vi-* to make this sound: *The tractor* clanked *along the concrete road.* *vt-*: *He* clanked *the pipe with a hammer.*
clan·nish (klăn′ĭsh) *adj-* **1** tending to associate with others of similar background, interests, or sympathies; exclusive: *the* clannish *ways of car enthusiasts.* **2** having, and often showing, prejudice against outsiders. *adv-* **clan′nish·ly.** *n-* **clan′nish·ness.**
clans·man (klănz′mən) *n-* [*pl.* **clans·men**] member of a clan.
clap (klăp) *vt-* [**clapped, clap·ping**] **1** to strike together with a quick, sharp sound: *The teacher* clapped *her hands for attention.* **2** to strike or slap, usually in a friendly way: *to* clap *one on the back.* **3** to put or place with great speed: *He* clapped *the lid on the pot.* *vi-* **1** to strike the hands together as in applause: *The audience* clapped *with enthusiasm.* **2** to strike or move with a sudden sharp noise: *The door* clapped *shut.* *n-* **1** short, sharp, loud noise: *a* clap *of thunder.* **2** a slap.
clap·board (klăb′ərd) *n-* long, narrow board, often thicker at one edge than at the other, used to cover the outside of wooden houses. *vt-* to cover with such boards: *to* clapboard *a house.* *adj-*: *a white* clapboard *house.*
clap·per (klăp′ər) *n-* **1** tongue of a bell. **2** person or things that claps.
clap·trap (klăp′trăp′) *Informal* *n-* any pretentious device; nonsense: *The candidate's talk was mostly* claptrap.
claque (klăk) *n-* **1** group of hired applauders at a performance, especially in the theater. **2** group of self-seeking followers. *Hom-* clack.

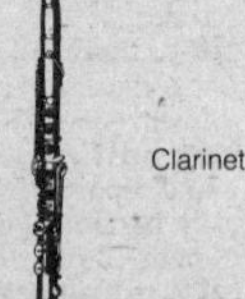
Clapper

clar·et (klăr′ət) *n-* **1** a red wine. **2** deep purplish-red color. *adj-*: *a* claret *velvet robe.*
clar·i·fi·ca·tion (klăr′ə fə kā′shən) *n-* the act of making clear, or the process of becoming clear: *a* clarification *of ideas.*
clar·i·fy (klăr′ə fī′) *vt-* [**clar·i·fied, clar·i·fy·ing**] **1** to make clear, transparent, or pure, as with a liquid, butter, or air. **2** to make plain or intelligible: *to* clarify *a statement.* *vi-*: *The syrup* clarified *as it heated.*
clar·i·net (klăr′ə nĕt′) *n-* mellow-toned woodwind musical instrument with a single-reed mouthpiece.—*n-* **clar′i·net′ist.**
clar·i·on (klăr′ē ən) *n-* small medieval trumpet having a shrill, clear sound. *adj-* clear and rousing; heraldic: *Patrick Henry's* clarion *call for liberty.*

Clarinet

clar·i·ty (klăr ə tē) *n-* clearness: *his* clarity *of speech*; *the* clarity *of water in a stream.*
clash (klăsh) *vi-* **1** to make a loud, metallic, reverberating sound by striking together: *The cymbals* clashed. **2** to come into conflict; be in opposition or discord: *The armies* clashed *on the plain. Pink and orange* clash. *vt-*: *They* clashed *their swords together.* *n-* **1** any sudden, discordant sound. **2** opposition; conflict; discord: *a* clash *of opinions*; *a* clash *of colors.*

clasp (klăsp) ***n-*** **1** fastening device that grips or hooks two parts or things together: *a tie* clasp. **2** a firm hold or grasp, as in shaking hands; close embrace. ***vt-*** **1** to fasten: *to* clasp *a bracelet.* **2** to grasp or hold close: *He* clasped *the handle of the door.*

clasp knife ***n-*** pocket knife, especially one with a clasp to hold the blade open.

class (klăs) ***n-*** **1** group of persons or things similar in various ways; sort; kind. **2** section of society having the same social or economic level; rank: *the middle* class. **3** group of students receiving instruction together, or ranked together, or graduating in the same year: *a science* class. **4** quality, grade of service, etc.: *mail sent second*-class. **5** *Biology* a category in the system of classifying animals and plants. A class is made up of orders; and several classes, in turn, form a phylum. **6** *Informal* style; tone; exclusiveness: *This hotel has* class! ***vt-*** to put in a group; rate; place: *He* classed *Churchill among the world's greatest men.*

in a class by itself (or **oneself**) the only one of its kind; unmatched; unique.

clas·sic (klăs′ĭk) ***adj-*** **1** serving as a model or standard of its kind: *a* classic *example of colonial architecture*; *a* classic *case of smallpox.* **2** of or in the style of ancient Greek or Roman art or literature. **3** restrained; simple: *The pump is a* classic *shoe design.* ***n-*** **1** anything, especially in art and literature, of such excellence that it is recognized as a permanent model or standard. **2** any person whose works are so regarded. **3 the classics** the literature of ancient Greece and Rome.

clas·si·cal (klăs′ĭ kəl) ***adj-*** **1** classic. **2** having to do with ancient Greece or Rome: *a map of the* classical *world.* **3** following the style or principles of the writers and artists of ancient Greece or Rome: *a building with* classical *lines and proportion.* **4** concerned with studies of the Greek and Roman classics: *a* classical *education; a* classical *scholar.* **5** standard; traditional; not new: *Euclid's geometry is* classical *geometry.* **6** relating to music by composers of accepted value and lasting fame, as distinguished from popular music, folk music, jazz, etc.—***adv-*** **clas′si·cal·ly**

clas·si·ci·sm (klăs′ĭ sĭz′əm) ***n-*** **1** the principles of simplicity, balance, formality, etc., used by ancient Greeks and Romans in literature, art, architecture, etc.; the opposite of romanticism. **2** agreement with, or the following of, these principles: *the* classicism *of his sculpture.*

clas·si·cist (klăs′ə sĭst′) ***n-*** **1** person who supports the principles of classicism. **2** person who urges the study of the classics. **3** person who is an authority on ancient Greece and Rome.

clas·si·fi·ca·tion (clăs′ə fə kā′shən) ***n-*** an arranging in groups or classes; also, the arrangement so made.

clas·si·fied (klăs′ə fīd′) ***adj-*** kept secret except to certain people: *a* classified *report on rocket research.*

classified ad ***n-*** short advertisement that appears, especially in newspapers, with other such advertisements on the same subject.

clas·si·fy (klăs′ə fī′) ***vt-*** [**clas·si·fied, clas·si·fy·ing**] **1** to arrange into groups or classes according to a system: *You can* classify *a collection of shells according to shape, color, or size.* **2** to declare (information) of value to an enemy and allow only certain people to have it: *to* classify *a report on missile research.*

class·mate (klăs′māt′) ***n-*** a member of the same class at school.

class·room (klăs′rōōm′) ***n-*** a room in a school where classes are held.

clat·ter (klăt′ər) ***n-*** **1** a rattling noise. **2** noisy talk; commotion. ***vi-***: *The forks* clattered *in the drawer.*

clause (klȯz) ***n-*** **1** *Grammar* a sentence or division of a sentence containing a finite verb or verb phrase and its subject. The sentence "He left yesterday, and they will leave tomorrow" has two clauses. See also *dependent clause, independent clause.* **2** a distinct part of a written agreement, contract, or treaty: *There is a* clause *in my contract which allows a month's vacation a year.*

claus·tro·pho·bi·a (klȯs′trə fō′bē ə) ***n-*** extreme fear of being shut in, as in closed or narrow places.

clav·i·chord (klăv′ə kȯrd′, -kôrd′) ***n-*** keyboard musical instrument, forerunner of the modern piano.

clav·i·cle (klăv′ĭ kəl) ***n-*** either of two bones that connect the breastbone and the shoulder blades; collarbone.

cla·vier (klə vêr′, klăv′ē ər) ***n-*** **1** keyboard of a musical instrument; also a "silent keyboard" used for practice. **2** any stringed instrument having a keyboard, such as a harpsichord, clavichord, or piano. *as* ***modifier***: *a score of* clavier *music.*

claw (klȯ) ***n-*** **1** a sharp, hooked, horny nail on a toe of an animal or bird; also, the toe and the nail. **2** the pincers of a shellfish such as a crab or lobster. **3** any hooked or pointed tool, such as the curved end of some hammer heads. ***vt-*** to scratch, tear, dig, or pull with the toes or fingers, especially the nails: *The cat* clawed *my arm.*

Bird's claw

clay (klā) ***n-*** soft, fine-grained earth that may be molded when moist and becomes stone-hard when baked. Bricks and pottery are made of clay. —***adj-*** **clay′ey.**

clay pigeon ***n-*** a disk, usually made of baked clay, hurled into the air as a target for trapshooting.

clean (klēn) ***adj-*** [**cleaner, clean·est**] **1** free from dirt; not filthy; unsoiled: *A food handler must have* clean *hands.* **2** free from guilt, sin, wrong, etc.; morally pure: *a* clean *life*; *a* clean *record.* **3** made or used for the first time; fresh: *a* clean *start*; *a* clean *sheet of paper.* **4** free from flaws or irregularities; smooth and even: *a* clean *jump*; *the* clean *motion of his arm*; *the* clean *lines of the car.* **5** not violating the rules of good sportsmanship; fair: *a* clean *fight.* ***vt-*** **1** to remove dirt, trash, etc., from: *to* clean *one's house.* **2** to prepare (fish, chicken, etc.) for cooking. ***adv-*** completely; thoroughly: *The bullet went* clean *through the tree.* —***n-*** **clean′ness.**

clean out **1** to make neat and orderly by removing dirt, trash, useless items, etc.: *to* clean out *one's attic.* **2** *Informal* to remove everything from: *The burglars* cleaned out *the safe.*

clean up **1** to remove dirt and filth from oneself: *to* clean up *for supper.* **2** to make (something) tidy and orderly: *to* clean up *the house.* **3** to finish; put in final form: *to* clean up *one's work.* **4** *Slang* to make a great amount of money.

clean-cut (klēn′kŭt′) ***adj-*** **1** clear; sharply defined; precise: *a* clean-cut *statement.* **2** having a neat, wholesome appearance: *a* clean-cut *stranger.*

clean·er (klē′nər) ***n-*** person, substance, or machine that removes dirt from things.

[1]**clean·ly** (klĕn′lē) ***adj-*** [**clean·li·er, clean·li·est**] careful to keep clean: *A* cleanly *cook washes her hands before preparing food.* [from Old English **clǣnlic** meaning "pure."] —***n-*** **clean′li·ness.**

[2]**clean·ly** (klĕn′ lē) ***adv-*** in a sharp or smooth way: *The diver cut the water* cleanly. [from Old English **clænlīce.**]

cleanse (klĕnz) ***vt-*** **[cleansed, cleans·ing]** to make clean or pure: *to* cleanse *one's hands.*

cleans·er (klĕn′ zər) ***n-*** substance used for cleaning, especially a scouring powder for sinks, floors, etc.

clean·up (klēn′ ŭp′) ***n-*** **1** a complete cleaning or ridding of dirt, vice, corruption, etc. **2** *Slang* unusually large profit; big haul; killing. ***adj-*** in baseball, fourth in the batting order of a team: *the* cleanup *position.*

clear (klêr) ***adj-*** **[clear·er, clear·est] 1** free of clouds, mud, or any other obstacle that blocks or reduces vision: *a* clear *day*; clear *water*; clear *glass.* **2** free of any obstacle to physical passage: *a* clear *road.* **3** distinct to the ear, eye, or mind; not vague nor blurred: *a* clear *voice*; *a* clear *explanation.* **4** free from moral or physical blemishes: *a* clear *conscience*; *a* clear *diamond*; *a* clear *complexion.* **5** free of confusion or vagueness: *a* clear *head*; *a* clear *purpose.* **6** without further cost to be deducted; net: *He made a* clear *$10,000 on that deal.* ***adv-*** completely; entirely: *The bullet passed* clear *through the target.* ***vt-*** **1** to free of (clouds, mud, or other obstacle to vision): *The fan* cleared *the smoke from the room.* **2** to free of (any physical obstacles): *to* clear *a field of stumps*; *to* clear *one's throat.* **3** to pass closely over or by without touching: *to* clear *a hurdle*; *to* clear *a corner by an inch.* **4** to pass or permit to pass (an examination as to legal or moral suitability): *We* cleared *customs. The committee* cleared *the appointment.* **5** to make as profit; to net: *to* clear *$5,000 on a sale.* ***vi-*** to become free of any obstacles or any blemishes: *The weather* cleared.

in the clear *Informal* free of guilt or blame.

clear away to finish up (work, affairs, etc.); dispose of; settle: *There is work to* clear away *before we go.*

clear out 1 to empty so as to make clean: *to* clear out *one's desk.* **2** *Informal* to leave a place, often quickly.

clear up 1 to become free of cloudiness, fog, etc.: *The day* cleared up *after the rain.* **2** to clarify or solve: *to* clear up *a mystery.* **3** to put in order; settle.

clear·ance (klêr′ əns) ***n-*** **1** the space or amount of space between a moving vehicle, ship, etc., and another object: *a* clearance *of 25 feet between the ship and the dock.* **2** permission granted a ship, plane, passenger, etc., to enter or leave a place: *The plane received* clearance *from the control tower.* **3** the exchanging of checks and other notes from banks and the settling of accounts at a clearinghouse. **4** official approval given to a person to handle restricted material or information.

clear-cut (klêr′ kŭt′) ***adj-*** **1** having a distinct outline: *a* clear-cut *profile.* **2** clear; direct; definite: *a* clear-cut *statement.*

clear·ing (klêr′ ĭng) ***n-*** piece of land from which trees and underbrush have been removed.

clear·ing·house (klêr′ ĭng hous′) ***n-*** office which serves banks by exchanging checks and other notes and settling accounts.

clear·ly (klêr′ lē) ***adv-*** plainly; distinctly: *I hear you quite* clearly.

cleat (klēt) ***n-*** **1** one of the blocks or spikes put on the soles of some athletes' shoes to prevent slipping. **2** strip of wood or metal fastened across a board to give support, hold something in place, prevent slipping, etc. **3** a kind of hook used for temporary fastening of ropes, particularly on ships.

Cleat

cleav·age (klē′ vĭj) ***n-*** **1** act of splitting or dividing. **2** the natural tendency of a crystal or rock to split along definite planes. **3** cleft.

[1]**cleave** (klēv) ***vt-*** **[cleft** (klĕft) or **cleaved** or **clove** (klōv), **cleft** or **cleaved** or **cloven** (klō′ vən), **cleav·ing] 1** to split or cut open: *The lightning* cleft *the tree.* **2** to cut a way through: *The destroyer* cleaved *the water.* ***vi-*** to come or split apart, especially along a crack or line of weakness: *Dry wood* cleaves *easily.* [from Old English **cleofan** meaning "to split."]

[2]**cleave** (klēv) ***vi-*** **[cleaved, cleav·ing]** to cling; hold fast or be faithful: *to* cleave *to one's principles.* [Old English **clifian, clēofian** meaning "to stick."]

cleav·er (klē′ vər) ***n-*** a butcher's heavy hatchet or chopper for cutting meat or bone.

clef (klĕf) *Music* ***n-*** any of several signs placed at the beginning of the staff to indicate the range of pitch of the notes. See *bass clef* and *treble clef.*

[1]**cleft** (klĕft) *p.t. & p.p.* of [1]**cleave.**

[2]**cleft** (klĕft) ***n-*** crack; crevice; fissure: *a* cleft *in the rock.* ***adj-*** partly divided; appearing to be split: *a* cleft *chin.*

cleft palate ***n-*** birth defect in which the roof of the mouth is split.

clem·a·tis (klĕm′ ə təs, klə măt′ əs) ***n-*** a vine of the buttercup family with showy purple, blue, or red flowers.

clem·en·cy (klĕm′ ən sē) ***n-*** **1** mercy; leniency: *The court showed* clemency *toward the young prisoner.* **2** mildness, as of the weather or climate.

clem·ent (klĕm′ ənt) ***adj-*** **1** forgiving; kind: *a* clement *judge.* **2** mild: *the* clement *weather.* ***—adv-*** **clem′ ent·ly.**

clench (klĕnch) ***vt-*** **1** to press closely together: *He* clenched *his teeth.* **2** to grasp firmly: *He* clenched *the sword in his hand.*

cler·gy (klûr′ jē) ***n-*** [*pl.* **cler·gies]** all persons ordained for religious service as ministers, priests, rabbis, etc.

cler·gy·man (klûr′ jē mən) ***n-*** [*pl.* **cler·gy·men]** an ordained minister, priest, rabbi, etc.

cler·ic (klĕr′ ĭk) ***n-*** clergyman.

cler·i·cal (klĕr′ ĭ kəl) ***adj-*** **1** having to do with the clergy: *a* clerical *collar.* **2** connected with the work of a clerk, typist, bookkeeper, etc.: *Filing is a* clerical *task.* ***—adv-*** **cler′ i·cal·ly.**

cler·i·cal·ism (klĕr′ ĭ kə lĭz′ əm) ***n-*** policy of defending or advancing the power of the clergy in either political or religious matters.

clerk (klûrk) ***n-*** **1** salesman or saleswoman in a store. **2** person who does the routine work of an office, especially keeping records: *a file* clerk. **3** public official who keeps records and does routine business.

clev·er (klĕv′ ər) ***adj-*** **[clev·er·er, clev·er·est] 1** mentally quick or alert: *A* clever *fox can escape the hounds.* **2** skillfull: *I wish I were* clever *enough to make my own clothes.* **3** showing skill or mental quickness: *a* clever *scheme.* ***—adv-*** **clev′ er·ly.** ***n-*** **clev′ er·ness.**

clev·is (klĕv′ əs) ***n-*** a U-shaped metal device drilled at the two ends to receive a pin or bolt, and used to connect machine parts, attach a chain, etc.

clew (klo͞o) clue.

cli·ché (klē shā′) ***n-*** **1** trite or overused expression such as "to get down to brass tacks." **2** any overworked idea, theme, or situation, as in room decoration, a song, a movie plot, etc.

click (klĭk) ***n-*** slight, sharp sound: *the* click *of a key in a lock.* ***vi-***: *Her high heels* clicked *on the pavement.* ***vt-***: *He* clicked *the metal balls.*

cli·ent (klī′ ənt) ***n-*** **1** person who engages the professional services of another, especially of a lawyer. **2** a good customer: *an antique dealer's* clients.

cli·en·tele (klī′ ən tĕl′, klē′-) ***n-*** all the habitual customers, clients, or patients of a merchant, lawyer, doctor, etc.

cliff (klĭf) ***n-*** high, steep face of rock or earth; precipice.

cliff dweller ***n-*** **1** any one of an early group of people, forerunners of the Pueblo Indians, who built dwellings on the cliffs and canyon walls of the southwestern United States. **2** any person who dwells on or in a cliff.

cliff-hang·er (klĭf′ hăng′ ər) *Informal* ***n-*** **1** melodrama presented as a serial with each installment ending in suspense, as in old cowboy films. **2** a game in which the outcome is in doubt to the very end.

cliff swallow ***n-*** square-tailed American swallow that builds its mud nest on cliff faces or under the eaves of buildings.

cli·mac·tic (klə măk′ tĭk) ***adj-*** relating to or forming a climax: *a* climactic *scene in the play.*

cli·mate (klī′ mət) ***n-*** **1** the weather conditions of a place over a period of time: *the warm* climate *of Florida in the winter.* **2** the prevailing outlook or attitude: *a favorable* climate *of opinion.*

cli·mat·ic (klī măt′ ĭk) ***adj-*** of or having to do with climate or weather. ***—adv-*** **cli·mat′ i·cal·ly.**

cli·ma·tol·o·gy (klī′ mə tŏl′ ə jē) ***n-*** branch of meteorology that studies climates.

cli·max (klī′ măks′) ***n-*** **1** highest and most important point in the development of events, ideas, etc.; turning point; culmination: *the* climax *of a play.* **2** last of a series of events: *The victory was a* climax *to a week of fighting.* ***vt-***: *His election* climaxed *a brilliant career.*

climb (klīm) ***vt-*** **1** to go up or over (something) by using hands and feet; scale: *to* climb *a cliff*; *to* climb *a tree.* **2** to mount; ascend: *The car easily* climbed *the hill.* **3** of a vine or shrub, to grow up (a wall, trellis, etc.) by twining or clinging with tendrils. ***vi-*** **1** to rise: *The plane* climbs *rapidly. Prices* climbed *higher.* **2** to go (up, over, or through) something by scaling or ascending: *to* climb *over the ridge*; *to* climb *through the window.* ***n-*** **1** a going up with effort; ascent: *a* climb *up Mt. Everest*; *a* climb *to fame.* **2** a place to be climbed: *Mt. Everest is a dangerous* climb. ***Hom-*** clime.

climb·er (klī′ mər) ***n-*** **1** person or thing that climbs. **2** in botany, a climbing plant. **3** *Informal* person who is very ambitious about getting ahead socially.

clime (klīm) *Archaic* ***n-*** a place; region. ***Hom-*** climb.

clinch (klĭnch) ***vt-*** **1** to fasten tightly, especially a nail by bending its end over. **2** to settle a matter: *to* clinch *a deal.* **3** to grasp and hold tightly: *The boxer* clinched *his opponent around the shoulders.* ***vi-*** to grapple; seize one another, as in boxing. ***n-*** a grasping and holding tightly: *The fighters are in a* clinch.

clinch·er (klĭnch′ ər) *Informal* ***n-*** an argument, act, or circumstance that settles or decides: *Of all the arguments for buying that car, the* clincher *is its low price.*

cling (klĭng) ***vi-*** **[clung** (klŭng), **cling·ing]** to hold fast or stick to someone or something: *to* cling *to a rope.*

clin·ic (klĭn′ ĭk) ***n-*** **1** an institution where specialists help people with a particular type of medical or personal problem: *heart* clinic; *dental* clinic; *reading* clinic. **2** infirmary where a group of doctors offer a wide range of medical services. **3** medical course in which students learn by observing the treatment of patients.

clin·i·cal (klĭn′ ĭ kəl) ***adj-*** **1** having to do with or carried out in a clinic. **2** scientifically detached; cooly analytical; not emotional: *a* clinical *approach to politics.* **3** dealing with the observation and treatment of patients rather than with laboratory experiments: *a* clinical *psychologist.* ***—adv-*** **clin′ i·cal·ly.**

clinical thermometer ***n-*** thermometer for taking body temperature.

clink (klĭngk) ***n-*** light tinkling or ringing sound: *the* clink *of coins.* ***vt-***: *He* clinked *a spoon against the glass.* ***vi-***: *The coins* clinked *in his pocket.*

clink·er (klĭng′ kər) ***n-*** partly fused stony mass left after burning coal in a stove or furnace.

Cli·o (klī′ ō) ***n-*** in Greek mythology, the Muse of history.

[1]**clip** (klĭp) ***vt-*** **[clipped, clip·ping]** to hold tightly together with a clasp. ***n-*** **1** a clasp, especially for holding papers: *a paper* clip. **2** ornament which is held by a clasp: *She wore a diamond* clip. **2** in automatic firearms, a metal container for holding cartridges and from which they are fed into the chamber. [from Old English word **clyppan** meaning "to embrace, fondle."]

Clip

[2]**clip** (klĭp) ***vt-*** **[clipped, clip·ping]** **1** to cut or trim with shears: *to* clip *wool from sheep.* **2** to cut short: *He* clips *his words when he talks fast.* ***n-*** **1** a cut or a snip: *With a* clip *of the shears, the barber finished the haircut.* **2** amount of wool cut from a sheep at one time. [from earlier English **clippen,** from Old Norse **klippa.**]

[3]**clip** (klĭp) ***n-*** a rate or pace: *He walks at a good* clip. [special use of [2]**clip.**]

clip·board (klĭp′ bôrd′) ***n-*** small board with a strong spring clip at the top to hold papers in place.

HAIR
NAIL
HEDGE
Clippers

[1]**clip·per** (klĭp′ ər) or **clip·pers** (-ərz) ***n-*** any of various tools for trimming hair, finger nails, hedges, etc. [from [2]**clip.**]

[2]**clip·per** (klĭp′ ər) ***n-*** a sailing vessel built for speed: *China* clipper. [from [3]**clip.**]

clip·ping (klĭp′ ĭng) ***n-*** piece cut off or out of something: *fingernail* clippings; *a newspaper* clipping.

clique (klēk) ***n-*** small group of people who stick closely together for common interests, usually rejecting outsiders: *a political* clique.

clo·a·ca (klō′ ā′ kə) ***n-*** [*pl.* **clo·a·cae** (-sē)] **1** sewer. **2** *Biology* body chamber in fish, reptiles, birds, etc., into which the intestinal, urinary, and reproductive canals all empty.

cloak (klōk) ***n-*** **1** loose, usually sleeveless, outer garment. **2** a covering or disguise: *His sweet words were a* cloak *for his treachery.* ***vt-*** to cover; conceal: *Fog* cloaks *the city buildings.*

Man in cloak

cloak·room (klōk′ ro͞om′) ***n-*** room where coats, hats, umbrellas, etc., are left temporarily; coatroom.

clob·ber (klŏb′ ər) *Slang* ***vt-*** **1** to pound or beat severely; to maul. **2** to defeat completely.

cloche (klōsh) ***n-*** deep, close-fitting woman's hat.

[1]**clock** (klŏk) ***n-*** device for measuring and indicating time, especially one larger than a watch, with a pair of pointers, or hands, that move around a dial marked to show hours and minutes. ***vt-*** to time (somebody or something), usually with a stopwatch: *to* clock *a race.* [from early Dutch **clocke** meaning "bell," from Medieval Latin **clocca** meaning "hand bell."]

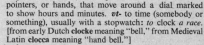

[2]**clock** (klŏk) ***n-*** long, narrow design extending upward from the ankle of a sock or stocking. [of unknown origin.] ***—adj-*** **clocked.**

clock·wise (klŏk'wīz') *adj-* in the same direction as that in which the hands of a clock move: *to turn* clockwise. *adj-*: *a* clockwise *direction.*

clock·work (klŏk'wûrk') *n-* the machinery of a clock. *as modifier: the* clockwork *regularity of his habits.*
like clockwork with regularity and exactness.

clod (klŏd) *n-* **1** lump of earth or clay. **2** stupid person.

clod·hop·per (klŏd'hŏp'ər) *n-* **1** an awkward country youth; rustic. **2 clodhoppers** heavy, sturdy shoes.

clog (klŏg) *vt-* **[clogged, clog·ging] 1** to obstruct; stop up; block: *Leaves* clogged *the drain.* **2** to hinder the movement of by blocking or obstructing: *Lint* clogged *the gears of the machine. vi-* to become obstructed or stopped up: *The fountain pen* clogged *and wouldn't write. n-* **1** a shoe with a wooden sole. **2** (also called **clog dance**) a dance by a person wearing heavy shoes that clatter in rhythm.

Bath clog

cloister (klois'tər) *n-* **1** a covered walk with open arches on one side, usually built around a courtyard. **2** a monastery or convent. *vt-* to confine, as in a monastery or convent; seclude.

Cloister

clois·tered (klois'tərd) *adj-* **1** with cloisters. **2** secluded.

clone (klōn) *Biology n-* a multicellular living organism that has been produced asexually from a single cell. *vt-* **[cloned, clon·ing]** to cause to grow as a clone: *The scientist* cloned *the carrot from a single carrot cell.*

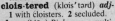

[1]close (klōz) *vt-* **[closed, clos·ing] 1** to shut: *Please* close *the window.* **2** to stop up; obstruct: *Fallen rocks had* closed *the mine entrance.* **3** to bring to an end; conclude: *to* close *a meeting.* **4** to bring together: *The doctor* closed *the wound. vi-* **1** to come together: *The curtains* closed *at the end of the play.* **2** to come to an end: *The season* closes *on Labor Day.* **3** to agree to a contract, sale, etc., as binding both parties. *n-* the end: *at the* close *of day.* [from Old French **clos** meaning "closed (space)," from Latin **clausum** also meaning "closed (space)."] *Hom-* clothes.

[2]close (klōs) *adj-* **[clos·er, clos·est] 1** without much space between; narrow; snug; fitting tightly: *a* close *weave*; *a* close *fit.* **2** stuffy: *The air was* close *in the room.* **3** strict and careful: *under* close *guard*; *a* close *translation.* **4** stingy: *The miser was* close *with his money.* **5** almost equal, often with the outcome in doubt: *a* close *race. adv-* very near: *He parked* close *to the curb.* [probably a later meaning of **[1]close** as an adjective.] **—*adv-* close'ly. *n-* close'ness.**

close call (klōs) *Informal n-* narrow escape.

closed season *n-* any time of year when hunting or fishing is illegal.

closed shop *n-* a factory or other business in which only union members may be hired. See also *open shop.*

closed syllable *n-* syllable that ends with a consonant.

close·fist·ed (klōs'fĭs'təd) *adj-* stingy.

close-grained (klōs'grānd') *adj-* **1** having a fine, smooth texture: *a* close-grained *rock.* **2** of wood, having closely packed fibers, as in spruce or pine. **3** of wood, having the annual rings close together.

close·mouthed (klōs'moutht') *adj-* discreet; careful about giving away any information.

close quarters *n-* **1** crowded and confined space: *They lived in* close quarters *in the barracks.* **2** close range: *They fought at* close quarters.

clos·et (klŏz'ĭt) *n-* **1** small room or cupboard for storing things. **2** small, private room, especially one for prayer or study. *vt-* to shut up in a private place: *The two leaders* closeted *themselves to discuss their plans.*

close·up (klōs'ŭp') *n-* a picture taken at short range.

clo·sure (klō'zhər) *n-* **1** a shutting up; ending. **2** something that closes, especially a lid or a cap. **3** in parliamentary procedure, the bringing of debate to an end by calling for a vote on the measure considered. **4** *Mathematics* property of an operation such that the result of the operation on any two members of a set is also a member of the set.

clot (klŏt) *n-* thickened mass of something that was liquid: *a blood* clot. *vi-* **[clot·ted, clot·ting]** to form such masses: *Blood* clots *when exposed to air. vt-* to cause to coagulate.

cloth (klȯth) *n-* **1** fabric made from wool, cotton, silk, linen, etc. **2** piece of such fabric used for a special purpose: *a dust* cloth. **3 the cloth** the clergy.

clothe (klōth) *vt-* **[clothed** or **clad** (klăd), **cloth·ing] 1** to dress; put clothes on. **2** to provide clothing for. **3** to cover with, or as with, a garment: *Flowers* clothed *the field in white. Age* clothed *him with dignity.*

clothes (klōz, klōthz) *n- pl.* garments; clothing. *Hom-* [1]close.

clothes·horse (klōz'hȯrs', -hôrs') *n-* **1** folding frame on which to dry or air clothes. **2** *Slang* person who has many clothes and likes to display them.

clothes·line (klōz'līn', klōthz'-) *n-* a rope or wire on which clothes are hung to dry.

clothes·pin (klōz'pĭn', klōthz') *n-* clamp or forked piece of wood used to fasten clothes to a clothesline.

clothes tree *n-* upright stand with hooks for clothes.

cloth·i·er (klōth'yər, -ē ər) *n-* one whose business is making or selling cloth or clothing.

cloth·ing (klō'thĭng) *n-* garments of any sort; clothes.

clo·ture (klō'chər) *n-* in the U.S. Senate and other legislatures, a rule that limits debate in order to get an immediate vote on a question.

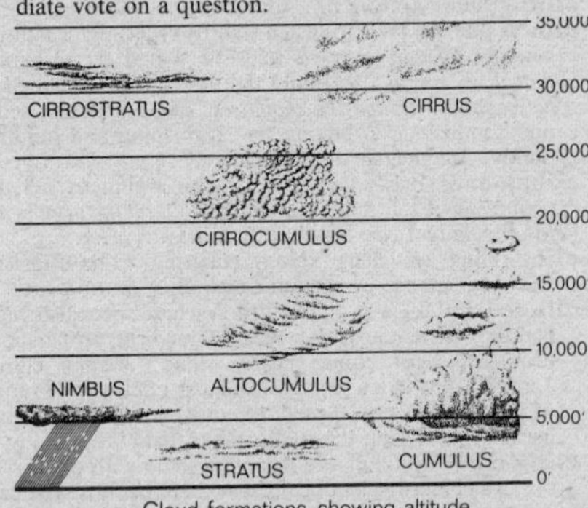

Cloud formations, showing altitude

cloud (kloud) *n-* **1** visible mass of condensed water floating above the earth. **2** similar mass of smoke or dust. **3** anything that moves in or like a mass, such as a large number of arrows, insects, horsemen, etc. **4** anything that threatens or obscures; a cause of trouble or confusion: *the* clouds *of war; an issue veiled in a* cloud *of controversy. vt-* **1** to cover with a mist, smoke, etc.: *Smoke* clouded *his vision.*

A heavy fog clouded *the streets.* **2** to trouble, darken, sully, etc.: *Grief* clouded *his face. A bad record* clouds *his reputation.* ***vi-***: *The sky* clouded *over.*

cloud·burst (kloud′ bûrst′) ***n-*** sudden heavy rainfall.

cloud chamber ***n-*** enclosure containing a gas supersaturated with water vapor, used to study atomic particles. When suddenly cooled, the vapor condenses on ions formed by a passing particle, thus making its path visible as a vapor trail.

cloud·less (kloud′ ləs) ***adj-*** free from clouds; not overcast; clear: *a* cloudless *sky.* ***—adv-*** **cloud′ less·ly.** ***n-*** **cloud′ less·ness.**

cloud seeding ***n-*** the release of tiny crystals of silver iodide, dry ice, etc., in clouds, to bring about rain.

cloud·y (klou′ dē) ***adj-*** **[cloud·i·er, cloud·i·est] 1** covered with clouds; overcast: *a* cloudy *sky.* **2** not transparent: *a* cloudy *liquid.* **3** not clear; obscure: *his* cloudy *notions.* ***—adv-*** **cloud′ i·ly.** ***n-*** **cloud′ i·ness.**

clout (klout) ***n-*** **1** strong blow. **2** in archery, a white cloth target used in long-distance shooting. **3** arrow that hits such a target. **4** *Archaic* a patch; rag. ***vt-*** to hit; strike: *to* clout *a home run.*

[1]**clove** (klōv) ***n-*** the dried flower bud of a tropical evergreen tree, used as a spice or in medicine. [from Middle English **cloue** meaning "nail," from the appearance of the dried spice.]

[2]**clove** (klōv) ***n-*** one of the segments of a garlic bulb. [from Old English **clufu,** related to [1]**cleave.**]

[3]**clove** (klōv) *p.t.* of [1]**cleave.**

clove hitch ***n-*** knot used to secure horses, boats, etc. For picture, see *knot.*

clo·ven (klō′ vən) ***adj-*** divided; split: *a* cloven *hoof.*

cloven hoof or **cloven foot** ***n-*** **1** a divided hoof such as that of cattle, deer, etc. **2** the sign of Satan, who is often represented as having such feet. ***—adj-*** **clo′ ven-hoofed′** or **clo′ ven-foot′ ed.**

Red clover

clo·ver (klō′ vər) ***n-*** any of various plants that grow close to the ground and have three leaflets in each leaf cluster and round, sweet-smelling flower heads of red, white, and purple.

in clover prosperous; having everything: *When Jason comes into his inheritance, he will be* in clover.

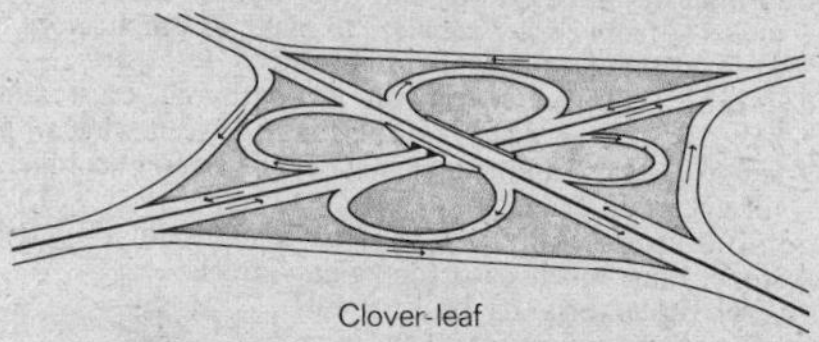

Clover-leaf

clo·ver-leaf (klō′ vər lēf′) ***n-*** kind of highway intersection in which two highways cross at different levels. They are connected by a series of ramps which outline the form of a four-leaf clover and allow cars to move from one highway to the other without making a left turn.

clown (kloun) ***n-*** **1** comedian, often dressed in an outlandish costume, who performs in a circus or other entertainment. **2** person who frequently acts like a fool and plays pranks: *the school* clown. **3** *Archaic* rude, clumsy man; boor. ***vi-***: *He* clowned *in circuses for thirty years. The boy* clowns *when he should be studying.*

clown·ish (klou′ nĭsh) ***adj-*** like a clown: *a* clownish *fellow.* ***—adv-*** **clown′ ish·ly.** ***n-*** **clown′ ish·ness:** *His* clownishness *is getting to be annoying.*

cloy (kloi) ***vt-*** to make weary by too much of anything pleasant: *Too much candy* cloys *his appetite.* ***vi-*** to cause a feeling of weariness, boredom, etc.: *Constant pleasure soon begins to* cloy.

club (klŭb) ***n-*** **1** heavy stick, usually thick at one end, especially one used as a weapon. **2** any of certain sticks or bats for hitting a ball: *a golf* club. **3** group of people united for some common purpose: *an athletic* club. **4** building or room occupied by such a group. **5** any one of a suit of playing cards (**clubs**) marked with black designs [♣] resembling clover leaves. ***vt-*** **[clubbed, club·bing]** to beat with a heavy stick, fist, etc.

club together to join together for a common purpose: *The boys* clubbed together *to buy a basketball.*

club·foot (klŭb′ fo͝ot′) ***n-*** birth deformity in which the foot is out of position or shape. ***—adj-*** **club′ foot′ ed.**

club moss ***n-*** any of a family of low-growing, evergreen, nonflowering plants, most of which bear spore sacs shaped like clubs.

cluck (klŭk) ***n-*** sound made by a hen calling her chickens. ***vi-*** to make such a sound.

clue (klo͞o) ***n-*** something that helps solve a problem or a mystery: *The footprints were a* clue. Also **clew.**

clump (klŭmp) ***n-*** **1** thick cluster: *a* clump *of bushes.* **2** thick mass; lump: *a* clump *of earth.* ***vi-*** to tread heavily: *The horses* clumped *along.* ***—adj-*** **clump′ y.**

clum·sy (klŭm′ zē) ***adj-*** **[clum·si·er, clum·si·est] 1** lacking in ease or grace; awkward: *a* clumsy *fellow; a* clumsy *excuse.* **2** hard to handle; unwieldy: *a* clumsy *rake.* ***—adv-*** **clum′ si·ly.** ***n-*** **clum′ si·ness.**

clung (klŭng) *p.t. & p.p.* of **cling.**

clus·ter (klŭs′ tər) ***n-*** group of persons or things close together; assemblage: *a* cluster *of grapes; a* cluster *of islands; a* cluster *of people.* ***vi-***: *The girls* clustered *around him.*

[1]**clutch** (klŭch) ***vt-*** to hold or grasp tightly; grip: *to* clutch *a knife.* ***n-*** **1** tight hold; grasp; grip: *a* clutch *on one's arm.* **2** in mechanics, a machine coupling used to connect an engine to a drive shaft, as in an automobile; also, the lever or pedal that operates this coupling. **3 clutches** possession; power; control: *They fell into the* clutches *of the enemy.* [from Old English **clyccan** meaning "to bend; clench."]

clutch at to try to snatch or seize.

[2]**clutch** (klŭch) ***n-*** **1** brood of chickens. **2** amount of eggs laid at one time. [from a dialectal form **cletch,** from Old Norse **klekja.**]

clut·ter (klŭt′ ər) ***n-*** disorderly state; confusion; jumble: *Please tidy up the* clutter *in your room.* ***vt-***: *Heaps of books* cluttered *her room.*

Clydes·dale (klīdz′ dāl′) ***n-*** big, strong work horse originally bred in the Clyde valley region of Scotland.

Cm symbol for curium.

cm. or **cm** centimeter or centimeters.

CNS or **C.N.S.** central nervous system.

Co symbol for cobalt.

co- *prefix* with; together; joint: *to co-operate.*

Co. 1 company. **2** county.

c.o. or **c/o** care of.

C.O. commanding officer.
coach (kōch) *n-* **1** large, enclosed, horse-drawn vehicle with four wheels. **2** formerly, a two-door sedan. **3** railroad passenger car, especially one without sleeping accommodations. **4** person who instructs or trains athletes, singers, dancers, etc. *vt-* to instruct or train (an athlete, singer, etc.): *He* coaches *the track team. vi-*: *He* coaches *for Notre Dame.*
coach-and-four (kōch′ən fôr′) *n-* carriage drawn by four horses.
coach dog *n-* dalmatian.
coach·man (kōch′ mən) *n-* [*pl.* **coach·men**] person who drives a horse-drawn carriage for a living.
co·ad·ju·tor (kō ăj′ ə tər, -ə jōō′ tər) *n-* assistant; especially a bishop appointed to assist another bishop.
co·ag·u·lant (kō ăg′ yə lənt) *n-* substance that causes a liquid to coagulate.
co·ag·u·late (kō ăg′ yə lāt′) *vi-* [**co·ag·u·lat·ed, co·ag·u·lat·ing**] to become clotted; to change from a liquid to a pasty solid: *When the blood from a cut* coagulates, *the bleeding stops. vt-* to cause such a change. *—n-* **co·ag′ u·la′ tion.**
coal (kōl) *n-* **1** a hard, black mineral fuel formed deep in the earth from buried vegetable matter by the action of heat and great pressure. **2** a glowing or charred bit of solid fuel; an ember. *vt-* to furnish with coal: *to* coal *a ship. vi-*: *The ship* coaled *at Lisbon.* ***Hom-*** cole.
coal·er (kō′ lər) *n-* ship that transports coal.
co·a·lesce (kō′ ə lĕs′) *vi-* to come together so as to be united; blend; fuse: *The grievances of the people* coalesced *into rebellious rage. —n-* **co′ a·les′ cence:** *the* coalescence *of ice crystals. adj-* **co′ a·les′ cent.**
coal gas *n-* **1** a fuel gas, chiefly a mixture of hydrogen, methane, and carbon monoxide, obtained by heating soft coal without air. **2** poisonous gas, chiefly carbon monoxide, given off by a coal furnace without enough draft.
co·a·li·tion (kō′ ə lĭsh′ ən) *n-* in politics, a temporary alliance of persons, parties, or countries for a special purpose. *as* ***modifier***: *a* coalition *government.*
coal oil *n-* kerosene.
coal tar *n-* thick, black, sticky substance obtained from soft coal by heating without air, and used to make many drugs, dyes, and other chemicals.
coarse (kôrs) *adj-* [**coars·er, coars·est**] **1** lacking in refinement; crude; vulgar: *a* coarse *manner*; *his* coarse *language.* **2** lacking fineness of texture or shape; composed of large or rough particles, features, etc.: *a* coarse *complexion*; coarse *features*; *a pile of* coarse *gravel.* **3** *Archaic* of poor or inferior quality. *—adv-* **coarse′ ly.** *n-* **coarse′ ness.** ***Hom-*** course.
coars·en (kôr′ sən) *vt-* to make coarse: *The rain and wind* coarsened *his face. vi-*: *His face had* coarsened *with age.*
coast (kōst) *n-* the land or region next to the sea; seashore. *vi-* **1** to ride along by the force of gravity or by the force of one's momentum after power has been cut off. **2** to drift along without working: *He worked hard at the beginning of the term and then* coasted *along.* **3** *Archaic* to sail along a coast, or from port to port.
coast·al (kōs′ təl) *adj-* of, on, or along a coast: *the* coastal *shipping lanes.*
Coastal Plain *n-* the broad, low plain stretching along the Atlantic and Gulf coasts of North America from New York to Texas.
coast·er (kōs′ tər) *n-* **1** small, shallow tray placed under a glass to protect a table from heat or dampness. **2** a ship engaged in trade along a coast.
coast guard *n-* **1** the branch of a nation's military defense that guards the coast, enforces shipping and immigration laws, and carries out rescue operations. **2 Coast Guard** (1) the coast guard of the United States, operating under the Treasury Department in peacetime and under the Navy during war. (2) *Informal* the U.S. Coast Guard Academy at New London, Connecticut.
coast·line (kōst′ līn′) *n-* outline of a seashore.
coast·ward (kōst′ wərd) *adj-* facing or directed toward a coast: *a* coastward *current. adv-* (also **coast′ wards**) toward a coast: *The ship turned* coastward.
coast·wise (kōst′ wīz′) *adv-* along a coast: *to sail* coastwise. *adj-*: *a* coastwise *current*; coastwise *trade.*
coat (kōt) *n-* **1** outer garment with sleeves, especially one for winter wear reaching to or below the knees. **2** the hair or fur of an animal: *Collies have a long* coat, *dachshunds a short* coat. **3** any outer layer that covers, especially a layer of paint: *The room needs two* coats. *vt-* to cover with a layer: *to* coat *furniture with wax.*
co·a·ti (kō ä′ tē) *n-* tropical American animal that looks like the raccoon but is larger and has a longer, flexible snout. Also **co·a′ ti·mun′ di** (-mŭn′ dē).
coat·ing (kō′ tĭng) *n-* layer; covering.
coat of arms *n-* **1** emblem of a person, family, etc., marked on a shield or similar surface. **2** shield marked with such an emblem; escutcheon.
coat of mail *n-* suit of mail.
coat·room (kōt′ rōōm′) *n-* cloakroom.
coax (kōks) *vt-* **1** to persuade or influence by gentleness, flattery, etc.: *Tom* coaxed *his father to let him borrow the car.* **2** to obtain by such means: *to* coax *a smile from the baby.*
co·ax·i·al cable (kō ăk′ sē əl) *n-* special cable for long-distance telephone, television, and telegraph transmission, usually made up of eight copper tubes, each with an insulated wire running through its center.
cob (kŏb) *n-* **1** corncob. **2** strong horse with short legs.
co·balt (kō′ bȯlt′) *n-* **1** silvery metallic element used to make very hard alloys. Symbol Co, At. No. 27, At. Wt. 58.93. **2** (also called **cobalt blue**) deep-blue coloring matter, an oxide of this metal.
cobalt 60 *n-* radioactive isotope of cobalt having an atomic weight of 60, and used in medicine and industry as a source of gamma rays. Half-life: 5.3 years.
cobalt bomb *n-* **1** apparatus in which cobalt 60 is the source of a strong beam of gamma rays for treating cancer or for other uses. **2** atomic bomb, theoretically designed to produce large amounts of deadly cobalt 60 fallout.
[1]**cob·bler** (kŏb′ lər) *n-* person who repairs shoes; shoemaker. [from earlier **cobble,** "to make or patch shoes," from **cob(be)** meaning "a lump; wad."]
[2]**cob·bler** (kŏb′ lər) *n-* **1** fruit pie with one crust and baked in a deep dish. **2** drink made of iced wine with lemon, sugar, and other flavorings: *sherry* cobbler. [of uncertain origin.]
cob·ble·stone (kŏb′ əl stōn′) *n-* a naturally rounded stone, once much used for paving streets.
co·bel·lig·er·ent (kō′ bə lĭj′ ər ənt) *n-* nation aiding another in a war.
co·bra (kō′ brə) *n-* any of various closely related poisonous snakes of Africa and Asia, including the spectacled or Indian cobra, the Egyptian cobra, and the king cobra of southeastern Asia. Cobras flatten their necks into a hood when alarmed.

King cobra, about 12 ft. long

cob·web (kŏb′ wĕb′) *n-* **1** web spun by a spider. **2** something flimsy or entangling, like a spider's web.

co·ca (kō′ kə) ***n-*** **1** any of several South American shrubs from whose leaves cocaine and other powerful drugs are obtained. **2** the leaves of this plant, chewed by some Andean Indians to keep them from feeling hunger and exhaustion.

co·caine or **co·cain** (kō′ kān′) ***n-*** powerful, habit-forming narcotic drug obtained from the leaves of the coca shrub and used in medicine as an anesthetic.

coc·cus (kŏk′ əs) ***n-*** [*pl.* **coc·ci** (kŏk′ ī, -sī)] a spherical bacterium.

coc·cyx (kŏk′ sĭks) ***n-*** [*pl.* **coc·cy·ges** (kŏk sī′ jēz′)] the lowermost bone of the spinal column.

coch·i·neal (kŏch′ ə nēl′) ***n-*** **1** a bright-red dye obtained from the dried bodies of insects found in Mexico, Central America, etc. **2** the insect itself.

coch·le·a (kŏk′ lē ə) ***n-*** [*pl.* **coch·le·ae** (-lē ē, -lē ī) or **coch·le·as**] spiral tube of the inner ear which contains the ends of the auditory nerve. For picture, see [1]*ear*.

[1]**cock** (kŏk) ***n-*** **1** grown male chicken. **2** any male bird. **3** water or gas tap; faucet. **4** hammer of a gun; also, its position when drawn back: *The pistol is at half* cock. **5** weathercock. ***vt-*** to pull back the hammer of (a gun) to firing position. [from Old English **cocc,** probably imitating the rooster's cry.]

[2]**cock** (kŏk) ***vt-*** to tilt or turn up: *He* cocked *his hat at a jaunty angle.* [a later meaning of [1]**cock**].

cock an eye at (or **toward**) to turn one's attention to.

[3]**cock** (kŏk) ***n-*** small, cone-shaped pile of hay. ***vt-*** to stack in such piles. [probably from a Danish word.]

cock·ade (kŏk′ ād′) ***n-*** **1** knot or rosette of ribbon or leather worn on a hat as a badge, insignia, etc. **2** ornament on a bridle.

cock-a-doo·dle-doo (kŏk′ ə dōō′ dəl dōō′) ***n-*** traditional word to represent the cry of a rooster.

cock-and-bull story ***n-*** an absurd, improbable tale.

cock·a·too (kŏk′ ə tōō′) ***n-*** [*pl.* **cock·a·toos**] large, noisy parrot of Indonesia and Australia, often white with a colored crest and markings.

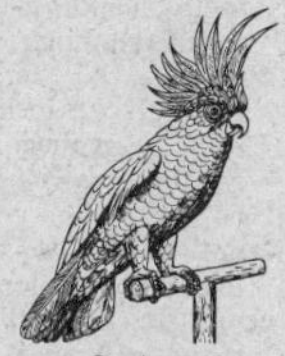

Cockatoo

cock·a·trice (kŏk′ ə trəs, -trīs′) ***n-*** a mythological monster, part cock and part serpent, whose glance was supposed to kill; basilisk.

cock·cha·fer (kŏk′ chā′ fər) ***n-*** any of a group of large beetles, including the June bug, rose chafer, and scarab, that feed on plant leaves.

cock·crow (kŏk′ krō′) ***n-*** time of day when roosters first crow; dawn.

cock·er·el (cŏk′ ər əl) ***n-*** young rooster.

cock·er spaniel (kŏk′ ər) ***n-*** small black, red-brown, or tan spaniel with a long, silky coat, originally bred for bird hunting.

cock-eyed (kŏk′ īd′) *Slang* ***adj-*** **1** cross-eyed. **2** tilted; crooked. **3** absurd; foolish.

cock·fight (kŏk′ fīt′) ***n-*** **1** fight between cocks. **2** fight, staged in a pit, between two cocks equipped with steel spurs on their legs. It is now generally illegal in the United States. **3** contest in which boys, jumping about on one leg, try to knock one another off balance.

cock·horse (kŏk′ hôrs′, -hôrs′) ***n-*** rocking horse.

[1]**cock·le** (kŏk′ əl) ***n-*** edible shellfish related to clams, with two heart-shaped fluted shells. [from Old French **coquille,** from Greek **konchē** meaning "conch."]

warm the cockles of (one's) heart to cheer; gladden.

[2]**cock·le** (kŏk′ əl) ***n-*** weed that grows among grain; especially, the **corn cockle.** [from Old English **coccel.**]

cock·le·bur (kŏk′ əl bûr′) ***n-*** **1** any of several coarse weeds whose seeds are enclosed in cases covered with long, hooked burs. **2** the burdock.

cock·le·shell (kŏk′ əl shĕl′) ***n-*** **1** shell of a cockle. **2** shell of a scallop, especially when worn on a pilgrim's hat. **3** a frail, light boat.

cock·ney (kŏk′ nē) ***n-*** [*pl.* **cock·neys**] **1** person of the eastern part of London. **2** the characteristic dialect or accent of these Londoners. ***adj-:*** *a* cockney *accent.*

cock·pit (kŏk′ pĭt′) ***n-*** **1** space for the pilot and copilot in some airplanes. **2** small, enclosed space used in cockfights.

cock·roach (kŏk′ rōch′) ***n-*** any of a group of insects, closely related to grasshoppers and crickets. Cockroaches are among the oldest kinds of living insects, and some kinds are common kitchen pests that live near water pipes and run about mostly at night.

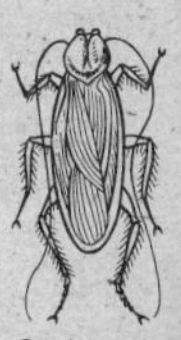

Cockroach

cocks·comb (kŏks′ kōm′) ***n-*** **1** the comb or crest of a cock. **2** garden plant with red or yellow flowers in a dense cluster that somewhat resemble the comb of a cock. **3** coxcomb.

cock·sure (kŏk′ shŏŏr′) ***adj-*** overly sure of oneself; overconfident.

cock·tail (kŏk′ tāl′) ***n-*** **1** chilled, mixed drink made of alcoholic liquors or fruit or vegetable juices. **2** shellfish or mixed fruit, served as an appetizer: *a shrimp* cocktail.

cock·y (kŏk′ ē) ***adj-*** [**cock·i·er, cock·i·est**] arrogantly sure of oneself; conceited: *Jim was very* cocky *about his chances of winning first prize in the contest.* **—*adv-* cock′ i·ly.**

co·co (kō′ kō) ***n-*** [*pl.* **co·cos**] the coconut palm.

[1]**co·coa** (kō′ kō) ***n-*** **1** powder made from the roasted seeds of the cacao tree; chocolate. **2** chocolate beverage made from this powder. **3** brownish color of this powder. ***adj-:*** *a* cocoa *leather.*

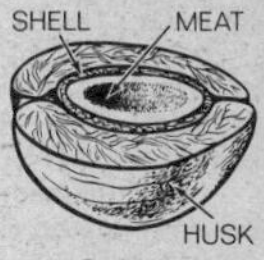

SHELL MEAT HUSK

Coconut

[2]**co·coa** (kō′ kō) coco.

cocoa butter ***n-*** hard, yellow fat from cacao seeds used to make soap, cosmetics, etc. Also **cacao butter.**

co·co·nut or **co·coa·nut** (kō′ kə nŭt′) ***n-*** **1** rounded fruit of the coconut palm. The coconut is made up of a thick husk containing a hard-shelled nut which is lined with edible white meat and filled with sweet, milky fluid. **2** the white meat of the fruit, often used as food.

coconut oil ***n-*** oil pressed from the dried meat of the coconut. It is used in cooking, manufacturing soap, etc.

coconut palm ***n-*** the tall tropical palm tree which bears the coconut. Also **coco palm.**

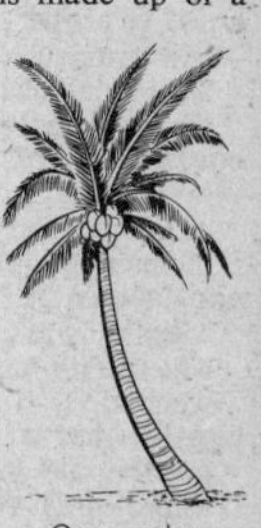

co·coon (kə kōōn′) ***n-*** the silk case spun by many insect larvae, such as caterpillars and silkworms, as a protection while they are developing into butterflies, moths, or the like.

Coco palm

cod (kŏd) ***n-*** [*pl.* **cod**; **cods** (kinds of cod)] any of several deep-sea food fishes of the northern Atlantic and Pacific.

C.O.D. (sē′ō′dē′) collect on delivery.

co·da (kō′ də) *Music* ***n-*** a passage of a movement or composition which brings it to a close.

Cod, 10-35 pounds

cod·dle (kŏd′əl) ***vt-*** [**cod·dled, cod·dling**] 1 to care for indulgently; pamper. 2 to cook gently in a liquid kept below the boiling point: *to* coddle *eggs.*

code (kōd) ***n-*** 1 system of symbols, letters, words, numbers, etc., used to stand for the letters and words of messages. Codes are used for secret messages or for brevity. 2 system, especially an alphabet, of dots and dashes, signs, etc., used for sending messages by telegraph, wigwag, etc. 3 a collection of laws or rules arranged in a clear and orderly fashion: *a building* code. 4 principles and rules of conduct generally accepted by a group of people: *the social* code; *the* code *of honor.* ***vt-*** [**cod·ed, cod·ing**]: *to* code *a message.*

co·deine (kō′dēn′) ***n-*** mild narcotic drug obtained from opium, used to relieve pain and coughing and to produce sleep.

co·dex (kō′dĕks′) ***n-*** [*pl.* **co·di·ces** (kō′də sez′)] an ancient manuscript of a book, especially of the Scriptures or classics.

cod·fish (kŏd′fĭsh′) ***n-*** the cod or its flesh, especially when cured and salted.

cod·ger (kŏj′ər) **n-** an odd, quaint, or eccentric man: *a lovable old* codger.

cod·i·cil (kŏd′ə səl) ***n-*** in law, a supplement to a will which changes it by explaining, adding to, or revoking any of its provisions.

cod·i·fy (kŏd′ə fī′, kō′də-) ***vt-*** [**cod·i·fied, cod·i·fy·ing**] to reduce to a system or code: *to* codify *laws.* **—*n-* cod′i·fi·ca′tion** (-fə kā′shən).

cod·ling (kŏd′lĭng) ***n-*** 1 small unripe apple. 2 any of several varieties of elongated greenish cooking apples.

codling moth ***n-*** a small moth whose larvae damage apples, pears, etc. Also **cod′lin moth.**

cod-liver oil ***n-*** (kŏd′lĭv′ər oil′) ***n-*** oil obtained from the liver of the cod, rich in vitamins A and D.

co·ed or **co-ed** (kō′ĕd′) *Informal* ***n-*** a woman student at a coeducational college.

co·ed·u·ca·tion (kō′ĕj′ə kā′shən) ***n-*** the education of both males and females in the same school. **—*adj-* co′ed′u·ca′tion·al:** *a* coeducational *college.*

co·ef·fi·cient (kō′ə fĭsh′ənt) ***n-*** 1 in algebra, a multiplier in a term, such as 2 or y in 2y, or 2, a, x, 2a, ax, or 2x in 2ax. 2 a number expressing a ratio of increase or decrease: *the* coefficient *of expansion of copper.*

coefficient of expansion ***n-*** mathematical expression for the rate of change in length, area, or volume of a solid or liquid when its temperature is raised one degree while the pressure is kept constant.

coe·la·canth (sē′lə kănth′) ***n-*** large, blue, primitive fish with fleshy fins, which is identical to the ancient fish from which four-legged animals are thought to have descended.

coe·len·ter·ate (sə lĕn′tə rāt′) ***n-*** any of a phylum of invertebrate sea animals (**Coelenterata**), such as jellyfishes, corals, sea anemones, and hydras, with thin walled bodies, a large body cavity, and only one opening, the mouth.

co·erce (kō ûrs′) ***vt-*** [**co·erced, co·erc·ing**] to compel by force or threats: *He* coerced *the prisoner into confessing.*

co·er·cion (kō ûr′shən) ***n-*** the act of compelling someone to do something against his will.

co·e·val (kō ē′vəl) ***adj-*** 1 of the same age. 2 living at the same time; contemporary. 3 lasting to the same age.

co·ex·ist (kō′ĭg zĭst′) ***vi-*** 1 to exist at the same time. 2 to live beside each other at peace although opposed in principle.

co·ex·ist·ence (kō′ĭg zĭs′təns) ***n-*** 1 an existing at the same time. 2 a living beside each other at peace although opposed in principle.

co·ex·ist·ent (kō′ĭg zĭs′tənt) ***adj-*** existing together at the same time; contemporaneous.

co·ex·ten·sive (kō′ĭk stĕn′sĭv) ***adj-*** having the same limits in time or space; extending equally.

cof·fee (kô′fē, kŏf′-) ***n-*** 1 a drink brewed from the roasted and ground seeds (called beans) of the coffee tree. 2 the seeds themselves, whole or ground. 3 the flavor of this drink, or its pale-brown color when mixed with milk. ***adj-*** *a dish of* coffee *ice cream.*

coffee house ***n-*** 1 place that serves coffee and other light refreshments. 2 coffee shop.

cof·fee·pot (kô′fē pŏt′, kŏf′-) ***n-*** pot in which coffee is made or served.

coffee shop ***n-*** restaurant serving coffee and simple meals.

coffee table ***n-*** low table, usually in front of a sofa.

coffee tree ***n-*** any of the several shrubs of the madder family which produce coffee.

cof·fer (kô′fər, kŏf′-) ***n-*** 1 money box; treasure chest. 2 **coffers** treasury; funds.

cof·fer·dam (kô′fər dăm′, kŏf′-) ***n-*** temporary watertight enclosure, open at the top and serving as a dam, which may be pumped dry to permit persons to work inside it on a sea or river bottom.

cof·fin (kô′fən) ***n-*** a box or case in which a corpse is buried; casket.

cog (kŏg) ***n-*** one of a series of teeth on the rim of a wheel that mesh with teeth on another wheel to transmit or receive motion.

COG

Cogwheel and cog

co·gent (kō′jənt) ***adj-*** compelling; forceful; convincing: *a* cogent *reason.* **—*n-* co′gen·cy:** *The* cogency *of his reasons demands action.* ***adv-*** **co′gent·ly.**

cog·i·tate (kŏj′ə tāt′) ***vi-*** [**cog·i·tat·ed, cog·i·tat·ing**] to reflect; ponder; think intently. **—*n-* cog′i·ta′tion.**

co·gnac (kōn′yăk′, kŏn′-) ***n-*** brandy made in the Cognac region of France.

cog·nate (kŏg′nāt′) ***adj-*** related by descent from a common source (used especially to refer to languages or words): *Latin "frater" and English "brother" are* cognate *words.* ***n-***: *English is a* cognate *of German. "Frater" and "brother" are* cognates.

cog·ni·tion (kŏg nĭsh′ən) ***n-*** the process of knowing or perceiving: *the* cognition *of one's surroundings.*

cog·ni·zance (kŏg′nə zəns) ***n-*** 1 understanding; notice: *to take* cognizance *of a fact.* 2 range of knowledge: *within a child's* cognizance.

cog·ni·zant (kŏg′nə zənt) ***adj-*** having knowledge; aware.

cog·no·men (kŏg nō′mən) ***n-*** 1 last or family name, especially in ancient Rome. 2 an identifying nickname, such as "Old Hickory" for Andrew Jackson.

cog·wheel (kŏg′hwēl′) ***n-*** a wheel with teeth or cogs in its rim for transmitting or receiving motion.

co·hab·it (kō hăb′ət) ***vi-*** to live together as husband and wife. **—*n-* co′hab′i·ta′tion.**

co·here (kō hêr′) ***vi-*** [**co·hered, co·her·ing**] to stick together in a mass, as mud; to hold together, as cement and stone.

co·her·ence (kō hêr′ əns) *n-* a holding together, especially logically, as in a speech: *He argued with* coherence. Also **co·her′ en·cy.**

co·her·ent (kō hêr′ ənt) *adj-* **1** sticking together: *a* coherent *mass of mud, gravel, and straw.* **2** logically connected and developed; consistent: *a* coherent *speech.* —*adv-* **co·her′ ent·ly.**

co·he·sion (kō hē′ zhən) *n-* the force by which particles of the same material are held together.

co·he·sive (kō hē′ sĭv) *adj-* sticking together: *Clay is* cohesive, *but gravel is not.* —*adv-* **co·he′ sive·ly.** *n-* **co·he′ sive·ness:** *A good modeling clay has* cohesiveness.

co·hort (kō′ hȯrt′, -hôrt′) *n-* **1** in ancient Rome, a body of soldiers of 300 to 600 men, or one of the ten divisions of a legion. **2** any band of soldiers or followers of someone. **3** *Informal* a follower or companion.

[1]**coif** (koif) *n-* **1** hood-shaped cap worn by a nun under her veil. **2** close-fitting cap; skull cap. **3** white cap worn formerly by English lawyers. [from Old French **coiffe,** from Late Latin **cofia,** from Germanic.] —*adj-* **coifed.**

[2]**coif** (kwŏf) *n-* coiffure. [from [1]**coif.**]

coif·feur (kwä fûr′) *French* hairdresser.

coif·fure (kwä fyo͞or′) *n-* style in which hair is arranged

coil (koil) *n-* **1** anything wound in a series of circles or spirals: *a* coil *of rope.* **2** one of the circles of a spiral, or a series of circles. **3** length of pipe wound in spirals for carrying water, etc. **4** electrical conducting wire, wound in spirals to provide an electrical effect, as in an electro-magnet. *vt-* to wind (something) in spirals or circles. *vi-*: *The snake* coiled *quickly.*

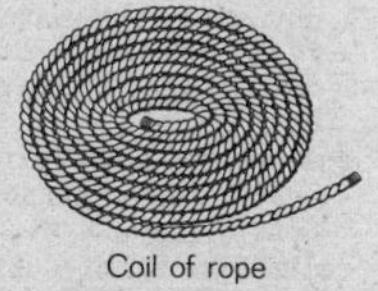
Coil of rope

coin (koin) *n-* **1** piece of metal, stamped by a government, used for money. **2** metal money: *Change the dollar bill for* coin. **3** any stamped piece of metal: *Souvenir* coins *were given away to advertise the new store.* *vt-* **1** to make metal into money. **2** to invent or make up: *The space age has* coined *words like "astronaut."* ***Hom-*** quoin.

coin·age (koi′ nĭj) *n-* **1** method of stamping pieces of money. **2** coins. **3** system of metal money used in a country. **4** invention or making up: *a* coinage *of new words.*

co·in·cide (kō′ ĭn sīd′) *vi-* [**co·in·cid·ed, co·in·cid·ing**] **1** to occur at the same time: *The two television broadcasts* coincide. **2** to occupy the same space exactly: *The federal and state highways* coincide *for twenty miles.* **3** to be alike; to agree (with): *Our opinions* coincide. *His ideas* coincide *with mine.*

co·in·ci·dence (kō ĭn′ sə dəns) *n-* **1** a remarkable occurrence of events, ideas, etc., at the same time by mere chance: *By* coincidence *the dress my cousin wore was exactly like mine.* **2** a coinciding; a happening at the same time or occupying the same space: *the* coincidence *of the State and Federal routes.*

co·in·ci·dent (kō ĭn′ sə dənt) *adj-* occurring at the same time, location, or extent (with): *the discomfort* coincident *with a bad cold.*

co·in·ci·den·tal (kō ĭn′ sə dĕn′ təl) *adj-* **1** occurring at the same time by chance. **2** coincident. —*adv-* **co·in′ ci·den′ tal·ly.**

coke (kōk) *n-* hard, clean-burning fuel left after coal has been heated without air.

Col. 1 Colonel. **2** Colombia.

col·an·der (kŏl′ ən dər, kŭl′-) *n-* a strainer; vessel with holes in the sides and bottom, used to drain water from vegetables, etc.

cold (kōld) *adj-* [**cold·er, cold·est**] **1** having or feeling little or no warmth; chilly: *The night is* cold *and stormy. I'm* cold *in this room.* **2** having little or no feeling: *a* cold *greeting*; *a* cold, *calculated scheme.* **3** not fresh; stale: *a* cold *scent*; *a* cold *trail.* **4** *Informal* far from a goal or answer. **5** *Slang* insensible. *n-* **1** lack of heat; also, the feeling caused by this: *I don't mind the* cold *when I'm dressed properly.* **2** common illness, usually marked by a running or congested nose, inflamation of the mucous membranes, and a sore throat. —*adv-* **cold′ ly.**

Colander

have cold feet to lack courage; be timid. **have** or **know (something) cold** *Informal* to know (something) thoroughly. **in cold blood** without feeling: *to kill* in cold blood. **out in the cold** thrust away; left out of something or out of consideration: *When the new manager came, George found himself* out in the cold. **throw cold water on** to discourage; dash: *to* throw cold water on *hopes and plans.*

cold-blood·ed (kōld′ blŭd′ əd) *adj-* **1** unfeeling; cruel; without pity: *a* cold-blooded *criminal.* **2** *Biology* having blood that stays at or near the temperature of the surrounding air or water, as fish, frogs, and snakes. **3** *Informal* overly sensitive to cold. —*n-* **cold′-blood′ ed·ness.**

cold-blood·ed·ly (kōld′ blŭd′ əd lē) *adv-* in a cruel and unfeeling way: *to kill* cold-bloodedly.

cold cream *n-* a thick, creamy cosmetic used to soften and cleanse the skin.

cold frame *n-* bottomless wooden box with a glass, plastic, or cloth top placed over plants to protect them from wind and cold.

cold front *n-* the forward edge of a cold air mass as it moves into a region of warmer air.

cold-heart·ed (kōld′ här′ təd) *adj-* not kind or warm; unfeeling; unsympathetic; callous. —*adv-* **cold′-heart′ ed·ly.** *n-* **cold′-heart′ ed·ness.**

cold shoulder *Informal n-* deliberate disregard; snub.

cold sore *n-* sore that appears around the mouth or nostrils during a cold or fever; fever blister; fever sore.

cold storage *n-* storage of foods, furs, or other perishables in refrigerated rooms.

cold war *n-* conflict between nations by any means short of actual fighting; especially, such conflict between Communist and non-Communist powers.

cold wave *n-* period of especially cold weather.

cole (kōl) *n-* any of certain plants of the mustard family, such as cabbage, kale, etc. ***Hom-*** coal.

co·le·op·ter·on (kō′ lē ŏp′ tər ŏn′) *n-* [*pl.* **co·le·op·te·ra**] any one of an order of insects **(Coleoptera),** that have an outer hard pair of wings covering a delicate inner pair; beetle. —*adj-* **co·le·op·ter·ous** (kō′ lē ŏp′- tər əs).

cole·slaw (kōl′ slȯ′) *n-* salad made of shredded cabbage with a dressing. [American word from Dutch **kool sla** meaning literally "cabbage salad."]

co·le·us (kō′ lē əs) *n-* any of a large group of garden and house plants of the mint family having large, showy, heart-shaped leaves of many colors.

cole·wort (kōl′ wûrt′) *n-* **1** cole. **2** a young cabbage. **3** a cabbage which does not have a compact head.

---

fāte, făt, dâre, bärn; bē, bĕt, mêre; bīte, bĭt; nōte, hŏt, môre, dȯg; fŭn, fûr; to͞o, bo͝ok; oil; out; tar; thin; then; hw for wh as in *wh*at; zh for s as in u*s*ual; ə for a, e, i, o, u, as in *a*go, lin*e*n, per*i*l, at*o*m, min*u*s

col·ic (kŏl′ĭk) *n-* severe pains in the abdomen or bowels. *—adj-* **col′ick·y.**

col·i·se·um (kŏl′ə sē′əm) *n-* 1 large stadium or hall for sports events, exhibitions, entertainment, etc. 2 **Coliseum** the Colosseum.

co·li·tis (kə lī′təs, kō-) *n-* inflammation of the large intestine.

col·lab·o·rate (kə lăb′ər āt′) *vi-* [**col·lab·o·rat·ed, col·lab·o·rat·ing**] 1 to work or cooperate with another in some activity: *to* collaborate *in the writing of a book.* 2 to aid or cooperate with an enemy that is occupying one's country. *—n-* **col·lab′o·ra′tion.**

col·lab·o·ra·tion·ist (kə lăb′ə rā′shən ĭst) *n-* person who collaborates with enemy occupation forces.

col·lab·o·ra·tor (kə lăb′ə rā′tər) *n-* 1 person who works with another in some activity. 2 collaborationist.

col·lage (kə läzh′) *n-* 1 work of art made by pasting scraps of paper, cloth, metal, string, etc., on a background. 2 art of making such designs. [from a French word meaning " a gluing," from **coller,** "to glue."]

col·lapse (kə lăps′) *vi-* [**col·lapsed, col·laps·ing**] 1 to fall down or in; cave in: *The roof* collapsed *under the weight of the snow.* 2 to fold, deflate, or otherwise assume a less bulky form: *The tripod* collapses *when you fold its legs. The rubber life raft* collapses *for storage.* 3 to break down completely or suddenly; fail: *The truce talks* collapsed *before a settlement was reached. The runner* collapsed *after crossing the finish line. vt-* 1 to cave in: *The flood* collapsed *the wall.* 2 to fold or otherwise cause to assume a less bulky form: *They* collapsed *the tent and packed it away. n-* 1 a caving in: *the sudden* collapse *of the bridge.* 2 breakdown; failure: *the* collapse *of truce talks; a total physical* collapse.

col·lap·si·ble (kə lăp′sə bəl) *adj-* of a nature that allows folding or otherwise being made less bulky: *a* collapsible *stove; a* collapsible *chair.*

col·lar (kŏl′ər) *n-* 1 the part of a shirt, dress, coat, etc., that fits around the neck. 2 ornamental band of cloth, lace, or jewels worn around the neck. 3 a band of leather or metal for the neck of an animal. 4 the part of a harness that fits over the neck of a horse. 5 metal ring on a machine shaft that keeps it in place. *vt- Informal* to seize; lay hold of; capture: *The police* collared *the thief.*

SHAFT
BRACKET
COLLAR

Collars, shirt and machine

col·lar·bone (kŏl′ər bōn′) *n-* either of two bones that connect the breastbone with the shoulder blades.

col·late (kŏl′āt′, kə lāt′) *vt-* [**col·lat·ed, col·lat·ing**] 1 to compare closely: *to* collate *lists.* 2 to arrange in the proper order.

col·lat·er·al (kə lăt′ər əl) *adj-* 1 connected with something, but usually of secondary importance: *the* collateral *results of an experiment; a piece of* collateral *evidence.* 2 side by side; parallel: *two* collateral *objectives of a space capsule.* 3 guaranteed or secured by property, stocks, bonds, etc.: *a* collateral *loan.* 4 descended from the same ancestors, but not in the direct line: *a* collateral *branch of the family. n-* property pledged as security for the repayment of a loan. *—adv-* **col·lat′er·al·ly.**

col·la·tion (kə lā′shən) *n-* 1 a collating or comparing; comparison. 2 a light meal, usually cold.

col·league (kŏl′ēg′) *n-* fellow member of a profession, committee, etc.; associate.

[1]**col·lect** (kə lĕkt′) *vt-* 1 to bring together; gather: *They* collected *the scraps into a heap.* 2 to pick up and remove: *to* collect *the test papers; to* collect *the trash.* 3 to gather and keep for study or as part of a hobby: *to* collect *stamps.* 4 to secure payment of: *to* collect *taxes.* 5 to regain control of: *to* collect *one's thoughts. vi-* 1 to come together; gather: *Many people* collected *outside his house. Scum* collects *on stagnant water.* 2 to secure payment of rent, taxes, etc.: *The landlord* collects *on the first of the month. adj-* paid for by the receiver: *a* collect *call. adv-: to call* collect. *—adj-* **col·lect′a·ble** or **col·lect′i·ble:** *a* collectable *debt; a tax that is not* collectable.

[2]**col·lect** (kŏl′ĕkt′) *n-* any of various short prayers used in certain church services.

col·lect·ed (kə lĕk′təd) *adj-* under control; calm; undisturbed: *calm, cool, and* collected. *—adv-* **col·lect′ed·ly.**

col·lec·tion (kə lĕk′shən) *n-* 1 a collecting or gathering: *The hospital organized the* collection *of old clothes.* 2 something gathered together: *a* collection *of dust in the corner.* 3 things of some special kind brought together as a hobby, or for display or study: *a stamp* collection. 4 the taking in of money as a payment or donation: *the* collection *of taxes; a church* collection.

col·lec·tive (kə lĕk′tĭv) *adj-* 1 done or attempted together; in common: *to achieve a goal by* collective *action.* 2 representing the whole; accumulated: *the* collective *wisdom of mankind. n-* an organization operated by a group cooperatively: *a* collective *factory.* *—adv-* **col·lec′tive·ly.**

collective bargaining *n-* process by which representatives of a union and an employer discuss and settle questions of wages, hours, working conditions, etc.

collective farm *n-* in the Soviet Union and other countries, a farm that is owned and managed by the government.

collective noun *n-* singular noun that names a group or collection. It can take either a singular or plural verb, depending on whether it refers to the group or the individual members acting separately. Examples: The committee is in session. The committee are disagreed on the question.

col·lec·tiv·ism (kə lĕk′tə vĭz′əm) *n-* system of government in which the means of economic production and distribution are owned by the state or by the people as a whole.

col·lec·tiv·ist (kə lĕk′tə vĭst′) *adj-* of or relating to collectivism. *n-* person who believes in or supports collectivism.

col·lec·ti·vi·za·tion (kə lĕk′tə və zā′shən) *n-* a bringing under governmental control or supervision.

col·lec·ti·vize (kə lĕk′tə vīz′) *vt-* [**col·lec·ti·vized, col·lec·ti·viz·ing**] to organize (agriculture, industry, etc.) under collective control.

col·lec·tor (kə lĕk′tər) *n-* person, thing, or device that collects: *an art* collector; *a tax* collector; *a dust* collector.

col·leen (kŏl′ēn′) *Irish n-* girl; young woman.

col·lege (kŏl′ĭj) *n-* 1 educational institution more advanced than the high school and giving bachelor degrees to its students when they have finished certain courses of study; also, a unit of a university. 2 school in which a special subject is taught: *a business* college; *a* college *of engineering.* 3 a junior college or community college. 4 association of persons in the same profession: *a* college *of surgeons.* 5 any of various groups of clerics: *the* college *of cardinals. as* **modifier**: *a* college *education; a* college *woman.*

col·le·gi·an (kə lē′jən) *n-* college student.

col·le·giate (kə lē′jət) *adj-* having to do with a college or with college students: *a* collegiate *program.*

col·lide (kə līd′) ***vi-*** **[col·lid·ed, col·lid·ing] 1** to meet and strike together with force; crash: *The cars* collided. **2** to clash: *He* collided *with me over politics.*

col·lie (kŏl′ ē) ***n-*** a large sheep dog with a long, thick coat and bushy tail.

col·lier (kŏl′ yər) ***n-*** **1** *chiefly Brit.* coal miner. **2** ship for carrying coal; coaler.

col·lier·y (kŏl′ yə rē) ***n-*** [*pl.* **col·lier·ies**] coal mine.

col·li·sion (kə lĭzh′ ən) ***n-*** **1** a coming or striking together with force; crash. **2** clash of interests, ideas, etc.

col·lo·cate (kŏl′ ə kāt′) ***vt-*** **[col·lo·cat·ed, col·lo·cat·ing]** to set or place side by side or in relation; juxtapose; arrange: *to* collocate *ideas.* **—*n-*** **col′ lo·ca′ tion.**

col·lo·di·on (kə lō′ dē ən) ***n-*** solution of guncotton in ether and alcohol, which dries quickly and leaves a tough, elastic film.

col·loid (kŏl′ oid′) ***n-*** substance made of invisibly small clusters of molecules which can remain suspended in liquids, solids, or gases for long periods of time. **—*adj-*** **col·loid′ al.** ***adv-*** **col·loid′ al·ly.**

col·lo·qui·al (kə lō′ kwē əl) ***adj-*** used in ordinary conversation or other circumstances where formal language is less appropriate; informal: *"Movies" is a* colloquial *word for "moving pictures."* **—*adv-*** **col·lo′ qui·al·ly** ***n-*** **col·lo′ qui·al·ness.**

col·lo·qui·al·ism (kə lō′ kwē ə lĭz′ əm) ***n-*** colloquial word or expression; also, the use of these.

col·lo·quy (kŏl′ ə kwē) ***n-*** [*pl.* **col·lo·quies**] conversation or discussion; conference.

col·lu·sion (kə lōō′ zhən) ***n-*** secret cooperation for an unlawful or harmful purpose.

col·lu·sive (kə lōō′ sĭv, -zĭv) ***adj-*** done with or acting in collusion: *a* collusive *agreement*; *the* collusive *partners.* **—*adv-*** **col·lu′ sive·ly.** ***n-*** **col·lu′ sive·ness.**

Colo. Colorado.

co·logne (kə lōn′) ***n-*** lightly scented perfume.

[1]**co·lon** (kō′ lən) ***n-*** punctuation mark [:] used to introduce a list or series, a long quotation, or anything else closely related to what has just been said. It sometimes follows the greeting in a letter. In this dictionary, a colon is used to introduce examples. [from Greek **kôlon** meaning "limb; part; clause," then "the mark that sets off the clause."]

[2]**co·lon** (kō′ lən) ***n-*** the large intestine, which in the human body is about six feet long. For picture, see *intestine.* [from Greek **kolon.**]

[3]**co·lon** (kō lōn′) ***n-*** [*pl.* **co·lons** or **co·lo·nes** (-lō′ nās)] the basic unit of money in Costa Rica and El Salvador. [from Spanish **colón,** from Cristóbal Colón, the Spanish name of Christopher Columbus.]

colo·nel (kûr′ nəl) ***n-*** in the Army, Air Force, or Marine Corps, a commissioned officer who ranks next below a brigadier general and next above a lieutenant colonel. ***Hom-*** kernel. **—*n-*** **colo′ nel·cy** (kûr′ nəl sē).

co·lo·ni·al (kə lō′ nē əl) ***adj-*** **1** relating to a colony or colonies. **2** relating to the thirteen British colonies which eventually became the United States, or to that period of our history: *our* colonial *heritage*; *an example of* colonial *architecture.* **—*adv-*** **co·lo′ ni·al·ly.**

co·lo·ni·al·ism (kə lō′ nē ə lĭz′ əm) ***n-*** policy of a nation that seeks to acquire and rule overseas territories.

co·lo·ni·al·ist (kə lō′ nē ə lĭst′) ***n-*** person who believes in or practices colonialism: *The prime minister was a* colonialist. ***adj-***: *a* colonialist *policy.*

col·o·nist (kŏl′ ə nĭst) ***n-*** **1** person who founds or settles a colony. **2** person who lives in a colony.

col·o·nize (kŏl′ ə nīz′) ***vt-*** **[col·o·nized, col·o·niz·ing]** **1** to found a colony in; send colonists to: *Lord Baltimore* colonized *Maryland.* **2** to migrate to and settle in: *Quakers* colonized *Pennsylvania.* ***vi-***: *The Spanish* colonized *vigorously in the New World.* **—*n-*** **col′ o·ni·za′ tion:** *the* colonization *of Australia.* ***n-*** **col′ o·niz′er.**

col·on·nade (kŏl′ ə nād′) ***n-*** a row of columns regularly spaced, usually supporting a roof or series of arches.

col·o·ny (kŏl′ ə nē) ***n-*** [*pl.* **col·o·nies**] **1** territory settled or conquered by people of a distant country and then governed by it. **2** group of people who leave their country to settle in another land, but remain subject to their home country: *A* colony *of Puritans settled in Massachusetts.* **3** group of persons drawn together in a locality by common nationality, religion, interests, etc. **4** *Biology* group of plants or animals of the same kind growing or living together: *ant* colony; *bacteria* colony; *a* colony *of pines.* **5 the Colonies** the thirteen British colonies that became the first States of the United States.

col·or (kŭl′ ər) ***n-*** **1** property of the light reaching the eyes which determines whether an individual with normal vision sees something as red, blue, green, etc. Color depends upon the wavelength of the light. **2** any hue, tint, or shade, sometimes including black and white. **3** a paint, dye, or pigment. **4** hue or tint of the skin; complexion: *Her good* color *indicated robust health.* **5** vividness and liveliness in a story, scene, place, period, etc.: *The* color *of cockney London.* **6** one or more hues or shades used as a symbol or badge: *my school* colors. **7 the colors** the flag, especially the national flag carried by a military unit. ***vt-*** **1** to give a hue, tint, or shade with an agent like paint, dye, pigment, etc. **2** to give a special or vivid quality to, often by telling more or less than the truth; slant: *His pride made him* color *his stories of the war.* ***vi-*** to blush; flush.

show (one's) true colors to show what one really is.

col·or·a·tion (kŭl′ ə rā′ shən) ***n-*** arrangement of colors and color strengths; coloring: *a flower's* coloration.

col·o·ra·tu·ra (kŭl′ ə rə tŏŏr′ ə, -tyŏŏr′ ə) *Music* ***n-*** **1** brilliant music for voice, with trills and complicated phrasing. **2** the runs and trills of such music. **3** coloratura soprano. ***adj-***: *a* coloratura *passage.* ***adv-***: *Please sing this* coloratura.

coloratura soprano *Music* ***n-*** high-pitched female voice having great range and flexibility; also, a singer having such a voice.

color bearer ***n-*** person who carries the colors, or the flag, especially in the armed forces.

col·or-blind (kŭl′ ər blīnd′) ***adj-*** unable to distinguish between certain colors, or, sometimes, to perceive any color. **—*n-*** **col′ or-blind′ ness.**

col·or·cast (kŭl′ ər kăst′) ***n-*** television program broadcast in color. ***vt-*** **[col·or·cast·ed** or **col·or·cast, col·or·cast·ing]**: *Channel 3* colorcasts *baseball games.*

col·ored (kŭl′ ərd) ***adj-*** **1** having color other than solid white or black. **2** Negro; also, of any race other than Caucasian (sometimes considered offensive). **3** biased or distorted: *a highly* colored *account of a riot.*

color film ***n-*** photographic film used to make color photographs and slides.

col·or·ful (kŭl′ ər fəl) ***adj-*** **1** rich with color. **2** vivid; fascinating; exciting the imagination: *The opening up of the West was a* colorful *period in our history.* **—*adv-*** **col′ or·ful·ly.** ***n-*** **col′ or·ful·ness.**

col·or·ing (kŭl′ ər ĭng) ***n-*** **1** act, art, or style of producing or using color. **2** appearance as to color; coloration:

the pale coloring *of a winter landscape.* **3** substance used to give color to something: *She put pink* coloring *in the cake icing.*

col·or·less (kŭl′ ər ləs) ***adj-*** **1** without color: *a* colorless *liquid.* **2** with little color; pale: *a* colorless *room.* **3** not vivid or interesting; dull: *a* colorless *story.* ***—adv-*** **col′ or·less·ly.** ***n-*** **col′ or·less·ness.**

color line ***n-*** barrier, chiefly social but often economic and political as well, set up by some members of one race to exclude other races.

co·los·sal (kə lŏs′ əl) ***adj-*** like a colossus; huge; immense; vast; tremendous: *a* colossal *city*; *the* colossal *expanse of the ocean.* ***—adv-*** **co·los′ sal·ly.**

Col·os·se·um (kŏl′ ə sē′ əm) ***n-*** amphitheater in ancient Rome in which gladiators fought, built 75-80 A.D. Much of it still stands. Also **Col′ i·se′ um.**

Co·los·sians (kə lŏsh′ ənz) ***n-*** a book of the New Testament consisting of St. Paul's epistle to the Christians at **Colossae,** an ancient city of Asia Minor.

co·los·sus (kə lŏs′ əs) ***n-*** [*pl.* **co·los·si** (-sī, -sē) or **co·los·sus·es**]. **1** an immense statue. **2** any person or thing of tremendous size or power.

Colossus of Rhodes ***n-*** huge bronze statue of Apollo erected in the harbor of Rhodes about 285 B.C. It was one of the seven wonders of the ancient world.

col·our (kŭl′ ər) *Brit.* color.

colt (kōlt) ***n-*** **1** young horse, especially a male less than a year old. **2** foal. **3** an inexperienced youth. ***—adj-*** **colt′ ish.** ***adv-*** **colt′ ish·ly.** ***n-*** **colt′ ish·ness.**

col·ter (kōl′ tər) ***n-*** blade or disk attached to a plow to cut the sod in front of the plowshare.

Co·lum·bi·an (kə lŭm′ bē ən) ***adj-*** of or relating to Christopher Columbus or to his time.

col·um·bine (kŏl′ əm bīn′) ***n-*** any of various closely related plants with showy, drooping flowers that have long, tubular projections.

Columbine

co·lum·bi·um (kə lŭm′ bē əm) ***n-*** niobium.

Co·lum·bus Day ***n-*** October 12, observed as a holiday in most of the United States to commemorate the discovery of America by Christopher Columbus in 1492.

col·umn (kŏl′ əm) ***n-*** **1** an upright pillar serving as a support or ornament for a building, or standing alone as a monument. **2** anything that resembles such a pillar in function or shape: *the spinal* column; *a* column *of smoke.* **3** one of two or more vertical divisions of type on a printed page. **4** a piece of writing contributed regularly to a newspaper or magazine by one person: *a society* column. **5** a line of figures, letters, or words arranged one above the others: *Add up that* column. **6** a line of troops or ships following one after the other. ***—adj-*** **col′ umned:** *a stately white-*columned *porch.*

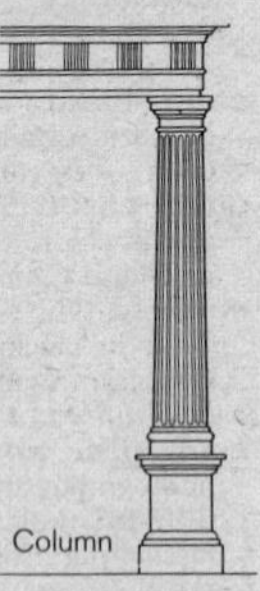

Column

co·lum·nar (kə lŭm′ nər) ***adj-*** shaped like or built with columns.

col·um·nist (kŏl′ əm nĭst′) ***n-*** person who writes a newspaper column.

co·ma (kō′ mə) ***n-*** a state of unconsciousness and insensibility, produced by disease, injury, or poison.

Co·man·che (kə măn′ chē, kō-) ***n-*** [*pl.* **Co·man·ches,** also **Co·man·che**] member of a tribe of Plains Indians who once ranged between Kansas and Mexico, and now are found only in northwestern Texas. ***adj-:*** *the* Comanche *hair style.*

com·a·tose (kō′ mə tōs′, kŏm′ ə-) ***adj-*** **1** in a coma: *The patient is still* comatose. **2** resembling a coma: *a* comatose *sleep.* ***—adv-*** **com′ a·tose′ ly.**

comb (kōm) ***n-*** **1** a thin piece of hard rubber, plastic, metal, or the like, cut so as to have many thin projections, and used to smooth, arrange, or hold the hair. **2** a similar metal instrument used to separate and clean the fibers of flax or wool. **3** a currycomb. **4** the fleshy, red growth on the head of a hen, rooster, or other fowl; crest. **5** honeycomb. ***vt-*** **1** to smooth or arrange the hair. **2** to search through: *They* combed *the woods for the child.*

Comb of rooster

[1]**com·bat** (kəm băt′) ***vt-*** [**com·bat·ed** or **com·bat·ted, com·bat·ing** or **com·bat·ting**] to fight; oppose: *Vaccines help* combat *disease.*

[2]**com·bat** (kŏm′ băt′) ***n-*** **1** conflict or struggle, especially a direct physical struggle: *a fierce* combat *between two swordsmen*; *the* combat *of ideas.* **2** military engagement with an enemy; action. *as* ***modifier:*** *the* combat *zone.*

[1]**com·bat·ant** (kŏm′ bə tənt) ***n-*** fighter, especially a member of an armed force who takes part in battle.

[2]**com·bat·ant** (kəm băt′ ənt) ***adj-*** fighting or ready and willing to fight.

combat fatigue ***n-*** psychological reaction to the strain of warfare, marked by depression, loss of self-control, and great anxiety; battle fatigue.

com·ba·tive (kəm băt′ ĭv) ***adj-*** quarrelsome; ready to give battle. ***—adv-*** **com·bat′ ive·ly.** ***n-*** **com·bat′ ive·ness:** *His* combativeness *is embarrassing to his family.*

combe (kōōm) coomb.

comb·er (kō′ mər) ***n-*** **1** machine or person that combs wool, cotton, etc. **2** long, steep, white-capped wave.

com·bi·na·tion (kŏm′ bə nā′ shən) ***n-*** **1** a putting, joining, or mixing together: *a new Boy Scout troop formed by the* combination *of two older ones*; *an unlucky* combination *of events.* **2** something made by putting or mixing together other things; union; conjunction: *Green is a* combination *of blue and yellow.* **3** series of numbers to which a dial must be moved to open a keyless lock.

[1]**com·bine** (kəm bīn′) ***vt-*** [**com·bined, com·bin·ing**] **1** to join; unite: *The two boys* combined *their efforts to solve the problem.* **2** to mix: *to* combine *ingredients to make a cake.* ***vi-:*** *Oxygen* combines *with iron to form rust.*

[2]**com·bine** (kŏm′ bīn′) ***n-*** **1** machine that harvests and threshes grain. **2** group of companies acting together to achieve mutual business goals; trust.

combining form *Grammar* ***n-*** word or stem of a word, usually from Greek or Latin, which can be combined with other words or stems to make new words. Example: "microphotograph" is composed of three combining forms, "micro-" (very small) plus "photo-" (light) plus "-graph" (picture). Some combining forms, such as "-less," "mid-," and "over-," are purely English in origin, but since they tend to become standard prefixes and suffixes, they are treated as such in this dictionary.

com·bus·ti·bil·i·ty (kəm bŭs′ tə bĭl′ ə tē) ***n-*** the ease with which a substance catches fire and burns.

com·bus·ti·ble (kəm bŭs′ tə bəl) ***adj-*** **1** able to catch fire and burn: *Wood is* combustible. **2** excitable: *a* combustible *temper.* ***n-*** a flammable substance.

com·bus·tion (kəm bŭs′ chən) ***n-*** **1** burning; the combining of a substance with oxygen so rapidly that heat and light are produced: *the* combustion *of oil in a furnace.* **2** the oxidation of food by living cells during metabolism.

Comdr. Commander.

Comdt. Commandant.

come (kŭm) ***vi-*** [**came** (kām), **come, com·ing**] **1** to draw near; approach: *Cold weather is* coming. **2** to arrive: *He will* come *tomorrow.* **3** to reach (to a certain point): *Her hair* comes *to her shoulders.* **4** to happen: *How did you* come *to know that*? **5** to occur to one in the mind: *A new idea* came *to me.* **6.** to happen as a result: *This accident* comes *of your carelessness.* **7** to become: *The knot* came *untied.* **8** to issue from; descend: *to* come *from a famous family.* **9** to be furnished or sold: *Telephones* come *in several colors.*

come about to happen; occur.

come across 1 to meet with or find by chance: *I* came across *an old friend.* **2** *Informal* to pay up (with); give.

come back to return, especially to the mind.

come by to get; acquire: *He* comes by *his wealth honestly.*

come down 1 to lose rank or standing: *He* came down *in the world after the loss of his business.* **2** to be handed down through tradition.

come in to arrive: *The train* came in *on time.*

come into to inherit: *She* came into *a fortune.*

come off 1 to become detached: *The cap* came off. **2** *Informal* to turn out to be: *The play* came off *well.*

come on 1 to meet or find by chance: *He* came on *the cabin while wandering through the woods.* **2** to progress: *How are you* coming on *at your new job?* **3** to enter on stage: *The actress* came on *dressed as a queen.*

come out 1 to be shown; to become evident: *It* came out *that they had friends in common.* **2** to be published or released: *Many books and movies* come out *every year.* **3** to turn out: *Did everything* come out *as planned?* **4** of a young lady, to be introduced into society.

come out with 1 to say frankly: *If anything bothers you* come out with *it.* **2** to bring out: *The automobile company* came out with *a new model.*

come to 1 to amount to: *The bill* came to *five dollars.* **2** to become conscious again: *He* came to *quickly.*

come up to arise: *The question* came up *at the meeting.*

come·back (kŭm′ băk′) ***n-*** **1** a recovery (of health, former standing in a profession, etc.): *the* comeback *of a patient*; *an actress's* comeback. **2** *Informal* a quick retort.

co·me·di·an (kə mē′ dē ən) ***n-*** **1** male actor who plays in comedies. **2** person who acts a comic sketch, tells jokes, does funny stunts, and the like; clown. ***n- fem.*** **co·me′ di·enne′** (kə mē′ dē ĕn′).

come·down (kŭm′ doun′) *Informal* ***n-*** a descent in position, status, or assurance.

com·e·dy (kŏm′ ə dē) ***n-*** [*pl.* **com·e·dies**] **1** a play, situation, or other happening that is funny. **2** in dramatic literature, a work which has a happy ending for the main characters. **3** the whole body of dramatic literature that includes such plays.

come·ly (kŭm′ lē) ***adj-*** [**come·li·er, come·li·est**] of pleasing appearance; attractive: *a* comely *woman.* **—*n-* come′ li·ness.**

com·er (kŭm′ ər) ***n-*** *Informal* person or thing that is on the way to success.

co·mes·ti·ble (kə mĕs′ tə bəl) ***n-*** something that is edible; a food.

com·et (kŏm′ ət) ***n-*** an immense body of matter, loosely held together, that travels in a long parabolic or, sometimes, elliptical path and develops a glowing fuzzy head and long tail when it comes near the sun.

Comet

com·fit (kŭm′ fĭt, kŏm′-) ***n-*** piece of candied fruit or sweetmeat.

com·fort (kŭm′ fərt) ***vt-*** to console, soothe, or cheer (a person, pet, etc.) in pain, grief, or trouble. ***n-*** **1** state of mental or spiritual ease; contentment: *Good health is a source of* comfort. *Serenity is a sign of* comfort. **2** relief or solace in distress: *Your kind thoughts gave me* comfort *in a difficult time.* **3** ability to give physical ease and well-being: *Springs add to the* comfort *of a car. He enjoyed the* comfort *of his favorite chair.* **4** someone or something that gives ease, contentment, or relief: *Heat and hot water are domestic* comforts. **—*adj-* com′ fort·less.**

com·fort·a·ble (kŭm′ fər tə bəl) ***adj-*** **1** free from any distress; at ease: *to feel* comfortable *with new acquaintances.* **2** giving ease or contentment; giving no distress: *a* comfortable *chair*; *a* comfortable *pair of shoes.* **—*adv-* com′ fort·a·bly.**

com·fort·er (kŭm′ fər tər) ***n-*** **1** person who consoles, soothes, or cheers another in grief, pain, or trouble. **2** a thick, quilted bed covering.

com·ic (kŏm′ ĭk) ***adj-*** **1** funny; humorous; comical: *a* comic *song.* **2** of or having to do with comedy: *a* comic *writer.* ***n-*** **1** a comedian. **2 comics** comic strips.

com·i·cal (kŏm′ ə kəl) ***adj-*** funny; causing laughter or amusement: *Dressed in his sister's clothes, he was a* comical *sight.* **—*adv-* com′ i·cal·ly.**

comic book ***n-*** small magazine containing comic strips.

comic opera ***n-*** opera or operetta with happy ending, funny plot, and spoken dialogue. See also *grand opera.*

comic strip ***n-*** series of drawings, usually in a newspaper, telling an adventure or a funny story, with speech shown in the drawings themselves.

com·ing (kŭm′ ĭng) ***adj-*** approaching: *the* coming *storm.* ***n-*** arrival; approach: *the* coming *of spring.*

com·i·ty (kŏm′ ə tē) ***n-*** [*pl.* **com·i·ties**] civility or politeness; courtesy and mutual respect between nations.

com·ma (kŏm′ ə) ***n-*** punctuation mark [,] used to show a slight interruption in thought, to separate words and ideas in a series, and to set off some grammatical constructions such as independent clauses or short quotations. In reading aloud or speaking, a slight pause and a change in voice pitch will usually be heard in the place of the comma.

com·mand (kə mănd′) ***vt-*** (in senses 1, 2, and 3 considered intransitive when the direct object is implied but not expressed) **1** to have authority and control over; rule; govern: *to* command *an army*; *to* command *a ship.* **2** to order (a person, group, etc.) to do what one wishes done: *They* commanded *her to leave.* **3** to order (something) to be done, not done, etc.: *The colonel* commanded *a retreat.* **4** to be in a position that controls; overlook: *The fort* commands *the entrance to the harbor.* **5** to merit and get: *to* command *respect*; *to* command *a high price.* ***n-*** **1** an order; directive: *The sergeant barked out a* command. **2** right to give orders; authority: *Who has* command *here*? **3** control; mastery: *a good* command *of English.* **4** persons or things subject to an officer's authority: *The general is proud of his* command.

com·man·dant (kŏm′ ən dănt′, -dänt′) ***n*** -commanding officer, especially of a military district, navy yard, etc.

---

fāte, făt, dâre, bärn; bē, bĕt, mêre; bīte, bĭt; nōte, hŏt, môre, dȯg; fŭn, fûr; to͞o, bo͝ok; oil; out; tar; thin; then; hw for wh as in *wh*at; zh for s as in u*s*ual; ə for a, e, i, o, u, as in *a*go, lin*e*n, per*i*l, at*o*m, min*u*s

com·man·deer (kŏm′ ən dêr′) *vt-* to seize or confiscate, especially for military use.

com·mand·er (kə măn′ dər) *n-* **1** military leader or chief; also, a leader in a similar position: *the* commander *of the expedition.* **2** in the Navy and Coast Guard, a commissioned officer who ranks next below a captain and next above a lieutenant commander. **3 commander in chief** [*pl.* **commanders in chief**] person in supreme control over a nation's armed forces.

com·mand·ing (kə măn′ dĭng) *adj-* **1** in charge: *the* commanding *officer.* **2** forcing one's attention; impressive; dominating: *a* commanding *personality*; *a* commanding *tone of voice.*

com·mand·ment (kə mănd′ mənt) *n-* **1** an order; a command. **2** a law, especially one of the Ten Commandments in the Bible.

com·man·do (kə măn′ dō) *n-* [*pl.* **com·man·dos** or **com·man·does**] member of an armed force trained to make surprise raids in enemy territory; also, the force itself. *as* ***modifier***: *a* commando *officer.*

com·mem·o·rate (kə mĕm′ ə rāt′) *vt-* [**com·mem·o·rat·ed, com·mem·o·rat·ing**] to honor or keep alive the memory of: *The names of many cities* commemorate *men who built our country.* **—*n-* com·mem′ o·ra′ tion:** *a speech of* commemoration. ***adj-* com·mem′ o·ra′ tive:** *a* commemorative *medal.*

com·mence (kə mĕns′) *vt-* [**com·menced, com·menc·ing**] to begin; start: *to* commence *work.* ***vi-***: *We'll* commence *tomorrow.*

com·mence·ment (kə mĕns′ mənt) *n-* **1** a beginning; origin. **2** ceremony in which students are given their diplomas; graduation exercises.

com·mend (kə mĕnd′) *vt-* **1** to praise; express approval of: *I* commend *you for being on time.* **2** to entrust: *to* commend *one's soul to God.* **3** to convey greetings and regards of: *Please* commend *me to your aunt.*

com·mend·a·ble (kə mĕn′ də bəl) *adj-* praiseworthy. **—*adv-* com·mend′ a·bly.**

com·men·da·tion (kŏm′ ən dā′ shən) *n-* **1** a praising or approving; also, an instance of this: *His teacher's* commendation *encouraged the student.* **2** official recognition and praise: *The soldier received a* commendation *for bravery.* **—*adj-* com·mend′ a·to′ ry** (kə mĕn′ də tôr′ ē): *a* commendatory *speech.*

com·men·su·ra·ble (kə mĕn′ shər ə bəl) *adj-* **1** measurable by the same units or standard: *Mileage and depth are* commensurable*; loudness and color are not.* **2** in proper proportion (to): *Punishment should be* commensurable *to the crime.* **—*adv-* com·men′ sur·a·bly.**

com·men·su·rate (kə mĕn′ shər ət) *adj-* **1** equal in extent or measure: *Six yards is* commensurate *with eighteen feet.* **2** commensurable. **—*adv-* com·men′ su·rate·ly.**

com·ment (kŏm′ ĕnt) *n-* **1** written or spoken remark, especially one that gives a personal reaction or opinion. **2** talk; gossip: *His unexpected departure caused* comment. ***vi-***: *to* comment *on the news.*

com·men·tar·y (kŏm′ ən tĕr′ ē) *n-* [*pl.* **com·men·tar·ies**] explanation or opinion, either direct or indirect; also, a broadcast, book, etc., containing this.

com·men·ta·tor (kŏm′ ən tā′ tər) *n-* person who gives opinion and explanation, especially of the news.

com·merce (kŏm′ ərs) *n-* the buying and selling of goods; trade; business transactions.

com·mer·cial (kə mûr′ shəl) *adj-* **1** having to do with trade or business: *a* commercial *enterprise*; *the* commercial *interests of the town.* **2** made to be sold in quantity: *a* commercial *pie.* ***n-*** advertising message on radio or television. **—*adv-* com·mer′ cial·ly.**

com·mer·cial·ism (kə mûr′ shə lĭz′ əm) *n-* attitude that emphasizes making money: *Some sports suffer from* commercialism.

com·mer·cial·ize (kə mûr′ shə līz′) *vt-* [**com·mer·cial·ized, com·mer·cial·iz·ing**] to put on a money-making or business basis: *to* commercialize *football.*

com·min·gle (kə mĭng′ gəl) *vi-* [**com·min·gled, com·min·gling**] to mix; mingle: *The older children did not* commingle *with the younger.* ***vt-***: *They* commingled *their herds.*

com·mis·er·ate (kə mĭz′ ə rāt′) *vt-* [**com·mis·er·at·ed, com·mis·er·at·ing**] to feel and express pity for: *to* commiserate *someone who is ill.* ***vi-*** to feel or express sympathy (with): *to* commiserate *with a beaten man.*

com·mis·er·a·tion (kə mĭz′ ə rā′ shən) *n-* a feeling of sympathy; also, an expression of this.

com·mis·sar·i·at (kŏm′ ə sĕr′ ē ət) *n-* **1** quartermaster or supply corps of an army; also, the officers of this corps. **2** supplies furnished by this department.

com·mis·sar·y (kŏm′ ə sâr′ ē) *n-* [*pl.* **com·mis·sar·ies**] **1** a store or other place selling food and equipment to employes of a company, members of an army, etc. **2** officer of an army commissariat. **3** a deputy or agent.

com·mis·sion (kə mĭsh′ ən) *n-* **1** the doing or performing (of some illegal, immoral, or inept act): *a* commission *of a crime.* **2** part of a selling price, paid as a fee to a salesman or agent: *The* commission *on the sale was $25.* **3** job or duty entrusted to someone: *Mr. Allen's* commission *was to persuade the mob to go home.* **4** appointment to create a work of art: *He got a* commission *for a new symphony.* **5** group of persons appointed to perform certain duties: *The mayor established a traffic* commission. **6** appointment to one of certain military ranks: *a captain's* commission. ***vt-*** **1** to appoint (someone) to do a certain thing: *President Jefferson* commissioned *Lewis and Clark to explore the western lands.* **2** to confer officer's rank upon. **3** to order (a work) from a composer, artist, etc.: *The city* commissioned *a cantata for the centennial.* **4** to put officially into service: *The navy* commissioned *the new cruiser today.*

in commission 1 officially in service: *The navy has six aircraft carriers* in commission. **2** in working condition. **on commission** receiving part of the selling price as payment: *He is selling refrigerators* on commission. **out of commission 1** not in working condition: *My car is* out of commission. **2** officially not in service.

commissioned officer *Military* ***n-*** officer of the rank of second lieutenant or above in the Army, Air Force, or Marine Corps, or of the rank of ensign or above in the Navy or Coast Guard. See also *noncommissioned officer* and *warrant officer.*

com·mis·sion·er (kə mĭsh′ ən ər) *n-* **1** public official in charge of a specified governmental department: *the* Commissioner *of Public Works.* **2** member of a commission. **3** supreme judge and arbitrator of an organized professional sport: *the baseball* commissioner.

com·mit (kə mĭt′) *vt-* [**com·mit·ted, com·mit·ting**] **1** to do or perform (something illegal, immoral, or inept): *to* commit *a crime*; *to* commit *an error.* **2** to give (someone) into another's care, custody, etc.: *to* commit *a criminal to jail*; *to* commit *a mental patient to an asylum.* **3** to register or record (something) in a certain form: *to* commit *an address to memory*; *to* commit *thoughts to writing.* **4** to pledge (oneself) to someone or something; involve or identify (oneself) with someone or something: *He* committed *himself to our cause.*

com·mit·ment (kə mĭt′ mənt) *n-* **1** an entrusting or giving in charge; also, an instance of this: *the* commitment *of a criminal to jail.* **2** pledge, promise, or duty regarded as a solemn responsibility: *a* commitment *to one's job.* Also **com·mit'tal.**

com·mit·tee (kə mĭt'ē) ***n-*** group of persons appointed or elected for a special purpose: *the finance* committee.

com·mit·tee·man (kə mĭt'ē mən) ***n-*** [*pl.* **com·mit·tee·men**] member of a committee. **—*n-*** *fem.* **com·mit'tee·wom'an** [*pl.* **com·mit·tee·wom·en**].

com·mode (kə mōd') ***n-*** **1** a bureau or chest of drawers. **2** an old-fashioned movable washstand. **3** toilet.

com·mo·di·ous (kə mō'dē əs) ***adj-*** roomy; spacious: *a* commodious *house.* **—*adv-*** **com·mo'di·ous·ly.** ***n-*** **com·mo'di·ous·ness:** *The* commodiousness *of the house.*

com·mod·i·ty (kə mŏd'ə tē) ***n-*** [*pl.* **com·mod·i·ties**] article of commerce, such as wheat, copper, silk, etc.

com·mo·dore (kŏm'ə dôr') ***n-*** **1** a naval officer ranking above a captain and below a rear admiral. This rank has not been used since World War II. **2** title given to a fleet or squadron commander, head of a yacht club.

com·mon (kŏm'ən) ***adj-*** [**com·mon·er, com·mon·est**] **1** frequently seen, heard, etc.; usual; familiar: *Snow is a* common *sight in northern countries.* **2** shared by or usual for many or all people; general: *That law is a matter of* common *knowledge. National parks are* common *property.* **3** of the ordinary kind; average: *the* common *people*; *a* common *clerk.* **4** of inferior quality; low; vulgar: *his* common *manners.* ***n-*** **1** land shared by all the people of a community. **2 commons** (1) *chiefly Brit.* common people. (2) dining hall, especially in a university, where food is served at common tables; also, the food served in this way. **3 Commons** House of Commons.

in common shared with another; jointly: *They held the property* in common. *She has much* in common *with her friend.*

com·mon·al·ty (kŏm'ə nəl tē) ***n-*** [**com·mon·al·ties**] the common people, especially as a political body.

common carrier ***n-*** company, such as a railroad or steamship line, whose business is the transportation of persons or goods.

common denominator ***n-*** a denominator which can be divided evenly by all the denominators in a set of fractions: *12 is a* common denominator *for 1/2, 1/3, 1/4, 1/6.*

common divisor ***n-*** a number that divides two or more numbers with zero remainders: *3 is the* common divisor *of 6, 12, and 24.*

com·mon·er (kŏm'ə nər) ***n-*** in Britain and other monarchies, one of the common people, as distinguished from one of the nobility.

common factor ***n-*** number which is a factor of any two or more numbers: *6 is a* common factor *of 12 and 24.*

common fraction ***n-*** fraction whose denominator and numerator are both integers.

common law ***n-*** system of law, sometimes unwritten, based on custom, usage, and court decisions, as distinct from statute law.

com·mon·ly (kŏm'ən lē) ***adv-*** usually; generally.

Common Market ***n-*** in Europe, an economic union organized to remove tariffs among member nations and to regulate tariffs between them and other countries; European Economic Community.

common multiple ***n-*** number that can be divided by two or more other numbers with zero remainders: *20 is a* common multiple *of 2, 4, 5, and 10.*

common noun See *noun.*

com·mon·place (kŏm'ən plās') ***n-*** **1** common, everyday thing or event: *Poverty is a* commonplace *among many people.* **2** dull and unoriginal remark, viewpoint, etc.: *His talk was full of* commonplaces. ***adj-***: *a* commonplace *occurrence*; *a* commonplace *speech.*

common school ***n-*** elementary school.

common sense ***n-*** practical way of looking at things; judgment based on experience.

common stock ***n-*** corporation stock which has voting rights but no fixed rate of dividends. It also has last claim to the assets of the company when it is dissolved.

common time or **common meter** *Music* ***n-*** pattern of note values and accents having four beats to the measure, each beat having the duration of a quarter note, with accents on the first and third beats.

com·mon·weal (kŏm'ən wēl') ***n-*** **1** public or general welfare; common good. **2** *Archaic* commonwealth.

com·mon·wealth (kŏm'ən wĕlth') ***n-*** **1** a state or free democratic nation; a republic. **2** the whole body of self-governing people in a state or nation. **3** one of several states of the United States: *the* Commonwealth *of Virginia.* **4 The Commonwealth** the British Commonwealth of Nations.

com·mo·tion (kə mō'shən) ***n-*** disturbance or disorder; confusion; turmoil: *The news caused a* commotion.

com·mu·nal (kə myōō'nəl, kŏm'yə nəl) ***adj-*** **1** of property, shared in common: *a plot of* communal *land.* **2** of or relating to a commune.

com·mu·nal·ism (kŏm'yə nə lĭz'əm) ***n-*** social system based on common or communal ownership of property. ►Should not be confused with COMMUNISM.

[1]**com·mune** (kə myōōn') ***vi-*** [**com·muned, com·mun·ing**] **1** to have an intimate talk or relationship (with): *to* commune *with oneself*; *to* commune *with nature.* **2** to take Holy Communion. [from Old French **communer,** from **comun** meaning "[2]commune" and "common".]

[2]**com·mune** (kŏm'yōōn') ***n-*** **1** society in which property is owned in common. **2** in some European countries, the smallest unit of local government. **3 the Commune** in the French Revolution, the committee which governed Paris, and later France, from 1789 to 1794. [from Old French **comu(g)ne,** from Late Latin **communia** meaning "duties in common."]

com·mu·ni·ca·ble (kə myōō'nĭ kə bəl) ***adj-*** liable to be transmitted from person to person: *a* communicable *disease.* **—*adv-*** **com·mu'ni·ca·bly.**

com·mu·ni·cant (kə myōō'nə kənt) ***n-*** **1** a person who imparts or communicates. **2** one who receives the Eucharist.

com·mu·ni·cate (kə myōō'nə kāt') ***vt-*** [**com·mu·ni·cat·ed, com·mu·ni·cat·ing**] to pass on to another; convey; impart; transmit: *to* communicate *a message*; *to* communicate *a disease.* ***vi-*** to send and receive information, ideas, etc.: *They* communicate *easily.*

communicate with to be connected with; also, to adjoin.

com·mu·ni·ca·tion (kə myōō'nə kā'shən) ***n-*** **1** exchange of information, ideas, etc.: *People speaking different languages often find* communication *difficult.* **2** a passing on; a transmitting: *the* communication *of news by radio.* **3** message; something communicated: *What was in that* communication *from headquarters?* **4 communications** telephone, telegraph, radio, and TV.

communications satellite ***n-*** satellite developed by scientists that sends or reflects radio signals between two points on earth.

com·mun·ion (kə myōōn'yən) ***n-*** **1** a sharing of experience; fellowship: *a close* communion *between friends.*

2 a group of persons sharing the same religious beliefs. 3 **Communion** or **Holy Communion** (1) a sacrament that commemorates Christ's last supper with the Apostles; the Eucharist. (2) the last part of the Mass in which the sacrament is received.

com·mu·ni·qué (kə myōō′ nə kā′) ***n-*** official announcement or bulletin.

com·mu·nism (kŏm′ yə nĭz′ əm) ***n-*** 1 economic and political idea, advanced by Karl Marx and modified by Nikolai Lenin and others, that the community as a whole should own all property and run all business and industry, and that this can be brought about only by armed revolution. 2 **Communism** system of government which claims to put this idea into practice through the dictatorship of a single party, the Communist Party, as in the Soviet Union. ►Should not be confused with COMMUNALISM.

com·mu·nist (kŏm′ yə nĭst) ***n-*** 1 person who advocates communism. 2 **Communist** member of the Communist Party. ***adj-*** 1 of or relating to communism. 2 **Communist** of or relating to Communism or the Communist Party.

Communist Party ***n-*** any of various political parties that follow Communist doctrines.

com·mu·ni·ty (kə myōō′ nə tē) ***n-*** [*pl.* **com·mu·ni·ties**] 1 all the people living in one place, such as a town or district, and subject to the same laws; also, the place itself: *a small New England* community. 2 group of persons bound together by common beliefs or interests: *a religious* community; *the scientific* community. 3 *Biology* group of plants or animals which share a particular environment and are more or less dependent on each other, especially for food. 4 a holding in common; a sharing: *a* community *of interests. as* ***modifier***: *This park is* community *property.*

community center ***n-*** place in which members of a community may meet for recreational and social activities.

community chest ***n-*** fund raised by voluntary contributions to support local welfare and charities.

community college ***n-*** school giving freshman and sophomore college courses and certain two-year training courses, and usually serving a specific community.

com·mu·ta·tion (kŏm′yə tā′ shən) ***n-*** a commuting of a payment or penalty: *the* commutation *of the high interest rate to a lower one.*

commutation ticket ***n-*** transportation ticket sold at a reduced rate, good for a certain number of trips, or for a certain period, over a given route.

com·mu·ta·tive (kə myōō′ tə tĭv′, *also* kŏm′ yə tā′tĭv) ***adj-*** *Mathematics* of an operation such as addition, producing the same result independent of the order or sequence of the members of the set. Example: a + b = b + a.

com·mu·ta·tor (kŏm′ yə tā′tər) ***n-*** device on the armature of a motor to allow it to use direct current, or one on the armature of a generator to produce direct current.

com·mute (kə myōōt′) ***vi-*** [**com·mut·ed, com·mut·ing**] to travel regularly back and forth over a distance, usually from one's home to work in another city. ***vt-*** to change (a legal sentence) to one less severe: *The governor* commuted *his sentence from ten years to five.*

com·mut·er (kə myōō′ tər) ***n-*** person who travels regularly from his home to his work in another city.

comp. 1 compound. 2 compare. 3 comparative.

[1]**com·pact** (kəm păkt′, kŏm′ păkt′) ***adj-*** 1 tightly packed; dense; compressed: *soil too* compact *for growing anything*; *a* compact *sentence.* 2 taking up relatively little space; small and solid; not bulky: *a* compact *bundle*; *a* compact *body.* ***vt-*** (kəm păkt′ *only*) to compress or pack close; make solid. ***n-*** (kŏm′păkt′ *only*) 1 small, flat cosmetic case. 2 automobile somewhat smaller than standard size. [from Latin **compactus** meaning "joined," from Latin **compingere** meaning "to join."] ***—adv-*** **com·pact′ly.** ***n-*** **com·pact′ness.**

[2]**com·pact** (kŏm′ păkt′) ***n-*** a solemn agreement; contract; pact. [from Latin **compactum** from Latin **compacisci** meaning "to make an agreement with," related to [1]**compact.**]

com·pac·tor (kəm păk′ tər) ***n-*** device that compacts or compresses garbage or rubbish into small packs for easy disposal.

[1]**com·pan·ion** (kəm păn′ yən) ***n-*** 1 person who regularly shares the work, play, interests, etc., of another; comrade: *He was my close* companion *all through school.* 2 person who accompanies another or others: *He found that his* companion *in the next seat was also going to Canada.* 3 thing that matches another; one of a pair: *I broke the* companion *to that vase.* [from Old French **compagnon,** from Late Latin **companionem** meaning "messmate."]

[2]**com·pan·ion** (kəm păn′ yən) ***n-*** companionway. [short for **companionway,** from Dutch **kompanje,** from Old French **compaigne,** from Late Latin **compania** meaning "company; group of messmates."]

com·pan·ion·a·ble (kəm păn′ yə nə bəl) ***adj-*** sociable; agreeable; pleasant to be with. ***—adv-*** **com·pan′ion·a·bly.**

com·pan·ion·ship (kəm păn′ yən shĭp′) ***n-*** fellowship; agreeable association.

com·pan·ion·way (kəm păn′ yən wā′) ***n-*** stairway leading below from the deck of a ship; companion.

com·pa·ny (kŭm′ pə nē) ***n-*** [*pl.* **com·pan·ies**] 1 guest or guests: *My* company *came for dinner.* 2 business or commercial firm. 3 group of people gathered together: *She guided a* company *of tourists.* 4 companions; associates: *He keeps bad* company. 5 companionship; society: *The lone trapper missed the* company *of others.* 6 body of soldiers; military unit made up of a headquarters and two or more platoons. 7 troupe of performers. 8 the officers and crew of a ship. *as* ***modifier***: *a* company *pension plan*; *the* company *commander.*

company union ***n-*** union of the employees of a single company, especially such a union controlled by the employer.

compar. comparative.

com·pa·ra·ble (kŏm′ pə rə bəl) ***adj-*** 1 of a nature that permits comparison: *Airplanes and birds are* comparable *because both fly.* 2 worthy or fit to be compared: *Rhinestones are hardly* comparable *to diamonds.* ***—adv-*** **com′pa·ra·bly.**

com·par·a·tive (kəm păr′ ə tĭv) ***adj-*** 1 making a comparison; comparing: *a* comparative *study of the weights of boys and girls.* 2 measured by comparison; not absolute; relative: *to live in* comparative *comfort.* ***n-*** *Grammar* The form of an adjective that normally fits the pattern: The table is ______ than the chair. Most comparatives are formed by adding the ending -er to the adjective or its root: taller, larger. Some, however, are completely different from their adjectives: good, better. Many adjectives do not have comparatives, but are compared by adding "more": *Dogs are* more intelligent *than turtles.* Some adverbs also have comparatives: well, better. ***—adv-*** **com·par′a·tive·ly.**

com·pare (kəm pâr) ***vt-*** [**com·pared, com·par·ing**] 1 to examine in order to find out, or show, likeness or difference in: *Before buying, she* compared *the two watches.* 2 to describe as similar; liken: *The writer* compared *the sound of guns to thunder.* 3 *Grammar* to give the positive, comparative, and superlative of (an adjective or adverb). ***vi-*** to be capable or worthy of comparison: *His cooking* compares *with mine.*

beyond compare above comparison; incomparable: *Her beauty was* beyond compare.

►If we COMPARE X with Y we are looking for similarities and differences. If we COMPARE X to Y, we are looking for similarities only. If we CONTRAST X with Y, we are looking for differences only.

com·par·i·son (kəm păr′ ə sən) ***n-*** **1** act of comparing; examination to find out or show likeness and difference: *a* comparison *of one car with another.* **2** likeness; similarity: *There is no* comparison *between these brands.* **3** statement that one thing is like another in some way; simile. Example: Life is like a game. **4** inflection of adjectives and adverbs showing differences of degree.

com·part·ment (kəm pärt′ mənt) ***n-*** a separate part, division, or section of an enclosed space: *a separate* compartment *for paper clips*; *a glove* compartment *in a car.* **—*adj-* com·part′ men·ted.**

com·part·men·tal·ize (kŏm′ pärt′ mĕn′ tə līz) ***vt-*** [**com·part·men·tal·ized, com·part·men·tal·iz·ing**] **1** to divide (something) into compartments. **2** to group or arrange in a single compartment or division: *We* compartmentalized *all the accounting work.*

Magnetic compass

com·pass (kŭm′ pəs, kŏm-) ***n-*** **1** instrument used for determining direction, such as a free-swinging magnetic needle that always points to the north magnetic pole, or a gyrocompass that always points to the true north. **2** (often **compasses** or **pair of compasses**) instrument having two pointed movable legs hinged at one end and used for drawing circles, taking measurements, etc. **3** range; extent: *the* compass *of a voice.* **4** bounds; boundary: *within the* compass *of a city.* ***vt-*** **1** to encircle, surround, or go around. **2** to accomplish; achieve: *to* compass *a goal.* **3** to grasp mentally; comprehend.

Drawing compass

compass card ***n-*** thin disk, marked with the 32 points of the compass and the 360 degrees of the circle, which turns on the pivot of a ship's compass to show direction.

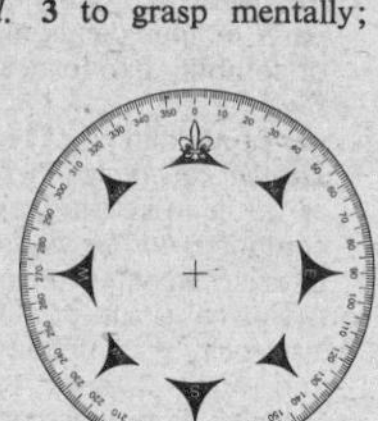
Compass card

com·pas·sion (kəm păsh′ ən) ***n-*** sympathy for the sorrow or suffering of others, with a desire to help.

com·pas·sion·ate (kəm-păsh′ ən ət) ***adj-*** feeling or showing compassion; sympathetic: **—*adv-* com·pas′ sion·ate·ly.**

com·pat·i·ble (kəm păt′ ə bəl) ***adj-*** able to exist together; harmonious; not inimical: *a* compatible *couple*; *a lamp* compatible *with the style of the room.* **—*n-* com·pat′ i·bil′ i·ty. *adv-* com·pat′ i·bly.**

com·pa·tri·ot (kəm pā′ trē ət) ***n-*** person of the same country; fellow citizen.

com·peer (kŏm′ pêr′) ***n-*** **1** person of equal rank or standing. **2** an associate or companion.

com·pel (kəm pĕl′) ***vt-*** [**com·pelled, com·pel·ling**] **1** to force; oblige: *The bandit's conscience* compelled *him to return.* **2** to get or exact by force: *to* compel *obedience.*

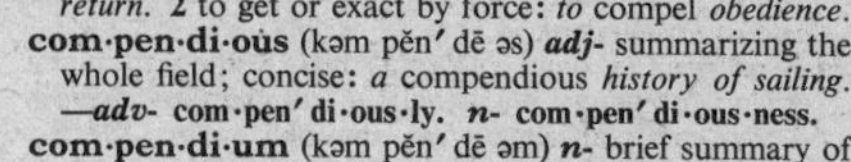

com·pen·di·ous (kəm pĕn′ dē əs) ***adj-*** summarizing the whole field; concise: *a* compendious *history of sailing.* **—*adv-* com·pen′ di·ous·ly. *n-* com·pen′ di·ous·ness.**

com·pen·di·um (kəm pĕn′ dē əm) ***n-*** brief summary of a large work or field of study; an abstract.

com·pen·sate (kŏm′ pən sāt′) ***vt-*** [**com·pen·sat·ed, com·pen·sat·ing**] to pay: *to* compensate *employees for overtime.* ***vi-*** to be a remedy (for); make up (for): *Glasses* compensate *for weak eyes.* **—*adj-* com·pen′ sa·tive′** (kəm pĕn′ sə tĭv′) or **com·pen′ sa·to′ ry** (-sə tôr′ ē).

com·pen·sa·tion (kŏm′ pən sā′ shən) ***n-*** **1** whatever makes good any lack or loss; payment; amends: *He received* compensation *for his injuries.* **2** something given in return for a service or something of value: *He receives inadequate* compensation *for the work he does.*

com·pete (kəm pēt′) ***vi-*** [**com·pet·ed, com·pet·ing**] to oppose or strive against another in a contest, business, etc.; contend; vie: *Three runners will* compete *in the race. The two companies* competed *for the contract.*

com·pe·tence (kŏm′ pə təns) ***n-*** **1** fitness; capability; ability: *No one questions her* competence *as a teacher.* **2** enough money for comfort; adequate means: *Income from investments assured him a lifelong* competence. Also **com′ pe·ten·cy.**

com·pe·tent (kŏm′ pə tənt) ***adj-*** having skill or knowledge in a particular field; qualified; fit: *A* competent *worker makes few mistakes.* **—*adv-* com′pe·tent·ly.**

com·pe·ti·tion (kŏm′ pə tĭsh′ ən) ***n-*** **1** a competing or contending; rivalry: *There is strong* competition *among auto manufacturers.* **2** contest or match, especially in sports: *a skiing* competition.

com·pet·itive (kəm pĕt′ ə tĭv) ***adj-*** involving competition or rivalry: *Football is a* competitive *sport.* **—*adv-* com·pet′ i·tive·ly. *n-* com·pet′ i·tive·ness.**

com·pet·i·tor (kəm pĕt′ ə tər) ***n-*** person or group that competes with another; rival or contestant: *The two automobile companies are* competitors.

com·pi·la·tion (kŏm′ pə lā′ shən) ***n-*** **1** a compiling: *the* compilation *of scientific data.* **2** something that has been compiled, such as a collection of notes, an anthology, etc.

com·pile (kəm pīl′) ***vt-*** [**com·piled, com·pil·ing**] **1** to put together (facts, articles, etc.) into a collection. **2** to compose from various sources: *to* compile *a history.*

com·pla·cen·cy (kəm plā′ sən sē) ***n-*** feeling of well-being and satisfaction, so strong as to be without any awareness of danger or the problems of others; self-satisfaction: *Lee's early victories jarred the North out of its* complacency. Also **com·pla′ cence.**

com·pla·cent (kəm plā′ sənt) ***adj-*** **1** uncritically, often smugly, satisfied with oneself or one's lot; self-satisfied: *He was quite* complacent *about his good fortune.* **2** showing or expressing this feeling: *a gentle,* complacent *smile.* **—*adv-* com·pla′ cent·ly.**

►Should not be confused with COMPLAISANT.

com·plain (kəm plān′) ***vi-*** **1** to express dissatisfaction or discontent because of a pain, sorrow, nuisance, etc.: *He* complained *of a headache.* **2** to report a wrong or injury: *He* complained *to the landlord about the noise.*

com·plain·ant (kəm plā′ nənt) ***n-*** person who makes a formal complaint, usually in court.

com·plaint (kəm plānt′) ***n-*** **1** expression of unhappiness, grief, dissatisfaction, etc.; grumbling. **2** something causing pain or discomfort: *He went to the doctor with a stomach* complaint. **3** formal charge or accusation against a person: *The tenant swore out a* complaint *against his landlord.*

com·plai·sant (kəm plā′zənt) ***adj-*** willing to please others; obliging; agreeable: *a* complaisant *manner.* —***adj-*** **com·plai′sant·ly.** ***n-*** **com·plai′sance:** *She was delighted with the* complaisance *of her hosts.*

►Should not be confused with COMPLACENT.

com·ple·ment (kŏm′plə mənt) ***n-*** **1** something added that makes a thing complete: *In a race horse, stamina is the* complement *of speed.* **2** the required number or amount; a complete set: *The task force now had its full* complement *of ships.* **3** one of two complementary angles. **4** one of two complementary colors. **5** *Grammar* (1) the word or group of words that follows the linking verb to complete a sentence. In "My sister is very beautiful," "very beautiful" is a complement. (2) in traditional grammar, also an object of a verb or preposition. ***vt-*** of a color or angle, to be complementary to: *Red* complements *green. Angle X* complements *Angle Y.* ***Hom-*** compliment.

com·ple·men·ta·ry (kŏm′plə mĕnt′ə rē, -mĕn′trē) ***adj-*** completing; filling out: *A* complementary *platoon of troops brought the company up to full strength.* ***Hom-*** complimentary.

complementary angles ***n-*** *pl.* two angles whose measures add up to 90°.

complementary colors ***n-*** a pair of colors consisting of one primary color and the secondary color obtained from the other two primary colors. Mixing complementary colors produces gray pigment or white light.

com·plete (kəm plēt′) ***adj-*** **1** lacking nothing; entire; whole; full: *a* complete *deck of cards.* **2** absolute: *a* complete *surprise.* **3** finished: *Her work is now* complete. ***vt-*** **[com·plet·ed, com·plet·ing] 1** to make whole or perfect: *I need several stamps to* complete *my collection.* **2** to bring to an end; finish: *to* complete *one's work.* —***adv-*** **com·plete′ly.** ***n-*** **com·plete′ness.**

com·ple·tion (kəm plē′shən) ***n-*** **1** a completing or finishing: *He is responsible for the* completion *of the job.* **2** condition of being completed: *The work is nearing* completion.

[1]**com·plex** (kŏm′plĕks, kəm plĕks′) ***adj-*** **1** made up of many parts; intricate: *a* complex *piece of machinery.* **2** hard to understand or explain: *a* complex *argument.* —***adv-*** **com′plex·ly** or **com·plex′ly.**

[2]**com·plex** (kŏm′plĕks′) ***n-*** **1** a whole made up of diverse and intricately related parts: *an industrial* complex. **2** in psychology, a group of related emotions, impulses, desires, etc., forming a part of one's personality and, sometimes, leading to abnormal behavior: *a guilt* complex.

complex fraction ***n-*** fraction in which the numerator or denominator or both are themselves fractions.

Examples: $\frac{1/4}{1/2}$, $\frac{2}{3/4}$, $\frac{1\,3/4}{1/2}$.

com·plex·ion (kəm plĕk′shən) ***n-*** **1** color, texture, and general appearance of the skin, especially of the face: *a smooth* complexion. **2** general character; nature: *The new evidence changes the* complexion *of the case.*

com·plex·ioned (kəm plĕk′shənd) ***adj-*** having a particular complexion (used only in compound words): *a smooth-*complexioned *girl.*

com·plex·i·ty (kəm plĕk′sə tē) ***n-*** [*pl.* **com·plex·i·ties**] **1** condition of being complex or complicated: *He was baffled by the* complexity *of the problem.* **2** something complex; intricacy: *Chess has many* complexities.

complex sentence ***n-*** *Grammar* a sentence that contains at least one independent clause and at least one dependent clause.

com·pli·ance (kəm plī′əns) ***n-*** a complying or yielding; acquiescence. Also **com·pli′an·cy.**

in compliance with in agreement with; in obedience to: *He quit smoking* in compliance with *his doctor's orders.*

com·pli·ant (kəm plī′ənt) ***adj-*** inclined to agree or consent; complying. —***adv-*** **com·pli′ant·ly.**

com·pli·cate (kŏm′plə kāt′) ***vt-*** **[com·pli·cat·ed, com·pli·cat·ing]** to make hard to handle, explain, or understand; make complex or involved: *His return really* complicates *matters.*

com·pli·cat·ed (kŏm′plə kā′təd) ***adj-*** hard to handle, explain, or understand: *a* complicated *machine; a* complicated *argument.* —***adv-*** **com′pli·cat′ed·ly.**

com·pli·ca·tion (kŏm′plə kā′shən) ***n-*** **1** thing that complicates; thing that increases difficulty or confusion: *There were so many* complications *in the rules that we couldn't understand the game.* **2** condition of being complicated; a tangle or confusion: *a* complication *of worries.*

com·plic·i·ty (kəm plĭs′ə tē) ***n-*** [*pl.* **com·plic·i·ties**] partnership in wrongdoing or crime: *He was charged with* complicity *in the theft.*

[1]**com·pli·ment** (kŏm′plə mənt) ***n-*** **1** expression of praise or approval: *She received many* compliments *on her new dress.* **2 compliments** polite, usually formal, greetings: *The new ambassador paid his* compliments *to the President.* ***Hom-*** complement.

[2]**com·pli·ment** (kŏm′plə mĕnt′) ***vt-*** to express admiration or praise for: *The guests* complimented *their hostess on her cooking. I* compliment *you on your good taste in decoration.* ***Hom-*** complement.

com·pli·men·ta·ry (kŏm′plə mĕnt′ə rē, -mĕn′trē) ***adj-*** **1** giving approval or praise: *Her remarks on the new house were* complimentary. **2** given free: *a* complimentary *ticket.* ***Hom-*** complementary. —***adv-*** **com′pli·men′ta·ri·ly.**

com·ply (kəm plī′) ***vi-*** **[com·plied, com·ply·ing]** to act in accordance (with a request, order, etc.): *to* comply *with traffic rules.*

com·po·nent (kəm pō′nənt, kŏm′pō-) ***n-*** one of the parts or ingredients making up a whole. ***adj-*** forming or combining to form a whole: *the* component *parts of a sentence.*

com·port (kəm pôrt′) ***vt-*** to conduct or behave (oneself): *He did not know how to* comport *himself at the party.* ***vi-*** to be in keeping; agree: *His lack of dignity does not* comport *with his position as a judge.* —***n-*** **com·port′ment:** *His* comportment *was most dignified.*

com·pose (kəm pōz′) ***vt-*** **[com·posed, com·pos·ing] 1** to form by combining: *This paste is* composed *of flour and water.* **2** to put together; make up: *to* compose *a letter.* **3** to produce or create (music to be performed). **4** to settle or arrange in an orderly, calm fashion: *Try to* compose *yourself. Let me* compose *my thoughts.* **5** to reconcile: *The opposing leaders* composed *their differences.* **6** to set (type) for printing. ***vi-*** to create musical works: *He* composes *as a hobby.*

►Where COMPOSE and COMPRISE both have the sense of constitute or be made up of, use COMPOSE in more concrete and immediate instances and COMPRISE in more abstract or general situations: *The cake is* composed *of many ingredients. The proposal* comprises *several points of view.* COMPRISE is awkward when used in the passive voice.

com·posed (kəm pōzd′) ***adj-*** not flustered or excited; calm; self-possessed. —***adv-*** **com·pos′ed·ly.**

com·pos·er (kəm pō′ zər) ***n-*** person who composes, especially one who writes music.

com·pos·ite (kəm pŏz′ət) ***adj-*** **1** made up of different parts that form a whole: *a* composite *picture made from several photographs.* **2** belonging to a large family of plants, including the daisy and the dandelion, having flowers that appear to be single blooms but are really formed of two kinds of smaller flowers. ***n-*** a blend or mixture; combination.

composite number ***n-*** any whole number that has one or more factors other than itself and 1. Example: 6 is a composite number since 2 and 3 are also factors of 6.

com·po·si·tion (kŏm′pə zĭsh′ən) ***n-*** **1** an artistic work, especially a piece of music. **2** story, essay, etc., written as a school assignment, especially for practice in a language. **3** the act of producing a piece of writing or music. **4** combination of parts or substances forming a whole: *the* composition *of the figures in a drawing; soil of a rich* composition. **5** a mixture of substances. **6** the setting up of type for printing.

com·pos·i·tor (kəm pŏz′ə tər) ***n-*** person who sets type for printing.

com·post (kŏm′pōst′) ***n-*** a mixture of decomposed substances, such as leaf mold and manure, used to fertilize soil.

com·po·sure (kəm pō′ zhər) ***n-*** calmness of mind or spirit; self-possession: *to keep one's* composure *in a crisis.*

com·pote (kŏm′pōt′) ***n-*** **1** stewed fruit, often of different kinds, usually served as a dessert. **2** stemmed dish used for serving candy, nuts, fruit, etc.

[1]**com·pound** (kŏm′pound′) ***n-*** **1** substance formed by the chemical combination of elements: *Salt (sodium chloride) is a* compound *of chlorine and sodium.* **2** a combination of two or more parts, ingredients, characteristics, etc.; mixture. **3** word composed of two or more other words, such as "horseback" and "half-hour." ***adj-*** consisting of two or more separate parts forming a single whole: *a* compound *word.*

[2]**com·pound** (kəm pound′) ***vt-*** **1** to prepare by mixing or combining ingredients: *A druggist* compounds *medicines prescribed by a doctor.* **2** to add to; increase: *His troubles were* compounded *by new problems.*

compound eye ***n-*** an eye made up of many separate units, each having a lens and a group of cells sensitive to light. Compound eyes occur in insects and shellfish.

compound fraction ***n-*** complex fraction.

compound fracture ***n-*** bone fracture in which the ends of the broken bone stick out through the skin. See also *simple fracture.*

compound interest ***n-*** interest computed periodically on the sum of the original principal and the accumulated interest.

compound leaf ***n-*** leaf, such as that of the sumac or the horse chestnut, consisting of several leaflets attached to a single leaf stem.

compound sentence ***n-*** *Grammar* a sentence that contains at least two independent clauses. It may also contain one or more dependent clauses.

com·pre·hend (kŏm′prĭ hĕnd′) ***vt-*** **1** to understand: *I heard his speech but did not* comprehend *his meaning.* **2** to include; take in: *Science* comprehends *the study of chemistry, physics, and biology.*

com·pre·hen·si·ble (kŏm′prĭ hĕn′sə bəl) ***adj-*** of such nature as to be comprehended; understandable. **—*n-*** **com′pre·hen′si·bil′i·ty.** ***adv-*** **com′pre·hen′si·bly.**

com·pre·hen·sion (kŏm′prĭ hĕn′shən) ***n-*** ability to understand; understanding: *The lecture was beyond our* comprehension.

com·pre·hen·sive (kŏm′prĭ hĕn′sĭv) ***adj-*** including or covering much; full; complete: *a* comprehensive *description;* comprehensive *studies.* **—*adv-*** **com′pre·hen′sive·ly.** ***n-*** **com′pre·hen′sive·ness.**

[1]**com·press** (kəm prĕs′) ***vt-*** to press, squeeze, or force tightly together or into a confined space: *to* compress *cotton into bales; to* compress *ideas into a paragraph.*

[2]**com·press** (kŏm′prĕs′) ***n-*** pad of gauze or other cloth, applied to a wound, sprain, etc.

com·pressed (kəm prĕst′) ***adj-*** **1** reduced in size or volume by or as if by squeezing. **2** flattened sideways, as the body of a flounder.

compressed air ***n-*** air whose volume has been decreased by force to give it greater pressure than atmospheric air. Its pressure is used to operate machines such as jackhammers, brakes, and spray guns.

com·press·i·ble (kəm prĕs′ə bəl) ***adj-*** of a nature that allows squeezing into a smaller volume: *Air is a* compressible *substance.* **—*n-*** **com·press′i·bil′i·ty.**

com·pres·sion (kəm prĕsh′ən) ***n-*** act or process of compressing.

compression ratio ***n-*** of an internal-combustion engine, the ratio of the volume of a fuel mixture before combustion to its volume after combustion but before exhaust.

com·pres·sor (kəm prĕs′ər) ***n-*** something that compresses, especially a machine for compressing air or a gas, such as that in an electric refrigerator. *as* ***modifier:*** *a* compressor *tank.*

com·prise (kəm prīz′) ***vt-*** [**com·prised, com·pris·ing**] to consist of; include: *This volume* comprises *all her work.* ►For usage note see COMPOSE.

com·pro·mise (kŏm′prə mīz′) ***n-*** settlement of differences in which each side yields something: *The strike was settled by* compromise. ***vi-*** [**com·pro·mised, com·pro·mis·ing**] to settle differences by yielding on each side: *They* compromised *on the amount of salary to be paid.* ***vt-*** to expose to suspicion or mistrust; endanger: *to* compromise *one's good name by cheating.*

comp·trol·ler (kən trōl′ər) ***n-*** person who supervises financial accounts; controller.

com·pul·sion (kəm pŭl′shən) ***n-*** **1** a compelling by force, fear, custom, etc.: *to govern by* compulsion; *to act under* compulsion. **2** very strong and usually unreasonable impulse: *a* compulsion *to avoid stepping on cracks in the pavement.*

com·pul·sive (kəm pŭl′sĭv) ***adj-*** **1** having power to compel; compelling: *a* compulsive *force.* **2** resulting from or influenced by a very strong impulse: *a* compulsive *talker; a* compulsive *eater.* **—*adv-*** **com·pul′sive·ly.** ***n-*** **com·pul′sive·ness.**

com·pul·so·ry (kəm pŭl′sə rē) ***adj-*** required by rule or law: *Attendance at school is* compulsory.

com·punc·tion (kəm pŭngk′shən) ***n-*** uneasiness of conscience; twinge of regret or remorse: *I felt some* compunction *at having kept him waiting.*

com·pu·ta·tion (kŏm′pyə tā′shən) ***n-*** the act or process of computing; calculation.

com·pute (kəm pyo͞ot′) ***vt-*** [**com·put·ed, com·put·ing**] to determine by mathematics; calculate: *Scientists can* compute *the distance from the earth to distant stars.*

com·put·er (kəm pyo͞o′ tər) ***n-*** complex electronic device for solving mathematical problems. Some kinds

fāte, făt, dâre, bärn; bē, bĕt, mêre; bīte, bĭt; nōte, hŏt, môre, dòg; fŭn, fûr; to͞o, bo͝ok; oil; out; tar; thin; then; hw for wh as in *wh*at; zh for s as in u*s*ual; ə for a, e, i, o, u, as in *a*go, lin*e*n, per*i*l, at*o*m, min*u*s

store, sort, and compare information given to them, and then use it to control industrial machinery and to navigate space vehicles.

com·put·er·ize (kəm pyōō′tə rīz) *vt-* [**com·put·er·ized, com·put·er·i·zing**] **1** to operate or control by means of a computer. **2** to equip with computers or a computer system. *—n-* **com·put·er·i·za′tion.**

com·rade (kŏm′răd′) *n-* friend or companion, especially one who shares one's interests and activities.

comrade in arms *n-* a fellow soldier.

com·rade·ly (kŏm′răd′lē) *adj-* typical of comrades; friendly: *a* comradely *greeting.*

com·rade·ship (kŏm′răd′shĭp′) *n-* companionship.

[1]**con** (kŏn) *vt-* [**conned, con·ning**] to study carefully, especially so as to learn by heart: *He* conned *each page.* [variant of [1]**can** in its meaning "learn to know how."]

[2]**con** (kŏn) *n-* reason or argument against something; used in the phrase **pros and cons:** *He weighed all the pros and* cons *before starting out on the expedition.* **adv-** against: *She can argue both pro and* con. [from Latin **contra** meaning "against."]

con·cave (kŏn′kāv′) *adj-* curved inward like the inside of a saucer. *—adv-* **con′cave′ly.**

Concave

con·cav·i·ty (kŏn′kăv′ə tē) *n-* [*pl* **con·cav·i·ties**] **1** the condition of being concave. **2** the inner surface of a rounded, hollow body.

con·ceal (kən sēl′) *vt-* to hide or keep secret: *to* conceal *a book; to* conceal *one's anger.*

con·ceal·ment (kən sēl′mənt) *n-* **1** a hiding or concealing: *The* concealment *of facts by a witness is a criminal offense.* **2** condition of being hidden: *He came out of* concealment *for brief periods of time.*

con·cede (kən sēd′) *vt-* [**con·ced·ed, con·ced·ing**] **1** to admit the truth of; acknowledge: *to* concede *a point in a debate.* **2** to give up or grant, often reluctantly: *to* concede *a raise in wages.* *vi-* to admit defeat; yield: *The candidate* conceded *early in the evening.*

con·ceit (kən sēt′) *n-* excessive or flattering belief in oneself; vanity: Conceit *blinds people to their faults.*

con·ceit·ed (kən sē′təd) *adj-* having too high an opinion of oneself; vain. *—adv-* **con·ceit′ed·ly.** *n-* **con·ceit′ed·ness.**

con·ceiv·a·ble (kən sē′və bəl) *adj-* thought of or imagined as possible; imaginable; possible: *It is* conceivable *that man will reach Mars.* *—adv-* **con·ceiv′a·bly.**

con·ceive (kən sēv′) *vt-* [**con·ceived, con·ceiv·ing**] **1** to form (a plan, project, etc.) in the mind: *They* conceived *a plot to overthrow the king.* **2** to form a mental picture of; imagine: *I cannot* conceive *his owning all that property.* **3** to become pregnant with (young). *vi-* to become pregnant.

conceive of to imagine: *I cannot* conceive of *her lying.*

con·cen·trate (kŏn′sən trāt′) *vt-* [**con·cen·trat·ed, con·cen·trat·ing**] (in sense 1 considered intransitive when the direct object is implied but not expressed) **1** to fix or focus (mind, feeling, or other faculty) on something: *He* concentrated *his efforts on the problem.* **2** to bring together at one point or place: *to* concentrate *an army.* **3** to increase the strength of (a solution): *to* concentrate *orange juice by removing water.* *vi-* to come together in one place: *The crowd* concentrated *near the gate.* *n-* something produced by purification: *a* concentrate *of vitamin C.*

con·cen·tra·tion (kŏn′sən trā′shən) *n-* **1** fixed attention on one object: *It requires* concentration *to study during a thunderstorm.* **2** group or mass brought together in one place or thing: *a* concentration *of enemy troops along the border.*

concentration camp *n-* prison of huts or barracks in a strongly fenced and guarded enclosure, especially such a prison used by the Nazi regime.

con·cen·tric (kən sĕn′trĭk) *adj-* having a common center: *several* concentric *circles or spheres.* *—adv-* **con·cen′tri·cal·ly.**

con·cept (kŏn′sĕpt′) *n-* a mental image; general idea or notion: *a* concept *of the solar system; a* concept *of a word's meaning.*

con·cep·tion (kən sĕp′shən) *n-* **1** a mental conceiving; forming of ideas, images, etc.: *The job requires great powers of* conception. **2** something conceived, such as an idea, plan, etc.: *It's a bold* conception, *but we will need help.* **3** fertilization of the egg and the beginning of a new life in the body of the mother.

con·cep·tu·al (kən sĕp′chōō əl) *adj-* relating to or involving mental conception or concepts: *Thinking is a* conceptual *process.* *—adv-* **con·cep′tu·al·ly.**

con·cern (kən sûrn′) *vt-* **1** to be of interest or importance to; have to do with; relate to; affect: *This doesn't* concern *the schedule.* **2** to make anxious or uneasy; worry; trouble: *His poor health* concerns *me.* *n-* interest or regard, especially anxious interest or worry: *a matter of deep* concern *to the nation.* **2** something that closely affects or relates to one; business; affair: *This is no* concern *of yours.* **3** business firm.

concern (oneself) with to be interested in; pay attention to.

con·cerned (kən sûrnd′) *adj-* **1** worried; troubled: *I'm* concerned *about him.* **2** taking part, engaged, or involved (in): *You are* concerned *in the new plans.*

con·cern·ed·ly (kən sûr′ nəd lē) *adv-* in a worried manner.

con·cern·ing (kən sûr′nĭng) *prep-* relating to; regarding; about: *Please give me the facts* concerning *this case.*

con·cert (kŏn′sərt) *n-* musical performance by singers, or players, or both. *as* ***modifier:*** *a* concert *hall.*

in concert in agreement; together.

con·cert·ed (kən sûr′təd) *adj-* planned, agreed upon, or carried out together; combined; joint: *a* concerted *effort.*

con·cert·ed·ly (kən sûr′təd lē) *adv-* together; jointly; in concert.

con·cer·ti·na (kŏn′sər tē′nə) *n-* a small musical instrument somewhat like an accordion.

con·cert·mas·ter (kŏn′sərt măs′tər) *n-* the leading first violinist of an orchestra.

con·cer·to (kən chĕr′tō) *n-* [*pl.* **con·cer·tos** or **con·cer·ti** (-tē)] musical composition, usually in three movements, for solo instruments and an orchestra.

concert pitch *n-* pitch to which instruments are tuned for performance, the A above middle C.

con·ces·sion (kən sĕsh′ən) *n-* **1** a yielding or conceding: *The argument can be settled only by* concession. **2** something yielded: *The stronger side demanded several* concessions. **3** right granted to conduct a business; also, the business itself: *the soft-drink* concession.

con·ces·sion·aire (kən sĕsh′ən âr′) *n-* person or company holding or operating a business concession.

con·ces·sive (kən sĕs′ĭv) *adj-* having the nature of a concession or admission; yielding: *a* concessive *act.* *—adv-* **con·ces′sive·ly.**

Conch

conch (kŏngk, kŏnch) *n-* [*pl.* **conchs** or **conch·es**] **1** any of a group of ocean shellfish related to snails. Conchs have a single, large, spiral shell that is often beautifully colored. **2** the shell itself.

con·cil·i·ate (kən sĭl′ē āt′) *vt-* [**con·cil·i·at·ed, con·cil·i·at·ing**] to gain the good will of; overcome the hostility of; placate: *The boy's apology* conciliated *his angry father.* —*n-* **con·cil′i·a′tion.**

con·cil·i·a·tor (kən sĭl′ē ā′tər) *n-* **1** person who conciliates. **2** person appointed to settle disputes between labor and management; arbitrator.

con·cil·i·a·tor·y (kən sĭl′ē ə tôr′ē) *adj-* intended to conciliate, reconcile, or pacify: *a* conciliatory *talk.*

con·cise (kən sīs′) *adj-* expressing much in few words; short and to the point; terse: *a* concise *and witty remark.* —*adv-* **con·cise′ly.** *n-* **con·cise′ness.**

con·clave (kŏn′klāv′) *n-* **1** private meeting of cardinals, especially for the election of a pope. **2** the rooms in which such a meeting is held. **3** any private or secret meeting: *a political* conclave.

con·clude (kən klōōd′) *vt-* [**con·clud·ed, con·clud·ing**] **1** to end; finish: *As he* concluded *his speech, there was loud applause.* **2** to settle; arrange after discussion or argument: *The two nations* concluded *a trade agreement.* **3** to arrive at an opinion by reasoning; decide: *After study, I have* concluded *that Russian is a difficult language.* *vi-* to come to an end: *His speech* concluded *with an appeal for unity.*

con·clu·sion (kən clōō′zhən) *n-* **1** opinion arrived at by reasoning: *What* conclusion *did you reach after your discussion?* **2** final part; end: *The* conclusion *of the book was exciting.* **3** settlement or arrangement after discussion: *the* conclusion *of a treaty.*

con·clu·sive (kən klōō′sĭv) *adj-* settling a problem or point; decisive; final: *a* conclusive *piece of evidence.* —*adv-* **con·clu′sive·ly.** *n-* **con·clu′sive·ness.**

con·coct (kən kŏkt′, kŏn′-) *vt-* **1** to make out of various parts or things: *Wanda* concocted *a salad of fruit and nuts.* **2** to make up; invent: *to* concoct *a story.*

con·coc·tion (kən kŏk′shən) *n-* **1** a concocting: *the* concoction *of a new dessert.* **2** something concocted: *His story is just a* concoction *of rumors.*

con·com·i·tant (kən kŏm′ə tənt) *n-* something that accompanies something else: *Happiness is not always a* concomitant *of wealth.* *adj-*: *a* concomitant *effect.* —*adv-* **con·com′i·tant·ly.**

con·cord (kŏng′kòrd′, -kôrd′) *n-* **1** agreement; harmony. **2** peaceful and friendly relations, as between nations.

con·cord·ance (kən kòr′dəns, -kôr′dəns) *n-* **1** agreement; harmony: *a* concordance *of aims.* **2** book consisting of an alphabetical list giving the location of all the important words in a single work or in the collected works of an author: *a* concordance *to Shakespeare.*

con·cor·dant (kən kòr′dənt, -kôr′dənt) *adj-* having the same opinions, attitudes, etc.; agreeing; harmonious: *views that are* concordant *with mine.* —*adv-* **con·cor′dant·ly.**

con·cor·dat (kŏn kòr′dăt′, -kôr′dăt′) *n-* formal agreement, especially between a country and the pope on church matters.

Con·cord grape (kŏng′kərd) *n-* large, dark blue American grape.

con·course (kŏn′kôrs) *n-* **1** a running, flowing, or coming together; confluence: *St. Louis is located at the* concourse *of the Mississippi and Missouri.* **2** crowd or assembly. **3** open place where crowds gather, as in a railroad station.

[1]**con·crete** (kŏn′krēt) *n-* a hardened mixture of cement, sand, gravel, and water, used in building and paving. *adj-*: *a* concrete *walk.*

[2]**con·crete** (kən krēt′, kŏn′krēt′) *adj-* **1** of a nature such that it can be seen, heard, touched, measured, etc.; belonging to the physical world; real: *A table is a* concrete *object.* **2** relating to actual things or events: *a* concrete *discussion of the effects of a tax.*

con·cre·tion (kŏn krē′shən) *n-* **1** an accumulating and growing together of ideas, things, matter, etc.: *Scientific research often depends on a* concretion *of facts over the years.* **2** a hardened mass such as a gall stone, formed in living tissue. **3** in geology, a solid, rounded mass of rock formed inside a rock of a different kind: *Small lime* concretions *were found throughout the shale.*

con·cu·bine (kŏng′kyə bīn′) *n-* woman living with a man who is not legally married to her; mistress.]

con·cur (kən kûr′) *vi-* [**con·curred, con·cur·ring**] **1** to agree: *All the judges* concurred *in the decision.* **2** to happen or work together; coincide: *Careful planning and good luck* concurred *to bring about victory.*

con·cur·rence (kən kûr′əns) *n-* **1** an agreeing; accord: *a* concurrence *of opinions.* **2** a happening or coming together: *a* concurrence *of events; a* concurrence *of lines.*

con·cur·rent (kən kûr′ənt) *adj-* **1** acting together; cooperating: *the* concurrent *effort of two political parties.* **2** agreeing; harmonious: *the* concurrent *views of several observers.* **3** happening at the same time or place: *His illness was* concurrent *with his financial troubles.*

con·cur·rent·ly *adv-* at the same time; simultaneously: *His novel appeared* concurrently *with his play.*

concurrent resolution *n-* resolution adopted by both houses of Congress. It is not a law and does not require the signature of the President.

con·cus·sion (kən kŭsh′ən) *n-* **1** a violent jarring; shock: *the* concussion *of an explosion.* **2** brain injury due to a blow or fall.

con·demn (kən dĕm′) *vt-* **1** to express strong disapproval of; censure: *The board* condemned *his harsh measures.* **2** to declare guilty in court; also, to sentence: *The judge* condemned *him to five years at hard labor.* **3** to declare unfit for use: *to* condemn *a slum dwelling.* **4** to take for public use; appropriate: *to* condemn *land for a state road.* —*adj-* **con·dem′na·ble.**

con·dem·na·tion (kŏn′dĕm nā′shən) *n-* the act of condemning; also, an instance of this.

con·dem·na·tor·y (kən dĕm′nə tôr′ē) *adj-* intended to or seeming to condemn: *a* condemnatory *ruling against an offender; a* condemnatory *frown.*

con·demned (kən dĕmd′) *adj-* **1** declared to be unfit, dangerous, etc.: *a* condemned *building.* **2** convicted of or sentenced for crime, especially capital crime. **3** reserved for convicted persons: *the* condemned *cell.* *n-* **the condemned** those sentenced to death.

con·den·sa·tion (kŏn′dĕn sā′shən) *n-* **1** the change from vapor into a liquid: *Rain forms by the* condensation *of water vapor.* **2** the liquid so formed: *the* condensation *ran down the window pane.* **3** a reducing in size; also, the thing so reduced: *the* condensation *of a report.* **4** removal of water from a liquid to produce a concentrated liquid: *the* condensation *of orange juice.*

con·dense (kən dĕns′) *vt-* [**con·densed, con·dens·ing**] **1** to change a gas or vapor to a liquid: *to* condense *steam to water.* **2** to reduce the volume of (a liquid) by removing water; to concentrate: *to* condense *milk or orange juice.* **3** to express in fewer words: *The newspaper* condensed *the long speech to a paragraph.* *vi-* **1** to become dense. **2** to change from a gas or vapor to a liquid. —*adj-* **con·den′sa·ble.**

condensed milk *n-* canned, sweetened milk from which part of the water has been removed, so that it has a thick, syrupy consistency. See also *evaporated milk.*

con·dens·er (kən dĕn′sər) *n-* **1** coiled tube, glass pipe, or other device for cooling gases to condense them into liquids. **2** device for holding and storing a charge of electricity; capacitor.

con·de·scend (kŏn′də sĕnd′) *vi-* **1** to stoop or come down willingly to the level of one's inferiors: *The king* condescended *to eat with the people.* **2** to do something with a superior or patronizing air: *Though Tom thought it beneath him, he* condescended *to walk the dog.*

con·de·scend·ing (kŏn′də sĕn′dĭng) *adj-* having a superior air; patronizing: *a* condescending *smile.* *—adv-* **con′de·scend′ing·ly.**

con·de·scen·sion (kŏn′də sĕn′shən) *n-* **1** a stooping to the level of one's inferiors, often with a superior air. **2** superior or patronizing attitude.

con·di·ment (kŏn′də mənt) *n-* spicy seasoning for food.

con·di·tion (kən dĭsh′ ən) *n-* **1** state in which a person or thing is: *to be in a healthy* condition; *to be in working* condition. **2** something that must exist before something else can happen or exist: *Hard work is a* condition *of success.* **3** one part in an agreement or set of circumstances: *a contract having six* conditions; *good working* conditions. *vt-* **1** to make (someone) fit: *to* condition *a boxer for a fight.* **2** to limit or restrict; affect: *Health often* conditions *one's success.* **3** to develop a conditioned reflex in (a person or animal).

in condition in good physical tone. **on condition that** provided that. **out of condition** in poor physical tone.

con·di·tion·al (kən dĭsh′ən əl) *adj-* **1** depending on a condition, circumstance, or certain terms; conditioned. **2** *Grammar* of a clause, tense, etc., expressing a condition. Example: "If it rains, we won't go." The part of the sentence before the comma is a conditional clause. *—adv-* **con·di′tion·al·ly.**

con·di·tioned (kən dĭsh′ənd) *adj-* **1** depending on a condition or conditions; conditional: *a* conditioned *agreement.* **2** having a specified physical tone: *a well-*conditioned *boxer.* **3** resulting from psychological conditioning: *a* conditioned *reflex.*

conditioned reflex *n-* reaction to a stimulus that has been repeatedly associated with another stimulus that usually causes that reaction. For example, a dog's mouth waters at the sight of food. If the food is repeatedly accompanied by the sound of a bell, the dog's mouth will finally begin to water just at the sound of the bell, without his seeing any food. Also **conditioned response.**

con·dole (kən dōl′) *vi-* [**con·doled, con·dol·ing**] to express sympathy (with): *We* condoled *with him over his loss.*

Condor, 8 1/2—11 ft. wingspread

con·do·lence (kən dō′ ləns) *n-* expression of sympathy for another's grief.

con·do·min·i·um (kŏn′ də mĭn′ ē əm) *n-* **1** apartment house in which the residents own their apartments instead of renting them. **2** individual apartment in such a building.

con·done (kən dōn′) *vt-* [**con·doned, con·don·ing**] to forgive or overlook (a fault or offense): *I cannot* condone *your rudeness.* *—n-* **con′do·na′tion** (kŏn′də nā′shən).

con·dor (kŏn′dər) *n-* large vulture with dull black feathers and a white neck ruff. Condors live in the mountains of California and South America.

con·duce to or **toward** (kən dōōs′, -dyōōs′) *vt-* [**con·duced to, con·duc·ing to**] to contribute to; lead to; promote: *Exercise* conduces to *health.*

con·du·cive (kən dōō′sĭv, kən dyōō′-) *adj-* tending to bring about; promoting; contributory (to): *Regular exercise is* conducive *to good health.*

[1]con·duct (kən dŭkt′) *vt-* (in senses 1, 2, and 3 considered intransitive when the direct object is implied but not expressed) **1** to guide. **2** to manage; direct, as an orchestra. **3** to transmit (electricity, heat, etc.). **4** to carry: *The canal* conducts *water.*

conduct oneself to behave: *Mr. Klyde always* conducts himself *with dignity.*

[2]con·duct (kŏn′dŭkt) *n-* **1** way in which a person acts; behavior; deportment: *to be praised for good* conduct. **2** general management or direction (of): *the* conduct *of one's business affairs.*

con·duc·tance (kən dŭk′təns) *n-* the ability of matter to conduct electricity, measured in mhos.

con·duc·tion (kən dŭk′shən) *n-* **1** transmission of heat, sound, or electricity through matter. **2** the act or process of conveying, as water by the roots of plants. **3** transmission of an impulse along the nerves.

con·duc·tive (kən dŭk′tĭv) *adj-* able to conduct heat, light, sound, electricity, etc.

con·duc·tiv·i·ty (kŏn′dək tĭv′ə tē) *n-* the power of an object or body to transmit heat, electricity, etc.

con·duc·tor (kən dŭk′tər) *n-* **1** guide; leader: *the* conductor *of an orchestra.* **2** person in charge of passengers on a train, bus, or street car. **3** a material that transmits sound, electricity, etc.

con·duit (kŏn′dōō ĭt) *n-* **1** canal or pipe for carrying water, etc. **2** a tube or other enclosed passage for electric wires.

cone (kōn) *n-* **1** solid body or figure which narrows evenly to a point from a flat base of circular or elliptical cross section. **2** anything having such a shape: *an ice-cream* cone; *the nose* cone *of a rocket.* **3** seed case of pine, fir, or some other evergreens. **4** in anatomy, cone-shaped nerve cells in the retina of the eye, involved in seeing color and fine detail.

Cones

con·el·rad (kŏn′əl răd′) *n-* civilian defense system of broadcasting at random on only two frequencies to prevent enemy aircraft and missiles from homing to their targets on radio signals. [shortened from *con*trol of *el*ectromagnetic *rad*iation.]

Con·es·to·ga wagon (kŏn′ə stō′gə) *n-* heavy, broad-wheeled covered wagon, first made in Conestoga, Pennsylvania, used by American pioneers in migration to the West. For picture, see *covered wagon.*

co·ney (kō′nē) cony.

con·fec·tion (kən fĕk′shən) *n-* **1** something very sweet, such as candy or crystallized fruit; sweetmeat.

con·fec·tion·er (kən fĕk′shən ər) *n-* person who makes or sells candy, cakes, and other sweet things.

confectioners' sugar *n-* very fine powdered sugar, used especially for icings, candy, etc.

con·fec·tion·er·y (kən fĕk′shən ĕr′ē) *n-* [*pl.* **con·fec·tion·er·ies**] **1** shop which sells candies, cakes, etc. **2** the things sold.

con·fed·er·a·cy (kən fĕd′ər ə sē) *n-* [*pl.* **con·fed·er·a·cies**] **1** union of persons or states joined together for mutual help; league; alliance. **2 the Confederacy** the Confederate States of America.

[1]**con·fed·er·ate** (kən fĕd′ ər ət) ***n-*** an ally, especially an accomplice in a plot, conspiracy, crime, etc.: *The bank robber and his* confederates *escaped.*

[2]**con·fed·er·ate** (kən fĕd′ ə rāt′) ***vi-*** [**con·fed·er·at·ed, con·fed·er·at·ing**] to join together in a confederacy; ally.

Con·fed·er·ate (kən fĕd′ ər ət) ***n-*** person who supported or fought for the Confederate States of America. ***adj-*** of or relating to the Confederate States of America.

Confederate States of America ***n-*** league of eleven Southern States that seceded from the United States in 1860 and 1861. In order of secession they were: South Carolina, Mississippi, Florida, Alabama, Georgia, Louisiana, Texas, Virginia, Arkansas, North Carolina, and Tennessee.

con·fed·er·a·tion (kən fĕd′ ə rā′ shən) ***n-*** **1** league; confederacy. **2** a joining together; confederating: *The 13 colonies first tried* confederation.

con·fer (kən fûr′) ***vi-*** [**con·ferred, con·fer·ring**] to consult; have a conference: *The two umpires* conferred. ***vt-*** to bestow: *to* confer *a medal.*

con·fer·ence (kŏn′ fər əns) ***n-*** meeting for discussing and exchanging ideas: *a* conference *on taxes.*

con·fer·ral (kən fûr′ əl) ***n-*** a bestowing or granting; presentation: *a* conferral *of honors.* Also **con·fer′ ment.**

con·fess (kən fĕs′) ***vt-*** **1** to admit or acknowledge (a fault, crime, debt, etc.): *to* confess *a robbery.* **2** to hear a telling of sins from: *The priest* confessed *my sister.* ***vi-*** **1** to make an acknowledgement or admission; admit (to): *He* confessed *to the robbery.* **2** to disclose the state of one's conscience to a priest.

con·fess·ed·ly (kən fĕs′ əd lē) ***adv-*** by confession.

con·fes·sion (kən fĕsh′ ən) ***n-*** **1** an admitting or acknowledging: *a* confession *of one's true feelings.* **2** formal statement admitting a crime: *The prisoner signed a* confession. **3** a telling of one's sins to a priest in order to obtain absolution.

con·fes·sion·al (kən fĕsh′ ən əl) ***n-*** booth in which a priest hears confessions.

con·fes·sor (kən fĕs′ ər) ***n-*** **1** priest who hears confessions. **2** person who confesses.

con·fet·ti (kən fĕt′ ē) ***n-*** (takes singular verb) small pieces of paper scattered at carnivals, parades, etc.

con·fi·dant (kŏn′ fə dănt′, -dänt′) ***n-*** intimate friend to whom private affairs are told. ***—n- fem.*** **con′fi·dante′.**

con·fide (kən fīd′) ***vt-*** [**con·fid·ed, con·fid·ing**] **1** to tell as a secret: *She* confided *her problems to her mother.* **2** to entrust; commit: *We* confided *the children to their grandmother's care.*

confide in 1 to tell secrets to. **2** to have trust in: *to* confide in *God.*

con·fi·dence (kŏn′ fə dəns) ***n-*** **1** trust; belief: *I have* confidence *in your ability to pass the test.* **2** belief in oneself; self-assurance; self-confidence: *His* confidence *makes him a fine actor.* **3** a secret: *The girl and her best friend exchanged* confidences.

in confidence as a secret.

confidence game ***n-*** trick or method of a swindler who gains a person's trust in order to defraud him.

con·fi·dent (kŏn′ fə dənt) ***adj-*** **1** self-assured; self-confident; bold: *The boxer had a jaunty,* confident *air.* **2** sure; convinced: *We are* confident *of victory.* ***—adv-*** **con′ fi·dent·ly.**

con·fi·den·tial (kŏn′ fə dĕn′ shəl) ***adj-*** **1** secret; private: *The agent turned in a* confidential *report.* **2** trusted with secret matters: *A* confidential *secretary must have good judgment.* ***—adv-*** **con′ fi·den′ tial·ly.**

con·fid·ing (kən fī′ dĭng) ***adj-*** trustful; unsuspicious: *a* confiding *disposition.* ***—adv-*** **con·fid′ ing·ly.**

con·fig·u·ra·tion (kən fĭg′ yə rā′ shən) ***n-*** **1** shape; outline; contour: *the* configuration *of the American continent.* **2** relative arrangement and spacing of parts: *the* configuration *of a molecule.*

con·fine (kən fīn′) ***vt-*** [**con·fined, con·fin·ing**] **1** to restrict within limits: *The banks could not* confine *the swollen river.* **2** to keep indoors; imprison: *Illness* confined *him to his room.*

con·fine·ment (kən fīn′ mənt) ***n-*** **1** imprisonment: *His* confinement *lasted two years.* **2** a staying indoors or in bed because of illness or childbirth.

cón·fines (kŏn′ fīnz′) ***n- pl.*** limits; boundaries: *the* confines *of a park.*

con·firm (kən fûrm′) ***vt-*** **1** to assure the truth of; verify: *The doctor* confirmed *the reports about the polio vaccine.* **2** to approve formally: *The Senate* confirmed *his appointment as a judge.* **3** to establish more firmly; strengthen: *The book* confirms *my belief.* **4** in some churches, to admit to full membership by a special rite. ***—adv-*** **con·firm′ ed·ly.**

con·firm·a·ble (kən fûr′ mə bəl) ***adj-*** such as can be confirmed. ***—adv-*** **con·firm′ a·bly.**

con·fir·ma·tion (kŏn′ fər mā′ shən) ***n-*** **1** a making sure or establishing; verification: *We awaited* confirmation *of his report.* **2** something that confirms or verifies; proof: *This is a* confirmation *of your discovery.* **3** formal approval: *the* confirmation *of his appointment.* **4** in some churches, a rite reaffirming faith and admitting one to full membership. **5** in Judaism, bar mitzvah.

con·firmed (kən fûrmd′) ***adj-*** firmly settled in a habit, way of life, etc.: *a* confirmed *bachelor.*

con·fis·cate (kŏn′ fĭs kāt′) ***vt-*** [**con·fis·cat·ed, con·fis·cat·ing**] to seize (property), especially for public use: *The police* confiscated *the smuggled goods.* ***—n-*** **con′ fis·ca′ tion.** ***adj-*** **con·fis′ ca·tor′ y** (kən fĭs′ kə tôr′ ē): *He said that the new tax is* confiscatory.

con·fla·gra·tion (kŏn′ flə grā′ shən) ***n-*** large and destructive fire.

[1]**con·flict** (kŏn′ flĭkt′) ***n-*** **1** a battle; fight; struggle. **2** a clash; failure to be in agreement or harmony: *a* conflict *between the two accounts of the accident.*

[2]**con·flict** (kən flĭkt′) ***vi-*** to be in opposition; clash (with): *One account of the accident* conflicts *with the other. The two accounts* conflict.

con·flu·ence (kŏn′ flo͞o′ əns) ***n-*** a flowing together of streams; also, the place where they join. Also **con′ flux′** (kŏn′ flŭks′). ***—adj-*** **con′ flu′ ent:** *two* confluent *streams.*

con·form (kən fôrm′, -fôrm′) ***vi-*** **1** to be in agreement with a set pattern or form; correspond (to): *These measurements* conform *to the blueprints.* **2** to act in accordance with rules, customs, etc.; obey; comply: *The army* conformed *to the rules of war.* ***vt-***: *Should I* conform *my habits to yours?*

con·form·a·ble (kən fôr′ mə bəl, kən fôr′-) ***adj-*** **1** similar or corresponding (to): *results* conformable *to our hopes.* **2** obedient or submissive (to): *He is* conformable *to his father's wishes.* ***—adv-*** **con·form′ a·bly.**

con·form·ance (kən fôr′ məns, kən fôr′-) ***n-*** conformity.

con·for·ma·tion (kŏn′ fər mā′ shən) ***n-*** form; structure; configuration; especially, the orderly arrangement of the parts of a thing: *the* conformation *of a molecule.*

con·form·ist (kən fôr′ mĭst, kən fôr′-) ***n-*** **1** one who conforms or adapts to the attitudes and practices of the group. **2** *Brit.* member of the Church of England.

con·form·i·ty (kən fôr′ mə tē, kən fôr′-) ***n-*** **1** agreement or accord; harmony: *a* conformity *of opinion.* **2** obedience (to); compliance (with): *to live in* conformity *with the law.* **3** behavior in accord with the common attitudes and practices of society.

con·found (kən found′) ***vt-*** **1** to bewilder or perplex; amaze: *The child's answers* confounded *the experts.* **2** to throw into disorder; make chaotic: *Their demands* confounded *the situation even more.* **3** to mistake for something else: *to* confound *dreams with reality.*

con·found·ed (kən found′ əd) ***adj-*** **1** bewildered; perplexed. **2** (*also* kŏn′ foun′ dəd) outrageous; accursed; blasted: *What a* confounded *nuisance!* **—*adv-*** **con·found′ ed·ly.**

con·frere (kōn′ frâr′, kŏn′-) ***n-*** fellow member of a profession, society, etc.; associate; colleague.

con·front (kən frŭnt′) ***vt-*** **1** to meet boldly and squarely; face up to: *to* confront *the enemy.* **2** to present (a person, group, etc.) squarely (with): *This* confronts *me with the need to make a quick decision.*

Con·fu·cian·ism (kən fyōō′ shən ĭz′ əm) ***n-*** moral teachings of the Chinese philosopher Confucius, emphasizing devotion to parents, ancestor worship, and the maintenance of justice and peace. **—*n-*** **Con·fu′ cian·ist.**

con·fuse (kən fyōōz′) ***vt-*** **[con·fused, con·fus·ing] 1** to throw into disorder; make chaotic: *Don't* confuse *the issue.* **2** bewilder; perplex: *Don't let all those questions* confuse *you.* **3** to mix up in the mind; mistake one thing for another: *The announcer* confused *the dates of the two events.* **—*adv-*** **con·fus′ ing·ly.**

con·fus·ed·ly (kən fyōō′ zəd lē) ***adv-*** in a confused or bewildered manner: *He ran about* confusedly. **—*n-*** **con·fus′ ed·ness.**

con·fu·sion (kən fyōō′ zhən) ***n-*** **1** disorder: *The room was in total* confusion. **2** perplexity; distraction: *The new event increased his* confusion. **3** embarrassment; discomfiture: *I couldn't hide my* confusion. **4** a mistaking or mixing up: *the* confusion *of "their" with "there."*

con·fute (kən fyōōt′) ***vt-*** **[con·fut·ed, con·fut·ing] 1** to prove (a statement) to be false: *to* confute *a claim.* **2** to prove (a person) to be wrong: *to* confute *an opponent.*

Cong. 1 Congregational. **2** Congress. **3** Congressional.

con·ga (kŏng′ gə) ***n-*** **1** Afro-Cuban dance in which the dancers follow one another in a snaky line. **2** tall, narrow African drum beaten with the hands.

con·geal (kən jēl′) ***vi-*** **1** to change from a fluid to a solid by cooling or freezing. **2** to thicken or coagulate; become viscous: *The oil* congealed. ***vt-***: *The cold air* congealed *the liquid.*

con·gen·ial (kən jēn′ yəl) ***adj-*** **1** having the same tastes and interests: *a* congenial *roommate.* **2** suited to one's nature; agreeable: *a* congenial *job.* **3** sociable; genial: *a* congenial *host.* **—*n-*** **con·ge′ ni·al′ i·ty** (kən jēn′ ē-ăl′ ə tē). ***adv-*** **con·gen′ ial·ly.**

con·gen·i·tal (kən jĕn′ ə təl) ***adj-*** existing at birth and not caused by later influences. **—*adv-*** **con·gen′ i·tal·ly.**

con·ger eel (kŏng′ gər) ***n-*** ocean eel which grows to as long as ten feet. It is an important food fish in Europe.

con·gest (kən jĕst′) ***vt-*** **1** to cause (an organ or part of the body) to become too full of blood or other fluid. **2** to make too crowded; clog: *Parades* congest *traffic.* ***vi-***: *His lungs* congested *overnight.*

con·ges·tion (kən jĕs′ chən) ***n-*** **1** overcrowded condition: *traffic* congestion. **2** excessive accumulation of blood or other fluid in an organ of the body: *a* congestion *of the lungs.*

[1]**con·glom·er·ate** (kən glŏm′ ə rāt′) ***vt-*** **[con·glom·er·at·ed, con·glom·er·at·ing]** to gather into a mass. ***vi-***: *These rocks* conglomerated *during millions of years.*

[2]**con·glom·er·ate** (kən glŏm′ ər ət) ***n-*** **1** mass of varied materials or elements. **2** a rock composed of pebbles, gravel, etc., held together by hardened clay or the like. ***adj-*** massed together; clustered: *a* conglomerate *substance*; conglomerate *flowers.*

con·glom·er·a·tion (kən glŏm′ ə rā′ shən) ***n-*** **1** a gathering into a mass. **2** a cohering mass; cluster. **3** mixed collection; hodgepodge.

con·go snake (kŏng′ gō) ***n-*** large, eelllike salamander of the southeastern United States. It lives both on land and in water. Also **congo eel.**

con·grat·u·late (kən grăch′ ə lāt′) ***vt-*** **[con·grat·u·lat·ed, con·grat·u·lat·ing]** to express sympathetic pleasure to (a person or persons) on account of an achievement of his, an honor, or a happy event. **—*adj-*** **con·grat′ u·la·to′ ry** (-ə lə tôr′ ē): *We sent the newlyweds a* congratulatory *message.*

con·grat·u·la·tion (kən grăch′ ə lā′ shən) ***n-*** **1** a congratulating. **2 congratulations** an expression of pleasure to another about his success or good fortune.

con·gre·gate (kŏng′ grə gāt′) ***vi-*** **[con·gre·gat·ed, con·gre·gat·ing]** to come together; assemble: *People* congregated *to watch the inauguration.*

con·gre·ga·tion (kŏng′ grə gā′ shən) ***n-*** a gathering of people, especially a group meeting for religious worship or instruction.

con·gre·ga·tion·al (kŏng′ grə gā′ shən əl) ***adj-*** **1** of or relating to a congregation. **2 Congregational** of or relating to Congregationalism or to Congregationalists.

con·gre·ga·tion·al·ism (kŏng′ grə gā′ shən ə lĭz′ əm) ***n-*** **1** form of church government in which each congregation governs itself. **2 Congregationalism** the faith and constitution of a Protestant denomination practicing congregationalism. **—*n-*** **con′ gre·ga′ tion·al·ist** or **Con′ gre·ga′ tion·al·ist.**

con·gress (kŏng′ grəs) ***n-*** **1** a meeting of representatives to discuss a particular thing; conference. **2** chief lawmaking body of some republics. **3 Congress** national lawmaking body of the United States, made up of the Senate and the House of Representatives.

con·gres·sion·al or **Con·gres·sion·al** (kən grĕsh′ ən-əl) ***adj-*** of or relating to the Congress of the United States: *the Fourth* Congressional *District.*

con·gress·man (kŏng′ grəs mən) ***n-*** [*pl.* **con·gress·men**] member of Congress, especially of the House of Representatives. ***n-*** *fem.* **con′ gress·wom′ an.**

con·gru·ent (kən grōō′ ənt, kŏng′ grōō-) ***adj-*** **1** agreeing; harmonizing; in accordance; congruous (with): *The plan is* congruent *with our aims.* **2** of geometric figures, coinciding exactly when placed one upon another. **—*n-*** **con·gru′ ence.** ***adv-*** **con·gru′ ent·ly.**

con·gru·i·ty (kən grōō′ ə tē) ***n-*** [*pl.* **con·gru·i·ties**] agreement; suitability; congruence; congruousness.

con·i·cal (kŏn′ ĭ kəl) ***adj-*** having to do with or resembling a cone: *Fujiyama has a* conical *shape.* Also **con′ ic.**

con·i·fer (kŏn′ ə fər) ***n-*** kind of tree that bears cones, such as the pine, fir, and spruce.

co·nif·er·ous (kə nĭf′ ər əs) ***adj-*** **1** bearing cones: *Pines are* coniferous *trees.* **2** made up of or relating to conifers: *the* coniferous *forests of Maine.*

conj. 1 conjugation. **2** conjunction. **3** conjunctive.

con·jec·tur·al (kən jĕk′ chər əl) ***adj-*** based on conjecture: *The discussion was* conjectural. **—*adv-*** **con·jec′ tur·al·ly.**

con·jec·ture (kən jĕk′ chər) ***n-*** **1** the forming of an opinion with little or no evidence; guesswork: *a book based on* conjecture *rather than research.* **2** a guess. ***vt-*** **[con·jec·tured, con·jec·tur·ing]**: *Columbus* conjectured *that the earth was round.* **—*n-*** **con·jec′ tur·er.**

con·join (kən join′) *vt-* to join together; connect; unite: *History* conjoined *their names.* *vi-*: *The generals* conjoined *to fight the king.*

con·joint (kən joint′) *adj-* united; combined; conjoined: *a* conjoint *attempt.* *—adv-* **con·joint′ ly.**

con·ju·gal (kŏn′ jə gəl) *adj-* having to do with marriage or with the relationship of husband and wife; connubial. *—n-* **con′ ju·gal′ i·ty.** *adv-* **con′ ju·gal·ly.**

[1]**con·ju·gate** (kŏn′ jə gāt′) *Grammar vt-* **[con·ju·gat·ed, con·ju·gat·ing]** to give the inflected forms of (a verb) in a set order. Example: I am, you are, he is, we are, you are, they are. *vi- Biology* to unite temporarily.

[2]**con·ju·gate** (kŏn′ jə gət) *adj-* joined, especially in pairs; coupled. *n-* one of a coupled pair.

con·ju·ga·tion (kŏn′ jə gā′ shən) *n-* **1** *Grammar* a conjugating of a verb; also, a class of verbs that are conjugated in the same way. **2** *Biology* (1) the act or process of joining together; the temporary uniting or fusing of two cells. (2) result of this process; union.

con·junc·tion (kən jŭngk′ shən) *n-* **1** a joining or occurring together; combination; union: *The* conjunction *of fog and icy roads made driving impossible.* **2** *Grammar* word, such as *and, but, or, if, when,* etc., that connects two other words, phrases, or clauses. Conjunctions also show the intended relationships between parts of a sentence. **3** *Astronomy* (1) position of a planet when lying on a straight line connecting the earth and the sun. (2) the apparent meeting of heavenly bodies. (3) the configuration in which two heavenly bodies are closest together. **4** *Mathematics* sentence made of two or more other sentences joined by the word "and," which is true only when all of its parts are true. Example: The sentence, $x + 3 = y$ and $y = 5$, is a conjunction.

con·junc·ti·va (kŏn′ jŭngk′ tī′ və) *n-* [*pl.* **con·junc·ti·vas** or **con·junc·ti·vae** (-vē, -vī)] membrane that covers the eye and the inside of the eyelids.

con·junc·tive (kən jŭnkg′ tĭv) *adj-* connecting; joining; uniting. *—adv-* **con·junc′ tive·ly.**

con·junc·ti·vi·tis (kən jŭngk′ tə vī′ təs) *n-* **1** highly contagious infection and inflammation of the conjunctiva; pinkeye. **2** any inflammation of the conjunctiva.

con·ju·ra·tion (kŏn′ jə rā′ shən) *n-* a conjuring; making of magic; also, a spell used in conjuring.

con·jure (kŭn′ jər, kŏn′-) *vt-* **[con·jured, con·jur·ing]** to make appear or disappear as if by magic: *The magician* conjured *a rabbit out of a hat.* *vi-* to perform magic: *The stranger claimed he could* conjure. *—n-* **con′ jur·er** or **con′ jur·or.**

conjure up to call up; bring into existence: *The old sailor's story* conjured up *scenes of pirate raids and buried treasure.*

Conn. Connecticut.

con·nect (kə nĕkt′) *vt-* **1** to join, link, or fasten together; unite: *A bus line* connects *the two towns.* *Twist the wires to* connect *them.* **2** to place in relationship; associate: *to* connect *names with faces.* *vi-* **1** to join: *The rooms* connect. **2** of trains, ships, etc., to arrive in time for passengers to make another scheduled departure: *The bus* connects *with the noon train.* **3** *Informal* to hit something: *When he* connects, *the ball goes out of the park.*

con·nec·tion (kə nĕk′ shən) *n-* **1** a joining or being joined; linking: *The* connection *of the business district with the airport is important.* **2** anything that joins or links other things together: *a broken* connection *in a pipe.* **3** relationship: *the* connection *of hard work with success.* **4** context; reference: *In this* connection, *his remark seems less important.* **5** relationship or link through marriage, common interests, or occupation: *a* connection *with the Steins on my grandmother's side*; *a good business* connection. **6** in transportation, the meeting of trains, buses, etc., that enables passengers to transfer without great delay: *poor train* connections.

con·nec·tive (kə nĕk′ tĭv) *adj-* serving to join or connect. *n-* **1** something that joins or connects. **2** *Grammar* a connecting word, such as a conjunction. *—adv-* **con·nec′ tive·ly:** *a phrase used* connectively.

connective tissue *n-* tough, fibrous white tissue that connects and supports the organs, muscles, bones, and other tissues of the body.

conn·ing tower (kŏn′ ĭng) *n-* **1** tall structure on a submarine deck, used for observation and as entrance to the interior. **2** armored pilothouse on a battleship.

con·niv·ance (kə nī′ vəns) *n-* silent assent to secret co-operation in a wrongdoing.

con·nive (kə nīv′) *vi-* **[con·nived, con·niv·ing]** **1** to permit or condone a wrongdoing by remaining silent and inactive: *The jailer* connived *at the prisoner's escape.* **2** to co-operate secretly; conspire: *He* connived *with others to force the chairman out of office.* *—n-* **con·niv′ er.**

con·nois·seur (kŏn′ ə sûr′) *n-* person who knows enough about an art, food, etc., to be a judge of it.

con·no·ta·tion (kŏn′ ə tā′ shən, kŏn′ ō-) *n-* meaning added to the literal or dictionary meaning of a word or phrase by frequent association with other ideas, the feelings of the user, etc.: *"Gluttony" and "filth" are* connotations *of "pig."* See also *denotation.*

con·no·ta·tive (kŏn′ ə tā′ tĭv) *adj-* **1** connoting. **2** having to do with connotation. *—adv-* **con′ no·ta′ tive·ly.**

con·note (kə nōt′) *vt-* **[con·not·ed, con·not·ing]** to imply or suggest in addition to the simple or literal meaning: *The word "equator" often* connotes *heat.*

con·nu·bi·al (kə nōō′ bē əl) *adj-* relating to marriage: *their* connubial *happiness.* *—adv-* **con·nu′ bi·al·ly.**

con·quer (kŏng′ kər) *vt-* to overcome or defeat: *to* conquer *a country*; *to* conquer *one's fear.* *vi-*: *The strongest do not always* conquer.

con·quer·or (kŏng′ kər ər) *n-* person who conquers, especially one who subdues a country by war.

con·quest (kŏng′ kwĕst′) *n-* **1** a winning or conquering, especially by war: *the* conquest *of Mexico by the Spanish.* **2** that which is won or conquered.

con·qui·sta·dor (kŏn kwĭs′ tə dòr′, -dôr′) *n-* **[con·qui·sta·dors** or **con·qui·sta·do·res]** one of the Spanish conquerors of parts of North and South America in the sixteenth century.

con·san·guin·i·ty (kŏn′ săng′ gwĭn′ ə tē) *n-* relationship by common ancestry.

con·science (kŏn′ shəns) *n-* sense of the rightness or wrongness of one's own acts: *Trust your* conscience.

con·sci·en·tious (kŏn′ shē ĕn′ shəs) *adj-* **1** careful and diligent; painstaking: *a* conscientious *worker.* **2** following one's conscience or sense of right; scrupulous: *a* conscientious *objection to war.* *—adv-* **con′ sci·en′ tious·ly.** *n-* **con′ sci·en′ tious·ness.**

conscientious objector *n-* person who refuses to serve in an armed force as a combatant because of religious or moral principles.

con·scious (kŏn′ shəs) *adj-* **1** able to feel and understand what is happening; in possession of one's senses; awake: *Is the patient* conscious *now?* **2** aware: *He was* conscious *of being watched.* **3** deliberate; intentional: *He made a* conscious *effort to be kind.* *—adv-* **con′ scious·ly.**

---

con·scious·ness (kŏn′ shəs nəs) ***n-*** **1** a being conscious; possession of one's senses: *A person who faints loses* consciousness. **2** awareness: *a* consciousness *of impending danger.* **3** total of one's thoughts and feelings; mind: *A new idea entered his* consciousness.

¹con·script (kən scrĭpt′) ***vt-*** to draft or force (a person) into service, especially into military service.

²con·script (kŏn′ scrĭpt′) ***n-*** person drafted into service; especially, one drafted into the army or navy. *as **modifier**: a* conscript *army.*

con·scrip·tion (kən skrĭp′ shən) ***n-*** forced enrollment in military or naval service; draft: *to raise troops by* conscription.

con·se·crate (kŏn′ sə krāt′) ***vt-*** [**con·se·crat·ed, con·se·crat·ing**] **1** to set apart or dedicate as sacred: *to* consecrate *a chapel.* **2** to devote to some worthy purpose: *She* consecrated *her life to the care of the sick.*

con·se·cra·tion (kŏn′ sə krā′ shən) ***n-*** **1** a consecrating; dedication. **2** devotion to a cause. **3** ordination, as of a bishop. *as **modifier**: the* consecration *ceremony.*

con·sec·u·tive (kən sĕk′ yə tĭv) ***adj-*** following without a break; coming in order; successive: *Four, five, and six are* consecutive *numbers.* **—*adv-* con·sec′ u·tive·ly.** ***n-*** **con·sec′ u·tive·ness.**

con·sen·sus (kən sĕn′ səs) ***n-*** general agreement; collective opinion: *The* consensus *was for adjournment of the meeting.*

con·sent (kən sĕnt′) ***vi-*** to give assent or approval; agree: *They* consented *to let him drive the car.* ***n-***: *He asked his parents'* consent *to use their car.*

con·se·quence (kŏn′ sə kwĕns′) ***n-*** **1** outcome; result: *The* consequences *were not foreseen.* **2** importance: *a person of no* consequence.

con·se·quent (kŏn′ sə kwĕnt) ***adj-*** resulting: *The storm and* consequent *flood caused great damage.*

con·se·quen·tial (kŏn′ sə kwĕn′ shəl) ***adj-*** **1** important; vital: *very* consequential *matters.* **2** consequent.

con·se·quent·ly (kŏn′ sə kwĕnt′ lē) ***adv-*** as a result; therefore: *I overslept;* consequently, *I missed the bus.*

con·ser·va·tion (kŏn′ sûr vā′ shən) ***n-*** careful use and protection, especially of natural resources such as soil, forest, and game; preservation.

con·ser·va·tion·ist (kŏn′ sər vā′ shən ĭst) ***n-*** person who advocates conservation of natural resources.

conservation of energy ***n-*** principle that energy can be neither created nor destroyed, but can only be changed from one form to another. See also *conservation of mass-energy.*

conservation of mass ***n-*** conservation of matter.

conservation of mass-energy ***n-*** principle that matter and energy are interchangeable according to Albert Einstein's equation, $E = mc^2$, but the total amount of matter and energy in the universe remains the same. E represents energy, m is the amount of matter (mass), and c is the velocity of light.

conservation of matter ***n-*** principle that matter can be neither created nor destroyed, now known to be true only if matter is not converted to energy or vice versa. See also *conservation of mass-energy.*

con·serv·a·tism (kən sûr′ və tĭz′ əm) ***n-*** tendency to oppose change and keep things as they are.

con·serv·a·tive (kən sûr′ və tĭv) ***adj-*** **1** inclined to keep things as they are; opposed to change. **2 Conservative** (1) having to do with a political party holding such views. (2) of or relating to a branch of Judaism that recognizes the authority of the Mosaic Law but maintains that precise interpretation of the Law should not divide Jews. It allows for modified rituals and other changes considered to be appropriate to the present time. **3** moderate; cautious; in the low range: *the* conservative *use of antibiotics; a* conservative *estimate.* ***n-*** **1** person who favors existing conditions or traditional ways, and opposes change. **2 Conservative** member of the **Conservative Party,** the major right-wing party of Great Britain. **—*adv-* con·serv′ a·tive·ly.**

con·serv·a·tor·y (kən sûr′ və tôr′ ē) ***n-*** [*pl.* **con·serv·a·tor·ies**] **1** greenhouse or glassed-in room; especially, a private one for the display of plants. **2** school for study of one of the fine arts, especially music.

¹con·serve (kən sûrv′) ***vt-*** [**con·served, con·serv·ing**] to keep from decay, destruction, loss, waste, or depletion; preserve: *Scientific farming* conserves *the soil.*

²con·serve (kŏn′ sûrv′) ***n-*** mixture of fruits, sugar, and usually nuts, cooked until thick: *plum* conserve.

con·sid·er (kən sĭd′ ər) ***vt-*** (in sense 1 considered intransitive when the direct object is implied but not expressed.) **1** to think over carefully: *to* consider *an offer.* **2** to bear in mind; allow for: *We should* consider *the traffic and start early.* **3** to be thoughtful of: *The selfish boy never* considered *his brother's feelings.* **4** to regard as: *I* consider *him our best player.*

con·sid·er·a·ble (kən sĭd′ ər ə bəl) ***adj-*** **1** fairly large: *a* considerable *sum of money.* **2** much: *He had* considerable *trouble.* **—*adv-* con·sid′ er·a·bly:** *Her game has improved* considerably *since she took lessons.*

con·sid·er·ate (kən sĭd′ ər ət) ***adj-*** thoughtful of others; kindly. **—*adv-* con·sid′ er·ate·ly.** ***n-*** **con·sid′ er·ate·ness.**

con·sid·er·a·tion (kən sĭd′ ə rā′ shən) ***n-*** **1** careful thought; deliberation: *After much* consideration, *he decided which car to buy.* **2** something to be taken into account; matter of concern: *The cost of the car was a major* consideration. **3** thoughtfulness or regard: *He showed no* consideration *for his neighbors.* **4** payment; compensation: *What* consideration *did he demand for his work?*

con·sid·ered (kən sĭd′ ərd) ***adj-*** carefully thought out: *a* considered *opinion.*

con·sid·er·ing (kən sĭd′ ər ĭng) ***prep-*** taking into account; allowing for; in view of: *He did well,* considering *his lack of preparation.*

con·sign (kən sīn′) ***vt-*** **1** to hand over; deliver formally: *They* consigned *her to a guardian.* **2** to send or address (a shipment, merchandise, etc.). **3** to set apart; devote: *The host* consigned *the room to our use.* **—*n-* con·sign′ or** or **con·sign′ er.**

con·sign·ee (kŏn′ sī′ nē′, kən sī′ nē′) ***n-*** person to whom goods are shipped or addressed.

con·sign·ment (kən sīn′ mənt) ***n-*** **1** a consigning or delivering. **2** something consigned: *The trucker lost a* consignment *of pots.*

on consignment to be paid for by the retailer only when sold: *He took a load of baseballs* on consignment.

con·sist (kən sĭst′) ***vi-*** **1** to be made up or composed (of): *Water* consists *of hydrogen and oxygen.* **2** to have as foundation or source (in): *The success of democracy* consists *in our responsibility as citizens.*

con·sist·en·cy (kən sĭs′ tən sē) ***n-*** [*pl.* **con·sist·en·cies**] **1** degree of density or thickness: *the* consistency *of molasses.* **2** steadiness and uniformity; evenness: *the* consistency *of his taste in music.* **3** agreement; harmony: *a* consistency *between words and actions.* Also **con·sist′ ence.**

con·sist·ent (kən sĭs′ tənt) ***adj-*** **1** continuing without change; constant; uniform: *bread of* consistent *quality.* **2** in agreement; in accord (with): *His last report was not* consistent *with his usual good work.* **—*adv-* con·sist′ ent·ly.**

con·sis·to·ry (kən sĭs′tə rē) ***n-*** [*pl.* **con·sis·to·ries**] **1** governing assembly of a church; especially, a session of the cardinals of the Roman Catholic Church, presided over by the pope. **2** place where such a meeting is held.

con·so·la·tion (kŏn′ sə lā′ shən) ***n-*** **1** comfort in time of distress: *The hurt child received* consolation *from his mother.* **2** person who or thing that consoles: *She was his* consolation.

con·sol·a·tor·y (kən sō′ lə tôr′ ē, kən sŏl′-) ***adj-*** consoling; giving comfort: *a* consolatory *letter.*

[1]**con·sole** (kən sōl′) ***vt-*** [**con·soled, con·sol·ing**] to comfort; solace; cheer up. [from Latin **consolari** meaning "to comfort greatly."]

[2]**con·sole** (kŏn′ sōl) ***n-*** **1** floor-model radio or television cabinet. **2** the desklike part of an organ, containing the keyboard and pedals. **3** table supported on a wall by brackets, or designed to stand against a wall. [from French **console** meaning "self-supporting," from an original meaning "wall bracket; support," from the same source as [1]**console.**

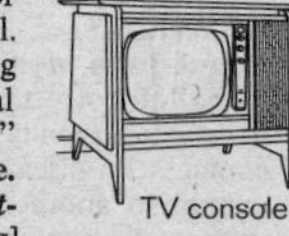
TV console

con·sol·i·date (kən sŏl′ ə dāt′) ***vt-*** [**con·sol·i·dat·ed, con·sol·i·dat·ing**] **1** to unite; combine; merge: *to* consolidate *several schools; to* consolidate *packages for shipment.* **2** to make secure; strengthen: *The company* consolidated *its gains.* ***vi-*** to unite; merge: *The two airlines* consolidated. ***—n-*** **con·sol′ i·da′ tion.**

con·som·mé (kŏn′ sə mā′) ***n-*** a clear soup made by boiling meat a long time to extract all its food value.

con·so·nance (kŏn′ sə nəns) ***n-*** **1** agreement; harmony. **2** *Music* (1) a combination of notes regarded as pleasant or harmonious. (2) the sound produced when these notes are played simultaneously. **3** in poetry, a kind of rhyme in which the rhyme words have the same sound in the final consonants or the same sound before and after the vowel. Examples: sti*ll* and fa*ll*, mu*ff* and cou*gh*, ra*te* and wri*te*.

con·so·nant (kŏn′ sə nənt) ***n-*** **1** a sound made by closing or narrowing the mouth or throat. **2** symbol of such a sound, such as "b," "c," and "d" in the English alphabet. ***adj-*** **1** consonantal. **2** *Music* harmonious. **3** consistent; agreeing: *an act* consonant *with one's beliefs.* ***—adv-*** **con′ so·nant·ly.**

con·so·nan·tal (kŏn′ sə nĕn′ təl) ***adj-*** made up of, resembling, or relating to a consonant or consonants.

[1]**con·sort** (kŏn′ sòrt′, -sôrt′) ***n-*** husband or wife; spouse.

[2]**con·sort** (kən sòrt′, -sôrt′) ***vi-*** to keep company (with); associate (with): *He habitually* consorts *with criminals.*

con·spic·u·ous (kən spĭk′ yōō əs) ***adj-*** **1** plainly visible: *a* conspicuous *spot.* **2** attracting attention; striking: *to be* conspicuous *for bad manners; a* conspicuous *success.* ***—adv-*** **con·spic′ u·ous·ly.** ***n-*** **con·spic′ u·ous·ness.**

con·spir·a·cy (kən spĭr′ ə sē) ***n-*** [*pl.* **con·spir·a·cies**] **1** secret agreement to do something unlawful or evil; a plot: *a* conspiracy *to rob a bank.* **2** group of conspirators.

con·spir·a·tor (kən spĭr′ ə tər) ***n-*** person who takes part in a secret plot.

con·spire (kən spīr′) ***vi-*** [**con·spired, con·spir·ing**] **1** to plan together secretly to do something unlawful or evil; plot. **2** to act or work together: *All things* conspired *for a happy day.*

con·sta·ble (kŏn′ stə bəl, kŭn′ stə bəl) ***n-*** **1** public peace officer with some minor judicial duties. **2** *Brit.* policeman of the lowest rank; patrolman.

con·stab·u·lar·y (kən stăb′ yə lĕr′ ē) ***n-*** **1** all the constables of a district; also, their district. **2** military police force not part of the regular army.

con·stan·cy (kŏn′ stən sē) ***n-*** **1** steadfastness; firmness of purpose; faithfulness: *to serve with* constancy *and devotion.* **2** freedom from change; uniformity; stability: *the* constancy *of the hot water supply.*

con·stant (kŏn′ stənt) ***adj-*** **1** always present; continual: *the* constant *noise of the street traffic.* **2** unchanging; invariable; uniform: *to walk at a* constant *pace.* **3** steadfast; faithful: *a* constant *friend.* ***n-*** **1** something which never changes. **2** *Mathematics* (1) a quantity that has a fixed value, such as pi (π). (2) a quantity whose value does not change throughout a problem and its solution. ***—adv-*** **con′ stant·ly.**

con·stel·la·tion (kŏn′ stə lā′ shən) ***n-*** **1** *Astronomy* group of stars, often named for a mythological person or thing whose outline it suggests; also, the region in the heavens occupied by such a group. **2** group of distinguished persons or things.

con·ster·na·tion (kŏn′ stər nā′ shən) ***n-*** terrified astonishment; paralyzing amazement; dismay: *To my* consternation *my wallet had disappeared.*

con·sti·pate (kŏn′ stə pāt′) ***vt-*** [**con·sti·pat·ed, con·sti·pat·ing**] to cause constipation in.

con·sti·pa·tion (kŏn′ stə pā′ shən) ***n-*** condition in which the bowels do not move freely enough.

con·stit·u·en·cy (kən stĭch′ ōō ən sē) ***n-*** [*pl.* **con·stit·u·en·cies**] body of voters which elects a representative, as to Congress; also, the district represented.

con·stit·u·ent (kən stĭch′ ōō ənt) ***adj-*** needed in the makeup of something: *Hydrogen is a* constituent *element of water.* ***n-*** **1** necessary ingredient or part. **2** voter in a political district.

con·sti·tute (kŏn′ stə tōōt′, -tyōōt′) ***vt-*** [**con·sti·tut·ed, con·sti·tut·ing**] **1** to make up or form: *Twelve eggs* constitute *a dozen.* **2** to appoint: *The will* constituted *him guardian.*

con·sti·tu·tion (kŏn′ stə tōō′ shən, -tyōō′ shən) ***n-*** **1** the basic law and principles of a nation, state, or other organized body. **2** composition or makeup, especially physical makeup: *to have a healthy* constitution. **3** an establishing or setting up: *to urge the* constitution *of a peace commission.* **4 the Constitution** written document setting forth the basic law and principles of the United States.

con·sti·tu·tion·al (kŏn′ stə tōō′ shən əl, -tyōō′ shən-əl) ***adj-*** **1** of, relating to, or regulated by a constitution of laws and principles: *a* constitutional *amendment; a* constitutional *crisis.* **2** in accordance with or permitted by such a constitution: *This law is* constitutional. **3** inherent in the makeup: *a* constitutional *weakness.* ***n-*** a walk taken for one's health. ***—adv-*** **con′ sti·tu′ tion·al·ly.**

con·sti·tu·tion·al·i·ty (kŏn′ stə tōō′ shə năl′ ə tē, -tyōō′ shə năl′ ə tē) ***n-*** agreement with, or validity under, the constitution: *We will test the* constitutionality *of the new law.*

con·sti·tu·tive (kən stĭch′ ə tĭv) ***adj-*** **1** essential; basic. **2** having authority to enact or establish. ***—adv-*** **con·sti′ tu·tive·ly.**

con·strain (kən strān′) ***vt-*** **1** to urge; force; compel: *to* constrain *a child to eat.* **2** to imprison; confine. **3** to hold in check; restrain: *to* constrain *one's temper.*

con·straint (kən strānt′) ***n-*** **1** force; compulsion: *to keep silent under* constraint. **2** a keeping back of natural feeling or behavior: *The boys were usually noisy, but they showed* constraint *when visitors came.*

con·strict (kən strĭkt′) ***vt-*** to squeeze tightly; compress; cramp: *to* constrict *a vein.*

con·stric·tion (kən strĭk′ shən) ***n-*** **1** a tightening or narrowing; contraction; compression: *the* constriction *of a blood vessel.* **2** anything that binds or cramps.

con·stric·tor (kən strĭk′ tər) ***n-*** **1** anything that constricts, especially certain surgical instruments and body muscles. **2** snake that kills its prey by strangling or crushing it in its coils.

con·struct (kən strŭkt′) ***vt-*** **1** to build; put together: *to* construct *a house*; *to* construct *a short story.* **2** *Mathematics* to draw geometric figures with such instruments as compass, protractor, straightedge, etc.

con·struct·tion (kən strŭk′ shən) ***n-*** **1** a putting together; building: *the* construction *of a bridge.* **2** way of building: *fireproof* construction. **3** thing built: *That new* construction *is the bank.* **4** explanation; interpretation: *He puts a wrong* construction *on my words.* **5** *Grammar* (1) the way in which words are related to one another in a sentence. (2) grammatically meaningful group or arrangement of words. *as* ***modifier****: a* construction *worker.*

con·struc·tive (kən strŭk′ tĭv) ***adj-*** building up; helping to improve or develop: *a* constructive *suggestion.* **—*adv-*** **con·struc′ tive·ly.** ***n-*** **con·struc′ tive·ness.**

con·strue (kən strōō′) ***vt-*** [**con·strued, con·stru·ing**] **1** to explain the meaning of; interpret: *They* construed *his shyness as snobbery.* **2** *Grammar* to analyze or explain (a sentence, clause, etc.) gramatically; parse.

con·sul (kŏn′ səl) ***n-*** **1** official appointed by a government to live in a foreign country, look after trade, and help any citizens of his own country who live or travel there. **2** either of two chief officials of the ancient Roman republic.

con·su·lar (kŏn′ sə lər) ***adj-*** of or relating to a consul or consulate: *The official has many* consular *duties.*

con·su·late (kŏn′ sə lət) ***n-*** **1** the office or residence of a consul. **2** consulship.

con·sul·ship (kŏn′ səl shĭp′) ***n-*** the position or term of a consul.

con·sult (kən sŭlt′) ***vt-*** to seek advice or information from: *to* consult *a lawyer*; *to* consult *a dictionary.* ***vi-*** to exchange opinions; confer: *The doctors* consulted *before operating.*

con·sult·ant (kən sŭl′ tənt) ***n-*** **1** person called upon for expert or professional advice. **2** one who consults.

con·sul·ta·tion (kŏn′ səl tā′ shən) ***n-*** **1** a consulting. **2** conference or meeting of consultants.

con·sume (kən sōōm′, -syōōm′) ***vt-*** [**con·sumed, con·sum·ing**] **1** to eat or drink up; devour. **2** to destroy: *Fire* consumed *the barn.* **3** to spend; exhaust; use up, often wastefully: *The job* consumes *all his energy. Television* consumes *his spare time.* **4** to absorb or overwhelm: *Curiosity* consumed *her.* **—*adj-*** **con·sum′ a·ble:** *a* consumable *resource.*

con·sum·er (kən sōō′ mər, -syōō′ mər) ***n-*** **1** person who buys and uses food, clothing, services, etc. **2** person or thing that uses up or consumes: *Television is often a* consumer *of time.*

[1]**con·sum·mate** (kŏn′ sə māt′) ***vt-*** [**con·sum·mat·ed, con·sum·mat·ing**] to bring to completion or perfection.

[2]**con·sum·mate** (kən sŭm′ ət) ***adj-*** perfect; carried to the highest degree: *a man of* consummate *skill.* **—*adv-*** **con·sum′ mate·ly.**

con·sum·ma·tion (kŏn′ sə mā′ shən) ***n-*** a completing or perfecting; fulfillment: *the* consummation *of one's life work.*

con·sump·tion (kən sŭmp′ shən) ***n-*** **1** a using or using up: *the* consumption *of goods and services.* **2** eating or drinking: *my* consumption *of three hamburgers.* **3** destruction, especially by fire. **4** tuberculosis of the lungs.

con·sump·tive (kən sŭmp′ tĭv) ***adj-*** **1** tending to use up or destroy; destructive: *Mining is a* consumptive *industry.* **2** ill with tuberculosis of the lungs. ***n-*** person who has tuberculosis of the lungs. **—*adv-*** **con·sump′ tive·ly.**

cont. or **contd.** continued.

con·tact (kŏn′ tăkt) ***n-*** **1** a touching; touch: *the* contact *of two wires.* **2** connection: *The pilot made* contact *with the tower.* **3** *Informal* person who is in a position to be helpful: *a good business* contact. **4** metal point, strip, etc., through which an electrical connection is made and broken in a switch or other device. ***vt-*** **1** (*also* kən tăkt′) to touch. **2** *Informal* to get in touch with: *Please* contact *me later.*

contact lens ***n-*** tiny plastic lens worn directly on the eyeball to correct eyesight.

con·ta·gion (kən tā′ jən) ***n-*** **1** a spreading of a disease by contact. **2** a disease that can spread from one person or animal to another. **3** a spreading of a feeling or influence: *the* contagion *of fear.*

con·ta·gious (kən tā′ jəs) ***adj-*** **1** spreading by contact; catching: *Mumps is a* contagious *disease.* **2** easily spreading: *Laughter is often* contagious. **—*adv-*** **con·ta′ gious·ly.** ***n-*** **con·ta′ gious·ness.**

con·tain (kən tān′) ***vt-*** **1** to hold within itself: *The box* contained *candy.* **2** to include as a part: *Some paints* contain *lead.* **3** to hold in check; keep within bounds: *to* contain *one's excitement.* **4** to equal: *A quart* contains *two pints.* **—*adj-*** **con·tain′ a·ble.**

con·tain·er (kən tā′ nər) ***n-*** box, can, jar, etc., used to contain or hold something.

con·tain·ment (kən tān′ mənt) ***n-*** the holding in bounds or in check of a hostile and aggressive power.

con·tam·i·nate (kən tăm′ ə nāt′) ***vt-*** [**con·tam·i·nat·ed, con·tam·i·nat·ing**] to make bad; pollute; infect: *Sewage* contaminates *water.* **—*n-*** **con·tam′ i·na′ tion.**

contd. continued.

con·temn (kən tĕm′) ***vt-*** to treat or regard with contempt and scorn; despise.

con·tem·plate (kŏn′ təm plāt′) ***vt-*** [**con·tem·plat·ed, con·tem·plat·ing**] **1** to look at or think about long and carefully; meditate on: *to* contemplate *the beauty of the desert.* **2** to consider; intend: *to* contemplate *making a trip.* **3** to foresee; expect: *Do you* contemplate *any difficulty because of bad weather?* ***vi-*** to meditate: *The monk* contemplated *for hours.*

con·tem·pla·tion (kŏn′ təm plā′ shən) ***n-*** **1** a looking at or thinking about something long and seriously. **2** meditation on spiritual matters. **3** expectation: *The nation built up its army in* contemplation *of war.*

con·tem·pla·tive (kən tĕm′ plə tĭv′) ***adj-*** of or given to deep and careful thought; meditative: *a* contemplative *life*; *a* contemplative *person.* **—*adv-*** **con·tem′ pla·tive·ly.** ***n-*** **con·tem′ pla·tive·ness.**

con·tem·po·ra·ne·ous (kən tĕm′ pə rā′ nē əs) ***adj-*** existing or occurring at the same time; contemporary (used especially of events). **—*adv-*** **con·tem′ po·ra′ ne·ous·ly.** ***n-*** **con·tem′ po·ra′ ne·ous·ness.**

con·tem·po·ra·ry (kən tĕm′ pə rĕr′ ē) ***adj-*** **1** current; modern: *good* contemporary *furniture.* **2** existing or occurring at the same time; contemporaneous. ***n-*** [*pl.* **con·tem·po·ra·ries**] person living at the same time as another: *Lee and Grant were* contemporaries.

con·tempt (kən tĕmpt′) ***n-*** **1** a feeling that a person or act is mean or vile; scorn: *We have only* contempt *for a* *liar.* **2** condition of being despised: *The traitor was held in* contempt. **3** disregard of lawful orders: *to be in* contempt *of court*; contempt *of Congress.*

con·tempt·i·ble (kən tĕmp′ tə bəl) ***adj-*** deserving contempt; mean; low. ***—n-*** **con·tempt′ i·bil′ i·ty** or **con·tempt′ i·ble·ness.** ***adv-*** **con·tempt′ i·bly.**

con·temp·tu·ous (kən tĕmp′ cho͞o əs) ***adj-*** feeling or expressing contempt; scornful: *a* contemptuous *answer.* ***—adv-*** **con·temp′ tu·ous·ly.** ***n-*** **con·temp′ tu·ous·ness.**

con·tend (kən tĕnd′) ***vi-*** **1** to strive; compete; vie: *to* contend *for the prize.* **2** to struggle (with); put up (with): *to* contend *with rain and insects.* ***vt-*** **1** to argue; maintain: *He* contended *his innocence.* **2** to contest: *He* contended *every point raised.*

[1]**con·tent** (kŏn′ tĕnt) ***n-*** **1** the subject matter or thought of a speech, book, etc. **2** capacity: *The* content *of the jar is six ounces.* **3 contents** all that is contained: *the* contents *of a box*; *the table of* contents *of a book.* [from Latin **contentum,** from **continere** meaning "contain."]

[2]**con·tent** (kən tĕnt′) ***adj-*** **1** satisfied: *He is* content *with his job.* **2** resigned; willing: *I am* content *to go.* ***n-*** satisfaction; ease of mind: *The dog lolled by the fire in sleepy* content. ***vt-*** to satisfy: *The work does not* content *him.* [from Latin **contentum** meaning "satisfied," from Latin **continēre** meaning "contain, be bounded in one's desire."]

con·tent·ed (kən tĕn′ təd) ***adj-*** generally satisfied: *a quiet,* contented *baby.* ***—adv-*** **con·tent′ ed·ly.** ***n-*** **con·tent′ ed·ness.**

con·ten·tion (kən tĕn′ shən) ***n-*** **1** a quarreling; disputing: *constant* contention *in a family.* **2** idea a person believes in or argues for: *the* contention *that poverty causes crime.*

con·ten·tious (kən tĕn′ shəs) ***adj-*** inclined to argue about trifles; quarrelsome. ***—adv-*** **con·ten′ tious·ly.** ***n-*** **con·ten′ tious·ness.**

con·tent·ment (kən tĕnt′ mənt) ***n-*** peace of mind; satisfaction.

[1]**con·test** (kŏn′ tĕst′) ***n-*** competition; a struggle: *Games, debates, and lawsuits are* contests.

[2]**con·test** (kən tĕst′) ***vt-*** **1** to dispute; challenge: *to* contest *an election*; *to* contest *a will.* **2** to fight for: *Our troops* contested *every foot of the battlefield.*

con·test·ant (kən tĕs′ tənt) ***n-*** **1** person who takes part in a contest; competitor. **2** person who contests or disputes a will, election, etc.

con·text (kŏn′ tĕkst′) ***n-*** **1** those parts of a written or spoken passage that surround a given expression and help to fix its meaning. **2** framework; surrounding circumstances: *in the* context *of war.*

con·tex·tu·al (kən tĕks′ cho͞o əl, -chəl) ***adj-*** of or relating to context: *a* contextual *error.* ***—adv-*** **con·tex′ tu·al·ly.**

con·ti·gu·i·ty (kŏn′ tə gyo͞o′ ə tē) ***n-*** [*pl.* **con·ti·gu·i·ties**] **1** a condition of being in contact. **2** nearness; immediate proximity.

con·tig·u·ous (kən tĭg′ yo͞o əs) ***adj-*** **1** touching; adjoining: *two* contiguous *houses.* **2** very near (to): *The field is* contiguous *to the village.* ***—adv-*** **con·tig′ u·ous·ly.** ***n-*** **con·tig′ u·ous·ness.**

con·ti·nence (kŏn′ tən əns) ***n-*** self-control; self-restraint, especially as to passions and desires. Also **con′ ti·nen·cy.**

[1]**con·ti·nent** (kŏn′ tən ənt) ***adj-*** temperate; exercising self-restraint. ***—adv-*** **con′ ti·nent·ly.** [from Latin **continens,** a specialized use of [2]**continent.**]

[2]**con·ti·nent** (kŏn′ tən ənt) ***n-*** **1** one of the seven large divisions of land on the earth. North America, South America, Europe, Asia, Africa, Australia, and Antarctica are the continents. **2 the Continent** the mainland of Europe. [from Latin **continens, -entis,** meaning "a containing; withholding."]

con·ti·nen·tal (kŏn tə nĕn′ təl) ***adj-*** **1** of or belonging to a continent. **2 Continental** (1) having to do with the American side in the American Revolution: *the* Continental *Army.* (2) having to do with the mainland of Europe: *a* Continental *tour.*

Continental Congress ***n-*** legislative and governing body of the American colonies, 1774-81.

Continental Divide ***n-*** the divide in or between ranges of the Rocky Mountains in western North America that separates east-flowing streams from west-flowing streams.

continental shelf ***n-*** the gently sloping submerged edge of a continent, often bordered by the **continental slope,** which plunges steeply into the ocean depths.

con·tin·gen·cy (kən tĭn′ jən sē) ***n-*** [*pl.* **con·tin·gen·cies**] **1** condition of being contingent. **2** event which may or may not happen: *to be ready for any* contingency.

con·tin·gent (kən tĭn′ jənt) ***adj-*** **1** possible, but uncertain. **2** accidental. **3** depending (on): *Her coming is* contingent *on the weather.* ***n-*** any unit or group in a gathering of representative units: *the Idaho* contingent *at the convention.* ***—adv-*** **con·tin′ gent·ly.**

con·tin·u·al (kən tĭn′ yo͞o əl) ***adj-*** **1** often repeated; one time after another; frequent: *I make* continual *trips to the store.* **2** continuous. ***—adv-*** **con·tin′ u′ al·ly.**

►CONTINUAL refers to frequent repetitions, whereas CONTINUOUS means without interruption: *His singing was* continual. (He often sang.) *His singing was* continuous. (He never stopped singing.)

con·tin·u·ance (kən tĭn′ yo͞o əns) ***n-*** **1** a keeping on, lasting, or continuing; a going on with: *a* continuance *of stormy weather.* **2** in law, adjournment of court action to a later day.

con·tin·u·a·tion (kən tĭn′ yo͞o ā′ shən) ***n-*** **1** a carrying on without a break; a going on: *Commuters asked for a* continuation *of regular train service during the summer.* **2** a taking up again after an interruption: *a* continuation *of the story in next month's magazine.* **3** a new part that continues a story, movie, etc.; installment.

con·tin·ue (kən tĭn′ yo͞o) ***vt-*** [**con·tin·ued, con·tin·u·ing**] (considered intransitive when the direct object is implied but not expressed) **1** to keep up or go on with; persist in: *He* continued *working far into the night.* **2** to begin again after stopping: *We will* continue *the discussion after lunch.* ***vi-*** to remain in a particular condition or position: *The seas* continued *calm. He* continued *in office for three years.*

con·ti·nu·i·ty (kŏn′ tə nyo͞o′ ə tē) ***n-*** [*pl.* **con·ti·nu·i·ties**] **1** continuation without interruption; smooth succession: *The sudden noise broke the* continuity *of his thoughts.* **2** in motion pictures and television, script or dialogue.

con·tin·u·ous (kən tĭn′ yo͞o əs) ***adj-*** unbroken; going on without interruption: *There is one* continuous *line of traffic on Main Street.* ***—adv-*** **con·tin′ u·ous·ly.** ***n-*** **con·tin′ u·ous·ness.**

►For usage note see CONTINUAL.

continuous spectrum ***n-*** of light or other electromagnetic radiation, a spectrum consisting of all wavelengths between certain limits, and having no gaps or empty spaces.

con·tin·u·um (kən tĭn′ yo͞o əm) ***n-*** an unbroken whole, gradations of which pass smoothly into one another: *the* continuum *of space.*

con·tort (kən tôrt′, -tôrt′) *vt-* to bend or twist violently out of shape; distort: *to* contort *one's face.*

con·tor·tion (kən tôr′shən, -tôr′shən) *n-* an unnatural twisting, as of the face or body.

con·tour (kŏn′to͝or) *n-* outline of a figure, coast, mountain, etc.: *the even* contour *of a vase.* *vt-* **1** to give a smooth, curving outline or surface to. **2** to cause to follow a contour line, as in building a road on a mountainside.

contour farming *n-* farming based on contour plowing.

contour line *n-* line on a map connecting points that are equal in elevation.

contour map *n-* map showing the surface features of an area of land by means of contour lines.

contour plowing *n-* plowing across the slope so that the furrows follow the contour of the land, in order to reduce soil erosion.

Contour map

contra- *prefix* against; opposite: *to* contra*dict.*

con·tra·band (kŏn′trə bănd′) *n-* **1** anything that may not legally be brought into or sent out of a country, especially in time of war. **2** a bringing in or out of such goods; smuggling. *as* ***modifier***: *a shipment of* contraband *goods.*

con·tra·bass (kŏn′trə bās′) *Music* *n-* in several families of instruments, the instrument whose range is below the bass; especially, the double bass. ***adj-*** having a lower pitch than the normal bass: *a* contrabass *clarinet.*

con·tra·cep·tion (kŏn′trə sĕp′shən) *n-* voluntary prevention of conception.

con·tra·cep·tive (kŏn′trə sĕp′tĭv) *n-* device, agent, or method used for contraception. *as* ***modifier***: *a* contraceptive *substance.*

[1]**con·tract** (kŏn′trăkt) *n-* legal agreement between two or more persons or groups to do something; also, the document containing such an agreement: *a labor* contract; *a movie* contract.

[2]**con·tract** (kən trăkt′) *vt-* **1** to draw together; make smaller by shortening, thickening, etc.: *to* contract *one's brows; to* contract *"is not" to "isn't."* **2** to get; acquire: *to* contract *a cold.* **3** (*also* kŏn′trăkt′) to enter into or arrange by legal agreement: *to* contract *a partnership.* *vi-* **1** to become smaller in length, width, volume, etc. **2** (*also* kŏn′trăkt′) to make a legal agreement: *Mr. Jones* contracted *with the builder for a home.*

contract bridge (kŏn′trăkt′) *n-* card game differing from auction bridge in that only the number of tricks bid can be counted toward game.

con·trac·tile (kən trăk′təl) *adj-* able to contract or to cause contraction: *the* contractile *muscles.*

con·trac·tion (kən trăk′shən) *n-* **1** a drawing together; shrinking; shortening: *the* contraction *of a muscle*; *the* contraction *of a word.* **2** a word that has been contracted. **3** an entering into; incurring: *the* contraction *of a debt.* **4** a catching or getting: *the* contraction *of a disease.*

con·trac·tor (kŏn′trăk tər) *n-* person who agrees to supply something or do work for a certain price.

con·trac·tu·al (kən trăk′cho͞o əl) *adj-* of, like, or included in a contract: *a* contractual *agreement.* ***—adv-*** **con·trac′tu·al·ly.**

con·tra·dict (kŏn′trə dĭkt′) *vt-* **1** to assert the opposite of: *He* contradicted *his own story.* **2** to deny the words of.

con·tra·dic·tion (kŏn′trə dĭk′shən) *n-* **1** a statement that contradicts another; also, a statement containing facts, ideas, etc., that contradict each other. **2** a saying the opposite or contrary: *He hates any* contradiction *of his views.* **3** disagreement; opposition: *There is no* contradiction *between my words and my actions.*

con·tra·dic·to·ry (kŏn′trə dĭk′tə rē) ***adj-*** opposing; contrary: *a* contradictory *statement.* ***—adv-*** **con′tra·dic′to·ri·ly.** ***n-*** **con′tra·dic′to·ri·ness.**

con·tra·dis·tinc·tion (kŏn′trə dĭs tĭngk′shən) *n-* distinction based on contrast: *the sciences in* contradistinction *to the arts.*

con·tral·to (kən trăl′tō) *Music* *n-* [*pl.* **con·tral·tos**] the musical range of the lowest female singing voice; alto; also, a singer having this range or a musical part written for it. ***adj-***: *a* contralto *voice.*

con·trap·tion (kən trăp′shən) *Informal* *n-* device or gadget; contrivance.

con·tra·ri·wise (kən trâr′ĭ wīz′, kŏn′-) *adv-* **1** in the opposite direction: *One road runs west, the other* contrariwise. **2** on the contrary.

con·tra·ry (kŏn′trĕr′ē) *adj-* **1** opposed; conflicting: *They held* contrary *opinions.* **2** opposite in direction; adverse: *the* contrary *tides.* **3** (*also* kŏn′trə rē or kən trâr′ē) habitually opposing or contradicting: *The* contrary *child argued with everyone.* *n-* [*pl.* **con·tra·ries**] the opposite: *If he says one thing, I believe the* contrary. ***—adv-*** **con′tra·ri·ly.** ***n-*** **con′tra·ri·ness.**

on the contrary the truth is just the opposite; contrariwise: *He seems happy, but,* on the contrary, *he is sad.*

[1]**con·trast** (kən trăst′) *vt-* to compare in order to show unlikeness or difference: *to* contrast *black and white*; *to* contrast *his joy with my sorrow.* *vi-* to be distinct; be clearly different in comparison (with): *Black and white* contrast. *Black* contrasts *with white.*

►*For usage note see* COMPARE.

[2]**con·trast** (kŏn′trăst′) *n-* **1** a comparing to show up differences; a contrasting: *By* contrast *with Ed, Tom is well-behaved.* **2** difference or unlikeness between things: *a sharp* contrast *of tone.*

con·trib·ute (kən trĭ′byo͞ot′) *vt-* [**con·trib·ut·ed, con·trib·ut·ing**] (considered intransitive when the direct object is implied but not expressed) to give or provide; furnish: *to* contribute *one's time to a cause.* *vi-* to help or aid; be of benefit (to): *Exercise* contributes *to one's health.*

con·tri·bu·tion (kŏn′trə byo͞o′shən) *n-* a giving or bestowing of something; also, the thing given.

con·trib·u·tor (kən trĭb′yə tər) *n-* **1** person who gives to a cause: *a* contributor *to a building fund.* **2** person who writes an article for a newspaper or magazine.

con·trib·u·to·ry (kən trĭb′yə tôr′ē) *adj-* **1** helping to produce a result: *a* contributory *factor.* **2** giving aid; assisting: *a* contributory *grant of money.*

con·trite (kən trīt′, kŏn′trīt′) *adj-* showing sorrow or regret for faults or wrongs; repentant; remorseful: *He shed* contrite *tears.* ***—adv-*** **con·trite′ly.** ***n-*** **con·trite′ness.**

con·tri·tion (kən trĭsh′ən) *n-* sorrow for faults or wrongs; sincere repentance.

con·triv·ance (kən trī′vəns) *n-* **1** invention; device: *The electric eye is a* contrivance *for opening the door automatically.* **2** a contriving or planning; scheming: *a plan of his own* contrivance. **3** plan or scheme: *What* contrivance *was used to get Alice to her surprise party?*

con·trive (kən trīv′) *vt-* [**con·trived, con·triv·ing**] **1** to plan or create by some clever means; devise; invent: *to* contrive *a scheme*; *to* contrive *an underwater breathing device.* **2** to bring about; manage: *to* contrive *escape.*

con·trol (kən trōl′) *vt-* [**con·trolled, con·trol·ling**] **1** to command or regulate; direct: *to* control *a business.* **2** to hold back; restrain; check: *to* control *one's temper.* *n-* **1** effective authority to direct or regulate: *to have* control *over a group.* **2** means of holding steady or in check: *I am in favor of price* controls. **3** device for regulating and guiding a machine: *the* controls *of an airplane.* **—*adj*- con·trol′ la·ble.**

con·trol·ler (kən trō′ lər, kŏn′-) ***n*- 1** someone or something that controls, especially a device that controls the speed, pressure, etc., of a machine. **2** (also **comptroller**) person who supervises financial accounts and expenditures of a large business or government organization.

con·tro·ver·sial (kŏn′ trə vûr′ shəl) ***adj*-** likely to cause disagreement or discussion: *a* controversial *issue.* **—*adv*- con′ tro·ver′ sial·ly.**

con·tro·ver·sial·ist (kŏn′ trə vur′ shə lĭst) ***n*-** person who likes to carry on controversies or debates.

con·tro·ver·sy (kŏn′ trə vûr′ sē) ***n*-** [*pl.* **con·tro·ver·sies**] argument; dispute; disagreement.

con·tro·vert (kŏn′ trə vûrt′) ***vt*-** to oppose in an argument; contradict; dispute: *to* controvert *an opinion.* **—*adj*- con′ tro·vert′ i·ble.**

con·tu·ma·cious (kŏn′ tyo͞o mā′ shəs) ***adj*-** stubbornly refusing to obey authority; insubordinate; rebellious: *a* contumacious *prisoner.* **—*adj*- con′ tu·ma′ cious·ly. *n*- con′ tu·ma·cy** (-mə sē): *the* contumacy *of a hardened criminal.*

con·tu·me·ly (kən tyo͞o′ mə lē, kŏn′ təm lē) ***n*-** [*pl.* **con·tu·me·lies**] **1** scornful rudeness in speech or action; insolence: *One must often bear the* contumely *of lesser men.* **2** an insult. **—*adj*- con′ tu·me′ li·ous** (kŏn′ tyə mē′ lē əs). ***adv*- con′ tu·me′ li·ous·ly.**

con·tu·sion (kən to͞o′ zhən, -tyo͞o′ zhən) ***n*-** a bruise.

co·nun·drum (kə nŭn′ drəm) ***n*- 1** riddle or puzzle whose answer often involves a humorous play on words. Example: What has four wheels and flies? A garbage truck. **2** any difficult or perplexing problem.

con·va·lesce (kŏn′ və lĕs′) ***vi*-** [**con·va·lesced, con·va·lesc·ing**] to get better after sickness; to recover strength and health: *He is in Florida to* convalesce.

con·va·les·cence (kŏn′ və lĕs′ əns) ***n*- 1** a returning to good health after disease or injury. **2** period of time this takes.

con·va·les·cent (kŏn′ və lĕs′ ənt) ***adj*- 1** getting better after sickness; recovering: *He is* convalescent, *but still in the hospital.* **2** having to do with recovery from illness: *a* convalescent *diet.* ***n*-** person who is getting well.

con·vec·tion (kən vĕk′ shən) ***n*-** circular currents within a liquid or gas due to differences in density between hotter and cooler portions and resulting in the transfer of heat. *as* ***modifier***: *a* convection *current.*

con·vene (kən vēn′) ***vi*-** [**con·vened, con·ven·ing**] to come together; to assemble for a meeting: *The legislature* convened. ***vt*-**: *The mayor* convened *the council.*

con·ven·ience (kən vēn′ ē əns) ***n*- 1** ease in using, getting, changing, etc.; suitability: *the* convenience *of a telephone*; *the* convenience *of paperback books.* **2** ease or comfort: *to provide a car for one's* convenience. **3** something that adds to one's comfort and ease.

at one's convenience at a time, place, etc., that is suitable to one; at one's pleasure.

con·ven·ient (kən vēn′ ē ənt) ***adj*- 1** easy to use, reach, change, etc.: *a* convenient *appliance.* **2** suited to one's comfort or needs: *a* convenient *time and place.* **— *adv*- con·ven′ ient·ly.**

convenient to near to; within easy reach of.

con·vent (kŏn′ vĕnt′) ***n*-** building occupied by a society of women who live together and devote themselves to a religious life; also, the society itself.

con·ven·tion (kən vĕn′ shən) ***n*- 1** meeting for some special purpose: *a* convention *of doctors.* **2** generally accepted practice; custom: *It is a* convention *for men to shake hands when introduced.* **3** agreement between nations, persons, etc.: *the* conventions *for proper treatment of prisoners of war.*

con·ven·tion·al (kən vĕn′ shən əl) ***adj*- 1** following accepted practices and customs; customary: *"How do you do?" is a* conventional *greeting.* **2** not new or original; commonplace: *The furnishings in the room were* conventional. **—*n*- con·ven′ tion·al′ i·ty** (-shən ăl′ ə tē). ***adv*- con·ven′ tion·al·ly.**

con·verge (kən vûrj′) ***vi*-** [**con·verged, con·verg·ing**] to come together at one point; meet: *Five roads* converge.

con·ver·gence (kən vûr′ jəns) ***n*-** the meeting of separate things at a point: *the* convergence *of light rays at a focus.*

con·ver·gent (kən vûr′ jənt) ***adj*-** joining at a point; coming together; converging: *Two* convergent *roads.* **—*adv*- con·ver′ gent·ly.**

con·ver·sant (kən vûr′ sənt) ***adj*-** familiar (with): *to be* conversant *with music.* **—*adv*- con·ver′ sant·ly.**

con·ver·sa·tion (kŏn′ vər sā′ shən) ***n*-** informal or familiar talk between people.

con·ver·sa·tion·al (kŏn′ vər sā′ shən əl) ***adj*-** suited or related to familiar talk: *a* conversational *tone*; conversational *French.* **—*adv*- con′ ver·sa′ tion·al·ly.**

con·ver·sa·tion·al·ist (kŏn′ vər sā′ shən ə lĭst) ***n*-** person who is good at conversing.

¹con·verse (kən vûrs′) ***vi*-** [**con·versed, con·vers·ing**] to talk informally with a person or persons; hold a conversation: *to* converse *about the weather.* [from Old French **converser,** from Latin **conversāri** meaning "to live with; be engaged in or with."]

²con·verse (kŏn′ vûrs′) ***n*- 1** opposite of something: *Heat is the* converse *of cold.* **2** reversed form of something, especially of a statement in reasoning: *"All stupid men are helpless" is the* converse *of "All helpless men are stupid."* ***adj*-**: *The* converse *statement is not true.* [from Latin **conversus** meaning originally "having been turned (over or opposite)," a form of **convertere,** "to convert; turn."] **—*adv*- con·verse′ ly.**

con·ver·sion (kən vûr′ zhən) ***n*- 1** a changing from one form or use to another: *the* conversion *of a vacant lot into a playground.* **2** a change from one religion, belief, etc., to another: *the* conversion *of heathens.*

¹con·vert (kən vûrt′) ***vt*- 1** to change (something) from one form, use, or purpose to another: *A boiler* converts *water into steam.* **2** to cause (a person) to believe in a religion, a point of view, etc.

²con·vert (kŏn′ vûrt′) ***n*-** person who has changed from one religion to another, or is led to accept someone else's opinions, ideas, etc., that had not been his own.

con·vert·er (kən vûr′ tər) ***n*- 1** device for changing AC electricity into DC or vice versa. **2** device for changing radio signals from one range into another in a receiver. **3** device for enabling a television set to receive broadcasts in the ultrahigh-frequency range. **4** furnace used in the Bessemer process; Bessemer converter.

con·vert·i·ble (kən vûr′ tə bəl) ***adj*-** of a nature that allows changing or adapting: *a* convertible *raincoat.* ***n*-** automobile with a top that can be raised and lowered. **—*n*- con·vert′ i·bil′ i·ty. *adv*- con·vert′ i·bly.**

con·vert·i·plane (kən vûr′ tə plān′) ***n*-** airplane that changes in midair from the vertical flight of a helicopter to fixed-wing flight.

con·vex (kŏn′ vĕks′) ***adj*-** curved outward like the outside of a ball. **—*adv*- con·vex′ ly. *n*- con·vex′ ness.**

Convex

fāte, făt, dâre, bärn; bē, bĕt, mêre; bīte, bĭt; nōte, hŏt, môre, dôg; fŭn, fûr; to͞o, bo͝ok; oil; out; tar; thin; then; hw for wh as in *wh*at; zh for s as in u*s*ual; ə for a, e, i, o, u, as in *a*go, lin*e*n, per*i*l, at*o*m, min*us*

con·vex·i·ty (kən vĕk′ sə tē) ***n-*** [*pl.* **con·vex·i·ties**] **1** a curving outward of a surface. **2** convex surface.

con·vey (kən vā′) ***vt-*** **1** to carry from one place to another; transmit; transport: *A truck will* convey *the equipment to the boat.* **2** to make known: *Her expression* conveyed *her disappointment.* **3** to transfer (property) from one person to another.

con·vey·ance (kən vā′ əns) ***n-*** **1** the carrying (of persons or things) from one place to another: *Trucks and trains are used for the* conveyance *of goods from factories to stores.* **2** vehicle used for carrying, such as a truck, car, etc. **3** a written title or deed to property.

con·vey·er or **con·vey·or** (kən vā′ ər) ***n-*** **1** someone or something that conveys. **2** mechanical device, such as a set of rollers or an endless belt, used in factories, mines, stores, etc., for moving materials and products.

conveyor belt ***n-*** continuous moving belt used to transport things from one place to another.

[1]**con·vict** (kən vĭkt′) ***vt-*** to prove or declare to be guilty: *The court* convicted *him of theft.*

[2]**con·vict** (kŏn′ vĭkt′) ***n-*** person in prison, or sentenced to prison for a crime.

con·vic·tion (kən vĭk′ shən) ***n-*** **1** a declaring, proving, or finding that someone is guilty: *The trial ended in the* conviction *and imprisonment of the thief.* **2** firm belief; definite opinion: *We hold strong* convictions.

con·vince (kən vĭns′) ***vt-*** [**con·vinced, con·vinc·ing**] to make (someone) certain; cause (someone) to believe: *I* convinced *him that he was wrong.* —***adv-*** **con·vinc′ ing·ly.** ***n-*** **con·vinc′ ing·ness.**

con·viv·i·al (kən vĭv′ ē əl) ***adj-*** **1** fond of merry-making with friends; jovial; gay. **2** like a feast; festive. —***n-*** **con·viv·i·al′ i·ty** (kən vĭv′ ē ăl′ ə tē).

con·vo·ca·tion (kŏn′ vō kā′ shən) ***n-*** a calling together of persons for a meeting or assembly; also, the meeting itself: *a* convocation *of clergymen.*

con·voke (kən vōk′) ***vt-*** [**con·voked, con·vok·ing**] to call together for a meeting: *to* convoke *Congress.*

con·vo·lute (kŏn′ və lo͞ot′) ***adj-*** rolled up or folded upon itself; coiled: *a* convolute *seashell.* —***adv-*** **con′ vo·lute′ ly.**

con·vo·lu·tion (kŏn′ və lo͞o′ shən) ***n-*** **1** a coiling or winding together. **2** coil or fold, especially any of the folds on the surface of the brain.

con·voy (kŏn′ voi′) ***n-*** **1** group (of ships, vehicles, etc.) led or guarded by an armed escort: *a* convoy *of troopships.* **2** the escort itself. ***vt-*** (*also* kən voi′): *Two destroyers* convoyed *the supply ship.*

con·vulse (kən vŭls′) ***vt-*** [**con·vulsed, con·vuls·ing**] **1** to shake or affect with spasms of laughter, pain, or emotion: *The comedian* convulsed *the audience.* **2** to agitate or disturb violently; shake.

con·vul·sion (kən vŭl′ shən) ***n-*** **1** violent jerking or contortion caused by spasmodic tightening of muscles; a fit; paroxysm. **2** violent disturbance: *Earthquakes are* convulsions *of the earth.*

con·vul·sive (kən vŭl′ sĭv) ***adj-*** like a convulsion: *The jokes threw her into* convulsive *laughter.* —***adv-*** **con·vul′ sive·ly.** ***n-*** **con·vul′ sive·ness.**

co·ny (kō′ nē) ***n-*** [*pl.* **co·nies**] **1** rabbit, especially the European rabbit. **2** any of several rabbitlike animals of Asia, Africa, and North America, especially the Old World hyrax. **3** rabbit fur. Also **coney.**

coo (ko͞o) ***n-*** soft, murmuring sound like that made by doves and pigeons. ***vi-***: *The doves* coo *in their cotes.*

cook (ko͝ok) ***vt-*** to prepare (food) by the use of heat, as by boiling, baking, or frying: *to* cook *a ham.* ***vi-***: *The ham* cooked. ***n-*** person who prepares food.
cook up to invent; concoct: *He* cooked up *an excuse.*

cook·book (ko͝ok′ bo͝ok′) ***n-*** book of recipes and other information for cooking.

cook·er (ko͝ok′ ər) ***n-*** special apparatus or vessel for cooking food: *a steam* cooker; *a pressure* cooker.

cook·er·y (ko͝ok′ ə rē) ***n-*** art or work of preparing food; cuisine: *Mrs. McGillicuddy is noted for her excellent Italian* cookery.

cook·ie (ko͝ok′ ē) ***n-*** [*pl.* **cook·ies**] small, flat, sweet cake. Also **cook′ y.**

cook·out (ko͝ok′ out′) ***n-*** picnic at which a meal is cooked.

cook·stove (ko͝ok′ stōv′) ***n-*** stove used for cooking.

cool (ko͞ol) ***adj-*** [**cool·er, cool·est**] **1** slightly or moderately cold; nearly chilly: *a* cool *breeze.* **2** not letting in or keeping heat: *a* cool *summer suit.* **3** not excited; calm: *the only* cool *one in the confusion.* **4** lacking warmth and friendliness; not cordial: *to get a* cool *reception.* ***vt-*** **1** to make slightly cold: *Please* cool *the wine.* **2** to make less excited; calm: *to* cool *one's anger.* ***vi-***: *The dessert* cooled *in the refrigerator. His anger* cooled. ***n-*** time or place that is moderately cold: *in the* cool *of the evening.* —***adv-*** **cool′ ly.** ***n-*** **cool′ ness.**

cool·ant (ko͞ol′ ənt) ***n-*** liquid or gas circulated through a cooling system of an engine, machine tool, etc.

cool·er (ko͞o′ lər) ***n-*** **1** device for keeping foods or liquids cool: *a water* cooler. **2** *Slang* jail.

cool-head·ed (ko͞ol′ hĕd′ əd) ***adj-*** not easily upset or disturbed; calm. —***n-*** **cool′ -head′ ed·ness.**

coo·lie (ko͞o′ lē) ***n-*** in the Orient, an unskilled laborer. ***Hom-*** coulee.

coomb (ko͞om) *Brit.* ***n-*** deep and narrow valley.

coon (ko͞on) ***n-*** raccoon.

coop (ko͞op) ***n-*** cage or enclosure for fowl, rabbits, etc. ***vt-*** to confine; shut (up): *They* cooped *him up in a tiny room.* ***Hom-*** coupe.

co-op (kō′ ŏp′) ***n-*** co-operative.

coop·er (ko͞o′ pər) ***n-*** maker or mender of barrels.

coop·er·age (ko͞op′ ər ĭj) ***n-*** **1** the work of a cooper; also, the charge for this. **2** his place of work.

co-op·er·ate or **co·op·er·ate** (kō ŏp′ ə rāt′) ***vi-*** [**co-op·er·at·ed** or **co·op·er·at·ed, co-op·er·at·ing** or **co·op·er·at·ing**] to work or act with others for a common purpose: *If everyone* co-operates, *we will finish on time.*

co-op·er·a·tion or **co·op·er·a·tion** (kō ŏp′ ə rā′ shən) ***n-*** a working together for the same end; mutual help; joint effort: *We would appreciate your* co-operation.

co-op·er·a·tive or **co·op·er·a·tive** (kō ŏp′ ər ə tĭv, -ə rā′ tĭv) ***adj-*** **1** working or willing to work with others for the same ends: *The project was successful because everyone was* co-operative. **2** of or having to do with co-operation: *a* co-operative *effort.* ***n-*** apartment house, store, or other facility collectively owned by its users. —***adv-*** **co-op′ er·a·tive·ly** or **co·op′ er·a·tive·ly.** ***n-*** **co-op′ er·a·tive·ness** or **co·op′ er·a·tive·ness.**

[1]**co-or·di·nate** or **co·or·di·nate** (kō ôr′ də nāt′) ***vt-*** [**co-or·di·nat·ed** or **co·or·di·nat·ed, co-or·di·nat·ing** or **co·or·di·nat·ing**] to harmonize; fit together; make work in a smooth and efficient manner: *to* co-ordinate *the departments of a business.* ***vi-***: *An athlete's muscles must* co-ordinate *well.* —***n-*** **co-or′ di·na′ tion** or **co·or′ di·na′ tion.**

[2]**co-or·di·nate** or **co·or·di·nate** (kō ôr′ dən ət) ***n-*** *Mathematics* one of a set of numbers, representing distances, which locate a point in space with regard to a fixed position. See also *Cartesian coordinates, polar coordinates,* and *spherical coordinates.* ***adj-*** of equal importance: *Mercy and justice are* co-ordinate *virtues.*

coot (ko͞ot) ***n-*** **1** a swimming and diving bird somewhat like a duck. **2** scoter. **3** *Slang* a man, especially an old man.

cop (kŏp) *Informal* ***n-*** policeman.

co·pal (kō′ păl′) ***n-*** natural resin obtained from certain tropical trees and used mainly for making varnishes.

[1]**cope** (kōp) ***vi-*** **[coped, cop·ing]** to contend (with); struggle successfully (with): *One clerk could not* cope *with their demands.* [from French **couper** meaning "to strike."]

[2]**cope** (kōp) ***n-*** long cloak or mantle worn by priests on certain occasions. [from Late Latin **capa** or **cappa** from earlier Latin word **caput** meaning "head." It is related to "[1]cape."]

Co·per·ni·can (kō pûr′ nĭ kən) ***adj-*** having to do with or following Copernicus's theory that the sun, not the earth, is the center of the solar system.

cop·i·er (kŏp′ ē ər) ***n-*** person or thing that copies, especially a machine for copying letters, photos, etc.

co·pi·lot (kō′ pī′ lət) ***n-*** assistant pilot who helps or relieves the chief pilot of an aircraft.

cop·ing (kō′ pĭng) ***n-*** the top covering of a wall, often of brick or stone and sloping so as to shed water.

coping saw ***n-*** saw with a narrow blade set in an open frame, used for cutting curves in wood.

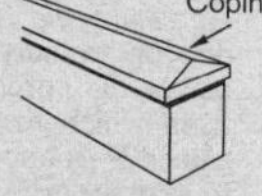

co·pi·ous (kō′ pē əs) ***adj-*** plentiful; ample; abundant: *a* copious *supply.* **—*adv-*** **co′ pi·ous·ly.** ***n-*** **co′ pi·ous·ness.**

cop·per (kŏp′ ər) ***n-*** **1** reddish-brown, metallic chemical element. Symbol Cu, At. No. 29, At. Wt. 63.54. **2** the reddish-brown color of this metal. **3** coin, such as a penny, made of this metal. ***adj-***: *a* copper *pot*; copper *hair.* **—*adj-*** **cop′ per·y.**

cop·per·as (kŏp′ ər əs) ***n-*** green, odorless chemical used in dyeing, making ink, etc.; green vitriol.

cop·per·head (kŏp′ ər hĕd′) ***n-*** **1** poisonous snake of the eastern United States, mostly reddish brown with darker or yellowish markings. **2 Copperhead** person from the North who sympathized with the South during the Civil War.

cop·per·plate (kŏp′ ər plāt′) ***n-*** **1** flat piece of engraved copper, used in printing. **2** print made from such a plate.

cop·per·smith (kŏp′ ər smĭth′) ***n-*** person who works in copper.

co·pra (kōp′ rə) ***n-*** dried meat of the coconut, from which coconut oil is obtained.

copse (kŏps) ***n-*** thick grove of bushes and small trees; thicket. Also **cop′ pice** (kŏp′ əs).

Copt (kŏpt) ***n-*** **1** Egyptian descended from the ancient Egyptians. **2** member of the ancient Christian church of Egypt.

Cop·tic (kŏp′ tĭk) ***adj-*** of or relating to the Copts, to their language, or to the **Coptic Church,** a very early Christian sect. ***n-*** the language of the Copts, now used only in the services of this church.

cop·u·la (kŏp′ yə lə) ***n-*** linking verb. Also **cop′ u·la′ tive verb** (kŏp′ yə lā′ tĭv).

cop·y (kŏp′ ē) ***vt-*** **[cop·ied, cop·y·ing]** (considered intransitive when the direct object is implied but not expressed) **1** to make or produce something that is exactly like something else or contains the same words, ideas, details, etc.: *to* copy *a drawing*; *to* copy *a letter.* **2** to imitate; mimic: *to* copy *a dancer's movements.* ***n-*** [*pl.* **cop·ies**] **1** duplicate, imitation, or reproduction of the contents of something else: *a* copy *of a picture*; *a neat* copy *of a manuscript.* **2** a single one of a number of identically printed books, magazines, pictures, etc. **3** typed or written material to be set in type and printed.

cop·y·book (kŏp′ ē bo͝ok′) ***n-*** book containing examples of handwriting for students to copy.

copy boy ***n-*** boy or man employed in a newspaper office or printing plant to carry copy and run errands.

cop·y·ist (kŏp′ ē ĭst) ***n-*** person who makes a copy or copies, especially of written material or music.

cop·y·right (kŏp′ ē rīt′) ***n-*** exclusive right of a creator of a literary, artistic, or musical work to distribute it to the public or to permit others to do so. Copyrights are permitted by law for a term of years. ***vt-*** to exercise and secure such a right for (a book, play, picture, musical composition, etc.).

co·quet (kō kĕt′) ***vi-*** **[co·quet·ted, co·quet·ting]** to pretend to be attracted to or in love with someone; flirt.

co·quet·ry (kō′ kə trē′, kō kĕt′ ə rē) ***n-*** [*pl.* **co·quet·ries**] flirtatious action, manner, behavior, etc.

co·quette (kō kĕt′) ***n-*** woman or girl who tries to attract men by insincerely affectionate behavior; flirt. **—*adj-*** **co·quet′ tish:** *a* coquettish *glance.* ***adv-*** **co·quet′ tish·ly.**

cor·a·cle (kôr′ ə kəl, kŏr′-) ***n-*** small, wide boat made of waterproof cloth or hide stretched over a frame.

cor·al (kôr′ əl, kŏr′-) ***n-*** **1** hard substance, somewhat like limestone, built up of the skeletons of great numbers of tiny sea animals called polyps. Coral is found in a great variety of shapes and colors. Some kinds are used in making jewelry. **2** one of the tiny animals forming this substance, or the distinctively shaped mass formed by them. **3** a deep, yellowish pink. ***adj-***: *a* coral *necklace*; *a* coral *dress.*

coral snake ***n-*** any of several small American poisonous snakes having bright bands of red, yellow, and black. They are related to the cobras.

cord (kôrd, kōrd) ***n-*** **1** string or narrow rope made of strands twisted together. **2** thin, flexible cable of insulated wires connecting electrical equipment to a source of electricity: *a lamp* cord. **3** stringlike part of the body, such as the spinal cord. **4** measure of cut firewood, equal to a pile 4 feet high, 4 feet wide, and 8 feet long. **5** fabric woven with raised strands or ridges; also, one of the ridges in such fabric. **—*adj-*** **cord′ ed:** *a* corded *fabric.* ***Hom-*** chord.

cord·age (kôr′ dĭj, kōr′-) ***n-*** cords and ropes in general, especially when forming the rigging of a ship.

cor·dial (kôr′ jəl, kōr′-) ***adj-*** warm and sincere; hearty: *a* cordial *welcome.* ***n-*** **1** sweet alcoholic drink; liqueur. **2** stimulating medicine; tonic. **—*adv-*** **cor′ dial·ly.**

cor·di·al·i·ty (kôr′ jē ăl′ ə tē, kōr′-) ***n-*** friendly sincerity; warmth: *the* cordiality *of her smile.*

cor·dil·ler·a (kôr′ dĭl yâr′ ə, kōr′-) ***n-*** large system of mountain ranges.

cor·don (kôr′ dən, kōr′-) ***n-*** **1** line or circle of persons, ships, forts, etc., surrounding and guarding something: *A* cordon *of detectives protected the bank.* **2** band or cord worn as a decoration of honor.

cor·do·van (kôr′ də vən, kōr′-) ***n-*** fine leather, now made chiefly from split horsehide, originally tanned at Cordova, Spain. Also **cordovan leather.**

cor·du·roy (kôr′ də roi′, kōr′-) ***n-*** **1** sturdy cotton fabric with a surface of velvety ridges. **2 corduroys** trousers made of this material. ***adj-***: *a* corduroy *jacket.* [probably adapted from French **corde du roi,** to mean "king's cord (corded material)."]

corduroy road ***n-*** road made of logs laid crosswise.

fāte, făt, dâre, bärn; bē, bĕt, mêre; bīte, bĭt; nōte, hŏt, môre, dòg; fŭn, fûr; to͞o, bo͝ok; oil; out; tar; thin; then; hw for wh as in *wh*at; zh for s as in us*u*al; ə for a, e, i, o, u, as in *a*go, lin*e*n, per*i*l, at*o*m, min*u*s

cord·wood (kȯrd′ wo͝od′, kôrd′-) ***n-*** cut firewood piled in a cord or sold by the cord.

core (kôr) ***n-*** **1** tough or fibrous central part that contains the seeds of certain fruits, such as apples and pears. **2** central or essential part: *the* core *of an argument.* **3** bar of soft iron or steel forming the central part of an electromagnet. ***vt-*** **[cored, cor·ing]** to remove the seeds and central part from (fruit). ***Hom-*** corps.

cor·e·op·sis (kôr′ ē ŏp′ səs) ***n-*** any of several plants related to the daisy and sunflower, often cultivated for their showy, yellow or reddish flowers.

cor·er (kôr′ ər) ***n-*** implement for removing cores from fruit.

co·ri·an·der (kôr′ ē ăn′ dər) ***n-*** plant related to the parsley and carrot, with aromatic seeds used as a spice.

Co·rin·thi·an (kə rĭn′ thē ən) ***adj-*** **1** of or relating to ancient Corinth. **2** of or belonging to an order of classical architecture having slender columns and bell-shaped capitals surrounded by acanthus leaves. ***n-*** a native or resident of Corinth.

Corinthian capital

Corinthians ***n-*** either of two epistles addressed by St. Paul to the Christians at Corinth. Each forms a book of the New Testament.

cork (kȯrk, kôrk) ***n-*** **1** the light, porous, resilient outer bark of the **cork oak,** a tree growing chiefly in Mediterranean countries. Cork is used to make bottle stoppers, rafts, life preservers, etc., and as an insulating or flooring material. **2** stopper, especially one made of this substance. **3** protective outer bark of woody plants. ***vt-*** to close or seal (a bottle, container, etc.) with a stopper. ***adj-***: *a* cork *raft.* ***—adj-*** **cork′ y [cork·i·er, cork·i·est]**: *a light,* corky *substance.*

Corkscrew

cork·er (kȯr′ kər, kôr′-) *Slang* ***n-*** remarkable or first-rate person or thing; dilly.

cork·screw (kȯrk′ skro͞o′, kȯrk′-) ***n-*** implement consisting of a pointed metal spiral with a handle, used to remove corks from bottles. ***adj-*** winding; spiral: *a* corkscrew *path.* ***vi-*** to follow a twisted, winding course.

Cormorant, about 2 1/2 ft. long

corm (kȯrm, kôrm) ***n-*** bulb-like lower part of the stem of plants such as the crocus and gladiolus, in which food is stored and from which a new plant may grow.

cor·mo·rant (kȯr′ mər ənt, kȯr′-) ***n-*** sea bird with dark feathers, webbed feet, and an elastic pouch under its bill in which it can hold fish.

[1]**corn** (kȯrn, kôrn) ***n-*** **1** widely cultivated cereal plant native to America, which produces large ears of grain on tall stalks; Indian corn; maize. **2** ears or kernels of this plant, used for food. **3** *Brit.* any food grain, especially wheat. **4** *Slang* trite, outmoded humor, sentiment, etc. ***vt-*** to preserve in spiced brine: *to* corn *beef.* [from Old English **corn** meaning "wheat; grain."]

Ear of corn

[2]**corn** (kȯrn, kôrn) ***n-*** a horny thickening of the skin, especially on a toe. [from Latin **cornu** meaning "horn." "Corn" and "horn" have a common origin.]

corn borer ***n-*** destructive moth larva that feeds on the ears and stalks of corn.

corn bread ***n-*** bread made from cornmeal.

corn·cob (kȯrn′ kŏb′, kôrn′-) ***n-*** the woody center of an ear of corn. *as* ***modifier****: a* corncob *pipe.*

corn cockle ***n-*** hairy plant with purplish-red flowers, often growing as a weed in grain fields.

corn·crib (kȯrn′ krĭb′, kôrn′-) ***n-*** bin or small building with slatted sides, in which ears of corn are stored.

Corncrib

cor·ne·a (kȯr′ nē ə, kôr′-) ***n-*** tough, transparent outer layer of tissue that covers the iris and pupil of the eye. For picture, see *eye.* ***—adj-*** **cor′ ne·al.**

corned (kȯrnd, kôrnd) ***adj-*** preserved in spiced brine: *a dinner of* corned *beef and cabbage.*

cor·ner (kȯr′ nər, kôr′-) ***n-*** **1** place or angle where two lines, sides, or edges meet: *a chair in the* corner *of the room*; *the* corner *of Elm and Pine streets.* **2** hidden or secluded place; nook: *a quiet* corner. **3** far place: *the* corners *of the earth.* **4** place or situation from which escape is difficult. **5** position of control gained by monopolizing a supply of something in order to raise the price: *to have a* corner *on wheat. as* ***modifier****: the* corner *house.* ***vt-*** **1** to drive (someone or something) into a space or situation from which escape is difficult: *The cat* cornered *the mouse.* **2** to gain control of by buying up in large quantities: *to* corner *a food supply.*

cut corners to save on expenses; economize.

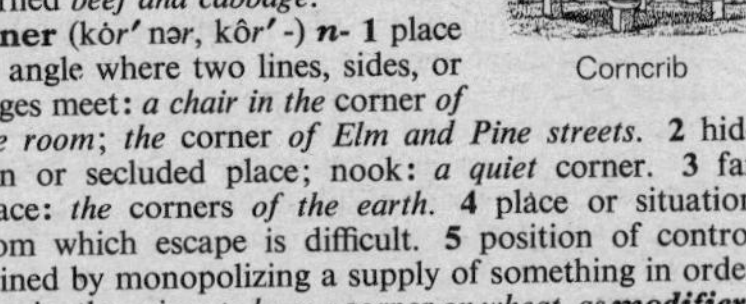

cor·nered (kȯr′ nərd, kôr′-) ***adj-*** **1** having a stated number of corners: *a three-*cornered *hat.* **2** having a stated kind of corner or corners: *a sharp-*cornered *frame.* **3** driven or hemmed into a corner: *a* cornered *animal.*

cor·ner·stone (kȯr′ nər stōn′, kȯr′-) ***n-*** **1** stone at a corner of the foundation of a building, often put in place at a special ceremony. **2** chief basis; foundation.

cor·net (kȯr nĕt′, kȯr-) ***n-*** brass musical instrument similar to a trumpet. ***—n-*** **cor·net′ ist** or **cor·net′ tist.**

Cornet

corn·field (kȯrn′ fēld′, kôrn′-) ***n-*** field in which corn is grown.

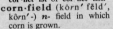

corn·flow·er (kȯrn′ flou′ ər, kȯrn′-) ***n-*** plant related to the thistle and dandelion, with bright blue, pink, or white flowers; bachelor's button.

corn·husk (kôrn′ hŭsk′, kôrn′-) ***n-*** leafy covering of an ear of corn. Also **corn shuck.**

cor·nice (kȯr′ nəs, kôr′-) ***n-*** projecting decorative strip of stone, molding, etc., at the top of a wall or column or just below the ceiling of a room.

Cor·nish (kȯr′ nĭsh, kôr′-) ***adj-*** of or relating to Cornwall or to its people. ***n-*** a Celtic language extinct since the eighteenth century.

corn·meal ***n-*** coarsely ground corn.

corn pone ***n-*** in southern United States, corn bread.

corn·stalk (kȯrn′ stȯk′, kôrn′-) ***n-*** stalk of the corn plant.

corn·starch (kȯrn′ stärch′, kôrn′-) ***n-*** very fine flour made from corn, used in making puddings and as a thickening for sauces.

Cornucopia

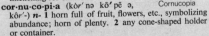

cor·nu·co·pi·a (kȯr′ nə kō′ pē ə, kôr′-) ***n-*** **1** horn full of fruit, flowers, etc., symbolizing abundance; horn of plenty. **2** any cone-shaped holder or container.

corn·y (kôr′ nē, kôr′-) *Slang adj-* **[corn·i·er, corn·i·est]** trite and outmoded; foolishly sentimental.

co·rol·la (kə rŏl′ ə) ***n-*** the inner envelope of a flower, often brightly colored, made up of the petals or a single flaring part, as in the morning-glory.

cor·ol·lar·y (kôr′ ə lĕr′ ē, kôr′-) ***n-*** [*pl.* **cor·ol·lar·ies**] statement that follows naturally from a statement which has already been proved, without requiring further proof.

Corolla

CALYX

co·ro·na (kə rō′ nə) ***n-*** **1** outer atmosphere of the sun, made up of hot gases. It is seen as a patch or circle of light around the moon during an eclipse of the sun. **2** halo of light seen around the moon, a bright light, or other shining body. ***—adj-*** **co·ro′ nal:** *a* coronal *spectrum.*

co·ro·na·graph (kə rō′ nə grăf′) ***n-*** special telescope used to study the sun's corona, in effect creating an artificial eclipse of the sun.

cor·o·nar·y (kôr′ ə nĕr′ ē, kŏr′-) ***adj-*** of or relating to the arteries or veins of the heart, especially to one of two arteries that rise from the aorta and supply blood to the heart. ***n-*** [*pl.* **cor·o·nar·ies**] coronary thrombosis.

coronary thrombosis ***n-*** a blocking by a blood clot of one of the two arteries that supply the blood to heart muscles.

cor·o·na·tion (kôr′ ə nā′ shən, kŏr′-) ***n-*** act or ceremony of crowning a king, queen, or other ruler.

cor·o·ner (kôr′ ə nər, kŏr′-) ***n-*** public officer who investigates death by unnatural or unknown causes.

cor·o·net (kôr′ ə nĕt′, kŏr′-) ***n-*** **1** small crown worn by nobles of a rank just below that of a king. **2** any band or ornament resembling this: *a* coronet *of braids.*

Coronet

Corp. **1** corporal. **2** corporation.

[1]**cor·po·ral** (kôr′ pər əl, kôr′-) ***adj-*** of the body; physical: *harsh* corporal *punishment.* [from Latin **corporalis,** from Latin **corpus** meaning "body." From this Latin word we also get "corpse" and "corps."]

[2]**cor·po·ral** (kôr′ pər əl, kôr′-) ***n-*** noncommissioned officer ranking next above private first class and next below sergeant. [from Italian **caporale** from Latin **caput** meaning "head." "[2]corporal" has no connection whatever with "[1]corporal."]

cor·po·rate (kôr′ pər ət, kôr′-) ***adj-*** **1** forming or belonging to a corporation: *the* corporate *members.* **2** of or by a group of individuals acting as a single body: *a* corporate *action*; corporate *efforts.* ***—adv-*** **cor′ po·rate·ly.** ***n-*** **cor′ po·rate·ness.**

cor·po·ra·tion (kôr′ pə rā′ shən, kôr′-) ***n-*** group of persons acting under law as one person to carry on a business, perform a public service, etc.

cor·por·e·al (kôr pôr′ ē əl, kôr-) ***adj-*** bodily; physical: *to have* corporeal *existence.* ***—adv-*** **cor·por′ e·al·ly.**

corps (kôr) ***n-*** [*pl.* **corps** (kôrs)] **1** large unit of an army, made up of two or more divisions. **2** body of troops trained for special duties: *the medical* corps. **3** group of persons working together: *the diplomatic* corps. ***Hom-*** core.

corps de ballet (kôr′ də bă lā′) ***n-*** dancers in a ballet company who do not perform as soloists. [from French, meaning literally "body (that is, permanent group) of the ballet."]

corpse (kôrps, kôrps) ***n-*** dead body, especially of a human being. ***—adj-*** **corpse′ like.**

cor·pu·lent (kôr′ pyə lənt, kôr′-) ***adj-*** having a large, stout body; fat. ***—n-*** **cor′ pu·lence.**

cor·pus·cle (kôr′ pŭs′ əl, kôr′-) ***n-*** **1** a red or white blood cell. **2** any minute particle or quantity of energy.

cor·pus de·lic·ti (kôr′ pəs də lĭk′ tī′, kôr′-) ***n-*** [*pl.* **cor·por·a·** (-pər ə) **de·lic·ti**] in law, the body of essential facts that establish whether a crime has been committed; especially, the dead body in a murder case.

cor·ral (kə răl′) ***n-*** **1** pen or enclosure for horses, cattle, or other livestock. **2** in earlier times, a circle of wagons drawn up for defense. ***vt-*** **[cor·ralled, cor·ral·ling] 1** to drive or shut (animals) into a pen. **2** to arrange (wagons) in a circle for defense. ***Hom-*** chorale.

Corral

cor·rect (kə rĕkt′) ***vt-*** **1** to remove errors from or indicate errors in; make or set right: *to* correct *a composition*; *to* correct *a watch that runs fast.* **2** to get rid of by curing or setting right: *to* correct *errors*; *to* correct *a bad habit.* ***adj-*** **1** right; exact; accurate: *Is this the* correct *answer*? **2** right according to a standard of judgment, taste, etc.: *to know* correct *manners.* ***—adv-*** **cor·rect′ ly.** ***n-*** **cor·rect′ ness.**

cor·rec·tion (kə rĕk′ shən) ***n-*** **1** a correcting or setting right. **2** a change, addition, etc., made in correcting something. **3** discipline or punishment intended to correct faults.

cor·rec·tion·al (kə rĕk′ shən əl) ***adj-*** for correction.

cor·rec·tive (kə rĕk′ tĭv) ***adj-*** tending or aiming to correct or cure faults, defects, etc.: *to offer* corrective *criticism.* ***n-*** something that corrects or tends to correct. ***—adv-*** **cor·rec′ tive·ly.** ***n-*** **cor·rec′ tive·ness.**

cor·re·late (kôr′ ə lāt′, kŏr′-) ***vt-*** **[cor·re·lat·ed, cor·re·lat·ing]** to show or establish a relationship or likeness between: *to* correlate *literature and history.* ***vi-*** have a connection or relationship with one another.

cor·re·la·tion (kôr′ ə lā′ shən, kŏr′-) ***n-*** **1** relationship or connection. **2** act or process of correlating.

cor·rel·a·tive (kə rĕl′ ə tĭv) ***adj-*** dependent upon or naturally related to something else: *The size and the weight of a stone are* correlative *qualities.* ***n-*** **1** either of two things related to each other. **2** correlative conjunction. ***—adv-*** **cor·rel′ a·tive·ly.**

correlative conjunction *Grammar* ***n-*** either word in several pairs of words used to connect two other words or phrases in the following pattern: *I saw* neither *the teacher* nor *the students. She gave Sally* both *the dress* and *the coat. He was on his way* either *to the store* or *to the bakery.* (In these examples the pairs of correlative conjunctions are: neither, nor; both, and; either, or.)

cor·re·spond (kŏr′ ə spŏnd′, kôr′-) ***vi-*** **1** to agree; match: *My answer* corresponds *with yours.* **2** to be like or similar to in position, use, character, or amount: *The wings of a bird* correspond *to the arms of a man.* **3** to exchange letters: *Do you* correspond *with her?*

cor·re·spond·ence (kŏr′ ə spŏn′ dəns, kȯr′ -) *n-* 1 agreement; likeness; close similarity: *a* correspondence *between two faces.* 2 the sending and receiving of letters; also, the letters themselves.

cor·re·spond·ent (kŏr′ ə spŏn′ dənt, kȯr′ -) *n-* 1 person with whom one exchanges letters. 2 person who writes news from a certain place for a newspaper or magazine.

cor·re·spond·ing (kŏr′ ə spŏn′ dĭng, kȯr′ -) *adj-* similar; in agreement: *statements* corresponding *in every detail.* *—adv-* **cor′ re·spond′ ing·ly.**

cor·ri·dor (kŏr′ ə dər, kȯr′ ə dər, -dȯr′) *n-* long hallway onto which rooms open: *a school* corridor.

cor·rob·o·rate (kə rŏb′ ə rāt′) *vt-* [**cor·rob·o·rat·ed, cor·rob·o·rat·ing**] to add to the certainty or reliability of; confirm: *These facts* corroborate *his account of the accident.* *—n-* **cor·rob′ o·ra′ tion.**

cor·rob·o·ra·tive (kə rŏb′ ər ə tĭv′) *adj-* serving to corroborate something. Also **cor·rob′ o·ra·to′ ry.**

cor·rode (kə rōd′) *vt-* [**cor·rod·ed, cor·rod·ing**] to eat away or destroy gradually by or as if by chemical action: *Some acids* corrode *metal.* *vi-* to be eaten away by chemical action: *Iron* corrodes *when exposed to air and water.*

cor·ro·sion (kə rō′ zhən) *n-* a corroding or eating away.

cor·ro·sive (kə rō′ sĭv, -zĭv) *adj-* 1 corroding or tending to corrode other substances. 2 bitter and cruel; cutting: *harsh,* corrosive *satire.* *n-* something that corrodes other substances. *—adv-* **cor·ro′ sive·ly.** *n-* **cor·ro′ sive·ness.**

corrosive sublimate *n-* mercuric chloride.

cor·ru·gate (kȯr′ ə gāt′, kŏr′-) *vt-* [**cor·ru·gat·ed, cor·ru·gat·ing**] to shape in wrinkles or alternate ridges and grooves. *vi-* to contract into wrinkles or folds.

corrugated paper *n-* cardboard pressed into narrow grooves and ridges, often with a layer of paper pasted over one or both surfaces, and used to make cartons, to pack merchandise, etc. Also **corrugated board.**

cor·ru·ga·tion (kȯr′ ə gā′ shən, kŏr′ -) *n-* 1 a shaping into wrinkles or regular grooves. 2 ridge or groove.

cor·rupt (kə rŭpt′) *adj-* 1 deviating from true or proper conduct; dishonest; depraved: *a* corrupt *government*; corrupt *morals.* 2 not accurate; full of errors: *a* corrupt *translation.* *vt-*: to cause to become dishonest or evil, especially by bribery or other improper influences: *to* corrupt *a witness.* *—adv-* **cor·rupt′ ly.** *n-* **cor·rupt′ ness.**

cor·rupt·i·ble (kə rŭp′ tə bəl) *adj-* likely to be corrupted; open to bribery or bad influences: *a* corruptible *witness.* *—n-* **cor·rupt′ i·bil′ i·ty.** *adv-* **cor·rupt′ i·bly.**

cor·rup·tion (kə rŭp′ shən) *n-* 1 a making, being, or becoming corrupt. 2 change that spoils or makes wrong: *a* corruption *of the original meaning.* 3 rottenness.

cor·rup·tive (kə rŭp′ tĭv) *adj-* tending or likely to corrupt: *a* corruptive *influence.* *—adv-* **cor·rup′ tive·ly.**

cor·sage (kȯr säzh′, kôr-) *n-* flower or cluster of flowers worn by a girl or woman, usually for a festive occasion.

cor·sair (kȯr′ sâr′, kôr′ -) *n-* pirate or privateer, especially one who marauded along the Barbary Coast.

[1]**corse·let** or **cors·let** (kȯrs′ lət, kôrs′ -) *n-* armor worn by a knight or soldier in earlier times; also, the breastplate of such armor. [from French, from **cor(p)s** meaning "body," related to **corpse** and **corps.**]

[2]**cor·se·let** or **cor·se·lette** (kôr′ sə lĕt′) *n-* woman's undergarment similar to a corset but less confining. [from [1]**corselet.**]

cor·set (kȯr′ sət, kôr′ -) *n-* tight-fitting undergarment extending from the thighs to the chest, worn chiefly by women to support or shape the figure. *vt-* to clothe or confine in such a garment.

cor·tege or **cor·tège** (kȯr tĕzh′, kôr-) *n-* train or procession of followers, attendants, etc.

cor·tex (kȯr′ tĕks′, kôr′ -) *n-* [*pl.* **cor·ti·ces** (-tə sēz′)] 1 the bark or rind of plants or fruits. 2 the outer layer of tissue of an organ, especially the **cerebral cortex** of the brain and the **adrenal cortex** of the adrenal glands.

cor·ti·cal (kȯr′ tĭ kəl, kôr′ -) *adj-* of or having to do with a cortex.

cor·ti·sone (kȯr′ tə sōn′, kôr′ -, -zōn′) *n-* powerful hormone secreted by the adrenal cortex and also made synthetically. It is used in the treatment of arthritis and other diseases.

co·run·dum (kə rŭn′ dəm) *n-* aluminum oxide (Al_2O_3), a hard mineral that occurs in various forms including sapphire and ruby. It is second only to diamond in hardness and is used for polishing and grinding.

cor·vette or **cor·vet** (kȯr vĕt′, kôr-) *n-* 1 in earlier times, a warship that had one tier of guns and was smaller than a frigate. 2 fast warship smaller than a destroyer. It is used chiefly to attack submarines.

co·sine (kō′ sīn′) *n-* of an acute angle in a right triangle, the ratio between the side adjacent to the angle and the hypotenuse.

cos·met·ic (kŏz mĕt′ ĭk) *n-* preparation such as lipstick or powder, used to beautify the skin, hair, etc. *adj-* intended to beautify one's appearance.

cos·mic (kŏz′ mĭk) *adj-* 1 having to do with the universe and the laws which govern it: *the* cosmic *order.* 2 in, of, or from outer space: *a patch of* cosmic *dust.* 3 vast; mighty. *—adv-* **cos′ mi·cal·ly.**

cosmic dust *n-* fine particles of solid matter in space.

cosmic rays *n-* highly penetrating radiation that reaches the earth from outer space and consists mainly of positively charged atomic nuclei.

cos·mog·o·ny (kŏz mŏg′ ə nē) *n-* [*pl.* **cos·mog·o·nies**] theory or account of the creation of the universe.

cos·mog·ra·phy (kŏz mŏg′ rə fē) *n-* [*pl.* **cos·mog·ra·phies**] the science that describes the general physical features of the universe.

cos·mol·o·gy (kŏz mŏl′ ə jē) *n-* [*pl.* **cos·mol·o·gies**] the branch of philosophy dealing with the origin and structure of the universe and the laws governing it.

cos·mo·naut (kŏz′ mə nȯt′) *n-* astronaut.

cos·mo·pol·i·tan (kŏz′ mə pŏl′ ə tən) *adj-* 1 at home anywhere; having broad interests and sympathies. 2 belonging to or characteristic of the whole world; not restricted to one region, nation, etc. *n-* well-informed, adaptable person who is at home everywhere.

cos·mo·pol·i·tan·ism (kŏz′ mə pŏl′ ə tən ĭz′ əm) *n-* condition of being cosmopolitan.

cos·mop·o·lite (kŏz mŏp′ ə līt′) *n-* a cosmopolitan.

cos·mos (kŏz′ məs) *n-* 1 the universe considered as an orderly system. 2 [*pl.* **cos·mos**] tall garden plant with variously colored flowers resembling those of the daisy.

Cos·sack (kŏs′ăk′) *n-* member of a group of frontiersmen of southern Russia, skilled in horsemanship.

cost (kȯst) *n-* 1 price charged or paid for something: *the* cost *of a purchase.* 2 expense; loss; sacrifice: *to be successful at the* cost *of one's health.* 3 **costs** the expenses of a lawsuit. *vt-* [**cost, cost·ing**] 1 to have as a price; require the expenditure of: *This book* costs *a dollar. Politeness* costs *little effort.* 2 to cause the loss of; to cause to lose: *The battle* cost *many lives.*

at all costs no matter what the cost may be.

cost (one) dear to result in a serious loss to.

cos·tal (kŏs′ təl) *adj-* having to do with or located near the ribs.

cos·ter·mon·ger (kŏs′ tər mŭng′ gər) *n-* *Brit.* peddler of fruit, vegetables, fish, etc.

cos·tive (kŏs′ tĭv) *adj-* constipated. *—adv-* **cos′ tive·ly.** *n-* **cos′ tive·ness.**

cost·ly (kȯst′lē) ***adj-*** [**cost·li·er, cost·li·est**] expensive in terms of money, time, losses, etc.: *a* costly *necklace*; *a* costly *mistake.* **—*n-* cost′li·ness.**

cost of living ***n-*** average price paid for food, housing, clothing, and other necessities by a person or family within a specific time period.

cos·tume (kŏs′to͞om′, -tyo͞om′) ***n-*** **1** clothes worn for a particular occasion, especially for a party or for performing on the stage: *a Halloween* costume; *the* costumes *for Hamlet.* **2** clothing or style of dress of a certain people or period: *Eskimo* costume; *medieval* costume. ***vt-*** [**cos·tumed, cos·tum·ing**]: *to* costume *actors.*

cos·tum·er (kŏs′to͞o′mər, -tyo͞o′mər) ***n-*** person who makes or provides costumes for actors, masquerades, etc.

co·sy (kō′zē) cozy.

¹cot (kŏt) ***n-*** narrow bed, especially one made of canvas stretched over a frame. [from Hindi **khat.**] ***Hom-*** caught.

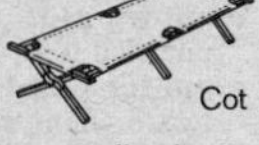
Cot

²cot (kŏt) ***n-*** **1** cottage. **2** shelter for birds or small animals; cote. [from Old English **cot.**] ***Hom-*** caught.

cote (kōt) ***n-*** coop, shed, or pen for birds or other small animals: *a dove* cote. ***Hom-*** coat.

co·ter·ie (kō′tə rē′) ***n-*** intimate group of people who share an interest; clique: *an art* coterie.

co·til·lion (kō tĭl′yən) ***n-*** **1** in earlier times, a lively social dance. **2** formal ball.

cot·tage (kŏt′ĭj) ***n-*** small house, often simple or rustic.

cottage cheese ***n-*** soft, white cheese usually made from curds of sour skim milk.

cottage pudding ***n-*** pudding resembling a plain cake, usually served warm with a sweet sauce.

cot·tag·er (kŏt′ĭ jər) ***n-*** person who lives in a cottage; especially, a rural tenant in England.

cot·ter (kŏt′ər) ***n-*** **1** (also **cotter key**) slightly tapered piece of wood or metal inserted into a slot to lock parts of a machine or other structure in place. **2** cotter pin. [of uncertain origin.]

Cotter pin

cotter pin ***n-*** double pin that is put through a hole in a shaft or bolt to hold a nut, wheel, etc., in place; cotter. It is spread at one end to keep it in the hole.

cot·ton (kŏt′ən) ***n-*** **1** a plant with soft white fibers attached to its seeds. **2** the fibers of this plant; also thread made from them. **3** cloth made from such thread. ***adj-:*** *a* cotton *shirt.* **—*adj-* cot′ton·like′.**

cotton gin ***n-*** machine for separating cotton fibers from seeds, hulls, and other material in the boll.

cot·ton·mouth (kŏt′ən mouth′) ***n-*** water moccasin; so called because the inside of its mouth is white.

cot·ton·seed (kŏt′ən sēd′) ***n-*** seed of the cotton plant.

Cotton flower and boll

cottonseed cake ***n-*** compressed mass remaining after the oil has been pressed out of cottonseeds. It is dried and ground into **cottonseed meal,** used for cattle feed and fertilizer.

cottonseed oil ***n-*** oil pressed from cottonseed and used in cooking and paints and as a lubricant.

cot·ton·tail (kŏt′ən tāl′) ***n-*** a small wild American rabbit with a fluffy, tuftlike, white tail.

cot·ton·wood (kŏt′ən wo͝od′) ***n-*** an American poplar having a fluffy, cottony tuft about the seed.

cot·ton·y (kŏt′ən ē) ***adj-*** soft, fluffy, and white, like cotton; also, covered with cottonlike down.

cot·y·le·don (kŏt′ə lē′dən) ***n-*** part of a seed containing food for the young root, stem, and first true leaves. It often appears above ground at germination as the seed leaf, and later shrivels up. **—*adj-* cot′y·le′don·ous.**

Cotyledons

couch (kouch) ***n-*** long upholstered seat; sofa. ***vt:*** to put into words; phrase: *The diplomat* couched *his request formally.*

couch·ant (kouch′ənt) ***adj-*** in heraldry, crouching, but with the head up: *a lion* couchant.

cou·gar (ko͞o′gər) ***n-*** mountain lion.

cough (kȯf) ***n-*** **1** spasmodic forcing of air from the lungs with a sharp or wheezing noise. **2** habit or illness accompanied by this: *He has a bad* cough. ***vi-:*** *The child* coughed *all night.* ***vt-:*** *to* cough *blood.*

could (ko͝od) *p.t.* of **can.** ***auxiliary verb*** **1** were able to; had the power or freedom to: *If he* could *buy them all, he would.* **2** would be able to; has the power or ability to under certain conditions: *She* could *climb the tower if they would let her.*

could·n't (ko͝od′ənt) could not.

cou·lee (ko͞o′lē) ***n-*** in the western United States, a deep gulch with sloping sides, usually the valley of a stream that is dry in summer. ***Hom-*** coolie.

cou·lomb (ko͞o′lŏm′, -lōm′) ***n-*** electrical unit equal to the electric charge carried by 6.25×10^{18} electrons.

coun·cil (koun′səl) ***n-*** **1** group of persons called together to discuss and settle problems, give advice, etc.: *a* council *of teachers.* **2** lawmaking or governing body, as of a city or town. **3** the deliberation of such a body: *to be deep in* council. ***Hom-*** counsel.

coun·cil·man (koun′səl mən) ***n-*** [*pl.* **coun·cil·men**] member of an assembly, especially of the lawmaking body of a city or town. **—*n-* *fem.* coun′cil·wom′an.**

coun·ci·lor or **coun·cil·lor** (koun′sə lər) ***n-*** member of a council. ***Hom-*** counselor.

coun·sel (koun′səl) ***n-*** **1** advice; instruction: *the* counsel *of an experienced person.* **2** lawyer or lawyers: *the* counsel *for the defense.* ***vt-*** to advise. ***Hom-*** council.

take counsel to confer; consult.

coun·se·lor or **coun·sel·lor** (koun′sə lər) ***n-*** **1** adviser: *a guidance* counselor. **2** lawyer. **3** person who supervises activities at a summer camp. ***Hom-*** councilor.

¹count (kount) ***vt-*** **1** to find the total number or amount of (a group of separate things) by adding; sum up; tally: *Please* count *your change.* **2** to say the numbers in order up to: *You should* count *ten before answering.* **3** to take into account; include: *If we* count *me, there are ten of us.* **4** to consider; judge: *I* count *myself lucky to be here.* ***vi-*** **1** to say numbers in order: *to* count *from 1 to 100.* **2** to be of value or effect: *This doesn't* count *much. Every dollar* counts. ***n-*** **1** an adding to find a total; a reckoning: *a* count *of votes.* **2** the total itself: *Should we add his vote to the* count? [from Old French **cunter,** from Latin **computare.**] **—*adj-* count′a·ble.**

count in to include: *Don't* count *me* in.

count off **1** to call out a number representing one's place in a line, beginning with number one at the front or an end. **2** to make or indicate a group of by counting: *He* counted off *a hundred books.*

fāte, făt, dâre, bärn; bē, bĕt, mêre; bīte, bĭt; nōte, hŏt, môre, dȯg; fŭn, fûr; to͞o, bo͝ok; oil; out; tar; thin; then; hw for wh as in what; zh for s as in usual; ə for a, e, i, o, u, as in ago, linen, peril, atom, minus

count on to rely on: *You can't* count on *a liar.*
count out 1 to omit; exclude: *I don't think I'd like that party.* Count *me* out. **2** to declare (a downed boxer) the loser by counting to ten.

[2]**count** (kount) ***n-*** in some European countries, a title of nobility, about the same as an English earl. [from Old French **conte,** an older form of French **comte,** from Latin **comes,** "companion of the emperor."]

count·down (kount′ doun′) ***n-*** a counting backward from some number to zero to indicate the precise time remaining before firing a rocket, guided missile, etc.

coun·te·nance (koun′ tən əns) ***n-* 1** the face: *a wrinkled* countenance. **2** expression of the face showing feeling or character: *a happy* countenance. **3** approval; encouragement: *I won't give aid or* countenance *to such a scheme.* ***vt-*** [**coun·te·nanced, coun·te·nanc·ing**] to give approval to; condone: *to* countenance *dishonesty.*

[1]**coun·ter** (koun′ tər) ***n-* 1** narrow table or flat surface at which goods are sold and money is handled. **2** small disk or other object used in games for keeping score. [from Old French **counteour,** from **counter** "to count."]

[2]**count·er** (koun′ tər) ***adv-*** in the contrary or opposite way: *to act* counter *to orders.* ***adj-*** contrary; opposing: *an idea* counter *to my own.* ***vt-*** (considered intransitive when the direct object is implied but not expressed) **1** to oppose: *to* counter *a plan.* **2** to return (a blow) with another blow. ***n-* 1** opposite; contrary: *the* counter *of my idea.* **2** in fighting, arguing, competing, etc., a stroke or thrust given in return. **3** piece of leather or other material used to stiffen the back of a shoe. [from French, from Latin **contrā,** "against."]

[3]**count·er** (koun′ tər) ***n-*** person or thing that counts. [from [1]**count.**]

counter- *prefix* **1** in the opposite direction: *to go* counter*clockwise*; counter*march.* **2** in opposition to: *a* counter*claim.* **3** so as to cancel: *to* counter*act.* **4** matching or corresponding: *a* counter*part*; counter*sign.*

coun·ter·act (koun′ tə răkt′) ***vt-*** to act against; offset the effect of. **—*n-* coun′ ter·ac′ tion.**

coun·ter·at·tack (koun′ tər ə tăk′) ***n-*** attack made to counteract an enemy attack. ***vt-*** to make such an attack: *to* counterattack *the enemy.* ***vi-***: *to* counterattack *along a broad front.*

coun·ter·bal·ance (koun′ tər băl′ əns) ***n-* 1** counterweight. **2** any power, influence, or effect that offsets another: *Religion is a* counterbalance *to fear.* ***vt-*** [**coun·ter·bal·anced, coun·ter·bal·anc·ing**]: *His cleverness* counterbalances *his strange appearance.*

coun·ter·check (koun′ tər chĕk′) ***n-* 1** something that checks or thwarts something else. **2** confirmation on a previous check to make sure; double check. ***vt-***: *to* countercheck *an enemy*; *to* countercheck *a claim.*

coun·ter·claim (koun′ tər klām′) ***n-*** claim set up by a defendant in a lawsuit to oppose the plaintiff's claim.

coun·ter·clock·wise (koun′ tər klŏk′ wīz′) ***adj-*** in the opposite direction to that in which the hands of a clock move: *a* counterclockwise *turn.* ***adv-***: *to turn* counterclockwise.

coun·ter·cur·rent (koun′ tər kûr′ ənt) ***n-*** current moving opposite to a nearby current.

coun·ter·es·pi·o·nage (koun′ ter ĕs′ pē ə näj′, -näzh′, -nĭj) ***n-*** espionage to uncover or oppose enemy espionage.

coun·ter·ex·am·ple (koun′ tər ĕg zăm′ pəl) *Mathematics* ***n-*** example which proves that a property is not true for all possible cases.

coun·ter·feit (koun′ tər fĭt) ***n-*** a copy, especially of money, made with intent to deceive or defraud. ***adj-***: *a* counterfeit *dollar bill*; *a* counterfeit *passport.* ***vt-***: *to* counterfeit *money*; *to* counterfeit *grief.*

coun·ter·in·tel·li·gence (koun′ tər ĭn′ tĕl′ ə jəns) ***n-*** activities and methods to uncover or oppose enemy spying, sabotage, etc.

coun·ter·mand (koun′ tər mănd′) ***vt-*** to issue instructions canceling or reversing (an order, plan, or the like): *The general* countermanded *the march.* ***n-*** a contrary order.

coun·ter·march (koun′ tər märch′) ***n-*** a marching back, usually along a previous line of advance. ***vi-***: *The troops* countermarched *during the night.*

coun·ter·of·fen·sive (koun′ tər ə fĕn′ sĭv) ***n-*** large-scale attack made to counter an enemy attack.

coun·ter·pane (koun′ tər pān′) ***n-*** bedspread or quilt

coun·ter·part (koun′ tər pärt′) ***n-*** person or thing that matches or corresponds closely to another: *An admiral in the navy is the* counterpart *of a general in the army.*

coun·ter·plot (koun′ tər plŏt′) ***n-*** plot or scheme intended to oppose another.

coun·ter·point (koun′ tər point′) ***n-* 1** combination of two or more related but independent melodies. **2** the melody that is added to the basic or primary melody. **3** the art of composing such an arrangement. **4** contrast or interplay of elements in a work of art, such as a drama. *as* ***modifier***: *a* counterpoint *rhythm.*

coun·ter·poise (koun′ tər poiz′) ***n-* 1** weight or force that balances or offsets another. **2** condition of balance: *two weights in* counterpoise. ***vt-*** [**coun·ter·poised, coun·ter·pois·ing**] to oppose with an equal force so as to balance; counterbalance.

coun·ter·rev·o·lu·tion (koun′ tər rĕv′ ə lōō′ shən) ***n-*** revolution opposed to the government, society, etc., established by a previous revolution.

coun·ter·rev·o·lu·tion·ar·y (koun′ tər rĕv′ ə lōō′ shən ĕr ē) ***adj-*** favoring or having to do with a counterrevolution. ***n-*** [*pl.* **coun·ter·rev·o·lu·tion·ar·ies**] person engaging in or inciting a counterrevolution.

coun·ter·shaft (koun′ tər shăft′) ***n-*** in machines, a secondary shaft between a main shaft and a working part.

coun·ter·sign (koun′ tər sīn′) ***n-*** password or secret signal: *If you give the* countersign *tonight, the guard will admit you.* ***vt-*** to add a signature to (a document already signed) to make it of value: *to* countersign *a check.*

coun·ter·sink (koun′ tər sĭngk′) ***vt-*** [**coun·ter·sank, coun·ter·sunk, coun·ter·sink·ing**] **1** to enlarge (the top of a hole) so that the head of a screw or bolt will fit flush with the surface. **2** to sink or fit (a screw, bolt, etc.) into such a hole. ***n-* 1** tool for drilling such a hole. **2** the hole itself.

coun·ter·spy (koun′ tər spī′) ***n-*** [*pl.* **coun·ter·spies**] counterespionage agent.

coun·ter·weight (koun′ tər wāt′) ***n-*** a weight used to counterbalance the weight of something, such as a window or elevator, so that it can easily be moved; counterbalance. ***vt-*** to counterbalance.

count·ess (koun′ təs) ***n-* 1** wife or widow of a count or earl. **2** woman with a rank of her own equal to that of a count or earl.

count·ing·house (koun′ tĭng hous′) *Archaic* ***n-*** building or room where business is done and accounts are kept.

count·less (kount′ ləs) ***adj-*** too many to be counted; innumerable: *the* countless *stars.*

coun·tri·fied (kŭn′ trĭ fīd′) ***adj-*** of or like country people in manners or appearance; rustic.

coun·try (kŭn′ trē) ***n-*** [*pl.* **coun·tries**] **1** state having its own government and definite boundaries and, usually, a single language and common customs; nation: *France and England are* countries. **2** the territory occupied by such a state: *The* country *of Switzerland is small.* **3** the people inhabiting such a state: *The* country *will vote* *tomorrow.* 4 place of one's birth or citizenship. 5 land and other resources of a region: *fertile* country. **6 the country** the area outside of cities or towns; rural region. *as* ***modifier***: *a* country *school not far from the city.*

country club ***n-*** club, usually private, located in the country, where one may swim, golf, etc.

coun·try·folk (kŭn′ trē fōk′) ***n-*** (takes plural verb) people who live in the country or rural areas.

coun·try·man (kŭn′ trē mən, -măn′) ***n-*** [*pl.* **coun·try·men**] **1** man who was born or lives in the same country as another; compatriot. **2** man who lives in a rural place. —***n-*** *fem.* **coun′ try·wom·an** [*pl.* **coun·try·wom·en**].

coun·try·seat (kŭn′ trē sēt′) ***n-*** mansion or estate located in the country.

coun·try·side (kŭn′ trē sīd′) ***n-*** **1** rural region or landscape: *The* countryside *glowed with color in the fall.* **2** people living in a rural district: *The whole* countryside *turned out for the celebration.*

coun·ty (koun′ tē) ***n-*** [*pl.* **coun·ties**] **1** definite political district of a country. **2** in all States of the United States except Louisiana, the largest political subdivision; also, its people. *as* ***modifier***: *a* county *official.*

county agent ***n-*** government official who provides people in rural areas with information and advice on farming and home economics.

county farm ***n-*** county-supported farm for persons who are unable to maintain and care for themselves.

county seat ***n-*** city or town at which a county government is located.

coup (kōō) ***n-*** a sudden, unexpected, and sometimes brilliantly successful, move or stroke. ***Hom-*** coo.

coup de grâce (kōō′ də gräs′) *French* [*pl.* **coups de grâce** (kōō′-)] deathblow or final stroke that puts an end to someone or something in extreme difficulty or suffering. (The literal meaning is "stroke of mercy.")

coup d'état (kōō′ dā tä′) ***n-*** [*pl.* **coups d'état** (kōō′-)] sudden overthrow of a government.

coupe (kōōp, *also* kōō pā′) ***n-*** **1** closed, two-door automobile with two wide seats for the driver and five passengers. **2** formerly, a closed, two-door automobile with one wide seat for the driver and two passengers. ***Hom-*** coop.

cou·pé (kōō pā′) ***n-*** closed, four-wheeled carriage for two with an outside driver's seat.

cou·ple (kŭp′ əl) ***n-*** **1** two things of the same kind; pair: *a* couple *of dimes.* **2** two persons of the opposite sex who are joined in some way: *a married* couple; *a dancing* couple. ***vt-*** [**cou·pled, cou·pling**] to join; connect: *to* couple *railroad cars.* ***vi-***: *The tractor and trailer* couple.

coup·ler (kŭp′ lər) ***n-*** **1** device on a keyboard instrument that links two or more keys or keyboards to be played together. **2** device that connects railroad cars; coupling. **3** transformer, resistor, or other device for transferring electrical energy from one circuit to another.

cou·plet (kŭp′ lət) ***n-*** two successive lines of verse which rhyme. Example: "Know then thyself, presume not God to scan;/The proper study of mankind is man."

cou·pling (kŭp′ lĭng) ***n-*** **1** a joining; a connection. **2** device that joins things together, especially one that joins railroad cars, one that joins pipes or hoses, or one that joins electronic circuits.

Car coupling

cou·pon (kyōō′ pŏn′, kōō′-) ***n-*** **1** ticket or part of a printed advertisement that can be exchanged for prizes, samples, etc. **2** small part of a bond that can be detached and given in to collect interest that is due.

cour·age (kûr′ ĭj) ***n-*** strength of mind and spirit that enables one to control fear when facing danger; bravery.

cou·ra·geous (kə rā′ jəs) ***adj-*** having courage; brave. —***adv-*** **cou·ra′ geous·ly.**

cour·i·er (kŏŏr′ ē ər, kûr′-) ***n-*** messenger, especially one carrying military or diplomatic material intended for quick delivery and for certain persons only.

course (kôrs) ***n-*** **1** onward motion; progress: *the* course *of history.* **2** direction; path: *the* course *of a ship*; *the* course *of a river.* **3** way of proceeding: *Your only proper* course *is to write the paper over.* **4** set of things in a series: *a* course *of X-ray treatments.* **5** lessons and classes in a certain subject: *a three-year* course *in nursing.* **6** piece of land laid out for a sport: *a golf* course; *a racing* course. **7** part of a meal served at one time: *The last* course *was dessert.* ***vi-*** [**coursed, cours·ing**] to run; flow: *The water* coursed *over the rapids.* ***Hom-*** coarse.
of course naturally; certainly.

cours·er (kôr′ sər) *Archaic* ***n-*** swift horse.

court (kôrt) ***n-*** **1** courtyard. **2** place marked and fitted for a game: *a* tennis *court.* **3** place for administering justice or holding trials; courtroom: *The witness was brought to* court. **4** judge or group of judges and officials who administer justice, hold trials, etc.: *The* court *is now in session.* **5** assembly for legal trial: *The case will be heard at the next* court. **6** official residence of a king or other sovereign. **7** attendants and retainers of a sovereign; also, the sovereign and his attendants. **8** official meeting of a sovereign and his advisers: *The king held* court *yesterday.* ***vt-*** **1** to seek the favor of: *A good politician will always* court *the voters.* **2** to woo; seek to win in marriage. **3** to try to get; seek; invite: *A good politician* courts *votes.* ***vi-*** to see each other often with the hope of marriage: *George and Mary* courted *for two years.*

cour·te·ous (kûr′ tē əs) ***adj-*** polite: *a* courteous *reply.* —***adv-*** **cour′ te·ous·ly.**

cour·te·san or **cour·te·zan** (kôr′ tə zən, kûr′-) ***n-*** a prostitute, especially at a royal court.

cour·te·sy (kûr′ tə sē) ***n-*** [*pl.* **cour·te·sies**] **1** politeness. **2** act of politeness or respect. **3** kindness or generosity: *Ice cream was given through the* courtesy *of the dairy.*

court·house (kôrt′ hous′) ***n-*** building where courts of law are held.

cour·ti·er (kôr′ tē ər) ***n-*** attendant at a royal court.

court·ly (kôrt′ lē) ***adj-*** [**court·li·er, court·li·est**] very courteous and dignified. —***n-*** **court′ li·ness.**

court-mar·tial (kôrt′ mär′ shəl) ***n-*** [*pl.* **courts-mar·tial**] court made up of military or naval personnel to try offenses against military or naval law; also, a trial by such a court. ***vt-***: *They* court-martialed *Sgt. Jones.*

Court of St. James ***n-*** royal court of Great Britain.

court plaster ***n-*** adhesive tape.

court·room (kôrt′ rōōm′) ***n-*** room where law cases are tried.

court tennis See *tennis.*

court·ship (kôrt′ shĭp′) ***n-*** a courting; wooing.

court·yard (kôrt′ yärd′) ***n-*** open place enclosed by buildings or walls; court.

cous·in (kŭz′ ən) ***n-*** son or daughter of one's aunt or uncle. ***Hom-*** cozen.

cou·ture (kōō tŏŏr′) ***n-*** art and business of designing and making fashionable clothes for women, usually to order. [from French.]

cou·tu·ri·er (ko͞o to͝or′ ē ā′, -ē ər) *n-* man who is the designer for or the owner of a firm that makes women's clothing to order. [from French.] *—n- fem.* **cou·tu·ri·ère** (ko͞o to͝or′ ē âr′).

co·va·lent bond (kō vā′ lənt) *n-* the chemical bond formed when two atoms share a pair of electrons.

cove (kōv) *n-* small bay; inlet of the sea; mouth of a creek.

cov·e·nant (kŭv′ ə nənt) *n-* solemn agreement or compact; contract. *vi-* to promise by solemn agreement (to).

cov·er (kŭv′ ər) *vt-* **1** to put or lay over: *Use this cloth to* cover *the table.* **2** to spread over: *Water slowly* covered *the basement floor.* **3** to lie or be placed over: *A lid* covers *a box.* **4** to hide: *to* cover *a mistake.* **5** to include: *That book* covers *the geography of America.* **6** to go or travel over: *We* covered *seven miles on our bicycles.* **7** to report: *The newspapers* covered *the mine disaster.* *n-* **1** something made or used to fit over something else to protect or enclose it: *a lens* cover; *a book* cover. **2** something that lies over something else; covering: *a* cover *of snow.* **3** concealment: *The bushes made good* cover *for the escaping men.* **4** blanket or quilt: *Put a* cover *on her when she falls asleep.* **5** dishes, silverware, etc., for one person at a meal.

cov·er·age (kŭv′ ər ĭj) *n-* **1** amount or extent of what is included: *good insurance* coverage. **2** a gathering and reporting of news: *TV's* coverage *of the wedding.*

cov·er·all (kŭv′ ər ȯl′) *n-* one-piece outer garment combining shirt and trousers, worn to protect the clothes.

cover charge *n-* fixed charge included in one's bill at a nightclub, restaurant, etc., usually when entertainment is furnished.

cover crop *n-* crop planted to prevent erosion through the winter and plowed under in spring to fertilize the soil.

covered wagon *n-* large wagon with a canvas top, used by pioneers traveling westward to the central and western parts of the United States; Conestoga wagon; prairie schooner.

Covered wagon

cov·er·ing (kŭv′ ər ĭng) *n-* something that covers.

cov·er·let (kŭv′ ər lət) *n-* bedspread.

cov·ert (kŭv′ ərt) *adj-* secret; hidden: *I took a* covert *glance at the note.* *n-* **1** protected place; shelter. **2** underbrush, thicket, etc., where animals may hide. *—adv-* **cov′ ert·ly.** *n-* **cov′ ert·ness.**

cov·et (kŭv′ət) *vt-* to desire eagerly (something, especially that which belongs to someone else).

cov·et·ous (kŭv′ ə təs) *adj-* desiring too greatly something that belongs to another; avaricious; greedy: *a* covetous *glance.* *—adv-* **cov′ et·ous·ly.** *n-* **cov′ et·ous·ness.**

cov·ey (kŭv′ ē) *n-* brood or flock of game birds: *a* covey *of quail*; covey *of grouse.*

¹cow (kou) *n-* **1** full-grown female bovine mammal, domesticated for its milk. **2** female moose, elephant, whale, etc. [from Old English **cu.**]

Cow, about 5 ft. high

²cow (kou) *vt-* to subdue by frightening; intimidate: *He* cowed *them with a show of strength.* [from Old Norse **kūga** having no connection whatever with **¹cow.**]

cow·ard (kou′ ərd) *n-* person who lacks courage; one who is shamefully timid.

cow·ard·ice (kou′ ər dəs) *n-* lack of courage; shameful timidity.

cow·ard·ly (kou′ ərd lē) *adj-* showing lack of courage; shamefully timid; contemptible: *a* cowardly *retreat.* *—n-* **cow′ ard·li·ness.**

cow·bell (kou′ bĕl′) *n-* small bell, often made of sheet metal, hung about a cow's neck, to indicate where she is.

cow·bird (kou′ bûrd′) *n-* small blackbird with a brown head, often seen near cattle. Cowbirds often lay their eggs in the nests of other birds.

cow·boy (kou′ boi′) *n-* in western United States and Canada, a cattle herder working mostly on horseback.

cow·catch·er (kou′ kăch′ er, -kĕch′ ər) *n-* metal framework on the front of a locomotive, for sweeping obstacles from the track.

cow·er (kou′ ər) *vi-* to crouch in fear, shame, or misery.

cow·girl (kou′ gûrl′) *n-* girl who helps herd and care for cattle on a ranch.

cow·hand (kou′ hănd′) *n-* cowboy.

cow·herd (kou′ hûrd′) *n-* person who herds or tends cattle.

cow·hide (kou′ hīd′) *n-* **1** the skin of a cow. **2** leather made by preparing such skin. *adj-*: *a* cowhide *belt.*

cowl (koul) *n-* **1** monk's hood that covers the head and shoulders; also, a long robe with a hood. **2** forward section of an automobile to which the dashboard and instrument panel are connected.

Cowl

cow·lick (kou′ lĭk′) *n-* tuft of hair growing upright, often above the forehead.

cowl·ing (kou′ lĭng) *n-* removable metal cover to streamline an airplane engine; also, a similar engine cover.

co-work·er (kō′ wûrk′ ər) *n-* fellow worker.

cow·pea (kou′ pē′) *n-* **1** widely cultivated vine closely related to the bean and producing seed pods up to two feet long. **2** the seed of this plant, eaten as a vegetable; black-eyed pea.

cow·poke (kou′ pōk′) *Slang n-* cowboy.

cow·pox (kou′ pŏks′) *n-* contagious disease of cows. Its germs are used in vaccinating people against smallpox.

cow·punch·er (kou′ pŭn′ chər) *Informal n-* cowboy.

cow·rie or **cow·ry** (kou′ rē) *n-* [*pl.* **cow·ries**] **1** the glossy, smooth, and often beautifully marked shell of any of a group of mollusks found in warm seas, especially the **money cowry,** used as money in parts of Africa and Asia. **2** the mollusk itself.

cow·slip (kou′ slĭp′) *n-* **1** marsh marigold. **2** any of various other flowering plants, especially, in England, a wild plant with fragrant yellow flowers.

cox·comb (kŏks′ kōm′) *n-* **1** the red peaked crest on a jester's hat; also, the hat itself. **2** vain, conceited, and foolish fellow; fop. **3** cockscomb.

cox·swain (kŏk′ sən) *n-* man who steers a boat, especially a racing shell.

coy (koi) *adj-* [**coy·er, coy·est**] **1** bashful; shy. **2** pretending to be shy; coquettish. *—adv-* **coy′ ly.** *n-* **coy′ ness.**

coy·ote (kī′ ōt′, kī ō′ tē) *n-* small wolf of western North America; prairie wolf. [American word from Mexican Spanish **coyote,** from Mexican Indian **koyotl.**]

Coyote, about 3 1/2 ft. long

coy·pu (koi′ po͞o′) *n-* [*pl.* **coy·pus**] a South American aquatic rodent that closely resembles the beaver and is valued for its fur; nutria.

coz (kŭz) *Informal n-* cousin.

coz·en (kŭz′ ən) *Archaic vt-* to cheat or deceive in a petty way. *Hom-* cousin. *—n-* **coz′ en·age.**

co·zy (kō′ zē) ***adj-*** **[co·zi·er, co·zi·est]** comfortable; snug: *a* cozy *corner by the fire.* ***n-*** padded cover for a teapot to keep the tea warm. Also **cosy.** ***—adv-*** **co′ zi·ly.** ***n-*** **co′ zi·ness.**

cp. compare.

c.p. candle power.

CPA or **C.P.A.** Certified Public Accountant.

Crab

cpd. compound.

Cpl. Corporal.

cps or **c.p.s.** cycles per second.

Cr symbol for chromium.

[1]**crab** (krăb) ***n-*** any of various crustaceans having a flattened body, four pairs of legs, a pair of grasping claws, and a small abdomen, or so-called tail, curled under the body. ***vi-*** **[crabbed, crab·bing]** to fish for these crustaceans. [from Old English **crabbe.**]

[2]**crab** (krăb) *Informal* ***vi-*** **[crabbed, crab·bing]** to find fault; be irritable; gripe; complain. [from [1]**crab,** probably influenced by [3]**crab** in the sense of "sour."]

[3]**crab** (krăb) ***n-*** crab apple. [of uncertain origin.]

crab apple ***n-*** **1** kind of small, sour apple. **2** thorny tree that bears this apple.

crab·bed (krăb′ əd) ***adj-*** **1** of handwriting, tiny, stiff, and hard to read. **2** crabby. ***—adv-*** **crab′ bed·ly.** ***n-*** **crab′ bed·ness.**

crab·by (krăb′ ē) *Informal* ***adj-*** **[crab·bi·er, crab·bi·est]** surly; irritable; crabbed. ***—adv-*** **crab′ bi·ly.**

crab grass ***n-*** any of several coarse grasses considered lawn pests because of their unsightly appearance and rapid growth and spread.

crack (krăk) ***n-*** **1** thin line showing a break without separation of parts: *a long* crack *in the wall.* **2** long, narrow opening between parts; crevice. **3** sharp, snapping sound: *the* crack *of a pistol.* **4** sharp blow: *a* crack *on the cheek.* ***vt-*** **1** to break or split without completely separating: *I* cracked *the cup.* **2** to cause to make a sharp, snapping sound: *He* cracked *the whip.* **3** *Chemistry* to break the molecules of (a compound, especially a petroleum compound) into simpler molecules by means of heat and, sometimes, a catalyst. ***vi-:*** *The cup* cracked *when she dropped it, but did not break. The whip* cracked *loudly.* ***adj-*** *Informal* excellent; first-rate; elite: *a* crack *company of marines.*

crack a joke to tell or make a joke.

crack up **1** to have a nervous breakdown. **2** to crash.

crack·brained (krăk′ brānd′) ***adj-*** crazy; senseless; crackpot: *a* crackbrained *scheme.*

crack·down (krăk′ doun′) ***n-*** a swift disciplinary action.

cracked (krăkt) ***adj-*** **1** broken without separation of parts: *He drank from a* cracked *glass.* **2** *Slang* crazy.

crack·er (krăk′ ər) ***n-*** **1** a dry, crisp, baked wafer made chiefly of flour and water. **2** disparaging term applied to a poor white person of the rural southeastern United States. **3** firecracker.

crack·er·jack (krăk′ ər jăk) *Informal* ***n-*** person or thing that is remarkably good; humdinger: *The skipper was a* crackerjack. ***adj-:*** *a* crackerjack *team.*

crack·ing (krăk′ ĭng) ***n-*** process for breaking (by heat, pressure, and catalysis) the large molecules of compounds containing hydrogen and carbon, such as petroleum, into the smaller, lighter molecules of substances such as gasoline. *as* ***modifier:*** *a* cracking *tower.*

crack·le (krăk′ əl) ***vi-*** **[crack·led, crack·ling]** to make repeated sharp, snapping, cracking noises: *The fire* crackled. ***n-*** **1** a repeated sharp, snapping, cracking noise. **2** finely cracked glaze of a kind of ceramic ware; also, the ware itself. **3** crackling.

crack·ling (krăk′ lĭng) ***n-*** crisp, browned skin of roast pork; crackle.

crack·ly (krăk′ lē) ***adj-*** likely to crackle; crisp.

crack·pot (krăk′ pŏt′) *Slang* ***n-*** person with wild or strange ideas. ***adj-:*** *They dismissed her* crackpot *schemes.*

crack-up (krăk′ ŭp′) ***n-*** **1** a crash; smash; collision. **2** *Informal* mental breakdown.

-cracy *combining form* government or rule by: *demo*cracy (rule by the people); *pluto*cracy (rule by the wealthy). [from Latin **-cratia,** from Greek **-krateia,** from **kratos** meaning "strength."]

cra·dle (krā′ dəl) ***n-*** **1** small bed on rockers, for a baby or doll. **2** birthplace: *the* cradle *of liberty.* **3** period of infancy: *insurance from the* cradle *to the grave.* **4** frame or jig for holding something being built or repaired. **5** curved, forklike frame attached to a scythe so that cut grain can be laid down in small bundles; also, a scythe with such an attachment. **6** in placer mining, a trough on rockers used to wash the metal-bearing earth. ***vt-*** **[cra·dled, cra·dling]** **1** to hold or keep (something) in or as if in a baby's bed on rockers. **2** to mow (grain, a field, etc.) with a cradle scythe. **3** to wash (metal-bearing earth) in a trough fitted with rockers.

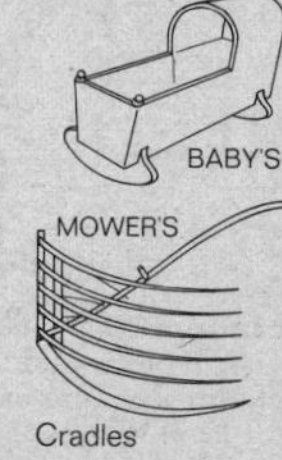

Cradles

cradle scythe ***n-*** scythe fitted with a cradle.

craft (krăft) ***n-*** **1** art or trade requiring personal skill: *the* craft *of fine printing.* **2** craftsmanship. **3** [*pl.* **craft**] boat, ship, or aircraft. **4** deceit; cunning.

crafts·man (krăfts′ mən) ***n-*** [*pl.* **crafts·men**] skilled workman, especially at a craft; artisan.

crafts·man·ship (krăfts′ mən shĭp′) ***n-*** skill in a craft; also, the quality of a product resulting from such skill.

craft·y (krăf′ tē) ***adj-*** **[craft·i·er, craft·i·est]** skillful at planning and carrying out underhanded schemes; cunning; wily; tricky. ***—adv-*** **craft′ i·ly.** ***n-*** **craft′ i·ness.**

crag (krăg) ***n-*** a steep, jagged rock. ***—adj-*** **crag′ gy.**

crake (krāk) ***n-*** any of various short-billed, long-legged European birds of the rail family, especially the **corn crake,** which frequents grain fields.

cram (krăm) ***vt-*** **[crammed, cram·ming]** **1** to stuff (something) forcibly with more than it has space for: *to* cram *a room with desks.* **2** to stuff (something) into too small a space: *to* cram *desks into the room.* ***vi-*** *Informal* to study intensively, especially at the last minute, for an examination.

[1]**cramp** (krămp) ***n-*** **1** iron bar bent at the ends, used to hold together blocks of stone, timber, or the like. **2** clamp. ***vt-*** to restrict or confine; hem in: *I don't want to* cramp *his enthusiasm.* [from early Dutch **kramp(e).**]

[2]**cramp** (krămp) ***n-*** **1** sudden, sharp, painful contraction of the muscles; muscle spasm. **2** **cramps** sharp abdominal pains. ***vi-:*** *His leg* cramped *and he was in agony.* ***vt-:*** *Fear* cramped *his stomach.* [from Old French, from early Dutch **kramp(e),** and related to [1]**cramp.**]

cram·pon (krăm′ pŏn′) ***n-*** **1** spiked iron plate strapped to boots to aid in climbing or walking on ice. **2** one of a pair of metal grappling hooks to raise heavy objects.

cran·ber·ry (krăn′ bĕr′ ē) ***n-*** [*pl.* **cran·ber·ries**] **1** a small, tart, red berry that grows in bogs. **2** the trailing vine it grows on. ***adj-:*** *We had turkey with* cranberry *sauce.*

---

fāte, făt, dâre, bärn; bē, bĕt, mêre; bīte, bĭt; nōte, hŏt, môre, dòg; fŭn, fûr; to͞o, bo͝ok; oil; out; tar; thin; then; hw for wh as in *wh*at; zh for s as in u*s*ual; ə for a, e, i, o, u, as in *a*go, lin*e*n, per*i*l, at*o*m, min*u*s

[American word from Dutch **kraanbere** and German **kranbeere,** meaning literally "crane berry."]

crane (krān) ***n-* 1** a wading bird with very long legs, a long straight bill, and a long neck. **2** machine for raising and moving heavy weights. **3** mechanical arm or support that swings on a pivot. ***vt-*** **[craned, cran·ing]** to stretch (the neck) to see better. ***vi-*:** *The crowd* craned *to see.*

Hoisting crane

Whooping crane, 5 ft. tall

cra·ni·al (krā′ nē əl) ***adj-*** belonging or relating to the skull or cranium: *the* cranial *nerves.*

cra·ni·um (krā′ nē əm) ***n-*** [*pl.* **cra·ni·ums** or **cra·ni·a** (-nē ə)] skull, especially the part enclosing the brain.

crank (krăngk) ***n-* 1** lever used to give rotary motion to some machine part and usually consisting of an arm with a handle at right angles on one end. **2** grouchy or cross person. **3** *Informal* person with odd ideas or one fixed idea: *This strange letter came from a* crank. ***vt-*** to start or operate with a rotary lever: *to* crank *an engine*; *to* crank *a windlass.*

crank·case (krăngk′ kās′) ***n-*** metal case that encloses the crankshaft of an engine and holds the lubricating oil.

crank·shaft (krăngk′ shăft′) ***n-*** shaft that is part of, drives, or is driven by a crank or cranks.

crank·y (krăng′ kē) ***adj-*** **[crank·i·er, crank·i·est]** ill-tempered; easily annoyed; surly; irritable. ***—adv-*** **crank′ i·ly.** ***n-*** **crank′ i·ness.**

cran·ny (krăn′ ē) ***n-*** [*pl.* **cran·nies**] small opening in a wall, rock, etc.; a crack; a chink. ***—adj-*** **cran′ nied.**

crape (krāp) crepe.

crap·pie (krăp′ ē) ***n-*** a fresh-water fish of North America related to the sunfish.

craps (krăps) ***n-*** (takes singular verb) game of chance played with a pair of dice.

¹crash (krăsh) ***vi-* 1** to fall down with great noise and usually with damage: *The vase* crashed *to the floor.* **2** to break one's way noisily (through something): *to* crash *through a wall.* **3** to make a loud noise like that of things falling and smashing: *The thunder* crashed. **4** to collide: *The two cars* crashed. **5** of an airplane, to smash violently into the ground, a building, etc. **6** of a business, the stock market, etc., to fail. ***vt-* 1** to break something to bits with noise and violence; smash. **2** to pilot (an airplane) in such a way as to wreck or destroy it. ***n-* 1** a smashing or shattering. **2** a sudden or loud sound, as of violent breakage: *The* crash *of an orchestra.* **3** violent smashing of an airplane into the ground or some other obstacle. **4** a collision. **5** failure of a business; also, general business and financial collapse. [from a Middle English word which probably imitates the sound.]

²crash (krăsh) ***n-*** coarse linen or cotton used for toweling, summer suits, etc. [probably a short form of Russian **krashenina** meaning "colored linen."]

crash dive ***n-*** very rapid emergency dive by a submarine.

crash-dive (krăsh′ dīv′) ***vi-*** **[crash-dived, crash-div·ing]** to make a crash dive. ***vt-*:** *They* crash-dived *the new submarine.*

crash-land (krăsh′ lănd′) ***vt-*** to land (a plane) in an emergency, usually elsewhere than at a landing field. ***vi-*:** *The little two-seater* crash-landed *on the highway.* ***—n-*** **crash′-land′ ing.**

crass (krăs) ***adj-*** stupid; insensitive; dense: *his* crass *ignorance.* ***—adv-*** **crass′ ly.** ***n-*** **crass′ ness.**

-crat *combining form* **1** supporter of a kind of government: *demo*crat (supporter of rule by the people). **2** person belonging to a group or class: *aristo*crat (member of the upper or privileged class). [from Greek **-kratēs** meaning "a ruler," from **kratos** meaning "power."]

crate (krāt) ***n-*** box or case made of wooden slats and used for shipping goods. ***vt-*** **[crat·ed, crat·ing]** to pack in such a box.

Orange crate

cra·ter (krā′ tər) ***n-* 1** bowl-shaped depression at the mouth of a volcano. **2** gaping hole in the ground, such as one made by a bomb or meteorite. **3** circular depression of uncertain origin on the surface of the moon, usually surrounded by a high uneven ridge.

Volcanic crater

cra·vat (krə văt′) ***n-*** necktie.

crave (krāv) ***vt-*** **[craved, crav·ing] 1** to want badly; long or yearn for: *to* crave *food.* **2** to ask or beg for: *to* crave *a favor.*

cra·ven (krā′ vən) ***adj-*** cowardly: *a* craven *fear.* ***n-*** contemptible coward. ***—adv-*** **cra′ ven·ly.** ***n-*** **cra′ ven·ness.**

crav·ing (krā′ vĭng) ***n-*** intense longing; strong desire.

craw (krò) ***n-* 1** the crop of a bird or insect. **2** the stomach, especially that of a lower animal.

craw·dad (krò′ dăd′) ***n-*** crayfish.

craw·fish (krò′ fĭsh′) ***n-*** crayfish. ***vi-*** *Informal* to retreat physically or verbally while pretending defiance.

crawl (kròl) ***vi-* 1** to move on hands and knees or by dragging the body along on the ground: *The baby* crawls. **2** to move or progress very slowly: *The cars* crawled *along. Time* crawled *that afternoon.* **3** to be filled or covered (with creeping, unpleasant things): *The house* crawls *with roaches.* **4** to tingle and shiver as if covered with creeping things: *Her flesh* crawled *as she looked at the centipede.* **5** to be cowed and servile: *Free men do not* crawl. ***n-* 1** slow movement or progress: *a baby's* crawl. **2** swimming stroke performed face down, with the arms raised alternately out of the water on each stroke.

cray·fish (krā′ fĭsh′) ***n-* 1** crustacean found in fresh water. It looks somewhat like a lobster, but is much smaller; crawfish; crawdad. **2** spiny lobster.

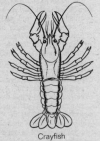

Crayfish

cray·on (krā′ ŏn) ***n-* 1** stick of wax material, colored chalk, or charcoal, shaped like a pencil and used for drawing. **2** a drawing made with such material. ***vt-*** to mark or draw (something) with one or more crayons: *to* crayon *a picture.*

craze (krāz) ***n-*** strong but passing interest; fad: *Large hats are the* craze *this year.* ***vt-*** **[crazed, craz·ing]** to make insane: *He was* crazed *by money troubles.*

cra·zy (krā′ zē) ***adj-*** **[cra·zi·er, cra·zi·est] 1** insane; mad; demented: *They acted as if they were* crazy. **2** *Informal* very fond of or excited (over); very enthusiastic (about): *I'm* crazy *about dogs.* **—*adv-*** **cra′ zi·ly.** ***n-*** **cra′ zi·ness.**

crazy bone ***n-*** funny bone.

crazy quilt ***n-*** a kind of patchwork quilt made with odd pieces of cloth sewn together without a design.

creak (krēk) ***vi-*** to make a sharp squeaking or grating sound, especially because of age or unfit condition: *That old gate* creaks *in the wind.* ***n-*** a harsh, squeaky sound. ***Hom-*** creek.

creak·y (krē′ kē) ***adj-*** **[creak·i·er, creak·i·est]** creaking; squeaky: *The door was no longer* creaky *after the hinges were oiled.*

cream (krēm) ***n-*** **1** the rich, fatty part of milk that rises to the top; hence, the best part; elite: *the* cream *of the crop; the* cream *of society.* **2** dessert or food made of this substance: *a butter* cream. **3** a yellowish-white color. **4** thick liquid preparation, often oily, for the skin: *hand* cream; *cold* cream. ***vt-*** **1** to prepare with a white sauce: *to* cream *carrots.* **2** to mix together into a paste: *to* cream *sugar and butter.*

cream·er (krē′ mər) ***n-*** **1** small pitcher for cream. **2** machine for separating cream from whole milk; separator.

cream·er·y (krē′ mə rē) ***n-*** [*pl.* **cream·er·ies**] **1** place where cream is separated from milk, and butter and cheese are made; dairy. **2** place where milk, butter, and cheese are bought and sold; dairy.

cream of tarter ***n-*** white powder used in baking and in commercial baking powder.

cream·y (krē′ mē) ***adj-*** **[cream·i·er, cream·i·est]** of, like, or full of cream. **—*n-*** **cream′ i·ness.**

crease (krēs) ***n-*** mark or line left by folding; a fold; ridge: *a* crease *in trousers.* ***vt-*** **[creased, creas·ing]** to make a fold or wrinkle in: *to* crease *trousers with an iron; to* crease *a dress.* ***vi-***: *The dress* creased *in the suitcase.*

cre·ate (krē āt′) ***vt-*** **[cre·at·ed, cre·at·ing] 1** to bring into being; cause to come into existence: *A painter* creates *art.* **2** to cause; bring about: *to* create *trouble.*

cre·a·tion (krē ā′ shən) ***n-*** **1** a creating; an originating: *The* creation *of a great poem requires inspiration and hard work.* **2** anything created or brought into being: *Shakespeare's plays are great* creations. **3** the universe, the world, and its creatures; all created things and beings: *On a beautiful morning, all* creation *seems to rejoice.* **4** the beginning of the world: *an Indian myth of* creation. **5 the Creation** the beginning of the world as described in the first book of the Bible.

cre·a·tive (krē ā′ tĭv) ***adj-*** having or showing the power to create: *a* creative *writer; the* creative *arts.* **—*adv-*** **cre·a′ tive·ly.** ***n-*** **cre·a′ tive·ness.**

cre·a·tor (krē ā′ tər) ***n-*** **1** person who creates: *Stephen Foster was the* creator *of many songs.* **2 the Creator** God.

crea·ture (krē′ chər) ***n-*** **1** any animal or human being. **2** person who is the mere tool of another.

crèche (krĕsh, krāsh) ***n-*** the Nativity represented with modeled figures as a Christmas decoration or display. **2** a foundling home. **3** a day nursery.

cre·dence (krē′ dəns) ***n-*** belief: *This rumor is not worthy of* credence.

cre·den·tials (krə dĕn′ shəlz) ***n-*** *pl.* **1** documents that prove one's identity, authority, professional status, etc.: *to present one's* credentials. **2** anything that upholds a person's claim to authority, trust, status, etc.: *He has good* credentials *as a critic.*

cred·i·ble (krĕd′ ə bəl) ***adj-*** **1** trustworthy: *a* credible *witness.* **2** believable: *a* credible *story.* **—*n-*** **cred′ i·bil′ i·ty.** ***adv-*** **cred′ i·bly.**

►Should not be confused with CREDITABLE or CREDULOUS.

cred·it (krĕd′ət) ***n-*** **1** acknowledgement of achievement, merit, etc.; recognition: *The Wright brothers get* credit *for inventing the airplane.* **2** honor; good reputation: *to be of good* credit *in the community.* **3** belief; credence: *I gave* credit *to her statements.* **4** record of satisfactory academic performance: *college* credit. **5** reputation for paying debts; financial standing: *Your* credit *must be good to open a charge account.* **6** arrangement to obtain goods and services with deferred payment; charge account: *The department store gave us* credit. **7** amount of money in a bank account or similar depository. **8** amount paid on a debt and entered on a business account: *a* credit *of $25 this month.* **9** in bookkeeping, the righthand side of an account. See also *debit.* ***vt-*** **1** to give belief to; put confidence in; trust: *Who would* credit *that ridiculous story?* **2** to ascribe (some achievement) to; attribute to: *We* credit *T. A. Edison with many inventions.* **3** to enter a financial record in favor of; give financial credit to: *to* credit *one for returned goods.* **4** to enter (a sum of money) in one's favor.

on credit without immediate, full cash payment.

cred·it·a·ble (krĕd′ ət ə bəl) ***adj-*** worthy of belief or praise. **—*n-*** **cred′ it·a·bil′ i·ty.** ***adv-*** **cred′ it·a·bly.**

►Should not be confused with CREDIBLE or CREDULOUS.

credit card ***n-*** personal card which authorizes purchases on credit.

cred·i·tor (krĕd′ ə tər) ***n-*** person to whom money is owed.

cre·do (krē′ dō, krā′-) ***n-*** [*pl.* **cre·dos**] **1** creed; set o beliefs; statement of faith. **2** (also **Credo**) the Nicene Creed or the Apostle's Creed; also, a musical setting for either.

cre·du·li·ty (krə dyōō′ lə tē, krə dōō′-) ***n-*** readiness to believe what one is told without proof.

cred·u·lous (krĕj′ ə ləs) ***adj-*** ready to believe almost anything. **—*adv-*** **cred′ u·lous·ly.** ***n-*** **cred′ u·lous·ness.**

►Should not be confused with CREDIBLE or CREDITABLE.

Cree (krē) ***n-*** [*pl.* **Crees,** also **Cree**] member of an Algonquian tribe of American Indians who formerly lived in the forests of Manitoba and Saskatchewan. ***adj-***: *the* Cree *system of writing.*

creed (krēd) ***n-*** **1** a set of beliefs or principles on any subject; credo: *a soldier's* creed. **2** a brief, summarizing statement of religious belief; credo: *the Apostle's* Creed.

creek (krēk, krĭk) ***n-*** **1** stream smaller than a river, to which it is often tributary; brook. **2** *chiefly Brit.* narrow inlet or bay. ***Hom-*** creak or crick.

Creek (krēk) ***n-*** [*pl.* **Creeks,** also **Creek**] member of a confederacy of American Indians who once ranged through Florida, Alabama, and Georgia. ***adj-***: *the* Creek *land.* ***Hom-*** creak.

creel (krēl) ***n-*** **1** wicker basket used for carrying fish. **2** wicker trap used for catching lobsters or fish.

Creel

creep (krēp) ***vi-*** **[crept** (krĕpt), **creep·ing] 1** to move with the body close to the ground; crawl: *The baby has just learned to* creep. **2** to move

fāte, făt, dâre, bärn; bē, bĕt, mêre; bīte, bĭt; nōte, hŏt, môre, dȯg; fŭn, fûr; tōō, bŏŏk; oil; out; t*a*r; thin; then; hw for wh as in *wh*at; zh for s as in u*s*ual; ə for a, e, i, o, u, as in *a*go, lin*e*n, per*i*l, at*o*m, min*u*s

slowly, imperceptibly, or carefully. **3** to grow along the ground or a surface by sending out clinging tendrils. **4** to feel as if something were crawling on one's skin, or as if one's skin were crawling itself. ***n-*** **1** a slow or imperceptible movement: *The slow* creep *of traffic.* **2 the creeps** *Informal* a sensation of fear.

creep·er (krē′ pər) ***n-*** **1** person or thing that moves slowly, or close to, or touching the ground. **2** plant, such as ivy, that grows along a surface and roots or attaches itself at intervals. **3** bird which creeps up and down tree trunks in search of insects. **4** grapnel. **5 creepers** baby's coveralls.

creep·y (krē′ pē) ***adj-*** [**creep·i·er, creep·i·est**] **1** causing a shivering sense of dread; scary: *a* creepy *house.* **2** frightened; shuddering: *a* creepy *sensation.* ***—adv-*** **creep′ i·ly.** ***n-*** **creep′ i·ness.**

cre·mate (krē′ māt′) ***vt-*** [**cre·mat·ed, cre·mat·ing**] to burn (a dead body) to ashes. ***—n-*** **cre·ma′ tion.**

cre·ma·tor·y (krē′ mə tôr′ ē) ***n-*** [*pl.* **cre·ma·tor·ies**] a furnace for cremating dead bodies; also, the establishment housing such a furnace. Also **cre′ ma·to′ ri·um.**

cre·ole (krē′ ōl′) ***adj-*** of food, cooked with a pungent sauce containing tomatoes, okra, peppers, etc.

Cre·ole (krē′ ōl′) ***n-*** **1** person of European descent, born in Latin America or the West Indies. **2** person descended from the original French settlers of Louisiana; also, the French dialect spoken by these people. **3** descendant of Spanish or Portuguese settlers along the Gulf of Mexico. ***adj-***: *a* Creole *word.*

cre·o·sol (krē′ ə sōl′, -sŏl′) ***n-*** colorless aromatic oily liquid chemical, distilled from beechwood tar.

cre·o·sote (krē′ ə sōt′) ***n-*** heavy, oily liquid with a smoky smell, obtained from coal tar or wood tar. It is used chiefly as a wood preservative.

crepe or **crêpe** (krāp) ***n-*** **1** soft, light fabric of silk, wool, cotton, or rayon, with a crinkled or wavy surface. **2** similar fabric, usually black, used as a veil, an armband, etc., to show mourning. Also **crape.**

crepe paper ***n-*** tissue paper having a crinkly surface, used for decoration, paper napkins, etc.

crept (krĕpt) *p.t. & p.p.* of **creep.**

cres. or **cresc.** crescendo.

cre·scen·do (krə shĕn′ dō) ***n-*** [*pl.* **cre·scen·dos**] a gradual increase in force or loudness, especially in music. ***adj- & adv-*** *Music* gradually growing louder.

Crescent

cres·cent (krĕs′ ənt) ***n-*** **1** figure shaped like the moon in its first or last quarter. **2** part of the moon visible at this time. ***adj-*** **1** having a shape like the first- or last-quarter moon. **2** increasing; growing in size: *the* crescent *moon.*

cre·sol (krē′ sōl, -sŏl) ***n-*** colorless, caustic, and poisonous liquid similar to carbolic acid. It is used as a disinfectant.

cress (krĕs) ***n-*** water cress.

cres·set (krĕs′ ət) ***n-*** torch or lantern in which the fuel burns in a mounted metal pot or basket.

Cres·si·da (krĕs′ ə də) ***n-*** in medieval legend, the Trojan woman who was unfaithful to her lover, Troilus.

Crest of peacock

crest (krĕst) ***n-*** **1** tuft or other growth on the top of an animal's head. **2** plume or other decoration on the top of a helmet. **3** ridge or top; summit: *the* crest *of a wave.* **4** figure at the top of a coat of arms or the figure itself used as a decoration or seal. ***vt-*** **1** to crown or top: *Green woods* crest *the hills.* **2** to reach the top of: *The climbers* crested *the final ridge.* ***vi-*** to reach the highest point: *The waves* crested *near shore.* ***—adj-*** **crest′ ed.**

crest·fall·en (krĕst′ fôl′ ən) ***adj-*** dejected; let down; discouraged. ***—adv-*** **crest′ fall′ en·ly.**

cre·ta·ceous (krĭ tā′ shəs) ***adj-*** resembling or containing chalk.

Cre·ta·ceous (krĭ tā′ shəs) ***n-*** last of the three periods of the Mesozoic era. The Cretaceous was marked by the spread of flowering plants and the extinction of dinosaurs. ***adj-***: *a* Cretaceous *limestone.*

cre·tin (krē′ tən) ***n-*** person suffering from cretinism.

cre·tin·ism (krē′ tən ĭz′ əm) ***n-*** diseased condition in which a lack of thyroid gland secretion prevents normal growth and mental development.

cre·tonne (krē′ tŏn′) ***n-*** strong cotton, linen, or rayon printed fabric, used for chairs, draperies, etc.

cre·vasse (krə văs′) ***n-*** **1** deep crack or chasm in an ice field or glacier, or in the earth after an earthquake. **2** a break in a levee.

crev·ice (krĕv′ əs) ***n-*** narrow crack or split; fissure.

[1]**crew** (kro͞o) ***n-*** **1** the persons manning a ship or aircraft, rowing a boat, etc. **2** all the men, except officers, manning a ship or aircraft: *The officers and* crew *of the submarine.* **3** group or gang or people who work together usually as a team: *a repair* crew *on a road*; *a gun* crew *on a ship.* [from Old French **accrëue** meaning "reinforcement," from a Late Latin word related to "increase."]

[2]**crew** (kro͞o) *p.t.* of [2]**crow.**

crew cut ***n-*** man's short haircut which leaves hair standing straight up like the bristles of a brush.

crib (krĭb) ***n-*** **1** small bed with enclosed sides for a child or doll. **2** rack or trough for feeding animals. **3** corncrib. **4** *Informal* unfair aid, as a key or translation, used by students. ***vi-*** [**cribbed, crib·bing**] *Informal* to use an unfair aid in a recitation or test. ***vt-*** to plagiarize; copy unethically: *He* cribbed *the essay from Addison.*

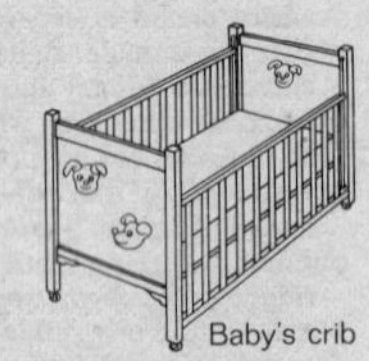
Baby's crib

crib·bage (krĭb′ ĭj) ***n-*** card game for two, three, or four players. The score is kept by means of pegs and a board.

crick (krĭk) ***n-*** painful spasm, stiffness, or cramp of the muscles, especially in the neck or back. ***vt-*** to twist so as to cause such a condition. ***Hom-*** creek.

[1]**crick·et** (krĭk′ ət) ***n-*** British outdoor game played with bats, balls, and wickets. There are eleven players on each side. ***—n-*** **crick′ et·er.** [from Old French **criquet** meaning "a bat used in a ball game," from early Dutch **kricke** meaning "crutch."]

[2]**crick·et** (krĭk′ ət) ***n-*** small, black or green hopping insect. The male makes a shrill, chirping sound by rubbing its wings together. [from Old French **criquet,** from early Dutch **krīke,** which was probably an imitation of the insect's sound.]

Cricket, about 1 in. long

[3]**crick·et** (krĭk′ ət) ***n-*** small wooden footstool. [of uncertain origin.]

cried (krīd) *p.t. & p.p.* of **cry.**

cri·er (krī ər) ***n-*** **1** an officer who publicly utters or cries announcements: *a town* crier. **2** person who cries.

cries (krīz) **1** plural of the noun **cry.** **2** form of the verb **cry** used with "he," "she," "it," or singular noun subjects, in the present tense.

crime (krīm) ***n-*** **1** an act forbidden by law, or omission of an act required by law. A crime is considered to endanger the public as a whole and not merely the individual victim. See also *felony, misdemeanor.* **2** sum of such illegal acts: *the rising rate of* crime. **3** *Informal* anything considered wrong; a shame: *It's a* crime *to sell it so cheaply. as* ***modifier***: *the* crime *rate.*

crim·i·nal (krĭm′ ə nəl) ***n-*** person guilty of crime. ***adj-*** **1** involving guilt for crime: *a* criminal *record; a* criminal *act.* **2** relating to crime: *the study of* criminal *law.* **3** *Informal* wrong; disgraceful: *His indifference is* criminal. **—*n-* crim′ i·nal′ i·ty.** ***adv-*** **crim′ i·nal·ly.**

crim·i·nol·o·gy (krĭm′ ə nŏl′ ə jē) ***n-*** social science concerned with crime and criminals.

crimp (krĭmp) ***vt-*** to press or bend into ridges, folds, or pleats; corrugate; flute. ***n-*** **1** ridge or fold made in this manner. **2** *Informal* something that hinders, delays, or inhibits: *The accident put a* crimp *in her plans.*

crimp·y (krĭm′ pē) ***adj-*** **[crimp·i·er, crimp·i·est]** crinkled; frizzly, as is hair or certain fabrics.

crim·son (krĭm′ zən) ***n-*** deep red. ***adj-***: *a* crimson *sky.* ***vi-*** to turn deep red in color: *Her face* crimsoned *with embarrassment.* ***vt-***: *Sunset* crimsons *the lake.*

cringe (krĭnj) ***vi-*** **[cringed, cring·ing]** **1** to crouch down or shrink back in fear: *The pup* cringed *at the noise.* **2** to act in a humble timid manner; abase oneself.

crin·kle (krĭng′ kəl) ***vt-*** **[crin·kled, crin·kling]** to wrinkle, crease, or crumple: *Try not to* crinkle *the paper.* ***vi-*** **1** to form fine ripples or creases. **2** to rustle; make a slight tinkling or crackling sound. ***n-*** a wrinkle. **—*adj-* crin′ kly:** *The candy was wrapped in* crinkly *paper.*

cri·noid (krī′ noid′) ***n-*** any of a group of stalked invertebrate sea animals that somewhat resemble flowers.

crin·o·line (krĭn′ ə lən) ***n-*** **1** loosely woven, stiffened fabric used to expand or stiffen clothes made with it or worn over it. **2** petticoat which makes the skirt over it stand out. **3** hoop skirt.

crip·ple (krĭp′ əl) ***n-*** person or animal handicapped by bodily injury, deformity, or the loss of a part; lame person. ***vt-*** **[crip·pled, crip·pling]** **1** to injure so as to handicap, often permanently: *The fall* crippled *him.* **2** to disable; damage: *The strike* crippled *the steel industry.*

cri·sis (krī′ səs) ***n-*** [*pl.* **cri·ses** (-sēz′)] **1** time of unusual difficulty or danger. **2** event that is a turning point; decisive moment: *Lincoln's election was a* crisis *in the struggle over slavery.* **3** turning point toward life or death in an illness.

crisp (krĭsp) ***adj-*** **[crisp·er, crisp·est]** **1** stiff, dry, and brittle: *a sandwich of* crisp *bacon and toast.* **2** fresh, firm, and crunchy: *a salad of* crisp *vegetables.* **3** brisk: *the* crisp *October air; a* crisp *manner of speaking.* **4** stiff and tight: *the child's* crisp *curls.* ***vt-***: *She* crisped *the bread in the oven.* ***vi-***: *The bread* crisped *in the oven.* **—*adv-* crisp′ ly.** ***n-*** **crisp′ ness.**

criss·cross (krĭs′ krŏs′) ***adj-*** crossed like lines of an X: *Eileen covered the paper with* crisscross *lines as she talked.* ***n-***: *A lattice is a* crisscross *of narrow slats.* ***vt-*** to mark or cover with crossing lines: *Wavy lines* crisscross *the fabric.* ***vi-***: *She* crisscrossed *over the error.*

cri·te·ri·on (krī têr′ ē ən) ***n-*** [*pl.* **cri·te·ri·a**] standard or rule by which to form a judgment; test: *A person's acts are* criteria *of his character.*

crit·ic (krĭt′ ĭk) ***n-*** **1** person who makes a reasoned judgment of the worth of anything, especially of literary, artistic, or scholarly works: *Jones is a professional art* critic. **2** person who finds fault or judges harshly; caviler; carper.

crit·i·cal (krĭt′ĭ kəl) ***adj-*** **1** inclined to find fault with or judge harshly: *Why are you so* critical *of everyone?* **2** of a critic or critics: *The book did not sell well, but received* critical *acclaim.* **3** important as a turning point; coming as a crisis; decisive: *a* critical *battle; a* critical *step in the experiment.* **—*adv-* crit′ i·cal·ly.**

critical mass ***n-*** the minimum amount or mass of fissionable material, such as uranium-235, that will sustain a chain reaction.

crit·i·cism (krĭt′ ə sĭz′ əm) ***n-*** **1** the occupation and judgments of critics: *literary* criticism. **2** a particular critical opinion or review; evaluation: *His* criticism *is in today's paper.* **3** faultfinding; disapproval; blame.

crit·i·cize (krĭt′ ə sīz′) ***vt-*** **[crit·i·cized, crit·i·ciz·ing]** **1** to make judgments on; point out the good and bad features of (something); evaluate: *It helps a music student to have an expert* criticize *his playing.* **2** to find fault with: *The candidate* criticized *his opponent.* ***vi-***: *It is a mistake to* criticize *before one understands.*

cri·tique (krĭ tēk′) ***n-*** a critical analysis; evaluation.

crit·ter (krĭt′ ər) ***n-*** *Informal* creature; living thing.

croak (krōk) ***n-*** low, harsh sound made by a frog, crow, or raven. ***vi-*** **1** to utter such a sound. **2** *Slang* to die. ***vt-*** to speak in a rasping voice: *He* croaked *a greeting.*

croak·er (krō′ kər) ***n-*** **1** any of several fishes that make grunting sounds when caught; a grunt. **2** any animal that croaks.

cro·chet (krō shā′) ***vt-*** **[cro·cheted** (krō shād′), **cro·chet·ing** (krō shā′ ĭng)**]** to make a piece of needlework by looping thread with one hooked needle.

Crocheting

crock (krŏk) ***n-*** heavy earthenware jar or pot.

crock·er·y (krŏk′ ə rē) ***n-*** earthenware.

croc·o·dile (krŏk′ ə dīl′) ***n-*** a tough-skinned, flesh-eating aquatic reptile with a long tail, a long narrow head, and a pointed snout, found in warm regions of Africa, Asia, Australia, and North America.

Nile crocodile, 16 ft. or more long

crocodile tears ***n-*** false, insincere grief. Crocodiles were thought to weep as they devoured their prey.

croc·o·dil·i·an (krŏk′ ə dĭl′ yən) ***n-*** any one of an order of reptiles **(Crocodilia)** that includes crocodiles, alligators, etc. ***adj-*** **1** belonging to the order, Crocodilia. **2** resembling, or having to do with, a crocodile.

cro·cus (krō′ kəs) ***n-*** [*pl.* **cro·cus·es** or **cro·ci** (-sī′)] one of the earliest spring-flowering plants, bearing purple, yellow, or white flowers.

Croe·sus (krē′ səs) ***n-*** a sixth-century B.C. king of Asia Minor, noted for his great wealth.

croft (krŏft) *chiefly Brit.* ***n-*** **1** small, enclosed field near a house. **2** very small tenant farm.

crois·sant (krwä sä^{n}′) *French* ***n-*** rich, flaky, crescent-shaped breakfast roll.

Cro-Mag·non (krō măg′ nən) ***n-*** member of a Stone Age people who lived in Europe about 25,000 years ago and are thought to be of the same species as modern man. ***adj-***: *a* Cro-Magnon *skull.*

crone (krōn) ***n-*** withered old woman.

cro·ny (krō′ nē) ***n-*** [*pl.* **cro·nies**] close friend or companion; chum; buddy.

crook (krŏŏk) ***n-*** **1** the bent, curved, or hooked part of anything: *the* crook *of the elbow.* **2** a stick with a bent or curved end: *shepherd's* crook. **3** *Informal* thief or swindler. ***vt-*** to bend or curve: *to* crook *a finger.* ***vi-***: *The stem of the flower* crooked *to the left.*

Crook

crook·ed (krŏŏk′ əd) ***adj-*** **1** not straight; bent; curved: *a* crooked *road*; *a* crooked *back.* **2** *Informal* not honest: *a* crooked *business.* **—*adv-* crook′ ed·ly.** ***n-*** **crook′ ed·ness.**

crook·neck (krŏŏk′ nĕk′) ***n-*** a squash.

croon (krōōn) ***vi-*** **1** to wail or moan softly; murmur. **2** to sing in a sentimental, murmuring manner. ***vt-***: *He* crooned *a song into the microphone.*

croon·er (krōōn′ ər) ***n-*** person who croons, especially a singer of popular songs in the 1920's and 1930's.

crop (krŏp) ***n-*** **1** amount of produce grown or gathered: *We had a big* crop *of potatoes this year.* **2** a lot of people or things thought of together as if they were harvested: *a* crop *of new writers.* **3** short haircut. **4** a pouch in some birds' gullets where food is made ready to be digested; craw. **5** short riding whip. ***vt-*** **[cropped, crop·ping] 1** to cut short; clip; trim: *to* crop *the tail of a horse.* **2** to cut or bite off: *The goat* cropped *the grass.* **3** to raise produce on: *He* cropped *most of his land.*
crop up to appear unexpectedly.

[1]crop·per (krŏp′ ər) ***n-*** sharecropper. [from **crop** in the meaning "to grow or harvest a crop."]

[2]crop·per (krŏp′ ər) ***n-*** bad fall. [of uncertain origin.]
come a cropper 1 to fall headlong, as from a horse. **2** to suffer a sudden disaster.

crop rotation ***n-*** system of planting a crop which enriches the soil after one or two crops that deplete it. Example: corn, then oats, then alfalfa.

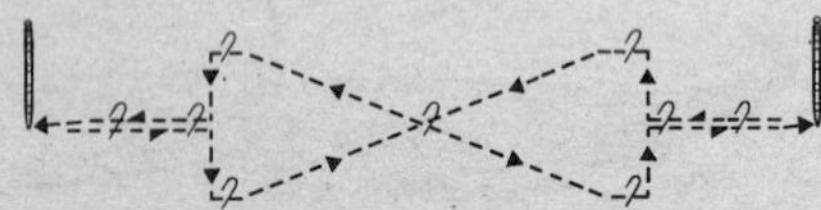
Croquet ground. Dotted lines and arrows show route.

cro·quet (krō kā′) ***n-*** lawn game in which wooden balls are driven by mallets from a starting stake through a number of low wire arches to a turning stake, and back to the starting point.

cro·quette (krō kĕt′) ***n-*** small ball of minced meat, fish, or other cooked food dipped in egg and crumbs and fried.

cro·sier or **cro·zier** (krō′ zhər) ***n-*** ornate shepherd's crook that is the symbol of office of a bishop, archbishop, or abbot.

Crosier

[1]cross (krȯs) ***n-*** **1** upright stake bearing a horizontal bar near the top, a form of which was used by the ancient Romans as an instrument of torture and execution. **2 the Cross** (1) the instrument of this type upon which Christ was crucified. (2) the Southern Cross. **3** such a figure as the symbol of Christ or of Christianity, in the form of a crucifix, a grave marker, a church decoration, etc. **4** ornament or medal in this shape, awarded as an honor or decoration: *the Navy* Cross. **5** a suffering or affliction: *He has a heavy* cross *to bear.* **6** mark (× or +) made by drawing one straight line across another. **7** such a mark used as a signature by one who cannot write. **8** mixture of breeds or varieties; hybrid: *A mule is a* cross *between a horse and a donkey.*

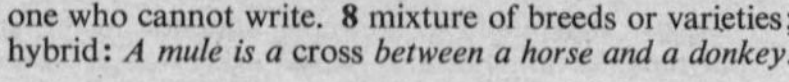

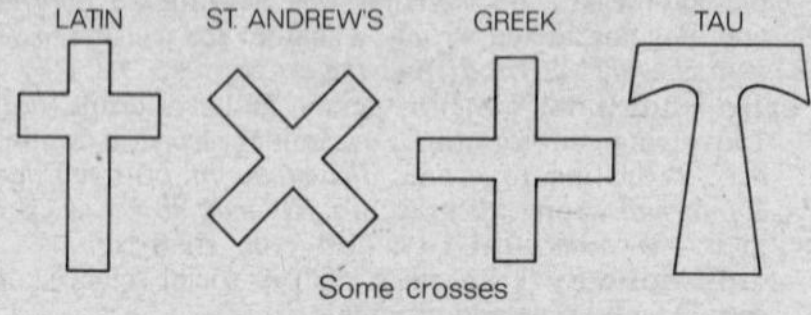
Some crosses

vt- (in senses 1, 2, and 4 considered intransitive when the direct object is implied but not expressed) **1** to go over or from one side to the other of: *A bridge* crosses *the river. Let's* cross *the street.* **2** to intersect: *Where one road* crosses *the other.* **3** to place or lay across or crosswise: *He* crossed *his legs.* **4** to pass while going in different directions: *My letter* crossed *his in the mail.* **5** to go against; oppose; contradict: *Don't* cross *him when he's angry.* **6** to crossbreed. **7** to draw a line through: *to* cross *a T.* ***vi-*** to interbreed. ***adj-*** lying or moving across; intersecting: *a* cross *street.* [from Old English **cros,** from Old Irish **cross,** from Latin **crux.**]
cross (oneself) to make the sign of the cross on oneself.
cross out to mark out or mark over; cancel.
cross up to baffle by acting contrary to expectation: *He thought I was going, but I* crossed *him* up *and stayed.*

[2]cross (krȯs) ***adj-*** **[cross·er, cross·est]** ill-tempered; peevish; grumpy; cranky. **—*adv-* cross′ ly.** ***n-*** **cross′ ness.** [from [1]**cross** in the sense of "athwart" or "contrary."]

cross·bar (krȯs′ bär′) ***n-*** a bar, line, or stripe going crosswise: *a* crossbar *on a hurdle.*

cross·beam (krȯs′ bēm′) ***n-*** **1** large beam that crosses from one wall to another. **2** any beam that crosses another.

cross·bones (krȯs′ bōnz′) See *skull and crossbones.*

cross·bow (krȯs′ bō′) ***n-*** a weapon of the Middle Ages consisting of a bow across a wooden stock with a groove to guide a heavy dart. **—*n-* cross′ bow′man.**

Crossbow

cross·breed (krȯs′ brēd′) ***vt-*** **[cross·bred** (-brĕd′), **cross·breed·ing]** to breed (plants or animals of different varieties or species) in order to obtain a stronger or otherwise more useful hybrid.

cross-country (krȯs′ kŭn′ trē) ***adj-*** **1** going across the countryside without regard to roads or trails or to obstacles: *a* cross-country *race.* **2** from one side of a country to the other: *a* cross-country *airplane trip.* ***adv-***: *They dashed* cross-country.

cross·cut (krȯs′ kŭt′) ***n-*** **1** direct route from one main route to another. **2** a mine tunnel branching from a main shaft or tunnel into the ore vein, or to another tunnel.

crosscut saw ***n-*** **1** carpenter's handsaw with teeth shaped and set for cutting across the grain. **2** two-man lumberman's saw.

cross-ex·am·ine (krȯs′ ĕg zăm′ ən) ***vt-*** **[cross-ex·am·ined, cross-ex·am·in·ing] 1** to question (a witness in a legal procedure) further and on behalf of the other side of the case in order to clarify or challenge his previous testimony. **2** to submit (someone) to close questioning from various persons or various points of view. **—*n-* cross′- ex·am′ i·na′ tion. —*n-* cross′ -ex·am′ in·er.**

cross-eyed (krȯs′ īd′) ***adj-*** having one or both eyes turned toward the nose.

cross-fer·ti·li·za·tion (krŏs′ fûr′tə lə zā′shən) *Biology* ***n-*** 1 fertilization of an organism by the union of a male and a female gamete. 2 cross-pollination.

cross-grained (krŏs′ grānd′) ***adj-*** 1 with diagonal or irregular grain or fiber. 2 contrary; perverse.

cross-hatch (krŏs′ hăch′) ***vt-*** to mark with straight parallel lines in one direction and cross them with lines in another direction, forming a closely checkered pattern.

cross·ing (krŏs′ĭng) ***n-*** 1 place where lines, paths, courses, rights of way, etc., intersect, especially where a street crosses a railroad. 2 place where a street, river, or railroad may be crossed. 3 a trip across a body of water, especially an ocean. 4 a crossbreeding.

cross·o·ver (krŏs′ō′vər) ***n-*** 1 place or passage for crossing from one side or level to another; especially, a short track for switching trains from one track to another. 2 (also **crossover network**) in electricity, a circuit, as in a radio or phonograph, that separates the higher and lower frequencies and feeds them into different speakers.

cross·patch (krŏs′păch′) *Informal* ***n-*** cranky person; grouch.

cross·piece (krŏs′pēs′) ***n-*** horizontal bar, beam, etc., crossing or connecting parts of a structure; crossbar.

cross-pol·li·na·tion (krŏs′pŏl′ə nā′shən) ***n-*** the fertilization of one plant by pollen from another.

cross-pur·pos·es (krŏs′pûr′pə səz) **at cross-purposes** against one another through misunderstanding.

cross-ques·tion (krŏs′kwĕs′chən) ***vt-*** to question closely and repeatedly; cross-examine.

cross reference ***n-*** note or statement in one part of a book directing the reader to another part.

cross·road (krŏs′rōd′) ***n-*** 1 road that crosses a main road, or runs from one main road to another. 2 **crossroads** (1) place, usually in the country, where two or more roads cross each other. (2) point at which an important decision must be made.

cross section ***n-*** 1 surface produced by slicing something at right angles to its length. 2 view or drawing made to represent such a real or theoretical surface: *a* cross section *of the airplane.* 3 group of people or things representative or typical of a larger group; a sampling.

Cross section

cross-stitch (krŏs′stĭch′) ***n-*** an X-shaped embroidery stitch. ***vt-:*** *The tailor* cross-stitched *the shirt.*

cross·trees (krŏs′trēz′) ***n-*** *pl.* short pieces of timber set crosswise at the tops of masts, to support the rigging.

cross·walk (krŏs′wŏk′) ***n-*** path marked out on a street or road to show pedestrians where to cross.

cross·way (krŏs′wā) ***n-*** place where two or more roads cross each other; crossroad. Also **cross′ways′**.

cross·wise (krŏs′wīz′) ***adj-*** 1 from side to side; across. 2 one crossing another: *The logs of a cabin are laid* crosswise *at the corners.* Also **cross′ways′**.

cross·word puzzle (krŏs′wûrd′) ***n-*** puzzle in which clues are given for words to be written in a diagram of small numbered squares. The words intersect each other, some reading down and others reading across.

crotch (krŏch) ***n-*** point of separation into parts, branches, or legs; fork.

Crotch

crotch·et (krŏch′ət) ***n-*** 1 whim or fancy; eccentricity. 2 kind of small hook or hook-like instrument.

crotch·et·y (krŏch′ə tē) ***adj-*** full of odd whims or fancies; eccentric.

Cro·ton bug (krō′tən) ***n-*** small, light brown cockroach common in the eastern United States.

crouch (krouch) ***vi-*** 1 to stoop or bend low, as if ready to spring. 2 to cringe, as if in fear. ***n-:*** *The leopard went into a* crouch, *ready to attack.*

[1]**croup** (kro͞op) ***n-*** kind of laryngitis marked by harsh coughing, hoarseness, and difficult noisy breathing. [of unknown origin.] *—**adj-*** **croup′y.**

[2]**croup** (kro͞op) ***n-*** rump of a horse. [from Old French **croupe,** probably from an early Germanic language.]

crou·ton (kro͞o′tŏn′) ***n-*** small toasted or fried cube of bread, eaten in soups and salads.

[1]**crow** (krō) ***n-*** 1 large black bird with a harsh voice. 2 a rook, raven, or other bird closely related to the crow. 3 crowbar. [from Old English **crawe.**]

as the crow flies in a direct cross-country course.

eat crow to humiliate oneself by having to withdraw a statement; back down.

[2]**crow** (krō) ***vi-*** [*p.t.* sometimes in sense 1, **crew** (kro͞o); otherwise **crowed**] 1 to make the shrill cry of a rooster. 2 to boast in triumph: *to* crow *over a victory.* 3 to utter a joyous cry, as a baby does. ***n-:*** *the rooster's* crow; *the baby's* crow *of joy.* [from Old English **crāwan** meaning "to crow like a cock," related to [1]**crow.**]

Crow (krō) ***n-*** [*pl.* **Crows,** also **Crow**] member of a Siouan Indian tribe which formerly lived near the Yellowstone River. ***adj-:*** *a* Crow *encampment.*

crow·bar (krō′bär′) ***n-*** long, straight iron bar, pointed or wedge-shaped at the working end and used as a lever; pinch bar. See also *wrecking bar.*

crowd (kroud) ***n-*** 1 number of persons or things collected closely together. 2 people in general; the masses. 3 set; clique: *the college* crowd. ***vt-*** 1 to fill by thronging or massing together: *People* crowded *the beaches. He* crowded *the showcase with toys.* 2 to press into a small space; cram (into): *He* crowded *the toys into the showcase.* ***vi-*** to gather together; press: *to* crowd *into a room.*

crow·foot (krō′fo͝ot′) ***n-*** any of a large family of plants, including the buttercups, anemones, columbines, etc.

crown (kroun) ***n-*** 1 headdress of gold and jewels, worn by kings or queens on ceremonial occasions. 2 the monarch himself, or his power. 3 anything likened to a king's headdress, such as a wreath for the head. 4 the top part: *the* crown *of a hill; the* crown *of the head.* 5 the exposed part of a tooth; also, an artificial replacement for it. For picture, see *tooth.* 6 completion; perfection: *Wisdom is the* crown *of age.* 7 a former British coin. 8 the heavy end of the shank of an anchor. 9 **the Crown** the government of Great Britain or of another constitutional monarchy. ***vt-*** 1 to put a royal headdress upon the head of; hence, to invest with regal power; reward; honor. 2 to be the topmost part of: *A dome* crowns *the building.* 3 to complete: *Success* crowns *a career.* 4 to put an artificial top on (a tooth). 5 *Informal* to hit on the head.

Crown

Crown Colony ***n-*** colony in the British Commonwealth over which the Crown keeps some control, usually through an appointed governor.

crown prince ***n-*** the first or immediate male heir to the throne.

crown princess ***n-*** 1 woman or girl who is next in succession to a throne. 2 wife of a crown prince.

crow's feet ***n-*** wrinkles near the outer corners of the eyes resembling the imprint of a crow's foot.
crow's·nest (krōz′ nĕst′) ***n-*** platform or box high on the mast of a ship, where a lookout is stationed.
cro·zier (krō′ zhər) crosier.
cru·cial (krōō′ shəl) ***adj-*** important because it marks a turning point: *a* crucial *battle.* **—*adv-* cru′ cial·ly.**
cru·ci·ble (krōō′ sə bəl) ***n-*** pot or other vessel, usually of earthenware, in which metals and ores are melted for refining at great heat.

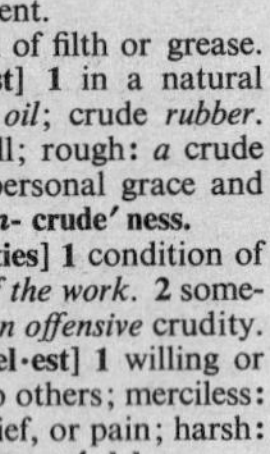
Crucible

cru·ci·fix (krōō′ sə fĭks′) ***n-*** figure of Christ on the cross.
cru·ci·fix·ion (krōō′ sə fĭk′ shən) ***n-*** **1** a crucifying or being crucified. **2** extreme persecution. **3 the Crucifixion** the execution of Christ on the cross.
cru·ci·form (krōō′ sə fôrm′, -fôrm′) ***adj-*** cross-shaped.
cru·ci·fy (krōō′ sə fī′) ***vt-*** **[cru·ci·fied, cru·ci·fy·ing] 1** to put (a person) to death by nailing or binding the hands and feet to a cross. **2** to torture; torment.
crud (krŭd) ***n-*** deposit or encrustation of filth or grease.
crude (krōōd) ***adj-*** **[crud·er, crud·est] 1** in a natural state; unrefined: *a barrel of* crude *oil;* crude *rubber.* **2** done or made without special skill; rough: *a* crude *drawing; a* crude *effort.* **3** lacking personal grace and refinement; rude. **—*adv-* crude′ ly. *n-* crude′ ness.**
cru·di·ty (krōō′ də tē) ***n-*** [*pl.* **cru·di·ties**] **1** condition of being crude; crudeness: *the* crudity *of the work.* **2** something that is crude: *His remark was an offensive* crudity.
cru·el (krōō′ əl) ***adj-*** **[cru·el·er, cru·el·est] 1** willing or inclined to cause suffering and pain to others; merciless: *a* cruel *tyrant.* **2** causing suffering, grief, or pain; harsh: *a* cruel *disease; a* cruel *winter.* **—*adv-* cru′ el·ly.**
cru·el·ty (krōō′ əl tē) ***n-*** [*pl.* **cru·el·ties**] **1** willingness or inclination to cause pain and suffering: *a streak of* cruelty *in his nature.* **2** cruel act or acts: *Torture is a* cruelty.
cru·et (krōō′ ət) ***n-*** small glass bottle for vinegar, oil, etc.

Cruet

cruise (krōōz) ***vi-*** **[cruised, cruis·ing] 1** to sail or move about unhurriedly, often without special destination: *The police car* cruised *through the park.* **2** to travel at cruising speed. ***vt-:*** *The pirates* cruised *the China Sea.* ***n-*** a sea voyage, especially a pleasure trip. ***Hom-*** cruse.
cruis·er (krōō′ zər) ***n-*** **1** fast warship smaller than and less heavily armed than a battleship. **2** powerboat with a cabin equipped for cooking, sleeping, etc.
cruising speed ***n-*** rate of travel below maximum speed, which an airplane, boat, etc., can safely maintain for long periods.
crul·ler (krŭl′ ər, krōl′-) ***n-*** small, sweetened cake made of twisted strips and fried in deep fat.
crumb (krŭm) ***n-*** **1** tiny piece of bread, cake, etc. **2** a bit; scrap; fragment: *mere* crumbs *of knowledge.*
crum·ble (krŭm′ bəl) ***vt-*** **[crum·bled, crum·bling]** to break into small pieces: *He* crumbled *bread to feed to the birds.* ***vi-*** to fall to pieces: *The general's hopes* crumbled *as his soldiers retreated.*
crum·bly (krŭm′ blē) ***adj-*** **[crum·bli·er, crum·bli·est]** apt to crumble: *The cake was too* crumbly *to slice.*
crum·pet (krŭm′ pət) ***n-*** small, round, unsweetened cake baked on a griddle and served toasted and buttered.
crum·ple (krŭm′ pəl) ***vt-*** **[crum·pled, crum·pling]** to press or crush (something), making irregular creases or wrinkles in it: *to* crumple *a sheet of paper.* ***vi-:*** *The clothes* crumpled *in the suitcase.*
crunch (krŭnch) ***n-*** a noisy chewing or grinding; also, the sound this produces. ***vt-*** to chew, grind, or crush noisily: *to* crunch *celery.* ***vi-:*** *The gravel* crunched *under our feet.* **—*adj-* crunch′y [crunch·i·er, crunch·i·est]:** *dry,* crunchy *snow.*
crup·per (krŭp′ ər, krōōp′-) ***n-*** in a harness, the leather loop passing under a horse's tail.
cru·sade (krōō sād′) ***n-*** any campaign for reform or improvement: *a* crusade *against crime; a* crusade *for women's rights.* ***vi-*** **[cru·sad·ed, cru·sad·ing]:** *He* crusaded *for better housing.* **—*n-* cru·sad′ er.**
Cru·sade (krōō sād′) ***n-*** any of the holy wars or expeditions undertaken by Christians during the Middle Ages to recover the Holy Land from the Muslims. **—*n-* Cru·sad′ er.**
cruse (krōōz, krōōs) ***n-*** small vessel, such as a jar or bottle, for holding oil, water, etc. ***Hom-*** cruise.
crush (krŭsh) ***vt-*** **1** to press out of shape; crumple; squash: *The car* crushed *the ball.* **2** to break into small or very fine pieces: *to* crush *ice; to* crush *rocks.* **3** to destroy; subdue; overwhelm: *The ruler* crushed *the rebellion. Losing the job* crushed *his spirit.* **4** to press close; squeeze: *The running mob* crushed *her against the wall.* ***vi-:*** *A linen dress* crushes *easily.* ***n-*** **1** dense crowd: *a great* crush *of people.* **2** great pressure or squeezing. **3** fruit-flavored soft drink. **4** an infatuation, usually brief. **—*n-* crush′ er:** *a rock* crusher.
crust (krŭst) ***n-*** **1** hard outer layer of bread, or of rolls, biscuits, etc. **2** a piece of this or of stale bread. **3** the pastry forming the outside of a pie. **4** any similar hard outer layer: *An icy* crust *formed on the snow. We live on the* crust *of the earth.* **5** *Slang* impudence. ***vt-:*** *Freezing rain* crusted *the snow.* ***vi-:*** *The cold gravy* crusted *over.*
crus·ta·cean (krə stā′ shən) ***n-*** any of a class of tough-shelled animals **(Crustacea)**, most of which live in water, such as crabs, lobsters, shrimps, etc.
crust·y (krŭs′ tē) ***adj-*** **[crust·i·er, crust·i·est] 1** having or resembling a crust. **2** surly; snappish. **—*adv-* crust′ i·ly. *n-* crust′ i·ness.**
crutch (krŭch) ***n-*** **1** wooden or metal staff usually fitting under the armpit and used by lame or injured persons in walking. **2** anything that serves as a mental or emotional support or partial remedy: *Eating is a* crutch *to him during his unhappy periods.*

Crutches

crux (krŭks) ***n-*** **1** the important point on which something depends; the pivotal point. **2** hard point to settle; difficult problem.
cry (krī) ***vi-*** **[cried, cry·ing] 1** to shout or call loudly: *to* cry *out in pain; to* cry *for help.* **2** to weep; shed tears. **3** of an animal or bird, to call loudly. ***vt-*** to announce publicly: *The peddler* cries *his wares.* ***n-*** [*pl.* **cries**] **1** loud or passionate utterance, as of joy, fear, anger, pain, etc. **2** outcry; clamor; demand: *a* cry *for vengeance.* **3** a calling out: *the watchman's* cry. **4** the characteristic call of an animal or bird. **5** fit of weeping. **6** rallying call; slogan: *a battle* cry.
far cry a long way: *This is a* far cry *from what we expected.* **in full cry** in full pursuit, as with a pack of hounds.
cry down 1 to belittle. **2** to silence by outshouting.
cry up to praise highly; extol.
cry·ba·by (krī′ bā′ bē) ***n-*** [*pl.* **cry·ba·bies**] child who cries a great deal, often for no good reason.
cry·ing (krī′ ĭng) ***adj-*** requiring immediate remedy: *a* crying *shame; a* crying *need.*

cry·o·gen·ics (krī'ə jĕn'ĭks) ***n-*** (takes singular verb) branch of physics having to do with very cold materials or processes (usually near absolute zero). ***—adj-*** **cry'o·gen'ic.**

crypt (krĭpt) ***n-*** underground vault, especially one under a church. Crypts are often used for tombs.

cryp·tic (krĭp'tĭk) ***adj-*** puzzling; mysterious. ***—adv-*** **cryp'ti·cal·ly:** *to speak* cryptically.

cryp·to·gram (krĭp'tə grăm') ***n-*** message in a secret code or cipher.

cryp·to·graph (krĭp'tə grăf') ***n-*** **1** cryptogram. **2** device for putting writing into code or cipher.

cryp·tog·ra·phy (krĭp tŏg'rə fē) ***n-*** science and use of codes and ciphers. ***—n-*** **cryp·tog'ra·pher.**

crys·tal (krĭs'təl) ***n-*** **1** clear, transparent type of quartz; rock crystal. **2** jewel or other ornament cut from this quartz or from fine glass. **3** very fine glass containing lead to increase its brilliance; also tableware made from this glass. **4** transparent cover of a watch dial. **5** *Physics* solid object having flat sides and a symmetrical form due to the arrangement of its atoms and molecules. **6** in electricity, thin piece of crystalline mineral that exhibits the piezoelectric effect. ***adj-*** **1** made of quartz or very fine glass. **2** resembling very fine glass, especially in clarity; transparent.

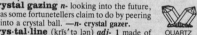

SNOW

SUGAR

QUARTZ

Crystals

crystal gazing ***n-*** looking into the future, as some fortunetellers claim to do by peering into a crystal ball. ***—n-*** **crystal gazer.**

crys·tal·line (krĭs'tə lən) ***adj-*** **1** made of crystals: *a* crystalline *rock.* **2** having the structure of a crystal. **3** resembling crystal, especially in clarity; transparent: *his* crystalline *prose.*

crystalline lens ***n-*** the small, clear lens of the eye, located behind the iris.

crys·tal·lize (krĭs'tə līz') ***vt-*** **[crys·tal·lized, crys·tal·liz·ing]** **1** to cause to form grains or become crystalline: *Low temperature* crystallizes *water.* **2** to give a fixed shape to: *He* crystallized *his plans.* ***vi-:*** *The sugar* crystallized. ***—n-*** **crys'tal·li·za'tion.**

crys·tal·log·ra·phy (krĭs'tə lŏg'rə fē) ***n-*** the branch of physics that studies the geometric forms, internal structure, and other properties of crystals.

Cs symbol for cesium.

C.S.A. Confederate States of America.

CST or **C.S.T.** Central Standard Time.

cu. cubic.

Cu symbol for copper.

cub (kŭb) ***n-*** **1** young of the fox, bear, lion, etc. **2** beginner; apprentice. ***as modifier:*** *a* cub *reporter.*

cub·by·hole (kŭb'ē hōl') ***n-*** small enclosed space: *He has a* cubbyhole *in his desk.* Also **cub'by** **[*pl.* cub·bies]**.

cube (kyo͞ob) ***n-*** **1** solid body with six square faces. **2** any block having six sides: *ice* cube; *sugar* cube. **3** *Mathematics* the product that results when a number is used three times as a factor. The cube of 3 is 27 (3 × 3 × 3 = 27). ***vt.*** **[cubed, cub·ing]** **1** to form into blocks: *to* cube *potatoes.* **2** *Mathematics* to use a number three times as a factor.

cube root ***n-*** a number that when used three times as a factor produces a given number. For example, 3 is the cube root of 27 (3 × 3 × 3 = 27).

cubic (kyo͞o'bĭk) ***adj-*** **1** (also **cu'bi·cal**) having the form of a cube. **2** of units of volume, having three dimensions: *a* cubic *foot.* **3** containing or having to do with the cube of a number: *a* cubic *equation.*

cubic foot ***n-*** unit of volume equal to that of a cube one foot long, one foot wide, and one foot deep.

cubic inch ***n-*** unit of volume equal to that of a cube one inch long, one inch wide, and one inch deep.

cu·bi·cle (kyo͞o'bĭ kəl) ***n-*** very small room or walled off area: a *telephone* cubicle; *a voter's* cubicle.

cubic measure ***n-*** system for measuring volume in three-dimensional units such as cubic inches or feet.

cub·ism (kyo͞o'bĭz'əm) ***n-*** style of modern art that portrays the subject matter in geometric forms, rather than realistically, and often from several angles at once.

cu·bit (kyo͞o'bĭt) ***n-*** **1** unit of length used by the ancient Egyptians, Hebrews, Romans, etc., based on the distance from the elbow to the tip of the middle finger. **2** in English measure, eighteen inches.

cub scout ***n-*** member of the junior division of the Boy Scouts.

cuck·oo (ko͞o'ko͞o', ko͞o'-) ***n-*** **[*pl.* cuck·oos]** **1** gray European bird having a characteristic two-noted call that sounds like its name. It lays its eggs in the nests of other birds and abandons them to be hatched there. **2** American bird having a similar call. ***adj-*** *Slang* crazy.

Cuckoo, about 12 in. long

cu. cm. cubic centimeter or cubic centimeters.

cu·cum·ber (kyo͞o'kŭm'bər) ***n-*** long, fleshy vegetable with a green rind, used in salads and for making pickles; also, the vine it grows on.

cud (kŭd) ***n-*** among ruminants such as cows, unchewed food which is brought back into the mouth from the first stomach to be chewed at leisure.

cud·dle (kŭd'əl) ***vt-*** **[cud·dled, cud·dling]** to hold close and tenderly: *to* cuddle *a baby.* ***vi-*** to lie close together; nestle. ***n-*** a close embrace; a hug.

cud·dly (kŭd'lē) ***adj-*** **[cud·dli·er, cud·dli·est]** **1** tending to cuddle or enjoy cuddling: *a* cuddly *child.* **2** pleasant to cuddle: *a* cuddly *pup.* Also **cud'dle·some** (-əl səm).

cudg·el (kŭj'əl) ***n-*** short thick stick used as a weapon; club. ***vt-*** to hit with a club.

[1]cue (kyo͞o) ***n-*** **1** on the stage, a word or an action that indicates the time for the next actor or actress to speak, act, or enter. **2** signal; hint: *That's my* cue *to leave.* ***vt-*** **[cued, cu·ing]:** *The prompter* cued *the actor.* [probably the spelling of the letter "q," the first letter of a Latin word **quando** meaning "when." This Latin word was often used in stage directions.] ***Hom-*** queue.

[2]cue (kyo͞o) ***n-*** **1** long tapering stick used to strike the ball in playing pool or billiards. **2** queue. ***vt-*** **[cued, cu·ing]** to strike (a pool or billiard ball) with a long, tapering stick. ***vi-*** to form a line; queue. [from French **queue,** from earlier **coue** meaning "tail," from Latin **cauda** also meaning "tail."] ***Hom-*** queue.

[1]cuff (kŭf) ***n-*** **1** the part of a glove or sleeve, or any wide band, covering the wrist. **2** the hem or fold of cloth on the bottom of a trouser leg. **3** handcuff. ***vt-:*** *The tailor* cuffed *the sleeves with white linen.* [from earlier English **coffe** meaning "glove," of uncertain origin.]

off the cuff *Slang* with little preparation; extemporaneously. **on the cuff** *Slang* on credit.

[2]cuff (kŭf) ***vt-*** to hit with the open hand; slap. ***n-*** a slap. [probably of Scandinavian origin.]

cuff·links (kŭf'lĭngks') ***n-*** *pl.* fastenings for shirt cuffs.

cu. ft. cubic foot or cubic feet.

cu. in. cubic inch or cubic inches.

cui·rass (kwĭ răs′, kyōō-) ***n-*** **1** piece of armor covering the body from neck to waist. **2** breastplate.

cui·sine (kwĭ zēn′) ***n-*** **1** style of cooking; cookery: *the* cuisine *of north Italy.* **2** kitchen, as of a hotel.

cul-de-sac (kŭl′ də săk′) ***n-*** [*pl.* **culs-de-sac** or **cul-de-sacs**] a blind alley; a passage with an opening only at one end; hence, a trap. [from French, meaning literally "bottom of the sack."]

cu·lex (kyōō′ lĕks′) ***n-*** [**cu·li·ces** (-lə sēz′)] mosquito belonging to a large genus (**Culex**) that includes the common house mosquito of Europe and North America.

cu·li·nar·y (kŭl′ ə nĕr′ ē, kyōō′ lə-) ***adj-*** having to do with the kitchen or with cooking: *his* culinary *talents.*

cull (kŭl) ***vt-*** to pick out; select and gather: *The draft* culled *the best of our youth. She* culled *out the bad peaches.* ***n-*** something picked out as inferior.

culm (kŭlm) ***n-*** the jointed, usually hollow, stem of a grass or sedge.

cul·mi·nate (kŭl′ mə nāt′) ***vi-*** [**cul·mi·nat·ed, cul·mi·nat·ing**] **1** to reach the highest point; end at the top (in): *The tower* culminated *in a cupola. His career* culminated *in the presidency.* **2** to come to a climax or turning point (in): *The dispute* culminated *in war.* **—*n-* cul′ mi·na′ tion.**

cu·lotte (kyōō lŏt′, kōō-) ***n-*** (often **culottes**) garment for women, like trousers but designed to resemble a skirt. *as* ***modifier****: a* culotte *dress.*

cul·pa·ble (kŭl′ pə bəl) ***adj-*** deserving blame: *Reckless driving is a* culpable *offense.* **—*n-* cul′ pa·bil′ i·ty** or **cul′ pa·ble·ness. *adv-* cul′ pa·bly.**

cul·prit (kŭl′ prĭt) ***n-*** guilty person; offender: *I caught the* culprit *who robbed the cookie jar.*

cult (kŭlt) ***n-*** **1** particular system of worship, or the people following it: *the* cult *of Apollo.* **2** devotion to a person, idea, theory, etc.: *the bullfighting* cult. **3** group of people so devoted: *a nudist* cult.

cul·ti·vate (kŭl′ tə vāt′) ***vt-*** [**cul·ti·vat·ed, cul·ti·vat·ing**] **1** to prepare (soil) for the planting and care of crops. **2** to raise (plants): *to* cultivate *roses.* **3** to loosen the soil around (plants). **4** to improve or develop: *to* cultivate *the mind by reading*; *to* cultivate *good habits.* **5** to seek the friendship of: *He* cultivates *only rich people.*

cul·ti·va·ted (kŭl′ tə vā′ təd) ***adj-*** **1** prepared for growing crops: *an acre of* cultivated *land.* **2** planted and tended by man, rather than growing wild: *a* cultivated *rosebush.* **3** cultured; refined: *a* cultivated *man*; cultivated *tastes.*

cul·ti·va·tion (kŭl′ tə vā′ shən) ***n-*** a cultivating: *the* cultivation *of land*; cultivation *of the mind.* **2** culture; refinement.

cul·ti·va·tor (kŭl′ tə vā′ tər) ***n-*** **1** person who cultivates. **2** farm or garden tool with long, pointed blades, used to loosen the soil and dig up weeds around growing plants.

Cultivator

cul·tur·al (kŭl′ chər əl) ***adj-*** **1** having to do with culture: *a* cultural *similarity between Japan and China.* **2** tending to improve or develop the mind: *a* cultural *activity.* **—*adv-* cul′ tur·al·ly.**

cul·ture (kŭl′ chər) ***n-*** **1** result of improving the mind, tastes, and manners; refinement. **2** a training and developing of the mind or body: *a class in physical* culture. **3** knowledge, customs, and arts of a people or group at a certain time: *the* culture *of ancient Greece.* **4** cultivation of land. **5** the raising and care of certain plants or animals: *rose* culture; *silkworm* culture. **6** a growth of bacteria in a special laboratory preparation.

cul·tured (kŭl′ chərd) ***adj-*** **1** cultivated, as in a bacteria culture. **2** refined; educated; well-bred.

cultured pearl ***n-*** pearl grown inside an oyster around a tiny object inserted by man.

cul·ver·in (kŭl′ vər ən) ***n-*** type of musket or cannon used in earlier times.

Culvert

cul·vert (kŭl′ vərt) ***n-*** a drain or passage for water under a road or railroad.

cum·ber (kŭm′ bər) ***vt-*** to burden; encumber.

cum·ber·some (kŭm′ bər səm) ***adj-*** heavy, bulky, or unwieldy; burdensome: *a* cumbersome *package.* **—*adv-* cum′ ber·some·ly. *n-* cum′ ber·some·ness.**

cum·brous (kŭm′ brəs) ***adj-*** troublesome; heavy; weighty: *a* cumbrous *load of responsibilities.* **—*adv-* cum′ brous·ly. *n-* cum′ brous·ness.**

cum·in (kŭm′ ən) ***n-*** **1** plant related to the carrot and parsley, with spicy seeds used as a seasoning in cooking. **2** the seeds of this plant. Also **cum′ min.**

cum lau·de (kōōm′ lou′ də) *Latin* with praise: *He graduated* cum laude.

cum·mer·bund (kŭm′ ər bŭnd′) ***n-*** wide sash or waistband, especially one worn by men with formal dress.

cum·quat (kŭm′ kwät′) kumquat.

cu·mu·la·tive (kyōōm′ yə lə tĭv) ***adj-*** growing in number, volume, strength, etc., by repeated additions; increasing steadily: *a* cumulative *effort.* **—*adv-* cu′mu·la·tive·ly. *n-* cu′ mu·la·tive·ness.**

cu·mu·lo·nim·bus (kyōōm′ yə lō nĭm′ bəs) ***n-*** thick, massive cloud billowing upward in the form of mountains or towers, and often producing thunderstorms.

cu·mu·lus (kyōōm′ yə ləs) ***n-*** [*pl.* **cu·mu·li** (-lē, -lī)] massive, rounded cloud billowing upward from a flat base. For picture, see *cloud.* [from Latin **cumulus** meaning "a heap."]

cu·ne·i·form (kyōō′ nə fôrm′, -fôrm′) ***adj-*** wedge-shaped, like the marks in the writing of the ancient Babylonians, Persians, etc. ***n-*** this type of writing.

Cuneiform writing

cun·ner (kŭn′ər) ***n-*** small, edible sea fish found along the northern Atlantic coast of North America.

cun·ning (kŭn′ ĭng) ***adj-*** **1** clever at deceiving; crafty; sly: *as* cunning *as a fox.* **2** *Informal* appealing; charming; cute: *What a* cunning *baby!* ***n-*** **1** cleverness at deceiving; craftiness. **2** skill in workmanship: *the* cunning *of his hand.* **—*adv-* cun′ ning·ly.**

cup (kŭp) ***n-*** **1** small container, often bowl-shaped and with a handle, used for drinking, measuring, etc. **2** the amount such a container holds; cupful. In cooking, a cup equals eight ounces or sixteen tablespoonfuls. **3** any of various hollow, rounded objects such as a vaselike or bowl-shaped trophy, or the blossom of a flower. **4** food or beverage served in a bowl-shaped container: *a fruit* cup. ***vt-*** [**cupped, cup·ping**] to form or enclose (something) in a hollow, rounded shape: *to* cup *one's hands*; *to* cup *one's chin in one's hands.* **—*adj-* cup′ like′.**

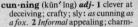

Cup

in (one's) cups intoxicated; drunk.

cup·bear·er (kŭp′ bâr′ ər) ***n-*** in earlier times, person who filled and served cups at banquets.

cup·board (kŭb′ ərd) ***n-*** closet or enclosed storage space with shelves for dishes, food, etc.; also, any small closet.

cup·cake (kŭp′ kāk′) ***n-*** small cake baked in a cup-shaped container.

cup·ful (kŭp′ fo͝ol′) ***n-*** the amount held by any cup; in cooking, half a pint: *a* cupful *of molasses.*
►In writing, always use CUPFULS for the plural. *She used two* cupfuls *of flour in the cake.*
Cu·pid (kyo͞o′ pĭd) ***n-*** **1** in Roman mythology, the god of love and son of Venus, identified with the Greek Eros. **2 cupid** a winged, naked baby represented with a bow and arrow as a symbol of love.
cu·pid·i·ty (kyo͞o pĭd′ ə tē) ***n-*** eager desire for possession; greed.
cu·po·la (kyo͞o′ pə lə) ***n-*** **1** small dome of a building; small tower raised above a roof. **2** similar windowed structure on the roof of a railroad car.

Cupola

cur (kûr) ***n-*** **1** mongrel dog. **2** nasty, hateful fellow.
cur·a·ble (kyo͝or′ ə bel) ***adj-*** such as can be cured: *a* curable *disease.* ***—n-*** **cur·a·bil′ i·ty.** ***adv-*** **cur′ a·bly.**
cu·ra·cy (kyo͝or′ ə sē) ***n-*** [*pl.* **cur·a·cies**] the job or duties of a curate, or the area under his care.
cu·ra·re (ko͞o rä′ rē) ***n-*** powerful poison that paralyzes the nerves, obtained from certain South American plants. It is used on arrow tips for hunting, and medically to relax muscles and relieve muscle spasms. Also **cu·ra′ ri.**
cu·ras·sow (kyo͝or′ ə sō′) ***n-*** any of several large turkey-like birds of Central and South America that are sometimes domesticated for food.
cu·rate (kyo͝or′ ət) ***n-*** clergyman who assists a pastor or vicar.
cur·a·tive (kyo͝or′ ə tĭv) ***adj-*** serving to remedy or correct: *a* curative *treatment*; curative *measures.* ***n-*** something that cures; remedy. ***—adv-*** **cur′ a·tive·ly.**
cu·ra·tor (kyo͝or′ ā′ tər) ***n-*** person in charge of a museum, art gallery, etc.
curb (kûrb) ***vt-*** **1** to keep within bounds; restrain: *to* curb *one's temper.* **2** to walk (a dog) along the edge of a street to keep him from soiling the sidewalk. ***n-*** **1** protecting rim of stone or cement along the edge of a sidewalk, pavement, etc.: *to park a car close to the* curb. **2** something that holds back, checks, or restrains: *to put a* curb *on extravagant spending.* **3** chain or strap on a horse's bit, used to hold back the horse when the reins are pulled.
curb·stone (kûrb′ stōn′) ***n-*** one of a row of stones laid along the edge of a street or sidewalk.
curd (kûrd) ***n-*** soft, thick substance that separates from the whey when milk turns sour. Curd is used in making cheese.
cur·dle (kûr′ dəl) ***vi-*** **[cur·dled, cur·dling] 1** to thicken into curds: *The milk* curdled *in the hot sun.* **2** to seem to thicken and stop as a result of fear, shock, disgust, etc.: *My blood* curdled *at the sound of his shrieks.* ***vt-***: *The hot sun* curdled *the milk.*
cure (kyo͝or) ***vt-*** **[cured, cur·ing] 1** to make well; remedy or heal: *This medicine will* cure *your cough. The doctor* cured *him.* **2** to get rid of or rid (someone) of; correct: *to* cure *one's fear of the dark*; *to* cure *someone of a bad habit.* **3** to preserve by salting, drying, etc.: *to* cure *meat.* ***vi-*** to undergo treatment or aging so as to keep well, to mature, etc.: *The hams are* curing *in the smokehouse. This paint takes two days to* cure. ***n-*** **1** medicine or procedure used to restore health or correct an undesirable condition; remedy: *a cold* cure. **2** a getting well; restoration to health: *a complete* cure *after long illness.*
cu·ré (kyo͝or′ ā) *French* ***n-*** parish priest.
cure-all (kyo͝or′ ȯl′) ***n-*** something claimed or intended to be a remedy for all illnesses, evils, etc.; panacea.
cur·few (kûr′ fyo͞o′) ***n-*** **1** officially set hour or signal at which persons, usually children, must be indoors and at home for the night. **2** in medieval times, the ringing of a bell at a fixed evening hour as a warning that fires and lights were to be put out; also, the law requiring this, or the hour at which the bell was rung.
Cu·ri·a (kyo͝or′ ē ə) ***n-*** central administrative body of the Vatican; the papal court at Rome. Also **Roman Curia.**
cu·rie (kyo͝or′ ē′) ***n-*** unit of radioactivity. One curie equals the quantity of radioactive material that undergoes 37 billion disintegrations per second.
cu·ri·o (kyo͝or′ ē ō) ***n-*** [*pl.* **cu·ri·os**] object valued as a curiosity because it is odd, interesting, or rare: *old shaving mugs and other* curios.
cu·ri·os·i·ty (kyo͝or′ ē ŏs′ ə tē) ***n-*** [*pl.* **cu·ri·os·i·ties**] **1** eager desire to know or learn: *An almanac can satisfy one's* curiosity *about many subjects. The puppy's* curiosity *got him into trouble.* **2** something unusual or rare: *A dirigible is a* curiosity *nowadays.*
cu·ri·ous (kyo͝or′ē əs) ***adj-*** **1** eager to know or find out: *a child's* curious *mind.* **2** odd; strange; unusual: *a collection of* curious *old coins*; *a* curious *accident.* ***—adv-*** **cu′ ri·ous·ly.** ***n-*** **cu′ ri·ous·ness.**
cu·ri·um (kyo͝or′ ē əm) ***n-*** man-made, silvery-white, radioactive element. Symbol Cm, At. No. 96.
curl (kûrl) ***n-*** **1** coiled or curved lock of hair; ringlet. **2** something resembling this: *a* curl *of smoke*; *wood shavings twisted into* curls. **3** manner in which something curves or coils: *Damp weather affects the* curl *of her hair.* ***vt-*** to form into curves or ringlets: *She* curled *her hair for the party.* ***vi-***: *Her hair* curls *naturally.*
curl up to sit or lie in a curved position.
cur·lew (kûr′ lo͞o, -lyo͞o) ***n-*** long-legged shore bird with a long, downward-curving bill.
cur·li·cue (kûr′ lə kyo͞o′) ***n-*** decorative or fanciful curve, swirl, or flourish.
curl·ing (kûr′ lĭng) ***n-*** game of Scottish origin played on ice with large, rounded stones, called **curling stones,** which players slide toward either of two circles.
curling iron ***n-*** metal tool, usually a rod-shaped pair of tongs, heated and used to curl the hair.
curl·y (kûr′ lē) ***adj-*** **[curl·i·er, curl·i·est] 1** having curls: *a* curly *head.* **2** in the shape of a curl: *a pig's* curly *tail.*
cur·mudg·eon (kûr mŭj′ ən) ***n-*** surly, ill-tempered fellow, especially an old man who is so.
cur·rant (kûr′ ənt) ***n-*** **1** small, seedless raisin used in puddings, cakes, etc. **2** small, sour, usually red, berry that grows in clusters on a prickly bush and is used in making jelly; also, the bush it grows on. ***Hom-*** current.
cur·ren·cy (kûr′ ən sē) ***n-*** [*pl.* **cur·ren·cies**] **1** coins, bills, etc., generally used as money: *Dimes and dollars are among the* currency *of the United States.* **2** general acceptance or circulation: *The rumor quickly gained* currency.
cur·rent (kûr′ ənt) ***n-*** **1** a flow in one direction; stream: *an ocean* current; *an air* current. **2** flow of electricity in a circuit: *a weak* current *in a poor conductor.* **3** general course; trend: *the* current *of public opinion.* ***adj-*** **1** of the present time; today's; contemporary; latest: *the* current *idea of comfort*; *the* current *issue of a magazine.* **2** widespread at the time: *a* current *usage.* **3** passing from

person to person; widely circulated: *A rumor of an invasion was widely* current. ***Hom-*** currant.

cur·rent·ly (kûr′ ənt lē) ***adv-*** at this time; now: *a movie* currently *being shown at a nearby theater.*

cur·rent·ness (kûr′ ənt nəs) ***n-*** a being recent, up-to-date, or generally accepted: *the* currentness *of this theory.*

cur·ric·u·lar (kə rĭk′ yə lər) ***adj-*** of or having to do with a curriculum.

cur·ric·u·lum (kə rĭk′ yə ləm) ***n-*** [*pl.* **cur·ric·u·lums** or **cur·ric·u·la** (-lə)] the subjects or course of study regularly taught at a school, college, etc.: *Music and French are included in our* curriculum.

cur·rish (kûr′ ĭsh) ***adj-*** like or behaving like a cur. ***—adv-*** **cur′ rish·ly.** ***n-*** **cur′ rish·ness.**

[1]**cur·ry** (kûr′ ē) ***vt-*** **[cur·ried, cur·ry·ing]** to rub down or clean (an animal) with a ridged or toothed implement called a **currycomb:** *to* curry *a horse.* [perhaps from Old French **correier, conreder** meaning "prepare," "make ready," related to "ready."]

curry favor to try to win favor by flattery, special attention, etc.: *He* curried favor *with the cook.*

[2]**cur·ry** (kûr′ ē) ***n-*** [*pl.* **cur·ries**] **1** highly seasoned powder made from various spices; also, a sauce made from it. **2** a dish of meat, rice, etc., seasoned with this powder. ***vt-*** **[cur·ried, cur·ry·ing]** to prepare (food) with this powder: *to* curry *meat.* [from Tamil **kari** "sauce."]

curse (kûrs) ***vt-*** **[cursed, curs·ing] 1** to call down evil or harm on: *The witch* cursed *her tomentors.* **2** to trouble severely; torment; afflict: *He was* cursed *with a bad temper. Some power* cursed *him all his short and miserable life.* ***vi-*** to use bad language; swear: *The villain* cursed *and twirled his mustache.* ***n-*** **1** oath, prayer, spell, etc., for evil or harm to befall someone or something. **2** something that causes harm, trouble, or suffering: *the* curse *of war.*

curs·ed (kûr′ səd) ***adj-*** **1** under a curse. **2** deserving a curse; hateful; detestable. ***adv-*** (*also* kûrst) (intensifier only): *This is* cursed *hard work.* ***—adv-*** **curs′ ed·ly.** ***n-*** **curs′ed·ness.**

cur·sive (kûr′ sĭv) ***adj-*** joined together by flowing lines, as the letters in handwriting. ***n-*** handwriting so joined; script. ***—adv-*** **cur′ sive·ly.**

cur·so·ry (kûr′ sə rē) ***adj-*** hasty; careless: *He gave the book a* cursory *reading.* ***—adv-*** **cur′ so·ri·ly.**

curt (kûrt) ***adj-*** **[curt·er, curt·est]** short and offhand, often with the effect of seeming rude: *a* curt *nod; a* curt *answer.* ***—adv-*** **curt′ ly.** ***n-*** **curt′ ness.**

cur·tail (kər tāl′) ***vt-*** to make shorter or less; cut down; reduce: *to* curtail *a speech because of lack of time; to* curtail *expenses.* ***—n-*** **cur·tail′ ment.**

cur·tain (kûr′ tən) ***n-*** **1** hanging drapery or screen, usually of cloth, used to cover or decorate, or to separate one place from another: *the* curtains *at a window; the* curtain *across the stage in a theater.* **2** anything resembling this: *a* curtain *of fog.* **3** the lowering or closing of such a drapery in a theater at a break in or the end of a performance: *the second-act* curtain. ***vt-*** to cover, separate, or provide with hangings, draperies, or similar partitions: *to* curtain *the windows.*

curtain call ***n-*** the opening of the curtain or the bowing of performers before the curtain in response to applause at the end of a show.

curtain raiser ***n-*** short piece presented before the main performance in a theater, concert hall, etc.; hence, any relatively unimportant introductory part.

curt·sy (kûrt′ sē) ***n-*** [*pl.* **curt·sies**] respectful bow which girls and women make by bending the knees and lowering the body. ***vi-*** **[curt·sied, curt·sy·ing]**: *She* curtsied *to the queen.* Also **curt′ sey.**

cur·va·ture (kûr′ və chər) ***n-*** **1** a bending or curving; also, the amount of bending, as of a curved line or surface. **2** *Medicine* an abnormally curved condition, especially of the spine.

curve (kûrv) ***n-*** **1** a line no part of which is straight. **2** rounded shape, bend, etc.: *the* curve *of her cheek; a* curve *in the road.* **3** in baseball, ball pitched so it swerves from a straight course. **4** *Mathematics* a set of points: *A straight line is a* curve. ***vi-*** **[curved, curv·ing]** to be rounded, arched, or bent: *The road* curves *to the right.* ***vt-***: *She* curved *her lips in a smile.*

cur·vet (kər vĕt′) ***n-*** springy leap which a horse makes by raising the front legs and then, before they touch the ground, raising the hind legs. ***vi-*** **[cur·vet·ted, cur·vet·ting]**: *His lively steed* curvetted *friskily.*

cur·vi·lin·e·ar (kûr′ və lĭn′ ē ər) ***adj-*** **1** bounded by a curved line or surface: *a* curvilinear *figure.* **2** curved: *the* curvilinear *trajectory of a rocket.*

cush·ion (ko͝osh′ ən) ***n-*** **1** pillow or soft pad to sit, lie, or rest on. **2** any covering resembling such a pillow or pad: *a* cushion *of pine needles.* **3** anything serving as a safeguard against harm; buffer. ***vt-*** **1** to act as a padding or buffer against: *A pile of hay* cushioned *his fall.* **2** to provide padding, protection, or comfort to: *His faith and good spirits* cushioned *him.*

cusp (kŭsp) ***n-*** a point or pointed end, as on the crown of a tooth or on the new moon.

cus·pid (kŭs′ pĭd) ***n-*** a canine tooth.

cus·pi·dor (kŭs′ pə dôr′, -dôr′) ***n-*** spittoon.

cuss (kŭs) *Informal* ***vt- & vi-*** to curse. ***n-*** odd person or animal: *a good-natured* cuss.

cuss·ed (kŭs′ əd) *Informal* ***adj-*** mean; stubborn; cantankerous; ornery. ***—adv-*** **cuss′ ed·ly.** ***n-*** **cuss′ ed·ness.**

cuss·word (kŭs′ wûrd′) *Informal* ***n-*** vulgar word or oath; profanity.

cus·tard (kŭs′ tərd) ***n-*** baked or boiled mixture of eggs, milk, and sugar, often with added flavoring.

custard apple ***n-*** **1** soft, pulpy, heart-shaped fruit of a small tree native to tropical America; also, the tree itself. **2** papaw.

cus·to·di·an (kəs tō′ dē ən) ***n-*** **1** person appointed to guard and take care (of): *A county clerk is the* custodian *of public records.* **2** person who takes care of a building; janitor.

cus·to·dy (kŭs′ tə dē) ***n-*** protective care; guardianship: *The children were in their grandmother's* custody.

take into custody to arrest and put under guard.

cus·tom (kŭs′ təm) ***n-*** **1** habit or generally accepted way of doing things: *It is her* custom *to get up at dawn.* **2** regular buying of goods or services from a store or business: *Most of our* custom *is with that store.* **3 customs** taxes or duties on goods brought into a country; also, the government agency that collects these taxes. ***adj-*** **1** producing work or merchandise to order only: *a* custom *tailor.* **2** (also **cus′ tom-made′**) made to order: *a* custom *suit.*

cus·tom·ar·y (kŭs′ tə mĕr′ ē) ***adj-*** according to or based on custom; usual: *It is* customary *for people to shake hands when they are introduced.* ***—adv-*** **cus′ tom·ar′ i·ly.** ***n-*** **cus′ tom·ar′ i·ness.**

cus·tom-built (kŭs′ təm bĭlt′) ***adj-*** built especially for the buyer at his order: *a* custom-built *TV set.*

cus·tom·er (kŭs′ təm ər) ***n-*** **1** person who buys goods or services, especially as a regular purchaser. **2** *Informal* person; fellow: *He's a* tough *customer.*

cus·tom·house (kŭs′ təm hous′) ***n-*** government building where taxes or duties are collected on imported and exported goods.

cut (kŭt) ***vt-*** **[cut, cut·ting]** (in senses 1, 4, 6, and 9 considered intransitive when the direct object is implied but not expressed) **1** to divide, separate, shorten, or make an opening in with a knife or sharp tool: *to* cut *a ribbon in two*; *to* cut *the grass.* **2** to make or shape with or as if with a sharp tool: *to* cut *a hole in the ice.* **3** to reduce or make less: *to* cut *prices, expenses, etc.* **4** to remove; eliminate: *She had to* cut *two songs from her program.* **5** to put an end to; interrupt: *The storm* cut *all telephone service.* **6** to go through; cross: *The railroad* cuts *the highway at that point.* **7** to dissolve: *a soap that* cuts *grease.* **8** to have (a tooth or teeth) appear through the gums: *The baby is* cutting *his first teeth.* **9** to pierce, wound, or hurt as if with something sharp: *His cruel remarks* cut *her deeply. The wind* cuts *sharply.* **10** to pretend not to recognize; snub: *I nodded to her but she* cut *me without a word.* **11** *Informal* to be absent from without official permission: *to* cut *a class.* ***vi-*** **1** to permit being sliced, divided, etc., by a sharp instrument: *This meat* cuts *easily.* **2** to go directly or abruptly: *The driver ahead of us* cut *sharply to the left.* ***n-*** **1** division, opening, wound, etc., made with something sharp: *a* cut *in a tree trunk made by an ax*; *a* cut *on the finger.* **2** piece, slice, etc., especially of meat, separated from a larger part by a sharp instrument: *a tender* cut *of beef.* **3** sharp, slashing blow, stroke, or movement. **4** a lowering or reduction: *a* cut *in prices.* **5** the removal of a part, especially to shorten or improve something: *to make* cuts *in a story.* **6** passage made by digging, blasting, etc.: *the railroad* cut. **7** style or shape, especially of clothing. **8** remark or action that wounds someone's feelings. **9** engraved block from which a picture is printed.

cut and dried brief and uninteresting. **cut out** suited; fit: *He's not* cut out *to be a soldier.*

cut down to bring down by or as if by means of a sharp tool; fell: *to* cut down *a tree.*

cut up *Informal* **1** to behave mischievously or boisterously. **2** to sadden or distress.

cu·ta·ne·ous (kyōō tān′ ē əs) ***adj-*** of or having to do with the skin: *a* cutaneous *irritation.*

cut·a·way (kŭt′ ə wā′) ***n-*** man's suit coat with the edges slanting outward and downward from the waist, worn chiefly for formal daytime occasions; morning coat.

cut·back (kŭt′ băk′) ***n-*** reduction or curtailment: *a* cutback *in government expenses.*

cute (kyōōt) ***adj-*** **[cut·er, cut·est] 1** *Informal* appealingly pretty, charming, etc.: *What a* cute *kitten!* **2** clever; shrewd: *a very* cute *device.* **—*adv-* cute′ ly. *n-* cute′ ness.**

cut glass ***n-*** glassware ornamented with designs cut into its surface.

cu·ti·cle (kyōō′ tĭ kəl) ***n-*** outer layer of skin, especially the thickened skin around the base of the fingernails or toenails.

cut·lass (kŭt′ ləs) ***n-*** short, heavy sword with a broad, curving blade.

Cutlass

cut·ler·y (kŭt′ lə rē) ***n-*** cutting instruments, especially implements used in cutting or serving food.

cut·let (kŭt′ lət) ***n-*** thin slice of meat, usually veal, cut from the ribs or leg and fried or broiled; also, a mixture of ground meat, fish, etc., shaped like this.

cut·off (kŭt′ ôf′) ***n-*** **1** route that shortens the traveling distance between two points; short cut. **2** device for stopping a flow of steam, water, gas, etc.; valve. **3** a stopping or ending; termination: *The* cutoff *for this project is in two weeks.* *as* ***modifier***: *a* cutoff *date.*

cut·out (kŭt′ out′) ***n-*** **1** design or figure to be cut out: *paper doll* cutouts. **2** space from which something was cut and removed. **3** device used to let the exhaust gases of an automobile engine bypass the muffler and pass directly into the air.

cut·purse (kŭt′ pûrs′) ***n-*** in earlier times, a thief who cut people's purses from their belts; hence, a pickpocket.

cut·ter (kŭt′ ər) ***n-*** **1** person or thing that cuts, especially a person whose job is cutting cloth, fur, etc., to be made into clothing. **2** small fast vessel used by the Coast Guard. **3** fast single-masted sailboat of narrow beam and deep draft formerly used by customs officials to chase smugglers. **4** sleigh for two persons.

cut·throat (kŭt′ thrōt′) ***n-*** a murderous villain. ***adj-*** murderous; ruthless: *to face* cutthroat *competition.*

cut·ting (kŭt′ ĭng) ***n-*** a shoot or branch cut from a plant for rooting or grafting.

cut·tle·bone (kŭt′ əl bōn′) ***n-*** the internal bony plate of the cuttlefish, often put into birds' cages to provide the birds with calcium salts.

cut·tle·fish (kŭt′ əl fĭsh′) ***n-*** ocean creature related to and resembling the squid, and having a long body and two long and eight shorter tentacles. Cuttlefish are classified as mollusks.

cut·worm (kŭt′ wûrm′) ***n-*** any of various caterpillars that destroy young stalks of cabbage, corn, etc., by eating through them at or near ground level.

cwt. hundredweight.

-cy *suffix* (used to form nouns) **1** condition or state: bankrupt*cy*. **2** rank or position: captain*cy*.

cy·a·nide (sī′ ə nīd′) ***n-*** extremely poisonous compound of the cyanogen radical (CN) and a metallic element or radical, especially potassium cyanide (KCN).

cy·an·o·gen (sī ăn′ ə jən) ***n-*** extremely poisonous, colorless, flammable gas (C_2N_2) having the odor of almonds.

cy·a·no·sis (sī′ ə nō′ səs) ***n-*** a blue coloring of the skin due to lack of oxygen in the blood.

cy·ber·net·ics (sī′ bər nĕt′ ĭks) ***n-*** (takes singular verb) science that deals with the principles of control and communication that apply both to electronic machines such as computers and to living organisms.

cy·cad (sī′ kəd) ***n-*** any of a group of mostly tropical plants that have existed from earliest times and now resemble palm trees or large ferns.

cycl- or **cyclo-** *combining form* circle: *a* cyclo*tron* (machine that accelerates nuclear particles in a circular chamber). [from Greek **kýklos** meaning "circle."]

cyc·la·men (sī′ klə mən) ***n-*** hothouse plant cultivated for its showy red, pink, or white flowers with petals turned sharply backward and upward.

cy·cle (sī′ kəl) ***n-*** **1** series of events, processes, actions, etc., that occur over and over again in regular order: *the* cycle *of the seasons.* **2** series of poems or stories about a central person or event: *the* cycle *of legends about King Arthur.* **3** a bicycle, tricycle, or motorcycle. **4** of an alternating current, one complete alteration (two reversals) in the direction of flow of the electricity. ***vi-*** **[cy·cled, cy·cling]** to ride a bicycle, tricycle, etc.

cy·clic (sī′ klĭk) ***adj-*** **1** occurring in cycles; hence, recurrent. **2** of organic chemical compounds, having a closed ring or chain of atoms in the molecular structure. Also **cy′cli·cal.** **—*adv-* cy′cli·cal·ly.**

cy·clist (sī′klĭst) ***n-*** person who rides a bicycle, tricycle, or motorcycle.

cy·clom·e·ter (sī klŏm′ ə tər) ***n-*** **1** instrument which counts the revolutions a wheel makes. It is often used to measure the distance a wheeled vehicle has traveled. 2 device used to measure circular arcs.

cy·clone (sī′ klōn′) *n-* **1** weather condition in which winds whirl around a center of low air pressure. **2** any destructive storm, such as a tornado or hurricane. *—adj-* **cy·clon′ ic** (sī klŏn′ ĭk).

cyclone cellar *n-* underground shelter for protection from tornadoes and similar destructive storms.

cy·clo·pe·di·a or **cy·clo·pae·di·a** (sī′ klō pē′ dē ə) *n-* encyclopedia. *—adj-* **cy′ clo·pe′ dic.**

Cy·clops (sī′ klŏps′) *n-* [*pl.* **Cy·clo·pes** (-klō′ pēz′)] in Homer's "Odyssey," one of a group of one-eyed giants. *—adj-* **Cy′ clo′ pe·an.**

cy·clo·ra·ma (sī′ klə răm′ ə) *n-* series of pictures arranged in a circle so as to appear in natural perspective to someone standing in the center.

cy·clo·tron (sī′ klə trŏn′) *n-* atom smasher in which electrically charged atomic particles are accelerated to very high speeds in a circular vacuum chamber.

cyg·net (sĭg′ nət) *n-* young swan. *Hom-* signet.

cyl·in·der (sĭl′ ən dər) *n-* **1** solid geometric figure described by the circumference of a circle as it moves along a straight line. The ends of this figure are equal parallel circles. **2** any body having this form, such as a piston chamber of a gasoline or steam engine, a barrel of a pump, or a roller used in a printing press or typewriter.

Cylinder

cy·lin·dri·cal (sə lĭn′ drə kəl) *adj-* shaped like a cylinder. *—adv-* **cy·lin′ dri·cal·ly.**

cym·bal (sĭm′ bəl) *n-* musical percussion instrument consisting of a circular metal plate that is struck with a drumstick or against another cymbal to produce a clashing or ringing sound. *Hom-* symbol.

Cymbals

cyn·ic (sĭn′ ĭk) *n-* person who doubts the goodness of human nature and believes that all people act from selfish interests.

cyn·i·cal (sĭn′ ĭ kəl) *adj-* doubting or expressing mistrust in the sincerity of people's motives: *a* cynical *person*; *a* cynical *remark*. *—adv-* **cyn′ i·cal·ly.**

cyn·i·cism (sĭn′ ə sĭz′ əm) *n-* **1** the attitude or beliefs of a cynic. **2** cynical statement, opinion, etc.

cy·no·sure (sī′ nə shŏŏr′, sĭn′-) *n-* **1** center or object of general attraction: *She was the* cynosure *of all eyes.* **2 Cynosure** in earlier times, the star Polaris, used as a guide by sailors and travelers.

cy·pher (sī′ fər) cipher.

cy·press (sī′ prəs) *n-* **1** any of several evergreen trees related to the pines, with fragrant needles and durable wood. **2** (usually **bald cypress**) related tree that sheds its needles, growing in swamps in southern United States. **3** the wood of these trees.

Cyp·ri·ote (sĭp′ rē ət) *n-* **1** a native or inhabitant of Cyprus. **2** the ancient or modern Greek dialect of Cyprus. *adj-*: *a* Cypriote *town*; *a* Cypriote *patriot.* Also **Cyp′ ri·ot.**

Cy·ril·lic (sə rĭl′ ĭk) *adj-* of or pertaining to the old Slavic alphabet based on the Greek and attributed to St. Cyril (827-69), versions of which are still used to write Russian, Bulgarian, and some other Slavic languages.

cyst (sĭst) *n-* **1** liquid-filled sac or pouch that forms in both plants and animals, especially a sac in the body containing diseased matter. **2** protective capsule enclosing certain one-celled animals during their inactive or resting stage.

cyst·ic (sĭs′ tĭk) *adj-* **1** relating to a cyst. **2** enclosed in a cyst. **3** relating to the bladder or gall bladder.

cyt- or **cyto-** *combining form* cell: *the* cyto*plasm.* [from scientific Latin **cyto** meaning "cell," from Greek **kýtos** meaning "a hollow."]

-cyte *combining form* cell: *leuco*cyte (white cell). [from Greek **kýtos** meaning "a cell; receptacle."]

cy·tol·o·gist (sī tŏl′ ə jĭst) *n-* person trained in and usually working in cytology.

cy·tol·o·gy (sī tŏl′ ə jē) *n-* branch of biology that deals with the study of cells.

cy·to·plasm (si′ tə plăz′ əm) *n-* all of the protoplasm outside the nucleus in a cell. *—adj-* **cy′ to·plas′ mic.**

C.Z. Canal Zone.

czar (zär) *n-* **1** (also **tsar**) the title of the former emperors of Russia. **2** person in a position of highest authority: *From his very poor beginnings he made his way up the ladder to become an industrial* czar.

cza·ri·na (zä rē′ nə) *n-* the wife of a czar; also, an empress of Russia. Also **tsarina.**

Czech (chĕk) *n-* **1** member of the western branch of Slavs which includes Bohemians, Moravians, and some Silesians. **2** the West Slavic language of the Czechs, formerly called Bohemian. *adj-*: *the* Czech *newspaper.* Also **Czech′ ish.** *Hom-* check.

Czech·o·slo·va·ki·an (chĕk′ ō slə väk′ ē ən) *n-* a citizen of Czechoslovakia. *adj-* of or pertaining to Czechoslovakia, its people, or their languages.

D

D, d (dē) *n-* [*pl.* **D's, d's**] **1** the fourth letter of the English alphabet. **2** Roman numeral for 500. **3** *Music* the second note of the C-major scale.

d. **1** died; dead. **2** in British currency, penny or pence (from Latin **denarius, denarii**).

[1]**dab** (dăb) *vt-* **[dabbed, dab·bing]** **1** to pat or brush (something) without great care, usually in applying some material: *She* dabbed *her face with powder.* **2** to pat, brush, or smear (some material), usually in applying it to a surface: *He* dabbed *paint on the wall.* *vi-*: *He* dabbed *lazily at the table with his brush.* *n-* **1** light brushing or patting stroke: *Give it a* dab *with the sponge.* **2** small amount or mass; bit: *a* dab *of butter*; *a* dab *of grease*; *a* dab *of color.* [from Middle English **dabben,** of unknown origin.]

[2]**dab** (dăb) *n-* any of various flatfish, including some soles, plaices, and flounders. [apparently same as [1]**dab.**]

dab·ble (dăb′ əl) *vt-* **[dab·bled, dab·bling]** to dip (the hands or feet) lazily in and out: *He* dabbled *his feet in the sand.* *vi-* **1** to paddle and splash about in water: *The children* dabbled *in the brook.* **2** to do something in a lazy or casual way: *He* dabbled *in art. Edward* dabbled *at gardening.*

dace (dās) *n-* [*pl.* **dace; dac·es** (kinds of dace)] **1** small European fresh-water fish, like the chub. **2** a related North American fish.

dachs·hund (däks′ hoo͝nt′, -hoo͝nd′) ***n-*** small hound with very short legs, long body, pointed nose, and drooping ears.

Dachshund, about 18 in. long

Da·cron (dā′krŏn′, dăk′rŏn′) ***n-*** trademark name of a strong man-made fiber and of cloth woven from it.

dac·tyl (dăk′ təl) ***n-*** **1** measure or foot in poetry made up of one accented syllable followed by two unaccented syllables. **2** line of poetry made up of such measures. Example: "Take′ her up/ tend′ er ly." ***—adj-*** **dac·tyl′ ic** (dăk tĭl′ ĭk): *a* dactylic *line.*

dad (dăd) *Informal* ***n-*** father.

dad·dy (dăd′ ē) *Informal* ***n-*** father.

dad·dy-long·legs (dăd′ ē lòng′lĕgz′) ***n-*** [*pl.* **dad·dy-long·legs**] spiderlike animal with very long legs and a small, round body; harvestman.

Daddy-long-legs

da·do (dā′ dō) ***n-*** [*pl.* **da·does**] **1** face of a pedestal between the base and the cornice. **2** (also **dado head**) set of circular blades fitted to a power saw to cut out a rectangular groove. **3** (also **dado plane**) narrow woodworking plane for the same purpose. **4** a rectangular groove. ***vt-*** to cut such a groove in.

Daed·a·lus (dĕd′ ə ləs) ***n-*** in Greek legend, a great creator and inventor who devised, among other things, the Labyrinth in Crete and the wings of Icarus.

daf·fo·dil (dăf′ ə dĭl′) ***n-*** garden plant that blossoms in spring with showy, usually yellow flowers; also, the flower.

Daffodil

daf·fy (dăf′ ē) *Informal* ***adj-*** **[daf·fi·er, daf·fi·est] 1** crazy; daft. **2** foolish; silly.

daft (dăft) *chiefly Brit.* ***adj-*** **1** weak-minded or simple; foolish. **2** insane; crazy. ***—adv-*** **daft′ ly.** ***n-*** **daft′ ness.**

dag·ger (dăg′ ər) ***n-*** **1** short, pointed, double-edged sword or knife, used to stab. **2** in printing, a reference mark (†).

da·guerre·o·type (də gĕr′ ə tīp′) ***n-*** **1** an early method of taking photographs on silver-coated plates. **2** a photograph made by this method.

dahl·ia (däl′ yə, dăl′-) ***n-*** any of several garden plants that flower in the autumn with showy single or double flowers; also, the flower itself.

dai·ly (dā′ lē) ***adj-*** happening, appearing, or done every day or every weekday: *a* daily *nap*; *a* daily *newspaper.* ***adv-*** every day; day by day: *This train leaves* daily. ***n-*** [*pl.* **dai·lies**] newspaper published every day.

dain·ty (dān′ tē) ***adj-*** **[dain·ti·er, dain·ti·est] 1** pretty in a delicate or graceful way: *a thin,* dainty *dress of pink.* **2** having delicate feelings or tastes; fastidious: *one's* dainty *eating habits.* **3** delicious: *a* dainty *morsel.* ***n-*** [*pl.* **dain·ties**] bit of delicious food: *a box of* dainties *from the bakery.* ***—adv-*** **dain′ ti·ly.** ***n-*** **dain′ ti·ness.**

dair·y (dâr′ ē) ***n-*** [*pl.* **dair·ies**] **1** building or room in which milk and cream are kept and made into butter and cheese; creamery. **2** shop or company that sells or serves milk and milk products; creamery. *as* ***modifier:*** *a* dairy *farm*; *a* dairy *restaurant.*

dair·y·maid (dâr′ ē mād′) ***n-*** girl or woman employed in a dairy; milkmaid.

dair·y·man (dâr′ ē mən) ***n-*** [*pl.* **dair·y·men**] man who owns, manages, or is employed in a dairy or a dairy farm.

da·is (dā′ ĭs) ***n-*** slightly raised platform for a throne, speaker's desk, etc.

Dais

dai·sy (dā′ zē) ***n-*** [*pl.* **dai·sies**] any of several plants with flowers having narrow petals radiating from a center of tiny flowers, especially the yellow and white **oxeye daisy** common in North America, and the smaller, low-growing **English daisy.**

Da·ko·ta (də kō′ tə) ***n-*** [*pl.* **Da·ko·tas,** also **Da·ko·ta**] **1** member of a Siouan tribe of American Indians inhabiting the upper Mississippi valley; Sioux. **2** the language of these Indians. ***—adj-*** **Da·ko′ tan:** *a* Dakotan *rite.*

Da·lai Lama (dä′ lī′ lä′ mə) ***n-*** religious leader of the Tibetan Buddhists and, until 1950, the ruler of Tibet.

dale (dāl) ***n-*** small valley; glen.

dal·li·ance (dăl′ ē əns) ***n-*** **1** play; trifling; flirtation. **2** a wasting of time; loitering.

dal·ly (dăl′ ē) ***vi-*** **[dal·lied, dal·ly·ing] 1** to play; amuse oneself; trifle; flirt. **2** to waste time; loiter.

Dal·ma·tian (dăl mā′ shən) ***n-*** kind of white dog with black spots, traditionally a mascot of firemen; coach dog.

¹dam (dăm) ***n-*** **1** barrier that holds back a body of water. **2** the water thus held back. ***vt-*** **[dammed, dam·ming]** to hold back with such a barrier; check the flow of: *Beavers* dammed *the river.* [from Middle English, perhaps from old Norse **dammr.**] ***Hom-*** damn.
dam up to hold back; control: *to* dam up *one's hatred.*

Dam

²dam (dăm) ***n-*** female parent of any four-footed animal, such as a horse, sheep, or deer. [a variation of the word **dame.**] ***Hom-*** damn.

dam·age (dăm′ ĭj) ***n-*** **1** injury; harm: *How much* damage *did the fire cause?* **2 damages** in law, amount that is claimed or allowed in court for harm or injury. ***vt-*** **[dam·aged, dam·ag·ing]:** *The fire* damaged *the building.*

dam·a·scene (dăm′ ə sēn′) ***vt-*** **[dam·a·scened, dam·a·scen·ing]** to decorate (metal) with etching or inlaid designs. ***n-*** decorative inlaid or etched work in iron or steel. *as* ***modifier:*** *a* damascene *sword.*

Da·mas·cus steel (də măs′ kəs) ***n-*** hard, elastic steel, formerly made in Damascus for sword blades.

dam·ask (dăm′ əsk) ***n-*** **1** patterned fabric, usually linen or silk, used for table linens, draperies, dresses, etc. **2** deep, rose-pink color. **3** Damascus steel. **4** damascene. *as* ***modifier:*** *a* damask *tablecloth*; damask *cheeks.*

dame (dām) ***n-*** **1** in earlier times, the mistress of a household; lady. **2** an old woman; beldam. **3** *Slang* woman. **4 Dame** *Brit.* (1) lady member of a British honorary order; also, her title. (2) title of a knight's or baronet's wife.

damn (dăm) ***vt-*** **1** to judge and condemn as bad, faulty, or as a failure: *The critics* damned *the book.* **2** to doom to eternal punishment. **3** to curse; swear at; call down a curse upon. ***Hom-*** dam.

dam·na·ble (dăm′ nə bəl) ***adj-*** deserving to be condemned; detestable: *a* damnable *lie.* ***—adv-*** **dam′ na·bly.** ***n-*** **dam′ na·ble·ness.**

fāte, făt, dâre, bärn; bē, bĕt, mêre; bīte, bĭt; nōte, hŏt, môre, dòg; fŭn, fûr; to͞o, bo͝ok; oil; out; tar; thin; then; hw for wh as in *wh*at; zh for s as in u*s*ual; ə for a, e, i, o, u, as in *a*go, lin*e*n, per*i*l, at*o*m, min*u*s

dam·na·tion (dăm nā′ shən) ***n-*** condemnation, especially to eternal punishment; also, eternal punishment.

damned (dămd) ***adj-*** [*superl.* **damned·est**] **1** condemned to eternal punishment. **2** *Slang* cursed; detestable.

Dam·o·cles (dăm′ ə klēz′) ***n-*** in Greek legend, a courtier of ancient Syracuse, who was made to sit at a banquet under a sword suspended by a single hair.

Da·mon and Pyth·i·as (dā′ mən ənd pĭth′ ē əs) ***n-*** in Roman legend, a pair of devoted friends. Damon offered his own life as a pledge for Pythias.

dam·o·zel (dăm′ ə zĕl′) *Archaic* ***n-*** young girl; damsel. Also **dam′ o·sel.**

damp (dămp) ***adj-*** **[damp·er, damp·est]** slightly or moderately wet; moist: *a* damp *cloth.* ***n-*** **1** moisture: *The cold and* damp *penetrated his bones.* **2** poisonous vapor or gas: *coal* damp. ***vt-*** **1** to reduce the intensity of; weaken; check: *to* damp *a fire*; *to* damp *a sound*; *to* damp *one's enthusiasm.* **2** to dampen. ***—adv-*** **damp′ly.** ***n-*** **damp′ ness.**

damp·en (dăm′ pən) ***vt-*** **1** to moisten: *to* dampen *a rag.* **2** to damp: *The accident* dampened *our spirits.*

damp·er (dăm′ pər) ***n-*** **1** movable plate, usually inside a flue, used to regulate the draft of a stove, furnace, etc. **2** device that lessens or stops vibrations or oscillations. Dampers are used on the strings of pianos, on the pointer needles of electrical instruments, etc. **3** something which depresses or discourages: *It put a* damper *on our fun.*

dam·sel *Archaic* ***n-*** young girl.

dam·sel·fly (dăm′ zəl flī′) ***n-*** [*pl.* **dam·sel·flies**] insect similar to the dragonfly, having a long slender body and four long wings folded over its back when at rest.

dam·son (dăm′ zən) ***n-*** **1** small purple plum, originally from Damascus. **2** tree that bears this plum.

dance (dăns) ***n-*** **1** a rhythmical movement of the body and feet, usually in time to music: *a school for learning* dance. **2** particular form of this, with certain steps and hand movements, such as the fox trot, waltz, etc. **3** a turn at performing such a movement: *May I have the next* dance? **4** social gathering at which persons perform such movements: *a Saturday night* dance. *as* ***modifier***: *a* dance *band.* ***vi-*** **[danced, danc·ing] 1** to move the body and feet in time to music: *I could* dance *all night.* **2** to move about lightly: *He* danced *with joy.* ***vt-*** **1** to perform (a waltz, jig, ballet, etc.). **2** to cause (a person) to move to music: *He* danced *her around the room.*

danc·er (dăn′ sər) ***n-*** **1** person who dances. **2** person who makes his living by dancing to entertain others.

dan·de·li·on (dăn′ də lī′ ən) ***n-*** **1** a common weed with yellow flowers and a rosette of jagged leaves that can be eaten. **2** the flower of this plant. *as* ***modifier***: *a salad of* dandelion *greens.*

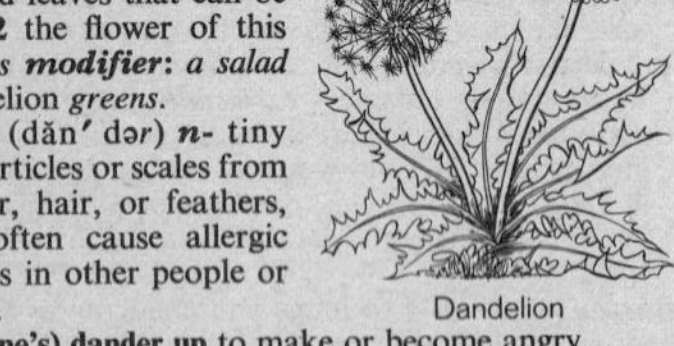
Dandelion

dan·der (dăn′ dər) ***n-*** tiny loose particles or scales from skin, fur, hair, or feathers, which often cause allergic reactions in other people or animals.

get (one's) dander up to make or become angry.

dan·dle (dăn′ dəl) ***vt-*** **[dan·dled, dan·dling]** to move (a baby) up and down on the knee, or in the arms.

dan·druff (dăn′ drəf) ***n-*** tiny scales of dead skin that flake off the scalp.

dan·dy (dăn′ dē) ***n-*** [*pl.* **dan·dies**] **1** man who gives too much attention to his clothes and appearance; fop. **2** *Informal* something good. ***adj-*** **[dan·di·er, dan·di·est]** *Informal* good; nice; fine.

Dane (dān) ***n-*** **1** person who was born in, or is a citizen of, Denmark. **2** person of Danish descent. ***Hom-*** deign.

dan·ger (dān′ jər) ***n-*** **1** chance of harm; risk; peril: *A fireman faces* danger *every day.* **2** possible cause of loss, injury, or death; hazard: *Ice is a* danger *to ships.*

dan·ger·ous (dān′ jər əs) ***adj-*** **1** unsafe; risky; perilous: *Handling explosives is* dangerous *work.* **2** likely to do harm: *A mad dog is* dangerous. ***—adv-*** **dan′ ger·ous·ly.** ***n-*** **dan′ ger·ous·ness.**

dan·gle (dăng′ əl) ***vi-*** **[dan·gled, dan·gling]** to hang or swing loosely: *The puppet* dangled *on a string.* ***vt-***: *The boy* dangled *his legs over the edge of the pool.*

Dan·iel (dăn′ yəl) ***n-*** **1** in the Bible, a Hebrew prophet, captive in Babylon. **2** a book of the Old Testament containing the story of this prophet.

Dan·ish (dā′ nĭsh) ***adj-*** of or relating to Denmark, its people, or their language: *a* Danish *custom.* ***n-*** the Germanic language of the Danes.

dank (dănk) ***adj-*** **[dank·er, dank·est]** unpleasantly damp; sodden: *a* dank *cellar.* ***—adv-*** **dank′ ly.** ***n-*** **dank′ ness.**

dan·seuse (dăn sōōz′) ***n-*** female ballet dancer.

Daph·ne (dăf′ nē) ***n-*** in Greek mythology, a nymph who escaped from Apollo by changing into a laurel tree.

daph·ni·a (dăf′ nē ə) ***n-*** tiny, insectlike, fresh-water crustacean with a transparent shell; water flea.

dap·per (dăp′ ər) ***adj-*** neat and smart in appearance; trim; spruce: *a* dapper *dresser.*

dap·ple (dăp′ əl) ***n-*** **1** spotted or mottled marking, such as one on the skin of an animal. **2** animal with such marking. ***adj-***: *a* dapple *cow.* ***vt-*** **[dap·pled, dap·pling]**: *The sunlight* dappled *the grass.*

D.A.R. Daughters of the American Revolution.

dare (dâr) ***auxiliary verb-*** to have enough courage to: *He didn't* dare *jump from a height.* ***vt-*** **[dared, dar·ing] 1** to have courage for; meet boldly: *Columbus* dared *the perils of an uncharted ocean.* **2** to challenge: *He* dared *me to climb the pole.* ***vi-*** to have enough courage: *When courage was needed, he* dared. ***n-*** a challenge.

take a dare to do what one is dared to do.

dare·dev·il (dâr′ dĕv′ əl) ***n-*** person who takes great risks recklessly. *as* ***modifier***: *a* daredevil *driver.*

dar·ing (dâr′ ĭng) ***n-*** bravery; boldness. ***adj-***: *a* daring *deed*; *a* daring *attempt*; *a* daring *aviator.* ***—adv-*** **dar′ ing·ly.** ***n-*** **dar′ ing·ness.**

dark (därk) ***adj-*** **[dark·er, dark·est] 1** having little or no light: *a* dark *room.* **2** not light in color: *a* dark *blue*; dark *complexion.* **3** gloomy; sullen: *a* dark *mood.* **4** mysterious; puzzling: *a deep,* dark *secret.* **5** evil; sinister: *a* dark *deed.* ***n-*** **1** absence of light: *the* dark *of night.* **2** nightfall: *after* dark. ***—adj-*** **dark′ ish.** ***adv-*** **dark′ ly.** ***n-*** **dark′ ness.**

in the dark in ignorance; lacking the relevant facts.

Dark Ages ***n-*** **1** period in history between the fall of the Roman Empire and the beginning of the Middle Ages. **2** the Middle Ages. Also **dark ages.**

dark·en (där′ kən) ***vt-*** to make darker: *to* darken *a color.* ***vi-***: *The sky* darkened *as the clouds rolled in.*

dark horse ***n-*** little-known entrant in a horse race, election, etc.

dark·ling (därk′ lĭng) *Archaic* ***adj-*** dimly seen. ***adv-*** in the darkness.

dark·room (därk′ rōōm′) ***n-*** room that has been darkened and protected from outside light and is used for developing and handling photographic films, plates, etc.

dar·ling (där′ lĭng) ***n-*** much loved person; object of deep affection: *the* darling *of her father's heart.* ***adj-*** *Informal* very attractive: *a* darling *dress.*

darn (därn) ***vt-*** to mend by weaving thread or yarn back and forth across a hole. ***n-*** a place thus mended.

darning needle *n-* 1 long needle with a large eye, used for darning. 2 dragonfly.

dart (därt) *vi-* to move in a quick, sudden way: *The dog* darted *after the rabbit.* *vt-* to shoot out: *She* darted *a glance at me.* *n-* 1 sudden movement: *a* dart *to the left.* 2 small, pointed missile meant to be thrown, or shot from a blowgun, crossbow, or the like; especially, such a missile with feathered tail thrown at a target in the game of **darts.**

Dart

dash (dăsh) *vi-* to rush violently: *to* dash *outside.* *vt-* 1 to throw violently: *to* dash *a cup to the floor.* 2 to destroy; ruin: *She* dashed *all my hopes.* 3 splatter; splash: *They* dashed *him with cold water.* *n-* 1 sudden rush or run: *a* dash *for freedom.* 2 short race: *a hundred-yard* dash. 3 little bit: *a* dash *of pepper.* 4 spirited energy; éclat: *a person of great* dash *and vigor.* 5 punctuation mark [—], used to show a pause or break in a sentence. A shorter form [–] is used to show a span of pages (1-15), years (1732-1799), etc. 6 dashboard. 7 the longer of the two sounds used in Morse Code.

dash off to do with haste: *to* dash off *a letter.*

dash·board (dăsh'bôrd') *n-* 1 instrument panel of an automobile; dash. 2 screen at the front of a carriage, boat, etc., used as protection against splashing.

dash·ing (dăsh'ĭng) *adj-* 1 lively; bold: *a* dashing *knight.* 2 showy; bright: *a* dashing *costume.*

das·tard (dăs'tərd) *n-* a sneaking and malicious coward.

das·tard·ly (dăst'tərd lē) *adj-* cowardly, sly, and evil: *His betrayal of his comrades was a* dastardly *act.*

da·ta (dā'tə, dăt'ə) *n- pl.* [*sing.* **da·tum**] facts and figures; information: *The* data *for a report.*

►DATA is now often used with a singular verb.

data bank *n-* that part of a computer in which information is stored; any filing system.

data processing *n-* conversion of raw information into a form that a computer can use and the handling and storage of that information by a computer. **—*n-* data processor.**

[1]date (dāt) *n-* 1 a particular time expressed as the day of the month, or the year, or both: *Abraham Lincoln's birth* date *is February 12, 1809.* 2 statement on a letter, coin, etc., giving such a time: *The* date *of a building is often on the cornerstone.* 3 period of time to which something belongs: *an invention of early* date. 4 *Informal* appointment or social engagement; also, the person with whom one has such an engagement. *vt-* [**dat·ed, dat·ing**] 1 to mark with the day of the month, etc.: *to* date *a letter.* 2 to find out or fix the time of: *Can you* date *that castle?* 3 *Informal* to escort socially (a person of the opposite sex). *vi- Informal* to have or keep social appointments as a couple. [from Old French, from Latin **data** meaning "(a letter or document) given (at a certain time)."] **—*adj-* date'less.**

out of date no longer in use or style; old-fashioned.

up to date 1 in fashion. 2 (also **to date**) up to now.

date from to belong to the time of; have origin in.

[2]date (dāt) *n-* 1 king of palm tree which bears clusters of oblong, one-seeded fruit. 2 the sweet fruit, usually dried, of this tree. *adj-:* *a* date *palm.* [from Old French (through Latin), from Greek **daktylos** meaning "finger."]

dat·ed (dā'təd) *adj-* 1 having a date: *a* dated *letter.* 2 old-fashioned: *a* dated *custom.*

date line *n-* 1 line at the beginning or end of a news article, letter, etc., giving the date and place of origin. 2 International Date Line.

da·tive (dā'tĭv) *Grammar* *n-* in Latin and other languages, a word or expression in the form used for indirect objects.

da·tum (dā'təm, dăt'əm) *n-* [*pl.* **da·ta**] 1 a fact, figure, or other single item of information; piece of data. 2 something such as a point or plane used as a basis for measuring or calculating elevation, depth, etc.: *Sea level is often used as a* datum. *as* ***modifier*****:** *a* datum *plane.*

daub (dôb) *n-* 1 a smear; smudge: *a* daub *of mud on her cheek.* 2 picture that is poorly painted. *vt-* 1 to cover or smear with mud, plaster, or the like. 2 to paint crudely: *He* daubed *the canvas.* *vi-:* *He's no painter; he just* daubs.

daugh·ter (dô'tər) *n-* 1 girl or woman in relation to her parents. 2 female descendant: *the* daughters *of Abraham.* 3 woman who belongs to or is closely related to a particular place, group, cause, etc.: *a true* daughter *of Ireland.*

daugh·ter-in-law (dô'tər ĭn lô') *n-* [*pl.* **daugh·ters-in-law**] wife of one's son.

daunt (dônt) *vt-* frighten; dishearten; make less courageous: *Even the risk of death did not* daunt *him.*

daunt·less (dônt'ləs) *adj-* fearless; brave: *a* dauntless *explorer.* **—*adv-* daunt'less·ly. *n-* daunt'less·ness.**

dau·phin (dô'fĭn) *n-* title for the oldest son of the king of France, used from 1349 to 1830.

dav·en·port (dăv'vən pôrt') *n-* large sofa.

Da·vid (dā'vəd) *n-* in the Bible, a son of Jesse and father of Solomon. David killed the giant Goliath, charmed Saul with a harp, and reigned over Israel for more than 40 years.

da·vit (dăv'ət, dā'vət) *n-* one of a pair of cranes for lowering boats into the water and recovering them.

Davits, holding a boat

Da·vy Jones (dā'vē jōnz') *n-* the spirit of the sea; the sailors' devil.

Davy Jones's locker *n-* the bottom of the sea, regarded as the grave of the drowned.

daw·dle (dô'dəl) *vi-* [**daw·dled, daw·dling**] to loiter; waste time; be lazy and casual: *He* dawdled *all day.*

dawn (dôn) *n-* 1 the coming of daylight in the morning. 2 the beginning or earliest appearance of something. *The invention of the airplane marked the* dawn *of a new age.* *vi-* 1 to begin to grow light in the morning: *The day* dawns *in the east.* 2 to begin to appear or develop.

dawn on to begin to be understood by; become clear to.

day (dā) *n-* 1 the period of light between sunrise and sunset. 2 period of 24 hours. 3 period in which a planet or other celestial body makes one complete rotation about its axis. 4 particular age or period: *in the* days *of hoop skirts.* 5 particular 24-hour period on which some special event takes place: *Thanksgiving* Day; *a wedding* day. 6 the number of hours given to work or school: *the eight-hour* day.

Day·ak (dī'ăk') *n-* one of a people living in Borneo. 2 the language of these people. Also **Dyak.**

day·break (dā'brāk') *n-* first appearance of light in the morning; dawn.

day coach *n-* ordinary railroad passenger car as distinct from a sleeping car, dining car, etc.

day·dream (dā'drēm') *n-* a dreamy, idle imagining; reverie; woolgathering. *vi-:* *Joey often* daydreams.

day·light (dā'līt') *n-* 1 the light of day. 2 the time between dawn and dusk when the sun gives light; daytime. 3 daybreak: *We will sail before* daylight.

see daylight to begin to see the solution of a problem, the end of a confused or very busy period, etc.

---

fāte, făt, dâre, bärn; bē, bĕt, mêre; bīte, bĭt; nōte, hŏt, môre, dóg; fŭn, fûr; tōō, bŏŏk; oil; out; tar; thin; then; hw for wh as in *wh*at; zh for s as in u*s*ual; ə for a, e, i, o, u, as in *a*go, lin*e*n, per*i*l, at*o*m, min*u*s

Daylight Saving Time ***n-*** system of keeping time in the summer. Clocks are set one hour ahead of standard time so that people will have an extra hour of daylight in the evening for recreation, gardening, etc.

day school ***n-*** primary or secondary school held during the daytime; especially, a private school attended by students who live at home.

day·star (dā′ stär′) ***n-*** **1** morning star. **2** *Archaic* sun.

day·time (dā′ tīm′) ***n-*** time between sunrise and sunset.

daze (dāz) ***vt-*** **[dazed, daz·ing]** to confuse or bewilder with a blow, a shock, etc.; stun: *The news of his friend's death* dazed *him.* ***n-*** confused or bewildered condition: *He came out of his* daze *three hours later.*

daz·zle (dăz′ əl) ***vt-*** **[daz·zled, daz·zling]** **1** to bewilder with a very bright light; blind temporarily. **2** to surprise or overcome by brilliant performance, speech, etc.: *Her singing* dazzled *us.* ***n-*** glare: *the* dazzle *of lights.*

daz·zling (dăz′ lĭng) ***adj-*** **1** so bright as to prevent clear vision: *a* dazzling *light.* **2** overwhelming: *a* dazzling *wit.* —***adv-*** **daz′ zling·ly.**

d.c. or **D.C.** or **DC** direct current.

D.C. District of Columbia.

D.D. Doctor of Divinity.

D-day (dē′ dā′) ***n-*** day set for the beginning of a military or other carefully planned operation; especially, June 6, 1944, when the Allies invaded France.

D.D.S. Doctor of Dental Surgery.

DDT (dē′ dē′ tē′) ***n-*** powerful chemical insect killer.

de- *prefix* **1** the opposite or the reverse: de*compress*; de*vitalize*; de*sensitize.* **2** an undoing: de*code*; de*form.* **3** removal or removal from: de*frost*; de*rail*; de*horn*; de*throne.* **4** down: de*value*; de*mote.* [from Middle English **de-**, from Old French **de-, des,** from Latin **de-**, "down; away" and **dis-**, "from."]

dea·con (dē′ kən) ***n-*** **1** church officer who does not preach but assists in certain ceremonies, in caring for the poor, etc. **2** in some churches, an ordained member of the clergy next below a priest in rank. —***n-*** *fem.* **dea′ con·ess.**

dead (dĕd) ***adj-*** **[dead·er, dead·est]** **1** no longer living: *a* dead *animal.* **2** without any life; inorganic: *A rock is* dead *matter.* **3** without force, motion, etc.; inactive: *a* dead *tennis ball*; *a* dead *party.* **4** no longer used; extinct: *a* dead *language.* **5** complete; entire: *a* dead *silence*; *a* dead *loss.* **6** exact: *at* dead *center.* ***adv-*** **1** *Informal* completely: *He's* dead *right.* **2** exactly; directly: *Steer* dead *ahead.* ***n-*** the time of the greatest quietness, inactivity, etc.: *the* dead *of night.* —***n-*** **dead′ ness.**

dead·beat (dĕd′ bēt′) *Slang* ***n-*** loafer or sponger.

dead·en (dĕd′ ən) ***vt-*** **1** to make less forceful or active; damp: *to* deaden *a sound*; deaden *a spring.* **2** to take away feeling or keenness from; numb: *The drug* deadened *his pain. Grief* deadened *her mind.*

dead end ***n-*** street, alley, etc., that is closed off at one end. *as* ***modifier*** **(dead-end)**: *a* dead-end *street.*

dead·eye (dĕd′ ī′) ***n-*** **1** on ships, a circular wooden block with three eyes through which lanyards are passed. For picture, see *ratline.* **2** *Informal* sharpshooter.

dead·fall (dĕd′ fôl′) ***n-*** **1** animal trap which kills or holds the prey by means of a heavy weight that falls on it. **2** mass of fallen trees, branches, etc.

dead heat ***n-*** a race which ends in a tie.

dead letter ***n-*** **1** letter that cannot be delivered or returned. Such letters are sent to the **dead-letter office** in the post office for further attempts at delivery. **2** something that has lost its former importance.

dead·line (dĕd′ līn′) ***n-*** the latest time set for something to be finished; time limit.

dead·lock (dĕd′ lŏk′) ***n-*** situation in which opposing sides are even in strength and neither will give in; stand-off; stalemate. ***vt-*** to bring about such a situation in: *Their endless arguments* deadlocked *the issue.* ***vi-***: *They* deadlocked *over the question of higher wages.*

dead·ly (dĕd′ lē) ***adj-*** **[dead·li·er, dead·li·est]** **1** causing or tending to cause death; lethal; fatal: *the* deadly *bite of the cobra.* **2** very hostile; aiming to kill or destroy: *a* deadly *enemy.* ***adv-*** in a manner resembling death; like death: *She is* deadly *pale.*

deadly nightshade ***n-*** **1** poisonous plant of the Old World; belladonna. **2** (also **black nightshade**) related plant with small white flowers and black berries considered to be poisonous.

deadly sins ***n-*** pride, lust, envy, anger, covetousness, gluttony, and sloth, the seven sins regarded as promoting other sins and as very dangerous to the soul; capital sins.

dead·pan (dĕd′ păn′) *Informal* ***adj-*** having little or no facial expression; impassive.

dead pan *Slang* ***n-*** expressionless face.

dead reckoning ***n-*** navigation by calculating distance covered in a certain time under certain conditions of wind, drift, etc., without astronomical sights or tables.

dead weight ***n-*** **1** the weight of something felt in full, without the lightness that a living thing seems to have. **2** any heavy, oppressive, or unbearable burden: *the* dead weight *of illiteracy.* **3** weight of a box car, ship, truck, or other carrier when not loaded.

deaf (dĕf) ***adj-*** **[deaf·er, deaf·est]** unable or partly unable to hear. —***adv-*** **deaf′ ly.** ***n-*** **deaf′ ness.**

deaf to unwilling to listen: *She was* deaf to *his pleas.*

deaf·en (dĕf′ ən) ***vt-*** **1** to make unable to hear. **2** to overpower or stun with noise: *Shrieks* deafened *me.*

deaf-mute (dĕf′ myōōt′) ***n-*** deaf person who cannot speak, usually as a result of deafness from early childhood. *as* ***modifier***: *a* deaf-mute *boy.*

[1]deal (dēl) ***vi-*** **[dealt, deal·ing]** **1** to be concerned (with): *History* deals *with the past.* **2** to behave; act: *He* deals *fairly with his partner.* **3** to trade; do business: *That jewelry store* deals *mainly in watches.* ***vt-*** **1** to give out; distribute: *Please* deal *the cards.* **2** to give; deliver: *We* dealt *the enemy a hard blow.* ***n-*** **1** a single passing out of playing cards. **2** *Informal* an instance of luck or of treatment by other persons: *to get a raw* deal. **3** *Informal* transaction or arrangement, especially in business or politics. **4** fairly large number or amount. [from Old English **dælan**] —***n-*** **deal′ er.**

[2]deal (dēl) ***n-*** a board of pine or fir. ***adj-***: *a* deal *table.* [probably from early Dutch **dele,** "board; plank."]

deal·ings (dē′ lĭngs) ***n-*** relations or connections, especially in commerce: *honest* dealings.

dean (dēn) ***n-*** **1** official of a college or university, often head of the faculty and in charge of instruction. **2** member of a college or school faculty in charge of student affairs and discipline. **3** the member of a group or organization who has served the longest: *the* dean *of newspaper columnists.* **4** head of a group of clergymen connected with a cathedral.

dean·er·y (dē′ nə rē) ***n-*** [*pl.* **dean·er·ies**] **1** position or authority of a dean. **2** residence of a dean.

dear (dêr) ***adj-*** **[dear·er, dear·est]** **1** loved; precious: *a* dear *friend.* **2** highly valued; esteemed (often used in letters as a polite form of address): *My* dear *John.* Dear *Sir.* **3** expensive; costly: *It's very* dear *at that price.* ***n-*** darling; loved one. ***interj-*** an exclamation of surprise or dismay. ***Hom-*** deer. —***adv-*** **dear′ly.** ***n-*** **dear′ ness.**

dearth (dûrth) ***n-*** shortage; scarcity: *a* dearth *of food.*

death (dĕth) ***n-*** **1** the end of life; dying. **2** the ending of anything; destruction: *the* death *of hope*; *the* death *of*

local industries. **3** the state of being dead: *In* death *he looked serene.* **4** a cause of dying; something that kills: *These stairs will be the* death *of me.*
at death's door near death. **put to death** to kill.
to death very much; to the last degree: *scared* to death.
death·bed (dĕth′bĕd′) *n-* **1** the bed in which a person dies. **2** the last hours of a person's life.
death·blow (dĕth′blō′) *n-* blow, event, etc., that causes death or an end of existence: *a* deathblow *to my hopes.*
death cup or **death angel** *n-* extremely poisonous mushrom, an amanita, having a white or olive cap, white gills, and a growth shaped like a cup at the base of the stem; destroying angel.
death·less (dĕth′ləs) *adj-* never dying; immortal; eternal. **—*n-* death′less·ness.**
death·like (dĕth′līk′) *adj-* like death or its aspects; deathly: *a* deathlike *trance*; *a* deathlike *pallor.*
death·ly (dĕth′lē) *adj-* [**death·li·er, death·li·est**] **1** deadly; causing death; lethal; fatal: *a* deathly *blow.* **2** deathlike: *a* deathly *silence.* *adv-* **1** in a manner like death: *His skin felt* deathly *cold.* **2** extremely; utterly: *Many animals are* deathly *afraid of fire.*
death mask *n-* mask made from a plaster mold of a dead person's face.
death rate *n-* the number of deaths within a particular group in a given time, usually stated as so many deaths per thousand inhabitants.
de·ba·cle (dĭ băk′əl) *n-* sudden and complete collapse; downfall; rout: *The defeat at the river was a* debacle.
de·bar (dĭ bär′, dē-) *vt-* [**de·barred, de·bar·ring**] to rule out; exclude; prohibit; bar: *They* barred *him.*
de·bark (dĭ bärk′, dē-) *vi-* to go ashore from a ship; disembark. *vt-*: *to* debark *troops.* **—*n-* de′bar·ka′tion.**
de·base (dĭ bās′) *vt-* [**de·based, de·bas·ing**] to lower in value or quality: *to* debase *oneself by cheating*; *to* debase *gold by adding copper.* **—*n-* de·base′ment.**
de·bat·a·ble (dĭ bā′tə bəl) *adj-* open to discussion or debate; not decided; moot: *a* debatable *question.*
de·bate (dĭ bāt′) *vt-* [**de·bat·ed, de·bat·ing**] to discuss or argue by giving reasons for and against: *We* debated *several questions.* *vi-*: *The council* debated *all night.* *n-* **1** argument; discussion: *after much* debate, *Congress passed the bill.* **2** formal contest in argumentation: *Our school team won the* debate. **—*n-* de·bat′er.**
de·bauch (dĭ bóch′) *vt-* to lead (someone) away from virtue; corrupt; seduce. *vi-* to overindulge in eating, drinking, etc; dissipate. *n-* drunken orgy; also, any excessive indulgence in sensual pleasures. **—*n-* de·bauch′er·y:** *the* debauchery *of many Roman emperors.*
de·bil·i·tate (dĭ bĭl′ə tāt′) *vt-* [**de·bil·i·tat·ed, de·bil·i·tat·ing**] to weaken; make feeble; impair the strength of: *A humid climate* debilitates *one who is not used to it.*
de·bil·i·ty (dĭ bĭl′ə tē) *n-* [*pl.* **de·bil·i·ties**] weakness; lack of energy or strength; feebleness.
deb·it (dĕb′ət) *n-* **1** entry in an account book showing a sum due. **2** the left-hand side of an account, where money owed is entered; opposite of credit. *vt-* **1** to enter (money due) in an account. **2** to charge with a debt: *Please* debit *Mr. Lee's account with $5.00.*
deb·o·nair or **deb·o·naire** (dĕb′ə nâr′) *adj-* carefree; gay; nonchalant; urbane. **—*adv-* deb′o·nair′ly.**
de·bouch (dĭ bo͞osh′, -bouch′) *vi-* to emerge or burst (from), or discharge (into something): *The men* debouched *from the car. Lake Victoria* debouches *into the Nile.*
de·brief (dē brēf′) *vt-* to question (as an astronaut) after a mission in order to obtain information.
de·bris (də brē′) or **dé·bris** (dā brē′) *n-* broken pieces; rubbish: *a street littered with* debris.
debt (dĕt) *n-* something owed, especially money owed: *a $600* debt; *a* debt *of gratitude for kindness.*
in debt having an obligation.
debt·or (dĕt′ər) *n-* person, group, country, etc., that owes a debt; someone with a debt to pay.
de·bunk (dĭ bŭngk′) *Informal vt-* to expose or ridicule sham, falseness, or exaggerated claims: *The politician* debunked *the theories of his opponent.* [American word drom **de-**, "away" and [2]**bunk,** "nonsense."]
de·but (dā′byo͞o′) *n-* **1** first public appearance on the stage: *the* debut *of an opera singer.* **2** formal introduction of a young girl into society. **3** beginning or opening.
deb·u·tante (dĕb′ yo͞o tänt′) *n-* young woman making her formal appearance in society, usually at a ball.
dec. deceased.
Dec. December.
deca- or **dec-** *prefix* ten: a deca*liter*; dec*athlon.* [from Greek **deka-**, from **deka** meaning "ten."]
dec·ade (dĕk′ād′) *n-* period of ten years.
de·ca·dent (dĕk′ə dənt, dĭ kā′-) *adj-* declining; deteriorating: *a* decadent *society.* *n-* person in a state of intellectual or moral decay. **—*adv-* de′ca·dent·ly** or **de·ca′dent·ly.** *n-* **de′ca·dence** or **de·ca′dence.**
de·caf·fein·at·ed (dē kăf′ə nā′təd) *adj-* having the caffeine removed.
dec·a·gon (dĕk′ə gŏn′) *n-* polygon with ten sides and ten angles.
dec·a·he·dron (dĕk′ə hē′drən) *n-* geometric solid having ten plane faces.
dec·a·li·ter or **dec·a·li·tre** (dĕk′ə lē′tər) *n-* unit of volume equal to ten liters.

Decahedron

Dec·a·logue (dĕk′ə lóg′, -lŏg′) *n-* the Ten Commandments. Also **Dec′a·log′.**
de·camp (dĭ kămp′, dē-) *vi-* **1** to leave a camp; break camp. **2** to depart quickly or secretly; run away. **—*n-* de·camp′ment.**
de·cant (dĭ kănt′, dē-) *vt-* to pour liquid, especially wine, carefully from one vessel into another without disturbing the sediment.
de·cant·er (dĭ kăn′tər) *n-* ornamental glass bottle with a stopper, used for wine or liquor.
de·cap·i·tate (dē kăp′ə tāt′) *vt-* [**de·cap·i·tat·ed, de·cap·i·tat·ing**] to cut off the head of; behead. **—*n-* de·cap′i·ta·tion.**
dec·a·pod (dĕk′ə pŏd′) *n-* **1** a crustacean, such as a lobster or crab, with five pair of legs. **2** one of a group of mollusks which resemble octopuses and have ten arms, such as the squid and the cuttlefish.
de·cath·lon (dĭ kăth′lŏn′) *n-* athletic contest consisting of ten different track or field events in which the contestant having the highest total score is the winner. The events are the 100, 400, and 1500 meter runs. 110 meter high hurdles, broad jump, high jump, discus throw, javelin throw, pole vault, and shot-put.
de·cay (dĭ kā′) *vi-* **1** to rot or decompose: *Plants that have died* decay *and make the soil rich.* **2** to lose strength or quality gradually; fail; waste away. *n-* **1** decomposition; rotting. **2** loss of strength or quality by degrees; decline: *the* decay *of a business*; *the* decay *of health with age.* **3** *Physics* disintegration of radioactive material.
de·cease (dĭ sēs′) *n-* death.
de·ceased (dĭ sēst′) *adj-* dead. *n-* **the deceased** dead person or persons.
de·ce·dent (dĭ sē′dənt) *n-* in law, a dead person.

fāte, făt, dâre, bärn; bē, bĕt, mêre; bīte, bĭt; nōte, hŏt, môre, dóg; fŭn, fûr; to͞o, bo͝ok; oil; out; tar; thin; then; hw for wh as in *wh*at; zh for s as in u*s*ual; ə for a, e, i, o, u, as in *a*go, lin*e*n, per*i*l, at*o*m, min*u*s

de·ceit (dĭ sēt′) *n-* **1** habit or practice of misleading or cheating: *His* deceit *lost him the trust of his friends.* **2** an attempt or device to mislead; trick.

de·ceit·ful (dĭ sēt′ fəl) *adj-* lying; cheating; insincere; false; given to fraud and trickery. *—adv-* **de·ceit′ ful·ly.** *—n-* **de·ceit′ ful·ness.**

de·ceive (dĭ sēv′) *vt-* [**de·ceived, de·ceiv·ing**] **1** to cause (a person) to believe what is untrue. **2** to mislead: *His strong appearance* deceived *me.* *—n-* **de·ceiv′ er.**

de·cel·er·ate (dē sĕl′ ə rāt′) *vt-* [**de·cel·er·ated, de·cel·er·ating**] to cause (a car, train, etc.) to move at a slower speed. *vi-* to decrease in speed. *n-* **de·cel′ er·a′ tion.**

De·cem·ber (dĭ sĕm′ bər) *n-* the twelfth and last month of the year, having 31 days.

de·cen·cy (dē′ sən sē) *n-* [*pl.* **de·cen·cies**] **1** proper behavior in speech, action, or dress; decorum. **2 decencies** the requirements of a respectable or proper life, including courtesy, cleanliness, and reasonable comfort.

de·cen·ni·al (də sən′ ē əl) *adj-* **1** of ten years. **2** occurring every ten years. *n-* a tenth anniversary.

de·cent (dē′ sənt) *adj-* **1** proper; suitable; appropriate: *to wear* decent *clothes; to have* decent *manners.* **2** respectable: *He comes from a* decent *home.* **3** passable; good enough; fair: *He makes a* decent *salary.* **4** kind; understanding. *—adv-* **de′ cent·ly.**

de·cen·tral·i·za·tion (dē sĕn′ trə lə zā′ shən) *n-* a reorganizing or spreading (of authority, activities, etc.) from one center to many branches: *the* decentralization *of industries into the suburbs.*

de·cen·tral·ize (dē sĕn′ trə līz′) *vt-* [**de·cen·tral·ized, de·cen·tral·iz·ing**] to transfer (control, operation, etc.) from a central point to outlying points.

de·cep·tion (dĭ sĕp′ shən) *n-* **1** act of deceiving; cheating. **2** something that fools or deceives; trickery; fraud.

de·cep·tive (dĭ sĕp′ tĭv) *adj-* deceiving; giving a false appearance or impression: *a* deceptive *calm before the storm.* *—adv-* **de·cep′ tive·ly.** *n-* **de·cep′ tive·ness.**

deci- *prefix* tenth: *a* deci*gram* (one tenth of a gram).

dec·i·bel (dĕs′ ə bĕl′, -bəl) *n-* unit for measuring the loudness of sounds.

de·cide (dĭ sīd′) *vi-* [**de·cid·ed, de·cid·ing**] **1** to determine or conclude; make up one's mind: *I* decided *to leave early.* **2** to give a judgment or decision: *The court* decided *in our favor.* *vt-* **1** to settle (a question, doubt, issue, etc.): *We* decided *the question of size.* **2** to cause the outcome of: *That one battle* decided *the war.*

de·cid·ed (dĭ sī′ dəd) *adj-* **1** definite; clear; unmistakable: *a* decided *improvement.* **2** not showing hesitation; determined: *very* decided *opinions.* *—adv-* **de·cid′ ed·ly.**

de·cid·u·ous (də sĭj′ o͞o əs) *adj-* shedding leaves yearly.

dec·i·gram (dĕs′ ə grăm′) *n-* unit of mass or weight equal to one-tenth of a gram.

dec·i·li·ter or **dec·i·li·tre** (dĕs′ ə lē′ tər) *n-* unit of volume equal to one-tenth of a liter.

dec·i·mal (dĕs′ ə məl) *n-* **1** a decimal fraction. **2** any numeral written with a decimal point. *adj-* having to do with or based on the number ten. *—adv-* **dec′ i·mal·ly.**

decimal fraction *n-* a proper fraction whose (unwritten) denominator is a power of ten. It is written as a whole number preceded by a dot (**decimal point**). The number of digits to the right of this dot determines the power of the denominator. Examples: .3 (decimal fraction) = 3/10 (denominator, ten to the first power); .09 = 9/100 (denominator, ten to the second power).

decimal number system *n-* system of numbers having the number ten as its base.

dec·i·mate (dĕs′ ə māt′) *vt-* [**dec·i·mat·ed, dec·i·mat·ing**] **1** to destroy a large part of. **2** to destroy one tenth of.

dec·i·me·ter or **dec·i·me·tre** (dĕs′ ə mē′ tər) *n-* unit of length equal to one tenth of a meter.

de·ci·pher (dĭ sī′ fər) *vt-* **1** to make out or interpret the meaning of (something that is not plain or clear): *to* decipher *someone's bad handwriting.* **2** to change from a code or cipher to ordinary words: *to* decipher *a code.*

de·ci·sion (dĭ sĭzh′ ən) *n-* **1** a deciding or making up one's mind; judgment. **2** opinion or judgment reached: *The court's* decision *is final.* **3** firmness; determination: *a man of* decision.

de·ci·sive (dĭ sī′ sĭv) *adj-* **1** settling something once and for all; conclusive: *A* decisive *battle ended the war.* **2** showing decision; positive; firm; determined: *a* decisive *answer.* *—adv-* **de·ci′sive·ly.** *n-* **de·ci′ sive·ness.**

deck (dĕk) *n-* **1** any of the floors or levels of a ship. **2** any flat surface or platform like a ship's deck: *a sun* deck; *an observation* deck. **3** pack of playing cards. *vt-* to decorate; array; adorn: *to* deck *the halls with holly.*

on deck ready for action; next in turn.

deck·hand (dĕk′ hănd′) *n-* sailor employed on the deck of a vessel rather than in the engine room or other special station; ordinary seaman.

de·claim (dĭ klām′) *vi-* **1** to speak or recite in public; deliver an oration. **2** to speak in a broad theatrical way: *He* declaims *all the time.* *vt-* to recite (something) in a theatrical manner: *to* declaim *a poem.* *—n-* **de·claim′ er.**

dec·la·ma·tion (dĕk′ lə mā′ shən) *n-* **1** a declaiming; also, an instance of this. **2** a public speech.

de·clam·a·tor·y (dĭ klăm′ ə tôr′ ē) *adj-* **1** relating to declamation. **2** loud and emotional; bombastic: *long,* declamatory *tirades.*

dec·la·ra·tion (dĕk′ lə rā′ shən) *n-* **1** statement; announcement. **2** public statement; proclamation: *a* declaration *of war.* **3** document listing goods liable to tax or duty: *a customs* declaration.

Declaration of Independence *n-* document of July 4, 1776, by which the 13 American colonies declared themselves to be free and independent of Great Britain.

de·clar·a·tive (dĭ klăr′ ə tĭv, dĭ klĕr′-) *adj-* making a statement; declaring, rather than asking or ordering: *"The cat is black." is a* declarative *sentence.*

de·clare (dĭ klâr′) *vt-* [**de·clared, de·clar·ing**] **1** to proclaim; announce publicly: *The President* declared *a holiday. He* declared *that he would not surrender.* **2** to affirm solemnly before a witness: *The prisoner* declared *his innocence.* **3** to list (goods on which duty is to be paid). *vi-* to make a declaration: *It was the first newspaper to* declare *for the senator.*

declare (oneself) to state one's belief or one's position in an argument or on a question.

de·clen·sion (dĭ klĕn′ shən) *Grammar n-* **1** all the forms showing the cases of a certain noun, pronoun, or adjective; paradigm. **2** group of words with the same or similar case forms.

de·clin·a·ble (dĭ klī′ nə bəl) *adj-* such as can be gramatically declined as a noun, pronoun, or adjective.

dec·li·na·tion (dĕk′ lə nā′ shən) *n-* **1** the deviation of the needle of a magnetic compass from true north. **2** a refusal. **3** a downward slope.

de·cline (dĭ klīn′) *vt-* [**de·clined, de·clin·ing**] **1** (considered intransitive when the direct object is implied but not expressed) to refuse: *to* decline *an invitation.* **2** *Grammar* to give the declension of (nouns, pronouns, or adjectives). *vi-* **1** to slope, bend, or lean downward. **2** to decay; fail: *His vigor began to* decline. **3** to go down; diminish: *The stock market* declined. *n-* **1** downward slope. **2** a lessening; deterioration: *a* decline *of prices; a* decline *in health.*

de·cliv·i·ty (dĭ klĭv′ ə tē) *n-* [*pl.* **de·cliv·i·ties**] a slope.

de·coc·tion (dĭ kŏk′shən) ***n-*** extract, flavor, etc., obtained by boiling, or boiling down, an animal or vegetable substance.
de·code (dē kōd′) ***vt-*** **[de·cod·ed, de·cod·ing]** to convert (a message) from a code or cipher to ordinary language.
dé·col·le·té (dā′ kŏl′ ə tā′) ***adj-*** **1** cut low at the neck: *a* décolleté *dress.* **2** having the neck and shoulders bare; wearing a low-necked dress.
de·com·pose (dē′ kəm pōz′) ***vi-*** **[de·com·posed, de·com·pos·ing]** **1** to decay; rot: *Dead plants gradually* decompose *and enrich the soil.* **2** to separate into basic parts. ***vt-***: *Heat* decomposes *certain chemical compounds.* **—*n-* de′ com′ po·si′ tion** (dē kŏm′ pə zĭsh′ ən).
de·com·press (dē′ kəm prĕs′) ***vt-*** **1** to free from pressure or compression. **2** to subject (a diver, caisson worker, etc.) to decompression.
de·com·pres·sion (dē′ kəm prĕsh′ ən) ***n-*** a decompressing; especially, the gradual decreasing of air pressure on deep-sea divers or caisson workers to prevent caisson disease. *as* ***modifier***: *a* decompression *process.*
de·con·tam·i·nate (dē′ kən tăm′ ə nāt′) ***vt-*** **[de·con·tam·i·nated, de·con·tam·i·nat·ing]** to remove or destroy poisons, bacteria, radioactive wastes, or other dangerous materials that contaminate (water, food, air, a place, an object, etc.). **—*n-* de′ con·tam′ i·na′ tion.**
de·con·trol (dē′ kən trōl′) ***vt-*** **[de·con·trolled, de·con·trol·ling]** to end government control of: *to* decontrol *rents.* ***n-*** removal of control: *a* decontrol *of housing.*
dé·cor or **de·cor** (dā′ kôr′, -kôr′) ***n-*** **1** pattern of decoration in a room, house, etc.; ornamentation. **2** stage scenery and furnishings.
dec·o·rate (dĕk′ ə rāt′) ***vt-*** **[dec·o·rat·ed, dec·o·rat·ing]** **1** to put ornaments on; adorn; embellish: *to* decorate *a Christmas tree.* **2** to paint or paper (a room, house, etc.). **3** to give (someone) a mark of distinction such as a medal or badge: *The general* decorated *four soldiers for bravery.*
dec·o·ra·tion (dĕk′ ə rā′ shən) ***n-*** **1** the adding of ornaments; adornment: *the* decoration *of the room for the party.* **2** thing used for decorating; an ornament. **3** medal; honorary ribbon or pin.
Decoration Day ***n-*** Memorial Day.
dec·o·ra·tive (dĕk′ ər ə tĭv, dĕk′ ə rā′ -) ***adj-*** serving to beautify or adorn; ornamental: *a* decorative *table setting.* **—*adv-* dec′ o·ra·tive·ly.** ***n-*** **dec′ o·ra·tive·ness.**
dec·o·ra·tor (dĕk′ ə rā′ tər) ***n-*** one who decorates, especially one who makes a business of planning and arranging interiors of houses.
dec·o·rous (dĕk′ ər əs) ***adj-*** suitable; fit; proper or dignified: *her* decorous *behavior.* **—*adv-* dec′ o·rous·ness.**
de·co·rum (dĭ kôr′ əm) ***n-*** that which is proper and fitting in behavior and language; dignity; propriety.
1**de·coy** (dē′ koi′) ***n-*** **1** a deceptive trick or snare. **2** a real or imitation bird used to lure live birds within gunshot. **3** person or thing used to lead someone into danger.
2**de·coy** (dĭ koi′, dē′ koi′) ***vt-*** to lead into a trap by means of a trick; entice; entrap.

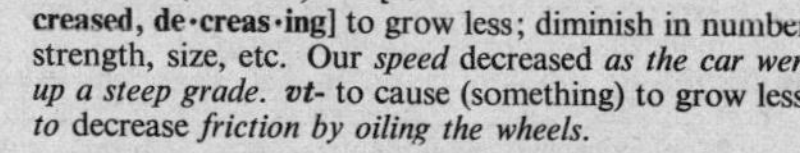

Decoy

1**de·crease** (dĭ krēs′) ***vi-*** **[de·creased, de·creas·ing]** to grow less; diminish in number, strength, size, etc. Our *speed* decreased *as the car went up a steep grade.* ***vt-*** to cause (something) to grow less: *to* decrease *friction by oiling the wheels.*
2**de·crease** (dē′ krēs′, dĭ krēs′) ***n-*** a lessening; decline; falling off: *a* decrease *in the number of accidents.*
de·cree (dĭ krē′) ***n-*** **1** official command or ordinance; law; edict: *a* decree *of the government.* **2** judgment or order given by a court: *a* divorce *decree.* ***vt-*** to establish by law: *to* decree *an amnesty.*
dec·re·ment (dĕk′ rə mənt) *Mathematics* ***n-*** the amount by which a variable quantity decreases.
de·crep·it (dĭ krĕp′ ət) ***adj-*** broken down by age or long use; feeble: *a* decrepit *car.* **—*adv-* de·crep′ it·ly.**
de·crep·i·tude (dĭ krĕp′ ə tōōd′, -tyōōd′) ***n-*** feebleness and poor condition, usually from old age or long use.
de·cre·scen·do (dā′ krə shĕn′ dō′, dē-) *Music* ***n-*** [*pl.* **de·cre·scen·dos**] a gradual decrease in loudness. ***adj- & adv-*** gradually decreasing in loudness.
de·cry (dē krī′) ***vt-*** **[de·cried, de·cry·ing]** **1** to condemn; censure: *to* decry *the latest dances.* **2** to belittle; try to lower the value of: *He* decried *the value of learning.*
ded·i·cate (dĕd′ ə kāt′) ***vt-*** **[ded·i·cat·ed, ded·i·cat·ing]** **1** to set apart for a special purpose, often by a ceremony: *The bishop will* dedicate *the new church.* **2** to devote; commit: *He* dedicated *his life to peace.* **3** to inscribe or address (a book or other artistic work) to a patron or friend. **—*adj-* ded′ i·ca·tor′ y** (dĕd′ ĭ kə tôr′ ē): *a* dedicatory *preface.*
ded·i·ca·tion (dĕd′ ə kā′ shən) ***n-*** **1** a devoting to a religious or other special purpose: *the* dedication *of a new church*; *the* dedication *of a doctor to his work.* **2** inscription to someone, expressing gratitude or respect, often prefixed to a book.
de·duce (dĭ dōōs′, -dyōōs′) ***vt-*** **[de·duced, de·duc·ing]** to reach a conclusion from known facts; infer: *I* deduce *from your remarks that you disagree with me.* **—*adj-* de·duc′ i·ble:** *This statement is not* deducible *from the evidence.*
de·duct (dĭ dŭkt′) ***vt-*** to take away (an amount or part); *I* deducted *$10 from the total.*
de·duc·ti·ble (dĭ dŭk′ tə bəl) ***adj-*** **1** of a type that permits deducting. **2** allowable as a deduction from total income in calculating income tax.
de·duc·tion (dĭ dŭk′ shən) ***n-*** **1** a taking away; subtraction: *the* deduction *of taxes from a salary.* **2** amount taken away: *After* deductions *there was not much left.* **3** deductive reasoning. **4** conclusion based on deductive reasoning.
de·duc·tive (dĭ dŭk′ tĭv) ***adj-*** arriving at a conclusion by deduction: *The crime was solved by* deductive *methods.* **—*adv-* de·duc′tive·ly.**
deductive reasoning ***n-*** orderly thinking based upon accepted facts or statements called "premises." In its traditional form **(deductive logic),** it uses the syllogism. The new facts or conclusions will be correct if the premises are correct and the method is proper. See also *inductive reasoning.*
deed (dēd) ***n-*** **1** something done; instance of behavior; act; action: *a heroic* deed; *an unfortunate* deed. **2** legal document showing the ownership of real estate. ***vt-*** to make over or transfer (real estate).
deem (dēm) ***vt-*** to judge; consider: *He* deemed *it wise.*
deep (dēp) ***adj-*** **[deep·er, deep·est]** **1** going far down from or below the top or surface: *a* deep *hole*; *a* deep *cut*; *a* deep *dive*; *a* deep *insight into the problem.* **2** going far back from the front or the nearest edge: *a* deep *shelf*; *a* deep *forest.* **3** intense; extraordinary; profound: *a* deep *sleep*; deep *feeling*; *a* deep *sigh*; *a* deep *breath.* **4** having strong and complex feelings, thoughts, etc.: *a* deep

---

fāte, făt, dâre, bärn; bē, bĕt, mêre; bīte, bĭt; nōte, hŏt, môre, dòg; fŭn, fûr; tōō, bŏŏk; oil; out; tar; thin; then; hw for wh as in *what*; zh for s as in *usual*; ə for a, e, i, o, u, as in *ago*, *linen*, *peril*, *atom*, *minus*

person. 5 absorbed; involved: *She was* deep *in thought.* 6 of colors, dark and rich: *a* deep *blue.* 7 of sounds; low in pitch: *a* deep *voice.* 8 hard to understand; obscure: *the* deep *sayings of the prophets.* ***adv-*** far down or into: *to dig* deep. ***n-*** place in an ocean or sea where the depth of the water exceeds 3000 fathoms. **—*adv-* deep'ly.**

deep·en (dē'pən) ***vt-*** to make (something) deeper: *to* deepen *a well*; *to* deepen *a color*; *to* deepen *one's understanding.* ***vi-*** to become darker or deeper: *The shadows* deepened. *The water* deepened *offshore.*

deep-root·ed (dēp'rōō'təd) ***adj-*** firmly planted or set; deeply implanted; profound: *a* deep-rooted *loyalty.*

deep-sea (dēp'sē') ***adj-*** of or in the deeper parts of the sea: *a* deep-sea *diver.*

deep-seat·ed (dēp'sē'təd) ***adj-*** found or planted deep within; firm and lasting: *a* deep-seated *tradition.*

deep-set (dēp'sĕt') ***adj-*** deeply placed or fixed: *She had* deep-set *blue eyes.*

deer (dêr) ***n-*** [*pl.* **deer**] any of several hoofed, cud-chewing mammals, the males of which have antlers. ***Hom-*** dear. **—*adj-* deer'like'.**

White-tail deer, 3½ ft. high at shoulder

deer·hound (dêr'hound') ***n-*** large dog with long, coarse coat, related to the Irish wolfhound and formerly used in deer hunting.

deer mouse ***n-*** any of a group of very common North American mice with buff-colored coat and white feet; white-footed mouse.

deer·skin (dêr'skĭn') ***n-*** 1 the skin of a deer. 2 leather made from this. ***adj-***: *a* deerskin *jacket.*

def. definition.

de·face (dĭ fās') ***vt-*** [**de·faced, de·fac·ing**] to spoil the appearance of (something) by marking or damaging: *to* deface *a wall with crayon marks.* **—*n-* de·face'ment.**

de fac·to (dē făk'tō, dā-) *Latin* actually existing, whether legally or not; in actual fact: *a* de facto *ruler.*

de·fal·cate (dĭ făl'kāt', dĭ fôl'-) ***vi-*** [**de·fal·cat·ed, de·fal·cat·ing**] to steal or misuse money entrusted to one's charge; embezzle. **—*n-* de'fal·ca'tion.**

def·a·ma·tion (dĕf'ə mā'shən) ***n-*** malicious injuring of a person's reputation. In law, defamation is called slander if spoken, and libel if written.

de·fam·a·tor·y (dĭ făm'ə tôr'ē) ***adj-*** slanderous; libelous.

de·fame (dĭ fām') ***vt-*** [**de·famed, de·fam·ing**] to injure or destroy the good name of; speak evil of; slander; libel: *This article* defames *me.*

de·fault (dĭ fôlt') ***n-*** failure to do something required; especially, failure to appear for a game or contest in which one is scheduled to play. ***vi-*** to fail to fulfill a contract, agreement, or obligation: *He* defaulted *in his payments on the loan.* ***vt-***: *He* defaulted *his contract.* **—*n-* de·fault'er.**

in default in the condition of having failed to meet some obligation: *She was* in default *by two payments.*

de·feat (dĭ fēt') ***vt-*** 1 to overthrow; overcome; win a victory over: *to* defeat *an enemy.* 2 to cause to fail; bring to nothing: *to* defeat *a purpose*; *to* defeat *one's hopes.* ***n-*** failure; condition of being overthrown.

de·feat·ism (dĭ fēt'ĭz'əm) ***n-*** attitude or state of mind of those who expect and accept defeat.

de·feat·ist (dĭ fēt'ĭst) ***n-*** person who expects and accepts being defeated. ***adj-*** having the attitude or state of mind associated with defeatism.

def·e·cate (dĕf'ə kāt') ***vi-*** [**def·e·cat·ed, def·e·cat·ing**] to expel waste from the intestines; move the bowels.

¹de·fect (dē'fĕkt', dĭ fĕkt') ***n-*** lack of a thing necessary to completeness; imperfection; flaw: *a* defect *in character*; *a* physical *defect*; *a* defect *in a tile floor.*

²de·fect (dĭ fĕkt') ***vi-*** to desert a party or cause, especially to join another: *The sailor* defected *to the enemy.*

de·fec·tion (dĭ fĕk'shən) ***n-*** a renouncing of allegiance, duty, loyalty, etc.; desertion: *the* defection *of a dancer.*

de·fec·tive (dĭ fĕk'tĭv) ***adj-*** 1 imperfect; incomplete; faulty: *a* defective *switch*; *a* defective *copy*; defective *hearing.* 2 below normal in mental or physical growth; retarded. 3 *Grammer* lacking one or more inflectional forms. "Must" and "ought" are defective because they lack infinitives and participles. ***n-*** person who is below normal in mental or physical growth. **—*adj-* de·fec'tive·ly. *n-* de·fec'tive·ness.**

de·fec·tor (dĭ fĕk'tər) ***n-*** person who defects.

de·fend (dĭ fĕnd') ***vt-*** 1 to protect from harm or danger; guard. 2 to argue or state a case for: *to* defend *a point of view.* **—*n-* de·fen'der.**

de·fend·ant (dĭ fĕn'dənt) ***n-*** person accused or sued in a law court.

de·fense (dĭ fĕns') ***n-*** 1 resistance to attack: *to help in the* defense *of one's country.* 2 person or thing that protects; protector; protection: *Cleanliness is one* defense *against disease.* 3 in law, the reply of the defendant to the charge against him. 4 (*also* dē'fĕns) the defending side or players in a game. Also, *Brit.*, **defence.**

de·fense·less (dĭ fĕns'ləs) ***adj-*** helpless; unprotected; having no defense. Also **de·fence·less. —*adv-* de·fense'less·ly. *n-* de·fense'less·ness.**

de·fen·si·ble (dĭ fĕn'sə bəl) ***adj-*** 1 of a kind that allows being protected or held by force: *a* defensible *beachhead.* 2 worthy of some defense or support; not beyond reason or morality: *a* defensible *point of view.* **—*n-* de·fen'si·bil'i·ty.**

de·fen·sive (dĭ fĕn'sĭv) ***adj-*** 1 designed to guard or protect: *a* defensive *alliance; a* defensive *weapon.* 2 of or relating to defense: *a* defensive *attitude.* **—*adv-* de·fen'sive·ly. *n-* de·fen'sive·ness.**

on the defensive resisting or expecting attack: *The army was* on the defensive.

¹de·fer (dĭ fûr') ***vt-*** [**de·ferred, de·fer·ring**] to put off or hold over until a later time; postpone: *Congress* deferred *action on the bill for a week.* [from Old French **differer,** from Latin **differre,** "put off."] **—*adj-* de·fer'ra·ble.**

²de·fer (dĭ fûr') ***vi-*** [**de·ferred, de·fer·ring**] to yield (to) or give in respectfully (to) someone or something: *We gladly* defer *to the judgment of a wise person.* [from French **déférer,** from Latin **deferre** meaning "hand over."]

def·er·ence (dĕf'ər əns) ***n-*** a yielding to the opinions or wishes of other persons because of respect for their authority, age, ability, etc.: *a* deference *for one's elders.*

def·er·en·tial (dĕf'ər ĕn'shəl) ***adj-*** showing respect: *a* deferential *bow.* **—*adj-* def·er·en'tial·ly.**

de·fer·ment (dĭ fûr'mənt) ***n-*** a putting off or delaying; postponement: *a draft* deferment. Also **de·fer'ral.**

de·fi·ance (dĭ fī'əns) ***n-*** 1 a going against; open resistance; scornful refusal to obey or respect: *The children climbed the cliff in* defiance *of all common sense.* 2 hostile challenge: *The trapped bear snarled his* defiance.

de·fi·ant (dĭ fī'ənt) ***adj-*** showing or expressing bold opposition: *a* defiant *reply.* **—*adj-* de·fi'ant·ly.**

de·fi·cien·cy (dĭ fĭsh'ən sē) ***n-*** [*pl.* **de·fi·cien·cies**] 1 shortage; lack; dearth; insufficiency: *a vitamin* deficiency. 2 defectiveness; abnormality: *a case of mental and physical* deficiency. 3 amount by which something falls short: *There's a* deficiency *of $10 in our club funds.*

deficiency disease *n-* illness, such as beriberi, caused by the lack of certain vitamins or other nutrients in the diet.

de·fi·cient (dĭ fĭsh′ ənt) *adj-* **1** not having enough of something; insufficient: *an army* deficient *in supplies.* **2** below standard; imperfect; defective: *to be mentally* deficient. *—adv-* **de·fi′ cient·ly.**

def·i·cit (def′ ə sĭt) *n-* **1** amount of money by which a required or expected sum falls short; shortage: *a $10* deficit *in the cash register.* **2** loss in business operation: *The store had a* deficit *last year.* **3** any deficiency in amount.

deficit spending *n-* government policy of spending large amounts of borrowed money to stimulate business and thus create jobs. Also **deficit financing.**

de·fied (dĭ fīd′) *p.t. & p.p.* of **defy.**

de·fi·er (dĭ fī′ ər) *n-* person who defies.

[1]**de·file** (dĭ fīl′) *vt-* **[de·filed, de·fil·ing] 1** to make dirty, foul, or impure; pollute: *to* defile *the air with smog*; *to* defile *a river with refuse.* **2** to spoil the purity of; profane; sully: *to* defile *a church or temple*; *to* defile *one's clean record.* [from Old English **befylan** meaning "to befoul," from **fūl,** "foul."] *—n-* **de·file′ ment.**

[2]**de·file** (dĭ fīl′, dē′ fīl′) *n-* narrow pass or passage between cliffs or mountains. *vi-* **[de·filed, de·fil·ing]** to march in single file: *The soldiers* defiled *to the barracks.* [from French **défilé,** from French **défiler** meaning "to march in a file; to unroll thread."]

de·fine (dĭ fīn′) *vt-* **[de·fined, de·fin·ing] 1** to give the meaning or meanings of (a word or phrase). **2** to describe in an exact manner, especially by showing the limits of: *to* define *their duties.* **3** to fix or give the limits of: *The treaty* defined *the borders of the two countries.* **4** to show clearly in outline: *The sky sharply* defined *the peaks.*

def·i·nite (dĕf′ ə nĭt) *adj-* **1** exact; precise; having specific limits: *The buyer made John a* definite *offer of $10.* **2** clear; not doubtful: *Frayed wire is a* definite *fire hazard.* *—adv-* **def′ i·nite·ly.** *n-* **def′ i·nite·ness.**

definite article *n-* the determiner "the," used to introduce a noun phrase.

def·i·ni·tion (dĕf′ ə nĭsh′ ən) *n-* **1** explanation of the meaning of a word or phrase: *Look up the* definition *of "jet" in this dictionary.* **2** a describing of the nature or limits of something: *the* definition *of the mayor's duties.* **3** sharpness of outline: *a photo with clear* definition.

de·fin·i·tive (də fĭn′ ə tĭv) *adj-* final and decisive; conclusive: *a* definitive *biography.* *—adv-* **de·fin′ i·tive·ly.** *n-* **de·fin′ i·tive·ness.**

de·flate (dĭ flāt′, dē-) *vt-* **[de·flat·ed, de·flat·ing] 1** to let air or gas out of: *to* deflate *a rubber raft.* **2** to make smaller; reduce the amount of: *to* deflate *prices.* **3** to reduce (a pompous or conceited person, an exaggerated tale or idea, etc.) to reasonable proportions.

de·fla·tion (dĭ flā′ shən, dē-) *n-* **1** a releasing of gas or air. **2** fall in prices and a rise in the value of money, caused by a decrease in the amount of money available to buy the consumer goods and services being produced. **3** the reducing of a pompous person, a snob, a wild story, etc., to proper size. *—adj-* **de·fla′ tion·ar′ y.**

de·flect (dĭ flĕkt′) *vt-* to turn aside; change from a straight course: *A spectator reached out and* deflected *the ball.* *vi-*: *The ball* deflected *to the left.*

de·flec·tion (dĭ flĕk′ shən) *n-* **1** a bending or turning away; deviation. **2** the number of units a needle or other pointer moves on the scale of an instrument during a measurement.

de·for·est (dē fòr′ əst, -fŏr′ əst) *vt-* to clear (a region) of its trees. *—n-* **de·for′ est·a′ tion.**

de·form (dĭ fòrm′, -fôrm′) *vt-* **1** to force out of shape; distort: *Tight shoes can* deform *your feet.* **2** to make ugly; disfigure; mar: *The accident* deformed *his face.*

de·formed (dĭ fòrmd′, -fôrmd′) *adj-* out of shape; distorted; disfigured: *a* deformed *back.*

de·for·ma·tion (dĕf′ ər mā′ shən, dē′ fòr′-) *n-* a deforming or being deformed; also, an instance of this.

de·form·i·ty (dĭ fòr′ mə tē, dĭ fôr′-) *n-* [*pl.* **de·form·i·ties**] **1** part of a human or animal body not properly shaped. **2** condition of being disfigured. **3** moral defect.

de·fraud (dĭ fròd′) *vt-* to cheat; commit a fraud against; swindle: *To make a false tax return is to* defraud *the government.*

de·fray (dĭ frā′) *vt-* to pay (cost or expenses): *Each camper must* defray *his own expenses.* *—n-* **de·fray′ al.**

de·frost (dĭ fròst′, dē-) *vt-* **1** to remove frost from: *to* defrost *a refrigerator.* **2** to thaw: *to* defrost *frozen foods.* *—n-* **de·frost′ er.**

deft (dĕft) *adj-* skillful and clever: *a* deft *dressmaker*; *a* deft *phrase.* *—adv-* **deft′ ly.** *n-* **deft′ ness.**

de·funct (dĭ fŭngkt′) *adj-* no longer living or active; dead; extinct: *a* defunct *idea*; *a* defunct *business.*

de·fy (dĭ fī′) *vt-* **[de·fied, de·fy·ing] 1** to challenge or dare openly and boldly: *This store* defies *all others to beat its prices.* **2** to treat as of no account or with contempt; scorn: *to* defy *the law*; *to* defy *a parent's wishes.* **3** to resist successfully: *The door* defies *attempts to open it.*

deg. degree.

de·gen·er·a·cy (dĭ jĕn′ ər ə sē) *n-* **1** very low and inferior condition, especially of moral behavior; rottenness; depravity. **2** degeneration.

[1]**de·gen·er·ate** (dē jĕn′ ə rāt′) *vi-* **[de·gen·er·at·ed, de·gen·er·at·ing]** to sink into a lower or worse condition; grow inferior.

[2]**de·gen·er·ate** (dĭ jĕn′ər ət) *adj-* very much below a former level or standard; inferior; worse: *Are these* degenerate *times?* *n-* morally debased person. *—adv-* **de·gen′ er·ate·ly.**

de·gen·er·a·tion (dĭ gĕn′ ə rā′ shən) *n-* a growing worse or inferior; also, an instance of this; degeneracy: *the* degeneration *of muscles through long disuse.*

de·gen·er·a·tive (dĭ jĕn′ ər ə tĭv) *adj-* showing, causing, or tending to cause degeneration: *a* degenerative *influence*; degenerative *disease.*

deg·ra·da·tion (dĕg′ grə dā′ shən) *n-* **1** a lowering in rank, morals, reputation, etc.; act of degrading. **2** very low moral condition; disgrace; dishonor; shame.

de·grade (dĭ grād′) *vt-* **[de·grad·ed, de·grad·ing]** to lower the character of; debase: *Anyone who cheats* degrades *himself.*

de·grad·ed (dĭ grā′ dəd) *adj-* morally corrupt; weak and sinful. *—adv-* **de·grad′ ed·ly.** *n-* **de·grad′ ed·ness.**

de·gree (dĭ grē′) *n-* **1** one of the equal unit divisions on a temperature scale: *Water boils at 212* degrees *(212°) Fahrenheit.* **2** unit used in measuring angles and parts of circles. **3** title of bachelor, master, or doctor given by a college or university for passing a certain course of study, or as a mark of honor.

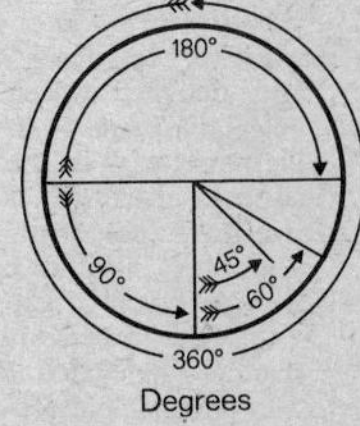

Degrees

4 a step or stage in progress: *to climb a steep hill by easy* degrees. 5 amount; extent: *a high* degree *of skill in dancing.* 6 social rank: *men of high* degree. 7 *Mathematics* (1) of an algebraic term, the sum of the exponents of the variable factors: x^3y *is of* degree *four.* (2) of a polynomial, the sum of the exponents of the term with the highest sum of exponents: $x^2y + 2x$ *is of* degree *three.*

degree day ***n-*** unit used in calculating fuel needs for heating. The number of degree days for one day equals the number of degrees the mean temperature of that day falls below a standard temperature, usually 65°F.

de·horn (dē hórn′, -hôrn′) ***vt-*** to remove the horns of (cattle); also, to prevent the growth of (horns).

de·hu·man·ize (dē hyōō′ mə nīz′) ***vt-*** **[de·hu·man·ized, de·hum·an·iz·ing]** to make inhuman, brutish, or coldly mechanical. ***—n-*** **de·hu′ man·i·za′ tion.**

de·hu·mid·i·fy (dē′ hyōō mĭd′ ə fī′) ***vt-*** **[de·hu·mid·i·fied, de·hu·mid·i·fy·ing]** to remove moisture from (air or other gases).

de·hy·drate (dē hī′ drāt′) ***vt-*****[de·hy·drat·ed, de·hy·drat·ing]** to remove the water from; dry out: *We* dehydrate *milk and pack it as a powder. Some diseases* dehydrate *the body.* ***vi-***: *The heat caused the mixture to* dehydrate.

de·hy·dra·tion (dē′ hī drā′ shən) ***n-*** 1 condition of being without water or moisture. 2 the removing of water from a substance by heat, chemical, or other means.

de·i·fi·ca·tion (dē′ ə fə kā′ shən) ***n-*** a deifying or being deified: *the* deification *of a king*; *the* deification *of money.*

de·i·fy (dē′ ə fī′) ***vt-*** **[de·i·fied, de·i·fy·ing]** to make into or worship as a god: *to* deify *a man*; *to* deify *success.*

deign (dān) ***vt-*** 1 to think (some action) worthy of one's dignity; condescend: *The governor* deigned *to grant us an audience.* 2 to give; grant. ***Hom-*** Dane.

de·ism (dē′ ĭz′ əm) ***n-*** the belief that God exists and created the world, but has since remained indifferent to its operation and problems. ***—n-*** **de′ ist.**

de·i·ty (dē′ ə tē) ***n-*** [*pl.* **de·i·ties**] 1 god or goddess: *Many ancient peoples worshipped the sun as a* deity. 2 **the Deity** God.

de·ject·ed (dĭ jĕk′ təd) ***adj-*** depressed; low-spirited; downcast: *The coach was* dejected *after the defeat.* ***—adv-*** **de·ject·ed·ly.** ***n-*** **de·ject′ ed·ness.**

de·jec·tion (dĭ jĕk′ shən) ***n-*** lowness of spirits; depression; sadness.

Del. Delaware.

Del·a·ware (dĕl′ ə wâr′) ***n-*** [*pl.* **Del·a·wares,** also **Del·a·ware**] member of a group of American Indians who formerly lived in the forests of the Delaware River valley and now live with the Cherokees in Oklahoma. ***adj-***: *the* Delaware *treaties.*

de·lay (dĭ lā′) ***vt-*** 1 to put off until later; postpone: *Rain* delayed *the game twenty minutes.* 2 to make (someone) late; detain: *The accident* delayed *him.* ***vi-***: *He* delayed *until it was too late.* ***n-***: *The rain caused a short* delay.

de·lec·ta·ble (dĭ lĕk′ tə bəl) ***adj-*** causing great pleasure and delight, especially to one's taste; delicious: *a* delectable *dish.* ***—n-*** **de·lec′ ta·bil′ i·ty** or **de·lec′ ta·ble·ness.** ***adv-*** **de·lec′ ta·bly.**

de·lec·ta·tion (dē′ lĕk tā′ shən) ***n-*** pleasure; delight.

[1]**del·e·gate** (dĕl′ ə gət, -gāt′) ***n-*** person chosen to act for a group or another person; spokesman; representative.

[2]**del·e·gate** (dĕl′ ə gāt′) ***vt-*** **[de·le·gat·ed, del·e·gat·ing]** 1 to select (a person or persons) as agent or representative: *We* delegated *Ron to speak for us at the meeting.* 2 to entrust; hand over: *to* delegate *authority.*

del·e·ga·tion (dĕl′ ə gā′ shən) ***n-*** 1 a delegating: *The* delegation *of duties to others is part of an executive's job.* 2 group of representatives: *a* delegation *of students.*

de·lete (dĭ lēt′) ***vt-*** **[de·let·ed, de·let·ing]** to cross out; eliminate: *The editor* deleted *the story from the paper.*

del·e·te·ri·ous (dĕl′ ə têr′ ē əs) ***adj-*** tending to cause harm or injury; hurtful: *a* deleterious *effect on one's health.* ***—adv-*** **del′ e·te′ ri·ous·ly.** ***n-*** **del′ e·te′ ri·ous·ness.**

de·le·tion (dĭ lē′ shən) ***n-*** 1 a deleting or taking out of a word, story, etc.: *the* deletion *of unnecessary words.* 2 word, story, etc., that has been deleted.

delft·ware (dĕlft′ wâr′) ***n-*** pottery having a white glaze with a blue pattern, first made in Delft, Holland.

[1]**de·lib·er·ate** (dĭ lĭb′ ər ət) ***adj-*** 1 thought out beforehand; intentional: *He told a* deliberate *lie.* 2 leisurely in action; unhurried: *a* deliberate *pace.* 3 careful; cautious: *a* deliberate *judgment.* ***—adv-*** **de·lib′ er·ate·ly.** ***n-*** **de·lib′ er·ate·ness.**

[2]**de·lib·er·ate** (dĭ lĭb′ ə rāt′) ***vi-*** **[de·lib·er·at·ed, de·lib·er·at·ing]** to think about, discuss, or debate something carefully: *The jury* deliberated *all day.* ***vt-***: *They* deliberated *the verdict.*

de·lib·er·a·tion (dĭ lĭb′ ə rā′ shən) ***n-*** 1 calm, careful thought: *The judge gave his decision after long* deliberation. 2 slowness and care: *The chess player moved with the utmost* deliberation. 3 a discussion or weighing up of reasons for and against action.

de·lib·er·a·tive (dĭ lĭb′ ər ā′ tĭv, -ə tĭv′) ***adj-*** meant for or tending to the careful consideration and debating of issues, policies, etc.: *The Senate is a* deliberative *body.* ***—adv-*** **de·lib′ er·a′ tive·ly.** ***n-*** **de·lib′ er·a′ tive·ness.**

del·i·ca·cy (dĕl′ ĭ kə sē) ***n-*** [*pl.* **del·i·ca·cies**] 1 something pleasing to the taste; delicious food. 2 fineness of quality, texture, etc.; daintiness: *the* delicacy *of lace.* 3 fineness of skill or touch: *the* delicacy *of an artist's brush strokes.* 4 fineness of feeling as to what is proper, fitting, or pleasing. 5 physical weakness; lack of vigor.

del·i·cate (dĕl′ ĭ kət) ***adj-*** 1 fine; dainty in quality, form, texture, or to the taste: *a* delicate *flavor.* 2 of a soft, pale tint: *a* delicate *pink.* 3 easily injured or damaged; fragile: *a* delicate *child*; *a* delicate *cup.* 4 finely sensitive: *a* delicate *touch*; *a* delicate *instrument.* 5 requiring skill; difficult to handle: *a* delicate *diplomatic mission.* ***—adv-*** **del′ i·cate·ly.** ***n-*** **del′ i·cate·ness.**

del·i·ca·tes·sen (dĕl′ ĭ kə tĕs′ ən) ***n-*** 1 store that sells and often serves prepared foods such as smoked meats, salads, cheeses, pickles, etc. 2 these foods collectively: *to have* delicatessen *for supper.* [American word from German **delikatessen** meaning "delicacies," from French **delicatesse** meaning "delicacy."]

de·li·cious (dĭ lĭsh′ əs) ***adj-*** pleasing ; delightful, especially to taste and smell. ***—adv-*** **de·li′ cious·ly.** ***n-*** **de·li′ cious·ness.**

de·light (dĭ līt′) ***vt-*** to please greatly; give enjoyment and pleasure to: *Toys* delight *a child.* ***n-*** 1 a great amount of pleasure; joy: *A vacation is a time of ease and* delight. 2 something that causes pleasure.

delight in to take great pleasure in.

de·light·ed (dĭ lī′ təd) ***adj-*** highly pleased; gratified: *I am* delighted *to meet you.* ***—adv-*** **de·light′ ed·ly.**

de·light·ful (dĭ līt′ fəl) ***adj-*** giving enjoyment; pleasing; charming: *a* delightful *evening.* ***—adv-*** **de·light′ ful·ly.** ***n-*** **de·light′ ful·ness.**

De·li·lah (də lī′ lə) ***n-*** Philistine woman who betrayed Samson to the Philistines by cutting off his hair, thereby depriving him of his strength.

de·lim·it (dĭ lĭm′ ət) ***vt-*** to mark the limits or bounds of; demarcate: *to* delimit *a topic for discussion.*

de·lin·e·ate (dĭ lĭn′ ē āt′) ***vt-*** **[de·lin·e·at·ed, de·lin·e·at·ing]** 1 to draw with lines; sketch. 2 to describe carefully and accurately in words; depict: *The reporter* delineated *every detail of the fire.*

de·lin·e·a·tion (dĭ lĭn′ ē ā′ shən) ***n-*** **1** a delineating; a picturing or describing: *the* delineation *of a battle.* **2** picture, story, etc., that describes something.

de·lin·e·a·tor (dĭ lĭn′ ē ā′ tər) ***n-*** person who delineates.

de·lin·quen·cy (də lĭng′ kwən sē) ***n-*** [*pl.* **de·lin·quen·cies**] **1** failure in one's duties; neglect. **2** any misdeed; fault. **3** juvenile delinquency.

de·lin·quent (də lĭng′ kwənt) ***adj-*** **1** failing in duty or responsibility: *a* delinquent *parent.* **2** past due: *a* delinquent *bill.* ***n-*** **1** person who does not observe his duties and responsibilities. **2** person, especially a juvenile, who breaks the law repeatedly or habitually. ***—adv-*** **de·lin′ quent·ly.**

del·i·ques·cence (dĕl′ ə kwĕs′ əns) *Chemistry* ***n-*** absorption of water from the air by certain compounds to such an extent as to dissolve them.

de·lir·i·ous (də lêr′ ē əs) ***adj-*** **1** in delirium; out of one's head; raving. **2** caused by or occurring with delirium: *a* delirious *dream.* **3** wildly excited or enthusiastic: *She was* delirious *with joy.* ***—adv-*** **de·lir′ i·ous·ly.** ***n-*** **de·lir′ i·ous·ness.**

de·lir·i·um (də lêr′ ē əm) ***n-*** **1** mental disturbance characterized by confused speech, hallucinations, restlessness, and frenzied excitement; a wandering and confused state of mind. Delirium is caused by fever, nervous shock, etc. and is usually temporary. **2** wild excitement: *a* delirium *of joy followed the home run.*

delirium tre·mens (trē′ mənz) ***n-*** violent form of delirium characterized by trembling, sweating, anxiety, etc. It is usually caused by excessive use of alcoholic liquors or narcotics.

de·liv·er (dĭ lĭv′ ər) ***vt-*** **1** to take (something) to a certain person or place; also, to hand over: *He* delivers *groceries for a living. The lawyer promised to* deliver *his client at the courthouse tomorrow.* **2** to utter: *to* deliver *a speech.* **3** to launch; aim: *to* deliver *a blow.* **4** to give birth to or assist in the birth of (a child or young animal). **5** to set free; rescue: *to* deliver *one from the threat of serious illness.* ***vi-*** *Informal* to give what is required or expected. **deliver (oneself) of** to utter or give forth with vigor.

de·liv·er·ance (dĭ lĭv′ ər əns) ***n-*** a rescue; release; a setting free: *to pray for* deliverance *from pain and trouble.*

de·liv·er·er (dĭ lĭv′ ər ər) ***n-*** person who delivers; especially, one who rescues or frees another.

de·liv·er·y (dĭ lĭv′ ə rē) ***n-*** [*pl.* **de·liv·er·ies**] **1** distribution; a handing over: *mail* delivery; *the* delivery *of the ransom money.* **2** what is delivered: *This* delivery *consists of a refrigerator.* **3** a releasing; a setting free: *the* delivery *of prisoners from jail.* **4** manner of speaking: *His forceful* delivery *made the speech effective.* **5** way of throwing a ball. **6** birth or a giving of birth.

dell (dĕl) ***n-*** small, secluded valley; glen.

Del·phic oracle (dĕl′ fĭk) ***n-*** in ancient Greece, the oracle of Apollo at Delphi, a woman whose sayings were interpreted by the priests.

del·phin·i·um (dĕl fĭn′ ē əm) ***n-*** tall garden plant with spikes of showy blue, lavender, or white flowers.

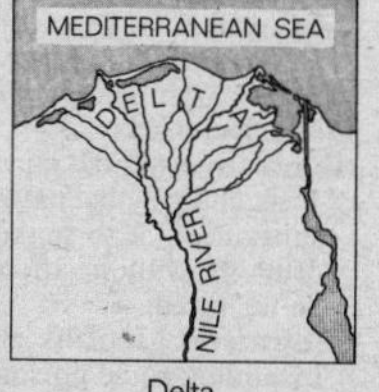

Delta

del·ta (dĕl′ tə) ***n-*** **1** more or less triangular accumulation of earth and sand at a river's mouth. **2** fourth letter of the Greek alphabet [△], equivalent to English "d."

del·ta-wing (dĕl′ tə wĭng′) ***adj-*** of an airplane, having two wings that, together with the fuselage, form a triangle, with the rear edge at right angles to the fuselage.

Airplane with delta-wings

de·lude (dĭ lo͞od′) ***vt-*** [**de·lud·ed, de·lud·ing**] to mislead; deceive: *He* deludes *himself with lies.*

del·uge (dĕl′ yo͞oj′) ***n-*** **1** heavy downpour; an overflowing of water; flood. **2** anything that overwhelms like a flood: *a* deluge *of fan letters*; *a* deluge *of visitors.* ***vt-*** [**del·uged, del·ug·ing**]: *The rains* deluged *the village. The audience* deluged *him with questions.*

de·lu·sion (dĭ lo͞o′ zhən) ***n-*** idea or belief that is contrary to facts or reason: *a* delusion *of grandeur.*

de·lu·sive (dĭ lo͞o′ sĭv, -zĭv) ***adj-*** tending to delude or mislead; deceptive: *a* delusive *scheme.* ***—adv-*** **de·lu′ sive·ly.**

de luxe (dĭ lŭks′, -lo͝oks′) ***adj-*** of the highest quality and elegance; luxurious: *a* de luxe *hotel suite.*

delve (dĕlv) ***vi-*** [**delved, delv·ing**] **1** to seek carefully for information; look diligently (into): *to* delve *in a library*; *to* delve *into an applicant's record.* **2** *Archaic* to dig.

Dem. Democrat; Democratic.

de·mag·net·ize (dē′ măg′ nə tīz′) ***vt-*** [**de·mag·net·ized, de·mag·net·iz·ing**] to remove the magnetism of (a substance, object, device, etc.).

dem·a·gog or **dem·a·gogue** (dĕm′ ə gŏg′) ***n-*** leader or agitator who gains and keeps power by appealing to the passion, prejudice, and ignorance of the people. ***—n-*** **dem′ a·gog′ ue·ry** (-gŏg′ ə rē) or **dem′ a·gog′ y** (-gŏj′ ē, -gŏg′ ē).

dem·a·gog·ic (dĕm′ ə gŏj′ ĭk) ***adj-*** of or in the manner of a demagog: *a* demagogic *appeal to the voters' prejudices.* ***—adv-*** **dem′ a·gog′ i·cal·ly.**

de·mand (dĭ mănd′) ***vt-*** **1** to ask for with authority; claim as a right; exact: *to* demand *instant obedience.* **2** to ask for urgently: *to* demand *to be paid*; demand *to be told.* **3** to have need for; require: *His business* demanded *his full time.* ***n-*** **1** strong request: *a* demand *for an answer.* **2** requirement or claim: *the* demands *of a job.* **3** a desire to own or use; call: *A* demand *for houses.*

de·mar·cate (dē′ mär kāt, dĭ mär′-) ***vt-*** [**de·mar·cat·ed de·mar·cat·ing**] to mark or fix the limits or bounds of; delimit; also, to distinguish clearly: *to* demarcate *my land from his.*

de·mar·ca·tion (dē′ mär kā′ shən) ***n-*** a marking out or delimiting; also, a resulting boundary.

[1]**de·mean** (dĭ mēn′) ***vt-*** to behave or conduct (oneself): *He* demeaned *himself well in public.* [from Old French **demener,** from **de-** meaning "on; away," and **mener** "to lead," from Latin **mināre** "to drive."]

[2]**de·mean** (dĭ mēn′) ***vt-*** to lower in dignity or character; debase: *He* demeaned *himself and his family by his cowardly behavior.* [from **de-** meaning "down to," and **mean** in the sense of "low; poor."]

de·mean·or (dĭ mē′ nər) ***n-*** the way one behaves; conduct; manner: *an even and composed* demeanor.

de·ment·ed (dĭ mĕn′ təd) ***adj-*** out of one's mind; insane; mad; crazed. ***—adv-*** **de·ment′ ed·ly.**

de·mer·it (dĭ mĕr′ ət) ***n-*** **1** something that calls for blame; fault; wrong act. **2** mark against one for failure or bad conduct.

fāte, făt, dâre, bärn; bē, bĕt, mêre; bīte, bĭt; nōte, hŏt, môre, dȯg; fŭn, fûr; to͞o, bo͝ok; oil; out; tar; thin; then; hw for wh as in *wh*at; zh for s as in u*s*ual; ə for a, e, i, o, u, as in *a*go, lin*e*n, per*i*l, at*o*m, min*u*s

de·mesne (də mān′, -mēn′) ***n*-** **1** in earlier times, a lord's manor house and the land attached to it or reserved for his use. **2** region, especially one under the control of a ruler or state; domain.

De·me·ter (də mē′ tər) ***n*-** in Greek mythology, the goddess of agriculture, fertility, and marriage. She is identified with the Roman Ceres.

demi- *prefix* less than full or complete; half: *a* demi*god.* [from Old French **demi** meaning "half," which goes back ultimately to Latin **dimidius,** "half," and literally, "apart (at the) middle."]

dem·i·god (dĕm′ĭ gŏd′) ***n*-** **1** lesser or minor god. **2** son of a god or goddess and a mortal. **3** man who is regarded as having godlike qualities. **—*n*-** *fem.* **dem′i·god′dess.**

dem·i·john (dĕm′ ĭ jŏn′) ***n*-** glass or stoneware bottle of one to ten gallon capacity and encased in wicker.

de·mise (dĭ mīz′) ***n*-** **1** death: *At her* demise *she was 75 years old.* **2** end; a ceasing: *the* demise *of ancient Rome.*

dem·i·tasse (dĕm′ĭ tăs′, -täs′) ***n*-** small cup in which after-dinner coffee, usually strong and black, is served; also, the coffee such a cup holds. [from French **demitasse,** meaning "half cup."]

de·mo·bi·lize (dē mō′ bə līz′) ***vt*-** [**de·mo·bi·lized, de·mo·bi·liz·ing**] to disband or dismiss from military service: *to* demobilize *troops.* **—*n*-** **de·mo′ bi·li·za′ tion.**

de·moc·ra·cy (də mŏk′ rə sē) ***n*-** [*pl.* **de·moc·ra·cies**] **1** form of government in which the people rule directly by assembling in meetings in order to vote on issues, or indirectly by going to the polls in order to elect representatives who will so act for them. **2** nation or state so governed: *The United States is a* democracy. **3** the treating of others as equals.
►Should not be confused with REPUBLIC.

dem·o·crat (dĕm′ ə krăt′) ***n*-** **1** person who believes that all should have an equal voice in government. **2** person who believes and acts on the belief that all others are his equals. **3 Democrat** member of the Democratic Party in the United States.

dem·o·crat·ic (dĕm′ ə krăt′ ĭk) ***adj*-** **1** of or like a democracy: *a* democratic *form of government.* **2** treating people as one's equals: *The Prince had a* democratic *manner that put us at ease.* **3 Democratic** of or relating to the Democratic Party. **—*adv*-** **dem′ o·crat′ i·cal·ly.**

Democratic Party ***n*-** one of the two chief political parties in the United States.

de·moc·ra·tize (də mŏk′ rə tīz′) ***vt*-** [**de·moc·ra·tized, de·moc·ra·tiz·ing**] to make democratic or more democratic: *to* democratize *a society.* **—*n*-** **de·moc′ ra·ti·za′ tion.**

de·mol·ish (dĭ mŏl′ ĭsh) ***vt*-** to wreck or ruin completely; tear down or apart; destroy: *to* demolish *old houses.*

dem·o·li·tion (dĕm′ ə lĭsh′ ən, dē′ mə-) ***n*-** a demolishing or destroying; also, an instance of this: *the* demolition *of a bridge.*

de·mon (dē′ mən) ***n*-** **1** evil spirit; devil; fiend. **2** very cruel and wicked person. **3** person with exceptional skill or energy: *a* demon *for work.* **4** in ancient Greek mythology and thought, a spirit that accompanies and guards over a human being; attendant spirit; genius. **—*adj*-** **de·mon′ ic** (dē mŏn′ ĭk). ***adv*-** **de·mon′ ic·al·ly.**

de·mo·ni·ac (dĭ mō′ nē ăk′) or **de·mo·ni·a·cal** (dē′ mə nī′ ə kəl) ***adj*-** **1** of or like a demon. **2** caused by a demon: *a* demoniac *frenzy.* ***n*-** (**demoniac** only) person possessed by a demon. **—*adv*-** **de′ mo ni′ a·cal·ly:** *He laughed* demoniacally.

de·mon·stra·ble (də mŏn′ strə bəl) ***adj*-** such as can be demonstrated: *a* demonstrable *truth.* **—*adv*-** **de·mon′ stra·bly.**

dem·on·strate (dĕm′ ən strāt′) ***vt*-** [**dem·on·strat·ed, dem·on·strat·ing**] **1** to teach or show (a way of doing something) by actual performance: *Mary will* demonstrate *how to solve the problem by working it on the board.* **2** to indicate or reveal: *These figures* demonstrate *a need for caution.* **3** to prove: *An experiment will* demonstrate *that wood cannot burn without oxygen.* **4** to exhibit and explain the good points of (a product): *The salesman* demonstrated *the sewing machine.* ***vi*-** to hold a meeting, parade, etc., to show public feelings: *The people* demonstrated *for a cleaner government.*

dem·on·stra·tion (dĕm′ ən strā′ shən) ***n*-** **1** a teaching or showing by actual performance: *Our teacher gave a* demonstration *of the new dance step.* **2** proof: *The experiment was clear* demonstration *that wood needs oxygen to burn.* **3** outward expression; show: *Crying is a* demonstration *of grief. A kiss is a* demonstration *of affection.* **4** a showing of the good points of a product: *the* demonstration *of a vacuum cleaner.* **5** a meeting, parade, etc., to show public feelings.

de·mon·stra·tive (də mŏn′ strə tĭv′) ***adj*-** **1** showing the feelings, especially affection, openly and strongly: *The* demonstrative *pup wagged its tail in joy.* **2** serving to demonstrate or show. ***n*-** *Grammar* a determiner that points out. English has four demonstratives: this, that, these, those. A demonstrative may introduce a noun phrase: These *two boys are my children.* It may also take the place of a noun phrase: These *are my children.* **—*adv*-** **de·mon′ stra·tive·ly.** ***n*-** **de·mon′ stra·tive·ness.**

demonstrative adjective ***n*-** a demonstrative that introduces a noun phrase.

demonstrative pronoun ***n*-** a demonstrative that takes the place of a noun phrase.

dem·on·stra·tor (dĕm′ ən strā′ tər) ***n*-** **1** person who demonstrates. **2** machine used for demonstrating the performance of its kind.

de·mor·al·ize (dĭ môr′ ə līz′, dĭ mŏr′-) ***vt*-** [**de·mor·al·ized, de·mor·al·iz·ing**] **1** to weaken the morale, spirit, or self-discipline of: *An attack on the rear guard* demoralized *the army.* **2** to weaken the morals of; corrupt. **—*n*-** **de·mor′ al·i·za′ tion.**

de·mote (dĭ mōt′) ***vt*-** [**de·mot·ed, de·mot·ing**] to reduce to a lower rank or grade: *to* demote *an army officer.* **—*n*-** **de·mo′ tion:** *His* demotion *was a blow to his pride.*

de·mur (dĭ mûr′) ***vi*-** [**de·murred, de·mur·ring**] **1** to take exception; object (followed by "at"): *He* demurred *at going so far.* **2** to hesitate; delay: *He* demurs *when he should act at once.* ***n*-** **1** demurral. **2** hesitation.

de·mure (dĭ myŏŏr′) ***adj*-** **1** quiet and modest: *In her* demure *way she was delighted also.* **2** pretending to be shy; coy. **—*adv*-** **de·mure′ ly.** ***n*-** **de·mure′ ness.**

de·mur·ral (dĭ mûr′ əl) ***n*-** objection or exception; demur.

den (dĕn) ***n*-** **1** home of a wild animal; lair. **2** a haunt: *a* den *of thieves.* **3** cozy private room for study or work: *Father's* den *is filled with books.*

Den. Denmark.

de·na·ture (dē nā′ chər) ***vt*-** [**de·na·tured, de·na·tur·ing**] **1** to change the natural qualities or properties of (a substance). **2** to make (something) unfit for eating or drinking without affecting its other properties. **—*adj*-** **de·na′ tured.**

denatured alcohol ***n*-** alcohol made unfit for drinking by adding some poisonous or obnoxious liquid.

den·drite (dĕn′ drīt′) ***n*-** **1** rock or mineral with markings in patterns on its surface resembling shrubs or tree branches. **2** one of the patterns. **3** a crystal that has a branching form. **4** *Biology* the branching part of a nerve cell that conducts impulses toward the cell body (for picture, see *neuron*).

den·gue (dĕng′ gē, -gā) ***n-*** infectious tropical disease marked by fever, headache, and severe pains in the joints. Dengue is transmitted by certain mosquitos.

de·ni·al (dĭ nī′ əl) ***n-*** a refusing to grant, admit, believe, etc.: *a* denial *of one's request*; *a* denial *of one's guilt.*

de·nier (dĕn′ yər) ***n-*** unit of fineness or coarseness of cotton, rayon, or silk yarn. A yarn has a fineness of one denier if 450 meters of it weigh 5 centigrams.

den·im (dĕn′ əm) ***n-*** **1** coarse, twilled cotton used for overalls, work jackets, etc. **2 denims** overalls, pants, etc., made of this cotton. [American word from a shortening of French **serge de Nimes** meaning "serge of Nimes."]

den·i·zen (dĕn′ ə zən) ***n-*** person or thing that lives in a place; dweller: *The bear is a* denizen *of the forest.*

de·nom·i·nate (dĭ nom′ ə nāt′) ***vt-*** **[de·nom·i·nat·ed, de·nom·i·nat·ing]** to name; designate: *The term "mammals"* denominates *a certain class of animals.*

de·nom·i·na·tion (dĭ nom′ ə nā′ shən) ***n-*** **1** a name, especially a general name: *Music, literature, and painting come under the* denomination *of fine arts.* **2** religious group; sect: *a church of the Presbyterian* denomination. **3** unit of value or measure: *He was paid with three bills of the same* denomination.

de·nom·i·na·tion·al (dĭ nŏm′ ə nā′ shən əl) ***adj-*** of, related to, or controlled by a religious group; sectarian: *a* denominational *school.* **—*adv-*** **de·nom′ i·na′ tion·al·ly.**

de·nom·i·na·tor (dĭ nŏm′ ə nā′ tər) ***n-*** the number named below the line in a fraction. A denominator shows how many equal parts a whole thing or unit is divided into. In the fraction 4/5, 5 is the denominator.

de·no·ta·tion (dē′ nō tā′ shən) ***n-*** **1** a denoting. **2** meaning; especially, the exact and literal meaning of a word or expression. See also *connotation.* **3** a name; designation.

de·note (dĭ nōt′) ***vt-*** **[de·not·ed, de·not·ing]** to mean; be a sign of; signify: *An SOS signal* denotes *distress.*

dé·noue·ment (dā′ nōō mäⁿ′) *French* ***n-*** final solution or unraveling of the plot of a novel or play, or of some complex situation.

de·nounce (dĭ nouns′) ***vt-*** **[de·nounced, de·nounc·ing]** **1** to speak against publicly; condemn: *The minister* denounced *gambling.* **2** to accuse; inform against: *to* denounce *a cheat.* **—*n-*** **de·nounce′ ment.**

dense (dĕns) ***adj-*** **[dens·er, dens·est]** **1** having the parts crowded thickly or tightly together; compact: *a* dense *forest*; *a* dense *fog*; *a* dense *gas.* **2** *Informal* dull; stupid. **—*adv-*** **dense′ ly.** ***n-*** **dense′ ness.**

den·si·ty (dĕn′ sə tē) ***n-*** [*pl.* **den·si·ties**] **1** closeness or compactness: *the* density *of a forest.* **2** *Physics* mass per unit of volume; the amount of matter in a given volume: *The* density *of iron is greater than that of wood.* **3** *Informal* stupidity.

dent (dĕnt) ***n-*** sunken place in a surface caused by a blow or by pressure: *We hit a tree and made a* dent *in the car fender.* ***vt-*** to make a small hollow in: *to* dent *a fender.* ***vi-*** to become damaged in this way: *Tin* dents *easily.*

den·tal (dĕn′ təl) ***adj-*** **1** pertaining to the teeth or to dentistry: *a* dental *clinic.* **2** pronounced with the tip of the tongue just behind or near the upper front teeth: *(d) and (t) are* dental *sounds.* ***n-*** a sound made in this way. **—*adv-*** **den′ tal·ly.**

dental floss ***n-*** waxed thread used for cleaning between the teeth.

den·ti·frice (dĕn′ tə frĭs) ***n-*** powder, paste, or liquid for cleaning the teeth.

den·tine (dĕn′ tēn′) ***n-*** hard substance that forms most of a tooth. It is beneath the enamel and around the pulp. Also **den′ tin** (dĕn′ tən).

den·tist (dĕn′ tĭst) ***n-*** doctor who treats the teeth and surrounding tissues, pulls teeth when necessary, and replaces them with false teeth.

den·tist·ry (dĕn′ tə strē) ***n-*** the branch of medical science that deals with the teeth and the mouth cavity.

den·ti·tion (dĕn tĭsh′ ən) ***n-*** **1** process or period of cutting and growing teeth. **2** number, kind, and arrangement of teeth.

den·ture (dĕn′ chər) ***n-*** false tooth or a set of false teeth; dental bridge or plate.

de·nude (dĭ nōōd′, -nyōōd′) ***vt-*** **[de·nud·ed, de·nud·ing]** to strip all covering from; make bare: *to* denude *a hillside of trees.* **—*n-*** **de′ nu·da′ tion.**

de·nun·ci·a·tion (dĭ nŭn′ sē ā′ shən, dē′-) ***n-*** public accusation or condemnation: *the candidate's* denunciation *of his opponent.* **—*adj-*** **de·nun′ ci·a·to′ ry** (dĭ nŭn′ sē ə tôr′ ē): *a* denunciatory *speech.*

de·ny (dĭ nī′) ***vt-*** **[de·nied, de·ny·ing]** **1** to refuse to admit or believe; say that (something) is not true; contradict: *I* denied *his accusation.* **2** to withhold; refuse to give: *to* deny *aid.* **3** to refuse; turn down: *to* deny *a request.*

de·o·dor·ant (dē ō′ də rənt) ***n-*** substance that destroys or disguises unpleasant odors, especially body odors. *as* ***modifier***: *a cake of* deodorant *soap.*

de·o·dor·ize (dē ō′ də rīz′) ***vt-*** **[de·o·dor·ized, de·o·dor·iz·ing]** to remove or disguise the unpleasant odors of. **—*n-*** **de·o′ dor·iz′ er.**

de·ox·i·dize (dē ŏk′ sə dīz′) *Chemistry* ***vt-*** **[de·ox·i·dized, de·ox·i·diz·ing]** **1** to remove oxygen from (a compound). **2** to cause (an oxide) to undergo reduction. **—*n-*** **de·ox′ i·diz′ er.**

de·ox·y·ri·bo·nu·cle·ic acid (dē ŏk′ sē rī′ bō nōō klē′ ĭk) ***n-*** DNA.

de·part (dĭ pärt′) ***vi-*** **1** to go away; leave: *The bus* departs *at 10 o'clock.* **2** to change; deviate; turn aside (from) something: *The builders* departed *from the original plan and put in more windows.*

de·part·ed (dĭ pär′ təd) ***n-*** **1** person who has died: *The family mourned the* departed. **2** the dead collectively.

de·part·ment (dĭ pärt′ mənt) ***n-*** **1** a division or branch of a government, business, or other organization: *the police* department *of the city government*; *the toy* department *of a store*; *the history* department *of a school.* **2** in France, a division of local government. **—*adj-*** **de′ part·men′ tal:** *a* departmental *matter.*

department store ***n-*** large store selling many kinds of goods arranged in separate departments.

de·par·ture (dĭ pär′ chər) ***n-*** **1** a going away; leaving: *He scheduled his* departure *for Friday.* **2** a turning away from customary methods or ways of thinking or acting; deviation; divergence: *The bright red dress was quite a* departure *for her.* **3** *Archaic* death.

de·pend (dĭ pĕnd′) ***vi-*** **1** to trust and count (on or upon): *I* depend *on you to be on time.* **2** to rely for support (on or upon): *to* depend *on relatives.* **3** to hinge or rest (on or upon): *His answer* depends *upon his mood.* **4** to hang down (from).

it depends the outcome, the facts, the best method, etc., cannot be known until other things happen or are known; it is contingent.

de·pen·da·ble (dĭ pĕn′ də bəl) ***adj-*** unlikely to fail; reliable; trustworthy: *a* dependable *friend.* **—*n-*** **de·pend′ a·bil′ i·ty.** ***adv-*** **de·pend′ a·bly.**

---

de·pen·dence (dĭ pĕn′ dəns) ***n-*** **1** condition of being influenced or determined by something: *the* dependence *of crops upon rainfall.* **2** reliance (on) or need (of) for support: *a child's* dependence *on its parents.* **3** a trustful relying (on); trust: *His* dependence *on his lawyer.*

de·pend·en·cy (dĭ pĕn′ dən sē) ***n-*** [*pl.* **de·pend·en·cies**] **1** country or territory controlled by another country from which it is geographically separated. **2** dependence.

de·pen·dent (dĭ pĕn′ dənt) ***adj-*** **1** relying on someone or something else for support. **2** conditioned by something: *Skill is* dependent *on practice.* **3** hanging down. ***n-*** person who relies on another for support.

dependent clause *Grammar* ***n-*** a clause used to modify another expression or word in it or to take the place of a noun. Examples: *The book* I want *is there. I know* who stole the cake. A dependent clause cannot be made to stand alone without change or loss of meaning. See also *independent clause.*

de·pict (dĭ pĭkt′) ***vt-*** to show by a picture or sculpture, or in words; portray; describe: *The book* depicted *life in Tibet.* **—*n-* de·pic′ tion.**

de·pil·a·tor·y (dĭ pĭl′ ə tôr′ē) ***n-*** [*pl.* **de·pil·a·tor·ies**] substance for removing hair. ***adj-***: *a* depilatory *cream.*

de·plete (dĭ plēt′) ***vt-*** [**de·plet·ed, de·plet·ing**] to reduce in amount to a danger point; exhaust; sap: *Illness* depleted *his strength.* **—*n-* de·ple′ tion.**

de·plor·a·ble (dĭ plôr′ ə bəl) ***adj-*** **1** making one sorry or sad; lamentable; grievous: *a* deplorable *accident.* **2** shameful; wretched: *his* deplorable *behavior.* **—*n-* de·plor′ a·ble·ness.** ***adv-*** **de·plor′ a·bly.**

de·plore (dĭ plôr) ***vt-*** [**de·plored, de·plor·ing**] to be very sorry about; regret strongly; lament: *to* deplore *the rise of crime.*

de·ploy (dĭ ploi′) ***vt-*** **1** to spread out in a line of battle: *to* deploy *troops for a charge.* **2** to assign position and duties to: *He* deployed *his assistants in a new and simpler way.* ***vi-***: *The brigade* deployed *and swept across the plain.* ***n-*** movement by which a body of troops is spread out in battle line. **—*n-* de·ploy′ ment.**

de·pop·u·late (dē pŏp′ yə lāt′) ***vt-*** [**de·pop·u·lat·ed, de·pop·u·lat·ing**] to remove the inhabitants of; reduce the number of people in: *Plague* depopulated *the countryside.* ***vi-***: *The center of the city* depopulated *rapidly.* **—*n-* de·pop′ u·la′ tion.**

[1]**de·port** (dē pôrt′) ***vt-*** to send out of a country by legal action; banish: *to* deport *a spy.* **—*n-* de′ por·ta′ tion.**

[2]**de·port** (dĭ pôrt′) ***vt-*** to behave or conduct (followed by "yourself," "himself," etc.): *He* deported *himself well.*

de·port·ment (dĭ pôrt′ mənt) ***n-*** **1** behavior; conduct: *to praise a child for polite* deportment. **2** the way one holds oneself in standing and walking; bearing; carriage.

de·pose (dĭ pōz′) ***vt-*** [**de·posed, de·pos·ing**] **1** to remove from a throne or high office: *to* depose *a king.* **2** to say under oath; declare in a sworn statement: *The witness* deposed *that he had seen the crime committed.*

de·pos·it (dĭ pŏz′ ĭt) ***vt-*** **1** to put or set down; place: *The postman* deposited *the package on the doorstep. A giant wave* deposited *us on the beach.* **2** to put (money or valuable things) in a bank or other safe place: *to* deposit *a pay check.* ***n-*** **1** sum of money placed in a bank. **2** part payment in advance: *He made a hundred dollar* deposit *on the car.* **3** natural mass or accumulation of coal, ore, etc.; also, any layer of material that has accumulated through natural processes: *an ore* deposit.

dep·o·si·tion (dĕp′ ə zĭsh′ ən) ***n-*** **1** a putting out of office or power; dethronement: *the* deposition *of a ruler.* **2** testimony under oath; affidavit: *The witness filed a* deposition *with the court.* **3** a laying down; a depositing: *Rivers build deltas by* deposition *of mud and silt.*

de·pos·i·tor (dĭ pŏz′ ə tər) ***n-*** person who places money in a bank.

de·pos·i·tor·y (dĭ pŏz′ ə tôr′ ē) ***n-*** [*pl.* **de·pos·i·tor·ies**] place where anything is deposited for safekeeping: *He built a vault as a* depository *for his gems.*

[1]**de·pot** (dē′ pō′, *also* dĕ′ pō′) ***n-*** a railroad station or bus terminal. [an American use of [2]**depot.**]

[2]**de·pot** (dĕp′ ō′, dē′ pō′) ***n-*** **1** warehouse. **2** place where military supplies are stored. **3** place where troops are assembled before being assigned to various military units. [from French **dépot,** from Latin **depositum** meaning "a deposit," or literally, "a thing put down."]

de·prave (dĭ prāv′) ***vt-*** [**de·praved, de·prav·ing**] to make bad morally; corrupt.

de·praved (dĭ prāvd′) ***adj-*** morally bad; corrupt; perverted: *a* depraved *criminal.* **—*adv-* de·pra′ved·ly.**

de·prav·i·ty (dĭ prăv′ ə tē) ***n-*** [*pl.* **de·prav·i·ties**] **1** immorality; corruptness; wickedness. **2** wicked act; immoral practice.

dep·re·cate (dĕp′ rə kāt′) ***vt-*** [**dep·re·cat·ed, dep·re·cat·ing**] to feel or say that (something) has little value or importance; disapprove of: *to* deprecate *modern art*; *to* deprecate *an award.* **—*n-* dep′ re·ca′ tion.** ***adj-*** **dep′ re·ca·tor′ y** (dĕp′ rĭ kə tôr′ ē).

►Should not be confused with DEPRECIATE.

de·pre·ci·ate (dĭ prē′ shē āt′) ***vt-*** [**de·pre·ci·at·ed, de·pre·ci·at·ing**] to lower the price or value of: *to* depreciate *the currency.* ***vi-*** to fall in value: *A house* depreciates *rapidly if not kept in repair.*

►Should not be confused with DEPRECATE.

de·pre·ci·a·tion (dĭ prē′ shē ā′ shən) ***n-*** a lessening in value because of deterioration, age, use, etc.

dep·re·da·tion (dĕp′ rə dā′ shən) ***n-*** a laying waste; a plundering; a ravaging.

de·press (dĭ prĕs′) ***vt-*** **1** to press down; also, to cause to sink: *She* depressed *an organ key. The heavy trucks* depressed *the road in several places.* **2** to make gloomy or sad: *The gray weather* depresses *me.* **3** to reduce in activity, strength, or vigor: *The pill* depressed *his heart action. The slump* depressed *trade.*

de·pres·sant (dĭ prĕs′ ənt) ***n-*** **1** anything that causes depression. **2** drug or other substance that soothes or lessens tension of the muscles or nerves; sedative.

de·pres·sion (dĭ prĕsh′ ən) ***n-*** **1** sunken place; hollow: *a* depression *in the lawn.* **2** low spirits; melancholy. **3** period marked by a decrease in trade, production, and employment. **4** act of pressing down.

de·prive (dĭ prīv′) ***vt-*** [**de·prived, de·priv·ing**] to strip, rob, or dispossess: *to* deprive *the experience of all its joy*; *to* deprive *a man of his privileges*; *to* deprive *the family of sleep.* **—*n-* dep′ ri·va′ tion** (dĕp′ rə vā′shən).

dept. department.

depth (dĕpth) ***n-*** **1** distance from top to bottom or from front to back: *the* depth *of a well*; *the* depth *of a shelf.* **2** distance below the surface: *He dived to a* depth *of 130 feet.* **3** great amount, degree, or intensity: *a* depth *of despair*; *rich* depth *of color*; depth *of silence.* **4** strength and complexity of feeling: *a man of* depth. **5** lowness of pitch: *the* depth *and resonance of his voice.* **6 depths** (1) the deep parts of the ocean, the earth, etc. (2) the most remote part: *the* depths *of the forest.* (3) the extreme degree: *the* depths *of gloom.* (4) very low moral or social condition: *I'll never sink to such* depths!

depth charge ***n-*** bomb designed to destroy submarines by exploding under water at preset depths. Also **depth bomb.**

dep·u·ta·tion (dĕp′ yə tā′ shən) ***n-*** **1** an appointing of someone to act as one's agent. **2** group of people appointed to act for others: *a* deputation *of leading citizens.*

de·pute (dĭ pyōōt′) *vt-* [**de·put·ed, de·put·ing**] to send (a person or persons) with authority to act, inquire, etc.
dep·u·tize (dĕp′ yə tīz′) *vt-* [**dep·u·tized, dep·u·tiz·ing**] to appoint as a deputy or agent.
dep·u·ty (dĕp′ yə tē) *n-* [*pl.* **dep·u·ties**] **1** person who is appointed to act for, or in the place of, another: *The sheriff has six* deputies. **2** in some countries, a member of a legislative body. *as* ***modifier****: a* deputy *marshal.*
de·rail (dĭ rāl′, dē-) *vt-* to force off a rail or rails: *A stone on the track* derailed *the train.* ***vi-*** to go off the rails: *The train* derailed *on a sharp curve.* **—*n-* de·rail′ ment.**
de·range (dĭ rānj′) *vt-* [**de·ranged, de·rang·ing**] **1** to upset the normal state or functioning of; cause to act abnormally: *The magnetic rock* deranged *the compass. Shell shock* deranged *his mind.* **2** disorganize; disarrange.
de·ranged (dĭ rānjd′) *adj-* **1** mentally disturbed; insane; psychotic. **2** upset; disordered.
de·range·ment (dĭ rānj′ ment) *n-* **1** a putting out of order; also, a condition of disorder. **2** insanity.
der·by (dŭr′ bē) *n-* [*pl.* **der·bies**] **1** man's hat of stiffened felt, having a narrow rolled brim and a rounded crown; bowler. **2 Derby** (*Brit.* där′ bē) championship race for three-year-old horses.

Man wearing derby

der·e·lict (dĕr′ ə lĭkt′) *adj-* **1** abandoned; run-down. **2** negligent; neglectful: *to be* derelict *in one's duty.* ***n-*** **1** anything cast away or forsaken; especially, a ship abandoned at sea. **2** person sunk to the lowest depths of degradation; tramp; bum.
der·e·lic·tion (dĕr′ ə lĭk′ shən) *n-* an abandoning or failure of responsibility; delinquency: *His failure to investigate was a serious* dereliction *of duty.*
de·ride (dĭ rīd′) *vt-* [**de·rided, de·rid·ing**] to mock; laugh at; jeer: *The boys* derided *him for his vanity.*
de·ri·sion (də rĭzh′ ən) *n-* ridicule; scorn; mockery.
de·ri·sive (də rī′ sĭv, -zĭv) *adj-* expressing ridicule or scorn; jeering; mocking: *an outburst of* derisive *laughter.* **—*adv-* de·ri′ sive·ly. *n-* de·ri′ sive·ness.**
der·i·va·tion (dĕr′ ə vā′ shən) *n-* **1** origin; source: *a tune of Turkish* derivation. **2** an obtaining of one thing from another by change or development: *the* derivation *of French law from Roman law.* **3** a recording or tracing of the development of a word from its original form and first meaning; etymology: *This dictionary gives the* derivation *of many words.* **4** *Grammar* a deriving of words from other words by adding prefixes and suffixes. The noun "darkness" may be derived from the adjective "dark" by adding the suffix "-ness"; the adjective "enjoyable" may be derived from the verb "enjoy" by adding the suffix "-able."
de·riv·a·tive (də rĭv′ ə tĭv) *adj-* obtained from an earlier or primary source: *a list of* derivative *words*; derivative *products*; *the* derivative *benefits of a job abroad.* ***n-****: The word "canal" is a* derivative *of a Latin word (canalis) meaning "channel." Paper is a* derivative *of wood.*
de·rive (dĭ rīv′) *vt-* [**de·rived, de·riv·ing**] **1** to get or obtain (from): *to* derive *pleasure from a hobby.* **2** to trace the history of (a word) as far back as possible. ***vi-****: The word* derives *from French.*
der·mal (dûr′ məl) *adj-* of or relating to the skin, especially to the dermis; cutaneous.
der·ma·tol·o·gist (dŭr′ mə tŏl′ ə jĭst) *n-* doctor specializing in skin diseases.
der·ma·tol·o·gy (dŭr′ mə tŏl′ ə jē) *n-* branch of medicine that deals with skin diseases.

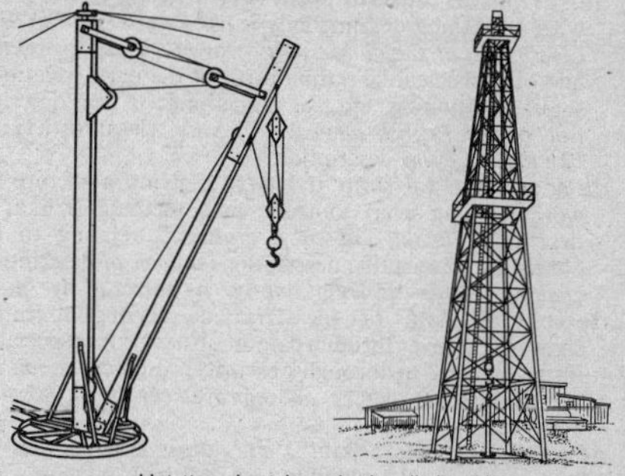
Hoisting derrick and oil-well derrick

der·mis (dûr′ məs) *n-* the layer of skin just beneath the epidermis, often called the true skin. For picture, see *skin.* Also **der′ ma.**
der·o·gate (dĕr′ ə gāt′) *vt-* [**der·o·gat·ed, der·o·gat·ing**] to detract from; lower in estimation; disparage; belittle: *He* derogated *his co-worker's ability.* ***vi-*** to detract or take away (from) something. **—*n-* der′ o·ga′ tion.**
de·rog·a·to·ry (də rŏg′ ə tôr′ ē) *adj-* harsh and critical; unflattering; disparaging; belittling: *He made* derogatory *statements about us.* **—*adv-* de·rog′ a·tor′ i·ly.**
der·rick (dĕr′ ĭk) *n-* **1** lifting machine consisting of a tall mast and hinged boom on the end of which weights are lifted and moved by means of pulleys. **2** framework above an oil well to hold drilling or hoisting machinery.
der·ring-do (dĕr′ ĭng dōō′) *n-* swashbuckling bravery.
der·rin·ger (dĕr′ ən jər) *n-* pocket pistol with a short barrel of large caliber. Also **der′ in·ger.** [American word from the name of H. **Deringer**, the inventor.]
der·vish (dûr′ vĭsh) *n-* member of any of several Muslim religious orders, some of which practice howling or whirling in order to induce a trance.
[1]**des·cant** (dĕs′ kănt′) *n-* **1** a discourse or series of remarks on some topic. **2** *Music* song or melody; also, a counterpoint to a melody.
[2]**des·cant** (dĭ skănt′) *vi-* **1** to comment freely; hold forth. **2** *Music* to sing a melody or counterpoint.
de·scend (dĭ sĕnd′) *vi-* **1** to go or come down from a higher to a lower level: *The rain* descended. *The lawn* descended *to the lake.* **2** to come in force: *Relatives* descended *upon us Saturday.* **3** to pass by inheritance: *The estate* descended *from father to son.* **4** to come or be derived: *This custom* descends *from the ancient Greeks.* ***vt-****: We* descended *the stairs.*
be descended from to have as an ancestor or ancestry.
de·scend·ant (dĭ sĕn′ dənt) *n-* person who is descended from a certain ancestor or family line.
de·scent (dĭ sĕnt′) *n-* **1** a going or coming down; movement to a lower level: *The airplane made a rapid* descent. **2** downward slope: *That hill has a sharp* descent *that is good for sledding.* **3** sudden attack or visit: *a* descent *by the hordes of locusts*; *a* descent *of week-end guests.* **4** ancestry: *She was of Spanish* descent. ***Hom-*** dissent.
de·scribe (dĭ skrīb′) *vt-* [**de·scribed, de·scrib·ing**] **1** to give an account or picture of in words: *She* described

her coat so well that I found it right away. **2** to draw or trace the outline of: *He* described *a circle in the air.*

de·scrip·tion (dĭ skrĭp′ shən) ***n-*** **1** a telling in words of what something or somebody is like; word picture: *His* description *of the dinner party was hilarious.* **2** orderly and careful scientific setting forth of the parts, relationships, functioning, etc., of something: *a new* description *of the English language.* **3** sort; class; variety: *I like food of every* description.

de·scrip·tive (dĭ skrĭp′ tĭv) ***adj-*** **1** giving a picture in words; telling what someone or something is like: *a* descriptive *booklet about a cruise.* **2** relating to or consisting of scientific description: *a book of* descriptive *zoology.* **—*adv-* de·scrip′ tive·ly.** ***n-*** **de·scrip′ tive·ness.**

de·scry (dĭ skrī′) ***vt-*** **[de·scried, de·scry·ing]** to catch sight of; discover through careful observation, especially in the distance or through obscurity: *to* descry *a sail on the horizon*; *to* descry *an improvement in a person's manners.*

des·e·crate (dĕs′ ə krāt′) ***vt-*** **[des·e·crat·ed, des·e·crat·ing]** to treat (something sacred) with contempt or irreverence; also, to put to a sacrilegious use. **—*n-* des′ e·cra′ tion.**

de·seg·re·gate (dē sĕg′ rə gāt′) ***vt-*** **[de·seg·re·gat·ed, de·seg·re·gat·ing]** to put an end to the forced separation of races in (public schools, housing, employment, public facilities, etc.). **—*n-* de·seg′ re·ga′ tion.**

de·sen·si·tize (dē sĕn′ sə tīz′) ***vt-*** **[de·sen·si·tized, de·sen·si·tiz·ing]** to make less sensitive; make insensitive: *to* desensitize *a nerve.* **—*n-* de·sen′ si·ti·za′ tion.**

[1]**de·sert** (dĭ zûrt′) ***vt-*** **1** to forsake; abandon: *to* desert *a house.* **2** *Military* to quit or run away from without leave or discharge: *The sergeant* deserted *his platoon.* ***vi-***: *The GI* deserted. [from French **deserter,** from Latin **desertāre,** "to abandon."] ***Hom-*** dessert. **—*n-* de·sert′ er.**

[2]**des·ert** (dĕz′ ərt) ***n-*** **1** dry land, usually receiving less than 10 inches annual rainfall. Deserts usually have scattered hardy plants with bare ground in between and, sometimes, shifting sand dunes. **2** empty, uncultivated area; wasteland. ***adj-*** **1** having to do with dry land or its vegetation: *the* desert *sands.* **2** uninhabited: *a* desert *island.* [from Old French, from Late Latin use of **desertum,** "(place) having been abandoned," from **deserere** and related to [1]**desert.**]

[3]**de·sert** (dĭ zûrt′) ***n-*** deserved reward or punishment: *He received his just* desert. Also **de·serts′.** [from Old French **deserte,** from **deservir** meaning "to deserve," from Latin **deservīre** "to serve well."] ***Hom-*** dessert.

de·ser·tion (dĭ zûr′ shən) ***n-*** **1** act of deserting; a leaving of one's post: *a* desertion *from the army.* **2** a being abandoned: *a wife's* desertion *by her husband.*

de·serve (dĭ zûrv′) ***vt-*** **[de·served, de·serv·ing]** to earn by service; be worthy of; merit: *to* deserve *promotion.*

de·serv·ed·ly (dĭ zûr′ vəd lē) ***adv-*** justly: *He was* deservedly *blamed for the accident.*

de·serv·ing (dĭ zûr′ vĭng) ***adj-*** worthy: *a* deserving *employee*; *to be* deserving *of recognition.*

des·ha·bille (dĕz′ ə bēl′) dishabille.

des·ic·cat·ed (dĕs′ ə kā′ təd) ***adj-*** **1** dried up: *a box of* desiccated *leaves.* **2** drained of vitality or vigor; withered and faded: *a* desiccated *personality.*

de·sign (dĭ zīn′) ***vt-*** **1** to draw or plan; also, to plan and draw in detail: *to* design *a house.* **2** to plan (something) for a specific purpose or end: *to* design *a car for speed.* ***n-*** **1** outline or sketch to serve as a guide or pattern. **2** arrangement of details according to a plan; pattern: *a book-jacket* design; *a flower* design. **3** (also **designs**) purpose or intention, usually destructive or immoral: *the party's* designs *against the government.*

des·ig·nate (dĕz′ ĭg nāt′) ***vt-*** **[des·ig·nat·ed, des·ig·nat·ing]** **1** to point out; show; mark: *The cross on the map* designates *where the troops landed.* **2** to name; choose; select: *She* designated *three bridesmaids to attend her.* **3** to call by a name: *Certain stones are* designated *gems.*

des·ig·na·tion (dĕz′ ĭg nā′ shən) ***n-*** **1** act of pointing out or indicating. **2** act of appointing; naming: *They approved his* designation *of George as his assistant.* **3** distinctive title or name: *What is the proper* designation *for a member of Congress?*

de·sign·ed·ly (dĭ zīn′ əd lē) ***adv-*** intentionally; purposely: *a* designedly *injurious remark.*

de·sign·er (dĭ zī′ nər) ***n-*** person who creates plans, patterns, or original sketches, especially of clothing, stage settings, or machines.

de·sign·ing (dĭ zī′ nĭng) ***n-*** **1** art of originating or planning designs. **2** act of scheming or plotting. ***adj-*** scheming; artful: *a* designing *person, not to be trusted.*

de·sir·a·ble (dĭ zīr′ ə bəl) ***adj-*** **1** such as to arouse desire; pleasing; worth having: *a* desirable *friend.* **2** advantageous; wise: *a* desirable *job.* **—*n-* de·sir′ a·ble·ness** or **de·sir′ a·bil′ i·ty.** ***adv-*** **de·sir′ a·bly.**

de·sire (dĭ zīər′) ***vt-*** **[de·sired, de·sir·ing]** **1** to wish or long for; crave. **2** to express a wish for; ask: *They* desired *us to go.* ***n-*** **1** a strong longing; wish: *to have a* desire *for chocolate.* **2** the thing longed for: *My chief* desire *is to go home.*

de·sir·ous (dĭ zīər′ əs) ***adj-*** full of desire; eager: *He was* desirous *of learning. He was* desirous *to learn.*

de·sist (dĭ zĭst′) ***vi-*** to discontinue; leave off; cease (from) some action: *He was told to* desist *from smoking.*

desk (dĕsk) ***n-*** **1** piece of furniture with a flat top on which to write, and drawers and compartments to hold writing materials. **2** a cabinet or stand with a sloping top to hold a book for a reader. **3** place or working station reserved for some special work: *the complaint* desk; *the city editor's* desk. **—*adj-* desk′ like′.**

Desk

[1]**des·o·late** (dĕs′ ə lāt′) ***vt-*** **[des·o·lat·ed, des·o·lat·ing]** **1** to lay waste to; make unfit for inhabitants: *An earthquake* desolated *the city.* **2** to overwhelm with sorrow: *Loss of her dog* desolated *the child.*

[2]**des·o·late** (dĕs′ ə lət) ***adj-*** **1** without inhabitants; empty; abandoned: *a* desolate *beach.* **2** in a condition of neglect or ruin: *a* desolate *castle.* **3** forlorn; miserable; dreary: *a* desolate *life.* **—*adv-* des′ o·late·ly.** ***n-*** **des′ o·late·ness.**

des·o·la·tion (dĕs′ ə lā′ shən) ***n-*** **1** a laying waste: *widespread* desolation *by an earthquake.* **2** wasted or ruined state: *The city lay in* desolation *after the bombing.* **3** barren land: *the* desolation *of central Asia.* **4** sadness; forlornness; also loneliness.

de·spair (dĭ spâr′) ***vi-*** to lose all hope (of) some outcome or event: *She* despaired *of ever starting the car.* ***n-*** **1** total loss of hope: *The shipwrecked men were in* despair. **2** that which causes hopelessness or for which there is no hope: *His asthma was the* despair *of his life.* **—*adj-* de·spair′ ing.** ***adv-*** **de·spair′ ing·ly.**

des·patch (dĭ spăch′) dispatch.

des·per·a·do (dĕs′ pə rä′ dō, -rā′ dō) ***n-*** [*pl.* **des·per·a·does** or **des·per·a·dos**] bold and reckless criminal, especially one of the western U.S. frontier.

des·per·ate (dĕs′ pər ət) ***adj-*** **1** in an unbearable situation and ready to take any action to relieve it: *a* desperate *criminal.* **2** extreme because of fear, danger, or suffering: *a* desperate *attempt to swim to shore*; *a* desperate *need.*

3 almost beyond hope; causing despair: *a* desperate *illness.* **—*adj*- des′per·ate·ly. *n*- des′per·ate·ness.**

des·per·a·tion (dĕs′pə rā′shən) ***n***- extreme impulse to act, due to fear, danger, suffering, or hopelessness: *In* desperation *he left his worn-out farm and went west.*

des·pi·ca·ble (də spĭk′ə bəl, dĕs′pĭk′ə bəl) ***adj***- contemptible; mean; vile. **—*n*- des·pi′ca·ble·ness. *adv*- des·pi′ca·bly.**

de·spise (dĭ spīz′) ***vt***- [**de·spised, de·spis·ing**] to regard as worthless; scorn: *to* despise *traitors.*

de·spite (dĭ spīt′) ***prep***- in spite of; heedless of: *to go sailing* despite *the storm warnings.*

de·spoil (dĭ spoil′) ***vt***- to rob; take away all belongings from: *The vandals* despoiled *the house.*

de·spond (dĭ spŏnd′) ***vi***- to be cast down in spirits; be greatly depressed; lose heart.

de·spond·en·cy (dĭ spŏn′dən sē) ***n***- dejection; feeling of depression or hopelessness. Also **de·spond′ence.**

de·spond·ent (dĭ spŏn′dənt) ***adj***- in low spirits; very depressed or discouraged: *He was* despondent *over his poor health.* **—*adj*- de·spond′ent·ly.**

des·pot (dĕs′pət, -pŏt′) ***n***- ruler who has complete power and uses it as he or she pleases; tyrant.

des·pot·ic (dĭ spŏt′ĭc) ***adj***- like a despot; tyrannical: *a* despotic *ruler.* **—*adv*- des·pot′i·cal·ly.**

des·pot·ism (dĕs′pə tĭz′əm) ***n***- 1 despotic use of power; tyranny: *The captain's* despotism *resulted in a mutiny.* 2 system of absolute government.

des·sert (dĭ zûrt′) ***n***- a course of fruits, pastry, pudding, etc., served at the end of a meal. ***Homs***- [1]desert, [3]desert.

des·ti·na·tion (dĕs′tə nā′shən) ***n***- place to which a person or thing is going.

des·tine (dĕs′tən) ***vt***- [**des·tined, des·tin·ing**] to set apart or determine beforehand: *Family tradition* destined *her for the medical profession.*

des·tined (dĕs′tənd) ***adj***- caused by destiny: *his* destined *defeat*; *our* destined *meeting.*

destined for bound for; intended for; certain to come to: *a train* destined for *New York*; *a car* destined for *the scrap heap*; *a man* destined for *high office.*

des·ti·ny (dĕs′tə nē) ***n***- [*pl.* **des·ti·nies**] 1 final lot or fortune of a person, country, or thing: *Death in a foreign land was his* destiny. 2 the succession of events in life considered as something beyond the power or control of man: *He thinks it folly to rebel against* destiny.

des·ti·tute (dĕs′tə to͞ot′, -tyo͞ot′) ***adj***- without means; extremely poor; penniless: *a* destitute *family.*

destitute of wholly without; lacking *The fire left them* destitute of *clothing. He is* destitute of *honor.*

des·ti·tu·tion (dĕs′tə to͞o′shən, -tyo͞o′shən) ***n***- extreme poverty; want.

de·stroy (dĭ stroi′) ***vt***- 1 to wreck; ruin; make useless: *The flood* destroyed *the village.* 2 to kill; also, to put an end to: *The scandal has* destroyed *the business.*

de·stroy·er (də stroi′ər) ***n***- 1 person or thing that destroys. 2 swift, light, heavily-armed warship smaller than a cruiser.

destroyer escort ***n***- warship smaller and slower than a destroyer and used to protect convoys.

de·struct (də strŭkt′) *Space* ***n***- the deliberate destroying of a missile or rocket after it is launched, by a radio signal that sets off an explosive charge carried by the missile itself. **—*vt*-:** *to* destruct *the missile.*

de·struct·i·ble (də strŭk′tə bəl) ***adj***- of a nature that allows being destroyed. **—*n*- de·struct′i·bil′i·ty.**

de·struc·tion (də strŭk′shən) ***n***- 1 a destroying or being destroyed: *The hurricane caused the* destruction *of many homes.* 2 cause of ruin or downfall.

de·struc·tive (də strŭk′tĭv) ***adj***- 1 harmful; causing destruction or ruin: *a* destructive *drought*; *a* destructive *child.* 2 tearing down without building up: *a* destructive *critic.* **—*adj*- de·struc′tive·ly *n*- de·struc′tive·ness.**

destructive distillation ***n***- process of decomposing organic substances such as wood and coal by heating them in the absence of air or oxygen and collecting the distilled products.

des·ue·tude (dĕs′o͞o ə to͞od′, -tyo͞od′) ***n***- state of disuse, as of a custom or fashion; obsolescence.

des·ul·tor·y (dĕs′əl tôr′ē) ***adj***- passing from one thing to another without order or method; disconnected; aimless: *his* desultory *reading.* **—*adj*- des′ul·tor′i·ly. *n*- des′ul·tor′i·ness.**

de·tach (dĭ tăch′) ***vt***- 1 to separate; disengage; disconnect: *to* detach *buttons from a coat.* 2 to detail for a special duty: *to* detach *soldiers to guard a pass.*

de·tach·a·ble (dĭ tăch′ə bəl) ***adj***- of a nature that allows being detached: *a* detachable *coat lining.* **—*n*- de·tach′a·bil′i·ty or de· tach′a·ble·ness.**

de·tached (dĭ tăcht′) ***adj***- 1 separate; unconnected: *a* detached *garage.* 2 withdrawn; aloof; indifferent: *He behaved with a* detached *coldness.* 3 impartial; unbiased; disinterested: *a* detached *view.* **—*adv*- de·tach′ed·ly.**

de·tach·ment (dĭ tăch′mənt) ***n***- 1 separation: *the* detachment *of a key from a chain.* 2 a standing apart; preoccupation; indifference; aloofness: *His* detachment *makes him difficult to know.* 3 absence of bias: *a judge's* detachment. 4 group of troops or ships separated from the main body and sent on special service.

de·tail (dĭ tāl′, dē′tāl′) ***vt***- 1 to relate minutely; enumerate; give particulars of: *She* detailed *the problems.* 2 to appoint for special duty: *He* detailed *two men for guard duty.* ***n***- 1 small or unimportant part or item: *a mere* detail. 2 such items considered together: *The* detail *in the painting was extraordinary.* 3 small body of troops assigned to special duty: *the kitchen* detail.

in detail item by item; with much minute information; fully: *He answered the question* in detail.

de·tain (dĭ tān′) ***vt***- 1 to delay; hold back: *A tardy patient* detained *the doctor.* 2 to keep in custody: *The police* detained *him.*

de·tect (dĭ tĕkt′) ***vt***- 1 to find out; discover; uncover: *to* detect *a criminal*; *to* detect *a leak in the gas main.* 2 to sense the existence of (someting not obvious); discern: *to* detect *a new sound.* 3 in electronics, to separate a modulated signal from a radio carrier wave. **—*adj*- de·tect′a·ble or de·tect′i·ble. *n*- de·tec′tion.**

de·tec·tive (dĭ tĕk′tĭv) ***n***- a person, usually a police officer, who investigates and obtains information about crimes. *as* ***modifier***: *a* detective *story.*

de·tec·tor (dĭ tĕk′tər) ***n***- 1 an electronic device that separates a modulated signal from a radio carrier wave: *a crystal* detector. 2 any device that indicates the presence of an electric current, radioactivity, etc.

dé·tente (dā tänt′) ***n***- lessening of strained relations or tensions, especially between nations.

de·ten·tion (dĭ tĕn′shən) ***n***- 1 a keeping back or withholding. 2 confinement; restraint. *as* ***modifier***: *a* detention *barracks*; *a* detention *ward.*

de·ter (dĭ tûr′) ***vt***- [**de·terred, de·ter·ring**] to discourage or hinder, especially by fear; restrain; dishearten: *Previous failures did not* deter *us from trying again.*

de·ter·gent (dĭ tûr′ jənt) ***n-*** any cleanser that acts like soap but is not made of natural fats and oils.

de·te·ri·o·rate (dĭ têr′ ē ə rāt′) ***vi-*** **[de·te·ri·o·rat·ed, de·te·ri·o·rat·ing]** to decline in quality or value; grow worse: *The economic situation* deteriorated. ***vt-***: *The dry heat* deteriorated *the leather.* **—*n-* de·te′ ri·o·ra′ tion.**

de·ter·mi·na·ble (dĭ tûr′ mə nə bəl) ***adj-*** of a nature that allows being discovered, found out, or established: *a* determinable *number of accidents.*

de·ter·mi·nant (dĭ tûr′ mə nənt) ***n-*** something which influences, limits, or conditions; factor: *Cost and location are often* determinants *in choosing a college.*

de·ter·mi·nate (dĭ tûr′ mə nət) ***adj-*** **1** having definite limits. **2** *Mathematics* having a known or fixed value. **—*adv-* de·ter′ mi·nate·ly. *n-* de·ter′ mi·nate·ness.**

de·ter·mi·na·tion (dĭ tûr′ mə nā′ shən) ***n-*** **1** a deciding or settling upon: *The* determination *of a name for the club took hours.* **2** firm resolution: *He spoke with* determination. **3** a calculating or fixing of position, degree, amount, character, etc.

de·ter·mine (dĭ tûr′ mən) ***vt-*** **[de·ter·mined, de·ter·min·ing]** **1** to decide firmly; resolve: *He* determined *to go to college.* **2** to cause (someone) to want very much: *The art award* determined *him to become a painter.* **3** to be the cause or reason for: *The pull of the moon* determines *the tides.* **4** to decide upon; agree upon: *to* determine *a name for a club.* **5** to find out; establish.

de·ter·mined (dĭ tûr′ mənd) ***adj-*** **1** firm; decided; resolute: *a very* determined *person.* **2** known; established: *at a* determined *height.* **—*adv-* de·ter′ mined·ly. *n-* de·ter′ mined·ness.**

de·ter·min·er (dĭ tûr′ mə nər) *Grammar* ***n-*** a word that occupies the first position in a noun phrase, or the second or third position after another determiner. Determiners include articles, demonstratives, possessive adjectives, and a few other words such as "any," "both," "several," and "whose," which are sometimes called adjectives. Determiners differ from adjectives in that determiners cannot be compared and cannot follow adjectives in a noun phrase (we say "both young people," not "young both people"). Many determiners may be used in place of the noun phrase which they introduce. Examples: These *books belong here.* These *belong here.* Several *people are going.* Several *are going.*

de·ter·rence (dĭ tûr′ əns, dĭ tĕr′-) ***n-*** a deterring.

de·ter·rent (dĭ tûr′ ənt, dĭ tĕr′-) ***adj-*** serving to deter or restrain: *a* deterrent *force.* ***n-*** person or thing that deters.

de·test (dĭ tĕst′) ***vt-*** to hate; dislike violently; loathe.

de·test·a·ble (dĭ tĕs′ tə bəl) ***adj-*** deserving to be detested; hateful: *Cruelty to animals is* detestable. **—*n-* de·test′ a·ble·ness. *adv-* de·test′ a·bly.**

de·tes·ta·tion (dē′ tĕs tā′ shən) ***n-*** feeling of extreme hatred; abhorrence: *a* detestation *of lying.*

de·throne (dĭ thrōn′) ***vt-*** **[de·throned, de·thron·ing]** to remove from a throne or other high position; depose: *to* dethrone *a champion.* **—*n-* de·throne′ ment.**

det·o·nate (dĕt′ ə nāt′) ***vt-*** **[det·o·nat·ed, det·o·nat·ing]** to cause (a high explosive) to explode. ***vi-*** to explode. **—*n-* det·o·na′ tion.**

det·o·na·tor (dĕt′ ə nā′ tər) ***n-*** small quantity of a high explosive, or a device containing it, used to set off another explosive.

de·tour (dē′ to͝or′, dĭ to͝or′) ***n-*** **1** roundabout route temporarily replacing a main route: *Take this* detour. **2** a turning aside from the main route: *We had to make a* detour. ***vi-***: *to* detour *around a road block.* ***vt-***: *to* detour *a truck convoy.*

de·tract (dĭ trăkt′) ***vi-*** to take a part away (from) something: *His vanity* detracts *from his personal appeal.*

de·trac·tion (dĭ trăk′ shən) ***n-*** a belittling or attacking of the reputation or worth of another; disparagement.

de·trac·tor (dĭ trăk′ tər) ***n-*** person who attacks the reputation or worth of another; defamer; slanderer.

det·ri·ment (dĕ′ trə mənt) ***n-*** something that harms or injures; also, injury or damage: *Overeating is a* detriment *to health. He overcame the* detriment *of a bad lisp.*

det·ri·men·tal (dĕ′ trə mĕn′ təl) ***adj-*** causing damage or loss; injurious: *an act that is* detrimental *to our cause.* **—*adv-* det′ ri·men′ tal·ly.**

de·tri·tus (də trī′ təs) ***n-*** any loose material, such as sand or gravel, produced by the wearing away of rocks.

[1]**deuce** (do͞os, dyo͞os) ***n-*** **1** playing card having two spots: *the* deuce *of hearts.* **2** in tennis, a tie score of 40 in a game or a tie score of five games or more each in a set. **3** a throw of two dice in which each die shows a single dot. [from Old French **deus** meaning "two," from Latin **duos,** a form of **duo** meaning "two."]

[2]**deuce** (do͞os, dyo͞os) ***n-*** the devil (used as an oath to express annoyance): *What the* deuce! Deuce *take it!* [probably from early German **duus** meaning "[1]deuce; the lowest throw in dice."]

deu·ced (do͞o′ səd, dyo͞o′-) ***adj-*** confounded; devilish: *It's a* deuced *trap!* **—*adv-* deu′ ced·ly.**

Deut. Deuteronomy.

deu·te·ri·um (do͞o têr′ ē əm, dyo͞o-) ***n-*** isotope of hydrogen with a neutron as well as a proton in its nucleus; heavy hydrogen.

Deu·ter·on·o·my (do͞o′ tə rŏn′ ə mē) ***n-*** fifth book of the Old Testament.

deut·sche mark (doi′ chə) ***n-*** the mark of West Germany.

de·val·u·a·tion (dē val′ yo͞o ā′ shən) ***n-*** a reducing in value, especially of money.

de·val·ue (dē văl′ yo͞o′) ***vt-*** **[de·val·ued, de·val·u·ing]** **1** to reduce the value of (money): *to* devalue *the dollar.* **2** to reduce the importance of (a person, idea, achievement, etc.) in people's minds. Also **de·val′ u·ate [de·val·u·at·ed, de·val·u·at·ing].**

dev·as·tate (dĕv′ ə stāt′) ***vt-*** **[dev·as·tat·ed, dev·as·tat·ing]** **1** to lay waste; make desolate: *War* devastated *the country.* **2** *Informal* to crush or destroy the vanity, pretensions, or composure of (a person). **—*adv-* dev′ as·tat′ ing·ly. *n-* dev′ as·tat′ or.**

dev·as·ta·tion (dĕv′ ə stā′ shən) ***n-*** a laying waste; destruction: *the* devastation *of the country by war.*

de·vel·op (də vĕl′ əp) ***vt-*** **1** to cause to grow and mature: *Water, sunlight, and air help to* develop *plants.* **2** to bring into being: *You should try to* develop *the reading habit.* **3** to work out in detail: *The candidate* developed *his plan of campaign.* **4** to put to use: *to* develop *a country's natural resources.* **5** to build houses on (a tract of land). **6** to treat (a photographic plate, print, or film) with chemicals to make the picture visible. ***vi-*** to grow and mature; progress: *Buds* develop *into blossoms. The mind* develops *from year to year.*

de·vel·op·er (də vĕl′ ə pər) ***n-*** someone or something that develops or causes developing; especially, a chemical substance or solution used in developing photographs.

de·vel·op·ment (də vĕl′ əp mənt) ***n-*** **1** a growing and maturing: *the* development *of a bud into a flower.* **2** a beginning or starting: *the* development *of new habits.* **3** an improving: *the* development *of a person's talents or mind.* **4** a putting to use: *the* development *of water power.* **5** treatment of exposed photographic films or paper to show the image. **6** an event or result: *an unfortunate* development. **7** a working out; a taking or giving shape: *the* development *of a plan.* **8** group of houses constructed in a similar manner, usually by the same builder **—*adj-* de·vel′ op·men′ tal.**

De·vi (dā′ vē′) ***n-*** in Hinduism, the mother goddess, consort of Siva.

de·vi·ant (dē′ vē ənt) ***adj-*** departing or varying from what is usual or correct: *a* deviant *tendency*; *a* deviant *pronunciation.* ***n-*** person or thing that departs or varies from the usual or normal.

de·vi·ate (dē′ vē āt′) ***vi-*** **[de·vi·at·ed, de·vi·at·ing]** to turn aside or stray (from) a course, way of action, belief, custom, etc.; swerve; diverge: *to* deviate *from truth.*

de·vi·a·tion (dē′ vē ā′ shən) ***n-*** **1** a turning aside from a course, belief, etc.; divergence. **2** the amount of this.

de·vi·a·tion·ist (dē′ vē ā′ shən ĭst) ***n-*** one who turns away or strays from the principles and practices of a political party; political heretic.

de·vice (dĭ vīs′) ***n-*** **1** tool or machine designed for a special use: *a* device *for cutting paper*; *a* device *for opening jars.* **2** trick; scheme: *The fox knows clever* devices *to throw the hounds off his trail.* **3** sign or symbol, especially a coat of arms on a shield or banner.

leave (someone) to (his) own devices to allow someone to do as he wishes, without benefit of help or advice.

dev·il (dĕv′ əl) ***n-*** **1** evil spirit. **2** wicked person. **3** pitiful or unfortunate person: *The poor* devil *was cold and hungry.* **4 the Devil** Satan, prince of hell and the personification of evil. ***vt-*** **1** to tease; pester. **2** of some foods, to chop fine, season, mix with a sauce, and sometimes bake: *to* devil *eggs*; *to* devil *crabs.*

dev·il·fish (dĕv′ əl fish′) ***n-*** **1** manta. **2** a giant octopus.

dev·il·ish (dĕv′ ə lĭsh) ***adj-*** **1** naughty; implike: *a* devilish *gleam in his eye.* **2** very wicked; evil; fiendish. ***—adv-*** **dev′ il·ish·ly.** ***n-*** **dev′ il·ish·ness.**

dev·il-may-care (dĕv′ əl mā kâr′) ***adj-*** very casual or careless; happy-go-lucky; reckless.

dev·il·ment (dĕv′ əl mənt) ***n-*** impish or roguish conduct; playful mischief: *a baby full of* devilment.

devil's advocate ***n-*** person who argues for a bad or unpopular cause, either to force a proving of the other side or because he likes to argue.

dev·il's-food cake (dĕv′ əlz fo͞od′) ***n-*** very rich dark chocolate cake.

dev·il·try (dĕv′ əl trē) ***n-*** [*pl.* **dev·il·tries]** **1** reckless mischief. **2** wickedness; cruelty. Also **dev′ il·ry.**

de·vi·ous (dē′ vē əs) ***adj-*** **1** turning away or differing from the usual or direct way; roundabout; circuitous: *a* devious *route to the lake*; *a* devious *line of thought*; *a* devious *way of solving a problem.* **2** using tricky and hidden methods; shrewdly vague: *a* devious *man.* ***—adv-*** **de′ vi·ous·ly.** ***n-*** **de′ vi·ous·ness.**

de·vise (dĭ vīz′) ***vt-*** **[de·vised, de·vis·ing]** to think up; contrive; invent; make: *to* devise *new ways of extracting coal*; *to* devise *a temporary shelter.* ***—n-*** **de·vis′ er.**

de·vi·tal·ize (dē vī′ tə līz′) ***vt-*** **[de·vi·tal·ized, de·vi·tal·iz·ing]** to weaken or destroy the vitality or vigor of: *The poor cast* devitalized *a fine play.*

de·void of (dĭ void′) ***prep-*** completely without; empty of: *She is* devoid of *sense. That is* devoid of *interest.*

de·volve (dĭ vŏlv′) ***vi-*** **[de·volved, de·volv·ing]** of duties, to pass or be settled (on or upon) a successor: *At the death of the president the presidency* devolves *on the vice-president.* ***vt-***: *to* devolve *the presidency on the vice-president.*

De·vo·ni·an (də vō′ nē ən) ***n-*** the fourth of the six periods of the Paleozoic era. Animal life (amphibians) first appeared on land in the Devonian. ***adj-***: *a* Devonian *limestone.*

de·vote (dĭ vōt′) ***vt-*** **[de·vot·ed, de·vot·ing]** **1** to set apart for a special reason: *They agreed to* devote *part of the park to a playground.* **2** to give (oneself) completely to some cause, work, etc.: *She* devoted *herself to art.*

de·vot·ed (dĭ vō′ təd) ***adj-*** wholly given up to some object, cause, or person; loyal; dedicated: *a* devoted *nurse*; *a* devoted *father.* ***—adv-*** **de·vot′ ed·ly.**

dev·o·tee (dĕv′ ə tē′, -tā′) ***n-*** person who is devoted to or very enthusiastic about something; follower; fan.

de·vo·tion (dĭ vō′ shən) ***n-*** **1** strong love or loyalty: *a mother's* devotion. **2** a giving of oneself to a person or a cause: *His* devotion *to his work leaves him little time for fun.* **3** religious devoutness. **4 devotions** prayers.

de·vo·tion·al (dĭ vō′ shən əl) ***adj-*** of or related to religious devoutness and worship: *a* devotional *life.* ***—adv-*** **de·vo′ tion·al·ly..**

de·vour (dĭ vouər′) ***vt-*** **1** to eat up greedily: *The lion* devoured *its prey.* **2** to destroy or lay waste: *Fire* devoured *the building.* **3** to take in eagerly with the eyes, ears, or mind: *to* devour *an adventure story.* **4** to overwhelm or occupy completely; consume: *Anxiety* devoured *him.*

de·vout (dĭ vout′) ***adj-*** **1** devoted to or showing very sincere religious thoughts and practices; very pious: *the* devout *life of a saint*; *a* devout *prayer.* **2** sincere; earnest: *a* devout *wish for success.* ***—adv-*** **de·vout′ ly.** ***n-*** **de·vout′ ness.**

dew (do͞o, dyo͞o) ***n-*** **1** moisture from the atmosphere that condenses in small drops on cool surfaces at night: *morning* dew *on the flowers.* **2** freshness; youthful glow: *the* dew *of youth.* ***vt-*** to wet with or as with dew; moisten: *Tears* dewed *her cheeks.* ***Homs-*** do, due.

dew·ber·ry (do͞o′ bĕr′ ē, dyo͞o′-) ***n-*** [*pl.* **dew·ber·ries]** **1** a kind of blackberry. **2** the running or trailing plant that bears this fruit.

dew·claw (do͞o′ clô′, dyo͞o′-) ***n-*** the little inner toe on the foot of certain dogs and other animals.

dew·drop (do͞o′ drŏp′, dyo͞o′-) ***n-*** drop of dew.

Dew·ey decimal system (do͞o′ ē, dyo͞o′-) ***n-*** system for classifying and cataloging books, periodicals, and other library materials. It uses three-digit whole numbers for major fields, and decimal additions for smaller subdivisions.

dew·lap (do͞o′ lăp′, dyo͞o′-) ***n-*** the fold of loose skin that hangs from the neck of cattle, dogs, and other animals.

DEW line (do͞o, dyo͞o) ***n-*** *d*istant *e*arly *w*arning line, a 3000-mile-long chain of radar stations located north of the Arctic Circle as part of a detection system against enemy missiles, planes, etc.

dew point ***n-*** the temperature at which a vapor condenses to form a liquid; especially, the temperature of the air at which dew forms.

dew·y (do͞o′ē, dyo͞o′-) ***adj-*** **[dew·i·er, dew·i·est]** **1** moist with dew. **2** fresh and sparkling as if with dew; glowing.

dex·ter (dĕk′ stər) ***adj-*** on a coat of arms, on the right-hand side (the viewer's left).

dex·ter·i·ty (dĕk stĕr′ ə tē) ***n-*** ease and skill, especially in using the hands and other parts of the body.

dex·ter·ous (dĕk′ stər əs) or **dex·trous** (dĕks′ trəs) ***adj-*** skilled, especially in using the hands: *a* dexterous *juggler.* ***—adv-*** **dex′ter·ous·ly.** ***n-*** **dex′trous·ness.**

dex·tral (dĕks′ trəl) ***adj-*** **1** of or on the right-hand side. **2** right-handed.

dex·trin (dĕk′ strĭn) or **dex·trine** (-strēn′) ***n-*** gummy substance obtained from various starches by heating or treating with acids. It is used as a glue.

dex·trose (dĕk′strōs′) ***n-*** crystalline sugar used for making jams, jellies, etc.; grape sugar.

---

fāte, făt, dâre, bärn; bē, bĕt, mêre; bīte, bĭt; nōte, hŏt, môre, dôg; fŭn, fûr; to͞o, bo͝ok; oil; out; t*a*r; thin; *th*en; hw for wh as in *wh*at; zh for s as in u*s*ual; ə for a, e, i, o, u, as in *a*go, lin*e*n, per*i*l, at*o*m, min*u*s

dhow (dou) ***n-*** sailboat, usually having one mast and a lateen sail, used along the east coast of Africa.

di- *combining form* two; double: *a* di*oxide*; di*cotyledon.* [from Greek **di-**, from **dis** meaning "twice."]

dia- *combining form* (**di-** before vowels) through or across: dia*thermy* (heating through); dia*meter* (measurement through or across). [from a Greek prefix meaning "through (and through); across."]

di·a·be·tes (dīʹ ə bēʹ tēz, -təs) ***n-*** disease characterized by an inability of the body to use carbohydrates, and due to the failure of the pancreas to produce sufficient insulin. Abnormally high amounts of unused sugar appear in the blood and the urine.

di·a·bet·ic (dīʹ ə bĕtʹ ĭk) ***adj-*** **1** of or relating to diabetes: *a* diabetic *symptom.* **2** having diabetes: *a* diabetic *child.* ***n-*** person having diabetes.

di·a·bol·ic (dīʹ ə bŏlʹ ĭk) or **di·a·bol·i·cal** (-ĭ kəl) ***adj-*** like a devil or his work; fiendish and inhuman: *a* diabolic *murder.* **—*adv-* diʹ a·bolʹ i·cal·ly.**

di·a·crit·ic (dīʹ ə krĭtʹ ĭk) ***n-*** diacritical mark. ***adj-*** diacritical.

di·a·crit·i·cal (dīʹ ə krĭtʹ ĭ kəl) ***adj-*** of a mark or sign, serving to indicate the sound value of a letter in the pronunciation of a word; diacritic. ***n-*** diacritical mark; diacritic. **—*adv-* diʹ a·critʹ i·cal·ly.**

diacritical mark ***n-*** mark or sign that indicates the sound value of a letter in the pronunciation of a word; diacritic; diacritical. In the pronunciation of "cat," the diacritical mark [˘] over the "a" indicates a sound value similar to that in "fat," "sat," etc.

di·a·dem (dīʹ ə dĕmʹ) ***n-*** **1** crown. **2** ornamental headband worn by royalty.

di·aer·e·sis (dī ĕrʹ ə səs) dieresis.

di·ag·nose (dīʹ əg nōsʹ) ***vt-*** [**di·ag·nosed, di·ag·nos·ing**] to identify or find out the nature of (a disease or other harmful condition) on the basis of certain signs or symptoms: *to* diagnose *measles*; *to* diagnose *an emotional difficulty.* **—*adj-* diʹ ag·nosʹ tic** (-nŏsʹ tĭk.)

di·ag·no·sis (dīʹ əg nōʹ səs) ***n-*** [*pl.* **di·ag·no·ses** (-sēzʹ)] **1** investigation of the nature of a disease or other trouble: *According to the doctor's* diagnosis *it was mumps.* **2** the report of such an investigation: *The doctor sent his* diagnosis *of his patient's condition to a surgeon.*

di·ag·nos·ti·cian (dīʹ əg nŏs tĭshʹ ən) ***n-*** person who makes diagnoses, especially a doctor skilled in this.

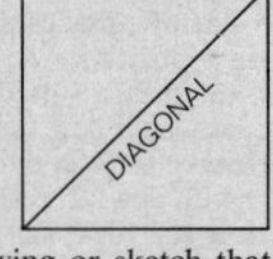

di·ag·o·nal (dī ăgʹ ə nəl) ***n-*** in a polygon or polyhedron, a straight line that connects any two corners that are not adjacent or consecutive. ***adj-*** from corner across to corner; slanting; oblique: *Fay took a* diagonal *course across the field.* **—*adv-* di·agʹ o·nal·ly.**

di·a·gram (dīʹ ə grămʹ) ***n-*** line drawing or sketch that shows how something is put together or how it works. ***vt-*** [**di·a·gramed** or **di·a·grammed, di·a·gram·ing** or **di·a·gram·ming**]: *to* diagram *a sentence.*

di·a·gram·mat·ic (dīʹ ə grə mătʹ ĭk) ***adj-*** in the form of a diagram or sketch: *a* diagrammatic *representation of the digestive organs.* **—*adv-* diʹ a·gram·matʹ i·cal·ly.**

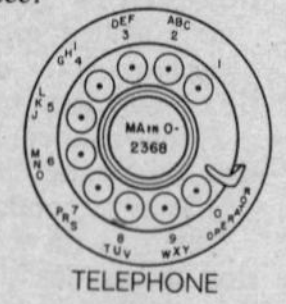

TELEPHONE Dials

di·al (dīʹ əl) ***n-*** **1** circle or part of a circle, such as the face of a clock, gauge, compass, etc., marked with units of measure to be indicated by a moving needle or other pointer. **2** lettered or numbered set of disks on a telephone, for signaling the number being called. **3** knob and indicator on a radio or television set for tuning to stations. ***vt-*** to operate such a device to get (a telephone connection, radio station, etc.): *to* dial *a number.* ***vi-***: *To get your number, please* dial *again.*

dial. dialect; dialectal.

di·a·lect (dīʹ ə lĕktʹ) ***n-*** form of a language peculiar to a locality, region, or group. ***adj-*** (also **diʹ a·lecʹ tal**) belonging to such a language.

di·a·logue (dīʹ ə lŏgʹ) ***n-*** **1** conversation, especially in a play, novel, etc. **2** exchange of views between groups over a period of time and on many occasions: *the* dialogue *between management and labor.* **3** essay in the form of a conversation, used by several philosophers.

dial tone ***n-*** steady buzz heard in a telephone, indicating that a number may be dialed.

diam. diameter.

di·am·e·ter (dī ămʹ ə tər) ***n-*** **1** length of a straight line that passes from one side of a circle or sphere, through the center, to the other side. For picture, see *circle.* **2** the line itself. **3** of a cylindrical object, twice the radius of a circular cross-section: *the* diameter *of a tube.*

di·a·met·ric (dīʹ ə mĕʹ trĭk) or **di·a·met·ri·cal** (-ĭ kəl) ***adj-*** **1** pertaining to a diameter. **2** completely opposite.

di·a·met·ri·cal·ly (dīʹə mĕʹ trĭk lē) ***adv-*** **1** along a diameter. **2** as one extreme is to its opposite: *This was* diametrically *opposed to what I said.*

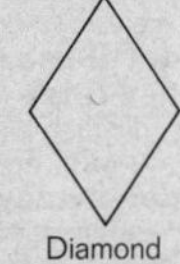
Diamond

di·a·mond (dīʹ mənd, dīʹ ə-) ***n-*** **1** extremely hard and nearly colorless precious mineral formed of pure crystallized carbon. **2** piece of this stone cut for use as jewelry or as a drilling or scraping point. **3** plane figure having four equal straight lines, and two acute and two obtuse angles. **4** in baseball, the part of the playing field having the four bases as its corners; infield. **5** any one of a suit of playing cards called **diamonds** that is marked with a red figure [♦]. ***as modifier***: *a* diamond *ring*; diamond *tiara.* **—*adj-* diʹ a·mond·likeʹ.**

di·a·mond·back (dīʹ mənd băkʹ) ***n-*** any of several large rattlesnakes having diamond-shaped markings on its back and found in the southern United States.

diamondback terrapin ***n-*** turtle found in salt marshes along the Atlantic and Gulf coasts. It has diamond markings on its back. For picture, see *terrapin.*

Di·an·a (dī ănʹ ə) ***n-*** in Roman mythology, the goddess of the moon and of the hunt. She is identified with the Greek Artemis.

di·a·pa·son (dīʹ ə pāʹ zən) ***n-*** **1** one of the two stops on an organ that affect all the tones of the instrument. **2** a swelling sound of harmonious notes or parts. **3** the entire range or compass of a voice or instrument. **4** a standard pitch given by a tuning fork. **5** the tuning fork itself.

di·a·per (dīʹ pər, dīʹ ə pər) ***n-*** **1** cloth or thick absorbent paper usually folded several times and used as or in a baby's underpants. **2** cloth woven in a geometric pattern that is repeated over and over. ***vt-***: *to* diaper *a baby.*

di·aph·a·nous (dī ăfʹ ə nəs) ***adj-*** transparent or translucent; sheer: *a* diaphanous *scarf.* **—*adv-* di·aphʹ a·nous·ly. *n-* di·aphʹ a·nous·ness.**

Diaphragm

di·a·phragm (dīʹ ə frămʹ) ***n-*** **1** muscular membrane inside the body that separates the chest from the abdomen. **2** in a telephone, loudspeaker, or the like, the vibrating disk or cone that produces sound waves. **3** device to regulate the size of a camera's lens opening. **4** any thin membrane that separates or divides.

di·a·rist (dī′ ə rĭst) ***n-*** person who keeps a diary.

di·ar·rhe·a or **di·ar·rhoe·a** (dī′ ə rē′ ə) ***n-*** unusual liquidity and frequency of the bowel movements.

di·a·ry (dī′ ə rē) ***n-*** [*pl.* **di·a·ries**] **1** day-to-day record of one's experiences, opinions, etc.; journal. **2** book in which such a record is kept.

Di·as·po·ra (dī ăs′ pər ə) ***n-*** **1** in Jewish history, the dispersion of the Jews among the Gentiles. **2** in the New Testament, Jewish Christians outside of Palestine. **3 diaspora** people of one country or faith dispersed among others.

di·as·to·le (dī ăs′ tə lē) ***n-*** rhythmic expansion and relaxation of the heart, following each contraction, during which the heart chambers are filled with blood. See also *systole.*

di·as·tol·ic (dī′ ə stŏl′ ĭk) ***adj-*** measured during, or having to do with, the diastole: *the* diastolic *blood pressure.*

di·as·tro·phism (dī ăs′ trə fĭz′ əm) ***n-*** in geology, any movement of the earth's solid parts, especially the very slow movements of the earth's crust that produce mountains, seas, islands, etc.

di·a·ther·my (dī′ ə thûr′ mē) ***n-*** **1** the heating of body tissues by a high-frequency electric current. **2** a machine for this purpose, used in medicine.

di·a·tom (dī′ ə tŏm′) ***n-*** one of a large group of very tiny one-celled algae, living in water and having beautifully marked, glasslike shells.

di·a·ton·ic scale (dī′ ə tŏn′ĭk) *Music* ***n-*** any one of the major or minor scales consisting of eight tones and having no chromatic tones.

di·a·tribe (dī′ ə trīb′) ***n-*** bitter and abusive speech or writing against a person, group, policy, etc.

dib·ble (dĭb′ əl) ***n-*** pointed gardening tool for making holes to plant seeds, bulbs, etc. ***vt-*** **[dib·bled, dib·bling]**: *to* dibble *the soil*; *to* dibble *seeds.*

dice (dīs) ***n-pl.*** [*sing.* **die**] small cubes of bone, plastic, etc., having sides marked with from one to six spots, and used in playing certain games. ***vt-*** **[diced, dic·ing] 1** to cut (vegetables, fruit, etc.) into small cubes. **2** to ornament or mark with cubes or squares.
in the dice destined to happen.

Dice

dick·ens (dĭk′ ənz) ***n-*** devil; deuce (used as an oath): *What the* dickens *do you mean?*

dick·er (dĭk′ ər) ***vi-*** to bargain in a petty way; haggle; chaffer. [American word from an obsolete noun **dicker** meaning "a lot or bundle of ten hides."]

dick·ey (dĭk′ ē) ***n-*** [*pl.* **dick·eys**] **1** partial front of a shirt or blouse for wear under sweaters and jackets. **2** shirt collar. **3** child's bib or pinafore. **4** (also **dick′ey·bird′**) small bird.

Dick test *Medicine* ***n-*** test, made by injecting scarlet-fever toxins into the skin, to determine whether one is susceptible or immune to scarlet fever.

di·cot·y·le·don (dī′ kŏt ə lē′ dən) ***n-*** plant that has two seed leaves (cotyledons). See also *monocotyledon.* Also **di′ cot′** (dī′ kŏt′). ***—adj-*** **di′ cot·y·le′ don·ous.**

dict. dictionary.

dic·ta (dĭk′ tə) *pl.* of **dictum.**

Dic·ta·phone (dĭk′ tə fōn′) ***n-*** trademark name of an office machine used for recording and reproducing what is spoken into it for later typing.

dic·tate (dĭk′ tāt′) ***vt-*** **[dic·tat·ed, dic·tat·ing]** (considered intransitive when the direct object is implied but not expressed) **1** to command flatly; prescribe absolutely: *Tyrants* dictate *the lives of their subjects. Conscience* dictates *obedience to law.* **2** to speak (something) for someone to write down: *The manager* dictated *two letters this morning.* ***n-*** something flatly commanded or prescribed: *the* dictates *of one's conscience.*

dic·ta·tion (dĭk tā′ shən) ***n-*** **1** a speaking of words to be written down; also, the words that are written down: *The stenographer read the* dictation *back to him.* **2** a telling someone what to do; a commanding.

dic·ta·tor (dĭk′ tā tər), dĭk tā′-) ***n-*** **1** ruler who has unlimited power; absolute head of a government: *Caesar made himself* dictator. **2** person whose authority is accepted in some special field: *a* dictator *of fashion.*

dic·ta·tor·i·al (dĭk′ tə tôr′ ē əl) ***adj-*** of or like a dictator or his practices; autocratic; absolute: *a* dictatorial *policy.* ***—adv-*** **dic′ ta·tor′ i·al·ly.**

dic·ta·tor·ship (dĭk′ tā tər shĭp′, dĭk tā′-) ***n-*** **1** rule by a dictator or in the absolute manner of a dictator. **2** country, organization, etc., so ruled.

dic·tion (dĭk′ shən) ***n-*** **1** pronunciation and rhythm in speaking or singing; enunciation. **2** one's choice of words in speaking and writing; wording.

dic·tion·ar·y (dĭk′ shə nĕr′ ē) ***n-*** [*pl.* **dic·tion·ar·ies**] **1** book that lists words of a language in alphabetical order and explains them in the same language. A dictionary tells what words mean, how to pronounce them, and how to spell them, and may also show how words are used and where they come from. **2** book that lists words of one language and explains them in another language: *a French-English* dictionary.

dic·tum (dĭk′ təm) ***n-*** [*pl.* **dic·ta**] **1** formal or authoritative statement; dogmatic assertion: *Some people believe in the* dictum *that might makes right.* **2** any popular or current saying; maxim.

did (dĭd) *p.t.* of [1]**do.**

di·dac·tic (dī dăk′ tĭk) ***adj-*** **1** intended to teach or guide: *a* didactic *essay.* **2** overly inclined to moralize: *a priggish,* didactic *man.* ***—n-*** **di·dac′ ti·cism′** (tə sĭz′ əm).

did·n't (dĭd′ ənt) did not.

Di·do (dī′ dō) ***n-*** in Roman legend, a queen of Carthage. According to the "Aeneid," she fell in love with Aeneas and stabbed herself to death when he left her.

didst (dĭdst) *Archaic* form of **did** (used only with "thou").

[1]**die** (dī) ***vi-*** **[died, dy·ing] 1** to stop living; suffer death: *John Adams and Thomas Jefferson both* died *on July 4, 1825.* **2** to fade; disappear; lose strength: *The breeze* died *toward evening.* **3** to yearn; be impatiently eager: *I'm* dying *to know.* [from Old English **dieyan,** probably from Old Norse **deyja.**] ***Hom-*** dye.

[2]**die** (dī) ***n-*** **1** device for stamping designs on coins, making raised patterns on paper, or cutting and shaping leather, sheet metal, etc. **2** tool for cutting threads on bolts, pipes, etc. **3** [*pl.* **dice**] one of a pair of dice. [from earlier English **de,** from Old French **dē(z),** from Latin **datum** meaning "given; thrown."] ***Hom-*** dye.
the die is cast the decision is made and there is no turning back from it.

Die for stamping cent

die-hard (dī′ härd′) ***n-*** person who stubbornly resists changing his views or principles. ***adj-***: *a* die-hard *political conservative.*

di·er·e·sis (dī ĕr′ ə səs) ***n-*** [*pl.* **di·er·e·ses** (-sēz)] two dots [¨] placed over a vowel to indicate its sound. Example: far, pronounced (fär).

►The dieresis is sometimes placed over the second of two adjoining vowels to show that each vowel is pronounced separately, but this practice is no longer widely used. Example: coöperate.

die·sel (dē′ zəl) ***adj-*** **1** powered by a Diesel engine: *a* diesel *truck.* **2** relating to or intended for a Diesel engine: *a barrel of* diesel *fuel.*

Diesel engine ***n-*** engine that burns oil in its cylinders. The oil is ignited by the heat of air compressed in the cylinders, instead of by an electric spark as in the gasoline engine.

Di·es I·rae (dē′ äs′ êr′ ī′, -ē′) ***n-*** title and beginning of a famous Latin hymn that is used in the Requiem Mass.

[1]**di·et** (dī′ ət) ***n-*** **1** one's usual food and drink: *The prisoner's* diet *was coarse and dry.* **2** a special choice of food, eaten to gain or lose weight, correct or ease an ailment, etc.: *a reducing* diet. ***vi-*** to eat or drink according to certain prescribed rules. [from **diete,** through Medieval Latin, from Greek **diaita** meaning "a way of life."]

[2]**di·et** (dī′ ət) ***n-*** formal or legislative assembly. [from Old French **diete,** from Medieval Latin **dieta,** apparently meaning "day" in the sense of "day of assembly."]

di·e·tar·y (dī′ ə tĕr′ ē) ***adj-*** having to do with diet or eating habits: *a new* dietary *fad.* ***n-*** [*pl.* **di·e·tar·ies**] **1** a certain fixed allowance of food: *the prison* dietary. **2** rules for, or a system of, regulating food.

di·e·tet·ic (dī′ ə tĕt′ ĭk) ***adj-*** **1** of or relating to diet; dietary. **2** acceptable or intended for special diets: *a* dietetic *dessert.*

di·e·tet·ics (dī′ ə tĕt′ iks) ***n-*** *pl.* (takes singular verb) branch of hygiene that deals with diet and its effects.

di·e·ti·tian or **di·e·ti·cian** (dī′ ə tĭsh′ ən) ***n-*** person trained in the field of dietetics and usually engaged in it as a profession.

dif·fer (dĭf′ ər) ***vi-*** **1** to be unlike: *Wrens and buzzards* differ *greatly in size.* **2** to be of opposite opinion; disagree: *We* differed *sharply over the amount to be spent.*

dif·fer·ence (dĭf′ rəns, -ər əns) ***n-*** **1** way or respect in which things are unlike; lack of similarity: *What is the* difference *between living and nonliving substances?* **2** the extent by which one thing differs from another: *a height* difference *of 2 inches.* **3** the result of a subtraction; also, the amount of this result: *The* difference *between 10 and 8 is 2.* **4** disagreement: *They had a serious* difference *of opinion.*

dif·fer·ent (dĭf′ rənt, -ər ənt) ***adj-*** **1** unlike; not alike; dissimilar: *boys of* different *ages*; *a coat* different *from mine.* **2** separate; distinct; not the same: *The boy had the same excuse for being late on three* different *occasions.* **3** not the same as others; unusual: *She has a very* different *way of dressing.* —***adv-*** **dif′ fer·ent·ly.**

►DIFFERENT is often used with "from," "than," or "to" in conversation, but DIFFERENT FROM is preferred in writing: *His bicycle is* different from *mine in color and weight.* See also VARIOUS.

dif·fer·en·tial (dĭf′ ə rĕn′ shəl) ***adj-*** of, related to, or involving a difference: *a* differential *rate.* ***n-*** differential gear. —***adv-*** **dif′fer·en′ tial·ly.**

differential gear ***n-*** device in a machine or an automobile that allows one shaft or driving wheel to turn faster than the other. In automobiles it compensates for the fact that the driving wheels are turning at different rates in rounding curves.

dif·fer·en·ti·ate (dĭf′ ə rĕn′ shē āt′) ***vt-*** [**dif·fer·en·ti·at·ed, dif·fer·en·ti·at·ing**] **1** to mark off; single out as unlike: *Aging* differentiates *a really good cheese from an ordinary one.* **2** to observe an unlikeness or difference between; distinguish between; discriminate: *to* differentiate *the warbles of various birds.* ***vi-*** **1** to see or discover a difference; distinguish: to differentiate *between two similar colors.* **2** to become different: *Boys and girls* differentiate *more and more as they grow older.*

dif·fer·en·ti·a·tion (dĭf′ ə rĕn′ shē ā′ shən) ***n-*** **1** act of differentiating; a causing, observing, or marking out of difference between things. **2** change from likeness to unlikeness between things.

dif·fi·cult (dĭf′ ĭ kəlt, -kŭlt′) ***adj-*** **1** not easy; hard to do or understand: *a* difficult *problem*; *a* difficult *language.* **2** arduous; rigorous; trying: *Weather conditions were* difficult. **3** hard to get along with; not easily managed: *a* difficult *child*; *a* difficult *situation.*

dif·fi·cul·ty (dĭf′ ə kŭl′ tē) ***n-*** [*pl.* **dif·fi·cul·ties**] **1** hardness of doing; lack of easiness; rigor: *the* difficulty *of learning German*; *a task of great* difficulty. **2** source of trouble; unfortunate circumstance; obstacle: *The* difficulty *is that he's too small.* **3** conflict; trouble: *He's in* difficulty *with the law.* **4 difficulties** disagreement; friction; quarrels.

be in difficulties to be short of money. **make difficulties** to raise objections; cause trouble. **with difficulty** only with great effort or hard work: *to read* with difficulty.

dif·fi·dence (dĭf′ ə dəns) ***n-*** lack of self-confidence; shyness; timidity: *Her* diffidence *makes her hard to talk with.*

dif·fi·dent (dĭf′ ə dənt) ***adj-*** lacking self-confidence; shy; timid: *a* diffident *smile.* —***adv-*** **dif′ fi·dent·ly.**

dif·fract (dĭ frăkt′) ***vt-*** **1** to separate or break into parts. **2** to cause (light rays, X rays, etc.) to undergo diffraction.

dif·frac·tion (dĭ frăk′ shən) *Physics* ***n-*** **1** the bending or spreading of light or other radiation as it passes through a narrow slit or around the edges of an object. **2** a similar phenomenon of sound waves.

diffraction grating *Physics* ***n-*** device for diffracting light, X rays, and other electromagnetic waves. It is a glass or metal plate etched with many parallel grooves.

[1]**dif·fuse** (dĭ fyo͞oz′) ***vt-*** [**dif·fused, dif·fus·ing**] to spread out or abroad from a source; send widely. ***vi-***: *The dye* diffused *slowly through the water.*

[2]**dif·fuse** (dĭ fyo͞os′) ***adj-*** **1** long and wordy: *a* diffuse *speech.* **2** spread thinly out or about; scattered: *a* diffuse *gas.* —***adv-*** **dif·fuse′ ly.** ***n-*** **dif·fuse′ ness.**

dif·fu·sion (dĭ fyo͞o′ zhən) ***n-*** **1** a spreading: *the* diffusion *of knowledge by means of low-priced books*; *the* diffusion *of pollen by wind and insects.* **2** a natural spreading of one substance through another; the intermingling of molecules. **3** diffuseness. —***adj-*** **dif·fu′ si·ble.**

dig (dĭg) ***vt-*** [**dug, dig·ging**] **1** to break or turn up (soil) with a spade or other instrument. **2** to make (a hole, excavation, etc.) by removing earth: *He* dug *a well in the garden.* **3** to get (something) out by turning up the ground: *to* dig *potatoes*; *to* dig *worms.* **4** to poke or prod: *He* dug *the horse with his spurs.* ***vi-*** **1** to make a way (through): *He* dug *through the pile of old letters.* **2** to seek; search for: *to* dig *for information*; *to* dig *out the truth.* ***n-*** **1** a thrust; a prod: *a* dig *in the ribs.* **2** *Informal* a biting remark.

[1]**di·gest** (dĭ jĕst′, dī-) ***vt-*** **1** to change (food) into a form that the body can use: *We* digest *some foods more easily than others.* **2** to absorb in the mind; think over; understand: *He* digested *his father's advice.* **3** (*also* dī′ jĕst) to summarize: *to* digest *a long article.* ***vi-*** to undergo change for use in the body: *Fats do not* digest *easily.*

[2]**di·gest** (dī′ jĕst′) ***n-*** condensed account; summary: *a book* digest; *a news* digest.

di·gest·i·ble (dĭ jĕs′ tə bəl, dī-) ***adj-*** of a nature that allows being digested: *Lamb is more* digestible *than pork.* ***—adv-*** **di·gest′ i·bly.** ***n-*** **di·ges′ ti·bil′ i·ty.**

di·ges·tion (dĭ jĕs′ chən, dī-) ***n-*** **1** the digesting of food: *A short rest after a meal aids* digestion. **2** the ability to digest food: *A nervous person often has poor* digestion.

di·ges·tive (dĭ jĕs′ tĭv, dī-) ***adj-*** having to do with digesting food; performing or helping digestion: *the* digestive *system*; *to prescribe* digestive *aids.* ***—adv-*** **di·ges′ tive·ly.**

digestive system ***n-*** the mouth, stomach, pancreas, intestines, and other body parts that aid in digestion.

dig·ger (dĭg′ ər) ***n-*** **1** person or animal that digs. **2** tool or machine that digs.

Dig·ger (dĭg′ ər) ***n-*** contemptuous name formerly given to Paiutes who were farmers rather than hunters.

dig·gings (dĭg′ ĭngz) ***n-*** *pl.* **1** place where the operation of digging, especially mining, is carried on. **2** the materials, especially minerals, that are being dug out.

dig·it (dĭj′ ĭt) ***n-*** **1** finger or toe. **2** any of the numerals 0, 1, 2, 3, 4, 5, 6, 7, 8, 9.

dig·i·tal (dĭj′ ĭ təl) ***adj-*** **1** of, having to do with, or resembling digits. **2** having digits: *a* digital *code.* ***n-*** a key on a musical instrument such as a piano or an organ.

digital computer ***n-*** machine that performs mathematical operations using numbers to represent all quantities involved in the calculation.

dig·i·ta·lis (dĭj′ ə tăl′ əs) ***n-*** **1** any of a group of plants bearing spikes of tubular flowers, especially the foxglove. **2** drug made from the leaves of the purple foxglove and used as a heart stimulant.

dig·ni·fied (dĭg′ nə fīd′) ***adj-*** calm and serious in manner; stately; noble in bearing: *the governor's* dignified *air.*

dig·ni·fy (dĭg′nə fī′) ***vt-*** **[dig·ni·fied, dig·ni·fy·ing]** **1** to make worthy or noble; show honor to: *By his achievements, the president* dignified *his office.* **2** to make appear worthy or noble: *Do not* dignify *the job by calling it a position.*

dig·ni·tar·y (dĭg′ nə tĕr′ ē) ***n-*** [*pl.* **dig·ni·tar·ies**] person of rank, position, or standing.

dig·ni·ty (dĭg′ nə tē) ***n-*** [*pl.* **dig·ni·ties**] **1** worthiness; nobleness: *the* dignity *of honest labor.* **2** poise; nobility of bearing; calm and serious manner: *to keep one's* dignity *through hardship.* **3** a high office; honorable rank.

di·graph (dī′ grăf′) ***n-*** group of two letters representing one sound, as "ea" in "head" or "th" in "that." See also *diphthong, ligature.*

di·gress (dĭ grĕs′, dī-) ***vi-*** to turn aside or get away from the main subject or line of argument.

di·gres·sion (dĭ grĕsh′ ən) ***n-*** a turning aside or wandering from the main subject: *a long* digression *on fate.*

di·gres·sive (dĭ grĕs′ ĭv) ***adj-*** tending to wander or turn aside from the main subject. ***—adv-*** **di·gress′ive·ly.** ***n-*** **di·gress′ ive·ness.**

dike (dīk) ***n-*** wall or bank built to hold back water and protect land from flooding: *In Holland,* dikes *hold back the sea.* ***vt-*** **[diked, dik·ing]** to protect from floods with a wall or bank: *Farmers along a river often* dike *their fields.*

Dike

di·lap·i·dat·ed (dĭ lăp′ ə dā′ təd) ***adj-*** run-down from neglect or hard use; fallen into ruin: *a* dilapidated *house*; *a* dilapidated *car.*

di·lap·i·da·tion (dĭ lăp′ ə dā′ shən) ***n-*** ruined or neglected condition; disrepair: *the* dilapidation *of an old house.*

di·late (dī lāt′, dī′ lāt′) ***vi-*** **[di·lat·ed, di·lat·ing]** **1** to become larger or wider: *The pupils of a cat's eyes* dilate *in the dark.* **2** to speak or write at length (on or upon) some topic: *The speaker* dilated *on his favorite subject.* ***vt-*** to make larger or wider: *The doctor* dilated *the pupil of my eye to examine it.* ***—n-*** **di·la′ tion.**

dil·a·tor·y (dĭl′ ə tôr′ ē) ***adj-*** **1** tending to delay or hold back: *the general's* dilatory *tactics.* **2** tardy; neglectful: *a* dilatory *student.* ***—adv-*** **dil′ a·tor′ i·ly.** ***n-*** **dil′ a·tor′ i·ness.**

di·lem·ma (dĭ lĕm′ ə) ***n-*** situation in which one must make an uneasy and difficult choice, often between two or more evils.

on the horns of a dilemma faced with a dilemma; forced to make a very difficult choice.

dil·et·tan·te (dĭl′ ə tănt′) ***n-*** [*pl.* **dil·et·tan·ti** (-tăn′ tē) or **dil·et·tantes**] person who pursues the fine arts, literature, or science merely for amusement; dabbler; amateur.

dil·et·tan·tism (dĭl′ ə tăn′ tĭz′ əm) ***n-*** the attitude or behavior of a dilettante.

[1]**dil·i·gence** (dĭl′ ə jəns) ***n-*** constant, earnest effort; care; zeal: *to perform one's tasks with* diligence. [from Latin **diligentia,** from **diligens, -entis** meaning "diligent."]

[2]**dil·i·gence** (dĭl′ə jəns) ***n-*** a horse-drawn carriage for public use, especially in France. [a special use in French of [1]**diligence** in the meaning of "haste."]

dil·i·gent (dĭl′ ə jənt) ***adj-*** steady, careful, and painstaking: *a* diligent *student.* ***—adv-*** **dil′ i·gent·ly.**

dill (dĭl) ***n-*** plant with finely cut, feathery leaves and spicy seeds, both of which are used to season foods; also, the leaves or seeds of this plant.

dill pickle ***n-*** a pickled cucumber flavored with dill.

dil·ly·dal·ly (dĭl′ ə dăl′ ē) ***vi-*** **[dil·ly·dal·lied, dil·ly·dal·ly·ing]** *Informal* to waste time; linger idly: *to* dilly-dally *over a job.*

di·lute (dĭ lo͞ot′, dī-) ***vt-*** **[di·lut·ed, di·lut·ing]** to weaken or thin by adding or mixing with something, especially water: *to* dilute *grape juice with water*; *to* dilute *the force of an argument.* ***adj-***: *a* dilute *solution of soda.*

di·lu·tion (dĭ lo͞o′ shən, dī-) ***n-*** **1** a diluting or becoming diluted. **2** something that has been diluted.

dim (dĭm) ***adj-*** **[dim·mer, dim·mest]** **1** not bright or clear; having or giving little light: *the* dim *light of evening*; dim *headlights.* **2** not clearly or sharply seen; hazy; faint: *a* dim *figure in the shadows*; *to have only a* dim *idea of the truth.* **3** not seeing or perceiving clearly: *eyes* dim *with tears.* ***vt-*** **[dimmed, dim·ming]** to make less bright, clear, distinct, etc.: *The driver* dimmed *his headlights. Tears* dimmed *her eyes.* ***vi-***: *The stars* dimmed *as dawn approached.* ***—adv-*** **dim′ ly.** ***n-*** **dim′ ness.**

dim. diminuendo.

dime (dīm) ***n-*** small silver coin of the United States or Canada, worth ten cents. [American word from French **dîme,** from Old French **disme** meaning "a tithe," from Latin meaning "a tenth."]

di·men·sion (dĭ mĕn′ shən) ***n-*** **1** size in a particular direction; also, its measurement in linear units. **2** any of the three properties associated with length, area, and volume. Anything having length only is said to be of one dimension. Anything having area and not volume is said to be of two dimensions. Anything having volume is said to be of three dimensions, corresponding to the length, width, and depth of a rectangular box. **3** (also **dimensions**) importance; scope: *a plan of vast* dimensions.

di·men·sion·al (dĭ mĕn′ shən əl, dī-) ***adj-*** of or having a dimension or dimensions such as length, breadth, or

fāte, făt, dâre, bärn; bē, bĕt, mêre; bīte, bĭt; nōte, hŏt, môre, dôg; fŭn, fûr; to͞o, bo͝ok; oil; out; tar; thin; then; hw for wh as in *wh*at; zh for s as in u*s*ual; ə for a, e, i, o, u, as in *a*go, lin*e*n, per*i*l, at*o*m, min*u*s

Several kinds of dinosaur

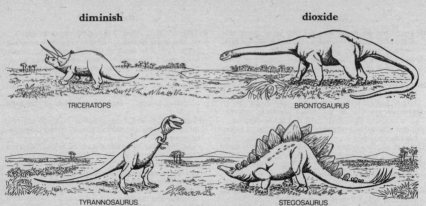

thickness: *a three-*dimensional *figure such as a cube*; dimensional *measurements.* ***—adv-*** **di·men′ sion·al·ly.**

di·min·ish (dĭ mĭn′ ĭsh) ***vt-*** to make less in amount, size, number, intensity, importance, etc.; decrease: *Rain* diminishes *the danger of forest fires. Illness* diminished *his strength.* ***vi-***: *The water supply* diminished.

di·min·u·en·do (dĭ mĭn′ yōō ĕn′ dō) *Music* ***n-*** [*pl.* **di·min·u·en·dos**] a gradual decrease in loudness. ***adj- & adv-*** gradually increasing in loudness.

dim·i·nu·tion (dĭm′ ĭn yōō′ shən, -ōō′ shən) ***n-*** a growing less; decrease: *a* diminution *of strength.*

di·min·u·tive (dĭ mĭn′ yə tĭv) ***adj-*** **1** very small; tiny: *a* diminutive *child.* **2** of a suffix, expressing or indicating smallness or affection or both. "-kin" and "-y" are diminutive suffixes. ***n-*** word formed by adding such a suffix: *"Lambkin" is a* diminutive *of "lamb."* ***—adv-*** **di·min′ u·tive·ly.** ***n-*** **di·min′ u·tive·ness.**

dim·i·ty (dĭm′ ə tē) ***n-*** [*pl.* **dim·i·ties**] thin cotton fabric with raised threads forming a striped or checked weave. *as* ***modifier***: *a* dimity *dress.*

dim·mer (dĭm′ ər) ***n-*** switch, rheostat, or other device for dimming automobile headlights, theater lights, etc.

di·mor·phism (dī′ môr′ fĭz əm, dī môr′-) ***n-*** **1** *Biology* (1) normal occurrence of two types of leaves, flowers, etc., on the same plant or on different plants of the same species. (2) of a particular species of animals, the normal occurrence of two types that differ in color, structure, etc. **2** *Chemistry* of a compound, the property of crystallizing into two different forms. ***—adj-*** **di′ mor′ phic.**

dim·ple (dĭm′ pəl) ***n-*** small hollow in the surface of something: *a* dimple *in her cheek.* ***vi-*** **[dim·pled, dim·pling]** to show or form such marks: *Her cheeks* dimpled *as she smiled.* ***vt-***: *The breeze* dimpled *the lake.*

dim·wit·ted (dĭm′ wĭt′ əd) *Informal* ***adj-*** stupid; foolish.

din (dĭn) ***n-*** loud, continued noise; confused uproar: *the* din *of city traffic.* ***vt-*** **[dinned, din·ning]** to teach or impart by saying emphatically over and over: *to* din *lessons into a child's mind.* ***vi-*** to make a loud noise: *The thunder* dinned *in his ears.*

di·nar (dĭ när′) ***n-*** **1** gold coin of early Islam, used in Persia and other countries of the Near East. **2** any of several monetary units used by some modern countries.

dine (dīn) ***vi-*** **[dined, din·ing]** to eat dinner. ***vt-*** to give a dinner for: *to wine and* dine *a guest.* ***Hom-*** dyne.

din·er (dī′ nər) ***n-*** **1** person eating dinner. **2** dining car. **3** small restaurant, especially one built to look somewhat like such a car.

di·nette (dī nĕt′) ***n-*** small room or area near a kitchen, used for eating meals.

ding (dĭng) ***n-*** high or tinkly sound made by a bell or chime. ***vi-*** to ring or chime shrilly.

ding-dong (dĭng′ dòng′, -dŏng′) ***n-*** the sound of repeated strokes of a bell.

din·ghy (dĭng′ gē) ***n-*** [*pl.* **din·ghies**] any of various types of small boats, especially a small rowboat.

din·gle (dĭng′ gəl) ***n-*** small wooded valley; dell.

din·go (dĭng′ gō) ***n-*** [*pl.* **din·goes**] wild dog of Australia.

din·gy (dĭn′ jē) ***adj-*** **[din·gi·er, din·gi·est]** not bright, fresh, or clean; dull; dirty: *a* dingy *house*; dingy *colors.* ***—adv-*** **din′ gi·ly.** ***n-*** **din′ gi·ness.**

dining car ***n-*** railroad car in which meals are served.

dining room ***n-*** room in which meals are usually served in a home, or in a hotel or other public place.

dink·ey (dĭng′ kē) ***n-*** [*pl.* **din·keys**] small locomotive used in logging, in railroad yards, etc. ***Hom-*** dinky.

din·ky (dĭng′ kē) *Informal* ***adj-*** **[din·ki·er, din·ki·est]** small and insignificant. ***Hom-*** dinkey.

din·ner (dĭn′ ər) ***n-*** **1** main meal of the day, generally the evening meal on weekdays but the midday meal on holidays and among country people. **2** formal meal given in honor of some person or occasion. *as* ***modifier***: *a* dinner *table*; dinner *dress.*

di·no·saur (dī′ nə sòr′) ***n-*** any of several kinds of reptiles that lived millions of years ago, especially certain giant reptiles, the largest land animals that ever lived.

dint (dĭnt) *Archaic* ***vt-*** to dent. ***n-*** a dent.

by dint of by force or exertion of: *We finished the task on time* by dint of *great effort.*

di·o·cese (dī′ ə səs, -sēs′) ***n-*** the church district under the authority of a bishop.

di·ode (dī′ ōd′) ***n-*** **1** electron tube that has two electrodes (a cathode and an anode) and is used especially to change alternating current into direct current. **2** rectifier or other device using a semiconductor that operates like a two-electrode electron tube.

Di·o·ny·sus (dī′ ə nī′ səs) ***n-*** in Greek mythology, a son of Zeus and god of wine and fertility. He is identified with the Roman Bacchus.

di·o·ra·ma (dī′ ə răm′ ə) ***n-*** an arrangement, usually for exhibit, of lifelike models of plants, animals, human figures, etc., shown in a setting that blends into a realistic painted background.

di·ox·ide (dī ŏk′ sīd′) ***n-*** oxide containing two atoms of oxygen per molecule.

dip (dĭp) ***vt-*** **[dip·ped, dip·ping]** **1** to put quickly into a liquid and take out again: *to* dip *one's finger in water*; *to* dip *a garment in dye.* **2** to scoop up with a ladle, spoon, cup, etc.: *to* dip *water from a spring.* **3** to lower and raise again quickly: *to* dip *the wings of a plane*; *to* dip *a flag.* **4** to make (a candle) by repeatedly putting a wick in melted wax. ***vi-*** **1** to go into water or other liquid and come out quickly: *gulls* dipping *in the ocean.* **2** to slope or sink downward: *The road* dips. **3** to reach into and take something out: *to* dip *into the cookie jar.* ***n-*** **1** a short plunge, immersion, or swim: *a* dip *in the lake.* **2** a short downward slope: *a* dip *in the road.* **3** a quick lowering and raising: *a* dip *of the head.* **4** creamy food intended to be scooped up on crackers, bread, etc. **5** liquid into which something may be plunged for cleaning, disinfecting, etc.: *a* dip *for sheep.*
dip into to read, study, or enter into briefly and superficially: *to* dip into *a book*; *to* dip into *politics.*

diph·the·ri·a (dĭf thêr′ ē ə, dĭp-) ***n-*** dangerous and contagious disease marked by high fever and a suffocating membrane that forms in the throat.

diph·thong (dĭf′ thŏng′, dĭp′-) ***n-*** two vowel sounds said together as one continuous sound, such as "oi" in "coil," or "ou" in "doubt." See also *digraph, ligature.*

di·plo·ma (dĭ plō′ mə) ***n-*** official document showing that some degree has been given or that a required course of study has been completed: *a college* diploma.

di·plo·ma·cy (dĭ plō′ mə sē) ***n-*** **1** the art or practice of managing relations between nations. **2** skill and tact in dealing with people.

dip·lo·mat (dĭp′ lə măt′) ***n-*** **1** person trained in and usually engaged in handling problems and relations between nations. **2** tactful and persuasive person. Also **di·plo′ ma·tist** (dĭ plō′ mə tĭst′).

dip·lo·mat·ic (dĭp′ lə măt′ ĭk) ***adj-*** **1** of or having to do with peacetime affairs between nations. **2** showing or using skill in peaceful and pleasant dealings with others; tactful: *a* diplomatic *refusal.* —***adv-*** **dip′ lo·mat′ i·cal·ly.**

diplomatic corps ***n-*** the officials such as ambassadors, envoys, etc., who conduct the diplomacy of a nation.

diplomatic immunity ***n-*** exemption from certain local laws, granted to diplomats stationed in a foreign country.

dip·per (dĭp′ ər) ***n-*** **1** person or thing that dips: *a* dipper *in a chocolate factory.* **2** long-handled cup for scooping up liquids. **3** either of two groups of stars suggesting the outline of such a cup, Big Dipper or Little Dipper.

Dipper

dip·so·ma·ni·a (dĭp′ sə mā′ nē ə) ***n-*** uncontrollable desire for alcoholic drink.

dip·so·ma·ni·ac (dĭp′ sə mā′ nē ăk′) ***n-*** an alcoholic.

dip·ter·ous (dĭp′ tər əs) ***adj-*** of or belonging to an order **(Diptera)** of insects having a single pair of wings, including the flies, mosquitoes, and gnats.

dip·tych (dĭp′ tĭk′) ***n-*** set of paintings, carvings, etc., made on two panels hinged together.

dire (dīər) ***adj-*** **[dir·er, dir·est]** extremely bad; dreadful; grave: *in* dire *need.* —***adv-*** **dire′ ly.** ***n-*** **dire′ ness.**

di·rect (dĭ rĕkt′, dī-) ***vt-*** **1** to manage the work or operation of; control; conduct: *to* direct *the affairs of a nation*; *to* direct *traffic*; *to* direct *a play.* **2** to order or instruct; command: *to* direct *the troops to advance.* **3** to show or tell the way to; lead or guide: *Can you* direct *me to the post office?* **4** to aim or address: *to* direct *one's energies toward one's work*; *to* direct *one's remarks to the class.* **5** to write the address on (a letter, package, etc.). ***adj-*** **1** straight; not roundabout: *a* direct *route.* **2** straightforward; frank; honest: *a* direct *answer.* **3** not through an intervening medium or source: *in* direct *contact*; *to have* direct *knowledge*; *a* direct *quotation.* **4** absolute; complete; exact: *the* direct *opposite.* **5** in an unbroken line of descent: *the* direct *heir to the throne.* ***adv-*** without intervening stops; directly: *This plane flies* direct *to Chicago.* — ***n-*** **di·rect′ ness.**

direct current ***n-*** electric current, such as that from batteries and certain generators, that flows continuously in the same direction. *Abbr.* D.C. See also *alternating current.*

direct discourse ***n-*** exact quotation of what has been said or written. Example: She said, "I am going to the park." See also *indirect discourse.*

directed number ***n-*** any member of the set of integers.

direct evidence ***n-*** evidence that deals with the main facts to be proved, given by a witness who testifies directly of his own knowledge. An eye-witness account is direct evidence. See also *circumstantial evidence.*

di·rec·tion (dĭ rĕk′ shən, dī-) ***n-*** **1** course or line of motion, attention, purpose, etc.: *to travel in an easterly* direction; *much progress in many* directions. **2** a directing or controlling; management; guidance: *to work under another's* direction. **3** (usually **directions**) instruction; order: *Read the* directions. **4** address on a letter, package, etc.

di·rec·tion·al (dĭ rĕk′ shən əl, dī-) ***adj-*** **1** having to do with or indicating direction. **2** sending or receiving sound or radio signals in a specified direction only: *a* directional *antenna*; *a* directional *microphone.*

direction finder ***n-*** receiving device for finding the direction toward radio transmitters.

di·rec·tive (dĭ rĕk′ tĭv, dī-) ***n-*** an order, regulation, instruction, etc.: *a military* directive.

di·rect·ly (dĭ rĕkt′ lē, dī-) ***adv-*** **1** in a direct line or manner; straight: *Travel* directly *north.* **2** *Informal* immediately; at once: *I'll take the medicine* directly.

direct object See [2]*object.*

di·rec·tor (dĭ rĕk′ tər, dī-) ***n-*** **1** person who directs or manages. **2** person who guides and controls the performance of a play, motion picture, etc. **3** member of the board that controls a business corporation. **4** device that points or aims a gun, telescope, etc.

di·rec·to·rate (dĭ rĕk′ tər ət, dī-) ***n-*** **1** group of directors. **2** the position or authority of a director.

di·rec·to·ry (dĭ rĕk′ tə rē, dī-) ***n-*** [*pl.* **di·rec·to·ries**] list or collection of names, addresses, etc., usually in alphabetical order: *a telephone* directory.

direct primary ***n-*** primary election at which the nominees of a political party are chosen directly by the voters instead of by delegates to a nominating convention.

direct proportion ***n-*** relation between two variables such that their ratio always remains the same.

direct tax ***n-*** tax, such as one on income or inherited property, that must be paid directly by the taxpayer to the government. See also *indirect tax.*

direct variation ***n-*** the keeping of a constant ratio between the values of two variables; the variation that satisfies the equation y = kx, where k is a constant; variation in direct proportion.

dire·ful (dīər′ fəl) ***adj-*** resulting in or suggesting dire happenings; ominous: *the* direful *croak of the raven.* —***adv-*** **dire′ ful·ly.** ***n-*** **dire′ ful·ness.**

dirge (dûrj) *n-* sad piece of music, such as a funeral hymn or song of mourning.

dir·i·gi·ble (dĭr′ ə jə bəl, də rĭj′ ə-) *n-* aircraft consisting of an elongated, gas-filled balloon or a rigid structure with gas-filled compartments, and having motors and rudders to drive and guide it.

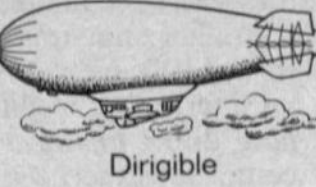
Dirigible

dirk (dûrk) *n-* a dagger or short sword.

dirn·dl (dûrn′ dəl) *n-* dress with a fitted bodice and a full skirt gathered at the waist; also, a skirt made in this style. *as* ***modifier****: a* dirndl *dress.* [from a German dialect word meaning "girl."]

dirt (dûrt) *n-* **1** dust, mud, or anything that makes something unclean; filth: *to wash the* dirt *from one's hands.* **2** loose earth or soil: *They covered the front lot with new* dirt. **3** any unclean or indecent action, writing, or talk. **4** *Informal* scandalous news; gossip.

dirt·y (dûr′ tē) *adj-* **[dirt·i·er, dirt·i·est] 1** not clean; soiled: *a* dirty *coat.* **2** mean; unfair: *a* dirty *trick.* **3** not decent: *to use* dirty *words.* **4** not clear in color: *a* dirty *green.* **5** stormy and unpleasant; foul: *the* dirty *weather.* *vt-* **[dirt·ied, dirt·y·ing]** to make unclean; soil: *to* dirty *one's hands.* **—*adv-* dirt′ i·ly.** ***n-*** **dirt′i·ness.**

dis- *prefix* **1** not; the opposite of: *a* dis*obedient child; sharp* dis*agreement.* **2** fail to; cease to; refuse to: *to* dis*satisfy; to* dis*agree; to* dis*obey.* **3** do the reverse of: *to* dis*entangle.* **4** lack of: *a* dis*union.* [from Latin **dis-** meaning "apart; away; opposite."]

dis·a·bil·i·ty (dĭs′ ə bĭl′ ə tē) *n-* [*pl.* **dis·a·bil·i·ties**] **1** loss or lack of physical or mental powers: *partial* disability *as a result of an injury.* **2** something that disables or handicaps: *His lack of training was a* disability.

dis·a·ble (dĭs ā′ bəl) *vt-* **[dis·a·bled, dis·a·bling]** to deprive of power or ability; cripple; incapacitate: *The injury to his knee* disabled *him for many weeks.* **—*n-* dis·a′ ble·ment.**

dis·a·bled (dĭs ā′ bəld) *adj-* having a disability; injured.

dis·a·buse (dĭs′ ə byōōz′) *vt-* **[dis·a·bused, dis·a·bus·ing]** to rid or free (someone) of a mistaken belief, idea, etc.; undeceive: *You must* disabuse *yourself of that notion.*

dis·ad·van·tage (dĭs′ əd văn′ tĭj) *n-* **1** unfavorable condition; obstacle; handicap: *Fear of water is a* disadvantage *in learning to swim.* **2** harm; detriment: *We heard rumors to his* disadvantage.

at a disadvantage in an unfavorable situation with relation to others: *The poor are* at a disadvantage.

dis·ad·van·taged (dĭs′ əd văn′ tĭjd) *adj-* lacking opportunities for improvement, recreation, etc., in one's daily life; underprivileged.

dis·ad·van·ta·geous (dĭs′ ăd′ vən tā′ jəs) *adj-* of a sort that harms or handicaps; unfavorable. **—*adv-* dis′ ad′- van·ta′ geous·ly.** ***n-*** **dis′ ad′ van·ta′ geous·ness.**

dis·af·fect (dĭs′ ə fĕkt′) *vt-* to turn (one or more persons) away from or against a person, cause, or organization that had their loyalty and adherence: *The Hungarian revolt* disaffected *many Communists.* **—*n-* dis′af·fec′tion.**

dis·a·gree (dĭs′ ə grē′) *vi-* **[dis·a·greed, dis·a·gree·ing] 1** to fail to agree; be unlike; conflict: *Your account* disagrees *with hers.* **2** to differ in opinion; quarrel: *They* disagreed *about the price.* **3** to have bad effects; be unsuitable: *The hot climate* disagrees *with him.*

dis·a·gree·a·ble (dĭs′ ə grē′ ə bəl) *adj-* **1** causing annoyance, discomfort, etc.; unpleasant: *a harsh,* disagreeable *voice;* disagreeable *weather.* **2** ill-tempered or rude. **—*n-* dis′ a·gree′ a·ble·ness.** ***adv-*** **dis′ a·gree′ a·bly.**

dis·a·gree·ment (dĭs′ ə grē′ ment) *n-* **1** difference of opinion; failure to agree: *a* disagreement *among members of the jury.* **2** argument; quarrel. **3** lack of similarity; difference: *a* disagreement *of details.*

dis·al·low (dĭs′ ə lou′) *vt-* to refuse to admit or allow the truth, reliability, etc., of; reject: *to* disallow *his claim.* **—*n-* dis′ al·low′ ance:** *the* disallowance *of his claim.*

dis·ap·pear (dĭs′ ə pêr′) *vi-* **1** to go out of sight; become invisible; vanish: *The ship* disappeared *over the horizon.* **2** to cease to exist: *Many old customs have* disappeared.

dis·ap·pear·ance (dĭs′ ə pêr′ əns) *n-* a passing from sight or existence; a vanishing.

dis·ap·point (dĭs′ ə point′) *vt-* **1** to fail to satisfy the hopes or expectations of: *The bad performance* disappointed *his admirers.* **2** to thwart or put an end to (hopes, aims, etc.). **—*adv-* dis′ ap·point′ ing·ly.**

dis·ap·point·ed (dĭs′ ə poin′ təd) *adj-* **1** saddened or disturbed because one's hopes or expectations have not been fulfilled: *a* disappointed *suitor.* **2** not fulfilled; thwarted.

dis·ap·point·ment (dĭs′ ə point′ mənt) *n-* **1** a disappointing: *his* disappointment *of their hopes.* **2** a feeling of being disappointed: *They couldn't hide their* disappointment. **3** person or thing that disappoints.

dis·ap·pro·ba·tion (dĭs′ ăp′ rə bā′ shən) *n-* disapproval.

dis·ap·prov·al (dĭs′ ə prōō′ vəl) *n-* the act of disapproving; dislike; unfavorable feeling.

dis·ap·prove (dĭs′ ə prōōv′) *vi-* **[dis·ap·proved, dis·ap·prov·ing]** to refuse to approve; have a bad or unfavorable opinion (of) someone or something: *She* disapproved *of his new necktie.* *vt-*: *to* disapprove *a request.* **—*adv-* dis′ ap·prov′ ing·ly.**

dis·arm (dĭs ärm′) *vt-* **1** to take a weapon or weapons from: *He* disarmed *the bandit.* **2** to remove doubts or unfriendly feelings of; win over: *He* disarmed *me with his smile.* *vi-* to reduce one's armed forces and weapons. **—*adv-* dis·arm′ ing·ly:** *He smiled* disarmingly.

dis·ar·ma·ment (dĭs är′ mə mənt) *n-* a ceasing to use or a putting aside of weapons, especially the reduction of weapons and men in the armed forces.

dis·ar·range (dĭs′ ə rānj′) *vt-* **[dis·ar·ranged, dis·ar·rang·ing]** to disturb the arrangement of; put in disorder. **—*n-* dis′ ar·range′ ment.**

dis·ar·ray (dĭs′ ə rā′) *n-* condition of disorder, untidiness, or confusion. *vt-* to throw into disorder.

dis·as·sem·ble (dĭs′ ə sĕm′ bəl) *vt-* **[dis·as·sem·bled, dis·as·sem·bling]** to take apart; separate into component parts: *to* disassemble *a machine.*

►Should not be confused with DISSEMBLE.

dis·as·so·ci·ate (dĭs′ ə sō′ sē āt′, -shē āt′) *vt-* **[dis·as·so·ci·at·ed, dis·as·so·ci·at·ing]** to dissociate. **—*n-* dis′- as·so′ ci·a′ tion.**

dis·as·ter (dĭ zăs′ tər) *n-* something that causes great trouble or suffering; great misfortune; calamity.

dis·as·trous (dĭ zăs′ trəs) *adj-* causing great misfortune, destruction, trouble, etc.: *a* disastrous *flood; a* disastrous *accident.* **—*adv-* dis·as′ trous·ly.** ***n-*** **dis·as′ trous·ness.**

dis·a·vow (dĭs′ ə vou′) *vt-* to refuse to claim or accept as one's own; deny; disown: *to* disavow *a belief.*

dis·a·vow·al (dĭs′ ə vou′ əl) *n-* a disavowing; denial.

dis·band (dĭs bănd′) *vt-* to break up and dismiss (an organized group of people): *to* disband *a regiment.* *vi-*: *The marchers* disbanded *after the parade.*

dis·bar (dĭs bär′) *vt-* **[dis·barred, dis·bar·ring]** to deprive (a lawyer) of the right to practice his profession. **—*n-* dis·bar′ ment.**

dis·be·lief (dĭs′ bĭ lēf′) *n-* a refusal to believe.

►For usage note see UNBELIEF.

dis·be·lieve (dĭs′ bĭ lēv′) *vt-* **[dis·be·lieved, dis·be·liev·ing]** to refuse to accept as true: *to* disbelieve *his story.* *vi-* to have no belief (in): *to* disbelieve *in the theory that there is life on Mars.* **—*n-* dis′ be·liev′ er.** ***adv-*** **dis′ be·liev′ ing·ly.**

dis·bur·den (dĭs bûr′ dən) ***vt-*** to relieve of a burden: *to* disburden *one's mind by confiding one's troubles.*

dis·burse (dĭs bûrs′) ***vt-*** **[dis·bursed, dis·burs·ing]** to pay out; issue (money, funds, etc.): *The treasurer* disburses *their salaries.* **—*n-*** **dis·burs′ er.**
►Should not be confused with DISPERSE.

dis·burse·ment (dĭs bûrs′ment) ***n-*** the paying out of money, funds, etc.; also, an amount thus paid out.

disc (dĭsk) disk.

[1]**dis·card** (dĭs kärd′) ***vt-*** to throw away or cast aside as useless: *to* discard *old clothes.* ***vi-*** (*also* dĭs′ kärd′) in card games, to throw off an unwanted card or play a card that is neither a trump nor of the suit led.

[2]**dis·card** (dĭs′ kärd′) ***n-*** **1** something thrown away: *These damaged boxes are* discards. **2** card that is discarded in a game. **3 the discard** place for, or condition of, something cast aside as useless: *clothes thrown into* the discard.

dis·cern (dĭ sûrn′, -zûrn′) ***vt-*** **1** to make out clearly; perceive: *I* discerned *his plan. We can* discern *stars in the sky.* **2** to distinguish: *to* discern *truth from falsehood.*

dis·cern·i·ble (dĭ sûr′ nə bəl, dĭ zûr′-) ***adj-*** such as can be seen or separately picked out: *hills barely* discernible *in the mist.* **—*adv-*** **dis·cern′ i·bly.**

dis·cern·ing (dĭ sûr′ nĭng, dĭ zûr′-) ***adj-*** having the ability to judge clearly and see small differences: *a* discerning *taste in music.* **—*adv-*** **dis·cern′ ing·ly.**

dis·cern·ment (dĭ sûrn′ mənt, dĭ zûrn′-) ***n-*** **1** ability to judge clearly and pick out small differences: *a woman of great* discernment. **2** act of perceiving or distinguishing.

[1]**dis·charge** (dĭs chärj′) ***vt-*** **[dis·charged, dis·charg·ing]** **1** to release from employment, service, etc.; dismiss: *to* discharge *a worker; to* discharge *a soldier from the army.* **2** to get rid of (passengers, cargo, etc.); unload: *The ship* discharged *its cargo at the wharf.* **3** to fire or shoot (a firearm); also, to shoot forth (an arrow, bullet, etc.). **4** to let flow or escape; give off: *a wound that* discharges *pus; an outlet that* discharges *water from a tank.* **5** to carry out; complete; *to* discharge *an errand.* **6** to pay off; settle: *to* discharge *a debt.* **7** to cause to release a charge of electricity: *to* discharge *a battery.* ***vi-*** **1** to flow forth or out; empty: *The stream* discharges *into the lake.* **2** to lose a charge of electricity. **3** of a gun, to fire; shoot.

[2]**dis·charge** (dĭs′ chärj′) ***n-*** **1** a dismissal or release from service, employment, etc.; also, a certificate of dismissal: *He received his* discharge *from the army.* **2** a firing or shooting off: *The* discharge *of the gun startled us.* **3** something that flows forth or escapes: *a watery* discharge *from the eyes.* **4** an unloading: *the* discharge *of cargo.* **5** a carrying out; performance: *the* discharge *of one's duty.* **6** a paying off or settling: *the* discharge *of one's debts.* **7** *Physics* (1) the release or emission of energy: *the* discharge *of electricity from a battery.* (2) the flow of an electric current through a gas.

dis·ci·ple (dĭ sī′ pəl) ***n-*** person who accepts the teachings of a leader and helps to spread them. The earliest followers of Jesus were called his disciples.

dis·ci·pli·nar·i·an (dĭs′ ə plə nĕr′ ē ən) ***n-*** person responsible for enforcing rules or keeping order: *The captain is a harsh* disciplinarian.

dis·ci·pli·nary (dĭs′ ə plə nĕr′ ē) ***adj-*** having to do with discipline; corrective: *strict* disciplinary *measures.*

dis·ci·pline (dĭs′ ə plĭn) ***n-*** **1** strict training of mind, body, character, etc.: *military* discipline. **2** obedience, self-control, or order resulting from this: *to maintain* discipline *in a classroom.* **3** punishment given in order to train or correct. **4** a field of learning or study: *Mathematics and astronomy are related* disciplines. ***vt-*** **[dis·ci·plined, dis·ci·plin·ing] 1** to train to be obedient or efficient; keep in order or under control: *to* discipline *troops.* **2** to punish in order to train or correct.

disc jockey *Informal* ***n-*** person who broadcasts a program of music from records.

dis·claim (dĭs klām′) ***vt-*** to refuse to claim or accept; deny; disown: *to* disclaim *responsibility for an action.*

dis·claim·er (dĭs klā′ mər) ***n-*** statement denying responsibility, knowledge, connection, etc.; denial.

dis·close (dĭs klōz′) ***vt-*** **[dis·closed, dis·clos·ing] 1** to uncover and make visible; bring to light: *Their digging* disclosed *a buried treasure.* **2** to make known; reveal: *to* disclose *secret information.*

dis·clo·sure (dĭs klō′ zhər) ***n-*** **1** a revealing or disclosing; also, an instance of this: *The* disclosure *of the epidemic frightened many.* **2** means of disclosing: *The speech was a* disclosure *of bribery.*

dis·col·or (dĭs kŭl′ ər) ***vt-*** to change or spoil the color of; stain: *The acid* discolored *his skin.* ***vi-***: *cloth guaranteed not to* discolor *in strong sunlight.*

dis·col·or·a·tion (dĭs kŭl′ ə rā′ shən) ***n-*** **1** a discolored mark or condition; stain. **2** a making or becoming discolored.

dis·com·fit (dĭs kŭm′ fət) ***vt-*** **1** to throw into confusion; disconcert; embarrass; dismay. **2** to defeat; rout.

dis·com·fi·ture (dĭs kŭm′ fə chər) ***n-*** a discomfiting or a being discomfited; confusion; dismay; embarrassment.

dis·com·fort (dĭs kŭm′ fərt) ***n-*** lack of comfort; uneasy or uncomfortable feeling; distress. ***vt-*** to make uncomfortable.

dis·com·mode (dĭs′ kə mōd′) ***vt-*** **[dis·com·mod·ed, dis·com·mod·ing]** to inconvenience; disturb; bother.

dis·com·pose (dĭs′ kəm pōz′) ***vt-*** **[dis·com·posed, dis·com·pos·ing]** to disturb the calm or composure of; upset; ruffle: *Heckling* discomposed *the speaker.*

dis·com·po·sure (dĭs′ kəm pō′ zhər) ***n-*** uneasy state; agitation: *his* discomposure *at the remark.*

dis·con·cert (dĭs′ kən sûrt′) ***vt-*** to disturb the calm or self-possession of; throw into confusion; upset: *His teasing* disconcerts *her.* **—*adv-*** **dis′ con·cert′ ing·ly:** *The question was* disconcertingly *sharp.*

dis·con·nect (dĭs′ kə nĕkt′) ***vt-*** to break or undo the connection of: *to* disconnect *an electric iron by removing the plug from the socket.* **—*n-*** **dis′ con·nec′ tion.**

dis·con·nect·ed (dĭs′ kə nĕk′ təd) ***adj-*** not connected, especially in the flow of ideas; disjointed: *a rambling,* disconnected *speech.* **—*adv-*** **dis′con·nect′ed·ly.** ***n-*** **dis′-con·nect′ ed·ness.**

dis·con·so·late (dĭs kŏn ′ sə lət) ***adj-*** unhappy; without cheer or comfort; desolate; gloomy: *a* disconsolate *man.* **—*adv-*** **dis·con′ so·late·ly.** ***n-*** **dis·con′ so·late·ness,**

dis·con·tent (dĭs′ kən tĕnt′) ***n-*** lack of ease and calm; dissatisfaction; restlessness. Also **dis·con·tent′ ment.**

dis·con·tent·ed (dĭs′ kən tĕn′ tĕd) ***adj-*** not happy or content; not satisfied: *He was* discontented *with his salary.* **—*adv-*** **dis′ con·tent′ ed·ly.** ***n-*** **dis′ con·tent′ ed·ness.**

dis·con·tin·u·a·tion (dĭs′ kən tĭn′ yo͞o ā′ shən) ***n-*** a stopping, ending, or breaking off. Also **dis′ con·tin′ u·ance.**

dis·con·tin·ue (dĭs′ kən tĭn′ yo͞o) ***vt-*** **[dis·con·tin·ued, dis·con·tin·u·ing]** to put an end to; stop; cease: *He had to* discontinue *work.* ***vi-***: *Boating* discontinued *in winter.*

dis·con·ti·nu·i·ty (dĭs′ kŏn′ tə no͞o′ ə tē, -nyo͞o′ ə tē) ***n-*** [*pl.* **dis·con·ti·nu·i·ties**] **1** break or gap; place where something stops and something quite different begins. **2** lack of continuity.

fāte, făt, dâre, bärn; bē, bĕt, mêre; bīte, bĭt; nōte, hŏt, môre, dóg; fŭn, fûr; to͞o, bo͝ok; oil; out; tar; thin; then; hw for wh as in *wh*at; zh for s as in u*s*ual; ə for a, e, i, o, u, as in *a*go, lin*e*n, per*i*l, at*o*m, min*u*s

dis·con·tin·u·ous (dĭs′ kən tĭn′ yōō əs) ***adj-*** stopping or breaking off; having gaps; sporadic: *The signals on the screen were* discontinuous. ***—adv-*** **dis′ con·tin′ u·ous·ly.**

dis·cord (dĭs′ kȯrd′, -kôrd′) ***n-*** **1** argument; disagreement; strife: *The group was too full of* discord *to work together.* **2** *Music* lack of harmony; dissonance: *The* discord *in modern music startles many people.* **3** harsh noise.

dis·cord·ant (dĭs kȯr′ dənt, -kôr′ dənt) ***adj-*** not agreeing; clashing; out of harmony: *a* discordant *meeting; a* discordant *musical chord.* ***—n-*** **dis·cord′ance.** ***adv-*** **dis·cord′ant·ly.**

dis·co·theque (dĭs′ kō tĕk′) ***n-*** nightclub or dance hall where patrons dance to recorded music.

dis·count (dĭs′ kount) ***n-*** (also **discount rate**) an allowance for cash payment, dealer's rate, etc.: *All catalog prices are subject to a 25%* discount. ***vt-*** **1** to give such a price reduction on: *We* discount *all bills paid within 30 days.* **2** (*also* dĭs kount′) to take (something) as not entirely true; allow for exaggeration in: *to* discount *a rumor.*

dis·coun·te·nance (dĭs koun′ tən əns) ***vt-*** **[dis·coun·te·nanced, dis·coun·te·nanc·ing] 1** to disconcert or abash: *The harshness of the rebuke* discountenanced *me.* **2** to disapprove of: *to* discountenance *a proposal.*

dis·cour·age (dĭs kûr′ ĭj) ***vt-*** **[dis·cour·aged, dis·cour·ag·ing] 1** to take away the hope or confidence of; dishearten: *Don't* discourage *the child.* **2** to try to prevent or deter: *Law enforcement* discourages *crime.* ***vi-*** to lose confidence: *Some people* discourage *easily.*

dis·cour·age·ment (dĭs kûr′ ĭj mənt) ***n-*** **1** a discouraging; rebuff: *He tried to make friends but met with* discouragement. **2** a feeling of being discouraged; disheartenment: *In his* discouragement *he gave up.* **3** something that discourages: *Lack of money is a big* discouragement.

dis·cour·ag·ing (dĭs kûr′ ə jĭng) ***adj-*** **1** tending to lessen hope and confidence; disheartening. **2** deterrent: *a* discouraging *effect on crime.* ***—adv-*** **dis·cour′ ag·ing·ly.**

[1]**dis·course** (dĭs′ kôrs′) ***n-*** **1** spoken or written treatment of some subject; treatise; lecture: *a* discourse *on astronomy.* **2** utterance; communication: *Poetry is a form of* discourse.

[2]**dis·course** (dĭs kôrs′) ***vi-*** **[dis·coursed, dis·cours·ing]** to talk at length on a subject: *He* discoursed *all day!*

dis·cour·te·ous (dĭs kûr′ tē əs) ***adj-*** rude; impolite: *It is* discourteous *to interrupt when someone is talking.* ***—adv-*** **dis·cour′ te·ous·ly.** ***n-*** **dis·cour′ te·ous·ness.**

dis·cour·te·sy (dĭs kûr′ tə sē) ***n-*** [*pl.* **dis·cour·te·sies**] **1** rudeness; bad manners; incivility. **2** a rude, ill-mannered, or uncivil act: *To ignore her invitation would be a* discourtesy.

dis·cov·er (dĭs kŭv′ ər) ***vt-*** to find or come upon anything for the first time: *Priestley* discovered *oxygen. George* discovered *music early.* ***—n-*** **dis·cov′ er·er.**

dis·cov·er·y (dĭs kŭv′ ə rē) ***n-*** [*pl.* **dis·cov·er·ies**] **1** a finding out about or a coming upon something for the first time: *the* discovery *of gold.* **2** the thing found, or found out: *Penicillin was a great* discovery.

dis·cred·it (dĭs krĕd′ ĭt) ***vt-*** **1** to throw doubt on; to destroy belief in: *to* discredit *the belief that toads cause warts.* **2** to refuse to believe: *I* discredit *all those stories.* ***n-*** **1** loss of good name or reputation: *to bring* discredit *on the whole family.* **2** person who causes loss of reputation: *He was a* discredit *to the family.* **3** doubt or disbelief: *Science brings old beliefs into* discredit.

dis·cred·it·a·ble (dĭs krĕd′ ĭ tə bəl) ***adj-*** bringing discredit; damaging to the reputation; disgraceful. ***—adv-*** **dis·cred′ it·a·bly.**

dis·creet (dĭs krēt′) ***adj-*** careful and tactful in speech and action; prudent; guarded: *Secrets are safe with a* discreet *friend.* ***—adv-*** **dis·creet′ ly.** ***n-*** **dis·creet′ ness.** ***Hom-*** discrete.

dis·crep·an·cy (dĭs krĕp′ ən sē) ***n-*** [*pl.* **dis·crep·an·cies**] difference; variance; lack of agreement: *the* discrepancy *between the two stories.* Also **dis·crep′ ance.**

dis·crep·ant (dĭs krĕp′ ənt) ***adj-*** differing; disagreeing; at variance: *two* discrepant *explanations.*

dis·crete (dĭs krēt′) ***adj-*** separate and distinct: *When sugar is melted, its* discrete *grains melt into a mass.* ***Hom-*** discreet.

dis·cre·tion (dĭs krĕsh′ ən) ***n-*** **1** ability or habit of being discreet; good judgement; prudence; tact. **2** freedom of choice or action: *Let's leave that to his* discretion.

dis·cre·tion·ar·y (dĭs krĕsh′ ən ĕr′ ē) ***adj-*** meant to be used by choice when needed: *In some matters the police have* discretionary *powers.*

dis·crim·i·nate (dĭs krĭm′ ə nāt′) ***vi-*** **[dis·crim·i·nat·ed, dis·crim·i·nat·ing] 1** to note small differences; distinguish or make a distinction: *to* discriminate *between good and inferior writers.* **2** to treat people differently and often badly because of race, religion, etc.; apply prejudice: *to* discriminate *against minority groups.* ***vt-***: *to* discriminate *good books from bad.*

dis·crim·i·nat·ing (dĭs krĭm′ ə nā′ tĭng) ***adj-*** **1** able to make small distinctions; discerning: *a* discriminating *taste in music.* **2** serving to identify or single out; differentiating. ***—adv-*** **dis·crim′ i·nat′ ing·ly.**

dis·crim·i·na·tion (dĭs krĭm′ ə nā′ shən) ***n-*** **1** a noting of fine differences; discernment: *to buy without* discrimination. **2** a distinction made or noted: *I agree with that* discrimination. **3** ability to discriminate. **4** difference in treatment or attitude: *without* discrimination *as to creed or color.*

dis·crim·i·na·tive (dĭs krĭm′ ə nə tĭv′) ***adj-*** making or noting distinctions. ***—adv-*** **dis·crim′ i·na·tive·ly.**

dis·crim·i·na·tor (dĭs krĭm′ ə nā′ tər) ***n-*** **1** person who discriminates. **2** radio circuit used in FM receivers to change variations of frequency into variations in the strength of a current.

dis·crim·i·na·to·ry (dĭs krĭm′ ə nə tôr′ ē) ***adj-*** making distinctions, especially unfair ones based on prejudice.

dis·cus (dĭs′ kəs) ***n-*** heavy metal and wood disk that is thicker at the center than at the rim. It is thrown for distance in athletic contests.

dis·cuss (dĭs′ kŭs′) ***vt-*** to talk over thoughtfully; consider; debate: *He will* discuss *the political situation.*

dis·cus·sant (dĭs kŭs′ ənt) ***n-*** person who takes part in a discussion, especially as an authority on a particular subject.

dis·cus·sion (dĭs kŭsh′ ən) ***n-*** **1** exchange of ideas among persons: *The article stimulated a* discussion. **2** a handling or presentation of a subject; lecture: *His* discussion *was illustrated by charts.*

dis·dain (dĭs dān′) ***vt-*** to show contempt for; look down upon: *She* disdained *everyone outside her set.* ***n-*** a looking down upon; contempt; scorn: *to treat with* disdain.

dis·dain·ful (dĭs dān′ fəl) ***adj-*** showing disdain; haughty: *His* disdainful *attitude made many enemies.* ***—adv-*** **dis·dain′ ful·ly.** ***n-*** **dis·dain′ ful·ness.**

dis·ease (dĭ zēz′) ***n-*** **1** disorder of mind or body marked by definite symptoms; illness; sickness. **2** any particular instance or kind of such disorder: *Measles and tuberculosis are* diseases.

dis·eased (dĭ zēzd′) ***adj-*** **1** suffering from a disease. **2** showing the effects of a disease.

dis·em·bark (dĭs′ ĕm bärk′) ***vi-*** to leave a ship or aircraft; to land; debark: *The students* disembarked *at New York.* ***vt-***: *We shall* disembark *the passengers at Pier 23.* ***—n-*** **dis·em′ bar·ka′ tion.**

dis·em·bod·y (dĭs′əm bŏd′ē) ***vt-*** **[dis·em·bod·ied, dis·em·bod·y·ing]** to separate from the body; make bodiless: *Death* disembodies *the soul.* **—*n-* dis′em·bod′i·ment.**

dis·em·bow·el (dĭs′əm bou′əl) ***vt-*** to remove the entrails or bowels from; to eviscerate.

dis·en·chant (dĭs′ən chănt′) ***vt-*** to strip (someone) of pleasant illusions: *We admired him at first, but his dishonesty soon* disenchanted *us.* **—*n-* dis′en·chant′ment.**

dis·en·cum·ber (dĭs′ən kŭm′bər) ***vt-*** to relieve (someone or something) of a burden or hindrance: *He* disencumbered *himself of his heavy coat.*

dis·en·fran·chise (dĭs′ən frăn′chīz′) ***vt-*** **[dis·en·fran·chised, dis·en·fran·chis·ing]** to disfranchise. **—*n-* dis′en·fran′chise′ment.**

dis·en·gage (dĭs′ən gāj′) ***vt-*** **[dis·en·gaged, dis·en·gag·ing]** to set free; detach; sever connections: *He* disengaged *himself from the corrupt regime.* ***vi-***: *The two armies* disengaged. **—*n-* dis′en·gage′ment.**

dis·en·tan·gle (dĭs′ən tăng′gəl) ***vt-*** **[dis·en·tan·gled, dis·en·tan·gling]** to free from or take out of a tangle or confusion; unravel. **—*n-* dis′en·tan′gle·ment.**

dis·es·teem (dĭs′ə stēm′) ***vt-*** to place a low value upon; hold in disfavor. ***n-***: *He expressed* disesteem *for the plan.*

dis·fa·vor (dĭs fā′vər) ***n-*** **1** dislike; disapproval: *to view with* disfavor. **2** a state of being out of favor: *The government was in* disfavor *with the people.*

dis·fig·ure (dĭs fĭg′yər) ***vt-*** **[dis·fig·ured, dis·fig·ur·ing]** to mar or spoil the form or appearance of: *Billboards* disfigure *the highways.*

dis·fig·ure·ment (dĭs fĭg′yər mənt) ***n-*** **1** a disfiguring or defacing: *We regret the* disfigurement *of the statue.* **2** something that disfigures: *The scar is a* disfigurement.

dis·fran·chise (dĭs frăn′chīs′) ***vt-*** **[dis·fran·chised, dis·fran·chis·ing]** to deprive of a right or rights of citizenship, especially of the right to vote; disenfranchise. **—*n-* dis·fran′chise′ment.**

dis·gorge (dĭs gŏrj′, -gôrj′) ***vt-*** **[dis·gorged, dis·gorg·ing]** (considered intransitive when the object is implied but not expressed) **1** to throw up or out; vomit; eject: *The volcano* disgorged *lava, fire, and smoke.* **2** to give (something) up unwillingly: *The army* disgorged *its spoils.*

dis·grace (dĭs grās′) ***n-*** **1** shame; loss of honor or good name. **2** cause of shame or discredit: *These dirty streets are a* disgrace *to the city.* ***vt-*** **[dis·graced, dis·grac·ing]** to bring shame, reproach, or dishonor upon: *He* disgraced *his mother by being rude to her guests.*

in disgrace not viewed with favor; no longer accepted: *The former prime minister is now* in disgrace.

dis·grace·ful (dĭs grās′fəl) ***adj-*** shameful; unworthy: *their* disgraceful *behavior.* **—*adv-* dis·grace′ful·ly.**

dis·grun·tle (dĭs grŭn′təl) ***vt-*** **[dis·grun·tled, dis·grun·tling]** to make dissatisfied or cross; put in a bad humor.

dis·guise (dĭs gīz′) ***vt-*** **[dis·guised, dis·guis·ing]** **1** to change the appearance of in order to hide identity: *The spy* disguised *himself as a sailor.* **2** to mask; cover up: *He* disguised *his anger with a smile.* ***n-*** an unusual manner or dress, put on to hide identity or feelings: *Despite his* disguise, *he was quickly recognized. Her calm manner was merely a* disguise.

dis·gust (dĭs gŭst′) ***n-*** very strong distaste; sickening dislike; loathing: *They turned away in* disgust. ***vt-*** to cause strong distaste or loathing in; sicken: *His table manners* disgusted *us.* **—*adv-* dis·gust′ing·ly**: *The room is* disgustingly *filthy.*

dis·gust·ed (dĭs gŭs′təd) ***adj-*** filled with disgust, resentment, or violent dislike. **—*adv-* dis·gust′ed·ly.**

dish (dĭsh) ***n-*** **1** plate or shallow bowl, generally used for holding food. **2** (also **dish′ful′**) amount held by such a container. **3** a particular food: *Lobster is his favorite* dish. **4** radio, radar, or television antenna having a reflector shaped like a bowl or plate. ***vt-*** to put in a plate or shallow bowl: *to* dish *ice cream.*

dish up *Informal* to serve, give, or deliver.

dis·ha·bille (dĭs′ə bēl′, -bē′) ***n-*** incompleteness or negligence of dress. Also **deshabille.**

dis·heart·en (dĭs här′tən) ***vt-*** to discourage; cause to lose hope: *They were* disheartened *by their many failures.* **—*adj-* dis·heart′en·ing.** ***adv-*** **dis·heart′en·ing·ly.**

di·shev·eled (dĭ shĕv′əld) ***adj-*** thrown into disorder; untidy; mussed: *her* disheveled *hair.*

dis·hon·est (dĭs ŏn′əst) ***adj-*** not honest. **—*adv-* dis·hon′est·ly.**

dis·hon·es·ty (dĭs ŏn′əs tē) ***n-*** [*pl.* **dis·hon·es·ties**] **1** lack of honesty. **2** a dishonest act or saying.

dis·hon·or (dĭs ŏn′ər) ***n-*** disgrace or shame; loss of good name: *to prefer death to* dishonor. ***vt-*** **1** to bring shame upon; show disrespect to: *By living an evil life he* dishonored *the family name.* **2** to refuse to pay (a bill or note).

dis·hon·or·a·ble (dĭs ŏn′ər ə bəl) ***adj-*** not honorable. **—*n-* dis·hon′or·a·ble·ness.** ***adv-*** **dis·hon′or·a·bly.**

dis·il·lu·sion (dĭs′ə lo͞o′shən) ***vt-*** to set free from a mistaken belief in the goodness or value of some person or thing: *We were* disillusioned *by his dishonesty.* **—*n-* dis′il·lu′sion·ment.**

dis·in·clined (dĭs′ĭn klīnd′) ***adj-*** not feeling like or wanting to; loath; unwilling: *A lazy person is* disinclined *to work.* **—*n-* dis·in′cli·na′tion** (-klə nā′shən).

dis·in·fect (dĭs′ĭn fĕkt′) ***vt-*** to make free from harmful germs. **—*n-* dis′in·fec′tion.**

dis·in·fec·tant (dĭs′ĭn fĕk′tənt) ***n-*** substance that kills disease germs. ***adj-***: *a* disinfectant *powder.*

dis·in·her·it (dĭs′ĭn hĕr′ət) ***vt-*** to cut off (an heir) from receiving property or money at someone's death.

dis·in·te·grate (dĭs ĭn′tə grāt′) ***vi-*** **[dis·in·te·grat·ed, dis·in·te·grat·ing]** **1** to break or come apart into bits and fragments; crumble: *The quilt* disintegrated *in the washing machine.* **2** *Physics* to undergo change from one element or isotope to another because of radioactive emission of nuclear particles. ***vt-*** to cause (something) to break or come apart: *The constant vibration* disintegrated *the glass.*

dis·in·te·gra·tion (dĭs ĭn′tə grā′shən) ***n-*** **1** a disintegrating; crumbling; a coming apart: *the* disintegration *of rock by weathering*; disintegration *of our hopes.* **2** *Physics* (1) change of atomic structure because of radioactive emission of nuclear particles. (2) a single emission of a nuclear particle.

dis·in·te·gra·tor (dĭs ĭn′tə grā′tər) ***n-*** something that causes disintegration.

dis·in·ter (dĭs′ĭn tûr′) ***vt-*** **[dis·in·terred, dis·in·ter·ring]** to dig up (a body) from a grave; exhume. **—*n-* dis′in·ter′ment.**

dis·in·ter·est·ed (dĭs ĭn′trəs təd, -tə rĕs′təd) ***adj-*** not in a position to gain or lose personally by the outcome of a given affair; free from bias; impartial; objective: *A trial judge must be* disinterested. **—*adv-* dis·in′ter·est′ed·ly.** ***n-*** **dis·in′ter·est′ed·ness.**

►DISINTERESTED means fair, objective, or having no private interest, whereas UNINTERESTED means bored or without any interest at all. *A judge or referee should be* disinterested, *but he should never be* uninterested.

dis·join (dĭs join′) *vt-* to part, separate, or detach (something). *vi-*: *We watched the two cells* disjoin.

dis·joint (dĭs joint′) *vt-* 1 to separate at the joints: *to* disjoint *a turkey*. 2 to put out of joint; dislocate.

dis·joint·ed (dĭs join′ təd) *adj-* 1 unconnected; incoherent: *a* disjointed *speech*. 2 dislocated. 3 taken apart at the joints. *—adv-* **dis·joint′ ed·ly.**

disk (dĭsk) *n-* 1 circular object, usually thin and flat. 2 *Astronomy* the flat appearance of a heavenly body when viewed from the earth: *the sun's* disk. 3 central part of the flower head of the daisy, aster, etc. bearing tiny, tubular flowers. 4 *Informal* a phonograph record. Also **disc.**

Disk

disk harrow *n-* farm implement having rows of disks which cut up the soil. For picture, see *harrow*.

dis·like (dĭs līk′) *vt-* **[dis·liked, dis·lik·ing]** to have a feeling against; not like: *She* dislikes *visiting the dentist*. *n-* a feeling against someone or something; distaste.

dis·lo·cate (dĭs′ lō kāt′) *vt-* **[dis·lo·cat·ed, dis·lo·cat·ing]** 1 to force out of place; especially, to put (a bone) out of joint. 2 to upset; throw into confusion: *The depression* dislocated *the normal workings of the economy*.

dis·lo·ca·tion (dĭs′ lō kā′ shən) *n-* a dislocating; a forcing out of place; also, the result of this: *a* dislocation *of the shoulder*.

dis·lodge (dĭs lŏj′) *vt-* **[dis·lodged, dis·lodg·ing]** to move or force out of position: *The earthquake* dislodged *massive boulders*.

dis·loy·al (dĭs loi′ əl) *adj-* not loyal: *to be* disloyal *to one's friends*. *—adv-* **dis·loy′ al·ly.**

dis·loy·al·ty (dĭs loi′ əl tē) *n-* [*pl.* **dis·loy·al·ties**] falseness to duty, government, friends etc.; faithlessness.

dis·mal (dĭz′ məl) *adj-* 1 gloomy; dreary; cheerless: *a* dismal *swamp*. 2 depressed; sad: *a* dismal *mood*. *—adv-* **dis′ mal·ly.**

dis·man·tle (dĭs măn′ təl) *vt-* **[dis·man·tled, dis·man·tling]** 1 to strip of furniture, equipment, etc.: *to* dismantle *a house*. 2 to take apart: *to* dismantle *a machine*.

dis·may (dĭs mā′) *vt-* to take away the courage of; frighten; dishearten; daunt: *The surprise attack* dismayed *them*. *n-* sudden loss of courage; frightened amazement: *our* dismay *at finding our car missing*.

dis·mem·ber (dĭs mĕm′ bər) *vt-* 1 to cut or tear off one part from another, especially limb from body. 2 to sever into parts and distribute; divide: *to* dismember *a country*. *—n-* **dis·mem′ ber·ment.**

dis·miss (dĭs mĭs′) *vt-* 1 to send away; direct or allow to leave: *to* dismiss *a class*. 2 to discharge; remove from office or employment: *to* dismiss *a clerk*. 3 to refuse to consider further: *The judge* dismissed *the case*.

dis·miss·al (dĭs mĭs′ əl) *n-* a dismissing: *the* dismissal *of the class*; *a* dismissal *from employment*; *the judge's* dismissal *of the case*.

dis·mount (dĭs mount′) *vi-* to get off or down (from) something: *to* dismount *from a horse*. *vt-* 1 to remove (something) from its setting, mounting, support, etc.: *to* dismount *a cannon*. 2 to take apart; dismantle: *to* dismount *a watch*.

dis·o·be·di·ence (dĭs′ ə bē′ dē əns) *n-* refusal to obey; failure to follow a rule or command.

dis·o·be·di·ent (dĭs′ ə bē′ dē ənt) *adj-* not obedient: *a* disobedient *child*. *—adv-* **dis′ o·be′ di·ent·ly.**

dis·o·bey (dĭs′ ə bā′) *vt-* to refuse or fail to obey: *to* disobey *parents*; *to* disobey *rules*. *vi-*: *He often* disobeys.

dis·o·blige (dĭs′ ə blīj′) *vt-* **[dis·o·bliged, dis·o·blig·ing]** to refuse or neglect to help or please (someone): *I hate to* disoblige *you, but I must leave now*.

dis·or·der (dĭs ȯr′ dər, dĭs ôr′-) *n-* 1 a commotion, especially a riot or other public disturbance. 2 lack of order or system; confusion: *Great* disorder *is common when children play*. 3 a mental or physical disease: *to suffer from a heart* disorder. *vt-* to disarrange badly; to throw into confusion.

dis·or·dered (dĭs ȯr′ dərd, dĭs ôr′-) *adj-* 1 damaged or upset; deranged; abnormal: *a* disordered *mind*; *a* disordered *condition of society*. 2 disorderly.

dis·or·der·ly (dĭs ȯr′ dər lē, dĭs ôr′-) *adj-* 1 not orderly; untidy: *a* disorderly *desk*. 2 lawless; unruly: *the* disorderly *mob*. *—n-* **dis·or′ der·li·ness.**

dis·or·gan·ize (dĭs ȯr′ gə nīz′, dĭs ôr′-) *vt-* **[dis·or·gan·ized, dis·or·gan·iz·ing]** to throw into confusion or disorder: *Fog* disorganized *the airplane schedule*. *—n-* **dis·or′ gan·i·za′ tion** (-nə zā′ shən).

dis·o·ri·ent (dĭs ôr′ ē ənt) *vt-* to cause (someone) to lose his ordinary sense of time, place, direction, etc.; confuse; mix up: *The shock of the accident* disoriented *him*. *—n-* **dis·o′ ri·en·ta′ tion.**

dis·own (dĭs ōn′) *vt-* to refuse to recognize or claim as one's own; reject: *to* disown *a leader*; *to* disown *one's flag*; *to* disown *a child*.

dis·par·age (dĭ spăr′ ĭj) *vt-* **[dis·par·aged, dis·par·ag·ing]** to belittle; criticize; run (something or someone) down; speak slightingly of: *to* disparage *a rival*. *—adv-* **dis·par′ ag·ing·ly**: *to speak* disparagingly *of one's rivals*. *n-* **dis·par′age·ment.**

dis·pa·rate (dĭs′ pər ət) *adj-* markedly different; not equal or similar: *two* disparate *points of view*; disparate *plans*. *—adv-* **dis·par′ ate·ly.**

dis·par·i·ty (dĭ spăr′ ə tē) *n-* [*pl.* **dis·par·i·ties**] inequality; difference; disproportion: *a* disparity *in ages*; *a* disparity *in character*.

dis·pas·sion·ate (dĭs păsh′ ə nət) *adj-* free from strong feelings that influence judgment; detached; impartial: *a* dispassionate *evaluation*. *—adv-* **dis·pas′ sion·ate·ly.**

dis·patch (dĭ spăch′) *vt-* 1 to send off quickly to some person, place, etc.: *to* dispatch *a message*; *to* dispatch *a taxicab*. 2 to finish quickly; settle: *to* dispatch *a business deal*. 3 to put to death; kill. *n-* 1 message, especially an official one: *a* dispatch *from the President*. 2 quick action and efficiency: *He handled our applications with* dispatch. 3 news report: *a* dispatch *from London*.

dis·patch·er (dĭ spăch′ ər) *n-* 1 official who directs the movements, especially the departures, of trains, taxicabs, buses, etc. 2 one who dispatches.

dis·pel (dĭ spĕl′) *vt-* **[dis·pel·led, dis·pel·ling]** to drive away; cause to disappear; scatter; disperse: *The sun* dispelled *the fog*.

dis·pen·sa·ble (dĭ spĕn′ sə bəl) *adj-* 1 such as can be done without; unnecessary; superfluous: *Luxuries and frills are* dispensable. 2 pardonable; subject to dispensation: *a* dispensable *fault*. *—n-* **dis·pen′ sa·bil′ i·ty.**

dis·pen·sa·ry (dĭ spĕn′ sə rē) *n-* [*pl.* **dis·pen·sa·ries**] place where medical treatment, medicines, etc., are provided; clinic.

dis·pen·sa·tion (dĭs′ pən sā′ shən) *n-* 1 a giving out; distribution. 2 a setting aside of rules or penalties in a special case, especially by a church official.

dis·pense (dĭ spĕns′) *vt-* **[dis·pensed, dis·pens·ing]** 1 to deal out in portions; distribute: *They* dispensed *clothing to the needy*. 2 to prepare and give out: *The druggist* dispenses *medicine*. 3 to carry out; apply: *to* dispense *justice*.

dispense with to do without; get rid of.

dis·pens·er (dĭ spĕn′ sər) *n-* person or thing that gives or deals out specified things: *a* dispenser *of gifts*; *a* dispenser *for paper towels*.

dis·pers·al (dĭ spûr′ səl) ***n-*** a sending or going away in various directions; a breaking up; a scattering: *the* dispersal *of a mob*; *the* dispersal *of a cloud of smoke.*

dis·perse (dĭ spûrs′) ***vt-*** **[dis·persed, dis·pers·ing]** to send in different directions; scatter: *The police* dispersed *the mob.* ***vi-*** to go off in different directions; separate: *The crowd* dispersed *after the meeting.*
►Should not be confused with DISBURSE.

dis·per·sion (dĭ spûr′ zhən) ***n-* 1** a dispersing; a scattering. **2** *Physics* separation of radiation into its components, especially the separation of light into colors by passing it through a prism. **3** the result of a dispersing.

dis·pir·it (dĭ spĭr′ ət) ***vt-*** to lower the spirits of; dishearten; depress: *His failure* dispirited *him.* **—*adj-* dis·pir′ i·ted.** ***adv-*** **dis·pir′ it·ed·ly.**

dis·place (dĭs plās′) ***vt-*** **[dis·placed, dis·plac·ing] 1** to take the place of; replace: *The jet plane is* displacing *the propeller-driven plane.* **2** to put out of the usual place. **3** of a floating object, to occupy the space of (a certain weight or volume of fluid).

displaced person ***n-*** person forced from his own country by war or upheaval, especially with loss of citizenship.

dis·place·ment (dĭs plās′ mənt) ***n-* 1** a putting out of place; a displacing. **2** the distance anything has moved from its original position. **3** *Physics* the amount of fluid displaced by a floating object, usually expressed in units of weight: *The ship's* displacement *is 38,000 tons.*

dis·play (dĭ splā′) ***vt-*** to show; exhibit; reveal: *to* display *talent*; *to* display *fear.* ***n-*** a showing or an exhibition: *a* display *of automobiles*; *a* display *of fear.*
on display arranged to show to best advantage.

dis·please (dĭs plēz′) ***vt-*** **[dis·pleased, dis·pleas·ing]** (considered intransitive when the object is implied but not expressed) to offend; annoy; make angry: *His bad manners* displease *his friends.*

dis·pleas·ure (dĭs plĕzh′ ər) ***n-*** displeased feeling; disapproval; annoyance: *my* displeasure *at loud commercials.*

dis·port (dĭ spôrt′) ***vt-*** to amuse or entertain (oneself), especially by frolicsome play.

dis·pos·a·ble (dĭ spō′ zə bəl) ***adj-* 1** such as can be thrown away after use: *a* disposable *container*; disposable *paper towels.* **2** of a kind that can be financially disposed of: *He sold his* disposable *assets.*

dis·pos·al (dĭ spō′ zəl) ***n-* 1** a getting rid of: *the* disposal *of refuse.* **2** a getting rid of by sale or transfer: *his* disposal *of the car.* **3** settlement; conclusion: *their final* disposal *of the matter.*
at (one's) disposal available for use at any time as one pleases: I *had my father's car* at my disposal.

dis·pose (dĭ spōz′) ***vt-*** **[dis·posed, dis·pos·ing]** to put in a certain position; arrange: *They* disposed *the shrubs attractively about the garden.*
disposed to subject to; inclined to: *He is* disposed to *colds. I am* disposed to *hear your request.*
dispose of 1 to get rid of: *to* dispose of *rubbish.* **2** to finish with; settle: *to* dispose of *a quarrel.*

dis·po·si·tion (dĭs′ pə zĭsh′ ən) ***n-* 1** a person's natural attitude or habit of mind; temperament: *a generous* disposition; *a jealous* disposition. **2** a liking; preference: *a* disposition *for quiet places.* **3** a putting in position; arrangement; distribution: *the* disposition *of furniture in a room.* **4** final settling or outcome: *the* disposition *of a lawsuit.* **5** power to settle or deal with; jurisdiction.

dis·pos·sess (dĭs′ pə zĕs′) ***vt-*** to put out of possession by legal action: *to* dispossess *a family of an apartment.*
one line short

dis·proof (dĭs pro͞of′) ***n-*** a proving that something claimed or asserted is not true; refutation: *the partial* disproof *of a statement.*

dis·pro·por·tion (dĭs′ prə pôr′ shən) ***n-*** lack of balance or symmetry; lack of proper relation in form, size, etc.

dis·pro·por·tion·ate (dĭs′ prə pôr′ shən ət) ***adj-*** lacking suitable size in relation to something else; unsymmetrical; out of proportion. **—*adv-* dis′ pro·por′ tion·ate·ly.** ***n-*** **dis′ pro·por′ tion·ate·ness.**

dis·prove (dĭs pro͞ov′) ***vt-*** **[dis·proved, dis·prov·ing]** to prove to be false or wrong: *to* disprove *a story by facts.*

dis·pu·ta·ble (dĭ spyo͞o′ tə bəl, dĭs′ pyə tə-) ***adj-*** open to question; debatable; arguable: *The existence of germs is no longer* disputable. **—*n-* dis·pu′ ta·bil′ i·ty.**

dis·pu·tant (dĭs′pyo͞o′ tənt, dĭs′ pyə-) ***n-*** person who takes part in a debate or argument.

dis·pu·ta·tion (dĭs′ pyo͞o tā′ shən) ***n-*** debate or argument.

dis·pute (dĭ spyo͞ot′) ***vi-*** **[dis·put·ed, dis·put·ing]** to argue; debate; quarrel in words: *They* disputed *over politics.* ***vt-* 1** to deny or question: *They* disputed *his authority.* **2** to fight for; contest: *The Marines* disputed *every inch of the beach when enemy boats landed.* ***n-* 1** argument; debate; difference of opinion. **2** quarrel: *a violent* dispute *over a boundary.*

dis·qual·i·fi·ca·tion (dĭs′ kwŏl′ ə fə kā′ shən) ***n-* 1** something that makes a person unable or unfit to do a certain thing: *Having no* disqualifications, *he was appointed to the court.* **2** a declaring that someone is not fitted for or entitled to privilege, position, participation, etc.

dis·qual·i·fy (dĭs kwŏl′ ə fī′) ***vt-*** **[dis·qual·i·fied, dis·qual·i·fy·ing] 1** to make unfit: *Deafness* disqualified *him for military service.* **2** to declare unfit or unsuitable: *The judge* disqualified *himself for the particular case.* **3** to deny (someone) the privilege of competing, winning a prize, etc.: *The judges* disqualified *the runner for a foul.*

dis·qui·et (dĭs kwī′ ət) ***vt-*** to make uneasy, anxious, or restless; disturb: *The sudden silence* disquieted *him.* ***n-*** uneasiness; anxiety: *A feeling of* disquiet *spread through the waiting crowd.*

dis·qui·e·tude (dĭs kwī′ ə to͞od′, -tyo͞od′) ***n-*** uneasiness of mind; anxiety; restlessness: *Her* disquietude *increased when she found she was alone in the house.*

dis·qui·si·tion (dĭs′ kwə zĭsh′ ən) ***n-*** a formal and thorough discussion; dissertation.

dis·re·gard (dĭs′ rĭ gärd′) ***vt-*** to pay no attention to; ignore: *He* disregarded *the traffic lights.* ***n-* 1** refusal to pay attention: *his* disregard *for traffic lights.* **2** lack of respect: *his* disregard *of my feelings.*

dis·re·mem·ber (dĭs′ rĭ mĕm′ bər) *Informal* ***vt-*** to forget; be unable to recall. ***vi-***: *He told me his name, but I* disremember.

dis·re·pair (dĭs′ rĭ pâr′) ***n-*** poor or unmended condition: *The century-old house was in* disrepair.

dis·rep·u·ta·ble (dĭs rĕp′ yə tə bəl) ***adj-* 1** of bad reputation; shady: *Not all* disreputable *people are in jail.* **2** not respectable: *a* disreputable *old coat.* **—*n-* dis·rep′ u·ta·ble·ness.** ***adv-*** **dis·rep′ u·ta·bly.**

dis·re·pute (dĭs′ rĭ pyo͞ot′) ***n-*** bad reputation; discredit: *Imperialism is now in* disrepute.

dis·re·spect (dĭs′ rĭ spĕkt′) ***n-*** lack of respect; rudeness.

dis·re·spect·ful (dĭs′ rĭ spĕkt′ fəl) ***adj-*** rude; lacking in respect. **—*adv-* dis·re·spect′ ful·ly.** ***n-*** **dis·re·spect′ ful·ness.**

dis·robe (dĭs rōb′) ***vi-*** **[dis·robed, dis·rob·ing]** to take one's clothes off: *He slowly* disrobed. ***vt-***: *She* disrobed *the child.*

---

fāte, făt, dâre, bärn; bē, bĕt, mêre; bīte, bĭt; nōte, hŏt, môre, dòg; fŭn, fûr; to͞o, bo͝ok; oil; out; tar; thin; then; hw for wh as in *wh*at; zh for s as in u*s*ual; ə for a, e, i, o, u, as in *a*go, lin*e*n, per*i*l, at*o*m, min*u*s

dis·rupt (dĭs rŭpt′) *vt-* **1** to break up or apart; to throw into disorder: *A riot* disrupted *the rally.* **2** to make unworkable and confused: *The enemy bombardment* disrupted *communications.* —*n-* **dis·rup′tion:** *the* disruption *of communications.*

dis·rup·tive (dĭs rŭp′ tĭv) *adj-* tending to disrupt; causing disruption. —*adv-* **dis·rup′tive·ly.** *n-* **dis·rup′tive·ness.**

dis·sat·is·fac·tion (dĭs′ săt′ əs făk′ shən) *n-* discontent; lack of satisfaction: *a* dissatisfaction *with one's life.*

dis·sat·is·fied (dĭs săt′ əs fīd′) *adj-* not pleased; discontented: *He is a* dissatisfied *man.*

dis·sat·is·fy (dĭs săt′ əs fī′) *vt-* [**dis·sat·is·fied, dis·sat·is·fy·ing**] to displease or cause discontent to (someone), especially by the lack of something: *The layout of the house* dissatisfied *her.*

dis·sect (dĭ sĕkt′, dī′-) *vt-* **1** to cut (an animal or plant) in pieces in order to study or examine the inner parts: *The biology class* dissected *frogs last week.* **2** to study or analyze part by part: *The teacher* dissected *my report.*

dis·sem·ble (dĭ sĕm′ bəl) *vt-* [**dis·sem·bled, dis·sem·bling**] to hide under a false appearance: *to* dissemble *one's feelings. vi-*: *Some people cannot* dissemble. —*n-* **dis·sem′bler.**

►Should not be confused with DISASSEMBLE.

dis·sem·i·nate (dĭ sĕm′ ə nāt′) *vt-* [**dis·sem·i·nat·ed, dis·sem·i·nat·ing**] to scatter; diffuse; give out; spread abroad: *to* disseminate *news.* —*n-* **dis·sem′i·na′tion.**

dis·sen·sion (dĭ sĕn′ shən) *n-* quarreling; angry disagreement because of difference of opinion; ill feeling: *A border dispute caused lasting* dissension.

dis·sent (dĭ sĕnt′) *vi-* to disagree; to have a different opinion: *Only one person* dissented *from the agreement. n-* difference in opinion: *a* dissent *from the majority. Hom-* descent.

dis·sent·er (dĭ sĕn′ tər) *n-* **1** one who disagrees with the majority or with established ideas, especially in religion or politics. **2 Dissenter** in Great Britain, a person not in conformity with the state church.

dis·ser·ta·tion (dĭ′ sər tā′ shən) *n-* formal, spoken, or written discussion of a subject; especially, a thesis written by a candidate for the Ph.D. degree.

dis·ser·vice (dĭs sûr′ vəs) *n-* harm; injury: *to do someone a great* disservice.

dis·sev·er (dĭ sĕv′ ər) *vt-* to sever completely.

dis·si·dent (dĭs′ ə dənt) *adj-* dissenting; differing; disagreeing: *a* dissident *voice. n-* one who differs or disagrees; a dissenter. —*n-* **dis′si·dence.**

dis·sim·i·lar (dĭ sĭm′ ə lər) *adj-* different; unlike: *two brothers with* dissimilar *tastes.* —*adv-* **dis·sim′i·lar·ly.**

dis·sim·i·lar·i·ty (dĭ sĭm′ ə lăr′ ə tē, -lĕr′ə tē) *n-* [*pl.* **dis·sim·i·lar·i·ties**] **1** unlikeness; difference. **2** something unlike; point of difference.

dis·sim·u·late (dĭ sĭm′ yə lāt′) *vi-* [**dis·sim·u·lat·ed, dis·sim·u·lat·ing**] to hide one's true feelings, plans, etc.; dissemble: *He* dissimulates *without any outward sign.* —*n-* **dis·sim′u·la′tion.**

dis·si·pate (dĭs′ ə pāt′) *vt-* [**dis·si·pat·ed, dis·si·pat·ing**] **1** to break up; drive away: *The sun rose and* dissipated *the fog.* **2** to spend foolishly; waste: *The prodigal son* dissipated *his money in almost no time. vi-* **1** to spread out so as to vanish: *The fog* dissipated *by noon.* **2** to waste one's energy and money in pursuit of pleasure; especially, to drink too much alcohol.

dis·si·pat·ed (dĭs′ ə pā′ təd) *adj-* **1** scattered; dispersed. **2** wasting one's energies, time, etc., on useless or foolish pleasures; intemperate; dissolute.

dis·si·pa·tion (dĭs′ ə pā′ shən) *n-* **1** a scattering; dispersal. **2** wasteful spending of one's energies, time, etc.; intemperate living; dissoluteness.

dis·so·ci·ate (dĭ sō′ sē āt′, dĭ sō′ shē-) *vt-* [**dis·so·ci·at·ed, dis·so·ci·at·ing**] to separate; disconnect; disassociate: *to* dissociate *two elements in a solution.*

dis·so·ci·a·tion (dĭ sō′ sē ā′ shən, dĭ sō′ shē-) *n-* **1** a breaking up or disconnecting; separation. **2** *Chemistry* (1) decomposition or breaking up of a complex substance into two or more simpler substances by applying heat, pressure, etc. (2) in a solution, the splitting of molecules into positive and negative ions.

dis·so·lute (dĭs′ ə lo͞ot′) *adj-* morally loose; dissipated; wanton: *a* dissolute *person; a* dissolute *life.* —*adv-* **dis′so·lute′ly.** *n-* **dis′so·lute′ness.**

dis·so·lu·tion (dĭs′ ə lo͞o′ shən) *n-* **1** a breaking up or ending: *the* dissolution *of a partnership.* **2** decay. **3** process of changing from a solid to a liquid or gas.

dis·solve (dĭ zŏlv′) *vi-* [**dis·solved, dis·solv·ing**] **1** to be absorbed into a liquid; pass into solution: *Salt* dissolves *in water.* **2** to become liquid; melt: *The snowman* dissolved *in the afternoon sun.* **3** to break up; end: *The partnership* dissolved *after many arguments.* **4** to disappear; vanish: *His dream of quick success* dissolved *after several defeats. vt-* **1** to cause to enter into solution: *He* dissolved *salt in water. Water will* dissolve *salt.* **2** to cause to break up or vanish; terminate: *They* dissolved *their partnership.* —*adj-* **dis·solv′a·ble.**

dis·so·nance (dĭs′ ə nəns) *n-* lack of harmony or agreement; discord: *the* dissonance *of his piano playing.*

dis·so·nant (dĭs′ ə nənt) *adj-* not harmonious; discordant: *the* dissonant *sounds from my brother's battered trumpet; our* dissonant *views.* —*adv-* **dis′so·nant·ly.**

dis·suade (dĭ swād′) *vt-* [**dis·suad·ed, dis·suad·ing**] to persuade or advise (someone) against doing something: *We* dissuaded *him from going.* —*n-* **dis·sua′sion.**

dis·sua·sive (dĭ swā′ sĭv, -zĭv) *adj-* tending to dissuade: *a* dissuasive *argument.* —*adv-* **dis·sua′sive·ly.** *n-* **dis·sua′sive·ness.**

dis·taff (dĭ′ stăf′) *n-* a stick around which wool, flax, etc., is wound for use in spinning.

distaff side *n-* female side of a family.

dis·tance (dĭ′ stəns) *n-* **1** a being distant. **2** amount of separation, along a particular path, between two points, lines, objects, places, etc.: *The* distance *between the two cities is 300 miles.*

in the distance far away from here.

dis·tant (dĭ′ stənt) *adj-* **1** far away: *The sun is* distant *from the earth.* **2** long ago; remote: *Dinosaurs lived in the* distant *past.* **3** not close in relationship: *Third cousins are* distant *relatives.* **4** not friendly: *Jane has been very* distant *since our argument.* **adv-** away: *two blocks* distant. —*adv-* **dis′tant·ly.**

dis·taste (dĭs tāst′) *n-* a dislike; aversion: *a* distaste *for chocolate; a* distaste *for hard work.*

dis·taste·ful (dĭs tāst′ fəl) *adj-* disagreeable; unpleasant: *a* distasteful *medicine; a* distasteful *conversation.* —*adv-* **dis·taste′ful·ly.** *n-* **dis·taste′ful·ness.**

dis·tem·per (dĭs tĕm′ pər) *n-* disease, especially an infection in dogs and other animals, in which there is fever, coughing, and loss of appetite.

dis·tend (dĭ stĕnd′) *vi-* to swell out: *The horse's nostrils* distended *in fear. vt-*: *The horse's belly was* distended *by colic.*

dis·ten·sion or **dis·ten·tion** (dĭ stĕn′ shən) *n-* a distending or being distended; inflation; dilation: *A* distension *of the stomach from colic.*

dis·till or **dis·til** (dĭ stĭl′) *vt-* [**dis·tilled, dis·till·ing**] **1** to purify or refine (a substance) by distillation. **2** to separate out by distillation: *to* distill *alcohol from grain. vi-* **1** to undergo distillation; also, to condense. **2** to appear slowly or in drops, as if by distillation.

dis·til·late (dĭs′ tə lāt′, -lət) ***n-*** product obtained by the process of distillation.

dis·til·la·tion (dĭs′ tə lā′ shən) ***n-*** **1** the process of heating a liquid or a solid until it forms a vapor, leading the vapor into a separate vessel, and condensing it by cooling. **2** a distillate.

dis·till·er (dĭ stĭl′ ər) ***n-*** person or thing that distills, especially an individual or company that makes liquors by distillation.

dis·til·ler·y (dĭ stĭl′ ə rē) ***n-*** [*pl.* **dis·til·ler·ies**] **1** industrial plant designed to carry out distillation. **2** factory for making and distilling alcoholic liquors.

dis·tinct (dĭ stĭngkt′) ***adj-*** **1** different; separate: *two* distinct *kinds of animals.* **2** clear; plain: *a* distinct *pronunciation.* **3** very definite; unmistakable: *a* distinct *improvement.* **—*adv-*** **dis·tinct′ly**: *a* distinctly *helpful suggestion.* ***n-*** **dis·tinct′ness.**

dis·tinc·tion (dĭ stĭngk′ shən) ***n-*** **1** the making of a difference: *to treat everybody alike without* distinction *as to race or creed.* **2** difference; point of difference: *to note the* distinction *between mice and rats.* **3** excellence; superiority: *a writer of* distinction. **4** mark of favor or honor: *A Nobel Prize is among his* distinctions.

dis·tinc·tive (dĭ stĭngk′ tĭv) ***adj-*** marking a difference from others: *They wore* distinctive *uniforms.* **—*adv-*** **dis·tinc′tive·ly.** ***n-*** **dis·tinc′tive·ness.**

dis·tin·guish (dĭ stĭng′ gwĭsh) ***vt-*** **1** to mark as different; to set apart: *Their uniforms* distinguish *soldiers, sailors, and marines from each other.* **2** to see clearly the difference between (two things): *He could not* distinguish *right from wrong.* **3** to perceive; recognize: *The captain could* distinguish *a lighthouse through the fog.* **4** to bring fame or honor on (oneself): *He* distinguished *himself by his courage on the battlefield.* ***vi-*** to note or make differences (between or among): *Can you* distinguish *between the two sets of instructions?* **—*adj-*** **dis·tin′guish·a·ble.** ***adv-*** **dis·tin′guish·a·bly.**

dis·tin·guished (dĭ stĭng′ wĭsht) ***adj-*** **1** famous for outstanding achievement; celebrated; eminent: *a* distinguished *statesman.* **2** showing distinction.

dis·tort (dĭ stôrt′, -stôrt′) ***vt-*** **1** to change the shape of; twist: *Pain* distorted *his face.* **2** to twist the original meaning of; misrepresent: *They* distorted *my speech.*

dis·tor·tion (dĭ stôr′ shən, dĭ stôr′-) ***n-*** **1** a distorting or being distorted: *a* distortion *of the truth.* **2** something distorted: *a newspaper filled with* distortions.

dis·tract (dĭ străkt′) ***vt-*** **1** to draw away the mind or attention of; divert: *Music* distracts *her from troubles.* **2** to confuse or bewilder; perplex: *All my directions serve only to* distract *him.* **3** to make crazy; drive mad: *That constant noise must stop before it* distracts *me entirely.*

dis·tract·ed (dĭ străk′ təd) ***adj-*** **1** harassed; confused. **2** insane; mad. **—*adv-*** **dis·tract′ed·ly.**

dis·trac·tion (dĭ străk′ shən) ***n-*** **1** something that turns the attention from something: *Television is a* distraction *when you are also trying to read.* **2** amusement; diversion: *Alice needed some* distraction *after her examinations.* **3** confusion; perplexity: *In his* distraction *after the accident, he forgot his name.* **4** madness; frenzy: *That noise drives me to* distraction. **—*adj-*** **dis·trac′tive.**

dis·trait (dĭ strā′) ***adj-*** absent-minded.

dis·traught (dĭ strôt′) ***adj-*** **1** deeply troubled and confused; distressed; agitated: *a* distraught *mother.* **2** insane; mad. **—*adv-*** **dis·traught′ly.**

dis·tress (dĭ strĕs′) ***n-*** **1** misery; sorrow; pain: *She is is great* distress *over the illness of her son.* **2** danger; serious trouble: *a ship in* distress. ***vt-***: *The sudden illness of her son* distressed *Mrs. Jones.* **—*adv-*** **dis·tress′ing·ly**: *Our team made a* distressingly *poor showing today.*

dis·tress·ful (dĭ strĕs′ fəl) ***adj-*** causing or full of distress, misery, anxiety, etc. **—*adv-*** **dis·tress′ful·ly.**

dis·trib·ute (dĭ strĭb′ yət) ***vt-*** **[dis·trib·ut·ed, dis·trib·ut·ing]** **1** to hand out or send out: *Pamphlets were* distributed *among the crowd.* **2** to spread out; scatter; strew: *He* distributed *the ointment evenly over the wound.* **3** to arrange; sort; put into groups: *to* distribute *mail.* **4** to sell, especially as a wholesaler to retailers.

dis·tri·bu·tion (dĭs′ trə byōō′ shən) ***n-*** **1** a giving or dealing out: *the* distribution *of food and clothing to the victims.* **2** the way something is spread out or distributed: *an uneven* distribution *of resources.* **3** a marketing, especially at wholesale.

dis·trib·u·tive (dĭ strĭb′ yə tĭv) ***adj-*** **1** of, related to, or involving distribution. **2** *Mathematics* of an operation such as multiplication, producing the same result when applied to a set as when applied to all members of the set separately. Example: $a \times (b + c) = a \times b + a \times c$. **—*adv-*** **dis·trib′u·tive·ly.**

dis·trib·u·tor (dĭ strĭb′ yə tər) ***n-*** **1** someone or something that distributes. **2** a merchant, especially a person or company that sells goods wholesale. **3** device that directs electric current to the spark plugs of an engine, making them fire in the proper order.

dis·trict (dĭs′ trĭkt′) ***n-*** **1** region or area: *a slum* district *in the older part of the city.* **2** a part of a country, state, or county marked out for a special purpose: *a school* district; *a voting* district.

district attorney ***n-*** lawyer who acts as the prosecuting attorney of a district.

dis·trust (dĭs trŭst′) ***n-*** lack of confidence; suspicion; mistrust: *He looked at the friendly stranger with* distrust. ***vt-***: *They* distrusted *his answers.*

dis·trust·ful (dĭs trŭst′ fəl) ***adj-*** having doubt and suspicion; mistrustful. **—*adv-*** **dis·trust′ful·ly.** ***n-*** **dis·trust′ful·ness.**

dis·turb (dĭ stûrb′) ***vt-*** **1** to break in upon; bother; interrupt: *The noise will* disturb *my work.* **2** to interfere with: *Don't* disturb *the books on that shelf.* **3** to upset; worry; make uneasy: *That rumor* disturbs *us.*

dis·turb·ance (dĭ stûr′ bəns) ***n-*** **1** a disturbing; interruption: *a* disturbance *of her privacy.* **2** something that disturbs: *The radio can be a great* disturbance. **3** public disorder: *a* disturbance *in the crowd.* **4** anxiety; worry; upset: *Her* disturbance *was plain to see.*

dis·turbed (dĭ stûrbd′) ***adj-*** mentally troubled or ill.

di·sul·fide or **di·sul·phide** (dĭ sŭl′ fīd′) ***n-*** a sulfide that contains two atoms of sulfur in each molecule: *carbon* disulfide *(CS_2).*

dis·un·ion (dĭs yōōn′ yən) ***n-*** **1** lack of agreement or union. **2** a breaking apart; separation.

dis·u·nite (dĭs′ yōō nīt′) ***vt-*** **[dis·u·nit·ed, dis·u·nit·ing]** to break up the unity of; separate; divide.

dis·u·ni·ty (dĭs yōō′ nə tē) ***n-*** [*pl.* **dis·u·ni·ties**] lack of unity or agreement; disunion.

dis·use (dĭs yōōs′) ***n-*** condition of not being used or practiced; neglect: *a custom that has fallen into* disuse.

di·syl·lab·ic (dĭs′ ə lăb′ ĭk, dī′ sə-) ***adj-*** of a word, having two syllables.

ditch (dĭch) ***n-*** long, narrow trench dug in the earth. ***vt-*** **1** to dig a trench in or around: *to* ditch *a garden for drainage.* **2** to throw into a ditch. **3** *Slang* to get rid of. ***vi-*** to bring an airplane to a forced landing on water.

dith·er (dĭth′ ər) ***n-*** condition of nervous excitement or confusion; agitation: *I'm in a* dither *about the party.*

dit·to (dĭt′ ō) ***n-*** [*pl.* **dit·tos**] **1** the same as before, represented in writing by ditto marks. *Abbr.* do. **2** any duplicate.

ditto marks ***n-pl.*** two marks ["] placed under something written or printed to indicate that it is to be repeated. Example: Add 5 and 10
" 3 " 4

dit·ty (dĭt′ ē) ***n-*** [*pl.* **dit·ties**] short, light song.

di·ur·nal (dī ûr′ nəl) ***adj-*** **1** occurring every day; daily: *the* diurnal *rotation of the earth*; diurnal *chores.* **2** occurring or active in the daytime: *a* diurnal *insect.* **3** opening in the daytime and closing at night: *a* diurnal *flower.* ***—adv-*** **di·ur′ nal·ly.**

di·van (dĭ′ văn, dĭ văn′) ***n-*** long, low, cushioned seat, usually having no back or ends.

dive (dīv) ***vi-*** [**dived** or **dove** (dōv), **div·ing**] **1** to plunge headfirst: *She* dived *from the prow of the boat into the waves.* **2** to go under water; submerge: *to* dive *seven fathoms*; *to* dive *for coins.* **3** to go quickly and deeply into something: *to* dive *into one's pocket*; *to* dive *into a book*; *to* dive *into a hallway.* ***vt-***: *to* dive *a plane.* ***n-*** sudden downward plunge: *The market took a* dive.

dive bomber ***n-*** type of warplane that releases its bombs while diving at the target.

div·er (dī′ vər) ***n-*** **1** person or animal who dives into the water; especially, a person who dives in diving competitions. **2** person who makes a living by going beneath water for pearls, sponges, treasure, etc.

Diver

di·verge (dĭ vûrj′, dī-) ***vi-*** [**di·verged, di·verg·ing**] **1** to go out from a point; branch out: *The road* diverges *around the lake.* **2** to differ: *Our opinions* diverge *on politics.*

di·ver·gence (dĭ vûr′ jəns, dī-) ***n-*** **1** a branching out from a common point: *the* divergence *of two roads.* **2** a turning aside from a main course or standard: *a* divergence *from one's principles.* **3** difference: *a* divergence *of opinion.*

di·ver·gent (dĭ vûr′ jənt, dī-) ***adj-*** **1** diverging from a point: *the two* divergent *forks of a stream.* **2** differing: *two* divergent *opinions.* ***—adv-*** **di·ver′ gent·ly.**

di·vers (dī′ vərz) ***adj-*** several or various: *He has lived in* divers *places in the world.*

di·verse (dĭ vûrs′, dī′-) ***adj-*** **1** clearly different: *They have* diverse *views.* **2** varied; diversified: *She has* diverse *interests.* ***—adv-*** **di·verse′ ly.** ***n-*** **di·verse′ ness.**

di·ver·si·fi·ca·tion (dĭ vûr′ sə fə kā′ shən) ***n-*** a diversifying: *the* diversification *of a business.*

di·ver·si·fy (dĭ vûr′ sə fī′) ***vt-*** [**di·ver·si·fied, di·ver·si·fy·ing**] to give variety to; vary: *to* diversify *one's reading.* ***vi-*** in business, to invest in several different lines or products.

di·ver·sion (dĭ vûr′ zhən, dī-) ***n-*** **1** pastime; recreation; amusement: *Her favorite* diversion *was dancing.* **2** a turning something aside or in a different direction: *the* diversion *of a stream from its original course.* **3** a turning of attention in a different direction: *A* diversion *was created by a surprise attack from another point.*

di·ver·sion·a·ry (dĭ vûr′ zhə nĕr′ ē, dī-) ***adj-*** turning the attention in a different direction: *a* diversionary *enemy attack.*

di·ver·si·ty (dĭ vûr′ sə tē, dī-) ***n-*** [*pl.* **di·ver·si·ties**] variety or difference: *a* diversity *of opinion*; *a* diversity *of color.*

di·vert (dĭ vûrt′, dī-) ***vt-*** **1** to turn aside or in a different direction: *Traffic was* diverted *until the highway was repaired. The band* diverted *our attention from the game.* **2** to amuse; entertain: *The movie* diverted *us.*

di·vert·ing (dĭ vûr′ tĭng, dī-) ***adj-*** serving to amuse or entertain; amusing: *a* diverting *pastime.* ***—adv-*** **di·vert′ ing·ly.**

di·vest (dĭ vĕst′, dī-) ***vt-*** to remove clothes, possessions, rights, etc., from (oneself or someone); strip: *He was* divested *of his rank and privileges.*

di·vide (dĭ vīd′) ***vt-*** [**di·vid·ed, di·vid·ing**] **1** to separate; keep apart: *A high fence* divides *their farm from ours.* **2** to separate into parts; share: *The money was* divided *equally among the boys.* **3** to arrange in groups; classify: *The books were* divided *according to subjects.* ***vi-*** **1** *Mathematics* to perform the operation of division. **2** to separate: *The river* divides *near the sea.* **3** to split up; part: *They* divided *over the question of salary.* ***n-*** line of high land between two river systems.
divide by to use as a factor in dividing.

di·vid·ed (dĭ vī′ dəd) ***adj-*** **1** separated into portions or parts: *a* divided *drawer.* **2** shared or passed out; distributed: *a* divided *responsibility.* **3** conflicting or disagreeing: *to be* divided *in our opinions.* **4** of the leaves of plants, having indentations from the base or midrib.

div·i·dend (dĭv′ ə dĕnd′) ***n-*** **1** number to be divided: *In 238 ÷ 2, the* dividend *is 238.* **2** money divided from time to time among people who own stock in a company or corporation as their share of the profits. **3** a share of anything divided.

di·vid·er (dĭ vī′ dər) ***n-*** **1** someone or something that divides: *a screen used as a room* divider. **2 dividers** pair of compasses with two sharp points, used for dividing lines, measuring distances, etc.

div·i·na·tion (dĭv′ ə nā′ shən) ***n-*** **1** act or process of divining: *his* divination *of my purpose.* **2** something divined; a prophecy or guess.

[1]**di·vine** (dĭ vīn′) ***adj-*** **1** of, coming from, or having to do with God: *His* divine *purpose*; divine *worship.* **2** seemingly more than human; godlike. **3** *Informal* delightful; glorious: *What* divine *weather!* ***n-*** clergyman; priest. [from Old French **divin,** from Latin **dīvīnus** meaning "godlike."] ***—adv-*** **di·vine′ ly**: *a* divinely *planned universe.*

[2]**di·vine** (dĭ vīn′) ***vt-*** [**di·vined, di·vin·ing**] **1** to foresee or foretell: *to* divine *the future.* **2** to guess by intuition or insight: *He* divined *my plans.* [from Latin **dīvīnāre,** "to perform like a god; to consult the god(s)," from **dīvīnus,** "divine."] ***—n-*** **di·vin′ er**: *a* diviner *of the future.*

diving bell ***n-*** large, hollow chamber, open at the bottom, used for work under water. It is kept free from water by the pressure of air pumped into it.

Diving bell

divining rod ***n-*** forked stick or branch that is held in the hands at the forked end, and supposedly dips downward when carried over underground water or minerals.

di·vin·i·ty (dĭ vĭn′ ə tē) ***n-*** [*pl.* **di·vin·i·ties**] **1** divine or godlike nature: *Most Christians believe in the* divinity *of Christ.* **2** a god; a divine being. **3** the study of religion; theology: *He has a degree of Doctor of* Divinity. **4 the Divinity** God.

di·vis·i·ble (dĭ vĭz′ əb əl) ***adj-*** **1** such as can be divided. **2** *Mathematics* of a given number, such that it can be divided (by a specified number) leaving 0 as a remainder: *18 is* divisible *by 2.* ***—adv-*** **di·vis′ i·bly.** ***n-*** **di·vis′ i·bil′ i·ty.**

di·vi·sion (dĭ vĭzh′ ən) ***n-*** **1** process of dividing; separation of a whole thing into parts: *the* division *of a house into rooms*; *the* division *of a play into acts.* **2** portion or part; department: *a company's sales* division; divisions *of a book.* **3** something that separates; partition. **4** difference of opinion; lack of agreement: *There was a* division *among the members on the choice of a name for the club.* **5** army unit usually made up of several regiments, with supporting troops, and commanded by a major general. **6** *Mathematics* operation that determines how many times one number (the divisor) is contained in another number (the dividend). It is the opposite of multiplication.

di·vi·sion·al (dĭ vĭzh′ə nəl) ***adj-*** of or related to a division, especially a military divison.

di·vi·sor (dĭ vī′zər) ***n-*** number by which another number is divided: *In 96 ÷ 3, the* divisor *is 3.*

di·vorce (dĭ vôrs′) ***n-*** **1** legal ending of a marriage: *to sue for* divorce. **2** complete separation: *a* divorce *between intentions and acts.* ***vt-*** **[di·vorced, di·vorc·ing]**: *to* divorce *one's wife or husband*; *to* divorce *the two subjects entirely.*

di·vor·cée (də vôr′sā′, -sē′, *also* də vôr′sā′) ***n-*** a divorced woman.

div·ot (dĭv′ət) ***n-*** small piece of turf torn up by a golf stroke.

di·vulge (dĭ vŭlj′) ***vt-*** **[di·vulged, di·vulg·ing]** to make known; reveal; disclose: *to* divulge *a secret.*

Dix·ie (dĭk′sē) ***n-*** **1** those States that made up the Confederacy during the Civil War; southern United States. **2** song about the South written in 1859, popular especially in the Confederate States.

Dix·ie·land (dĭk′sē lănd′) ***n-*** **1** style of jazz that originated in New Orleans. **2** southern United States; Dixie.

diz·zy (dĭz′ē) ***adj-*** **[diz·zi·er, diz·zi·est]** **1** feeling as if one were whirling and falling; giddy. **2** causing or seeming to cause giddiness: *a* dizzy *height*; *a* dizzy *pace.* ***vt-*** **[diz·zied, diz·zy·ing]**: *Heights* dizzy *her.* ***—adv-*** **diz′zi·ly.** ***n-*** **diz′zi·ness.**

DNA (dē′ĕn′ā′) ***n-*** deoxyribonucleic acid, a complex substance that controls the activities of chromosomes. Genes form a part of the DNA molecule, which is found in the nuclei of living cells.

[1]**do** (do͞o) ***vt-*** **[did** (dĭd), **done** (dŭn), **do·ing]** **1** to perform or carry out; accomplish: *to* do *a job.* **2** to produce; execute: *to* do *a painting*; *to* do *a play.* **3** to give; grant: *to* do *a favor.* **4** to work on; set in order: *to* do *one's hair*; *to* do *one's room.* **5** to reach or cover (a speed, distance, etc.); achieve: *to* do *55 miles an hour*; *to* do *300 miles in a day.* ***vi-*** **1** to fare: *to* do *well in business.* **2** to be good enough; be satisfactory: *Those shoes won't* do *for hiking.* ***auxiliary verb*** (1) used as an intensifier: *I* do *like that color!* (2) used with "not" to make a negative statement: *I* did *not say that.* (3) used to ask a question: Do *you need these papers?* (4) used to replace a verb or verbal statement instead of repeating it: *Who owns this jacket? I* do. *He walks as his father* does. [from Old English **don.**] ***Homs-*** dew, due.

do away with to kill; also, to put an end to: *to* do away with *unnecessary expenses.*

do in *Informal* to kill.

do (someone) out of *Informal* to cheat someone of.

do up to wrap or tie up: *to* do up *a parcel.*

do without to proceed in spite of not having.

[2]**do** (dō) *Music* ***n-*** the first note of a musical scale of the type "do, re, mi, fa, etc." (from Italian **do,** probably made up from Latin **dominus.**] ***Homs-*** doe, dough.

do. ditto.

dob·bin (dŏb′ən) ***n-*** a horse, especially an old or wornout workhorse.

Do·ber·man pin·scher (dō′bər mən pĭn′chər) ***n-*** fairly large, short-haired dog, originally from Germany, that is sometimes used in police work.

doc·ile (dŏs′əl) ***adj-*** easily trained, led, or managed; tractable: *a* docile *horse*; *a* docile *child.* ***—adv-*** **doc′ile·ly.** ***n-*** **do·cil′i·ty** (dŏ sĭl′ə tē, dō-).

Dock

[1]**dock** (dŏk) ***n-*** **1** waterway between piers, where ships may tie up to load and unload; slip. **2** *Informal* pier; wharf. ***vt-*** to bring (a boat) to a pier or wharf: *The captain* docked *his boat beside Pier 36.* ***vi-***: *The Queen Mary* docked *three hours late.* [probably from early Dutch **docke,** "channel."]

[2]**dock** (dŏk) ***vt-*** **1** to cut off the end of (a tail or something similar); cut short. **2** to make a deduction from the wages of: *They* docked *everyone a week's pay.* ***n-*** stump of an animal's tail. [probably from Old Norse **dockr,** "a short, thick tail," related to [4]**dock.**]

[3]**dock** (dŏk) ***n-*** place in a courtroom for a prisoner who is on trial. [from Flemish **docke, dok,** "a pen; cage."]

[4]**dock** (dŏk) ***n-*** any of several coarse weeds with clusters of small greenish or reddish flowers. [from Old English **docce,** related to [2]**dock.**]

dock·et (dŏk′ət) ***n-*** **1** list of cases to be tried by a court; also, any list or calendar of matters to be acted on: *The problem of raising more money is on the* docket *for March.* **2** a list of legal decisions. **3** label or tag attached to a package and listing its contents. ***vt-*** **1** to enter on a list of matters for consideration. **2** to mark or label.

dock·yard (dŏk′yärd′) ***n-*** place where ships are built, repaired, or outfitted; shipyard.

doc·tor (dŏk′tər) ***n-*** **1** person who is licensed to practice medicine or surgery. **2** person who holds the highest degree given by a university. ***vt-*** **1** to try to cure: *to* doctor *a cold.* **2** *Informal* to tamper with: *to* doctor *an account.*

doc·tor·al (dŏk′tər əl) ***adj-*** related to or studying for a doctorate: *a* doctoral *thesis*; *a* doctoral *candidate.*

doc·tor·ate (dŏk′tər ət) ***n-*** university degree or rank of doctor: *to study for a* doctorate *in English.*

doc·tri·naire (dŏk′trə nâr′) ***adj-*** typical of a person who has theoretical ideas on politics or other matters, and disregards facts and practical considerations.

doc·trine (dŏk′trĭn) ***n-*** something taught as the deeply held belief or principles of a church, political party, or other group: *the* doctrines *of the church*; *the* doctrine *of states' rights.* ***—adj-*** **doc′trin·al:** *a* doctrinal *sermon.*

doc·u·ment (dŏk′yə mənt) ***n-*** official paper that gives information or proof of something; a record: *Birth and marriage certificates are* documents *of importance.* ***vt-*** to support or prove (a point, theory, etc.) with facts or evidence.

doc·u·men·ta·ry (dŏk′yo͞o mĕn′tə rē) ***adj-*** **1** supported by or made up of such facts as may be found in documents or official records: *Give me* documentary *proof of your accusations!* **2** dealing with real events and people in a factual way: *a* documentary *motion picture.* ***n-*** [*pl.* **doc·u·men·ta·ries**] motion picture of this kind.

doc·u·men·ta·tion (dŏk′yo͞o mĕn tā′shən) ***n-*** a supplying or preparing of documentary evidence, records, etc.; also, the evidence, records, etc., prepared or supplied.

fāte, făt, dâre, bärn; bē, bĕt, mêre; bīte, bĭt; nōte, hŏt, môre, dȯg; fŭn, fûr; to͞o, bo͝ok; oil; out; tar; thin; then; hw for wh as in what; zh for s as in usual; ə for a, e, i, o, u, as in ago, linen, peril, atom, minus

1**dod·der** (dŏd′ ər) ***vi-*** to move feebly and unsteadily, as a person weakened by old age does; tremble or totter. [of uncertain origin, but perhaps related to **dither.**]

2**dod·der** (dŏd′ ər) ***n-*** leafless plant with tiny flowers and threadlike, twining stems that attach themselves to and weaken or destroy other plants. [perhaps from early German **doder.**]

do·dec·a·gon (dō′ dĕk′ ə gŏn) ***n-*** polygon with 12 sides.

do·dec·a·he·dron (dō′ dĕk′ ə hē′ drən) ***n-*** polyhedron with 12 faces.

dodge (dŏj) ***vt-*** **[dodged, dodg·ing] 1** to avoid by moving aside quickly: *to* dodge *a blow.* **2** to avoid by deception or cunning; evade: *to* dodge *an issue.* ***vi-***: *to* dodge *through traffic.* ***n-*** **1** sudden move aside; twist or turn. **2** a trick: *I know that old* dodge.

dodge·ball (dŏj′ bòl′) ***n-*** game in which a group of players throw a large ball at another group, who try to avoid being hit by it.

dodg·er (dŏj′ ər) ***n-*** **1** person who uses trickery and evasion to avoid doing something: *a draft* dodger. **2** (usually **corn dodger**) small cake made from corn meal.

do·do (dō′ dō) ***n-*** [*pl.* **do·does** or **do·dos**] large, extinct bird with very short legs, a large hooked beak, and wings too small for flight.

Dodo

doe (dō) ***n-*** the female of the deer, antelope, rabbit, and some other animals. ***Homs-*** 2do, dough.

Doe, John (dō) See *John Doe.*

do·er (do͞o′ ər) ***n-*** person who does something, especially a person of action and energy: *a* doer, *not a thinker.*

does (dŭz) form of 1**do** used with "he," "she," "it," or singular noun subjects, in the present tense.

doe·skin (dō′ skĭn′) ***n-*** **1** fine, soft leather made from the skin of a female deer, or from the skin of a sheep or lamb. **2** closely-woven cloth, usually of wool, with a soft, napped surface.

does·n't (dŭz′ ənt) does not.

doff (dŏf) ***vt-*** to take off (clothing, especially a hat).

dog (dòg) ***n-*** **1** four-footed animal of which there are many domesticated breeds used as pets, for hunting, police work, etc. **2** the male of this animal or of the fox, wolf, etc. **3** *Informal* fellow: *He's a gay* dog. ***vt-*** **[dogged, dog·ging]** to follow closely; trail: *to* dog *someone's footsteps.* **—*adj-* dog′ like′.**

dog·bane (dòg′ bān′) ***n-*** any of several shrubby plants with small pink or white flowers and milky juice.

dog·cart (dòg′ kärt′) ***n-*** **1** light, two-wheeled, horse-drawn carriage with seats back to back. **2** cart drawn by dogs.

Dogcart

dog days ***n-*** period of hot, sultry weather in late summer.

doge (dōj) ***n-*** in the former republics of Venice and Genoa, the chief magistrate.

dog-ear (dòg′ êr′) ***n-*** corner of a page that is turned down or folded over. **—*adj-* dog′-eared′**: *a* dog-eared *book.*

dog·face (dòg′ fās′) *Slang* ***n-*** U.S. Army infantryman.

dog·fight (dòg′ fīt′) ***n-*** **1** *Military* battle between fighter planes. **2** fight between dogs, or any rough brawl.

dog·fish (dòg′ fĭsh′) ***n-*** [*pl.* **dog·fish** or **dog·fish·es**] any of various small sharks, found in North American waters.

Dogfish

dog·ged (dòg′ əd) ***adj-*** stubborn and persevering: *his* dogged *courage.* **—*adv-* dog′ ged·ly.** ***n-*** **dog′ ged·ness.**

dog·ger·el (dŏg′ ər əl, dòg′-) ***n-*** trivial, silly, or poorly constructed verse. *as* ***modifier:*** *a bit of* doggerel *verse.*

dog·house (dòg′ hous′) ***n-*** small house for a dog. **in the doghouse** *Informal* in someone's bad graces; in disfavor.

do·gie (dō′ gē) ***n-*** in the western United States, a motherless or stray calf.

dog in the manger ***n-*** person who prevents others from using something he cannot use or does not want.

dog·ma (dòg′ mə) ***n-*** principle, belief, or doctrine that is accepted as authoritative, especially by a religion.

dog·mat·ic (dòg măt′ ĭk) or **dog·mat·i·cal** (-ĭ kəl) ***adj-*** **1** of or related to dogma. **2** stating or expressing beliefs or opinions in a positive, often arrogant manner: *The professor is very* dogmatic. **—*adv-* dog·mat′ i·cal·ly.**

dog·ma·tism (dòg′ mə tĭz′ əm) ***n-*** a positive, authoritative, often arrogant asserting of opinions or beliefs; also, the opinion or belief itself. **—*n-* dog′ ma·tist′.**

do-gooder (do͞o′ go͝od′ ər) *Informal* ***n-*** person who is extremely eager to right wrongs; overanxious reformer.

dog paddle ***n-*** clumsy swimming stroke in which the hands move like the forepaws of a swimming dog.

Dog Star ***n-*** Sirius.

dog·tooth violet (dòg′ to͞oth′) ***n-*** early spring-flowering plant with mottled leaves and nodding, usually yellow flowers; adder's tongue; trout lily. It is not related to the true violets. Also **dog's-tooth violet.**

dog·trot (dòg′ trŏt′) ***n-*** a slow, gentle trot.

dog·watch (dòg′ wăch′) ***n-*** either of two shortened watches aboard a ship, one from 4 to 6 P.M., the other from 6 to 8 P.M.

dog·wood (dòg′ wo͝od′) ***n-*** small tree or shrub with blossoms consisting of clusters of tiny flowers surrounded by four petallike, pink or white bracts.

Dogwood

doi·ly (doi′ lē) ***n-*** [*pl.* **doi·lies**] small mat of linen, lace, paper, etc., often placed under a vase, serving dish, etc.

do·ings (do͞o′ ĭngz) ***n-*** *pl.* **1** actions; behavior. **2** activities; events.

dol·drums (dōl′ drəmz, *also* dòl′-) ***n-*** *pl.* **1** region of calms near the equator, where sailing ships are often becalmed. **2** dull and depressed state of mind or spirits.

dole (dōl) ***vt-*** **[doled, dol·ing]** to give out sparingly or in small quantities: *to* dole *out an allowance.* ***n-*** a giving out of money, food, etc., as assistance for people in need; also, the necessities thus given.

dole·ful (dōl′ fəl) ***adj-*** sad; gloomy; mournful: *a* doleful *wail.* **—*adv-* dole′ ful·ly.** ***n-*** **dole′ ful·ness.**

doll (dòl, dŏl) ***n-*** **1** toy made to resemble a baby, child, or grown person. **2** a pretty child or young woman. **doll up** *Informal* to dress up.

dol·lar (dŏl′ ər) ***n-*** **1** the unit of money in the United States and some other countries. **2** paper note or silver coin equal to 100 cents. *as* ***modifier***: *a* dollar *bill.*

dol·lop (dŏl′ əp) ***n-*** portion or serving of a soft substance or liquid: *a* dollop *of ice cream.*

dol·ly (dòl′ ē, dŏl′-) ***n-*** [*pl.* **dol·lies**] **1** child's word for a doll. **2** small platform on wheels, used for moving heavy objects.

Dolman sleeve

dol·man (dōl′ mən, dŏl′-) ***n-*** **1** long Turkish robe or similar garment. **2 dolman sleeve** sleeve that is wide and loose at the armhole and narrower toward the wrist.

dol·o·mite (dō′ lə mīt′, dŏl′ ə-) ***n*-** **1** mineral of calcium magnesium carbonate, $CaMg(CO_3)_2$, commonly found as gray or pale pink crystals. **2** hard rock that consists mainly of this mineral.

do·lor (dō′ lər, dŏl′ ər) ***n*-** sorrow; grief, pain.

dol·or·ous (dō′ lər əs, dŏl′ ər-) ***adj*-** expressing or causing pain or sorrow: *She uttered a* dolorous *cry.* **—*adv*- do′ lor·ous·ly.** ***n*-** **dol′ or·ous·ness.**

dol·phin (dŏl′ fĭn) ***n*-** small, toothed whale with a long snout and a hook-shaped fin on its back.

Dolphin, 6—8 ft. long

dolt (dōlt) ***n*-** dull, stupid person; dunce; blockhead.

dolt·ish (dōl′ tĭsh) ***adj*-** of or like a dolt; stupid. **—*adv*- dolt′ ish·ly.** ***n*-** **dolt′ ish·ness.**

-dom *suffix* **1** office, territory, or domain of: *earl*dom; *king*dom; *film*dom. **2** all of a given class or rank: *official*dom; *cat*dom. **3** state or condition of being: *free*dom; *wis*dom. **4** process or condition of being a: *martyr*dom.

do·main (dō mān′) ***n*-** **1** lands owned by one person or family; estate. **2** region under the control of one ruler or government; dominion; realm. **3** field or sphere of thought or action: *the* domain *of natural science.*

dome (dōm) ***n*-** **1** large rounded roof on a circular base. **2** something high and rounded: *the* dome *of the sky.* ***vt*-** **[domed, dom·ing]** to top or form with a high, rounded roof or similar part.

Dome

do·mes·tic (də mĕs′ tĭk) ***adj*-** **1** relating to home or household affairs: *busy with* domestic *chores.* **2** fond of home and household affairs: *a* domestic *type of woman.* **3** relating to or made in one's own country; not foreign: *a* domestic *product*; domestic *trade.* **4** living with and cared for by man; not wild; tame: *Household pets and cattle are* domestic *animals.* ***n*-** a household servant. **—*adv*- do·mes′ ti·cal·ly.**

do·mes·ti·cate (də mĕs′ tə kāt′) ***vt*-** **[do·mes·ti·cat·ed, do·mes·ti·cat·ing]** **1** to tame or adapt to live with and be useful to man: *to* domesticate *cattle.* **2** to make (a person) fond of home life or skillful in domestic affairs. **—*n*- do·mes′ ti·ca′ tion.**

do·mes·tic·i·ty (dō′ mĕs tĭs′ ə tē) ***n*-** [*pl.* **do·mes·tic·i·ties**] home life; also, a liking for or settling into home life.

domestic science ***n*-** training and instruction in household arts such as cooking and sewing.

dom·i·cile (dŏm′ ə sīl′, dō′ mə-) ***n*-** a home; dwelling; residence. ***vt*-** **[dom·i·ciled, dom·i·cil·ing]** to establish in a fixed residence.

dom·i·nant (dŏm′ ə nənt) ***adj*-** **1** most important or influential; ruling; controlling: *the* dominant *member of a partnership*; *the* dominant *influence in his life.* **2** most prominent or outstanding: *Red is the* dominant *color in this painting.* **3** *Biology* of a pair of inherited factors (or genes), relating to the one which suppresses or dominates the other, and therefore appears more often in the offspring (see also *recessive*): *The gene for brown eyes is* dominant *over that for blue eyes.* **4** *Music* consisting of or based on the fifth note of a scale. ***n*-** *Music* the fifth note of a scale. **—*n*- dom′ i·nance.** ***adv*-** **dom′ i·nant·ly.**

dom·i·nate (dŏm′ ə nāt′) ***vt*-** **[dom·i·nat·ed, dom·i·nat·ing]** **1** to rule or control by will or strength: *The Romans once* dominated *Europe.* **2** to occupy a commanding position over: *The cliff* dominates *the town.* ***vi*-** to exercise influence or control: *The strong* dominate *over the weak.* **—*n*- dom′ i·na′ tion.**

dom·i·neer (dŏm′ ə nêr′) ***vi*-** to exercise authority arrogantly or tyrannically; be overbearing: *The manager* domineered *over his timid clerk.*

dom·i·neer·ing (dŏm′ ə nêr′ ĭng) ***adj*-** bossy and overbearing; tyrannical; dictatorial: *a haughty,* domineering *woman.* **—*adv*- dom′ i·neer′ ing·ly.**

Do·min·i·can (də mĭn′ ĭ kən) ***n*-** **1** member of the religious order founded by St. Dominic in 1215. **2** a native or citizen of the Dominican Republic. ***adj*-**: *a* Dominican *priest*; *the* Dominican *president.*

dom·i·nie (dŏm′ ə nē, dō′ mə-) *Scottish* ***n*-** **1** schoolmaster. **2** clergyman; minister.

do·min·ion (də mĭn′ yən) ***n*-** **1** supreme authority or control; rule. **2** territory under the authority of a ruler or government: *the Queen's* dominions. **3** (usually **Dominion**) self-governing nation of the British Commonwealth that is outside the United Kingdom and that acknowledges the British sovereign as chief of state.

dom·i·no (dŏm′ ə nō′) ***n*-** [*pl.* **dom·i·noes** or **dom·i·nos**] **1** thin block of wood, bone, etc., marked with two groups of spots, and used in playing a game called **dominoes.** **2** loose cloak with a hood and mask covering the upper part of the face, formerly worn at masquerades.

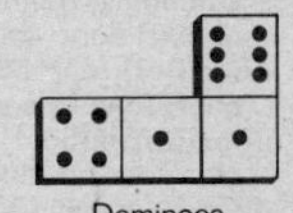
Dominoes

¹don (dŏn) ***vt*-** **[donned, don·ning]** to put on; dress in: *The judge* donned *his robe.* [a contraction of "do on."]

²don (dŏn) ***n*-** **1** Spanish lord or gentleman: *the noble* don. **2 Don** Spanish title and form of address similar to "Sir" or "Mr.," and used before the first name or full name: *That is* Don *Pedro.* **3** *Brit.* teacher or professor in a college or university. [from Spanish **don,** from Latin **dominus** meaning "master."]

do·nate (dō′ nāt′) ***vt*-** **[do·nat·ed, do·nat·ing]** to give (money, necessities, one's services, etc.) to a charitable or worthwhile cause; contribute. **—*n*- do′ na′ tor.**

do·na·tion (dō nā′ shən) ***n*-** a charitable gift; grant.

done (dŭn) *p.p.* of **do.** ***adj*-** cooked to a certain degree: *He likes his steaks well* done.

don·jon (dŏn′ jən, dŭn′-) ***n*-** main tower of a medieval castle; keep. ***Hom*-** dungeon.

Don Juan (dŏn wän′, *also* -jōō′ ən) ***n*-** in Spanish legend, a nobleman who had many love affairs.

don·key (dŏng′ kē, dŭng′-) ***n*-** [*pl.* **don·keys**] **1** strong, surefooted animal related to the horse, but having a smaller body, longer ears, and a shorter mane; ass. **2** stupid or obstinate person.

Donkey, 4—5 ft. high

donkey engine ***n*-** a small, movable steam engine, used for pumping, hoisting, etc.

don·na (dŏn′ ə) ***n*-** Italian title and form of address similar to "lady" or "madam," used before the first name.

don·ny·brook (dŏn′ ē brŏŏk′) ***n*-** noisy brawl.

do·nor (dō′ nər) ***n*-** one who gives or donates something: *a* donor *of blood to a blood bank.*

---

fāte, făt, dâre, bärn; bē, bĕt, mêre; bīte, bĭt; nōte, hŏt, môre, dòg; fŭn, fûr; tōō, bŏŏk; oil; out; tar; thin; then; hw for wh as in *wh*at; zh for s as in u*s*ual; ə for a, e, i, o, u, as in *a*go, lin*e*n, per*i*l, at*o*m, min*u*s

Don Qui·xo·te (dŏn′ kē hō′ tē, *also* dŏn kwĭk′ sət′) ***n-*** **1** novel by Cervantes, satirizing outmoded chivalry. **2** the idealistic but impractical hero of this novel. **3** any person who attempts impossible romantic deeds.

don't (dōnt) do not.

►DON'T is the contraction for "do not." *I* don't *know.* Do not use DON'T when you mean "doesn't."

doo·dad (dōō′ dăd′) *Informal* ***n-*** small article; gadget.

doo·dle (dōō′ dəl) *Informal* ***n-*** a drawing or scribble made in an aimless, absent-minded way. ***vi-*** **[doo·dled, doo·dling]** to draw or scribble in this way: *She* doodles *constantly.* ***vt-***: *He* doodled *circles.* **—*n-* doo′ dler.**

doo·dle·bug (dōō′ dəl bŭg′) ***n-*** the larva of the ant lion and several other insects.

doom (dōōm) ***n-*** **1** destiny that cannot be escaped, especially destruction, ruin, or death: *He met his* doom *on the battlefield.* **2** a sentence or judgment, especially the Last Judgment. ***vt-*** **1** to condemn; sentence: *The judge* doomed *him to lifelong imprisonment.* **2** to destine: *The project was* doomed *to fail.*

dooms·day (dōōmz′ dā′) ***n-*** day of the Last Judgment; hence, any day of final judgment.

door (dôr) ***n-*** **1** movable barrier that swings on hinges, slides, or revolves, and provides a means of entrance to a building, room, vehicle, etc. **2** any means of entrance or exit; doorway: *the* door *to success.*

door·bell (dôr′ bĕl′) ***n-*** bell or buzzer at the outside of a door, rung by someone who wishes to enter.

door·jamb (dôr′ jăm′) ***n-*** upright piece forming the side of a door opening.

door·keep·er (dôr′ kē′ pər) ***n-*** person who guards an entrance.

door·knob (dôr′ nŏb′) ***n-*** knob on a door, turned or pulled to open it.

door·man (dôr′ mən) ***n-*** [*pl.* **door·men**] attendant at the entrance of an apartment house, hotel, etc., who opens the door for people and often acts as a guard.

door·mat (dôr′ măt′) ***n-*** mat placed at a door and used for wiping dirt from the shoes.

door·nail (dôr′ nāl′) ***n-*** a nail with a large head.

dead as a doornail *Informal* unquestionably dead.

door·step (dôr′ stĕp′) ***n-*** step or steps leading up to an outside door.

door·stop (dôr′ stŏp′) ***n-*** device or object used to keep a door open, or to keep it from slamming or swinging too far back.

door·way (dôr′ wā′) ***n-*** the opening in which a door is hung; also, the entrance to a building or room.

door·yard (dôr′ yärd′) ***n-*** yard at a house entrance.

dope (dōp) ***n-*** **1** preparation painted or sprayed on the fabric surfaces of an airplane to strengthen and waterproof them. **2** *Informal* narcotics. **3** *Slang* secret or special information. **4** *Slang* stupid person. ***vt-*** **[doped, dop·ing]** *Slang* to treat or affect with narcotics.

dope out *Slang* to figure out.

Dop·pler effect (dŏp′ lər) ***n-*** change in frequency of sound, light, etc., due to the motion of the source with respect to the observer or listener. Thus, when a train moves toward an observer, its whistle seems to be higher in pitch than when the train is moving away. Also called **Doppler shift.**

Doric capital

Dor·ic (dŏr′ ĭk, dŏr′-) ***adj-*** **1** of or belonging to the oldest and simplest order of classical Greek architecture. **2** of or relating to Doris, a region of ancient Greece. ***n-*** the dialect spoken in this region.

dor·mant (dŏr′ mənt, dôr′-) ***adj-*** sleeping or temporarily inactive: *a* dormant *volcano.* **—*n-* dor′ man·cy.**

dor·mer (dŏr′ mər, dôr′-) ***n-*** **1** (usually **dormer window**) upright window built so as to project from a sloping roof. **2** gabled structure containing such a window.

dor·mi·to·ry (dŏr′ mə tôr′ē, dôr′-) ***n-*** [*pl.* **dor·mi·to·ries**] **1** a building containing a number of rooms used for sleeping. **2** room containing a number of beds, especially in a school or institution.

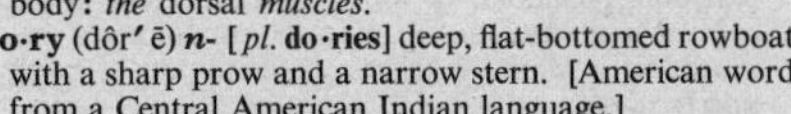

Dormer window

dor·mouse (dŏr′ mous′, dôr′-) ***n-*** [*pl.* **dor·mice**] small, hibernating squirrellike animal of Europe, Asia, and Africa.

dor·sal (dŏr′ səl, dôr′-) ***adj-*** of or having to do with the back of the body: *the* dorsal *muscles.*

do·ry (dôr′ ē) ***n-*** [*pl.* **do·ries**] deep, flat-bottomed rowboat with a sharp prow and a narrow stern. [American word from a Central American Indian language.]

dos·age (dō′ sĭj) ***n-*** **1** the amount of medicine, radiation, etc., to be given at one time. **2** the giving of medicine in doses. **3** process of adding one or more ingredients to a product to improve it.

dose (dōs) ***n-*** **1** amount of medicine to be given or taken at one time. **2** *Informal* amount of unpleasant treatment: *a* dose *of punishment.* ***vt-*** **[dosed, dos·ing]** to give medicine to: *to* dose *a cold.*

do·sim·e·ter (dō sĭm′ ə tər) ***n-*** device for measuring the strength and total amount of radiation absorbed by a person in a given period of time.

dos·si·er (dŏs′ yā′, dŏs′ ē ā′) ***n-*** collection of documents or papers containing a detailed report or information on a person or particular matter.

dost (dŭst) *Archaic* form of [1]**do** used with "thou" in the present tense. ***Hom-*** dust.

[1]**dot** (dŏt) ***n-*** small, rounded spot or mark. ***vt-*** **[dot·ted, dot·ting]** to mark with or as if with such spots: *Be sure to* dot *your "i's." Daisies* dotted *the hillside.* [from Old English **dott** meaning "the head of a boil."]

[2]**dot** (dŏt) ***n-*** property which a bride brings to her husband; dowry. [from French **dot,** from Latin **dos,** "a dowry."]

dot·age (dō′ tĭj) ***n-*** foolish or childish condition sometimes caused by old age: *an old man in his* dotage.

do·tard (dō′ tərd) ***n-*** person made weak and childish by extreme old age.

dote (dōt) ***vi-*** **[dot·ed, dot·ing]** **1** to lavish great or excessive love or fondness (on or upon) a person, pet, etc.: *to* dote *on a grandchild.* **2** to be weak and childish from old age.

doth (dŭth) *Archaic* form of [1]**do** used with "he," "she," "it," or singular noun subjects, in the present tense.

dotted swiss ***n-*** fine cotton or similar fabric with a pattern of small, raised dots.

dou·ble (dŭb′ əl) ***adj-*** **1** having or forming two identical or similar parts; paired: *the* double *"t" in "butter"; a* double *door.* **2** twice the usual size, amount, value, etc.; multiplied by two: *a* double *portion; a solution of* double *strength.* **3** having two uses, applications, intentions, etc.: *a* double *meaning; to serve a* double *purpose.* **4** of a flower, having more than a single row of petals: *a* double *rose.* ***vt-*** **[dou·bled, dou·bling]** **1** to make twice as much; multiply by two: *to* double *one's income.* **2** to fold over so as two form two layers or thicknesses: *to* double *a piece of paper.* **3** of a ship, to pass around (a projecting piece of land): *to* double *a cape.* ***vi-*** **1** to increase to twice as much: *Prices have* doubled. **2** to be a replacement or substitute: *He* doubles *for the star.* **3** to turn sharply and trace the same or a similar course:

to double *on one's tracks.* **4** in baseball, to make a two-base hit. ***n-*** **1** number or amount that is twice as much. **2** someone or something that looks exactly like another: *She is Sally's* double. **3** in baseball, a hit enabling the batter to reach second base. **4 doubles** game, such as tennis, played with two players on each side instead of one. ***adv-*** in twos or pairs: *to see* double.
double up 1 to bend sharply or suddenly: *He* doubled up *with pain.* **2** to share quarters with someone.

double bar *Music* ***n-*** two vertical lines placed close together on a staff to indicate the end of a composition or a section of it.

dou·ble-bar·reled (dŭb′ əl băr′ əld) ***adj-*** **1** of a gun, having two barrels. **2** having a double purpose: *a* double-barreled *question.*

double bass (bās) ***n-*** member of the violin family of musical instruments that is largest in size and lowest in pitch; bass viol.

Man playing double bass

double bassoon ***n-*** largest and deepest-toned musical instrument of the oboe family, pitched an octave lower than the bassoon.

dou·ble-breast·ed (dŭb′ əl brĕs′- təd) ***adj-*** of a coat, jacket, etc., having a wide overlap and two rows of buttons.

double chin ***n-*** sagging fold of flesh under the chin.

dou·ble-cross (dŭb′ əl krŏs′) *Slang* ***vt-*** to deceive or betray (someone) by acting contrary to promises. **—*n-* dou′ ble-cross′ er.**

double cross *Slang* ***n-*** an act of cheating or treachery.

dou·ble-deal·ing (dŭb′ əl dē′ lĭng) ***n-*** treacherous, deceitful behavior. ***adj-*** : *a* double-dealing *scoundrel.* **—*n-* dou′ ble-deal′ er.**

dou·ble-deck·er (dŭb′ əl dĕk′ ər) ***n-*** something having two sections, parts, or layers one above the other. *as* ***modifier***: *a* double-decker *bus.*

double eagle ***n-*** former gold coin of the United States, having a value of twenty dollars.

dou·ble-edged (dŭb′əl ĕjd′) ***adj-*** **1** having two cutting sides: *a* double-edged *sword.* **2** acting both ways: *a* double-edged *argument.*

dou·ble en·ten·dre (dōōb′ lŏⁿtŏⁿ′drə) ***n-*** statement, joke, etc., that can be interpreted as having two meanings, one of which is, usually, indecent. [from French **double entente** meaning "double meaning."]

dou·ble-head·er (dŭb′ əl hĕd′ ər) ***n-*** two games played in succession on the same day for the price of one.

double jeopardy ***n-*** the subjection of a person to a second trial for an offense for which he has already been tried and judged.

dou·ble-joint·ed (dŭb′ əl join′ təd) ***adj-*** having extremely flexible joints that enable the limbs, fingers, spine, etc., to bend in unusual ways.

double negative ***n-*** occurrence in the same statement of two negative words or expressions. Example: I don't never go there.
►DOUBLE NEGATIVES are not considered proper in English.

dou·ble-park (dŭb′əl pârk′) ***vt-*** to park (a motor vehicle) in the street alongside another already parked parallel to the curb. ***vi-***: *Please don't* double-park.

double play ***n-*** in baseball, the putting out of two base runners in one connected series of plays.

dou·ble-quick (dŭb′ əl kwĭk′) ***adj-*** done with the quickest possible step, action, etc. ***n-*** very quick step used in marching; double time.

double standard ***n-*** two sets of rules for moral behavior applied to two different groups of people, especially when one set is applied to men and another to women.

double star ***n-*** two stars so close together that they look like one except when viewed through a telescope.

dou·blet (dŭb′ lət) ***n-*** close-fitting jacket worn by men from about 1400 to about 1650.

Doublet

double take ***n-*** failure to react to a surprise, joke, etc., followed by a sudden flash of understanding or recognition: *to do a* double take *on unexpectedly meeting an old friend.*

double talk ***n-*** rapid flow of words consisting of a mixture of sense and nonsense, intended to amuse, deceive, confuse, etc.

double time ***n-*** **1** a rapid step, twice as fast as usual marching time, usually equal to 180 paces per minute. **2** payment of twice the usual hourly wages.

dou·ble·tree (dŭb′ əl trē′) ***n-*** crossbar on a wagon, plow, etc., used when two horses are harnessed abreast.

dou·bloon (dŭb lōōn′) ***n-*** former Spanish gold coin.

dou·bly ***adv-*** in twice the quantity or degree.

doubt (dout) ***vt-*** to be uncertain or undecided about; distrust or question: *I* doubt *his honesty. I* doubt *whether it will rain.* ***vi-***: *He who* doubts *may learn the truth for himself.* ***n-*** **1** feeling of disbelief or mistrust: *I have some* doubt *about that.* **2** a state or condition of uncertainty: *Their fate is still in* doubt. **—*n-* doubt′ er.**
no doubt or **without doubt** certainly; without question.

doubt·ful (dout′ fəl) ***adj-*** **1** feeling or showing doubt; undecided; hesitating: *a* doubtful *expression*; *to be* doubtful *about making a decision.* **2** not clear or sure; uncertain: *the outcome is* doubtful. **3** of questionable character: *a* doubtful *reputation.* **—*adv-* doubt′ ful·ly. *n-* doubt′ ful·ness.**

doubt·less (dout′ ləs) ***adv-*** without doubt; certainly: *He was* doubtless *the smartest.* Also **doubt′ less·ly.**

douche (dōōsh) ***n-*** **1** spray of water for cleansing a part of the body, especially an internal part. **2** device used for cleansing in this manner. ***vt-*** **[douched, douch·ing]** to cleanse or treat with a spray of water.

dough (dō) ***n-*** thick, spongy mixture of flour and other ingredients, such as butter, eggs, or milk, used for making bread or pastry. ***Homs-*** ²do, doe.

dough·nut (dō′ nŭt′) ***n-*** small cake of sweetened dough, often in the shape of a ring, fried in deep fat.

dough·ty (dou′ tē) ***adj-*** **[dough·ti·er, dough·ti·est]** strong and bold; brave: *a* doughty *warrior.*

dough·y (dō′ ē) ***adj-*** **[dough·i·er, dough·i·est]** of or like dough in consistency or appearance; pasty.

Doug·las fir (dŭg′ ləs) ***n-*** **1** tall cone-bearing evergreen tree of western North America, having durable wood much used in plywood. **2** the wood of this tree.

dour (dour, dōōr) ***adj-*** **[dour·er, dour·est]** gloomy and forbidding in appearance or manner: *his* dour *expression.* **—*adv-* dour′ ly. *n-* dour′ ness.**

douse (dous) ***vt-*** **[doused, dous·ing] 1** to plunge into water or other liquid: *to* douse *a flaming torch.* **2** to throw water over; drench: *He* doused *me with the hose.*

¹**dove** (dŭv) ***n-*** any of a group of related birds that includes the common pigeon and the mourning dove. [from Old English **dūfe-**, found in compounds.]

[2]**dove** (dōv) *p.t.* of **dive**.

dove·cote (dŭv′ kōt′, -kŏt′) ***n-*** small house or boxlike shelter for doves or pigeons. Also **dove′ cot** (dŭv′ kŏt′).

dove·tail (dŭv′ tāl′) ***vt-*** to join the ends of (two pieces of wood) by means of a dovetail joint. ***vi-*** to interlock smoothly in a harmonious whole: *Our plans* dovetailed *neatly.* ***n-*** one of the wedge-shaped projections in a dovetail joint.

dovetail joint ***n-*** an interlocking joint made of boards or timbers, one of which has dovetails that fit into slots of the same shape in the other board.

dow·a·ger (dou′ ə jər) ***n-*** **1** widow who holds property or a title from her husband, especially the widow of a king, duke, etc. **2** a dignified elderly woman.

dow·dy (dou′ dē) ***adj-*** **[dow·di·er, dow·di·est]** lacking style or smartness in dress or appearance: *a* dowdy *woman.* **—*adv-* dow′ di·ly.** ***n-*** **dow′ di·ness.**

dow·el (dou′ əl) ***n-*** peg or projection that fits into a corresponding hole, and is used to join two pieces of wood, metal, etc. ***vt-*** to fasten or equip with such pegs.

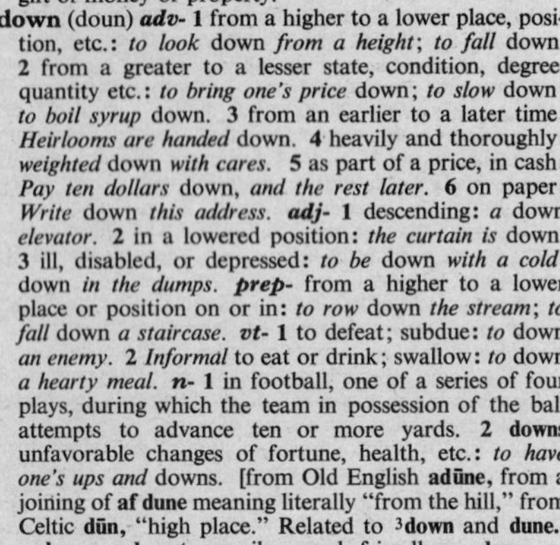

dow·er (dou′ ər) ***n-*** part of a deceased husband's estate which the law gives to his widow for life. ***vt-*** to provide with an inheritance or gift of money or property.

[1]**down** (doun) ***adv-*** **1** from a higher to a lower place, position, etc.: *to look* down *from a height*; *to fall* down. **2** from a greater to a lesser state, condition, degree, quantity etc.: *to bring one's price* down; *to slow* down; *to boil syrup* down. **3** from an earlier to a later time: *Heirlooms are handed* down. **4** heavily and thoroughly: *weighted* down *with cares.* **5** as part of a price, in cash: *Pay ten dollars* down, *and the rest later.* **6** on paper: *Write* down *this address.* ***adj-*** **1** descending: *a* down *elevator.* **2** in a lowered position: *the curtain is* down. **3** ill, disabled, or depressed: *to be* down *with a cold*; down *in the dumps.* ***prep-*** from a higher to a lower place or position on or in: *to row* down *the stream*; *to fall* down *a staircase.* ***vt-*** **1** to defeat; subdue: *to* down *an enemy.* **2** *Informal* to eat or drink; swallow: *to* down *a hearty meal.* ***n-*** **1** in football, one of a series of four plays, during which the team in possession of the ball attempts to advance ten or more yards. **2 downs** unfavorable changes of fortune, health, etc.: *to have one's ups and* downs. [from Old English **adūne,** from a joining of **af dune** meaning literally "from the hill," from Celtic **dūn,** "high place." Related to [3]**down** and **dune.**]

down and out penniless and friendless. **down on** bearing a grudge against: *Why are you* down on *him?* **Down with (someone)**! Throw (someone) out of office!

[2]**down** (doun) ***n-*** **1** soft, fluffy feathers: *a pillow stuffed with* down. **2** any similar soft fuzz or hair: *the* down *on a peach.* [from an earlier Old Norse word **dūnn.**]

[3]**down** (doun) *chiefly Brit.* ***n-*** (often **downs**) open, grassy, rolling country. [from Old English **dūn** meaning "hill;" related to **dune.**]

down·beat (doun′ bēt′) *Music* ***n-*** downward stroke made by a conductor's baton or hand to indicate the first accented beat of each measure; also, the first beat or the first accented beat in a measure.

down·cast (doun′ kăst′) ***adj-*** **1** sad; discouraged; dejected: *The team was* downcast *over the loss of the game.* **2** directed downward: *with* downcast *eyes.*

down·draft (doun′drăft′) ***n-*** strong current of air in a downward direction, especially one in the open air due to heat convection or the presence of mountains. Downdrafts affect the flight of airplanes, gliders, birds, etc.

down·fall (doun′ fôl′) ***n-*** **1** sudden fall from power, rank, good standing, or good fortune: *the* downfall *of the government.* **2** a fall of rain, snow, etc.

down·grade (doun′ grād′) ***n-*** a downward slope. ***vt-*** **[down·grad·ed, down·grad·ing]** **1** to put into a lower rank, position, etc.: *to* downgrade *an employee.* **2** to belittle: *to* downgrade *his accomplishments.*

on the downgrade gradually declining; becoming worse: *His health is* on the downgrade.

down·heart·ed (doun′ här′ təd) ***adj-*** sad; unhappy; downcast. **—*adv-* down′ heart′ ed·ly.**

down·hill (doun′ hĭl′) ***adv-*** down a slope; downward: *He went* downhill *on his sled. His health has been going* downhill *for some time.* ***adj-***: *a* downhill *ride.*

Down·ing Street (dou′ nĭng) ***n-*** short street in London, on which the principal government buildings are located; hence, the British government or cabinet.

down·pour (doun′ pôr′) ***n-*** heavy fall of rain.

down·right (doun′ rīt′) ***adj-*** **1** complete; thorough: *That's* downright *nonsense!* **2** straightforward; plain; blunt: *an honest and* downright *man*; *a* downright *answer.* ***adv-*** completely; utterly: *That's* downright *silly!*

down·stairs (doun′ stârz) ***adv-*** on, to, or toward a lower floor or the foot of a staircase: *He ran* downstairs. *Meet me* downstairs. ***n-*** the lower floor of a house: *She has the whole* downstairs. ***adj-***: *a* downstairs *room.*

down·stream (doun′ strēm′) ***adv-*** in the direction of the current or flow of the stream: *We waded* downstream. ***adj-***: *a* downstream *position.*

down·town (doun′ toun′) ***adv-*** in or toward the business center or lower part of a city: *Let's go* downtown. ***adj-***: *a* downtown *office*; downtown *traffic.*

down·trod·den (doun′ trŏd′ ən) ***adj-*** kept in poverty, bondage, etc.; oppressed: *a* downtrodden *nation.*

down under *Informal* ***adv-*** in or from Australia or New Zealand. ***n-*** Australia or New Zealand.

down·ward (doun′ wərd) ***adj-*** moving from a higher to a lower level: *the* downward *flight of a bird.* ***adv-*** (also **down′ wards**) **1** from a higher to a lower level or condition: *The kite* glided *downward.* **2** from an earlier time: *a custom handed* downward *through the ages.*

down·y (dou′ nē) ***adj-*** **[down·i·er, down·i·est]** made of, covered with, or resembling fine, soft, feathers; soft, fluffy, or fuzzy. **—*n-* down′ i·ness.**

dow·ry (dou′ rē) ***n-*** [*pl.* **dow·ries**] money or property a woman brings to her husband at marriage.

dowse (douz) ***vi-*** **[dowsed, dows·ing]** to attempt to find (water or minerals) with a divining rod. **—*n-* dows′ er.**

dox·ol·o·gy (dŏk sŏl′ ə jē) ***n-*** [*pl.* **dox·ol·o·gies**] any of several short hymns or verses in praise of God.

doz. dozen.

doze (dōz) ***vi-*** **[dozed, doz·ing]** to sleep lightly: *Father* dozed *in his chair.* ***n-*** a light sleep; nap.

doze off to begin to fall asleep.

doz·en (dŭz′ ən) ***n-*** **1** [*pl.* **doz·en**] set of twelve: *Give me a* dozen *of those brown eggs. I want three* dozen *of the red roses.* **2 dozens** *Informal* a large number: *I have* dozens *of reasons. as* ***determiner*** (always preceded by another determiner): *There are a* dozen *boxes here and two* dozen *there.*

doz·enth (dŭz′ ənth) ***adj-*** twelfth.

DP displaced person.

dpt. department.

D.P.W. Department of Public Works.

dr. dram or drams.

Dr. **1** Doctor. **2** Drive.

drab (drăb) ***adj-*** **[drab·ber, drab·best]** **1** dull; cheerless; monotonous: *a* drab *existence.* **2** having a dull, grayish brown color: *wispy,* drab *hair.* ***n-*** **1** dull, grayish brown color. 2 thick woolen cloth of this color. *—adv-* **drab′ly.** ***n-*** **drab′ness.**

drach·ma (drăk′ mə) ***n-*** [*pl.* **drach·mas** or **drach·mae** (-mē)] 1 in ancient Greece, a coin; also, a small unit of weight. 2 standard monetary unit of Greece. 3 one of several modern weights, such as the dram.

draft or **draught** (drăft) ***n-*** 1 sketch, outline, or version of something: *the first* draft *of a speech.* 2 written order for the payment or drawing out of money: *a bank* draft. 3 method of selecting men for compulsory military service; conscription. 4 group of men so selected. 5 stream of air: *to feel a* draft *around the shoulders.* 6 device for controlling the air stream in a stove, furnace, etc. 7 line drawing or plan, as for an engine or building. 8 the pulling of a load by beasts: *to use oxen for* draft. 9 depth of a floating ship's bottom beneath the surface of the water, especially when the ship is loaded. 10 (usually **draught**) the hauling in of a net of fish; also, a catch of fish. 11 (usually **draught**) a drink: *a* draught *of water.* ***adj-*** 1 used for pulling loads: *a team of* draft *horses.* 2 (usually **draught**) drawn from a keg: *cold* draught *beer.* ***vt-*** 1 to write or draw the outlines or plan of. 2 to select for some special purpose: *to* draft *men into the army.*

draft·ee (drăf tē′) ***n-*** person who has been drafted for military service; conscript.

drafts·man (drăfts′ mən) ***n-*** [*pl.* **drafts·men**] one who draws mechanical drawings, building plans, etc. Also, *chiefly Brit.,* **draughts′man.** *—n-* **drafts′man·ship.**

draft·y (drăf′ tē) ***adj-*** [**draft·i·er, draft·i·est**] exposed to or admitting currents of air: *a* drafty *place*; *a* drafty *room.* Also, *chiefly Brit.,* **draugh′ty.** *—n-* **draft′i·ness.**

drag (drăg) ***vt-*** [**dragged, drag·ging**] 1 to draw along by force; haul. 2 to search the bottom of with a grapnel or similar device: *They* dragged *the lake for the sunken motor.* 3 to harrow (a field). ***vi-*** 1 to trail along the ground: *Her skirt* dragged. 2 to move or go too slowly: *The speech* dragged. ***n-*** 1 device for searching the bottom of a river or lake. 2 sledge for hauling loads. 3 harrow for breaking up soil. 4 anything that hinders or slows down. 5 *Slang* influence; pull. 6 *Physics* combination of forces such as friction and turbulence that retard the motion of an object (such as a plane or missile) through a fluid.

drag (one's) feet to fail to act promptly.

drag·gle (drăg′ əl) ***vi-*** [**drag·gled, drag·gling**] to become wet or soiled by trailing in the mud or along damp ground: *The clothes* draggled *in the wet grass.* ***vt-*** to wet or soil by dragging on the ground.

Dragon

drag·net (drăg′ nĕt′) ***n-*** 1 a net drawn along a river or sea bottom to catch fish, or along the ground to catch small game. 2 police hunt in which every resource is used.

drag·on (drăg′ ən) ***n-*** imaginary animal, usually thought of as a large, winged reptile that breathes fire and has terrible fangs and claws.

drag·on·fly (drăg′ ən flī′) ***n-*** [*pl.* **drag·on·flies**] slender insect with four gauzy wings and a long green, blue, or brown body, usually found near water; darning needle.

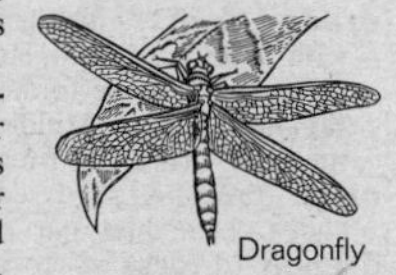
Dragonfly

dra·goon (drə gōōn′) ***n-*** heavily armed mounted soldier; cavalryman. ***vt-*** to force; coerce: *They* dragooned *him into doing slave labor.*

drain (drān) ***vt-*** 1 to draw off (a liquid) gradually: *to* drain *water from a reservoir.* 2 to make empty: *to* drain *the bathtub.* 3 to use up; exhaust: *The operation* drained *the doctor's energy.* ***vi-*** 1 to discharge a liquid: *The street* drains *into the sewer.* 2 to become dry or empty: *She left the dishes to* drain. ***n-*** 1 channel, pipe, sewer, etc., for carrying away unwanted liquids. 2 a continuous demand: *a* drain *on one's time.*

drain·age (drā′ nĭj) ***n-*** 1 a drawing or flowing off, especially of water or waste: *the* drainage *of a piece of land.* 2 system of pipes for drawing off water. 3 material that drains away. *as* ***modifier***: *a* drainage *canal.*

drain·pipe (drān′ pīp′) ***n-*** pipe for drainage.

drake (drāk) ***n-*** male duck.

dram (drăm) ***n-*** 1 one eighth of an ounce in apothecaries' weight, or one sixteenth of an ounce in avoirdupois weight. 2 small drink of alcoholic liquor.

dra·ma (drăm′ ə, drä′ mə) ***n-*** 1 a work in prose or verse, intended for acting on a stage; play. 2 field of dramatic art or literature: *a student of* drama; *Greek* drama. 3 any series of events leading to a climax: *the* drama *of a murder trial.* 4 dramatic or striking quality or effect: *the* drama *of the pounding waves.*

dra·mat·ic (drə măt′ ĭk) ***adj-*** 1 having to do with plays or the study of plays. 2 having the exciting quality of a play: *the* dramatic *events of the Civil War.* 3 striking; vivid; theatrical: *a* dramatic *skyline*; *a* dramatic *costume*; *a* dramatic *gesture.* *—adv-* **dra·mat′i·cal·ly.**

dra·ma·tics (drə măt′ ĭks) ***n-*** 1 (takes singular verb) the art of performing or producing plays. 2 exaggerated or theatrical behavior.

dram·a·tis per·so·nae (drăm′ ə təs pər sō′ nē) *Latin* the characters in a play.

dram·a·tist (drăm′ ə tĭst) ***n-*** person who writes plays; playwright.

dram·a·tize (drăm′ ə tīz′) ***vt-*** [**dram·a·tized, dram·a·tiz·ing**] 1 to make into a play: *to* dramatize *a novel.* 2 to make (a report, story, etc.) dramatic, vivid, or spectacular: *The newspaper* dramatized *the wedding.* *—n-* **dram′a·ti·za′tion.**

drank (drăngk) *p.t.* of **drink.**

drape (drāp) ***vt-*** [**draped, drap·ing**] 1 to cover or adorn gracefully with, or as if with, cloth: *to* drape *a window*; *to* drape *a statue.* 2 to arrange in folds: *to* drape *the skirt of a dress.* 3 to spread or sprawl casually: *He* draped *himself across the chair.* ***vi-*** to hang softly and gracefully: *Silk jersey* drapes *well.* ***n-*** 1 a window drapery. 2 way in which something hangs: *The* drape *of the dress was faulty.*

drap·er (drā′ pər) ***n-*** dealer in cloth or clothing.

dra·per·y (drā′ pə rē) ***n-*** [*pl.* **dra·per·ies**] 1 artistic arrangement of a fabric or garment so that it falls in loose, graceful folds. 2 material hung in this fashion.

dras·tic (drăs′ tĭk) ***adj-*** very forceful; having a powerful effect: *to take* drastic *measures.* *—adv-* **dras′ti·cal·ly.**

draught (drăft) draft.

on draught from a barrel or cask: *beer* on draught.

draughts (drăfts) *Brit.* ***n-*** (takes singular verb) the game of checkers.

draughts·man (drăfts′ mən) draftsman.

draught·y (drăf′ tē) drafty.

Dra·vid·i·an (drə vĭd′ ē ən) ***n-*** 1 member of a people of southern India that has lived in the region since very

---

fāte, făt, dâre, bärn; bē, bĕt, mêre; bīte, bĭt; nōte, hŏt, môre, dòg; fŭn, fûr; tōō, bŏŏk; oil; out; tar; thin; then; hw for wh as in *wh*at; zh for s as in u*s*ual; ə for a, e, i, o, u, as in *a*go, lin*e*n, per*i*l, at*o*m, min*u*s

ancient times. 2 group of related languages of southern India, Ceylon, and West Pakistan. ***adj-***: *a* Dravidian *custom.*

draw (drȯ) ***vt-*** **[drew** (drōō), **drawn, draw·ing]** (in senses 1, 2, 4, 6, 10, and 15, considered intransitive when the object is implied but not expressed) **1** to pull or drag: *to* draw *a cart.* **2** to pull out; haul up: *to* draw *water from a well.* **3** to steer or lead in some direction: *I* drew *him aside.* **4** to attract: *The game* drew *a crowd.* **5** to arouse: *to* draw *criticism*; *to* draw *applause.* **6** to extract; bring out: *to* draw *a cork*; *to* draw *a gun.* **7** to take out: *to* draw *money from a bank*; *to* draw *facts from a book.* **8** to get; gain; win: *to* draw *a salary*; *to* draw *interest*; *to* draw *a prize.* **9** to reach by reasoning: to draw *a conclusion.* **10** to form (a picture, likeness, or diagram) with pen or pencil, chalk, etc. **11** to write out in suitable form: *to* draw *a will.* **12** to close: *to* draw *the curtains.* **13** to inhale: *to* draw *fresh air into the lungs.* **14** to cause to come forth: *to* draw *blood*; *to* draw *bath water.* **15** to cause to shrink; pucker, or contract: *Hot water* draws *wool. The burn* drew *the skin.* **16** to require a certain depth in which to float: *The boat* draws *fifteen feet.* **17** to disembowel: *to* draw *a chicken.* ***vi-*** **1** to approach or recede; move: *Morning* draws *near. He* drew *back suddenly.* **2** to cause or allow a current of air to pass: *The chimney* draws *well.* **3** to contract or pucker: *The astringent made her skin* draw. **4** to take a chance, as in a lottery: *to* draw *for a prize.* ***n-*** **1** act of bringing out and aiming a gun: *The bandit had a fast* draw. **2** a chance or turn to take a playing card, slip, straw, etc., where the outcome depends on chance; also, the thing taken: *That was a lucky* draw. **3** contest left undecided; tie; toss-up. **4** movable section of a drawbridge. **5** gully into which water drains.

draw a blank to be unsuccessful; get no response.

draw away to move ahead: *The horse* drew away *from the others and won the race.*

draw off 1 to withdraw; depart. **2** to drain off.

draw on to make a demand on; use as a source: *to* draw on *one's memory for an answer.*

draw out 1 to prolong: *to* draw out *a speech.* **2** to persuade someone to talk about himself: *to* draw out *a shy new student.*

draw the line to set a limit.

draw up 1 to write in suitable form: *to* draw up *a contract.* **2** to bring or come to a halt: *He* drew up *his horse and dismounted. The carriage* drew up *at the inn.* **3** to straighten up; bring oneself up to full height: *He* drew *himself* up *in indignation as he denied the charge.* **4** to arrange: *The colonel* drew *the regiment* up *in battle order.*

draw·back (drȯ′ bak′) ***n-*** disadvantage; hindrance: *It is a* drawback *not to have binoculars at the races.*

draw·bar (drȯ′ bär′) ***n-*** bar used to couple railroad cars, or for hitching implements to a tractor.

draw·bridge (drȯ′ brĭj′) ***n-*** bridge that can be raised or turned to prevent someone from crossing it or to permit boats to pass.

Medieval drawbridge

[1]**draw·er** (drȯ′ ər) ***n-*** person who draws.

[2]**draw·er** (drȯr) ***n-*** box (with handles) that slides in and out of a bureau, table, etc.

draw·ers (drȯrz) ***n-*** (takes plural verb) undergarment for the lower part of the body.

draw·ing (drȯ′ ĭng) ***n-*** **1** a dragging or pulling of something: *the* drawing *of a load*; *the* drawing *of a gun.* **2** picture or sketch made with pen, pencil, chalk, etc. **3** the art of making such a picture. **4** a picking of slips, tickets, etc., at a lottery.

drawing room ***n-*** room for receiving and entertaining guests; living room or parlor.

drawl (drȯl) ***vt-*** to utter in a leisurely, drawn-out way: *He* drawled *a reply.* ***n-***: *He has a Texas* drawl.

drawn (drȯn) *p.p.* of **draw.** ***adj-*** twisted out of shape; haggard: *a face* drawn *with pain.*

drawn butter ***n-*** melted butter, used as a sauce for shellfish, vegetables, etc.

draw·string (drȯ′ strĭng′) ***n-*** cord or tape threaded through a hem, casing or eyelets and used to close or tighten an opening.

dray (drā) ***n-*** low, strong cart without sides, for carrying heavy loads. ***vt-*** to transport by such a cart.

dray·man (drā′ mən) ***n-*** [*pl.* **dray·men**] person whose work is draying.

dread (drĕd) ***vt-*** to look forward to with fear: *He* dreads *going to the dentist.* ***n-*** fear, especially of harm to come: *his* dread *of storms.* ***adj-*** causing fear, terror, or awe: *a* dread *ruler*; dread *omens.*

dread·ful (drĕd′ fəl) ***adj-*** **1** terrible; causing fear or awe: *a* dreadful *hurricane.* **2** very bad; unpleasant: *a* dreadful *error.* **—*adv-* dread′ ful·ly.** ***n-*** **dread′ ful·ness.**

dread·nought or **dread·naught** (drĕd′ nȯt′) ***n-*** large battleship heavily armed with big guns.

dream (drēm) ***n-*** **1** thoughts, emotions, or pictures experienced or seen during sleep. **2** something fancied while awake; daydream. **3** state of mind during which a person fancies; reverie: *He mowed the grass in a* dream. **4** something more perfect than could be hoped for: *a* dream *of a day.* **5** goal; hope: *His* dream *is to buy an island.* ***vi-*** **[dreamed** or **dreamt** (drĕmt), **dream·ing] 1** to have ideas or mental images during sleep: *She* dreamed *all night.* **2** to think hopefully and habitually (of) something one desires keenly: *He* dreamed *of glory.* **3** to have idle fancies while awake: *He* dreamed *as he mowed the lawn.* ***vt-***: *Did you* dream *anything?* **—*n-* dream′ er.**

dream·land (drēm′ lănd′) ***n-*** land seen in dreams; hence, a land of fancy or world of dreams.

dream·y (drē′ mē) ***adj-*** **[dream·i·er, dream·i·est] 1** like a dream; dim; vague: *a* dreamy *recollection.* **2** likely to daydream often; impractical: *a* dreamy *person.* **3** *Informal* like something in a dream; charming: *a* dreamy *tune.* **—*adv-* dream′ i·ly.** ***n-*** **dream′ i·ness.**

drear (drêr) *Archaic* ***adj-*** dreary.

drear·y (drêr′ ē) ***adj-*** **[drear·i·er, drear·i·est]** gloomy; cheerless; causing low spirits: *a* dreary *day.* **—*adv-* drear′ i·ly.** ***n-*** **drear′ i·ness.**

[1]**dredge** (drĕj) ***n-*** **1** ship or barge equipped with machinery to deepen ship channels, clean harbors, etc. **2** device with a net, used for gathering shellfish. ***vt-*** **[dredged, dredg·ing]**: *The city will* dredge *the river.* [from early Dutch **dregghe** or **dregge.**] **—*n-* dredg′ er.**

Dredge

[2]**dredge** (drĕj) ***vt-*** **[dredged, dredg·ing]** to sprinkle (food) with flour, corn meal, etc. ***n-*** (also **dredg′ er**) small container with a perforated lid used for this; shaker. [apparently from Middle English **drage** meaning "grain mixture," from Old French **dragie.**]

dregs (drĕgz) ***n-*** *pl.* **1** sediment of a liquid: *the* dregs *of coffee.* **2** worthless part of anything: *the* dregs *of society.*

drench (drĕnch) ***vt-*** to soak; to wet thoroughly: *The heavy rain* drenched *the earth.*

Dres·den (drĕz′ dən) ***n-*** fine porcelain manufactured in Dresden, Germany. Also **Dresden china.**

dress (drĕs) ***vt-* 1** to clothe: *to* dress *a child.* **2** to deck out: *to* dress *a window.* **3** to make ready for use: *to* dress *a chicken*; *to* dress *a wooden beam.* **4** to treat or bind up: *to* dress *a wound.* **5** to arrange (hair); also, to curry (a horse). **6** to straighten (a line of soldiers) in military drill. ***vi-* 1** to put on clothes. **2** to put on formal clothes: *to* dress *for a reception.* **3** to select and wear clothes: *She* dresses *well.* **4** in drilling, to form into a straight line: "*Right,* dress!" ***n-* 1** clothes; attire; apparel. **2** outer garment worn by a woman, girl, or small child. **3** any outer garb or appearance: *trees in autumn* dress. ***adj-* 1** relating to women's clothing: *a* dress *pattern.* **2** designed for formal or ceremonial wear: *his* dress *shoes*; dress *uniform.* **3** requiring formal wear: *a* dress *occasion.*

dress down to scold severely.

dress up to put on one's best clothes.

dres·sage (drĕ säzh′) ***n-*** art of directing a horse through changes of pace and gait for exhibition purposes, by barely noticeable hand, leg, and weight-shifting movements of the rider.

[1]**dress·er** (drĕs′ ər) ***n-* 1** chest of drawers or bureau, often with a mirror. **2** cupboard for dishes, glasses, etc. [from Old French **dresseur,** from Old French **dresser** meaning "make straight; arrange; dress."]

[2]**dress·er** (drĕs′ ər) ***n-* 1** person who assists another to dress; a valet: *He is a* dresser *in a theater.* **2** person who dresses something: *a* dresser *of leather*; *a* dresser *of wounds*; *a window* dresser. **3** person who dresses in a certain way: *He is a flashy* dresser. [from **dress.**]

dress·ing (drĕs′ ĭng) ***n-* 1** act of putting on clothes, treating a wound, etc. **2** substance for stiffening fabrics. **3** bandage and medicine for a wound. **4** sauce for a salad. **5** stuffing for a roast fowl, fish, etc.

dress·ing-down (drĕs′ ĭng doun′) ***n-*** a severe scolding.

dressing gown ***n-*** loose robe worn while dressing or lounging.

dressing station ***n-*** battlefield station set up to give medical aid to the wounded.

dress·mak·ing (drĕs′ mā′ kĭng) ***n-*** the craft of making dresses for women. **—*n-* dress′mak′ er.**

dress rehearsal ***n-*** final rehearsal of a play or other performance, in costume and with all the sound and lighting effects to be used in actual performance.

dress·y (drĕs′ ē) ***adj-*** **[dress·i·er, dress·i·est] 1** given to smart and stylish dressing: *a* dressy *actor.* **2** stylish; smart: *a* dressy *social event.* **—*n-* dress′ i·ness.**

drew (drōō) *p.t.* of **draw.**

drib·ble (drĭb′ əl) ***vi-*** **[drib·bled, drib·bling] 1** to fall or let fall in drops; trickle: *Water is* dribbling *from the leaky faucet.* **2** to drip saliva from the mouth; to drool: *A baby* dribbles *when it's teething.* **3** to move a ball by a series of bounces or kicks, as in basketball or soccer. ***vt-*:** *The faucet* dribbled *hot water. The baby* dribbled *saliva. Joe* dribbled *the ball.* **—*n-* drib′ bler.**

drib·let (drĭb′ lət) ***n-*** small amount; bit.

dried (drīd) *p.t. & p.p.* of **dry.** ***adj-*** with the moisture removed: *sweet* dried *prunes.*

dri·er or **dry·er** (drī′ ər) ***n-* 1** person or thing that removes moisture. **2** (usually **dryer**) machine that removes water by the use of heat or air; especially, an appliance that dries laundry. **3** substance added to paint or varnish to make it dry more quickly.

dri·er (drī′ ər) *compar.* of **dry.**

dries form of the verb **dry** used with "he," "she," "it," or a singular noun subject, in the present tense.

dri·est (drī′ əst) *superl.* of **dry.**

drift (drĭft) ***n-* 1** slow movement caused by air or water currents; also, the direction or rate of movement: *the* drift *of an iceberg.* **2** very slow ocean current: *the North Atlantic* Drift. **3** something driven along, drawn together, or piled up, as by wind or water: *a smoke* drift; *snow* drift. **4** direction in which anything is driven; tendency; meaning: *the* drift *of a speech.* **5** distance a ship, airplane, missile, etc., is carried from its course by ocean or air currents. **6** in geology, loose rocks, earth, etc., carried by a glacier. ***vi-* 1** to be carried along aimlessly by or as if by a current or by circumstances: *The clouds* drifted. *His thoughts* drifted. *He* drifted *through life.* **2** to gather or collect in heaps: *The snow* drifted *against the barn.* ***vt-*:** *The wind* drifted *the snow.*

drift·er (drĭf′ tər) ***n-*** person who moves aimlessly from one job or place to another.

drift·wood (drĭft′ wŏŏd′) ***n-*** wood washed ashore by the waves and tide.

[1]**drill** (drĭl) ***n-* 1** tool for boring holes in wood, metal, or other hard substances. **2** drill press. **3** mollusk which feeds on oysters by piercing their shells with holes. **4** military exercises, especially the prescribed ways of marching, turning, forming ranks, etc. **5** thorough training by frequent repetition: *to teach arithmetic by* drill. ***vt-* 1** to pierce or bore with a tool designed for the purpose. **2** to train in or put through military exercises. **3** to instruct by frequent repetition. ***vi-*:** *The pupils* drilled *on arithmetic. The platoon has* drilled *all day.* [from Dutch **dril.**]

Drill

[2]**drill** (drĭl) ***n-* 1** machine for making furrows and planting seeds. **2** furrow in which the seeds are sown. ***vt-*** to sow in rows: *to* drill *corn.* [of uncertain origin.]

[3]**drill** (drĭl) ***n-*** strong cotton cloth with a twill weave. [from earlier **drilling,** from German **drillich,** from Latin **trilix** meaning literally "three-threaded."]

[4]**drill** (drĭl) ***n-*** West African baboon closely related to the mandrill but smaller. [perhaps from an African language.]

drill·mas·ter (drĭl′ măs′ tər) ***n-*** person who trains or teaches by drilling, as in military exercises.

drill press ***n-*** drilling machine in which the tool is pressed down on the work, usually with a hand lever.

dri·ly (drī′ lē) dryly.

drink (drĭngk) ***vt-*** **[drank** (drăngk), **drunk** (drŭngk), **drink·ing] 1** to take in or absorb (a liquid): *I* drink *milk. Plants* drink *water.* **2** to participate in (a toast): *We* drink *a toast to your health.* ***vi-* 1** to swallow a liquid. **2** to take alcoholic liquors habitually. **3** to take part in a toast (to) some person, event, etc.: *We* drink *to your health.* ***n-* 1** a liquid to be swallowed; beverage: *a soft* drink. **2** a quantity of liquid swallowed: *to have a* drink *of water.* **3** excessive use of liquor: *It drove him to* drink. **—*adj-* drink′ a·ble. *n-* drink′ er.**

drip (drĭp) ***vi-*** **[dripped, drip·ping]** to fall in drops: *Rain* dripped *from the roof.* ***vt-*** (considered intransitive when the direct object is implied but not expressed) to let fall in drops: *The roof* dripped *rain. The spigot* drips. ***n-* 1** a falling of a liquid in drops; also, the drops themselves: *a steady* drip *from the roof.* **2** a projecting part, as in a window sill, shaped to throw off rain.

drip-dry (drĭp′ drī′) ***adj-*** made of certain synthetic fibers or of treated cotton, and drying without wrinkles if hung without wringing. ***vt-*** **[drip-dried, drip-dry·ing]** to dry by hanging without wringing.

drip·pings (drĭp′ ĭngz) ***n-*** *pl.* juice from roasting meat.

drive (drīv) ***vt-*** [**drove** (drōv), **driven** (drĭv′ ən), **driving**] **1** to urge forward; make move: *to* drive *cattle.* **2** to put in motion and guide; steer; also, to carry in a vehicle: *to* drive *a car*; *to* drive *a friend home.* **3** to move by hitting: *to* drive *a golf ball*; *to* drive *a nail.* **4** to make by digging: *to* drive *a well.* **5** to set or keep in motion: *Steam* drives *the engine.* **6** to urge along by force; overwork: *He* drives *his employees.* **7** to carry through forcefully; conclude: *to* drive *a bargain.* **8** to force into a particular state or action: *The noise* drives *me mad. Ambition* drove *him to run for office.* ***vi-*** **1** to press, aim, or be moved forward steadily or with violence: *The waves* drove *toward the shore.* **2** to travel in a carriage or motor car. **3** in golf, to strike the ball from a tee. ***n-*** **1** swift hard blow or hit: *a* drive *to left field.* **2** trip in an automobile or carriage: *a Sunday* drive. **3** road for vehicles: *a winding* drive *to the house.* **4** effort to carry out some purpose; campaign: *a clothing* drive. **5** forceful effort; energy: *a man of* drive *and ambition.* **6** a gathering together, or rounding up, as of cattle for branding, logs for floating, etc. **7** mechanism that sets something in motion or transmits motion: *an electric* drive *for a telescope*; *chain* drive *on a truck.*

drive at to mean; intend: *What is he* driving at?

drive-in (drīv′ ĭn′) ***n-*** restaurant, outdoor theater, etc., where customers can remain in their cars. *as* ***modifier:*** *a* drive-in *bank.*

driv·el (drĭv′ əl) ***vi-*** **1** to let saliva drip from the mouth; slobber. **2** to talk like a fool. ***n-*** **1** saliva flowing from the mouth. **2** idiotic talk. **—*n-* driv′ el·er.**

driv·er (drī′ vər) ***n-*1** person who drives a vehicle, animals, logs, etc. **2** a golf club with a wooden head for striking the ball from a tee. **3** the part of a machine that transmits power.

driver ant ***n-*** any of various African or South American stinging ants that travel in large groups devouring insects and small animals in their path.

drive shaft ***n-*** shaft in a machine or an automobile that transmits mechanical power from one part to another, especially from the engine to a working part such as a wheel.

drive·way (drīv′ wā′) ***n-*** private road leading from a garage, house, or other building to the street.

driz·zle (drĭz′ əl) ***vi-*** [**driz·zled, driz·zling**] to rain slightly or mistily. ***n-*** fine, misty rain.

driz·zly (drĭz′ lē) ***adj-*** raining slightly and continuously.

drogue (drōg) ***n-*** **1** sea anchor. **2** (also **drogue chute**) small parachute used to make a space capsule or other craft more stable, or to slow it down.

droll (drōl) ***adj-*** amusing and strange; quaint; odd: *The men told* droll *stories.* **—*adv-* drol′ ly.** ***n-*** **droll′ ness.**

droll·er·y (drō′ lə rē) ***n-*** [*pl.* **droll·er·ies**] dry or quaint humor; jesting; also, a quaint story.

drom·e·dar·y (drŏm′ ə dĕr′ ē) [*pl.* **drom·e·dar·ies**] See *camel.*

Dromedary, 7 ft. high

¹drone (drōn) ***vi-*** [**droned, dron·ing**] **1** to make a dull, monotonous sound; hum: *The airplanes* droned *overhead.* **2** to speak or read in a monotonous tone: *A few people fell asleep as the speaker* droned *on.* ***vt-:*** *He always* drones *his speeches.* ***n-*** **1** monotonous tone; humming: *the* drone *of mosquitoes.* **2** pipe of a bagpipe that sounds a sustained bass tone. [of uncertain origin, perhaps from **²drone.**]

²drone (drōn) ***n-*** **1** the male of the honeybee, which produces no honey and does no work. **2** lazy person who will not do his share of the work. **3** radio-controlled airplane or boat without a pilot, used as a target for gunnery or missiles. [from Old English **dran.**]

drool (dro͞ol) ***vi-*** **1** to let saliva dribble from the mouth, as a hungry animal at the sight of food.

droop (dro͞op) ***vi-*** **1** to sink, bend, or hang down: *The flowers are* drooping *with the heat.* **2** to weaken; languish: *His spirits* drooped. ***vt-*** to let sink or hang down: *to* droop *the head.* ***n-:*** *a* droop *in a hem*; *a* droop *of the head.* **—*adv-* droop′ ing·ly:** *The stalks grew* droopingly.

droop·y (dro͞o′ pē) ***adj-*** [**droop·i·er, droop·i·est**] **1** drooping or tending to droop: *a* droopy *skirt.* **2** low in spirits: *a* droopy *manner.* **—*adv-* droop′ i·ly.** ***n-*** **droop′ i·ness.**

drop (drŏp) ***vi-*** [**dropped, drop·ping**] **1** to fall to a lower position, rank, degree, price, etc.: *The sun* dropped *out of sight. He* dropped *to fifth place. Prices* dropped. **2** to grow lower in sound or pitch: *Her voice* dropped *to a whisper.* **3** to cease or end: *There the matter* dropped. **4** to become less; slacken: *Book sales* dropped. ***vt-*** **1** to let fall in tiny masses: *to* drop *medicine from a spoon.* **2** to let fall: *to* drop *a book.* **3** to lower: *to* drop *the eyes*; *to* drop *a blind.* **4** to fell with a blow or weapon: *to* drop *a deer.* **5** of animals, to give birth to: *to* drop *a calf.* **6** to have done with; end: *to* drop *an argument.* **7** to send, deliver, or set down: *to* drop *a note*; *to* drop *a passenger.* **8** to utter casually: *to* drop *a suggestion.* **9** to omit: *to* drop *a letter from a word.* **10** to demote to a lower class, or remove from an organization: *to* drop *a student from the football squad.* ***n-*** **1** small rounded mass of liquid: *a* drop *of water.* **2** anything shaped or hanging like a small rounded mass of liquid: *a crystal* drop *on an earring.* **3** any very small quantity: *a* drop *of truth.* **4** sudden descent or fall: *a* drop *in prices.* **5** something arranged to fall or be lowered: *the* drop *in a gallows*; *a curtain* drop. **6** receptacle or slot for mail.

a drop in the bucket tiny portion of what is needed.
let (something) drop to let (a secret, remark, etc.) slip out.
drop behind to fall behind; lag behind; fail to keep up.
drop in, over, or **by** to visit informally.
drop off to fall asleep: *Timmy* dropped off *right away.*
drop out withdraw; quit: *He* dropped out *of the contest.*

drop cloth ***n-*** large cloth spread over floors and furniture to protect them while the room is painted.

drop kick ***n-*** football kick in which the ball is dropped and then kicked just as it rebounds from the ground.

drop·out (drŏp′ out′) ***n-*** person who chooses to leave school or college before graduating, especially one who leaves school when attendance is no longer compulsory.

drop·per (drŏp′ ər) ***n-*** small, thin glass tube with a rubber bulb at one end, used to measure and eject a liquid, such as medicine, in small drops.

drop·pings (drŏp′ ĭngz) ***n-*** *pl.* animal dung.

drop·sy (drŏp′ sē) ***n-*** unnatural collection of watery fluid in cavities or tissues of the body.

dro·soph·i·la (drō sŏf′ ə lə) ***n-*** a common fruit fly, whose species have been used for studies in heredity.

dross (drŏs) ***n-*** **1** the scum or refuse of melted metal; slag. **2** any worthless matter; refuse; waste.

drought (drout) or **drouth** (drouth) ***n-*** continued absence of rain; dryness. **—*adj-* drought′ y** or **drouth′ y.**

¹drove (drōv) *p.t.* of **drive.**

²drove (drōv) ***n-*** **1** herd of animals driven in a group: *a* drove *of oxen.* **2** a crowd of people: *Visitors came to the fair in* droves. [from Old English **drāf** meaning "a drove; a driving," and closely related to **¹drove.**]

dro·ver (drō′ vər) ***n-*** **1** person who drives cattle, sheep, etc., to market. **2** cattle dealer.

drown (droun) ***vi-*** to die from having the breath cut off by water or other liquid. ***vt-*** **1** to kill by keeping under water. **2** to overpower: *Their chatter* drowned *the music.*

drowse (drouz) ***vi-*** **[drowsed, drows·ing]** to be half asleep; doze: *He* drowsed *during class.* ***n-*** a sleepy or half-asleep condition; doze.

drow·sy (drou′ zē) ***adj-*** **[drow·si·er, drow·si·est] 1** sleepy; inclined to sleep: *Everyone felt* drowsy *after the feast.* **2** making one sleepy: *the* drowsy *sound of rain.* **—*adv-* drow′ si·ly.** ***n-*** **drow′ si·ness.**

drub (drŭb) ***vt-*** **[drubbed, drub·bing]** to beat or whip soundly; thrash.

drub·bing (drŭb′ ĭng) ***n-*** severe beating or defeat.

drudge (drŭj) ***n-*** **1** person who does routine, slavish, uninteresting work. **2** person who works hard for small pay. ***vi-*** **[drudged, drudg·ing]** to work hard at disagreeable tasks; slave away.

drudg·er·y (drŭj′ə rē) ***n-*** [*pl.* **drudg·er·ies**] hard, disagreeable, uninteresting work: *a life spent in* drudgery.

drug (drŭg) ***n-*** **1** a medicine or substance used in making medicine. **2** a substance used to lessen pain or cause sleep; especially, a habit-forming narcotic. ***vt-*** **[drugged, drug·ging] 1** to make dull or sleepy with a medicinal substance: *to* drug *a patient before an operation.* **2** to put such a substance in: *to* drug *wine.*

drug·gist (drŭg′ ĭst) ***n-*** **1** pharmacist. **2** person who owns a drugstore.

drug·store (drŭg′ stôr′) ***n-*** store where medicines are sold.

dru·id (dro͞o′ ĭd) ***n-*** Celtic priest of ancient Britain.

drum (drŭm) ***n-*** **1** musical instrument, most often consisting of a hollow cylinder with skin or some other membrane stretched tightly over one or both ends, and played by beating with sticks. **2** anything shaped like this instrument: *an oil* drum. **3** eardrum. ***vi-*** **[drummed, drum·ming] 1** to beat; play percussion instruments. **2** to tap monotonously with the fingers or feet. **3** to make a hollow beating sound by rapidly flapping the wings, as some birds do. ***vt-*** to cause to tap against something rhythmically.

Kettledrum

Snare drum

drum into to teach or convey by repetition.

drum (someone) out to expel in disgrace, especially from a military unit.

drum up to create or enliven: *to* drum up *trade.*

drum·lin (drŭm′ lən) ***n-*** long, low mound of glacial till, rounded at one end and pointed at the other.

drum major ***n-*** leader of a band or drum corps. **—*n-*** *fem.* **drum ma′ jor·ette′** (mā′ jə rĕt′).

drum·mer (drŭm′ ər) ***n-*** **1** person who plays the drum. **2** traveling salesman.

drum·stick (drŭm′ stĭk′) ***n-*** **1** stick for beating a drum. **2** the lower part of the leg of a cooked fowl.

drunk (drŭngk) *p.p.* of **drink.** ***adj-*** overcome by alcohol, or as if by alcohol; intoxicated: *to be* drunk. ***n-*** **1** intoxicated person. **2** drunkard; sot. **3** drinking spree.

drunk·ard (drŭngk′ ərd) ***n-*** person who has the habit of getting drunk; an alcoholic.

drunk·en (drŭngk′ ən) ***adj-*** **1** intoxicated; drunk. **2** caused by intoxication: *a* drunken *rage*; *a* drunken *sleep.* **—*adv-* drunk′ en·ly.** ***n-*** **drunk′ en·ness.**

dry (drī) ***adj-*** **[dri·er, dri·est] 1** not wet or moist: *the* dry *air*; dry *eyes.* **2** having little or no rainfall: *India has a* dry *season and a rainy season.* **3** not under or in water: *They pulled the boat onto* dry *land.* **4** empty of its water supply; drained away: *a* dry *river*; *a* dry *well.* **5** thirsty: *He felt* dry *after working in the sun.* **6** quiet but shrewd: *The joke was made funnier by the* dry *manner in which he told it.* **7** not sweet: *a* dry *wine.* **8** uninteresting; dull: *a* dry *book.* **9** of solid, rather than liquid, substances: *a* dry *measure.* **10** forbidding the sale of intoxicants: *a* dry *city.* ***n-*** person who favors the prohibition of alcoholic beverages. ***vt-*** **[dried, dry·ing]:** *to* dry *dishes.* ***vi-***: *The ink* dried *quickly.* **—*n-* dry′ ness.**

dry·ad (drī′ ăd′) ***n-*** a nymph supposed to live in a tree.

dry cell ***n-*** sealed electric cell in which the opposite poles (negative and positive) are separated by a paste.

dry-clean (drī′ klēn′) ***vt-*** to clean (fabrics) with a solvent such as benzine and not with water.

dry cleaner ***n-*** **1** person who dry-cleans. **2** solvent used for dry-cleaning.

dry-dock (drī′ dŏk′) ***vt-*** to put (a ship) in dry dock.

dry dock ***n-*** artificial basin where ships are repaired or cleaned. The ship is floated in and the water pumped out.

dry·er (drī′ ər) ***n-*** a drier.

dry-farm (drī′ fârm′) ***vi-*** to grow crops by the methods of dry-farming. **—*n-* dry-farmer.**

dry-farm·ing (drī′ fär′ mĭng) ***n-*** the farming of dry land without irrigation, using special methods of conserving soil moisture and raising crops resistant to drought.

dry goods ***n-*** *pl.* textiles and textile products such as clothes and household linens.

Dry Ice ***n-*** trademark name of carbon dioxide gas frozen solid, resembling blocks of snow but passing directly from the solid to the gaseous state. Also **dry ice.**

dry·ly (drī′ lē) ***adv-*** **1** quietly but shrewdly: *to comment* dryly *on events.* **2** dully; uninterestingly. Also **drily.**

dry measure ***n-*** system for measuring solid commodities by volume, in which two pints equal a quart, eight quarts equal a peck, and four pecks equal a bushel.

dry rot ***n-*** **1** decay of seasoned timber, caused by certain fungi. **2** any of various fungous diseases affecting vegetables, especially potatoes; also, the rot caused by such a disease.

dry run ***n-*** practice or rehearsal of a planned event.

dry-shod (drī′ shŏd′) ***adj-*** with shoes kept dry.

D.S.T. or **DST** Daylight Saving Time.

du·al (do͞o′ əl, dyo͞o′-) ***adj-*** having two parts; twofold; double: *a* dual *purpose.* ***Hom-*** duel. **—*adv-* du′ al·ly.**

[1]**dub** (dŭb) ***vt-*** **[dubbed, dub·bing] 1** to make (a man) a knight by touching the shoulder with a sword. **2** to give a title or nickname to: *We* dubbed *him "Silent Sam."* [from Old English **dubbian,** from Old French **adober.**]

[2]**dub** (dŭb) ***vt-*** **[dubbed, dub·bing]** to add new sounds or vary previously recorded sounds on (the sound track of a film or some other recording). [short for **double.**]

[3]**dub** (dŭb) *Informal* ***n-*** awkward fellow. [American word of uncertain origin.]

du·bi·e·ty (do͞o bī′ ə tē, dyo͞o-) ***n-*** [*pl.* **du·bi·e·ties**] **1** condition of being dubious; dubiousness; doubtfulness; uncertainty: *the* dubiety *of his remarks.* **2** something doubtful or uncertain.

du·bi·ous (do͞o′ bē əs, dyo͞o′-) ***adj-*** **1** doubtful; uncertain: *a* dubious *venture* **2** to be mistrusted; questionable: *a* dubious *friend.* **—*adv-* du′ bi·ous·ly.** ***n-*** **du′ bi·ous·ness.**

du·cal (do͞o′ kəl, dyo͞o′-) ***adj-*** of or related to a duke or dukedom: *a* ducal *estate.*

duc·at (dŭk′ət) ***n-*** **1** in earlier times, any of various gold or silver coins used in Europe, especially a coin of Venice. **2** *Slang* ticket of admission.

duch·ess (dŭch′əs) ***n-*** **1** wife or widow of a duke. **2** woman with the rank or authority of a duke.

duch·y (dŭch′ē) ***n-*** [*pl.* **duch·ies**] land governed by or associated with the title of a duke or duchess; dukedom.

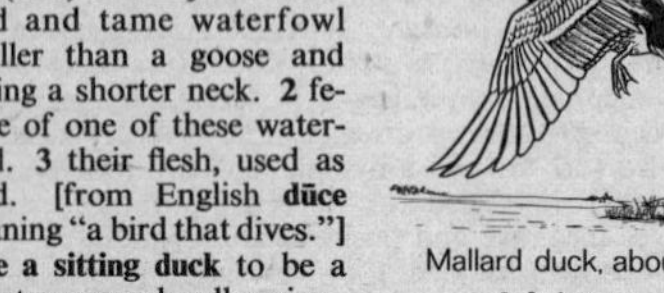
Mallard duck, about 2 ft. long

[1]**duck** (dŭk) ***n-*** **1** any of several wild and tame waterfowl smaller than a goose and having a shorter neck. **2** female of one of these waterfowl. **3** their flesh, used as food. [from English **dūce** meaning "a bird that dives."]

be a sitting duck to be a target one can hardly miss.

[2]**duck** (dŭk) ***vi-*** to move or crouch quickly to avoid being hit: *When the shots were fired, everybody* ducked. ***vt-*** **1** to avoid; evade: *to* duck *a blow*; *to* duck *a question.* **2** to lower or bend (the head, shoulder, etc.) to avoid being hit. **3** to plunge or thrust under water: *The winning team* ducked *their captain.* ***n-*** **1** a brief plunging into water. **2** quick movement made to avoid something: *a* duck *to the right.* [from Old English **douken.**]

[3]**duck** (dŭk) ***n-*** **1** coarse linen or cotton cloth, used for outer clothing, tents, sails, and awnings. **2 ducks** trousers made of this material. [from Dutch **doek,** "cloth."]

duck·bill (dŭk′ bĭl′) ***n-*** **1** beak or implement shaped like the bill of a duck. **2** (also **duck′billed′ platypus**) platypus. **3** paddlefish.

ducking stool ***n-*** in earlier times, a stool used for ducking persons in water as a form of punishment.

duck·ling (dŭk′ lĭng) ***n-*** young duck.

duck·pins (dŭk′pĭnz′) ***n-*** *pl.* **1** (takes singular verb) bowling game similar to tenpins but using smaller balls and pins. **2** pins used in this game.

duck soup *Slang* ***n-*** something that is easy to do.

duck·weed (dŭk′ wēd′) ***n-*** any of various water plants floating on ponds and having no stems or true leaves.

duct (dŭkt) ***n-*** **1** tube or canal for carrying a liquid or gas, especially a tube in the body that carries glandular secretions. **2** pipe through which electric wires or cables are led.

duc·tile (dŭk′ təl) ***adj-*** such as can be drawn out thin without breaking: *Heated glass becomes* ductile *before it melts.* **—*n-* duc′ til′ i·ty** (dŭk′ tĭl′ ə tē).

duct·less gland (dŭkt′ ləs) ***n-*** endocrine gland.

dud (dŭd) ***n-*** **1** bomb or shell that fails to explode when it should. **2** *Slang* person or thing that is a failure.

dude (do͞od) ***n-*** **1** man who is too concerned with his clothing or appearance. **2** in western United States, a tourist, especially one from the East who visits a ranch. [American word, perhaps from **dud up,** "dress up."]

dude ranch ***n-*** ranch at which vacationers ride horseback and play at ranching.

dudg·eon (dŭj′ ən) ***n-*** anger; displeasure.

duds (dŭdz) *Informal* ***n-*** *pl.* clothing.

due (do͞o, dyo͞o) ***adj-*** **1** owed; payable: *a fine is* due *on the library book.* **2** proper or fit; appropriate: *They showed* due *respect to the distinguished visitor.* **3** required or expected to arrive: *The plane is* due *in ten minutes.* ***adv-*** directly; exactly: *The ship traveled* due *north.* ***n-*** **1** that which is owed; that which must be given to another: *Pay the man his* due. **2 dues** fee or charge, as for membership in a club. ***Homs-*** dew, do.

due to owing to; caused by: *The poor harvest was* due to *lack of rain.* **fall due** to become payable: *The bill* falls due *the first of each month.* **in due course** in the natural course of events: *He will decide* in due course.
►Some traditionalists object to the use of DUE TO to introduce adverbial phrases of cause. In the sentence *The game was canceled* due to *rain* they would prefer "because of," "owing to," or "on account of." Nevertheless, many good writers now use DUE TO in this way. Traditionalists have never objected to DUE TO in phrases that modify nouns: *The cancellation was* due to *rain.*

du·el (do͞o′ əl, dyo͞o′-) ***n-*** **1** private fight arranged according to rules between two persons, with swords or pistols, in the presence of witnesses called "seconds." **2** any contest between two opponents: *The rival politicians had a* duel *of words.* ***vt-***: *to* duel *an enemy.* ***vi-***: *to* duel *with swords.* ***Hom-*** dual. **—*n-* du′ el·er.**

du·el·ist (do͞o′ ə lĭst, dyo͞o′-) ***n-*** either person in a duel.

du·en·na (do͞o ĕn′ ə) ***n-*** **1** elderly woman who acts as a guardian to a girl in a Spanish or Portuguese family. **2** a chaperone.

due process of law ***n-*** legal procedure that is sufficient and proper to protect the private rights guaranteed by law. Also **due process.**

du·et (do͞o ĕt′, dyo͞o-) ***n-*** musical composition for two voices or instruments.

duff (dŭf) ***n-*** thick flour pudding boiled in a bag.

duf·fel (dŭf′ əl) ***n-*** **1** coarse woolen fabric with a thick nap. **2** outfit or equipment for camping.

duffel bag ***n-*** large bag, usually of canvas, for carrying clothes and personal equipment.

[1]**dug** (dŭg) *p.t. & p.p.* of **dig.**

[2]**dug** (dŭg) ***n-*** teat or udder. [apparently from an old Scandinavian word similar to Swedish **dagga,** "suckle."]

du·gong (do͞o′ gȯng′) ***n-*** large plant-eating sea mammal having two forelimbs and a paddlelike tail; sea cow.

dug·out (dŭg′ out′) ***n-*** **1** hole dug in a hillside or in the ground and roofed over with logs, sod, etc., to form a shelter. **2** canoe or boat made by hollowing out a tree trunk. **3** in baseball, either of the long, low shelters at the side of the infield for the players.

dui·ker (dī′ kər) ***n-*** small South African antelope. The male has short straight horns. Also **dui′ ker·bok′** (-bŏk′).

duke (do͞ok, dyo͞ok) ***n-*** **1** ruler of a duchy. **2** in Great Britain, a nobleman who ranks next below a prince.

duke·dom (do͞ok′ dəm, dyo͞ok′-) ***n-*** **1** rank or title of a duke. **2** duchy.

dul·cet (dŭl′ sət) ***adj-*** sweet and pleasant to the ear: *her* dulcet *tones.* ***n-*** organ stop of sweet tone.

dul·ci·mer (dŭl′ sə mər) ***n-*** **1** musical instrument with wire strings, played with two light hammers. **2** homemade zither, plucked with the fingers.

Man playing modern dulcimer

dull (dŭl) ***adj-*** **[dull·er, dull·est] 1** not sharp or pointed; blunt: *a* dull *pencil*; *a* dull *razor.* **2** not felt acutely; not intense: *a* dull *pain.* **3** slow to learn or understand: *a* dull *boy*; *a* dull *student.* **4** not interesting: *a* dull *book.* **5** not clear or bright; vague: *a* dull *yellow*; *a* dull *suit*; *a* dull *sound.* **6** not lively: *a* dull *party*; *a* dull *look.* **7** not active: *Business is* dull *this summer.* ***vt-***: *to* dull *the pain*; *to* dull *the blade.* **—*adv-* dul′ ly. *n-* dull′ness.**

dull·ard (dŭl′ ərd) ***n-*** stupid or slow-witted person.

dulse (dŭls) ***n-*** a coarse red seaweed, sometimes eaten as a relish or spice.

du·ly (do͞o′ lē, dyo͞o′-) ***adv***- in a suitable and proper way; at the proper time and place: *He was* duly *sworn in.*

dumb (dŭm) ***adj***- [**dumb·er, dumb·est**] **1** unable to speak; mute: *a deaf and* dumb *person*; *our* dumb *animal friends.* **2** not speaking; silent: *He remained* dumb *with grief.* **3** *Informal* stupid. **—*adv*- dumb′ ly. *n*- dumb′ ness.**

dumb·bell (dŭm′ bĕl′) ***n***- **1** exercising device consisting of two wooden or metal balls connected by a bar. **2** *Slang* stupid person.

dumb·found or **dum·found** (dŭm′found′) ***vt***- to make speechless with surprise, fear, etc.; amaze.

dumb show ***n***- gestures that express meaning without sounds; pantomime.

dumb-wait·er (dŭm′ wā′ tər) ***n***- small elevator for conveying dishes, garbage, etc., from floor to floor.

dum·dum bullet (dŭm′ dŭm′) ***n***- bullet with a soft nose or with its jacket stripped back so that the lead beneath will spread on hitting.

dum·my (dŭm′ ē) ***n***- [*pl.* **dum·mies**] **1** copy or imitation, especially of the human figure, made to resemble or work like the real object: *a ventriloquist's* dummy; *a football* dummy; *a wooden* dummy *of a rifle.* **2** *Slang* stupid or thick-witted person. **3** in bridge, a person whose cards are laid on the table and played by his partner. **4** model of a page or book to be printed. *as* ***modifier***: *a* dummy *door on a stage.*

dump (dŭmp) ***vt***- **1** to let fall or throw away in a mass; unload: *to* dump *sand from a truck.* **2** to put up (goods, stock, etc.) for sale in large amounts and below the market price. ***n***- **1** a place where trash may be thrown out: *the city* dump. **2** a place where military supplies are kept: *an ammunition* dump.

dump·ling (dŭmp′ lĭng) ***n***- **1** dough boiled or steamed and served with meat: *stew with* dumplings. **2** shell of dough wrapped around a piece of fruit which is then boiled or baked: *apple* dumplings.

dumps (dŭmps) **down in the dumps** gloomy; low in spirits; depressed.

dump·y (dŭm′ pē) ***adj***- [**dump·i·er, dump·i·est**] short and stout; squat. **—*adv*- dump′ i·ly. *n*- dump′ i·ness.**

1**dun** (dŭn) ***adj***- dull grayish brown. [from Old English **dunn,** apparently from Celtic.] ***Hom***- done.

2**dun** (dŭn) ***n***- **1** repeated demand for the payment of a debt. **2** person who continually demands the payment of a debt. ***vt***- [**dunned, dun·ning**]: *The restaurant* dunned *him for the bill.* [a form of **din.**] ***Hom***- done.

dunce (dŭns) ***n***- **1** stupid person. **2** backward pupil.

dunce cap ***n***- in earlier times, a cone-shaped paper cap put on the head of a slow or lazy pupil. Also **dunce's cap.**

dun·der·head (dŭn′ dər hĕd′) ***n***- stupid or dull person; blockhead. **—*adj*- dun′ der·head′ ed.**

dune (do͞on, dyo͞on) ***n***- low sand hill formed by the wind, especially near a shore.

dung (dŭng) ***n***- excrement from animals; manure.

dun·ga·ree (dŭng′ gə rē′) ***n***- **1** coarse, durable cotton material; denim. **2 dungarees** trousers or work clothes made from this material; jeans.

Dunes

dung beetle ***n***- any of various beetles that breed in and feed upon dung.

dun·geon (dŭn′ jən) ***n***- dark, underground prison. ***Hom***- donjon.

dung·hill (dŭng′ hĭl′) ***n***- heap of manure.

dunk (dŭngk) ***vt***- to dip (a doughnut, bread, etc.) into a liquid, such as coffee; sop. ***vi***-: *to* dunk *daintily.* [American word from German **dunken,** "to dip."]

dun·nage (dŭn′ ĭj) ***n***- **1** any loose, bulky material placed around or under ship's cargo to prevent damage. **2** baggage or personal belongings.

du·o (do͞o′ ō) ***n***- [*pl.* **du·os**] **1** duet. **2** *Informal* pair; couple.

du·o·dec·i·mal (do͞o′ ə dĕs′ ə məl) ***adj***- having to do with or based on the number twelve.

duodecimal number system ***n***- system of numerals having the number twelve as its base.

du·o·de·num (do͞o′ ə dē′ nəm, do͞o ŏd′ ə nəm) ***n***- [*pl.* **du·o·de·na**] the first part of the small intestine, just below the stomach. For picture, see *intestine.* **—*adj*- du′ o·de′ nal** or **du·o′ de·nal:** *a* duodenal *ulcer.*

dupe (do͞op, dyo͞op) ***n***- person who is easily tricked or believes everything he is told. ***vt***- [**duped, dup·ing**] to deceive by tricking: *They* duped *him into telling.*

du·plex (do͞o′ plĕks′, dyo͞o′-) ***adj***- having two similar parts; double; twofold. ***n***- a duplex apartment or house.

duplex apartment ***n***- apartment whose rooms are on two floors.

duplex house ***n***- house designed for two families.

1**du·pli·cate** (do͞o′ plə kāt′, dyo͞o′) ***vt***- [**du·pli·cat·ed, du·pli·cat·ing**] **1** to make an exact or nearly exact copy of: *She* duplicated *the dress she had admired at the fashion show.* **2** to repeat exactly or nearly so: *He* duplicated *his former triumphs.* **—*n*- du′ pli·ca′ tion.**

2**du·pli·cate** (do͞o′ plə kət, dyo͞o′-) ***n***- something exactly like something else; twin: *This print is a* duplicate *of the original. as* ***modifier***: *a* duplicate *key.*
in duplicate with an original and one copy; double.

dup·li·ca·tor (do͞o′ plə kā′ tər) ***n***- office machine for making exact rapid copies of papers, notices, etc.

du·plic·i·ty (do͞o plĭs′ ə tē, dyo͞o-) ***n***- [*pl.* **du·plic·i·ties**] deception; deceit; double-dealing: *It is often hard to see through the* duplicity *of a cunning man.*

du·ra·ble (do͝or′ ə bəl, dyo͝or′-) ***adj***- lasting; not breaking down or wearing out easily: *a* durable *pair of shoes*; *a* durable *friendship.* **—*adv*- du′ ra·bly. *n*- du′ ra·bil′ i·ty.**

du·ra ma·ter (do͝or′ ə mā′ tər) ***n***- outermost membrane that covers the brain and the spinal cord. It is tougher and more fibrous than either of the other two membranes.

dur·ance (do͝or′ əns, dyo͝or′-) *Archaic* ***n***- imprisonment.

du·ra·tion (do͝or ā′ shən, dyo͝or-) ***n***- amount of time during which anything lasts: *a storm of short* duration.

du·ress (do͝or ĕs′, dyo͝or-) ***n***- **1** force used to get someone to do something; compulsion; coercion: *The prisoner signed a confession under* duress. **2** *Law* unlawful confinement or imprisonment.

dur·ing (do͝or′ ĭng, dyo͝or′-) ***prep***- **1** throughout the time of: *We do not go to school* during *the summer.* **2** in the course of: *He called sometime* during *the evening.*

dur·ra (do͝or′ ə) ***n***- canelike grass grown for its grain.

durst (dûrst) *Archaic* form of **dare** used in the past tense.

du·rum wheat (do͝or′ əm, dûr′ əm) ***n***- a hard wheat widely used in making flour for macaroni, spaghetti, etc.

dusk (dŭsk) ***n***- **1** the time of day when darkness comes on; twilight. **2** darkness; gloom: *in the* dusk *of the forest.*

dusk·y (dŭs′ kē) ***adj***- [**dusk·i·er, dusk·i·est**] **1** somewhat dark in color. **2** lacking light; shadowy. **—*adv*- dusk′ i·ly. *n*- dusk′ i·ness.**

dust (dŭst) ***n***- fine, dry particles of earth or other powder-like material: *a cloud of* dust. ***vt***- **1** (considered intransitive when the direct object is implied but not expressed) to brush or wipe away such particles from: *Susie* dusted *the furniture.* **2** to cover or sprinkle: *She* dusted *the cake with sugar.* **—*adj-*** **dust′ less.** ***Hom-*** dost.

bite the dust to fall in battle; be defeated. **throw dust in (someone's) eyes** to mislead; to fool.

dust bowl ***n-*** dry region swept by dust storms.

dust·er (dŭs′ tər) ***n-*** **1** person or thing that removes dust; especially a cloth, appliance, bunch of feathers, etc., for removing dust from objects. **2** light outer garment formerly worn in open vehicles to protect clothing from road dust. **3** woman's loose, knee-length housecoat. **4** any device for sprinkling a powderlike substance.

dust jacket ***n-*** detachable heavy paper cover for a book.

dust·pan (dŭst′ păn′) ***n-*** small shovel with a short handle, used with a brush to collect floor sweepings.

dust·proof (dŭst′ prōōf′) ***adj-*** capable of keeping out dust or protecting from dust: *a* dustproof *clothes bag.*

dust storm ***n-*** windstorm that carries clouds of dust.

dust·y (dŭs′ tē) ***adj-*** **[dust·i·er, dust·i·est] 1** covered with dust or containing much dust: *a* dusty *attic.* **2** like dust in appearance: *a* dusty *gray.* **—*n-*** **dust′ i·ness.**

Dutch (dŭch) ***n-*** **1** the language of the Netherlands. **2 the Dutch** the people of the Netherlands. ***adj-*** **1** of or relating to the Netherlands, its people, or their language. **2** *Archaic* German.

go Dutch *Informal* to have a Dutch treat. **in Dutch** *Informal* to be in disfavor or in trouble.

Dutch·man (dŭch′ mən) ***n-*** [*pl.* **Dutch·men**] **1** a Hollander. **2** *Archaic* a German.

dutch·man's-breech·es (dŭch′ mənz brĭch′ əz) ***n-*** [*pl.* **dutch·man's-breech·es**] plant having sprays of white, pale yellow, or pinkish flowers that resemble tiny pairs of breeches hanging upside down.

Dutch oven ***n-*** **1** cast-iron or heavy aluminum cooking pot with a cover that fits tightly, used on top of the stove for braising, steaming, or baking. **2** sheet-metal oven used for roasting or baking before an open fire.

Dutch treat *Informal* ***n-*** an entertainment or outing at which each person pays his own share.

Dutch uncle *Informal* ***n-*** someone who severely rebukes or scolds another.

du·te·ous (dōō′ tē əs, dyōō′-) ***adj-*** dutiful; obedient. **—*adv-*** **du′ te·ous·ly.** ***n-*** **du′ te·ous·ness.**

du·ti·a·ble (dōō′ tē ə bəl, dyōō′-) ***adj-*** subject to the payment of a duty or tax: *a shipment of* dutiable *goods.*

du·ti·ful (dōō′ tə fəl, dyōō′-) ***adj-*** doing one's duty; obedient: *a* dutiful *son.* **—*adv-*** **du′ ti·ful·ly.** ***n-*** **du′ ti·ful·ness.**

du·ty (dōō′ tē, dyōō′-) ***n-*** [*pl.* **du·ties**] **1** what one ought to do; obligation: *a sense of* duty; *a man's* duty *to his country.* **2** service required by one's work or position: *the* duties *of a secretary.* **3** a tax, especially on goods brought into a country; tariff: *a* duty *on perfume.*

dwarf (dwȯrf) ***n-*** **1** person, animal, or plant greatly below normal size, often deformed in some way. **2** in fairy tales, a tiny person with unusual or magical powers. **3** dwarf star. *as* ***modifier***: *a* dwarf *rose.* ***vt-*** **1** to prevent from growing to natural size: *The lack of rain* dwarfed *the flowers.* **2** to make look small by comparison.

dwarf·ish (dwȯrf′ ĭsh) ***adj-*** like a human dwarf.

dwarf star *Astronomy* ***n-*** star of average or less than average brightness and mass. The sun is a dwarf star. See also *white dwarf.*

dwell (dwĕl) ***vi-*** **[dwelled** or **dwelt, dwell·ing]** to live in a place; reside: *The princess* dwells *in yonder castle.* **—*n-*** **dwell′ er.**

dwell on to think, speak, or write about at length; linger on: *His mind* dwells on *unhappy memories.*

dwell·ing (dwĕl′ ĭng) ***n-*** house; place of residence: *a two-story* dwelling.

dwin·dle (dwĭn′ dəl) ***vi-*** **[dwin·dled, dwin·dling]** to become smaller or less; to shrink: *The water supply* dwindled *from lack of rain.*

dwt. pennyweight.

Dy symbol for dysprosium.

Dy·ak (dī′ ăk′) Dayak.

dyb·buk (dĭb′ ək) ***n-*** in Jewish legend, a demon or spirit of a dead person that was believed to take control of and dwell in a living man or woman.

dye (dī) ***vt-*** **[dyed, dye·ing]** to give color to, usually by dipping into a liquid containing coloring matter: *She* dyed *her dress blue.* ***n-*** **1** coloring matter; dyestuff. **2** color produced by dyeing. ***Hom-*** die. **—*n-*** **dy′ er.**

dyed-in-the-wool (dīd′ ĭn thə wŏŏl′) ***adj-*** complete; thorough: *a* dyed-in-the-wool *political conservative.*

dye·ing (dī′ ĭng) ***n-*** act or process of using dye to give color to yarn, cloth, hair, etc. ***Hom-*** dying.

dye·stuff (dī′ stŭf′) ***n-*** any coloring matter; dye.

dy·ing (dī′ ĭng) ***adj-*** **1** passing from life: *the last wish of the* dying *man.* **2** said or done at the time of death: *a* dying *wish.* **3** becoming weaker. ***Hom-*** dyeing.

dyke (dīk) dike.

dy·nam·ic (dī năm′ ĭk) ***adj-*** **1** full of energy; forceful. **2** having to do with the energy of motion: *a* dynamic *current of air.* **—*adv-*** **dy·nam′ i·cal·ly.**

dy·nam·ics (dī năm′ ĭks) ***n-*** (takes singular verb) branch of physics that deals with the motion of particles or objects in relation to the forces that cause the motion.

dy·na·mite (dī′ nəmīt′) ***n-*** high explosive made of nitroglycerin in an absorbent material and packed in cylindrical sticks. ***vt-*** **[dy·na·mit·ed, dy·na·mit·ing]** to destroy or damage with high explosives. **—*n-*** **dy′ na·mit′ er.**

dy·na·mo (dī′ nə mō′) ***n-*** [*pl.* **dy·na·mos**] **1** machine that converts mechanical energy into electrical energy; generator. **2** *Informal* a very energetic or active person.

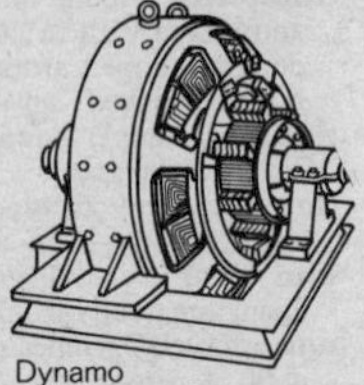
Dynamo

dy·na·mo·e·lec·tric (dī′ nə mō ə lĕk′ trĭk) ***adj-*** operating by or having to do with the conversion of mechanical energy into electrical energy, or vice versa.

dy·na·mom·e·ter (dī′ nə mŏm′ ə tər) ***n-*** **1** device, such as a spring balance, to measure mechanical force. **2** instrument that measures the mechanical power of an engine, an electric motor, etc.

dy·nast (dī′ năst′) ***n-*** ruler, especially one of a dynasty.

dy·nas·tic (dī năs′ tĭk) ***adj-*** of or related to a dynasty.

dy·nas·ty (dī′ nəs tē) ***n-*** [*pl.* **dy·nas·ties**] a line or succession of rulers who belong to the same family.

dyne (dīn) ***n-*** unit of force equal to the force required to give a mass of one gram an acceleration of one centimeter per second for each second the force acts. ***Hom-*** dine.

dy·sen·ter·y (dĭs′ ən tĕr′ ē) ***n-*** painful disease of the bowels, marked by severe inflammation and by mucous, and bloody discharges. Some forms are very contagious.

dys·gen·ic (dĭs jĕn′ ĭk) ***adj-*** having to do with or causing the degeneration of a species or type.

dys·pep·sia (dĭs pĕp′ shə, -sē ə) ***n-*** poor, impaired, or painful digestion; indigestion.

dys·pep·tic (dĭs pĕp′ tĭk) ***adj-*** **1** having to do with indigestion. **2** gloomy or ill-tempered. ***n-*** person with chronic indigestion. **—*adv-*** **dys·pep′ ti·cal·ly.**

dys·pro·si·um (dĭs prō′ zē əm) ***n-*** lustrous, metallic, strongly magnetic chemical element, found in certain minerals. Symbol Dy, At. No. 66, At. Wt. 162.50.

dz. dozen or dozens.

E

E, e (ē) ***n-*** [*pl.* **E's, e's**] **1** the fifth letter of the English alphabet. **2 E** *Music* the third note of the C-major scale.
E symbol for energy.
E. **1** east. **2** eastern. **3** engineer. **4** English. **5** earl.
ea. each.
each (ēch) ***determiner*** (traditionally called adjective or pronoun) **1** every separate: *We allowed* each *student to take his turn.* **2** all, but one by one: *They* each *took turns.* ***n-*** every one: Each *of the cities had a power plant.*
each other of two, every one (to, with, against, toward, etc.) every other; reciprocally: *The two girls waved to* each other *across the room.*
►In writing, reserve EACH OTHER for use with two persons and ONE ANOTHER for several: *Harry and Tom were shouting to* each other. *In the playground the children were shouting to* one another, *causing a great deal of noise.*
ea·ger (ē′ gər) ***adj-*** full of keen desire: *He was* eager *to play football.* **—*adv-* ea′ ger·ly.** ***n-*** **ea′ ger·ness.**
►For usage note see ANXIOUS.
ea·gle (ē′ gəl) ***n-*** any of various large, sharp-sighted birds of prey. For picture, see *bald eagle.*
ea·gle-eyed (ē′ gəl īd′) ***adj-*** having very keen eyesight.
ea·glet (ē′ glət) ***n-*** young eagle.

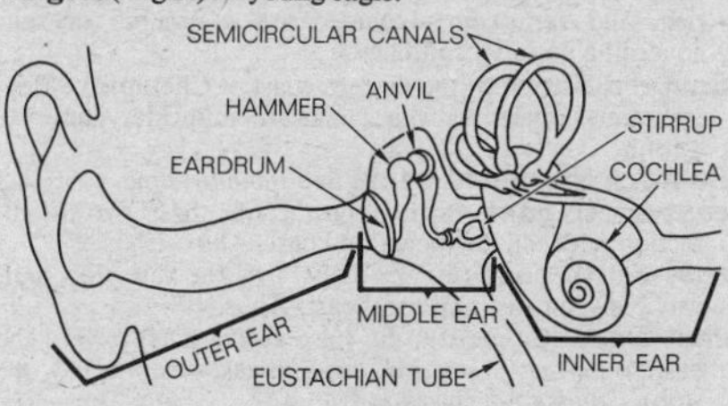

Human ear

[1]**ear** (êr) ***n-*** **1** the entire organ of hearing. **2** the outer, visible part of this organ: *A cat has pointed* ears *that stand up.* **3** sense of hearing: *George has a sharp* ear. **4** particular ability to hear and understand various sounds in music, poetry, etc.: *A good singer must have a good* ear. **5** attention; heed: *Give* ear *to what I say.* **6** anything resembling the outer part of the ear, such as the handle of a pitcher. [from Old English word **ēare** of the same meaning.] **—*adj-* ear′ like′.**
be all ears to listen with all one's attention.
[2]**ear** (êr) ***n-*** seed-bearing spike of a cereal plant such as corn or wheat. [unchanged form of an Old English word.]
ear·ache (êr′ āk′) ***n-*** pain in the inner part of the ear.
ear·drum (êr′ drŭm′) ***n-*** **1** cavity within the ear; tympanum. **2** less correctly, the thin membrane of skin between the outer and the middle ear that vibrates when sound waves strike it; tympanic membrane.
ear·flap (êr′ flăp′) or **ear·lap** (-lăp′) ***n-*** part of a hat or cap that hangs over the ears or folds down to cover them.
earl (ûrl) ***n-*** British nobleman, below a marquis and above a viscount in rank.

Ear of corn

earl·dom (ûrl′ dəm) ***n-*** the rank of an earl, or the land or possessions associated with his title.
ear·lobe (êr′ lōb′) ***n-*** soft, fleshy, lower portion of the external part of the human ear. For picture, see *lobe.*
ear·ly (ûr′ lē) ***adv-*** [**ear·li·er, ear·li·est**] **1** before the usual or required time: *Snow fell* early *this year. He arrived at school* early. **2** at or near the beginning: *These events occurred* early *in his career.* ***adj-*** **1** coming, occurring, or doing something before the normal or expected time: *We had an* early *spring this year. He is an* early *riser.* **2** long before the present; ancient: *a superstition going back to* early *times.* **—*n-* ear′ li·ness.**
early bird *Informal* ***n-*** person who arrives or starts doing things before most others do.
ear·mark (êr′ märk′) ***n-*** mark, such as a slit in the ear of a sheep, cow, etc., used to identify it; hence, any distinguishing mark or characteristic: *Your remark has all the* earmarks *of an insult.* ***vt-*** **1** to mark the ear of (an animal), **2** to set aside for a special purpose, often with an identifying mark: *He* earmarked *the book for you.*
ear·muffs (êr′ mŭfs′) ***n- pl.*** pair of warm coverings for the ears, usually held by a flexible band over the head.
earn (ûrn) ***vt-*** **1** to receive as payment for labor, service, etc.: *He* earns *a large salary.* **2** to gain as a result of one's behavior, efforts, etc.; deserve: *to* earn *someone's praise.* **3** to produce (interest, dividends, etc.). ***Hom-*** urn.
[1]**ear·nest** (ûr′ nəst) ***adj-*** filled with deep and sincere feeling, intentions, or purpose; serious: *an* earnest *apology*; *an* earnest *student.* [from Old English **eornost.**] **—*adv-* ear′ nest·ly.** ***n-*** **ear′ nest·ness.**
in earnest with sincere or serious intent.
[2]**ear·nest** (ûr′ nəst) ***n-*** **1** token or pledge of something: *an* earnest *of my good will.* **2** (also **earnest money**) money given in advance to show honest intentions. [from earlier **ernes**, apparently from an alteration of **erres**, an Old French plural form, from Latin singular **arra**, from Greek **arrhabon**, from Hebrew **'ērābōn.**]
earn·ings (ûr′ nĭngz) ***n- pl.*** **1** payment received for work, services, etc. **2** profits.
ear·phone (êr′ fōn′) ***n-*** **1** small telephone or radio speaker, usually one of a pair, held to the ear by a band over the head. **2** a similar device used as part of an electronic hearing aid.
ear·ring (êr′ rĭng′) ***n-*** ornament worn on the earlobe.
ear·shot (êr′ shŏt′) ***n-*** range within which a sound can be heard; hearing distance: *He was out of* earshot.
ear·split·ting (êr′ splĭt′ ĭng) ***adj-*** very loud and piercing.
earth (ûrth) ***n-*** **1** (usually **Earth**) our planet, fifth largest in the solar system, and the third in order of distance from the sun. **2** the world we inhabit: *Peace on* earth, *good will to men.* **3** the people who inhabit it: *All the* earth *rejoices.* **4** the solid matter that composes it; the land: *"The waters covered the face of the* earth." **5** soil; ground: *Some pine trees grow best in sandy* earth.
down to earth sensible; practical.
[1]**earth·bound** (ûrth′ bound′) ***adj-*** confined to or unable to move from the earth; hence, worldly and materialistic: *an airplane* earthbound *because of heavy fog*; earthbound *interests.* [from **earth** plus [2]**bound.**]
[2]**earth·bound** (ûrth′ bound′) ***adj-*** headed or coming toward the earth: *an* earthbound *meteorite.* [from **earth** plus [4]**bound.**]

earth·en (ûr′thən, -*th*ən) *adj-* **1** made of earth: *an* earthen *mound.* **2** made of earthenware: *an* earthen *jar.*
earth·en·ware (ûr′thən wâr′, -*th*ən wâr′) *n-* dishes and containers made of clay hardened by fire. Earthenware is usually thicker and heavier than fine china or porcelain. *as modifier: an* earthenware *jug.*
earth·ly (ûrth′lē) *adj-* **1** of or having to do with this world; not heavenly or spiritual: *our* earthly *possessions.* **2** possible; imaginable: *no* earthly *use.*
earth·quake (ûrth′kwāk′) *n-* sudden trembling of the ground, usually caused by a shifting of rock layers along a fault or fissure under the earth's surface.
earth science *n-* any of the sciences, such as geology or oceanography, dealing with the earth or part of the earth.
earth·ward (ûrth′wərd) *adv-* (also **earth′wards**) toward the earth. *adj-: an* earthward *dive.*
earth·work (ûrth′wûrk′) *n-* wall or hill of earth piled up for defense.
earth·worm (ûrth′wûrm′) *n-* worm with a ringed or segmented body that burrows in the soil and eats decaying organic matter; angleworm.
earth·y (ûrth′ē) *adj-* [**earth·i·er, earth·i·est**] **1** resembling or containing earth or soil: *dull,* earthy *colors.* **2** natural, simple, and often crude or vulgar: *an* earthy *sense of humor.* —*n-* **earth′i·ness.**
ear·wig (êr′wĭg′) *n-* any of various small harmless insects that have a pair of strong pincers at the end of the body.
ear·worm (êr′wûrm′) *n-* any caterpillar that feeds on the developing ears of corn.
ease (ēz) *n-* **1** freedom from pain, toil, effort, or worry; comfort: *a life of* ease. **2** freedom from strain; naturalness: *the* ease *of her manner.* *vt-* [**eased, eas·ing**] **1** to relieve; lighten: *medicine that* eases *pain.* **2** to make less tight; loosen: *to* ease *a snug waistband.* **3** to move slowly and carefully: *He* eased *the car into the garage.*
at ease **1** relaxed; comfortable: *to be* at ease *with strangers.* **2** *Military* standing with the legs apart, the hands clasped behind the back, and with strict silence maintained (often used as a command). **take (one's) ease** to lounge comfortably; relax.
ea·sel (ē′zəl) *n-* stand or frame, often with a movable prop at the back, used to hold a picture, painter's canvas, etc., in an upright position.

Easel

eas·i·ly (ē′zə lē) *adv-* **1** without trouble or difficulty; comfortably: *The patient is resting* easily. **2** by any estimate; without doubt: *He is* easily *the tallest man here.*
eas·i·ness (ē′zē nəs) *n-* lack of difficulty, effort, etc.
east (ēst) *n-* **1** the direction halfway between north and south and generally toward the rising sun; also, the point of the compass indicating this direction; opposite of *west.* **2** the region or part of a country or continent in this direction: *the* east *of England.* **3** **the East** (1) Asia; the Orient. (2) the eastern part of the United States, especially the area from Maine through Maryland. *adj-* **1** in or to the east: *the* east *side of town.* **2** of winds, from the east. *adv-* toward the east: *He faced* east.

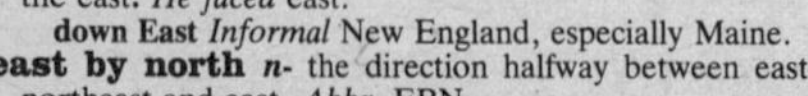

down East *Informal* New England, especially Maine.
east by north *n-* the direction halfway between east-northeast and east. *Abbr.* EBN.

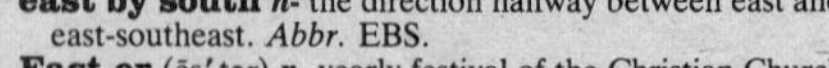

east by south *n-* the direction halfway between east and east-southeast. *Abbr.* EBS.
East·er (ēs′tər) *n-* yearly festival of the Christian Church to celebrate the rising from the dead of Jesus Christ, observed on the first Sunday after the first full moon of spring; Pasch. Also **Easter Sunday.**
east·er·ly (ēs′tər lē) *adj-* **1** generally toward the east: *an* easterly *direction.* **2** of winds, generally from the east: *an* easterly *breeze.* *adv-* generally eastward: *a ship going* easterly. *n-* [*pl.* **eas·ter·lies**] wind from the east.
east·ern (ēs′tərn) *adj-* **1** in or toward the east: *an* eastern *port; an* eastern *view.* **2** characteristic of or from the east: *an* eastern *custom.* **3 Eastern** (1) of or in the eastern part of the United States. (2) of or relating to the Christian churches of the eastern Roman Empire. (3) of or relating to the Orient.
East·ern·er (ēs′tər nər) *n-* person who lives in or comes from the eastern part of the United States or the countries of the East.
Eastern Hemisphere *n-* the half of the earth that extends from pole to pole and includes Europe, Asia, and Africa, and the surrounding oceans.
east·ern·most (ēs′tərn mōst′) *adj-* farthest east.
Eastern Orthodox Church *n-* group of Eastern Christian churches that variously recognize as their spiritual heads the patriarchs of Constantinople, Alexandria, Antioch, and Jerusalem. Included are a number of self-governing national churches.
Eastern Shore *n-* the eastern coast of Chesapeake Bay, sometimes including the Delaware and Maryland peninsula.
Eastern Standard Time See *standard time.*
east-north·east (ēst′nôr′thēst′, -nôr′thēst′) *n-* the direction between northeast and east. *Abbr.* ENE.
east-south·east (ēst′sou′thēst′) *n-* the direction halfway between east and southeast. *Abbr.* ESE.
east·ward (ēst′wərd) *adv-* (also **east′wards**) toward the east: *to journey* eastwards. *adj-: an* eastward *journey.* *n-: storm clouds to the* eastward.
eas·y (ē′zē) *adj-* [**eas·i·er, eas·i·est**] **1** requiring little effort; not difficult: *an* easy *task; an* easy *book to read.* **2** free from trouble or worry: *an* easy *life; to be* easy *in one's mind.* **3** permitting ease and relaxation; comfortable: *an* easy *seat.* **4** not stiff or self-conscious; relaxed: *an* easy *manner; an* easy *style of writing.* **5** gentle; moderate: *an* easy *pace.* **6** not strict or demanding: *an* easy *course.* *adv-* *Informal* comfortably; peacefully.
go easy *Informal* **1** to be careful or sparing: *Please* go easy *with the gravy!* **2** to be lenient or sympathetic (with or on). **take it easy** *Informal* to relax.
easy chair *n-* large, comfortable, upholstered armchair.
eas·y·go·ing (ē′zē gō′ĭng) *adj-* calm, relaxed, and good-humored: *an* easygoing *manner; an* easygoing *employer.*
eat (ēt) *vt-* [**ate** (āt), **eat·en, eat·ing**] **1** to take into the mouth and swallow, usually after chewing: *to* eat *a peach; to* eat *a meal.* **2** to use habitually as food: *Seals* eat *fish.* *vi-* **1** to have a meal: *We* eat *at noon.* **2** to wear (away); gnaw (into); erode; corrode: *The flood* ate *away the dike. Acids* eat *into metal.*
eat up to consume; destroy.
eat (one's) words to wish (one) had never said what he did; strongly regret some statement.
eat·a·ble (ē′tə bəl) *adj-* fit or safe to be eaten; edible. *n-* (often **eatables**) thing suitable for food.
eaves (ēvz) *n-* (takes plural verb) overhanging edge of a sloping roof.

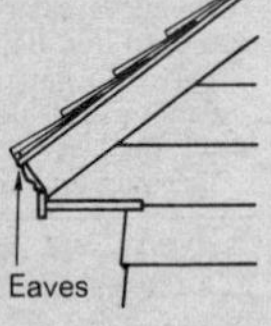
Eaves

eaves·drop (ēvz′ drŏp′) ***vi-*** [**eaves·dropped, eaves·drop·ping**] to listen secretly to the private conversation of others. **—*n-* eaves′ drop′ per.**

ebb (ĕb) ***n-*** **1** the going out of the tide. **2** low state: *His courage was at its* ebb. ***vi-*** **1** to flow back; recede: *The tide* ebbed. **2** to weaken; decline: *Hope* ebbed.

ebb tide ***n-*** the receding tide; also, the point or time of lowest tide.

eb·on (ĕb′ ən) ***adj-*** **1** black as ebony: *her flowing* ebon *tresses.* **2** *Archaic* made of ebony.

eb·on·ite (ĕb′ ə nīt′) ***n-*** black, hard rubber that has been specially treated with chemicals; vulcanite.

eb·on·y (ĕb′ ə nē) ***n-*** [*pl.* **eb·on·ies**] hard, black wood of various tropical trees, used chiefly for decorative work, piano keys, etc.; also, any of the trees from which this wood is obtained. ***adj-*** **1** made of this wood: *an* ebony *table.* **2** black: *her* ebony *hair.*

e·bul·lient (ĭ bo͝ol′ yənt, ĭ bŭl′-) ***adj-*** full of enthusiasm and high spirits; bubbling. **—*n-* e·bul′ lience** or **e·bul′ lien·cy.** ***adv-*** **e·bul′ lient·ly.**

eb·ul·li·tion (ĕ′ bə lĭ′ shən) ***n-*** **1** a bubbling or boiling up. **2** a sudden surge or outburst of feeling.

ec·ce ho·mo (ĕk′ ē hō′ mō′, ĕk′ sē-) *Latin* behold the man. These words, spoken by Pontius Pilate in surrendering Jesus for crucifixion, are often used as the title of paintings or statues of Jesus crowned with thorns.

ec·cen·tric (ĕk sĕn′ trĭk) ***adj-*** **1** odd, peculiar, or unconventional: *Hermits are* eccentric *persons. His behavior was quite* eccentric. **2** not having the same center; not concentric: *two* eccentric *circles.* **3** turning about a point or axis not at the center: *an* eccentric *wheel.* **4** not quite circular in shape: *the* eccentric *orbit of a satellite.* ***n-*** **1** odd, peculiar, or unconventional person. **2** machine part that turns on an axis not at the center.

ec·cen·tric·i·ty (ĕk′ sən trĭs′ ə tē) ***n-*** [*pl.* **ec·cen·tric·i·ties**] **1** odd and unusual behavior, action etc.: *my aunt's little* eccentricities. **2** condition of being eccentric. **3** the amount or degree by which something is eccentric.

Eccl. or **Eccles.** Ecclesiastes.

Ec·cle·si·as·tes (ĭ klē′ zē ăs′ tēz) ***n-*** a book of the Old Testament.

ec·cle·si·as·tic (ĭ klē′ zē ăs′ tĭk) ***adj-*** (also **ec·cle′ si·as′ ti·cal**) of or having to do with the church or with church organization and government. ***n-*** a clergyman. **—*adv-* ec·cle′ si·as′ ti·cal·ly.**

Ec·cle·si·as·ti·cus (ĭ klē′ zē ăs′ tĭ kəs) ***n-*** one of the books of the Old Testament Apocrypha, accepted as authentic by the Roman Catholic Church. In the CCD Bible it is called the **Book of Sirach.**

Ecclus. Ecclesiasticus.

ech·e·lon (ĕsh′ ə lŏn′) ***n-*** **1** part of an organization, especially of a military unit, thought of as a level from the top down or a step from the front to the rear: *a high* echelon *of command*; *the rear* echelon. **2** formation of aircraft, ships, etc., with each member behind, above or below, and to one side of the one ahead.

e·chid·na (ĭ kĭd′ nə) ***n-*** one of two kinds of anteaters that are covered with sharp spines; spiny anteater. Echidnas are among the few mammals whose young are hatched from eggs.

Spiny echidna, 14—20 in. long

e·chi·no·derm (ĭ kī′ nə dûrm′) ***n-*** one of a large group of sea animals (**Echinodermata**), including starfishes, sea urchins, etc. Most echinoderms have a tough spiny skin and are made up of several similar segments extending from a center.

ech·o (ĕk′ ō) ***n-*** [*pl.* **ech·oes**] **1** repetition of a sound due to the reflection of sound waves. **2** the repeated sound itself. **3 Echo** in Greek mythology, a nymph who, because of her love for Narcissus, pined away until only her voice remained. ***vi-*** to give back or repeat sound; resound: *The corridors* echoed *with footsteps.* ***vt-*** to repeat or imitate the words or actions of (another).

e·clair (ā klâr′) ***n-*** small, long, hollow shell of light pastry filled with custard or whipped cream and usually covered with frosting.

e·clat (ā klä′) ***n-*** **1** striking or sensational effect; brilliance; dash: *to perform with* éclat. **2** loud applause: *The audience responded with* éclat. [from French **éclat,** from **éclater,** meaning "to burst forth."]

ec·lec·tic (ĭ klĕk′ tĭk) ***adj-*** choosing or making use of what one considers the best ideas in various sources or systems of thought, learning, art, etc.: *his* eclectic *philosophy of life.* ***n-*** person who so chooses and selects. **—*adv-* ec·lec′ ti·cal·ly.**

ec·lec·ti·cism (ĭ klĕk′ tə sĭz′ əm) ***n-*** eclectic philosophy, style, methods, etc.

e·clipse (ĭ klĭps′) ***n-*** complete or partial apparent darkening of the sun by the passage of the moon between it and the earth, or of the moon by the shadow of the earth. ***vt-*** [**e·clipsed, e·clips·ing**] to throw into the shade; outshine: *Alan's last role* eclipsed *all his others.*

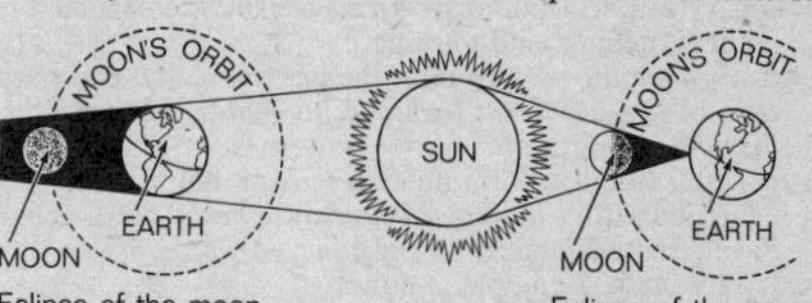

Eclipse of the moon. Eclipse of the sun.

The eclipse of the sun is seen where the moon's shadow touches the earth

e·clip·tic (ĭ klĭp′ tĭk) *Astronomy* ***n-*** imaginary circle formed by the intersection of the plane of the earth's orbit with the celestial sphere. The ecliptic is also the path the sun appears to travel in a year, as seen from the earth. ***adj-*** (also **e·clip′ ti·cal**) **1** having to do with this circle or path. **2** having to do with an eclipse. **—*adv-* e·clip′ ti·cal·ly.**

ec·logue (ĕk′ lŏg′) ***n-*** poem about ideal country life, originally consisting of a dialogue between shepherds.

e·col·o·gy (ĭ kŏl′ ə jē) ***n-*** branch of biology that deals with the relationships of organisms to each other and to their environment.

e·co·nom·ic (ĕk′ ə nŏm′ ĭk, ē′ kə-) ***adj-*** having to do with the production, distribution, and use of wealth, goods, and services: *the* economic *history of the country.*

e·co·nom·i·cal (ē′ kə nŏm′ ĭ kəl, ĕk′ ə nŏm′-) ***adj-*** wise in the use of money, materials, effort, etc.; practical and thrifty: *an* economical *wife.* **—*adv-* e′ co·nom′ i·cal·ly.**

e·co·nom·ics (ĕk′ ə nŏm′ ĭks, ē′ kə-) ***n-*** **1** (takes singular verb) science of the production, distribution, and use of wealth, goods, and services. **2** (takes plural verb) management and use of money, goods, etc.: *The* economics *of running a household are often complicated.*

e·con·o·mist (ĭ kŏn′ ə mĭst) ***n-*** person trained or skilled in economics.

---

fāte, făt, dâre, bärn; bē, bĕt, mêre; bīte, bĭt; nōte, hŏt, môre, dȯg; fŭn, fûr; to͞o, bo͝ok; oil; out; tar; thin; then; hw for wh as in *wh*at; zh for s as in u*s*ual; ə for a, e, i, o, u, as in *a*go, lin*e*n, per*i*l, at*o*m, min*u*s

e·con·o·mize (ĭ kŏn′ə mīz′) *vi-* [**e·con·o·mized, e·con·o·miz·ing**] to cut down on waste or expenses; be thrifty and sparing. *vt-* to use sparingly and to the best advantage: *to* economize *one's efforts.*

e·con·o·my (ĭ kŏn′ə mē) *n-* [*pl.* **e·con·o·mies**] **1** thrifty use of money, goods, etc; also, an instance of this: *We must practice* economy. *She thought of several small* economies *in running the family.* **2** system of organizing production, distribution, and consumption of goods and services of a region or state; economic system.

e·co·sys·tem (ĕk′ō sĭs′təm) *n-* the ecological community of all the organisms in a given area together with their physical and chemical environment, considered as a unit of function and activity.

ec·ru (ĕ′kro͞o′, ā′kro͞o′) *n-* a pale, yellowish brown. *adj-*: *curtains of* ecru *linen.*

ec·sta·sy (ĕks′stə sē) *n-* [*pl.* **ec·sta·sies**] feeling or state of deep emotion, especially of rapturous joy.

ec·stat·ic (ĕks stăt′ĭk) *adj-* feeling, producing, or expressing rapturous joy. *—adv-* **ec·stat′i·cal·ly.**

ec·to·derm (ĕk′tə dûrm′) *n-* outermost layer of an animal embryo. It later develops into the skin, the nervous system, and the various sense organs.

ec·u·men·i·cal (ĕk′yə mĕn′ĭ kəl) *adj-* **1** of or having to do with the Christian churches throughout the world: *an* ecumenical *council.* **2** worldwide in scope; universal. *—adv-* **ec′u·men′i·cal·ly.**

ec·ze·ma (ĕg zē′mə, ĕk′sə mə) *n-* skin disease in which watery blisters and crusts form, usually accompanied by redness, itching, and burning.

[1]**-ed** *word ending* used to form the past tense and past participle of regular verbs: *I wash*ed *my hands. I have wash*ed *the dishes.*

[2]**-ed** *suffix* (used to form adjectives from nouns) **1** having; equipped with: *a bowlegged cowboy*; *a belt*ed *dress.* **2** like; having the characteristics of: *honey*ed *words.*

ed. 1 edited. 2 edition. 3 editor.

E·dam cheese (ē′dəm, -dăm′) *n-* mild, yellow curd cheese, originally made in Edam, the Netherlands.

Ed·da (ĕd′ə) *n-* either of two collections of Old Icelandic literature, the **Elder Edda** of about 1200, a collection of Norse poetry, and the **Younger** or **Prose Edda** of about 1230, a summary of Norse mythology.

ed·dy (ĕd′ē) *n-* [*pl.* **ed·dies**] **1** current of air, water, etc., that runs opposite to the main current, thus causing whirlwinds or whirlpools. **2** small whirlwind or whirlpool. *vi-* [**ed·died, ed·dy·ing**] to move with a circular motion; whirl: *The smoke* eddied *from the chimney.*

e·del·weiss (ā′dəl wīs′, -vīs′) *n-* small plant that grows on high mountains and has blossoms consisting of tiny, yellow flowers surrounded by white, petallike leaves.

e·de·ma (ĭ dē′mə) *n-* any swelling of the body caused by an unusual accumulation of fluid in the spaces between tissues, organs, etc.

E·den (ē′dən) *n-* **1** Garden of Eden; Paradise. **2** any delightful place or condition.

e·den·tate (ē dĕn′tāt′) *n-* any member of the small order of mammals (**Edentata**) that includes the sloth, armadillo, and giant anteater. Edentates have few or no teeth. *adj-* **1** of, relating to, or belonging to this order. **2** toothless: *an* edentate *leaf.*

edge (ĕj) *n-* **1** extreme or outermost border; rim; margin: *the* edge *of the brook.* **2** thin, sharp, cutting part of a knife, tool, etc. **3** *Informal* margin or advantage: *to win by a slight* edge; *to have an* edge *on one's opponents. vt-* [**edged, edg·ing**] **1** to form or put a border on: *Reeds* edged *the pond.* **2** to sharpen (a blade, cutting tool, etc.) **3** to push carefully into a narrow place: *He* edged *the tool into the crevice. vi-* to move carefully, little by little: *The hikers* edged *along the cliff.*

on edge tense, nervous, or impatient.

edged (ĕjd) *adj-* having an edge or edges of a stated kind, number, etc.: *a double-*edged *sword.*

edge·wise (ĕj′wīz′) *adv-* **1** with the edge foremost. **2** standing or resting on an edge. Also **edge′ways′.**

edg·ing (ĕj′ĭng) *n-* decorative border along an edge: *an* edging *of lace on a petticoat.*

edg·y (ĕj′ē) *adj-* [**edg·i·er, edg·i·est**] tense and uneasy; nervous; apprehensive. *—adv-* **edg′i·ly.** *n-* **edg′i·ness.**

ed·i·ble (ĕd′ə bəl) *adj-* fit or safe to be used for food; eatable: *Some fish are* edible. *—n-* **ed′i·bil′i·ty.**

e·dict (ē′dĭkt′) *n-* command from an official authority that has the strength of a law; decree.

ed·i·fi·ca·tion (ĕd′ə fə kā′shən) *n-* mental or moral improvement: *A speech intended for our* edification.

ed·i·fice (ĕd′ə fəs) *n-* a large and impressive building.

ed·i·fy (ĕd′ə fī′) *vt-* [**ed·i·fied, ed·i·fy·ing**] to instruct and benefit, especially in morals, religion, etc.

Ed·i·son effect (ĕd′ə sən) *n-* in vacuum tubes, the flow of current from a hot, negatively charged filament to a positively charged metal plate.

ed·it (ĕd′ĭt) *vt-* **1** to correct, revise, and prepare (manuscript) for publication. **2** to review, select, and arrange (motion-picture film, electronic tape, etc.) before offering to the public. **3** to select, arrange, and comment on (poems, essays, etc.) published as a single work or collection. **4** to direct the editorial policies and preparation of (a newspaper, magazine, etc.).

edit. 1 edition. 2 edited. 3 editor.

e·di·tion (ĭ dĭsh′ən) *n-* **1** particular published form of a literary or musical work: *a new* edition *of "Little Women"; the third* edition *of an encyclopedia.* **2** all the copies of a newspaper or magazine printed at one time.

ed·i·tor (ĕd′ə tər) *n-* **1** person who corrects, revises, or prepares a manuscript, film, tape, etc., for publication or performance. **2** person who directs the policies of a newspaper, magazine, etc.

ed·i·tor·i·al (ĕd′ə tôr′ē əl) *n-* article in a newspaper, magazine, etc. expressing the official opinions or viewpoint of the editor or publisher on some topic; also, a similar statement broadcast on radio or television. *adj-* **1** of, resembling, or contained in such an article or statement: *his* editorial *opinions.* **2** of or having to do with an editor or editing: *her* editorial *duties. —adv-* **ed′i·tor′i·al·ly.**

ed·i·tor·i·al·ize (ĕd′ə tôr′ē ə līz′) *vi-* [**ed·i·tor·i·al·ized, ed·i·tor·i·al·iz·ing**] **1** to express opinions in or as if in an editorial. **2** to present such opinions as if facts.

ed·i·tor·ship (ĕd′ə tər shĭp′) *n-* **1** the position or work of an editor. **2** editorial control: *the magazine under Jean Toll's* editorship.

ed·u·ca·ble (ĕj′ə kə bəl) *adj-* such as can be educated or instructed. *—n-* **ed′u·ca·bil′i·ty.**

ed·u·cate (ĕj′ə kāt′, ĕd′yo͞o-) *vt-* [**ed·u·cat·ed, ed·u·cat·ing**] to develop and improve by teaching or training; add to the knowledge or experience of: *to* educate *children*; *to* educate *one's mind.*

ed·u·ca·tion (ĕj′ə kā′shən, ĕd′yo͞o-) *n-* **1** act or process of teaching or training, especially by a system of study or discipline. **2** knowledge or skill gained from training or learning. **3** study of the methods of teaching and learning: *a school of* education.

ed·u·ca·tion·al (ĕj′ə kā′shən əl, ĕd′yo͞o-) *adj-* **1** of, having to do with, or used in teaching or learning: *books, maps, and other* educational *materials; modern* educational *methods.* **2** providing information or knowledge; instructive. *—adv-* **ed′u·ca′tion·al·ly.**

ed·u·ca·tive (ĕj′ ə kə tĭv, ĕd′ yōō-) ***adj-*** tending to educate; instructive.

ed·u·ca·tor (ĕj′ ə kā′ tər, ĕd′ yōō-) ***n-*** **1** teacher or other official of a school. **2** expert on education.

e·duce (ē dyōōs′, -dōōs′) ***vt-*** [**e·duced, e·duc·ing**] to draw forth; bring out; elicit: *to* educe *desired information by skillful questioning.* **—*adj-*** **e·duc′ i·ble.**

►Should not be confused with ADDUCE.

-ee *suffix* (used to form nouns) **1** person who is affected by an action or process: *employ*ee; *pay*ee. **2** receiver of a: *licens*ee; *grant*ee. **3** one who does or is: *stand*ee.

eel (ēl) ***n-*** any of various snakelike fishes with slippery skin. **—*adj-*** **eel′ like′.**

Eel, 2—3 ft. long

eel·grass (ēl′ grăs′) ***n-*** underwater plant with long, narrow leaves, commonly found in sandy or muddy waters near North Atlantic shores.

e′en (ēn) *Archaic* ***adv-*** even; indeed. ***n-*** evening.

e′er (âr) *Archaic* ***adv-*** ever. ***Homs-*** air, ere, heir, [2]are.

ee·rie or **ee·ry** (êr′ ē) ***adj-*** [**ee·ri·er, ee·ri·est**] **1** strange and frightening: *the* eerie *cry of an owl.* **2** uneasy; edgy: *an* eerie *feeling.* **—*adv-*** **ee′ ri·ly.** ***n-*** **ee′ ri·ness.**

ef·face (ĭ fās′) ***vt-*** [**ef·faced, ef·fac·ing**] to erase; wipe out; destroy. **—*n-*** **ef·face′ ment.** ***n-*** **ef·fac′ er.**

efface (oneself) to keep (oneself) in the background.

ef·fect (ĭ fĕkt′) ***n-*** **1** result of the action or influence of one thing, person, etc., on another or others; consequence: *the* effect *of a medicine*; *the* effect *of poverty.* **2** convincing illusion: *Sound* effects *are important in TV. The new plastic gives the* effect *of real leather.* **3 effects** personal possessions; movable goods: *one's household* effects. ***vt-*** to cause; bring about; accomplish: *He tried to* effect *an end to the quarrel.*

for effect for show; for the sake of impressing: *to talk merely* for effect. **give effect to** to put into action. **in effect 1** in force or action: *The law is* in effect. **2** actually: *He was,* in effect, *dismissed.* **take effect** to begin to operate or have results: *The pill* takes effect *quickly.*

►For usage note see AFFECT.

ef·fect·ive (ĭ fĕk′ tĭv) ***adj-*** **1** having the power to produce a result, especially a desired result: *an* effective *medicine*; *an* effective *argument.* **2** in force: *The law will be* effective *next week.* **—*adv-*** **ef·fect′ ive·ly.** ***n-*** **ef·fect′ ive·ness.**

ef·fec·tu·al (ĭ fĕk′ chōō əl) ***adj-*** producing or able to produce desired results: *an* effectual *law*; *an* effectual *person.* **—*adv-*** **ef·fec′ tu·al·ly.** ***n-*** **ef·fec′ tu·al·ness** or **ef·fec′ tu·al′ i·ty** (-chōō ăl′ ə tē).

ef·fec·tu·ate (ĭ fĕk′ chōō āt′) ***vt-*** [**ef·fec·tu·at·ed, ef·fec·tu·at·ing**] to bring about; accomplish; effect: *to* effectuate *desired results.* **—*n-*** **ef·fec′ tu·a′ tion.**

ef·fem·i·nate (ĭ fĕm′ ə nət) ***adj-*** of a man or boy, having more feminine qualities than are suitable to a male; womanish; unmanly. **—*n-*** **ef·fem′ i·na·cy** or **ef·fem′ i·nate·ness.** ***adv-*** **ef·fem′ i·nate·ly.**

ef·fen·di (ĕ fĕn′ dē) ***n-*** in Turkey and Arab countries, a title or respectful form of address equivalent to "sir" or "gentleman."

ef·fer·vesce (ĕf′ ər vĕs′) ***vi-*** [**ef·fer·vesced, ef·fer·vesc·ing**] **1** to give off gas in bubbles, as a carbonated drink does. **2** to be lively, gay, and full of enthusiasm.

ef·fer·ves·cent (ĕf′ ər vĕs′ ənt) ***adj-*** **1** forming or giving off bubbles of gas: *Champagne is an* effervescent *wine.* **2** full of bubbling enthusiasm: *her* effervescent *personality.* **—*n-*** **ef′ fer·ves′ cence**: *That ginger ale has lost its* effervescence. ***adv-*** **ef′ fer·ves′ cent·ly.**

ef·fete (ĕ fēt′) ***adj-*** no longer productive or vigorous; exhausted in power, effectiveness, etc.: *an* effete *civilization.* **—*adv-*** **ef·fete′ly.** ***n-*** **ef·fete′ness.**

ef·fi·ca·cious (ĕf′ ə kā′ shəs) ***adj-*** able to do what is expected or required; successful in desired function; effective: *an* efficacious *remedy*; *an* efficacious *person.* **—*adv-*** **ef′ fi·ca′ cious·ly.** ***n-*** **ef′ fi·ca′ cious·ness.**

ef·fi·ca·cy (ĕf′ ĭ kə sē) ***n-*** [*pl.* **ef·fi·ca·cies**] the power to produce results, especially desired results.

ef·fi·cien·cy (ĭ fĭsh′ ən sē) ***n-*** [*pl.* **ef·fi·cien·cies**] **1** ability to produce desired results with the least amount of time, expense, or labor; effective use of effort or energy. **2** *Physics* of an engine or other machine, the ratio of the useful work delivered by it to the amount of energy supplied to it.

ef·fi·cient (ĭ fĭsh′ ənt) ***adj-*** producing the desired results with the least output of time, expense, and labor. **—*adv-*** **ef·fi′ cient·ly.**

ef·fi·gy (ĕf′ ə jē) ***n-*** [*pl.* **ef·fi·gies**] portrait, statue, or other likeness of a person; especially, a crude image representing a hated person.

in effigy symbolically, in the form of a crude image.

ef·flo·res·cence (ĕ′ flə rĕs′ əns) ***n-*** **1** act, state, or season of flowering. **2** *Chemistry* loss of water of crystallization by certain crystals when exposed to air. **3** any rash, eruption, or lesion of the skin. **—*adj-*** **ef′ flo·res′ cent.**

ef·flu·vi·um (ĕ flōō′ vē əm) ***n-*** [*pl.* **ef·flu·vi·a** (-ə) or **ef·flu·vi·ums**] vapor or odor, especially one that is foul-smelling or poisonous.

ef·fort (ĕf′ ərt) ***n-*** **1** a putting forth of physical or mental power; exertion: *With great* effort, *he held back an angry reply.* **2** a try; an attempt: *The dog made an* effort *to get through the opening.* **3** something produced by work; achievement: *his latest literary* effort.

ef·fort·less (ĕf′ ərt ləs) ***adj-*** requiring or showing little or no effort; easy: *an* effortless *victory.* **—*adv-*** **ef′ fort·less·ly.** ***n-*** **ef′ fort·less·ness.**

ef·fron·ter·y (ĭ frŭn′ tə rē) ***n-*** [*pl.* **ef·fron·ter·ies**] shameless boldness or impudence; insolence; audacity.

ef·ful·gence (ĭ fŭl′ jəns) ***n-*** great brightness or splendor; radiance. **—*adj-*** **ef·ful′ gent.** ***adv-*** **ef·ful′ gent·ly.**

ef·fu·sion (ĭ fyōō′ zhən) ***n-*** **1** a pouring or gushing forth, especially an unrestrained outpouring of ideas or feelings. **2** *Medicine* (1) escape of fluid into a part or tissue of the body. (2) such escaped fluid. **3** *Chemistry* passage of gas under pressure through small openings.

ef·fu·sive (ĭ fyōō′ sĭv) ***adj-*** showing or expressing excessive enthusiasm or feeling; gushing: *his* effusive *thanks.* **—*adv-*** **ef·fu′ sive·ly.** ***n-*** **ef·fu′ sive·ness.**

eft (ĕft) ***n-*** newt, especially an immature newt.

e.g. for example [from Latin **exempli gratia**].

[1]**egg** (ĕg) ***n-*** **1** the oval or round body produced by hens and used as food; also, a similar body produced by the females of many animals, from which the young develop. Birds, insects, fish, and most reptiles hatch from eggs. **2** (also **egg cell**) reproductive cell produced by female animals and many plants. **3** *Informal* person; fellow: *He's a good* egg. [from an Old Norse word.]

[2]**egg** (ĕg) ***vt-*** to urge or goad (often used with "on"): *She* egged *him on to mischief.* [from Old Norse **eggja,** originally meaning "to give an edge to."]

egg·beat·er (ĕg′ bē′ tər) ***n-*** device, usually having rotary blades, used to beat eggs, whip cream, etc.

egg·head (ĕg′ hĕd′) *Slang* ***n-*** a highbrow; intellectual.

egg·nog (ĕg′ nŏg′) ***n-*** a drink made of eggs beaten up with milk, sugar, spices, and often wine or other liquor.

[American word from [1]**egg** plus British **nog** meaning "strong ale."]

egg·plant (ĕg′ plănt′) ***n*- 1** plant that bears a large, oval, purple-skinned fruit. **2** its fruit, eaten as a vegetable.

Eggplant

egg·shell (ĕg′ shĕl′) ***n*- 1** the shell of an egg, especially a bird's egg. **2** a very light tan. ***adj*- 1** very light tan. **2** having a slight gloss: *an* eggshell *enamel.* **3** thin and fragile: *fine* eggshell *china.*

e·gis (ē′ jəs) aegis.

eg·lan·tine (ĕg′ lən tīn′, -tēn′) ***n*-** wild rose with fragrant pink or white flowers; sweetbrier.

e·go (ē′ gō) ***n*-** [*pl.* **e·gos**] **1** the self or individual personality, especially as it is aware of being distinct from other selves and other things; separate identity. **2** *Informal* strong approval of oneself; egotism; conceit.

e·go·ism (ē′ gō ĭz′ əm) ***n*-** the habit or tendency of considering or valuing everything from one's own self.

e·go·ist (ē′ gō ĭst) ***n*-** person who considers or values everything in terms of his own preferences, interests, etc. **—*adj*- e′ go·is′ tic** or **e′ go·is′ ti·cal.** ***adv*- e′ go·is′ ti·cal·ly.**

e·go·tism (ē′ gə tĭz′ əm, *also* ĕg′ ə-) ***n*-** the habit of thinking, talking, or writing too much about oneself; conceit.

e·go·tist (ē′ gə tĭst, *also* ĕg′ ə-) ***n*-** one who makes excessive and boastful references to himself; a conceited person. **—*adj*- e′ go·tis′ ti·cal** or **e′ go·tis′ tic.** ***adv*- e′ go·tis′ ti·cal·ly.**

e·gre·gious (ĭ grē′ jəs) ***adj*-** shockingly bad; flagrant; outrageous: *an* egregious *blunder.* **—*adv*- e·gre′ gious·ly.** ***n*- e·gre′ gious·ness.**

e·gress (ē′ grĕs′) ***n*- 1** a going out; departure. **2** a means of leaving; place through which to leave; exit. **3** *Astronomy* emergence of a heavenly body from eclipse. ***vi*-** to emerge: *The astronauts will soon* egress *from the capsule.*

e·gret (ē′ grət) ***n*- 1** white wading bird related to the heron and having long, decorative outer plumes in the breeding season. **2** one of these plumes; aigrette.

E·gyp·tian (ĭ jĭp′ shən) ***adj*-** of or pertaining to Egypt, its people, or their culture. ***n*- 1** a native of Egypt or one of his descendants. **2** the language of ancient Egypt up to about the third century B.C.

Egyptian cotton ***n*-** fine cotton with long fibers, grown chiefly in Egypt.

eh (ā, ĕ) ***interj*-** exclamation expressing a question, surprise, uncertainty, etc.

ei·der (ī′ dər) or **eider duck** ***n*-** large sea duck of northern latitudes, valued for its soft breast feathers.

ei·der·down (ī′ dər doun′) ***n*- 1** soft breast feathers of the eider duck. **2** bed covering stuffed with these.

eight (āt) ***n*- 1** amount or quantity that is one greater than 7; 8. **2** *Mathematics* (1) the cardinal number that is the sum of 7 and 1. (2) a numeral such as 8 that represents this cardinal number. *as* ***determiner*** (traditionally called adjective or pronoun): *There are* eight *people here and* eight *there.* ***Hom*-** ate.

eight·een (ā′ tēn′) ***n*- 1** amount or quantity that is one greater than 17. **2** *Mathematics* (1) the cardinal number that is the sum of 17 and 1. (2) a numeral such as 18 that represents this cardinal number. *as* ***determiner*** (traditionally called adjective or pronoun): *There are* eighteen *dogs here and* eighteen *there.*

eight·eenth (ā′ tēnth′) ***adj*- 1** next after seventeenth. **2** the ordinal of 18; 18th. ***n*- 1** the next after the seventeenth; 18th. **2** one of eighteen equal parts of a whole or group. **3** the last term in the name of a fraction having a denominator of 18: 1/18 *is one* eighteenth. ***adv*-:** *His boat finished* eighteenth *in the race.*

eight·fold (āt′ fōld′) ***adj*- 1** eight times as many or as much. **2** having eight parts. ***adv*-:** *They increased their output* eightfold.

eighth (ātth) ***adj*- 1** next after seventh. **2** the ordinal of 8; 8th. ***n*- 1** the next after the seventh; 8th. **2** one of eight equal parts of a whole or group. **3** the last term in the name of a fraction having a denominator of 8: 1/8 *is one* eighth. ***adv*-:** *He spoke of you* eighth.

eighth note *Music* ***n*-** note held one eighth as long as a whole note. For picture, see *note.*

eight·i·eth (ā′ tē əth) ***adj*- 1** next after seventy-ninth. **2** the ordinal of 80; 80th. ***n*- 1** the next after the seventy-ninth; 80th. **2** one of eighty equal parts of a whole or group. **3** the last term in the name of a fraction having a denominator of 80: 1/80 *is one* eightieth. ***adv*-:** *He stood* eightieth *in line.*

eight·y (ā′ tē) ***n*-** [*pl.* **eight·ies**] **1** amount or quantity that is one greater than 79; 80. **2** *Mathematics* (1) the cardinal number that is the sum of 79 and 1. (2) a numeral such as 80 that represents this cardinal number. *as* ***determiner*** (traditionally called adjective or pronoun): *There are* eighty *birds here and* eighty *there.*

ein·stein·i·um (īn stī′ nē əm) ***n*-** radioactive metal element. Symbol Es, At. No. 99.

ei·ther (ē′ thər, ī′ thər) ***determiner*** (traditionally called adjective or pronoun) **1** one or the other of two: *You may take* either *seat. He looked at two cars, but didn't buy* either. **2** each of two: *Trees lined* either *side of the street.* ***adv*-** also (used only after a negative): *I didn't go, and he didn't go,* either. ***n*-** any of two: *We'll take* either *of them.* ***conj*-** (used with "or" to introduce two alternatives): *He said,* "Either *you go or I go." They will leave* either *today or tomorrow. I want* either *a pear or an apple.*

e·jac·u·late (ĭ jăk′ yə lāt′) ***vt*-** [**e·jac·u·lat·ed, e·jac·u·lat·ing**] **1** to exclaim; blurt out. **2** to eject or discharge (a stream or flow of fluid).

e·jac·u·la·tion (ĭ jăk′ yə lā′ shən) ***n*- 1** a sudden exclamation or cry. **2** act or process of ejaculating.

e·ject (ĭ jĕkt′) ***vt*-** to push, throw, or force out; expel: *to* eject *a used cartridge.* **—*n*- e·jec′ tion.**

e·jec·tor (ĭ jĕk′ tər) ***n*-** someone or something that ejects; especially, a mechanical device that expels used material.

[1]**eke** (ēk) [**eked, ek·ing**] **eke out 1** to just manage to make (a living): *He* eked out *a living by writing.* **2** to add enough to (something) to make do; supplement: *to* eke out *a meal of leftovers by adding rice.* [from Old English **ēcan.**]

[2]**eke** (ēk) *Archaic* also. [from Old English **ēc.**]

[1]**e·lab·o·rate** (ĭ lăb′ ər ət) ***adj*-** carefully worked out in great detail; painstakingly prepared; intricate: *to make* elaborate *plans;* elaborate *costumes for a play.* **—*adv*- e·lab′ o·rate·ly.** ***n*- e·lab′ o·rate·ness.**

[2]**e·lab·o·rate** (ĭ lăb′ ə rāt′) ***vt*-** [**e·lab·o·rat·ed, e·lab·o·rat·ing**] to work out with great care and detail: *The general* elaborated *his plan.* **—*n*- e·lab′ o·ra′ tion.**
elaborate on to give more details about.

Eland, 3 1/2—6 ft. high at shoulder

e·lan (ā lä^{n}′) ***n*-** dash and enthusiasm; vivacity; ardor. [from French.]

e·land (ē′ lənd) ***n*-** large South African antelope having twisted horns on both the male and the female.

el·a·pid (ĕl′ ə pĭd′) ***n-*** any of a large group of poisonous snakes with grooved fangs.

e·lapse (ĭ lăps′) ***vi-*** [**e·lapsed, e·laps·ing**] of time, to go by; pass: *Many days* elapsed *before they returned.*

e·las·mo·branch (ĭ lăz′ mə brăngk′) ***n-*** member of a primitive group of fishlike animals **(Elasmobranchii)** that have skeletons of cartilage. Elasmobranchs include sharks and rays.

e·las·tic (ĭ lăs′ tĭk) ***adj-*** **1** able to spring back to normal size, shape, or position after being stretched or pressed together: *Rubber is an* elastic *substance.* **2** easily changed or adapted to fit circumstances; flexible: *an* elastic *foreign policy*; ***n-*** **1** stretchable cloth or tape woven with strands of rubber or similar material. **2** a rubber band. ***—adv-*** **e·las′ ti·cal·ly.**

e·las·tic·i·ty (ĭ lăs′ tĭs′ ə tē, ē′ lăs′-) ***n-*** **1** condition or quality of being elastic: *the* elasticity *of a rubber band*; *the* elasticity *of his temperament.* **2** *Physics* property of matter that causes an object or substance to return to its original form or shape after a stretching, bending, or otherwise deforming force has been removed.

elastic limit ***n-*** in engineering, the maximum point to which a structural material can be stretched, bent, etc., without causing it to be permanently deformed.

e·late (ĭ lāt′) ***vt-*** [**e·lat·ed, e·lat·ing**] to make excited with joy or pride; raise the spirits of: *Winning first prize* elated *her.* ***—adv-*** **e·lat′ ed·ly.**

el·a·ter (ĕl′ ə tər) ***n-*** any of several related beetles that turn over suddenly with a loud, clicking noise after falling on their backs.

e·la·tion (ĭ lā′ shən) ***n-*** feeling of exultant joy or pride.

E layer ***n-*** Heaviside layer.

el·bow (ĕl′ bō) ***n-*** **1** the joint in the arm between wrist and shoulder; also, the outer part of the arm at this point. **2** something bent at an angle, such as a curved section of pipe. ***vt-*** to nudge, jostle, or push with or as if with the outer part of the arm: *She* elbowed *the other shoppers aside.*

Pipe elbow

elbow grease *Slang* ***n-*** physical effort; hard work.

el·bow·room (ĕl′ bō ro͞om′) ***n-*** enough room for one's work or activities; ample space or scope.

eld (ĕld) *Archaic* ***n-*** ancient times.

[1]**eld·er** (ĕl′ dər) ***adj-*** older: *Which is the* elder *sister?* ***n-*** **1** older or more experienced person: *Young Indians respected the* elders *of the tribe.* **2** an officer of certain churches. [from Old English **eldra.**]

[2]**el·der** (ĕl′ dər) ***n-*** shrub with flat clusters of white flowers, and small black, reddish, or purple berries. [from Old English **ellern.**]

el·der·ber·ry (ĕld′ ər bĕr′ ē) ***n-*** [*pl.* **el·der·ber·ries**] **1** the small, round berry of the elder. **2** the elder bush. ***as modifier***: *He made* elderberry *wine.*

eld·er·ly (ĕl′ dər lē) ***adj-*** of a person, somewhat old; past middle age: *an* elderly *gentleman.*

elder statesman ***n-*** older person retired from public life, who acts as an unofficial consultant on government problems.

eld·est (ĕl′ dəst) ***adj-*** oldest; first born: *the* eldest *child.*

El Do·ra·do (ĕl′ də rä′ dō, -rā′ dō) ***n-*** fabled region rich in gold and precious stones, sought by early explorers in the New World; hence, any rich region.

e·lect (ĭ lĕkt′) ***vt-*** **1** to choose or select by vote: *The club* elects *officers in May.* **2** to decide; prefer: *Tom* elected *to stay at home last night.* ***adj-*** chosen for an office but not yet serving: *the governor-*elect.

e·lec·tion (ĭ lĕk′ shən) ***n-*** **1** an electing or a being elected: *his* election *to office.* **2** the process of choosing a person or persons for office by voting: *a presidential* election.

e·lec·tion·eer (ĭ lĕk′ shə nêr′) ***vi-*** to work to secure votes for a party or candidate during an election.

e·lec·tive (ĭ lĕk′ tĭv) ***adj-*** **1** chosen by election: *an* elective *official.* **2** filled by election: *an* elective *office.* **3** open to choice; not compulsory: *an* elective *course of study.* ***n-*** school course not included in a student's required subects.

e·lec·tor (ĭ lĕk′ tər) ***n-*** **1** voter, especially a qualified voter. **2** member of the electoral college.

e·lec·tor·al (ĭ lĕk′ tər əl) ***adj-*** of, having to do with, or consisting of electors: *the* electoral *vote.*

electoral college ***n-*** group of citizens chosen by the voters of each State to elect the president and vice-president of the United States.

electoral vote ***n-*** the number of votes cast by members of the electoral college.

e·lec·tor·ate (ĭ lĕk′ tər ət) ***n-*** all the persons entitled to vote in an election; the qualified voters.

e·lec·tric (ĭ lĕk′ trĭk) ***adj-*** **1** of or produced by electricity; producing, transmitting, or using electricity: *an* electric *generator*; *an* electric *current*; *an* electric *train.* **2** thrilling; exciting: *An* electric *quiver ran through the crowd.*

e·lec·tri·cal (ĭ lĕk′ trĭ kəl) ***adj-*** **1** operated by electricity: *new* electrical *appliances.* **2** concerned or working with electricity. ***—adv-*** **e·lec′ tri·cal·ly.**

electrical transcription ***n-*** an electronic recording of a performance, usually for a radio broadcast later.

electric chair ***n-*** **1** device for executing condemned prisoners by electricity. **2** *Informal* execution by this means.

electric eel ***n-*** eellike fish of South America that has special organs which produce strong electric shocks.

electric eye ***n-*** photoelectric cell used to turn switches on and off in order to open doors, start fans, etc.

electric field ***n-*** **1** region surrounding an electric charge, a charged object, or a moving magnet, in which a force acts on a charge brought into the region. **2** the electric force itself that acts at a particular point in the region.

e·lec·tri·cian (ĭ lĕk′ trĭsh′ ən) ***n-*** person who installs, repairs, or works with electrical wiring or appliances.

e·lec·tric·i·ty (ĭ lĕk′ trĭs′ ə tē) ***n-*** **1** transfer of energy in a flow of electrons from one place to another. For example, energy in falling water drives a generator which drives electrons through a wire. The electrons in turn drive motors in homes and factories. **2** potential energy of a stationary electric charge; static electricity. **3** branch of science that deals with the theory and principles that explain electrical phenomena.

electric storm or **electrical storm** ***n-*** thunderstorm.

e·lec·tri·fi·ca·tion (ĭ lĕk′ trə fə kā′ shən) ***n-*** a supplying of electricity; also, an equipping to use it.

e·lec·tri·fy (ĭ lĕk′ trə fī′) ***vt-*** [**e·lec·tri·fied, e·lec·tri·fy·ing**] **1** to charge with electricity. **2** to equip (a house, railway, etc.) for the use of electricity. **3** to thrill: *His speech* electrified *the audience.*

electro- *combining form* of or having to do with electricity; electric: *an* electro*magnet.* [from Greek **elektron** meaning "amber," associated with static electricity.]

e·lec·tro·car·di·o·graph (ĭ lĕk′ trō kär′ dē ə grăf′) ***n-*** instrument used to detect abnormalities of the heart by recording on a graph, called an **e·lec′ tro·car′ di·o·gram′**, the electric impulses produced by the heartbeats.

---

fāte, făt, dâre, bärn; bē, bĕt, mêre; bīte, bĭt; nōte, hŏt, môre, dȯg; fŭn, fûr; to͞o, bo͝ok; oil; out; ta*r*; thin; *th*en; hw for wh as in *wh*at; zh for s as in u*s*ual; ə for a, e, i, o, u, as in *a*go, lin*e*n, per*i*l, at*o*m, min*u*s

e·lec·tro·chem·is·try (ĭ lĕk′ trō kĕm′ ĭs trē) ***n-*** branch of chemistry that deals with the study of chemical changes caused by electrical action, and the production of electricity by chemical reactions. **—*adj-* e·lec′ tro·chem′ i·cal:** *an* electrochemical *reaction.*

e·lec·tro·cute (ĭ lĕk′ trə kyōōt′) ***vt-*** **[e·lec·tro·cut·ed, e·lec·tro·cut·ing]** to kill by electric shock. **—*n-* e·lec′ tro·cu′ tion.**

e·lec·trode (ĭ lĕk′ trōd′) ***n-*** **1** either pole of an electric battery or any other source of electricity. **2** in an electron tube, transistor, etc., any one of the parts that give off, collect, or control the flow of electrons.

e·lec·tro·dy·nam·ics (ĭ lĕk′ trō dī năm′ ĭks) ***n-*** branch of physics studying the interactions among electrical, magnetic, and mechanical events and forces. It deals with magnetic fields generated by currents, behavior of charged particles in electric and magnetic fields, etc.

e·lec·trol·y·sis (ĭ lĕk′ trŏl′ ə səs) ***n-*** **1** process of decomposing a chemical compound by passing an electric current through its solution. **2** the destruction of hair roots by means of an electric current.

e·lec·tro·lyte (ĭ lĕk′ trə līt′) ***n-*** **1** any substance that conducts electricity when in solution or in a liquid state. **2** a solution that conducts electricity. **—*adj-* e·lec′ tro·lyt′ ic** (-trə lĭt′ ĭk). ***adv-*** **e·lec′ tro·lyt′ i·cal·ly.**

e·lec·tro·lyze (ĭ lĕk′ trə līz′) ***vt-*** **[e·lec·tro·lyzed, e·lec·tro·lyz·ing]** to decompose or separate into different parts by electrolysis.

e·lec·tro·mag·net (ĭ lĕk′ trō măg′ nət) ***n-*** piece of soft iron made into a magnet by passing an electric current through a coil of wire wrapped around it.

Electromagnet

electromagnetic wave ***n-*** wave of energy characterized by electric and magnetic fields that spread outward from it. Light waves and radio waves are examples of electromagnetic waves.

e·lec·tro·mag·net·ism (ĭ lĕk′ trō măg′ nə tĭz′ əm) ***n-*** **1** magnetism that is produced by an electric current. **2** branch of science that deals with the relationship between electricity and magnetism, and with related phenomena. **—*adj-* e·lec′ tro·mag·net′ ic.**

e·lec·trom·e·ter (ĭ lĕk′ trŏm′ ə tər) ***n-*** any instrument that detects or measures the voltage of an electric current by measuring forces of attraction or repulsion between two charged bodies.

e·lec·tro·mo·tive (ĭ lĕk′ trō mō′ tĭv) ***adj-*** producing or tending to produce an electric current.

electromotive force ***n-*** **1** force which tends to cause electricity to flow from one point to another. **2** in an electrical circuit, a difference of potential between two points; voltage.

e·lec·tron (ĭ lek′ trŏn) ***n-*** tiny particle of matter that has one unit of negative charge and a mass equal to 1/1837 of the mass of a proton (or 9.1×10^{-25} grams). Electrons move around the nucleus of the atom, which has a positive charge. They also move in a stream from one atom to another as an electric current.

electron gun ***n-*** device used in an electron tube for producing and focusing a stream of electrons.

e·lec·tron·ic (ĭ lĕk′ trŏn′ ĭk) ***adj-*** **1** of or having to do with electrons. **2** of, having to do with, or functioning by the principles of electronics: *Radios and computers are* electronic *devices.* **—*adv-* e·lec′ tron′ i·cal·ly.**

electronic brain ***n-*** *Informal* an electronic computing or translating machine.

e·lec·tron·ics (ĭ lĕk′ trŏn′ ĭks) ***n-*** (takes singular verb) branch of science that deals with the production, behavior, and use of electrons, especially in vacuum tubes, photoelectric cells, and similar devices.

electron microscope ***n-*** extremely high-powered microscope in which beams of electrons instead of light are used to produce an enlarged image.

electron tube ***n-*** sealed glass or metal tube, usually with a vacuum inside it, containing a negatively charged electrode that emits a stream of electrons when heated; vacuum tube. Electron tubes are used in many ways, especially to select and amplify electric signals.

electron volt ***n-*** unit of energy needed to move an electron between two points having a potential difference of 1 volt. It is equal to 1.602×10^{-12} ergs.

e·lec·tro·plate (ĭ lĕk′ trō plāt′) ***vt-*** **[e·lec·tro·plat·ed, e·lec·tro·plat·ing]** to cover (something) with a coating of metal by electrolysis.

e·lec·tro·pos·i·tive (ĭ lĕk′ trō pŏz′ ə tĭv) ***adj-*** **1** having a positive electric charge. **2** of a solution, basic; not acid.

e·lec·tro·scope (ĭ lĕk′ trə skōp′) ***n-*** instrument that can detect very small electric charges and show whether they are positive or negative.

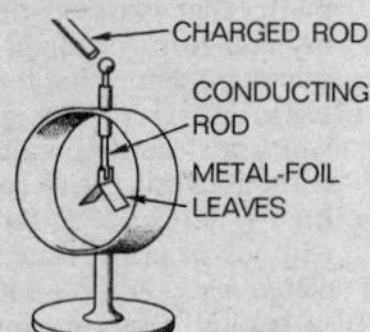

Electroscope

e·lec·tro·stat·ic (ĭ lĕk′ trō stăt′ ĭk) ***adj-*** of or having to do with electrostatics or with static electricity.

electrostatic generator ***n-*** apparatus that produces high-voltage electrical discharges.

e·lec·tro·stat·ics (ĭ lĕk′ trō stăt′ ĭks) ***n-*** (takes singular verb) branch of physics that deals with phenomena caused by the attractions and repulsions of stationary electric charges.

e·lec·tro·ther·a·py (ĭ lĕk′ trō thĕr′ ə pē) ***n-*** treatment of disease with heat generated by an electric current.

e·lec·tro·type (ĭ lĕk′ trō tīp′) ***n-*** **1** plate for use in printing, made by covering a wax or lead mold of the original type with a thin metal shell by electroplating, and then backing it with molten metal. **2** a print made from a plate of this kind. ***vt-*** **[e·lec·tro·typed, e·lec·tro·typ·ing]** to make a printing plate of, by this process.

el·ee·mos·y·na·ry (ĕl′ ə mŏs′ ə nĕr′ ē) ***adj-*** related to, relying on, or given as charity.

el·e·gance (ĕl′ ə gəns) ***n-*** refinement and good taste.

el·e·gant (ĕl′ ə gənt) ***adj-*** **1** having or showing good taste and refinement: *courtly,* elegant *manners.* **2** *Informal* very pleasing. **—*adv-* el′ e·gant·ly.**

el·e·gi·ac (ĕl′ ə jī′ ək) ***adj-*** of, or in the form of an elegy.

el·e·gize (ĕl′ ə jīz′) ***vt-*** **[el·e·gized, el·e·giz·ing]** to describe or lament in an elegy; write mournfully about.

el·e·gy (ĕl′ ə jē) ***n-*** [*pl.* **el·e·gies**] poem of a mournful or serious nature, often lamenting the dead.

el·e·ment (ĕl′ ə mənt) ***n-*** **1** (also **chemical element**) substance that cannot be broken down into simpler substances by ordinary chemical means. Gold, iron, hydrogen, and oxygen are elements. **2** one of the main principles or steps of a subject; necessary part of a whole: *to learn the* elements *of arithmetic*; *to have all the* elements *of a good story.* **3** circumstances or surroundings best suited to one's nature or abilities: *Water is the natural* element *of a fish.* **4 the elements** the forces of nature, such as rain, wind, or snow. **5** *Mathematics* any member of a set.

el·e·men·tal (ĕl′ ə mĕn′ təl) ***adj-*** of or having to do with basic principles or characteristics, especially of the physical world: *an* elemental *force.*

el·e·men·ta·ry (ĕl′ ə mĕn′ tə rē) ***adj-*** of or having to do with first steps or principles; introductory.

elementary charge' ***n-*** fundamental quantity of positive or negative electricity, equal in magnitude to the charge on the electron (1.6×10^{-19} coulomb).

elementary school ***n-*** school which provides the first six or eight years of formal education and sometimes includes kindergarten.

el·e·phant (ĕl′ ə fənt) ***n-*** largest living land animal, native to Africa and Asia and having a thick, gray, wrinkled hide, two curved ivory tusks, and a trunk.

Asian elephant, 8—10 ft. high

el·e·phan·ti·a·sis (ĕl′ ə fən-tī′ ə səs) ***n-*** filariasis.

el·e·phan·tine (ĕl′ ə fən tēn′, -tīn′) ***adj-*** of, like, or suggestive of an elephant; slow and heavy.

el·e·vate (ĕl′ ə vāt′) ***vt-*** **[el·e·vat·ed, el·e·vat·ing] 1** to raise to a higher level; lift: *to* elevate *a window shade.* **2** to raise to a higher rank or status: *He was* elevated *to the peerage.* **3** to improve the mental or moral quality of: *Great ideas* elevate *the mind.*

el·e·vat·ed (ĕl′ ə vā′ təd) ***adj-*** **1** raised to or placed at a high level: *an* elevated *platform.* **2** noble and inspired; lofty: *a sermon filled with* elevated *thoughts.* ***n-*** railroad raised high above street level.

el·e·va·tion (ĕl′ ə vā′ shən) ***n-*** **1** raised place: *The house is built on a slight* elevation. **2** height, especially above sea level: *The* elevation *of the land at that point is 958 feet.* **3** a raising or a being raised.

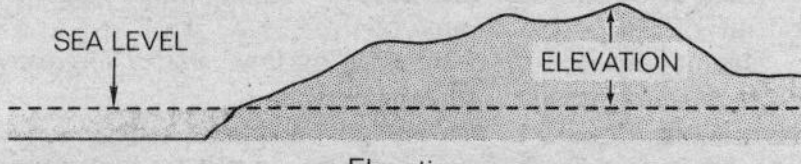

Elevation

el·e·va·tor (ĕl′ ə vā′ tər) ***n-*** **1** anything that lifts up. **2** movable platform or enclosed car that carries people, freight, etc., up and down between different levels or floors, usually inside a building. **3** in aeronautics, either of two flaps or control surfaces that are hinged to the horizontal parts of an airplane's tail and are used to make the tail go up or down. For picture, see *airplane.* **4** building equipped to store and process grain; grain elevator.

Grain elevator

e·lev·en (ĭ lĕv′ ən) ***n-*** **1** amount or quantity that is one greater than ten; 11. **2** *Mathematics* (1) the cardinal number that is the sum of 10 and 1. (2) a numeral such as 11 that represents this cardinal number. **3** a football team. *as* ***determiner*** (traditionally called adjective or pronoun): *There are* eleven *ships here and* eleven *there.*

e·lev·enth (ĭ lĕv′ ənth) ***adj-*** **1** next after tenth. **2** the ordinal of 11; 11th. ***n-*** **1** the next after the tenth; 11th. **2** one of eleven equal parts of a whole or group. **3** the last term in the name of a fraction having a denominator of 11: *1/11 is one* eleventh. ***adv-***: *He finished* eleventh *in the contest.*

eleventh hour ***n-*** the last possible time before it is too late: *The strike was called off at the* eleventh hour.

elf (ĕlf) ***n-*** [*pl.* **elves** (ĕlvz)] small goblin, fairy, or sprite, sometimes mischievous, sometimes helpful.

elf·in (ĕl′ fĭn) ***adj-*** suggestive of an elf; odd and charming: *her* elfin *laughter.*

elf·ish (ĕl′ fĭsh) ***adj-*** like an elf; impish: *his* elfish *pranks.* **—*adv-* elf′ ish·ly. *n-* elf′ ish·ness.**

e·lic·it (ĭ lĭs′ ĭt) ***vt-*** to draw out; bring forth; evoke: *to* elicit *a reply.* ***Hom-*** illicit.

e·lide (ĭ līd′) ***vt-*** **[e·lid·ed, e·lid·ing]** to omit or slur (a syllable or vowel) in pronouncing a word or words.

el·i·gi·ble (ĕl′ ə jə bəl) ***adj-*** **1** qualified or entitled to participate in or receive: *to be* eligible *for promotion;* eligible *to play;* eligible *for citizenship.* **2** suitable for marriage. **—*n-* el′ i·gi·bil′ ity. *adv-* el′ i·gi·bly.**

E·li·jah (ĭ lī′ jə) ***n-*** ninth century B.C. prophet. In the CCD Bible, **E·li′ a.**

e·lim·i·nate (ĭ lĭm′ ə nāt′) ***vt-*** **[e·lim·i·nat·ed, e·lim·i·nat·ing] 1** to get rid of; dispose of; remove: *to* eliminate *all possibility of error; to* eliminate *contestants in a race.* **2** to leave out of consideration; omit.

e·lim·i·na·tion (ĭ lĭm′ ə nā′ shən) ***n-*** **1** act or process of eliminating: *the* elimination *of wastes from the body.* **2** a being eliminated: *his* elimination *from the race.*

E·li·sha (ĭ lī′ shə) ***n-*** ninth century B.C. Hebrew prophet who succeeded Elijah.

e·li·sion (ĭ lĭzh′ ən) ***n-*** **1** the omission or slurring over of a syllable or vowel sound in pronouncing a word or words. Example: the omission of the sound of the "i" of "is" in "What's that?", or of the "e" of "de" in French "louis d'or." **2** an omitting or dropping out of a word, paragraph, passage, etc. ***Hom-*** Elysian.

e·lite (ə lēt′) ***n-*** **1** the best or most esteemed members of a society, profession, etc.: *Colonel Curtis is among the military* elite. **2** a type size for typewriters. *as* ***modifier***: *an* elite *regiment; an* elite *typewriter.*

e·lix·ir (ĭ lĭk′ sər) ***n-*** **1** sweet solution, usually of water and alcohol, that is used as a medium for medicine. **2** in alchemy, the philospher's stone, the substance that was supposed to change metals into gold; also, the substance that was supposed to restore and prolong youth. **3** remedy for all troubles; cure-all.

E·liz·a·be·than (ə lĭz′ ə bē′-thən) ***adj-*** of or pertaining to Queen Elizabeth of England (1533-1603), her reign, or the culture of her age. ***n-*** person who lived during this time.

elk (ĕlk) ***n-*** [*pl.* **elk** or **elks**] **1** large European deer related to the American moose. **2** large American deer related to the red deer of Europe; wapiti.

American elk, about 5 ft. high at shoulder

[1]ell (ĕl) ***n-*** old measure of length, chiefly for cloth, varying from 27 to 45 inches. [from Old English **eln.**]

[2]ell (ĕl) ***n-*** an addition to a building, constructed at right angles to the main structure; L. [from the letter "L."]

el·lipse (ĭ lĭps′) ***n-*** **1** closed plane curve, similar to an oval but having both ends equal in size. **2** *Mathematics* closed plane curve drawn so that, for any point P on the curve, the sum of the distances from P to two fixed points called foci is constant.

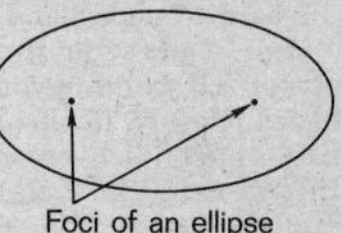
Foci of an ellipse

el·lip·sis (ĭ lĭp′ səs) ***n-*** [*pl.* **el·lip·ses** (-sēz′)] **1** in grammar, the omission of a word or words strictly required by grammatical rule but unnecessary for the sense of the statement. Example: "It is warmer today than yesterday" instead of "It is warmer today than it was yesterday." **2** series of marks [. . . or * * *] used in printing or writing to show that a word or words have been omitted.

el·lip·tic (ĭ lĭp′ tĭk) or **el·lip·ti·cal** (-tĭ kəl) ***adj-*** **1** of, having to do with, or shaped like an ellipse or part of an ellipse. **2** in grammar, showing or using ellipsis. ***—adv-*** **el·lip′ ti·cal·ly.**

elm (ĕlm) ***n-*** **1** tall shade tree with arching or outspread branches. **2** the hard, tough wood of this tree.

Elm

el·o·cu·tion (ĕl′ ə kyōō′ shən) ***n-*** art or style of reciting or speaking in public, especially a stilted or pompous style no longer popular.

E. long. east longitude.

e·lon·gate (ē lòng′ gāt′) ***vt-*** [**e·lon·gat·ed, e·lon·gat·ing**] to lengthen; extend: *to* elongate *a line*; *to* elongate *a story.* ***vi-***: *Earthworms* elongate *and contract at will.*

e·lon·ga·tion (ē′ lòng gā′ shən) ***n-*** **1** a making or becoming longer. **2** *Astronomy* angle between two celestial bodies as viewed from Earth, especially the angle between a planet or the moon and the sun.

e·lope (ĭ lōp′) ***vi-*** [**e·loped, e·lop·ing**] to go or run away secretly to be married. ***—n-*** **e·lope′ment.** ***n-*** **e·lop′ er.**

el·o·quence (ĕl′ ə kwəns) ***n-*** **1** ability to convey the intended meaning very well; power of expression: *the preacher's* eloquence. **2** good ordering and expression; expressiveness: *the* eloquence *of his appeal.* **3** art of effective speaking; oratory; elocution.

el·o·quent (ĕl′ ə kwənt) ***adj-*** conveying or expressing the intended meaning very well; expressive: *an* eloquent *speaker*; *an* eloquent *sermon.* ***—adv-*** **el′ o·quent·ly.**

else (ĕls) ***adv-*** **1** instead; otherwise: *How* else *could I do it*? *I asked him where* else *our club could meet.* **2** in addition; next: *What* else *do you want*? **3** if not; if this advice or command is ignored: *Do as I do, or* else *you may fall.* ***adj-*** different; other: *You looked like someone* else.

else·where (ĕls′ hwâr) ***adv-*** in, at, or to some other place; somewhere else: *I'll meet you* elsewhere.

e·lu·ci·date (ĭ lōō′ sə dāt′) ***vt-*** [**e·lu·ci·dat·ed, e·lu·ci·dat·ing**] to make clear; clarify; explain: *to* elucidate *a difficult point.* ***—n-*** **e·lu′ ci·da′ tion.**

e·lude (ĭ lōōd′, -lyōōd′) ***vt-*** [**e·lud·ed, e·lud·ing**] **1** to escape by being quick or clever; evade: *to* elude *one's pursuers.* **2** to evade the memory or recognition of (someone): *Her name* eludes *me.*

►Should not be confused with ALLUDE.

e·lu·sion (ĭ lōō′ zhən, -lyōō′ zhən) ***n-*** act of eluding: *his* elusion *of his pursuers.* ***Hom-*** illusion.

e·lu·sive (ĭ lōō′ sĭv, -lyōō′ sĭv) ***adj-*** **1** hard to catch; tending to escape or slip away: *an* elusive *butterfly.* **2** hard to understand, remember, or express: *an* elusive *idea.* ***—adv-*** **e·lu′ sive·ly.** ***n-*** **e·lu′ sive·ness.**

el·ver (ĕl′ vər) ***n-*** a young eel.

elves (ĕlvs) *pl.* of **elf.**

E·ly·si·an (ĭ lĭzh′ ən) ***adj-*** heavenly. ***Hom-*** elision.

E·ly·si·um (ĭ lĭz′ ē əm) ***n-*** in Greek mythology, the land of the blessed dead. Also **Elysian Fields.**

em- *prefix* See *en-*.

e·ma·ci·ate (ĭ mā′ shē āt′) ***vt-*** [**e·ma·ci·a·ted, e·ma·ci·a·ting**] to cause to waste away; make thin: *Hunger* emaciated *the survivors.* ***—adj-*** **e·ma′ ci·a′ ted.**

em·a·nate (ĕm′ ə nāt′) ***vi-*** [**em·a·na·ted, em·a·na·ting**] to flow out from a source: *Light* emanates *from the sun.*

em·a·na·tion (ĕm′ ə nā′ shən) ***n-*** **1** a flowing forth or an issuing: *a sudden* emanation *of noise.* **2** something that flows forth: *a foul* emanation *from a swamp.*

e·man·ci·pate (ĭ măn′ sə pāt′) ***vt-*** [**e·man·ci·pat·ed, e·man·ci·pat·ing**] to set free from slavery or strict control; liberate. ***—n-*** **e·man′ ci·pa′ tion.**

Emancipation Proclamation ***n-*** proclamation made by President Lincoln, on January 1, 1863, giving freedom to Negro slaves living in those States still in active rebellion against the United States.

[1]**e·mas·cu·late** (ĭ măs′ kyə lāt′) ***vt-*** [**e·mas·cu·lat·ed, e·mas·cu·lat·ing**] **1** to remove the masculinity of. **2** to deprive of strength and vigor: *Too much luxury can* emasculate *a nation.*

[2]**e·mas·cu·late** (ĭ măs′ kyə lət) ***adj-*** **1** deprived of masculinity. **2** stripped of strength and vigor: *an* emasculate *nation.*

em·balm (ĕm bäm′, -bälm′) ***vt-*** to preserve (a dead body) with spices, chemicals, etc.

em·bank (ĕm băngk′) ***vt-*** to build an embankment for (a river bank, highway, etc.).

em·bank·ment (ĕm băngk′ mənt) ***n-*** man-made slope or bank, especially one built to support a highway or hold back the waters of a river.

Embankment

em·bar·go (ĕm bär′ gō) ***n-*** [*pl.* **em·bar·goes**] **1** official prohibition by a government of ocean trade into and out of its ports. **2** any restraint imposed on commerce by law. ***vt-***: *The government* embargoed *all foreign vessels.*

em·bark (ĕm bärk′) ***vi-*** to go on board ship as a passenger: *to* embark *for France.* ***vt-*** to put on board ship: *to* embark *cargo.*

embark on to begin: *to* embark on *a law career.*

em·bar·ka·tion (ĕm′ bär kā′ shən) ***n-*** act or process of going on board a ship or aircraft or of beginning a new venture.

em·bar·rass (ĕm băr′ əs) ***vt-*** **1** to cause (a person) to feel self-conscious; fluster; disconcert: *His teacher's praise* embarrassed *Tom.* **2** to worry; hinder: *Lack of money* embarrassed *him.* ***—adv-*** **em·bar′ rass·ing·ly.**

em·bar·rassed (ĕm băr′ əst) ***adj-*** feeling or showing embarrassment. ***—adv-*** **em·bar′ rassed·ly.**

em·bar·rass·ment (ĕm băr′ əs mənt) ***n-*** **1** flustered or ruffled state of mind; chagrin; humiliation: *To my* embarrassment *I spilled my coffee.* **2** something that impedes or hinders: *a* financial *embarrassment.*

em·bas·sy (ĕm′ bə sē) ***n-*** [*pl.* **em·bas·sies**] **1** residence or office of an ambassador. **2** an ambassador and his assistants.

em·bat·tled (ĕm băt′ əld) ***adj-*** **1** drawn up in battle order; armed and ready to fight. **2** fortified: *an* embattled *frontier.*

em·bed (ĕm bĕd′) ***vt-*** [**em·bed·ded, em·bed·ding**] to set (something) firmly in surrounding matter: *They* embedded *the posts in concrete.* Also **imbed.**

em·bel·lish (ĕm bĕl′ ĭsh) ***vt-*** **1** to adorn; ornament; beautify: *They* embellished *the altar with carvings of roses.* **2** to add fanciful details to, especially a story; elaborate. ***—n-*** **em·bel′ lish·ment.**

em·ber (ĕm′ bər) ***n-*** **1** a glowing piece of wood or coal in the ashes of a fire. **2 embers** smoldering ashes.

Ember days ***n-*** *pl.* in Anglican and Roman Catholic churches, the Wednesday, Friday, and Saturday after the first Sunday of Lent, after Whitsunday, after September 14, and after December 13, set aside for fasting and prayer.

em·bez·zle (ĕm bĕz′ əl) ***vt-*** **[em·bez·zled, em·bez·zling]** to steal (money) entrusted to one: *The cashier* embezzled *a sum of money from the bank.* **—*n-* em·bez′zle·ment:** *The* embezzlement *was discovered.* ***n-*** **em·bez′zler.**

em·bit·ter (ĕm bĭt′ ər) ***vt-*** to make bitter, morose, or resentful; sour: *The death of her only son* embittered *the woman.*

em·bla·zon (ĕm blā′ zən) ***vt-*** **1** to inscribe or adorn with heraldic symbols. **2** to adorn or light up with bright colors: *Stars* emblazoned *the sky.*

em·blem (ĕm′ bləm) ***n-*** something that stands for something else; also, symbol that can be seen: *He wore the* emblem *of a famous regiment.*

em·blem·at·ic (ĕm′ blə măt′ ĭk) or **em·blem·at·i·cal** (-ĭkəl) ***adj-*** symbolic; serving as an emblem: *The laurel wreath is* emblematic *of victory.*

em·bod·i·ment (ĕm bŏd′ ĭ mənt) ***n-*** **1** an embodying. **2** a perfect example of something; epitome; personification: *He was the* embodiment *of helpfulness.*

em·bod·y (ĕm bŏd′ ē) ***vt-*** **[em·bod·ied, em·bod·y·ing]** **1** to put into a form that can be touched or seen: *to* embody *an idea in marble.* **2** to collect into a united whole: *The bylaws are* embodied *in this pamphlet.* **3** to include or incorporate: *The new law will be* embodied *in the present code.*

em·bold·en (ĕm bōl′ dən) ***vt-*** to make bold; give courage to: *The cheers* emboldened *the boxer.*

em·bo·lism (ĕm′ bə lĭz′ əm) ***n-*** sudden blocking of a blood vessel by an embolus.

em·bo·lus (ĕm′ bə ləs) ***n-*** [*pl.* **em·bo·li** (-lē′, -lī′)] blood clot, air bubble, bit of tissue, or other plug that blocks a blood vessel.

em·boss (ĕm bȯs′, -bŏs′) ***vt-*** **1** to raise above a surface by pressure of a die: *to* emboss *a border on a paper napkin.* **2** to decorate with raised figures: *The printer* embossed *the paper with my monogram.*

em·bow·er (ĕm bou′ ər) ***vt-*** to enclose or shelter with a bower of flowers, vines, etc.

em·brace (ĕm brās′) ***vt-*** **[em·braced, em·brac·ing]** **1** to grasp in the arms; hug: *Mitzi ran down the path and* embraced *her father.* **2** to take up; adopt: *The class gladly* embraced *the museum's offer of a tour.* **3** to include: *Biology* embraces *botany and zoology.* ***n-*** a hug.

em·bra·sure (ĕm brā′ zhər) ***n-*** an opening in the wall of a fortification from which to fire guns.

em·broi·der (ĕm broi′ dər) ***vt-*** **1** to decorate by sewing colored threads into a design: *to* embroider *a scarf.* **2** to add imaginary details to; exaggerate: *to* embroider *a story.* ***vi-***: *She* embroiders *beautifully.*

em·broi·der·y (ĕm broi′ də rē) ***n-*** [*pl.* **em·broi·der·ies**] **1** ornamental needlework. **2** embellishment or exaggeration of something told or written.

em·broil (ĕm broil′) ***vt-*** to involve (a person or persons) in difficulties, quarrels, etc.: *His pride* embroiled *him in squabbles.*

em·bry·o (ĕm′ brē ō) ***n-*** [*pl.* **em·bry·os**] **1** early form of an animal during development from a fertilized egg and before being hatched or born. **2** an unsprouted plant germ in a seed. **3** an early stage of growth or development: *A frontier fort was the* embryo *of the city of Pittsburgh.*

Embryo of fish

em·bry·ol·o·gist (ĕm′ brē ŏl′ ə jĭst) ***n-*** person trained in embryology and usually working in this field.

em·bry·ol·ogy (ĕm′ brē ŏl′ ə jē) ***n-*** branch of biology that deals with the structure and development of embryos. **—*adj-* em′bry·o·log′i·cal** (ĕm′ brē ə lŏj′ ĭ kəl): *an* embryological *study of fertile hen's eggs.*

em·bry·on·ic (ĕm′ brē ŏn′ ĭk) ***adj-*** **1** of or having to do with an embryo. **2** immature; not yet fully developed.

em·cee (ĕm′ sē′) *Informal* ***n-*** master of ceremonies. ***vt-*** to perform as master of ceremonies of: *to* emcee *a banquet.* ***vi-***: *He* emceed *at the banquet.*

e·mend (ĭ mĕnd′) ***vt-*** to correct, usually by making changes in: *to* emend *a text.*

►For usage note see AMEND.

e·men·da·tion (ē′ mĕn dā′ shən) ***n-*** a correction, especially of written material.

em·er·ald (ĕm′ ər əld) ***n-*** **1** a precious stone of a clear, deep-green color. **2** the color of this stone. ***adj-***: *The sea was* emerald *and calm.*

Emerald Isle ***n-*** Ireland.

e·merge (ĭ mûrj′) ***vi-*** **[e·merged, e·merg·ing]** **1** to come forth into view: *The sun* emerged *from a bank of clouds.* **2** to become known; appear: *The facts* emerged *slowly.*

e·mer·gence (ĭ mûr′ jəns) ***n-*** an emerging; a coming forth into view or knowledge: *an* emergence *of facts.*

e·mer·gen·cy (ĭ mûr′ jən sē) ***n-*** [*pl.* **e·mer·gen·cies**] sudden or unexpected happening that makes quick action necessary. *as* ***modifier***: *an* emergency *exit*; *an* emergency *light.*

e·mer·gent (ĭ mûr′ jənt) ***adj-*** coming forth; appearing: *an* emergent *nationalism*; *an* emergent *maturity.*

e·mer·i·tus (ĭ mĕr′ ə təs) ***adj-*** retired from service with honorary rank and title: *professor* emeritus.

em·er·y (ĕm′ ə rē) ***n-*** very hard dark corundum used in powdered form for grinding or polishing.

e·met·ic (ĭ mĕt′ ĭk) ***n-*** a medicine that causes vomiting. *as* ***modifier***: *an* emetic *drug.*

E.M.F. or **e.m.f.** electromotive force.

em·i·grant (ĕm′ ə grənt) ***n-*** person who leaves his country to settle in another. *as* ***modifier***: *an* emigrant *Hungarian.*

►Should not be confused with IMMIGRANT.

em·i·grate (ĕm′ ə grāt′) ***vi-*** **[em·i·grat·ed, em·i·grat·ing]** to leave one's own country to settle in another: *He* emigrated *to Mexico.* **—*n-* em′i·gra′tion.**

►Should not be confused with IMMIGRATE.

ém·i·gré (ĕm′ ə grā′, *Fr.* ā′ mĭ grā′) ***n-*** an emigrant, especially a political refugee. *as* ***modifier***: *an* émigré *statesman.* Also **em′i·gre′.**

em·i·nence (ĕm′ ə nəns) ***n-*** **1** high standing; great distinction: *He has achieved* eminence *in the medical profession.* **2** high ground; an elevation. **3 Eminence** in the Roman Catholic Church, a title of honor given to a cardinal (preceded by "Your" or "His").

em·i·nent (ĕm′ ə nənt) ***adj-*** outstanding; distinguished: *an* eminent *writer.* **—*adj-* em′i·nent·ly.**

eminent domain ***n-*** in law, the right or power of a government to take possession or control of private property for public use, usually on paying what is judged to be a fair price.

e·mir (ĭ mêr′) ***n-*** **1** Arabian prince or chieftain. **2** title of certain Arab officials. **3** title given to certain persons descended from Mohammed.

em·is·sar·y (ĕm′ ə sĕr′ ē) ***n-*** [*pl.* **em·is·sar·ies**] person sent on a mission or errand, especially one of a confidential nature: *the President's* emissary *to the new nation.*

fāte, făt, dâre, bärn; bē, bĕt, mêre; bīte, bĭt; nōte, hŏt, môre, dȯg; fŭn, fûr; tōō, bŏŏk; oil; out; tar; thin; then; hw for wh as in what; zh for s as in usual; ə for a, e, i, o, u, as in ago, linen, peril, atom, minus

e·mis·sion (ĭ mĭsh′ ən, ē-) ***n-*** **1** act or process of emitting: *the* emission *of light.* **2** something emitted: *Heat is one of the* emissions *from a light bulb.* **—*adj-*** **e·mis′ sive:** *an* emissive *source of light.*

e·mit (ĭ mĭt′, ē-) ***vt-*** **[e·mit·ted, e·mit·ting]** to send forth; discharge: *A volcano* emits *lava.*

Em·man·u·el (ĭ măn′ yōō ĕl′, -əl) ***n-*** name for the Messiah. Also **Immanuel.**

e·mol·li·ent (ĭ mŏl′ yənt, -ē ənt) ***adj-*** softening; soothing to the skin: *an* emollient *oil.* ***n-*** a softening substance.

e·mol·u·ment (ĭ mŏl′ yə mənt) ***n-*** pay; wages; salary.

e·mote (ē mōt′) ***vi-*** **[e·mot·ed, e·mot·ing]** to express emotion, especially for theatrical effect.

e·mo·tion (ĭ mō′ shən) ***n-*** **1** strong feeling: *to speak with* emotion. **2** any particular feeling, such as joy, fear, etc.

e·mo·tion·al (ĭ mō′ shən əl) ***adj-*** **1** having to do with the emotions; based on feeling: *a silly,* emotional *quarrel.* **2** stirring the emotion: *His talk on loyalty was full of* emotional *appeal for the audience.* **3** easily stirred; excitable: *an* emotional *person.* **—*adv-*** **e·mo′ tion·al·ly.**

e·mo·tion·al·ism (ĭ mō′ shən əl ĭz′ əm) ***n-*** **1** conscious indulgence in emotion, especially in displaying it. **2** an emotional outlook.

e·mo·tion·al·ize (ə mō′ shən əl īz′) ***vt-*** **[e·mo·tion·al·ized, e·mo·tion·al·iz·ing]** to give an emotional bias or quality to: *Certain newspapers* emotionalize *the news.*

e·mo·tive (ĭ mō′ tĭv) ***adj-*** **1** relating to the emotions. **2** showing the emotions or appealing to them. **—*adv-*** **e·mo′ tive·ly.**

em·pa·thy (ĕm′ pə thē) ***n-*** the ability to feel with another and to see the world through his eyes; identification.

em·per·or (ĕm′ pər ər) ***n-*** ruler of an empire.

em·pha·sis (ĕm′ fə sĭs) ***n-*** [*pl.* **em·pha·ses** (-sēz′)] **1** strong attention or stress; concentration (on): *an* emphasis *on correct spelling.* **2** stress of the voice, given to one or more words or syllables.

em·pha·size (ĕm′ fə sīz′) ***vt-*** **[em·pha·sized, em·pha·siz·ing]** to stress; place special value or importance on.

em·phat·ic (ĕm făt′ ĭk) ***adj-*** **1** said or done with special force or emphasis: *an* emphatic *reply.* **2** striking; forceful; definite: *the* emphatic *contrast between black and white.* **—*adv-*** **em·phat′ i·cal·ly.**

em·phy·se·ma (ĕm′ fə sē′ mə) ***n-*** abnormal puffing of body tissue by air or other gases, especially one that reduces the size of the air sacs in the lungs and makes breathing more and more difficult.

em·pire (ĕm′ pīər′) ***n-*** **1** group of countries under the control of one ruler. **2** country of which the ruler bears the title of emperor. **3** absolute power or authority. **4** power; sovereignty: *the responsibilities of* empire.

em·pir·i·cal (ĕm pĭr′ ĭ kəl) ***adj-*** based on what has actually happened and been observed rather than on theory or supposed rules: *an* empirical *opinion.* Also **em·pir′ ic. —*adv-*** **em·pir′ i·cal·ly.**

em·pir·i·cism (ĕm pĭr′ ə sĭz′ əm) ***n-*** **1** action based entirely on knowledge of what has actually happened and been observed. **2** in philosophy, the theory that all human knowledge is of this sort. See also *rationalism.* **—*n-*** **em·pir′ i·cist.**

em·place·ment (ĕm plās′ mənt) *Military* ***n-*** place and mounting for a heavy gun or guns.

em·plane (ĕm plān′) ***vi-*** **[em·planed, em·planing]** to board an airplane. ***vt-*** to place or load (passengers or cargo) aboard an airplane.

em·ploy (ĕm ploi′) ***vt-*** **1** to give work to (a person) for pay; hire: *We hope to* employ *a new secretary tomorrow.* **2** to make use of: *He* employed *his spare time to good advantage.* **3** to occupy; take up: *Driving* employs *much of my time.* ***n-*** service: *He is in my uncle's* employ.

em·ploy·ee (ĕm ploi′ ē′, -ploi′ ē) ***n-*** person employed by another person or a business concern. Also **employe.**

em·ploy·er (ĕm ploi′ ər) ***n-*** person or business concern that employs another person.

em·ploy·ment (ĕm ploi′ mənt) ***n-*** **1** the act of hiring: *He was busy with the* employment *of new help.* **2** a being employed; having work: *Full* employment *keeps a country prosperous.* **3** a use: *the* employment *of harsh measures.* **4** work; occupation: *His regular* employment *is welding. as* ***modifier****: the* employment *office.*

em·por·i·um (ĕm pôr′ ē əm) ***n-*** [*pl.* **em·por·i·ums** or **em·por·i·a** (-ē ə)] **1** store with varied merchandise (often used humorously). **2** trade center; marketplace.

em·pow·er (ĕm pou′ ər) ***vt-*** to give power or authority to; authorize: *The sheriff* empowered *the posse to act.*

em·press (ĕm′ prəs) ***n-*** the wife of an emperor, or a woman ruling an empire.

emp·ty (ĕmp′ tē, ĕm′ tē) ***adj-*** **[emp·ti·er, emp·ti·est]** **1** containing nothing; unoccupied; void: *an* empty *closet; an* empty *house.* **2** without meaning; barren: *an* empty *promise; an* empty *dream; his* empty *words.* ***vt-*** **[emp·tied, emp·ty·ing]** **1** to remove the contents from: *She* emptied *her desk.* **2** to pour out; drain: *to* empty *the water from a tank.* ***vi-*** to become vacant or drained; discharge itself: *The room* emptied *at noon. The river* empties *into the bay.* **—*adv-*** **emp′ ti·ly.** ***n-*** **emp′ ti·ness.**

empty set *Mathematics* ***n-*** set that is null.

em·py·re·an (ĕm pĭr′ ē ən, ĕm′ pī′ rē′ ən) ***n-*** **1** the heavens. **2** the highest heaven in ancient astronomy, consisting of fire or light. ***adj-*** heavenly; celestial. **—*adj-*** **em·pyr′ e·al** or **em′py·re′ al.**

e·mu (ē′ myōō′) ***n-*** large, three-toed Australian bird resembling the ostrich.

em·u·late (ĕm′ yə lāt′, -yōō lāt′) ***vt-*** **[em·u·lat·ed, em·u·lat·ing]** to strive to equal or surpass (someone): *We* emulate *people we admire.* **—*n-*** **em·u·la′ tion.**

em·u·la·tive (ĕm′ yə lā′ tĭv, ĕm′ yōō-) ***adj-*** showing a desire to equal or surpass someone else; admiringly imitative (of): *an* emulative *act; to be* emulative *of someone.* **—*adv-*** **em′ u·la′ tive·ly.**

em·u·la·tor (ĕm′ yə lā′ tər, -ĕm′ yōō-) ***n-*** person who emulates.

em·u·lous (ĕm′ yə ləs) ***adj-*** emulative; striving to equal or surpass someone. **—*adv-*** **em′ u·lous·ly.** ***n-*** **em′ u·lous·ness.**

e·mul·si·fi·ca·tion (ĭ mŭl′ sə fə kā′ shən) ***n-*** process of emulsifying.

e·mul·si·fy (ĭ mŭl′ sə fī′) ***vt-*** **[e·mul·si·fied, e·mul·si·fy·ing]** to make or convert (something) into an emulsion.

e·mul·sion (ĭ mŭl′ shən) ***n-*** **1** liquid mixture in which one liquid, usually a fat, is suspended throughout another in the form of very fine drops that do not dissolve or cluster together. See also *suspension.* **2** a coating applied to photographic films, plates, etc., to make them sensitive to light.

en- *prefix* **1** to place or go into, upon, or onto: *to* en*cradle*; en*throne.* **2** to cover or surround with: *to* en*circle*; en*case*; en*tangle*; en*wrap.* **3** to cause to be or resemble; make: *to* en*slave*; en*feeble*; en*able*; en*act.* Also **em-** before "b," "p," and sometimes "m": *to* em*bank*; em*plane.* [from Greek **en-**, from Latin **in-** meaning "in; into."]

¹-en *suffix* **1** (used to form verbs from adjectives) to make or become: *hard*en; *straight*en. **2** (used to form verbs from nouns) to cause to have more or to acquire more: *length*en; *strength*en. **3** (used to form adjectives from nouns) made of; resembling: *gold*en; *wheat*en; *earth*en.

²-en *word ending* **1** for many past participles: *giv*en; *brok*en. **2** to form some noun plurals: *ox*en; *child*ren.

en·a·ble (ĭn ā′ bəl) ***vt-*** **[en·a·bled, en·a·bling]** to give (one or something) power or ability to do something: *The scholarship* enabled *her to go to college.*

en·act (ĭn ăkt′) ***vt-*** **1** to make into law: *Congress* enacted *a bill to lower tariffs.* **2** to act the part of: *He* enacted *the hero.* **3** to represent dramatically: *They* enacted *the Nativity.*

en·act·ment (ĭn ăkt′ mənt) ***n-*** **1** an enacting; a making into law: *the* enactment *of labor legislation.* **2** law or decree.

e·nam·el (ĭ năm′ əl) ***n-*** **1** any of various substances used to coat the surface of metal, glass, or pottery for protection and decoration. It forms a hard glossy surface. **2** paint that dries with a glossy surface. **3** hard, white outer surface of the teeth. ***vt-*** to cover with a hard, glossy substance or paint.

e·nam·el·ware (ĭ năm′ əl wâr′) ***n-*** pottery, art objects, kitchenware, etc., coated with enamel.

en·am·or (ĭ năm′ ər) ***vt-*** to inspire with love; charm. **enamored of** in love with.

en·camp (ĕn kămp′) ***vi-*** to settle in or make a camp: *The legion* encamped *across the Rhone.* ***vt-***: *The officer* encamped *his troops in the valley.*

en·camp·ment (ĕn kămp′ mənt) ***n-*** **1** the making of a camp; settlement in a camp. **2** a camp.

en·case (ĕn kās′) ***vt-*** **[en·cas·ed, en·cas·ing]** to enclose (something) in or as in a box or case. Also **incase.**

-ence *suffix* See *-ance.*

en·ceph·a·li·tis (ĕn sĕf′ ə lī′ təs) ***n-*** **1** inflammation of the brain. **2** sleeping sickness.

en·ceph·a·lon (ĕn sĕf′ ə lŏn′, -lən) *Biology* ***n-*** the brain.

en·chain (ĕn chān′) ***vt-*** to bind with or as with chains.

en·chant (ĕn chănt′) ***vt-*** **1** to bewitch; overcome by magic: *Merlin* enchanted *the knight's sword.* **2** to delight greatly: *Her voice* enchanted *us.*

en·chant·er (ĕn chăn′ tər) ***n-*** one who enchants. ***—n-*** *fem.* **en·chant′ress.**

en·chant·ing (ĕn chăn′ tĭng) ***adj-*** so charming as to bewitch; causing great delight. ***—adv-*** **en·chant′ ing·ly.**

en·chant·ment (ĕn chănt′ mənt) ***n-*** **1** great delight: *a child's* enchantment *with toys.* **2** magic spell.

en·chase (ĕn chās′) ***vt-*** **[en·chased, en·chas·ing]** to ornament, as by carving in relief or inlaying.

en·chi·la·da (ĕn′ chə lä′ də) ***n-*** a meat- or cheese-stuffed tortilla, served with a sauce usually flavored with chili. [from Mexican Spanish, ultimately from Spanish **en-**, "in," plus American Indian **chili,** "chili pepper."]

en·ci·pher (ĕn sī′ fər) ***vt-*** to change (a message, signal, etc.) into a cipher to keep it secret.

en·cir·cle (ĕn sûr′ kəl) ***vt-*** **[en·cir·cled, en·cir·cling]** **1** to make a circle around; surround: *The crowd* encircled *the winning team.* **2** to go completely around: *Satellites can* encircle *the earth.* ***—n-*** **en·cir′ cle·ment.**

en·clave (ĕn′ klāv′) ***n-*** **1** territory enclosed by land to which it is not politically subject: *The Vatican is an* enclave *within Italy.* **2** district of a country or city inhabited by a minority group: *the Christian* enclave *in a Muslim city.*

en·close (ĕn klōz′) ***vt-*** **[en·closed, en·clos·ing]** **1** to close in on all sides: *We* enclosed *the baby's crib with mosquito netting.* **2** to surround with a fence or wall: *We* enclosed *the lot with a wire fence.* **3** to place in an envelope for mailing, delivery, safekeeping, etc., usually along with a letter: *I* enclose *my check for $10.* Also **inclose.**

en·clo·sure (ĕn klō′ zhər) ***n-*** **1** a closing or shutting in: *The* enclosure *of the porch with glass was done quickly.* **2** something that closes in; fence; wall. **3** place that is closed in by a fence, wall, etc.: *an* enclosure *for elephants.* **4** something that is put in with something else: *an* enclosure *in a letter.* Also **inclosure.**

en·co·mi·um (ĕn kō′ mē əm) ***n-*** [*pl.* **en·co·mi·ums** or **en·co·mi·a** (-mē ə)] a formal statement of praise; eulogy.

en·com·pass (ĕn kŭm′ pəs) ***vt-*** **1** to surround; encircle: *Enemy forces* encompassed *the camp.* **2** to include: *His education* encompasses *many branches of knowledge.*

en·core (äng′ kôr) ***interj-*** again! once more! (a cry to a performer for a repetition or for something additional). ***n-*** a response to such a request: *She played two* encores.

en·coun·ter (ĕn koun′ tər) ***n-*** **1** unexpected meeting: *Our* encounter *with the famous actor was exciting.* **2** a fight or battle: *a frightening* encounter *between two gangs.* ***vt-*** **1** to meet unexpectedly: *We* encountered *an old friend yesterday.* **2** to meet in conflict; fight.

en·cour·age (ĕn kûr′ ĭj) ***vt-*** **[en·cour·aged, en·cour·ag·ing]** **1** to give hope or courage to: *The medical report* encouraged *us.* **2** to urge by showing approval: *Her parents* encouraged *her to study the piano.* **3** to aid; foster: *to* encourage *a plant's growth.*

en·cour·age·ment (ĕn kûr′ ĭj mənt) ***n-*** **1** a giving of hope or courage: *Constant* encouragement *helped the crippled child to learn to walk again.* **2** something that gives courage or hope: *Talking to the successful violinist was an* encouragement *to the music student.* **3** a fostering: *money for the* encouragement *of research.*

en·cour·ag·ing (ĕn kŭr′ ə jĭng) ***adj-*** **1** giving hope; inspiring. **2** aiding; helping. ***—adv-*** **en·cour′ ag·ing·ly.**

en·croach (ĕn krōch′) ***vi-*** **1** to infringe or intrude upon another's domain or privileges: *The enemy* encroached *upon our waters.* **2** to spread or pass beyond the natural limits: *The flooding river* encroached *on the land.* ***—n-*** **en·croach′ ment.**

en·crust (ĕn krŭst′) ***vt-*** to cover over with a hard coat; overlay: *to* encrust *a crown with gems.* Also **incrust.**

en·cum·ber (ĕn kŭm′ bər) or **in·cum·ber** (ĭn kŭm′- bər) ***vt-*** **1** to impede; hinder: *The girl's tight skirt* encumbered *her when she tried to hurry.* **2** to weigh down; burden: *to be* encumbered *with debts.*

en·cum·brance (ĕn kŭm′ brəns) ***n-*** something that hinders or holds back; a burden: *Too much luggage is an* encumbrance.

-ency *suffix* See *-ancy.*

en·cy·cli·cal (ĕn sĭ′ klĭ kəl) ***n-*** letter addressed by the Pope to the bishops of the Roman Catholic Church. Also **encyclical letter.**

en·cy·clo·pe·di·a (ĕn sī′ klə pē′ dē ə) ***n-*** a book or set of books containing articles, usually arranged in alphabetical order, on all branches of knowledge or on some special subject. Also **en·cy′clo·pae′ di·a.** ***as modifier***: *an* encyclopedia *salesman.*

en·cy·clo·pe·dic (ĕn sī′ klə pē′ dĭk) ***adj-*** very broad and factual, like an encyclopedia: *His learning is truly* encyclopedic. Also **en·cy′clo·pae′ dic.**

en·cyst (ĕn sĭst′) ***vt-*** to enclose in a membranous sac or cyst. ***vi-*** to form or become enclosed in a cyst.

end (ĕnd) ***n-*** **1** point or part at which something begins or leaves off: *both* ends *of the stick.* **2** farthest or last part of anything: *the* end *of the road*; *the* end *of a rope.* **3** point at which something ceases to exist; final limit: *I'm at the* end *of my patience. His life came to an* end. **4** aim; purpose; object: *His family's happiness was the* end *for which he worked.* ***vt-*** to bring to a conclusion:

The fight ended *the party*. **2** to be part of the conclusion of: *That scene* ends *the play*. ***vi-***: *The play* ended.

at the end at last. **end to end** lengthwise. **in the end** finally; ultimately. **on end** **1** in an upright position. **2** one after another: *We stood in line for hours* on end.

end up to arrive, or become in time: *He'll* end up *in jail.*

en·dan·ger (ĕn dān′ jər) ***vt-*** to put in danger; jeopardize: *He* endangered *his life by careless driving. as* ***modifier***: *an* endangered *species.*

en·dear (ĕn dêr′) ***vt-*** to make (someone) dear (to someone): *Her kindness* endeared her to us all.

en·dear·ment (ĕn dêr′ mənt) ***n-*** a spoken expression of affection, especially a phrase or single word.

en·deav·or (ĕn dĕv′ ər) ***vt-*** to attempt; strive; try hard: *She will* endeavor *to swim across the channel.* ***n-*** effort; attempt: *He made every* endeavor *to win her friendship.*

en·dem·ic (ĕn dĕm′ ĭk) ***adj-*** belonging or restricted to a given people or region: *a disease* endemic *in India.*

end·ing (ĕnd′ ĭng) ***n-*** conclusion; last part.

en·dive (ĕn′ dīv′) ***n-*** **1** (*also* ä^{n} dēv′) salad plant with broad, whitish leaves in a tight cluster. Also **Belgian endive.** **2** related plant with wavy leaves; escarole.

end·less (ĕnd′ ləs) ***adj-*** **1** lasting forever; having no end. **2** joined at the ends; continuous: *an* endless *chain.* —***adv-*** **end′less·ly.** ***n-*** **end′less·ness.**

end·most (ĕnd′ mōst′) ***adj-*** hindmost; farthest; located at the extreme limit.

en·do·car·di·um (ĕn′dō kär′ dē əm) ***n-*** thin, protective layer of tissue that lines the heart.

en·do·crine (ĕn′ də krĭn′) ***adj-*** **1** of or having to do with an endocrine gland or its secretion. **2** secreting directly into the blood or the lymph. ***n-*** endocrine gland.

endocrine gland ***n-*** any gland that secretes hormones directly into the bloodstream or the lymph; ductless gland.

en·do·cri·nol·o·gy (ĕn′də krĭ nŏl′ ə jē) ***n-*** branch of medicine that deals with the endocrine glands and their secretions.

en·dorse (ĕn dórs′, -dôrs′) ***vt-*** **[en·dorsed, en·dors·ing]** **1** to approve; support; sanction: *Congress* endorsed *the President's plan.* **2** to write one's name on the back of (a check or other document) as a legal sign that one approves or acknowledges payment of money or some other transaction. Also **indorse.** —***n-*** **en·dors′er.**

en·dorse·ment (ĕn dórs′ mənt, ĕn dôrs′-) ***n-*** **1** something written to endorse a check or other document. **2** approval; support; sanction: *The mayor's* endorsement *helped the senator win the election.* Also **indorsement.**

en·do·skel·e·ton (ĕn′ dō skĕl′ ə tən) ***n-*** any rigid, supportive body structure found inside many animals. Man has an endoskeleton. See also *exoskeleton.*

en·do·sperm (ĕn′ dō spûrm′) ***n-*** the part of a seed that contains stored food material.

en·do·ther·mic (ĕn′ dō thûr′ mĭk) ***adj-*** having to do with the absorption of heat by chemical reactions. See also *exothermic.*

en·dow (ĕn dou′) ***vt-*** **1** to provide with a permanent fund or source of income by gift (often followed by "with"): *Ms. Allen generously* endowed *her college.* **2** to equip; furnish (always followed by "with"): *She* endowed *her children with her keen sense of humor.*

en·dow·ment (ĕn dou′ mənt) ***n-*** **1** money or other property given an institution for its support: *The college received an* endowment *from the Jones family.* **2** the act of making such a gift. **3** person's abilities or talents: *Good looks are his only* endowment.

end point ***n-*** **1** final point, such as 0° on the Kelvin temperature scale. **2** point that marks the conclusion of a process.

en·dur·a·ble (ĕn dŏŏr′ ə bəl, ĕn dyŏŏr′-) ***adj-*** such as can be endured; bearable. —***adv-*** **en·dur′a·bly.**

en·dur·ance (ebn dŏŏr′ əns, ĕn dyŏŏr′-) ***n-*** **1** ability to bear up under strain, suffering, fatigue, or hardship: *A long-distance swimmer needs great* endurance. **2** ability to withstand hard wear or use: *to test the* endurance *of a car, as* ***modifier***: *an* endurance *record.*

en·dure (ĕn dŏŏr′, -dyŏŏr′) ***vt-*** **[en·dured, en·dur·ing]** **1** to bear bravely; suffer: *The pioneers* endured *many hardships.* **2** to put up with; tolerate; bear: *They cannot* endure *the cold.* ***vi-*** **1** to remain in existence; persist: *Lincoln's name will* endure *forever.* **2** to suffer patiently without yielding: *They* endured *through all hardships.*

end·ways (ĕnd′ wāz′) or **end·wise** (ĕnd′ wīz′) ***adv-*** **1** on end. **2** with the end forward. **3** lengthwise. **4** end to end.

ENE or **E.N.E.** east-northeast.

en·e·ma (ĕn′ ə mə) ***n-*** liquid injected into the lower bowel through the rectum as a purgative, a food, etc.

en·e·my (ĕn′ ə mē) ***n-*** [*pl.* **en·e·mies**] **1** person who harbors hatred or works actively against another; unfriendly opponent; foe; adversary. **2** hostile military force, nation, etc. **3** anything that harms or injures: *Cancer is an* enemy *of humanity. as* ***modifier***: *a fleet of* enemy *warships.*

en·er·get·ic (ĕn′ ər jĕt′ ĭk) ***adj-*** very active; industrious; vigorous. —***adv-*** **en′er·get′i·cal·ly.**

en·er·gize (ĕn′ ər jīz′) ***vt-*** **[en·er·gized, en·er·giz·ing]** **1** to give energy or animation to (someone or something): *His fear* energized *him.* **2** to apply an electric voltage to (a circuit, a piece of equipment, etc.).

en·er·gy (ĕn′ ər jē) ***n-*** [*pl.* **en·er·gies**] **1** material power of the universe; ability to do work: *Einstein studied the relation of* energy *to matter.* **2** ability to put forth muscular effort; vigor: *He needed all his* energy *to win.* **3** mental or physical force: *She spoke with* energy.

en·er·vate (ĕn′ ər vāt′) ***vt-*** **[en·er·vat·ed, en·er·vat·ing]** to sap the force and vitality of; weaken physically or mentally. —***n-*** **en′er·va′tion.**

en·fant ter·ri·ble (ä^{n}′fä^{n} tə rē′blə) *French* terrible child; hence, any young person whose brash and bold behavior upsets others.

en·fee·ble (ăn fē′ bəl) ***vt-*** **[en·fee·bled, en·fee·bling]** to weaken; make feeble: *Sickness* enfeebled *him.*

en·fi·lade (ĕn′fə lād′) *Military* ***vt-*** **[en·fi·lad·ed, en·fi·lad·ing]** to fire or be able to fire weapons at (a line of troops, a road, a trench, etc.) from the side in a raking pattern. ***n-*** situation in which such fire can be delivered.

en·fold (ĕn fōld′) ***vt-*** **1** to wrap up; enclose: *I* enfolded *the vase in cloth to protect it.* **2** to clasp; embrace: *She* enfolded *the child in her arms.* Also **infold.**

en·force (ĕn fôrs′) ***vt-*** **[en·forced, en·forc·ing]** **1** to compel obedience to: *The police* enforce *the law.* **2** to impose by force; compel: *to* enforce *silence.*

en·force·ment (ĕn fôrs′ mənt) ***n-*** act or process of enforcing: *Law* enforcement *is necessary to keep order.*

en·fran·chise (ĕn frăn′chīz′) ***vt-*** **[en·fran·chised, en·fran·chis·ing]** **1** to give (a person) the right to vote: *Wyoming* enfranchised *women in 1890.* **2** to free, as from slavery. —***n-*** **en·fran′chise′ment.**

eng. engineer.

Eng. **1** England. **2** English.

en·gage (ĕn gāj′) ***vt-*** **[en·gaged, en·gag·ing]** **1** to be the concern or subject of; occupy: *Work* engaged *most of her time.* **2** to get the right to use; reserve for use: *to* engage *a suite of rooms.* **3** to hire; employ: *to* engage *a new gardener.* **4** to attract and hold: *The squabble* engaged his *attention.* **5** to bind or pledge (oneself): *He* engaged himself *to pay the debt.* **6** to promise; vow:

They engaged *that they would meet again in ten years.* **7** to fight: *to* engage *the enemy.* **8** to send into battle: *They* engaged *eight divisions of troops.* **9** to make a mechanical connection or contact with or between: *to* engage *the clutch*; *to* engage *the gears.* ***vi-*** **1** to take part or involve oneself (in something): *to* engage *in a long discussion*; *to* engage *in sports.* **2** to begin to fight: *The armies* engaged *at once.* **3** to become mechanically connected, in contact, or interlocked: *The gears* engaged.

en·gaged (ĕn gājd′) ***adj-*** **1** bound by a promise to marry; betrothed (to): *Bill and May are* engaged. *Bill is* engaged *to May.* **2** busy; occupied: *The telephone is* engaged. **3** of machine parts, connected, in contact, or interlocked. **4** fighting: *Two divisions are* engaged.

en·gage·ment (ĕn gāj′ mənt) ***n-*** **1** a promise to marry; betrothal. **2** appointment; promise to meet someone somewhere at a fixed time: *I have a three o'clock* engagement *with my lawyer.* **3** employment: *The actress had a six weeks'* engagement *in a summer theater.* **4** battle; conflict. **5** of machine parts, a connecting, contact, or interlocking. *as* ***modifier***: *an* engagement *ring for May.*

en·gag·ing (ĕn gā′ jĭng) ***adj-*** winning; attractive; pleasing: *an* engaging *pastime.* **—*adv-* en·gag′ ing·ly.**

en·gen·der (ĕn jĕn′ dər) ***vt-*** to give birth to; bring into being; create: *Truthfulness* engenders *confidence.*

en·gine (ĕn′ jən) ***n-*** **1** machine that changes energy into mechanical power by using the pressure of hot steam, burning gasoline, hydrazine, etc., or by electrically accelerating a stream of ions, as in one type of rocket engine. **2** any machine or instrument: *an* engine *of war.* **3** a locomotive. *as* ***modifier***: *an* engine *part.*

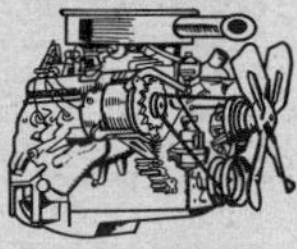

Steam and internal-combustion (gasoline) engines

en·gi·neer (ĕn′ jə nêr′) ***n-*** **1** person who designs, develops, and helps to build machines, structures, electrical systems, etc. Most engineers are graduates of colleges of engineering, with degrees in mechanical engineering, civil engineering, electrical engineering, etc. **2** driver of a locomotive. **3** officer whose concern is the engines and other mechanisms of a ship. ***vt-*** **1** to design, develop, or help to build (some technical device, system, project, etc.). **2** to plan and direct: *to* engineer *an election campaign.*

en·gi·neer·ing (ĕn′ jə nêr′ ĭng) ***n-*** **1** field of scientific and technical study dealing with the designing, development, and building of machinery, bridges, electrical and electronic equipment, airplanes, etc. **2** a use of such study: *the* engineering *of the Panama Canal.*

Eng·lish (ĭng′ glĭsh) ***adj-*** of or pertaining to England, its people, or their language: *the* English *countryside.* **1** the English language, including Old English or Anglo-Saxon (up to about 1100), Middle English (about 1100 to about 1500), and Modern English (from about 1500 to the present). Also, the language of the people of the United States and many areas now or formerly under British control. **2** spin given to a ball when it is thrown or driven. **3 the English** (takes a plural verb) the people of England.

English horn ***n-*** woodwind instrument with a double reed, similar to the oboe. It is larger and lower in a pitch than the oboe, and has a richer and fuller tone.

Man playing English horn

Eng·lish·man (ĭng′ glĭsh mən) ***n-*** [*pl.* **Eng·lish·men**] a native or citizen of England. **—*n-* *fem.* Eng′ lish·wom′ an.**

English muffin ***n-*** round, flat muffin made of yeast dough, baked on a griddle, and usually toasted before eating.

English walnut ***n-*** walnut.

en·gorge (ĕn gȯrj′, -gôrj′) ***vt-*** **[en·gorged, en·gorging]** to devour; swallow greedily.

en·graft or **in·graft** (ĕn grăft′) ***vt-*** to graft.

en·grave (ĕn grāv′) ***vt-*** **[en·graved, en·grav·ing] 1** to cut letters or designs into the surface of (wood, metal, stone, etc.) for display or for printing: *to* engrave *a silver cup*; *to* engrave *plates for a new dollar bill.* **2** to print (cards, bills, etc.) from blocks or plates cut in this way. **3** to cut (letters, figures, etc.) into something: *to* engrave *the date on a cornerstone.* **4** to prepare (a picture, plate, etc.) by photoengraving. **5** to fix (something) in one's mind or memory. **—*n-* en·grav′ er.**

en·grav·ing (ĕn grā′ vĭng) ***n-*** **1** the act or occupation of cutting letters or designs into stone, hard wood, or metal for display or printing. **2** a design cut in this way. **3** a print made from a block or plate cut in this way.

en·gross (ĕn grōs′) ***vt-*** **1** to occupy wholly; fill the mind or time of: *His hobby* engrosses *him.* **2** to prepare the official copy of (a state document).

en·gulf (ĕn gŭlf′) ***vt-*** to swallow up; overwhelm; bury: *High waves* engulfed *the swimmers.*

en·hance (ĕn hăns′) ***vt-*** **[en·hanced, en·hanc·ing]** to add to; increase: *Flowers* enhanced *her beauty.*

e·nig·ma (ĭ nĭg′ mə) ***n-*** person or thing not easily understood; puzzle; riddle: *His intentions remained an* enigma.

en·ig·mat·ic (ĕn′ ĭg măt′ ĭk) or **en·ig·mat·i·cal** (-ĭ kəl) ***adj-*** like an enigma; puzzling; difficult to understand; mysterious: *an* enigmatic *smile*; *an* enigmatic *remark.* **—*adv-* en′ig·mat′ i·cal·ly.**

en·join (ĕn join′) ***vt-*** **1** to order emphatically; direct; urge: *to* enjoin *someone to leave*; *to* enjoin *silence.* **2** to issue a legal injunction against: *The court* enjoined *the defendant to pay his taxes.*

en·joy (ĕn joi′) ***vt-*** **1** to take pleasure or delight in: *We* enjoyed *the picnic.* **2** to possess; have the use of: *I* enjoy *good health.*

enjoy oneself to have a good time.

en·joy·a·ble (ĕn joi′ ə bəl) ***adj-*** pleasing; delightful. **—*adv-* en·joy′ a·bly. *n-* en·joy′ a·ble·ness.**

en·joy·ment (ĕn joi′ mənt) ***n-*** **1** pleasure; delight; satisfaction: *He finds* enjoyment *in reading.* **2** pleased or gratifying possession: *the* enjoyment *of a good reputation.*

en·kin·dle (ĕn kĭn′ dəl) ***vt-*** **[en·kin·dled, en·kin·dling]** to kindle.

en·lace (ĕn lās′) ***vt-*** **[en·laced, en·lac·ing] 1** to encircle or enfold as if in laces: *to* enlace *one in red tape*; *to* enlace *a city in new roads.* **2** to entwine; interlace; entangle: *to* enlace *strands of rope in splicing.*

en·large (ĕn lärj′) ***vt-*** **[en·larged, en·larg·ing]** to make larger; add to; increase in quantity, extent, etc.: *to* enlarge *a house*; enlarge *a photograph.* ***vi-*** to grow larger: *The population gradually* enlarges.

enlarge on (or **upon**) to speak or write more fully upon.

en·large·ment (ĕn lärj′ mənt) ***n-*** **1** an increasing or growing; a making larger. **2** a thing that is added: *The* *new wing is an* enlargement *to our house.* **3** something made larger, especially a photographic print made with an enlarger.

en·larg·er (ĕn lär′ jər) ***n-*** device that magnifies the image of a photographic negative and is used to make prints larger than the negative.

en·light·en (ĕn lī′ tən) ***vt-*** to furnish with knowledge; free from ignorance; instruct; inform: *Let me* enlighten *you as to your duties.* **—*n-* en·light′ en·ment.**

en·list (ĕn lĭst′) ***vt-*** **1** to enroll, especially for military service: *to* enlist *men for the army.* **2** to attract and gain (someone's help) for a cause: *We* enlisted *his services for the Red Cross.* ***vi-*** **1** to enter the armed forces without being drafted. **2** to join any cause.

enlisted man ***n-*** male member of the armed forces who is not a commissioned officer or a warrant officer.

en·list·ment (ĕn lĭst′ mənt) ***n-*** **1** the period of time for which a man or woman signs up for service in the armed forces. **2** an enlisting or being enlisted.

en·liv·en (ĕn lī′ vən) ***vt-*** to put life into; invigorate; brighten: *Edgar's new records* enlivened *the party.*

en masse (än′ măs′, *Fr.* ä^n-) ***adv-*** all together; in a group.

en·mesh (ĕn mĕsh′) ***vt-*** to catch in or as in a net or meshes; entangle.

en·mi·ty (ĕn′ mə tē) ***n-*** [*pl.* **en·mi·ties**] hatred; ill will; hostility: *an* enmity *between two nations.*

en·no·ble (ĕn nō′ bəl) ***vt-*** [**en·no·bled, en·no·bling**] **1** to make noble and dignified; exalt: *His life was* ennobled *by his generosity.* **2** to raise to the nobility.

en·nui (än′ wē′) ***n-*** boredom resulting from inactivity; discontent; weariness.

E·noch (ē′ nək) ***n-*** **1** eldest son of Cain. **2** father of Methuselah.

e·nor·mi·ty (ĭ nôr′ mə tē, ĭ nôr′ -) ***n-*** [*pl.* **e·nor·mi·ties**] hugeness in wickedness: *the* enormity *of his offense.* **2** a great wrong or crime: *Hitler's many* enormities.

►Should not be confused with ENORMOUSNESS, which means great size of anything.

e·nor·mous (ĭ nôr′ məs, ĭ nôr′ -) ***adj-*** very large; huge. **—*adv-* e·nor′ mous·ly.** ***n-*** **e·nor′ mous·ness.**

en·ough (ĭ nŭf′) ***determiner*** (traditionally called adjective or pronoun) sufficient; as much or as many as necessary or desirable: *Do we have* enough *food for tomorrow? Yes, we have* enough. ***n-*** a sufficient amount; an ample supply: *I have had* enough *of this bad weather.* ***adv-*** **1** sufficiently; adequately: *Have you practiced* enough? *He didn't run fast* enough. **2** fully; quite: *He is willing* enough *to work.* ***interj-*** stop; no more.

well enough fairly well: *I liked the movie* well enough.

en·quire (ĕn kwīər′) inquire.

en·qui·ry (ĭn′ kwə rē) inquiry.

en·rage (ĕn rāj′) ***vt-*** [**en·raged, en·rag·ing**] to make very angry; infuriate: *Teasing* enraged *the dog.*

en rap·port (ä^n ră pôr′) *French* in agreement; in sympathy.

en·rapt (ĕn răpt′) ***adj-*** rapt; in a state of rapture.

en·rap·ture (ĕn răp′ chər) ***vt-*** [**en·rap·tured, en·rap·tur·ing**] to move to rapture; fill with delight.

en·rich (ĕn rĭch′) ***vt-*** **1** to make better or more effective by desirable additions: *to* enrich *flour*; *to* enrich *soil.* **2** to make (one's mind, an experience, one's life, etc.) fuller and more satisfying. **3** to make more beautiful; adorn. **4** to make wealthy: *Grandfather's investments* enriched *the whole family.* **—*n-* en·rich′ment.**

en·roll or **en·rol** (ĕn rōl′) ***vt-*** [**en·rolled, en·roll·ing**] **1** to put the name (of a person or persons) on a list or register: *to* enroll *students for a special class.* **2** to make a member: *The club* enrolled *him.* ***vi-*** to become a member; register: *He* enrolled *yesterday.*

en·roll·ment or **en·rol·ment** (ĕn rōl′ mənt) ***n-*** **1** number of persons admitted to a group: *The* enrollment *of the school is one thousand.* **2** admission to membership: *her* enrollment *in the Girl Scouts.*

en route (än ro͞ot′, ĕn-) ***adv-*** on the way: *The plane is* en route *to London.*

en·sconce (ĕn skŏns′) ***vt-*** [**en·sconced, en·sconc·ing**] **1** to place; settle comfortably: *We* ensconced *her in the sofa with a book.* **2** to establish in a secret place; hide: *The boys* ensconced *themselves in the cave.*

en·sem·ble (än säm′ bəl) ***n-*** **1** all the parts of a thing viewed together as a whole; total effect. **2** things selected as a set for some purpose; outfit: *a camping* ensemble *including a folding table*; *an* ensemble *of lightweight luggage.* **3** group of musicians playing or singing together. **4** supporting performers in a play, ballet, etc.

en·shrine (ĕn shrīn′) ***vt-*** [**en·shrined, en·shrin·ing**] **1** to place or preserve on an altar or in a holy place. **2** to cherish; keep sacred: *They* enshrined *his memory in their hearts.* **—*n-* en·shrine′ ment.**

en·shroud (ĕn shroud′) ***vt-*** to cover completely; conceal; wrap; envelop; shroud: *Fog* enshrouds *the city.*

en·sign (ĕn′ sīn′, -sən) ***n-*** **1** a national flag or banner used on ships. **2** pennant showing office, rank, or authority: *the general's* ensign. **3** (ĕn′ sən) in the U.S. Navy, a commissioned officer next below a lieutenant (junior grade) and next above a warrant officer.

Norwegian ensign

en·si·lage (ĕn′ sə lĭj) ***n-*** silage.

en·slave (ĕn slāv′) ***vt-*** [**en·slaved, en·slav·ing**] **1** to make a slave of; place in bondage. **2** to dominate completely: *Fear of poverty* enslaved *him.* **—*n-* en·slave′ ment.**

en·snare (ĕn snâr′) ***vt-*** [**en·snared, en·snar·ing**] to trap; snare; trick: *to* ensnare *birds in a net.*

en·sue (ĕn so͞o′, -syo͞o′) ***vi-*** [**en·sued, en·su·ing**] to follow in order; result; come afterward: *The ship ran aground and panic* ensued.

en·sure (ĕn sho͝or′) ***vt-*** [**en·sured, en·sur·ing**] **1** to make sure or certain: *This reservation* ensures *your seat.* **2** to secure; guarantee: *The new law* ensures *more protection.*

►Should not be confused with INSURE.

-ent *suffix* See *-ant.*

en·tab·la·ture (ĕn tăb′ lə chər) ***n-*** in classical architecture, the horizontal parts of a structure that rest directly on the columns.

en·tail (ĕn tāl′) ***vt-*** **1** to impose; require; make necessary: *Success* entails *hard work.* **2** to bequeath (land, property, etc.) in such a way that the heirs cannot give or will it away. **—*n-* en·tail′ ment.**

en·tan·gle (ĕn tăng′ gəl) ***vt-*** [**en·tan·gled, en·tan·gling**] **1** to ensnare; enmesh: *I* entangled *my fishing line in the reeds. They* entangled *me in their plot.* **2** to cause a tangle in; confuse; muddle: *His interference further* entangled *the dispute.*

en·tan·gle·ment (ĕn tăng′ gəl mənt) ***n-*** **1** a tangling. **2** condition of being caught in or as in a snare or net: *He fought against legal* entanglement. **3** trap or snare made of something tangled, especially barbed wire.

en·tan·gling (ĕn tăng′ glĭng) ***adj-*** serving to entangle, involve, or embarrass: *an* entangling *alliance.*

en·tente (än tänt′, *Fr.* ä^n tä^{n}t′) ***n-*** **1** an agreement or understanding between governments. **2** governments that have made such an agreement.

en·ter (ĕn′ tər) ***vt-*** (in senses 1, 3, and 5 considered intransitive when the direct object is implied but not expressed) **1** to go or come into: *He* entered *the house.*

2 to record: *The clerk* entered *the name in the register.* 3 to join: *to* enter *the army.* 4 to enroll: *to* enter *a horse in a race*; *to* enter *a pupil in school.* 5 to become a competitor in: *to* enter *a contest.* ***vi-*** to come upon the stage in a play, opera, etc.

enter into to go into; take part in: *to* enter into *a discussion.*

enter on (or **upon**) to begin: *to* enter upon *a new life.*

en·ter·i·tis (ĕn′ tə rī′ təs) ***n-*** inflammation of the intestines, especially of the small intestine.

en·ter·prise (ĕn′ tər prīz′) ***n-*** 1 an undertaking; project: *a difficult* enterprise; *a business* enterprise. 2 willingness or energy to start new projects; initiative: *a spirit of* enterprise; *man of* enterprise. See also *free enterprise.*

en·ter·pris·ing (ĕn′ tər prī′ zĭng) ***adj-*** willing to start new and untried projects; venturesome; energetic: *The Wright brothers were* enterprising *men.* ***—adv-*** **en′ ter·pris′ ing·ly.**

en·ter·tain (ĕn′ tər tān′) ***vt-*** 1 to receive as a guest; give food and drink to: *They will* entertain *friends at dinner tonight.* 2 to amuse; divert; interest: *That magician has* entertained *many audiences.* 3 to consider; keep in mind: *He is* entertaining *the offer of a new job.* ***vi-*** to receive guests: *We* entertained *in the garden.*

en·ter·tain·er (ĕn′ tər tān′ ər) ***n-*** singer, dancer, actor, etc., who performs in public.

en·ter·tain·ing (ĕn′ tər tān′ ĭng) ***adj-*** amusing; diverting; pleasing; interesting. ***—adv-*** **en′ ter·tain′ ing·ly.**

en·ter·tain·ment (ĕn′ tər tān′ mənt) ***n-*** 1 an entertaining or being entertained: *the* entertainment *of guests*; *the* entertainment *of a new idea.* 2 something that amuses, interests, diverts, etc., such as a play or a circus.

en·thrall or **en·thral** (ĕn thrôl′) ***vt-*** [**en·thralled, en·thral·ling**] to hold under a spell; charm; captivate: *The singer* enthralled *his audience.*

en·throne (ĕn thrōn′) ***vt-*** [**en·throned, en·thron·ing**] 1 to place on a throne or in a position of power: *to* enthrone *a king.* 2 to place in a position of reverence or devotion: *to* enthrone *a hero.* ***—n-*** **en·throne′ ment.**

en·thuse (ĕn thōōz′) *Informal* ***vi-*** [**en·thused, enthus·ing**] to become enthusiastic; show enthusiasm. ***vt-*** to make enthusiastic; fill with enthusiasm.

►Most educated people avoid this word.

en·thu·si·asm (ĕn thōō′ zē ăz′ əm) ***n-*** strong and joyous feeling of interest or admiration (for): *Rain did not affect our* enthusiasm.

en·thu·si·ast (ĕn thōō′ zē ăst′) ***n-*** person with keen interest in or feeling for something; a fan; buff: *a tennis* enthusiast.

en·thu·si·as·tic (ĕn thōō′ zē ăs′ tĭk) ***adj-*** full of enthusiasm; keenly interested: *an* enthusiastic *baseball fan.* ***—adv-*** **en·thu′ si·as′ ti·cal·ly.**

en·tice (ĕn tīs′) ***vt-*** [**en·ticed, en·tic·ing**] to lead on by arousing hope or desire; lure; tempt: *He* enticed *the dog with a bone.* ***—n-*** **en·tice′ ment.** ***adv-*** **en·tic′ ing·ly.**

en·tire (ĕn tīər′) ***adj-*** 1 whole; complete: *the* entire *family*; *the* entire *program.* 2 unbroken: *an* entire *series.* 3 total: *his* entire *ignorance of the matter.*

en·tire·ly (ĕn tīər′ lē) ***adv-*** wholly; completely.

en·tire·ty (ĕn tīər′ tē) ***n-*** the whole; the total.

in its entirety as a whole; completely.

en·ti·tle (ĕn tī′ təl) ***vt-*** [**en·ti·tled, en·ti·tling**] 1 to give (someone) a right or privilege (to): *The law* entitles *every person accused of a crime to a trial.* 2 to give a title to: *Mark Twain* entitled *a book "The Adventures of Tom Sawyer."*

en·ti·ty (ĕn′ tə tē) ***n-*** [*pl.* **en·ti·ties**] 1 independent being or existence: *Some Indian tribes try to preserve their* entity. 2 something real in itself or distinct in character: *The United States is an* entity *rather than a loose confederation. Love and beauty are* entities *in themselves.*

en·tomb (ĕn tōōm′) ***vt-*** 1 to place in a grave or tomb; bury. 2 to serve as a tomb for. ***—n-*** **en·tomb′ ment.**

en·to·mol·o·gist (ĕn tə mŏl′ ə jĭst) ***n-*** person trained in and usually working in entomology.

en·to·mo·log·i·cal (ĕn′ tə mə lŏj′ ĭ kəl) ***adj-*** of or having to do with entomology.

en·to·mol·o·gy (ĕn′ tə mŏl′ ə jē) ***n-*** branch of zoology that deals with insects.

en·tou·rage (än′ tōō räzh, -räj) ***n-*** attendants, associates, or followers, especially of a person of rank.

en·trails (ĕn′ trəlz, -trālz′) ***n-*** *pl.* the internal parts of man or animals, especially the bowels.

en·train (ĕn trān′) ***vi-*** to board a train: *We* entrained *at noon.* ***vt-*** to put aboard a train: *to* entrain *troops.*

[1]**en·trance** (ĕn′ trəns) ***n-*** 1 door or passage through which one enters: *the* entrance *to a tunnel.* 2 an entering: *The actress makes a dramatic* entrance *wherever she goes.* 3 permission to enter: *He gained* entrance *to the place.* [from Old French **entrance,** from **entrer** meaning "to enter," from Latin **intrare,** from **intrō,** "within."]

[2]**en·trance** (ĕn trăns′) ***vt-*** [**en·tranced, en·tranc·ing**] 1 to put under a spell. 2 to fill with delight; enrapture: *The ballet* entranced *her.* [from **en-** meaning "in" plus **trance** meaning "a spell."] ***—n-*** **en·trance′ ment.**

en·tranc·ing (ĕn trăn′ sĭng) ***adj-*** causing delight or rapture: *an* entrancing *melody.* ***—adv-*** **en·tranc′ ing·ly.**

en·trant (ĕn′ trənt) ***n-*** one who enters; especially, one who becomes a competitor in a contest.

en·trap (ĕn trăp′) ***vt-*** [**en·trapped, en·trap·ping**] to lure into a trap, especially into a bad moral or legal situation. ***—n-*** **en·trap′ ment.**

en·treat (ĕn trēt′) ***vt-*** to ask earnestly; beg; beseech: *to* entreat *a favor.* ***—adv-*** **en·treat′ ing·ly.**

en·treat·y (ĕn trē′ tē) ***n-*** [*pl.* **en·treat·ies**] earnest request; prayer: *He was deaf to her* entreaties.

en·tree (än′ trā′) ***n-*** 1 entrance; privilege of entering; access: *He gained* entree *to the exclusive club.* 2 the main dish of a meal. Also **entrée.**

en·trench (ĕn trĕnch′) ***vt-*** 1 to surround or protect by digging deep ditches: *The soldiers* entrenched *themselves near the enemy lines.* 2 to establish firmly: *He strongly* entrenched *himself in the company.* Also **intrench.**

en·trench·ment (ĕn trĕnch′ mənt) ***n-*** 1 system of trenches and earthworks, used for protection and defense: *The* entrenchment *extended along the riverbank.* 2 any fortified position. 3 an entrenching or being entrenched.

en·tre·pre·neur (än′ trə prə nûr′) ***n-*** person who establishes a business enterprise or a series of them.

en·trust (ĕn trŭst′) ***vt-*** to turn (someone or something) over for safekeeping or care: *to* entrust *money to a bank.*

entrust (someone) with to trust or be willing to trust (someone) to do something, care for something, etc.

en·try (ĕn′ trē) ***n-*** [*pl.* **en·tries**] 1 a going into; entering: *Their* entry *into the country was illegal.* 2 place through which one goes or comes in, such as a vestibule. 3 item recorded in a list, diary, etc.: *an* entry *in the ship's log.* 4 person or thing entered in a contest.

en·twine (ĕn twīn′) ***vt-*** [**en·twined, en·twin·ing**] 1 to wind or twine around: *Ivy* entwined *the cottage.* 2 to twist together: *They* entwined *their hands as they walked.*

e·nu·mer·ate (ĭ nōō′ mə rāt′, ĭ nyōō′-) ***vt-*** [**e·nu·mer·at·ed, e·nu·mer·at·ing**] **1** to list or name one by one. **2** to count; number. ***—n-*** **e·nu′ mer·a′ tion.**

e·nu·me·ra·tive (ĭ nōō′ mə rə tĭv′, ĭ nyōō′-) ***adj-*** of or having to do with enumerating.

e·nun·ci·ate (ĭ nŭn′ sē āt′) ***vt-*** [**e·nun·ci·at·ed, e·nun·ci·at·ing**] **1** (considered intransitive when the direct object is implied but not expressed) to pronounce or utter (words, sounds, etc.): *to* enunciate *one's "t's" clearly.* **2** to proclaim; announce: *to* enunciate *a theory.*

e·nun·ci·a·tion (ĭ nŭn′ sē ā′ shən) ***n-*** **1** manner of pronouncing words or sounds: *her clear* enunciation. **2** statement; announcement: *an* enunciation *of policy.*

en·vel·op (ĕn vĕl′ əp) ***vt-*** to enfold in or as in a wrapper, so as to cover or conceal: *Fog* enveloped *the city.*

en·ve·lope (ĕn′ və lōp′, än′-) ***n-*** **1** flat paper wrapper for enclosing letters. **2** any outer covering, especially that of a dirigible or balloon.

en·ven·om (ĕn vĕn′ əm) ***vt-*** **1** to poison. **2** to embitter; fill with hate: *Envy* envenomed *him.*

en·vi·a·ble (ĕn′ vē ə bəl) ***adj-*** admirable or desirable enough to cause envy: *He has an* enviable *school record.* ***—adv-*** **en′ vi·a·bly.**

en·vi·ous (ĕn′ vē əs) ***adj-*** feeling or showing envy; jealous: *to be* envious *of someone's success.* ***—adv-*** **en′ vi·ous·ly.** ***n-*** **en′ vi·ous·ness.**

en·vi·ron (ĕn vī′ rən, -ərn) ***vt-*** to form a circle or ring around; encircle: *Forests* environ *the city.*

en·vi·ron·ment (ĕn vī′ ərn mənt, ĕn vī′ rən-) ***n-*** **1** all the things that are around or in the neighborhood of a person, building, etc.; physical surroundings: *the* environment *of the new school.* **2** all the influences, ideas, conditions, etc., among which a person lives: *a good family* environment. **3** a place with particular conditions: *a forest* environment; *an arctic* environment. ***—adj-*** **en·vi′ ron·men′ tal:** *an* environmental *influence.* ***adv-*** **en·vi′ ron·men′ tal·ly.**

en·vi·rons (ĕn vī′ rənz, -ərnz) ***n- pl.*** the surroundings of a city; suburbs; outskirts.

en·vis·age (ĕn vĭz′ ĭj) ***vt-*** [**en·vis·aged, en·vis·ag·ing**] **1** to form a mental picture of; visualize: *to* envisage *a better world.* **2** to expect or plan on in advance; contemplate: *Do you* envisage *a rise in taxes?*

en·voy (ĕn′ voi, än′-) ***n-*** **1** messenger. **2** government official sent on a mission to another government. **3** a diplomat ranking next below an ambassador. **4** l'envoi, the last stanza of a ballade.

en·vy (ĕn′ vē) ***n-*** [*pl.* **en·vies**] **1** feeling of discontent aroused by the advantages or possessions of another; resentful jealousy: *He was filled with* envy *at his friend's accomplishment.* **2** the object of such a feeling: *Her beauty was the* envy *of all the girls.* ***vt-*** [**en·vied, en·vy·ing**] to feel resentment toward or because of: *He* envied *his friend's success.*

en·wrap (ĕn răp′) ***vt-*** [**en·wrapped, en·wrap·ping**] to enclose; envelop; enfold.

en·wreathe (ĕn rēth′) ***vt-*** [**en·wreathed, en·wreath·ing**] to wreathe around; surround; encircle.

en·zyme (ĕn′ zīm′) ***n-*** protein that starts or speeds up chemical action in other substances without undergoing any permanent change itself. Enzymes are made by the cells of all living organisms.

E·o·cene (ē′ ə sēn′) ***n-*** the second of the five epochs of the Tertiary period. ***adj-***: *the* Eocene *epoch.*

e·o·hip·pus (ē′ ō hĭp′ əs) ***n-*** small primitive horse having four toes on its forefeet and three toes on its hindfeet. It was an ancestor of the horse of modern times.

E·o·lith·ic (ē′ ō lĭth′ ĭk) ***adj-*** of or relating to the earliest period of the Stone Age.

e·on (ē′ ŏn′, -ən) ***n-*** extremely long period of time; an eternity; age: *rocks lasting through* eons. Also **aeon.**

ep·au·let or **ep·au·lette** (ĕp′ ə lĕt′) ***n-*** shoulder ornament on a uniform, usually signifying rank.

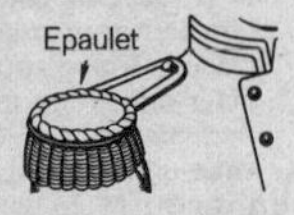

e·phed·rine (ĭ fĕd′ rĭn) ***n-*** drug extracted from certain Chinese plants or made synthetically, and used to raise the blood pressure, to treat asthma and hay fever, and to dilate the pupil of the eye.

e·phem·er·al (ĭ fĕm′ ər əl) ***adj-*** **1** lasting for only a short time; fleeting; transitory: *When compared to the age of the earth, man's life is* ephemeral. **2** living for only one day, as certain insects do.

E·phe·sians (ĭ fē′ zhənz) ***n-*** (takes singular verb) tenth book of the New Testament consisting of St. Paul's epistle to the church at Ephesus.

eph·od (ĕf′ ŏd′) ***n-*** in ancient times, a garment worn by a Hebrew high priest.

E·phra·im (ē′ frəm) ***n-*** **1** in the Old Testament, the younger son of Joseph. **2** the tribe of Israel descended from him; hence, the kingdom of Israel.

epi- *prefix* on; above; over: *the* epi*dermis*; epi*glottis*; epi*center.* [from Greek **epi-** meaning "upon; on; at."]

ep·ic (ĕp′ ĭk) ***n-*** long narrative poem in a lofty style that tells of heroes and heroic deeds. The "Iliad" is an epic. ***adj-*** **1** of or related to such a poem: *an* epic *hero.* **2** grand; majestic; noble: *an* epic *achievement.*

ep·i·cen·ter (ĕp′ ə sĕn′ tər) ***n-*** place on the surface of the earth directly above the place an earthquake starts.

ep·i·cure (ĕp′ ə kyŏŏr′) ***n-*** person who is devoted to refined pleasures, especially eating and drinking.

ep·i·cu·re·an (ĕp′ ə kyŏŏr ē′ ən) ***n-*** **1** follower of Epicurus. **2** epicure; gourmet. ***adj-*** fit for an epicure.

ep·i·dem·ic (ĕp′ ə dĕm′ ĭk) ***n-*** **1** general attack of a disease in a particular area: *The town had an* epidemic *of measles.* **2** widespread occurrence of anything: *an* epidemic *of robberies.* ***adj-*** attacking many people at the same time and spreading from person to person: *Influenza is an* epidemic *disease.*

ep·i·der·mis (ĕp′ ə dûr′ məs) ***n-*** **1** outermost layer of an animal's skin. For picture, see *skin.* **2** outer layer of cells on the leaf or bark of a plant. ***—adj-*** **ep′ i·der′ mal.**

ep·i·glot·tis (ĕp′ ə glŏt′ əs) ***n-*** leaf-shaped lid of cartilage that covers the upper part of the windpipe during the act of swallowing. For picture, see *throat.*

ep·i·gram (ĕp′ ə grăm′) ***n-*** terse, witty saying. Example: "All men are equal, but some are more equal than others."

ep·i·gram·mat·ic (ĕp′ ə grə măt′ ĭk) or **ep·i·gram·mat·i·cal** (-măt′ ĭ kəl) ***adj-*** **1** of or like an epigram; short and witty: *an* epigrammatic *observation.* **2** of a person, fond of using epigrams. ***—adv-*** **ep′ i·gram·mat′ i·cal·ly.**

ep·i·lep·sy (ĕp′ ə lĕp′ sē) ***n-*** disease of the nervous system marked by fits of fainting with or without convulsive jerking of the muscles.

ep·i·lep·tic (ĕp′ ə lĕp′ tĭk) ***adj-*** of, having to do with, or affected with epilepsy. ***n-*** person having epilepsy.

ep·i·log or **ep·i·logue** (ĕp′ ə lŏg′, -lŏg′) ***n-*** **1** concluding part of a story, poem, etc., usually giving added information or comment. **2** speech recited at the end of a play.

E·piph·a·ny (ĭ pĭf′ ə nē) ***n-*** church festival on January 6 commemorating the visit of the three Magi to the Christ child, the first manifestation of Christ to the Gentiles.

ep·i·phyte (ĕp′ ə fīt′) ***n-*** plant, such as a fern or orchid, that grows on another plant but does not receive nourishment from the supporting plant. See also *parasite.* ***—adj-*** **ep′ i·phy′ tic** (ĕp′ ə fĭt′ ĭk).

Epis. or **Episc.** **1** Episcopal. **2** Epistle or Epistles.

e·pis·co·pa·cy (ĭ pĭsʹ kə pə sē) ***n-*** [*pl.* **e·pis·co·pa·cies**] **1** church government by bishops. **2** office, rank, or term of office of a bishop. **3** bishops as a group.

e·pis·co·pal (ĭ pĭsʹ kə pəl) ***adj-*** **1** of, relating to, or governed by a bishop. **2 Episcopal** belonging to, or referring to the Protestant Episcopal Church, which represents the Anglican communion in the United States. ***—adv-*** **e·pisʹ co·pal·ly.**

E·pis·co·pa·li·an (ĭ pĭsʹ kə pālʹ yən, -pālʹ ē ən) ***n-*** member of the Protestant Episcopal Church. ***adj-***: *the* Episcopalian *version of the text.*

ep·i·sode (ĕpʹ ə sōdʹ) ***n-*** **1** section or incident in a literary work: *the* episode *of whitewashing the fence in "Tom Sawyer."* **2** outstanding incident in a person's life, in history, etc. **3** an installment of a story or play published or performed serially.

ep·i·sod·ic (ĕpʹ ə sŏdʹ ĭk) ***adj-*** **1** of or like an episode. **2** broken up into a series of separate incidents, usually in a loose and aimless way. ***—adv-*** **epʹ i·sodʹ i·cal·ly.**

e·pis·tle (ĭ pĭsʹ əl) ***n-*** **1** letter, especially a formal one. **2 Epistle** one of the letters or collections of letters written by the Apostles and forming part of the New Testament.

e·pis·to·lar·y (ĭ pĭsʹ tə lĕrʹ ē) ***adj-*** **1** of or related to letters or letter writing: *an* epistolary *style.* **2** in the form of letters: *an* epistolary *novel.*

ep·i·taph (ĕpʹ ə tăfʹ) ***n-*** writing inscribed on a tomb, tombstone, etc., in memory of the person buried there.

ep·i·tha·la·mi·um (ĕpʹ ə thə lāʹ mē əm) ***n-*** [*pl.* **ep·i·tha·la·mi·ums** or **ep·i·tha·la·mi·a** (-mē ə)] song or poem honoring a bride and bridegroom; nuptial song or poem. Also **epʹ i·tha·laʹ mi·on** (-mē ən).

ep·i·the·li·um (ĕpʹ ə thēʹ lē əm) ***n-*** [*pl.* **ep·i·the·liums** or **ep·i·the·lia** (-lē ə)] thin sheet or layer of tissue that serves as a protective lining or covering for the tubes, cavities, and organs of the body. This tissue also forms the secretory part of most glands. ***—adj-*** **epʹ i·theʹ li·al.**

ep·i·thet (ĕpʹ ə thĕtʹ) ***n-*** **1** adjective or other descriptive term used to express some characteristic quality. Examples: "fleet-footed" in "fleet-footed Achilles," or "the Fat" in "Charles the Fat." **2** insulting name: *to hurl* epithets *at someone.*

e·pit·o·me (ə pĭtʹ ə mē) ***n-*** **1** most typical or ideal representative of something; embodiment: *Samson is the* epitome *of courage.* **2** short summary of a writing; synopsis; abstract.

e·pit·o·mize (ə pĭtʹ ə mīzʹ) ***vt-*** [**e·pit·o·mized, e·pit·o·miz·ing**] **1** to be the most typical or ideal representative of; embody most perfectly: *Samson* epitomizes *courage.* **2** to summarize; abridge.

e plu·ri·bus u·num (ēʹ plŏŏrʹ ə bəs yōōʹ nəm) *Latin* one out of many. As a motto of the United States, it means one nation made up of many sovereign States.

ep·och (ĕpʹ ək) ***n-*** **1** period of time in which unusual or important events take place; era: *The* epoch *of space exploration began with the launching of the first earth satellite.* **2** the beginning of such a period: *The launching of the satellite marked an* epoch *in space exploration.* **3** a minor division of geologic time, shorter than a period. ***—adj-*** **epʹ och·al.** ***adv-*** **epʹ och·al·ly.**

e·pox·y (ə pŏkʹ sē) ***n-*** [*pl.* **e·pox·ies**] any of various synthetic resins used to make extremely strong adhesives and plastics. *as* ***modifier***: *an* epoxy *cement.*

Ep·som salts (ĕpʹ səm) ***n-*** white or colorless crystalline salt used in medicine as a cathartic and, externally, in a soaking bath to reduce soreness and swelling.

eq. **1** equal. **2** equivalent. **3** equation. **4** equator.

eq·ua·ble (ĕkʹ wə bəl, ēʹ kwə-) ***adj-*** **1** steady and unchanging; even: *an* equable *climate.* **2** not readily upset; serene and tranquil: *an* equable *disposition.* ***—n-*** **eʹ qua·bilʹ i·ty.** ***adv-*** **eqʹ ua·bly.**

e·qual (ēʹ kwəl) ***adj-*** **1** having the same size, amount, value, rank, etc.; alike; identical: *I want an* equal *share*; *men* equal *before the law.* **2** fairly matched; even: *an* equal *contest.* **3** belonging to all; shared: *our* equal *rights*; equal *duties.* ***n-*** person or thing of the same size, amount, value, etc., as another: *As a swimmer he has few* equals. ***vt-*** **1** to be the same as, in size, amount, value, etc.: *Sixteen ounces* equal *one pound.* **2** to achieve the same as: *He* equaled *his rival.* ***—adv-*** **eʹ qual·ly.**

equal to **1** the same as: *Four plus four is* equal to *eight.* **2** sufficiently able for; enough for.

e·qual·i·ty (ē kwŏlʹ ə tē) ***n-*** [*pl.* **e·qual·i·ties**] **1** sameness; identity. **2** treatment, rights, etc., that are the same for all persons. **3** *Mathematics* statement that two variables, quantities, etc. are equal, usually in the form of an equation.

e·qual·ize (ēʹ kwə līzʹ) ***vt-*** [**e·qual·ized, e·qual·iz·ing**] to make equal or even. ***—n-*** **eʹ qual·i·zaʹ tion.**

e·qua·nim·i·ty (ĕkʹ wə nĭmʹ ə tē, ēʹ kwə-) ***n-*** evenness of mind or temper; calmness; serenity.

e·quate (ĭ kwātʹ) ***vt-*** [**e·quat·ed, e·quat·ing**] to make treat, or consider as equal: *to* equate *two quantities.*

e·qua·tion (ĭ kwāʹ zhən) ***n-*** **1** a statement that two quantities are equal: $3 + 3 = 6$ *is an* equation. **2** in arithmetic, any sentence with "equals" for its verb. Example: $x + 3 = 7$.

e·qua·tor (ĭ kwāʹ tər) ***n-*** **1** an imaginary circle around the earth that is equally distant from the North and South Poles and divides the earth into the northern and southern hemispheres. **2** any similar circle around another planet or the sun. **3** the celestial equator.

e·qua·to·ri·al (ĕkʹ wə tôrʹ ē əl, ēʹ kwə-) ***adj-*** **1** having to do with or located near the earth's equator. **2** like conditions near the earth's equator: *a week of* equatorial *heat.* ***—adv-*** **eʹ qua·toʹ ri·al·ly.**

eq·uer·ry (ĕkʹ wə rē, ĭ kwĕrʹ ē) ***n-*** [*pl.* **eq·uer·ries**] **1** officer in charge of the horses of a prince or nobleman. **2** in England, a personal attendant of any member of the sovereign's family.

e·ques·tri·an (ĭ kwĕsʹ trē ən) ***n-*** **1** man or boy riding a horse. **2** man or boy regarded as a rider of horses: *Tom's a good* equestrian. ***adj-*** **1** of or related to horses or horsemanship: *his* equestrian *training.* **2** performing with horses, as in a circus: *an* equestrian *artist.* **3** showing a figure on horseback: *an* equestrian *statue.* ***—n-*** ***fem.*** **e·quesʹ tri·enneʹ** (-ĕnʹ).

equi- *combining form* equal; equally: *an* equi*lateral triangle*; equi*valent.* [from Latin **æqui-**, from **aeguus** meaning "equal."]

e·qui·dis·tant (ēʹ kwə dĭsʹ tənt) ***adj-*** separated by equal distances; equally distant.

e·quilat·er·al (ē kwə lătʹ ər əl) ***adj-*** in geometry, having all sides of the same length: *an* equilateral *triangle.* ***—adv-*** **eʹ qui·latʹ er·al·ly.**

e·qui·lib·ri·um (ēʹ kwə lĭbʹ rē əm) ***n-*** **1** balance: *A tightrope walker keeps his* equilibrium *with a pole.* **2** evenness of mind and emotions; aplomb.

e·quine (ĕkʹ wīnʹ, ēʹ kwīnʹ) ***adj-*** of or like a horse.

e·qui·noc·tial (ēʹ kwə nŏkʹ tē əl, ĕkʹ wə-) ***adj-*** **1** pertaining to the equinoxes, or having day and night of equal length. **2** occurring at the time of an equinox.

equinoctial line *n-* the celestial equator.

e·qui·nox (ē′ kwə nŏks′, ĕk′ wə-) *n-* **1** either of the two days each year on which the sun is directly above the equator. On these days, day and night are of equal length everywhere on earth. The **vernal equinox** occurs about March 21, and the **autumnal equinox** occurs about September 22. **2** either of the two points on the celestial sphere where the celestial equator and the ecliptic intersect.

e·quip (ĭ kwĭp′) *vt-* [**e·quipped, e·quip·ping**] to supply with something needed or useful; fit out: *to* equip *a polar expedition.*

eq·ui·page (ĭ kwĭp′ ĭj) *n-* **1** equipment or outfit of an army, vessel, camp, etc. **2** carriage fitted out with horses and liveried servants.

e·quip·ment (ĭ kwĭp′ mənt) *n-* **1** things or supplies needed for a particular purpose; outfit: *Camping* equipment *includes tents and sleeping bags.* **2** a fitting out; an equipping: *the* equipment *of a bicycle with lights.*

e·qui·poise (ĕk′ wə poiz′, ē′ kwə-) *n-* **1** equality of weight or force; equilibrium; balance. **2** weight or force that counterbalances another; counterpoise.

eq·ui·ta·ble (ĕk′ wə tə bəl) *adj-* just; fair; impartial: *an* equitable *decision.* **—*adv-*** **eq′ ui·ta·bly.**

eq·ui·ty (ĕk′ wə tē) *n-* [*pl.* **eq·ui·ties**] **1** fairness; justice: *No one questions the* equity *of this transaction.* **2** in law, a body of rules based on natural principles of justice, administered in special courts, and distinct from statutes. **3** portion actually owned by a buyer after all debts, mortgages, etc., are subtracted: *He has a $4000* equity *in his house.*

e·quiv·a·lence (ĭ kwĭv′ ə ləns) *n-* sameness in value, amount, meaning, etc.; equality. Also **e·quiv′ a·len·cy.**

e·quiv·a·lent (ĭ kwĭv′ ə lənt) *adj-* **1** equal in value, amount, meaning etc.: *Cheating is* equivalent *to lying.* **2** *Mathematics* (1) having the same solution set: equivalent *equations.* (2) having equal areas or volumes: equivalent *figures.* (3) having the same value: equivalent *fractions.* (4) naming the same number for all replacements: equivalent *phrases.* (5) being true together or false together: equivalent *sentences.* (6) having the same number of elements: equivalent *sets.* ***n-***: *Two nickels are the* equivalent *of a dime.* **—*adv-*** **e·quiv′ a·lent·ly.**

e·quiv·o·cal (ĭ kwĭv′ ə kəl) *adj-* of doubtful or uncertain meaning, value, etc.; ambiguous: *an* equivocal *reply.* **—*adv-*** **e·quiv′ o·cal·ly.** ***n-*** **e·quiv′ o·cal·ness.**

e·quiv·o·cate (ĭ kwĭv′ ə kāt′) *vi-* [**e·quiv·o·cat·ed, e·quiv·o·cat·ing**] to deceive by making equivocal or ambiguous statements: *He would rather* equivocate *than give a direct, truthful answer.* **—*n-*** **e·quiv′ o·ca′ tion.** ***n-*** **e·quiv′ o·ca′ tor:** *An* equivocator *makes me uneasy.*

Er symbol for erbium.

[1]**-er** *suffix* (used to form nouns) **1** person or thing that does: *danc*er; *roll*er. **2** person who is interested in or concerned with: *philosoph*er; *astronom*er. **3** person who lives in or comes from: *New York*er.

[2]**-er** *word ending* used to form the comparative of many adjectives and adverbs, carrying the meaning "to a higher degree": *great*er; *strong*er; *earli*er.

e·ra (êr′ ə, ĕr′ ə) *n-* **1** period of time measured from a particular event: *The Christian* era *dates from the birth of Christ.* **2** period of history characterized by certain events, men, etc.: *the* era *of Napoleon*; *the jazz* era. **3** one of the five major divisions of geologic time.

e·rad·i·cate (ĭ răd′ ə kāt′) *vt-* [**e·rad·i·cat·ed, e·rad·i·cat·ing**] to destroy completely; annihilate; wipe out: *Vaccination has nearly* eradicated *smallpox.* **—*adj-*** **e·rad′ i·ca·ble** (-kə bəl). ***n-*** **e·rad′ i·ca′ tion.** ***n-*** **e·rad′ i·ca′ tor:** *I need ink* eradicator *to correct this error.*

e·rase (ĭ rās′) *vt-* [**e·rased, e·ras·ing**] **1** to remove (a mark, word, etc.); rub out: *Please* erase *that misspelled word.* **2** to remove markings from: *Please* erase *the blackboard.* ***vi-*** to permit rubbing out or removing: *This paper* erases *easily.* **—*adj-*** **e·rase′ a·ble.**

e·ras·er (ĭ rā′ sər) *n-* anything used for rubbing out written marks.

e·ras·ure (ĭ rā′ shər) *n-* **1** an erasing: *the* erasure *of all misspellings.* **2** the result of an erasing, especially the mark or smudge left: *an unsightly* erasure.

er·bi·um (ûr′ bē əm) *n-* lustrous metal element found in certain minerals. Symbol Er, At. No. 68, At. Wt. 167.26.

ere (âr) *Archaic* ***conj-*** **1** before. **2** rather than. ***prep-*** before. ***Homs-*** air, e'er, heir, [2]are.

e·rect (ĭ rĕkt′) *vt-* **1** to construct or build: *They will* erect *a new building.* **2** to set up; establish; found: *to* erect *a new government.* **3** to set upright; raise: *to* erect *a flagpole.* ***adj-*** directed upward; upright; vertical: *Sit* erect *in your chair. He has an* erect *posture.* **—*adv-*** **e·rect′ ly.** ***n-*** **e·rect′ ness.**

e·rec·tion (ĭ rĕk′ shən) *n-* **1** an erecting; a raising or setting up: *The* erection *of a new school will be expensive.* **2** structure; building.

er·e·mite (ĕr′ ə mīt′) *n-* religious hermit.

erg (ûrg) *n-* unit of work equal to the work done in lifting one gram one centimeter.

er·go (ĕr′ gō′, ûr′ -) *Latin* therefore; hence.

er·got (ûr′ gŏt′, -gət) *n-* poisonous fungus on rye, wheat, and other grasses. It is the source of several alkaloids used to stop hemorrhage and to treat migraine.

erl·king (ûrl′ kĭng′) *n-* in Germanic folklore, an evil spirit that is especially harmful to children.

er·mine (ûr′ mən) *n-* **1** any of various weasels valued for their white winter fur. **2** the winter fur of these animals.

Ermine, about 14 in. long

e·rode (ĭ rōd′) *vt-* [**e·rod·ed, e·rod·ing**] **1** to wear away by rubbing or by the washing or blowing away of particles; eat away: *Rain and wind* eroded *the hillside. The wiring was* eroded *by acid.* **2** to form by wearing away: *Water* eroded *gullies in the hill.*

Er·os (êr′ ŏs′, ĕr′-) *n-* in Greek mythology, god of love, son of Aphrodite. He is identified with Roman Cupid.

e·ro·sion (ĭ rō′ zhən) *n-* a gradual wearing or eating away: *the* erosion *of rocks by running water.*

e·ro·sive (ĭ rō′ sĭv, -zĭv) *adj-* causing erosion; eroding.

e·rot·ic (ĭ rŏt′ ĭk) *adj-* of, related to, or causing sexual passion. **—*adv-*** **e·rot′ i·cal·ly.**

e·rot·i·cism (ĭ rŏt′ ə sĭz′ əm) *n-* erotic nature.

err (ĕr, ûr) *vi-* to make a mistake; do wrong; be incorrect: *To* err *is human.*

er·rand (ĕr′ ənd) *n-* **1** trip for a special purpose: *an* errand *of mercy.* **2** thing to be done on such a trip: *I've finished my* errands.

er·rant (ĕr′ ənt) *adj-* **1** roving in search of adventure: *an* errant *knight.* **2** mistaken; wrong: *his* errant *behavior.*

er·ra·ta (ĭ rä′ tə, ĭ rā′ tə) *n- pl.* [*sing.* **er·ra·tum** (-təm)] errors in printing or writing, often given in a list at the beginning or end of a book.

er·rat·ic (ĭ răt′ ĭk) *adj-* **1** wandering; straying: *an* erratic *journey.* **2** odd; eccentric: *her* erratic *behavior.* ***n-*** in geology, a large boulder deposited by glacial action, whose composition is unlike that of the native bedrock. **—*adv-*** **er·rat′ i·cal·ly.**

er·ro·ne·ous (ĭ rō′ nē əs) *adj-* incorrect; mistaken: *an* erroneous *belief.* **—*adv-*** **er·ro′ ne·ous·ly.** ***n-*** **er·ro′ ne·ous·ness.**

er·ror (ĕr′ ər) ***n-*** **1** mistake; inaccuracy: *an* error *in spelling*; *an* error *of 5 per cent in his total.* **2** wrongness of conduct or belief: *the* error *of his ways.* **3** in baseball, a misplay by a member of the team in the field that permits the batting team to gain a base, score a run, etc. **4** *Mathematics* the difference between the measured value and the true value of a quantity.

er·satz (ĕr′ zäts′) ***adj-*** serving as a substitute, and usually an inferior one: *an* ersatz *coffee.* [from German.]

erst·while (ûrst′ hwīl′) ***adj-*** former. ***adv-*** *Archaic* formerly; in times past.

eru·dite (ĕr′ ə dīt′ ĕr′ yə-) ***adj-*** learned; scholarly: *an* erudite *lecture.* **—*adv-* er′ u·dite′ ly.**

er·u·di·tion (ĕr′ ə dĭsh′ ən, ĕr′ yə-) ***n-*** scholarly knowledge; learning: *a man of great* erudition.

e·rupt (ĭ rŭpt′) ***vi-*** to burst forth: *The volcano* erupted. *Steam* erupted *from the geyser. The meeting* erupted *into a din of angry voices.* ***vt-***: *The volcano* erupts *lava.* ►Should not be confused with IRRUPT.

e·rup·tion (ĭ rŭp′ shən) ***n-*** **1** a bursting out or forth; outbreak: *the* eruption *of a volcano*; *an* eruption *of violence.* **2** rash on the skin.

e·rup·tive (ĭ rŭp′ tĭv) ***adj-*** **1** erupting or bursting forth: *an* eruptive *volcano.* **2** formed by volcanic eruption: *a mass of* eruptive *rock.*

-ery *suffix* (used to form nouns) **1** place of business, establishment, or dwelling: *tann*ery; *nurs*ery; *nunn*ery. **2** qualities, conduct, or practices: *snobb*ery; *trick*ery; *prud*ery. **3** class or collection: *millin*ery; *fin*ery. **4** art or occupation: *arch*ery; *surg*ery. **5** condition: *slav*ery.

er·y·sip·e·las (ĕr′ ə sĭp′ ə ləs, ĭr′-) ***n-*** acute, infectious disease of the skin and underlying tissues, marked by fever, redness, swelling, and other symptoms.

e·ryth·ro·my·cin (ə rĭth′ rə mī′ sən) ***n-*** antibiotic drug produced from a mold found in soil.

E·sau (ē′ sò′) ***n-*** in the Old Testament, the older of the twin sons of Isaac and Rebecca. He sold his birthright to his brother Jacob.

es·cad·rille (ĕs′ kə drĭl′) ***n-*** squadron of warplanes in the French air force, especially in World War I.

es·ca·late (ĕs′ kə lāt′) ***vt-*** **[es·ca·lat·ed, es·ca·lat·ing]** to cause (something) to increase in scale, intensity, etc.: *to* escalate *a skirmish into a battle.* ***vi-***: *The border clash* escalated *into a war.* **—*n-* es′ ca·la′ tion.**

es·ca·la·tor (ĕs′ kə lā′ tər) ***n-*** moving stairway used to convey passengers from floor to floor.

es·cal·lop (ĭ skăl′ əp, ĭ skäl′-) ***vt-*** to scallop.

es·ca·pade (ĕs′ kə pād′) ***n-*** brief, wild break from restraint; reckless adventure; spree.

es·cape (ĭ skāp′) ***vi-*** **[es·caped, es·cap·ing]** **1** to get away or get free; break loose: *to* escape *from prison.* **2** to avoid capture, harm, etc.: *He* escaped *by hiding in a cellar.* **3** to flow out; issue: *Gas is* escaping *from that pipe.* ***vt-*** **1** to get away from: *to* escape *prison.* **2** to avoid: *to* escape *capture.* **3** to issue from (a person) unawares: *A sigh* escaped *him.* **4** to be forgotten or unnoticed by; slip by: *His name* escapes *me now.* ***n-*** **1** a getting away; successful flight: *an* escape *from prison.* **2** means of getting away: *a fire* escape. ***as modifier***: *an* escape *route.*

es·cape·ment (ĭ skāp′ mənt) ***n-*** **1** device used in most timepieces to ensure uniform motion. It consists of a toothed wheel driven by the spring or weights, and an oscillating lever with two projecting parts, which alternately engage the wheel in time with the motion of the balance wheel or pendulum. **2** a similar device in a typewriter that regulates the horizontal movement of the carriage.

escape velocity ***n-*** velocity to which an object, such as a rocket or spacecraft, must be accelerated before the power is cut off, in order for it to overcome the gravitational pull of the primary body. The escape velocity from Earth is about 25,000 m.p.h.

es·cap·ism (ĭ skā′ pĭz əm) ***n-*** an avoiding of unpleasant feelings and thoughts associated with everyday life, by daydreaming, excessive recreation, etc. **—*n-* es·cap′ ist.**

es·ca·role (ĕs′ kə rōl′) ***n-*** salad plant with crisp, wavy leaves; endive.

es·carp·ment (ĭ skärp′ mənt) ***n-*** steep slope or cliff.

es·chew (ĕs chōō′) ***vt-*** to avoid; shun: *to* eschew *wine.*

[1]**es·cort** (ĕs′ kòrt′, -kôrt′) ***n-*** **1** group of persons, ships, or planes that accompanies and safeguards another: *An* escort *of destroyers accompanied the aircraft carrier.* **2** man or boy who attends or accompanies a woman or girl: *He will be my* escort *at the dance.*

[2]**es·cort** (ĕs kòrt′, -kôrt′) ***vt-*** to attend or accompany: *Jet fighters* escorted *the bombers. He* escorted *her home.*

es·cu·do (ĕs kōō′ dō) ***n-*** [*pl.* **es·cu·dos**] the basic unit of money in Chile and in Portugal.

es·cutch·eon (ĭ skŭch′ ən) ***n-*** surface, usually shield-shaped, on which a coat of arms is displayed.

-ese *suffix* (used to form adjectives and nouns) **1** pertaining to the country or region of; also, an inhabitant of: *Japan*ese; *Senegal*ese; *Canton*ese. **2** language or jargon of: *Japan*ese; *Portugu*ese; *journal*ese.

es·ker (ĕs′ kər) ***n-*** in geology, a winding ridge composed of layers of gravel and sand, deposited by streams that ran under or through glacial ice.

Es·ki·mo (ĕs′ kə mō′) ***n-*** [*pl.* **Es·ki·mos,** also **Es·ki·mo**] a member of a Mongoloid people living on the Arctic shores of North America, Greenland, and northeastern Asia. ***adj-***: *an* Eskimo *boot.*

Eskimos

Es·ki·mo·an (ĕs′ kə mō′ ən) ***n-*** a family of languages spoken along the shores of Greenland and Labrador, in the Hudson Bay area, along the Arctic coast of North America, and in western and northern Alaska. Also called **Eskimo-Aleut.**

Eskimo dog ***n-*** breed of wolflike dogs with a heavy gray coat, used by Eskimos to draw sleds; husky.

e·soph·a·gus (ĭ sŏf′ ə gəs) ***n-*** the part of the digestive tract between the throat and the stomach; gullet. For picture, see *intestine.*

es·o·ter·ic (ĕs′ ə tĕr′ ĭk) ***adj-*** **1** intended for or understood by a small, select group of persons: *an* esoteric *philosophy.* **2** secret; confidential: *an* esoteric *club.* **—*adv-* es′ o·ter′ i·cal·ly.**

es·pe·cial (ə spĕsh′ əl) ***adj-*** special. **—*adv-* es·pe′ cial·ly.**

Es·pe·ran·to (ĕs′ pə rän′ tō) ***n-*** an invented international language based on words common to the main European languages.

es·pi·o·nage (ĕs′ pē ə nĭj, -ə näzh′) ***n-*** **1** spying; the work of a government spy. **2** the systematic use of spies.

es·pla·nade (ĕs′ plə nād′, -näd′) ***n-*** open, level space, especially along a shore, for public use as a walk or road.

es·pous·al (ĕs pou′ zəl) ***n-*** **1** an espousing of a cause, principle, etc.; advocacy. **2** betrothal. **3** wedding.

es·pouse (ə spouz′) ***vt-*** **[es·poused, es·pous·ing] 1** to be a follower of; advocate; support: *to* espouse *the cause of liberty.* **2** to give or take in marriage.

es·pres·so (ĕs prĕs′ o) ***n-*** [*pl.* **es·pres·sos**] dark, strong coffee, usually served black in a small cup.

es·prit (ĕs prē′) *French* ***n-*** spirit; mind; intelligence; wit.

es·prit de corps (ĕs prē′ də kȯr′) *French* ***n-*** spirit of unity, pride, etc., among the members of a group.

es·py (ĭ spī′) ***vt-*** **[es·pied, es·py·ing]** to catch sight of (something that is far away or hidden); detect; descry: *to* espy *a ship on the horizon.*

Esq. or **Esqr.** Esquire.

es·quire (ĕs′ kwīər′) ***n-*** **1** in the Middle Ages, a young aspirant for knighthood who served as the personal attendant and armor-bearer of a knight; squire. **2** member of the English gentry ranking next below a knight. **3 Esquire** *chiefly Brit.* title of courtesy or respect, often written after a man's name.

-ess *suffix* (used to form nouns) female: *count*ess; *tigr*ess.

1**es·say** (ĕs′ ā) ***n-*** **1** short piece of writing on a single subject, generally giving the personal views of the author. **2** (*also* ĕ sā′) an attempt; an experiment.

2**es·say** (ĭ sā′) ***vt-*** to try: *Tom* essayed *the high jump.*

es·say·ist (ĕs′ ā′ ĭst) ***n-*** writer of essays.

es·sence (ĕs′ əns) ***n-*** **1** that which makes a thing what it is; true inward nature: *A friendly attitude is the very* essence *of peace.* **2** concentrated extract of a plant, food, etc.; also, such an extract dissolved in alcohol: *the* essence *of roses.* **3** a perfume.

es·sen·tial (ə sĕn′ shəl) ***adj-*** necessary; not to be done without; basic: *Food is* essential *for life.* ***n-*** something basic and necessary. ***—adv-*** **es·sen′ tial·ly.**

essential oil ***n-*** any of various fragrant oils extracted from plants and used to make essences and perfumes.

-est *word ending* used to form the superlative of many adjectives and some adverbs and carrying the meaning "to the highest degree": *great*est; *fair*est; *earl*iest.

est. 1 established. **2** estimated. **3** estate.

EST or **E.S.T.** Eastern Standard Time.

es·tab·lish (ĭ stăb′ lĭsh) ***vt-*** **1** to found; set up: *to* establish *a school.* **2** to settle; place firmly: *He* established *his son in business.* **3** to cause to be accepted: *to* establish *a rule.* **4** to prove legally or beyond any doubt: *to* establish *a fact.*

established church ***n-*** church that is officially recognized and partly supported by the government.

es·tab·lish·ment (ĭ stăb′ lĭsh mənt) ***n-*** **1** an establishing or being established: *the* establishment *of a new town.* **2** something, such as a business, household, etc., that is founded or organized for a certain purpose: *That clothing* establishment *has been on Maple Street for 60 years.* **3 the Establishment** all the persons who have high and important positions in a government or some portion of it; controlling class.

es·tate (ĭ stāt′) ***n-*** **1** large house and the large area of land belonging to it: *an* estate *in the country.* **2** everything owned by a person; property: *His* estate *was divided among his children.* **3** position or stage in life: *He reached man's* estate *at the age of 21.*

es·teem (ĭ stēm′) ***vt-*** **1** to think highly of; regard as valuable: *The staff officers* esteem *the general.* **2** to consider; look upon as: *I shall* esteem *it an honor.* ***n-*** high opinion; respect: *to enjoy great* esteem.

es·ter (ĕs′ tər) ***n-*** any of a large group of organic compounds formed when acids and alcohols react. The fats and oils found in living organisms are esters.

Es·ther (ĕs′ tər) ***n-*** **1** in the Old Testament, the Jewish wife of King Ahasuerus (Xerxes) of Persia who saved her people from massacre. **2** a book of the Old Testament relating this story.

es·thete (ĕs′ thēt′) ***n-*** **1** one who is deeply sensitive to the beauty of art or nature. **2** one who pretends to love beauty or art, or is excessive about it. Also **aesthete.**

es·thet·ic (ĕs thĕt′ ĭk) ***adj-*** **1** of or related to beauty in art or nature: *the* esthetic *appeal of a magnificent sunset.* **2** deeply aware of or sensitive to beauty: *an* esthetic *personality.* Also **aesthetic.** ***—adv-*** **es·thet′ i·cal·ly.**

es·thet·i·cism (ĕs thĕt′ ə sĭz′ əm) ***n-*** **1** belief that artistic beauty is the most important human value and standard. **2** excessive devotion to art. Also **aestheticism.**

es·thet·ics (ĕs thĕt′ ĭks) ***n-*** (takes singular verb) the study of the nature of beauty, especially in art; philosophy of beauty and art. Also **aesthetics.**

es·ti·ma·ble (ĕs′ tə mə bəl) ***adj-*** **1** worthy of respect or honor; deserving esteem: *an* estimable *contribution to science.* **2** such as can be estimated or reckoned; calculable: *an* estimable *cost.* ***—adv-*** **es′ ti·ma·bly.**

1**es·ti·mate** (ĕs′ tə māt′) ***vt-*** **[es·ti·mat·ed, es·ti·mat·ing]** to form an opinion or judgment about (value, amount, size, etc.): *to* estimate *a man's character; to* estimate *the size of a room.*

2**es·ti·mate** (ĕs′ tə mət) ***n-*** **1** calculation of cost or value: *The carpenter gave an* estimate *of $45 for the job.* **2** written statement of such a calculation. **3** judgment; opinion: *a rough* estimate *of his qualifications.*

es·ti·ma·tion (ĕs′ tə mā′ shən) ***n-*** **1** judgment; opinion: *In my* estimation *this book is very well written.* **2** regard; esteem; respect: *a man held in high* estimation *by all.* **3** an estimating or reckoning: *an* estimation *of costs.*

es·ti·vate (ĕs′ tə vāt′) ***vi-*** **[es·ti·vat·ed, es·ti·vat·ing] 1** to spend the summer. **2** to lie dormant during the summer, as certain animals do. See also *hibernate.* Also **aestivate.** ***—n-*** **es′ ti·va′ tion.**

es·trange (ĭ strānj′) ***vt-*** **[es·tranged, es·trang·ing] 1** to make (someone who has been friendly or affectionate) feel indifferent or unfriendly: *to* estrange *one's friends through neglect.* **2** to remove or separate (oneself) from family, friends, etc.; alienate. ***—n-*** **es·trange′ ment.**

es·tro·gen (ĕs′ trə jən) ***n-*** any of a small group of hormones that promote female secondary sex characteristics, such as the growth and development of the womb, milk glands, etc.

es·tu·ar·y (ĕs′ cho͞o ĕr′ ē) ***n-*** [*pl.* **es·tu·ar·ies**] wide mouth of a river that flows into the sea and into which the tide flows.

ESTUARY

Estuaries of some rivers along the Atlantic

-et *suffix* (used to form nouns) small: *an eagl*et; *an isl*et.

et al. 1 and elsewhere [from Latin **et alibi**]. **2** and others [from Latin **et alii**].

etc. (ĕt′ sĕt′ ər ə) et cetera.

et cet·er·a (ĕt′ sĕt′ ər ə) *Latin* and others; and so forth.

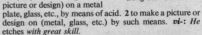

etch (ĕch) ***vt-*** **1** to engrave (a picture or design) on a metal plate, glass, etc., by means of acid. **2** to make a picture or design on (metal, glass, etc.) by such means. ***vi-***: *He* etches *with great skill.*

etch·ing (ĕch′ ĭng) ***n-*** **1** the process or art of making pictures or designs on metal plates, glass, etc., by means of acid. **2** picture or design printed from a metal plate engraved by such means; also, the plate itself.

e·ter·nal (ĭ tûr′ nəl) ***adj-*** **1** without beginning or end; timeless: *an* eternal *universe.* **2** without stopping; perpetual; unending: *her* eternal *chatter.* **3** always the same; unchanging; immutable: *an* eternal *principle.* ***—adv-*** **e·ter′ nal·ly.**

e·ter·ni·ty (ĭ tûr′ nə tē) ***n-*** [*pl.* **e·ter·ni·ties**] **1** time without beginning or end; everlasting time. **2** time that seems endless: *I've waited an* eternity *for an answer.* **3** life after death: *He hovered between life and* eternity.

[1]**-eth** *suffix* See *-th.*

[2]**-eth** *Archaic verb ending* used with "he," "she," or "it" in the present tense: *He go*eth.

eth·ane (ĕth′ ān′) ***n-*** colorless, odorless gas, a compound of carbon and hydrogen (C_2H_6). Ethane occurs in natural gas and crude petroleum and is used as a fuel.

eth·a·nol (ĕth′ ə nŏl′) ***n-*** ethyl alcohol.

e·ther (ē′ thər) ***n-*** **1** light, colorless, sweet-smelling, volatile, and flammable liquid compound of carbon, hydrogen, and oxygen, [$(C_2H_5)_2O$]. Ether is used as a solvent and as an anesthetic in surgery. **2** in early science, a thin invisible material believed to fill all the unoccupied space of the universe. It is now popularly referred to as the medium through which radio waves are transmitted. **3** the clear, purer air of the upper atmosphere. **4** *Chemistry* any compound containing two carbon atoms bonded to an oxygen atom.

e·the·re·al (ĭ thêr′ ē əl) ***adj-*** **1** light; airy; delicate: *What* ethereal *music!* **2** heavenly; unearthly: *Angels are* ethereal. ***—adv-*** **e·the′re·al·ly.** ***n-*** **e·the′re·al·ness.**

eth·i·cal (ĕth′ ĭ kəl) ***adj-*** **1** in keeping with moral principles or standards of proper action: *It is not* ethical *for a lawyer to reveal confidences.* **2** of or having to do with ethics. ***—adv-*** **eth′i·cal·ly.** ***n-*** **eth′i·cal·ness.**

eth·ics (ĕth′ ĭks) ***n-*** **1** (takes singular verb) branch of philosophy that deals with the principles of right and wrong action. **2** (takes plural verb) standards of right conduct or proper action, often within a particular profession: *His legal* ethics *are questionable.*

eth·nic (ĕth′ nĭk) ***adj-*** of, having to do with, or typical of a group or division of mankind with similar traits, customs, historical background, etc. ***—adv-*** **eth′ni·cal·ly:** *tribes that are* ethnically *similar.*

eth·nol·o·gist (ĕth nŏl′ ə jĭst) ***n-*** person trained in ethnology and usually engaged in it as a profession.

eth·nol·o·gy (ĕth nŏl′ ə jē) ***n-*** branch of anthropology that deals with the historical background, geographical distribution, and customs of groups or divisions of mankind. ***—adj-*** **eth′no·log′i·cal.** ***adv-*** **eth′no·log′i·cal·ly.**

eth·yl (ĕth′ əl) ***n-*** chemical radical (C_2H_5), composed of carbon and hydrogen, with a valence of one..

ethyl alcohol ***n-*** colorless alcohol (C_2H_5OH), a product of fermentation; ethanol; grain alcohol; alcohol. It is the intoxicating ingredient in alcoholic beverages, and is also widely used in medicines and in the manufacture of chemical products.

eth·y·lene (ĕth′ ə lēn′) ***n-*** colorless, flammable gas, a compound of carbon and hydrogen (C_2H_4).

ethylene gly·col (glī′ kŏl′) ***n-*** colorless, poisonous alcohol ($C_2H_4(OH)_2$) that is used as an antifreeze and as a germicide. Also **gly′col′.**

et·i·quette (ĕt′ ĭ kət, -kĕt′) ***n-*** rules and customs of correct behavior, especially on social occasions.

E·trus·can (ĭ trŭs′ kən) ***adj-*** of or relating to ancient Etruria, its people, or their language. ***n-*** **1** an inhabitant of Etruria. **2** the extinct language of Etruria.

-ette *suffix* (used to form nouns) **1** little: *a kitchen*ette. **2** girl or woman engaging in a certain activity: *a drum major*ette. **3** resembling or imitating: *flannel*ette.

e·tude (ā′ tōōd′, -tyōōd′) *Music* ***n-*** piece that provides practice in some point of performing technique.

et·y·mol·o·gist (ĕt′ ə mŏl′ ə jĭst) ***n-*** person who is a student of or expert in etymology.

et·y·mol·o·gy (ĕt′ ə mŏl′ ə jē) ***n-*** [*pl.* **et·y·mol·o·gies**] **1** the scientific study of word origins and histories. **2** origin and history of a word; especially, a statement or brief description showing the changing forms and meanings of a word. This dictionary gives many etymologies at the ends of the main definitions, before idioms or derived words, as follows: [from Greek **etymologia,** from **etymon,** "the original form of a word," plus **-logia,** "science of."]. ***—adj-*** **et′y·mo·log′i·cal** (ĕt′ ə mə lŏj′ ĭ kəl). ***adv-*** **et′y·mo·log′i·cal·ly.**

Eu symbol for europium.

eu- *prefix* good; well; pleasing: eu*phony* (pleasing and harmonious sound). [from Greek **eu-**, variant **ev-**, meaning "well; good."]

eu·ca·lyp·tus (yōō′ kə lĭp′ təs) ***n-*** [*pl.* **eu·ca·lyp·ti** (-tī), or **eu·ca·lyp·tus·es**] any of several tall trees, mostly native to Australia, that are valued for their timber and for a fragrant oil used in medicine.

Eucalyptus

Eu·cha·rist (yōō′ kə rĭst) ***n-*** **1** in the Christian Church, Holy Communion; the sacrament of the Lord's Supper. **2** consecrated bread and wine of this sacrament. ***—adj-*** **Eu′cha·ris′tic:** *the* Eucharistic *wine.*

eu·chre (yōō′ kər) ***n-*** card game popular in former times.

eu·gen·ic (yōō jĕn′ ĭk) ***adj-*** of or having to do with the principles of eugenics or their application: *a* eugenic *marriage.* ***—adv-*** **eu·gen′i·cal·ly.**

eu·gen·ics (yōō jĕn′ ĭks) ***n-*** (takes singular verb) science or theory of improving the human species by applying knowledge of the laws of heredity to produce children with outstanding mental or physical qualities.

Eu·gle·na (yōō glē′ nə) ***n-*** in zoology, any of a large genus of green, one-celled, aquatic protozoans with one or more flagella. Euglenas move about like animals, but contain granules of chlorophyll with which they synthesize food like plants.

eu·lo·gist (yōō′ lə jĭst) ***n-*** person who delivers a eulogy.

eu·lo·gis·tic (yōō′ lə jĭs′ tĭk) ***adj-*** of or like a eulogy; full of praise; flattering. Also **eu′lo·gis′ti·cal.** ***—adv-*** **eu′lo·gis′ti·cal·ly.**

eu·lo·gize (yōō′ lə jīz′) ***vt-*** [**eu·lo·gized, eu·lo·giz·ing**] to praise highly, especially in a formal speech or piece of writing.

eu·lo·gy (yōō′ lə jē) ***n-*** [*pl.* **eu·lo·gies**] formal praise of a person's character, accomplishments, etc., either in a speech or in writing: *to deliver a funeral* eulogy.

Eu·men·i·des (yōō mĕn′ ə dēz′) ***n-*** in Greek mythology, the avenging Furies.

eu·nuch (yōō′ nək) ***n-*** man whose sex glands have been removed, especially one who is an attendant in a harem.

eu·phe·mism (yōō′ fə mĭz′ əm) ***n-*** mild or less offensive expression used instead of one that is plainer or more accurate. Examples: "pass on" for "die"; "throw up" for "vomit." ***—adj-*** **eu′phe·mis′tic.** ***adv-*** **eu′phe·mis′sti·cal·ly.**

eu·pho·ni·ous (yōō fō′ nē əs) ***adj-*** pleasing in sound; agreeable to hear: *a* euphonious *voice.* ***—adv-*** **eu·pho′ni·ous·ly.** ***n-*** **eu·pho′ni·ous·ness.**

---

eu·pho·ny (yōō′ fə nē) ***n-*** pleasantness of sound, especially in the use of words.

eu·pho·ri·a (yōō fôr′ ē ə) ***n-*** a feeling of health and well-being.

eu·re·ka (yōō rē′ kə) ***interj-*** exclamation of triumph upon making a discovery, solving a problem, etc. [from Greek **heurēka** meaning "I have found (it)!", said to have been shouted by Archimedes when he discovered a method of determining the purity of gold.]

Eu·ro·pe·an (yŏŏr′ ə pē′ ən) ***adj-*** of or pertaining to Europe or its inhabitants. ***n-*** native or citizen of a country in Europe.

European Economic Community See *Common Market.*

European plan ***n-*** in hotels, a system by which lodging and service are provided at a fixed price, while meals, if desired, are paid for separately. See also *American plan.*

eu·ro·pi·um (yōō rō′ pē əm) ***n-*** gray, malleable, metal element. Symbol Eu, At. No. 63, At. Wt. 151.96.

Eu·ryd·i·ce (yōō rĭd′ ə sē) ***n-*** wife of Orpheus.

Eu·sta·chi·an tube (yōō stā′ shən) ***n-*** slender tube or canal that connects the middle ear and the throat, and serves to equalize the air pressure on the inner and outer surfaces of the eardrum. For picture, see *ear.*

eu·tha·na·sia (yōō′ thə nā′ zhə, -zhē ə) ***n-*** the causing of a painless, easy death for a person suffering from a painful, incurable disease or injury.

e·vac·u·ate (ĭ văk′ yōō āt′) ***vt-*** [**e·vac·u·at·ed, e·vac·u·at·ing**] **1** to leave (a place) empty; abandon: *to* evacuate *a burning building.* **2** to remove or withdraw (people) from a place: *to* evacuate *troops from a fort.* ***vi:*** to expel wastes from the bowels. ***—n-*** **e·vac′ u·a′ tion.**

e·vac·u·ee (ĭ văk′ yōō ē′) ***n-*** person removed from a dangerous place, especially in a war or other disaster.

e·vade (ĭ vād′) ***vt-*** [**e·vad·ed, e·vad·ing**] to avoid or escape from by a trick, deceptive action, etc.; elude: *to* evade *pursuers; to* evade *responsibility.*

e·val·u·ate (ĭ văl′ yōō āt′) ***vt-*** [**e·val·u·at·ed, e·val·u·at·ing**] **1** to declare or estimate the value or worth of; appraise: *A judge must carefully* evaluate *all evidence presented at a trial.* **2** *Mathematics* to replace a variable or variables in (an algebraic expression) by a permissible number or numbers and perform the operation indicated in the expression: *If* $x = 4$, *one* evaluates $3x$ *as* 3×4, *or 12.*

e·val·u·a·tion (ĭ văl′ yōō ā′ shən) ***n-*** **1** an evaluating; estimate; appraisal. **2** periodic review of a person's work, or of an overall program, in order to judge effectiveness and suitability.

ev·a·nes·cent (ĕv′ ə nĕs′ ənt) ***adj-*** tending to disappear or fade away; fleeting: *an* evanescent *memory of early childhood.* ***—n-*** **ev′ a nes′ cence.** ***adv-*** **ev′ a·nes′ cent·ly.**

e·van·gel·i·cal (ē′ văn′ jĕl′ ĭ kəl, ē′ vən-) ***adj-*** **1** of or according to the four Gospels of the New Testament. **2** founded on or holding the belief that faith in Jesus Christ is the only means of religious salvation: *an* evangelical *church.* **3** showing the fervor of an evangelist.

e·van·ge·lism (ĭ văn′ jə lĭz′ əm) ***n-*** earnest efforts to win followers to the gospel of Jesus Christ, especially by an intense and emotional style of preaching.

e·van·ge·list (ĭ văn′ jə lĭst) ***n-*** **1** person who preaches the gospel of Jesus Christ, especially a traveling preacher who holds revival meetings. **2 Evangelist** any one of the four writers of the Gospels of the New Testament; Matthew, Mark, Luke, or John. ***—adj-*** **e·van′ ge·lis′ tic.** ***adv-*** **e·van′ ge·lis′ ti·cal·ly.**

e·van·ge·lize (ĭ văn′ jə līz′) ***vt-*** [**e·van·ge·lized, e·van·ge·liz·ing**] to preach the Christian gospel to; also, to convert to Christianity by such preaching.

e·vap·o·rate (ĭ văp′ ə rāt′) ***vi-*** [**e·vap·o·rat·ed, e·vap·o·rat·ing**] **1** to change from solid or liquid into vapor: *Gasoline* evaporates *faster than water.* **2** to disappear like vapor; fade: *Their hopes* evaporated. ***vt-*** **1** to cause to change to vapor. **2** to concentrate by heating or drying to remove moisture. ***—n-*** **e·vap′ o·ra′ tion.**

evaporated milk ***n-*** milk thickened by evaporation of some of its water and then usually canned. See also *condensed milk.*

evaporating dish ***n-*** shallow, porcelain dish used in laboratories to evaporate solutions.

e·vap·o·ra·tor (ĭ văp′ ə rā′ tər) ***n-*** **1** apparatus for evaporating liquid in order to concentrate or purify some substance. **2** part of a refrigerator where the refrigerant evaporates as it absorbs heat.

e·va·sion (ĭ vā′ zhən) ***n-*** the act of evading; clever escape, avoidance, or putting off: *an* evasion *of one's pursuers.*

e·va·sive (ĭ vā′ sĭv, -zĭv) ***adj-*** seeking to avoid or escape; also, not frank or straightforward: *to give an* evasive *answer.* ***—adv-*** **e·va′ sive·ly.** ***n-*** **e·va′ sive·ness.**

eve (ēv) ***n-*** **1** time or day just before an important or significant event: *the* eve *of the battle; the* eve *of their departure.* **2** (often **Eve**) the evening or day before a holiday, especially a religious holiday: *Christmas* Eve. **3** *Archaic* evening.

Eve (ēv) ***n-*** in the Old Testament, the first woman created. She was the wife of Adam, and is regarded as the mother of the human race.

[1]**e·ven** (ē′ vən) ***adj-*** [**e·ven·er, e·ven·est**] **1** level; smooth: *an* even *surface.* **2** on the same line; at a level: *water* even *with the top of the bucket.* **3** not having or showing marked differences or variation; steady; uniform: *an* even *pulse; an* even *temper; an* even *tone of voice.* **4** equal in quantity, standing, etc.: *Take flour and sugar in* even *amounts.* **5** exact: *an* even *mile.* **6** with no accounts left to settle: *If I pay you a quarter, we'll be* even. **7** of a number, divisible by two with a zero remainder; also, marked or counted by such a number: *such* even *numbers as 4, 16, and 328.* ***vt-*** **1** to make level, smooth, or uniform: *to* even *the ground with a rake; to* even *a hem.* **2** to make equal: *to* even *the score.* ***adv-*** **1** at the same time; just: *She answered* even *as I spoke.* **2** so much as; at all: *He isn't* even *angry.* **3** in comparison, still: *You can do* even *better.* **4** in fact; indeed: *She is pretty,* even *beautiful.* [from Old English **efen.**] ***—adv-*** **e′ ven·ly.** ***n-*** **e′ ven·ness.**

even if regardless of whether: *I'll go,* even if *it rains.*

[2]**e·ven** (ē′ vən) *Archaic* ***n-*** evening. [from Old English **aefen.**]

eve·ning (ēv′ nĭng) ***n-*** the close of day and early part of the night; late hours of daylight and early hours of darkness. *as* ***modifier:*** *the* evening *meal.*

evening star ***n-*** bright planet, especially Venus, seen in the western sky shortly after sunset.

even number ***n-*** any integer that is divisible by 2 with a zero remainder.

e·ven·song (ē′ vən sòng′) ***n-*** a late afternoon or evening church service, especially in the Anglican or Episcopal Church; vespers.

e·vent (ĭ vĕnt′) ***n-*** **1** a happening; occurrence: *When did the* event *take place?* **2** item in a program, especially in a series of sports activities: *a track* event.

at all events or **in any event** whatever happens; in any case. **in the event of** in case of; if a specified thing should happen: *We'll stay at home* in the event of *rain.*

e·vent·ful (ĭ vĕnt′ fəl) ***adj-*** full of happenings or incidents, especially, interesting or important ones: *an* eventful *day.* ***—adv-*** **e·vent′ ful·ly.** ***n-*** **e·vent′ ful·ness.**

e·ven·tide (ē′ vən tīd′) *Archaic* ***n-*** evening.

e·ven·tu·al (ĭ vĕn′ chōō əl) ***adj-*** happening as the result of events or circumstances; ultimate: *His* eventual *success is certain.* ***—adv-*** **e·ven′ tu·al·ly.**

e·ven·tu·al·i·ty (ĭ vĕn′ chōō ăl′ ə tē) ***n-*** [*pl.* **e·ven·tu·al·i·ties**] possible occurrence or circumstance: *I'll be there in any* eventuality.

e·ven·tu·ate (ĭ vĕn′ chōō āt′) ***vi-*** [**e·ven·tu·at·ed, e·ven·tu·at·ing**] to happen in the end; result: *The quarrel* eventuated *in open warfare.*

ev·er (ĕv′ ər) ***adv-*** **1** at any time: *Did you* ever *ride a horse? Will he* ever *come back?* **2** always; forever: *It was* ever *thus. They were happy* ever *after.* **3** (intensifier only) *How did you* ever *finish so quickly?*

ever so *Informal* very: *I feel* ever so *much better.*

ev·er·glade (ĕv′ ər glād′) ***n-*** low, swampy area.

ev·er·green (ĕv′ ər grēn′) ***adj-*** bearing leaves or needles throughout the year; not deciduous. ***n-***: *Holly and most pines are* evergreens.

Evergreens

ev·er·last·ing (ĕv′ ər lăs′ tĭng) ***adj-*** lasting or seeming to last forever; eternal: *our* everlasting *gratitude; that* everlasting *noise.* ***n-*** plant having flowers that keep their form and color when dried. ***—adj-*** **ev′ er·las′ ting·ly.**

ev·er·more (ĕv′ ər môr′) ***adv-*** always; forever.

eve·ry (ĕv′ rē) ***determiner-*** (traditionally called adjective) **1** all the individual members or parts of a group, category, kind, etc.; each: *I expect* every *man to do his duty. He comes* every *day.* **2** all or any possible: *I have* every *confidence in him. He has had* every *opportunity.*

every now and then or **every once in a while** from time to time; occasionally. **every other** each alternating one of a series: *He comes* every other *day.*

eve·ry·bod·y (ĕv′ rē bŏd′ ē, -bŭd′ ē) ***pron-*** everyone.

eve·ry·day (ĕv′ rē dā′) ***adj-*** ordinary; not special or festive: *an* everyday *matter; her* everyday *dresses.*

eve·ry·one (ĕv′ rē wŭn′) ***pron-*** every person of a group; everybody: *Is* everyone *here?*

►Should not be confused with EVERY ONE, which means every unit (of any set of persons or things): Every one *of the peaches was rotten.*

eve·ry·thing (ĕv′ rē thĭng′) ***pron-*** all things; all that relates to a particular subject, occasion, etc.

eve·ry·where (ĕv′ rē hwâr′) ***adv-*** in every place; in all places or parts: *We looked* everywhere *for my lost cat.* ***n-*** all places: *letters from* everywhere.

e·vict (ĭ vĭkt′) ***vt-*** to put out (a person or persons) from a place, especially by legal force; expel: *to* evict *a family from a house.* ***—n-*** **e·vic′ tion.**

ev·i·dence (ĕv′ ə dəns) ***n-*** **1** facts from which to judge or draw a conclusion: *What* evidence *do you have that he was here?* **2** in law, the facts, testimony, objects, etc., that are admitted according to certain rules as proper for consideration in a trial, hearing, etc.: *Three witnesses gave* evidence. *A pistol was admitted in* evidence. ***vt-*** [**ev·i·denced, ev·i·denc·ing**] to make evident or plain; show; indicate: *His smile* evidenced *his good will.*

in evidence visible or perceptible; to be seen: *He is nowhere* in evidence.

ev·i·dent (ĕv′ ə dənt) ***adj-*** easy to see or understand; plain; obvious: *His earnest intentions are* evident *to all.* ***—adv-*** **ev′ i·dent′ ly:** *He is* evidently *earnest.*

e·vil (ē′ vəl) ***n-*** **1** the causing of suffering, fear, death, etc.; opposite of good. **2** any cause of suffering, etc.; especially, intentional cruelty; wickedness: *The peddling of narcotics is a great* evil. *War is an* evil, *whoever wins.* ***adj-*** **1** very harmful; wicked: *to have* evil *intentions.* **2** indicating or connected with great suffering, disaster, etc.: *an* evil *prophecy;* evil *times.*

e·vil·do·er (ē′ vəl dōō′ ər) ***n-*** person who does evil intentionally or habitually.

evil eye ***n-*** supposed power to cause harm by a stare or glance. Belief in the evil eye is an old superstition.

e·vil-mind·ed (ē′ vəl mīn′ dəd) ***adj-*** having evil or obscene thoughts or intentions.

e·vince (ĭ vĭns′) ***vt-*** [**e·vinced, e·vinc·ing**] to show; make evident: *to* evince *great bravery; to* evince *displeasure.*

e·vis·ce·rate (ĭ vĭs′ ə rāt′) ***vt-*** [**e·vis·ce·rat·ed, e·vis·ce·rat·ing**] to remove the intestines or internal organs of. ***—n-*** **e·vis′ ce·ra′ tion.**

ev·o·ca·tion (ĕv′ ō kā′ shən) ***n-*** an evoking or calling forth: *the* evocation *of a memory by a song.*

e·voke (ĭ vōk′) ***vt-*** [**e·voked, e·vok·ing**] to call forth; call up; produce: *His letter* evoked *an angry answer.*

ev·o·lu·tion (ĕv′ ə lōō′ shən) ***n-*** **1** growth; gradual development, especially through a series of forms or stages: *the* evolution *of the modern university.* **2** *Biology* theory that plants and animals of types now living have developed from earlier and simpler forms of life by the process of natural selection. **3** *Mathematics* the operation of extracting a root.

ev·o·lu·tion·ar·y (ĕv′ ə lōō′ shə nĕr′ ē) ***adj-*** of, having to do with, or resulting from evolution.

ev·o·lu·tion·ist (ĕv′ ə lōō′ shən ĭst) ***n-*** person who believes in evolution, especially biological evolution.

e·volve (ĭ vŏlv′) ***vi-*** [**e·volved, e·volv·ing**] to grow or develop gradually: *An oak tree* evolves *from a tiny acorn.* ***vt-*** to work out or produce in gradual stages: *to* evolve *a new method.* ***—n-*** **e·volve′ ment.**

ewe (yōō) ***n-*** female sheep. ***Homs-*** yew, you.

ew·er (yōō′ ər) ***n-*** large jug or water pitcher.

ex- *prefix* **1** out; out from: *to* ex*hale* (to breathe out; opposite of in*hale*). **2** (followed by a hyphen) at one time but not now; former: *an* ex-*president.*

ex. 1 example. **2** except. **3** exception. **4** examined.

ex·ac·er·bate (ĕk săs′ ər bāt′, ĕg zăs′-) ***vt-*** [**ex·ac·er·bat·ed, ex·ac·er·bat·ing**] to make (feelings, symptoms, ills, etc.) sharper or more severe; make worse; aggravate. ***—n-*** **ex·ac′ er·ba′ tion.**

►For usage note see AGGRAVATE.

ex·act (ĕg zăkt′) ***adj-*** **1** accurate and correct in all parts or details: *an* exact *copy;* exact *measurements.* **2** strict and precise in regard to facts, details, etc.: *an* exact *mind.* ***vt-*** to insist upon; require: *to* exact *payment of a loan; to* exact *strict obedience.* ***—n-*** **ex·act′ ness.**

ex·act·ing (ĕg zăk′ tĭng) ***adj-*** **1** requiring great skill, precision, or concentration: *an* exacting *task.* **2** making many or unreasonable demands; severe: *an* exacting *employer.* ***—adv-*** **ex·act′ ing·ly.**

ex·ac·tion (ĕg zăk′ shən) ***n-*** a requiring or demanding of payment, especially an unjust or difficult payment.

ex·act·i·tude (ĕg zăk′ tə tōōd′, -tyōōd′) ***n-*** process or habit of being exact; precision: *the* exactitude *of his reasoning.*

ex·act·ly (ĕg zăkt′ lē) ***adv-*** **1** in an exact manner; without error; accurately: *to follow directions* exactly. **2** precisely; quite; entirely: *It's* exactly *as you say.*

exact sciences ***n-*** sciences such as physics, chemistry, and astronomy, whose laws, data, etc., can be stated accurately in numerical or other mathematical terms.

ex·ag·ger·ate (ĕg zăj′ ə rāt′) ***vt-*** [**ex·ag·ger·at·ed, ex·ag·ger·at·ing**] to enlarge beyond truth or reason; overstate: *to* exaggerate *one's exploits.* ***vi-***: *Herbert always* exaggerates.

ex·ag·ger·a·tion (ĕg zăj′ ə rā′ shən) ***n-*** **1** an exaggerating; misleading enlargement or overemphasis. **2** statement that exaggerates: *a story full of* exaggerations.

ex·alt (ĕg zòlt′) ***vt-*** **1** to raise in rank and dignity: *The people* exalted *him to the office of President.* **2** to praise highly; glorify: *They* exalted *God in their hymns.*
►Should not be confused with EXULT.

ex·al·ta·tion (ĕg′ zòl′ tā′ shən, ĕk′ sòl′-) ***n-*** **1** an exalting or a being exalted. **2** feeling of being emotionally or spiritually uplifted; elation.

ex·am (ĕg zăm′) *Informal* ***n-*** examination; test.

ex·am·i·na·tion (ĕg zăm′ ə nā′ shən) ***n-*** **1** a careful studying or investigating: *the* examination *of the evidence.* **2** a checking or inspecting of the body or part of it by a doctor, dentist, etc. **3** a test of knowledge or skill: *an* examination *in French.* **4** a questioning of a witness, especially under oath in court.

ex·am·ine (ĕg zăm′ ən) ***vt-*** [**ex·am·ined, ex·am·in·ing**] **1** to look at carefully; inspect; investigate: *He* examined *the ameba under the microscope.* **2** to question in order to find out information, etc.: *to* examine *a witness.*

ex·am·ple (ĕg zăm′ pəl) ***n-*** **1** one part of a group, category, collection, etc., that shows what the whole is like; sample; specimen: *This painting is an* example *of her best work.* **2** an exercise or problem that illustrates a process, method, or rule: *an* example *in arithmetic.* **3** person, thing, or behavior worthy of being copied or imitated: *to follow the* example *of a great man.* **4** incident or circumstance used as a warning: *Let his punishment be an* example *to you.*
for example by way of illustration; as a typical instance. **set an example** to act in a manner likely to be imitated.

ex·as·per·ate (ĕg zăs′ pə rāt′) ***vt-*** [**ex·as·per·at·ed, ex·as·per·at·ing**] to irritate greatly; annoy keenly: *Her folly* exasperated *him.* ***—adv-*** **ex·as′ per·at′ ing·ly.**
►For usage note see AGGRAVATE.

ex·as·per·a·tion (ĕg zăs′ pə rā′ shən) ***n-*** keen annoyance; great irritation; great vexation.

ex ca·the·dra (ĕks′ kə thē′ drə) *Latin* from one's official position; authoritative: *an* ex cathedra *judgment.*

ex·ca·vate (ĕks′ kə vāt′) ***vt-*** [**ex·ca·vat·ed, ex·ca·vat·ing**] **1** to dig or hollow out: *to* excavate *a cave in a hillside.* **2** to uncover by digging: *They* excavated *the ruins of an ancient city.* ***vi-*** to dig.

ex·ca·va·tion (ĕks′ kə vā′ shən) ***n-*** **1** act or process of excavating. **2** hole made by excavating.

ex·ca·va·tor (ĕks′ kə vā′ tər) ***n-*** person or thing that excavates; especially, a tool or machine used for digging.

ex·ceed (ĕk sēd′) ***vt-*** **1** to go beyond the limit of; overdo: *to* exceed *one's authority.* **2** to excel; surpass: *His courage* exceeds *mine.*

ex·ceed·ing (ĕk sē′ dĭng) ***adv-*** *Archaic* very.

ex·ceed·ing·ly (ĕk sē′ dĭng lē) ***adv-*** very; remarkably.

ex·cel (ĕk sĕl′) ***vi-*** [**ex·celled, ex·cel·ling**] to be superior to others in ability or quality: *Arthur* excels *in sports.* ***vt-***: *Carlo* excels *Arthur in arithmetic.*

ex·cel·lence (ĕk′ sə ləns) ***n-*** superior quality; outstanding ability or worth.

ex·cel·len·cy (ĕk′ sə lən sē) ***n-*** [*pl.* **ex·cel·len·cies**] **1** excellence. **2 Excellency** title of honor or form of address for certain officials of high rank (used with "His," "Her," or "Your"): *His* Excellency *the Governor.*

ex·cel·lent (ĕk′ sə lənt) ***adj-*** of unusually high quality; very good: *an* excellent *player.* ***—adv-*** **ex′ cel·lent·ly.**

ex·cel·si·or (ĕk sĕl′ sē ər, -sĕl′ shər) ***n-*** thin, very narrow wood shavings used to pack breakable objects or to stuff toys, furniture, etc.

Ex·cel·si·or (ĕk sĕl′ sē ôr′) *Latin* ***interj-*** higher; ever upward: *a banner with the motto* "Excelsior."

ex·cept (ĕk sĕpt′) ***prep-*** outside of; apart from; barring: *He ate everything* except *dessert.* ***conj-*** (also **except that**) apart from the fact that: *I could go* except *I don't want to.* ***vt-*** to leave out; omit; exclude: *He* excepted *their names from his list of guests.*
except for but for; apart from.
►For usage note see ACCEPT.

ex·cep·ting (ĕk sĕp′ tĭng) ***prep-*** *Informal* except.

ex·cep·tion (ĕk sĕp′ shən) ***n-*** **1** a leaving out of a person or thing; omission: *Every boy without* exception *must be there.* **2** something that differs from others of the same class or group: *an* exception *to the rule.*
take exception to object; protest.

ex·cep·tion·a·ble (ĕk sĕp′ shən ə bəl) ***adj-*** causing or likely to cause objection or criticism.

ex·cep·tion·al (ĕk sĕp′ shən əl) ***adj-*** unusual; outstanding; extraordinary: *a pianist of* exceptional *talent.* ***—adv-*** **ex·cep′ tion·al·ly.**

1**ex·cerpt** (ĕk′ sûrpt′, ĕg′ zûrpt′) ***n-*** part or passage taken from a longer work: *some* excerpts *from an opera.*

2**ex·cerpt** (ĕk sûrpt′, ĕg zûrpt′) ***vt-*** to take out or select (a part or passage) from a longer work.

ex·cess (ĕk′ sĕs′, ĕk sĕs′) ***n-*** **1** quantity that is more than is usual or desirable; overabundance: *He has an* excess *of energy.* **2** amount by which one thing is more than another or more than required: *an* excess *of rolls over frankfurters.* **3** indulgence in anything to a degree greater than is healthy or otherwise desirable: *to avoid* excess *in eating.* ***adj-*** over and above what is usual or required; extra; surplus: *to carry* excess *baggage.*
to excess too much; immoderately: *to eat* to excess.

ex·ces·sive (ĕk sĕs′ ĭv) ***adj-*** beyond what is usual or reasonable; extreme; immoderate: *his* excessive *demands.* ***—adv-*** **ex·ces′ sive·ly.** ***n-*** **ex·ces′ sive·ness.**

ex·change (ĕks chānj′) ***vt-*** [**ex·changed, ex·chang·ing**] **1** to give (something) for something else; trade; barter: *to* exchange *a toy for a book.* **2** to give and receive; interchange: *to* exchange *ideas.* **3** to return (a purchase) and take something else: *to* exchange *a dress for a larger one.* ***n-*** **1** a giving of one thing for another: *the* exchange *of goods for cash.* **2** a giving and receiving; interchange: *an* exchange *of greetings.* **3** substitution: *the* exchange *of city life for country life.* **4** place where trading is carried on: *the stock* exchange. **5** central office of a telephone system. ***—n-*** **ex·chang′ er.**

ex·change·a·ble (ĕks chānj′ ə bəl) ***adj-*** such as can be exchanged for or replaced by something else: *Is this jacket* exchangeable? ***—n-*** **ex·change′ a·bil′ i·ty.**

ex·cheq·uer (ĕks chĕk′ ər) ***n-*** **1** treasury, especially of a government. **2 Exchequer** in Great Britain, the department of the government in charge of national funds.

1**ex·cise** (ĕk sīz′) ***vt-*** [**ex·cised, ex·cis·ing**] to remove by or as if by cutting out: *to* excise *a tumor*; *to* excise *a paragraph.* [from Latin **excisus** meaning "having been cut out."] ***—n-*** **ex·ci′ sion** (ĕk sĭzh′ ən).

2**ex·cise** (ĕk′ sīz′) or **excise tax** ***n-*** tax imposed on certain articles within the country where they are manufactured, sold, or used. *as* ***modifier***: *to collect* excise *duties.* [from early Dutch **excijis,** from Old French **acceis,** which goes back to Latin **ad-**, "to," plus **cēnsus** meaning "a tax; census."]

ex·cit·a·ble (ĕk sī′ tə bəl) ***adj-*** easily roused or stirred up: *an* excitable *person*; *his* excitable *temper.* ***—n-*** **ex·cit′ a·bil′ i·ty.** ***adv-*** **ex·cit′ a·bly.**

ex·ci·ta·tion (ĕk′sī tā′shən, ĕk′sə-) ***n-*** **1** a being or causing to be excited. **2** *Physics* process in which an atom absorbs energy; also, the state resulting from the process. **3** *Biology* effect of a stimulus on an organism.

ex·cite (ĕk sīt′) ***vt-*** **[ex·cit·ed, ex·cit·ing] 1** to stir the mind or emotions of: *The President's stirring speech* excited *us.* **2** to call forth; arouse: *to* excite *pity.* **3** to cause to become active; stimulate: *The odor of food* excites *the salivary glands.* **4** *Physics* to cause (an atom) to absorb energy. ***—adv-*** **ex·cit′ ing·ly.**

ex·cit·ed (ĕk sī′təd) ***adj-*** **1** stirred up; animated; agitated; stimulated. **2** *Physics* in a state of excitation. ***—adv-*** **ex·cit′ ed·ly.**

ex·cite·ment (ĕk sīt′mənt) ***n-*** **1** condition of being excited; enthusiasm; agitation. **2** an arousing or stirring up; stimulation: *the* excitement *of emotions.* **3** commotion: *What's all the* excitement *up the street?*

ex·cit·ing (ĕk sī′tĭng) ***adj-*** causing excitement; stirring; moving: *an* exciting *story.* ***—adv-*** **ex·cit′ ing·ly.**

ex·claim (ĕks klām′) ***vt-*** to speak or cry out suddenly in surprise, anger, pleasure, etc.: *"Aha!" he* exclaimed.

ex·cla·ma·tion (ĕks′ klə mā′shən) ***n-*** sudden or excited utterance expressing strong feeling, a warning, etc.

exclamation point or **exclamation mark** ***n-*** punctuation mark [!] used to indicate surprise, sorrow, or other strong feeling.

ex·clam·a·to·ry (ĕks klăm′ə tôr′ē) ***adj-*** using, consisting of, or containing an exclamation.

ex·clude (ĕks kloo͞d′) ***vt-*** **[ex·clud·ed, ex·clud·ing] 1** to shut or keep out; prevent from entering: *to* exclude *someone from a club*; *to* exclude *sound.* **2** to leave out; omit: *to* exclude *unnecessary material from a report.*

ex·clu·sion (ĕks kloo͞′zhən) ***n-*** an excluding or a being excluded: *the* exclusion *of women from certain jobs.*

ex·clu·sive (ĕks kloo͞′siv) ***adj-*** **1** not shared with any others; sole: *his* exclusive *control of the company*; exclusive *right to a patent.* **2** open or available only to a chosen or privileged group: *an* exclusive *club.* **3** undivided; complete: *his* exclusive *devotion to his work.* ***n-*** *Informal* item, product, etc., offered by one source only. ***—adv-*** **ex·clu′ sive·ly.** ***n-*** **ex·clu′ sive·ness.**

exclusive of not including: *There are sixteen men on the team,* exclusive of *the manager.* **mutually exclusive** each not capable of including the other: *"Prejudice" and "tolerance" are* mutually exclusive *terms.*

ex·com·mu·ni·cate (ĕks′kə myoo͞′nə kāt′) ***vt-*** **[ex·com·mu·ni·cat·ed, ex·com·mu·ni·cat·ing]** to cut off officially from the membership or communion of a church. ***—n-*** **ex′ com·mu′ ni·ca′ tion.**

ex·co·ri·ate (ĕk skôr′ē āt′) ***vt-*** **[ex·co·ri·at·ed, ex·co·ri·at·ing]** to strip or rub away the skin of; hence, to criticize or scold with harsh severity.

ex·cre·ment (ĕks′krə mənt) ***n-*** waste matter discharged from the body, especially by way of the intestinal tract.

ex·cres·cence (ĕks krĕs′əns) ***n-*** any unusual, conspicuous, or unsightly outgrowth, protruding lump, etc. ***—adj-*** **ex·cres′ cent:** *an* excrescent *lump on his nose.*

ex·crete (ĕks krēt′) ***vt-*** **[ex·cret·ed, ex·cret·ing]** to throw off (waste matter) from the body or its tissues.

ex·cre·tion (ĕks krē′shən) ***n-*** **1** act or process of excreting. **2** something excreted.

ex·cre·to·ry (ĕks′krə tôr′ē) ***adj-*** of or having to do with excretion: *an* excretory *duct.*

ex·cru·ci·at·ing (ĕks kroo͞′shē ā′tĭng) ***adj-*** extremely painful; torturing: *an* excruciating *toothache*; excruciating *embarrassment.* ***—adv-*** **ex·cru′ ci·at′ ing·ly.**

ex·cul·pate (ĕks′kəl pāt′, ĕks kŭl′pāt′) ***vt-*** **[ex·cul·pat·ed, ex·cul·pat·ing]** to free from blame; absolve from a charge of guilt; exonerate. ***—n-*** **ex′ cul·pa′ tion.**

ex·cur·sion (ĕks kûr′zhən) ***n-*** **1** a short trip generally made by a group of people for a special purpose or for pleasure. **2** a special round trip at a reduced fare.

ex·cur·sion·ist (ĕks kûr′zhən ĭst) ***n-*** person who goes on an excursion.

ex·cus·a·ble (ĕks kyoo͞′zə bəl) ***adj-*** deserving to be pardoned: *an* excusable *delay.* ***—adv-*** **ex·cus′ a·bly.**

[1]**ex·cuse** (ĕks kyoo͞z′) ***vt-*** **[ex·cused, ex·cus·ing] 1** to pardon; forgive: *He* excused *his brother's mistake.* **2** to free from duty, obligation, attendance, etc.: *She* excused *him from the test.* **3** to explain or justify: *Her shyness* excuses *her awkwardness.*

excuse (oneself) 1 to make an apology for oneself: *She* excused herself *for being late.* **2** to ask to be released or permitted to leave: *He* excused himself *from the meeting.*

[2]**ex·cuse** (ĕks kyoo͞s′) ***n-*** **1** reason given as an explanation: *an* excuse *for being late.* **2** a release, as from a duty, promise, etc.

ex·e·cra·ble (ĕk′sə krə bəl) ***adj-*** **1** hateful; outrageous; abominable: *his* execrable *wickedness.* **2** very bad; of vile quality: *her* execrable *taste.* ***—n-*** **ex′ e·cra·ble·ness.** ***adv-*** **ex′ e·cra·bly.**

ex·e·crate (ĕk′sə krāt′) ***vt-*** **[ex·e·crat·ed, ex·e·crat·ing] 1** to declare to be evil; denounce violently; damn. **2** to detest; abhor. ***vi-*** to curse; swear.

ex·e·cra·tion (ĕk′sə krā′shən) ***n-*** **1** act of cursing or swearing. **2** expression of loathing; curse.

ex·e·cute (ĕk′sə kyoo͞t′) ***vt-*** **[ex·e·cut·ed, ex·e·cut·ing] 1** to carry out, perform, or make :*to* execute *a plan.* **2** to put to death according to law. **3** to make legal by signing or sealing: *to* execute *a lease.*

ex·e·cu·tion (ĕk′sə kyoo͞′shən) ***n-*** **1** a carrying out or putting into effect: *the proper* execution *of a plan.* **2** manner or style of doing something; performance: *his* execution *of a piano solo.* **3** punishment by death.

ex·e·cu·tion·er (ĕk′sə kyoo͞′shən ər) ***n-*** person who puts a condemned person to death.

ex·ec·u·tive (ĕg zĕk′yə tĭv) ***n-*** **1** person who directs, manages, or supervises the affairs of a business, institution, or organization. **2** person, group, or branch of government responsible for putting laws into effect. ***adj-*** **1** of or having to do with the work or responsibilities of a manager or director: *an* executive *position in the company*; *his* executive *ability.* **2** having to do with the execution of laws: *the* executive *powers of the President.*

Executive Mansion ***n-*** **1** the White House. **2** in some States, the official residence of the governor.

ex·ec·u·tor (ĕg zĕk′yə tər) ***n-*** in law, a person who is appointed in a will to see that its terms are carried out. ***—n-*** *fem.* **ex·ec′ u·trix′** (-trĭks′).

ex·em·plar (ĕg zĕm′plär′, -plər) ***n-*** something or someone worthy of being copied or imitated; model; example.

ex·em·pla·ry (ĕg zĕm′plə rē) ***adj-*** **1** worthy to serve as a model; praiseworthy: *The boy's conduct was* exemplary. **2** serving as a warning: *to administer* exemplary *punishment.* ***—adv-*** **ex·em′ pla·ri·ly.** ***n-*** **ex·em′ pla·ri·ness.**

ex·em·pli·fi·ca·tion (ĕg zĕm′plə fə kā′shən) ***n-*** **1** showing or making plain by example. **2** an example or model: *He is the* exemplification *of courage.*

ex·em·pli·fy (ĕg zĕm′plə fī′) ***vt-*** **[ex·em·pli·fied, ex·em·pli·fy·ing]** to show or serve as an example of; illustrate; demonstrate: *This picture* exemplifies *the artist's style.*

ex·empt (ĕg zĕmpt′) ***vt-*** to free from a tax, duty, obligation, etc., to which others are subject; excuse: *to* exempt *a student from a test.* ***adj-***: *He is* exempt *from the test.*

ex·emp·tion (ĕg zĕmp′shən) ***n-*** **1** an exempting or a being exempt; freedom from an obligation, tax, etc. **2** an amount the government allows a person, for himself and for each dependent, as a deduction from his total income for a year when he determines his income tax.

ex·er·cise (ĕk′ sər sīz′) ***vt-*** **1** [**ex·er·cised, ex·er·cis·ing**] **1** to put into action; use: *to* exercise *authority, care, or self-control.* **2** to use in order to train or develop: *to* exercise *the muscles or the mind.* ***vi-*** to perform some bodily activity for physical fitness: *to* exercise *every day.* ***n-*** **1** physical or mental activity that improves the body or mind: *Swimming is good* exercise. **2** performance: *the* exercise *of duty.* **3** active use: *the* exercise *of power.* **4** lesson or example for practice: *a piano* exercise. **5 exercises** formal program; ceremony: *graduation* exercises.

ex·ert (ĕg zûrt′) ***vt-*** to put forth; bring to bear; to put to use: *to* exert *one's influence.*
exert (oneself) to make an effort.

ex·er·tion (ĕg zûr′ shən) ***n-*** **1** use of strength or force; effort: *Football requires a lot of* exertion. *Their* exertions *were in vain.* **2** active use: *by* exertion *of his will.*

ex·fo·li·a·tion (ĕks′ fō′ lē ā′ shən) ***n-*** **1** a separation or falling off in layers or scales; especially, in geology, a weathering process in which curved scales or thin flakes peel off the exposed surfaces of rocks. **2** the peeled material.

ex·ha·la·tion (ĕk′ sə lā′ shən, ĕks′ hə-) ***n-*** **1** a breathing out or giving forth as if by breathing out: *the* exhalation *of perfume from a flower.* **2** something thus breathed or given forth.

ex·hale (ĕks′ hāl′) ***vt-*** [**ex·haled, ex·hal·ing**] to breathe out or give off as if by breathing forth: *He* exhaled *a deep breath. The swamp* exhaled *an unpleasant odor.* ***vi-***: *He* exhaled *deeply.*

ex·haust (ĕg zòst′) ***vt-*** **1** to tire out completely: *The game* exhausted *him.* **2** to use up; drain: *He* exhausted *my patience.* **3** to discuss or treat thoroughly: *to* exhaust *a subject.* **4** to draw or force out: *to* exhaust *air from a chamber.* ***n-*** **1** discharged steam or gas fumes, especially from an engine. **2** the discharging of such fumes. **3** (also **exhaust pipe**) pipe through which such fumes escape. ***as modifier***: *an* exhaust *outlet.* **—*adj-* ex·haust′ i·ble.**

ex·haust·ed (ĕg zòs′ təd) ***adj-*** completely tired; worn out: *He came home* exhausted *after the long hike.* **—*adv-* ex·haust′ ed·ly:** *He yawned* exhaustedly.

ex·haus·tion (ĕg zòs′ chən) ***n-*** **1** the draining or using up of something: *the* exhaustion *of the water supply.* **2** condition of being worn out; extreme fatigue: *the* exhaustion *that follows long exercise.*

ex·haus·tive (ĕg zòs′ tĭv) ***adj-*** omitting or neglecting nothing; thorough; complete: *an* exhaustive *study.* **—*adv-* ex·haus′ tive·ly. *n-* ex·haus′ tive·ness.**

ex·hib·it (ĕg zĭb′ ĭt) ***vt-*** **1** to show; display: *to* exhibit *the symptoms of a cold; to* exhibit *great courage.* **2** to show publicly; put on display: *to* exhibit *paintings.* ***n-*** **1** object or collection of objects put on public display. **2** in law, an object marked to be used as evidence.

ex·hi·bi·tion (ĕk′ sə bĭsh′ ən) ***n-*** **1** an exhibiting; display. *His* exhibition *of strength impressed us.* **2** a public showing: *an* exhibition *of sculpture.*
on exhibition being displayed publicly.

ex·hi·bi·tion·ism (ĕk′ sə bĭsh′ ən ĭz′ əm) ***n-*** behavior to attract attention to oneself. **—*n-* ex′ hi·bi′ tion·ist.**

ex·hib·i·tor (ĕg zĭb′ ə tər) ***n-*** person or organization that holds or displays an exhibit. Also **ex·hib′ i·ter.**

ex·hil·a·rate (ĕg zĭl′ ə rāt′) ***vt-*** [**ex·hil·a·rat·ed, ex·hil·a·rat·ing**] to make cheerful or joyous; enliven: *The news that he had won the contest* exhilarated *him.* **—*adv-* ex·hil′ a·rat′ ing·ly:** *an* exhilaratingly *fine day.*

ex·hil·a·ra·tion (ĕg zĭl′ ə rā′ shən) ***n-*** a feeling of joy or lively well-being.

ex·hort (ĕg zòrt′, -zôrt′) ***vt-*** to urge by appeal or argument; advise strongly: *He* exhorted *the jury to make a just decision.* ***vi-***: *The lawyer* exhorted *earnestly.*

ex·hor·ta·tion (ĕg′ zòr tā′ shən, ĕg′ zôr-) ***n-*** an exhorting; strong and earnest appeal: *the preacher's* exhortations.

ex·hu·ma·tion (ĕks′ hyōō mā′ shən) ***n-*** an exhuming; also, an instance of this: *the* exhumation *of a body.*

ex·hume (ĕg zyōōm′) ***vt-*** **1** [**ex·humed, ex·hum·ing**] to dig up (a buried corpse); disinter. **2** to bring to light (something forgotten or hidden); uncover; reveal.

ex·i·gen·cy (ĕk′ sə jən sē, ĕg zĭj′ ən sē) ***n-*** [*pl.* **ex·i·gen·cies**] **1** situation that needs immediate attention. **2** pressing necessity; urgency. Also **ex′ i·gence.**

ex·i·gent (ĕk′ sə jənt) ***adj-*** demanding instant attention; urgent: *an* exigent *need; his* exigent *demands.*

ex·ile (ĕg′ zīl′, ĕk′ sīl′) ***n-*** **1** absence, usually compulsory, from one's home or country; banishment: *They demanded the* exile *of the king. The writer lived in* exile. **2** person who is banished or goes away from his country for a long time: *The* exile *returned after many years.* ***vt-*** [**ex·iled, ex·il·ing**] to send away from home or country; banish: *They* exiled *their former ruler.*

ex·ist (ĕg zĭst′) ***vi-*** **1** to have actual being; be: *He believes goblins really* exist. **2** to live or continue to go on living: *Plants cannot* exist *without water.* **3** to be found; occur: *Such conditions* exist *only in large cities.*

ex·ist·ence (ĕg zĭs′ təns) ***n-*** **1** state or fact of existing: *The microscope reveals the* existence *of many tiny things.* **2** life: *Man's* existence *depends on oxygen.* **3** way of life: *He leads a peaceful* existence *in the country.*

ex·ist·ent (ĕg zĭs′ tənt) ***adj-*** **1** existing; living: *Dinosaurs are no longer* existent. **2** present or occurring now; current: *the* existent *traffic conditions.*

ex·is·ten·tial·ism (ĕg′ zə stĕn′ shəl ĭz′ əm) ***n-*** philosophy of the 19th and 20th centuries which says that human existence is unique and cannot be described or explained. It stresses the absence of any ordained purpose or meaning in human life, and therefore the importance of each man's own judgments and decisions.

ex·it (ĕg′ zĭt, ĕk′ sĭt) ***n-*** **1** way or passage through which to go out: *The building has several* exits. **2** a going out or departure, especially of an actor from the stage. ***vi-***: *They* exited *through the side door.*

ex lib·ris (ĕks lē′ brĭs) *Latin* from the books of (an inscription often written or pasted on the inside cover of a book, together with the owner's name).

Exod. Exodus.

Ex·o·dus (ĕk′ sə dəs) ***n-*** **1** second book of the Old Testament, relating the departure (**the Exodus**) of the Israelites from Egypt under the guidance of Moses. **2 exodus** any mass departure.

ex of·fi·ci·o (ĕk′ sə fĭsh′ ē ō) *Latin* because of or by right of the office one holds: *The President of the United States is* ex officio *Commander in Chief of the Army.*

ex·on·er·ate (ĕg zŏn′ ə rāt′) ***vt-*** [**ex·on·er·at·ed, ex·on·er·at·ing**] to free from blame; acquit or clear of an accusation or responsibility: *The jury* exonerated *the accused man.* **—*n-* ex·on′ er·a′ tion.**

ex·or·bi·tant (ĕg zòr′ bə tənt, ĕg zôr′-) ***adj-*** going beyond the expected limits; excessive; out of all reason: *an* exorbitant *price.* **—*n-* ex·or′ bi·tance:** *The* exhorbitance *of his demand astounds me.* ***adv-*** **ex·or′ bi·tant·ly.**

ex·or·cise (ĕk′ sôr′ sīz′, ĕk sôr′-) *vt-* [**ex·or·cised, ex·or·cis·ing**] 1 to expel (an evil spirit) by prayers or magic ceremonies. 2 to deliver or free from evil spirits. Also **ex′ or′ cize′**. —*n-* **ex′ or·cis′ er**

ex·or·cism (ĕk′ sôr′ sĭz′ əm, ĕk′ sôr′-) *n-* act, process, or ritual of expelling evil spirits. —*n-* **ex′ or·cist′**.

ex·o·skel·e·ton (ĕk′ sō skĕl′ ə tən) *n-* any rigid, protective body structure found on the outside or just beneath the surface of many animals; external skeleton: *The fly has a jointed* exoskeleton. See also *endoskeleton*.

ex·o·sphere (ĕk′ sō sfêr′) *n-* outermost portion of the earth's atmosphere, lying beyond the ionosphere, and starting at about 500 miles above the earth's surface. —*adj-* **ex′ o·spher′ ic.**

ex·o·ther·mic (ĕk′ sō thûr′ mĭk) *adj-* having to do with, characterized by, or produced by the giving off of heat. See also *endothermic*.

ex·ot·ic (ĕg zŏt′ ĭk) *adj-* 1 from another part of the world; not native; strange: *an* exotic *plant.* 2 having the charm of strangeness: *an* exotic *Spanish dance.* —*adv-* **ex·ot′ ic·al·ly.**

ex·pand (ĕk spănd′) *vi-* to increase in size or volume; grow larger; swell: *Metals* expand *when heated.* *vt-* 1 to make larger, wider, or broader; enlarge: *to* expand *one's nostrils*; *to* expand *a short story into a novel.* 2 to open or spread out: *to* expand *a folded bag*.

ex·pand·a·ble (ĕk spăn′ də bəl) *adj-* of a nature that allows being expanded. Also **ex·pan′ si·ble** (ĕk spăn′- sə bəl).

expanding universe *n-* theory of the material universe that states that all parts of the universe began moving out from a central point or mass. It is based on the observed differences in velocity of stars, galaxies, etc., such that the farther away a galaxy is from the earth, the faster it appears to be moving. Also **big bang theory.**

ex·panse (ĕk spăns′) *n-* 1 wide, open space or area: *the great* expanse *of the ocean.* 2 the extent to which a thing has been spread out: *the* expanse *of her skirt*.

ex·pan·sion (ĕk spăn′ shən) *n-* 1 an increasing in size, scope, etc. 2 something thus enlarged: *This book is the* expansion *of a short story.* 3 *Physics* process in which a constant amount of a substance increases in volume: *the* expansion *of metals or gases when heated.* 4 *Mathematics* a number expressed as a sum of terms, or as a continued product. Example: $72 = 2 \times 4 \times 9$.

ex·pan·sive (ĕk spăn′ sĭv) *adj-* 1 widely spread or extended; broad: *an* expansive *stretch of desert.* 2 genial and outgoing; free and easy: *an* expansive *manner.* 3 causing expansion. 4 tending to expand. —*adv-* **ex·pan′ sive·ly.** *n-* **ex·pan′ sive·ness.**

ex·pa·ti·ate (ĕk spā′ shē āt′) *vi-* [**ex·pa·ti·at·ed, ex·pa·ti·at·ing**] to talk or write freely and at length: *to* expatiate *upon the beauty of the place*.

1**ex·pa·tri·ate** (ĕk spā′ trē āt′) *vt-* [**ex·pa·tri·at·ed, ex·pa·tri·at·ing**] to banish (a person) from his native country; exile. *vi-* to withdraw oneself from one's native land: *He* expatriated *before the war.* —*n-* **ex·pa′ tri·a′ tion.**

2**ex·pa·tri·ate** (ĕk spā′ trē ət) *n-* person exiled from or living permanently away from his native land. *as modifier: an* expatriate *writer*.

ex·pect (ĕk spĕkt′) *vt-* 1 to look forward to as likely or certain to come or happen: *to* expect *to go on a trip*; *to* expect *a storm.* 2 to consider necessary or desirable; require: *I* expect *you to do a good job.* 3 *Informal* to think likely; suppose: *I* expect *he can do it*.

ex·pect·an·cy (ĕk spĕk′ tən sē) *n-* [*pl.* **ex·pect·an·cies**] 1 an expecting; a looking forward to something. 2 something expected or anticipated, especially on the basis of known facts or statistics: *life* expectancy.

ex·pect·ant (ĕk spĕk′ tənt) *adj-* 1 expecting or seeming to expect something: *an* expectant *look.* 2 awaiting a planned or likely event. —*adv-* **ex·pect′ ant·ly.**

ex·pec·ta·tion (ĕk′ spĕk tā′ shən) *n-* 1 a looking forward to something; anticipation: *We waited in* expectation *of a good dinner.* 2 (usually **expectations**) prospect, plan, or hope, especially for future wealth or success: *His* expectations *are good*.

ex·pec·to·rant (ĕk spĕk′ tər ənt) *adj-* helping the discharge of mucus or other fluids from the lungs and throat. *n-* medicine that does this.

ex·pec·to·rate (ĕk spĕk′ tə rāt′) *vt-* [**ex·pec·to·rat·ed, ex·pec·to·rat·ing**] to eject (phlegm, saliva, etc.) from the throat or lungs by coughing or spitting; also, to spit. *vi-*: *to* expectorate *into a basin.* —*n-* **ex·pec′ to·ra′ tion.**

ex·pe·di·en·cy (ĕk spē′ dē ən sē) *n-* [*pl.* **ex·pe·di·en·cies**] 1 suitableness; fitness for a purpose. 2 the doing of what promises to be useful for gaining a certain end, rather than what is right. Also **ex·pe′ di·ence.**

ex·pe·di·ent (ĕk spē′ dē ənt) *adj-* 1 useful and practical without reference to right; based on narrow self-interest; politic: *In a crisis, much that we do is merely* expedient. 2 proper and fit for a special purpose: *It would now be* expedient *to ask for help.* 3 serving as a quick and necessary step in a pressing situation: *an* expedient *maneuver.* *n-* a means to a particular end: *to use a hasty* expedient. —*adv-* **ex·pe′ di·ent·ly.**

ex·pe·dite (ĕk′ spə dīt′) *vt-* [**ex·pe·dit·ed, ex·pe·dit·ing**] 1 to hasten; help forward; quicken: *to* expedite *progress.* 2 to carry out quickly: *He* expedited *the stowing of the cargo.* —*n-* **ex′ pe·dit′ er.**

ex·pe·di·tion (ĕk′ spə dĭsh′ ən) *n-* 1 trip for a special purpose: *a hunting* expedition. 2 group of people making such a trip: *The* expedition *departed for the South Pole.* 3 efficiency and promptness: *to do a task with* expedition.

ex·pe·di·tion·ar·y (ĕk′ spə dĭsh′ ə nĕr′ ē) *adj-* having to do with or forming an expedition.

ex·pe·di·tious (ĕk′ spə dĭsh′ əs) *adj-* speedy and efficient: *an* expeditious *filing system.* —*adv-* **ex′ pe·di′ tious·ly.** *n-* **ex′ pe·di′ tious·ness.**

ex·pel (ĕk spĕl′) *vt-* [**ex·pelled, ex·pel·ling**] 1 to force out: *to* expel *an enemy*; *to* expel *one's breath.* 2 to send away permanently: *to* expel *an ambassador*.

ex·pend (ĕk spĕnd′) *vt-* to use up; spend.

ex·pend·a·ble (ĕk spĕn′ də bel) *adj-* such as can be used, sacrificed, or lost in the course of accomplishing an aim, especially in warfare: *an* expendable *supply of ammunition*; expendable *troops*.

ex·pen·di·ture (ĕk spĕn′ də chər) *n-* 1 a spending, as of money, time, labor, etc. 2 something spent; outlay: *heavy* expenditures *for college tuition*.

ex·pense (ĕk spĕns′) *n-* 1 a spending of money, time, labor, etc.: *He was educated at considerable* expense. 2 cost: *the* expense *of an education.* 3 cause of spending: *Food, rent, and clothing are our chief* expenses. 4 loss, injury, or sacrifice: *a victory won at terrible* expense.

ex·pen·sive (ĕk spĕn′ sĭv) *adj-* 1 high-priced. 2 gained at high cost: *an* expensive *victory.* —*adv-* **ex·pen′ sive·ly.** *n-* **ex·pen′ sive·ness.**

ex·pe·ri·ence (ĕk spêr′ ē əns) *n-* 1 knowledge or skill gained by direct action, observation, participation, etc.: *to gain* experience *by practice.* 2 a living through, feeling, or participating in something: *the* experience *of being snowbound*; *a soldier's war* experiences; *the* experience *of grief*. ***vt-*** **[ex·pe·ri·enced, ex·pe·ri·enc·ing]** to know by feeling or encountering personally; live through: *to* experience *hardship*.

ex·pe·ri·enced (ĕk spêr′ ē ənst) ***adj-*** having skill or knowledge gained through doing and seeing things; practiced: *an* experienced *doctor*.

ex·pe·ri·en·tial (ĕk spêr′ ē ĕn′ shəl) ***adj-*** having to do with or based on experience: *his* experiential *skill*.

ex·per·i·ment (ĕk spĕr′ ə mənt) ***n-*** a test or trial to discover something or to confirm or disprove something: *The chemist's* experiments *proved his theory to be correct*. ***vi-*** to make a test or tests to find out something: *to* experiment *with electricity*. **—*n-* ex·per′ i·ment′ er.**

ex·per·i·men·tal (ĕk spĕr′ ə mĕn′ təl) ***adj-* 1** of or having to do with experiments: *an* experimental *science*. **2** used in or tried as an experiment: *an* experimental *rocket*. **—*adv-* ex·per′ i·men′ tal·ly.**

ex·per·i·men·ta·tion (ĕk spĕr′ ə mĕn′ tā′ shən) ***n-*** act or process of experimenting.

ex·pert (ĕk′ spûrt′) ***n-*** person who has special skill or knowledge; authority; specialist: *an* expert *in mathematics*; *a* financial *expert*. ***adj-*** (*also* ĕk′ spûrt′) having special skill or knowledge; trained by practice; skillful: *an* expert *swimmer*; *his* expert *knowledge*. **—*adv-* ex′ pert′ ly. *n-* ex′ pert′ ness.**

ex·per·tise (ĕk′ spûr tēz′) ***n-*** expert knowledge.

ex·pi·ate (ĕk′ spē āt′) ***vt-*** **[ex·pi·at·ed, ex·pi·at·ing]** to atone for; make amends for: *to* expiate *one's sins*.

ex·pi·a·tion (ĕk′ spē ā′shən) ***n-* 1** a making amends for an offense; atonement. **2** the act of making amends.

ex·pi·ra·tion (ĕk′ spə rā′ shən) ***n-* 1** a coming to an end or close; termination: *to renew a lease at its* expiration. **2** the act of breathing out.

ex·pire (ĕk spīər′) ***vi-*** **[ex·pired, ex·pir·ing] 1** to come to an end; cease to be in effect; terminate: *My driver's license has* expired. **2** to breathe out; exhale. **3** to die.

ex·plain (ĕk splān′) ***vt-*** (considered intransitive when the direct object is implied but not expressed) **1** to make plain or clear; tell the meaning of: *to* explain *the solution of a problem*. **2** to account for; give the reason or cause of: *to* explain *one's conduct*. **—*adj-* ex·plain′ a·ble.**

ex·pla·na·tion (ĕk′ splə nā′ shən) ***n-* 1** a making clear or plain; interpretation: *This lesson requires a great deal of* explanation *to be understood*. **2** statement or fact which makes plain or accounts for something: *to give an* explanation *for lateness*.

ex·plan·a·to·ry (ĕk splăn′ ə tôr′ ē) ***adj-*** serving to explain or make clear: *an* explanatory *footnote*.

ex·ple·tive (ĕk′ splə tĭv′) ***n-* 1** emphatic exclamation or oath. **2** *Grammar* word such as "it" or "there" used to fill the subject position in sentences which have no true subject word or in which the true subject has been placed after the verb. Examples: It *is raining*. (no true subject) There *are three men in the room*. (the subject, "three men," placed after the verb) It *is hard to swim upstream*. (the subject, "to swim upstream," placed after the verb).

ex·pli·ca·ble (ĕk′ splĭ kə bəl, ĕk splĭk′ ə-) ***adj-*** of a nature that allows being explained; explainable.

ex·pli·cate (ĕk′ splə kāt′) ***vt-*** **[ex·pli·cat·ed, ex·pli·cat·ing]** to explain carefully and in detail.**—*n-* ex′ pli·ca′ tion.**

ex·plic·it (ĕk splĭs′ ĭt) ***adj-*** clear and unmistakable in meaning or intent: *brief but* explicit *instructions*; *to be* explicit *in stating one's viewpoint*. See also *implicit*. **—*adv-* ex·plic′ it·ly. *n-* ex·plic′ it·ness.**

ex·plode (ĕk splōd′) ***vi-*** **[ex·plod·ed, ex·plod·ing] 1** to undergo a quick and violent change, accompanied by an intense discharge of heat and usually a large volume of gas. **2** to burst with sudden loud noise: *The pressure tank* exploded. **3** to break forth suddenly: *to* explode *with laughter*. **4** to increase suddenly and rapidly: *World population has* exploded *in recent years*. ***vt-* 1** to cause to undergo an explosion: *to* explode *dynamite*. **2** to cause to burst suddenly with a loud noise. **3** to show to be false; refute: *to* explode *a popular notion*.

[1]**ex·ploit** (ĕk sploit′) ***vt-* 1** to put to use; develop: *to* exploit *our natural resources*. **2** to make unfair use of for one's own gain or advantage: *to* exploit *one's friends*. **—*adj-* ex·ploit′ a·ble. *n-* ex·ploit′ er.**

[2]**ex·ploit** (ĕk′ sploit′) ***n-*** bold, adventurous act or deed.

ex·ploi·ta·tion (ĕk′ sploi tā′ shən) ***n-* 1** the working and using of something, such as lands, mines, etc. **2** the use of a person, thing, or occasion for personal profit.

ex·plo·ra·tion (ĕk′ splôr ā′ shən, ĕk′ splə rā′-) ***n-* 1** a searching out of unknown things or places: *an* exploration *of the sea*. **2** investigation: *an* exploration *of facts*.

ex·plo·ra·to·ry (ĕk splôr′ ə tôr′ ē) ***adj-*** of or for exploring: *an* exploratory *expedition*.

ex·plore (ĕk splôr′) ***vt-*** **[ex·plored, ex·plor·ing] 1** to travel over or in (a region) to learn more about it. **2** to examine or investigate thoroughly: *to* explore *all possibilities*. ***vi-***: *He likes to* explore.

ex·plor·er (ĕk splôr′ ər) ***n-*** person who travels in unknown or far places to find out about them.

ex·plo·sion (ĕk splō′ zhən) ***n-* 1** an exploding; the rapid and violent change of some substances, which is accompanied by an intense discharge of heat and usually a large volume of gas. **2** sudden, violent bursting with a loud noise: *the* explosion *of an oil tank*. **3** sudden, furious outburst: *an* explosion *of anger*. **4** sudden, rapid increase: *the recent* explosion *in world population*.

ex·plo·sive (ĕk splō′ sĭv, -zĭv) ***adj-* 1** likely to explode: *an* explosive *substance*; *an* explosive *situation*. **2** like an explosion: *an* explosive *burst of laughter*. ***n-*** substance that can explode, such as dynamite. **—*adv-* ex·plo′ sive·ly. *n-* ex·plo′ sive·ness.**

ex·po·nent (ĕk′ spō′ nənt, ĕk′ spō′ -) ***n-* 1** person who explains or interprets something: *an* exponent *of modern jazz*. **2** person who champions or symbolizes an idea, cause, etc. **3** *Mathematics* numeral written above and to the right of a term and indicating a power of the term. In x^3, the 3 is an exponent.

ex·po·nen·tial (ĕk′ spə nĕn′ shəl) ***adj-* 1** of or having to do with one or more mathematical exponents. **2** defined by a mathematical expression that contains at least one exponent different from 1: *an* exponential *curve*.

exponential notation ***n-*** any number phrase or numeral in which exponents are used: $6^2 \cdot 6^3 = 6^5$.

ex·port (ĕk′ spôrt′) ***vt-*** (*also* ĕk spôrt′) to send or carry out (goods, products, etc.) to another country for sale: *The United States* exports *cotton to Great Britain* ***n-* 1** article or commodity sold and sent to a foreign country: *Wool is an important* export *of Australia*. **2** the sending of goods to another country for sale: *the* export *of tin from Bolivia*. *as* **modifier**: *the* export *trade*. **—*adj-* ex·port′ a·ble. *n-* ex·port′ er.**

ex·por·ta·tion (ĕk′ spôr tā′ shən) ***n-*** an exporting.

ex·pose (ĕk spōz′) ***vt-*** **[ex·posed, ex·pos·ing] 1** to make known; reveal: *to* expose *a crime*; *to* expose *someone's guilt*. **2** to leave unprotected from risk, danger, etc.: *to* expose *a child to a contagious disease*. **3** to lay bare; uncover: *to* expose *one's back to the sun*. **4** to allow light to reach (a photographic film or plate). **—*n-* ex·pos′ er.**

ex·po·sé (ĕk′ spō zā′) ***n-*** the publication of something unworthy or shameful; also, the thing published.

ex·po·si·tion (ĕk′ spə zĭsh′ ən) ***n-* 1** large exhibition of products, industrial or scientific equipment, art, etc.

2 a setting forth of facts or ideas, especially in writing. 3 *Music* the first statement of a theme.

ex·pos·i·tor (ĕk spŏs′ ə tər) ***n-*** person who explains or expounds something.

ex·pos·i·tor·y (ĕk spŏz′ ə tôr′ ē) ***adj-*** setting forth or explaining facts, ideas, etc.: *pages of* expository *writing.*

ex post fac·to (ĕks′ pōst′ făk′ tō) ***adj- & adv-*** of a rule of law, applying to an event that happened before the enactment of the rule or law. [from Latin, meaning "from after the deed."]

ex·pos·tu·late (ĕk spŏs′ chə lāt′) ***vi-*** [**ex·pos·tu·lat·ed, ex·pos·tu·lat·ing**] to plead earnestly (with), especially about something one disapproves of: *to* expostulate *with a friend who intends to drop out of school.* ***—n-*** **ex·pos′ tu·la′ tion.** ***adj-*** **ex·pos′ tu·la·to′ ry** (-chə lə tôr′ ē): *an* expostulatory *letter.*

ex·po·sure (ĕk spō′ zhər) ***n-*** **1** an exposing or being exposed: *the* exposure *of a plot*; exposure *to the sun.* **2** outlook: *a room with a western* exposure. **3** the exposing of a photographic film or plate to light; also, a portion of film that is thus exposed.

exposure meter ***n-*** light meter.

ex·pound (ĕk spound′) ***vt-*** to set forth in detail; explain or interpret: *to* expound *the law.* ***—n-*** **ex·pound′ er.**

ex·press (ĕk sprĕs′) ***vt-*** **1** to make known, especially by the use of language; show; reveal: *to* express *an idea clearly*; *to* express *joy.* **2** to represent; symbolize: *The statue* expresses *the belief in freedom.* **3** to send (something) by a speedy means of transportation. **4** to press or squeeze out: *to* express *toothpaste from a tube.* ***n-*** **1** fast train or other conveyance stopping only at principal stations. **2** system of rapid transportation for mail, packages, goods, etc. ***adj-*** **1** plainly stated; explicit: *his* express *wish.* **2** of or having to do with quick or direct transportation: *an* express *train*; *an* express *company.* ***adv-*** by a quick and direct system of transportation: *Send it* express. ***—n-*** **ex·press′ er.**
express (oneself) 1 to use language in a certain way: *to* express oneself *clearly.* **2** to show or communicate deeply felt emotion: *to* express oneself *in dancing.*

ex·press·i·ble (ĕk sprĕs′ ə bəl) ***adj-*** such as can be expressed: *easily* expressible *ideas.*

ex·pres·sion (ĕk sprĕsh′ ən) ***n-*** **1** an expressing or representing in language or art: *the forceful* expression *of ideas*; *an algebraic* expression. **2** something which conveys or shows an idea, emotion, etc.: *The gift was an* expression *of thanks.* **3** a look on the face that shows feeling or thought: *a worried* expression. **4** voice quality or intonation that conveys feeling: *to speak with* expression. **5** a saying; phrase. ***—adj-*** **ex·pres′ sion·less.**

ex·pres·sion·ism (ĕk sprĕsh′ ən ĭz′ əm) ***n-*** a style of art that uses bold line and color to express emotion.

ex·pres·sive (ĕk sprĕs′ ĭv) ***adj-*** serving to express or reveal; full of meaning: *a look* expressive *of sadness.* ***—adv-*** **ex·pres′ sive·ly.** ***n-*** **ex·pres′ sive·ness.**

ex·press·ly (ĕk sprĕs′ lē) ***adv-*** **1** particularly; especially: *These instructions are meant* expressly *for you.* **2** in clear terms; plainly: *She told us* expressly *to come early.*

ex·press·man (ĕk sprĕs′ mən) ***n-*** [*pl.* **ex·press·men**] person who works in the express business.

ex·press·way (ĕk sprĕs′ wā′) ***n-*** road built for direct, rapid travel between major towns and cities.

ex·pro·pri·ate (ĕk sprō′ prē āt′) ***vt-*** [**ex·pro·pri·at·ed, ex·pro·pri·at·ing**] to take away (property, possessions, etc.), especially by official authority: *to* expropriate *land to build a railroad.* ***—n-*** **ex·pro′ pri·a′ tion.**

ex·pul·sion (ĕk spŭl′ shən) ***n-*** an expelling or a being expelled: *the* expulsion *of air*; *his* expulsion *from school.*

ex·punge (ĕk spŭnj′) ***vt-*** [**ex·punged, ex·pung·ing**] to blot or rub out; erase; wipe out: *to* expunge *a mark.*

ex·pur·gate (ĕk′ spər gāt′) ***vt-*** [**ex·pur·gat·ed, ex·pur·gat·ing**] to alter by taking out whatever seems offensive to good taste or morality: *to* expurgate *a book.* ***—n-*** **ex′ pur·ga′ tion.**

ex·qui·site (ĕk′ skwĭz ət, ĕk skwĭz′-) ***adj-*** **1** pleasing because of great beauty, delicacy, refinement, etc.: *an* exquisite *rose*; exquisite *cabinet work.* **2** keenly felt; intense: *an* exquisite *joy.* ***—adv-*** **ex′ qui·site·ly** or **ex·qui′ site·ly.** ***n-*** **ex′ qui·site·ness** or **ex·qui′ site·ness.**

ex·tant (ĕk′ stənt) ***adj-*** in existence; not extinct, destroyed, or lost: *Some ancient fish are still* extant.

ex·tem·po·ra·ne·ous (ĕks′ tĕm′ pə rā′ nē əs) ***adj-*** made or done on the spur of the moment, or with little planned preparation: *an* extemporaneous *speech.* ***—adv-*** **ex′ tem′ po·ra′ ne·ous·ly.** ***n-*** **ex′ tem′ po·ra′ ne·ous·ness.**

ex·tem·po·rar·y (ĕk stĕm′ pə rĕr′ ē) ***adj-*** extemporaneous. ***—adv-*** **ex·tem′ po·rar′ i·ly.**

ex·tem·po·re (ĕk stĕm′ pə rē′) ***adj-*** without preparation; impromptu: *an* extempore *recitation.* ***adv-***: *to speak* extempore.

ex·tend (ĕk stĕnd′) ***vt-*** **1** to lengthen: *to* extend *a road*; *to* extend *a visit.* **2** to stretch out: *to* extend *an arm.* **3** to enlarge; increase; expand: *to* extend *one's power.* **4** to give; offer: *to* extend *a warm welcome*; *to* extend *credit.* ***vi-*** **1** to continue in time or distance; stretch out: *The plains* extend *for miles.*

ex·ten·sion (ĕk stĕn′ shən) ***n-*** **1** a making longer or larger. **2** a stretching or reaching out. **3** part attached to and extending from a main part: *an* extension *of the roof above the driveway.* **4** telephone connected with a main switchboard or another phone. *as* ***modifier***: *an* extension *cord.*

ex·ten·sive (ĕk stĕn′ sĭv) ***adj-*** wide; broad; far-reaching: *an* extensive *area*; *his* extensive *interests.* ***—adv-*** **ex·ten′ sive·ly:** *to travel* extensively. ***n-*** **ex·ten′ sive·ness.**

ex·ten·sor (ĕk stĕn′ sər) ***n-*** muscle that extends or straightens out a joint in an arm or leg. See also *flexor.*

ex·tent (ĕk stĕnt′) ***n-*** size, space, amount, or degree to which a thing is extended; length; limit: *the* extent *of his knowledge*; *to agree with someone to a certain* extent.

ex·ten·u·ate (ĕk stĕn′ yo͞o āt′) ***vt-*** [**ex·ten·u·at·ed, ex·ten·u·at·ing**] to show as less serious by offering explanations or excuses for; lessen the blame for.

ex·ten·u·a·tion (ĕks tĕn′ yo͞o ā′ shən) ***n-*** **1** an extenuating. **2** explanation or excuse making a wrong less serious.

ex·te·ri·or (ĕk stêr′ ē ər) ***n-*** **1** outer part; outside: *The* exterior *of the house is white.* **2** outward or visible appearance: *His gruff* exterior *is misleading.* ***adj-*** on, for, or coming from the outside; outer: *an* exterior *door*; *a good* exterior *paint*; exterior *assistance.*

ex·ter·mi·nate (ĕk stûr′ mə nāt′) ***vt-*** [**ex·ter·mi·nat·ed, ex·ter·mi·nat·ing**] to get rid of by killing; wipe out: *to* exterminate *harmful insects.* ***—n-*** **ex·ter′ mi·na′ tion.**

ex·ter·mi·na·tor (ĕk stûr′ mə nā′ tər) ***n-*** person or thing that exterminates, especially a person employed to get rid of insects, rats, etc.

ex·ter·nal (ĕk stûr′ nəl) ***adj-*** **1** on, of, or from the outside: *an* external *layer*; *an* external *force.* **2** visible or apparent to an observer: *the* external *appearance of success.* **3** on or for the outer part of the body: *medicine for* external *use.* ***n-*** (usually **externals**) outward form or appearance: *the mere* externals *of wealth.* ***—adv-*** **ex·ter′ nal·ly.**

external skeleton *n-* exoskeleton.

ex·tinct (ĕk stĭngkt′) *adj-* 1 no longer existing as a form of life: *the dinosaur is an* extinct *animal.* 2 no longer active or burning: *an* extinct *volcano.*

ex·tinc·tion (ĕk stĭngk′ shən) *n-* 1 a making or becoming extinct; total destruction: *attempts to prevent the* extinction *of rare birds.* 2 a putting out or extinguishing.

ex·tin·guish (ĕk stĭng′ gwĭsh) *vt-* 1 to put out: *to* extinguish *a fire.* 2 to put an end to; destroy: *to* extinguish *hope.* —*adj-* **ex·tin′ guish·a·ble.** *n-* **ex·tin′ guish·er:** *a fire* extinguisher.

ex·tir·pate (ĕk′ stər pāt′) *vt-* [**ex·tir·pat·ed, ex·tir·pat·ing**] to root out; remove or destroy completely: *to* extirpate *an evil.* —*n-* **ex′ tir·pa′ tion.**

ex·tol (ĕk stōl′) *vt-* [**ex·tolled, ex·tol·ling**] to praise highly: *to* extol *another's virtues* —*n-* **ex·tol′ ler.**

ex·tort (ĕk stôrt′, -stôrt′) *vt-* to obtain by force, threats, blackmail, etc.: *to* extort *money*; *to* extort *a confession.*

ex·tor·tion (ĕk stôr′ shən, -stôr′ shən) *n-* act or obtaining money, etc., by force, threats, etc.; especially, the crime of doing this.

ex·tor·tion·ate (ĕk stôr′ shə nət, ĕk stôr′-) *adj-* 1 too high; excessive: *an* extortionate *interest rate.* 2 having the purpose of extortion or as bad as extortion: *an* extortionate *demand.* —*adv-* **ex·tor′ tion·ate·ly.**

ex·tor·tion·ist (ĕk stôr′ shən ĭst, ĕk stôr′-) *n-* person who extorts from another; especially, a criminal whose specialty is extortion. Also **ex·tor′ tion·er.**

ex·tra (ĕk′ strə) *adj-* more than what is usual or expected; additional: *I need* extra *time to finish this test.* *n-* 1 something added: *Use your allowance for* extras, *such as books.* 2 special edition of a newspaper. 3 in motion-picture making, a person hired on a day-to-day basis for small, non-talking parts, as in crowd scenes. *adv- Informal* especially: *an* extra *good meal.*

extra- *prefix* outside; beyond; besides: *an* extra*ordinary event*; extra*curricular activities.* [from Latin **extra-**, from **extra** meaning "outside of; outside."]

[1]**ex·tract** (ĕk străkt′) *vt-* 1 to pull out; draw out with effort: *to* extract *a tooth*; *to* extract *information.* 2 to obtain by pressing, cooking, or some other special process: *to* extract *oil from olives*; *to* extract *gold from ore.* 3 to get; take out: *to* extract *a letter from a file.* —*adj-* **ex·tract′ a·ble** or **ex·tract′ i·ble.**

[2]**ex·tract** (ĕk′ străkt′) *n-* something taken out or obtained: *vanilla* extract; *an* extract *from a book.*

ex·trac·tion (ĕk străk′ shən) *n-* 1 act or process of extracting. 2 origin; descent: *a person of Irish* extraction.

ex·trac·tive (ĕk străk′ tĭv) *adj-* 1 of, relating to, or produced by extraction. 2 tending to exhaust or extract without replacing: *Mining is an* extractive *industry.*

ex·trac·tor (ĕk străk′ tər) *n-* person or thing that extracts; especially, part of a gun that removes empty cartridges from the firing chamber.

ex·tra·cur·ric·u·lar (ĕk′ strə kə rĭk′ yə lər) *adj-* not part of a school's curriculum or regular course of study.

ex·tra·dite (ĕk′ strə dīt′) *vt-* [**ex·tra·dit·ed, ex·tra·dit·ing**] 1 to surrender (someone) in one State or country to the legal agents of another State or country where the person is accused of a crime. 2 to obtain the surrender of (an accused person in another State or country).

ex·tra·di·tion (ĕk′ strə dĭsh′ ən) *n-* act or process of extraditing; also, an instance of this. *as* ***modifier****: an* extradition *hearing*; extradition *attempts.*

ex·tra·mu·ral (ĕk′ strə myŏŏr′ əl) *adj-* between different schools: *a program of* extramural *athletics.* See also *intramural.*

ex·tra·ne·ous (ĕk strā′ nē əs) *adj-* not related or essential to the matter at hand; irrelevant: *His questions were* extraneous *to the discussion.* —*adv-* **ex·tra′ ne·ous·ly.** *n-* **ex·tra′ ne·ous·ness.**

ex·traor·di·nar·y (ĕk strôrd′ ən ĕr′ ē, ĕk strôrd′ -) *adj-* beyond the usual size, shape, course, etc.; unusual; very special. —*adv-* **ex·traor′ di·nar′ i·ly.**

ex·trap·o·late (ĕk străp′ ə lāt′) *vi-* [**ex·trap·o·lat·ed, ex·trap·o·lat·ing**] 1 *Mathematics* to extend a curve or function beyond the range of known values, using the values that have already been determined as a basis for the extension. 2 to predict or estimate anything on a similar basis. —*n-* **ex·trap′ o·la′ tion.**

ex·tra·sen·so·ry (ek′ strə sĕn′ sə rē) *adj-* beyond the normal range of human sensory perception.

ex·tra·ter·res·tri·al (ĕk′ strə tə rĕs′ trē əl) *adj-* not on or in the earth; in outer space; on another planet.

ex·tra·ter·ri·to·ri·al (ĕk′ strə tĕr′ ə tôr′ ē əl) *adj-* outside the authority of the local government.

ex·trav·a·gance (ĕk străv′ ə gəns) *n-* 1 excess or lack of moderation, especially in spending money: *His* extravagance *will put him in debt.* 2 something excessive, something unduly costly: *His car is an* extravagance.

ex·trav·a·gant (ĕk străv′ ə gənt) *adj-* going beyond reasonable limits; excessive, especially in spending: *an* extravagant *spender.* —*adv-* **ex·trav′ a·gant·ly.**

ex·trav·a·gan·za (ĕk străv′ ə găn′ zə) *n-* theatrical or movie production, usually a musical show, that is lavishly staged and costumed; spectacular.

ex·treme (ĕk strēm′) *adj-* 1 highest; greatest; utmost: *with* extreme *joy*; *in* extreme *danger.* 2 excessive: *his* extreme *modesty.* 3 severe; drastic: *to take* extreme *measures.* 4 farthest: *The* extreme *end of the yard.* *n-* 1 the greatest possible degree: *the* extreme *of courage.* 2 drastic or extraordinary kind or degree: *an* extreme *of behavior.* 3 **extremes** (1) things as different as possible; complete opposites: *Love and hate are* extremes. (2) *Mathematics* first and fourth terms of a proportion (see also *means*). —*adv-* **ex·treme′ ly.** *n-* **ex·treme′ ness.**
go to extremes to do or say drastic or severe things.

extreme unction *n-* former term for the anointing of the sick, a Roman Catholic sacrament administered to a person who is seriously ill or dying.

ex·trem·ist (ĕk strē′ mĭst) *n-* person who holds or advocates extreme or radical views, especially in politics. *adj-*: *an* extremist *political viewpoint.*

ex·trem·i·ty (ĕk strĕm′ ə tē) *n-* [*pl.* **ex·trem·i·ties**] 1 very end; last point or stage; tip: *the southern* extremity *of Greenland.* 2 greatest or highest degree: *the* extremity *of misery.* 3 extreme measure or action. 4 **extremities** hands and feet.

ex·tric·a·ble (ĕk′ strĭk ə bəl, ĕk strĭk′-) *adj-* such as can be extricated or set free.

ex·tri·cate (ĕk′ strə kāt′) *vt-* [**ex·tri·cat·ed, ex·tri·cat·ing**] to release or set free from danger or difficulty: *to* extricate *oneself from danger.* —*n-* **ex′ tri·ca′ tion.**

ex·trin·sic (ĕk strĭn′ zĭk, -sĭk) *adj-* 1 not belonging or necessary to the nature of something; extraneous; unessential: *His questions are* extrinsic *to the argument.* 2 outside of something; external: *an* extrinsic *force acting on an object.* —*adv-* **ex·trin′ si·cal·ly.**

ex·tro·ver·sion (ĕk′ strə vûr′ shən) *n-* concentration of one's thoughts and emotions on outside activities rather than on one's inner self. See also *introversion.*

ex·tro·vert (ĕk′ strə vûrt′) *n-* person who tends toward extroversion. See also *introvert.*

ex·trude (ĕk strōōd′) *vt-* [**ex·trud·ed, ex·trud·ing**] 1 to push or force out: *Strong pressure* extruded *the mud.* 2 to shape (plastic, metal, rubber, etc.) by forcing while soft through special openings. *vi-*: *Hot lava* extruded *from the fissure.*

ex·tru·sion (ĕk strōō′zhən) *n-* 1 the act or process of extruding or forcing out: *the* extrusion *of lava from a fissure.* 2 the process of extruding plastic, metal, rubber, etc. 3 something extruded.

ex·u·ber·ance (ĕg zōō′bər əns) *n-* 1 overflowing joy and vitality; high spirits: *No amount of discipline could lessen his* exuberance. 2 abundant growth or fertility: *the* exuberance *of the area's plant life.* —*adj-* **ex·u′ber·ant:** *an* exuberant *crowd.* *adv-* **ex·u′ber·ant·ly.**

ex·ude (ĕg zōōd′, -zyōōd′) *vt-* [**ex·ud·ed, ex·ud·ing**] to give forth; send out; emit: *to* exude *sweat; to* exude *confidence.* *vi-*: *Sweat* exuded *from every pore.* —*n-* **ex′u·da′tion.**

ex·ult (ĕg zŭlt′) *vi-* to feel great joy or triumph; rejoice (at): *The team* exulted *at winning.* —*adv-* **ex·ult′ing·ly.**
►Should not be confused with EXALT.

ex·ult·ant (ĕg zŭl tənt) *adj-* showing or feeling great joy; triumphant. —*adv-* **ex·ult′ant·ly.**

ex·ul·ta·tion (ĕg′zŭl tā′shən) *n-* great joy; triumphant rejoicing: *The crowd cheered in* exultation *at the news.*

ex·ur·bi·a (ĕks ûr′bē ə) *n-* area between a city's suburbs and the country.

-ey *suffix* See ²-*y*.

eye (ī) *n-* 1 the bodily organ with which a person or animal sees. 2 a gaze; look: *Archie cast a longing* eye *at the puppy.* 3 close watch: *Keep an* eye *on the baby.* 4 something thought to resemble an eye, such as the hole where a needle is threaded or the bud of a potato. 5 in meterology, the calm, central region of a hurricane or cyclone. 6 **eyes** judgment; opinion: *Bert's work had little worth in the* eyes *of the teacher.* *vt-* [**eyed, ey·ing**] to look at; gaze at. *Homs-* ²ay or aye, I.

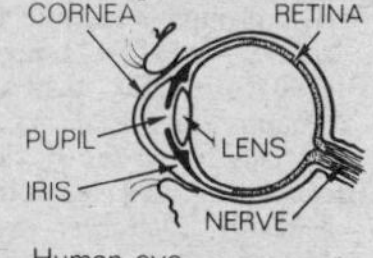

Human eye

catch (someone's) eye to get (someone's) attention. **have an eye for** to be a keen and appreciative judge of: *to* have an eye for *beauty.* **make eyes at** to flirt with. **see eye to eye** to agree perfectly. **set eyes on** to see. **with an eye to** with the aim or purpose of.

eye·ball (ī′bòl′) *n-* the globe of the eye enclosed in the bony socket behind the eyelids and connected to the optic nerve.

eye·brow (ī′brou′) *n-* 1 the ridge above either eye. 2 the hair that grows on this ridge.

eye·cup (ī′kŭp′) *n-* small cup with a curved rim that fits over the eye, used for washing the eyes or applying medicine to them.

eye dropper *n-* small glass tube with a rubber bulb, used to apply drops of medicine to the eye.

eye·ful (ī′fo͝ol′) *n-* 1 amount that fills the eye: *an* eyeful *of dust.* 2 *Informal* full or satisfying look: *You doubt me? Come to my house and get an* eyeful.

eye·glass (ī′glăs′) *n-* 1 any lens, such as a monocle, used to improve faulty eyesight. 2 in an optical instrument, the eyepiece. 3 **eyeglasses** pair of glass lenses used to improve or correct eyesight; spectacles.

eye·lash (ī′lăsh′) *n-* 1 protective fringe of hair that grows on the edge of the eyelid. 2 one of the hairs of this fringe.

eye·less (ī′ləs) *adj-* without eyes; blind: *an* eyeless *fish.*

eye·let (ī′lət) *n-* 1 small hole in leather or cloth for a lace or cord. 2 metal ring to strengthen such a hole; grommet. *Hom-* islet.

eye·lid (ī′lĭd′) *n-* the movable upper or lower cover of skin that opens or closes the eye.

eye opener *n- Informal* startling or revealing news, experience, discovery, etc.

eye·piece (ī′pēs′) *n-* in a telescope, microscope, etc., the lens or system of lenses nearest the eye of the user.

eye·sight (ī′sīt′) *n-* 1 power or ability to see. 2 range of vision or sight: *The house is within* eyesight.

eye·sore (ī′sôr′) *n-* something unpleasant or ugly to one's eye; offensive sight: *That old hat is an* eyesore.

eye·spot (ī′spŏt′) *n-* simple organ of vision that consists of pigment cells covering a nerve ending that is sensitive to light.

eye splice *n-* splice made by turning back the end of a rope and splicing it into the rope to form a loop.

eye·stalk (ī′stòk′) *n-* movable stalk with a compound eye at its tip, found on lobsters, crabs, etc.

eye strain *n-* tired or strained condition of the eyes caused by poor eyesight, reading in bad light, etc.

eye·tooth (ī′to͞oth′) *n-* [*pl.* **eye·teeth**] either one of the two canine teeth in the upper jaw; the third tooth from the front on either side.

eye·wit·ness (ī′wĭt′nəs) *n-* one who has seen something happen, and is thus able to testify to it: *an* eyewitness *to a robbery.* *as* ***modifier***: *an* eyewitness *account.*

E·ze·ki·el (ĭ zē′kē əl) *n-* 1 in the Old Testament, a major Hebrew prophet of the sixth century B.C. 2 a book of the Old Testament which contains his prophecies. In the CCD Bible, **E·ze′chi·el.**

Ez·ra (ĕz′rə) *n-* 1 in the Old Testament, a Hebrew scribe and high priest who led the Jews out of the Babylonian captivity. 2 historical book of the Old Testament written by him. In the CCD Bible, **Es′dra** (ĕz′drə).

F

F, f (ĕf) *n-* [*pl.* **F's, f's**] 1 the sixth letter of the English alphabet. 2 **F** *Music* the fourth note of the C-major scale.

f *Music* forte.

F 1 *Mathematics* symbol for function. 2 *Chemistry* symbol for fluorine.

f. 1 female; feminine. 2 franc. 3 following.

F. 1 February. 2 Friday. 3 Fahrenheit. 4 French.

fa (fä) *Music n-* the fourth note of a musical scale.

fa·ble (fā′bəl) *n-* 1 story that teaches a moral or lesson, especially one in which animals talk and act like people: *the* fable *of the fox and the grapes.* 2 legend or myth: *the* fables *of Scandinavia.* 3 a statement or tale that is not true; falsehood. *as* ***modifier***: *a* fable *writer.*

fa·bled (fā′bəld) *adj-* told about in a fable or fables.

fab·ric (făb′rĭk) *n-* 1 woven or knitted cloth. 2 structure: *the* fabric *of society.*

fab·ri·cate (făb′rə kāt′) *vt-* [**fab·ri·cat·ed, fab·ri·cat·ing**] 1 to make up or invent (a story, lie, etc.). 2 to construct or assemble; manufacture: *to* fabricate *airplane parts.* —*n-* **fab′ri·ca′tion.**

fab·ri·ca·tor (făb′rə kā′tər) *n-* 1 liar. 2 one who makes or constructs things.

fāte, făt, dâre, bärn; bē, bĕt, mêre; bīte, bĭt; nōte, hŏt, môre, dòg; fŭn, fûr; to͞o, bo͝ok; oil; out; tar; thin; then; hw for wh as in *what*; zh for s as in *usual*; ə for a, e, i, o, u, as in *ago*, *linen*, *peril*, *atom*, *minus*

Fa·bri·koid (fă′ brə koid′) ***n-*** trade name for a fabric resembling leather and used for bookbinding, luggage, and upholstery.

fab·u·list (făb′ yə lĭst) ***n-*** person, such as Aesop, who makes up fables.

fab·u·lous (fă′ byə ləs) ***adj-*** amazing; incredible; astounding: *his* fabulous *wealth.* **—*adv-* fab′ u·lous·ly.** ***n-*** **fab′ u·lous·ness.**

fa·cade (fə säd′) ***n-*** **1** entire outer side of a building, especially the main front or the side facing the street. **2** appearance put on in order to deceive others; false front; pretense: *A* facade *of calmness hid her terror.*

face (fās) ***n-*** **1** the front of the head; visage: *The eyes, nose, and mouth are parts of the* face. **2** front, principal, or usable side of something, such as that of a playing card, a clock, or a coin. **3** look or expression: *a sour* face. **4** public reputation and dignity; personal worth: *to lose* face; *to save one's* face. **5** *Informal* impudence; nerve. **6** (1) in printing, the surface of a type or plate that makes the impression. (2) the size or style of the letters or characters; also, the letters or characters themselves. **7** *Mathematics* a plane surface of a solid figure. *as* ***modifier***: *tan* face *powder.* ***vt-*** **[faced, fac·ing] 1** to turn toward; be opposite to: *She* faced *me.* **2** to stand bravely against; confront: *to* face *the enemy.* **3** to be threatened with; expect to suffer: *Unless we act, we* face *ruin and defeat.* **4** to put an outer layer on: *to* face *a house with shingles.* ***vi-*** to stand with the front toward a certain direction: *The windows* face *east.* Face *left.*

face to face with faces turned toward one another; in confrontation: *They stood* face to face. **in the face of** in the presence of; threatened by: *He showed courage* in the face of *danger.* **make a face** to twist the features to show disgust, disapproval, etc.; grimace. **put a (certain) face on** to speak or behave so as to give a (certain) impression of something: *He* put a good face on *our efforts.* **to (someone's) face** openly; in (someone's) presence: *He didn't dare say it* to my face.

face out to withstand (a crisis) boldly until it has passed.

face up to to confront bravely: *to* face up to *danger.*

face card ***n-*** in a deck of playing cards, the king, queen, or jack.

face-lift·ing (fās′ lĭf′ tĭng) ***n-*** **1** process of removing wrinkles or tightening sagging muscles in the face by plastic surgery. **2** process of renovating a building or other construction.

fac·et (făs′ ət) ***n-*** **1** any of the small, flat surfaces on a cut gem. For picture, see *gem.* **2** side or aspect: *the many* facets *of his character.*

fa·ce·tious (fə sē′ shəs) ***adj-*** humorous and frivolous: *a* facetious *remark.* **—*adv-* fa·ce′ tious·ly.** ***n-*** **fa·ce′ tious·ness.**

face value ***n-*** **1** number showing value and printed on a banknote, bond, etc., as distinct from market value. **2** apparent or seeming value.

fa·cial (fā′ shəl) ***adj-*** of or for the face: *a* facial *expression; a* facial *cream.* ***n-*** *Informal* treatment to beautify the face with massage, lotions, etc. **—*adv-* fa′ cial·ly.**

fac·ile (făs′ əl) ***adj-*** **1** quick and skillful; smooth; fluent: *a* facile *writer.* **2** demanding little work or effort; easily done: *a* facile *task.* **3** easily influenced; yielding; agreeable: *a* facile *personality.* **—*adv-* fac′ ile·ly.**

fa·cil·i·tate (fə sĭl′ ə tāt′) ***vt-*** **[fa·cil·i·tat·ed, fa·cil·i·tat·ing]** to make easy or easier: *Airplanes* facilitate *travel.* **—*n-* fa·cil′ i·ta′ tion.**

fa·cil·i·ty (fə sĭl′ ə tē′) ***n-*** [*pl.* **fa·cil·i·ties**] **1** ease; skill: *She dances with* facility. **2** (usually **facilities**) device or means which makes something easier: *Good kitchen* facilities *are a help in cooking.* **3** site; establishment: *a military* facility *at Watertown.*

fac·ing (fā′ sĭng) ***n-*** **1** covering in front of a building, wall, etc., for ornament or protection. **2** decorative or protective lining applied along the inner or outer edge of a garment. **3 facings** trimmings, collar, and cuffs of a military coat.

fac·sim·i·le (făk sĭm′ ə lē) ***n-*** exact copy of a document, book, etc.; reproduction.

in facsimile as an exact copy.

fact (făkt) ***n-*** **1** something true, real, and actual: *A scientist needs* facts. **2** reality; actuality: *Can you tell* fact *from fancy in this situation?* **3** thing, event, etc., that is said to be true or real: *Check the* facts *in the report.*

as a matter of fact, in fact, in point of fact in truth; really; actually.

fac·tion (făk′ shən) ***n-*** group of people within a political party, company, etc., who oppose another group, usually to advance their own interests. **—*adj-* fac′ tion·al:** *an organization torn by* factional *strife.*

fac·tion·al·ism (făk′ shən əl ĭz′ əm) ***n-*** spirit or tendency of breaking up into factions: *a party split by* factionalism. **—*n-* fac′ tion·al·ist.**

fac·tious (făk′ shəs) ***adj-*** **1** given to forming factions or rival groups: *a* factious *leader.* **2** quarrelsome: *a* factious *spirit.* **—*adv-* fac′ tious·ly.** ***n-*** **fac′ tious·ness.**

fac·ti·tious (făk tĭsh′ əs) ***adj-*** not natural or spontaneous; artificial: *a* factitious *smile.* **—*adv-* fac·ti′ tious·ly.** ***n-*** **fac·ti′ tious·ness.**

fac·tor (făk′ tər) ***n-*** **1** something that helps to bring about a result: *Diet and exercise are important* factors *in healthy living.* **2** in arithmetic, any number which can be multiplied by another number to get a given product: *The* factors *of 10 are 2 and 5.* ***vt-*** *Mathematics* to resolve or separate (a number or an expression) into factors.

fac·tor·i·za·tion (făk′ tər ə zā′ shən) ***n-*** expression which shows results of factoring. Example: $10 = 2 \times 5$.

fac·to·ry (făk′ tə rē) ***n-*** [*pl.* **fac·to·ries**] place in which goods are manufactured.

fac·to·tum (făk′ tō′ təm) ***n-*** person employed to do various tasks, usually minor; handyman.

fac·tu·al (făk′ cho͞o əl) ***adj-*** of, based on, or consisting of facts; real: *a* factual *report.* **—*adv-* fac′ tu·al·ly.**

fac·ul·ty (făk′ əl tē) ***n-*** [*pl.* **fac·ul·ties**] **1** special ability or skill to do something; talent: *She has a* faculty *for saying the right thing.* **2** a power of the mind or body: *the* faculty *of sight.* **3** staff of teachers.

fad (făd) ***n-*** brief fashion or craze: *a mah-jongg* fad.

fad·dist (făd′ ĭst) ***n-*** person who follows new fads.

fade (fād) ***vi-*** **[fad·ed, fad·ing] 1** to grow dim or faint: *Some colors* fade *easily. The sound of drums* faded *away.* **2** to wither: *The flowers* fade *in autumn.* ***vt-***: *Sunlight* fades *the colors in most cloths.*

fade in (or **out**) in the movies, television, etc., to increase (or decrease) gradually in brightness or sound.

fade-out (fād′ out′) ***n-*** a gradual decrease or disappearance.

faer·ie or **faer·y** (fâr′ ē) *Archaic* fairy.

[1]**fag** (făg) ***vt-*** **[fagged, fag·ging]** to tire out or exhaust (usually followed by "out"): *The long climb* fagged *us out.* ***n-*** in English public schools, a boy who runs errands, etc., for an older boy. [of uncertain origin.]

[2]**fag** (făg) *Brit. Slang* ***n-*** cigarette. [apparently from **fag end,** from earlier **flag end,** from [2]**flag,** "to droop."]

fag end ***n-*** **1** the unfinished end of a piece of cloth or the frayed, untwisted end of a rope. **2** the last or poorest part of anything: *the* fag end *of a hard day.*

Fa·gin (fā′ gən) ***n-*** in Dickens' "Oliver Twist," an obnoxious old man who trained children to become thieves.

fa·got or **fag·got** (făg′ət) ***n-*** bundle of sticks tied together for firewood.

fag·ot·ing (făg′ə tĭng) ***n-*** **1** interlocking cross-stitch used to join ribbons or bands in an open seam. **2** hemstitch.

Fahr. Fahrenheit.

Fahr·en·heit (făr′ən hīt′) ***adj-*** naming or relating to a temperature scale on which 32° is the freezing point and 212° the boiling point of water. It is used in thermometers for cooking, weather forecasts, etc. *Abbr.* F. For picture, see *thermometer.*

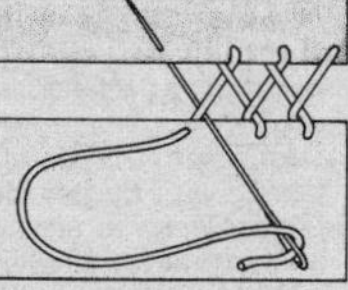
Fagoting

fail (fāl) ***vi-*** **1** to be unsuccessful (in) doing, making, or becoming something: *to* fail *in one's exams; to* fail *in one's duty.* **2** to fall short of what is expected or desired: *The crop* failed. **3** to cease to function; stop working: *The engine* failed. *His heart* failed. **4** to become weaker or sicker: *He is* failing *fast and may not survive the night.* **5** to become bankrupt: *The business* failed *last year.* **6** to receive a mark of failure in a course of study: *Did you pass or* fail? ***vt-*** **1** to give no help to; desert: *Her friends* failed *her when she needed them most.* **2** to neglect or not do (something): *He* failed *to come,* **3** to give a mark of failure to (a student); also, to receive a mark of failure in (a course of study).

without fail certainly; surely: *Be there* without fail.

fail·ing (fā′lĭng) ***n-*** weakness; fault: *Habitual tardiness was one of his chief* failings. ***prep-*** in the absence of; without: *She said,* "Failing *an answer, I will go.*"

faille (fīl) ***n-*** soft fabric of cotton, rayon, or silk, with narrow, flat, horizontal ribs. ***Hom-*** file.

fail-safe (fāl′sāf′) ***adj-*** relating to a system or technique for absolute control of bombers flying in an alert.

fail·ure (fāl′yər) ***n-*** **1** lack of success; unsuccessful effort: *a* failure *in a history examination.* **2** a falling short of something expected, desired, or needed: *the* failure *of this year's crops.* **3** a neglecting; omission: *his* failure *to write.* **4** unsuccessful person or thing: *He was a* failure *in business.* **5** a becoming bankrupt: *the* failure *of his business.* **6** accidental ceasing to function: *the* failure *of the motor.*

fain (fān) *Archaic* ***adv-*** willingly: *He would* fain *go.* ***adj-*** willing: *She was* fain *to go.* ***Homs-*** fane, feign.

faint (fānt) ***vi-*** to lose consciousness briefly. ***n-*** brief loss of consciousness. ***adj-*** **[faint·er, faint·est]** **1** weak; exhausted; dizzy of sick. **2** indistinct; dim: *a* faint *noise; a* faint *light.* **3** feeble; halfhearted: *a* faint *attempt at courtesy.* **—*adv-*** **faint′ly.** ***n-*** **faint′ness.** ***Hom-*** feint.

faint·heart·ed (fānt′här′təd) ***adj-*** lacking courage; cowardly; timid. **—*adv-*** **faint′heart′ed·ly.** ***n-*** **faint′heart′ed·ness.**

[1]**fair** (fâr) ***adj-*** **[fair·er, fair·est]** **1** honest or just: *a* fair *decision;* fair *play.* **2** light in color; blond: *to have* fair *skin;* fair *hair.* **3** clear; not rainy or stormy, favorable: *in* fair *weather.* **4** average; reasonably satisfactory: *His spelling is only* fair. *He has a* fair *chance of success.* **5** pleasing to the sight; lovely: *this land so green and* fair. ***adv-*** in an honest and just manner: *Play* fair. [from Old English **fæger** meaning "light," originally "pleasing."] ***Hom-*** fare. **—*adj-*** **fair′ish.** ***n-*** **fair′ness.**

bid fair to appear likely or favorable. **fair and square** just and honest.

[2]**fair** (fâr) ***n-*** **1** large exhibition of industrial, commercial, and agricultural products, often with cultural and educational displays, amusements, etc.: *the New York World's* Fair *of 1964-5.* **2** gathering of persons for the display and sale of goods: *a book* fair. [from Old French **feire,** from Latin **fēria** meaning "a holiday."] ***Hom-*** fare.

fair ball ***n-*** in baseball, a ball that is batted so as to fall withing the area marked off by the foul lines, and that does not cross a base line leading from home plate.

fair game *Informal* ***n-*** person or thing that is properly open to attack, pursuit, etc.

fair·ground (fâr′ground′) ***n-*** (often **fairgrounds**) place where fairs are held.

fair·ly (fâr′lē) ***adv-*** **1** justly; in an honest manner: *The games were judged* fairly. *They treated us* fairly. **2** somewhat; moderately; rather: *Mike plays the piano* fairly *well.* **3** completely; really: *She* fairly *burst with joy.*

fair-mind·ed (fâr′mīn′dəd) **adj-** not prejudiced; just and impartial: *a* fair-minded *juror.* **—*n-*** **fair′mind′ed·ness.**

fair trade ***n-*** trade under a law or agreement which allows manufacturers to set a minimum price for their products, and forbids distributors to sell for less.

fair-trade (fâr′trād′) ***vt-*** **[fair-trad·ed, fair-trad·ing]** to fix a price on or sell according to a law or agreement requiring fair trade. ***adj-***: *a* fair-trade *law.*

fair·way (fâr′wā′) ***n-*** in golf, the grassy space between the tee and the green and within fixed boundaries.

fair-weath·er (fâr wĕth′ər) ***adj-*** suitable only in good weather: *a* fair-weather *road.*

fair-weather friend ***n-*** friend who is dependable and helpful only when one has no trouble or grief.

fair·y (fâr′ē) ***n-*** [*pl.* **fair·ies**] an imaginary being of tiny, human shape, usually having magical powers. *as* ***modifier:*** *a* fairy *tale.*

fair·y·land (fâr′ē lănd′) ***n-*** **1** the country of the fairies. **2** any beautiful, enchanting place.

fairy ring ***n-*** ring of mushrooms produced from the extensions of the mushroom-mycelia underground.

fairy tale ***n-*** **1** a story about fairies, witches, or unreal beings, as "Puss-in-Boots." **2** highly fanciful lie: *He told a* fairy tale *about having been an army captain.*

fait ac·com·pli (fĕ′tə kō^{n} plē′) *French* accomplished fact; something that can no longer be changed.

faith (fāth) ***n-*** **1** trust; confidence: *Do you have* faith *in his word?* **2** belief in God. **3** system of religious belief: *the Christian* faith; *the Jewish* faith. **4** promise of loyalty: *to keep or break* faith.

bad faith dishonesty; insincerity. **break faith** to fail to fulfull one's principles, a promise, etc. **in faith** indeed; really and truly. **in good faith** honestly. **keep faith** to stick to one's principles, a vow, etc.

faith·ful (fāth′fəl) ***adj-*** **1** loyal; trustworthy: *a* faithful *dog; a* faithful *friend.* **2** without mistakes; accurate: *a* faithful *copy of a picture.* ***n-*** **the faithful** followers or adherents, especially of a religion. **—*adv-*** **faith′ful·ly.** ***n-*** **faith′ful·ness.**

faith·less (fāth′ləs) ***adj-*** disloyal; false: *He proved to be a* faithless *friend.* **—*adv-*** **faith′less·ly.** ***n-*** **faith′less·ness.**

fake (fāk) ***vt-*** **[faked, fak·ing]** to imitate in order to deceive; pretend: *to* fake *blindness.* ***adj-*** false; counterfeit: *a* fake *dollar bill.* ***n-*** something or someone that is not as represented: *The dealer sold a* fake *as a painting by Rembrandt.* **—*n-*** **fak′er.**

fak·er·y (fā′kə rē) ***n-*** [*pl.* **fak·er·ies**] **1** act or process of faking. **2** something faked; a fake: *This is another of the clever* fakeries.

fa·kir (fə kêr′) ***n-*** in the Muslim religion, a begging monk. [from Arabic **faqīr** meaning "a poor man."]

fal·chion (fòl′ chən) ***n-*** in the Middle Ages, a short sword with a wide, curved blade.

fal·con (făl′ kən, fòl′ -) ***n-*** any of several small, swift hawks that can be trained to hunt birds and small game.

Falcon, about 18 in. long

fal·con·er (făl′ kən ər, fòl′ -) ***n-*** person who trains, hunts with, or breeds falcons.

fal·con·ry (făl′ kən rē, fòl′ -) ***n-*** **1** the art of training falcons to hunt. **2** the sport of hunting with falcons.

fal·de·ral (făl′ də răl′) folderol.

fall (fòl) ***vi-*** **[fell** (fĕl), **fall·en, fall·ing] 1** to come down; drop: *He* fell *off the chair. Rain* fell *heavily.* **2** to lessen; decrease: *The temperature* fell *to zero. Her voice* fell *to a whisper.* **3** to be wounded or killed: *to* fall *in battle.* **4** to be defeated or overthrown: *The city* fell *after a siege of three months.* **5** to yield to a moral error or fault; sin: *Adam* fell *through disobedience to God.* **6** to lose dignity, reputation, etc.: *He* fell *in her estimation.* **7** to happen; occur: *Christmas* fell *on Sunday last year.* **8** to come or happen by right or chance, or at a particular place: *The estate* fell *to the eldest son. The accent mark* falls *on the first syllable.* **9** to pass into a certain physical or mental condition: *to* fall *ill; to* fall *asleep.* **10** to be uttered: *A sigh* fell *from his lips.* **11** to be divided or classified: *His writings* fall *into three types: novels, plays, and essays.* ***n-*** **1** a coming down; a dropping: *a* fall *of rain.* **2** amount that comes down: *There'll be a heavy* fall *of snow.* **3** distance covered by something dropping: *It's only a short* fall. **4** a lessening; decrease: *a* fall *in prices.* **5** capture; overthrow; loss of power: *the* fall *of a city.* **6** a yielding to moral error; sin: *the* fall *of Adam.* **7** loss of dignity, reputation, etc.: *a* fall *from favor.* **8** autumn. **9** in wrestling, a victory attained by pinning an opponent's shoulders to the floor; also, one of the parts of a match that comes to an end with such a victory or a time limit. **10 falls** waterfall. **11 the Fall** the sin of Adam and Eve. *as* ***modifier:*** *a brisk* fall *day.*

fall back to withdraw; move back or away.

fall back on to go back to.

fall behind to be unable to keep up.

fall flat to fail to have the intended effect: *The best joke can* fall flat *if not told properly.*

fall for *Informal* **1** to fall in love with. **2** to be tricked by.

fall in 1 to take the proper place in a line: *The soldiers* fell in *for inspection.* **2** to meet or join by chance. **3** to agree: *We* fell in *with his plan.*

fall off to lessen; decrease: *Attendance* fell off.

fall on (or **upon) 1** to come or descend upon: *A hush* fell on *the audience.* **2** to attack: *The bandits* fell on *him.*

fall out 1 to quarrel; disagree: *They* fell out *over the placement of the fence.* **2** to drop out of line.

fall short 1 to be not enough: *Our supplies* fell short. **2** to fail to reach the place aimed at or the standard required: *The arrow* fell short.

fall through to fail; come to nothing: *Our plans* fell through.

fall to 1 to begin an attack. **2** to begin to eat.

fall under 1 to be found or included as part of: *His powers* fall under *my jurisdiction.* **2** to come under the power of (a spell, someone's influence, etc.).

fal·la·cious (fə lā′ shəs) ***adj-*** based on false or unsound reasoning: *a* fallacious *conclusion.* **—*adv-* fal·la′ cious·ly. *n-* fal·la′ cious·ness.**

fal·la·cy (făl′ ə sē) ***n-*** [*pl.* **fal·la·cies] 1** mistaken idea, opinion, or belief: *the* fallacy *that wealth always means happiness.* **2** false or unsound reasoning.

fall·en (fòl′ ən) ***adj-*** **1** dropped: *a* fallen *leaf.* **2** ruined; overthrown: *a* fallen *nation.* **3** killed in battle: *a* fallen *soldier.*

fallen angel ***n-*** one of the angels who were cast out of heaven with Lucifer for rebelling against God.

fall guy *Slang* ***n-*** person who is left to take the blame or punishment for a failure.

fal·li·ble (făl′ ə bəl) ***adj-*** liable to be wrong or deceived; capable of error: *All men are* fallible. **—*n-* fal′ li·bil′ i·ty. *adv-* fal′ li·bly.**

falling star ***n-*** shooting star; meteor.

fall line ***n-*** in geology, a region marking the boundary between a coastal plain and the older land mass, marked by an abrupt change in elevation and, therefore, rapids and waterfalls.

fal·lo·pi·an tube (fə lō′ pē ən) ***n-*** one of two long narrow tubes in a female animal, through which the reproductive egg cells pass from the ovary to the uterus.

fall-out (fòl′ out′) ***n-*** radioactive particles and dust that fall to earth after the explosion of a nuclear bomb.

fal·low (făl′ ō) ***adj-*** plowed up, but left unseeded or without crops for a season: *the* fallow *land.*

fallow deer ***n-*** small European deer having very broad antlers, and, usually, white spots on a pale coat in the summer.

false (fòls) ***adj-*** **[fals·er, fals·est] 1** untrue or incorrect; wrong: *He had a* false *idea of her character.* **2** misleading; deceitful: *a* false *promise.* **3** not natural; artificial: *to wear* false *teeth.* **4** disloyal; unfaithful: *a* false *friend.* **5** lying. **—*adv-* false′ ly. *n-* false′ ness.**

play false to cheat or betray.

false bottom ***n-*** thin partition in a suitcase, trunk, etc., which conceals a secret compartment at the bottom.

false colors ***n-*** *pl.* **1** flag or ensign of a nation other than one's own, flown to deceive an enemy. **2** sham; pretense.

false face ***n-*** mask.

false·hood (fòls′ hŏŏd′) ***n-*** a lie.

false imprisonment ***n-*** unlawful jailing of a person.

false pride ***n-*** pride based on unworthy reasons.

false rib ***n-*** a rib that is not connected directly to the breastbone.

fal·set·to (fòl sĕt′ ō) *Music* ***n-*** [*pl.* **fal·set·tos] 1** artificial way of singing, used especially by tenors to produce notes above the normal range of their voices. **2** person who sings in such a way. ***adj-:*** *a* falsetto *note.* ***adv-:*** *to sing* falsetto.

fal·si·fy (fòl′ sə fī′) ***vt-*** **[fal·si·fied, fal·si·fy·ing] 1** to alter or tamper with (a document, records, etc.) so as to deceive someone. **2** to lie or distort the truth about; misrepresent: *He* falsified *his motives.* ***vi-*** to tell falsehoods; lie. **—*n-* fal′ si·fi′ er. *n-* fal′ si·fi·ca′ tion.**

fal·si·ty (fòl′ sə tē) ***n-*** [*pl.* **fal·si·ties] 1** quality or condition of being untrue or dishonorable; falseness. **2** an error; falsehood.

Fal·staff (fòl′ stăf′), **Sir John** ***n-*** a fat, jolly old knight of Shakespeare's plays. **—*adj-* Fal·staff′ i·an.**

fal·ter (fòl′ tər) ***vi-*** **1** to move or act in an uncertain or unsteady way; waver; hesitate: *He* faltered *at the door, wondering if he should go in.* **2** to speak with hesitation; stammer: *He* faltered *as he tried to find the right words.* **—*n-* fal′ ter·er. *adv-* fal′ ter·ing·ly.**

fame (fām) ***n-*** widespread reputation, especially of a favorable kind; renown: *Edison's* fame *as an inventor.*

famed (fāmd) ***adj-*** famous.

fa·mil·iar (fə mĭl′ yər) ***adj-*** **1** well-known; often seen or heard: *I recognized the* familiar *voice on the telephone.* **2** well-acquainted: *Are you* familiar *with the facts in the case?* **3** having close acquaintance; personally close; intimate: *He has few* familiar *friends.* **4** easy; informal: *to write in a* familiar *style*; *in* familiar *language.* **5** unduly forward; bold: *He is much too* familiar *with people he meets for the first time.* **—*adv-*** **fa·mil′ iar·ly.**

fa·mil·i·ar·i·ty (fə mĭl′ yăr′ ə tē, -ē ĕr′ ə tē) ***n-*** [*pl.* **fa·mil·i·ar·i·ties**] **1** close acquaintance or knowledge: *His* familiarity *with Hopi customs made him well liked.* **2** freedom from formality: *to be on terms of* familiarity *with someone.* **3** undue forwardness in speech or manner: *his undue* familiarity *toward his superiors.*

fa·mil·iar·ize (fə mĭl′ yə rīz′) ***vt-*** [**fa·mil·iar·ized, fa·mil·iar·iz·ing**] to make (someone) feel well acquainted or at ease with something. **—*n-*** **fa·mil′ iar·i·za′ tion.**

fam·i·ly (făm′ lē, -ə lē) ***n-*** [*pl.* **fam·i·lies**] **1** parents and their children: *The Brown* family *lives next door.* **2** the children of a married couple: *Mr. and Mrs. Brown have a large* family. **3** persons closely related by birth; all people descended from the same ancestor: *The Nelson* family *has been in New York for 250 years.* **4** group of related plants, animals, languages, etc.: *Lions and tigers belong to the cat* family. *as* ***modifier***: *a* family *resemblance*; family *Bible.*

family name ***n-*** last name; surname.

family skeleton ***n-*** something shameful or scandalous which a family keeps secret.

family tree ***n-*** ancestors or descendants of a family; lineage; also, a diagram or chart of this.

fam·ine (făm′ ən) ***n-*** **1** extreme scarcity of food. **2** starvation. **3** shortage of some one thing, especially a crop.

fam·ished (făm′ ĭsht) ***adj-*** very hungry; starving: *The* famished *dogs snarled over a scrap of meat.*

fa·mous (fā′ məs) ***adj-*** widely known; renowned; famed: *Admiral Byrd was a* famous *explorer.*

fa·mous·ly (fā′ məs lē) *Informal* ***adv-*** wonderfully.

[1]**fan** (făn) ***n-*** anything used to stir or drive air, especially a motor-driven set of revolving blades, or a piece of paper or cloth moved back and forth in the hand. ***vt-*** [**fanned, fan·ning**] **1** to wave something to cast a breeze on: *to* fan *oneself*; *to* fan *a fire.* **2** to stir up; excite: *to* fan *enthusiasm.* **3** in baseball, to strike out (a batter). ***vi-*** in baseball, to strike out. [from Old English **fann,** from Latin **vannus** meaning "a fan for winnowing grain."]

Fans

fan out to spread apart while moving forward: *The hunters* fanned out *to cover the whole field.*

[2]**fan** (făn) ***n-*** enthusiastic supporter; buff: *a baseball* fan; *a movie* fan. [American word partly from **fanatic** and partly from **the fancy** meaning "followers of a certain hobby."]

fa·nat·ic (fə năt′ ĭk) ***n-*** person having unduly strong and unreasonable beliefs about something: *a* fanatic *about diet.* ***adj-*** (also **fa·nat′ ic·al**) wild and unreasonable: *a* fanatic *belief in witchcraft.* **—*adv-*** **fa·nat′ ic·al·ly.**

fa·nat·i·cism (fə năt′ ə sĭz′ əm) ***n-*** strong and unreasonable enthusiasm for some cause, principle, etc.

fan·cied (făn′ sēd) ***adj-*** imagined; unreal: *He was beset by* fancied *enemies.*

fan·ci·er (făn′ sē ər) ***n-*** person who has a special interest in or fondness for something: *a bird* fancier.

fan·ci·ful (făn′ sə fəl) ***adj-*** **1** imaginary; not real: *Her story was about goblins, dragons, and other* fanciful *creatures.* **2** imaginative: *a* fanciful *writer.* **3** showing fancy; strangely designed: *a* fanciful *dress.* **—*adv-*** **fan′ ci·ful·ly.** ***n-*** **fan′ ci·ful·ness.**

fan·cy (făn′ sē) ***n-*** [*pl.* **fan·cies**] **1** imagination, especially of an odd or extravagant sort: *Such strange tales show a lively* fancy. **2** notion; whim: *His head was filled with wild ideas and* fancies. **3** fondness: *They took a* fancy *to each other.* ***adj-*** [**fan·ci·er, fan·ci·est**] **1** not plain; ornamental: *a* fancy *dress.* **2** superior; choice: *to sell* fancy *groceries.* **3** *Informal* of prices, very high: *to charge* fancy *rates.* **4** *Informal* highly skillful or graceful: *to show* fancy *footwork.* ***vt-*** [**fan·cied, fan·cy·ing**] **1** to imagine: *I can't* fancy *his doing that.* **2** to like: *Which dress do you* fancy *most?* **—*adv-*** **fan′ ci·ly.**

fancy (oneself) to regard (oneself) as: *He* fancied himself *an expert.*

fancy dress ***n-*** dress or costume for a masquerade.

fan·cy-free (făn′ sē frē′) ***adj-*** free of cares or responsibilities; especially, free to fall in love with another.

fan·cy·work (făn′ sē wûrk′) ***n-*** ornamental needlework, such as embroidery or crocheting.

fan·dan·go (făn dăng′ gō) ***n-*** [*pl.* **fan·dan·gos**] **1** lively Spanish dance, usually accompanied by a guitar and castanets. **2** music written for such a dance.

fane (fān) *Archaic* ***n-*** temple. ***Homs-*** fain, feign.

fan·fare (făn′ fâr′) ***n-*** **1** musical flourish, especially of trumpets. **2** loud or showy display: *What's all the* fanfare *about?*

fang (făng) ***n-*** long, sharp tooth. **—*adj-*** **fanged:** *a* fanged *serpent.*

FANGS

Fangs of a tiger

fan mail ***n-*** letters of praise to an actor, writer, etc., from fans.

fan·tail (făn′ tāl′) ***n-*** **1** any tail, structure, or end shaped like an open fan. **2** any of various birds having fan-shaped tails. **3** a goldfish with double tail fins. **4** a Pacific flatfish. **5** the overhanging part of the stern of a ship.

fan-tan (făn′ tăn′) ***n-*** **1** card game in which the first player to get rid of his cards is the winner. **2** Chinese gambling game played with coins or tokens.

fan·ta·si·a (făn tā′ zhə, -zē ə) ***n-*** **1** musical composition written according to no fixed or set form. **2** medley of various tunes or themes.

fan·tas·tic (făn tăs′ tĭk) ***adj-*** **1** (also **fan·tas′ ti·cal**) imaginative; unreal: *He told some* fantastic *story about riding a subway in the desert.* **2** odd; queer; grotesque: *a* fantastic *shape.* **—*adv-*** **fan·tas′ ti·cal·ly.**

fan·ta·sy (făn′ tə sē, -zē) ***n-*** [*pl.* **fan·ta·sies**] **1** imagination; unrestrained fancy. **2** thing imagined or not real; daydream; fanciful idea: *Her wealth is sheer* fantasy. **3** poem, play, or story showing much imagination or having fanciful ideas: *"Peter Pan" is a* fantasy.

far (fär) ***adj-*** [**far·ther, far·thest,** or **fur·ther, fur·thest** (See note at *farther.*)] **1** not near; distant: *a* far *land*; *a* far *past.* **2** more distant of two: *the* far *side of the street.* **3** covering a long distance or time: *a* far *journey.* ***adv-*** **1** to or at a great or definite distance: *He came* far *before he rested. I will go only so* far. **2** beyond what is right and proper: *Don't go too* far *with your accusations.* **3** by a great deal; very much: *He is* far *wiser than I.*

as far as or **so far as** to the extent that: *You may go now,* as far as *I'm concerned.* **by far** or **far and away** very much: *He is* by far *the worst speaker I've ever heard.* **far and near** or **far and wide** everywhere: *They came from* far and near *to hear him.* **go far** to be successful. **how far** to what distance or extent: How far *will you go to stop him?* **so far** up to now: *We've had no danger* so far. **so far so good** up to now there has been no trouble.

far·ad (făr′ ăd′) ***n-*** in electricity, unit of electrical capacitance, equal to the capacitance of a condenser which retains a charge of one coulomb with a difference in potential of one volt.

far·a·day (făr′ ə dā′) ***n-*** unit of electricity equal to about 96,500 coulombs; in electrochemistry, the amount of electricity needed to deposit or liberate an amount of an element equal to its atomic weight divided by its valence, expressed in grams.

far·a·way (fär′ ə wā′) ***adj-*** **1** distant; remote: *He wants to travel to* faraway *places.* **2** dreamy: *a* faraway *look.*

farce (färs) ***n-*** **1** play filled with absurd and exaggerated comic situations. **2** absurd or useless proceeding: *The election was a* farce.

far·ci·cal (fär′ sĭ kəl) ***adj-*** of or like farce: *The nomination was a* farcical *event.* **—*adv-*** **far′ ci·cal·ly.**

far cry ***n-*** long way: *His behavior is a* far cry *from what I expected.*

fare (fâr) ***n-*** **1** money paid for a trip: *bus* fare; *train* fare. **2** food and drink: *How is the* fare *at the lodge?* ***vi-*** **[fared, far·ing] 1** to do; get along: *How did you* fare *on your visit?* **2** to happen; turn out. ***Hom-*** fair.

fare·thee·well (fâr′ thē wĕl′) **to a fare-the-well** completely; utterly.

fare·well (fâr′ wĕl′) ***n-*** a good-by. ***interj-*** good-by. *as* ***modifier***: *a* farewell *dinner.*

far-fetched (fär′ fĕcht′) ***adj-*** hardly believable; offered frivolously or desperately: *a* far-fetched *excuse.*

far-flung (fär′ flŭng′) ***adj-*** **1** distant and far apart: *the* far-flung *outposts.* **2** covering great distances: *a* far-flung *battlefield.*

fa·ri·na (fə rē′ nə) ***n-*** **1** a flour or meal obtained mainly from corn and other grains, potatoes, and nuts. It is cooked in puddings and as a breakfast cereal. **2** starch.

far·i·na·ceous (făr′ ə nā′ shəs) ***adj-*** **1** made of or containing farina. **2** having a mealy texture. **3** rich in starch.

farm (färm) ***n-*** **1** land used for growing crops or raising animals: *a dairy* farm; *a wheat* farm. **2** such land and the buildings on it: *Peter lived on a* farm. *as* ***modifier***: *a* farm *implement.* ***vi-*** to work or use land for crops or livestock: *Some of the pioneers* farmed, *while others hunted.* ***vt-*** to cultivate (land): *We* farm *300 acres.*

farm out to lease; to let: *The work was* farmed out *to another company.*

farm club ***n-*** in baseball, a minor-league team subsidized by a major-league team to develop and train new players.

farm·er (fär′mər) ***n-*** person who operates a farm, either as owner or tenant.

farm hand ***n-*** farm worker.

farm·house (färm′ hous′) ***n-*** house, especially the farmer's home, on a farm.

farm·ing (fär′ mĭng) ***n-*** the cultivation of crops and the raising of livestock; agriculture.

farm·stead (färm′ stĕd′) ***n-*** farm land and its buildings.

farm·yard (färm′ yärd′) ***n-*** area around farm buildings.

far·o (fâr′ ō, fâr′ ō) ***n-*** a gambling game played with cards and chips.

far-off (fär′ ŏf′) ***adj-*** far away; distant; remote: *travel in* far-off *places.*

far-reach·ing (fär′ rē′ chĭng) ***adj-*** having an influence or effect that extends over a wide range: *a decision with* far-reaching *results.*

far·row (făr′ ō) ***n-*** a litter of pigs. ***vi-*** to give birth to a litter of pigs: *The prize sow* farrowed.

far-see·ing (fär′ sē′ ĭng) ***adj-*** using or showing good judgment in planning for the future; foresighted.

far-sight·ed (fär′ sī′ təd) ***adj-*** **1** able to see distant objects more clearly than near ones. **2** having or showing good judgement in planning and making decisions: *a* far-sighted *statesman*; *a* far-sighted *policy.* **—*adv-*** **far-sight′ ed·ly.** ***n-*** **far-sight′ ed·ness.**

far·ther (fär′ thər) *compar.* of **far.** ***adj-*** more distant: *the* farther *end of the field.* ***adv-*** at or to a greater distance: *He walked* farther *than I did.*

►Either FARTHER or FURTHER is correct as the comparative of "far." However, FARTHER usually refers only to actual distance. *Your house is* farther *away than mine. Every year he gets* further *into debt.*

far·ther·most (fär′ thər mōst′) ***adj-*** most distant; farthest.

far·thest (fär′ thəst) *superl.* of **far.** ***adj-*** most distant: *the* farthest *planet.* ***adv-*** at or to the greatest distance: *Who can run* farthest?

►See usage note at FARTHER.

far·thing (fär′ thĭng) ***n-*** former British coin worth one fourth of a British penny.

far·thin·gale (fär′thən gāl′) ***n-*** skirt supported by a circular hoop or pad, worn in the 16th and 17th centuries; also, the supporting framework itself.

Farthingale

fas·ces (făs′ ēz′) ***n-pl.*** symbol of the power and authority of the ancient Roman state, consisting of a bundle of rods bound around an axe.

fas·ci·nate (făs′ ə nāt′) ***vt-*** **[fas·ci·nat·ed, fas·ci·nat·ing]** to attract and hold the attention of (a person or animal) by or as if by a mysterious power; hold spellbound; enchant.

fas·ci·nat·ing (făs′ə nā′ tĭng) ***adj-*** attracting and holding the attention; very interesting; enchanting: *a* fascinating *subject.* **—*adv-*** **fas′ ci·nat·ing·ly.**

fas·ci·na·tion (făs′ ə nā′ shən) ***n-*** **1** a fascinating or a being fascinated. **2** strong attraction; charm.

fas·ci·na·tor (făs′ə nā′ tər) ***n-*** person or thing that fascinates.

fas·cism (făsh′ ĭz′ əm) ***n-*** political philosophy or system of government that advocates central control, often under the leadership of a dictator, has rigid censorship, and suppresses opposition.

fas·cist (făsh′ ĭst′) ***n-*** believer in or supporter of fascism. ***adj-***: *a* fascist *government.*

fash·ion (făsh′ ən) ***n-*** **1** way; manner: *to behave in a strange* fashion. **2** style, habit, or custom of a time: *the* fashions *of the colonial period.* ***vt-*** to make; form; shape: *He* fashioned *a boat from wood.* **—*n-*** **fash′ ion·er.**

after (or **in**) **a fashion** in some sort of manner; partly; incompletely: *to succeed* after a fashion.

fash·ion·a·ble (făsh′ ən ə bəl) ***adj-*** following the fashions of the times; stylish. **—*adv-*** **fash′ ion·a·bly.**

fashion plate ***n-*** illustration showing current styles of clothing; hence, a stylishly dressed person.

¹fast (făst) ***adj-*** **[fast·er, fast·est] 1** quick; swift; rapid: *a* fast *runner.* **2** securely fixed; firm; steady: *The stake is* fast *in the ground.* **3** staunch; faithful: *They are* fast *friends.* **4** fixed; nonfading: *cloth dyed with* fast *colors.*

5 ahead of the correct time: *The clock is ten minutes* fast. 6 wild; dissipated: *to lead a* fast *life*. ***adv-*** **1** quickly; swiftly; rapidly. **2** firmly; steadily: *to hold* fast *to a support*. **3** in a wild and dissipated manner. **4** soundly: *He is* fast *asleep*. [from Old English **fæst** meaning "firm(ly)"; used in such phrases as "drink fast (hard)," "follow fast (closely on)," from Old Norse.]

2**fast** (făst) ***vi-*** to eat little or no food; also, go without food or without certain foods as a religious duty. ***n-*** a period of going without food: *He ended his* fast *with a light meal*. [from Old English **fæstan** meaning originally "observe strictly; hold firmly (to rules)."]

fast day ***n-*** day on which people fast, especially as a religious observance.

fas·ten (făs′ ən) ***vt-*** **1** to join; attach: *to* fasten *a shelf to a wall*. **2** to close or cause to close securely: *to* fasten *the lock*. **3** to keep fixed steadily: *to* fasten *attention on*.

fas·ten·er (făs′ ən ər) ***n-*** device that closes an opening, or attaches one thing to another.

fas·ten·ing (făs′ ən ĭng) ***n-*** something that fastens or holds things together, such as a bolt, clasp, or chain.

fas·tid·i·ous (făs tĭd′ ē əs) ***adj-*** hard to please; very critical or particular: *to be* fastidious *about food or clothes*. ***—adv-*** **fas·tid′ i·ous·ly.** ***n-*** **fas·ti′ di·ous·ness.**

fast·ness (făst′ nəs) ***n-*** **1** fortified, secure place; stronghold: *a mountain fastness*. **2** a condition of being fast.

fat (făt) ***n-*** oily substance found in animals and plants. Fats are compounds of carbon, hydrogen, and oxygen. ***adj-*** **[fat·ter, fat·test] 1** having much of this substance: *This meat is* fat. **2** heavy with flesh; plump. **3** well-filled. ***vt-*** **[fat·ted, fat·ting]** to fatten. ***—n-*** **fat′ ness.**
the fat of the land the best of everything.

fa·tal (fā′ təl) ***adj-*** **1** causing death: *a* fatal *accident*. **2** causing great harm or ruin: *a* fatal *mistake*. ***—adv-*** **fa′ tal·ly.**

fa·tal·ism (fā′ tə lĭz′ əm) ***n-*** philosophic principle or belief that all events are determined in advance, and that therefore one cannot control or change what will happen. ***—n-*** **fa′ ta·list.** ***adj-*** **fa′ ta·lis′ tic:** *a* fatalistic *attitude*. ***adv-*** **fa′ ta·lis′ ti·cal·ly:** *to think* fatalistically.

fa·tal·i·ty (fə tăl′ ə tē) ***n-*** [*pl.* **fa·tal·i·ties**] **1** death in a disaster: *There were two* fatalities *in the plane crash*. **2** tendency or likeliness to be doomed: *There is a* fatality *in all his undertakings*. **3** deadly effect or influence: *the* fatality *of a disease*.

fat·back (făt′ băk′) ***n-*** fatty, unsmoked salt pork from the back of a hog.

fate (fāt) ***n-*** **1** power that is believed to control and decide what will happen; destiny. **2** what happens to someone; one's lot: *We wondered about the* fate *of the missing pilot*. **3 the Fates** in classical mythology, the three goddesses who controlled human destiny. ***Hom-*** fete. ***—adj-*** **fat′ ed:** *a man* fated *to succeed*.

fate·ful (fāt′ fəl) ***adj-*** **1** decisive: *a* fateful *day*. **2** foretelling or seeming to foretell disaster; ominous: *a* fateful *prophecy*. **3** deadly; bringing death: *a* fateful *arrow*. ***—adv-*** **fate′ ful·ly.** ***n-*** **fate′ ful·ness.**

fa·ther (fä′ thər) ***n-*** **1** male parent. **2** male ancestor; forefather. **3** founder or important leader: *the Pilgrim* Fathers. **4** one of the chief writers and teachers of the early Christian church. **5 Father** form of address for an ordained priest. **6 the Father** (also **our Father**) God. ***vt-*** **1** to be the male parent of; beget. **2** to originate or invent. ***—n-*** **fa′ ther·less.**

fa·ther·hood (fä′ thər hŏŏd′) ***n-*** condition of being a father.

fa·ther-in-law (fä′ thər ĭn lò′) ***n-*** [*pl.* **fa·thers-in-law**] father of one's husband or wife.

fa·ther·land (fä′ thər lănd′) ***n-*** country of one's birth.

fa·ther·ly (fä′ thər lē) ***adj-*** of or like a father: *to give a young man* fatherly *advice*. ***—n-*** **fa′ ther·li·ness.**

fath·om (făth′ əm) ***n-*** a measure equal to six feet, used mostly in measuring the depth of water. ***vt-*** **1** to find the depth of. **2** to get to the bottom of; understand: *I can't* fathom *his meaning*. ***—adj-*** **fath′ om·able.**

Fa·thom·e·ter (fă thŏm′ ə tər, făth′ ə mē′ tər) ***n-*** trademark name for a device that indicates water depth by means of sonar.

fath·om·less (făth′ əm ləs) ***adj-*** **1** too deep to measure. **2** impossible to understand. ***—adv-*** **fath′ om·less·ly.**

fa·tigue (fə tēg′) ***n-*** **1** weariness; tiredness; exhaustion of body or mind: *Poor nutrition can result in* fatigue. **2** (also **fatigue duty**) heavy work, such as digging, assigned to military personnel. **3 fatigues** work clothes, especially a uniform worn by soldiers for heavy work. ***vt-*** **[fa·tigued, fa·ti·guing]** to make tired; weary: *That work* fatigues *him*. ***vi-***: *He* fatigues *quickly*.

fat·ten (făt′ ən) ***vt-*** to make fat. ***vi-*** to become fat.

fat·ty (făt′ ē) ***adj-*** **[fat·ti·er, fat·ti·est]** having much fat; oily; greasy: *too many* fatty *foods*. ***—n-*** **fat′ ti·ness.**

fatty acid ***n-*** any of a group of organic acids of which plant and animal fats are largely composed.

fa·tu·i·ty (fə tōō′ ə tē, fə tyōō′-) ***n-*** [*pl.* **fa·tu·i·ties**] **1** smug silliness. **2** smugly foolish remark or action.

fat·u·ous (făch′ ōō əs) ***adj-*** smugly stupid or silly. ***—adv-*** **fat′ u·ous·ly.** ***n-*** **fat′ u·ous·ness.**

fau·cet (fò′ sət) ***n-*** device for turning on or off the flow of liquids from a pipe or container; tap.

fault (fòlt) ***n-*** **1** a mistake or defect: *a* fault *in grammar*. **2** weakness; shortcoming: *Carelessness is a* fault. **3** blame; responsibility: *The accident was your* fault. **4** in geology, a fracture of the earth's crust along which some movement takes place, causing a displacement of the original rock layers. **5** in tennis, a failure to serve correctly. ***vt-*** to criticize or blame.

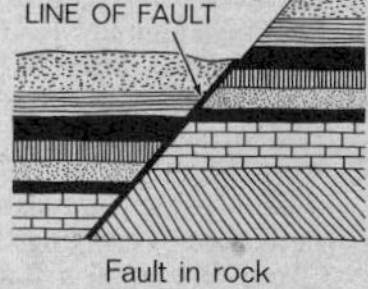

Fault in rock

be at fault to be to blame: *He is not* at fault. **find fault** to be critical or disapproving. **find fault with** to blame or criticize. **to a fault** to an excessive degree.

fault·find·ing (fòlt′ fīn′ dĭng) ***n-*** habit or practice of criticizing or blaming. ***—n-*** **fault′ find′ er.**

fault·less (fòlt′ ləs) ***adj-*** having no faults or defects; flawless; perfect: *a* faultless *performance*. ***—adv-*** **fault′ less·ly.** ***n-*** **fault′ less·ness.**

fault·y (fòl′ tē) ***adj-*** **[fault·i·er, fault·i·est]** having faults; imperfect. ***—adv-*** **fault′ i·ly.** ***n-*** **fault′ i·ness.**

faun (fòn) ***n-*** in Roman mythology, a minor woodland god, often pictured as having a goat's horns and hind legs. ***Hom-*** fawn.

fau·na (fò′ nə) ***n-*** the animals of a particular region, environment, or period of time. See also *flora*.

Fau·nus (fò′ nəs) ***n-*** in Roman mythology, a god of nature and agriculture. He is identified with the Greek Pan.

Faun

Faust (foust) ***n-*** in medieval legend, a philosopher who sold his soul to a devil for wisdom and wordly pleasure.

faux pas (fō pä′) ***n-*** [*pl.* **faux pas** (fō pä′, -päz′)] error or blunder, especially in manners or propriety.

fa·vor (fā′ vər) ***n-*** **1** act of kindness: *Will you do me a* favor? **2** partiality; special consideration: *We haven't asked any* favors. **3** approval: *The singer won the* favor *of the audience.* **4** small gift or souvenir: *a party* favor. ***vt-*** **1** to like; approve: *I* favor *that plan.* **2** to show partiality or give unfair advantage to: *to* favor *one employee over another.* **3** to show consideration for; oblige: *Please* favor *us with a prompt reply.* **4** to make possible or easy: *Good weather* favors *our plans.* **5** *Informal* to look like (a relative): *She* favors *her mother.*
in favor of giving approval or support for. **in (someone's) favor** to (someone's) advantage.

fa·vor·a·ble (fā′ vər ə bəl) ***adj-*** **1** expressing approval: *a* favorable *account of his progress.* **2** helpful; advantageous: *a* favorable *breeze.* **—*n-*** **fa′ vor·a·ble·ness.** ***adv-*** **fa′ vor·a·bly.**

fa·vored (fā′ vərd) ***adj-*** **1** treated or considered with favor: *a* favored *friend.* **2** having a specified appearance: *ill-*favored.

fa·vor·ite (fā′ vər ət) ***adj-*** best liked: *My* favorite *book is "Tom Sawyer."* ***n-*** **1** person given the preference; the one best liked. **2** contestant thought most likely to win.

fa·vor·it·ism (fā′ vər ə tĭz′ əm) ***n-*** unfair preference or partiality.

[1]**fawn** (fȯn) ***n-*** **1** young deer less than a year old. **2** a light tan color. ***adj-*** light tan. [from Old French word **faon** that goes back to Latin **fetus**, "young animal."] ***Hom-*** faun. **—*adj-*** **fawn′ like′.**

Fawn

[2]**fawn** (fȯn) ***vi-*** **1** to show fondness or submission by wagging the tail, whining, etc.: *This dog* fawns *on his master.* **2** to try to win favor by flattery or by cringing: *Some people* fawn *on rich relatives.* [from Old English **fagnian** meaning "to rejoice," from **fægen,** "fain."] ***Hom-*** faun.

fay (fā) ***n-*** a fairy or elf. ***Hom-*** fey.

faze (fāz) *Informal* ***vt-*** [**fazed, faz·ing**] to upset; disconcert. ***Hom-*** phase.

FBI Federal Bureau of Investigation.

FCC or **F.C.C.** Federal Communications Commission.

F clef *Music* ***n-*** bass clef.

Fe symbol for iron.

fe·al·ty (fē′ əl tē) ***n-*** **1** in feudal times, the pledge of a vassal to be faithful to his lord. **2** loyalty; allegiance.

fear (fêr) ***n-*** **1** feeling of fright, alarm, or extreme anxiety; dread; terror: *a* fear *of ghosts*; *to tremble with* fear. **2** awe; reverence: *a* fear *of God.* ***vt-*** **1** to be afraid of; be alarmed by; be frightened by: *Cats* fear *water.* **2** to feel awe toward: *to* fear *God.* ***vi-*** to be afraid.
fear for to be afraid or apprehensive about (someone or something that is threatened): *to* fear for *one's life.*

fear·ful (fêr′ fəl) ***adj-*** **1** causing alarm or fright; awful; terrible: *That was a* fearful *storm.* **2** afraid; apprehensive: *The passengers were* fearful *of an accident.* **—*adv-*** **fear′ ful·ly.** ***n-*** **fear′ ful·ness.**

fear·less (fêr′ ləs) ***adj-*** unafraid; courageous; brave. **—*adv-*** **fear′ less·ly.** ***n-*** **fear′ less·ness.**

fear·some (fêr′ səm) ***adj-*** frightening; alarming; terrifying. **—*adv-*** **fear′ some·ly.** ***n-*** **fear′ some·ness.**

fea·si·ble (fē′ zə bəl) ***adj-*** **1** possible to do or accomplish: *a* feasible *project.* **2** such as can be used or dealt with: *a* feasible *route up a mountain.* **3** reasonable; possible to accept: *a* feasible *explanation.* **—*n-*** **fea′ si·bil′ i·ty.** ***adv-*** **fea′ si·bly.**

feast (fēst) ***n-*** **1** large, elaborate meal. **2** religious festival in memory of a saint or an event: *the* feast *of St. John.* ***vt-*** **1** to honor or entertain with a rich meal: *to* feast *a war hero.* **2** to give pleasure to; delight: *to* feast *one's eyes.* ***vi-*** to eat heartily: *We* feasted *well.*

feat (fēt) ***n-*** deed or action which shows great courage, skill, strength, etc.; exploit: *Climbing that mountain was a remarkable* feat. ***Hom-*** feet.

feath·er (fĕth′ ər) ***n-*** one of the outgrowths on a bird's skin that form its coat and flying equipment. ***vt-*** **1** to provide, cover, or line with one or some of these: *to* feather *the inside of a nest.* **2** to turn (the blade of an oar) parallel with the surface of the water while holding it out of the water. **3** to turn (the blade of an airplane propeller) parallel to the line of flight. **—*adj-*** **feath′ er·less.** ***adj-*** **feath′ er·like′.**

Feather

a feather in (one's) cap an achievement to be proud of. **in fine (good,** or **high) feather** in excellent condition. **feather (one's) nest** to gain wealth or profit.

feather bed ***n-*** mattress filled with feathers, or a bed having such a mattress.

feath·er·bed·ding (fĕth′ ər bĕd′ ĭng) ***n-*** practice of requiring an employer to hire more workers than are actually used, or to accept limits on the production of each worker.

feath·er·brain (fĕth′ ər brān′) *Informal* ***n-*** frivolous or silly person. **—*adj-*** **feath′ er·brained′.**

feather·edge (fĕth′ ər ĕj′) ***n-*** **1** any sharp tapering edge that is easily bent back or broken. **2** the edge on an incorrectly sharpened cutting tool, which is curled back and broken off. **—*adj-*** **feath′ er·edged′.**

feath·er·stitch (fĕth′ ər stĭch′) ***n-*** type of embroidery using a series of short stitches extending alternately to the right and left. ***vt-*** to embroider (something) with this stitch.

feath·er·weight (fĕth′ ər wāt′) ***n-*** **1** boxer or wrestler who weighs more than 118 pounds and less than 127 pounds. **2** very light or unimportant person or thing.

feath·er·y (fĕth′ ə rē) ***adj-*** **1** filled or covered with feathers. **2** resembling light, fine feathers: *soft,* feathery *snowflakes*; *delicate,* feathery *ferns.* **—*n-*** **feath′ er·i·ness.**

fea·ture (fē′ chər) ***n-*** **1** something distinct or noticeable about a thing: *The clock tower is a* feature *of the new building.* **2** chief or special attraction of a performance, exhibit, etc. **3** part of the face: *His nose was his most prominent* feature. ***vt-*** [**fea·tured, fea·tur·ing**] to give special prominence to. **—*adj-*** **fea′ ture·less.**

Feb. February.

Feb·ru·ar·y (fĕb′ ro͞o ĕr ē, *also* fĕb′ yo͞o-) ***n-*** the second month of the year, having 28 days (29 in leap years).

fe·ces (fē′ sēz′) ***n-*** (takes plural verb) solid waste material eliminated from the body; excrement.

feck·less (fĕk′ ləs) ***adj-*** weak and irresponsible.

fe·cund (fē′ kənd, fĕk′ ənd) ***adj-*** fruitful; fertile; productive: *a* fecund *mind.* **—*n-*** **fe·cun′ di·ty** (fə kŭn′ də tē).

fed (fĕd) *p.t. & p.p.* of **feed.**
fed up *Slang* disgusted; bored; wearied.

fed·er·al (fĕd′ ər əl) ***adj-*** of, belonging to, or making up a nation formed by the union of smaller states.

Fed·er·al (fĕd′ ər əl) ***adj-*** **1** of or relating to the government of the United States, as distinguished from that of any individual State. **2** relating to someone favoring the

Union armies during the Civil War. ***n-*** supporter of the Union during the Civil War.

Federal Bureau of Investigation ***n-*** branch of the U.S. Department of Justice charged with investigating violations of Federal laws and presenting evidence concerning them.

fed·er·al·ism (fĕd′ər əl iz′əm) ***n-*** **1** system, principle, or doctrine of federal union. **2** belief in or support of this.

fed·er·a·list (fĕd′ər əl ĭst) ***n-*** **1** person who advocates a union of states into one nation. **2 Federalist** in early U.S. history, a person who urged a federal union of the American colonies and a strong central government. ***adj-***: *a* federalist *policy*; *the* Federalist *Party*.

fed·er·al·ize (fĕd′ər ə līz′) ***vt-*** **[fed·er·al·ized, fed·er·al·iz·ing]** to form into a federal union; federate.

fed·er·ate (fĕd′ə rāt′) ***vt-*** **[fed·er·at·ed, fed·er·at·ing]** to combine (states or societies) into a union.

fed·er·a·tion (fĕd′ə rā′shən) ***n-*** **1** a union by agreement of states or other units, in which the units delegate part or all of their authority to the governing body of the whole. **2** act or process of forming such a union.

fee (fē) ***n-*** **1** charge or payment, as for service by a professional person, or for a right to do something: *a doctor's* fee. **2** fief. **3** (also **fee simple**) land estate inherited or held by a person in his own right.

fee·ble (fē′bəl) ***adj-*** **[fee·bler, fee·blest]** lacking strength or vigor; very weak. ***—n-*** **fee′ble·ness.** ***adv-*** **fee′bly.**

fee·ble-mind·ed (fē′bəl mīn′dəd) ***adj-*** mentally subnormal; having very little power to think or to learn. ***—adv-*** **fee′ble-mind′ed·ly.** ***n-*** **fee′ble-mind′ed·ness.**

feed (fēd) ***vt-*** **[fed** (fĕd), **feed·ing]** **1** to supply food for: *to* feed *the poor.* **2** to give food to; put food into the mouth of: *to* feed *a baby.* **3** to give as food: *to* feed *meat to a dog.* **4** to add to or supply with something: *to* feed *fuel to a fire.* ***vi-*** to take food; eat: *The dogs* fed *hungrily.* ***n-*** **1** food for animals; fodder. **2** *Informal* a meal.

feed on (or **upon**) to draw nourishment from; eat.

feed·back (fēd′băk′) ***n-*** in an electronic device, machine, living organism, etc., process in which a portion of the output is returned to the input in order to control or change the output.

feed·er (fē′dər) ***n-*** **1** person or thing that feeds. **2** device that supplies material to a machine. **3** a branch stream, railway, etc., supplying a main channel or line.

feeder line ***n-*** **1** a conductor or series of conductors that supply electricity to a certain point in a system for distribution to other parts. **2** gas or water main, railway, etc., that supplies a main line.

feel (fēl) ***vt-*** **[felt** (fĕlt), **feel·ing]** **1** to examine by touch: *to* feel *someone's pulse*; *to* feel *a piece of cloth.* **2** to be aware of (something) by touch: *I* felt *the rain on my face.* **3** to have a sense of; be moved or affected by: *to* feel *pity*; *to* feel *an insult.* **4** to be sure of without proof: *I* feel *it to be so.* ***vi-*** **1** to search by touch; grope: *to* feel *for a match.* **2** to be aware of being in some definite condition of mind or body: *to* feel *faint.* **3** to have sympathy: *to* feel *deeply for someone.* **4** to seem to the touch: *The air* feels *damp.* ***n-*** a quality perceived by touch.

feel like **1** *Informal* to have a desire for: *I* feel like *taking a walk.* **2** to seem to the touch: *It* feels like *silk.*

feel out to find out what (someone) thinks about something.

feel up to *Informal* to feel well enough to.

feel·er (fē′lər) ***n-*** **1** part of an animal that gives it information by touch, such as a cat's whisker or an insect's antenna. **2** something said or done to find out the opinions or purposes of others.

feel·ing (fē′lĭng) ***n-*** **1** the sense of touch by which a person tells hot from cold, rough from smooth, etc. **2** sensation: *a* feeling *of pain; a* feeling *of hunger.* **3** emotion: *a* feeling *of anger*; *a* feeling *of joy.* **4** sympathy; pity: *Has he any* feeling *for the suffering of others?* **5** effect made on mind or emotions: *a* feeling *of achievement*; *the* feeling *produced by a poem.* **6** opinion; impression: *What is your* feeling *on this subject?* **7 feelings** sensitive part of one's nature: *It hurt his* feelings.

feel·ing·ly (fē′lĭng lē) ***adv-*** sympathetically.

feet (fēt) *pl.* of **foot.** ***Hom-*** feat.

feign (fān) ***vt-*** to pretend; put on an appearance of: *to* feign *friendship.* ***Homs-*** fain, fane. ***—n-*** **feign′er.**

feint (fānt) ***n-*** a deceptive action, gesture, etc; especially, in boxing, fencing, or combat, a pretense of attacking at one point or place while really intending to attack at another. ***vi-***: *to* feint *with the left hand and strike with the right hand.* ***Hom-*** faint.

feld·spar (fĕld′spär′) ***n-*** crystalline mineral, usually white or pink, found in many common rocks.

fe·lic·i·tate (fə lĭs′ə tāt′) ***vt-*** **[fe·lic·i·tat·ed, fe·lic·i·tat·ing]** to congratulate; wish happiness to. ***—n-*** **fe·lic′i·ta′tion.**

fe·lic·i·tous (fə lĭs′ə təs) ***adj-*** **1** well chosen; apt and graceful: *a* felicitious *phrase.* **2** showing skill, tact, and grace: *a* felicitious *speaker.* ***—adv-*** **fe·lic′i·tous·ly.** ***n-*** **fe·lic′i·tous·ness.**

fe·lic·i·ty (fə lĭs′ə tē) ***n-*** [*pl.* **fe·lic·i·ties]** **1** great happiness. **2** pleasing and appropriate choice of words.

fe·line (fē′līn′) ***adj-*** **1** of or pertaining to the cat family. **2** catlike: *his* feline *grace.* ***n-*** animal of the cat family.

[1]**fell** (fĕl) *p.t.* of **fall.**

[2]**fell** (fĕl) ***vt-*** to cause to fall; shoot, knock, or cut down: *to* fell *a tree.* [from Old English **fellan,** "to cause to fall," from **feallan** "to fall."] ***—n-*** **fell′er.**

[3]**fell** (fĕl) ***adj-*** **[fell·er, fell·est]** **1** cruel and vicious; totally wicked: *a* fell *villain.* **2** *Archaic* deadly. [from Old French **fel,** from **felon** meaning "[1]felon."]

[4]**fell** (fĕl) ***n-*** **1** animal's hide. **2** thin, tough membrane between the skin and muscles of many animals. [from Old English.]

fel·lah (fĕl′ə) ***n-*** [*pl.* **fel·la·hin** (fĕl′ə hēn′), **fel·la·heen]** peasant or agricultural worker in Egypt and other Arab countries.

fel·loe (fĕl′ō) ***n-*** felly. ***Hom-*** fellow.

fel·low (fĕl′ō) ***n-*** **1** man or boy: *a friendly* fellow. **2** companion; associate: *a* fellow *in misfortune.* **3** one of a matched pair. **4** member of a learned society, or the governing body of a college or university. **5** a graduate student who receives an annual sum from a college or university for a stated period of study. *as* ***modifier***: *a* fellow *worker*; fellow *students.* ***Hom-*** felloe.

hail fellow well met having a hearty greeting for everybody.

fellow man ***n-*** a human being like oneself: *esteem for one's* fellow man.

fel·low·ship (fĕl′ō shĭp′) ***n-*** **1** friendliness; companionship: *a feeling of warm* fellowship. **2** group of persons having similar beliefs, interests, or tastes. **3** membership in such a group: *He was admitted into the* fellowship *of the club.* **4** money given to a person by a college or foundation to further his studies or training.

fellow traveler ***n-*** person who sympathizes with and supports the aims of a group or political party, especially the Communist Party, without actually being a member.

fel·ly (fĕl′ ē) ***n-*** [*pl.* **fel·lies**] wooden rim of a wheel, into which the outer ends of the spokes are fitted. Also **felloe.**

[1]**fel·on** (fĕl′ ən) ***n-*** person who has committed a felony; criminal. [from Old French, from Late Latin **fellonis.**]

[2]**fel·on** (fĕl′ ən) ***n-*** red, painful swelling on a finger or toe, near or under the nail. [possibly a special use of [1]**felon.**]

fe·lo·ni·ous (fə lō′ nē əs) ***adj-*** classed as a felony: *a* felonious *assault.* **—*adv-* fe·lo′ ni·ous·ly.**

fel·o·ny (fĕl′ ə nē) ***n-*** [*pl.* **fel·on·ies**] major crime, such as murder and burglary, for which the law provides a greater punishment than for a misdemeanor.

[1]**felt** (fĕlt) *p.t.* of **feel.**

[2]**felt** (fĕlt) ***n-*** a kind of cloth made of wool, hair, or fur pressed together instead of woven. ***adj-*** made of this material: *a* felt *hat.* ***vt-*** **1** to mat or press into this kind of cloth. **2** to cover with this kind of cloth. [from Old English.]

felt·ing (fĕl′ tĭng) ***n-*** **1** process by which felt is made. **2** material used to make felt, or the cloth itself.

fem. feminine.

fe·male (fē′ māl′) ***n-*** **1** a living thing, especially a woman or girl, of the sex that bears offspring. ***adj-*** **1** of or belonging to the sex that produces young. **2** of or having to do with a plant whose flowers have only pistils; pistillate. **3** in mechanics, having to do with a hollow fitting, plug, etc., threaded or bored to receive a corresponding part within it.

fem·i·nine (fĕm′ ə nĭn) ***adj-*** **1** of, relating to, typical of, or suitable for females: *a* feminine *fashion*; *a* feminine *voice.* **2** having the characteristics of a woman: *her* feminine *ways.* **3** *Grammar* belonging to a class of words that in English name people, animals, or things that are or are considered female, and in other languages name or describe many words without regard to female characteristics. **—*adv-* fem′ i·nine·ly.**

fem·i·nin·i·ty (fĕm′ ə nĭn′ ə tē) ***n-*** womanly or girlish characteristics, behavior, etc.

fem·i·nism (fĕm′ ə nĭz′ əm) ***n-*** **1** belief that men and women are intellectually and socially equal and that women should be given all the privileges, advantages, and opportunities enjoyed by men. **2** organized activity based on this principle.

fem·i·nist (fĕm′ ə nĭst) ***n-*** a believer in feminism, especially one who works for women's rights.

femme fa·tale (făm′ fă tăl′) *French* woman who charms men and lures them into danger.

fe·mur (fē′ mər) ***n-*** long bone of the leg, connecting the hip and knee; thighbone.

fen (fĕn) ***n-*** low, marshy land.

fence (fĕns) ***n-*** **1** barrier of stone, wood, wire, etc., constructed around or along a piece of land. **2** a receiver of stolen goods. ***vt-*** [**fenced, fenc·ing**] to enclose with a barrier. ***vi-*** to fight with swords or foils as a sport; also, to thrust and parry with words. **—*n-* fen′ cer.**

on the fence undecided; neutral.

fence in to surround or confine with or as if with a fence.

fence off to separate (from something) with a fence.

fenc·ing (fĕn′ sĭng) ***n-*** **1** the art or sport of fighting with swords. **2** material for a fence.

fend (fĕnd) ***vt-*** to push away from; protect against impact; repel (usually followed by "off"): *to* fend *off branches from one's face.*

Men fencing

fend·er (fĕn′ dər) ***n-*** **1** protective piece of metal over the wheel of an automobile, bicycle, etc. **2** metal guard in front of an open fireplace. **3** device on the front of a locomotive or streetcar to catch or push aside anything hit.

fen·es·tra·tion (fĕn′ ə strā′ shən) ***n-*** **1** the arrangement of the windows and doors in a building, especially in respect to design. **2** an opening, such as in a surface. **3** *Medicine* act or operation of forming an opening in bone, tissue, etc., especially in treating deafness.

fen·nel (fĕn′ əl) ***n-*** plant with a sweetish flavor and odor, having leaves and stalks eaten as a salad or vegetable, and aromatic seeds used as flavoring.

F.E.P.C. ***adj-*** of or relating to fair employment practices as outlined by the federal Committee on Fair Employment Practices (1941-46).

fe·ral (fêr′ əl, fĕr′ -) ***adj-*** like a wild beast; untamed; undomesticated. ***Homs-*** ferrule, ferule.

fer-de-lance (fĕr′ də lăns′) ***n-*** large and poisonous brown and gray snake, inhabiting Central and South America. The fer-de-lance is a pit viper.

[1]**fer·ment** (fûr mĕnt′) ***vi-*** to go through a chemical change because of the action of tiny living plants such as yeasts, certain bacteria, etc. ***vt-*:** **1** to cause to undergo this change: *The bacteria* fermented *the milk.* **2** to stir up; agitate.

[2]**fer·ment** (fûr′ mĕnt′) ***n-*** **1** substance containing yeasts, molds, bacteria, etc., that cause fermentation. **2** state of unrest, agitation, or excitement: *The whole nation was in a* ferment *over the election.*

fer·men·ta·tion (fûr′ mĕn tā′ shən) ***n-*** **1** the chemical changing of organic substances through the action of enzymes produced by certain yeasts and bacteria, especially through the action of yeasts on fruit sugar to produce alcohol. **2** process of causing or undergoing this change.

fer·mi·um (fĕr′ mē əm) ***n-*** man-made, radioactive, metal element. Symbol Fm, At. No. 100.

Fern frond

fern (fûrn) ***n-*** any of a large group of plants that have featherlike or leafy fronds and do not produce flowers or seeds. **—*adj-* fern′ like′.** ***adj-*** **fern′ y [fern·i·er, fern·i·est]:** *a* ferny *glade.*

fe·ro·cious (fə rō′ shəs) ***adj-*** fierce; savage: *a* ferocious *lion*; *a* ferocious *attack.* **—*adv-* fe·ro′ cious·ly.** ***n-*** **fe·ro′ cios·ness.**

fe·roc·i·ty (fə rŏs′ ə tē) ***n-*** [*pl.* **fe·roc·i·ties**] fierceness; savage cruelty: *The wolves attacked with* ferocity.

fer·ret (fĕr′ ət) ***n-*** a fierce, slender weasel with a long body, sometimes used to destroy rats and mice or to hunt rabbits. ***vt-*** (usually followed by "out") to hunt down; search perseveringly for: *We* ferreted *out the criminals.* **—*n-* fer′ ret·er.**

Ferret, about 18 in. long

fer·ric (fĕr′ ĭk) *Chemistry* ***adj-*** **1** of, having to do with, or containing iron. **2** naming or pertaining to an iron compound in which iron has its higher valence.

Fer·ris wheel (fĕr′ əs) ***n-*** an amusement park attraction consisting of a huge wheel with passenger cars hanging freely on rods between twin rims.

ferro- *combining form* **1** of, having to do with, or combined with iron: *a* ferro*alloy.* **2** containing iron in its lower valence, or ferrous, state of iron: ferro*maganese.* [from modern Latin **ferro-**, from Latin **ferrum,** "iron."]

fer·ro·mag·net·ic (fĕr′ ō măg nĕt′ ĭk) ***adj-*** functioning like iron in a magnetic field: *Cobalt is* ferromagnetic.

fer·rous (fĕr′ əs) *Chemistry* ***adj-*** **1** of, having to do with, or containing iron. **2** naming or pertaining to an iron compound in which iron has its lower valence.

fer·rule (fĕr′ əl) ***n-*** metal ring or cap placed around the end of a stick, tool handle, etc., to strengthen it or to join it to something else. ***Homs-*** feral, ferule.

fer·ry (fĕr′ ē) ***n-*** [*pl.* **fer·ries**] **1** (also **fer′ry·boat**) boat that carries passengers, and usually vehicles, across a narrow body of water. **2** place where this is done. ***vt-*** [**fer·ried, fer·ry·ing**] **1** to carry on such a boat: *to* ferry *troops across the river.* **2** to deliver (aircraft) by flying to a particular destination. ***vi-***: *We* ferried *over to the island.* **—*n-* fer′ry·man.**

fer·tile (fûr′ təl) ***adj-*** **1** producing abundantly; causing productiveness: *our* fertile *land.* **2** able to bear seeds, fruit, or young: *a* fertile *plant.* **3** able to grow into a plant or animal: *a* fertile *seed*; *a* fertile *egg.* **—*n-* fer·til′ i·ty** (fər tĭl′ ə tē).

Fertile Crescent

Fertile Crescent ***n-*** arc-shaped fertile area on the eastern shore of the Mediterranean, where farming was supposedly first carried on.

fer·ti·lize (fûr′ tə līz′) ***vt-*** [**fer·ti·lized, fer·ti·liz·ing**] **1** to add substances to (soil) to make it richer and more productive. **2** to give (an egg cell) the ability to grow by combining it with a male cell. **—*n-* fer′ ti·li·za′ tion** (fûr′ tə lə zā′ shən).

fer·ti·liz·er (fûr′ tə lī′ zər) ***n-*** material, such as a chemical or manure, used to make soil more productive.

fer·ule (fĕr′ əl) ***n-*** a rod or flat stick, formerly used to punish children in school. ***Homs-*** feral, ferrule.

fer·vent (fûr′ vənt) ***adj-*** strong or warm in feeling; intense; earnest. **—*n-* fer′ ven·cy. *adv-* fer′ vent·ly.**

fer·vid (fûr′ vĭd) ***adj-*** fiery in feeling; earnest; impassioned: *a* fervid *loyalty*; fervid *oratory.* **—*adv-* fer′ vid·ly. *n-* fer′ vid·ness.**

fer·vor (fûr′ vər) ***n-*** warmth and earnestness of feeling.

-fest *combining form Slang* occasion when a type of activity is performed: *sing*fest; *talk*fest. [probably from German **Fest** meaning "a feast; fete."]

fes·tal (fĕs′ təl) ***adj-*** of or relating to a feast, holiday, or festival. **—*adv-* fes′ tal·ly.**

fes·ter (fĕs′ tər) ***vi-*** **1** to form or become filled with pus: *The wound* festered. **2** to linger painfully; cause a sore feeling; rankle: *The insult* festered *in his mind.*

fes·ti·val (fĕs′ tə vəl) ***n-*** **1** time of rejoicing and feasting, usually in memory of some special event. **2** periodic entertainment or cultural activity: *a music* festival.

Festival of Lights ***n-*** Hanukkah.

fes·tive (fĕs′ tĭv) ***adj-*** of or having to do with a feast or festival; gay; joyous; merry: *a* festive *occasion*; *a* festive *scene.* **—*adv-* fes′ tive·ly.**

fes·tiv·i·ty (fĕs tĭv′ ə tē) ***n-*** [*pl.* **fes·tiv·i·ties**] merry-making; rejoicing; celebration.

Festoon

fes·toon (fĕs to͞on′) ***n-*** decorative chain, rope, garland, etc., often of leaves or flowers draped in curves; also, a sculptured copy of such a decoration. ***vt-*** to decorate with such ornaments: *Workmen* festooned *City Hall.*

fe·tal (fē′ təl) ***adj-*** of or relating to a fetus.

fetch (fĕch) ***vt-*** **1** to go after and bring; go and get: *Please* fetch *me the book from my desk.* **2** to sell for.

fetch·ing (fĕch′ ĭng) ***adj-*** charming; pretty; attractive: *What a* fetching *hat!* **—*adv-* fetch′ ing·ly.**

fete (fāt) ***n-*** festival; celebration. ***vt-*** [**fet·ed, fet·ing**] to entertain or honor with a celebration: *He was* feted *in every town that he visited.* Also **fête. *Hom-*** fate.

fet·id (fĕt′ ĭd) ***adj-*** having or giving forth a very bad odor; stinking. **—*adv-* fet′ id·ly. *n-* fet′ id·ness.**

fe·tish (fĕt′ ĭsh) ***n-*** **1** any object, such as a wooden image, supposed to have magic power. **2** anything to which one is unreasonably devoted: *Money is a miser's* fetish.

fet·ish·ism (fĕt′ ĭsh ĭz′ əm) ***n-*** **1** the practice of attaching magical powers to objects, or of worshiping them. **2** unreasonable devotion to something. **—*n-* fet′ ish·ist.**

fet·lock (fĕt′ lŏk′) ***n-*** a projection on a horse's leg just above and behind the hoof; also, a tuft of hair growing on this projection.

fet·ter (fĕt′ ər) ***n-*** **1** chain to bind the feet so as to prevent freedom of motion. **2** anything that limits, checks, or holds back. ***vt-*** **1** to chain the feet of. **2** to restrain.

fet·tle (fĕt′ əl) ***n-*** working or performing condition: *The athlete is in fine* fettle.

fe·tus or **foe·tus** (fē′ təs) ***n-*** the stage of an unborn mammal in which the major body features have appeared. The human embryo is a fetus from about the eighth week of pregnancy until birth.

[1]feud (fyo͞od) ***n-*** bitter quarrel or hatred which has gone on for a long time, especially between families or clans. ***vi-*** to carry on such a quarrel or hatred. [from Middle English **fede,** from Old French **fe(i)de,** "hostility."]

[2]feud (fyo͞od) ***n-*** a fief. [from Medieval Latin **feudum,** from a Germanic word related to English **fee.**]

feu·dal (fyo͞o′ dəl) ***adj-*** of or having to do with feudalism.

feu·dal·ism (fyo͞o′ də lĭz′ əm) ***n-*** the social, political, and economic system in Europe during the Middle Ages. Under this system a vassal had to perform military and other services for the lord from whom he held the fief. Also **feudal system. —*adj-* feu′ dal·is′ tic.**

feu·da·tor·y (fyo͞o′ də tôr′ ē) ***n-*** [*pl.* **feu·da·tor·ies**] a vassal. ***adj-*** owing feudal service to an overlord.

fe·ver (fē′ vər) ***n-*** **1** condition in which the body temperature is higher than normal, usually accompanied by rapid pulse, weakness, etc. **2** any of various diseases having this condition as a symptom: *typhoid* fever. **3** state of intense activity or nervous excitement: *a* fever *of anxiety. as* ***modifier***: *a* fever *chart.* **—*adj-* fe′ vered.**

fever blister or **fever sore** ***n-*** blister on or near the mouth, often accompanying a cold or fever.

fe·ver·ish (fē′ vər ĭsh) ***adj-*** **1** having a fever: *He was* feverish *from his cold.* **2** caused by a fever: *wild,* feverish *dreams.* **3** excited; restless: *in* feverish *haste.* **—*adv-* fe′ ver·ish·ly. *n-* fe′ ver·ish·ness.**

few (fyo͞o) ***determiner*** (traditionally called adjective or pronoun) a small number of; not many: *There are* few *people here. Many are called but* few *are chosen.* ***n-*** **1** a small number only; small minority: *In that village,* few *of the houses are white.* **2 the few** the minority: *He is among* the few.

a few a small, indefinite number: *I saw* a few *people today.* **quite a few** more than a small number.

few·er (fyo͞o′ ər) ***determiner*** (traditionally called adjective or pronoun) a smaller number of; not so many: *I see* fewer *stars now. More tried, but* fewer *succeeded.* ***n-*** a smaller number: *I see that* fewer *of my friends have had colds this year than last.*

►For usage note see LESS.

few·est (fyo͞o′ əst) ***determiner*** (traditionally called adjective) the smallest number of: *Of the whole team, he had the* fewest *hits.*

---

fāte, făt, dâre, bärn; bē, bĕt, mêre; bīte, bĭt; nōte, hŏt, môre, dȯg; fŭn, fûr; to͞o, bo͝ok; oil; out; tar; thin; then; hw for wh as in *wh*at; zh for s as in u*s*ual; ə for a, e, i, o, u, as in *a*go, lin*e*n, per*i*l, at*o*m, min*u*s

fey (fā) ***adj-*** strange, elfin, and unearthly in appearance or manner: *a fey sense of humor.* ***Hom-*** fay.

fez (fĕz) ***n-*** [*pl.* **fez·zes**] high, red cap with a tassel, originally worn by men in the Middle East.

Fez

ff fortissimo.

ff. 1 following (pages, paragraphs, etc.). 2 folios.

FHA Federal Housing Administration.

fi·an·cé (fē′än sā′) ***n-*** a man engaged to be married. ***—n-*** *fem.* **fi′an·cée′.**

fi·as·co (fē ăs′ kō) ***n-*** [*pl.* **fi·as·cos** or **fi·as·coes**] complete failure, especially one ending in laughter or contempt.

fi·at (fī′ ət) ***n-*** **1** an official command or decree: *a royal* fiat. **2** authorization; sanction.

fib (fĭb) ***n-*** a lie, especially about something unimportant. ***vi-*** [**fibbed, fib·bing**] to tell such a lie. ***—n-*** **fib′ber.**

fi·ber (fī′ bər) ***n-*** **1** one of many thin threadlike strands that form certain plant and animal substances: *muscle* fibers; *wood* fibers. **2** substance containing such strands: *wool* fiber; *hemp* fiber. **3** nature; quality: *moral* fiber.

fi·ber·board (fī′ bər bôrd′) ***n-*** a tough, somewhat pliable building material made of compressed wood or other plant fibers and rolled into flat sheets.

Fi·ber·glas (fī′ bər glăs′) ***n-*** trademark name for very fine, strong filaments of glass that are used to make textile materials, reinforced plastics, insulation, etc.; spun glass. Also **Fi′ber·glass′, fi′ber·glass′.**

fi·bril (fī′ brəl) ***n-*** small, slender fiber, especially one of the fine hairs on the roots of some plants.

fi·bril·la·tion (fĭb′ rə lā′ shən) ***n-*** rapid, spasmodic contraction of the heart muscles, resulting in a weak and irregular heartbeat.

fi·brin (fī′ brən) ***n-*** white, threadlike, insoluble substance that forms when blood clots.

fi·brin·o·gen (fī brĭn′ ə jən) ***n-*** either of two proteins involved in the clotting of blood, especially the soluble protein in the blood plasma.

fi·brous (fī′ brəs) ***adj-*** having, made of, or resembling fibers: *the* fibrous *trunk of a coconut palm.*

fib·u·la (fĭb′ yə lə) ***n-*** the outer, smaller bone of the leg between the knee and the ankle.

-fication *suffix* (used to form nouns from, or corresponding to, verbs ending in -fy) act or process of (the meaning of the verb); also, the result: *electrify, electri*fication; *beautify, beauti*fication.

fick·le (fĭk′ əl) ***adj-*** uncertain; changeable; unsteady: *He is too* fickle *to be relied upon.* ***—n-*** **fick′le·ness.**

fic·tion (fĭk′ shən) ***n-*** **1** literary works, such as novels and short stories, which tell of imaginary events and characters. **2** anything made up or imagined; hence, not fact: *His excuse was pure* fiction. ***—adj-*** **fic′tion·al.**

fic·tion·al·ize (fĭk′ shən əl īz′) ***vt-*** [**fic·tion·al·ized, fic·tion·al·iz·ing**] to make into fiction: *to* fictionalize *history in a novel.* ***—n-*** **fic′tion·al·i·za′tion.**

fic·ti·tious (fĭk tĭsh′ əs) ***adj-*** **1** imagined; not real: *a* fictitious *character.* **2** made up in order to deceive; false. ***—adv-*** **fic·ti′tious·ly.** ***n-*** **fic·ti′tious·ness.**

fid·dle (fĭd′ əl) *Informal* ***n-*** violin. ***vi-*** [**fid·dled, fid·dling**] **1** to play or tinker (with something) idly or without skill: *Please stop* fiddling *with the dial.* **2** to play the fiddle. ***—n-*** **fid′dler.**

Fiddler crab

fiddler crab ***n-*** small burrowing crab of Atlantic coastal waters. The male has an enlarged claw.

fid·dle·sticks (fĭd′ əl stĭks′) ***interj-*** nonsense! rubbish!

fi·del·i·ty (fə dĕl′ ə tē) ***n-*** [*pl.* **fi·del·i·ties**] **1** faithfulness; trustworthiness. **2** accuracy; exactness: *to report the news with* fidelity. **3** ability of a phonograph or similar device to reproduce sound without distortion.

fid·get (fĭj′ ət) ***vi-*** to move about restlessly; make nervous movements; be uneasy. ***n-*** **the fidgets** restlessness; uneasiness. ***—adj-*** **fidg′et·y.**

fi·du·ci·ar·y (fĭ do͞o′ shē ĕr′ ē, fə dyo͞o′-) ***n-*** [*pl.* **fi·du·ci·ar·ies**] person appointed to manage property for another; trustee. ***adj-*** **1** of or relating to a trust: *a* fiduciary *agent.* **2** depending on public confidence for its value: *Paper money is* fiduciary *currency.*

fie (fī) ***interj-*** for shame; shame: *Oh,* fie *on you!*

fief (fēf) ***n-*** in the feudal system, land held by a vassal in return for service to an overlord; fee; feud.

field (fēld) ***n-*** **1** piece of open land used for planting, pasture, etc.: *a corn*field. **2** land yielding some product: *an oil* field. **3** piece of land which has a special use: *a football* field. **4** an open space: *a* field *of snow.* **5** place of military operations or battle: *headquarters in the* field; *battle*field. **6** area or sphere of special interest or activity: *the* field *of medicine.* **7** background against which something is seen: *a flag with stars on a* field *of blue.* **8** participants in a contest or sport: *to be sixth in a* field *of nine.* **9** area of work away from a central office or headquarters: *We now have six salesmen in the* field. **10** area that can be seen, especially through a microscope, telescope, etc. **11** *Physics* (1) region in which a force acts on an object that is brought into the region: *an electric* field; *a magnetic* field. (2) the force itself that acts at any particular point in the region. ***as modifier:*** *a* field *hospital.* ***vt-*** **1** in baseball, to catch and properly dispose of (the ball, a fly, a grounder, etc.). **2** to enter (a team, players, etc.) in an athletic event. ***vi-*** in baseball, to play as an infielder or outfielder.

take the field to go on the field for a game, battle etc.
sweep the field to win in all events or contests.

field artillery ***n-*** readily movable artillery used by troops in the field against enemy troops, buildings, etc.

field day ***n-*** **1** day devoted to outdoor sports, competitions, etc., among the members of a group: *the firemens'* field day. **2** *Informal* any exciting occasion, especially one marked by enjoyment or easy success.

field·er (fēl′ dər) ***n-*** in baseball, an infielder or outfielder.

field glass ***n-*** **1** small telescope for use in the field. **2 field glasses** binoculars for outdoor use.

field goal ***n-*** **1** in football, a goal counting three points, usually made by a place kick that puts the ball over the crossbar between the uprights of the goal post in regular play. **2** in basketball, a goal scored while the ball is in play, counting two points.

field gun ***n-*** cannon mounted on a wheeled carriage for use in the field; fieldpiece.

field hospital ***n-*** temporary military hospital near a combat zone.

field house ***n-*** building on an athletic field, with lockers, showers, etc., for the players.

field magnet ***n-*** magnet used to produce a magnetic field in an electric motor or generator, a cyclotron, etc.

field marshal ***n-*** in certain armies, an officer next below the commander in chief.

field mouse ***n-*** mouse that lives in fields and meadows, either habitually or only during the warm season.

field·piece (fēld′ pēs′) ***n-*** field gun.

field trip ***n-*** trip away from the classroom for observation and investigation.

field winding ***n-*** winding of the field magnet in an electric generator or motor.

field work ***n-*** work done away from a central office, laboratory, factory, etc.

fiend (fēnd) ***n-*** **1** devil; demon; evil spirit; also, any extremely wicked or cruel person. **2** *Informal* addict: *a* bridge *fiend.* **3 the Fiend** the Devil. **—*adj-* fiend′like′.**

fiend·ish (fēn′dĭsh) ***adj-*** devilish; savage; cruel: *a* fiendish *crime.* **—*adv-* fiend′ish·ly. *n-* fiend′ish·ness.**

fierce (fêrs) ***adj-*** **[fierc·er, fierc·est]** furiously violent and intense: *a* fierce *fighter*; fierce *resistance.* **2** savage: *a* fierce *animal.* **—*adv-* fierce′ly. *n-* fierce′ness.**

fi·er·y (fī′ə rē) ***adj-*** **[fi·er·i·er, fi er·i·est]** **1** flaming; burning. **2** resembling a fire: *a* fiery *sunset.* **3** spirited; passionate; ardent: *a* fiery *speech.* **4** easily aroused: *a* fiery *temper.* **—*n-* fi′er·i·ness.**

fi·es·ta (fē ĕs′tə) ***n-*** festival, especially a saint's day as celebrated in Spain or Latin America with parades and music.

fife (fīf) ***n-*** small, shrill-toned musical instrument resembling the flute. ***vt-*** **[fifed, fif·ing]** to play on a fife: *He* fifed *a tune.* ***vi-:*** *He* fifed *happily.* **—*n-* fif′er.**

Fife

fif·teen (fĭf′tēn′) ***n-*** **1** amount or quantity that is one greater than 14. **2** *Mathematics* (1) the cardinal number that is the sum of 14 and 1. (2) a numeral such as 15 that represents this cardinal number. *as* ***determiner*** (traditionally called adjective or pronoun): *There are* fifteen *girls here and* fifteen *there.*

fif·teenth (fĭf′tēnth′) ***adj-*** **1** next after fourteenth. **2** the ordinal of 15; 15th. ***n-*** **1** the next after the fourteenth; 15th. **2** one of fifteen equal parts of a whole or group. **3** the last term in the name of a fraction having a denominator of 15: *1/15 is one* fifteenth. ***adv-:*** *Tim finished* fifteenth *in the swimming race.*

fifth (fĭfth) ***adj-*** **1** next after fourth. **2** the ordinal of 5; 5th. ***n-*** **1** the next after the fourth; 5th. **2** one of five equal parts of a whole or group. **3** the last term in the name of a common fraction having a denominator of 5: *1/5 is one* fifth. **4** *Music* an interval of five tones on the scale counting the extremes, as from A to E in the tuning of a violin, and the harmonic combination of these tones. **5** a quantity of alcoholic liquor equal to one-fifth of a gallon or four-fifths of a quart; also the bottle holding this much. ***adv-:*** *He spoke of you* fifth.

fifth column ***n-*** in wartime, civilians within a country who secretly aid its enemies. **—*n-* fifth columnist.**

fifth·ly (fĭfth′lē) ***adv-*** as fifth in a series.

fifth wheel ***n-*** **1** an extra, superfluous wheel for a four-wheeled vehicle. **2** *Informal* superfluous thing or person.

fif·ti·eth (fĭf′tē əth) ***adj-*** **1** next after forty-ninth. **2** the ordinal of 50; 50th. ***n-*** **1** the next after the forty-ninth; 50th. **2** one of fifty equal parts of a whole or group. **3** the last term in the name of a fraction having a denominator of 50: *1/50 is one* fiftieth. ***adv-:*** *He stood* fiftieth *in his class.*

fif·ty (fĭf′tē) ***n-*** [*pl.* **fif·ties**] **1** amount or quantity that is one greater than 49. **2** *Mathematics* (1) the cardinal number that is the sum of 49 and 1. (2) a numeral such as 50 that represents this cardinal number. *as* ***determiner*** (traditionally called adjective or pronoun): *There are* fifty *rabbits here and* fifty *there.*

fif·ty-fif·ty (fĭf′tē fĭf′tē) *Informal* ***adj-*** **1** as likely to go one way as another; even: *to have a* fifty-fifty *chance of success.* **2** half-and-half; equal: *a* fifty-fifty *division of profits.* ***adv-*** equally: *Let's share it* fifty-fifty.

fig (fĭg) ***n-*** **1** sweet, pear-shaped fruit with many seeds, usually eaten dried or preserved. **2** tree wich bears this fruit. **3** something of no value; farthing: *I don't care a* fig *for your ideas.*

Fig

fig. figure.

fight (fīt) ***n-*** **1** a struggle with fists or weapons: *The quarrel led to a* fight. **2** any struggle: *the* fight *against disease*; *the* fight *for freedom.* **3** the will and ability to struggle: *The raccoon was full of* fight *when caught.* ***vi-*** **[fought** (fôt), **fight·ing]** **1** to take part in a struggle: *He* fought *long and hard.* **2** to strive against difficulties or opponents: *to* fight *for a goal.* ***vt-*** **1** to struggle against; make war on; combat: *to* fight *the enemy.* **2** to engage in (a battle, conflict, duel, etc.): *to* fight *a battle.*

fight off to defend oneself successfully against.

fight shy of to avoid.

fight·er (fī′tər) ***n-*** **1** person who engages in physical conflict with another. **2** person who struggles or battles for a cause: *Abigail Adams was a* fighter *for liberty.* **3** professional boxer. **4** (also **fighter plane**) fast, maneuverable aircraft used mainly to attack enemy planes.

fig·ment (fĭg′mənt) ***n-*** something merely imagined; fiction: *Ghosts are a* figment *of the imagination.*

fig·ur·a·tive (fĭg′yər ə tĭv) ***adj-*** **1** using figures of speech: *a* figurative *style of writing.* **2** metaphorical; not literal: *a figurative* meaning *of a word.* **3** showing by a recognizable figure; emblematic; representational: *Much drawing is not* figurative, *but abstract.* **—*adv-* fig′ur·a·tive·ly. *n-* fig′ur·a·tive·ness.**

fig·ure (fĭg′yər) ***n-*** **1** shape; outline: *a* figure *in the darkness*; *a slim* figure. **2** person as he appears to others: a *pitiful* figure. **3** a likeness of something, especially one that is molded or carved: *a* figure *of Lincoln on a coin.* **4** an illustrative drawing: *The note refers to* Figure *6.* **5** a design or pattern, as in fabrics. **6** pattern made by movement in skating or dancing. **7** figure of speech. **8** symbol for a number: *to write letters and* figures. **9** price: *to buy at a low* figure. **10** *Mathematics* (1) flat surface bounded by lines (plane figure). (2) space bounded by lines (solid figure). **11 figures** arithmetic; use of numbers: *Are you good at* figures? ***vi-*** **[fig·ured, fig·ur·ing]** **1** to appear or play a part (in) something: *Her name* figures *in the news.* **2** to make calculations: *I don't just guess, I* figure. ***vt-*** *Informal* to calculate; reason: *He* figured *that it was time to leave.*

figure on to take into consideration or account.

figure out to understand by reasoning or calculating.

fig·ured (fĭg′yərd) ***adj-*** **1** having a design or pattern; not plain: *a* figured *silk.* **2** *Music* richly ornamented; florid.

Ship's figurehead

fig·ure·head (fĭg′yər hĕd′) ***n-*** **1** person in a position of authority who has no real power: *Most European kings are* figureheads. **2** ornamental statue or carving on a ship's bow.

figure of speech ***n-*** one or more words used in an unexpected and imaginative way to increase the force and meaning of an expression. Metaphors and similes are figures of speech.

fig·u·rine (fĭg′ yə rēn′) ***n-*** small statue.

fil·a·ment (fĭl′ ə mənt) ***n-* 1** hairlike strand of material; very slender, delicate fiber. **2** fine wire in an electric bulb, electron tube, etc. **3** slender stem of a flower stamen.

Filament
1 of thread
2 of stamen

fil·a·ri·a·sis (fĭl′ə rī′ə səs) ***n-*** disease caused by the blockage of the lymph vessels by roundworms, which enormously enlarges and thickens the feet, legs, etc.; elephantiasis.

fil·bert (fĭl′ bərt) ***n-*** sweet, edible nut of the hazel tree.

filch (fĭlch) ***vt-*** to steal, especially something of small value; pilfer. **—*n-* filch′ er.**

[1]**file** (fīl) ***n-*** tool, usually of metal, with raised teeth or sharp ridges on its surface and used for smoothing, cutting, shaping, etc. ***vt-*** **[filed, fil·ing]** to use such a tool on: *to* file *one's nails.* ***vi-*:** *He* filed *through iron.* [from Old English **fīl.**] ***Hom-*** faille.

File

[2]**file** (fīl) ***n-* 1** case, drawer, or folder in which papers are kept in order. **2** papers arranged in order. **3** row of people or objects one behind the other: *The soldiers marched in double* file. ***vt-*** **[filed, fil·ing] 1** to arrange (papers, letters, etc.) in order, especially in a case. **2** to hand in for consideration or record: *to* file *an application.* ***vi-*** to march in line, one behind the other: *They* filed *out.* [from French **fil,** from Latin **filum,** "thread."] ***Hom-*** faille.

Card file

on file recorded: *We have his report* on file.

file clerk ***n-*** person who files papers, letters, etc., in an office, and finds them when they are wanted.

fi·let (fĭ lā′, fĭl′ ā) ***n-* 1** slice of meat or fish without bone; fillet: *a* filet *of sole.* **2** net lace with a square mesh. ***vt-*** (also **fillet**) **[fi·leted** (fĭ lād′, fĭl′ ād), **fi·let·ing** (fĭ lā′ ĭng, fĭl′ ā ĭng)**]** to cut or draw the bones from.

filet mi·gnon (mēn′yōⁿ′) ***n-*** [*pl.* **fi·lets mi·gnons** (fĭ lā′ mēn′ yōⁿ′)] round, boneless cut of meat from the thick end of a beef tenderloin. [from French, meaning literally "good little cut."]

fil·i·al (fĭl′ ē əl) ***adj-*** due to a parent from a child: *his* filial *love*; filial *respect.* **—*adv-* fil′ i·al·ly.**

fil·i·bus·ter (fĭl′ ə bŭs′ tər) ***n-* 1** attempt to defeat a bill on the floor of a legislature by using the privilege of debate to give long and irrelevant speeches until the bill is dropped in fatigue and desperation. **2** adventurer who lawlessly invades a foreign country and attempts to stir up a revolution. ***vi-* 1** to give long and irrelevant speeches in a legislature in order to cause a bill to be dropped. **2** to invade a foreign country and attempt to stir up a revolution. ***vt-*:** *The opposition* filibustered *the money bill for two weeks.* **—*n-* fil′ i·bus′ ter·er.**

fil·i·gree (fĭl′ ə grē′) ***n-*** ornamental lacelike work in gold or silver wire; also, any delicate tracery: *The frost made a beautiful* filigree *on the trees.* ***as modifier*:** *a* filigree *pin.* ***vt-*** **[fil·i·greed, fili·gree·ing]** to decorate with such work.

Filigree earring

fil·ing (fī′ lĭng) ***n-*** small fragment rubbed off by a file.

Fil·i·pi·no (fĭl′ ə pē′ nō) ***n-*** [*pl.* **Fil·i·pi·nos**] a native of the Philippine Islands, or his descendants. ***adj-*:** *a* Filipino *custom.*

fill (fĭl) ***vt-* 1** to make full: *to* fill *a glass.* **2** to stop up holes or openings of: *to* fill *teeth.* **3** to supply fully: *to* fill *a person's needs.* **4** to supply what is needed: *to* fill *an order.* **5** to perform the duties or requirements of: *He* fills *the position of president.* **6** to take up all the space in: *The crowd* filled *the room.* **7** to spread throughout: *Music* filled *the air.* ***vi-*** to become full: *Her eyes* filled *with tears.* ***n-* 1** enough to satisfy: *I ate my* fill. **2** stone, gravel, etc., used to build up low ground.

fill in 1 to put in missing or additional details. **2** to be a substitute: *The singer* filled in *for her friend.*

fill out 1 to grow larger. **2** to complete by inserting something in: *to* fill out *an application.*

fill the bill *Informal* to meet requirements.

fill·er (fĭl′ ər) ***n-* 1** person or thing that fills. **2** thing or substance used to fill a space, cavity, etc. **3** preparation put on wood before painting it.

fil·let (fĭl′ ət) ***n-* 1** ribbon or band worn around the head. **2** narrow band or strip of any material. **3** (also **filet**) slice of meat or fish without bone. ***vt-* 1** to bind or decorate with a narrow band, strip, etc. **2** to filet.

fill·ing (fĭl′ ĭng) ***n-* 1** material used to fill something: *a pie* filling. **2** a making full. **3** material put into a tooth to fill a cavity.

filling station ***n-*** place where gasoline, and often other supplies or services, are provided for vehicles.

fil·lip (fĭl′ əp) ***n-* 1** sharp tap or snap with a fingertip. **2** a slight, sharp stimulus that excites or arouses.

fil·ly (fĭl′ ē) ***n-*** [*pl.* **fil·lies**] young female horse.

film (fĭlm) ***n-* 1** thin layer or coating: *a* film *of oil on water.* **2** haze; blur: *a* film *of mist.* **3** thin sheet or roll of transparent and flexible material coated with an emulsion sensitive to light and used for making photographs. **4** motion picture. ***vt-* 1** to cover with a thin coating: *Ice* filmed *the window.* **2** to make a motion picture of: *to* film *a play.* ***vi-* 1** to become covered or obscured with mist or haze: *His eyes* filmed *with tears.* **2** to be suitable for use in a motion picture: *The script* films *well. His face* films *badly.* **—*adj-* film′ like′.**

film·strip (fĭlm′ strĭp′) ***n-*** strip of photographic film that is projected one frame or picture at a time.

film·y (fĭl′ mē) ***adj-*** **[film·i·er, film·i·est] 1** very thin; sheer. **2** covered with a thin layer of something; hazy; dim. **—*adv-* film′ i·ly. *n-* film′ i·ness.**

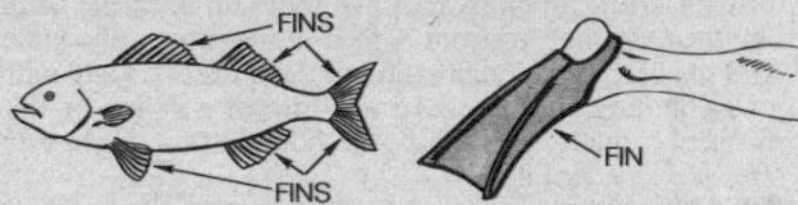

Fins of a fish and of a skin diver

fil·ter (fĭl′ tər) ***n-*** material or device used to permit the passage of certain things while stopping others. Filters are made for liquids, light rays, gases, radio or sound signals, etc. ***vt-* 1** to stop the passage of by use of such material or device: *to* filter *impurities from oil.* **2** to pass through such a device: *to* filter *oil to remove impurities.* ***vi-*** to pass or move slowly through something.

fil·ter·a·ble (fĭl′ tər ə bəl) or **fil·tra·ble** (fĭl′ trə bəl) ***adj-*** **1** such as can be held back by a filter. **2** of microorganisms, such as can pass through a filter.

filth (fĭlth) ***n-* 1** offensive dirt. **2** foulness; obscenity.

filth·y (fĭl′ thē) ***adj-*** **[filth·i·er, filth·i·est] 1** covered with or containing filth; dirty; foul. **2** nasty; underhanded: *a* filthy *trick.* **3** offensive; obscene: *a* filthy *word.* **—*adv-* filth′ i·ly. *n-* filth′ i·ness.**

fil·trate (fĭl′ trāt′) ***n-*** liquid that passes through a filter. ***vt-*** **[fil·trat·ed, fil·trat·ing]** to filter. **—*n-* fil·tra′ tion.**

fin (fĭn) ***n-* 1** any of the thin, bony, skin-covered parts of a fish's body by which it balances, steers, and drives itself.

through the water; also, anything of similar shape and function. 2 broad shoe, usually of rubber, used in skin diving; flipper. *Hom-* Finn. *—adj-* **fin′ less.** *adj-***fin′like′.**

fi·na·gle (fə nā′ gəl) *Informal vi-* **[fi·na·gled, fi·na·gling]** to practice deception or fraud. *vt-* **1** to cheat or trick (someone). **2** to get by guile or trickery. *—n-* **fi·na′ gler.**

fi·nal (fī′ nəl) *adj-* **1** coming at the end; last: *the* final *act of a play.* **2** settling the matter; deciding: *the* final *word on the subject.* *n-* **1** the last examination in a course. **2 finals** the last events or games in a tournament.

fi·na·le (fĭ năl′ ē, fĭ näl′ ē) *n-* **1** last movement of a long piece of music. **2** closing scene of an opera or play; the end.

fi·nal·ist (fī′ nəl ĭst) *n-* in games, competitions, etc., person who takes part in the finals.

fi·nal·i·ty (fī năl′ ə tē) *n-* [*pl.* **fi·nal·i·ties**] condition of being final, finished, or settled; conclusiveness: *There was an air of* finality *about the decision.*

fi·na·lize (fī′ nəl īz′) *vt-* **[fi·na·lized, fi·na·liz·ing]** to put into final form.

►This relatively new word is widely used in government and business because it has no exact synonym. However, many writers and speakers still avoid it.

fi·nal·ly (fī′ nə lē) *adv-* **1** at last: *The work is* finally *done.* **2** in or at the end; lastly: *I wish,* finally, *to thank you all.* **3** in a final manner; conclusively: *It has* finally *ended.*

fi·nance (fĭ năns′, fī′ năns′) *n-* **1** management of money affairs: *A banker is skilled in* finance. **2 finances** income; funds; revenue: *The firm's* finances *are in good shape.* *vt-* **[fi·nanced, fi·nanc·ing]** to provide money or credit for: *The bank* financed *the factory.*

fi·nan·cial (fĭ năn′ shəl, fī-) *adj-* having to do with money matters: *He needs* financial *help.* *—adv-* **fi·nan′ cial·ly.**

fin·an·cier (fĭn′ ăn sêr′, fī′ năn-) *n-* **1** person skilled in money management. **2** person who makes investment his business.

fin·back whale (fĭn′ băk′) *n-* large whalebone whale that has long grooves on the outer skin of the throat.

finch (fĭnch) *n-* any of several small songbirds. Buntings, canaries, and sparrows are finches.

find (fīnd) *vt-* **[found** (found), **find·ing] 1** to look for and get back: *Did you* find *your pen*? **2** to discover by chance or accident: *He* found *a dime in the street.* **3** to learn or discover: *to* find *the answer.* **4** to reach; get to: *The bullet* found *its mark.* **5** to determine; declare: *The jury* found *him guilty.* **6** to set aside: *to* find *time for play.* **7** *Archaic* to furnish or provide. *n-* valuable or pleasing discovery: *The ancient manuscript was quite a* find.

find oneself to discover one's abilities.

find out to discover.

find·er (fīn′ dər) *n-* **1** person or thing that finds. **2** small lens on a camera or telescope that is used to locate the area to be photographed or observed.

find·ing (fīn′ dĭng) *n-* **1** discovery. **2** something found or ascertained. **3 findings** (1) conclusion reached as the result of an investigation: *The committee published its* findings. (2) small supplies or tools of a workman.

[1]**fine** (fīn) *adj-* **[fin·er, fin·est] 1** of high or superior grade or quality; excellent: *a* fine *silk*; *a* fine *voice.* **2** thin; sharp: *a* fine *needle*; *a* fine *edge on a knife.* **3** elegant; refined: *He has* fine *manners.* **4** excellent in character: *a* fine *boy.* **5** pleasant; bright: *a* fine *day.* **6** not coarse or heavy; delicate: *grains of* fine *sand*; *a* fine *piece of embroidery.* **7** subtle: *to make a* fine *distinction.* **8** *Informal* in good condition; contented; not ill or unhappy: *I feel* fine. *adv-* *Informal* well; properly: *My toaster works* fine. [from Old French **fin** meaning "perfected," from Latin **fīnītus.**] *—adv-* **fine′ ly.** *n-* **fine′ ness.**

[2]**fine** (fīn) *n-* money paid as a penalty for breaking a law or rule. *vt-* **[fined, fin·ing]** to punish by making a person pay money: *The judge* fined *him $15 for speeding.* [from Old French **fin** or Medieval Latin **finis,** "a quit payment; final arrangement," from a former meaning "an end."]

fine art *n-* **1** one of the arts, such as painting, music, sculpture, poetry, etc., usually thought to be concerned with creating beauty. **2** any skill requiring delicacy.

fine·drawn (fīn′ drȯn′) *adj-* drawn to extreme subtlety or fineness: *a* fine-drawn *distinction.*

fin·er·y (fī′ nə rē) *n-* [*pl.* **fin·er·ies**] showy dress or ornaments: *The girls came to the party in their best* finery.

fi·nesse (fĭ nĕs′) *n-* **1** skill; delicacy of execution: *to play a flute with* finesse. **2** skillful management; subtle strategy: *to handle a situation with* finesse. **3** in card games, an attempt to take a trick by playing the lower of two cards not in sequence, on the chance or knowledge that the opponent who has already played has the card in between. *vi-* **[fi·nessed, fi·nes·sing]** to make such a play in a card game. *vt-* to play (a certain card) for such a reason.

fin·ger (fĭng′ ər) *n-* **1** one of the five separate parts of the end of the hand, especially one of the four besides the thumb; digit. **2** part of a glove made to hold one of these. **3** anything that resembles one of these in form or use. *vt-* to use one or more fingers to touch, press, or play on: *to* finger *cloth*; *to* finger *a guitar.*

THUMB
FOREFINGER
MIDDLE FINGER
RING FINGER
PINKIE

Fingers

put (one's) finger on to point out exactly: *He* put his finger on *the answer.* **twist (someone) around (one's) little finger** to manage (someone) easily; control (someone) completely.

finger bowl *n-* small bowl to hold water for rinsing the fingers during or after a meal.

fin·ger·ing (fĭng′ ər ĭng) *n-* **1** a touching or feeling with the fingers. **2** the placing of the fingers on a musical instrument in playing it; also, notation on a piece of music showing this.

fin·ger·ling (fĭng′ ər lĭng) *n-* small salmon or trout.

fin·ger·nail (fĭng′ gər nāl′) *n-* hard, protective, hornlike covering at the end of a finger. For picture, see *nail.*

finger painting *n-* **1** the making of pictures on a specially prepared paper by applying a thick paint with the fingers and palms. **2** picture created in this way.

fin·ger·print (fĭng′ gər prĭnt′) *n-* an impression left on something by the lines on the end of the finger: *Police examined the gun for* fingerprints. *vt-* to cause a person to make inked prints with his fingers so that he may be identified: *The police* fingerprinted *the prisoner.*

Fingerprint

fin·ick·y (fĭn′ ĭ kē) *adj-* too particular or fussy; exacting; precise: *He's* finicky *about food.* Also **fin′ i·cal, fin′ ick·ing.** *—adv-* **fin′ i·cal·ly.**

fi·nis (fĭn′ ĭs) *n-* the end; conclusion. [from Latin.]

fin·ish (fĭn′ ĭsh) *vt-* **1** to bring to an end; complete; conclude: *to* finish *a piece of work.* **2** to treat the surface of (something) in some way: *to* finish *wood.* **3** to use up completely: *to* finish *a glass of milk.* *vi-*: *The mystery story* finished *abruptly.* *n-* **1** completion; end: *the* finish *of a race.* **2** surface or texture: *a glossy* finish; *a* *smooth* finish. **3** material for use on surfaces: *to use varnish as a* finish. ***Hom-*** Finnish. **—*n-* fin′ish er.**

finish off **1** complete. **2** to overcome; also, to kill.

finish with **1** complete. **2** to stop having anything to do with: *I* finished with *that crowd last year.*

fin·ished (fĭn′ĭsht) ***adj-*** **1** ended; completed. **2** perfected; polished: *a* finished *piece of work.* **3** highly accomplished or skilled: *a* finished *performer.*

fi·nite (fī′nīt′) ***adj-*** **1** having a limit or limits; not infinite: *Our solar system is* finite. **2** *Mathematics* (1) completely countable: *a* finite *number.* (2) neither infinite nor infinitesimal: *a* finite *length.* **3** *Grammar* of a verb or verb phrase, definite as to past, present, or future time, as in the following sentences:

He walked *slowly into the room.* (finite verb)
He normally walks *fast.* (finite verb)
He will walk *tomorrow.* (finite verb phrase)

—*adv-* fi′nite·ly.

Finn (fĭn) ***n-*** **1** a native or inhabitant of Finland. **2** a person of Finnish ancestry. ***Hom-*** fin.

fin·nan had·die (fĭn′ən hăd′ē) ***n-*** smoked haddock.

finned (fĭnd) ***adj-*** **1** having a fin or fins. **2** having a fin or fins of a specified number, type, etc.: *sharp-*finned.

Finn·ish (fĭn′ĭsh) ***adj-*** of or relating to Finland, its people, or its culture. ***n-*** the language of Finland, Karelia, and parts of Norway and Sweden. ***Hom-*** finish.

fiord (fyôrd) ***n-*** a long, narrow, deep arm of the sea between high cliffs, as on the coast of Norway. Fiords are glacial valleys flooded by the sea when the shoreline sank.

Fiords on the coast of Norway

fir (fûr) ***n-*** **1** any of several cone-bearing evergreen trees related to the pines. **2** the wood of these trees. ***adj-***: *a* fir *grove*; fir *logs.* ***Hom-*** fur.

fire (fīər′) ***n-*** **1** flames produced by burning; combustion. **2** burning wood, coal, or other fuel: *to build a* fire. **3** a destructive burning; conflagration: *a forest* fire. **4** a discharging of weapons: *The attack was met by heavy* fire. **5** excitement; inspiration: *Her speech had* fire. **6** brightness; light: *the* fire *of a sunset.* ***as modifier***: *a* fire *alarm.* ***vt-*** **[fired, fir·ing]** **1** to cause to shoot or explode: *to* fire *a gun.* **2** to add fuel to: *to* fire *a furnace.* **3** to animate; excite: *Ambition* fires *his genius.* **4** to apply intense heat to: *to* fire *bricks.* **5** to set aflame: *to* fire *fallen leaves.* **6** *Informal* to dismiss from a job. ***vi-*** to discharge a weapon or weapons.

between two fires attacked from both sides. **catch fire** begin to burn. **hang fire** be slow in acting; be slow in going off; be delayed. **on fire** **1** burning. **2** full of a flaming spirit, like fire. **open fire** to begin to shoot. **take fire** begin to burn. **under fire** under attack.

fire away to ask questions rapidly.

fire up to start a fire, as in a furnace.

fire·arm (fīər′ärm′) ***n-*** weapon such as a rifle, pistol, shotgun, etc., that uses gunpowder to fire projectiles and is small enough to be carried.

fire·ball (fīər′bŏl′) ***n-*** **1** meteor. **2** ball of lightning or fire. **3** the hot, glowing cloud of vapor, debris, etc., that develops around the center of a nuclear explosion.

fire·boat (fīər′bōt′) or **fire boat** ***n-*** boat equipped with apparatus for fighting fires.

fire·brand (fīər′brănd′) ***n-*** **1** piece of burning wood. **2** person who stirs up trouble. **3** hot-tempered person.

fire·brick (fīər′brĭk′) ***n-*** brick made to withstand high temperature, used to line furnaces, fireplaces, etc.

fire·bug (fīər′bŭg′) ***n-*** *Informal* a pyromaniac.

fire control ***n-*** **1** the control or putting out of fires. **2** *Military* the control of gunfire, rockets, missiles, etc., especially by the use of special equipment.

fire·crack·er (fīər′krăk′ər) ***n-*** small roll of paper which contains gunpowder and a fuse; cracker. Firecrackers explode loudly and are used at celebrations.

fire·damp (fīər′dămp′) ***n-*** dangerous, explosive gas formed in coal mines.

fire·dog (fīər′dȯg′) ***n-*** andiron.

fire-eat·er (fīər′ē′tər) ***n-*** **1** performer who pretends to eat fire. **2** someone eager to fight or quarrel.

fire engine ***n-*** truck equipped to fight fires.

fire escape ***n-*** a device, such as a ladder, metal stairway, or chute, to provide escape from a burning building.

fire extinguisher ***n-*** any portable apparatus, such as a small tank containing chemicals, used for smothering small fires with water or chemicals.

fire·fight·er (fīər′fī′tər) ***n-*** person whose work is to put out fires.

fire·fly (fīər′flī′) ***n-*** [*pl.* **fire·flies**] small flying beetle that periodically gives off a glowing light.

fire·house (fīər′hous′) ***n-*** building in which firemen and equipment for fighting fires are housed; fire station.

fire irons ***n-*** *pl.* implements such as poker, shovel, and tongs, used in tending a fire in a fireplace.

fire·less cooker (fīər′ləs) ***n-*** insulated container, which seals in heat, for cooking food or keeping it warm.

fire·light (fīər′līt′) ***n-*** light from the flames of a fire.

fire·man (fīər′mən) ***n-*** [*pl.* **fire·men**] **1** firefighter. **2** person who tends to the fire in a furnace, an engine, etc.; stoker. **3** enlisted person in the navy who handles engineering machinery. **4** member of a locomotive crew who tends the engines.

fire·place (fīər′plās′) ***n-*** place for building an open fire. An indoor fireplace usually has a chimney and, often, a mantel.

Fireplace

fire·plug (fīər′plŭg′) ***n-*** hydrant for supplying water in case of fire.

fire·power (fīər′pou′ər) *Military* ***n-*** **1** ability to deliver gunfire, rockets, missiles, etc. **2** amount of fire that a weapon or unit delivers.

fire·proof (fīər′pro͞of′) ***adj-*** made of material which does not burn or does not burn easily: *a* fireproof *building.* ***vt-*** to treat with a substance or furnish with a material which does not burn easily.

fire screen ***n-*** metal screen to keep sparks from flying out of a fireplace.

fire·side (fīər′sīd′) ***n-*** **1** place near the fire; hearth. **2** home or home life; domesticity.

fire station ***n-*** firehouse.

fire tower ***n-*** tower in which a person is stationed to report fires, especially forest fires.

fire·trap (fīər′trăp′) ***n-*** structure apt to catch fire and not having proper means of escape.

fire truck ***n-*** fire engine.

fire·war·den (fīər′wȯr′dən) ***n-*** official in charge of preventing or fighting fires, especially forest fires.

fire·wa·ter (fīər′wȯt′ər) ***n-*** strong alcoholic drink (term first used by the North American Indians).

fire·wood (fīər′wo͝od′) ***n-*** wood for use as fuel.

fire·works (fīər′wûrks′) ***n-*** *pl.* **1** devices which burn or explode, used in celebrations to make loud noises or displays of light. **2** display of such devices; pyrotechnics.

firing line ***n-*** **1** position from which troops fire upon the enemy or at targets. **2** the foremost position in a campaign, controversy, etc.

firing pin ***n-*** in a firearm, the part that strikes the cap or primer of the cartridge to fire it.

fir·kin (fûr′ kən) ***n-*** **1** small wooden vessel or cask for butter, lard, etc. **2** unit of capacity, usually equal to about one quarter of a barrel.

[1]**firm** (fûrm) ***adj-*** **[firm·er, firm·est] 1** solid; not yielding easily; not soft. **2** fixed in place; not easily moved: *a* firm *post*; *a* firm *foundation.* **3** steady; not shaking: *a* firm *voice.* **4** not easily changed; steadfast: *a* firm *belief.* **5** not varying; also, not subject to change: *a* firm *price.* ***vt-*** to fix; make secure or compact: *to* firm *a pole in the ground.* ***vi-***: *The cheese* firmed *nicely.* [from Old French **ferme,** "steadfast."] ***—adv-*** **firm′ ly.** ***n-*** **firm′ ness.**
firm up 1 to become more solid or steadier: *The stock market* firmed up *tonight.* **2** to strengthen or complete.

[2]**firm** (fûrm) ***n-*** business concern, house, or company, especially a business partnership. [from Italian and Spanish **firma** meaning "signature; firm name," from **firmar,** "to sign," from Latin **firmare,** "to confirm."]

fir·ma·ment (fûr′ mə mənt) ***n-*** the sky; the heavens.

first (fûrst) ***adj-*** **1** coming before all others in time, place, order, quality, importance, etc.: *He was* first *in his class,* **2** ordinal of 1; 1st: *He lived on* 1st *Avenue.* ***adv-*** **1** before all others in time, place, order, etc.: *He spoke of you* first. **2** rather than do (something); before doing (something); sooner: *I would die* first. ***n-*** **1** person or thing that is before all others in time, place, order, etc.: *We were the* first *to go.* **2** the slowest and most powerful forward driving gear in most motor vehicles; low. **3** in baseball, first base: *He's safe on* first!
at first in the beginning: *She didn't want to go* at first. **first and last** altogether; all in all: *He was* first and last *a scientist.* **from the first** since the beginning: *She was a nuisance* from the first. **in the first place** to start with.

first aid ***n-*** treatment or help given a sick or hurt person before regular medical treatment from a doctor is obtained. *as* ***modifier*** **(first-aid):** *a* first-aid *kit.*

first-born (fûrst′ bôrn′) ***adj-*** born first; oldest. ***n-*** the first child born to a couple.

first class ***n-*** **1** the highest or best type: *a mind of the* first class. **2** most expensive class of cabin, seating, service, etc., on a ship, train, or airplane. **3** mail consisting of letters, postcards, and sealed matter. ***—adj-*** **(first-class):** *a* first-class *cabin*; first-class *mail.* ***adv-*** **(first-class):** *to travel* first-class.

first fruits ***n-*** *pl.* **1** the earliest harvest of a crop. **2** the earliest results of any undertaking.

first-hand (fûrst′ hănd′) ***adj-*** direct from the original source: *a* first-hand *account.* ***adv-***: *I heard it* first-hand.

first lady ***n-*** **1** the wife of the President of the United States or of the governor of a State. **2** the leading woman of a profession.

first lieutenant See *lieutenant.*

first·ly (fûrst′ lē) ***adv-*** as first in a series.

first offender ***n-*** person who has been legally declared guilty of breaking the law for the first time.

first papers ***n-*** documents filed by a foreigner declaring intention to become a citizen of the United States.

first person *Grammar* ***n-*** form of a pronoun or verb used to indicate the speaker or speakers. Example: I, me, my, we, us, our, I go, we have. *as* ***modifier*** **(first-person):** *a* first-person *pronoun.*

first-rate (fûrst′ rāt′) ***adj-*** excellent; very good; of the best quality: *a* first-rate *book.*

first sergeant ***n-*** in the Army and Marine Corps, the highest ranking noncommissioned officer in a company.

first string ***n-*** the regular first team or lineup of a sports organization. ***—adj-*** **(first-string):** *a* first-string *fullback.*

first violin ***n-*** violinist who plays the higher-pitched of two violin parts in an orchestra, string quartet, etc.; also, the part played. ***—n-*** **first violinist.**

firth (fûrth) *Scottish* ***n-*** a narrow arm of the sea; mouth of a river.

fis·cal (fĭs′ kəl) ***adj-*** **1** relating to money matters; financial. **2** having to do with the public treasury or revenues: *U.S.* fiscal *policy.* ***—adv-*** **fis′ cal·ly.**

fiscal year ***n-*** any twelve-month period on which the accounting of a business or government is based

fish (fĭsh) ***n-*** [*pl.* **fish; fish·es** (kinds of fish)] **1** any of a variety of cold-blooded water animals having a backbone, fins, and gills. They usually have scaly bodies. **2** the flesh of water animals, used for food. ***vi-*** **1** to catch, or try to catch water animals: *Dad* fishes *for recreation.* **2** to search (inside something): *He* fished *in his pocket for a dime.* **3** to seek to gain something by indirect means: *to* fish *for an invitation*; *to* fish *for a compliment.* ***vt-*** **1** to catch or try to catch. **2** to try to catch water animals in: *to* fish *a stream for rainbow trout.* ***—adj-*** **fish′ like′.**

fish-and-chips (fĭsh′ ən chĭps′) *Brit.* ***n-*** *pl.* fried fish fillets and French-fried potatoes.

fish·er (fĭsh′ ər) ***n-*** **1** person who fishes; fisherman. **2** fur-bearing, flesh-eating animal, related to the weasel, with short legs and a long bushy tail. ***Hom-*** fissure.

fish·er·man (fĭsh′ ər mən) ***n-*** [*pl.* **fish·er·men**] person who fishes for sport or for a living.

fish·er·y (fĭsh′ ə rē) ***n-*** [*pl.* **fish·er·ies**] **1** the business of catching fish: *Sardine* fishery *is an important Maine industry.* **2** establishment equipped to catch fish: *the Pacific salmon* fisheries. **3** fishing ground.

fish hawk ***n-*** osprey.

fish·hook (fĭsh′ ho͝ok′) ***n-*** barbed hook, to be attached to a line and baited, for catching fish.

fish·ing (fĭsh′ ĭng) ***n-*** the catching of fish for money or sport.

fishing ground ***n-*** place where fish are found.

fishing rod ***n-*** long, flexible pole with a line, hook, and often a reel, used to catch fish.

fishing tackle ***n-*** hooks, lines, rods, etc., used in catching fish.

fish meal ***n-*** meal or flour made by grinding up whole fish, such as menhaden, and drying the mash. It is used chiefly as a fertilizer and a food for animals.

fish·mon·ger (fĭsh′ mŭng′ gər, -mŏng′ gər) *Brit.* ***n-*** dealer in fish.

fish·pond (fĭsh′ pŏnd′) ***n-*** a pond in which fish are kept.

fish story ***n-*** an exaggerated tale.

fish·wife (fĭsh′ wīf′) ***n-*** [*pl.* **fish·wives**] **1** coarse, loud, abusive woman. **2** woman who sells fish.

fish·y (fĭsh′ ē) ***adj-*** **[fish·i·er, fish·i·est] 1** like fish; tasting or smelling of fish. **2** abounding in fish. **3** lacking expression; dull: *a* fishy *stare.* **4** *Informal* questionable, doubtful, suspicious.

fis·sion (fĭsh′ ən) ***n-*** **1** a splitting into parts. **2** *Biology* process of cell reproduction in which the nucleus undergoes mitosis and then the entire cell splits into usually two complete cells. **3** *Physics* the breakdown or disintegration of the nucleus of an atom, with the release of large quantities of energy.

fis·sion·a·ble (fĭsh′ ən ə bəl) ***adj-*** of a nature that allows fission.

fission bomb *n-* atom bomb.

fis·sure (fĭsh′ ər) *n-* narrow opening; crack: *a* fissure *in the earth.* *vt-* [**fis·sured, fis·sur·ing**] to cleave; split: *Earthquakes had* fissured *the plateau.* *vi-*: *The hot rock* fissured. *Hom-* fisher.

fist (fĭst) *n-* closed hand with the fingers tightly bent.

fist·i·cuffs (fĭs′ tə kŭfs′) *n-* fighting with fists.

fis·tu·la (fĭs′ chə lə) *n-* an abnormal opening or passage, often caused by disease, leading into some internal organ of the body. *—adj-* **fis′ tu·lous**: *a* fistulous *condition.*

[1]**fit** (fĭt) *adj-* [**fit·ter, fit·test**] **1** suitable; proper; appropriate; right (for): *a banquet* fit *for a king*; *weather* fit *for flying.* **2** in good physical condition: *to feel* fit. *vt-* [**fit·ted, fit·ting**] **1** to be suitable, proper, or right for; befit: *The music* fitted *the occasion.* **2** to be right for in size, shape, function, etc.: *Does this light bulb* fit *the socket?* **3** to make the right size, shape, etc.; adapt: *to* fit *a suit for a customer.* **4** to put carefully into place: *to* fit *a piece into a jigsaw puzzle.* **5** to supply: *to* fit *a ship for a long voyage.* *vi-* to be of the right size, shape, etc.: *Your coat* fits *well. The two parts* fit *together.* *n-* adjustment of one thing to another: *a perfect* fit; *a loose* fit. [from earlier English **fyt** of doubtful origin.] *—adv-* **fit′ ly.** *n-* **fit′ ness.**

see (or **think**) **fit to** to decide to; choose to.

fit in 1 to have a suitable place or position: *She doesn't* fit in *with that crowd.* **2** to agree; be in keeping.

fit out (or **up**) to supply with what is suitable for a purpose: *to* fit *oneself* out *for a journey.*

[2]**fit** (fĭt) *n-* **1** sudden, violent attack of disease or illness: *a* fit *of epilepsy*; *a* fit *of indigestion.* **2** sudden outburst: *a* fit *of laughter.* [from Old English **fitt,** "a struggle."]

by (or **in**) **fits and starts** in efforts that start and stop irregularly: *He does his homework* by fits and starts.

fitch (fĭch) *n-* the European polecat; also, its fur. Also **fitch′ ew** (fĭch′ o͞o).

fit·ful (fĭt′ fəl) *adj-* not regular; stopping for a short time and then starting again; spasmodic: *a baby's* fitful *crying*; fitful *sleep.* *—adv-* **fit′ ful·ly.** *n-* **fit′ ful·ness.**

fit·ter (fĭt′ ər) *n-* **1** person who adjusts or puts together pipes or parts of machinery. **2** person who adjusts and alters clothing to make it fit.

fit·ting (fĭt′ ĭng) *adj-* suitable; proper: *a* fitting *moment for a word of praise.* *n-* **1** session with a tailor or seamstress to have a garment made or altered to fit. **2** anything used in adjusting or connecting: *a pipe* fitting. **3 fittings** the equipment or necessary fixtures of a house, shop, car, etc. *—adv-* **fit′ ting·ly.**

five (fīv) *n-* **1** amount or quantity that is one greater than 4. **2** *Mathematics* (1) the cardinal number that is the sum of 4 and 1. (2) a numeral such as 5 that represents this cardinal number. *as* ***determiner*** (traditionally called adjective or pronoun): *There are* five *boys here and* five *there.*

five-and-ten (fīv′ ən tĕn′) *n-* variety store which sells inexpensive items including many which cost only five or ten cents. Also **five-and-dime.**

five·fold (fīv′ fōld′) *adj-* **1** five times as many or as much. **2** having five parts: *a* fivefold *solution to the problem.* *adv-*: *Mechanization increased factory output* fivefold.

Five Nations *n-* confederacy, formed about 1570, of Iroquoian Indians of the Mohawk Valley, New York, including the Mohawks, Onondagas, Cayugas, Oneidas, and Senecas. See also *Six Nations.*

fix (fĭks) *vt-* **1** to make firm; fasten: *The sailors* fixed *a new mast on the boat.* **2** to set definitely; establish: *He* fixed *a time and place for our meeting.* **3** to repair: *A plumber* fixed *the leaky pipe.* **4** to arrange; prepare: *Mother* fixed *lunch.* **5** to place (blame, responsibility, etc.) definitely on a person. **6** to make fast or permanent: *to* fix *the color of a dyed fabric.* **7** to direct or hold steadily: *to* fix *one's eyes*; *to* fix *one's attention.* **8** to bathe (film, paper, etc.) in a chemical solution that removes compounds still sensitive to light to ensure the permanence of the photographic image. **9** *Slang* to determine the outcome of a contest in advance, often by bribing one or more of the contestants. *n-* in navigation, the determined position of a ship or aircraft. *—adj-* **fix′ a·ble.** *n-* **fix′ er.**

in a fix in a bad situation; in a predicament.

fix on (or **upon**) to choose; decide: *to* fix on *a date.*

fix up *Informal* **1** to provide or supply with something: *to* fix *someone* up *with a job.* **2** to put in order: *to* fix up *a house.*

fix·a·tion (fĭk sā′ shən) *n-* **1** act or process of making permanent: *the* fixation *of dyes.* **2** condition of being permanent: *the* fixation *of a habit.* **3** in psychology, a constant preoccupation with some idea.

fix·a·tive (fĭk′ sə tĭv′) *n-* a preparation that serves to make something permanent or to protect the surface of a painting, film, drawing, etc.

fixed (fĭkst) *adj-* firmly established; set; unchanging: *a* fixed *purpose.* *—adv-* **fix′ ed·ly.** *n-* **fix′ ed·ness.**

fixed star *n-* star whose position in relation to other stars always seems the same, as distinguished from a planet.

fix·ings (fĭk′ sĭngz) *n- pl.* the things needed in any preparation; furnishings; trimmings.

fix·i·ty (fĭk′ sə tē) *n-* condition of being fixed; stability; permanence.

fix·ture (fĭks′ chər) *n-* **1** something permanently fastened in place: *a light* fixture. **2** person permanently placed.

fizz (fĭz) *n-* **1** hissing sound. **2** effervescent or bubbling beverage: *a lime* fizz. *vi-*: *The soda* fizzed *when it was poured.* *—adj-* **fizz′ y** [**fizz·i·er, fizz·i·est**].

fiz·zle (fĭz′ əl) *vi-* [**fiz·zled, fiz·zling**] to make a spluttering, hissing sound: *Wet firecrackers* fizzle. *n-* person or attempt that comes to nothing: *That's a* fizzle!

fizzle out to fail; come to nothing.

fjord (fyôrd) fiord.

fl. 1 fluid. **2** flourished.

Fla. Florida.

flab·ber·gast (flăb′ ər găst′) *Informal* *vt-* to astonish: *His ignorance will* flabbergast *you.*

flab·by (flăb′ ē) *adj-* [**flab·bi·er, flab·bi·est**] yielding to slight pressure; not firm; soft and weak: *his* flabby *muscles.* *—adv-* **flab′ bi·ly.** *n-* **flab′ bi·ness.**

flac·cid (flăk′ sĭd, flăs′ ĭd) *adj-* lacking firmness; weak; flabby: *his* flaccid *jowls.* *—n-* **flac·cid′ i·ty** or **flac′ cid·ness.** *adv-* **flac′ cid·ly.**

fla·con (flăk′ ən, flă kōn′) *n-* bottle, often ornamental, with a tight cap or stopper: *a* flacon *of perfume.*

[1]**flag** (flăg) *n-* piece of cloth bearing marks or patterns that give it a certain meaning; banner; pennant: *a signal* flag; *a school* flag. *vt-* [**flagged, flag·ging**] **1** to signal with or as if with such a piece of cloth: *to* flag *a train.* **2** to place a banner or pennant on. [from an Old Norse form similar to Danish **flag,** "to flutter (as in the wind)"; part of the meaning comes from [2]**flag.**]

United States flag

[2]**flag** (flăg) *vi-* [**flagged, flag·ging**] to lose strength; grow weak; droop: *Our energy* flagged. *Their interest in the movie* flagged. [perhaps a combination of early English **flakken,** "to flap about; fly" and Old French **flaquir,** "to droop," from Latin **flaccus,** "slack; flaccid."]

[3]**flag** (flăg) ***n-*** an iris, especially any of several wild irises such as the **blue flag** and the **yellow flag.** [of similar origin to [1]**flag,** in the sense of "flutter."]

[4]**flag** (flăg) ***n-*** flagstone. ***vt-*** **[flagged, flag·ging]** to pave with flagstones. [from Old Norse **flaga** meaning "slab," and the verb **flagna,** "to flake off."]

Flag Day ***n-*** June 14, the anniversary of the day in 1777 on which the U.S. national flag was adopted.

[1]**flag·el·late** (flăj′ ə lāt′) ***vt-*** **[flag·el·lat·ed, flag·el·lat·ing]** to whip, especially as a punishment. ***—n-*** **flag′ el·la′ tion.**

[2]**flag·el·late** (flăj′ ə lət) ***adj-*** having or producing whiplike strands or branches: *a* flagellate *animal.* ***n-*** any of the protozoans having such strands.

fla·gel·lum (flə jĕl′ əm) ***n-*** [*pl.* **fla·gel·la** (-ə)] in biology, a long thin, movable strand or thread that projects singly or in groups from a cell and is the major organ of movement of many micro-organisms.

flag·eo·let (flăj′ ə lĕt′) ***n-*** small musical instrument like a flute, but blown into from the end, not the side.

flag·ging (flăg′ ĭng) ***n-*** pavement of flagstones, or flagstones used for paving.

flag·man (flăg′ mən) ***n-*** [*pl.* **flag·men**] person who signals with a flag or lights, especially on a railroad.

flag officer ***n-*** in the navy, any officer above the rank of a captain and entitled to display a flag showing his rank.

flag of truce ***n-*** white flag shown to the enemy to signal willingness to surrender or a desire to confer.

flag·on (flăg′ ən) ***n-*** a metal or earthenware container for holding liquids. It has a spout, handle, and often a lid.

Flagon

flag·pole (flăg′ pōl′) ***n-*** pole from which a flag is flown.

fla·grant (flā′ grənt) ***adj-*** bad in a way that draws attention; outrageous: *his* flagrant *misconduct.* ***—n-*** **fla′ gran·cy.** ***adv-*** **fla′ grant·ly.**

flag·ship (flăg′ shĭp′) ***n-*** ship that carries the commander of a fleet and flies his flag.

flag·staff (flăg′ stăf′) ***n-*** pole on which a flag is flown.

flag·stone (flăg′ stōn′) ***n-*** large, flat stone, or slab of stone, used especially for paving walks.

flag-wav·ing (flăg′ wā′ vĭng) ***n-*** emotional show of or appeal to patriotic sentiment.

flail (flāl) ***n-*** device consisting of two sticks, one of which is a handle, joined by a thong or link, and used to beat ripe grain from the stalks. ***vt-*** to beat with or as if with such a device: *to* flail *the air with one's arms.*

Flail

flair (flâr) ***n-*** **1** ability to select what is good or distinctive; discernment: *to show* flair *in choosing clothes.* **2** talent; aptitude: *his* flair *for drawing.* ***Hom-*** flare.

flak (flăk) ***n-*** anti-aircraft fire. [from German **Fliegerabwehrkanonen,** "aircraft protection cannons."]

flake (flāk) ***n-*** small, thin particle of something: *a* flake *of soap*; *a* flake *of snow.* ***vi-*** **[flaked, flak·ing]** to break or separate into small, thin particles; scale: *The paint* flaked *off.* ***vt-***: *to* flake *dried codfish.*

flak·y (flā′ kē) ***adj-*** **[flak·i·er, flak·i·est]** consisting of or tending to form flakes; light; crisp: *a* flaky *pie crust.* ***—adv-*** **flak′ i·ly.** ***n-*** **flak′ i·ness.**

flam·beau (flăm′ bō′) ***n-*** [*pl.* **flam·beaux** (-bōz′) or **flam·beaus**] **1** flaming torch. **2** large and often elaborate candlestick.

flam·boy·ant (flăm boi′ ənt) ***adj-*** **1** suggesting flames in color or brilliance: *a* flamboyant *sunset.* **2** showy; ornate: *a* flamboyant *piece of jewelry*; *a* flamboyant *style.* **3** having wavy, flamelike lines, as in some Gothic architecture. ***—n-*** **flam·boy′ ance.** ***adv-*** **flam·boy′ ant·ly.**

flame (flām) ***n-*** **1** burning gas or vapor coming up from a fire: *the* flame *of a candle.* **2** strong feeling: *a* flame *of rage.* **3** *Informal* a sweetheart. ***vi-*** **[flamed, flam·ing]** to blaze: *The logs* flamed *quickly.* ***—adj-*** **flame′ like′.**

fla·men·co (flə mĕng′ kō) ***n-*** style of dancing and singing of the Gypsies of Andalusia, Spain; also, music in this style. *as* ***modifier***: *a* flamenco *guitarist.*

flame·out (flām′ out′) ***n-*** the sudden shutting down of a jet engine, especially because of lack of fuel or incomplete combustion of fuel.

flame thrower ***n-*** military weapon that throws a stream of burning fuel under pressure.

flam·ing (flā′ mĭng) ***adj-*** **1** burning in flames. **2** like a flame in color: *the* flaming *autumn foliage.* **3** violent; passionate: *a* flaming *rage.*

fla·min·go (flə mĭng′ gō) ***n-*** [*pl.* **fla·min·gos** or **fla·min·goes**] pink or red wading bird with long legs and neck, found in warm climates.

Flamingo, about 5 ft. tall

flam·ma·ble (flăm′ ə bəl) ***adj-*** easily set afire; likely to burst into flame; inflammable: *Gas is* flammable. ***—n-*** **flam′ ma·bil′ i·ty.**

►Both FLAMMABLE and INFLAMMABLE mean "such as can be easily inflamed or ignited." However, because the prefix "in-" often means "not," use FLAMMABLE for easily ignitable and NONFLAMMABLE for fireproof.

flange (flănj) ***n-*** raised or projecting rim on a wheel, pipe, etc., serving to hold or attach the object to another object or surface.

flank (flăngk) ***n-*** **1** fleshy part of an animal between the hip and ribs. **2** side of anything: *the* flank *of a building*; *the* flank *of a mountain.* **3** right or left side of a fleet, army, football line, etc. ***vt-*** **1** to be located by the side of: *Trees* flanked *the road.* **2** to attack or go around the side of: *to* flank *enemy troops.*

flank·er (flăng′ kər) ***n-*** person or group that protects or goes around a flank; especially, a football player lined up nearer the sidelines than an opposing player.

flan·nel (flăn′ əl) ***n-*** **1** fabric, usually made of wool, having a plain or twill weave with a soft, flat nap. **2 flannels** trousers, underwear, etc., made of this material. ***adj-***: *a warm* flannel *skirt.*

flan·nel·ette (flăn′ ə lĕt′) ***n-*** soft cotton material like flannel, used for baby garments, nightclothes, etc.

flap (flăp) ***n-*** **1** anything broad and flat that is attached on one side with the rest hanging loose: *the* flap *of an envelope*; *a tent* flap. **2** a light blow from, or a movement made by, something broad and flat; also, the sound made by this: *a* flap *of a beaver's tail*; *the* flap *of wings.* **3** in aeronautics, a hinged section attached to the rear edge of an airplane's wing, used to increase lift and decrease speed. ***vt-*** **[flapped, flap·ping]** to move to and fro or up and down: *The geese* flapped *their wings.* ***vi-*** to sway about loosely, often with a beating noise.

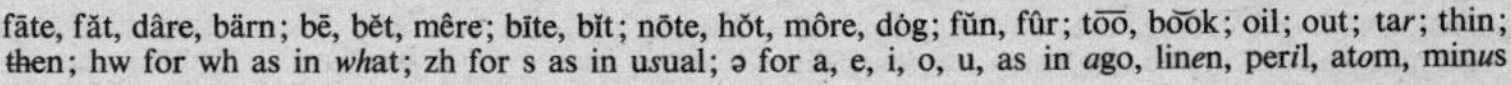
fāte, făt, dâre, bärn; bē, bĕt, mêre; bīte, bĭt; nōte, hŏt, môre, dȯg; fŭn, fûr; tōō, bŏŏk; oil; out; tar; thin; then; hw for wh as in *wh*at; zh for s as in u*s*ual; ə for a, e, i, o, u, as in *a*go, lin*e*n, per*i*l, at*o*m, min*u*s

flap·jack (flăp′ jăk′) ***n-*** pancake; griddlecake.

flap·per (flăp′ ər) ***n-*** **1** something that flaps, such as the flipper of a seal. **2** in the 1920's, a young woman who followed the latest fashions in dress and behavior.

flare (flâr) ***vi-*** **[flared, flar·ing] 1** to burn brightly with a sudden or unsteady flame or light: *The match* flared *and then went out. Light* flared *from the windows.* **2** to burst out or leap up like a flame: *Anger* flared *in his eyes.* **3** to spread outward: *The vase* flares *at the top.* ***n-*** **1** bright, unsteady flame or light. **2** fire or blaze used as a signal: *road* flares. **3** sudden outburst: *a* flare *of temper.* **4** a spreading outward: *the* flare *of a skirt.* ***Hom-*** flair.
flare up 1 of a chronic disease, to become acute. **2** (also **flare out**) to express sudden anger.

flare-up (flâr′ ŭp′) ***n-*** **1** a sudden bursting into flame. **2** a sudden bursting out: *a* flare-up *of violence.*

flash (flăsh) ***n-*** **1** sudden burst of light: *a* flash *of lightning.* **2** sudden outburst: *a* flash *of temper.* **3** showy display: *the* flash *of cheap jewelry.* ***vt-*** **1** to send forth swiftly or suddenly: *to* flash *a light*; *to* flash *a look.* **2** to send out in short bursts of light: *to* flash *a signal.* **3** to make a show of: *She* flashed *her diamonds.* ***vi-*** **1** to shine suddenly for a moment: *A light* flashed *on the dark shore.* **2** to appear suddenly; pass at great speed: *A train* flashed *by.* ***adj-*** done quickly: *a* flash *success.*
flash in the pan person or thing that seems promising at first but turns out to be a failure. **in a flash** in an instant; very quickly: *It happened* in a flash.

flash·back (flăsh′ băk′) ***n-*** interruption in a story, motion picture, etc., to describe earlier events.

flash bulb ***n-*** electric bulb which gives a very strong light for a short time, used in photography. Also **flash′ lamp′.**

flash card ***n-*** card with a word, phrase, arithmetic example, etc., on it, held up by a teacher in front of a class for rapid review or an aid in learning.

flash flood ***n-*** sudden flood caused by a heavy rainfall in the surrounding area.

flash·gun (flăsh′ gŭn′) ***n-*** device used to hold and set off a flash bulb.

flash·ing (flăsh′ ĭng) ***n-*** sheet metal used for waterproofing, especially at roof angles, chimney bases, etc.

flash·light (flăsh′ līt′) ***n-*** **1** small, portable electric light that uses batteries for power. **2** flash of light, used to take a photograph.

flash point ***n-*** the lowest temperature at which the vapor from a combustible substance will ignite when exposed to a flame.

flash·y (flăsh′ ē) ***adj-*** **[flash·i·er, flash·i·est]** showy and often cheap-looking; gaudy: *He wears* flashy *clothes or jewelry.* **—*adv-*** **flash′ i·ly.** ***n-*** **flash′ i·ness.**

flask (flăsk) ***n-*** glass or metal bottle for holding liquids, especially a narrow-necked bottle used in laboratories.

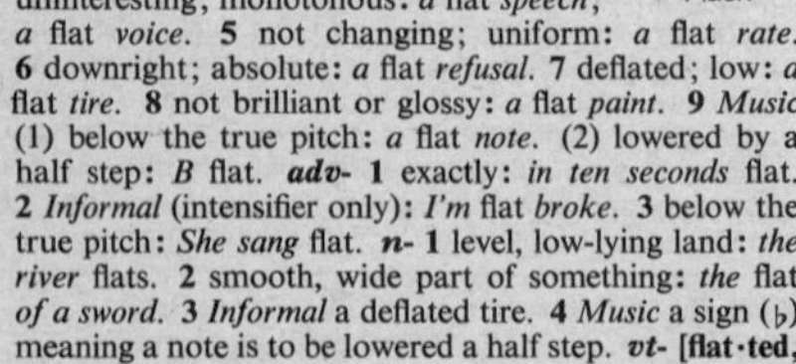
Flask

[1]**flat** (flăt) ***adj-*** **[flat·ter, flat·test] 1** having an even, smooth surface: *the* flat *face of a cliff*; flat *country.* **2** evenly stretched or spread out: *The carpet is not* flat. **3** smooth but not thick or deep: *a* flat *pan.* **4** dull; uninteresting; monotonous: *a* flat *speech*; *a* flat *voice.* **5** not changing; uniform: *a* flat *rate.* **6** downright; absolute: *a* flat *refusal.* **7** deflated; low: *a* flat *tire.* **8** not brilliant or glossy: *a* flat *paint.* **9** *Music* (1) below the true pitch: *a* flat *note.* (2) lowered by a half step: *B* flat. ***adv-*** **1** exactly: *in ten seconds* flat. **2** *Informal* (intensifier only): *I'm* flat *broke.* **3** below the true pitch: *She sang* flat. ***n-*** **1** level, low-lying land: *the river* flats. **2** smooth, wide part of something: *the* flat *of a sword.* **3** *Informal* a deflated tire. **4** *Music* a sign (♭) meaning a note is to be lowered a half step. ***vt-*** **[flat·ted, flat·ting]** to lower in pitch: *The composer* flatted *that note.* ***vi-***: *The tenor* flatted *several times.* [probably from Old Norse **flatr.**] **—*n-*** **flat′ ness.**
fall flat to fall short of success; fail.

[2]**flat** (flăt) ***n-*** apartment having all its rooms on the same floor. [from Old English **flet** meaning "floor." It was probably influenced in its spelling by the related [1]**flat.**]

flat·boat (flăt′ bōt′) ***n-*** large boat with a flat bottom and square ends, used especially to float goods down a river or on shallow waters.

flat·car (flăt′ kär′) ***n-*** railroad car without roof or sides, for carrying freight.

flat·fish (flăt′ fĭsh′) ***n-*** [*pl.* **flat·fish; flat·fish·es** (kinds of flatfish)] any of a number of flat, broad fishes, such as the halibut, sole, and flounder, whose eyes travel to one side of their bodies while they are still small. They swim on their sides with the eyeless side down.

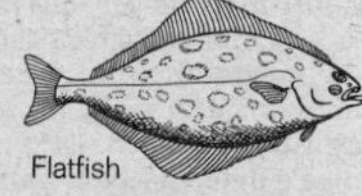
Flatfish

flat·foot (flăt′ fo͝ot′) *Slang* ***n-*** [*pl.* **flat·feet**] policeman, especially one who walks a regular beat.

flat-foot·ed (flăt′ fo͝ot′ əd) ***adj-*** having a foot in which the arch of the instep is flattened so that the entire sole rests on the ground. **—*n-*** **flat′-foot′ ed·ness.**

Flat·head (flăt′ hĕd′) ***n-*** [*pl.* **Flat·heads** or **Flat·head**] **1** member of one of several Indian groups, especially the Chinook, so named because of their custom of deforming their heads. **2** the Salish tribe of Montana which did not practice this custom. ***adj-***: *a* Flathead *family.*

flat·i·ron (flăt′ ī′ ərn) ***n-*** heavy iron with a flat, wedge-shaped surface used for pressing clothes, etc.

flat·ly (flăt′ lē) ***adv-*** emphatically; absolutely: *He* flatly *refuses to go.*

flat silver ***n-*** silverware such as knives and forks.

flat·ten (flăt′ ən) ***vt-*** to cause to become flat or prone; make level: *The steamroller* flattened *the road surface.* ***vi-***: *The cake* flattened *instead of rising.* **—*n-*** **flat′ ten·er.**
flatten out 1 to become flat. **2** of aircraft, to resume horizontal flight; level off: *The plane* flattened out *at 15,000 feet.*

flat·ter (flăt′ ər) ***vt-*** **1** to compliment highly; also, to praise too much: *Your invitation* flatters *me. He* flattered *his employer in the hope of a raise.* **2** to show very favorably: *The snapshot* flatters *him.* **—*n-*** **flat′ ter·er.** ***adv-*** **flat′ ter·ing·ly:** *He spoke to her* flatteringly.

flat·ter·y (flăt′ ə rē) ***n-*** [*pl.* **flat·ter·ies**] excess praise.

flat·tish (flăt′ ĭsh) ***adj-*** rather flat; somewhat flat.

flat·top (flăt′ tŏp′) ***n-*** *Slang* aircraft carrier.

flat·u·lent (flăch′ ə lənt, flăt′ yo͞o-) ***adj-*** **1** affected by or tending to cause gas in the stomach or intestines. **2** pretentious; pompous; conceited. **—*n-*** **flat′ u·lence.**

flat·ware (flăt′ wâr′) ***n-*** tableware that is more or less flat, such as plates, knives, and forks, as distinguished from bowls, pitchers, etc.

flat·work (flăt′ wûrk′) ***n-*** laundry such as sheets, towels, napkins, etc., which can be pressed by a machine rather than by a hand iron.

flat·worm (flăt′ wûrm′) ***n-*** any of various flat-bodied worms, most of which are parasitic on vertebrate animals, including man.

flaunt (flònt) ***vt-*** to show off; display arrogantly: *to* flaunt *one's superior knowledge.* ***vi-*** **1** to go about boldly or impudently: *to* flaunt *through the streets.* **2** to wave showily: *flags* flaunting *in the breeze.* **—*adv-*** **flaunt′ ing·ly:** *He* flauntingly *showed his contempt.*

flau·tist (flò′ tĭst, flou′ -) ***n-*** flutist.

fla·vor (flā′ vər) ***n-*** **1** taste of something that is eaten or drunk: *stew with a spicy* flavor. **2** substance that gives a particular taste to food or drink: *Chocolate is a good* flavor. **3** distinctive quality: *stories with a quaint* flavor. ***vt*****:** *to* flavor *a pie with lemon.* ***—adj-*** **fla′ vor·less.**

fla·vor·ing (flā′ vər ĭng) ***n-*** substance or extract used to give a special taste to food or drink: *chocolate* flavoring.

flaw (flȯ) ***n-*** damaged or weak point; defect; fault: *a* flaw *in a glass*; *a* flaw *in character.* ***—adj-*** **flawed:** *a* flawed *ruby.*

flaw·less (flȯ′ ləs) ***adj-*** without a defect; perfect: *a* flawless *diamond.* ***—adv-*** **flaw′ less·ly.** ***n-*** **flaw′ less·ness.**

flax (flăks) ***n-*** **1** plant with blue flowers, grown for its fibers and seeds. The fibers are spun into threads and then woven into linen, and the seeds yield linseed oil. **2** the threadlike fibers from the stem of this plant.

Flax

flax·en (flăk′ sən) ***adj-*** **1** like flax or made of flax. **2** the color of flax straw; pale yellow: *her* flaxen *hair.*

flax·seed (flăk′ sēd′) ***n-*** the seeds of flax, used in medicine and for making linseed oil.

flay (flā) ***vt-*** **1** to strip off the skin from. **2** to scold severely; criticize harshly. ***—n-*** **flay′ er.**

flea (flē) ***n-*** **1** wingless insect that sucks blood from birds and mammals, including man. The flea, although only about a fifth of an inch long, is noted for its ability to make long jumps. **2** any of various other small animals that jump like fleas. ***Hom-*** flee.

fleck (flĕk) ***n-*** small spot, mark, or particle: *a* fleck *of dust.* ***vt-*** to spot or mark: *Clouds* flecked *the sky.*

Flea

flec·tion (flĕk′ shən) ***n-*** act of bending, especially an arm or leg.

fledge (flĕj) ***vi-*** **[fledged, fledg·ing]** of a young bird, to grow feathers necessary for flight. ***vt-*** to furnish (an arrow) with feathers.

fledg·ling (flĕj′ lĭng) ***n-*** young bird just able to fly; hence, a young and inexperienced person.

flee (flē) ***vi-*** **[fled** (flĕd), **flee·ing] 1** to hurry or run away, especially from danger: *The deer* fled *as we approached.* **2** to disappear quickly; vanish: *His troubles* fled. ***vt-*** **1** to run away from: *to* flee *a burning house.* **2** to avoid; shun: *to* flee *evil.* ***Hom-*** flea.

fleece (flēs) ***n-*** **1** the woolly coat that covers a sheep; also, all the wool shorn or cut off a sheep at one time. **2** anything like the coat of a sheep. ***vt-*** **[fleeced, fleec·ing] 1** to cut wool off a sheep. **2** to rob, cheat, or swindle (someone). ***—n-*** **fleec′ er.**

fleec·y (flē′ sē) ***adj-*** **[fleec·i·er, fleec·i·est]** of or like fleece; soft and light: *a* fleecy *cloud.* ***—n-*** **fleec′ i·ness.**

[1]**fleet** (flēt) ***n-*** **1** group of warships under one command. **2** group of boats or vehicles moving or working together, or under the same management. [from Old English **flēot** meaning "ship," from **flēotan,** "to float; swim."]

[2]**fleet** (flēt) ***adj-*** **[fleet·er, fleet·est] 1** fast; swift: *a* fleet *horse.* ***vi-*** to pass swiftly: *The hours* fleeted *by.* [from Old English **flēot(e)** meaning "a stream; creek; any moving water," and **flēotan,** "to float; swim." The idea of moving gives the sense of "swift."] ***—adv-*** **fleet′ ly.** ***n-*** **fleet′ ness.**

fleet admiral ***n-*** Admiral of the Fleet.

fleet·ing (flē′ tĭng) ***adj-*** passing quickly; lasting a short time; brief: *a* fleeting *glimpse.* ***—adv-*** **fleet′ ing·ly.**

Flem·ing (flĕm′ ĭng) ***n-*** a Belgian whose language is Flemish.

Flem·ish (flĕm′ ĭsh) ***adj-*** of or pertaining to Flanders, its people, or their language. ***n-*** language spoken by the Flemings, closely related to Dutch.

flense (flĕns) ***vt-*** **[flensed, flens·ing]** to strip blubber or skin from: *to* flense *a whale.*

flesh (flĕsh) ***n-*** **1** the soft parts of the body between the skin and bones, consisting chiefly of muscle and fat. **2** the meat of animals, birds, or fish used as food. **3** soft pulp of fruits and vegetables used as food. **4** the body, as distinguished from the mind and soul: *The spirit is willing, but the* flesh *is weak.* **5** a light, pinkish tan. ***—adj-*** **flesh′ less.**

flesh and blood kin: *Your brothers and sisters are your own* flesh and blood. **in the flesh** in the actual, living state, rather than as a picture or image.

flesh-col·ored (flĕsh′ kŭl′ ərd) ***adj-*** light pinkish tan.

flesh·ly (flĕsh′ lē) ***adj-*** **1** of or having to do with the body: *our* fleshly *ills.* **2** worldly rather than spiritual. ***—n-*** **flesh′ li·ness.**

flesh·pots (flĕsh′ pots′) ***n-*** *pl.* physical luxuries and comforts; high living; also, places providing them.

flesh wound ***n-*** wound not affecting a bone or vital organ.

flesh·y (flĕsh′ ē) ***adj-*** **[flesh·i·er, flesh·i·est] 1** having much flesh or pulp: *a* fleshy *fruit.* **2** plump; fat. ***—n-*** **flesh′ i·ness.**

fleur-de-lis (flûr′ də lē′) ***n-*** [*pl.* **fleurs-de-lis** (-lēz′)] **1** design resembling an iris flower, used especially as the emblem of the former royal family of France. **2** the iris. Also **fleur′ -de-lys′.**

Fleur-de-lis

flew (flōō) *p.t.* of **fly.** ***Homs-*** flu, flue.

flex (flĕks) ***vt-*** **1** to bend: *to* flex *one's knees*; *to* flex *a bow by tightening the bowstring.* **2** to tighten or contract (a muscle).

flex·i·ble (flĕk′ sə bəl) ***adj-*** **1** easily bent: *a* flexible *fishing rod.* **2** capable of fitting to new conditions; adaptable: *a* flexible *person*; *a* flexible *form of government.* ***—n-*** **flex′ i·bil′ i·ty.** ***adv-*** **flex′ i·bly.**

flex·ion (flĕk′ shən) ***n-*** a bending or turning, as of an arm or muscle.

flex·or (flĕk′ sər) ***n-*** muscle that bends or flexes a joint in an arm or a leg. See also *extensor.*

flex·ure (flĕk′ shər) ***n-*** **1** a bending or a being bent. **2** the part bent.

flick (flĭk) ***n-*** light, quick stroke or motion: *to give a horse a* flick *with the whip*; *a* flick *of the wrist.* ***vt-*** to strike or move lightly and quickly: *He* flicked *the horse gently.*

[1]**flick·er** (flĭk′ ər) ***vi-*** **1** to shine or burn unsteadily; waver: *A candle* flickers *in the breeze.* **2** to move back and forth; tremble; quiver: *The shadows* flickered *on the wall.* ***n-*** unsteady light or movement; flutter: *the* flicker *of a candle*; *the* flicker of an eyelid. [from Old English **flicorian** meaning "to flutter."] ***—adv-*** **flick′ er·ing·ly:** *The candle burned* flickeringly. ***adj-*** **flick′ er·y.**

[2]**flick·er** (flĭk′ ər) ***n-*** North American woodpecker with a bright red mark at the neck and yellow under the wings and tail. [probably an imitation of the cry.]

flied (flīd) *p.t. & p.p.* of **fly** (to hit a baseball).

fli·er (flī′ ər) ***n-*** **1** aviator. **2** anything that flies or moves very rapidly, such as an express train. **3** daring or risky investment intended to make money quickly: *a* flier *in stocks.* **4** advertising leaflet.

flies (flīz) **1** plural of the noun **fly.** **2** form of the verb **fly** used with "he," "she," "it," or singular noun subjects in the present tense.

fāte, făt, dâre, bärn; bē, bĕt, mêre; bīte, bĭt; nōte, hŏt, môre, dȯg; fŭn, fûr; tōō, bŏŏk; oil; out; tar; thin; then; hw for wh as in what; zh for s as in usual; ə for a, e, i, o, u, as in ago, linen, peril, atom, minus

¹flight (flīt) ***n-*** **1** act, process, or manner of flying: *The bat has a zigzag* flight. **2** the passage or distance flown: *the London-New York* flight; *a short* flight. **3** swift passage: *the* flight *of time.* **4** a flying group: *a* flight *of geese*; *a* flight *of arrows.* **5** a group or series of steps: *He lived three* flights *up.* **6** a passing beyond the usual: *a* flight *of imagination.* [from Old English **flyht,** "a flying."]
take flight to begin flying; rise in flight.

²flight (flīt) ***n-*** hasty departure: *his* flight *from the burning building.* [from earlier English **fliht,** "a fleeing," from **flēon,** related to English **flee.**]
put to flight to cause to flee. **take flight** or **take to flight** to flee; run away.

flight attendant ***n-*** person employed to care for passengers on airplanes.

flight·less (flīt′ləs) ***adj-*** unable to fly: *The ostrich is a* flightless *bird.*

flight path ***n-*** path or route taken by an aircraft, guided missile, or spacecraft in flight.

flight·y (flī′tē) ***adj-*** [**flight·i·er, flight·i·est**] shifting rapidly and aimlessly in interest and enthusiasm; giddy; frivolous: *a* flighty *young girl*; flighty *conversation.* ***—adv-*** **flight′i·ly.** ***n-*** **flight′i·ness.**

flim·flam (flĭm′flăm′) *Informal* ***n-*** a cheating by deception; trickery. ***vt-*** [**flim·flammed, flim·flam·ming**] to cheat or trick. ***—n-*** **flim′flam′mer.**

flim·sy (flĭm′zē) ***adj-*** [**flim·si·er, flim·si·est**] **1** fragile; not solid; poorly made: *The* flimsy *boat was crushed like an eggshell.* **2** weak; not convincing: *a* flimsy *excuse.* ***—adv-*** **flim′si·ly.** ***n-*** **flim′si·ness.**

flinch (flĭnch) ***vi-*** to draw back or away from pain, danger, an unpleasant duty, etc.: *He* flinches *at noise.*

fling (flĭng) ***vt-*** [**flung** (flŭng), **fling·ing**] **1** to throw or hurl with force: *to* fling *a stone*; *to* fling *a burden down.* **2** to move or jerk suddenly: *to* fling *one's head back.* ***vi-*** to rush headlong or impatiently: *to* fling *out of the room.* ***n-*** **1** a toss or throw: *She gave her hat a* fling. **2** sneer or gibe: *a* fling *at politicians.* **3** a lively dance. See also *Highland fling.*
have a fling to indulge in a period of unrestrained pleasure. **have a fling at** to have a try at; attempt briefly.

flint (flĭnt) ***n-*** **1** very hard quartz, usually dull gray, that produces sparks when struck against steel. **2** a piece of this quartz; also, a piece of metal alloy used to produce sparks in cigarette lighters.

flint·lock (flĭnt′lŏk′) ***n-*** old-fashioned gun fired by a spark from a flint and steel attached to it.

Flintlock

flint·y (flĭn′tē) ***adj-*** [**flint·i·er, flint·i·est**] **1** made of or like flint. **2** hard; unyielding: *a* flinty *look.* ***—adv-*** **flint′i·ly.** ***n-*** **flint′i·ness.**

¹flip (flĭp) ***vt-*** [**flipped, flip·ping**] **1** to flick with the fingers; tap or push lightly: *to* flip *a switch.* **2** to turn rapidly: *to* flip *the pages of a book.* **3** to toss with a quick motion of a finger and thumb: *to* flip *a coin.* ***vi-*** to turn: *The fish* flipped *over.* ***n-*** **1** short, quick turning movement: *She gave the egg a* flip. **2** somersault. [origin uncertain.]

²flip (flĭp) *Informal* ***adj-*** [**flip·per, flip·pest**] saucy; flippant: *a* flip *remark.* [probably from Old Norse **fleipa** or **flipa,** "to babble."]

flip·pant (flĭp′ənt) ***adj-*** not showing proper respect or seriousness: *her* flippant *attitude*; *a* flippant *reply.* ***—n-*** **flip′pan·cy.** ***adv-*** **flip′pant·ly.**

flip·per (flĭp′ər) ***n-*** **1** finlike limb of a seal, sea turtle, etc. **2** fin worn by a skin diver (for picture, see *fin*).

flirt (flûrt) ***vi-*** **1** to be insincerely or playfully romantic with a member of the opposite sex: *He* flirted *with all the girls.* **2** to toy or play: *to* flirt *with danger.* ***vt-*** to toss, move, or open and close briskly: *to* flirt *a fan.* ***n-*** person who playfully acts the lover.

Flippers

flir·ta·tion (flûr tā′shən) ***n-*** **1** act of flirting. **2** brief, light romance.

flir·ta·tious (flûr tā′shəs) ***adj-*** playfully romantic; coquettish: *a* flirtatious *girl*; *a* flirtatious *glance.* ***—adv-*** **flir·ta′tious·ly.** ***n-*** **flir·ta′tious·ness.**

flit (flĭt) ***vi-*** [**flit·ted, flit·ting**] **1** to move or fly lightly and quickly; dart: *The bird* flitted *about.* **2** to pass quickly.

flit·ter (flĭt′ər) ***vi-*** to flutter.

float (flōt) ***vi-*** **1** to be held up by liquid or air: *Wood* floats *on water. A balloon* floats *in the air.* **2** to move or drift freely: *A cloud* floated *across the sky.* ***vt-*** **1** to cause to rest on, move along, or rise to the surface of a liquid: *to* float *a raft.* **2** to plan and set going, especially as a financial venture: *to* float *a business*; *to* float *a loan.* ***n-*** **1** something that floats or helps something else to float: *a* float *on a fishline.* **2** an exhibit on a platform with wheels, used in a parade. ***—adj-*** **float′a·ble.**

float·er (flō′tər) ***n-*** **1** person or thing that floats. **2** person who moves aimlessly from place to place or job to job.

floating decimal ***adj-*** using a system of expressing a number as a product of a decimal and a particular power of 10: *He bought a calculator with a* floating decimal *system.*

floating island ***n-*** soft custard pudding topped with meringue or whipped cream.

floating rib ***n-*** in human beings, one of the two lowest pairs of ribs, which are attached only to the vertebrae.

floc·cu·lent (flŏk′yə lənt) ***adj-*** having or resembling soft, fluffy tufts or shreds of wool or similar material. ***—n-*** **floc′cu·lence.**

¹flock (flŏk) ***n-*** **1** a group of animals or birds of one kind which travel or feed together: *a* flock *of sheep*; *a* flock *of geese.* **2** large number of people together, especially the members of a single church: *The minister greeted his* flock. ***vi-*** to come together or move in crowds: *People* flocked *to the beaches.* [from Old English **flocc.**]

²flock (flŏk) ***n-*** small tuft or mass of very short, woolly fibers. ***vt-*** to cover (a fabric or wallpaper) with such tufts. [from Old French **floc,** from Latin **floccus.**]

flock·ing (flŏk′ĭng) ***n-*** short, woolly fibers applied to wallpaper or fabric in an ornamental design.

floe (flō) ***n-*** large sheet or mass of ice drifting on the sea. ***Hom-*** flow.

flog (flŏg) ***vt-*** [**flogged, flog·ging**] to beat hard with a stick or whip. ***—n-*** **flog′ger.**

flood (flŭd) ***n-*** **1** great flow of water; especially, a body of water overflowing its banks. **2** a great outpouring or abundance resembling a deluge: *a* flood *of tears*; *a* flood *of letters.* **3 the Flood** in the Bible, a great deluge in the days of Noah. ***vt-*** **1** to cover or cause to be covered with water: *The heavy rain* flooded *the basement.* **2** to supply in large quantity. ***vi-*** to rise and overflow.

flood·gate (flŭd′gāt′) ***n-*** gate or sluice in a waterway to keep out or let in water.

flood·light (flŭd′līt′) ***n-*** **1** broad beam of light covering a large area. **2** a lamp that gives such a light. ***vt-*** to light by such means: *to* floodlight *a football field.*

flood plain *n-* plain bordering a river and frequently flooded by it, especially such a plain formed by deposits of soil left by floods.

flood tide *n-* the incoming tide; also, the point or time of highest tide.

floor (flôr) *n-* 1 the part of a room that one walks on, or a surface resembling this: *a wooden* floor; *the ocean* floor. 2 all the rooms on one level in a building; story. 3 the main part of an assembly hall, where members sit and speak. 4 the right to speak in such an assembly: *He has the* floor. *vt-* 1 to build a walking surface in: *to* floor *a house.* 2 to knock down: *The boxer* floored *his opponent.* 3 *Informal* to dumbfound; baffle.

floor·ing (flôr′ĭng) *n-* 1 materials for floors. 2 a floor or floors.

floor leader *n-* in either of the houses of Congress, a person who is chosen by his political party to direct its business and strategy on the floor.

floor show *n-* series of performances by singers, dancers, or comedians in a nightclub.

floor·walk·er (flôr′wȯk′ər) *n-* person employed in a large store to supervise clerks and direct customers.

flop (flŏp) *vi-* [**flopped, flop·ping**] 1 to drop or fall heavily or clumsily: *She* flopped *into a chair.* 2 to move or flap about: *to* flop *like a fish out of water.* 3 *Slang* to fail. *vt-*: *He* flopped *his suitcase on the floor.* *n-* 1 act or sound of flopping. 2 *Slang* a failure.

flop·py (flŏp′ē) *adj-* [**flop·pi·er, flop·pi·est**] tending to flap or move loosely about: *a rabbit with* floppy *ears.* *—adv-* **flop′pi·ly.** *n-* **flop′pi·ness.**

floppy disc *n-* flexible plastic disk on which information is recorded magnetically.

flor·a (flôr′ə) *n-* the plants of a particular region, environment, or period of time. See also *fauna.*

flo·ral (flôr′əl) *adj-* of or like flowers: *a* floral *design*; *a* floral *fragrance.* *—adv-* **flo′ral·ly.**

Flor·en·tine (flôr′ən tēn′, flȯr′-) *n-* a native of Florence, Italy. *adj-* 1 of or relating to Florence or its inhabitants. 2 relating to a dull, brushed finish used on gold or silver jewelry.

flo·res·cence (flôr ĕs′əns, flə rĕs′-) *n-* a blossoming or period of blossoming. *—adj-* **flo·res′cent.**

flo·ret (flôr′ət) *n-* small flower, especially one of many forming a dense cluster of a single flowering head.

flor·id (flŏr′ĭd, flȯr′-) *adj-* 1 bright in color; flushed: *a* florid *complexion.* 2 full of flowery ornamentation; elaborate and showy: *a* florid *style of writing.* *—adv-* **flor′id·ly.** *n-* **flor′id·ness.**

flor·in (flôr′ən, flŏr′-) *n-* any of various European coins.

flo·rist (flôr′ĭst, flŏr′-) *n-* a person who grows or sells flowers as a business.

floss (flŏs, flȯs) *n-* 1 soft, glossy silk or cotton thread used in embroidering, crocheting, etc. 2 soft, silky fibers in certain plant pods or husks, such as the milkweed.

floss·y (flŏs′ē, flȯ′sē) *adj-* [**floss·i·er, floss·i·est**] 1 of or like floss; soft and silky. 2 *Slang* showy and pretentious in an effort to be elegant.

flo·ta·tion (flō tā′shən) *n-* 1 act or process of floating. 2 the sale of stock in a new business to get enough money to start operation. 3 in mining, a method of spearating crushed or powdered ores by putting them in a special liquid which will float only certain particles. *as modifier*: *a* flotation *process.*

flo·til·la (flō tĭl′ə) *n-* 1 fleet of small vessels; also, a small fleet. 2 in the U.S. Navy, a unit of two or more squadrons of vessels of the same type.

flot·sam (flŏt′səm) *n-* the wreckage of a ship or its cargo found floating in the sea. See also *jetsam.*

[1]**flounce** (flouns) *vi-* [**flounced, flounc·ing**] to move or go in a jerky, impatient, or angry manner: *She* flounced *out of the room.* *n-* jerky, impatient, motion. [of uncertain origin; perhaps from Old Norse, and related to Swedish **flunsa** meaning "to plunge."]

[2]**flounce** (flouns) *n-* strip of cloth gathered and sewn along an edge of something; ruffled border. *vt-* [**flounced, flounc·ing**] to add such a border to (something). [from earlier **frounce,** probably from Old French **froncer,** "to wrinkle (the brow, etc.)," from Latin **frons,** "brow."]

[1]**floun·der** (floun′dər) *vi-* to make awkward, blundering efforts to get through or out of something; struggle clumsily: *to* flounder *about in a swamp*; *to* flounder *through a speech.* [apparently from [2]**flounder,** from the motion of the fish.]

[2]**floun·der** (floun′dər) *n-* [*pl.* **floun·der; floun·ders** (kinds of flounder)] any of various flatfishes used for food. [from Old French **flondre,** from Old Norse, as in Swedish **flundra.**]

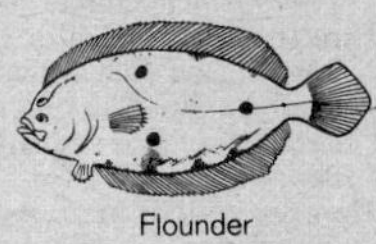
Flounder

flour (flou′ər) *n-* fine meal of ground wheat or other grain. *vt-* to sprinkle or cover with this. *Hom-* flower.

flour·ish (flûr′ĭsh) *vi-* 1 to grow; prosper; thrive; be successful: *Citrus fruits* flourish *in warm climates. Business* flourished *last year.* 2 to reach a high point in achievement or development: *Egyptian civilization* flourished *over 2000 years ago.* *vt-* to wave or swing about in the air: *to* flourish *a sword.* *n-* 1 showy waving: *a* flourish *of flags, hats, etc.* 2 decoration in handwriting: *He signed his name with a* flourish. 3 showy passage of music, often played by trumpets, bugles, etc.

flour·y (flou′rē) *adj-* 1 of or resembling flour. 2 smeared or covered with flour.

flout (flout) *vt-* to mock; scoff at; treat with scorn: *to* flout *the authorities.* *—n-* **flout′er.**

flow (flō) *vi-* 1 to move or run along as fluids do: *Water* flows. *Blood* flows *in a vein.* 2 to abound; be plentiful: *Wine* flowed *at the feast.* 3 to move or pour forth like a stream: *Goods* flowed *into the stores. The words* flowed. 4 to appear to move in a pleasing, continuous motion. 5 to hang loose; stream: *Her hair* flows *to her waist.* 6 of the tide, to rise. *n-* 1 act of running or streaming: *to stop the* flow *of blood.* 2 the amount of fluid passing through an opening or by a certain point in a given time. 3 any continuous, uninterrupted movement or procedure; a current: *the* flow *of a river*; *a* flow *of talk. the* flow *of traffic.* 4 the coming in of the tide. *Hom-* floe.

flow·er (flou′ər) *n-* 1 in seed-bearing plants, a part which contains the organs of reproduction and from which the seeds develop. Most flowers have petals and are often brightly colored, but some are tiny and inconspicuous. 2 any plant grown for, or noticeable because of, its blossoms: *to plant* flowers. 3 the best part: *the* flower *of the country's youth*; *in the* flower *of life.* *vi-* to bloom. *Hom-* flour. *—adj-* **flow′er·less.** *adj-* **flow′er·like′.**

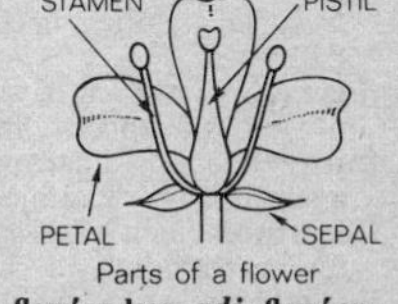

Parts of a flower

flow·ered (flou′ərd) *adj-* having flowers or a design resembling flowers: *a* flowered *dress.*

fāte, făt, dâre, bärn; bē, bĕt, mêre; bīte, bĭt; nōte, hŏt, môre, dȯg; fŭn, fûr; tōō, bŏŏk; oil; out; tar; thin; then; hw for wh as in *wh*at; zh for s as in u*s*ual; ə for a, e, i, o, u, as in *a*go, lin*e*n, per*i*l, at*o*m, min*u*s

flow·er·et (flou′ ər ət) ***n-*** little flower; floret.

flowering plant ***n-*** any of a large and major group of highly evolved plants whose seeds are enclosed in a fruit; angiosperm.

flow·er·pot (flou′ ər pŏt′) ***n-*** container, usually of baked clay, in which to plant or keep growing plants.

flow·er·y (flou′ ə rē) ***adj-*** [**flow·er·i·er, flow·er·i·est**] **1** full of or resembling flowers: *a* flowery *meadow*; *a* flowery *fragrance*. **2** full of or using showy, ornate words or phrases; florid. **—*n-* flow′ er·i·ness.**

flown (flōn) *p.p.* of [1]**fly.**

flu (flōō) ***n-*** influenza. ***Homs-*** flew, flue.

flub (flŭb) *Informal* ***vt-*** [**flubbed, flub·bing**] to fail clumsily at (doing something); bungle. ***n-*** a bungling error.

fluc·tu·ate (flŭk′ chōō āt′) ***vi-*** [**fluc·tu·at·ed, fluc·tu·at·ing**] to rise and fall; also, to vary unsteadily; waver: *Prices may* fluctuate. **—*n-* fluc′ tu·a′ tion.**

flue (flōō) ***n-*** **1** pipe or passage for carrying off smoke, hot air, etc., such as that in a chimney. **2** (also **flue pipe**) an organ pipe that produces a tone when a current of air strikes the lip or opening in the side of the pipe. ***Homs-*** flew, flu.

flu·en·cy (flōō′ ən sē) ***n-*** ease and smoothness, especially in speaking.

flu·ent (flōō′ ənt) ***adj-*** **1** spoken or produced with ease; smooth and flowing: *to speak* fluent *Spanish*; *the* fluent *motions of a dancer*. **2** using words in a smooth, flowing manner: *a* fluent *speaker*. **—*adv-* flu′ ent·ly.**

fluff (flŭf) ***n-*** **1** soft, light, downy material: *The kitten looked like a ball of* fluff. **2** *Informal* a mistake in making a speech, acting a part, etc. ***vt-*** **1** to shake or puff out into a soft mass: *The bird* fluffed *its feathers*. **2** *Informal* to make a mistake in speaking or saying (something).

fluff·y (flŭf′ ē) ***adj-*** [**fluff·i·er, fluff·i·est**] resembling, consisting of, or covered with fluff. **—*n-* fluff′ i·ness.**

flu·id (flōō′ ĭd) ***n-*** substance that will flow; a liquid or a gas. ***adj-*** **1** able to flow; not solid; liquid or gaseous: *Molten steel is* fluid. **2** not fixed or settled; likely to change: *My plans are* fluid. **—*adv-* flu′ id·ly.**

fluid dram ***n-*** unit of liquid measure equal to 1/8 fluid ounce or about 3.7 cubic centimeters; about a teaspoonful.

fluid drive ***n-*** in an automobile transmission, a kind of clutch, consisting of two platelike turbine blades enclosed in an oil-filled case. Engine power rotates one blade, setting the oil in motion, thus causing the other blade to rotate. Also **fluid clutch.**

flu·id·i·ty (flōō ĭd′ ə tē) ***n-*** condition of being fluid.

fluid ounce ***n-*** unit of liquid measure equal to 1/16 pint.

[1]**fluke** (flōōk) ***n-*** **1** flattened, pointed end of an arm of an anchor. **2** one of the two lobes of a whale's tail. **3** barbed or pointed head of a harpoon, arrow, lance, etc. [origin uncertain; perhaps from [3]**fluke.**]

[2]**fluke** (flōōk) ***n-*** stroke of good or bad luck: *He won by a lucky* fluke. [origin uncertain.] **—*adj-* fluk′ y [flu·ki·er, flu·ki·est].**

[3]**fluke** (flōōk) ***n-*** **1** any of various parasitic flatworms. **2** any of various flounders. [from Old English **floc.**]

flume (flōōm) ***n-*** **1** narrow gorge or ravine through which a stream flows. **2** artificial channel for water.

flum·mox (flŭm′ əks) *Informal* ***vt-*** to throw into confusion; bewilder.

flung (flŭng) *p.t. & p.p.* of **fling.**

flunk (flŭngk) *Informal* ***vt-*** **1** to fail (a subject, test, etc.). **2** to give a failing mark to. ***vi-***: *He* flunked *in English*.

flunk out to be discharged from a school because of bad marks.

flunk·y (flŭng′ kē) ***n-*** [*pl.* **flunk·ies**] **1** person who meekly serves and tries to please another; toady. **2** footman or similar uniformed servant (now considered derogatory). Also **flunk′ ey.**

flu·o·resce (flōō′ ə rĕs′, flôr ĕs′) ***vi-*** [**flu·o·resced, flu·o·res·ing**] to show fluorescence.

flu·o·res·cence (flōō′ ə rĕs′ əns, flôr ĕs′-) ***n-*** **1** the emitting of electromagnetic radiation, usually as light, by certain substances when exposed to radiation of another wavelength. See also *phosphorescence*. **2** the emitted radiation. **—*adj-* flu·o′ res′ cent.**

fluorescent lamp ***n-*** tubular electric lamp in which glowing filaments produce ultraviolet light in reaction with mercury vapor, and this light in turn causes the inner coating of phosphor to fluoresce brightly.

flu·o·ri·date (flōō′ ə rə dāt′, flôr′ ə-) ***vt-*** [**flu·o·ri·dat·ed, flu·o·ri·dat·ing**] to treat with fluorides; especially, to add fluorides to (drinking water) in order to prevent tooth decay. **—*n-* flu′ o·ri·da′ tion.**

flu·o·ride (flōō′ ə rīd′, flôr′ īd′) ***n-*** any chemical compound that consists of fluorine combined with another element or radical.

flu·o·rine (flōō ə rēn′, flôr′ ēn′) ***n-*** pale yellow poisonous gas that is one of the most reactive elements. Symbol F, At. No. 9, At. Wt. 18.9984.

flu·o·rite (flōō′ ə rīt′, flôr′ īt′) ***n-*** mineral calcium fluoride (CaF_2), found in various colors. It is used to make metals melt more easily in soldering, making steel, etc. Also **flu′ or·spar′** (flōō′ ər spär′, flôr′-).

fluor·o·scope (flōō′ ər ə skōp′, flôr′-) ***n-*** device for studying the shadows cast on a fluorescent screen by an object placed between the screen and a source of X rays; especially, such a machine used to examine people.

flur·ry (flŭr′ ē) ***n-*** [*pl.* **flur·ries**] **1** confusion or bustle; commotion: *a* flurry *of excitement*. **2** light, brief fall of snow, or a sudden gust of wind. ***vt-*** [**flur·ried, flur·ry·ing**] to confuse; agitate; fluster.

[1]**flush** (flŭsh) ***vi-*** **1** to become red; glow; blush: *Her cheeks* flushed *with excitement. He* flushed *with embarrassment*. **2** to flow and spread rapidly: *Water* flushed *into the room*. ***vt-*** **1** to cleanse or wash out with a strong flow of water: *to* flush *a clogged pipe*. **2** to make red; cause to glow. **3** to fill with elation and excitement. ***n-*** **1** a blush or glow. **2** sudden flow or rush. **3** feeling of excitement or elation: *the first* flush *of victory*. ***adj-*** **1** at the same line or level; even: *doors* flush *with the walls*. **2** abundantly supplied, especially with money. **3** prosperous: *a* flush *age*. [of uncertain origin.]

flush out to clean or unclog: *to* flush out *a drain*.

[2]**flush** (flŭsh) ***n-*** in some card games, especially poker, a hand in which all the cards are of the same suit. [from French **flux,** from earlier **flus** in the sense of "a flowing," from Latin **fluxus.**]

[3]**flush** (flŭsh) ***vt-*** to startle into flight or from a hiding place: *to* flush *a partridge*. ***vi-***: *The birds* flushed *when the dog approached*. [from Middle English **flusschen.**]

flus·ter (flŭs′ tər) ***vt-*** to upset or excite; confuse: *Teasing* flusters *me*. ***n-*** confused or agitated condition.

Man playing a flute

flute (flōōt) ***n-*** **1** wind instrument with a high, clear tone, played by blowing across a mouthpiece near one end. **2** shallow, decorative groove: *the* flutes *in the columns of a temple*. ***vi-*** [**flut·ed, flut·ing**] to play on a flute, or to make a sound like that of a flute. ***vt-*** **1** to make decorative grooves or folds in: *to* flute *a ruffle*. **2** to speak or sing (something) high and clear.

flut·ing (flo͞o′ tĭng) ***n-*** series of decorative grooves: *to ornament the legs of a table with* fluting.

flut·ist (flo͞o′ tĭst) ***n-*** person who plays the flute. Also **flautist.**

flut·ter (flŭt′ ər) ***vi-*** **1** to fly or move with an irregular flapping of the wings: *The wounded bird* fluttered *along the ground.* **2** to flap, wave, or beat rapidly: *The leaves* fluttered *in the breeze. My heart* fluttered *with excitement.* **3** to move about nervously and excitedly: *The anxious hostess* fluttered *from guest to guest.* ***vt-*** to cause to move with a flapping or rapid motion: *The bird* fluttered *its wings. She* fluttered *her eyelashes at him.* ***n-*** **1** rapid, irregular motion or change. **2** state of nervous excitement. **—*n-* flut′ ter·er.** ***adj-*** **flut′ ter·y.**

flu·vi·al (flo͞o′ vē əl) ***adj-*** of or produced by a stream.

flux (flŭks) ***n-*** **1** constant flowing; continuous change: *Conditions are in* flux. **2** any flow or discharge, especially an abnormal flow of matter from the body. **3** substance used to make metals melt more easily. **4** substance such as rosin or an acid, used in soldering and brazing to clean surfaces and improve the joining of metals. **5** *Physics* (1) rate of flow of a fluid or of particles across a given area. (2) magnetic flux.

[1]**fly** (flī) ***vi-*** [**flew** (flo͞o), **flown** (flōn), **fly·ing**] **1** to move through the air with or as if with wings: *Birds* fly *south in the fall. The arrow* flew *to the target.* **2** to move or go very swiftly; speed: *He* flew *to her aid. The hours* flew *quickly by.* **3** to move through or in the air: *The flag* flew *in the breeze.* **4** to travel in or pilot an aircraft: *He has* flown *often.* **5** [*p.t. & p.p.* **flied**] in baseball, to bat the ball high in the air. ***vt-*** **1** to pilot (an aircraft); also, to transport (passengers, goods, etc.) in an aircraft. **2** to cause to move through or float in the air: *to* fly *a kite*; *to* fly *a flag.* ***n-*** [*pl.* **flies**] **1** strip of cloth covering a zipper or row of buttons on a garment, especially trousers. **2** in baseball, a ball batted high in the air. **3** door or side flap of a tent; also, a canvas sheet used to form a roof over an area next to or near a tent. [from Old English **flēogan.**]

flying high *Informal* very elated or confident of success. **let fly** to hurl or shoot forth with great force. **on the fly** **1** while something is still in the air: *He caught the ball* on the fly. **2** *Informal* very quickly or briefly, because pressed for time: *to eat* on the fly.

fly at to attack or rush at suddenly and violently.

fly blind to fly an aircraft entirely by instruments, as in heavy fog or clouds.

fly in the face (or **teeth**) **of** to be openly defiant of.

[2]**fly** (flī) ***n-*** [*pl.* **flies**] **1** any of various insects with a single pair of gauzy wings, especially the common housefly. For picture, see *housefly.* **2** a fishhook fitted with feathers to look like an insect. [from Old English **flēoge, flyge.** It is of course from [1]**fly.**]

fly in the ointment something that spoils an otherwise happy or profitable situation.

fly·blown (flī′ blōn′) ***adj-*** covered with maggots or blowfly eggs; hence, rotten, dirty, or corrupt.

fly-by-night (flī′ bī nīt′) ***n-*** shifty or untrustworthy person, especially one who sets up a shaky or dishonest business for a quick profit. ***adj-***: *a* fly-by-night *business.*

fly·cast·ing (flī′ kăs′ tĭng) ***n-*** skill or practice of fishing with artificial flies. **—*n-* fly′ cast′ er.**

fly·catch·er (flī′ kăch′ ər) ***n-*** any of several related birds that catch insects in flight.

fly dope ***n-*** substance used to make artificial fishing flies waterproof.

fly·er (flī′ ər) flier.

fly·ing (flī′ ĭng) ***adj-*** **1** able to fly or move through the air as if with wings. **2** brief and hurried; fleeting: *a* flying *visit.* **3** moved by or streaming in the air: *gay,* flying *banners.*

flying boat ***n-*** seaplane having a body like a boat hull and a small float under each wing.

flying buttress ***n-*** arched support whose top rests against and strengthens a wall, used in Gothic architecture.

flying colors ***n-*** striking success or honor; triumph: *to pass a test with* flying colors.

flying field ***n-*** level area where airplanes land or take off; small airport.

flying fish ***n-*** any of several fishes found mainly in warm seas and having long winglike fins that enable them to make gliding leaps above the surface of the water.

Flying fish, 8—18 in. long

flying fox ***n-*** any of various large, fruit-eating bats native to warm areas of Asia, Africa, and America.

flying jib ***n-*** in a sailing ship, a small sail at the foremost part, attached to an extension of the bowsprit called the **flying jib boom.**

flying machine ***n-*** in earlier times, an airplane or similar flying craft.

flying saucer or **flying disk** ***n-*** any of various unidentified disk-shaped objects which people say they have seen flying in the sky at great speeds.

flying squirrel ***n-*** an American squirrel that makes long, gliding leaps by stretching out the loose folds of skin connecting its front and hind legs.

flying start ***n-*** in a race, a getaway from the starting position at top speed; hence, any swift beginning seemingly destined for success.

fly·leaf (flī′ lēf′) ***n-*** [*pl.* **fly·leaves**] blank sheet of paper at the beginning or end of a book.

fly·pa·per (flī′ pā′ pər) ***n-*** paper covered with a sticky or poisonous substance, hung to trap and kill flies.

fly·speck (flī′ spĕk′) ***n-*** small spot of dirt left by a fly; hence, any similar small spot.

fly·trap (flī′ trap′) ***n-*** **1** any device for catching flies. **2** any plant that traps insects; Venus's-flytrap.

fly·way (flī′ wā) ***n-*** route along which birds travel in their regular migrations.

fly·weight (flī′ wāt′) ***n-*** boxer who weighs 112 pounds or less.

fly·wheel (flī′ hwēl′) ***n-*** heavy wheel used in a machine to help regulate and make more uniform the speed of the working parts.

Fm symbol for fermium.

FM frequency modulation.

f-number ***n-*** in photography, a number obtained by dividing the focal length of a lens by its diameter as regulated by the diaphragm. The smaller the number, the larger the opening is.

foal (fōl) ***n-*** the young of the horse or other closely related animal, especially one less than a year old. ***vi-*** to bring forth such young.

foam (fōm) ***n-*** frothy mixture of many tiny bubbles, such as that formed on a liquid by shaking, constant movement, fermentation, etc.: *the* foam *formed by the breaking waves.* ***vi-*** to form or produce a mass of tiny bubbles; froth. **—*adj-* foam′ y [foam·i·er, foam·i·est].**

foam at the mouth **1** to produce a mass of frothy saliva, as a dog with rabies does. **2** *Informal* to be furious.

foam rubber ***n-*** rubber made soft and resilient by filling it with tiny bubbles while it is in a liquid state.

[1]**fob** (fŏb) ***n-*** ornamental chain, ribbon, or brooch to which a watch, locket, seal, etc., may be attached. [probably from German **fuppe** meaning "pocket."]

[2]**fob** (fŏb) ***vt-*** **[fobbed, fob·bing]** (followed by "off") to deceive (someone) or use (something) as a means of deceiving someone: *to* fob *him off with a trick*; *to* fob *off a fake.* [from Middle English **fobbe,** "a trickster."]

f.o.b. or **F.O.B.** free on board.

fo·cal (fō′ kəl) ***adj-*** of, at, or having to do with a focus: *the* focal *point.*

focal infection ***n-*** infection in a particular part of the body, such as a tooth, which may spread to other parts.

fo·cal·ize (fō′ kə līz′) ***vt-*** **[fo·cal·ized, fo·cal·iz·ing]** to concentrate or confine (an infection, disorder, etc.) to a limited area of the body. **—*n-* fo′ cal·i·za′ tion.**

focal length ***n-*** in optics, the distance from the center of a lens or curved mirror to the point where parallel rays from an object are brought to a point; focus.

fo'c'sle (fōk′ səl) forecastle.

fo·cus (fō′ kəs) ***n-*** [*pl.* **fo·cus·es** or **fo·ci** (-sī)] **1** point at which rays of light, sound waves, electron beams, etc., meet after being bent by a lens, curved mirror, sound reflector, etc. **2** focal length. **3** the adjustment of the eyes, a camera, lens, etc., in order to produce clear images; also, the condition of being sharp and clear to the sight: *good* focus. **4** the central point or center of interest. **5** of a geometric figure such as an ellipse, a fixed point or one of two fixed points used in constructing or drawing the figure. For picture, see *ellipse.* **6** of an earthquake, the point from which the shock waves originate. ***vt-* 1** to adjust (the eyes, a camera, etc.) in order to produce clear images: *He* focused *the camera on the dog.* **2** to center; concentrate: *She* focused *her attention on dancing.* ***vi-* 1** to meet; converge: *Light passing through this lens* focuses *at six inches.* **2** to produce a sharp image: *This projector* focuses *when you turn the lens.* **3** to center or concentrate (on).

fod·der (fŏd′ ər) ***n-*** coarse food, such as hay, for horses, cattle, and sheep.

foe (fō) ***n-*** enemy; adversary.

foe·tal (fē′ təl) fetal.

foe·tus (fē′ təs) fetus.

fog (fŏg, fôg) ***n-* 1** cloud or mass of water vapor near the surface of the earth or water; thick mist. **2** any haziness or blurred condition: *the* fog *on a photographic film.* **3** confused or bewildered state: *Her mind is in a* fog. ***vt-*** **[fogged, fog·ging]** to cover, blur, or obscure with or as if with a thick mist. ***vi-*** to become foggy.

fog bank ***n-*** dense, low mass of fog, especially over a body of water.

fog·bound (fŏg′ bound′, fôg′-) ***adj-*** surrounded by fog that obscures visibility and makes traveling unsafe.

fog·gy (fŏg′ ē, fôg′-) ***adj-*** **[fog·gi·er, fog·gi·est] 1** full of or obscured by fog: *a* foggy *day.* **2** hazy; blurred: *a* foggy *photograph.* **3** not clear; confused: *such* foggy *notions.* **—*adv-* fog′ gi·ly. *n-* fog′ gi·ness.**

fog·horn (fŏg′ hôrn′, fôg′ hôrn′, -hôrn′) ***n-*** horn or similar device that sends warning signals to ships in a fog.

fo·gy (fō′ gē) ***n-*** [*pl.* **fo·gies**] person having old-fashioned or stuffy ideas and habits. Also **fo′ gey.**

foi·ble (foi′ bəl) ***n-*** minor failing or weakness.

[1]**foil** (foil) ***vt-*** to interfere with and prevent from being successful; thwart; balk: *to* foil *an attempt to escape.* [from Old French **fouler,** "trample under foot," from Latin **fullāre,** from **fullō,** "a fuller (of cloth)."]

[2]**foil** (foil) ***n-* 1** metal rolled or beaten into a very thin, flexible sheet: *aluminum* foil. **2** person or thing that sets off another by contrast: *Her simple dress was a perfect* foil *for her diamond necklace.* [from Old French **foille,** from Latin **folia** meaning "leaves."]

[3]**foil** (foil) ***n-*** slender sword with a blunt point, used in fencing. [apparently from [1]**foil** because the blunted end prevented injury.]

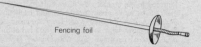

Fencing foil

foist (foist) ***vt-*** to pass off (something false or defective) as genuine or desirable; palm off: *to* foist *a fake gem.*

[1]**fold** (fōld) ***vt-* 1** to bend, double, or arrange (something) so that one part overlaps another: *to* fold *a letter*; *to* fold *a shirt after ironing it.* **2** to place close to the body: *The bird* folded *its wings.* **3** to embrace, clasp, or envelop: *She* folded *the puppy in her arms.* **4** in cooking, to blend (beaten egg whites, whipped cream, etc.) gently into a mixture. ***vi-* 1** to become doubled, bent, or creased: *Cardboard does not* fold *easily.* **2** *Slang* of a theatrical performance, business enterprise, etc., to be unsuccessful; fail. ***n-* 1** part doubled or lapped over another: *the* folds *of the heavy curtains.* **2** crease made by bending or doubling something: *Cut along the* fold. [from Old English **faldan.**]

[2]**fold** (fōld) ***n-* 1** pen or enclosure for sheep. **2** group of those who think or act alike, such as a religious sect, political party, etc.: *After many years he returned to the* fold. [from Old English **falod.**]

-fold *suffix* (used to form adjectives) **1** multiplied by; times: *a two*fold *increase.* **2** consisting of a specified number of parts: *a three*fold *plan.*

folded mountain ***n-*** a mountain formed by inner forces of the earth's crust, which uplift and fold underlying rock layers. See also *block mountain.*

fold·er (fōl′ dər) ***n-* 1** outer cover, often a sheet of heavy paper folded double, for holding papers. **2** booklet, circular, etc., made by folding a large sheet. **3** device or machine that folds, especially one used in binding books.

fol·de·rol (fŏl′ də rŏl′) ***n-*** foolish or pointless talk, trifling, or ornamentation; nonsense.

fo·li·age (fō′ lē ĭj) ***n-*** the leaves of a plant; also, leaves in general: *a plant with evergreen* foliage; *autumn* foliage.

fo·li·a·tion (fō′ lē ā′ shən) ***n-* 1** of a plant, the producing of leaves, or a being in leaf. **2** the numbering of pages in a book, manuscript, etc.; pagination.

fo·li·o (fō′ lē ō′) ***n-*** [*pl.* **fo·li·os**] **1** book of the largest standard size, made from sheets of paper folded only once; also, the size of a book thus made. **2** in printing, the number of a page. *as **modifier**: a* folio *edition of Shakespeare's works.* ***vt-*** to number (book pages).

folk (fōk) ***n-* 1** [*pl.* **folk**] a people having, or assumed to have, the same customs, traditions, historical background, etc.: *the Celtic* folk; *country* folk. **2** (often **folks**) *Informal* people: *Some* folks *are always on the go.* **3 folks** *Informal* one's relatives; especially, parents; family. *as **modifier**: ancient* folk *customs.*

folk dance ***n-* 1** a dance that is handed down from generation to generation among a people. **2** music for this kind of dance. **—*n-* folk dancer. *n-* folk dancing.**

folk·lore (fōk′ lôr′) ***n-*** traditions, beliefs, etc., originating in earlier times among a people and kept alive by them.

folk music ***n-*** music created and preserved by the common people. The composer is not usually known.

folk singer ***n-*** singer who specializes in the performance of folk songs.

folk song ***n-*** song created and preserved by the common people, and of which the composer is not usually known; also, a song imitating this type. ***—n-*** **folk singing.**

folk·sy (fōk′sē) *Informal* ***adj-*** **[folk·si·er, folk·si·est] 1** friendly; neighborly. **2** informal or casual; also, self-consciously unpretentious. ***—n-*** **folk′si·ness.**

folk tale ***n-*** old story, often about a local hero, originating among the people of a region or among those working at the same occupation, and handed on from generation to generation.

folk·way (fōk′wā′) ***n-*** (usually **folkways**) one of the traditional customs or attitudes of a people or group.

fol·li·cle (fŏl′ĭ kəl) ***n-*** **1** small cavity, sac, or gland of the body. **2** in botany, a dry fruit that develops from a simple pistil and opens along only one side.

fol·low (fŏl′ō) ***vt-*** (in sense 1 considered intransitive when the direct object is implied but not expressed) **1** to come or go after: *Please* follow *me. Lead, and we'll* follow. **2** go along: *to* follow *a path.* **3** to act according to; accept as a guide; comply with: *to* follow *advice*; *to* follow *the rules.* **4** to pursue, physically or with the eyes, ears, attention, understanding, etc.: *to* follow *a criminal closely*; *to* follow *someone's reasoning.* **5** to result from; be the consequence of: *Illness may* follow *neglect.* **6** to make a living from: *to* follow *a trade.* ***vi-*** to come as a logical conclusion: *Your second statement does not* follow *from your first.*

follow through to carry through to the end; especially, in golf or tennis, to continue the motion of a stroke after hitting the ball.

follow up 1 to pursue or check thoroughly: *to* follow up *on a rumor.* **2** to make sure that a proposed action is carried out.

fol·low·er (fŏl′ō ər) ***n-*** person who follows another person, or a belief, theory, etc., as a supporter, disciple, or admirer.

fol·low·ing (fŏl′ō ĭng) ***adj-*** **1** coming after; next: *the* following *day.* **2** about to be mentioned, listed, etc: *The* following *guests were there.* ***n-*** **1** body of followers, supporters, or admirers: *a popular actor with a large* following. **2 the following** those about to be mentioned: *Among the winners are the* following: *John, Sue, Lil.*

fol·ly (fŏl′ē) ***n-*** [*pl.* **fol·lies**] **1** lack of good sense; foolishness. **2** silly or reckless idea, behavior, etc.

fo·ment (fō mĕnt′) ***vt-*** to stir up; incite: *to* foment *a revolution.* ***—n-*** **fo·ment′er.**

fo·men·ta·tion (fō′mĕn tā′shən) ***n-*** **1** a stirring up or inciting to rebellion, unrest, etc. **2** the applying of warm or moist substances to the body to relieve a painful or diseased condition; also, the substance thus applied.

fond (fŏnd) ***adj-*** **[fond·er, fond·est] 1** loving or affectionate; sometimes, foolishly or excessively so: *a* fond *look*; *his* fond *parents.* **2** deeply felt; cherished: *my* fondest *hopes.* ***—adv-*** **fond′ly.**

fond of having a strong liking for.

fon·dant (fŏnd′dənt) ***n-*** sweet, creamy sugar mixture used for making candy, icings, etc.; also, a candy made from such a mixture.

fon·dle (fŏn′dəl) ***vt-*** **[fon·dled, fon·dling]** to stroke or touch lovingly; caress. ***—n-*** **fon′dler.**

fond·ness (fŏnd′nəs, fŏn′-) ***n-*** liking; affection.

fon·due (fŏn dyōō′) ***n-*** dish made from melted cheese, usually served with food to be dipped into it.

[1]font (fŏnt) ***n-*** **1** basin or other container for holy water or for water used in baptizing. **2** a spring; source: *She is a* font *of knowledge.* [from Old English meaning "basin," and from Old French meaning "spring." Both are from Latin **fons, fontis** meaning "spring; fountain."]

[2]font (fŏnt) ***n-*** in printing, a full assortment of one size and style of type. [from Old French **fonte,** from **fondre** meaning "to melt."]

Font

fon·ta·nel (fŏn′tən ĕl′) ***n-*** any spot on an infant's head not covered by bone, especially the large one at the top of the head where a pulse can be observed.

food (fōōd) ***n-*** **1** any substance eaten or taken in by a plant or animal to help it live and grow; especially, solid nourishment in contrast to liquid. **2** something that provides aid, stimulation, etc., especially for the mind: *This is* food *for thought.*

food chain ***n-*** succession in which various organisms feed upon one another and thus depend upon one another.

food processor ***n-*** small appliance used to chop or purée foods; it often has attachments for slicing or blending.

food stamp ***n-*** government-issued coupon that can be used instead of money to buy food. *as* ***modifier:*** food stamp *program.*

food·stuff (fōōd′stŭf′) ***n-*** anything used as food.

fool (fōōl) ***n-*** **1** person who lacks sense, insight, or judgment; silly or unwise person. **2** in former times, a jester. ***vt-*** to trick; deceive. ***vi-*** to act silly; play or joke foolishly. ***—adj-*** *Informal* silly; senseless: *That was a* fool *thing to do!*

fool around *Informal* **1** to spend time idly or foolishly. **2** to tamper, interfere, or trifle.

fool away to spend wastefully or unwisely.

fool with 1 to play or putter idly with. **2** to interfere unwisely with.

fool·har·dy (fōōl′här′dē) ***adj-*** **[fool·har·di·er, fool·har·di·est]** having or showing courage without judgment; heedless of consequences; rash; reckless. ***—adv-*** **fool′har′di·ly.** ***n-*** **fool′har′di·ness.**

fool·ish (fōō′lĭsh) ***adj-*** **1** lacking sense or judgment; unwise. **2** silly; ridiculous. ***—adv-*** **fool′ish·ly.** ***n-*** **fool′ish·ness.**

fool·proof (fōōl′prōōf′) ***adj-*** so simple, easy, and safe as to make bungling or failure impossible.

fools·cap (fōōl′skăp′) ***n-*** **1** paper in sheets measuring about 16 by 13 inches. **2** (also **fool's cap**) tall, pointed hat decorated with bells and formerly worn by jesters.

fool's gold ***n-*** mineral, especially iron pyrite, that resembles and is sometimes mistaken for gold.

foot (fŏŏt) ***n-*** [*pl.* **feet** (fēt)] **1** part forming the end of the leg, on which man or other animals stand or walk. **2** something resembling this in position, appearance, or use; lowest part; base: *the* foot *of a table leg*; *the* foot *of a sail*; *the* foot *of a hill.* **3** lowest place in rank or order; bottom: *the* foot *of the list*; *the* foot *of the class.* **4** part of a bed or similar resting place opposite to the end where the head rests. **5** lowest part of a stocking, boot, etc. **6** measure of length equal to twelve inches. *Abbr.* ft. **7** one of the rhythmic units of a line of verse, consisting of a combination of accented and unaccented syllables. The line "Twinkle, twinkle, little star" has four

Foot of a goblet

fāte, făt, dâre, bärn; bē, bĕt, mêre; bīte, bĭt; nōte, hŏt, môre, dòg; fŭn, fûr; tōō, bŏŏk; oil; out; tar; thin; then; hw for wh as in *wh*at; zh for s as in u*s*ual; ə for a, e, i, o, u, as in *a*go, lin*e*n, per*i*l, at*o*m, min*u*s

feet. **8** in former times, unmounted soldiers; infantry. ***vt-*** *Informal* to pay (a bill, costs, expenses, etc.).

one foot in the grave such poor health or great age as to be near death. **on foot 1** by walking or running: *to go* on foot. **2** under way: *new plans* on foot. **put (one's) foot down** to act with firmness and determination; assert oneself. **put (one's) foot in it** to make an embarrassing mistake. **under foot** in the way; apt to be tripped over. **foot it** to walk, run, or dance.

foot·age (fo͝ot′ ĭj) ***n-*** amount, as of lumber or motion picture film, measured in feet.

foot-and-mouth disease (fo͝ot′ən mouth′) ***n-*** contagious disease of cattle, sheep, and other hoofed animals, marked by fever and the appearance of blisters around the mouth and hoofs.

foot·ball (fo͝ot′ bòl′) ***n-*** **1** leather, air-filled ball, usually oval with pointed ends. **2** game played with such a ball; especially, in the United States, a game played by two teams of eleven men each on a field 100 yards long with goal posts, joined by a crossbar, at each end. **3** *Brit.* soccer or rugby.

foot·board (fo͝ot′ bôrd′) ***n-*** **1** board for resting or supporting the feet. **2** crosswise board at the foot end of a bed.

foot·bridge (fo͝ot′ brĭj′) ***n-*** bridge for crossing on foot.

foot-can·dle (fo͝ot′ kăn′ dəl) ***n-*** unit of brightness or illumination on a surface. One foot-candle is the amount of light or illumination that strikes a surface having an area of one square foot and located at a distance of one foot from a source with a strength of one candle.

foot·ed (fo͝ot′ əd) ***adj-*** having a foot or feet of a certain number or kind: *a four-*footed *animal.*

foot·fall (fo͝ot′ fòl′) ***n-*** sound of a footstep.

foot·gear (fo͝ot′ gêr′) ***n-*** footwear.

foot·hill (fo͝ot′ hĭl′) ***n-*** one of the low hills at the base of a mountain or mountain range.

foot·hold (fo͝ot′ hōld′) ***n-*** **1** place on which to stand or step; footing: *a* foothold *on a narrow ledge.* **2** position from which to proceed in any undertaking.

foot·ing (fo͝ot′ ĭng) ***n-*** **1** firm placing of the feet: *He lost his* footing *and fell on the ice.* **2** foothold. **3** position or standing; basis: *to start out on an equal* footing.

foot·less (fo͝ot′ ləs) ***adj-*** **1** lacking a foot or feet. **2** pointless; ineffectual: *idle,* footless *fancies.* ***—adv-*** **foot′ less·ly.** ***n-*** **foot′ less·ness.**

foot·lights (fo͝ot′ līts′) ***n-*** *pl.* row of lights along the front of the floor of the stage in a theater.

foot·loose (fo͝ot′ lo͞os′) ***adj-*** free to travel about or live as one wishes.

foot·man (fo͝ot′ mən) ***n-*** [*pl.* **foot·men**] male servant, usually in uniform, who answers the door, waits on table, opens car doors, etc.

foot·note (fo͝ot′ nōt′) ***n-*** note of explanation at the bottom of a page, usually indicated in the body of the text by a number or symbol referring to it.

foot·pad (fo͝ot′ păd′) ***n-*** in former times, an unmounted robber who robbed people traveling on foot.

foot·path (fo͝ot′ păth′) ***n-*** trail where people may walk.

foot-pound (fo͝ot′ pound′) ***n-*** the work done when a force of one pound acts through a distance of one foot.

foot·print (fo͝ot′ prĭnt′) ***n-*** mark or impression left by a foot: *a* footprint *on the rug*; footprints *in sand.*

foot·race (fo͝ot′ rās′) ***n-*** race in which the contestants walk or run rather than ride.

foot·rest (fo͝ot′ rĕst′) ***n-*** something on which to rest or support the feet.

foot rule ***n-*** ruler twelve inches long.

foot soldier ***n-*** soldier in the infantry.

foot·sore (fo͝ot′ sôr′) ***adj-*** having aching or tired feet, especially from walking: *a weary,* footsore *traveler.*

foot·step (fo͝ot′ stĕp′) ***n-*** **1** a step or stride made in walking or running: *his faltering* footsteps. **2** sound of a step. **3** mark made by a foot; footprint.

follow in (someone's) footsteps to take the same route or course someone else has taken.

foot·stool (fo͝ot′ sto͞ol′) ***n-*** low stool on which to rest the feet when sitting down.

foot·wear (fo͝ot′ wâr′) ***n-*** shoes, boots, slippers, rubbers, and other coverings for the feet; footgear.

foot·work (fo͝ot′ wûrk′) ***n-*** use or movement of the feet in sports, dancing, etc.: *fast* footwork.

foot·worn (fo͝ot′ wôrn′) ***adj-*** **1** wearied by walking. **2** worn down by being walked upon.

fop (fŏp) ***n-*** man who wears dressy, stylish clothes and is vain about his appearance; dandy.

fop·per·y (fŏp′ ə rē) ***n-*** [*pl.* **fop·per·ies**] the behavior, appearance, or fancy clothing of a fop.

fop·pish (fŏp′ ĭsh) ***adj-*** resembling or typical of a fop. ***—adv-*** **fop′ pish·ly.** ***n-*** **fop′ pish·ness.**

for (fòr, fôr, fər) ***prep-*** **1** useful or needed in the case of; suited to: *a bag* for *potatoes*; *a knife* for *cutting.* **2** meant to belong to; directed to: *a gift* for *you*; *a letter* for *Maria.* **3** to have or to do: *It's time* for *tea. He was hired* for *the job.* **4** including the extent or time of: *We can see* for *miles. He was gone* for *three days.* **5** with the purpose or intention of having, reaching, getting, etc.: *to go* for *a walk*; *to leave* for *New York*; *to try* for *a prize.* **6** because of: *to shout* for *joy.* **7** in place of; instead of: *Use this table* for *a desk. Jones batted* for *Wagner.* **8** in support of; in the interest of: *to fight* for *one's rights.* **9** on behalf of: *Say hello* for *me.* **10** as or at the price of; also, in the amount of: *a check* for *ten dollars.* **11** regarding; in respect to: *I'm worried* for *his safety.* **12** regardless of; despite: *I don't believe him,* for *all his boasting.* **13** in spite of being: *He is very quick,* for *a fat man.* **14** as being; as: *We accepted her* for *a friend.* **15** when done by; on the part of: *Swimming is easy* for *you.* **16** to take care of: *enough* for *all.* ***conj-*** because; since: *Let's go,* for *it's cold.* ***Homs-*** fore, four.

O! for . . . (or **Oh! for . . .**) I wish I (or we) had . . .: O! for *a fudge sundae!*

for·age (fòr′ ĭj, fŏr′-) ***n-*** **1** food for animals, especially horses and cattle. **2** a search for food or provisions. ***vi-*** [**for·aged, for·ag·ing**] to search about for something, especially food: *to* forage *in the refrigerator.* ***vt-*** to get (food) by searching or ransacking: *to* forage *a meal.*

for·ay (fôr′ ā) ***n-*** a sudden raid or invasion, especially for the purpose of taking supplies or plunder. ***vi-***: *to* foray *into the enemy camp.*

[1]**for·bear** (fòr bâr′, fôr-) ***vi-*** [**for·bore** (-bôr′), **for·borne** (-bôrn′), **for·bear·ing**] **1** to keep or hold oneself back; refrain: *to* forbear *from quarreling.* **2** to be patient: *I must ask you to* forbear *a while longer.* ***vt-*** to refrain from (doing something): *He could not* forbear *to interrupt.* [from Old English **forberan** meaning literally "bear (back) from."] ***—adv-*** **for·bear′ ing·ly.**

[2]**for·bear** (fôr′ bâr′) forebear. [from earlier **fore-**, plus **be**, plus [1]**-er.**]

for·bear·ance (fòr bâr′ əns, fôr-) ***n-*** a forbearing; exercise of restraint or self-control; patience.

for·bid (fòr bĭd′, fər-) ***vt-*** [**for·bade** (-băd′, -bād′) or **for·bad** (-băd′), **for·bid·den, for·bid·ding**] **1** to command (a person) not to do something; refuse to allow: *My father* forbade *me to go.* **2** to ban; prohibit.

for·bid·ding (fòr bĭd′ ĭng, fər-) ***adj-*** seeming to be hostile, threatening, or dangerous: *his* forbidding *manner*; forbidding *clouds.* ***—adv-*** **for·bid′ ding·ly.**

force (fôrs) ***n-*** **1** a push or pull that can produce a change in the motion of something; that which causes or tends to cause an object to accelerate or decelerate. **2** strength; power; vigor: *the* force *of the wind*; *the* force *of a blow*; *the* force *of his character.* **3** the use of physical strength, superior power, or compulsion: *to arrest someone by* force. **4** (often **forces**) particular group of persons, especially one organized in a military fashion: *the police* force; *the labor* force *of a factory*; *the armed* forces. **5** power to convince or persuade: *the* force *of the evidence.* **6** powerful influence: *a* force *for social improvement.* ***vt-*** **[forced, forc·ing] 1** to compel: *to* force *a person to do something against his will.* **2** to cause to open, give way, etc., by using physical strength: *to* force *a lock*; *to* force *one's way through a crowd.* **3** to produce by special or unnatural effort: *to* force *a smile.* **4** to press or impose: *to* force *a gift on someone.* **5** to cause (a plant) to grow or bloom faster than usual.

in force 1 in use or operation: *The new traffic law is now* in force. **2** in great numbers: *The class came out* in force *to watch the football game.*

forced (fôrst) ***adj-*** **1** done because one cannot do otherwise; under duress or threat: *a* forced *landing*; forced *labor.* **2** strained and unnatural: *a* forced *laugh.*

force·ful (fôrs′ fəl) ***adj-*** having force or vigor; strong; powerful: *a* forceful *argument*; *his* forceful *manner.* **—*adv-* force′ ful·ly. *n-* force′ ful·ness.**

for·ceps (fòr′ sĕps′, fôr′-) ***n-*** (takes plural verb) pincers with specially shaped jaws, used in dentistry, surgery, etc.

Surgical forceps Dental forceps

force pump ***n-*** pump that uses a piston to force a liquid through valves under strong pressure.

for·ci·ble (fôr′ sə bəl) ***adj-*** **1** done by force or violence: *The police made a* forcible *entry into the room.* **2** energetic; powerful; forceful; effective: *to take* forcible *measures.* **—*n-* for′ ci·ble·ness. *adv-* for′ ci·bly.**

ford (fôrd) ***n-*** shallow part of a stream, where one can cross by walking, riding, or driving through the water. ***vt-*** to cross (a stream) by walking, riding, or driving through a shallow part. **—*adj-* ford′ a·ble.**

[1]fore (fôr) ***adj-*** at or toward the front: *the* fore *part of a ship.* ***adv-***: *The whale rammed us* fore *of the mast.* For picture, see *aft.* [from Old English.] ***Homs-*** for, four.

to the fore to a leading position; into full view or play: *He came* to the fore *as a leader.*

[2]fore (fôr) ***interj-*** shout used on a golf course to warn players who are in danger of being hit by the ball. [probably short for **before.**] ***Homs-*** for, four.

fore- *prefix* **1** before in time or order: *the* fore*noon*; *to* fore*tell.* **2** situated in front: *a* fore*paw*; *the* fore*lock.* **3** front part of: *the* fore*arm*; *the* fore*deck.*

fore-and-aft (fôr′ ənd ăft′) ***adj-*** following or in a line with the direction of a ship's length: *a vessel with* fore-and-aft *sails.* ***adv-*** **fore and aft** lengthwise; from stem to stern.

[1]fore·arm (fôr′ ärm′) ***n-*** part of the arm between the elbow and the wrist. [from **fore-**, plus **[1]arm.**]

[2]fore·arm (fôr ärm′) ***vt-*** to provide protection to (a person or persons) before danger comes: *His knowledge* forearmed *him and he won.* [from **fore-**, plus **[2]arm.**]

fore·bear (fôr′ bâr′) ***n-*** one of the persons from whom one is descended; ancestor. Also **forbear.**

fore·bode (fôr bōd′) ***vt-*** **[fore·bod·ed, fore·bod·ing]** to be a sign or warning of (trouble, misfortune, etc.): *feelings that* forbode *disaster.* **—*adv-* fore·bod′ ing·ly.**

fore·bod·ing (fôr bō′ dĭng) ***n-*** a feeling that something bad is going to happen: *He had a* foreboding *of disaster.*

fore·cast (fôr′ kăst′) ***vt-*** **[fore·cast** or **fore·cast·ed, fore·cast·ing]** to tell, estimate, or indicate ahead of time, especially on the basis of known information; predict: *to* forecast *the results of an election*; *to* forecast *the weather.* ***n-*** prediction made in this manner: *tomorrow's weather* forecast. **—*n-* fore′ cast′ er.**

fore·cas·tle (fōk′ səl, *also* fôr′ kăs′ əl) ***n-*** **1** the part of a ship's upper deck in front of the forward mast. **2** the crew's quarters in the fore part of a ship. Also **fo'c'sle.**

fore·close (fôr klōz′) ***vt-*** **[fore·closed, fore·clos·ing] 1** to subject (a mortgage or the holder of a mortgage) to the process of foreclosure. **2** to prevent or put an end to; bar: *to* foreclose *all discussion.*

fore·clo·sure (fôr klō′ zhər) ***n-*** legal proceeding in which the holder of a mortgage or lien seeks to collect what is owed to him when the regular payments are not made. In the case of a mortgage he is often entitled to sell the property for this purpose.

fore·deck (fôr′ dĕk′) ***n-*** forward part of a ship's main deck.

fore·doom (fôr do͞om′) ***vt-*** to doom in advance; destine.

fore·fa·ther (fôr′ fä thər) ***n-*** ancestor.

fore·fend (fòr fĕnd′, fôr-) forfend.

fore·fin·ger (fôr′ fĭng′ gər) ***n-*** finger next to the thumb; index finger. For picture, see *finger.*

fore·foot (fôr′ fo͝ot′) ***n-*** [*pl.* **fore·feet**] one of the front feet of a four-legged animal.

fore·front (fôr′ frŭnt′) ***n-*** place or part in front; most advanced position; vanguard: *the* forefront *of the army.*

fore·gath·er (fôr gath′ ər) forgather.

fore·go (fôr gō′) forgo.

fore·go·ing (fôr′ gō′ ĭng) ***adj-*** stated, written, or appearing just before; preceding: *the* foregoing *quotation.* ***n-*** **the foregoing** what has been stated or written just before: *the* foregoing *from the Bible.*

fore·gone conclusion (fôr′ gòn , -gŏn′) ***n-*** event, outcome, etc., that is known or settled in advance: *His promotion was a* foregone conclusion.

fore·ground (fôr′ ground′) ***n-*** **1** part of a scene, picture, etc., that is or seems closest to the observer. **2** place or position that receives the most attention or recognition: *Fine work keeps him in the* foreground.

fore·hand (fôr′ hănd′) ***n-*** stroke in tennis, ping-pong, etc., made with the arm extended outward from the body and the inside of the wrist moving toward the net. *as **modifier**: a powerful* forehand *stroke.*

fore·hand·ed (fôr′ hănd′ əd) ***adj-*** mindful of future needs; thrifty; prudent: *Be* forehanded *and save regularly.* **—*adv-* fore′ hand′ ed·ly. *n-* fore′ hand′ ed·ness.**

fore·head (fôr′ hĕd′, fŏr′ əd) ***n-*** the part of the face above the eyes; brow.

for·eign (fòr′ ən, fŏr′-) ***adj-*** **1** belonging to or coming from another country or nation: *She speaks a* foreign *language.* **2** having to do with other nations or countries: *a* foreign *correspondent*; *the President's* foreign *policy.* **3** not related or not belonging: *Dishonesty is* foreign *to his nature.* **—*n-* for′ eign·ness.**

foreign affairs ***n-*** the dealings or diplomatic relations between a nation and other nations.

for·eign-born (fòr′ ən bôrn′, fŏr′-) ***adj-*** born in a foreign country: *a* foreign-born *neighbor.*

---

fāte, făt, dâre, bärn; bē, bĕt, mêre; bīte, bĭt; nōte, hŏt, môre, dòg; fŭn, fûr; to͞o, bo͝ok; oil; out; tar; thin; then; hw for wh as in *wh*at; zh for s as in u*s*ual; ə for a, e, i, o, u, as in *a*go, lin*e*n, per*i*l, at*o*m, min*u*s

for·eign·er (fòr′ ən ər, fŏr′ -) ***n-*** person who was born in or is a citizen of another country.
foreign exchange ***n-*** **1** the settling of debts between persons, corporations, etc., that are not located in the same country. **2** bills of exchange used in such dealings.
Foreign Legion ***n-*** branch of the French Army that enlists foreigners, under French officers, and has traditionally been used in the French colonies.
foreign office ***n-*** in Great Britain and certain other countries, the government bureau that conducts relations with foreign countries.
fore·know (fôr nō′) ***vt-*** **[fore·knew, fore·know·ing, fore·known]** to know beforehand.
fore·knowl·edge (fôr′ nŏl′ ĭj) ***n-*** advance knowledge.
fore·leg (fôr′ lĕg′) ***n-*** one of the front legs of an animal.
fore·limb (fôr′ lĭm′) ***n-*** a front leg, wing, fin, or arm.
fore·lock (fôr′ lŏk′) ***n-*** a tuft or bunch of hair growing on the front part of the head.
fore·man (fôr′ mən) ***n-*** [*pl.* **fore·men**] **1** person in charge of a group of workers. **2** chairman and spokesman of a jury. ***—n-*** *fem.* **fore′ wom·an.**
fore·mast (fôr′ măst′) ***n-*** mast nearest a ship's bow.
fore·most (fôr′ mōst′) ***adj-*** first in position or importance: *the* foremost *singer of his day.*
fore·named (fôr′ nāmd′) ***adj-*** named, mentioned, or cited earlier: *the* forenamed *occurrences.* ***n-*** **the forenamed** person or persons named before.
fore·noon (fôr′ nōōn′) ***n-*** time between sunrise and midday; the morning.
fo·ren·sic (fə rĕn′ sĭk, -zĭk) ***adj-*** relating to or used in court trials, public debate, or other cases of formal argumentation: *a* forensic *style*; forensic *language.*
fore·or·dain (fôr′ òr′ dān′, fôr′ ôr′ -) ***vt-*** to decree or destine beforehand: *His talents* foreordained *success.*
fore·or·di·na·tion (fôr′ òr′ də nā′ shən, fôr′ ôr′ -) ***n-*** a foreordaining.
fore·part (fôr′ pärt′) ***n-*** the first or front part of something.
fore·paw (fôr′ pò′) ***n-*** a front foot of any animal that has claws.
fore·quar·ter (fôr′ kwòr′ tər) ***n-*** **1** the front part of a side of beef, lamb, etc. **2 forequarters** the front legs, chest, etc., of an animal.
fore·run·ner (fôr′ rŭn′ ər) ***n-*** something which precedes or foreshadows something else: *a* forerunner *of disaster.*
fore·sail (fôr′ sāl′, -səl) ***n-*** **1** the largest and lowest sail on the foremast of a square-rigged vessel. **2** the large fore-and-aft sail on the foremast of a schooner.
fore·see (fôr sē′) ***vt-*** **[fore·saw** (fôr sò′), **fore·seen, fore·see·ing]** to know beforehand; anticipate; expect: *I* foresee *a hard battle.* ***—adj-*** **fore·see′ able.**
fore·shad·ow (fôr shăd′ ō) ***vt-*** to give signs of or indicate beforehand. ***—n-*** **fore·shad′ ow·er.**
fore·sheet (fôr′ shēt′) ***n-*** **1** one of the ropes used to adjust the tightness of a foresail. **2 foresheets** front part of an open boat.
fore·short·en (fôr shòr′ tən, -shôr′ tən) ***vt-*** to shorten, lengthen, widen, or narrow (lines and shapes) in drawing so as to make such things as extended arms, headlong bodies, etc., appear as an observer might see them.
fore·sight (fôr′ sīt′) ***n-*** **1** a knowing or seeing beforehand. **2** careful planning; heedful thought for the future; prudence: *Lack of* foresight *caused a shortage.*
fore·sight·ed (fôr′ sī′ təd) ***adj-*** having or marked by foresight: *a* foresighted *approach to the problem.* ***—adv-*** **fore′ sight′ ed·ly.** ***n-*** **fore′ sight′ ed·ness.**
fore·skin (fôr′ skĭn′) ***n-*** fold of skin that covers the end of the male sex organ in human beings, part or all of which is removed in circumcision.

for·est (fòr′ əst, fŏr′ -) ***n-*** a growth of trees covering a large tract of land; large woods. *as* ***modifier:*** *the* forest *animals.* ***vt-*** to cover with trees or forest. ***—adj-*** **for′ est·ed:** *a heavily* forested *region.*
fore·stall (fôr stòl′) ***vt-*** to prevent or thwart by action taken in advance: *His quick stop* forestalled *an accident.* ***—n-*** **fore·stall′ er.**
for·est·a·tion (fòr′ ə stā′ shən, fŏr′ -) ***n-*** extensive planting and care of trees to make or restore a forest.
fore·stay (fôr′ stā′) ***n-*** strong rope or cable from the foremast to the bow of a ship, to support the foremast.
for·est·er (fòr′ ə stər, fŏr′ -) ***n-*** **1** person whose work is taking care of a forest and the wildlife in it. **2** forest dweller.
for·est·ry (fòr′ ə strē, fŏr′ -) ***n-*** science of planting and caring for forests, including good lumbering practice and conservation.
fore·taste (fôr′ tāst′) ***n-*** sample of what something will be like later: *The early frost was a* foretaste *of winter.*
fore·tell (fôr tĕl′) ***vt-*** **[fore·told, fore·tell·ing]** to tell in advance; predict: *Who can* foretell *what will happen?* ***—n-*** **fore·tell′ er.**
fore·thought (fôr′ thòt′) ***n-*** planning in advance; prudence; heed for the future; foresight: *His* forethought *in saving enabled him to buy a house.*
fore·top (fôr′ tŏp′) ***n-*** platform at the top of the lowest section of the foremast of a ship.
for·ev·er (fòr ĕv′ ər, fər-) ***adv-*** **1** always; eternally; without ever ending. **2** continually; most of the time: *He is* forever *watching television.*
for·ev·er·more (fòr ĕv′ ər môr′, fər-) ***adv-*** from now on; forever.
fore·warn (fôr wòrn′) ***vt-*** to caution in advance: *The weather bureau* forewarned *us of the hurricane.*
fore·went (fôr wĕnt′) *p.t.* of **forego.** See *forgo.*
fore·word (fôr′ wûrd′) ***n-*** preface; introductory matter, especially to a book.
for·feit (fòr′ fət, fôr′ -) ***vt-*** to lose or give up because of neglect or fault: *The team failed to show up and* forfeited *the game.* ***n-*** something lost as the result of neglect, fault, etc; forfeiture. ***—n-*** **for′ feit·er.**
for·fei·ture (fòr′ fĭ chər, fôr′-) ***n-*** **1** the losing of something as a punishment or because of neglect or wrongdoing: *He paid for careless driving with the* forfeiture *of his license.* **2** a forfeit.
for·fend (fòr fĕnd′, fôr-) ***vt-*** *Archaic* prevent.
for·gath·er or **fore·gath·er** (fòr găth′ ər, fôr-) ***vi-*** to assemble; come together.
for·gave (fòr gāv′, fôr-, fər-) *p.t.* of **forgive.**
1**forge** (fôrj) ***n-*** **1** hearth for heating metals, consisting of a fire fanned by a forced draft of air. **2** blacksmith shop; smithy. ***vt-*** **[forged, forg·ing] 1** to shape (heat-softened metal) with a hammer or other tool, either by hand or by machine. **2** to write or copy (a document or another's name) with intent to deceive; counterfeit: *to* forge *a signature*; *to* forge *a check.* [from Old French, from Latin **fabrica** meaning "workshop."]

Forge

2**forge** (fôrj) ***vi-*** **[forged, forg·ing]** to move forward steadily, but with difficulty: *to* forge *ahead*; *to* forge *through a crowd.* [of uncertain origin.]
forg·er (fôr′ jər) ***n-*** person who counterfeits checks, signatures, documents, paintings, etc.
for·ger·y (fôr′ jə rē) ***n-*** [*pl.* **for·ger·ies**] **1** a copying or imitating of something with intent to deceive. **2** a false signature. **3** anything counterfeit.

for·get (fôr gĕt′, fôr-, fər-) ***vt-*** [**for·got** (-gŏt′), **for·got·ten** (-gŏt′ ən), **for·get·ting**] (considered intransitive when the direct object is implied but not expressed) **1** to be unable to remember: *I* forgot *the title.* **2** to cease to think of: *I will try to* forget *the incident.* **3** neglect or fail to remember: *When he is playing football, he sometimes* forgets *his studies.* **—*adj-* for·get′ ta·ble.** ***n-*** **for·get′ter. forget oneself** be off guard; lose control of oneself.

for·get·ful (fôr gĕt′ fəl, fôr-, fər-) ***adj-*** **1** in the habit of forgetting; having a poor memory; absent-minded: *I write things down because I'm* forgetful. **2** neglectful: *He is* forgetful *of his duties.* **—*adv-* for·get′ ful·ly.**

for·get·ful·ness (fôr gĕt′ fəl nəs, fôr-, fər-) ***n-*** **1** habit of forgetting; absent-mindedness. **2** loss or lack of memory.

for·get-me-not (fôr gĕt′ mē nŏt′, fôr) ***n-*** small plant with tiny blue flowers.

for·giv·a·ble (fôr gĭv′ ə bəl, fôr-, fər-) ***adj-*** of a kind that can be forgiven; not very serious: *a* forgivable *offense.* **—*adv-* for·giv′ a·bly.**

for·give (fôr gĭv′, fôr-, fər-) ***vt-*** [**for·gave** (-gāv′), **for·giv·en, for·giv·ing**] **1** to pardon; excuse: *She* forgave *his clumsiness. He* forgave *his attackers.* **2** to require no repayment of (a debt); remit. **—*n-* for·giv′ er.**

for·give·ness (fôr gĭv′ nəs, fôr-, fər-) ***n-*** **1** pardon: *He asked* forgiveness. **2** act of forgiving or pardoning.

for·giv·ing (fôr gĭv′ ĭng, fôr′-, fər-) ***adj-*** **1** showing forgiveness: *a* forgiving *gesture.* **2** tending to forgive: *a* forgiving *nature.* **—*adv-* for·giv′ ing·ly.** ***n-*** **for·giv′ ing·ness.**

for·go (fôr gō′) ***vt-*** [**for·went** (-wĕnt′), **for·gone** (-gôn′, -gŏn′), **for·go·ing**] to give up; do without: *Ann decided to* forgo *candy to lose weight.*

for·got (fôr gŏt′, fôr-, fər-) *p.t.* of **forget.**

for·got·ten (fôr gŏt′ ən, fôr-, fər-) *p.p.* of **forget.** ***adj-*** no longer remembered: *a* forgotten *book.*

fork (fôrk, fôrk) ***n-*** **1** instrument with two or more long points, prongs, or tines, such as a table fork, a pitchfork, a tuning fork, or a trident. **2** a branching; point of separation: *a* fork *of a tree; a* fork *in the road.* **3** one of the branches in such a separation: *the* fork *to the left.* ***vt-*** to pitch or lift with, or as with an instrument with several points: *Ted* forked *the hay onto the wagon.* ***vi-*** to divide; separate: *The road to Devon* forks *to the left. The tree branch* forks *again and again.* **—*adj-* fork′ like′. fork over** (or **out**) *Slang* to give; hand over or out.

Table fork — Pitchfork — Tuning fork

fork·lift (fôrk′ lĭft′, fôrk′-) ***n-*** wheeled machine which lifts, carries, and stacks loads with a set of steel prongs.

forked (fôrkt, fôrkt) ***adj-*** **1** having prongs. **2** opening into two or more parts: *a* forked *road.* **3** zigzag; jagged: *the* forked *lightning.*

for·lorn (fôr lôrn′, fôr lôrn′) ***adj-*** **1** lonely or wretched: *He felt* forlorn *at his pet's death.* **2** neglected; deserted: *a* forlorn *old house.* **—*adv-* for·lorn′ ly.** ***n-*** **for·lorn′ness.**

forlorn hope ***n-*** **1** a vain hope. **2** an extremely difficult or improbable undertaking.

form (fôrm, fôrm) ***n-*** **1** the outward shape, structure, or contour of something: *a rounded* form; *the pointed* form *of a cone.* **2** a body, especially the human body: *the tall* form *of Mr. Brown.* **3** kind or variety: *A tree is a* form *of plant life.* **4** state or character in which a thing appears: *water in the* form *of ice.* **5** special arrangement or method of composition: *the sonnet* form; *symphonic* form. **6** a mold or pattern: *a* form *for ice cream.* **7** established practice or ritual: *a* form *of worship; the* form *for introductions.* **8** standard of conduct; custom. An accepted manner of doing something is called **good form**; an unacceptable manner is **bad form. 9** fitness or condition for doing something, especially athletic: *He is in excellent* form *today.* **10** a typewritten or printed blank with spaces left to be filled in; also, a typewritten or printed letter to be sent out in great numbers. **11** in printing, type locked in a frame ready for printing. **12** *chiefly Brit.* long bench without a back; hence, a class or grade in some schools. **13** *Grammar* any of the ways in which a word is written or pronounced to show its meaning: *"Cactuses" and "cacti" are* forms *of "cactus."* **14** in linguistics, a unit of speech that has meaning, such as a morpheme, word, clause, etc. ***vt-*** **1** to give shape to; make: *to* form *a bowl of clay.* **2** to develop; train: *to* form *good habits.* **3** to serve to make up; to compose: *Four students* form *the committee.* **4** *Grammar* to add an ending or make some other change in a word: *to* form *plurals from singulars.* ***vi-*** to take shape; to become.

for·mal (fôr′ məl, fôr′-) ***adj-*** **1** according to strict rules, customs, or usage: *a* formal *dinner.* **2** authoritative; official: *to give* formal *permission.* **3** requiring full dress to be worn: *a* formal *dance.* ***n-*** **1** a dance at which men are expected to wear tuxedos, tails, full dress, etc., and women to wear gowns. **2** woman's gown worn at such dances and other full-dress affairs. **—*adv-* for′ mal·ly.**

form·al·de·hyde (fôr măl′ də hīd′, fər-) ***n-*** colorless gas, a compound of carbon, hydrogen, and oxygen (CH_2O), having a suffocating odor. It is used in water solution as a disinfectant and preservative.

For·ma·lin (fôr′ mə lĭn, fôr′-) ***n-*** trademark name for a water solution of formaldehyde and methyl alcohol.

for·mal·ism (fôr′ mə lĭz′ əm, fôr′-) ***n-*** a strict following of forms, rites, or customs, especially in religion or art. **—*n-* for′ mal·ist.** ***adj-*** **for′ mal·is′ tic.** ***adv-*** **for′ mal·is′ ti·cal·ly.**

for·mal·i·ty (fôr măl′ ə tē, fər-) ***n-*** [*pl.* **for·mal·i·ties**] **1** careful attention to forms, rules, and customs: *All the guests were greeted with* formality *at the reception.* **2** something required by custom, rule, or social practice: *legal* formalities; *the* formalities *of a wedding.* **3** something done only for the sake of form or custom.

for·mal·ize (fôr′ mə līz′, fôr′-) ***vt-*** [**for·mal·ized, for·mal·iz·ing**] **1** to put into proper form: *Let's* formalize *our agreement.* **2** to make formal or more formal.

for·mat (fôr′ măt′, fôr′-) ***n-*** **1** the whole style and size of a book or magazine, including paper, type faces, and binding. **2** the general makeup of any presentation, such as a television show or a political campaign.

for·ma·tion (fôr mā′ shən, fər-) ***n-*** **1** a shaping; molding: *the* formation *of good habits.* **2** an originating; starting: *the* formation *of a business.* **3** way in which a thing is formed in the arrangement of its parts, etc.: *We studied the* formation *of a tooth in class.* **4** arrangement: *troops in marching* formation; *a new* formation *for football.* **5** certain natural pattern or arrangement; a structure.

for·ma·tive (fôr′ mə tĭv, fôr′-) ***adj-*** **1** giving shape to; helping to form: *the* formative *duties of a parent.* **2** of or relating to growth: *one's* formative *years.* **—*adv-* for′ ma·tive·ly.** ***n-*** **for′ ma·tive·ness.**

for·mer (fôr′ mər, fôr′-) ***adj-*** coming before in time or order; past; earlier: *the sailing ships of* former *days.* ***n-*** **the former** the first (of two) mentioned: *He raises horses and cows,* the former *for riding, the latter for milk.*

for·mer·ly (fôr′ mər lē, fôr′-) *adv-* in past time; once: *People* formerly *traveled in carriages.*

form·fit·ting (fôrm′ fĭt′ ĭng, fôrm′-) *adj-* closely fitted to the body: *a* formfitting *dress.*

for·mic (fôr′ mĭk, fôr′-) *adj-* **1** having to do with, or made from, formic acid. **2** of or having to do with ants.

For·mi·ca (fôr′ mī′ kə) *n-* trade name for a strong, synthetic resin used to make counter tops, paneling, etc. Also **formica.**

formic acid *n-* colorless acid (HCOOH) having a strong odor and found in plants and certain insects such as the ant. It is used for dyeing and finishing cloth.

for·mi·da·ble (fôr′ mĭ də bəl, fôr′-) *adj-* **1** causing fear or cautious respect: *a* formidable *army*; *a* formidable *danger.* **2** hard to deal with, overcome, or accomplish: *To climb the mountain was a* formidable *task.* **—n- for′ mi·da·bil′ i·ty.** ***adv-*** **for′ mi·da·bly.**

form·less (fôrm′ ləs, fôrm′-) *adj-* lacking a regular or definite shape; amorphous. **—*adv-* form′ less·ly.** ***n-*** **form′ less·ness.**

for·mu·la (fôrm′ yə lə, fôrm′-) *n-* [*pl.* **for·mu·las** or **for·mu·lae** (-lē)] **1** a set of rules; detailed instructions; recipe: *the* formula *for a cough medicine*; *a* formula *for international peace.* **2** a certain set of words habitually used at certain times: *the* formula *"sincerely yours" at the end of a letter.* **3** in chemistry, a statement that tells the elements that make up something: *H_2O is the* formula *for water.* **4** in mathematics, a statement of a rule or process: *$A = lw$ is the* formula *for finding the area of a rectangle (area equals length times width).*

for·mu·late (fôrm′ yə lāt′, fôrm′-) *vt-* [**for·mu·lat·ed, for·mu·lat·ing**] to put into definite form; to state in an orderly way: *to* formulate *plans.* **—n- for′ mu·la′ tion.**

for·ni·cate (fôr′ nə kāt′, fôr-) *vi-* [**for·ni·cat·ed, for·ni·cat·ing**] to have unlawful sexual intercourse. **—n- for·ni·ca′ tion.**

for·sake (fər sāk′, fôr-) *vt-* [**for·sook** (-sŏŏk′), **for·sak·en, for·sak·ing**] to give up; abandon. **—n- for·sak′ er.**

for·sooth (fər sōōth′) *Archaic* ***adv-*** indeed; in truth.

for·swear (fôr swâr′, fôr-) *vt-* [**for·swore** (fôr swôr′, fôr swôr′), **for·sworn** (fôr swôrn′, fôr swôrn′), **for·swear·ing**] to give something up: *to* forswear *smoking.*

for·syth·i·a (fər sĭth′ ē ə, fôr-) *n-* cultivated shrub that bears bright yellow flowers in early spring.

fort (fôrt) *n-* **1** an area or structure built to withstand attack. **2** a permanent military camp or station. ***Hom-*** [1]forte.

[1]**forte** (fôrt) *n-* special talent; field of best effort: *My* forte *is music.* [from earlier French, from Old French **fort,** "strong," from Latin **fortis,** "strong."] ***Hom-*** fort.

[2]**for·te** (fôr′ tā, -tē) *Music* ***adv- & adj-*** loudly; loud; with power: *Play this passage* forte. *Listen to the* forte *passage.* [from Italian, from Latin **fortis,** "strong."]

forth (fôrth) ***adv-*** **1** onward; forward (in time, place, or order): *to go* forth *to battle*; *from this day* forth. **2** out, as from hiding or concealment: *The plants put* forth *tender new shoots.* ***Hom-*** fourth.

and so forth and so on; and the like; et cetera: *They were singing, dancing,* and so forth.

forth·com·ing (fôrth′ kŭm′ ĭng) *adj-* **1** about to appear or happen; approaching: *We put notices of* forthcoming *activities on the bulletin board.* **2** available; at hand: *Money for the project will be* forthcoming *when needed.*

forth·right (fôrth′ rīt′) *adj-* honest and direct; straightforward; frank: *a* forthright *reply.* **—*adv-* forth′ right′ ly.** ***n-*** **forth′ right′ ness.**

forth·with (fôrth′ wĭth′, -wĭth′) ***adv-*** at once.

for·ti·eth (fôr′ tē əth, fôr′-) *adj-* **1** next after thirty-ninth. **2** the ordinal of 40; 40th. ***n-*** **1** the next after the thirty-ninth; 40th. **2** one of forty equal parts of a whole or group. **3** the last term in the name of a fraction having a denominator of 40: 1/40 *is one* fortieth. ***adv-:*** *His boat finished* fortieth *in the race.*

for·ti·fi·ca·tion (fôr′ tə fə kā′ shən) *n-* **1** a making strong; preparation against attack: *the* fortification *of a canal*; fortification *against sickness.* **2** a protective wall, mound of earth, or other structure, sometimes temporary, as on a battlefield. **3** a fort or system of forts.

for·ti·fy (fôr′ tə fī′) *vt-* [**for·ti·fied, for·ti·fy·ing**] **1** to strengthen against attack by building forts, walls, etc.: *to* fortify *a city.* **2** to make strong: *Vitamins help to* fortify *us against colds.* **—n- for′ ti·fi·er.**

for·tis·si·mo (fôr tĭs′ ə mō) *Music* ***adv- & adj-*** very loudly; very loud: *Play this passage* fortissimo. *Listen to the* fortissimo *passage.*

for·ti·tude (fôr′ tə tōōd′, fôr′ tə tyōōd′, fôr′-) *n-* courage or firmness in meeting pain, danger, or trouble.

fort·night (fôrt′ nīt′) *chiefly Brit.* ***n-*** two weeks.

fort·night·ly (fôrt′ nīt′ lē) *chiefly Brit.* ***adv-*** every two weeks: *to meet* fortnightly. ***adj-*** occurring every two weeks: *a* fortnightly *meeting.* ***n-*** magazine, journal, etc., that appears every two weeks.

for·tress (fôr′ trəs) *n-* stronghold; fort or fortification.

for·tu·i·tous (fôr tyōō′ ə təs, -tōō′ ə təs) *adj-* **1** happening by chance; accidental: *our* fortuitous *meeting.* **2** lucky; fortunate: *a* fortuitous *accident.* **—*adv-* for·tu′ i·tous·ly.** ***n-*** **for·tu′ i·tous·ness.**

for·tu·nate (fôr′ chə nət, fôr′-) *adj-* favored by chance; lucky. **—*adv-* for′ tu·nate·ly.**

for·tune (fôr′ chən, fôr′-) *n-* **1** what happens to a person, either for good or ill; chance; luck: *He had the bad* fortune *to lose his bicycle.* **2** destiny; fate: *It was his* fortune *to rise to fame.* **3** a large amount of money; wealth; riches: *He made a* fortune *in the steel business.*

fortune cookie *n-* crisp, thin, folded cookie containing a slip of paper with a prediction or piece of advice.

fortune hunter *n-* a seeker of wealth, especially by means of marriage.

for·tune·tell·er (fôr′ chən tĕl′ ər, fôr′-) *n-* one who attempts or pretends to predict another's future by looking at playing cards, gazing at a crystal ball, etc. **—n- for′ tune·tell′ ing.**

for·ty (fôr′ tē, fôr′-) *n-* [*pl.* **for·ties**] **1** the amount or quantity that is one greater than 39. **2** *Mathematics* (1) the cardinal number that is the sum of 39 and 1. (2) a numeral such as 40 that represents this cardinal number. *as* ***determiner*** (traditionally called adjective or pronoun): *There are* forty *pigs here and* forty *there.*

for·ty-five (fôr′ tē fīv′, fôr′-) *n-* **1** amount or quantity that is one greater than 44. **2** *Mathematics* (1) the cardinal number that is the sum of 44 and 1. (2) a numeral such as 45 that represents this cardinal number. **3** a .45-caliber pistol. *as* ***determiner*** (traditionally called adjective or pronoun): *There are* forty-five *cars here* forty-five *there.*

for·ty-nin·er (fôr′ tē nī′ nər, fôr′) *n-* person who went to California to seek gold in 1849.

forty winks *Informal* ***n-*** a quick nap.

fo·rum (fôr′ əm) *n-* **1** in ancient Rome, the place where public meetings and assemblies were held. **2** any place or medium of communication in which matters are discussed publicly: *The United Nations is a* forum *of world opinion.* **3** a discussion open to the public.

for·ward (fôr′ wərd, fôr′-) ***adv-*** (also **for′ wards**) **1** to or toward the front; to the fore; onward; ahead: *to leap* forward; *to run* forward *on a ship*; *to pass papers* forward. **2** toward the future: *from this time* forward. ***adj-*** **1** placed in the front: *the* forward *defense line.*

2 toward the front; ahead; onward: *a* forward *leap.* 3 toward the future: *a* forward *look.* 4 advanced; well ahead of others: *the most* forward *position*; forward *ideas.* 5 impudent; bold: *a* forward *manner.* ***vt-*** 1 to send (letters, packages, etc.) on to someone who has moved to a new address. 2 to send (freight) on from one point to the next. 3 to refer (papers, inquiries, etc.) to someone else: *to* forward *a request to the proper authority.* 4 to cause (something) to progress; advance: *to* forward *the party's cause.* ***n-*** player stationed in a scoring position in certain games, such as hockey, basketball, or volleyball. **—*n-* for'ward·er.**

for·ward·ly (fȯr'wərd lē, fôr'-) ***adv-*** impudently; boldly.

for·ward·ness (fȯr'wərd nəs, fôr'-) ***n-*** 1 condition of being advanced or in front. 2 impudence; boldness.

forward pass ***n-*** in football, a throwing of the ball toward the opponent's goal line.

for·went (fȯr wĕnt', fôr-) *p.t.* of **forgo.**

fosse (fŏs) ***n-*** moat; ditch surrounding a castle.

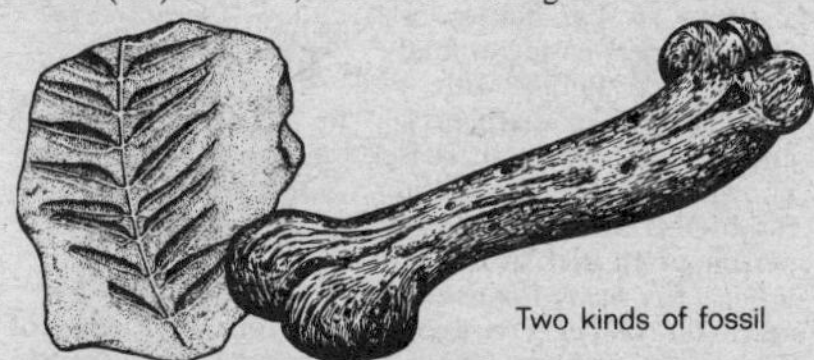
Two kinds of fossil

fos·sil (fŏs'əl) ***n-*** 1 actual remains of ancient animals and plants found buried in the earth or imbedded in rock, as fossil ferns in coal, fossil shells in mountain shale, etc. 2 a preserved indication of the existence of a living organism, such as dinosaur footprints in mud that has turned to rock. 3 *Informal* person or thing which is out of date or old fashioned. *as* ***modifier:*** *a* fossil *fern.*

fossil fuel ***n-*** fuel derived from fossil material such as oil and coal.

fos·sil·ize (fŏs'əl īz') ***vt-*** [**fos·sil·ized, fos·sil·iz·ing**] to change into a fossil; petrify. ***vi-*** to become a fossil. **—*n-* fos'sil·i·za'tion.**

fos·ter (fŏs'tər, fŏs'-) ***vt-*** 1 to advance; promote; encourage: *The children's concerts* foster *an appreciation of music.* 2 to nurture; nourish; bring up; care for: *to* foster *a child.* ***adj-*** belonging to a family though not related by blood: *a* foster *child.* **—*n-* fos'ter·er.**

foster brother ***n-*** male foster child in a family having another child or children.

foster child ***n-*** child who is raised or cared for by parents who are not its own either by blood relation or legal adoption.

foster father ***n-*** man who serves as father of a foster child.

foster mother ***n-*** woman who serves as mother of a foster child.

foster parent ***n-*** a foster father or foster mother.

foster sister ***n-*** female foster child in a family having another child or children.

fought (fȯt) *p.t. & p.p.* of **fight.**

foul (foul) ***adj-*** [**foul·er, foul·est**] 1 offensive; disgusting: *a* foul *smell.* 2 evil; wicked; vile: *a* foul *deed.* 3 stormy; inclement: *a* foul *day*; foul *weather.* 4 unfair; underhanded: *to succeed by fair means or* foul. 5 in baseball, batted outside the foul lines: *He hit a long* foul *fly.* ***adv-*** in baseball, becoming a foul ball: *The ball rolled* foul. ***n-*** 1 in some sports, an action which breaks the rules. 2 foul ball. ***vt-*** 1 to make dirty or impure; pollute: *Smoke* fouls *the air.* 2 to tangle or snag: *The sloppy sailor* fouled *the rope.* ***vi-***: *The fishing line* fouled *in the branches.* ***Hom-*** fowl. **—*adv-* foul'ly. *n-* foul'ness.**

run foul (or **afoul**) **of** to collide with; come into conflict with: *to* run foul of the law.

foul up *Informal* to mix or mess up; confuse; bungle.

fou·lard (fo͞o lärd') ***n-*** satiny fabric with a twill weave, usually of silk and either plain or printed.

foul ball ***n-*** in baseball, a ball hit or tipped so as to fall outside the foul lines or to roll or bounce across either base line between first or third base and home plate.

foul line ***n-*** in baseball, a line coinciding with a base line and extending to the wall.

foul mouthed (foul'moutht', -mouthd') ***adj-*** using vulgar or profane language.

foul play ***n-*** 1 treachery, especially a resort to violence: *The marchers met with* foul play. 2 dishonest dealing.

foul tip ***n-*** in baseball, a ball hit glancingly so that it continues toward the catcher or backstop, hits the plate or the ground behind the plate, etc.

[1]**found** (found) ***vt-*** to begin; establish; set up: *to* found *a colony*; *to* found *a new business.* [from Old French **fonder,** from Latin **fundāre,** from **funda,** "bottom."]

[2]**found** (found) ***vt-*** to form, especially metal, by melting and pouring into a mold; cast. [from Old French **fondre,** from Latin **fundere,** "to pour."]

foun·da·tion (foun dā'shən) ***n-*** 1 the part of a building or other structure, often partly underground, which bears the weight; also, the surface or underground rock, soil, etc., on which something is built. 2 basis: *His philosophy has a firm* foundation. 3 believable or valid evidence: *The story of Washington and the cherry tree has no* foundation. 4 beginning; founding; establishment: *the* foundation *of a college.* 5 endowed institution, especially one that gives money grants to support scholarly and scientific work. 6 fund used to endow such an institution.

[1]**found·er** (foun'dər) ***vi-*** 1 to become filled with water and sink: *Our boat leaked and began to* founder. 2 of a horse, to become lame or otherwise disabled. 3 to collapse; fail: *The business* foundered. [from Old French **fondrer,** meaning "go to the bottom," from Old French **fond,** from Latin **funda.**]

[2]**found·er** (foun'dər) ***n-*** person who establishes or founds: *the* founders *of a colony.* [from [2]**found.**]

[3]**found·er** (foun' dər) ***n-*** person who makes metal castings, especially type. [from [3]**found.**]

found·ling (found'lĭng) ***n-*** baby or child that is found after having been deserted.

found·ry (foun'drē) ***n-*** [*pl.* **found·ries**] 1 place where metal castings are made. 2 the process of casting metal.

fount (fount) ***n-*** 1 source: *a* fount *of wisdom*; *a* fount *of knowledge.* 2 *Archaic* fountain.

foun·tain (foun'tən) ***n-*** 1 a spring of water. 2 a place or machine where water or other drinks may be had: *a drinking* fountain; *a soda* fountain. 3 a jet or jets of water: *The* fountain *rose in feathery plumes of water.* 4 the structure, often ornamental, from which these jets come: *This* fountain *is made of bronze.* 5 a source or reservoir: *A library is a* fountain *of knowledge.*

Fountain

fāte, făt, dâre, bärn; bē, bĕt, mêre; bīte, bĭt; nōte, hŏt, môre, dȯg; fŭn, fûr; to͞o, bo͝ok; oil; out; tar; thin; then; hw for wh as in *wh*at; zh for s as in u*s*ual; ə for a, e, i, o, u, as in *a*go, lin*e*n, per*i*l, at*o*m, min*u*s

foun·tain·head (foun′ tən hĕd′) ***n-*** 1 spring from which a stream flows. 2 a first source: *a* fountainhead *of truth.*

fountain pen ***n-*** pen which feeds ink automatically to the writing point from a reservoir in the barrel.

four (fôr) ***n-*** 1 amount or quantity that is one greater than 3. 2 *Mathematics* (1) the cardinal number that is the sum of 3 and 1. (2) a numeral such as 4 that represents this cardinal number. *as* ***determiner*** (traditionally called adjective or pronoun): *There are* four *jars here and* four *there.* ***Homs-*** for, fore.

on all fours on hands and knees; in a crawling position.

four-flush·er (fôr′ flŭsh′ ər) ***n-*** person who bluffs or pretends, like a poker player who has only four cards of the same suit but plays as if he had a flush.

four·fold (fôr′ fōld′) ***adj-*** 1 four times as many or as much. 2 having four parts: *a* fourfold *leaf.* ***adv-***: *They increased their output* fourfold.

four-foot·ed (fôr′ fŏŏt′ əd) ***adj-*** having four feet: *A dog is a* four-footed *animal.*

four freedoms ***n-*** freedom of speech and religion and freedom from want and fear. These were set forth as the goals of U.S. foreign policy in early 1941.

four-hand·ed (fôr′ hăn′ dəd) ***adj-*** 1 needing or using four hands: *a* four-handed *sonata.* 2 made for four players, such as a game: *a* four-handed *card game.*

Four-H clubs (fôr′ āch′) ***n-*** youth organization sponsored by the Department of Agriculture and offering instruction in agriculture and home economics. The name means that it attempts to help the head, hands, heart, and health of its members.

four hundred ***n-*** the established inner social circle of a community: *My neighbors belong to the* four hundred.

four-in-hand (fôr′ ĭn hănd′) ***n-*** 1 necktie tied with a slipknot and having ends that hang down over each other. 2 a team of four horses driven by a single driver.

four-leaf clover ***n-*** a clover having four leaflets instead of the usual three. It is thought to bring good luck to those who find it or keep it.

four-o'clock (fôr′ ə klŏk′) ***n-*** bushy, cultivated plant with variously colored flowers that open in cloudy weather or the late afternoon and close in the morning.

four-post·er (fôr′ pōs′ tər) ***n-*** bedstead with four posts, usually tall and often with a canopy and curtains.

four·score (fôr′ skôr′) ***n-*** four times twenty; eighty.

four·some (fôr′ səm) ***n-*** 1 a group of four, especially two mixed couples. 2 game or players in a game, especially golf, in which two pairs of partners play each other.

four·square (fôr′ skwâr′) ***adj-*** 1 honest; forthright. 2 having four equal sides; square.

four·teen (fôr′ tēn′) ***n-*** 1 amount or quantity that is one greater than 13. 2 *Mathematics* (1) the cardinal number that is the sum of 13 and 1. (2) a numeral such as 14 that represents this cardinal number. *as* ***determiner*** (traditionally called adjective or pronoun): *There are* fourteen *goats here and* fourteen *there.*

four·teenth (fôr′ tēnth′) ***adj-*** 1 next after thirteenth. 2 the ordinal of 14; 14th. ***n-*** 1 the next after the thirteenth; 14th. 2 one of fourteen equal parts of a whole or group. 3 the last term in the name of a fraction having a denominator of 14: 1/14 *is one* fourteenth. ***adv-***: *His boat finished* fourteenth *in the race.*

fourth (fôrth) ***adj-*** 1 next after third. 2 the ordinal of 4; 4th. ***n-*** 1 the next after the third; 4th. 2 one of four equal parts of a whole or group. 3 the last term in the name of a common fraction having a denominator of 4: 1/4 *is one* fourth. 4 *Music* an interval of four tones on the scale counting the extremes, as from C to F, and the harmonic combination of these tones. ***adv-***: *He spoke of you* fourth. ***Hom-*** forth.

fourth dimension ***n-*** 1 a dimension that is assumed to be added to length, width, and height, in an effort to solve a mathematical problem, develop a physical theory, write fiction, etc. 2 in the theory of relativity, the time co-ordinate in the concept of space-time.

fourth estate ***n-*** the press; journalism; newspapers and magazines and their staffs and publishers.

fourth·ly (fôrth′ lē) ***adv-*** as fourth in a series.

Fourth of July ***n-*** Independence Day; anniversary of signing the Declaration of Independence in 1776.

fo·ve·a (fō′ vē ə) ***n-*** [*pl.* **fo·ve·ae** (-vē ē, -vēī)] *Biology* a shallow pit or depression; especially, the area of sharp vision and color vision in the retina of the eye.

fowl (foul) ***n-*** [*pl.* **fowl** or **fowls**] 1 bird. 2 barnyard bird, such as a chicken, goose, duck, turkey, or guinea hen, raised for its meat or eggs. 3 meat of such a bird when served as food. 4 a full-grown chicken or rooster; also its meat. ***Hom-*** foul.

fowl·er (foul′ ər) ***n-*** one who catches or kills wild birds.

fowl·ing piece (foul′ ĭng) ***n-*** *Archaic* light shotgun.

fox (fŏks) ***n-*** [*pl.* **fox·es** or **fox**] 1 a meat-eating animal of the dog family with a pointed muzzle, sharp ears, and a long bushy tail. It is known for its cunning. 2 the fur of this animal. 3 a sly person. ***vt-*** to trick shrewdly. ***adj-***: *a* fox *hunt*; fox *collar.*

Red fox, about 3 1/2 ft. long

Fox (fŏks) ***n-*** [*pl.* **Fox·es,** also **Fox**] one of a tribe of Algonquian Indians who formerly lived in Wisconsin around Lake Winnebago and the Fox River. They now live on a reservation in Iowa. ***adj-***: *a* Fox *village.*

fox fire ***n-*** phosphorescent light given off by rotten wood that has been attacked by certain types of fungus.

fox·glove (fŏks′ glŭv′) ***n-*** plant which has a one-sided spike of showy, tubular flowers. It is the source of the drug digitalis.

fox·hole (fŏks′ hōl′) ***n-*** a hole dug by a soldier in battle as shelter from enemy fire.

fox·hound (fŏks′ hound′) ***n-*** any of several hounds with a keen sense of smell and great endurance, bred and trained to hunt foxes.

fox·tail (fŏks′ tāl′) ***n-*** 1 tail of a fox; brush. 2 any of various grasses having blossoms in the form of a brush.

fox terrier ***n-*** a small, active, alert dog of the terrier family, either smooth or wire-haired.

fox trot ***n-*** 1 a ballroom dance in two-four or four-four time with combinations of quick and slow steps. 2 the music for this dance. **—*adj-* (fox-trot):** *a* fox-trot *step.*

fox·y (fŏk′ sē) ***adj-*** [**fox·i·er, fox·i·est**] 1 like a fox; sly. 2 (also **foxed**) stained; discolored. **—*adv-* fox′ i·ly. *n-* fox′ i·ness.**

foy·er (foi′ ər) ***n-*** lobby or entrance hall; vestibule.

Fr symbol for francium.

fr. 1 franc. 2 from.

Fr. 1 French. 2 Father. 3 Friday.

fra·cas (frā′ kəs) ***n-*** wild, noisy fight or quarrel; row.

frac·tion (frăk′ shən) ***n-*** 1 part or fragment: *to complete only a* fraction *of one's assigned work.* 2 *Mathematics* any number written so as to show that it is the quotient of two numbers; ratio. The fraction ¾ is the quotient of 3 divided by 4. A **proper fraction** is one with the numerator smaller than the denominator, and an **improper fraction** is one with the numerator equal to or greater than the denominator.

frac·tion·al (frăk′ shən əl) ***adj-*** 1 of, having to do with, or consisting of a fraction. 2 small or insignificant in size or importance. 3 *Chemistry* having to do with processes in which the parts of a mixture can be separated according to differences in their physical or chemical properties. —*adv*- **frac′tion·al·ly.**

fractional distillation *n*- process of separation of liquids, in which the temperature of a mixture of liquids is slowly raised so that each liquid vaporizes as its boiling point is reached.

fractional numeral *n*- numeral composed of two numerals with a horizontal bar between them, such as $\frac{3}{8}$.

frac·tious (frăk′shəs) *adj*- 1 unruly; rebellious. 2 irritable; cross; fretful. —*adv*- **frac′tious·ly.** *n*- **frac′tious·ness.**

frac·ture (frăk′chər) *n*- 1 process of breaking or cracking. 2 a break or crack, especially in a bone. *vt*- [**frac·tured, frac·tur·ing**] to break or crack: *to* fracture *one's arm.* *vi*-: *His bones* fracture *easily.*

frag·ile (frăj′əl) *adj*- frail; easily broken: *a* fragile *vase.* —*adv*- **frag′ile·ly.** *n*- **fra·gil′i·ty** (frə jĭl′ə tē).

[1]**frag·ment** (frăg′mənt) *n*- 1 part broken off or separated from a whole; portion; piece: *the* fragments *of the broken jar.* 2 incomplete or unfinished part: *sentence* fragment.

[2]**frag·ment** (frăg mĕnt′) *vt*- to break into pieces: *to* fragment *rocks.* *vi*-: *Glass* fragments *easily.*

frag·men·tar·y (frăg′mən tĕr′ē) *adj*- broken and incomplete; disconnected: *a* fragmentary *report.*

frag·men·ta·tion (frăg′mən tā′shən) *n*- act or process of breaking, shattering, especially of rocks.

fra·grance (frā′grəns) *n*- pleasant odor; sweet smell.

fra·grant (frā′grənt) *adj*- pleasing in odor; sweet-smelling. —*adv*- **fra′grant·ly.**

frail (frāl) *adj*- [**frail·er, frail·est**] 1 physically weak: *a* frail *child.* 2 delicate; fragile; easily broken; unsubstantial. —*adv*- **frail′ly.** *n*- **frail′ness.**

frail·ty (frāl′tē) *n*- [*pl.* **frail·ties**] 1 weakness, especially moral weakness: *the* frailty *of his character.* 2 fault or failing due to moral weakness: *human* frailties.

frame (frām) *n*- 1 the supporting or shaping part of a structure: *The skeleton is the* frame *of the body.* 2 surrounding part or border: *a picture* frame; *a door* frame. 3 bodily construction; build. 4 general structure; system: *The Constitution established our* frame *of government.* 5 in bowling, one of the ten divisions of the game. 6 one of the successive exposures or pictures on a strip of motion-picture film. *vt*- [**framed, fram·ing**] 1 to put together; construct; assemble: *John* framed *his reply carefully.* 2 to surround or enclose in a border: *to* frame *a picture.* 3 *Slang* to cause to be accused falsely. —*n*- **fram′er.**

Frame of a boat

frame house *n*- house built with a wooden framework.

frame of mind *n*- mental or emotional state.

frame of reference *n*- 1 set of facts, experiences, or values within which a subject, idea, etc., has meaning: *a problem within one's own* frame of reference. 2 *Physics* set of reference points by which relative motion is judged.

frame-up (frām′ŭp′) *Slang* *n*- a plot to place the guilt for a crime on an innocent person.

frame·work (frām′wûrk′) *n*- structure that supports, gives shape, or holds together: *a house's* framework.

fram·ing (frā′mĭng) *n*- 1 frame or framework. 2 material used for frames or framework.

franc (frăngk) *n*- the basic unit of money in France, Belgium, Switzerland, and some other countries. *Hom*- frank.

fran·chise (frăn′chīz′) *n*- 1 right to vote. 2 right or privilege granted to a person or group, especially by a government or company; *a* franchise *to operate buses.*

Fran·cis·can (frăn sĭs′kən) *adj*- of or pertaining to St. Francis of Assisi, or to the three religious orders founded by him. *n*- member of any one of these orders.

fran·ci·um (frăn′sē əm) *n*- radioactive metal element. Symbol Fr, At. No. 87, At. Wt. 223.

Franco- *combining form* French.

fran·gi·ble (frăn′jə bəl) *adj*- easily broken; brittle.

[1]**frank** (frăngk) *adj*- [**frank·er, frank·est**] showing thoughts or feelings openly and honestly; candid: *a* frank *look*; *a* frank *opinion.* [from Old French **franc,** "free; freeborn."] *Hom*- franc. —*adv*- **frank′ly.** *n*- **frank′ness.**

[2]**frank** (frăngk) *n*- 1 the right to send mail without paying postage on it. 2 a mark that indicates this right. *vt*- 1 to mark (mail) in this manner. 2 to send (mail) free of postal charges. [from [1]**frank.**] *Hom*- franc.

[3]**frank** (frăngk) *Informal* *n*- frankfurter. *Hom*- franc.

Frank (frăngk) *n*- member of a Germanic tribe that lived along the Rhine in the third century A.D., and later conquered what is now France. *Hom*- franc.

Frank·en·stein (frăngk′ən stīn′) *n*- 1 character in a novel of the same name, who creates a monster that finally destroys him. The name is mistakenly used for the monster itself. 2 anything that becomes dangerous to its creator.

frank·furt·er (frăngk′fər tər) *n*- spiced sausage of beef or beef and pork. [American word from the German town of **Frankfurt.**]

frank·in·cense (frăngk′ĭn sĕns′) *n*- fragrant, spicy resin from certain African and Asiatic trees, burned as incense.

Frank·ish (frăngk′ĭsh) *adj*- of or relating to the Franks. *n*- the West Germanic language of the Franks.

fran·tic (frăn′tĭk) *adj*- wildly excited; frenzied: *her* frantic *cries for help*; *a scene of* frantic *activity.* —*adv*- **fran′ti·cal·ly** or **fran′tic·ly.** *n*- **fran′tic·ness.**

frappe (frăp) *n*- 1 thick milk shake made with ice cream. 2 frappé.

frap·pé (fră pā′) *adj*- chilled; iced. *n*- beverage, such as fruit juice or liqueur, that is served half frozen or over shaved ice; frappe.

fra·ter·nal (frə tûr′nəl) *adj*- 1 of or like a brother or brothers: *a* fraternal *relationship*; fraternal *affection.* 2 consisting of or having to do with people having a brotherly relationship. —*adv*- **fra·ter′nal·ly.**

fraternal twins *n*- human twins of the same or opposite sex, developed from separately fertilized ova and, as a result, having different hereditary characteristics. See also *identical twins.*

fra·ter·ni·ty (frə tûr′nə tē) *n*- [*pl.* **fra·ter·ni·ties**] 1 society or group of men or boys joined by a common interest, especially such an organization in high schools and colleges. 2 brotherhood.

frat·er·nize (frăt′ər nīz′) *vi*- [**frat·er·nized, frat·er·niz·ing**] to associate in a friendly or brotherly way (with): *The soldiers* fraternized *with the people of the conquered town.* —*n*- **frat·er·ni·za′tion.**

frat·ri·cide (fră′trə sīd′) *n*- 1 the killing of one's own brother or sister. 2 person who kills his brother or sister.

Frau (frou) *German* *n*- [*pl.* **Frau·en** (frou′ən)] 1 title used before a surname, equivalent to "Mrs." 2 married woman.

fraud (frȯd) *n*- 1 deceit or trickery, especially when used to cheat others of money or property. 2 *Informal* person or thing that is not what is claimed or represented.

fraud·u·lent (frȯ′ jə lənt, frȯd′ yo͞o-) ***adj***- of, obtained by, or using fraud: *guilty of* fraudulent *practices.* **—*n*- fraud′ u·lence.** ***adv*- fraud′ u·lent·ly.**

fraught (frȯt) ***adj***- filled; laden: *It's* fraught *with danger.*

Fräu·lein (froi′ līn′) *German* ***n***- [*pl.* **Frau·lein**] **1** title used before a surname, equivalent to "Miss." **2** unmarried woman.

[1]**fray** (frā) ***n***- battle; brawl; rough-and-tumble fight. [short for **affray.**] ***Hom***- Frey.

[2]**fray** (frā) ***vt***- to cause to ravel or wear out, especially at the edge: *Constant wear* frayed *his shirt cuffs.* ***vi***-: *His cuffs* frayed *at the edges.* [from Old French **freier,** from Latin **fricāre,** "to rub away."] ***Hom***- Frey.

fraz·zle (frăz′ əl) *Informal* ***vt***- [**fraz·zled, fraz·zling**] **1** to fray. **2** to wear out; exhaust. ***vi***- **1** to become frayed. **2** to become weary or exhausted. ***n***- **1** frayed or ragged end. **2** state of complete exhaustion.

freak (frēk) ***n***- **1** abnormal animal or plant (offensive when applied to persons). **2** strange, sudden whim. ***adj***- abnormal and unusual; bizarre: *a* freak *accident.*

freak·ish (frē′ kĭsh) ***adj***- abnormal or unnatural; odd: *a* freakish *event.* **—*adv*- freak′ ish·ly.** ***n*- freak′ ish·ness.**

freck·le (frĕk′ əl) ***n***- small tan or brown spot on the skin. ***vt***- [**freck·led, freck·ling**] to mark with such spots. ***vi***- to become marked with such spots.

freck·led (frĕk′ əld) ***adj***- covered with freckles: *a* freckled *face.* Also **freck′ ly.**

free (frē) ***adj***- [**fre·er, fre·est**] **1** not controlled or dominated by others; having or showing liberty; independent: *a* free *people*; *a* free *country*; *a* free *choice.* **2** not confined or restricted in action: *a prisoner happy to be* free; *his* free *stride.* **3** unattached; loose: *the* free *end of a rope.* **4** abundant; profuse: *a* free *flow of blood.* **5** without cost or charge: *a* free *ticket*; *a* free *show.* **6** not busy; unoccupied: *a* free *telephone line*; *to be* free *all afternoon.* **7** unrestrained, often in a bold and forward manner: *You are too* free *with your language.* ***adv***- **1** into an unrestricted or unconfined state: *The cable swung* free. *The prisoner broke* free. **2** without charge: *The children were admitted* free. ***vt***- [**freed, free·ing**] **1** to set at liberty; release: *to* free *a man from prison*; *to* free *the slaves.* **2** to rid or clear of some trouble or burden: *to* free *him from debt.* **—*adv*- free′ ly.** ***n*- free′ ness:** *a* freeness *of manner.*

free and easy not formal or strained; relaxed: *a* free and easy *manner.* **free from** (or **of**) without: *to be* free from *pain*; free of *debt*; free of *prejudice.* **free with** generous; liberal: *to be* free with *one's money.* **make free with** to be overly familiar with; take liberties with.

free association ***n***- **1** conscious or unconscious association by a person of one idea, image, memory, etc., with another. **2** technique in psychoanalysis in which such associations are studied.

free·board (frē′ bôrd′) ***n***- ship's side between the water line and the deck or gunwale.

free·boot·er (frē′ bo͞o′ tər) ***n***- pirate. **—*n*- free′ boot′ ing.**

free·born (frē′ bôrn′) ***adj***- **1** born free, rather than in slavery or servitude. **2** of or for those born free.

free city ***n***- city, such as certain ones in the Middle Ages, that is an independent, sovereign state.

freed·man (frēd′ mən) ***n***- [*pl.* **freed·men**] man freed from slavery. **—*n*-** *fem.* **freed′ wom′ an.**

free·dom (frē′ dəm) ***n***- **1** the state of being free; liberty: *to fight for* freedom. **2** free or complete use: *He was given the* freedom *of the city.* **3** familiarity; outspokenness: *to ask personal questions with too much* freedom. **4** ease: *clothes that allow* freedom *of motion.*

freedom from condition of being free from.

free energy ***n***- in a physical or chemical system, that part of the energy that is available to do work.

free enterprise ***n***- the economic principle or system of minimum government control or regulation of business.

free fall ***n***- **1** the fall of an object when the only force acting on it is gravity. **2** the portion of a parachute jump before the parachute is opened.

free flight ***n***- flight of a rocket, after the engine is turned off.

free-for-all (frē′ fər ȯl′) ***n***- wild, noisy fight or quarrel.

free·hand (frē′ hănd′) ***adj***- done or drawn by hand without a ruler, compasses, etc. ***adv***-: *to draw* freehand.

free hand ***n***- **1** freedom or permission to do as one pleases: *a* free hand *in running a business.* **2** generosity.

free·hand·ed (frē′ hăn′ dəd) ***adj***- generous; liberal: *a* freehanded *benefactor.* **—*adv*- free′ hand′ ed·ly.**

free·hold (frē′ hōld′) ***n***- **1** property held by the owner for life. **2** possession of such property, usually including the right to pass it on to one's heirs. **—*n*- free′ hold′ er.**

free lance ***n***- writer, artist, actor, etc., who does not work regularly for any one employer, but sells his services to anyone interested in buying them. **—*adj*- (free-lance):** *a* free-lance *writer.* ***vi*- (free-lance)** [**free-lanced, free-lanc·ing**]: *He* free-lances *for a living.*

free·man (frē′ mən) ***n***- [*pl.* **free·men**] person who is not a slave.

Free·ma·son (frē′ mā′ sən) ***n***- member of a secret society professing brotherly love, charity, and mutual aid; Mason.

Free·ma·son·ry (frē′ mā′ sən rē) ***n***- **1** the beliefs and principles of the Freemasons. **2 freemasonry** spirit of fellowship among those with common interests.

free on board ***adv***- commercial term meaning that the stated price covers delivery to a common carrier, but no further shipment costs. *Abbr.* f.o.b. or F.O.B.

free port ***n***- seaport where few or no customs duties are imposed on imported goods intended to be carried or shipped elsewhere.

free press ***n***- the right or freedom to publish newspapers, books, etc., without government control or censorship.

fre·er (frē′ ər) *compar.* of **free.**

free·si·a (frē′ zhə, -zhē ə) ***n***- plant cultivated for its fragrant, tubular, white, yellow, or purplish flowers.

free silver ***n***- **1** free and unlimited minting of silver coins, especially at a fixed ratio to gold. **2** economic policy that favors this practice.

free soil ***n***- territory in which slavery is prohibited, especially such territory in the United States before the Civil War.

Free-Soil Party ***n***- U.S. political party formed in 1848 to prevent the extension of slavery into the territories.

free-spo·ken (frē′ spō′ kən) ***adj***- speaking freely and openly; outspoken; frank.

fre·est (frē′ əst) *superl.* of **free.**

free·stone (frē′ stōn′) ***n***- **1** any stone, such as limestone, that may be cut in any direction without splitting. **2** a fruit, such as certain peaches, whose flesh does not stick to the stone. *as* ***modifier***: *a* freestone *peach.*

free·think·er (frē′ thĭngk′ ər) ***n***- person whose ideas and opinions, especially about religion, are based on independent judgment and not on tradition or authority. **—*adj*- free′ think′ ing.**

free throw ***n***- in basketball, an unopposed chance to throw a basket from the foul line, given to a player who has been fouled by an opponent.

free trade ***n***- import and export trade that is not restricted by tariffs or customs duties.

free·trad·er (frē′ trā′ dər) ***n***- person who believes in or is engaged in free trade.

free verse ***n***- poetry, usually unrhymed, having irregular meter or rhythm.

free·way (frē′wā′) ***n-*** superhighway designed for smooth and rapid movement of vehicles.

free·wheel·ing (frē′hwē′lĭng) ***adj-*** **1** turning or coasting free, as a car or bicycle does when fitted with a special device. **2** marked by or behaving with unchecked energy and abandon: *a* freewheeling *political campaign*; *a* freewheeling *dealer in oil stocks.*

free·will (frē′wĭl′) ***adj-*** made or done of one's own accord; voluntary: *a* freewill *gift.*

free will ***n-*** **1** freedom from force, restraints, or outside influences in making choices or decisions. **2** the doctrine that man has such freedom of choice.

of (one's) own free will without being forced or coerced; voluntarily: *He did it* of his own free will.

free world ***n-*** **1** the parts of the world that are free from Communist or any other dictatorship. **2** the United States and its allies.

freeze (frēz) ***vt-*** [**froze** (frōz), **froz·en** (frō′zən), **freez·ing**] **1** to cause a liquid to become solid either by cooling it or by cooling and compressing it at the same time. **2** to change the liquids in (a container or substance) to solids by cooling. **3** to damage or kill with cold. **4** to fix officially at a given level: *to* freeze *prices.* ***vi-*** **1** to become solid in response to cooling or cooling and compressing. **2** to become hard or solid because of cold: *The meat* froze *rapidly in the freezer.* **3** to be chilled, damaged, or killed by cold or frost: *The unprotected plant* froze *during the night.* **4** to become closed or clogged by ice: *The pipes* froze *and then burst.* **5** to become motionless or unable to move: *to* freeze *with terror.* ***n-*** period of extremely cold weather; frost. ***Hom-*** frieze.

freeze out to force out or drive away by unfriendliness, competition, etc.

freeze-dry (frēz′drī′) ***vt-*** [**freeze-dried, freeze-dry·ing**] to dry (food) in a frozen state under high vacuum for preservation. **—*adj-* freeze-dried.**

freez·er (frē′zər) ***n-*** **1** cabinet in which foods or other perishable materials are kept frozen to preserve them. **2** machine for freezing liquids: *an ice cream* freezer.

freezing point ***n-*** temperature at which a liquid freezes or becomes solid. At sea level, the freezing point of fresh water is 0°C. of 32°F.

freight (frāt) ***n-*** **1** goods transported by means of truck, train, ship, or aircraft; cargo. **2** transportation of goods by such means. **3** charge or price for such transportation. ***as modifier***: *a* freight *train.* ***vt-*** **1** to transport (goods) as cargo. **2** to load (a vehicle, vessel, etc.) with cargo.

freight·age (frāt′ĭj) ***n-*** the transportation of freight; also, the goods transported, or the charge for transporting them.

freight·er (frā′tər) ***n-*** ship for carrying goods rather than passengers; cargo vessel.

French (frĕnch) ***adj-*** of or pertaining to France, its people, language, or culture. ***n-*** **1** the Romance language spoken in France and some other countries. **2 the French** (takes a plural verb) the people of France collectively.

French and Indian War ***n-*** conflict in North America between the English and the French (1754-63), in which most of the Indians involved aided the French.

French door ***n-*** one of a pair of full-length glass doors hinged on the outer sides and opening in the middle.

French fries *Informal* ***n- pl.*** strips of potatoes fried in deep fat.

French fry ***vt-*** to fry (potatoes, onions, etc.) in deep fat.

French horn ***n-*** brass wind instrument with a long, coiled tube and flaring end. It has a mellow tone.

French horn

French leave *Slang* ***n-*** hasty, unceremonious departure, often in secret.

French·man (frĕnch′mən) ***n-*** [*pl.* **French·men**] man who is a native or inhabitant of France. **—*n-*** *fem.* **French′wom′an.**

French Revolution ***n-*** revolution that began in France in 1789 and led to the overthrow of the French monarch and the proclamation of a republic in 1792.

French toast ***n-*** slices of bread dipped in egg and milk and fried quickly.

French window ***n-*** **1** French door through which one can leave or enter a house. **2** a casement window.

fre·net·ic (frə nĕt′ĭk) ***adj-*** wildly excited; frenzied; frantic. **—*adv-* fre·net′ic·al·ly.**

fren·zied (frĕn′zēd) ***adj-*** wildly excited; frantic.

fren·zy (frĕn′zē) ***n-*** [*pl.* **fren·zies**] state of intense or violent excitement, rage, fury, etc.: *The bad news caused the king to go into a* frenzy.

fre·quen·cy (frē′kwən sē) ***n-*** [*pl.* **fre·quen·cies**] **1** an occurring over and over within a short period of time: *the* frequency *of snowstorms in winter.* **2** number of times that a certain action happens in a given time; rate of occurrence: *a pulse with a* frequency *of eighty beats to the minute.* **3** *Physics* number of vibrations or oscillations that take place in a given unit of time. **4** *Mathematics* the number of times a value occurs or is observed to occur in relation to the total number of possible occurrences.

frequency modulation ***n-*** way of radio broadcasting in which the frequency of the radio wave is changed according to the sound being broadcast. *Abbr.* FM. See also *amplitude modulation.*

[1]fre·quent (frē′kwənt) ***adj-*** happening or appearing often: *his* frequent *trips.* **—*adv-* fre′quent·ly.**

[2]fre·quent (frē kwĕnt′ *or* frē′kwənt) ***vt-*** to go to often or habitually: *He* frequents *the museum.* **—*n-* fre·quent′er** or **fre′quent·er.**

fres·co (frĕs′kō) ***n-*** [*pl.* **fres·coes** or **fres·cos**] **1** painting made on wet plaster, covering a wall, ceiling, etc. **2** the art of making such paintings.

fresh (frĕsh) ***adj-*** [**fresh·er, fresh·est**] **1** recently made, used, gathered, etc.: *a vase of* fresh *flowers*; *a cup of* fresh *coffee*; fresh *footprints.* **2** new; not made, used, or known before: *a* fresh *approach*; *a* fresh *sheet of paper*; fresh *news.* **3** additional or different: *There's still time to make a* fresh *start.* **4** not stale or spoiled: *a loaf of* fresh *bread.* **5** of food, not preserved. **6** not faded; vivid: *memories still* fresh *in the mind.* **7** of air, uncontaminated. **8** of water, not salty. **9** not tired; lively; vigorous: *He is* fresh *after his nap.* **10** of a wind, moderately strong. **11** *Slang* impudent; saucy. **—*adv-* fresh′ly. *n-* fresh′ness.**

fresh up *Informal* to freshen up.

fresh·en (frĕsh′ən) ***vt-*** to make clearer, stronger, more lively, etc.: *to* freshen *faded colors.* ***vi-*** to become stronger: *The breeze* freshened.

freshen up *Informal* to make oneself comfortable or presentable by washing, changing clothes, etc.

fresh·et (frĕsh′ət) ***n-*** **1** sudden swelling of a stream by melting snow or heavy rain. **2** a fresh-water stream that runs into the sea.

fresh·man (frĕsh′mən) ***n-*** [*pl.* **fresh·men**] student in the first year of high school or college.

fresh·wa·ter (frĕsh′ wŏt′ ər, -wŏt′ ər) ***adj-*** of or living in water that is not salty: *a* fresh-water *fish.*

1**fret** (frĕt) ***vi-*** **[fret·ted, fret·ting]** to be worried or irritated: *She* frets *over little things.* ***vt-*** **1** to annoy, worry, or irritate. **2** to rub or wear away: *The stream* fretted *a channel in the rock.* ***n-*** irritation; annoyance: *the* frets *and cares of life.* [from Old English **fretan,** "to eat up."]

2**fret** (frĕt) ***n-*** ornamental design made of short straight lines. ***vt-*** **[fret·ted, fret·ting]** to decorate with such a design. [from Old French **frettes,** "grill," from **frete,** "a ferrule; iron support."]

Fret

3**fret** (frĕt) ***n-*** one of the ridges on the neck of a banjo, guitar, etc. [special use of 2**fret.**] ***—adj-*** **fret′ ted.**

fret·ful (frĕt′ fəl) ***adj-*** irritable; peevish: *the* fretful *child.* ***—adv-*** **fret′ ful·ly.** ***n-*** **fret′ ful·ness.**

fret saw ***n-*** saw with a narrow, fine-toothed blade mounted on a frame, used for delicate ornamental work.

fret·work (frĕt′ wûrk′) ***n-*** ornamental carving or openwork, usually of frets or interlacing lines.

Freud·i·an (froi′ dē ən) ***adj-*** relating or conforming to the theories or teachings of Sigmund Freud. ***n-*** believer in or follower of Freud's theories of psychology.

Frey (frā) ***n-*** in Norse mythology, the god of fertility, peace, and agriculture. ***Hom-*** fray.

Frey·a (frā′ ə) ***n-*** in Norse mythology, goddess of love.

Fri. Friday.

fri·a·ble (frī′ ə bəl) ***adj-*** easily crumbled or reduced to powder; *soft,* friable *rock.* ***—n-*** **fri′ a·bil′ i·ty** or **fri′ a·ble·ness.**

fri·ar (frī′ ər) ***n-*** man who is a member of any of several Roman Catholic orders, especially the Dominicans, Franciscans, Carmelites, and Augustinians. ***Hom-*** fryer.

fri·ar·y (frī′ ə rē) ***n-*** [*pl.* **fri·a·ries**] monastery for friars.

fric·as·see (frĭk′ ə sē′) ***n-*** chicken, veal, etc., that has been cut up, sauteed, stewed, or steamed, and served in a thickened gravy. ***vt-*** **[fric·as·seed, fric·as·see·ing]**: *to* fricassee *a chicken.*

fric·tion (frĭk′ shən) **1** the rubbing of one object against another: *the* friction *of a towel on the skin.* **2** the force of resistance that acts to oppose the motion of one object along or across the surface of another: *to wax skis to reduce* friction. **3** disagreement or irritation between two or more people. *as* ***modifier:*** *a* friction *clutch.* ***—adj-*** **fric′ tion·less.**

fric·tion·al (frĭk′ shən əl) ***adj-*** of or having to do with friction. ***—adv-*** **fric′ tion·al·ly.**

friction tape ***n-*** cloth or plastic tape coated with an adhesive, and used in electrical work to protect and insulate an electrical conductor.

Fri·day (frī′ dā, -dē) ***n-*** the sixth day of the week.

fried (frīd) *p.t. & p.p.* of 1**fry.**

fried·cake (frīd′ kāk′) ***n-*** small cake, such as a doughnut or cruller, that is fried in deep fat.

friend (frĕnd) ***n-*** **1** person one knows and likes. **2** ally. **3** person who gives support to someone or something. **make friends with** to become friendly with.

Friend (frĕnd) ***n-*** member of the Society of Friends; Quaker.

friend·less (frĕnd′ ləs) ***adj-*** without any friends. ***—n-*** **friend′ less·ness.**

friend·ly (frĕnd′ lē) ***adj-*** **[friend·li·er, friend·li·est]** **1** like a friend; kind; amiable: *a* friendly *person; a* friendly *gesture.* **2** not hostile; amicable; peaceable: *a* friendly *country on the border.* **3** favorable: *a* friendly *wind.* ***—n-*** **friend′ li·ness.**

friend·ship (frĕnd′ shĭp) ***n-*** relationship between persons who like and respect each other; warm affection.

fries (frīz) form of the verb **fry** used with "he," "she," "it," or singular noun subjects in the present tense.

1**frieze** (frēz) ***n-*** **1** band, often decorated with carved figures, between the cornice and architrave of a building. **2** any similar decorative band around the walls of a room. [from earlier French **frize.**] ***Hom-*** freeze.

Frieze

2**frieze** (frēz) ***n-*** coarse, woolen cloth with a shaggy nap on one side. [from earlier French **drap de frise,** "cloth of Friesland."] ***Hom-*** freeze.

fri·gate (frĭg′ ət) **1** in former times, a type of square-rigged sailing warship with three masts. **2** light modern warship used chiefly for escort duty.

frigate bird ***n-*** long-winged tropical sea bird with a hooked beak and forked tail; man-o'-war bird.

fright (frīt) ***n-*** **1** violent, sudden fear or alarm. **2** *Informal* something ugly or ridiculous in appearance.

Frigate

fright·en (frī′ tən) ***vt-*** to fill with terror or alarm: *The strange noises* frightened *her.* ***vi-***: *He* frightens *easily.*

fright·ful (frīt′ fəl) ***adj-*** **1** horrible; causing fear or terror: *a* frightful *disaster.* **2** unpleasant; disagreeable; ugly: *a* frightful *noise.* ***—adv-*** **fright′ ful·ly.** ***n-*** **fright′ ful·ness.**

frig·id (frĭj′ ĭd) **1** freezing; very cold: *a* frigid *climate.* **2** very unfriendly; hostile; chilly: *a* frigid *silence.* ***—n-*** **fri·gid′ i·ty** or **frig′ id·ness.** ***adv-*** **frig′ id·ly.**

Frigid Zone ***n-*** former term for the north and south polar regions.

fri·jol (frē hōl′) *Spanish* ***n-*** [*pl.* **fri·jo·les** (frē hō′ lās)] bean used widely as food by Mexicans and the Spanish-speaking people of southwestern United States.

frill (frĭl) ***n-*** **1** narrow, gathered or pleated strip of decorative trimming; ruffle: *a* frill *on a dress.* **2 frills** *Informal* useless or excessive ornaments, activities, etc. ***—adj-*** **frill′ y [frill·i·er, frill·i·est].**

fringe (frĭnj) ***n-*** **1** decorative band or border on a strip of tape, edge of cloth, etc., consisting of many single strands, often knotted. **2** anything resembling this: *a* fringe *of grass along a walk.* **3** outer edge or limit: *the* fringe *of the town; the* fringes *of society.* ***vt-*** **[fringed, fring·ing]** to put or form a decorative edge or border on.

frip·per·y (frĭp′ ə rē) ***n-*** [*pl.* **frip·per·ies**] **1** cheap, showy clothing or ornaments. **2** pretense or showiness in speech, manners, etc.

frisk (frĭsk) ***vi-*** to run, dance, or skip playfully; frolic: *The squirrels* frisked *about the park.* ***vt-*** *Slang* to search (someone) for a concealed weapon, stolen loot, etc.

frisk·y (frĭs′ kē) ***adj-*** **[frisk·i·er, frisk·i·est]** lively; playful; frolicsome: *a* frisky *kitten.* ***—adv-*** **frisk′ i·ly.** ***n-*** **frisk′ i·ness.**

1**frit·ter** (frĭt′ ər) ***n-*** small cake consisting of some fruit, vegetable, or other food that has been dipped in or added to a batter, and then fried. [from Old French **friture,** "a fried dish (usually fish)," from **frit,** "fried," from Latin **frīgere** "to fry."]

2**frit·ter** (frĭt′ ər) **fritter away** to waste bit by bit; squander: *to* fritter away *time; to* fritter away *money.* [from an older meaning of **fritter** "a fragment," from Old French **freture,** from Latin **fractūra,** "a broken thing; fracture."] ***—n-*** **frit′ ter·er.**

fri·vol·i·ty (frĭ vŏl′ ə tē) ***n-*** [*pl.* **fri·vol·i·ties**] **1** quality of being frivolous. **2** frivolous thing or act.

friv·o·lous (frĭv′ ə ləs) ***adj-*** **1** not serious; giddy: *a* frivolous *girl who never thinks about serious matters.* **2** unimportant; trivial; insignificant: *his* frivolous *activities.* **—*adv-*** **friv′ o·lous·ly.** ***n-*** **friv′ o·lous·ness.**

frizz (frĭz) ***vt-*** to crimp into small, tight curls: *to* frizz *one's hair.* ***vi-***: *Her hair* frizzes *at the top.* ***n-*** hair that forms small, tight curls. Also **friz.**

[1]**friz·zle** (frĭz′ əl) ***vt- & vi-*** [**friz·zled, friz·zling**] to frizz. ***n-*** small, tight curl. [of uncertain origin, perhaps from French **friser** meaning "to curl."] **—*adj-*** **friz′ zly.**

[2]**friz·zle** (frĭz′ əl) ***vi-*** [**friz·zled, friz·zling**] to make a sputtering or sizzling noise while cooking, especially frying: *The bacon* frizzled *in the pan.* ***vt-*** to make (food) crisp by frying. [perhaps from **fry** and **sizzle.**]

frizz·y (frĭz′ ē) ***adj-*** [**frizz·i·er, frizz·i·est**] forming or having tight curls; kinky. **—*adv-*** **frizz′ i·ly.** ***n-*** **frizz′ i·ness.**

fro (frō) **to and fro** back and forth.

frock (frŏk) ***n-*** **1** woman's or child's dress. **2** long robe or outer garment, especially one worn by a monk or clergyman.

frock coat ***n-*** tight-fitting, double-breasted man's dress coat extending to the knees, worn chiefly in the 19th century.

frog (frŏg, frȯg) ***n-*** **1** small, tailless amphibian with smooth skin and webbed feet, noted for its long leaps and its swimming ability. **2** wedge-shaped horny growth in the middle of the sole of a horse's foot. **3** decorative fastener on clothes, consisting of a corded or braided loop and a button. **4** device that permits a railroad car's wheels to move smoothly across different tracks at an intersection or switch. **5** holder to keep flower stems in place in a bowl or display

Leopard frog, 2—4 in. long

frog in (one's) throat hoarseness in speaking, caused by a cold, temporary irritation, etc.

frog·man (frŏg′ mən′, frȯg′-) ***n-*** [*pl.* **frog·men**] navy man who is specially trained and equipped to work underwater.

frol·ic (frŏl′ ĭk) ***vi-*** [**frol·icked, frol·ick·ing**] to play or romp merrily. ***n-*** **1** burst of merry, playful activity; romp: *to have a* frolic *in the snow.* **2** merrymaking; gaiety: *an air of fun and* frolic. **—*n-*** **frol′ ick·er.**

frol·ic·some (frŏl′ ĭk səm) ***adj-*** full of fun and gaiety.

from (frŭm, frŏm) ***prep-*** **1** beginning with; starting at: *to work* from *noon until three o'clock.* **2** at a distance measured in relation to: *a mark three inches* from *the end of the board.* **3** originating in or with: *tin* from *South America*; *a letter* from *my cousin.* **4** out of: *He took some change* from *his pocket.* **5** out of reach of; out of the possession of: *Take the candy away* from *the baby.* **6** as being unlike: *I don't know one flower* from *another.* **7** because of: *weak* from *hunger.*

frond (frŏnd) ***n-*** long, fringed leaf of a fern or palm tree. **—*adj-*** **frond′ ed.**

front (frŭnt) ***n-*** **1** first or foremost part of any thing or place: *The* front *of the bus was empty.* **2** land which faces a body of water: *The cottage was on the lake* front. **3** actual scene of fighting during a war: *The captain was at the* front *during the campaign.* **4** large group or movement united for a common goal: *a labor* front. **5** *Informal* person, thing, or manner used to present a desired image to the public: *to put on a brave* front; *to be a* front *for thieves.* **6** in meteorology, the irregular but definite boundary between warm and cold air masses. See also *warm front*; *cold front.* ***adj-*** located at the foremost part: *the* front *wall of a house.* ***vt-*** to stand opposite; face: *The hotel* fronts *the ocean.*

front on to face: *The hotel* fronts on *the ocean.*

front·age (frŭn′ tĭj) ***n-*** **1** front part of a building or piece of land; also, its length, or the direction in which it faces. **2** land lying beside a public street or road; especially, the length of such land along the street or road: *a* frontage *of 100 feet.* **3** land beside a body of water: *lake* frontage; *ocean* frontage.

fron·tal (frŭn′ təl) ***adj-*** **1** of or having to do with the front. **2** of or having to do with the forehead. ***n-*** (also **frontal bone**) in anatomy, the bone which forms the forehead and the first part of the top of the head.

fron·tier (frŭn têr′) ***n-*** **1** the most remote settled area of a country beyond which lies wild, unsettled territory: *The* frontier *of America moved slowly west.* **2** boundary; border: *the northern* frontier *of the United States.* **3** (usually **frontiers**) new, unexplored fields of learning: *the* frontiers *of space.* *as* ***modifier***: *a* frontier *town.*

fron·tiers·man (frŭn têrz′ mən) ***n-*** [*pl.* **fron·tiers·men**] man who lives at the edge of a settled, civilized area.

fron·tis·piece (frŭn′ təs pēs′) ***n-*** picture on the page which faces the title page of a book.

front·let (frŭnt′ lət) ***n-*** **1** band or object worn on the forehead. **2** forehead of an animal.

front page ***n-*** the first page of a newspaper, usually reserved for the most important or sensational news. *as* ***modifier*** **(front-page)**: *It was* front-page *news.*

frosh (frŏsh) *Slang* ***n-*** freshman.

frost (frȯst, frŏst) ***n-*** **1** small, featherlike ice crystals formed on the ground and exposed objects when dew or water vapor freezes. **2** freezing weather; freezing temperature: *The first* frost *came in early November.* ***vt-*** **1** to treat so as to give a dull, whitish surface to: *to* frost *light bulbs.* **2** to put frosting on. **3** to cover with ice crystals. ***vi-*** to become covered with ice crystals. **—*adj-*** **frost′ less.** ***adj-*** **frost′ like′.**

frost·bite (frȯst′ bīt′, frŏst′-) ***n-*** frozen or partially frozen condition of some part of the body.

frost·bit·ten (frȯst′ bĭt′ ən, frŏst′-) ***adj-*** suffering from or affected by frostbite.

frost·ed (frȯst′ əd, frŏst′-) ***adj-*** **1** having a dull, whitish surface: *a* frosted *glass.* **2** covered with frosting. **3** frozen.

frost·ing (frȯs′ tĭng, frŏs′-) ***n-*** **1** mixture of sugar, egg whites, and liquid used for covering cakes or pastry. **2** dull finish on glass or metal that looks like frost.

frost·y (frŏs′ tē, frŏs′-) ***adj-*** [**frost·i·er, frost·i·est**] **1** cold with frost: *a* frosty *morning.* **2** covered with frost: *the* frosty *grass.* **3** cold and unfriendly: *a* frosty *smile*; *a* frosty *stare.* **—*adv-*** **frost′ i·ly.** ***n-*** **frost′ i·ness.**

froth (frȯth, frŏth) ***n-*** **1** mass of small bubbles, such as that formed on top of some liquids after they have been shaken or poured: *the foaming* froth *on a glass of root beer.* **2** shallow, worthless ideas, talk, etc. ***vi-*** to foam: *Mad dogs often* froth *at the mouth.*

froth·y (frȯ′ thē, -t͟hē) ***adj-*** [**froth·i·er, froth·i·est**] **1** of, covered with, or resembling froth: *a* frothy *layer of soapsuds.* **2** without substance; frivolous; trivial. **—*adv-*** **froth′ i·ly.** ***n-*** **froth′ i·ness.**

fāte, făt, dâre, bärn; bē, bĕt, mêre; bīte, bĭt; nōte, hŏt, môre, dȯg; fŭn, fûr; to͞o, bo͝ok; oil; out; tar; thin; t͟hen; hw for wh as in *wh*at; zh for s as in u*s*ual; ə for a, e, i, o, u, as in *a*go, lin*e*n, per*i*l, at*o*m, min*u*s

fro·ward (frō′ərd) ***adj-*** disobedient and stubborn; contrary. **—*adv-* fro′ ward·ly. *n-* fro′ ward·ness.**

frown (froun) ***n-*** a drawing together of the brows when one is displeased or in thought; stern look. ***vi-*** to have such an expression on one's face. **—*adv-* frown′ ing·ly.**
frown on to disapprove of: *to* frown on *gambling.*

frow·zy (frou′ zē) ***adj-*** **[frow·zi·er, frow·zi·est]** having a sloppy appearance; slovenly; untidy. **—*n-* frow′ zi·ness.**

froze (frōz) *p.t.* of **freeze.**

fro·zen (frō′ zən) *p.p.* of **freeze.**

fruc·tose (frŭk′ tōs′, fro͝ok′-) ***n-*** very sweet, yellowish-white sugar, occurring in many fruits and in honey; fruit sugar; levulose.

fru·gal (fro͞o′ gəl) ***adj-*** **1** not wasteful; thrifty; economical: *a* frugal *housewife.* **2** not plentiful and not expensive: *a* frugal *supper.* **—*n-* fru·gal′ i·ty** (fro͞o găl′ ə tē) also **fru′ gal·ness. *adv-* fru′ gal·ly.**

fruit (fro͞ot) ***n-*** **1** the fleshy part of a plant that contains the seeds and is often good to eat. **2** the seed or seed-bearing part of a plant. Acorns, grains, and strawberries are fruits. **3** product or result: *the* fruit *of hard work.*

fruit cake ***n-*** rich cake with raisins, nuts, citron, etc.

fruit fly ***n-*** small, two-wing fly that lays its eggs on ripe fruit. It has been used in many studies of inheritance.

fruit·ful (fro͞ot′ fəl) ***adj-*** **1** producing fruit: *a* fruitful *tree.* **2** yielding results; productive: *a* fruitful *discussion.* **—*adv-* fruit′ ful·ly. *n-* fruit′ ful·ness.**

fru·i·tion (fro͞o ĭsh′ ən) ***n-*** **1** realization or attainment; fulfillment: *the* fruition *of my most cherished hopes.* **2** the bearing of fruit.

fruit·less (fro͞ot′ ləs) ***adj-*** **1** without result; unsuccessful: *We made a* fruitless *search for the lost money.* **2** bearing no fruit. **—*adv-* fruit′ less·ly. *n-* fruit′ less·ness.**

fruit sugar ***n-*** fructose.

fruit·y (fro͞o′ tē) ***adj-*** **[fruit·i·er, fruit·i·est]** having the taste or smell of fruit.

frump (frŭmp) ***n-*** dowdy, slovenly woman. **—*adj-* frump′ ish** or **frump′ y [frump·i·er, frump·i·est].**

frus·trate (frŭs′ trāt′) ***vt-*** **[frus·trat·ed, frus·trat·ing]** to foil; baffle; defeat. **—*n-* frus·tra′ tion.**

frus·tum (frŭs′ təm) ***n-*** [*pl.* **frus·tums** or **frus·ta** (-tə)] remainder of a pyramid or cone when the top is cut off along a plane parallel to the base.

Frustum of a cone

[1]fry (frī) ***vt-*** **[fried, fry·ing]** to cook in hot fat: *We* fried *eggs.* ***vi-*:** *The eggs are* frying *in this pan.* [from Old French **frire,** from Latin **frigere.**]

[2]fry (frī) ***n-*** [*pl.* **fry**] young fish. [from Old Norse **frjo** meaning "offspring," and Old French **froi,** "fish eggs."]

fry·er (frī′ ər) ***n-*** **1** young, tender chicken for frying. **2** deep pan for frying food. ***Hom-*** friar.

frying pan ***n-*** shallow pan with a handle, used for frying food.

ft. foot or feet.

FTC Federal Trade Commission. Also **F.T.C.**

fuch·sia (fyo͞o′ shə) ***n-*** **1** low shrub with drooping, tubelike flowers, usually deep red or pink. **2** deep purplish-red color. ***adj-*:** *a* fuchsia *wool.*

fud·dle (fŭd′ əl) ***vt-*** **[fud·dled, fud·dling]** to stupefy or confuse with drink, or as if with drink; intoxicate. ***n-*** state of confusion, as from drink.

[1]fudge (fŭj) ***n-*** **1** kind of candy with a soft, creamy consistency, flavored usually with chocolate or maple. **2** made-up story; humbug. [of uncertain origin.]

[2]fudge (fŭj) ***vt-*** **[fudged, fudg·ing] 1** to make or make do with (something improvised): *to* fudge *an answer to an embarrassing question.* **2** to fake; falsify: *to* fudge *the accounts.* ***vi-*** to avoid a decision or promise; hedge. [perhaps from earlier **fadge (out),** "to fill out."]

Fuehr·er (fyo͝or′ ər) *German* ***n-*** title meaning "leader," given to Adolf Hitler by his followers. Also **Führ′ er** (fʏ′ rər).

fuel (fyo͞o′ əl) ***n-*** **1** anything burned to give heat or to operate an engine. Coal, wood, and oil are fuels. **2** anything that stirs up or keeps alive anger, resentment, or the like. ***vt-*:** *They* fueled *the plane.*

fu·gi·tive (fyo͞o′ jə tĭv) ***adj-*** **1** fleeing from danger, pursuit, or duty: *a* fugitive *convict.* **2** fleeting; not lasting very long: *a* fugitive *idea.* ***n-*** person who flees from danger, pursuit, or duty: *a* fugitive *from a police state.*

fugue (fyo͞og) ***n-*** musical composition in which a tune or theme is repeated by the various voices or parts and is intricately developed in counterpoint.

-ful *suffix* **1** full of; having or showing the quality of: *hope*ful; *wonder*ful. **2** likely to; able to: *forget*ful; *help*ful. **3** amount that will fill: *hat*ful.

ful·crum (fo͝ol′ krəm, fŭl′-) ***n-*** [*pl.* **ful·crums** or **ful·cra** (-krə)] the point on which a lever turns when it is used.

Fulcrum

ful·fill (fo͝ol fĭl′) ***vt-*** **1** to complete or accomplish: *to* fulfill *an assignment.* **2** meet; satisfy: *to* fulfill *a requirement.* **3** to bring about; bring to actuality; realize: *to* fulfill *a promise.* **—*n-* ful·fill′ ment.**

[1]full (fo͝ol) ***adj-*** **[full·er, full·est] 1** filled; able to hold no more: *a* full *pail.* **2** complete; whole; entire; maximum: *a* full *hour*; full *moon*; full *speed ahead.* **3** filling entirely some definite space: *The ship has a* full *load.* **4** rich and well-endowed in some special way: *a* full *flavor*; *a* full *tone*; *a* full *life.* **5** rounded out: *a* full *figure.* **6** generous in the amount of material; not skimpy: *a* full *skirt*; full *draperies.* **7** having the same parents: *They are* full *brothers.* ***adv-*** **1** completely; entirely: *The dog is* full *grown.* **2** squarely: *struck* full *on the target.* [from Old English.] **—*n-* full′ ness.**
full of having plenty of; well supplied with: *The story is* full of *excitement.* **in full** completely: *He paid the bill* in full. **to the full** to the highest extent; thoroughly.

[2]full (fo͝ol) ***vt-*** to shrink and thicken (cloth) by dampening and pressing it. [from Old French **fouler,** "to trample on," from Late Latin **fullāre,** from **fullō,** "a fuller."]

full·back (fo͝ol′ băk′) ***n-*** **1** in football, a back usually lining up slightly behind the halfbacks, and often used for direct plunges through the line. **2** in rugby and soccer, a player whose role is primarily defensive.

full-blood·ed (fo͝ol′ blŭd′ əd) ***adj-*** **1** full of vigor; hearty. **2** thoroughbred; of a pure, unmixed strain.

full-blown (fo͝ol′ blōn′) ***adj-*** blossomed out; at the height of bloom; matured: *a* full-blown *rose.*

full-bod·ied (fo͝ol′ bŏd′ ēd) ***adj-*** rich and strong in tone or flavor; not thin or weak: *a* full-bodied *wine.*

full dress ***n-*** clothing required for formal or ceremonial occasions. **—*adj-* (full-dress):** *a* full-dress *reception.*

full·er (fo͝ol′ ər) ***n-*** one who thickens cloth by moistening, heating, and pressing.

fuller's earth ***n-*** soft clay used for filtering fats and oils and for cleaning woolen cloth before fulling.

full-fledged (fo͝ol′ flĕjd′) ***adj-*** **1** with all its feathers grown; mature: *a* full-fledged *bird.* **2** fully developed or qualified; having full status: *a* full-fledged *doctor.*

full-grown (fo͝ol′ grōn′) ***adj-*** having reached full size; mature.

full house ***n-*** **1** capacity audience in a theater. **2** in poker, a hand consisting of three cards of one value and two of another, such as three aces and two nines.

full-length (fo͝ol′lĕngth′) ***adj-*** **1** showing or covering the entire length of something, especially a person: *a* full-length *snapshot*; *a* full-length *gown.* **2** of a standard length; not shortened: *a* full-length *movie.*

full moon ***n-*** the moon at the end of the second quarter, when it is seen as a fully lighted disk; also, the time of month when this occurs. For picture, see *moon.*

full-scale (fo͝ol′skāl′) ***adj-*** **1** of the same size as the original: *a* full-scale *drawing.* **2** fully developed; not limited: *a* full-scale *war.*

full-time (fo͝ol′ tīm′) ***adj-*** **1** taking up all of one's working time: *a* full-time *job.* **2** working or serving as such during one's whole working time: *a* full-time *employee*; *a* full-time *fireman.* ***adv-***: *to work* full-time.

ful·ly (fo͝ol′ ē) ***adv-*** **1** completely; entirely: *to be* fully *dressed*; *to be* fully *aware of danger.* **2** not less than.

ful·mi·nate (fo͝ol′ mə nāt′, fŭl′-) ***vi-*** **[ful·mi·nat·ed, ful·mi·nat·ing] 1** to make loud or strong statements of condemnation: *to* fulminate *against corruption.* **2** to explode with a loud noise. ***vt-*** **1** to utter or issue (a threat, rebuke, etc.). **2** to cause to explode. ***n-*** a material easily exploded by a blow. ***—n-*** **ful′ mi·na′ tion.**

ful·some (fo͝ol′ səm) ***adj-*** excessive; immoderate: *his* fulsome *flattery.* ***—adv-*** **ful′ some·ly.** ***n-*** **ful′ some·ness.**

fu·ma·role (fyo͞o′ mə rōl′) ***n-*** small hole or fissure in the earth near a volcano that emits steam and volcanic gases.

fum·ble (fŭm′ bəl) ***vi-*** **[fum·bled, fum·bling]** to grope or feel about in a search: *He* fumbled *in his pocket for a match.* ***vt-*** to handle clumsily or drop through clumsiness: *to* fumble *a ball.* ***n-*** act of dropping a ball accidentally; also, the ball after it has been dropped: *to recover a* fumble. ***—n-*** **fum′ bler.** ***adv-*** **fum′ bling·ly.**

fume (fyo͞om) ***n-*** smoke, vapor, or gas, especially if offensive: *strong* fumes *from ammonia*; *exhaust* fumes. ***vi-*** **[fumed, fum·ing] 1** to give off smoke or vapor. **2** to be very angry: *He* fumed *because the bus was late.* ***vt-*** to treat or process by exposure to smoke or vapors.

fu·mi·gate (fyo͞o′ mə gāt′) ***vt-*** **[fu·mi·gat·ed, fu·mi·gat·ing]** to disinfect with poisonous fumes in order to destroy germs or insects: *to* fumigate *a sickroom.* ***—n-*** **fu′ mi·ga′ tion.** ***n-*** **fu′ mi·ga′ tor:** *to use a new type of* fumigator; *to go into business as a* fumigator.

fun (fŭn) ***n-*** amusement; sport; pleasure.
in fun in jest. **make fun of** or **poke fun at** to ridicule.

func·tion (fŭngk′ shən) ***n-*** **1** proper or natural work; purpose: *The* function *of the heart is to pump blood.* **2** formal social gathering or official ceremony. **3** *Mathematics* (1) set of ordered pairs with no two first elements alike. (2) quantity whose value depends on the value of another quantity. ***vi-*** to work; operate: *This typewriter* functions *poorly. When he is out I* function *in his place.*

func·tion·al (fŭngk′ shən əl) ***adj-*** **1** of or relating to the functioning or working of something: *a* functional *disorder.* **2** favoring usefulness; efficient; practical: *a* functional *plan*; functional *design.* ***—adv-*** **func′ tion·al·ly.**

func·tion·ar·y (fŭngk′ shən ĕr′ ē) ***n-*** [*pl.* **func·tion·ar·ies**] person who holds an office; an official.

function word *Grammar* ***n-*** word used in sentences to relate other words, phrases, or clauses. Conjunctions are function words.

fund (fŭnd) ***n-*** **1** money set aside for a special use: *a* fund *for library books.* **2** supply; stock: *a* fund *of information.* **3 funds** money: *Lack of* funds *halted the work.* ***vt-*** **1** to provide money for: *to* fund *a medical plan.* **2** to arrange a longer period of payment for (a debt).

fun·da·men·tal (fŭn′ də mĕn′ təl) ***n-*** **1** an essential or basic part: *Learning to recognize letters is a* fundamental *of reading.* **2** *Physics* the lowest frequency or tone produced when an object vibrates as a whole; the frequency on which a harmonic is based. ***adj-*** basic; essential. ***—adv-*** **fun′ da·men′ tal·ly.**

fun·da·men·tal·ism (fŭn′ də mĕn′ tə lĭz′ əm) ***n-*** belief that everything related in the Bible happened exactly as described; also, a movement in Protestantism based on this belief. ***—n-*** **fun′ da·men′ tal·ist.**

fu·ner·al (fyo͞o′ nər əl) ***n-*** the final disposing of the body of a dead person; also, the rites and services connected with this. *as* ***modifier***: *a* funeral *bouquet.*

funeral home ***n-*** an undertaker's establishment, where dead bodies are prepared for burial and where funeral services may be held; mortuary. Also **funeral parlor.**

fu·ner·ar·y (fyo͞o′ nə rĕr′ ē) ***adj-*** having to do with or used for a funeral or funerals: *a* funerary *custom.*

fu·ne·re·al (fyo͞o nêr′ ē əl) ***adj-*** **1** suitable for a burial. **2** mournful; gloomy. ***—adv-*** **fu·ne′ re·al·ly.**

fun·gi (fŭn′ jī, -gī) *pl.* of **fungus.**

fun·gi·cide (fŭn′ jə sīd′, fŭng′ gə-) ***n-*** anything that kills fungus growths. ***—adj-*** **fun′ gi·cid′ al.**

fun·gous (fŭng′ gəs) ***adj-*** **1** of, relating to, or caused by a fungus. **2** growing and spreading rapidly, as some funguses do. ***Hom-*** fungus.

fun·gus (fŭng′ gəs) ***n-*** [*pl.* **fun·gi** (fŭn′ jī, -gī) or **fun·gus·es**] one of a group of plants, without leaves or green color, which feed upon plants or animal matter. Bacteria, molds, mushrooms, toadstools, and mildews are fungi. *as* ***modifier***: *a* fungus *disease.* ***Hom-*** fungous.

Fungi

fu·nic·u·lar (fyo͞o nĭk′ yə lər) ***n-*** (also **funicular railway**) railway in which the cars are pulled up and let down a slope by ropes or cables, especially one in which a car going up counterweights one going down.

funk (fŭngk) *chiefly Brit. Informal* ***vi-*** to be in a state of cowardly fear. ***vt-*** to evade or shrink from: *to* funk *a test.* ***n-*** panic; fright.

fun·nel (fŭn′ əl) ***n-*** **1** cone-shaped vessel ending in a tube. It is used for filling bottles. **2** smokestack of a ship. ***vt-*** to pass (something) through or as if through a cone-shaped vessel.

KITCHEN
SHIP'S
Funnels

fun·nies (fŭn′ ēz) ***n-*** *pl.* comic strips; also, the section of a newspaper carrying them.

fun·ny (fŭn′ ē) ***adj-*** **[fun·ni·er, fun·ni·est] 1** amusing; comical: *a* funny *clown*; *a* funny *joke.* **2** strange; peculiar: *He gave me a* funny *look.* **3** *Informal* involving deception or fraud. ***—adv-*** **fun′ ni·ly.** ***n-*** **fun′ ni·ness.**

funny bone ***n-*** inner point of the elbow where the ulnar nerve is near the surface; crazy bone. A blow here causes a painful, numb, or tingling sensation to run along the forearm.

fur (fûr) ***n-*** **1** thick, soft hair that covers certain animals. **2** skin of an animal with the hair on it; pelt. **3** garment made of such skins: *We put our* furs *in storage for the summer.* **4** any light, fuzzy covering, such as a coating on the tongue. ***adj-***: *a* fur *hat.* ***vt-*** **[furred, fur·ring]**

1 to cover or clothe with fur: *She* furred *herself with mink.* 2 to apply an outer surface to (a wall, floor, etc.) over flat strips of wood, in order to renew, to provide an air space, or to level. ***Hom-*** fir.

fur·be·low (fûr′bə lō) ***n-*** 1 ruffle, flounce, or other trim on women's clothing. 2 **furbelows** showy ornamentation, such as spangles on a dancer's costume.

fur·bish (fûr′bĭsh) ***vt-*** to make bright by rubbing or polishing; renew. **—*n-* fur′bish·er.** ***n-*** **fur′bish·ment.**

Fu·ries (fyŏŏr′ēz) ***n-*** in Greek and Roman mythology, the three goddesses who avenge unpunished crimes.

fu·ri·ous (fyŏŏr′ē əs) ***adj-*** 1 very angry: *He was* furious *at the insult.* 2 violent: *a* furious *storm.* **—*adv-* fu′ri·ous·ly.** ***n-*** **fu′ri·ous·ness.**

furl (fûrl) ***vt-*** to roll up and fasten to a spar, pole, etc.
►Should not be confused with REEF.

fur·long (fûr′lŏng) ***n-*** one eighth of a mile; 220 yards.

fur·lough (fûr′lō) ***n-*** leave of absence, especially for an enlisted man in military service. ***vt-*** to give leave of absence to.

fur·nace (fûr′nəs) ***n-*** an enclosed structure in which fuel is burned to produce heat for heating a building, separating metal from ore, baking pottery, etc.

fur·nish (fûr′nĭsh) ***vt-*** 1 to supply; provide: *Jane will* furnish *cookies for the party.* 2 to equip with furniture: *to* furnish *a house.* **—*n-* fur′nish·er.**

fur·nish·ings (fûr′nĭsh ĭngz) ***n-*** *pl.* 1 the necessary furniture and fittings of a house. 2 articles of clothing and accessories of dress.

fur·ni·ture (fûr′nə chər) ***n-*** movable articles such as tables, desks, chairs, beds, etc.

fu·ror (fyŏŏr′ər, -ôr) ***n-*** 1 great outburst of excitement or enthusiasm spreading among many people; stir: *The news caused a* furor. 2 rage; fury: *He said things he did not mean in his* furor.

fur·ri·er (fûr′ē ər) ***n-*** person who prepares or sells furs; also, person who makes or repairs fur garments.

fur·ring (fûr′ĭng) ***n-*** material used to fur a wall, ceiling, etc.; also, the process of applying it.

fur·row (fûr′ō) ***n-*** 1 groove in which to plant seed; rut made by a plow. 2 groove; wrinkle. ***vt-***: *He* furrowed *a field. Age* furrows *his brow.*

Furrows

fur·ry (fûr′ē) ***adj-*** [**fur·ri·er, fur·ri·est**] 1 covered with fur: *a* furry *animal.* 2 like fur or made of fur. **—*n-* fur′ri·ness.**

fur·ther (fûr′thər) *compar.* of **far.** ***adj-*** 1 additional; more: *to need* further *help*; *to say one thing* further. 2 farther. ***adv-*** 1 in addition; moreover; furthermore: *She remarked,* further, *that you were late.* 2 to a greater extent or degree: *He spoke* further *about his plans.* 3 farther. ***vt-*** to promote; help forward.
►For usage note see FARTHER.

fur·ther·ance (fûr′thər əns) ***n-*** a furthering; advancement: *the* furtherance of a health program.

fur·ther·more (fûr′thər môr′) ***adv-*** besides; also.

fur·ther·most (fûr′thər mōst′) ***adj-*** farthermost.

fur·thest (fûr′thəst) *superl.* of **far.**

fur·tive (fûr′tĭv) ***adj-*** sly; stealthy: *a* furtive *glance;* furtive *behavior.* **—*adv-* fur′tive·ly.** ***n-*** **fur′tive·ness.**

fu·ry (fyŏŏr′ē) ***n-*** [*pl.* **fu·ries**] 1 great anger; rage: *He was in a* fury *over the ruling.* 2 violence; fierceness: *the* fury *of a storm.* 3 stormy, furious person, especially a woman.
like fury furiously.

furze (fûrz) ***n-*** gorse.

[1]**fuse** (fyōōz) ***n-*** any of various devices, such as a tube filled with gunpowder, a cord covered with something that burns rapidly, a clockwork or trigger that works on impact, used to set off an explosive charge or weapon. ***vt-*** [**fused, fus·ing**] to equip with such a device. Also **fuze.** [from Italian **fuso,** from Latin **fūsus,** "spindle."]

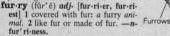

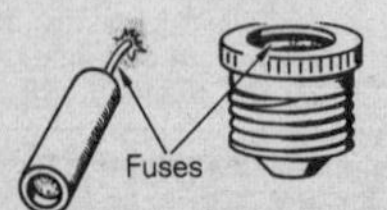
Fuses

[2]**fuse** (fyōōz) ***vt-*** [**fused, fus·ing**] 1 to melt, especially by heating. 2 to blend or combine by melting: *to* fuse *copper and tin.* ***vi-*** 1 to melt. 2 to blend and intermix as if melted together: *My ideas* fuse *with his.* ***n-*** piece of metal which fills a gap in an electric circuit. The metal melts and breaks the circuit when the current is too strong for safety. [from Latin **fusus** meaning literally "poured," from **fundere** "to pour; found."]

fu·see (fyōō′zē′) ***n-*** 1 kind of friction match that will burn in the wind. 2 bright red flare that burns for a certain length of time, used chiefly as a railroad signal.

fu·se·lage (fyōō′sə läzh′, -lĭj′) ***n-*** the body of an airplane to which the wings, rudder, etc., are attached. For picture, see *airplane.*

fu·sel oil (fyōō′zəl) ***n-*** poisonous, oily, colorless mixture of various alcohols that is used as a solvent in chemical processes. It is a by-product of fermentation.

fu·si·ble (fyōō′zə bəl) ***adj-*** of a nature that allows being melted without change in chemical composition. **—*n-* fu′si·bil′i·ty.**

fu·sil (fyōō′zəl) ***n-*** kind of flintlock musket.

fu·sil·ier or **fu·sil·eer** (fyōō′zə lêr′) ***n-*** 1 formerly, a soldier armed with a fusil. 2 member of any of several British regiments.

fu·sil·lade (fyōō′zə lād′) ***n-*** 1 the firing of many guns at once or in quick succession. 2 a number of questions or comments made in rapid order. ***vt-*** [**fu·sil·lad·ed, fu·sil·lad·ing**]: *to* fusillade *enemy troops.*

fu·sion (fyōō′zhən) ***n-*** 1 a melting as a result of heat: *the* fusion *of iron in a furnace.* 2 a mixing or blending by melting: *Bronze is made by the* fusion *of copper and tin.* 3 a blending or union of separate things into one. 4 the combining of two light atomic nuclei to form a heavier nucleus.

fusion bomb ***n-*** bomb in which the nuclei of a light element fuse to form a heavier element, resulting in the release of huge amounts of energy.

fuss (fŭs) ***n-*** 1 needless activity; unnecessary stir, especially in small matters: *to make a* fuss *about entertaining.* 2 gushing praise or attention: *a* fuss *over an important guest.* 3 complaint: *a* fuss *over the weather.* ***vi-*** to make an unnecessary stir: *to* fuss *over dinner.* **—*n-* fuss′er.**

fuss·y (fŭs′ē) ***adj-*** [**fuss·i·er, fuss·i·est**] 1 painstaking in a nervous way; fastidious; finicky: *a* fussy *housekeeper.* 2 requiring delicate and patient work; exacting: *Watch repairing is a* fussy *job.* 3 petulant; irritable: *a* fussy *baby.* **—*adv-* fuss′i·ly.** ***n-*** **fuss′i·ness.**

fus·tian (fŭs′chən) ***n-*** 1 kind of coarse twilled cotton cloth, such as corduroy or velveteen. 2 napped cloth of linen and cotton or wool. 3 high-sounding speech; empty wordiness. ***adj-*** 1 made of such cloth. 2 pretentious; pompous.

fust·y (fŭs′tē) ***adj-*** [**fust·i·er, fust·i·est**] 1 moldy; musty; stuffy. 2 antiquated. **—*adv-* fust′i·ly.** ***n-*** **fust′i·ness.**

fu·tile (fyōō′təl, -tīl′) ***adj-*** useless and hopeless; not getting anywhere: *He made a* futile *attempt to save the patient.* **—*adv-* fu′tile·ly.** ***n-*** **fu·til′i·ty** (fyōō tĭl′ə tē).

fu·ture (fyōō′chər) ***n-*** time, events, etc., that are yet to come: *The* future *looks bright.* ***adj-*** yet to happen; coming: *to predict* future *events.* **—*adj-* fu′ture·less.**

future perfect tense *Grammar* ***n-*** verb tense, formed with the auxiliary verb "shall" or "will," and "have," indicating action to take place before a specified future time. Example: *When you come tomorrow, I* shall have finished *this task.* Also **future perfect.**

future tense *Grammar* ***n-*** verb tense, formed with the auxiliary verb "shall" or "will," indicating action in time to come. Example: *I* shall see *you soon.*

fu·tur·ism (fyōō′ chə rĭz′ əm) ***n-*** movement in art, literature, and music, beginning about 1910, that stressed the forceful qualities of the present age. **—*n-* fu′ tur·ist.**

fu·tur·is·tic (fyōō′ chə rĭs′ tĭk) ***adj-*** **1** of or relating to the future or to futurism. **2** very much advanced in design or idea; suited to the future; ahead of its time: *a* futuristic *building.* **—*adv-* fu′ tur·is′ ti·cal·ly.**

fu·tu·ri·ty (fyōō tŏŏr′ ə tē, fyōō tyŏŏr′-) ***n-*** [*pl.* **fu·tu·ri·ties**] **1** the future. **2** condition of being future.

fuze (fyōōz) [1]fuse.

fuzz (fŭz) ***n-*** fine, light particles of hair, down, etc.: *the* fuzz *on a peach.*

fuzz·y (fŭz′ ē) ***adj-*** [**fuzz·i·er, fuzz·i·est**] **1** covered with or resembling fuzz or down: *a* fuzzy *peach.* **2** vague; blurred; not clear: *the* fuzzy *outline of hills through the fog.* **—*adv-* fuzz′ i·ly. *n-* fuzz′ i·ness.**

-fy *suffix* **1** (used to form verbs from adjectives) to cause to be; also, to become: to *simpli*fy; *lique*fy. **2** (used to form verbs from nouns) to make similar to or typical of: *to citi*fy. [from Old French **-fier,** from Latin **-ficāre,** from **facere,** "to make, do."]

G

G, g (jē) ***n-*** [*pl.* **G's, g's**] **1** the seventh letter of the English alphabet. **2 G** *Music* the fifth note of the C-major scale. **3** *Physics* (1) **g** symbol for the acceleration caused by gravity, about 32 feet per second per second. (2) **g's** expression, in multiples of the earth's gravitational force, for the inertial force a body is subjected to when accelerating or deaccelerating: *The astronauts experienced a force of 8* g's *during liftoff.*

g. 1 gram or grams. **2** goalie. **3** goalkeeper. **4** guard.

Ga symbol for gallium.

Ga. Georgia.

gab (găb) *Informal* ***vi-*** [**gabbed, gab·bing**] to talk idly and much; chatter. ***n-*** idle talk; prattle.

gab·ar·dine (găb′ ər dēn′) ***n-*** twilled fabric with a hard surface and a sheen, made of wool, cotton, or rayon, and used for raincoats, suits, etc. Also **gab′ er·dine′.**

gab·ble (gă′ bəl) ***vi-*** [**gab·bled, gab·bling**] **1** to talk disconnectedly, or without meaning; jabber. **2** to make a clatter of meaningless sounds. ***n-*** rapid, meaningless sounds: *the* gabble *of geese.* **—*n-* gab′ bler.**

gab·by (găb′ ē) *Informal* ***adj-*** [**gab·bi·er, gab·bi·est**] talkative: *a* gabby *neighbor.* **—*n-* gab′ bi·ness.**

ga·ble (gā′ bəl) ***n-*** **1** the section of an outside wall in the shape of a vertical triangle between the slopes of a ridged roof. **2** any similar construction, as over a window. **—*adj-* ga′ bled:** *a* gabled *window.*

[1]gad (găd) ***n-*** **1** sharp rod or switch; goad for driving cattle. **2** pointed iron or steel tool for loosening ore. [from Old Norse **gaddr,** "a goad."]

[2]gad (găd) ***vi-*** [**gad·ded, gad·ding**] to go from place to place; ramble: *to* gad *about town.* [from Middle English **gadden,** of uncertain origin.] **—*n-* gad′ der.**

gad·a·bout (găd′ ə bout′) *Informal* ***n-*** person who wanders or rushes about idly.

gad·fly (găd′ flī′) ***n-*** [*pl.* **gad·flies**] **1** kind of fly that stings horses and cattle. **2** person who annoys or goads.

gadg·et (găj′ ət) *Informal* ***n-*** **1** small device or tool having a special use: *a* gadget *for coring apples.* **2** an object whose name and use one does not know.

gad·o·lin·i·um (găd′ ə lĭn′ ē əm) ***n-*** metallic rare-earth element. Symbol Gd, At. No. 64, At. Wt. 157.25.

Gael (gāl) ***n-*** **1** a Celt of Ireland, Scotland, or the Isle of Man, especially one who speaks Gaelic. **2** Scottish Highlander. ***Hom-*** gale.

Gael·ic (gā′ lĭk) ***n-*** a Celtic language formerly spoken in different dialects by the people of Ireland, western Scotland and the Highlands, and the Isle of Man. It is still spoken by some of these. ***adj-*** of or relating to this language or to the Gaels.

gaff (găf) ***n-*** **1** large hook with a handle, used for getting large fish out of the water. **2** spar to which is attached the head of a fore-and-aft sail. ***vt-*** to seize (a fish) with a large hook.

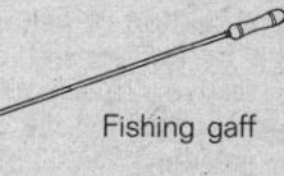

Fishing gaff

stand the gaff to endure a hardship or ordeal.

gaf·fer (găf′ ər) ***n-*** respectable and good old man, especially a countryman (now used humorously).

gag (găg) ***n-*** **1** something forcibly put into or on a person's mouth to keep him from talking or crying out; also, something put into the mouth to hold it open. **2** strategy or rule to prevent or limit freedom of discussion. **3** *Slang* a remark or act designed to get a laugh. ***vt-*** [**gagged, gag·ging**] **1** to stop up the mouth. **2** to silence by force or law. **3** to cause to retch: *The medicine* gagged *him.* ***vi-*** **1** to choke; strain as in vomiting: *to* gag *on a bone.* **2** *Slang* to tell a joke.

[1]gage (gāj) *Archaic* ***n-*** **1** a promise; pledge. **2** challenge to combat or pledge to fight indicated by throwing down or picking up a glove; also, the object thrown down. ***vt-*** [**gaged, gag·ing**] **1** to pledge. **2** to risk or stake in combat. **3** to wager. [from Old French **gage,** of Germanic origin. It is very closely related to **wage.**]

[2]gage (gāj) gauge. [from Old French **gauger** meaning "to measure."]

[3]gage (gāj) ***n-*** greengage. [from Sir William **Gage,** an Englishman who first brought this fruit to his country.]

gai·e·ty (gā′ ə tē) ***n-*** [*pl.* **gai·e·ties**] **1** merriment; cheerfulness; gay spirits: *a time of* gaiety. **2** gay, bright appearance: *the* gaiety *of the room.* Also **gayety.**

gai·ly (gā′ lē) ***adv-*** **1** merrily; happily. **2** brightly; strikingly: *the* gaily *painted walls.*

gain (gān) ***vt-*** **1** to get; earn: *to* gain *a profit.* **2** to win: *to* gain *an advantage.* **3** to increase in: *to* gain *weight.* **4** to improve in value, position, etc., by: *He* gained *ten yards.* **5** to arrive at: *to* gain *the shore.* **6** of a clock or watch, to run fast by (a certain amount). ***vi-*** **1** to increase (in): *to* gain *in wisdom.* **2** to grow heavier in body weight: *When he found he had* gained *he went on a diet.* **3** to improve one's position in a race or chase. ***n-*** **1** desirable improvement or increase: *a ten-yard* gain; *a* gain *in wisdom.* **2** (often **gains**) profit; earnings; winnings.

gain on (or **upon**) to draw nearer to; overtake.

gain over to win the support of; win over to one's side.

gain·er (gā′ nər) ***n-*** **1** person or thing that gains. **2** dive in which the person jumps forward, does a complete backward somersault, and enters the water feet first.

gain·ful (gān′ fəl) ***adj-*** profitable; paid: *to find some* gainful *occupation.* **—*adv-*** **gain′ ful·ly.** ***n-*** **gain′ ful·ness.**

gain·say (gān′ sā′) ***vt-*** **[gain·said, gain·say·ing]** to deny or dispute: *I can't* gainsay *that.* **—*n-*** **gain′ say·er.**

gainst or **'gainst** (gĕnst, gānst) against.

gait (gāt) ***n-*** **1** way a person or animal walks or runs. **2** any of the several foot movements of a horse, such as a walk, trot, or canter. ***vt-*** to train to step at a regular pace: *to* gait *a horse.* ***Hom-*** gate.

gait·ed (gā′ təd) ***adj-*** **1** stepping in a particular way: *fast*-gaited. **2** trained to a gait or gaits: *a* gaited *horse.*

gai·ter (gā′ tər) ***n-*** **1** covering of cloth or leather for the lower leg or ankle, fitting over the top of the shoe. **2** shoe with an elastic strip on each side. **3** a kind of overshoe with a cloth top.

Gaiter

gal (găl) *Slang* ***n-*** girl or young woman.

gal. gallon or gallons.

ga·la (gā′ lə, găl′ ə) ***n-*** festival; gay celebration. ***adj-*** festive: *Their party was a* gala *affair.*

ga·lac·tic (gə lăk′ tĭk) ***adj-*** of or relating to a galaxy or galaxies.

Gal·a·had (găl′ ə hăd′) ***n-*** in Arthurian legend, the noblest and purest knight of the Round Table, who was successful in his quest of the Holy Grail.

Gal·a·te·a (găl′ ə tē′ ə) ***n-*** in Greek mythology, an ivory statue of a maiden brought to life by Aphrodite after the sculptor, Pygmalion, had fallen in love with it.

Ga·la·tians (gə lā′ shənz) ***n-*** **1** inhabitants of ancient Galatia. **2** (takes singular verb) book of the New Testament, written by St. Paul and known as the **Epistle to the Galatians.**

gal·ax·y (găl′ ək sē) ***n-*** [*pl.* **gal·ax·ies**] **1** vast separate system of stars, dust and gas clouds, distinct clusters of stars, etc. Each galaxy contains billions of stars, and millions of galaxies make up the universe. **2** any brilliant group: *a* galaxy *of great pianists.* **3 Galaxy** the Milky Way Galaxy.

gale (gāl) ***n-*** **1** strong wind, especially one with a velocity between about 30 and 60 miles per hour. **2** outburst: *a* gale *of laughter.* ***Hom-*** Gael.

ga·le·na (gə lē′ nə) ***n-*** a blueish-gray mineral lead sulfide, which is the chief ore of lead.

Gal·i·le·an (găl′ ə lē′ ən) ***adj-*** of or relating to Galilee. ***n-*** **1** native of Galilee. **2** contemptuous term for Christians in ancient times. **3 the Galilean** Jesus Christ.

[1]**gall** (gȯl) ***n-*** **1** bitter fluid made by the liver and stored in the gall bladder; bile. **2** anything bitter or distasteful. **3** spite; rancor. **4** *Slang* insolence; impudence. [from Old English **galla.**] ***Hom-*** Gaul.

[2]**gall** (gȯl) ***n-*** sore on the skin caused by chafing, especially on a horse. ***vt-*** **1** to make sore by chafing. **2** to annoy; vex; irritate: *He* galled *me by his constant criticism.* [probably from special uses of [1]**gall** and [3]**gall.**] ***Hom-*** Gaul.

[3]**gall** (gȯl) ***n-*** abnormal swelling or growth on a leaf or stem, caused by the attack of certain insects, bacteria, or fungi; gallnut. [from French **galle,** from Latin **galla,** "a gall of the oak tree, shaped like a nut."] ***Hom-*** Gaul.

Galls on oak leaf

gal·lant (găl′ ənt, gə lănt′, gə länt′) ***adj-*** **1** (găl′ ənt *only*) brave; high-spirited. **2** (găl′ ənt *only*) of splendid or stately appearance. **3** respectful and courteous with women; chivalrous. **4** very attentive to the ladies. ***n-*** **1** man of fashion. **2** ladies' man; suitor. **—*adv-*** **gal′ lant·ly** or **gal·lant′ ly.** ***n-*** **gal′ lant·ness** or **gal·lant′ ness.**

gal·lant·ry (găl′ ən trē) ***n-*** [*pl.* **gal·lant·ries**] **1** bravery; heroic courage. **2** chivalrous behavior with or attention to women; also, an instance of this: *His* gallantries *were not gladly received.*

gall bladder ***n-*** small pear-shaped muscular sac which stores bile from the liver.

gal·le·on (găl′ ē ən) ***n-*** large sailing vessel, used mainly by the Spanish in the 15th and 16th centuries. It had several decks, and its high stern was often armed.

Galleon

gal·ler·y (găl′ ə rē) ***n-*** [*pl.* **gal·ler·ies**] **1** balcony for spectators in a theater, assembly hall, etc.; especially, the highest balcony with the cheapest seats. **2** audience in the top balcony. **3** group of spectators at some sports events. **4** building or room for exhibiting works of art. **5** long, narrow passage or hall. **6** outdoor balcony or platform, such as a porch or the platform around an engine.

gal·ley (găl′ ē) ***n-*** [*pl.* **gal·leys**] **1** ship driven by both oars and sails, used in ancient times and in the Middle Ages. **2** the kitchen of a ship or airplane. **3** tray for holding metal type set up in words, sentences, etc.; also, a proof from such type.

Roman galley

galley slave ***n-*** **1** slave or convict forced to row a galley. **2** one who does dreary, routine work; drudge.

gall·fly (gȯl′ flī′) ***n-*** [*pl.* **gall·flies**] any of various insects that deposit their eggs on plants and cause galls.

Gal·lic (găl′ ĭk) ***adj-*** of or pertaining to ancient Gaul or modern France.

Gal·li·cism or **gal·li·cism** (găl′ ə sĭz′ əm) ***n-*** **1** a French word, phrase, or manner of speech used in other languages. **2** a French trait or habit.

gall·ing (gȯl′ ĭng) ***adj-*** chafing; exasperating; vexing.

gal·li·um (găl′ ē əm) ***n-*** rare silvery-gray metal element. Symbol Ga, At. No. 31, At. Wt. 69.72.

gal·li·vant (găl′ ə vănt′) *Informal* ***vi-*** to gad about joyfully.

gall·nut (gȯl′ nŭt′) ***n-*** [3]gall.

gal·lon (găl′ ən) ***n-*** unit of liquid measurement. The **standard gallon** in the United States equals four quarts or 231 cubic inches; the **imperial gallon** in the United Kingdom and the Commonwealth equals 277.420 cubic inches or five U.S. quarts.

gal·lop (găl′ əp) ***n-*** **1** a springing run; especially, the fastest gait of a horse. **2** a horseback ride at this gait: *Shall we go for a* gallop? ***vi-*** to run or ride at this gait: *The horse* galloped. *We* galloped *along.* ***vt-***: *They* galloped *the horses.* **—*n-*** **gal′ lop·er.**

gal·lows (găl′ ōz) ***n-*** [*pl.* **gal·lows**] **1** framework with a crossbar holding a suspended noose from which criminals are hanged. **2 the gallows** death by hanging: *to sentence a man to* the gallows.

Gallows

gall·stone (gȯl′ stōn′) ***n-*** lump of waxy or stony matter formed in the gall bladder or the bile passages.

ga·lore (gə lôr′) ***adj-*** very many; in abundance (used after the noun it modifies): *pretty girls* galore.

ga·losh (gə lŏsh′) ***n-*** [*pl.* **ga·losh·es**] high protective overshoe, usually made of rubber or plastic. **—*adj-* ga·loshed′**: *bundled up and* galoshed *for the snow.*

ga·lumph (gə lŭmf′, -lŭmp′) ***vi-*** **1** to move along with a heavy, clumsy tread; clump: *The bashful boys* galumphed *across the stage.* **2** originally, to ride along in triumph.

gal·van·ic (găl văn′ ĭk) ***adj-*** **1** of or relating to electricity produced by chemical action; also, producing such electricity: *a* galvanic *cell.* **2** stimulating; electrifying: *a* galvanic *personality.* **—*adv-* gal·van′ i·cal·ly.**

gal·va·nize (găl′ və nīz′) ***vt-*** [**gal·va·nized, gal·va·niz·ing**] **1** to coat (iron or steel) with zinc to prevent rusting. **2** to excite; stir up; arouse, as if by an electric shock: *He* galvanized *us into action.* **—*n-* gal′ va·ni·za′ tion.**

gal·va·nom·e·ter (găl′ və nŏm′ ə tər) ***n-*** instrument used to detect the presence of an electric current, measure its intensity, and determine its direction.

gam·bit (găm′ bĭt) ***n-*** **1** chess move, especially an opening move, in which a player sacrifices a piece in order to gain a favorable position. **2** any opening action.

gam·ble (găm′ bəl) ***vi-*** [**gam·bled, gam·bling**] **1** to play for money or a prize: *to* gamble *at cards.* **2** to take a risk on something uncertain, especially for gain: *They* gambled *on good weather for the early flight.* ***vt-*** to risk or squander for uncertain gain: *to* gamble *one's reputation.* ***n-*** any risk or act that does not have a sure result. ***Hom-*** gambol. **—*n-* gam′ bler.**

gamble away to lose by the risking of stakes: *to* gamble away *a fortune.*

gam·bling (găm′ blĭng) ***n-*** betting or risking something for uncertain gain; playing at cards, roulette, etc.; gaming; wagering. *as* ***modifier***: *a* gambling *debt.*

gam·bol (găm′ bəl) ***n-*** a dancing or skipping about for joy or sport; frolic. ***vi-*** [**gam·boled, gam·bol·ing**]: *The lambs* gamboled *in the meadow.* ***Hom-*** gamble.

gam·brel roof (găm′ brəl) ***n-*** ridged, two-sided roof with each side having a steeply sloped lower section and a flatter upper section.

[1]**game** (gām) ***n-*** **1** form of play, especially a contest, played according to rules: *Football is a popular* game. **2** single contest played according to rules: *a* game *of checkers.* **3** unit or division of a match, as in tennis. **4** materials or equipment needed for such play: *The store sells toys and* games. **5** amusement; joke; playful trick; also, jest. **6** *Informal* plan; scheme: *I can see through your* game. **7** wild animals, fish, or birds that are hunted for sport; also, the flesh used for food. **8** *Slang* business; profession. ***adj-*** **1** having to do with wildlife hunted for sport: *to enforce* game *laws.* **2** plucky; courageous: *a* game *fighter.* ***vi-*** [**gamed, gam·ing**] to play for a stake or prize. [from Old English **gamen** meaning "sport; joy."] **—*adv-* game′ ly. *n-* game′ ness.**

make game of to make fun of; ridicule. **play the game** to play according to the rules; be straightforward. **the game is up** the plan, intrigue, etc., has failed.

[2]**game** (gām) *Informal* ***adj-*** lame: *a* game *leg.* [perhaps from dialectal French **cambi,** "bent."]

game bird ***n-*** any bird commonly and legally hunted for sport and food, such as partridge or pheasant.

game·cock (gām′ kŏk′) ***n-*** rooster trained for cockfights.

game fish ***n-*** any fish usually caught for sport.

game·keep·er (gām′ kē′ pər) ***n-*** person in charge of animals or birds that are to be bred or protected as game, especially on a private estate.

game of chance ***n-*** any game whose outcome depends entirely or chiefly upon chance; gambling game.

game·some (gām′ səm) ***adj-*** merry; gay. **—*adv-* game′ some·ly.**

game·ster (gām′ stər) ***n-*** person who gambles often.

gam·ete (găm′ ēt′, gə mēt′) ***n-*** either of the two reproductive cells (egg and sperm) that can unite to form a new individual. Most gametes have half the number of chromosomes that all other body cells have; germ cell.

ga·me·to·phyte (gə mē′ tə fīt′) ***n-*** in the life cycle of plants, the phase or generation that produces the sex cells. See also *sporophyte.*

game warden ***n-*** official responsible for the enforcement of laws that restrict hunting and fishing.

gam·in (găm′ ən) ***n-*** **1** child of the streets; urchin. **2** elfin child. ***Hom-*** gammon. **—*n-*** *fem.* **gam·ine′** (gă mēn′).

gam·ing (gā′ mĭng) ***n-*** gambling.

gam·ma (găm′ ə) ***n-*** **1** third letter of the Greek alphabet, similar to G. **2** unit of mass and weight equal to one-millionth of a gram; a microgram. **3** *Physics* unit used to express the intensity of a magnetic field. One gamma equals 1/100,000 gauss.

gamma globulin ***n-*** one of the globulins extracted from human blood plasma. It contains antibodies and is used in the treatment of measles and hepatitis.

gamma rays ***n-*** very penetrating electromagnetic radiation of shorter wavelength than X rays.

gam·mon (găm′ ən) ***n-*** cured ham or strip of bacon; the lower end of a flitch. ***Hom-*** gamin.

gam·ut (găm′ ət) ***n-*** **1** the whole series of recognized musical notes. **2** the entire range of anything: *to run the* gamut *of emotion from joy to despair.*

gam·y (gā′ mē) ***adj-*** [**gam·i·er, gam·i·est**] **1** plucky; ready; spirited. **2** having the flavor of game, especially of nearly spoiled game. **—*adv-* gam′ i·ly. *n-* gam′ i·ness.**

gan·der (găn′ dər) ***n-*** **1** male goose. **2** simpleton.

gang (găng) ***n-*** **1** group of persons, especially a working crew: *a* gang *of laborers.* **2** neighborhood group of boys and young men often organized along racial or ethnic lines and sometimes fighting other such groups; street gang. **3** criminal organization; mob. **4** large group or set of anything: *a whole* gang *of troubles.* **5** a set of tools or machines arranged for use together: *a* gang *of snowplows.* ***vt-*** to put together or operate as a group: *to* gang *machines; to* gang *switches.* ***vi-*** to form a group: *The boys* ganged *around the cheerleader.* ***Hom-*** gangue.

gang together to go around habitually in a group.

gang up on to attack (someone) as a group.

gang·ling (găng′ glĭng) ***adj-*** spindling and awkward: *a* gangling *youth.* Also **gang′ ly.**

gan·gli·on (găng′ glē ən) ***n-*** [*pl.* **gan·gli·a** (-glē ə) or **gan·gli·ons**] knot of nerve-cell bodies outside of the central nervous system.

gang·plank (găng′ plăngk′) ***n-*** movable bridge used at a pier for entering or leaving a ship.

gang plow ***n-*** plow designed to make several parallel rows of furrows at once.

gan·grene (găng′ grēn′) ***n-*** death or decay of tissue in a living animal body because the blood supply has been cut off. **—*adj-* gan′ gre·nous** (găng′ grə nəs).

gang·ster (găng′ stər) ***n-*** member of a criminal gang.

gangue (găng) ***n-*** in mining, the worthless rock found in a vein of ore. ***Hom-*** gang.

gang·way (găng′ wā′) ***n-*** **1** gangplank; also, the opening in the side of a ship used to admit passengers or freight. **2** passageway; aisle. ***interj-*** Stand aside and make room!

gan·net (găn′ ət) ***n-*** any of a family of large, fish-eating sea birds; especially, a bird of the North Atlantic which breeds in colonies on cliffs and rocky islands.

¹gant·let (gônt′ lət, gănt′-) ***n-*** **1** stretch of railroad track where two separate lines of track come close together or overlap through tunnels or over bridges. **2** gauntlet, the passage used for punishment. [from **²gauntlet.**]

²gant·let (gônt′ lət, gănt′-) ***n-*** gauntlet, the glove. [from **¹gauntlet.**]

gan·try (găn′ trē) ***n-*** [*pl.* **gan·tries**] **1** overhead, bridgelike structure that moves on parallel tracks and supports a traveling crane. **2** large, movable, many-layered scaffold used to service a large rocket on its launching pad. **3** overhead structure that straddles several railroad tracks and carries signal lights.

Gan·y·mede (găn′ ə mēd′) ***n-*** in Greek mythology, a beautiful youth whom Zeus carried to Olympus to be his cupbearer.

gaol (jāl) *Brit.* jail.

gaol·er (jā′ lər) *Brit.* jailer.

gap (găp) ***n-*** **1** open break; also, any unfilled space in something otherwise continuous: *a* gap *in a fence*; *a* gap *in the conversation*; *a* gap *in his education.* **2** pass through a mountain ridge. **3** separation between ideas, attitudes, etc., of two people or groups. **4** spark gap.

gape (gāp) ***vi-*** **[gaped, gap·ing] 1** to open the mouth wide, as from sleepiness; yawn. **2** to stare with open mouth in amazement: *The country boy* gaped *at the city sights.* **3** to spread or be apart: *The zipper* gaped *open.* ***n-*** **1** a staring with open mouth. **2** opening between the jaws of birds or of fishes. **3 the gapes** (1) disease of poultry. (2) fit of yawning. **—*n-* gap′ er.** ***adv-*** **gap′ ing·ly.**

gar (gär) ***n-*** [*pl.* **gar**] any of several fresh-water fishes resembling the pike and having long, narrow jaws; garfish.

G.A.R. Grand Army of the Republic.

ga·rage (gə räj′, -räzh′) ***n-*** building or shed in which automobiles are sheltered, stored, or repaired.

garb (gärb) ***n-*** clothing, especially of a distinct style: *the* garb *of a nurse.* ***vt-*** to dress; clothe.

gar·bage (gär′ bĭj) ***n-*** waste material, usually food, thrown out from a kitchen, market, etc.; hence, any worthless or offensive stuff.

gar·ble (gär′ bəl) ***vt-*** **[gar·bled, gar·bling]** to confuse or distort with or without intention to mislead: *to* garble *a report.* **—*n-* gar′ bler.**

gar·çon (găr sōⁿ′) *French* ***n-*** **1** waiter. **2** boy or youth.

gar·den (gär′ dən) ***n-*** **1** piece of ground set aside for growing flowers, fruits, vegetables, etc. **2** place where plants or animals are displayed to the public: *a zoological* garden. *as* ***modifier***: *a* garden *plant.* ***vi-*** to raise or work with plants, especially as a hobby.

gar·den·er (gär′ dən ər) ***n-*** person who works in a garden, especially a person hired to care for a garden.

gar·de·ni·a (gär dē′ nē ə, -dē′ nyə) ***n-*** shrub or tree of warm climates, having large, very fragrant white flowers; also, the flower itself.

Garden of Eden ***n-*** in the Bible, the garden in which Adam and Eve first lived; Paradise.

gar·fish (gär′ fĭsh′) ***n-*** [*pl.* **gar·fish; gar·fish·es** (kinds of garfish)] gar.

Gar·gan·tu·a (gär găn′ chōō ə) ***n-*** gluttonous giant hero of a satire of the same name, written by Rabelais in 1534.

Gar·gan·tu·an (gär găn′ chōō ən) ***adj-*** suggestive of Gargantua; hence, gigantic: *a* Gargantuan *appetite.*

gar·gle (gär′ gəl) ***vi-*** **[gar·gled, gar·gling]** to rinse the throat with a liquid, such as an antiseptic, that is kept in motion by forcing the breath out through it. ***vt-*** to use (a liquid) in this way. ***n-*** **1** liquid used for this purpose. **2** bubbling sound in the throat so produced.

gar·goyle (gär′ goil′) ***n-*** a spout jutting from a building to carry off water. Gargoyles are often in the shape of grotesque human beings or animals.

Gargoyle

gar·ish (gâr′ ĭsh, gär′-) ***adj-*** unpleasantly showy; too bright or glaring; gaudy: *The beautiful road was spoiled by a string of* garish *billboards.* **—*adv-* gar′ ish·ly.** ***n-*** **gar′ ish·ness.**

gar·land (gär′ lənd) ***n-*** wreath or strand of intertwined leaves, flowers, etc., worn or used as decoration. ***vt-*** to decorate with such an ornament.

gar·lic (gär′ lĭk) ***n-*** **1** plant related to the onion, having a bulb with a strong taste and odor. **2** the bulb of this plant, used to flavor food.

gar·ment (gär′ mənt) ***n-*** any article of clothing. *as* ***modifier***: *the* garment *industry.* ***vt-*** to clothe; dress.

gar·ner (gär′ nər) ***vt-*** to gather in; store away: *to* garner *grain*; *to* garner *sayings from a book.*

gar·net (gär′ nət) ***n-*** **1** crystalline mineral, usually deep red in color, used as a semiprecious gem and as an abrasive. **2** a deep red color. ***adj-***: *a* garnet *ring*; garnet *taffeta.*

garnet paper ***n-*** paper coated with crushed garnet and used as an abrasive.

gar·nish (gär′ nĭsh) ***vt-*** to decorate, adorn, or embellish, especially a dish of food: *to* garnish *a steak with parsley.* ***n-*** decoration, especially on food. **—*n-* gar′ nish·er.**

gar·nish·ee (gär′ nə shē′) ***vt-*** **[gar·nish·eed, gar·nish·ee·ing] 1** in law, to claim and hold (property, money, etc.) from a person who owes money, until the settlement of the debt. **2** in law, to issue a garnishment to.

gar·nish·ment (gär′ nĭsh mənt) ***n-*** **1** in law, legal warning that a person's property is to be given to a creditor because of debt. **2** subtraction of a definite sum from someone's salary to pay a creditor.

gar·ni·ture (gär′ nə chər) ***n-*** something used as decoration, especially on food.

gar·ret (găr′ ət) ***n-*** attic.

gar·ri·son (găr′ ə sən) ***n-*** **1** group of soldiers stationed in a fort or in a town for defense. **2** fort or town where soldiers are stationed for defense. ***vt-*** to station soldiers in (a fort or town) for defense: *to* garrison *a town.*

gar·rote or **ga·rotte** (gə rŏt′) ***vt-*** **[gar·rot·ed** or **ga·rott·ed, gar·rot·ing** or **ga·rott·ing]** to strangle (someone) with a metal strip, rope, wire, etc. ***n-*** **1** a strangling in this manner, formerly used as a method of execution. **2** implement used for this. **—*n-* gar·rot′ er.**

gar·ru·lous (găr′ ə ləs, *also* găr′ yə-) ***adj-*** very talkative; chattering. **—*adv-* gar′ ru·lous·ly.** ***n-*** **gar′ ru·lous·ness** or **gar·ru′ li·ty** (gə rōō′ lə tē).

gar·ter (gär′ tər) ***n-*** **1** band or strap, often elastic and having a fastener, used to hold up a sock or stocking. **2 Garter** Order of the Garter.

garter snake ***n-*** any of a group of harmless American snakes that are striped along the back. Garter snakes bring forth live young.

gas (găs) ***n-*** [*pl.* **gas·es** or **gas·ses**] **1** any substance in the gaseous state under the general conditions of temperature and pressure existing on earth. **2** vapor. **3** any mixture of gases that will burn and be used for heating and cooking. **4** *Informal* any of various vapors used as anesthetics. **5** a gaseous substance or mist used as a weapon: *tear* gas; *poison* gas. **6** *Informal* gasoline. *as* ***modifier***: *a* gas *mask.* ***vt-*** **[gassed, gas·sing]** to injure or poison with gas.

gas chamber ***n-*** room in which people or animals are killed by poison gas.

Gas·con (găs′kən) ***adj-*** of or relating to Gascony or its inhabitants. ***n-*** a native of Gascony.

gas·e·ous (găs′ē əs, găsh′əs) ***adj-*** **1** in the form of gas; *Steam is water in its* gaseous *state.* **2** *of or like gas: a* gaseous *mixture.*

gaseous state ***n-*** the one of the three physical states of matter in which a substance has no definite shape or volume and tends to expand without limit. A gas will expand to fill a larger space and can be compressed into a smaller space. See also *liquid state* and *solid state.*

gash (găsh) ***n-*** long, narrow cut or wound. ***vt-*** to make such a cut or wound in.

gas·house (găs′hous′) ***n-*** gasworks.

gas jet ***n-*** nozzle or other fixture with an opening through which gas may flow.

gas·ket (găs′kət) ***n-*** **1** thin piece of rubber, metal, etc., used to make a joint or seal through which liquids or gases will not flow. **2** rope used to tie furled sails fast.

gas·light (găs′līt′) ***n-*** **1** light made by burning gas. **2** lamp or fixture for producing such a light. ***—adj*** **gas′lit:** *The shadows flickered in the* gaslit *room.*

gas mantle ***n-*** perforated cone or sheath of a heat-resisting material that gives light by incandescence when it is put over a gas flame.

gas mask ***n-*** covering for the face connected to an air filter and used to protect against poisonous gases.

gas·o·hol (găs′ə hôl′) ***n-*** mixture of ethanol and gasoline used in place of gasoline; usually 10% ethanol to 90% gasoline.

gas·o·line or **gas·o·lene** (găs′ə lēn′) ***n-*** colorless liquid mixture of hydrocarbons refined from petroleum. Gasoline turns to vapor easily, and the vapor burns violently. It is used chiefly as a fuel for engines.

gasp (găsp) ***vi-*** to catch one's breath in surprise, distress, or the like. **2** to struggle for breath: *The ill child was* gasping. ***vt-*** to utter in a breathless manner: *to* gasp *an urgent message.* ***n-*** a short, sudden breath: *He gave a* gasp *when he saw the tiger.*

the (or **one's**) **last gasp** the very end; dying breath.

gas station ***n-*** filling station.

gas·sy (găs′ē) ***adj-*** **[gas·si·er, gas·si·est] 1** filled with gas. **2** of or like gas. ***—n-*** **gas′si·ness.**

gas·tric (găs′trĭk) ***adj-*** of or relating to the stomach.

gastric juice ***n-*** the acid mixture of digestive juices secreted by the cells of the stomach lining.

gastric ulcer ***n-*** ulcer on the stomach lining, usually related to an excess secretion of hydrochloric acid, often caused by anxiety.

gas·tri·tis (găs′trī′təs) ***n-*** inflammation of the stomach.

gastro- or gastr- *combining form* **1** stomach or belly: *a* gastr*itis* (inflammation of the stomach); gastro*pod* (belly foot. **2** stomach and: *a* gastro*intestinal X ray.* [from Greek **gastr-** from **gastēr,** meaning "stomach."]

gas·tro·in·tes·ti·nal (găs′trō ĭn tĕs′tə nəl) ***adj-*** of or having to do with the stomach and intestines.

gas·tron·o·my (găs′trŏn′ə mē) ***n-*** the art of preparing or enjoying good food. ***—adj-*** **gas′tro·nom′ic** (găs′trə nŏm′ĭk) or **gas′tro·nom′i·cal.**

gas·tro·pod (găs′trə pŏd′) ***n-*** any of a large group of water and land mollusks **(Gastropoda),** including snails, limpets, etc., which usually have a single spiral shell and a muscular creeping organ called a foot.

gas·works (găs′wûrks′) ***n-*** *pl.* industrial plant where gas is manufactured or processed; gashouse.

gat (găt) *Archaic p.t.* of **get.**

gate (gāt) ***n-*** **1** opening in a fence or wall. **2** movable part or framework that closes such an opening. **3** valve or door for controlling the flow of water in a canal, irrigation ditch, pipe, etc. ***Hom-*** gait.

gate crasher *Informal* ***n-*** person who enters a place without being invited or without paying.

gate·house (gāt′hous′) ***n-*** house at an entrance or gateway of an estate, park, etc.

gate·post (gāt′pōst′) ***n-*** either of the two posts between which a gate swings.

gate·way (gāt′wā′) ***n-*** **1** opening fitted with a gate. **2** way of entering or achieving: *The Panama Canal is a* gateway *to the Pacific. Reading is a* gateway *to knowledge.*

gath·er (găth′ər) ***vt-*** **1** to bring to oneself: *He* gathered *a crowd around him. She* gathered *the child in her arms.* **2** to pick and collect: *to* gather *sea shells.* **3** to gain slowly; pick up: *to* gather *speed.* **4** to draw together in small folds: *to* gather *a skirt at the waist.* **5** to conclude; understand (usually takes a clause as object): *I* gather *that you have trouble with grammar.* ***vi-*** to come together: *A crowd* gathered *at the gate.* ***n-*** in sewing, one of a series of small folds or puckers.

be gathered to one's fathers of a person, to die.

gather up to draw together; pick up.

gath·er·er (găth′ər ər) ***n-*** person who gathers, especially a member of a tribe of people who gather plants, grains, etc., for their needs.

gath·er·ing (găth′ər ĭng) ***n-*** meeting or social function at which people come together.

gauche (gōsh) ***adj-*** awkward or inept, especially in social behavior. [from French **gauche,** "left" with the meaning "left-hand" or "awkward."] ***—n-*** **gauche′ness.**

gau·che·rie (gō′chə rē) ***n-*** gauche manner or act.

gau·cho (gou′chō) ***n-*** [*pl.* **gau·chos**] South American cowboy, usually of Spanish and Indian ancestry.

gaud (gȯd) ***n-*** cheap or showy trinket or ornament.

gaud·y (gȯ′dē) ***adj-*** **[gaud·i·er, gaud·i·est]** bright and gay in a flashy or showy way: *a* gaudy *orange and purple necktie.* ***—adj-*** **gaud′i·ly.** ***n-*** **gaud′i·ness.**

gauge (gāj) ***n-*** **1** a standard measurement: *Wire is available in various* gauges. **2** any of various instruments for measuring size, quantity, force, etc.: *a wire* gauge, *a wind* gauge. **3** any means or standard for making a comparison, judgment, etc. ***vt-*** **[gauged, gaug·ing]** to measure, estimate, or judge with or as if with a measuring device: *to* gauge *the diameter of wire; to* gauge *a person's character.* Also **gage.** ***—adj-*** **gauge′a·ble.** ***n-*** **gaug′er.**

Wire gauge

Gaul (gȯl) ***n-*** **1** ancient name of the part of Europe west of the Alps and north of the Pyrenees. **2** native or inhabitant of this region. **3** a Frenchman. ***Hom-*** gall.

gaunt (gȯnt) ***adj-*** **[gaunt·er, gaunt·est] 1** very thin; bony; emaciated: *to be weak and* gaunt *after a long illness.* **2** barren and desolate; grim. ***—adj-*** **gaunt′ly.** ***n-*** **gaunt′ness.**

[1]**gaunt·let** (gȯnt′lət) ***n-*** **1** in the Middle Ages, a mailed glove to protect wrists and hands from wounds. **2** glove with a flaring cuff, especially

MODERN

MEDIEVAL

Gauntlets

a canvas or leather working glove with a deep, stiff cuff to protect the wrist. **3** the cuff itself. [from French **gantelet,** from **gant,** "glove," from an earlier Germanic word.]

take up the gauntlet to assume a challenge; espouse a cause, especially a controversial one. **throw down the gauntlet** to challenge someone.

[2]**gaunt·let** (gȯnt′ lət) ***n-*** double line of men who strike out at a person who is forced to run between them as a punishment. Also **gantlet.** [from earlier **gantlope,** from Swedish **gatlopp,** "a running down a lane."]

run the gauntlet 1 to undergo such punishment. **2** to be exposed to severe criticism, extreme danger, etc.

Gau·ta·ma (gȯ′ tə mə, gou′-) ***n-*** Buddha.

gauze (gȯz) ***n-*** thin, transparent, loosely woven fabric, often used for bandages. **—*adj-* gauze′ like′.**

gauz·y (gȯ′ zē) ***adj-*** [**gauz·i·er, gauz·i·est**] like gauze; soft, delicate, and insubstantial. **—*n-* gauz′ i·ness.**

gave (gāv) *p.t.* of **give.**

gav·el (găv′ əl) ***n-*** small mallet used by presiding officers, judges, etc., to call a group to order.

Gavel

gav·i·al (gā′ vē əl) ***n-*** large, fish-eating crocodilian of India. The gavial has long, slender jaws and webbed feet.

ga·votte (gə vŏt′) ***n-* 1** dance popular in the 17th and 18th centuries somewhat resembling the minuet. **2** music for this dance.

Ga·wain (gə wān′, gă′ wən) ***n-*** in Arthurian legend, a knight of the Round Table, nephew of King Arthur.

gawk (gȯk) *Informal* ***vi-*** to stare stupidly or in astonishment. ***n-*** clumsy, stupid person.

gawk·y (gȯ′ kē) ***adj-*** [**gawk·i·er, gawk·i·est**] clumsy; awkward. **—*adv-* gawk′ i·ly. *n-* gawk′ i·ness.**

gay (gā) ***adj-*** [**gay·er, gay·est**] **1** merry; lighthearted; lively: *a* gay *party*; *the* gay *music.* **2** bright and cheerful: *a* gay *color.* **—*n-* gay′ ness.**

gay·e·ty (gā′ ə tē) gaiety.

gay·ly (gā′ lē) gaily.

gaz. gazette.

gaze (gāz) ***vi-*** [**gazed, gaz·ing**] to look long and steadily: *Janet* gazed *at the scenery as the train sped on.* ***n-*** a long, steady look. **—*n-* gaz′ er.**

ga·ze·bo (gə zē′ bō) ***n-*** [*pl.* **ga·ze·bos** or **ga·ze·boes**] small, outdoor pavilion or summerhouse.

ga·zelle (gə zĕl′) ***n-*** any of several small, brown to white antelopes of Africa, Arabia, and Asia, having short curving horns and large dark eyes. The gazelle is known for its speed and grace.

Gazelle, 20—35 in. high at shoulder

ga·zette (gə zĕt′) ***n-*** newspaper or other periodical, especially an official journal.

gaz·et·teer (găz′ ə têr′) ***n-*** a list of geographical terms with explanations, appearing as a separate work or as an appendix to another.

G.B. Great Britain.

G.C.D. or **g.c.d.** greatest common divisor.

G clef *n-* treble clef.

Gd symbol for gadolinium.

Ge symbol for germanium.

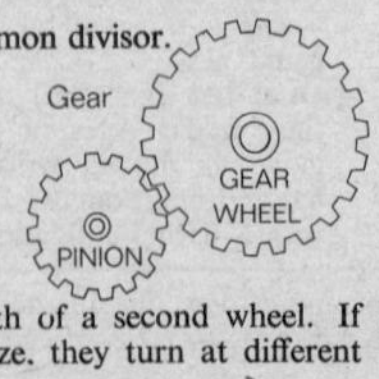

gear (gêr) ***n-* 1** set of toothed wheels working together in a machine, to transmit power at chosen speeds. The teeth of one wheel fit into the teeth of a second wheel. If the wheels are of different size, they turn at different speeds. The engine of a car is connected to the wheels by means of gears. **2** (also called **gear wheel**) any wheel of a set of gears. **3** any arrangement of parts used for a special purpose: *the steering* gear *of a ship*; *landing* gear *of an airplane.* **4** equipment in general: *hunting* gear. ***vt-* 1** to equip with gears. **2** to adjust; fit: *We have* geared *our organization to this type of work.*

Gear
GEAR WHEEL
PINION

in gear having the gear wheels connected with the engine. **out of gear 1** having the gear wheels disconnected from the engine. **2** not working smoothly. **shift gears** to connect or disconnect the gears in a power-transmission system.

gear·ing (gêr′ ĭng) ***n-* 1** all the gears of a machine. **2** act of equipping with gears.

gear·shift (gêr′ shĭft′) ***n-* 1** mechanism, usually operated by a lever, designed to connect and disconnect gears. **2** the lever itself, especially in motor vehicles.

geck·o (gĕk′ ō) ***n-*** [*pl.* **geck·os, geck·oes**] small, harmless house lizard, useful in destroying insects. Geckos have toe pads and can run along walls and ceilings.

Gecko, about 6 in. long

gee (jē) ***interj-* 1** *Informal* exclamation of surprise, pleasure, etc. **2** command given to a horse or ox to turn right (see also [3]*haw*). ***vi-*** [**geed, gee·ing**] to turn to the right: *The horses* geed. ***vt-***: *He* geed *the team of horses.*

geese (gēs) *pl.* of **goose.**

ge·fil·te fish (gə fĭl′ tə) ***n-*** mixture of chopped fish, crumbs, eggs, and seasoning, formed into balls or patties, and cooked in a fish stock.

Ge·hen·na (gə hĕn′ ə) ***n-* 1** in the Bible, a valley outside Jerusalem. **2** in the New Testament, hell; hence, any place of torment.

Gei·ger counter (gī′ gər koun′ tər) ***n-*** instrument that consists of a Geiger-Müller tube and an electronic counting device that registers one count whenever an ionization takes place in the tube. It is used to detect and measure the intensity of ionizing radiation. Also **Geiger-Müller counter.**

Gei·ger-Mül·ler tube (gī′ gər myl′ ər) ***n-*** sealed, thin-walled, glass tube filled with gas and containing two electrodes between which a current flows when charged particles ionize the gas.

gei·sha (gā′ shə) ***n-*** [*pl.* **gei·sha** or **gei·shas**] Japanese woman educated to provide entertainment and companionship for men.

gel (jĕl) ***n-*** mixture formed when particles of a certain size are evenly dispersed in a liquid. Gels flow like liquids, or become firm and jellylike, depending on the temperature. Raw egg white and the protoplasm of all living cells are gels. ***vi-*** [**gelled, gel·ling**] to become such a mixture. ***Hom-*** jell.

gel·a·tin (jĕl′ ə tən) ***n-*** clear, jellylike substance made from the bones, hoofs, and skin of animals or from some vegetables. It is sold in the form of a powder and used in making jellies, marshmallows, and ice cream, as well as in glue, medicine, etc. Also **gel′ a·tine.**

ge·lat·i·nous (jə lăt′ ə nəs) ***adj-*** of, like, or containing gelatin; jellylike.

geld (gĕld) ***vt-*** to castrate (a horse or other animal.)

geld·ing (gĕl′ dĭng) ***n-*** castrated animal, especially a horse.

gel·id (jĕl′ ĭd) ***adj-*** frigid; frozen.

gem (jĕm) ***n-* 1** precious stone, especially one cut or set as an ornament. **2** anything of great value or beauty: *This Toscanini album is the* gem *of my entire record collection.* **—*adj-* gem′ like′.**

FACET BEZEL
Gem

[1]gem·i·nate (jĕm′ ə nāt′) *vt-* [**gem·i·na·ted, gem·i·na·ting**] to double or arrange in identical pairs. *vi-: The chromosomes* geminated. *—n-* **gem·i·na′ tion.**

[2]gem·i·nate (jĕm′ ə nət) *adj-* arranged in pairs or doubled: *the* geminate *chromosomes.*

Gem·i·ni (jĕm′ ə nī′, -ə nē) *n-* constellation thought to outline the figure of the twin brothers, Castor and Pollux.

gems·bok (gĕmz′ bŏk′) *n-* large African antelope with long, tapered horns, a tufted tail, and striking markings.

Gemsbok, about 3 ft. high at shoulder

-gen *combining form* producer of: *aller*gen (producer of allergy); *carcino*gen (producer of cancer). [from a modern active modification of Greek **-genes** meaning "formed; produced."]

gen. 1 gender. 2 general. 3 genus. 4 genitive.

Gen. 1 Genesis. 2 General.

gen·darme (zhän′ därm′) *French n-* policeman who has had special military training.

gen·der (jĕn′ dər) *n-* 1 sex, male or female. 2 *Grammar* (1) the distinction between words or forms of a word that corresponds roughly to that between male, female, and sexless things. (2) any of the three types of this distinction: masculine, feminine, and neuter. In English, gender is shown chiefly by the personal pronouns. "He," "his," and "him" are masculine. "She," "her," and "hers" are feminine. "It" and "its" are neuter. Some English nouns have feminine suffixes such as "-ess."

gene (jēn) *n-* the part of a chromosome that is responsible for the transmission of a particular trait from parent to child. The color of a child's eyes is determined by some of the genes of his parents. ***Hom-*** jean.

ge·ne·al·o·gist (jē′ nē ŏl′ ə jĭst, jĕn′ ē-) *n-* maker of genealogies; specialist in genealogy.

gen·e·al·o·gy (jē′ nē ŏl′ ə jē, jĕn′ ē-) *n-* [*pl.* **gen·e·al·o·gies**] 1 method or system of investigating the descent of a person or family from an ancestor. 2 an account of such a descent; pedigree. *—adj-* **gen′ e·a·log′ i·cal** (-ə lŏj′ ĭ kəl). *adv-* **gen′ e·a·log′ i·cal·ly.**

gen·e·ra (jĕn′ ə rə) *pl.* of **genus.**

gen·er·al (jĕn′ rəl, jĕn′ ər əl) *adj-* 1 having to do with all or nearly all: *a* general *panic.* 2 widespread: *Afternoon tea is a* general *custom in England.* 3 not limited to one thing, class, or region: *the* general *public*; *a physician with a* general *practice.* 4 not definite; not in detail: *I have a* general *idea how rockets work.* 5 chief or head: *postmaster* general. *n-* 1 in the Army and Air Force, a commissioned officer who ranks next below a General of the Army or a General of the Air Force and next above a lieutenant general. 2 in the Marine Corps, a commissioned officer of the highest grade, ranking above a lieutenant general. 3 form of address for a brigadier general, major general, lieutenant general, and General of the Army or Air Force.

in general for the most part; usually.

general assembly *n-* 1 representatives of a State, organization, etc., meeting together as a legislative group. 2 school assembly attended by the entire school. 3 **General Assembly** deliberative body of the United Nations, made up of delegates of all member states.

General Court *n-* the legislature of the States of Massachusetts or New Hampshire.

general delivery *n-* 1 postal department which handles mail for persons who call for it instead of having it delivered to a street address. 2 mail so delivered.

gen·er·al·is·si·mo (jĕn′ ər ə lĭs′ ə mō′) *n-* [*pl.* **gen·er·al·is·si·mos**] in certain countries, the supreme commander of the armed forces.

gen·er·al·i·ty (jĕn′ ə răl′ ə tē) *n-* [*pl.* **gen·er·al·i·ties**] 1 general statement that may be too broad to be useful: *to talk in* generalities. 2 the large part of; the mass: *The* generality *of citizens in the United States eat well.*

gen·er·al·i·za·tion (jĕn′ rə lə zā′ shən) *n-* 1 a generalizing. 2 generalizing statement: *to make* generalizations.

gen·er·al·ize (jĕn′ rə līz′) *vi-* [**gen·er·al·ized, gen·er·al·iz·ing**] 1 to treat a subject as a whole rather than in parts; be vague, superficial, or casual by emphasizing a general aspect: *The speaker* generalized *on the need for better housing but neglected to offer any program.* 2 to make a general rule from facts or specific instances.

gen·er·al·ly (jĕn′ rə lē) *adv-* 1 most of the time; usually: *We* generally *have dinner at six o'clock.* 2 in most places or by most people; widely: *The new styles have been* generally *accepted.* 3 without being definite about particular things or persons: *to speak* generally.

General of the Air Force *n-* in the Air Force, the highest rank; also, a commissioned officer holding this rank. A General of the Air Force ranks above a general.

General of the Army *n-* in the Army, the highest rank; also, a commissioned officer holding this rank. A General of the Army ranks above a general.

general practitioner *n-* doctor who does not limit his practice to any special field of medicine.

gen·er·al·ship (jĕn′ rəl shĭp′) *n-* 1 rank or office of a general. 2 leadership and skill; especially in war.

general staff *n-* 1 group of the highest-ranking officers, who direct the military affairs of a nation: *the German* general staff. 2 group of officers who assist and advise the commander of a division or higher military unit.

general store *n-* comparatively small retail store that carries a large variety of merchandise.

gen·er·ate (jĕn′ ə rāt′) *vt-* [**gen·er·at·ed, gen·er·at·ing**] to produce; bring into existence: *Water power often is used to* generate *electricity. A friendly smile* generates *good will.* *—adj-* **gen′ er·a·tive** (jĕn′ ər ə tĭv).

gen·er·a·tion (jĕn′ ə rā′ shən) *n-* 1 all the people who are born at about the same time: *Our* generation *is producing many scientists.* 2 one step in the line of family descent. Grandparents, their children, and grandchildren make up three generations. 3 period of time, about 30 years, between the birth of one generation and the next. 4 act or process of producing: *the* generation *of power.*

gen·e·ra·tor (jĕn′ ə rā′ tər) *n-* 1 *Physics* machine that produces electricity from mechanical energy, usually by means of a rotating armature between the poles of a magnet; dynamo. 2 *Chemistry* apparatus used to produce a gas or vapor. 3 person or thing that generates.

ge·ner·ic (jə nĕr′ ĭk) *adj-* 1 of or including an entire kind or class; general, not specific. 2 of or relating to a genus: *the* generic *name of a plant.* *—adv-* **ge·ner′ i·cal·ly.**

gen·er·os·i·ty (jĕn′ ə rŏs′ ə tē) *n-* [*pl.* **gen·er·os·i·ties**] 1 willingness to share or give; unselfishness. 2 freedom from spitefulness or meanness; nobility: *He showed* generosity *in praising his opponent.* 3 a generous act.

gen·er·ous (jĕn′ ər əs) *adj-* 1 unselfish; free in giving or sharing: *to be* generous *to people in need.* 2 noble; not mean or spiteful: *a* generous *nature.* 3 large; plentiful: *a* generous *supply of paper.* **—*adv*- gen′ er·ous·ly.** ***n*- gen′ er·ous·ness.**

gen·e·sis (jĕn′ ə sĭs) ***n*-** [*pl.* **gen·e·ses** (-sēz)] **1** a beginning; the coming into being of anything: *We can see the* genesis *of this novel in an early short story of his.* **2 Genesis** the first book of the Bible, in which the creation of the world is described.

ge·net·ic (jə nĕt′ ĭk) ***adj*-** of, relating to, or resulting from heredity through genes; hereditary.

genetic code ***n*-** the arrangement of chemical bases in the DNA molecule that controls the traits of an organism.

ge·net·i·cist (jə nĕt′ ə sĭst) ***n*-** one trained or skilled in genetics, and usually engaged in it as a profession.

ge·net·ics (jə nĕt′ ĭks) ***n*-** branch of biology dealing with heredity and the genes.

Geneva Convention ***n*-** an international agreement, drawn up at Geneva in 1864, on the treatment and care of prisoners, the sick, and the wounded during war.

gen·ial (jēn′ yəl) ***adj*- 1** smilingly pleasant; warmly friendly: *a* genial *greeting.* **2** favorable to comfort and growth; warm or mild: *a* genial *climate.* **—*n*- gen·i·al′ i·ty** (jēn ē ăl′ ə tē). ***adv*-* gen′ ial·ly.**

ge·nie (jē′ nē) ***n*-** [*pl.* **ge·nies** or **ge·ni·i** (jē′ nē ī′)] jinn.

gen·i·tal (jĕn′ ə təl) ***adj*-** of or having to do with the reproductive process or organs.

gen·i·tals (jĕn′ ə təlz) ***n*-** *pl.* the sex organs.

gen·i·tive (jĕn′ ə tĭv) *Grammar* ***adj*-** in some languages, such as Latin, belonging to or naming a case resembling the possessive case in English and used to indicate possession, origin, or source. ***n*-** this case; also, a word in this case.

gen·i·to·u·ri·nar·y (jĕn′ ə tō yŏŏr′ ə nĕr′ ē) ***adj*-** of or having to do with the genital and urinary organs.

gen·ius (jēn′ yəs) ***n*- 1** outstanding ability to think, create, or invent: *Mozart showed* genius *in music almost from infancy.* **2** person who has this ability: *Einstein was a mathematical* genius. **3** a special talent or aptitude: *He has a* genius *for figures.* **4** person of high mental powers, especially one with a very high intelligence quotient. **5** [*pl.* **gen·i·i** (jē′ nē ī′)] guardian spirit.

gen·o·cide (jĕn′ ə sīd′) ***n*-** destruction of a national, racial, or religious group. **—*adj*- gen′ o·ci′ dal.**

Gen·o·ese (jĕn′ ō ēz′) ***n*-** [*pl.* **Gen·o·ese**] a native or citizen of Genoa. ***adj*-**: *a* Genoese *sailor.*

gen·re (zhän′ rə, *Fr.* zhä^n^r) ***n*- 1** a kind, sort, or class, especially in literature, art, etc. **2** style of realistic painting or sculpture that portrays everyday life, events, and manners. *as* ***modifier***: *a* genre *painting.*

gen·teel (jĕn tēl′) ***adj*-** polite and correct in manners and behavior, especially in a self-conscious way. **—*adv*- gen·teel′ ly.** ***n*- gen·teel′ ness.**

gen·tian (jĕn′ shən) ***n*-** any of several related plants with deep blue flowers, such as the **fringed gentian.**

gen·tile or **Gen·tile** (jĕn′ tīl′) ***n*- 1** person who is not a Jew. **2** among Mormons, anyone not a Mormon. ***adj*- 1** not Jewish. **2** not Mormon.

gen·til·i·ty (jĕn tĭl′ ə tē) ***n*-** [*pl.* **gen·til·i·ties**] **1** good manners or refinement of a well-bred person. **2** traditions, background, etc., of persons of distinguished family or ancestry.

Fringed gentian

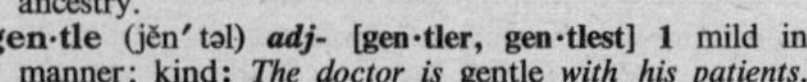

gen·tle (jĕn′ təl) ***adj*-** [**gen·tler, gen·tlest**] **1** mild in manner; kind: *The doctor is* gentle *with his patients.* **2** light; not rough; soft: *a* gentle *breeze; a* gentle *touch.* **3** having a mild or good temper: *a* gentle *dog.* **4** gradual; not extreme: *The driveway has a* gentle *slope.* **5** of or from a family of distinguished ancestry: *a man of* gentle *birth.* **—*n*- gen′ tle·ness.** ***adv*- gen′ tly** (jĕnt′ lē).

gen·tle·folk (jĕn′ təl fōk′) ***n*-** *pl.* in England, people of wealth and property ranking below the nobility; gentry.

gen·tle·man (jĕn′ təl mən) ***n*-** [*pl.* **gen·tle·men**] **1** a well-bred, considerate man. **2** a man: *There is a* gentleman *to see you.* **3 gentlemen** formal salutation in a business letter. **4** in England, a man of wealth or property ranking below a nobleman. **—*n*- gen′tle·man·like′.**

gen·tle·man·ly (jĕn′ təl mən lē) ***adj*-** courteous and well-bred; gentlemanlike. **—*n*- gen′ tle·man·li·ness**

gentleman's agreement ***n*-** arrangement or decision agreed to without formal contract, signature, etc.

gen·tle·wom·an (jĕn′ təl wŏŏm′ ən) ***n*-** [*pl.* **gen·tle·wom·en**] **1** a well-bred, considerate woman; lady. **2** in England, a woman from a family of wealth and property having a rank below that of the nobility.

gen·try (jĕn′ trē) ***n*-** gentlefolk.

gen·u·flect (jĕn′ yə flĕkt′) ***vi*-** to bend the knee,especially in religious worship. **—*n*- gen·u·flec′ tion.**

gen·u·ine (jĕn′ yōō ən) ***adj*-** real; not false; true: *a* genuine *pearl.* **—*adv*- gen′ u·ine·ly.** ***n*- gen′ u·ine·ness.**

ge·nus (jē′ nəs) ***n*-** [*pl.* **gen·er·a** (jĕn′ ər ə)] one of the groupings or categories that is used in the classification of living organisms. A genus belongs to a family and is made up of one or more species.

geo- *combining form* earth; surface of the earth: geo*physics*; geo*centric*; geo*morphology.* [from Greek **gê,** meaning "the earth."]

ge·o·cen·tric (jē′ ō sĕn′ trĭk) ***adj*- 1** having to do with, measured, or apparently seen in relation to the earth's center. **2** relating to or based on the idea that the earth, not the sun, is the center of the solar system and the universe: *a* geocentric *theory.*

ge·ode (jē′ ōd′) ***n*- 1** a round rock having a cavity or hollow space lined with small crystals. **2** the cavity itself.

ge·o·des·ic (jē′ ə dĕs′ ĭk, -dē′ sĭk) ***n*-** (also **geodesic line**) the shortest line on a curved surface that connects two points on that surface. A great circle is a geodesic line. ***adj*-** of or having to do with the geometry of such lines.

geodesic dome ***n*-** light, strong, hemispherical dome made up of many triangular units covered with a thin, tough material, and capable of enclosing large areas.

ge·od·e·sy (jē ŏd′ ə sē) ***n*-** science that deals with the methods used to determine the size, shape, curvature, and area of the earth. Geodesy includes the mapping of large parts of the earth's surface, and the study of the earth's gravitational and magnetic fields.

ge·o·det·ic (jē ə dĕt′ ĭk) ***adj*-** of, having to do with, or determined by geodesy; geodesic.

ge·og·ra·pher (jē ŏg′ rə fər) ***n*-** person who specializes in geography.

ge·o·graph·ic (jē′ ə grăf′ ĭk) or **ge·o·graph·i·cal** (-ĭ kəl) ***adj*-** having to do with geography: *a* geographic *chart.* **—*adv*- ge′ o·graph′ i·cal·ly.**

geographical mile See *mile.*

ge·og·ra·phy (jē ŏg′ rə fē) ***n*- 1** the study of the earth and the distribution of living things on the earth. Geography includes the study of the natural and political boundaries of the earth's land and water areas, surface features, climates, animal and plant life, resources, peoples, agriculture, and industries. **2** [*pl.* **ge·og·ra·phies**] the surface features of an area: *The* geography *of the Mediterranean is noted particularly for its contrasting features.*

geol. 1 geology. 2 geologist.
ge·o·log·ic (jē′ə lŏj′ĭk) or **ge·o·log·i·cal** (-ĭ kəl) ***adj-*** of or relating to geology. **—*adv-* ge′·o·log′i·cal·ly.**
ge·ol·o·gist (jē ŏl′ə jĭst) ***n-*** person trained or skilled in geology, and usually engaged in it as a profession.
ge·ol·o·gy (jē ŏl′ə jē) ***n-*** science that studies the earth, especially its crust and the changes brought about in the crust by natural processes such as erosion and mountain-building.
geom. geometry.
ge·o·met·ric (jē′ə mĕ′trĭk) ***adj-*** 1 of, having to do with, or based on the principles and methods of geometry. 2 made up of or exhibiting a pattern of straight lines or simple curves: *a* geometric *figure*; *a* geometric *design.* Also **ge′o·met′ri·cal. —*adv-* ge′o·met′ri·cal·ly.**
ge·om·e·tri·cian (jē′ə mə trĭsh′ən) ***n-*** person who specializes in geometry.
geometric progression ***n-*** sequence of related numbers in which the ratio between succeeding numbers remains constant. Example: 1, 2, 4, 8, 16, etc.
ge·om·e·try (jē′ŏm′ə trē) ***n-*** 1 branch of mathematics dealing with space, especially the properties, measurement, and relationships of points, lines, angles, figures, surfaces, and solids. 2 form or system of logic that derives a group of theorems from an initial set of axioms. Neither the axioms nor the theorems are necessarily concerned with the space or truth known in everyday experience: *Euclid used certain axioms to formulate a* geometry. 3 the arrangement of objects in a scene, painting, etc., or the elements in a design.
ge·o·mor·phol·o·gy (jē′ō mór′fŏl′ə jē, jē′ō môr′-) ***n-*** science that studies the features of the earth's surface, especially the way in which they are formed and develop. **—*adj-* ge′o·mor′pho·log′i·cal** (-fə log′ĭ kəl).
ge·o·phys·ics (jē′ō fĭz′ĭks) ***n-*** branch of science that uses the methods and techniques of physics to study the earth's motion, size, shape, internal structure, magnetic field, etc. **—*adj-* ge·o·phys′i·cal.**
ge·o·pol·i·ti·cian (jē′ō pŏl′ə tĭsh′ən) ***n-*** person who specializes in geopolitics.
ge·o·pol·i·tics (jē′ō pŏl′ə tĭks) ***n-*** (takes singular verb) study of the interactions of economics, geography, etc., upon politics. **—*adj-* ge′o·pol′i·tic** or **ge′o·po·li′ti·cal. *adv-* ge′o·pol·i′ti·cal·ly.**
Geor·gian (jór′jən, jôr′-) ***adj-*** 1 of or pertaining to any of the kings of England named George, or to the art, styles, customs, etc., of their reign. 2 of or relating to the State of Georgia or to its citizens. 3 of or relating to Georgia, a constituent republic of the Soviet Union, or to the language of its people. ***n-*** 1 a person living during the reign of any one of the Georges of England, or characterized by the ideas and manners current then. 2 a native of the State of Georgia in the United States. 3 a native of Georgia in the Soviet Union.
ge·o·ther·mal (jē′ō thûr′məl) ***adj-*** of or produced by the heat of the earth's interior: geothermal *energy;* geothermal *steam.*
Ger. 1 German. 2 Germany.
ge·ra·ni·um (jə rā′nē əm) ***n-*** 1 any of several wild plants having deeply cut leaves and lavender or pinkish flowers. 2 any of several plants cultivated for their showy clusters of bright red, pink, or white blossoms.

Wild geranium

ger·fal·con (jûr′făl′kən, -fól′ken, -fó′kən) gyrfalcon.
ger·i·at·rics (jĕr′ē ă′trĭks) ***n-*** (takes singular verb) branch of medicine that studies and treats the diseases and problems of old age.
germ (jûrm) ***n-*** 1 tiny living organism that causes disease; microbe. Germs can be seen only with a microscope. 2 tiny mass of living matter that may develop into an animal or plant: *Wheat* germ *is the living part of the wheat grain.* 3 a spore. 4 something minor or undeveloped that may grow; a beginning: *the* germ *of war*; *the* germ *of an idea.*
Ger·man (jûr′mən) ***adj-*** of or relating to Germany, its people or their language. ***n-*** 1 the language of Germany, spoken also in Austria and part of Switzerland. 2 a native of Germany.
ger·mane (jər mān′) ***adj-*** relevant; pertinent; related: *Your remarks are not* germane *to the subject.*
Ger·man·ic (jər măn′ĭk) ***n-*** branch of the Indo-European language family including German, English, Dutch, Afrikaans, Flemish, and the Scandinavian tongues. ***adj-*** of or pertaining to the Teutonic peoples, or to the languages spoken by them.
ger·ma·ni·um (jər mā′nē əm) ***n-*** metallic, grayish-white element used to make transistors. Symbol Ge, At. No. 32, At. Wt. 72.59.
German measles ***n-*** (takes singular verb) contagious virus disease characterized by a sore throat, fever, and a skin rash, and dangerous to the fetus during the first three months of pregnancy; rubella.
German shepherd ***n-*** breed of dog often used in police work and for guiding blind people.
German silver ***n-*** nickel silver.
germ cell ***n-*** a reproductive cell; gamete.
ger·mi·ci·dal (jûr′mə sī′dəl) ***adj-*** deadly to germs.
ger·mi·cide (jûr′mə sīd′) ***n-*** substance used to kill germs, especially germs causing disease.
ger·mi·nal (jûr′mə nəl) ***adj-*** 1 of or having to do with a germ cell or germ. 2 having to do with an early stage of growth or development; coming into being: *a* germinal *thought.*
ger·mi·nate (jûr′mə nāt′) ***vi*** [**ger·mi·nat·ed, ger·mi·nat·ing**] to sprout; start to grow. ***vt-*** to cause to grow: *Warmth and moisture* germinate *seeds.* **—*n-* ger·mi·na′tion.**
germ theory ***n-*** 1 theory that infectious diseases are caused by the activities of tiny living organisms inside the body. 2 theory that all living organisms originate only from previously existing living organisms.
germ warfare ***n-*** use of bacteria and other disease-causing organisms as weapons of war.
ger·ry·man·der (jĕr′ē măn′dər) ***vt-*** to divide (a state, voting district, etc.) in such a way as to give an unfair advantage to a particular political party or group. ***n-*** 1 the act of making such a district. 2 a district so formed.
ger·und (jĕr′ənd) *Grammar* ***n-*** English verb form ending in "-ing" and used as a noun. In the sentence "Seeing is believing," "seeing" and "believing" are gerunds. A gerund can take a direct object and can be modified by an adverb: Believing *him was easy.* ("Him" is the direct object.) Seeing *poorly is better than not* seeing *at all.* ("Poorly" and "at all" are adverbs.)
Ge·sta·po (gə stä′pō) ***n-*** the Nazi secret police, which operated especially against those opposing the regime

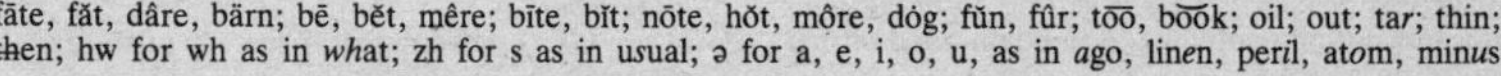
fāte, făt, dâre, bärn; bē, bĕt, mêre; bīte, bĭt; nōte, hŏt, môre, dóg; fŭn, fûr; tōō, bŏŏk; oil; out; tar; thin; then; hw for wh as in what; zh for s as in usual; ə for a, e, i, o, u, as in ago, linen, peril, atom, minus

ges·ta·tion (jĕs tā′ shən) ***n-*** **1** development and growth of the young in the uterus. **2** development of an idea or concept, especially in the mind. *as* ***modifier:*** *The* gestation *period of an elephant is about 20 months.*
ges·tic·u·late (jə stĭk′ yə lāt) ***vi-*** **[ges·tic·u·lat·ed, ges·tic·u·lat·ing]** to make movements, often while speaking, that express or emphasize one's thoughts. **—*n-* ges·tic′ u·la′ tion.** ***adj-*** **ges·tic′ u·la′ tive.**
ges·ture (jĕs′ chər) ***n-*** **1** a movement of the body, arms, hands, or face, to express an idea or feeling, or to stress what is being said: *a dancer's expressive* gestures. **2** something said or done to impress other people, or as a courtesy: *Inviting new neighbors to visit is a friendly* gesture. ***vi-*** **[ges·tured, ges·tur·ing]** to make expressive or emphatic motions.
get (gĕt) ***vt-*** **[got** (gŏt) or **got·ten** (gŏt′ ən), **get·ting] 1** to gain or obtain possession of; acquire: *to* get *books at the library*; *to* get *one's parents' permission.* **2** to receive: *Did you* get *my letter? He* got *the worst of it.* **3** to take, remove, transfer, etc.: *to* get *one's hat from the closet*; *to* get *the cat out of the room*; *to* get *a message to someone.* **4** to understand; grasp: *to* get *the meaning of a poem*; *to* get *the point of a joke.* **5** to obtain or produce by some effort, process, calculation, etc.: *to* get *power from a waterfall*; *to multiply and* get *the correct answer*; *to* get *breakfast.* **6** to cause to do something; bring into a certain state or condition: *to* get *one's hair cut*; *to* get *oneself ready*; *to* get *a friend to do you a favor.* **7** to come down with; contract: *to* get *the measles.* **8** *Informal* to catch, strike, strike down, overpower, etc.: *The police* got *their man. The bullet* got *him in the leg.* **9** *Informal* annoy; trouble: *Don't let their teasing* get *you.* ***vi-*** **1** to become: *to* get *hungry*; *to* get *tired.* **2** to bring oneself into a certain state: *to* get *ready.* **3** to arrive: *to* get *there on time.* **4** to move, come, go, etc.: *Please* get *in the car.*
has (or **have**) **got to** *Informal* must: *I've* got to *go now.*
get about 1 to move around. **2** to become known: *News* gets about *quickly.*
get across *Informal* to make understood: *He* got *his meaning* across.
get along 1 to be on good terms. **2** to succeed moderately: *He's not rich but he* gets along. **3** to move on.
get around *Informal* **1** to move around and observe: *We ought to listen to him because he* gets around. **2** of news, to spread about. **3** to bypass (a difficulty). **4** to win over: *I can always* get around *Mother.*
get at to reach: *Put it where the dog can't* get at *it.*
get away 1 to leave; depart. **2** to escape.
get away with *Informal* to escape punishment for.
get back 1 to move backwards: *He* got back *out of the path of the car.* **2** to return: *When will you* get back?
get back at to take revenge on.
get behind to fail to maintain an expected pace or progress.
get by 1 to move past. **2** *Informal* to manage; get along.
get down to 1 to begin. **2** to find and consider: *to* get down to *facts.*
get in 1 to arrive: *Did the train* get in *on time?* **2** to put in; manage to say: *to* get in *a word.*
get into to become involved in: *to* get into *trouble.*
get off 1 to get down from: *to* get off *a bicycle.* **2** to start: *to* get off *early to school.* **3** to escape: *He* got off *with only a scratch from the accident.*
get on 1 to go up on; board: *to* get on *a bus.* **2** to continue; move along: *Let's* get on *with this lesson.* **3** to succeed or manage: *He is* getting on *in the company.* **4** to put on (clothing). **5** to be on good terms: *They* get on *very well.* **6** to grow older.
get out 1 to leave a closed place; escape. **2** to become known: *Sometimes a secret* gets out.
get out of to escape; avoid: *I can't* get out of *going.*
get over to recover from.
get there to arrive.
get through to finish.
get through to to make contact with.
get together 1 to come together; meet: *Let's* get together *soon.* **2** to collect: Get *your books* together.
get up 1 to get out of bed. **2** to stand up.
get·a·way (gĕt′ ə wā′) ***n-*** **1** an escape, such as that of criminals after a crime. **2** a going into motion from a standstill: *The runner made a quick* getaway.
Geth·sem·a·ne (gĕth sĕm′ ə nē) ***n-*** garden near Jerusalem, the scene of Christ's suffering and arrest; hence, any mental or spiritual agony.
get-to·geth·er (gĕt′ tə gəth′ ər) *Informal* ***n-*** a social gathering of any kind.
get-up (gĕt′ ŭp′) *Informal* ***n-*** **1** outfit o costume, especially an unusual one. **2** general appearance.
gew·gaw (gyōō′ gȯ′) ***n-*** decorative object or trinket of slight value: *Her house was filled with* gewgaws.
gey·ser (gī′ zər) ***n-*** a hot spring that throws a jet of steam and hot water into the air, often at regular intervals.

Geyser

ghast·ly (găst′ lē) ***adj-*** **[ghast·li·er, ghast·li·est] 1** horrible; shocking: *The survivors told* ghastly *stories of the disaster.* **2** like a ghost; deathly pale: *The sick man's face looked* ghastly. **3** *Informal* very bad or unpleasant: *a* ghastly *mistake.* ***adv-***: *His face turned* ghastly *pale.* **—*n-* ghast′ li·ness.**
ghee (gē) ***n-*** in India, an oil prepared from melted butter made from buffalo milk, and used in cooking and in medicine.
gher·kin (gûr′ kən) ***n-*** small cucumber used for pickling.
ghet·to (gĕt′ ō) ***n-*** [*pl.* **ghet·tos**] **1** section of a city in which Jews were formerly forced to live. **2** any section where a minority group lives together, often under crowded or undesirable conditions.
ghost (gōst) ***n-*** **1** the spirit of a dead person, thought of as appearing or making its presence known to the living. **2** any faint, shadowy thing or appearance: *the* ghost *of a smile*; ghosts *on a television screen.* **—*adj-* ghost′like′.**
give up the ghost to die.
ghost·ly (gōst′ lē) ***adj-*** **[ghost·li·er, ghost·li·est] 1** of or like a ghost; spectral. **2** *Archaic* of or having to do with spiritual or religious matters. **—*n-* ghost′ li·ness.**
ghost town ***n-*** deserted town or village that was formerly busy or prosperous.
ghost writer ***n-*** person who writes a speech, book, etc., for someone else whose name appears as the author.
ghoul (gōōl) ***n-*** **1** robber of dead bodies or of graves. **2** in Muslim folklore, an evil spirit who robs graves and preys on the dead. **3** one who enjoys corrupt or loathsome things. **—*adj-* ghoul′ ish.** ***adv-*** **ghoul′ ish·ly.** ***n-*** **ghoul′ ish·ness.**
G.H.Q. general headquarters.
GI (jē′ ī′) *Informal* ***n-*** [*pl.* **GIs** or **GI's**] enlisted man in the U.S. Army: *He was a* GI *all through the war.* ***adj-*** **1** of or relating to army enlisted men: *the* GI *sort of humor.* **2** issued, used, or required by the army: *a pair of* GI *shoes.*
G.I. or **GI 1** government issue. **2** (also **g.i.**) gastrointestinal.

gi·ant (jī′ ənt) ***n-*** **1** in myth, legend, and fairy tale, a man of huge size and great strength. **2** unusually large example of something. **3** person of great power or achievement in anything: *Darwin and Einstein were* giants *of science.* **4** giant star. ***adj-*** **1** very large; huge. **2** very powerful: *a* giant *mind.* ***—n-*** *fem.* **gi′ ant·ess.**

giant panda See *panda.*

giant star *Astronomy* ***n-*** any of a class of red or orange stars, each of which is about 100 times brighter than our sun and 20 to 100 times larger.

gib·ber (jĭb′ ər) ***vi-*** to chatter foolishly or without making sense; babble. ***n-*** **1** foolish chatter. **2** gibberish.

gib·ber·ish (jĭb′ ər ĭsh) ***n-*** garbled speech or writing.

gib·bet (jĭb′ ət) ***n-*** a kind of gallows. ***vt-*** to execute by hanging.

gib·bon (gĭb′ ən) ***n-*** a small ape of Southeast Asia, having very long arms and no tail.

Gibbon, about 3 ft. tall

gib·bous (jĭb′ əs, gĭb′-) ***adj-*** **1** of the moon or a planet, being more than half full but not having all the apparent disk illuminated. **2** swollen or protuberant on one side; also, humpbacked. ***—adv-*** **gib′ bous·ly.** ***n-*** **gib′ bous·ness.**

gibe (jīb) ***n-*** remark expressing scorn or contempt; taunt. ***vt-*** **[gibed, gib·ing]** to sneer at; taunt: *They* gibed *him for his mistakes.* ***vi-*** to jeer (at); scoff (at): *They* gibed *at his speech.* ***—adv-*** **gib′ ing·ly:** *He answered the critics* gibingly.

gib·lets (jĭb′ ləts) ***n-*** *pl.* the heart, liver, and gizzard of poultry.

gid·dy (gĭd′ ē) ***adj-*** **[gid·di·er, gid·di·est]** **1** dizzy; lightheaded; having the feeling of spinning about. **2** causing dizziness: *a* giddy *height.* **3** not serious; frivolous: *a* giddy *young girl.* ***—adv-*** **gid′ di·ly.** ***n-*** **gid′ di·ness.**

Gid·e·on (gĭd′ ē ən) ***n-*** a hero of Israel who delivered his people from slavery and idolatry.

gift (gĭft) ***n-*** **1** a present; a thing given: *The girls exchanged Christmas* gifts. **2** natural ability; talent: *a* gift *for singing.*
in (one's) gift in (one's) power to give or bestow.

gift·ed (gĭf′ təd) ***adj-*** having ability; talented.

[1]**gig** (gĭg) ***n-*** **1** an open, two-wheeled carriage pulled by a horse. **2** a fast and light boat carried on shipboard for the captain's use. [from earlier **gig(ge)** meaning "a child's top; a whirling contrivance," of uncertain origin.]

[2]**gig** (gĭg) ***n-*** set of barbed hooks drawn through a school of fish to hook them through the body. ***vt-*** **[gigged, gig·ging]** to catch fish by this method. [from earlier **fizgig,** from Spanish **fisga** meaning "a harpoon."]

gi·gan·tic (jī găn′ tĭk) ***n-*** of giant size, power, etc.; huge; enormous. ***—adv-*** **gi·gan′ ti·cal·ly.**

gig·gle (gĭg′ əl) ***vi*** **[gig·gled, gig·gling]** **1** to laugh in a nervous, mischievous, or silly way. ***n-*** a light, silly, or mischievous laugh. ***—n-*** **gig′ gler.** ***adj-*** **gig′ gly.**

Gi·la monster (hē′ lə) ***n-*** large, venomous orange and black lizard of southwestern United States and northern Mexico.

Gila monster, up to 20 in. long

[1]**gild** (gĭld) ***vi-*** **[gild·ed** or **gilt, gild·ing]** **1** to cover with gold or with any gold-colored substance: *to* gild *a picture frame.* **2** to make golden: *The setting sun* gilded *the sky.* **3** to make (something unpleasant) seem more attractive; gloss over: *It is a lie, no matter how he* gilds *it.* [from Old English **gyldan,** from **gold,** "golden."] ***Hom-*** guild.

[2]**gild** (gĭld) guild. [from Old Norse **gildi.**]

gild·ing (gĭl′ dĭng) ***n-*** **1** thin layer of gold or similar material used to cover something. **2** surface produced in this way. **3** a deceptively pleasing appearance.

[1]**gill** (gĭl) ***n-*** **1** bodily organ of young amphibians, fish, and other aquatic animals, which takes up oxygen from the surrounding water and gives up carbon dioxide to it. **2** one of the many soft, thin vertical plates on the underside of a mushroom cap. [from earlier English **gille,** perhaps from a Scandinavian word.]

[2]**gill** (jĭl) ***n-*** unit of liquid measure equal to one fourth of a pint. [from Old French **gelle** meaning a "wine measure," from Late Latin **gillo,** "a receptacle."]

gill slit ***n-*** one of the several pairs of vertical slits in the throats of young amphibians and fish through which water passes from the mouth over the gills.

gil·ly·flow·er (jĭl′ ē flou′ ər) ***n-*** any of various related plants, such as the wallflower or the stock.

gilt (gĭlt) ***adj-*** covered with, or of the color of, gold; gilded: *a* gilt *statue.* ***n-*** paint made from powdered gold or something resembling it. ***Hom-*** guilt.

gilt-edged (gĭlt′ ĕjd′) ***adj-*** **1** having gilded edges: *a* gilt-edged *book.* **2** of the highest standard or quality.

gim·bals (gĭm′ bəlz, jĭm′-) ***n-*** *pl.* kind of instrument mounting consisting of two concentric rings pivoted to each other. Gimbals are used to keep compasses, gyroscopes, etc., horizontal no matter how the base or platform tilts. For picture, see *gyroscope.*

gim·crack (jĭm′ krăk′) ***n-*** a bright and showy object of little use or value; gew·gaw.

gim·let (gĭm′ lət) ***n-*** tool with a screw point for making small holes.

Gimlet

gim·let-eyed (gĭm′ lət īd′) ***adj-*** having keen and piercing eyes: *a* gimlet-eyed *detective.*

gim·mick (gĭm′ ĭk) *Informal* ***n-*** **1** gadget. **2** clever trick or idea, especially one used to make some plan or undertaking succeed. ***—adj-*** **gim′ mick·y.**

[1]**gimp** (gĭmp) ***n-*** narrow cord or flat braid, used as trimming for clothing, curtains, upholstery, etc. [from French **guimpe,** earlier **guimple,** "a blouse's wimple," from early German **wimpal,** "wimple."]

[2]**gimp** (gĭmp) *Slang* ***vi-*** to limp. [of uncertain origin.] ***—adv-*** **gimp′ i·ly.** ***adj-*** **gimp′ y [gimp·i·er, gimp·i·est].**

[1]**gin** (jĭn) ***n-*** a clear alcoholic liquor flavored with juniper berries. [short for **geneva** meaning "Holland gin." It comes from Dutch **genever,** from Old French **genevre,** from Latin **jūniperus,** "juniper; juniper berry."]

[2]**gin** (jĭn) ***n-*** machine for separating cotton fibers from seeds. ***vt-*** **[ginned, gin·ning]** to clear (cotton) of seeds with such a machine. [an early shortening of **engine,** from Old French **engin,** meaning "any type of device," from Latin **ingenium,** "talent."] ***—n-*** **gin′ ner.**

gin·ger (jĭn′ jər) ***n-*** **1** tropical plant cultivated for its spicy, sharp-tasting root. **2** powder obtained by grinding these roots, used as a spice or medicine. **3** these roots, coated with sugar and made into candy. **4** *Informal* pep; high spirits. ***—adj-*** **gin′ ger·y.**

ginger ale ***n-*** bubbly soft drink flavored with ginger.

ginger beer ***n-*** bubbly soft drink made with yeast and strongly flavored with ginger.

---

fāte, făt, dâre, bärn; bē, bĕt, mêre; bīte, bĭt; nōte, hŏt, môre, dòg; fŭn, fûr; too͞, bo͝ok; oil; out; tar; thin; then; hw for wh as in *wh*at; zh for s as in u*s*ual; ə for a, e, i, o, u, as in *a*go, lin*e*n, per*i*l, at*o*m, min*u*s

gin·ger·bread (jĭn′ jər brĕd′) ***n-*** **1** cake or cookie flavored with ginger and molasses. **2** gaudy, elaborate ornamentation, especially on a house or furniture.

gin·ger·ly (jĭn′ jər lē) ***adv-*** very carefully; timidly: *She* gingerly *fingered the vase.* ***adj-*** very cautious or careful: *She took a* gingerly *step forward.* **—*n-* gin′ger·li·ness.**

gin·ger·snap (jĭn′ jər snăp′) ***n-*** small, crisp molasses cookie flavored with ginger.

ging·ham (gĭng′ əm) ***n-*** cloth made of dyed yarn, usually of cotton with a pattern of checks.

gink·go (gĭng′ kō′) ***n-*** [*pl.* **gink·goes**] large shade tree with fan-shaped leaves, native to China and Japan.

gin rummy ***n-*** card game for two, in which each player is dealt ten cards and attempts to end the hand by matching them with drawn cards to make sets or by laying down his hand when his unmatched cards, less one for discarding, add up to ten or fewer points.

gin·seng (jĭn′ sĕng′) ***n-*** **1** herb, native to China and North America, having a thick root that is used in oriental medicine. **2** root of this plant; also, a preparation extracted from it.

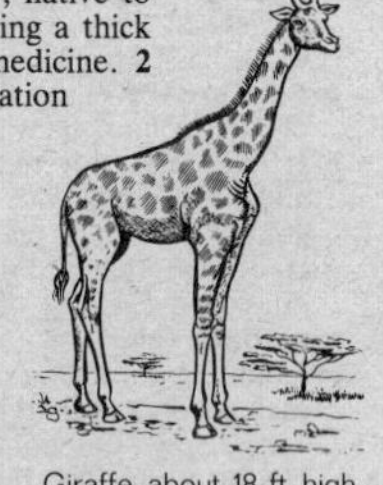
Giraffe, about 18 ft. high

Gip·sy (jĭp′ sē) Gypsy.

gipsy moth gypsy moth.

gi·raffe (jə răf′) ***n-*** African animal with long legs and a very long neck. it is the tallest of all mammals and feeds on the leaves of tall trees, and chews a cud.

gird (gûrd) ***vt-*** [**gird·ed** or **girt** (gûrt), **gird·ing**] **1** to surround; encircle: *Mountains* girded *the valley.* **2** to make ready; prepare: *to* gird *oneself for battle.* ***vi-*** **1** to make oneself ready; prepare: *to* gird *for action.* **2** to fasten something (on) with a belt or cord: *to* gird *on a sword.*

gird up (one's) loins to prepare for action or battle.

gird·er (gûr′ dər) ***n-*** strong, horizontal beam, often of steel, which supports the floor of a building or bridge.

gir·dle (gûr′ dəl) ***n-*** **1** sash or belt worn about the waist. **2** light, elastic undergarment worn to support the back and slim the waist and hips. **3** anything that surrounds like a belt: *a* girdle *of green around a city.* ***vt-*** [**gir·dled, gird·ling**] **1** to bind with or as with a belt. **2** to encircle: *Clouds* girdled *the moon.* **3** to cut off a strip of bark in a complete circle around (a tree or branch).

girl (gûrl) ***n-*** female child or young woman. **2** female servant (now considered offensive).

girl·friend (gûrl′ frĕnd′) ***n-*** **1** sweetheart. **2** girl or woman who is a friend.

girl·hood (gûrl′ hŏŏd) ***n-*** the time or condition of being a girl.

girl·ish (gûr′ lĭsh) ***adj-*** like a girl; of a girl. **—*adv-* girl′ish·ly.** ***n-*** **girl′ish·ness.**

Girl Scouts ***n-*** **1** (takes singular or plural verb) organization for training girls in physical fitness, good citizenship, and helpfulness to others. **2 girl scout** member of the Girl Scouts.

girt (gûrt) *p.t. & p.p.* of **gird.**

girth (gûrth) ***n-*** **1** distance around: *a man's* girth *at the waist; the* girth *of a tree trunk.* **2** strap fastened around an animal to hold a saddle, blanket, etc., in place. ***vt-*** to fasten with a strap or band.

gist (jĭst) ***n-*** the main point or idea of a matter; essence: *the* gist *of a story or speech.*

give (gĭv) ***vt-*** [**gave** (gāv), **giv·en, giv·ing**] **1** to hand over to another freely or as a present: *I* gave *him a pencil.* **2** to pay in exchange for something received: *I* gave *five dollars for this pin.* **3** to sacrifice; devote: *he* gave *his time for others.* **4** to administer: *to* give *a dose of medicine.* **5** to deal; inflict (a blow, beating, etc.). **6** to deliver: *to* give *a speech.* **7** to state; utter: *to* give *an opinion; to* give *a shout.* **8** to perform; present: *to* give *a play.* **9** to provide; furnish: *to* give *heat; to* give *advice; to* give *joy.* **10** to furnish as entertainment: *to* give *a party.* **11** to transmit; communicate: *He* gave *me the measles.* Give *her the news.* **12** to allot; assign: *to* give *homework.* **13** to grant: *to* give *permission.* **14** to entrust: *I* give *it into your charge.* **15** to pledge: *to* give *one's word.* **16** to execute (a bodily movement): *he* gave *a leap for joy.* ***vi-*** **1** to present gifts; contribute: *He* gave *freely to the hospital.* **2** to yield, as to force, pressure, motion, etc.: *The old floor* gave *under my feet.* ***n-*** a yielding to pressure; elasticity; flexibility: *An airplane wing must have a certain amount of* give. **—*n-* giv′er.**

give and take to make mutual concessions.

give away **1** to give up possesssion of. **2** to make known; reveal: *to* give away *a secret.*

give back to return.

give in to yield; surrender.

give it to (someone) *Informal* to punish (someone).

give off send out; emit: *to* give off *a strange sound.*

give out **1** to send out; distribute. **2** to make known. **3** to become exhausted, worn out, or used up.

give over **1** to surrender; yield. **2** to set apart for a purpose; devote: *to* give over *land for a park.*

give rise to to cause or produce; result in.

give up **1** to surrender; yield. **2** to stop doing something: *to* give up *smoking.* **3** to stop trying; admit failure.

give way **1** to retreat; withdraw; yield the right of way. **2** to yield or submit (to): *Don't* give way *to despair.* **3** to collapse, as a bridge under a heavy load.

give-and-take (gĭv′ ən tāk′) ***n-*** **1** compromise. **2** conflict and rivalry: *the* give-and-take *of daily life.*

give·a·way (gĭv′ ə wā′) *Informal* ***n-*** **1** clear evidence of something. **2** something given away.

giv·en (gĭv′ ən) ***adj-*** **1** stated; specified: *What can we judge from the* given *facts?* **2** granted: *a God-*given *talent.*

given to in the habit of: *He is* given to *bragging.*

given name ***n-*** name given at birth; first name.

giz·zard (gĭz′ ərd) ***n-*** muscular second stomach of birds, in which food is crushed and ground.

Gk. Greek

gla·cé (glă sā′) *French* ***adj-*** **1** coated with a sugar glaze; candied. **2** iced; frosted. **3** having a glossy surface.

gla·cial (glā′ shəl) ***adj-*** **1** of, relating to, or caused by a glacier or glaciation: *a* glacial *stream;* glacial *landscape.* **2** icy; frigid: *a* glacial *wind.* **3** unfriendly: *a* glacial *look.* **—*adv-* gla′cial·ly.**

glacial period ***n-*** **1** any of the four times in the earth's history, beginning about 800 million years ago, during which ice sheets covered large areas of the earth's surface. The latest of the four was the Pleistocene. **2** one of the four times during the Pleistocene epoch when ice advances occurred. **3** the Pleistocene epoch. Also **glacial epoch.**

gla·ci·ate (glā′ shē āt′, -sē āt′) ***vt-*** [**gla·ci·at·ed, gla·ci·at·ing**] to form glaciers or ice sheets on: *The ice* glaciated *half the continent.* **—*n-* gla·ci·a′tion.**

gla·ci·at·ed (glā′ shē ā′ təd, glā′ sē-) ***adj-*** **1** covered with an ice sheet or glaciers. **2** scraped, scoured, filled, or otherwise changed by glaciers: *a* glaciated *valley.*

gla·cier (glā′ shər) ***n-*** huge, moving mass of ice, on land, formed by the pressure of many snowfalls. At the present time glaciers are found only in high mountains or polar regions.

glad (glăd) ***adj-*** **[glad·der, glad·dest] 1** joyous; cheerful: *Easter is a* glad *season.* **2** happy; pleased: *I am* glad *that you could come.* **3** causing, bringing, or showing joy: *This is* glad *news.* ***—adv-*** **glad′ly.** ***n-*** **glad′ness.**

glad·den (glăd′ən) ***vt-*** to make happy.

glade (glād) ***n-*** small open space in a forest.

glad·i·a·tor (glăd′ē ā′ tər) ***n-*** a man, usually a slave, who fought with a sword or other weapon to entertain the people in the public arenas of ancient Rome. ***—adj-*** **glad′i·a·tor′i·al** (glăd′ē ə tôr′ē əl).

glad·i·o·lus (glăd′ē ō′ ləs, also glə dī′ ə ləs) ***n-*** [*pl.* **glad·i·o·li** (-lē) or **glad·i·o·lus·es**] cultivated plant having long, slender leaves and spikes of showy, variously colored flowers; also, its flower. Also **glad′i·o′la** or **glad·i′o·la.**

Gladiolus

glam·o·rize (glăm′ ə rīz′) ***vt-*** **[glam·o·rized, glam·o·riz·ing]** to add or assign glamor to: *to* glamorize *a bedroom*; *to* glamorize *an author.*

glam·or·ous (glăm′ ər əs) ***adj-*** enchanting; filled with magical charm: *a* glamorous *actress.* ***—adv-*** **glam′or·ous·ly.** ***n-*** **glam′or·ous·ness.**

glam·our or **glam·or** (glăm′ər) ***n-*** enchantment; mysterious charm; fascination: *the* glamour *of the East.*

glance (glăns) ***vi-*** **[glanced, glanc·ing] 1** to take a quick look: *He* glanced *at the passing car.* **2** to strike at a slant and fly (off): *The bullet* glanced *off the target.* **3** *Archaic* to flash. ***n-*** **1** quick or brief look: *a* glance *at the newspaper.* **2** rebound; carom. **3** gleam.

gland (glănd) ***n-*** bodily organ or other specialized tissue that secretes certain substances, such as enzymes and hormones, which are used in many places in the body.

glan·ders (glăn′ dərz) ***n-*** contagious disease of horses, mules, etc., marked by mucus discharges from the nose and swelling of the glands of the lower jaw.

glan·du·lar (glăn′ jə lər) ***adj-*** relating to, resembling, or having a gland or glands.

glare (glâr) ***n-*** **1** uncomfortable hot light; dazzling brightness: *the* glare *of the sun.* **2** fierce look: *an* angry *glare.* ***vi-*** **[glared, glar·ing]** to cast an uncomfortable light or hostile stare: *The sun* glared. *The librarian* glared *at the noisy girls.* ***—adj-*** **glar′y [glar·i·er, glar·i·est.]**

glar·ing (glâr′ ĭng) ***adj-*** **1** unpleasantly bright; dazzling: *the* glaring *headlights of a car.* **2** of colors, gaudy; too bright. **3** very easily seen; impossible to miss or ignore: *a* glaring *mistake.* **4** angry or fierce: *the maniac's* glaring *eyes.* ***—adv-*** **glar′ing·ly.**

glass (glăs) ***n-*** **1** hard, brittle substance, usually transparent or translucent, made from sand mixed with soda, potash, and other chemicals, and shaped at high heat by pressing, blowing, extruding, etc. **2** an article made of this substance, such as a mirror, drinking vessel, etc. **3** instrument for seeing, such as a telescope or microscope. **4** glassful. **5 glasses** eyeglasses; spectacles. *as* ***modifier***: *a* glass *bowl*; glass *windows.*

glass blowing ***n-*** the shaping of molten glass by forcing air into it through a tube. ***—n-*** **glass blower.**

glass·ful (glăs′ fo͝ol′) ***n-*** the amount held by a drinking glass.

glass·mak·ing (glăs′ mā′ kĭng) ***n-*** the art or process of making glass.

glass snake ***n-*** any of several legless lizards having tails that break off very easily; especially, the small and pretty insect-eating **American glass snake** of southern United States and northern Mexico.

glass·ware (glăs′ wâr′) ***n-*** articles made of glass.

glass·y (glăs′ē) ***adj-*** **[glass·i·er, glass·i·est] 1** very smooth and shiny: *the* glassy *surface of calm water.* **2** lifeless; without expression: *a dull,* glassy *stare.* ***—adv-*** **glass′i·ly.** ***n-*** **glass′i·ness.**

glau·co·ma (glò kō′ mə, glou-) *Medicine* ***n-*** disease of the eye marked by increasing pressure of the fluids within the eyeball that may lead to gradual loss of sight.

glaze (glāz) ***vt-*** **[glazed, glaz·ing] 1** to furnish or fit (a window, case, frame, or the like) with glass. **2** to cover or overlay with a thin coating of glass, or a substance resembling glass; hence, to make smooth, hard, and glossy: *to* glaze *pottery.* **3** in cooking, to coat with something, such as melted sugar, that becomes hard and shiny: *to* glaze *a ham*; *to* glaze *fruit.* ***vi-*** to become glassy: *His eyes* glazed *from fatigue.* ***n-*** **1** substance used to make a glossy surface, especially on pottery. **2** smooth, glasslike surface: *a* glaze *of ice.*

gla·zier (glā′ zhər) ***n-*** person whose work is to provide and install glass for windows, showcases, etc.

glaz·ing (glā′ zĭng) ***n-*** **1** the work of a glazier. **2** glass set or to be fitted in frames. **3** any substance used to make a smooth, glassy surface. **4** the applying of such a surface: *the* glazing *of pottery.*

gleam (glēm) ***n-*** **1** flash or beam of light. **2** something resembling a brief flash or glint: *a* gleam *of hope.* **3** brightness; glow: *the* gleam *of polished silver.* ***vi-*** to send out rays of light; shine: *The* stars *gleamed.*

glean (glēn) ***vt-*** **1** to pick or gather (what the reapers have left in a field): *to* glean *corn.* **2** to gather bit by bit: *to* glean *facts by careful reading.* ***—n-*** **glean′er.**

glean·ings (glē′ nĭngz) ***n-*** *pl.* things acquired by gleaning.

glee (glē) ***n-*** **1** gaiety; joy; merriment. **2** song for male voices in three or more parts, without accompaniment.

glee club ***n-*** a chorus, especially a male chorus at a school or college.

glee·ful (glē′ fəl) ***adj-*** full of glee; merry; gay. ***—adv-*** **glee′ful·ly.** ***n-*** **glee′ful·ness.**

glen (glĕn) ***n-*** narrow, secluded valley.

glen·gar·ry (glĕn găr′ē) ***n-*** [*pl.* **glen·gar·ries**] Scottish cap with creased top and straight sides.

glib (glĭb) ***adj-*** **[glib·ber, glib·best]** quick and ready; without much thought or sincerity; facile: *a* glib *talker*; *a* glib *excuse.* ***—adv-*** **glib′ly.** ***n-*** **glib′ness.**

glide (glīd) ***vi-*** **[glid·ed, glid·ing] 1** to move smoothly and easily without apparent effort: *Skaters* glided *on the ice.* **2** to pass imperceptibly: *The years* glide *by.* **3** to fly or soar on wings while not applying driving power. ***n-*** **1** smooth, sliding movement. **2** movement through the air on wings while no driving power is being applied. **3** in phonetics, sound produced while the organs of speech are shifting from the position for one sound to that for another.

glid·er (glī′ dər) ***n-*** **1** winged aircraft without an engine, designed to be towed behind an airplane or launched into flight. **2** outdoor seat that swings backward and forward on chains within a low supporting framework.

Glider

fāte, făt, dâre, bärn; bē, bĕt, mêre; bīte, bĭt; nōte, hŏt, môre, dòg; fŭn, fûr; to͞o, bo͝ok; oil; out; tar; thin; then; hw for wh as in *wh*at; zh for s as in u*s*ual; ə for a, e, i, o, u, as in *a*go, lin*e*n, per*i*l, at*o*m, min*u*s

glim·mer (glĭm′ ər) ***n-*** **1** faint, flickering light: *the* glimmer *of dying embers.* **2** faint glimpse or hint: *a* glimmer *of hope.* ***vi-*** **1** to flicker; shine unsteadily: *The candle* glimmered *and went out.* **2** to appear faintly or indistinctly: *Lights* glimmered *in the fog.*

glim·mer·ing (glĭm′ ər ĭng) ***n-*** **1** faint, unsteady light. **2** faint glimpse; inkling; glimmer.

glimpse (glĭmps) ***n-*** short look; quick view: *I caught a* glimpse *of her in the passing car.* ***vt-*** **[glimpsed, glimps·ing]** to get a quick view of: *to* glimpse *a shooting star.* ***vi-*** to look briefly; glance (at): *to* glimpse *at a painting.*

glint (glĭnt) ***n-*** a gleam; sparkle: *the* glint *of silver*; *a merry* glint *in his eye.* ***vi-***: *The lake* glinted *in the sun.*

glis·san·do (glĭ sän′ dō) *Music* ***n-*** a rapid sliding up or down the scale. ***adj- & adv-*** with such sliding.

glis·ten (glĭs′ ən) ***vi-*** to sparkle; shine: *The street* glistened *after the rain.*

glis·ter (glĭs′ tər) *Archaic* ***vi-*** to glisten.

glit·ter (glĭt′ ər) ***vi-*** **1** to sparkle coldly; shine with bright, flashing light: *Her diamonds* glittered. **2** to be bright and showy: *The actress* glittered *with wit and temperament.* ***n-***: *the* glitter *of gold*; *the* glitter *of a palace ballroom.* **—*adj-* glit′ ter·y.**

gloam·ing (glō′ mĭng) ***n-*** twilight; dusk.

gloat (glōt) ***vi-*** to gaze or dwell upon something with a feeling of triumph, greed, or spite: *The miser* gloats *over his gold. He* gloated *over my misfortunes.* **—*n-* gloat′ er. *adj-* gloat′ ing. *adv-* gloat′ ing·ly.**

glob·al (glō′ bəl) ***adj-*** **1** covering or including the whole world; worldwide: *a* global *conflict.* **2** shaped like a globe. **—*adv-* glob′ al·ly.**

globe (glōb) ***n-*** **1** a body shaped like a ball; sphere. **2** sphere representing the earth, with a map of the world upon it, or a sphere representing the sky, showing the heavenly bodies in their relative positions. **3 the globe** the earth.

Globe

globe·fish (glōb′ fĭsh′) ***n-*** [*pl.* **globe·fish; globe·fish·es** (kinds of globefish)] any of various spiny-finned tropical fishes that inflate themselves into globular form; puffer.

globe·trot·ter (glōb′ trŏt′ ər) ***n-*** person who travels over the world, especially for pleasure.

glob·u·lar (glŏb′ yə lər) ***adj-*** **1** shaped like a globe or globule; round. **2** made up of globe-shaped particles.

glob·ule (glŏb′ yo͞ol′) ***n-*** small globe; drop: *a* globule *of liquid.*

glob·u·lin (glŏb′ yə lĭn′) ***n-*** any of a group of proteins found in many plants and animals, including man. Antibodies and certain proteins of seeds are globulins.

glock·en·spiel (glŏk′ ən spēl′) *Music* ***n-*** instrument with tuned metal bars, bells, or tubes, set in a frame and played by striking with two small hammers.

gloom (glo͞om) ***n-*** **1** sadness; low spirits; depression: *to relieve one's* gloom. **2** dimness; partial darkness: *in the* gloom *of an old building.* ***vi-*** to be or look gloomy: *He* gloomed *over his failure.*

gloom·y (glo͞o′ mē) ***adj-*** **[gloom·i·er, gloom·i·est]** **1** sad; depressed: *a* gloomy *picture*; *a* gloomy *mood.* **2** dim; partially dark: *a* gloomy *corridor.* **—*adv-* gloom′ i·ly. *n-* gloom′ i·ness.**

Glo·ri·a (glôr′ ē ə) ***n-*** **1** one of several Latin hymns of praise to God, beginning in the original with the word "Gloria." **2** a section of the Mass in which such a hymn is said or sung; also, the musical setting of the hymn.

glor·i·fi·ca·tion (glôr′ ə fə kā′ shən) ***n-*** a glorifying or being glorified; exaltation.

glo·ri·fy (glôr′ ə fī′) ***vt-*** **[glo·ri·fied, glo·ri·fy·ing]** **1** to honor and exalt: *to* glorify *a hero.* **2** to praise and worship: *to* glorify *God.* **3** to make something appear better, grander, or more beautiful: *to* glorify *a building with a gilded dome.* **—*n-* glor′ i·fi·er.**

glo·ri·ous (glôr′ ē əs) ***adj-*** **1** splendid; magnificent: *a* glorious *show of fireworks.* **2** having or bringing honor and glory; worthy of praise: *a* glorious *victory.* **—*adv-* glo′ ri·ous·ly.**

glo·ry (glôr′ ē) ***n-*** [*pl.* **glo·ries**] **1** fame and honor: *Scientific achievements bring* glory *to a nation.* **2** praise; credit: *the* glory *of a distinguished career.* **3** reason for pride: *The Colosseum was the* glory *of ancient Rome.* **4** highest state of magnificence or prosperity: *Greece in her* glory. **5** radiant beauty; splendor: *the* glory *of a sunset.* **6** halo. ***vi-*** **[glor·ied, glor·y·ing]** to rejoice in; be proud of (usually followed by "in" or "at").

go to glory to die. **in one's glory** at one's happiest or most successful.

[1]**gloss** (glôs) ***n-*** **1** smooth shining surface; luster: *the* gloss *of satin.* **2** a deceptive appearance: *the* gloss *of respectability.* ***vt-*** to make smooth and lustrous. [from Old Norse **glossi,** "a blaze," or **glys,** "luster."]

gloss over to cover up or excuse a mistake or wrong act; gild: *to* gloss over *an error.*

[2]**gloss** (glôs) ***n-*** **1** word or words that translate or explain some word or passage in a text, especially when these are added in the margin or between lines. **2** glossary. ***vt-*** to explain (a text, word, etc.). [from earlier **gloze,** from Old French **glose,** through Latin from Greek **glôssa,** "a language; tongue."] **—*n-* gloss′ er.**

glos·sa·ry (glôs′ ə rē, glŏs′-) ***n-*** [*pl.* **glos·sa·ries**] list of special or technical words with explanations.

gloss·y (glôs′ ē) ***adj-*** **[gloss·i·er, gloss·i·est]** smooth and shiny: *a* glossy *table.* **—*adv-* gloss′ i·ly. *n-* gloss′ i·ness.**

glot·tis (glŏt′ əs) ***n-*** [*pl.* **glot·tis·es** or **glot·ti·des** (-ə dēz′)] narrow opening at the upper end of the windpipe, between the vocal cords.

glove (glŭv) ***n-*** **1** covering for the hand with a separate sheath for each finger and the thumb. **2** padded covering to protect the hand: *a baseball* glove. **—*adj-* gloved:** *a* gloved *hand.*

hand in glove with in close agreement or cooperation with. **handle with kid gloves** to treat gently.

glov·er (glŭv′ ər) ***n-*** person who makes gloves.

glow (glō) ***vi-*** **1** to give off intense light and heat without flame: *Embers* glowed *after the fire died.* **2** to give off light but not heat: *The face of the clock* glows *in the dark.* **3** to shine with brilliant color: *The trees* glow *with autumn splendor.* **4** to be warm or flushed, as from exercise. **5** to have the appearance, color, etc., of good health. **6** to radiate; be suffused (with): *to* glow *with pride.* ***n-*** **1** a giving off of light from something that is red-hot or white-hot. **2** brightness; light: *the* glow *of a firefly*; *a red* glow *at sunset.* **3** special appearance or tone: *a* glow *of happiness*; *a* glow *of health.*

glow·er (glou′ ər) ***vi-*** to stare threateningly or angrily; scowl: *The boxer* glowered *at his opponent.* ***n-*** an angry or sullen stare. **—*adv-* glow′ er·ing·ly:** *He looked* gloweringly *at the pile of work.*

glow·ing (glō′ ĭng) ***n-*** **1** burning; incandescent: *a* glowing *furnace.* **2** bright; vivid: *the* glowing *colors of the rainbow.* **3** having the appearance of health, excitement, etc.: *a* glowing *complexion.* **4** eager; animated: *a* glowing *description.* **—*adv-* glow′ ing·ly.**

glow·worm (glō′ wûrm′) ***n-*** any of various insects or larvae which glow or flicker in the dark.

glox·in·i·a (glŏk sĭn′ ē ə) ***n-*** cultivated plant, related to the African violet, having large bell-shaped flowers of white, red, or purple.

gloze (glōz) **[glozed, gloz·ing] gloze over** to explain away.

glu·cose (glo͞o′ kōs′) ***n-*** **1** sugar ($C_6H_{12}O_6$) produced in living organisms from starch and other sugars. Glucose is the major source of energy for metabolism, and in plants it plays an important part in photosynthesis. **2** thick syrup containing a mixture of dextrose, maltose, dextrin, and water, used in baking, candy making, etc.

glue (glo͞o) ***n-*** **1** substance used to join and bond things together, made from animal hides, hooves and horns, sinews, etc. **2** any of various substances made from rubber, casein, blood, synthetic resin, etc., and used for the same purpose; cement; adhesive. ***as modifier***: *a* glue *pot*; *a* glue *joint*. ***vt-*** **[glued, glu·ing]** to join or bond together with such a substance.

glu·ey (glo͞o′ ē) ***adj-*** **[glu·i·er, glu·i·est] 1** like glue; sticky. **2** smeared with glue.

glum (glŭm) ***adj-*** **[glum·mer, glum·mest]** silent and gloomy; sullen. ***—adv-*** **glum′ ly.** ***n-*** **glum′ ness.**

glut (glŭt) ***n-*** an oversupply: *a* glut *of wheat on the market*. ***vt-*** **[glut·ted, glut·ting] 1** to more than satisfy; overstuff: *He* glutted *his appetite with rich food.* **2** to oversupply with goods in excess of the demand: *to* glut *the market*.

glu·ten (glo͞o′ tən) ***n-*** a sticky protein substance found in the flour of certain grains, especially wheat.

glu·ti·nous (glo͞o′ tən əs) ***adj-*** like glue; sticky. ***—adv-*** **glu′ tin·ous·ly.**

[1]**glut·ton** (glŭt′ ən) ***n-*** **1** person who eats too much; pig. **2** person who is very greedy (for something): *a* glutton *for reading*. [from Old French **glutun,** from Latin **glut(t)ōn-,** from **glutire,** "to swallow; gulp."]

glutton for punishment person who habitually drives or pushes himself very hard.

[2]**glut·ton** (glŭt′ ən) ***n-*** wolverine. [from [1]**glutton.**]

glut·ton·ous (glŭt′ən əs) ***adj-*** given to overeating. ***—adv-*** **glut′ ton·ous·ly.** ***n-*** **glut′ ton·ous·ness.**

glut·ton·y (glŭt′ ən ē) ***n-*** [*pl.* **glut·ton·ies**] **1** excess in eating. **2** greed for something: *a* gluttony *for books*.

glyc·er·ol (glĭs′ ə rȯl′, -rōl′) ***n-*** colorless, sweet, pale-yellow alcohol ($C_3H_5(OH)_3$), found combined with fats and used as a solvent and in the manufacture of explosives. Also **glyc′ er·in** or **glyc′ er·ine.**

gly·co·gen (glī kə jən) ***n-*** white insoluble sugar that is the only carbohydrate stored in the animal body. Glycogen is readily changed into glucose by the liver, thus helping to maintain the proper blood-sugar level.

gm. or **gm** gram or grams.

G-man (jē′ măn′) *Informal* ***n-*** [*pl.* **G-men**] agent of the Federal Bureau of Investigation.

GMT or **G.M.T.** Greenwich mean time.

gnarl (närl) ***n-*** knot on a tree or in wood. ***vt-*** to make knotty or twisted: *Hard work had* gnarled *his hands.*

gnarled (närld) ***adj-*** twisted; knotty. Also **gnar′ ly.**

gnash (năsh) ***vt-*** to grind or strike (the teeth) together in rage or pain. ***n-*** a snap or bite of the teeth.

gnat (năt) ***n-*** any of several tiny biting or stinging flies, such as the midge. ***—adj-*** **gnat′ ty.**

Gnat

gnaw (nȯ) ***vt-*** **[gnawed, gnawed** or **gnawn, gnaw·ing] 1** to bite and wear away: *A dog* gnaws *a bone. Rats* gnawed *a hole.* **2** to trouble; torment: *The lie* gnawed *his guilty conscience.* ***vi-*** to bite or nibble repeatedly: *Ruth* gnawed *on a pretzel.* ***—n-*** **gnaw′ er.**

gneiss (nīs) ***n-*** rock composed of layers of quartz, mica, and feldspar. It is like granite in composition, but not in structure. ***Hom-*** nice.

gnome (nōm) ***n-*** in fable and myth, dwarf that lives underground to guard treasures of precious metals and stones. ***—adj-*** **gnome′ like′** or **gnom′ ish.**

gnu (no͞o, nyo͞o) ***n-*** South African antelope with a mane, a flowing tail, and curved horns. ***Homs-*** knew, new.

Gnu, about 4 ft. high at shoulder

go (gō) ***vi-*** **[went** (wĕnt), **gone** (gȯn, gŏn), **go·ing] 1** to pass from one place to another; move; travel: *to* go *from New York to Boston*; *to* go *shopping*. **2** to move away; leave; depart: *The train* goes *at five. The bus had already* gone. **3** to follow or be guided: *to* go *by the rule.* **4** to be in a certain condition: *to* go *prepared.* **5** to work, run, or operate: *The motor won't* go. **6** to extend; lead: *This wire* goes *to the basement.* **7** to make a particular motion, sound, etc.: *The song* goes *like this.* **8** to proceed; result: *The election* went *in his favor.* **9** to have a specific place or position: *This chair* goes *there.* **10** to adopt certain views or a course of action: *The government decided to* go *to war.* **11** to pass by; elapse: *An hour* goes *quickly.* **12** to be given, sold, or spent: *The ring* goes *to Sue. The house* went *at auction. My money* went *for food.* **13** to disappear; be abolished or lost: *Crime must* go. **14** to pass from one person to another: *Mumps* went *through the whole school.* **15** to fail; collapse: *Her hearing* went. *The scaffolding* went. **16** to participate in: *Will you* go *swimming*? **17** to be or become: *to* go *hungry*; *to* go *blind.* **18** to fit; belong: *The boot* goes *on this foot.* **19** to continue or appear in a certain state or condition: *to* go *unpunished*; *to* go *without a coat.* **20** *Archaic* to walk. ***n-*** [*pl.* **goes**] **1** success: *He made a* go *of it.* **2** *Informal* a try. **3** *Informal* vigor; energy: *He has plenty of* go. ***—n-*** **go′ er.**

let go to give up; stop trying. **let (oneself) go 1** to give way to one's feelings or desires. **2** to become careless of one's appearance, behavior, etc. **no go** *Slang* impossible; useless. **on the go** *Informal* always active; busy.

go about 1 to begin and do (something): *How do you* go about *joining?* **2** to be busy at: *He* goes about *his business.* **3** in sailing, to tack.

go after to seek; pursue.

go ahead 1 to proceed: *I told him to* go ahead. **2** to make progress; succeed: *He is* going ahead *fast.*

go along with to agree with: *I* go along with *his idea.*

go around or **go round 1** to be enough: *The cake will just* go around. **2** to make a detour. **3** to pay a visit to.

go at to begin and do: *to* go at *one's work.*

go back on 1 to betray. **2** to break (a promise).

go begging to be in little demand.

go beyond to exceed: *to* go beyond *the speed limit.*

go by 1 to be guided by; conform to: *I'll* go by *what you say.* **2** to be known by: *He* goes by *the name of Harry.*

go by the board to be discarded.

go down 1 to be defeated; lose. **2** to be recorded or written down: *to* go down *in history.*

go for 1 to reach for; try to get. **2** to favor; support.

go in for *Informal* to take part in; engage in.

go into 1 to be contained in: *Three* goes into *nine.* **2** to deal with; take up as a topic: *to* go into *the reasons* *for an act.* **3** to investigate thoroughly. **4** to enter as an occupation: *to* go into *law.*

go in with to join; share with.

go it alone to tackle something by oneself.

go off **1** to explode. **2** to begin, proceed, and end: *The program* went off *well.*

go on **1** to happen: *What is* going on? **2** to begin to work or operate: *The lights are* going on. **3** to approach; near: *He is* going on *twenty.*

go out **1** to be extinguished; end. **2** to go away from one's house for entertainment. **3** to strike: *The men* went out *for higher wages.* **4** to give sympathy: *My heart* went out *to him.* **5** to become a candidate for a team: *to* go out *for track.*

go over **1** to examine carefully. **2** to repeat; review.

go steady *Informal* to date one person exclusively.

go through **1** to go to the end of; do thoroughly. **2** to undergo; experience. **3** to search: *to* go through *a desk.* **4** to perform; take part in: *to* go through *a ceremony.* **5** to reach the end of.

go through with to complete; endure to the end.

go to to attend: *He* goes to *Yale.*

go together **1** to harmonize: *two colors that* go together. **2** to keep company; date.

go under **1** to sink; be overwhelmed. **2** to fail; be ruined.

go with **1** *Informal* to date. **2** to be in harmony with.

go without to get along without.

goad (gōd) ***n-*** **1** sharp-pointed stick used to drive cattle. **2** anything that drives or urges a person to action: *The scholarship was a* goad *to his ambition.* ***vt-*** to drive or urge on; incite: *to* goad *cattle; to* goad *one to anger.*

go-a·head (gō′ ə hed′) *Informal* ***n-*** authority or permission to begin or proceed with something.

goal (gōl) ***n-*** **1** place at either end of a field or other playing area where the score is made in football, basketball, hockey, lacrosse, etc. **2** a score: *Our team made a* goal. **3** line or mark at the end of a race: *The winner will be the first person to cross the* goal. **4** aim; purpose. *What is your* goal *in life?* **5** planned destination: *His* goal *was Paris.*

goal·ie (gō′ lē) *Informal* ***n-*** goalkeeper.

goal·keep·er (gōl′ kē′ pər) ***n-*** player who protects the goal for his team.

goal line ***n-*** line marking the goal in a game.

goal post ***n-*** one of a pair of posts with a crossbar, forming the goal in football, soccer, etc.

goat (gōt) ***n-*** **1** cud-chewing animal about the size of, and related to, the sheep, usually having short horns and a beard. It is valued for its milk, skin, meat, and, in some varieties, for its hair. **2** *Informal* innocent person made to take blame or punishment, or to seem a fool; butt; scapegoat. ***—adj-*** **goat′ like′.**

get (someone's) goat *Slang* to anger; annoy.

Goat, about 3 ft. long

goat·ee (gō′ tē′) ***n-*** small, pointed beard on the chin or on the lower lip.

goat·herd (gōt′ hûrd′) ***n-*** one who tends goats, especially while at pasture.

goat·skin (gōt′ skĭn′) ***n-*** **1** the skin of a goat. **2** leather made from this. **3** container for wine or water made of this leather. *as* ***modifier:*** *a* goatskin *cloak.*

goat·suck·er (gōt′ sŭk′ ər) ***n-*** any of various insect-eating birds that fly by night, such as the whippoorwill or nighthawk.

[1]**gob** (gŏb) *Slang* ***n-*** sailor in the United States navy. [an American word of uncertain origin.]

[2]**gob** (gŏb) ***n-*** mass or lump: *a* gob *of ice cream.* [partly from Old French **gobe,** "mouthful; gulp," partly from Gaelic **gob** meaning "mouth; beak."]

[1]**gob·ble** (gŏb′ əl) ***vt-*** **[gob·bled, gob·bling]** to eat fast and greedily; devour: *He* gobbled *his food.* [from Old French **gober,** "to swallow," from **gobe,** "[2]gob."]

[2]**gob·ble** (gŏb′ əl) ***n-*** noise made by a male turkey. ***vi-*** **[gob·bled, gob·bling]** to make this noise. [from [1]**gobble.**]

gob·ble·dy·gook (gŏb′ əl dē go͝ok′) *Informal* ***n-*** writing or speech that is meant to be serious and impressive, but is actually pompous, repetitive, and full of jargon.

gob·bler (gŏb′ lər) ***n-*** male turkey.

go-be·tween (gō′ bə twēn′) ***n-*** person who makes peace, does business, or settles difficulties between two parties who do not meet during the arrangements.

gob·let (gŏb′ lət) ***n-*** drinking glass with a slender stem and a flat base.

gob·lin (gŏb′ lĭn) ***n-*** in fable or myth, an evil or mischievous spirit having the form of an ugly, grotesque dwarf.

go-by (gō′ bī′) *Informal* ***n-*** a deliberate ignoring or rejection; refusal to act or consider: *He gave the plan the* go-by.

Goblet

go·cart (gō′ kärt′) ***n-*** **1** a frame rolling on casters and used for teaching children to walk; walker. **2** light, open baby carriage; stroller. **3** small handcart. **4** a light horse-drawn carriage.

God (gŏd) ***n-*** the Creator and Ruler of the universe; the Lord; the Supreme Being; the Almighty; Jehovah.

god (gŏd) ***n-*** **1** a male being who is thought of and worshiped as having greater than human powers over nature and human affairs. **2** image, object, etc., worshipped as having divine powers. **3** something that takes all of a person's interest or devotion: *Money is his* god.

god·child (gŏd′ chīld′) ***n-*** [*pl.* **god·chil·dren**] child for whose religious training a godfather or godmother promises to assume responsibility.

god·daugh·ter (gŏd′ dò′ tər) ***n-*** female godchild.

god·dess (gŏd′ əs) ***n-*** **1** female deity. **2** woman greatly admired for her charm, beauty, etc.

god·fa·ther (gŏd′ fä′ thər) ***n-*** man who promises at the baptism or confirmation of someone else's child to assume responsibility for the child's religious training.

god·head (gŏd′ hĕd′) ***n-*** **1** divine nature; divinity. **2 Godhead** God; Supreme Being.

god·hood (gŏd′ ho͝od′) ***n-*** the state or quality of being a god; divinity.

god·less (gŏd′ ləs) ***adj-*** **1** not believing in or worshiping God. **2** wicked. ***—n-*** **god′ less·ness.**

god·like (gŏd′ līk′) ***adj-*** like or suitable to a god; divine.

god·ly (gŏd′ lē) ***adj-*** **[god·li·er, god·li·est]** obeying and loving God; pious: *a* godly *man.* ***—n-*** **god′ li·ness.**

god·moth·er (gŏd′ mŭth′ ər) ***n-*** woman who promises at the baptism or confirmation of someone else's child to assume responsibility for the child's religious training.

god·par·ent (gŏd′ pâr′ ənt, -păr′ ənt) ***n-*** godfather or godmother.

God's acre ***n-*** churchyard or cemetery.

god·send (gŏd′ sĕnd′) ***n-*** something unexpected and very welcome, as if sent by God.

god·son (gŏd′ sŭn′) ***n-*** male godchild.

God·speed (gŏd′ spēd′) ***n-*** a wish for good luck and success, especially on a journey.

god·wit (gŏd′ wĭt′) ***n-*** bird with a long bill and long legs, related to the snipes and curlews.

goes (gōz) **1** form of the verb **go** used with "he," "she," "it," or singular noun subjects, in the present tense. **2** plural of the noun **go.**

go-get·ter (gō′ gĕt′ ər) *Informal* ***n-*** energetic or aggressive person who goes after what he wants.

gog·gle (gŏg′ əl) ***vi-*** **[gog·gled, gog·gling]** to stare with wide-open or bulging eyes. ***n-*** a bulging or rolling of the eyes. **2 goggles** glasses worn to protect the eyes against wind, glaring light, flying chips, etc.

goggle eyes ***n-*** eyes that bulge or stare in or as if in amazement. **—*adj-* gog′ gle-eyed:** *a* goggle-eyed *stare.*

go·ing (gō′ ĭng) ***n-*** **1** a moving away; departure: *They all regretted his* going. **2** condition of a road, path, etc., as it affects travel or progress: *The* going *is very rough on that trail.* ***adj-*** **1** operating or conducting business successfully: *a* going *concern.* **2** *Informal* now in existence: *He is the best shortstop* going.

be going to to be about to or intending to: *I* am going to *wash my hair. When* are *you* going to *finish?*

go·ings-on (gō′ ĭngz ŏn′) ***n-*** *pl.* actions or behavior, usually when regarded with disapproval.

goi·ter (goi′ tər) ***n-*** swelling in the front of the neck, caused by a diseased condition of the thyroid gland. Also **goi′ tre.**

gold (gōld) ***n-*** **1** heavy, precious, metal element, of a yellow color in its pure state, used for making coins and jewelry and kept in reserve by governments to give value to their currencies. Symbol Au, At. No. 79, At. Wt. 196.967. **2** color of this metal. **3** money; wealth: *He has lots of* gold. **4** that which is the highest or best in quality: *a heart of* gold. ***adj-***: *a* gold *watch.*

gold·brick (gōld′ brĭk′) *Slang* ***n-*** person, especially a soldier, who tries to avoid work, duties, etc. ***vi-*** to shirk or avoid work or responsibility.

gold·en (gōl′ dən) ***adj-*** **1** made of gold: *a* golden *ring.* **2** resembling gold in color, luster, etc.: *her* golden *hair*; *the* golden *dawn.* **3** extremely good, favorable, successful, etc.; splendid: *a* golden *voice*; *a* golden *opportunity*; *the* golden *years of one's life.* **—*adv-* gold′ en·ly.**

golden age ***n-*** in Greek and Roman legend, the first age of the world, a period of perfect human happiness and innocence; hence, a period of greatest glory in the history of a nation, literature, etc.

golden anniversary ***n-*** golden wedding.

golden calf ***n-*** **1** in the Old Testament, a golden idol worshiped by the Israelites. **2** mammon.

golden eagle ***n-*** large eagle of the northern hemisphere, with golden-brown feathers on the back of its neck.

Golden Fleece ***n-*** in Greek legend, a fleece of gold which, although guarded by a sleepless dragon, was carried away by Jason and the Argonauts.

golden glow ***n-*** tall, branching plant cultivated for its showy, yellow, double flowers.

golden mean ***n-*** the middle point or way between extremes of behavior, feelings, etc.; moderation.

gold·en·rod (gōl′ dən rŏd′) ***n-*** tall, autumn-blooming plant with sprays of tiny yellow flowers.

Goldenrod

golden rule ***n-*** **1** rule of conduct urging people to treat others as they themselves would wish to be treated. **2** any basic rule of conduct: *The* golden rule *of boating is "Watch the sky."*

golden wedding ***n-*** the fiftieth anniversary of a wedding; golden anniversary.

gold-filled (gōld′ fĭld′) ***adj-*** made of metal covered with gold.

gold·finch (gōld′ fĭnch′) ***n-*** **1** American songbird with a yellow body and black crown, wings, and tail. **2** European songbird with a crimson face and wings marked with yellow.

gold·fish (gōld′ fĭsh′) ***n-*** [*pl.* **gold·fish**; **gold·fishes** (kinds of goldfish)] small, golden-yellow or orange fresh-water fish native to China, and raised and kept as an aquarium fish.

gold leaf ***n-*** gold beaten very thin, used in gilding.

gold rush ***n-*** sudden rush of people to a place where gold has just been discovered.

gold·smith (gōld′ smĭth′) ***n-*** person who makes or sells articles of gold.

gold standard ***n-*** use of gold as the standard of value for the money of a country. The basic unit of money is declared to be equal to and exchangeable for a certain quantity of gold.

golf (gȯlf, gŏlf) ***n-*** outdoor game in which a small, hard ball is driven with special clubs into a series of holes distributed over a course, the object being to get the ball into each hole in as few strokes as possible. ***vi-*** to play this game. ***vt-*** *Informal* to hit (a ball) with an underhand swing. **—*n-* golf′ er.**

golf club ***n-*** **1** one of a set of long-handled clubs having metal or wooden heads, and used in playing golf. **2** an organization of golfers; also, its golf course, buildings, etc.

golf course ***n-*** tract of ground used for playing golf, and having nine or eighteen holes, greens, natural or artificial obstacles, etc. Also **golf links.**

Gol·go·tha (gŏl′ gə thə) ***n-*** in the Bible, the place near Jerusalem where Jesus was crucified; Calvary.

Go·li·ath (gə lī′ əth) ***n-*** in the Bible, a giant Philistine who was slain by David with a sling.

gol·ly (gŏl′ ē) *Informal* ***interj-*** exclamation of surprise, annoyance, etc.

Go·mor·rah (gə mȯr′ ə, -mŏr′ ə) See *Sodom and Gomorrah.*

-gon *combining form* plane figure having (the indicated number of) angles and, therefore, sides: *hexa*gon (six angles and six sides). [from Greek **gōniā** meaning "angle."]

go·nad (gō′ năd′) ***n-*** male or female reproductive gland; testis or ovary.

gon·do·la (gŏn′ də lə) ***n-*** **1** narrow, sharp-pointed boat, with high, ornamental ends, rowed with a single oar by a standing boatman. It is used for transportation in Venice. **2** freight car with low sides and no top. **3** the cabin of a dirigible.

Gondola

gon·do·lier (gŏn′ də lêr′) ***n-*** man who rows a gondola.

gone (gȯn, gŏn) *p.p.* of **go.** ***adj-*** **1** used up; exhausted: *The cookies are all* gone. **2** departed or dead: *He is* gone *but not forgotten.* **3** faint; weak: *a* gone *feeling.*

be gone on *Informal* to be in love with. **far gone** much advanced; deeply involved: *He is* far gone *in love.*

gon·er (gȯn′ ər, gŏn′-) *Informal* ***n-*** person or thing that is dead, lost, beyond help, etc.

gong (gŏng, gȯng) ***n-*** flat or saucer-shaped metal disk which produces a ringing tone when struck.

gon·or·rhea (gŏn′ ə rē′ ə) ***n-*** contagious, inflammatory venereal disease of the mucous membranes of the genitourinary system. It is caused by a bacterium, the **gonococcus.** Also **gon′ or·rhoe′ a.**

goo (gōō) *Slang* ***n-*** anything sticky, such as glue.

goo·ber (gōō′ bər) *Informal* ***n-*** peanut.

fāte, făt, dâre, bärn; bē, bĕt, mêre; bīte, bĭt; nōte, hŏt, môre, dȯg; fŭn, fûr; tōō, bŏŏk; oil; out; tar; thin; then; hw for wh as in *wh*at; zh for s as in u*s*ual; ə for a, e, i, o, u, as in *a*go, lin*e*n, per*i*l, at*o*m, min*u*s

good (gŏŏd) ***adj-*** [**bet·ter** [bĕt′ ər), **best** (bĕst)] **1** above average in quality: *some* good *food*; *a* good *book.* **2** suited to the purpose; producing favorable results: *a* good *day for swimming*; *drugs* good *for a fever.* **3** well-behaved: *a* good *child.* **4** morally excellent: *He tried to live a* good *life.* **5** kind; friendly: *God is* good. **6** enjoyable; pleasant: *a* good *time.* **7** fresh; not spoiled: *two* good *eggs.* **8** proper; becoming: *to show* good *manners.* **9** thorough; complete: *a* good *scolding.* **10** fairly great; more than a little: *a* good *supply.* **11** able; skilled: *a* good *surgeon.* **12** valid; sound: *a* good *excuse.* **13** real; not counterfeit: *a* good *five-dollar bill.* ***n-*** **1** whatever is desirable, beneficial, etc.: *He did more harm than* good. **2** merit; worth: *There is some* good *in everyone.* **3** profit; advantage; benefit: *I tell you for your own* good. ***interj-*** exclamation of pleasure, satisfaction, etc.

a good thing a bargain. **as good as** almost; practically: *The job is* as good as *done.* **for good** or **for good and all** forever; finally; permanently: *He is leaving town* for good. **good and** *Informal* thoroughly: *He is* good and *mad. He'll leave when he's* good and *ready.* **make good 1** to make up for; repay or replace. **2** to succeed. **3** to keep (a promise). **no good** useless; worthless. **to the good** as a profit or advantage; extra: *a pound* to the good.

►In uneducated speech GOOD is often used for WELL. Instead of "*He swims* good," you should write. "*He swims* well." "*He is a* good *boy*" means that he isn't naughty. "*He is a* well *boy*" means that he is not sick.

good afternoon ***interj-*** a conventional expression used on meeting or parting during the afternoon.

good-by or **good·by** (gŏŏd′ bī′) ***interj-*** farewell. ***n-*** [*pl.* **good-bys** or **good·bys**] a farewell: *a fond good-by.* *as* ***modifier***: *a* good-by *kiss.* Also **good-bye.**

good day ***interj-*** a conventional expression used on meeting or parting during the day.

good evening ***interj-*** a conventional expression used on meeting or parting in the evening.

good-for-noth·ing (gŏŏd′ fər nŭth′ ĭng) ***adj-*** useless; worthless. ***n-*** idle, rascally, or inept person.

Good Friday ***n-*** the Friday before Easter Sunday, observed as the anniversary of the Crucifixion.

good-heart·ed (gŏŏd′ här′ təd) ***adj-*** kind; generous. ***—adv-*** **good′-heart′ ed·ly.** ***n-*** **good′-heart′ ed·ness.**

good humor ***n-*** cheerful or pleasant mood. ***—adj-*** **(good′-hu′ mored):** *a* good-humored *smile.* ***adv-*** **good′-hu′ mored·ly.**

good·ish (gŏŏd′ ĭsh) *chiefly Brit.* ***adj-*** fairly good.

good-look·ing (gŏŏd′ lŏŏk′ ĭng) ***adj-*** attractive; handsome in appearance.

good·ly (gŏŏd′ lē) ***adj-*** [**good·li·er, good·li·est**] **1** large; considerable; abundant: *a* goodly *amount of money.* **2** pleasing; attractive: *a* goodly *land.* ***—n-*** **good′ li·ness.**

good·man (gŏŏd′ mən) *Archaic* ***n-*** [*pl.* **good·men**] **1** head of a household; husband. **2** title of courtesy used for a man ranking below a gentleman.

good morning ***interj-*** conventional expression used on meeting or parting in the morning.

good nature ***n-*** pleasant or easygoing disposition. ***—adj-*** **good′ -na′ tured:** *his* good-natured *patience.* ***adv-*** **good′-na′ tured·ly.** ***n-*** **good′-na′ tured·ness**

good·ness (gŏŏd′ nəs) ***n-*** condition or quality of being good; excellence. ***interj-*** exclamation of surprise.

good night ***interj-*** expression used on parting at night. *as* ***modifier*** **(good-night):** *a* good-night *kiss.*

goods (gŏŏdz) ***n- pl.*** **1** things that are bought and sold; merchandise. **2** things owned; belongings, especially things that can be moved: *household* goods. **3** cloth.

get (or **have**) **the goods on (someone)** *Slang* to get or have proof that someone has done wrong.

goods and chattels ***n-*** in law, property other than land.

Good Samaritan ***n-*** in one of Christ's parables in the New Testament, the kindly rescuer of a victim of highway robbers; hence, any kindly, helpful person.

good-sized (gŏŏd′ sīzd′) ***adj-*** large; of considerable size.

good temper ***n-*** pleasant mood or disposition. ***—adj-*** **good′-tem′ pered.** ***adv-*** **good′-tem′ pered·ly.**

good turn ***n-*** friendly, helpful deed; favor.

good·wife (gŏŏd′ wīf′) *Archaic* ***n-*** [*pl.* **good·wives**] wife, or mistress of a household, used as a title of courtesy.

good will ***n-*** **1** kind and friendly feeling. **2** the extra value that a business has because of its good reputation.

[1]**good·y** (gŏŏd′ ē) *Informal* ***n-*** [*pl.* **good·ies**] something very good to eat, such as candy or cake. ***interj-*** exclamation of childlike pleasure. [from **good.**]

[2]**good·y** (gŏŏd′ ē) *Archaic* ***n-*** [*pl.* **good·ies**] old woman or housewife of humble station, used as a title of courtesy. [a contraction of **goodwife.**]

good·y-good·y (gŏŏd′ ē gŏŏd′ ē) *Informal* ***n-*** [*pl.* **good·y-good·ies**] person who is, or pretends to be, nore virtuous than others. ***adj-***: *his* goody-goody *attitude.*

goo·ey (gōō′ ē) *Slang* ***adj-*** [**goo·i·er, goo·i·est**] **1** sticky; gluey: *a* gooey *paint.* **2** chewy and rich: *a* gooey *candy.*

goof (gōōf) ***n-*** **1** *Informal* a blunder. **2** *Slang* stupid or silly person. ***vi-*** *Informal* to make a mistake; blunder.

goof off *Slang* **1** to pass the time doing nothing. **2** to neglect or avoid an assigned task or work.

goof·y (gōō′ fē) *Slang* ***adj-*** [**goof·i·er, goof·i·est**] stupid or silly; also, insane. ***—n-*** **goof′ i·ness.**

goon (gōōn) *Slang* ***n-*** **1** stupid person. **2** hoodlum, especially one hired to attack workers on strike.

goose (gōōs) ***n-*** [*pl.* **geese** (gēs)] **1** any of several water birds, larger than a duck, with webbed feet, stout bodies, and a long neck. See also *gander, gosling.* **2** the female of this bird, as distinguished from the male, or gander. **3** flesh of this bird, used as food. **4** silly person. ***—adj-*** **goose′ like′.**

Wild goose, 2-3 ft. long

cook (someone's) goose *Informal* to ruin someone's chances, plans, hopes, etc.

goose·berry (gōōs′ bĕr′ ē, gōōz′ bə rē) ***n-*** [*pl.* **goose·ber·ries**) **1** round, juicy berry, usually picked while it is still green. **2** the prickly bush it grows on.

goose egg *Informal* ***n-*** zero; score of zero in a game.

goose·flesh (gōōs′ flĕsh′) ***n-*** temporary roughness of the skin as the result of cold, fear, etc., caused by the erection of tiny hairs on the skin. Also **goose pimples.**

goose·neck (gōōs′ nĕk′) ***n-*** anything long and curved like a goose's neck, such as a movable support for a desk lamp. *as* ***modifier***: *a* gooseneck *lamp.*

goose-step (gōōs′ stĕp′) ***vi-*** [**goose·stepped, goose·step·ping**] to march using the goose step.

goose step ***n-*** parade step in which the leg is swung high with a straight, stiff knee.

G.O.P. the U.S. Republican Party. [short for Grand Old Party.]

go·pher (gō′ fər) ***n-*** **1** burrowing animal with large cheek pouches and long-clawed forefeet, such as the **pocket gopher.** **2** striped ground squirrel of western North America.

Pocket gopher, about 9 in. long

Gor·di·an knot (gȯr′dē ən, gôr′-) *n-* 1 a knot tied by Gordius, legendary king of Phrygia, and thought to be so intricate that it could only be untied by the future ruler of Asia. Alexander the Great cut it through with his sword. 2 any problem requiring bold measures to solve it.

[1]**gore** (gôr) *n-* thick, sticky blood coming from a cut or wound. [from Old English **gor,** "dung; clotted filth."]

[2]**gore** (gôr) *vt-* [**gored, gor·ing**] to pierce with a horn or tusk. [from Middle English **gore,** from Old English **gār** meaning "a spear," and related to [3]**gore.**]

[3]**gore** (gôr) *n-* wedge-shaped piece of cloth, such as those sewn together to make umbrellas or some skirts. [from Old English **gāra** meaning "triangular piece (of land); corner; point," and related to [2]**gore.**] *—adj-* **gored:** *a* gored *skirt.*

Gorge

gorge (gȯrj, gôrj) *n-* steep, narrow passage, especially between rocks; ravine. *vt-* [**gorged, gorg·ing**] to stuff with food: *The boy* gorged *himself with cake. vi-* to eat greedily. *—n-* **gorg′er.**

make (one's) gorge rise to cause (one) to feel disgusted.

gor·geous (gȯr′jəs, gôr′-) *adj-* rich or brilliant in color; splendid: *a* gorgeous *sunset. —adv-* **gor′geous·ly.** *—n-* **gor′ geous·ness.**

gor·get (gȯr′jət, gôr′-) *n-* piece of armor for the throat.

Gor·gon (gȯr′gən, gôr′-) *n-* 1 in Greek mythology, any one of three sisters, of whom Medusa is best known, whose appearance was so terrifying that any person who looked at her was turned to stone. 2 **gorgon** a hideous or terrifying woman.

go·ril·la (gə rĭl′ə) *n-* the largest of the manlike apes, native to Africa. *Hom-* guerrilla.

Gorilla about 6 ft. tall

gor·mand·ize (gȯr′mən dīz′, gôr′-) *vi-* [**gor·mand·ized, gor·mand·iz·ing**] to stuff oneself with food; eat greedily. *—n-* **gor′mand·iz′er.**

gorse (gȯrs, gôrs) *n-* spiny shrub bearing yellow flowers and found on wasteland in Europe; furze.

gor·y (gôr′ē) *adj-* [**gor·i·er, gor·i·est**] bloody. *—adv-* **gor′i·ly.** *n-* **gor′i·ness.**

gosh (gŏsh) *Informal interj-* exclamation of surprise, distress, etc.

gos·hawk (gŏs′hȯk′) *n-* any of several powerful, short-winged hawks. For picture, see *hawk.*

Go·shen (gō′shən) *n-* 1 region in Egypt allotted to the Israelites. 2 any place of peace and plenty.

gos·ling (gŏs′lĭng) *n-* young goose.

gos·pel (gŏs′pəl) *n-* 1 the teachings of Jesus and the Apostles. 2 **Gospel** (1) any of the first four books of the New Testament, by Matthew, Mark, Luke, and John. (2) part of one of these books read at a religious service. 3 anything believed as absolutely true.

gos·sa·mer (gŏs′ə mər) *n-* 1 fine, silky thread or web made by a spider. 2 any thin, light, delicate fabric: *a scarf of* gossamer. *adj-* (also **gos′sa·mer·y**) light and thin: *a* gossamer *cloud.*

gos·sip (gŏs′əp) *n-* 1 idle talk, often unfriendly, about people and their affairs. 2 person fond of such talk. *vi-: They were* gossiping *about me when I walked in. —n-* **gos′sip·er.** *adj-* **gos′sip·y.**

got (gŏt) *p.t. & p.p.* of **get.**

►Both GOT and GOTTEN are used as past participles. *I have already* got(ten) *the tickets.* Only GOT is used in questions asking "Do you have?": *Have you* got *a pen?*

Goth (gŏth) *n-* member of a Germanic people who invaded the Roman Empire in the third and fourth centuries A.D.

Goth·ic (gŏth′ĭk) *adj-* 1 of or relating to the Goths or to their language. 2 of or referring to a style of architecture prevalent in western Europe from 1200 to 1500 A.D., with pointed arches, ribbed vaulting, and the lavish use of ornamental carving. 3 **gothic** in literature, reflecting medieval influence; characterized by grotesqueness and violence. *n-* the extinct Germanic language of the Goths.

got·ten (gŏt′ən) *p.p.* of **get.**

►For usage note see GOT.

Gouge

gouge (gouj) *n-* 1 curved, hollow chisel for scooping out grooves or holes in wood. 2 groove or hole made with or as if with such a tool. *vt-* [**gouged, goug·ing**] 1 to cut or scoop with or as if with a grooved cutting tool. 2 *Slang* to charge too high a price; cheat. *—n-* **goug′er.**

gou·lash (gōō′läsh′) *n-* stew made of beef or veal and vegetables, and seasoned with paprika.

gourd (gôrd, gŏŏrd) *n-* 1 fruit of various plants related to the cucumber and the melon, which harden when dried, and are used as bowls, dippers, rattles, etc. 2 plant on which this fruit grows.

Gourds

gour·mand (gŏŏr mänd′, gŏŏr′mənd) *n-* 1 person who likes fine food and drink 2 one who is greedy about eating and drinking.

gour·met (gŏŏr mā′) *n-* person who likes and is expert in judging and choosing fine foods and drinks. as ***modifier:*** *a* gourmet *dinner.*

gout (gout) *n-* 1 disease that causes painful inflammation of the joints, especially of the big toe. 2 large blob.

gout·y (gou′tē) *adj-* [**gout·i·er, gout·i·est**] 1 diseased with gout. 2 of, relating to, or caused by gout.

gov. or **Gov.** 1 governor. 2 government.

gov·ern (gŭv′ərn) *vt-* 1 to manage, direct, or regulate the operation or workings of; control: *to* govern *a nation; to* govern *one's temper.* 2 to decide; determine; influence: *The financial report* governed *their decision.* 3 to require to be in a particular grammatical mood, case, etc.: *A subject* governs *the number of its verb. —adj-* **gov′ern·a·ble.**

gov·ern·ess (gŭv′ərnəs) *n-* woman who teaches someone else's children in their own home.

gov·ern·ment (gŭv′ərn mənt, -ər mənt) *n-* 1 control; direction; management: *the* government *of a city, state, or country.* 2 person or group of persons who govern. 3 system of governing: *a republican* government. 4 *in grammar, the influence of one word in determining the number or mood of another.* as ***modifier:*** *a* government *agency. —adj-* **gov′ern·men′tal** (gŭv′ərn mĕn′təl).

gov·er·nor (gŭv′ər nər) *n-* 1 person elected head of a State in the United States. 2 person appointed to be the head of government of a colony, province, etc. 3 *chiefly Brit.* person who directs or manages something: *the*

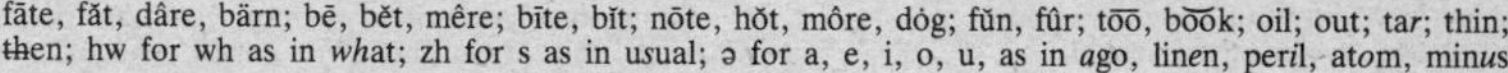

fāte, făt, dâre, bärn; bē, bĕt, mêre; bīte, bĭt; nōte, hŏt, môre, dȯg; fŭn, fûr; tōō, bŏŏk; oil; out; tar; thin; then; hw for wh as in *wh*at; zh for s as in u*s*ual; ə for a, e, i, o, u, as in *a*go, lin*e*n, per*i*l, at*o*m, min*u*s

governors *of a bank.* 4 device attached to an engine or machine to keep it going at an even speed.

governor general ***n-*** governor who has deputy governors under him.

gov·er·nor·ship (gŭv′ər nər shĭp′) ***n-*** position, duties, or term of office of a governor.

govt. or Govt. government.

gown (goun) ***n-*** **1** woman's dress, especially a long one. **2** loose outer garment worn by graduating students, judges, clergy, etc. **3** loose, informal garment.

Academic gown

gr. or **gr 1** gram or grams. **2** grade. **3** grain or grains. **4** gross.

Gr. 1 Greece. **2** Greek.

grab (grăb) ***vt-*** **[grabbed, grab·bing]** to seize or take suddenly; snatch: *Don't* grab *all the cookies for yourself.* ***n-*** a quick, snatching movement: *He made a* grab *for the ball.* ***—n-*** **grab′ber.**

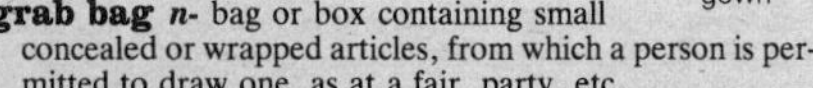

grab bag ***n-*** bag or box containing small concealed or wrapped articles, from which a person is permitted to draw one, as at a fair, party, etc.

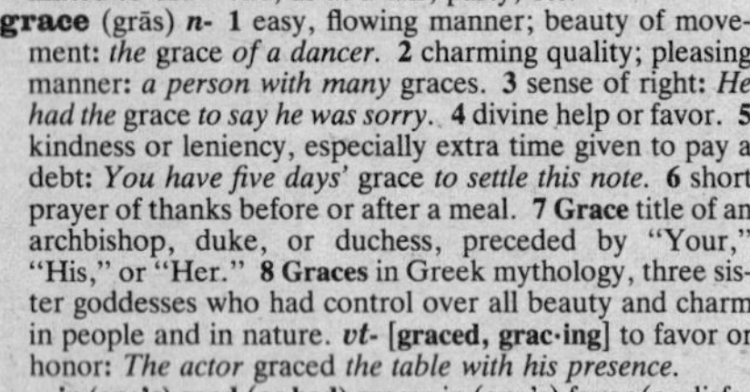

grace (grās) ***n-*** **1** easy, flowing manner; beauty of movement: *the* grace *of a dancer.* **2** charming quality; pleasing manner: *a person with many* graces. **3** sense of right: *He had the* grace *to say he was sorry.* **4** divine help or favor. **5** kindness or leniency, especially extra time given to pay a debt: *You have five days'* grace *to settle this note.* **6** short prayer of thanks before or after a meal. **7 Grace** title of an archbishop, duke, or duchess, preceded by "Your," "His," or "Her." **8 Graces** in Greek mythology, three sister goddesses who had control over all beauty and charm in people and in nature. ***vt-*** **[graced, grac·ing]** to favor or honor: *The actor* graced *the table with his presence.*

in (one's) good (or **bad**) **graces** in (one's) favor (or disfavor): *He is* in *her* good graces.

grace·ful (grās′fəl) ***adj-*** showing or having charm and elegance of movement, posture, form, or expression: *a* graceful *dancer; a* graceful *letter of thanks.* ***—adv-*** **grace′ful·ly.** ***n-*** **grace′ful·ness.**

grace·less (grās′ləs) ***adj-*** **1** without grace; clumsy. **2** not caring for what is right or proper. ***—adv-*** **grace′less·ly.** ***n-*** **grace′less·ness.**

grace note *Music* ***n-*** note added as an ornament.

gra·cious (grā′shəs) ***adj-*** full of grace and charm; pleasant and courteous: *A* gracious *host makes the guests feel at home.* **2** merciful or kindly: *Be* gracious, *O king!* ***—adv-*** **gra′cious·ly.** ***n-*** **gra′cious·ness.**

grack·le (grăk′əl) ***n-*** any of several long-tailed American blackbirds with glossy, iridescent feathers.

gra·da·tion (grā dā′shən, grə-) ***n-*** **1** a dividing or being divided into a continuous series of values, colors, etc.: *the* gradation *of sounds between a shout and a whisper.* **2** one of the parts, markings, etc., of such a series.

grade (grād) ***n-*** **1** class or year in school: *the fourth* grade. **2** letter or number showing how well one has done school work; mark. **3** one of a series of degrees or stages in rank, quality, advancement, etc.: *to sell meat of good* grade; *to reach the* grade *of general manager.* **4** rate or degree of slope, especially of a road: *a steep* grade. **5 the grades** elementary school. ***vt-*** **[grad·ed, grad·ing] 1** to give a mark to: *to* grade *papers.* **2** to sort into categories, levels, etc.: *These eggs have been* graded *by size.*

make the grade *Informal* to succeed.

grade crossing ***n-*** a place where a railroad crosses a highway or another railroad on the same level.

grad·er (grā′dər) ***n-*** **1** pupil in a certain grade at school: *a sixth* grader. **2** person or thing that grades.

grade school ***n-*** elementary school.

gra·di·ent (grā′dē ənt) ***n-*** **1** degree of slope or of change in level: *the* gradient *of the face of a cliff.* **2** sloping part of a road, railroad, etc.; grade; ramp. **3** rate of change of such variable factors as temperature, pressure, etc.; also, a diagram showing such change.

grad·u·al (grăj′o͞o əl) ***adj-*** proceeding little by little; moving or changing slowly or by degrees: a gradual *improvement;* a gradual *slope.* ***—adv-*** **grad′u·al·ly.** ***n-*** **grad′u·al·ness.**

grad·u·a·lism (grăj′o͞o ə lĭzm) ***n-*** the principle or practice of going by degrees toward a desired end. ***—n-*** **grad′u·al·ist.**

[1]**grad·u·ate** (grăj′o͞o āt′) ***vt-*** **[grad·u·at·ed, grad·u·at·ing] 1** to give a degree or diploma for finishing work at a school or college: *Our high school* graduated *200 students last year.* **2** to mark (a glass, tube, etc.) with lines for measuring. ***vi-*** **1** to receive a degree or diploma: *He* graduated *from college.* **2** to change or shift gradually: *stripes that* graduate *from light to dark.*

►The form "*He was* GRADUATED *from high school*" has become very stiff and old-fashioned. Write "*He* GRADUATED *from high school.*"

[2]**grad·u·ate** (grăj′o͞o ət) ***n-*** **1** person who has finished a course of study in a school and has received a diploma. **2** tube, flask, or other container marked with lines or numbers for measuring liquids or solids. as ***modifier:*** *a* graduate *school; to take* graduate *courses.*

grad·u·a·tion (grăj′o͞o ā′shən) ***n-*** **1** ceremony at which diplomas are given to students of a school; commencement exercises. **2** a mark showing spaces, degrees, amounts, etc., on an instrument or container used for measuring; also, a series of such marks. **3** gradual change or shift: *the* graduation *from light to dark.*

graf·fi·ti (grə fēt′ē) ***—n-*** *pl.* [*sing.* **graf·fi·to**] (takes singular verb) inscriptions or drawings on walls or other surfaces.

[1]**graft** (grăft) ***n-*** **1** twig or branch of one plant set into another of which it will become a living part. **2** plant or tree resulting from such an operation. **3** piece of skin, bone, etc., transplanted from one part of the body to another, or from one body to another. ***vt-*** (also **engraft, ingraft**) to transfer or implant (a living branch, piece of tissue, etc.) into another living organism: *to* graft *a branch of white rose into a red rose bush.* [from earlier **graff,** from Old French **graffe** meaning "a writing tool," from Latin and Greek **graphion,** "stylus," because a twig inserted in a tree trunk was thought to resemble a writing instrument held in the hand.] ***—n-*** **graft′er.**

Graft

[2]**graft** (grăft) ***n-*** the gaining of money or advantages thus through dishonest use of one's position; also, the money or advantages thus gained. ***vi-*** to use one's position to gain money or advantages dishonestly. [of uncertain origin.] ***—n-*** **graft′er.**

gra·ham (grā′əm) ***adj-*** made from coarsely ground whole-wheat: *a box of* graham *crackers;* graham *flour.*

Grail (grāl) ***n-*** in medieval legend, the cup used by Christ at the Last Supper. Also **Holy Grail.**

grain (grān) ***n-*** **1** seed of wheat, rice, oats, corn, and other cereal plants. **2** plant or plants bearing such seeds: *a field of* grain. **3** tiny, hard particle of sugar, salt, sand, etc. **4** a tiny bit: *There isn't a* grain *of truth in the story* **5** very small unit of weight. One pound is equal to 7,000 grains. **6** lines and patterns in wood or stone caused by the way the fibers or layers are arranged.

go against the grain to be contrary to one's nature.

grain alcohol ***n-*** alcohol.

grained (grănd) ***adj-*** **1** having grains or a granular appearance: *fine-*grained *sugar.* **2** painted in imitation of the grain in wood, stone, etc.

grain elevator ***n-*** tall building where grain is stored.

grain·y (grā' nē) ***adj-*** **[grain·i·er, grain·i·est]** consisting of or like grains; granular. ***—n-*** **grain' i·ness.**

gram (grăm) ***n-*** the basic unit of mass and weight in the metric system. One ounce is equal to about 28 grams. Also, *chiefly Brit.,* **gramme.** *Abbr.* gm.

-gram *combining form* something written, traced, or otherwise marked out: *crypto*gram (something written in secret code or cipher); *tele*gram (printed or written message sent electrically over wires). [from Greek **gramma,** "a thing written down," related to **graph.**]

gram atom ***n-*** amount of an element that has a weight in grams numerically equal to the atomic weight. Also **gram-atomic weight.**

gra·mer·cy (grə mûr' sē) *Archaic* ***interj-*** thank you.

gram·mar (grăm' ər) ***n-*** **1** branch of language study that deals with the forms of words, their relation to each other, and their arrangement in phrases, clauses, and sentences to convey meaning. **2** book or other work that describes these in an orderly way. **3** the way in which a person speaks or writes, as compared with accepted or standard usage: *His* grammar *was bad.*

gram·mar·i·an (grə mâr' ē ən) ***n-*** person who is an expert in or teacher of grammar.

grammar school ***n-*** **1** in the United States, an elementary school. **2** in England, a school preparing students for college.

gram·mat·i·cal (grə măt' ĭ kəl) ***adj-*** according to the rules of grammar. ***—adv-*** **gram·mat' i·cal·ly.**

gram molecule *Chemistry* ***n-*** amount of an element or compound that has a weight in grams numerically equal to the molecular weight. Also **gram-molecular weight.**

gram·o·phone (grăm' ə fōn') ***n-*** **1** *chiefly Brit.* phonograph. **2 Gramophone** *Trademark* a make of phonograph.

gram·pus (grăm' pəs) ***n-*** sea mammal related to the dolphins and the killer whale.

gran·a·ry (grăn' ə rē, grān'-) ***n-*** [*pl.* **gran·a·ries**] storehouse for grain; hence, region producing much grain.

grand (grănd) ***adj-*** **[grand·er, grand·est]** **1** great in size or general effect; impressive: *a* grand *spectacle*; *a* grand *palace.* **2** full of dignity, pride, or authority: *a* grand *lady*; grand *manners.* **3** including everything; complete: *the* grand *total.* **4** most important; main: *the* grand *ballroom.* **5** *Informal* very good or satisfying: *We had a* grand *time.* ***n-*** *Slang* a thousand dollars. ***—adv-*** **grand' ly.** ***n-*** **grand' ness.**

gran·dam (gran' dăm', -dəm) *Archaic* ***n-*** an old woman, especially a grandmother. Also **gran·dame.**

grand·aunt (grănd' ănt', -änt') ***n-*** aunt of one's father or mother; great-aunt.

grand·child (grăn' chīld') ***n-*** [*pl.* **grand·chil·dren**] child of one's son or daughter.

grand·dad (grăn' dăd') *Informal* ***n-*** grandfather.

grand·daugh·ter (grăn' dȯ' tər) ***n-*** daughter of one's son or daughter.

grand duke ***n-*** **1** in certain European countries, a sovereign duke who is next below a king in rank. **2** formerly, in Russia, a prince of the royal family. ***—n-*** *fem.* **grand duchess.**

gran·dee (grăn dē') ***n-*** Spanish or Portuguese nobleman of the highest rank; hence, any person of importance.

gran·deur (grăn' jər) ***n-*** greatness; splendor: *the* grandeur *of mountain scenery.*

grand·fa·ther (grăn' fä*th*' ər) ***n-*** father of one's father or mother.

grandfather clock ***n-*** large clock with a pendulum, contained in a tall case. Also **grandfather's clock.**

grand·fa·ther·ly (grăn' fä' thər lē) ***adj-*** like or typical of a grandfather: *to give* grandfatherly *advice.*

gran·dil·o·quent (grăn dĭl' ə kwənt) ***adj-*** using high-sounding or pompous language, means of expression, etc. ***—n-*** **gran·dil' o·quence.** ***adv-*** **gran·dil' o·quent·ly.**

gran·di·ose (grăn' dē ōs') ***adj-*** **1** imposing; impressive; magnificent. **2** trying to seem great or grand; pompous. ***—adv-*** **gran' di·ose' ly.** ***—n-*** **gran' di·os' i·ty** (grăn' dē ŏs' ə tē) or **gran' di·ose' ness.**

grand jury See *jury.*

grand·ma (grăn' mä', grä'-) *Informal* ***n-*** grandmother.

grand·moth·er (grăn' mŭ*th*' ər) ***n-*** mother of one's father or mother.

grand·moth·er·ly (grăn' mŭ*th*' ər lē) ***adj-*** like or typical of a grandmother: *a* grandmotherly *hug.*

grand·neph·ew (grăn' nef' yōō) ***n-*** son of one's nephew or niece.

grand·niece (grăn' nēs') ***n-*** daughter of one's nephew or niece.

grand opera ***n-*** opera in which all the words are set to music. See also *comic opera.*

grand·pa (grăm' pä', grăn'-) *Informal* ***n-*** grandfather.

grand·par·ent (grăn' pâr' ənt, -păr' ənt) ***n-*** father or mother of either of one's parents.

grand piano ***n-*** large piano with the strings extended horizontally. For picture, see *piano.*

grand·sire (grăn' sīər') *Archaic* ***n-*** one's grandfather or forefather.

grand slam ***n-*** **1** in bridge, the winning of all the tricks in a hand. **2** (also **grand slam home run**) in baseball, a home run hit with runners on all bases.

grand·son (grăn' sŭn') ***n-*** son of one's son or daughter.

grand·stand (grăn' stănd') ***n-*** rows of seats, often roofed, at an athletic field, race course, along a parade route, etc. ***vi-*** *Informal* to show off to attract attention.

grandstand play *Informal* ***n-*** showy action, especially in sports, intended to attract attention.

grand·un·cle (grănd' ŭng' kəl) ***n-*** uncle of one's father or mother; great-uncle.

grange (grānj) ***n-*** **1** *chiefly Brit.* a farm and its buildings. **2** (usually **Grange**) in the United States, an association of farmers, founded to promote their interests.

Grang·er ***n-*** **1** member of a Grange. **2 granger** in the early West, any farmer.

gran·ite (grăn' ĭt) ***n-*** hard, crystalline rock, usually gray, composed mainly of quartz, feldspar, and mica. Granite is used for buildings and monuments.

gran·ite·ware (grăn' ət wâr') ***n-*** ironware, such as pots or similar utensils, coated with hard enamel.

gran·ny or **gran·nie** (grăn' ē) ***n-*** [*pl.* **gran·nies**] *Informal* **1** grandmother. **2** an old woman.

grant (grănt) ***vt-*** **1** to give (something asked for); allow: *He* granted *us permission to leave early.* **2** to agree; admit as true: *I* grant *that you are right.* **3** to give or confer (property, a right or privilege, etc.) by a formal act. ***n-*** **1** something given, such as a right, sum of money, tract of land, etc. **2** act or procedure of formally giving or conferring something: *the king's* grant *of land*

---

fāte, făt, dâre, bärn; bē, bĕt, mêre; bīte, bĭt; nōte, hŏt, môre, dȯg; fŭn, fûr; tōō, bŏŏk; oil; out; ta*r*; thin; *th*en; hw for wh as in *wh*at; zh for s as in u*s*ual; ə for a, e, i, o, u, as in *a*go, lin*e*n, per*i*l, at*o*m, min*u*s

to the colonists. —*adj-* **grant′a·ble**: *a* grantable *request*; *a* grantable *assumption*. *n-* **grant′er.**

take for granted 1 to suppose to be true; assume: *He* took it for granted *that he was going with us.* 2 to be offhand or careless about something familiar or expected: *to* take *one's family* for granted.

grant·ee (grăn tē′) *n-* in law, the receiver of a grant.

grant·or (grăn′ tôr′) *n-* in law, a person who makes a grant.

gran·u·lar (grăn′ yə lər) *adj-* composed of or resembling grains or granules. —*n-* **gran′u·lar′i·ty** (grăn′ yə lăr′ ə tē, -lĕr′ ə tē): *the* granularity *of some candy.*

gran·u·late (grăn′ yə lāt′, -yōō lāt′) *vt-* **[gran·u·lat·ed, gran·u·lat·ing]** 1 to make into small grains: *Wind and rain* granulate *rock into sand.* 2 to roughen the surface of. *vi-* to form into granules: *The sugar* granulated.

gran·u·la·tion (grăn′ yə lā′ shən) *n-* 1 a granulating or being granulated. 2 roughened or granular surface.

gran·ule (grăn′ yōōl′) *n-* small grain or particle.

grape (grāp) *n-* 1 any of various edible, juicy berries that grow in clusters on a vine, and are used to make wine, raisins, etc. 2 the vine this fruit grows on. 3 grapeshot. *as* ***modifier***: *a jar of* grape *jam.* —*adj-* **grape′like′** or **grap′y [grap·i·er, grap·i·est].**

grape·fruit (grāp′ frōōt′) *n-* 1 round, pale-yellow citrus fruit, larger than an orange, and with a pleasantly sour taste. 2 the thorny broadleaf evergreen tree that bears this fruit. *as* ***modifier***: *a glass of* grapefruit *juice.*

grape·shot (grāp′ shŏt′) *n-* cluster of small iron balls that scatter when fired from a cannon.

grape sugar *n-* dextrose.

grape·vine (grāp′ vīn′) *n-* 1 vine that bears grapes. 2 *Informal* network of rumor and hearsay.

graph (grăf) *n-* 1 diagram that shows by lines, bars, etc., the relationship between two or more things. 2 *Mathematics* representation of a given equation as a set of points in relation to coordinates.

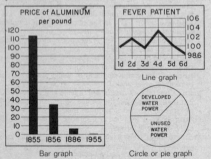

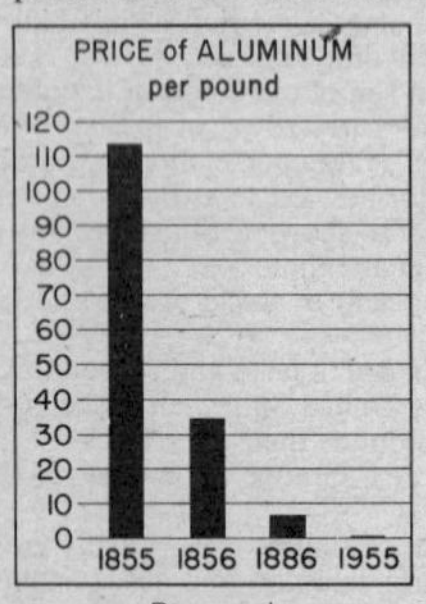

Bar graph

Line graph

Circle or pie graph

-graph *combining form* 1 something that writes or records: *tele*graph. 2 something written or otherwise recorded: *auto*graph; *photo*graph. [from Greek **-graphos** meaning "a writing down," from **graphein**, "to write."]

graph·ic (grăf′ ĭk) *adj-* 1 having to do with graphs, diagrams, or the use of charts and pictures instead of words. 2 vividly described, written, etc.: *This book gives a* graphic *description of a roundup.* 3 of or related to drawing, painting, etc. —*adv-* **graph′i·cal·ly.**

graphic arts *n-* arts or processes such as drawing, painting, engraving, or photography, in which objects, designs, etc., are shown on a flat surface; especially, some methods of making prints from blocks or plates.

graph·ite (grăf′ īt′) *n-* black, soft form of carbon used in lead pencils, as a lubricant, etc.

graph·ol·o·gy (grăf ŏl′ ə jē) *n-* the study of handwriting, especially as an indication of a person's character.

graph paper *n-* paper having a pattern of lines forming small squares and used for making graphs, diagrams, etc.

-graphy *combining form* 1 art or system of writing or recording: *steno*graphy; *photo*graphy. 2 a writing on a subject or in a field of learning: *bio*graphy. 3 descriptive science: *geo*graphy. [from Greek **-graphia** meaning "a writing down," from **graphein.**]

grap·nel (grăp′ nəl) *n-* 1 light anchor with several hooked arms, used for seizing or holding. 2 grappling iron.

Grapnel

grap·ple (grăp′ əl) *vi-* **[grap·pled, grap·pling]** to struggle; wrestle: *to* grapple *with an opponent*; *to* grapple *with a problem.* *vt-* to seize or hold onto with or as if with a hooked tool. *n-* grapnel. —*n-* **grap′pler.**

grappling iron *n-* 1 tool with several hooks for clutching something. 2 grapnel.

grasp (grăsp) *vt-* 1 to hold firmly in the hand: *to* grasp *a baseball bat.* 2 to hold in the mind; understand: *to* grasp *a problem.* *n-* 1 firm hold: *Get a* grasp *on the rope.* 2 understanding: *to have a firm* grasp *of subtraction.*

grasp at 1 to try to grab: *to* grasp at *a rope.* 2 to take or accept eagerly: *to* grasp at *any suggestion.*

grasp·ing (grăs′ pĭng) *adj-* greedy. —*adv-* **grasp′ing·ly.**

grass (grăs) *n-* 1 any of a large family of plants having jointed stems and narrow leaves called blades. Wheat, corn, bamboo, and sugar cane are all grasses. 2 lawn or turf. 3 green herbage eaten by grazing animals. —*adj-* **grass′less.** *adj-* **grass′like′.**

grass·hop·per (grăs′ hŏp′ ər) *n-* leaping insect with wings and long, powerful hind legs, related to the locust and katydid.

Grasshopper, about 1 1/4 in. long

grass·land (grăs′ lănd′) *n-* land, usually without trees, on which grass grows abundantly.

grass roots *n- pl.* voters who speak for themselves rather than through a political organization.

grass snake *n-* 1 any of various small, harmless European snakes that live in marshes. 2 garter snake.

grass widow *n-* woman who is divorced or otherwise separated from her husband. —*n- masc.* **grass widower.**

grass·y (grăs′ ē) *adj-* **[grass·i·er, grass·i·est]** 1 covered with grass. 2 of or like grass. —*n-* **grass′i·ness.**

[1]**grate** (grāt) *vt-* **[grat·ed, grat·ing]** 1 to make into bits or powder by rubbing on a rough surface: *to* grate *cheese.* 2 to irritate: *to* grate *someone's feelings.* *vi-* (often followed by "on," "upon," or "against") 1 to rub or scrape so as to produce a harsh, irritating sound: *The chalk* grated *on the blackboard.* 2 to cause an irritating effect, as if by scraping: *Her shrill voice* grates *on my nerves.* [from Old French **grater**, meaning "to scratch; scrape," from an earlier Germanic word.] ***Hom-*** great.

[2]**grate** (grāt) *n-* 1 frame of metal bars to hold fuel in a fireplace, or a frame that can be rocked to dislodge ashes in a stove. 2 frame of crossed or parallel bars, as at a window to prevent escape or entrance; a grating. *vt-* **[grat·ed, grat·ing]** to furnish with iron bars: *to* grate *a store window.* [from Late

Grate

Latin **grata** or **crāta** meaning a "grating," from Latin **crūtis** meaning "a hurdle; frame."] ***Hom-*** great.

grate·ful (grāt′ fəl) ***adj-*** **1** thankful; showing thanks: *I am* grateful *to you for all your help.* **2** agreeable; welcome: *a* grateful *relief from the heat.* **—*adv-*** **grate′ ful·ly.** ***n-*** **grate′ ful·ness.**

grat·er (grā′ tər) ***n-*** kitchen utensil with a rough surface, used to grate vegetables, cheese, etc.

grat·i·fi·ca·tion (grăt′ ə fə kā′ shən) ***n-*** **1** satisfaction; a being pleased: *The painter looked upon his completed work with* gratification. **2** source of satisfaction: *Your happiness is a great* gratification *to me.*

grat·i·fy (grăt′ ə fī′) ***vt-*** **[grat·i·fied, grat·i·fy·ing] 1** to please; give pleasure to: *He was* gratified *by his son's success.* **2** to give satisfaction to: *to* gratify *someone's thirst for knowledge.* **—*adv-*** **grat′ i·fy′ ing·ly.**

[1]**grat·ing** (grā′ tĭng) ***adj-*** **1** harsh in sound; scraping: *The rusty door opened with a* grating *sound.* **2** getting on one's nerves; irritating: *a* grating *habit.* [from [1]**grate.**] **—*adv-*** **grat′ ing·ly.**

[2]**grat·ing** (grā′ tĭng) ***n-*** framework of bars side by side or crossed, used to cover a window, sewer, etc.; grate. [from [2]**grate.**]

Grating

gra·tis (grăt′ əs, grā′ təs) ***adv-*** free of cost.

grat·i·tude (grăt′ ə to͞od′, -tyo͞od′) ***n-*** thankfulness for help, kindness, or good fortune.

gra·tu·i·tous (grə to͞o′ ə təs, grə tyo͞o′-) ***adj-*** **1** without cost: *to give* gratuitous *advice to a client.* **2** without cause; unwarranted: *a* gratuitous *insult.* **—*adv-*** **gra·tu′ i·tous·ly.** ***n-*** **gra·tu′ i·tous·ness.**

gra·tu·i·ty (grə to͞o′ ə tē, grə tyo͞o′-) ***n-*** [*pl.* **gra·tu·i·ties**] extra money given for services; tip.

Gr. Br. or **Gr. Brit.** Great Britain.

[1]**grave** (grāv) ***n-*** **1** hole in the ground in which a dead body is placed for burial. **2** any place of burial: *The sea was his* grave. **3** death. [from Old English **græf,** "a place dug out; a grave," and related to [3]**grave.**]

[2]**grave** (grāv) ***adj-*** **[grav·er, grav·est] 1** serious; solemn; thoughtful: *Everyone was* grave *at the inauguration.* **2** needing serious thought; important: *The President has* grave *responsibilities.* ***n-*** grave accent. [from French, from Latin **gravis** meaning "heavy."] **—*adv-*** **grave′ ly.** ***n-*** **grave′ ness.**

[3]**grave** (grāv) ***vt-*** **[graved, grav·en, grav·ing]** to shape, carve, or engrave with or as if with a chisel or other pointed tool. [from Old English **grafan,** and related to [1]**grave** and **engrave.**]

grave accent (grāv, gräv) ***n-*** accent mark [`] placed over certain vowels to indicate a particular sound of the vowel, as in the French "mère." In English it is sometimes used to show that the ending **-ed** is pronounced as a separate syllable, as in "agèd."

grave·dig·ger (grāv′ dĭg′ ər) ***n-*** person who digs graves for a living.

grav·el (grăv′ əl) ***n-*** mixture of small stones and pebbles. ***vt-*** to cover with this mixture: *to* gravel *a road.*

grav·el·ly (grăv′ ə lē) ***adj-*** **1** of, like, or full of gravel. **2** harsh and rough in sound: *a* gravelly *voice.*

graven image ***n-*** carved statue, especially an idol.

grav·er (grā′ vər) ***n-*** **1** any of various tools used by engravers. **2** engraver or sculptor.

grave·stone (grāv′ stōn′) ***n-*** tombstone.

grave·yard (grāv′ yärd′) ***n-*** cemetery.

grav·i·tate (grăv′ ə tāt′) ***vi-*** **[grav·i·tat·ed, grav·i·tat·ing] 1** to move, or tend to move, in response to a gravitational force. **2** to move as if drawn by such a force. ***vt-*** in mining, to cause to move by the force of gravity.

grav·i·ta·tion (grăv′ ə tā′ shən) ***n-*** **1** *Physics* the force of attraction between any two objects in the universe. The larger the product of the masses of the two objects, the greater the force, and the further apart the objects are, the weaker the force. **2** a gravitating. **—*adj-*** **grav′ i·ta′ tion·al.**

grav·i·ty (grăv′ ə tē) ***n-*** [*pl.* **grav·i·ties**] **1** the attractive force that draws all objects at or near the surface of the earth toward its center; also, the similar force of any other heavenly body. **2** seriousness; solemnity; importance: *The child quickly sensed the* gravity *of the occasion.*

gra·vy (grā′ vē) ***n-*** [*pl.* **gra·vies**] fat and juices that come from cooking meat, or a sauce made from these.

gravy train *Slang* ***n-*** easy job that is well paid.

gray (grā) ***n-*** any shade that is a mixture of black and white. ***adj-*** **[gray·er, gray·est] 1** of this shade: *a* gray *dress.* **2** having hair of this shade; hence, old: *He is* gray *before his time.* **3** dull; cheerless: *a* gray *day.* ***vt-***: *Time* grayed *the linens.* ***vi-***: *The linens* grayed. Also, *chiefly Brit.,* **grey. —*adv-*** **gray′ ly.** ***n-*** **gray′ ness.**

gray·beard (grā′ bêrd′) ***n-*** old man; also, one who has gained much wisdom and experience.

gray·ish (grā′ ĭsh) ***adj-*** somewhat gray.

gray·lag (grā′ lăg′) ***n-*** a common wild goose of the Old World.

gray·ling (grā′ lĭng) ***n-*** [*pl.* **gray·ling; gray·lings** (kinds of grayling)] fresh-water fish related to the trout.

gray matter ***n-*** a grayish tissue of the nervous system, composed of nerve cell bodies and certain nerve fibers. See also *white matter.*

[1]**graze** (grāz) ***vi-*** **[grazed, graz·ing]** to eat growing grass, as sheep and cattle do. ***vt-*** to put into a pasture or on a range to feed: *to* graze *cattle.* [from Old English **grasian,** from Old English **græs** meaning "grass."]

[2]**graze** (grāz) ***vt-*** **[grazed, graz·ing]** to touch, rub, or scrape lightly against: *A bullet* grazed *his arm.* ***n-*** a slight rub or scrape. [probably from [1]**graze,** in a possible early sense of "coming close to the grass."]

graz·ing (grā′ zĭng) ***n-*** the raising of sheep, cattle, or other domestic animals that require pasture: *a nomadic tribe that lives by* grazing. *as* ***modifier***: *ten acres of* grazing *land; a* grazing *culture.*

grease (grēs, grēz) ***n-*** **1** melted or softened animal fat. **2** any thick, oily substance, especially one used as a lubricant. ***vt-*** **[greased, greas·ing] 1** to cover with fat: *to* grease *a baking dish.* **2** to lubricate. ***Hom-*** Greece.

grease the hand (or **palm**) **of** *Informal* to bribe or tip.

grease·paint (grēs′ pānt′) ***n-*** any of the various creams or pastes of different colors, used as theatrical makeup.

grease·wood (grēs′ wo͝od′) ***n-*** any of several spiny shrubs that grow on the dry plains of western United States. The wood contains some oil and is sometimes used locally for fuel.

greas·y (grē′ sē, -zē) ***adj-*** **[greas·i·er, greas·i·est] 1** covered with or containing grease: *His hands were* greasy. *The food was* greasy. **2** feeling or looking like grease; smooth and slippery. **—*adv-*** **greas′ i·ly.** ***n-*** **greas′ i·ness.**

great (grāt) ***adj-*** **[great·er, great·est] 1** large in size; vast: *a* great *forest.* **2** large in number: *a* great *crowd.* **3** more than usual in degree, intensity, etc.: *a* great *clap of thunder; to be in* great *pain.* **4** long in time or extent: *a*

---

fāte, făt, dâre, bärn; bē, bĕt, mêre; bīte, bĭt; nōte, hŏt, môre, dóg; fŭn, fûr; to͞o, bo͝ok; oil; out; tar; thin; then; hw for wh as in *wh*at; zh for s as in u*s*ual; ə for a, e, i, o, u, as in *a*go, lin*e*n, per*i*l, at*o*m, min*u*s

great *distance*; *a* great *gap*. **5** of unusual skill, intelligence, etc.; distinguished: *a* great *leader*; *a* great *mind*. **6** important; significant: *a* great *event*. **7** *Informal* excellent; very good: *That's just* great! ***Hom-*** grate.

great-aunt (grāt′ ănt′, -änt′) ***n-*** grandaunt.

Great Bear ***n-*** Ursa Major.

great circle ***n-*** circle formed by the intersection of the earth's surface with an imaginary plane that passes through the center of the earth. The shortest distance between any two points on the earth lies on a great circle.

great city ***n-*** a city which, with its suburbs, has more than a million inhabitants.

great·coat (grāt′ kōt′) ***n-*** heavy overcoat.

Great Dane ***n-*** one of a breed of tall, powerful, short-haired dogs.

Great Divide ***n-*** Continental Divide.

great-grand·child (grāt′ grăn′ chīld′) ***n-*** [*pl.* **great-grand·chil·dren**] grandchild of one's son or daughter.

great-grand·daugh·ter (grāt′ grăn′ dò′ tər) ***n-*** daughter of one's grandchild.

great-grand·fa·ther (grāt′ grăn′ fä′ thər) ***n-*** father of one's grandfather or grandmother.

great-grand·moth·er (grāt′ grăn′ mŭ′ thər) ***n-*** mother of one's grandfather or grandmother.

great-grand·par·ent (grāt′ grănd′ pâr′ ənt, -păr′ ənt) ***n-*** father or mother of a grandparent.

great-grand·son (grāt′ grăn′ sŭn′) ***n-*** son of one's grandchild.

great·heart·ed (grāt′ här′ təd) ***adj-*** **1** generous; noble. **2** high-spirited; brave; fearless.

great horned owl ***n-*** large owl of North America, with pointed tufts of feathers that resemble ears or horns.

great·ly (grāt′ lē) ***adv-*** much; highly: *He was* greatly *pleased at the success of the project.*

great·ness (grāt′ nəs) ***n-*** **1** hugeness; vastness: *The* greatness *of the Grand Canyon is overwhelming.* **2** high distinction; lasting importance: *He achieved* greatness *as an artist.* **3** natural dignity or nobility: *He showed true* greatness *by his generosity to his enemies.*

great seal ***n-*** principal seal of a nation or other state, used on official documents.

Great Spirit ***n-*** the deity worshiped by many North American Indians.

great-un·cle (grāt′ ŭng′ kəl) ***n-*** granduncle.

Great War *Archaic* ***n-*** World War I.

greaves (grēvz) ***n-*** *pl.* armor to protect the legs from ankle to knee.

grebe (grēb) ***n-*** any of several water birds related to the loon, and having partially webbed feet. Some species have earlike tufts of feathers.

Grebe

Gre·cian (grē′ shən) ***adj-*** of, relating to, or resembling the art, architecture, facial characteristics, etc., of the ancient Greeks: *her* Grecian *profile*; *a* Grecian *temple.*

Gre·co-Ro·man (grē′ kō rō′ mən) ***adj-*** of or pertaining to both ancient Greece and Rome.

greed (grēd) ***n-*** intense, selfish craving; desire for more than one's share: *a miser's* greed *for money.*

greed·y (grē′ dē) ***adj-*** [**greed·i·er, greed·i·est**] **1** having or showing an extremely keen desire for food and drink: *That* greedy *fellow has eaten all the ice cream!* **2** wanting more than one's share; desiring or wanting too much. ***—adv-*** **greed′ i·ly.** ***n-*** **greed′ i·ness.**

Greek (grēk) ***adj-*** of or pertaining to Greece, its people, their language, or their culture. ***n-*** **1** the Indo-European language of ancient or modern Greece. **2** a native or inhabitant of Greece.

Greek cross ***n-*** plain cross whose four arms are of the same length. For picture, see *cross.*

Greek Orthodox Church ***n-*** the church of Greece, a self-governing branch of the Eastern Orthodox Church.

green (grēn) ***n-*** **1** the color of growing grass and leaves. Green is between blue and yellow on the spectrum. **2** a grassy area. **3** in golf, smooth grass around a hole. **4 greens** (1) leaves, wreaths, etc., used as decoration. (2) leafy vegetables used for food: *beet* greens; *dandelion* greens. ***adj-*** [**green·er, green·est**] **1** having the color of growing grass and leaves: *a* green *felt.* **2** unripe: *The fruit is still* green. **3** untrained; inexperienced: *He is still* green *at his job.* **4** not dried; unseasoned: *The lumber is still* green. **5** having a sickly color: *Her face turned* green, *and she fainted.* ***—n-*** **green′ ness.**

green with envy extremely envious.

green·back (grēn′ băk′) ***n-*** piece of paper money with its back printed in green ink.

green corn ***n-*** sweet corn.

green·er·y (grēn′ ər ē) ***n-*** [*pl.* **green·er·ies**] green plants or leaves.

green-eyed (grēn′ īd′) ***adj-*** **1** having green eyes. **2** jealous; envious.

green·gage (grēn′ gāj′) ***n-*** sweet, greenish-yellow plum.

green·gro·cer (grēn′ grō′ sər) *chiefly Brit.* ***n-*** person who sells fresh vegetables and fruit.

green·horn (grēn′ hòrn′, -hôrn′) ***n-*** **1** inexperienced person; newcomer. **2** person easily fooled; dupe.

green·house (grēn′ hous′) ***n-*** hothouse.

greenhouse effect ***n-*** process in which the atmosphere admits heat rays from the sun but partially blocks the passage of the heat rays of longer wavelength that are given off by the earth's surface.

green·ing (grē′ nĭng) ***n-*** type of green-skinned apple, usually used for cooking or baking.

green·ish (grē′ nĭsh) ***adj-*** somewhat green.

green light ***n-*** **1** green traffic light, which, when lit, gives persons or vehicles the right to go ahead. **2** *Informal* approval or permission to go ahead with any plan or activity.

green manure ***n-*** any crop, such as clover, beans, etc., plowed under to make the soil more fertile.

green·sward (grēn′ swòrd′) ***n-*** area densely covered with green grass.

green thumb ***n-*** talent for making plants grow.

Green·wich time (grĕn′ ĭch) ***n-*** the time at the prime meridian (0° longitude), which passes through Greenwich, England. Greenwich time is used as the basis of standard time around the world. Also **Greenwich mean time.**

green·wood (grēn′ wŏŏd′) ***n-*** forest or wood when the leaves are green.

greet (grēt) ***vt-*** **1** to address or welcome (a person, group, etc.) in a courteous, friendly manner: *He* greeted *his guests at the door.* **2** to receive; meet: *The crowd* greeted *the President with cheers.* **3** to appear before: *A wondrous sight* greeted *us in this strange land.* ***—n-*** **greet′ er.**

greet·ing (grē′ tĭng) ***n-*** word, message, gesture, etc., expressing courtesy, friendship, or welcome.

gre·gar·i·ous (grə gâr′ ē əs) ***adj-*** **1** fond of being with groups of people; seeking the company of others; sociable. **2** living in herds or flocks, as sheep do. ***—adv-*** **gre·gar′ i·ous·ly.** ***n-*** **gre·gar′ i·ous·ness.**

Gre·go·ri·an calendar (grĕ gôr′ ē ən) ***n-*** calendar introduced by Pope Gregory XIII in 1582. It corrected and superseded the Julian calendar and was based on the astronomical year. In 1752 it was adopted in England and the American colonies and is now used in most of the world.

Gregorian chant ***n-*** type of plainsong used in Roman Catholic Church services, introduced under Pope Gregory I (590-604). See *plainsong*.

grem·lin (grĕm′ lĭn) ***n-*** small, imaginary creature whose mischievous acts are said to cause mechanical and other troubles, especially in airplanes.

gre·nade (grə nād′) ***n-*** small bomb thrown by hand or fired from a rifle.

gren·a·dier (grĕn′ ə dêr′) ***n-*** **1** in former times, a foot soldier who threw grenades. **2** member of a special British army regiment called the **Grenadier Guards.**

gren·a·dine (grĕn′ ə dēn′) ***n-*** syrup made from pomegranates, used as a flavoring.

Greyhound, about 2 ft high at shoulder

grew (grōō) *p.t.* of **grow.**

grey (grā) *chiefly Brit.* gray.

grey·beard (grā′ bêrd′) graybeard.

grey·hound (grā′ hound′) ***n-*** a slender, sharp-faced, long-legged dog, famous for its grace and speed, used in racing and sometimes in hunting.

grid (grĭd) ***n-*** **1** a grating of parallel iron bars; gridiron. **2** in electronics, an electrode that controls the flow of electrons from cathode to anode in a vacuum tube.

grid·dle (grĭd′ əl) ***n-*** flat, heavy pan or similar utensil, used for cooking pancakes.

grid·dle·cake (grĭd′ əl kāk′) ***n-*** pancake baked on a griddle.

Gridiron

grid·i·ron (grĭd′ ī′ ərn) ***n-*** **1** rack of parallel bars on which to broil meat, etc. **2** something that looks like this, especially a football field.

grief (grēf) ***n-*** **1** deep sorrow; great sadness. **2** cause or source of sorrow.

come to grief to meet with disaster; fail.

griev·ance (grē′ vəns) ***n-*** real or imagined wrong considered as a source of annoyance or resentment; cause for complaint.

grieve (grēv) ***vi-*** **[grieved, griev′·ing]** to feel sorrow: *I* grieve *over your misfortune.* ***vt-*** to cause sorrow to; distress: *Your misfortune* grieves *me.*

griev·ous (grē′ vəs) ***adj-*** **1** causing physical or mental suffering; severe: *a* grievous *wrong.* **2** full of grief or anguish: *a* grievous *moan.* **3** outrageous; glaring: *a* grievous *mistake.* **—*adv-*** **griev′ ous·ly.** ***n-*** **griev′ ous·ness.**

grif·fin or **grif·fon** (grĭf′ ĭn) ***n-*** mythical monster with the head and wings of an eagle and the body of a lion. Also **gryphon.**

Griffin

grill (grĭl) ***n-*** **1** gridiron or similar device used for broiling food. **2** dish of food cooked over a gridiron: *We had a mixed* grill *for dinner.* **3** restaurant that specializes in food cooked this way. **4** grille. ***vt-*** **1** to cook on a gridiron. **2** to put to severe questioning: *to* grill *a prisoner.* ***Hom-*** grille. **—*n-*** **grill′ er.**

grille (grĭl) ***n-*** metal grating, used as a gate, decorative screen, protective barrier, etc. ***Hom-*** grill.

grill·work (grĭl′ wûrk′) ***n-*** metalwork for a grille.

grilse (grĭls) ***n-*** [*pl.* **grilse**] young salmon that has returned to fresh water from the sea for the first time.

grim (grĭm) ***adj-*** **[grim·mer, grim·mest]** **1** cruel; fierce: *a* grim *battle.* **2** unyielding: *a* grim *determination.* **3** forbidding; threatening: *a* grim *cliff.* **4** frightening; horrible: *a* grim *tale.* **—*adv-*** **grim′ ly.** ***n-*** **grim′ ness.**

gri·mace (grĭ mās′, grĭm′ əs) ***n-*** a twisting or distortion of the face especially to show pain, disgust, or disapproval: *to make a* grimace. ***vi-*** **[gri·maced, gri·mac·ing]**: *He* grimaced *when I said I'd be late.*

grime (grīm) ***n-*** dirt that is rubbed or ground into the skin or other surface.

grim·y (grī′ mē) ***adj-*** **[grim·i·er, grim·i·est]** covered with grime; dirty: *The plumber's hands were* grimy. **—*adv-*** **grim′ i·ly.** ***n-*** **grim′ i·ness.**

grin (grĭn) ***n-*** broad smile produced by drawing back the lips so as to show one's teeth. ***vi-*** **[grinned, grin·ning]**: *He didn't just smile; he* grinned.

grind (grīnd) ***vt-*** **[ground** (ground), **grind·ing]** **1** to crush into small pieces or a powder: *to* grind *wheat; to* grind *coffee beans.* **2** to make or produce by this process: *to* grind *flour.* **3** to grate; rub harshly: *to* grind *one's teeth.* **4** to smooth or sharpen by rubbing against a rough surface: *to* grind *an ax.* **5** to oppress; crush: *The tyrant* ground *the people under his heel.* **6** to operate by turning a crank: *to* grind *a pepper mill.* ***n-*** **1** something produced by crushing or powdering: *a coarse* grind *of coffee.* **2** *Informal* long, continuous, monotonous activity: *the daily* grind *at the office.* **3** *Informal* student who works hard, taking little time for recreation.

grind out to produce or make by long, strenuous effort: *to* grind out *a living.*

grind·er (grīn′ dər) ***n-*** **1** person who sharpens tools, utensils, etc. **2** machine for grinding.

grind·stone (grīnd′ stōn′) ***n-*** disk of fine-grained stone, turned by a crank or treadle, and used for sharpening tools.

have (or **keep**) **one's nose to the grindstone** to work long and hard at something.

Grindstone

grip (grĭp) ***vt-*** **[gripped, grip·ping]** **1** to grasp tightly: *If you* grip *the side of the cart, you won't fall out.* **2** to appeal strongly to; interest very much: *this story* grips *the imagination.* ***n-*** **1** tight grasp; strong hold or handclasp. **2** manner in which something is grasped: *the proper* grip *for a fencing foil.* **3** handle or other part of a tool, racket, golf club, firearm, etc., meant to be grasped. **4** valise; suitcase. ***Hom-*** grippe. **—*adj-*** **grip′ less.** ***n-*** **grip′ per.** ***adv-*** **grip′ ping·ly.**

come to grips **1** to fight; enter into combat: *The two armies finally* came to grips. **2** to confront; become involved (with): *We must* come to grips *with this problem.*

gripe (grīp) ***vt-*** **[griped, grip·ing]** **1** *Informal* to irritate; annoy: *Your antics* gripe *me.* **2** to cause pain in the bowels of (someone). ***vi-*** **1** *Informal* to complain. ***n-*** **1** *Informal* complaint. **2** **gripes** pain in the bowels.

grippe (grĭp) ***n-*** influenza. ***Hom-*** grip. **—*adj-*** **grip′ py:** *a* grippy *cold.*

gris·ly (grĭz′ lē) ***adj-*** **[gris·li·er, gris·li·est]** horrible; gruesome; ghastly. ***Hom-*** grizzly. **—*n-*** **gris′ li·ness.**

grist (grĭst) ***n-*** **1** grain to be ground. **2** flour or meal.

grist for (one's) mill something that can be turned to good use.

gris·tle (grĭs′ əl) ***n-*** cartilage.

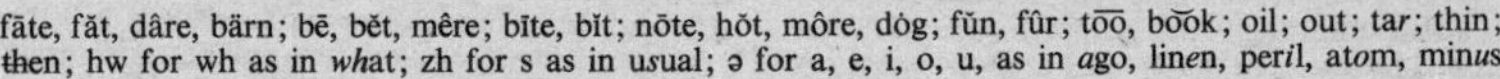

gris·tly (grĭs′ lē) ***adj-*** [**grist·li·er, grist·li·est**] partly or wholly made up of gristle: *A* gristly *bear makes tough chewing.*

grist·mill (grĭst′ mĭl′) ***n-*** mill for grinding grain.

grit (grĭt) ***n-* 1** small, hard particles of sand, stone, etc. **2** ability to endure hardships; firm spirit: *It took* grit *to start a farm in Alaska.* ***vt-*** [**grit·ted, grit·ting**] to press or grind together: *to* grit *one's teeth.*

grits (grĭts) ***n-*** *pl.* coarsely ground grain or meal; especially, coarsely ground hominy.

grit·ty (grĭt′ ē) ***adj-*** [**grit·ti·er, grit·ti·est**] **1** like, containing, or made of grit. **2** brave and determined; plucky. **—*n-* grit′ ti·ness.**

griz·zled (grĭz′ əld) ***adj-* 1** streaked with gray: *a* grizzled *beard.* **2** gray-haired: *a* grizzled *old man.*

griz·zly (grĭz′ lē) ***adj-*** [**griz·zli·er, griz·zli·est**] grayish; grizzled. ***n-*** [*pl.* **griz·zlies**] grizzly bear. ***Hom-*** grisly.

Grizzly bear, 8-10 ft. long

grizzly bear *n-* large bear of the mountains of northwestern North America, having brown, white-tipped hair.

groan (grōn) ***n-*** low, sad sound of pain, suffering, etc.; moan: *a* groan *of pain.* ***vi-*** to make this or a similar sound: *He* groaned *when he lost. The old house* groaned *in the storm.* ***Hom-*** grown. **—*n-* groan′ er.**

groat (grōt) ***n-*** English coin worth four pennies, used from the 14th to the 17th centuries.

groats (grōts) ***n-*** *pl.* hulled, coarsely crushed grain such as barley, buckwheat, etc.

gro·cer (grō′ sər) ***n-*** person who sells groceries.

gro·cer·y (grō′ sə rē) ***n-*** [*pl.* **gro·cer·ies**] **1** food store. **2 groceries** foods, such as flour, sugar, butter, etc.

grog (grŏg) ***n-*** any alcoholic liquor, especially rum or whiskey that has been mixed with water.

grog·gy (grŏg′ ē) ***adj-*** [**grog·gi·er, grog·gi·est**] *Informal* dazed or unsteady from lack of sleep, a severe blow, etc. **—*adv-* grog′ gi·ly. *n-* grog′ gi·ness.**

groin (groin) ***n-* 1** fold or hollow where the thigh is joined to the lower part of the abdomen. **2** in architecture, the curved ridge where two vaults intersect. **—*adj-* groined:** *a* groined *ceiling in a cathedral.*

Grommets

grom·met (grŏm′ ət) ***n-* 1** ring of metal or other durable material, used to reinforce a hole through which a rope or lacing is passed, as on a sail or tent. **2** ring of rope, used especially on a ship or boat.

groom (grōōm) ***n-* 1** man about to be married or one just married; bridegroom. **2** man or boy who takes care of horses. ***vt-* 1** to clean and feed (horses). **2** to make neat in appearance: *to* groom *one's hair carefully.* **3** *Informal* to prepare (someone) for a position or office: *to* groom *a boy for politics.*

grooms·man (grōōmz′ mən) ***n-*** [*pl.* **grooms·men**] man who attends the bridegroom at a wedding.

groove (grōōv) ***n-* 1** narrow track or channel; furrow; rut: *A window slides up and down in* grooves. *Running water made a* groove *in the rock.* **2** unchanging way of thinking or of doing things: *to get into a* groove. ***vt-*** [**grooved, groov·ing**] to form a narrow track or channel in: *to* groove *a stone.*

in the groove *Slang* **1** performed or done with great ease and skill. **2** up-to-date; aware.

grope (grōp) ***vi-*** [**groped, grop·ing**] to feel, reach, or search about uncertainly: *He* groped *for the doorknob. She* groped *for the right words.* ***vt-***: *to* grope *one's way.*

gros·beak (grōs′ bēk) ***n-*** any of several birds related to the finches, such as the **rose-breasted grosbeak,** the male of which is black and white, with a rose-colored breast.

gros·grain (grō′ grān′) ***n-*** fabric of heavily corded silk or rayon. *as **modifier**: a* grosgrain *hatband.*

gross (grōs) ***adj-* 1** including everything; total: *the* gross *profits of a business.* **2** thick; heavy: *the* gross *body of a hippopotamus.* **3** very bad and easily seen; glaring: *a* gross *mistake.* **4** coarse; vulgar: *Her* gross *manners offended her companions.* ***n-*** [*pl.* **gross**] 12 dozen; 144. ***vt-*** to earn as a total sum, without deductions: *He* grosses *$500,000 a year.* **—*adv-* gross′ ly. *n-* gross′ ness.**

gross national product *n-* total value of all the goods and services produced in a nation in a year.

gross ton *n-* in Great Britain, 2,240 pounds; long ton.

Gros Ventre (grō′ vä^n′ trə) ***n-*** [*pl.* **Gros Ventres,** also **Gros Ventre**] either of two American Indian tribes, the Atsina and the Hidatsa, especially the Atsina, a Plains tribe of Montana related to the Arapahoes.

grot (grŏt) *Archaic* ***n-*** grotto.

gro·tesque (grō tĕsk′) ***adj-*** distorted and odd; fantastic. **—*adv-* gro·tesque′ ly. *n-* gro·tesque′ ness.**

grot·to (grŏt′ ō) ***n-*** [*pl.* **grot·toes** or **grot·tos**] man-made or natural cave.

grouch (grouch) ***n-* 1** ill-tempered, complaining person. **2** fit of ill-temper. ***vi-*** to complain; grumble.

grouch·y (grou′ chē) ***adj-*** [**grouch·i·er, grouch·i·est**] sullen; irritable. **—*adv-* grouch′ i·ly. *n-* grouch′ i·ness.**

[1]**ground** (ground) ***n-* 1** surface of the earth; land; soil: *to touch* ground; *fertile* ground; *frozen* ground **2** land for a particular use: *hunting* grounds. **3** land beneath a body of water: *The ship hit* ground. **4** in electricity, a conductor or connection that leads an electric current into the earth. **5 grounds** (1) land around a building or house. (2) basis; reasons: *the* grounds *for his defense.* (3) sediment or dregs, especially of coffee, left over after brewing. ***vt-* 1** to establish; found: *to* ground *a government on democratic principles.* **2** to run (a ship) aground. **3** to teach (someone) the fundamentals of a subject: *to* ground *someone in algebra.* **4** to connect (an electrical conductor) with the earth. **5** to force (an airplane or pilot) to stay on land. ***vi-* 1** to fall to or reach the earth; land: *The astronauts have* grounded *safely.* **2** to run aground: *The ship* grounded. **3** in electricity, to become connected with or lead into the earth. **4** in baseball, to hit a grounder. [from Old English **grūnd.**]

above ground alive. **break ground 1** to start constructing a building. **2** to begin anything. **common ground** point of agreement or harmony. **cover ground 1** to cover a certain distance. **2** to cover a certain amount of work, ideas, etc. **cut the ground from under (someone's) feet** to destroy the major points of (someone's) argument or defense. **from the ground up** completely; thoroughly: *He has mastered his subject* from the ground up. **gain ground** to make progress; advance. **give ground** to move back; retreat. **hold** or **stand (one's) ground** to refuse to give up or yield; hold one's position. **lose ground** to be forced back; fail. **run into the ground 1** to criticize or blame severely. **2** to overdo. **shift (one's) ground** to change one's position, point of view, etc.

ground out in baseball, to be put out after hitting a grounder.

[2]**ground** (ground) *p.t. & p.p.* of **grind.**

ground cover *n-* any of various low-growing plants that form a dense mass close to the surface of the earth.

ground crew *n-* crew at an airport or military airbase responsible for the repair and maintenance of aircraft.

ground·er (groun′ dər) ***n-*** in baseball, a ball that is hit so that it bounces along the ground. Also **ground ball.**

ground floor ***n-*** floor of a building or house that is on or near the level of the ground.

get in on the ground floor *Informal* to join something at its start, when the chance for profit is best.

ground glass ***n-*** **1** glass with its surface roughened to make it translucent but not transparent. **2** glass that has been crushed to a very fine powder.

ground·hog (ground′hŏg′, -hȯg′) ***n-*** woodchuck. According to tradition, on **Groundhog Day,** February 2, the groundhog comes out of his hole; if he sees his shadow, winter will continue for six more weeks.

ground·less (ground′ləs) ***adj-*** without cause or reason; unjustified; baseless: *a* groundless *accusation.* **—*adv-*** **ground′ less·ly.** ***n-*** **ground′ less·ness.**

ground·ling (ground′lĭng) ***n-*** in Shakespeare's time, a person who paid for admission to the cheapest part of a theater, which was on the ground below stage level.

ground loop ***n-*** sharp swerving of an aircraft that goes out of control on the ground.

ground·nut (ground′nŭt′) *chiefly Brit.* ***n-*** peanut.

ground pine ***n-*** any of various trailing, evergreen club mosses, often used for Christmas decorations.

ground squirrel ***n-*** any of various small, burrowing animals related to the gophers and the chipmunks.

ground swell ***n-*** slow rise and fall of the ocean in deep long waves, caused by a distant storm or earthquake.

ground water ***n-*** water below the earth's surface, forming the source of wells, springs, etc.

ground wave ***n-*** radio wave that travels along the surface of the earth rather than through the sky.

ground wire ***n-*** wire connecting an electrical apparatus to the ground or to an object that is grounded.

ground·work (ground′ wûrk′) ***n-*** foundation; basis.

ground zero ***n-*** the ground exactly below or above the center of a nuclear explosion.

group (grōōp) ***n-*** **1** number of persons or things clustered together or considered as a whole: *a* group *of people on the street corner*; *the science* group. **2** *Biology* any number of plants or animals considered to have common qualities. **3** *Chemistry* two or more atoms, forming a part of a molecule, that react as a single unit: *the hydroxyl* group *(OH^-)* **4** *Mathematics* a set of elements that satisfy the conditions of closure, identity, inverse, and the associative law, when a given operation is performed. *as* ***modifier***: *a* group *activity.* ***vi-*** to gather together: *The people* grouped *slowly.* ***vt-*** to arrange or place together: *to* group *chairs in circles.*

group·er (grōō′ pər) ***n-*** [*pl.* **group·er**; **group·ers** (kinds of grouper)] any of various large fishes of warm seas, related to the sea basses.

group·ing (grōō′ pĭng) ***n-*** arrangement in a group: *the* grouping *of people in a photo.*

[1]**grouse** (grous) ***n-*** [*pl.* **grouse**] any of several wild birds related to and resembling the domestic chicken and the pheasant. [probably from Old French **griesche** or **greoches** meaning "gray."]

Ruffed grouse about 18 in. long

[2]**grouse** (grous) *Informal* ***vi-*** [**groused, grous·ing**] to complain; grouch. ***n-*** complaint. **—*n-*** **grous′ er.** [of uncertain origin.]

grove (grōv) ***n-*** group of trees growing together: *a* grove *of birches*; *an orange* grove; *a pine* grove.

grov·el (grŏv′ əl, grŭv′-) ***vi-*** **1** to lie flat or crawl on the ground, as if begging for mercy: *to* grovel *in the dust.* **2** to act in a cringing, servile manner. **—*n-*** **grov′ el·er.**

grow (grō) ***vi-*** [**grew** (grōō), **grown** (grōn), **grow·ing**] **1** of a living organism, to become bigger by natural development; increase in size by the multiplication of cells. **2** to spring up naturally; come from seed: *Daisies* grow *in meadows.* **3** to increase: *The volume of their shouts* grew *to a roar.* **4** to become: *The sky began to* grow *dark.* ***vt-*** **1** to plant and care for; cultivate: *He* grows *tomatoes in his garden.* **2** to develop: *to* grow *a mustache.*

grow on (or **upon**) to become gradually more attractive to: *This painting* grows on *me.*

grow out of **1** to be a result of: *Most prejudices* grow out of *ignorance.* **2** to get too big or mature for: *to* grow out of *one's clothes*; *to* grow out of *bad habits.*

grow up to become an adult.

grow·er (grō′ ər) ***n-*** **1** something that grows in a certain way: *That plant is a fast* grower. **2** person who cultivates a particular kind of plant: *a* grower *of tomatoes.*

growl (groul) ***n-*** low, threatening sound, such as that made by an angry dog, or a surly or irritated person. ***vi-***: *The bear* growled *at the crowd.* ***vt-***: *Jack* growled *an answer to his roommate.* **—*n-*** **growl′ er.**

grown (grōn) *p.p.* of **grow.** ***adj-*** fully developed; mature. ***Hom-*** groan.

grown·up (grōn′ ŭp′) *Informal* ***n-*** an adult; mature person.

grown-up (grōn′ ŭp′) ***adj-*** of or suitable for an adult: *He has* grown-up *manners.*

growth (grōth) ***n-*** **1** natural development: *He has reached his full* growth. *This plant has had a slow* growth. **2** increase in quantity, number, size, etc.: *There has been a large* growth *in population this past year.* **3** something growing or that has grown: *a day's* growth *of beard*; *a season's* growth *of wheat.* **4** abnormal lump on an animal or plant. *as* ***modifier***: *a* growth *rate.*

[1]**grub** (grŭb) ***vi-*** [**grubbed, grub·bing**] **1** to dig in the ground: *Pigs* grub *in the forest for food.* **2** to toil endlessly at a dreary job; drudge. ***vt-*** to dig up by the roots: *to* grub *a stump from the ground.* [from Middle English **grubben.**] **—*n-*** **grub′ ber.**

[2]**grub** (grŭb) ***n-*** **1** soft, wormlike larva of some insects. **2** *Informal* food, especially that taken on a camping trip. [from Middle English **grubbe,** from **grubben.**]

grub·by (grŭb′ ē) ***adj-*** [**grub·bi·er, grub·bi·est**] **1** dirty and sloppy; slovenly. **2** infested with insect larvae. **—*adv-*** **grub′ bi·ly.** ***n-*** **grub′ bi·ness.**

grub hoe ***n-*** heavy hoe for digging up roots.

grub·stake (grŭb′ stāk′) ***n-*** **1** food, supplies, etc., given to a mining prospector in return for a share of anything of value he may find. **2** money or support given to advance any undertaking. ***vt-*** [**grub·staked, grub·stak·ing**]: *to* grubstake *a prospector.* **—*n-*** **grub′ stak′ er.**

grudge (grŭj) ***n-*** feeling of envy, spite, or ill will: *He has a* grudge *against me because I voted against his plan.* ***vt-*** [**grudged, grudg·ing**] to begrudge: *to* grudge *someone his wealth.* **—*adv-*** **grudg′ ing·ly**: *to share* grudgingly.

gru·el (grōō′ əl) ***n-*** thin porridge, made by boiling cereal in milk or water.

gru·el·ing (grōō′ lĭng) ***adj-*** very tiring; exhausting.

grue·some (grōō′ səm) ***adj-*** horrible and repulsive; grisly. **—*adv-*** **grue′ some·ly.** ***n-*** **grue′ some·ness.**

gruff (grŭf) ***adj-*** **1** harsh; hoarse: *a* gruff *voice.* **2** rough; rude; surly: *He had a good heart but a* gruff *manner.* **—*adv-*** **gruff′ ly.** ***n-*** **gruff′ ness.**

grum·ble (grŭm′ bəl) *vi-* [**grum·bled, grum·bling**] to mutter, murmur, or growl discontentedly: *He was always* grumbling *about the weather.* *vt-*: *He* grumbled *a reply.* *n-*: *a* grumble *of discontent.* —*n-* **grum′ bler.**

grump·y (grŭm′ pē) *adj-* [**grump·i·er, grump·i·est**] irritable; ill-tempered; grouchy: *a* grumpy *old man.* —*adv-* **grump′ i·ly.** *n-* **grump′ i·ness.**

Grun·dy (grŭn′ dē), **Mrs.** *n-* any prudish person.

grunt (grŭnt) *n-* **1** gruff, deep sound made by hogs, or a similar sound made by persons who are annoyed, working hard, etc. **2** any of various edible marine fishes that make a low, gruff sound. *vi-*: *He* grunted *with each tug on the rope.* *vt-*: *He was so tired he could only* grunt *his answers.* —*n-* **grunt′ er.**

gry·phon (grĭf′ ən) griffin.

Gt. Br. or **Gt. Brit.** Great Britain.

gua·na·co (gwə nä′ kō) *n-* [*pl.* **gua·na·cos**] South American animal related to and larger than the llama.

gua·no (gwä′ nō) *n-* [*pl.* **gua·nos**] hardened waste matter of sea birds, especially that found on islands near Peru.

Gua·ra·ni (gwär′ ə nē′) *n-* [*pl.* **Gua·ra·nis** or **Gua·ra·ni**] **1** one of several Indian tribes of Bolivia, Brazil, and Paraguay; also, a member of one of these tribes. **2** the language of these people, one of the two official languages of Paraguay. **3 guarani** the basic unit of money of Paraguay. —*adj-*: *a* Guarani *custom.*

guar·an·tee (găr′ ən tē′) *n-* **1** pledge or assurance that something is what it is said to be, or will give a certain amount of service; warranty: *a money-back* guarantee. **2** anything that assures some outcome or condition: *Wealth is not a* guarantee *of happiness.* **3** guaranty. **4** person who receives a guaranty. **5** person who makes himself responsible for another; guarantor. *vt-* [**guar·an·teed, guar·an·tee·ing**] **1** to vouch for: *to* guarantee *a watch.* **2** to assure: *to* guarantee *success.* **3** in law, to be legally responsible for: *to* guarantee *a friend's debt.*

guar·an·tor (găr′ ən tȯr′, -tôr′) *n-* person who acts as surety for another.

guar·an·ty (găr′ ən tē′) *n-* [*pl.* **guar·an·ties**] **1** agreement or promise to answer for the payment of another's debt or obligation. **2** property pledged for the performance of an agreement. *vt-* [**guar·an·tied, guar·an·ty·ing**] **1** to vouch for; warrant. **2** to be responsible for.

guard (gärd) *vt-* **1** to protect or defend from harm, theft, etc.: *to* guard *a city*; *to* guard *a collection of gems.* **2** to watch over: *to* guard *a prisoner*; *to* guard *one's speech.* **3** in some games, to protect (a card or piece); also, to prevent (an opponent) from scoring. *n-* **1** protection; defense: *Vaccination is our best* guard *against smallpox.* **2** man or body of men employed to control or protect: *a prison* guard; *the President's* guard. **3** a device for protection: *mud*guard; *shoulder* guard. **4** in fencing, a position of defense. **5** either of two football players on each side of the center of a forward line. **6** one of the defensive players in basketball.

keep guard to watch over. **off guard** unprepared to defend oneself or respond: *The teacher caught him* off guard *with a question.* **on guard** wary; in position to defend oneself. **on (one's) guard** prepared against danger or surprise: *Be* on your guard *against hitchhikers.* **stand guard** to act as a sentry.

guard against to prevent by being careful and watchful: *to* guard against *colds*; *to* guard against *mistakes.*

guard cell *n-* one of the two crescent-shaped cells that control the flow of gases into and out of the stomata of plants by regulating the size of the opening.

guard·ed (gär′ dəd) *adj-* **1** protected: *a heavily* guarded *fort.* **2** careful; cautious: *a* guarded *answer.* —*adv-* **guard′ ed·ly.** *n-* **guard′ ed·ness.**

guard hair *n-* on some animals, one of the coarse, longer hairs protecting the soft coat of fur beneath.

guard·house (gärd′ hous′) *n-* **1** military jail. **2** house occupied by police or soldiers acting as guards.

guard·i·an (gär′ dē ən) *n-* **1** person or thing that protects: *The Bill of Rights is the* guardian *of our liberties.* **2** person who, by law, has the care of another person or his property or both.

guard·i·an·ship (gär′ dē ən shĭp′) *n-* position, duties, and rights of a guardian.

guard·rail (gärd′ rāl′) *n-* **1** handrail or bar placed alongside some dangerous area or valuable object to prevent accidents or damage. **2** safety rail or beam laid parallel to railway tracks to help keep the wheels in position at dangerous points.

guard·room (gärd′ ro͞om′) *n-* **1** the room occupied by a military guard on duty. **2** place of temporary imprisonment for soldiers.

gua·va (gwä′ və) *n-* tree or shrub of tropical America, yielding a pear-shaped fruit from which various preserves are made; also, the fruit.

gua·yu·le (gwī o͞o′ lē) *n-* shrub of Mexico and southwestern United States that yields a rubber; also, the rubber produced from this plant.

gu·ber·na·to·ri·al (go͞o′ bər nə tôr′ ē əl) *adj-* of or relating to a governor or to his office: *a* gubernatorial *election.*

gudg·eon (gŭj′ ən) *n-* [*pl.* **gudg·eon**; **gudg·eons** (kinds of gudgeon)] **1** any of several small European fishes related to the carp and used for bait. **2** any of various other fishes, including some minnows.

guer·don (gûr′ dən) *n-* a reward for courage.

guer·ril·la or **gue·ril·la** (gə rĭl′ ə) *n-* person who carries on irregular warfare; especially, one of an independent band engaged in harassing an enemy in wartime; partisan. *as* ***modifier***: *in* guerrilla *warfare.* ***Hom-*** gorilla.

guess (gĕs) *vt-* **1** to form an opinion of without certain knowledge: *Historians* guess *that the Gypsies originated in India.* **2** to estimate; surmise: *to* guess *one's weight.* **3** to solve correctly by surmising: *He* guessed *it!* **4** to think; suppose: *I* guess *we should hurry.* *vi-*: *He doesn't know*; *he is only* guessing. *n-*: *His* guess *about the weather was wrong.* —*n-* **guess′ er.**

guess·work (gĕs′ wûrk′) *n-* result obtained by guessing; conjecture.

guest (gĕst) *n-* **1** person who is entertained by a host. **2** person who stays temporarily at a hotel, inn, etc.

guff (gŭf) *Slang* *n-* stuff and nonsense; baloney.

guf·faw (gə fȯ′) *n-* coarse or loud burst of laughter. *vi-*: *He* guffawed *over the crude joke.*

guid·ance (gī′ dəns) *n-* **1** a guiding: *the policeman's* guidance *of traffic.* **2** advice given to a person about what studies or job he should choose, or about personal problems; also, the profession and study of such counseling. **3** the controlling of a guided missile's route. *as* ***modifier***: *a* guidance *counselor*; *a* guidance *system.*

guide (gīd) *n-* **1** person who shows the way or directs; especially, a person hired or paid to conduct hunting or fishing trips, visits through museums, etc. **2** thing that shows the way: *A compass was our* guide. **3** device that regulates or directs the position or motion of something: *a paper* guide *on a typewriter.* **4** person or thing taken as a model. **5** a guidebook. *vt-* [**guid·ed, guid·ing**] **1** to lead; steer: *Tugs* guided *the ship into the dock.* *The President* guided *us to peace.* **2** to direct; instruct: *The book* guided *us in the repair of the car.*

guide·book (gīd′ bo͝ok′) *n-* book of directions, information, etc., about a museum, travel, etc.

guided missile ***n-*** missile whose course may be changed during flight either by radio, by a preset program, or by its response to surrounding forces.

guide·line (gīd′ līn) ***n-*** [usually *pl.* **guide·lines**] outline or standard for future policy or conduct: guidelines *for a project.*

guide·post (gīd′ pōst′) ***n-*** post or marker to direct travelers.

guide word ***n-*** in a reference work, one of the two words at the top of a page, over the columns of text, which show the first and last entries on that page.

gui·don (gī′ dən) ***n-*** **1** small standard or flag for a single company of troops. **2** the person who carries it.

guild (gĭld) ***n-*** **1** in the Middle Ages, an organization of men in the same trade or craft whose aim was to keep their standards high and protect their interests. **2** organization of people for a common purpose. ***Hom-*** gild.

guild·er (gĭl′ dər) ***n-*** Dutch silver coin; also, the monetary unit of the Netherlands; gulden.

guild·hall (gĭld′ hȯl′) ***n-*** meeting place of a guild.

guile (gīl) ***n-*** sly trickery; deceit; cunning: *He used* guile *to get his way.* ***—adj-*** **guile′ful.** ***adv-*** **guile′ful·ly.** ***n-*** **guile′ful·ness.**

guile·less (gīl′ ləs) ***adj-*** free from guile; innocent; frank; open. ***—adv-*** **guile′less·ly.** ***n-*** **guile′less·ness.**

guil·le·mot (gĭl′ ə mŏt′) ***n-*** any of several narrow-billed auks found in northern seas.

guil·lo·tine (gĭl′ ə tēn′) ***n-*** apparatus for beheading a person by means of a heavy, slanted knife dropping between two upright guides. ***vt-*** [**guil·lo·tined, guil·lo·tin·ing**] to behead with this instrument.

Guillotine

guilt (gĭlt) ***n-*** **1** the fact of having done something wrong, especially of having broken a law: *to establish the* guilt *of the accused.* **2** the feeling of having done wrong, whether real or imaginary. ***Hom-*** gilt. ***—adj-*** **guilt′less.** ***adv-*** **guilt′less·ly.**

guilt·y (gĭl′ tē) ***adj-*** [**guilt·i·er, guilt·i·est**] **1** deserving of blame: *Who was* guilty *of singing off key?* **2** responsible for a crime; convicted: *The jury found him* guilty *of the crime.* **3** showing guilt; having to do with guilt: *a* guilty *look; a* guilty *conscience.* ***—adv-*** **guilt′i·ly.** ***n-*** **guilt′i·ness.**

guin·ea (gĭn′ ē) ***n-*** a former British monetary unit equal to 21 shillings.

guinea fowl ***n-*** **1** gray-and-white speckled domestic fowl having a small featherless head with a bright-red comb. **2** flesh of this fowl, as food. Also **guinea hen.**

Guinea fowl, about 18 in. long

guinea pig ***n-*** small, plump, gentle animal of the rat family, with short legs and short ears. The guinea pig is kept for a pet.

Guinea pig about 9 in. long

Guin·e·vere (gwĭn′ ə vêr′, -vər) ***n-*** in Arthurian legend, wife of King Arthur. She was in love with Lancelot.

guise (gīz) ***n-*** **1** external appearance; likeness: *Henry arrived in the* guise *of a sailor.* **2** cloak; pretense: *to cheat a person under the* guise *of friendship.*

gui·tar (gĭ tär′) ***n-*** musical instrument having six strings and a hollow wooden body. It is played by plucking the strings with the fingers or a pick.

Guitar

gulch (gŭlch) ***n-*** ravine; gorge.

gul·den (gōōl′ dən) ***n-*** guilder.

gulf (gŭlf) ***n-*** **1** large area or arm of a sea or ocean, partly enclosed by land. **2** deep hollow in the earth; abyss. **3** wide separation: *The quarrel left a* gulf *between them.*

gulf·weed (gŭlf′ wēd′) ***n-*** sargasso.

[1]gull (gŭl) ***n-*** large, light-colored, web-footed sea bird of graceful, often hovering, flight, found everywhere near coasts. It is a valuable scavenger and is protected by law in many places. [perhaps from Welsh **gwylan** or Cornish **gullan.**]

Herring gull, about 2 ft. long

[2]gull (gŭl) ***vt-*** to cheat; deceive; outwit. ***n-*** person easily cheated or deceived; dupe. [of uncertain origin.]

gul·let (gŭl′ ət) ***n-*** **1** the tube by which food travels from the mouth to the stomach; esophagus. **2** *Informal* the throat.

gul·li·ble (gŭl′ ə bəl) ***adj-*** easily fooled or deceived. ***—n-*** **gul′li·bil′i·ty.** ***adv-*** **gul′li·bly.**

gul·ly (gŭl′ ē) ***n-*** [*pl.* **gul·lies**] ditch or channel worn by water. ***vt-*** [**gul·lied, gul·ly·ing**]: *Heavy rains* gullied *the hillside.*

gulp (gŭlp) ***vt-*** **1** to swallow quickly or greedily: *The horse* gulped *the water.* **2** to hold back as if by swallowing; stifle: *to* gulp *back a sob.* ***vi-*** to catch one's breath as if swallowing: *He* gulped *with relief.* ***n-*** big swallow: *to empty a glass in one* gulp. ***—n-*** **gulp′er.**

[1]gum (gŭm) ***n-*** **1** sticky substance obtained from trees. **2** this or a similar substance prepared for some industrial use, as in drugs. **3** chewing gum. **4** natural rubber. **5** gum tree. **6 gums** rubber overshoes. ***vt-*** [**gummed, gum·ming**] to smear or stick with mucilage or glue. ***vi-*** to become stiff or sticky. [from Old French **gomme,** from Latin **gummi,** from Greek **kommi.**]

[2]gum (gŭm) ***n-*** firm, pink flesh around the roots of the teeth. [from Old English **gōma** meaning "palate."]

gum ammoniac ***n-*** ammoniac.

gum ar·a·bic (ăr′ ə bĭk′) ***n-*** gum obtained from certain species of acacia, and used in the manufacture of mucilage, ink, candies, medicine, etc.

gum·bo (gŭm′ bō) ***n-*** [*pl.* **gum·bos**] **1** the okra plant or its edible pods. **2** thick soup containing okra. **3** in western United States, a kind of fine soil which becomes very sticky when wet.

gum·boil (gŭm′ boil′) ***n-*** small abscess on the gums.

gum·drop (gŭm′ drŏp′) ***n-*** jellylike candy in a molded shape, made with flavored gelatin or gum arabic, and coated with sugar crystals.

gum·my (gŭm′ ē) ***adj-*** **[gum·mi·er, gum·mi·est]** like gum; covered or filled with a sticky substance; sticky. **—*n-* gum′ mi·ness.**

gump·tion (gŭmp′ shən) ***n-*** energy; initiative; spirit: *He hasn't the* gumption *to find a job.*

gum resin ***n-*** dried mixture of gum and resin, from the sap of various trees and plants.

gum·shoe (gŭm′ shōō′) ***n-*** **1** a rubber overshoe. **2** a rubber-soled shoe. **3** *Slang* detective. ***vi-*** *Slang* **[gum·shoed, gum·shoe·ing]** to go silently or sneakily.

gum trag·a·canth (trăg′ ə kănth) ***n-*** a gum obtained from certain Asiatic or European trees which is used as a stiffening agent in textiles and as an emulsifier in the manufacture of medicines, food, etc. It is often used as a substitute for gum arabic. Also **tragacanth.**

gum tree ***n-*** any of various trees which exude gum.

gum·wood (gŭm′ wŏŏd′) ***n-*** wood of a gum tree.

gun (gŭn) ***n-*** **1** weapon that shoots a projectile by the force of exploding gunpowder or compressed air; firearm. Rifles, pistols, and cannons are guns. **2** tool that shoots something out: *a grease* gun; *a spray* gun. **3** a shooting of a gun as a salute or signal: *a salute of twenty-one* guns; *a starting* gun. **4** *Slang* a throttle. ***vi-*** **[gunned, gun·ning]** to shoot or hunt with a firearm. ***vt-*** **1** to shoot (a person). **2** to open up the throttle of.

give (something) the gun *Slang* to speed something up. **go great guns** *Slang* to go along or perform at a top level of speed and efficiency. **spike (someone's) guns** to spoil another's plans. **stick to one's guns** to be firm; not yield or retreat.

gun down to shoot and destroy.

gun for 1 to pursue in order to harm or kill. **2** to aim for (a favor, position, etc.); seek for.

gun·boat (gŭn′ bōt′) ***n-*** small warship for use on rivers and coastal waters.

gun carriage ***n-*** the structure, often with wheels, upon which a cannon is mounted.

gun·cot·ton (gŭn′ kŏt′ ən) nitrocellulose.

gun·fire (gŭn′ fīr′) ***n-*** the shooting off of guns; firing.

gun·lock (gŭn′ lŏk′) ***n-*** mechanism of a gun that controls the hammer or firing pin to fire the charge, especially in old types of guns such as the flintlock.

gun·man (gŭn′ mən) ***n-*** [*pl.* **gun·men]** man armed with a gun, usually for criminal purposes.

gun metal ***n-*** **1** variety of bronze, formerly used in making cannon, etc. **2** metal alloy treated to look like this bronze. **3** the color of this bronze, dark gray with a blue or purple tinge. ***adj-*** **(gun-metal):** *a* gun-metal *plate*; *a* gun-metal *sky.*

gun moll *Slang* ***n-*** armed female gangster.

gun·nel (gŭn′ əl) gunwale.

gun·ner (gŭn′ ər) ***n-*** **1** man whose duty is firing a gun, especially on a military ship or airplane. **2** in the Navy and Marine Corps, a warrant officer in charge of guns and gunnery supplies. **3** person who hunts with a gun.

gun·ner·y (gŭn′ ə rē) ***n-*** science of artillery; the knowledge and use of guns.

gun·ning (gŭn′ ĭng) ***n-*** the hunting of game, especially small game, with a gun.

gun·ny (gŭn′ ē) ***n-*** [*pl.* **gun·nies]** **1** strong, coarse material made of jute or hemp fiber, used in baling. **2** (also **gunny sack**) bag or sack made of this material: *The* gunny *of flour split open.*

gun pit ***n-*** an excavation in which artillery is placed for concealment.

gun·pow·der (gŭn′ pou′ dər) ***n-*** explosive powder used in guns, fireworks, blasting, etc.; especially, a mixture of potassium nitrate, charcoal, and sulfur.

gun·shot (gŭn′ shŏt′) ***n-*** **1** shot fired from a gun. **2** range of a gun: *The bear was within* gunshot.

gun-shy (gŭn′ shī′) ***adj-*** afraid of a gun or the sound of gunfire: *a* gun-shy *horse.*

gun·smith (gŭn′ smĭth′) ***n-*** person who makes or repairs firearms.

gun·stock (gŭn′ stŏk′) ***n-*** shaped or molded part of a gun, usually of wood, by which it is held.

gun·wale (gŭn′ əl) ***n-*** upper edge of the side of a boat.

gup·py (gŭp′ ē) ***n-*** [*pl.* **gup·pies]** tiny fresh-water fish often kept in aquariums because of its bright coloring.

gur·gle (gûr′ gəl) ***vi-*** **[gur·gled, gur·gling]** **1** to flow with a bubbling sound: *The brook* gurgled. **2** to make this sound: *The baby* gurgled. ***n-:*** *the* gurgle *of milk poured from a bottle.*

gush (gŭsh) ***vi-*** **1** to burst out violently; pour forth suddenly: *Oil* gushed *from the well.* **2** *Informal* to speak with too much enthusiasm, admiration, etc.: *The caller* gushed *over the baby.* ***vt-:*** *The volcano* gushed *lava.* ***n-*** **1** sudden bursting out: *a* gush *of blood*; *a* gush *of anger.* **2** *Informal* silly, sentimental talk or display of affection.

gush·er (gŭsh′ ər) ***n-*** **1** oil well with a strong, natural flow that makes pumping unnecessary. **2** *Informal* person who speaks sentimentally and effusively.

gush·ing (gŭsh′ ĭng) ***adj-*** **1** pouring out. **2** *Informal* sentimental; effusive: *a* gushing *manner.* **—*adv-* gush·ing·ly.**

gush·y (gŭsh′ ē) *Informal* ***adj-*** **[gush·i·er, gush·i·est]** given to being effusive or sentimental: *a* gushy *person.* **—*adv-* gush′ i·ly. *n-* gush′ i·ness.**

gus·set (gŭs′ ət) ***n-*** **1** small, triangular or diamond-shaped piece of cloth inserted in a garment to ease or widen a part, or strengthen a seam. **2** metal bracket for strengthening an angle.

gust (gŭst) ***n-*** **1** sudden rush or strong puff of wind. **2** outburst of feeling, as of laughter or rage.

gus·ta·tor·y (gŭs′ tə tôr′ ē) ***adj-*** having to do with the sense of taste: *Dinner was a* gustatory *joy.*

gus·to (gŭs′ tō) ***n-*** zest; relish; enjoyment.

gust·y (gŭs′ tē) ***adj-*** **[gust·i·er, gust·i·est]** **1** marked by bursts of wind: *a* gusty *day.* **2** given to sudden outbursts: *his* gusty *laughter.* **—*adv-* gust′ i·ly. *n-* gust′ i·ness.**

gut (gŭt) ***n-*** **1** alimentary canal; especially, the intestine. **2** catgut. **3** narrow channel or passage. **4 guts** (1) bowels; entrails. (2) *Slang* courage; grit; also, impudence. ***vt-*** **[gut·ted, gut·ting]** **1** to extract the entrails from. **2** to plunder or destroy the inside of: *Fire* gutted *the building.*

gut·ta-per·cha (gŭt′ ə pûr′ chə) ***n-*** grayish or yellowish substance similar to rubber, made of the juice of a tree of Malaysia, and used as insulation and in dentistry; also, the tree itself.

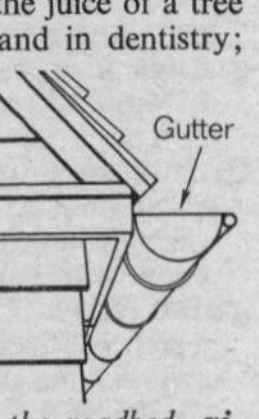

gut·ter (gŭt′ ər) ***n-*** **1** trough to carry off water, such as a trough along the eaves of a building to catch water from the roof, a ditch along a road, or the part of a roadway close to the curb. **2** impoverished and degraded level of life. ***as modifier:*** *profane,* gutter *language.* ***vt-*** **1** to supply with troughs. **2** to form channels in: *The flood* guttered *the roadbed.* ***vi-*** of a candle, to melt so that the wax runs down the sides in channels.

gut·ter·snipe (gŭt′ ər snīp′) *n-* poor and tattered person, especially a child, who spends much time in the streets.

gut·tur·al (gŭt′ ər əl) *adj-* **1** having to do with the throat. **2** harsh and grating, as when formed in the throat: *his* guttural *speech. n-* a sound formed or modified in the throat. Example: (g) as in "go." *—adv-* **gut′ tur·al·ly.**

gut·ty (gŭt′ ē) *Slang adj-* **[gut·ti·er, gut·ti·est]** showing or having vitality or impudence.

[1]**guy** (gī) *n-* wire or rope used to keep something steady: *the* guys *of a tent pole vt-* to steady with such a wire or rope. [from Old French **guie,** from **guier,** "to guide."]

[2]**guy** (gī) *Informal n-* man; fellow. *vt-* to ridicule: *His friends* guyed *him good-naturedly.* [from an effigy (called a **guy**) which is burned in England every year on November 5 to commemorate the failure of **Guy Fawkes** to blow up the Houses of Parliament in 1605.]

guz·zle (gŭz′ əl) *Informal vt-* **[guz·zled, guz·zling]** to drink greedily: *to* guzzle *a lemonade. vi-: He* guzzled *all evening. —n-* **guz′zler.**

gym (jĭm) *n-* gymnasium.

gym·na·si·um (jĭm nā′ zē əm) *n-* **1** large room or building for athletic practice or indoor sports. **2 Gymnasium** in some European countries, a secondary school equivalent to high school and the first two years of college in the United States. *as modifier: the* gymnasium *floor.*

gym·nast (jĭm′ năst′) *n-* person skilled in gymnastics.

gym·nas·tics (jĭm năs′ tĭks) *n- pl.* **1** (takes singular verb) special physical exercises such as tumbling, rope climbing, etc., for developing the body. **2** vigorous exercise or twistings of the body. *—adj-* **gym·nas′ tic.**

gym·no·sperm (jĭm′ nō spûrm′) *n-* any of a group of plants, **(Gymnospermae),** producing seeds without a seed case or true fruit. See also *angiosperm.*

gy·ne·col·o·gist (jĭn′ ə kŏl′ ə jĭst, gī′ nə-) *n-* doctor who specializes in the treatment of women's diseases and disorders. *—n-* **gy′ ne·col′ o·gy.**

gyp (jĭp) *Slang vt-* **[gypped, gyp·ping]** to cheat or defraud. *n-* **1** fraud; swindle. **2** (also **gypper**) a cheat; swindler.

gyp·sum (jĭp′ səm) *n-* mineral calcium sulfate ($CaSO_4 \cdot 2H_2O$), used in making plaster of Paris.

Gyp·sy (jĭp′ sē) *n-* [*pl.* **Gyp·sies**] **1** member of a wandering Caucasian people with dark skin and black hair, who probably migrated from India to Europe around 1500. **2** the language of these people; Romany. *adj-: a* Gypsy *violinist; a* Gypsy *fortuneteller.* Also **Gip′ sy.**

gypsy moth *n-* moth of European origin, the caterpillars of which are very destructive to trees.

gy·rate (jī′ rāt′) *vi-* **[gy·rat·ed, gy·rat·ing] 1** to revolve around a fixed point or axis. **2** to move in a circle or spiral. *—n-* **gy·ra′ tion.** *adj-* **gy′ ra·tor′ y** (jī′ rə tôr′ ē).

gyr·fal·con (jûr′ făl′ kən, -fôl′ kən, -fò′ kən) *n-* any of several large, powerful falcons found in northern or arctic regions. Also **gerfalcon.**

gy·ro (jī′ rō) *n-* **1** gyroscope. **2** gyrocompass.

gyro- *combining form* functioning by means of a gyroscope: *a* gyro*stabilizer.* [from Greek **gyros** meaning "a ring; circle."]

gy·ro·com·pass (jī′ rō kŭm′ pəs) *n-* a compass that is kept pointing north by a gyroscope.

gy·ro·ho·ri·zon (jī′ rō hə rī′ zən) *n-* gyroscopic instrument in an airplane that shows whether the plane is pointing up or down or tilting left or right.

gy·ro·pi·lot (jī′ rō pī′ lət) *n-* mechanism in an airplane or boat, controlled by a gyroscope, and which automatically holds the craft on a preset line of travel.

gy·ro·scope (jī′ rə skōp′) *n-* device consisting of a heavy wheel mounted on gimbals. When the wheel is spinning rapidly, its axis tends to point in the same direction, no matter how the mounting is titled. Gyroscopes are used in navigational instruments, rocket guidance systems, and as toys, etc.

Gyroscope

gy·ro·scop·ic (jī′ rə skŏp′ ĭk) *adj-* **1** of or relating to a gyroscope or its action. **2** controlled by a gyroscope.

gy·ro·sta·bi·liz·er (jī′ rō stā′ bə līz′ ər) *n-* gyroscopic mechanism designed to reduce the rolling motion of a ship or airplane.

gyve (jīv) *Archaic n-* fetter for the leg. *vt-* **[gyved, gyv·ing]** to fetter or shackle. *Hom-* jive.

H

H, h (āch) *n-* [*pl.* **H's, h's**] eighth letter of the English alphabet.

H 1 symbol for hydrogen. **2** symbol for henry.

ha (hä) *interj-* exclamation expressing wonder, suspicion, doubt, mirth, joy, etc.

Ha·bak·kuk (hăb′ ə kŭk′, hə băk′ ək) *n-* **1** Hebrew prophet of the seventh century B.C. **2** book of the Old Testament by him. In the CCD Bible, **Ha′ bac·uc.**

ha·be·as cor·pus (hā′ bē əs kȯr′ pəs, -kôr′ pəs) *n-* in law, a writ or order to produce a prisoner before a court to decide whether he is being justly held.

hab·er·dash·er (hăb′ ər dăsh′ ər) *n-* shopkeeper who sells men's furnishings, such as socks, shirts, hats, etc.

hab·er·dash·er·y (hăb′ ər dăsh′ ə rē) *n-* [*pl.* **hab·er·dash·er·ies**] **1** goods sold by a haberdasher. **2** shop where they are sold.

hab·er·geon (hăb′ ər jən) *n-* in medieval armor, a jacket of mail shorter than a hauberk; also, a hauberk.

ha·bil·i·ments (hə bĭl′ ə mənts) *n- pl.* clothing; attire; dress; garb. Also **ha·bil′ i·ment.**

hab·it (hăb′ ĭt) *n-* **1** action repeated so often that one does it automatically: *the* habit *of nail biting.* **2** usual practice; custom: *the* habit *of a daily walk.* **3** addiction: *the tobacco* habit. **4** usual mental or moral pattern or make-up: *the scientist's* habit *of mind.* **5** type of dress worn for a certain activity or by members of a religious group, or the like. *vt-* to dress (oneself): *They* habited *themselves in black.*

Habits
NUN'S RIDING

hab·it·a·ble (hăb′ ə tə bəl) *adj-* fit or suitable for living in: *a* habitable *house.*

---

hab·i·tant (hăb′ə tənt) ***n-*** dweller; inhabitant.

hab·i·tat (hăb′ə tăt) ***n-*** 1 natural environment of a plant or animal: *The ocean is the* habitat *of the whale.* 2 place where a person or animal is usually found.

hab·i·ta·tion (hăb′ə tā′shən) ***n-*** 1 an occupying or inhabiting; occupancy: *a shack not fit for human* habitation. 2 place to live in; residence. 3 settlement.

ha·bit·u·al (hə bĭch′o͞o əl) ***adj-*** 1 occurring regularly; customary; usual: *her* habitual *promptness.* 2 given over to a habit: *a* habitual *smoker.* ***—adv-*** **ha·bit′u·al·ly.**

ha·bit·u·ate (hə bĭch′o͞o āt′) ***vt-*** [**ha·bit·u·at·ed, ha·bit·u·at·ing**] to accustom or adapt: *Frontier life* habituated *them to hardship.* ***—n-*** **ha·bit′u·a′tion.**

ha·bi·tude (hăb′ə to͞od′, -tyo͞od′) ***n-*** customary manner, behavior, or state of mind; habit.

ha·bit·u·é (hə bĭch′o͞o ā′) ***n-*** frequent visitor: *They are* habitués *of the theater.*

ha·chure (hə sho͞or′) ***n-*** short line used for shading, and in map-making to show hills and slopes.

ha·ci·en·da (hä′sē ĕn′də, *Sp.* ä′sē ĕn′dä) ***n-*** 1 house and land of a ranch, estate, or plantation in parts of Latin America settled by Spaniards, 2 in southwestern United States, a low ranch house with wide verandas. [American word from Spanish, meaning originally "something to be worked on or done," ultimately from Latin **facere,** "to do."]

[1]**hack** (hăk) ***vt-*** to cut unevenly or irregularly: *He* hacked *the loaf of bread into chunks.* ***vi-*** 1 to make rough cuts: *He* hacked *at the tree.* 2 to give short dry coughs. ***n-*** 1 a cut or gash. 2 short, dry cough. [from Old English **haccian.**]

[2]**hack** (hăk) ***n-*** 1 coach, carriage, or taxi for hire. 2 horse for hire. 3 all-purpose horse. 4 one who does dull work for hire: *a literary* hack. ***adj-*** 1 of or for a taxi or hired carriage, etc.: *a* hack *stand.* 2 done, or working, merely for money; hired: *to do* hack *work*; *a* hack *writer.* [short for **hackney,** from **Hackney,** England, a town where people would hire horses for a journey outbound from London. Some horses were worn-out nags.]

hack·a·more (hăk′ə môr′) ***n-*** rawhide or rope halter used chiefly for breaking horses. [American word, probably from Spanish **jáquima** meaning "halter."]

hack·ber·ry (hăk′bĕr′ē) ***n-*** [*pl.* **hack·ber·ries**] 1 any of several U.S. trees or coarse shrubs related to the elm. 2 the sweet, red or dark-purple edible berry of these.

hack·le (hăk′əl) ***n-*** neck plumage of a domestic fowl.

hack·man (hăk′mən) ***n-*** [*pl.* **hack·men**] driver of a carriage or cab.

hack·ney (hăk′nē) ***n-*** [*pl.* **hack·neys**] 1 horse used chiefly for riding or driving. 2 carriage or hack kept for hire. ***vt-*** to wear out by common use; hence, to make trite. ***adj-*** let out for hire: *a* hackney *coach.*

hack·neyed (hăk′nēd) ***adj***: commonplace; trite.

hack·saw (hăk′sò′) ***n-*** close-toothed saw with a narrow blade, used for cutting metals, plastics, etc. For picture, see [1]*saw.*

had (hăd) *p.t. & p.p.* of **have.**

had·dock (hăd′ək) ***n-*** [*pl.* **had·dock**; rarely, **had·docks**] North Atlantic food fish related to the cod.

Ha·des (hā′dēz) ***n-*** 1 in Greek mythology, ruler of the world of the dead and a brother of Zeus; Pluto; also, his realm. 2 **hades** *Informal* hell.

had·n't (hăd′ənt) had not.

haf·ni·um (hăf′nē əm) ***n-*** metal element used in the manufacture of tungsten filaments and in nuclear reactors. Symbol Hf, At. No. 72, At. Wt. 178.49.

haft (hăft) ***n-*** handle of a knife, sword, etc.

hag (hăg) ***n-*** 1 ugly old woman. 2 witch.

hag·fish (hăg′fĭsh′) ***n-*** [*pl.* **hag·fish**; **hag·fish·es** (kinds of hagfish)] any of several eellike ocean fishes related to the lampreys, that bore into the bodies of other fish.

Hag·ga·dah (hə gä′də, -gò′də) ***n-*** story of the Jews' exodus from Egypt, included as part of the Seder ceremony at Passover; also, a book including this story and other parts of the Seder ritual.

Hag·ga·i (hăg′ī′, hăg′ē ī′) ***n-*** 1 Hebrew prophet. 2 a book of the Old Testament written by him. In the CCD Bible, spelled **Ag·gai′** (ă gī′).

hag·gard (hăg′ərd) ***adj-*** having a worn and worried look; tired: *my* haggard *eyes.* ***—n-*** **hag′gard·ness.**

hag·gis (hăg′əs) ***n-*** Scottish dish made of the heart, liver, lungs, etc., of a sheep or calf, seasoned, mixed with oatmeal, and boiled in a sheep's stomach.

hag·gle (hăg′əl) ***vi-*** [**hag·gled, hag·gling**] to argue or dispute, especially over prices. ***—n-*** **hag′gler.**

hag·rid·den (hăg′rĭd′ən) ***adj-*** harassed; oppressed.

Hai·da (hī′də) ***n-*** [*pl.* **Hai·das,** also **Hai·da**] 1 a member of any one of the North American Indian tribes inhabiting Queen Charlotte Islands and the Prince of Wales Island, Alaska. 2 the language of these people.

hai·ku (hī′ko͞o) ***n-*** [*pl.* **hai·ku**] poem containing a total of seventeen syllables in three lines. [from Japanese **haiku,** from **hai** meaning "sport, play," and **ku** meaning "poem, verse."]

[1]**hail** (hāl) ***n-*** 1 rounded bits of ice, usually small, that fall in showers like rain; hailstones. 2 anything that falls like hailstones: *a* hail *of rocks*; *a* hail *of curses.* ***vi-*** to rain hailstones. ***vt-*** to shower; pour down: *to* hail *blows upon someone.* [from Old English **hægel** of the same meaning.] ***Hom-*** hale.

[2]**hail** (hāl) ***vt-*** 1 to call out to in greeting: *to* hail *a friend.* 2 to signal: *to* hail *a taxi.* ***n-*** 1 a greeting. 2 a shout. [from an ancient greeting **be heil(l)** meaning "be hale; be of good health." **Heill** is an Old Norse word related to [1]**hale.**] ***Hom-*** hale. ***—n-*** **hail′er.**

within hail within shouting distance.

hail from to come from: *He* hails from *Omaha.*

hail-fel·low (hāl′fĕl′ō) ***adj-*** comradely: friendly and informal: *The convention was a* hail-fellow *affair.* Also **hail-fel′low-well-met.**

hail·stone (hāl′stōn′) ***n-*** ball or pellet of ice that is formed in thunder clouds.

hail·storm (hāl′stórm′, -stôrm′) ***n-*** storm of hail.

hair (hâr) ***n-*** 1 mass of threadlike growths forming the coat or fur of an animal, or such natural growth on a person's skin. 2 any one of these threadlike growths. 3 something resembling these growths, such as the fibers on some plants. 4 very small distance, space, or degree: *The baseball missed him by a* hair. ***Hom-*** hare. ***—adj-*** **haired:** *a long-*haired *dog.* ***adj-*** **hair′like′.**

not turn a hair to remain absolutely calm. **split hairs** to make tiny distinctions in an argument.

hair·breadth (hâr′brĕdth′) or **hair's·breadth** (hârz′-) ***n-*** width no greater than that of a hair; very small distance. ***adj-*** very narrow: *a* hairbreadth *escape.*

hair·brush (hâr′brŭsh′) ***n-*** brush for the hair.

hair·cloth (hâr′klòth′, -klŏth′) ***n-*** wiry fabric of horsehair or camel's hair, with a cotton or linen warp, used in upholstering or for stiffening garments.

hair·cut (hâr′kŭt′) ***n-*** a cutting of, or a style of cutting, the hair. ***—n-*** **hair′cut′ter.** ***n-*** **hair′cut′ting.**

hair·do (hâr′do͞o′) ***n-*** [*pl.* **hair·dos**] style of arranging hair; coiffure.

hair·dress·er (hâr′drĕs′ər) ***n-*** 1 person who cuts or arranges hair. 2 *Brit.* barber. ***—n-*** **hair′dress′ing.**

hair·less (hâr′ləs) ***adj-*** without hair.

hair·line (hâr′līn′) ***n-*** 1 edge of the area of the head covered by hair: *a receding* hairline. 2 *very thin line* or margin. *as* ***modifier:*** *a* hairline *scar*; *a* hairline *decision by the umpire.*

hair·pin (hâr′pĭn′) ***n-*** metal or plastic pin with two prongs, used to hold the hair in place. ***adj-*** U-shaped; doubling back on itself like such a pin: *a* hairpin *turn.*

hair-rais·ing (hâr′rā′zing) ***adj-*** terrifying.

hair·split·ter (hâr′splĭt′ər) ***n-*** person who insists upon petty and unimportant distinctions in reasoning; quibbler. **—*n-* hair′split′ting.**

hair·spring (hâr′spring′) ***n-*** delicate, hairlike spring which regulates the balance wheel in a watch.

hair-trig·ger (hâr′trĭg′ər) or **hair-trig·gered** (-ərd) ***adj-*** **1** reacting quickly to the slightest pressure or stimulus: *a* hair-trigger *temper.* **2** very quick; split-second: *He swerved in a* hair-trigger *response to danger.*

hair trigger ***n-*** gun trigger so adjusted that a mere touch discharges the weapon.

hair·y (hâr′ē) ***adj-*** [**hair·i·er, hair·i·est**] **1** covered with hair: *a* hairy *animal.* **2** of or like hair: *the* hairy *husk of coconuts.* **—*n-* hair′i·ness.**

Hai·tian (hā′shən) ***n-*** **1** a native or inhabitant of Haiti **2** the French dialect spoken by most of the people of Haiti, ***adj-***: *a* Haitian *official.*

Haj or **Hadj** (hăj) ***n-*** pilgrimage to Mecca required of every Muslim at least once in his lifetime, after which he is called **Haj·i** or **Hadj·i** (hăj′ē), and can use that title.

hake (hāk) ***n-*** [*pl.* **hake; hakes** (kinds of hake)] any of several ocean food fishes related to the cod.

hal·berd (hăl′bərd) ***n-*** weapon of the 15th and 16th centuries combining spear and battle-ax. Also **hal′bert** (hăl′bərt).

hal·ber·dier (hăl′bər dêr′) ***n-*** soldier armed with a halberd.

hal·cy·on (hăl′sē ən) ***n-*** a fabled bird identified with the kingfisher and supposedly able to bring calm weather so that it might nest at sea. ***adj-*** peaceful; happy; calm: *summer's* halcyon *days.*

[1]**hale** (hāl) ***adj-*** strong; healthy; robust. [from Old English **hāl,** related to **whole.**] ***Hom-*** *hail.*

[2]**hale** (hāl) ***vt-*** [**haled, hal·ing**] to pull or drag by, or as by, force: *to* hale *a man into court.* [from Old French haler, from an early Germanic word. It is related to **haul.**] ***Hom-*** hail.

half (hăf) ***n-*** [*pl.* **halves** (hăvz)] **1** either one of the two equal parts or groups into which an object or collection of objects can be divided: *He bought* half *of a cake. He sold* half *of his stamp collection.* **2** number that represents such a part. **3** thirty minutes: *It is* half *past nine.* **4** in football, basketball, etc., either of the two equal periods of a game, usually separated by an interval. **5** *Informal* a halfback. ***adj-*** **1** being either of the two equal, or roughly equal, parts: *a* half *pound*; *a* half *share in the company.* **2** partial; incomplete: *a* half *truth.* ***adv-*** partly; partially: *He was* half *asleep.*

do (something) by halves to do something badly or in an incomplete way. **go halves** *Informal* to share equally. **in half** into halves. **not by half** almost not at all; hardly at all. **not half bad** rather good.

half-and-half (hăf′ən hăf′) ***n-*** something, especially a mixture, that is half one thing and half another. ***adv-***: *to mix* half-and-half. ***adj-***: *a* half-and-half *mixture.*

half·back (hăf′băk′) ***n-*** in football, either of two players having a position behind the line of scrimmage, and halfway between the quarterback and the fullback; also, in field hockey, soccer, etc., any of several players who line up between the fullbacks and the forwards.

half-baked (hăf′bākt′) ***adj-*** **1** not baked thoroughly **2** *Informal* showing bad or incomplete planning, judgment, etc.: *a* half-baked *idea.*

half-boot ***n-*** boot reaching about halfway to the knee.

half-breed (hăf′brēd′) ***n-*** person whose parents are of different racial divisions. (Considered an offensive word.)

half brother ***n-*** brother related through one parent only.

half-caste (hăf′kăst′) ***n-*** half-breed, especially one having one parent of Asian and the other of European ancestry. (Now considered an offensive word.)

half cock ***n-*** position of the hammer of a gun pulled back halfway and locked so that it cannot be fired **—*adj-* half′-cocked′**: *a* half-cocked *pistol.*

go off half-cocked (or **at half cock**) *Informal* to act or speak impulsively or rashly.

half crown ***n-*** former British silver coin worth two and a half shillings.

half dollar ***n-*** silver coin of the United States and Canada, worth fifty cents.

half eagle ***n-*** former gold coin of the United States worth five dollars.

half gainer ***n-*** dive made by leaping forward while doing half of a backward somersault and plunging into the water headfirst, facing the board.

half·heart·ed (hăf′här′təd) ***adj-*** lacking enthusiasm or interest: *a* halfhearted *attempt.* **—*adv-* half′heart′ed·ly.** ***n-*** **half′heart′ed·ness.**

half-hour (hăf′our′) ***n-*** **1** a period of thirty minutes. **2** the point thirty minutes after the beginning of an hour. *as* ***modifier:*** *a* half-hour *program.*

half-hour·ly (hăf′our′lə) ***adj-*** occurring once every thirty minutes, or at intervals of a half-hour: *a* half-hourly *signal.* ***adv-***: *The clock* struck *half-hourly.*

half-life (hăf′līf′) *Physics* ***n-*** amount of time during which half of the atoms in a given sample of a radioactive element disintegrate.

half-mast (hăf′măst′) **at half-mast** of a flag, flying at some distance below the top of its staff as a sign of mourning or a signal of distress. Also **at half-staff.**

half moon ***n-*** the moon at the end of the first quarter or the beginning of the last quarter.

half nel·son (nĕl′sən) ***n-*** wrestling hold applied from behind, in which an arm is put under the opponent's armpit and hooked upwards around his neck, which is thus pressed forcibly down.

half note *Music* ***n-*** note held half as long as a whole note. For picture, see *note.*

half·pen·ny (hā′pə nē) *British* ***n-*** **1** [*pl.* **half·pen·nies**] former British coin worth half a penny. **2** [*pl.* **half·pence** (-pəns)] amount of money this coin is worth.

half sister ***n-*** sister related through one parent only.

half slip ***n-*** skirt worn under outer clothing; petticoat.

half-sole (hăf′sōl′) ***vt-*** [**half-soled, half-sol·ing**] to repair (shoes, boots, etc.) by attaching half soles.

half sole ***n-*** patch used to repair the sole of a shoe or boot and extending from the toe to the instep.

half-staff (hăf′stăf′) See *half-mast.*

half step ***n-*** **1** *Music* difference in pitch between any two adjacent tones in a chromatic scale; semitone. **2** *Military* quick marching step 15 inches long.

half time ***n-*** interval between the halves of a game.

half·tone (hăf′tōn′) ***n-*** **1** picture made by an engraving process which reproduces shades of light and dark **2** in painting, photography, etc., any tone between the lightest and the darkest. 3 *Music* (also **half tone**) half step; interval equal to half a tone on the scale.

half-track or **half·track** (hăf′ trăk′) ***n-*** type of military vehicle that has treads like those of a tractor in the rear and two front wheels.

half·way (hăf′ wā′) ***adj-*** 1 located midway between two points: *the* halfway *mark.* 2 partial; incomplete: *a* halfway *measure.* ***adv-*** 1 midway; at half the distance: *They met* halfway *between the two towns.* 2 partially: *He* halfway *consented to go.*

go (or **meet**) **halfway** to compromise with, in order to reach an agreement.

half-wit (hăf′ wĭt′) ***n-*** feeble-minded or very stupid person. **—*adj-* half′-wit′ted.**

hal·i·but (hăl′ ə bət) ***n-*** [*pl.* **hal·i·but; hal·i·buts** (kinds of halibut)] the largest of the flatfish, used as food.

hal·ite (hā′ līt, hăl′ īt) ***n-*** rock salt; sodium chloride (NaCl) as it is found in rocky deposits in the earth.

hal·i·to·sis (hăl′ ə tō′ səs) ***n-*** bad or unpleasant breath.

hall (hȯl) ***n-*** 1 passageway leading to rooms in a building. 2 room, vestibule, etc., at the entrance of a building. 3 large room, especially one used for public gatherings. 4 public building: *the town* hall. 5 one of the buildings of a college, university, etc. 6 *chiefly Brit.* large, impressive home; manor house. ***Hom-*** haul.

hal·lah (KHä′ lə) chalah.

hal·le·lu·jah or **hal·le·lu·iah** (hăl′ ə lo͞o′ yə) ***n-*** cry or song of praise to God. ***interj-*** "Praise be to God."

hall·mark (hȯl′ märk′) ***n-*** mark stamped on gold or silver articles to testify to their purity; hence, any distinguishing characteristic or mark of genuineness. ***vt-*** to stamp with such a mark.

hal·loo (hə lo͞o′) ***n-*** a shout to attract attention, to urge on hounds in a hunt, etc.: *loud* halloos *for help.* ***interj-***: *He shouted* "Halloo!" *to his hounds.* ***vi-***: *The hunter* hallooed *to his hounds.*

hal·low (hăl′ ō) ***vt-*** to make sacred; set apart or honor as holy; consecrate.

hal·lowed (hăl′ ōd′) ***adj-*** 1 made holy; consecrated: *Parts of Jerusalem are* hallowed *ground.* 2 honored or regarded as sacred: *our* hallowed *traditions.*

Hal·low·een (hăl′ ō ēn′) ***n-*** evening of October 31; eve of All Saints' Day. Also **Hal·low·e'en.**

hal·lu·ci·na·tion (hə lo͞o′ sə nā′ shən) ***n-*** a seeming to see, hear, or experience something which is not there, especially as a result of illness, stimulation by a drug, etc.; also, something seen or experienced thus.

hal·lu·cin·o·gen (hə lo͞o′ sə nə jĕn, hăl′ yo͞o sĭn′ ə jĕn) ***n-*** substance that induces or tends to induce hallucinations. **—*adj-* hal·lu′cin·o·gen′ic:** *an* hallucinogenic *drug.*

hall·way (hȯl′ wā′) ***n-*** entrance hall or passageway in a building; corridor.

ha·lo (hā′ lō) ***n-*** [*pl.* **ha·los** or **ha·loes**] 1 circle of light around a shining body, such as the sun or moon. 2 in pictures, a ring, disk, or burst of light, surrounding or above the heads of holy persons; also, anything resembling this. 3 glory or splendor with which one endows a person or an object highly prized. ***vt-*** to surround with, or as if with, a circle of light.

hal·o·gen (hăl′ ə jən) ***n-*** any of four elements, fluorine, chlorine, bromine, and iodine, that have similar chemical properties and atomic structures.

[1]halt (hȯlt) ***n-*** a stop or pause: *After a short* halt *the parade moved forward.* ***vi-*** to come to a stop: *The train* halted *at the crossroads.* ***vt-*** to bring to a stop: *to* halt *the advance of an army.* [ultimately from older Germanic **Halt!** meaning "Stop!", from **halten,** "to stop," and related to **[1]hold.**]

[2]halt (hȯlt) ***vi-*** to waver; falter; hesitate: *He began his speech briskly, but then* halted *nervously.* ***adj-*** *Archaic* lame; crippled. ***n-*** *Archaic* **the halt** those who are lame. [from Old English **healt,** "lamed by a wound."]

halt·ing·ly (hȯl′ tĭng lē) ***adv-*** waveringly; falteringly.

hal·ter (hȯl′ tər) ***n-*** 1 rope or strap by which an animal is led or tied. 2 noose for hanging criminals. 3 backless blouse that ties around the neck.

Halter

halve (hăv) ***vt-*** [**halved, halv·ing**] 1 to divide something into two equal parts: *to* halve *the melon.* 2 to lessen something by half: *This machine* halves *the work.* ***Hom-*** have.

halves (hăvz) *pl.* of **half.**

hal·yard (hăl′ yərd) ***n-*** rope or tackle on a ship, for hoisting or lowering a sail, yard, or flag.

ham (hăm) ***n-*** 1 thigh of a hog, especially this part smoked and salted, used as food. 2 the back of the thigh and the buttock. 3 *Slang* actor or performer who overacts. 4 *Informal* amateur radio operator. ***vi-*** [**hammed, ham·ming**] *Slang* to perform in a showy, exaggerated manner; overact.

Ham (hăm) ***n-*** in the Bible, the youngest son of Noah.

Ha·man (hā′ mən) ***n-*** in the Old Testament, a Persian high official who plotted to destroy the Jews, and was hanged when his plot was disclosed to the king.

ham·burg·er (hăm′ bûr′ gər) ***n-*** 1 finely ground beef. 2 small pat of such meat, especially one served on a sliced roll or bun. Also **ham′burg.** [American word, a special use of German **Hamburger** meaning "coming from (the city of) Hamburg."]

hame (hām) ***n-*** one of the two curved bars on the collar of a horse's harness, to which the traces are fastened.

ham·let (hăm′ lət) ***n-*** small village.

Ham·let (hăm′ lət) ***n-*** in Shakespeare's play of this name, the hero, a prince of Denmark, who seeks to avenge his father's murder.

ham·mer (hăm′ ər) ***n-*** 1 tool having a head of metal, wood, etc., attached crosswise at the end of a handle, and used for driving nails, beating metals, etc. 2 anything resembling this in action or use, such as a part of a gun that strikes to detonate the ammunition, or one of the parts that strikes the strings of a piano. 3 the outer one of the three tiny, sound-transmitting bones in the middle ear (for picture, see *[1]ear*). ***vt-*** 1 to pound or beat with or as if with a heavy tool: *to* hammer *iron into horseshoes; to* hammer *the table with one's fist.* 2 to drive, force, etc., by or as if by pounding: *to* hammer *nails; to* hammer *a lesson into someone's mind.* ***vi-*** to strike with heavy blows; pound; bang: *to* hammer *against the door.* **—*n-* ham′mer·er. *adj-* ham′mer·less. *adj-* ham′mer·like′.**

Hammers

hammer and tongs *Informal* with all one's strength or energy: *to go at a task* hammer and tongs.

hammer away to work hard and persistently.

hammer out to work out by thought or effort.

hammer and sickle ***n-*** emblem consisting of a crossed hammer and sickle, shown on the flag of the Soviet Union, and symbolizing the worker and the peasant.

ham·mer·head (hăm′ ər hĕd′) ***n-*** fierce shark having a long head at right angles to its body, and eyes at the ends of the head. For picture, see *shark.*

ham·mer·lock (hăm′ ər lŏk′) ***n-*** wrestling hold in which an opponent's arm is bent and held behind his back.

ham·mock (hăm′ək) ***n-*** swinging bed made of heavy cloth or a network of cords, and suspended by cords at both ends.

[1]**ham·per** (hăm′ pər) ***n-*** large basket or similar container, having a cover and often made of wicker: *a picnic* hamper; *a clothes* hamper. [from Old French **hanapier,** "a case to hold a cup," from early Germanic **knap(p),** "a beaker."]

Hammock

[2]**ham·per** (hăm′ pər) ***vt-*** to obstruct or hinder the motion of; impede: *His heavy equipment* hampered *his progress.* [from Middle English **hampren** of the same meaning.]

ham·ster (hăm′ stər) ***n-*** small rodent with a short tail and cheek pouches.

ham·string (hăm′ strĭng′) ***n-*** **1** in man, either of two groups of tendons at the back of the knee. **2** in animals, the large tendon above and behind the hock. ***vt-*** [**ham·strung** (hăm′ strŭng′), **ham·string·ing**] **1** to lame or cripple by cutting this tendon. **2** to hamper; frustrate: *His rivals* hamstrung *him.*

hand (hănd) ***n-*** **1** the part of the arm below the wrist, including the fingers. **2** a pointer on a dial. **3** skill; deftness: *Try your* hand *at this game.* **4** handwriting: *I recognized his* hand *on the envelope.* **5** workman; assistant: *a hired* hand; *a farm* hand. **6** side: *to meet trouble on every* hand; *to stand at the king's right* hand. **7** (often **hands**) control; power: *The matter is in your* hands. **8** assistance: *Give me a* hand *in moving this desk.* **9** active part: *He had a* hand *in making this decision.* **10** in card playing, (1) a round of a game. (2) the cards held by a player. (3) an individual player. **11** *Informal* applause: *Give him a big* hand. **12** way of handling or doing something; touch: *a light* hand *on the reins*; *the* hand *of an artist.* **13** source: *knowledge at first* hand. **14** pledge of assurance; promise: *He gave me his* hand *on the bargain.* **15** promise to marry or permit marriage with. **16** measure of about four inches, used chiefly in determining the height of horses. ***vt-*** to pass, give, etc., by, or as if by, holding with the fingers: *to* hand *someone a book.* *as* ***modifier***: *a* hand *drill.* ***—adj-*** **hand′ like′.**

at hand near; within reach in distance or time. **at the hand (or hands) of** through the action of. **by hand** using the hands rather than machines. **change hands** to pass from one person to another. **clean hands** freedom from blame or turpitude; innocence. **force (someone's) hand** to compel (someone) into hasty or rash action: *His sudden offer to sell* forced my hand. **from hand to hand** passing from one person to another. **from hand to mouth** with nothing saved for the future: *They live* from hand to mouth. **hand and foot 1** with both hands and feet tied: *He was bound* hand and foot. **2** completely; totally: *He waited on her* hand and foot. **hand in glove** in close connection with: *They worked* hand in glove. **hand in hand 1** holding hands. **2** close together. **hand over fist** quickly; in large amounts: *He made money* hand over fist. **hands down** easily: *He won* hands down. **Hands off!** Don't touch or interfere. **Hands up!** command to raise one's hands in the air, especially as a sign of surrender. **hand to hand 1** from one person to the next. **2** at very close quarters: *They battled* hand to hand. **have (one's) hands full** be very busy; have all one can do. **in hand** under control: *He has the situation well* in hand. **join hands** become partners. **keep (one's) hand in** to pursue an activity or interest so as not to lose knowledge and ability. **lay hands on** to do physical violence to. **off (one's) hands** out of (one's) care or responsibility. **on hand** close by; ready for use. **on (one's) hands** in one's care or charge. **on the other hand** from the opposite point of view. **out of hand** out of control. **show (one's) hand** reveal (one's) intentions. **take in hand** deal with; bring under control. **tie (someone's) hands** frustrate; prevent from acting. **to hand** within reach; readily available: *to use whatever materials come* to hand. **try (one's) hand** to make an attempt. **turn (one's) hand to** to work at. **upper hand** advantage; control: *the* upper hand *in the argument.* **wash (one's) hands of** to refuse further responsibility for. **with a heavy hand** sternly; unmercifully.

hand down 1 to pass along from one generation to another: *to* hand down *a wedding gown.* **2** to make and transmit (a ruling, decision, etc.).

hand in to give to someone in authority; submit: *to* hand in *a prisoner*; *to* hand in *an examination paper.*

hand it to *Slang* to give praise or recognition to.

hand on to pass along to the next in succession.

hand out to give out; distribute.

hand over to give to someone; deliver.

hand·bag (hănd′ băg′) ***n-*** **1** small suitcase or traveling bag. **2** woman's purse.

hand·ball (hănd′ bôl′) ***n-*** **1** game in which the players bat a ball against a wall with the hand. **2** small ball used in this game.

hand·bar·row (hănd′ băr′ ō) ***n-*** flat frame with two handles at each end, used for carrying loads.

hand·bill (hănd′ bĭl′) ***n-*** printed advertisement distributed by hand.

hand·book (hănd′ bo͝ok′) ***n-*** small reference book, such as a guidebook or manual.

hand·breadth (hănd′ brĕdth′) or **hands·breadth** (hăndz′-) ***n-*** measure of length approximately equal to the width of the hand.

hand·car (hănd′ kär′) ***n-*** small, open car or platform propelled along railroad tracks by a hand lever.

hand·cart (hănd′ kärt′) ***n-*** cart moved by hand.

hand·clasp (hănd′ klăsp′) ***n-*** a clasping or grasping of another's hand as a greeting, sign of sympathy, etc.

hand·craft (hănd′ krăft′) ***n-*** skilled use of the hands in making useful objects; also, an art or process requiring such skill; handicraft. ***—adj-*** **hand′ craft′ ed:** *a* hand-crafted *cabinet.*

hand·cuff (hănd′ kŭf′) ***n-*** one of a pair of hinged metal bracelets joined by a short chain and locked about a prisoner's wrist or wrists. ***vt-***: *He* handcuffed *the prisoner.*

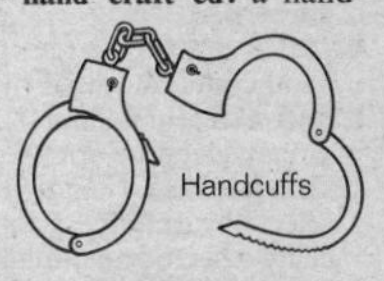
Handcuffs

hand·ed (hăn′ dəd) ***adj-*** **1** having or using a certain hand: *a left-*handed *pitcher.* **2** using hands in a certain way: *He was heavy-*handed *at the piano.* **3** requiring or using a certain number of hands: *a one-*handed *operation.*

hand·ful (hănd′ fo͝ol′) ***n-*** **1** amount one hand can hold: *a* handful *of clay*; *several* handfuls *of nails.* **2** very small number or amount: *Only a* handful *of people came.*

hand·grip (hănd′ grĭp′) ***n-*** **1** grip or clasp of the hand. **2** handle.

hand·i·cap (hăn′ dĭ kăp′) ***n-*** **1** something that hinders or prevents activities that are normal for others in the group; defect; disability; disadvantage; hindrance: *Poor* *eyesight is a* handicap. **2** in sports, an adjustment of points or scores, starting times or positions, etc., in order to make chances more or less equal among stronger and weaker entrants in a tournament, game, or race. **3** game or contest in which such conditions exist. ***vt-*** **[hand·i·capped, hand·i·cap·ping]** **1** to hinder or hold back: *Bad eyesight* handicaps *him.* **2** in sports, to assign or arrange the competitive conditions of, in order to give weaker contestants a better chance against stronger ones: *The coach* handicapped *the runners.* **—*n-* hand'i·cap'per.**

hand·i·craft (hăn'dĭ krăft') ***n-*** **1** skillful use of the hands in making things. **2** any art, such as pottery, weaving, etc., using the hands. **—*n-* hand'i·craft'er.**

hand·i·ly (hăn'də lē) ***adv-*** **1** in a handy or deft manner; skillfully. **2** easily; comfortably: *to win a race* handily.

hand·i·ness (hăn'dē nəs) ***n-*** **1** deftness or skill with the hands. **2** the ease of use; convenience.

hand·i·work (hăn'dĭ wûrk') ***n-*** **1** work done with the hands; manual craftsmanship. **2** anything done by personal effort: *This garden is Mary's* handiwork.

hand·ker·chief (hăng'kər chĭf) ***n-*** **1** square piece of cloth for wiping the face, nose, or eyes. **2** kerchief.

han·dle (hăn'dəl) ***n-*** part of a tool, container, door, etc., designed to be grasped by the hand. ***vt-*** **[han·dled, han·dling]** **1** to hold, touch, or move with the hand. **2** to manage; control: *She* handled *the car with skill.* **3** to deal with or treat: *He* handles *complaints tactfully.* **4** to buy and sell: *A broker* handles *stocks and bonds.* ***vi-*** to act or behave in a certain way: *The car* handles *well.*

fly off the handle to lose one's temper.

han·dle·bar (hăn'dəl bär') ***n-*** **1** curved steering bar of a bicycle, motorcycle, etc. **2** (also **handlebar mustache**) wide mustache curving down, then up at the ends.

han·dled (hăn'dəld) ***adj-*** having a handle or handles, especially of a certain kind or number: *a pearl-*handled *knife*; *a two-*handled *saw.*

hand·ler (hănd'lər) ***n-*** **1** person who handles. **2** person who trains animals, especially one who displays and tends animals in a show or competition. **3** trainer of a boxer who acts as his second during a fight.

hand·made (hănd'mād') ***adj-*** made by hand.

hand·maid (hănd'mād') ***n-*** in former times, a female servant or attendant. Also **hand'maid'en.**

hand-me-down (hănd'mē doun') *Informal* ***n-*** something used by one person and then given to another; especially, a garment given to a younger person after the wearer outgrows it.

hand organ ***n-*** large, portable music box operated by a hand crank and used by street musicians.

hand·out (hănd'out') *Informal* ***n-*** **1** food, clothing, or money given to or as if to a beggar. **2** press release.

hand-picked (hănd'pĭkt') ***adj-*** **1** gathered by hand. **2** selected carefully. **3** chosen for a particular reason, especially a secret one: *a* hand-picked *candidate.*

hand·rail (hand'rāl') ***n-*** rail at the side of a stairway, platform, etc., to be grasped with the hand for safety.

hand·saw (hănd'sȯ') ***n-*** saw used with one hand.

hand·shake (hănd'shāk') ***n-*** a clasping of someone's right hand, as in greeting, parting, etc.

hand·some (hăn'səm) ***adj-*** **[hand·som·er, hand·som·est]** **1** of pleasing appearance; good-looking. **2** ample; generous: *a* handsome *reward.* **3** gracious; impressive: *a* handsome *gesture.* ***Hom-*** hansom. **—*adv-* hand'some·ly.** ***n-*** **hand'some·ness.**

hand·spike (hănd'spīk') ***n-*** bar used as a lever for lifting heavy weights.

hand·spring (hănd'sprĭng') ***n-*** somersault in which only the hands touch the ground.

hand-to-hand (hăn'tə hănd') ***adj-*** involving physical contact: *a* hand-to-hand *fight.*

hand-to-mouth (hăn'tə mouth') ***adj-*** having nothing to spare; not providing for the future: *The young actor led a* hand-to-mouth *existence.*

hand·work (hănd'wûrk') ***n-*** work done by hand, especially fine and skillful work.

hand·writ·ing (hănd'rī'tĭng) ***n-*** **1** way a person writes; penmanship. **2** writing done by hand.

hand·y (hăn'dē) ***adj-*** **[hand·i·er, hand·i·est]** **1** skillful; deft: *He is* handy *with tools.* **2** convenient: *a* handy *basket for carrying groceries.* **3** conveniently located.

han·dy·man (hăn'dē măn') ***n-*** [*pl.* **han·dy·men**] man hired to do odd jobs; factotum.

hang (hăng) ***vt-*** **[hung** (hŭng), **hang·ing]** **1** to suspend from a nail, hook, or the like: *to* hang *curtains*; *to* hang *a picture.* **2** to attach by hinges so that the object can swing to and fro: *to* hang *a door.* **3** [*p.p.* & *p.t.* **hanged**] to execute on the gallows. **4** to cause to droop: *He* hung *his head in shame.* **5** to decorate or cover with suspended things: *to* hang *a wall with pictures.* ***vi-*** **1** to dangle; be suspended: *a lamp* hung *from the ceiling.* **2** to loom (over) something threateningly: *The danger of a flood* hung *over the village.* **3** to depend (on or upon): *My decision* hangs *on your answer.* **4** to float: *Clouds* hang *over the city.* **5** to die by execution on the gallows. **6** to fall or drape in a certain way: *This curtain* hangs *well.* **7** to hold (on or onto) something for support: *to* hang *on to the banister.* ***n-*** **1** manner in which a thing falls or drapes: *the* hang *of a skirt.* **2** *Informal* right manner of doing or using; knack: *to get the* hang *of a new dance.*

hang around *Informal* to loiter or linger about.

hang back to be unwilling or reluctant.

hang fire to delay or be delayed, usually temporarily.

hang on **1** to keep trying, struggling, etc.; persist; not give up: *to* hang on *in spite of troubles.* **2** to listen very carefully to: *He* hung on *her words.*

hang out at *Slang* to frequent; hang around in.

hang over to be about to happen; threaten.

hang together to stick together; be of a piece.

hang up to put a telephone receiver back in place, and so end a telephone conversation.

►HANG has two past tense forms. HANGED is used only to refer to executions. *He was* hanged *this morning at dawn.* For all other meanings use HUNG.

hang·ar (hăng'ər) ***n-*** shed for housing airplanes and other aircraft. ***Hom-*** hanger.

hang·dog (hăng'dȯg') ***adj-*** having an ashamed, cringing appearance: *a* hangdog *look.*

hang·er (hăng'ər) ***n-*** **1** device such as a hook, peg, or wire frame upon which something may be hung: *a coat* hanger. **2** person who hangs something. ***Hom-*** hangar.

hang·er-on (hăng'ər ŏn') ***n-*** [*pl.* **han·gers-on**] follower chiefly interested in his own profit; parasite.

hang glider ***n-*** a large, kite-shaped device with a harness from which a person hangs while soaring or gliding from a high place.

hang gliding ***n-*** sport of riding a hang glider.

hang·ing (hăng'ĭng) ***n-*** **1** execution in which a person is suspended by the neck until dead. **2 hangings** drapery for walls, windows, etc. ***adj-*** **1** suspended: *a* hanging *fixture.* **2** situated on a steep slope: *a* hanging *garden.*

hanging offense ***n-*** a crime punishable by death.

hang·man (hăng'mən) ***n-*** [*pl.* **hang·men**] public officer whose duty it is to hang condemned criminals.

hang·nail (hăng'nāl') ***n-*** shred of loose skin close to the fingernail.

hang·out (hăng'out') *Slang* ***n-*** residence or place frequently visited.

hang·o·ver (hăng′ ō′ vər) *Informal* ***n-*** **1** something remaining from an earlier time or condition. **2** headache, fatigue, nausea, etc., sometimes following drunkenness.

hank (hăngk) ***n-*** **1** skein, especially of yarn. **2** coil; knot; loop: *a* hank *of hair.*

han·ker (hăng′ kər) ***vi-*** to yearn or crave: *to* hanker *after money.* **—*n-* hank′ er·er.**

han·ker·ing (hăng′ kər ĭng) ***n-*** desire; yearning; craving: *a* hankering *to own a car.*

han·ky (hăng′ kē) *Informal* ***n-*** [*pl.* **han·kies**] handkerchief.

han·ky-pan·ky (hăng′ kē păng′ kē) *Informal* ***n-*** trickery; deceit; underhanded dealings.

Han·sen's disease (hăn′ sənz) ***n-*** leprosy.

han·som (hăn′ səm) ***n-*** a two-wheeled, covered, horse-drawn cab, with an outside seat for the driver at the back. Also **hansom cab.** For picture, see *cab.* ***Hom-*** handsome.

Ha·nuk·kah or **Cha·nu·kah** (KHän′ ə kə, hän′-) ***n-*** Jewish festival, usually in December, commemorating the restoration of the Temple at Jerusalem after the victory of the Maccabees in 164 B.C. Hanukkah is celebrated by lighting candles on eight successive days.

hap (hăp) *Archaic* ***n-*** chance; lot; fortune. ***vi-*** **[happed, hap·ping]** to happen; befall.

hap·haz·ard (hăp′ hăz′ ərd) ***adj-*** happening by chance; not planned; aimless: *a* haphazard *conversation.* **—*adv-* hap′ haz′ ard·ly. *n-* hap′ haz′ ard·ness.**

hap·less (hăp′ ləs) ***adj-*** unlucky. **—*adv-* hap′ less·ly. *n-* hap′ less·ness.**

hap·ly (hăp′ lē) *Archaic* ***adv-*** perhaps; by chance.

hap·pen (hăp′ ən) ***vi-*** **1** to take place; occur: *How did the accident* happen? **2** to act by chance so as; chance: *We* happened *to meet on the street.*

happen on (or **onto**) to find by chance; meet with: *We* happened on *a house in the woods.*

happen to **1** to be the experience of: *What* happened to *John to make him so happy?* **2** to be the fate or disposition of; become of: *What* happened to *Jane?*

hap·pen·ing (hăp′ ən ĭng) ***n-*** event; occurrence.

hap·pen·stance (hăp′ ən stăns′) *Informal* ***n-*** an occurrence due to chance; accident.

hap·pi·ly (hăp′ ə lē) ***adv-*** **1** in a happy manner; joyfully. **2** luckily; fortunately: *The date,* happily, *has been changed.* **3** skillfully; appropriately: *The two styles mix very* happily.

hap·pi·ness (hăp′ ĭ nəs) ***n-*** **1** condition of being glad or contented; joyfulness; contentment. **2** good fortune: *We wished him every* happiness.

hap·py (hăp′ ē) ***adj-*** **[hap·pi·er, hap·pi·est]** **1** having or showing joy, pleasure, contentment, etc.: *a* happy *person*; *a* happy *smile.* **2** lucky; fortunate: *a* happy *turn of events.* **3** very apt; good: *a* happy *selection of colors.*

hap·py-go-luck·y (hăp′ ē gō lŭk′ ē) ***adj-*** gay; lighthearted; trusting to luck.

ha·ra-ki·ri (hăr′ ə kĭ′ rē) ***n-*** suicide by cutting open the abdomen with a dagger.

ha·rangue (hə răng′) ***n-*** long, noisy speech; tirade. ***vt-*** **[ha·rangued, ha·rangu·ing]** to address in this manner: *He* harangued *me about my poor showing.* ***vi-***: *The speaker* harangued *for hours on the Senate floor.*

har·ass (hăr′ əs, hə răs′) ***vt-*** **1** to annoy or worry constantly: *The daily complaints* harassed *her.* **2** to trouble by raids or pillage. **—*n-* har′ ass·ment** or **har·ass′ ment**

har·bin·ger (här′ bĭn jər) ***n-*** person or thing that announces what is coming: *a* harbinger *of doom.*

har·bor (här′ bər) ***n-*** **1** protected part of a sea, lake, or river which can serve as a shelter for ships. **2** any place of shelter or safety. ***vt-*** **1** to shelter or lodge: *He was forced to* harbor *an escaped convict.* **2** to keep in one's mind: *to* harbor *a grudge.* **—*adj-* har′ bor·less.**

hard (härd) ***adj-*** **[hard·er, hard·est]** **1** solid; firm; rigid: *a* hard *bone.* **2** not easy; difficult: *a* hard *problem.* **3** strong; forceful; vigorous: *a* hard *blow on the chin.* **4** industrious: *a* hard *worker.* **5** harsh; unsympathetic: *a* hard *face.* **6** heavy; severe: *a* hard *winter.* **7** containing a high percentage of alcohol: *Rum is* hard *liquor.* **8** of the letters "c" and "g," pronounced as in "cat" and "go." **9** of money, metal rather than currency; also, exchangeable for gold. ***adv-*** **1** with effort and energy: *He studied* hard. *He was breathing* hard. **2** with strength or violence: *to hit* hard. **3** in a painful manner: *He was hit* hard *by her deceit.* **4** so as to be solid: *to freeze* hard.

hard and fast fixed; unchangeable. **hard by** close; near. **hard of hearing** deaf or partially deaf. **hard put to it** to have great difficulty. **hard up** *Informal* to be in great need of money.

hard-bit·ten (härd′ bĭt′ ən) ***adj-*** tough; unyielding: *a* hard-bitten *negotiator.*

hard-boiled (härd′ boild′) ***adj-*** **1** of an egg, boiled until white and yolk become solid. **2** *Informal* unfeeling; hardened by experience; tough: *a* hard-boiled *judge.*

hard coal ***n-*** anthracite.

hard·en (här′ dən) ***vi-*** **1** to become hard: *The mixture* hardened *as it dried.* **2** to become firm; steady: *The market* hardened *toward the end of the day.* **3** to become rigid, unbending, or unyielding: *Their courage* hardened *as the battle went against them.* **4** to become cruel and forbidding: *His heart* hardened *toward his nephews. Her face* hardened *in scorn.* ***vt-***: *He* hardened *his muscles. The good news* hardened *the stock market.*

hard·head·ed (härd′ hĕd′ əd) ***adj-*** **1** not easily swayed by feeling; practical; shrewd: *a* hardheaded *businessman.* **2** stubborn; obstinate. **—*adv-* hard′ head′ ed·ly. *n-* hard′ head′ ed·ness.**

hard·heart·ed (härd′ här′ təd) ***adj-*** not showing pity or sympathy. **—*adv-* hard′ heart′ ed·ly. *n-* hard′ heart′ ed·ness.**

har·di·hood (här′ dĭ ho͝od′) ***n-*** boldness; daring.

har·di·ness (här′ dĭ nəs) ***n-*** **1** strength; robustness. **2** hardihood; boldness.

hard·ly (härd′ lē) ***adv-*** **1** barely; scarcely: *There is* hardly *enough food.* **2** not likely: *That is* hardly *the case.*

hard-mouthed (härd′ moutht′) ***adj-*** of a horse, not sensitive to a bit in the mouth.

hard·ness (härd′ nəs) ***n-*** condition of being unyielding or hard; resistance to being dented, penetrated, or scratched: *The* hardness *of the diamond is such that it can cut glass.* See also *Moh's scale.*

hard palate ***n-*** bony part of the palate; the front part of the roof of the mouth. For picture, see *palate.*

hard·pan (härd′ păn′) ***n-*** **1** compact layer in soil, often clayey, that roots cannot penetrate. **2** solid foundation.

hard sauce ***n-*** creamed mixture of butter, powdered sugar, and flavoring, used on puddings.

hard sell *Informal* ***n-*** high-pressure advertising or salesmanship, often loud and fast-talking.

hard·ship (härd′ shĭp′) ***n-*** something that is hard to endure, such as hunger, privation, cold, etc.

hard·tack (härd′ tăk′) ***n-*** hard, unsalted biscuit.

hard·top (härd′ tŏp′) ***n-*** automobile designed like a convertible but having a rigid top of metal or plastic.

---

hard·ware (härd′ wâr′) *n-* **1** tools, nails and screws, kitchen utensils, electrical fittings, etc., usually made of metal. **2** equipment that is solid and durable: *military* hardware. **3** side arms.
hard water *n-* water containing dissolved salts of calcium and magnesium, especially magnesium carbonate. Unless removed, these salts react with soap to form an insoluble scum in water.
hard·wood (härd′ wŏŏd′) *n-* **1** strong, heavy wood from certain broadleaf trees such as the maple or oak. **2** tree that yields such wood. *adj-*: *a* hardwood *floor.*
har·dy (här′ dē) *adj-* **[har·di·er, har·di·est] 1** strong; robust; able to bear suffering or hardship: *A* hardy *soldier can march all night.* **2** daring; bold: *a* hardy *adventurer.* **3** of plants, able to endure extremes of temperature, moisture, etc. *—adv-* **hard′ i·ly.**
hare (hâr) *n-* member of the rabbit family that jumps rather than runs. It has longer ears and more powerful legs than the rabbit and does not burrow. Some hares, such as the jackrabbit, are called rabbits. *Hom-* hair.

Varying hare, about 18 in. long

hare·bell (hâr′ bĕl′) *n-* plant with a slender stalk and blue flowers shaped like bells.
hare·brained (hâr′ brānd′) *adj-* silly; rash.
hare·lip (hâr′ lĭp′) *n-* divided condition of the upper lip, existing from birth. *—adj-* **hare′ lipped′.**
ha·rem (hăr′ əm, hâr′-) *n-* **1** part of a Muslim house where the women live. **2** women who live in this area.
hark (härk) *vi-* to listen; listen closely (used especially as an exclamation).
hark back to to go back or refer to: *This superstition* harks back to *the Middle Ages. He is always* harking back to *his war service.*
hark·en (här′ kən) *vi-* to listen closely; pay attention to.
Har·le·quin (här′ lə kwĭn′) *n-* **1** comic character in pantomime, with shaven head and masked face, who wears a parti-colored costume. **2 harlequin** clown; buffoon. *adj-* **harlequin** parti-colored: *a* harlequin *pattern.*
har·lot (här′ lət) *n-* prostitute.
harm (härm) *n-* **1** injury; damage. **2** moral evil or wrongdoing. *vt-* to hurt; damage; injure.
harm·ful (härm′ fəl) *adj-* hurtful; causing damage; injurious: *a* harmful *habit.* *—adv-* **harm′ ful·ly.** *n-* **harm′ ful·ness.**
harm·less (härm′ ləs) *adj-* having no power to damage or hurt: *a* harmless *drug.* *—adv-* **harm′ less·ly.** *n-* **harm′ less·ness.**
har·mon·ic (här mŏn′ ĭk) *adj-* **1** in tune; concordant; harmonious. **2** *Music* (1) of or relating to harmony. (2) relating to a tone whose rate of vibration is two times, three times, etc., the rate of a certain primary tone. **3** *Physics* having harmonic motion. *n- Music* overtone.
har·mon·i·ca (här mŏn′ ĭ kə) *n-* small musical instrument with metal reeds, played by blowing and sucking air through a set of holes; mouth organ.
harmonic motion *Physics n-* the simplest type of vibratory motion in which there is a regular, periodic movement about a midpoint. The motion of a pendulum is approximately harmonic. Also **simple harmonic motion.**
har·mo·ni·ous (här mō′ nē əs) *adj-* **1** pleasant and unruffled; friendly; peaceable: *a* harmonious *family life.* **2** combining to form a pleasing and agreeable whole: *a* harmonious *color scheme.* **3** pleasing to the ear; melodious: *a* harmonious *string ensemble.* *—adv-* **har·mo′ ni·ous·ly.**
har·mo·ni·um (här mō′ nē əm) *n-* small keyboard instrument in which tones are produced by air passing over reeds; reed organ.
har·mo·ni·za·tion (här′ mə nə zā′ shən) *n-* a putting or bringing into harmony: *the* harmonization *of ideas.*
har·mo·nize (här′ mə nīz′) *vt-* **[har·mo·nized, har·mo·niz·ing] 1** to bring into agreement or accord: *to* harmonize *colors.* **2** to cause to agree; reconcile: *to* harmonize *conflicting opinions.* **3** to arrange in musical harmony, as a melody. *vi-* **1** to play or sing in parts. **2** to be in agreement; blend: *The two styles of furniture* harmonized. *—n-* **har′ mo·niz′ er.**
har·mo·ny (här′ mə nē) *n-* [*pl.* **har·mo·nies**] **1** pleasing combination or arrangement of parts, things, etc.: *the* harmony *of a color scheme.* **2** agreement in feelings, opinions, etc.: *the* harmony *between the two parties.* **3** pleasing combination of musical sounds. **4** *Music* combination of musical tones to form chords; also, the study of this.

Harness

har·ness (här′ nəs) *n-* **1** arrangement of straps and metal pieces by which an animal is hitched to a vehicle or, sometimes, controlled for riding. **2** any such arrangement of straps. *vt-* **1** to put such an arrangement on (a horse, dog, etc.). **2** to make useful in a controlled way: *to* harness *a waterfall*; *to* harness *one's strength.*
harp (härp) *n-* large triangular musical instrument with many strings, played by plucking the strings with the fingers. *vi-* to play on such an instrument. *—n-* **harp′ er.**
harp on (or **about**) to repeat or talk about at great length.

Woman playing harp

harp·ist (här′ pĭst) *n-* person who plays a harp.
har·poon (här pōōn′) *n-* barbed spear with a rope attached, either shot from a gun or thrown, and used to catch whales, large fish, etc. *vt-* to strike or kill with a harpoon: *He* harpooned *a seal.* *—n-* **har·poon′ er.**

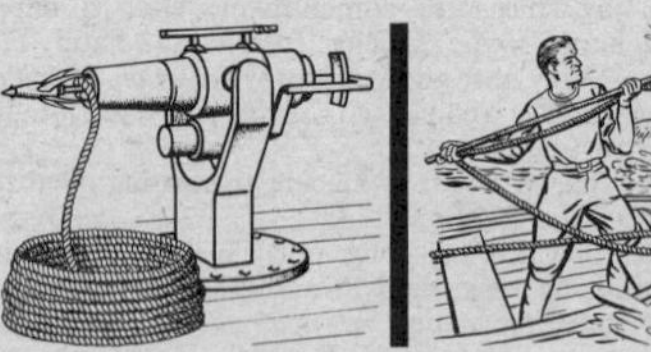
Harpoons

harpoon gun *n-* gun that fires a harpoon.
harp·si·chord (härp′ sə kòrd′, -kôrd′) *n-* keyboard instrument, developed before the piano, having wire strings that are plucked by quill or leather points.
Har·py (här′ pē) *n-* [*pl.* **Har·pies**] **1** in Greek mythology, one of several filthy, winged monsters who are part woman and part bird. **2 harpy** shrewish woman.

har·que·bus (här′kwə bəs) ***n-*** portable gun of the 15th and 16th centuries, later replaced by the musket.

Harquebus

har·ri·dan (hăr′ə dən) ***n-*** scolding, cross old woman.
har·ri·er (hăr′ē ər) ***n-*** **1** cross-country runner. **2** small dog used to hunt hares. [from **hare.**]
har·ri·er (hăr′ē ər) ***n-*** **1** person who harries. **2** any of various long-legged hawks. [from **harry.**]
har·row (hăr′ō) ***n-*** farm implement with sharp iron teeth or sharp steel disks. It is drawn by a horse or tractor over plowed land to break up the soil or cover up seed. ***vt-*** **1** to cultivate (land, a field, etc.) with such an implement. **2** to distress; trouble; disturb painfully: *Fear of failure* harrowed *him.* **—*n-* har′row·er.**

Disk harrow

har·row·ing (hăr′ō ĭng) ***adj-*** causing pain, fear, or torment: *The crash was a* harrowing *experience.*
har·ry (hăr′ē) ***ve-*** **[har·ried, har·ry·ing] 1** to torment; vex: *He* harried *the speaker with many questions.* **2** to keep raiding; plunder: *Pirates* harried *the galleons.*
harsh (härsh) ***adj-*** **[harsh·er, harsh·est] 1** unkind; hard; severe: *a* harsh *command.* **2** rough; coarse: *a* harsh *wool.* **3** unpleasant; disagreeable: *a* harsh *sound.* **—*adv-* harsh′ly. *n-* harsh′ness.**
hart (härt) ***n-*** male red deer over five years old; stag. ***Hom-*** heart.
harte·beest (här′tə bēst′) ***n-*** any of several large African antelopes with ringed horns.
harts·horn (härts′hôrn′, -hôrn′) ***n-*** **1** antler of a hart, formerly the chief source of ammonia. **2** preparation of ammonia, used mainly for smelling salts.
har·um-scar·um (hâr′əm skâr′əm, hăr′əm skăr′-) *Informal* ***adj-*** reckless; rash; irresponsible. ***adv-*** in a reckless manner; rashly: *He ran* harum-scarum *into the fight.* ***n-*** person who behaves recklessly.
har·vest (här′vəst) ***n-*** **1** a ripe crop of grain, fruit, etc.: *a large* harvest *of apples.* **2** the gathering of a crop: *The farmer hired men for the wheat* harvest. **3** the season when crops are gathered, usually late summer or early fall. **4** result or reward: *Her success is the* harvest *of her efforts.* ***vt-*** to gather in; reap: *to* harvest *corn.* ***vi-***: *They* harvested *last week.*
har·vest·er (här′vəs tər) ***n-*** **1** person who gathers a crop; reaper. **2** machine for gathering crops, especially grain.
har·vest·man (här′vəst mən) ***n-*** [*pl.* **har·vest·men**] **1** daddy-longlegs. **2** man who harvests; harvester.
harvest moon ***n-*** full moon in late September, when it often appears unusually large and bright.
has (hăz) form of **have** used with "he," "she," "it," or singular noun subjects, in the present tense.
has-been (hăz′bĭn′) *Informal* ***n-*** person who was once famous, popular, or effective, but is no longer so.
hash (hăsh) ***n-*** **1** mixture of meat and vegetables chopped into small pieces and fried together. **2** *Informal* hashish. ***vt-*** **1** to chop into small pieces. **2** *Informal* to review; reconsider: *They* hashed *and rehashed the problem.*
make a hash of *Informal* to make a mess of. **settle (someone's) hash** *Slang* to deal with someone severely.

hash·ish or **hash·eesh** (hăsh′ēsh′) ***n-*** sprouts and tops of the hemp plant, smoked or chewed for an intoxicating effect; marijuana.
has·n't (hăz′ənt) has not.
hasp (hăsp) ***n-*** hinged metal clasp which fits over a staple and is fastened with a pin or padlock to keep a door or box closed.
has·sle (hăs′əl) *Informal* ***n-*** heated argument; fight; squabble. ***vi-*** **[has·sled, has·sling]** to squabble; fight.
has·sock (hăs′ək) ***n-*** **1** upholstered cushion used to kneel or sit upon; footstool. **2** tuft of coarse grass.
hast (hăst) *Archaic* form of **have** used with "thou" in the present tense.
haste (hāst) ***n-*** a hurry; speed; rush: *to leave in* haste.
make haste to hurry: *Please* make haste; *we are late.*
has·ten (hā′sən) ***vi-*** to go quickly; hurry: *He* hastened *to the bank.* ***vt-*** to cause to move faster or be done more quickly: *We* hastened *the children across the street.*
hast·y (hās′tē) ***adj-*** **[hast·i·er, hast·i·est] 1** quick; speedy; hurried: *a* hasty *exit.* **2** carelessly said or done; rash: *a* hasty *remark.* **3** quick to become angry; fiery. **—*adv-* hast′i·ly. *n-* hast′i·ness.**
hasty pudding ***n-*** a mush or pudding made by stirring corn meal, oatmeal, or flour into boiling water or milk.
hat (hăt) ***n-*** a covering for the head, usually with a crown and a brim. **—*adj-* hat′less.**
pass the hat to ask for contributions; take up a collection. **take (one's) hat off to** to show respect for or honor by or as if by removing one's hat. **talk through (one's) hat** to talk of something one knows nothing about; talk foolishly. **toss (one's) hat in the ring** to run for political office. **under (one's) hat** as a secret; in confidence.
hat·band (hăt′bănd′) ***n-*** cloth band worn around the crown of a hat, just above the brim.
[1]**hatch** (hăch) ***vt-*** **1** to cause young to come out of (eggs). **2** to produce (young) from eggs: *to* hatch *a brood of chickens.* **3** to plan in secret; plot: *The rebels* hatched *a scheme to get arms.* ***vi-*** **1** to produce living young: *All the eggs* hatched. **2** to come out of the egg: *These chicks* hatched *yesterday.* ***n-*** the brood produced at one time: *a* hatch *of chicks.* [of unknown origin.]
[2]**hatch** (hăch) ***n-*** **1** an opening in a deck, roof, or floor, often with a removable cover or trap door; hatchway. **2** the cover or trap door for such an opening. [from Old English **hæcc** meaning "a grating."]

Hatch

[3]**hatch** (hăch) ***vt-*** to mark (a drawing) with closely spaced parallel lines running in one or more directions, as a means of shading, marking off a certain area, etc.; crosshatch. ***n-*** one of the lines used for this. [from Old French **hacher** meaning "to cut (across); chop up," and related to **hash** and **hatchet.**]
hatch·er·y (hăch′ə rē) ***n-*** [*pl.* **hatch·er·ies**] place where eggs, especially those of fish or poultry, are hatched.
hatch·et (hăch′ət) ***n-*** small, light ax with a head like a hammer and a short handle, used with one hand.
bury the hatchet to end a quarrel or fight; make peace.
dig up the hatchet to start fighting; make war.
hatchet face ***n-*** face with long, sharp, and thin features. **—*adj-* hatch′et-faced′** (hăch′ət fāst′).
hatch·et·man (hăch′ət măn′) ***n-*** [*pl.* **hatch·et·men**] **1** hired killer. **2** person whose job is to carry out ruthless schemes of his superior. **3** critic who specializes in severe attack.

hatch·ing (hăch′ ĭng) ***n-*** hachures on a map, chart, etc.

hatch·way (hăch′ wā′) ***n-*** opening in a ship's deck, or in a roof or floor, for passage below.

hate (hāt) ***vt-*** **[hat·ed, hat·ing] 1** to have very strong feelings against; detest; loathe: *Most people* hate *war or the thought of it.* **2** to regard as unpleasant; dislike: *She* hates *to wash dishes.* ***vi-***: *You have to be taught to* hate. ***n-*** **1** extreme or intense dislike; hatred: *He was consumed with* hate *for his tormentors.* **2** *Informal* a person or thing hated: *a pet* hate. **—*n-* hat′ er.**

hate·ful (hāt′ fəl) ***adj-*** **1** full of hate; showing hate: *a* hateful *remark*; *a* hateful *look.* **2** deserving or causing hate; detestable; loathsome: *Murder is a* hateful *crime.* **—*adv-* hate′ ful·ly. *n-* hate′ ful·ness.**

hath (hăth) *Archaic* form of **has** used with "he," "she," "it," or singular noun subjects in the present tense.

hat·pin (hăt′ pĭn′) ***n-*** long, sharp pin worn to fasten a woman's hat to her hair.

hat·rack (hăt′ răk′) ***n-*** framework of pegs or hooks, standing on the floor or hung on a wall to hold hats.

ha·tred (hā′ trəd) ***n-*** extreme or intense dislike; hate.

hat·ter (hăt′ ər) ***n-*** person who sells or makes men's hats.

hau·berk (hȯ′ bərk) ***n-*** knee-length coat of armor made of mail and worn by soldiers in the Middle Ages.

haugh·ty (hȯ′ tē) ***adj-*** **[haugh·ti·er, haugh·ti·est] 1** extremely proud of oneself or one's rank, social position, etc., and scornful of others; arrogant: *Cinderella had two* haughty *stepsisters.* **2** showing such pride and scorn: *a* haughty *look.* **—*adv-* haugh′ ti·ly. *n-* haugh′ ti·ness.**

haul (hȯl) ***vt-*** **1** to pull with force; tug with effort: *The dogs will* haul *the sled.* **2** to transport: *The moving van* hauled *our furniture away.* **3** to change the course of (a sailing ship) more directly into the wind. ***vi-*** to change course or direction: *The sailboat* hauled *into the wind.* ***n-*** **1** act of transporting: *a hard* haul *up the mountain.* **2** distance over which something is transported: *a long* haul *from St. Louis to California.* **3** the amount taken, caught, or won at one time: *a big* haul *of sardines*; *a fine* haul *of prizes.* ***Hom-*** hall. **—*n-* haul′ er.**

haul off 1 to turn a ship's course away from something. **2** *Slang* to draw the arm back in a position to strike.

haunch (hȯnch) ***n-*** **1** fleshy hind part of the hip of a person or animal: *The dog sat on his* haunches. **2** hindquarter of an animal, used for food: *a* haunch *of mutton.*

haunt (hȯnt) ***vt-*** **1** to visit or inhabit in a supernatural way: *They thought ghosts* haunted *the abandoned house.* **2** to trouble or bother persistently: *The memory of the accident* haunted *him for many years.* **3** to visit often or repeatedly: *He used to* haunt *the second-hand bookstores.* ***n-*** **1** place visited frequently: *The lake is a favorite summer* haunt. **2** *Informal* ghost.

haunt·ing (hȯn′ tĭng) ***adj-*** often coming back to the mind: *the* haunting *refrain.* **—*adv-* haunt′ ing·ly.**

haut·boy (ō′ boi′) ***n-*** oboe.

hau·teur (hō tûr′, *Fr.* ō tûr′) ***n-*** haughtiness; arrogance.

have (hăv) ***vt-*** **[had, hav·ing] 1** to hold; possess; own: *He* has *a ticket to the game. They* have *a new car. She* has *both charm and tact.* **2** to get; obtain; receive: *I* had *a letter from her yesterday.* **3** to take; accept: *I'll* have *toast and coffee.* **4** to hold or harbor in the mind: *He* has *a grudge against his brother. I* have *a new plan.* **5** to experience or undergo: *She* had *a good time. He* had *an accident. George* has *a bad cold.* **6** to put up with; allow; tolerate: *I won't* have *bad manners at this table.* **7** to cause to do or be done: *He* had *his sister help him with the chores.* **8** *Informal* to get the better of; beat: *He really* had *me in that argument.* **9** to state as a fact; assert: *Gossip* has *it that they were secretly married.* **10** to bear; be the parent of: *My sister* had *a baby last week. The dog* had *pups.* ***auxiliary verb-*** used with past participles to form the present perfect, past perfect, and future perfect tenses, and the perfect participle. Examples: I have made; I had made; I will have made; having made. ***Hom-*** halve.

have at to attack; hit; strike: *Let's* have at *them!*

have done to get through; finish: *Pay the man off and* have done *with him.*

have it in for to have a grudge against; seek revenge on.

have it out to fight or argue to a conclusion: *They* had it out *in the state tournament.*

have on to wear; be dressed in: *She* had on *a pink party dress with matching gloves.*

have to to be forced to; be obliged; must: *He* has to *work late every Thursday night.*

have to do with 1 to be connected with; be related to: *History* has to do with *events and peoples of the past.* **2** to be associated with; deal with: *If you're wise, you won't* have *anything* to do with *them.*

ha·ven (hā′ vən) ***n-*** **1** a sheltered harbor or port for ships. **2** any place of shelter or safety; refuge: *The weary travelers found* haven *at the inn.*

have-not (hăv′ nŏt′) ***n-*** person, group, or country with very little wealth or few resources. *as* ***modifier***: *a* have-not *nation.*

have·n't (hăv′ ənt) have not.

hav·er·sack (hăv′ ər săk′) ***n-*** soldier's or hiker's canvas bag for carrying provisions, worn over the shoulders or hung by a strap from a shoulder.

hav·oc (hăv′ ək) ***n-*** wide and general destruction; ruin; devastation: *The hurricane caused* havoc *in the town.*

cry havoc to give the signal to an army for pillage and destruction. **play havoc with** to destroy; ruin; devastate.

[1]**haw** (hȯ) ***n-*** **1** the small, red, berrylike fruit of a hawthorn. **2** hawthorn. [from Old English **haga** meaning "a hawthorn fruit; a hedge."]

[2]**haw** (hȯ) ***n-*** sound made by a speaker who is unsure of himself or is searching for words. See also [2]*hem.* [perhaps an imitation of the sound.]

[3]**haw** (hȯ) ***interj-*** command given to a horse, oxen, etc., to turn left. See also *gee.* ***vi-***: *The horses* hawed. ***vt-***: *He* hawed *the team of horses.* [of unknown origin.]

Ha·wai·ian (hə wī′ ən) ***n-*** **1** a native or naturalized citizen of Hawaii. **2** the Polynesian language of the Hawaiian Islands. ***adj-***: *the* Hawaiian *guitar.*

[1]**hawk** (hȯk, hŏk) ***n-*** any of several swift, powerful birds of prey having a curved beak and sharp talons. Some kinds of hawks are trained to hunt other birds and small game. ***vi-*** to hunt with a hawk or falcon. [an alteration of Old English **hafuc.**] ***Hom-*** hock. **—*adj-* hawk′ like′.**

Goshawk, about 2 ft long

[2]**hawk** (hȯk, hŏk) ***vt-*** to call out (goods) for sale while going from place to place; peddle: *They* hawked *ice cream along the beach.* [shortened from [1]**hawker.**] ***Hom-*** hock.

[3]**hawk** (hȯk, hŏk) ***vi-*** to clear the throat noisily by coughing hard. ***vt-*** to bring up (phlegm) from the throat by coughing. [probably an imitation of the sound made when the throat is cleared in this way.] ***Hom-*** hock.

[1]**hawk·er** (hȯ′ kər) ***n-*** a person who calls out goods for sale in the streets; peddler. [from early German **hocker,** "huckster," from **hocken** meaning "to bend over (under the weight of a pack")).]

[2]**hawk·er** (hȯ′ kər) ***n-*** falconer. [from [1]**hawk.**]

hawk-eyed (hȯk′ īd′) ***adj-*** having keen sight.

hawk·ing (hȯ′ kĭng) ***n-*** the hunting of wild birds or game with the help of hawks; falconry.

hawks·bill (hȯks′ bĭl′) ***n-*** small sea turtle whose shell yields the most valuable tortoise shell for commerce.

hawse·hole (hȯz′ hōl′) ***n-*** opening in the upper bow of a ship, through which a cable, chain, or hawser is passed. Also **hawse.**

haw·ser (hȯ′ zər) ***n-*** thick rope or cable for towing and mooring ships.

haw·thorn (hȯ′ thȯrn′, -thôrn′) ***n-*** thorny shrub or tree which has fragrant white, pink, or red blossoms in the spring, and red or orange berries in the fall; haw.

hay (hā) ***n-*** grass, clover, alfalfa, etc., cut and dried for food for cattle or horses. ***vi-*** to cut and dry grass, alfalfa, etc., for hay. ***Hom-*** hey.

hit the hay *Slang* to go to bed. **make hay** to take advantage of one's opportunities.

hay·cock (hā′ kŏk′) ***n-*** small, dome-shaped pile of hay stacked in a field.

hay fever ***n-*** sneezing, watery eyes, running nose, headache, etc., caused by an allergic reaction to the pollen of certain plants, especially ragweed.

hay·fork (hā′ fȯrk′, -fôrk′) ***n-*** **1** long-handled pitchfork. **2** motor-driven mechanical fork for turning and moving hay.

hay·loft (hā′ lȯft′, -lŏft′) ***n-*** the upper part of a barn or stable, where hay is stored; haymow.

hay·mak·er (hā′ mā′ kər) *Slang* ***n-*** hard, swinging punch with the fist intended as a knockout blow.

hay·mow (hā′ mou′) ***n-*** **1** hayloft. **2** a pile of hay in a barn or stable.

hay·rack (hā′ răk′) ***n-*** **1** rack mounted on a wagon body for hauling hay. **2** rack for holding hay so that animals can eat it (for picture, see *rack*).

hay·rick (hā′ rĭk′) ***n-*** haystack.

hay·ride (hā′ rīd′) ***n-*** pleasure ride by a group in a wagon partly filled with hay.

hay·seed (hā′ sēd′) ***n-*** **1** grass seed that falls from hay when it is shaken. **2** *Slang* country person; yokel.

hay·stack (hā′ stăk′) ***n-*** large pile of hay stacked in the open air.

hay·wire (hā′ wīər′) ***n-*** wire for tying up bales of hay or straw. ***adj-*** *Informal* **1** poorly made, improvised, or repaired, as if hastily wired together: *a* haywire *contraption.* **2** not working properly; also, crazy: *The clock is* haywire. *He is* haywire.

haz·ard (hăz′ərd) ***n-*** **1** the chance of harm, damage, or loss; danger; risk: *Arctic exploration is full of* hazards. **2** person, thing, or condition that can cause damage or destruction: *Reckless drivers and speeding cars are* hazards *to other motorists.* **3** on a golf course, a sand pit, pond, or other obstacle in which a ball may be trapped. **4** an old game played with dice, from which craps developed. ***vt-*** **1** to leave to chance; expose to danger; risk: *People who are careless with fire* hazard *their lives.* **2** to offer; venture: *He* hazarded *a guess.*

haz·ard·ous (hăz′ ər dəs) ***adj-*** dangerous; risky: *Shooting rapids in a canoe is a* hazardous *sport.* ***—adv-*** **haz′ ard·ous·ly.** ***n-*** **haz′ ard·ous·ness.**

[1]**haze** (hāz) ***n-*** **1** a light fog, mist, or smoke in the air. **2** confusion of thought; daze: *His mind was in a* haze. [of uncertain origin.]

[2]**haze** (hāz) ***vt-*** **[hazed, haz·ing]** to make (someone) do unpleasant tasks or foolish tricks: *The fraternity members* hazed *the pledges as part of their initiation.* [from an Old French **haser** meaning "to irritate."]

ha·zel (hā′ zəl) ***n-*** **1** shrub or small tree of the birch family that bears an edible nut. **2** the wood of this tree. **3** light, reddish brown, the color of the hazelnut shell. ***adj-***: *a* hazel *twig*; *her* hazel *eyes.*

ha·zel·nut (hā′ zəl nŭt′) ***n-*** the nut of the hazel; filbert.

ha·zy (hā′ zē) ***adj-*** **[ha·zi·er, ha·zi·est]** **1** full of fog, mist, or smoke: *a* hazy *sky.* **2** unclear: *a* hazy *view*; hazy *ideas.* ***—adv-*** **ha′ zi·ly.** ***n-*** **ha′ zi·ness.**

H-bomb (āch′ bŏm′) ***n-*** hydrogen bomb.

H.C.F. or **h.c.f.** highest common factor.

hdqrs. headquarters.

he (hē) ***pron-*** (used as a singular subject in the third person) **1** male person or animal that has been named or is being pointed out: *Where is Charles?* He *is upstairs.* He*'s coming with me now!* **2** any person or animal (often followed by "who" or "that"): He *who hesitates is lost.* ***n-*** a male: *Is that hamster a* he *or a she? as* ***modifier***: *a* he*-goat.*

He symbol for helium.

HE or **H.E.** high explosive.

head (hĕd) ***n-*** **1** the part of the body of man and most animals that contains the brain, mouth, eyes, ears, etc., and is located at the top of an upright body or the front of a four-legged or crawling body in ordinary motion. **2** the enlarged top part of something resembling this: *the* head *of a nail*; *the* head *of a hammer.* **3** top or upper part: *the* head *of a staircase*; *the* head *of a river*; *the* head *of a sail.* **4** front end: *the* head *of a parade*; *the train's* head. **5** the round, firm, top part of a plant: *a* head *of lettuce.* **6** of a bed, cot, bunk, etc., the end at which the upper part of the body lies. **7** top or highest position of rank, authority, etc.: *at the* head *of the government*; *at the* head *of the table.* **8** person of highest rank; chief; ruler: *the* head *of a company.* **9** picture or sculpture of the face and top part of a person; portrait: *a marble* head *of Caesar.* **10** topic or title: *He arranged his report under three* heads. **11** headline. **12** [*pl.* **head**] a single animal or person: *ten* head *of cattle*; *seats at ten dollars a* head. **13** (often **heads**) the main side of a coin, often stamped with the image of the face and top part of a person: *If it's* heads *I win, tails you win.* **14** mental ability; mind: *to have a good* head *for figures.* **15** foam or froth on top of a glass of beer, ale, etc. **16** the raised, middle, and sorest part of a pimple, boil, etc. **17** pressure or amount of pressure: *a good* head *of steam.* **18** the tight membrane of a drum, tambourine, etc., that one strikes to produce sound. *as* ***modifier***: *the* head *man of a firm*; *the* head *car of the motorcade.* ***vt-*** **1** to be in charge of; lead; direct (often with "up"): *Our teacher* heads *the history department.* **2** to be at the front or top of; precede: *The honored guests* headed *the parade. Her name* heads *the honor roll.* **3** to cause to go in a certain direction: *The pilot* headed *his plane toward the sea.* **4** in soccer, to hit (the ball) with the head. ***vi-*** to go or move in a certain direction: *to* head *west*; *to* head *for danger.* ***—adj-*** **head′ less.**

bring to a head to bring to a climax or crisis: *The committee's new petition* brought *the entire matter* to a head. **come to a head** **1** to come to a climax or crisis. **2** to fill with pus, as a boil does. **give (someone) his head** to let someone go or do as he chooses. **go to (one's) head** **1** to make one conceited: *His quick success* went to his head. **2** to make one intoxicated. **hang (one's) head** to show that one is ashamed by or as if by lowering the head. **head and shoulders above** much better than: *Bill is* head and shoulders above *Tom in tennis.* **head over heels** **1** in a somersault: *He stumbled and fell* head over heels. **2** completely; thoroughly: *They* *were* head over heels *in love.* **hide (one's) head** to show that one is ashamed by or as if by lowering the head or concealing the face. **keep (one's) head** to remain calm and self-controlled; not get excited: *He* kept his head *during the riot.* **keep (one's) head above water** to survive; avoid disaster: *Some poor families can barely* keep their heads above water. **lose (one's) head** to lose self-control; become excited: *The fans* lost their heads *and threw things at the umpire.* **make head or tail of** to make sense of; understand (usually expressed negatively): *He couldn't* make head or tail of *that poem.* **off** (or **out of**) **one's head** crazy; insane; irrational. **on** (or **upon**) **one's head** as one's total responsibility: *Let success or failure be* on my head. **(one's) head off** very much; excessively: *to laugh* your head off; *to talk* his head off. **over (one's) head** 1 too hard or strange to understand: *Nuclear physics is* over my head. 2 over the authority of another without consulting him: *He went* over the *supervisor's* head *and brought the matter to the president.* **put** (or **lay**) **heads together** to discuss or plan together; scheme. **take it into (one's) head** to get the idea or notion: *He* took it into his head *that he should be the manager.* **turn (one's) head** to cause to become conceited: *Popularity* turned her head.

head off 1 to get in front of and turn aside: *The posse* headed off *the rustlers at the pass.* 2 to prevent; avert: *Quick thinking* headed off *a collision.*

head·ache (hĕd′ āk′) ***n-*** 1 a continuous pain in the head. 2 *Informal* a cause of trouble or bother; annoyance.

head·board (hĕd′ bôrd′) ***n-*** board or frame at or forming the head of a bed.

head·cheese (hĕd′ chēz′) ***n-*** soft, jellied loaf of meat made of chopped parts of the head and feet of a pig or calf and usually served cold.

head·dress (hĕd′ drĕs′) ***n-*** 1 a covering or decoration worn on the head. 2 the way the hair is worn or arranged; coiffure.

head·ed (hĕd′ əd) ***adj-*** 1 having a head of a certain kind: *a large-*headed *dog*; *a light*headed *feeling.* 2 having a certain number of heads: *a three-*headed *statue.*

head·er (hĕd′ ər) ***n-*** 1 person or machine that puts on or removes the heads of barrels, nails, etc. 2 farm machine that cuts off and loads heads of grain. 3 *Informal* a fall, dive, or headlong plunge.

head·first (hĕd′ fûrst′) ***adv-*** 1 with the head in front: *He dived* headfirst *into the pool.* 2 in thoughtless haste; rashly: *He jumped* headfirst *into the argument.* ***adj-***: *a* headfirst *plunge.* Also **head′ fore′ most′**.

head·gate (hĕd′ gāt′) ***n-*** 1 gate at the upstream end of a canal lock. 2 gate that controls the flow of water into a sluice, irrigation ditch, etc.

head·gear (hĕd′ gêr′) ***n-*** 1 anything worn on the head, especially a protective helmet. 2 the part of a horse's harness that fits over the head.

head-hun·ter (hĕd′ hŭn′ tər) ***n-*** warrior in a primitive tribe who cuts off the head of an enemy he has killed and keeps it as a trophy. **—*n-* head′ -hunt′ ing.**

head·ing (hĕd′ ĭng) ***n-*** 1 title, subtitle, topic, etc., put at the beginning of something written or printed. 2 direction of travel, especially of a ship or airplane.

head·land (hĕd′ lənd) ***n-*** high point of land jutting into a body of water, especially a cliff; cape; promontory.

head·light (hĕd′ līt′) ***n-*** bright light on the front of an automobile, train, etc., to illuminate the road ahead.

head·line (hĕd′ līn′) ***n-*** line or lines in large type at the top of a news story, telling what it is about. ***adj-*** worthy of a headline; important: *a bit of* headline *gossip.*

head·lin·er (hĕd′ lī′ nər) ***n-*** 1 writer of headlines for a newspaper. 2 *Informal* star actor, athlete, etc.

head·lock (hĕd′ lŏk′) ***n-*** in wrestling, a tight hold with the arm or arms around the head of an opponent.

head·long (hĕd′ lòng′) ***adv-*** 1 with the head first; headfirst: *Alice fell* headlong *down the rabbit hole.* 2 without thinking; recklessly; rashly: *He dashed* headlong *into the street chasing the ball.* ***adj-*** 1 headfirst: *a* headlong *dive.* 2 reckless; rash: *a* headlong *attack.*

head·man (hĕd′ mən) ***n-*** [*pl.* **head·men**] leader or chief; highest official: *We met the* headman *of the African village.* Also **head man.**

head·mas·ter (hĕd′ măs′ tər) ***n-*** man in charge of a private school; principal. **—*n-*** *fem.* **head′ mis·tress.**

head-on (hĕd′ ŏn′) ***adj-*** between two things going in opposite directions and meeting front to front: *a* head-on *collision.* ***adv-*** front to front from opposite directions: *to crash* head-on.

head·phone (hĕd′ fōn′) ***n-*** 1 small radio or telephone speaker held to the ear by a band over the head. 2 **headphones** two of these, one for each ear, on a single band.

head·piece (hĕd′ pēs′) ***n-*** 1 covering for the protection of the head; also, a cap or hat. 2 in printing, a design at the beginning of a chapter or other large section.

head·quar·ters (hĕd′ kwòr′ tərz) ***n-*** (takes singular or plural verb) place from which orders are sent out; center of control or authority; main office: *army* headquarters; *police* headquarters; *the* headquarters *of the Republican Party.*

head·rest (hĕd′ rĕst′) ***n-*** any device, such as one on a barber's or dentist's chair, for supporting the head.

head·room (hĕd′ ro͞om′) ***n-*** clear space overhead for passing under a bridge or arch, through a doorway or tunnel, etc.

head·ship (hĕd′ shĭp′) ***n-*** position or authority of a head or leader; leadership; command.

heads·man (hĕdz′ mən) ***n-*** [*pl.* **heads·men**] executioner who beheads persons sentenced to death.

head·stand (hĕd′ stănd′) ***n-*** the position of being upside down with one's weight resting on the top of the head.

head·stone (hĕd′ stōn′) ***n-*** tombstone.

head·strong (hĕd′ stròng′) ***adj-*** 1 determined to have one's way; stubborn; willful: *He's too* headstrong *to be a good chairman.* 2 marked by stubborn determination; rash: *a* headstrong *decision.*

head·wait·er (hĕd′ wā′ tər) ***n-*** man in charge of the dining room at a hotel, restaurant, etc.; maître d'hôtel.

head·wa·ters (hĕd′ wò′ tərz, -wŏt′ ərz) ***n-*** *pl.* the small stream or streams that are the source of a river; upper waters of a stream.

head·way (hĕd′ wā′) ***n-*** 1 forward motion; progress: *to make* headway *against a current*; *to make* headway *with one's plans.* 2 the time interval between two trains or other vehicles passing a point on the same route in the same direction; also, the distance between the two vehicles. 3 headroom.

head wind ***n-*** wind that blows opposite to the direction in which a ship, airplane, etc., is moving: *Strong* head winds *delayed the arrival of the plane.*

head work ***n-*** work done with the head or mind; mental effort; thought.

head·y (hĕd′ ē) ***adj-*** **[head·i·er, head·i·est]** 1 able to make one feel light-headed or giddy; intoxicating: *a* heady *wine*; *a* heady *aroma.* 2 slightly dizzy or intoxicated: *a* heady *feeling.* 3 headstrong; rash. **—*n-* head′ i·ness.**

heal (hēl) ***vt-*** 1 to make well; help to become whole or sound: *to* heal *the sick*; *to* heal *a wound.* 2 to settle; reconcile: *Discussion* healed *their bad feelings.* ***vi-*** to get well; become healthy: *The cut* healed *quickly in the fresh air.* ***Homs-*** heel, he'll. **—*n-* heal′ er.**

health (hĕlth) ***n-*** **1** freedom from sickness, deformity, etc.: Health *is a blessing.* **2** condition of the parts and the functioning of something, especially of the body or mind: *good* health; *failing* health; *the* health *of the steel industry.* **3** a toast to (a person's) happiness and good bodily condition: *to drink his* health. *as* ***modifier:*** *a* health *problem*; health *education*; *a* health *commissioner.*

health·ful (hĕlth′ fəl) ***adj-*** good for the health; giving health; wholesome: *a* healthful *food*; *a* healthful *climate.* **—*adv-*** **health′ ful·ly.** ***n-*** **health′ ful·ness.**
►Should not be confused with HEALTHY.

health insurance ***n-*** insurance coverage or policy that entitles one to medical care, hospitalization, etc., for the payment of a fixed periodic fee.

health·y (hĕl′ thē) ***adj-*** **[health·i·er, health·i·est] 1** having good health: *a* healthy *child.* **2** showing good health or welfare: *a* healthy *appetite*; *a* healthy *glow in one's cheeks.* **3** contributing to safety or welfare: *a* healthy *respect for tigers.* **—*adv-*** **health′ i·ly.** ***n-*** **health′ i·ness.**
►Should not be confused with HEALTHFUL.

heap (hēp) ***n-*** **1** many things lying one on another; pile: *a* heap *of rocks.* **2** *Informal* a large amount; a lot: *a* heap *of money*; *a* heap *of trouble.* ***vt-*** **1** to put into a pile: *He* heaped *the baggage in one corner.* **2** to fill up; load: *The cook* heaped *each plate with meat and potatoes.* **3** to give in large amounts: *He* heaped *gifts on his grandchildren. They* heaped *insults on the enemy.* ***vi-*** to become piled: *Drifting snow* heaps *up quickly.*

hear (hêr) ***vt-*** **[heard** (hûrd), **hear·ing] 1** to become aware of (sound waves or their source) through the ears: *I* hear *the crying of a baby. I* heard *the coyotes last night.* **2** to become informed of: *He* heard *the news on the radio.* **3** to pay attention to; listen to: *Please* hear *what I have to say.* **4** to give a chance to be heard, especially in a formal situation: *The king* heard *the petitioners. The judge* heard *three cases today.* **5** to grant: *Lord,* hear *our plea.* ***vi-*** **1** to be aware of sound through the ears: *A deaf person can't* hear. **2** to be told; get news; learn: *I never* heard *of it.* ***Hom-*** here. **—*n-*** **hear′ er.**

hear from 1 to get a message from. **2** to be dealt with or punished by: *Don't do it or you'll* hear from *me.*

hear out to listen to (someone) until he has finished.

will not hear of will not permit or agree to.

hear·ing (hêr′ ĭng) ***n-*** **1** the sense by which sound is perceived; ability to hear: *His* hearing *was impaired by the explosion.* **2** the distance over which sound can be heard: *In the park they kept the children within* hearing. **3** chance to be heard: *The mayor gave him a* hearing. **4** a formal meeting to discuss or investigate something.

hearing aid ***n-*** small battery-operated sound amplifier and speaker, worn in or near the ear to improve hearing.

heark·en (här′ kən) harken.

hear·say (hêr′ sā) ***n-*** something heard about from the talk of other persons; rumor; gossip. ***adj-*** based on what is heard from someone else, and not on personal knowledge: *a* hearsay *account*; hearsay *evidence.*

hearse (hûrs) ***n-*** vehicle for carrying a coffin at a funeral.

AORTA
PULMONARY ARTERY
AURICLES
VENTRICLES
Human heart

heart (härt) ***n-*** **1** the hollow, muscular organ in the chest that pumps blood through the body. **2** the innermost part; center; core: *the* heart *of the jungle*; hearts *of lettuce.* **3** one's deepest being or beliefs; true nature: *I knew in my* heart *that I was wrong. His* heart *was not in his work.* **4** state of mind; mood: *a heavy* heart. **5** tender feelings; sympathy; compassion: *His loneliness touched our* hearts. **6** courage: *the* heart *of a lion.* **7** energy; spirit; enthusiasm: *Put more* heart *into your work.* **8** a design [♥] pointed at the bottom and divided at the top into two equal lobes. **9** any one of a suit of playing cards marked with this design in red. **10 hearts** (1) a suit of cards marked in this way. (2) a card game whose object is to win all or none of the cards so marked. ***Hom-*** hart.

after (one's) own heart that suits or pleases one perfectly: *She is a girl* after my own heart. **at heart** in one's inmost being: *He is a religious man* at heart. *We have your best interests* at heart. **break (one's) heart** to cause one deep grief or disappointment. **by heart** by memory: *He knows that poem* by heart. **change of heart** a change of mind or attitude: *He had a* change of heart *and decided not to punish the boy.* **do (one's) heart good** to be very pleasing and gratifying to one: *The news* did my heart good. **eat (one's) heart out** to feel great sadness, regret, or longing. **have a heart** to be kind and merciful. **have (one's) heart in (one's) mouth** to be afraid. **have (one's) heart in the right place** to have good intentions; mean well. **heart and soul** with all one's energy, spirit, etc. **in (one's) heart of hearts** in the deepest and most serious part of one's knowledge and feelings. **lay to heart** to give serious thought to: *He heard the warning and* laid *it* to heart. **set (one's) heart on** to want very much; long for: *He* set his heart on *a sailboat.* **take to heart** to be deeply impressed or affected by: *Don't* take *the defeat too much* to heart. **to (one's) heart's content** as much as one wishes: *Eat* to your heart's content. **wear (one's) heart on (one's) sleeve** to show one's feelings too openly: *The sentimental girl* wore her heart on her sleeve. **with all (one's) heart. 1** with all one's being: *He loved her* with all his heart. **2** gladly; willingly.

heart·ache (härt′ āk′) ***n-*** sorrow; grief.

heart·beat (härt′ bēt′) ***n-*** **1** a single contraction and relaxation of the heart muscles. **2** the rate or type of these: *a rapid* heartbeat; *a fluttery* heartbeat.

heart·break (härt′ brāk′) ***n-*** very great sorrow or grief.

heart·break·ing (härt′brā′ kĭng) ***adj-*** causing or marked by great sorrow or grief.

heart·bro·ken (härt′ brō′ kən) ***adj-*** overwhelmed by sorrow or grief. **—*adv-*** **heart′ bro′ ken·ly.**

heart·burn (härt′ bûrn′) ***n-*** burning or otherwise painful sensation in the middle of the chest, usually caused by too much acid in the stomach.

heart·ed (här′ təd) ***adj-*** having a specified kind of feeling, nature, etc.: *broken*-hearted; *hard*-hearted; *kind*-hearted.

heart·en (här′ tən) ***vt-*** to cheer up; encourage.

heart·felt (härt′ fĕlt′) ***adj-*** deeply felt; sincere; genuine.

hearth (härth) ***n-*** **1** flat stone or brick floor of a fireplace, often extending into the room. **2** the fireplace as a symbol of home; fireside: *the comfort of one's* hearth. **3** the part of a stove, oven, or furnace on which the fire is built. **4** the floor of a forge or furnace where ore is exposed to the action of heat.

Hearth

hearth·side (härth′ sīd′) ***n-*** the area in a room just around the hearth; hence, one's home. *as* ***modifier:*** *the* hearthside *stories told by grandfather.*

hearth·stone (här*th*′ stōn′) ***n-*** **1** flat stone forming a hearth. **2** the center of a home; fireside.

heart·i·ly (här′ tə lē) ***adv-*** **1** in a warm, friendly way; cordially: *She greeted us* heartily. **2** enthusiastically: *They laughed* heartily. **3** with a good appetite. **4** completely; thoroughly: *I* heartily *agree with you.*

heart·i·ness (här′ tĭ nəs) ***n-*** **1** warmth; cordiality. **2** strength; vigor. **3** enthusiasm; zest. **4** abundance of appetite or food.

heart·land (här*t*′ lănd′) ***n-*** **1** most important region or center of some activity: *The Midwest is the* heartland *of American farming.* **2** in geopolitics, a region that gives its possessor control over surrounding regions and a position of great military strength.

heart·less (här*t*′ ləs) ***adj-*** without sympathy or pity; cruel; callous: *It is* heartless *to mistreat animals.* **—*adv-*** **heart′ less·ly.** ***n-*** **heart′ less·ness.**

heart-rend·ing (här*t*′ rĕn′ dĭng) ***adj-*** causing extreme grief; very distressing: *a* heart-rending *bit of news*; heart-rending *cries for help.* **—*adv-*** **heart′ rend′ ing·ly.**

hearts·ease or **heart's-ease** (här*ts*′ ēz′) ***n-*** **1** any of various violets. **2** ease of mind; tranquility.

heart·sick (här*t*′ sĭk′) ***adj-*** very unhappy; despondent.

heart·strings (här*t*′ strĭngz′) ***n- pl.*** the deepest feelings; strongest emotions: *Sick babies tug at my* heartstrings.

heart-to-heart (här*t*′ tōō här*t*′) ***adj-*** frank and direct; intimate; sincere: *a* heart-to-heart *talk.*

heart·wood (här*t*′ wŏŏd′) ***n-*** the hard, tough, inner wood of a tree.

heart·y (här′ tē) ***adj-*** **[heart·i·er, heart·i·est] 1** warm and sincere; friendly; cordial: *a* hearty *welcome.* **2** in excellent health; strong; vigorous: *a* hearty *old man.* **3** full of enthusiasm; not restrained: *a* hearty *laugh.* **4** abundant and nourishing; satisfying: *a* hearty *meal.* **5** needing much food to be satisfied: *a* hearty *appetite.* ***n-*** [*pl.* **heart·ies**] good fellow; comrade; mate: *Keep a lookout for whales, my* hearties.

heat (hēt) ***n-*** **1** warmth, especially great warmth: *the* heat *of a fire*; *the* heat *of the sun.* **2** high temperature: *He doesn't mind the* heat. **3** *Physics* form of energy associated with the rapid, random motion of molecules. Heat is transferred from one substance to another by conduction, convection, or radiation and usually produces a rise in temperature. **4** the cost of warming a house, building, or apartment: *We include* heat *in the tenant's rent.* **5** intense feeling; excitement: *He says rash things in the* heat *of an argument.* **6** in sports, a single race or contest in a series, especially to eliminate the poorest competitors from the finals. **7** periodic condition of a female animal when she is ready for mating. ***vt-*** to make hot or warm: *A furnace* heats *the house.* ***vi-***: *The soup is* heating *on the stove.*

heat up 1 to make or become hot or warm: *Please* heat up *the baby's bottle.* **2** to become warmer than is proper or desired: *This engine* heats up *quickly.*

heat·ed (hē′ təd) ***adj-*** hot; inflamed; hence, angry; vehement: *a* heated *argument.* **—*adv-*** **heat′ ed·ly.**

heat·er (hē′ tər) ***n-*** a stove, furnace, or radiator for warming a room or automobile.

heat exchanger ***n-*** device that transfers heat from a liquid or gas on one side of a wall or barrier to another fluid on the other side, thereby increasing the temperature of one fluid while cooling the other.

heath (hēth) ***n-*** **1** in Great Britain, flat wasteland, often overgrown with shrubs; moor. **2** any one of several low-growing shrubs found on wasteland. Heather belongs to this family of plants.

hea·then (hē′ *th*ən) ***n-*** **1** person who does not believe in the Christian, Jewish, or Muslim God. **2** person who worships many gods or has no god; pagan. **3** uncivilized person; barbarian; savage. **4 the heathen** such persons collectively. ***adj-***: *a* heathen *idol*; heathen *customs.* **—*adj-*** **hea′ then·ish.**

hea·then·dom (hē′ *th*ən dəm) ***n-*** heathen peoples, countries, beliefs, or practices.

heath·er (hĕ*th*′ ər) ***n-*** tiny-leaved shrub with stalks of small, pale-purple blossoms, common in Scotland and England. **—*adj-*** **heath′ er·y.**

heating element ***n-*** electric wire that becomes hot when current passes through it. Heating elements are used in electric toasters, blankets, percolators, etc.

heat of fusion ***n-*** of a unit mass of a solid substance that is already at its melting point, the amount of heat necessary to bring about the change from solid to liquid, without changing the temperature.

heat of vaporization ***n-*** of a unit mass of a liquid that is already at its normal boiling point, the amount of heat necessary to cause the change from liquid to gas or vapor, without changing the temperature.

heat·stroke (hēt′ strōk′) ***n-*** extreme fatigue or collapse, accompanied by fever and dryness of the skin, caused by long exposure to high heat.

heat wave ***n-*** period of very hot weather.

heave (hēv) ***vt-*** **[heaved** or (chiefly nautical) **hove** (hōv), **heav·ing] 1** to lift or raise with effort; hoist: *The masons* heaved *the last stone to the top of the wall.* **2** to throw (something heavy); hurl: *He can* heave *the shot over 50 feet.* **3** to force out with an effort; utter with exertion: *He* heaved *a sigh of relief. She* heaved *a sob.* **4** *Informal* to vomit: *The sick boy* heaved *his supper.* ***vi-*** **1** to rise and fall repeatedly: *The waves* heaved *during the storm. His chest* heaved *for several minutes after the race.* **2** to swell upward; bulge: *The ground* heaved *during the blast. His chest* heaved *with pride.* **3** *Informal* to vomit or try to vomit; retch. ***n-*** **1** effort in lifting or throwing: *With a mighty* heave, *he put the crate on the truck.* **2** a throw or the distance thrown: *a record-breaking* heave *of the ball.* **3** a rising and falling movement, as the waves of the sea. **4 heaves** (takes singular verb) a disease of horses, marked by heavy breathing and coughing, and heaving of the flanks. **—*n-*** **heav′ er.**

heave ho! call used by sailors when pulling up anchor or doing other hard work.

heave in sight to rise into view, as a ship or land does.

heave to to stop a ship's forward motion by setting the sails so that they counteract one another.

heav·en (hĕv′ ən) ***n-*** **1** in some religions, the dwelling place of God and the angels and of the souls of good people after death. **2** any place or period of great happiness; state of bliss: *Our vacation in the Rockies was* heaven. **3 the heavens** the sky; place where the sun, moon, and stars appear. **4 Heaven** the Deity; God; Providence: *We pray* Heaven *grant us lasting peace.*

move heaven and earth to do everything within one's power: *I* moved heaven and earth *to get you here.*

heav·en·ly (hĕv′ ən lē) ***adj-*** **1** of or relating to the dwelling place of God; divine: *the* heavenly *choirs.* **2** fit for heaven; beyond compare; very beautiful: *a* heavenly *day.* **3** of the sky; celestial: *The sun, moon, and stars are* heavenly *bodies.* **—*n-*** **heav′ en·li·ness.**

heav·en·ward (hĕv′ ən wərd) ***adj-*** directed or going toward heaven: *a* heavenward *gaze.* ***adv-*** (also **heav′ en·wards**) toward heaven.

Heav·i·side layer (hĕv′ ĭ sīd′) ***n-*** layer of the ionosphere closest to the earth; E layer.

heav·y (hĕv′ ē) ***adj-*** **[heav·i·er, heav·i·est] 1** having much weight; hard to lift, carry, or move: *a* heavy *man*;

a heavy *bag of groceries*; *a* heavy *trunk.* **2** of greater than average weight, thickness, or density for its kind: *a* heavy *winter jacket*; heavy *socks*; heavy *legs*; heavy *cream*; heavy *oil for summer driving*; *a* heavy *fog.* **3** of great amount or force: *a* heavy *rain*; heavy *traffic*; *a* heavy *blow to the head.* **4** using or dealing in large quantities: *a* heavy *buyer*; *a* heavy *smoker.* **5** weighed down; loaded; full: *trees* heavy *with apples*; *sleepy children with* heavy *eyes.* **6** weighed down with sorrow; very sad: *Her heart was* heavy *at leaving home.* **7** hard to bear; harsh; oppressive: *a* heavy *fine*; heavy *taxes.* **8** hard to digest; rich; fatty: *to eat* heavy *foods.* **9** very cloudy and dark; overcast; gloomy: *a* heavy *sky.* **10** hard to travel over; full of obstacles; rough: *a* heavy *road*; heavy *going*; heavy *seas.* **11** hard to read or understand; not clear and flowing: *a* heavy *book*; *a* heavy *style of writing.* **12** loud and deep; powerful: *a* heavy *bass voice.* **13** of large size or capacity compared with others of its general type: *a* heavy *cruiser*; heavy *artillery.* ***—adv-*** **heav′i·ly.** ***n-*** **heav′i·ness.**

hang heavy to pass slowly and monotonously; drag on: *His evenings* hang heavy *on his hands.*

heav·y-du·ty (hĕv′ē dōō′tē, -dyōō′tē) ***adj-*** able to stand hard use, great strain, or wear: *a* heavy-duty *tire.*

heav·y-hand·ed (hĕv′ē hăn′dəd) ***adj-*** **1** clumsy in doing things with the hands; awkward: *The new boy was* heavy-handed *with the dishes.* **2** unreasonably severe or harsh in dealing with others; oppressive; tyrannical: *a* heavy-handed *ruler.* ***—adv-*** **heav′y-hand′ed·ly.** ***n-*** **heav′y-hand′ed·ness.**

heav·y-heart·ed (hĕv′ē här′təd) ***adj-*** sad; unhappy; depressed. ***—adv-*** **heav′y-heart′ed·ly.** ***n-*** **heav′y-heart′ed·ness.**

heavy hydrogen ***n-*** deuterium.

heav·y·set (hĕv′ē sĕt′) ***adj-*** having a short, stout body; stocky; thickset: *a* heavyset *wrestler.*

heavy water ***n-*** water in which all, or a relatively large amount of, the hydrogen is deuterium.

heav·y·weight (hĕv′ē wāt′) ***n-*** a person of more than average weight; especially, a boxer or wrestler over 175 pounds. *as* ***modifier***: *the* heavyweight *champion.*

He·be (hē′bē) ***n-*** in Greek mythology, the goddess of youth and cupbearer to the gods.

He·bra·ic (hē brā′ĭk) ***adj-*** of or relating to the Hebrew people, their language, or their customs; Hebrew.

He·brew (hē′brōō) ***n-*** **1** member or descendant of the Semitic group who were the chief inhabitants of ancient Palestine; Israelite; Jew. **2** the Semitic language of the ancient Hebrews. **3** the official language of modern Israel. ***adj-***: *a book of* Hebrew *songs.*

Hebrews, Epistle to the (hē′brōōz′) ***n-*** book of the New Testament addressed to Hebrew Christians.

Hec·a·te (hĕk′ə tē, also hĕk′ət) ***n-*** in Greek mythology, the goddess of the underworld. She was later associated with sorcery.

hec·a·tomb (hĕk′ə tōm′) ***n-*** in ancient Greece, public sacrifice of 100 oxen to the gods; hence, any great slaughter.

heck·le (hĕk′əl) ***vt-*** **[heck·led, heck·ling]** to interrupt and try to confuse (a public speaker) with annoying questions or remarks. ***—n-*** **heck′ler.**

hect·are (hĕk′târ′) ***n-*** in the metric system, a unit of land measure equal to 100 ares (10,000 square meters or 2.471 acres.)

hec·tic (hĕk′tĭk) ***adj-*** **1** very exciting; full of activity or commotion: *a* hectic *day at the fair.* **2** flushed and hot; feverish: *People with tuberculosis often look* hectic. ***—adv-*** **hec′ti·cal·ly.**

hec·to·graph (hĕk′tə grăf′) ***n-*** device for making copies of letters, drawings, etc., by taking the impression off of a gelatin pad. ***vt-*** to copy (a letter, drawing, etc.) with such a device.

hec·tor (hĕk′tər) ***vt-*** **1** to threaten; bully; intimidate. **2** to tease; torment. ***—n-*** swaggering or blustering fellow; bully.

Hec·tor (hĕk′tər) ***n-*** in the "Iliad," a Trojan hero killed by Achilles. He was the son of Priam and Hecuba.

Hec·u·ba (hĕk′yə bə) ***n-*** in Homer's "Iliad," the wife of Priam and mother of Hector, Paris, and others.

he'd (hēd) **1** he had: *If* he'd *wanted to come, he could have.* **2** he would: *He said* he'd *go.* ***Hom-*** heed.

hedge (hĕj) ***n-*** **1** thick row of bushes or small trees serving as a fence: *a hawthorn* hedge *between the two houses.* **2** any boundary or barrier. **3** something that protects against loss or disaster: *His savings were a* hedge *against unemployment.* ***vt-*** **[hedged, hedg·ing]** **1** to put a fence of bushes or trees around: *We* hedged *the garden with flowering plants.* **2** to make (a bet or investment) in addition to another one to counteract or reduce the chance of loss. ***vi-*** to avoid being frank or direct: *He* hedged *when asked about it.* ***—n-*** **hedg′er.**

hedge in to surround; hem in.

hedge·hog (hĕj′hŏg′) ***n-*** **1** small insect-eating animal whose back is covered with fur and stiff hairs which harden into spines at the ends. It can defend itself by rolling into a ball. **2** porcupine.

Hedgehog
about 10 1/2 in. long

hedge·hop (hĕj′hŏp′) ***vi-*** **[hedge·hopped, hedge·hop·ping]** to fly an airplane close to the ground, especially for dusting crops, trees, etc. ***—n-*** **hedge′hop′per.**

hedge·row (hĕj′rō′) ***n-*** tall, heavily entangled row of trees and thick bushes, growing on a low mound, that borders fields and pastures in some parts of Europe.

he·don·ism (hē′də nĭz′əm) ***n-*** **1** in philosophy, the idea that pleasure or happiness is the chief good and the proper goal of all human activity. **2** a living for pleasure; self-indulgence. ***—n-*** **he′don·ist.** ***adj-*** **he′don·ist′ic.**

heed (hēd) ***vt-*** to pay careful attention to; mind; observe: *to* heed *advice*; *to* heed *traffic regulations.* ***vi-***: *Some boys just won't* heed. ***n-*** careful attention; notice: *He gave no* heed *to the warning.* ***Hom-*** he'd.

heed·ful (hēd′fəl) ***adj-*** careful; attentive; watchful; mindful. ***—adv-*** **heed′ful·ly.** ***n-*** **heed′ful·ness.**

heed·less (hēd′ləs) ***adj-*** not careful or attentive; thoughtless; neglectful; inconsiderate. ***—adv-*** **heed′less·ly.** ***n-*** **heed′less·ness.**

hee·haw (hē′hô′) ***n-*** the harsh, loud cry of a donkey, or any silly laugh sounding like this. ***vi-*** to make such a cry or silly laugh.

[1]**heel** (hēl) ***n-*** **1** the back part of the human foot; also, the part of a shoe, boot, or stocking that covers it. **2** the block of leather, rubber, etc., under the rear of a shoe or boot. **3** anything like a heel in shape, position, or function: *a* heel *of bread*; *the* heel *of a golf club.* ***vt-*** **1** to put (lower rear parts) on shoes, boots, etc.: *He had his shoes soled and* heeled. **2** to follow closely in the tracks of. **3** to strike with the lower rear part of a golf club or tool. ***vi-*** **1** to follow close to someone's legs, as a dog does. **2** to tap with or extend the lower rear

part of the foot, as one sometimes does in dancing. [from Old English **hēla.**] ***Homs-*** heal, he'll.

at heel at the heels of another; close behind. **cool (one's) heels** *Informal* to wait or be kept waiting. **down at the heel** (or **heels**) with one's shoes worn down at the heels; hence, shabby; run-down. **kick up (one's) heels** to throw off ordinary reserve and dignity; have a good time without restraint. **on the heels of** following just after: *The rain came* on the heels of *the wind.* **show (one's) heels to** to run away from and keep ahead of. **take to (one's) heels** to run away.

[2]**heel** (hēl) ***vi-*** to lean to one side; list: *The ship* heeled *over when the cargo shifted.* ***vt-*** to cause (a ship) to lean to one side. [from Old English **h(i)eldan** meaning "to slope."] ***Homs-*** heal, he'll.

[3]**heel** (hēl) *Slang* ***n-*** a low, contemptible person. [a special use of [1]**heel.**] ***Homs-*** heal, he'll.

heft (hĕft) *Informal* ***n-*** **1** heaviness; weight: *the* heft *of a stone*; *a man of considerable* heft. **2** the greater part; main part; gist: *the* heft *of a story.* ***vt-*** **1** to lift: *to* heft *an iron bar.* **2** to test the weight of by lifting.

heft·y (hĕf′ tē) *Informal* ***adj-*** **[heft·i·er, heft·i·est]** heavy and bulky; big and powerful: *a* hefty *load*; *a* hefty *football player.*

he·gem·o·ny (hə jĕm′ ə nē) ***n-*** [*pl.* **he·gem·o·nies**] dominant leadership or influence of one nation or state over another, or over others in a confederation.

He·gi·ra or **He·ji·ra** (hə jī′ rə) ***n-*** **1** the flight of Mohammed from Mecca to Medina in 622 A.D. **2** the Muslim era dating from that time. **3 hegira** any such flight.

heif·er (hĕf′ ər) ***n-*** young cow that has not yet given birth to a calf.

height (hīt) ***n-*** **1** measurement from the head to the foot; stature: *a man of average* height. **2** distance from the ground or bottom to the top: *the* height *of a figure or building.* **3** the distance something rises above the earth or above sea level; altitude; elevation: *the* height *of an airplane*; *the* height *of a mountain.* **4** the state of being high: *Some people are afraid of* height. **5** a high place; hill: *a house on the* height *overlooking the river*; *to be afraid of* heights. **6** the highest point; top; summit: *The writer reached the* height *of his career at thirty.* **7** the extreme; utmost degree: *the* height *of popularity or of ignorance.* ***Hom-*** hight.

height·en (hī′ tən) ***vt-*** **1** to make higher; raise; elevate: *They* heightened *the fence around the backyard.* **2** to increase in strength, degree, or effect: *His sarcastic tone only* heightened *her anger.* ***vi-*** to become higher, stronger, or greater: *The suspense* heightened.

hei·nous (hā′ nəs) ***adj-*** very wicked; hateful; atrocious. **—*adv-*** **hei′ nous·ly.** ***n-*** **hei′ nous·ness.**

heir (âr) ***n-*** **1** person who receives or has the right to receive money, property, or title at the death of the owner. In law, an **heir apparent** [*pl.* **heirs apparent**] is one who will become an heir if he outlives the person from whom the inheritance will pass; an **heir presumptive** [*pl.* **heirs presumptive**] is one who will become an heir if his right is not canceled by the birth of another more closely related. **2** a person or group that inherits qualities from others who have lived before: *We are the* heirs *of Greek and Roman civilization.* ***Homs-*** air, [2]are, e'er, ere.

fall heir to to inherit: *He* fell heir to *his uncle's farm.*

heir·ess (âr′ əs) ***n-*** a woman or girl who inherits, or is in line to inherit, money, property, or a title.

heir·loom (âr′ lo͞om′) ***n-*** piece of personal property handed down in a family from generation to generation.

He·ji·ra (hə jī′ rə) Hegira.

held (hĕld) *p.t. & p.p.* of **hold.**

Hel·en of Troy (hĕl′ ən əv troi′) ***n-*** in Greek mythology, the beautiful wife of Menelaus, king of Sparta. Her elopement with Paris caused the Trojan War.

hel·i·cal (hĕl′ ĭ kəl, hē′ lĭ-) ***adj-*** of, relating to, or in the form of a helix; spiral.

hel·i·con (hĕl′ ĭ kŏn′) ***n-*** large, coiled brass instrument similar to a tuba, used by marching bands.

hel·i·cop·ter (hĕl′ ə kŏp′ tər) ***n-*** aircraft with rotary wings mounted on a vertical drive shaft and turned by an engine or by jets in the wing-tips.

Helicopter

helio- *combining form* sun: helio*graph.* [from Greek **helio-** from **helios,** "sun."]

he·li·o·cen·tric (hē′ lē ō sĕn′ trĭk) ***adj-*** **1** as if seen from the center of the sun (used of the position of a celestial object). **2** having the sun as a center: *The solar system is* heliocentric. Also **he′ li·o·cen′ tri·cal.**

he·li·o·graph (hē′ lē ə grăf′) ***n-*** **1** signaling device that flashes a beam of sunlight from point to point by means of a mirror. **2** instrument for photographing the sun.

He·li·os (hē′ lē ŏs′) ***n-*** in Greek mythology, the sun god who drove his chariot across the sky.

he·li·o·trope (hē′ lē ə trōp′) ***n-*** **1** any of several related plants, especially one cultivated for its clusters of small, fragrant white or purple flowers. **2** a reddish purple. **3** any plant that reacts to sunlight by turning toward the sun. **4** bloodstone. **—*adj-*:** *a* heliotrope *ribbon.*

he·li·o·tro·pism (hē′ lē ŏt′ rə pĭz′ əm) ***n-*** orientation of the movements of plants or their parts toward or away from sunlight.

hel·i·port (hĕl′ ə pôrt′) ***n-*** landing field for helicopters.

he·li·um (hē′ lē əm) ***n-*** very light odorless and colorless gas that is one of the elements. It is inert under ordinary conditions, and is used in weather balloons, by divers, etc. Symbol He, At. No. 2, At. Wt. 4.0026.

he·lix (hē′ lĭks) ***n-*** [*pl.* **he·lix·es** or **he·li·ces** (hĕl′ ə sēz′, hē′ lə-)] **1** curve traced by a point as it moves lengthwise at constant speed along the surface of a rotating cylinder or cone. **2** in architecture, a spiral ornament.

Conical helix

hell (hĕl) ***n-*** **1** in some religions, the place where the wicked are punished forever after death. **2** any place or condition of misery or evil. **3** *Slang* harsh treatment.

he'll (hēl) he will; he shall. ***Homs-*** heal, heel.

hell·bend·er (hĕl′ bĕn′ dər) ***n-*** large salamander found commonly in the streams of the Ohio River valley.

hell·cat (hĕl′ kăt′) ***n-*** **1** shrewish woman. **2** witch; hag.

hel·le·bore (hĕl′ ə bôr′) ***n-*** **1** (also **false hellebore**) plant related to the lilies, with small greenish or white flowers and very poisonous roots. **2** any of several plants related to the buttercup, with large, showy flowers.

Hel·lene (hĕl′ ēn′) ***n-*** a Greek.

Hel·len·ic (hə lĕn′ ĭk) ***adj-*** of or relating to Greece, especially to the social and cultural aspects of classical Greek civilization, art, or literature. ***n-*** a subfamily of the Indo-European languages, including both ancient and modern Greek.

Hel·le·nism (hĕl′ ə nĭz′ əm) ***n-*** **1** admiration or imitation of ancient Greek thought, manners, or style. **2** the body of classic ideals associated with ancient Greece.

hell·gram·mite (hĕl′ grə mīt′) ***n-*** the aquatic larva of an insect resembling a dragonfly, often used as fish bait.

hell·hound (hĕl′ hound′) ***n-*** hound from hell or the underworld, such as Cerberus; hence, a fiendish person.

hel·lion (hĕl′yən, *also* hĕl′-) *Informal* ***n-*** person who likes to stir up trouble and confusion; mischief-maker.

hell·ish (hĕl′ĭsh) ***adj-*** of, from, or characteristic of hell; fiendish; horrible. ***—adv-*** **hell′ish·ly.** ***n-*** **hell′ish·ness.**

hel·lo (hĕ lō′) ***interj-*** **1** exclamation of greeting. **2** exclamation of surprise. ***n-*** [*pl.* **hel·los**]: *He gave me a cheerful* "Hello" *as we passed.*

1**helm** (hĕlm) ***n-*** **1** the complete steering gear of a ship, especially the tiller or wheel. **2** position of control or command: *Mr. Green took the* helm *of the business.* [from Old English **helma.**]

Helm

2**helm** (hĕlm) *Archaic* ***n-*** helmet. [from Old English **helm** meaning "helmet; any protection or cover."]

hel·met (hĕl′mət) ***n-*** protective head covering of metal, plastic, or other tough, resistant material: *a soldier's* helmet; *a fireman's* helmet.

ROMAN

MODERN INDUSTRIAL

Helmets

helms·man (hĕlmz′mən) ***n-*** [*pl.* **helms·men**] person who steers or guides a ship or boat; pilot.

Hel·ot (hĕ′lət) ***n-*** **1** member of the lowest social class of ancient Sparta. **2 helot** a serf or slave.

help (hĕlp) ***vt-*** **1** to aid; assist: *to* help *a friend in trouble.* **2** to keep from; avoid: *He could not* help *dropping the glass.* **3** to be a remedy or cure for: *Nothing* helps *my headache.* ***vi-*** to give aid or support; be helpful: *They offered to* help. *It didn't make him completely happy, but it* helped. *Tom* helped *start the car.* ***n-*** **1** support; aid; assistance: *to give* help *in time of disaster.* **2** person or people who work for one: *the hired* help. **3** person or thing that aids or assists: *You were a big* help *at the party.* **4** remedy or solution: *There is no* help *for her illness.* ***—n-*** **help′er.**

cannot help but cannot avoid doing something: *I* cannot help but *laugh at him.*

help (oneself) to to serve oneself with; take: *Please* help yourself to *more meat.*

help·ful (hĕlp′fəl) ***adj-*** giving aid; useful: *Jane was* helpful *around the house.* ***—adv-*** **help′ful·ly.** ***n-*** **help′ful·ness.**

help·ing (hĕl′pĭng) ***n-*** portion of food served at table.

helping verb ***n-*** auxiliary verb.

help·less (hĕlp′ləs) ***adj-*** **1** unable to take care of oneself: *a* helpless *invalid.* **2** unable to help; unavailing; useless: *a* helpless *gesture.* ***—adv-*** **help′less·ly.** ***n-*** **help′less·ness.**

help·mate (hĕlp′māt′) ***n-*** person one depends on for help, especially one's wife. Also **help′meet′** (-mēt′).

hel·ter-skel·ter (hĕl′tər skĕl′tər) ***adv-*** pellmell; in confused haste or disorder: *He threw them* helter-skelter *into the suitcase.* ***adj-***: *her* helter-skelter *manner.*

helve (hĕlv) ***n-*** handle of an ax, hammer, etc.

1**hem** (hĕm) ***n-*** **1** edge of material folded back on itself and stitched down. **2** hemline. ***vt-*** **[hemmed, hem·ming]**: *to* hem *a skirt*; *to* hem *curtains.* [from Old English **hem(m)** of the same meaning.]

hem in to surround; enclose; encircle: *Steep hills* hemmed in *the tiny village.*

2**hem** (hĕm) ***interj-*** sound made in clearing the throat, to attract attention, or express doubt. ***vi-*** **[hemmed, hem·ming]** to make such a sound. [probably an imitation of the sound.]

hem and haw 1 to speak in a hesitating way. **2** to try to avoid giving an answer.

he·ma·tite (hē′mə tīt′, hĕm′ə) ***n-*** the chief ore of iron. It consists of ferric oxide and is blackish or rusty-red.

hemi- *combining form* half: *a* hemi*sphere.* [from Greek **hemi-**, "half."]

hem·ip·ter·ous (hĭ mĭp′ter əs) ***adj-*** of or having to do with the order of true bugs **(Hemiptera),** which include bedbugs, chinch bugs, etc.

hem·i·sphere (hĕm′ə sfêr′) ***n-*** **1** half of the globe of the earth. **2** half of any sphere. **3** either the right or the left half of the cerebrum.

hem·i·spher·ic (hĕm′ə sfêr′ĭk, -sfĕr′ĭk) or **hem·i·spher·i·cal** (-ĭ kəl) ***adj-*** **1** of, or relating to a hemisphere: *a* hemispheric *alliance.* **2** (usually **hemispherical**) having the shape of a hemisphere.

hem·line (hĕm′līn′) ***n-*** lower edge of a skirt.

hem·lock (hĕm′lŏk′) ***n-*** **1** any of several evergreen trees related to the pines. **2** the wood of such a tree. **3** any of several poisonous plants related to the carrot and parsley.

hemo- *combining form* blood: *a* hemo*philiac*; hemo*globin.* Also **haemo-.** [from Greek **haîma,** "blood."]

he·mo·glo·bin (hē′mə glō′bən) ***n-*** protein and iron pigment contained in the red blood cells. Hemoglobin transfers oxygen from the lungs to the body tissues and brings carbon dioxide from the tissues to the lungs.

he·mol·y·sis (hē mŏl′ə səs) ***n-*** destruction of red blood cells, resulting in the release of hemoglobin into the plasma. ***—adj-*** **hem′o·ly′tic.** (hē′mə lĭt′ĭk).

he·mo·phil·i·a (hē′mə fĭl′yə) ***n-*** hereditary blood disorder of males, marked by the failure of the blood to coagulate normally, and by prolonged bleeding from even a very small wound.

he·mo·phil·i·ac (hē′mə fĭl′ē ăk′) ***n-*** person with hemophilia; bleeder.

hem·or·rhage (hĕm′ər ĭj) ***n-*** bleeding from a damaged artery, vein, etc., especially a great or continuous flow of blood. ***vi-*** **[hem·or·rhaged, hem·or·rhag·ing.]** to bleed profusely.

hem·or·rhoids (hĕm′ə roidz′) ***n-*** *pl.* painful swellings of the veins in the anal region; piles.

hemp (hĕmp) ***n-*** **1** tall Asiatic plant having tough fibers used for making rope and coarse cloth. **2** hashish.

hemp·en (hĕm′pən) ***adj-*** made of or resembling hemp.

hem·stitch (hĕm′stĭch′) ***n-*** ornamental stitch often used to trim hems. It is made by pulling out several parallel threads from the cloth and gathering the cross threads into small, uniform bundles to form an open design. ***vt-***: *to* hemstitch *a cloth.* ***—n-*** **hem′stitch′er.**

hen (hĕn) ***n-*** **1** adult female of the domestic fowl. See also *rooster, cock, chicken, chick.* **2** female of other birds. **3** female of various other animals, such as the lobster and certain fishes. **4** *Slang* a woman, especially a fussy old woman.

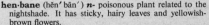

Hen

hen·bane (hĕn′bān′) ***n-*** poisonous plant related to the nightshade. It has sticky, hairy leaves and yellowish-brown flowers.

hence (hĕns) ***adv-*** **1** from this time: *School starts two weeks* hence. **2** from this place: *a mile* hence. **3** there-

fāte, făt, dâre, bärn; bē, bĕt, mêre; bīte, bĭt; nōte, hŏt, môre, dȯg; fŭn, fûr; to͞o, bo͝ok; oil; out; ta*r*; thin; then; hw for wh as in *wh*at; zh for s as in u*s*ual; ə for a, e, i, o, u, as in *a*go, lin*e*n, per*i*l, at*o*m, min*u*s

fore; for this reason: *The tortoise moved very slowly, and* hence *lost the race with the hare.* ***interj-*** *Archaic* Go away! Begone!

hence·forth (hĕns′fôrth′) ***adv-*** from this time on. Also **hence′ for′ ward.**

hench·man (hĕnch′ mən) ***n-*** [*pl.* **hench·men**] assistant or supporter, usually for personal gain, of a powerful or influential person: *a political boss and his* henchmen.

hen·e·quen or **hen·e·quin** (hĕn′ ə kən) ***n-*** **1** fiber from the leaves of a Mexican agave, used for making ropes, coarse cloth, etc. **2** the plant itself.

hen·house (hĕn′ hous′) ***n-*** coop for hens. Also **hen′ coop′.**

hen·na (hĕn′ ə) ***n-*** **1** reddish-brown cosmetic or dye made from the leaves of a small Asiatic tree. **2** the tree itself. **3** a reddish-brown color. ***adj-*** reddish brown. ***vt-*** [**hen·naed** (hĕn′ əd), **hen·na·ing**] to dye reddish brown.

hen·ner·y (hĕn′ ə rē) ***n-*** [*pl.* **hen·ner·ies**] place in which poultry is kept or raised.

hen·peck (hĕn′ pĕk′) ***vt-*** to bully or nag (one's husband).

hen·ry (hĕn′ rē) *Physics* ***n-*** a unit of inductance. One henry is the inductance of a circuit in which an electromotive force of one volt is induced by an electric current that changes at the rate of one ampere per second.

he·pat·i·ca (hə păt′ ĭ kə) ***n-*** spring-blooming plant with leathery, three-lobed leaves and lavender, pink, or white flowers; liverwort.

hep·a·ti·tis (hĕp′ ə tī′ təs) ***n-*** inflammation of the liver.

hep·ta·gon (hĕp′ tə gŏn′) ***n-*** polygon with seven sides and seven angles.

hep·tag·o·nal (hĕp tăg′ ə nəl) ***adj-*** having seven sides. —***adv-*** **hep·tag′ o·nal·ly.**

her (hûr) ***pron-*** objective case of **she**: *I see* her. *Pass* her *the bread. I did it for* her. ***determiner*** (possessive case of the pronoun "she," now usually called possessive adjective) of, belonging to, or done by a certain girl, woman, or female animal: *Sue saw* her *friends.* Her *eyes are blue.* Her *work is very neat. The cow chewed* her *cud.*

He·ra (hêr′ ə) ***n-*** in Greek mythology, the queen of the gods, sister and wife of Zeus, and goddess of marriage. She is identified with the Roman Juno.

Her·a·cles (hĕr′ ə klēz′) Hercules. Also **Her′ a·kles.**

her·ald (hĕr′ əld) ***n-*** **1** in former times, an official who made public announcements or carried messages for a ruler. **2** person or thing which announces or foretells the coming of another person or event: *The robin is the* herald *of spring.* ***vt-*** to tell of or announce the coming of: *Trumpets* heralded *the opening of the festival.*

he·ral·dic (hə răl′ dĭk) ***adj-*** of or related to heralds or heraldry.

her·ald·ry (hĕr′ əl drē) ***n-*** art or science dealing with coats of arms and the tracing of family histories.

herb (ûrb, *also* hûrb) ***n-*** **1** any plant that has a soft, juicy stem rather than a woody one. Most herbs wither to the ground or die completely after flowering. **2** any such plant used as a medicine or for seasoning.

her·ba·ceous (hûr′ bā′ shəs, ûr′-) ***adj-*** **1** having the characteristics of herbs: *a* herbaceous *plant.* **2** consisting of herbs: *a* herbaceous *border in a garden.*

herb·age (ûr bĭj, *also* hûr′-) ***n-*** growing grass and herbs, especially when used for pasturage.

herb·al (ûr′ bəl, hûr′-) ***adj-*** of or having to do with herbs. ***n-*** book about herbs or plants.

herb·al·ist (ûr′ bə lĭst, hûr′-) ***n-*** person who grows, collects, or deals in herbs, especially medicinal plants.

her·bar·i·um (hûr′ bâr′ ē əm, ûr′-) ***n-*** [*pl.* **her·bar·i·ums** or **her·bar·i·a** (-ē ə)] **1** collection of dried plants, usually scientifically classified. **2** room or building where such a collection is kept.

herb·i·cide (hûr′ bə sīd, ûr′-) ***n-*** chemical used to kill plants or inhibit their growth. —***adj-*** **herb′ i·ci′ dal:** *a* herbicidal *compound.*

herb·i·vore (hûr′ bə vôr′, ûr′-) ***n-*** a herbivorous animal.

her·biv·or·ous (hər bĭv′ ər əs) ***adj-*** feeding on vegetable matter; plant-eating.

her·cu·le·an (hûr′ kyə lē′ ən) ***adj-*** **1** having, showing, or requiring great strength: *a* herculean *task.* **2 Herculean** of or relating to Hercules.

Her·cu·les (hûr′ kyə lēz′) ***n-*** **1** in Greek and Roman mythology, a son of Jupiter known for his great strength and for doing twelve gigantic tasks imposed on him by Juno. **2 hercules** any man of great strength and size.

herd (hûrd) ***n-*** **1** group of animals, especially cattle or sheep, that travel and feed together; flock; drove. **2** flock or mob of people. ***vt-*** **1** to gather, keep, or drive together: *He* herded *the cattle toward the gate.* **2** to tend (cattle, sheep, etc.). ***vi-*** to come together in a group or flock. —***n-*** **herd′ er.**

herds·man (hûrdz′ mən) ***n-*** [*pl.* **herds·men**] man who owns or tends a herd of cattle, sheep, etc.

here (hêr) ***adv-*** **1** to or toward this place: *Please come* here. **2** in or at this place or spot: *The vase is* here *on the table. Is it* here *that we turn?* **3** at this point: *I disagree with you* here. *The audience interrupted him* here. ***pron-*** this place or point: *Where do we go from* here? ***interj-*** exclamation to indicate that one is present in a roll call, to attract attention, etc. ***Hom-*** hear.

here and there scattered about; in various places.
neither here nor there unrelated to the point; irrelevant.

►HERE and THERE are often used unnecessarily, as in *"Read this* here *book. Sharpen that* there *pencil." "Read this book"* is sufficient. However, if you wish to emphasize a particular object, you may use these words after the noun or pronoun. *Read that book* there; *don't read this one* here.

here·a·bout (hêr′ ə bout′) or **here·a·bouts** (-bouts′) ***adv-*** near here; around this place.

here·af·ter (hêr ăf′ tər) ***adv-*** after this time; in the future. ***n-*** **the hereafter** life after death; world to come.

here·by (hêr′ bī′) ***adv-*** by this means: *The mayor announced, "I* hereby *declare a holiday."*

he·red·i·tar·y (hə rĕd′ ə tĕr′ ē) ***adj-*** **1** passed from parent to child by means of genes. **2** passed from generation to generation in a group: *the* hereditary *rights of the American citizen.* **3** passed from possessor to heir: *a* hereditary *fortune.* —***adv-*** **he·red′ i·tar′ i·ly.**

he·red·i·ty (hə rĕd′ ə tē) ***n-*** [*pl.* **he·red·i·ties**] **1** the passing on of traits from parent to offspring by means of genes: *Eye color is a result of* heredity. **2** all the traits passed on in this way, such as blood group.

Here·ford (hûr′ fərd) ***n-*** a breed of beef cattle originally from England, and usually having a reddish-brown coat with white markings.

here·in (hêr′ ĭn′) ***adv-*** in this place, matter, situation, etc.; in this: *He said,* "Herein *lies the solution.*"

here·of (hêr ŏv′, -ŭv′) ***adv-*** of or regarding this.

here·on (hêr ŏn′) ***adv-*** on this; hereupon.

here's (hêrz) here is.

her·e·sy (hĕr′ ə sē) ***n-*** [*pl.* **her·e·sies**] belief contrary to accepted or official doctrine, especially of a religion.

her·e·tic (hĕr′ ə tĭk) ***n-*** person whose beliefs are contrary to accepted or official doctrine, especially in religion.

he·ret·i·cal (hə rĕt′ ĭ kəl) ***adj-*** expressing or resulting from heresy. —***adv-*** **he·ret′ i·cal·ly.**

here·to (hêr′ tōō′) ***adv-*** to this thing, subject, etc.

here·to·fore (hêr′ tə fôr′) ***adv-*** before this time; until now· formerly.

here·un·to (hêr′ ən tōō′) ***adv-*** to this; hereto.

here·up·on (hêr′ə pŏn′) ***adv-*** upon this; hereon.
here·with (hêr′wĭth′, -wĭth′) ***adv-*** with this; together with this.
her·it·a·ble (hĕr′ĭ tə bəl) ***adj-*** such as can be inherited. **—*n-* her′i·ta·bil′i·ty.**
her·i·tage (hĕr′ə tĭj) ***n-*** something, such as property or a right or privilege, belonging to one by inheritance or tradition: *a rich* heritage; *a* heritage *of freedom.*
her·maph·ro·dite (hər măf′rə dīt′) ***n-*** animal or plant with both male and female sexual organs.
Her·mes (hûr′mēz′) ***n-*** in Greek mythology, the messenger of the gods. He is identified with the Roman Mercury.
her·met·ic (hər mĕt′ ĭk) or **her·met·i·cal** (-ĭ kəl) ***adj-*** airtight. **—*adv-* her·met′i·cal·ly.**
her·mit (hûr′mĭt) ***n-*** person who withdraws from society and lives alone, especially to lead a holy life; recluse.
her·mit·age (hûr′mə tĭj) ***n-*** **1** home of a hermit. **2** any secluded place to live; retreat.
hermit crab ***n-*** any of several sea crabs that live in empty mollusk shells to protect their soft bodies.
her·ni·a (hûr′nē ə) ***n-*** the protrusion of an organ or part of an organ, such as the intestine, through a break in the tissue that surrounds it; rupture.
he·ro (hêr′ō) ***n-*** [*pl.* **he·roes**] **1** man who does, or is admired for, a courageous or noble deed. **2** leading male character in a story, poem, or play. **—*n-fem.* her′o·ine. 3** (also **hero sandwich**) sandwich made from a long roll or loaf sliced lengthwise, and filled with meat, cheese, relishes, etc.
He·ro (hêr′ō) ***n-*** in Greek legend, a priestess whose lover, Leander, nightly swam the Hellespont to join her.
he·ro·ic (hĭ rō′ĭk) ***adj-*** **1** of, fit for, or worthy of a hero; courageous; noble: *a* heroic *rescue*; heroic *deeds.* **2** having to do with a hero or heroes: *a* heroic *age*; heroic *poetry.* **3** larger or grander than usual: *a* heroic *statue.* Also **he·ro′i·cal. —*adv-* he·ro′i·cal·ly.**
he·ro·ics (hə rō′ĭks) ***n-*** *pl.* actions, words, etc., intended to impress others by their bravery or grandeur.
her·o·in (hēr′ō ĭn) ***n-*** dangerous habit-forming narcotic made from morphine. ***Hom-*** heroine.
her·o·ism (hĕr′ō ĭz′əm) ***n-*** conduct or spirit worthy of a hero; great courage, daring, etc.
her·on (hĕr′ən) ***n-*** any of various wading birds with a long neck and a long pointed bill. Herons live in marshes and feed on fish, frogs, and insects.

Great blue heron, about 4 ft. high

her·pes (hûr′pēz) ***n-*** any of several skin diseases caused by a virus, and marked by patches of small blisters which tend to spread.
her·pe·tol·o·gist (hûr′pə tŏl′ə jĭst) ***n-*** person who is a student of or expert in herpetology.
her·pe·tol·o·gy (hûr′pə tŏl′ə jē) ***n-*** the branch of zoology that deals with reptiles and amphibians.
Herr (hĕr) *German* ***n-*** [*pl.* **Her·ren** (hĕr′ən)] title of courtesy equivalent to "Mr."
her·ring (hĕr′ĭng) ***n-*** [*pl.* **her·ring; her·rings** (kinds of herring)] **1** any of several small food fishes caught in North Atlantic waters. **2** any of various related fishes, such as the sardine.
her·ring·bone (hĕr′ĭng bōn′) ***n-*** pattern or weave in which rows of short parallel lines slant in opposite directions from a series of long central lines. *as **modifier**: a* herringbone *suit.*
hers (hûrz) ***pron-*** (possessive pronoun) thing or things belonging to her: *It is* hers. *That cat of* hers *is cute.*
her·self (hər sĕlf′) ***pron-*** **1** reflexive form of **her**; her own self: *She cut* herself *with the knife. She is ashamed of* herself. **2** her normal or true self: *Laura isn't* herself *today.* **3** intensive form of **she**: *She* herself *told me about it.* **4** *Irish* she: *I am sure* herself *will not deny it.*
by herself 1 alone: *She came* by herself. **2** without any help: *She made that dress* by herself.
hertz (hûrts) ***n-*** [*pl.* **hertz**] unit of frequency equal to one cycle per second.
he's (hēz) **1** he is. **2** he has (auxiliary verb only).
hes·i·tan·cy (hĕz′ə tən sē, -tĕn′sē) ***n-*** [*pl.* **hes·i·tan·cies**] indecision; hesitation. Also **hes′i·tance.**
hes·i·tant (hĕz′ə tənt) ***adj-*** pausing, wavering, or proceeding slowly because of uncertainty, indecision, etc.: *a* hesitant *person*; hesitant *speech.* **—*adv-* hes′i·tant·ly.**
hes·i·tate (hĕz′ə tāt′) ***vi-*** [**hes·i·tat·ed, hes·i·tat·ing**] **1** to pause or stop because of doubt, uncertainty, or unwillingness: *He* hesitated *before diving into the icy water.* **2** to be unwilling: *I* hesitate *to take this risk.* **—*adv-* hes′i·tat·ing·ly:** *He advanced* hesitatingly.
hes·i·ta·tion (hĕz′ə tā′shən) ***n-*** **1** a pausing in uncertainty or doubt; a wavering: *After some* hesitation, *she bought the blue car.* **2** a faltering in speech.
Hes·per·i·des (hĕs pĕr′ə dēz) ***n-*** *pl.* in Greek mythology, the nymphs who guarded the golden apples of Hera.
Hes·per·us (hĕs′pə rəs) ***n-*** the evening star, especially Venus.
Hes·sian (hĕsh′ən) ***n-*** **1** a native of Hesse, Germany. **2** soldier of Hesse hired by the British to fight in the American Revolution. ***adj-*** of or from Hesse.
Hessian fly ***n-*** small fly whose larvae or young are very destructive to wheat.
hetero- *combining form* other; different: hetero*geneous* (of different kinds). [from Greek **heteros,** "other."]
het·er·o·dox (hĕt′ər ə dŏks′) ***adj-*** differing from, or holding views that differ from, accepted doctrine or belief, especially in religion; not orthodox.
het·er·o·dox·y (hĕt′ər ə dŏk′sē) ***n-*** [*pl.* **het·er·o·dox·ies**] **1** disagreement with or denial of accepted doctrine or belief; lack of orthodoxy. **2** unorthodox doctrine or belief.
het·er·o·ge·ne·i·ty (hĕt′ə rō′jə nē′ə tē) ***n-*** [*pl.* **het·er·o·ge·ne·i·ties**] condition of being heterogeneous.
het·er·o·ge·ne·ous (hĕt′ər ə jĕn′ē əs) ***adj-*** **1** made up of different and varied parts, members, etc.: *a* heterogeneous *mixture*; *a* heterogeneous *group.* **—*adv-* het′er·o·ge′ne·ous·ly.**
het·er·o·sex·u·al (hĕt′ər ə sĕk′shōō əl) ***adj-*** *Biology* **1** of the different sexes. **2** relating to or showing sexual feeling toward members of the opposite sex. ***n-*** a heterosexual person.
hew (hyōō) ***vt-*** [**hewed, hewed** or **hewn, hew·ing**] (considered intransitive when the object is implied but not expressed) **1** to chop; hack: *to* hew *a path through the forest.* **2** to shape by chopping or chipping with, or as if with, an ax or adz: *to* hew *beams from logs.* ***Hom-*** hue. **hew to the line** to conform strictly.
hewn (hyōōn) *p.p.* of **hew.** ***adj-*** shaped with a broad ax or adz: *The floor was supported by* hewn *beams.*

hex (hĕks) *Informal* ***n-*** evil spell; jinx. ***vt-*** to cast an evil spell on. [American word from Pennsylvania German, from German **hexe.**]

hexa- *combining form* six: *a hexa*gon; *hexa*pod. [from Greek **hexa-**, from **hex**, "six."]

hex·a·gon (hĕk′ sə gŏn′) ***n-*** polygon with six sides and six angles.

hex·ag·o·nal (hĕk săg′ ə nəl) ***adj-*** having six sides. ***—adv-*** **hex·ag′ o·nal·ly.**

hex·am·e·ter (hĕk săm′ ə tər) ***n-*** verse consisting of lines having six poetic feet or measures; also, a line in such meter. *as* ***modifier***: *lines of* hexameter *verse.*

hex·a·pod (hĕk′ sə pŏd′) ***n-*** insect; member of the class of insects **(Insecta)** which includes all the true or six-legged insects, such as bees, flies, etc.

hey (hā) ***interj-*** exclamation to attract someone's attention, express surprise, etc. ***Hom-*** hay.

hey·day (hā′ dā′) ***n-*** time of greatest power, glory, vigor, etc.: *He was greatly admired in his* heyday.

Hf symbol for hafnium.

Hg symbol for mercury.

H.H. 1 His Highness. **2** Her Highness. **3** His Holiness.

hhd. hogshead.

hi (hī) ***interj-*** **1** *Informal* exclamation of greeting. **2** shout to attract attention. ***Homs-*** hie, high.

H.I. Hawaiian Islands (unofficial).

hi·a·tus (hī ā′ təs) ***n-*** gap, blank space, or break, especially in a manuscript.

hi·ba·chi (hē bä′ chē) *Japanese* ***n-*** portable pot-shaped container covered with a heavy wire grill in which charcoal is burned to warm a room, broil foods, etc.

hi·ber·nate (hī′ bər nāt′) ***vi-*** **[hi·ber·nat·ed, hi·ber·nat·ing]** to spend the winter in a state resembling sleep, as do bears, raccoons, etc. See also *estivate.*

hi·ber·na·tion (hī′ bər nā′ shən) ***n-*** **1** the act of hibernating. **2** sleeplike state of an animal that hibernates.

hi·bis·cus (hī bĭs′ kəs, hī-) ***n-*** any of a group of plants, shrubs, or trees with large colorful flowers. The red hibiscus is the state flower of Hawaii.

hic·cup (hĭk′ ŭp′) ***n-*** **1** short, sharp sound resembling a gasp, caused by a spasm of the diaphragm that pushes air against the vocal cords. **2 hiccups** condition in which this sound is produced repeatedly. ***vi***: *He* hiccuped *loudly.* Also **hic·cough** (hĭk′ ŭp′).

hick·o·ry (hĭk′ ə rē) ***n-*** [*pl.* **hick·o·ries**] **1** any of several North American trees having hard wood and producing edible nuts. **2** the wood of this tree. [an American word from **pohickery,** from an American Indian language.]

hi·dal·go (hĭ dăl′ gō) ***n-*** [*pl.* **hi·dal·gos**] Spanish nobleman who ranks below a grandee.

Hi·dat·sa (hĭ dät′ sə) ***n-*** [*pl.* **Hi·dat·sas,** also **Hi·dat·sa**] one of a tribe of American Indians who lived near the Missouri and were related to the Dakota Sioux.

hid·den (hĭd′ ən) *p.p.* of [1]**hide.** ***adj-*** out of sight; concealed: *to dig for* hidden *treasure.*

[1]**hide** (hīd) ***vt-*** **[hid, hidden** or **hid, hid·ing] 1** to put or keep out of sight: *to* hide *the candy in the cupboard.* **2** to keep secret; conceal: *He tried to* hide *the truth from us.* **3** to block the sight of; obstruct: *Tall trees* hid *the view of the river.* ***vi-*** to conceal oneself; be concealed: *Quick,* hide *in the closet!* [from Old English **hydan.**]

[2]**hide** (hīd) ***n-*** the skin of an animal, either untreated or made ready for use. ***vt-*** **[hid·ed, hid·ing]** *Informal* to whip; flog. [from Old English **hyd.**]

hide-and-seek (hīd′ ənd sēk′) ***n-*** children's game in which one player tries to find the others, who are hiding.

hide·a·way (hīd′ ə wā′) ***n-*** place for hiding or remaining in concealment; secret or secluded retreat.

hide·bound (hīd′ bound′) ***adj-*** **1** stubbornly holding on to one's opinions and ideas; obstinate and unchanging: *a* hidebound *conservative in politics.* **2** of cattle, having the skin too tight as a result of poor feeding.

hid·e·ous (hĭd′ ē əs) ***adj-*** extremely ugly; horrible; frightful: *a* hideous *grimace*; *a* hideous *crime.* ***—adv-*** **hid′ e·ous·ly.** ***n-*** **hid′ e·ous·ness.**

hide-out (hīd′ out′) *Informal* ***n-*** place for hiding, especially from the police or those in authority.

[1]**hid·ing** (hī′ dĭng) ***n-*** state of being concealed; concealment: *to remain in* hiding. [from [1]**hide.**]

[2]**hid·ing** (hī′ dĭng) *Informal* ***n-*** a beating; thrashing. [from [2]**hide.**]

hie (hī) *Archaic* ***vt-*** **[hied, hy·ing** or **hie·ing]** to betake; hurry (followed by "me," "him," "myself," "himself," etc.): *He* hied *himself to the castle.* ***Homs-*** hi, high.

hi·er·ar·ch·y (hī′ ə rär′ kē) ***n-*** [*pl.* **hi·er·ar·chies**] **1** organization or system in which standing is based on rank, grade, etc.: *a business* hierarchy; *the church* hierarchy. **2** governing body or group of officials, clergymen, etc., organized in this way.

hi·er·o·glyph (hī′ ər ə glĭf′) ***n-*** one of the characters making up a system of hieroglyphic writing, usually a more or less recognizable image of an animal, a man, the sun, a stalk of grain, etc.

Hieroglyphics

hi·er·o·glyph·ic (hī′ ər ə glĭf′ ĭk) ***n-*** **1** a hieroglyph. **2** system of writing using hieroglyphs; especially, that used by the ancient Egyptians. **3** writing that resembles this in being hard to read or decipher: *It was written in George's* hieroglyphic. ***adj-***: *a* hieroglyphic *inscription.* ***—adv-*** **hi′ er·o·glyph′ i·cal·ly.**

hi-fi (hī′ fī′) ***n-*** **1** high fidelity. **2** *Informal* phonograph using high-fidelity equipment. ***adj-***: *a* hi-fi *set.*

hig·gle·dy-pig·gle·dy (hĭg′ əl dē pĭg′ əl dē) ***adj-*** confused and jumbled; topsy-turvy. ***adv-*** in a confused or untidy manner.

high (hī) ***adj-*** **[high·er, high·est] 1** elevated or extending far above the ground or other surface: *a* high *shelf*; *a* high *cloud*; *a* high *tower.* **2** measured from the ground or surface to a certain height; tall: *a building 200 feet* high. **3** made to or from a great height: *a* high *dive, a* high *climb.* **4** important; chief: *a* high *government official.* **5** noble in character, aims, etc.; lofty: *his* high *ambitions.* **6** above the usual amount, intensity, degree, etc.: *a* high *fever*; high *speed*; high *prices.* **7** very good; excellent: *to be in* high *spirits*; *to have a* high *opinion of someone.* **8** of sounds, above the middle or usual pitch: *a* high *tone*; *a* high *voice.* ***adv-*** **1** to or at a great height, position, etc.: *to climb* high; *to sit* high *in the grandstand.* **2** in an extravagant or luxurious manner: *to live* high. ***n-*** **1** the uppermost level or point for a certain time, condition, etc.: *The temperature reached a new* high *today.* **2** in meteorology, a mass of air having a barometric pressure greater than the average or that of surrounding regions; anticyclone. **3** (also **high gear**) in the transmission of an automobile, the setting of gears that affords the greatest speed. ***Homs-*** hi, hie.

high and dry alone and deserted: *He left her* high and dry. **high and low** in all possible places; everywhere: *I looked for him* high and low. **on high** at a great height; in the air: *The flags waved* on high.

high·ball (hī′ bôl′) ***n-*** **1** drink made with alcoholic liquor and soda, and served with ice in a tall glass. **2** signal for a railroad train to go ahead. ***vi-*** *Slang* to move ahead at great speed.

high·born (hī′ bôrn′) ***adj-*** of noble birth or descent.

high·boy (hī′boi′) ***n-*** high chest of drawers.

high·brow (hī′brou′) *Informal* ***n-*** person with educated tastes and interests; intellectual (often used to show disfavor). ***adj-***: highbrow *tastes.*

high chair ***n-*** high-legged chair in which a baby sits.

High Church ***n-*** group in the Anglican Communion that generally favors church authority and traditional rites. See also *Low Church.* **—*adj-*** **(High-Church):** *a* High-Church *ritual.* ***n-*** **High′-Church′man.**

high·er (hī′ər) *compar.* of **high.** ***adj-*** more advanced, complex, etc., than something in the same category: *the* higher *animals*; higher *education.*

high·er-up (hī′ər ŭp′) *Informal* ***n-*** person of important rank or position.

high explosive ***n-*** any of a group of explosives, including TNT and dynamite, that explode with extreme force and rapidity.

high fidelity ***n-*** the reproduction of sound by a radio, phonograph, etc., so that it sounds very much like the original. **—*adj-*** **(high-fidelity);** *a* high-fidelity *phonograph; a* high-fidelity *system.*

high-flown (hī′flōn′) ***adj-*** full of extravagant and pretentious ideas, expressions, etc.: high-flown *language.*

high fre·quen·cy ***n-*** any radio frequency in the range of 3 to 30 megacycles, used in the transmission of radio and television signals. **—*adj-*** **(high-frequency):** *a* high-frequency *receiver.*

high-grade (hī′grād′) ***adj-*** of high quality.

high·hand·ed (hī′hăn′dəd) ***adj-*** overbearing; domineering; arrogant: *the* highhanded *manner of a dictator.* **—*adv-*** **high′hand′ed·ly.** ***n-*** **high′hand′ed·ness.**

high hat ***n-*** top hat.

high-hat (hī′hăt′) *Informal* ***vt-*** **[high-hat·ted, high-hat·ting]** to treat in a snobbish manner; snub. ***adj-***: high-hat *manner.*

high·jack (hī′jăk′) hijack.

high jinks ***n-*** *pl.* boisterous, good-natured fun or pranks.

high jump ***n-*** athletic contest in which the contestants attempt to jump over a horizontal bar that is raised slightly after each successful try.

high·land (hī′lənd) ***n-*** **1** (often **highlands**) high or mountainous land, region, etc. **2 the Highlands** mountainous region in northern and western Scotland.

High·land·er (hī′lən dər) ***n-*** **1** a native of the Scottish Highlands. **2 highlander** inhabitant of a highland.

Highland fling ***n-*** lively dance of the Scottish Highlands.

high·light (hī′līt′) ***n-*** **1** part or point from which light is brightly reflected, especially the brightest part or point of a painting, photograph, etc. **2** the most outstanding or interesting event, part, etc.: *Her performance was the* highlight *of the evening.* ***vt-*** **1** to light brightly or show as brightly lit. **2** to give emphasis, prominence, or interest to: *He* highlighted *his speech with quotations.*

high·ly (hī′lē) ***adv-*** **1** in a great degree; very much; extremely: *a taste for* highly *seasoned food*; *a* highly *educated person.* **2** favorably; with approval: *The man's employer spoke* highly *of his work.* **3** at a high price or rate: *a* highly *paid worker.*

high-mind·ed (hī′mīn′dəd) ***adj-*** noble or lofty in character, feelings, etc.: *his* high-minded *sentiments.* **—*adv-*** **high′-mind′ed·ly.** ***n-*** **high′-mind′ed·ness.**

high·ness (hī′nəs) ***n-*** **1** nobility; loftiness: *a* highness *of purpose.* **2 Highness** title for people of royal families, preceded by "Your," "His," or "Her."

high-octane (hī′ŏk′tān′) ***adj-*** of engine fuels, producing little knock.

high-pitched (hī′pĭcht′) ***adj-*** **1** high in pitch; shrill; piping: *a* high-pitched *voice.* **2** steep in slope: *a* high-pitched *roof.*

high-pow·ered (hī′pou′ərd) ***adj-*** having great power.

high-pres·sure (hī′prĕsh′ər) ***adj-*** **1** having or dealing with high pressure: *a* high-pressure *valve.* **2** having high atmospheric pressure: *a* high-pressure *air mass.* **3** aggressive; stubborn: *a* high-pressure *salesman.* ***vt-*** **[high-pres·sured, high-pres·sur·ing]** *Informal* to attempt to sell or persuade, using aggressive methods.

high priest ***n-*** chief priest.

high-rise (hī′rīz′) ***adj-*** having many stories: *a* high-rise *office building.* ***n-*** a building with many stories: *My aunt lives in a* high-rise.

high·road (hī′rōd′) ***n-*** main road; highway.

high school ***n-*** a school that is above elementary school and below college. *as* ***modifier:*** *his* high school *graduation.*

high seas ***n-*** *pl.* the part of any ocean or sea that is beyond the legal authority of any one country.

high-sound·ing (hī′soun′dĭng) ***adj-*** impressive or pretentious when spoken: *a* high-sounding *title.*

high-spir·it·ed (hī′spĭr′ə təd) ***adj-*** having a bold or fiery spirit; mettlesome: *a* high-spirited *horse.* **—*adv-*** **high′-spir′it·ed·ly.** ***n-*** **high′-spir′it·ed·ness.**

high-strung (hī′strŭng′) ***adj-*** tense; excitable; nervous.

high·tail (hī′tāl′) *Slang* ***vi-*** to run or move quickly.

high-ten·sion (hī′tĕn′shən) ***adj-*** having a high voltage: high-tension *wires.*

high-test (hī′tĕst′) ***adj-*** of gasoline; having an unusually low boiling point.

high tide ***n-*** **1** highest point of a tide; also, the time this point is reached. **2** peak or high point of something.

high time ***n-*** the latest time without serious consequences for someone to do something.

high-toned (hī′tōnd′) *Informal* ***adj-*** having or showing superiority in morals, quality, etc., especially in a pretentious way: high-toned *sentiments.*

high-water mark ***n-*** **1** the highest point reached by a rising body of water. **2** the highest or most advanced point reached in a person's career, a battle, etc.

high·way (hī′wā′) ***n-*** any public road, especially a main road between towns for motor vehicles.

high·way·man (hī′wā′mən) ***n-*** [*pl.* **high·way·men**] in former times, a thief, usually mounted on horseback, who robbed persons on public roads.

high·wire (hī′wīər′) ***n-*** tightrope.

hi·jack (hī′jăk′) *Slang* ***vt-*** to rob a truck or other carrier of (merchandise) en route to its destination; also, to take the truck and contents illegally. **—*n-*** **hi′jack′er.**

hike (hīk) ***n-*** long walk or march: *The Boy Scout troop went for a* hike *in the country.* ***vi-*** **[hiked, hik·ing]:** *They* hiked *for five miles.* **—*n-*** **hik′er.**

hi·lar·i·ous (hə lâr′ē əs) ***adj-*** gay and merry in a noisy way. **—*adv-*** **hi·lar′i·ous·ly.**

hi·lar·i·ty (hə lăr′ə tē) ***n-*** [*pl.* **hi·lar·i·ties**] noisy mirth.

hill (hĭl) ***n-*** **1** elevation of the earth that is not as high as a mountain. **2** heap or mound of earth: *an ant* hill. **3** a heap of earth around a plant, or the heap and the plant: *a* hill *of beans.*

hill·bil·ly (hĭl′bĭl′ē) ***n-*** [*pl.* **hill·bil·lies**] person from the mountain regions of southern United States (often used to show disfavor).

hill·ock (hĭl′ək) ***n-*** small hill.

hill·side (hĭl′sīd′) ***n-*** side or slope of a hill.

hill·top (hĭl′ tŏp′) ***n-*** the top part of a hill.
hill·y (hĭl′ ē) ***adj-*** [**hill·i·er, hill·i·est**] having many hills; not level: *through* hilly *country.*
hilt (hĭlt) ***n-*** handle of a dagger or sword.
to the hilt completely; entirely: *It pleased me* to the hilt.

Hilt

hi·lum (hī′ ləm) ***n-*** [*pl.* **hi·la** (-lə)] **1** in botany, scar left on a seed at the point where it was attached to the ovule. **2** in anatomy, notch or opening where ducts, nerves, etc., enter or leave an organ.
him (hĭm) ***pron-*** objective case of **he**: *I see* him. *Pass* him *the bread. I did it for* him. ***Hom-*** hymn.
him·self (hĭm sĕlf′) ***pron-*** **1** reflexive form of **him**; his own self: *He hid* himself *under the table. He is proud of* himself. **2** his normal or true self: *After a moment of dizziness, he came to* himself. **3** intensive form of **he**: *He* himself *will come.* **4** *Irish* he: *I am sure* himself *will not deny it.*
by himself 1 alone: *He came by* himself. **2** without any help: *He built the shed* by himself.
[1]**hind** (hīnd) ***adj-*** [**hind·er, hind·most** or **hind·er·most**] at the back; rear: *the* hind *legs of a dog.* [from earlier **hinder,** from Old English **hindan,** "from behind."]
[2]**hind** (hīnd) ***n-*** female of the deer, especially the red deer. See also *hart.* [from Old English.]
[3]**hind** (hīnd) ***n-*** **1** in Scotland and northern England, a farm worker. **2** *Archaic* peasant. [alteration of earlier **hine,** short for Old English **hīne man** meaning "member of a household; household servant."]
[1]**hin·der** (hĭn′ dər) ***vt-*** to get in the way of; put obstacles in the way of; impede; prevent: *The sand* hindered *our walking.* [from Old English **hindrian,** from [2]**hinder.**]
[2]**hind·er** (hīn′ dər) *compar.* of [1]**hind.** [from Old English, meaning "backwards."]
Hin·di (hĭn′ dē) ***n-*** the principal language of northern India, belonging to the Indo-European family of languages.
hind·most (hīnd′ mōst′) or **hind·er·most** (hīn′ dər-) *superl.* of [1]**hind.**
hind·quar·ter (hīnd′ kwôr′ tər) ***n-*** **1** either side of the hind part of a carcass of beef, veal, lamb, etc. **2 hindquarters** haunches.
hin·drance (hĭn′ drəns) ***n-*** **1** person or thing that hinders; obstacle. **2** a hindering: *the* hindrance *of one's plans.*
hind·sight (hīnd′ sīt′) ***n-*** **1** ability to look back and see what should have been done. **2** rear sight of a gun.
Hin·du (hĭn′ dōō) ***n-*** native or inhabitant of India whose religion is Hinduism. ***adj-*** of or relating to such persons or to Hinduism: *a* Hindu *festival*; *a* Hindu *god.*
Hin·du·ism (hĭn′ dōō ĭz′ əm) ***n-*** chief religion of India, based upon the worship of Brahma but recognizing many other gods and goddesses. Hinduism also includes various schools of philosophy and a system of social organization and customs.
hinge (hĭnj) ***n-*** **1** jointed pieces of metal on which a gate, door, lid, etc., swings to open and close. **2** natural movable joint, such as the knee or the joining cartilage of a clamshell.
hinge on or **upon** to depend on.

Hinges

hint (hĭnt) ***n-*** indirect or slight indication; roundabout suggestion: *I might guess the riddle if you give me a* hint. *A* hint *of spring was in the air.* ***vt-*** to suggest or refer to in a roundabout way: *She* hinted *that I should polish my shoes.* **—*n-* hint′ er.**
hint at to suggest or refer to indirectly.

hin·ter·land (hĭn′ tər lănd′) ***n-*** **1** region lying inland from the lands bordering the sea or a large river. **2** region that supplies a city and uses it for a trade center. **3** region remote from towns or cities.
[1]**hip** (hĭp) ***n-*** **1** part of the body that curves outward on each side below the waist, formed by the hipbones and their fleshy covering. **2** hipbone. **3** hip joint. [from Old English **hype.**]
[2]**hip** (hĭp) ***n-*** seedcase of the rose. [from Old English **hēope.**]
hip·bone (hĭp′ bōn′) ***n-*** either of the two large, flat, irregular bones that form the sides of the pelvis. Each hipbone is made up of the ilium, ischium, and pubis.
hip joint ***n-*** the ball-and-socket joint between the hipbone and the femur.
Hip·po·crat·ic oath (hĭp′ ə krăt′ ĭk) ***n-*** the ethical guide for the medical profession, based on an oath attributed to Hippocrates.
hip·po·drome (hĭp′ ə drōm′) ***n-*** **1** in ancient Greece or Rome, a race course for horses and chariots. **2** arena for circuses, sports events, etc.
hip·po·pot·a·mus (hĭp′ ə pŏt′ ə məs) ***n-*** [*pl.* **hip·po·pot·a·mus·es** or **hip·po·pot·a·mi** (-mī, -mē)] large African plant-eating river animal with a tough hide, a huge mouth, and short legs.

Hippopotamus, about 14 ft. long

hire (hīər) ***vt-*** [**hired, hir·ing**] **1** to employ for pay: *The manager* hired *a secretary.* **2** to pay for the use of: *to* hire *a truck.* ***n-*** money paid as wages or as rent: *That man is not worth his* hire.
for hire available in return for payment.
hire out 1 to give services for pay: *She* hires out *as a maid.* **2** to allow others to use for pay: *He* hired out *his truck for $10 a day.*
hire·ling (hīər′ lĭng) ***n-*** person who will serve anyone or do any task for money; hack.
hir·sute (hûr′ sōōt′, -syōōt′) ***adj-*** hairy.
his (hĭz) ***determiner*** (possessive case of the pronoun "he," now usually called possessive adjective) **1** of or belonging to him: *Fortunately* his *fall wasn't serious.* **2** made or done by him: *He did* his *homework.* **3** inhabited by him: *I called* his *room at the hotel.* ***pron-*** (possessive pronoun) thing or things belonging to him: *This is* his. *That tie of* his *is worn out.*
His·pa·ni·a (hĭ spā′ nē ə, hĭ spăn′-) ***n-*** Latin name for Spain and Portugal. **—*adj-* His·pan′ ic.**
hiss (hĭs) ***n-*** **1** sound of a prolonged /s/, such as that made by escaping steam, a snake, etc. **2** similar sound uttered by persons expressing dislike, anger, etc. ***vi-*** to make such a sound: *The steam* hissed *in the radiator. The crowd* hissed *during the speech.* ***vt-***: *to* hiss *one's words*; *to* hiss *a performance.*
his·ta·mine (hĭs′ tə mēn′) *Medicine* ***n-*** chemical compound that occurs in all animal tissues and has the ability to make blood vessels dilate. It is thought to cause the unpleasant symptoms in many allergies.
his·tol·o·gy (hĭ stŏl′ ə jē) ***n-*** **1** branch of biology that deals with the very tiny features of plant and animal tissue visible only with a microscope. **2** such features of a certain kind of tissue: *the* histology *of the lung.*
his·tol·o·gist (hĭ stŏl′ ə jĭst) ***n-*** person who is an expert in, and usually occupied with, histology.
his·to·ri·an (hĭ stôr′ ē ən) ***n-*** a writer of or an expert in history.
his·tor·ic (hĭ stôr′ ĭk) ***adj-*** **1** important in history or in human events; decisive; famous: *a* historic *spot*; *a* historic *meeting.* **2** historical.

his·tor·i·cal (hĭ stôr′ ĭ kəl) ***adj-*** **1** of or relating to history: *a* historical *event*; *a* historical *study.* **2** based on history: *a* historical *novel.* **3** historic. **—*adv-* his·tor′ i·cal·ly.**

his·to·ry (hĭs′ tə rē, hĭs′ trē) ***n-*** [*pl.* **his·tor·ies**] **1** record of past facts and events: *We shall read a* history *of the United States.* **2** past events or facts connected with a thing, person, nation, etc.: *the weird* history *of that family.* **3** branch of learning which deals with past events: *a class in* history.

his·tri·on·ic (hĭs′ trē ŏn′ ĭk) ***adj-*** **1** overly dramatic or emotional in one's speech or manner; artificial; affected. **2** of or relating to actors or acting.

his·tri·on·ics (hĭs′ trē ŏn′ ĭks) ***n-*** **1** (takes plural verb) display of dramatic and affected behavior: *Her* histrionics *offend me.* **2** (takes singular verb) the art of stage performance.

hit (hĭt) ***vt-*** **[hit, hit·ting]** (in senses 1, 3, and 4 considered intransitive when the direct object is implied but not expressed) **1** to give a blow to; strike: *to* hit *someone on the chin*; *to* hit *a ball.* **2** to bump or crash forcibly: *He* hit *his head on the door.* **3** to fly into or dash against forcibly: *The arrow* hit *the target. The car* hit *the railing.* **4** to become suddenly clear or known to: *The answer just now* hit *me.* **5** in baseball, to make (a specified base hit): *to* hit *a double.* **6** to reach; come up to: *He* hit *his stride. We* hit *eighty miles an hour.* ***vi-*** **1** to crash (against something). **2** in baseball, to make a base hit. ***n-*** **1** stroke, blow, etc., that reaches its mark: *I have three* hits *and two misses.* **2** successful or popular song, play, etc. **3** in baseball, a base hit. **—*n-* hit′ ter.**

hard hit affected deeply: *He was* hard hit *by his* father's death. **hit or miss** without worrying about the outcome; in an aimless or haphazard manner.

hit and run in baseball, to make a hit-and-run play.

hit it off to get along well with one another.

hit on (or **upon**) to come or light on; happen on: *He finally* hit on *the right answer.*

hit out at to attack wildly with blows or harsh words.

hit-and-run (hĭt′ ən rŭn′) ***adj-*** **1** done by or involving someone who immediately drives or runs away: *a* hit-and-run *accident*; *a* hit-and-run *driver*; *a* hit-and-run *attack.* **2** in baseball, having to do with a play in which a base-runner starts for the next base when the pitcher starts his throw to the batter, and the batter tries to hit the ball, preferably behind the runner.

hitch (hĭch) ***vt-*** to attach; tie; fasten: *Please* hitch *the horse to the wagon.* ***vi-*** to pull (up) with a short jerk: *Tom* hitched *up his trousers.* ***n-*** **1** short jerk: *Tom gave his trousers a* hitch. **2** obstacle; delay; halt: *There was a sudden* hitch *in the program.* **3** kind of knot; especially, a temporary knot.

TIMBER HITCH
HALF HITCH
Hitches

hitch·hike (hĭch′ hīk′) ***vi-*** **[hitch·hiked, hitch·hik·ing]** to travel by asking for rides along the way: *He* hitch-hiked *across the United States.* **—*n-* hitch′ hik′ er.**

hitching post ***n-*** post for hitching horses.

hith·er (hĭth′ ər) ***adv-*** here: *Come* hither!

hith·er·to (hĭth′ ər tōō′) ***adv-*** up to this time.

hith·er·ward (hĭth′ ər wərd) or **hith·er·wards** (-wərdz) ***adv-*** hither.

Hit·tite (hĭ′ tīt′) ***n-*** member of an ancient people whose powerful empire lasted from 2000-1200 B.C. in Asia Minor and northern Syria. ***adj-***: *a* Hittite *king.*

hive (hīv) ***n-*** **1** box or house for honeybees. For picture, see *beehive.* **2** swarm of bees living in this place. **3** place where there are crowds of busy people: *The big store was a* hive *of activity.* ***vt-*** **[hived, hiv·ing]** to put (bees) into a hive. ***vi-*** to live together in or as in a hive.

hives (hīvz) ***n-*** *pl.* (takes singular or plural verb) an itching skin rash, often caused by an allergy.

H.M.S. **1** His (or Her) Majesty's Ship. **2** His (or Her) Majesty's Service.

ho (hō) ***interj-*** exclamation used to attract attention, express delight, surprise, etc. ***Hom-*** hoe.

Ho symbol for holmium.

hoar (hôr) ***adj-*** hoary. ***Hom-*** whore.

hoard (hôrd) ***n-*** supply of things that is stored up or hidden away: *a* hoard *of gold.* ***vt-***: *to* hoard *valuable coins.* ***Hom-*** horde. **—*n-* hoard′ er.**

hoar·frost (hôr′ frŏst′, -frŏst′) ***n-*** tiny drops of dew frozen on plants, trees, the ground, etc.; rime.

hoar·hound (hôr′ hound′) horehound.

hoarse (hôrs) ***adj-*** **[hoars·er, hoars·est]** **1** rough, harsh, or gruff in sound: *A cold had made Jane's voice* hoarse. **2** having a rough, harsh voice: *Jane was* hoarse *from a cold.* ***Hom-*** horse. **—*adv-* hoarse′ ly.** ***n-*** **hoarse′ ness.**

hoar·y (hôr′ ē) ***adj-*** **[hoar·i·er, hoar·i·est]** **1** white or gray. **2** old; venerable. **—*n-* hoar′ i·ness.**

hoax (hōks) ***n-*** mischievous trick or fraud; especially, a practical joke to deceive the public. **—*n-* hoax′ er.**

¹hob (hŏb) ***n-*** ledge at the back or sides of the inside of a fireplace on which food is kept warm. [a form of **hub**, originally meaning "a projection."]

²hob (hŏb) ***n-*** elf or goblin. [probably from **Hob**, an old nickname for Robin (Goodfellow) or Robert.]

play (or **raise**) **hob** *Informal* to make mischief.

hob·ble (hŏb′ əl) ***vi-*** **[hob·bled, hob·bling]** to limp or walk with difficulty: *The old man* hobbled *along on his cane.* ***vt-*** **1** to tie two legs of (an animal) loosely together to hinder its movements. **2** to hinder; hamper: *to* hobble *our progress.* ***n-*** **1** limping or halting walk. **2** rope, strap, etc., used to hobble an animal.

Hobble

hob·ble·de·hoy (hŏb′ əl dē hoi′) ***n-*** **1** adolescent boy. **2** awkward, gawky boy.

hob·by (hŏb′ ē) ***n-*** [*pl.* **hob·bies**] subject or interest pursued mainly for pleasure in one's spare time; avocation: *His* hobby *is boating.*

hob·by·horse (hŏb′ ē hôrs′, -hôrs′) ***n-*** **1** toy made of a stick with a horse's head, on which children pretend to ride. **2** wooden horse on rockers or on a merry-go-round. **3** favorite or pet idea, subject, etc.

hob·gob·lin (hŏb′ gŏb′ lĭn) ***n-*** **1** troublesome elf. **2** imaginary thing that causes fear; bogey.

hob·nail (hŏb′ nāl′) ***n-*** **1** large-headed nail on the sole of a heavy shoe to lessen wear or prevent slipping. **2** pattern of closely spaced tufts or bosses on glass, fabrics, etc. **—*adj-* hob′ nailed′.**

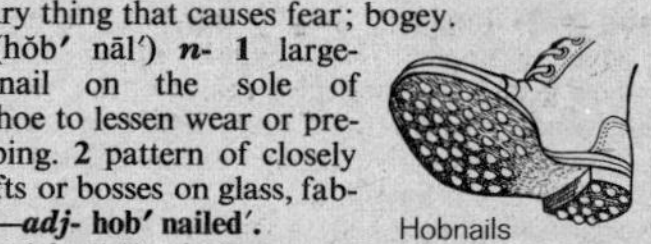
Hobnails

hob·nob (hŏb′ nŏb′) ***vi-*** **[hob·nob·bed, hob·nob·bing]** to be on close or friendly terms (with): *He* hobnobs *with the rich.*

ho·bo (hō′ bō) ***n-*** [*pl.* **ho·bos** or **ho·boes**] person without regular work who wanders from place to place; tramp.

Hob·son's choice (hŏb′ sənz) ***n-*** choice without alternative. [from the English liveryman Thomas **Hobson's** rule that every customer take the horse nearest the door.]

1**hock** (hŏk) ***n-*** the joint in the hind leg of some animals, such as the horse, cow, etc., corresponding to the ankle in man. ***vt-*** to lame by cutting the tendons of such a joint; hamstring. [from Old English **hōh.**] ***Hom-*** hawk.

2**hock** (hŏk) *Slang* ***vt-*** to pawn. ***n-*** condition of being in pawn. [American word of uncertain origin, perhaps akin to Dutch **hok,** "prison; animal pen."] ***Hom-*** hawk.

3**hock** (hŏk) ***n-*** any white Rhine wine. [from **Hochheim,** Germany, where a type of Rhine wine was first produced.] ***Hom-*** hawk.

hock·ey (hŏk′ ē) ***n-*** **1** (also **ice hockey**) game played on ice between two teams of six players each wearing skates and carrying curved sticks which are used to drive a hard rubber disk called a "puck" into the opponent's goal. **2** (also **field hockey**) similar game played on an outdoor field between teams of eleven players each, with a ball instead of a puck.

MASON'S

COAL

Hods

ho·cus-po·cus (hō′ kəs pō′ kəs) ***n-*** **1** meaningless words and phrases used in magic. **2** trickery of a magician or juggler; sleight of hand; also, any trickery used to cover up deception. ***vt-*** *Informal* to trick.

hod (hŏd) ***n-*** **1** bucket for carrying coal. **2** V-shaped trough on a long handle, for carrying bricks or mortar.

hodge·podge (hŏj′ pŏj′) ***n-*** jumble; confused mixture: *a* hodgepodge *of toys.*

hoe (hō) ***n-*** tool with a flat blade on a long handle, used for digging up weeds, loosening soil, etc. ***vt-*** **[hoed, hoe·ing]**: *Early in the morning Barney* hoed *his garden.* ***vi-***: *Barney* hoed *all afternoon.* ***Hom-*** ho. **—*n-*** **ho′ er.**

Hoe

hoe·cake (hō′ kāk′) ***n-*** small cornmeal cake.

hog (hŏg, hȯg) ***n-*** **1** full-grown pig. **2** greedy or dirty person.

go the whole hog *Slang* to go all the way.

ho·gan (hō′ găn′) ***n-*** dwelling of the Navaho Indians usually made of wooden posts and branches covered with earth.

hog·back (hŏg′ băk′, hȯg′-) ***n-*** **1** in geology, a sharp ridge formed by the edge of a tilted layer of hard rock which has been laid bare by the erosion of a layer of softer rock close to it. **2** any sharp, steep ridge.

hog·gish (hŏg′ ĭsh, hȯg′-) ***adj-*** like a hog; filthy or greedy; coarse: *his* hoggish *eating habits.* **—*adv-*** **hog′ gish·ly.** ***n-*** **hog′ gish·ness.**

hog·nose snake (hŏg′ nōz′, hȯg′-) ***n-*** any of several nonpoisonous North American snakes with stout bodies and a flat snout.

hogs·head (hŏgz′ hĕd′, hȯgz′-) ***n-*** **1** large cask. **2** a liquid measure equal to 63 gallons.

hog·wash (hŏg′ wŏsh′, hȯg′ wȯsh′) ***n-*** **1** kitchen refuse or garbage fed to hogs; swill. **2** *Informal* worthless or meaningless talk, ideas, etc.; nonsense.

hoi pol·loi (hoi′ pə loi′) ***n-*** the common people regarded as without culture or breeding; the masses or herd.

hoist (hoist) ***vt-*** to lift up; raise, especially by means of tackle, cranes, etc.: *to* hoist *the sails of a ship.* ***n-*** **1** apparatus for raising things: *The elevator is a* hoist. **2** a lifting; push upward; boost: *a* hoist *over the wall.*

hoist with (one's) own petard to be caught or hurt by a scheme one has made against someone else.

hoi·ty-toi·ty (hoi′ tē toi′ tē) ***interj-*** exclamation of surprise and contempt. ***adj-*** haughty; arrogant.

ho·kum (hō′ kəm) *Slang* ***n-*** meaningless talk or writing; claptrap; bunk.

1**hold** (hōld) ***vt-*** **[held, hold·ing] 1** to have or keep in the hand; grasp; grip; clasp: *to* hold *a bouquet.* **2** to keep in a certain pose or manner: *She* held *her head erect.* **3** to contain: *This jug* holds *one gallon.* **4** to keep by force; protect; defend: *to* hold *a fort.* **5** to control; keep back; check: *It is better to* hold *your temper before you speak out angrily.* **6** to believe; accept: *Most Americans* hold *the opinion that democracy is desirable.* **7** to carry on; conduct: *to* hold *a meeting*; *to* hold *a church service.* **8** to occupy; keep: *He* held *the office of secretary.* ***vi-*** **1** to grasp or grip; clasp: *You must* hold *tightly to the rope.* **2** to remain or continue: *Please* hold *still. Our ranks* held *despite the withering fire. My promise still* holds. *The wind* held *from the south.* **3** to be faithful or loyal (to): *to* hold *to one's promise.* **4** to be true or in force: *The same rule* holds *for everyone.* ***n-*** **1** a grasp; grip: *Take a good* hold *on the handle.* **2** something that may be grasped for support. **3** influence; control: *She has some sort of* hold *over him.* **4** *Music* symbol placed over [𝄐] or under [𝄑] a note or rest to show that it is to be prolonged; pause. [from Old English **h(e)aldan.**]

get (or **take**) **hold of 1** to get a grip on; take or seize. **2** to get control of: *You ought to* get hold of *yourself.*

hold forth to speak at length; lecture or preach: *He* held forth *for two hours.*

hold good to be accepted as true or valid: *Will his statements* hold good *in court?*

hold in to check; keep back; restrain.

hold off 1 to keep at a distance. **2** to keep from capturing, advancing, etc.: *We* held off *the enemy for days.* **3** to put off; delay: *He* held off *calling me.*

hold on 1 to retain a grip or grasp on something. **2** to continue or persist: *They* held on *until help came.* **3** *Informal* wait! stop!

hold (one's) own to retain one's present position; not fall behind.

hold (one's) peace to refrain from speaking or interfering.

hold out to last; remain firm; stand: *The pioneers* held out *against hunger and cold all winter.*

hold over 1 to postpone for later consideration: *We will* hold over *the new business.* **2** to keep for an additional period: *The movie is being* held over *another week.*

hold up 1 to delay; hinder: *He* held up *our departure.* **2** to rob by force, usually with a gun.

hold water *Informal* to be true or valid.

hold with to approve of; agree with: *Grandma does not* hold with *all the new cooking methods.*

2**hold** (hōld) ***n-*** space below the main deck of a ship, in which cargo is stored. [from **hole** and Dutch **hol,** "ship's cavity."]

hold·back (hōld′ băk′) ***n-*** **1** something that restrains or hinders; check. **2** on a horse-drawn vehicle, the strap or iron on the shaft attached to the harness that permits the horse to stop or push back the vehicle.

hold·er (hōl′ dər) ***n-*** **1** person who owns or possesses something: *He was the* holder *of many awards.* **2** a device for holding on to something or keeping something in: *He used the box as a* holder *for pencils.*

hold·ing (hōl′dĭng) ***n-*** (often **holdings**) something owned; property, especially real estate or stocks.

holding company ***n-*** corporation which holds enough stock to control the operation of another company.

hold·up (hōld′ŭp) ***n-*** **1** armed robbery or attempt to rob. **2** a delay: *a traffic* holdup *due to an accident.*

hole (hōl) ***n-*** **1** opening in or through something: *a* hole *in the tablecloth.* **2** cavity in a solid body or mass: *a* hole *in a tooth.* **3** place hollowed in the ground by an animal; burrow: *A woodchuck lives in a* hole. **4** on a golf course, a sunken cup into which a ball is driven. ***vt-*** **[holed, hol·ing] 1** to drive or dig an opening, excavation, etc., into: *They* holed *the mountain for a tunnel. The rock* holed *the ship.* **2** in golf, to hit into the cup: *He* holed *the ball in four strokes.* ***Hom-*** *whole.*

burn a hole in one's pocket of money, to make one anxious to spend it. **pick holes in,** to pick out mistakes or flaws in.

hole up to go into seclusion or hiding; also, to hibernate.

hol·i·day (hŏl′ə dā′) ***n-*** **1** day of no work, fixed by law or custom to celebrate a famous event: *Thanksgiving is a* holiday. **2** period of time which a person takes off from work; vacation: *We will spend a month's* holiday *at the lake.* ***adj-*** **1** *of or relating to a holiday or holidays*: *the* holiday *schedule.* **2** gay; carefree: *a* holiday *mood.*

ho·li·ness (hō′lē nəs) ***n-*** **1** air or aura of sacredness; presence of divinity: *The pilgrim felt the* holiness *of the shrine.* **2** saintliness; godliness: *the* holiness *of his life.* **3 His Holiness** title and form of address for the Pope.

hol·lan·daise (hŏl′ən dāz′) ***n-*** rich sauce made of egg yolks, butter, and lemon juice, and served hot over vegetables, fish, or egg dishes.

Hol·land·er (hŏl′ən dər) ***n-*** native or citizen of the Netherlands; Dutchman.

hol·ler (hŏl′ər) *Informal* ***n-*** a shout; yell. ***vi-*** **1** to yell: *He* hollered *loudly.* **2** to complain. ***vt-***: *He* hollered *my name.*

hol·low (hŏl′ō) ***adj-*** **[hol·low·er, hol·low·est] 1** empty inside; not solid. **2** having a cuplike shape; concave. **3** sunken: *She had* hollow *cheeks after her illness.* **4** deep, muffled, and echoing: *We heard* hollow *sounds from the cave.* **5** unreal; insincere; false: *He spoke* hollow *words of praise.* ***n-*** **1** empty space; cavity. **2** valley. ***vt-*** to scoop (out): *The children* hollowed *out the pumpkin.* ***—adv-*** **hol′low·ly.** ***n-*** **hol′low·ness.**

hol·ly (hŏl′ē) ***n-*** [*pl.* **hol·lies**] **1** shrub or small tree with stiff, prickly, glossy evergreen leaves and bright-red berries. **2** branches of this shrub used as a decoration: *Decorate the halls with* holly.

Holly

hol·ly·hock (hŏl′ē hŏk′) ***n-*** tall plant with hairy leaves and large flowers of various colors growing from the main stem.

Holmes, Sherlock (hōlmz, shûr′lŏk′) See *Sherlock Holmes.*

hol·mi·um (hōl′mē əm) ***n-*** metallic rare-earth element. Symbol Ho, At. No. 67, At. Wt. 164.930.

hol·o·caust (hŏl′ə kŏst′, hō′lə-) ***n-*** **1** great destruction or loss of life by fire. **2** in earlier times, a sacrifice wholly consumed by fire.

Hol·o·caust (häl′ə kôst′, hō′lə-) ***n-*** destruction of European Jews by Nazis during the 1930's and 1940's.

hol·o·gram (hŏl′ə grăm′, hō′lə-) ***n-*** the plate on which the light patterns produced by holography are recorded.

hol·o·graph (hō′lə grăf′, hŏl′ə-) ***n-*** letter, will, etc., of a person that is entirely in his own handwriting. ***as modifier:*** *a* holograph *manuscript.*

hol·o·gra·phy (hə lŏg′rə fē) ***n-*** a method that uses laser light to create three-dimensional images.

Hol·stein (hōl′stēn′, *also* -stīn′) ***n-*** breed of large black and white dairy cattle, originally from Schleswig-Holstein, Germany.

hol·ster (hōl′stər) ***n-*** **1** leather pistol case usually worn on a belt around the waist. **2** similar case for a rifle, attached to the saddle of a horse.

Holster

ho·ly (hō′lē) ***adj-*** **[ho·li·er, ho·li·est] 1** of or related to God or religious use; sacred: *the* Holy *Bible*; *a* holy *day.* **2** morally good; saintly: *a* holy *man.* ***Hom-*** wholly.

Holy City ***n-*** city such as Jerusalem, Rome, or Mecca, that is a sacred center of religious worship.

Holy Communion See *Communion.*

holy day ***n-*** day set apart as a religious festival, day of fasting, etc.

Holy Father ***n-*** a title of the Pope.

Holy Ghost ***n-*** Holy Spirit.

Holy Grail ***n-*** Grail.

Holy Land ***n-*** Palestine.

holy orders ***n-*** **1** the rite or sacrament of ordination to the priesthood. **2** the rank of an ordained minister or priest, or other various church officials.

Holy Roman Empire ***n-*** loose confederation of German and Italian territories in central and western Europe, established in 962 and ended in 1806.

Holy See ***n-*** the seat of the papacy; the papal court.

Holy Spirit ***n-*** in Christianity, the third person of the Trinity, the Holy Ghost.

ho·ly·stone (hō′lē stōn′) ***n-*** piece of soft sandstone used for scouring a ship's deck. ***vt-*** **[ho·ly·stoned, ho·ly·ston·ing]** to scrub with such a stone.

Holy Thursday ***n-*** the day before Good Friday; Maundy Thursday.

holy water ***n-*** water blessed by a priest and used for the ceremonial cleansing of persons and things.

Holy Week ***n-*** the week before Easter.

Holy Writ ***n-*** the Bible; the Scriptures.

hom·age (hŏm′ĭj) ***n-*** **1** reverence; respect: *We pay* homage *to his memory.* **2** in medieval times, an act by which a vassal promised faithful service to his lord.

hom·bre (ŏm′brā′, -brē) *Slang* ***n-*** fellow; man.

home (hōm) ***n-*** **1** place where a person lives; residence; house; domicile. **2** family group: *He kept his* home *together.* **3** country, State, town, etc., where one was born or raised, or where one lives. **4** place where an animal is commonly found; habitat: *The polar bear's* home *is the Arctic.* **5** institution for care or relief: home *for the aged.* **6** the goal in some games; especially, home plate in baseball. ***as modifier:*** *a happy* home *life*; *her* home *town.* ***adv-*** **1** to or at one's residence, native place, etc.: *to go* home. **2** to the point aimed at; to the heart: *to drive a nail* home; *to say something that strikes* home. ***vi-*** **[homed, hom·ing] 1** to move or aim toward a certain point from which signals radiate: *The planes* home *on the radio beacon.* **2** to return to base, residence, house, etc., from a distance, as some

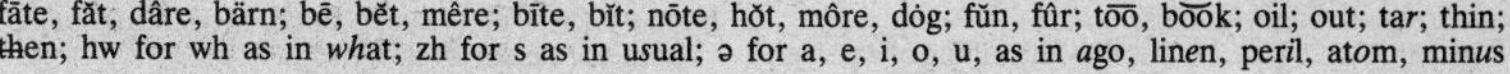
fāte, făt, dâre, bärn; bē, bĕt, mêre; bīte, bĭt; nōte, hŏt, môre, dòg; fŭn, fûr; tōō, bŏŏk; oil; out; tar; thin; then; hw for wh as in what; zh for s as in usual; ə for a, e, i, o, u, as in ago, linen, peril, atom, minus

pigeons do. ***vt-*** to cause (an airplane, guided missile, etc.) to seek a certain point or target that radiates waves or signals: *We can* home *a rocket on the heat from engine exhausts.* **—*adj-* home′less.**

at home 1 at ease; comfortable: *They feel* at home *with each other.* 2 willing to see or entertain: *The Allens are* at home *to all their neighbors.* **bring home** to convey or teach forcibly: *The sight of wounds and death* brings home *the horror of war.*

home base ***n-*** home plate.

home·bred (hōm′brĕd′) ***adj-*** bred at home; native; domestic: *a* homebred *strain of wheat.*

home economics ***n-*** the study of home management, including cooking, clothing, child care, etc.

home·land (hōm′lănd′) ***n-*** nation of one's birth or allegiance.

home·like (hōm lĭk′) ***adj-*** comfortable, friendly, etc., like a home.

home·ly (hōm′lē) ***adj-*** **[home·li·er, home·li·est]** 1 homelike; plain; simple: *The speaker used* homely *everyday words.* 2 having plain features; not handsome or beautiful: *Lincoln had a* homely *but noble face.* 3 not polished or refined: *the* homely *but hospitable manners of this part of the country.* **—*n-* home′li·ness.**

home·made (hōm′mād′) ***adj-*** made, or as if made, at home: *to like* homemade *food.*

home·mak·er (hōm′mā′kər) ***n-*** person in a home who cooks the food, takes care of the children, etc. **—*n-* home′mak′ing.**

home plate ***n-*** in baseball, the five-sided slab at which a player stands while batting and which marks the last of the four bases a player must touch to score a run; home base.

ho·mer (hō′mər) ***n-*** in baseball, a home run.

Ho·mer·ic (hō mĕr′ĭk) ***adj-*** of or pertaining to Homer, his poems, his style, or the civilization and times about which he wrote.

home·room (hōm′ro͞om′) ***n-*** daily session in a school during which a class meets to have its attendance checked, hear bulletins, etc.; also, the room in which it meets.

home rule ***n-*** administration of its own local or internal affairs by a dependent country, colony, etc.

home run ***n-*** in baseball, a hit which allows the batter to go from home plate around the diamond without stopping and reach home plate safely.

home·sick (hōm′sĭk′) ***adj-*** longing for home; sad because of being away from home: *He was* homesick *during the first weeks at college.* **—*n-* home′sick′ness.**

home·spun (hōm′spŭn′) ***n-*** cloth made from yarn spun at home; coarse, loosely woven cloth. ***adj-*** 1 made of such cloth, as a dress. 2 plain; simple; unpolished.

home·stead (hōm′stĕd′) ***n-*** 1 house with its surrounding land and buildings. 2 under the **Homestead Act** of 1862, a 160-acre tract of public land given to a settler on condition that he live on it and improve it.

home·stead·er (hōm′stĕd′ər) ***n-*** person who has a homestead, especially under the Homestead Act.

home·stretch (hōm′strĕtch′) ***n-*** 1 the part of a racetrack between the last turn and the finish line. See also *back stretch.* 2 the final stage or part of any effort.

home·ward (hōm′wərd) ***adv-*** (also **home′wards**) toward home: *We started* homeward. ***adj-*** bound for home: *a* homeward *journey.*

home·work (hōm′wûrk′) ***n-*** school lessons to be done at home.

home·y (hō′mē′) ***adj-*** **[home·i·er, home·i·est]** warm, friendly, cozy, etc., like one's home; homelike: homey *personality.* **—*n-* home′y·ness.**

hom·i·cide (hŏm′ə sīd′, hō′mə-) ***n-*** the killing of a person by another.

hom·i·ci·dal (hŏm′ə sī′dəl, hōm′-) ***adj-*** 1 likely or intending to kill; murderous: *a* homicidal *maniac.* 2 causing one to kill or wish to kill: *a* homicidal *hatred.* **—*adv-* hom′i·ci′dal·ly.**

hom·i·ly (hŏm′ə lē) ***n-*** [*pl.* **hom·i·lies**] 1 religious discourse or sermon, usually based on the Bible. 2 solemn talk, usually long and tiresome, on morals or conduct.

homing pigeon ***n-*** pigeon raised to find its way home from great distances.

hom·i·nid (hŏm′ə nĭd) ***n-*** member of a family **(Hominidae)** of two-footed, erect mammals, of which modern man is the only survivor.

hom·i·ny (hŏm′ə nē) ***n-*** hulled corn, bleached and puffed up by soaking in a weak lye solution and used as food. [American word shortened from **rockahominy,** from an American Indian language.]

homo- *combining form* same; equal; like: homo*phone* (same sound); homo*graph* (same written form). [from Greek **homo-,** from **homos** meaning "the same."]

ho·mo·ge·ne·i·ty (hō′mə jə nē′ə tē, hŏm′ə-) ***n-*** condition of being homogeneous.

ho·mo·gen·e·ous (hō′mə jē′nē əs) ***adj-*** 1 similar or identical; alike: *two* homogeneous *organs.* 2 having the same parts, composition, etc., throughout; uniform: *a* homogeneous *liquid.* **—*adv-* ho′mo·ge′ne·ous·ly.**

ho·mog·en·ize (hə mŏj′ə nīz′) ***vt-*** **[ho·mog·en·ized, ho·mog·en·iz·ing]** 1 to make homogeneous. 2 to reduce (a substance) to very fine particles which distribute themselves evenly, especially as the fat is in **homogenized milk.**

hom·o·graph (hŏm′ə grăf′) ***n-*** word that is spelled the same as one or more other words, but differs in meaning, origin, or pronunciation. Examples: "bear" (to carry) and "bear" (the animal); "cape" (point of land) and "cape" (cloak); "lead" (to conduct) and "lead" (the metal). In this dictionary homographs are indicated by raised numbers at the beginning of the entry words.

ho·mol·o·gous (hə mŏl′ə gəs) *Biology* ***adj-*** corresponding in structure and origin, as the arm of a man and the wing of a bat do.

hom·o·nym (hŏm′ə nĭm) ***n-*** 1 homophone. 2 word that is spelled and pronounced the same as one or more other words, but differs in meaning and usually in origin. Examples: "miss" (to fail to hit) and "miss" (unmarried girl); "peck" (measure) and "peck" (to strike with the beak).

hom·o·phone (hŏm′ə fōn′) ***n-*** word that is pronounced the same as one or more other words, but differs in spelling and meaning. Examples: "Hair" and "hare"; "real" and "reel." In this dictionary homophones are indicated at the ends of definitions after the label ***Hom-*.**

ho·mop·ter·ous (hō mŏp′tər əs) ***adj-*** of or relating to the order **(Homoptera)** of insects, which includes cicadas, aphids, etc.

Ho·mo sa·pi·ens (hō′mō sā′pē ənz) ***n-*** scientific name for modern humans.

Hon. Honorable.

hone (hōn) ***n-*** fine-grained stone for sharpening razors, tools, etc. ***vt-*** **[honed, hon·ing]**: *to* hone *a razor.*

hon·est (ŏn′ĭst) ***adj-*** 1 not in the habit of lying, cheating, or stealing; trustworthy: *an* honest *man.* 2 not false or deceptive; true: *an* honest *report.* 3 open; frank: *an* honest *face.* 4 genuine; without fraud: *an* honest *price.* **—*adv-* hon′est·ly.**

hon·es·ty (ŏn′ĭs tē) ***n-*** truthfulness; sincerity; uprightness: *Their* honesty *is unquestionable.*

hon·ey (hŭn′ē) ***n-*** sweet, thick, sticky liquid made by bees from the nectar of flowers.

hon·ey·bee (hŭn′ ē bē′) ***n-*** bee that makes honey. Large colonies are kept in hives to produce honey.

hon·ey·comb (hŭn′ ē kōm′) ***n-*** framework of six-sided cells with walls of wax, built by bees to hold honey and eggs. ***vt-*** to pierce with many holes or tunnels: *The beam was* honeycombed *with ant tunnels.*

Honeybee, about 3/4 in. long

hon·ey·dew (hŭn′ ē do͞o′, -dyo͞o′) ***n-*** **1** sweet, sticky substance found on the stems and leaves of certain trees and plants in hot weather. **2** sweet substance secreted on the leaves of plants by certain insects, such as aphids, scale insects, etc.

honeydew melon ***n-*** smooth-skinned white melon with a sweet, light-green flesh.

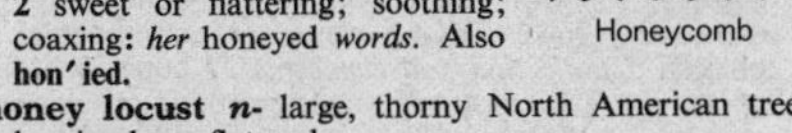

Honeycomb

hon·eyed (hŭn′ ēd) ***adj-*** **1** covered, filled with, or made of honey. **2** sweet or flattering; soothing; coaxing: *her* honeyed *words.* Also **hon′ ied.**

honey locust ***n-*** large, thorny North American tree bearing long, flat pods.

hon·ey·moon (hŭn′ ē mo͞on′) ***n-*** holiday taken by a man and woman just after their wedding. ***vi-***: *They will* honeymoon *in Canada.* **—*n-* hon′ ey·moon′ er.**

hon·ey·suck·le (hŭn′ ē sŭk′ əl) ***n-*** vine or bush with dark green leaves and sweet-smelling, tubular flowers that are usually white, yellow, or pink.

Honeysuckle

honk (hŏngk) ***n-*** **1** call of a wild goose. **2** any sound like this call: *the* honk *of a horn.* ***vi-*** to make such a sound: *We heard the geese* honk. ***vt-*** to sound or blow (a horn). **—*n-* honk′ er.**

hon·ky·tonk (hŏng′ kē tŏngk′) *Slang* ***n-*** cheap, noisy saloon, nightclub, etc. *as* ***modifier***: *a* honkytonk *neighborhood*; honkytonk *music.*

hon·or (ŏn′ ər) ***n-*** **1** high esteem; great respect: *to show* honor *to one's parents.* **2** high rank; distinction; dignity: *the* honor *of being president*; *the* honor *of knighthood.* **3** excellent reputation; good name: *to defend one's* honor. **4** strong feeling for right or justice; uprightness; integrity: *a man of* honor. **5** glory; fame; renown: *to seek* honor *by engaging in daring adventures.* **6** cause of respect or esteem; source of credit: *Sheila is an* honor *to her family.* **7** act of respect or social courtesy: *It is an* honor *to be invited to this ceremony. He did her the* honor *of attending her party.* **8** virtue or chastity, especially of women. **9** in card games such as bridge, an ace, king, queen, jack, or ten. **10 Honor** title for a high official such as a judge or mayor, preceded by "Your," "His," or "Her." **11 honors** (1) public acts or ceremonies of respect: *funeral* honors. (2) distinguished standing in school or college. (3) recognition of merit; award: *He won first* honors *in the exhibition.* ***vt-*** **1** to treat with respect or deference: *to* honor *one's parents.* **2** to show respect or esteem to: *They* honored *him by making him captain of the team.* **3** to accept and pay when due: *The bank will* honor *my check.* Also, *chiefly Brit.*, **honour.**

do the honors act as host or hostess. **on one's honor** pledged and trusted to do something.

hon·or·a·ble (ŏn′ ər ə bəl) ***adj-*** **1** worthy of respect: *His behavior is always* honorable. **2** having and showing regard for truth and high principles: *an* honorable *man.* **3** with merit and good name: *an* honorable *discharge.* **4** done or accompanied with signs of honor or respect: *an* honorable *burial.* **5 the Honorable** courtesy title for persons holding high office, or for the children of members of the British nobility. **—*n-* hon′ or·a·ble·ness. *adv-* hon′ or·a·bly.**

hon·o·rar·i·um (ŏn′ ə râr′ ē əm) ***n-*** [*pl.* **hon·o·rar·i·ums** or **hon·o·rar·i·a** (-ē ə)] honorary fee paid to a professional man as a courtesy, in recognition of a service on which custom forbids a price to be set.

hon·or·ar·y (ŏn′ ə rĕr′ ē) ***adj-*** **1** bestowed as a courtesy or mark of respect, without requiring the usual duties, fees, etc.: *an* honorary *degree from a college.* **2** holding a title or position as an honor only, without pay or regular duties: *an* honorary *vice-president.*

honor roll ***n-*** record of the names of persons who have won honor or distinction, such as a list of students who have achieved high academic standing.

honor system ***n-*** system of trusting people in schools and other institutions to obey the rules and to do their work, take examinations, etc., without supervision.

[1]hood (ho͝od) ***n-*** **1** head covering that leaves only the face exposed, sometimes attached to a robe or coat. **2** anything like this in appearance or use. **3** a fold hanging at the back of a gown worn by a graduate of a college or university, and indicating by its color the wearer's degree. **4** the cover of an automobile engine. ***vt-*** to cover or furnish with or as if with such a covering. [from Old English **hōd.**] **—*adj-* hood′ less. *adj-* hood′ like′.**

Hood

[2]hood (ho͝od, ho͞od) *Slang* ***n-*** hoodlum. ***Hom-*** who'd.

-hood *suffix* (used to form nouns) **1** state, quality, character, or condition of being: *child*hood, *hardi*hood, *mother*hood, *likeli*hood. **2** an instance or example of being: *false*hood. **3** group of; also, membership in the group: *brother*hood; *priest*hood.

hood·ed (ho͝od′ əd) ***adj-*** having a hood or a part resembling a hood: *a* hooded *cloak*; *the* hooded *cobra.*

hood·lum (ho͝od′ ləm, ho͞od′-) ***n-*** **1** member of a criminal gang; mobster. **2** young ruffian; street tough.

hoo·doo (ho͞o′ do͞o′) ***n-*** **1** voodoo. **2** *Informal* bad luck, an evil spell, etc., or a person or thing that causes any of these; jinx. ***vt-*** *Informal* to bring or cause bad luck to.

hood·wink (ho͝od′ wĭngk′) ***vt-*** to mislead by a trick; deceive; cheat. **—*n-* hood′ wink′ er.**

hoof (ho͝of, ho͞of) ***n-*** [*pl.* **hoofs** or **hooves** (ho͝ovz, ho͞ovz)] the horny covering of the toes of some animals, such as the horse or cow. It is the part of the foot that rests on the ground and supports the weight of the animal in walking or running. ***vi-*** *Informal* to go on foot; walk, dance, etc. (often followed by "it"). **—*adj-* hoof′ less. *adj-* hoof′ like′.**

HORSE'S
DEER'S
Hooves

on the hoof alive; not butchered: *The price of steers was 12 cents a pound* on the hoof.

hoof·beat (ho͝of′ bēt′, ho͞of′-) ***n-*** sound made by an animal's hoof in running, galloping, etc.

hoofed (ho͝oft, ho͞oft) ***adj-*** having hoofs.

hoof·er (ho͝of′ ər) *Slang* ***n-*** professional dancer.

hook (hŏŏk) ***n-*** **1** curved piece of metal, bone, wood, etc., designed to catch, hold, or fasten something: *a crochet* hook; *a door* hook; *a coat* hook. **2** something curved like this, such as a narrow cape that turns inland at the outer end. **3** in boxing, a short swinging blow. **4** in golf, baseball, etc., a ball's path of flight curving to the left away from a right-handed hitter (see also *slice*). ***vt-*** **1** to catch or fasten with or as if with a curved implement: *to* hook *a fish*; *to* hook *the door*. **2** to make with a hooked implement: *to* hook *a rug*. **3** in sports, to hit or throw a ball so that it curves to the left if one is right-handed or to the right if one is left-handed. ***vi-*** **1** to bend or curve sharply: *This road* hooks *to the left*. **2** to become fastened: *This* hooks *in back*. **—*adj-* hook′ like′. *adj-* hook′ less.**

Hook

by hook or by crook by fair means or foul. **on (one's) own hook** *Informal* on (one's) own responsibility.

hook up to put together and connect the parts of (a radio set, telephone, etc.).

hook·ah or **hook·a** (hŏŏk′ ə) ***n-*** Oriental tobacco pipe in which the smoke is drawn through water to cool it.

hook and eye ***n-*** a fastening consisting of a hook and an eye or loop into which the hook fits.

hooked (hŏŏkt) ***adj-*** **1** curved or bent like a hook: *a* hooked *nose*. **2** made with a hook: *a* hooked *rug*. **3** having a hook or hooks. **4** *Slang* caught; trapped.

Hook and eye

hooked rug ***n-*** rug made by pulling yarn or strips of cloth through a piece of canvas, burlap, etc., with a hooked tool.

hook·up (hŏŏk′ ŭp′) ***n-*** **1** arrangement and connection of parts and circuits such as those of a radio set, telephone system, network of radio or television stations, or a set of mechanical parts. **2** *Informal* partnership; alliance.

hook·worm (hŏŏk′ wûrm′) ***n-*** small worm, most common in warm climates, that causes weakness and loss of weight. It bores through the skin of the bare foot and makes its way to the intestine.

hook·y (hŏŏk′ ē) **play hooky** *Informal* to be absent from school without permission or good reason; be a truant.

hoo·li·gan (hōō′ lə gən) *Informal* ***n-*** hoodlum.

hoo·li·gan·ism (hōō′ lə gə nĭz′ əm) ***n-*** destructive or irresponsible behavior like that of hooligans.

hoop (hōōp, hŏŏp) ***n-*** **1** circular band or ring for holding together the staves of a barrel, tub, etc. **2** similar ring rolled along the ground by children. **3** anything shaped like such a band or ring. **4** (often **hoops**) circular framework of whalebone or wire used in former times to expand a woman's skirt. ***vt-*** to bind or secure with a curved band; encircle. **—*adj-* hoop′ like′.**

hoop skirt ***n-*** wide skirt worn in former times over a hoop or similar framework.

hoo·ray (hə rā′) hurrah.

hoose·gow (hōōs′ gou′, hōōz′-) *Slang* ***n-*** jail. [American word from Spanish **juzgado** meaning "courtroom," ultimately from Latin **judicare**, "to judge."]

Hoo·sier (hōō′ zhər) ***n-*** a native or resident of Indiana.

hoot (hōōt) ***n-*** **1** the cry of an owl, or any sound like it. **2** a shout showing dislike, disapproval, contempt, etc. ***vi-*** **1** to utter the cry of an owl, or make a similar sound. **2** to shout to show dislike, disapproval, etc.: *The crowd* hooted *at the speaker*. ***vt-*** **1** to show disapproval of or scorn for by shouting: *to* hoot *an unpopular speaker*. **2** to drive away by jeering: *to* hoot *an actor off the stage*. **—*n-* hoot′ er.**

hoot·en·an·ny (hōōt′ ən ăn′ ē) ***n-*** [*pl.* **hoot·en·an·nies**] an informal performance by a group of folk singers, in which the audience often participates.

hooves (hŏŏvz, hōōvz) *pl.* of **hoof.**

[1]**hop** (hŏp) ***vi-*** **[hopped, hop·ping]** **1** to move by short jumps, using both or all feet at once: *Frogs and birds* hop. **2** to move by short jumps, using only one leg: *He hurt his foot and* hopped *about in pain*. **3** *Informal* to make a quick trip, especially by plane. ***vt-*** to jump over or onto: *to* hop *a fence*; *to* hop *a train*. ***n-*** **1** a short jump, especially on one leg. **2** *Informal* a kind of dance, or a party at which there is dancing. **3** *Informal* a flight in an airplane. [from Old English **hoppian.**]

[2]**hop** (hŏp) ***n-*** **1** vine with green flowers shaped like small pine cones. **2 hops** dried flowers of this vine, used to flavor beer and ale. [from early Dutch **hoppe.**]

hope (hōp) ***n-*** **1** desire for something with a feeling that the desire may be fulfilled; desire accompanied by expectation: *He has* hopes *of making money*. **2** the thing desired: *Success in business was his constant* hope. **3** feeling of trust and confidence that the future will turn out well: *Never lose* hope. **4** cause or source of such a feeling: *He is the* hope *of the family*. ***vt-*** **[hoped, hop·ing]** to wish and expect; desire confidently or expectantly (takes only a clause or an infinitive as object): *I* hope *that you can come. I* hope *to come*. ***vi-*** **1** to have a strong wish (for) something one expects may occur: *We* hope *for the best*. **2** to wish and expect that things will turn out well: *He continued to* hope.

hope against hope to go on having hope although fulfillment seems unlikely.

hope chest ***n-*** chest or box in which a young woman collects articles to use when she is married.

hope·ful (hōp′ fəl) ***adj-*** **1** full of hope; full of confident expectation: *He is* hopeful *that he will be able to go*. **2** expressing hope: *a few* hopeful *words*. **3** giving hope; promising success or a good outcome: *a* hopeful *sign*. ***n-*** person who expects or is expected to succeed. **—*adv-* hope′ ful·ly. *n-* hope′ ful·ness.**

hope·less (hōp′ ləs) ***adj-*** **1** without hope. **2** having or showing little likelihood of success: *a* hopeless *task*. **—*adv-* hope′ less·ly. *n-* hope′ less·ness.**

Ho·pi (hō′ pē) ***n-*** [*pl.* **Ho·pis,** also **Ho·pi**] one of a group of American Pueblo Indians who now live in northeastern Arizona. ***adj-***: *a* Hopi *rug*.

hop·per (hŏp′ ər) ***n-*** **1** person or thing that hops. **2** any of various hopping insects, such as the leaf hopper. **3** container or chute from which something is fed to a machine, mill, bin, process, etc.

Hopper

hop·scotch (hŏp′ skŏch′) ***n-*** children's game, in which the players toss a small object into a series of numbered spaces of a diagram drawn on the ground, and then hop from space to space to pick it up.

horde (hôrd) ***n-*** **1** crowd; swarm; multitude. **2** a wandering tribe of people. ***Hom-*** hoard.

hore·hound (hôr′ hound′) ***n-*** **1** plant related to the mints, with small white flowers and aromatic leaves from which an extract is taken. **2** candy or cough medicine flavored with this extract. Also **hoarhound.**

ho·ri·zon (hə rī′ zən) ***n-*** **1** the line where the earth and sky seem to meet. **2** the limit of one's knowledge, interest, experience, etc.

Horizontal

hor·i·zon·tal (hŏr′ ə zŏn′ təl) ***adj-*** parallel to the plane of the horizon; at right angles to a vertical line; flat; level. ***n-*** line, surface, plane, etc., that is parallel to the horizon. **—*adv-* hor′ i·zon′ tal·ly.**

hor·mone (hȯr′ mōn′, hôr′-) ***n-*** **1** secretion produced by a gland, such as the pituitary gland, and carried by the blood to other parts of the body, where it may regulate growth, other glands, etc. **2** a similar substance in plants.

horn (hȯrn, hôrn) ***n-*** **1** hard, bony, often pointed and curved growth or projection on the heads of certain animals, such as the cow or goat. **2** the substance or material of which such growths are made. **3** anything pointed and curved like such projections, such as the points of the crescent moon. **4** container or wind instrument made by hollowing out such growths: *a powder* horn. **5** *Music* any of a group of brass wind instruments: *a French* horn. **6** something that sticks up on the head of an animal, such as the eyestalk of a snail. **7** device that makes a loud sound as a warning signal: *an automobile* horn. *as* ***modifier***: *a* horn *spoon*; *the* horn *rims of eyeglasses.* **—*adj-*** **horn′ less.** ***adj-*** **horn′ like′.**

draw (or **pull**) **in one's horns** to hold oneself back.

horn in *Slang* to intrude or meddle.

horn·beam (hȯrn′ bēm′, hôrn′-) ***n-*** small tree related to the birch and alder, with very hard wood.

horn·bill (hȯrn′ bĭl′, hôrn′-) ***n-*** any of several Asian or African birds with a very large bill having a hollow, horny projection on top.

horn·blende (hȯrn′ blĕnd′, hôrn′-) ***n-*** common hard mineral, usually black or greenish black, and containing iron and various silicates.

horn·book (hȯrn′ bo͝ok′, hôrn′-) ***n-*** in former times, page with the alphabet, table of numbers, etc., on it, protected by a sheet of transparent horn and fastened in a frame with a handle. It was used in teaching children to read.

horned (hȯrnd, hôrnd) ***adj-*** having a horn, horns, or a hornlike projection.

horned owl ***n-*** any of several owls having hornlike tufts of feathers on their heads. For picture, see *owl.*

horned toad ***n-*** harmless, flat-bodied lizard with scales and hornlike growths on the head and body. Also **horned lizard.**

hor·net (hȯr′ nət, hôr′ nət) ***n-*** large wasp that can give a painful sting.

Hornet, about 3/4 in. long

horn of plenty ***n-*** cornucopia.

horn·pipe (hȯrn′ pīp′, hôrn′-) ***n-*** **1** lively dance, usually performed by a single person, formerly popular among sailors. **2** music for this dance.

horn·y (hȯr′ nē, hôr′-) ***adj-*** **[horn·i·er, horn·i·est]** **1** hardened like horn; calloused: *his* horny *hands.* **2** made of horn or a hornlike substance. **3** having horns or hornlike projections. **—*n-*** **horn′ i·ness.**

ho·rol·o·gy (hôr ŏl′ ə jē) ***n-*** **1** the science of measuring time. **2** the art of making watches, clocks, etc.

hor·o·scope (hȯr′ ə skōp′, -hŏr′-) ***n-*** **1** the position of the planets and stars at any moment, especially at the hour of a person's birth, regarded by some as influencing his life. **2** diagram representing the twelve divisions of the heavens, used by astrologers to tell a person's future.

hor·ren·dous (hŏr ĕn′ dəs, hȯr-) ***adj-*** horrible; terrible; frightful. **—*adv-*** **hor·ren′ dous·ly.**

hor·ri·ble (hŏr′ ə bəl, hȯr′-) ***adj-*** **1** causing horror; terrible; dreadful: *a* horrible *accident*; *a* horrible *disease.* **2** *Informal* very bad, unpleasant, etc.: *a* horrible *noise.* **—*n-*** **hor′ ri·ble·ness.** ***adv-*** **hor′ ri·bly.**

hor·rid (hŏr′ əd, hȯr′-) ***adj-*** **1** causing disgust or horror; fearsome. **2** *Informal* extremely unpleasant, disagreeable, etc.: *He's a* horrid *person. What a* horrid *thing to say!* **—*adv-*** **hor′ rid·ly.** ***n-*** **hor′ rid·ness.**

hor·rif·ic (hŏr ĭf′ ĭk, hȯr-) ***adj-*** causing horror or alarm.

hor·ri·fy (hŏr′ ə fī, hȯr′-) ***vt-*** **[hor·ri·fied, hor·ri·fy·ing]** to cause to feel horror; fill with great terror, fear, or alarm; shock greatly: *The news* horrified *the town.*

hor·ror (hŏr′ ər, hȯr′-) ***n-*** **1** strong feeling of terror or dread. **2** strong dislike or aversion: *She has a* horror *of dirt.* **3** anything that causes great terror, suffering, etc.: *the* horrors *of a nuclear war.* **4** *Informal* something extremely bad, ugly, unpleasant, etc.

hors de com·bat (ȯr′ də kōⁿ bä′) *French* out of the fight; disabled.

hors d'oeu·vre (ȯr dûrv′, *Fr.* ȯr dûv′ rə) ***n-*** [*pl.* **hors d'oeuvres** or **hors d'oeuvre** (*Fr.* ȯr dûv′ rə)] any of various relishes or appetizers. [from French, meaning literally "outside of (the main) work."]

horse (hȯrs, hôrs) ***n-*** **1** large, plant-eating animal with four legs, solid hoofs, and a long mane and tail, used for drawing vehicles and for riding. **2** the full-grown male of this animal. See also *colt, filly, gelding, mare, stallion.* **3** movable frame, usually consisting of two pairs of legs joined by a crossbar, used as a support. **4** in gymnastics, a padded or wooden block used for vaulting. **5** mounted soldiers; cavalry: *a regiment of* horse. *as* ***modifier***: *a* horse *race.* ***vt-*** **[horsed, hors·ing]** to mount on or supply with a steed. ***Hom-*** hoarse.

horse of another color *Informal* an entirely different matter, situation, etc.

horse around *Slang* to engage in horseplay.

horse·back (hȯrs′ băk′, hôrs′-) ***n-*** the back of a horse: *He rode the range on* horseback. ***adv-*** on the back of a horse: *He rides* horseback.

horse·car (hȯrs′ kär, hôrs′-) ***n-*** **1** streetcar drawn by a horse or horses. **2** car for transporting horses.

horse chestnut ***n-*** **1** large tree with pointed clusters of white or pink blossoms, and reddish-brown, inedible nuts enclosed in burs. **2** nut of this tree.

horse·flesh (hȯrs′ flĕsh′, hôrs′-) ***n-*** **1** meat from a horse. **2** horses in general: *He is a good judge of* horseflesh.

horse·fly (hȯrs′ flī′, hôrs′-) ***n-*** [*pl.* **horse·flies**] large black fly that bites horses and cattle.

horse·hair (hȯrs′ hâr′, hôrs′-) ***n-*** **1** hair of a horse, especially from the mane and tail. **2** stiff cloth made from this hair.

horse·hide (hȯrs′ hīd′, hôrs′-) ***n-*** the hide of a horse, or leather made from it.

horse latitudes ***n-*** nautical term for either of two regions situated at latitudes of about 30 degrees north or south of the equator. The horse latitudes are noted for light, changeable winds, and occasional calms.

horse·laugh (hȯrs′ lăf′, hôrs′-) ***n-*** loud, coarse laugh.

horse·less carriage (hȯrs′ ləs, hôrs′-) ***n-*** automobile, especially an early model.

horse mackerel ***n-*** **1** the common tuna. **2** fish of the Pacific Ocean, related to the jacks and pompanos.

horse·man (hȯrs′ mən, hôrs′-) ***n-*** [*pl.* **horse·men**] **1** rider on horseback. **2** person who is skilled in riding or managing horses. **—*n-*** *fem.* **horse′ wom′ an** [*pl.* **horse·wom·en**].

horse·man·ship (hȯrs′ mən shĭp′, hôrs′-) ***n-*** art or skill of riding and managing horses.

horse opera *Slang* ***n-*** motion picture or television show, with a western setting and much riding.

horse pistol ***n-*** large pistol formerly carried by riders on horseback.

horse·play (hôrs′ plā′, hôrs′-) ***n-*** rough, boisterous, playful behavior.

horse·pow·er (hôrs′ pou′ ər, hôrs′-) ***n-*** a unit of power. One horsepower is the amount of power required to raise 33,000 pounds one foot in one minute.

Horseshoe

horse·rad·ish (hôrs′ răd′ ĭsh, hôrs′-) ***n-*** **1** plant related to the radish, and having a large, coarse root with a sharp, spicy flavor. **2** a relish made from this root.

horse sense *Informal* ***n-*** common sense.

horse·shoe (hôrs′ shōō, hôrs′-) ***n-*** **1** flat, U-shaped, protective iron plate nailed to the bottom of a horse's hoof. **2** something shaped like this. **3 horseshoes** game played with such plates or similar pieces of metal, the object being to throw the plate over or near a stake. ***—n-*** **horse′ shoe·er.**

horseshoe crab ***n-*** large marine animal related to the spiders, with a shell shaped like a horseshoe; king crab.

horse·whip (hôrs′ hwĭp′, hôrs′-) ***n-*** leather whip for managing horses. ***vt-*** **[horse·whipped, horse·whip·ping]** to flog with such a whip.

hors·y (hôr′ sē, hôr′-) ***adj-*** **[hors·i·er, hors·i·est] 1** of or resembling a horse. **2** fond of horses, horse racing, etc. ***—adv-*** **hors′ i·ly.** ***n-*** **hors′ i·ness.**

Horseshoe crab

hor·ta·tor·y (hôr′ tə tôr′ ē, hôr′-) ***adj-*** serving or tending to urge and encourage. Also **hor′ ta·tive** (-tə tĭv′).

hor·ti·cul·tur·al (hôr′ tə kŭl′ chər əl, hôr′-) ***adj-*** of or relating to horticulture. ***—adv-*** **hor′ ti·cul′ tur·al·ly.**

hor·ti·cul·ture (hôr′ tə kŭl′ chər, hôr′-) ***n-*** the art or science of raising and developing flowering plants, fruits, vegetables, etc.

hor·ti·cul·tur·ist (hôr′ tə kul′ chər ĭst, hôr′-) ***n-*** person who is trained in or specializes in horticulture.

ho·san·na (hō zăn′ ə) ***interj-*** exclamation of praise to God. ***n-***: *to praise God with loud* hosannas.

hose (hōz) ***n-*** **1** [*pl.* **hos·es**] flexible tubing of rubber, plastic, etc., used for piping water or other liquid. **2** [*pl.* **hose**] stockings or socks. ***vt-*** **[hosed, hos·ing]** to supply, wash, or drench with water or liquid piped through flexible tubing.

Ho·se·a (hō zā′ ə, -zē′ ə) ***n-*** **1** Hebrew prophet of the eighth century B.C. **2** a book of the Old Testament bearing his name. In the CCD Bible **O·see′** (ō zē′).

ho·sier·y (hō′ zhər ē) ***n-*** stockings or socks.

hos·pice (hŏs′ pĭs) ***n-*** place of shelter for travelers, especially one kept by a religious order.

hos·pi·ta·ble (hŏs′ pĭ tə bəl, hŏ spĭt′ ə-) ***adj-*** **1** generous and friendly in welcoming guests and strangers: *a* hospitable *hostess*; *a* hospitable *greeting*. **2** very receptive; open: *to be* hospitable *to new ideas*. ***—adv-*** **hos′ pi·ta·bly.**

hos·pi·tal (hŏs′ pĭ təl) ***n-*** place, usually having a trained staff and special equipment, for the care and treatment of the sick and injured. *as* ***modifier***: *a* hospital *ward*; hospital *patient*; hospital *building*.

hos·pi·tal·i·ty (hŏs′ pə tăl′ ə tē) ***n-*** [*pl.* **hos·pi·tal·i·ties**] warm, generous reception of guests and strangers.

hos·pi·tal·i·za·tion (hŏs′ pĭ tə lə zā′ shən) ***n-*** **1** a hospitalizing or being hospitalized. **2** period of stay in a hospital. **3** form of insurance that provides complete or partial coverage against hospital expenses.

hos·pi·tal·ize (hŏs′ pə tə līz′) ***vt-*** **[hos·pi·tal·ized, hos·pi·tal·iz·ing]** to place in a hospital for treatment.

[1]**host** (hōst) ***n-*** **1** person who receives and entertains guests in his home or somewhere else: *Our* host *took us to a restaurant for dinner*. **2** person, such as an innkeeper, who provides food and lodging for pay. **3** *Biology* any living animal or plant that provides nourishment or lodgment to a parasite. [from Latin **hospes** meaning "guest; host." "Hospitality" is related to this word.]

[2]**host** (hōst) ***n-*** great army, multitude, or throng: *a conquering* host; host *of daffodils covered the hillside*. [from Old French, from Latin **hostis,** related to **hostile.**]

[3]**host** (hōst) ***n-*** (usually **Host**) bread or wafer used in celebration of the Eucharist. [from Latin **hostia.**]

hos·tage (hŏs′ tĭj) ***n-*** person handed over to or held by force by another as security or guarantee that certain things asked for will be done.

hos·tel (hŏs′ təl) ***n-*** **1** lodging place, especially one of a system of supervised lodgings for young people on bicycle trips, hikes, etc. **2** *Archaic* inn. ***Hom-*** hostile.

hos·tel·er (hŏs′ təl ər) ***n-*** **1** traveler, hiker, etc., who stops at hostels overnight. **2** *Archaic* innkeeper.

hos·tel·ry (hŏs′ təl rē) *Archaic* ***n-*** [*pl.* **hos·tel·ries**] inn; lodging place.

hos·tess (hō′ stəs) ***n-*** **1** girl or woman who receives and entertains guests in her home or somewhere else. **2** woman employed by a restaurant, hotel, airline, etc., to welcome and seat guests.

hos·tile (hŏs′ təl, -tīl′) ***adj-*** **1** of or like an enemy; warlike: *The* hostile *army was preparing to attack*. **2** unfriendly; opposed: *He is* hostile *to new ideas*. ***Hom-*** hostel. ***—adv-*** **hos′ tile·ly.**

hos·til·i·ty (hŏs tĭl′ ə tē) ***n-*** [*pl.* **hos·til·i·ties**] **1** unfriendliness; hatred; dislike: *The campaign was marked by* hostility. **2 hostilities** warfare: *to cease* hostilities.

hos·tler (hŏs′ lər, ŏs′-) ***n-*** man or boy who takes care of horses; groom.

hot (hŏt) ***adj-*** **[hot·ter, hot·test] 1** of high temperature: *a* hot *stove*; hot *soup*. **2** fiery; excitable; violent: *a* hot *temper*. **3** having a sharp or biting taste: *Pepper and mustard are* hot. **4** fresh; new: *a* hot *scent*; hot *news*. **5** close in pursuit of a person or object sought for: *They were* hot *on his trail*. **6** in constant use: *The cables are* hot *with news reports*. **7** electrically charged: *a* hot *wire*. **8** radioactive. **9** *Informal* much in demand; currently popular: *a* hot *item in a sale*. **10** in jazz, exciting and full of rhythmic effects and melodic improvisations. **11** *Informal* good; excellent: *That movie was not so* hot. **12** *Informal* very uncomfortable or difficult: *He can make it* hot *for you*. **13** *Slang* stolen. **14** *Slang* in danger of capture, arrest, etc. ***—n-*** **hot′ ness.**

hot air *Slang* ***n-*** empty talk; foolish ideas.

hot·bed (hŏt′ bĕd′) ***n-*** **1** bed of earth covered with glass and artificially warmed to force the growth of plants. **2** any place or condition that promotes growth or activity of something: *a* hotbed *of crime*.

hot-blood·ed (hŏt′ blŭd′ əd) ***adj-*** easily excited or angered; fiery; impetuous.

hot·box (hŏt′ bŏks′) ***n-*** an axle bearing in a railroad car, locomotive, etc., that has become overheated by friction.

hot·cake (hŏt′ kāk′) ***n-*** griddlecake.

sell (or **go**) **like hotcakes** *Informal* be very much in demand; be disposed of rapidly.

hot cross bun ***n-*** bun marked with a cross of frosting, eaten during Lent or on Good Friday.

hot·dog (hŏt′ dôg′) *Informal* ***n-*** frankfurter, especially a hot frankfurter served in a soft roll.

ho·tel (hō′ tĕl′) ***n-*** an establishment that furnishes food and lodging to the public for pay.

hot·foot (hŏt′ fo͝ot′) *Informal* ***adv-*** in great haste. ***vi-*** to hurry; run (often followed by "it").

hot·head (hŏt′ hĕd′) ***n-*** rash, excitable, quick-tempered person.

hot·head·ed (hŏt′ hĕd′ əd) ***adj-*** quick-tempered; excitable; impetuous. —***adv-*** **hot′ head′ ed·ly.** ***n-*** **hot′ head′ ed·ness.**

hot·house (hŏt′ hous′) ***n-*** a building with glass sides and a glass roof, heated for growing plants; greenhouse. *as* ***modifier:*** *a* hothouse *plant.*

hot·ly (hŏt′ lē) ***adv-*** in a fiery manner; violently; passionately; ardently: *to reply* hotly *to an accusation.*

hot plate ***n-*** small, portable cooking stove, especially an electric one, with one or two burners.

hot rod *Slang* ***n-*** automobile, especially a jalopy, with a stripped-down body and a souped-up engine, usually driven by a teen-age boy. —***n-*** **hot′-rod′ der.**

hot·shot (hŏt′ shŏt′) *Slang* ***n-*** person who does something very well; expert. *as* ***modifier:*** *a* hotshot *golfer.*

Hot·ten·tot (hŏt′ ən tŏt′) ***n-*** **1** member of a South African people native to Cape of Good Hope Province and now living mainly in central Africa. **2** the language of these people.

hot water *Informal* ***n-*** trouble: *to be in* hot water.

hound (hound) ***n-*** **1** any of several breeds of dog used for hunting, especially those that hunt by scent and have large, drooping ears and short hair. **2** *Informal* any dog. ***vt-*** to pursue with, or as if with, such dogs.

hour (our) ***n-*** **1** amount of time equal to 1/24 of the length of time from one noon to the next; sixty minutes. **2** time of day indicated by a clock, watch, etc.: *The* hour *is three o'clock.* **3** one of the twelve numbers on a clock: *This clock chimes the* hours. **4** loosely reckoned period of time: *the children's* hour. **5** any particular time: *in the* hour *of danger.* **6** a class session, 60 minutes or less; also, a unit of college or university credit covering one such session per week. **7** unit of distance reckoned by the time taken to travel it: *three* hours *distant.* **8 hours** fixed or stated times for work, school, etc.: *office* hours; *school* hours. **9 Hours** (1) a time for daily liturgical devotion; canonical hours. (2) the book containing the prayers for these daily periods. ***Hom-*** our.

after hours after the regular hours for business, work, school, etc. **of the hour** of the present; of the day: *man of the* hour.

hour·glass (our′ glăs′) ***n-*** device for measuring the passage of one hour, consisting of two rounded glass sections connected by a narrow neck through which sand trickles. The passage of sand from one section to the other takes one hour.

Hourglass

hou·ri (ho͝or′ ē) ***n-*** one of the beautiful maidens of the Muslim paradise.

hour·ly (our′ lē) ***adj-*** **1** occurring every hour, or at intervals of an hour: *an* hourly *time signal*; hourly *bus service.* **2** computed in terms of an hour's work, operation, etc.: *his* hourly *wages.* ***adv-:*** *The chimes ring* hourly.

[1]**house** (hous) ***n-*** [*pl.* **hous·es** (houz′ əz)] **1** building or other structure made to live in; dwelling. **2** building made for a particular purpose: *a* house *of worship*; *a fraternity* house; *the opera* house. **3 House** division of a lawmaking body or group: *the* House *of Representatives.* **4** family, especially a ruling family: *a prince of the ruling* house. **5** number of people at a performance: *There was a full* house *to see the show.*

bring down the house *Informal* to be enthusiastically applauded by the audience. **clean house 1** to do the chores of cleaning a home. **2** to get rid of undesirable people, inefficient practices, etc. **keep house** to manage a house and its affairs; do housework. **on the house** free; at the expense of the management.

[2]**house** (houz) ***vt-*** **[housed, hous·ing] 1** to provide with a home, lodging, or shelter: *to* house *guests*; *to* house *a boat for the winter.* **2** to enclose in a protective covering: *to* house *an automobile engine.*

house·boat (hous′ bōt′) ***n-*** barge or other boat equipped and used as a dwelling.

Houseboat

house·boy (hous′ boi′) ***n-*** male servant who does household chores.

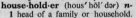

house·break (hous′ brāk′) ***vt-*** **[house·broke, house·broken, house·break·ing]** to train (an animal) to control its bodily functions so that it can live indoors.

house·break·er (hous′ brā′ kər) ***n-*** person who breaks into a house; burglar. —***n-*** **house′ break′ ing.**

house·coat (hous′ kōt′) ***n-*** comfortable robe worn by women or girls as informal indoor clothing.

house·fly (hous′ flī′) ***n-*** [*pl.* **house·flies**] common fly, dangerous as a carrier of germs, found in all parts of the world.

house·hold (hous′ hōld′) ***n-*** a house and all the persons living in it. *as* ***modifier:*** *a* household *pet.*

house·hold·er (hous′ hōl′ dər) ***n-*** **1** head of a family or household. **2** person who occupies a house, especially its owner.

Housefly

household word ***n-*** very familiar word or phrase.

house·keep·er ***n-*** woman who manages the affairs of a household or hotel, especially one hired to do so.

house·keep·ing (hous′ kē′ pĭng) ***n-*** care and management of a household.

house·maid (hous′ mād′) ***n-*** female servant who does housework.

housemaid's knee ***n-*** painful swelling of the tissue around the kneecap, usually afflicting persons who work a great deal upon their knees.

house·moth·er (hous′ mŭth′ ər) ***n-*** woman who takes charge of a group of young girls living together and acts as chaperon, in a dormitory, sorority house, etc.

House of Commons ***n-*** the lower house and main lawmaking body of the British or Canadian parliaments.

house of correction ***n-*** place of confinement for persons convicted of minor offenses.

House of Lords ***n-*** the upper house of the British Parliament, made up of the nobility and high-ranking clergy.

House of Representatives ***n-*** **1** the lower branch of the United States Congress. Its members are elected for two-year terms on the basis of population. **2** a similar body in many State and national legislatures.

house party ***n-*** party of guests invited for a few days to a country home, college fraternity or sorority, etc.

house·top (hous′ tŏp′) ***n-*** top or roof of a house.

shout (something) from the housetops to tell or announce (something) loudly and publicly.

house·warm·ing (hous′ wȯr′ mĭng) ***n-*** party celebrating a family's moving into a new house.

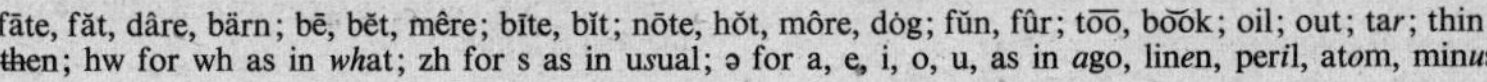
fāte, făt, dâre, bärn; bē, bĕt, mêre; bīte, bĭt; nōte, hŏt, môre, dȯg; fŭn, fûr; to͞o, bo͝ok; oil; out; tar; thin; then; hw for wh as in *wh*at; zh for s as in u*s*ual; ə for a, e, i, o, u, as in *a*go, lin*e*n, per*i*l, at*o*m, min*u*s

house·wife (hous′wīf′) *n-* [*pl.* **housewives**] 1 woman who manages a home for her family. 2 (*also* hŭz′ əf) small case for sewing items. *—adj-* **house′wife′ly.**
house·work (hous′wûrk′) *n-* cleaning, washing, ironing, cooking, and other work to be done in a house.
[1]**hous·ing** (hou′zĭng) *n-* 1 lodging. 2 the providing of homes for people: *The mayor has promised better* housing *for the city.* 3 protective cover or container for a machine or a machine part. [from [2]**house.**]
[2]**hous·ing** (hou′zĭng) *n-* 1 a decorative saddlecloth. 2 **housings** decorative trappings, especially for a horse. [from Old French **houce,** from a Germanic word.]
hove (hōv) *p.t. & p.p.* of **heave,** chiefly in nautical use.
hov·el (hŭv′əl, hŏv′-) *n-* small, wretched cottage or hut.
hov·er (hŭv′ər, hŏv′-) *vi-* 1 to stay in the air over one place: *The bird* hovered *over its nest. The helicopter* hovered *over the highway.* 2 to stay or wait nearby: *The children* hovered *around the toy counter.* 3 to waver: *to* hover *between life and death.*
Hov·er·craft (hŭv′ər krăft′, hŏv′ər-) [*pl.* **Hov·er·craft**] *n-* trademark name for a vehicle that travels a few inches above water or ground on a cushion of air from air jets blowing downward. Also **hovercraft.**
how (hou) *adv-* 1 in what way or manner: *Tell me* how *you did that trick.* How *are we to interpret her remarks?* 2 by what means: *Just* how *do you plan to get here?* 3 to what extent, degree, or amount: *We don't know* how *serious his injuries are.* How *much paper do you need?* 4 in what state or condition: *Find out* how *he is today.* 5 for what reason; why: *I wonder* how *he could laugh at such a time.* 6 at what price: *Mr. Danton,* how *do you sell those oranges? n-* manner, means, method, etc.: *I don't understand the* how *or why of it.*
how about *Informal* 1 what do you say to or think of: *She asked,* "How about *going to the theater?*" 2 would you like to have: *Our host said,* "How about *some more ice cream?*" **how come** *Informal* why is it that.
how·be·it (hou′bē′ĭt) *Archaic adv-* nevertheless; be this as it may. *conj-* although.
how·dah (hou′də) *n-* a seat, usually decorated and with a canopy, for riding an elephant or camel.

Howdah

how·ev·er (hou ĕv′ər) *adv-* no matter how; in whatever way: *Every effort,* however *small, will be a help. conj-* nevertheless, yet; in spite of that: *I cannot,* however, *agree. Later,* however, *he agreed.*
how·itz·er (hou′ĭt sər) *n-* short cannon for firing shells in a higher trajectory than an ordinary cannon does.
howl (houl) *n-* 1 long, wailing cry of a wolf or dog. 2 cry of pain, rage, distress, or contempt. *vi-* 1 to give a long, wailing cry as a dog does. 2 to make a wailing sound: *The wind* howls. 3 to shout; yell.
howl down to drown out the voice or the words of a speaker with shouts of contempt, anger, etc.
howl·er (houl′ər) *n-* 1 person or thing that howls. 2 (also **howler monkey**) long-tailed New World monkey that utters a loud, howling cry. 3 *Informal* foolish or laughable blunder.
how·so·ev·er (hou′sō ĕv′ər) *adv-* in whatever manner or degree; however.
hoy·den (hoi′dən) *n-* rough, boisterous girl; tomboy. *—adj-* **hoy′den·ish.**
HP, H.P., hp., or **h.p.** 1 horsepower. 2 high pressure.
H.Q. or **h.q.** headquarters.
hr. hour.
H.R. House of Representatives.
H.R.H. 1 Her Royal Highness. 2 His Royal Highness
ht. height.
hub (hŭb) *n-* 1 central part of a wheel, from which the spokes spread out. 2 center of interest or activity: *The downtown area is the* hub *of our city.*

Hub

hub·bub (hŭb′ŭb) *n-* loud confused noise; uproar.
hub·cap (hŭb′căp′) *n-* disk-shaped piece of metal clamped over the center of an automobile wheel.
huck·a·back (hŭk′ə băk′) *n-* coarse linen or cotton cloth, used for toweling. Also **huck.**
huck·le·ber·ry (hŭk′əl bĕr′ē) *n-* [*pl.* **huck·le·ber·ries**] 1 shiny, purplish-black berry related to the blueberry 2 the shrub on which it grows.
huck·ster (hŭk′stər) *n-* 1 peddler, especially one who deals in fruit and vegetables. 2 *Slang* person in the advertising business.
hud·dle (hŭd′əl) *vi-* [**hud·dled, hud·dling**] 1 to gather or crowd together in a close-pressed group: *The chilly campers* huddled *around the fire.* 2 to hunch or draw oneself together: *He* huddled *in a corner..* 3 *Informal* to gather together to consult, make a decision, etc. *vt-* to crowd or push together in a confused group or mass: *He* huddled *his clothes in a heap. n-* 1 in football, a group of players gathered together behind the line of scrimmage to decide on the next play. 2 group of things crowded together.
[1]**hue** (hyōō) *n-* color; tint; shade of color: *flowers of every* hue. [from Old English **hīw** meaning "appearance; shape; color."] *Hom-* hew.
[2]**hue** (hyōō) **hue and cry** general outcry of alarm or protest. [from Old French **hü!,** a hunting call and a shout indicating danger. **Hue and cry** refers to an Old French and Middle English exclamation meaning "Stop him! Sound the alarm!" Everyone who heard it was obliged to drop everything and chase the wrongdoer.]
huff (hŭf) *n-* fit of anger or ill-humor, especially as a result of being offended. *vi-* to blow; puff: *The cyclists* huffed *and puffed as they pedaled to the top of the hill. vt-* to make angry: *She was* huffed *by his rudeness.*
huff·y (hŭf′ē) *adj-* [**huff·i·er, huff·i·est**] 1 easily offended; touchy. 2 in a surly mood; ill-humored. *—adv-* **huff′i·ly.** *n-* **huff′i·ness.**
hug (hŭg) *vt-* [**hugged, hug·ging**] 1 to hold tightly or as if in the arms; squeeze. 2 to hold fast to; cling to: *to* hug *a cherished belief.* 3 to keep close to: *The swimmers* hugged *the shore just to be safe. n-* a close embrace.
huge (hyōōj) *adj-* [**hug·er, hug·est**] 1 very large; enormous: *The elephant is a* huge *animal.* 2 very great: *The party was a* huge *success. —adv-* **huge′ly:** *We enjoyed ourselves* hugely. *n-* **huge′ness.**
Hu·gue·not (hyōō′gə nŏt′) *n-* a French Protestant of the sixteenth or seventeenth century.
hu·la (hōō′lə) *n-* Hawaiian dance which tells a story. The dancers move their arms and hands to describe different things and events, and sway their hips in time to the music. Also **hu′la-hu′la.**
hulk (hŭlk) *n-* 1 wreck of an old ship; dismantled hull. 2 heavy, clumsy ship. 3 overgrown, awkward person or thing: *a* hulk *of a man.*
hulk·ing (hŭl′kĭng) *adj-* big and clumsy: *The giant's* hulking *form filled the doorway.*
[1]**hull** (hŭl) *n-* body or framework of a ship, seaplane, etc., without rigging or upper structures. [from Dutch **hul,** from **hol,** "the hold of a ship," and influenced by [2]**hull.**]
hull down of a ship, so far away that only the part above the hull is visible.

[2]hull (hŭl) *n-* **1** outer covering or case enclosing certain seeds or fruits. **2** leaflets at the base of the stem of certain berries, such as the strawberry. **3** any outer case or covering. *vt-* to remove the outer covering, leaves, etc., from: *to* hull *peas; to* hull *strawberries.* [from Old English **hulu.**]

hul·la·ba·loo (hŭl′ ə bə lo͞o′) *n-* noisy tumult; uproar.

hum (hŭm) *vi-* [**hummed, hum·ming**] **1** to make a continuous murmuring or buzzing sound; drone: *Bees* hummed *in the garden.* **2** to make musical sounds with the lips closed: *The boys sang the words and the girls* hummed. **3** *Informal* to be full of energetic action or movement: *The busy office* hummed *with activity. vt-* **1** to sing with closed lips: *to* hum *a melody.* **2** to produce an effect on (someone) by so doing: *to* hum *a baby to sleep. n-*: *the* hum *of an engine.*

hu·man (hyo͞o′ mən) *adj-* **1** of, belonging to, or having the qualities of man or mankind: *the* human *species;* human *nature.* **2** having to do with mankind: *the study of* human *affairs.* **—*n-* hu′ man·ness.**

human being *n-* member of the human species; person.

hu·mane (hyo͞o mān′) *adj-* **1** showing mercy, kindness, and compassion toward others: *a* humane *man;* humane *laws.* **2** believed to have a civilizing or refining influence: *Literature and music are* humane *studies.* **—*adv* hu·mane′ ly. *n-* hu·mane′ ness.**

hu·man·ism (hyo͞o′ mə nĭz′əm) *n-* any system of thought or action concerned primarily with human interests and ideals.

hu·man·ist (hyo͞o′mən ĭst′) *n-* **1** person with a deep interest in human affairs or human nature. **2** student of the humanities. **—*adj-* hu′man·is′ tic.**

hu·man·i·tar·ian (hyo͞o măn′ə târ′ ē ən) *n-* person who is devoted to the welfare of human beings. *adj-*: *the* humanitarian *career of a medical missionary.*

hu·man·i·tar·i·an·ism (hyoo măn′ə târ′ ē ə nĭz′əm) *n-* philosophy or actions of a humanitarian.

hu·man·i·ty (hyo͞o măn′ə tē) *n-* [*pl.* **hu·man·i·ties**] **1** human beings in general. **2** human nature. **3** kindness of heart; feeling for others: *They showed* humanity *in their generous treatment of the poor.* **4 the humanities** studies of a cultural nature, such as literature, languages, and philosophy.

hu·man·ize (hyo͞o′mə nīz′) *vt-* [**hu·man·ized, hu·man·iz·ing**] to make humane; refine; civilize. **—*n-* hu′man·i·za′ tion. *n-* hu′ man·iz′er.**

hu·man·ly (hyo͞o′ mən lē) *adv-* **1** in a human way or manner: *Animals cannot be expected to think* humanly. **2** within human power or knowledge: *We will do whatever is* humanly *possible.*

hu·man·oid (hyü′mən oid) *adj-* having human form or characteristics: *a* humanoid *skeleton. n-* **1** a being with these characteristics, especially earliest man: Humanoids *first appeared on earth millions of years ago.* **2** *Science fiction* an extraterrestrial creature with the ability to reason.

hum·ble (hŭm′bəl) *adj-* [**hum·bler, hum·blest**] **1** not proud or boastful; modest; meek. **2** not grand or important: *Abraham Lincoln had a* humble *beginning. vt-* [**hum·bled, hum·bling**]: *He* humbled *himself in true repentance.* **—*n-* hum′ble·ness. *adv-* hum′bly.**

hum·bug (hŭm′bŭg′) *n-* **1** thing or act intended to deceive; sham; fraud. **2** person who makes false claims or pretensions; deceiver; imposter. **3** nonsense. *vt-* [**hum·bugged, hum·bug·ging**] to deceive; cheat.

hum·din·ger (hŭm′ dĭng′ ər) *Slang n-* person or thing of remarkable excellence.

hum·drum (hŭm′ drŭm′) *adj-* dull; monotonous: *a* humdrum *life. n-* dull routine; monotony.

hu·mer·us (hyo͞o′ mər əs) *n-* **1** in humans, bone of the upper arm, from the shoulder to the elbow. **2** corresponding bone in the forelimb of animals. ***Hom-*** humorous.

hu·mid (hyo͞o′ mĭd) *adj-* damp; moist: *The air is* humid *before a rain.* **—*n-* hu′ mid·ness.**

hu·mid·i·fy (hyo͞o mĭd′ ə fī′) *vt-* [**hu·mi·di·fied, hu·mid·di·fy·ing**] to give dampness to. **—*n-* hu·mid′ i·fi′er.**

hu·mid·i·ty (hyo͞o mĭd′ ə tē) *n-* **1** dampness; moisture. **2** amount of moisture or water vapor in the air: *a day of high* humidity. **3** relative humidity.

hu·mi·dor (hyo͞o′ mə dôr′, -dôr′) *n-* container which keeps cigars or tobacco fresh and moist.

hu·mil·i·ate (hyo͞o mĭl′ ē āt′) *vt-* [**hu·mil·i·at·ed, hu·mil·i·at·ing**] to put to shame; cause to lose dignity and pride: *Jack was* humiliated *when his classmate outran him.* **—*adv-* hu·mil′ i·a·ting·ly.**

hu·mil·i·a·tion (hyo͞o mĭl′ē ā′shən) *n-* a lowering or injuring of pride; a putting or being put to shame: *The child's tantrum caused the family great* humiliation.

hu·mil·i·ty (hyo͞o mĭl′ə tē) *n-* modest sense of one's own importance; meekness: *to accept with* humility.

hum·ming·bird (hŭm′ ĭng bûrd′) *n-* any of various tiny, bright-colored, long-billed birds that feed upon the nectar of flowers. The rapid movement of their wings in flight makes a hum.

Ruby-throated hummingbird, about 3 1/2 in. long

hum·mock (hŭm′ək) *n-* small hill or rounded mound. **—*adj-* hum′ mock·y.**

hu·mor (hyo͞o′ mər) *n-* **1** cause of laughter or amusement; funniness: *the* humor *in a good joke; the* humor *of the incident.* **2** ability to be amusing; wit; also, writings, lectures, etc., showing this: *Mark Twain's immortal* humor. **3** mood; state of mind: *Don't bother him when he is in a bad* humor. *vt-* to yield to the whims of; indulge. **—*adj-* hu′ mor·less.**

out of humor not in a good mood; cross or irritable.

hu·mor·ist (hyo͞o′ mər ĭst) *n-* person who writes or says amusing things.

hu·mor·ous (hyo͞o′ mər əs) *adj-* funny; amusing; comical: *a* humorous *story; a* humorous *situation.* ***Hom-*** humerus. **—*adv-* hu′ mor·ous·ly. *n-* hu′ mor·ous·ness.**

hump (hŭmp) *n-* rounded or bulging lump or mass: *a camel's* hump. *vi-* **1** to rise up in a bump; form a lump (often followed by "up"): *The ground* humps *up about sixty feet from the door.* **2** *Slang* to make a great effort; hustle. **—*adj-* hump′ like′.**

hump·back (hŭmp′băk′) *n-* hunchback. **—*adj-* hump′ backed.**

hump·y (hŭmp′ ē) *adj-* [**hump·i·er, hump·i·est**] **1** full of or covered with humps: *a* humpy *field.* **2** like a hump.

hu·mus (hyo͞o′ məs) *n-* rich black or brown substance in the soil formed by the decay of leaves or other vegetable matter and providing food for plant life.

---

fāte, făt, dâre, bärn; bē, bĕt, mêre; bīte, bĭt; nōte, hŏt, môre, dóg; fŭn, fûr; to͞o, bo͝ok; oil; out; tar; thin; then; hw for wh as in *wh*at; zh for s as in u*s*ual; ə for a, e, i, o, u, as in *a*go, lin*e*n, per*i*l, at*o*m, min*u*s

Hun (hŭn) ***n-*** member of a barbarous nomadic people who invaded Europe in the fifth century under Attila, their powerful king and general.

hunch (hŭnch) ***n-*** **1** a feeling or suspicion; premonition: *to have a* hunch; *to follow a* hunch. **2** a hump. ***vt-*** to bend (the back or shoulders) to form a hump. ***vi-*** **1** to bend (over): *He* hunched *over his desk. He* hunched *over to avoid the blow.* **2** to pull one's arms, shoulders, and legs tightly against one's body: *He* hunched *into a ball to keep warm.*

hunch·back (hŭnch′ băk′) ***n-*** **1** person whose back is warped into a hump at the shoulders. **2** crooked back that forms a hump at the shoulders. Also **humpback.** ***—adj-*** **hunch′ backed.**

hun·dred (hŭn′ drəd) ***n-*** amount or quantity that is one greater than 99; 100.

hun·dred·fold (hŭn′ drəd fōld′) ***n-*** hundred times: *This is larger by a* hundredfold. *We must increase our output by a* hundredfold. ***adj-*** amounting to a hundred times: *a* hundredfold *increase in production.*

hun·dredth (hŭn′ drədth) ***adj-*** **1** next after 99th. **2** the ordinal of 100; 100th. ***n-*** **1** the next after the 99th; 100th. **2** one of a hundred equal parts of a whole or group. **3** the last term in the name of a common fraction having a denominator of 100 or of the corresponding decimal fraction. 1/100 and .01 are each one hundredth.

hun·dred·weight (hŭn′ drəd wāt′) ***n-*** unit of weight equal to 100 pounds. *Abbr.* cwt.

hung (hŭng) *p.t. & p.p.* of **hang.**
►For usage note see HANG.

Hun·gar·i·an (hŭng gâr′ ē ən) ***n-*** **1** a native or inhabitant of Hungary; especially, a Magyar. **2** the language of the people of Hungary; Magyar. ***adj-***: *a* Hungarian *wine.*

hun·ger (hŭng′ gər) ***n-*** **1** a craving or need for food: *She satisfies her* hunger *with a candy bar.* **2** strong or eager desire: *He has a* hunger *for friendship.* ***vi-*** **1** to feel hungry: *He* hungered *for a good meal.* **2** to long (for); yearn (for): *He* hungered *for a sight of home.*

hunger strike ***n-*** refusal to eat until certain conditions are met; self-imposed fast.

hung jury ***n-*** jury that cannot agree on a verdict.

hun·gry (hŭng′ grē) ***adj-*** **[hun·gri·er, hun·gri·est]** **1** wanting food: *He was* hungry *at lunchtime.* **2** eager; desirous: *That child is* hungry *for attention.* **3** showing or feeling hunger or need: *a lean and* hungry *look.* ***—adv-*** **hun′ gri·ly.** ***n-*** **hun′ gri·ness.**

hunk (hŭngk) *Informal* ***n-*** large piece or lump; chunk.

hun·ky-do·ry (hŭng′ kē dôr′ ē) *Slang* ***adj-*** fine; good.

hunt (hŭnt) ***vt-*** **1** to pursue something, such as wild animals, for food or sport: *He* hunts *deer. We* hunted *butterflies for the collection.* **2** to look for; search for; try to find: *They* hunted *the lost ball.* ***vi-***: *We* hunt *on weekends. They* hunted *for gold.* ***n-*** **1** pursuit of wild animals or game: *We went on a duck* hunt. **2** a search: *After a long* hunt, *we found the right house.*

hunt down to track down; pursue until captured; look for until found: *Federal troops* hunted down *the bandits.*

hunt up to search out; look for and find.

hunt·er (hŭn′ tər) ***n-*** **1** person who pursues game; huntsman: *The* hunter *fired his gun at the rabbit.* **2** one who seeks something. **3** horse or hound trained for hunting.

hunt·ing (hŭn′ tĭng) ***n-*** **1** the stalking and killing of game. **2** a search: *Weeks of* hunting *uncovered the mine.*

hunting ground ***n-*** area in which one may hunt.

hunt·ress (hŭn′ trəs) ***n-*** woman who hunts.

hunts·man (hŭnts′ mən) ***n-*** [*pl.* **hunts·men**] **1** man who pursues game; hunter. **2** one who has charge of a hunt, especially of the hounds.

hur·dle (hûr′ dəl) ***n-*** **1** kind of fence in movable sections. **2** frame or other barrier over which runners or horses jump in a kind of race. **3** obstacle. **4 hurdles** race in which runners must jump over frames. ***vt-*** **[hur·dled, hur·dling]** **1** to surmount an obstacle. **2** to leap over with a running stride. ***—n-*** **hur′ dler.**

Hurdle

hur·dy-gur·dy (hûr′ dē gûr′ dē) ***n-*** [*pl.* **hur·dy-gur·dies**] mechanical musical instrument played by turning a handle, often in the streets.

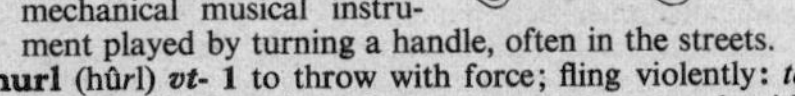

hurl (hûrl) ***vt-*** **1** to throw with force; fling violently: *to* hurl *a rock through a window.* **2** to utter or speak with violence: *They* hurled *insults.* ***—n-*** **hurl′ er.**

hurl·y-burl·y (hûr′ lē bûr′ lē) ***n-*** confusion.

Hu·ron (hyŏŏr′ ŏn′) ***n-*** [*pl.* **Hu·rons,** also **Hu·ron**] one of a group of Iroquoian Indians who lived in Ontario and the St. Lawrence River valley. ***adj-***: *a* Huron *canoe.*

hur·rah (hə rä′) ***interj-*** shout expressing joy, applause, or triumph. ***vi-*** to utter such a shout. Also **hur·ray′** (hə rā′).

hur·ri·cane (hûr′ ə kān′) ***n-*** vast and destructive tropical storm with very heavy rains and violent winds, exceeding 73 miles per hour, that spiral around a calm center of low atmospheric pressure.

hur·ried (hûr′ ēd) ***adj-*** showing haste; hasty; done in a hurry: *It was a* hurried *trip.* ***—adv-*** **hur′ ried·ly.**

hur·ry (hûr′ ē) ***vi-*** **[hur·ried, hur·ry·ing]** to move or act quickly: *I have to* hurry *or I shall be late.* ***vt-*** to cause to move or act quickly; rush: *Please don't* hurry *me. Let's* hurry *this job.* ***n-*** [*pl.* **hur·ries**] impatient or needless haste: *No need for* hurry, *we have all day.*

hurt (hûrt) ***vt-*** **[hurt, hurt·ing]** **1** to cause pain to: *That hangnail* hurts *my finger.* **2** to grieve or offend: *She was* hurt *by those spiteful remarks.* **3** to damage; harm: *It won't* hurt *this watch to wear it in water.* ***vi-*** to cause pain: *That bruise* hurts. *Not being accepted for the team* hurts. ***n-*** injury; wound; harm: *a* hurt *to one's pride.*

hurt·ful (hûrt′ fəl) ***adj-*** harmful; causing pain or injury. ***—adv-*** **hurt′ ful·ly.**

hur·tle (hûr′ təl) ***vi-*** **[hur·tled, hur·tling]** **1** to rush, speed, shoot, or fly wildly or at great speed: *The jet* hurtled *through the air.* **2** to dash; throw oneself; rush recklessly: *The boys* hurtled *out of the door.*

hus·band (hŭz′ bənd) ***n-*** man who has a wife. ***vt-*** to use carefully; save: *to* husband *one's supplies.*

hus·band·man (hŭz′ bənd mən) ***n-*** [*pl.* **hus·band·men**] farmer.

hus·band·ry (hŭz′ bən drē) ***n-*** **1** farming; agriculture; especially, the raising of farm animals. **2** careful management: *By good* husbandry *Mr. White amassed a considerable fortune.*

hush (hŭsh) ***vt-*** to make quiet: *to* hush *a crying child.* ***vi-***: *We were asked to* hush *during the music.* ***n-*** silence; stillness: *Not a sound broke the* hush *of the evening.*

hush money *Informal* ***n-*** bribe offered to persuade someone not to talk.

hush puppy ***n-*** fried ball of cornmeal dough.

husk (hŭsk) ***n-*** outermost covering of certain nuts and grains, such as corn and coconuts; also, any worthless outer covering. ***vt-*** to remove such a covering from: *to* husk *corn.* ***—n-*** **husk′ er.**

Butternut husks

husking bee ***n-*** gathering of friends and neighbors to help a farmer husk his corn. Also **husking.**

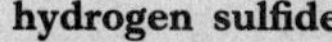

[1]husk·y (hŭs′ kē) ***adj-*** **[husk·i·er, husk·i·est]** somewhat hoarse; almost like a whisper: *a* husky *voice.* [perhaps from **husk,** with reference to the dry, rough qualities of husks.] —***adv-*** **husk′ i·ly.** ***n-*** **husk′ i·ness.**

[2]husk·y (hŭs′ kē) ***adj-*** **[husk·i·er, husk·i·est]** big and strong: *a* husky *boy.* —***n-*** **husk′ i·ness.** [of uncertain origin, perhaps from the toughness of husks.]

[3]husk·y (hŭs′ kē) ***n-*** [*pl.* **husk·ies]** Eskimo dog. Also **Husky.** [American word of uncertain origin.]

hus·sar (hə zär′) ***n-*** soldier of the light cavalry.

hus·sy (hŭz′ ē, *also* hŭs′-) ***n-*** [*pl.* **hus·sies]** **1** an indecent or forward woman. **2** pert, mischievous girl.

hus·tings (hŭs′ tĭngz) *chiefly Brit.* ***n-*** platform for making election speeches; stump.

hus·tle (hŭs′ əl) ***vi-*** **[hus·tled, hus·tling]** **1** to hurry; move or act with speed: *We'll have to* hustle *to get there.* **2** to make a living in a shady way, especially by taking advantage of the greed or innocence of one's victims. ***vt-*** **1** to push, crowd, or shove roughly; jostle: *The police* hustled *the thieves into the police station.* **2** *Informal* to get by rapid and tireless work: *The salesman went out to* hustle *some new business.* —***n-*** **hust′ ler.**

hustle and bustle energetic and confusing activity: *the* hustle and bustle *of a great metropolis.*

hut (hŭt) ***n-*** small, roughly built house.

hutch (hŭch) ***n-*** **1** cupboard with a set of open shelves above it; also, the open shelves alone. **2** chest for storage. **3** pen for animals, especially for rabbits.

hy·a·cinth (hī′ ə sĭnth′) ***n-*** spring flowering plant grown from a bulb and having fragrant flowers of various colors.

hy·brid (hī′ brĭd) ***n-*** **1** offspring produced by the mating of two different varieties or species of plants or animals: *Some roses are* hybrids. **2** anything formed of parts of unlike origin, especially a compound word, such as "cablegram." ***adj-*** produced by two different species or elements.

hy·brid·ism (hī′ brĭd ĭz′ əm) ***n-*** the production of hybrids.

hy·brid·ize (hī′ brə dīz′) ***vt-*** **[hy·brid·ized, hy·brid·iz·ing]** to subject (a species, race, etc.) to crossbreeding; interbreed. ***vi-*** to produce hybrids. —***n-*** **hy′ brid·i·za′ tion.**

Hyacinth

hy·dra (hī′ drə) ***n-*** **1** [*pl.* **hy·dras** or **hy·drae** (-drē)] any of several small, fresh-water animals having a flexible, tubelike body and a mouth surrounded by tentacles. **2 Hydra** in Greek mythology, a nine-headed sea serpent that grew two heads for each one cut off, but was finally killed by Hercules.

hy·dran·gea (hī drăn′ jə) ***n-*** shrub with large rounded clusters of white, blue, or pink flowers; also, the flower cluster of this plant.

hy·drant (hī′ drənt) ***n-*** **1** short, thick, upright pipe, usually on a curb, to which firemen attach hoses for their water supply; fireplug. **2** water faucet; tap.

hy·drate (hī′ drāt′) ***n-*** chemical compound into which water molecules have been absorbed and which form part of the chemical structure. ***vt-*** **[hy·drat·ed, hy·drat·ing]** to cause (a compound) to absorb water molecules into its chemical structure.

Hydrant

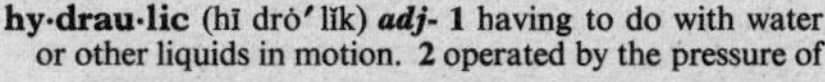

hy·drau·lic (hī drò′ lĭk) ***adj-*** **1** having to do with water or other liquids in motion. **2** operated by the pressure of liquid or by the force of liquid in motion. **3** hardening under water: *a* hydraulic *cement.* —***adv-*** **hy′ drau′ li·cal·ly.**

hydraulic brakes ***n-*** brakes operated by the pressure of fluid in cylinders.

hydraulic mining ***n-*** mining by the direct use of a powerful stream of water.

hy·drau·lics (hī′ drò′ lĭks) ***n-*** (takes singular verb) branch of science that deals with the principles and practical engineering applications of water and other liquids in motion.

hy·dra·zine (hī′ drə zēn′) ***n-*** liquid compound of hydrogen and nitrogen (N_2H_4) that is a rocket fuel.

hy·dride (hī′ drīd′) ***n-*** compound of hydrogen and an element or radical.

hydro- *combining form* **1** water: hydro*graphy*; hydro*phone.* **2** *Chemistry* indicating a compound of hydrogen: hydro*fluoric acid.* [from Greek **hydro-,** from **hydor,** "water."]

hy·dro·bro·mic acid (hī′ drō brō′ mĭk) ***n-*** strong colorless acid which is a solution of hydrogen bromide gas (HBr) in water.

hy·dro·car·bon (hī′ drə kär′ bən) ***n-*** any of a vast number of organic compounds, such as butane and benzene, that contains only hydrogen and carbon.

hy·dro·chlo·ric acid (hī′ drə klôr′ ĭk) ***n-*** strong, colorless acid (HCl) that is a water solution of hydrogen chloride gas. It is the acid in gastric juice.

hy·dro·cy·an·ic acid (hī′ drō sī ăn′ ĭk) ***n-*** very poisonous, colorless, volatile, liquid compound (HCN) having the odor of almonds; prussic acid.

hy·dro·dy·nam·ics (hī′ drō dī năm′ ĭks) ***n-*** (takes singular verb) branch of science that studies the motion of liquids, and the forces interacting between a liquid and a solid object that moves through it or is immersed in it. —***adj-*** **hy′ dro·dy·nam′ic.** ***adv-*** **hy′dro·dy·nam′i·cal·ly.**

hy·dro·e·lec·tric (hī′ drō ə lĕk′ trĭk) ***adj-*** of or having to do with electricity produced from water power.

hy·dro·fluor·ic acid (hī′ drə flôr′ ĭk, -flŏŏ′ ər ĭk) ***n-*** corrosive water solution of hydrogen fluoride (HF) used in the etching and frosting of glass.

hy·dro·foil (hī′ drə foil′) ***n-*** **1** vane mounted on struts beneath the hull of a boat and designed to raise the boat above water when it reaches a certain speed. **2** boat having such vanes.

One type of hydrofoil

hy·dro·gen (hī′ drə jən) ***n-*** odorless, colorless, flammable gas that is the lightest of the elements. It combines with oxygen to form water and with many other elements to form acids and most organic compounds. Symbol H, At. No. 1, At. Wt. 1.00797. —***adj-*** **hy·drog′ e·nous** (hī drŏj′ ə nəs).

hy·dro·gen·ate (hī drŏj′ ə nāt′) ***vt-*** **[hy·dro·gen·at·ed, hy·dro·gen·at·ing]** **1** to treat with hydrogen in a chemical reaction. **2** to combine with hydrogen. —***n-*** **hy′ dro·gen·a′ tion.**

hydrogen bomb ***n-*** thermonuclear bomb of tremendous explosive power resulting from the fusion of hydrogen atoms; H-bomb.

hydrogen peroxide or **peroxide** ***n-*** colorless, unstable liquid (H_2O_2) used especially in water solutions of varying strengths as a bleaching or disinfecting agent and as a rocket propellant.

hydrogen sulfide ***n-*** poisonous, colorless, flammable gas (H_2S), having an odor of rotten eggs.

hy·drog·ra·phy (hī drŏg′ rə fē) ***n-*** science that deals with the describing, surveying, and mapping of seas, lakes, rivers, etc. ***—n-*** **hy·drog′ ra·pher.** ***adj-*** **hy·dro·graph′ ic** (hī′ drə grăf′ ĭk).

hy·droid (hī′ droid′) ***adj-*** of or having to do with the group of hydrozoans that includes the hydras. ***n-*** a hydrozoan.

hy·drol·y·sis (hī drŏl′ ə səs) ***n-*** process in which the ions of a salt react with ions of water to produce a solution that is either acidic or basic.

hy·drom·e·ter (hī drŏm′ ə tər) ***n-*** instrument consisting of a long glass tube weighted at one end so that it floats vertically when immersed in a liquid. Hydrometers are used to determine the approximate specific gravities of liquids. ***—adj-*** **hy′ dro·met′ ric** (hī′ drə mĕ′ trĭk).

hy·dro·ni·um (hī drō′ nē əm) ***n-*** ion made up of a hydrogen ion combined with a water molecule (H_3O^+). Hydrogen ions are present in water only as hydronium ions.

hy·dro·pho·bi·a (hī′ drə fō′ bē ə) ***n-*** rabies.

hy·dro·phone (hī′ drə fōn′) ***n-*** device for listening to underwater sounds.

hy·dro·plane (hī′ drə plān′) ***n-*** **1** light motorboat with a flat bottom on which it skims along the surface of the water at high speed. **2** kind of airplane that can land on or take off from the surface of water; seaplane.

Hydroplanes

hy·dro·pon·ics (hī′ drə pŏn′ ĭks) ***n-*** (takes singular verb) the science of growing plants without soil but with their roots in chemical solutions containing proper plant food. ***—adj-*** **hy′ dro·pon′ ic.**

hy·dro·sphere (hī′ drə sfêr′) ***n-*** all of the water and ice on earth and in the atmosphere.

hy·dro·stat·ics (hī′ drō stăt′ ĭks) ***n-*** (takes singular verb) branch of science that deals with the study of liquids at rest and their pressures on objects in them. ***—adj-*** **hy′ dro·stat′ ic.**

hy·dro·ther·a·py (hī′ drō ther′ ə pē) *Medicine* ***n-*** the use of water in the treatment of various diseases.

hy·dro·trop·ism (hī drŏ′ trə pĭz′ əm) ***n-*** tendency of a plant to grow towards water.

hy·drous (hī′ drəs) ***adj-*** containing water, especially in chemical combination.

hy·drox·ide (hī drŏk′ sīd′) ***n-*** compound containing the hydroxyl group (OH^-).

hy·drox·yl (hī drŏk′ səl) ***n-*** chemical radical (OH^-) made up of a single atom of oxygen and hydrogen, and having a single negative charge.

hy·dro·zo·an (hī drə zō′ ən) ***n-*** any of a group of aquatic coelenterates **(Hydrozoa)** that includes hydras, corals, and the Portugese man-of-war.

hy·e·na (hī ē′ nə) ***n-*** night-prowling, meat-eating animal of Africa and Asia, somewhat like a large dog.

Laughing hyena, 2 1/2–3 ft. high at shoulder

hy·giene (hī′ jēn) ***n-*** **1** study of good health practices; principles of good health. **2** practice of good health rules.

hy·gi·en·ic (hī′ jē ĕn′ ĭk, hī jĕn′ ĭk, -jē′ nĭk) ***adj-*** **1** of or having to do with hygiene. **2** not injurious to health; sanitary; healthful. ***—adv-*** **hy′ gi·en′ i·cal·ly.**

hy·gien·ist (hī jē′ nĭst, hī jĕn′ ĭst) ***n-*** person who is a student of or expert in hygiene.

hy·gro·graph (hī′ grə grăf′) ***n-*** a hygrometer that automatically records its readings on a chart.

hy·grom·e·ter (hī grŏm′ ə tər) ***n-*** instrument that measures the humidity or amount of moisture in the air. ***—adj-*** **hy′ gro·met′ ric.**

hy·gro·scop·ic (hī′ grə skŏp′ ĭk) ***adj-*** **1** having the property of taking up and holding moisture from the air, as salt does in damp weather. **2** of or relating to this property or process.

hy·men (hī′ mən) ***n-*** membrane partly closing the vagina.

Hy·men (hī′ mən) ***n-*** in Greek mythology, the god of marriage.

hy·me·ne·al (hī′ mə nē′ əl) ***adj-*** of or relating to marriage; nuptial: *a* hymeneal *celebration.*

hy·men·op·ter·ous (hī′ mə nŏp′ tər əs) ***adj-*** of, having to do with, or belonging to the large group of insects **(Hymenoptera),** including the ants, bees, and wasps, that have four wings and usually live in colonies.

hymn (hĭm) ***n-*** **1** song of praise to God. **2** any song of praise, thanksgiving, or the like. ***Hom-*** him. ***—adj-*** **hymn′ like.**

hym·nal (hĭm′ nəl) ***n-*** book of hymns.

hymn·book (hĭm′ bo͝ok′) ***n-*** hymnal.

hyper- *prefix* **1** abnormally great; excessive: hyper*acidity.* **2** excessively: hyper*critical.* [from Greek **hyper-**, meaning "over; above; exceedingly."]

hy·per·a·cid·i·ty (hī′ pər ə sĭd′ ə tē) ***n-*** excess acid, especially in the stomach.

hy·per·bo·la (hī pûr′ bə lə) ***n-*** **1** a curve formed by the intersection of a double right-circular cone with a plane that cuts both parts of the cone and is parallel to the axis of the cone but does not contain it. A hyperbola thus has two branches. ***—adj-*** **hy·per·bol′ ic.**

Hyperbola

hy·per·bo·le (hī pûr′ bə lē) ***n-*** figure of speech that states much more than the truth; exaggeration for effect. Examples: The day was endless. The driver was about ten feet tall.

hy·per·bol·ic (hī′ pər bol′ ĭk) ***adj-*** **1** extreme or inordinate: *a really* hyperbolic *exaggeration.* **2** greatly exaggerated or overstated: *his* hyperbolic *praise of the book.* **3** of, related to, or having the form of a hyperbola: *a* hyperbolic *surface.*

hy·per·cri·ti·cal (hī′ pər krĭt′ ĭ kəl) ***adj-*** tending to complain about trivial things; overly sensitive to the faults of others. ***—adv-*** **hy′ per·cri′ ti·cal·ly.**

Hy·per·i·on (hī pêr′ ē ən) ***n-*** **1** in Greek mythology, the son of Uranus and the father of Helios. **2** in Homer's "Iliad," Helios himself. **3** in later times, Apollo.

hy·per·o·pi·a (hī′ pə rō′ pē ə) ***n-*** farsightedness.

hy·per·sen·si·tive (hī′ pər sĕn′ sə tĭv) ***adj-*** very sensitive; especially, having very tender feelings that are easily wounded or offended. ***—n-*** **hy·per·sen′ si·tive·ness.** ***n-*** **hy·per·sen′ si·tiv′ i·ty.**

hy·per·son·ic (hī′ pər sŏn′ ĭk) ***adj-*** of, having to do with, or characterized by speeds that are at least 5 times the speed of sound.

hy·per·ten·sion (hī′ pər tĕn′ shən) ***n-*** abnormally high blood pressure.

hy·per·thy·roid·ism (hī′ pər thī′ roid ĭz′ əm) ***n-*** condition resulting from excessive activity of the thyroid gland. It is marked by an increased metabolic rate, weight loss, increased heart rate, and nervousness.

hy·per·tro·phy (hī pûr′ trə fē) ***n-*** increased size of a part or organ, due to growth instead of a tumor.

hy·phen (hī′ fən) ***n-*** punctuation mark [-] used to join two or more words to make a compound word, as in *self-denial,* or to divide a word at the end of a line of writing or printing.

hy·phen·ate (hī′ fə nāt′) ***vt-*** [**hy·phen·a·ted, hy·phen·a·ting**] to write or print with a hyphen: *The word "great-grandmother" is* hyphenated *in this sentence. Oscar's family* hyphenates *its last name Blake-Jones.* **—*n-* hy′ phen·a′ tion.**

hyp·no·sis (hĭp nō′ səs) ***n-*** [*pl.* **hyp·no·ses** (-sēz)] artificially produced trance which resembles sleep, but in which a person is extremely sensitive to suggestions made by the person who put him into the condition.

hyp·not·ic (hĭp nŏt′ ĭk) ***adj-*** having to do with or producing hypnosis. ***n-*** something that produces sleep, as a drug. **—*adv-* hyp·not′ i·cal·ly.**

hyp·no·tism (hĭp′ nə tĭz′ əm) ***n-*** act or process of inducing hypnosis in a person. **—*n-* hyp′ no·tist.**

hyp·no·tize (hĭp′ nə tīz′) ***vt-*** [**hyp·no·tized, hyp·no·tiz·ing**] **1** to put (someone) into a condition of hypnosis. **2** to captivate or fascinate. **—*n-* hyp′ no·tiz′ er.**

[1]**hy·po** (hī′ pō) ***n-*** sodium thiosulfate. [short for **hyposulfite.**]

[2]**hy·po** (hī′ pō) *Informal* ***n-*** [*pl.* **hy·pos**] **1** hypodermic needle. **2** hypodermic injection. [short for **hypodermic.**]

hy·po·chon·dri·a (hī′ pə kŏn′ drē ə) ***n-*** **1** continual anxiety about one's health, accompanied by concern with usually imaginary symptoms of illness. **2** *Archaic* severe depression; low spirits.

hy·po·chon·dri·ac (hī′ pə kŏn′ drē ăk′) ***adj-*** having to do with or affected with hypochondria. ***n-*** person affected with hypochondria.

hy·po·cot·yl (hī′ pə kŏt′ əl) ***n-*** the part of the embryo of a seed plant which becomes the stem of the mature plant. It is located between the cotyledons and the radicle.

hy·poc·ri·sy (hĭ pŏk′ rə sē) ***n-*** [*pl.* **hy·poc·ri·sies**] pretense of being what one is not or feeling what one does not feel: *His sympathy is just* hypocrisy.

hy·po·crite (hĭp′ ə krĭt′) ***n-*** person who puts on a false appearance of being good, kind, honest, etc.; one who is insincere in word or action.

hy·po·crit·i·cal (hĭp′ ə krĭt′ ĭ kəl) ***adj-*** of or like a hypocrite; insincere. **—*adv-* hy′ po·crit′ i·cal·ly.**

hy·po·der·mic (hī′ pə dûr′ mĭk) ***n-*** **1** (also **hypodermic injection**) medicine or other substance injected beneath the skin; injection; shot. **2** (also **hypodermic syringe**) tube with a plunger and needle, used to inject substances beneath the skin. ***adj-*** under or beneath the skin.

hypodermic needle ***n-*** needle of a hypodermic syringe.

hy·po·sul·fite (hī′ pō sŭl′ fīt) ***n-*** sodium thiosulfate.

hy·pot·e·nuse (hī pŏt′ ə no͞oz′) ***n-*** of a right triangle, the name of the side that is opposite the right angle. For picture, see *right triangle.*

hy·poth·e·sis (hī pŏth′ ə sĭs) ***n-*** [*pl.* **hy·poth·e·ses** (-sēz)] statement or proposition that is based on observation and reasoning and is used as a basis for further investigation, even though little supporting evidence is known for it. See also *theory.*

hy·poth·e·size (hī pŏth′ ə sīz′) ***vi-*** [**hy·poth·e·sized, hy·poth·e·siz·ing**] to form a hypothesis.

hy·po·thet·i·cal (hī′ pə thĕt′ ĭ kəl) ***adj-*** **1** based on a hypothesis. **2** based on supposition: *a* hypothetical *location.* Also **hy′ po·thet′ ic. —*adv-* hy′ po·thet′ i·cal·ly.**

hy·po·thy·roid·ism (hī′ pō thī′ roi dĭz′ əm) ***n-*** condition resulting from too little thyroxin being produced by the thyroid gland, and marked by a lowered metabolic rate and a weakening of muscles.

hy·rax (hī′ răks′) ***n-*** any of various small, hoofed, Old World mammals resembling a rabbit; cony.

hys·sop (hĭs′ əp) ***n-*** **1** any of several plants related to the mints, with aromatic leaves and small blue or purple flowers. **2** any of various other plants, especially an unidentified plant mentioned in the Bible.

hys·ter·ec·to·my (hĭs′ tə rĕk′ tə mē) ***n-*** surgical removal of the uterus.

hys·te·ri·a (hĭ stĕr′ ē ə, hĭ stêr′ ē ə) ***n-*** **1** emotional disorder usually marked by disturbances in the normal functioning of the muscles, senses, etc. Example: a soldier who is afraid of being killed may become temporarily unable to walk, even though nothing is organically wrong with him. **2** uncontrollable excitement; frenzy.

hys·ter·ic (hĭ stĕr′ ĭk) ***adj-*** hysterical. ***n-*** person given to hysteria.

hys·ter·i·cal (hĭ stĕr′ ĭ kəl) ***adj-*** **1** lacking emotional control; violently emotional: *the* hysterical *throng.* **2** *Informal* very funny. **—*adv-* hys·ter′ i·cal·ly.**

hys·ter·ics (hĭ stĕr′ ĭks) ***n-*** (takes plural verb) fit of uncontrolled emotion, such as laughing and crying together.

I

I, i (ī) ***n-*** [*pl.* **I's, i's**] **1** the ninth letter of the English alphabet. **2** Roman numeral for the number one.

[1]**I** (ī) ***pron-*** (used as a singular subject in the first person) the person who is speaking or writing. [a reduced form of Old English **ic** of the same meaning.] ***Homs-*** [2]ay or aye, eye.

[2]**I** symbol for iodine.

I. **1** Island. **2** Islands. **3** Isle; Isles.

Ia. Iowa.

i·amb (ī′ ămb′) ***n-*** **1** a measure or foot in poetry made up of one unaccented syllable followed by one accented syllable. **2** a line in poetry made up of such measures. Example: "Was this′/the face′/that launched′/a thou′/sand ships′?" **—*adj-* i·am′ bic.**

ian *suffix* See *-an.*

i·bex (ī′ bĕks′) ***n-*** [*pl.* **i·bex** or **i·bex·es**] European or Asiatic wild goat with large, backward-curving horns.

ibid. or **ib.** in the same place [from Latin **ibidem.**]

-ibility *suffix* See *-ability.*

i·bis (ī′ bĭs′) ***n-*** [*pl.* **i·bis·es** or **i·bis**] any of several large, flesh-eating wading birds, related to herons.

White ibis

-ible *suffix* See *-able*

-ic *suffix* (used to form adjectives) **1** having the nature of: *angel*ic; *anem*ic. **2** being a; belonging to: *Copt*ic; *Celt*ic. **3** having to do with:

poetic; *volcanic*. 4 *Chemistry* with a valence relatively higher than in compounds or ions having an adjective ending in -ous: *nitric*; *ferric*.

-ical *suffix* alternate form of the adjective suffix **-ic** (except for chemical compounds).

Ic·a·rus (ĭk′ ər əs) ***n-*** in Greek legend, the son of Daedalus, who escaped from Crete by flying with wings made by his father. He flew so near the sun that it melted the wax fastening his wings, and he drowned in the sea.

ICBM Intercontinental Ballistic Missile.

I.C.C. Interstate Commerce Commission.

ice (īs) ***n-*** **1** solid frozen water. **2** something which looks, feels, or acts like this. **3** frozen dessert made with fruit flavoring or juice and water: *Orange* ice *is good in hot weather.* *as* **modifier**: *six* ice *cubes*; *an* ice *skate.* ***vt-*** [**iced, ic·ing**] **1** to cool with frozen water: *to* ice *drinks.* **2** to cover with frosting or icing: *to* ice *a cake.* ***vi-*** to become covered with frozen water (often followed by "up"): *The wings of the airplane were* icing *up rapidly.*
break the ice to overcome formality and reserve.

ice age ***n-*** **1** a time when large areas of the earth were covered by sheets of ice and glaciers. **2 Ice Age** the Pleistocene epoch in geology, noted for its glaciation.

ice bag ***n-*** rubberized cloth container designed to hold ice and to be applied to the body as a cold pack.

ice·berg (īs′ bûrg′) ***n-*** **1** mass of floating ice, often of great size, detached from the base of a glacier. Only about one ninth of its mass shows above water. **2** person with a cold disposition.

PART BELOW WATER

Iceberg

ice·boat (īs′ bōt′) ***n-*** sailing vehicle for use on ice. It is shaped like a cross, with runners at each end of the crosspiece and one at the stern for steering.

ice·bound (īs′ bound′) ***adj-*** **1** surrounded by ice so as to be unable to move: *an* icebound *ship.* **2** unusable because of ice: *an* icebound *harbor.*

ice·box (īs′ bŏks′) ***n-*** refrigerator, especially one that uses ice but does not make it.

ice·break·er (īs′ brāk′ ər) ***n-*** a ship with strong engines and prow that cuts channels in frozen rivers, lakes, or harbors to permit the passage of ships.

ice·cap (īs′ kăp′) ***n-*** ice sheet.

ice cream ***n-*** frozen dessert made with milk, cream, sugar, flavoring, and sometimes gelatin and eggs.

ice field ***n-*** very large sheet of floating sea ice.

ice·house (īs′ hous′) ***n-*** building where ice is stored.

Ice·land·ic (īs lăn′ dĭk) ***adj-*** of or relating to Iceland, its people, or their language. ***n-*** the North Germanic language of the people of Iceland. The older forms of this language are known as **Old Icelandic** or Old Norse.

Iceland spar ***n-*** calcite.

ice·man (īs′ măn′) ***n-*** [*pl.* **ice·men**] person who supplies and delivers ice.

ice pack ***n-*** **1** floating ice mass consisting of separate pieces jammed together and frozen solid. **2** ice bag.

ice pick ***n-*** hand tool with a needlelike spike, used for chipping blocks of ice into smaller pieces.

ice sheet ***n-*** **1** either of the two immense, permanent masses of ice, thousands of feet deep, that cover most of Greenland and Antarctica. The ice in an ice sheet moves slowly outward in all directions from the regions of greatest thickness; ice cap. **2** any flat mass of covering ice, such as the large ice floes in the Arctic.

ice-skate (īs′ skāt′) ***vi-*** [**ice-skat·ed, ice-skat·ing**] to skate with ice skates. **—*n-* ice skater.**

ice skate ***n-*** blade mounted on a shoe or attaching to a shoe, for skating on ice.

ich·neu·mon (ĭk nōō′ mən, ĭk nyōō′-) ***n-*** small, flesh-eating animal of the Old World that looks like a weasel and is related to the mongooses and civets.

ichneumon fly ***n-*** any of a large group of insects which lay their eggs upon the larvae of other insects.

ichthy- or **ichthyo-** *combining form* fish: ichthy*ology* [from Greek **ichthys**, meaning "fish."]

ich·thy·ol·o·gist (ĭk′ thē ŏl′ ə jĭst) ***n-*** person expert in and usually working in ichthyology.

ich·thy·ol·o·gy (ĭk′ thē ŏl′ ə jē) ***n-*** branch of zoology dealing with fish.

ich·thy·o·saur (ĭk′ thē ə sôr′) ***n-*** any of various extinct marine fishlike reptiles of the Mesozoic era. They had long jaws and paddlelike limbs.

i·ci·cle (ī′ sĭk′ əl, -sə kəl) ***n-*** hanging spike of ice.

ic·i·ly (ī′ sə lē) ***adv-*** in a cold or icy manner.

ic·i·ness (ī′ sē nəs) ***n-*** condition of being frozen, icy, or chilly.

ic·ing (ī′ sĭng) ***n-*** **1** coating for cakes and cookies made usually with sugar, butter, milk or water, and flavoring, etc.; frosting. **2** formation of layers of ice on airplane wings, ship decks, etc.

Icicles

i·con (ī′ kŏn′) ***n-*** **1** in the Eastern Orthodox Church, a sacred picture of Christ, the Virgin, etc., usually brightly painted on a wooden panel. **2** any image, especially a picture. Also **ikon.**

i·con·o·clast (ī kŏn′ ə klăst′) ***n-*** **1** person who attacks popular beliefs or traditions. **2** person who destroys images or icons, or who is opposed to their use in religion. **—*adj-* i·con′ o·clas′ tic.**

i·con·o·scope (ī kŏn′ ə skōp′) ***n-*** electron tube used in earlier television cameras. See also *image orthicon.*

-ics *suffix* (used to form nouns usually in substitution for the adjective suffix "-ic.") **1** a science or system: *econom*ics; *mathemat*ics. **2** actions having to do with: *hyster*ics; *atmospher*ics.

ic·y (ī′ sē) ***adj-*** [**ic·i·er, ic·i·est**] **1** like ice; very cold: *an* icy *wind.* **2** covered with ice: *an* icy *road.* **3** of ice: *an* icy *film.* **4** cold and unfriendly: *She has an* icy *manner.*

I'd (īd) **1** I had. **2** I would. **3** I should.

i·de·a (ī dē′ ə) ***n-*** **1** thought; notion; inkling; understanding: *Have you any* idea *what he is talking about?* **2** plan or scheme: *It would be a good* idea *to plant some trees in front.* **3** impression or picture formed in the mind: *She found the house quite different from her* idea *of it.* **4** purpose or meaning of something: *What was the main* idea *of that story?* **—*adj-* i·de′ a·less.**

i·de·al (ī dē′ əl) ***adj-*** **1** existing in imagination only; not real or practical. **2** equal to one's highest wish; perfect: *an* ideal *day.* ***n-*** **1** highest standard of excellence or beauty. **2** person or thing regarded as worthy of imitation; model. **3** mental image representing the perfect type: *No girl measured up to his* ideal *of a perfect wife.* **4** goal. **—*adj-* i·de′ al·less.** ***adv-*** **i·de′ al·ly.**

i·de·al·ism (ī dē′ ə lĭz′ əm) ***n-*** **1** the tendency to see things as they should be instead of as they are. **2** the effort to arrange one's life and surroundings according to one's own standard of perfection. **3** in art and literature, the effort to depict beauty and perfection rather than fact. **4** in philosophy, any of various systems or schools generally agreeing that truth and reality are not to be found in the common-sense world outside the mind, but either in the mind itself or in some realm beyond the mind. **—*n-* i·de′ al·ist.** ***adj-*** **i·de′ al·is′ tic.** ***adv-*** **i·de′ al·is′ ti·cal·ly.**

i·de·al·ize (ī dē′ ə līz′) ***vt-*** **[i·de·al·ized, i·de·al·iz·ing]** to look upon or represent as perfect, regardless of fact: *to* idealize *marriage.* **—*n-* i·de′ al·i·za′ tion.**

i·den·ti·cal (ī dĕn′ tə kəl) ***adj-*** **1** the very same: *the* identical *spot.* **2** exactly alike: *No two faces are* identical. **—*adv-* i·den′ ti·cal·ly. *n-* i·den′ ti·cal·ness.**

identical twins ***n-*** human twins of the same sex, developed from a single fertilized ovum and, as a result, having identical hereditary characteristics. See also *fraternal twins.*

i·den·ti·fi·ca·tion (ī dĕn′ tə fə kā′ shən) ***n-*** **1** an identifying or being identified: *the* identification *of criminals.* **2** proof that someone or something is what is claimed: *He showed his driver's license as* identification.

i·den·ti·fy (ī dĕn′ tə fī′) ***vt-*** **[i·den·ti·fied, i·den·ti·fy·ing]** **1** to discover or state the identity of; recognize; name: *He* identified *the bridge in the snapshot.* **2** to make, consider, or treat as identical: *to* identify *wealth with success.* **3** to associate: *He refused to* identify *himself with their scheme.* ***vi-*** to feel a kinship or oneness with another person: *The girl* identified *with the heroine of the story.* **—*adj-* i·den′ ti·fi′ a·ble′:** *The ship was not* identifiable. ***adv-* i·den′ ti·fi′ a·bly. *n-* i·den′ ti·fi·er.**

i·den·ti·ty (ī dĕn′ tə tē) ***n-*** [*pl.* **i·den·ti·ties**] **1** who a person is; what a thing is: *The* identity *of the author* is unknown. **2** sameness; oneness: *She* noticed *the* identity *of their papers.* **3** particular personality; individuality: *to assert one's* identity. **4** *Mathematics* (1) element in a set that, when combined in an operation with any other element, does not change that element. For addition, the identity element is 0, and for multiplication, it is 1: $7 + 0 = 7$; $9 \times 1 = 9$. (2) expression stating the equivalence of two terms: $6 = 6$.

i·de·o·graph (ĭd′ ē ə grăf′) ***n-*** picture or symbol used in a writing system to represent an idea or thing rather than the particular word or phrase for it. For example, a picture of a lion might be used to suggest power. Also **i′ de·o·gram′** (ĭd′ ē ə grăm′). **—*adj-* i′ de·o·graph′ ic. *adv-* i′ de·o·graph′ i·cal·ly.**

i·de·ol·o·gy (ĭd′ ē ŏl′ ə jē, ī′ dē-) ***n-*** [*pl.* **i·de·ol·o·gies**] system of ideas and theories about human life, especially that of some political party, nation, etc. **—*adj-* i′ de·o·log′ i·cal** (ĭd′ ē ə lŏj′ ĭ kəl). ***adv-* i′ de·o·log′ i·cal·ly.**

ides (īdz) ***n-*** *pl.* (takes singular or plural verb) in the ancient Roman calendar, the 15th of March, May, July, and October; the 13th of the other months.

id·i·o·cy (ĭd′ ē ə sē) ***n-*** [*pl.* **id·i·o·cies**] **1** almost total lack of intelligence; extreme mental deficiency. **2** very foolish act; extreme foolishness.

id·i·om (ĭd′ ē əm) ***n-*** **1** a group of words whose meaning must be known as a whole because it cannot be learned from the meanings of the same words used separately. "To go back on" doesn't only mean "to move backward onto," but also "to betray or fail." **2** the language used by the people of a certain region, group, class, etc.: *the American* idiom; *the* idiom *of sailors.* **3** a particular person's way of using words: *Shakespeare's* idiom.

id·i·o·mat·ic (ĭd′ ē ə măt′ ĭk) ***adj-*** **1** given to, or marked by, the use of idiom: *to speak* idiomatic *French.* **2** peculiar to the language of a country or region; colloquial. **3** having the nature of an idiom: *an* idiomatic *phrase.* **—*adv-* id′ i·o·mat′ i·cal·ly.**

id·i·o·syn·cra·sy (ĭd′ ē ə sĭn′ krə sē) ***n-*** [*pl.* **id·i·o·syn·cra·sies**] a peculiarity in behavior, speech, dress, etc.: *my uncle's* idiosyncrasies. **—*adj-* id′ i·o·syn·crat′ ic** (-sĭn krăt′ ĭk). ***adv-* id′ i·o·syn·crat′ ic·al·ly.**

id·i·ot (ĭd′ ē ət) ***n-*** **1** person born with almost no mental powers, and unable to learn. **2** *Informal* silly person.

id·i·ot·ic (ĭd′ ē ŏt′ ĭk) ***adj-*** stupid; silly; senseless. **—*adv-* id′i·ot′ic·al·ly.**

i·dle (ī′ dəl) ***adj-*** **1** not employed; not used; not working: *an* idle *workman*; idle *machinery.* **2** not willing to work; lazy: *He is an* idle *boy and will not do his chores.* **3** useless; of no importance or worth: *to waste time in* idle *talk.* ***vi-*** **[i·dled, i·dling]** **1** to run slowly without doing work, as an engine does in neutral gear when the throttle is not applied. **2** to waste time; do nothing. ***vt-*** *Informal* to cause (employes) to stop working: *The strike* idled *300 workers.* ***Homs-*** idol, idyll. **—*n-* i′ dle·ness. *adv-* i′ dly.**
idle away to pass (time) idly: *We* idled away *the afternoon.*

i·dler (īd′ lər) ***n-*** **1** person who is lazy or wastes time and does nothing. **2** (also **idler pulley**) loose pulley pressing against a belt to guide it or to tighten it. **3** (also **idler wheel)** gear wheel placed between two others to transfer motion from one of these to the other without changing the direction of rotation.

Idler wheel

i·dol (ī′ dəl) ***n-*** **1** image of a god used as an object of worship. **2** person or thing greatly loved or admired. ***Homs-*** idle, idyll.

i·dol·a·ter (ī dŏl′ ə tər) ***n-*** person who idolizes. **—*n-* *fem.* i·dol′ a·tress.**

i·dol·a·try (ī dŏl′ ə trē) ***n-*** [*pl.* **i·dol·a·tries**] an idolizing. **—*adj-* i·dol′ a·trous. *adv-* i·dol′ a·trous·ly.**

i·dol·ize (ī′ də līz′) ***vt-*** **[i·dol·ized, i·dol·iz·ing]** **1** to love or admire beyond reason: *to* idolize *a movie star.* **2** to worship as an idol. **—*n-* i′ dol·i·za′ tion.**

i·dyll or **i·dyl** (ī′ dəl) ***n-*** **1** prose piece describing a peaceful scene or event in country life. **2** episode or scene suitable for such a piece. ***Homs-*** idle, idol.

i·dyl·lic (ī dĭl′ ĭk) ***adj-*** **1** having to do with, or of the nature of, the idyll. **2** having country charm and simplicity. **—*adv-* i·dyl′ li·cal·ly.**

-ie or **-y** *suffix* (used to form nouns) **1** little and appealing to the affections: *birdie*; *dolly*. **2** *Informal* of a certain nature: *toughie*.

i.e. that is. [from Latin **id est**].

if (ĭf) ***conj-*** **1** on the condition that: *I'll go* if *you will.* **2** in case that; in the event that; supposing that: *I'm not going* if *it rains.* **3** whether: *I wonder* if *the plane will be on time.* **4** even though: *an attractive,* if *awkward, girl.* **5** used to introduce an exclamation expressing (1) a wish: *Oh,* if *it were only payday!* (2) surprise: *Well,* if *it isn't Mack himself!* ***n-*** condition; supposition: *There are many* ifs *in our summer plans.*

►IF is used to show a condition. If *he comes, I will be happy.* Either IF or WHETHER is used to express doubt. *I don't know* whether *he is ill. I don't know* if *he is ill.*

-iferous *combining form* producing; yielding; bearing: *odori*ferous; *carboni*ferous. [from Latin **-(i)fer,** from **ferre,** "to bear," plus English **-ous.**]

ig·loo (ĭg′ lo͞o) ***n-*** [*pl.* **ig·loos**] Eskimo hut, especially a dome-shaped one built with blocks of snow. Also **ig′ lu.**

ig·ne·ous (ĭg′ nē əs) ***adj-*** **1** having to do with fire. **2** produced by fire, intense heat, or volcanic action: *an* igneous *rock.*

Igloo

fāte, făt, dâre, bärn; bē, bĕt, mêre; bīte, bĭt; nōte, hŏt, môre, dóg; fŭn, fûr; to͞o, bo͝ok; oil; out; tar; thin; then; hw for wh as in *wh*at; zh for s as in u*s*ual; ə for a, e, i, o, u, as in *a*go, lin*e*n, per*i*l, at*o*m, min*u*s

ig·nite (ĭg nīt′) ***vt-*** [**ig·nit·ed, ig·nit·ing**] to set fire to; set on fire: *to* ignite *twigs.* ***vi-*** to catch fire; take fire: *The dry leaves* ignited *from a spark.* **—*n-* ig·nit′ er.**

ig·ni·tion (ĭg nĭsh′ ən) ***n-*** **1** act of catching fire or lighting a fire. **2** system in an internal-combustion engine that ignites the fuel. *as **modifier**: an* ignition *engine.*

ig·no·ble (ĭg nō′ bəl) ***adj-*** **1** of low character; mean; base: *A cheat is an* ignoble *man.* **2** shameful; disgraceful: *an* ignoble *defeat.* **—*n-* ig·no′ ble·ness. *adv-* ig·no′ bly.**

ig·no·min·i·ous (ĭg′ nə mĭn′ ē əs) ***adj-*** **1** disgraceful; shameful; dishonorable: *an* ignominious *act.* **2** humiliating: *an* ignominious *punishment.* **—*adv-* ig′ no·min′ i·ous·ly. *n-* ig′·no·min′ i·ous·ness.**

ig·no·min·y (ĭg′ nə mĭn′ ē, ĭg nŏm′ ə nē) ***n-*** [*pl.* **ig·no·min·ies**] disgrace or dishonor; also, a cause of this.

ig·no·ra·mus (ĭg nə răm′ əs, -rā′ məs) ***n-*** [*pl.* **ig·no·ra·mus·es**] ignorant person.

ig·no·rance (ĭg′ nə rəns) ***n-*** lack of knowledge.

ig·no·rant (ĭg′ nə rənt) ***adj-*** **1** lacking in knowledge or education: *He is* ignorant *of the customs in other countries.* **2** unaware: *He was* ignorant *of the facts.* **3** based on ignorance: *an* ignorant *answer.* **—*adv-* ig′ no·rant·ly.**

ig·nore (ĭg nôr′) ***vt-*** [**ig·nored, ig·nor·ing**] to pay no attention to; refuse to notice.

i·gua·na (ĭ gwä′ nə) ***n-*** any of several long-tailed lizards, especially a tropical American lizard with a crest of scales along its back and a puffed out throat.

Iguana, different kinds vary from a few inches to 6 ft long

IGY (ī′ jē′ wī′) International Geophysical Year.

i·kon (ī′ kŏn′) icon.

il·e·um (ĭl′ ē əm) ***n-*** lowest division of the small intestine. ***Hom-*** ilium.

Il·i·ad (ĭl′ ē əd) ***n-*** ancient Greek epic poem, by Homer, telling some of the events of the siege of Ilium (Troy).

il·i·um (ĭl′ ē əm) ***n-*** the large upper portion of either of the hipbones. For picture, see *pelvis.* ***Hom-*** ileum.

ilk (ĭlk) ***n-*** breed; sort; kind: *thieves and others of that* ilk.

ill (ĭl) ***adj-*** [**worse, worst**] **1** sick; not well; diseased: *The child is* ill. **2** disagreeable; hostile: *his* ill *humor*; ill *will.* **3** harmful: *an* ill *turn.* **4** immoral; bad: *a person of* ill *repute.* **5** improper; unacceptable: *his* ill *manners.* ***adv-*** **1** unkindly; with hostility: *to treat someone* ill. **2** hardly; scarcely: *They can* ill *afford such a car.* **3** badly: *to fare* ill. ***n-*** **1** an evil: *War is one of the great* ills *of the world.* **2** something unfavorable or injurious: *to work* ill *to one's neighbors.* **3** misfortune; trouble.

ill at ease uneasy; nervous; uncomfortable.

I'll (īl) **1** I shall. **2** I will. ***Homs-*** aisle, isle.

ill. 1 illustrated. **2** illustration.

Ill. Illinois.

ill-ad·vised (ĭl′ əd vīzd′) ***adj-*** poorly or harmfully advised; unwise; imprudent; rash: *an* ill-advised *scheme.*

ill-bred (ĭl′ brĕd′) ***adj-*** badly brought up; impolite.

ill-con·sid·ered (ĭl′ kən sĭd′ ərd) ***adj-*** poorly considered; showing lack of thought: *an* ill-considered *opinion.*

ill-dis·posed (ĭl′ dĭ spōzd′) ***adj-*** unfavorable: *He was* ill-disposed *toward the idea.*

il·le·gal (ĭ lē′ gəl) ***adj-*** not lawful; forbidden by law. **—*n-* il′ le·gal′ i·ty** (ĭl′ ə găl′ ə tē). ***adv-*** **il·le′ gal·ly.**

il·leg·i·ble (ĭ lĕj′ ə bəl) ***adj-*** not readable; difficult to read: *an* illegible *date on a coin*; illegible *handwriting.* **—*n-* il·leg′ i·bil′ i·ty. *adv-* il·leg′ i·bly.**

il·le·git·i·mate (ĭl′ ə jĭt′ ə mət) ***adj-*** **1** born to an unmarried woman. **2** unlawful; illegal: *an* illegitimate *act.* **—*n-* il′ le·git′ i·ma·cy. *adv-* il′ le·git′ i·mate·ly.**

ill-fat·ed (ĭl′ fā′ təd) ***adj-*** **1** destined to misfortune; doomed: *an* ill-fated *marriage.* **2** bringing, or resulting in, misfortune: *an* ill-fated *meeting.*

ill-fa·vored (ĭl′ fā′ vərd) ***adj-*** unattractive; ugly.

ill-got·ten (ĭl′ gŏt′ ən) ***adj-*** obtained by evil or unlawful methods: *an* ill-gotten *fortune.*

ill-hu·mored (ĭl′ hyōō′ mərd) ***adj-*** bad-tempered; disagreeable: *an* ill-humored *man.* **—*adv-* ill′ -hu′ mored·ly.**

il·lib·er·al (ĭ lĭb′ ər əl) ***adj-*** **1** narrow-minded. **2** stingy; close; ungenerous: *an* illiberal *allowance.* **—*n-* il·lib′ er·al′ i·ty** (-ăl′ ə tē).

il·lic·it (ĭ lĭs′ ĭt) ***adj-*** illegal; forbidden: *an* illicit *trade.* ***Hom-*** elicit. **—*adv-* il·lic′ it·ly. *n-* il·lic′ it·ness.**

il·lim·it·a·ble (ĭ lĭm′ ə tə bəl) ***adj-*** without limits; boundless; vast: *his* illimitable *ambition.* **—*adv-* il·lim′ it·a·bly.**

Il·li·nois (ĭl′ ə noi′, -noiz′) ***n-*** [*pl.* **Il·li·nois**] a member of a confederacy of Algonquian Indians who lived in Illinois, Iowa, and Wisconsin.

il·lit·er·a·cy (ĭ lĭt′ ər ə sē) ***n-*** [*pl.* **il·lit·er·a·cies**] inability to read and write.

il·lit·er·ate (ĭ lĭt′ ər ət) ***adj-*** **1** unable to read and write. **2** showing lack of education: *an* illiterate *letter.* ***n-*** person unable to read and write. **—*adv-* il·lit′ er·ate·ly.**

ill-man·nered (ĭl′ măn′ ərd) ***adj-*** impolite; rude. **—*adv-* ill-man′ nered·ly.**

ill-na·tured (ĭl′ nā′ chərd) ***adj-*** cross; disagreeable; surly. **—*adv-* ill′ na′ tured·ly.**

ill·ness (ĭl′ nəs) ***n-*** **1** condition of being sick: *She stayed home because of* illness. **2** disease; malady.

il·log·i·cal (ĭ lŏj′ ĭ kəl) ***adj-*** not logical; contrary to reason. **—*adv-* il·log′ i·cal·ly. *n-* il·log′ i·cal·ness.**

ill-spent (ĭl′ spĕnt′) ***adj-*** badly spent; wasted: *an* ill-spent *hour.*

ill-starred (ĭl′ stärd′) ***adj-*** ill-fated and unlucky, as if born with a bad horoscope.

ill-suit·ed (ĭl′ sōō′ təd, -syōō′ təd) ***adj-*** not fitting; unsuitable: *a man* ill-suited *for the job.*

ill-tem·pered (ĭl′ tĕm′ pərd) ***adj-*** having a bad temper; cranky: *an* ill-tempered *bull.* **—*adv-* ill-tem′ pered·ly.**

ill-timed (ĭl′ tīmd′) ***adj-*** happening at the wrong time; done at an unsuitable time: *an* ill-timed *remark*; *an* ill-timed *sale of stock.*

ill-treat (ĭl′ trēt′) ***vt-*** to treat badly or cruelly; abuse; mistreat: *to* ill-treat *an animal.* **—*n-* ill′ -treat′ ment.**

il·lu·mi·nate (ĭ lōō′ mə nāt′) ***vt-*** [**il·lu·mi·nat·ed, il·lu·mi·nat·ing**] **1** to furnish with light: *Floodlights* illuminated *the ball park.* **2** to explain; make clear: *His lecture* illuminated *the subject of space flight.* **3** to ornament (a capital letter or the border of a page) with colored designs. **—*n-* il·lu′ mi·na′ tion. *adj-* il·lu′ mi·na·tive.**

il·lu·mine (ĭ lōō′ mən) ***vt-*** [**il·lu·mined, il·lu·min·ing**] to light up; brighten; illuminate: *The moon* illumined *the niggt. A smile* illumined *her face.*

illus. or **illust. 1** illustrated. **2** illustration. **3** illustrator.

ill-us·age (ĭl′ yōō′ sĭj) ***n-*** wrong treatment; abuse.

ill-use (ĭl′ yōōz′) ***vt-*** [**ill-used, ill-using**] to treat badly.

il·lu·sion (ĭ lōō′ zhən, ĭ lyōō′-) ***n-*** **1** an impression of sight, hearing, or another sense, that is different from what actually is; mistaken perception: *The shadow of the rock created the* illusion *of an animal standing there.* **2** false or mistaken idea or belief; delusion. ***Hom-*** elusion.

►Should not be confused with ALLUSION.

Illusion: crown and brim same length

il·lu·sive (ĭ lōō′ sĭv, ĭ lyōō′-) ***adj-*** deceptive; illusory: *The war produced a period of* illusive *prosperity.* **—*adv-* il·lu′ sive·ly. *n-* il·lu′ sive·ness.**

il·lu·so·ry (ĭ lo͞o′ zə rē, ĭ lyo͞o′-) ***adj-*** deceptive; misleading; unreal: *to have* illusory *hopes for fame.*

il·lus·trate (ĭl′ ə strāt′, *also* ĭ lŭs′ trāt′) ***vt-*** **[il·lus·trat·ed, il·lus·trat·ing] 1** to make clear: *The film* illustrates *the hardships faced by the whalers.* **2** to make clear or explain by using examples or comparisons: *to* illustrate *a spelling rule with an example.* **3** to make clear or ornament with pictures, diagrams, etc.: *to* illustrate *a lecture*; *to* illustrate *a story.* **4** to be an example, instance, picture, etc., of: *The building* illustrates *our best work in architecture.*

il·lus·tra·tion (ĭl′ ə strā′ shən) ***n-*** **1** a picture, diagram, map, etc., used to explain or decorate: *an* illustration *of a Roman aqueduct.* **2** example or comparison: *His conduct was an* illustration *of courage.* **3** an explaining by the use of examples or pictures: *The teacher gave an* illustration *of the use of levers.*

il·lus·tra·tive (ĭ lŭs′ trə tĭv′) ***adj-*** tending to explain or make clear. ***—adv-*** **il·lus′ tra·tive·ly.**

il·lus·tra·tor (ĭl′ əs trā′ tər) ***n-*** person who makes pictures for a book, magazine, etc.

il·lus·tri·ous (ĭ lŭs′ trē əs) ***adj-*** **1** famous for greatness, courage, nobility, etc.; celebrated: *an* illustrious *statesman.* **2** bestowing glory and fame: *an* illustrious *deed.* ***—adv-*** **il·lus′ tri·ous·ly** ***n-*** **il·lus′ tri·ous·ness.**

ill will ***n-*** unfriendly feeling; hate.

I'm (īm) I am.

im·age (ĭm′ ĭj) ***n-*** **1** object made in the likeness of a person, animal, etc.: *an* image *of a cat carved in jade.* **2** thing seen in a mirror, or through a magnifying glass, camera lens, etc.: *A microscope gives a large* image *of tiny things.* **3** copy; close likeness: *He is the* image *of his father.* **4** a picture in the mind: *His dreams were full of vivid* images. ***vt-*** **[im·aged, im·ag·ing] 1** to reflect, as in a mirror: *The still pond* imaged *the trees.* **2** to picture in the mind; imagine. **3** to describe or portray.

image or·thi·con (ôr′ thə kŏn′, ôr′-) ***n-*** electron tube used in most television cameras.

im·age·ry (ĭm′ ĭj rē) ***n-*** [*pl.* **im·age·ries**] **1** mental pictures collectively, especially those formed in the imagination of an artist, poet, etc. **2** language which causes the mind to form pictures.

im·ag·i·na·ble (ĭ măj′ ə nə bəl) ***adj-*** such as can be imagined or pictured in the mind; conceivable: *the greatest joy* imaginable. ***—adv-*** **im·ag′ i·na·bly.**

im·ag·i·nar·y (ĭ măj′ ə nĕr′ ē) ***adj-*** existing only in the mind or imagination; not real.

im·ag·i·na·tion (ĭ măj′ ə nā′ shən) ***n-*** **1** the power of the mind to form pictures; ability to form mental pictures of things not actually present or seen: *His* imagination *carried him to exotic, far-away places.* **2** product of this power; mental picture or idea; a fancy: *He thought he heard a prowler, but it was just* imagination. **3** power to create through mental images new things or new ideas: *Only à good* imagination *can produce original art.* **4** resourcefulness: *To get out of that scrape will take some* imagination.

im·ag·i·na·tive (ĭ măj′ ə nə tĭv) ***adj-*** **1** having imagination or creative ability: *an* imaginative *artist.* **2** coming from the imagination; fanciful. ***—adv-*** **im·ag′ i·na·tive·ly.**

im·ag·ine (ĭ măj′ ən) ***vt-*** **[im·ag·ined, im·ag·in·ing] 1** to form an idea or mental picture of: *Try to* imagine *living in a castle.* **2** to suppose; guess: *I* imagine *it's late.*

i·ma·go (ĭ mā′ gō) ***n-*** [*pl.* **i·ma·goes** or **i·ma·gi·nes** (ĭ măj′ ə nēz′)] adult, fully developed form of an insect.

i·mam (ĭ mäm′) ***n-*** **1** in the Muslim religion, the prayer leader of a mosque. **2** Muslim ruler who claims to be descended from Mohammed and holds power in both religious and political affairs.

im·bal·ance (ĭm băl′ əns) ***n-*** lack of balance.

im·be·cile (ĭm′ bə səl) ***n-*** **1** person with a weak mind, having less intelligence than a moron but more than an idiot. **2** *Informal* silly or stupid person. ***adj-*** **1** weak-minded. **2** stupid; foolish: *an* imbecile *remark.*

im·be·cil·ic (ĭm′ bə sĭl′ ĭk) ***adj-*** imbecile.

im·be·cil·i·ty (ĭm′ bə sĭl′ ə tē) ***n-*** [*pl.* **im·be·cil·i·ties**] **1** weakness of mind. **2** folly; absurdity.

im·bed (ĭm bĕd′) embed.

im·bibe (ĭm bīb′) ***vt-*** **[im·bibed, im·bib·ing] 1** to drink. **2** to absorb into the mind: *to* imbibe *knowledge.* ***—n-*** **im·bib′ er.**

im·bro·glio (ĭm brōl′ yō) ***n-*** [*pl.* **im·bro·glios**] perplexing or confused situation.

im·bue (ĭm byo͞o′) ***vt-*** **[im·bued, im·bu·ing] 1** to cause to absorb; tinge deeply; dye: *The sunset* imbued *the lake with rose.* **2** to pervade; fill the mind of; permeate: *Desire for freedom* imbued *the people.*

im·i·ta·ble (ĭm′ ə tə bəl) ***adj-*** of a nature that allows being copied or imitated.

im·i·tate (ĭm′ ə tāt′) ***vt-*** **[im·i·tat·ed, im·i·tat·ing] 1** to follow as a model or pattern; copy: *She* imitated *her older sister. The young artist* imitated *the painting of the old master.* **2** to impersonate; mimic: *He* imitated *a Japanese wrestler.* **3** to look like; counterfeit.

im·i·ta·tion (ĭm′ ə tā′ shən) ***n-*** **1** a copying; imitating: *By* imitation *one may learn.* **2** a mimicking: *The comedian did* imitations *of famous people.* **3** a copy: *The carving is an* imitation *of an old Chinese piece.* **4** a counterfeit: *The alloy was a good* imitation *of gold.* ***adj-*** made to resemble something; fake: *an* imitation *wood finish.*

im·i·ta·tive (ĭm′ ə tā′ tĭv) ***adj-*** meant to or tending to imitate. ***—adv-*** **im′ i·ta′ tive·ly.** ***n-*** **im′ i·ta′ tive·ness.**

im·i·ta·tor (ĭm′ ə tā′ tər) ***n-*** person who copies or mimics.

im·mac·u·late (ĭ măk′ yə lət) ***adj-*** **1** spotless; absolutely clean: *His clothes were* immaculate. **2** pure; faultless. ***—adv-*** **im·mac′ u·late·ly.** ***n-*** **im·mac′ u·late·ness.**

Immaculate Conception ***n-*** in the Roman Catholic Church, the doctrine that the Virgin Mary, through divine intervention, was conceived without sin.

im·ma·nent (ĭm′ ə nənt) ***adj-*** dwelling within; inherent; intrinsic: *the* immanent *force of his character.* ***Hom-*** imminent. ***—n-*** **im′ ma·nence.**

Im·man·u·el (ĭ măn′ yo͞o əl, -ĕl′) Emmanuel.

im·ma·te·ri·al (ĭm′ ə têr′ ē əl) ***adj-*** **1** not consisting of matter; without physical form: *Ghosts are* immaterial. **2** unimportant: *What you do is* immaterial *to me.* ***—adv-*** **im′ ma·te′ ri·al·ly.** ***n-*** **im′ ma·te′ ri·al·ness.**

im·ma·ture (ĭm′ ə cho͝or′, -tyo͝or′) ***adj-*** **1** not ripe; not fully grown or developed; not finished or perfected: *an* immature *ear of corn*; immature *plans.* **2** behaving in a childish way: *an* immature *man.* ***—adv-*** **im′ ma·ture′ ly.**

im·ma·tu·ri·ty (ĭm′ ə cho͝or′ ə tē, -tyo͝or′ ə tē) ***n-*** condition of being immature; unripeness; childishness.

im·meas·ur·a·ble (ĭ mĕzh′ ər ə bəl) ***adj-*** boundless; impossible to measure. ***—adv-*** **im·meas′ ur·a·bly.**

im·me·di·a·cy (ĭ mē′ dē ə sē) ***n-*** [*pl.* **im·me·di·a·cies**] **1** condition of being free from anything coming in between; direct relationship; closeness: *the* immediacy *of the school to his house*; *the* immediacy *of danger at the front.* **2** present necessity: *the* immediacy *of their needs.*

im·me·di·ate (ĭ mē′ dē ət) ***adj-*** **1** happening or coming at once; instant: *an* immediate *reply*; *our* immediate *needs.* **2** having to do with the present: *the* immediate *question*;

no immediate *plans.* **3** with nothing intervening; direct: *the* immediate *cause or effect.* **4** near or close by in space or time: *the* immediate *neighborhood*; *the* immediate *future.* **5** next in line or relation: *the* immediate *family.* **—*adv-* im·me′ di·ate·ly.** ***n-*** **im·me′ di·ate·ness.**

im·me·mo·ri·al (ĭm′ ə môr′ ē əl) ***adj-*** beyond reach of memory or record. **—*adv-* im′ me·mo′ ri·al·ly.**

im·mense (ĭ mĕns′) ***adj-*** enormous; huge; great: *an* immense *building*; *an* immense *success.* **—*adv-* im·mense′ ly.** ***n-*** **im·mense′ ness** or **im·men′ si·ty.**

im·merse (ĭ mûrs′) ***vt-*** **[im·mersed, im·mers·ing] 1** to plunge or dip into a liquid: *to* immerse *a dress in dye.* **2** to baptize by plunging (a person) entirely under water. **3** to engage deeply; absorb: *He was* immersed *in his work.*

im·mer·sion (ĭ mûr′ zhən) ***n-*** **1** an immersing or being immersed; especially, a baptism by immersing. **2** *Astronomy* disappearance of a heavenly body behind another, or into its shadow.

im·mi·grant (ĭm′ ə grənt) ***n-*** person who comes into a country to make it his permanent home.
►Should not be confused with EMIGRANT.

im·mi·grate (ĭm′ ə grāt′) ***vi-*** **[im·mi·grat·ed, im·mi·grat·ing]** to enter a foreign country intending to settle there permanently. **—*n-* im′ mi·gra′ tion.**
►Should not be confused with EMIGRATE.

im·mi·nent (ĭm′ ə nənt) ***adj-*** about to happen; threatening: *an* imminent *storm*; imminent *death.* ***Hom-*** immanent. **—*n-* im′ mi·nence.** ***adv-*** **im′ mi·nent·ly.**

im·mo·bile (ĭ mō′ bəl) ***adj-*** immovable; also, motionless: *his* immobile *features.* **—*n-* im′ mo·bil′ i·ty.**

im·mo·bi·lize (ĭ mō′ bə līz′) ***vt-*** **[im·mo·bi·lized, im·mo·bi·liz·ing]** to make unable or difficult to move or use: *Illness* immobilized *him.* **—*n-* im·mo′ bi·li·za′ tion.**

im·mod·er·ate (ĭ mŏd′ ər ət) ***adj-*** not moderate; extreme; excessive: *an* immoderate *appetite for sweets.* **—*adv-* im·mod′ er·ate·ly.** ***n-*** **im·mod′ er·ate·ness** or **im·mod′ er·a·cy** or **im·mod′ er·a′ tion.**

im·mod·est (ĭ mŏd′ əst) ***adj-*** not modest; especially, not decent or proper: *an* immodest *dress*; immodest *behavior.* **—*adv-* im·mod′ est·ly.** ***n-*** **im·mod′ est·y.**

im·mo·late (ĭm′ ō lāt′) ***vt-*** **[im·mo·lat·ed, im·mo·lat·ing]** to offer in sacrifice; especially, to kill as a victim for sacrifice. **—*n-* im′ mo·la′ tion.**

im·mor·al (ĭ mȯr′ əl, ĭ mŏr′-) ***adj-*** **1** contrary to conscience or what is considered right: *their* immoral *conduct.* **2** wicked; unscrupulous. **—*adj-* im·mor′ al·ly.**

im·mo·ral·i·ty (ĭm′ ȯ răl′ ə tē, ĭm′ ə-) ***n-*** [*pl.* **im·mo·ral·i·ties**] **1** reverse of morality; immoral nature or condition. **2** immoral behavior; wickedness.

im·mor·tal (ĭ mȯr′ təl, ĭ môr′-) ***adj-*** **1** living forever; freed from death: *the* immortal *soul.* **2** never to be forgotten; of everlasting fame. **3** having to do with something more than human; divine; heavenly: *an* immortal *vision.* ***n-*** **1** person who never dies. **2** person whose fame is undying. **3 the immortals** in mythology, the gods. **—*adv-* im·mor′ tal·ly.**

im·mor·tal·i·ty (ĭm′ ȯr tăl′ ə tē, im′ ər tăl′ ə tē) ***n-*** **1** individual life that never ends. **2** everlasting fame.

im·mor·tal·ize (ĭ mȯr′ tə līz′, ĭ môr′-) ***vt-*** **[im·mor·tal·ized, im·mor·tal·iz·ing] 1** to give everlasting fame to; cause to be remembered. **2** to give unending life to. **—*n-* im·mor′ tal·i·za′ tion.**

im·mov·able (ĭ mōō′ və bəl) ***adj-*** **1** not movable; firmly fixed: *an* immovable *object.* **2** firm; unchanging or unyielding: *an* immovable *stubborness.* ***n-*** **immovables** in law, property such as land or buildings. **—*n-* im·mov′ a·bil′ i·ty.** ***adv-*** **im·mov′ a·bly.**

im·mune (ĭ myōōn′) ***adj-*** **1** safe (from); protected (against): *to be* immune *from harm.* **2** not susceptible (to); totally resistant (to): *She is* immune *to polio since her shots. He is* immune *to persuasion.*

immune reaction ***n-*** **1** complex reaction in which the animal body produces antibodies against an invading foreign protein, such as a virus or bacterium. The antibodies combine with and render harmless the invader. **2** similar reaction of the human body that results in the destruction of a skin graft or organ transplant from another person.

im·mu·ni·ty (ĭ myōō′ nə tē) ***n-*** [*pl.* **im·mu·ni·ties**] **1** freedom from duties, burdens, obligation, etc.: *to claim* immunity *from jury duty.* **2** total resistance (to a disease) because of antibodies or lysins in the blood.

im·mu·nize (ĭm′ yə nīz′) ***vt-*** **[im·mu·nized, im·mu·niz·ing]** to make immune; especially, to protect by vaccination or inoculation. **—*n-* im′ mu·ni·za′ tion.**

im·mu·nol·o·gy (ĭm′ yə nŏl′ ə jē) ***n-*** the branch of medicine concerned with immunity to disease.

im·mu·nol·o·gist (ĭm′ yə nŏl′ ə jĭst) ***n-*** person who is expert in, and usually occupied with, immunology.

im·mure (ĭ myŏŏr′) ***vt-*** **[im·mured, im·mur·ing]** to confine or seal within walls; shut up in. **—*n-* im·mure′ment.**

im·mu·ta·ble (ĭ myōō′ tə bəl) ***adj-*** unchangeable; unalterable. **—*n-* im·mu′ ta·bil′ i·ty** or **im·mu′ ta·ble·ness.** ***adv-*** **im·mu′ ta·bly.**

imp (ĭmp) ***n-*** **1** young or small devil; little demon. **2** mischievous child.

Imp

imp. 1 imperial. **2** imperative. **3** imported. **4** importer. **5** imperfect.

im·pact (ĭm′ păkt′) ***n-*** **1** the blow of one thing hitting another; collision: *the* impact *of baseball and bat.* **2** startling or impressive effect: *the* impact *of the news.*

im·pact·ed (ĭm păk′ təd) ***adj-*** **1** of a tooth, so deeply wedged in the jawbone that it will not come through the gum. **2** wedged firmly.

im·pair (ĭm pâr′) ***vt-*** to lessen the quantity, excellence, value, or strength of; weaken; damage; harm: *Dim light* impairs *the eyesight.* **—*n-* im·pair′ ment.**

im·pale (ĭm pāl′) ***vt-*** **[im·paled, im·pal·ing]** to pierce through with something pointed; especially, to kill by piercing with a sharp stake. **—*n-* im·pale′ ment.**

im·pal·pa·ble (ĭm păl′ pə bəl) ***adj-*** **1** impossible to feel by touch: *the still,* impalpable *air*; *the* impalpable *shadows.* **2** not easily grasped by the mind: *to make* impalpable *distinctions.* **—*n-* im·pal′ pa·bil′ i·ty.** ***adv-*** **im·pal′ pa·bly.**

im·pan·el (ĭm păn′ əl) ***vt-*** **1** to enter upon a list for jury duty. **2** to select (a jury) from such a list. **—*n-* im·pan′ el·ment.**

im·part (ĭm pärt′) ***vt-*** **1** to give; bestow: *Flowers* impart *beauty to a room.* **2** to disclose: *to* impart *a secret.*

im·par·tial (ĭm pär′ shəl) ***adj-*** not favoring either side; not biased; fair; just; disinterested: *an* impartial *referee.* **—*adv-* im·par′ tial·ly.**

im·par·ti·al·i·ty (ĭm pär′ shē ăl′ ə tē) ***n-*** freedom from partiality or favoritism; fairness.

im·pass·a·ble (ĭm păs′ ə bəl) ***adj-*** such as cannot be crossed or passed over, through, or along; not passable: *an* impassable *swamp.* **—*n-* im·pass′ a·bil′ i·ty:** *the* impassability *of the swamp.* ***adv-*** **im·pass′ a·bly.**

im·passe (ĭm′ păs′) ***n-*** position or situation from which there is no obvious or logical way out; deadlock.

im·pas·sioned (im păsh′ ənd) ***adj-*** showing strong emotion: *an* impassioned *speaker.*

im·pas·sive (ĭm păs′ ĭv) ***adj-*** showing or feeling no emotion; unmoved; calm: *an* impassive *audience.* **—*adv-* im·pas′ sive·ly.** ***n-*** **im·pas′ sive·ness** or **im′ pas·siv′ i·ty** (ĭm′ pə sĭv′ ə tē).

im·pa·tience (ĭm pā′ shəns) ***n-*** **1** lack of patience; inability to tolerate or endure delay, restraint, etc.: *to feel* impatience *toward carelessness.* **2** restless eagerness: *her* impatience *to be off on the trip.* **3** a cultivated flowering plant related to the jewelweed.

im·pa·tient (ĭm pā′ shənt) ***adj-*** **1** not patient; feeling or showing annoyance with delay, opposition, etc.: *an* impatient *reply.* **2** restlessly eager: *She is* impatient *to grow up.* **—*adv-* im·pa′ tient·ly.**

im·peach (ĭm pēch′) ***vt-*** **1** to charge (a person in public office) before a court, with misconduct in office. **2** to question or challenge (a person's honor, motives, etc.). **—*adj-* im·peach′ a·ble.**

im·peach·ment (ĭm pēch′ mənt) ***n-*** an impeaching; especially, the calling to trial of a public official for misconduct.

im·pec·ca·ble (ĭm pĕk′ ə bəl) ***adj-*** **1** not capable of sin or error. **2** free from fault or flaw: *a suit of* impeccable *cut.* **—*n-* im·pec′ ca·bil′ i·ty:** *the* impeccability *of his manners.* ***adv-*** **im·pec′ ca·bly.**

im·pe·cu·ni·ous (ĭm′ pə kyōō′ nē əs) ***adj-*** lacking money; poor. **—*adv-* im′ pe·cu′ ni·ous·ly.**

im·pede (ĭm pēd′) ***vt-*** **[im·ped·ed, im·ped·ing]** to hold back; obstruct; hinder: *Fog* impeded *our progress.*

im·ped·i·ment (ĭm pĕd′ ə mənt) ***n-*** **1** something that holds back or obstructs; a hindrance. **2** a speech defect.

im·ped·i·men·ta (ĭm pĕd′ ə mĕn′ tə) ***n-*** *pl.* things which hinder progress; baggage; especially, army supplies and equipment.

im·pel (ĭm pĕl′) ***vt-*** **[im·pelled, im·pel·ling]** to drive forward; push on; force to motion or action: *Wind* impelled *us along the street. Fear* impelled *him to lie.*

im·pel·ler (ĭm pĕl′ ər) ***n-*** **1** person or thing that impels. **2** rotor of a pump or air blower; also, a blade of such a rotor. **3** compressor of a jet engine.

im·pend (ĭm pĕnd′) ***vi-*** to be about to happen; threaten to happen: *A storm* impends. *Death* impends.

im·pen·e·tra·bil·i·ty (ĭm′ pĕn′ ə trə bĭl′ ə tē) ***n-*** property of matter that makes it impossible for two bodies to occupy the same space at the same time.

im·pen·e·tra·ble (ĭm pĕn′ ə trə bəl) ***n-*** **1** such as cannot be penetrated, pierced, or passed through: *an* impenetrable *stone wall.* **2** impossible to understand: *an* impenetrable *theory.* **3** closed to reason, sympathy, etc.: *an* impenetrable *bias.* **—*adv-* im·pen′ e·tra·bly.**

im·pen·i·tent (ĭm pĕn′ ə tənt) ***adj-*** not sorry for one's sin or wrongdoing; unrepentant. ***n-*** person who is not repentant; hardened sinner. **—*n-* im·pen′ i·tence:** *his strong-willed* impenitence. ***adv-*** **im·pen′ i·tent·ly.**

im·per·a·tive (ĭm pĕr′ ə tĭv) ***adj-*** **1** not to be disobeyed or avoided; commanding; authoritative: *an* imperative *gesture.* **2** urgent; essential: *It is* imperative *to leave at once.* **3** *Grammar* expressing command or exhortation: *an* imperative *sentence.* ***n-*** **1** a command or order. **2** *Grammar* (1) mood of the verb expressing command or exhortation. In "Go away!" and "Stop, thief!" the verbs are in the **imperative mood.** (2) verb or verb form in this mood. **—*adv-* im·per′ a·tive·ly. *n-* im·per′ a·tive·ness.**

im·per·cep·ti·ble (ĭm′ pər sĕp′ tə bəl) ***adj-*** too small, gradual, or subtle to be aware of or to grasp: *a tree's* imperceptible *growth; an* imperceptible *shade of meaning.* **—*n-* im′ per·cep′ ti·bil·i·ty. *adv-* im′ per·cep′ ti·bly.**

imperf. imperfect.

im·per·fect (ĭm pûr′ fĭkt) ***adj-*** not perfect; faulty; defective. ***n-*** the imperfect tense. **—*adv-* im·per′ fect·ly. *n-* im·per′ fect·ness.**

im·per·fec·tion (ĭm′ pər fĕk′ shən) ***n-*** **1** lack of perfection. **2** a blemish; defect; fault; flaw.

imperfect tense *Grammar* ***n-*** tense of a verb which indicates action in the past, and going on, but not completed. Example: *He* was walking.

im·pe·ri·al (ĭm pêr′ ē əl) ***adj-*** having to do with or suitable to an empire, emperor, or empress: *an* imperial *policy;* imperial *robes.* ***n-*** small, pointed beard. **—*adv-* im·pe′ ri·al·ly.**

im·pe·ri·al·ism (ĭm pêr′ ē ə lĭz′ əm) ***n-*** **1** policy of extending the rule or control of a nation over other countries; also, support of such a policy. **2** power or system of government of an emperor. **—*n-* im·pe′ ri·al·ist′.** ***adj-*** **im·pe′ ri·al·ist′ ic.** ***adv-*** **im·pe′ ri·al·ist′ ic·al·ly.**

im·per·il (ĭm pĕr′ əl) ***vt-*** to put in danger; endanger: *Floods* imperiled *the lowlands.*

im·pe·ri·ous (ĭm pêr′ ē əs) ***n-*** haughty; domineering; masterful: *With an* imperious *gesture, she ordered us to leave.* **—*adv-* im·pe′ ri·ous·ly. *n-* im·pe′ ri·ous·ness.**

im·per·ish·a·ble (ĭm pĕr′ ĭsh ə bəl) ***adj-*** not perishable; not subject to decay. **—*n-* im·per′ ish·a·bil′ i·ty** or **im·per′ ish·a·ble·ness.** ***adv-*** **im·per′ ish·a·bly.**

im·per·ma·nent (ĭm pûr′ mə nənt) ***adj-*** not lasting; temporary. **—*n-* im·per′ ma·nence.** ***adv-*** **im·per′ ma·nent·ly.**

im·per·me·a·ble (ĭm pûr′ mē ə bəl) ***adj-*** not permitting permeation; impervious: *an* impermeable *layer of rock.* **—*n-* im·per′ me·a·bil′ i·ty. *adv-* im·per′ me·a·bly.**

im·per·son·al (ĭm pûr′ sən əl) ***adj-*** **1** not aimed at or referring to any particular person: *an* impersonal *discussion of student problems.* **2** not prejudiced; not influenced by personal feeling: *an* impersonal *approach to a subject.* **3** not existing as a person: *the* impersonal *forces of nature.* **—*n-* im·per′ son·al′ i·ty** (-ăl′ ə tē): *the* impersonality *of a court.* ***adv-*** **im·per′ son·al·ly.**

im·per·son·ate (ĭm pûr′ sə nāt′) ***vt-*** **[im·per·son·at·ed, im·per·son·at·ing]** **1** to act the character of; mimic; play the part of, especially on the stage. **2** to pretend to be (another person) in order to deceive: *The spy* impersonated *an officer.* **—*n-* im·per′ son·a′tion.**

im·per·son·a·tor (ĭm pûr′ sə nā′ tər) ***n-*** person who mimicks or pretends to be another person; especially, an entertainer who mimicks: *a clever* impersonator.

im·per·ti·nence (ĭm pûr′ tə nəns) ***n-*** **1** insolence; impudence. **2** impudent act or remark: *his rude* impertinences. **3** lack of relevance or pertinence.

im·per·ti·nent (ĭm pûr′ tə nənt) ***adj-*** **1** insolent; disrespectful: *an* impertinent *retort.* **2** not pertinent; irrelevant. **—*adv-* im·per′ ti·nent·ly.**

im·per·turb·a·ble (ĭm′ pər tûr′ bə bəl) ***adj-*** not excitable; calm; unshaken. **—*n-* im′ per·turb′ a·bil′ i·ty. *adv-* im′ per·turb′ a·bly.**

im·per·vi·ous (ĭm pûr′ vē əs) ***adj-*** **1** not permitting entrance or passage (to): *a tent* impervious *to rain.* **2** closed (to); not receptive (to): *She is* impervious *to criticism.* **—*adv-* im·per′ vi·ous·ly. *n-* im·per′ vi·ous·ness.**

im·pe·ti·go (ĭm′ pə tī′ gō) ***n-*** contagious skin disease marked by pus spots which later become crusted.

im·pet·u·os·i·ty (ĭm pĕch′ ōō ŏs′ ə tē) ***n-*** [*pl.* **im·pet·u·os·i·ties**] **1** impetuous nature or behavior: *the* impetuosity *of youth.* **2** impetuous act.

im·pet·u·ous (ĭm pĕch′ ōō əs) ***adj-*** **1** given to or marked by sudden, unthinking actions; impulsive; headlong; rash: *an* impetuous *person; an* impetuous *decision to quit.* **2** moving fast or with violent force: *an* impetuous *current.* **—*adv*- im·pet′u·ous·ly.** ***n*- im·pet′u·ous·ness:** *He means no harm, but his* impetuousness *causes trouble.*

im·pe·tus (ĭm′ pə təs) ***n*- 1** forward push; stimulus: *The tax decrease gave an* impetus *to industry.* **2** force or momentum by which a moving body tends to overcome resistance.

im·pi·e·ty (ĭm pī′ ə tē) ***n*- [*pl.* im·pi·e·ties] 1** lack of religious reverence. **2** irreverent or profane act.

im·pinge (ĭm pĭnj′) ***vi*- [im·pinged, im·ping·ing] 1** to strike or press (on, upon, or against): *Light rays* impinge *on the retina.* **2** to encroach; infringe (on): *to* impinge *upon our liberties.* **—*n*- im·pinge′ment.**

im·pi·ous (ĭm′ pē əs, *also* ĭm′ pī′-) ***adj*-** not pious; irreverent toward God and sacred things; profane. **—*adv*- im′pi·ous·ly** or **im′pi′ous·ly.** ***n*- im′pi·ous·ness** or **im′pi′ous·ness.**

imp·ish (ĭm′ pĭsh) ***adj*-** like, or suitable to, an imp; mischievous. **—*adv*- imp′ish·ly.** ***n*- imp′ish·ness.**

im·pla·ca·ble (ĭm plăk′ ə bəl, im plā′ kə-) ***adj*-** such as cannot be pacified, appeased, or reconciled; relentless: *an* implacable *hatred.* **—*n*- im·pla′ca·bil′i·ty.** ***adv*- im·pla′ca·bly.**

im·plant (ĭm plănt′) ***vt*-** to plant or set in deeply; hence, to fix firmly in the consciousness: *to* implant *an idea.* **—*n*- im′plan·ta′tion.**

[1]im·ple·ment (ĭm′ plə mənt) ***n*-** tool or instrument with which work is done: *Hoes are garden* implements.

[2]im·ple·ment (ĭm′ plə mĕnt′) ***vt*-** to carry out by concrete means and acts; put into practical effect: *to* implement *a plan.*

im·pli·cate (ĭm′ plə kāt′) ***vt*- [im·pli·ca·ted, im·pli·ca·ting]** to show or say that (someone or something) has caused or aided in something harmful: *The thief* implicated *two helpers.*

im·pli·ca·tion (ĭm′ plə kā′ shən) ***n*- 1** something that is implied: *The* implications *are more important than the direct statements.* **2** an implicating in something harmful: *the thief's* implication *of his two helpers.*

im·plic·it (ĭm plĭs′ ĭt) ***adj*- 1** understood though not expressed; implied: *an* implicit *threat.* **2** trusting in the word or authority of another without question; complete; unreserved: *an* implicit *faith.* **—*adv*- im·plic′it·ly.**

im·plode (ĭm plōd′) ***vi*- [im·plod·ed, im·plod·ing]** to cave in with explosive violence because external pressure is greater than internal pressure.

im·plore (ĭm plôr′) ***vt*- [im·plored, im·plor·ing]** to ask earnestly; beg; entreat: *to* implore *aid and protection.* **—*n*- im·plor′er.** ***adv*- im·plor′ing·ly.**

im·ply (ĭm plī′) ***vt*- [im·plied, im·plying]** to mean without saying directly; suggest indirectly; hint: *He didn't say he would vote for us, but he* implied *that he would.*

►For usage note see INFER.

im·po·lite (ĭm′ pə līt′) ***adj*-** discourteous; showing bad manners; not polite. **—*adv*- im·po·lite′ly.** ***n*- im·po·lite′ness.**

im·pol·i·tic (ĭm pŏl′ ə tĭk) ***adj*-** not showing shrewd and careful judgment; unwise: *an* impolitic *decision.*

im·pon·der·a·ble (ĭm pŏn′ dər ə bəl) ***n*-** something that cannot be exactly known, predicted, or measured: *the* imponderables *of war.* **—*adv*- im·pon′der·a·bly.** ***n*- im·pon′der·a·ble·ness.**

[1]im·port (ĭm′ pôrt′) ***vt*- (*also* ĭm pôrt′)** to bring in (merchandise, products, etc.) from another country: *The United States* imports *tea from India.* ***n*-** something so brought in: *Coffee is one of our* imports *from Brazil.* [from Latin **importāre**, "to carry; bring in or about."]

[2]im·port (ĭm pôrt′) ***vi*-** to mean; signify; imply: *What does that cloud* import? ***n*- (*also* ĭm′ pôrt) 1** meaning; significance: *the* import *of an act.* **2** importance: *a matter of no* import. [from Medieval Latin **importāre** meaning "to be important; to signify."]

im·por·tance (ĭm pôr′ təns, ĭm pôr′-) ***n*-** condition of being meaningful, necessary, powerful, or otherwise important: *the* importance *of reading.*

im·por·tant (ĭm pôr′ tənt, ĭm pôr′-) ***adj*- 1** filled with meaning or possible consequences; serious; valuable: *an* important *test*; *an* important *day in history.* **2** having power or authority: *The governor of a state is an* important *man.* **—*adv*- im·por′tant·ly.**

im·por·ta·tion (ĭm′ pôr tā′ shən) ***n*- 1** a bringing in of goods from other countries. **2** something brought in from another country; an import.

im·port·er (ĭm pôr′ tər, ĭm′ pôr′ tər) ***n*-** one who imports; one who brings goods into a country from abroad.

im·por·tu·nate (im′ pôr′ chə nət, ĭm pôr′ tyo͞o-) ***adj*-** insistent; persistently demanding; clamoring: *We have heard their* importunate *demands for justice and aid.* **—*adv*- im·por′tu·nate·ly.** ***n*- im·por′tu·nate·ness.**

im·por·tune (ĭm pər tyo͞on′, -to͞on′) ***vt*- [im·por·tuned, im·por·tun·ing]** to insist; demand; entreat; implore: *He* importuned *me for help.* **—*n*- im·por·tu′ni·ty.**

im·pose (ĭm pōz′) ***vt*- [im·posed, im·pos·ing] 1** to put on as a tax, burden, penalty, charge, etc.: *The judge* imposed *a fine.* **2** to force: *He didn't* impose *his advice on me, but I listened to him willingly.* **—*n*- im·pos′er.**

impose on or **upon** to take advantage of.

im·pos·ing (ĭm pō′ zĭng) ***adj*-** worthy of notice; demanding attention; impressive. **—*adv*- im·pos′ing·ly.**

im·po·si·tion (ĭm′ pə zĭsh′ ən) ***n*- 1** the act of imposing something: *the* imposition *of a tax.* **2** tax, punishment, etc., that is imposed: *an* imposition *on imports.* **3** intrusion or demand upon someone's time, hospitality, etc. **4** trick or deception.

im·pos·si·bil·i·ty (ĭm pos′ ə bĭl′ ə tē) ***n*- [*pl.* im·pos·si·bil·i·ties] 1** condition of not being possible: *the* impossibility *of knowing what will happen next week.* **2** something impossible: *To live twice is an* impossibility.

im·pos·si·ble (ĭm pŏs′ ə bəl) ***adj*- 1** such as cannot be done or cannot happen; not possible: *It is* impossible *to be in two places at the same time.* **2** not easy or not convenient: *It is* impossible *for me to be there on time.* **3** hard to endure; objectionable: *an* impossible *person.* **—*adv*- im·pos′si·bly.**

im·post (ĭm′ pōst′) ***n*-** tax or duty, especially one levied by the government on goods brought into a country.

im·pos·tor (ĭm pŏs′ tər) ***n*-** person who tries to deceive others by pretending to be someone or something else.

im·pos·ture (ĭm pŏs′ chər) ***n*-** a fraud or deception; especially, a deceitful impersonation.

im·po·tent (ĭm′ pə tənt) ***adj*-** lacking power; weak; unable to act. **—*n*- im′po·tence.** ***adv*- im′po·tent·ly.**

im·pound (ĭm pound′) ***vt*- 1** to take by law; confiscate. **2** to shut up or confine: *to* impound *stray cattle.* **3** to collect (water) in a reservoir.

im·pov·er·ish (ĭm pŏv′ ər ĭsh) ***vt*- 1** to make poor. **2** to exhaust (natural resources, fertility, etc.): *Bad farming methods* impoverished *the soil.* **—*n*- im·pov′er·ish·er.** ***n*- im·pov′er·ish·ment:** *the* impoverishment *of the soil.*

im·prac·ti·ca·ble (ĭm prăk′ tĭ kə bəl) ***adj*-** such as cannot be put into effect or operation; unworkable: *an* impracticable *plan.* **—*n*- im·prac′ti·ca·bil′i·ty.** ***adv*- im·prac′ti·ca·bly.**

im·prac·ti·cal (ĭm prăk′ tĭ kəl) ***adj*-** not practical; not concerned with realities: *an* impractical *scheme*; *an* impractical *man.* **—*n*- im·prac′ti·cal′i·ty (-kăl′ ə tē).** ***adv*- im·prac′ti·cal·ly.**

im·pre·ca·tion (ĭm′ prə kā′ shən) ***n*-** a curse; a calling down of evil on someone.

im·preg·na·ble (ĭm prĕg′ nə bəl) ***adj-*** secure against attack; not to be overcome or taken by force; unconquerable; invincible: *an* impregnable *fortress in the hills.* **—*n-* im·preg′ na·bil′ i·ty. *adv-* im·preg′ na·bly.**

im·preg·nate (ĭm prĕg′ nāt′) ***vt-*** [**im·preg·nat·ed, im·preg·nat·ing**] **1** to make pregnant; fertilize. **2** to cause to be saturated with. **—*n-* im′ preg·na′ tion.**

im·pre·sa·ri·o (ĭm′ prə săr′ ē ō, -sär′ ē ō) ***n-*** [*pl.* **im·pre·sa·ri·os**] person who arranges or directs concerts, operas, etc.

[1]**im·press** (ĭm′ prĕs′) ***n-*** mark made by, or as by, a stamp; impression. [from Latin **impressum,** from **imprimire,** "to seal; press into or upon."]

[2]**im·press** (ĭm prĕs′) ***vt-*** **1** to strike (someone) as remarkable and memorable, especially in a favorable way: *His wit* impressed *me. The candidate does not* impress *me.* **2** to mark by, or as if by, pressing with a stamp or die; stamp: *to* impress *a seal in wax*; *to* impress *an idea on one's audience.* [from [1]**impress.**] **—*n-* im·press′ er.**

[3]**im·press** (ĭm prĕs′) ***vt-*** to force into military or naval service by seizing and holding, once a customary practice: *to* impress *a new crew for the frigate.* [from [2]**in-,** plus [2]**press.**] **—*n-* im·press′ ment.**

im·pres·sion (ĭm prĕsh′ ən) ***n-*** **1** an effect or impact on the mind or feelings: *Her first airplane ride made a strong* impression *on her.* **2** idea that is not clear or certain; especially, a judgment made quickly without strong factual basis: *I had the* impression *that he was in a hurry. It's only an* impression, *but I think this is a very good car.* **3** mark made by pressing: *the* impression *of a seal on wax.* **4** a mimicking; imitation: *Tom gave his* impression *of Winston Churchill.*

im·pres·sion·a·ble (ĭm prĕsh′ ən ə bəl) ***adj-*** easily influenced; very sensitive to impressions. **—*n-* im·pres′ sion·a·bil′ ity. *adv-* im·pres′ sion·a·bly.**

im·pres·sion·ism (ĭm prĕsh′ ən ĭz′ əm) ***n-*** **1** style of painting that tries to capture impressions of light on surfaces with short strokes of varied colors and no clear outlines. **2** in music and literature, a style based on this, in which the total impression of a moment, scene, etc., is built by a series of sounds or words that suggest it. **—*n-* im·pres′ sion·ist. *adj-* im·pres′ sion·is′ tic.**

im·pres·sive (ĭm prĕs′ ĭv) ***adj-*** strongly affecting the mind, feelings, or actions, especially in a favorable way: *The new government buildings are* impressive. **—*adv-* im·pres′ sive·ly. *n-* im·pres′ sive·ness.**

im·pri·ma·tur (ĭm′ prə mā′ tər) ***n-*** consent of an authority, especially a bishop of the Roman Catholic Church, for the publication of printed matter.

[1]**im·print** (ĭm prĭnt′) ***vt-*** to print; impress: *They* imprinted *the birth certificate with an official seal.*

[2]**im·print** (ĭm′ prĭnt′) ***n-*** **1** a mark; impression: *the* imprint *of a foot in the sand.* **2** printer's or publisher's name, and the place and date of publication, printed on the title page or at the end of a book.

im·pris·on (ĭm prĭz′ ən) ***vt-*** **1** to put or keep in prison. **2** to keep shut up; confine: *to* imprison *a tiger in a cage.* **—*n-* im·pris′ on·ment.**

im·prob·a·ble (ĭm prŏb′ ə bəl) ***adj-*** not probable; not likely to happen, exist, or be true: *an* improbable *result*; *an* improbable *story.* **—*adv-* im·prob′ a·bly. *n-* im·prob′ a·bil′ i·ty.**

im·promp·tu (ĭm prŏmp′ to͞o) ***adj-*** without preparation; offhand: *an* impromptu *picnic.* ***adv-***: *to speak* impromptu. ***n-*** something, such as a musical composition, that is made, done, or performed without preparation.

im·prop·er (ĭm prŏp′ ər) ***adj-*** **1** not proper; not suitable: *to use* improper *tools.* **2** contrary to good taste: *It is* improper *to eat peas with a knife.* **3** wrong; incorrect: *the* improper *use of a word.* **—*adv-* im·prop′ er·ly.**

improper fraction See *fraction.*

im·pro·pri·e·ty (ĭm′ prə prī′ ə tē) ***n-*** [*pl.* **im·pro·pri·e·ties**] **1** lack of propriety. **2** something as in language or conduct that is incorrect or indecent.

im·prove (ĭm pro͞ov′) ***vt-*** [**im·proved, im·prov·ing**] to make better: *Exercise* improves *the posture.* ***vi-*** to become better: *Her health* improved *in the milder climate.* **—*adj-* im·prov′ a·ble. *n-* im·prov′ er.**

improve on to make or do something better than.

im·prove·ment (ĭm pro͞ov′ mənt) ***n-*** **1** a making or becoming better: *Much* improvement *of roads is necessary.* **2** a change or addition that makes something better or more valuable: *a household* improvement.

im·prov·i·dent (ĭm prŏv′ ə dĕnt′, -dənt) ***adj-*** **1** lacking in thrift or foresight. **2** not providing for the future. **—*n-* im·prov′ i·dence. *adv-* im·prov′ i·dent·ly.**

im·prov·i·sa·tion (ĭm prŏv′ ə zā′ shən) ***n-*** **1** an improvising: *the hasty* improvisation *of a shelter.* **2** something improvised: *This shelf is an* improvisation.

im·pro·vise (ĭm′ prə vīz′) ***vt-*** [**im·pro·vised, im·pro·vis·ing**] **1** to make up as one goes along: *As he sang, he* improvised *words to fit the music.* **2** to invent or construct to fit an immediate need: *The scouts* improvised *a shelter for the night.* **—*n-* im′ pro·vi′ ser.**

im·pru·dent (ĭm pro͞o′ dənt) ***adj-*** not wise or prudent; heedless; rash: *It is* imprudent *to cross against the lights.* **—*n-* im·pru′ dence. *adv-* im·pru′ dent·ly.**

im·pu·dence (ĭm′ pyo͝o dəns) ***n-*** disrespect; sauciness.

im·pu·dent (ĭm′ pyo͝o dənt) ***adj-*** disrespectful; saucy; not very well mannered. **—*adv-* im′ pu·dent·ly.**

im·pugn (ĭm pyo͞on′) ***vt-*** **1** to raise questions about: *to* impugn *someones motives.* **2** to attack by arguments as false: *to* impugn *a claim for damages.* **—*n-* im·pugn′ er.**

im·pulse (ĭm′ pŭls′) ***n-*** **1** sudden desire to do something: *Henrietta acts on* impulse, *without stopping to think.* **2** sudden push or driving force: *The* impulse *of the storm drove waves high up on the shore.* **3** sudden increase or peak; surge; pulse: *electrical* impulses.

im·pul·sion (ĭm pŭl′ shən) ***n-*** **1** an impelling: *This engine is moved by the* impulsion *of expanding steam.* **2** something that drives or forces: *Duty was his main* impulsion. **3** tendency to move forward; impetus: *the* impulsion *given to science by Pasteur.* **4** strong impulse to act or do something; compulsion.

im·pul·sive (ĭm pŭl′ sĭv) ***adj-*** **1** coming from an impulse: *an* impulsive *smile.* **2** moved by or likely to act on sudden feeling: *She is so* impulsive *she is always speaking out of turn.* **3** pushing forward: *an* impulsive *force.* **—*adv-* im·pul′ sive·ly. *n-* im·pul′ sive·ness.**

im·pu·ni·ty (ĭm pyo͞o′ nə tē) ***n-*** freedom from punishment, injury, or loss: *You cannot steal with* impunity.

im·pure (ĭm pyo͝or′) ***adj-*** **1** unclean; unwholesome; contaminated; dirty: *to purify* impure *water.* **2** mixed with another substance, especially something inferior: *There are laws against* impure *drugs.* **3** bad; corrupt in thought or action. **—*adv-* im·pure′ ly. *n-* im·pure′ ness.**

im·pu·ri·ty (ĭm pyo͝or′ ə tē) ***n-*** [*pl.* **im·pu·ri·ties**] **1** something that makes a substance impure: *the* impurities *in water.* **2** lack of moral purity.

im·pu·ta·tion (ĭm′ pyə tā′ shən, ĭm′ pyo͞o-) ***n-*** **1** an imputing, especially of guilt or wrongdoing. **2** something imputed.

---

fāte, făt, dâre, bärn; bē, bĕt, mêre; bīte, bĭt; nōte, hŏt, môre, dóg; fŭn, fûr; to͞o, bo͝ok; oil; out; ta*r*; thin; *th*en; hw for wh as in *wh*at; zh for s as in u*s*ual; ə for a, e, i, o, u, as in *a*go, lin*e*n, per*i*l, at*o*m, min*u*s

im·pute (ĭm pyo͞ot′) *vt-* [**im·pu·ted, im·pu·ting**] to set to the account of; attribute; ascribe: *to* impute *one's failure to poor health.* —*adj-* **im·pu′ta·ble.**

in (ĭn) *prep-* **1** inside: *to put clothes* in *a trunk*; *to live* in *a town.* **2** subjected to a situation, condition, etc.: *I am* in *pain.* **3** into: *She has just gone* in *the house.* **4** during: *He came* in *the evening.* **5** after: *Call back* in *an hour.* **6** at the time of: *He left* in *the middle of May.* **7** for: *a parade* in *honor of the returning heroes.* **8** with the use of: *a note scribbled* in *pencil.* **9** wearing: *a woman* in *a flowered hat.* **10** arranged so as to make: *houses* in *a row.* **11** for the purpose of: *used* in *baking.* **12** according to: *This is wrong* in *my opinion.* **13** regarding; in respect to: *People vary* in *ability.* **14** influenced or affected by: *to squeal* in *delight*; *never* in *doubt.* *adv-* **1** toward the inside: *He went* in. **2** inside a place; at home: *My mother is* in. *Is the doctor* in? **3** into an activity or function: *Join* in *the fun. I got* in *by one vote.* **4** into a condition, position, or place: *Throw it* in *with the rest. We have just moved* in. **5** *Informal* preferred or fashionable: *Large hats are* in *this year.* *adj-* **1** incoming: *the* in *line of traffic.* **2** having power: *the* in *party.* *n- Informal* **1** means of entering or reaching a desirable situation: *He has an* in *with the agency.* **2** **ins** those in power or influence. *Hom-* inn.

in for due for, especially something unpleasant: *We are* in for *a long, hot summer.* **ins and outs** all the details: *He knows the* ins and outs *of the business.* **in that** because; since; for the reason that.

In symbol for indium.

[1]**in-** *prefix* not; lack of: in*audible*; in*ability.* Also **-im; -ir; -il:** im*practical*; ir*regular*; il*logical.* [from Latin **in-**, "not."]

[2]**in-** *prefix* in or on: in*side*; in*land.* Also **-im; -ir; -il:** im*part*; ir*rigate*; il*lusion.* [from Latin **in-**, "on; in; into."]

[3]**in-** *prefix* **1** into: in*ject.* **2** toward: in*cline.* **3** within: in*door.* [from Old English **in-**, from **in**, "in; into; toward."]

in. 1 inch. 2 inches.

in·a·bil·i·ty (ĭn′ ə bĭl′ ə tē) *n-* [*pl.* **in·a·bil·i·ties**] lack of power or means: *an* inability *to sleep*; inability *to pay.*

in ab·sen·tia (ăb sĕn′ chə) *Latin* when the person concerned is absent: *to convict him* in absentia.

in·ac·ces·si·ble (ĭn′ ək sĕs′ ə bəl) *adj-* impossible or difficult to reach or get to: *a place* inaccessible *by car.* —*n-* **in′ac·ces′si·bil′i·ty.** *adv-* **in′ac·ces′si·bly.**

in·ac·cu·ra·cy (ĭn ăk′ yər ə sē) *n-* [*pl.* **in·ac·cu·ra·cies**] **1** lack of accuracy or exactness: *the* inaccuracy *of a statement.* **2** an error: *a page full of* inaccuracies.

in·ac·cu·rate (ĭn ăk′ yər ət) *adj-* not correct; not accurate; not exact. —*adv-* **in·ac′cu·rate·ly.**

in·ac·tion (ĭn ăk′ shən) *n-* lack of motion, especially of effort; idleness: *His* inaction *was his undoing.*

in·ac·tive (ĭn ăk′ tĭv) *adj-* **1** not moving about; not active: *Sickness made the patient* inactive. **2** not in use or action: *an* inactive *bank account*; *an* inactive *volcano.* —*adv-* **in·ac′tive·ly.** *n-* **in′ac·tiv′i·ty.**

in·ad·e·qua·cy (ĭn ăd′ ə kwə sē) *n-* [*pl.* **in·ad·e·qua·cies**] **1** lack of what is needed or the amount needed: *an* inadequacy *of funds.* **2** defect; fault.

in·ad·e·quate (ĭn ăd′ ə kwət) *adj-* not sufficient; not enough to meet some need: *The dining space is* inadequate *for our large group.* —*adv-* **in·ad′e·quate·ly.**

in·ad·mis·si·ble (ĭn′ əd mĭs′ ə bəl) *adj-* such as cannot be admitted or allowed, especially as evidence: *Hearsay evidence is* inadmissible. —*n-* **in′ad·mis′si·bil′i·ty.**

in·ad·vert·ence (ĭn′ əd vûr′ təns) *n-* **1** lack of proper care or attention: *The mistake was due to* inadvertence. **2** error caused by such a lack: *It was an* inadvertence.

in·ad·vert·ent (ĭn′ əd vûr′ tənt) *adj-* due to heedlessness; unintended; thoughtless: *an* inadvertent *slight.* —*adv-* **in′ad·ver′tent·ly.**

in·ad·vis·a·ble (ĭn′ əd vī′ zə bəl) *adj-* not recommended; not wise or sensible: *It is* inadvisable *to skate on thin ice.* —*n-* **in′ad·vis′a·bil′i·ty.** *adv-* **in′ad·vis′a·bly.**

in·al·ien·a·ble (ĭn āl′ yən ə bəl) *adj-* such as cannot be taken away or transferred: *an* inalienable *right.* —*n-* **in·al′ien·a·bil′i·ty.** *adv-* **in·al′ien·a·bly.**

in·ane (ĭn ān′) *adj-* empty; foolish; silly: *He makes* inane *remarks.* —*adv-* **in·ane′ly.** *n-* **in·ane′ness.**

in·an·i·mate (ĭn ăn′ ə mət) *adj-* **1** lifeless; nonliving: *the* inanimate *stones.* **2** dull; spiritless: *an* inanimate *conversation.* —*adv-* **in·an′i·mate·ly.** *n-* **in·an′i·mate·ness.**

in·an·i·tion (ĭn′ ə nĭsh′ ən) *n-* emptiness; weakness; exhaustion from hunger.

in·an·i·ty (ĭ năn′ ə tē) *n-* [*pl.* **in·an·i·ties**] **1** foolishness; silliness; stupidity. **2** emptiness. **3** something foolish, stupid, or empty.

in·ap·pli·ca·ble (ĭn ăp′ lĭ kə bəl) *adj-* such as cannot be suited or applied to a definite purpose; not to be used or applied: *This answer is* inapplicable *to the problem.* —*n-* **in·ap′pli·ca·bil′i·ty.** *adv-* **in·ap′pli·ca·bly.**

in·ap·pre·ci·a·ble (ĭn′ ə prē′ shə bəl) *adj-* too small to be important; negligible: *an* inappreciable *difference in tone.* —*adv-* **in′ap·pre′ci·a·bly.**

in·ap·pro·pri·ate (ĭn′ ə prō′ prē ət) *adj-* not correct or suitable: *A party dress is* inappropriate *for a hike.* —*adv-* **in′ap·pro′pri·ate·ly.** *n-* **in′ap·pro′pri·ate·ness.**

in·apt (ĭn ăpt′) *adj-* **1** not suitable: *an* inapt *remark.* **2** inept. —*adv-* **in·apt′ly.** *n-* **in·apt′ness.**

► For usage note see INEPT.

in·apt·i·tude (ĭn ăp′ tə to͞od′, -tyo͞od′) *n-* lack of special fitness or skill; unfitness: *an* inaptitude *for mathematics.*

in·ar·tic·u·late (ĭn′ är tĭk′ yə lət) *adj-* **1** incapable of speaking; dumb: *the* inarticulate *animals*; *almost* inarticulate *with surprise.* **2** not speaking easily or fluently: *a flustered and* inarticulate *man.* **3** not expressed in words: *an* inarticulate *rage.* **4** not jointed. —*adv-* **in′ar·tic′u·late·ly.** *n-* **in′ar·tic′u·late·ness.**

in·ar·tis·tic (ĭn′ är tĭs′ tĭk) *adj-* not artistic. —*adv-* **in′ar·tis′ti·cal·ly.**

in·as·much as (ĭn′ əz mŭch′) *conj-* since; because: *You may leave now,* inasmuch as *you wish to.*

in·at·ten·tion (ĭn′ ə tĕn′ shən) *n-* failure to put one's mind on something; heedlessness: *A moment's* inattention *caused the accident.*

in·at·ten·tive (ĭn′ ə tĕn′ tĭv) *adj-* not paying attention. —*adv-* **in′at·ten′tive·ly.** *n-* **in′at·ten′tive·ness.**

in·au·di·ble (ĭn ȯd′ ə bəl) *adj-* such as cannot be heard; not audible: *an* inaudible *remark.* —*adv-* **in·aud′i·bly.** *n-* **in·aud′i·bil′i·ty.**

in·aug·u·ral (ĭn ȯg′ yo͝or əl, ĭn ȯ′ gər-) *adj-* **1** having to do with an inauguration: *an* inaugural *parade.* **2** opening; initial; first: *His* inaugural *remark.* *n-* speech made at the beginning of a term of office.

in·au·gu·rate (ĭn ȯ′ gə rāt′, -gyə rāt′) *vt-* [**in·au·gu·rat·ed, in·au·gu·rat·ing**] **1** to place in office with formal ceremony; install: *to* inaugurate *a president.* **2** to make a formal beginning of; commence: *to* inaugurate *a policy.* **3** to open formally for use: *to* inaugurate *a park.*

in·au·gu·ra·tion (in ȯ′ gə rā′ shən, -gyə rā′ shən) *n-* an inaugurating, especially a placing in office with formal ceremony: *the impressive Presidential* inauguration.

Inauguration Day *n-* the January 20 following a Presidential election in the United States, the day on which the winner is inaugurated.

in·aug·u·ra·tor (ĭn ȯ′ gə rā′ tər, -gyə rā′ tər) *n-* person who inaugurates.

in·aus·pi·cious (ĭn′ ȯ spĭsh′ əs) ***adj-*** unlucky; unfavorable: *an* inauspicious *beginning.* **—*adv-* in′ aus·pi′ cious·ly.** ***n-*** **in′ aus·pi′ cious·ness.**

in·board (ĭn′ bôrd′) ***adv-*** **1** inside the hull of a ship or boat: *They heaved the net* inboard. **2** toward the center line of the fuselage of an aircraft. ***adj-*** **1** located inside the hull: *an* inboard *engine.* **2** on an aircraft, nearest the center line of the fuselage: *the* inboard *port engine.* **3** of boats, powered by an inboard engine. ***n-*** a small boat powered by an inboard engine: *a 20-foot* inboard.

in·born (ĭn′ bôrn′) ***n-*** present in a person at birth; natural: *Musicianship is often an* inborn *talent.*

in·bound (ĭn′ bound′) ***adj-*** approaching a destination: *That is the* inbound *plane.*

in·bred (ĭn′ brĕd′) ***adj-*** **1** descended from closely related ancestors: *Many royal families are* inbred. **2** natural; innate: *an* inbred *kindness.*

in·breed (ĭn′ brēd′) ***vt-*** **[in·bred, in·breed·ing]** to mate (closely related animals). ***vi-*** to mate or breed within a closely related group.

in·breed·ing (ĭn′ brē′ dĭng) ***n-*** **1** the systematic mating of successive generations of plants or animals in order to improve the breed. Inbreeding can also damage the breed if any of the original stock is defective. **2** marriage between people who are closely related.

inc. **1** incorporated. **2** inclosure. **3** inclusive. **4** including.

In·ca (ĭng′ kə) ***n-*** **1** the ruler or a member of the ruling family of the great Andean Indian empire destroyed by Pizarro in 1532. **2** [*pl.* **In·cas,** also **In·ca**] a member of the leading people of this Indian empire. **—*adj-* In′ can** or **In·ca′ ic** (ĭng kā′ ĭk).

in·cal·cu·la·ble (ĭn kăl′ kyə lə bəl) ***adj-*** **1** beyond estimate; very great: *His mistake did* incalculable *harm.* **2** not dependable; unpredictable: *a person of* incalculable *moods.* **—*n-* in·cal′ cu·la·bil′ i·ty.** ***adv-*** **in·cal′ cu·la·bly.**

in·can·des·cent (ĭn′ kən dĕs′ ənt) ***adj-*** glowing with intense heat; bright; brilliant. **—*n-* in′ can·des′ cence.**

incandescent lamp ***n-*** lamp with a metal filament that gives off light when an electric current makes it hot.

in·can·ta·tion (ĭn′ kăn tā′ shən) ***n-*** **1** the use of charms or spells, sung or spoken, as a part of a magic ritual. **2** the words used.

in·ca·pa·ble (ĭn kā′ pə bəl) ***adj-*** **1** not having the power or ability (of): *to be* incapable of *speaking.* **2** lacking ability: *an* incapable *man.* **—*n-* in·ca′ pa·bil′ i·ty.**

incapable of not able to undergo; not susceptible of: *His style is* incapable of *improvement.*

in·ca·pac·i·tate (ĭn′ kə păs′ ə tāt′) ***vt-*** **[in·ca·pa·ci·ta·ted, in·ca·pa·ci·ta·ting]** to make powerless or unfit; disable: *Old age* incapacitates *one for hard labor.*

in·ca·pac·i·ty (ĭn′ kə păs′ ə tē) ***n-*** [*pl.* **in·ca·pac·i·ties**] **1** lack of ability or aptitude: *an* incapacity *for work.* **2** disability; defect: *to suffer from an* incapacity.

in·car·cer·ate (ĭn kär′ sə rāt′) ***vt-*** **[in·car·cer·at·ed, in·car·cer·at·ing]** to shut up in a prison; confine; imprison. **—*n-* in·car′ cer·a′ tion.**

in·car·na·dine (ĭn kär′ nə dīn′, *also* -dēn′) ***vt-*** **[in·car·na·dined, in·car·na·din·ing]** to dye or stain red.

[1]**in·car·nate** (ĭn kär′ nāt′) ***vt-*** **[in·car·nat·ed, in·car·nat·ing]** **1** to give a body to; clothe with flesh: *Medieval belief* incarnated *the devil in many animal forms.* **2** to give a real or material form to: *This policy* incarnates *modern theory.*

[2]**in·car·nate** (ĭn kär′ nət, -nāt′) ***adj-*** personified; embodied in human form.

in·car·na·tion (ĭn′ kär nā′ shən) ***n-*** **1** the taking on of a material form, especially human. **2** person or thing considered to represent an ideal or principle: *He is the* incarnation *of honesty.* **3 the Incarnation** the birth and life of Jesus Christ as a human being.

in·case (ĭn kās′) ***vt-*** **[in·cased, in·cas·ing]** to enclose in a box or other solid covering; surround with anything: *to* incase *oneself in armor.* **—*n-* in·case′ ment.**

in·cau·tious (ĭn kȯ′ shəs) ***adj-*** not careful or prudent; heedless. **—*adv-* in·cau′ tious·ly.** ***n-*** **in·cau′ tious·ness.**

in·cen·di·a·rism (ĭn sĕn′ dē ə rĭz′ əm) ***n-*** incendiary behavior or action.

in·cen·di·ar·y (ĭn sĕn′ dē ĕr′ ē) ***adj-*** **1** stirring up strife, violence, or emotion: *an* incendiary *speech.* **2** likely to or designed to set things on fire: *a man with an* incendiary *tendency*; *an* incendiary *bomb.* ***n-*** [*pl.* **in·cen·di·ar·ies**] **1** person who stirs up strife or violence. **2** person who sets destructive fires; pyromaniac. **3** bomb or grenade designed to set fires.

[1]**in·cense** (ĭn′ sĕns′) ***n-*** **1** substance that produces a sweet odor when burned. **2** perfume or smoke given off by such a substance when burned. **3** any pleasant odor: *the sweet* incense *of blossoms.* [from Old French **encens** meaning "burnt spices; something burned or set on fire," from the same Latin word as [2]**incense.**]

[2]**in·cense** (ĭn sĕns′) ***vt-*** **[in·censed, in·cens·ing]** to infuriate; make extremely angry. [from Old French **incenser** from Latin **incensum** from Latin **incendere** meaning "to set on fire; inflame."]

in·cen·tive (ĭn sĕn′ tĭv) ***n-*** a motive for action, effort, etc.: *Love of country was his* incentive.

in·cep·tion (ĭn sĕp′ shən) ***n-*** beginning; first stage: *The movement was successful from its* inception.

in·ces·sant (ĭn sĕs′ ənt) ***adj-*** constant; not stopping: *an* incessant *chirping of insects.* **—*adv-* in·ces′ sant·ly.**

in·cest (ĭn′ sĕst′) ***n-*** sexual relationship between persons so closely related that their marriage is forbidden by law.

in·ces·tu·ous (ĭn sĕs′ chōō əs) ***adj-*** between persons too closely related for lawful marriage. **—*adv-* in·ces′ tu·ous·ly.** ***n-*** **in·ces′ tu·ous·ness.**

inch (ĭnch) ***n-*** measure of length, twelve of which make a foot. *Abbr.* in. ***vi-*** to move little by little.

by inches by a slender margin: *That car missed me* by inches. **every inch** in all ways; entirely: *She was* every inch *a lady.* **inch by inch** little by little; bit by bit: *I climbed* inch by inch. **not yield an inch** not surrender the slightest bit. **within an inch of** extremely close to.

in·cho·ate (ĭn kō′ ət) ***adj-*** just beginning; not yet fully formed or in order; incipient: *to have a vague,* inchoate *idea.* **—*adv-* in·cho′ ate·ly.** ***n-*** **in·cho′ ate·ness.**

inch·worm (ĭnch′ wûrm′) ***n-*** measuring worm.

in·ci·dence (ĭn′ sə dəns) ***n-*** **1** the rate of separate cases or events of something; occurrence: *A high* incidence *of crime.* **2** the meeting of a ray of light, a bullet, line, etc., with a surface. **3** angle of incidence.

in·ci·dent (ĭn′ sə dənt) ***n-*** a happening; event; episode: *He told us* incidents *from his childhood.* ***adj-*** **1** coming along with something else; accompanying: *skiing and its* incident *risks.* **2** hitting against something, especially at an angle: *an* incident *light ray.*

incident to likely to happen in connection with (something else): *Risks are* incident to *a soldier's life.*

in·ci·den·tal (ĭn′ sə dĕn′ təl) ***adj-*** **1** happening in connection with something more important: *the* incidental *expenses of a trip*; incidental *music for a play.* **2** made or added casually; thrown in: *an* incidental

---

fāte, făt, dâre, bärn; bē, bĕt, mêre; bīte, bĭt; nōte, hŏt, môre, dóg; fŭn, fûr; tōō, bŏŏk; oil; out; tar; thin; then; hw for wh as in *wh*at; zh for s as in u*s*ual; ə for a, e, i, o, u, as in *a*go, lin*e*n, per*i*l, at*o*m, min*u*s

remark. **3 incidentals** small, unimportant items. ***—adv-* in′ ci·den′ tal·ly.**

in·cin·er·ate (ĭn sĭn′ ə răt′) ***vt-*** **[in·cin·er·at·ed, in·cin·er·at·ing]** to burn to ashes; dispose of by burning: *to* incinerate *garbage.* ***—n-* in·cin′ er·a′ tion.**

in·cin·er·a·tor (ĭn sĭn′ ə rā′ tər) ***n-*** person or thing that incinerates, especially a furnace for burning trash.

in·cip·i·ent (ĭn sĭp′ ē ənt) ***adj-*** beginning to be or appear: *an* incipient *revolution.* ***—n-* in·cip′ i·ence** or **in·cip′ i·en·cy**: *the* incipience *of war.* ***adv-* in·cip′ i·ent·ly.**

in·cise (ĭn sīz′) ***vt-*** **[in·cis·ed, in·cis·ing]** to engrave; carve; cut into: *to* incise *a design.*

in·cised (ĭn sīzd′) ***adj-*** engraved; carved.

in·ci·sion (ĭn sĭzh′ ən) ***n-*** **1** act of cutting into or engraving something. **2** thin cut, especially one made by a scalpel in surgery: *to close an* incision *with stitches.*

in·ci·sive (ĭn sī′ sĭv) ***adj-*** **1** sharp; penetrating: *an* incisive *study of water pollution.* **2** cutting; biting: *an* incisive *wit.* ***—adv-* in·ci′ sive·ly.** ***n-* in·ci′ sive·ness.**

in·ci·sor (ĭn sī′ zər) ***n-*** any one of the chisel-shaped cutting teeth in the front of both jaws of all mammals, including man. For picture, see *tooth.*

in·ci·ta·tion (ĭn′ sī tā′ shən) ***n-*** a stirring up or provoking: *the* incitation *of the mob to violence.*

in·cite (ĭn sīt′) ***vt-*** **[in·cit·ed, in·cit·ing]** to rouse; stir up: *The sailor* incited *the crew to mutiny.* ***—n-* in·cit′ er.**

in·cite·ment (ĭn sīt′ mənt) ***n-*** **1** an inciting; stirring up; incitation: *his* incitement *of the crowd.* **2** something that incites: *Hunger was a powerful* incitement *to the crime.*

in·ci·vil·i·ty (ĭn′ sə vĭl′ ə tē) ***n-*** **[*pl.* in·ci·vil·i·ties]** **1** rude act; discourtesy: *His failing to come was an* incivility. **2** impoliteness: *He is notorious for his* incivility.

incl. 1 including. **2** inclosure.

in·clem·ent (ĭn klĕm′ ənt) ***adj-*** **1** stormy; not mild: *December's* inclement *weather.* **2** harsh; severe: *an* inclement *act.* ***—n-* in·clem′ en·cy.** ***adv-* in·clem′ ent·ly.**

in·cli·na·tion (ĭn′ klə nā′ shən) ***n-*** **1** a leaning, sloping, or bending: *He showed his agreement by a slight* inclination *of the head.* **2** degree of slope: *The* inclination *of the roof is great enough to allow water to run off.* **3** a liking; choice; preference: *His present* inclinations *are toward a singing career.*

[1]**in·cline** (ĭn klīn′) ***vi-*** **[in·clined, in·clin·ing]** **1** to lean or tilt: *The post* inclines *slightly to the left.* **2** to slant or slope upward: *The field* inclines *steeply toward the north.* **3** to favor; be disposed: *She* inclines *more toward the old than the new.* ***vt-*** **1** to cause to lean or tilt: *to* incline *a post to the right.* **2** to bow or nod: *to* incline *one's head in agreement.* **3** to cause (someone) to favor or be disposed toward an opinion, conclusion, etc.: *Your manner* inclines *me to believe what you say.*

[2]**in·cline** (ĭn′ klīn′) ***n-*** sloping plane or surface; slope.

in·clined (ĭn klīnd′) **1** (*often* ĭn′ klīnd′) slanting; sloping: *an* inclined *surface.* **2** leaning. **3** disposed by feeling or wish: *Come see us when you are so* inclined.

inclined plane ***n-*** **1** a plane that makes an angle other than 90° with a horizontal plane. **2** *Physics* one of the basic "simple machines."

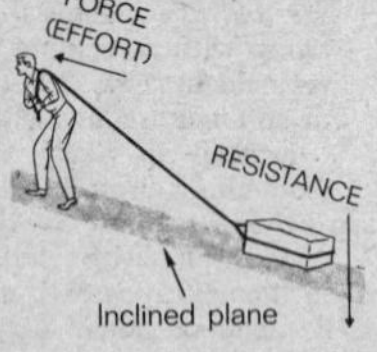

Inclined plane

in·cli·nom·e·ter (ĭn′ klə nŏm′ ə tər) ***n-*** **1** instrument used to show the direction of the earth's magnetic field at a given point by the amount of deviation from the horizontal. **2** device to measure angles of elevation or slope. **3** instrument that measures the amount by which an airplane or ship tilts from the horizontal.

in·close (ĭn klōz′) enclose.

in·clo·sure (ĭn klō′ zhər) enclosure.

in·clude (ĭn klōōd′) ***vt-*** **[in·clud·ed, in·clud·ing]** **1** to contain as part of the whole: *Does this price* include *the tax?* **2** to put in with others; enter: *Please* include *me on your list.*

in·clud·ing (ĭn klōō′ dĭng) ***prep-*** taking or counting in as part of a whole: *All of us,* including *the dog, got wet.*

in·clu·sion (ĭn klōō′ zhən) ***n-*** a taking into or being taken into: *The* inclusion *of Roger was a mistake.*

in·clu·sive (ĭn klōō′ sĭv) ***adj-*** **1** including or taking in the first- and last-mentioned things in a group: *The figures zero to nine,* inclusive, *are called digits.* **2** containing a great deal; comprehensive: *an* inclusive *survey.* ***—adv-* in·clu′ sive·ly.** ***n-* in·clu′ sive·ness.**

inclusive of taking in; taking into account; including.

incog. incognito.

in·cog·ni·to (ĭn′ kŏg nē′ tō, ĭn kŏg′ nə tō′) ***adv-*** in disguise; under an assumed name: *to travel* incognito. ***adj-***: *an* incognito *celebrity.*

in·co·her·ent (ĭn′ kō hêr′ ənt) ***adj-*** **1** not clinging together; loose. **2** without logical connection in thought or language: *an* incoherent *essay.* ***—n-* in′ co·her′ ence.** ***adv-* in′ co·her′ ent·ly.**

in·com·bus·ti·ble (ĭn′ kəm bŭs′ tə bəl) ***adj-*** such as cannot catch fire or be burned; nonflammable.

in·come (ĭn′ kŭm′) ***n-*** amount of money one gets from labor, business, property, etc.; wages; salary.

income tax ***n-*** tax on net personal or business income.

in·com·ing (ĭn′ kŭm′ ĭng) ***adj-*** **1** coming in: *the* incoming *tide.* **2** coming into office: *the* incoming *mayor.*

in·com·men·su·ra·ble (ĭn′ kə mĕn′ shər ə bəl) ***adj-*** not commensurable; lacking a common unit or basis for comparison: *Love and money are* incommensurable. ***—n-* in′ com·men′ su·ra·bil′ i·ty.** ***adv-* in·com·men′ su·ra·bly.**

in·com·men·su·rate (ĭn′ kə mĕn′ shər ət) ***adj-*** **1** unequal; inadequate: *His strength is* incommensurate *to his duties.* **2** incommensurable. ***—adv-* in·com·men′ su·rate·ly.**

in·com·mode (ĭn′ kə mōd′) ***vt-*** **[in·com·mod·ed, in·com·mod·ing]** to inconvenience; disturb; put out: *The lack of a room seriously* incommoded *me.*

in·com·mo·di·ous (ĭn′ kə mō′ dē əs) ***adj-*** **1** inconvenient; uncomfortable. **2** uncomfortably small or cramped.

in·com·mu·ni·ca·ble (ĭn′ kə myōō′ nĭ kə bəl) ***adj-*** such as cannot be communicated.

in·com·mu·ni·ca·do (ĭn′ kə myōō′ nə kä′ dō) ***adj-*** not allowed or unable to communicate with others: *The prisoner was kept* incommunicado.

in·com·mun·i·ca·tive (ĭn′ kə myōō′ nĭ kə tĭv′) ***adj-*** not given to speaking freely; reserved; reticent.

in·com·pa·ra·ble (ĭn kŏm′ pə rə bəl) ***adj-*** **1** such as cannot be equaled or surpassed; matchless: *an* incomparable *beauty.* **2** such as cannot be compared; not comparable. ***—adv-* in·com′ pa·ra·bly.**

in·com·pat·i·ble (ĭn′ kəm păt′ ə bəl) ***adj-*** not compatible: *an* incompatible *couple; desires* incompatible *with one's income.* ***—n-* in′ com·pat′ i·bil′ i·ty.** ***adv-* in′ com·pat′ i·bly.**

in·com·pe·tence (ĭn kŏm′ pə təns) ***n-*** **1** lack of ability or fitness: *the* incompetence *of a worker.* **2** in law, lack of qualification.

in·com·pe·tent (ĭn kŏm′ pə tənt) ***adj-*** **1** lacking enough ability, skill, etc.; not competent: *an* incompetent *carpenter.* **2** in law, not legally qualified. ***—adv-* in·com′ pe·tent·ly.**

in·com·plete (ĭn′ kəm plēt′) ***adj-*** with some part or parts missing; not finished; not complete: *an* incomplete *deck of cards*; *an* incomplete *book report.* **—*adv*- in′ com·plete′ ly. *n*- in′ com·plete′ ness.**

in·com·pre·hen·si·ble (ĭn′ kŏm′ prĭ hĕn′ sə bəl) ***adj***- such as cannot be understood. **—*n*- in′ com′ pre·hen′ si·bil′ i·ty. *adv*- in′ com′ pre·hen′ si·bly.**

in·com·press·i·ble (ĭn′ kəm prĕs′ ə bəl) ***adj***- not compressible. **—*n*- in′ com·press′ i·bil′ i·ty.**

in·con·ceiv·a·ble (ĭn′ kən sē′ və bəl) ***adj***- **1** impossible to conceive or imagine: *A square circle is* inconceivable. **2** hard to believe or understand: *Light travels at an* inconceivable *speed.* **—*n*- in′ con·ceiv′ a·bil′ i·ty. *adv*- in′ con·ceiv′ a·bly.**

in·con·clu·sive (ĭn′ kən klo͞o′ sĭv) ***adj***- proving nothing; unconvincing; indecisive: *an* inconclusive *argument*; *an* inconclusive *experiment.* **—*adv*- in′ con·clu′ sive·ly. *n*- in′ con·clu′ sive·ness.**

in·con·gru·i·ty (ĭn′ kən gro͞o′ ə tē) ***n***- [*pl.* **in·con·gru·i·ties**] **1** lack of agreement, harmony, or, sometimes, appropriateness; incongruousness: *the* incongruity *of his presence in the palace.* **2** something incongruous: *The book is full of* incongruities *of expression.*

in·con·gru·ous (ĭn kŏng′ gro͞o əs) ***adj***- **1** unsuitable; not appropriate; out of place: *His solemn face was* incongruous *with the gaiety of the party.* **2** lacking in agreement or harmony: *two* incongruous *colors.* **—*adv*- in·con′ gru·ous·ly. *n*- in·con′ gru·ous·ness.**

in·con·se·quen·tial (ĭn kŏn′ sə kwĕn′ shəl) ***adj***- **1** unrelated to the subject; irrelevant. **2** trivial; unimportant. **—*adv*- in·con′ se·quen′ tial·ly.**

in·con·sid·er·a·ble (ĭn′ kən sĭd′ ər ə bəl) ***adj***- not deserving consideration; slight; trivial. **—*adv*- in′ con·sid′ er·a·bly.**

in·con·sid·er·ate (ĭn′ kən sĭd′ ər ət) ***adj***- thoughtless; without proper regard for others: *an* inconsiderate *remark.* **—*adv*- in′ con·sid′ er·ate·ly. *n*- in′ con·sid′ er·ate·ness.**

in·con·sist·en·cy (ĭn′ kən sis′ tən sē) ***n***- [*pl.* **in·con·sist·en·cies**] **1** lack of sameness or agreement: *the* inconsistency *of two stories.* **2** contradiction: *a testimony full of* inconsistencies.

in·con·sist·ent (ĭn′ kən sĭs′ tənt) ***adj***- **1** not in keeping or agreement; at variance: *His actions are* inconsistent *with his words.* **2** having contradictions within itself; not logical: *an* inconsistent *argument.* **3** not holding to the same principles, practices, etc.; changeable; fickle: *an* inconsistent *person.* **—*adv*- in′ con·sist′ ent·ly.**

in·con·sol·a·ble (ĭn′ kən sō′ lə bəl) ***adj***- of a nature that doesn't allow being consoled or cheered; disconsolate: *He was* inconsolable *over his friend's death.* **—*adv*- in′ con·sol′ a·bly.**

in·con·spic·u·ous (ĭn′ kən spĭk′ yo͞o əs) ***adj***- not easily seen or noticed; not striking or showy: *an* inconspicuous *part in a play*; *an* inconspicuous *hat.* **—*adv*- in′ con·spic′ u·ous·ly. *n*- in′ con·spic′ u·ous·ness.**

in·con·stant (ĭn kŏn′ stənt) ***adj***- likely to change; not constant; undependable: *an* inconstant *friend.* **—*n*- in·con′ stan·cy. *adv*- in·con′ stant·ly.**

in·con·test·a·ble (ĭn′ kən tĕs′ tə bəl) ***adj***- such as cannot be questioned or challenged; indisputable: *our* incontestable *rights.* **—*n*- in′ con·test′ a·bil′ i·ty. *adv*- in′ con·test′ a·bly.**

in·con·ti·nent (ĭn kon′ tə nənt) ***adj***- lacking control, especially of the passions and desires; unrestrained. **—*n*- in·con′ ti·nence. *adv*- in·con′ ti·nent·ly.**

in·con·tro·vert·i·ble (ĭn′ kŏn′ trə vûr′ tə bəl) ***adj***- such as cannot be denied; undeniable; indisputable: *an* incontrovertible *fact.* **—*n*- in′ con′ tro·vert′ i·bil′ i·ty. *adv*- in′ con′ tro·vert′ i·bly.**

in·con·ven·ience (ĭn′ kən vēn′ ē əns) ***n***- **1** trouble, bother, or annoyance: *A water shortage causes* inconveniences. **2** a cause of trouble, bother, or annoyance: *A water shortage is an* inconvenience. ***vt***- **[in·con·ven·ienced, in·con·ven·ienc·ing]** to cause bother or annoyance to: *The water shortage* inconvenienced *us.*

in·con·ven·ient (ĭn′ kən vēn′ ē ənt) ***adj***- causing bother or annoyance; not convenient: *an* inconvenient *location*; *an* inconvenient *choice.* **—*adv*- in′ con·ven′ ient·ly.**

in·cor·po·rate (ĭn kôr′ pə rāt′) ***vt***- **[in·cor·po·rat·ed, in·cor·po·rat·ing]** **1** to put in; include; add: *to* incorporate *an idea into a story.* **2** to bring together into a whole; blend; merge. **3** to form into a corporation: *to* incorporate *a business.* ***vi***- **1** to unite into a single body. **2** to form a corporation. **—*n*- in·cor′ po·ra′ tion.**

in·cor·po·re·al (ĭn′ kôr pôr′ ē əl) ***adj***- not made of matter. **—*adv*- in′ cor·po′ re·al·ly.**

in·cor·rect (ĭn′ kə rĕkt′) ***adj***- **1** not according to fact; not true or accurate: *an* incorrect *report.* **2** not according to model or rule; faulty; wrong: *an* incorrect *approach to a problem.* **3** not in keeping with good usage or standards; improper: *very* incorrect *behavior.* **—*adv*- in′ cor·rect′ ly. *n*- in′ cor·rect′ ness.**

in·cor·ri·gi·ble (ĭn kŏr′ ĭj ə bəl, ĭn kôr′-) ***adj***- beyond reform or correction: *an* incorrigible *liar*; incorrigible *lying.* **—*n*- in·cor′ ri·gi·bil′ i·ty. *adv*- in·cor′ ri·gi·bly.**

in·cor·rupt·i·ble (ĭn′ kə rŭp′ tə bəl) ***adj***- not corruptible; honest: *an* incorruptible *witness.* **—*n*- in′ cor·rupt′ i·bil′ i·ty. *adv*- in′ cor·rupt′ i·bly.**

[1]**in·crease** (ĭn krēs′) ***vt***- **[in·creased, in·creas·ing]** to make greater; augment; add to: *Trade* increased *the country's wealth.* ***vi***-: *His sales* increased *last week.* **—*adv*- in·creas′ ing·ly.**

[2]**in·crease** (ĭn′ krēs′) ***n***- **1** growth or enlargement: *an* increase *in business.* **2** amount that is added: *an* increase *of ten dollars in the price.*

on the increase increasing; rising.

in·cred·i·ble (ĭn krĕd′ ə bəl) ***adj***- hard to believe; beyond belief: *an* incredible *adventure.* **—*n*- in·cred′ i·bil′ i·ty. *adv*- in·cred′ i·bly.**

►Should not be confused with INCREDULOUS.

in·cre·du·li·ty (ĭn′ krə dyo͞o′ lə tē, -do͞o′ lə tē) ***n***- unwillingness to believe; lack of belief; skepticism; doubt.

in·cred·u·lous (ĭn krĕj′ ə ləs) ***adj***- **1** doubting; skeptical; questioning as to truth and accuracy; not willing or able to believe: *to be* incredulous *of the statement.* **2** showing doubt: *an* incredulous *smile.* **—*adv*- in·cred′ u·lous·ly.**

►Should not be confused with INCREDIBLE.

in·cre·ment (ĭng′ krə mənt) ***n***- **1** increase; enlargement. **2** amount that is added; especially, one of a series of small or regular additions: *an* increment *of $5 a year.*

in·crim·i·nate (ĭn krĭm′ ə nāt′) ***vt***- **[in·crim·i·nat·ed, in·crim·i·nat·ing]** to charge with, or involve in, a crime; show to be guilty: *His words* incriminated *him.* **—*n*- in·crim′ i·na′ tion. *adj*- in·crim′ i·na·to′ ry.**

in·crust (ĭn krŭst′) encrust.

in·crus·ta·tion (ĭn′ krŭs tā′ shən) ***n***- **1** an encrusting or being encrusted. **2** crust or hard coating. **3** ornamental layer, inlay, etc.: *a diadem with* incrustations *of diamonds.*

in·cu·bate (ĭng′ kyə bāt′) ***vt***- **[in·cu·bat·ed, in·cu·bat·ing]** **1** to sit upon (eggs) in order to hatch them. **2** to keep (eggs, bacteria, etc.) under conditions favorable for hatching, development, etc.: *to* incubate *a bacterial culture.* **3** to give form to or develop gradually: *He* incubated *a new idea in his mind for weeks.* ***vi*-**: *The eggs* incubated *for two weeks. The idea* incubated *slowly in his mind.* **—*n*- in′cu·ba′tion.**

in·cu·ba·tor (ĭng′kyə bā′tər) ***n*-** **1** heated box for hatching eggs. **2** heated box or cabinet used to help the growth of very small babies or prematurely born babies.

in·cu·bus (ĭng′kyə bəs) ***n*-** [*pl.* **in·cu·bus·es, in·cu·bi** (-bē, -bī)] **1** in the Middle Ages, an evil spirit believed to lie heavily on persons in their sleep. **2** nightmare. **3** any depressing weight or burden: *the* incubus *of poverty.*

in·cul·cate (ĭn kŭl′kāt′, ĭn′kəl-) ***vt*-** [**in·cul·cat·ed, in·cul·cat·ing**] to impress into the mind by repetition; instill: *The mother tried to* inculcate *honesty in her children.* **—*n*- in′cul·ca′tion.**

in·cum·bent (ĭn kŭm′bənt) ***adj*-** lying or leaning with its weight on something else. ***n*-** person who holds office. **—*n*- in·cum′ben·cy.** ***adv*-** **in·cum′bent·ly.**

incumbent on (or **upon**) resting upon as a duty: *It is* incumbent upon *every good citizen to vote.*

in·cum·ber (ĭn kŭm′bər) encumber.

in·cum·brance (ĭn kŭm′brəns) encumbrance.

in·cur (ĭn kûr′) ***vt*-** [**in·curred, in·cur·ring**] to fall into; bring upon oneself: *to* incur *debts*; *to* incur *punishment.*

in·cur·a·ble (ĭn kyŏŏr′ə bəl) ***adj*-** not curable; such as cannot be cured: *an* incurable *disease.* ***n*-** person having a disease that cannot be cured. **—*n*- in·cur′a·bil′i·ty.** ***adv*-** **in·cur′a·bly.**

in·cur·sion (ĭn kûr′zhən) ***n*-** **1** inroad; raid; invasion: *an* incursion *into enemy territory.* **2** a running in: *an* incursion *of water.* **—*adj*- in·cur′sive** (-sĭv).

Ind. Indiana.

in·debt·ed (ĭn dĕt′əd) ***adj*-** owing money or gratitude; under obligation: *We are* indebted *to you for your help.* **—*n*- in·debt′ed·ness.**

in·de·cen·cy (ĭn dē′sən sē) ***n*-** [*pl.* **in·de·cen·cies**] **1** lack of decency; want of modesty, propriety, delicacy, etc. **2** word, act, picture, etc., offensive to modesty.

in·de·cent (ĭn dē′sənt) ***adj*-** **1** not proper; in bad taste: *He spoke and left in* indecent *haste.* **2** not modest; unfit to be seen or heard; obscene: *to use* indecent *language*; indecent *pictures.* **—*adv*- in·de′cent·ly.**

in·de·ci·pher·a·ble (ĭn′dĭ sī′fər ə bəl) ***adj*-** such as cannot be deciphered: *an* indecipherable *signature.*

in·de·ci·sion (ĭn′də sĭzh′ən) ***n*-** inability to decide.

in·de·ci·sive (ĭn′dĭ sī′sĭv) ***adj*-** **1** not settling a matter; inconclusive: *to give* indecisive *evidence.* **2** not positive or certain; hesitating; irresolute: *an* indecisive *reply.* **—*adv*- in′de·ci′sive·ly.** ***n*-** **in′de·ci′sive·ness.**

in·de·clin·a·ble (ĭn′dĭ klī′nə bəl) *Grammar* ***adj*-** of a word, keeping the same form in all cases.

in·dec·o·rous (ĭn dĕk′ər əs) ***adj*-** in bad taste; not suitable; improper: *her* indecorous *behavior*; indecorous *speech.* **—*adv*- in·dec′o·rous·ly.** ***n*-** **in·dec′o·rous·ness.**

in·deed (ĭn dēd′) ***adv*-** in fact; really: *We were* indeed *pleased by his success.*

indef. indefinite.

in·de·fat·i·ga·ble (ĭn′dĭ făt′ĭ gə bəl) ***adj*-** not giving in easily to fatigue; untiring: *an* indefatigable *worker.* **—*n*- in′de·fat′i·ga·bil′i·ty.** ***adv*-** **in′de·fat′i·ga·bly.**

in·de·fen·si·ble (ĭn′dĭ fĕn′sə bəl) ***adj*-** not defensible: *an* indefensible *beachhead*; *an* indefensible *point of view.* **—*n*- in′de·fen′si·bil′i·ty.** ***adv*-** **in′de·fen′si·bly.**

in·de·fin·a·ble (ĭn′dĭ fī′nə bəl) ***adj*-** such as cannot be described or explained clearly; subtle; vague: *an* indefinable *charm.* **—*n*- in′de·fin′a·bil′i·ty.** ***adv*-** **in′de·fin′a·bly.**

in·def·i·nite (ĭn dĕf′ə nət) ***adj*-** **1** having no fixed or exact limit: *an* indefinite *period of time.* **2** not clear or certain; vague: *his* indefinite *plans.* **3** *Grammar* not defining or specifying precisely, such as certain determiners, verb forms, etc. **—*adv*- in·def′i·nite·ly.** ***n*-** **in·def′i·nite·ness.**

indefinite article *Grammar* ***n*-** either of the determiners "a" or "an," used to introduce a noun phrase.

indefinite pronoun *Grammar* ***n*-** pronoun that refers to an unspecified person or thing or an unspecified number or group. Examples: anybody, everybody, nothing.

in·del·i·ble (ĭn dĕl′ə bəl) ***adj*-** **1** impossible to remove or erase; permanent: *an* indelible *ink.* **2** leaving a mark that is impossible to remove or erase: *an* indelible *pencil.* **—*n*- in·del′i·bil′i·ty.** ***adv*-** **in·del′i·bly.**

in·del·i·cate (ĭn dĕl′ĭ kət) ***adj*-** lacking in refinement or good taste; coarse; crude: *an* indelicate *remark.* **—*n*- in·del′i·ca·cy.** ***adv*-** **in·del′i·cate·ly.**

in·dem·ni·fi·ca·tion (ĭn dĕm′nə fə kā′shən) ***n*-** **1** an indemnifying or being indemnified. **2** compensation or repayment for loss, damage, injury, or expense.

in·dem·ni·fy (ĭn dĕm′nə fī′) ***vt*-** [**in·dem·ni·fied, in·dem·ni·fy·ing**] **1** to repay or compensate for loss, expense, or damage: *to* indemnify *the farmers for loss of crops.* **2** to secure against loss or damage; insure.

in·dem·ni·ty (ĭn dĕm′nə tē) ***n*-** [*pl.* **in·dem·ni·ties**] **1** repayment or compensation for loss, damage, injury, etc. **2** security against loss, damage, etc.; insurance.

in·dent (ĭn dĕnt′) ***vt*-** **1** to make a dent, notch, or other impression in: *to* indent *the sand with footsteps.* **2** to begin (a line, especially the first line of a paragraph) with a blank space. ***n*-** (*also* ĭn′dĕnt′) indentation.

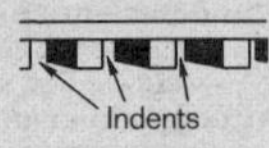

in·den·ta·tion (ĭn′dĕn tā′shən) ***n*-** **1** an indenting or being indented. **2** dent or notch. **3** blank space that sets a written or printed line in from a margin.

in·den·tion (ĭn dĕn′shən) ***n*-** **1** a setting in from a margin, such as at the beginning of a paragraph. **2** dent or notch.

in·den·ture (ĭn dĕn′chər) ***n*-** **1** written agreement, especially one binding a servant or an apprentice to a master. **2** a dent; indentation. ***vt*-** [**in·den·tured, in·den·tur·ing**] to bind (a servant, apprentice, etc.) by a written agreement.

in·den·tu·red (ĭn dĕn′chərd) ***adj*-** bound by a written contract to work for the same master for a certain length of time: *an* indentured *servant.*

in·de·pend·ence (ĭn′dĭ pĕn′dəns) ***n*-** **1** freedom from influence, support, control, or government by others. **2** income or a sum of money sufficient for one's needs.

Independence Day ***n*-** July 4th, celebrated in the United States as the anniversary of the day on which the Declaration of Independence was adopted in 1776.

in·de·pend·ent (ĭn′dĭ pĕn′dənt) ***adj*-** **1** not depending on or controlled by others: *an* independent *country.* **2** not willing to accept help from others: *a poor but* independent *man.* **3** not easily influenced; not biased: *an* independent *mind.* **4** not connected with others; separate: *an* independent *store.* **5** *Grammar* such as can stand alone as a sentence. **—*adv*- in′de·pen′dent·ly.**

independent of aside or apart from.

independent clause *Grammar* ***n*-** clause that can stand alone as a sentence. The following sentence has two independent clauses: I can go today, *but* I can't go tomorrow. See also *dependent clause.*

in·de·scrib·a·ble (ĭn′dĭ skrī′bə bəl) ***adj*-** impossible to describe; beyond expression: *an* indescribable *fear of the dark.* **—*adv*- in′de·scrib′a·bly.**

in·de·struct·i·ble (ĭn′dĭ strŭk′tə bəl) ***adj*-** not destructible; durable; lasting: *Energy is* indestructible. **—*n*- in′de·struct′i·bil′i·ty.** ***adv*-** **in′de·struct′i·bly.**

in·de·ter·min·a·ble (ĭn′ dĭ tûr′ mə nə bəl) ***adj*- 1** such as cannot be determined or ascertained: *an* indeterminable *number of accidents.* **2** such as cannot be settled or decided. **—*n*- in′ de·ter′ min·a·ble·ness.**

in·de·ter·mi·nate (ĭn′ dĭ tûr′ mə nət) ***adj*- 1** not settled or fixed; indefinite; vague: *an* indeterminate *amount*; *an* indeterminate *result.* **2** of a cluster of flowers, having stems not ending in a flower or bud. **—*adv*- in′ de·ter′ mi·nate·ly. *n*- in′ de·ter′ mi·nate·ness.**

in·de·ter·mi·na·tion (ĭn′ dĭ tûr′ mə nā′ shən) ***n*-** unsettled or indecisive state of mind; lack of decision.

in·dex (ĭn′ dĕks′) ***n*-** [*pl.* **in·dex·es** or **in·di·ces** (-də sēz′)] **1** alphabetical list of the names and topics in a book, with the page on which each is treated. **2** something that points out; sign or indication: *an* index *of a country's prosperity.* **3** in printing, a mark [☞] used to call attention. **4** index finger; forefinger. **5** in science, number expressing the ratio of one amount or dimension to another. **6** *Mathematics* the numeral that shows the root to be extracted. The numeral 3 is the index in the expression $\sqrt[3]{27}$. ***vt*-** to furnish (a book) with, or enter (a word) into, an alphabetical reference.

In·dex (ĭn′ dĕks′) ***n*-** in the Roman Catholic Church, a list of books regarded as harmful to the faith and morals of its members, who are asked not to read them without permission.

index finger ***n*-** finger next to the thumb; forefinger.

index of refraction ***n*-** number that represents the relationship between the speed of light in a vacuum and its speed in a given transparent substance. Light travels in water about three-fourths as fast as it does in a vacuum. Water's index of refraction is 4/3.

india ink ***n*-** black, heavy-bodied, drawing ink.

In·di·an (ĭn′ dē ən) ***adj*- 1** of or pertaining to the original inhabitants of the Americas at the time of its discovery, or their descendants: *an* Indian *peace council.* **2** pertaining to India, its people, or their language. **3** made by or used by the American Indians, or made in India. ***n*- 1** one of the original inhabitants of the Americas or their descendants. **2** native or citizen of the Republic of India or a person of Indian descent. **3** any of the languages of the American Indians.

Indian paintbrush

Indian club ***n*-** club shaped like a bottle, swung by the hands in gymnastic exercises.

Indian corn ***n*-** corn; maize.

Indian file ***n*-** single file.

Indian giver *Informal* ***n*-** person who takes back a gift he has given.

Indian meal ***n*-** cornmeal.

Indian paintbrush ***n*-** one of a group of plants with showy flowers, growing in western United States. It is the state flower of Wyoming.

Indian pipe ***n*-** leafless, waxy-white plant with a single nodding, bell-shaped flower, growing chiefly in dense woods.

Indian pipe

Indian pudding ***n*-** pudding made of cornmeal, milk, and molasses.

Indian summer ***n*-** period of mild weather following autumn frosts.

Indian Territory ***n*-** formerly, a territory of the United States set aside for the Indians; now, a part of Oklahoma.

India paper ***n*-** thin, absorbent yellow paper made in China and Japan of vegetable fiber and used in the printing of fine engravings.

India rubber or **india rubber** ***n*-** caoutchouc.

indic. indicative.

in·di·cate (ĭn′ də kāt′) ***vt*-** [**in·di·cat·ed, in·di·cat·ing**] **1** to be a sign of; suggest: *Fever* indicates *illness.* **2** to show; mark: *Signposts* indicate *the road.* **3** to make known briefly; point out: *Please* indicate *your intentions.*

in·di·ca·tion (ĭn′ də kā′ shən) ***n*- 1** a showing or pointing out. **2** something that serves to point out or show; sign; symptom: *Fever is an* indication *of illness.* **3** degree or amount indicated, as on a graduated instrument.

in·dic·a·tive (ĭn dĭk′ ə tĭv) ***adj*- 1** pointing out; showing; suggestive (of): *His opinions are* indicative *of prejudice.* **2** *Grammar* designating, or having to do with, a verb or verb phrase that states a fact or asks a direct question in a sentence. Such a verb or phrase is said to be in the **indicative mood.** In the sentences "Mary plays the piano" and "Did you go?" the verbs are in the indicative mood. ***n*-** verb in the indicative mood. **—*adv*- in·dic′ a·tive·ly.**

in·di·ca·tor (ĭn′ də kā′ tər) ***n*- 1** someone or something that indicates: *Facial expression is often an* indicator *of the feelings.* **2** any device, such as a needle or pointer on a dial or gauge, that indicates heat, pressure, speed, etc. **3** *Chemistry* chemical, such as litmus, that changes color at a particular stage of acidity or other condition.

in·di·ces (ĭn′ də sēz′) *pl.* of **index.**

in·dict (ĭn dīt′) ***vt*- 1** to charge with an offense; accuse. **2** in law, to charge formally with a crime after a grand jury has considered the evidence: *to* indict *a person for theft.* ***Hom*-** indite. **—*n*- in·dict′ er** or **in·dict′ or.**

in·dict·able (ĭn dī′ tə bəl) ***adj*- 1** liable to be indicted, or charged with a crime in due form of law. **2** of an offense, giving cause for indictment.

in·dict·ment (ĭn dīt′ mənt) ***n*- 1** an indicting or being indicted. **2** written accusation of a crime, presented to the court by a grand jury after it has considered the evidence.

In·dies (ĭn′ dēz) ***n*-** *pl.* the East Indies; also, formerly, the West Indies.

in·dif·fer·ence (ĭn dĭf′ rəns, -ər əns) ***n*- 1** lack of interest or feeling: *to* regard *suffering with indifference.* **2** lack of importance: *a matter of complete* indifference *to us.*

in·dif·fer·ent (ĭn dĭf′ rənt, -ər ənt) ***adj*- 1** not caring or concerned about something; without any strong feeling one way or the other: *an* indifferent *audience*; indifferent *to the suffering of others.* **2** neither good nor bad; mediocre: *an* indifferent *book.* **—*adv*- in·dif′ fer·ent·ly.**

in·dig·e·nous (ĭn dĭj′ ə nəs) ***adj*-** native; born, growing, or produced naturally in certain locations, regions, or climates: *Tobacco is* indigenous *to America.* **—*adv*- in·dig′ e·nous·ly.**

in·di·gent (ĭn′ də jənt) ***adj*-** very poor; needy: *an* indigent *widow.* **—*n*- in′ di·gence. *adv*- in′ di·gent·ly.**

in·di·gest·i·ble (ĭn′ də jĕs′ tə bəl, ĭn′ dī-) ***adj*-** impossible to digest or not easily digested. **—*n*- in′ di·gest′ i·bil′ i·ty. *adv*- in′ di·gest′ i·bly.**

in·di·ges·tion (ĭn′ də jĕs′ chən) ***n*-** difficulty in digesting food; also, the discomfort resulting from such difficulty.

in·dig·nant (ĭn dĭg′ nənt) ***adj*-** angry at something considered unfair, mean, or cruel: *to be* indignant *over cruelty*; *an* indignant *letter.* **—*adv*- in·dig′ nant·ly.**

in·dig·na·tion (ĭn′ dĭg nā′ shən) ***n*-** anger at something considered unfair, mean, or cruel: *His lies aroused my* indignation.

fāte, făt, dâre, bärn; bē, bĕt, mêre; bīte, bĭt; nōte, hŏt, môre, dȯg; fŭn, fûr; to͞o, bo͝ok; oil; out; t*a*r; thin; *th*en; hw for wh as in *wh*at; zh for s as in u*s*ual; ə for a, e, i, o, u, as in *a*go, lin*e*n, per*i*l, at*o*m, min*u*s

in·dig·ni·ty (ĭn dĭg′ nə tē) ***n-*** [*pl.* **in·dig·ni·ties**] thing or act that humiliates, lowers the dignity, or wounds the pride; insult; slight: *to suffer* indignities.

in·di·go (ĭn′ də gō′) ***n-*** [*pl.* **in·di·gos** or **in·di·goes**] **1** plant related to the peas and beans from which a blue dye can be obtained. **2** (also **indigo blue**) blue dye, formerly obtained from such a plant, but now made chiefly from coal tar; also, its deep, violet-blue color. ***adj-***: *an* indigo *band on the rainbow.*

indigo bunting ***n-*** North American songbird related to the finches, the male of which is a brilliant blue.

indigo snake ***n-*** large, blue-black, nonpoisonous snake of southern United States.

in·di·rect (ĭn′ də rĕkt′) ***adj-*** **1** not in a straight line; roundabout: *an* indirect *route.* **2** not closely connected; not immediate; secondary: *an* indirect *cause*; *an* indirect *result.* **3** not straight to the point: *an* indirect *answer.* **4** not straightforward; dishonest: *his* indirect *methods.* **—*adv-*** **in′ di·rect′ ly.** ***n-*** **in′ di·rect′ ness.**

indirect discourse ***n-*** statement which gives what one has said or written without quoting it exactly. Example: She said she was going to the park.

in·di·rec·tion (ĭn′ də rĕk′ shən) ***n-*** roundabout means or methods; deviousness.

indirect measurement ***n-*** the determination of the value of a desired quantity by actually measuring a different but related quantity and then computing.

indirect object See ²*object.*

indirect tax ***n-*** tax, such as one on manufactured goods, imports, etc., that is paid indirectly in the form of higher prices for the taxed goods. See also *direct tax.*

in·dis·cern·i·ble (ĭn′ də sûr′ nə bəl) ***adj-*** not discernible; imperceptible: *an* indiscernible *difference.* **—*adv-*** **in′ dis·cern′ i·bly.**

in·dis·creet (ĭndĭ skrēt′) ***adj-*** not careful or cautious; unwise: *an* indiscreet *remark.* **—*adv-*** **in′ dis·creet′ ly.** ***n-*** **in′ dis·creet′ ness.**

in·dis·cre·tion (ĭn′ dĭ skrĕsh′ ən) ***n-*** **1** imprudent act or step: *His free and easy behavior with the judge was an* indiscretion. **2** condition or habit of being indiscreet.

in·dis·crim·i·nate (ĭn′ dĭ skrĭm′ ə nət) ***adj-*** **1** not discriminating; not choosing carefully: *an* indiscriminate *reader.* **2** confused; jumbled: *an* indiscriminate *mixture of several styles.* **—*adv-*** **in′ dis·crim′ i·nate·ly.**

in·dis·pens·a·ble (ĭn′ dĭ spĕn′ sə bəl) ***adj-*** absolutely necessary; essential: *Machinery is* indispensable *in industry.* ***n-*** something essential. **—*n-*** **in′ dis·pens·a·bil′ i·ty.** ***adv-*** **in·dis·pens′ a·bly.**

in·dis·posed (ĭn′ dĭ spōzd′) ***adj-*** **1** not willing: *to be* indisposed *to help.* **2** mildly sick: *Mother is* indisposed.

in·dis·po·si·tion (ĭn′ dĭs′ pə zĭsh′ ən) ***n-*** **1** slight illness. **2** aversion; unwillingness.

in·dis·pu·ta·ble (ĭn′ dĭ spyōō′ tə bəl, ĭn dĭs′ pyə-) ***adj-*** absolutely true; beyond question; not to be disputed: *an* indisputable *victory.* **—*n-*** **in′ dis·pu′ ta·bil′ i·ty.** ***adv-*** **in′ dis·pu′ ta·bly.**

in·dis·so·lu·ble (ĭn′ dĭ sŏl′ yə bəl) ***adj-*** such as cannot be dissolved, broken up, or destroyed; indestructible: *an* indissoluble *friendship.* **—*n-*** **in′ dis·sol′ u·bil′ i·ty.** ***adv-*** **in′ dis·sol′ u·bly.**

indis·tinct (ĭn′ dĭ stĭngkt′) ***adj-*** not clear or distinct; blurred; faint: *an* indinstinct *murmur*; *an* indistinct *mark.* **—*adv-*** **in′ dis·tinct′ ly.** ***n-*** **in′ dis·tinct′ ness.**

in·dis·tin·guish·a·ble (ĭn′ dĭ stĭng′ gwĭsh ə bəl) ***adj-*** such as cannot be distinguished or perceived; imperceptible: *an* indistinguishable *difference.* **—*adv-*** **in′ dis·tin′ guish·a·bly.**

in·dite (ĭn dīt′) *Archaic* ***vt-*** [**in·dit·ed, in·dit·ing**] to compose or express in writing; write. ***Hom-*** indict.

in·di·um (ĭn′ dē əm) ***n-*** rare, soft, silvery metal element that occurs in some zinc ores and is used in jewelry and dental alloys. Symbol In, At. No. 49, At. Wt. 114.82.

in·di·vid·u·al (ĭn′ də vĭj′ ōō əl) ***adj-*** **1** belonging to or intended for a single person or thing: *an* individual *locker*; *an* individual *plate.* **2** particular; separate: *to give* individual *help*; *an* individual *report.* **3** having features that belong to it alone: *an* individual *hair style.* ***n-*** **1** person: *He is a kind* individual. **2** single person, animal, or thing: *the freedom of the* individual.

in·di·vid·u·al·ism (ĭn′ də vĭj′ ōō ə lĭz′ əm) ***n-*** **1** personal independence or freedom in thought or action; also, self-reliance. **2** economic or political belief that the interest of the individual is higher than that of the group.

in·di·vid·u·al·ist (ĭn′ də vĭj′ ōō ə list) ***n-*** **1** person who acts and thinks on his own without relying on the thoughts or actions of others. **2** one who believes in or supports individualism. **—*adj-*** **in′ di·vid′ u·al·is′ tic.**

in·di·vid·u·al·i·ty (ĭn′ də vĭj′ ōō ăl′ ə tē) ***n-*** [*pl.* **in·di·vid·u·al·i·ties**] **1** all the characteristics that make a person different from other persons: *a man of marked* individuality. **2** condition of being different from all others; personality: *Keep your* individuality. **3** condition or quality of existing separately; separate existence.

in·di·vid·u·al·ize (ĭn′ də vĭj′ ōō ə līz′) ***vt-*** [**in·di·vid·u·al·ized, in·di·vid·u·al·iz·ing**] **1** to give a distinct or individual character to: *to* individualize *one's performance.* **2** to adapt or relate to the specific needs, abilities, etc., of the individual: *to* individualize *language instruction.*

in·di·vid·u·al·ly (ĭn′ də vĭj′ ōō ə lē) ***adv-*** one by one; separately; personally: *to see them* individually.

in·di·vis·i·ble (ĭn′ də vĭz′ ə bəl) ***adj-*** **1** such as cannot be divided; not divisible **2** *Mathematics* admitting of no further division; leaving a remainder other than zero. **—*n-*** **in′ di·vis′ i·bil′ i·ty.** ***adv-*** **in′ di·vis′ i·bly.**

in·doc·tri·nate (ĭn dŏk′ trə nāt′) ***vt-*** [**in·doc·tri·nat·ed, in·doc·tri·nat·ing**] **1** to instruct in principles or doctrines. **2** to teach (someone) partisan or sectarian ideas, principles, etc.: *He wants to* indoctrinate *young people, not to teach them to think.* **—*n-*** **in·doc′ tri·na′ tion.**

In·do-Eu·ro·pe·an (ĭn′ dō yoor′ ə pē′ ən) ***adj-*** of or relating to the world's largest family of languages, those spoken in most of Europe and the countries colonized by Europeans, as well as in southwestern Asia and India.

in·do·lent (ĭn′ də lənt) ***adj-*** avoiding or disliking work or exertion; lazy. **—*n-*** **in′ do·lence.** ***adv-*** **in′ do·lent·ly.**

in·dom·i·ta·ble (ĭn dŏm′ ə tə bəl) ***adj-*** unconquerable; unyielding; steadfast: *an* indomitable *will.* **—*n-*** **in·dom′ i·ta·bil′ i·ty.** ***adv-*** **in·dom′ i·ta·bly.**

in·door (ĭn′ dôr′) ***adj-*** belonging to or done inside a house or building: *Chess is an* indoor *sport.*

in·doors (ĭn′ dôrz′) ***adv-*** inside or into a building: *When it rains, we play* indoors. *Please take them* indoors.

in·dorse (in dôrs′) endorse. **—*n-*** **in·dorse′ ment.** ***n-*** **in·dors′ er.**

in·du·bi·ta·ble (ĭn dōō′ bə tə bəl, ĭn dyōō′-) ***adj-*** too clear or certain to be doubted; unquestionable: *an* indubitable *triumph.* **—*n-*** **in·du′ bi·ta·ble·ness.** ***adv-*** **in·du′ bi·ta·bly.**

in·duce (ĭn dōōs′, -dyōōs′) ***vt-*** [**in·duced, in·duc·ing**] **1** to persuade; prevail upon: *Money will* induce *him to go.* **2** to produce; bring on or about: *to* induce *sleep by drugs.* **3** to arrive at (a conclusion or principle) from the observation or study of particular cases. **4** to produce (an electric current or magnetic effect) by induction.

in·duce·ment (ĭn dōōs′ mənt, ĭn dyōōs′-) ***n-*** something that persuades or influences; incentive: *The prize was an* inducement *to study.*

in·duct (ĭn dŭkt′) *vt-* **1** to place officially in office; install: *to* induct *a mayor.* **2** to enroll into military service.

in·duct·ance (ĭn dŭk′ təns) *n-* the producing, by a varying current, of an induced electromotive force, either in the current-carrying circuit or a magnetically linked circuit. This is the basic process in transformers.

in·duct·ee (ĭn dŭk′ tē) *n-* person who is inducted.

in·duc·tion (ĭn dŭk′ shən) *n-* **1** act or ceremony of installing a person in office. **2** the process of reasoning by which a general conclusion is reached from a study of particular facts. **3** procedure by which a civilian is enrolled into military service. **4** (also **electromagnetic induction**) the producing of an electromotive force in a conductor that moves through a magnetic field so as to cut the magnetic flux. **5** (also **electrostatic induction**) the producing of an electric charge in a neutral body when it is brought near a charged object. **6** (also **magnetic induction**) process in which a ferromagnetic substance becomes magnetic when placed in a magnetic field.

induction coil *n-* kind of transformer that produces a high-voltage alternating current from a low-voltage direct current. It consists of a primary coil carrying an interrupted direct current that induces a high electromotive force in a secondary coil of many fine turns.

in·duc·tive (ĭn dŭk′ tĭv) *adj-* **1** of or having to do with logical induction; reasoning by induction. **2** *Physics* relating to, produced, or causing induction or inductance. *—adv-* **in·duc′ tive·ly.** *n-* **in·duc′ tive·ness.**

inductive reasoning *n-* orderly thinking or predicting based upon what has happened before and therefore is likely to happen again. Inductive reasoning is often used to make general rules or theories that account for facts or events that have been observed. Also **inductive logic.** See also *deductive reasoning.*

in·dulge (ĭn dŭlj′) *vt-* **[in·dulged, in·dulg·ing] 1** to humor by giving in to: *to* indulge *a child.* **2** to yield to; gratify: *to* indulge *a liking for candy.*

indulge in to do, take part in, or treat oneself to: *He* indulges in *friendly bridge parties.*

in·dul·gence (ĭn dŭl′ jəns) *n-* **1** the humoring or satisfying of another: *I request your* indulgence *in this matter.* **2** a giving way to one's own likings: *Too much* indulgence *in sweets is bad for us.* **3** something in which a person indulges: *Smoking was his only* indulgence. **4** indulgent act; favor. **5** in the Roman Catholic Church, the remission of punishment still due for sins, the guilt of which is already forgiven.

in·dul·gent (ĭn dŭl′ jənt) *adj-* yielding easily to whims or desires of others; lenient; not very strict: *an* indulgent *parent.* *—adv-* **in·dul′ gent·ly.**

in·dus·tri·al (ĭn dŭs′ trē əl) *adj-* **1** relating to or engaged in industry, especially manufacturing: *an* industrial *worker; a small* industrial *output.* **2** not agricultural or commercial; having highly developed industries: *an* industrial *nation.* **3** used in industry: *an* industrial *diamond;* industrial *alcohol.* *—adv-* **in·dus′ tri·al·ly.**

in·dus·tri·al·ist (ĭn dŭs′ trē ə lĭst′) *n-* manager or owner of a manufacturing enterprise.

in·dus·tri·al·ize (ĭn dŭs′ trē ə līz′) *vt-* **[in·dus·tri·al·ized, in·dus·tri·al·iz·ing]** to make industrial; to develop industries in: *to* industrialize *a country.* *—n-* **in·dus′ tri·al·i·za′ tion.**

Industrial Revolution *n-* the social and economic change from an agricultural to an industrial civilization that took place in England from the mid-eighteenth to mid-nineteenth century and is still continuing.

in·dus·tri·ous (ĭn dŭs′ trē əs) *adj-* working hard and steadily; diligent: *an* industrious *farmer.* *—adv-* **in·dus′ tri·ous·ly.** *n-* **in·dus′ tri·ous·ness.**

in·dus·try (ĭn′ də strē) *n-* **1** all forms of business dealing with production, transportation, and communication, especially manufacturing: *America's* industry. **2** specific form or branch of such business: *the fishing* industry. **3** hard work; diligence.

[1]**in·e·bri·ate** (ĭ nē′ brē āt′) *vt-* **[in·e·bri·at·ed, in·e·bri·at·ing]** to make drunk; intoxicate. *—n-* **in·e′ bri·a′ tion.**

[2]**in·e·bri·ate** (ĭ nē′ brē ət) *adj-* drunken; intoxicated. *n-* drunkard, especially one who is a habitual drunkard.

in·ed·i·ble (ĭn ĕd′ ə bəl) *adj-* not fit to be eaten; not edible: *an* inedible *mushroom.* *—n-* **in·ed′ i·bil′ i·ty.**

in·ef·fa·ble (ĭn ĕf′ ə bəl) *adj-* too great or overwhelming to be expressed in words; beyond description: *an* ineffable *grief.* *—n-* **in·ef′ fa·bil′ i·ty.** *adv-* **in·ef′ fa·bly.**

in·ef·face·a·ble (ĭn′ ĭ fā′ sə bəl) *adj-* such as cannot be blotted or rubbed out; indelible. *—n-* **in′ ef·face′ a·bil′ i·ty.** *adv-* **in′ ef·face′ a·bly.**

in·ef·fec·tive (ĭn′ ə fĕk′ tĭv) *adj-* **1** not producing the desired result; not effective: *an* ineffective *argument.* **2** incompetent; inefficient: *an* ineffective *person.* *—adv-* **in′ ef·fec′ tive·ly.** *n-* **in′ ef·fec′ tive·ness.**

in·ef·fec·tu·al (ĭn′ ĭ fĕk′ chōō əl) *n-* **1** having no effect; futile; useless: *The rescue efforts were* ineffectual. **2** lacking power, ability, vigor, and impressiveness; weak and harmless: *an* ineffectual *little man.* *—n-* **in′ ef·fec′ tu·al′ i·ty.** *adv-* **in′ ef·fec′ tu·al·ly.**

in·ef·fi·ca·cious (ĭn ĕf′ ə kā′ shəs) *adj-* not producing what is desired; not efficacious: *an* inefficacious *remedy.*

in·ef·fi·ca·cy (ĭn ĕf′ ĭ kə sē) *n-* inability to produce what is desired: *the* inefficacy *of a treatment.*

in·ef·fi·cient (ĭn′ ĭ fĭsh′ ənt) *adj-* **1** requiring unnecessary time, energy, or work: *an* inefficient *process.* **2** wasteful of time and energy: *an* inefficient *worker.* *—n-* **in′ ef·fi′ cien·cy:** *He was finally discharged for* inefficiency. *adv-* **in′ ef·fi′ cient·ly.**

in·e·las·tic (ĭn′ ə lăs′ tĭk) *adj-* **1** not elastic: *Ice is an* inelastic *substance.* **2** not easily changed or adapted to fit circumstances; inflexible: *an* inelastic *supply of steel.* *—n-* **in′ e·las·tic′ i·ty.**

in·el·e·gant (ĭn ĕl′ ə gənt) *adj-* lacking in elegance, refinement, or good taste; coarse; crude: *an* inelegant *style.* *—n-* **in·el′ e·gance.** *adv-* **in·el′ e·gant·ly.**

in·el·i·gi·ble (ĭn ĕl′ ə jə bəl) *adj-* not eligible; unqualified for a certain position, activity, etc. *n-* person who is not eligible. *—n-* **in·el′ i·gi·bil′ i·ty.**

in·ept (ĭn ĕpt′) *adj-* **1** not fit or suited; out of place; inappropriate: *an* inept *remark.* **2** awkward; clumsy: *an* inept *carpenter.* *—adv-* **in·ept′ ly.** *n-* **in·ept′ ness.**

►INEPT means clumsy or unfit: *He is an* inept *doctor.* INAPT refers to suitability: *His words were* inapt.

in·ept·i·tude (ĭn ĕp′ tə tōōd′, -tyōōd′) *n-* **1** lack of suitability; inappropriateness. **2** awkwardness; incompetence. **3** foolish or inappropriate act or remark: *a book full of* ineptitudes.

in·e·qual·i·ty (ĭn′ ĭ kwŏl′ ə tē) *n-* [*pl.* **in·e·qual·i·ties**] **1** lack of equality; difference in quality, standing, etc.: *an* inequality *of opportunity for education.* **2** lack of evenness or uniformity, or an instance of this: *marked* inequalities *in temperature.* **3** *Mathematics* statement that one quantity is either less than or more than another quantity.

in·eq·ui·ta·ble (ĭn ĕk′ wə tə bəl) *adj-* not equitable; unfair or unjust. *—adv-* **in·eq′ ui·ta·bly.**

in·eq·ui·ty (ĭn ĕk′ wə tē) ***n-*** [*pl.* **in·eq·ui·ties**] **1** lack of equity or fairness; injustice. **2** unfair or unjust act, condition, etc.

in·e·rad·i·ca·ble (ĭn′ ə răd′ ə kə bəl) ***adj-*** such as cannot be erased or removed: *an* ineradicable *mistake.* —***adv-*** **in′ e·rad′ i·ca·bly.**

in·ert (ĭ nûrt′) ***adj-*** **1** having no power to act or move: *an* inert *lump of clay.* **2** slow; sluggish. **3** not entering into chemical reaction under ordinary circumstances: *an* inert *gas.* —***adv-*** **in·ert′ ly.** ***n-*** **in·ert′ ness.**

inert gas ***n-*** any of a group of six gases that are not chemically reactive under ordinary conditions of temperature and pressure. The inert gases are helium, neon, argon, krypton, xenon, and radon.

in·er·tia (ĭ nûr′ shə) ***n-*** **1** *Physics* property of matter by which an object tends to remain at rest or, if in motion, to continue moving uniformly in the same direction until it is acted upon by an external force. The quantitative measure of inertia is mass. **2** unwillingness to change or act: *A feeling of* inertia *often follows a long illness.*

inertial guidance ***n-*** navigation of a rocket, submarine, etc., by a self-contained, automatic system requiring no information from outside the vehicle. By means of gyroscopes, accelerometers, and a computer, the system senses and compensates for any changes in direction and speed from a predetermined course.

in·es·ca·pa·ble (ĭn′ ə skā′ pə bəl) ***adj-*** such as cannot be escaped or avoided: *the* inescapable *consequences of one's errors.* —***adv-*** **in′ es·ca′ pa·bly.**

in·es·ti·ma·ble (ĭn ĕs′ tə mə bəl) ***adj-*** too great to be estimated or measured: *a gift of* inestimable *value*; *an* inestimable *distance.* —***adv-*** **in·es′ ti·ma·bly.**

in·ev·i·ta·ble (ĭn ĕv′ ə tə bəl) ***adj-*** not to be avoided, escaped, or averted; sure to happen; certain: *With our team so far in the lead, victory seems* inevitable. —***n-*** **in·ev′ i·ta·bil′i·ty.** ***adv-*** **in·ev′ i·ta·bly.**

in·ex·act (ĭn′ ĕg zăkt′) ***adj-*** not accurate; not exact; not absolutely correct: *He earned a low mark on the test for his* inexact *answers.* —***adv-*** **in′ ex·act′ ly.** ***n-*** **in′ ex·act′ ness.**

in·ex·cus·a·ble (ĭn′ ĕks kyōō′ zə bəl) ***adj-*** not to be forgiven, pardoned, or justified; not to be explained away: *That boy's continued carelessness is* inexcusable. —***n-*** **in′ ex·cus′ a·bil′ i·ty.** ***adv-*** **in′ ex·cus′ a·bly.**

in·ex·haust·i·ble (ĭn′ ĕg zŏs′ tə bəl) ***adj-*** without end or limits; impossible to use up. —***n-*** **in′ ex·haust′ i·bil′ i·ty.** ***adv-*** **in′ ex·haust′ i·bly.**

in·ex·o·ra·ble (ĭn ĕk′ sər ə bəl, ĭn ĕg′ zĕr-) ***adj-*** **1** not changed or influenced by pleas; unyielding: *an* inexorable *enemy.* **2** such as cannot be changed, stopped, prevented, etc.: *the* inexorable *advance of the tide.* —***n-*** **in·ex′ o·ra·bil′ i·ty.** ***adv-*** **in·ex′ o·ra·bly.**

in·ex·pe·di·ent (ĭn′ ĕk spē′ dē ənt) ***adj-*** not expedient; inadvisable; unwise: *It is* inexpedient *to raise prices now.* —***n-*** **in′ ex·pe′ di·en·cy.** ***adv-*** **in′ ex·pe′ di·ent·ly.**

in·ex·pen·sive (ĭn′ ĕk spĕn′ sĭv) ***adj-*** not expensive; cheap. —***adv-*** **in′ ex·pen′ sive·ly.** ***n-*** **in′ ex·pen′ sive·ness.**

in·ex·pe·ri·ence (ĭn′ ĕk spêr′ ē əns) ***n-*** lack of experience, or of the skill and ability that come from first-hand knowledge or practice. —***adj-*** **in′ ex·pe′ ri·enced.**

in·ex·pert (ĭn ĕk′ spûrt′) ***adj-*** not expert. —***adv-*** **in·ex′ pert·ly** ***n-*** **in·ex′ pert·ness.**

in·ex·pi·a·ble (ĭn ĕk′ spē ə bəl) ***adj-*** such as cannot be expiated or atoned for; unpardonable: *an* inexpiable *sin.*

in·ex·pli·ca·ble (ĭn ĕk′ splĭ kə bəl, ĭn′ ĭk splĭk′ ə bəl) ***adj-*** not to be explained; impossible to account for; beyond understanding: *an* inexplicable *act.* —***n-*** **in·ex′ pli·ca·bil′ i·ty.** ***adv-*** **in·ex′ pli·ca·bly.**

in·ex·press·i·ble (ĭn′ ĕk sprĕs′ ə bəl) ***adj-*** such as cannot be put into words; beyond one's ability to express: *an* inexpressible *longing.* —***n-*** **in′ ex·press′ i·bil′ i·ty.** ***adv-*** **in′ ex·press′ i·bly.**

in·ex·pres·sive (ĭn′ ĕk sprĕs′ ĭv) ***adj-*** not expressive: *an* inexpressive *face.* —***n-*** **in′ ex·pres′ sive·ness.**

in·ex·tin·guish·a·ble (ĭn′ ĕk stĭng′ gwĭsh ə bəl) ***adj-*** such as cannot be extinguished or put out; unquenchable. —***adv-*** **in′ ex·tin′ guish·a·bly.**

in·ex·tri·ca·ble (ĭn ĕk′ strĭ kə bəl) ***adj-*** so entangled or confused as to be difficult or impossible to untie, escape from, solve, etc.: *an* inextricable *difficulty.* —***adv-*** **in·ex′ tri·ca·bly.**

in·fal·li·ble (ĭn făl′ ə bəl) ***adj-*** incapable of failing or being wrong; unerring: *He claims his remedy is* infallible. *Weather forecasts are not* infallible. —***n-*** **in·fal′ i·bil′ i·ty.** ***adv-*** **in·fal′ li·bly.**

in·fa·mous (ĭn′ fə məs) ***adj-*** **1** having a reputation for wickedness: *an* infamous *pirate.* **2** shameful; disgraceful: *an* infamous *day in history.* —***adv-*** **in′ fa·mous·ly.** ***n-*** **in′ fa·mous·ness.**

in·fa·my (ĭn′ fə mē) ***n-*** [*pl.* **in·fa·mies**] **1** public shame, disgrace, and scorn: *The traitor brought ruin and* infamy *upon himself.* **2** great wickedness or evil, or an instance of this: *a life of* infamy; *hated for his* infamies.

in·fan·cy (ĭn′ fən sē) ***n-*** [*pl.* **in·fan·cies**] **1** babyhood; very early childhood. **2** first stages of development: *Fifty years ago the airplane was still in its* infancy.

in·fant (ĭn′ fənt) ***n-*** **1** very young child; baby. **2** in law, person under the age of 21; minor. *as* ***modifier***: *an* infant *diet*; infant *care*; *an* infant *industry.*

in·fan·ta (ĭn făn′ tə) ***n-*** daughter of a Spanish or Portuguese king.

in·fan·ti·cide (ĭn făn′ tə sīd′) ***n-*** **1** the killing of an infant, especially a newborn baby. **2** person who kills an infant.

in·fan·tile (ĭn′ fən tīl′) ***adj-*** **1** of or related to babies: *an* infantile *disease.* **2** typical of a baby; childish: *her* infantile *behavior.*

infantile paralysis ***n-*** poliomyelitis.

in·fan·til·ism (ĭn′ fən tə lĭz′ əm, -tī lĭz′ əm) ***n-*** abnormal continuation or appearance of childlike traits in adults.

in·fan·try (ĭn′ fən trē) ***n-*** [*pl.* **in·fan·tries**] soldiers who are armed, equipped, and trained to fight on foot; foot soldiers. —***n-*** **in′ fan·try·man.**

in·fat·u·ate (ĭn făch′ ōō āt′) ***vt-*** [**in·fat·u·at·ed, in·fat·u·at·ing**] to arouse an unreasonable passion in (someone).
infatuated with foolishly or unreasonably in love with or devoted to (someone or something): *She is* infatuated with *her own beauty.*

in·fat·u·a·tion (ĭn făch′ ōō ā′ shən) ***n-*** state of being infatuated; foolish or unreasonable love for or devotion to someone or something.

in·fect (ĭn fĕkt′) ***vt-*** to cause disease, unhealthiness, or pollution in by the introduction of germs, viruses, etc.: *Escaping sewage may* infect *drinking water. Janet's cold* infected *the entire family.*

in·fec·tion (ĭn fĕk′ shən) ***n-*** **1** an infecting or becoming infected; especially, a causing of disease by contact with germs or viruses: *to protect a cut against* infection. **2** disease caused by germs or viruses: *a chronic* infection.

in·fec·tious (ĭn fĕk′ shəs) ***adj-*** **1** caused or spread by germs, viruses, etc.: *an* infectious *disease.* **2** tending to spread to others: *Enthusiasm is* infectious. —***adv-*** **in·fec′ tious·ly**: *She giggled* infectiously. ***n-*** **in·fec′ tious·ness.**

in·fe·lic·i·tous (ĭn′ fə lĭs′ ə təs) ***adj-*** not felicitous.

in·fe·lic·i·ty (ĭn′ fə lĭs′ ə tē) ***n-*** [*pl.* **in·fe·lic·i·ties**] **1** lack of felicity. **2** infelicitous act or remark.

in·fer (ĭn fûr′) ***vt-*** [**in·ferred, in·fer·ring**] to understand or conclude on the basis of various facts, impressions, judgments, etc.; deduce from evidence and experience:

From the way the mice acted, he inferred *that they were hungry. I* infer *that you are angry.*

► In cases where meaning is not directly stated, the listener or reader INFERS, and the speaker or writer IMPLIES: *He* implied *that I was a liar. I* inferred *from his statement that he thought I was a liar.*

in·fer·ence (ĭn′ fər əns) ***n*-** **1** an inferring or deducing: *to use* inference *in making up one's mind.* **2** something inferred: *His* inferences *are based on errors of fact.*

in·fer·en·tial (ĭn′ fə rĕn′ shəl) ***adj*-** of or related to inference. **—*adv*- in′ fer·en′ tial·ly.**

in·fe·ri·or (ĭn fêr′ ē ər) ***adj*-** **1** lower in place, rank, quality, importance, etc.: *to occupy an* inferior *position; to feel* inferior *because of lack of education.* **2** of poor quality: *to sell* inferior *merchandise;* inferior *workmanship.* ***n*-** person who ranks below another.

inferior to lower in quality, importance, etc., than.

in·fe·ri·or·i·ty (ĭn′ fêr′ ē ŏr′ ə tē) ***n*-** **[in·fe·ri·or·i·ties]** inferior or lower rank, quality, or importance.

inferiority complex ***n*-** in psychology, a complex based on a person's beliefs, feelings, etc., about his real or imagined handicaps. For instance, if he believes himself weak, he may act overly aggressive.

in·fer·nal (ĭn fûr′ nəl) ***adj*-** **1** of or characteristic of hell: *the* infernal *regions;* infernal *heat.* **2** *Informal* hateful; outrageous: *his* infernal *impudence.* **—*adv*- in·fer′ nal·ly.**

infernal machine ***n*-** explosive device, often disguised as a harmless object, for destroying life or property.

in·fer·no (ĭn fûr′ nō) ***n*-** [*pl.* **in·fer·nos**] **1** hell. **2** any place of terror or misery, especially one of intense heat: *The fire department found the house was an* inferno.

in·fer·tile (ĭn fûr′ təl) ***adj*-** not fertile.

in·fest (ĭn fĕst′) ***vt*-** to swarm in or over so as to cause trouble or harm; overrun: *Pirates* infest *the coast.*

in·fes·ta·tion (ĭn′ fĕs tā′ shən) ***n*-** act of infesting, or the condition of being infested.

in·fi·del (ĭn′ fə dəl) ***n*-** person who does not believe in a certain religion; especially, in former times among Christians, one who was not a Christian or, among Muslims, one who did not believe in Islam.

in·fi·del·i·ty (ĭn fə dĕl′ ə tē) ***n*-** [*pl.* **in·fi·del·i·ties**] violation of faith or trust; unfaithfulness.

in·field (ĭn′ fēld′) ***n*-** **1** the part of a baseball field generally bounded by the base lines. **2** players of the defending team stationed in this area; the infielders. *as* ***modifier***: *an* infield *hit.*

in·field·er (ĭn′ fēl′ dər) ***n*-** in baseball, any of the four players, the first, second, and third baseman, and the shortstop, who play near the three bases.

in·fil·trate (ĭn′ fĭl′ trāt′) ***vt*-** **[in·fil·trat·ed, in·fil·trat·ing]** **1** to move gradually and secretly into or through (enemy lines, a government, etc.), especially so as to gain control or disrupt normal procedures. **2** to filter or seep into or through; permeate. **—*n*- in′ fil·tra′ tion. *n*- in′ fil·tra′ tor:** *Communist* infiltrators *ruined the reform group.*

infin. infinitive.

in·fi·nite (ĭn′ fə nət) ***adj*-** **1** without limits; endless: *stars scattered through* infinite *space.* **2** seemingly endless; vast; inexhaustible: *to act with* infinite *care.* **3** *Mathematics* having a magnitude that is larger than any fixed magnitude that can be assigned. **—*adv*- in′ fi·nite·ly. *n*- in′ fi·nite·ness.**

in·fin·i·tes·i·mal (ĭn′ fĭn′ ə tĕs′ ə məl, -tĕz′ məl) ***adj*-** **1** too small to be measured or considered significant: *an* infinitesimal *speck.* **2** *Mathematics* of a variable quantity, having a smaller magnitude than any magnitude that can be assigned, except zero. ***n*-** *Mathematics* such a variable quantity. **—*adv*- in′ fin·i·tes′ i·mal·ly.**

in·fin·i·tive (ĭn fĭn′ ə tĭv) *Grammar* ***n*-** **1** base form of a verb when not used to show time. The infinitive is used in verb phrases introduced by "to" or by one of the modal auxiliaries "will," "should," "may," etc. Examples: *Mary likes to* sing *folk songs. John will* play *on the A team this year.* **2** verb phrase introduced by "to."

in·fin·i·tude (ĭn fĭn′ ə to͞od′, -tyo͞od′) ***n*-** infinite amount, extent, etc.; boundlessness: *the* infinitude *of space; an* infinitude *of patience.*

in·fin·i·ty (ĭn fĭn′ ə tē) ***n*-** [*pl.* **in·fin·i·ties**] **1** space, time, distance, etc. that has or seems to have no limit or boundary. **2** state of being infinite; boundlessness. **3** amount or number that is immeasurably large. **4** *Mathematics* (1) quantity having an infinite magnitude, represented by the symbol [∞]. (2) the position of points in space that are assumed to be at an infinite distance from a reference point.

in·firm (ĭn fûrm′) ***adj*-** weak, unsteady, or feeble, especially from old age or sickness. **—*adv*- in·firm′ ly.**

in·fir·ma·ry (ĭn fûr′ mə rē) ***n*-** [*pl.* **in·fir·ma·ries**] building or room in a school, factory, etc., for medical care.

in·fir·mi·ty (ĭn fûr′ mə tē) ***n*-** [*pl.* **in·fir·mi·ties**] **1** state of being infirm; weakness; feebleness: *the* infirmity *of old age.* **2** a personal flaw: *He tolerates my* infirmities.

in·flame (ĭn flām′) ***vt*-** **[in·flamed, in·flam·ing]** **1** to stir up; arouse: *His fiery speech* inflamed *the people.* **2** to make red, swollen, and painful: *The smoke from the bonfire* inflamed *her eyes.*

in·flam·ma·ble (ĭn flăm′ ə bəl) ***adj*-** **1** flammable. **2** easily excited or aroused: *an* inflammable *temper.* **—*n*- in·flam′ ma·bil′ i·ty. *adv*- in·flam′ ma·bly.**

► For usage note see FLAMMABLE.

in·flam·ma·tion (ĭn′ flə mā′ shən) ***n*-** **1** condition of being inflamed; redness, swelling, etc., of some part of the body. **2** act of stirring up, or the condition of being stirred up: *the* inflammation *of public feeling.*

in·flam·ma·tor·y (ĭn flăm′ ə tôr′ ē) ***adj*-** **1** tending to excite or arouse anger, violence, revolt, etc.: *an* inflammatory *speech.* **2** related to or causing inflammation: *an* inflammatory *infection.*

in·flate (ĭn flāt′) ***vt*-** **[in·flat·ed, in·flat·ing]** **1** to swell by filling with air or gas; distend: *to* inflate *a balloon.* **2** to puff up with pride or self-satisfaction: *David's new honors helped to* inflate *his already high opinion of himself.* **3** to increase (prices, values, etc.) beyond the usual degree. ***vi*-** to become blown up or puffed up. **—*adj*- in·flat′ a·ble. *n*- in·flat′ er** or **in·fla′ tor.**

in·fla·tion (ĭn flā′ shən) ***n*-** **1** process of inflating, or the condition of being inflated. **2** a rise in prices and a fall in the value of money, caused by an increase in the amount of money available to buy goods and services, or by a scarcity of goods and services.

in·fla·tion·ary (ĭn flā′ shən ĕr′ ē) ***adj*-** of, related to, or caused by an economic inflation: *an* inflationary *price.*

in·flect (ĭn flĕkt′) ***vt*-** **1** to change the pitch or tone of (the voice). **2** *Grammar* to vary the form of (a word) so as to show changes in person, case, tense, etc.; decline or conjugate. "Him," "his," "gave," and "given" are inflected forms of the pronoun "he" and the verb "give."

in·flec·tion (ĭn flĕk′ shən) ***n*-** **1** the rise and fall in the voice; change in pitch or tone of voice: *His* inflection *showed that he was asking a question, not making a statement.* **2** *Grammar* (1) process by which the form of a word changes to show tense (go, going, gone, went), number (go, goes; man, men), case (man, man's, men's), or degree (small, smaller, smallest). (2) any of these changes of form: *the* inflections *of the verb.*

in·flex·i·ble (ĭn flĕk′ sə bəl) ***adj*-** 1 not bending easily; rigid: *an* inflexible *iron rod.* 2 not to be turned from a set plan or purpose; unyielding: *Once he has decided, he is* inflexible. 3 unchanging; immutable: *an* inflexible *law.* **—*n*- in·flex′i·bil′i·ty. *adv*- in·flex′i·bly.**

in·flict (ĭn flĭkt′) ***vt*-** 1 to lay on (a blow); cause (wounds, pain, etc.): *The angry lion attacked the trainer and* inflicted *many wounds.* 2 to put on or impose (a punishment or something not welcome): *He* inflicts *his troubles on everyone.* **—*n*- in·flic′tion.**

in·flo·res·cence (ĭn′ flə rĕs′ əns) ***n*-** a cluster or group of flowers that has a particular kind of arrangement.

in·flow (ĭn′flō′) ***n*-** 1 action or process of flowing in. 2 something, such as water, air, etc., that flows in.

in·flu·ence (ĭn′ flo͞o əns) ***n*-** 1 power to persuade others or or to produce results, especially by suggestion and other indirect means: *His* influence *is limited to this department.* 2 effect produced by such power: *Florence Nightingale had a great* influence *on the development of nursing.* 3 person who or thing that produces such an effect: *Florence Nightingale was a great* influence *in improved medical care.* 4 power that comes from wealth, social position, connections, etc.: *Will you use your* influence *to help me?* ***vt*-** **[in·flu·enced, in·flu·enc·ing]** to have an effect on: *Weather* influences *our lives.*

in·flu·en·tial (ĭn′ flo͞o ĕn′ shəl) ***adj*-** having influence; exerting power: *an* influential *man.* **—*adv*- in′ flu·en′ tial·ly.**

in·flu·en·za (ĭn′ flo͞o ĕn′ zə) ***n*-** contagious virus disease marked by an inflamed nose and throat, headache, fever, muscular pains, etc.; flu.

in·flux (ĭn′ flŭks′) ***n*-** a flowing or steady moving in; inflow: *an* influx *of water*; *an* influx *of tourists.*

in·fold (ĭn fōld′) enfold.

in·form (ĭn fôrm′, -fôrm′) ***vt*-** to tell; make known to; give information to: *Please* inform *me when she arrives.* ***vi*-** to give information that causes another to be accused or suspected (usually followed by "against" or "on"): *The thief* informed *on his accomplices.*

in·for·mal (ĭn fôr′ məl, ĭn fôr′-) ***adj*-** 1 not formal; not following set rules, customs, or ceremonies: *an* informal *conference of the committee members*; *to give an* informal *talk*; *an* informal *party.* 2 casual and relaxed, or suitable for casual and relaxed occasions: *an* informal *mood*; informal *clothes.* 3 of language, suitable for most conversation and casual writing, but lacking the dignity, care, and accuracy of formal speech and writing. Informal language is not considered wrong or substandard, even though it is not suitable for every language situation. **—*adv*- in·for′ mal·ly.**

in·for·mal·i·ty (ĭn fər măl′ ə tē) ***n*-** [*pl.* **in·for·mal·i·ties**] 1 lack of formality. 2 informal act.

in·form·ant (ĭn fôr′ mənt, ĭn fôr′-) ***n*-** person who gives information.

in·for·ma·tion (ĭn′ fər mā′ shən) ***n*-** 1 knowledge, facts, news, etc., communicated to or learned by another or others: *Much* information *can be gained by reading. Can you give me any* information *about the new bus schedules?* 2 communication or learning of such knowledge or facts: *This booklet is for your* information. 3 signals, messages, or data that go into or come out of a computer. **—*adj*- in′ for·ma′ tion·al.**

in·form·a·tive (ĭn fôr′ mə tĭv, ĭn fôr′-) ***adj*-** giving or providing information: *an* informative *booklet.*

in·formed (ĭn fôrmd′, -fôrmd′) ***adj*-** 1 having special or authoritative information: *an* informed *news source.* 2 having or showing learning or knowledge; educated: *an* informed *mind*; informed *tastes.*

in·form·er (ĭn fôr′ mər, ĭn fôr′-) ***n*-** person who gives information, especially one who incriminates another.

in·frac·tion (ĭn frăk′ shən) ***n*-** the breaking or violation of a law, rule, etc.; infringement.

in·fra·red rays (ĭn′ frə rĕd′) ***n*-** electromagnetic waves that have a longer wavelength than visible red light but are shorter than radio waves. Infrared rays cannot be seen but can usually be felt as heat.

in·fre·quent (ĭn frē′ kwənt) ***adj*-** not frequent; rare: *his* infrequent *visits*; *an* infrequent *visitor.* **—*n*- in·fre′ quence** or **in·fre′ quen·cy. *adv*- in·fre′ quent·ly.**

in·fringe (ĭn frĭnj′) ***vt*-** **[in·fringed, in·fring·ing]** to violate; disregard or break (a law, patent, etc.) **—*n*- in·fringe′ ment. *n*- in·fring′ er.**

infringe on (or **upon**) to trespass or encroach on.

in·fu·ri·ate (ĭn fyo͝or′ ē āt′) ***vt*-** **[in·fu·ri·at·ed, in·fu·ri·at·ing]** to enrage; make furious; madden. **—*adv*- in·fu′ ri·at′ ing·ly:** *an* infuriatingly *sarcastic voice.*

in·fuse (ĭn fyo͞oz′) ***vt*-** **[in·fused, in·fus·ing]** 1 to put in by, or as if by, pouring; instill: *The coach* infused *enthusiasm into the team.* 2 to inspire: *to* infuse *a team with spirit.* 3 to steep (a plant, tea leaves, etc.) in a liquid.

in·fus·i·ble (ĭn fyo͞o′ zə bəl) ***n*-** such as cannot be fused or melted; not fusible. **—*n*- in·fus′ i·bil′ i·ty.**

in·fu·sion (ĭn fyo͞o′ zhən) ***n*-** 1 act or process of infusing, or an instance of this. 2 preparation obtained by steeping a substance in a liquid.

[1]-ing *word ending* used to form the present participle of verbs: *I am go*ing. *You are driv*ing. *It is dropp*ing. *He was rac*ing. [from Old English **-end(e).**]

[2]-ing *suffix* 1 (used to form nouns from verbs) (1) action or process indicated by the verb: *our walk*ing; *its buzz*ing; *their meet*ing. (2) result or product of such action: *a draw*ing; *a build*ing. (3) something that is used for a certain purpose indicated by the verb: *seat cover*ing; *stuff*ing for a cushion; *cake frost*ing. 2 (used to form nouns of the verbal type from words other than verbs): *to enjoy bullfight*ing. [from Old English **-ing.**]

in·gen·ious (ĭn jēn′ yəs) ***adj*-** 1 clever; inventive; resourceful: *an* ingenious *mechanic.* 2 showing ingenuity; skillfully invented, made or done: *an* ingenious *machine.* **—*adv*- in·gen′ ious·ly. *n*- in·gen′ ious·ness.**

►Should not be confused with INGENUOUS.

in·ge·nue (ăn′ jə no͞o′, *Fr.* ăn′ zhə nʏ′) ***n*-** naive or unsophisticated young girl; especially, in the theater, the role of such a girl, or the actress who plays such a role.

in·ge·nu·i·ty (ĭn′ jə no͞o′ ə tē) ***n*-** [*pl.* **in·ge·nu·i·ties**] cleverness or skill in inventing, devising, etc.: *to use* ingenuity *in escaping*; *built with great* ingenuity.

in·gen·u·ous (ĭn jĕn′ yo͞o əs) ***adj*-** simple and natural; without guile: *the* ingenuous *questions of a child.* **—*adv*- in·gen′ u·ous·ly. *n*- in·gen′ u·ous·ness.**

►Should not be confused with INGENIOUS.

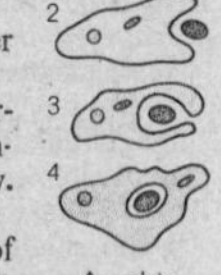

Amebic ingestion

in·gest (ĭn jĕst′) ***vt*-** to take food into the body for digestion. **—*n*- in·ges′ tion.**

in·gle·nook (ĭng′ gəl no͝ok′) ***n*-** corner beside a fireplace.

in·glor·i·ous (ĭn glôr′ ē əs) ***adj*-** dishonorable or disgraceful; shameful: *an* inglorious *defeat.* **—*adv*- in·glor′ i·ous·ly. *n*- in·glor′ i·ous·ness.**

in·got (ĭng′ gət) ***n*-** bar or other mass of cast metal produced at a refinery, smelting plant, etc.

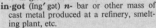

in·graft (ĭn grăft′) engraft.

in·grain (ĭn grān′, ĭn′-) ***vt*-** to fix deeply, especially in the mind or spirit: *to* ingrain *a belief in someone's mind.*

in·grained (ĭn′ grānd′) ***adj-*** deeply or permanently fixed; deep-rooted: *an* ingrained *prejudice*; ingrained *dirt that will not wash off.*

in·grate (ĭn′ grāt′) ***n-*** ungrateful or thankless person.

in·gra·ti·ate (ĭn grā′ shē āt′) ***vt-*** **[in·gra·ti·at·ed, in·gra·ti·at·ing]** to make one's way into a person's favor; endear (oneself) to someone: *He tried to* ingratiate *himself with his rich uncle.* **—*adv-* in·gra′ ti·at′ ing·ly.**

in·grat·i·tude (ĭn grăt′ ə to͞od′, -tyo͞od′) ***n-*** lack of gratitude or appreciation; thankless or ungrateful conduct: *He resented her* ingratitude.

in·gre·di·ent (ĭn grē′ dē ənt) ***n-*** any one of the things that make up a mixture or other product made by mixing or combining substances: *Eggs and butter are among the* ingredients *of this cake.*

in·gress (ĭn′ grĕs′) ***n-*** **1** act or right of entering a building, office, etc. **2** way by which to enter; entrance.

in·grow·ing (ĭn′ grō′ ĭng) ***adj-*** growing inward.

in·grown (ĭn′ grōn′) ***adj-*** grown into or within something, especially the flesh: *an* ingrown *toenail.*

in·hab·it (ĭn hăb′ ət) ***vt-*** to live in or on; dwell in: *Manlike creatures may* inhabit *distant planets. Seals* inhabit *these islands.* **—*n-* in·hab′ i·ta′ tion.**

in·hab·it·a·ble (ĭn hăb′ ə tə bəl) ***adj-*** such as can be inhabited; suitable for living in or occupying: *an* inhabitable *island.*

in·hab·it·ant (ĭn hăb′ ə tənt) ***n-*** permanent or habitual dweller in a place: *The town has 6,000* inhabitants.

in·hab·it·ed (ĭn hăb′ ə təd) ***adj-*** lived in, having dwellers or residents: *This island is* inhabited.

in·hal·ant (ĭn hā′ lənt) ***n-*** medicine to be inhaled.

in·ha·la·tor (ĭn′ hə lā′ tər) ***n-*** device from which one can inhale air, medicine, etc.

in·hale (ĭn hāl′) ***vt-*** **[in·haled, in·hal·ing]** to draw into the lungs; breathe in: *to* inhale *fresh air.* ***vi-***: *He* inhales *with difficulty because he has a cold.* **—*n-* in′ ha·la′ tion** (ĭn′ hə lā′ shən).

in·hal·er (ĭn hā′ lər) ***n-*** **1** device from which something is inhaled, such as an inhalator. **2** one that inhales.

in·har·mo·ni·ous (ĭn′ här mō′ nē əs) ***adj-*** not harmonious; lacking harmony or agreement. **—*adv-* in′ har·mo′ ni·ous·ly.** ***n-*** **in′ har·mo′ ni·ous·ness.**

in·her·ent (ĭn hêr′ ənt, ĭn hĕr′-) ***adj-*** existing as a natural or basic part of a person or thing; intrinsic: *the* inherent *hardness of steel*; *his* inherent *generosity*; *the danger* inherent *in this situation.* **—*n-* in·her′ ence.** ***adv-*** **in·her′ ent·ly.**

in·her·it (ĭn hĕr′ ĭt) ***vt-*** **1** to come into possession of at the death of a former owner; succeed to: *She* inherited *a fortune in jewels.* **2** to receive by birth from one's parents or ancestors: *He* inherited *his brown hair from his father.* **3** to get from a former time, condition etc.: *We* inherited *these traditions from our ancestors.*

in·her·it·a·ble (ĭn hĕr′ ə tə bəl) ***adj-*** such as can be inherited; heritable: *an* inheritable *characteristic.*

in·her·it·ance (ĭn hĕr′ ə təns) ***n-*** **1** something inherited: *His* inheritance *was a million dollars.* **2** an inheriting: *His fortune came to him by* inheritance, *not by hard work.*

in·her·i·tor (ĭn hĕr′ ə tər) ***n-*** person who inherits something; heir: *He is the* inheritor *of his aunt's estate.*

in·hib·it (ĭn hĭb′ ĭt) ***vt-*** **1** to restrain or hold in check: *The presence of the police* inhibited *the crowd.* **2** to suppress (a feeling, thought, wish, etc.) within oneself: *A sense of duty causes us to* inhibit *our desire for pleasure.* **—*adj-* in·hib′ i·to′ ry**: *Being watched has an* inhibitory *effect on most people.*

in·hi·bi·tion (ĭn′ hə bĭsh′ ən) ***n-*** **1** act or process of inhibiting: *the* inhibition *of an impulse.* **2** something inhibited: *He has few* inhibitions.

in·hos·pi·ta·ble (ĭn hŏs′ pĭt ə bəl) ***adj-*** **1** not hospitable; unfriendly toward visitors or guests: *an* inhospitable *host.* **2** not providing food, shelter, or other resources; barren: *an* inhospitable *region.* **—*adv-* in·hos′ pi·ta·bly.**

in·hos·pi·tal·i·ty (ĭn hŏs′ pə tăl′ ə tē) ***n-*** lack of hospitality.

in·hu·man (ĭn′ hyo͞o′ mən) ***adj-*** **1** not humane; cruel; ruthless: *the enemy's* inhuman *treatment of prisoners.* **2** not resembling or typical of a human being: *strange,* inhuman *monsters.* **—*adv-* in′ hu′ man·ly.**

in·hu·mane (ĭn′ hyo͞o mān′) ***adj-*** not humane; merciless; cruel. **—*adv-* in′ hu·mane′ ly.**

in·hu·man·i·ty (ĭn′ hyo͞o măn′ ə tē) ***n-*** [*pl.* **in·hu·man·i·ties**] **1** lack of mercy or sympathy; cruelty: *man's* inhumanity *to man.* **2** inhuman or cruel act.

in·im·i·cal (ĭ nĭm′ ĭ kəl) ***adj-*** **1** opposed or unfriendly; hostile: *For some reason he is* inimical *to me.* **2** showing hostility: *an* inimical *gesture.* **3** harmful; injurious: *Narcotics are* inimical *to health.* **—*adv-* in·im′ i·cal·ly.**

in·im·i·ta·ble (ĭ nĭm′ ə tə bəl) ***adj-*** impossible to imitate; matchless: *an* inimitable *performance.* **—*n-* in·im′ i·ta·bil′ i·ty.** ***adv-*** **in·im′ i·ta·bly.**

in·iq·ui·tous (ĭ nĭk′ wə təs) ***adj-*** very unjust or wicked. **—*adv-* in·iq′ ui·tous·ly.** ***n-*** **in·iq′ ui·tous·ness.**

in·iq·ui·ty (ĭ nĭk′ wə tē) ***n-*** [*pl.* **in·iq·ui·ties**] **1** great injustice or wickedness. **2** unjust or wicked act or deed.

in·i·tial (ĭ nĭsh′ əl) ***n-*** (often **initials**) first letter of each part of a name: *Sam Allen's* initials *are S.A.* ***adj-*** **1** of, at, or related to the beginning or first part: *the* initial *letters of his name*; *the* initial *stages of an experiment.* **2** done or occurring for the first time: *our* initial *visit to the new museum.* ***vt-*** to mark or sign with the first letters of one's name: *He* initialed *the papers.*

in·i·tial·ly (ĭ nĭsh′ ə lē) ***adv-*** at the beginning.

Initial Teaching Alphabet ***n-*** set of forty-three letters or symbols, each representing a sound of the English language, used to teach reading in some schools.

[1]**in·i·ti·ate** (ĭ nĭsh′ ē āt′) ***vt-*** **[in·i·ti·at·ed, in·i·ti·at·ing]** **1** to begin; start on its way; introduce: *to* initiate *a drive to raise money*; *to* initiate *a new law.* **2** to help or instruct (a person) in something new: *to* initiate *a student into the study of Spanish.* **3** to admit or introduce (a person) to a club, society, etc., with formal ceremonies.

[2]**in·i·ti·ate** (ĭ nĭsh′ ē ət) ***n-*** person who has been recently initiated into a club, society, etc.

in·i·ti·a·tion (ĭ nĭsh′ ē ā′ shən) ***n-*** **1** an initiating or being initiated; also, an instance of this: *the* initiation *of a new rule.* **2** the ceremonies with which a person is made a member of a group, club, etc.

in·i·ti·a·tive (ĭ nĭsh′ ə tĭv) ***n-*** **1** first or introductory step in an undertaking: *He took the* initiative *in producing the play.* **2** ability to see and readiness to undertake what must be done, without detailed instructions, urging, etc.; enterprise: *He has plenty of* initiative *and would do well in this job.* **3** the right of citizens to introduce new laws, or the method of doing so.

in·i·ti·a·tor (ĭ nĭsh′ ē ā′ tər) ***n-*** person who initiates, especially one who starts or introduces something new.

in·ject (ĭn jĕkt′) ***vt-*** **1** to force (a liquid) into, especially into a body cavity with a syringe, or into the flesh with a needle. **2** to throw in; introduce: *to* inject *a comment.*

in·jec·tion (ĭn jĕk′ shən) ***n-*** **1** act or process of injecting something: *the* injection *of vaccine into the body*; *the* injection *of some humor into the conversation.* **2** substance, such as a vaccine, injected into the body.

in·ju·di·cious (ĭn′ jə dĭsh′ əs) ***adj-*** not judicious. ***—adv-*** **in′ ju·di′ cious·ly.** ***n-*** **in′ ju·di′ cious·ness.**

in·junc·tion (ĭn jŭngk′ shən) ***n-*** **1** order; command; instruction: *He obeyed his father's* injunction. **2** in law, order from a court directing a person or group to do or not do something: *to issue an* injunction *against a strike.*

in·jure (ĭn′ jər) ***vt-*** **[in·jured, in·jur·ing]** to damage; harm: *to* injure *a leg*; *to* injure *one's reputation.*

in·ju·ri·ous (ĭn jŏŏr′ ē əs) ***adj-*** causing injury or harm; harmful: *infection from* injurious *bacteria*; *an* injurious *habit.* ***—adv-*** **in·ju′ ri·ous·ly.** ***n-*** **in·ju′ ri·ous·ness.**

in·ju·ry (ĭn′ jə rē) ***n-*** [*pl.* **in·ju·ries**] hurt or damage; harm: *an* injury *to one's eyes*; *an* injury *to one's pride.*

in·jus·tice (ĭn jŭs′ təs) ***n-*** **1** unfairness; lack of justice. **2** unjust act; wrong: *You do him an* injustice *to believe such gossip about him.*

ink (ĭngk) ***n-*** **1** colored fluid used for writing, drawing, and printing. **2** dark fluid ejected by certain marine animals, such as the squid or cuttlefish, to keep from being seen by an enemy. ***vt-*** to mark or cover with such fluid: *to* ink *type.* ***—n-*** **ink′ er.**

ink·horn (ĭngk′ hôrn′, -hôrn′) ***n-*** formerly, an inkwell made of horn or similar material.

ink·ling (ĭngk′ lĭng) ***n-*** slight idea or faint suggestion; hint: *Constance had no* inkling *of their plans.*

ink·stand (ĭngk′ stănd′) ***n-*** small rack or holder for a container of ink, pens, etc.

ink·well (ĭngk′ wĕl′) ***n-*** small container for ink, usually on a desk.

ink·y (ĭng′ kē) ***adj-*** **[ink·i·er, ink·i·est] 1** spotted or covered with ink: *Mike's* inky *fingers.* **2** dark as black ink: *an* inky *sky.* ***—n-*** **ink′ i·ness.**

in·laid (ĭn′ lād′) ***adj-*** **1** set into the surface as decoration: *an* inlaid *design of gold in a silver bracelet.* **2** decorated with a design set into the surface: *an* inlaid *box.*

in·land (ĭn′ lənd) ***adj-*** of, having to do with, or located in the interior part of a country or region; away from the sea: *an* inland *journey*; *an* inland *town.* ***adv-*** toward the interior; away from the sea: *to travel* inland.

in·land·er (ĭn′ lən dər) ***n-*** person living inland.

in-law (ĭn′ lŏ′) *Informal* ***n-*** a relative by marriage.

in·lay (ĭn′ lā′) ***n-*** **1** pieces of ivory, wood, metal, etc., set into the surface of something to form a design; also, a design made with such materials. **2** filling of gold, porcelain, etc., shaped and cast to fit snugly into a cavity in a tooth. ***vt-*** (*also* ĭn′ lā′) **[in·laid, in·lay·ing] 1** to set (pieces of ivory, wood, etc.) into a surface to form a design. **2** to decorate with such designs.

in·let (ĭn′ lĕt′) ***n-*** **1** small bay, cove, or arm of the sea. **2** entrance: *the* inlet *of a water main.*

Inlets on Maine coast

in·mate (ĭn′ māt′) ***n-*** one of a group living in the same place, especially in a prison or other institution.

in me·mo·ri·am (ĭn mə môr′ ē əm) *Latin* in or to the memory of a particular person.

in·most (ĭn′ mōst′) ***adj-*** **1** most personal, private, or intimate; deepest: *a person's* inmost *thoughts*; *a person's* inmost *longings.* **2** farthest in; innermost.

inn (ĭn) ***n-*** **1** small hotel, usually in the country. **2** restaurant or tavern. ***Hom-*** in.

in·nate (ĭ nāt′) ***adj-*** arising from or belonging to the inner nature of a person or thing; not acquired; intrinsic: *an* innate *love of freedom.* ***—adv-*** **in·nate′ ly.**

in·ner (ĭn′ ər) ***adj-*** **1** farther in; interior: *to withdraw to an* inner *room*; *the* inner *lining of a coat.* **2** having to do with the mind or soul: *man's* inner *life.* **3** private; personal; secret: *one's* inner *feelings.*

inner ear ***n-*** the innermost part of each ear, which contains the semicircular canals and the cochlea. For picture see [1]*ear.*

Inner Light ***n-*** in the Quaker religion, the presence of God in the human soul.

in·ner·most (ĭn′ ər mōst′) ***adj-*** farthest in from the outside; inmost: *the* innermost *depths of a cave.*

inner sanctum ***n-*** place, such as a private study, where one is free from disturbance or distraction.

inner tube ***n-*** rubber tube that can be inflated with air, used inside the tire of a motor vehicle.

in·ning (ĭn′ ĭng) ***n-*** **1** period in a baseball game or similar game during which each team has a turn at batting while the other plays in the field. **2 innings** turn or opportunity to accomplish something: *Our party will have its* innings *after the next election.*

inn·keep·er (ĭn′ kē′ pər) ***n-*** person who owns or manages an inn.

in·no·cence (ĭn′ ə səns) ***n-*** **1** freedom from guilt or blame: *We accept a person's* innocence *until he is proved guilty.* **2** freedom from evil or sin; purity. **3** freedom from trickery or deceit; simplicity; openness: *the* innocence *of a child.*

in·no·cent (ĭn′ ə sənt) ***adj-*** **1** free from guilt or wrongdoing; blameless: *The jury declared him* innocent. *She was* innocent *of spreading gossip.* **2** harmless in meaning and effect: *an* innocent *little prank.* **3** not worldly; free from deceit; simple or pure in thought: *as* innocent *as a baby.* ***—adv-*** **in′ no·cent·ly.**

in·noc·u·ous (ĭ nŏk′ yŏŏ əs) ***adj-*** harmless: *an* innocuous *remark.* ***—adv-*** **in·noc′ u·ous·ly.** ***n-*** **in·noc′ u·ous·ness.**

in·no·vate (ĭn′ ə vāt′) ***vt-*** **[in·no·vat·ed, in·no·vat·ing]** to introduce (something) that is new or that makes a change. ***vi-*** to make innovations. ***—n-*** **in′ no·va′ tor:** *He is an* innovator *in the field of fashion.*

in·no·va·tion (ĭn′ ə vā′ shən) ***n-*** **1** something new or different, such as a change in customs or ways of doing things: *The automobile was a great* innovation *in transportation.* **2** an introducing or bringing in something new: *the* innovation *of plastics into industry.*

in·nu·en·do (ĭn′ yŏŏ ĕn′ dō) ***n-*** [*pl.* **in·nu·en·does**] suggestion or hint, usually unfavorable; insinuation: *His conversation is full of sly* innuendoes.

in·nu·mer·a·ble (ĭ nōō′ mər ə bəl, ĭ nyōō′-) ***adj-*** too many to be counted; countless: *the* innumerable *stars.* ***—n-*** **in·nu′ mer·a·ble·ness.** ***adv-*** **in·nu′ mer·a·bly.**

in·oc·u·late (ĭ nŏk′ yə lāt′) ***vt-*** **[in·oc·u·lat·ed, in·oc·u·lat·ing] 1** to produce a mild case of disease in (a person or animal) by injecting or swallowing its bacteria or virus, usually in order to prevent future attacks: *to* inoculate *a child against typhoid.* **2** to introduce germs, molds, etc., into, usually for a scientific purpose. **3** to implant or instill (ideas, opinions, etc.) in the mind of.

in·oc·u·la·tion (ĭ nŏk′ yə lā′ shən) ***n-*** **1** an inoculating. **2** something injected or put in by inoculating.

in·of·fen·sive (ĭn′ ə fĕn′ sĭv) ***adj-*** **1** not offensive or unpleasant. **2** not harmful; innocuous. **3** not warlike, threatening, or dangerous; peaceable. ***—adv-*** **in′ of·fen′ sive·ly.** ***n-*** **in′ of·fen′ sive·ness.**

in·op·er·a·ble (ĭn ŏp′ ər ə bəl) ***adj-*** such as cannot be corrected or treated by surgery.

in·op·er·a·tive (ĭn ŏp′ ər ə tĭv′) ***adj-*** not in working condition: *The radio was* inoperative.

in·op·por·tune (ĭn ŏp′ ər tōōn′, -tyōōn′) ***adj-*** **1** happening at the wrong time: *an* inopportune *remark.* **2** in-

convenient. —*adv*- **in·op′ por·tune′ ly.** *n*- **in·op′ por·tune′ ness.**

in·or·di·nate (ĭn ôr′ də nət, ĭn ôr′-) *adj*- excessive; immoderate: *His anger was* inordinate. —*adv*- **in·or′ di·nate·ly.** *n*- **in·or′ di·nate·ness.**

in·or·gan·ic (ĭn′ ôr găn′ ĭk, ĭn′ ôr-) *adj*- made up of or relating to matter that is neither animal nor vegetable. Rocks are inorganic. —*adv*- **in′ or·gan′ i·cal·ly.**

in·pa·tient (ĭn′ pā′ shənt) *n*- patient who stays in a hospital or clinic while under medical treatment. *as modifier*: *the* inpatient *facilities of a hospital.*

in·put (ĭn′ po͝ot′) *n*- **1** quantity of energy that is put into a machine, electrical circuit, etc., in order to do work or overcome resistance. **2** the terminal through which the energy is introduced. **3** the information fed into a computer.

in·quest (ĭn′ kwĕst′) *n*- an official inquiry, especially one made with the help of a jury into the cause of a sudden death.

in·quire (ĭn kwīər′) *vi*- [**in·quired, in·quir·ing**] **1** to seek information by asking; ask (about): *to* inquire *about train schedules.* **2** to make an investigation (into): *The committee* inquired *into the causes of crime.* **3** to ask (after) the welfare or whereabouts of a person: *to* inquire *after a friend.* *vt*-: *I* inquired *the way to the station.* Also **enquire.** —*n*- **in·quir′ er.** *adv*- **in·quir′ ing·ly.**

in·quir·y (ĭng′ kwə rē, ĭn kwīr′ ē) *n*- [*pl.* **in·quir·ies**] **1** an inquiring: *Details will be given on* inquiry. **2** investigation: *an* inquiry *into the cause of the accident.* **3** question: *She made several* inquiries *about the subject.*

in·qui·si·tion (ĭn′ kwə zĭsh′ ən) *n*- **1** severe questioning or investigation, especially one that disregards the rights and feelings of the subject. **2 Inquisition** in the Roman Catholic Church of former days, an agency established for seeking out heresy and punishing heretics.

in·quis·i·tive (ĭn kwĭz′ ə tĭv) *adj*- **1** eager to learn; curious: *an* inquisitive *mind.* **2** too curious; prying; disregardful of another's privacy: *an* inquisitive *gossip.* —*adv*- **in·quis′ i·tive·ly.** *n*- **in·quis′ i·tive·ness.**

in·quis·i·tor (ĭn kwĭz′ ə tər) *n*- **1** person who conducts an inquisition. **2 Inquisitor** an officer of the Inquisition. —*adj*- **in·qui·si·to′ ri·al:** *an* inquisitorial *committee.*

in·road (ĭn′ rōd′) *n*- **1** sudden invasion; entry by force: *an* inroad *into the enemy's line.* **2** an advance that destroys the thing attacked: *Disease made great* inroads *on his reserve of strength.*

in·rush (ĭn′ rŭsh′) *n*- a pouring in; sudden invasion: *an* inrush *of waters*; *an* inrush *of campers.*

in·sane (ĭn sān′) *adj*- **1** not sane; seriously ill mentally; crazy; psychotic. **2** used by or for persons who are not sane: *an* insane *ward in a hospital.* —*adv*- **in·sane′ ly.**

in·san·i·tar·y (ĭn săn′ ə tĕr′ ē) *adj*- so unclean as to be a risk to health; contaminated: *the* insanitary *drinking water*; *the* insanitary *living conditions.*
►Should not be confused with UNSANITARY.

in·san·i·ty (ĭn săn′ ə tē) *n*- [*pl.* **in·san·i·ties**] **1** severe mental illness; madness; psychosis. **2** in law, mental condition that prevents one from knowing the difference between right and wrong. **3** extreme folly or senselessness: *Climbing an icy cliff alone is sheer* insanity.

in·sa·ti·a·ble (ĭn sā′ shə bəl, -shē ə bəl) *adj*- not to be satisfied: *The child's* insatiable *curiosity often got him in trouble.* —*n*- **in·sa′ ti·a·bil′ i·ty.** *adv*- **in·sa′ ti·a·bly.**

in·sa·ti·ate (ĭn sā′ shət, -shē ət) *adj*- never satiated or satisfied: *an* insatiate *appetite.* —*adv*- **in·sa′ ti·ate·ly.** *n*- **in·sa′ ti·ate·ness.**

in·scribe (ĭn skrīb′) *vt*- [**in·scribed, in·scrib·ing**] **1** to write or engrave: *to* inscribe *one's initials on the wall.* **2** to write on or engrave on: *to* inscribe *a ring with one's initials.* **3** to sign or dedicate (a book, picture, etc.) when giving it to someone. **4** *Mathematics* to draw (a figure) inside the boundary or outline of a second figure, so that the two figures are tangent at every possible point. The figure thus drawn on the inside is called an **inscribed figure.** —*n*- **in·scrib′ er.**

The circle is inscribed in the square. The triangle is inscribed in the circle.

in·scrip·tion (ĭn skrĭp′ shən) *n*- **1** something written, especially the painted, carved, engraved, or embossed words on a wall, tombstone, ring, coin, or the like. **2** the dedication or note written on a book, photograph, etc., when giving it to someone. **3** the act of inscribing.

in·scru·ta·ble (ĭn skro͞o′ tə bəl) *adj*- not to be understood easily; baffling: *an* inscrutable *expression.* —*n*- **in·scru′ ta·bil′ i·ty.** *adv*- **in·scru′ ta·bly.**

in·sect (ĭn′ sĕkt′) *n*- any of the huge class of arthropods (**Insecta**) that have six legs, one or two wing pairs, and a body divided into head, thorax, and abdomen. Grasshoppers and fleas are insects. —*adj*- **in′ sect·like′.**

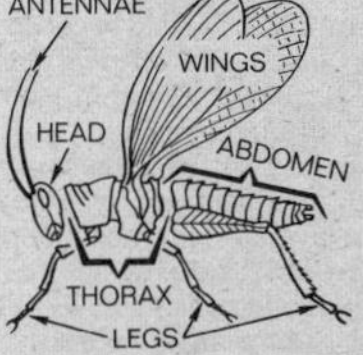

Parts of an insect

in·sec·ti·cide (ĭn sĕk′ tə sīd′) *n*- poisonous preparation for killing insects.

in·sec·ti·vore (ĭn sĕk′ tə vôr′) *n*- **1** any of an order of small, burrowing, and mostly nocturnal mammals (**Insectivora**) that includes the moles, shrews, and hedgehogs. **2** any animal or plant that feeds on insects.

in·sec·tiv·o·rous (ĭn′ sĕk tĭv′ ər əs) *adj*- **1** insect-eating. **2** belonging or pertaining to the insectivores.

in·se·cure (ĭn′ sə kyo͝or′) *adj*- **1** not free from care, fear, or worry: *an* insecure *person.* **2** not free from danger; unsafe: *an* insecure *hideout.* **3** not confident; not certain or assured. —*adv*- **in′ se·cure′ ly.** *n*- **in′ se·cur′ i·ty.**

in·sem·i·nate (ĭn sĕm′ ə nāt′) *vt*- [**in·sem·i·nat·ed, in·sem·i·nat·ing**] **1** to introduce the male reproductive cell into. **2** to sow (seed) in something; also, to implant or instill (ideas, opinions, etc.). —*n*- **in·sem′ i·na′ tion.**

in·sen·sate (ĭn sĕn′ sāt′) *adj*- **1** unfeeling; brutal: *an* insensate *fury.* **2** without good sense: *an* insensate *fool.* **3** without sensation; lifeless: *the* insensate *rocks.* —*adv*- **in·sen′ sate′ ly.**

in·sen·si·ble (ĭn sĕn′ sə bəl) *adj*- **1** unconscious: *He was knocked* insensible *by a rock.* **2** without feeling; numb: *His arm was* insensible *for an hour after the accident.* **3** indifferent: *He is* insensible *to the beauties of nature.* **4** unaware: *to be* insensible *of danger.* —*n*- **in·sen′ si·bil′ i·ty.** *adv*- **in·sen′ si·bly.**

in·sen·si·tive (ĭn sĕn′ sə tĭv) *adj*- **1** without sensation; numb: *The dentist made Tom's tooth* insensitive *before he filled it.* **2** unmoved by beauty, suffering, etc.; unsympathetic: *He was* insensitive *to the sea's grandeur.* —*adv*- **in·sen′ si·tive·ly.** *n*- **in·sen′ si·tive·ness.**

in·sep·a·ra·ble (ĭn sĕp′ə rə bəl) ***adj-*** impossible to separate or part: *two* inseparable *friends.* ***n-*** **inseparables** things or persons that cannot be parted or divided. ***—n-*** **in·sep′a·ra·ble·ness** or **in·sep′a·ra·bil′i·ty.** ***adv-*** **in·sep′a·ra·bly.**

1**in·sert** (ĭn sûrt′) ***vt-*** to put in; introduce: *to* insert *a coin in a slot.*

2**in·sert** (ĭn′ sûrt′) ***n-*** something put in, especially a page slipped in between the pages of a book or magazine.

in·ser·tion (ĭn sûr′ shən) ***n-*** **1** a putting in: *The* insertion *of advertisements in a newspaper often gets results.* **2** something put in; insert. **3** piece of fabric set in a garment.

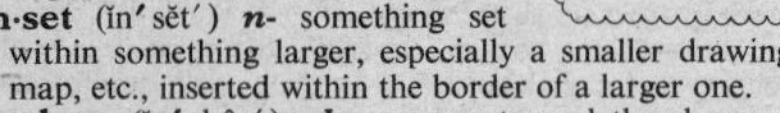

Insertion

1**in·set** (ĭn sĕt′) ***vt-*** **[in·set, in·set·ting]** to put in; insert; also, to inlay.

2**in·set** (ĭn′ sĕt′) ***n-*** something set within something larger, especially a smaller drawing, map, etc., inserted within the border of a larger one.

in·shore (ĭn′ shôr′) ***adv-*** near or toward the shore: *to head* inshore. ***adj-*** near, or moving toward, the shore: *an* inshore *current*; inshore *sailing.*

1**in·side** (ĭn′ sīd′) ***n-*** inner part; interior: *Clean the* inside *of the tub.* ***adj-*** **1** inner: *the* inside *pages of a newspaper.* **2** private or secret: *some* inside *information.* **3 insides** inner organs of the body, especially those of the abdomen; entrails.

inside out with the wrong side outward: *to turn a glove* inside out.

2**in·side** (ĭn′ sīd′) ***prep-*** within: *Look* inside *the box.* ***adv-***: *You will find your friend* inside.

inside of within (something): *The small box is* inside of *the large one.*

in·sid·er (ĭn sī′ dər) ***n-*** person in the ruling group of some organization, or one who can get information not available to most people.

in·sid·i·ous (ĭn sĭd′ ē əs) ***adj-*** doing harm secretly or in a hidden manner: *an* insidious *disease*; insidious *gossip.* ***—adv-*** **in·sid′i·ous·ly.** ***n-*** **in·sid′i·ous·ness.**

in·sight (ĭn′ sīt′) ***n-*** **1** ability to see (into) and to understand: *a good teacher's* insight *into the problems of the students.* **2** an instance of this.

in·sig·ni·a (ĭn sĭg′ nē ə) ***n-*** **1** *pl.* [*sing.* **in·sig·ne** (ĭn sĭg′ nē)] emblems of rank or honor: *A colonel with all his* insignia. **2** [*pl.* **in·sig·ni·as**] one such emblem: *the* insignia *of a commander.*

Insignia

in·sig·nif·i·cant (ĭn′ sĭg nĭf′ ə kənt) ***adj-*** of small or no importance; having little meaning or value: *an* insignificant *sum*; *an* insignificant *person.* ***—n-*** **in′sig·nif′i·cance.** ***adv-*** **in′sig·nif′i·cant·ly.**

in·sin·cere (ĭn′ sĭn sêr′) ***adj-*** not sincere; not truly meant or felt. ***—adv-*** **in′sin·cere′ly.** ***n-*** **in′sin·cer′i·ty** (ĭn′ sĭn sĕr′ ə tē).

in·sin·u·ate (ĭn sĭn′ yo͞o āt′) ***vt-*** **[in·sin·u·a·ted, in·sin·u·a·ting]** **1** to hint slyly; imply: *The lawyer* insinuated *that the witness was lying.* **2** to put in by clever, indirect means: *As he spoke he* insinuated *his critical comments.*

in·sin·u·a·tion (ĭn sĭn′ yo͞o ā′ shən) ***n-*** indirect or sly hint; implied meaning; innuendo: *to be slandered by* insinuations; *to resent* insinuations.

in·sip·id (ĭn sĭp′ ĭd) ***adj-*** **1** without flavor; tasteless: *the* insipid *food.* **2** uninteresting; dull: *an* insipid *novel.* ***—n-*** **in′sip·id′i·ty** or **in·sip′id·ness.** ***adv-*** **in·sip′id·ly.**

in·sist (ĭn sĭst′) ***vt-*** **1** to make an urgent demand: *I* insist *that you go.* **2** to state firmly and immovably: *He* insists *that he is right.*

insist on to demand or require: *I* insist on *the best.*

in·sist·ence (ĭn sĭs′ təns) ***n-*** **1** a demanding without letup: *His* insistence *finally wore down my opposition.* **2** the taking of a firm stand: *Please forgive my* insistence.

in·sist·ent (ĭn sĭs′ tənt) ***adj-*** **1** demanding: *I did not want to go, but he was* insistent. **2** continuing to demand attention or action; urgent: *the* insistent *ringing of the telephone.* ***—adv-*** **in·sis′tent·ly.**

in·so·bri·e·ty (ĭn′ sə brī′ ə tē) ***n-*** lack of sobriety.

in·so·far as (ĭn′ sō fär′ ăz) ***adv-*** to the extent that; to the degree that: *He is working,* insofar as *I can tell.*

in·sole (ĭn′ sōl′) ***n-*** **1** inner sole of a shoe. **2** extra inner sole, worn for comfort or protection.

in·so·lence (ĭn′ sə ləns) ***n-*** rude and contemptuous disrespect: *The gesture was pure* insolence.

in·so·lent (ĭn′ sə lənt) ***adj-*** not respectful; rude and arrogant: *The witness's* insolent *replies angered the judge.* ***—adv-*** **in′so·lent·ly.**

in·sol·u·ble (ĭn sŏl′ yə bəl) ***adj-*** **1** impossible to dissolve: *Grease is* insoluble *in cold water.* **2** impossible to solve or explain: *an* insoluble *problem.* ***—n-*** **in·sol′u·bil′i·ty,** also **in·sol′u·ble·ness.** ***adv-*** **in·sol′u·bly.**

►For usage note see SOLUBLE.

in·solv·a·ble (ĭn sŏl′ və bəl) ***adj-*** not solvable.

►For usage note see SOLUBLE.

in·sol·vent (ĭn sŏl′ vənt) ***adj-*** unable to pay all debts; bankrupt. ***n-*** person who cannot pay all his debts. ***—n-*** **in·sol′ven·cy.**

in·som·ni·a (ĭn sŏm′ nē ə) ***n-*** inability to sleep.

in·so·much (ĭn′ sō mŭch′) ***adv-*** to such a degree or extent: *If a man lies often, he is* insomuch *untrustworthy.*

insomuch as inasmuch as.

in·sou·ci·ance (ĭn so͞o′ sē əns) ***n-*** lack of concern or caring; indifference; lightheartedness.

in·spect (ĭn spĕkt′) ***vt-*** **1** to examine carefully, especially to check for faults, errors, etc.: *Each morning the foreman* inspected *our work.* **2** to examine or review (troops, military equipment, etc.) officially.

in·spec·tion (ĭn spĕk′ shən) ***n-*** **1** an inspecting; careful examination for faults, errors, etc.: *In some States,* inspection *of automobiles must be made twice a year.* **2** official review or examination of troops, military equipment, etc.

in·spec·tor (ĭn spĕk′ tər) ***n-*** **1** person who inspects. **2** high-ranking officer in a police department.

in·spi·ra·tion (ĭn′ spə rā′ shən) ***n-*** **1** a stirring of mind, feelings, or imagination that leads to action or creation: *The artist's* inspiration *came from his everyday surroundings.* **2** person or thing that inspires: *The music of the band was an* inspiration *to the marchers.* **3** bright idea; impulse or sudden thought that leads to action or creation: *Your suggesting that we take an extra canteen was an* inspiration. **4** a drawing of air into the lungs. ***—adj-*** **in′spir·a′tion·al.** ***adv-*** **in′spi·ra′tion·al·ly.**

in·spire (ĭn spīər′) ***vt-*** **[in·spired, in·spir·ing]** **1** to stir deeply; breathe life into; arouse to action. **2** to be the cause of; arouse; call forth: *Honesty* inspires *respect. Her beauty* inspired *the poem.* ***vi-*** to draw air into the lungs. ***—adv-*** **in·spired′ly.** ***n-*** **in·spir′er.** ***adv-*** **in·spir′ing·ly.**

in·spir·it (ĭn spĭr′ ət) ***vt-*** to give life or vitality to; cheer; inspire: *The leader's speech* inspirited *his followers.*

inst. **1** this present month (from "instant," formerly used in writing letters). **2** institute; institution.

in·sta·bil·i·ty (ĭn′ stə bĭl′ ə tē) ***n-*** lack of stability.

in·stall (ĭn stŏl′) ***vt-*** **1** to put into place and make ready for use: *The plumber* installed *a hot water unit.* **2** to put into office with ceremony: *They* installed *the mayor yesterday.* **3** to place or settle: *The cat* installed *itself near the fire.* ***—n-*** **in·stall′er.**

in·stal·la·tion (ĭn′ stə lā′ shən) ***n-*** **1** a setting up in position for service: *the* installation *of a telephone.* **2** machine or apparatus set up or ready to be set up. **3** a putting into office or position, especially with ceremony; installment: *We were present at the* installation *of the mayor.* **4** a base; camp, usually military.

[1]**in·stall·ment** (ĭn stȯl′ mənt) ***n-*** an establishing in position or office; installation. [from Medieval Latin **installāre,** from Latin **in-,** "in; into," plus **stallum,** "a position; seat; [1]stall," from a Germanic word.]

[2]**in·stall·ment** (ĭn stȯl′ mənt) ***n-*** **1** any one of several parts that follow in a series: *The second* installment *of the story will appear next month.* **2** any one of several partial payments made in settlement of a bill: *The third* installment *on the car is due Tuesday. as* ***modifier****: an* installment *plan*; installment *buying.* Also, *chiefly Brit.,* **in·stal′ ment.** [from an archaic English **(e)stall** meaning "to arrange payments (for a debt, etc.)," from Old French **estaler,** from **estal,** "position," from an older German **stall,** "[1]stall."]

in·stance (ĭn′ stəns) ***n-*** a case; example: *There have been many* instances *of people failing.* ***vt-*** [**in·stanced, in·stanc·ing**] to offer as an example: *I can* instance *four cases.*
for instance as an example.
►Should not be confused with INSTANT.

in·stant (ĭn′ stənt) ***n-*** moment; space of time almost too short to measure: *He stopped the car not an* instant *too soon.* ***adj-*** **1** immediate: *an* instant *remedy.* **2** of foods, drinks, soups, etc., so prepared that one need only add water or some other fluid before cooking or eating: *an* instant *cake mix*; instant *coffee*; instant *vegetable soup.*
►Should not be confused with INSTANCE.

in·stan·ta·ne·ous (ĭn′ stən tā′ nē əs) ***adj-*** happening or following in an instant: *an* instantaneous *reply.* ***—adv-*** **in′ stan·ta′ ne·ous·ly.** ***n-*** **in′ stan·ta′ ne·ous·ness.**

in·stant·ly (ĭn′ stənt lē) ***adv-*** immediately; at once: *The dog obeyed the order* instantly. *I shall come* instantly.

in·stead (ĭn stĕd′) ***adv-*** as a substitute or alternative: *They didn't come to our house, so we went to theirs* instead.
instead of in place of: *I will go* instead of *you.*

in·step (ĭn′ stĕp′) ***n-*** **1** arched upper side of the foot between the toes and the ankle. **2** part of a shoe, slipper, stocking, etc., that covers this part of the foot.

Instep

in·sti·gate (ĭn′ stə gāt′) ***vt-*** [**in·sti·gat·ed, in·sti·gat·ing**] to cause by prompting, urging, or incitement: *to* instigate *a revolt.* ***—n-*** **in′ sti·ga′ tion.**

in·sti·ga·tor (ĭn′ stə gā′ tər) ***n-*** person who instigates.

in·still or **in·stil** (ĭn stĭl′) ***vt-*** [**in·stilled, in·still·ing**] to add little by little; put in gradually; impart; implant; infuse: *to* instill *respect for the rights of others.*

[1]**in·stinct** (ĭn′ stĭngkt′) ***n-*** **1** inborn urge to do things in a certain way; natural untaught way of acting: *Squirrels gather food for winter by* instinct. **2** talent; natural ability: *He has a happy* instinct *for saying the right thing.*

[2]**in·stinct** (ĭn stĭngkt′) ***adj-*** filled or infused (with): *to be* instinct *with love*; *to be* instinct *with joy.*

in·stinc·tive (ĭn stĭngk′ tĭv) ***adj-*** not gained through learning or experience; inborn; natural: *an* instinctive *fear of loud noises.* ***—adv-*** **in·stinc′ tive·ly.**

in·sti·tute (ĭn′ stə to͞ot′, -tyo͞ot′) ***n-*** **1** school, museum, or other such institution: *an art* institute; *California* Institute *of Technology.* **2** building or group of buildings that houses one of these. ***vt-*** [**in·sti·tut·ed, in·sti·tut·ing**] **1** to begin; start; originate: *We* instituted *a search for him.* **2** to establish: *The club* instituted *new laws.*

in·sti·tu·tion (ĭn′ stə to͞o′ shən, -tyo͞o′ shən) ***n-*** **1** an established custom, law, etc.: *Thanksgiving Day is an American* institution. **2** a setting up; an establishing: *the* institution *of new traffic regulations.* **3** organization, corporation, or establishment set up for a certain purpose. These include schools, hospitals, prisons, etc. **4** building or buildings used by such organizations. ***—adj-*** **in′ sti·tu′ tion·al.** ***adv-*** **in′ sti·tu′ tion·al·ly.**

in·sti·tu·tion·al·ize (ĭn′ stə to͞o′ shən ə līz′, ĭn′- stə tyo͞o′-) ***vt-*** **1** to establish in organized form: *Men* institutionalize *their religions.* **2** to place in a hospital, special school, asylum, etc., for care and treatment.

in·struct (ĭn strŭkt′) ***vt-*** **1** to teach: *He* instructs *two classes.* **2** to direct; order: *We* instructed *him to report.*

in·struc·tion (ĭn strŭk′ shən) ***n-*** **1** an instructing; education: *Ann got her early* instruction *at home, but Ralph went to school.* **2** lessons: *Some grade schools give* instruction *in foreign languages.* **3 instructions** directions or orders: *We couldn't understand the* instructions. ***—adj-*** **in·struc′ tion·al:** *an* instructional *manual.*

in·struc·tive (ĭn strŭk′ tĭv) ***adj-*** informative; giving knowledge: *an* instructive *talk on art.* ***—adv-*** **in·struc′ tive·ly.** ***n-*** **in·struc′ tive·ness.**

in·struc·tor (ĭn strŭk′ tər) ***n-*** teacher, especially a college teacher holding the lowest rank of full-time appointment. ***—n-*** *fem.* **in·struc′ tress.**

[1]**in·stru·ment** (ĭn′ strə mənt) ***n-*** **1** tool used for some particular kind of work: *a surgeon's* instruments. **2** means by which something is accomplished: *The army was the dictator's* instrument *for controlling the country.* **3** person who is someone else's tool: *Jones was merely an* instrument *of the criminal gang.* **4** device used to measure, control, or examine: *Airplanes carry many* instruments. *A thermostat is an* instrument *to control a furnace. The telescope and microscope are scientific* instruments. **5** device by which musical sounds are made, such as the harp, flute, etc. **6** legal or financial document such as a deed, writ, check, mortgage, etc. *as* ***modifier****: an* instrument *panel*; *an* instrument *case.*

[2]**in·stru·ment** (ĭn′ strə mənt′) ***vt-*** **1** to provide with devices for measuring and controlling: *to* instrument *a guided missile.* **2** *Music* to orchestrate.

in·stru·men·tal (ĭn′ strə mĕn′ təl) ***adj-*** **1** helping to bring about; serving as a means: *He was* instrumental *in our finding a new home.* **2** performed on or written for a musical instrument. ***—adv-*** **in′ stru·men′ tal·ly.**

in·stru·men·tal·ist (ĭn′ strə mĕn′ tə lĭst) ***n-*** person who plays a musical instrument, especially as a professional.

in·stru·men·ta·tion (ĭn′ strə mən tā′ shən) ***n-*** **1** the instrumenting of some vehicle, device, apparatus, etc.; also, the field of science and engineering specializing in this. **2** all the instruments of a particular vehicle, apparatus, etc.

instrument landing ***n-*** landing of an aircraft by means of its instruments and with the help of ground radio and radar devices, usually made in a fog or storm.

instrument panel ***n-*** panel on which instruments for measuring, navigating, etc., are mounted.

in·sub·or·di·nate (ĭn′ sə bȯr′ də nət, -bôr′ də nət) ***adj-*** rebelling against authority; disobedient; mutinous: *an* insubordinate *soldier.* ***—adv-*** **in′ sub·or′ di·nate·ly.** ***n-*** **in′ sub·or′ di·na′ tion.**

in·sub·stan·tial (ĭn′ səb stăn′ shəl) ***adj-*** **1** unreal; lacking substance; imaginary: *an* insubstantial *hope.* **2** lacking solidity; frail. ***—adv-*** **in′ sub·stan′ tial·ly.**
►Should not be confused with UNSUBSTANTIAL.

fāte, făt, dâre, bärn; bē, bĕt, mêre; bīte, bĭt; nōte, hŏt, môre, dȯg; fŭn, fûr; to͞o, bo͝ok; oil; out; tar; thin; then; hw for wh as in *wh*at; zh for s as in u*s*ual; ə for a, e, i, o, u, as in *a*go, lin*e*n, per*i*l, at*o*m, min*u*s

in·suf·fer·a·ble (ĭn sŭf′ər ə bəl) *adj-* intolerable; unbearable: *his* insufferable *rudeness.* **—*adv-* in·suf′fer·a·bly.** ***n-*** **in·suf′fer·a·ble·ness.**

in·suf·fi·cient (ĭn′sə fĭsh′ənt) *adj-* not enough; inadequate; not sufficient: *The time allowed for the job was* insufficient. **—*n-* in′suf·fi′cien·cy:** *an* insufficiency *of food.* ***adv-*** **in′suf·fi′cient·ly.**

in·su·lar (ĭn′sə lər, -syə lər) *adj-* **1** of or relating to an island or its people: *an* insular *custom.* **2** living or situated on an island: *an* insular *city.* **3** forming an island: *an* insular *reef.* **4** detached; isolated: *an* insular *location.* **5** narrow-minded; prejudiced; provincial: *an* insular *attitude.*

in·su·lar·i·ty (ĭn′sə lăr′ə tē, ĭn′syə-) *n-* **1** condition of being an island or islands: *the* insularity *of Hawaii.* **2** condition of living on an island or isolated from other people; hence, narrowness of mind, opinions, views, etc.

in·su·late (ĭn′sə lāt′) *vt-* **[in·su·lat·ed, in·su·lat·ing]** **1** to cover, line, or surround with a material or device that will not conduct electricity, heat, sound, etc.: *to* insulate *a wire; to* insulate *a roof.* **2** to set apart; isolate: *to* insulate *one's mind from disturbing ideas.*

in·su·la·tion (ĭn′sə lā′shən) *n-* **1** material used to prevent the passage of heat, sound, electricity, etc. **2** an insulating: *Let's start the* insulation *of the attic.* **3** condition of being insulated: *The rock wool in the walls provides heat* insulation.

in·su·la·tor (ĭn′sə lā′tər) *n-* something that prevents the passage of heat, electricity, sound or other influences.

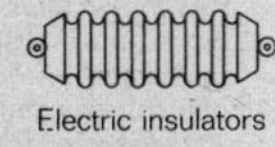

Electric insulators

in·su·lin (ĭn′sə lĭn) *n-* hormone given off by certain cells in the pancreas, which helps the body to use sugar and protein.

[1]in·sult (ĭn sŭlt′) *vt-* to treat a person or thing rudely or scornfully; affront: *to* insult *with vile names.*

[2]in·sult (ĭn′sŭlt′) *n-* a rude or scornful action or speech; an affront: *To question a person's honesty is an* insult.

in·sult·ing (ĭn sŭl′tĭng) *adj-* **1** showing rudeness, scorn, or contempt: *an* insulting *manner.* **2** giving offense to another: *an* insulting *question.* ***adv-*** **in·sul′ting·ly.**

in·su·per·a·ble (ĭn sōō′ pər ə bəl) *adj-* not to be surmounted or overcome: *These are* insuperable *difficulties.* **—*adv-* in·su′per·a·bly.**

in·sup·port·a·ble (ĭn′sə pôr′tə bəl) *adj-* unbearable; intolerable. ***adv-*** **in′sup·port′a·bly.**

in·sur·a·ble (ĭn shōōr′ə bəl) *adj-* able, proper, or suitable to be insured: *The staff was not* insurable *because of its dangerous occupation.*

in·sur·ance (ĭn shōōr′əns) *n-* **1** system of guarding against loss by the paying of small, regular amounts to a company in exchange for a promise to pay an agreed amount in case of death, accident, theft, illness, etc. **2** the contract by which such an agreement is made. **3** regular amount paid for this service; premium: *John's sister pays $75 a month life* insurance. **4** amount for which a person or thing is insured; also, the amount paid by an insurance company to cover a loss.

in·sure (ĭn shōōr′) *vt-* **[in·sured, in·sur·ing]** **1** to compensate for the loss of (life; health, property, etc.) by buying insurance. **2** to sell insurance to cover: *The company will not* insure *him.*

►Should not be confused with ENSURE.

in·sured (ĭn shōōrd′) *adj-* protected by insurance: *The boat is* insured *for a large sum.*

in·sur·er (ĭn shōōr′ər) *n-* company which insures a person or thing: *Our firm was the* insurer *for the cargo.*

in·sur·gence (ĭn sûr′jəns) *n-* act of rebelling or revolting: *an* insurgence *against the royal power.*

in·sur·gen·cy (ĭn sûr′jən sē) *n-* [*pl.* **in·sur·gen·cies**] **1** spirit of revolt; rebelliousness. **2** rebellion that is not considered a full-scale revolution. **3** insurgence.

in·sur·gent (ĭn sûr′jənt) *adj-* rising in revolt; rebellious: *The* insurgent *troops were defeated.* *n-* a rebel.

in·sur·mount·a·ble (ĭn′sər moun′tə bəl) *adj-* such as cannot be overcome: *an* insurmountable *evil.* **—*adv-* in′sur·mount′a·bly.**

in·sur·rec·tion (ĭn′sə rĕk′shən) *n-* active revolt against authority, especially against a government.

in·sur·rec·tion·a·ry (ĭn′sə rĕk′shən ĕr′ē) *adj-* of or relating to insurrection: *the* insurrectionary *forces.*

in·sur·rec·tion·ist (ĭn′sə rĕk′shən ĭst) *n-* person who takes part in an insurrection.

in·tact (ĭn tăkt′) *adj-* untouched; whole; uninjured: *After the bombing, only a few buildings remained* intact.

in·tag·lio (ĭn tăg′lē ō, -tăl′yō) *n-* [*pl.* **in·tag·li·os**] **1** an engraving or carving cut into or below the surface of any hard material. **2** a gem so ornamented.

in·take (ĭn′tăk′) *n-* **1** a taking in: *an* intake *of money; an* intake *of water.* **2** the amount taken in: *The* intake *of each boiler is 3,000 gallons an hour.* **3** pipe or channel through which a fluid is brought in, or the opening where a fluid enters.

in·tan·gi·ble (ĭn tăn′jə bəl) *adj-* **1** such as cannot be touched: *Time, hope, and darkness are* intangibie. **2** difficult to grasp with the mind; vague; hazy: *an* intangible *fear;* intangible *suspicions.* **—*n-* in·tan′gi·bil′i·ty:** *I recognize the* intangibility *of my suspicions.* ***adv-*** **in·tan′gi·bly.**

in·te·ger (ĭn′tə jər) *n-* any positive or negative whole number, or zero.

in·te·gral (ĭn′tə grəl) *adj-* **1** helping to make up something whole: *Sincerity is an* integral *part of friendship.* **2** making a unit; whole; complete: *an* integral *arrangement.* **—*adv-* in′te·gral·ly.**

in·te·grate (ĭn′tə grāt′) *vt-* **[in·te·gra·ted, in·te·gra·ting]** **1** to bring parts together to make a whole: *to* integrate *studies with athletics in the school day.* **2** to make schools, housing, transportation, etc., open to all races on an equal basis. *vi-* to become open or accessible to all races on an equal basis.

integrated circuit *n-* solid object in which patterns of impurities have been designed to perform serveral different electronic functions.

in·te·gra·tion (ĭn′tə grā′shən) *n-* an integrating or being integrated: *the* integration *of parts of an automobile; the* integration *of races in a school.*

in·teg·ri·ty (ĭn tĕg′rə tē) *n-* **1** honesty; uprightness; moral soundness: *The mayor's* integrity *was questioned during the scandal.* **2** wholeness; completeness.

in·teg·u·ment (ĭn tĕg′yə mənt) *n-* a covering, such as a skin or husk, that encloses; tegument.

in·tel·lect (ĭn′tə lĕkt′) *n-* **1** the understanding and reasoning power of the mind: *She has* intellect *as well as feeling.* **2** great intelligence: *a man of* intellect.

in·tel·lec·tu·al (ĭn′tə lĕk′chōō əl) *adj-* **1** having to do with the mind and its reasoning powers: *Winning a scholarship is an* intellectual *achievement.* **2** having or showing intellect: *an* intellectual *person.* *n-* person devoted to the pursuits of the intellect. **—*n-* in′tel·lec·tu·al′i·ty** (-ăl′ə tē): *the* intellectuality *of their interests.* ***adv-*** **in′tel·lec′tu·al·ly.**

in·tel·lec·tu·al·ism (ĭn′tə lĕk′chōō ə lĭz′əm) *n-* **1** concern with intellectual interests. **2** use or application of the intellect. **—*n-* in′tel·lec′tu·al·ist.**

in·tel·li·gence (ĭn tĕl′ə jəns) *n-* **1** ability to learn, understand, or know: *He shows high* intelligence *for a* *boy of his age.* **2** ability to learn from experience and to handle new situations. **3** news or information, especially secret information gathered by a government.

intelligence quotient ***n-*** number describing a person's level of intelligence as measured by a particular intelligence test. It is derived by multiplying the tested mental age by 100 and dividing the result by age in years, with 16 years the highest divisor used. *Abbr.* IQ or I.Q.

intelligence test ***n-*** test or series of tests used in measuring intelligence in a person or animal.

in·tel·li·gent (ĭn tĕl′ ə jənt) ***adj-*** having or showing a keen and able mind: *An* intelligent *child learns quickly.* —***adv-*** **in·tel′ li·gent·ly.**

in·tel·li·gent·si·a (ĭn tĕl′ ə jĕn′ sē ə) ***n-*** intellectuals as a group.

in·tel·li·gi·ble (ĭn tĕl′ ə jə bəl) ***adj-*** such as can be understood; clear: *His words were* intelligible. —***n-*** **in·tel′ li·gi·bil′ i·ty.** ***adv-*** **in·tel′ li·gi·bly.**

in·tem·per·ance (ĭn tĕm′ pər əns) ***n-*** **1** lack of moderation and restraint; excess: *the* intemperance *of his speech.* **2** excessive use of alcoholic liquor.

in·tem·per·ate (ĭn tĕm′ pər ət) ***adj-*** **1** not moderate; not restrained; excessive: *his* intemperate *language.* **2** given to excessive use of alcoholic liquors. —***adv-*** **in·tem′ per·ate·ly.** ***n-*** **in·tem′ per·ate·ness**: *The* intemperateness *of his speech startled the audience.*

in·tend (ĭn tĕnd′) ***vt-*** **1** to have as a purpose; mean: *He did not* intend *to go away.* **2** to design for a purpose or group: *The author* intended *this book for adults.*

in·tend·ed (ĭn tĕn′ dəd) ***adj-*** meant; planned; had in mind as a purpose or a meaning: *the* intended *meaning of a remark.* ***n-*** *Archaic* person to whom one is engaged to be married.

in·tense (ĭn tĕns′) ***adj-*** **1** extreme; very great: *an* intense *pain.* **2** strong in feeling: *an* intense *person.* —***adv-*** **in·tense′ ly.** ***n-*** **in·tense′ ness.**

in·ten·si·fi·er (ĭn tĕn′ sə fī′ ər) *Grammar* ***n-*** **1** word or phrase such as "so," "too," "very," "a little," "a bit," which modifies adjectival or adverbial modifiers. Examples:

This wood is too *soft.* (modifying an adjective)
He works very *hard* indeed. (modifying an adverb)
Bill worked a little *harder lately.* (modifying an adverb)

2 as used in this dictionary, a word that has no meaning but serves to strengthen the word it modifies. Example: *He's a* precious *fool.*

in·ten·si·fy (ĭn tĕn′ sə fī′) ***vt-*** **[in·ten·si·fied, in·ten·si·fy·ing]** to make more intense: *He* intensified *his studies before examinations.* ***vi-***: *He was given medicine when the pain* intensified. —***n-*** **in·ten′ si·fi·ca·tion.**

in·ten·si·ty (ĭn tĕn′ sə tē) ***n-*** [*pl.* **in·ten·si·ties**] **1** strength or degree (of heat, sound, etc.): *The sound increased in* intensity. **2** a being intense; great degree, strength, or force: *the* intensity *of his anger; the* intensity *of the storm.*

in·ten·sive (ĭn tĕn′ sĭv) ***adj-*** thorough; concentrated; carried out with the greatest care: *An* intensive *search turned up the missing key.* —***adv-*** **in·ten′ sive·ly.** ***n-*** **in·ten′ sive·ness.**

in·tent (ĭn tĕnt′) ***adj-*** determined; bent on: *to be* intent *on what one is doing; an* intent *look.* ***n-*** purpose; aim; intention: *an* intent *to learn.* —***adv-*** **in·tent′ ly.**

in·ten·tion (ĭn tĕn′ shən) ***n-*** **1** something intended; purpose; plan; resolve: *It is my* intention *to build a new house next year. They acted with good* intention. **2 intentions** purposes; motives; wishes: *Their* intentions *are not the best.*

in·ten·tion·al (ĭn tĕn′ shən əl) ***adj-*** done deliberately or on purpose; not accidental. —***adv-*** **in·ten′ tion·al·ly.**

in·tent·ness (ĭn tĕnt′ nəs) ***n-*** quality or state of being intent; earnest attention or mental application: *great* intentness *of purpose; an* intentness *of thought.*

in·ter (ĭn tûr′) ***vt-*** **[in·terred, in·ter·ring]** to bury; especially, to bury a dead person.

inter- *prefix* **1** between or among: inter*planetary*; inter*continental.* **2** together or one with the other: inter*weave.* [from Latin **inter-**, from **inter**, "among; during."]

►INTER- has the sense of "between." Inter*state commerce is business carried on between two or more states.* INTRA- means "within." Intra*state commerce is carried on within one state.*

in·ter·act (ĭn′ tər ăkt′) ***vi-*** to influence or act on each other; have mutual effect: *These two chemicals* interact. —***n-*** **in·ter·act′ tion.**

in·ter·breed (ĭn′ tər brēd′) ***vt-*** **[in·ter·bred, in·ter·breed·ing]** to breed by crossing different kinds of stocks. ***vi-*** to breed with each other, as animals or plants of different species do.

in·ter·cede (ĭn′ tər sēd′) ***vi-*** **[in·ter·ced·ed, in·ter·ced·ing]** to make a plea for someone else: *to* intercede *on behalf of a friend's request for a job.* —***n-*** **in′ ter·ced′ er.**

in·ter·cel·lu·lar (ĭn′ tər sĕl′ yə lər) ***adj-*** located between cells: *an* intercellular *fluid.*

in·ter·cept (ĭn′ tər sĕpt′) ***vt-*** **1** to seize, catch, or stop on the way: *to* intercept *a message; to* intercept *a forward pass.* **2** *Mathematics* to bound or delimit (a line, surface, etc.) by marking off. ***n-*** *Mathematics* **1** the distance from the origin to the point where a given curve cuts a coordinate axis; also, the point of interception. **2** an intercepted segment or part. —***n-*** **in′ ter·cep′ tion.**

in·ter·cep·tor (ĭn′ tər sĕp′ tər) ***n-*** **1** person or thing that intercepts: *the* interceptor *of the message.* **2** kind of fighter plane used to attack bombers.

in·ter·ces·sion (ĭn′ tər sĕsh′ ən) ***n-*** an interceding. ***Hom-*** intersession.

in·ter·ces·sor (ĭn′ tər sĕs′ ər) ***n-*** person who intercedes.

[1]**in·ter·change** (ĭn′ tər chānj′) ***vt-*** **[in·ter·changed, in·ter·chang·ing]** **1** to put persons or things in the place of each other: *You can* interchange *the parts of these machines.* **2** to exchange. ***vi-*** to exchange partners or positions: *The dancers continually* interchanged.

[2]**in·ter·change** (ĭn′ tər chānj′) ***n-*** **1** a putting of persons or things in the other's place: *an* interchange *of notes or goods.* **2** an exchanging: *an* interchange *of ambassadors.* **3** place where one may enter or leave a superhighway.

in·ter·change·a·ble (ĭn′ tər chān′ jə bəl) ***adj-*** designed so as to be put in place of one another: *Tires on an automobile are* interchangeable. —***n-*** **in′ ter·change·a·bil′ i·ty.** ***adv-*** **in′ ter·change′ a·bly.**

in·ter·col·le·gi·ate (ĭn′ tər kə lē′ jət) ***adj-*** carried on among or between colleges: *four* intercollegiate *sports.*

in·ter·com (ĭn′ tər kŏm′) ***n-*** wired system of voice communication between rooms, desks, buildings, etc., in which each station has both a microphone and a speaker. Also **intercommunication system.**

in·ter·com·mu·ni·cate (ĭn′ tər kə myo͞o′ nə kāt′) ***vi-*** **[in·ter·com·mu·ni·cat·ed, in·ter·com·mu·ni·cat·ing]** **1** to have free passage from one to another: *The dining room and kitchen* intercommunicate. **2** to communicate with each other. —***n-*** **in′ ter·com·mu′ ni·ca·tion.**

in·ter·con·nect (ĭn′ tər kə nĕkt′) ***vt-*** to connect one with another: *to* interconnect *the two loudspeakers.* ***vi-***: *The roads* interconnect. —***n-*** **in′ ter·con·nec′ tion.**

in·ter·con·ti·nen·tal (ĭn'tər kŏn'tə nĕn'təl) ***adj-*** 1 traveling or capable of traveling from one continent to another: *an* intercontinental *flight.* 2 of or relating to things existing between continents.

in·ter·cos·tal (ĭn'tər kŏs'təl) ***adj-*** between the ribs.

in·ter·course (ĭn'tər kôrs') ***n-*** 1 dealings, relations, and communications: *The* intercourse *between the two countries has been peaceful.* 2 sexual relations.

in·ter·de·nom·i·na·tion·al (ĭn'tər dĭ nŏm'ə nā'shən əl) ***adj-*** of or relating to mutual action among several religious denominations.

in·ter·de·part·men·tal (ĭn'tər dĭ pärt'mĕn'təl) ***adj-*** existing or carried on between departments.

in·ter·de·pen·dence (ĭn'tər dĭ pĕn'dəns) ***n-*** dependence on each other or one another.

in·ter·de·pend·ent (ĭn'tər dĭ pĕn'dənt) ***adj-*** dependent on each other or one another: *an* interdependent *group*; interdependent *nations.* **—*adv-* in'ter·de·pen'dent·ly.**

[1]in·ter·dict (ĭn'tər dĭkt') ***vt-*** 1 to prohibit or forbid; restrain; prevent: *to* interdict *the use of drugs*; *to* interdict *an enemy attack.* 2 to cut off from the spiritual services of a church. **—*n-* in'ter·dict'ion.**

[2]in·ter·dict (ĭn'tər dĭkt) **—*n-*** a formal prohibition.

in·ter·est (ĭn'trəst, ĭn'tər əst) ***n-*** 1 desire to take part in, work at, or hear about: *Beth shows an* interest *in sports.* 2 the cause of such desire; attraction, hobby: *Tennis is her chief* interest. 3 power to hold attention: *Suspense adds* interest *to a story.* 4 well-being; welfare: *a club working for the public* interest. 5 money paid by a person for the use of borrowed money. 6 share; investment; part ownership: *an* interest *in a shoe factory.* 7 **interests** group of people concerned with the same activity: *the farming* interests. ***vt-*** to cause or arouse desire, enthusiasm, or curiosity: *The story* interests *me.*

in the interest of for the good of.

in·ter·est·ed (ĭn'tər ĕs'təd, -trĭs təd) ***adj-*** 1 attracted; curious; intrigued: *an* interested *audience.* 2 showing interest: *an* interested *look.* 3 having a share or part in: *the* interested *persons.* **—*adv-* in'ter·est·ed·ly.**

in·ter·est·ing (ĭn'tər ĕs'tĭng, -trĭs tĭng) ***adj-*** holding attention; arousing interest. **—*adv-* in'ter·est·ing·ly.**

in·ter·face (in'tər fās') ***vi-*** **[in·ter·faced, in·ter·fac·ing]** to have interreactions with one or more people or groups of people: *Teachers will* interface *with students at the meeting tonight.* ***n-*** border between two different substances: *A meniscus forms at the* interface *of water and air.*

in·ter·fere (ĭn'tər fêr') ***vi-*** **[in·ter·fered, in·ter·fer·ing]** 1 to obstruct; hamper; conflict with; clash: *Absence* interferes *with school work.* 2 to meddle: *This doesn't concern you, so don't* interfere. **—*n-* in·ter·fer'er.**

in·ter·fer·ence (ĭn'tər fêr'əns) ***n-*** 1 a coming into conflict, clashing. 2 thing that stops or hampers; a block. 3 a meddling. 4 unwanted noise, static, etc., that hampers radio or telephone communication. 5 in some sports, a violation of the rules by interfering with another player. 6 in football, the blocking or blockers running ahead of the ball carrier. 7 *Physics* interaction between two or more waves (of sound, light, etc.) in which there is a periodic reinforcing and weakening of the waves as they get into and out of phase with each other.

in·ter·fuse (ĭn'tər fyōōz') ***vt-*** **[in·ter·fus·ed, in·ter·fus·ing]** 1 to cause to flow together or blend. 2 to spread through. **—*n-* in·ter·fu'sion**

in·ter·im (ĭn'tər ĭm) ***n-*** time or period between events; the meantime. *as* ***modifier:*** *an* interim *event.*

in·te·ri·or (ĭn têr'ē ər) ***n-*** 1 the inside: *the* interior *of a building.* 2 inland part of a country: *deep in the* interior *of Africa.* 3 domestic or internal affairs of a nation as opposed to foreign affairs: *a ministry of the* interior. ***adj-*** 1 having to do with rooms, furniture, curtains, etc., in a building: *an* interior *decorator;* interior *design.* 2 inland; away from the coast or border: *the* interior *regions of a country.* 3 on the inside; inner; internal: *the* interior *mechanism of a machine.*

interj. interjection.

in·ter·ject (ĭn'tər jĕkt') ***vt-*** to insert or introduce suddenly; interpose: *to* interject *a question.*

in·ter·jec·tion (ĭn'tər jĕk'shən) ***n-*** 1 an inserting or interjecting. 2 question, remark, or other expression that is interjected. 3 *Grammar* word or phrase expressing strong emotion such as anger, fear, or surprise, or calling attention to what follows, but having no grammatical connection with the rest of the sentence. Examples: "say!", "oh!", "darn it!", "what!".

in·ter·lace (ĭn'tər lās') ***vt-*** **[in·ter·laced, in·ter·lac·ing]** to lace or weave together; intertwine: *to* interlace *strips of cloth.* ***vi-:*** *The brown threads and the green* interlaced.

in·ter·lard (ĭn'tər lärd') ***vt-*** to mix or vary with something different or irrelevant, often in order to give variety; intersperse: *to* interlard *a speech with jokes.*

[1]in·ter·line (ĭn'tər līn') ***vt-*** **[in·ter·lined, in·ter·lin·ing]** to fit (a garment) with an extra inner lining. [from **inter-** plus **[2]line.**]

[2]in·ter·line (ĭn'tər līn') ***vt-*** **[in·ter·lined, in·ter·lin·ing]** 1 to write or insert between the lines of: *The editor* interlined *the manuscript with his corrections.* 2 to write or print (comments, translations, etc.) between the lines of a book or other document. [from Medieval Latin **interlineāre,** from Latin **inter-** plus **linea,** "[1]line."]

in·ter·lin·e·ar (ĭn'tər lĭn'ē ər) ***adj-*** 1 written or situated between lines: *an* interlinear *translation.* 2 having different languages or texts in alternate lines.

in·ter·lin·ing (ĭn'tər lī'nĭng) ***n-*** extra inner lining placed between the lining and the outer fabric.

in·ter·link (ĭn'tər lĭngk') ***vt-*** to link together.

in·ter·lock (ĭn'tər lŏk') ***vt-*** 1 to fit (pieces, parts, etc.) closely together. 2 to lock together or interlace tightly with something else: *The two deer* interlocked *horns.* 3 to arrange (switches, signals, etc.) in such a way that they must be operated in a certain order or together, to prevent accidents. ***vi-:*** *The branches of the tree* interlocked *in a dense hedge. The pieces of the puzzle* interlocked.

in·ter·loc·u·tor (ĭn'tər lŏk'yə tər) ***n-*** person who asks questions or takes part in a conversation with another.

in·ter·loc·u·to·ry (ĭn'tər lŏk'yə tôr'ē) ***adj-*** 1 in law, not final; pronounced during the course of an action: *an* interlocutory *divorce.* 2 of or having to do with questions or conversation.

in·ter·lop·er (ĭn'tər lō'pər) ***n-*** outsider who interferes; intruder; meddler: *an* interloper *in one's affairs.*

in·ter·lude (ĭn'tər lōōd') ***n-*** 1 period or action between events, differing from what comes before and after: *an* interlude *of sunshine.* 2 piece of music played between the acts of a play, parts of a church service, etc.

in·ter·lu·nar (ĭn'tər lōō'nər) ***adj-*** of or relating to the time between the old and new moon, when the moon is invisible.

in·ter·mar·riage (ĭn'tər măr'ĭj) ***n-*** 1 marriage between persons of different racial or religious groups. 2 marriage between persons who are closely related.

in·ter·mar·ry (ĭn'tər măr'ē) ***vi-*** **[in·ter·mar·ried, in·ter·mar·ry·ing]** to become connected by marriage with someone of a different racial, religious, or tribal group.

in·ter·me·di·ar·y (ĭn'tər mē'dē ĕr ē) ***n-*** [*pl.* **in·ter·me·di·ar·ies**] person who acts as a mediator or go-between. ***adj-*** 1 intermediate: *an* intermediary *step in a process.* 2 serving to mediate: *an* intermediary *proposal.*

in·ter·me·di·ate (ĭn′tər mē′dē ət) *adj-* being or coming between two points, stages, things, or persons: *The tadpole is an* intermediate *stage of a frog's growth. n-* go-between; mediator. *—adv-* **in·ter·me′di·ate·ly.**

in·ter·ment (ĭn tûr′mənt) *n-* burial.

in·ter·mez·zo (ĭn′tər mĕt′sō) *n-* [*pl.* **in·ter·mez·zos** or **in·ter·mez·zi** (-sē)] short piece of music played between the acts or scenes of an opera or drama.

in·ter·mi·na·ble (ĭn tûr′mə nə bəl) *adj-* lasting or seeming to last forever; endless: *an* interminable *speech. —adv-* **in·ter′mi·na·bly.**

in·ter·min·gle (ĭn′tər mĭng′gəl) *v-* [**in·ter·min·gled, in·ter·min·gling**] to mix together; join together; mingle: *The visitors soon* intermingled *with the crowd. vt-: The author* intermingled *tragedy and comedy in her play.*

in·ter·mis·sion (ĭn′tər mĭsh′ən) *n-* **1** interval of time between two parts of a performance or other proceeding. **2** pause; interruption: *He worked without* intermission.

in·ter·mit·tent (ĭn′tər mĭt′ənt) *adj-* alternately starting and stopping; repeated at intervals; coming and going: *an* intermittent *rain. —adv-* **in′ter·mit′tent·ly.**

in·ter·mix (ĭn′tər mĭks′) *vi-* to mix or blend together: *Joy and sorrow* intermixed *in her life. vt-: He* intermixes *humor and pathos in his writing. —n-* **in′ter·mix′ture.**

[1]**in·tern** (ĭn tûrn′) *vt-* to confine or detain (enemy or belligerent persons, ships, etc.), especially during a war.

[2]**in·tern** (ĭn′tûrn′) *n-* recently graduated physician who is getting final training in a hospital. *vi-: Sue* interned *at the county hospital.* Also **interne.**

in·ter·nal (ĭn tûr′nəl) *adj-* **1** existing or situated within the surface or boundary of something; inner: *The heart is an* internal *organ.* **2** within a country; domestic: *the* internal *affairs of a country. —adv-* **in·ter′nal·ly.**

internal-combustion engine *n-* engine in which the fuel burns inside the engine itself, most often in a cylinder. Gasoline engines and jet engines are examples.

in·ter·na·tion·al (ĭn′tər năsh ən əl) *adj-* having to do with, or going on between, two or more nations or their people: *an* international *organization*; international *trade. —adv-* **in′ter·na′tion·al·ly.**

International Date Line *n-* imaginary line, situated at about the 180th meridian, at which it is internationally agreed that the time changes abruptly by a day. A calendar day is added when crossing the line from east to west, and subtracted when going west to east.

International Date Line

in·ter·na·tion·al·ism (ĭn′tər năsh′ən ə lĭz′əm) *n-* **1** international character, principles, or outlook. **2** cooperation among nations to promote a common outlook. **3** doctrine or belief fostering such an attitude. *—n-* **in′ter·na′tion·al·ist.**

in·ter·na·tion·al·ize (ĭn′tər năsh′ən ə līz′) *vt-* to make international; especially, to put under international control: *to* internationalize *a port.*

in·terne (ĭn′tûrn′) [2]intern.

in·ter·ne·cine (ĭn′tər nĕs′ēn′, -nēs′ĭn′, -nē′sĭn′) *adj-* with much mutual killing: *an* internecine *feud.*

in·tern·ee (ĭn′tûr′nē′) *n-* prisoner of war, enemy alien, etc., who has been interned.

in·tern·ist (ĭn tûr′nĭst) *n-* doctor who specializes in diseases of the internal organs.

in·tern·ment (ĭn tûrn′mənt) *n-* an interning of a belligerent ship, person, etc.; also, the period of this.

in·tern·ship (ĭn′tûrn′shĭp′) *n-* period during which one is a medical intern; also, the training received.

in·ter·pen·e·trate (ĭn′tər pĕn′ə trāt′) *vt-* to penetrate thoroughly or between. *—n-* **in′ter·pen′e·tra′tion.**

in·ter·phase (ĭn′tər fāz′) *n-* stage in mitosis between successive cell divisions, in which the DNA molecules of the nucleus replicate themselves in preparation for the next division. During interphase, the cell grows and matures. Interphase is the usual stage of body cells.

in·ter·plan·e·tar·y (ĭn′tər plăn′ə tĕr′ē) *adj-* between the planets of the solar system: *an* interplanetary *rocket.*

in·ter·play (ĭn′tər plā′) *n-* action of things, ideas, etc. on each other; interaction: *the* interplay *of minds.*

in·ter·po·late (ĭn tûr′pə lāt′) *vt-* [**in·ter·po·lat·ed, in·ter·po·lat·ing**] **1** to insert (new or unauthorized matter) into a book or writing. **2** to alter (a book or writing) by putting in such matter. **3** to insert between other things or parts: *to* interpolate *a remark.* **4** *Mathematics* of a series or table, to derive or estimate the value of an unknown quantity that lies between two known quantities. *—n-* **in·ter′po·la′tion.**

in·ter·pose (ĭn′tər pōz′) *vt-* [**in·ter·posed, in·ter·pos·ing**] **1** to place or set between other things: *to* interpose *a fence between two fields.* **2** to put forth in order to interfere; thrust in: *to* interpose *annoying questions.* **3** to introduce (a remark, comment, etc.) in a conversation *vi-* to come between parties in a quarrel; mediate. *—n-* **in′ter·pos′er.** *n-* **in′ter·po·si′tion** (-pə zĭ′shən).

in·ter·pret (ĭn tûr′prət) *vt-* **1** to translate (conversation, speeches, etc.) for people who speak different languages. **2** to explain the meaning of: *Can you* interpret *the poem in your own words?* **3** in acting or performing, to bring out the meaning of or give a special meaning to: *This actor is noted for* interpreting *historic personalities.* **4** to read a meaning into: *He* interpreted *my look as one of anger. vi-* to translate conversation, speeches, etc., for people who speak different languages.

in·ter·pre·ta·tion (ĭn tûr′prə tā′shən) *n-* **1** explanation: *an* interpretation *of a speech*; *an* interpretation *of a poem.* **2** a bringing out or giving a special meaning to in acting or performing: *a conductor's* interpretation *of French music.* **3** oral translation. *—adj-* **in·ter′pre·ta′tive** or **in·ter′pre·tive.**

in·ter·pret·er (ĭn tûr′prə tər) *n-* **1** person who translates conversation, speeches, etc., for people who speak different languages. **2** person who explains some subject.

in·ter·ra·cial (ĭn′tər rā′shel) *adj-* related to, for, or between persons of different races.

in·ter·reg·num (ĭn tər rĕg′nəm) *n-* **1** time between two successive governments or regimes, especially between the reigns of two kings. **2** break or pause; interruption.

in·ter·re·late (ĭn′tər rē lāt′) *vt-* [**in·ter·re·lat·ed, in·ter·re·lat·ing**] to bring (something) into a mutual relationship: *to* interrelate *two plans. vi-: Their ideas do not* interrelate *well. —n-* **in′ter·re·la′tion.**

in·ter·re·lat·ed (ĭn′tər rē lā′təd) *adj-* having a connection between each other; mutually related.

in·ter·re·la·tion·ship (ĭn′tər rē lā′shən shĭp′) *n-* mutual relationship.

in·ter·ro·gate (ĭn tĕr′ə gāt′) *vt-* [**in·ter·ro·gated, in·ter·ro·gat·ing**] to question, especially question closely or systematically; examine: *to* interrogate *a spy. —n-* **in·ter′ro·ga′tor.**

---

in·ter·ro·ga·tion (ĭn tĕr′ ə gā′ shən) ***n-*** **1** an interrogating or questioning, especially official questioning. **2** question; query.

interrogation mark or **point** ***n-*** question mark.

in·ter·rog·a·tive (ĭn′ tə rŏg′ ə tĭv) ***adj-*** **1** containing or asking a question: *an* interrogative *sentence.* **2** questioning: *an* interrogative *look.* ***n-*** *Grammar* word used to ask a question. Examples: "why," "where," "who," "when," "what." ***—adv-*** **in′ ter·rog′ a·tive·ly.**

interrogative pronoun ***n-*** pronoun used as an interrogative to ask a question. The interrogative pronouns are "who," "whom," and "what."

in·ter·rog·a·tor·y (ĭn′ tə rŏg′ ə tôr′ ē) ***adj-*** questioning: *an* interrogatory *remark.*

in·ter·rupt (ĭn′ tə rŭpt′) ***vt-*** **1** to stop or hinder by breaking in upon: *to* interrupt *a speaker*; *to* interrupt *a speech*; *to* interrupt *one's sleep.* **2** to cut off: *to* interrupt *a circuit.* **3** to obstruct: *A wall* interrupts *our view.* ***vi-*** to break in upon an action, speech, etc.: *Please stop* interrupting *constantly.* ***—n-*** **in′ ter·rupt′ er.**

in·ter·rup·tion (ĭn′ tə rŭp′ shən) ***n-*** **1** a being broken in upon or a breaking in upon: *There was an* interruption *in the program for a special announcement.* **2** temporary pause: *He worked without* interruption *all morning.*

in·ter·scho·las·tic (ĭn tər skə lăs′ tĭk) ***adj-*** between or among different schools: *an* interscholastic *game.*

in·ter·sect (ĭn′ tər sĕkt′) ***vt-*** **1** to cut across at the same level or in the same plane: *Elm Street* intersects *Second Avenue.* **2** in geometry, to divide (a line, surface, etc.) by cutting across. ***vi-*:** **1** to cut across each other at the same level or in the same plane: *The lines of an* × intersect. **2** *Mathematics* in the theory of sets, to overlap; to have elements in common.

in·ter·sec·tion (ĭn′ tər sĕk′ shən) ***n-*** **1** point of crossing; place where things, especially streets, cross at one level. **2** a cutting across: *The* intersection *of three main roads caused traffic jams.* **3** *Mathematics* a set consisting entirely of elements common to two or more sets; also, the set of points common to two or more geometric figures.

Intersection

in·ter·ses·sion (ĭn′ tər sĕsh′ ən) ***n-*** period between sessions or school semesters. ***Hom-*** intercession.

in·ter·sperse (ĭn′ tər spûrs′) ***vt-*** **[in·ter·spersed, in·ter·spers·ing] 1** to place here and there among other things: *to* intersperse *leaves among the flowers.* **2** to give variety to by inserting things here and there: *to* intersperse *a play with comments.* ***—n-*** **in′ ter·sper′ sion** (-spûr′ zhən).

in·ter·state (ĭn′ tər stāt′) ***adj-*** between States.

in·ter·stel·lar (ĭn′ tər stĕl′ ər) ***adj-*** among the stars.

in·ter·stice (ĭn tûr′ stəs) ***n-*** [*pl.* **in·ter·stic·es** (-stə sēz′)] narrow space or crevice; chink.

in·ter·sti·tial (ĭn′ tər stĭsh′ əl) ***adj-*** **1** of or having to do with an interstice. **2** *Biology* situated between the cells of a tissue: *Lymph is an* interstitial *fluid.*

in·ter·trib·al (ĭn′ tər trī′ bəl) ***adj-*** taking place or existing between tribes: *an* intertribal *war.*

in·ter·twine (ĭn′ tər twīn′) ***vi-*** **[in·ter·twined, in·ter·twin·ing]** to twine and twist together; interlace: *Ivy and wisteria vines* intertwined *above the door.* ***vt-*:** *to* intertwine *multicolored strips of cloth.*

in·ter·ur·ban (ĭn′ tər ûr′ bən) ***adj-*** between cities or towns: *an* interurban *railroad.*

in·ter·val (ĭn′ tər vəl) ***n-*** **1** period of time between events: *After a brief* interval *the program continued.* **2** space between objects, etc.: *the* interval *between two lawns.* **3** *Music* difference of pitch between tones.

at intervals 1 at regular distances: *He spread out his men* at intervals. **2** now and then; here and there.

in·ter·vene (ĭn′ tər vēn′) ***vi-*** **[in·ter·vened, in·ter·ven·ing] 1** to come or be (between): *The years that* intervene *between grade school and college bring many changes.* **2** to get in the way; interfere: *If nothing unexpected* intervenes, *we shall go as planned.* **3** to step in to settle: *to* intervene *in a quarrel.* ***—n-*** **in′ ter·ven′ er.**

in·ter·ven·tion (ĭn′ tər vĕn′ shən) ***n-*** **1** an interfering: *an* intervention *in the affairs of another.* **2** a coming between: *A friend's* intervention *prevented a fight.*

in·ter·view (ĭn′ tər vyōō′) ***n-*** **1** personal meeting to discuss something: *the foreman's* interviews *with job seekers.* **2** account or record of such a discussion: *Smith's* interview *with the governor was published in the papers.* ***vt-*:** *The reporter* interviewed *the visiting diplomat.* ***—n-*** **in′ ter·view·er.**

in·ter·weave (ĭn′ tər wēv′) ***vt-*** **[in·ter·wove, in·ter·wov·en** or **in·ter·wove, in·ter·weav·ing]** to twist or weave together; intertwine: *to* interweave *silk with cotton.* ***vi-*:** *Yarn* interweaves *easily.*

in·tes·tate (ĭn tĕs′ tāt′) ***adj-*** **1** not having made a will: *to die intestate.* **2** not disposed of by a will.

in·tes·ti·nal (ĭn tĕs′ tĭn əl) ***adj-*** having to do with the intestines: *an* intestinal *tract.* ***—adv-*** **in·tes′ ti·nal·ly.**

in·tes·tine (ĭn tĕs′ tən) ***n-*** **1** muscular, gland-lined tube extending from the stomach to the anus. It is composed of a long, narrow section, the **small intestine,** and a thicker, shorter section, the **large intestine** (colon). In the small intestine, food is completely digested and absorbed, and in the large intestine, water is absorbed and feces are formed. **2** the entire alimentary canal.

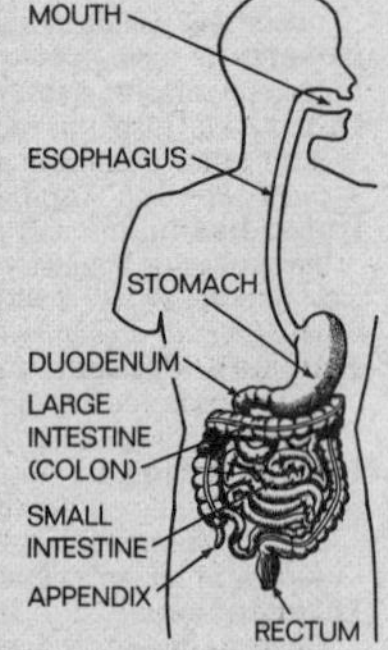

Intestine

in·ti·ma·cy (ĭn′ tə mə sē) ***n-*** [*pl.* **in·ti·ma·cies.**] close friendship; confidential relationship.

[1]**in·ti·mate** (ĭn′ tə mət) ***adj-*** **1** close; confidential: *his* intimate *friend.* **2** innermost; private; personal: *her* intimate *thoughts.* **3** coming from close study and experience: *an* intimate *knowledge of the country.* ***n-*** close friend; confidant: *Bess had many acquaintances, but no* intimates. [from French **intime,** "private; secret; dear," from Latin **intimus,** "inmost" or "dear friend."] ***—adv-*** **in′ ti·mate·ly.**

[2]**in·ti·mate** (ĭn′ tə māt′) ***vt-*** **[in·ti·mat·ed, in·ti·mat·ing]** to make (something) known indirectly; hint; imply. [from Latin **intimāre** meaning "to announce," from **intimus,** "inmost."] ***—n-*** **in′ ti·mat·er.**

in·ti·ma·tion (ĭn′ tə mā′ shən) ***n-*** a hint; indirect suggestion: *He gave no* intimation *of leaving.*

in·tim·i·date (ĭn tĭm′ ə dāt′) ***vt-*** **[in·tim·i·dat·ed, in·tim·i·dat·ing]** to make afraid by threats; frighten; cow. ***—n-*** **in·tim′ i·da′ tion.**

in·tim·i·da·tor (ĭn tĭm′ ə dā′ tər) ***n-*** one who intimidates.

in·to (ĭn′ tōō) ***prep-*** **1** to the inside of: *to fall* into *a pond*; *to walk* into *a building.* **2** to a time in: *He worked all night and* into *the next day.* **3** to the form or state of: *The water changed* into *steam.* **4** against: *He crashed* into *the wall. He walked* into *the wind.*

in·tol·er·a·ble (ĭn tŏl′ ər ə bəl) ***adj-*** very hard to endure; unbearable: *the* intolerable *heat.* ***—adv-*** **in·tol′er·a·bly.**

in·tol·er·ance (ĭn tŏl′ ər əns) ***n-*** **1** unwillingness to allow customs, behavior, opinions, beliefs, etc., not like one's own; lack of tolerance: *Religious* intolerance *in their homelands brought many early settlers to America.* 2 inability to endure: *an* intolerance *to certain drugs.*

in·tol·er·ant (ĭn tol′ ər ənt) ***adj-*** not willing to allow opinions, beliefs, customs, or behavior different from one's own. ***—adv-*** **in·tol′ er·ant·ly.**

intolerant of not able or willing to endure.

in·to·na·tion (ĭn′ tə nā′ shən) ***n-*** **1** manner of speaking, especially as it depends on the pitch of the voice and the pauses between words. **2** an intoning. **3** *Music* ability to sing or play notes of accurate pitch; also, pitch itself.

in·tone (ĭn tōn′) ***vt-*** **[in·toned, in·ton·ing]** to recite in a singing tone; chant: *to* intone *a church service.* ***vi-***: *to* intone *in a low voice.*

in to·to (tō′ tō) *Latin* totally; completely.

in·tox·i·cant (ĭn tŏk′ sə kənt) ***n-*** **1** that which intoxicates, especially alcohol. **2** anything that excites or elates.

in·tox·i·cate (ĭn tŏk′ sə kāt′) ***vt-*** **[in·tox·i·cat·ed, in·tox·i·cat·ing]** **1** to make drunk. **2** to fill with wild excitement; elate: *The warm spring air* intoxicated *the colt.* ***—adv-*** **in·tox′ i·cat′ ing·ly.** ***n-*** **in·tox′ i·ca′ tion.**

intra- *prefix* within: intra*mural*; intra*state*. [from Latin **intrā,** "within; inside; inside of."]

►For usage note see INTER-.

in·trac·ta·ble (ĭn trăk′ tə bəl) ***adj-*** unmanageable; not easily controlled: *an* intractable *temper*; *an* intractable *metal.* ***—n-*** **in·trac′ ta·bil′ i·ty.** ***adv-*** **in·trac′ ta·bly.**

in·tra·mu·ral (ĭn′ trə myŏŏr′ əl) ***adj-*** **1** entirely within the walls or limits of a city, university, etc. **2** limited to the members of a school, college, or other organization.

in·tran·si·gent (ĭn trăn′ sĭ jənt) ***adj-*** uncompromising; not reconcilable: *an* intransigent *rebel.* ***n-*** one who is uncompromising. ***—n-*** **in·tran′ si·gence.** ***adv-*** **in·tran′ si·gent·ly.**

in·tran·si·tive (ĭn trăn′ sə tĭv) *Grammar* ***adj-*** of verbs, not having an object. Examples: *He* sits. *He* laughed. *John* rode *down the street.* ***n-***: *That verb is an* intransitive. ***—adv-*** **in·tran′ si·tive·ly.**

in·tra·state (ĭn′ trə stāt′) ***adj-*** within a State.

in·tra·ve·nous (ĭn′ trə vē′ nəs) ***adj-*** within or into a vein: *an* intravenous *drug.* ***—adv-*** **in′ tra·ve′ nous·ly.**

in·treat (ĭn trēt′) entreat.

in·trench (ĭn trĕnch′) entrench. ***—n-*** **in·trench′ ment.**

in·trep·id (ĭn trĕp′ ĭd) ***adj-*** fearless; bold; brave. ***—n-*** **in′ tre·pid′ i·ty** (ĭn′ trə pĭd′ ə tē). ***adv-*** **in′ trep′ id·ly.**

in·tri·ca·cy (ĭn′ trĭ kə sē) ***n-*** [*pl.* **in·tri·ca·cies.**] **1** involvement or complexity of form, design, etc. **2** a twist or turn; complication: *the* intricacies *of the process.*

in·tri·cate (ĭn′ trĭ kət) ***adj-*** involved; complicated: *an* intricate *plot.* ***—adv-*** **in′ tri·cate·ly.** ***n-*** **in′ tri·cate·ness.**

in·trigue (ĭn trēg′) ***n-*** **1** secret plotting and scheming; underhanded deviousness: *She enjoys* intrigue. **2** a secret plot or scheme: *to take part in an* intrigue. ***vi-*** **[in·trigued, in·tri·guing]** to carry on secret plots or schemes: *He was disgraced because he* intrigued *with the enemy.* ***vt-*** to arouse the curiosity of; interest; fascinate: *His way of living* intrigues *us.*

in·tri·guer (ĭn trē′ gər) ***n-*** person who takes part in or begins an intrigue; schemer; plotter.

in·tri·guing (ĭn trē′ gĭng) ***adj-*** interesting; fascinating: *an* intriguing *suggestion.* ***—adv-*** **in·tri′ guing·ly.**

in·trin·sic (ĭn trĭn′ zik, -sĭk) ***adj-*** relating to the essential nature or makeup of a thing or person; inherent: *a man's* intrinsic *worth.* ***—adv-*** **in·trin′ si·cal·ly.**

intro- *prefix* into; within: intro*duce*; intro*spection*; intro*vert*. [from Latin **intro-,** from **intrō,** "within; inside."]

in·tro·duce (ĭn′ trə dōōs′, -dyōōs′) ***vt-*** **[in·tro·duced, in·tro·duc·ing]** **1** to make known formally: *He* introduced *us to his family.* **2** to bring into use, notice, etc.: *to* introduce *new fashions*; *to* introduce *new procedures in the office.* **3** to give (someone) knowledge of something for the first time: *to* introduce *one to the poetry of Keats.* **4** to present for debate, a vote, etc.; propose: *to* introduce *a bill into Congress.* **5** to begin; open: *A short overture* introduced *the opera.* **6** to put in; inject; insert: *to* introduce *a probe into a wound.* ***—n-*** **in′ tro·duc′ er.**

in·tro·duc·tion (in′ trə dŭk′ shən) ***n-*** **1** an introducing or being introduced. **2** beginning section of a book, speech, etc., meant to prepare the audience for what is to follow. **3** book that introduces beginners to a subject.

in·tro·duc·to·ry (ĭn′ trə dŭk′ tə rē) ***adj-*** serving to introduce; prefatory: *an* introductory *paragraph.*

in·tro·spec·tion (in′ trə spĕk′ shən) ***n-*** examination of one's own thoughts and feelings.

in·tro·spec·tive (ĭn′ trə spĕk′ tĭv) ***n-*** examining or inclined to examine one's own thoughts and feelings; subjective. ***—adv-*** **in′ tro·spec′ tive·ly.**

in·tro·ver·sion (ĭn′ trə vûr′ zhən) ***n-*** **1** act of looking inward or within. **2** tendency to be chiefly occupied with one's own mental or emotional processes.

in·tro·vert (ĭn′ trə vûrt′) *Biology* ***vt-*** to turn (an organ) inward or within. ***n-*** person who tends toward introversion.

in·trude (ĭn trōōd′) ***vi-*** **[in·trud·ed, in·trud·ing]** to enter without invitation or welcome; break in (on): *A loud crash* intruded *on the silence of the night.* ***vt-***: *He* intruded *his opinion into the conversation.* ***—n-*** **in·trud′ er.**

in·tru·sion (in trōō′ zhən) ***n-*** **1** an entering without being invited; a forcing or breaking in; trespass. **2** a thrusting of advice, opinion, etc., upon another: *The card players resented his advice as an* intrusion.

in·tru·sive (ĭn trōō′ sĭv) ***adj-*** inclined to enter without invitation; forward. ***—adv-*** **in·tru′ sive·ly.**

in·trust (ĭn trŭst′) entrust.

in·tu·i·tion (ĭn′ tōō ĭsh′ ən, ĭn′ tyōō-) ***n-*** **1** power to perceive something immediately without special information or reasoning: *to know someone's troubles by* intuition. **2** something perceived in this way.

in·tu·i·tive (ĭn tōō′ ə tĭv, ĭn′ tyōō′-) ***adj-*** **1** perceiving by intuition: *an* intuitive *judge of persons.* **2** based on intuition: *an* intuitive *dislike.* ***—adv-*** **in·tu′ i·tive·ly.**

in·un·date (ĭn′ ən dāt′) ***vt-*** **[in·un·dat·ed, in·un·dat·ing].** **1** to overflow; flood: *Heavy rains* inundated *the fields.* **2** to spread over or cover, as by a flood: *On holidays the visitors* inundated *the studio.* ***—n-*** **in′ un·da′ tion.**

in·ure (ĭ nyŏŏr′, -nŏŏr′) ***vt-*** **[inured, inur·ing]** to harden; toughen: *to* inure *oneself to danger.* ***vi-*** to come into use or advantage; take effect: *The fund* inured *to his benefit.*

in·vade (ĭn vād′) ***vt-*** **[in·vad·ed, in·vad·ing]** **1** to enter in order to attack: *An enemy* invaded *the country and conquered it.* **2** to infringe upon; violate; encroach on: *to* invade *one's privacy.* **3** to enter in force: *Swarms of children* invaded *the swimming pool.* ***—n-*** **in·vad′ er.**

[1]**in·va·lid** (ĭn′ və lĭd′) ***n-*** sick or weak person; especially someone constantly ill. [from Old French **invalide,** from Latin **invalidus,** from **in-,** "not," plus **validus,** "strong."]

[2]**in·val·id** (ĭn văl′ ĭd) ***adj-*** of no force, authority, or value; not valid. [from Latin **invalidus** meaning "not valid."] ***—adv-*** **in·val′ id·ly.**

in·val·i·date (ĭn văl′ ə dāt′) ***vt-*** **[in·val·i·dat·ed, in·val·i·dat·ing]** to weaken or destroy the force or authority of; to make null and void: *The last will* invalidates *all others.* ***—n-*** **in·val′ i·da′ tion.**

---

fāte, făt, dâre, bärn; bē, bĕt, mêre; bīte, bĭt; nōte, hŏt, môre, dȯg; fŭn, fûr; tōō, bŏŏk; oil; out; ta*r*; thin; then; hw for wh as in *wh*at; zh for s as in u*s*ual; ə for a, e, i, o, u, as in *a*go, lin*e*n, per*i*l, at*o*m, min*u*s

in·va·lid·i·ty (ĭn′ və lĭd′ ə tē) ***n-*** lack of validity.

in·val·u·a·ble (ĭn văl′ yōō ə bəl) ***adj-*** having a worth or value beyond measure; priceless: *an* invaluable *friend*; *an* invaluable *jewel.* **—*adv-* in·val′ u·a·bly.**

in·var·i·a·ble (ĭn vâr′ ē ə bəl, ĭn văr′-) ***adj-*** never changing; constant; not variable: *a man of* invariable *habits.* **—*n-* in·var′ i·a·bil′ i·ty. *adv-* in·var′ i·a·bly.**

in·va·sion (ĭn vā′ zhən) ***n-*** an invading or being invaded.

in·vec·tive (ĭn vĕk′ tĭv) ***n-*** violent, bitter accusation or attack in words; abusive language.

in·veigh (ĭn vā′) ***vi-*** to speak violently and bitterly (against): *The lawyer* inveighed *bitterly against the accused criminal.* ***n-* in·veigh′ er.**

in·vei·gle (ĭn vā′ gəl) ***vt-*** **[in·vei·gled, in·vei·gling]** to persuade by deception or flattery; lure: *to* inveigle *him into going.* **—*n-* in·vei′ gle·ment. *n-* in·vei′ gler.**

in·vent (ĭn vĕnt′) ***vt-*** **1** to make or devise (something new): *James Watt* invented *the steam engine.* **2** to make up; fabricate: *to* invent *an excuse.*

in·ven·tion (ĭn vĕn′ shən) ***n-*** **1** a making or devising something new; creation: *The* invention *of automatic machines has created serious labor problems.* **2** device, process, etc., that has been invented: *The lightning rod is one of Benjamin Franklin's* inventions. **3** something made up or false: *The story of George Washington and the cherry tree is pure* invention. **4** creative imagination; ingenuity.

in·ven·tive (ĭn vĕn′ tĭv) ***adj-*** creative; ingenious; original: *an* inventive *mind*; *an* inventive *design.* **—*adj-* in·ven′ tive·ly. *n-* in·ven′ tive·ness.**

in·ven·tor (ĭn vĕn′ tər) ***n-*** person who invents; one who finds new ways of doing things or creates new devices.

in·ven·to·ry (ĭn′ vən tôr′ ē) ***n-*** [*pl.* **in·ven·to·ries**] list of items in a store or other institution: *The library made an* inventory *of its books.* ***vt-*** **[in·ven·to·ried, in·ven·to·ry·ing]**: *to* inventory *the books in a library.*

in·verse (ĭn′ vûrs′) ***adj-*** opposite in tendency, direction or effect. ***n-*** **1** *Mathematics* an operation that undoes what another operation did. Addition and subtraction are **inverse operations. Inverse elements** of a set are the pairs of elements that, when combined according to a given operation, yield the identity for that operation. Examples: $3 + (-3) = 0$ (for addition), and $1/4 \times 4 = 1$ (for multiplication). **2** the direct opposite. **—*adv-* in·verse′ ly.**

inverse variation ***n-*** relationship of two quantities in which an increase in one produces a corresponding decrease in the other, or vice versa, such that the product of the two quantities is constant. Such a relationship is described by the equation $xy = k$, where k is a constant.

in·ver·sion (ĭn vûr′ zhən) ***n-*** an inverting or being inverted.

in·vert (ĭn vûrt′) ***vt-*** **1** to turn upside down: *If we* invert *a capital "M" it looks like a "W."* **2** to reverse the order or position of: *We* inverted *the order of numbers, and counted from ten to one.* **—*adj-* in·vert′ i·ble.**

in·ver·te·brate (ĭn vûr′ tə brāt′, -brət) ***adj-*** without a backbone. ***n-*** animal without a backbone, such as an earthworm, snail, etc.

in·vest (ĭn vĕst′) ***vt-*** **1** to put (money or other resources) into something in the expectation of profit from dividends or increasing value: *He* invested *$5,000 in railroad stock.* **2** to install in office. **3** to give power or authority to: *to* invest *a person with the right to vote.* ***vi-*** to put money into something for profit: *He* invests *wisely.*

in·ves·ti·gate (ĭn vĕs′ tə gāt′) ***vt-*** **[in·ves·ti·gat·ed, in·ves·ti·gat·ing]** to look into thoroughly and systematically; probe: *Police* investigated *the cause of the accident.* **—*adj-* in·ves′ ti·ga′ tive:** *an* investigative *branch of government.*

in·ves·ti·ga·tion (ĭn vĕs′ tə gā′ shən) ***n-*** thorough inquiry: *an* investigation *of the fire.*

in·ves·ti·ga·tor (ĭn vĕs′ tə gāt′) ***n-*** person who investigates; especially, one whose job is to investigate.

in·ves·ti·ture (ĭn vĕs′ tə chər) ***n-*** **1** ceremony of installing a person in office. **2** garment or covering.

in·vest·ment (ĭn vĕst′ mənt) ***n-*** **1** an investing: *an* investment *in oil stocks*; *an* investment *of one's time.* **2** amount invested: *The original* investment *doubled in value.* **3** something in which money is invested: *The new house was a valuable* investment.

in·ves·tor (ĭn vĕs′ tər) ***n-*** person who invests money in hope of profit.

in·vet·er·ate (ĭn vĕt′ ər ət) ***adj-*** **1** of long standing; deep-rooted: *an* inveterate *hatred.* **2** habitual: *an* inveterate *liar.* **—*adv-* in·vet′ er·ate·ly.**

in·vid·i·ous (ĭn vĭd′ ē əs) ***adj-*** **1** likely to provoke ill will or envy; offensive: *an* invidious *remark.* **2** unfairly partial or biased: *an* invidious *criticism.* **—*adv-* in·vid′ i·ous·ly. *n-* in·vid′ i·ous·ness.**

in·vig·or·ate (ĭn vĭg′ ə rāt′) ***vt-*** **[in·vig·or·at·ed, in·vig·or·at·ing]** to give strength and energy to; animate. **—*adv-* in·vig′ or·at′ ing·ly. *n-* in·vig′ or·a′ tion.**

in·vin·ci·ble (ĭn vĭn′ sə bəl) ***adj-*** such as cannot be conquered or overcome; unconquerable: *an* invincible *army.* **—*n-* in·vin′ ci·bil′ i·ty. —*adv-* in·vin′ ci·bly.**

in·vi·o·la·ble (ĭn vī′ ə lə bəl) ***adj-*** **1** such as must not be violated; sacred: *an* inviolable *vow*; inviolable *laws.* **2** such as cannot be destroyed: *an* inviolable *spirit.* **—*n-* in·vi′ o·la·bil′ i·ty. *adv-* in·vi′ o·la·bly.**

in·vi·o·late (ĭn vī′ ə lət) ***adj-*** not violated; undefiled and unbroken: *He kept his oath* inviolate.

in·vis·i·ble (ĭn vĭz′ ə bəl) ***adj-*** concealed from view; not visible: *Clouds make the stars* invisible. *The magician's magic cloak made him* invisible. **—*n-* in·vis′ i·bil′ i·ty. *adv-* in·vis′ i·bly.**

in·vi·ta·tion (ĭn′ və tā′ shən) ***n-*** written or spoken request to attend or take part in: *a wedding* invitation.

in·vite (ĭn vīt′) ***vt-*** **[in·vit·ed, in·vit·ing]** **1** to ask (a person) to come somewhere or to take part in something: *to* invite *one to a banquet.* **2** to request; ask for: *The speaker* invites *your comments following his speech.* **3** to demand; call for: *A good performance* invites *applause.* **4** to tend to bring about: *Carelessness* invites *injury.*

in·vit·ing (ĭn vī′ tĭng) ***adj-*** tempting; attractive: *an* inviting *offer of a new job.* **—*adv-* in·vit′ ing·ly.**

in·vo·ca·tion (ĭn′ və kā′ shən) ***n-*** **1** a calling upon for help or support; also, the words used for doing this: *an* invocation *to the Muse.* **2** prayer at the opening of a church service or formal public meeting. **3** a conjuring up of devils; also, the magic words for doing so.

in·voice (ĭn′ vois′) ***n-*** **1** itemized list of merchandise sent to a buyer, usually giving prices, quantity, shipping charges, etc. **2** the merchandise listed. ***vt-*** **[in·voiced, in·voic·ing]**: *to* invoice *a shipment of electrical appliances.*

in·voke (ĭn vōk′) ***vt-*** **[in·voked, in·vok·ing]** **1** to call on for help or support; plead for: *to* invoke *God's blessing.* **2** to call forth by magic; conjure: *to* invoke *a genie.*

in·vol·un·tar·y (ĭn vŏl′ ən tĕr′ ē) ***adj-*** not voluntary: *an* involuntary *cry.* **—*adv-* in·vol′ un·tar′ i·ly.**

in·volve (ĭn vŏlv′) ***vt-*** **[in·volved, in·volv·ing]** **1** to entangle; draw into; mix up with or in: *His remark* involved *him in the argument.* **2** to require; demand; include as a necessary part: *Success always* involves *effort.* **3** to occupy; engage: *School work* involves *most of my time.* **—*n-* in·volve′ ment.**

in·vul·ner·a·ble (ĭn vŭl′ nər ə bəl) ***adj-*** not vulnerable: *an* invulnerable *fortress*; *an* invulnerable *argument.* **—*n-* in·vul′ ner·a·bil′ i·ty. *adv-* in·vul′ ner·a·bly.**

in·ward (ĭn′ wərd) ***adj-*** **1** toward the inside or center: *an* inward *push.* **2** at or near the center; inner. ***adv-*** (also **in′ wards**) **1** into or toward the inner self: *His thoughts turned* inward. **2** toward the inside or center.

in·ward·ly (ĭn′ wərd lē) ***adv-*** internally; especially, in the mind or feelings: *He was* inwardly *ashamed.*

in·ward·ness (ĭn′ wərd nəs) ***n-*** tendency to be inward in one's thinking and feeling; introspective behavior.

i·o·dide (ī′ ə dīd′) ***n-*** compound of iodine and another element or radical.

i·o·dine (ī′ ə dīn′) ***n-*** grayish-black, solid element that gives off a purple vapor when heated. It is used with alcohol as a general antiseptic, and its compounds are used in medicine, photography, and many industries. Symbol I, At. No. 53, At. Wt. 126.9044.

i·o·dize (ī′ ə dīz′) ***vt-*** [**i·o·dized, i·o·diz·ing**] to treat or saturate with iodine or an iodide.

i·o·do·form (ī ō′ də fôrm′, -fôrm′) ***n-*** yellow crystalline compound of iodine, (CHI_3), used as an antiseptic.

i·on (ī′ ən, ī′ ŏn′) ***n-*** an atom or group of chemically bonded atoms that has gained or lost one or more electrons, thus acquiring a negative or positive electrical charge. When a neutral atom gains one or more electrons it becomes a **negative ion** (anion), but when it loses one or more electrons it becomes a **positive ion** (cation).

-ion *suffix* (used to form nouns) **1** act or process of: *erupt*ion; *immers*ion. **2** condition or state of: *deject*ion; *tens*ion; *confus*ion. **3** that which performs the action of: *restrict*ion; *transmiss*ion. **4** the result of: *object*ion; *collis*ion. (Many words ending in *-ion* can have three or all four of these meanings. Examples: *direct*ion; *dispers*ion; *restrict*ion. See *-ation*; *-ition.*

ion engine ***n-*** a small rocket engine that produces thrust by electrically accelerating a stream of ions. Although the amount of thrust is very small, the engine can continuously operate for months.

i·on·ic (ī ŏn′ ĭk) ***adj-*** of or having to do with ions.

I·on·ic (ī ŏn′ ĭk) ***adj-*** **1** of or relating to ancient Ionia or its people. **2** of or relating to an order of classical architecture distinguished by scroll-like decorations on the capitals of pillars. ***n-*** dialect of ancient Ionia or Attica; classic Greek.

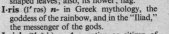

Ionic capital and column

i·on·i·za·tion (ī′ ə nə zā′ shən) ***n-*** **1** *Chemistry* the dissociation of certain compounds into ions when they are dissolved. **2** *Physics* process in which ions are formed when atoms lose their outer electrons under the impact of radiation or when an electrical current passes through a gas.

i·on·ize (ī′ ə nīz′) ***vi-*** [**i·on·ized, i·on·iz·ing**] to dissociate into ions. ***vt-*** to cause ionization.

i·on·o·sphere (ī ŏn′ ə sfêr′) ***n-*** region of ionized air in the upper atmosphere that reflects certain radio waves, thus making possible radio broadcasting over long distances. It has several different layers and lies about 50 to 400 miles above the earth, its height varying with time of day, season, and solar activity.

i·o·ta (ī ō′ tə) ***n-*** **1** small or insignificant amount or degree; jot: *a rumor without an* iota *of truth.* **2** letter of the Greek alphabet which corresponds to "i."

I.O.U. or **IOU** (ī′ ō′ yōō′) ***n-*** signed notice that "I owe you" so much: *Here is my* I.O.U. *for ten dollars.*

-ious *suffix* (added to the stems of nouns ending in *-ion* to form the adjective) characterized by or full of: *ambit*ious; *relig*ious; *infect*ious.

i·pe·cac (ĭp′ ə kăk′) ***n-*** **1** tropical South American creeping plant; also, its root. **2** extract or tincture of its root, used in medicine to cause vomiting. [American word from South American Indian **ipe-kaa-guéne** meaning "a small plant which causes vomiting."]

Iph·i·ge·ni·a (ĭf′ ə jə nī′ ə) ***n-*** in Greek legend, the daughter of Agamemnon, who offered her as a sacrifice.

ip·so fac·to (ĭp′ sō făk′ tō) *Latin* by the fact itself.

IQ or **I.Q.** intelligence quotient.

Ir symbol for iridium.

I·ran·i·an (ĭ rā′ nē ən) ***n-*** **1** a native or inhabitant of Iran (Persia). **2** the modern Persian language. **3** branch of the Indo-European family of languages that includes Persian and several other languages.

I·ra·qi (ĭ răk′ ē, ĭ răk′-) ***n-*** **1** a native or inhabitant of Iraq. **2** the Arabic dialect spoken in Iraq.

i·ras·ci·ble (ĭ răs′ ə bəl) ***adj-*** easily angered; hot-tempered. **—*n-*** **i·ras′ ci·bil′ i·ty.** ***adv-*** **i·ras′ ci·bly.**

i·rate (ī′ rāt′) ***adj-*** angry; enraged. **—*adv-*** **i′ rate′ ly.**

IRBM intermediate range ballistic missile.

ire (īər) ***n-*** anger; wrath: *to arouse a person's* ire. **—*adj-*** **ire′ ful.** ***adv-*** **ire′ ful·ly.**

ir·i·des·cent (ĭr′ ə dĕs′ ənt) ***adj-*** having a shimmering play of colors, as soap bubbles, opals, or some fabrics do. **—*n-*** **ir′ i·des′ cence.** ***adv-*** **ir′ i·des′ cent·ly.**

i·rid·i·um (ĭ rĭd′ ē əm) ***n-*** silvery, hard, brittle metal element found in platinum ores. Iridium is used in the manufacture of bearings. Symbol, Ir, At. No. 77, At. Wt. 192.2.

i·ris (ī′ rəs) ***n-*** [*pl.* **i·ris·es**] **1** the circular, colored part of the eye located between the cornea and the lens. For picture, see *eye.* **2** plant with large flowers and sword-shaped leaves; also, its flower; flag.

Iris

I·ris (ī′ rəs) ***n-*** in Greek mythology, the goddess of the rainbow, and in the "Iliad," the messenger of the gods.

I·rish (ī′ rĭsh) ***n-*** **1** a native or citizen of Ireland. **2** the ancient or modern language of the people of Ireland; also, the dialect of English spoken there. **3 the Irish** the people of Ireland and their ancestors and descendants, collectively. ***adj-***: *a tablecloth of* Irish *linen.*

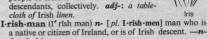

I·rish·man (ī′ rĭsh mən) ***n-*** [*pl.* **I·rish·men**] man who is a native or citizen of Ireland, or is of Irish descent. **—*n-*** *fem.* **I·rish·wom·an.**

Irish potato ***n-*** the ordinary potato, used as food.

irk (ûrk) ***vt-*** to annoy; weary; bore: *He* irks *me.*

irk·some (ûrk′ səm) ***adj-*** tiresome; tedious: *an* irksome *task.* **—*adv-*** **irk′ some·ly.** ***n-*** **irk′ some·ness.**

i·ron (ī′ ərn) ***n-*** **1** silver-white, metal element used commercially as wrought iron, cast iron, and a component of steel. Symbol Fe, At. No. 26, At. Wt. 55.847. **2** any of several tools, such as one used for branding cattle and one used to pry tires onto and off of wheels; especially, an appliance used for pressing clothes and cloth after washing. **3** firmness; rigidity; strength: *a man of* iron. **4** golf club with a metal head. **5 irons** chains or fetters. *as* ***modifier***: *an* iron *gate*; *an* iron *stove*; *to rule with an* iron *hand*; *an* iron *will.* ***vt-*** **1** to smooth (clothes, etc.) with an appliance. **2** to fetter.

have too many irons in the fire to be involved in too many plans or activities at the same time. **strike while the iron is hot** to seize a good opportunity.

iron out to straighten out (problems, difficulties, etc.).

Iron Age *n-* stage of human progress marked by the use of iron tools and weapons. It succeeds the Bronze Age.

i·ron·clad (ī′ərn klăd′) *adj-* 1 covered and protected with iron plates. 2 unbreakable; strict: *an* ironclad *rule.* *n- Archaic* warship cased with iron or steel plates.

Iron Curtain *n-* condition of censorship, secrecy, and strict border regulations imposed by the Soviet Union between their zone of influence and Western Europe.

i·ron·i·cal (ī rŏn′ĭ kəl) or **i·ron·ic** (ī rŏn′ĭk) *adj-* marked by or full of irony. *—adv-* **i·ron′i·cal·ly.**

iron lung *n-* steel cylinder or airtight covering for the chest fitted with a bellows that applies rhythmic air pressure to the chest of a patient inside it, and enables breathing by persons whose chest muscles are paralyzed.

iron oxide *n-* black, magnetic compound of iron and oxygen (Fe_3O_4) used primarily as a pigment.

i·ron·stone (ī′ərn stōn′) *n-* 1 (also **ironstone china**) hard, usually white pottery with a glassy surface. 2 iron ore.

i·ron·ware (ī′ərn wâr′) *n-* articles made of iron.

i·ron·wood (ī′ərn wŏŏd′) *n-* any of various trees with very hard, heavy wood, such as acacias, ebonies, etc.

i·ron·work (ī′ərn wûrk′) *n-* 1 iron articles; also work in iron. 2 **ironworks** place where iron is smelted or articles are made from it.

i·ron·work·er (ī′ərn wûr′kər) *n-* person who works in iron or on steel construction jobs.

i·ro·ny (ī′rə nē) *n-* [*pl.* **i·ro·nies**] 1 humorous or sarcastic way of expressing the direct opposite of what is really meant. To say "That's good!" when someone makes a mistake is irony. 2 situation or happening that is the direct opposite of what was intended or expected.

Ir·o·quois (ĭr′ə kwoi′) *n-* [*pl.* **I·ro·quois**] 1 member of the American Indian confederacy including the Cayugas, Mohawks, Oneidas, Onondagas, and Senecas, and later the Tuscaroras, and others. 2 any of the languages of these people. *adj-*: *an* Iroquois *legend.*

ir·ra·di·ate (ĭ rā′dē āt′) *vt-* [**ir·ra·di·at·ed, ir·ra·di·at·ing**] 1 to direct light upon or through, illuminate. 2 to treat with or expose to electromagnetic radiation, etc.: *to* irradiate *milk with ultraviolet rays.* *—n-* **ir·ra′di·a′tion.**

ir·ra·tion·al (ĭ răsh′ən əl) *adj-* 1 not rational; lacking or not using reasoning powers. 2 contrary to reason; absurd: *an* irrational *fear.* *—adv-* **ir·ra′tion·al·ly.**

ir·ra·tion·al·i·ty (ĭ răsh′ən ăl′ə tē) *n-* [*pl.* **ir·ra·tion·al·i·ties**] 1 irrational behavior or condition. 2 something which shows lack of reason.

irrational number *n-* a real number that cannot be expressed in the form a/b, where "a" and "b" are integers. For example, $\sqrt{2}$ and π are irrational numbers.

ir·re·claim·a·ble (ĭ′rĭ klā′mə bəl) *adj-* such as cannot be reclaimed: *miles of* irreclaimable *land.* *—n-* **ir′re·claim′a·ble·ness.** *adv-* **ir′re·claim′a·bly.**

ir·rec·on·cil·a·ble (ĭ râk′ən sī′lə bəl) *adj-* such as cannot be reconciled: *two* irreconcilable *foes.* *n-* person who refuses to yield or accept compromises. *—n-* **ir·rec′on·cil′a·bil′i·ty** or **ir·rec′on·cil′a·ble·ness.** *adv-* **ir·rec′on·cil′a·bly.**

ir·re·cov·er·a·ble (ĭ′rĭ kŭv′ər ə bəl) *adj-* such as cannot be recovered: *an* irrecoverable *opportunity.* *—n-* **ir′re·cov′er·a·ble·ness.** *adv-* **ir′re·cov′er·a·bly.**

ir·re·deem·a·ble (ĭ′rĭ dē′mə bəl) *adj-* such as cannot be redeemed: *an* irredeemable *loss.* *—n-* **ir′re·deem′a·ble·ness.** *adv-* **ir′re·deem′a·bly.**

ir·re·duc·i·ble (ĭ′rĭ dōō′sə bəl, -dyōō′sə bəl) *adj-* 1 such as cannot be reduced: *their* irreducible *expenses.* 2 such as cannot be simplified: *an* irreducible *fraction.* *—n-* **ir′re·duc′i·bil′i·ty** or **ir′re·duc′i·ble·ness.** *adv-* **ir′re·duc′i·bly.**

ir·ref·u·ta·ble (ĭ rĕf′yə tə bəl, ĭ′rĭ fyōō′-) *adj-* such as cannot be refuted or disproved: *an* irrefutable *argument.* *—n-* **ir·ref′u·ta·bil′i·ty** or **ir·ref′u·ta·ble·ness.** *adv-* **ir·ref′u·ta·bly.**

ir·reg·u·lar (ĭ rĕg′yə lər) *adj-* 1 not regular or even; not uniform in shape, order, arrangement, etc.: *buses running at* irregular *intervals.* 2 not according to rule or to custom. 3 *Grammar* not following a regular pattern of inflection. Examples: The verb "to be" is irregular in conjugation. The adjective "good" is irregular in comparison. *—adv-* **ir·reg′u·lar·ly.**

ir·reg·u·lar·i·ty (ĭ rĕg′yə lăr′ə tē) *n-* [*pl.* **ir·reg·u·lar·i·ties**] 1 lack of regularity. 2 thing or place that is irregular: *Being late is an* irregularity *of conduct.*

ir·rel·e·vant (ĭ rĕl′ə vənt) *adj-* not relevant; not bearing upon the case: *to offer* irrelevant *evidence.* *—n-* **ir·rel′e·vance** or **ir·rel′e·van·cy.** *adv-* **ir·rel′e·vant·ly.**

ir·re·li·gious (ĭ rĭ lĭj′əs) *adj-* lacking religion or respect for religion; profane. *—adv-* **ir′re·li′gious·ly.**

ir·re·me·di·a·ble (ĭ′rĭ mē′dē ə bəl) *adj-* such as cannot be remedied. *—n-* **ir′re·me′di·a·ble·ness.** *adv-* **ir′re·me′di·a·bly.**

ir·rep·a·ra·ble (ĭ rĕp′ər ə bəl) *adj-* such as cannot be repaired, restored, or remedied: *his* irreparable *losses.* *—n-* **ir·rep′a·ra·ble·ness.** *adv-* **ir·rep′a·ra·bly.**

ir·re·place·a·ble (ĭ′rĭ plā′sə bəl) *adj-* such as cannot be relaced: *an* irreplaceable *employee.* *—n-* **ir′re·place′a·ble·ness.**

ir·re·pres·si·ble (ĭ′rĭ prĕs′ə bəl) *adj-* such as cannot be repressed: *a burst of* irrepressible *laughter.* *—n-* **ir′re·pres′si·bil′i·ty** or **ir′re·pres′si·ble·ness.** *adv-* **ir′re·pres′si·bly.**

ir·re·proach·a·ble (ĭ′rĭ prō′chə bəl) *adj-* not reproachable; faultless: *their* irreproachable *conduct.* *—n-* **ir′re·proach′a·ble·ness.** *adv-* **ir′re·proach′a·bly.**

ir·re·sist·i·ble (ĭ′rĭ zĭs′tə bəl) *adj-* such as cannot be resisted; too strong or desirable to be resisted: *an* irresistible *dessert.* *—n-* **ir′re·sist′i·bil′i·ty.** *adv-* **ir′re·sist′i·bly.**

ir·res·o·lute (ĭ rĕz′ə lōōt′, -lyōōt′) *adj-* not resolute: *He is* irresolute *in his decisions.* *—adv-* **ir·res′o·lute′ly.** *n-* **ir·res′o·lute′ness** or **ir·res′o·lu′tion.**

ir·re·spec·tive (ĭ′rĭ spĕk′tĭv) *adj-* independent (of); regardless (of): *Everyone was invited,* irrespective *of age.* *—adv-* **ir′re·spec′tive·ly.**

ir·re·spon·si·ble (ĭ′rĭ spŏn′sə bəl) *adj-* not responsible; not to be depended upon: *an* irresponsible *driver.* *—n-* **ir′re·spon′si·bil′i·ty.** *adv-* **ir′re·spon′si·bly.**

ir·re·triev·a·ble (ĭ′rĭ trē′və bəl) *adj-* such as cannot be retrieved: *The posted letter was* irretrievable. *—n-* **ir′re·triev′a·ble·ness.** *adv-* **ir′re·triev′a·bly.**

ir·rev·er·ence (ĭ rĕv′ər əns) *n-* lack of reverence or respect; also, an act or remark showing this.

ir·rev·er·ent (ĭ rĕv′ər ənt) *adj-* not reverent, especially toward sacred things. *—adv-* **ir·rev′er·ent·ly.**

ir·re·vers·i·ble (ĭ′rĭ vûr′sə bəl) *adj-* such as cannot be reversed. *—n-* **ir′re·vers′i·bil′i·ty** or **ir′re·vers′i·ble·ness.** *adv-* **ir′re·vers′i·bly.**

ir·rev·o·ca·ble (ĭ rĕv′ə kə bəl) *adj-* such as cannot be revoked or undone: *an* irrevocable *act.* *—n-* **ir·rev′o·ca·bil′i·ty** or **ir·rev′o·ca·ble·ness.** *adv-* **ir·rev′o·ca·bly.**

ir·ri·gate (ĭr′ə gāt′) *vt-* [**ir·ri·gat·ed, ir·ri·gat·ing**] 1 to supply (land) with water from a main source by means of ditches, canals, etc. 2 to wash out with a constant flow of liquid in order to clean or disinfect: *to* irrigate *an infected ear.*

ir·ri·ga·tion (ĭr′ə gā′shən) *n-* 1 the science and practice of furnishing water to land under cultivation. 2 the flushing of wounds with water.

ir·ri·ta·bil·i·ty (ĭr′ ə tə bĭl′ ə tē) ***n-*** **1** ease of being irritated or angered. **2** *Biology* a fundamental characteristic of living organisms and their cells that enables them to respond to changes in the environment.

ir·ri·ta·ble (ĭr′ ə tə bəl) ***adj-*** **1** easily annoyed or angered; cranky. **2** extremely sensitive: *an* irritable *skin condition.* **—*n-* ir′ ri·ta·ble·ness.** ***adv-*** **ir′ ri·ta·bly.**

ir·ri·tant (ĭr′ ə tənt) ***n-*** something that irritates; especially, that which causes sensitiveness or inflammation. ***adj-*** causing physical irritation.

ir·ri·tate (ĭr′ ə tāt′) ***vt-*** **[ir·ri·tat·ed, ir·ri·tat·ing]** **1** to make sore; cause to become inflamed: *Strong soap can* irritate *a baby's skin.* **2** to make impatient or angry; annoy: *He* irritates *me.* **—*adv-* ir′ ri·tat′ ing·ly.**

►For usage note see AGGRAVATE.

ir·ri·ta·tion (ĭr′ ə tā′ shən) ***n-*** **1** an irritating or being irritated: *He showed his* irritation *when we came late.* **2** something that irritates: *His lateness is a constant* irritation. **3** soreness; inflammation: *a small skin* irritation.

ir·rupt (ĭ rŭpt′) ***vi-*** **1** to rush in with force; appear suddenly: *The water* irrupted *through the dike.* **2** of an animal population, to increase suddenly in numbers.

►Should not be confused with ERUPT.

ir·rup·tion (ĭ rŭp′ shən) ***n-*** **1** a bursting or rushing in. **2** sudden increase in numbers. **—*adv-* ir·rup′ tive.**

is (ĭz) form of **be** used with "he," "she," "it," or singular noun subjects, in the present tense.

as is in the condition found in, whether damaged, soiled, etc.: *The chair sells for $30* as is.

I·saac (ī′ zək) ***n-*** in the Bible, a Hebrew patriarch, son of Abraham and father of Esau and Jacob.

I·sa·iah (ī zā′ ə) ***n-*** **1** in the Bible, a great Hebrew prophet of the eighth century B.C. **2** a book of the Bible attributed to him. In the CCD Bible, **I·sa′ ia.**

is·chi·um (ĭs′ kē əm) ***n-*** the lowest portion of either of the hipbones. For picture, see *pelvis.*

I·seult (ē so͝olt′) ***n-*** in Arthurian legend, wife of King Mark of Cornwall. She was beloved by Tristram.

-ish *suffix* (used to form adjectives) **1** somewhat; rather: *black*ish; *sweet*ish. **2** resembling; having the characteristics of: *hog*gish; *boy*ish. **3** having to do with (a national group): *Engl*ish; *Swed*ish. **4** *Informal & chiefly Brit.* approximately; about: *fifty*ish.

Ish·ma·el (ĭsh′ mā əl) ***n-*** in the Bible, the exiled son of Abraham; hence, an outcast.

Ish·tar (ĭsh′ tär′) ***n-*** in Assyrian and Babylonian mythology, the goddess of love and fertility. She was identified with the Phoenician Astarte.

i·sin·glass (ī′ zən glăs′) ***n-*** **1** a gelatin made from the dried air bladders of fish and used in glues, printing inks, etc. **2** mica, especially when used as a window in stoves.

I·sis (ī′ səs) ***n-*** in Egyptian mythology, the goddess of love and fertility; sister and wife of Osiris.

Is·lam (ĭs läm′) ***n-*** **1** the religion of the Muslims, first taught by the prophet Mohammed in the 7th century A.D. The Muslims worship one God, Allah, and consider Mohammed as the last of the true prophets. **2** the Muslims as a group, their culture, and their lands. **—*adj-* Is·lam′ ic** (-läm′ ĭk, -lăm′ ĭk): *an* Islamic *prophet.*

is·land (ī′ lənd) ***n-*** **1** piece of land completely surrounded by water. **2** something like such a piece of land: *a safety* island *in the street.*

is·land·er (ī′ lən dər) ***n-*** person who was born on or is living on an island.

isle (īl) ***n-*** small island. ***Homs-*** aisle, I'll.

is·let (ī′ lĭt) ***n-*** very small island. ***Hom-*** eyelet.

ism (ĭz′ əm) ***n-*** distinctive system or doctrine.

-ism *suffix* (used to form nouns) **1** action or practice of: *hero*ism; *cannibal*ism; *exhibition*ism; *critic*ism. **2** condition or quality of; also, a special or abnormal condition: *optim*ism. **3** characteristic or peculiarity (of a people, language, speech, etc.): *American*ism; *colloquial*ism. **4** system; doctrine; policy; set of principles, etc.: *pacif*ism.

is·n't (ĭz′ ənt) is not.

iso- *combining form* **1** equal: iso*bar* (equal pressure). **2** being an isomer of. [from Greek **isos,** "equal."]

i·so·bar (ī′ sə bär′) ***n-*** line on a weather map connecting places having the same atmospheric pressure at a particular time.

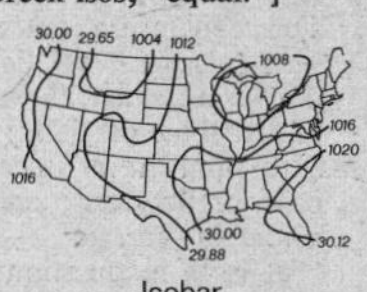

Isobar

i·so·gon·ic line (ī′ sə gŏn′ ĭk, -gòn′ ĭk) ***n-*** line on a map that joins points on the earth's surface having the same magnetic variation or declination.

i·so·late (ī′ sə lāt′) ***vt-*** **[i·so·lat·ed, i·so·lat·ing]** **1** to set apart or to cause to be apart from others: *The hospital* isolated *contagious cases. Lack of a telephone* isolated *him.* **2** to select or separate from others or from some substance: *to* isolate *a virus of the common cold.*

i·so·la·tion (ī′ sə lā′ shən) ***n-*** **1** an isolating or separating. **2** remoteness; loneliness: *the* isolation *of the farmhouse.*

i·so·la·tion·ism (ī′ sə lā′ shən ĭz′ əm) ***n-*** policy of avoiding political and economic entanglements with other nations. **—*n-* i′ so·la′ tion·ist.**

I·sol·de (ĭ sōl′ də) Iseult.

i·so·mer (ī′ sə mər) *Chemistry* ***n-*** one of two or more compounds that contain equal amounts of the same elements, but differ in structure and properties.

i·so·met·ric (ī′ sə mĕ′ trĭk) ***adj-*** of or having to do with a special kind of exercise in which the muscles are tensed without shortening or contracting them.

isometric projection ***n-*** system of accurately drawing a three-dimensional object by measurement along three axes that correspond to the three dimensions.

i·sos·ce·les triangle (ī sŏs′ ə lēz′) ***n-*** triangle having two equal sides.

i·sos·ta·sy (ī sŏs′ tə sē) ***n-*** **1** in geology, the theory that there is an equilibrium between the lighter and heavier parts of the earth's crust, which is maintained by a plastic flow of the underlying, supporting rock layers. **2** condition in which there is equal pressure on every side.

i·so·therm (ī′ sə thûrm′) ***n-*** line on a weather map connecting places which have the same temperature at a particular time, or the same average temperature for a certain period.

i·so·tope (ī′ sə tōp′) *Chemistry* ***n-*** one of two or more atoms of an element whose nucleus contains the same number of protons as the other atoms but a different number of neutrons. The isotopes of an element have the same atomic number but different atomic weights.

Is·ra·el (ĭz′ rē əl, ĭz′ rā′ əl, ĭz′ rəl) ***n-*** **1** the Hebrew patriarch Jacob. **2** the descendants of Jacob, the Jewish people. **3** the ancient northern kingdom after the division of the Jews. **4** a modern Jewish nation at the eastern end of the Mediterranean Sea.

Is·rae·li (ĭz rā′ lē) ***n-*** citizen of the modern country of Israel. ***adj-***: *the* Israeli *parliament.*

Is·ra·el·ite (ĭz′ rē ə līt′, ĭz′ rə līt′) ***n-*** a descendant of Israel or Jacob; a Hebrew.

is·su·ance (ĭsh′ o͞o əns) ***n-*** an issuing.

is·sue (ĭsh′ o͞o) ***n-*** **1** a coming, passing, or flowing out; also, that which emerges: *the* issue *of blood from a cut*; *an* issue *of lava from a volcano.* **2** an official putting forth, producing, or distributing; also, that which is distributed: *the* issue *of a coin.* **3** a printing or publishing of a book, magazine, etc.; also, the entire number, or edition, put out at one time, or a particular copy: *last week's* issue. **4** subject of concern or of dispute; point or question for debate: *the chief political* issues *of the day.* **5** offspring; children: *to die without* issue. **6** decision; conclusion; outcome: *What is the probable* issue *of such evidence?* ***vt-*** **[is·sued, is·su·ing] 1** to send out; discharge; emit: *The crater* issued *smoke.* **2** to give out or distribute officially: *to* issue *licenses*; *to* issue *supplies.* **3** to publish: *to* issue *a Sunday paper.* ***vi-*** to come, pass, or flow out; emerge: *Cold water* issued *from the mountain spring.* ***—adj-*** **is′su·a·ble.** ***n-*** **is′su·er.**
at issue in question; being discussed. **join** (or **take**) **issue with** to disagree or argue with.

-ist *suffix* (used to form nouns) **1** (often corresponds with the verb suffix "-ize") one who makes a practice of doing something: *moral*ist. **2** (often corresponds with the noun suffix "-y") one who pursues some branch of art or science; one whose profession is: *botan*ist; *zoolog*ist; *art*ist. **3** (usually corresponds with the noun suffix "-ism") follower of a system, doctrine, policy, set of principles, etc.: *Buddh*ist; *isolation*ist; *pacif*ist.

isth·mus (ĭs′ məs) ***n-*** narrow strip of land connecting two larger bodies of land.

Isthmus of Panama

it (ĭt) ***pron-*** (used as a singular subject or object in the third person) **1** thing, animal, happening, or idea talked about: *Where is the key?* It *is in the door.* **2** word of no meaning used to introduce a statement that something exists or is true: *He said* "It *is three o'clock.*" It *is warm in here.* ***n-*** **1** something that is neither male nor female: *Not a he or a she but an* it. **2** in certain games, the player picked out to find certain things, answer questions, guard a place, etc.: *We played hide-and-seek, and I was* it.

It. or **Ital. 1** Italian. **2** Italy.

ITA Initial Teaching Alphabet.

ital. 1 italic. **2** italics.

I·tal·i·an (ĭ tăl′ yən) ***n-*** **1** a native or inhabitant of Italy, or one of his descendants. **2** the Romance language of Italy. ***adj-***: *unforgettable* Italian *landscapes.*

i·tal·ic (ĭ tăl′ ĭk, ī-) ***adj-*** having to do with a type in which the letters slant to the right. ***n-*** **1** type of this style. **2 italics** letters in slanting type.

i·tal·i·cize (ĭ tăl′ ə sīz′) ***vt-*** **[i·tal·i·cized, i·tal·i·ciz·ing] 1** to print with letters that slant toward the right. **2** to underline (a letter or word) in writing.

itch (ĭch) ***n-*** **1** sensation of tingling and irritation in the skin. **2** contagious skin disease characterized by this sensation. **3** constant and craving desire; restless urge: *an* itch *to fly.* ***vi-*** **1** to have a feeling in the skin causing a desire to scratch; also, to be the cause of such a feeling. **2** to have a longing; feel an urge: *He* itches *to fight.* ***—n-*** **itch′ i·ness.** ***adj-*** **itch′ y [itch·i·er, itch·i·est].**

-ite *suffix* (used to form nouns) **1** inhabitant or native of: *Muscov*ite (native or inhabitant of Moscow). **2** follower of, sympathizer with, or believer in: *Labor*ite. **3** descendant of: *Israel*ite. **4** the name of a commercial product: *dynam*ite. **5** fossil organisms: *trilob*ite. **6** rock or mineral: *hemat*ite. **7** *Chemistry* the salt of an acid having a name that ends in -ous: *nitr*ite; *sulf*ite. **8** in anatomy, part, segment, or joint of a body: *dendr*ite.

i·tem (ī′ təm) ***n-*** **1** one thing among several: *What is the first* item *on the shopping list?* **2** piece of news: *several funny* items *in the paper.* **3** entry in an account book.

i·tem·ize (ī′ tə mīz′) ***vt-*** **[i·tem·ized, i·tem·iz·ing]** to list the separate items of: *to* itemize *a milk bill.*

it·er·ate (ĭt′ ər āt′) ***vt-*** **[it·er·at·ed, it·er·at·ing]** to repeat: *to* iterate *a threat.* ***—n-*** **it′ er·a′ tion.** ***adj-*** **it′er·a·tive**: *an* iterative *appeal for help.*

i·tin·er·ant (ī tĭn′ ər ənt, ĭ tĭn′-) ***adj-*** **1** wandering from place to place: *a troupe of* itinerant *musicians.* **2** traveling a circuit in one's duties: *an* itinerant *preacher.* ***n-*** wandering person. ***—adv-*** **i·tin′ er·ant·ly.**

i·tin·er·ar·y (ī tĭn′ ə rĕr′ ē, ĭ tĭn′-) ***n-*** [*pl.* **i·tin·er·ar·ies**] **1** proposed route for a journey, or a route actually taken. **2** record of a journey. **3** traveler's guidebook.

-ition *suffix* (used to form nouns) **1** act or process of: *defin*ition (act of defining); *oppos*ition; *compet*ition. **2** the condition or state of: *malnutr*ition; *amb*ition. **3** that which performs the action of: *prohib*ition; *pet*ition. **4** the result of: *compos*ition. (Many words ending in "-ition" can have two or all three of these meanings. Examples: *defin*ition; *compos*ition; *inhib*ition.)

-itious *suffix* (used to form adjectives) marked by; relating to; having the quality of: *fact*itious (not genuine; artificial); *fict*itious (invented or imagined).

-itis *suffix* (used to form nouns) **1** inflammation of: *bronch*itis; *appendic*itis; *mening*itis. **2** *Informal* excessive fondness for; weakness for: *telephon*itis; *television*itis.

it'll (ĭt əl) **1** it will. **2** it shall.

its (ĭts) ***determiner*** (possessive case of the pronoun "it," now usually called possessive adjective) **1** of or belonging to it: *The tree lost* its *leaves.* **2** inhabited by it: *The turtle returned to* its *pond.*

it's (ĭts) **1** it is. **2** it has (auxiliary verb only).

it·self (ĭt′ sĕlf′) ***pron-*** **1** its own self: *The cat was licking* itself. **2** word used for emphasis: *The frame* itself *is worth more than the picture.*
by itself 1 alone: *The owl perched* by itself. **2** without any help: *The door opened* by itself.

-ity *suffix* (used to form nouns) **1** state, condition, or quality: *inferior*ity; *superior*ity; *atroc*ity; *fratern*ity; *patern*ity (condition of being a father); *mortal*ity. **2** property of a substance: *dens*ity; *conductiv*ity.

-ive *suffix* (used to form adjectives) **1** relating to; having the nature, character, or quality of: *fest*ive (relating to a feast or festival); *attract*ive; *mass*ive. **2** having a tendency to; given to: *destruct*ive; *disrupt*ive; *explos*ive. (Many adjectives ending in "-ive" are also used as nouns. Examples: *explos*ive; *sedat*ive; *incent*ive.)

I've (īv) I have.

i·vo·ry (īv′ rē, ī′ və rē) ***n-*** [*pl.* **i·vo·ries**] **1** white, bonelike substance which forms the tusks of elephants, walruses, etc. **2** creamy white. ***adj-***: *an* ivory *box*; ivory *paper.*

ivory tower ***n-*** state or situation in which one ignores everyday problems and pursues his own pleasure and mental delights; retreat; escape.

i·vy (ī′ vē) ***n-*** [*pl.* **i·vies**] **1** any of several vines with glossy leaves. **2** any of several unrelated vines, such as poison ivy. ***—adj-*** **i·vied.**

English ivy

-ize *suffix* (used to form verbs) **1** to cause to be, become, or resemble; make conform with: *American*ize; *Anglic*ize. **2** to cause to be formed into: *union*ize. **3** to subject or to treat to a specified action: *satir*ize; *critic*ize. **4** to treat or combine with: *oxid*ize. **5** to treat like; act in the manner of: *tyrann*ize; *idol*ize. **6** to become like; change into: *crystall*ize. **7** to engage in; practice; follow a certain policy: *econom*ize.

J

J, j (jā) ***n-*** [*pl.* **J's, j's**] the tenth letter of the English alphabet.

jab (jăb) ***vt-*** [**jabbed, jab·bing**] to stab or poke: *He* jabbed *me with his elbow.* ***n-*** quick stab; sharp poke: *She gave the pillow a* jab *with her finger.*

jab·ber (jăb′ər) ***vi-*** to talk rapidly and indistinctly; chatter; babble. ***n-:*** *the* jabber *of monkeys.* ***n-*** **jab′ber·er.**

Jab·ber·wock (jă′bər wŏk′) ***n-*** imaginary monster in the nonsense poem "Jabberwocky," included in Lewis Carroll's "Through the Looking Glass."

ja·bot (zhă bō′) ***n-*** ruffle of lace or cloth down the front of a blouse, bodice, or shirt.

jack (jăk) ***n-*** **1** any of various portable mechanical or hydraulic devices that exert a powerful force and are used chiefly to raise cars or other heavy loads. **2** playing card with a picture of a young man; knave. It comes between the ten and the queen. **3** small flag flown on a ship to show its nationality. **4** electrical device in which a long, slim plug is inserted to make a connection. **5** male animal, especially a donkey. **6** man or boy, especially one employed in manual labor or as a sailor: jack-*of-all-trades*; Jack *Tar.* **7** *Slang* money. **8** bootjack. **9** small metal piece with six projections, used in a children's game. **10 jacks** children's game using such metal pieces and a rubber ball, in which the pieces are picked up in various ways as the ball bounces. ***vt-*** (often used with "up") **1** to raise or lift with or as if with a mechanical or hydraulic device: *to* jack *the car up*; *to* jack *up prices.* **2** to spur on; exhort: *to* jack *up a lazy student.*

Raising car with jack

jack·al (jăk′əl) ***n-*** **1** wild dog of Asia and Africa, about the size of a fox. It feeds on carrion and small game. **2** person who does base or menial work for another; lackey.

Jackal, about 15 in. high at shoulder

jack·a·napes (jăk′ə nāps′) ***n-*** saucy or conceited fellow; also, a pert child.

jack·ass (jăk′ăs′) ***n-*** **1** male donkey. **2** stupid person; blockhead.

jack boot or **jack·boot** (jăk′bo͞ot′). ***n-*** military boot reaching above the knee.

jack·daw (jăk′dȯ′) ***n-*** dusky, black, mischievous, European crow. It can learn to imitate human speech.

jack·et (jăk′ət) ***n-*** **1** short, coatlike garment. **2** life jacket. **3** any covering meant to insulate, protect, or toughen. ***—adj-*** **jack′et·ed.**

Jackdaw, about 14 in. long

Jack Frost ***n-*** frost or wintry weather thought of as a person.

jack·ham·mer (jăk′hăm′ər) ***n-*** rock drill powered by compressed air.

jack-in-the-box (jăk′ĭn thə bŏks′) ***n-*** doll on a spring attached to the bottom of a box so that the doll pops up when the lid is released.

jack-in-the-pul·pit (jăk′in thə po͝ol′pĭt) ***n-*** North American plant, growing in damp woods, with a spike of tiny yellow flowers arched over by a hoodlike spathe.

SPATHE

SPADIX

Jack-in-the-pulpit

jack·knife (jăk′nīf′) ***n-*** [*pl.* **jack·knives**] **1** large pocketknife with blades that can be folded back into the handle. **2** fancy dive in which the diver bends double, then straightens out.

jack-of-all-trades (jăk′ əv ȯl′ trādz′) ***n-*** man who can do all kinds of jobs; handyman.

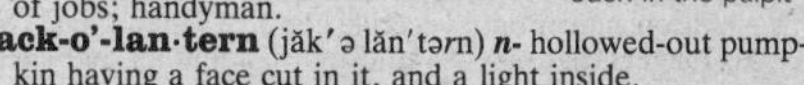

jack-o'-lan·tern (jăk′ə lăn′tərn) ***n-*** hollowed-out pumpkin having a face cut in it, and a light inside.

jack·pot (jăk′pŏt′) ***n-*** **1** everything gambled for, in one large prize or pot; especially, the whole contents of a gambling slot machine. **2** in poker, a deal in which all players enter, and in which a pair of jacks or better is needed to open the betting.

hit the jackpot **1** to win a jackpot. **2** to have a sweeping and important success.

jack rabbit ***n-*** long-eared western hare able to make 20-foot jumps.

jack·screw (jăk′skro͞o′) ***n-*** jack that increases or decreases its pressing force as a screw is turned.

Jack·so·ni·an (jăk sō′nē ən) ***adj-*** having to do with Andrew Jackson, his policies, or his era.

jack·straw (jăk′strȯ′) ***n-*** one of the light strips of wood or metal used in the child's game, **jackstraws,** in which a player tries to lift a strip out of a pile with a hook or magnet without moving other strips.

Ja·cob (jā′kəb) ***n-*** a Hebrew patriarch, son of Isaac, and ancestor of the twelve tribes of Israel.

Jac·o·bite (jăk′ə bīt′) ***n-*** in English history, a follower of James II after his dethronement in 1688, or a supporter of one of his descendants.

Jacob's ladder (jā′kəbz lăd′ər) ***n-*** **1** in the Bible, a ladder reaching from earth to heaven, seen by Jacob in a dream. **2** a rope ladder with wooden rungs.

jac·quard (jə kärd′) ***n-*** **1** fabric such as brocade or damask with an intricate figured weave. **2** loom equipped to weave such fabric.

[1]jade (jād) ***n-*** **1** hard stone, in a range of green, bluish-green, and greenish-white shades, used for jewelry and ornaments. **2** (also **jade green**) light bluish green. ***adj-:*** *a* jade *silk.* [a shortened form of earlier French **ejade,** from a Spanish phrase **piedra de ijada** meaning "stone for (curing pain) of the side."]

[2]jade (jād) ***n-*** **1** worthless or worn-out horse. ***vt-*** [**jad·ed, jad·ing**] to wear out or tire, as with overwork. [from Middle English **iade,** from Scottish **yawd** or **yald,** perhaps from Old Norse **jalda** meaning "a mare."]

jad·ed (jā′dəd) ***adj-*** **1** exhausted. **2** dulled by having too much of something; satiated: *a* jaded *appetite.*

jag (jăg) ***n-*** sharp, projecting point; a notch. ***vt-*** [**jagged, jag·ging**] to cut or tear making a ragged edge.

---

fāte, făt, dâre, bärn; bē, bĕt, mêre; bīte, bĭt; nōte, hŏt, môre, dȯg; fŭn, fûr; to͞o, bo͝ok; oil; out; tar; thin; then; hw for wh as in *wh*at; zh for s as in u*s*ual; ə for a, e, i, o, u, as in *a*go, lin*e*n, per*i*l, at*o*m, min*u*s

jag·ged (jăg'əd) ***adj-*** having a ragged edge; sharply notched: *The coast has a* jagged *outline.* ***—adv-*** **jag'ged·ly.** ***n-*** **jag'ged·ness.**

Jaguar, about 6 1/2 ft. long

jag·uar (jăg'wär') ***n-*** fierce and handsome wild cat of tropical America.

jai a·lai (hī'lī') ***n-*** game of Spanish and Basque origin, resembling handball and played by two or four men, each with a curved basket strapped to one wrist.

jail (jāl) ***n-*** prison, especially one where people are locked up as punishment for lesser crimes, or to wait for trial. ***vt-:*** *to* jail *a man for robbery.*

jail·break (jāl'brāk') ***n-*** an escape from jail.

jail·er or **jail·or** (jā'lər) ***n-*** person in charge of a jail.

ja·lop·y (jə lŏp'ē) *Slang* ***n-*** old, dilapidated automobile.

jal·ou·sie (jăl'ə sē) ***n-*** **1** blind made of overlapping horizontal slats that may be adjusted to let in light and air while keeping out sun or rain; venetian blind. **2** window made of glass louvers that may be adjusted to admit air and keep out rain. *as* ***modifier:*** *a* jalousie *door.*

[1]**jam** (jăm) ***vt-*** **[jammed, jam·ming]** **1** to pack tightly; cram: *He* jammed *all his clothes into one suitcase.* **2** to put or place forcibly; crush down: *He* jammed *his hat on his head.* **3** to make unworkable or unmovable by sticking or blocking some part. *An accident* jammed *traffic.* **4** to make (electronic signals) unintelligible by sending out interfering signals of approximately the same frequency: jam *a radio program.* ***vi-*** to become unworkable or unmovable because of a sticking or blocking: *the window* jammed. ***n-:*** *a log* jam; *a traffic* jam. [perhaps a changed form of **champ,** "to chew noisily."]

[2]**jam** (jăm) ***n-*** preserve made by boiling fruit with sugar until thick. [probably a special use of [1]**jam,** since in making jam, much fruit is packed tightly together.]

jamb (jăm) ***n-*** one of the upright sides of a doorway, window opening, or fireplace.

jam·bo·ree (jăm'bə rē') ***n-*** **1** noisy, lively party or spree. **2** large gathering of the Boy Scouts.

James (jāmz) ***n-*** in the Bible, either of two apostles, St. James the Greater, or St. James the Less. A book of the New Testament is attributed to James the Less.

jam session ***n-*** gathering of jazz musicians to improvise freely on various numbers for the fun of it.

Jan. January.

jan·gle (jăng'gəl) ***vi-*** **[jan·gled, jan·gling]** **1** to make a noise that is harsh or discordant: *The alarm clock* jangled. ***vt-*** **1** to cause to make such a sound: *He* jangled *the bunch of keys.* **2** to set on edge; irritate: *That banging door* jangled *my nerves.* ***n-:*** *the* jangle *of an alarm clock.* ***—n-*** **jan'gler.**

jan·i·tor (jăn'ə tər) ***n-*** person whose job it is to clean and take care of a building. ***—adj-*** **jan'i·tor'i·al.**

Jan·u·ar·y (jăn'yōō ĕr'ē) ***n-*** the first month of the year, having 31 days.

Ja·nus (jā'nəs) ***n-*** in Roman mythology, the god of portals, able to look into the past and the future. He is usually represented with two faces.

ja·pan (jə păn') ***n-*** **1** Japanese lacquer, a hard, brilliant varnish for wood or metal; also, any coating resembling it. **2** lacquered articles decorated in a Japanese style. ***vt-*** **[ja·panned, ja·pan·ning]:** *to* japan *a tray.*

Jap·a·nese (jăp'ə nēz') ***n-*** [*pl.* **Jap·a·nese**] **1** a native or inhabitant of Japan or his descendants. **2** the language of Japan. **3 the Japanese** the people of Japan and their ancestors and descendants, collectively. ***adj-:*** *a* Japanese *garden; a* Japanese *camera.*

Japanese beetle ***n-*** small, bronze-green beetle that was accidentally introduced into the United States from Japan and is very destructive to vegetation.

[1]**jar** (jär) ***vt-*** **[jarred, jar·ring]** **1** to cause to shake: *The blast* jarred *the house.* **2** to cause a shock to: *The news* jarred *him.* ***vi-*** **1** to produce a harsh sound or jolting motion: *The brakes* jarred *as the car stopped.* **2** to come into or be in conflict: *His ideas* jarred *with mine.* ***n-*** **1** sudden shake; jolt; shock. **2** harsh sound. [of uncertain origin.]
jar on to have an unpleasant effect on.

[2]**jar** (jär) ***n-*** **1** wide-mouthed container of pottery or glass. **2** contents of a jar; jarful. [from French **jarre,** from Arabic **jarrah,** "earthenware water vessel."]

Jar

jar·di·niere (zhär'də nyĕr', jär'də nêr') ***n-*** container or stand for holding plants or flowers.

jar·ful (jär'fŏŏl') ***n-*** **1** the amount held by a jar.

jar·gon (jär'gən) ***n-*** **1** specialized language of a group, trade, or profession; cant: *the* jargon *of space scientists.* **2** confused or meaningless speech or writing; gibberish. **3** mixed language, such as pidgin English, that simplifies communication between different peoples.

jas·mine or **jas·min** (jăz'mən) ***n-*** any of several climbing shrubs with very fragant white, red, or yellow flowers.

Ja·son (jā'sən) ***n-*** in Greek legend, the hero who led the Argonauts in search of the Golden Fleece.

jas·per (jăs'pər) ***n-*** cloudy quartz, usually red, brown, or yellow, used for ornamental objects.

ja·to unit (jā'tō') ***n-*** one or more small rocket motors attached to an aircraft to give extra power for takeoff.

jaun·dice (jòn'dəs, jŏn'-) ***n-*** **1** disease in which the skin and eyeballs turn yellow, caused by the abnormal presence of bile in the blood and body fluids. **2** mental condition, such as jealousy, which distorts the judgment. ***vt-*** **[jaun·diced, jaun·dic·ing]** to affect or prejudice (the mind of) by envy, jealousy, etc.

jaun·diced (jòn'dəst) ***adj-*** **1** affected by jaundice; yellowed: *his* jaundiced *skin.* **2** prejudiced or affected by envy, jealousy, etc.: *a* jaundiced *attitude.*

jaunt (jònt) ***n-*** short pleasure trip. ***vi-*** to make such a trip.

jaun·ty (jòn'tē) ***adj-*** **[jaun·ti·er, jaun·ti·est]** gay and carefree in manner, appearance, etc.; dashing: *his* jaunty *stride; a* jaunty *hat.* ***—adv-*** **jaun'ti·ly.** ***n-*** **jaun'ti·ness.**

Ja·va (jăv'ə) ***n-*** **1** a kind of coffee obtained from Java and other Indonesian islands. **2** a breed of black-and-white domestic fowl. **3** *Slang* any coffee.

Java man ***n-*** species of apelike men of the Pleistocene epoch, known from the fossil remains found in Java; Pithecanthropus.

Jav·a·nese (jăv'ə nēz') ***adj-*** of or pertaining to Java or its people, language or culture.

jave·lin (jă'lən) ***n-*** short, light spear thrown by hand, now cheifly thrown for distance in sports contests.

jaw (jò) ***n-*** **1** one of the two bones that frame the mouth and in which the teeth are set; also, the part of the face in the region of these bones. **2** (often **jaws**) anything suggesting the action or form of these two bones: *the* jaws *of a vise.* ***vi-*** *Slang* to talk idly. ***—adj-*** **jaw'less.**

jaw·bone (jò'bōn') ***n-*** one of the two bones in which the teeth are set; jaw.

jaw·break·er (jò'brā'kər) *Informal* ***n-*** **1** word that is difficult to pronounce. **2** round, very hard candy.

jay (jā) ***n-*** any of several noisy, often brightly colored birds related to the crows, such as the bluejay.

jay·walk (jā′ wôk′) *Informal* ***vi-*** to cross a street without obeying traffic rules and signals. **—*n-* jay′ walk′ er.**

jazz (jăz) ***n-* 1** kind of American popular music that uses odd combinations of rhythm. Jazz musicians like to make up their own treatment of tunes and harmonies as they go along. **2** *Slang* nonsense; foolishness. *as* **modifier:** *a* jazz *musician*; *a* jazz *band.* ***vt-*** to play or sing (music) in a jazzy manner. **—*n-* jazz′ man.**

jazz up *Slang* to make more lively or exciting.

jazz·y (jăz′ ē) ***adj-*** **[jazz·i·er, jazz·i·est] 1** resembling or typical of jazz. **2** *Slang* showy; flashy. **—*adv-* jazz′ i·ly.** ***n-*** **jazz′ i·ness.**

jeal·ous (jĕl′ əs) ***adj-* 1** afraid of losing someone's affection or love: *a* jealous *suitor.* **2** feeling ill will and envy: *She is* jealous *because she didn't win the prize.* **3** anxiously careful and watchful: *He is* jealous *of his good name.* **—*adv-* jeal′ ous·ly.** ***n-*** **jeal′ ous·ness.**

jeal·ous·y (jĕl′ ə sē) ***n-*** [*pl.* **jeal·ous·ies**] **1** the feeling, attitude, etc., of someone who is jealous: *He could not conceal his* jealousy *from his rival.* **2** an instance of jealous feeling: *their petty* jealousies.

jean (jēn) ***n-* 1** closely woven, heavy cotton cloth used for making work clothes, children's play clothes, etc. **2 jeans** trousers, usually dark blue, made from this cloth. ***Hom-*** gene.

jeep (jēp) ***n-*** small, powerful motorcar originally made for military use. It is now used where power and ruggedness are required.

Jeep

jeer (jêr) ***vt-*** to shout or rail mockingly at; taunt; deride: *The crowd* jeered *the losing team.* ***vi-:*** *The crowd* jeered *at the players.* ***n-*** derisive cry or remark; taunt. **—*n-* jeer′ er.** ***adv-*** **jeer′ ing·ly.**

Je·ho·vah (jĭ hō′ və) ***n-*** in the Old Testament, God.

Jehovah's Witnesses ***n-*** (takes plural verb) sect of Christians who are pacifists and who do not acknowledge the authority of the state in matters of conscience.

je·june (jə jo͞on′) ***adj-*** lacking interest or point; dull; empty: *a* jejune *tale*; jejune *ideas.*

je·ju·num (jə jo͞o′ nəm) ***n-*** the portion of the small intestine that extends from the duodenum to the ileum.

jell (jĕl) ***vi-* 1** to turn to jelly. **2** *Informal* to take shape; assume definite form: *His plans haven't* jelled. ***Hom-*** gel.

jel·ly (jĕl′ ē) ***n-*** [*pl.* **jel·lies**] **1** food consisting of fruit juice cooked with sugar and thickened by cooling to a soft, clear, substance that holds its shape when removed from a mold; also, any similar food made from meat juice, gelatin, etc. **2** any of various substances resembling this: *petroleum* jelly. ***vi-*** **[jel·lied, jel·ly·ing]** to thicken into a substance of this kind: *The soup* jellied *as it cooled.* ***vt-*** to cover with or cause to become such a substance: *to* jelly *fruits in a salad*; *to* jelly *soup by cooling it.* **—*adj-* jel′ ly·like′.**

jel·ly·fish (jĕl′ ē fĭsh′) ***n-*** [*pl.* **jel·ly·fish; jel·ly·fishes** (kinds of jellyfish)] any of several boneless sea creatures with an umbrella-shaped, partly transparent body that looks like jelly. Some kinds have slender, stinging threads on the underside.

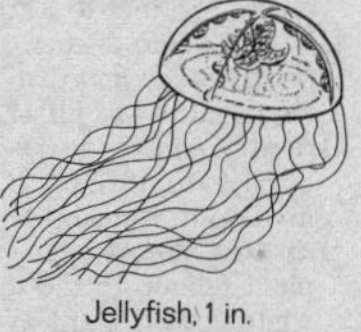
Jellyfish, 1 in. to 12 ft. across

jen·net (jĕn′ ət) ***n-* 1** small Spanish horse. **2** female donkey.

jen·ny (jĕn′ ē) ***n-*** [*pl.* **jen·nies**] **1** spinning jenny. **2** the female of some animals. *as* ***modifier:*** *the* jenny *wren.*

jeop·ard·ize (jĕp′ ər dīz′) ***vt-*** **[jeop·ard·ized, jeop·ard·iz·ing]** to put in danger; risk: *to* jeopardize *one's life.*

jeop·ard·y (jĕp′ ər dē) ***n-* 1** danger; peril: *His safety is in* jeopardy. **2** in law, the risk to which a defendant is exposed when he is on trial for a crime.

jer·bo·a (jər bō′ ə) ***n-*** any of various small, nocturnal animals of Asia and Africa, related to the rats, and having very long hind legs used for leaping.

jer·e·mi·ad (jĕr′ ə mī′ əd) ***n-*** long, mournful complaint or lamentation; sorrowful story.

Jer·e·mi·ah (jĕr′ ə mī′ ə) ***n-* 1** in the Old Testament, a Hebrew prophet during the seventh century B.C. **2** a book of the Bible containing his prophecies. In the CCD Bible, **Jer′ e·mi′ a.**

[1]jerk (jûrk) ***vt-* 1** to give a quick pull, twist, toss, or push to: *to* jerk *a coat off*; *to* jerk *a fish out of water.* **2** *Informal* to prepare (ice cream sodas) at a soda fountain. ***vi-*** to move abruptly, or with sudden starts and stops: *The train* jerked *along.* ***n-* 1** quick, sudden pull, twist, or similar motion. **2** *Slang* stupid or annoying person. [of uncertain origin.] **—*n-* jerk′ er.**

[2]jerk (jûrk) ***vt-*** to convert (meat) into jerky. [from **[2]jerky.**]

jer·kin (jûr′ kĭn) ***n-*** close-fitting, waist-length jacket without sleeves, often made of leather, and worn chiefly by men in former times.

Jerkin

jerk·wa·ter (jûrk′ wô′ tər, -wŏt′ ər) *Informal* ***adj-*** small and unimportant: *a* jerkwater *town.*

[1]jerk·y (jûr′ kē) ***adj-*** **[jerk·i·er, jerk·i·est]** moving abruptly, or with sudden starts and stops; not smooth: *a* jerky *motion.* [from **[1]jerk.**] **—*adv-* jerk′ i·ly.** ***n-*** **jerk′ i·ness.**

[2]jerk·y (jûr′ kē) ***n-*** meat, especially beef, that has been cut into thin strips and dried in the sun. Also **jerked beef.** [from Spanish **charqui,** from Peruvian Indian **ccharqui.**]

Jer·o·bo·am (jĕr′ ə bō′ əm) ***n-* 1** king who founded the kingdom of Israel. **2 jeroboam** large champagne bottle holding about four quarts.

jer·ry-built (jĕr′ ē bĭlt′) ***adj-*** built quickly and poorly.

jer·sey (jûr′ zē) ***n-*** [*pl.* **jer·seys**] **1** close-textured knitted fabric of wool, cotton, nylon, etc. **2** shirt, sweater, or similar garment made of this material. **3 Jersey** one of a breed of small dairy cattle that originated in the island of Jersey and is noted for the richness of its milk.

jes·sa·mine (jĕs′ ə mĭn) ***n-*** jasmine. The yellow jessamine is the State flower of South Carolina.

Jes·se (jĕs′ ē) ***n-*** in the Bible, the father of David.

jest (jĕst) ***n-* 1** funny remark intended to make people laugh. **2** an object of fun or joking. ***vi-*** to speak in a teasing or humorous way; joke.

in jest in a joking way; not seriously.

jest·er (jĕs′ tər) ***n-*** person who makes jokes; especially, in former times, a man who was expected to entertain a king or nobleman by jokes and odd actions.

Jes·u·it (jĕz′ o͞o ĭt, jĕzh′-) ***n-*** member of the Society of Jesus, an order of Roman Catholic priests.

Je·sus (jē′ zəs) ***n-*** Jesus of Nazareth, on whose life, death, and teachings the Christian religion is based; Christ. Also **Jesus Christ.**

[1]jet (jĕt) ***n-* 1** stream of gas, liquid, etc., gushing or squirting from an opening: *A jet of water spurted from the fountain.*

---

fāte, făt, dâre, bärn; bē, bĕt, mêre; bīte, bĭt; nōte, hŏt, môre, dòg; fŭn, fûr; to͞o, bo͝ok; oil; out; tar; thin; then; hw for wh as in *wh*at; zh for s as in u*s*ual; ə for a, e, i, o, u, as in *a*go, lin*e*n, per*i*l, at*o*m, min*u*s

2 spout or nozzle out of which such a stream comes: *a gas* jet. **3** jet engine or jet plane. *as* ***modifier:*** *a* jet *airport.* ***vi-*** [**jet·ted, jet·ting**] **1** to shoot, gush or spout out: *Steam* jetted *from the punctured pipe.* **2** to travel by jet plane. ***vt-*** to squirt or pour (liquid or gas) in a stream. [from Old French **jeter** meaning "to throw or fling out or about; push forward," from Latin **jactāre.**]

[2]jet (jĕt) ***n-*** **1** hard, black mineral similar to coal, which can be highly polished and is used for making ornaments, buttons, etc. **2** (usually **jet-black**) a deep, glossy black. ***adj-:*** *a string of* jet *beads.* [from Old French **jaiet,** from a Greek word **gagatēs,** that comes from **gagai,** a town in Asia near Greece where the mineral was mined.]

jet engine ***n-*** engine in which continuous burning of fuel forces a stream of compressed gas from the rear. The escaping gases push the craft forward in the same way that air escaping from an inflated balloon causes it to dart forward when it is released.

jet lag ***n-*** feeling of disorientation caused by crossing several time zones in a short time.

jet plane ***n-*** airplane driven by a jet engine. Also **jet airplane.**

jet-pro·pelled (jĕt′prə pĕld′) ***adj-*** driven by a jet engine.

jet propulsion ***n-*** the propelling of an aircraft, boat, car, etc., by jet engine.

jet·sam (jĕt′səm) ***n-*** cargo thrown overboard to lighten a ship in danger, especially such cargo that has been washed ashore. See also *flotsam.*

jet stream ***n-*** **1** in meteorology, a high-altitude, high-velocity wind that generally travels from west to east. **2** powerful stream of gas shot from a jet or rocket engine.

jet·ti·son (jĕt′ə sən) ***vt-*** **1** to throw (cargo) overboard to lighten a ship in danger. **2** to throw away; get rid of. ***n-*** the throwing overboard of cargo, especially to lighten a ship in danger.

jet·ty (jĕt′ē) ***n-*** [*pl.* **jet·ties**] **1** structure built out into the water to break the force of the waves. **2** landing pier.

Jew (jo͞o) ***n-*** **1** a descendant of the Hebrew people. **2** anyone whose religion is Judaism. **3** originally, a member of the tribe of Judah.

jew·el (jo͞o′əl) ***n-*** **1** precious stone; gem. **2** valuable ornament set with gems. **3** piece of precious stone or other hard material used as a bearing in the works of a watch. **4** person or thing that is highly valued: *This is the* jewel *of my collection.* **—*adj-* jew′eled:** *a* jeweled *pin.* ***adj-*** **jew′el·like′.**

jew·el·er (jo͞o′lər, jo͞o′ə lər) ***n-*** person who makes, repairs, or deals in jewelry.

jew·el·ry (jo͞o′əl rē, jo͞ol′-) ***n-*** ornaments of silver, gold, etc., set with gems; jewels.

jew·el·weed (jo͞ol′wēd′, jo͞o′əl-) ***n-*** tall plant with dangling orange or yellow flowers, and seed cases that burst open at a touch when they are ripe; touch-me-not.

Jew·ess (jo͞o′əs) ***n-*** Jewish woman or girl (term often considered offensive).

jew·fish (jo͞o′fĭsh′) ***n-*** [*pl.* **jew·fish; jew·fishes** (kinds of jewfish)] one of various large fish related to the sea basses and found in warm seas.

Jew·ish (jo͞o′ĭsh) ***adj-*** of, relating to, or characteristic of the Jews, their religion, or their customs. ***n-*** *Informal* Yiddish.

Jew·ry (jo͞o′rē) ***n-*** **1** the Jewish people. **2** *Archaic* [*pl.* **Jew·ries**] district inhabited by Jews.

jew's-harp or **jews'-harp** (jo͞oz′härp′) ***n-*** small musical instrument which is held between the teeth. It has a thin, flexible metal strip that produces twanging tones when it is struck with the fingers.

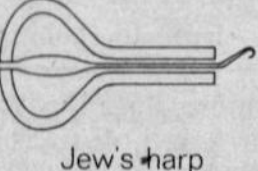
Jew's harp

Jez·e·bel (jĕz′ə bĕl′) ***n-*** in the Bible, the wicked wife of a king of Israel; hence, any bold, vicious woman.

[1]jib (jĭb) ***n-*** small three-cornered sail in front of the foremast. [of uncertain origin.]

cut of (someone's) jib *Informal* a person's outward appearance or manner.

[2]jib (jĭb) ***vi-*** *&* ***vt-*** **[jibbed, jib·bing]** [1]jibe.

[3]jib (jĭb) ***n-*** projecting arm of a crane, derrick, etc. [probably from **gibbet,** from Old French **gibet,** from an earlier Germanic word meaning "forked stick."]

jib boom ***n-*** a spar that serves to lengthen the bowsprit of a vessel, and to which a jib is attached.

Jib

[1]jibe (jīb) ***vi-*** [**jibed, jib·ing**] **1** to cause or permit a fore-and-aft rigged sail and its boom to swing suddenly from one side of a boat to the other when sailing before the wind. **2** to change the course of a boat by thus maneuvering the sail. ***vt-*** to maneuver (a sail or boat) in this manner. [from Dutch **gijben** or **gijpen.**] ***Hom-*** gibe.

[2]jibe (jīb) gibe. [a variation of **gibe,** perhaps from Old French **giber** meaning "to handle roughly."]

[3]jibe (jīb) *Informal* ***vi-*** [**jibed, jib·ing**] to be in agreement; coincide. [of uncertain origin.] ***Hom-*** gibe.

jif·fy (jĭf′ē) *Informal* ***n-*** [*pl.* **jif·fies**] moment; instant.

jig (jĭg) ***n-*** **1** quick, lively dance; also, the music for this dance: *an Irish* jig. **2** any of several kinds of fishhook that are drawn through the water with a jerky or twitching motion. **3** device used to guide, control, or hold a tool or piece of work in place during a mechanical operation. ***vi-*** [**jigged, jig·ging**] **1** to dance a quick, lively dance. **2** to move with a jerky or bobbing motion. **3** to fish by jerking a hook through the water.

[1]jig·ger (jĭg′ər) ***n-*** **1** person who jigs. **2** small glass or cup used to measure liquor. **3** quantity of liquor it holds, usually 1½ oz. **4** *Informal* any thing, device, or part whose name is unknown or cannot be remembered. **5** a jig for fishing. **6** any of various mechanical devices that operate with a jerky motion. [of uncertain origin.]

[2]jig·ger (jĭg′ər) chigger. [a variation of **chigger,** from **chigoe,** from a West Indian word.]

jig·gle (jĭg′əl) ***vi-*** [**jig·gled, jig·gling**] to move with short, quick jerks: *His feet* jiggled *in time to the music.* ***vt-:*** *He* jiggled *his feet.* ***n-*** slight, jerky motion; slight shake.

jig·gly (jĭg′ə lē) ***adj-*** [**jig·gli·er, jig·gli·est**] moving or tending to move with a jerky or bouncing motion.

jig·saw (jĭg′sȯ′) ***n-*** **1** a saw with a thin blade set in a C-shaped frame, used for cutting along curved or jagged lines. **2** saber saw.

jigsaw puzzle ***n-*** a puzzle made of a picture which has been cut into many irregular pieces. One must put the pieces together to form the original picture.

jilt (jĭlt) ***vt-*** to discard or desert (a lover, sweetheart, etc.): *She* jilted *her fiancé.* ***n-*** person who discards a lover, sweetheart, etc. **—*n-* jilt′er.**

jim·my (jĭm′ē) ***n-*** [*pl.* **jim·mies**] short crowbar used by burglars to open doors, windows, etc. ***vt-*** [**jim·mied, jim·my·ing**] to force open with such a crowbar.

jim·son weed (jĭm′sən) ***n-*** tall, coarse, very poisonous plant related to the nightshades, having trumpet-shaped white flowers and leaves with an unpleasant smell.

jin·gle (jĭng′gəl) ***n-*** **1** light tinkling or ringing sound: *the* jingle *of sleigh bells.* **2** pleasing or catchy succession of sounds in a poem, often with little sense. **3** simple poem or song, often using nonsense words, marked by catchy, repeated sounds. "Hickory, dickory, dock" is a jingle.

vi- [**jin·gled, jin·gling**] to make a light tinkling or ringing sound: *The bells* jingled. *vt-*: *He* jingled *the bells.*

jin·gly (jĭng′ glē) *adj-* [**jin·gli·er, jin·gli·est**] having or producing a tinkling, repeated sound.

jin·go (jĭng′ gō) *n-* [*pl.* **jin·goes**] person who favors a warlike policy in foreign affairs.

jin·go·ism (jĭng′ gō ĭz′ əm) *n-* attitude, belief, etc., supporting a warlike policy in foreign affairs. *—n-* **jin′ go·ist.** *adj-* **jin′ go·is′ tic.**

jinn (jĭn) *n-* [*pl.* **jinns** or **jinn**] in Muslim legend, a spirit appearing in both human and animal forms, and having a supernatural influence over mankind for good and evil; genie. Also **jin′ ni** (jĭn′ ē) or **jin′ nee.**

jin·rik·i·sha or **jin·rick·sha** (jĭn rĭk′ shò, -shä) *n-* light two-wheeled vehicle drawn by a man, originally used in Japan. Also **ricksha** or **rickshaw.**

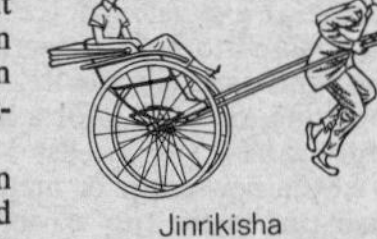
Jinrikisha

jinx (jĭngks) *Slang n-* person or thing that brings bad luck. *vt-* to bring bad luck to.

jit·ney (jĭt′ nē) *Slang n-* **1** a nickel. **2** bus or car that carries passengers for a small fare.

jit·ter·bug (jĭt′ ər bŭg′) *Slang n-* **1** a dance in which couples move rhythmically to swing music, twirling and using improvised acrobatic movements. **2** person who dances this dance. *vi-* [**jit·ter·bugged, jit·ter·bug·ging**] to dance in such a manner.

jit·ters (jĭt′ ərz) *Slang n-* (takes singular verb) extreme nervousness. *—adj-* **jit′ ter·y.**

jiu·jit·su or **jiu·ju·tsu** (jo͞o jĭt′ so͞o) jujitsu.

Ji·va·ro (hē′ vä′ rō) *n-* [*pl.* **Ji·va·ro** or **Ji·va·ros**] one of a group of South American Indians who live in Ecuador and eastern Peru, and are famous for head-hunting.

jive (jīv) *Slang n-* **1** swing music. **2** special vocabulary of jazz musicians or jazz fans. *vi-* [**jived, jiv·ing**] to dance or play swing music. *Hom-* gyve.

job (jŏb) *n-* **1** something a person has to do; duty; responsibility: *It is his* job *to empty the trash.* **2** paid position; employment; work: *He has a* job *as a teacher.* **3** piece of work: *Do a better* job. **4** *Informal* difficult task: *It is quite a* job *to clean the cellar.* *vt-* [**jobbed, job·bing**] **1** to buy up (goods) for resale in smaller quantities. **2** to sublet (work) to different contractors, workmen, etc. *vi-* to do an occasional piece of work for pay.

Job (jōb) *n-* **1** in an Old Testament book, a man who patiently suffered great adversity. **2** the book itself.

job·ber (jŏb′ ər) *n-* **1** person who buys a large amount of goods from manufacturers and sells it in smaller quantities to retail dealers. **2** person who does piecework.

job·hold·er (jŏb′ hōl′ dər) *n-* person with a regular job.

job·less (jŏb′ ləs) *adj-* without a job; unemployed.

job lot *n-* miscellaneous collection of goods, often of inferior quality, bought and sold together.

jock·ey (jŏk′ ē) *n-* man whose profession is riding race horses. *vt-* to move or shift (something) about to gain a good position: *The drivers* jockeyed *their cars.* *vi-* **1** to move or maneuver in this way: *to* jockey *for position.* **2** to ride a horse in a race.

jo·cose (jō kōs′) *adj-* humorous; playful; joking: *a* jocose *manner.* *—adv-* **jo·cose′ ly.** *n-* **jo·cose′ ness** or **jo·cos′ i·ty** (jō kŏs′ ə tē).

joc·u·lar (jŏk′ yə lər) *adj-* **1** given to joking: *a* jocular *person.* **2** humorous; funny; jesting: *a* jocular *reply.* *—n-* **joc′ u·lar′ i·ty** (-yə lăr′ ə tē). *adv-* **joc′ u·lar·ly.**

joc·und (jŏk′ ənd) *adj-* merry; pleasant; cheerful. *—n-* **jo·cun′ di·ty** (jō kŭn′ də tē). *adv-* **joc′ und·ly.**

jodh·purs (jŏd′ pərz) *n- pl.* riding breeches that fit loosely above the knee and closely between the knee and ankle.

Jo·el (jō′ əl) *n-* **1** in the Bible, a Hebrew prophet. **2** a book of the Old Testament attributed to him.

[1]**jog** (jŏg) *vt-* [**jogged, jog·ging**] **1** to push or shake slightly; jar; nudge: *to* jog *someone's elbow.* **2** to stir up; revive: *to* jog *someone's memory.* *vi-* to move at a slow, jolting pace or trot; *The old horse* jogged *along.* *n-* **1** slight shake; nudge. **2** (also **jog trot**) slow, steady gait that is faster than a walk. [of uncertain origin.] *—n-* **jog′ ger.**

[2]**jog** (jŏg) *n-* sharp, sudden bend, turn, or change of direction: *a* jog *in the road*; *a* jog *in a wall.* *vi-* [**jogged, jog·ging**] to make or have such a bend: *The road* jogs *to the left.* [a variation of **jag,** from Middle English **jagge,** from Old English **sceaga,** meaning "notch; uneven tear."]

jog·gle (jŏg′ əl) *vt-* [**jog·gled, jog·gling**] to give (something) a slight shake; nudge; jolt. *n-* slight shake; jolt.

John (jŏn) *n-* one of the twelve apostles, reputed to be the author of the fourth Gospel. Also **St. John the Divine.**

John Bull *n-* imaginary man thought to personify the English people; hence, a typical Englishman.

John Doe *n-* in legal papers, a made-up name for an unknown person; also, name for any unspecified person.

John Han·cock (jŏn hăn′ kŏk′) *Informal n-* a person's signature. [from John Hancock, whose signature on the Declaration of Independence is bold and legible.]

John Henry *n-* **1** in American Negro folklore, a railroad worker of unusually great strength. **2** *Informal* a person's signature; John Hancock.

john·ny·cake (jŏn′ ē kāk′) *n-* bread made of cornmeal mixed with milk or water, eggs, etc.

John·ny-jump-up (jŏn′ ē jŭmp′ ŭp′) *n-* garden plant related to the violets, and resembling a small pansy.

John·ny-on-the-spot (jŏn′ ē ŏn′ thə spŏt′) *n-* *Informal* person who is always on hand at the right time.

John the Baptist *n-* the forerunner and baptizer of Jesus. John was beheaded by Herod.

join (join) *vt-* **1** to put together; fasten; connect: *to* join *hands*; *to* join *a hose to a faucet.* **2** to come together with; meet and unite with: *The brook* joins *the river.* **3** to become a member of; become associated with: *to* join *a club.* **4** to make into one; unite: *to* join *a couple in marriage.* **5** to come into the company of: *He* joined *us for a swim.* *vi-* **1** to become associated or united: *The two roads* join *at this point.* **2** to take part with others; participate: *to* join *in a conversation.* *n-* joint.

join·er (join′ ər) *n-* **1** person or thing that joins. **2** skilled carpenter who finishes the inside woodwork for houses. **3** jointer. **4** *Informal* person who joins many clubs, organizations, etc.

join·er·y (joi′ nə rē) *n-* **1** skill or trade of a joiner; skilled work in wood. **2** things made by a joiner.

joint (joint) *n-* **1** part of an animal where two bones are joined, usually to allow motion. **2** in a plant, part of a stem from which branches and leaves grow. **3** connecting part between two things: *a pipe* joint. **4** place where two things are connected: *a* joint *in the woodwork.* **5** large piece of meat for a roast. **6** *Slang* cheap or disreputable place of entertainment; also, any house, building, etc. *adj-* **1** united; combined: *a* joint *declaration of policy.* **2** used, shared, or held by two or more persons: *a* joint *bank account.* *vt-* **1** to fit to-

Elbow joint

fāte, făt, dâre, bärn; bē, bĕt, mêre; bīte, bĭt; nōte, hŏt, môre, dȯg; fŭn, fûr; to͞o, bo͝ok; oil; out; tar; thin; then; hw for wh as in *wh*at; zh for s as in u*s*ual; ə for a, e, i, o, u, as in *a*go, lin*e*n, per*i*l, at*o*m, min*u*s

gether by means of a connecting part, hinge, etc. **2** to cut at the place where two bones are joined.

out of joint 1 out of place at the joint; dislocated. **2** in a state of disorder: *The times are* out of joint.

Joint Chiefs of Staff ***n-*** principal military advisory board of the United States, composed of a chairman, the Chiefs of Staff of the Army and Air Force, the Chief of Naval Operations, and, when necessary, the Commandant of the Marine Corps.

joint·er (join′ tər) ***n-* 1** person who joints. **2** a plane or a power-driven tool used to smooth and straighten the parts of wood that will make a joint. Also **joiner.**

joint·ly (joint′ lē) ***adv-*** together; in combination.

joint resolution ***n-*** resolution passed by both houses of Congress, which has the force of law when signed by the President.

joist (joist) ***n-*** a beam supporting a floor or ceiling.

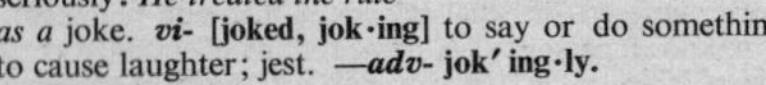

joke (jōk) ***n-* 1** something funny said or done to cause laughter. **2** object of laughter; something not taken seriously: *He treated the rule as a* joke. ***vi-*** **[joked, jok·ing]** to say or do something to cause laughter; jest. **—*adv-* jok′ ing·ly.**

no joke a serious matter.

jok·er (jō′ kər) ***n-* 1** person who jokes. **2** extra playing card in a deck of cards, used in some games as a card of the highest value. **3** clause which seems unimportant but actually changes the meaning of a document.

jol·li·fi·ca·tion (jŏl′ ə fə kā′ shən) *Informal* ***n-*** festivity; rejoicing; merrymaking.

jol·li·ty (jŏl′ ə tē) ***n-*** [*pl.* **jol·li·ties**] merriment; gaiety.

jol·ly (jŏl′ ē) ***adj-*** **[jol·li·er, jol·li·est]** merry; gay; full of fun or laughter. ***vt-*** **[jol·lied, jol·ly·ing]** *Informal* to tease, humor, or flatter with good-humored joking.

Jolly Roger ***n-*** the pirate flag, usually having a white skull and crossbones on a black field; the black flag.

jolt (jōlt) ***vt-*** to shake with jerky movements; jar: *The rough ride* jolted *us.* ***vi-*** to move along in a jerky manner: *The carriage* jolted *down the hill.* ***n-*** a sudden jerk, bump, shake, or shock: *The train stopped with a* jolt.

Jo·nah (jō′ nə) ***n-* 1** Hebrew prophet who was thrown overboard, swallowed by a great fish, and cast up alive after three days. **2** book of the Old Testament telling this story. In the CCD Bible, **Jo′ na. 3** anyone bringing bad luck.

Jon·a·than (jŏn′ ə thən) ***n-*** in the Bible, a son of Saul and close friend of David.

jon·quil (jŏng′ kwĭl, jŏn′ kwĭl) ***n-*** plant related to the narcissus and daffodil, with fragrant, trumpet-shaped, yellow or white flowers; also, the flower itself.

Jo·seph (jō′ zəf, -səf) ***n-* 1** in the Bible, a son of Jacob sold into slavery in Egypt by his brothers. **2** (also **Saint Joseph**) foster father of Jesus and husband of Mary. **3 Joseph of Arimathea** a wealthy disciple of Jesus who buried Him in his own tomb.

josh (jŏsh) *Informal* ***vt-*** to make fun of in a good-humored way; tease playfully. ***vi-*** to joke playfully.

Josh·u·a (jŏsh′ ə wə) ***n-*** in the Bible, the successor of Moses and leader of the Israelites. **2** book of the Old Testament. In the CCD Bible, **Jo′ su·e** (jŏs′ o͞o ē).

Joshua tree ***n-*** a yucca of southwestern United States, with short leaves and clusters of greenish-white flowers.

Jo·si·ah (jō sī′ ə) ***n-*** in the Bible, a king of Judah around the seventh century B.C. In the CCD Bible, **Jo·si′ a.**

joss stick (jŏs) ***n-*** thin stick of incense.

jos·tle (jŏs′ əl) ***vt-*** **[jos·tled, jos·tling]** to push roughly; elbow. ***n-*** a shove; push. **—*n-* jos′ tler.**

jot (jŏt) ***vt-*** **[jot·ted, jot·ting]** to write down briefly and quickly: *to* jot *down an address.* ***n-*** tiny bit; iota.

joule (jo͞ol) ***n-*** unit of work in the mks system defined as the work done when a force of one newton acts through a distance of one meter. A joule is equal to 10^7 ergs or 0.7375 foot-pounds.

jounce (jouns) ***vt-*** **[jounced, jounc·ing]** to shake up and down; jolt; bounce: *The old car* jounced *the passengers.* ***vi-*:** *The car* jounced. ***n-*** sudden jerk; jolt.

jour·nal (jûr′ nəl) ***n-* 1** daily record of news or events; diary. **2** daily record of acts of a legislature or transactions of a business. **3** newspaper or periodical appearing at regular intervals. **4** in machines, the part of a shaft or axle that turns in a bearing.

jour·nal·ese (jûr′ nə lēz′) ***n-*** careless style of writing supposed to be characteristic of newspapers.

jour·nal·ism (jûr′ nə lĭz′ əm) ***n-*** the work of publishing, editing, or writing for a newspaper or magazine.

jour·nal·ist (jûr′ nə lĭst′) ***n-*** person who writes for or edits a newspaper or magazine.

jour·nal·is·tic (jûr′ nə lĭs′ tĭk) ***adj-*** of or having to do with journalism or journalists. **—*adv-* jour′ nal·is′ ti·cal·ly:** *He writes* journalistically.

jour·ney (jûr′ nē) ***n-* 1** trip, especially a long one, or one taking considerable time. **2** distance traveled in a certain time: *a day's* journey. ***vi-*** to make a trip; travel.

jour·ney·man (jûr′ nē mən) ***n-*** [*pl.* **jour·ney·men**] person who has finished his apprenticeship in a trade or skill and works for another.

joust (joust, *also* jŭst) ***n-*** a combat, often in sport, between two mounted knights with lances. ***vi-*** to take part in such a contest. **—*n-* joust′ er.**

Jove (jōv) ***n-*** Jupiter. **—*adj-* Jo′ vi·an:** *a* Jovian *brow.*

jo·vi·al (jō′ vē əl) ***adj-*** full of laughter; jolly. **—*n-* jo′ vi·al′ i·ty** (jō′ vē ăl′ ə tē). ***adv-*** **jo′ vi·al·ly.**

jowl (joul) ***n-* 1** lower jaw. **2** cheek. **3** (usually **jowls**) slack, fleshy parts hanging under the lower jaw.

joy (joi) ***n-* 1** a feeling of great happiness, gladness, or pleasure. **2** that which causes this feeling: *Her thoughtfulness is a* joy *to her mother.*

joy·ful (joi′ fəl) ***adj-*** full of gladness; showing or causing joy; happy; joyous. **—*adv-* joy′ ful·ly.** ***n-*** **joy′ ful·ness.**

joy·less (joi′ ləs) ***adj-*** without joy; not causing joy; cheerless; dismal; dull: *a* joyless *home*; *a* joyless *future.* **—*adv-* joy′ less·ly.** ***n-*** **joy′ less·ness.**

joy·ous (joi′ əs) ***adj-*** happy; glad; joyful: *a* joyous *occasion.* **—*adv-* joy′ ous·ly.** ***n-*** **joy′ ous·ness.**

joy·ride (joi′ rīd′) ***n-*** automobile ride for pleasure, especially a reckless ride. **—*n-* joy′ rid′ er.**

J.P. justice of the peace.

Jr. or **jr.** junior.

ju·bi·lant (jo͞o′ bə lənt) ***adj-*** showing great joy; triumphantly joyful; exultant: *The crowd was* jubilant. **—*n-* ju′ bi·lance:** *the* jubilance *of the crowd.* ***adv-*** **ju′ bi·lant·ly.**

ju·bi·la·tion (jo͞o′ bə lā′ shən) ***n-*** triumphant rejoicing.

ju·bi·lee (jo͞o′ bə lē′) ***n-* 1** anniversary, especially the 50th or 25th. **2** any time of great and general rejoicing.

Ju·dah (jo͞o′ də) ***n-* 1** in the Old Testament, a son of Jacob. **2** the tribe descended from him. **3** the ancient Hebrew kingdom which included the tribe of Benjamin as well as Judah. In the CCD Bible, **Ju·da.**

Ju·da·ic (jo͞o dā′ ĭk) ***adj-*** of or relating to the Jews or Judaism.

Ju·da·ism (jo͞o′ dē ĭz′ əm, jo͞o′ dĭz′ əm) ***n-* 1** one of the world's great religions; the religion of the Jews. Judaism was among the first religions that taught a belief in one God, and was the ancestor of Christianity. **2** the traditions of thought, morality, and culture associated with this religion.

Ju·das (jo͞o′ dəs) ***n-*** **1** the disciple who betrayed Jesus. **2** any betrayer. Also **Judas Is·car′ i·ot** (ĭs kăr′ ē ət).

Judas tree ***n-*** tree bearing stemless, rose-pink flowers early in the spring, before the leaves appear.

Jude (jo͞od) ***n-*** disciple of Jesus who wrote the New Testament book called the Epistle of Jude. Also **St. Jude.**

Ju·de·o-Chris·tian (jo͞o dā′ ō krĭs′ chən) ***adj-*** of or relating to the ethical and cultural traditions common to Judaism and Christianity.

judge (jŭj) ***n-*** **1** official who presides in a court of law and hears cases, passes sentences, etc. **2** person who decides the winner in a contest: *a* judge *in a dog show.* **3** person who has enough experience or knowledge to decide on the quality, value, or extent of something: *a* judge *of cattle*; *a good* judge *of distance.* ***vt-*** **[judged, judg·ing]** (considered intransitive when the direct object is implied but not expressed) **1** to hear cases, pass sentences, etc., in a court of law. **2** to decide (a contest, argument, dispute, etc.). **3** to think; consider: *I* judged *this to be true.* **4** to form an opinion about: *to* judge *the merits of a play.* **5** to criticize and blame. **—*n-* judg′ er.**

Judg·es (jŭj′ əz) ***n-*** (takes singular verb) the seventh book of the Old Testament.

judge·ship (jŭj′ shĭp′) ***n-*** position, duties, or term of office of a judge.

judg·ment or **judge·ment** (jŭj′ mənt) ***n-*** **1** a judging; making a decision after careful consideration: *the* judgment *of a criminal.* **2** decision made after careful consideration: *The* judgment *of the court was in his favor.* **3** opinion; estimation: *In his* judgment *this car is the best buy.* **4** good sense: *a man of excellent* judgment. **5** misfortune considered as a punishment from God.

Judgment Day ***n-*** the day of the Last Judgment.

ju·di·ca·to·ry (jo͞o′ dĭ kə tôr′ ē) ***adj-*** of or relating to legal justice and courts of justice.

ju·di·ca·ture (jo͞o′ dĭ kə chər) ***n-*** system of courts of justice in a country; judiciary.

ju·di·cial (jo͞o dĭsh′ əl) ***adj-*** **1** having to do with a judge or court of law: *the* judicial *proceedings.* **2** ordered, enforced, or allowed by a judge or court of law: *a* judicial *decision.* **3** suited for judging or tending to judge: *a* judicial *mind.* **—*adv-* ju·di′ cial·ly.**

ju·di·ci·ar·y (jo͞o dĭsh′ ē ĕr ē, -dĭsh′ ə rē) ***n-*** [*pl.* **ju·di·ci·ar·ies**] **1** system of courts of justice in a country. **2** judges of these courts. **3** branch of government that administers justice. ***adj-*** having to do with judges, courts of law, or the procedures of a court; judicial.

ju·di·cious (jo͞o dĭsh′ əs) ***adj-*** showing good judgment; sensible. **—*adv-* ju·di′ cious·ly. *n-* ju·di′ cious·ness.**

Ju·dith (jo͞o′ dĭth) ***n-*** in the Old Testament Apocrypha, a Jewish woman who saved her people by slaying the Assyrian general, Holofernes.

ju·do (jo͞o′ dō′) ***n-*** sport and form of physical training based on jujitsu.

jug (jŭg) ***n-*** **1** glass or earthenware container with a small, short neck and a handle. **2** such a container and its contents: *a* jug *of cider.* **3** (also **jug′ ful′**) amount such a container holds when full.

Jug

jug·ger·naut (jŭg′ ər nôt′) ***n-*** **1** any slow, irresisitible force or object that destroys everything in its path. **2** anything demanding blind devotion and self-sacrifice.

jug·gle (jŭg′ əl) ***vt-*** **[jug·gled, jug·gling]** **1** to perform tricks with; especially, to toss (objects) in the air and catch them in rapid succession: *The clown* juggled *three oranges and a lemon.* **2** to change (facts or figures) so as to deceive: *The manager* juggled *the figures to show a profit.* ***vi-***: *The clown* juggles *with oranges. The manager* juggles *with figures.* ***n-*** **1** a tossing and catching of objects in the air in rapid succession. **2** deception; trickery.

jug·gler (jŭg′ lər) ***n-*** **1** person who performs the trick of keeping objects moving rapidly in the air. **2** trickster; deceiver. **—*n-* jug′ gler·y:** *His* jugglery *got him into trouble.*

jug·u·lar (jŭg′ yə lər) ***adj-*** having to do with the neck or throat, especially with two large veins **(the jugular veins)** that return blood from the head and run along either side of the neck.

juice (jo͞os) ***n-*** **1** liquid part of vegetables, fruits, meats, etc.: *tomato* juice. **2** (usually **juices**) natural fluids of the body: *gastric* juices. **3** *Slang* electricity. **4** *Slang* fuel.

juic·y (jo͞o′ sē) ***adj-*** **[juic·i·er, juic·i·est]** **1** full of juice: *a* juicy *orange.* **2** *Informal* full of interest; lively; colorful: *a* juicy *story.* **—*adv-* juic′ i·ly. *n-* juic′ i·ness.**

ju·jit·su (jo͞o jĭt′ so͞o) ***n-*** Japanese style of wrestling and self-defense that uses the strength and weight of an opponent in order to defeat him. Also **jiujitsu, jiujutsu.**

juke box (jo͝ok) *Informal* ***n-*** large automatic phonograph operated by dropping a coin in a slot and pushing a button to make the record selection.

ju·lep (jo͞o′ ləp) ***n-*** drink made of bourbon, sugar, fresh mint, and crushed ice.

Ju·li·an calendar (jo͞o′ lē ən) ***n-*** calendar introduced by Julius Caesar in 46 B.C., giving most years 365 days but every fourth year, 366 days. It has been superseded by the Gregorian calendar.

ju·li·enne (jo͞o′ lē ĕn′) ***n-*** clear soup containing vegetables cut into thin strips. ***adj-*** cut into thin strips: *served with* julienne *potatoes.*

Ju·li·et (jo͞o′ lē ĕt′) ***n-*** the young heroine of Shakespeare's "Romeo and Juliet."

Ju·ly (jo͞o lī′, jə-) ***n-*** the seventh month of the year, having 31 days.

jum·ble (jŭm′ bəl) ***vt-*** **[jum·bled, jum·bling]** to mix in a confused way; put together without order: *to* jumble *things together.* ***n-*** confused mass; disorder.

jum·bo (jŭm′ bō) *Informal* ***adj-*** large; huge: *a* jumbo *ice-cream cone.* ***n-*** [*pl.* **jum·bos**] large person, animal, or thing. [from **Jumbo,** a very large circus elephant.]

jump (jŭmp) ***n-*** **1** a leap, spring, or bound: *a* jump *off a diving board.* **2** distance covered by a leap: *a* jump *of six feet.* **3** something to be leaped or hurdled: *The third* jump *was a low hedge.* **4** in sports, a contest featuring a leap: *the high* jump. **5** sudden start or jerk: *a startled* jump. **6** sudden rise: *a* jump *in temperature.* ***vi-*** **1** to spring from the ground; leap; bound: *to* jump *over a puddle.* **2** to give a sudden start: *to* jump *in fright.* **3** to rise suddenly: *Prices* jumped. **4** to pass or change abruptly (from one thing to another): *to* jump *from one subject to another.* **5** to spring down from or out of a window, plane, etc.: *to* jump *from a plane.* ***vt-*** **1** to cause to leap, spring, or bound: *to* jump *a horse over a hurdle.* **2** to leap over; pass over; skip: *to* jump *a brook*; *to* jump *ten pages.* **3** *Informal* to leap upon: *to* jump *a train.* **4** *Informal* to leave or quit suddenly: *to* jump *town.*

get the jump on *Slang* to get an advantage over.

jump a claim to seize mining rights or a piece of land claimed by another.

jump at to accept eagerly and quickly.

jump off to begin; go into action.

jump the gun *Slang* to begin a race before the signal.

jump the track to leave the rails suddenly.

---

fāte, făt, dâre, bärn; bē, bĕt, mêre; bīte, bĭt; nōte, hŏt, môre, dȯg; fŭn, fûr; to͞o, bo͝ok; oil; out; t*a*r; thin; then; hw for wh as in *wh*at; zh for s as in u*s*ual; ə for a, e, i, o, u, as in *a*go, lin*e*n, per*i*l, at*o*m, min*u*s

jump area *Military* ***n-*** area assigned for the landing of paratroops, often behind enemy lines.

¹**jump·er** (jŭm′ pər) ***n-*** **1** person, animal, or thing that jumps. **2** piece of wire or other conductor used to make a temporary electrical connection, to bypass something in a circuit, etc. [from **jump.**]

²**jump·er** (jŭmp′ ər) ***n-*** **1** sleeveless dress, usually worn over a blouse. **2 jumpers** rompers. [from an earlier, dialectal **jump,** "short coat," from French **jup(p)e,** ultimately from Arabic **jubbah,** "loose garment."]

jumping bean ***n-*** seed of any of several related Mexican plants containing a larva whose movements cause the seed to move about jerkily.

jumping jack ***n-*** toy consisting of a little jointed figure of a man that can be made to jump by pulling a string.

jump-off (jŭmp′ ŏf′, -ōf′) ***n-*** beginning of action, especially in a planned campaign or attack.

jump seat ***n-*** folding seat between the front and back seats of an automobile, usually a limousine or taxi.

jump shot ***n-*** in basketball, a shot made by a player at the highest point of a jump.

jump·y (jŭm′ pē) ***adj-*** **[jump·i·er, jump·i·est] 1** moving in short, quick jumps. **2** nervous; easily made nervous.

jun·co (jŭng′ kō) ***n-*** [*pl.* **jun·cos** or **jun·coes**] any of various small North American birds that are related to the finches, are gray above and white underneath, and have white outer tail feathers; snowbird.

junc·tion (jŭngk′ shən) ***n-*** **1** a joining; a being joined: *the* junction *of two rivers.* **2** place where two or more things meet or cross: *an important railroad* junction.

junc·ture (jŭngk′ chər) ***n-*** **1** a joining or being joined; junction. **2** point or line at which things join; joint.
at this juncture at this point; at this time.

June (jo͞on) ***n-*** the sixth month of the year, having 30 days.

June bug ***n-*** reddish-brown beetle that begins to fly about the beginning of June.

jun·gle (jŭng′ gəl) ***n-*** **1** wild land covered with a thick growth of tropical plants, trees, and vines. **2** any place of fierce struggle for existence: *in the* jungle *of the slums.* ***as modifier****: a* jungle *animal.*

jungle fowl ***n-*** any of several wild birds of Asia supposed to be the ancestor of the domestic chicken.

jungle gym ***n-*** four-sided structure of horizontal and vertical bars upon which children can climb and play.

jun·ior (jo͞on′ yər) ***n-*** **1** person who is younger or of lower standing than another: *He is my* junior *by six years.* **2** in high schools and colleges, student of the next to last year: *he is a* junior *in college.* ***adj-*** **1** of lower standing or position: *a* junior *partner.* **2** of or having to do with the third year of a four-year course in high school or college: *the* junior *class.* **3 Junior** the younger (used by a son named for his father): *James Stone,* Junior.

junior college ***n-*** school offering only the first two years of a regular four-year college course, and usually certain two-year training courses.

junior high school ***n-*** school between the elementary school and the senior high school, usually including the 7th, 8th, and 9th grades.

ju·ni·per (jo͞o′ nə pər) ***n-*** any of several evergreen trees or shrubs related to the pines, having flat, branched leaves and purple berries.

¹**junk** (jŭngk) ***n-*** **1** old or discarded metal, paper, rags, etc. **2** *Informal* anything useless; trash. **3** *Slang* narcotic drug, especially heroin. ***vt-*** to discard as worthless or useless: *We finally* junked *our old car.* [from Old French **jonc** meaning "a plant with a hollow stem; a string; cord," from Latin **juncus** meaning "a reed." **Junk** used to mean "cord," then "old or discarded cord," and finally anything old or ready to be thrown away.]

²**junk** (jŭngk) ***n-*** kind of Chinese sailing vessel with a flat bottom, high stern, and lugsails. [from Portuguese **junco,** originally from Malay **jong.**]

Chinese junk

jun·ket (jŭng′ kət) ***n-*** **1** food made of curdled milk that has been sweetened and flavored. **2** feast or picnic. **3** pleasure trip or excursion, especially one made by a government official or committee at public expense and announced as a necessary business trip. ***vi-****: The senator* junketed *to Europe last summer.* **—*n-* jun′ ket·er.**

junk·ie (jŭng′ kē) *Slang* ***n-*** **1** junkman. **2** narcotic addict, especially a heroin addict. Also **junk′ y.**

junk·man (jŭngk′ măn′) ***n-*** [*pl.* **junk·men**] person who earns a living by buying and selling junk.

Ju·no (jo͞o′ nō′) ***n-*** in Roman mythology, the goddess of marriage, wife of Jupiter, and queen of the gods, identified with the Greek Hera.

Ju·no·esque (jo͞o′ nō ĕsk′) ***adj-*** of or having the stately beauty of Juno.

jun·ta (ho͝on′ tə, jŭn′ tə) ***n-*** **1** administrative or legislative council, especially in Spain or Latin America. **2** small group of persons in control of a government, especially after a revolution: *a country ruled by a military* junta. **3** (also **jun′ to**) conspiratorial group; cabal.

Ju·pi·ter (jo͞o′ pə tər) ***n-*** **1** in Roman mythology, the ruler of gods and men, identified with the Greek Zeus; Jove. **2** the largest planet in the solar system, fifth in order of distance from the sun.

Ju·ras·sic (jə răs′ ĭk) ***n-*** the second of the three periods of the Mesozoic era, marked by the existence of dinosaurs and many other reptiles. ***adj-****: a* Jurassic *reptile.*

ju·rid·i·cal (jo͝or ĭd′ ĭ kəl) ***adj-*** of or related to law or legal proceedings; legal. **—*adv-* ju·rid′ i·cal·ly.**

ju·ris·dic·tion (jo͝or′ əs dĭk′ shən) ***n-*** **1** lawful right to govern, make laws, or, especially, to administer justice: *the* jurisdiction *of Congress*; *the* jurisdiction *of Michigan*; *the* jurisdiction *of the county courts.* **2** the limits within which such a right may be exercised; range of authority or control: *This is not in my* jurisdiction. **3** right to represent certain workers in a labor union.

ju·ris·pru·dence (jo͝or′ əs pro͞o′ dəns) ***n-*** **1** science or philosophy of law. **2** any system or branch of law: *medical* jurisprudence; *English* jurisprudence.

ju·rist (jo͝or′ ĭst) ***n-*** **1** expert in jurisprudence. **2** any attorney or judge.

ju·ror (jo͝or′ ər) ***n-*** member of a jury.

ju·ry (jo͝or′ ē) ***n-*** [*pl.* **ju·ries**] **1** group of citizens sworn under oath to listen to testimony in a legal case and reach a verdict according to such testimony. A **grand jury** is a group of 12 to 23 persons selected to examine the evidence against supposed offenders and decide whether or not to indict or send them for trial. A **petty,** or **trial jury,** which is composed of 12 persons, hears the evidence in an actual trial and, if possible, gives a verdict. **2** any group of persons selected to judge a contest.

ju·ry·man (jo͝or′ ē mən) ***n-*** [*pl.* **ju·ry·men**] male juror. **—*n-* *fem.* ju′ ry·wom′ an** [*pl.* **ju·ry·wom·en**].

just (jŭst) ***adj-*** **1** not showing favor; fair; honest: *The judge handed down a* just *decision.* **2** having a sound or reasonable basis: *Ellen had a* just *dislike for the people who had mistreated her.* **3** rightly given; deserved; earned: *He received a* just *reward for his work.* ***adv-*** **1** exactly: *That is* just *what I wanted.* **2** a moment ago; very recently: *We* just *finished dinner.* **3** barely: *The* *ball* just *missed us.* **4** right now; at this moment: *He is* just *coming.* **5** only: *Give me* just *one.* **6** *Informal* simply; quite: *That's* just *wonderful.* ***—adv-*** **just′ ly.** ***n-*** **just′ness.**

just now a moment ago; very recently: *He finished* just now. **just the same** nonetheless; however.

jus·tice (jŭs′ təs) ***n-*** **1** fairness; right action: *We should use* justice *even in dealing with our enemies.* **2** legal administration: *a court of* justice. **3** judge; judicial officer.

bring (someone) to justice to cause (someone) to be tried or otherwise legally punished for wrongdoing. **do justice 1** to show or represent truly or well: *That photo does not* do *her* justice. *I can't* do justice *to the story.* **2** to administer legal justice.

justice of the peace ***n-*** local magistrate having limited jurisdiction, such as trying minor offenses, administering oaths, performing marriages, etc.

jus·ti·fi·a·ble (jŭs′ tə fī′ ə bəl) ***adj-*** such as can be justified or defended; defensible: *Is it* justifiable *for a starving man to steal bread?* ***—n-*** **jus′ ti·fi′ a·bil′ i·ty:** *the* justifiability *of his complaint.* ***adv-*** **jus′ ti·fi′ a·bly.**

jus·ti·fi·ca·tion (jŭs′ tə fə kā′ shən) ***n-*** **1** a justifying or being justified. **2** something that justifies: *Poverty is no* justification *for stealing.*

jus·ti·fy (jŭs′ tə fī′) ***vt-*** **[jus·ti·fied, jus·ti·fy·ing] 1** to show to be right or just; defend with good reason: *How do you* justify *your absence?* **2** to declare free from blame: *The verdict* justified *him in the eyes of the law.* **3** in printing, to give (lines) the proper length by spacing; also, to make the right-hand margin (of a page) straight and even.

jut (jŭt) ***vi-*** **[jut·ted, jut·ting]** to stick (out); thrust itself (out); project: *The peninsula* juts *out into the bay.*

jute (jo͞ot) ***n-*** **1** fiber of a tropical plant, used to make burlap and rope. **2** the plant itself.

Jute (jo͞ot) ***n-*** member of a Germanic tribe living in Jutland, some of whom, with the Angles and Saxons, invaded and settled in Britain during the fifth century.

ju·ve·nile (jo͞o′ və nĭl, -nīl′) ***adj-*** **1** young; youthful; childish; immature: *Pouting is a* juvenile *manner of getting your own way.* **2** of or for young people: *a* juvenile *book.* ***n-*** **1** young person. **2** book for young people. **3** actor who plays youthful parts.

juvenile court ***n-*** law court having jurisdiction in cases involving children under a certain age, usually 18.

juvenile delinquency ***n-*** criminal offenses or antisocial acts committed by children under a certain age, usually 18. ***—n-*** **juvenile delinquent.**

jux·ta·pose (jŭks′ tə pōz′) ***vt-*** **[jux·ta·posed, jux·ta·pos·ing]** to place close together or side by side: *to* juxtapose *light and dark paper.*

jux·ta·po·si·tion (jŭks′ tə pə zĭsh′ ən) ***n-*** a juxtaposing or a being juxtaposed: *the* juxtaposition *of two colors.*

K

K, k (kā) ***n-*** [*pl.* **K's, k's**] the eleventh letter of the English alphabet.

K symbol for potassium.

K. 1 kilogram. **2** king. **3** knight.

Kaa·ba (kä′ bə) ***n-*** sacred black stone in the courtyard of the great mosque at Mecca, thought to have been given to Abraham by the archangel Gabriel.

ka·bob (kə bŏb′) ***n-*** **1** shish kebab. **2** in India, roast meat.

ka·chi·na (kə chē′ nə) ***n-*** one of various mythical ancestral spirits worshipped by the Hopi and other Pueblo Indians; also, a carved and painted wooden doll representing one of these spirits.

Kad·dish (kä′ dĭsh) ***n-*** in Judaism, a prayer recited by mourners.

Kaf·fir (kăf′ ər) ***n-*** a Negro (used as a term of contempt by southern African white people). Also **Kaf′ ir.**

Kai·ser (kī′ zər) ***n-*** title applied to the emperors of the Holy Roman Empire and to the former emperors of Austria-Hungary and Germany.

kale (kāl) ***n-*** **1** vegetable similar to cabbage, having loose, curly leaves instead of a head. **2** leaves of this plant, eaten as a cooked vegetable or as a salad.

ka·lei·do·scope (kə lī′ də skōp′) ***n-*** tube-shaped optical toy lined with mirrors and containing loose bits of colored glass, which are reflected as changing geometrical patterns when the tube is rotated.

ka·lei·do·scop·ic (kə lī′ də skŏp′ ĭk) ***adj-*** like a kaleidoscope; continually and rapidly changing: *the* kaleidoscopic *events of our time.* ***—adv-*** **ka·lei′ do·scop′ i·cal·ly.**

kal·so·mine (kăl′ sə mīn′) calcimine.

ka·mi·ka·ze (kăm′ ə kăz′ ē) ***n-*** in World World II, a Japanese suicide attack in which planes loaded with high explosives dive into a target; also, the plane or pilot in such a suicide attack. *as* ***modifier:*** *a* kamikaze *attack*; kamikaze *pilot.*

kan·ga·roo (kăng′ gə ro͞o′) ***n-*** [*pl.* **kan·ga·roos**] any of various plant-eating mammals of Australia having short forelegs, powerful hind legs with which it leaps, and a long, strong tail. The female Kangaroo has a pouch for carrying her young. Adults of some types reach a height of over six feet. ***—adj-*** **kan′ ga·roo′ like′.**

kangaroo rat ***n-*** any of various gnawing animals of Mexico and southwestern United States, having strong, well-developed hind legs, and a long tail.

Kans. Kansas.

ka·o·lin or **ka·o·line** (kā′ ə lĭn) ***n-*** a fine, usually white clay that is a pure natural form of aluminum sulfate. It is used to make porcelain.

ka·pok (kā′ pŏk′) ***n-*** mass of silky fibers in the seed pods of a tropical tree called the **kapok tree,** used for stuffing cushions, mattresses, life preservers, etc.

ka·put (kə po͝ot′, kă-) *Informal* ***adj-*** defeated or destroyed.

ka·ra·kul (kăr′ ə kəl) ***n-*** **1** valuable pelt of the newborn lambs of the astrakhan, or curly-haired sheep of Russia and Asia. **2** this breed of sheep. Also **caracul.**

kar·at (kăr′ ət) ***n-*** unit of measure for stating the purity of gold. In commercial use, 24 karats is pure gold. ***Homs-*** carat, caret, carrot.

ka·ra·te (kə rä′ tē) ***n-*** method of self-defense, originating in Japan, in which sudden, sharp blows are given with the side of the hand and fingertips.

kar·ma (kär′ mə) ***n-*** **1** in Hinduism and Buddhism, the total of good and evil in one's previous life or incarnation, which determines one's next life or incarnation. **2** less correctly, one's fate or destiny.

kar·roo or **ka·roo** (kə ro͞o′) ***n-*** [*pl.* **kar·roos**] in South Africa, a dry tableland or plateau.

---

fāte, făt, dâre, bärn; bē, bĕt, mêre; bīte, bĭt; nōte, hŏt, môre, dȯg; fŭn, fûr; to͞o, bo͝ok; oil; out; tar; thin; then; hw for wh as in *wh*at; zh for s as in u*s*ual; ə for a, e, i, o, u, as in *a*go, lin*e*n, per*i*l, at*o*m, min*u*s

ka·ty·did (kā′ tē dĭd′) ***n-*** any of several green insects that resemble and are closely related to grasshoppers. The males produce shrill sounds with their front wings.

Katydid,1 1/2—2 in. long

kau·ri (kou′ rē) ***n-*** **1** any of several large, resinous New Zealand timber trees related to the pines. **2** wood of this tree. **3** resin obtained from such a tree, used in varnishes, for linoleum, etc.

kay·ak (kī′ ăk′) ***n-*** **1** single-seated Eskimo canoe, made of waterproof skins stretched over a light frame with a small opening in the middle for the canoeist. **2** similar canoe made of canvas, nylon, etc., stretched over a frame of aluminum or steel.

Kayak

kc. kilocycle.

kea (kē′ ə) ***n-*** large, greenish New Zealand parrot which normally feeds on insects, but which also kills sheep by tearing their backs to feed on the kidney fat.

ke·bab or **ke·bob** (kə bŏb′) ***n-*** **1** shish kebab. **2** kabob.

kedge (kĕj) ***n-*** light anchor used especially for pulling a grounded ship free. ***vt-*** **[kedged, kedg·ing]** to move (a ship) by reeling in an anchor that is embedded some distance away. ***vi-***: *We* kedged *until our boat was free.*

keel (kēl) ***n-*** **1** a strong timber or a bar, plate, or beam of metal, running the length of the bottom of a ship, and serving as the backbone of the ship's frame. **2** fin or other slim structure extending beneath the bottom of a sailboat to keep the boat from moving sideways when the wind comes from one side. **3** something resembling this, such as the bottom of an airship.

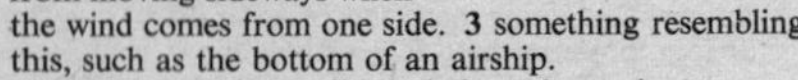
Keel

on an even keel not tilting; balanced; steady.

keel over **1** to capsize; turn bottom up. **2** to fall down: *She* keeled over *in a faint.*

keel·haul (kēl′ hȯl′) ***vt-*** **1** to punish or torture (a man) by hauling him through the water under the keel of a ship. **2** to scold severely; rebuke.

keel·son (kēl′ sən) ***n-*** a timber or a bar, beam, or plate of metal bolted above or alongside the keel of a ship to strengthen it.

[1]**keen** (kēn) ***adj-*** **[keen·er, keen·est]** **1** sharp; cutting. **2** stinging; bitter: *a* keen *wind.* **3** sensitive; highly developed: *He has* keen *sight and hearing.* **4** alert; quick; clever: *a* keen *mind.* **5** eager; enthusiastic: *a* keen *interest in sports.* **6** *Slang* excellent; great. [from Old English **cēne** meaning originally "wise; canny; experienced; capable," and later, "bold."] ***—adv-*** **keen′ ly.** ***n-*** **keen′ ness.**

[2]**keen** (kēn) *Irish* ***n-*** wailing lament for the dead. ***vi-***: *to* keen *for one's father.* [from Irish **caoine** meaning "a lamenting," from **caoinid,** "wails."] ***—n-*** **keen′ er.**

keep (kēp) ***vt-*** **[kept, keep·ing]** **1** to continue to have or hold; not give up; retain: *Will you* keep *the money you found? She* kept *her secret for years.* **2** to cause to continue in a certain condition, place, etc.; maintain: *to* keep *a motor running*; *to* keep *the two boxers apart*; *to* keep *one's hair short*; *to* keep *step.* **3** to save; store: *Where do you* keep *your bonds?* **4** to carry out; fulfill: *to* keep *a promise.* **5** to do over and over; continue: *She* kept *coming back. He* kept *shouting.* **6** to manage; conduct: *to* keep *house*; *to* keep *a flower shop.* **7** to take care of; look after: *to* keep *sheep*; *to* keep *valuable papers.* **8** to support (a person). **9** to prevent: *to* keep *the enemy from advancing.* **10** to detain: *to* keep *a boy after school.* **11** to observe; celebrate: *to* keep *the Sabbath.* **12** to maintain (a record, accounts, a diary, etc.). **13** to carry in stock: *We* keep *all kinds of dog food.* ***vi-*** **1** to continue; remain: *to* keep *cheerful*; *to* keep *indoors.* **2** of food, to remain fresh. **3** to refrain (from): *to* keep *from talking.* ***n-*** **1** means of subsistence; food, clothing, and shelter: *to work for one's* keep. **2** care; custody: *Her son is in my* keep. **3** strongest building of a castle; donjon.

Keep of Norman castle

for keeps *Informal* **1** seriously. **2** permanently.

keep in to prevent from going outside.

keep on **1** to continue without change: *to* keep on *doing the same work.* **2** to let stay; retain: *The maid was very lazy, but we* kept *her* on.

keep one's temper to refrain from getting angry.

keep to oneself **1** to avoid disclosing (something). **2** to remain aloof or alone.

keep up **1** to maintain an equal pace: *Johnny had trouble* keeping up *in his class.* **2** to continue: *The rain* kept up *all day.* **3** to maintain: *Can you* keep up *the house, now that you've lost your job?*

keep up with **1** to maintain an equal pace with. **2** to stay informed about: *to* keep up with *the latest news.*

keep·er (kē′ pər) ***n-*** **1** person who guards, watches, or takes care of something: *a* keeper *at the zoo*; *a store*keeper. **2** *Informal* fish large enough to be legally kept when caught.

keep·ing (kē′ pĭng) ***n-*** care; charge: *in his* keeping.

in keeping with in agreement with; in harmony with.

keep·sake (kēp′ sāk′) ***n-*** something kept in memory of the giver or of an occasion; memento.

keg (kĕg) ***n-*** **1** small cask or barrel. **2** amount one of these holds when full: *four* kegs *of water.* **3** unit of weight for nails, equal to 100 pounds.

Keg

kelp (kĕlp) ***n-*** **1** kind of large brown seaweed. **2** ashes of such seaweed, a source of iodine.

kel·pie or **kel·py** (kĕl′ pē) *Scottish* ***n-*** water spirit, usually in the shape of a horse, that is supposed to cause or warn of death by drowning.

Kel·vin (kĕl′ vən) ***adj-*** naming or relating to a temperature scale on which absolute zero (—273.16°C) is the zero point. The temperature intervals on the Kelvin scale are the same as on the centigrade thermometer.

ken (kĕn) ***n-*** range of sight or understanding; comprehension; perception: *That's beyond my* ken.

ken·nel (kĕn′ əl) ***n-*** **1** place where dogs are bred, raised for sale, or looked after. **2** doghouse.

ke·no (kē′ nō) ***n-*** game similar to bingo or lotto.

ke·pi (kā′ pē, kĕp′ ē) ***n-*** military cap having a round, flat top and a visor, worn by French soldiers and policemen.

kept (kĕpt) *p.t. & p.p.* of **keep.**

ker·a·tin (kĕr′ ə tən) ***n-*** tough, insoluble protein that forms the outer layers or substance of skin, hair, nails, feathers, horns, and scales of vertebrate animals.

ker·chief (kŭr′ chĭf) ***n-*** **1** piece of cloth used to cover the head or tie around the neck. **2** handkerchief.

kerf (kŭrf) ***n-*** **1** cut made by a saw or torch; also, the width of such a cut. **2** place where a felled tree is cut.

kern (kûrn) *Archaic* ***n-*** Irish foot soldier or peasant.

ker·nel (kûr′nəl) *n-* 1 soft, inner part of a nut or fruit, often used for food. 2 seed or grain of such plants as corn, wheat, and rye. 3 central or important part of a structure, plan, argument, etc.; core; nucleus. ***Hom-*** colonel.

ker·o·sene (kĕr′ə sēn) *n-* thin, oily hydrocarbon that is distilled from petroleum or coal and used as a heating and jet fuel.

Walnut kernel

Ker·ry blue terrier (kĕr′ē) *n-* breed of terriers originating in Ireland, having a soft, bluish-gray coat and a long head.

kes·trel (kĕs′trəl) *n-* small European falcon noted for hovering in the air with its head always to the wind.

ketch (kĕch) *n-* small fore-and-aft rigged sailboat having two masts, of which the shorter is nearest the stern.

ketch·up (kĕch′əp) *n-* sauce made of tomatoes and spices. Also **catchup, catsup.**

ket·tle (kĕt′əl) *n-* pot used to heat liquids; especially, a teakettle.

kettle of fish *Informal* situation; predicament.

ket·tle·drum (kĕt′əl drŭm′) *n-* large, bowl-shaped brass or copper drum with parchment stretched over the top; one of the tympani. For picture, see *drum.*

[1]key (kē) *n-* 1 piece of shaped metal used for turning the bolt in a lock to fasten or open something. 2 anything like this in shape or use: *a* key *to wind a toy; a* key *to open a can.* 3 place or position controlling entrance: *New Orleans is the* key *to the Mississippi.* 4 main clue; means of finding a solution or explanation: *This letter is the* key *to the whole mystery.* 5 list or table that explains a map, chart, etc.: *a color* key *to a map; a* key *to a test.* 6 any of a set of levers, buttons, etc., pressed down by the finger on a piano, typewriter, etc., to make it work. 7 series of musical tones related to one tone (keynote): *the* key *of F.* 8 tone or pitch: *She sang off* key. *adj-* important; necessary; vital: *Steel is a* key *industry. vt-* to make appropriate to; adjust: *to* key *a TV program to the interests of children.* [from Old English **cæg(e),** meaning "a key; a solution."] ***Hom-*** quay. —*adj-* **key′less.**

key up to stimulate; excite: *The players were all* keyed *up.*

[2]key (kē) *n-* in southeastern United States, a low island or reef. [from Spanish **cayo,** from a native West Indian word, influenced by **[1]key** and **quay.**] ***Hom-*** quay.

key·board (kē′bôrd′) *n-* complete series of keys by means of which a piano, organ, etc., is played, or a typewriter, adding machine, etc., is operated.

Keyboard of a piano

keyed (kēd) *adj-* 1 of musical instruments or certain machines, having keys. 2 *Music* set in a certain key. 3 of an arch, secured with a keystone. 4 of a map, test, etc., provided with an explanation or answers.

key·hole (kē′hōl′) *n-* small hole in a door or lock for inserting a key.

key·note (kē′nōt′) *n-* 1 first note of a musical scale. 2 main idea; chief theme.

keynote speech *n-* political speech, especially at a nominating convention, that outlines the basic policy of a party.

key punch *n-* machine with a keyboard like that of a typewriter, used to record and code information by punching patterns of holes in cards.

key·stone (kē′stōn′) *n-* 1 stone in the middle of an arch that holds the other stones in place. 2 essential thing upon which other things depend: *Freedom is the* keystone *of democracy.*

key word *n-* the main or essential word in a sentence, passage, puzzle, etc.

Keystone

kg. 1 kilogram. 2 keg.

khak·i (kăk′ē, kä′kē) *n-* 1 yellowish-brown color. 2 cloth of a dull yellow-brown color. *adj-* 1 having this color. 2 made of this cloth: *a* khaki *uniform.*

khan (kän) *n-* 1 in the Middle Ages, the title of Genghis Khan or any of his imperial successors who ruled most of Asia. 2 in Iran, Afghanistan, etc., a title of respect given to certain dignitaries. [from Turkish **khān.**]

khe·dive (kə dēv′) *n-* title of any of the Turkish viceroys who ruled Egypt from 1867 to 1914.

kib·butz (kĭ bo͞ots′) *n-* [*pl.* **kib·butz·es** or **kib·but·zim** (kĭ′bo͞ot sēm′)] Israeli farm settlement in which the property and labor are shared in common; collective farm.

kib·itz (kĭb′əts) **Informal** *vi-* to look on and give unwanted advice at a card game. —*n-* **kib′itz·er.**

kick (kĭk) *vt-* 1 to hit or strike with the foot: *to* kick *a rock.* 2 to move or drive by doing this: *to* kick *a ball across a field.* 3 in football, to make or score (an extra point or field goal) by kicking. *vi-* 1 to thrust out with the foot: *to* kick *and prance in a dance.* 2 to spring back; recoil;: *The shotgun* kicks *when it's fired.* 3 *Informal* to complain; grouse. 4 in football, to punt. *n-* 1 blow or thrust with the foot: *He gave the can a swift* kick. 2 a recoil: *That gun has some* kick *to it.* 3 *Slang* a thrill.

kick back 1 to recoil. 2 *Slang* to return a part of (one's salary, fee, etc.).

kick in *Informal* to contribute one's share of (money).

kick off 1 in football, to kick the ball toward the opposing team to begin play at the beginning of each half or after a touchdown or field goal. 2 *Slang* to die.

kick out *Informal* to eject forcibly from a place.

kick upstairs *Informal* to promote (someone) in order to remove him from a job of real responsibility.

kick over the traces to defy authority; have a fling.

kick·back (kĭk′băk′) *n-* 1 *Informal* sudden, strong reaction or recoil. 2 *Slang* a returning of a part of one's salary or fee; also, the amount returned.

kick·er (kĭk′ər) *n-* 1 person who kicks, especially a football player who specializes in kicking. 2 small marine engine, especially an outboard motor.

kick·off (kĭk′ôf′) *n-* in football, a place kick toward the opposing team, which begins the play at the beginning of each half or after a touchdown or field goal.

kid (kĭd) *n-* 1 young goat. 2 leather made from the skin of a young goat. 3 *Informal* child; youth. *adj-* 1 made of the skin of a young goat: *white* kid *gloves.* 2 *Informal* younger or youngest: *my* kid *sister. vt- Slang* [**kid·ded, kid·ding**] 1 to deceive; fool. 2 to play or fool with; tease: *I didn't mean it; I was just* kidding *you. vi- Slang* to make jokes and quips; be frivolous and amusing: *Please stop* kidding.

kid·dush (kĭd′əsh, kĭ do͞osh′) *n-* in Judaism, a prayer said over wine, especially to commence the Sabbath.

kid·nap (kĭd′năp′) *vt-* [**kid·naped** or **kid·napped, kid·nap·ing** or **kid·nap·ping**] to carry off and hold (someone, especially a child) by force or trickery, usually to collect a ransom. **—*n-* kid′nap·er** or **kid′nap·per.**

kid·ney (kĭd′nē) ***n-*** **1** either of the two glandular organs of the animal body located in the lower back near the spine. The kidney regulates the composition of the blood and eliminates waste products in the form of urine. **2** sort or kind: *a man of his* kidney.

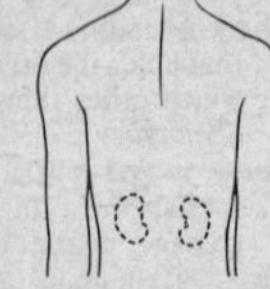

Kidneys, showing position from back

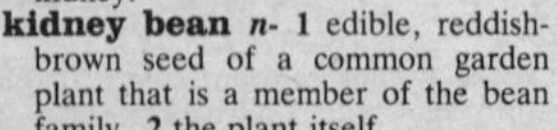

kidney bean ***n-*** **1** edible, reddish-brown seed of a common garden plant that is a member of the bean family. **2** the plant itself.

kid·skin (kĭd′skĭn′) ***n-*** leather made from the skin of a young goat, used especially for gloves and shoes.

¹kill (kĭl) ***vt-*** **1** to deprive of life; slay. **2** to destroy: *Frost* kills *crops.* **3** to defeat; reject; discard: *The senators* killed *the tax bill.* **4** spend (time) idly: *We* killed *an hour looking out the window.* ***vi-*** to cause death; slay: *He* killed *without conscience.* ***n-*** act of causing death, especially in hunting; also, the dead prey. [from Middle English **kyllen,** probably related to **quell.**] **—*n-* kill′er.**

²kill (kĭl) ***n-*** stream, creek, or channel (found in place names). [American word from Dutch **kil.**]

kill·deer (kĭl′dêr′) ***n-*** kind of plover with brown back and wings, orange-brown tail, and white breast crossed by two brown bands. For picture, see *plover.*

killer whale ***n-*** large, flesh-eating sea mammal.

kill·ing (kĭl′ĭng) ***n-*** *Informal* sudden gain or profit.

kill-joy (kil′joi′) ***n-*** person who ruins the joy of others.

kiln (kĭl, *also* kĭln) ***n-*** oven for baking pottery.

ki·lo (kĭl′ō, kē′lō) ***n-*** [*pl.* **ki·los**] **1** kilogram. **2** kilometer.

kilo- *combining form* thousand: *a* kilo*gram.*

kil·o·cy·cle (kĭl′ə sī′kəl) ***n-*** **1** unit of frequency equal to 1000 cycles per second. **2** 1000 cycles.

kil·o·gram (kĭl′ə grăm′) ***n-*** unit of mass and weight in the metric system equal to 1000 grams or about 2.2 pounds. Also **kil′o·gramme.**

kil·o·gram-me·ter (kĭl′ə grăm′mē′tər) ***n-*** unit of work equal to the work done in raising a mass of one kilogram through a distance of one meter against the force of gravity. One kilogram-meter equals about 9.8×10^7 ergs or about 7.2 foot-pounds.

kil·o·li·ter (kĭl′ə lē′tər) ***n-*** unit of volume or capacity equal to 1000 liters. Also **kil′o·li′tre.**

kil·o·me·ter (kə lŏm′ə tər, *also* kĭl′ə mē′-) ***n-*** unit of distance equal to 1000 meters or about 3,281 feet. Also **kil′o·me′tre.**

kil·o·ton (kĭl′ə tŭn′) ***n-*** **1** unit of weight equal to 1000 tons. **2** unit of explosive force or power, equal to that produced by 1000 tons of TNT.

kil·o·watt (kĭl′ə wŏt′) ***n-*** unit of electrical power equal to 1000 watts.

kil·o·watt-hour (kĭl′ə wŏt′our′) ***n-*** unit of energy equal to the energy expended by 1000 watts of electrical power during a time period of one hour.

kilt (kĭlt) ***n-*** short, pleated skirt worn by men of Celtic lands, especially by Scottish Highlanders.

kil·ter (kĭl′tər) **out of kilter** *Informal* not in working condition; out of order.

Kimono

ki·mo·no (kə mō′nə) ***n-*** [*pl.* **ki·mo·nos**] **1** loose outer garment bound with a broad sash, worn by men and women in Japan. **2** woman's dressing gown.

kin (kĭn) ***n-*** person's family; relatives. ***adj-*** **1** related: *John is* kin *to me.* **2** similar; alike: *This book is* kin *to that one in subject.*

next to kin person or persons most closely related; immediate family.

-kin *suffix* (used to form nouns) little; small: *lamb*kin.

¹kind (kīnd) ***adj-*** [**kind·er, kind·est**] **1** gentle and loving. **2** thoughtful; considerate: *It was* kind *of you to send flowers.* [from Old English **(ge)cynde,** "fitting; natural; inborn." related to **²kind.**]

²kind (kīnd) ***n-*** sort; class; variety: *What* kind *of apple is that? It takes all* kinds *of people.* [from English **cynd** meaning "natural character; class." It is related to **kin.**]

in kind 1 with something of the same sort: *to return an evil deed* in kind. **2** with goods rather than money: *to pay a debt* in kind. **kind of** *Informal* somewhat; rather: *This is* kind of *stupid.*

kin·der·gar·ten (kĭn′dər gär′tən, -gär′dən) ***n-*** school or class for children, usually between four and six years of age, in which children learn to work and play together and begin to develop their individual abilities.

kind·heart·ed (kīnd′här′təd) ***adj-*** generous and sympathetic; thoughtful of others. **—*adv-* kind′heart′ed·ly. *n-* kind′heart′ed·ness.**

kin·dle (kĭn′dəl) ***vt-*** [**kin·dled, kin·dling**] **1** to set fire to; light: *to* kindle *a fire.* **2** to make bright or shining: *Excitement* kindled *her face.* **3** to arouse; stir up: *The insult* kindled *his anger.* ***vi-*** **1** to catch fire: *The dry wood* kindled *immediately.* **2** to become aroused or stirred up: *to* kindle *with enthusiasm.* **3** to become bright and glowing: *Her eyes* kindled *with excitement.*

kin·dling (kĭnd′lĭng) ***n-*** material for starting a fire, such as small pieces of wood.

kind·ly (kīnd′lē) ***adj-*** [**kind·li·er, kind·li·est**] gentle and thoughtful of others; kind. *He is a* kindly *man who will help anyone.* ***adv-*** **1** in a kind, friendly way: *He treated me* kindly. **2** please be good enough to: *Will you* kindly *explain?* **—*n-* kind′li·ness.**

take kindly to to be pleasant or agreeable to.

kind·ness (kīnd′nəs) ***n-*** **1** gentleness to and thoughtfulness of others; a being kind: *She showed* kindness *by helping us.* **2** helpful or thoughtful act; kind act.

kin·dred (kĭn′drəd) ***n-*** relatives. ***adj-*** of the same kind; related: *Writing and spelling are* kindred *studies.*

kine (kīn) *Archaic* ***n-*** *pl.* cows; cattle.

kine·scope (kĭn′ə skōp′) ***n-*** **1** picture tube. **2** a movie of a television program.

kin·es·thet·ic (kĭn′ĭs thĕt′ĭk) ***adj-*** having to do with the sensation of bodily motion or position perceived by the nerve endings in the muscles and joints. **—*adv-* kin′es·thet′i·cal·ly. *n-* kin′es·the′sia** (-thē′zhə) or **kin′es·the′sis** (-thē′sĭs).

ki·net·ic (kĭ nĕt′ĭk) ***adj-*** of, having to do with, or due to motion.

kinetic energy ***n-*** energy that an object or particle has as a result of its motion. See also *potential energy.*

kin·folk (kĭn′fōk′) ***n-*** *pl.* one's relatives; kin. Also **kinsfolk.**

king (kĭng) ***n-*** **1** male sovereign of a country; monarch. **2** person or thing that is thought of as being very important or powerful: *The lion is the* king *of the jungle.* **3** playing card with the picture of a crowned male monarch. **4** in checkers, a piece which has been moved over to the opponent's last row on the board and can now move backwards or forwards. **5** in chess, the principal piece, whose imminent capture ends the game.

king·bird (kĭng′bûrd′) ***n-*** any of various quarrelsome birds related to the flycatchers.

king cobra ***n-*** large, very poisonous cobra of India and southeastern Asia; hamadryad. It is the world's largest venomous snake.

king crab ***n-*** **1** horseshoe crab. For picture, see *horseshoe crab.* **2** any of various large edible crabs of the northern Pacific, with a small body and very long legs.

king·dom (kĭng′ dəm) ***n-*** **1** country that has a king or queen; monarchy. **2** one of the three groups into which all natural things are divided: *the animal* kingdom. **3** domain; realm: *the* kingdom *of the mind.*

king·fish (kĭng′ fĭsh′) ***n-*** [*pl.* **king·fish; king·fishes** (kinds of kingfish)] any of various sea fishes, especially a large food fish of the North American Atlantic coast.

king·fish·er (kĭng′ fĭsh′ ər) ***n-*** a crested bird with a blue back and white breast and neckband. It catches fish with its long, black beak as it flies over the surface of the water.

Kingfisher, about 1 ft. long

king·ly (kĭng′ lē) ***adj-*** [**king·li·er, king·li·est**] of or suitable for a king: *a* kingly *treasure*; *his* kingly *rights.* **—*n-* king′ li·ness.**

king·mak·er (kĭng′ mā′ kər) ***n-*** one who is influential in the selection of a king or other powerful person.

king·pin (kĭng′ pĭn′) ***n-*** **1** in bowling, the foremost or center pin. **2** *Informal* the most important or influential person. **3** kingbolt.

Kings (kĭngz) ***n-*** (takes singular verb) **1** either of two historical books in the Old Testament, "I and II Kings." **2** in the CCD Bible, the four "King" books, corresponding to "I and II Samuel" and "I and II Kings."

king·ship (kĭng′ shĭp′) ***n-*** **1** power, office, or dignity of a king. **2** art or manner of ruling a kingdom.

king-size (kĭng′ sīz′) ***adj-*** larger than the usual: *a* king-size *sheet.*

king snake ***n-*** any of various large, nonpoisonous snakes of southern and central United States, which often feed on other snakes.

kink (kĭngk) ***n-*** **1** twist, curl, or sharp bend in a rope, wire, hair, etc. **2** stiffness in some part of the body; cramp: *a* kink *in the neck.* **3** odd twist of mind or character; strange notion. ***vt-*** to cause to form twists, curls, or bends: *to* kink *a hose.* ***vi-***: *Don't let that cord* kink.

kin·ka·jou (kĭngk′ ə jo͞o′) ***n-*** flesh-eating, tree-dwelling mammal of Central and South America related to the raccoons and having large eyes, soft, brownish fur, and a long tail capable of grasping.

kink·y (kĭng′ kē) ***adj-*** [**kink·i·er, kink·i·est**] full of curls or twists; frizzy.

kin·ni·ki·nic (kĭn′ ĭ kə nĭk′) ***n-*** mixture of dried leaves and bark of certain plants, formerly smoked by certain North American Indians.

kins·folk (kĭnz′ fōk′) ***n-*** *pl.* kinfolk.

kin·ship (kĭn′ shĭp′) ***n-*** **1** family relationship. **2** relatedness; connection; similarity.

kins·man (kĭnz′ mən) ***n-*** [*pl.* **kins·men**] male relative. **—*n-*** *fem.* **kins′ wom′ an.**

ki·osk (kē′ ŏsk′-, kī′-) ***n-*** **1** in Turkey and Iran, an open summerhouse or pavilion. **2** small, similar structure, used as a newsstand, refreshment booth, etc.

Ki·o·wa (kī′ ə wə) ***n-*** [*pl.* **Ki·o·was,** also **Ki·o·wa**] member of a small tribe of American Plains Indians who now live in southwestern Oklahoma.

kip (kĭp) ***n-*** untanned hide of a young or small animal.

kip·per (kĭp′ ər) ***vt-*** to cure (fish) by salting and drying or smoking. ***n-*** fish that has been thus cured.

kirk (kûrk) *Scottish* ***n-*** church.

kir·tle (kûr′ təl) *Archaic* ***n-*** **1** woman's dress, skirt, or petticoat. **2** man's coat or tunic.

kis·met (kĭz′ mət) ***n-*** destiny; fate.

kiss (kĭs) ***n-*** **1** to touch or press with the lips as a caress, greeting, or sign of respect. **2** to touch gently; caress: *The waves* kissed *the shore.* ***n-***: *a* kiss *on one's cheek*; *the* kiss *of the waves on the shore.* **—*adj-* kiss′ a·ble.**

kiss·er (kĭs′ ər) ***n-*** person who kisses.

kit (kĭt) ***n-*** **1** set or collection of tools, materials, etc., for a particular job or purpose: *a* kit *for building a model boat*; *a soldier's* kit. **2** case, box, or bag for holding these.

kitch·en (kĭch′ ən) ***n-*** **1** room in which food is prepared. **2** equipment for cooking: *a field* kitchen.

kitch·en·ette (kĭch′ ə nĕt′) ***n-*** small, compact kitchen.

kitchen midden ***n-*** a pile of shells and other refuse found at the site of an ancient shore-dwelling people.

kitchen police *Military* ***n-*** the duty of assisting the cooks, cleaning up after meals, etc. *Abbr.* K.P.

kitch·en·ware (kĭch′ ən wâr′) ***n-*** pots, pans, and other utensils used in cooking.

Swallow-tailed kite, 1 1/2 to 2 ft. long

[1]kite (kīt) ***n-*** any of several hawks with slender wings, noted for their graceful flight. Some kites have forked tails. [from Old English **cyta** having the same meaning.]

[2]kite (kīt) ***n-*** frame of light wood over which is stretched a silk or paper covering, flown at the end of a long string. [**[1]kite** in a later, special use, from the fact that a kite looks like a bird in the sky.]

Box kite and common kite

kith and kin (kĭth) ***n-*** *pl.* friends and relatives.

kith·a·ra (kĭth′ ər ə) cithara.

kit·ten (kĭt′ ən) ***n-*** young cat.

kit·ten·ish (kĭt′ ən ĭsh) ***adj-*** **1** lively and playful; frisky. **2** coy; coquettish. **—*adv-* kit′ ten·ish·ly.** ***n-*** **kit′ ten·ish·ness.**

[1]kit·ty (kĭt′ ē) ***n-*** [*pl.* **kit·ties**] pet name for a cat or kitten. [a variant of **kitten.**]

[2]kit·ty (kĭt′ ē) ***n-*** [*pl.* **kit·ties**] pool or fund of money accumulated for a specific purpose; especially, such a pool accumulated by the players in a card game to cover expenses, buy refreshments, etc. [of uncertain origin.]

kit·ty-cor·ner (kĭt′ ē kôr′ nər, -kôr′ nər) cater-corner.

ki·va (kē′ və) ***n-*** among the Pueblo Indians, a round ceremonial chamber entered through the roof.

ki·wi (kē′ wē′) ***n-*** grayish-brown, flightless New Zealand bird with hairlike feathers, undeveloped wings, and a long bill.

Kiwi

Kla·math (klăm′ əth) ***n-*** [*pl.* **Kla·maths,** also **Kla·math**] member of a tribe of American Indians who lived in southeastern Oregon and northern California.

klep·to·ma·ni·a (klĕp′ tə mā′ nē ə) ***n-*** very powerful impulse to steal, often when one has no need for the article in question. **—*n-* klep′ to·ma′ ni·ac.**

klieg light (klēg) ***n-*** powerful electric-arc floodlight used in motion picture studios.

---

fāte, făt, dâre, bärn; bē, bĕt, mêre; bīte, bĭt; nōte, hŏt, môre, dòg; fŭn, fûr; to͞o, bo͝ok; oil; out; tar; thin; then; hw for wh as in *wh*at; zh for s as in u*s*ual; ə for a, e, i, o, u, as in *a*go, lin*e*n, per*i*l, at*o*m, min*u*s

km. or **km** kilometer; kilometers.

knack (năk) ***n-*** **1** right or best way of doing something: *I want to dance well, but I can't get the* knack *of it.* **2** special skill; talent; aptitude: *a* knack *for carpentry.*

knap·sack (năp′ săk′) ***n-*** sturdy canvas bag for clothing, food, etc., carried on the back by straps fitting over the shoulders or attached to a carrying frame; rucksack.

Knapsack

knave (nāv) ***n-*** **1** in earlier times, a male servant or man of humble birth. **2** dishonest or deceitful person; scoundrel. **3** in card games, a jack. ***Hom-*** nave.

knav·er·y (nā′ və rē) ***n-*** [*pl.* **knav·er·ies**] dishonesty; treachery.

knav·ish (nā′ vĭsh) ***adj-*** deceitful; cunning in a dishonest way. ***—adv-*** **knav′ ish·ly.** ***n-*** **kna′ vish·ness.**

knead (nēd) ***vt-*** **1** to mix and work into a mass, usually with the hands: *to* knead *clay.* **2** to work over or treat with the hands or fingers; massage. ***Hom-*** need.

knee (nē) ***n-*** **1** joint of a human leg between the thigh and the lower leg; also, the corresponding part of a four-footed animal. **2** anything resembling this part, such as a sharply curved brace. **3** part of a pair of trousers or other garment covering this joint.

bring (someone) to (his) knees to conquer or cow (someone); make (someone) surrender.

knee·cap (nē′ kăp′) ***n-*** small, flat, movable bone that covers the front of the knee; patella. Also **knee′ pan.**

kneel (nēl) ***vi-*** **[knelt** (nĕlt) or **kneeled, kneel·ing]** to go down on one or both knees, usually as a sign of reverence or earnest pleading: *to* kneel *in prayer.*

knell (nĕl) ***n-*** the slow sounding of a bell to announce a death or a funeral. ***vt-*** to ring (a bell) slowly or solemnly. ***vi-***: *The church bells* knelled *all morning.*

knew (no͞o, nyo͞o) *p.t.* of **know.** ***Homs-*** gnu, new.

Knick·er·bock·er (nĭk′ ər bŏk′ ər) ***n-*** **1** a descendant of the early Dutch settlers of New York State. **2** a New Yorker.

knick·er·bock·ers (nĭk′ ər bŏk′ ərz) ***n-*** (takes plural verb) knickers, especially those worn by men in the 17th and 18th centuries.

Knickerbockers

knick·ers (nĭk′ ərz) ***n-*** (takes plural verb) full-cut breeches that gather and reach just below the knee.

knick·knack (nĭk′ năk′) ***n-*** any small decorative ornament. Also **nicknack.**

knife (nīf) ***n-*** [*pl.* **knives]** **1** cutting tool of many forms with a keen, usually single-edged blade. **2** sharp cutting blade in a machine. ***vt-*** **[knifed, knif·ing]** to cut or stab with such an implement: *to* knife *an enemy in a fight.* ***vi-*** to cut or slice (through). ***—adj-*** **knife′ like′.**

Carving knife Table knife

Pocket knife

knight (nīt) ***n-*** **1** during the Middle Ages, a mounted warrior in the service of his feudal superior; especially, such a man who has served as a squire and been ceremonially inducted into the order of chivalry. **2** today, a man honored by the British sovereign. He ranks below a baronet and is addressed with his given name preceded by "Sir." **3** in chess, the piece shaped like a horse's head. ***vt-*** to raise to the rank of knight. ***Hom-*** night.

knight-er·rant (nīt′ ĕr′ ənt) ***n-*** [*pl.* **knights-er·rant]** medieval knight who roamed in search of adventure.

knight-er·rant·ry (nīt ĕr′ ən trē) ***n-*** [*pl.* **knight-er·ran·tries]** **1** life and experience of a knight-errant. **2** exaggerated romantic adventure or scheme.

knight·hood (nīt′ ho͝od′) ***n-*** **1** character, rank, or dignity of a knight; chivalry. **2** whole body or class of knights.

knight·ly (nīt′ lē) ***adj-*** **[knight·li·er, knight·li·est]** like a knight; chivalric. ***Hom-*** nightly. ***—n-*** **knight′ li·ness.**

knish (knĭsh) ***n-*** rich crust folded over seasoned meat, cheese, or potato filling and baked or fried.

knit (nĭt) ***vt-*** **[knit** or **knit·ted, knit·ting]** **1** to make (a fabric or garment) by looping a single thread or yarn on needles either by hand or by machine: *to* knit *a sweater.* **2** to make a stitch in knitting of the type usually found on the right side of a garment. See also *purl.* **3** to unite closely; lock or draw together: *to* knit *one's fingers*; *to be* knit *together by common interests.* **4** to frown: *to* knit *one's brows.* ***vi-*** **1** to weave thread or yarn in loops by the use of needles: *Grandmother* knits. **2** to become closely joined or united: *The broken bone* knit *well.* ***—n-*** **knit′ter.**

knit·ting (nĭt′ ĭng) ***n-*** garment, fabric, etc., being knitted by hand.

knitting needle ***n-*** straight, slender, pointed rod, used in knitting by hand. For picture, see *needle.*

Knitting

knit·wear (nĭt′ wâr′) ***n-*** knitted clothing.

knives (nīvz) *pl.* of **knife.**

knob (nŏb) ***n-*** **1** rounded handle of a door, drawer, umbrella, etc. **2** rounded swelling, lump, or mass on a surface. **3** knoll. ***—adj-*** **knob′ like′.**

knob·by (nŏb′ ē) ***adj-*** **[knob·bi·er, knob·bi·est]** **1** bumpy; having protuberances: *a* knobby *hand.* **2** like a knob. ***—n-*** **knob′ bi·ness.**

knock (nŏk) ***vi-*** **1** to give a sharp blow; rap (on): *to* knock *with one's fist*; *to* knock *on the wall.* **2** to collide; bump: *He* knocked *into many people as he ran.* **3** to rap on a door in order to show one's presence outside. **4** of internal-combustion engines, to jar or pound noisily: *The engine* knocks. ***vt-*** **1** to strike or beat; give a blow to: *to* knock *a lamp down.* **2** to strike (something) against something else: *to* knock *one's head against a wall.* **3** *Slang* to criticize unfavorably; disparage. ***n-*** **1** sharp, quick blow; rap: *a* knock *at the door.* **2** a noisy banging: *a* knock *in the pipes.* **3** the pounding, pinging noise and vibration made by an internal-combustion engine when fuel burns faster than the pistons can move.

knock about (or **around)** **1** to toss (someone or something) here and there with blows: *The waves* knocked *the boat* about. **2** to wander about in search of adventure or pleasure: *He* knocked about *quite a lot in his youth.*

knock down **1** to sell to the highest bidder at an auction: *He* knocked *the antique vase* down *to a dealer.* **2** to take apart; disassemble.

knock off *Informal* **1** to stop what one is doing: *We'll* knock off *at 3 o'clock. Please* knock off *the noise.* **2** to do quickly: *We'll* knock *this job* off. **3** to kill or otherwise dispose of: *They* knocked off *their rivals.*

knock out **1** to cause (someone) to lose consciousness, especially by a blow. **2** to make quickly.

knock together to build or put together hastily.

knock·a·bout (nŏk′ ə bout′) ***n-*** small sloop. ***adj-*** **1** noisy and rough; boisterous: *a* knockabout *game.* **2** suitable for rough use: *an old* knockabout *car.*

knock·down (nŏk′ doun′) ***adj-*** **1** hard enough to knock someone or something down; rough; fierce: *a* knockdown *blow*; *a* knockdown *battle.* **2** made so as to be easily put together and taken apart: *a* knockdown *bookcase.* ***n-*** **1** a knocking down: *a* knockdown *in a boxing match.* **2** something easily put together or taken apart.

knock·er (nŏk′ ər) ***n-*** **1** person who knocks. **2** ring, knob, or the like, hinged to a metal plate on a door.

Knocker

knock-kneed (nŏk′ nēd′) ***adj-*** having the legs bent inward so that the knees touch.

knock·out (nŏk′ out′) ***n-*** **1** in boxing, the knocking of a fighter to the floor so that he does not get up before the referee counts ten; also, a victory scored in this way. **2** *Slang* something very attractive or spectacular. *as* ***modifier****: a* knockout *blow*; *a* knockout *dress.*

knoll (nōl) ***n-*** small, round hill.

[1]**knot** (nŏt) ***n-*** **1** any of many forms of interweaving or tying together a cord or cords. **2** enlargement of a muscle, gland, etc.; lump. **3** hard lump in wood, different in color and grain from surrounding wood, where a branch has grown. **4** group; gathering: *There was a* knot *of people on the street.* **5** complication or entanglement: *a problem full of* knots. **6** unit of speed used by ships and airplanes, equal to a rate of one nautical mile per hour. ***vt-*** **[knot·ted, knot·ting] 1** to tie or fasten together: *to* knot *a tie*; *to* knot *a rope.* **2** to entangle. ***vi-*** to become tangled: *Wet rope* knots. [from Old English **cnotta.**] ***Homs-*** naught, not. **—*adj-* knot′less.**

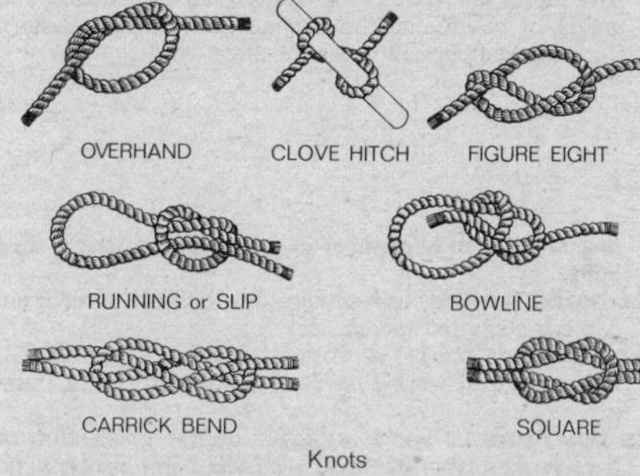

Knots

[2]**knot** (nŏt) ***n-*** sandpiper of northern regions that migrates south in winter. ***Homs-*** naught, not. [of uncertain origin.)

knot·hole (nŏt′ hōl′) ***n-*** round hole in a board where a knot has fallen out.

knot·ty (nŏt′ ē) ***adj-*** **[knot·ti·er, knot·ti·est] 1** full of knots: *a* knotty *cord.* **2** hard to solve or explain; difficult: *a* knotty *problem.*

know (nō) ***vt-*** **[knew** (no͞o, nyo͞o), **known** (nōn), **know·ing] 1** to perceive with the mind; understand clearly: *He* knows *his subject.* **2** to have a grasp of through study or practice: *to* know *music*; *to* know *French.* **3** to recognize: *I* knew *him instantly.* **4** to be familiar with: *to* know *the road.* **5** to have information about; be aware of: *I* know *his reasons.* **6** to have in the memory: *to* know *a song.* **7** to be certain of: *to* know *the truth.* **8** to distinguish: *to* know *right from wrong.* **9** to experience: *to* know *hardship.* ***Hom-*** no. **—*adj-* know′a·ble.**

be in the know to have inside or secret information.

know-how (nō′ hou′) *Informal* ***n-*** special ability to do something well; technical skill. ***Hom-*** nohow.

know·ing (nō′ ĭng) ***adj-*** astute: *a* knowing *smile.*

know·ing·ly (nō′ ĭng lē) ***adv-*** **1** fully aware of the facts, results, etc.; deliberately: *He would never insult you* knowingly. **2** in a knowing manner: *to smile* knowingly.

knowl·edge (nŏl′ ĭj) ***n-*** **1** what has been learned by study or observation; learning. **2** familiarity from study or experience: *a* knowledge *of the area*; *a* knowledge *of painting.*

to (or **to the best of) one's knowledge** as far as one knows; on the best information one has.

know·ledge·a·ble (nŏl′ ĭ jə bəl) ***adj-*** well informed; knowing a great deal. **—*adv-* know′ledge·a·bly.**

known (nōn) *p.p.* of **know.**

knuck·le (nŭk′ əl) ***n-*** **1** finger joint, especially one of the joints connecting the fingers to the hand. **2** a cut of meat from a joint of an animal. **3 knuckles** (also **brass knuckles**) set of metal finger rings or guards worn over the doubled fist for use as a weapon. ***vi-*** **[knuck·led, knuck·ling]** to keep the joints of the fingers close to the ground in shooting a marble.

knuckle down to apply oneself earnestly.

knuckle under to give in; submit.

knurl (nûrl) ***n-*** **1** knot; knob; lump. **2** small ridge such as on the edge of a thumbscrew or coin. **—*adj-* knurled.**

k.o. or **K.O.** (kā′ ō′) in boxing, a knockout.

ko·al·a (kō ä′ lə) ***n-*** Australian animal that looks like a small bear. It has soft gray fur and large ears and lives in trees, and the female carries her young in a pouch.

Koala, about 2 ft. long

ko·bold (kō′ bōld′, -bȯld′) ***n-*** in German folklore, a gnome or mischievous sprite that haunts houses and lives in caves or mines.

kohl (kōl) ***n-*** preparation used by Muslim and Hindu women to darken the edges of the eyelids.

kohl·ra·bi (kōl răb′ ē) ***n-*** type of cabbage that forms no head but has a fleshy, edible stem.

kola (kō′ lə) ***n-*** small tropical tree bearing a brownish, bitter nut that yields caffeine and is used in beverages as a stimulant.

Kol Ni·dre (kōl nĭd′ rā′, kȯl nĭd′ rē′, -rə) ***n-*** in Judaism, a prayer chanted in the service on the eve of Yom Kippur; also, the music to which the prayer is set.

koo·doo (ko͞o′ do͞o′) kudu.

kook·a·bur·ra (ko͝ok′ ə bûr′ ə) ***n-*** Australian bird of the kingfisher type, noted for its raucous call, which resembles loud laughter.

ko·peck or **ko·pek** (kō′ pĕk′) ***n-*** Russian coin, the hundredth part of a ruble.

Ko·ran (kôr′ ăn′, kə rän′, -răn′) ***n-*** the sacred writings of the Muslims, recording the revelations of Allah (God) to Mohammed. It is written in Arabic.

Ko·re·an (kə rē′ ən) ***adj-*** of or pertaining to Korea, its people, or their language. ***n-*** **1** a native of Korea, or his descendants. **2** the language of these people.

Korean War ***n-*** war between North and South Korea (1950-1953) in which the United Nations supported South Korea. It was the first time that the United Nations took police action in a conflict. Many United States soldiers were involved.

ko·sher (kō′ shər) ***adj-*** **1** sanctioned by Jewish law, especially by those laws pertaining to food and its preparation. **2** serving or dealing in such food.

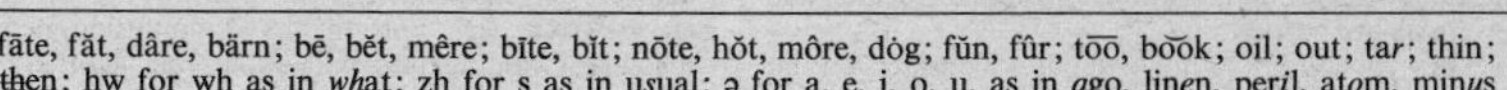
fāte, făt, dâre, bärn; bē, bĕt, mêre; bīte, bĭt; nōte, hŏt, môre, dȯg; fŭn, fûr; to͞o, bo͝ok; oil; out; tar; thin; then; hw for wh as in *wh*at; zh for s as in u*s*ual; ə for a, e, i, o, u, as in *a*go, lin*e*n, per*i*l, at*o*m, min*u*s

kow·tow (kou′tou′) ***n-*** traditional Chinese greeting of respect and worship, made by kneeling and touching the forehead to the ground. ***vi-*** to show deference by such an act; hence, to be humble, obsequious, servile.

K.P. 1 (also **KP**) kitchen police. 2 Knights of Pythias. 3 Knights of St. Patrick.

Kr symbol for krypton.

kraal (kräl) ***n-*** 1 South African village consisting of a group of huts surrounded by a stockade. 2 pen for livestock in South Africa.

K ration ***n-*** in the U.S. Army during World War II, a small package of food meant to be a full day's emergency ration for one soldier.

Krem·lin (krĕm′lən) ***n-*** 1 the citadel of Moscow, housing many of the Soviet Union's government offices. 2 the government of the Soviet Union. 3 **kremlin** the citadel of any Russian city.

krill (krĭl) ***n-*** [*pl.* **krill**] small shrimplike creature found in the Antarctic Ocean and other oceans in the same area.

kris (krēs) ***n-*** Malay or Indonesian dagger or short sword with a ridged and twisting blade.

Kriss Krin·gle (krĭs′krĭng′gəl) ***n-*** Santa Claus.

kryp·ton (krĭp′tŏn′) ***n-*** rare inert gaseous element present in the atmosphere. The spectral wavelength of a krypton isotope is used to define the meter's length. Symbol Kr, At. No. 36, At. Wt. 83.80.

ku·dos (kōō′dōs′, kyōō′dŏs′) ***n-*** praise; credit; glory.

ku·du (kōō′dōō′) ***n-*** large grayish-brown African antelope with large, spirally twisted horns. Also **koodoo.**

kud·zu (kōōd′zōō′) ***n-*** trailing Asiatic vine used for fodder and soil improvement.

ku·lak (kōō′lăk′) ***n-*** Russian peasant or farmer who opposed the Soviet collectivization of farms.

kum·quat (kŭm′kwŏt′) ***n-*** small citrus fruit with sour pulp and sweet, edible rind, used for making preserves. 2 tree or shrub bearing this fruit. Also **cumquat.**

Kurd (kûrd, kōōrd) ***n-*** a member of nomadic people living mainly in Kurdistan.

Kur·dish (kûr′dĭsh, kōōr′-) ***n-*** the Iranian language of the Kurds. ***adj-*** of or pertaining to the people of Kurdistan.

Ku·te·nai (kōō′tə nā′) ***n-*** [*pl.* **Ku·te·nais,** also **Ku·te·nai**] 1 one of a North American Indian people living on both sides of the United States-Canada border near the Pacific coast. 2 the language of these people. ***adj-:*** *many* Kutenai *camps.*

kw. or **kw** kilowatt; kilowatts.

Kwa·ki·utl (kwä′kē ōō′təl) ***n-*** [*pl.* **Kwa·ki·utls,** also **Kwa·ki·utl**] 1 one of a tribe of North American Indians living on the northwest coast of British Columbia and on Vancouver Island. 2 the language of these people. ***adj-:*** *a* Kwakiutl *fish dish.*

K.W.H. or **kwh** kilowatt-hour; kilowatt-hours.

Ky. Kentucky.

kym·o·graph (kī′mə grăf′) ***n-*** instrument for recording waves or periodic variations, such as of muscular contractions, pulse beats, etc., on a continuous graph. It often consists of a movable pen that traces a line on a moving paper scroll or cylinder.

Kyr·i·e e·le·i·son (kĭr′ē ä′ē lā′ə sŏn′) ***n-*** 1 "Lord have mercy on us," the first words of an ancient song and prayer of petition in the Roman Catholic and Eastern Christian churches. 2 music for these words.

L

L, l (ĕl) [*pl.* **L's, l's**] 1 the twelfth letter of the English alphabet. 2 Roman numeral for 50.

l. or **l** 1 left. 2 liter or liters.

L. or **£** pound sterling.

la (lä) *Music* ***n-*** the sixth note of a musical scale.

La symbol for lanthanum.

La. Louisiana.

lab (lăb) *Informal* ***n-*** laboratory.

la·bel (lā′bəl) ***n-*** 1 tag, sticker, words, etc., attached to or printed on an article and giving information about it: *a* label *in a dress; a* label *on a can.* 2 an identifying or descriptive phrase, word, or symbol: *"Adj-," "n-" are* labels *used to identify parts of speech.* ***vt-*** [**la·beled, la·bel·ing**] 1 to give an identifying mark to. 2 to call; describe: *to* label *someone a leader.* **—*n-* la′bel·er.**

la·bi·al (lā′bē əl) ***adj*** 1 of or relating to the lips. 2 formed by the lips in speaking, as the consonants /p/ and /b/ are. ***n-*** sound, or a letter representing a sound, formed by the lips.

la·bor (lā′bər) ***n-*** 1 physical or mental toil; work. 2 difficult task: *the* labors *of Hercules.* 3 workers, especially when considered as a class or as members of labor unions: *a law to benefit* labor. 4 process of giving birth to a child; especially, the contractions of the womb preceding the birth. ***vi-*** 1 to exert mental or physical effort; toil. 2 to be burdened or distressed: *to* labor *under a handicap.* 3 to move slowly and heavily. 4 of a ship, to pitch and roll. ***vt-*** to work out in detail: *to* labor *a topic.* Also *Brit.* **labour.**

lab·o·ra·to·ry (lăb′rə tôr′ē) ***n-*** [*pl.* **lab·o·ra·to·ries**] room, building, or buildings where scientific research and experiments are carried on.

Labor Day ***n-*** holiday to honor labor, celebrated on the first Monday of September in most States of the United States.

la·bored (lā′bərd) ***adj-*** produced with effort; forced; not natural: *a* labored *speech.*

la·bor·er (lā′bər ər) ***n-*** worker, especially one who does heavy physical work that does not require much training.

la·bor·i·ous (lə bôr′ē əs) ***adj-*** requiring great effort or hard work: *a* laborious *task.* **—*adv-* la·bor′i·ous·ly.** ***n-*** **la·bor′i·ous·ness.**

la·bor·ite (lā′bə rīt′) ***n-*** person who supports the interests of the working class or the labor unions. ***adj-:*** *a* laborite *point of view; a* laborite *tendency.*

labor party ***n-*** political party that supports the interests of labor or the labor unions.

la·bor-sav·ing (lā′bər sā′vĭng) ***adj-*** designed to replace or diminish human labor, especially manual labor: *a* labor-saving *device.*

labor union ***n-*** organization of workers joined to protect and further their mutual interests.

La·bour·ite (lā′bər īt′) ***n-*** member of the **Labour Party,** the major left wing party of Great Britain.

la·bur·num (lə bûr′nəm) ***n-*** poisonous tree or shrub, with clusters of yellow flowers.

Labyrinth

lab·y·rinth (lăb′ə rĭnth′) ***n-*** 1 confusing network of passages winding into and about one another, so it is almost impossible to find one's way through it; maze; hence, something extremely complex or tortuous. **2** the winding passages of the internal ear. **3 Labyrinth** in Greek mythology, the intricate structure built for King Minos in Crete as a prison for the Minotaur.

lab·y·rin·thine (lăb′ ə rĭn′ thən, -thīn′, -thēn′) ***adj-*** like a labyrinth; intricate; tortuous: *a* labyrinthine *network of trails.* Also **lab′ y·rinth′ i·an.**

lac (lăk) ***n-*** resinous substance secreted on certain kinds of trees by a scale insect and used in making shellac, lacquer, etc.

lace (lās) ***n-* 1** ornamental fabric of fine threads, such as those of linen, cotton, or silk, woven in a delicate open design. **2** cord or string, passed through eyelets or other holes to fasten together parts of a garment, shoe, etc. ***vt-* [laced, lac·ing] 1** to fasten with this kind of cord: *to* lace *a shoe.* **2** to weave or twine together. **3** to add a dash of alcoholic liquor to: *to* lace *lobster with sherry.* **4** *Informal* to beat; lash. ***vi-*** to be fastened with a string or cord: *This flap* laces *shut.* ***—adj-* lace′ like′.**

Needlepoint lace

lac·er·ate (lăs′ ə rāt′) ***vt-*** **[lac·er·at·ed, lac·er·at·ing] 1** to tear badly; mangle: *The shattered glass* lacerated *his hand.* **2** to distress; cause mental anguish to: *Sharp criticism* lacerated *his pride.*

lac·er·a·tion (lăs′ ə rā′ shən) ***n-* 1** a lacerating; tearing. **2** the jagged wound resulting from this.

lace·wing (lās′ wĭng′) ***n-*** any of various insects with four lacelike wings and brilliant eyes.

lach·ry·mal (lă′ krə məl) ***adj-*** of or relating to the glands that secrete tears: *the* lachrymal *ducts.* ***n-*** *pl.* **lachrymals** glands that produce tears. Also **lacrimal.**

lach·ry·mose (lă′ krə mōs′) ***adj-* 1** tearful; weeping. **2** tending to cause tears; sad; mournful: *a* lachrymose *tale of woe.* ***—adv-* lach′ ry·mose′ ly.**

lac·ing (lā′ sĭng) ***n-* 1** a fastening or holding together with a lace or cord. **2** braid, cord, string, or the like, to hold something together or serve as a trimming. **3** *Informal* a sound thrashing.

lack (lăk) ***n-* 1** a being deficient or wanting; shortage: *a* lack *of common sense.* **2** that which is missing or needed: *Honesty is one of the many* lacks *in his character.* ***vt-*** to be without (something wanted or needed); be denied or destitute of: *He* lacks *time to finish. We* lacked *the money to build the cottage.* ***vi-*** to have too little; be incomplete: *He* lacks *in ability and courage.*

lack·a·dai·si·cal (lăk′ ə dā′ zĭ kəl) ***adj-*** listless; lacking spark or spirit; languid: *a* lackadaisical *attitude toward work.* ***—adv-* lack′ a·dai′ si·cal·ly.**

lack·ey (lăk′ ē) ***n-*** [*pl.* **lack·eys**] in earlier times, a footman or male servant, usually in uniform or livery; hence, a servile follower: *a dictator and his* lackeys.

lack·ing (lăk′ ĭng) ***adj-*** not having enough; deficient; wanting: *Money is* lacking *for this project.*

lack·lus·ter (lăk′ lus′ tər) ***adj-*** lacking brightness, sparkle, or vitality: *a* lackluster *smile.*

la·con·ic (lə kon′ ĭk) ***adj-*** using few words; concise; terse; undemonstrative: *He has a* laconic *style of writing.* ***—adv-* la·con′ i·cal·ly.**

lac·quer (lăk′ ər) ***n-*** any of various glossy, quick-drying enamels that are not baked onto the surface they cover. Lacquer was originally made from lac.

lac·ri·mal (lă′ krə məl) lachrymal.

la·crosse (lə krós′) ***n-*** field game played by two teams of ten players each (boys or men) or twelve players each (girls or women), in which the object is to send the ball into the opponents' goal by means of a long-handled racket. [American word from Canadian French **la crosse** meaning literally "the crosier; hooked stick."]

lact-, lacti-, or **lacto-** *combining form* milk. [from Latin **lac, lactis** meaning "milk."]

lac·tase (lăk′ tās′) ***n-*** enzyme of the intestinal juice that accelerates the reaction in which lactose is split into two simpler sugars, including glucose. It also occurs in certain bacteria.

lac·tate (lăk′ tāt′) ***n-*** any salt of lactic acid. ***vi-*** **[lac·tat·ed, lac·tat·ing]** to secrete milk. ***—n-* lac′ ta′ tion.**

lac·te·al (lăk′ tē əl) ***adj-* 1** of or like milk; milky. **2** conveying or containing chyle. ***n-*** any of the tiny vessels that carry chyle.

lac·tic (lăk′ tĭk) ***adj-*** of milk; derived from milk.

lactic acid ***n-*** an organic acid ($C_3H_6O_3$) found in cells and muscle tissue. It is produced from carbohydrate fermentation and is present in sour milk, fermented vegetable juices, etc.

lac·tose (lăk′ tōs′) ***n-*** hard, white, crystalline sugar ($C_{12}H_{22}O_{11}$) that occurs in the milk of all mammals; milk sugar.

la·cu·na (lə kyōō′ nə, -kōō′ nə) ***n-*** [*pl.* **la·cu·nae** (-ē) or **la·cu·nas**] **1** an empty space; blank; gap: *a* lacuna *in the manuscript.* **2** a tiny pit or hollow in bones or tissues.

lac·y (lā′ sē) ***adj-*** **[lac·i·er, lac·i·est]** of or like lace; having a delicate, open pattern. ***—n-* lac′ i·ness.**

lad (lăd) ***n-*** boy or young man.

lad·der (lăd′ ər) ***n-* 1** device of parallel bars or ropes with evenly spaced crosspieces between them, used for climbing. **2** upward path: *the* ladder *of social success.*

ladder truck ***n-*** fire truck carrying ladders of various lengths; especially, an aerial ladder truck equipped with a hydraulically operated extension ladder.

lade (lād) ***vt-*** **[lad·ed, lad·ed** or **lad·en, lad·ing] 1** to load, especially with cargo. **2** to dip (liquid) with a ladle. ***vi-*** to take on cargo. ***Hom-*** laid.

lad·en (lā′ dən) ***adj-* 1** loaded: *a heavily* laden *ship.* **2** weighed down; burdened: *a man* laden *with grief.*

lad·ing (lā′ dĭng) ***n-* 1** the loading of cargo or freight. **2** cargo or freight loaded.

la·dle (lā′ dəl) ***n-*** long-handled bowl-shaped spoon or dipper. ***vt-*** **[la·dled, la·dling]** to use such a spoon; dip. ***—n-* la′ dler.**

Ladle

la·dy (lā′ dē) ***n-*** [*pl.* **la·dies**] **1** a woman: *the* lady *next door; the* lady *in the second row.* **2** woman who is especially polite, well-bred, etc.: *Mrs. Allen is a real* lady. **3** the wife of a man of high standing: *the colonel's* lady. **4 Lady** (1) in Great Britain, title and form of address for a woman of high social rank, either by birth or by marriage to a knight or nobleman. (2) Our Lady.

la·dy·bug (lā′ dē bŭg′) or **la·dy·bird** (lā′ dē bûrd′) ***n-*** round-backed beetle, usually reddish-brown with large black spots. It is valuable as an enemy of harmful insects.

Ladybug

la·dy·fin·ger (lā′ dē fĭng′ gər) ***n-*** small sponge cake of long, thin shape.

lady in waiting ***n-*** woman who attends a queen or princess.

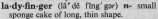

lady·like (lā′ dē līk′) ***adj-*** courteous and neat in a feminine way; well-bred; refined: *a* ladylike *appearance.*

la·dy·love (lā′ dē lŭv′) *n-* sweetheart.

La·dy·ship (lā′ dē shĭp′) *n-* title for Ladies (used with "Her" or "Your"): *Her* Ladyship *is not at home.*

la·dy's-slip·per or **la·dy·slip·per** (lā′ dē slĭp′ ər) *n-* any of a group of wild orchids with a flower that resembles a slipper.

lag (lăg) *vi-* **[lagged, lag·ging] 1** to fail to keep pace; fall back: *The slow runner* lagged *behind the others in the race.* **2** to fall off; slacken: *Interest* lagged *towards the end of the performance.* *vt-* to pitch or shoot (a marble) at a mark. *n-* a falling behind in movement or progress; also, the amount of such falling behind. *—n-* **lag′ ger.**

la·ger (lä′ gər) *n-* beer which is slowly fermented and stored for sedimentation at low temperature. [American word from **lager beer,** from German **lagerbier,** meaning literally "beer laid up (in storage)."]

lag·gard (lăg′ ərd) *n-* one who lags or falls behind; straggler. *adj-* slow; falling behind: *a* laggard *student.* *—adv-* **lag′ gard·ly.** *n-* **lag′ gard·ness.**

la·gniappe or **la·gnappe** (lăn′ yăp′) *Informal* *n-* small complimentary gift to a customer; something extra given for good measure. [American word from Louisiana French, from Spanish **la ñapa** meaning "the gift."]

la·goon (lə go͞on′) *n-* shallow bay or lake, usually connected with the sea; especially, the body of water inside an atoll. For picture, see *atoll.*

laid (lād) *p.t. & p.p.* of [1]**lay.** *Hom-* lade.

lain (lān) *p.t.* of [2]**lie.** *Hom-* lane.

lair (lâr) *n-* den or home of a wild animal.

laird (lârd) *Scottish* *n-* the owner of an estate; lord.

lais·sez faire (lĕs′ ā fâr′, lā′ zā-) *n-* **1** principle of noninterference. **2** in economics, the theory that a government should interfere as little as possible in trade, industry, labor, etc.

la·i·ty (lā′ ə tē) *n-* [*pl.* **la·i·ties**] laymen, especially as distinguished from the clergy.

[1]**lake** (lāk) *n-* large body of water, usually smaller than a sea, surrounded by land. *as* ***modifier***: *a* lake *fish.* [from Latin **lacus.**]

[2]**lake** (lāk) *n-* **1** deep-red pigment made from cochineal or lac; also, the color of this pigment. **2** any of numerous pigments made by combining organic coloring matter with metallic salts. [from French **laque,** from Persian **lāk** meaning originally "lac," from Sanskrit **lākshā.**]

lake dweller *n-* inhabitant of a **lake dwelling,** a house built on piles over a lake, especially in prehistoric times.

lake trout *n-* lake fish common in North America, fished both for sport and for sale.

la·ma (lä′ mə) *n-* Buddhist priest or monk of Tibet or Mongolia.

la·ma·ser·y (lä′ mə sĕr′ ē) *n-* [*pl.* **la·ma·ser·ies**] in Tibet and Mongolia, a monastery of lamas.

lamb (lăm) *n-* **1** young sheep. **2** flesh of this animal, used as food. **3** skin or hide of this animal. **4** gentle, innocent, or helpless person, especially a child. **5 the Lamb** Christ. *vi-* to give birth to lambs. *—adj-* **lamb′ like′.**

Lamb

lam·baste (lăm bāst′) *Slang* *vt-* **[lam·bast·ed, lam·bast·ing] 1** to beat; assault violently. **2** to scold; chastise severely.

lam·bent (lăm′ bənt) *adj-* **1** playing lightly over a surface; flickering: *a* lambent *flame.* **2** softly radiant: *the* lambent *light of stars.* **3** having lightness or brilliance: *a* lambent *sense of humor.* *—n-* **lam′ ben·cy:** *The* lambency *of a full moon.* *adv-* **lam′ bent·ly.**

lamb·kin (lăm′ kĭn) *n-* **1** little lamb. **2** cherished child.

lamb·skin (lăm′ skĭn) *n-* **1** the hide of a lamb, including the wool. **2** leather or parchment made from this skin.

lame (lām) *adj-* **[lam·er, lam·est] 1** crippled or disabled, especially in a leg or foot. **2** stiff; painful: *a* lame *shoulder.* **3** poor; weak: *a* lame *excuse.* *vt-* **[lamed, lam·ing]** to cripple. *—adv-* **lame′ ly.** *n-* **lame′ ness.**

la·mé (lä mā′) *n-* fabric woven of flat gold or silver thread, often brocaded, sometimes mixed with silk or other fiber. *as* ***modifier***: *a* lamé *evening dress.*

lame duck *n-* **1** elected office holder who continues in office for a time after his defeat for reelection and before his successor is installed. **2** ineffectual or inefficient person.

la·ment (lə mĕnt′) *vt-* to feel and express great sorrow over: *to* lament *the death of a friend.* *vi-* to feel and show grief, sorrow, or regret: *to* lament *over a lost cause.* *n-* **1** lamentation. **2** a sorrowful poem or song.

lam·en·ta·ble (lăm′ ən tə bəl) *adj-* **1** to be regretted; sorrowful; mournful: *a* lamentable *sight.* **2** inferior; pitiful: *a* lamentable *recital.* *—adv-* **lam′ en·ta·bly.**

lam·en·ta·tion (lăm′ ən tā′ shən) *n-* **1** expression of sorrow; lament. **2 Lamentations** (takes singular verb) poetical book of the Old Testament attributed to the prophet Jeremiah.

lam·i·na (lăm′ ə nə) *n-* [*pl.* **lam·i·nae** (-nē) or **lam·i·nas**] **1** thin plate, layer, or scale of metal, rock, bone, etc. **2** the blade, or expanded part, of a leaf.

lam·i·nate (lăm′ ə nāt′) *vt-* **[lam·i·nat·ed, lam·i·nat·ing] 1** to roll or compress (metal) into thin sheets. **2** to make by putting together thin layers of more than one material: *to* laminate *plywood.* *n-* (*also* lăm′ ə nət) a product made of many thin layers.

lam·i·na·tion (lăm′ ə nā′ shən) *n-* **1** the process of laminating. **2** laminated structure; arrangement in thin layers. **3** thin layer; lamina.

lamp (lămp) *n-* **1** device containing one or more electric light bulbs and focusing or diffusing their light; also, an electric light bulb. **2** any of various other devices that produce light by combustion, fluorescence, incandescence, etc. **3** vessel with a wick in which alcohol or oil is burned. **4** any of various devices for producing radiation, as a sun lamp. *as* ***modifier***: *a* lamp *shade.*

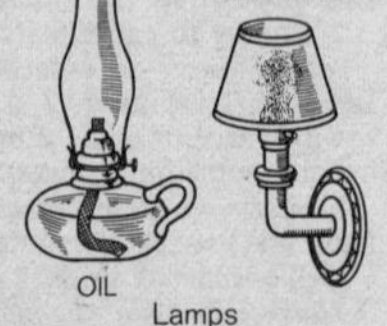

Lamps

lamp·black (lămp′ blăk′) *n-* fine, deep-black soot made by burning oil, gas, etc., and used especially as a pigment in paints and printing ink.

lamp·light·er (lămp′ lī′ tər) *n-* person who lights lamps; especially, in earlier times, someone employed to go about lighting street lamps.

lam·poon (lăm po͞on′) *n-* harsh or malicious piece of writing that attacks and ridicules a person; mocking satire. *vt-* to ridicule; assail: *The critic* lampooned *the play.* *—n-* **lam·poon′ er** or **lam·poon′ ist.**

lam·poon·er·y (lăm′ po͞on′ ə rē) *n-* [*pl.* **lam·poon·er·ies**] the satire of a lampooner: *The* lampoonery *in that cartoon offended many readers.*

lamp·post (lămp′ pōst′) *n-* post that holds a street lamp.

lam·prey (lăm′ prē) *n-* [*pl.* **lam·preys**] any of several eel-like water animals that prey upon fish by means of a round mouth lined with rasping teeth.

Lan·cas·ter (lăng′ kə stər) *n-* family of the English rulers from 1399 to 1461. *—adj-* **Lan′ cas′ tri·an** [lăng′ kăs′ trē ən]: *their* Lancastrian *ancestors.*

lance (lăns) ***n-*** **1** weapon consisting of a long pole or shaft with a sharp metal point. **2** soldier equipped with this weapon. **3** any sharp-pointed instrument resembling this, such as a fish spear, a surgeon's knife, etc. ***vt-*** **[lanced, lanc·ing] 1** to stab or pierce with a long, sharp spear. **2** to cut open (a boil, cyst, etc.).

lance corporal ***n-*** in the Marine Corps, an enlisted man who ranks next below a corporal and next above a private first class.

Lan·ce·lot (lăns′ ə lŏt′) ***n-*** in Arthurian legend, the bravest and ablest knight of the Round Table.

lanc·er (lăn′ sər) ***n-*** **1** mounted soldier armed with a lance. **2 lancers** (takes singular verb) a form of quadrille; also, the music for such a set of dances.

lan·cet (lăn′ sət) ***n-*** small, pointed, two-edged surgical knife.

lance·wood (lăns′ wo͝od′) ***n-*** **1** tough, elastic wood used for fishing rods, carriage shafts, etc. **2** any of various tropical trees yielding this wood.

land (lănd) ***n-*** **1** the surface of the globe not covered by water. **2** country or nation: *to be known throughout the* land; *my native* land. **3** the people of a country or nation: *The whole* land *prayed for him.* **4** soil; ground: *fertile* land. **5** ground held as property: *That* land *belongs to me.* ***vt-*** **1** to set on shore or bring to the ground: *to* land *troops*; *to* land *a plane.* **2** to capture and bring to shore: *to* land *a fish.* **3** *Informal* to win; obtain: *to* land *a prize.* **4** to bring to a destination: *The train will* land *you in New York on time.* **5** to bring to a condition or state: *His conduct* landed *him in trouble.* ***vi-*** **1** to come or go ashore; disembark: *The passengers* landed *at noon.* **2** to alight; come to earth: *The paratroopers* landed *safely.* **3** to arrive in or at a place, condition, or state: *to* land *in jail.* ***—adj-*** **land′ less.**

lan·dau (lăn′ dou′, -dȯ′) ***n-*** **1** four-wheeled carriage with a top in two sections that can be raised or lowered separately. **2** closed automobile having a back seat with a collapsible top.

land breeze ***n-*** breeze blowing from the land toward the sea; offshore breeze.

land·ed (lăn′ dəd) ***adj-*** **1** owning land: *a* landed *proprietor.* **2** consisting of land: *a* landed *estate.*

land·fall (lănd′ fȯl′) ***n-*** sighting of land from the sea or air; also, the land first sighted or reached.

land·form (lănd′ fȯrm′, -fôrm′) ***n-*** natural feature of the earth, such as a canyon, mountain range, etc.

land grant ***n-*** land given by the federal government for railroads, educational institutions, etc. *as* ***modifier*** **(land-grant)**: *a* land-grant *college.*

land·hold·er (lănd′ hōl′ dər) ***n-*** owner or holder of land.

land·hold·ing (lănd′ hōl′ dĭng) ***n-*** a holding or owning of land; also, property in land: *a large* landholding.

land·ing (lăn′ dĭng) ***n-*** **1** a wide step or platform at the end of, or between flights of, stairs. **2** a wharf or pier at which ships may discharge passengers or goods. **3** a coming to land from, or as from, a ship: *the* landing *of Columbus at San Salvador.* **4** the setting down of an airplane at the end of a flight.

landing craft *Military* ***n-*** type of naval craft designed for landing troops, weapons, supplies, etc.

landing field ***n-*** field for airplanes to land or take off.

landing gear ***n-*** apparatus on which a plane lands.

landing stage ***n-*** floating platform at the end of a pier or wharf, used for unloading passengers and freight.

landing strip ***n-*** runway without airport shops, hangars, etc., where planes land and take off; airstrip.

land·la·dy (lănd′ lā′ dē) ***n-*** [*pl.* **land·lad·ies**] **1** woman who runs an inn or rents rooms in her house. **2** woman who rents to others land or houses that she owns. **3** wife of a landlord.

land·locked (lănd′ lŏkt′) ***adj-*** **1** surrounded or nearly surrounded by land: *a* landlocked *bay.* **2** confined to waters shut off from the sea: *a* landlocked *fish.*

land·lord (land′ lȯrd′, -lôrd′) ***n-*** **1** man who rents to others land or houses that he owns. **2** man who runs an inn or rents rooms in a house.

land·lub·ber (lănd′ lŭb′ ər) ***n-*** person who is awkward or inexperienced on shipboard.

land·mark (lănd′ märk′) ***n-*** **1** object, such as a stone or post, that marks a boundary of a tract of land. **2** conspicuous and well-known object which serves as a guide or is characteristic of the area: *The Statue of Liberty is a* landmark. **3** event that is a turning point or is otherwise very important: *a* landmark *in history.*

land mine ***n-*** bomb placed in the ground and, most often, set to explode when it is run over or stepped on.

land office ***n-*** government office for receiving and handling claims to land, especially land being granted free. ***adj-*** **(land-office) 1** of or relating to such an office. **2** vigorous; rushing: *to do a* land-office *business.*

land·own·er (lănd′ ō′ nər) ***n-*** person who owns land.

land-poor (lănd′ po͝or′) ***adj-*** owning tracts of land that do not yield enough income for taxes and other charges.

land reform ***n-*** measures taken to bring about a fairer and wider distribution of farmland.

land·scape (lănd′ skāp′) ***n-*** **1** stretch of scenery that the eye can take in at a glance. **2** painting or other picture showing such a scene. ***vt-*** **[land·scaped, land·scap·ing]** to arrange (grounds, a garden, park, etc.) with trees, shrubs, flowers, etc.

landscape gardener ***n-*** person who designs and arranges pleasing landscapes in parks, around houses, etc. ***—n-*** **landscape gardening:** *to do* landscape gardening.

land·slide (lănd′ slīd′) ***n-*** **1** a slipping of a mass of earth or rock down a steep slope. **2** a mass of falling earth or rock. **3** victory in an election which one side wins by a great majority.

lands·man (lăndz′ mən) ***n-*** [*pl.* **lands·men**] man who lives and works on the land, as distinguished from a seaman.

Land theory ***n-*** theory that color may be perceived by the retina's responding to the differences between longer and shorter wavelengths of light, rather than its having three different color receptors. From these responses, the brain re-creates the full range of colors.

land·ward (lănd′ wərd) ***adj-*** lying or being toward the land; facing the mainland: *The house is on the* landward *side of the island.* ***—adv-*** (also **land′ wards**) to or toward the land: *The shark came* landward.

lane (lān) ***n-*** **1** narrow path or road, especially one between fences, hedges, or walls: *a green country* lane. **2** fixed route or course for ships or planes. **3** a section of a road used for one line of traffic. **4** any narrow way or track, such as a bowling alley. ***Hom-*** lain.

lan·guage (lăng′ gwĭj) ***n-*** **1** all of the systems by which human beings combine sounds into meaningful units, such as words, and these into larger patterns to convey ideas and feelings. **2** any of the several thousand such systems that are or have been used by people belonging to different groups: *the French* language; *the Cherokee* language; *the Hittite* language. (Most of these show family relationships with others.) **3** words and expressions chiefly used within a certain field of knowledge or activity; terminology: *the* language *of science*; *the* language *of baseball*; *the* language *of poetry*. **4** any way or means of communicating: *the* language *of the animals*. **5** the particular words, phrases, and sentences chosen or constructed by a person or group; diction: *to use simple* language; *to admire Shakespeare's* language. ***as modifier***: *a* language *instructor*.

lan·guid (lăng′ gwĭd) ***adj-*** **1** weak or drooping, as if from exhaustion; lacking energy or strength: *Hot weather makes people* languid. **2** lacking briskness, or quickness of movement; slow: *a* languid *walk*. ***—adv-*** **lan′ guid·ly.**

lan·guish (lăng′ gwĭsh) ***vi-*** **1** to lose health, strength, or animation; become weak; droop; fade: *The roses* languished *in the summer heat*. **2** to waste away or suffer under unfavorable conditions: *to* languish *in prison*; *to* languish *in poverty*. **3** to pine (for); long: *The exiles* languished *for their native land*. ***—n-*** **lan′ guish·er.**

lan·guish·ing (lăng′ gwĭsh′ ĭng) ***adj-*** **1** becoming languid; drooping; lacking strength, energy, or alertness. **2** sentimentally dreamy; melancholy: *a* languishing *look*. ***—adv-*** **lan′ guish·ing·ly.**

lan·guor (lang′ gər) ***n-*** **1** weakness; fatigue; listlessness; weariness of body or mind: *The intense heat filled the travelers with* languor. **2** sentimental dreaminess; a soft, tender mood: *a* pleasant *languor*. ***—adj-*** **lan′ guor·ous.** ***adv-*** **lan′ guor·ous·ly.**

lan·gur (läng go͝or′) ***n-*** any of various large, slender, long-tailed Asiatic monkeys.

lank (lăngk) ***adj-*** **1** tall and lean: *a* lank *figure*. **2** of hair, straight and limp. ***—n-*** **lank′ ness.**

lank·y (lăng′ kē) ***adj-*** **[lank·i·er, lank·i·est]** awkwardly tall and thin. ***—adv-*** **lank′ i·ly.** ***n-*** **lank′ i·ness.**

lan·o·lin or **lan·o·line** (lăn′ ə lĭn) ***n-*** natural fatty coating of sheep's wool. It is used in cosmetics, ointments, soaps, etc.

lan·tern (lăn′ tərn) ***n-*** **1** transparent case enclosing a light and protecting it. **2** top story of a lighthouse where the light is kept. **3** structure with open or glazed sides above an opening in a roof for light, ventilation, or decoration.

Electric lantern

lan·tha·nide series (lăn′ thə nīd′) ***n-*** the group of rare-earth elements.

lan·tha·num (lăn′ thə nəm) ***n-*** metallic rare-earth element. Symbol La, At. No. 57, At. Wt. 138.91.

lan·yard (lăn′ yərd) ***n-*** **1** short rope or line used on shipboard for tightening the lines that brace the masts. **2** cord with a hook, used for firing certain types of cannon. **3** cord worn around the neck by sailors for holding a knife or whistle, and by soldiers for attaching a sidearm.

La·oc·o·on (lā ŏk′ ō ŏn′) ***n-*** in Greek legend, a Trojan priest killed with his twin sons by sea serpents after he warned the Trojans against the wooden horse.

[1]**lap** (lăp) ***n-*** **1** the front of a person's body from waist to knees when he sits down; also, the part of the clothing covering this. **2** place or condition in which a person is raised and cared for: *to be reared in the* lap *of luxury*. **3** care or choosing: *His fate was in the* lap *of the gods*. [from Old English **laeppa,** "fold of a garment."]

[2]**lap** (lăp) ***n-*** **1** part of an object that extends over another: *The shingles have a four-inch* lap. *The coat has a wide* lap. **2** one part of a longer distance: *a* lap *of a journey*; *the first* lap *of a race*. ***vt-*** **[lapped, lap·ping]** **1** to lay or fold over, as cloth; wrap: *He* lapped *the coat around her*. **2** to cover something else partially; overlap: *to* lap *one shingle over another*. **3** to polish (a metal surface) to a high gloss. ***vi-*** **1** to extend beyond; partly cover something: *One session* lapped *over into the next*. **2** to be folded: *The cuffs* lap *back*. [from [1]**lap** in a later and different meaning.]

[3]**lap** (lăp) ***vt-*** **[lapped, lap·ping]** **1** to drink as an animal does by taking a liquid into the mouth with the tongue. **2** to splash gently against: *The sea* laps *the shore*. ***vi-*** to make a splashing, rippling sound: *The waves* lapped *against the side of the boat*. ***n-***: *the* lap *of water in a pool*. [from Old English **lapian.**] ***—n-*** **lap′ per.**

lap dog ***n-*** small pet dog.

la·pel (lə pĕl′) ***n-*** part of a coat, jacket, or dress formed by a continuation of the collar and turned back on the chest.

Lapel

lap·i·dar·y (lăp′ ə dĕr′ ē) ***n-*** [*pl.* **lap·i·dar·ies**] skilled workman who cuts and sets precious stones. ***adj-*** **1** of or relating to precious stones or the act of cutting them. **2** of or relating to engraved inscriptions, especially on stone monuments.

lap·in (lă′ pən) ***n-*** rabbit fur, usually sheared and dyed.

lap·is laz·u·li (lăp′ ĭs lăz′ ə lē, -lăz′ yə lī′) ***n-*** an opaque semiprecious stone, usually of bright azure blue.

Lapp (lăp) ***n-*** **1** (also **Lap′ land′ er**) a native or inhabitant of Lapland. **2** (also **Lapp′ ish**) the language of the Lapps.

lap robe ***n-*** blanket to keep the lap and legs warm.

lapse (lăps) ***n-*** **1** slight error or mistake; slip; momentary failure: *a* lapse *of the tongue*; *a* lapse *of memory*. **2** a slipping back; a return to wrong or sinful ways: *a* lapse *from true belief*; *a* lapse *into crime*; *a* lapse *into savagery*. **3** a falling, passing, or slipping away gradually; also, a falling into disuse: *a* lapse *into silence*; *the* lapse *of a local custom*. **4** passage (of time). **5** loss of a claim, right, etc., through failure to use or renew it: *the* lapse *of a contract*. ***vi-*** **[lapsed, laps·ing]** **1** to fall away from what is right or what is good; backslide: *to* lapse *into heresy*. **2** to glide or slip slowly away; fall or sink gradually: *to* lapse *into silence*; *to* lapse *into a coma*. **3** to fall into disuse; disappear: *Many local customs have* lapsed *in this century*. **4** to end or pass to another because of failure to fulfill certain conditions: *His lease* lapsed *when he didn't pay the rent*.

lap·wing (lăp′ wĭng′) ***n-*** crested plover of Europe and Asia with an iridescent green and violet back and a white breast, noted for its flapping flight and wailing cry.

lar·board (lär′ bərd) *Archaic* ***n-*** left side of the ship when one faces the bow; port. ***adj-*** pertaining to the left, or port, side of a ship.

lar·ce·nous (lär′ sə nəs) ***adj-*** **1** guilty of theft: *a* larcenous *act*. **2** having to do with larceny. ***—adv-*** **lar′ ce·nous·ly.**

lar·ce·ny (lär′ sə nē) ***n-*** [*pl.* **lar·cen·ies**] ***n-*** the unlawful taking away of another's property; theft; stealing.

larch (lärch) ***n-*** **1** any of several varieties of the pine tree with small cones and needlelike leaves that drop in the fall. **2** the tough, hard wood of this tree.

lard (lärd) ***n-*** white, greasy substance made from the fat of hogs and used in cooking. ***vt-*** **1** to smear with fat or grease. **2** to insert strips of fat, usually bacon, into (meat) before roasting. **3** to enrich: *to* lard *a story with jokes*.

lard·er (lär′ dər) ***n-*** **1** place where meat and other foods are kept; pantry. **2** a supply or stock of food.

large (lärj) ***adj-*** [**larg·er, larg·est**] **1** big; great in size, quantity, capacity, etc.: *a* large *dog; a* large *fortune.* **2** having greater size, capacity, quantity, etc. than another: *I want the* large *size.* **3** not small or petty; broad in understanding and sympathy: *a man of* large *and generous nature.* ***adv-***: *Write* large. ***—n-*** **large'ness.**

at large 1 free; out of prison: *The escaped convict is still* at large. **2** chosen to represent a whole section instead of one of its districts: *a congressman* at large.

large intestine See *intestine.*

large·ly (lärj'lē) ***adv-*** **1** to a great extent; for the most part: *He is* largely *to blame.* **2** generously; abundantly: *The foundation is* largely *endowed.*

large-scale (lärj'skāl') ***adj-*** **1** showing things at or nearly at their true size: *a* large-scale *drawing.* **2** of maps, showing a relatively short distance on the ground with a relatively long distance on the map, and thus permitting small details to be shown. **3** big in scope, size, or range.

lar·gess or **lar·gesse** (lär jĕs') ***n-*** **1** liberal giving; also a generous gift. **2** generosity of mind or spirit.

lar·go (lär'gō) *Music* ***adj- & adv-*** slow; stately; slower than lento.

lar·i·at (lăr'ē ət) ***n-*** long rope with a sliding noose, used to catch horses or cattle or to tether them; lasso. [American word from Spanish **la reata,** "the rope."]

¹lark (lärk) ***n-*****1** any of a group of small, European songbirds, especially the skylark. **2** a similar North American bird, the meadowlark. [from Old English **lœwerce, lāferce.** In Scotland "laverock" is still used for "lark."]

²lark (lärk) ***n-*** amusing adventure; frolic; prank. [apparently a variant of Middle English **lake, laik** meaning "to frolic," and influenced by **¹lark.**]

lark·spur (lärk'spûr') ***n-*** any of several wild or cultivated plants with finely divided clusters of leaves and small white, pink, or, especially, blue flowers in spikes.

lar·va (lär'və) ***n-*** [*pl.* **lar·vae** (**-vē**)] **1** The second stage in the life cycle of insects having a complete metamorphosis. A larva is wingless, immature and usually wormlike, completely unlike the adult. **2** the early form of certain other animals which change in form as they develop: *The tadpole is the* larva *of frogs and toads.* ***—adj-*** **lar'val.**

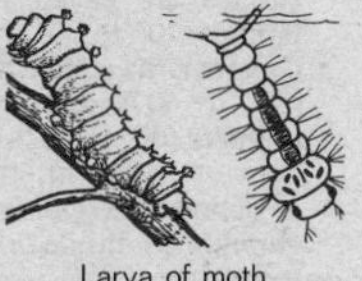

Larva of moth and mosquito

lar·yn·gi·tis (lăr'ən jī'təs) ***n-*** inflammation of the larynx, marked by hoarseness or loss of voice.

lar·ynx (lăr'ĭngks) ***n-*** [*pl.* **la·ryn·ges** (lə rĭn'jēz') or **lar·ynx·es**] enlargement of the upper part of the windpipe that in man and most mammals contains the vocal cords. ***—adj-*** **la·ryn'ge·al** (lə rĭn'jəl): *a* laryngeal *inflammation.*

la·sa·gna (lə zän'yə) ***n-*** baked dish of broad, flat noodles layered with tomato sauce, meat, and cheese. [from Italian **lasagna,** from Greek **lasanon** meaning "a cooking pot."]

las·civ·i·ous (lə sĭv'ē əs) ***adj-*** sensual; lewd; lustful ***—adv-*** **las·civ'i·ous·ly.** ***n-*** **las·civ'i·ous·ness.**

la·ser (lā'zər) ***n-*** device that generates a single frequency of intense, polarized light, all of whose waves are in phase with each other. [shortened from *l*ight *a*mplification by *s*timulated *e*mission *r*adiation.] ***Hom-*** lazar.

¹lash (lăsh) ***n-*** **1** the flexible part of a whip; thong. **2** stroke given with a whip. **3** one of the small hairs along the edge of the eyelid; eyelash. ***vt-*** **1** to strike with a whip: *It used to be common punishment to* lash *criminals.* **2** to switch to and fro: *The caged lion* lashed *its tail.* **3** to beat; strike violently: *The wind* lashed *the trees.* **4** to rebuke or scold severely; castigate: *He* lashed *me with a torrent of angry words.* **5** to stir up; arouse: *The speaker* lashed *the crowd into a frenzy.* [of uncertain origin.]

lash out to attack, especially with words; strike out.

²lash (lăsh) ***vt-*** to fasten with a cord or rope: *The Indians* lashed *poles together to make the framework for a tepee.* ***n-*** the cord or rope itself. [perhaps from Old French **lace** meaning "a lace; a tie."]

¹lash·ing (lăsh'ĭng) ***n-*** a whipping. [from **¹lash.**]

²lash·ing (lăsh'ĭng) ***n-*** **1** act of binding. **2** cord, rope, etc., used for binding. **3 lashings** bindings. [from **²lash.**]

lass (lăs) ***n-*** girl; young woman.

lass·ie (lăs'ē) ***n-*** girl; young woman; lass.

las·si·tude (lăs'ə tōōd', -tyōōd') ***n-*** weariness of mind or body; lack of energy; listlessness.

las·so (lăs'ō) ***n-*** [*pl.* **las·sos** or **las·soes**] noosed rope used by cowboys to catch cattle, etc.; lariat. ***vt-*** to catch with such a rope.

Cowboy twirling lasso

¹last (lăst) ***adj-*** **1** coming after all others in time, place, order, etc.; final: *The* last *letter of the alphabet is z.* **2** directly before the present: *the dance* last *night.* **3** most recent: *The* last *time I saw him was yesterday.* **4** being only one remaining: *the* last *cookie in the jar.* **5** least likely; least fitted: *He is the* last *man for such a job.* ***adv-*** **1** after all others: *The slowest runner comes in* last *in the race.* **2** most recently: *When did you* last *go to the dentist?* ***n-*** **1** person, thing, or part that is at the end: *the* last *of his family; the* last *of the story.* **2** end: *to be loyal to the* last. [from Old English **latost,** "latest."]

at last finally. **at the last minute** at the latest possible time. **breathe one's last** to die. **see the last of** to see for the last time.

²last (lăst) ***vi-*** **1** to go on; continue: *The rain* lasted *three days.* **2** to be enough; hold out: *This much bread ought to* last *for two days.* **3** to hold up; endure: *Stone buildings* last *longer than wooden ones.* [from Old English **læstan,** "follow in the track of; continue," from Old English **lāst,** "footstep; track." It is related to **³last.**]

³last (lăst) ***n-*** model or form in the shape of the foot, on which shoes are made or repaired. [from Old English **læst,** "a boot," from Old English **lāst,** "a footstep."]

stick to (one's) last to stay within (one's) own field of knowledge and skill; mind (one's) own business.

last·ing (lăs'tĭng) ***adj-*** keeping up or continuing a long time; enduring; permanent: *a* lasting *friendship.* ***—adv-*** **last'ing·ly.** ***n-*** **las'ting·ness.**

Last Judgment ***n-*** in some religions, the final judging of every person at the end of the world.

last·ly (lăst'lē) ***adv-*** finally; in conclusion; at the end: *And* lastly, *we shall sum up what we learned.*

last quarter ***n-*** the third phase of the moon, between the full moon and the new moon. For picture, see *moon.*

last rites ***n- pl.*** **1** in some religions, the last sacraments administered to the gravely ill or the dying. **2** religious observances proper to death or at funerals.

---

fāte, făt, dâre, bärn; bē, bĕt, mêre; bīte, bĭt; nōte, hŏt, môre, dȯg; fŭn, fûr; tōō, bŏŏk; oil; out; tar; thin; th̶en; hw for wh as in *wh*at; zh for s as in u*s*ual; ə for a, e, i, o, u, as in *a*go, lin*e*n, per*i*l, at*o*m, min*u*s

last straw ***n-*** the last of a series of irritations, which provokes a reaction from the sufferer.

Last Supper ***n-*** Christ's last meal with his disciples.

last word ***n-*** **1** final expression in an exchange of words. **2** final decision. **3** authoritative treatment or statement: *This book is the* last *word on politics.* **4** *Informal* the most up-to-date thing of its kind.

lat. latitude.

latch (lăch) ***n-*** **1** locking device consisting of a bar pivoted at one end, the free end of which may be raised from or lowered into a notch to fasten a door, etc. **2** any of several devices used for a similar purpose: *a window* latch. ***vt-*** to fasten; lock: *Please* latch *the screen door.*

Latch on door

on the latch fastened only with a latch; not locked.

latch·key (lăch′ kē′) ***n-*** key that unlocks a latch, especially at the main entrance of a dwelling.

latch·string (lăch′ strĭng′) ***n-*** string that, passed through a hole in a door, releases the inside latch from outside.

late (lāt) ***adj-*** **[lat·er, lat·est] 1** after the usual or expected time: *Spring is* late *this year.* **2** tardy: *He was* late *for work today.* **3** during the final or latter part; toward the end: *The leaves began to fall in* late *autumn.* **4** of recent time or date; happening not long ago: *the* late *floods; his* late *illness.* **5** no longer living: *the* late *Mr. Barnes.* ***adv-*** **1** after the usual or expected time; tardily: *She arrived* late. **2** at or toward an advanced time: *Spring came* late. **—*n-* late′ ness.**

of late lately: *He has been rather absent-minded* of late.

late·com·er (lāt′ kŭm′ ər) ***n-*** person or thing that arrives late, or after most others.

la·teen sail (lə tēn′) ***n-*** three-cornered sail attached to a yard that slants across a low mast.

Late Latin ***n-*** a form of Latin used by writers from the third to the sixth centuries A.D.

Lateen sails

late·ly (lāt′ lē) ***adv-*** not long ago; recently: *His work has improved* lately.

la·tent (lā′ tənt) ***adj-*** hidden; present but not active: *his* latent *strength; a* latent *talent for the theater; a* latent *disease.* **—*n-* la′ ten·cy**: *The disease remained undetected during the period of* latency. ***adv-*** **la′ tent·ly.**

lat·er·al (lăt′ ər əl) ***adj-*** of, at, or coming from the side: *a* lateral *pass.* **—*adv-* lat′ er·al·ly.**

la·tex (lā′ tĕks′) ***n-*** any of several milky juices found in various plants and trees, from which various products are made. Natural rubber is made from the latex of one kind of tropical tree.

lath (lăth) ***n-*** one of the thin, narrow strips of wood fastened to the frame of a building and used to support the plaster of walls and ceilings.

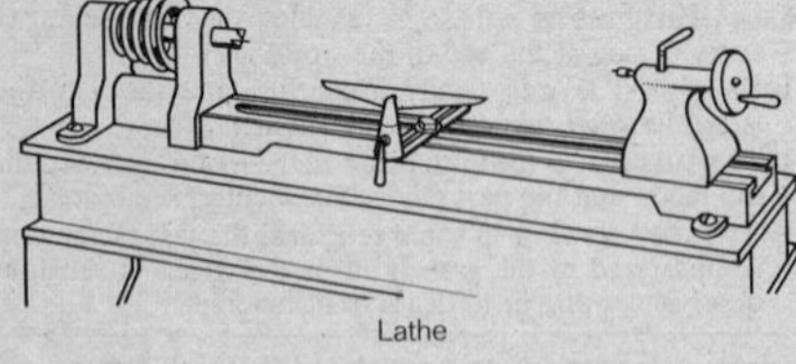

Lathe

lathe (lāth) ***n-*** machine for holding a piece of wood, metal, etc., and spinning it against a shaping tool.

lath·er (lăth′ ər) ***n-*** **1** foam made from soap and water. **2** foamy sweat of a horse. ***vt-*** to cover with a froth or foam: *She* lathered *her hair with shampoo.* ***vi-*** to make a froth or foam: *Most soap won't* lather *in salt water.* **—*n-* lath′ er·er.**

lath·ing (lăth′ ĭng, lāth′-) ***n-*** **1** framework of laths, used to support plaster on walls. **2** act of putting such a framework in place.

Lat·in (lăt′ ən) ***adj-*** **1** of or relating to ancient Rome (Latium), its people, their culture, or their language. **2** of or relating to people whose language is that of France, Italy, Portugal, and Spain. **3** of or belonging to the Roman Catholic Church, as distinguished from the Eastern Christian churches. ***n-*** **1** the language of ancient Rome, and until recently the principal language of the Catholic Church. **2** member of a people whose language is derived from Latin or who live in Latin America. **3** inhabitant of ancient Latium.

Latin American ***n-*** native or inhabitant of Latin America. ***adj-*** **(Latin-American)**: *in current* Latin-American *literature.*

Latin cross ***n-*** right-angle cross with the horizontal bar crossing a longer vertical bar near the top. For picture, see [1]*cross.*

Lat·in·ist (lăt′ ən ĭst) ***n-*** someone well versed or specializing in the Latin language; Latin scholar.

Latin Quarter ***n-*** section of Paris, south of the Seine, frequented by students and artists.

lat·i·tude (lăt′ ə to͞od′, -tyo͞od′) ***n-*** **1** distance north or south of the equator measured in degrees, represented on maps or globes by lines parallel to the equator. Regions of the earth's surface are called the **low latitudes** (0° to 30° from the equator), the **middle latitudes** (30° to 60°), and the **high latitudes** (60° to 90°). **2** freedom of judgment, thought, or action; freedom from restrictions: *The diplomat was given wide* latitude *in negotiating the treaty.*

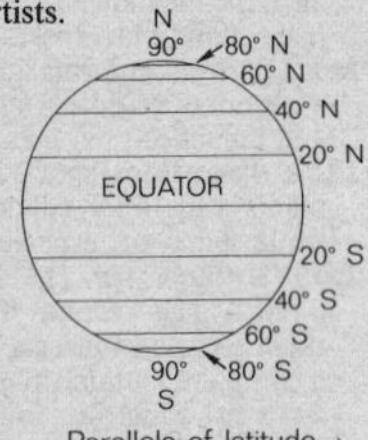

Parallels of latitude

la·trine (lə trēn′) ***n-*** toilet, especially one in a military camp.

lat·ter (lăt′ ər) ***adj-*** **1** the second of two people or things mentioned: *We measured Sam and Henry, and found the* latter *was taller.* **2** later; near the end: *I shall be going shopping the* latter *part of the week.*

►LATTER is used with "former" to mean the second of a pair: *I know both Professor James and Professor Eliot; I met the* former (i.e., Prof. James) *in Cambridge and the* latter (i.e., Prof. Eliot) *in Washington.* LATER is only used in a time sense: *It is* later *than you think.*

Lat·ter-day Saint (lăt′ ər dā′) ***n-*** Mormon.

lat·ter·ly (lat′ ər lē) ***adv-*** recently; of late; lately.

lat·tice (lăt′ əs) ***n-*** **1** framework of crossed parallel strips of wood, metal, etc., with space between them for air or light. **2** door, gate, window, etc., made of such a framework. ***vt-*** **[lat·ticed, lat·tic·ing]**: *to* lattice *a door; to* lattice *a porch.*

lat·ticed (lăt′ əst) ***adj-*** made of or having lattice: *a* latticed *gate.*

Lattice

lat·tice·work (lăt′ əs wûrk′) ***n-*** lattices collectively, especially those in doors, furniture, windows, etc. *as **modifier**: a* latticework *chair.*

laud (lȯd) ***vt-*** to praise; extol: *We* lauded *the writer for his excellent book.* ***n-*** **lauds** (or **Lauds**) prayers of praise, which, together with Matins, form the first of the canonical hours.

laud·a·ble (lȯd′ ə bəl) ***adj-*** praiseworthy; deserving of esteem: *a* laudable *achievement.* **—*adv-* laud′ a·bly.**

lau·da·num (lȯ′ də nəm) ***n-*** solution of opium in alcohol.

laud·a·tor·y (lȯ′ də tôr′ ē) ***adj-*** containing or giving praise; commendatory: *a* laudatory *remark.*

laugh (lăf) ***vi-*** **1** to make sounds and facial movements to express joy, amusement, scorn, etc. (at or over): *Everybody* laughed *at the joke.* ***vt-*** to move or affect (someone) by laughing; cause (something to happen) as a result of laughing: *We* laughed *him out of his bad mood. Just* laugh *your troubles away.* ***n-*** series of sounds and facial movements expressing joy, amusement, etc.

laugh off to disregard as unimportant; shrug off.

laugh on the other side of the mouth (or **face**) to regret one's amusement later.

laugh up one's sleeve to laugh secretly or privately, especially at someone's mistake.

laugh·a·ble (lăf′ ə bəl) ***adj-*** provoking laughter; amusing; comical (often used to show disfavor): *Her efforts to be sophisticated were* laughable. **—*adv-* laugh′ a·bly.**

laugh·ing (lăf′ ĭng) ***adj-*** **1** uttering laughter. **2** full of or calling forth laughter: *This is no* laughing *matter.*

laughing gas ***n-*** nitrous oxide.

laughing stock ***n-*** an object of laughter or scorn.

laugh·ter (lăf′ tər) ***n-*** act or sound of laughing.

[1]**launch** (lȯnch) ***n-*** **1** formerly, the largest boat carried by a warship. **2** motor-driven pleasure boat, usually without a deck or partly decked. [from Spanish **lancha** of the same meaning.]

Launch

[2]**launch** (lȯnch) ***vt-*** **1** to lower or cause (a vessel) to be lowered into the water, especially for the first time; set afloat. **2** to start off; begin: *to* launch *a new business*; *to* launch *an attack.* **3** to hurl; cause to go forth with force: *to* launch *a glider; to* launch *a rocket.* [from Old French **lancier** meaning "to throw a lance," from Latin **lancea,** "a lance."] **—*n-* launch′ er.**

launch into to begin with vigor.

launch out to begin something uncertain or hazardous.

launching pad ***n-*** platform from which a rocket or missile is launched.

laun·der (lȯn′ dər, lŏn′-) ***vt-*** to wash and iron: *to* launder *a dress.* ***vi-***: *This linen* launders *well.* **—*n-* laun′ der·er.**

laun·dress (lȯn′ drəs, lŏn′-) ***n-*** woman who makes a living by washing and ironing clothes.

laun·dro·mat (lȯn′ drə măt′) ***n-*** commercial laundry, usually self-service, with coin-operated washing and drying machines. [from **Laundromat,** trademark.]

laun·dry (lȯn′ drē, lŏn′-) ***n-*** [*pl.* **laun·dries**] **1** clothes and linens to be washed. **2** place where clothes and linens are washed; also, a business engaged in such work.

laun·dry·man (lȯn′ drē mən, lŏn′-) ***n-*** [*pl.* **laun·dry·men**] man who works for a laundry, especially to collect and deliver laundry.

laun·dry·wo·man (lȯn′ drē wo͝om′ ən) ***n-*** [*pl.* **laun·dry·wo·men**] laundress.

lau·re·ate (lȯr′ ē ət) ***n-*** person to whom an award or other honor has been given for achievement in arts or science; especially, a poet laureate.

lau·re·ate·ship (lȯr′ ē ət shĭp′) ***n-*** the position of poet laureate; also, the time during which one holds this.

lau·rel (lȯr′ əl) ***n-*** **1** evergreen shrub with glossy leaves, used by the ancient Greeks and Romans to make crowns of honor for heroes and poets. Its leaves, called bay leaves, are used to flavor food. **2** mountain laurel. **3 laurels** fame and honor. **—*adj-* lau′ reled:** *his* laureled *brow.*

look to (one's) laurels to beware of losing one's high position. **rest on (one's) laurels** to be satisfied with past achievements and not work for new ones.

la·va (lăv′ ə, lä′ və) ***n-*** **1** melted rock flowing from a volcano. **2** such rock when hardened.

la·va-la·va (lä′ və lä′ və) ***n-*** rectangular cotton printed cloth worn in Polynesia as a skirt.

la·va·liere (lăv′ ə lêr′) ***n-*** ornament strung on a fine chain and worn as a necklace.

lav·a·to·ry (lăv′ ə tôr′ ē) ***n-*** [*pl.* **la·va·to·ries**] **1** room with a basin or basins for washing the hands and face, and a toilet. **2** basin with faucets, for washing.

lave (lāv) *Archaic* ***vt-*** [**lav·ed, lav·ing**] to wash; bathe.

lav·en·der (lăv′ ən dər) ***n-*** **1** pale-purple or pale-violet color. **2** plant with pale-purple flowers and narrow woolly leaves, cultivated for its oil which is much used for perfume. **3** dried leaves and flowers of this plant, used to scent linens. ***adj-***: *a* lavender *dress*; *a* lavender *scent.*

lav·ish (lăv′ ĭsh) ***adj-*** giving freely or too freely: *to be* lavish *with money*; *to be* lavish *of praise.* ***vt-*** to give or spend freely and generously: *to* lavish *money on the poor.* **—*adv-* lav′ ish·ly. *n-* lav′ ish·ness.**

law (lȯ) ***n-*** **1** a rule or regulation set up by a government to be followed by all of the people under its authority; ordinance: *Congress makes* laws *for the nation.* **2** the body of laws and regulations set up by a government: *The Constitution is the basic* law *of the United States.* **3** the study or practice of law: *to choose* law *as a profession.* **4** the working of the law: *to keep* law *and order.* **5** any custom, rule, or regulation followed and generally accepted by a group of people. **6** in science and philosophy, statement of what happens under certain conditions: *the* law *of gravity.* **7** *Informal* the police. **8 the Law** first five books of the Old Testament. *as **modifier***: *a* law *student*; *a* law *firm.*

lay down the law to express one's wishes very firmly.

law-a·bid·ing (lȯ′ ə bī′ dĭng) ***adj-*** observing the laws and customs of society. **—*adv-* law′-a·bid′ ing·ly.**

law·break·er (lȯ′ brā′ kər) ***n-*** one who breaks the law. **—*n-* law′ break′ ing.**

law·ful (lȯ′ fəl) ***adj-*** **1** allowed or recognized by the law: *a* lawful *claim.* **2** according to law; right, not wrong: *his* lawful *acts.* **—*adv-* law′ ful·ly. *n-* law′ ful·ness.**

law·giv·er (lȯ′ gĭv′ ər) ***n-*** one who invents and enacts a code of law: *Solon was a famous Greek* lawgiver.

law·less (lȯ′ ləs) ***adj-*** **1** without laws: *a* lawless *country.* **2** not obeying the laws: *a* lawless *bandit.* **—*adv-* law′ less·ly. *n-* law′ less·ness.**

law·mak·er (lȯ′ mā′ kər) ***n-*** person who has a part in enacting laws; legislator.

law·mak·ing (lȯ′ mā′ kĭng) ***n-*** the enacting of laws; legislation. *as **modifier***: *a* lawmaking *assembly.*

law·man (lȯ′ mən) ***n-*** [*pl.* **law·men**] sheriff or other peace officer.

[1]**lawn** (lȯn) ***n-*** stretch of ground covered with grass that is kept closely cut, especially such ground near or around a house. [from earlier **laund,** from Old French **launde** meaning "wooded ground."]

[2]lawn (lôn) ***n-*** thin, fine cloth, usually of cotton or linen. [from an earlier English phrase, **laune lynen,** meaning "linen from Laon." Laon is the French town where it was first woven.]

lawn mower ***n-*** machine used to cut grass.

law·ren·ci·um (lô rĕn'sē əm) ***n-*** radioactive, metal, man-made element. Symbol Lw, At. No. 103.

law·suit (lô'sōōt') ***n-*** question or claim to be decided in a court of law.

law·yer (lô'yər) ***n-*** person trained in the law and engaged in it as a profession; attorney.

lax (lăks) ***adj-*** **1** careless; negligent; not strict: *to have* lax *morals;* lax *behavior;* lax *discipline.* **2** not tight or firm; loose; slack: *a* lax *rope.* ***—adv-*** **lax'ly.** ***n-*** **lax'ness.**

lax·a·tive (lăk'sə tĭv) ***n-*** medicine or remedy used to make the bowels move. ***adj-:*** *a* laxative *food.*

lax·i·ty (lăk'sə tē) ***n-*** [*pl.* **lax·i·ties**] lack of strictness or carefulness: *a* laxity *of discipline.*

[1]lay (lā) ***vt-*** [**laid** (lād), **lay·ing**] **1** to put or place: *to* lay *a book on the table*; *to* lay *one's hand on someone's shoulder; to* lay *great stress on education.* **2** to put down in a certain position or place: *to* lay *linoleum; to* lay *bricks*; *to* lay *a submarine cable.* **3** to bring or beat down: *One blow* laid *him on the floor.* **4** to put down or quiet; settle: *to* lay *the dust by sprinkling.* **5** to impose: *to* lay *a tax.* **6** to charge: *to* lay *an accusation*; *to* lay *the blame for an accident.* **7** to assert; put forward; to give for examination: *to* lay *claim to the fortune*; *to* lay *one's case before the authorities.* **8** to prepare: *to* lay *careful plans.* **9** to bring into a particular state: *The wind* laid *the branches bare.* **10** to produce (eggs): *Ants* lay *eggs.* **11** to bet: *to* lay *a wager.* **12** to set in time or place: *to* lay *a scene in colonial times.* ***vi-*** to produce eggs. [from Old English **lecgan** meaning literally "to make lie," from **licgan** meaning **[2]lie.**] ***Hom-*** lei.

lay of the land layout of the land or general situation.

lay about to strike out in all directions.

lay aside **1** to put down or away: *to* lay *one's work* aside. **2** to save for future needs: *to* lay *money* aside.

lay away **1** to save: *to* lay *money* away. **2** to set something aside until paid for.

lay by to save: *to* lay by *money for a vacation.*

lay down **1** to proclaim forcefully; assert: *to* lay down *the rules.* **2** to give up or sacrifice (one's life). **3** to give as partial payment: *Mr. Jones* laid down *$500 toward the purchase of a car.*

lay for *Slang* to wait for.

lay hold on to get a grip on.

lay in to store: *Squirrels* lay in *food for the winter.*

lay into *Slang* to attack (a person) verbally or physically.

lay off **1** to put out of work temporarily; discharge: *He* laid off *the workers while the factory was being rebuilt.* **2** to mark off. **3** *Slang* to refrain from.

lay low **1** to knock down. **2** to defeat or kill. **3** *Informal* lie low.

lay on **1** to apply; spread: *to* lay *the paint* on *in a thin coat.* **2** to strike; hit: *to* lay on *with blows.*

lay (oneself) out to take pains; make an effort.

lay open to cut open.

lay out **1** to mark off; plot: *to* lay out *a garden.* **2** to spend: *to* lay out *money.*

lay to to go at something; apply oneself with vigor.

lay up **1** to put aside; store: *to* lay up *a supply of groceries.* **2** to cause to stay in bed, or be inactive because of illness or injury.

►For usage note see LIE.

[2]lay (lā) *p.t.* of **[2]lie.** ***Hom-*** lei.

[3]lay (lā) ***adj-*** **1** having to do with a person who is not a clergyman: *a* lay *assistant to the minister.* **2** of a person, outside any profession: *In legal matters it is better to have expert advice than a* lay *opinion.* [from Old French **lai,** from Latin **lāicus,** from Greek **lāïkos,** from **lāos** meaning "people."] ***Hom-*** lei.

[4]lay (lā) ***n-*** short poem or song. [probably from Old French **lai,** of Celtic origin.] ***Hom-*** lei.

lay·er (lā'ər) ***n-*** **1** one thickness of a material spread over a surface: *the outer* layer *of skin; the* layers *of the earth.* **2** someone or something that lays: *a hen that's a good* layer; *a brick*layer. ***—adj-*** **lay'ered.** ***n-*** **lay'er·ing.**

layer cake ***n-*** a cake, usually frosted, made in layers held together by a sweet filling.

lay·ette (lā ĕt') ***n-*** outfit of clothes and equipment for a newborn baby.

lay·man (lā'mən) ***n-*** [*pl.* **lay·men**] **1** person who is not an expert on a subject: *Even a* layman *can understand this book on rockets.* **2** person who is a church member, but not a clergyman. ***—n-*** *fem.* **lay'wom'an.**

lay·off (lā'ôf') ***n-*** **1** temporary discharge of workers. **2** period of such unemployment.

lay·out (lā'out') ***n-*** **1** a planning or arranging. **2** the plan or arrangement itself. **3** design of written matter and illustrations which is prepared for printing. **4** *Informal* situation; setup; organization.

lay·o·ver (lā'ō'vər) ***n-*** stopover; an interruption of a particular length in a journey.

laz·ar (lā'zər, lăz'ər) *Archaic* ***n-*** beggar suffering from a disease; especially, a leper. ***Hom-*** laser.

Laz·a·rus (lăz'ər əs) ***n-*** **1** in the New Testament, the brother of Martha and Mary raised from the dead by Jesus. **2** in one of the parables, a sick beggar who after death was taken up into Abraham's bosom.

laze (lāz) ***vi-*** [**lazed, laz·ing**] to loaf: *to* laze *in the sun.*

la·zy (lā'zē) ***adj-*** [**laz·i·er, laz·i·est**] **1** not inclined to work; slothful. **2** slow moving; sluggish: *the* lazy *river.* **3** relaxing: *a* lazy *day.* ***—adv-*** **la'zi·ly.** ***n-*** **la'zi·ness.**

lb. pound; pounds.

l.c. **1** lower case. **2** left center.

L.D.S. Latter-day Saints.

lea (lē) *Archaic* ***n-*** meadow; pasture land. ***Hom-*** lee.

leach (lēch) ***vt-*** **1** to cause (a liquid) to drip or percolate through some material: *to* leach *water through wood ashes to obtain lye.* **2** to wash with water to extract the soluble substances. **3** to extract by percolation: *to* leach *lye from ashes.* ***vi-*** to be extracted or dissolved out by this process. ***Hom-*** leech.

[1]lead (lēd) ***vt-*** [**led** (lĕd), **lead·ing**] **1** to go before to show the way: *He* led *the troops through the valley.* **2** to guide or conduct, by either the hand or some connecting thing: *The boy* led *the horse by the reins.* **3** to go at the head of; be first in: *The color guard* leads *the parade.* **4** to command or direct: *A general* leads *an army. A conductor* leads *an orchestra.* **5** to influence or guide in an opinion or action: *What* led *you to do that?* **6** to live; pass; spend: *to* lead *a good life.* ***vi-*** **1** to guide along a way: *You* lead *and I'll follow.* **2** to extend or conduct: *This road* leads *to the river.* ***n-*** **1** the first place; the position ahead: *to take the* lead *in a race.* **2** the amount by which one is ahead: *a ten-foot* lead. **3** influence; guidance: *He usually follows his sister's* lead. **4** clue; tip; hint: *The footprints were a* lead *in solving the crime.* **5** chief part in a play; also, chief actor. **6** main electric power line to a house, appliance, etc. [from Old English **lædan,** "to cause to go," from **lithan,** "to go."] ***Hom-*** lied.

lead off to begin: *We* led off *the rally with songs.*

lead on to encourage someone in an unwise or mistaken course; to entice insincerely.

lead up to to bring about; pave the way for: *the events that* lead up to *a war.*

[2]lead (lĕd) ***n-*** **1** soft, gray, heavy metal element. Its chief ore is galena, and it is used in piping, solder, and radiation shielding. Symbol Pb, At. No. 82, At. Wt. 207.19. **2** the baked mixture of powdered graphite and clay used in the form of rods in pencils. **3** in printing, one of the thin strips of metal used for spacing between lines. **4** small mass of metal used on the end of a line for finding the depth of water. **5 leads** metal framework for windows with small panes of clear or stained glass. [from Old English **lēad.**] ***Hom-*** led.

lead·en (lĕd′ən) ***adj-*** **1** made of lead. **2** hard to move; heavy: *His legs were* leaden *from fatigue.* **3** sluggish; dull; depressed: *the team's* leaden *spirits after defeat.* **4** dull gray: *a* leaden *sky.* **—*adv-* lead′en·ly.**

lead·er (lē′dər) ***n-*** **1** person who guides, conducts, or directs: *an orchestra* leader. **2** person who holds the first place or is fitted to do so: *a born* leader. **3** length of gut, plastic, or wire used between a fishing line and the hook or lure. **—*adj-* lead′er·less.**

lead·er·ship (lē′dər shĭp′) ***n-*** **1** ability to lead. **2** guidance. **3** position of a leader.

lead·ing (lē′dĭng) ***n-*** a guiding or conducting; guidance; direction. ***adj-*** **1** guiding; directing. **2** first or among the first in achievement, quality, sales, etc.; foremost.

leading question ***n-*** question so expressed as to draw forth or suggest the answer desired by the asker.

Types of leaf

leaf (lēf) ***n-*** [*pl.* **leaves**] **1** one of the green, usually flat, parts that grow from the stem or roots of a plant and in which most photosynthesis takes place. **2** flower petal: *rose* leaves. **3** sheet of paper in a book, consisting of a page and its reverse side. **4** very thin sheet of metal: *gold* leaf. **5** any of various flat, movable parts: *a table* leaf. ***vi-*** **1** to put forth leaves: *Our lilac began to* leaf *in April.* **2** to turn, as sheets of paper: *I* leafed *through the new book.* ***Hom-*** lief. **—*adj-* leaf′less. *adj-* leafed.**

in leaf of deciduous plants, bearing leaves at the time. **take a leaf from (someone's) book** to follow someone's example. **turn over a new leaf** to reform; to change; to do things in a new and better way.

leaf hopper ***n-*** any of several small, leaping insects feeding on the juices of plants.

leaf·let (lēf′lət) ***n-*** **1** small leaf, especially a section of a compound leaf. **2** small pamphlet.

leaf mold ***n-*** fertilizing material or ground layer composed chiefly of decayed leaves.

leaf spring ***n-*** spring made of layers of curved metal strips or plates. For picture, see *spring.*

leaf stalk ***n-*** stem or stalk supporting a leaf; petiole.

leaf·y (lē′fē) ***adj-*** **[leaf·i·er, leaf·i·est] 1** covered with or having many leaves. **2** like leaves; simulating leaves: *a* leafy *design.* **—n- leaf′i·ness.**

[1]league (lēg) ***n-*** union or group formed by two or more countries, organizations, or persons for a common purpose: *the* League *of Nations*; *a baseball* league. ***vi-*** **[leagued, lea·guing]** to form such a union or group; unite or combine. [from Old French **ligue,** ultimately from Latin **ligare** meaning "bind."]

in league in close union; in association.

[2]league (lēg) ***n-*** measure of distance about three miles. [from Old French **legue,** of Celtic origin.]

League of Nations ***n-*** international organization (1920-46), founded primarily to preserve the peace of the world. It was superseded by the United Nations.

lea·guer (lē′gər) ***n-*** member of a league.

Le·ah (lē′ə) ***n-*** in the Old Testament, Jacob's first wife.

leak (lēk) ***n-*** **1** hole, crack, or other opening which lets something pass in or out accidentally: *The roof had a bad* leak. **2** a passing in or out accidentally: *The gas* leak *is serious.* ***vi-*** **1** to pass in or out accidentally: *Water is* leaking *from this pail.* **2** to let something pass in or out accidentally: *The boat* leaks *like a sieve.* **3** to be revealed accidentally or deliberately: *Plans for a surprise attack* leaked *out.* ***vt-***: *This pipe* leaks *gas.* ***Hom-*** leek.

leak·age (lē′kĭj) ***n-*** **1** the process of leaking in or out: *the* leakage *of gas; the* leakage *of military information.* **2** that which leaks in or out: *Gas* leakage *into the refrigerator spoiled the food.* **3** the quantity that leaks: *The broken faucet had a* leakage *of two gallons an hour.*

leak·y (lē′kē) ***adj-*** **[leak·i·er, leak·i·est]** permitting the accidental entrance or escape of a gas or liquid: *a* leaky *faucet*; *a* leaky *boat.* **—n- leak′i·ness.**

[1]lean (lēn) ***vi-*** **1** to slant, slope, or incline from a straight position: *There is a famous tower in Italy that* leans. **2** to bend the upper part of the body: *He* leaned *over the table.* **3** to rest on or against something for support: *Don't* lean *on your desk.* **4** to depend; rely on: *She* leans *on her experience.* **5** to be inclined; show a preference: *Her interests* lean *toward sports.* ***vt-*** to place (something) in a slanting position: *The painter* leaned *the ladder against the wall.* [from a blend of Old English **hlēonian** meaning "to lean," and **hlænan** meaning "to cause to lean."] ***Hom-*** lien.

[2]lean (lēn) ***adj-*** **[lean·er, lean·est] 1** thin; without fat: *the* lean *meat.* **2** not productive; scant: *a* lean *year.* **3** having economy of expression: *a* lean *style of writing.* [from Old English **hlæche,** "thin."] ***Hom-*** lien. **—*n-* lean′ness.**

Le·an·der (lē ăn′dər) ***n-*** in Greek legend, Hero's lover.

lean·ing (lē′nĭng) ***n-*** inclination; tendency; bent.

lean-to (lēn′to͞o′) ***n-*** [*pl.* **lean-tos**] **1** temporary shelter of sloping branches, thatch, etc., built by campers, hunters, etc. **2** small building with a roof sloping toward its free side, built against another building.

Camper's lean-to

leap (lēp) ***vi-*** **[leaped** or **leapt** (lĕpt, lēpt) **leap·ing] 1** to jump or spring: *He* leaped *from the rock. The salmon* leaped *up the falls.* **2** to move quickly, as if with a jump: *He* leaped *to his feet.* ***vt-*** **1** to pass over with a jump or bound: *The runner* leaped *the ditch.* **2** to cause to jump: *to* leap *a horse.* ***n-*** jump; bound. **—*n-* leap′er.**

leap at to seize at (something): *to* leap at *an opportunity.*

leap·frog (lĕp′frŏg′, -frŏg′) ***n-*** game in which each player takes turns running and jumping over the bent back of the player in front of him, and then bends over in his turn for the next runner.

leap year ***n-*** a year with 366 days, in which February has 29 instead of 28 days. The extra day is added every fourth year to make up for the fact that the calendar year is about 6 hours shorter than the tropical year.

Lear (lêr) ***n-*** legendary king of Britain; hero of Shakespeare's tragedy "King Lear." ***Hom-*** leer.

learn (lûrn) *vt-* [**learned** or **learnt** (lûrnt), **learn·ing**] **1** to gain knowledge of or skill in: *She is* learning *French. The baby has* learned *how to walk.* **2** to memorize: *to* learn *a poem and recite it.* **3** to become informed of; find out: *I regret to* learn *the sad news. vi-* **1** to become skillful, able, or informed: *She has never cooked, but she can* learn. **2** to find out: *He* learned *of her whereabouts from a friend.* —*n-* **learn′ er.**

►For usage note see TEACH.

learn·ed (lûr′ nəd) *adj-* having or showing much knowledge; scholarly: *a* learned *man.* —*adv-* **learn′ ed·ly.**

learn·ing (lûr′ nĭng) *n-* knowledge gained by study.

lease (lēs) *n-* **1** written agreement for the renting of land or buildings for a certain time: *We signed a two-year* lease *for this house.* **2** the period of time agreed upon in such an agreement: *How long is your* lease *on that land? vt-* [**leased, leas·ing**] to rent (something) according to the terms of an agreement: *He* leased *the land for a year.*

new lease on life new chance to enjoy oneself, make use of an opportunity, etc.

lease·hold (lēs′ hōld′) *n-* **1** a holding of land or other property by lease. **2** the land or other property so held.

leash (lēsh) *n-* a strap, chain, or cord for holding or leading a dog or other animal. *vt-* to fasten or hold with such a tether: *to* leash *a dog.*

hold in leash to keep in check; to hold back or under control. **on leash** held and controlled by a leash.

least (lēst) *adj-* (*superl.* of **little**) smallest in amount, size, degree, importance, etc.: *Who did the* least *work? He argues over the* least *thing. adv-* (*superl.* of **little**) to the smallest extent or degree: *to like something* least. *n-* the smallest: *the* least *of my worries.*

at least or **at the least** at any rate; as a minimum concession: *You could* at least *talk to him.* **not in the least** not at all: *"Do you mind doing this?"* "Not in the least!"

least common multiple *n- Mathematics* of a set of numbers, the smallest number that can be evenly divided (with zero remainder) by every number in the set. Example: *The* least common multiple *of 3, 6, and 9 is 18.*

least·ways (lēst′ wāz′) *Informal adv-* at any rate; at least. Also **least′ wise′.**

leath·er (lĕth′ ər) *n-* skin of an animal tanned and prepared for use. *as **modifier**: a* leather *belt.*

leath·ern (lĕth′ ərn) *Archaic adj-* made of or like leather.

leath·er·neck (lĕth′ ər nĕk′) *n- Slang* U.S. marine.

leath·er·y (lĕth′ ə rē) *adj-* like leather: *a* leathery *skin.*

[1]**leave** (lēv) *vi-* [**left, leav·ing**] to go away; depart: *All the guests* left *by ten o'clock. vt-* **1** to withdraw from; cease to remain in; abandon; quit: *to* leave *home*; *to* leave *a job*; *to* leave *school before graduating.* **2** to let (something or someone) stay or be: *We'll* leave *the chair where it is.* **3** to depart without taking; forget: *I* left *my books at the store, and had to go back for them.* **4** to deliver: *The postman* left *a letter.* **5** to hand over; entrust: *I will* leave *the decision to you.* **6** to have remaining after subtraction: *2 from 5* leaves *3.* **7** to give by a will; bequeath: *When he died he* left *everything to his wife.* [from Old English **læfan** meaning "to let remain."] ***Hom-*** lief.

leave alone to avoid bothering; leave in peace.

leave behind 1 to forget; fail to bring: *I* left *my bathing suit* behind, *so I can't go swimming.* **2** to go or draw ahead of: *One runner* left *the others* behind.

leave off 1 to omit. **2** to cease; stop.

leave out to omit: *Don't* leave out *my middle name.*

[2]**leave** (lēv) *n-* **1** permission to be absent from work or duty: *The soldier asked for* leave *to visit his family.* **2** period of time for which such permission is given: *a ten-day* leave. **3** permission. [from Old English **lēaf** meaning "permission."] ***Hom-*** lief.

by your leave with your permission. **leave of absence** permission to be absent from work or duty; also, the period of time covered by such permission. **take leave of** to say good-by to.

►LEAVE is sometimes misused for LET, as in: Leave *us go.* This sentence should be written as: Let *us go.* Either word may be used with "alone." Leave *me alone.* Let *me alone.*

[3]**leave** (lēv) *vi-* [**leaved, leav·ing**] to put out leaves: *This shrub* leaves *in April.* [from **leaf.**] ***Hom-*** lief.

lea·ven (lĕv′ ən) *n-* **1** yeast or other substance that causes dough to rise; leavening. **2** influence which cheers or lightens: *Humor is the* leaven *of life. vt-* **1** to make (dough) rise by adding yeast or a similar substance. **2** to mix with some modifying element: *One can* leaven *criticism with a little praise.*

leav·en·ing (lĕv′ ən ĭng) *n-* leaven.

leaves (lēvz) *pl.* of **leaf.**

leave-tak·ing (lēv′ tā′ kĭng) *n-* act or ceremony of departing; good-by; farewell: *a formal leave-taking.*

leav·ings (lē′ vĭngz) *n- pl.* remains; things left over.

lech·er·ous (lĕch′ ər əs) *adj-* excessively pursuing sexual activity. —*adv-* **leach′ er·ous·ly.** *n-* **lech′ er·ous·ness.**

lech·er·y (lĕch′ ə rē) *n-* excessive sexual indulgence.

lec·i·thin (lĕs′ ə thĭn′) *n-* one of a group of waxlike organic compounds found in all living organisms, especially in nervous tissue.

lec·tern (lĕk′ tərn) *n-* tall desk from which a minister, teacher, etc., reads or consults his notes while addressing an audience.

lec·ture (lĕk′ chər) *n-* **1** talk or address before an audience or class: *a series of* lectures *on art.* **2** lengthy reproof; also, a scolding: *She gave them a* lecture *on their bad manners. vi-* [**lec·tured, lec·tur·ing**] to give an address: *He* lectured *on modern literature. vt-* to reprove at length; also, to scold: *I had to* lecture *the children on their behavior.* —*n-* **lec′ tu·rer.**

led (lĕd) *p.t. & p.p.* of [1]**lead.** ***Hom-*** [2]lead.

Le·da (lē′ də) *n-* in Greek mythology, the beloved of Zeus and mother of Helen of Troy.

ledge (lĕj) *n-* **1** narrow shelf along a wall: *a window* ledge. **2** shelflike ridge of rock: *a* ledge *on the cliff.*

ledg·er (lĕj′ ər) *n-* the main account book of a business firm, in which the final summaries of receipts and payments are recorded.

lee (lē) *n-* side away from the wind; sheltered side: *the* lee *of a ship. adj-*: *the* lee *side of an island.* ***Hom-*** lea.

leech (lēch) *n-* **1** any of a group of segmented worms which fasten themselves to the skin and suck blood. Formerly, leeches were much used in medicine to draw blood from patients. **2** person who gets all he can out of another; parasite. **3** *Archaic* doctor. ***Hom-*** leach.

lee·chee (lē′ chē) litchi.

leek (lēk) *n-* plant of the onion family, used in seasoning. ***Hom-*** leak.

leer (lêr) *n-* a sly or nasty sidelong look which expresses a feeling of malice, lust, etc. *vi-*: *He* leered *at his helpless victim.* ***Hom-*** Lear.

leer·y (lêr′ ē) *Informal adj-* suspicious; hesitant about something: *I am somewhat* leery *of his sudden willingness to help.* —*adv-* **leer′ i·ly.** *n-* **leer′ i·ness.**

lees (lēz) *n- pl.* material that settles to the bottom during the fermentation and aging of wines; dregs.

lee shore *n-* shore that lies to the leeward of a ship and is therefore dangerous in a storm because the wind drives the ship toward it.

lee·ward (lo͞o′ ərd, lē′ wərd) ***n-*** side sheltered or away from the wind: *We anchored the boat to the* leeward *of the island.* ***adj-***: *It will be warmer on the* leeward *side of the deck.* ***adv-*** toward the leeward.

lee·way (lē′ wā′) ***n-*** **1** extra or allowable room, time, etc.; margin of variation or deviation: *There is little* leeway *between the ship and the pier.* **2** the lateral drift to leeward of a moving ship.

[1]**left** (lĕft) *p.t. & p.p.* of [1]**leave.**

left over remaining; not used.

[2]**left** (lĕft) ***n-*** **1** side from which one starts reading a page of English; the opposite of right: *Steering wheels of American cars are usually on the* left. **2** direction to this side: *to turn to the* left. **3 Left** (1) all the political parties or groups advocating progressive or democratic socialist policies in government, economics, etc. (2) Communists and Communist sympathizers. ***adj-*** on or to the left: *the* left *hand; a* left *turn.* ***adv-***: *to turn* left. [from Old English **lyfte** meaning "weak." The left hand was traditionally regarded as the weaker.]

left field ***n-*** section of the outfield behind third base and the shortstop position. **—*n-* left fielder.**

left-hand (lĕft′ hănd′) ***adj-*** **1** at or in the direction of one's left hand: *a* left-hand *turn.* **2** counterclockwise: *a screw with a* left-hand *thread.*

left-hand·ed (lĕft′ hăn′ dəd) ***adj-*** **1** of a person, using the left hand more naturally and with more skill than the right. **2** made to be used by such a person: *a* left-handed *golf club.* **3** counterclockwise. **4** in baseball, standing on the right side of the plate while batting. **5** insulting by what is not said; ironic and insincere: *He paid the singer a* left-handed *compliment by praising only his posture.* ***adv-***: *Can you write* left-handed? **—*adv-* left′-hand′ ed·ly.** ***n-*** **left′-hand′ ed·ness.**

left-hand·er (lĕft′ hăn′ dər) ***n-*** person who is left-handed; especially, a left-handed baseball pitcher.

left·ist (lĕf′ tĭst) ***n-*** **1** person who advocates progressive or democratic socialist policies in government, economics, etc. **2** Communist or Communist sympathizer. ***adj-***: *a speech full of* leftist *views.*

left·o·ver (lĕft′ ō′ vər) ***n-*** (usually **leftovers**) what remains; especially, food remaining unserved at a meal: *Mother made the* leftovers *into hash.* ***adj-***: *the* leftover *ham.*

left wing ***n-*** **1** all the political parties or groups that advocate radical, socialist, or Communist policies in government, economics, etc. **2** any faction within a group whose views or policies are more liberal than those of the group as a whole: *the* left wing *of the medical society.* **—*adj-* (left-wing)**: *a* left-wing *faction.* ***n-*** **left′-wing′ er.**

left·y (lĕf′ tē) *Slang* ***n-*** [*pl.* **left·ies**] left-handed person.

leg (lĕg) ***n-*** **1** one of the limbs of the body that give it support and by which men and animals walk and run. **2** part of a garment which covers one of these limbs: *a trouser* leg. **3** something like such a limb in use or appearance: *a table* leg. **4** stage of a journey or other undertaking: *the last* leg *of a trip.* **5** *Mathematics* one of two sides of a triangle, the third being the base. ***vi-*** [**legged, leg·ging**] to walk or run (usually followed by "it"). **—*adj-* leg′ less.**

not have a leg to stand on to have no support or proof whatever for one's opinion or action. **on (one's) last legs** *Informal* near exhaustion, death, etc. **pull (one's) leg** *Informal* tease; deceive jokingly.

leg·a·cy (lĕg′ ə sē) ***n-*** [*pl.* **leg·a·cies**] **1** property or money left to someone by a will. **2** something handed down from those who have gone before; heritage: *a* legacy *of honor; our* legacy *of freedom.*

le·gal (lē′ gəl) ***adj-*** **1** of or having to do with the law: *a* legal *matter.* **2** permitted or required by the law: *the* legal *age for obtaining a driver's license.* **—*adv-* le′ gal·ly.**

le·gal·ism (lē′ gə lĭz′ əm) ***n-*** strict following of the exact words of the law. **—*n-* le′ gal·ist.** ***adj-*** **le′ gal·is′ tic.**

le·gal·i·ty (lə găl′ ə tē) ***n-*** [*pl.* **le·gal·i·ties**] conformity to law; lawfulness: *the* legality *of a business merger.*

le·gal·ize (lē′ gə līz′) ***vt-*** [**le·gal·ized, le·gal·iz·ing**] to make legal.

legal tender ***n-*** currency or other form of money which by law must be accepted in payment of debts.

leg·ate (lĕg′ ət) ***n-*** ambassador or envoy; especially, a representative of the Pope.

leg·a·tee (lĕg′ ə tē′) ***n-*** person who receives a legacy.

le·ga·tion (lə gā′ shən) ***n-*** **1** group of diplomatic representatives whose chief does not have the rank of ambassador. **2** headquarters of such a group in the foreign country where it is stationed.

le·ga·to (lə gä′ tō) *Music* ***adj- & adv-*** in a flowing manner, with the notes tied smoothly together.

leg·end (lĕj′ ənd) ***n-*** **1** story handed down from the past and not regarded as true history, although partly based on actual events; also, the story of the life of a saint. **2** such stories as a group: *famous heroes in Greek* legend. **3** inscription on a coin, coat of arms, banner, etc. **4** title and description under a picture, or key explaining a map or chart.

le·gen·da·ry (lĕj′ ən dĕr′ ē) ***adj-*** **1** having to do with or told in legends or myths: *a* legendary *hero.* **2** famous; celebrated: *His deeds were* legendary.

leg·er·de·main (lĕj′ ər də mān′) ***n-*** **1** sleight of hand; quick, clever tricks with the hands. **2** any deception based on trickery.

leg·ged (lĕg′ əd) ***adj-*** having a specified kind or number of legs: *a four-*legged *stool; a bow*legged *boy.*

leg·gings (lĕg′ ĭngz) ***n-*** protective outer garments for the legs, reaching from foot to knee, or above.

Leggings

leg·gy (lĕg′ ē) ***adj-*** [**leg·gi·er, leg·gi·est**] having long, awkward legs: *a* leggy *colt.*

leg·horn (lĕg′ hôrn′, -hərn′) ***n-*** **1** a braid made of fine Italian wheat straw. **2** hat made of such a straw. **3** (usually **Leghorn**) any of a breed of small domestic fowl originally developed in Italy and valued for its large production of eggs.

leg·i·ble (lĕj′ ə bəl) ***adj-*** such as can be read; readable. **—*adv-* leg′ i·bly.** ***n-*** **leg′ i·bil′ i·ty.**

le·gion (lē′ jən) ***n-*** **1** large body of soldiers; army. **2** very great number of persons or things: *a* legion *of angels.* **3** in ancient Rome, an army unit consisting of 3,000 to 6,000 foot soldiers, with an auxiliary force of cavalry. **4** (often **Legion**) any of various military or honorary national organizations: *the American* Legion.

be legion to abound; to exist in large numbers: *New cold remedies* are legion.

le·gion·naire (lē′ jə nâr′) ***n-*** (often **Legionnaire**) a member of a military or honorary national organization.

le·gion·ar·y (lē′ jə nĕr′ ē) ***n-*** [*pl.* **le·gion·ar·ies**] a soldier or member of a legion. ***adj-*** **1** of or relating to a legion. **2** constituting a legion; very numerous.

Legion of Honor ***n-*** French honorary order founded by Napoleon Bonaparte in 1802, as a reward for distinguished service.

leg·is·late (lĕj′ əs lāt′) ***vi-*** [**leg·is·lat·ed, leg·is·lat·ing**] to make a law or laws: *Congress* legislates *for the United States.* ***vt-*** to require or impose by law: *to* legislate *moral conduct.*

leg·is·la·tion (lĕj′ əs lā′ shən) ***n-*** **1** the making or enacting of laws: *Congress is responsible for* legislation. **2** laws made or enacted: *new tax* legislation.

leg·is·la·tive (lĕj′ əs lā′ tĭv) ***adj-*** **1** having the power of making laws: *the* legislative *branch of the government.* **2** having to do with making laws: *new* legislative *measures.*

leg·is·la·tor (lĕj′ əs lā′ tər) ***n-*** member of a lawmaking group: *Senators and Representatives are* legislators.

leg·is·la·ture (lĕj′ əs lā′ chər) ***n-*** lawmaking group of a country or State.

[1]**le·git·i·mate** (lə jĭt′ ə mət) ***adj-*** **1** lawful; rightful; according to the rules: *to use tax money for* legitimate *purposes*; *a* legitimate *heir.* **2** reasonable; justifiable: *a* legitimate *excuse.* **3** born in wedlock: *a* legitimate *child.* **—*n-* le·git′ i·ma·cy:** *to prove the* legitimacy *of a claim*; *the* legitimacy *of an argument.* ***adv-*** **le·git′ i·mate·ly.**

[2]**le·git·i·mate** (lə jĭt′ ə māt′) ***vt-*** [**le·git·i·mat·ed, le·git·i·mat·ing**] to permit or recognize by law: *to* legitimate *a partnership.*

legitimate theater ***n-*** stage plays performed by actors in front of an audience rather than a camera, as distinguished from movies, TV, musical revues, etc.

le·git·i·mize (lə jĭt′ ə mīz′) ***vt-*** [**le·git·i·mized, le·git·i·miz·ing**] to legitimate. **—*n-* le·git′ i·mi·za′ tion.**

leg·man (leg′ mən) ***n-*** [*pl.* **leg·men**] **1** newspaperman or reporter assigned to gather information. **2** assistant who gathers information, runs errands, does small tasks, etc.

leg-of-mut·ton (lĕg′ əv mŭt′ ən) ***adj-*** shaped like the upper leg of a sheep; large and full at the top, small at the bottom: *a* leg-of-mutton *sleeve.*

leg·ume (lĕg′ yōōm′, lə gyōōm′) ***n-*** **1** plant bearing podlike fruit such as peas and beans. Legumes are important to agriculture because their roots harbor bacteria that perform nitrogen fixation. **2** fruit of such a plant. **3 legumes** the seed of such fruit used as food.

le·gu·mi·nous (lə gyōō′ mə nəs) ***adj-*** being, or relating to, legumes: *a* leguminous *plant*; leguminous *crops.*

leg work ***n-*** **1** work of a legman. **2** any errands, small tasks, etc., involving much walking.

le·hu·a (lā hōō′ ə) ***n-*** tree of the Pacific islands, with brilliant red flowers and hard wood.

lei (lā, lā′ ē) ***n-*** Hawaiian wreath of flowers. ***Hom-*** lay.

lei·sure (lē′ zhər, lĕzh′ ər) ***n-*** **1** freedom from work or duties. **2** time available for or devoted to recreation, relaxation, etc. ***as modifier***: *Her* leisure *time was spent in reading. The habits of the* leisure *classes have changed.* **—*adj-* lei′ sured:** *a* leisured *man.*

at leisure **1** having spare time. **2** not occupied. **3** with no hurry. **at (one's) leisure** at one's convenience; when one has free time.

lei·sure·ly (lē′ zhər lē, lĕzh′ ər lē) ***adj-*** **1** slow; not hurried: *a* leisurely *walk.* **2** free and restful: *a* leisurely *afternoon at the beach.* ***adv-*** slowly and without hurrying: *to stroll* leisurely. **—*n-* lei′ sure·li·ness.**

lem·ming (lĕm′ ĭng) ***n-*** small rodent of the arctic regions resembling a mouse. Periodically, millions of lemmings move in a mass into the sea and drown.

lem·on (lĕm′ ən) ***n-*** **1** small, oval, yellow fruit with a sour juice used to flavor foods and drinks. **2** the tree which bears this fruit. **3** a pale yellow. **4** *Slang* something or someone disappointing, undesirable, inadequate, etc. ***adj-***: *a* lĕmon *dress*; lemon *sherbet.*

lem·on·ade (lĕm′ ə nād′) ***n-*** a drink made of lemon juice, sugar, and water.

lemon balm ***n-*** a bushy European mint with lemon-flavored leaves.

le·mur (lē′ mər) ***n-*** any of various small, sharp-nosed, tree-dwelling mammals, related to the monkeys. They have soft, woolly fur and are found chiefly in Madagascar.

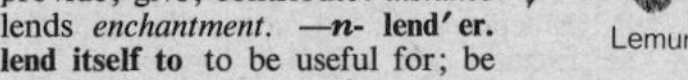
Lemur

lend (lĕnd) ***vt-*** [**lent, lend·ing**] (in senses 1 and 2 considered intransitive when the direct object is implied but not expressed) **1** to allow someone to have or to use a thing with the understanding that it is to be returned: *He* lends *his books freely.* **2** to give the use of (money) at a specified rate of interest. **3** to provide; give; contribute: *distance* lends *enchantment.* **—*n-* lend′ er.**

lend itself to to be useful for; be suitable for: *This tool* lends itself to *many uses.* **lend (oneself) to** to stoop to.

►For usage note see LOAN.

lend-lease (lĕnd′ lēs′) ***n-*** as authorized by the Congress, the furnishing of such articles as aircraft, ships, munitions, food, etc., to a friendly nation whose defense is vital to the safety of the United States. ***as modifier***: *a* lend-lease *program.* ***vt-*** [**lend-leased, lend-leas·ing**] to furnish (such articles): *to* lend-lease *food.*

length (lĕngkth) ***n-*** **1** the measure of a thing from end to end; the longer or longest measure of a thing, as distinguished from its width and thickness: *the* length *of a boat*; *the* length *of a board.* **2** extent in space or time: *the* length *of a race course*; *the* length *of an interview.* **3** a specified distance considered as a unit of measure: *an arm's* length. **4** piece of something, usually of a certain size, cut from a larger piece: *a* length *of rope.*

at full length stretched out. **at length** **1** in full; in detail: *to describe a trip* at length. **2** finally; at last. **go to any length** (or **lengths**) to do whatever is necessary; stop at nothing. **keep at arm's length** to avoid being friendly with; treat with coldness.

length·en (lĕngth′ ən) ***vt-*** to make longer: *to* lengthen *a skirt.* ***vi-***: *The days* lengthen *in spring.*

length·wise (lĕngkth′ wīz′) or **length·ways** (lĕngkth′ wāz′) ***adv-*** in the direction of the length: *to saw a board* lengthwise. ***adj-***: *a* lengthwise *measurement.*

length·y (lĕng′ thē) ***adj-*** [**length·i·er, length·i·est**] long; too long; drawn out: *a* lengthy *speech.* **—*adv-* length′ i·ly.** ***n-*** **length′ i·ness.**

le·ni·en·cy (lē′ nē ən sē, lēn′ yən sē) or **le·ni·ence** (-əns) ***n-*** mildness; mercifulness; gentleness.

le·ni·ent (lē′ nē ənt, lēn′ yənt) ***adj-*** mild; merciful; not severe or harsh: *a* lenient *judge.* **—*adv-* le′ ni·ent·ly.**

Len·i-Len·a·pe or **Len·ni-Len·a·pe** (lĕn′ ē lĕn′ ə pē′) See *Delaware.*

len·i·ty (lĕn′ ə tē) ***n-*** mildness; leniency; gentleness.

lens (lĕnz) ***n-*** **1** piece of transparent material curved on one or both sides. It spreads or focuses the light rays passing through it. **2** unit consisting of two or more such glass pieces cemented together, used in high-quality cameras, microscopes, etc. **3** crystalline lens of the eye. For picture, see *eye.* **4** any device that focuses radiation other than light, as in an electron microscope.

Lens as a burning glass

lent (lĕnt) *p.t. & p.p.* of **lend.**

Lent (lĕnt) ***n-*** period of penitence and self-denial observed in the Roman Catholic and other Christian churches from Ash Wednesday to Easter, excluding the Sundays.

Lent·en (lĕn′ tən) ***adj-*** **1** pertaining to or suitable for Lent. **2 lenten** meager; spare.

len·til (lĕn′ tĭl) ***n-*** **1** a pod-bearing plant. **2** the seeds of this plant, cooked and eaten like peas and beans.

len·to (lĕn′ tō) *Music* ***adj-*** & ***adv-*** slow; slower than adagio but faster than largo.

l'en·voi or **l'en·voy** (lĕn′ voi′, län voi′ *Fr.* lä^n vwä′) ***n-*** **1** a postscript to a poem or prose work, often as a dedication. **2** the concluding stanza of a ballade.

Le·o (lē′ ō) ***n-*** northern constellation thought to outline the figure of a lion.

le·o·nine (lē′ ə nīn′) ***adj-*** of or like a lion.

leop·ard (lĕp′ ərd) ***n-*** large tawny cat with black spots, or sometimes all black, found in Asia and Africa. ***adj-*** made of the skin of this animal. **—*n-*** *fem.* **leop′ard·ess.** ***adj-*** **leop′ard·like′.**

Leopard, 7—8 ft. long

lep·er (lĕp′ ər) ***n-*** person suffering from leprosy.

lep·i·dop·ter·an (lĕp′ ə dŏp′ tər ən) ***n-*** any member of an order of insects **(Lepidoptera)**, which includes moths, butterflies, etc.

lep·i·dop·ter·ous (lĕp′ ə dŏp′ tər əs) ***adj-*** belonging to or characteristic of the lepidopterans.

lep·re·chaun (lĕp′ rə kŏn′, -kòn′) ***n-*** in Irish folklore, an elf resembling a little old man, who knows of hidden treasure.

lep·ro·sy (lĕp′ rə sē) ***n-*** a germ disease causing gradual loss of feeling, swellings and sores on the skin, wasting away of the flesh, and deformities; Hansen's disease. **—*adj-*** **lep′rous.**

lese majesty (lēz) ***n-*** in law, a crime against the sovereign or ruling power; treason.

le·sion (lē′ zhən) ***n-*** **1** any abnormal condition of tissue or disability of an organ in any part of the body, caused by injury or disease. **2** injury; damage.

les·pe·de·za (lĕs′ pə dē′ zə) ***n-*** any of various shrubby leguminous plants used for forage.

less (lĕs) ***determiner*** (traditionally called adjective or pronoun) **1** smaller in quantity: *Mexico has* less *area than the United States.* **2** not so much: *Make* less *noise, please!* **3** *Informal* fewer. **4** shorter: *We'll get home in* less *time if we fly.* **5** lower in rank, degree, or importance: *no* less *a person than the king.* ***n-*** a smaller quantity: *He bought* less *of the fabric than I did.* ***adv-*** (*compar.* of **little**) to a smaller degree or extent; not so: *He was* less *scared than surprised. You should walk* less *and sleep more.* ***prep-*** minus: *four months* less *five days.* See also *lesser.*

none the less nevertheless. **the less** even less.

►Use LESS with things you do not count by units, such as water or color, and use FEWER with things you can count, such as gallons of water or shades of color: *This tank holds* less *water than that one. This tank holds a hundred gallons* fewer *than that one. This picture has* less *color than the other one. This picture has* fewer *shades of red than the other one.*

-less *suffix* (used to form adjectives) **1** without; lacking: *tree*less; *end*less; *value*less. **2** unable to do something specified: *sleep*less; *rest*less. **3** beyond any power or ability to: *count*less, *resist*less.

les·see (lĕs sē′) ***n-*** person who holds property under a lease; tenant.

less·en (lĕs′ ən) ***vt-*** **1** to reduce; make less: *to* lessen *the length of a rope; to* lessen *working hours.* **2** to cause (something) to appear less important, valuable, etc.; belittle; disparage: *Don't* lessen *his services to the state.* ***vi-*** to become less: *The rain* lessened. ***Hom-*** lesson.

less·er (lĕs′ ər) ***adj-*** smaller; inferior: *to choose the* lesser *evil; a* lesser *man.*

lesser panda See *panda.*

les·son (lĕs′ ən) ***n-*** **1** unit of study to be learned at one time; assignment: *The* lesson *begins on page 50.* **2** instruction given at one time: *My next* lesson *is at three o'clock.* **3** thing serving as an example of what is right or wrong; what is learned from experience: *That was a* lesson *to us.* **4** *Informal* reprimand; rebuke: *The principal gave him a good* lesson. **5** portion of the Bible read as part of a church service. **6 lessons** school work; studies. ***Hom-*** lessen.

les·sor (lĕs′ òr′, -ôr′) ***n-*** person who grants a lease; person who rents property to another.

lest (lĕst) ***conj-*** **1** for fear that: *We watched all night* lest *the bandits should return.* **2** that (used after words expressing fear or anxiety): *I feared* lest *I'd be too late.*

[1]let (lĕt) ***vt-*** **[let, let·ting] 1** to permit; allow: *He* let *no one enter the house.* **2** to allow to run out, flow out, or escape: *to* let *air out of a tire.* **3** to allow to pass, go, leave, etc. (often followed by "through," "by," etc.): *Please* let *me by.* **4** to give out; assign: *to* let *work to a contractor.* **5** *chiefly Brit.* to rent or hire; lease: *to* let *rooms by the week.* ***vi-*** *chiefly Brit.* to be hired or leased: *The house* lets *for $150 a month.* ***auxiliary verb*** (usually in the imperative and used with an infinitive without "to") **1** to introduce a proposal, request, or give an order: *"Boys,* let's *build a fire."* Let's *go.* Let *everyone stand up.* **2** to express a warning, often used ironically: *Just* let *him try.* **3** to introduce an assumption or suggestion: *Gentlemen,* let *six be the product of two numbers.* [from Old English **lætan.**] ***Hom-*** Lett.

let alone 1 *Informal* not to mention; to say nothing of: *He can't juggle two balls,* let alone *six.* **2** not to interfere with; leave undisturbed; not touch or trouble: *Just* let *him* alone *and stop bothering him.*

let be to stop bothering or interfering with: *He doesn't need your help;* let *him* be!

let down 1 to lower; cause to descend: *to* let *a bucket* down *into a well.* **2** to disappoint; fail: *to* let *a friend* down. **3** to stop making an effort: *Don't* let down *till the job is finished.* **4** to lengthen (a garment).

let drive at to whack; strike a heavy blow at.

let fly 1 to throw; hurl; shoot: *to* let fly *an arrow; to* let fly *a torpedo.* **2** to lash out; direct a verbal attack: *to* let fly *with a torrent of abuse.*

let go of to release; stop holding on to.

let in to allow to enter: *Please* let *me* in *the house.*

let know to inform: *Please* let *me* know *if you can't come.*

let loose to set free; release from restraint: *to* let loose *a chained animal; to* let loose *violent emotions.*

let off 1 to allow to escape, flow out, or run out: *The boiler* let off *steam.* **2** to allow to get off: *I asked the driver to* let *me* off *at the corner.* **3** to allow to go free; excuse from a punishment: *The judge* let *him* off *with a warning not to speed.* **4** to excuse from work or obligation: *The manager* let *the clerks* off *at noon.*

let on *Informal* **1** to allow to be known; admit: *Don't* let on *that you see him.* **2** to give the impression; pretend.

---

fāte, făt, dâre, bärn; bē, bĕt, mêre; bīte, bĭt; nōte, hŏt, môre, dòg; fŭn, fûr; to͞o, bo͝ok; oil; out; tar; thin; then; hw for wh as in *wh*at; zh for s as in u*s*ual; ə for a, e, i, o, u, as in *a*go, lin*e*n, per*i*l, at*o*m, min*u*s

let out 1 to loosen a garment by opening the seams: *to* let out *a coat.* 2 to permit to go out: *At night we* let *the cat* out. 3 to give forth; emit: *to* let out *a sigh.* 4 to reveal unintentionally: *to* let out *a secret.* 5 *Informal* to dismiss or be dismissed: *to* let *school* out.
let slide to neglect; fail to take care of: *His business failed because he* let *it* slide.
let the cat out of the bag to reveal a secret.
let up to stop or diminish: *The wind* let up *a little.*
►For usage note see LEAVE.

²let (lĕt) ***n-*** 1 in tennis and other racket games, a served ball that touches the top of the net before it drops fair. The serve is made again. 2 *Archaic* obstacle; hindrance. [from Old English **lettan,** "belated," from **læt,** "late."]
without let or hindrance without delay or difficulty.

-let *suffix* (used to form nouns) 1 small; little; short: *book*let; *play*let; *stream*let. 2 band or ornament to be worn on: *ank*let; *arm*let.

let·down (lĕt′doun′) ***n-*** 1 a slowing up; slackening; decrease: *a* letdown *in business*; *a* letdown *in effort.* 2 *Informal* disappointment: *His trip was a big* letdown.

le·thal (lē′thəl) ***adj-*** causing death; deadly: *a* lethal *gas.* ***—adv-*** **le′thal·ly.**

le·thar·gic (lə thär′jĭk) ***adj-*** 1 feeling or overcome by lethargy; sleepy; dull; sluggish. 2 having to do with or causing lethargy. ***—adv-*** **le·thar′gi·cal·ly.**

leth·ar·gy (lĕth′ər jē) ***n-*** [*pl.* **leth·ar·gies**] 1 unnatural drowsiness. 2 lack of interest; apathy; indifference.

Le·the (lē′thē) ***n-*** in Greek mythology, a river in Hades, a drink of whose water produced loss of memory; hence, oblivion. ***—adj-*** **Le′the′an.**

let's (lĕts) let us: *Turn off the TV and* let's *go.*

Lett (lĕt) ***n-*** one of a people living in Latvia and closely related to the Lithuanians. ***—adj-*** **Lett′ish.** ***Hom-*** let.

let·ter (lĕt′ər) ***n-*** 1 mark or character used in writing or printing to represent a speech sound; one of the characters or symbols of an alphabet. 2 written message, usually sent by mail: *a business* letter. 3 official document giving certain privileges or identifying the bearer: *a* letter *of credit.* 4 exact, word-for-word meaning: *to obey the spirit as well as the* letter *of the law.* 5 the initial or initials of a school, worn as an award for skill in sports or other activities: *Harry won his football* letter. 6 **letters** literature; literary culture; learning: *a man of* letters. ***vt-*** to mark with the characters or symbols of an alphabet: *to* letter *a sign.* ***—n-*** **let′ter·er.**
to the letter in every detail: *to follow rules* to the letter.

letter carrier ***n-*** person who delivers and collects mail; postman; mailman.

let·tered (lĕt′ərd) ***adj-*** 1 marked with letters. 2 literate; having education.

let·ter·head (lĕt′ər hĕd′) ***n-*** 1 printed heading at the top of a sheet of writing paper, usually containing the name and address of the sender. 2 sheet of paper so printed.

let·ter·ing (lĕt′ər ĭng) ***n-*** 1 act of drawing letters, such as those used in signs. 2 letters or words so made: *The* lettering *of a sign.*

let·ter-per·fect (lĕt′ər pûr′fĭkt) ***adj-*** without any mistakes; correct in every detail.

let·ter·press (lĕt′ər prĕs′) ***n-*** in printing, matter printed from type or similar raised and inked surfaces, rather than from offset plates or other engraved plates.

letters of marque ***n-*** *pl.* formerly, a government license or commission permitting a ship to seize enemy merchant ships.

letters patent ***n-*** *pl.* official document giving a person authority from a government to do some act or to enjoy some privilege.

let·tuce (lĕt′əs) ***n-*** leafy garden vegetable used mainly in salads and as a garnish.

let·up (lĕt′ŭp′) *Informal* ***n-*** 1 a lessening or slackening, such as of effort or intensity: *The wind blew without* letup. 2 a pause; stop: *A brief* letup *in our work.*

leu·co·cyte or **leu·ko·cyte** (lo͞o′kə sīt′) ***n-*** white blood cell.

leu·ke·mi·a (lo͞o kē′mē ə) *Medicine* ***n-*** disease marked by an excessive multiplication of the white blood cells; cancer of the blood.

Lev. Leviticus.

¹lev·ee (lĕv′ē) ***n-*** 1 high bank built along a river to prevent floods. 2 landing place or quay. [American word from Louisiana French **levée** meaning "something raised," and related to **²levee.**] ***Hom-*** levy.

²lev·ee (lĕv′ē) ***n-*** 1 morning reception once held by a king or other person of high rank on awakening from sleep. It was considered a great honor to be invited to a levee. 2 in England, an afternoon court assembly at which the king or queen receives only men. 3 any social reception. [from French **levé,** from Old French **lever,** from Latin **levare** meaning "to raise."] ***Hom-*** levy.

lev·el (lĕv′əl) ***n-*** 1 spirit level. 2 a specified height above some reference point: *The water rose to a* level *of 29 feet.* 3 place from which altitude is measured: *18 feet above sea* level; *three stories above ground* level. 4 relative place, degree, position, etc.; plane; rank: *to sink to the* level *of a common thief*; *a high* level *of intelligence*; *a formal* level *of usage in English.* 5 floor or story of a structure: *The refreshment stand is on the upper* level. ***adj-*** 1 horizontal; parallel to the surface of still water; smooth; flat: *a* level *floor*; *a* level *pasture.* 2 at the same height or plane: *a bracket* level *with my chin.* 3 steady; consistent; not wavering: *a* level *head*; *a* level *tone.* ***vt-*** 1 to smooth; make even; make horizontal: *to* level *a road*; *to* level *a floor.* 2 to tear down; raze: *to* level *a whole city.* 3 to knock down: *He* leveled *his opponent in two rounds.* 4 to make equal or the same; equalize: *Disaster* levels *us all.* 5 to aim: *to* level *a gun at a target*; *to* level *criticism at the government.* ***—n-*** **lev′el·er** ***adv-*** **lev′el·ly.** ***n-*** **lev′el·ness.**
(one's) level best *Informal* the best one can do; one's very best. **on a level** at the same height, plane, rank, etc.: *His work is* on a level *with the best.* **on the level** *Slang* 1 honest; fair. 2 honestly and fairly.
level off 1 to make flat or even. 2 to come or bring into a level position: *The plane* leveled off *at 8,000 feet.*

lev·el-head·ed (lĕv′əl hĕd′əd) ***adj-*** 1 having good common sense and sound judgment; sensible. 2 cool in stress and danger; unruffled.

lev·er (lĕv′ər, *also* lē′vər) ***n-*** 1 bar used to pry up or lift a heavy object. 2 a simple machine based on the fact that when light pressure is applied on the long end of a bar resting on a fixed point, it will lift a heavy weight on the short end. 3 projecting piece used to operate or adjust a mechanism: *a gearshift* lever.

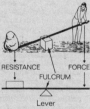

Lever

le·ver·age (lĕv′ər ĭj) ***n-*** 1 the action or use of a lever. 2 mechanical power gained by using a lever.

Le·vi (lē′vī′) ***n-*** in the Old Testament, the third son of Jacob and the founder of one of the tribes of Israel.

Le·vi·a·than (lə vī′ə thən) ***n-*** 1 in the Bible, a sea monster of enormous size. 2 anything huge, such as a whale or a large ship. Also **le·vi′a·than.**

le·vis or **Le·vis** (lē′ vīz′) ***n-*** tight-fitting pants of heavy denim, made stronger with copper rivets at points of strain. Also **le′ vi′s**′, or **Le′ vi′s**′. [from **Levi's,** trademark of **Levi Strauss,** U.S. maker of work clothes.]

lev·i·tate (lĕv′ ə tāt′) ***vi-*** **[lev·i·tat·ed, lev·i·tat·ing]** to rise and float in the air because of, or as if because of, lightness or supposed supernatural powers. ***vt-*** to cause to rise or float in the air.

Le·vit·i·cus (lə vĭt′ ĭ kəs) ***n-*** the third book of the Old Testament, containing the Jewish ceremonial laws.

lev·i·ty (lĕv′ ə tē) ***n-*** [*pl.* **lev·i·ties**] **1** lack of seriousness; frivolity. **2** fickleness; capriciousness.

lev·u·lose (lĕv′ yə lōs′) ***n-*** fructose.

lev·y (lĕv′ ē) ***vt-*** **[lev·ied, levy·ing]** **1** to impose, raise, or collect (a tax, fine, etc.) by force or authority: *to* levy *a tax.* **2** to draft or enlist for military service: *to* levy *an army.* **3** to wage (war). ***n-*** [*pl.* **lev·ies**] **1** the imposing or collection of taxes, fines, etc. **2** forced enlistment of men for military service: *the greatest* levy *of troops in history.* **3** money, troops, etc. collected by force or authority. ***Hom-*** levee.

levy on to seize by law in order to collect money.

lewd (lo͞od, lyo͞od) ***adj-*** **[lewd·er, lewd·est]** obscene; indecent: *a* lewd *song.* **—*adv-* lewd′ ly.** ***n-*** **lewd′ ness.**

lex (lĕks) *Latin* ***n-*** [*pl.* **le·ges** (lē′ jēz)] law.

lex·i·cal (lĕk′ sĭ kəl) ***adj-*** **1** of or having to do with words, especially with their meaning; semantic. **2** of or having to do with a lexicon or dictionary. **—*adv-* lex′ i·cal·ly.**

lex·i·cog·ra·pher (lĕk′ sə kŏ′ grə fər) ***n-*** person who makes or helps to make a dictionary.

lex·i·co·graph·ic (lĕk′ sĭ kə grăf′ ĭk) or **lex·i·co·graph·i·cal** (-ĭ kəl) ***adj-*** of or having to do with lexicography or with dictionaries. **—*adv-* lex′ i·co·graph′ i·cal·ly.**

lex·i·cog·ra·phy (lĕk′ sə kŏ′ grə fē) ***n-*** the art or occupation of making dictionaries.

lex·i·con (lĕk′ sə kŏn′) ***n-*** dictionary, especially one of an ancient language.

Ley·den jar (lī′ dən) ***n-*** early kind of capacitor consisting of a glass jar coated with a conducting material on its inner and outer sides. The jar has an insulated, one-hole stopper containing a metal rod that is connected to the inner coating by a metal chain.

Leyden jar

Li symbol for lithium.

li·a·bil·i·ty (lī′ ə bĭl′ ə tē) ***n-*** [*pl.* **li·a·bil·i·ties**] **1** legal responsibility. **2** tendency toward; susceptibility: *a person's* liability *to disease.* **3** something that handicaps; disadvantage; hindrance: *Poor eyesight is a* liability. **4** something owed; debt. **5 liabilities** sum of what a person or company owes.

li·a·ble (lī′ ə bəl) ***adj-*** legally responsible: *If the car is damaged, I will consider you* liable.

be liable to 1 *Informal* to have the tendency to: *He is* liable to *goof.* **2** to be subject to (a tax, punishment, etc.): *to* be liable to *arrest.* **be liable for** to be legally responsible for: *to* be liable for *one's debts.*

►LIABLE is sometimes used in conversation in the sense of "likely" or "probable." In careful writing and speaking, reserve LIABLE for the legal sense. *I am* liable *for damage done by my dog.* But: *It is* likely *to rain.*

li·ai·son (lē′ ə zŏn′, lē ā′ zŏn′) ***n-*** **1** a linking up of parts or groups; especially, communication and cooperation between units of an army. **2** a love affair. **3** in French and other languages, the pronouncing of an otherwise silent consonant when it occurs at the end of a word and immediately before another word beginning with a vowel. The consonant is pronounced as if it were the first letter of the second word. Examples: "l" and "t" in *Il est un gendarme* (ē lĕ tü^n zhä^n därm′) show liaison.

li·a·na or **li·ane** (lē än′ ə, -ăn′ ə) ***n-*** any of various tropical climbing vines with woody stems.

li·ar (lī′ ər, līər) ***n-*** person who knowingly says things that are not true; one who tells lies. ***Hom-*** lyre.

li·ba·tion (lī bā′ shən) ***n-*** **1** a pouring out of wine or other liquid in honor of a god. **2** the liquid poured out.

li·bel (lī′ bəl) ***n-*** **1** written or printed statement tending to defame or to injure a person's reputation. **2** the act or crime of writing or publishing such a statement. **3** any false or damaging statement. ***vt-*** to write or publish a malicious, injurious statement against; defame. **—*n-* li′ bel·er.**

li·bel·ous or **li·bel·lous** (lī′ bə ləs) ***adj-*** containing, or of the nature of, a libel: *a* libelous *statement.* **—*adv-* li′ bel·ous·ly.** ***n-*** **li′ bel·ous·ness.**

lib·er·al (lĭb′ ər əl) ***adj-*** **1** favoring social progress and democratic reform: *a* liberal *government.* **2** tolerant; free from prejudice: *a* liberal *attitude toward religious worship.* **3** generous; bountiful: *a* liberal *donation.* **4** ample; plentiful: *a* liberal *supply.* **5** broad; not limited: *a* liberal *education.* ***n-*** **1** person who favors social progress and democratic reform. **2 Liberal** member of a **Liberal Party,** especially that of Canada or of Great Britain. **—*adv-* lib′ er·al·ly.** ***n-*** **lib′ er·al·ness.**

liberal arts ***n-*** subjects or college courses, such as literature, philosophy, languages, etc., studied for culture rather than for immediate practical, technical, or professional use; the humanities.

liberal education ***n-*** education in the liberal arts rather than as a preparation for a specific profession.

lib·er·al·ism (lĭb′ ər ə lĭz′ əm) ***n-*** liberal ideas, opinions, or principles.

lib·er·al·i·ty (lĭb′ ər ăl′ ə tē) ***n-*** [*pl.* **lib·er·al·i·ties**] **1** generosity: *the* liberality *of the townspeople.* **2** a generous gift: *a millionaire famous for his* liberalities. **3** lack of prejudice; tolerance.

lib·er·al·ize (lĭb′ ər ə līz′) ***vt-*** **[lib·er·al·ized, lib·er·al·i·zing]** **1** to make liberal or more liberal in ideas, principles, attitudes, etc.; break away from tradition, established patterns, etc.: *to* liberalize *the curriculum.* **2** to make less severe or strict; make freer: *to* liberalize *the income tax laws.* **—*n-* lib′ er·al·i·za′ tion.**

lib·er·ate (lĭb′ ə rāt′) ***vt-*** **[lib·er·at·ed, lib·er·at·ing]** **1** to set free: *to* liberate *a slave.* **2** to free (a gas, radical, etc.) from chemical combination. **—*n-* lib′ er·a′ tion.**

lib·er·a·tor (lĭb′ ə rā′ tər) ***n-*** person who liberates, especially one who brings freedom to a people or nation.

lib·er·tar·i·an (lĭb′ ər târ′ ē ən) ***n-*** **1** supporter of the doctrine of free will. **2** person who advocates liberty, especially of thought and conduct.

lib·er·tine (lĭb′ ər tēn′) ***n-*** person who gives free rein to his lewd impulses and desires; rake. ***adj-*** loose in morals; lascivious; lewd.

lib·er·ty (lĭb′ ər tē) ***n-*** [*pl.* **lib·er·ties**] **1** freedom from foreign rule or harsh, unreasonable government: *The colonies fought to gain their* liberty. **2** freedom from captivity, prison, slavery, etc.: *The prisoner pleaded for his* liberty. **3** freedom from control: *Freedom of speech is a precious* liberty. **4** freedom of choice; right or power to do as one pleases: *to have much* liberty. **5** permission given to a sailor to go ashore.

at liberty 1 free; not confined: *The burglar is* at liberty *right now.* **2** allowed; permitted: *I'm not* at liberty *to tell you her secrets.* **3** not busy; unoccupied.

take liberties to be too bold or familiar.

Liberty Bell ***n-*** bell rung in Philadelphia, July 4, 1776, when the Continental Congress declared the independence of the thirteen American colonies.

li·bid·i·nous (lə bĭd′ ən əs) ***adj-*** lewd; lascivious; lustful. —***adv-*** **li·bid′ i·nous·ly.**

li·bi·do (lə bē′ dō) ***n-*** **1** sexual desire or instinct. **2** in psychoanalysis, driving forces or desires behind all human activities; vital impulse.

Li·bra (lī′ brə, lē′-) ***n-*** constellation of stars thought to outline the figure of a balance.

li·brar·i·an (lī brâr′ ē ən) ***n-*** person in charge of a library or doing library work as a profession.

li·brar·y (lī′ brâr′ ē) ***n-*** [*pl.* **li·brar·ies**] **1** room or building where books are kept to be used or borrowed. **2** room in a private house where books are kept. **3** collection of books, magazines, phonograph records, etc.

li·bret·tist (lĭ brĕt′ ĭst) ***n-*** writer of a libretto.

li·bret·to (lĭ brĕt′ ō) ***n-*** [*pl.* **li·bret·tos** or **li·bret·ti** (-ē)] **1** words or text of an opera or other long musical composition. **2** book containing these words.

lice (līs) *pl.* of **louse.**

li·cense (lī′ səns) ***n-*** **1** legal permission to do something; also, the document showing this permission: *a driver's* license; *a fishing* license. **2** freedom or right to ignore rules for the sake of effect: *poetic* license. **3** abuse of freedom; unrestrained liberty. **4** loose and lawless behavior; immoral action: *the unbelievable* license *of the invading soldiers.* ***vt-*** [**li·censed, li·cens·ing**] to give legal written permission (to do something): *to* license *a doctor to practice.* Also, *chiefly Brit.,* **li′cence.** —***n-*** **li′ cens·er** or **li′ cen·sor.**

li·cens·ee (lī′ sən sē′) ***n-*** person who receives a license.

li·cen·tious (lĭ sĕn′ chəs) ***adj-*** **1** unrestrained by law or morality; lawless; immoral. **2** lewd; dissolute; libertine. —***adv-*** **li·cen′ tious·ly.** ***n-*** **li·cen′ tious·ness.**

li·chee (lē′ chē) ***n-*** **1** edible fruit of an Asiatic tree related to the soapberries, having a thin, brittle shell and a single hard seed surrounded by a sweet pulp. **2** the tree itself. Also **litchi.**

li·chen (lī′ kən) ***n-*** small plant without flowers or true leaves that grows flat on rocks, trees, etc. Lichens are made up of fungi and algae growing cooperatively together. ***Hom-*** liken.

lick (lĭk) ***vt-*** **1** to pass the tongue over: *to* lick *a stamp.* **2** to move or pass over lightly: *The flames* licked *the meat on the grill.* **3** *Informal* to defeat; beat: *Our team can* lick *yours.* **4** *Informal* to whip; thrash: *to* lick *a bully.* ***n-*** **1** movement of the tongue (over something): *The cow gave her calf a* lick. **2** a salt lick. **3** *Informal* a small amount; a bit: *I don't care a* lick *about it.* **4** *Informal* a blow; slap. **5** *Informal* brief spell of work.

lick into shape to put into proper shape or condition.

lick·e·ty-split (lĭk′ ə tē splĭt′) *Informal* ***adv-*** rapidly; at full speed: *He ran* lickety-split *to the corner.*

lic·o·rice (lĭk′ ə rĭs, lĭk′ rĭsh) ***n-*** **1** dried root of a plant of the pea family, or an extract made from it, used in medicines and candy. **2** the plant itself. **3** candy flavored with such an extract.

lid (lĭd) ***n-*** **1** a movable top or cover to a container, box, etc.: *a pot* lid. **2** an eyelid. —***adj-*** **lid′ less.**

[1]**lie** (lī) ***n-*** untrue statement made in order to deceive; a deliberate untruth; falsehood: *He never tells a* lie. ***vi-*** [**lied, ly·ing**] **1** to make an untrue statement in order to deceive. **2** to give a misleading impression: *Figures never* lie. [from Old English **lyge.**] ***Hom-*** lye.

give the lie to 1 to accuse (someone) of not telling the truth. **2** to prove to be false.

[2]**lie** (lī) ***vi-*** [**lay** (lā), **lain** (lān), **ly·ing**] **1** to be in a flat or resting position: *The book* lies *on the table.* **2** to put oneself in a flat or resting position (often followed by "down"): *to* lie *on the sofa.* **3** to be situated: *Canada* lies *north of the United States.* **4** to remain in a certain condition: *His talent* lies *idle.* **5** to be; exist: *The trouble* lies *in the engine.* **6** to be buried: *His body* lies *in the churchyard.* ***n-*** **1** the way, position, or direction in which something is situated or arranged: *the sloping* lie *of the meadow; the* lie *of a golf ball.* **2** lair or hiding place of an animal. [from Old English **licgan.**] ***Hom-*** lye.

lie in to be confined in order to give birth to a child.

lie low to hide; stay out of sight.

►Confusion arises because LAY is both a transitive verb meaning to put (something) and the past tense of the intransitive verb LIE, meaning to recline; stretch out horizontally. Careful speakers and writers do not use LAY to mean LIE: *Read it to me as I* lie (*not* lay) *here. He read it to me as I* lay (*not* laid) *there. Please* lay *the box here. She* laid *the box carefully on the table.*

lied (lēd) *Music* ***n-*** [*pl.* **lie·der**] German art song. ***Hom-*** [1]lead.

lie detector ***n-*** instrument that records the bodily reactions of a person as he is being questioned. It is used to indicate a probable falsehood.

lief (lēv, lēf) *Archaic* ***adv-*** gladly. ***Hom-*** leaf or leave.

liege (lēj) ***n-*** **1** in medieval times, a lord, master, or ruler, called a **liege lord,** who had a right to services and loyalty from all of the people subject to him. **2** in medieval times, person, called a **liege′ man,** who owed services and loyalty to a lord, master, or ruler; vassal. ***adj-*** **1** having the right to devotion and service: *a* liege *lord.* **2** bound by feudal law to give service and allegiance. **3** faithful; loyal.

lien (lēn) ***n-*** legal claim upon the property of another as security for a debt. ***Hom-*** lean.

lieu (lo͞o, lyo͞o) **in lieu of** in place of; instead of.

Lieut. lieutenant.

lieu·ten·an·cy (lo͞o tĕn′ ən sē) ***n-*** office, term of office, rank, or authority of a lieutenant.

lieu·ten·ant (lo͞o tĕn′ ənt) ***n-*** **1** in the Army, Air Force, and Marine Corps, a **second lieutenant,** the officer of the lowest commissioned grade, or a **first lieutenant,** ranking next above this and next below a captain. **2** in the Navy and Coast Guard, either an officer ranking next below a lieutenant commander, or a **lieutenant (junior grade),** ranking next below this and just above an ensign. **3** officer next below a captain in a police or fire department. **4** person who acts for a superior; deputy.

lieutenant colonel ***n-*** in the Army, Air Force, and Marine Corps, an officer ranking next below a colonel and next above a major.

lieutenant commander ***n-*** in the Navy and Coast Guard, an officer ranking next below a commander and next above a lieutenant.

lieutenant general ***n-*** in the Army, Air Force, and Marine Corps, an officer ranking next below a general and next above a major general.

lieutenant governor ***n-*** an elected official next in rank to the governor of a State, who succeeds to the office in case of the governor's death or disability.

life (līf) ***n-*** [*pl.* **lives** (līvz)] **1** the particular quality which distinguishes animals and plants from rocks, earth, and other objects that do not grow and reproduce. **2** a being alive; existence. **3** a living person: *Two* lives *were lost in* *the accident.*. 4 period of a person's existence, between birth and death: *to be happy all one's* life. 5 living things: *animal* life. 6 report of a person's existence; biography: *The* life *of Washington.* 7 energy; vitality: *He's full of* life. 8 way of living: *a* life *of luxury.* 9 cheering influence; moving spirit: *the* life *of the party.* 10 period of existence or usefulness of something: *the* life *of a car. as* ***modifier***: *the* life *force*; life *sciences*; *a* life *appointment.*

bring to life 1 to bring back to the mind or senses. 2 to make lively. **come to life** 1 to regain consciousness. 2 to become lively or animated. **for dear life** in order to, or as if to, save one's life; with great and urgent effort, speed, etc. **for the life of me** *Informal* even if my life depended on it; by any means: *I couldn't go* for the life of me. **from life** from a living model. **not on your life** *Informal* definitely not; by no means. **to the life** exactly; perfectly imitated: *The portrait is Ferdy* to the life.

life belt ***n-*** life preserver made like a belt.

life·blood (līf′ blŭd′) ***n-*** 1 blood essential to life. 2 anything essential to life; source of vital strength and energy: *Research is the* lifeblood *of our society.*

life·boat (līf′ bōt′) ***n-*** boat for saving people at sea.

life buoy ***n-*** a float, usually a ring filled with light material or air, for keeping a person afloat in the water.

life cycle ***n-*** the entire series of changes in form and function that an organism undergoes from a specified stage to the same stage in the next generation.

life expectancy ***n-*** probable number of years of life of an individual, especially as determined statistically in terms of age, sex, environment, etc.

life·guard (līf′ gärd′) ***n-*** expert swimmer trained in rescue work, who looks after the safety of bathers.

life insurance ***n-*** 1 agreement by which a company insures a person's life in return for certain payments. The company agrees to pay a certain sum of money, at the purchaser's death, to a person he names. 2 amount of money to be received stated in such an agreement.

life jacket ***n-*** life preserver made like a jacket or vest.

life·less (līf′ ləs) ***adj-*** 1 dead: *a* lifeless *body.* 2 never having been alive; without life: *a* lifeless *statue.* 3 without living things: *a* lifeless *planet.* 4 not lively; dull. —***adv-*** **life′ less·ly.** ***n-*** **life′ less·ness.**

life·like (līf′ līk′) ***adj-*** seeming to be or closely imitating a living thing or real life. —***n-*** **life′ like′ ness.**

life·line (līf′ līn′) ***n-*** 1 any rope used for lifesaving, especially one shot by rocket to a ship in distress. 2 line attached to a lifeboat or life buoy for saving life. 3 signal rope used by a diver by which he is lowered or raised from the water. 4 route by which supplies can be sent to a place which cannot otherwise be reached.

life·long (līf′ lòng′) ***adj-*** lasting throughout life.

life net ***n-*** strong net or sheet of canvas used by firemen to catch persons jumping from high places without injuring them.

life preserver ***n-*** a ring, belt, or jacket, either inflatable or filled with material that floats, used to keep a person afloat in the water.

Life-preserver

life raft ***n-*** raft, often inflatable, used for saving people at sea.

life·sav·er (līf′ sā′ vər) ***n-*** 1 person or thing that saves people from drowning. 2 *Informal* person or thing that saves someone from a serious difficulty.

life·sav·ing (līf′ sā′ vĭng) ***n-*** rescue work, especially saving people from drowning. *as* ***modifier***: *a* lifesaving *course.*

life-size (līf′ sīz′) ***adj-*** of the same size as the object represented: *a* life-size *statue.*

life span ***n-*** length of time an organism lives.

life·time (līf′ tīm′) ***n-*** the length of time that a person lives; hence, the length of time that a thing lasts: *the* lifetime *of a car. as* ***modifier***: *a* lifetime *guarantee*; *a* lifetime *appointment.*

life·work (līf′ wûrk′) ***n-*** 1 work to which a person devotes a lifetime. 2 entire or main work of one's life.

lift (lĭft) ***vt-*** 1 to take hold of and raise to a higher place; take off the ground; hoist: *to* lift *a box.* 2 to raise upward: *to* lift *the head.* 3 to bring to a higher level; raise in rank, condition, value, etc.: *The good news* lifted *his spirits. Hard work* lifted *him out of poverty.* 4 *Informal* to steal. 5 *Informal* to plagiarize. 6 to change (a person's face) by surgery in order to remove wrinkles and other signs of age. ***vi-*** to seem to rise; disappear: *The fog* lifted. ***n-*** 1 a raising; an upward movement: *a* lift *of the hand.* 2 the amount that may be hoisted at one time; load. 3 aid; assistance, especially a ride: *He gave me a* lift *into town.* 4 a feeling of well-being: *The good news gave him a* lift. 5 elevated or erect bearing, carriage, etc.: *the proud* lift *of her head.* 6 *British* elevator. 7 layer that makes a shoe's heel higher. —***n-*** **lift′ er.**

lift off of a rocket or missile, to rise off the launching pad and begin flight.

lift one's voice to cry, speak, or sing out loudly.

lift·off (lĭft′ òf′, -ŏf′) ***n-*** take-off by a rocket or spacecraft from its launching pad.

lig·a·ment (lĭg′ ə mənt) ***n-*** band of tough tissue which connects bones or holds an organ of the body in place.

lig·a·ture (lĭg′ ə chər) ***n-*** 1 something that unites or binds, such as a bandage, cord, etc. 2 in surgery, a thread or wire used to tie blood vessels in order to stop bleeding. 3 in printing, two or more letters joined together to form a single character. The "ffl" in "sniffle" is a ligature. 4 *Music* a slur or a group of notes connected by a slur.

[1]light (līt) ***n-*** 1 the range of electromagnetic waves that stimulate the retina and by which human vision is made possible. The various colors have different wavelengths, ranging from the short violet to the longer red. 2 a source of brightness, such as an electric lamp, the sun, etc.; also, the brightness or radiance given off by these. 3 illumination from the sun; daylight; especially, daybreak or dawn. 4 source of mental or spiritual illumination; enlightenment. 5 way in which something appears or is viewed: *to put someone in a bad* light. 6 a setting afire or means of setting afire: *a* light *for a cigarette.* 7 gleam or glow; lively expression: *a* light *in her eyes.* 8 window or window pane. 9 famous person; luminary: *He is a shining* light. ***adj-*** **[light·er, light·est]** 1 clear; bright; not dark: *a* light, *airy room.* 2 of a color, pale or subdued rather than deep, dark, or intense: *a hazy,* light-*blue sky*; *the* light *yellow-brown of a sandbank.* ***vt-*** **[light·ed** or **lit** (lĭt), **light·ing]** 1 to set on fire; kindle: *to* light *a fire.* 2 to cause to shine and give forth brightness: *to* light *a lamp.* 3 to make bright and clear; illuminate: *Electric power* lights *the town at night.* 4 to show or guide by making bright and clear: *to* light *his way.* ***vi-*** to become bright; take fire; start to burn. [from Old English **lēoht,** "a light."]

according to one's lights according to one's beliefs and ideas: *Each acted* according to his lights. **bring to**

fāte, făt, dâre, bärn; bē, bĕt, mêre; bīte, bĭt; nōte, hŏt, môre, dòg; fŭn, fûr; to͞o, bo͝ok; oil; out; tar; thin; then; hw for wh as in *wh*at; zh for s as in u*s*ual; ə for a, e, i, o, u, as in *a*go, lin*e*n, per*i*l, at*o*m, min*u*s

light to reveal: *to* bring *facts* to light. **cast (throw,** or **shed) light on** to help in the understanding of; clarify: *to* throw light on *a problem.* **come to light** to be revealed; become known: *The facts* came to light. **in the light of** considering; taking into account: *to act quickly* in the light of *a new situation.* **to see the light** 1 to come into existence. 2 to come to public view. 3 to understand: *After the explanation he began to* see the light.

light up 1 to make bright or clear: *The lamp* lights up *the room.* 2 to brighten: *His face* lit up *with a smile.* 3 of lights, to come on together or one by one: *At nightfall, the city slowly* lighted up.

²**light** (līt) ***adj-*** **[light·er, light·est]** 1 not heavy; having little weight: *a* light *package*; light *as a feather.* 2 having less density, weight, bulk, power, etc., than others of its general type: *a* light *cloth*; *a* light *cruiser*; light *artillery*; *a* light, *pointed arch*; *a* light *soprano voice.* 3 slight or mild in comparison with others: *a* light *snow*; light *punishment.* 4 not serious or profound: *a book of* light *verse*; light *comedy*; *a* light *manner of dealing with a serious problem.* 5 not important; trivial: *The consequences were* light. 6 cheerful; gay: *a* light *heart*; *in a light* mood. 7 graceful; agile; nimble: *a* light *step.* 8 of foods, not rich or fatty. 9 of drinks, having a relatively mild and smooth taste: *a* light *whiskey*; light *wines.* 10 delicate; dainty; subtle: *a* light *touch on the keyboard*; *with a* light *hand.* ***adv-*** 1 lightly. 2 carrying little weight; without heavy equipment: *to travel* light. [from Old English **lighte,** meaning "not heavy."]

light in the head 1 slightly faint; dizzy. 2 foolish. **make light of** to treat as of little importance; disregard; pay little or no attention to: *to* make light of *one's troubles.*

³**light** (līt) ***vi-*** **[light·ed** or **lit** (lĭt), **light·ing]** 1 to settle; come to rest; alight: *The bird* lighted *on the bush.* 2 to come by chance: *to* light *on the right answer.* 3 to fall suddenly: *The blow* lighted *on his head.* [from Old English **līhtan,** meaning originally "to make (a load) less heavy; take the load off," thus "to dismount from a horse," and finally "to settle anywhere." It is closely related to ²**light** and ²**alight.**]

light into *Informal* to attack.

light out *Informal* to leave suddenly; depart in haste.

¹**light·en** (lī′ tən) ***vt-*** to make light, bright, or clear: *The sun* lightened *her hair.* ***vi-*** 1 to become light; grow brighter: *The sky* lightened *as the clouds lifted.* 2 to flash lightning: *It* lightened *and thundered all night.* [from Middle English **light(e)nen,** from ¹**light.**]

²**light·en** (lī′ tən) ***vt-*** 1 to make less heavy; reduce the load of: *to* lighten *a ship.* 2 to make less burdensome: *to* lighten *someone's troubles.* 3 to make more cheerful; enliven: *His jokes* lighten *any occasion.* [from Middle English **light(e)nen,** from ²**light.**]

¹**light·er** (lī′ tər) ***n-*** person or thing that causes something to give light or to burn; especially, a device for lighting cigarettes, cigars, etc. [from ¹**light,** "to set afire."]

²**light·er** (lī′ tər) ***n-*** large open barge used in loading and unloading vessels. ***vt-*** to carry (goods) in such a barge. [from Dutch **ligter** meaning literally "an unloader," from ²**light.**]

light-fin·gered (līt′ fĭng′ gərd) ***adj-*** 1 skillful at picking pockets. 2 having a deft, delicate touch.

light-foot·ed (līt′ fo͝ot′ əd) ***adj-*** stepping lightly; nimble.

light·head·ed (līt′ hĕd′ əd) ***adj-*** 1 dizzy or giddy on account of illness. 2 silly; foolish; thoughtless. ***—adv-*** **light′ head′ ed·ly.** ***n-*** **light′ head′ ed·ness.**

light·heart·ed (līt′ här′ təd) ***adj-*** 1 gay; cheerful. 2 free from worry. ***—adv-*** **light′ heart′ ed·ly.** ***n-*** **light′ heart′ ed·ness.**

light·house (līt′ hous′) ***n-*** a building, usually a tower, with a powerful light at the top to guide ships. It often marks dangerous rocks.

Lighthouse

light·ing (lī′ tĭng) ***n-*** 1 illumination; ignition. 2 system providing illumination, as in a theater; also, the apparatus providing it. 3 distribution of light and dark areas in a picture, photograph, etc.

light·ly (līt′ lē) ***adv-*** 1 with little weight, force, pressure, etc.; not heavily; gently: *to press* lightly *on a lever.* 2 to a small degree; moderately: *to season* lightly. 3 nimbly; swiftly: *to glide* lightly *over the ice.* 4 cheerfully; in a carefree manner: *to take a loss* lightly. 5 frivolously: *to behave* lightly. 6 slightingly; with indifference: *to think* lightly *of someone's efforts.* 7 with little or no reason: *He was not one to talk* lightly.

light meter ***n-*** device used in photography to measure the amount of light that falls on or is reflected from a scene to be photographed; exposure meter.

light-mind·ed (līt′ mīn′ dəd) ***adj-*** frivolous; silly. ***—adv-*** **light′-mind′ ed·ly.** ***n-*** **light′-mind′ ed·ness.**

¹**light·ness** (līt′ nəs) ***n-*** 1 brightness. 2 paleness of color. [from Old English **līhtnes,** from **līht,** "¹light."]

²**light·ness** (līt′ nəs) ***n-*** 1 smallness in amount or weight; lack of heaviness: *The* lightness *of the trunk made it easy to lift.* 2 lack of harshness or severity; mildness: *the* lightness *of the judge's sentence.* 3 nimbleness; grace: *the* lightness *of her step.* 4 frivolity; levity: *the* lightness *of his tone.* [from ²**light.**]

light·ning (līt′ nĭng) ***n-*** a flashing of light in the sky caused by electricity passing between clouds or from clouds to earth.

lightning ar·res·ter (ə rĕs′ tər) ***n-*** device that protects electrical equipment from sudden surges of high voltage caused by lightning bolts, often by grounding the surges through spark gaps.

lightning bug ***n-*** small beetle whose abdomen gives off flashes of light; a firefly.

lightning rod ***n-*** metal rod fastened on a building and connected with the earth to act as a ground conductor and protect the building from lightning.

lights (līts) ***n-*** *pl.* the lungs, especially of pigs, sheep, etc., used as food.

light·ship (līt′ shĭp′) ***n-*** vessel carrying a warning light and moored at sea to warn other ships of danger or to mark a channel.

light·some (līt′ səm) *Archaic* ***adj-*** 1 cheerful; gay. 2 frivolous. 3 nimble; lively. ***—adv-*** **light′ some·ly.** ***n-*** **light′ some·ness.**

light·weight (līt′ wāt′) ***n-*** 1 boxer who weighs between 127 and 135 pounds. 2 person or animal of less than average weight. 3 *Informal* stupid or unimportant person. ***adj-*** below average in weight.

light-year (līt′ yêr′) *Astronomy* ***n-*** unit of length equal to the distance light travels in one year, which is about 6×10^{12} miles.

lig·nin (lĭg′ nĭn) ***n-*** organic substance that forms the main part of woody tissue.

lig·nite (lĭg′ nīt′) ***n-*** soft, brownish-black coal in which the original wood has not been completely changed to coal and may still be recognized.

lig·num vi·tae (lĭg′ nəm vī′ tē) ***n-*** 1 any of several tropical American trees with very hard, heavy wood. 2 wood of these trees.

lik·a·ble (lī′ kə bəl) ***adj-*** pleasing and agreeable; inspiring friendly feelings or liking. ***—n-*** **lik′ a·ble·ness.**

[1]**like** (līk) ***prep-*** **1** similar to; having the characteristics of: *The town is* like *a place in the Alps.* **2** typical of: *It was* like *him to be kind.* **3** in the manner of: *He acted* like *a man.* **4** as if (something) is occurring or will occur: *It looks* like *rain. It sounds* like *war.* **5** such as: *green vegetables* like *beans and spinach.* **6** in the mood for; desirous of: *I feel* like *dozing.* ***adj-*** exactly or nearly the same; similar: *in a* like *manner.* ***n-*** the equal of a person or thing: *I have never seen its* like. [from Old English **gelic** meaning "similar; equal."]

and the like and others of the same kind: *books, newspapers, magazines,* and the like. **like as not** probably; the chances are: *Well,* like as not *we will see you there.*

[2]**like** (līk) ***vt-*** **[liked, lik·ing] 1** to find agreeable or pleasant; enjoy: *All his classmates* like *him. Do you* like *sports?* **2** to approve of or admire: *I* like *his spirit.* ***vi-*** to prefer; choose: *I will go when I* like. ***n-*** **likes** preferences: *What are your* likes *and dislikes?* [from Old English **lician,** "be pleasing to (someone)." Originally **lician** meant "be like or equal," thus "fitting and proper" and "pleasing."]

-like *suffix* meaning "resembling" or "similar to": *child*like.

like·li·hood (līk′ lē hŏŏd′) ***n-*** probability; chance.

like·ly (līk′ lē) ***adj-*** **[like·li·er, like·li·est] 1** reasonably expected (to); apt (to): *He is* likely *to make the All-Star team.* **2** suitable; promising: *a* likely *place to stop*; *a* likely *lad for the job.* **3** probable: *a* likely *consequence.* **4** hardly believable (used sarcastically): *a* likely *tale.* ***adv-*** probably: *They will* likely *be late.*

►For usage note see LIABLE.

lik·en (lī′ kən) ***vt-*** to say (anything) is like another; compare: *She* likened *me to a cat.* ***Hom-*** lichen.

like·ness (līk′ nəs) ***n-*** **1** picture; representation; portrait: *That photograph is a good* likeness *of you.* **2** appearance; form: *an enemy in the* likeness *of a friend.* **3** resemblance; similarity: *the* likeness *between the two sisters.*

like·wise (līk′ wīz′) ***adv-*** **1** in the same manner: *Go and do* likewise. **2** also; too: *He is tall and* likewise *strong.*

lik·ing (lī′ kĭng) ***n-*** **1** fondness: *I have a* liking *for books.* **2** taste: *This food is not to my* liking.

li·lac (lī′ lək, -lăk′) ***n-*** **1** shrub with clusters of fragrant white or pinkish-purple blossoms; also, the blossoms of this shrub. **2** the color of its blossom; a light, pinkish purple. ***adj-***: *a* lilac *and orange dress.*

lil·li·pu·tian (lĭl′ ə pyōō′ shən) ***n-*** **1** very small person. **2 Lilliputian** one of the tiny inhabitants of **Lilliput** (lĭl′ ə pət), an imaginary country described in Swift's "Gulliver's Travels." ***adj-***: *his* Lilliputian *strength.*

lilt (lĭlt) ***vi-*** to sing or speak with a light rhythm and fluctuating pitch. ***vt-***: *to* lilt *a tune.* ***n-*** **1** lively, gay song. **2** rhythmic flow; cadence: *He speaks with a Welsh* lilt. **3** light, springy movement: *On such a fine morning there was a* lilt *in her step.*

lilt·ing (lĭl′ tĭng) ***adj-*** **1** speaking or singing with a lilt: *a* lilting *voice.* **2** light and gay: *a* lilting *tune.*

lil·y (lĭl′ ē) ***n-*** [*pl.* **lil·ies**] plant grown from a bulb and having a trumpet-shaped blossom; also, its blossom.

lil·y-liv·ered (lĭl′ ē lĭv′ ərd) ***adj-*** cowardly; timid.

lily of the valley ***n-*** [*pl.* **lilies of the valley**] small plant with tiny white or pink bell-shaped flowers on a slender stalk; also, its sweet-smelling flowers.

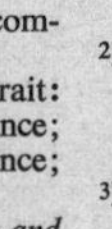
Lily

lily pad ***n-*** one of the large, rounded, floating leaves of the water lily.

lil·y-white (lĭl′ ē hwīt′) ***adj-*** **1** white as a lily. **2** *Informal* excluding, or discriminating against, Negroes.

li·ma bean (lī′ mə) ***n-*** any of several varieties of bean grown for their broad, flat, edible seeds; also, the green or greenish-white seed.

limb (lĭm) ***n-*** **1** arm or leg of a man or animal or the wing of a bird. **2** one of the main branches of a tree. **3** *Astronomy* the edge of a heavenly body, as seen from earth; also, the earth's edge, as seen from a spacecraft. ***—adj-*** **limb′ less.**

[1]**lim·ber** (lĭm′ bər) ***adj-*** able to bend and move easily; supple; flexible: *a* limber *tree branch*; *a* limber *body.* ***vt-*** to make supple or nimble: *Exercise* limbers *the body.* [from **limb.**] ***—n-*** **lim′ ber·ness.**

limber up to make or become supple and nimble through exercise, etc.: *The dancers* limbered up.

[2]**lim·ber** (lĭm′ bər) ***n-*** detachable front part of a gun carriage. [apparently from French **limoniere,** meaning literally "belonging to the shafts."]

lim·bo (lĭm′ bō) ***n-*** **1** a place of confinement or oblivion. **2** in some Christian theologies, an abode of the souls of just people born before Christ, and of unbaptized infants.

Lim·burg·er (lĭm′ bûr′ gər) ***n-*** a soft, white, and strong-smelling cheese. Also **Limburger cheese, Lim′ burg cheese.**

[1]**lime** (līm) ***n-*** chemical compound of calcium and oxygen, prepared by burning limestone, bones, or shells; calcium oxide (CaO_2). It is used for making cement, for improving acid soil, etc. [from Old English **līm.**]

[2]**lime** (līm) ***n-*** **1** yellowish-green citrus fruit, somewhat like a lemon. **2** the tree bearing this fruit. **3** a yellowish-green color. ***adj-***: *a* lime *pie*; *a* lime *silk.* [from French, from Spanish **lima,** from Persian **līmu(n),** "lemon."]

[3]**lime** (līm) ***n-*** linden [from earlier English **line,** from Old English **lind,** meaning "linden."]

lime·kiln (līm′ kĭl′ *also* -kĭln′) ***n-*** furnace in which limestone, shells, etc., are burned to obtain lime.

lime·light (līm′ līt′) ***n-*** **1** brilliant light produced by playing an intensely hot flame upon lime, formerly used as a spotlight in the theater. **2** prominent position before the public; glare of publicity.

lim·er·ick (lĭm′ ər ĭk) ***n-*** humorous poem of five lines. The first, second, and fifth lines rhyme, as do the third and fourth:

There once was an old man of Lyme
Who married three wives at a time.
When asked why a third,
He replied, "One's absurd,
And bigamy, sir, is a crime."

lime·stone (līm′ stōn′) ***n-*** rock used for building, road making, etc. It yields lime when burned.

lime·wa·ter (līm′ wôt′ ər, -wŏt′ ər) ***n-*** solution of lime and water, used in medicine.

lim·it (lĭm′ət) ***n-*** **1** that which confines, ends, or checks: *a speed* limit. **2** point not to be passed; furthest point: *to reach the* limit *of one's endurance.* **3** (usually **limits**) border or boundary: *the city* limits. **4** maximum or minimum allowed: *a* limit *of two chances per person.* **5** something nearly intolerable: *That is the* limit! ***vt-*** to restrict or confine: *to* limit *the amount of candy one eats.* ***—adj-*** **lim′ it·a·ble:** *his* limitable *authority.* ***n-*** **lim′ i·ter.** ***adj-*** **lim′ it·less:** *It has* limitless *possibilities.*

go the limit to go as far, or do as much, as one can.

lim·i·ta·tion (lĭm′ə tā′ shən) ***n-*** **1** a limiting or being limited. **2** something that bounds or holds back;

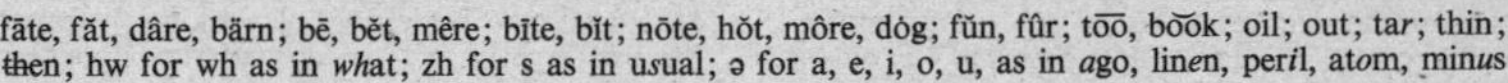
fāte, făt, dâre, bärn; bē, bĕt, mêre; bīte, bĭt; nōte, hŏt, môre, dòg; fŭn, fûr; tōō, bŏŏk; oil; out; tar; thin; then; hw for wh as in *wh*at; zh for s as in u*s*ual; ə for a, e, i, o, u, as in *a*go, lin*e*n, per*i*l, at*o*m, min*u*s

restriction or qualification, especially with regard to abilities or personality: *His height is a* limitation.

lim·it·ed (lĭm′ ə təd) ***adj***- **1** restricted; defined: *a* limited *amount of space available.* **2** of a train, carrying a restricted number of passengers and making only a few stops. **3** controlled by law or statute: *a* limited *monarchy*; *a* limited *partnership.* ***n***-: *the Chicago* limited.

limn (lĭm) *Archaic* ***vt***- **[limned, lim·ning] 1** to paint or draw. **2** to portray; depict. —***n***- **limn′ er** (lĭm′ ər, -nər).

lim·ou·sine (lĭm′ ə zēn′) ***n***- large, usually luxurious automobile, especially one in which the driver's seat is separated by a glass partition from the back seat.

[1]**limp** (lĭmp) ***n***- lame, halting walk. ***vi***-: *He* limped *off the tennis court.* [possibly from Old English **lemphealt,** meaning "lame."]

[2]**limp** (lĭmp) ***adj***- **1** lacking stiffness, firmness, or strength: *a* limp *shirt*; *to be* limp *with relief.* **2** weak in character. [of uncertain origin.] —***adv***- **limp′ ly.** ***n***- **limp′ ness.**

lim·pet (lĭm′ pət) ***n***- shellfish with a flat, cone-shaped shell, found clinging tightly to rocks or piling.

lim·pid (lĭm′ pĭd′) ***adj***- transparent; sparklingly clear: *a* limpid *pool.* —***adv***- **lim′ pid·ly.** ***n***- **lim·pid′ i·ty** or **lim′ pid·ness.**

linch·pin (lĭnch′ pĭn′) ***n***- iron pin through the end of an axle to keep the wheel from coming off; axle pin.

lin·den (lĭn′ dən) ***n***- any of several varieties of large shade trees with heart-shaped leaves and clusters of cream-colored flowers, such as the lime tree in Europe or the basswood in North America.

[1]**line** (līn) ***n***- **1** long, narrow mark made with a pencil, pen, tool, etc.: *Draw a* line *down the center.* **2** long, strong piece of string, rope, or wire used for a special purpose: *telephone* line; *fishing* line. **3** wrinkle or crease on the face or palm of the hand. **4** long row or series of persons or things: *a waiting* line; *a* line *of cars.* **5** row of printed or written words on a page or column: *This article takes ten* lines *in the paper.* **6** boundary; border: *The prisoner escaped across the state* line. **7** plan of thought or action: *Along what* line *will the story be written?* **8** path of travel; course: *The bird flew in a straight* line *across the sky.* **9** series of persons following one another, in a family: *He comes from a royal* line. **10** outline; contour: *The* line *of his back was stiff and straight.* **11** business; occupation: *What is his* line? **12** range of items: *The salesman showed his* line *to the shopkeeper.* **13** series of ships, trains, buses, etc., which give regular service; a transportation company: *Not many bus* lines *run in the country.* **14** in football, the line of scrimmage; also, the linemen. **15 lines** actor's words or dialogue in a play. **16** *Mathematics* a set of points; the union of two opposite rays with a common endpoint. See [1]*ray.* ***vt***- **[lined, lin·ing] 1** to draw long, straight, narrow marks on: *to* line *poster paper.* **2** to form or establish a row along: *Cars* lined *the curb.* [from Old English **līne,** "cord," and Old French **ligne,** "row; stroke made by a pen," both of which come from Latin **linea,** "flaxen thread or cord (used as a measuring device or marker)."]

all along the line at every point; everywhere: *He had success* all along the line. **bring into line** to persuade or cause (a person or group) to cooperate or agree. **come into line** to agree; cooperate. **draw the line** (or **a line**). See *draw.* **get** (or **have**) **a line on** to obtain (or have) information on. **hold the line** to stand firm; permit no retreat. **in line 1** in a long, straight row. **2** in agreement or harmony. **in line for** to be the next for; slated for: *He's* in line for *a vice-presidency.* **in line of duty** in the course or performance of duty. **on a line** evenly lined up; on the same level. **out of line 1** not conforming with accepted standards: *Her behavior was* out of line. **2** uncalled for; insubordinate: *His retort was* out of line. **read between the lines** to find a hidden meaning in a letter, speech, etc. **toe the line** to submit to discipline; obey orders; accept what is laid down.

line out in baseball, to be put out by hitting a line drive that is caught.

line up 1 to form a long straight row: *The soldiers* lined up *for inspection.* **2** to align: *to* line up *the wheels of a car.* **3** to rally; enlist the support of: *to* line up *volunteers.* **4** to assemble; amass.

[2]**line** (līn) ***vt***- **[lined, lin·ing]** to cover the inner surface of: *to* line *curtains*; *to* line *a box.* [from earlier **line** meaning "piece of linen cloth; flax," partly from [1]**line** and partly from Old English **līn,** "flax."]

lin·e·age (lĭn′ ē ĭj) ***n***- line of ancestors; also, all the descendants of one ancestor.

lin·e·al (lĭn′ ē əl) ***adj***- **1** pertaining to or in the direct descent from an ancestor: *his* lineal *heirs.* **2** linear. —***adv***- **lin′ e·al·ly.**

lin·e·a·ment (lĭn′ ē ə mənt) ***n***- (usually **lineaments**) outline or feature, especially of the face.

lin·e·ar (lĭn′ ē ər) ***adj***- **1** consisting of lines: *a* linear *drawing.* **2** having length only: *a straight line is a* linear *curve.* **3** along a line: *Light waves exhibit* linear *motion.* **4** of or having to do with straight-line equations.

linear equation ***n***- equation whose graph is a straight line. Example: 3x — 2 = 24.

linear measure ***n***- **1** measurement of length or distance. **2** system of measures for length; also, one such measure: *The mile and the inch are* linear measures.

line·back·er (līn′ băk′ ər) ***n***- in football, a defensive player stationed just behind the line of scrimmage.

line drive ***n***- in baseball, a batted ball that travels in a nearly straight line, usually not far from the ground.

line graph ***n***- graph in which the values represented by points are connected by straight lines.

line·man (līn′ mən) ***n***- [*pl.* **line·men**] **1** man who puts up and repairs telephone or telegraph wires. **2** inspector of railroad tracks. **3** in surveying, person who carries the tape, line, or chain. **4** in football, player, such as a guard or tackle, whose main position is in the line.

lin·en (lĭn′ ən) ***n***- **1** the thread spun from flax fibers. **2** the strong, loosely woven cloth made of this thread. **3 linens** articles once made of linen, but now made of cotton and other materials as well. They include sheets, tablecloths, towels, and sometimes shirts and underwear. *as **modifier**: a* linen *dress.*

line of fire ***n***- course within which gunfire is directed.

line of force or **line of flux** ***n***- one of a group of imaginary lines drawn to illustrate the field around a magnet.

line of scrimmage ***n***- in football, a line across the field and parallel with the goal lines, established at each point where the ball is placed.

line of sight ***n***- **1** line between a person's eye and the object or point at which he is looking. **2** line, unbroken by the horizon, between transmitting and receiving antennas.

[1]**lin·er** (lī′ nər) ***n***- **1** large, fast commercial ship belonging to a shipping line. **2** in baseball, a ball hit straight and low; line drive. **3** person who makes lines: *a road* liner. [from [1]**line.**]

[2]**lin·er** (lī′ nər) ***n***- **1** person who makes, fits, or attaches linings. **2** lining: *a helmet* liner. [from [2]**line.**]

line segment *Mathematics* ***n***- set of points made up of two given points and all the points between them.

lines·man (līnz′ mən) ***n***- [*pl.* **lines·men**] **1** in football, an official who has charge of marking the progress of the ball in play and the distance to be gained. **2** in tennis, an official who decides whether the ball in play strikes inside or outside the lines of the court. 3 telephone or telegraph lineman.

line-up or **line·up** (līn′ ŭp′) *n*- 1 persons arranged in a line, as for identification: *a police* line-up. 2 in team sports, the arrangement of a team's players before a game or play; also, the players themselves: *Dick is in today's* line-up. 3 *Informal* any grouping.

-ling *suffix* (used to form nouns) 1 one connected or related to: *nurse*ling; *hire*ling. 2 small; diminutive (often used contemptuously): *duck*ling; *prince*ling.

lin·ger (lĭng′ gər) *vi*- 1 to remain long or be reluctant to go; tarry: *They* lingered *at the beach.* 2 to delay; procrastinate: *to* linger *over a decision.* —*n*- **lin′ ger·er.**

lin·ge·rie (län′ jə rā′, län′ jə rē′, *French* lăn zhə rē′) *n*- women's undergarments and sleeping clothes.

lin·go (lĭng′ gō) *Informal n*- [*pl.* **lin·goes**] 1 language; dialect, used humorously or contemptuously of an unfamiliar speech. 2 special vocabulary of a profession or other field of interest; jargon: *baseball* lingo.

lin·gua fran·ca (lĭng′ gwə frăng′ kə) *n*- 1 mixture of Italian, French, Spanish, Greek, and Arabic, spoken in the Mediterranean area. 2 any language or jargon commonly used as a trade language.

lin·guist (lĭng′ gwĭst) *n*- 1 person skilled in several different languages. 2 student of language or linguistics.

lin·guis·tic (lĭng gwĭs′ tĭk) *adj*- of or pertaining to language or linguistics. —*adv*- **lin·guis′ ti·cal·ly.**

lin·guis·tics (lĭng gwĭs′ tĭks) *n*- (takes singular verb) the science that deals with the nature of language, the structure and history of individual languages and the relations among them, the exact sounds used in each language, and the arrangement of these sounds in larger structures such as words, phrases, and sentences.

lin·i·ment (lĭn′ ə mənt) *n*- liquid for rubbing on the skin to ease aches, sprains, etc.

lin·ing (lī′ nĭng) *n*- inside covering; also, the material used to cover an inner surface: *the stomach* lining; lining *for a coat.*

link (lĭngk) *n*- 1 one of a series of loops or connecting rings in a chain. 2 something that connects or joins; tie. 3 in land surveying, the hundredth part of a chain, equal to 7.92 inches. *vi*-: *The facts finally* linked *up.* *vt*- to join; unite; connect: *They* linked *arms.*

link·age (lĭngk′ ĭj) *n*- 1 a way of being linked. 2 system of links, especially the series of connecting rods transmitting power or motion in an engine. 3 *Biology* a grouping of two or more genes on the same chromosome, so that they tend to be inherited together. 4 *Chemistry* way that atoms or groups of atoms are associated to form a molecule; bond.

linking verb *Grammar n*- verb such as "be," "become," "seem," etc., which links a noun phrase with an adjective in the pattern: The black cat ——— small. The linking verb sometimes links two noun phrases, as in: *"That man* is *a senator."* or *"My father* became *the leader of the troop."* A few linking verbs link a noun phrase with an adverb or adverb phrase as in: *"The white car* is *here."* or *"The church* is *at the top of the hill."*

links (lĭngks) *n*- *pl.* golf course. *Hom*- lynx.

lin·net (lĭn′ ət) *n*- small European songbird.

li·no·le·um (lĭ nō′ lē əm) *n*- floor covering made of compressed cork and linseed oil on burlap or canvas.

Li·no·type (lī′ nə tīp′) *n*- trademark name for a machine that sets and casts a line of type in a single metal bar, called a slug. See also *Monotype.*

lin·seed (lĭn′ sēd′) *n*- seed of the flax plant, from which **linseed oil** is pressed. Linseed oil is used in making paints, linoleum, etc.

lin·sey-wool·sey (lĭn′ zē wŏŏl′ zē) *n*- coarse cloth of wool mixed with some linen or cotton.

lint (lĭnt) *n*- 1 fuzz of short fibers that works loose from some kinds of cloth. 2 fleecy fibers scraped from linen cloth and used in bandages for dressing wounds. 3 raw cotton after ginning. —*adj*- **lint′ y** [**lint·i·er, lint·i·est**]: *a* linty *blanket.*

lin·tel (lĭn′ təl) *n*- piece of stone or timber set into a wall above a door or window to support the wall above the opening.

lint·er (lĭn′ tər) *n*- machine for removing **linters**, the short fibers left sticking to cottonseed after one ginning.

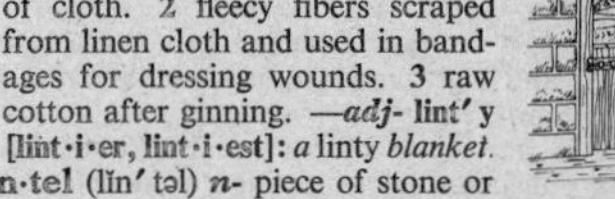
Lion, about 9 ft. long

li·on (lī′ ən) *n*- 1 large and powerful, tawny cat found in Africa and South Asia, called the King of Beasts for its strength and appearance. Adult males have dark, shaggy manes. 2 a man of strength and courage. 3 (also **social lion**) celebrated person who is much sought after by society. —*n*- *fem.* **li′on·ess.**

li·on·ize (lī′ ə nīz′) *vt*- [**li·on·ized, li·on·iz·ing**] to treat as a celebrity: *to* lionize *a new astronaut.*

lion's share *n*- the greater or greatest part.

lip (lĭp) *n*- 1 either of the fleshy edges of the mouth. 2 the rim or edge of a hollow opening or container.

li·pase (lī′ pās′, lĭp′ ās′) *n*- any of a group of enzymes that split fats into fatty acids and glycerol.

lip-read (lĭp′ rēd′) *vt*- [**lip-read, lip-read·ing**] to understand what is being said by watching the movements of the speaker's lips. —*n*- **lip′ -read′er.**

lip service *n*- statements of belief, agreement, etc., that are spoken but are not sincere.

lip·stick (lip′ stĭk′) *n*- cosmetic stick for coloring lips.

liq. 1 liquid. 2 liquor.

liq·ue·fac·tion (lĭ′ kwə făk′ shən) *n*- a liquefying.

li·que·fy (lĭ′ kwə fī′) *vi*- [**liq·ue·fied, liq·ue·fy·ing**] to become liquid; melt: *Ice cream* liquefies *quickly in heat.* *vt*- to change to a liquid: *to* liquefy *tin by melting.* —*adj*- **liq′ ue·fi′ a·ble.** *n*- **liq′ ue·fi′ er.**

li·queur (lĭ kûr′) *n*- sweet, strong, flavored, and often syrupy alcoholic beverage; cordial.

liq·uid (lĭ′ kwĭd) *adj*- 1 able to flow, as water, oil, and sap do; not solid or gaseous: *a* liquid *wax*; liquid *air.* 2 smooth, clear, and flowing in sound: *a sweet and* liquid *voice.* 3 in phonetics, pronounced without any blocking of the air stream, as the consonant /l/ is. 4 clear and shining: *the dog's* liquid *eyes.* 5 easily changed into cash: *bonds and other* liquid *assets.* *n*- 1 any substance in the liquid state under the conditions of temperature and pressure existing on earth. 2 substance, such as water, oil, sap, etc., that flows but is not a gas. 3 speech sound pronounced without any blocking of the air stream. The consonants /l/ and /r/ are liquids. —*n*- **li·quid′ i·ty** or **liq′ uid·ness.** *adv*- **liq′ uid·ly.**

liquid air *n*- air liquefied by extremely low temperatures and high pressures, used as a refrigerant.

liq·ui·date (lĭ′ kwə dāt′) *vt*- [**liq·ui·dat·ed, liq·ui·dat·ing**] 1 to pay off or settle: *to* liquidate *a debt.* 2 to settle

---

fāte, făt, dâre, bärn; bē, bĕt, mêre; bīte, bĭt; nōte, hŏt, môre, dȯg; fŭn, fûr; tōō, bŏŏk; oil; out; ta*r*; thin; then; hw for wh as in *wh*at; zh for s as in u*s*ual; ə for a, e, i, o, u, as in *a*go, lin*e*n, per*i*l, at*o*m, min*u*s

the affairs of (a business, estate, etc.) by turning the assets into cash, paying the debts, and dividing what is left among the owners or heirs. **3** to make harmless; especially, to kill quietly: *The dictator* liquidated *his enemies.* ***vi-***: *The company was badly in debt, so they decided to* liquidate. ***—n-*** **liq′ ui·da′ tion.**

liquid measure ***n-*** **1** system of measuring liquids. **2** any unit of such a system: *The pint and the liter are* liquid measures.

liquid oxygen ***n-*** oxygen liquefied by extremely low temperatures and high pressures, used in steel making, rocket propellants, etc.

liquid state ***n-*** one of the three physical states of matter in which a substance has a definite volume but not definite shape. A liquid takes the shape of a container with equal or greater volume. See also *gaseous state* and *solid state.*

liq·uor (lĭk′ ər) ***n-*** **1** any strong alcoholic drink, such as gin, whiskey, or brandy. **2** any liquid, such as broth, syrup, or brine.

li·ra (lêr′ ə) ***n-*** [*pl.* **li·re** (lē′ rā′) or **li·ras**] **1** monetary unit of Italy. **2** in Turkey and Syria, a pound.

lisle (līl) ***n-*** fine, hard-twisted cotton thread, or a fabric knitted from it, used especially for stockings.

lisp (lĭsp) ***vi-*** to pronounce (s) or (z) incorrectly as (th). A person who lisps would pronounce "sunspot" as "thŭnthpŏt," and "zip" as "thĭp." ***vt-***: *to* lisp *a poem.* ***n-***: *She spoke with a* lisp. ***—n-*** **lisp′ er.**

lis·some or **lis·som** (lĭs′ əm) ***adj-*** **1** lithe; supple: *a* lissome *young girl.* **2** nimble; swift and light in motion. ***—adv-*** **lis′ some·ly.**

[1]**list** (lĭst) ***n-*** series of names, items, titles, etc.; catalog; roll; register. ***vt-*** to name or write down, usually in some order: *to* list *the jobs one has held.* [from Old French **liste** meaning "list; border; strip," from an early Germanic **lista** of the same meaning.]

[2]**list** (lĭst) ***vi-*** to tilt or lean to one side in the water: *The ship* listed *to starboard.* ***n-***: *The ship developed a bad* list. [special use of [3]**list** in the sense of "inclination to."]

[3]**list** (lĭst) *Archaic* ***vi-*** to please; choose. [from Old English **lystan** meaning "to be pleasing (to someone); to incline (someone) toward."]

[4]**list** (lĭst) ***n-*** **1** edge or selvage of cloth. **2** band of cloth. **3** ridge alongside a plowed furrow. **4** slender strip of wood. ***vt-*** **1** to cover with strips of cloth. **2** to trim away a strip from the edge of (a board). **3** to plow with a lister. [from Old English **list,** related to [1]**list.**]

[5]**list** (lĭst) *Archaic* ***vi-*** to listen. [from Middle English **listen,** from Old English **hlystan,** "to hear."]

lis·ten (lĭs′ ən) ***vi-*** **1** to pay attention in order to hear; make an effort to hear: *to* listen *carefully for a footfall.* **2** to heed advice or instruction: *You'll never do that job right if you don't* listen. **3** to hear purposely for pleasure, instruction, etc.: *to* listen *to music.* ***—n-*** **lis′ ten·er.**

listen in 1 to tune in a radio station to hear a broadcast. **2** to eavesdrop, as on the telephone.

list·er (lĭs′ tər) ***n-*** **1** kind of plow that digs furrows for planting seeds. **2** (also **lister planter**) such a plow equipped with attachments for dropping seeds in the furrow and then covering the seeds.

list·less (lĭst′ ləs) ***adj-*** lacking energy or desire to move or act; indifferent; languid; lethargic: *Hot, humid weather made him* listless. ***—adv-*** **list′ less·ly.** ***n-*** **list′ less·ness.**

list price ***n-*** retail price for merchandise as quoted by a store or catalog.

lists (lĭsts) ***n- p.*** **1** in medieval days, the enclosure or the field in which tournaments were fought by knights in shining armor. **2** any place of contest.

lit (lĭt) *p.t. & p.p.* of [1]**light** and [3]**light.**

lit·a·ny (lĭt′ ə nē) ***n-*** [*pl.* **lit·a·nies**] form of prayer, led by the clergyman with responses from the congregation.

lit·chi (lē′ chē) lichee.

li·ter (lē′ tər) ***n-*** a measure of volume in the metric system, defined as the volume of one kilogram of water at 4° C. and under a standard pressure of 760 mm.

lit·er·a·cy (lĭt′ ər ə sē) ***n-*** **1** ability to read and write. **2** learning and culture; education.

lit·er·al (lĭt′ ər əl) ***adj-*** **1** word-for-word; verbatim: *a* literal *translation.* **2** following the exact truth; not exaggerated; precise: *a* literal *statement.* **3** inclined to follow the exact words; matter-of-fact: *a* literal *mind.* ***Hom-*** littoral. ***—n-*** **lit′ er·al·ness.**

lit·er·al·ly (lĭt′ ər ə lē) ***adv-*** **1** in a literal manner: *to* translate *literally*; *to speak* literally. **2** *Informal* (intensifier only): *I* literally *broke my back getting the job done.*

lit·er·ar·y (lĭt′ ə rĕr′ ē) ***adj-*** **1** of or relating to literature or to authors: *a* literary *masterpiece*; literary *studies.* **2** especially fit for writing: *a* literary *talent.*

lit·er·ate (lĭt′ ər ət) ***adj-*** **1** able to read and write. **2** marked by learning and culture, especially in literature. ***n-*** person who can read and write. ***—adv-*** **lit′ er·ate·ly.**

lit·er·a·ture (lĭt′ ər ə chər, -tyŏŏr′) ***n-*** **1** written works, especially such imaginative works as poems, plays, essays, and stories considered valuable for their style, form, and subject matter. **2** any collection or body of such works from a particular country, period of time, etc.: *American* literature; *modern* literature. **3** everything written on a single subject, considered as a whole: *medical* literature. *as* ***modifier***: *a* literature *course.*

-lith *combining form* (used to form nouns): *mono*lith (single stone). [from Greek **lithos,** "stone."]

lithe (līth, *also* līth) ***adj-*** [**lith·er, lith·est**] able to bend easily; supple. ***—adv-*** **lithe′ ly.** ***n-*** **lithe′ ness.**

lith·i·um (lĭth′ ē əm) ***n-*** soft, silver-white, metal element, the lightest metal known. It is used in making porcelain, medicines, etc. Symbol Li, At. No. 3, At. Wt. 6.939.

litho- *combining form* stone: litho*graphy* (printing from stone). [from Greek **lithos,** "stone."]

lith·o·graph (lĭth′ ə grăf′) ***n-*** a print made by the process of lithography. ***vt-*** to print from a stone. ***—n-*** **li·thog′ ra·pher** (lĭth ŏg′ rə fər). ***adj-*** **lith′ o·graph′ ic.** ***adv-*** **lith′ o·graph′ i·cal·ly.**

li·thog·ra·phy (lĭ thŏg′ rə fē) ***n-*** art or process of printing with a special kind of flat stone or metal plate, based on the fact that oily ink will not stick to the parts of the stone or plate treated with water or a special gum, but will stick to the design that is to be printed.

lith·o·sphere (lĭth′ ə sfêr′) ***n-*** the solid crust of the globe, as distinct from the layers of air and water.

lit·i·gant (lĭt′ ə gənt) ***n-*** either party in a lawsuit. *as* ***modifier***: *one of the* litigant *parties.*

lit·i·ga·tion (lĭt′ ə gā′ shən) ***n-*** act or process of carrying on a lawsuit; also, a lawsuit.

lit·mus (lĭt′ məs) ***n-*** violet-blue dye obtained from lichens, which is turned red by an acid and restored to blue by an alkali. It is used to make **litmus paper,** soft paper stained with litmus that is used to indicate whether something is acid or alkali.

li·tre (lē′ tər) *chiefly Brit.* liter.

Litt. D. 1 Doctor of Literature. **2** Doctor of Letters.

lit·ter (lĭt′ ər) ***n-*** **1** paper, scraps, etc., scattered carelessly about. **2** young born at one time to pigs, dogs, etc.: *a* litter *of puppies.* **3** straw, hay, etc., used as bedding for animals. **4** cot or stretcher for carrying a sick or wounded person. **5** couch with a canopy,

Roman litter

borne on men's shoulders by means of long shafts. ***vt-*** to make (a place) untidy by scattering odds and ends about. ***vi-* 1** to drop and strew trash about carelessly. **2** to give birth to young puppies, pigs, etc.

lit·ter·bug (lĭt′ ər bŭg′) *Informal* ***n-*** person who litters public areas with waste paper and other trash.

lit·tle (lĭt′ əl) ***adj-*** **[lit·tler, lit·tlest** or **least] 1** small in size or quantity; small by comparison: *a* little *box*; *a* little *river*; *a* little *man.* **2** small in dignity or importance; trivial: *to work at a* little *post*; *to fret about* little *things.* **3** short in time or distance; brief: *a* little *while*; *a* little *walk to the store.* **4** having the charm of smallness: *a dear* little *house.* **5** narrow; petty; mean: *He has a* little *mind.* ***adv-*** **[less, least] 1** slightly; hardly any or not at all: *She is* little *known. He* little *cares what happens.* **2** seldom; rarely: *He goes to the movies very* little. ***n-*** small or negligible amount: *I saw a* little *of the show. She gives* little *to charity.* **—*n-* lit′ tle·ness.**

a little to a small extent or degree; slightly: *It's* a little *warm here.* **little by little** gradually; by degrees. **little or nothing** hardly anything. **make little of** to treat as of little or no importance. **not a little** very; very much: *The problem gave us* not a little *trouble.* **think little of** to have a low regard for; consider of small value.

Little Dipper ***n-*** group of seven stars including the North Star, located in the Northern Hemisphere; Ursa Minor. Also **Little Bear.**

Little Dipper

Little League ***n-*** any one of many leagues belonging to an international organization of baseball teams for boys eight to twelve years old. Little-League baseball is sponsored by local businessmen, civic groups, etc., and has almost the same rules as regular baseball, except that the diamond is smaller and the games are six innings long instead of nine. *as* ***modifier*** **(Little-League):** *a* Little-League *champion.* **—*n-* Little Leaguer.**

lit·to·ral (lĭt′ ər əl) ***adj-*** relating to, near, or living on a shore. ***n-*** shore of a sea, lake, or other water, and the country lying near it. ***Hom-*** literal.

lit·ur·gy (lĭt′ ər jē) ***n-*** [*pl.* **lit·ur·gies]** set form of service for public worship; prescribed religious ritual and ceremonies. **—*adj-* li·tur′ gi·cal.** ***adv-*** **li·tur′ gi·cal·ly.**

liv·a·ble (lĭv′ ə bəl) ***adj-*** **1** fit or agreeable to live in or with: *a* livable *room.* **2** endurable: *a harsh but* livable *experience.* Also **live′ a·ble.**

[1]live (lĭv) ***vi-*** **[lived, liv·ing] 1** to exist; have life: *Dinosaurs* lived *a long time ago.* **2** to remain or continue alive: *He* lived *to be 100.* **3** to make one's home; reside; dwell: *He* lives *on Main Street.* **4** to conduct one's life: *to* live *extravagantly.* **5** to maintain oneself: *He* lives *on a small allowance.* **6** to enjoy life fully: *He knows how to* live! **7** to remain in memory, history, etc.: *His great words* live *in our hearts.* ***vt-*** **1** to experience or pass: *to* live *a gay life.* **2** to enact or practice: *to* live *a part*; *to* live *one's principles.* [from Old English **lifian,** "to live; dwell."]

live and let live to be tolerant; mind one's own business.
live down to live in such a way that past mistakes are forgotten: *to* live down *a shame.*
live in to live in the household where one is employed.
live off 1 to be supported by: *He* lived off *his parents.* **2** to take nourishment from: *to* live off *the land.*
live on 1 to continue to live: *He* lived on *for many years.* **2** to subsist on: *You can't* live on *candy alone.*
live through to survive the experience of: *She has* lived through *illness and poverty, and still she is cheerful.*
live up to to fulfill: *He didn't* live up to *our hopes.*
live with (something) to resign oneself to (something unpleasant or inconvenient).

[2]live (līv) ***adj-*** **1** alive; having life: *to buy a* live *chameleon at the circus.* **2** full of life, energy, interest, etc.: *a very* live *young man.* **3** important at this moment; current; not past or dead: *a* live *issue; a* live *question.* **4** burning; glowing: *We roasted corn in the* live *coals.* **5** not exploded: *a* live *bomb.* **6** charged with or carrying electricity: *a* live *wire.* **7** of cartridges and shells, having a bullet or other projectile; not blank. [shortened from **alive,** from Old English **on life,** "in life."]

live·li·hood (līv′ lĭ hŏŏd′) ***n-*** means of existence or support; living; subsistence: *The store is his* livelihood.

live·long (lĭv′ lông′) ***adj-*** whole; entire: *the* livelong *day.*

live·ly (līv′ lē) ***adj-*** **[live·li·er, live·li·est] 1** full of life; active; vigorous: *That horse is very* lively. **2** quick; gay; spirited: *a* lively *tune.* **3** exciting; eventful: *We had a* lively *day.* **4** alert; keen: *a* lively *interest.* **5** vivid; bright: *a* lively *color.* **6** bouncing back quickly: *a* lively *ball.* ***adv-*:** *Step* lively! **—*n-* live′ li·ness.**

liv·en (lī′ vən) ***vt-*** to put life into; wake up; enliven: *Music* livens *a party.* ***vi-*** to become cheerful or lively: *She* livened *after a nap.*

live oak ***n-*** evergreen oak of southern United States. For picture, see *oak.*

[1]liv·er (lĭv′ ər) ***n-*** **1** in man, a large glandular organ in the upper part of the right-hand side of the abdomen. The liver produces bile, and changes and stores certain substances from the blood. **2** similar organ in other vertebrate animals. [from Old English **lifer.]**

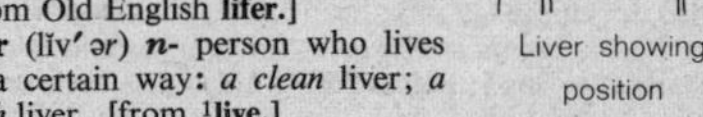

Liver showing position

[2]liv·er (lĭv′ ər) ***n-*** person who lives in a certain way: *a clean* liver; *a high* liver. [from **[1]live.]**

liver fluke ***n-*** any of various parasitic flatworms that invade the liver of mammals.

liv·er·ied (lĭv′ ər ēd′) ***adj-*** dressed in livery.

liv·er·wort (lĭv′ ər wərt′) ***n-*** **1** any of a class of mosslike plants. **2** hepatica.

liv·er·wurst (lĭv′ ər wûrst′) ***n-*** sausage containing cooked and ground liver and pork scraps.

liv·er·y (lĭv′ ə rē, lĭv′ rē) ***n-*** [*pl.* **liv·er·ies] 1** special uniform of male servants in a wealthy household. **2** the care and renting of horses, carriages, etc.

liv·er·y·man (lĭv′ rē mən) ***n-*** [*pl.* **liv·e·ry·men]** man who owns or works in a livery stable.

livery stable ***n-*** place where horses are boarded and where horses and carriages may be hired.

lives (līvz) *pl.* of **life.**

live steam ***n-*** steam coming direct from a boiler, under pressure and able to do work.

live·stock (līv′ stŏk′) ***n-*** horses, cattle, sheep, pigs, etc., kept or raised on a farm or ranch.

live wire *Informal* ***n-*** lively and energetic person.

liv·id (lĭv′ ĭd) ***adj-*** **1** black and blue from a bruise. **2** ashy pale: *a face* livid *with anger.* **3** furious. **—*adv-* liv′ id·ly.** ***n-*** **liv′ id·ness.**

liv·ing (lĭv′ ĭng) ***adj-*** **1** having life; alive at present: *a* living *author.* **2** now existent; now in use: *a* living *language.* **3** vigorous; active: *a* living *faith.* **4** true to life; exact: *the* living *image of his father.* **5** having to do with the way of life: *good* living *conditions.* ***n*- 1** state of existence. **2** way of life: *plain* living. **3** livelihood: *to earn a* living. **4** in England, a church appointment. **5 the living** all those who are alive.

Collared lizard, about 1 ft. long

living room ***n*-** room where a family spends most of its indoor leisure; sitting room.

living wage ***n*-** wage large enough to support a person and his family with modest comfort and security.

liz·ard (lĭz′ ərd) ***n*-** reptile usually having a slender body tapering into a long tail, four legs with five-toed feet, a scaly skin, ear holes, and movable eyelids. There are some 2,500 kinds. ***—adj*- liz′ ard·like′.**

ll. lines.

lla·ma (lä′ mə) ***n*-** South American cud-chewing mammal related to the camel but having no hump. It is often used as a beast of burden, and its long, light-brown or white hair is valued as a fiber for making cloth.

Llama, 4—5 ft. high at shoulder

lla·no (lä′ nō) ***n*-** [*pl.* **lla·nos**] in Spanish American countries, a treeless, grassy plain.

LL.D. (ĕl′ ĕl′ dē′) Doctor of Laws.

lo (lō) ***interj*-** look! see! behold!: *and,* lo! *he was turned into a frog.* ***Hom*-** low.

load (lōd) ***vt*- 1** to put into or upon: *to* load *a car*; *to* load *a donkey.* **2** to put (cargo) into or upon a vehicle, ship, etc.: *to* load *bananas.* **3** to burden; weigh down; also, to supply lavishly; heap: *to* load *a man with work*; *to* load *a person with gifts.* **4** to put ammunition in; charge: *to* load *a gun.* **5** to make heavier on one side: *to* load *dice.* ***vi*- 1** to receive a load: *The ship* loaded *at Recife.* **2** to put a cartridge into a gun. ***n*- 1** something put on a person or beast or into a conveyance to be carried: *to put a* load *of bananas on a ship.* **2** amount carried, or that can be carried at one time, especially by a particular means: *an arm*load *of groceries*; *a ship*load *of grain.* **3** amount of work a person, machine, factory, etc., is expected to carry, perform, or produce: *He has a full* load *of classes this term.* **4** burden: *a* load *of responsibility*; *a* load *of work.* **5** charge, or amount of ammunition, in a gun. **6** amount of electricity a circuit carries. **7 loads** *Informal* great amount; lots: *He ate* loads *of ice cream.* ***—n*- load′ er.**

load·ed (lō′ dəd) ***adj*- 1** having a full load. **2** *Slang* having a great deal of money. **3** *Slang* drunk.

load·star (lōd′ stär′) lodestar.

load·stone (lōd′ stōn′) lodestone.

1loaf (lōf) ***n*-** [*pl.* **loaves** (lōvz)] **1** mass of bread baked usually in a rectangular or round shape. **2** food prepared in a similar shape: *a* loaf *of pound cake*; *a meat* loaf. [from Old English **hlāf,** meaning originally "breadstuff," then later "a separate baking."]

2loaf (lōf) ***vi*-** to pass the time doing nothing; be lazy. [American word of uncertain origin.]

loaf·er (lō′ fər) ***n*- 1** lazy person. **2** a sporty shoe.

loam (lōm) ***n*-** rich, easily crumbled soil of clay and sand mixed with decayed leaves and plants.

loam·y (lōm′ ē) ***adj*-** [**loam·i·er, loam·iest**] containing or resembling loam. ***—n*- loam′ i·ness.**

loan (lōn) ***n*- 1** something lent, especially a sum of money: *a government* loan. **2** a lending or being lent: *to ask for the* loan *of something*; *give someone a* loan; *books on* loan. ***vt*-** to lend. ***Hom*-** lone.

►Both LOAN and LEND are correct as verbs, although some persons prefer to use LOAN as a verb only when speaking of money. *Please* loan *me five dollars. Please* lend *me five dollars.* Only LOAN is used as a noun. *I gave him a* loan *of five dollars.*

loan shark ***n*-** person who lends money at a very high, and often illegal, rate of interest.

loan word ***n*-** word taken from some other language and wholly or partly naturalized. Examples: ersatz, coupé, gusto, blitzkrieg. Also **loan′ word.**

loath (lōth) ***adj*-** unwilling: *I was* loath *to go.* Also **loth. nothing loath** quite willing.

loathe (lōth) ***vt*-** [**loathed, loath·ing**] to feel extreme dislike or disgust toward; detest: *to* loathe *spiders.*

loath·ing (lō′ thĭng) ***n*-** great disgust or dislike; aversion.

loath·ly (lōth′ lē, *also* lōth′-) ***adv*-** unwillingly. ***adj*-** *Archaic* loathsome.

loath·some (lōth′ səm) ***adj*-** detestable; disgusting: *a* loathsome *odor.* ***—adv*- loath′ some·ly.** ***n*- loath′ some·ness.**

loaves (lōvz) *pl.* of **loaf.**

lob (lŏb) ***vt*-** [**lobbed, lob·bing**] to throw, strike, or send (a ball or other object) in a high arc: *to* lob *a tennis ball.* ***vi*-**: *She* lobbed *into the back court.* ***n*- 1** in tennis and other sports, a ball sent in a high arc. **2** in cricket, a ball sent underhand.

lo·bate (lō′ bāt′) ***adj*- 1** having lobes. **2** resembling a lobe.

lob·by (lŏb′ ē) ***n*-** [*pl.* **lob·bies**] **1** hall, corridor, or room which is an entrance or a waiting room: *a hotel* lobby. **2** person or group that tries to influence members of a legislature for or against a measure. ***vi*-** [**lob·bied, lob·by·ing**] to try to influence members of a legislature for or against a measure: *to* lobby *for a law.*

lob·by·ist (lŏb′ ē ĭst) ***n*-** person who lobbies.

lobe (lōb) ***n*-** a rounded, projecting part of something, especially of a leaf or animal organ: *the* lobe *of the ear.* ***—adj*- lobed.**

Lobe of leaf Ear lobe

lo·be·lia (lō bēl′ yə) ***n*-** any of several herbaceous plants with red or blue, or occasionally white, flowers.

lob·lol·ly pine (lŏb′ lŏl′ ē) ***n*- 1** a pine of southern United States, having coarse bark. **2** the wood of this tree, valued as lumber.

lob·ster (lŏb′ stər) ***n*-** large sea crustacean with five pairs of legs, the first developed into powerful pincers; also, its flesh, used as food.

lobster pot ***n*-** cage with a funnel-shaped net inside, used as a trap for catching lobsters.

lo·cal (lō′ kəl) ***adj*- 1** having to do with a particular place: *the* local *news.* **2** limited to a single part of the body: *a* local *irritation*; *a* local *injury.* **3** stopping at all stations: *a* local *train.* ***n*-** train, bus, etc., that stops at all stations.

Lobster, about 1 ft. long

local anesthetic ***n*-** anesthetic that acts only on the part of the body immediately around the point of application.

local color ***n*-** tone or feeling given to writing, news reporting, etc., by describing the appearance of a locality, and the customs, speech, dress, and life of its population.

lo·cale (lō kăl′) ***n*-** place or setting of some event, development, work, etc.: *The tale's* locale *is Moose Jaw.*

lo·cal·ism (lō′ kəl ĭz′ əm) ***n-*** **1** attachment to, or interest in, one's own locality. **2** word, expression, or custom used in a particular region.

lo·cal·i·ty (lō kăl′ ə tē) ***n-*** [*pl.* **lo·cal·i·ties**] general region, place, or district; neighborhood.

lo·cal·ize (lō′ kə līz′) ***vt-*** [**lo·cal·ized, lo·cal·iz·ing**] to restrict to a particular place: *to* localize *an epidemic.* ***vi-*** to become local: *The pain* localized *after a time.* **—*n-* lo′ cal·i·za′ tion.**

lo·cal·ly (lō′ kə lē) ***adv-*** with respect to a particular place or region, especially to the place at hand.

local option ***n-*** power granted to a county, town, etc., to decide whether certain laws shall be carried out.

lo·cate (lō′ kāt′) ***vt-*** [**lo·cat·ed, lo·cat·ing**] **1** to seek out and fix the position of; find: *to* locate *a friend's house*; *to* locate *an oil leak.* **2** to determine the position, site, or limits of and mark: *to* locate *a gold mine*; *to* locate *a boundary.* **3** to place or establish in a particular spot; station: *He* located *his store on a busy corner.* ***vi-*** to settle: *The family* located *in Arizona finally.*

be located to have a special location or situation.

lo·ca·tion (lō kā′ shən) ***n-*** **1** a locating or being located: *the* location *of a missing person.* **2** position or place: *The bank is in a central* location. **3** piece of land marked out for a particular use; site: *a good* location *for a new school.* **4** place, outside a studio, where a motion picture is filmed.

loch (lŏKH) *Scottish* ***n-*** lake.

[1]**lock** (lŏk) ***n-*** **1** any device for fastening a door, window, lid, drawer, or the like, especially one operated by a key. **2** section of a canal or other waterway, with watertight gates at each end, for raising or lowering boats to another water level. **3** firing mechanism of a gun. ***vt-*** **1** to fasten or secure with, or as if with, a device: *to* lock *a safe.* **2** to shut up or in; confine or secure: *to* lock *in a criminal*; *to* lock *papers in a drawer.* **3** to make fast or rigid by the linking or jamming of parts: *to* lock *the wheels of a car*; *to* lock *the gears*; *to* lock *together pieces of a picture puzzle.* ***vi-*** **1** to become fastened by a device: *The door* locks *automatically.* **2** to become securely joined or linked; also, to jam: *The wheels* locked. [from Old English **loc,** "a fastening; bolt; bar; lock."]

Locks in the Panama Canal

lock, stock, and barrel in its entirety; completely.

under lock and key put securely away as in a safe.

lock on of the guidance systems of rockets, torpedos, etc., to detect and remain fixed on a target, by means of radio, heat, or sound waves.

lock out 1 to keep out by fastening a door on the inside. **2** to prevent (employees) from entering their place of work except on the employer's terms.

[2]**lock** (lŏk) ***n-*** **1** portion of hair that hangs together; tress or curl. **2 locks** all the hair of the head. [from Old English **locc,** of the same meaning.]

lock·er (lŏk′ ər) ***n-*** **1** drawer, chest, small trunk, or compartment with a lock; especially, one of a number of cupboards for individual use in a public building such as a gymnasium. **2** in a ship, a compartment or chest for clothes, ammunition, etc.

lock·et (lŏk′ ət) ***n-*** small, thin, ornamental case with a hinged cover for holding a portrait or keepsake, usually worn on a necklace.

lock·jaw (lŏk′ jŏ′) ***n-*** disease in which the jaws become firmly locked; a type of tetanus.

lock·nut (lŏk′ nŭt′) ***n-*** **1** nut that prevents the loosening of another nut. **2** nut that locks itself when screwed tight.

lock·out (lŏk′ out′) ***n-*** the shutdown of a factory, shop, etc., by an employer to force workers to accept his terms.

Locket

lock·smith (lŏk′ smĭth′) ***n-*** maker or repairer of locks.

lock step ***n-*** marching step in which the marchers follow very close behind one another.

lock stitch ***n-*** machine stitch using two threads, a top thread and a bobbin thread, that lock together.

lock·up (lŏk′ ŭp′) *Informal* ***n-*** jail.

lo·co (lō′ kō) ***adj-*** *Slang* crazy; mad. ***n-*** [*pl.* **lo·cos**] **1** locoweed. **2** disease of the nervous system of animals caused by eating locoweed. ***vt-*** [**lo·coed, lo·co·ing**] to poison (animals) with locoweed.

lo·co·mo·tion (lō′ kə mō′ shən) ***n-*** act or power of moving from place to place; motion: *Trains and planes are means of* locomotion. *Most animals have* locomotion.

Steam locomotive

lo·co·mo·tive (lō′ kə mō′ tĭv) ***n-*** engine that pulls railroad trains. ***adj-*** of, related to, or used in locomotion: *the* locomotive *parts of the body.*

lo·co·weed (lō′ kō wēd′) ***n-*** plant of western United States that causes a chronic nervous disease in cattle, sheep, etc., that have eaten it.

lo·cus (lō′ kəs) *Mathematics* ***n-*** [*pl.* **lo·ci** (lō′ sī′)] set of points, all of which satisfy a given condition or conditions. In a plane, the locus of all points that are the same distance from a given fixed point is a circle.

lo·cust (lō′ kəst) ***n-*** **1** a kind of grasshopper which flies in great swarms and is very destructive to plants of all kinds. **2** cicada. **3** tree with fernlike leaves, clusters of fragrant blossoms, and seed pods that look like bean pods.

Locust, about 2 in. long

lode (lōd) ***n-*** vein or other deposit of metal ore. ***Hom-*** load

lode·star (lōd′ stär′) ***n-*** **1** star used as a reference point for finding direction; especially, Polaris, the North Star. **2** anything fixed and constant, used as a guide.

lode·stone (lōd′ stōn′) ***n-*** **1** a piece of magnetite that acts like a magnet. **2** anything that attracts like a magnet.

lodge (lŏj) ***n-*** **1** country house or cabin, especially one used by hunters. **2** small house or cottage on the grounds of a large estate. **3** local branch or chapter of certain organizations; also, its meeting place. **4** American Indian hut or dwelling; also, those living in it. **5** den or shelter of some wild animals: *a beaver* lodge. ***vt-*** [**lodged, lodg·ing**] **1** to provide with a temporary shelter or place to sleep: *We* lodged *the flood victims in the schoolhouse.* **2** to put or fix in some particular place: *He* lodged *a bullet in the tree.* **3** to place formally before a judge or other official: *to* lodge *a complaint.* ***vi-*** **1** to take a temporary shelter or place to sleep. **2** to get stuck; catch: *The bone* lodged *in his throat.*

lodg·er (lŏj′ər) ***n-*** person who rents one or more rooms in another person's house.

lodg·ing (lŏj′ĭng) ***n-*** **1** temporary place to live or to sleep. **2 lodgings** room or rooms rented to live in.

lodg·ment or **lodge·ment** (lŏj′mənt) ***n-*** **1** a lodging or being lodged; also, an instance of this: *the* lodgment *of a complaint*; *the* lodgment *of a bone in the throat.* **2** firm or safe place for something. **3** something deposited or accumulated: *a* lodgment *of grime.*

loess (lûs) ***n-*** yellowish, fine-grained sediment forming deposits in many places throughout the world. It is thought to be eroded soil that is carried by the wind.

loft (lȯft, lŏft) ***n-*** **1** attic; garret. **2** storage place just below the roof of a barn; hayloft. **3** gallery; balcony: *a choir* loft. **4** upper floor in a warehouse, factory building, etc. **5** large open floor used to lay out full-scale plans, such as those for boats or sails.

loft·y (lȯf′tē, lŏf′-) ***adj-*** **[loft·i·er, loft·i·est] 1** very high: *the* lofty *mountain peaks.* **2** noble and dignified; elevated: *his* lofty *ambitions.* **3** proud; haughty: *a* lofty *manner.* **—*adv-* loft′i·ly.** ***n-*** **loft′i·ness.**

log (lŏg, lȯg) ***n-*** **1** length of wood cut from the trunk or a branch of a felled tree. **2** any of various devices for measuring the speed of a ship; especially, the **patent log,** which records the rotations of a small propeller towed on a long line behind the ship. **3** (also **log′book′**) book in which a regular and frequent record of operation is kept in a ship, airplane, radio station, etc. ***vt-*** **[logged, log·ging] 1** to fell and remove timber from (land); lumber. **2** to enter (facts) in the record book of a ship, airplane, etc. **3** to cover (a certain distance) in a ship or airplane: *They* logged *90 miles the second day.* **4** to travel at (a certain speed): *to* log *five knots for six hours.* ***vi-*** to cut and remove timber.

lo·gan·ber·ry (lō′gən bĕr′ē) ***n-*** [*pl.* **lo·gan·ber·ries**] **1** large, dark-red berry of a plant that is a cross between the raspberry and the blackberry. **2** the plant itself.

log·a·rithm (lŏg′ə rĭth′əm, lȯg′-) *Mathematics* ***n-*** of a given number, another number that indicates the power to which a fixed number called the base must be raised in order to obtain the given number. If the base is 10, the logarithm of 1000 is 3, since $10^3 = 1000$.

loge (lōzh) ***n-*** box or front of the mezzanine in a theater.

log·ger (lŏg′ər, lȯg′-) ***n-*** **1** person whose work is logging; lumberjack. **2** machine for handling logs.

log·ger·head (lŏg′ər hĕd′, lȯg′-) ***n-*** large sea turtle.

at loggerheads unable to agree; at odds.

log·ging (lŏg′ĭng, lȯg′-) ***n-*** the work or business of cutting trees, sawing the trunks and branches into logs, and moving the logs to a sawmill.

log·ic (lŏj′ĭk) ***n-*** **1** sound reasoning; clear thinking: *Be guided by* logic, *not by feelings.* **2** way or method of reasoning: *His* logic *is faulty.* **3** branch of philosophy that deals with reasoning; science of reason. **4** system or method of reasoning: *Aristotle's* logic; *deductive* logic.

log·i·cal (lŏj′ĭ kəl) ***adj-*** **1** in agreement with sound reasoning; sensible: *It is* logical *to look for a fire if you smell smoke.* **2** of or related to the science or study of logic. **—*adv-* log′i·cal·ly.**

lo·gi·cian (lə jĭsh′ən) ***n-*** person skilled in logic; especially, a philosopher who specializes in logic.

lo·gis·tics (lə jĭs′tĭks) ***n-*** (takes singular verb) the movement, supply, and maintenance of troops and military equipment.

log·jam (lŏg′jăm′, lȯg′-) ***n-*** tangled mass of floating logs that have blocked up a river.

log·roll·ing (lŏg′rō′lĭng, lȯg′-) ***n-*** **1** in politics, the practice of helping others further their policies in return for similar help or favors. **2** a moving or rolling of logs, as in clearing land. **3** sport or contest in which two persons stand on the same floating log and each tries, by spinning the log with his feet, to cause the other to lose his balance.

log·wood (lŏg′wŏŏd′, lȯg′-) ***n-*** **1** heavy, brownish-red wood of a Central American and West Indian tree, from which dyes are extracted. **2** the tree itself.

lo·gy (lō′gē) ***adj-*** **[lo·gi·er, lo·gi·est]** dull; lethargic.

-logy *combining form* science; study; theory: *bio*logy. [from Greek **-logia,** from **logos,** "word; reason; study."]

loin (loin) ***n-*** **1** the lower part of the back of the body between the ribs and the hip bones. **2** cut of meat from this part of an animal.

gird up (one's) loins to ready oneself for a difficult task, as if arming oneself for battle.

loin·cloth (loin′klȯth′, -klŏth′) ***n-*** piece of cloth worn as a garment about the loins.

loi·ter (loi′tər) ***vi-*** **1** to go slowly and stop frequently on the way; linger: *Don't* loiter *on your way home from school.* **2** to sit or stand idly; spend time idly; loaf: *No* loitering *is allowed in the courthouse.* **—*n-* loi′ter·er.**

loll (lŏl) ***vi-*** **1** to sit, lie, or stand in a lazy, very relaxed way: *He was so tired that he just* lolled *on the sofa.* **2** to hang or droop loosely: *The sick dog lay with his tongue* lolling *out of his mouth.*

lol·li·pop (lŏl′ē pŏp′) ***n-*** hard sugar candy on the end of a small stick; sucker. Also **lol′ly·pop′.**

lone (lōn) ***adj-*** **1** alone; isolated; solitary: *one* lone *tree.* **2** single; sole; only: *the* lone *survivor.* ***Hom-*** loan.

lone·ly (lōn′lē) ***adj-*** **[lone·li·er, lone·li·est] 1** unhappy from lack of companionship: *He was* lonely *on his first long trip by himself.* **2** remote; isolated; seldom visited: *a* lonely *mountain village.* **—*n-* lone′li·ness.**

lone·some (lōn′səm) ***adj-*** **1** sad because alone; lonely: *a* lonesome *widow.* **2** not often visited; desolate: *a* lonesome *road.* **—*adv-* lone′some·ly.** ***n-*** **lone′some·ness.**

¹long (lȯng) ***adj-*** **[long·er, long·est] 1** great or greater than usual in distance or time from beginning to end; not short or brief: *Get a* long *string for the kite. We had a* long *wait for the bus.* **2** having a great number of items: *a* long *list.* **3** extended to a specified measure in length or time: *a foot* long; *a week* long. **4** of vowels, pronounced with the same sound as the name of the letter representing the sound. This dictionary indicates long vowels in the pronunciations by the macron over the letter or letters. Examples: (ā) in "came," (ē) in "she," (ī) in "kite," (ō) in "smoke," and (o͞o) in "plume" and "fume." ***adv-*** **1** for or during a considerable time: *I can't stay* long. **2** at a very distant time; remotely: *That happened* long *ago.* **3** for the whole extent of a specified time: *all week* long. [from Old English **long, lang.**]

as long as or **so long as** provided that. **in the long run** in the end; over a period of time. **the long and short of** all there is to say about; a summary of: *That's* the long and short of *the matter.*

²long (lȯng) ***vi-*** to wish very much; yearn: *He* longs *to see his old friends again.* [from Old English **langian.**]

long. longitude.

long·boat (lȯng′bōt′) ***n-*** the largest boat carried on a sailing ship.

long·bow (lȯng′bō′) ***n-*** long bow held usually vertically, drawn back by hand, and released to project a long, feathered arrow. See also *crossbow.*

long-dis·tance (lȯng′dĭs′təns) ***adj-*** **1** of or related to telephone service between distant places: *a* long-distance *call*; *a* long-distance *operator.* **2** covering or able to cover a long distance: *a* long-distance *runner.* ***adv-:*** *He called* long-distance.

lon·gev·i·ty (lŏn jĕv′ ə tē) ***n-*** very long life.

long face ***n-*** sad or disappointed facial expression.

long·hand (lŏng′ hănd′) ***n-*** ordinary handwriting: *We sign our names in* longhand. See also *shorthand.*

long·horn (lŏng′ hŏrn′, -hôrn′) ***n-*** breed of cattle with long horns, formerly common in Mexico and southwestern United States.

long·ing (lŏng′ ĭng) ***n-*** strong desire: *a* longing *for candy.* ***adj-:*** *The children cast* longing *looks at the cake.* ***—adv-* long′ ing·ly.**

lon·gi·tude (lŏn′ jə tōōd′, lŏn′-, -tyōōd′) ***n-*** distance east or west of the prime meridian, measured in degrees, and represented on maps and globes by great circles that run between the North and South Poles.

PRIME MERIDIAN
N
90° 60° 30° W W W
30° 60° 90° E E E
S
Longitude

lon·gi·tu·di·nal (lŏn′ jə tōō′ də nəl, lŏn′-, -tyōō′ də nəl) ***adj-*** **1** of or having to do with length or longitude. **2** running lengthwise: *The planks of a boat are* longitudinal. ***—adv-* lon′ gi·tu′ di·nal·ly.**

long-lived (lŏng′ līvd′, -lĭvd′) ***adj-*** living or existing a long time: *a* long-lived *tree.*

long-play·ing (lŏng′ plā′ ĭng) ***adj-*** of phonograph records, made to be played at 33⅓ revolutions per minute.

long-range (lŏng′ rānj′) ***adj-*** **1** designed to cover a long distance: *a* long-range *missile.* **2** covering a long period of time in the future: *He has made* long-range *plans.*

long·shore·man (lŏng′ shôr′ mən) ***n-*** [*pl.* **long·shore·men**] man who is employed to load and unload ships at a seaport; stevedore.

long shot *Informal* ***n-*** something that has only a small chance of turning out well; anything that has heavy odds against it: *That bet is a* long shot.

by a long shot *Informal* by very much; by a great deal: *He missed* by a long shot. **not by a long shot** *Informal* emphatically not; certainly not.

long-stand·ing (lŏng′ stăn′ dĭng) ***adj-*** happening or lasting for a long time: *a* long-standing *dispute.*

long-suf·fer·ing (lŏng′ sŭf′ ər ĭng) ***adj-*** patiently bearing injury, insult, etc., for a long time: *a* long-suffering *victim of practical jokes.*

long suit ***n-*** **1** in card games, the suit in which a player holds the most cards. **2** something in which one is strongest; strong point; forte.

long ton ***n-*** gross ton.

long-wind·ed (lŏng′ wĭn′ dəd) ***adj-*** **1** long and tiresome; tedious: *a* long-winded *lecture.* **2** capable of continued exertion without becoming short of breath: *a* long-winded *runner.* **3** capable of holding the breath for a long time: *a* long-winded *diver.* ***—adv-* long′-wind′ ed·ly.** ***n-* long′-wind′ ed·ness.**

look (lŏŏk) ***vi-*** **1** to direct the eyes: *Please* look *at the blackboard.* **2** to search: *I've been* looking *everywhere for you.* **3** to appear; seem: *She* looks *happy.* **4** to face: *My window* looks *out on the road.* **5** *Informal* to expect: *I* look *to hear from you soon.* ***vt-*** **1** to appear to be or to fit: *He* looks *his age. She* looks *the part.* **2** *Informal* to pay attention to; watch: *You should* look *what you're doing.* ***n-*** **1** glance: *Take a* look *at this.* **2** appearance; expression: *He has a sad* look *lately.* **3 looks** appearance: *I like her* looks. *I don't care for the* looks *of this place.*

look after to take care of: *Please* look after *the baby.*

look alive to be alert; hurry up.

look at to examine: *Please* look at *the pump.*

look daggers at to look at with hostility; glare at.

look down on or **look down (one's) nose at** to feel superior to.

look for to expect: *I'll* look for *you about three o'clock.*

look forward to to expect (usually something pleasant): *I* look forward to *a wonderful party.*

look in on to visit briefly.

look in the eye (or **face**) to face with courage; stand up to; confront.

look into to investigate: *The school* looks into *the record of each new student.*

look on 1 (also **look upon**) to regard; consider: *I* look on *him as my best friend.* **2** to watch: *You two play and I'll* look on.

look (oneself) to look normal: *You don't* look yourself.

look out or **look out for** to watch out; be careful or on guard: *Please* look out for *the wet paint.* Look out! *The boat is tipping!*

look over to examine: *Please* look over *your papers before you hand them in.*

look to 1 to see to; be sure of: *You must* look to *it that you are on time.* **2** to count on: *I* look to *him for help.*

look up to search for; try to find: *We'll* look up *the time of the show in the newspaper.*

look up to to respect highly.

look·er-on (lŏŏk′ ər ŏn′, -ŏn′) ***n-*** [*pl.* **look·ers-on**] person who watches or looks on; onlooker.

looking glass ***n-*** mirror.

look·out (lŏŏk′ out′) ***n-*** **1** person who watches to guard against attack or to see what is happening: *The bandits posted a* lookout *on the hill.* **2** careful watch: *Keep a good* lookout *and let me know when you see the train coming.* **3** place from which to watch or look out. **4** *Informal* care; concern; business: *If he gets into trouble, it's his* lookout, *not mine.*

on the lookout watchful: *Be* on the lookout *for rattlesnakes while walking in the the desert.*

Hand loom

¹loom (lōōm) ***n-*** frame or machine on which cloth is woven. [from Old English **(ge)lōma** meaning "implement; tool."]

²loom (lōōm) ***vi-*** to appear in an indistinct way in a form that seems large and threatening: *The outline of a truck* loomed *out of the mist. Disaster* loomed *ahead.* [of uncertain origin.]

¹loon (lōōn) ***n-*** large, diving, fish-eating water bird with a short neck and pointed bill, noted for its uncanny call. [from Old Norse **lōmr** probably meaning "awkward."]

Loon, 2—3 ft. long

²loon (lōōn) ***n-*** crazy, silly, or ignorant person. [from Scottish **loon** or **loun.**]

loon·y (lōō′ nē) *Informal* ***adj-*** [**loon·i·er, loon·i·est**] **1** insane; mad. **2** foolish; silly. ***n-*** [*pl.* **loon·ies**] insane person; lunatic. [from **lunatic.**]

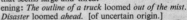

loop (lo͞op) ***n-*** **1** the shape of a noose. **2** anything bent, tied, or fastened in this shape: *a button* loop. **3** bend or curve in a stream, road, etc., suggesting this shape. **4** airplane stunt of flying a vertical circle. ***vt-***: *to* loop *a thread*; *to* loop *an airplane.* ***vi-***: *The airplane* looped *high in the air. The road* loops *near the monument.*

Decorative loops on a uniform

loop·hole (lo͞op′ hōl′) ***n-*** **1** small opening in the wall of a fortification through which a gun may be fired. **2** omission or lack of clearness in a law, contract, etc., which permits it to be broken or gotten around; basis for an evasion.

loose (lo͞os) ***adj-*** **[loos·er, loos·est]** **1** not firmly fixed, tied or bound: *a* loose *board*; loose *papers in a box.* **2** not tied up; not confined; free: *The dog got* loose *and ran away.* **3** not tightly or closely packed; not compact: *a* loose *weave*; *the* loose *sand.* **4** not tight or close-fitting: *a* loose *collar.* **5** not sufficiently controlled: *his* loose *talk*; loose *conduct.* **6** not exact or strict: *A* loose *count showed there were more than 50 people.* ***vt-*** **[loosed, loos·ing]** **1** to set free; release: *to* loose *one from any obligation.* **2** to make less tight; relax; loosen: *to* loose *one's grip.* **3** to untie; unfasten: *to* loose *one's hair.* **4** to shoot: *to* loose *an arrow.* ***—adv-*** **loose′ ly.** ***n-*** **loose′ ness.**

Loophole

break loose to get away or escape suddenly: *He* broke loose *from his captors.* **cut loose 1** to disconnect or separate; unfasten. **2** *Informal* to have fun in a wild, uncontrolled manner; go on a spree. **let** (or **set** or **turn**) **loose** to free; release. **on the loose** not confined or restrained; free.

loose end ***n-*** something that remains to be taken care of; unfinished or undecided matter. Also **loose thread.**

at loose ends confused or uncertain; unsettled.

loose-joint·ed (lo͞os′ join′ təd) ***adj-*** **1** having loose joints. **2** having free and easy movements; limber: *a* loose-jointed *runner.* ***—adv-*** **loose′-joint′ ed·ly.** ***n-*** **loose′-joint′ ed·ness.**

loose-leaf (lo͞os′ lēf′) ***adj-*** having, or designed to have, pages that can be easily inserted or taken out.

loos·en (lo͞o′ sən) ***vt-*** **1** to make loose or less tight: *to* loosen *a screw*; loosen *one's belt.* **2** to unfasten; undo: *Just* loosen *the halter and let the horse graze.* **3** to make less dense or compact: *One should* loosen *the soil before planting.* ***vi-***: *The jar lid may* loosen *if you heat it.*

loot (lo͞ot) ***n-*** things stolen or taken by force; plunder; booty: *The pirates buried their* loot *on an island.* ***vt-*** to rob by force; plunder: *The outlaws attacked and* looted *the train.* ***vi-***: *The thief* looted *as he went.* ***Hom-*** lute.

[1]**lop** (lŏp) ***vt-*** **[lopped, lop·ping]** to cut; chop (often followed by "off" or "from"): *to* lop *the branches from a tree*; *to* lop *off a large piece.* [from Old English **loppede** meaning "cut off."]

[2]**lop** (lŏp) ***vi-*** **[lopped, lop·ping]** to hang limply; flop. [probably a form of [1]**lap.**]

lope (lōp) ***n-*** easy swinging stride or gait; slow canter: *The horse went into a* lope. ***vi-*** **[loped, lop·ing]** to move with such a stride or gait: *We* loped *through the forest. We* loped *after the ball.* ***vt-***: *to* lope *one's horse.*

lop-eared (lŏp′ êrd′) ***adj-*** having ears that droop.

lop·sid·ed (lŏp′ sīd′ əd) ***adj-*** having one side lower than the other; heavier or larger on one side than on the other. ***—adv-*** **lop′ sid′ ed·ly.** ***n-*** **lop′ sid′ ed·ness.**

lo·qua·cious (lō kwā′ shəs) ***adj-*** talking too much; talkative; garrulous. ***—adv-*** **lo·qua′ cious·ly.** ***n-*** **lo·qua′ cious·ness** or **lo·quac′ i·ty** (lō kwăs′ ə tē).

lo·quat (lō′ kwăt′) ***n-*** **1** small tree of the rose family, native to China and Japan. **2** yellow, edible, plumlike fruit of this tree.

lo·ran (lôr′ ăn′) ***n-*** navigation system with which a ship or aircraft can determine its position on the basis of the different times required for synchronized radio signals to travel from several widely separated transmitting stations. [shortened from *lo*ng *ra*nge *n*avigation.]

lord (lòrd, lôrd) ***n-*** **1** person having authority to rule over others; ruler. **2** in Great Britain, a nobleman or a bishop or archbishop of the Church of England. **3 Lord** (1) God. (2) Jesus Christ (also **Our Lord**). (3) in Great Britain, a title of honor or nobility.

lord it over to act with absolute authority toward.

lord·ling (lòrd′ lĭng, lôrd′-) ***n-*** **1** minor or petty lord. **2** child who is or will be a lord.

lord·ly (lòrd′ lē, lôrd′-) ***adj-*** **[lord·li·er, lord·li·est]** **1** suitable for a lord; grand; magnificent: *a* lordly *mansion.* **2** haughty; scornful: *his* lordly *airs.* ***—n-*** **lord′ li·ness.**

lord·ship (lòrd′ shĭp′, lôrd′-) ***n-*** **1** authority; rule. **2 Lordship** (with "Your" or "His") in Great Britain, title used in speaking to or speaking of a nobleman, a bishop or archbishop of the Church of England, certain judges, and certain high civic officials.

Lord's Prayer ***n-*** prayer taught by Christ, beginning with the words "Our Father"; Paternoster.

Lord's Supper ***n-*** **1** the Last Supper. **2** the Eucharist; Holy Communion.

lore (lôr) ***n-*** **1** traditions, legends, tales, etc., of or about a special group: *Indian* lore; *Gypsy* lore. **2** learning or knowledge about a special subject: *bird* lore.

lor·gnette (lòr nyĕt′, lôr-) ***n-*** **1** eyeglasses fastened to a long handle. **2** long-handled opera glasses.

lorn (lòrn, lôrn) *Archaic* ***adj-*** forlorn; forsaken.

lor·ry (lŏr′ ē, lòr′-) *Brit.* ***n-*** [*pl.* **lor·ries**] truck.

lose (lo͞oz) ***vt-*** **[lost, los·ing]** **1** to have no longer, or be deprived of by accident, carelessness, death, etc.: *I* lost *my keys. He* lost *his leg. He* lost *his son in a car accident.* **2** to fail to keep: *Don't* lose *your patience. She* lost *her footing.* **3** to fail to win: *to* lose *the second race.* **4** to cause the loss of: *His mean remarks* lost *him many friends.* **5** to waste: *We* lost *hours in the heavy traffic.* **6** to fail to hear, see, or understand; miss: *I* lost *your last few sentences.* ***vi-*** to suffer a loss: *We* lost *on that deal. Our baseball team* lost *yesterday.* ***—n-*** **los′ er.**

lose (oneself) 1 to disappear: *The boy* lost himself *in the crowd.* **2** to be absorbed (in something).

lose (one's) heart to fall in love.

lose out *Informal* to be defeated; fail to win.

los·ings (lo͞o′ zĭngz) ***n-*** *pl.* money lost in gambling.

loss (lòs, lŏs) ***n-*** **1** a losing or being lost: *the* loss *of a ship*; *the* loss *of a football game.* **2** amount lost: *His business showed a* loss *this year instead of a profit.* **3** harm, sadness, etc., caused by losing something or someone. **4 losses** (1) the number of soldiers killed, wounded, or captured in battle. (2) losings.

at a loss in a puzzled or uncertain condition: *Your words of praise place me* at a loss. **at a loss to** puzzled or uncertain how to: *I am* at a loss to *say what I feel.*

lost (lòst, lŏst) *p.t. & p.p.* of **lose.** ***adj-*** **1** missing: *The police found the* lost *boy.* **2** off the right path; astray: *a* lost *calf.* **3** unseen; not visible: *That hill is* lost *in the distance.* **4** departed; no longer present: *a* lost *friend*; lost *hopes.* **5** destroyed; ruined: *The harvest was* lost *because of too much rain.* **6** wasted; useless: *a* lost *opportunity*; lost *time*. **7** not won: *the* lost *foot race*. **8** hopeless: *a* lost *cause*.

lost in absorbed or engrossed in: *to be* lost in *thought*. **lost on** wasted on: *All my advice was* lost on *him*. **lost to** insensitive to: *He is* lost to *any sense of honor*.

lot (lŏt) ***n*-** **1** piece or plot of ground: *an empty* lot. **2** *Informal* great deal; quite a bit: *We have a* lot *of work to do*. **3** group of things taken together: *A new* lot *of shoes just arrived in the store*. **4** number, piece of wood, straw, etc., used to decide something by chance: *We will draw* lots *for the prize*. **5** use of this method to decide something by chance: *The class chose their representative by* lot. **6** luck; fate; fortune: *Poverty is his* lot.

cast (or **throw**) **in (one's) lot with** to join and share the good or bad fortunes of.

►Either LOT or LOTS may be used in conversation. *He has* lots (*a* lot) *of money*. In writing, a more specific phrase is usually desirable. *He has a half million dollars*.

loth (lōth) loath.

lo·tion (lō′ shən) ***n*-** liquid preparation used to soothe, treat, or beautify the skin.

lots (lŏts) ***adv*-** considerably: *He is* lots *better*.

lot·ter·y (lŏt′ ə rē) ***n*-** [*pl.* **lot·ter·ies**] scheme of distributing prizes in which people buy numbered tickets, the winning ticket or tickets being selected by lot.

lo·tus (lō′ təs) ***n*-** **1** plant related to the water lily, found in Egypt and India. The lotus is a sacred and symbolic flower in the Buddhist and Hindu religions. **2** plant of the pea family, with red, pink, or white flowers. **3** in Greek legend, a fruit supposed to cause a dreamy languor in those who ate it.

Indian lotus

loud (loud) ***adj*-** **[loud·er, loud·est]** **1** having a strong and powerful sound: *a* loud *voice; a* loud *knocking*. **2** noisy: *a* loud *party*. **3** too bright; too colorful; gaudy: *a* loud *necktie*. ***adv*-**: *He spoke* loud *and clear*. **—*adv*- loud′ ly. *n*- loud′ ness.**

loud·speak·er (loud′ spē′ kər) ***n*-** part of a radio, phonograph, television set, etc., which changes electrical signals into sound waves.

lou·is d'or (lo͞o′ ē dôr′, -dôr′) ***n*-** French coin used in the 17th and 18th centuries. Also **lou′ is.**

Louisiana French ***n*-** French spoken in Louisiana since the seventeenth century and including words borrowed from the Spanish and Indian languages.

Louisiana Purchase ***n*-** French territory in the New World, extending from the Mississippi to the Rocky Mountains, and from Canada to the Gulf of Mexico, which the United States bought in 1803.

lounge (lounj) ***vi*-** **[lounged, loung·ing]** to move, act, or rest in a relaxed, lazy manner. ***n*-** **1** comfortable room to relax in; especially, a room for eating, drinking, or smoking in a hotel, on a train, etc.: *He watched TV in the airport* lounge. **2** couch or sofa. **—*n*- loung′ er.**

lour (lou′ ər) ²lower.

louse (lous) ***n*-** [*pl.* **lice** (līs)] **1** small, wingless insect that lives in the hair and on the bodies of men and animals. **2** insect that sucks the sap of plants; aphid. **3** *Slang* [*pl.* **lous·es**] mean, contemptible person.

Body louse

lous·y (lou′ zē) ***adj*-** **[lous·i·er, lous·i·est]** **1** infested with lice. **2** *Slang* mean or worthless. **—*n*- lous′ i·ness.**

lout (lout) ***n*-** stupid, awkward person; boor. **—*adj*- lout′ ish.**

lou·ver (lo͞o′ vər) ***n*-** **1** one of a series of horizontally slanting and overlapping boards arranged in a window, door, etc., so as to provide air and light while shedding rain. **2** one of a series of small openings, as in an automobile hood, to provide ventilation. *as* ***modifier***: *a* louver *door*. **—*adj*- lou′ vered.**

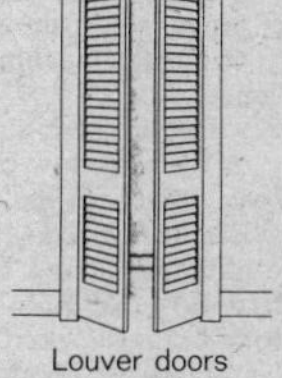

Louver doors

lov·a·ble (lŭv′ ə bəl) ***adj*-** of such a nature as to be loved; deserving or inspiring love: *a* lovable *disposition*; *a* lovable *baby*. **—*adv*- lov′ a·bly. *n*- lov′ a·ble·ness.**

love (lŭv) ***n*-** **1** strong feeling of affection for another: *a mother's* love; *the* love *between husband and wife*; love *for a friend*. **2** strong liking for something; fondness: *a* love *for music*. **3** sweetheart; someone dear: *She is my* love. **4** in tennis, no score. **5 Love** Cupid; Eros. ***vt*-** **[loved, lov·ing]** **1** to have a deep affection for. **2** to have a fondness for: *I* love *going to a baseball game*. ***vi*-** to feel deep affection: *He* loves *with all his heart*.

fall in love to begin to feel love for a person or thing. **for the love of** for the sake of. **in love** having or experiencing the feeling of love, especially for one of the opposite sex. **make love** to kiss, hug, etc., as lovers do.

love affair ***n*-** romantic attachment or union, especially between a man and woman not married to each other.

love apple *Archaic* ***n*-** tomato.

love·bird (lŭv′ bûrd′) ***n*-** **1** small parrot that appears to show great affection for its mate. Lovebirds are often kept as cage birds. **2 lovebirds** very affectionate couple.

love feast ***n*-** **1** any banquet or celebration held to promote or show good feeling and devotion among those present. **2** among early Christians, a meal eaten together as a symbol of brotherly love.

love knot ***n*-** knot regarded as a token of undying love.

love·less (lŭv′ ləs) ***adj*-** **1** feeling no love; unloving. **2** getting no love; unloved.

love·li·ness (lŭv′ lē nəs) ***n*-** beauty; also, great charm.

love·lorn (lŭv′ lôrn′, -lôrn′) ***adj*-** longing for or deserted by one's lover; pining because of love.

love·ly (lŭv′ lē) ***adj*-** **[love·li·er, love·li·est]** **1** beautiful in appearance or character. **2** *Informal* charming; delightful: *such* lovely *music*.

lov·er (lŭv′ ər) ***n*-** **1** person who is in love with another. **2** person who has a fondness or strong liking for something: *a* lover *of music*.

love seat ***n*-** sofa or chair for two persons.

love·sick (lŭv′ sĭk′) ***adj*-** sad, disturbed, inattentive, and otherwise in poor condition because of love.

lov·ing (lŭv′ ĭng) ***adj*-** showing or feeling love; affectionate: *She has a* loving *nature*. **—*adv*- lov′ ing·ly.**

¹**low** (lō) ***adj*-** **[low·er, low·est]** **1** below or of less than the usual or normal height, level, amount, etc.: *a* low *river*; low *costs*. **2** not loud; soft: *Speak in a* low *voice*. **3** deep in pitch; not shrill: *the* low *notes of a tuba*. **4** small: *a* low *number*. **5** feeble; weak: *The patient is very* low *today*. **6** gloomy; depressed: *to be in* low *spirits*. **7** unfavorable: *I have a* low *opinion of liars*. **8** mean; not kind: *a* low *trick*. **9** coarse; vulgar: *to use* low *talk*. **10** *Informal* having little or no money; broke: *I'm really* low *today*. **11** inferior: *glass of* low *quality*; *a* low *grade of meat*. ***adv*-**: *to fly* low; *to sink* low; *to aim* low; *to speak* low. ***n*-** **1** depressed level or condition: *Prices*

reached a new low *this year.* 2 gear coupling of an automobile, machine, etc., that gives the least speed and most power. 3 area having relatively reduced barometric pressure. [from earlier **louh, lah,** from Old Norse **lāgr** originally meaning "lie down."] ***Hom-*** lo. **—*n-* low′ness.**

low on having a little or inadequate supply of; short on: *We are* low on *water.*

[2]low (lō) ***vi-*** to make the sound that a cow makes; moo. ***n-:*** *He heard the* low *of a hungry cow.* [from Old English **hlōwan** meaning "bellow."] ***Hom-*** lo.

low·boy (lō′ boi′) ***n-*** low chest of drawers on legs.

low·bred (lō′ brĕd′) ***adj-*** 1 crude and vulgar in behavior; ill-bred. 2 coming from parents or ancestors in the lower ranks of society.

low·brow (lō′ brou′) *Informal* ***n-*** person who lacks culture or refinement; uncultivated person. ***adj-:*** *one's* lowbrow *taste in art.*

Low Church *n-* group in the Anglican Communion that emphasizes evangelical principles and favors simple ceremony. ***adj-* (Low-Church):** *a* Low-Church *service.* See also *High Church.* **—*n-* Low′-Church′man.**

low·down (lō′ doun′) *Slang* ***n-*** the truth; especially, facts that are not known to most people.

low-down (lō′ doun′) *Informal* ***adj-*** low and mean; contemptible: *He's a* low-down, *dirty rat.*

[1]low·er (lō′ ər) *compar.* of **[1]low.** ***vt-*** 1 to make less; reduce: *to* lower *the price of milk.* 2 to make less loud: *Please* lower *your voice.* 3 to reduce the height or level of: *to* lower *the water in a canal.* [from **[1]low.**]

[2]low·er (lou′ ər) ***vi-*** 1 to look sullen; scowl; frown. 2 to appear gloomy and threatening: *The sky* lowered *in the east.* ***n-*** scowl; frown. Also **lour.** [from Middle English **louren, luren,** from early Dutch **lūren,** "leer; frown."]

low·er·case (lō′ ər kās′) ***n-*** in printing, the small letters as distinct from the capital letters. **—*adj-*:** *a* lowercase *letter.*

low·er·most (lō′ ər mōst′) ***adj-*** lowest.

lowest terms *n-* of fractions, the form in which the numerator and the denominator have no common factor other than 1.

low frequency *n-* any radio frequency from 30 to 300 kilocycles, used to send radio and television signals. ***adj-* (low-frequency):** *a* low-frequency *receiver.*

low-keyed (lō′ kēd′) or **low-key** (lō′ kē′) ***adj-*** restrained; subdued: *a* low-keyed *novel.*

low·land (lō′ lənd) ***n-*** low, level country.

low·land·er (lō′ lən dər, lō′ lăn′-) ***n-*** person who was born or lives in a lowland.

low·ly (lō′ lē) ***adj-*** **[low·li·er, low·li·est]** low in rank, position, standard, etc.; humble: *The king was kind even to his* lowly *servants.* **—*n-* low′li·ness.**

low-mind·ed (lō′ mīn′ dəd) ***adj-*** having low and vulgar feelings, thoughts, etc.; coarse. **—*adv-* low′-mind′ed·ly. *n-* low′-mind′ed·ness.**

low-pitched (lō′ pĭcht′) ***adj-*** 1 having a low tone or range of tone. 2 slightly sloped: *a* low-pitched *roof.*

low-pressure (lō′ prĕsh′ ər) ***adj-*** 1 having or operating at the lower range of efficient pressure: *a* low-pressure *boiler.* 2 of atmospheric pressure, having a barometric reading lower than that of surrounding areas or lower than the average: *a* low-pressure *area.* 3 *Informal* easy and casual; not insistent: *a* low-pressure *salesman.*

low-spir·it·ed (lō′ spĭr′ ə təd) ***adj-*** sad and melancholy; downhearted. **—*adv-* low′-spir′it·ed·ly. *n-* low′-spir′it·ed·ness.**

low tide *n-* the tide at its lowest point at a particular place, occurring twice a day; also, the time at which this low point is reached.

low-water mark *n-* mark indicating the lowest level reached by water at a place.

[1]lox (lŏks) ***n-*** salty, smoked salmon. [from Yiddish, from earlier German **lachs** meaning "salmon."]

[2]lox (lŏks) ***n-*** *l*iquid *ox*ygen.

loy·al (loi′ əl) ***adj-*** faithful; true: *his* loyal *devotion; to be* loyal *to a creed.* **—*adv-* loy′al·ly.**

loy·al·ist (loi′ əl ĭst) ***n-*** 1 one who supports or defends his nation or government, especially during a revolt. 2 **Loyalist** (1) in the American Revolution, person loyal to England; Tory. (2) in the Spanish Civil War, one who supported the Republic against the uprising of Franco.

loy·al·ty (loi′ əl tē) ***n-*** [*pl.* **loy·al·ties**] devoted attachment; faithfulness: *a* loyalty *to one's country.*

loz·enge (lŏz′ ənj) ***n-*** 1 diamond-shaped figure or design. 2 small, often medicated, piece of candy.

LP (ĕl′ pē′) ***n-*** *Trademark* name of certain long-playing records.

LSD or **LSD-25** (ĕl′ ĕs′ dē′) ***n-*** an alkaloid obtained from ergot and able to produce hallucinations and other abnormal mental states. It has been used in psychological research. [short for **lysergic acid diethylamide.**]

Lt. lieutenant.

ltd. or **Ltd.** *chiefly Brit.* limited.

Lu symbol for lutetium.

lub·ber (lŭb′ ər) ***n-*** 1 slow, clumsy fellow. 2 landlubber.

lub·ber·ly (lŭb′ ər lē) ***adj-*** slow and clumsy; ungainly.

lu·bri·cant (lo͞o′ brĭ kənt) ***n-*** oil, grease, or similar substance applied to the moving parts of an automobile, machine, etc., to reduce friction.

lu·bri·cate (lo͞o′ brə kāt′) ***vt-*** **[lu·bri·cat·ed, lu·bri·cat·ing]** to use or apply a lubricant.

lu·bri·ca·tion (lo͞o′ brə kā′ shən) ***n-*** a lubricating or being lubricated; especially, the greasing of an automobile at a garage or gasoline station.

lu·bri·ca·tor (lo͞o′ brə kā′ tər) ***n-*** 1 person or device that applies a lubricant. 2 a lubricant.

lu·cent (lo͞o′ sənt) ***adj-*** 1 shining; luminous. 2 transparent.

lu·cerne (lo͞o sûrn′, *also* lo͞o′ sərn) *chiefly Brit.* ***n-*** alfalfa.

lu·cid (lo͞o′ sĭd) ***adj-*** 1 clear; easy to understand: *a* lucid *explanation.* 2 sane; mentally sound: *An insane person often has* lucid *moments.* 3 bright or transparent: *the* lucid *lake.* **—*adv-* lu′cid·ly. *n-* lu′cid·ness.**

lu·cid·i·ty (lo͞o sĭd′ ə tē) ***n-*** clarity; also, ease of understanding: *I like the* lucidity *of his writing.*

Lu·ci·fer (lo͞o′ sə fər) ***n-*** 1 rebellious archangel who was cast out of heaven. He is identified with Satan. 2 the planet Venus as morning star.

luck (lŭk) ***n-*** 1 fortune; chance: *That's his hard* luck. 2 good fortune: *My* luck *seems to have run out.*

down on (one's) luck having bad luck; unlucky. **in luck** lucky; fortunate. **out of luck** unlucky.

luck·i·ly (lŭk′ ə lē) ***adv-*** fortunately; happily.

luck·less (lŭk′ ləs) ***adj-*** unfortunate; not lucky. **—*adv-* luck′less·ly. *n-* luck′less·ness.**

luck·y (lŭk′ ē) ***adj-*** **[luck·i·er, luck·i·est]** 1 fortunate; having good luck: *He is usually* lucky *in card games.* 2 bringing good fortune; having a fortunate result: *a* lucky *charm; a* lucky *guess.*

lu·cra·tive (lo͞o′ krə tĭv) ***adj-*** making money or profit; profitable: *a* lucrative *business.*

lu·cre (lo͞o′ kər) ***n-*** money or wealth regarded as an evil.

lu·di·crous (lo͞o′ dĭ krəs) ***adj-*** causing laughter; laughable; comical: *a* ludicrous *attempt at a swan dive.* **—*adv-* lu′di·crous·ly. *n-* lu′di·crous·ness.**

luff (lŭf) ***n-*** 1 the forward edge of a fore-and-aft sail. 2 a shift in course to sail more directly into the wind. ***vi-*** 1 to sail more directly into the wind. 2 of a fore-and-aft sail, to flap and flutter along the forward edge as the wind strikes on both sides.

[1]**lug** (lŭg) ***vt-*** **[lug·ged, lug·ging]** to carry or drag by putting forth great effort: *He* lugged *the television set into the room.* [from Old Norse **lugga,** "to pull by the hair."]

[2]**lug** (lŭg) ***n-*** **1** something that sticks out more or less like an ear and is used as a handle or support. **2** *Informal* stupid fellow; lout; blockhead. [from an early English word perhaps related to Old Norse **lugg** meaning "forelock; hair of the head."]

lug·gage (lŭg′ĭj) ***n-*** bags, suitcases, trunks, and boxes a person takes on a trip; baggage.

lug·ger (lŭg′ər) ***n-*** sailboat with one or more lugsails.

lug·sail (lŭg′sāl′, -səl) ***n-*** four-sided sail that is tied to a spar crossing the mast at an angle, and has no boom.

Lugger with lugsails

lu·gu·bri·ous (lə gōō′ brē əs) ***adj-*** mournful or sad in an affected or exaggerated manner; woeful. ***—adv-*** **lu·gu′ bri·ous·ly.** ***n-*** **lu·gu′ bri·ous·ness.**

lug·worm (lŭg′wûrm′) ***n-*** any of various segmented worms found in sandy seashores and used for bait.

Luke (lo͝ok) ***n-*** disciple of Christ, physician and companion of St. Paul, reputed to be the author of the third Gospel and of the Acts of the Apostles in the New Testament. Also **St. Luke.**

luke·warm (lo͞ok′wórm′) ***adj-*** **1** fairly warm; not hot or cold; tepid: *a* lukewarm *bath.* **2** showing no enthusiasm; indifferent: *the* lukewarm *applause.* ***—adv-*** **luke′ warm′ ly.** ***n-*** **luke′ warm′ ness.**

lull (lŭl) ***vt-*** to quiet; calm: *The sound of the waves* lulled *me to sleep.* ***n-*** a quiet period; a temporary lessening of noise, activity, etc: *a* lull *in a storm*; *a* lull *in the talk.*

lul·la·by (lŭl′ə bī′) ***n-*** [*pl.* **lul·la·bies**] song to lull a baby to sleep.

lum·ba·go (lŭm bā′gō) ***n-*** pain in the lower part of the back, caused by injury, disease, etc.

lum·bar (lŭm′bər, -bär′) ***adj-*** of or having to do with the back and sides of the body between the ribs and hips. ***Hom-*** lumber.

[1]**lum·ber** (lŭm′bər) ***n-*** wood that has been cut into planks, boards, shingles, etc.: *I need some* lumber *to build a shelf.* ***vt-*** to cut down the trees of (an area) and saw them into planks, boards, etc.: *My grandfather* lumbered *that mountainside.* ***vi-*** to cut down and saw trees as a business or occupation. [from earlier **lumber-room** meaning "room for storing furniture, etc."] ***Hom-*** lumbar.

[2]**lum·ber** (lŭm′bər) ***vi-*** to move in a clumsy, heavy way: *The bear* lumbered *up to our car.* [from Middle English **lomeren,** from Old Norse **hlymar** meaning "a loud noise; rumbling."] ***Hom-*** lumbar. ***—adv-*** **lum′ ber·ing·ly.**

lum·ber·ing (lŭm′bər ĭng) ***n-*** business or occupation of cutting down trees, sawing them into lumber, etc.

lum·ber·jack (lŭm′bər jăk′) ***n-*** man who cuts down trees for lumber and moves them to a sawmill; logger.

lum·ber·man (lŭm′bər mən) ***n-*** [*pl.* **lum·ber·men**] **1** man who cuts trees and prepares and ships lumber. **2** man who buys and sells lumber.

lum·ber·yard (lŭm′bər yärd′) ***n-*** place where lumber is stored and sold.

lu·men (lo͞o′mən) ***n-*** **1** space or inside diameter of any tubular body structure, including an artery, vein, etc. **2** *Physics* unit that measures the amount of energy of visible light, per unit of time, that a one-candle source of light radiates onto a unit surface, all of whose points are a unit distance away from the source.

lu·mi·nar·y (lo͞o′mə nĕr′ē) ***n-*** [*pl.* **lu·mi·nar·ies**] **1** light-giving body such as the sun. **2** person who is very skilled and important in his field.

lu·mi·nes·cence (lo͞o′mə nĕs′əns) ***n-*** emission of light from a cool source, such as an insect or certain crystals. ***—adj-*** **lu′ mi·nes′ cent.**

lu·mi·nos·i·ty (lo͞o mə nŏs′ə tē) ***n-*** [*pl.* **lu·mi·nos·i·ties**] **1** a giving-off of light. **2** something luminous. **3** degree of brightness; quantity of light radiated.

lu·mi·nous (lo͞o′mə nəs) ***adj-*** **1** giving off light; shining; bright: *The stars are* luminous. **2** easy to understand; clear: *a* luminous *way of writing.* ***—adv-*** **lu′ mi·nous·ly.** ***n-*** **lu′ mi·nous·ness.**

lum·mox (lŭm′əks) ***n-*** clumsy, stupid person.

[1]**lump** (lŭmp) ***n-*** **1** small mass of solid material, usually without any special shape: *a* lump *of dough*; lumps *in mashed potatoes.* **2** a bump or swelling: *a* lump *on the head.* **3** a cube or small square (of sugar). **4** dull, stupid, and ungainly person. ***vi-*** to form into a lump or lumps: *Cooked cereal will* lump *unless well stirred.* ***vt-*** to put (things) together in one amount, mass, or pile. [from Middle English, probably from an earlier Danish word.]

[2]**lump** (lŭmp) **like it or lump it** in spite of (one's) wishes: *He had to go,* like it or lump it. [American word of uncertain origin.]

lump·ish (lŭm′pĭsh) ***adj-*** heavy; clodlike; dull: *He is a* lumpish *fool.* ***—adv-*** **lump′ ish·ly.** ***n-*** **lump′ ish·ness.**

lump·y (lŭm′pē) ***adj-*** **[lump·i·er, lump·i·est]** **1** full of or covered with lumps. **2** having an irregular or clumsy appearance.

Lu·na (lo͞o′nə) ***n-*** in Roman mythology, the goddess of the moon.

lu·na·cy (lo͞o′nə sē) ***n-*** [*pl.* **lu·na·cies**] **1** mental illness; madness. **2** wild, extreme folly or foolhardiness: *That stunt was pure* lunacy.

lu·na moth (lo͞o′nə) ***n-*** North American moth that has a whitish body and light-green wings which may have a spread of 3½ inches.

Luna moth

lu·nar (lo͞o′nər) ***adj-*** of or relating to the moon: *a* lunar *landscape.*

lunar eclipse ***n-*** the partial or total obstruction of the moon's reflected light when the moon passes through the earth's shadow. For picture, see *eclipse.*

lunar month ***n-*** the 28 days from one new moon to the next new moon.

lu·na·tic (lo͞o′nə tĭk′) ***n-*** insane person; madman. ***adj-*** **1** for or having to do with such persons: *a* lunatic *asylum.* **2** mad; crazy; wildly foolish: *a* lunatic *stunt.*

lunatic fringe ***n-*** persons whose social, political, or other views seem insane to most people.

lunch (lŭnch) ***n-*** midday meal, usually lighter than dinner, eaten between breakfast and dinner: *We eat* lunch *at school.* ***vi-*** to eat the midday meal.

lunch·eon (lŭn′chən) ***n-*** lunch, especially one to which guests are invited.

lunch·eon·ette (lŭn′chə nĕt′) ***n-*** restaurant which serves light meals, usually at a counter.

lunch·room (lŭnch′ro͞om′) ***n-*** **1** room in a school, factory, etc., where people eat, or where simple meals can be bought. **2** restaurant that serves light meals.

fāte, făt, dâre, bärn; bē, bĕt, mêre; bīte, bĭt; nōte, hŏt, môre, dȯg; fŭn, fûr; to͞o, bo͝ok; oil; out; tar; thin; then; hw for wh as in *wh*at; zh for s as in u*s*ual; ə for a, e, i, o, u, as in *a*go, lin*e*n, per*i*l, at*o*m, min*u*s

lung (lŭng) *n-* either of two spongelike organs in the chest of man and other air-breathing animals, used for breathing.

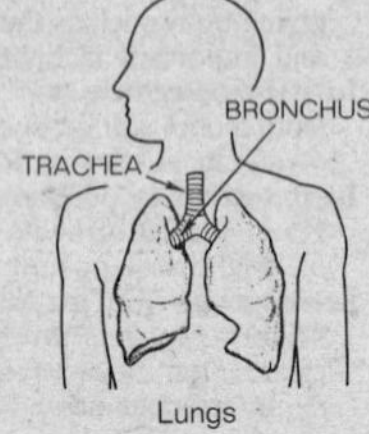

Lungs

lunge (lŭnj) *n-* [**lunged, lung·ing**] sudden forward movement; jump or leap forward, usually in order to strike or seize. *vi-* to make such a movement.

lung·fish (lŭng′ fĭsh′) *n-* [*pl.* **lung·fish; lung·fishes** (kinds of lungfish)] any of a group of fishes with gills plus an air bladder used like a lung. It can breathe in the air as well as in the water.

[1]**lu·pine** (lo͞o′ pən) *n-* **1** any of various garden plants related to the peas, with blue, white, or purple flowers; also, the flower of this plant. **2** the edible seeds of the white lupine. [from French **lupin,** from Latin **lupinum** or **lupinus,** ultimately of same origin as [2]**lupine.**]

[2]**lu·pine** (lo͞o′ pīn′) *adj-* **1** of or relating to a wolf. **2** ravenous; fierce. [from Latin **lupīnus,** "wolflike," from **lupus,** "wolf."]

[1]**lurch** (lûrch) *n-* a sudden leaning or swaying motion to one side: *The bus gave a* lurch *as one wheel went into a ditch.* *vi-* to make a lurch or lurches; stagger or sway: *As the boat pitched, the passengers* lurched *against the rail.* [apparently from the sense of "stoop" of a dialectal variant of **lurk.**]

[2]**lurch** (lûrch) **in the lurch** in a difficult or embarrassing situation. [from earlier French **lourche,** the name of a table game and a move in that game.]

lure (lo͝or, lyo͝or) *vt-* [**lured, lur·ing**] to attract or draw by promising profit or pleasure; tempt with promises; entice: *The sound of the circus parade* lured *the children away from their studies.* *n-* **1** thing that attracts by offering pleasure or profit; attraction; allurement: *Gold was the* lure *that started a rush to California in 1849.* **2** artificial minnow, piece of shiny metal, or other device used to attract and catch fish. *—n-* **lur′ er.**

lu·rid (lo͝or′ ĭd, lyo͝or′-) *adj-* **1** sensational; striking or shocking: *the* lurid *career of a criminal.* **2** glaring in color; gaudy: *The* lurid *posters attracted attention.* **3** shining with a fiery glow: *a* lurid *shape seen through the smoke.* *—adv-* **lu′ rid·ly.** *n-* **lur′ rid·ness.**

lurk (lûrk) *vi-* **1** to hide or remain secretly in or near a place: *The burglar* lurked *in the bushes until the watchman had passed.* **2** to sneak or slink; move furtively: *I saw a man* lurking *around the building.* *—n-* **lurk′ er.**

lus·cious (lŭsh′ əs) *adj-* **1** very pleasant and sweet to taste or smell; delicious: *a* luscious *ripe peach.* **2** pleasing to any of the senses: *the* luscious *music.* *—adv-* **lus′ cious·ly.** *n-* **lus′ cious·ness.**

lush (lŭsh) *adj-* **1** juicy and luxuriant in growth: *the* lush *grass.* **2** covered with rich growth: *a* lush *meadow.* *n- Slang* an alcoholic. *—adv-* **lush′ ly.** *n-* **lush′ ness.**

lust (lŭst) *n-* **1** intense sexual desire. **2** very strong craving or desire: *a* lust *for power*; *a* lust *for gold.* *vi-* **1** to have intense sexual desire. **2** to have a very strong craving or desire: *The dictator* lusted *for conquest.*

lus·ter or **lus·tre** (lŭs′ tər) *n-* **1** a shine or brilliance of a surface that reflects light; gloss: *New cars have a high* luster. **2** brightness; radiance: *Tinsel and colorful balls gave* luster *to the Christmas tree.* **3** glory; splendor: *The runner's victory added new* luster *to his fame.* **4** In ceramics, an iridescent, glossy, metallic glaze.

lus·ter·ware (lus′ tər wâr′) *n-* pottery having a lustrous, iridescent glaze.

lust·ful (lŭst′ fəl) *adj-* driven by, or full of, lust. *—adv-* **lust′ ful·ly.** *n-* **lust′ ful·ness.**

lus·trous (lŭs′ trəs) *adj-* shiny; glossy; gleaming: *a* lustrous *silk gown.* *—adv-* **lus′ trous·ly.**

lust·y (lŭs′ tē) *adj-* [**lust·i·er, lust·i·est**] strong and healthy; vigorous: *a* lusty *boxer*; *a* lusty *shout.* *—adv-* **lust′ i·ly.** *n-* **lust′ i·ness.**

lute (lo͞ot, lyo͞ot) *n-* musical instrument, popular in the sixteenth and seventeenth centuries, having a pear-shaped body, eleven to twenty-four strings, some in pairs, a fingerboard with frets, and pegs for tuning. *Hom-* loot.

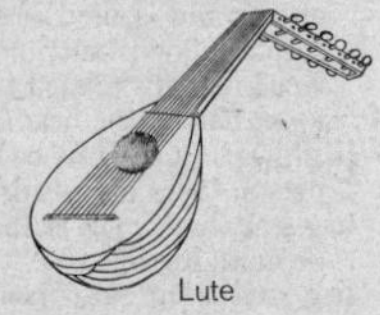
Lute

lu·te·ti·um or **lu·te·ci·um** (lo͞o tē′ shē əm) *n-* metallic rare-earth element. Symbol Lu, At. No. 71, At. Wt. 174.97.

Lu·ther·an (lo͞o′ thər ən) *adj-* of or relating to Martin Luther or to the church he founded. *n-* member of a Protestant church adhering to Luther's doctrines and principles.

Lu·ther·an·ism (lo͞o′ thər ə nĭz′ əm) *n-* the religious doctrines and system of worship of the Lutherans.

lux·u·ri·ance (lug zho͞or′ ē əns, lŭk sho͞or′-) *n-* richness and abundance, especially in growth.

lux·u·ri·ant (lŭg zho͞or′ ē ənt, lŭk sho͞or′-) *adj-* abundant, rich, or vigorous in growth: *the* luxuriant *vegetation of the tropics.* *—adv-* **lux·u′ ri·ant·ly.**
►Should not be confused with LUXURIOUS.

lux·u·ri·ate (lŭg zho͞or′ ē āt′, lŭk sho͞or′-) *vi-* **1** to enjoy or express oneself indulgently, especially in feeling or circumstance: *to* luxuriate *in grief*; *to* luxuriate *in a bubble bath.* **2** to grow richly and abundantly.

lux·u·ri·ous (lug zho͞or′ ē əs, lŭk sho͞or′-) *adj-* marked by or providing luxury: *the* luxurious *new theater.* *—adv-* **lux·u′ ri·ous·ly.** *n-* **lux·u′ ri·ous·ness.**
►Should not be confused with LUXURIANT.

lux·u·ry (lug′ zhə rē, lŭk′ shə-) *n-* [*pl.* **lux·u·ries**] **1** something that is not necessary for life but can make it more enjoyable or comfortable. Luxuries are often things that are expensive or difficult to get. **2** way or condition of life in which a person enjoys great comfort and many fine things: *Most Americans live in* luxury *compared to people of very poor countries.* **3** great comfort or pleasure: *the* luxury *of a soft easy chair.*

[1]**-ly** *suffix* (forming adjectives) **1** like; having the nature of; characteristic of: *brother*ly; *soldier*ly. **2** happening at particular intervals: *week*ly; *dai*ly; *hour*ly. [from Old English **-lic.**]

[2]**-ly** *suffix* (forming adverbs) **1** in a given manner: *weak*ly; *quiet*ly. **2** at every (particular interval): *week*ly; *hour*ly. [from Old English **-lice,** from **-lic,** [1]**-ly.**]

ly·ce·um (lī sē′ əm) *n-* **1** an association for literary study, popular lectures, debate, etc. **2** building where it meets.

ly·co·po·di·um (lī′ kə pō′ dē əm) *n-* **1** one of the two groups of club mosses, often used in Christmas decorations. **2** a fine, yellow, flammable powder, consisting of the spores of one club moss, which is used in the making of pills and fireworks.

lye (lī) *n-* **1** sodium hydroxide. **2** formerly, a strong alkali obtained by soaking wood ashes and used in soap making. *Hom-* lie.

[1]**ly·ing** (lī′ ĭng) *pres. p.* of [1]**lie.**

[2]**ly·ing** (lī′ ĭng) *pres. p.* of [2]**lie.**

lymph (lĭmf) *n-* the usually clear, yellowish fluid that circulates in the lymph vessels (lymphatics), contains lymphocytes, and bathes all the body cells.

lym·phat·ic (lĭm făt′ĭk) ***adj-*** **1** of or having to do with lymph, lymph vessels, or lymph nodes. **2** lacking energy; sluggish; indifferent. ***n-*** thin-walled vessel transporting lymph.

lymph node or **lymph gland** ***n-*** one of the many, bean-shaped enlargements of the lymph vessels that contain and produce lymphocytes.

lym·pho·cyte (lĭm′ fə sīt′) ***n-*** white blood cell, especially one of the phagocytes made in the lymph glands.

lynch (lĭnch) ***vt-*** to kidnap and kill (an accused or suspected wrongdoer), thus denying the right to legal trial. **—*n-* lynch′ er.**

Lynx, about 3 ft. long

lynch law ***n-*** practice of lynching instead of respecting the legal rights of those suspected of crime.

lynx (lĭngks) ***n-*** short-tailed wildcat with tufted ears and a light gray or brown speckled coat; especially, the larger gray variety called the **Canada lynx.** ***Hom-*** links.

ly·on·naise (lī′ ə nāz′) ***adj-*** prepared with finely sliced onions: *We ate* lyonnaise *potatoes.*

Ly·ra (lī′ rə) ***n-*** constellation of stars thought to outline the figure of a lyre.

lyre (līər) ***n-*** musical instrument like a small harp with three to ten strings. Lyres were used by the ancient Greeks to accompany singing and poetry. ***Hom-*** liar.

Lyre

lyre·bird (līər′ bûrd′) ***n-*** an Australian bird, the male of which has a very long tail that resembles the shape of a lyre when spread.

lyr·ic (lĭr′ ĭk) ***adj-*** **1** like a song; musical. **2** of or having to do with a kind of short poem that usually expresses very personal feelings. ***n-*** **1** a short poem expressing such feelings. **2 lyrics** words for a song.

lyr·i·cal (lĭr′ ĭ kəl) ***adj-*** **1** like a song; musical; lyric: *the* lyrical *call of a bird.* **2** showing great emotion; poetical: *She became quite* lyrical *in praising the picture.* **—*adv-* lyr′ i·cal·ly.**

ly·sin (lī′ sən) ***n-*** any of a group of antibodies that dissolve micro-organisms and foreign cells.

M

M, m (ĕm) ***n-*** [*pl.* **M's, m's**] **1** the thirteenth letter of the English alphabet. **2** Roman numeral for 1,000.

m. or **m** **1** meter or meters. **2** mile or miles. **3** minute or minutes. **4** male; masculine.

M **1** Medieval. **2** Middle.

M. monsieur.

ma (mä) *Informal* ***n-*** mother.

M.A. Master of Arts.

ma'am (măm) madam.

ma·ca·bre (mə kä′ brə, -bər) ***adj-*** **1** gruesome; ghastly; horrible: *The battlefield was a* macabre *sight.* **2** unduly interested in death; morbid: *a* macabre *love of funerals.*

mac·ad·am (mə kăd′əm) ***n-*** **1** pavement of crushed stone, closely packed and rolled. **2** the stone so used.

mac·ad·am·ize (mə kăd′ ə mīz′) ***vt-*** **[mac·ad·am·ized, mac·ad·am·iz·ing]** to cover (a road) with macadam.

ma·caque (mə kăk′, -kăk′) ***n-*** any of various short-tailed monkeys of Asia and North Africa.

mac·a·ro·ni (măk′ ə rō′ nē) ***n-*** food made of wheat-flour paste, shaped into hollow tubes and dried.

mac·a·roon (măk′ə ro͞on′) ***n-*** cookie made of sugar, egg whites, and almonds or coconut.

ma·caw (mə kȯ′) ***n-*** any of various large tropical American parrots with a strong, hooked bill, brilliant plumage, and a harsh voice.

Macaw, about 3 ft. long

Mac·beth (mək bĕth′) ***n-*** Scottish king; hero of Shakespeare's play "Macbeth."

Mac·ca·bees (măk′ ə bēz′) ***n-*** *pl.* **1** family of Jewish patriots who led a successful religious revolt against the Syrians (175-164 B.C.) **2** four books of the Old Testament Apocrypha. The first two are accepted as canonical by Roman Catholics. **—*adj-* Mac′ ca·be′ an.**

[1]**mace** (mās) ***n-*** **1** club with a spiked head, used as a weapon in medieval times. **2** ornamental club or staff carried by or before an official as a symbol of power. [from Old French **mace,** from Late Latin **mattea,** "a hacking or digging tool," and related to **mattock.**]

Mace

[2]**mace** (mās) ***n-*** a spice ground from the dried covering of the nutmeg occurring between the husk and the seed. [from Old French **mac(e)is,** from Greek **maker** meaning "the reddish rind of an Indian tree."]

mac·e·rate (măs′ ə rāt′) ***vt-*** **[mac·er·at·ed, mac·er·at·ing]** **1** to soften or separate the parts of (a solid substance) by soaking or digestion. **2** to weaken by, or as if by, fasting. **—*n-* ma′ cer·a′ tion.**

ma·che·te (mə shĕt′ ē, -chĕt′ ē) ***n-*** long, heavy blade used for cutting vegetation by hand. [from Spanish, from **macho,** "hammer; ax."]

Machete

Mach·i·a·vel·li·an (măk′ ē ə vĕl′ ē ən) ***adj-*** of or resembling the crafty, unscrupulous practices recommended by Niccolò Machiavelli for governing a principality. ***n-*** anyone using crafty or unscrupulous methods.

mach·i·nate (măk′ə nāt′, măsh′-) ***vi-*** **[mach·i·nat·ed, mach·i·nat·ing]** to form harmful plots; scheme.

mach·i·na·tion (măk′ ə nā′ shən, mash′-) ***n-*** scheme or plot; sly intriguing: *the lawyer's* machinations.

mach·i·na·tor (măk′ə nā′ tər, măsh′-) ***n-*** person who machinates.

ma·chine (mə shēn′) ***n-*** **1** device using applied energy to do work. Machines convert energy from one form to another, transfer energy from place to place, multiply force or speed, or change the direction of a force. The wheel and axle, pulley, lever, screw, wedge, and inclined plane are simple machines. **2** apparatus with moving parts, made up of simple machines: *a sewing* machine. **3** person who acts mechanically, without intelligence, or with unfailing regularity. **4** person very highly trained in or well adapted for a particular activity: *He's a real pitching* machine. **5** a highly organized political group or clique, usually run by a boss, that controls a political party in an area. *as **modifier**: a* machine *age; a* machine *boss.* ***vt-*** [**ma·chined, ma·chin·ing**] to shape, grind, finish, etc., with a machine or machine tools.

machine gun ***n-*** gun that keeps shooting as long as the trigger is pressed; fully automatic gun, especially one heavy enough to require a tripod or other mount. ***vt-*** (**machine-gun**) [**ma·chine-gunned, ma·chine-gun·ning**] to shoot (a person, troops, etc.) with such a gun.

ma·chin·er·y (mə shē′ nə rē) ***n-*** [*pl.* **ma·chin·er·ies**] **1** machines collectively: *new* machinery *for a factory.* **2** the parts of a machine: *the* machinery *of a clock.* **3** system and organization by which something works: *the* machinery *of government.*

machine tool ***n-*** power-driven machine used to shape, bore, mill, cut, or otherwise work metal.

ma·chin·ist (mə shē′ nĭst) ***n-*** person skilled in adjusting and operating machine tools to work metal.

ma·chis·mo (mä chēz′ mō) ***n-*** [*pl.* **ma·chis·mo**] **1** strong or aggressive sense of manliness. **2** excessive concern over one's masculinity. [from Spanish **macho** meaning "male."]

Mach number (măk, mäk) ***n-*** number that shows the relationship between the speed of an object and the speed of sound in the same medium. An aircraft flying at twice the speed of sound has a Mach number of 2.

ma·cho (mä′ chō) ***adj-*** aggressively masculine or virile. ***n-*** [*pl.* **ma·chos**] a man who exhibits machismo.

mack·er·el (măk′ ər əl) ***n-*** [*pl.* **mack·er·el; mack·er·els** (kinds of mackerel)] any of various marine food fishes related to the tunas and bonitos, especially a fish 12 to 18 inches long with a greenish back and blue stripes, found in the North Atlantic.

mackerel sky ***n-*** pattern of clouds made up of rows of small clouds resembling the markings on a mackerel's back; cirrocumulus.

mack·i·naw (măk′ ə nŏ′) ***n-*** **1** heavy jacket, often plaid. **2** heavy, napped, often plaid, woolen cloth.

mack·in·tosh (măk′ ən tŏsh′) ***n-*** **1** raincoat. **2** lightweight, waterproof fabric.

mac·ra·mé (măk′ rə mā′) ***n-*** the process of knotting thread or cord into a design. *as **modifier**: a* macramé *belt.*

mac·ro·cosm (măk′ rə kŏz′ əm) ***n-*** **1** the whole world; universe. **2** large thing or system when compared with a small thing or system that resembles or represents it in miniature: *American society as a* macrocosm *can be better understood by studying a typical American small town.* See also *microcosm.*

ma·cron (mā′ krŏn′, măk′ rŏn′) ***n-*** mark [-] written or printed over a vowel to show that it is long when pronounced.

mad (măd) ***adj-*** [**mad·der, mad·dest**] **1** out of one's mind; insane. **2** *Informal* angry: *He was so* mad *that his face was red.* **3** foolish; rash: *It was* mad *of her to try to swim in the icy water.* **4** *Informal* very enthusiastic: *to be* mad *about baseball.* **5** wild; excited; frantic: *a* mad *rush toward the exit.* **6** having rabies: *a* mad *dog.*

mad·am (măd′ əm) ***n-*** [*pl.* **mes·dames** (mā dăm′)] polite word used in speaking or writing to a woman.

mad·ame (mə dăm′) ***n-*** [*pl.* **mes·dames** (mā dăm′)] French title or form of address for a married woman, equivalent to "Mrs."

mad·cap (măd′ căp′) ***n-*** lively, spirited person who acts on impulse: *You never know what that* madcap *will do next!* ***adj-*** lively or rash: *the children's* madcap *tricks.*

mad·den (măd′ ən) ***vt-*** **1** to cause to become insane; craze. **2** to cause to become very angry; enrage.

mad·den·ing (măd′ ən ĭng) ***adj-*** **1** such as to drive one crazy or frantic with irritation. **2** infuriating; enraging. **—*adv-*** **mad′ den·ing·ly**: *a* maddeningly *long wait.*

mad·der (măd′ ər) ***n-*** **1** European plant with clusters of small, yellowish flowers, and roots from which a red dye is obtained; also, any of various related plants. **2** red dye obtained from this root; alizarin. **3** a brilliant red color. ***adj-***: *a* madder *crayon.*

made (mād) *p.t. & p.p.* of **make**. ***Hom-*** maid.

made of having as basic material or materials: *a table* made of *oak; a shelter* made of *boards and stones.*

Ma·dei·ra (mə dêr′ ə) ***n-*** sweet, amber-colored, fortified wine made on the island of Madeira.

mad·e·moi·selle (măd′ mwə zĕl′, măd′ mə-) ***n-*** [*pl.* **mes·de·moi·selles** (mād′ mwə zĕl′, mād′ mə-)] French title or form of address equal to "Miss."

made-to-order (mād′ too͞ ŏr′ dər, -ôr′ dər) ***adj-*** made at a person's request; custom-made; tailor-made.

made-up (mād′ ŭp′) ***adj-*** invented; fabricated, such as a story: *That is a* made-up *tale.*

mad·house (măd′ hous′) ***n-*** **1** *Informal* hospital or other institution for insane people. **2** noisy, disorderly place: *The children's room was a* madhouse.

mad·ly (măd′ lē) ***adv-*** in a wild and frenzied manner: *The crowd swarmed* madly *over the playing field.*

mad·man (măd′ măn′) ***n-*** [*pl.* **mad·men**] insane man; lunatic. **—*n-*** *fem.* **mad′ wom′ an.**

mad·ness (măd′ nəs) ***n-*** **1** illness of the mind; insanity. **2** wild or foolish behavior: *It's* madness *to go so fast.*

Ma·don·na (mə dŏn′ ə) ***n-*** **1** statue or painting representing Mary and the infant Jesus. **2 the Madonna** the Virgin Mary.

ma·dras (măd′ rəs, mə drăs′) ***n-*** cotton fabric originally made in India and usually having a plaid or striped pattern. *as **modifier**: a* madras *jacket.*

mad·ri·gal (măd′ rə gəl) ***n-*** unaccompanied song having parts for several voices in which the theme and its variations are interwoven.

mael·strom (māl′ strəm, -strŏm′) ***n-*** **1** whirlpool. **2** wild and dangerous force or place: *The battle was a* maelstrom *of flying steel.* **3 Maelstrom** whirlpool near the northwestern coast of Norway.

maes·tro (mī′ strō′) ***n-*** [*pl.* **maes·tros**] recognized master in music, such as a composer or conductor.

mag. **1** magazine. **2** magnet. **3** magnetism. **4** *Astronomy* magnitude.

mag·a·zine (măg′ ə zēn′, măg′ ə zēn′) ***n-*** **1** collection of stories, poems, or other reading matter issued at regular times. **2** in a firearm, a compartment for holding cartridges or shells so that they can be fed into the chamber for firing. **3** building or compartment for storing explosives, ammunition, weapons, etc.

Magazine of rifle

Mag·da·lene or **Mag·da·len** (măg′ də lēn, -lən) ***n-*** Mary Magdalene.

ma·gen·ta (mə jĕn′ tə) ***n-*** **1** purplish-red dye and pigment derived from coal tar. **2** purplish-red color given by this dye. ***adj-***: *a* magenta *dress.*

mag·got (măg′ ət) ***n-*** the soft, wormlike larva of a two-winged fly, such as the housefly.

Fly and maggot

Ma·gi (mā′ jī′) ***n-*** *pl.* [*sing.* **Ma·gus** (mā′ gəs)] **1** in the Bible, the three "wise men of the east" who brought gifts to the infant Jesus. **2** the priestly caste in Media and Persia.

mag·ic (măj′ĭk) ***n-*** **1** art or pretended art of using and controlling supernatural powers in the natural world, by means of spells, charms, rituals, etc., and with the assistance of demons and spirits; sorcery; witchcraft. **2** the spells, charms, etc., used in this art. **3** craft or skill by which one produces puzzling effects by tricks and illusions, usually for entertainment; sleight of hand; legerdemain. **4** special or mysterious charm or power: *The* magic *of the music made us feel like dancing.* ***adj-*** **1** having supernatural power: *a* magic *wand*; *a* magic *spell.* **2** done by supernatural power or sleight of hand: *a* magic *trick.* **3** enchanted: *a* magic *moment.* **4** supernatural; mysterious: *his* magic *powers.*

mag·i·cal (măj′ĭ kəl) ***adj-*** **1** of or relating to magic: *a* magical *spell.* **2** like magic; casting a mysterious spell: *the* magical *effect of moonlight.* **—*adv-*** **mag′i·cal·ly.**

ma·gi·cian (mə jĭsh′ən) ***n-*** **1** person who uses magic; sorcerer. **2** one who creates effects by deft tricks.

magic lantern ***n-*** an early type of slide projector.

magic square ***n-*** arrangement of numbers resembling a checkerboard, in which the sum of the numbers is identical for every row, column, and diagonal.

mag·is·te·ri·al (măj′ə stêr′ē əl) ***adj-*** **1** of or relating to a magistrate or judge. **2** having an air of authority; hence, overbearing; domineering; dictatorial: *a* magisterial *tone.* **—*adv-*** **mag′is·te′ri·al·ly.**

mag·is·tra·cy (măj′ĭs trə sē′) ***n-*** [*pl.* **mag·is·tra·cies**] **1** position, function, or term of a magistrate or judge. **2** a body of judges. **3** the district of a magistrate.

mag·is·trate (măj′ĭs trāt′) ***n-*** **1** government official with power to administer and enforce the law. **2** local judge.

mag·ma (măg′mə) ***n-*** the extremely hot rock material that occurs deep within the earth's crust, and from which igneous rocks and lava are formed.

Mag·na Char·ta or **Mag·na Car·ta** (măg′nə kär′tə) ***n-*** **1** the charter forming the basis of English civil liberty, which King John was forced by the feudal barons to sign in 1215. **2** any document that safeguards personal liberties.

mag·na cum lau·de (măg′nə ko͝om′lou′də, -lȯ′də) *Latin* with great honor, praise, or distinction: *He was graduated* magna cum laude.

mag·na·nim·i·ty (măg′nə nĭm′ə tē) ***n-*** [*pl.* **mag·na·nim·i·ties**] **1** largeness of heart and spirit that enables one to rise above and ignore mean, petty, and personal things; nobility. **2** generosity.

mag·nan·i·mous (măg năn′ə məs) ***adj-*** having or showing magnanimity. **—*adv-*** **mag·nan′i·mous·ly.** ***n-*** **mag·nan′i·mous·ness.**

mag·nate (măg′nāt′, -nət) ***n-*** person of importance, especially one of wealth and power in an industry: *an oil* magnate. ***Hom-*** magnet.

mag·ne·sia (măg nē′zhə, -shə) ***n-*** white tasteless powder (MgO) used as an antacid and a mild laxative, and also used in fertilizers, firebricks, etc.

mag·ne·si·um (măg nē′zē əm, -nē′zhəm) ***n-*** light, silver-white metal element that burns with a bright, dazzling light. Magnesium is used to make light airplane parts, flares, etc. Symbol Mg, At. No. 12, At. Wt. 24.312.

mag·net (măg′nət) ***n-*** **1** an object, such as a piece of metal, alloy, or ore, that exerts a force of attraction on iron and other materials. **2** a lodestone. **3** an electromagnet. **4** anything that attracts. ***Hom-*** magnate.

Horseshoe magnet

mag·net·ic (măg nĕt′ĭk) ***adj-*** **1** of or having the properties of a magnet or magnetism: *a* magnetic *needle.* **2** of or having to do with the earth's magnetism: *the North* Magnetic *Pole.* **3** having the power to charm and attract: *a* magnetic *personality.*

magnetic field ***n-*** **1** region that surrounds a magnetic body or a wire through which current flows, and which exhibits magnetic force. **2** the magnetic force itself, which acts at a particular point in the region.

magnetic flux ***n-*** the lines of flux (or force) in a magnetic field, considered collectively.

magnetic mine ***n-*** underwater explosive device detonated by the magnetic field around the steel hull of a passing ship.

magnetic needle ***n-*** thin bar of magnetized metal which, when hanging freely in a magnetic field, tends to point in the direction of the field.

magnetic north ***n-*** direction toward which the north-seeking end of a compass needle points. See also *true north.*

magnetic pole ***n-*** **1** either of the two poles of a magnet. **2** either of the two places, in the Arctic **(North Magnetic Pole)** and the Antarctic **(South Magnetic Pole),** that are the poles of the earth's magnetic field.

magnetic storm ***n-*** sudden, worldwide disturbance of the earth's magnetic field, caused by sunspot activities, and, especially, solar flares.

magnetic tape ***n-*** ribbon of plastic or paper coated on one side with iron oxide particles that are arranged into patterns by the varying electromagnetic impulses produced in a tape recorder.

mag·ne·tism (măg′nə tĭz′əm) ***n-*** **1** force that is shown by certain elements and alloys, a current-carrying conductor, and the earth itself, through which a metal is attracted and a magnetic field produced. **2** branch of science that deals with the study of magnetic phenomena. **3** power to attract others; personal charm.

mag·net·ite (măg′nə tīt′) ***n-*** black magnetic oxide (Fe_3O_4) of iron, one of the most important iron ores.

mag·ne·ti·za·tion (măg′nə tə zā′shən) ***n-*** a magnetizing or being magnetized.

mag·ne·tize (măg′nə tīz′) ***vt-*** [**mag·ne·tized, mag·ne·tiz·ing**] **1** to cause to be magnetic. **2** to attract as with a magnet; put under a spell: *His voice* magnetized *us.*

mag·ne·to (măg nē′tō) ***n-*** [*pl.* **mag·ne·tos**] generator that produces high-voltage alternating current, often used to provide the ignition spark in some engines.

Mag·ni·fi·cat (măg nĭf′ə kăt′, -kät′) ***n-*** **1** in the New Testament, the hymn of the Virgin Mary, beginning "My soul doth magnify the Lord." **2** any musical setting for this hymn.

mag·ni·fi·ca·tion (măg′nə fə kā′shən) ***n-*** an enlarging; especially, the apparent enlarging of something seen through a telescope, microscope, or magnifying glass.

mag·nif·i·cent (măg nĭf′ə sənt) ***n-*** **1** grand in appearance; richly ornamented; splendid: *a* magnificent *palace.* **2** excellent; very fine: *a* magnificent *idea.* **—*n-*** **mag·nif′i·cence.** ***adv-*** **mag·ni·fi′cent·ly.**

mag·ni·fy (măg′nə fī′) ***vt-*** [**mag·ni·fied, mag·ni·fy·ing**] **1** to make (something) appear larger: *The microscope* magnified *by 100 times the tiny cells on the slide.* **2** to exaggerate; make seem greater than what is true: *to* magnify *the difficulties of an undertaking.* **3** *Archaic* to glorify. **—*n-*** **mag′ni·fi′er.**

magnifying glass ***n-*** lens that causes objects to appear larger than they actually are.

mag·nil·o·quent (măg nĭl′ ə kwənt) ***adj-*** pompously eloquent in speaking or writing; boastful. **—*n-* mag·nil′ o·quence.** ***adv-*** **mag·nil′ o·quent·ly.**

mag·ni·tude (măg′ nə to͞od′, -tyo͞od′) ***n-*** **1** size; largeness: *the* magnitude *of the universe*; *the* magnitude *of a task.* **2** *Astronomy* brightness of a star or other heavenly body as expressed by a number on an accepted scale. **Apparent magnitude** refers to brightness as actually observed from the earth, and **absolute magnitude** to brightness as it would appear if the body were at a certain fixed distance from the observer.

Magnolia

mag·no·li·a (măg nō′ lē ə, -nōl′ yə) ***n-*** **1** ornamental tree with shiny leaves, and large white or pink, fragrant flowers. **2** the flower. It is the State flower of Louisiana and Mississippi.

mag·num o·pus (măg′ nəm ō′ pəs) *Latin* chief work; masterpiece: *"Paradise Lost" is Milton's* magnum opus.

mag·pie (măg′ pī′) ***n-*** **1** a large black-and-white bird of the crow family. Magpies gather in chattering flocks. **2** person who chatters.

Magpie, about 20 in. long

ma·guey (mə gā′) ***n-*** [*pl.* **ma·gueys**] **1** any of several Mexican agaves yielding fiber; especially, the century plant. **2** any of several hard fibers obtained from these plants and used for making rope, coarse cloth, etc.

Mag·yar (mŏ′ dyŏr, *also* măg′ yär) ***n-*** **1** a member of the main ethnic group of people living in Hungary. **2** the Hungarian language.

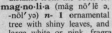

ma·ha·ra·ja or **ma·ha·ra·jah** (mä′ hə rä′ jə, -zhə) ***n-*** Hindu prince above a raja in rank.

ma·ha·ra·ni or **ma·ha·ra·nee** (mä′ hə rä′ nē) ***n-*** **1** wife of a maharaja. **2** ruling princess of India.

ma·hat·ma (mə hät′ mə, -hăt′ mə) ***n-*** **1** title of respect, meaning "great soul," given to a wise and holy man in Asian religions. **2** such a person.

Ma·hi·can (mə hē′ kən) ***n-*** [*pl.* **Ma·hi·cans,** also **Ma·hi·can**] one of a tribe of Algonquian Indians who formerly lived near the Hudson River and eastward. Also **Mohican.** ►Should not be confused with MOHEGAN.

mah-jongg or **mah-jong** (mä′ zhŏng′, -jŏng′) ***n-*** American version of a Chinese game of skill and chance, played with small tiles somewhat resembling dominoes.

ma·hog·a·ny (mə hŏg′ ə nē) ***n-*** [*pl.* **ma·hog·a·nies**] **1** any of several tropical trees having a hard wood, often used for making furniture. **2** the wood of this tree. **3** a reddish-brown color. ***adj-*:** *a* mahogany *stain.*

ma·hout (mə hout′) ***n-*** elephant driver and keeper.

maid (mād) ***n-*** **1** female servant. **2** *Archaic* unmarried woman; maiden. ***Hom-*** made.

maid·en (mā′ dən) ***n-*** girl; unmarried woman; maid. ***adj-*** **1** unmarried: *my* maiden *aunt.* **2** of or like a young girl. **3** first: *a* maiden *voyage*; *a* maiden *effort.*

maid·en·hair (mā′ dən hâr′) ***n-*** delicate fern found in deep and shady woods

maid·en·hood (mā′ dən ho͝od′) ***n-*** time when a girl is a maiden; also, the condition of being a maiden.

maid·en·ly (mā′ dən lē′) ***adj-*** like or suitable to a young girl; modest; gentle. **—*n-* mai′ den·li·ness.**

maiden name ***n-*** last name of a woman before marriage.

maid-in-wait·ing (mād′ ən wā′ tĭng) ***n-*** [*pl.* **maids-in-wait·ing**] girl or young woman who attends a queen or other great lady as part of her household.

maid of honor ***n-*** unmarried woman who acts as chief companion to the bride at a wedding.

Maid of Or·léans (mād′ əv ôr′ lĕnz′) ***n-*** Joan of Arc.

maid·serv·ant (mād′ sûr′ vənt) *Archaic* ***n-*** female servant.

Mai·du (mī′ do͞o) ***n-*** [*pl.* **Maidus,** also **Maidu**] member of a tribe of American Indians who lived in California between the Feather and American rivers. ***adj-*:** *a* Maidu *custom.*

[1]**mail** (māl) ***n-*** **1** letters, packages, magazines, etc., sent through the post office: *There was no* mail *today.* **2** government system of carrying and delivering letters, magazines, etc.: *Send that parcel by* mail. ***vt-*** to put into the mail: *to* mail *a package to a friend.* *as* ***modifier*:** *a* mail *train*; *a* mail *bag.* [from Middle English **male** meaning "a wallet; bag," from Old French, from Old High German **mal(a)ha.** Wallets and traveling bags were once used to carry mail.] ***Hom-*** male.

CHAIN

SCALE

Mail

[2]**mail** (māl) ***n-*** armor, especially garments made of or covered with interlocking metal links, metal rings, or overlapping metal scales. [from Old French **maille,** from Latin **macula** meaning "a spot; mesh of a net."] ***Hom-*** male. **—*adj-* mailed.**

mail·a·ble (mā′ lə bəl) ***adj-*** such as can conveniently be mailed or may legally be mailed: *a* mailable *package.*

mail·box (māl′ bŏks′) ***n-*** **1** box in which mail is placed when delivered. **2** box in which mail is placed to be collected by the post office.

mail drop ***n-*** slot or chute where mail can be inserted.

mail·er (mā′ lər) ***n-*** **1** person who mails. **2** an addressing or postage-stamping machine. **3** mailing container.

mail·man (māl′ măn′, -mən) ***n-*** [*pl.* **mail·men**] person who collects and delivers mail; postman.

mail order ***n-*** an order sent by mail for merchandise to be delivered and paid for by mail. A company set up to fill such orders is a **mail-order house.** *as* ***modifier*** **(mail-order):** *a* mail-order *electronics firm.*

maim (mām) ***vt-*** to deprive (someone) of the use of a part of the body; mutilate; cripple: *A leg wound* maimed *the soldier for life.*

main (mān) ***adj-*** most important; central; master; principal: *a* main *street*; *the* main *idea.* ***n-*** **1** pipe, line, cable, etc., from which lesser ones branch off: *Water and gas* mains *usually run under the streets.* **2** wide stretch of sea; the open sea: *Treasure ships sailed across the Spanish* Main *from South America to Spain.* ***Homs-*** Maine, mane.

by main force with sheer, unaided strength: *The boy lifted the weight* by main force. **in the main** for the most part: *I agree with you* in the main. **with might and main** with strength and application.

Maine (mān) ***n-*** U.S. battleship that blew up and sank in the harbor of Havana, Cuba, February 15, 1898.

main·land (mān′ lənd) ***n-*** continent or broad stretch of land, as distinct from the islands off its coast. **—*n-* main′ land·er.**

main·ly (mān′ lē) ***adv-*** chiefly; principally; for the most part.

main·mast (mān′ măst′, -məst) ***n-*** a ship's chief mast.

main·sail (mān′ səl, *also* -sāl′) ***n-*** the largest sail on the mainmast of a ship.

main·sheet (mān′ shēt′) *n-* rope used to flatten the mainsail and set it at the proper angle to the wind.

main·spring (mān′ spring′) *n-* 1 spring that makes a watch or clock go. 2 chief driving force: *Personal ambition was the* mainspring *of his career.*

main·stay (mān′ stā′) *n-* 1 strong rope or cable holding in place the mainmast of a sailing ship. 2 main support: *Bread is a* mainstay *of one's daily diet.*

main stem *n-* 1 *Informal* main street. 2 main railroad line.

main·stream (mān′ strēm′) *n-* chief current or tendency; most meaningful tradition or line of development: *the* mainstream *of American thought.*

Main Street *n-* the chief business street of a town or city; hence, a group or locality in which money and business are the only interests.

main·tain (mān tān′) *vt-* 1 to keep from declining or changing; especially, to keep in a desirable condition: *to* maintain *highways; to* maintain *a good reputation.* 2 to keep up; continue: *to* maintain *a fast pace.* 3 to keep possession of (something attacked, in danger, etc.); hold on to: *to* maintain *one's footing on an icy walk.* 4 to provide for the existence of; support: *He* maintains *a large family.* 5 to state firmly; assert; claim: *He* maintains *that he will never yield.* **—*adj-* main·tain′ a·ble.**

main·te·nance (mān′ tə nəns) *n-* 1 the act or process of maintaining: *the* maintenance *of highways; the* maintenance *of an opinion; the* maintenance *of life.* 2 means of support; food and other necessities.

main·top (mān′ tŏp′) *n-* platform at the head of the mainmast of a ship.

main yard *n-* on a ship, the spar from which the mainsail is hung.

maî·tre d'hô·tel (mĕ′ trə dō tĕl′, *also* mā′ trə-) *French* [*pl.* **maî·tres d'hô·tel**] headwaiter or chief steward of a restaurant, club, etc.

maize (māz) *n-* 1 Indian corn; corn. 2 the yellow of ripe corn kernels. ***adj-***: *a* maize *sweater.* ***Hom-*** maze.

Maj. major.

ma·jes·tic (mə jĕs′ tĭk) ***adj-*** full of majesty; dignified and impressive; stately: *a* majestic *procession.* Also **ma·jes′ ti·cal. —*adv-* ma·jes′ ti·cal·ly.**

maj·es·ty (măj′ ə stē) *n-* [*pl.* **maj·es·ties**] 1 quality that moves to awe by its greatness, size, power, etc.; grandeur; splendor: *the king in all his* majesty; *the* majesty *of the sea.* 2 **Majesty** title of a sovereign or royal ruler, preceded by "Your," "His," or "Her."

ma·jor (mā′ jər) *adj-* 1 greater than others or the rest in amount, extent, number, importance, effect, etc.: *to do a* major *part of the work; a* major *novelist; a* major *cause of accidents.* 2 *Music* relating to or based on the major scale: *a* major *chord.* *n-* 1 in the Army, Air Force, and Marine Corps, a commissioned officer who ranks next below a lieutenant colonel and next above a captain. 2 *Music* the major scale, or an arrangement or combination of notes based on this scale. 3 subject in which one concentrates one's studies, especially in college: *English is his* major. 4 person who concentrates his studies in such a subject: *He is an English* major. ***vi-*** to concentrate one's studies in a certain subject, especially in college: *He* majored *in English.*

ma·jor-do·mo (mā′ jər dō′ mō) *n-* [*pl.* **ma·jor-do·mos**] chief steward of a great household.

major general *n-* in the Army, Air Force, and Marine Corps, a commissioned officer who ranks next below a lieutenant general and next above a brigadier general.

ma·jor·i·ty (mə jŏr′ ə tē, mə jŏr′-) *n-* [*pl.* **ma·jor·i·ties**] 1 the greater of two numbers considered as parts of a whole: *a* majority *of the votes.* 2 difference between this greater number and the smaller: *In the class election she won by 24 to 18, a* majority *of six.* 3 full legal age of 21 years. *as* ***modifier***: *a* majority *vote;* majority *rule.* ▶Should not be confused with PLURALITY.

major league *n-* in certain sports, especially U.S. baseball, one of the organizations including the top-ranking professional teams. *as* ***modifier*** (**major-league**): *a* major-league *player.* **—*n-* major leaguer.**

major scale *Music n-* scale having half steps between the third and fourth notes and the seventh and eighth notes.

make (māk) ***vt-*** **[made, mak·ing]** 1 to produce or create; cause: *to* make *trouble; to* make *a noise.* 2 to bring into being; build; put together: *to* make *laws; to* make *a bookcase; to* make *an agreement.* 3 to gain; earn; win; acquire: *to* make *a living; to* make *friends or enemies.* 4 to win a position on: *to* make *the track team.* 5 to execute (an action, motion, etc.): *to* make *a bow; to* make *a speech; to* make *a journey.* 6 to prepare for use: *to* make *a bed; to* make *hay.* 7 to form or arrive at in one's mind: *to* make *plans; to* make *a guess.* 8 to cause to (act, feel, be, look, etc.): *You* make *me laugh. The fire* made *him warm. He* made *himself useful.* 9 *Informal* to cause to succeed: *His dance* makes *the show.* 10 to force or compel (to do something): *to* make *a child behave.* 11 to achieve or produce by exerting oneself: *to* make *an effort; to* make *another attempt.* 12 to reach; get to: *to* make *a train; to* make *home by sundown.* 13 to conclude to be the meaning or character (of): *What do you* make *of him?* 14 to consider; judge; estimate: *I* make *the total weight to be ten tons.* 15 in electricity, to complete or close (a circuit). ***vi-*** 1 to move; head: *They* made *toward the hills. The dog* made *for the door.* 2 to cause oneself to be in a certain state or condition: *to* make *certain of success.* 3 to constitute or amount to something specified: *That* makes *sense. Two and two* make *four.* 4 to have what is needed to be or develop into something specified: *He* makes *a fine mayor.* ***n-*** 1 brand or style: *a new* make *of automobile.* 2 manner of construction, workmanship, etc.: *an old cabinet of fine* make.

on the make *Informal* striving aggressively for success.

make after to pursue; chase.

make as if (or **as though**) to act as if.

make away with 1 to eat or consume completely; finish: *He* made away with *the whole pie.* 2 to steal. 3 to kill.

make it *Informal* to succeed in attaining something.

make off to leave in a hurry.

make off with to steal: *Someone* made off with *his hat.*

make out 1 to understand: *I can't* make *you* out. 2 to see clearly; distinguish. 3 to succeed; get along: *He'll* make out *all right.* 4 to fill out; complete: *to* make out *a form.* 5 to write: *to* make out *a list.*

make over 1 to remake; alter: *to* make over *an old dress.* 2 to transfer the ownership of.

make up 1 to invent: *Let's* make up *a good story.* 2 to form; compose: *Water* makes up *most of the earth's surface.* 3 to assemble; bring or put together: *to* make up *a team for softball.* 4 to become friendly again: *to* make up *after a quarrel.* 5 to catch up on: *to* make up *an assignment.* 6 to put makeup on.

make up for to compensate for: *to* make up for *lost time.*

make up to *Informal* to try to win favor with (someone) by flattery or a show of affection.

make-be·lieve (māk′ bə lēv′) ***adj-*** 1 imaginary; fictional: *a* make-believe *island.* 2 pretended; false: *a* make-believe *battle.* ***n-***: *the world of* make-believe.
mak·er (mā′ kər) ***n-*** 1 person or thing that makes something; creator or builder. 2 **Maker** God; the Creator.
make·shift (māk′ shĭft′) ***n-*** thing which can be used for the time being until something better is obtained. ***adj-*** temporary: *to use a box for a* makeshift *table.*
make·up (māk′ ŭp′) ***n-*** 1 way a thing is put together; composition; structure: *the* makeup *of a compound.* 2 arrangement; layout: *the* makeup *of the front page.* 3 disposition; nature: *Gloom is part of his* makeup. 4 cosmetics used by women or by actors making up for a part.
mak·ing (mā′ kĭng) ***n-*** 1 act of a person who, or thing that, makes; also, the process followed: *bread-*making. 2 influence, force, or happening that contributes to someone's advancement or success: *That job was his* making. 3 **makings** materials or qualities required: *He has the* makings *of a good businessman.*
mal- *prefix* ill; bad; poor; wrong: *to* mal*treat*; mal*adjusted.* [from Old French, from Latin **male-,** from **male,** "badly."]
Mal·a·chi (măl′ ə kī′) ***n-*** 1 fifth-century B.C. Hebrew prophet. 2 book of the Old Testament with his prophecies. In the CCD Bible, **Mal·a·chi′ a.**
mal·a·chite (măl′ ə kīt′) ***n-*** opaque, bright-green mineral that is an important ore of copper, and from which ornamental objects are made.
mal·ad·just·ed (măl′ ə jŭs′ təd) ***adj-*** poorly adjusted; not in harmony with one's associates or surroundings.
mal·ad·just·ment (măl′ ə jŭst′ mənt) ***n-*** poor or wrong adjustment.
mal·ad·min·is·ter (măl′ əd mĭn′ ə stər) ***vt-*** to administer or manage badly. —***n-*** **mal′ ad·min′ is·tra′ tion.**
mal·a·droit (măl′ ə droit′) ***adj-*** lacking skill; awkward; clumsy. —***adv-*** **mal′ a·droit′ ly.** ***n-*** **mal′ a·droit′ ness.**
mal·a·dy (măl′ ə dē) ***n-*** [*pl.* **mal·a·dies**] sickness; illness.
Mal·a·ga (măl′ ə gə) ***n-*** 1 rich, sweet wine originally produced in Malaga, Spain. 2 (also **Malaga grape**) type of sweet, light-green grape from which this wine is made.
mal·a·prop·ism (măl′ ə prŏp′ ĭz′ əm) ***n-*** ridiculous misuse of words. [from **Mrs. Malaprop,** a character in Sheridan's play "The Rivals."]
ma·lar·i·a (mə lâr′ ē ə) ***n-*** disease caused by a parasite introduced into the blood by the bite of the infected female anopheles mosquito, and characterized by spells of chills, weakness, and fever. —***adj-*** **ma·lar′ i·al.**
Ma·lay (mə lā′, mā′ lā′) ***n-*** 1 member of a people who live in Malaysia. 2 the language of these people. ***adj-***: *the* Malay *archipelago.* —***adj-*** **Ma·lay′ an.**
mal·con·tent (măl′ kən tĕnt′) ***adj-*** discontented, especially with established authority. ***n-*** person who is discontented with the established order of things.
male (māl) ***n-*** member of the sex that in mature animals becomes the father of offspring, or in plants has stamens and produces pollen. ***adj-*** 1 of or belonging to this sex. 2 consisting of men or boys: *a* male *chorus.* 3 typical of men or boys; masculine. 4 fitting into a corresponding part shaped to receive it: *a* male *plug.* ***Hom-*** mail.
mal·e·dic·tion (măl′ ə dĭk′ shən) ***n-*** the calling down of evil upon someone; curse.
mal·e·fac·tion (măl′ ə făk′ shən) ***n-*** evil deed; sin.
mal·e·fac·tor (măl′ ə făk′ tər) ***n-*** a criminal or evildoer. —***n-*** *fem.* **mal′ e·fac′ tress.**
male·ness (māl′ nəs) ***n-*** male traits or qualities; masculinity; virility.
ma·lev·o·lent (mə lĕv′ ə lənt) ***adj-*** wishing evil or injury to others; spiteful; malicious. —***n-*** **ma·lev′ o·lence.** ***adv-*** **ma·lev′ o·lent·ly.**

mal·fea·sance (măl′ fē′ zəns) ***n-*** wrongful conduct, especially wrongdoing by a public official.
mal·for·ma·tion (măl′ fər mā′ shən) ***n-*** faulty or abnormal structure, especially in a living body; deformity.
mal·formed (măl′ fôrmd′, -fôrmd′) ***adj-*** badly or abnormally formed.
mal·func·tion (măl′ fŭngk′ shən) ***vi-*** to fail to function in the normal or intended manner; function defectively. ***n-*** failure to function normally; defective operation.
mal·ic acid (măl′ ĭk, mā′ lĭk) ***n-*** colorless, mild, pleasant-tasting acid ($C_4H_6O_5$) found in some fruits.
mal·ice (măl′ əs) ***n-*** 1 desire to harm; spite or ill will directed against someone. 2 (also **malice aforethought**) in law, willful intent to injure or cause harm.
ma·li·cious (mə lĭsh′ əs) ***adj-*** arising from or bearing ill will; filled with spite: *her* malicious *gossip*; *a* malicious *person.* —***adv-*** **ma·li′ cious·ly.** ***n-*** **ma·li′ cious·ness.**
ma·lign (mə līn′) ***adj-*** 1 harmful; injurious: *a* malign *influence.* 2 malicious; evil: *the* malign *rule of a tyrant.* ***vt-*** to speak evil of; slander: *to* malign *an innocent person.* —***n-*** **ma·lign′ er.** ***adv-*** **ma·lign′ ly.**
ma·lig·nan·cy (mə lĭg′ nən sē) ***n-*** [*pl.* **ma·lig·nan·cies**] 1 a being malignant. 2 malignant tumor.
ma·lig·nant (mə lĭg′ nənt) ***adj-*** 1 wishing or causing harm or evil; filled with great hate or malice: *a* malignant *plot*; *his* malignant *fury.* 2 likely to cause death, especially by spreading and growing throughout the body; cancerous: *a* malignant *growth.* —***adv-*** **ma·lig′ nant·ly.**
ma·lig·ni·ty (mə lĭg′ nə tē) ***n-*** [*pl.* **ma·lig·ni·ties**] harmfulness or malice; also, an instance of these.
ma·lin·ger (mə lĭng′ ər) ***vi-*** to pretend to be sick or injured in order to escape duty. —***n-*** **ma·ling′ er·er.**
mall (mȯl) ***n-*** shaded public walk or promenade, often bordered by trees or lined with shops. ***Hom-*** maul.
mal·lard (măl′ ərd) ***n-*** common wild duck. The male has an iridescent green head. For picture, see *duck.*
mal·le·a·ble (măl′ ē ə bəl, măl′ ə bəl) ***adj-*** such as can be shaped by hammering or rolling: *Gold is a* malleable *metal.* —***n-*** **mal′ le·a·bil′ i·ty.**
mal·let (măl′ ət) ***n-*** 1 a short-handled hammer with a wooden head shaped like a barrel. 2 a similar long-handled implement for driving balls in croquet or polo.

Mallet

mal·low (măl′ ō) ***n-*** any of various plants with five-petaled, often very showy flowers. The hollyhock and the hibiscus are related to the mallows.
malm·sey (mäm′ zē) ***n-*** [*pl.* **malm·seys**] a rich, full-flavored, sweet wine.
mal·nu·tri·tion (măl′ no͞o trĭsh′ ən) ***n-*** inadequate nourishment of the body due to lack of food, a poorly balanced diet, or poor digestion.
mal·oc·clu·sion (măl′ ə klo͞o′ zhən) ***n-*** a faulty coming together of the upper and lower teeth.
mal·o·dor·ous (măl′ ō′ dər əs) ***adj-*** having a bad smell. —***adv-*** **mal·o′ dor·ous·ly.** ***n-*** **mal·o′ dor·ous·ness.**
mal·prac·tice (măl′ prăk′ təs) ***n-*** 1 wrong or neglectful treatment of a patient by a surgeon or physician. 2 conduct of any profession in an illegal or wrong way.
malt (mȯlt) ***n-*** barley or other grain made to sprout, then roasted and dried for use in beer and a food extract. ***vt-*** to change to or prepare with this substance.
malted milk ***n-*** 1 powder made with dried milk, malt, and sometimes other flavorings. 2 (also **malted**) drink made with this powder, milk, and chocolate or other flavoring, often whipped with ice cream.
Mal·tese (mȯl′ tēz′) ***n-*** [*pl.* **Mal·tese**] 1 native or inhabitant of Malta. 2 the language of these people, which is an Arabic dialect. ***adj-***: *a* Maltese *custom.*

Maltese cat *n-* a short-haired domestic cat with bluish-gray fur.

Maltese cross *n-* a cross having four arms which are equal and have wide, notched ends.

mal·tose (mȯl′tōs′) or **malt sugar** *n-* crystalline sugar ($C_{12}H_{22}O_{11}$), consisting of two molecules of glucose and formed when starch is digested.

mal·treat (măl′trēt′) *vt-* to treat cruelly or roughly; misuse. **—*n-* mal′treat′ment.**

ma·ma (mä′mə, *also Brit.* mə mä′) *n-* mother (used chiefly when speaking to or about one's own mother).

mam·bo (mäm′bō′) *n-* [*pl.* **mam·bos**] fast dance of Haitian origin, similar to a rumba; also, the music for this dance. *vi-* to perform this dance.

[1]**mam·ma** (mă′mə) *n-* [*pl.* **mam·mae** (-mē)] mammary gland. [from Latin **mamma** with the same meaning.]

[2]**mam·ma** (mä′mə) mama.

mam·mal (măm′əl) *n-* animal that has a backbone and, in the female, milk glands for feeding its young. Most mammals are four-footed furry or hairy animals. Human beings, bats, and whales are also mammals. **—*adj-* mam·mal′ian** (mə māl′ē ən).

mam·mo·gram (măm′ə grăm) *n-* X ray of a human breast, used to detect cancer and other tumors.

mam·mog·ra·phy (mə mäg′rə fē) *n-* process of making a mammogram.

mam·mon (măm′ən) *n-* **1** material wealth considered as a bad influence or unworthy goal. **2 Mammon** the personification of greed and worldly gain.

mam·moth (măm′əth) *n-* large, hairy elephant with curved tusks. Mammoths became extinct several thousand years ago. *adj-* gigantic; huge.

Mammoth, up to 13 ft high at shoulder

man (măn) *n-* [*pl.* **men** (mĕn)] **1** adult male of the human species. **2** mankind; the human race: *the progress of* man. **3** person; human being: *Every* man *to his own taste.* **4** person having qualities considered very manly, such as strength and bravery: *to act like a* man. **5** male employee; worker; hand: *The contractor has ten* men *on the job.* **6** playing piece in chess, checkers, or similar games. **7** husband or lover. *vt-* [**manned, man·ning**] **1** to furnish or staff with workers or helpers: *to* man *a ship.* **2** to take one's place for work or duty at: *He was ordered to* man *the gun.* **3** to brace or nerve (oneself): *He* manned *himself for the task.*

man and boy *Informal* during much of a person's life: *I've known him thirty years,* man and boy. **man and wife** husband and wife. **to a man** without exception.

man about town *n-* man who leads a very active social life, and is often seen at night clubs, the theater, etc.

man·a·cle (măn′ĭ kəl) *n-* handcuff; fetter. *vt-* [**man·a·cled, man·a·cling**] to place handcuffs or fetters on.

man·age (măn′ĭj) *vt-* [**man·aged, man·ag·ing**] **1** to be in charge of: *to* manage *a store*; *to* manage *a baseball team.* **2** to control: *to* manage *a wild horse.* **3** to contrive; succeed somehow: *I* managed *to get away.*

man·age·a·ble (măn′ə jə bəl) *adj-* such as can be managed or controlled: *a* manageable *horse*; *a* manageable *task.* **—*n-* man′age·a·bil′i·ty.**

man·age·ment (măn′ĭj mənt) *n-* **1** direction; control; handling: *good* management *of a business*; management *of a shop.* **2** those in charge of a business or enterprise; also, all such people collectively.

man·ag·er (măn′ĭj ər) *n-* **1** person who has control or direction; person in charge: *sales* manager; *the* manager *of a team.* **2** person skilled in conducting a business, household affairs, etc.: *Maureen is a good* manager.

man·a·ge·ri·al (măn′ə jêr′ē əl) *adj-* of or having to do with a manager or with management.

ma·ña·na (mä nyä′nä) *Spanish adv-* tomorrow or in the future. *n-* the next day, or some future time.

man-at-arms (măn′ət ärmz′) *n-* [*pl.* **men-at-arms**] soldier; especially, during the Middle Ages, a heavily armed, mounted soldier.

man·a·tee (măn′ə tē′) *n-* large, plant-eating mammal that lives in rivers and bays; sea cow.

Manatee

Man·chu (măn′chōō′) *n-* **1** one of a Mongolian people from Manchuria, who conquered China in 1643 and established a dynasty that lasted until 1912. **2** the language of these people. *adj-*: *the* Manchu *armies.*

man·da·mus (măn dā′məs) *n-* in law, a writ or document from a superior court, directing a person, corporation, or lower court to perform some public duty or act.

Man·dan (măn′dăn′) *n-* [*pl.* **Man·dans,** also **Man·dan**] one of an almost extinct tribe of American Indians who lived in North Dakota between the Heart and Little Missouri rivers. *adj-*: *a* Mandan *ceremony.*

man·da·rin (măn′də rĭn′, -rən) *n-* **1** member of one of the nine grades of highly educated public officials under the Chinese Empire. **2** (also **mandarin orange**) Chinese variety of orange with a sweet pulp and a rind that peels easily. **3 Mandarin** northern dialect of Chinese; also, formerly, the court language of the Chinese Empire.

man·da·tar·y (măn′də tĕr′ē) *n-* [*pl.* **man·da·tar·ies**] nation, person, etc., to which a mandate has been issued.

man·date (măn′dāt′) *n-* **1** official order; command; decree. **2** political instructions from voters to their representatives in a legislature, as expressed by the results of an election. **3** formerly, a charge from the League of Nations to a member nation, authorizing it to govern conquered territory. **4** a territory so governed (see also *trust territory*) *vt-* [**man·dat·ed, man·dat·ing**] to put (a territory) under supervisory control.

man·da·tor·y (măn′də tôr′ē) *adj-* **1** containing or required by an official command; compulsory; obligatory. **2** of or relating to a League of Nations mandate. *n-* [*pl.* **man·da·tor·ies**] mandatary.

man·di·ble (măn′də bəl) *n-* **1** bone of the lower jaw. **2** jawlike part, such as the upper or lower part of a bird's beak, or biting part of an insect's mouth.

man·do·lin (măn′də lĭn′) *n-* musical instrument with a rounded, tapering sound box and eight wire strings, played by plucking.

man·drake (măn′drāk′) *n-* **1** Old World plant with a very large, forked root, formerly believed to have magic powers. **2** the May apple.

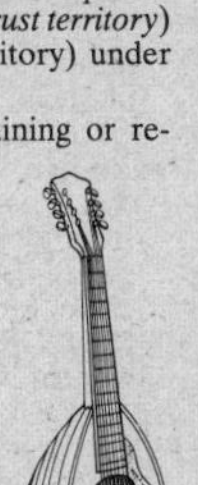

Mandolin

---

fāte, făt, dâre, bärn; bē, bĕt, mêre; bīte, bĭt; nōte, hŏt, môre, dȯg; fŭn, fûr; tōō, bŏŏk; oil; out; tar; thin; then; hw for wh as in *wh*at; zh for s as in u*s*ual; ə for a, e, i, o, u, as in *a*go, lin*e*n, per*i*l, at*o*m, min*u*s

man·drel (măn′ drəl) ***n-*** **1** snug-fitting cylindrical or conical piece of metal on which something can be held for shaping on a lathe or similar machine. **2** similar device around which metal, glass, etc., may be shaped or cast. ***Hom-*** mandrill.

man·drill (măn′ drəl) ***n-*** large, fierce western African monkey related to the baboons. It has conspicuous blue and red markings on its face. ***Hom-*** mandrel.

mane (mān) ***n-*** the long hair on the top of the head and on the neck of a horse, lion, zebra, and some other animals. ***Homs-*** main, Maine. —***adj-*** **maned.**

man-eat·ing (măn′ ē′ tĭng) ***adj-*** likely to attack and eat human beings: *a* man-eating *shark.* —***n-*** **man′ -eat′ er.**

ma·neu·ver (mə no͞o′ vər) ***n-*** **1** planned and supervised movement of troops or ships. **2** skillful action, move, etc.: *a clever* maneuver. **3 maneuvers** practice exercises carried out by military forces: *to send new recruits out on* maneuvers. ***vi-*** **1** to perform planned military movements: *Battleships* maneuvered *off the coast.* **2** to plan with art and skill; scheme: *He* maneuvered *for a seat next to the celebrity.* ***vt-*** **1** to move (troops, ships, etc.) according to a plan: *The admiral* maneuvered *his fleet into attack position.* **2** to move, manage, or manipulate in a clever, skillful way: *He* maneuvered *his car into a small space.* Also **maneuvre.**

ma·neu·ver·a·ble (mə no͞o′ vər ə bəl) ***adj-*** such as can be maneuvered; moved, operated, or managed with ease: *a fast,* maneuverable *airplane.* —***n-*** **ma·neu′ ver·a·bil′ i·ty:** *This device gives greater* maneuverability.

man Friday ***n-*** devoted and helpful assistant; right-hand man. [from the name of the servant and constant companion of Robinson Crusoe.]

man·ful (măn′ fəl) ***adj-*** manly; determined; brave. —***adv-*** **man′ ful·ly.** ***n-*** **man′ ful·ness.**

man·ga·nese (măng′ gə nēz′, -nēs′) ***n-*** hard, brittle, grayish-white metal element, used in glass, paint, and hard steel. Symbol Mn, At. No. 25, At. Wt. 54.938.

mange (mānj) ***n-*** contagious skin disease of domestic animals, caused by parasites.

man·ger (mān′ jər) ***n-*** box or trough in which food for horses or cattle is placed.

[1]**man·gle** (măng′ gəl) ***vt-*** **[man·gled, man·gling] 1** to mutilate by cutting or hacking; maim; crush: *A trap had* mangled *the raccoon's paw.* **2** to spoil in the making or doing; botch: *to* mangle *a piece of music.* [from an early legal term, **mangler,** from Old French **mahaignier** meaning "to maim," from **mahaigne,** "an injury; mayhem." Maim and mayhem come from these same Old French words.] —***n-*** **man′ gler.**

[2]**man·gle** (măng′ gəl) ***n-*** machine or electric appliance that presses cloth and clothes by means of rollers. ***vt-*** **[man·gled, man·gling]:** *to* mangle *sheets.* [from Dutch **mangel,** "machine for smoothing," ultimately from Greek **manganon,** "machine worked with a winch and pulley."]

man·go (măng′ gō) ***n-*** [*pl.* **man·goes or man·gos] 1** fruit with a thin, tough, yellow or reddish skin and sweet, juicy pulp. **2** the tropical tree that bears this fruit.

man·go·steen (măng′ gə stēn′) ***n-*** **1** East Indian fruit with a thick, brownish-red skin and white, juicy pulp. **2** tree that bears this fruit.

Mango

man·grove (măng′ grōv′, măn′-) ***n-*** tropical tree or shrub that grows in swampy ground. Its wide-spreading branches send down roots that look like tree trunks and form thickets.

man·gy (mān′ jē) ***adj-*** **[man·gi·er, man·gi·est] 1** having, resembling, or caused by mange. **2** worn, shabby, and untidy. —***n-*** **man′ gi·ness.**

man·han·dle (măn′ hăn′ dəl) ***vt-*** **[man·han·dled, man·han·dling]** to handle roughly; treat with brutality.

man·hole (măn′ hōl′) ***n-*** an opening that has a removable cover and is used to enter a sewer, tank, etc.

man·hood (măn′ ho͝od′) ***n-*** **1** the state of being an adult male human being: *to arrive at* manhood. **2** manly qualities, such as courage and bravery. **3** men as a group: *the* manhood *of the nation.*

man-hour (măn′ ou′ ər) ***n-*** amount of work that can be done by one man in one hour, used as a unit in estimating costs, wages, etc.

ma·ni·a (mā′ nē ə) ***n-*** **1** form of insanity characterized by spells of great excitement and disorganized behavior. **2** excessive enthusiasm; craze: *a* mania *for clothes.*

-mania *combining form* strong, often uncontrollable craving or obsession: *mono*mania (obsession with one idea). [from **mania,** from Greek **maniā,** "frenzy."]

ma·ni·ac (mā′ nē ăk′) ***n-*** insane person who is violent and uncontrollable. ***adj-*** violently insane.

ma·ni·a·cal (mə nī′ ə kəl) ***adj-*** of or characteristic of a violently insane person: *a* maniacal *rage.* —***adv-*** **ma·ni′ a·cal·ly:** *He laughed* maniacally.

man·ic-de·pres·sive (măn′ ĭk dĭ prĕs′ ĭv) ***adj-*** characterized by alternate periods of excessive excitement and excessive depression. ***n-*** person who undergoes such alternate emotional states.

man·i·cure (măn′ ə kyo͞or′) ***n-*** treatment for the care or grooming of the hands and fingernails. ***vt-*** **[man·i·cured, man·i·cur·ing]:** *She* manicured *her fingernails.*

man·i·cur·ist (măn′ ə kyo͞or′ ĭst) ***n-*** person who does manicuring.

man·i·fest (măn′ ə fĕst′) ***adj-*** clear and apparent to the sight or understanding: *The truth of the statement is* manifest. ***vt-*** to show plainly; reveal; display: *to* manifest *interest.* ***n-*** list of passengers or cargo carried by an airplane, ship, etc. —***adv-*** **man′ i·fest′ ly.**

man·i·fes·ta·tion (măn′ ə fĕs tā′ shən) ***n-*** a showing or displaying: *His whistling is a* manifestation *of joy.*

man·i·fes·to (măn′ ə fĕs′ tō) ***n-*** [*pl.* **man·i·fes·toes** or **man·i·fes·tos]** public declaration or proclamation setting forth the intentions, aims, or motives of a group.

man·i·fold (măn′ ə fōld′) ***adj-*** **1** many and varied; diverse: *his* manifold *duties.* **2** consisting of or including many parts or forms: *a* manifold *subject.* ***n-*** pipe or chamber with two or more outlets along its length, used for connecting one pipe with others. —***adv-*** **man′ i·fold′ly.**

man·i·kin (măn′ ə kən, -kĭn′) ***n-*** **1** little man; dwarf. **2** model of the human body, often with removable parts, used in the study of anatomy. Also **mannikin.** ***Hom-*** mannequin.

ma·nil·a (mə nĭl′ ə) ***adj-*** **1** made of Manila paper: *a* manila *folder.* **2 Manila** made of Manila hemp: *a* Manila *rope.* ***n-*** **Manila** Manila hemp or Manila paper.

Manila hemp ***n-*** abaca.

Manila paper ***n-*** heavy, durable, light-brown or yellow paper, originally made from Manila hemp, and used for making envelopes, folders, etc., and as wrapping paper.

ma·ni·oc (măn′ ē ŏk′) ***n-*** the bitter cassava, from which tapioca is made.

ma·nip·u·late (mə nĭp′ yə lāt′) ***vt-*** **[ma·nip·u·lat·ed, ma·nip·u·lat·ing] 1** to handle or operate skillfully, especially with the hands: *to* manipulate *puppets.* **2** to influence, manage, or control cleverly and shrewdly: *to* manipulate *public opinion.* **3** to twist to one's own advantage; falsify: *to* manipulate *expense accounts.* —***n-*** **ma·nip′ u·la′ tor:** *a* manipulator *of public opinion.*

ma·nip·u·la·tion (mə nĭp′ yə lā′ shən) ***n-*** **1** a manipulating or a being manipulated. **2** in the treatment of certain diseases or injuries, the moving of a joint or limb with the hands in order to improve its condition.

man·i·tou (măn′ ə to͞o′) ***n-*** in the religion of the Algonquian Indians, the power or spirit that rules nature. [American word from Algonquian **manitto** meaning "he is a god."] Also **man′ i·to′** or **man′ i·tu′**.

man·kind (măn′ kīnd′) ***n-*** the human species.

man·like (măn′ līk′) ***adj-*** **1** like or typical of a man. **2** resembling a human being: *a* manlike *ape.*

man·ly (măn′ lē) ***adj-*** [**man·li·er, man·li·est**] having the qualities befitting a man; courageous, honorable, resolute, etc. **—*n-* man′ li·ness.**

man-made (măn′ mād′) ***adj-*** made by man, rather than by the processes of nature: *Rayon is a* man-made *material.*

man·na (măn′ ə) ***n-*** **1** in the Bible, food miraculously supplied to the children of Israel during their wandering in the wilderness. **2** any much-needed thing that is unexpectedly supplied: *The praise was* manna *to him.*

man·ne·quin (măn′ ə kən, -kĭn′) ***n-*** **1** person, usually a woman, employed as a model to display clothes. **2** jointed model of the human figure, used especially to display clothes. ***Hom-*** manikin.

man·ner (măn′ ər) ***n-*** **1** habitual personal behavior; individual style: *a kind* manner; *a rapid* manner *of speaking.* **2** any way or style in which a thing is done: *a painting in the Chinese* manner; *the usual* manner *of handling a problem.* **3** sort; type; also, kinds or species: *What* manner *of man is he? We catch all* manner *of fish in the bay.* **4 manners** (1) social behavior: *He has good* manners. (2) habits and customs: *the* manners *of the ancient Romans.* ***Hom-*** manor.

man·nered (măn′ ərd) ***adj-*** **1** having a particular kind of manner or manners: *a well-*mannered *girl.* **2** having or marked by mannerisms: *a* mannered *style of writing.*

man·ner·ism (măn′ ə rĭz′ əm) ***n-*** distinctive or peculiar action, gesture, style, etc., especially if habitual or affected.

man·ner·less (măn′ ər ləs) ***adj-*** lacking good manners.

man·ner·ly (măn′ ər lē) ***adj-*** polite. ***adv-*** politely; respectfully. **—*n-* man′ ner·li·ness.**

man·ni·kin (măn′ ə kən, -kĭn′) manikin.

man·nish (măn′ ĭsh) ***adj-*** characteristic of or suitable for a man; masculine: *his* mannish *stride*; *her gruff,* mannish *voice.* **—*adv-* man′ nish·ly. *n-* man′ nish·ness.**

ma·noeu·vre (mə no͞o′ vər) maneuver.

man-of-war (măn′ əv wŏr′, -ə wŏr′) ***n-*** [*pl.* **men-of-war**] warship used in former times.

ma·nom·e·ter (mə nŏm′ ə tər) ***n-*** instrument for measuring the pressure of gases.

man·or (măn′ ər) ***n-*** **1** under the feudal system, a piece of land granted to a nobleman, part of which he occupied while the rest was occupied and farmed by serfs. **2** in later times, a piece of land similarly granted, but farmed by tenants. **3** mansion, especially one on a large farm or country estate. ***Hom-*** manner.

ma·nor·i·al (mə nôr′ ē əl) ***adj-*** of or belonging to a manor.

man-o'-war bird (măn′ ə wŏr′) ***n-*** frigate bird.

man·pow·er (măn′ pou′ ər) ***n-*** **1** total number of people working or available for work in an industry, nation, etc.; especially, the number of men available for military service. **2** (often **man power**) power supplied by the physical effort of a human being.

manse (măns) ***n-*** a parsonage; especially, the home of a Presbyterian minister.

man·serv·ant (măn′ sûr′ vənt) ***n-*** [*pl.* **men·serv·ants**] male servant, such as a butler or valet.

man·sion (măn′ shən) ***n-*** large house; stately residence.

man·slaugh·ter (măn′ slŏ′ tər) ***n-*** in law, the killing of a human being unlawfully but without intention.

man·ta (măn′ tə) ***n-*** **1** piece of cloth used as a cape, shawl, blanket, etc., in Latin American countries. **2** (also **manta ray**) any of several very large rays of tropical waters; devilfish. For picture, see ²*ray.*

man·tel (măn′ təl) ***n-*** **1** structure or facing of wood, marble, brick, etc., around and above a fireplace. **2** mantelpiece. ***Hom-*** mantle.

Mantel

man·tel·piece (măn′ təl pēs′) ***n-*** shelf above a fireplace; mantel.

man·til·la (măn tē′ yə) ***n-*** scarf, usually of lace or a sheer silk, worn over the head and shoulders by Spanish and Latin American women.

man·tis (măn′ təs) ***n-*** [*pl.* **man·tis·es** or **man·tes** (-tēz′)] (often **praying mantis**) any of several long, slender insects related to the grasshoppers, which prey on other insects. Mantises often take a position with the front legs bent as if in prayer.

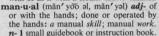

Praying mantis, 2—5 in. long

man·tle (măn′ təl) ***n-*** **1** long, loose cloak. **2** anything that covers or conceals: *night's* mantle *of darkness.* **3** layer of the earth located between the crust and core. The mantle is considered to be about 1800 miles thick. **4** protective membrane covering the body of a mollusk, which secretes the shell. **5** a gas mantle. **6** the back and upper part of the wings of a bird. ***vt-*** [**man·tled, man·tling**] to cover with or as if with a cloak. ***Hom-*** mantel.

Mantle

man·u·al (măn′ yo͞o əl, măn′ yəl) ***adj-*** of or with the hands; done or operated by the hands: *a* manual *skill*; manual *work.* ***n-*** **1** small guidebook or instruction book. **2** drill in the handling of a rifle, saber, or other weapon.

manual alphabet ***n-*** alphabet used by deaf-mutes, consisting of signs made with the fingers, each sign representing a letter.

man·u·al·ly (măn′ yo͞o ə lē, măn′ yə lē) ***adv-*** by hand or with the hands: *This machine is* manually *controlled.*

manual training ***n-*** training in work that is done with the hands, such as woodworking, metalwork, etc.

manuf. manufacture; manufacturer; manufacturing.

man·u·fac·ture (măn′ yə făk′ chər) ***vt-*** [**man·u·fac·tured, man·u·fac·tur·ing**] **1** to make by hand or by machinery, usually in large numbers: *to* manufacture *shoes in a large factory.* **2** to make or make up: *to* manufacture *an excuse.* ***n-*** **1** a making; production, especially by machinery and in large numbers: *the* manufacture *of household appliances.* **2** something produced by industrial means; product.

man·u·fac·tur·er (măn yə făk′ chər ər) ***n-*** person or company whose business is manufacturing.

man·u·mis·sion (măn′ yə mĭsh′ ən) ***n-*** a freeing or being freed from slavery; emancipation.

---

fāte, făt, dâre, bärn; bē, bĕt, mêre; bīte, bĭt; nōte, hŏt, môre, dŏg; fŭn, fûr; to͞o, bo͝ok; oil; out; tar; thin; then; hw for wh as in *wh*at; zh for s as in u*s*ual; ə for a, e, i, o, u, as in *a*go, lin*e*n, per*i*l, at*o*m, min*u*s

ma·nure (mə nyŏŏr′, -nŏŏr′) *n-* substance, especially animal waste, used to enrich the soil; fertilizer. *vt-* [**ma·nured, ma·nur·ing**] to put this substance on or in.

man·u·script (măn′ yə skrĭpt′) *n-* **1** book or paper written by hand or on the typewriter, such as an author's copy sent to a publisher or printer. Before the invention of printing, all books were handwritten manuscripts. **2** handwriting, as opposed to printing. **3** (also **manuscript writing**) handwriting in which each letter is formed like a printed letter.

Manx cat (măngks) *n-* a breed of short-haired domestic cat having no visible tail.

man·y (mĕn′ ē) ***determiner*** (traditionally called adjective or pronoun) a large number of; numerous: *There are* many *people here.* Many *are called but few are chosen.* *n-* **1** a large number: *In that village,* many *of the houses are white.* **2 the many** the majority.

a good many a fairly large number: *I saw* a good many *people today.* **a great many** a large number.

man·y-sid·ed (mĕn′ ē sī′ dəd) *adj-* **1** having many sides or surfaces: *a* many-sided *geometrical figure.* **2** having many parts or aspects; complex: *a* many-sided *problem.*

man·za·ni·ta (măn′ zə nē′ tə) *n-* any of several broadleaf evergreen shrubs of western North America.

Ma·o·ri (mou′ rē) *n-* [*pl.* **Ma·o·ri** or **Ma·o·ris**] **1** a member of a Polynesian people of New Zealand. **2** the language of these people. *adj-*: *a* Maori *chief.*

map (măp) *n-* **1** drawing, picture, or model of the surface of the earth or a part of it, showing the relative size and position of the features or places represented. **2** chart of the heavens. *vt-* [**mapped, map·ping**] **1** to represent or place on such a picture, model, or chart. **2** to plan in detail: *to* map *a cross-country trip*; *to* map *out a campaign.*

ma·ple (mā′ pəl) *n-* **1** any of various trees of the northern middle latitudes, with deeply indented leaves and two-winged seeds. **2** the hard, durable wood of these trees, used in making furniture. **3** a flavoring obtained from the sap of the sugar maple. *adj-*: *a* maple *table*; *a cake with* maple *frosting.*

Leaves and seeds of sugar maple

maple sugar *n-* sugar made by boiling down the sap of the sugar maple.

maple syrup *n-* syrup made by boiling sap from the sugar maple until it thickens.

mar (mär) *vt-* [**marred, mar·ring**] **1** to spoil the appearance of; flaw: *to* mar *a table top.* **2** to damage; impair: *to* mar *an excellent record.*

Mar. March.

mar·a·bou (măr′ ə bōō′) *n-* **1** large African stork. **2** the long, soft, wing or tail feathers, of this bird, used as trimming on women's clothes.

ma·ra·ca (mə rä′ kə) *n-* rattle made from a dried gourd or similar object containing seeds or beads, and used as a rhythm instrument.

Woman playing maracas

mar·a·schi·no (măr′ ə skē′ nō, -shē′ nō) *n-* [*pl.* **mar·a·schi·nos**] **1** alcoholic cordial made from European wild cherries and flavored with the crushed pits. **2** (also **maraschino cherry**) a cherry preserved in a syrup flavored with this cordial or an imitation of it.

mar·a·thon (măr′ ə thŏn′) *n-* **1** long-distance footrace. The official length is 26 miles, 385 yards. **2** any endurance contest: *a dance* marathon.

ma·raud (mə rȯd′) *vi-* to rove in search of plunder: *The gang* marauded *over the countryside.* *vt-* to plunder; raid: *A fox* marauded *the chicken coop.* —*n-* **ma·raud′er.**

mar·ble (mär′ bəl) *n-* **1** hard, close-grained rock composed of crystallized limestone and often streaked with various colors. Marble can be given a very smooth finish, and is used as building material, for sculpture, etc. **2** something made of or resembling this stone. **3** small, smooth ball made of glass, agate, etc., and used in playing the children's game of **marbles.** *adj-* **1** made of this stone. **2** smooth, white, or cold as polished marble: *her* marble *brow.* *vt-* [**mar·bled, mar·bling**] to give the appearance of marble to (something).

mar·ca·site (mär′ kə sīt′, -zīt′) *n-* **1** crystalline mineral, a compound of iron and sulfur, having a silvery, metallic appearance. **2** piece of this mineral, or of polished steel resembling it, used in ornaments.

mar·cel (mär sĕl′) *n-* deep, regular wave or series of such waves, put in the hair by means of a special curling iron. *vt-* [**mar·celled, mar·cel·ling**]: *to* marcel *the hair.*

[1]**march** (märch) *n-* **1** regular, measured step or walk, especially of soldiers. **2** distance passed over in walking with regular step from one place to another: *a day's* march *to camp.* **3** steady onward movement: *the* march *of years.* **4** musical composition or rhythm intended to accompany steady, measured walking. *vi-* **1** to move with regular steps, or in military form. **2** to move forward at a steady pace: *Time* marches *on.* *vt-* to cause to move at a steady pace: *to* march *troops.* [from French **marcher** originally meaning "to trample," probably from Late Latin **marcus,** "a hammer."] —*n-* **march′ er.**

on the march moving or advancing steadily. **steal a march on** to get an advantage over (someone) by a secret or unexpected action.

[2]**march** (märch) *n-* land next to the border between two regions, such as one of the counties near the border of England and Scotland. [from Old French **marche,** from Germanic **marca,** and related to [1]**mark.**]

March (märch) *n-* the third month of the year, having 31 days.

mar·chion·ess (mär′ shə nəs) *n-* wife or widow of a marquis, or a woman having a rank like a marquis.

Mar·di gras (mär′ dē grä′) *n-* Shrove Tuesday, the last day before Lent, celebrated in some cities with festivities.

[1]**mare** (mâr) *n-* female horse, donkey, zebra, etc. [from Old English **mere,** from **mearh** meaning "horse."]

[2]**ma·re** (mär′ ā) *n-* [*pl.* **ma·ri·a** (mär′ ē ə)] one of the large, relatively dark, circular areas seen on the moon's surface through a telescope, once thought to be seas. [from Latin **mare** meaning "sea."]

mare's nest *n-* **1** discovery which at first seems to be wonderful but which proves to be deceptive or a hoax. **2** state of confused disorder; hopeless tangle.

mare's tail *n-* long, narrow, cirrus cloud.

mar·ga·rine or **mar·ga·rin** (mär′ jə rən, -rēn′) *n-* substitute for butter usually made mostly of hydrogenated vegetable oils, and some cow's milk, vitamins A and D, flavorings, and coloring; oleo-margarine.

mar·gin (mär′ jən) *n-* **1** border around print or writing on a page, usually left blank. **2** extra amount allowed beyond what is needed: *to allow a* margin *of ten minutes to catch a train.* **3** edge; rim: *the* margin *of a pool.* **4** the difference between the cost of something and the price at which it is sold; markup. **5** the percentage of the price of a stock that a purchaser is required by law to deposit with a stockbroker in order to protect all parties from loss if the price of the stock later goes down.

mar·gin·al (mär′ jə nəl) *adj-* **1** of or forming a margin. **2** placed on or near a margin: *a* marginal *note.* **3** in business, making a very small profit: *a* marginal *operation.* **—*adv*- mar′ gin·al·ly.**

mar·gue·rite (mär′ gə rēt′, mär′ gyə-) ***n*-** daisy; also, any of several single chrysanthemums resembling daisies.

mar·i·gold (măr′ ə gōld′) ***n*- 1** garden plant having yellow, orange, or dark-red flowers. **2** any of various other flowering plants, such as the marsh marigold.

ma·ri·jua·na (măr′ ə wä′ nə) ***n*- 1** dried tops of the hemp plant. **2** a narcotic drug produced from hemp leaves. Also **ma′ ri·hua′ na.**

ma·rim·ba (mə rĭm′ bə) ***n*-** musical instrument consisting of strips of hardwood, each with a cylindrical resonating chamber under it. It is played by striking the strips with mallets.

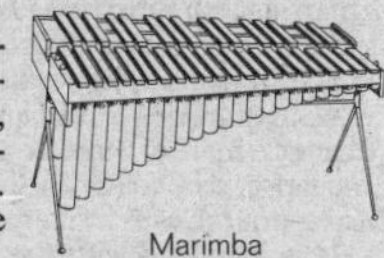

Marimba

ma·ri·na (mə rē′ nə) ***n*-** dock or area of a harbor where sailboats and motorboats are moored and serviced.

mar·i·nade (măr′ ə nād′) ***n*-** liquid, usually containing wine, oil, and seasonings, in which food is soaked in order to improve the flavor or to tenderize it.

mar·i·nate (măr′ ə nāt′) ***vt*- [mar·i·nated, mar·i·nat·ing]** to soak in a marinade before cooking or serving.

ma·rine (mə rēn′) ***adj*- 1** of, related to, or living in the sea: *a* marine *fish.* **2** of or having to do with navigation, shipping, etc.: *a* marine *compass*; marine *insurance.* ***n*- 1** one of a body of troops specially trained for making overseas landings. **2 marines** branch of a nation's military force composed of such troops. **3 Marines** the United States Marine Corps.

Marine Corps ***n*-** branch of the United States armed forces consisting of troops specially trained to make overseas landings. The Commandant of the Marine Corps is responsible to the Secretary of the Navy.

mar·i·ner (măr′ ə nər, mĕr-) ***n*-** sailor.

mar·i·o·nette (măr′ ē ə nĕt′, mĕr′-) ***n*-** jointed puppet made to move and gesture by manipulation of strings or wires attached to it.

Mar·i·po·sa lily (măr′ ə pō′ zə, -pŏ′ sə) ***n*- 1** plant of the lily family with showy flowers, found in California and Mexico. **2** the flower of this plant.

mar·i·tal (măr′ ə təl) ***adj*-** of or related to marriage: *a* marital *vow.* **—*adv*- mar′ i·tal·ly.**

Marionette

mar·i·time (măr′ ə tīm′) ***adj*- 1** of or related to the sea, boats, shipping, or navigation: *the study of* maritime *law.* **2** bordering on the sea; coastal.

mar·jo·ram (mär′ jə rəm) ***n*-** any of a group of plants of the mint family, especially **sweet marjoram,** used as a flavoring in cooking.

[1]**mark** (märk) ***n*- 1** line, dot, scratch, ring, etc., on a surface: *The wet glass left a* mark *on the table.* **2** object, design, number, etc., used as a sign or indicator; marker: *the ten-mile* mark; *the starting* mark; *an exclamation* mark. **3** feature or trait; token: *a* mark *of intelligence.* **4** something aimed at; goal; target: *He hit the* mark *with his first arrow.* **5** letter or number that show one's grade in a test or school course. **6 marks** grades in school or college: *He raised his* marks *last year.* ***vt*- 1** to make a line, dot, etc., on: *The wet glass* marked *the table.* **2** to indicate or show by some sign, symbol, gesture, etc.; designate: *X* marks *the spot.* **3** to be a feature or trait of; characterize: *Increased exploration of space will* mark *the future.* **4** to single out; select: *to* mark *a person for promotion.* **5** to pay attention to; heed: *You had better* mark *my warning.* **6** to determine the value of; evaluate; grade: *to* mark *a test.* [from Old English **mearc** meaning "boundary."] ***Hom*-** marque.

beside (or **wide of**) **the mark** not to the point: *The answers given by the witness were* beside the mark. **leave (one's) mark** to make a lasting impression. **make (one's) mark** to achieve success: *He* made *his* mark *in the world.* **of mark** of importance or distinction: *a man* of mark. **up to** (or **below**) **the mark** at (or below) a set standard or level of quality or achievement. **mark down 1** make a note of. **2** to lower the price of.

mark off to separate or divide with lines: *to* mark off *a distance on a map.*

mark out 1 to mark off completely. **2** to set apart.

mark time 1 to move the feet in marching time without going forward. **2** to stop operations while waiting for something: *to* mark time *in our sales campaign.*

mark up 1 to add (a certain amount) to the cost of an item in order to arrive at its selling price. **2** to raise the price of.

[2]**mark** (märk) ***n*-** the unit of money and a coin of Germany. See also *deutsche mark, ostmark.* [from German]. ***Hom*-** marque.

Mark (märk) ***n*-** the evangelist who is said to have written the second Gospel of the New Testament. Also **St. Mark.**

mark·down (märk′ doun′) ***n*-** a lowering of price, especially of retail price; also, amount it is reduced.

marked (märkt) ***adj*- 1** clear; plain; noticeable: *a* marked *improvement in health.* **2** having a mark or marks.

mark·ed·ly (mär′ kəd lē) ***adv*-** in a clear and obvious manner; noticeably: *He has* markedly *improved.*

marked man ***n*-** person singled out as an object of another's hatred, vengeance, etc.

mark·er (mär′ kər) ***n*- 1** something used as a sign or indicator: *a* marker *for the exact spot.* **2** person or device used to keep score in a game or to grade exams.

mar·ket (mär′ kət) ***n*- 1** place where goods are sold: *a food* market. **2** buying and selling; trade, especially in specific goods or services: *The used-car* market *is very active when new models come out.* **3** area or country where goods may be sold: *a foreign* market *for cars.* **4** demand: *There is a big* market *for warm clothing during the winter.* **5** stock market. ***vi*-** to buy food and other household items: *I* marketed *this morning.* ***vt*-** to sell; offer for sale: *We* market *tires.* **—*n*- mar′ ket·er.**

in the market for wanting to buy. **on the market** up for sale. **play the market** to buy and sell in, or speculate in, the stock market.

mar·ket·a·ble (mär′ kə tə bəl) ***adj*-** such as can be sold; suitable for sale: *His invention is not* marketable. **—*n*- mar′ ket·a·bil′ i·ty.**

mar·ket·ing (mär′ kə tĭng) ***n*-** branch of business study and practice that deals with all the processes involved in selling goods. Marketing includes advertising, transporting and storing, selling, getting information about possible products and sales, etc.

market·place (mär′ kət plās′) ***n*- 1** place where goods, especially food and household things, are sold. **2** the world of trade; commerce.

market value ***n*-** the current or prevailing price.

mark·ing (mär′ kĭng) ***n*-** mark or pattern of marks.

marks·man (märks′ mən) ***n*- [*pl.* marks·men]** person who is skilled in shooting.

---

fāte, făt, dâre, bärn; bē, bĕt, mêre; bīte, bĭt; nōte, hŏt, môre, dog; fŭn, fûr; to͞o, bo͝ok; oil; out; tar; thin; then; hw for wh as in *wh*at; zh for s as in u*s*ual; ə for a, e, i, o, u, as in *a*go, lin*e*n, per*i*l, at*o*m, min*u*s

marks·man·ship (mär*r*ks′ mən shĭp′) ***n-*** ability as a marksman.

mark·up (mär*r*k′ ŭp′) ***n-*** amount or percentage of the cost of an article, added to the cost to determine the selling price.

marl (mär*r*l) ***n-*** a crumbly soil consisting of clay, sand, and calcium carbonate in the form of shell fragments; also, any crumbly earth layer.

mar·lin (mär*r*′ lən) ***n-*** [*pl.* **mar·lin; mar·lins** (kinds of marlin)] any of various large deep-sea fishes with bills, related to the sailfish. ***Hom-*** marline.

mar·line (mär*r*′ lən) ***n-*** small, two-stranded cord used aboard sailing ships for binding the end of a rope to prevent fraying. ***Hom-*** marlin.

Marmoset, 18 in. long

mar·line·spike or **mar·lin·spike** (mär*r*′ lən spīk′) ***n-*** pointed iron tool used to separate the strands of rope or wire cable for splicing.

mar·ma·lade (mär*r*′ mə lād′) ***n-*** jellylike preserve made of the pulp and peel of fruits, especially oranges.

mar·mo·set (mär*r*′ mə sĕt′, -zĕt′) ***n-*** South American monkey about the size of a squirrel, with long silky fur.

mar·mot (mär*r*′ mət) ***n-* 1** any of various stout-bodied, gnawing animals with coarse fur and a short bushy tail, related to the squirrels. **2** woodchuck.

[1]**ma·roon** (mə ro͞on′) ***n-*** dark-red or reddish-brown color. ***adj-***: *a* maroon *cloak.* [from French **marron,** "chestnut," from Greek **máraon.**]

[2]**ma·roon** (mə ro͞on′) ***vt-*** to leave helpless and alone, especially on a desolate island or coast: *The loss of our boat* marooned *us for two nights.* [from French **marron,** "(escaped) slave of the West Indies", from Spanish **cimarron,** "wild."]

Marmot, about 27 in. long

marque (mär*r*k) *Archaic* ***n-*** seizure by a country of things, especially ships, belonging to its enemy; reprisal. ***Hom-*** mark.

mar·quee (mär*r* kē′) ***n-* 1** large, projecting canopy or shelter, often used as a signboard, over the entrance of a theater, hotel, etc. **2** *chiefly Brit.* large, open-sided tent, often used for an outdoor entertainment or party.

mar·quis (mär*r*′ kwĭs, *Fr.* mär kē′) ***n-*** nobleman ranking next below a duke. Also, *Brit.,* **mar′ quess** (mär*r*′ kwĭs).

mar·quise (mär*r* kēz′) ***n-* 1** wife or widow of a French marquis. **2** pointed oval shape of some cut gems; also, a ring or jewel having gems set in such a shape. ***as modifier***: *a* marquise *diamond.*

mar·qui·sette (mär*r*′ kwə sĕt′) ***n-*** very sheer fabric of cotton, silk, or synthetic, having a fine mesh weave.

mar·riage (măr′ ĭj) ***n-* 1** the relationship between a husband and wife; married life. **2** a marrying; wedding. ***as modifier***: *the* marriage *vows.*

mar·riage·a·ble (măr′ ĭj ə bəl) ***adj-*** suitable for marrying; unmarried, and above the legal age for marriage.

mar·ried (măr′ ēd) ***adj-* 1** of or related to marriage: *a* married *life.* **2** joined in marriage; wedded: *a* married *couple*; *a* married *woman.*

mar·row (măr′ ō) ***n-* 1** the soft, fatty tissue that is present in the cavities of most bones and produces the red blood cells. **2** the essence or best part of anything.

mar·row·bone (măr′ ō bōn′) ***n-* 1** bone containing edible marrow. **2 marrowbones** *Informal* the knees.

[1]**mar·ry** (măr′ ē) ***vt-*** **[mar·ried, mar·ry·ing] 1** to take for a husband or wife; wed: *John asked Ann to* marry *him.* **2** to join as husband and wife; perform the wedding ceremony for: *A minister* married *them.* **3** to give in marriage: *He* married *his youngest daughter to a writer.* ***vi-*** to enter into a marriage: *He* married *young.* (from Old French **marier,** from Latin **marītāre,** from **marīta** "woman having a husband," from **mas, maris,** "man."]

[2]**mar·ry** (măr′ ē) *Archaic* ***interj-*** exclamation of anger, surprise, etc. [oath on the name of the Virgin Mary.]

Mars (mär*r*z) ***n-* 1** in Roman mythology, the god of war. He is identified with the Greek Ares. **2** seventh largest planet in the solar system, and the fourth in order from the sun.

Mar·seil·laise (mär*r*′ sə lĕz′, *Fr.* mär sā yĕz′) ***n-*** the national anthem of France, composed during the French Revolution.

marsh (mär*r*sh) ***n-*** low wet land; swamp.

mar·shal (mär*r*′ shəl) ***n-* 1** federal officer having duties like those of a sheriff. **2** fire or police chief. **3** official in charge of ceremonies: *the* marshal *of a parade.* **4** in some armies and air forces, an officer higher than or equivalent to a general. ***vt-*** to put in order; organize: *to* marshal *ideas for a debate.* ***Hom-*** martial.

marsh gas ***n-*** methane.

marsh·mal·low (mär*r*sh′ mĕl′ ō, -măl′ ō) ***n-*** soft, spongy, white candy with a vanilla flavor.

marsh mallow ***n-*** tall mallow that grows in marshes and has large pink flowers.

marsh marigold ***n-*** plant that grows in wet places and has bright yellow flowers; cowslip.

marsh·y (mär*r*′ shē) ***adj-*** **[marsh·i·er, marsh·i·est]** of or like a marsh or swamp. **—*n-* marsh′ i·ness.**

mar·su·pi·al (mär so͞o′ pē əl) ***n-*** any of an order of mammals **(Marsupialia),** the females of which have an abdominal pouch in which the very immature young finish developing. Except for the oppossum, all marsupials are native to Australia.

mart (mär*r*t) ***n-*** market.

mar·ten (mär*r*′ tən) ***n-* 1** slender-bodied animal of the weasel family, valued for its dark-brown fur. **2** the fur of this animal. ***Hom-*** martin.

Mar·tha (mär*r*′ thə) ***n-*** in the New Testament, a sister of Lazarus and Mary.

American marten, about 2 ft. long

mar·tial (mär*r*′ shəl) ***adj-*** of, like, or suited to war or military life: *a* martial *spirit*; martial *music.* **—*adv-* mar′ tial·ly.** ***Hom-*** marshal.

martial law ***n-*** military rule or authority imposed on a country or region in place of civil law, during a war or other emergency.

Mar·tian (mär*r*′ shən) ***adj-*** of or relating to the planet Mars. ***n-*** a supposed inhabitant of Mars.

mar·tin (mär*r*′ tən) ***n-*** any of several birds related to the swallows. One of the most common is the **purple martin.** ***Hom-*** marten.

Purple martin, about 8 in. long

mar·ti·net (mär*r*′ tə nĕt′) ***n-*** person who requires strict obedience to rules; rigid disciplinarian: *The sergeant was too much of a* martinet.

mar·tin·gale or **mar·tin·gal** (mär′ tən gāl′) ***n***- **1** in a horse's harness, a forked strap which passes from the girth between the forelegs up to the headgear, for holding the head down. **2** in sailing ships, a spar extending downward from the point where the bowsprit and jib boom are joined, for holding the stays that brace the jib boom against upward stress.

mar·tyr (mär′ tər) ***n***- **1** person who suffers torture or death for the sake of his religion or principles. **2** one who endures great suffering, especially for a long time and without complaint. ***vt***- **1** to torture or put to death for loyalty to a belief. **2** to persecute; torture.
a martyr to a sufferer from: *For a long time he has been* a martyr to *her tantrums.*

mar·tyr·dom (mär′ tər dəm) ***n***- **1** a suffering of torture or death for the sake of one's principles or religion. **2** any long, intense suffering: *the* martyrdom *of arthritis.*

mar·vel (mär′ vəl) ***n***- extraordinary thing; amazing example; a wonder: *A large dam is a* marvel *of modern engineering.* ***vi***- to be struck with wonder (at): *We* marveled *at the Grand Canyon.*

mar·vel·ous (mär′ vəl əs) ***adj***- astonishing; wonderful. ***—adv***- **mar′ vel·ous·ly.** ***n***- **mar′ vel·ous·ness.**

Marx·ism (märk′ sĭz′ əm) ***n***- the social, political, and economic teachings of Karl Marx and Friedrich Engels.

Marx·ist (märk′ sĭst) ***adj***- of or pertaining to Karl Marx or his theories. ***n***- follower of Marx, his philosophy, or his doctrine.

Mar·y (mâr′ ē) ***n***- **1** the Virgin Mary. **2** a sister of Lazarus and Martha. **3** Mary Magdalene.

Mary Magdalene ***n***- in the New Testament, a woman of Magdala out of whom Jesus cast seven devils. She witnessed the Crucifixion, and Jesus appeared first to her after the Resurrection. She is traditionally identified with a penitent sinful woman whom Jesus forgave. Also **Magdalene** or **Magdalen.**

mar·zi·pan (mär′ zə păn′) ***n***- thick paste of crushed almonds mixed with sugar and egg whites, often used as a coating for wedding cakes or formed into various fruit shapes as a confection.

masc. masculine.

mas·ca·ra (mə skăr′ ə, mă-) ***n***- makeup for darkening or coloring the eyelashes and eyebrows.

mas·cot (măs′ kŏt′) ***n***- person, animal, or thing that is supposed to bring good luck: *Our* mascot *is a goat.*

mas·cu·line (măs′ kyə lən) ***adj***- **1** of or for boys or men: *John and Peter are* masculine *names.* **2** having the qualities of a man; manly: *a* masculine *handwriting.* **3** *Grammar* gender of adjectives and nouns that corresponds roughly to the male sex. ***—adv***- **mas′ cu·line·ly.**

mas·cu·lin·i·ty (măs′ kyə lĭn′ ə tē) ***n***- male traits or qualities; manliness; virility.

ma·ser (mā′ zər) ***n***- device that amplifies a particular frequency of electromagnetic radiation with very high fidelity to the original signal. It is used in radio astronomy. [shortened from *m*icrowave *a*mplification by *s*timulated *e*mission of *r*adiation.]

mash (măsh) ***vt***- **1** to squash; crush: *The elephant's heavy feet* mashed *the grass.* **2** to make into a soft, pulplike mixture: *Mother* mashed *the potatoes.* ***n***- **1** soft, pulplike mixture: *The baby ate a* mash *of bananas and water.* **2** warm mixture of bran or meal and water, used as food for animals. **3** crushed grain mixed with malt and fermented to make beer, whiskey, etc. ***—n***- **mash′ er.**

mash·ie (măsh′ ē) ***n***- in golf, a club with a sloping iron face, for making shots of medium length.

mask (măsk) ***n***- **1** a covering to hide or protect the face, eyes, breathing passages or lungs, etc.: *a Halloween* mask; *a welder's* mask; *a gas* mask. **2** anything that hides or conceals: *He escaped under the* mask *of darkness.* ***vt***-: *He* masked *his face. Clouds* masked *the moon.* ***Hom***- masque.

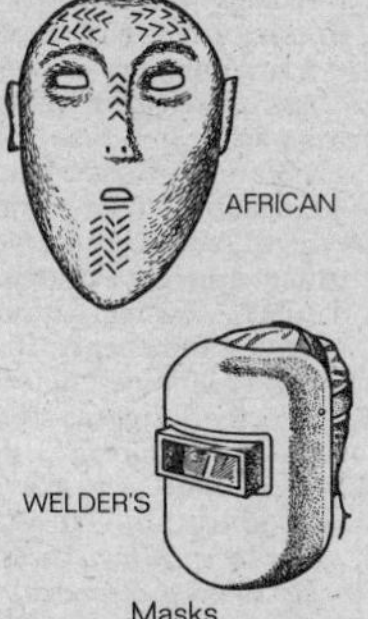

Masks

masked (măskt) ***adj***- **1** wearing a mask on the face: *a* masked *bandit.* **2** hidden or disguised: *a real but* masked *reason for his behavior.*

masked ball ***n***- ball or party at which masks and costumes are worn; masquerade.

mask·er (măs′ kər) ***n***- person who attends a masquerade or takes part in a masque. Also **mas′ quer.**

mas·o·chism (mas′ ə kĭz′ əm) ***n***- emotional disorder in which one gets pleasure from suffering or humiliation at the hands of another. ***—n***- **mas′ o·chist.**

ma·son (mā′ sən) ***n***- **1** person who works or builds with stone, brick, etc. **2 Mason** Freemason.

Ma·son-Dix·on line (mā′ sən dĭk′ sən) ***n***- the boundary line between Pennsylvania and Maryland, regarded as separating the North from the South.

Ma·son·ic (mə sŏn′ ĭk) ***adj***- of or pertaining to Freemasons or to their society or rites.

Mason jar ***n***- glass jar with a very tight screw top, used in preserving and canning food at home.

ma·son·ry (mā′ sən rē) ***n***- [*pl.* **ma·son·ries**] **1** brick, stone, concrete blocks, etc., laid by a mason: *the* masonry *of the foundation.* **2** the work or trade of a mason: *an apprentice in* masonry. **3 Masonry** Freemasonry. *as* ***modifier***: *a* masonry *wall.*

masque (măsk) ***n***- **1** form of entertainment, popular in the 16th and 17th centuries, consisting of pantomime and dance, sometimes with words. **2** masquerade; masked ball. ***Hom***- mask.

mas·quer·ade (măs′ kə rād′) ***n***- **1** party or dance at which masks and costumes are worn. **2** a disguise. ***vi***- [**mas·quer·ad·ed, mas·quer·ad·ing**]: *The children* masqueraded *as elves.* ***—n***- **mas′ quer·ad′ er.**

[1]**mass** (măs) ***n***- **1** quantity of matter without regular shape; lump: *a* mass *of dough.* **2** large number or quantity: *a* mass *of people*; *a* mass *of lava.* **3** size; bulk: *The huge* mass *of the pyramid amazed me.* **4** main or larger part: *The* mass *of voters want a new school.* **5 the masses** the ordinary working people and their families. **6** *Physics* quantity of matter in a body, as measured by the body's inertia; also, the body itself. See also *weight. as* ***modifier***: *the* mass *movement*; *a* mass *market.* ***vt***- to bring together into one group: *The general* massed *his troops for an attack.* ***vi***-: *The troops* massed *for an attack.* [from Latin **massa,** "lump (of dough); mass," ultimately from Greek **massein,** "to knead."]

[2]**mass** or **Mass** (măs) ***n***- **1** in the Roman Catholic Church and in some Anglican churches, a service of prayers and rituals celebrating the Eucharist. **2** a musical setting for such a service. [from Old English **mæsse,** from a Late Latin phrase uttered by the priest at the end of the service, "Ite, **missa** est," "Go, you are dismissed."]

Mass. Massachusetts.

---

fāte, făt, dâre, bärn; bē, bĕt, mêre; bīte, bĭt; nōte, hŏt, môre, dȯg; fŭn, fûr; to͞o, bo͝ok; oil; out; tar; thin; then; hw for wh as in *wh*at; zh for s as in u*s*ual; ə for a, e, i, o, u, as in *a*go, lin*e*n, per*i*l, at*o*m, min*u*s

Mas·sa·chu·set (măs′ ə cho͞o′ sət) *n-* [*pl.* **Mas·sa·chu·sets,** also **Mas·sa·chu·set**] one of a tribe of Algonquian Indians who formerly lived around Massachusetts Bay.

mas·sa·cre (măs′ ə kər) *n-* a brutal, wholesale killing of a large number of people; slaughter. *vt-* [**mas·sa·cred, mas·sa·cring**]: *to* massacre *settlers.*

mas·sage (mə säzh′, -säj′) *n-* a rubbing, kneading, or vibrating of some part of the body to increase blood circulation, relieve stiffness or soreness, etc. *vt-* [**mas·saged, mas·sag·ing**]: *to* massage *the scalp.*

mass-energy equation *n-* an equation, developed by Albert Einstein, expressing the interchangeability of matter and energy. In the equation, $E = mc^2$, E is the energy in joules, m is the mass in kilograms, and c is the velocity of light, 3×10^8 meters per second.

mas·seur (mă sûr′) *n-* man whose job is giving massages. *—n- fem.* **mas·seuse′** (mă so͞oz′).

mas·sive (măs′ ĭv) *adj-* **1** solid and heavy; bulky: *He was blocked by a* massive *door.* **2** strong and imposing: *his* massive *features*; massive *evidence.* *—adv-* **mas′ sive·ly.** *n-* **mas′ sive·ness.**

mass medium *n-* [*pl.* **mass media**] medium of communication, such as newspapers, radio, television, and motion pictures, that reaches and influences great numbers of peoples.

mass meeting *n-* meeting of a large number of people to learn about or act on some issue.

mass number *n-* atomic mass number.

mass-pro·duce (măs′ prə do͞os′, -dyo͞os′) *vt-* [**mass-pro·duced, mass-pro·duc·ing**] to manufacture in large quantities: *They* mass-produced *costume jewelry.*

mass production *n-* manufacture of goods in large quantities, especially by the use of assembly lines. *as modifier* (**mass-production**): *a* mass-production *process.*

[1]**mast** (măst) *n-* **1** on boats and ships, an upright pole for supporting sails, crow's-nest, radio antenna, hoisting tackle, etc. **2** any upright pole, such as a flagpole, a tall radio antenna, or the main post of a derrick. [from Old English **mæst** meaning originally "bough or trunk of a tree."] *—adj-* **mast′less.**

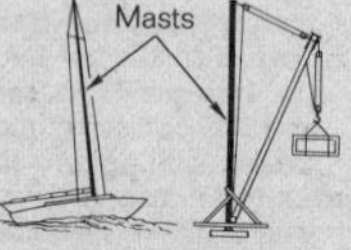

before the mast 1 formerly, the quarters of common sailors, situated forward of the foremast. **2** as a common sailor: *to sail* before the mast.

[2]**mast** (măst) *n-* chestnuts, beechnuts, etc., especially when used as feed for pigs. [from Old English **mæst** meaning "fattening material."]

mas·ter (măs′ tər) *n-* **1** person who rules, directs, or controls a person or thing: *a dog's* master; *a slave's* master. **2** person of great skill or ability; expert: *a* master *at storytelling.* **3** captain of a ship. **4** *chiefly Brit.* male teacher. **5 Master** (1) title used before a young boy's name, instead of Mr. (2) Master of Arts or Master of Science. *vt-* **1** to get control over; dominate: *to* master *one's temper.* **2** to become skillful or expert in: *to* master *a foreign language.* *adj-* **1** chief; main: *the* master *bedroom.* **2** controlling or operating everything: *a* master *switch*; *a* master *key.* **3** fully skilled and experienced; able to teach the occupation to and judge the ability of others: *a* master *carpenter.*

mas·ter-at-arms (măs′ tər ət ärmz′) *n-* [*pl.* **mas·ters-at-arms**] in the Navy, a petty officer whose duty aboard ship is enforcing law and order.

mas·ter·ful (măs′ tər fəl) *adj-* **1** expert; showing mastery: *The tennis champion had a* masterful *serve.* **2** domineering; authoritative: *his* masterful *tone.* *—adv-* **mas′ ter·ful·ly.** *n-* **mas′ ter·ful·ness.**

master key *n-* key which can open several different locks, or all the doors in a building; passkey.

mas·ter·ly (măs′ tər lē) *adj-* showing mastery: *a* masterly *touch on the piano.* *—n-* **mas′ ter·li·ness.**

mas·ter·mind (măs′ tər mīnd′) *n-* person of great ability and knowledge, who is the chief planner or director of large or complex projects: *the* mastermind *behind the revolt.* *vt-*: *to* mastermind *a revolt.*

Master of Arts *n-* **1** degree given by a college or university to a person who has completed a prescribed course of graduate work in literature, philosophy, history, etc. **2** person who has received this degree. *Abbr.* M.A. or A.M.

master of ceremonies *n-* **1** person, usually an entertainer, who presides over the activities and introduces performers or speakers in a show or at a formal dinner. **2** person who determines and supervises the formal procedures followed in a ceremony.

Master of Science *n-* **1** degree given by a college or university to a person who has completed a prescribed course of graduate work in one of the sciences. **2** person who has received this degree. *Abbr.* M.S. or M.Sc.

mas·ter·piece (măs′ tər pēs′) *n-* **1** something, especially a work of art, showing great skill or genius: *an artistic* masterpiece. **2** the best thing that a person has written, made, painted, etc.: *"Huckleberry Finn" is said to be Mark Twain's* masterpiece. Also **mas′ ter·work′.**

master sergeant *n-* **1** in the Army and Marine Corps, a noncommissioned officer who ranks next below a sergeant major and above all other sergeants. **2** in the Air Force, a noncommissioned officer ranking below warrant officers but above other sergeants and all airmen.

mas·ter·stroke (măs′ tər strōk′) *n-* masterly or ingenious act, decision, etc.; feat.

mas·ter·y (măs′ tə rē) *n-* **1** control or domination; rule: *to have* mastery *over one's own temper.* **2** skill and knowledge; command: *a* mastery *of arithmetic.*

mast·head (măst′ hĕd′) *n-* **1** top of a ship's mast, especially of the lower mast, used as a lookout. **2** the block of printing in a newspaper or magazine that gives the names of the publisher and editors, the address of the editorial offices, etc.

mas·tic (măs′ tĭk) *n-* **1** small evergreen tree of the Mediterranean region related to the cashews. **2** yellowish or greenish gum or resin that oozes from the bark of this tree and is used in making varnishes. **3** pasty, quick-drying cement.

mas·ti·cate (măs′ tə kāt′) *vt-* [**mas·ti·cat·ed, mas·ti·cat·ing**] **1** to chew (food). **2** to grind or knead (rubber, wood, etc.) to a pulp. *—n-* **mas′ ti·ca′ tion.**

mas·tiff (măs′ tĭf) *n-* large, short-haired dog with heavy jowls, usually light-brown in color.

Mastiff, about 3 1/2 ft. high at shoulder

mas·to·don (măs′ tə dŏn′, -dən) *n-* any of various large, extinct mammals related to present-day elephants but sometimes having tusks in the lower jaw.

mas·toid (măs′ toid′) *adj-* of or having to do with either of knobs of the skull that can be felt behind the ears.

[1]**mat** (măt) *n-* **1** flat piece of cloth, plastic, woven straw, etc., used mainly as covering for a floor or table: *a door* mat; *a place* mat *on the table.* **2** pad covering the floor for gymnasium exercises or wrestling. **3** anything entangled in a thick mass: *a* mat *of hair.* *vt-* [**mat·ted, mat·ting**] to tangle together in a thick mass: *The sea*

breeze matted *his hair.* ***vi-***: *His hair* matted *in the rain.* [from Old English **meatte,** from Late Latin **matta.**]

[2]**mat** (măt) ***n-*** border of cardboard, burlap, etc., either placed alone around a picture or between a picture and its frame. ***vt-*** [**mat·ted, mat·ting**]: *to* mat *an etching.* [from French.]

[3]**mat** or **matte** (măt) ***n-*** dull, lusterless finish on a surface. *as* ***modifier***: *a* mat *finish.* [from Old French **mat(te)** originally meaning "dull; dead; subdued."]

mat·a·dor (măt′ ə dôr′) ***n-*** in bullfighting, the man who taunts and manages the bull with a cape until it is tired and then kills it with a sword; torero.

[1]**match** (măch) ***n-*** small stick of wood or pasteboard with a tip that bursts into flame when rubbed or scratched. [from Old French **mesche** meaning "wick," from Greek **myxa** meaning "the hole in a lamp for the wick."]

[2]**match** (măch) ***n-*** **1** thing that is exactly like another: *I am looking for a* match *for this paint.* **2** person or thing that is suitable for another: *Tan shoes are a good* match *for a brown dress.* **3** person or animal that can compete with another on equal terms: *She is not yet a* match *for her mother in cooking.* **4** marriage. **5** person considered for marriage: *He is a good* match. **6** a contest: *a wrestling* match. ***vi-*** to be alike: *The two candlesticks* match *exactly.* ***vt-*** **1** to be similar or equal to: *This color* matches *that one.* **2** to put together (similar or equal things): *to* match *socks.* **3** to make correspond; suit: *to* match *supply to demand.* **4** to place in a contest with another: *The promoter* matched *the two fighters.* **5** to meet on equal terms: *I can't* match *him in tennis.* [from Old English **(ge)mæcce,** "an equal; a fitting companion," and related to **make.**] —***n-*** **match′ er.**

match·less (măch′ ləs) ***adj-*** not having an equal; peerless: *his* matchless *skill.* —***adv-*** **match′ less·ly.**

match·lock (măch′ lŏk′) ***n-*** in former times, a type of gunlock in which the powder charge was ignited by a slow-burning wick; also, a musket having such a lock.

match·mak·er (măch′ mā′ kər) ***n-*** **1** person who arranges marriages. **2** person who arranges athletic contests, especially prize fights. —***n-*** **match′ mak′ ing.**

match·wood (măch′ wŏŏd′) ***n-*** small splinters of wood.

[1]**mate** (māt) ***n-*** **1** the other of a pair: *the* mate *to a shoe.* **2** companion; associate: *He and his* mates *left the school grounds.* **3** husband or wife. **4** the male or female of a pair of animals. **5** officer on a merchant ship ranking below the captain. ***vt-*** [**mat·ed, mat·ing**] **1** to join or pair: *to* mate *shoes.* **2** to marry. **3** to breed: *to* mate *dogs.* ***vi-***: *Do those shoes* mate*? Birds* mate *in the spring and build their nests.* [from Middle English **mate** meaning "companion; messmate," from early Germanic **mate** or **maat,** and related to **meat.**]

[2]**mate** (māt) ***vt-*** [**mat·ed, mat·ing**] in chess, to checkmate. ***n-*** checkmate. [from Old French **(eschec) mat** meaning "the (chess king) is dead," from Persian or Arabic **(shāh) māta,** "the Shah is dead," and related to [3]**mat.**]

ma·té or **ma·te** (mä′ tā′) ***n-*** **1** Brazilian holly plant from which a tea is brewed. **2** the tea itself.

ma·te·ri·al (mə têr′ ē əl) ***n-*** **1** stuff of which something is made. **2** woven fabric; cloth. **3** one or more persons likely to be useful or good in some particular field: *splendid* material *for the team.* **4** information, such as facts and figures, to be used in a book, composition, report, etc. **5 materials** things needed to do something: *to secure building* materials. ***adj-*** **1** made of matter; physical; not spiritual or mental: *Stones, chairs, and the human body are* material *things.* **2** of or relating to the body: *one's* material *needs.* **3** relating to or chiefly interested in physical rather than spiritual or cultural things. **4** essential; important: *a* material *loss.*

►Should not be confused with MATÉRIEL.

ma·te·ri·al·ism (mə têr′ ē ə lĭz′ əm) ***n-*** **1** the doctrine that the entire universe, including man, is composed of matter, and that all actions, thoughts, etc., are the results of matter in motion. **2** the doctrine that physical pleasure, wealth, etc., make up the highest good or ideal of man. **3** excessive concern with physical pleasure, wealth, etc., rather than with spiritual and intellectual values. —***n-*** **ma·te′ ri·al·ist.**

ma·te·ri·al·is·tic (mə têr′ ē ə lĭs′ tĭk) ***adj-*** **1** of or related to the doctrines of materialism. **2** excessively concerned with physical pleasure, wealth, etc., rather than with spiritual and intellectual values. —***adv-*** **ma·te′ ri·al·is′ ti·cal·ly.**

ma·te·ri·al·ize (mə têr′ ē ə līz′) ***vi-*** [**ma·te·ri·al·ized, ma·te·ri·al·iz·ing**] **1** to become real and actual; become a fact: *Do you think our hopes will ever* materialize? **2** to take on physical or bodily form: *The spirit* materialized *at the séance.* **3** to appear suddenly: *He seemed to* materialize *out of thin air.*

ma·te·ri·al·ly (mə têr′ ē ə lē) ***adv-*** **1** considerably: *The music teacher's ideas helped* materially *in planning the play.* **2** in a physical or material way: *The enemy was strong* materially *but weak in leadership.*

ma·té·ri·el (mə têr′ ē ĕl′) ***n-*** equipment and supplies required in the operation of any organization.

►Should not be confused with MATERIAL.

ma·ter·nal (mə tûr′ nəl) ***adj-*** **1** of or like a mother; motherly: *her* maternal *love.* **2** on the mother's side of the family: *Your mother's father is your* maternal *grandfather.* —***adv-*** **ma·ter′ nal·ly.**

ma·ter·ni·ty (mə tûr′ nə tē) ***n-*** motherhood. ***adj-*** of or relating to pregnancy and childbirth: *a* maternity *dress*; maternity *care*; *a* maternity *ward in a hospital.*

math or **math.** mathematics.

math·e·mat·i·cal (măth′ ə măt′ ĭ kəl) ***adj-*** **1** of, having to do with, or based on mathematics: *Engineers need* mathematical *training.* **2** exact; carefully calculated: *The parts of a watch are made with* mathematical *precision.* —***adv-*** **math′ e·mat′ i·cal·ly.**

math·e·ma·ti·cian (măth′ ə mə tĭsh′ ən) ***n-*** **1** person trained in mathematics and usually engaged in it as a profession. **2** person skillful in mathematics.

math·e·mat·ics (măth′ ə măt′ ĭks) ***n-*** (takes singular verb) study that deals with the properties of and relationships between numbers, quantities, operations, sets, measurements, shapes, etc. Arithmetic and geometry are branches of mathematics.

mat·in (măt′ ən) ***n-*** **1** *Archaic* morning song, especially of birds. **2 matins** (1) the prayers traditionally said with lauds after midnight. They are the first of the canonical hours. (2) in the Anglican Communion, the service of morning prayers.

mat·i·née or **mat·i·nee** (măt′ ən ā′) ***n-*** afternoon performance of a play, movie, etc.

ma·tri·arch (mā′ trē ärk′) ***n-*** mother who, like a patriarch, rules over a family, tribe, etc. —***adj-*** **ma′ tri·arch′ al**: *a* matriarchal *society.*

ma·tri·arch·y (mā′ trē är′ kē) ***n-*** [*pl.* **ma·tri·arch·ies**] family, tribe, or other form of society in which the mother is ruler, with descent and succession being traced through her rather than the father.

mat·ri·ces (mā′ trə sēz′, mă′-) *pl.* of **matrix.**

ma·tri·cide (mă′ trə sīd′, mā′-) *n-* 1 murder of one's own mother. 2 one who murders his own mother.

ma·tric·u·late (mə trĭk′ yə lāt′) *vi-* [**ma·tric·u·lat·ed, ma·tric·u·lat·ing**] to register in a college or university as a candidate for a degree; enroll. *vt-*: *The college refused to* matriculate *him.* —*n-* **ma·tric′ u·la′ tion**

mat·ri·mo·ny (mă′ trə mō′ nē) *n-* [*pl.* **mat·ri·mon·ies**] marriage. —*adj-* **mat′ ri·mo′ ni·al**: *a* matrimonial *vow.* *adv-* **mat′ ri·mo′ ni·al·ly.**

ma·trix (mā′ trĭks) *n-* [*pl.* **ma·tri·ces** (-trĭ sēz′) or **ma·trix·es**] 1 substance, object, organ, etc., within which anything begins, forms, develops, or is contained: *Soil is the* matrix *in which seeds sprout.* 2 *Biology* (1) the substance between the cells of a tissue. (2) the cells that form a tooth or nail. 3 the womb. 4 any mold in which something is cast; especially, in printing, the mold in which type characters are cast. 5 in geology, rock in which fossils, crystals, etc., are imbedded.

ma·tron (mā′ trən) *n-* 1 married woman or widow, especially an older one. 2 woman attendant or guard in an institution: *the* matron *in a prison.*

ma·tron·ly (mā′ trən lē) *adj-* of, like, or suitable for an older married woman or widow.

matron of honor *n-* at a wedding, a married woman who serves as the chief attendant of the bride.

Matt. Matthew.

matte (măt) ³mat.

mat·ted (măt′ əd) *adj-* 1 covered with a mat or mats. 2 entangled in a thick mass: *the* matted *undergrowth.*

mat·ter (măt′ ər) *n-* 1 anything that takes up space and has mass; material substance: *Some of the* matter *in an atom bomb is changed to energy.* 2 the content or thought of something written or spoken: *The* matter *of the lecture was good, but the delivery was bad.* 3 affair; business: *Burglary is a* matter *for the police to handle.* 4 importance; significance: *an idea of little* matter. 5 printed material: *advertising* matter. 6 pus. *vi-* to be of importance: *It hardly* matters *one way or the other.*

as a matter of fact indeed; to tell the truth: *I talked with him this morning,* as a matter of fact. **for that matter** as far as that goes; in regard to that: *Well,* for that matter, *his schooling does not fit him for the job.* **matter of course** thing taken for granted; expected thing. **no matter** 1 of no importance. 2 in spite of; regardless of: *I will come* no matter *what happens.* **What is the matter?** What is wrong? What is the difficulty?

mat·ter-of-fact (măt′ ər əv făkt′) *adj-* literal and factual; unemotional: *a* matter-of-fact *tone.* —*adv-* **mat′ ter-of-fact′ ly.** *n-* **mat′ ter-of-fact′ ness.**

Mat·thew (mă′ thyōō′) *n-* one of the twelve apostles, believed to be the author of the first Gospel of the New Testament. Also **St. Matthew.**

mat·ting (măt′ ĭng) *n-* 1 coarse fabric of straw, hemp, grass, etc., used for making mats and for wrapping and packing. 2 mats collectively.

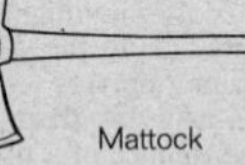
Mattock

mat·tock (măt′ ək) *n-* digging tool that resembles a pickax but has a broad, flat blade at one or both ends.

mat·tress (mă′ trəs) *n-* cloth-covered pad filled with resilient material such as cotton linters, wire springs, etc., used on or for a bed.

Mattress

ma·tur·a·tion (măch′ ə rā′ shən) *n-* a growing or coming to maturity. *as modifier*: *a* maturation *date.*

ma·ture (mə tyōōr′, -chōōr′, -tōōr′) *adj-* 1 of animals, fruit, plants, etc., fully grown or ripe. 2 grown-up; not silly or childish: *a* mature *mind.* 3 due and payable: *a* mature *debt.* 4 fully developed or completed: *His plans are not yet* mature. *vi-* [**ma·tured, ma·tur·ing**] 1 to become fully grown: *Most animals* mature *faster than human beings.* 2 to become ripe. 3 to develop fully or reach completion. 4 to become due for payment: *When your savings bond* matures, *you can collect its full value.* —*adv-* **ma·ture′ ly.**

ma·tu·ri·ty (mə tyōōr′ ə tē, -chōōr′-, mə tōōr′-) *n-* 1 full adult growth: *Many fish and frogs never reach* maturity. 2 balance and wisdom in mind feelings, etc., supposed to accompany full adult growth in human beings: *Even though he is thirty, he is far from true* maturity. 3 of bonds, the date at which the full face value is payable.

matz·o (mät′ sə) *n-* [*pl.* **matz·os** or **matz·oth** (-sōth′)] thin, flat piece of unleavened bread resembling a cracker, traditionally eaten by Jews during Passover.

maud·lin (mȯd′ lən) *adj-* overly or weakly sentimental.

maul (mȯl) *vt-* to strike and knock about; treat very roughly: *The lion* mauled *his trainer.* *n-* large, heavy hammer, usually with a broad wooden head. *Hom-* mall. —*n-* **maul′ er.**

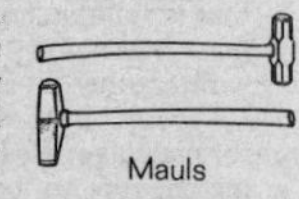
Mauls

maun·der (mȯn′ dər) *vi-* to talk or act aimlessly.

Maun·dy Thursday (mȯn′ dē) *n-* Holy Thursday.

mau·so·le·um (mȯ′ sə lē′ əm, mȯ′ zə-) *n-* large and imposing tomb.

mauve (mōv, mȯv) *n-* pale purple color. *adj-*: *a* mauve *dress.*

mav·er·ick (măv′ ər ĭk) *n-* 1 formerly, an unbranded or lost animal, especially a calf, that became the property of the first person to brand it. 2 *Informal* person who refuses to conform or agree with the policies, ways, etc., of his group; independent; dissenter. *as modifier*: *a* maverick *Senator.* [American word from Samuel **Maverick**, a Texan who did not brand his cattle.]

ma·vis (mā′ vəs) *n-* a European thrush.

maw (mȯ) *n-* the mouth, gullet, or stomach of an animal.

mawk·ish (mȯ′ kĭsh) *adj-* foolishly sentimental; maudlin. —*adv-* **mawk′ ish·ly.** *n-* **mawk′ ish·ness.**

max. maximum.

max·il·la (măk sĭl′ ə) *n-* [*pl.* **max·il·lae** (-sĭl′ ē) or **max·il·las**] 1 the upper jawbone of vertebrates, in which the upper teeth are rooted. 2 in arthropods, including insects, crabs, etc., either of a pair of accessory jaws behind the mandibles.

max·il·lar·y (măk sə lĕr′ ē) *adj-* of or having to do with the upper jaw. *n-* [*pl.* **max·il·lar·ies**] maxilla.

max·im (măk′ sĭm) *n-* general truth expressed as a wise saying. Example: "Honesty is the best policy."

max·i·mize (măk′ sə mīz′) *vt-* [**max·i·mized, max·i·miz·ing**] 1 to increase to the greatest possible proportion or amount; raise to the highest degree: *to* maximize *profits.* 2 to magnify; exaggerate: *He* maximized *the importance of what he had done.* —*n-* **max′ i·mi·za′ tion.**

max·i·mum (măk′ sə məm) *adj-* most, highest, or greatest; top: *The* maximum *temperature today was 80 degrees.* *n-* [*pl.* **max·i·ma** (-mə) or **max·i·mums**]: *We will pay a* maximum *of ten dollars for the present.*

may (mā) *auxiliary verb* [*p.t.* **might**] 1 am, is, or are allowed to: *You* may *come in.* 2 will possibly: *It* may *rain tonight.* 3 I wish or hope that: May *all your days be happy ones.* 4 would have the opportunity or possibility to: *He is willing to die so that we* may *live.*

►For usage note see CAN.

May (mā) *n-* the fifth month of the year, having 31 days.

Ma·ya (mä′ yə) *n-* [*pl.* **Ma·yas,** also **Ma·ya**] 1 one of an ancient tribe of highly civilized American Indians who still live in Yucatan, Guatemala, and Honduras; also, the Central American Indian civilization that reached its height between 600 and 900 A.D. 2 the language of these Indians. ***—adj-*** **Ma′yan:** *ancient* Mayan *temples.*

May apple ***n-*** plant of North America with large leaves, a large, white flower, and a small, yellow fruit.

may·be (mā′ bē) ***adv-*** perhaps; possibly.

May·day (mā′ dā′) ***n-*** the international radiotelephone distress signal used by ships or aircraft. [from French **m'aidez** meaning "Help me."]

May Day ***n-*** the first day of May, long celebrated as a spring festival with outdoor dances, games, and other activities, and now often marked by parades or other demonstrations of labor organizations. *as* ***modifier*** **(May-Day):** *this year's* May-Day *celebration.*

may·flow·er (mā′ flou′ ər) ***n-*** **1** any of several plants, such as the trailing arbutus, that flower in May or early spring. **2 Mayflower** the sailing ship that brought the Pilgrims from England to the New World in 1620.

may·fly (mā′ flī′) ***n-*** [*pl.* **may·flies**] any of various delicate, short-lived insects, with large, transparent front wings.

may·hap (mā′ hăp′) *Archaic* ***adv-*** perhaps.

may·hem (mā′ hĕm′) ***n-*** in law, the offense of injuring a person, violently and unlawfully, so as to mutilate.

May·ing (mā′ ĭng) ***n-*** the celebration of May Day.

mayn't (mānt) may not.

may·on·naise (mā′ ə nāz′) ***n-*** thick sauce or dressing of egg yolks, oil, lemon juice or vinegar, and seasoning.

may·or (mā′ ər) ***n-*** chief elected official of a city or town. ***—adj-*** **may′ or·al.**

may·or·al·ty (mā′ ər əl tē) ***n-*** [*pl.* **may·or·al·ties**] the office or term of office of a mayor.

may·pole (mā′ pōl′) ***n-*** tall pole, decorated with ribbons and flowers, around which people dance on May Day.

May queen ***n-*** girl chosen to be the queen of a May-Day celebration.

maze (māz) ***n-*** **1** confusing network of passageways, tunnels, etc. **2** confusion or indecision; bewilderment: *I was in such a* maze *I couldn't answer.* ***Hom-*** maize.

ma·zur·ka (mə zûr′ kə) ***n-*** lively Polish dance; also, the music for such a dance. Also **ma·zour′ ka.**

ma·zy (mā′ zē) ***adj-*** [**ma·zi·er, ma·zi·est**] like a maze; winding and confusing.

mb millibar.

mc or **m.c.** **1** megacycle. **2** millicurie.

M.C. or **MC** (ĕm′ sē′) ***n-*** master of ceremonies.

Md. Maryland.

M.D. or **MD** Doctor of Medicine.

me (mē) ***pron-*** objective case of I: *He saw* me. *Pass* me *the bread. He did it for* me. ***Hom-*** mi.

Me. Maine (unofficial).

M.E. **1** Methodist Episcopal. **2** mechanical engineer. **3** mining engineer. **4** Middle English.

me·a cul·pa (mā′ ə kŭl′ pə) *Latin* [*pl.* **me·a cul·pas**] It is my fault.

[1]**mead** (mēd) ***n-*** grassy field; meadow. [from Old English **mæd.**] ***Homs-*** Mede, meed.

[2]**mead** (mēd) ***n-*** intoxicating drink made of fermented honey, water, and spices. [from Old English **meodu** of the same meaning.] ***Homs-*** Mede, meed.

mead·ow (mĕd′ ō) ***n-*** grassy field used for grazing animals or growing hay.

mead·ow·lark (mĕ′ dō lärk′) ***n-*** North American songbird having a yellow breast with a black, V-shaped mark.

mea·ger (mē′ gər) ***adj-*** **1** scanty; insufficient; unsatisfactory: *a* meager *diet.* **2** lean; thin: *a* meager *face.* Also **mea′ gre.** ***—adv-*** **mea′ ger·ly.** ***n-*** **mea′ ger·ness.**

[1]**meal** (mēl) ***n-*** **1** breakfast, lunch, dinner, or supper; regular occasion when food is served: *to eat candy between* meals. **2** food eaten or served at a regular time: *three* meals *a day.* [from Old English **mæl** meaning "mark; fixed time; time when food is taken; the food itself."]

[2]**meal** (mēl) ***n-*** **1** coarsely ground grain, especially corn meal. **2** any ground material resembling this: *fish* meal. [from Old English **me(o)lu, mealu** meaning "that which is ground."]

meal·ie (mē′ lē) ***n-*** **1** in Africa, an ear of Indian corn. **2 mealies** in Africa, corn; maize. ***Hom-*** mealy.

meal·time (mēl′ tīm′) ***n-*** time fixed for a meal.

meal·y (mē′ lē) ***adj-*** [**meal·i·er, meal·i·est**] **1** dry and powdery; like meal: *a dish of* mealy *potatoes.* **2** of or containing meal: *a* mealy *dough.* **3** covered with meal. **4** mealy-mouthed. ***Hom-*** mealie. ***—n-*** **meal′ i·ness.**

meal·y-mouthed (mē′ lē moutht′, -mouthd′) ***adj-*** afraid or unwilling to use plain language; not outspoken; not sincere.

[1]**mean** (mēn) ***vt-*** [**meant** (mĕnt), **mean·ing**] **1** to express or indicate the idea of; have the sense of: *One word often* means *several things.* **2** to have in mind; intend: *He* means *to go. He* means *harm.* **3** to be a sign of: *Those black clouds* mean *rain.* **4** to design for or direct toward: *He* meant *those words for all of us.* ***vi-*** to have a specified value or importance: *His good name* means *everything to him.* [from Old English **mænan,** "tell; communicate by telling; moan," related to **moan.**] ***Hom-*** mien.

mean harm to to be unkindly disposed toward.

mean well to have good intentions: *He* means well, *although he sometimes behaves badly.*

mean well by to be kindly disposed toward.

[2]**mean** (mēn) ***adj-*** [**mean·er, mean·est**] **1** humble; low: *of* mean *birth.* **2** not generous: *as* mean *as a miser.* **3** shabby: *a* mean *slum area.* **4** inferior; poor: *clothes of* mean *quality.* **5** dishonorable; base; petty: *a* mean *motive.* **6** *Informal* spiteful; unkind: *a* mean *remark.* **7** dangerous; vicious: *a* mean *animal.* **8** *Informal* difficult: *a* mean *problem to solve.* **9** *Slang* excellent; first-rate: *to play a* mean *game of bridge.* [from Old English **(ge)mæne** meaning "common; general."] ***Hom-*** mien. ***—adv-*** **mean′ ly.** ***n-*** **mean′ ness.**

no mean not insignificant; not inferior; not ordinary: *He is an actor of* no mean *talent.*

[3]**mean** (mēn) ***n-*** **1** something that is midway between two things that are opposite: *Gray is the* mean *between black and white.* **2** *Mathematics* average. **3** in logic, middle term of a syllogism. **4 means** (1) way by which something is accomplished: *A boat was the* means *of rescue.* (2) wealth: *a man of* means. (3) *Mathematics* the second and third terms of a proportion. In the proportion a : b = c : d, b and c are the means (see also *extremes).* ***adj-*** **1** halfway between two extremes: *a* mean *height; a* mean *course.* **2** average; medium: *today's* mean *temperature.* [from Old French **mien,** from Latin **mediānus** meaning "in the middle," from **medius,** "middle."] ***Hom-*** mien.

by all means **1** at any cost; without fail: *You should* by all means *see the show.* **2** of course; certainly. **by means of** by the use of; through: *He won* by means of *clever tricks.* **by no means** in no way; not at all. **not by any means** not at all; in no way.

me·an·der (mē ăn′ dər) *vi-* **1** to follow a winding course: *The brook* meanders *across the meadow.* **2** to wander along in an aimless way. *n-* **1** a winding or turn of a stream. **2** (often **meanders**) a winding course; a rambling movement. **3** an ornamental, geometric pattern of winding lines. **4 Meander** winding river flowing past Troy to the Aegean Sea; the Menderes.

mean distance *Astronomy n-* the average of the minimum and maximum distances of a planet or satellite from the body around which it revolves.

mean·ing (mē′ nĭng) *n-* **1** way a thing can be understood; sense; significance: *the* meaning *of a word*; *the* meaning *of a dream.* **2** way in which a thing is meant; object; intention: *the* meaning *of her visit.* *adj-* expressive; full of significance: *a* meaning *glance.* —*adv-* **mean′ ing·ly.**

mean·ing·ful (mē′ nĭng fəl) *adj-* **1** having meaning: *A word is a* meaningful *unit of language.* **2** full of meaning; significant; important. —*adv-* **mean′ ing·ful·ly.**

mean·ing·less (mē′ nĭng ləs) *adj-* having no meaning or significance; making no sense: *a* meaningless *remark.* —*adv-* **mean′ ing·less·ly.**

meant (mĕnt) *p.t. & p.p.* of **mean.**

mean·time (mēn′ tīm′) *n-* **1** time between occasions: *He called yesterday and today, and in the* meantime *I thought it over.* **2** present time or time remaining: *I'll do as I've always done, for the* meantime. *adv-* meanwhile.

mean time *n-* time based on the average length of the day from midnight to midnight throughout the year. The exact length of the day varies because the earth's orbit is not a perfect circle; universal time.

mean·while (mēn′ hwīl′) *adv-* **1** in the time between two occasions; between now and then: *The test is tomorrow;* meanwhile, *we must study.* **2** during the same time: *The girls prepared lunch;* meanwhile, *the boys built a fire.*

mea·sles (mē′ zəlz) *n-* (takes singular verb) **1** contagious virus disease more common among children than grownups, marked by fever and red spots on the skin; rubeola. **2** German measles.

mea·sly (mēz′ lē) *adj-* [**mea·sli·er, mea·sli·est**] **1** having measles. **2** infested with trichina or tapeworm larvae. **3** *Slang* skimpy, insignificant, or worthless: *a* measly *tip.*

meas·ure (mĕzh′ ər) *n-* **1** size, amount, quantity, or capacity of a thing, as found by a rule or standard. **2** any unit of measurement, such as a foot, pint, pound, or minute; also, device for using such units, such as a foot rule, a pint cup, etc. **3** system of measurement: *dry* measure. **4** basis of comparison: *the* measure *of one's strength or weakness.* **5** extent or degree: *a small* measure *of success.* **6** legislative bill: *a* measure *before the Senate.* **7** means; course of action: *a preventive* measure. **8** verse meter or rhythm. **9** *Music* (1) group of notes between two bars. (2) time of a piece of music; tempo. *vt-* [**meas·ured, meas·ur·ing**] **1** to find the length, size, contents, weight, or length of time of anything in the standard units. **2** to estimate by comparison; appraise: *to* measure *the skill of an author.* **3** to serve as a standard for: *Inches* measure *length.* **4** to traverse; cover (a distance): *to* measure *twenty miles a day.* **5** to calculate and adjust; keep under control: *to* measure *one's actions.* *vi-* **1** to be of a certain size, weight, etc.: *The table* measures *three feet across.* **2** to take measurements.—*adj-* **meas′ ur·a·ble.** *adv-* **meas′ ur·a·bly.** *n-* **meas′ ur·er.**

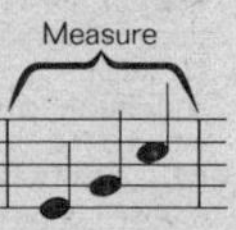

take measures to take action to accomplish or correct something. **take (someone's) measure** to estimate or make a judgment of character, competence, etc.
measure off to mark off; set the boundaries of.
measure one's length to fall or lie flat.
measure out to give out; allot: *to* measure out *rations.*
measure up to to meet the standards of.

meas·ured (mĕzh′ ərd) *adj-* **1** regulated or determined by some standard: *a* measured *distance.* **2** uniform; regular; slow and steady; rhythmical: *a* measured *verse.* **3** carefully considered: *to speak with* measured *words.*

meas·ure·less (mĕzh′ ər′ ləs) *adj-* too great to be measured; vast; immense; unlimited.

meas·ure·ment (mĕzh′ ər mənt) *n-* **1** a finding of size, dimensions, weight, distance, volume, etc.; measuring: *A yardstick is used in the* measurement *of length.* **2** size, dimensions, volume, weight, etc., found by measuring: *The tailor took Joe's* measurements. **3** system of units of measure: *cubic* measurement.

measuring worm *n-* any of several caterpillars, the larvae of various moths, which progress by humping the body into a loop and then reaching out with the front end; inchworm.

meat (mēt) *n-* **1** flesh of animals used as food; also, flesh of a particular animal: *Beef, pork, and lamb are popular* meats. **2** fleshy, edible part of anything: *the* meat *of a nut.* **3** the most important part; gist; substance: *the* meat *of the book.* **4** *Archaic* food. *as* ***modifier***: *a* meat *loaf.* ***Homs-*** meet, mete. —*adj-* **meat′ less.**

meat·y (mē′ tē) *adj-* [**meat·i·er, meat·i·est**] **1** of or like meat. **2** full of meat or nourishment. **3** full of substance or meaning: *a* meaty *book.* —*n-* **meat′ i·ness.**

mec·ca (mĕk′ ə) *n-* **1** any place visited by many people: *New York City is a* mecca *for tourists.* **2** any place of special attraction: *the* mecca *of serious tennis players.*

me·chan·ic (mə kăn′ ĭk) *n-* person who is skilled in building, using, or repairing machinery. *adj-* having to do with manual work or skill: *the* mechanic *trades.*

me·chan·i·cal (mə kăn′ ĭ kəl) *adj-* **1** operated by or using machines or machine parts: *a* mechanical *doll*; *a* mechanical *device.* **2** of or relating to machines or machinery: *a* mechanical *failure*; mechanical *drawing.* **3** of or relating to the science of mechanics: *a* mechanical *engineer.* **4** showing no thought or feeling; merely automatic; soulless: *The actor gave a* mechanical *performance.* —*adv-* **me·chan′ i·cal·ly.**

mechanical advantage *n-* of a machine, the ratio of the applied force to the produced force.

mechanical drawing *n-* **1** an exact scale drawing of a machine, machine part, etc., showing certain views and measurements and made as a guide for producing or reproducing what is shown. **2** the art, method, or work of making such drawings.

me·chan·ics (mə kăn′ ĭks) *n-* **1** (takes singular verb) the branch of physics that deals with the effects of forces on physical bodies. **2** (takes singular verb) the principles of machines and how they work: *the* mechanics *of an automobile engine.* **3** (takes plural verb) the principles or technical aspects of anything: *the* mechanics *of dance.*

me·chan·ism (mĕk′ ə nĭz′ əm) *n-* **1** machine: *A pulley is a simple* mechanism. **2**·working parts of a machine: *Sand in the* mechanism *will stop a watch.* **3** any system of parts working together: *the* mechanism *of government.* **4** any arrangement or device: *a* mechanism *for selecting candidates.* **5** any mechanistic philosophy.

mech·a·nis·tic (mĕk′ ə nĭs′ tĭk) *adj-* **1** of or having to do with mechanics. **2** having to do with or based on the theory that all events are explainable as results of mechanical forces only. —*adv-* **mech′ a·nis′ ti·cal·ly.**

mech·a·nize (mĕk′ ə nīz′) *vt-* [**mech·a·nized, mech·a·niz·ing**] **1** to introduce machinery into: *to* mechanize *mining coal.* **2** to furnish with tanks, trucks, etc. —*n-* **mech′ a·ni·za′ tion.**

med·al (mĕd'əl) *n-* flat metal badge, often coin-shaped, honoring an important event or given as a reward for a heroic or important act or service; decoration. ***Hom-*** meddle.

med·a·list (mĕd'əl ĭst) *n-* **1** designer or maker of medals. **2** person to whom a medal has been awarded. **3** in golf, winner of a kind of contest scored on the basis of total strokes rather than holes won or lost.

me·dal·lion (mə dăl'yən) *n-* **1** large medal. **2** an ornament consisting of a raised design or figures, used in decorating walls, fabrics, leather goods, etc.

Medal

Medal of Honor *n-* highest U.S. military decoration, awarded to persons who have shown extraordinary gallantry in action, at the risk of their lives and beyond the call of duty. It is given in the name of Congress, and is often called the **Congressional Medal of Honor.**

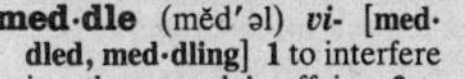

Medallion

med·dle (mĕd'əl) *vi-* [**med·dled, med·dling**] **1** to interfere in other people's affairs. **2** to touch, handle, or tamper with other people's possessions without permission. ***Hom-*** medal. **—*n-* med'dler.**

med·dle·some (mĕd'əl səm) *adj-* in the habit of meddling. **—*n-* med'dle·some·ness.**

Me·de·a (mĭ dē'ə) *n-* in Greek legend, Jason's wife, who helped him obtain the Golden Fleece.

me·di·a (mē'dē ə) *n-* [*pl.* of **medium**] newspapers, magazines, radio, television, and other means of communication and advertising, collectively.

►Careful writers and speakers do not use MEDIA as a singular noun. *Radio is a* medium *of communication, and one of the mass* media.

me·di·ae·val (mē'dē ē'vəl, mə dē'vəl) medieval.

me·di·al (mē'dē əl) *adj-* **1** of or having to do with the middle; situated in the middle. **2** having to do with the mean; average. **3** in phonetics, neither beginning nor ending a word, as the syllable "di" in "medial." **—*adv-* me'di·al·ly.**

me·di·an (mē'dē ən) *adj-* of, having to do with, or located in the middle; central. *n-* **1** the middle number in a series of numbers. The median in a series that has an even number of terms is the average of the two middle terms. **2** in geometry, the line drawn from any vertex of a triangle to the midpoint of the side opposite the vertex; also, the line joining the midpoints of the legs of a trapezoid.

[1]me·di·ate (mē'dē āt') *vt-* [**me·di·at·ed, me·di·at·ing**] **1** to bring about by acting as a mediator: *to* mediate *a settlement.* **2** to settle (a dispute, differences, etc.) by friendly intervention. *vi-* to act as a mediator to bring about peace or agreement. **—*n-* me'di·a'tion.**

[2]me·di·ate (mē'dē ət) *adj-* acting through or involving an intermediate agency or agent; indirect: *A disease transmitted by* mediate *contact.*

me·di·a·tor (mē'dē ā'tər) *n-* person or group that mediates to bring about peace or agreement.

med·ic (mĕd'ĭk) *Informal n-* **1** physician. **2** medical student or intern. **3** member of the military medical services, especially one assigned to a combat area.

Med·i·caid (mĕd'ĭ kād') *n-* program sponsored by federal, state, and local governments that provides medical benefits for those who are not covered by social security and who cannot afford regular medical care.

med·i·cal (mĕd'ĭ kəl) *n-* of or relating to the study and practice of medicine or the treatment of disease by the use of medicine. **—*adv-* med'i·cal·ly.**

me·dic·a·ment (mə dĭk'ə mənt) *n-* drug or other substance used for healing or curing; remedy; medicine.

Med·i·care (mĕd'ĭ kâr') *n-* government-sponsored program of medical care, especially for elderly people who are covered by social security.

med·i·cate (mĕd'ə kāt') *vt-* [**med·i·cat·ed, med·i·cat·ing**] **1** to treat with any curative or healing substance. **2** to put medicine into: *to* medicate *an ointment.*

med·i·ca·tion (mĕd'ə kā'shən) *n-* **1** a medicating; treatment with medicine. **2** medicament.

me·dic·i·nal (mə dĭs'ə nəl) *adj-* **1** having the power to prevent or cure disease, relieve pain, etc.: *a* medicinal *preparation.* **2** of or like a medicine: *a* medicinal *taste.* **—*adv-* me·dic'i·nal·ly.**

med·i·cine (mĕd'ə sən) *n-* **1** drug or other substance to prevent or cure disease, relieve pain, etc. **2** the scientific study that deals with the prevention, treatment, and cure of disease; the art of healing, especially the practices which are not chiefly surgical. **3** medical profession. **4** among North American Indians, any object thought to have magical powers of healing, protection, or the like; also, magical power.

take one's medicine to endure suffering, fatigue, punishment, etc.

medicine ball *n-* heavy, stuffed, leather-covered ball thrown from one person to another for physical exercise.

medicine man *n-* among North American Indians, a person supposed to have magic power over evil spirits, diseases, etc.; shaman.

me·di·e·val (mē'dē ē'vəl, mə dē'vəl) *adj-* of or relating to the Middle Ages, the period in European history from about 500 A.D. to about 1400 A.D. Also **mediaeval. —*adv-* me'di·e'val·ly.**

me·di·o·cre (mē'dē ō'kər) *adj-* not outstanding; neither very good nor very bad.

me·di·oc·ri·ty (mē'dē ŏk'rə tē) *n-* [*pl.* **me·di·oc·ri·ties**] **1** lack of either goodness or badness in skill or value. **2** mediocre person; person of average ability.

med·i·tate (mĕd'ə tāt') *vi-* [**med·i·tat·ed, med·i·tat·ing**] to think deeply, especially about morals and spiritual matters; contemplate; reflect: *to* meditate *upon morals. vt-* to consider; plan: *to* meditate *revenge.*

med·i·ta·tion (mĕd'ə tā'shən) *n-* deep thought; quiet, serious reflection and contemplation.

med·i·ta·tive (mĕd'ə tā'tĭv) *adj-* given to long and serious thought; pensive. **—*n-* med'i·ta'tive·ness.**

Med·i·ter·ra·ne·an (mĕd'ə tə rā'nē ən) *adj-* of or relating to the sea which separates Europe from Africa, or to the people and culture of the countries bordering it.

me·di·um (mē'dē əm) *n-* [*pl.* **me·di·ums** or **me·di·a** (-dē ə)] **1** (*pl.* **me·di·ums**) middle position: *a happy* medium *between extremes.* **2** means or agent through which something is accomplished: *an* advertising *medium.* **3** substance in which a thing exists: *pigment in an oil* medium. **4** substance through which something acts or is carried: *Air is a* medium *for sound.* **5** (*pl.* **me·di·ums**) person assumed to be a messenger between spirits and living persons. ***adj-*** occupying a middle position, condition, or state.

---

fāte, făt, dâre, bärn; bē, bĕt, mêre; bīte, bĭt; nōte, hŏt, môre, dóg; fŭn, fûr; to͞o, bo͝ok; oil; out; tar; thin; then; hw for wh as in *wh*at; zh for s as in u*s*ual; ə for a, e, i, o, u, as in *a*go, lin*e*n, per*i*l, at*o*m, min*u*s

medium frequency ***n-*** radio frequency ranging between 300 and 3000 kilocycles.

med·lar (mĕd lər) ***n-*** **1** small, European tree related to the roses and quinces. **2** its hard, bitter fruit.

med·ley (mĕd'lē) ***n-*** [*pl.* **med·leys**] **1** a mixture or confused mass; jumble: *a* medley *of sounds.* **2** musical piece made up of several different songs or pieces.

me·dul·la (mə dŭl'ə) ***n-*** [*pl.* **me·dul·las** or **me·dul·lae** (-ē)] **1** the soft, centrally located part of any organ or body structure, such as a bone, hair, etc.; also, in botany, the pith. **2** medulla oblongata.

medulla ob·lon·ga·ta (ŏb'lòng gŏt'ə) ***n-*** the cylindrical extension of the spinal cord into the brain, containing centers that regulate respiration and the heart rate.

med·ul·lar·y (mĕd'ə lĕr'ē, mə dŭl'ə rē) ***adj-*** of or relating to marrow or to a medulla.

me·du·sa (mə dōō'sə, -dyōō'sə) ***n-*** [*pl.* **me·du·sas** or **me·du·sae** (-sē, -zē)] **1** jellyfish. **2 Medusa** in Greek mythology, one of the Gorgons slain by Perseus.

meed (mēd) *Archaic* ***n-*** something well-deserved; reward; fit recompense. ***Hom-*** mead.

meek (mēk) ***adj-*** [**meek·er, meek·est**] **1** very patient, gentle, and mild; humble. **2** not inclined to assert oneself. ***—adv-*** **meek'ly.** ***n-*** **meek'ness.**

meer·schaum (mêr'shòm', -shəm) ***n-*** **1** white, soft, clayey mineral found chiefly in Asia Minor. **2** tobacco pipe having a bowl of this substance.

[1]**meet** (mēt) ***vt-*** [**met** (mĕt), **meet·ing**] **1** to come upon or face to face with; encounter: *I* met *her on the stairs. He overcame every obstacle he* met. **2** to be introduced to: *I want to* meet *your cousin.* **3** to be present at the arrival of: *to* meet *the late bus.* **4** to come into contact with; connect with: *The Missouri* meets *the Mississippi.* **5** to come or be brought to the attention of; be seen or heard by: *to* meet *the eye.* **6** to oppose in battle, fight, duel, etc.: *to* meet *the enemy.* **7** to answer or deal with in a satisfactory way: *to* meet *the board's objections.* **8** to satisfy; conform to; comply with: *to* meet *the demand for a product*; *to* meet *all the requirements.* **9** to pay: *to* meet *bills regularly.* ***vi-*** **1** to come together: *They* met *in the hall. Three rivers* meet *in the valley.* **2** to keep an appointment: *Let's* meet *at 3 o'clock.* **3** to become acquainted: *They* met *at school.* **4** to come together as a group; assemble: *The board of directors* meets *at* 10 *o'clock.* **5** to come together as rivals; fight; contend: *The two wrestlers* met *in the arena.* ***n-*** a gathering or assemblage for competition in sports: *a track* meet; *a swimming* meet. [from Old English **mētan** of the same meaning.] ***Homs-*** meat, mete.

meet with to experience; encounter: *to* meet with *disaster.*

[2]**meet** (mēt) *Archaic* ***adj-*** proper; fitting; right: *It is* meet *to give thanks.* [from Old English **gemāete, gemēte.**] ***Homs-*** meat, mete. ***—adv-*** **meet'ly.**

meet·ing (mē'tĭng) ***n-*** **1** a coming together; an encounter: *a chance* meeting *with a friend.* **2** a coming together of people for discussion or some common purpose; an assembly: *a* meeting *of the faculty.* **3** the people at such a gathering: *The town* meeting *voted to increase taxes.* **4** place where things come together.

meeting house ***n-*** a building for public worship, especially one used by Quakers.

mega- *combining form* **1** million: *a* mega*cycle.* **2** very large: mega*lith* (very large stone). [from Greek **mega-**, from **megas** meaning "large."]

meg·a·cy·cle (mĕg'ə sī'kəl) ***n-*** **1** unit used to express the frequency of electromagnetic waves, and equal to 1,000,000 cycles. **2** one million cycles.

meg·a·hertz (mĕg'ə hûrts) ***n-*** unit of frequency equal to one million hertz.

meg·a·lith (mĕg'ə lĭth') ***n-*** in archeology, huge stone or boulder used in certain prehistoric monuments.

meg·a·lo·ma·nia (mĕg'ə lō mā'nē ə) ***n-*** **1** form of mental disorder in which a person believes himself to be supremely powerful and important. **2** tendency toward exaggeration. ***—n-*** **meg'a·lo·ma'ni·ac.**

meg·a·lop·o·lis (mĕg'ə lŏp'ə ləs) ***n-*** **1** vast, densely populated area with several large cities. **2** metropolis.

meg·a·phone (mĕg'ə fōn') ***n-*** device, usually a funnel-shaped speaking trumpet, for increasing or directing the sound of the voice.

meg·a·ton (mĕg'ə tŭn') ***n-*** explosive power equal to the energy released by one million tons of TNT.

mei·o·sis (mī ō'sĭs) *Biology* ***n-*** process of germ-cell division in which the number of chromosomes is reduced to half the original number. See also *mitosis.* ***—adj-*** **mei·o·tic** (mī ŏt'ĭk)

mel·an·cho·lia (mĕl'ən kō'lē ə) ***n-*** mental disorder marked by severe emotional and physical depression.

mel·an·chol·ic (mĕl'ən kŏl'ĭk) ***adj-*** related to or affected with melancholy or melancholia.

mel·an·chol·y (mĕl'ən kŏl'ē) ***adj-*** **1** sad; downcast; gloomy: *a* melancholy *mood.* **2** causing sadness or gloom: *The abandoned house was a* melancholy *sight.* ***n-*** sad or gloomy state of mind; low spirits; depression.

Mel·a·ne·sian (mĕl'ə nē'zhən) ***n-*** one of the dark-skinned people of Melanesia. ***adj-****: a* Melanesian *hat.*

mé·lange (mā länzh') *French* mixture; medley.

mel·a·nin (mĕl'ə nən) ***n-*** dark-brown or black animal pigment which gives color to the hair, eyes, skin, etc.

mel·a·nism (mĕl'ə nĭz'əm) ***n-*** excessive pigmentation of the organs, hair, skin, etc.

mel·a·no·ma (mĕl'ə nō'mə) ***n-*** black mole or tumor.

Mel·ba toast (mĕl'bə) ***n-*** thinly sliced bread toasted till brown and crisp.

meld (mĕld) ***n-*** in pinochle and other card games, a combination of cards to be declared for a score; also, a declaring of such cards. ***vt-*** to declare and display (a combination of cards) for a score. ***vi-*** to display certain scoring cards.

me·lee (mā'lā') ***n-*** confused hand-to-hand fight among a number of persons; fray.

mel·lif·lu·ous (mə lĭf'lōō əs) ***adj-*** smooth and sweet; honeyed; dulcet: *a* mellifluous *voice.* ***—adv-*** **mel·lif'lu·ous·ly.** ***n-*** **mel·lif'lu·ous·ness**

mel·low (mĕl'ō) ***adj-*** [**mel·low·er, mel·low·est**] **1** soft, juicy, and fully ripe: *a* mellow *peach.* **2** of a delicate, rich flavor: *a* mellow *wine.* **3** rich; loamy: *a* mellow *soil.* **4** full; pure; not harsh or coarse: *a* mellow *sound; a* mellow *color.* **5** softened and made gentle by age, experiences, etc.: *a* mellow *gentleman.* ***vt-*** to make mature, gentle, or sweet: *Sorrow* mellowed *her nature.* ***vi-*** to become mellow by aging: *This wine has* mellowed *for two years.* ***—adv-*** **mel'low·ly.** ***n-*** **mel'low·ness.**

me·lo·de·on (mə lō'dē ən) ***n-*** **1** small reed organ supplied with air by a bellows worked by pedals. **2** a kind of accordion.

me·lod·ic (mə lŏd'ĭk) ***adj-*** **1** having to do with or full of melody. **2** melodious. ***—adv-*** **me·lod'i·cal·ly.**

me·lo·di·ous (mə lō'dē əs) ***adj-*** **1** containing or producing melody: *a* melodious *song; a* melodious *instrument.* **2** pleasing to hear; musical: *a* melodious *voice.* ***—adv-*** **me·lo'di·ous·ly.** ***n-*** **me·lo'di·ous·ness.**

mel·o·dra·ma (mĕl'ə drăm'ə, -drä'mə) ***n-*** **1** highly sensational or romantic play with a happy ending. **2** branch of dramatic art represented by such plays. **3** sensational behavior or language.

mel·o·dra·mat·ic (mĕl' ə drə mat' ĭk) ***adj-*** **1** of or having to do with melodrama. **2** highly sensational or emotional; exaggerated; lurid: *a* melodramatic *account of the escape.* —*adv-* **mel'o·dra·mat'i·cal·ly.**

mel·o·dy (mĕl'ə dē) *n-* [*pl.* **mel·o·dies**] 1 an arrangement of musical sounds making up a tune: *a familiar* melody. 2 chief part in a piece of music; air: *The sopranos carry the* melody. 3 any sound considered to be like the sound of music: *the* melody *of poetry.*

mel·on (mĕl'ən) *n-* the fleshy, juicy, round or oval fruit of any of several vines, such as the watermelon, muskmelon, or cantaloupe.

Melons

Mel·pom·e·ne (mĕl pŏm'ə nē) *n-* in Greek mythology, the Muse of tragedy.

melt (mĕlt) *vt-* 1 to change from a solid to a liquid state by heating: *to* melt *butter.* 2 to dissolve: *This detergent* melts *grease.* 3 to soften; make tender or gentle: *The baby's smile* melted *her heart.* *vi-*: *The snow* melted *quickly in the sun.* *n-* something changed from a solid to a liquid state; also, the amount so changed: *a* melt *of steel.* —*n-* **melt'er.**

melt away to disappear: *The fog* melted away.

melt into to pass or shade gradually into each other; blend; merge: *The blue sea seems to* melt into *the sky.*

melt·down (mĕlt'doun) *n-* accident in which the temperature in a nuclear reactor rises enough to melt the reactor and the surface underneath it.

melting point *n-* temperature at which a solid becomes liquid. Crystalline solids have specific melting points, while amorphous solids, like glass, do not.

melting pot *n-* 1 crucible. 2 place where differences of custom, nationality, etc., are fused into a common pattern: *New York has been a great* melting pot.

mem·ber (mĕm'bər) *n-* 1 one of a group or set: *a club* member. 2 a limb or other projecting part of the body. 3 *Mathematics* either of the sides of algebraic equation. *as modifier*: *a* member *nation.*

mem·ber·ship (mĕm'bər shĭp') *n-* 1 enrollment or participation: *a* membership *in a club.* 2 number of people who belong: *The* membership *in the art class is limited to 30. as modifier*: *a* membership *committee.*

mem·brane (mĕm'brān) *n-* thin, flexible sheet or layer of animal or vegetable tissue that serves as a cover or a lining of an organ: *mucous* membrane.

mem·bra·nous (mĕm'brə nəs, mĕm brā'-) *adj-* 1 of, like, or relating to a membrane: *a* membranous *tissue.* 2 forming a membrane: *a* membranous *throat disease.*

me·men·to (mə mĕn'tō) *n-* [*pl.* **me·men·tos** or **me·men·toes**] anything that serves as a reminder; souvenir.

mem·o (mĕm'ō) *Informal* *n-* [*pl.* **mem·os**] memorandum.

mem·oir (mĕm'wär') *n-* 1 record or account of events, written from the author's personal knowledge or experience. 2 biography; biographical sketch or notice. 3 **memoirs** (1) autobiography. (2) record of the activities of a club or society.

mem·o·ra·bi·lia (mĕm'ər ə bĭl'ē ə) *n-* 1 things worthy of remembrance or record. 2 the record of such things.

mem·o·ra·ble (mĕm'ə rə bəl) *adj-* worth being remembered; unforgettable: *a* memorable *day.* —*n-* **mem'o·ra·ble·ness.** *adv-* **mem'o·ra·bly.**

mem·o·ran·dum (mĕm'ə răn'dəm) *n-* [*pl.* **mem·o·ran·dums** or **mem·o·ran·da** (-də)] 1 brief note written to remind one of something. 2 a brief written report or communication, especially one of a business nature. 3 in law, informal document stating the terms of a contract or transaction. 4 in diplomacy, informal statement or summary regarding some subject of discussion between two governments.

me·mo·ri·al (mə môr'ĭ əl) *n-* 1 something that serves to commemorate: *the Lincoln* Memorial. 2 written statement of facts addressed to a public body, official, etc., usually accompanied by a request or protest. 3 (usually **memorials**) historical records; memoirs.

Memorial Day *n-* day set aside to honor soldiers and sailors killed in war. It is May 30 in most States.

me·mo·ri·al·ize (mə môr'ē ə līz') *vt-* [**me·mo·ri·al·ized, me·mo·ri·al·iz·ing**] 1 to address a petition or memorial to. 2 to commemorate.

mem·o·rize (mĕm'ə rīz') *vt-* [**mem·o·rized, mem·o·riz·ing**] to learn by heart; fix in the memory: *to* memorize *a speech.* —*n-* **mem'o·ri·za'tion.** *n-* **mem'o·riz'er.**

mem·o·ry (mĕm'ə rē) *n-* [*pl.* **mem·o·ries**] 1 power of remembering: *a poor* memory *for names.* 2 a remembering or being remembered: *to do something worthy of* memory. 3 person or thing remembered: *The old house is one of my earliest* memories. 4 what is remembered of someone: *to honor the* memory *of our heroes.* 5 length of time within which something is remembered: *within the* memory *of humans.* 6 in electronics, computer part that stores information; storage.

in memory of in honor or remembrance of: *a gift* in memory of *the late President.*

men (mĕn) *pl.* of **man.**

men·ace (mĕn'əs) *n-* 1 threat; danger: *a public* menace. 2 *Informal* annoying person; a pest. *vt-* [**men·aced, men·ac·ing**] to threaten; endanger: *The rising river* menaced *the town.* —*adv-* **men'ac·ing·ly.**

mé·nage (mā näzh') *n-* 1 household; domestic establishment. 2 household management.

me·nag·er·ie (mə năj'ə rē) *n-* 1 collection of wild animals in cages, kept for exhibition. 2 place where they are kept.

mend (mĕnd) *vt-* 1 to repair: *to* mend *a coat; to* mend *a harness.* 2 to reform; make right: *The thief promised to* mend *his ways.* *vi-* to return to good health; also, of a bone, to knit: *The child* mended *quickly.* —*n-* **mend'er.**

on the mend getting better.

men·da·cious (mĕn dā'shəs) *adj-* 1 given to lying; not truthful: *a* mendacious *person.* 2 false; not true: *a* mendacious *statement.* —*adv-* **men·da'cious·ly.** *n-* **men·da'cious·ness.**

men·dac·i·ty (mĕn dăs'ə tē) *n-* 1 untruthfulness; habitual lying. 2 a lie.

men·de·le·vi·um (mĕn'də lē'vē əm) *n-* short-lived, artificially produced, radioactive element. Symbol Md, At. No. 101.

men·di·cant (mĕn'dĭ kənt) *n-* beggar. *adj-* practicing begging; living on alms: *a* mendicant *religious order.*

Men·e·la·us (mĕn'ə lā'əs) *n-* in Greek legend, a king of Sparta, brother of Agamemnon and husband of Helen.

men·ha·den (mĕn hā'dən) *n-* [*pl.* **men·ha·den; men·ha·dens** (kinds of menhaden)] any of several fishes related to the herrings, used for fertilizer and oil.

me·ni·al (mē'nē əl, mēn'yəl) *adj-* 1 of, relating to, or suitable for servants: *a* menial *occupation.* 2 lowly; degrading: *a* menial *task.* *n-* 1 servant who performs lowly tasks. 2 servile person. —*adv-* **me'ni·al·ly.**

me·nin·ges (mə nĭn'jēz) *n-* *pl.* [*sing.* **me·ninx** (mē'nĭngks', mĕn'ĭngks')] the three membranes that envelop the brain and the spinal cord. —*adj-* **me·nin'ge·al.**

men·in·gi·tis (mĕn'ən jī'təs) *n-* inflammation of the membranes enveloping the spinal cord and brain.

---

fāte, făt, dâre, bärn; bē, bĕt, mêre; bīte, bĭt; nōte, hŏt, môre, dòg; fŭn, fûr; tōō, bŏŏk; oil; out; ta*r*; thin; *th*en; hw for wh as in *wh*at; zh for s as in u*s*ual; ə for a, e, i, o, u, as in *a*go, lin*e*n, per*i*l, at*o*m, min*u*s

me·nis·cus (mə nĭs′ kəs) ***n-*** [*pl.* **me·nis·cus·es** or **me·nis·ci** (-sī′, -kī′, -sē)] **1** crescent or crescent-shaped body. **2** curved surface of a liquid in a tube or other vessel. The surface curves up along the walls when the liquid wets them, and down when it does not. **3** a lens concave on one side and convex on the other.

Me·nom·i·nee (mə nŏm′ ə nē) ***n-*** [*pl.* **Me·nom·i·nees,** also **Me·nom·i·nee**] member of a tribe of Algonquian Indians who are still living in north-central Wisconsin. ***adj-***: *a* Menominee *chief.*

Men·non·ite (mĕn′ ə nīt′) ***n-*** a member of a Protestant sect that was established in Friesland in the sixteenth century and is still active in parts of Europe and the United States. They oppose military service, the taking of oaths, and the holding of public office.

me·no·rah (mə nôr′ ə) ***n-*** candlestick used in Jewish religious services and rituals, such as the seven-branched type used in temples or a Hanukkah candle-holder.

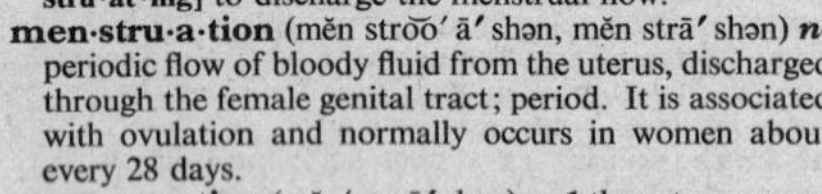
Menorah

menses (mĕn′ sēz′) ***n-*** *pl.* menstruation.

men·stru·al (mĕn′ stro͞o əl) ***adj-*** of or relating to menstruation.

men·stru·ate (mĕn′ stro͞o āt′, mĕn′ strāt′) ***vi-*** [**men·stru·at·ed, men·stru·at·ing**] to discharge the menstrual flow.

men·stru·a·tion (mĕn stro͞o′ ā′ shən, mĕn strā′ shən) ***n-*** periodic flow of bloody fluid from the uterus, discharged through the female genital tract; period. It is associated with ovulation and normally occurs in women about every 28 days.

men·su·ra·tion (mĕn′ sə rā′ shən) ***n-*** **1** the act or process of measuring. **2** the branch of mathematics dealing with the measurement of lengths, areas, and volumes.

-ment *suffix* (used to form nouns from verbs) **1** the act of: *enforce*ment; *infringe*ment. **2** the condition or state of being: *content*ment; *disappoint*ment. **3** the means or instrument of: *adorn*ment; *argu*ment. **4** the thing produced by or the result of: *pave*ment; *attach*ment.

men·tal (mĕn′ təl) ***adj-*** **1** of, in, or relating to the mind: *a* mental *process.* **2** of or relating to diseases of the mind: *a* mental *patient.* **—*adv-*** **men′ tal·ly.**

men·tal·i·ty (mĕn tăl′ ə tē) ***n-*** [*pl.* **men·tal·i·ties**] **1** amount or quality of mental powers; intellectual ability: *a person of average* mentality. **2** style or type of thinking: *a* child's *mentality.*

men·thol (mĕn′ thôl′) ***n-*** solid, white substance having the odor of mint, obtained from oil of peppermint and used in medicine, toilet preparations, etc.

men·tion (mĕn′ shən) ***vt-*** to touch on briefly in speech or writing; talk about: *He didn't* mention *you.* ***n-*** brief notice; light or chance remark: *a* mention *in the newspaper.* **—*adj-*** **men′ tion·a·ble.**

make mention of to refer to; remark on: *He* made mention of *the fact.* **not to mention** to say nothing of: *I enjoyed the meal,* not to mention *the conversation.*

men·tor (mĕn′ tôr′, -tər) ***n-*** wise and trusted teacher.

men·u (mĕn′ yo͞o′) ***n-*** **1** bill of fare; list of dishes that may be ordered in a restaurant. **2** foods served at a particular meal: *the* menu *of a banquet.*

me·ow (mē ou′) ***n-*** the mewing cry of a cat. ***vi-*** to make this sound.

Meph·is·toph·e·les (mĕf′ ə stŏf′ ə lēz′) ***n-*** in German legend, an evil spirit to whom Faust sold his soul for power and wisdom.

Meph·is·to·phe·li·an (mĕf′ ə stə fē′ lē ən, mə fĭs′ tə fē′-) ***adj-*** like Mephistopheles; crafty, wicked, and sardonic: *his* Mephistophelian *smile.* Also **Meph′ is·to′ phe·le′ an.**

mer·can·tile (mûr′ kən tēl′, -tīl′) ***adj-*** having to do with, or engaged in, trade; relating to merchants.

mer·can·til·ism (mûr′ kən tīl′ ĭz′ əm, ·tēl′ ĭz′ əm) ***n-*** economic system of Europe between 1500 and 1750, which sought to maintain an excess of exports over imports and to collect the difference in gold and silver.

Mer·ca·tor projection (mər kā′ tər) ***n-*** an often-used method of map-making in which the earth's surface is represented as a rectangle. Meridians are shown as parallel lines, and the parallels of latitude as straight lines that intersect the meridians at right angles, but are spaced farther apart as they get away from the equator.

mer·ce·nar·y (mûr′ sə nĕr′ ē) ***adj-*** greedy for money; prompted by love of money: *a* mercenary *person.* ***n-*** [*pl.* **mer·ce·nar·ies**] soldier hired by a foreign army.

mer·cer (mûr′ sər) ***n-*** a dealer in woven fabrics.

mer·cer·ize (mûr′ sə rīz′) ***vt-*** [**mer·cer·ized, mer·cer·iz·ing**] to treat (cotton thread or fabric) in such a way that it is made stronger, more lustrous, and more capable of absorbing dyes. **—*n-*** **mer′ cer·i·za′ tion.**

mer·chan·dise (mûr′ chən dīz′) ***vt-*** [**mer·chan·dised, mer·chan·dis·ing**] **1** to buy and sell. **2** to try to promote the sales of (goods, services, etc.) through advertising, attractive presentation, etc. ***vi-*** to carry on commerce. ***n-*** (*often* mûr′ chən dīs′) goods and articles that are bought and sold. **—*n-*** **mer′ chan·dis′ er.**

mer·chant (mûr′ chənt) ***n-*** person who buys and sells goods: *a hardware* merchant. ***adj-*** **1** of or having to do with trade: *a* merchant *ship.* **2** of or having to do with the merchant marine: *a* merchant *captain.*

mer·chant·man (mûr′ chənt mən) ***n-*** [*pl.* **mer·chant·men**] a trading ship; merchant vessel.

merchant marine ***n-*** **1** all the ships of a nation that are engaged in trade or commerce, as distinguished from warships. **2** the officers and crews of these vessels. Also, *chiefly Brit.,* **merchant navy.**

mer·ci·ful (mûr′ sə fəl) ***adj-*** feeling or showing mercy; kindhearted; clement; lenient; not cruel. **—*adv-*** **mer′ ci·ful·ly.** ***n-*** **mer′ ci·ful·ness.**

mer·ci·less (mûr′ sə ləs) ***adj-*** without mercy; cruel; not relenting: *a* merciless *tyrant; the sun's* merciless *heat.* **—*adv-*** **mer′ ci·less·ly.** ***n-*** **mer′ ci·less·ness.**

mer·cu·ri·al (mər kyo͝or′ ē əl) ***adj-*** lively; changeable; fickle; quick-witted: *a* mercurial *temperament; a* mercurial *actor.* **—*adv-*** **mer·cu′ ri·al·ly.**

mer·cur·ic chloride (mər kyo͝or′ ĭk, mûr′ kyə rĭk) ***n-*** very poisonous white powder ($HgCl_2$), used as a disinfectant; corrosive sublimate.

Mer·cu·ro·chrome (mûr kyo͝or′ ə krōm′) ***n-*** trademark name for a compound of mercury whose deep-red water solution is used as an antiseptic.

mer·cu·rous chloride (mər kyo͝or′ əs, mûr′ kyə rəs) ***n-*** white, tasteless, insoluble powder (HgCl) used in medicine as an antiseptic and laxative; calomel.

mer·cu·ry (mûr′ kyə rē) ***n-*** heavy metal element that is liquid at ordinary temperatures; quicksilver. It is used in thermometers and barometers. Symbol Hg, At. No. 80, At. Wt. 200.59.

Mer·cu·ry (mûr′ kyə rē) ***n-*** **1** in Roman mythology, the messenger of the gods, who presided over commerce, skill of hand, or quickness of wit. **2** the smallest planet of the solar system and the one nearest the sun.

mer·cy (mûr′ sē) ***n-*** [*pl.* **mer·cies**] **1** kindness shown a person who is in one's power; leniency; clemency: *to show* mercy *to a defeated enemy.* **2** something to be thankful for; a blessing: *It is a* mercy *that no one was hurt.*

at the mercy of completely in the power of.

[1]**mere** (mêr) ***adj-*** **1** slight: *a* mere *hint of spring.* **2** (intensifier only, expressing disapproval): *a* mere *hanger-on; a*

mere *copy of the original.* [from Old French **mier,** from Latin **merus** meaning "unmixed; pure."]

[2]**mere** (mêr) *Archaic* ***n-*** shallow lake; marsh. [from Old English **mere** meaning "lake; sea."]

mere·ly (mêr′ lē) ***adv-*** only; simply; just.

mer·est (mêr′ əst) ***adj-*** the very slightest; most trivial.

mer·e·tri·cious (mĕr′ ə trĭsh′ əs) ***adj-*** attracting by false show; deceitfully alluring; tawdry. ***—adv-*** **mer′ e·tri′ cious·ly.** ***n-*** **mer′ e·tri′ cious·ness.**

mer·gan·ser (mər găn′ sər) ***n-*** any of several fish-eating, often crested, wild ducks with a slender, hooked bill.

merge (mûrj) ***vt-*** **[merged, merg·ing]** to unite by fusing or intermingling; mingle; blend: *to* merge *two banks; to* merge *ideas.* ***vi-:*** *Two small banks* merged *with a larger one. Dawn* merged *into day. Traffic* merges *here.*

merg·er (mûr′ jər) ***n-*** a merging, especially the legal combination of two or more business firms into one.

me·rid·i·an (mə rĭd′ ē ən) ***n-* 1** either half of a great circle passing through the north and south poles; also, a line on a map or globe representing this. **2** zenith.

me·ringue (mə răng′) ***n-*** mixture of beaten egg white and sugar, used as an icing or baked as small shells.

me·ri·no (mə rē′ nō) ***n-*** [*pl.* **me·ri·nos**] **1** breed of sheep with short legs and long, silky wool. **2** fine cloth or yarn made from this wool.

mer·it (mĕr′ ət) ***n-* 1** quality that is valuable and deserves praise: *a novel of* merit; *the* merit *of honesty.* **2** (often **merits**) the condition of having or not having worth: *to be treated according to one's* merits. **3 merits** the right or wrong of anything: *to judge a case on its* merits. *as* ***modifier:*** *a* merit *badge.* ***vt-*** to deserve.

mer·i·to·ri·ous (mĕr′ ə tôr′ ē əs) ***adj-*** having merit; worthy of praise or reward: *a* meritorious *action.* ***—adv-*** **mer′ i·to′ ri·ous·ly.** ***n-*** **mer′ i·to′ ri·ous·ness.**

merit system ***n-*** system by which appointments and promotions are based on competence.

merl or **merle** (mûrl) ***n-*** European blackbird.

Mer·lin (mûr′ lən) ***n-*** in medieval legend, especially that of King Arthur, a magician and prophet.

mer·maid (mûr′ mād′) ***n-*** imaginary creature with the head and upper body of a woman and the tail of a fish. ***—n-*** *masc.* **mer′ man** (mûr′ mən) [*pl.* **mer·men**].

Mermaid

Mer·ri·mack (mĕr′ ə măk′) ***n-*** U.S. frigate that was rebuilt with iron-plated sides by the Confederacy and renamed the "Virginia." It fought the "Monitor," a Union armored warship, in the Civil War. See also *Monitor.*

mer·ri·ment (mĕr′ ĭ mənt) ***n-*** fun; gaiety; mirth.

mer·ry (mĕr′ ē) ***adj-*** **[mer·ri·er, mer·ri·est]** full of fun; bright and lively; gay; cheerful: *a* merry *chorus; a* merry *twinkle in his eye.* ***—adv-*** **mer′ ri·ly.**

make merry to have fun.

mer·ry-an·drew (mĕr′ ē ăn′ drōō′) ***n-*** a clown; buffoon.

mer·ry-go-round (mĕr′ ē gō′ round′) ***n-* 1** revolving circular platform with wooden animals or seats on which people may ride; carousel. **2** a number of activities in rapid succession: *a weekend* merry-go-round *of parties.*

Merry-go-round

mer·ry·mak·ing (mĕr′ ē mā′ kĭng ***n-*** enjoyment of fun and good fellowship; gaiety; festivity: *Sounds of* merrymaking *came from the house.* ***adj-:*** *a crowd of* merrymaking *picknickers.* ***—n-*** **mer′ ry·mak′ er.**

Mer·thi·o·late (mər thī′ ə lāt′) ***n-*** trademark name for a solution of a compound containing mercury, sulfur, and other elements, used as a germicide.

me·sa (mā′ sə) ***n-*** a flat-topped hill with steep, rocky sides, common in southwestern United States. [American word from Spanish **mesa,** "table," from Latin **mensa,** "table."]

Mesa

mes·cal (mĕ skăl′) ***n-* 1** alcoholic drink made from the juice of the agave plant. **2** cactus plant with rounded stems that bear knobs that resemble buttons. These knobs are chewed as a narcotic by certain Indians in Mexico. [American word from Spanish **mezcal,** from Nahuatl Indian **mexcalli.**]

mes·dames (mā däm′) *pl.* of **madam** or **madame.**

mes·de·moi·selles (mād′ mwə zĕl′) *pl.* of **mademoiselle.**

mes·en·ter·y (mĕs′ ən tĕr′ ē) ***n-*** [*pl.* **mes·en·ter·ies**] a membraneous fold of the peritoneum that envelops and supports most of the viscera, including the intestines. ***—adj-*** **mes′ en·ter′ ic.**

mesh (mĕsh) ***n-* 1** one of the open spaces between the cords of a net, the wire of a screen, etc. **2** fabric, network, etc., having such spaces. **3 meshes** a means of entangling; net; trap: *the* meshes *of a spider's web; caught in the* meshes *of circumstance. as* ***modifier:*** *a pair of* mesh *stockings.* ***vi-*** to fit together; engage; interlock: *The teeth of a zipper* mesh. ***vt-*** to enmesh.

in mesh fitted together; engaged; interlocked.

mes·mer·ism (mĕz′ mə rĭz′ əm, mĕs′-) ***n-*** hypnotism. ***—n-*** **mes′ mer·ist.**

mes·mer·ize (mĕz′ mə rīz′, mĕs′-) ***vt-*** **[mes·mer·ized, mes·mer·iz·ing] 1** to hypnotize. **2** to fascinate; charm; enchant: *The magician* mesmerized *us all with his tricks.* ***—n-*** **mes′ mer·iz′ er.**

meso- *combining form* in the middle: *the* meso*derm* (middle layer of germ cells). [from Greek **meso-,** from **mesos,** "middle."]

mes·o·derm (mĕz′ ə dûrm′, mĕs′-) ***n-*** the middle layer of cells of an animal embryo. Muscles, blood and blood vessels, and tendons develop from mesoderm.

Mes·o·lith·ic (mĕz′ ə lĭth′ ĭk, mĕs′-) ***adj-*** in anthropology, of or having to do with a period of early human culture in which the economy was intermediate between food gathering and agriculture.

me·son (mĕz′ ŏn′, mā′ sŏn′) *Physics* ***n-*** any of four known kinds of nuclear particles having a mass greater than an electron's, but less than a proton's. A meson may have a positive or negative charge, or be neutral.

Mes·o·zo·ic (mĕs′ ə zō′ ĭk, mĕz′-) ***n-*** era of geologic time lasting from about 200 million to 60 million years ago, during which reptiles were dominant and flowering plants developed and spread. ***adj-:*** *the* Mesozoic *era.*

mes·quite (mĕs kēt′, mĕs′ kēt′) ***n-*** low, thorny tree that grows in dry places in southwestern United States and Mexico. Its narrow, sweet pods are used as food for cattle. [American word from Spanish **mezquite,** from Nahuatl Indian **mizquitl.**]

mess (mĕs) ***n-* 1** state of being dirty or in disorder; also, someone or something in such a state: *His room is in a* mess. *She was* a mess *after that muddy walk.* **2** difficult situation; trouble; plight: *Cheating got him into a* mess. 3 bad job; bungle; botch: *She made a complete* mess *of her painting.* 4 quantity of something eaten as food: *He caught a* mess *of trout*; *a* mess *of porridge.* 5 group of people, especially soldiers or sailors, who eat together. 6 meal eaten by such a group. 7 place where they eat: *the officers'* mess. ***vi-*** to eat as a member of a group of soldiers, sailors, etc.: *The four will* mess *together.*

mess around (or **about**) 1 *Informal* to busy oneself with trifling jobs; putter: *He likes to* mess around *at home.* 2 *Slang* to interfere or trifle (with).

mess up 1 *Informal* to make dirty or untidy: *Don't* mess up *the living room.* 2 to spoil; ruin.

mes·sage (mĕs′ĭj) ***n-*** 1 communication directed to another or others, especially in the form of spoken or written words: *to telephone a* message *to a friend*; *a* message *in Morse code*; *the President's* message *to Congress.* 2 subject or idea intended to teach or influence: *a novel with a* message.

mes·sen·ger (mĕs′ən jər) ***n-*** person who carries messages or does errands: *a telegraph* messenger; *a diplomatic* messenger. *as* ***modifier***: *a* messenger *boy.*

mess hall ***n-*** room or building where a large group of people, especially soldiers or sailors, eat together.

Mes·si·ah (mə sī′ə) ***n-*** 1 in the Old Testament, the expected king and deliverer of the Jews; the Christ. 2 in the New Testament, Jesus, regarded as the savior of mankind. 3 **messiah** any expected leader or savior of a people, nation, etc.

Mes·si·an·ic (mĕs′ē ăn′ĭk) ***adj-*** of or relating to the Messiah.

mes·sieurs (mə syûr′) *pl.* of **monsieur.**

mess kit ***n-*** compact set of eating utensils, used by soldiers in the field, campers, etc.

mess·mate (mĕs′māt′) ***n-*** one of a group of persons who eat together regularly, as in the army or navy.

Messrs. (mĕs′ərz) Messieurs. (used as plural of **Mr.**).

mess·y (mĕs′ē) ***adj-*** [**mess·i·er, mess·i·est**] dirty or untidy; sloppy; unpleasant: *a* messy *kitchen*; *a* messy *job of cleaning up.* ***—adv-*** **mess′i·ly.** ***n-*** **mess′i·ness.**

mes·ti·zo (mĕs tē′zō) ***n-*** [*pl.* **mes·ti·zos**] person of mixed racial ancestry; especially, in Latin America, a descendant of American Indians and of Europeans. [from Spanish, ultimately from Latin **misctere** meaning "to mix."] ***—n-*** *fem.* **mes·ti′za** (-zə).

met (mĕt) *p.t. & p.p.* of [1]**meet.**

met·a·bol·ic (mĕt′ə bŏl′ĭk) ***adj-*** of or having to do with metabolism; caused or produced by metabolism. ***—adv-*** **met′a·bol′i·cal·ly.**

me·tab·o·lism (mə tăb′ə lĭz′əm) ***n-*** 1 the sum of all the chemical processes that occur in living organisms. See also *anabolism* and *catabolism.* 2 *Informal* rate at which the body consumes energy; basal metabolism. A person with **high metabolism** consumes energy at a faster rate than one with **low metabolism.**

met·a·car·pal (mĕt′ə kär′pəl) ***n-*** any of the five slender bones of the palm of the hand. *as* ***modifier***: *a* metacarpal *fracture.*

met·al (mĕt′əl) ***n-*** 1 chemical element that is usually solid and shiny when pure or polished, that can be melted by heat, and that can conduct electricity. Gold, silver, copper, tin, iron, and aluminum are metals. 2 mixture of such elements, such as brass or bronze; alloy. 3 basic or essential quality; spirit: *a man of fine* metal. 4 *Chemistry* any element that can replace the hydrogen of an acid to form a base. *as* ***modifier***: *a* metal *tip on an arrow.* ***Hom-*** mettle.

me·tal·lic (mə tăl′ĭk) ***adj-*** 1 consisting of or containing metal: *a* metallic *compound*; *a* metallic *thread.* 2 resembling metal in certain properties: *a* metallic *luster*; *the* metallic *sound of a bell.*

me·tal·loid (mĕt′ə loid′) ***n-*** chemical element having some of the properties of both a metal and a nonmetal. One metalloid is arsenic, which is both silvery gray and a poor conductor. *as* ***modifier***: *a* metalloid *element.*

met·al·lur·gy (mĕt′ə lûr′jē) ***n-*** science of separating metals from their ores and preparing them for use. ***—adj-*** **met′al·lur′gi·cal.**

met·al·lur·gist (mĕt′ə lûr′jĭst) ***n-*** person skilled in and usually occupied in metallurgy.

met·al·work (mĕt′əl wûrk′) ***n-*** 1 articles or decorations made of metal. 2 the making of such articles. ***—n-*** **met′al·work′er.**

met·al·work·ing (mĕt′əl wûr′kĭng) ***n-*** art or process of making things out of metal. *as* ***modifier***: *the* metalworking *trade.*

met·a·mor·phic (mĕt′ə mòr′fĭk, -môr′fĭk) ***adj-*** 1 produced by or showing a change of form, shape, or structure. 2 in geology, of, relating to, or formed by metamorphism: *a* metamorphic *rock.*

met·a·mor·phism (mĕt′ə mòr′fĭz′əm, -môr′fĭz′əm) ***n-*** the change in the composition, texture, and internal structure of rock by heat, pressure, the introduction of new materials, or the action of water.

met·a·mor·phose (mĕt′ə mòr′fōz′, -môr′fōz′) ***vt-*** [**met·a·mor·phosed, met·a·mor·phos·ing**] 1 to change into a different form or nature: *The wicked witch* metamorphosed *the princess into a bird.* 2 in geology, to cause to undergo metamorphism. ***vi-*** to undergo change of form, shape, or structure.

met·a·mor·pho·sis (mĕt′ə mòr′fə səs, -môr′fə səs) ***n-*** [*pl.* **met·a·mor·pho·ses** (-sēz′)] 1 a change in form or structure. 2 *Biology* changes in form, structure, or function as a result of development, especially the change of an insect larva into a pupa and then into the adult form. 3 transformation, especially by sorcery.

met·a·phase (mĕt′ə fāz′) ***n-*** the stage in mitosis during which the chromosomes first move to the equatorial plane, located midway between the poles of the spindle fibers, and then split lengthwise.

met·a·phor (mĕt′ə fòr′, -fôr′) ***n-*** figure of speech in which a name, action, or descriptive word ordinarily applied to a certain object is applied to another in order to suggest a likeness between them. A metaphor is distinguished from a simile by not having "as" or "like" to introduce it. Example: His fist is a hammer. ***—adj-*** **met′a·phor′i·cal.** ***adv-*** **met′a·phor′i·cal·ly.**

met·a·phys·i·cal (mĕt′ə fĭz′ĭ kəl) ***adj-*** 1 of or having to do with metaphysics. 2 hard to understand; abstract. ***—adv-*** **met′a·phys′i·cal·ly.**

met·a·phy·si·cian (mĕt′ə fə zĭsh′ən) ***n-*** person skilled in metaphysics; abstract philosopher.

met·a·phys·ics (mĕt′ə fĭz′ĭks) ***n-*** (takes singular verb) branch of philosophy that deals with such subjects as the basic or absolute nature, character, and causes of being and knowing.

me·tas·ta·sis (mə tă′stə səs) *Medicine* ***n-*** [*pl.* **me·tas·ta·ses** (-sēz′)] 1 the spread of a disease from one part or organ to another not directly connected with it. This may occur in certain types of cancer. 2 the disease in its new site.

me·tas·ta·size (mə tă′stə sīz′) *Medicine* ***vi-*** [**me·tas·ta·sized, me·tas·ta·siz·ing**] to spread through the body from one part or organ to another not directly connected with it, as certain malignancies do.

met·a·tar·sal (mĕt′ə tär′səl) ***n-*** any one of the five long bones of the foot between the ankle and the toes. *as* ***modifier***: *a* metatarsal *fracture*; *the* metatarsal *region.*

met·a·zo·an (mĕt' ə zō' ən) ***n-*** any of the group of animals **(Metazoa)** whose cells are differentiated into tissues, organs, etc. All multicellular animals are metazoans. See also *protozoan.*

mete (mēt) ***vt-*** [**met·ed, met·ing**] to give a share of, by or as if by measuring out; distribute; allot: *The judge* meted *out punishment to each criminal.* ***Homs-*** meat, meet.

me·tem·psy·cho·sis (mĕt' əm sī' kō' səs) ***n-*** [*pl.* **me·tem·psy·cho·ses** (-sēz')] passage of the soul after death into the body of another person or animal.

me·te·or (mē' tē ər) ***n-*** piece of matter that falls toward the earth at great speed from outer space; shooting star. Meteors burn with a bright glow when they hit the air around the earth, and are usually burned up before they reach the ground. See also *meteorite.*

me·te·or·ic (mē' tē ŏr' ĭk, -ŏr' ĭk) ***adj-*** **1** of meteors or a meteor: *a dazzling* meteoric *display.* **2** like a meteor; brilliant or dazzling for a short time: *the* meteoric *careers of some popular singers.*

me·te·or·ite (mē' tē ə rīt') ***n-*** mass of metal or stone that has fallen to earth from outer space. See also *meteor.*

me·te·or·o·log·i·cal (mē' tē ər ə lŏj' ĭ kəl) or **me·te·or·o·log·ic** (-lŏj' ĭk) ***adj-*** of or having to do with weather and climate or with meteorology. ***—adv-*** **me' te·or·o·log' i·cal·ly.**

me·te·o·rol·o·gist (mē' tē ə rŏl' ə jĭst) ***n-*** person skilled in and usually occupied in meteorology.

me·te·or·ol·o·gy (mē' tē ə rŏl' ə jē) ***n-*** the science of weather and climate.

[1]**me·ter** (mē' tər) ***n-*** **1** instrument that measures and shows a record of the measurement: *an electric* meter; *a parking* meter. **2** the basic unit of length in the metric system, defined as 1,650,763.73 times the wavelength of the light emitted by the excited atoms of the krypton-86 isotope. It is equivalent to 39.37 inches. ***vt-*** to control or regulate by means of a measuring instrument. [from French **mètre,** from Greek **métron,** "a measure."]

[2]**me·ter** (mē' tər) **1** particular way syllables are arranged in a line of poetry to produce a certain rhythm. **2** time, beat, or rhythm in music. Also, *chiefly Brit.,* **me' tre.** [from Latin **metrum,** from Greek **métron,** "measure."]

-meter *combining form* instrument for measuring: *alti*meter. [from French **-metre** from **mètre** from Greek **metron** meaning "measure; measuring instrument."]

meth·ane (mĕth' ān') ***n-*** colorless, odorless gas (CH_4) found in nature as natural gas and as marsh gas. It is highly flammable, and is used as fuel.

meth·a·nol (mĕth' ə nŏl', -nōl') ***n-*** methyl alcohol.

me·thinks (mē thĭngks') *Archaic* I think; it seems to me.

meth·od (mĕth' əd) ***n-*** **1** way of doing something, especially according to a system or established order: *a new* method *of multiplication.* **2** orderly arrangement of ideas, subjects, etc.: *His writing lacks* method.

me·thod·i·cal (mə thŏd' ĭ kəl) ***adj-*** **1** done, arranged, or presented in an orderly or systematic way: *a* methodical *outline*; *a* methodical *performance.* **2** inclined to be orderly or systematic: *a* methodical *housekeeper.* ***—adv-*** **me·thod' i·cal·ly.** ***n-*** **me·thod' i·cal·ness.**

Meth·o·dist (mĕth' ə dĭst') ***n-*** member of a Protestant denomination that developed from the teachings of John and Charles Wesley in England in the 18th century. ***adj-:*** *a* Methodist *minister.*

Meth·o·dism (mĕth' ə dĭz' əm) ***n-*** the doctrines and worship of the Methodists.

meth·o·dol·o·gy (mĕth' ə dŏl' ə jē) ***n-*** [*pl.* **meth·o·dol·o·gies**] **1** any orderly system of principles by which a body of knowledge, especially a science, is organized, studied, etc. **2** study or use of such principles.

me·thought (mē thŏt') *Archaic* I thought; it seemed to me.

Me·thu·se·lah (mə thōō' zə lə) ***n-*** in the Old Testament, a patriarch said to have lived 969 years; hence, any very old man. In the CCD Bible, **Ma·thu' sa·le.**

meth·yl alcohol (mĕth' əl) ***n-*** colorless, poisonous alcohol (CH_3OH), a product of the reaction between carbon monoxide and hydrogen gas; methanol; wood alcohol. It is used in antifreezes, denatured alcohol, and the manufacture of chemical products.

meth·yl·at·ed (mĕth' ə lā' təd) ***adj-*** mixed with methyl alcohol, often to render undrinkable.

me·tic·u·lous (mə tĭk' yə ləs) ***adj-*** very careful about details; very orderly and methodical: *a* meticulous *girl.* ***—adv-*** **me·tic' u·lous·ly.** ***n-*** **me·tic' u·lous·ness.**

me·tre (mē' tər) [2]meter.

met·ric (mĕ' trĭk) ***adj-*** **1** of or involving measurement, especially according to the metric system. **2** metrical.

met·ri·cal (mĕ' trĭ kəl) ***adj-*** **1** of or having to do with meter or rhythm in poetry; using or composed in meter: *a* metrical *translation.* **2** metric. ***—adv-*** **met' ri·cal·ly.**

metric system ***n-*** decimal system of weights and measures based on the meter for length and the kilogram for weight. The liter is used for capacity.

metric ton ***n-*** measure of weight equal to 1,000 kilograms or 2,204.62 pounds avoirdupois.

met·ro·nome (mĕ' trə nōm') ***n-*** a device that beats time in loud ticks, used especially for music practice.

me·trop·o·lis (mə trŏp' ə ləs) ***n-*** **1** large city, especially one that is a center of business and culture. **2** chief city of a country, state, or region. **3** in ancient Greece, the parent city of a colony.

met·ro·pol·i·tan (mĕ' trə pŏl' ə tən) ***adj-*** of or having to do with a large city: *the* metropolitan *police force.* ***n-*** **1** person who lives in and knows the ways of a large city. **2** bishop next in rank below patriarch in the Eastern Orthodox Church and other churches.

Metronome

metropolitan area ***n-*** a major city and its surrounding area, considered as a center of population and business.

met·tle (mĕt' əl) ***n-*** courage; spirit: *The hard trip to the West tested the* mettle *of the pioneers.* ***Hom-*** metal.
on (one's) mettle ready or eager to do (one's)best.

met·tle·some (mĕt' əl səm) ***adj-*** full of spirit; courageous; bold: *a* mettlesome *horse.*

mev or **Mev** or **m.e.v.** million electron volts.

[1]**mew** (myōō) ***n-*** the cry of a cat; meow. ***vi-:*** *The kittens* mewed *loudly.* [probably an imitation of the sound.]

[2]**mew** (myōō) ***n-*** a gull, especially the common European gull. [from Old English **mæw.**]

[3]**mew** (myōō) ***n-*** in former times, a cage for hawks. ***vt-*** to shut up or enclose in or as if in a cage. [from Old French **mue** meaning "a molting; a molting cage," from Latin **mutāre,** "to change."]

mewl (myōōl) ***vi-*** to cry weakly like a baby; whimper. ***n-*** a cry like this; whimper. ***Hom-*** mule.

mews (myōōz) *chiefly Brit.* ***n-*** (takes singular verb) **1** in former times, a stable or group of stables surrounding a court. **2** narrow street or alley with houses converted from such stables. [from the plural of [2]**mew.** The stables of Henry VIII were built on the site of old Royal Falconry.] ***Hom-*** muse.

Mex. 1 Mexico. 2 Mexican.
Mex·i·can (měk′sĭ kən) ***adj***- of or relating to Mexico or its people. ***n***- citizen of Mexico, or person of Mexican descent.
Mexican Spanish ***n***- the Spanish language as spoken and written in Mexico.
Mexican War ***n***- war fought between the United States and Mexico (1846-1848), through which the United States acquired large parts of the Southwest.
me·zu·zah (mə zo͞o′zə) ***n***- small metal tube containing a strip of parchment inscribed with certain passages from the Old Testament and one of the Hebrew names for God. A mezuzah may be fastened to the side of the doorway of a Jewish home or worn as an amulet.
mez·za·nine (měz′ə nēn′) ***n***- 1 in a building, an extra floor between two others, usually the first and second, often in the form of a gallery. 2 in a theater, the first balcony or the first few rows of this balcony.
mez·zo (mět′sō′, -měd′zō′) *Music* ***adv***- moderately: *a* mezzo *forte passage.* ***adj***- having a range between very high and very low: *She is a* mezzo-*soprano.* ***n***- [*pl.* **mez·zos**] singer who is a mezzo-soprano.
mez·zo-so·pran·o (mět′sō sə prăn′ō, měd′sō-) *Music* ***n***- [*pl.* **mez·zo-so·pran·os**] range of the female singing voice somewhat higher than contralto and somewhat lower than soprano; also, a singer having such a range, or a part written for it. ***adj***-: *a* mezzo-soprano *voice.*
mez·zo·tint (mět′sō tĭnt′, měd′zō-) ***n***- 1 process of engraving on copper or other metal that produces a soft-toned effect. 2 picture produced by this process.
Mg symbol for magnesium.
mg or **mg.** milligram or milligrams.
mho (mō) ***n***- [*pl.* **mhos**] unit of conductance, defined as the amount of conductance of a conductor whose resistance is 1 ohm.

$1 \text{ mho} = \frac{1}{1 \text{ ohm.}}$ [**ohm** spelled backwards.]

mi (mē) *Music* ***n***- third note of a musical scale. ***Hom***- me.
mi. mile or miles
Mi·a·mi (mī ăm′ē) ***n***- [*pl.* **Mi·a·mis,** also **Mi·am·i**] one of a tribe of Algonquian Indians who originally lived in Wisconsin, Ohio, and Indiana, but gradually moved southward into Oklahoma. ***adj***-: *a* Miami *chief.*
mi·as·ma (mī ăz′mə) ***n***- 1 poisonous vapor once believed to rise from decayed matter, especially in swamps, and to be the cause of malaria. 2 any harmful influence or effect: *a* miasma *of superstition.* **—*adj*- mi·as′mal.**
mi·ca (mī′kə) ***n***- mineral that is easily separated into thin, flexible sheets that look like transparent or cloudy glass. Mica can stand great heat and is a good insulator for electricity. ***Hom***- Micah.
Mi·cah (mī′kə) ***n***- 1 Hebrew prophet of the eighth century B.C. 2 book of the Old Testament. In the CCD Bible, **Mi·che′a** (mī kē′ə). ***Hom***- mica.
mice (mīs) *pl.* of **mouse.**
Mich. Michigan.
Mi·chael (mī′kəl) ***n***- one of the archangels, leader of a host of angels. Also **St. Michael the Archangel.**
Mich·ael·mas (mĭk′əl məs) ***n***- the feast of St. Michael the Archangel, celebrated on September 29, especially in England and on the Continent.
Mick·ey Finn (mĭk′ē fĭn′) *Slang* ***n***- any of several powerful drugs, especially chloral hydrate, that are secretly put into alcoholic drinks to produce unconsciousness; also, the drink itself.
Mic·mac (mĭk′măk′) ***n***- [*pl.* **Mic·macs,** also **Mic·mac**] member of an Algonquian tribe of American Indians living in Nova Scotia, New Brunswick, and Newfoundland. ***adj***-: *a* Micmac *camp.*
micro- *combining form* 1 very small: *a* micro*wave transmitter*; micro*photo.* 2 enlarging that which is very small: *a* micro*scope*; micro*phone.* 3 dealing with the very small with the aid of microscopes: *the study of* micro*biology*; micro*photography.* 4 in the metric system and other technical measurement, a millionth of a (stated unit): *a* micro*gram* (a millionth of a gram); micro*second.* [from Greek **mikros** meaning "small."]
mi·crobe (mī′krōb) ***n***- living plant or animal so small that it can be seen only through a microscope.
mi·cro·bi·o·log·i·cal (mī′krō bī′ə lŏj′ĭ kəl) or **mi·cro·bi·o·log·ic** (-lŏj′ĭk) ***adj***- having to do with microscopic organisms or with the study of microbiology. **—*adv*- mi′cro·bi′o·log′i·cal·ly.**
mi·cro·bi·ol·o·gist (mī′krō bī ŏl′ə jĭst) ***n***- person trained in microbiology.
mi·cro·bi·ol·o·gy (mī′krō bī ŏl′ə jē) ***n***- branch of biology that deals with microscopic organisms.
mi·cro·cop·y (mī′krō kŏp′ē) ***n***- [*pl.* **mi·cro·cop·ies**] very small photographic copy of a manuscript, picture, etc.; microfilm. ***vt***- [**mi·cro·cop·ied, mi·cro·cop·y·ing**]: *to* microcopy *a manuscript.*
mi·cro·cosm (mī′krə kŏz′əm) ***n***- a little world; universe in miniature; also, a community or person thought of as representing this. See also *macrocosm.*
mi·cro·fiche (mī′krə fēsh′) ***n***- [*pl.* **mi·cro·fiche** or **mi·cro·fich·es**] card containing microfilmed versions of printed pages.
mi·cro·film (mī′krə fĭlm′) ***n***- 1 narrow film for making very small photographs, for preserving and storing in a small space. 2 a single exposed frame of such film; microcopy. ***vt***-: *to* microfilm *a musical score.*
mi·cro·gram (mī′krə grăm′) ***n***- unit of weight in the metric system equal to one millionth of a gram.
mi·cro·graph (mī′krə grăf′) ***n***- 1 device for producing very tiny engraving or writing. 2 photomicrograph.
mi·cro·groove (mī′krō gro͞ov′) ***n***- very fine, narrow groove in a long-playing phonograph record.
mi·cro·me·te·or·ite (mī′krō mē′tē ə rīt′) ***n***- meteorite having a diameter usually of less than a millimeter.
mi·crom·e·ter (mī krŏm′ə tər) ***n***- 1 instrument for measuring very small distances, used with a microscope or telescope. 2 (also **micrometer caliper**) a gauge with a fine screw for precise measurement of screws, bolts, etc.
mi·cron (mī′krŏn′) ***n***- [*pl.* **mi·crons** or **mi·cra** (-krə)] unit of measurement equal to .001 millimeter.
mi·cro-or·gan·ism (mī′krō ŏr′gə nĭz′əm) ***n***- living plant or animal so small that it can be seen only through a microscope. Bacteria and most protozoans are micro-organisms. Also **mi′cro·or′gan·ism.**
mi·cro·phone (mī′krə fōn′) ***n***- instrument that changes sounds into corresponding electrical signals for recording, broadcasting, etc.
mi·cro·pho·to·graph (mī krō fō′tə grăf′) ***n***- photograph that has been reduced to a very small or microscopic size, and, hence, can only be viewed with special enlarging equipment. See also *photomicrograph.* **—*n*- mi′cro·pho·tog′ra·phy** (mī′krō fə tŏg rə fē).

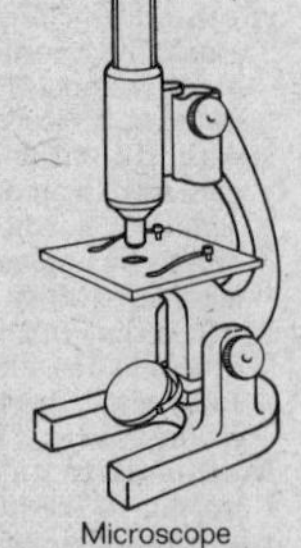
Microscope

mi·cro·scope (mī′krə skōp′) ***n***- instrument with an arrangement of lenses for making very tiny plant cells, animal cells, etc., look large enough to be seen and studied. See also *electron microscope.*

mi·cro·scop·ic (mī′ krə skŏp′ ĭk) ***adj*- 1** seen or perceived only through a microscope: *a* microscopic *animal.* **2** of or having to do with a microscope; made or done with a microscope: *a* microscopic *lens*; *a* microscopic *examination of a blood sample.* **3** like a microscope; able to see the smallest detail: *a* microscopic *eye.* **—*adv*- mi′ cro·scop′ i·cal·ly.**

mi·cros·co·py (mī krŏs′ kə pē) ***n*-** process or technique of using the microscope as a means of scientific study.

mi·cro·sec·ond (mī′ krō sĕk′ ənd) ***n*-** one millionth of a second in time.

mi·cro·wave (mī′ krō wāv′) ***n*-** any electromagnetic wave whose wavelength is less than 1 meter. Microwaves are used in radar and television.

[1]**mid** (mĭd) ***adj*- 1** in phonetics, pronounced with the tongue between high and low positions, as it is for vowels such as (ā), (ĕ), and (ə): *the* mid *vowels.* **2** middle: *the* mid *part of June.* [from Old English **midd,** "middle."]

[2]**mid** or **'mid** (mĭd) amid. [shortened from **amid.**]

mid- *prefix* **1** in the middle part of what is indicated: *a* mid-*Victorian style.* **2** occurring in the center among others; central: *the* mid*point*; mid*iron.*

mid·af·ter·noon (mĭd′ ăf′ tər nōōn′) ***n*-** middle part of the afternoon; time around 3 and 4 p.m. *as **modifier**: a* midafternoon *swimming party.*

mid·air (mĭd′ âr′) ***n*-** in the air above the earth: *The bomb exploded in* midair.

Mi·das (mī′ dəs) ***n*-** in Greek legend, a king of Phrygia who had the power to turn anything he touched into gold.

mid-chan·nel (mĭd′ chăn′ əl) ***n*-** middle part of a channel, measured from side to side.

mid-course (mĭd′ kôrs′) **in mid-course** at a point part way through a continuous motion, journey, etc.: *The rocket changed direction* in mid-course.

mid·day (mĭd′ dā′) ***n*-** middle of the day; noon. *as **modifier**: the* midday *meal*; *in the* midday *sun.*

mid·den (mĭd′ ən) ***n*-** See *kitchen midden.*

mid·dle (mĭd′ əl) ***n*- 1** approximate center of anything: *the* middle *of the room.* **2** point halfway between the beginning and the end: *the* middle *of the movie*; *the* middle *of the week.* **3** point halfway between two sides of something long and continuous, such as a road, river, etc. **4** part of the body between the chest and the hips: *The ball hit him square in the* middle. ***adj*- 1** halfway between two points, ends, sides, etc.; central: *the* middle *room.* **2** not at either extreme of a range; intermediate: *people of* middle *income.*

middle age *n*- time of a person's life between youth and old age, usually considered to include the years between 40 and 60. **—*adj*- (middle-aged):** *a* middle-aged *man.*

Middle Ages *n*- the medieval period of European history, from about 500 A.D. to about 1400 A.D.

middle C *Music* ***n*-** note written on the first line below the staff in the treble clef, or on the first line above the staff in the bass clef; also, the tone this represents.

middle class *n*- 1 in the United States, the economic class between the rich and the poor. It has usually been taken to include small businessmen, professional people, office workers, etc. **2** especially in countries having a hereditary nobility, the social class between the aristocracy and the laborers. **—*adj*- (middle-class):** *a* middle-class *family*; *a* middle-class *neighborhood.*

middle ear *n*- the cavity behind the eardrum; tympanum. It contains three tiny bones (anvil, hammer, and stirrup) that transmit sound waves from the eardrum to the inner ear. For picture, see [1]*ear.*

Middle English *n*- the English language as written and spoken from about 1100 to about 1500. In comparison with Old English, it has fewer inflectional endings, a different system of pronunciation, and many words borrowed from French.

mid·dle·man (mĭd′ əl măn′) ***n*-** [*pl.* **mid·dle·men**] person acting as a go-between or agent between buyer and seller, especially a dealer who buys goods from a producer to sell to a retail merchant or consumer.

mid·dle·weight (mĭd′ əl wāt′) ***n*- 1** person of average weight. **2** boxer who weighs between 147 and 160 pounds. *as **modifier**: the* middleweight *champion.*

Middle Westerner *n*- a native or long-time inhabitant of the Middle West; Midwesterner.

mid·dling (mĭd′ lĭng) ***adj*-** of average quality, size, or rank; neither good nor bad; ordinary. ***adv*-** *Informal* moderately; fairly: *in* middling *good health.* ***n*- middlings 1** a mixture of coarsely ground wheat flour and fine bran. **2** goods of average quality, size, etc.

mid·dy (mĭd′ ē) ***n*-** [*pl.* **mid·dies**] **1** *Informal* midshipman; naval cadet. **2** (also **middy blouse**) loose blouse like a sailor's, having a wide square collar.

Middy blouse

mid·field (mĭd′ fēld′) ***n*-** part of an athletic field midway between the goals. *as **modifier**: a* midfield *attempt at a field goal.*

mid-flight (mĭd′ flīt′) **in mid-flight** at a point part way through a continuous flight or other rapid movement: *The airplane lost an engine* in mid-flight. *The runner tripped and fell* in mid-flight.

midge (mĭj) ***n*-** very small fly, gnat, or similar flying insect; hence, a very small person.

midg·et (mĭj′ ət) ***n*- 1** very small person, not deformed but much below the normal size. **2** any thing very small of its kind. *as **modifier**: a* midget *racing car.*

mid·i·ron (mĭd′ ī′ ərn) ***n*-** golf club having an iron or steel head with a slightly slanted face. It is used for hitting the ball moderate distances.

mid·land (mĭd′ lənd) ***n*-** middle or central part of a country; the interior. *as **modifier**: the* midland *plains of the United States.*

mid-length (mĭd′ lĕngth′) ***adj*-** neither long nor short; of medium length: *a* mid-length *skirt.*

mid·mor·ning (mĭd′ môr′ nĭng, mĭd′ môr′-) ***n*-** middle part of the morning; time around 10 a.m. *as **modifier**: a* midmorning *conference.*

mid·most (mĭd′ mōst′) ***adj*-** exactly in the middle or nearest the middle.

mid·night (mĭd′ nīt′) ***n*-** the middle of the night; 12 o'clock at night. ***adj*- 1** of or at 12 o'clock at night: *a* midnight *supper.* **2** very dark: *a* midnight *blue.*

burn the midnight oil to study or work far into the night.

midnight sun *n*- the sun seen continuously for several months during the summer in arctic and antarctic regions. It is visible even at midnight.

mid-ocean ridge *n*- a series of interconnected, underwater mountain ranges that occur in the Atlantic Ocean, Indian Ocean, and the southern and eastern Pacific Ocean.

mid·point (mĭd′ point′) ***n*-** point or place exactly in the middle: *the* midpoint *of a line*; *the* midpoint *of his career.*

mid·rib (mĭd′ rĭb′) ***n-*** the vein along the center of a leaf.

mid·riff (mĭd′ rĭf′) ***n-*** **1** the muscular partition separating the cavity of the chest from that of the abdomen; diaphragm. **2** part of the body between the chest and the waist: *a fatty bulge at the* midriff.

mid·sec·tion (mĭd′ sĕk′ shən) ***n-*** **1** *Informal* part of the body between the chest and the hips; belly; midriff. **2** part of an airplane between the nose and the tail.

mid·se·mes·ter (mĭd′ sə mĕs′ tər) ***n-*** **1** examination given near the middle of a semester. **2** time around the middle of a semester. *as* ***modifier:*** *a* midsemester *grade.*

mid·ship·man (mĭd′ shĭp′ mən) ***n-*** [*pl.* **mid·ship·men**] **1** man in training to become an officer in the U.S. Navy or Coast Guard, especially at a naval academy. **2** junior officer in the British navy.

mid·ships (mĭd′ shĭps′) amidships.

[1]**midst** (mĭdst) ***n-*** middle place or part; middle; center. [from Middle English **middest,** based on [1]**mid.**]

in our (or **their** or **your**) **midst** among us, them, or you: *There is a stranger* in our midst. **in the midst of** **1** in the middle of: *He stood* in the midst of *the crowd.* **2** existing together with: *poverty* in the midst of *plenty.*

[2]**midst** or **'midst** (mĭdst) amidst. [from **amidst.**]

mid·stream (mĭd′ strēm′) ***n-*** the middle of a stream.

mid·sum·mer (mĭd′ sŭm′ ər) ***n-*** **1** the middle of the summer, halfway between spring and fall. **2** the day, occurring about June 21, that has the longest period of daylight in the year. *as* ***modifier:*** *the* midsummer *heat.*

mid·term (mĭd′ tûrm′) ***adj-*** taking place in the middle of a term: *a* midterm *examination.* ***n-*** (often **midterms**) examination in the middle of a school or college term; also, period in which these examinations are given.

mid·town (mĭd′ toun′) ***n-*** central part of a town or city. *as* ***modifier:*** *the* midtown *office of the bank.*

mid-Vic·to·ri·an (mĭd′ vĭk tôr′ ē ən) ***adj-*** **1** of or having to do with the middle portion of the reign of Queen Victoria, about 1850 to 1880. **2** relating to or characteristic of the art, fashions, ideas, or standards of morality and taste of this period; hence, prudish, conventional, or old-fashioned. ***n-*** **1** person who lived during this period. **2** person of prudishly old-fashioned tastes, ideas, or attitudes.

mid·way (mĭd′ wā′) ***adj-*** in the middle of the way or distance; occupying a middle place or position: *the* midway *point in a journey.* ***adv-*** in or to the middle of the way or distance; halfway: *He caught cold* midway *through the campaign.* ***n-*** part of a circus, carnival, or fair, where side shows and other amusements are located.

mid·week (mĭd′ wēk′) ***n-*** **1** middle of the week. **2 Midweek** among the Quakers, Wednesday. *as* ***modifier:*** *a* midweek *holiday.*

mid·week·ly (mĭd′ wēk′ lē) ***adj-*** happening or done in the middle of the week: *a* midweekly *report.* ***adv-:*** *They met* midweekly.

Mid·west·ern·er (mĭd wĕs′ tər nər) ***n-*** Middle Westerner.

mid·wife (mĭd′ wīf′) ***n-*** [*pl.* **mid·wives** (-wīvz′)] woman who assists women in childbirth.

mid·win·ter (mĭd′ wĭn′ tər) ***n-*** **1** middle of the winter, halfway between fall and spring. **2** the day, occurring about December 21, that has the shortest period of daylight in the year. *as* ***modifier:*** *a* midwinter *vacation.*

mid·year (mĭd′ yêr′) ***adj-*** taking place in the middle of a year: *a* midyear *sale*; *a* midyear *examination.* ***n-*** (often **midyears**) examination in the middle of a school or college year; also, the time of these examinations.

mien (mēn) ***n-*** person's appearance, especially as it reveals character, feeling, etc.; manner; air; bearing: *The prince's proud and noble* mien. ***Hom-*** mean.

miff (mĭf) *Informal* ***vt-*** to put in a bad mood; annoy; offend. ***n-*** trivial quarrel or annoyance; fuss.

[1]**might** (mīt) *p.t.* of **may:** *I told him he* might *go.* ***auxiliary verb.*** **1** am, is, or are allowed to: *And* might *I ask who you are?* **2** may possibly: *Be good and I* might *let you have my bicycle tomorrow.* **3** could possibly, but doubtfully: *If we had rushed, we* might *have caught the train.* **4** I wish for, but without much hope: *O,* might *this sad news prove untrue*! **5** could if acting properly: *You* might *at least say, "Thank you."* **6** would have the opportunity or possibility to: *He died so that we* might *live.* [from Old English **mihte** meaning "I was able," from **magan,** "may."] ***Hom-*** mite.

►MIGHT and MAY are used interchangeably to express possibility, permission, wish, hope, or request, but MIGHT implies less possibility of an outcome, or less expectation that a hope or wish will be fulfilled. "He might come" suggests less certainty than "He may come." "Might I have this?" suggests more of an expectation of a negative answer than "May I have this?"

[2]**might** (mīt) ***n-*** strength; power; force: *to push with all one's* might; *the* might *of the Roman Empire.* [from Old English **miht** meaning "bodily or spiritual strength; power."] ***Hom-*** mite.

might·y (mī′tē) ***adj-*** [**might·i·er, might·i·est**] **1** very strong; powerful: *a* mighty *warrior*; *a* mighty *effort.* **2** of unusual size, importance, etc.; great: *a* mighty *wave*; *a* mighty *ship.* ***adv-*** *Informal* very; greatly; extremely: *We are* mighty *glad to see you.* ***—adv-*** **might′ i·ly.** ***n-*** **might′ i·ness.**

mig·non·ette (mĭn′ yə nĕt′) ***n-*** fragrant garden plant with clusters of tiny, greenish-white flowers.

mi·graine (mī′ grān′) ***n-*** severe headache, often concentrated on one side of the head and accompanied by dizziness and nausea.

mi·grant (mī′ grənt) ***adj-*** moving from place to place, especially with the changes of season; migratory: *He hired* migrant *workers to harvest his peaches.* ***n-*** person, animal, or bird that migrates.

mi·grate (mī′ grāt′) ***vi-*** [**mi·grat·ed, mi·grat·ing**] **1** to travel from one region to another as the seasons change: *Ducks and geese* migrate *southward in the fall.* **2** to move to a new home in a different region: *The pioneers* migrated *to the West.*

mi·gra·tion (mī grā′ shən) ***n-*** **1** act of migrating: *the* migration *of birds.* **2** number of people, birds, or animals that migrate: *a large* migration *of ducks.*

mi·gra·tor·y (mī′ grə tôr′ ē) ***adj-*** moving from place to place; wandering; roving: *a* migratory *worker*; migratory *birds*; *the* migratory *life of a tramp.*

mi·ka·do (mə kä′ dō) ***n-*** [*pl.* **mi·ka·dos**] the emperor of Japan.

mike (mīk) *Informal* ***n-*** microphone.

mil (mĭl) ***n-*** unit of length equal to one thousandth of an inch. ***Hom-*** mill.

mi·la·dy (mə lā′ dē) ***n-*** [*pl.* **mi·la·dies**] my lady.

milch (mĭlch) ***adj-*** giving milk: *a* milch *cow.*

mild (mīld) ***adj-*** [**mild·er, mild·est**] **1** calm and gentle in disposition, temperament, or manner: *a* mild *man who wouldn't harm a soul*; *a* mild *tone of voice.* **2** not extreme or harsh; moderate; temperate: *a* mild *winter*; mild *punishment.* **3** not sharp or strong: *a* mild *cheese*; *a* mild *tobacco.* ***—adv-*** **mild′ ly.** ***n-*** **mild′ ness.**

mil·dew (mĭl′ do͞o′, -dyo͞o′) ***n-*** tiny fungus found on plants, decaying matter, cloth, leather, or paper. Mildew often appears during warm, damp weather as a whitish coating or as spots of mold. ***vt-*** to affect with such a fungus or mold: *The dampness* mildewed *my books.* ***vi-:*** *Leather left in a damp cellar will* mildew.

mile (mīl) ***n-*** a measure of length or distance. On land, a **statute mile** is equal to 5,280 feet. In the United States, a **geographical mile** (or **nautical mile** or **air mile**) is equal to 6,080.20 feet.

mile·age (mī′lĭj) ***n-*** **1** distance or number of miles covered in traveling. **2** use one gets from something, according to miles traveled: *high* mileage *from a gallon of gasoline.* **3** money allowed for traveling expenses, estimated at a certain rate per mile.

mile·post (mīl′ pōst′) ***n-*** signpost along a road, stating the distance in miles to a certain point.

mil·er (mī′ lər) ***n-*** runner or horse trained to compete in races of one mile.

mile·stone (mīl′ stōn′) ***n-*** **1** roadside stone used to mark distance. **2** important event: *a* milestone *in history.*

mi·lieu (mēl yōō′) ***n-*** surroundings; environment: *the familiar* milieu *of one's own home.*

mil·i·tant (mĭl′ ə tənt) ***adj-*** **1** ready to fight; warlike: *a* militant *nation.* **2** aggressive and prepared to fight in support of a cause: *a* militant *defender of freedom.* ***n-*** person who is aggressive in support of a cause. ***—adv-*** **mil′ i·tant·ly.** ***n-*** **mil′ i·tan·cy.**

mil·i·ta·rism (mĭl′ ə tə rĭz′ əm) ***n-*** **1** tendency to uphold a nation's power by means of a strong army and navy. **2** policy of being ready to fight on the slightest provocation. **3** government or rule by military interests; military ideals or spirit. ***—n-*** **mil′ i·ta·rist.**

mil·i·ta·ris·tic (mĭl′ ə tə rĭs′ tĭk) ***adj-*** of or having to do with militarism; having military ideals or spirit: *a* militaristic *government.* ***—adv-*** **mil′ i·ta·rist′ i·cal·ly.**

mil·i·ta·rize (mĭl′ ə tə rīz′) ***vt-*** **[mil·i·ta·rized, mil·i·ta·riz·ing]** **1** to prepare or equip for war; convert (a nation) to a military power: *Hitler* militarized *Germany after 1933.* **2** to fill with military ideals or spirit. ***—n-*** **mil′ i·ta·ri·za′ tion.**

mil·i·tar·y (mĭl′ ə tĕr′ ē) ***adj-*** **1** of or having to do with war, arms, or the armed forces: *to receive* military *training*; military *history.* **2** of, for, or by soldiers: *a* military *band*; *a* military *uniform.* ***n-*** **the military** the armed forces. ***—adv-*** **mil′ i·tar′ i·ly.**

military police ***n-*** (takes plural verb) soldiers whose duties are to keep order, arrest soldiers guilty of misconduct, protect civilians of an occupied area, guard prisoners of war, etc. See also *shore patrol.*

mil·i·tate (mĭl′ ə tāt′) ***vi-*** **[mil·i·tat·ed, mil·i·tat·ing]** to act, work, or operate (against) someone or something: *His obvious rashness* militated *against him.*

mi·li·tia (mə lĭsh′ ə) ***n-*** body of citizens who are trained for defense of their country in emergencies. In the United States the militia is called the National Guard.

mi·li·tia·man (mə lĭsh′ ə mən) ***n-*** [*pl.* **mi·li·tia·men**] member of the militia.

milk (mĭlk) ***n-*** **1** white fluid produced by female mammals for feeding their young. The milk of several domestic animals, such as cows and goats, is used for human food. **2** liquid resembling this, especially the juice of certain plants or fruits: *Coconut* milk *makes a refreshing drink.* ***as modifier***: *a* milk *carton*; *an old* milk *truck.* ***vt-*** **1** to draw milk from: *to* milk *a cow.* **2** to cheat; take unfair advantage of; exploit: *The swindler* milked *his unsuspecting victims.* ***vi-*** to draw milk from a cow, goat, etc.: *He likes to* milk. ***—adj-*** **milk′ like′.**

milk·er (mĭl′ kər) ***n-*** **1** person or machine that milks. **2** cow or goat that gives milk: *She's a good* milker.

milk·maid (mĭlk′ mād′) ***n-*** woman or girl who milks cows or works in a dairy.

milk·man (mĭlk′ măn′) ***n-*** [*pl.* **milk·men**] man who sells or delivers milk.

milk of magnesia ***n-*** chalky white liquid, chiefly magnesia, used as a laxative and an antacid.

milk shake or **milk·shake** (mĭlk′ shāk′) ***n-*** a drink of beaten milk, flavoring, and often ice cream.

milk snake ***n-*** small, gray or reddish-brown king snake with black markings, that feeds on mice, frogs, etc. It is harmless to people and easily tamed. Milk snakes were once thought to get their food by milking cows.

milk·sop (mĭlk′ sŏp′) ***n-*** weak, timid man or boy.

milk sugar ***n-*** lactose.

milk tooth ***n-*** in mammals, one of the temporary teeth that fall out before adulthood and are replaced by permanent teeth.

milk·weed (mĭlk′ wēd′) ***n-*** tall plant with oval leaves, clusters of small, purplish flowers, and sticky milklike juice.

milk·y (mĭl′ kē) ***adj-*** **[milk·i·er, milk·i·est]** **1** like milk in appearance, especially in color: *a* milky *sap*; *a* milky *complexion.* **2** containing milk: *a* milky *sauce.* ***—n-*** **milk′ i·ness.**

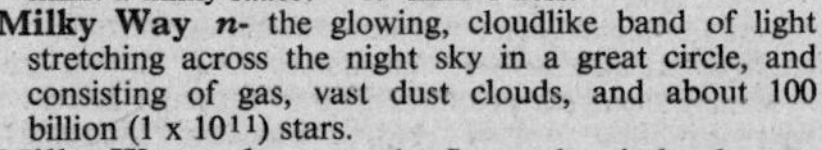

Milkweed

Milky Way ***n-*** the glowing, cloudlike band of light stretching across the night sky in a great circle, and consisting of gas, vast dust clouds, and about 100 billion (1 x 10^{11}) stars.

Milky Way galaxy ***n-*** the flattened, spiral galaxy to which the sun, solar system, and Milky Way belong; the Galaxy.

[1]**mill** (mĭl) ***n-*** **1** machine or implement for grinding or pulverizing: *a pepper* mill. **2** building containing such machinery, especially for grinding grain. **3** any factory: *a paper* mill; *a cotton* mill; *a steel* mill. ***vt-*** **1** to grind: *to* mill *flour.* **2** to cut or stamp ridges across the edge of (a coin). **3** to shape with a milling machine. ***vi-*** to surge around, as a restless crowd does. [from Old English **myl(e)n,** from Late Latin **molina,** from Latin **mola** meaning "millstone."] ***Hom-*** mil.

Mill

through the mill *Informal* through a hard and trying experience or period of training.

[2]**mill** (mĭl) ***n-*** the thousandth part of a dollar; one tenth of a cent. [from Latin **millesimus** meaning "thousandth," from **mille,** "one thousand."] ***Hom-*** mil.

mill·dam (mĭl′ dăm′) ***n-*** barrier built across a stream to form a mill pond.

mil·len·ni·um (mə lĕn′ ē əm) ***n-*** [*pl.* **mil·len·ni·ums** or **mil·len·ni·a** (-nē ə)] **1** a period of a thousand years. **2** according to the Bible, the time when Christ will return and reign on earth for a thousand years; hence, a period of perfection. ***—adj-*** **mil·len′ ni·al.**

mill·er (mĭl′ ər) ***n-*** **1** man who owns or runs a mill for grinding grain into flour or meal. **2** milling machine. **3** any moth with wings that seem dusted with flour.

---

fāte, făt, dâre, bärn; bē, bĕt, mêre; bīte, bĭt; nōte, hŏt, môre, dóg; fŭn, fûr; tōō, bŏŏk; oil; out; tar; thin; then; hw for wh as in *wh*at; zh for s as in u*s*ual; ə for a, e, i, o, u, as in *a*go, lin*e*n, per*i*l, at*o*m, min*u*s

mil·let (mĭl′ət) ***n-*** **1** a grass grown in Europe and Asia for its grain. In the United States it is used mainly as fodder. **2** the seed of this grass. **3** any of various other grasses resembling this grass.

milli- *combining form* **1** thousand: a milli*pede.* **2** a thousandth of (a stated unit): *a* milli*meter.* [from Latin **milli-**, from **mille** meaning "one thousand."]

mil·li·am·pere (mĭl′ ē ăm′ pêr′) ***n-*** electrical unit equal to one thousandth of an ampere.

mil·li·bar (mĭl′ ə bär′) ***n-*** unit for measuring atmospheric pressure, equal to a force of 1,000 dynes per square centimeter. Standard pressure at sea level is 1,013 millibars. *Abbr.* mb

mil·li·gram (mĭl′ ə grăm′) ***n-*** unit of weight in the metric system, equal to one thousandth of a gram. Also, *chiefly Brit.,* **mil′ li·gramme′.** *Abbr.* mg. or mg

mil·li·li·ter (mĭl′ ə lē′ tər) ***n-*** unit of capacity in the metric system, equal to one thousandth of a liter. Also *chiefly Brit.,* **mil′ li·li′ tre.** *Abbr.* ml. or ml

mil·li·me·ter (mĭl′ ə mē′ tər) ***n-*** unit of length in the metric system equal to one thousandth of a meter. Also, *chiefly Brit.,* **mil′ li·me′ tre.** *Abbr.* mm. or mm

mil·li·ner (mĭl′ ə nər) ***n-*** trimmer, maker, or seller of women's hats.

mil·li·ner·y (mĭl′ ə nĕr′ ē) ***n-*** **1** articles sold by a milliner, especially women's hats, but including laces, ribbons, and other trimmings. **2** the business of a milliner.

mill·ing (mĭl′ ĭng) ***n-*** **1** work in or of a mill, especially the making of flour and other cereal foods. **2** the ridges around a milled coin. **3** work of a milling machine.

milling machine ***n-*** machine tool for cutting and shaping metal by moving it against rotating cutters.

mil·lion (mĭl′ yən) ***n-*** **1** one thousand thousands; 1,000,000. **2** an indefinitely large number: *They asked* millions *of questions.* *as **modifier*** (always preceded by another determiner): *a* million *dollars here and a* million *there.*

mil·lion·aire (mĭl′ yə nâr′) ***n-*** a person having a million dollars or more, or property worth such an amount. **—*n-*** *fem.* **mil′ lion·air′ ess.**

mil·lion·fold (mĭl′ yən fōld′) ***n-*** million times: *This is larger by a* millionfold. ***adj-*** amounting to a million times: *a* millionfold *increase in production.*

mil·lionth (mĭl′ yənth) ***adj-*** **1** last in a series of a million. **2** the ordinal of 1,000,000. ***n-*** **1** the last in a series of a million. **2** one of a million equal parts of a whole or group. **3** the last term in the name of a common fraction having a denominator of 1,000,000, or of the corresponding decimal fraction .000001.

mil·li·pede (mĭl′ ə pēd′) ***n-*** any of a class of small wormlike animals resembling centipedes, but having more segments in the body, more legs, and no poison fangs.

mill·pond (mĭl′ pŏnd′) ***n-*** pond, usually formed by a dam, where water is stored to provide power for a mill.

mill·race (mĭl′ rās′) ***n-*** channel that leads water to a mill wheel; also, the current driving the wheel.

mill·stone (mĭl′ stōn′) ***n-*** either of a pair of large, grooved, circular stones used to grind grain.

Millstone

mill·stream (mĭl′ strēm′) ***n-*** stream that powers a mill; especially, the water in a millrace.

mill wheel ***n-*** water wheel that drives a mill.

mill·work (mĭl′ wûrk′) ***n-*** goods, especially woodwork, processed or finished in a mill.

mill·wright (mĭl′ rīt′) ***n-*** person who builds mills or installs their machinery.

mi·lord (mə lôrd′, -lôrd′) ***n-*** my lord.

milque·toast (mĭlk′ tōst′) ***n-*** shy or ineffectual person.

milt (mĭlt) ***n-*** the male reproductive glands of a fish when filled with seminal fluid; also, the fluid itself. ***vt-*** to impregnate (fish eggs) with milt.

mime (mīm, mēm) ***n-*** **1** (also **mim′ er**) an actor who portrays characters or narrates events through gesture and body movement, without speaking. **2** in classical times, an actor who performed in dramas that made fun of people or events. **3** such a performance. ***vt-*** **[mimed, mim·ing]** to imitate or mimic (someone or something) through gesture and body movement. ***vi-*** to perform as an actor without speaking.

Mim·e·o·graph (mĭm′ ē ə grăf′) ***n-*** trademark name for a machine that makes copies of drawings and typewritten or written material. ***vt-*** **mimeograph** to make copies of with such a machine: *to* mimeograph *a letter.*

mim·ic (mĭm′ ĭk) ***n-*** person who copies another's speech, actions, or looks, usually to entertain; imitator: *Some comedians are very skillful* mimics. ***vt-*** **[mim·icked, mim·ick·ing]** to copy in fun or mockery; imitate: *It is not easy to* mimic *a person without offending him.* ***adj-*** **1** imitative: *the* mimic *habits of a monkey.* **2** pretended; mock: *a* mimic *battle.*

mim·ic·ry (mĭm′ ə krē) ***n-*** [*pl.* **mim·ic·ries**] **1** the practice or art of mimicking. **2** close natural similarity of certain birds, animals, and insects to other natural objects, serving as concealment, protection, etc.

mi·mo·sa (mə mō′ sə, -zə) ***n-*** any of various plants related to the pea, including trees and shrubs, that grow in warm regions. The fernlike leaves of some of these fold or droop in the dark or when touched.

min. **1** minute or minutes. **2** minimum.

min·a·ret (mĭn′ ə rĕt′) ***n-*** slender tower of a mosque. From its balconies Muslims are called to prayers.

Twin minarets

mince (mĭns) ***vt-*** **[minced, minc·ing]** to chop or cut into fine pieces: *to* mince *an onion.* ***vi-*** to walk in a dainty, affected manner. ***n-*** mincemeat. *as **modifier:*** *a* mince *pie.*

not mince words (or **matters**) to speak or act in a direct and decisive way.

mince·meat (mĭns′ mēt′) ***n-*** mixture of finely chopped apples, raisins, currants, lemon peel, suet, and often meat, used as a pie filling.

minc·ing (mĭn′ sĭng) ***adj-*** speaking, walking, or behaving primly and affectedly. **—*adv-*** **minc′ ing·ly.**

mind (mīnd) ***n-*** **1** ability to think, reason, know, etc.; intellect; mentality: *to have a good* mind. **2** site or center of thought and reason, as distinguished from the body and the soul. **3** opinion; point of view: *to change one's* mind. **4** sound condition of the mental faculties; sanity: *He appeared to be losing his* mind. **5** person considered in terms of his mental ability: *He was one of the great* minds *of the age.* ***vt-*** (in senses 1 and 2 considered intransitive when the direct object is implied but not expressed) **1** to object to; resent: *I hope you don't* mind *being by yourself. He never seemed to* mind, *no matter how much we kidded him.* **2** to obey: *You must* mind *the policeman.* **3** to be careful of: *Please* mind *what you say.* **4** to take care of; care for: *to* mind *the baby.*

bear (or **keep) in mind** to remember. **be of one mind** to agree; share an opinion. **give (someone) a piece of (one's) mind** to express frankly and angrily. **have half a mind to** to be somewhat inclined to. **in (one's** or **the) mind's eye** as visualized or seen in the mind: *It remained vivid to him* in his mind's eye. **keep (one's) mind on** to concentrate (on something). **make up (one's) mind** to reach a decision. **never mind** pay no attention to; ignore or forget: *Something else has come up, so* never mind *that.* **on (one's) mind** in one's thoughts. **out of (one's) mind 1** mad; insane. **2** frantic or furious: *He's going* out of his mind *with worry.* **put (one) in mind of** to remind of; make one think of. **set (one's) mind on** to determine to do or get something: *Once he* sets his mind on *something he works tirelessly for it.* **slip (one's) mind** to be forgotten: *The exact date* slips my mind. **speak (one's) mind** to express frankly one's opinions, ideas, etc. **to (one's) mind** in one's opinion or judgment.

mind·ed (mīn′ dəd) ***adj-*** **1** having a mind of a certain kind or with a particular interest: *mathematics*-minded; *strong*-minded. **2** disposed or inclined; intending: *to be* minded *to swim.*

mind·ful (mīnd′ fəl) ***adj-*** aware (of); conscious (of); thoughtful: *Father was always* mindful *of the needs of the family.* **—*adv-*** **mind′ ful·ly.** ***n-*** **mind′ ful·ness.**

mind·less (mīnd′ ləs) ***adj-*** **1** showing no intelligence; dull-witted; stupid: *a* mindless *oaf.* **2** careless; heedless. **—*adv-*** **mind′ less·ly.** ***n-*** **mind′ less·ness.**

mind reader ***n-*** person who claims or is thought to be able to know another's thoughts. **—*n-*** **mind reading.**

[1]**mine** (mīn) ***pron-*** (possessive pronoun) thing or things belonging to me: *This hat is* mine. Mine *is green.* ***adj-*** *Archaic* my (used before words beginning with a vowel): *I will raise* mine *eyes unto the hills.* [from Old English **mīn** meaning "my; of me."]

[2]**mine** (mīn) ***n-*** **1** pit or excavation from which minerals, precious stones, etc., are dug; also, a deposit of ore or coal. **2** rich supply or source: *He is a* mine *of information.* **3** explosives placed underground or in the water to delay or destroy enemy troops, vehicles, or ships. ***vt-*** **[mined, min·ing] 1** to get by digging underground: *to* mine *coal.* **2** to dig into, as for ore or metals: *The company* mined *the entire hillside.* **3** to bury or place explosives in (a place where they will harm the enemy): *They* mined *the field.* ***vi-*** to work at digging up minerals. [from Old French **mine,** of Celtic origin.]

mine·field (mīn′ fēld′) ***n-*** an area, either on land or in water, in which explosive mines have been laid.

mine·layer (mīn′ lā′ ər) ***n-*** naval vessel that plants explosive mines in the water.

min·er (mī′ nər) ***n-*** person who works in or owns a mineral deposit. ***Hom-*** minor.

min·er·al (mĭn′ ər əl) ***n-*** substance that is neither animal nor vegetable; especially, a substance taken from the earth by mining: *Salt is a common* mineral. ***adj-***: *our* mineral *resources*; mineral *oil.*

min·er·al·o·gy (mĭn′ ə rŏl′ ə jē) ***n-*** science of minerals that deals with their origin, structure, classification, etc. **—*adj-*** **min′ er·a·log′ i·cal** (mĭn′ ər ə lŏj′ ĭ kəl).

min·er·al·o·gist (mĭn′ ə rŏl′ ə jĭst) ***n-*** person who is expert in and usually works in mineralogy.

mineral oil ***n-*** oil from a mineral source; especially, a clear oil used as a laxative.

mineral water ***n-*** water having a high mineral content; especially, water from springs and wells that is drunk and otherwise used for its supposed healthful effects.

Mi·ner·va (mĭ nûr′ və) ***n-*** in Roman mythology, the goddess of wisdom who presided over useful and ornamental arts. She is identified with the Greek Athena.

min·e·stro·ne (mĭn′ ə strōn′, -strō′ nē) ***n-*** thick vegetable soup of Italian type, having a meat stock as base.

mine·sweep·er (mīn′ swē′ pər) ***n-*** naval vessel that removes explosive mines from the water, or explodes them harmlessly, by sweeping their anchor lines with a long cable. **—*n-*** **mine′ sweep′ ing.**

Ming (mĭng) ***n-*** the Chinese dynasty that ruled from 1368 to 1644, a period noted for the skill of its artists and artisans, especially in porcelains. ***adj-***: *a* Ming *vase.*

min·gle (mĭng′ gəl) ***vi-*** **[min·gled, min·gling] 1** to mix: *The waters of the Missouri and Mississippi rivers* mingle *near St. Louis.* **2** to associate: *The soldiers were forbidden to* mingle *with their prisoners.* ***vt-*** to mix; intermingle: *One should not* mingle *sheep with tigers.*

ming tree (mĭng) ***n-*** **1** potted evergreen tree that has been artificially stunted. **2** an imitation dwarf tree made by combining various plant materials.

min·i·a·ture (mĭn′ ē ə chər, mĭn′ ə chər) ***adj-*** very small in scale; minute; tiny: *a* miniature *train*; *a* miniature *camera*; *a* miniature *Doberman pinscher.* ***n-*** **1** small model or reproduction: *a* miniature *of the Liberty Bell.* **2** a tiny portrait: *She wears a* miniature *in a brooch.*

in miniature in a tiny size or scale: *Rex is his father* in miniature.

min·i·a·tur·ize (mĭn′ ə chə rīz′, mĭn′ ē ə-) ***vt-*** **[min·i·a·tur·ized, min·i·a·tur·iz·ing]** to make (something) in small scale or size; especially, to design or make (radios, electron tubes, mechanisms, etc.) in very small size: *to* miniaturize *the guidance system of a rocket.*

min·im (mĭn′ əm) ***n-*** **1** smallest liquid measure, equal to one sixtieth of a fluid dram; about one drop. **2** in penmanship, a down stroke. **3** in music, a half note.

min·i·mal (mĭn′ ə məl) ***adj-*** pertaining to or being a minimum. **—*adv-*** **min′ i·mal·ly.**

min·i·mize (mĭn′ ə mīz′) ***vt-*** **[min·i·mized, min·i·miz·ing] 1** to reduce to the smallest degree, part, or proportion: *These devices* minimize *the danger of the flight.* **2** to make little of; deny the seriousness of: *He* minimized *the importance of what he had done.* **—*n-*** **min′ i·mi·za′ tion.** ***n-*** **min′ i·miz′ er.**

min·i·mum (mĭn′ ə məm) ***n-*** [*pl.* **min·i·mums** or **min·i·ma** (-mə)] **1** smallest amount possible or allowable: *Practice your music a* minimum *of an hour a day.* **2** lowest point or degree reached: *a* minimum *of 28° on the thermometer.* ***adj-*** **1** least possible or allowable; lowest possible: *the* minimum *mark for passing.* **2** lowest known or recorded: *a* minimum *rainfall of an inch a year.*

minimum wage ***n-*** wage fixed by law or contract as the lowest an employer may pay an employee.

min·ing (mī′ nĭng) ***n-*** **1** the work or business of taking ores, coal, etc., from the earth: *Coal* mining *is the chief industry of several states.* **2** the burying or planting of explosive mines. *as* ***modifier***: *a* mining *engineer.*

min·ion (mĭn′ yən) ***n-*** a flattering servant or follower: *He became the prince's* minion. ***Hom-*** minyan.

min·is·ter (mĭn′ ə stər) ***n-*** **1** clergyman, especially in a Protestant church. **2** diplomat sent to a foreign country to represent his government. **3** in some countries, the head of a major government department. ***vi-*** to give help, attention, or service: *Doctors* minister *to the sick.*

min·is·te·ri·al (mĭn′ ə stêr′ ē əl) ***adj-*** of or relating to a minister or to his office or duties.

min·is·trant (mĭn′ ə strənt) ***adj-*** serving; giving aid. ***n-*** one who serves or aids.

min·is·tra·tion (mĭn′ ə strā′ shən) ***n-*** **1** act of serving or aiding: *the* ministration *of a priest.* **2** service or aid given.

min·is·try (mĭn′ ə strē) ***n-*** [*pl.* **min·is·tries**] **1** the work, profession, or office of a clergyman: *He is studying for the* ministry. **2** in some countries, a major government department; also, the building this occupies. **3** service or length of service of a clergyman or officer of state: *During the* ministry *of Mr. Jones we built a new church.* 4 devoted service or help: *the* ministry *of nurses to the sick.* 5 church or government ministers as a group.

min·i·track (mĭn′ ĭ trăk′) *n-* electronic system that tracks the path of a rocket or earth satellite by means of radio signals.

American mink, about 20 in. long

mink (mĭngk) *n-* 1 a slender, aggressive, water-loving member of the weasel family. 2 the valuable fur of this animal. *as modifier: a* mink *stole; a* mink *muff.*

Minn. Minnesota.

min·now (mĭn′ ō) *n-* 1 any of several very small fresh-water fishes commonly used as bait. 2 any of several fishes, usually small, of the carp family.

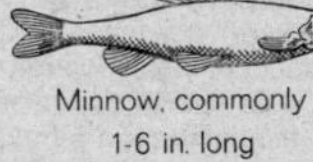

Minnow, commonly 1-6 in. long

Mi·no·an (mə nō′ ən) *adj-* of or relating to a Bronze Age civilization in Crete from about 3000-1100 B.C.

mi·nor (mī′ nər) *adj-* 1 small; insignificant: *a* minor *gain in the stock market*; *a* minor *incident.* 2 not dangerous or serious: *several* minor *injuries.* 3 lesser or smaller: *Land makes up the* minor *part of the earth's surface.* 4 less important; having secondary status: *a* minor *official*; *a* minor *poet.* 5 younger than the legal age of adulthood: *a* minor *child.* 6 *Music* relating to or based on a minor scale. *n-* 1 person younger than the legal age of adulthood. 2 college subject in which one concentrates, but to a lesser degree than one does in the major subject: *a major in history with a* minor *in sociology.* 3 *Music* a minor scale, or an arrangement or combination of notes based on such a scale. *vi-* to study or complete studies in a college subject in which one concentrates, but less than one does in a major subject: *to* minor *in Spanish.* ***Hom-*** miner.

mi·nor·i·ty (mə nŏr′ ə tē, mə nŏr′ ə tē, mī-) *n-* [*pl.* **mi·nor·i·ties**] 1 group or segment that is smaller in number than another group or segment with which it makes up a whole: *the* minority *of the votes cast*; *lefthanded people are in the* minority. 2 (also **minority group**) group of persons who are different in race, religion, etc., from most of the population. 3 period of time before one reaches the legal age of adulthood. *as modifier*: *a* minority *opinion*; *the* minority *vote.*

minor league *n-* in baseball, football, etc., a professional league in which the caliber of performance is generally below that of a major league, the rate of pay lower, etc. *as modifier* **(minor-league)**: *a* minor-league *team.* ***—n-*** **minor leaguer.**

minor scale *Music n-* any of several scales having half steps placed differently from those of the major scale.

Mi·nos (mī′ nŏs′) *n-* in Greek mythology, a king and lawgiver of Crete, and a son of Zeus.

Min·o·taur (mĭn′ ə tôr′) *n-* in Greek mythology, a monster, half man and half bull, confined by Minos to the Labyrinth.

min·ster (mĭn′ stər) *n-* 1 church of a monastery. 2 in England, a cathedral.

min·strel (mĭn′ strəl) *n-* 1 performer, usually one made up as a Negro, who sings, dances and jokes, in an entertainment called a **minstrel show,** popular in the United States after about 1850. 2 medieval entertainer who sang or recited stories, songs, ballads, etc., to music: *A band of* minstrels *amused the king and queen.*

min·strel·sy (mĭn′ strəl sē) *n-* the art of a minstrel; also, the songs of a minstrel.

¹mint (mĭnt) *n-* 1 any of several sweet-smelling herbs used for flavoring, such as the peppermint. 2 candy flavored with such an herb. [from Old English **minte**, from Latin **ment(h)a**, from Greek **minthē**.]

²mint (mĭnt) *n-* 1 place where coins are made by the government. 2 *Informal* vast amount, especially of money; fortune: *He made a* mint *in the iron and steel industries.* *vt-* 1 to make (coins) by stamping out of metal. 2 to make up or invent (a word, phrase, etc.). [from Old English **mynet**, from Latin **monēta**, which is also the source of the word **money**.]

in mint condition brandnew; fresh and unused: *an old book* in mint condition.

mint·age (mĭn′ tĭj) *n-* 1 act or process of coining money. 2 cost of coining. 3 imprint on a coin.

min·u·end (mĭn′ yōō ĕnd′) *n-* number from which another number, the subtrahend, is subtracted. In $4 - 2 = 2$, the minuend is 4.

min·u·et (mĭn′ yōō ĕt′) *n-* 1 slow, stately dance popular in the 17th and 18th centuries. 2 music for such a dance, often used as a movement in a larger composition.

mi·nus (mī′ nəs) *prep-* 1 less; decreased by: *Eight* minus *three is five.* 2 without: *He came home* minus *his tonsils.* *adj-* 1 negative; indicating a negative quantity: *a* minus *value*; *a* minus *three.* 2 and less; slightly below or lower than: *a grade of B* minus. 3 indicating subtraction: *a* minus *sign.* *n-* 1 sign [—] showing that the number following is to be subtracted. 2 a negative quantity; a subtraction; also, a negative thing or a disadvantage.

¹min·ute (mĭn′ ət) *n-* 1 sixty seconds; 1/60th of an hour. 2 1/60th of a degree in an angle or circle. 3 1/60th of a degree of latitude or longitude. 4 moment; very brief time: *I'll be back in a* minute. 5 specific point of time: *The doctor came the* minute *we sent for him.* 6 **minutes** official record of a meeting: *As secretary, Jim will read the* minutes *of our last meeting. Abbr.* min. [from Latin **minūta**, a form of **minūtus** meaning "²minute."]

up to the minute the very latest; the most modern.

²mi·nute (mī nōōt′; mī nyōōt′, mə-) *adj-* 1 extremely small; tiny: *Sand consists mainly of* minute *particles of rock.* 2 precise; detailed: *a* minute *description.* 3 trifling or insignificant: *It's of* minute *importance.* [from Latin **minūtus**, from **minuere** meaning "to make small," from **minor,** "less."] ***—adv-*** **mi·nute′ ly.** ***n-*** **mi·nute′ness.**

min·ute·man (mĭn′ ət măn′) *n-* [*pl.* **min·ute·men**] in the Revolutionary War, an American colonist ready for military service at a minute's notice.

mi·nu·ti·ae (mī nōō′ shē ī′, mə-) *n- pl.* [*sing.* **mi·nu·ti·a** (-ə)] small, precise, or trivial details.

minx (mĭngks) *n-* bold or saucy girl.

min·yan (mĭn′ yən) *n-* in Judaism, ten adult males, the minimum number that must be present to conduct lawful and valid services. ***Hom-*** minion.

Mi·o·cene (mī′ ə sēn′) *n-* the fourth of the five epochs of the Tertiary period. *adj-*: *the* Miocene *epoch.*

mir·a·cle (mĭr′ ə kəl) *n-* 1 event that cannot be explained by the laws of nature and is therefore believed to be caused by divine power: *The parting of the Red Sea is a* miracle *recorded in the Bible.* 2 wonder; marvel; highly unusual event: *It is a* miracle *that we won the game.*

miracle play *n-* a medieval drama enacting a miracle of some holy person, especially the Virgin Mary.

mi·rac·u·lous (mə răk′ yə ləs) *adj-* 1 in the nature of a miracle: *We read of the* miraculous *parting of the Red Sea.* 2 able to perform wonders; wonderful; marvelous: *a* miraculous *invention*; *a* miraculous *drug.* ***—adv-*** **mi·rac′ u·lous·ly.** ***n-*** **mi·rac′ u·lous·ness.**

mi·rage (mə räzh′) ***n-*** **1** optical illusion occurring on paved roads, deserts, etc., as a result of which images of lakes, distant scenes, etc., appear above or below the horizon, distorted, or inverted. It is caused by the refraction of light by layers of air of different temperatures that are near the ground. **2** something that seems real but is not; illusion: *His achievement was a* mirage.

mire (mīər) ***n-*** deep mud or slush: *We waded through the* mire *to reach the road.* ***vt-*** **[mired, mir·ing] 1** to soil with mud, slush, etc. **2** to cause to be stuck in or as if in mud: *to* mire *the wheels of a cart.*

mir·ror (mĭr′ ər) ***n-*** **1** implement having a reflecting surface, usually a piece of glass coated with silver on the back, and used for reflecting images or changing the direction of light rays. **2** a concave disk of glass or metal used to gather and focus light in an astronomical reflector. **3** something that helps give a clear impression or likeness: *Old newspapers are a* mirror *of past times.* ***vt-*** **1** to reflect: *The pond* mirrors *the house and garden.* **2** to show as if by reflection: *The book* mirrors *the life of a certain time.* ***—adj-*** **mir′ror·like′.**

mirth (mûrth) ***n-*** fun; merriment; jollity.

mirth·ful (mûrth′ fəl) ***adj-*** gay; jolly; merry: *a* mirthful *laugh.* ***—adv-*** **mirth′ ful·ly.** ***n-*** **mirth′ ful·ness.**

mirth·less (mûrth′ ləs) ***adj-*** having no gaiety, joy, or humor: *a* mirthless *smile.* ***—adv-*** **mirth′ less·ly.** ***n-*** **mirth′ less·ness.**

mir·y (mī′ ə rē, mī′ rē) ***adj-*** **[mir·i·er, mir·i·est]** muddy, slushy, or dirty: *a* miry *road.*

mis- *prefix* **1** bad or wrong: *a* mis*deed.* **2** badly or wrongly: *to* mis*spell*; mis*treat.*

mis·ad·ven·ture (mĭs′ əd vĕn′ chər) ***n-*** **1** bad luck; misfortune: *They failed through* misadventure, *not from lack of skill.* **2** mishap; piece of bad luck: *We had several* misadventures *on the trip.*

mis·al·li·ance (mĭs′ ə lī′ əns) ***n-*** harmful alliance, especially an improper or undesirable marriage.

mis·an·thrope (mĭs′ ən thrōp′) ***n-*** person who hates or distrusts mankind. Also **mis·an′ thro·pist** (mĭs ăn′- thrə pĭst).

mis·an·thro·py (mĭs ăn′ thrə pē) ***n-*** hatred or distrust of mankind. ***—adj-*** **mis′ an·throp′ ic** (mĭs′ ən thrŏp′ ĭk): *a bitter,* misanthropic *man.*

mis·ap·pli·ca·tion (mĭs′ ăp′ lə kā′ shən) ***n-*** a misapplying.

mis·ap·ply (mĭs′ ə plī′) ***vt-*** **[mis·ap·plied, mis·ap·ply·ing]** to use or apply (something) incorrectly or wrongfully: *to* misapply *one's skills.*

mis·ap·pre·hend (mĭs′ ăp′ rē hĕnd′) ***vt-*** to misunderstand; have a mistaken idea of: *to* misapprehend *an order*; *to* misapprehend *our motives.*

mis·ap·pre·hen·sion (mĭs′ ăp′ rə hĕn′ shən) ***n-*** **1** a misapprehending. **2** something wrongly understood: *Your belief is based on a* misapprehension.

mis·ap·pro·pri·ate (mĭs′ ə prō′ prē āt′) ***vt-*** **[mis·ap·pro·pri·at·ed, mis·ap·pro·pri·at·ing]** to take dishonestly for one's own use. ***—n-*** **mis′ ap·pro′ pri·a′ tion.**

mis·be·come (mĭs′ bĭ kŭm′) ***vt-*** **[mis·be·came, mis·be·come, mis·be·com·ing]** to be unsuitable or unbecoming to: *His acts* misbecome *him.*

mis·be·got·ten (mĭs′ bĭ gŏt′ ən) ***adj-*** wrongly or irregularly produced; especially, born out of wedlock.

mis·be·have (mĭs′ bĭ hāv′) ***vi-*** **[mis·be·haved, mis·be·hav·ing]** to behave badly. ***—n-*** **mis′ be·ha′ vior.**

mis·be·lief (mĭs′ bĭ lēf′) ***n-*** wrong or false belief.
►Should not be confused with UNBELIEF or DISBELIEF.

misc. 1 miscellaneous. **2** miscellany.

mis·cal·cu·late (mĭs′ kăl′ kyə lāt′) ***vt-*** **[mis·cal·cu·lat·ed, mis·cal·cu·lat·ing]** to make a mistake in; misjudge: *He* miscalculated *the amount.* ***vi-*** to make an error in judgment or foresight. ***—n-*** **mis′ cal′ cu·la′ tion.**

mis·called (mĭs′ kold′) ***adj-*** called by a wrong or unsuitable name.

mis·car·riage (mĭs′ kăr′ ĭj) ***n-*** **1** a failing or going wrong: *a* miscarriage *of justice.* **2** premature delivery of an embryo or a fetus that cannot survive.

mis·car·ry (mĭs′ kăr′ ē) ***vi-*** **[mis·car·ried, mis·car·ry·ing] 1** to go astray. **2** of plans, intentions, etc., to be unsuccessful. **3** of a woman, to deliver an embryo or a fetus that cannot survive.

mis·cast (mĭs′ kăst′) ***vt-*** **[mis·cast, mis·cast·ing] 1** to give an unsuitable role to (a performer). **2** to choose an unsuitable performer, or performers for.

mis·ceg·e·na·tion (mĭs′ ə jə nā′ shən) ***n-*** mating between persons of different races. [from Latin **miscere** meaning "to mix," plus Latin **genus,** "race."]

mis·cel·la·ne·ous (mĭs′ ə lā′ nē əs) ***adj-*** made up of more than one kind; mixed; heterogeneous: *a* miscellaneous *group*; *a* miscellaneous *catch of fish.* ***—adv-*** **mis′ cel·la′ ne·ous·ly.** ***n-*** **mis′ cel·la′ ne·ous·ness.**

mis·cel·la·ny (mĭs′ ə lā′ nē) ***n-*** [*pl.* **mis·cel·la·nies**] **1** group of things of different kinds: *a* miscellany *of goods in the shop window.* **2** book, periodical, or the like, containing a variety of literary compositions.

mis·chance (mĭs chăns′, mĭs′-) ***n-*** **1** bad luck; misfortune: *By* mischance, *he slipped and fell.* **2** piece of bad luck; mishap.

mis·chief (mĭs′ chəf) ***n-*** **1** foolish or thoughtless behavior that can harm or injure. **2** harm; injury: *People who carry tales about others can do great* mischief. **3** teasing; merry pranks: *She is full of* mischief *and is the life of every party.* **4** person who causes mischief, plays tricks, etc.: *That child is a little* mischief.

mis·chie·vous (mĭs′ chə vəs) ***adj-*** **1** playful in an annoying way; teasing: *That* mischievous *boy tied knots in my socks.* **2** harmful; causing injury: *a* mischievous *rumor.* ***—adv-*** **mis′ chie·vous·ly.** ***n-*** **mis′ chie·vous·ness.**

mis·ci·ble (mĭs′ ə bəl) ***adj-*** **1** such as can be mixed. **2** *Chemistry* of or having to do with liquids that are mutually soluble in each other: *Alcohol and water are* miscible.

mis·con·ceive (mĭs′ kən sēv′) ***vt-*** **[mis·con·ceived, mis·con·ceiv·ing]** to have a wrong understanding of; misunderstand: *He* misconceived *the problem.*

mis·con·cep·tion (mĭs′ kən sĕp′ shən) ***n-*** **1** failure of understanding: *Many mistakes result from* misconception. **2** mistaken idea or interpretation: *The belief that the earth is flat was a* misconception.

[1]**mis·con·duct** (mĭs kŏn′ dŭkt′) ***n-*** wrong behavior: *to punish for* misconduct.

[2]**mis·con·duct** (mĭs′ kən dŭkt′) ***vt-*** to manage badly: *to* misconduct *one's affairs.*
misconduct (oneself) to misbehave.

mis·con·struc·tion (mĭs′ kən strŭk′ shən) ***n-*** a misconstruing; failure to grasp the proper meaning.

mis·con·strue (mĭs′ kən stro͞o′) ***vt-*** **[mis·con·strued, mis·con·stru·ing]** to interpret wrongly or falsely; misunderstand; misconceive: *to* misconstrue *a road sign.*

[1]**mis·count** (mĭs′ kount′) ***vt-*** to count incorrectly.

[2]**mis·count** (mĭs′ kount′) ***n-*** a mistake in counting.

mis·cre·ant (mĭs′ krē ənt) ***n-*** villain. ***adj-*** villainous; unscrupulous.

mis·cue (mĭs′ kyōō′) ***n-*** **1** in billiards, a stroke in which the cue slips. **2** mistake or error; slip-up. ***vi-*** **[mis·cued, mis·cu·ing] 1** to make a billiards shot in which the cue slips. **2** to make a mistake. **3** in a play or other performance, to give or respond to the wrong cue. ***vt-*** to give (a performer) a wrong cue.

mis·date (mĭs′ dāt′) ***vt-*** **[mis·dat·ed, mis·dat·ing]** to give an incorrect date to.

mis·deal (mĭs′ dēl′) ***vi-*** **[mis·dealt, mis·deal·ing]** to deal cards wrongly. ***n-*** (*also* mĭs′ dēl′) a wrong dealing of a card or cards.

mis·deed (mĭs′ dēd′) ***n-*** wrong act; crime.

mis·de·mean·or (mĭs′ dĭ mē′ nər) ***n-*** **1** in law, any crime not punishable by death, by a term in a State prison, or by a prison term exceeding one year. See also *felony*. **2** any misbehavior.

mis·di·rect (mĭs′ də rĕkt′, -dī rĕkt′) ***vt-*** **1** to give false or incorrect instructions to: *He* misdirected *the tourist.* **2** to use or apply wrongly or foolishly: *to* misdirect *one's energies.* **3** to place a wrong address on (a letter, parcel, etc.). ***—n-*** **mis′ di·rec′ tion.**

mis·do·ing (mĭs′ dōō′ ĭng) ***n-*** wrongdoing.

mi·ser (mī′ zər) ***n-*** greedy and stingy person who loves money for its own sake; especially, one who hoards wealth and lives as though he were poor.

mis·er·a·ble (mĭz′ ər ə bəl) ***adj-*** **1** unhappy; wretched: *The dog gave a* miserable *howl when we left him alone.* **2** bad; worthless: *a* miserable *meal of stale bread and burnt meat.* **3** causing unhappiness, trouble, or annoyance: *a* miserable *headache.* ***—n-*** **mis′ er·a·ble·ness.** ***adv-*** **mis′ er·a·bly.**

Mi·se·re·re (mĭz′ ə rĕr′ ē, -rêr′ ē) ***n-*** **1** in the Bible, Psalm 51 (in the Vulgate and CCD version, Psalm 50). **2** musical setting for this psalm.

mi·ser·ly (mī′ zər lē) ***adj-*** greedy and tight-fisted; stingy; grasping. ***—n-*** **mi′ ser·li·ness.**

mis·er·y (mĭz′ ə rē) ***n-*** [*pl.* **mis·er·ies**] **1** great unhappiness, wretchedness, pain, etc.: *He is in* misery *with a bad toothache.* **2** wretched conditions: *Some people rise from* misery *to fortune.* **3** cause of distress or suffering: *toothaches and other* miseries.

mis·fire (mĭs′ fīər′) ***vi-*** **[mis·fired, mis·fir·ing] 1** of firearms, explosives, internal-combustion engines, etc., to fail to fire, explode, or ignite at the proper time. **2** of plans, endeavors, etc., to fail in reaching desired effects or results. ***n-***: *a* misfire *in an engine.*

mis·fit (mĭs′ fĭt′) ***n-*** **1** something that does not fit properly: *His coat was a* misfit *and his trousers baggy.* **2** person who is out of place among his associates or not properly adjusted to his environment: *Ned felt like a* misfit *in the new school.*

mis·for·tune (mĭs′ fôr′ chən, -fôr′ chən) ***n-*** **1** bad luck; adversity: *In spite of all his* misfortune *he had a cheerful* spirit. **2** stroke of bad luck; unlucky accident: *The hailstorm was a* misfortune *for the farmers.*

mis·give (mĭs gĭv′) *Archaic* ***vt- & vi-*** **[mis·gave, mis·giv·en, mis·giv·ing]** to fail in confidence or courage.

mis·giv·ing (mĭs gĭv′ ĭng) ***n-*** feeling of doubt, distrust, or worry: *He had no* misgivings *about his ability.*

mis·gov·ern (mĭs′ gŭv′ ərn) ***vt-*** to rule badly; mismanage. ***—n-*** **mis′ gov′ ern·ment.**

mis·guide (mĭs′ gīd′) ***vt-*** **[mis·guid·ed, mis·guid·ing]** to mislead; influence to wrong conduct or thought. ***—n-*** **mis′ guid′ ance.**

mis·guid·ed (mĭs′ gī′ dəd) ***adj-*** **1** incorrect; wrong; erroneous: *a* misguided *belief.* **2** under an improper influence: *a* misguided *boy.* ***—adv-*** **mis′ guid′ ed·ly.**

mis·han·dle (mĭs′ hăn′ dəl) ***vt-*** **[mis·han·dled, mis·han·dling]** to handle or treat badly; also, mismanage.

mis·hap (mĭs′ hăp′) ***n-*** minor accident or stroke of bad luck: *The spilling of the gravy was his only* mishap.

mish·mash (mĭsh′ măsh′) ***n-*** confused mixture; jumble; medley; hodgepodge.

mis·in·form (mĭs′ ĭn fôrm′, -fôrm′) ***vt-*** to give incorrect or false information to: *The clerk* misinformed *me.* ***—n-*** **mis′ in·for·ma′ tion.**

mis·in·ter·pret (mĭs′ ĭn tûr′ prət) ***vt-*** to form a wrong or false impression of; misconstrue; misconceive; misunderstand: *He* misinterpreted *the article.* ***—n-*** **mis′ in·ter′ pre·ta′ tion.**

mis·judge (mĭs′ jŭj′) ***vt-*** **[mis·judged, mis·judg·ing]** to make an error in judgment; make a wrong estimate of: *The baseball player* misjudged *the ball and dropped it.* ***vi-***: *Everyone* misjudges *at some time or another.* ***—n-*** **mis′ judg′ ment** or **mis′ judge′ ment.**

mis·lay (mĭs′ lā′) ***vt-*** **[mis·laid, mis·lay·ing] 1** to lose temporarily; put in a wrong place or place later forgotten: *Dad* mislaid *the key and can't unlock the door.* **2** to lay or set down incorrectly: *to* mislay *a carpet.*

mis·lead (mĭs′ lēd′) ***vt-*** **[mis·led, mis·lead·ing] 1** to deceive; give a false impression: *Her glowing account of the movie* misled *me.* **2** to lead astray: *Bad companions* misled *Joe and got him into trouble.*

mis·like (mĭs′ līk′) *Archaic* ***vt-*** **[mis·liked, mis·lik·ing]** to have an aversion to; dislike.

mis·man·age (mĭs′ măn′ ĭj) ***vt-*** **[mis·man·aged, mis·man·ag·ing]** to direct or administer (an organization, business, etc.) poorly. ***—n-*** **mis′ man′ age·ment.**

mis·match (mĭs′ măch′) ***vt-*** **1** to match (opponents in sports) unfairly or unsuitably: *to* mismatch *an amateur with a professional.* **2** to put together (things that do not belong together or go together well): *to* mismatch *a striped blouse with a plaid skirt.* ***n-*** a wrong or unsuitable matching or bringing together: *Their marriage was a* mismatch.

mis·name (mĭs′ nām′) ***vt-*** **[mis·named, mis·nam·ing]** to name wrongly or inappropriately; miscall.

mis·no·mer (mĭs′ nō′ mər) ***n-*** wrong name or term; incorrect use of a name: *It would be a* misnomer *to call a "bat" a "bird."*

mi·sog·a·mist (mə sŏg′ ə mĭst′) ***n-*** person who hates marriage.

mi·sog·y·nist (mə sŏj′ ə nĭst′) ***n-*** person who hates women.

mis·place (mĭs′ plās′) ***vt-*** **[mis·placed, mis·plac·ing] 1** to put somewhere and then forget where; mislay: *I have* misplaced *the letter with his new address.* **2** to put in the wrong place: *to* misplace *a comma.* **3** to give (trust, love, etc.) where it is not deserved. ***—n-*** **mis′ place′ ment.**

¹mis·play (mĭs′ plā′) ***n-*** in sports, a faulty play; error: *The* misplay *cost us the game.*

²mis·play (mĭs′ plā′) ***vt-*** in sports, to handle in a faulty manner: *He* misplayed *the ball.*

¹mis·print (mĭs′ prĭnt′) ***vt-*** to print (a letter, word, etc.) incorrectly.

²mis·print (mĭs′ prĭnt′) ***n-*** a mistake in printing.

mis·pro·nounce (mĭs′ prə nouns′) ***vt-*** **[mis·pro·nounced, mis·pro·nounc·ing]** to utter with a wrong sound or to accent a wrong syllable: *Clarence* mispronounces *"granted" as "granite."* ***—n-*** **mis′ pro·nun′ ci·a′ tion** (prə nŭn′ sē ā′ shən).

mis·quote (mĭs′ kwōt′) ***vt-*** **[mis·quot·ed, mis·quot·ing]** to quote the words of (a person, book, etc.) incorrectly. ***—n-*** **mis′ quo·ta′ tion.**

mis·read (mĭs′ rēd′) ***vt-*** **[mis·read, mis·read·ing] 1** to read incorrectly: *to* misread *directions.* **2** to misunderstand; interpret wrongly: *She sometimes* misreads *my expression and thinks I am angry.*

mis·rep·re·sent (mĭs′ rĕp′ rə zĕnt′) ***vt-*** to give a wrong impression of; report incorrectly, either willfully or through carelessness. ***—n-*** **mis′ rep′ re·sen·ta′ tion.**

mis·rule (mĭs′ ro͞ol′) ***vt-*** **[mis·ruled, mis·rul·ing]** to govern badly or unjustly. ***n-*** **1** disorder; unjust control; bad government. **2** confusion or tumult; disorder.

[1]**miss** (mĭs) ***vt-*** (in senses 1 and 2 considered intransitive when the direct object is clearly implied but not expressed) **1** to fail to hit, touch, or reach: *The boxer's punch* missed *its mark. He tried again but* missed. **2** to fail to catch or get: *I* missed *the bus and had to walk. He went for the fly ball but* missed *again.* **3** to fail to attend, hear, or watch: *He* missed *school for a week. She* missed *most of the show.* **4** to fail to find or recognize: *You can't* miss *my house.* **5** to fail to understand or appreciate: *She* missed *the point of the joke.* **6** to be sad at the absence or loss of: *We* miss *our friends when they go away.* **7** to realize the absence of: *I* missed *my purse when I went to buy a ticket.* **8** to overlook; fail to cover or deal with: *He* missed *several patches when he painted the wall.* **9** to fail to keep: *He* missed *his footing on the broken step.* **10** to avoid; escape: *He barely* missed *getting hurt.* **11** to fail to take advantage of; let go by: *to* miss *a good chance.* ***n-*** a failure to hit, touch, or reach: *His first shot was a* miss. [from Old English **missan** meaning "fail to hit (the mark)."]

[2]**miss** (mĭs) ***n-*** **1** young unmarried woman; girl: *She's a pretty little* miss. **2 Miss** title used before the name of a girl or unmarried woman: *She was* Miss *Cole before she married.* [a shortened form of **mistress.**]

Miss. Mississippi.

mis·sal (mĭs′ əl) ***n-*** in the Roman Catholic Church, a book containing the prayers read or sung during the Mass throughout the year. ***Hom-*** missile.

mis·shap·en (mĭs′ shā′ pən) ***adj-*** poorly shaped; deformed. ***—adv-*** **mis′ shap′ en·ly.**

mis·sile (mĭs′ əl) ***n-*** **1** guided missile. **2** any projectile, such as a bullet, mortar shell, spear, stone, etc. *as* ***modifier***: *a* missile *launcher.* ***Hom-*** missal.

mis·sile·man (mĭs′ əl mən) ***n-*** [*pl.* **mis·sile·men**] person who designs, builds, or operates guided missiles.

miss·ing (mĭs′ ĭng) ***adj-*** **1** lost; absent: *A page is* missing *from this history book. He is* missing *from class.* **2** not accounted for, in battle or other danger: *Six persons were dead and eight* missing.

mis·sion (mĭsh′ ən) ***n-*** **1** group of people sent to carry out a special task or assignment: *The United Nations sends* missions *to help countries with their problems.* **2** special task or assignment, especially of a military kind: *Our* mission *was to destroy the refinery.* **3** church, school, or building used by missionaries: *The Alamo was a Spanish* mission *before it was a fort.* **4** (also **mission in life**) person's lifework; calling. **5** attack in a bomber or other aircraft during a war: *He flew forty* missions *in Korea.* **6 missions** the establishment of churches and of schools, hospitals, and other services; missionary work.

mis·sion·ar·y (mĭsh′ ə nĕr′ ē) ***n-*** [*pl.* **mis·sion·ar·ies**] person who is sent to propagate a religion by attempting to convert others, especially in foreign lands. ***adj-*** of or relating to religious missions or to those who carry them out: *his* missionary *zeal.*

mis·sive (mĭs′ ĭv) ***n-*** letter or other written message.

mis·spell (mĭs′ spĕl′) ***vt-*** **[mis·spelled** or **mis·spelt, mis·spell·ing]** to spell incorrectly.

mis·spent (mĭs′ spĕnt′) ***adj-*** spent foolishly or for the wrong purposes; wasted.

mis·state (mĭs′ stāt′) ***vt-*** **[mis·stat·ed, mis·stat·ing]** to state falsely or incorrectly; misrepresent. ***—n-*** **mis′ state′ ment.**

mis·step (mĭs′ stĕp′) ***n-*** **1** a false step; stumble. **2** error in conduct.

miss·y (mĭs′ ē) *Informal* ***n-*** [*pl.* **miss·ies**] miss.

mist (mĭst) ***n-*** **1** visible, watery vapor in the atmosphere, at or near the earth's surface; fog; also, an accumulation of water in the atmosphere, either floating or falling in fine drops. **2** anything that dims the sight, either physically or mentally; dimness: *a* mist *of tears; a* mist *of confusion.* ***vi-*** to become misty or covered with tiny drops (often followed by "over"). ***vt-*** to cover with or as if with a fog; dim or obscure.

mis·take (mə stāk′) ***n-*** **1** error: *Your paper has six spelling* mistakes. **2** an error in judgment; defect; misunderstanding: *His conclusion was based on a* mistake. ***vt-*** **[mis·took, mis·tak·en, mis·tak·ing]** **1** to make an error in; misunderstand; be wrong about: *I* mistook *her joking and took it seriously.* **2** to take one person or thing for another: *I* mistook *you for Billy.*

mis·tak·en (mə stā′ kən) ***adj-*** wrong; incorrect: *a* mistaken *idea; a* mistaken *act.* ***—adv-*** **mis·tak′ en·ly.**

Mis·ter (mĭs′ tər) ***n-*** title of respect, usually written "Mr.," used before the name of a man or the name of his office: *my father,* Mr. *Smith;* Mr. *President.*

mis·tle·toe (mĭs′ əl tō′) ***n-*** parasitic evergreen plant that grows on the branches of trees and bears waxy, greenish-white berries. Sprigs of mistletoe are often used as Christmas decorations.

Mistletoe

mis·tral (mĭs′ trəl, mĭ străl′) ***n-*** dry, violent northwest wind in the Mediterranean provinces of France.

mis·trans·late (mĭs′ trăn′- slāt′) ***vt-*** **[mis·trans·lat·ed, mis·trans·lat·ing]** to translate incorrectly. ***—n-*** **mis′ trans′ la′ tion.**

mis·treat (mĭs′ trēt′) ***vt-*** to abuse; treat badly. ***—n-*** **mis′ treat′ ment.**

mis·tress (mĭs′ trəs) ***n-*** **1** woman at the head of a household, estate, etc. **2** woman who has a romantic affair with a man; sweetheart. **3** female owner of a horse, dog, or other animal. **4** in some schools, a title given to female teachers. **5 Mistress** a title once used before the name of any woman.

mis·tri·al (mĭs′ trī′ əl) ***n-*** court trial which is not finished or whose outcome is cancelled because of some error or irregularity of procedure.

mis·trust (mĭs′ trŭst′) ***n-*** lack of confidence; suspicion or doubt: *The situation filled him with* mistrust. ***vt-*** to doubt or suspect: *I* mistrust *his motives.* ***—adj-*** **mis′ trust′ ful.** ***adv-*** **mis′ trust′ ful·ly.**

mist·y (mĭs′ tē) ***adj-*** **[mist·i·er, mist·i·est]** **1** having mist; filled with mist; obscured by mist; slightly foggy: *a* misty *valley; the* misty *horizon; a* misty *morning.* **2** tearful; moist: *She didn't cry but her eyes were* misty. **3** not clear; vague: *a* misty *memory of a dream.* ***—adv-*** **mist′i·ly.** ***n-*** **mist′ i·ness.**

mis·un·der·stand (mĭs′ ŭn dər stănd′) ***vt-*** **[mis·un·der·stood, mis·un·der·stand·ing]** to take (a person, remark, etc.) in a wrong sense; mistake the meaning of. ***vi-***: *I think you've* misunderstood.

---

fāte, făt, dâre, bärn; bē, bĕt, mêre; bīte, bĭt; nōte, hŏt, môre, dȯg; fŭn, fûr; to͞o, bo͝ok; oil; out; tar; thin; then; hw for wh as in *wh*at; zh for s as in u*s*ual; ə for a, e, i, o, u, as in *a*go, lin*e*n, per*i*l, at*o*m, min*u*s

mis·un·der·stand·ing (mĭs′ ŭn′ dər stăn′ dĭng) ***n-*** **1** mistake as to meaning or motive: *Their* misunderstanding *of the recipe caused them to make a mess of the cake.* **2** disagreement; quarrel: *Their* misunderstandings *last only a little while.*

mis·us·age (mĭs′ yōō′ sĭj) ***n-*** **1** wrong or improper use of words. **2** ill-treatment; abuse.

[1]**mis·use** (mĭs′ yōōz′) ***vt-*** [**mis·used, mis·us·ing**] **1** to use wrongly: *to* misuse *a word; to* misuse *study time.* **2** to treat badly; to abuse: *to* misuse *a horse by making him run too fast.*

[2]**mis·use** (mĭs′ yōōs′) ***n-*** wrong use: *the* misuse *of privileges.*

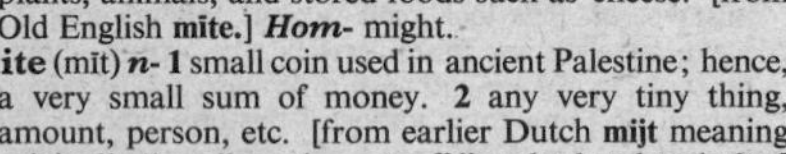
Mite (chigger larva)

[1]**mite** (mīt) ***n-*** any of several tiny, spiderlike creatures that live on plants, animals, and stored foods such as cheese. [from Old English **mīte.**] ***Hom-*** might.

[2]**mite** (mīt) ***n-*** **1** small coin used in ancient Palestine; hence, a very small sum of money. **2** any very tiny thing, amount, person, etc. [from earlier Dutch **mijt** meaning originally "small portion cut off," and related to [1]**mite.**] ***Hom-*** might.

mi·ter (mī′ tər) ***n-*** **1** tall, pointed headdress worn by popes, bishops, and abbots at special ceremonies. **2** (often **miter joint**) joint, such as those at the corners of picture frames, formed by fitting together two pieces cut at a slant. ***vt-*** to join or form in this manner. Also, *chiefly Brit.,* **mi′ tre.**

Miter joint

miter box ***n-*** device for guiding a handsaw in making miter joints.

mit·i·gate (mĭt′ ə gāt′) ***vt-*** [**mit·i·gat·ed, mit·i·gat·ing**] to make less severe or painful: *Time* mitigates *grief.* —***n-*** **mit′ i·ga′ tion.**

mi·to·chon·dri·a (mī′ tə kŏn′ drē ə) ***n-*** *pl.* [*sing.* **mi·to·chon·dri·on** (-ən)] tiny granular bodies found in the cytoplasm of all cells having a nucleus. They contain RNA and enzymes, which produce energy for the cell's processes.

mi·to·sis (mī tō′ səs) *Biology* ***n-*** process of cell division consisting of five stages (interphase, anaphase, metaphase, prophase, and telophase) in which the chromosomes replicate, the cell splits, and two new cells are produced, each having the same number of chromosomes as the original cell. See also *meiosis.*

mi·tral valve (mī′ trəl) ***n-*** valve of the heart that controls the flow of blood between the left auricle and left ventricle.

mitt (mĭt) ***n-*** **1** kind of glove without fingers or with half fingers. **2** mitten. **3** padded glove used in baseball.

mit·ten (mĭt′ ən) ***n-*** covering for the hand with one place for the fingers and a smaller place for the thumb.

mitz·vah (mĭts′ və) ***n-*** [*pl.* **mitz·vahs** or **mitz·voth** (-vōth)] **1** commandment or rule of conduct of the Jewish law. **2** good deed or generous act.

mix (mĭks) ***vt-*** **1** to unite or blend into one mass or substance: *to* mix *paint.* **2** to make by putting ingredients together: *to* mix *a cake.* ***vi-*** **1** to become united or blended: *Oil does not* mix *with water.* **2** to mingle; associate; take part: *to* mix *with the crowd; to* mix *well.* ***n-*** combination of ingredients: *a package of cake* mix. **mix up 1** to confuse: *He always* mixes up *our names.* **2** to be involved: *He is* mixed up *in the affair.*

mixed (mĭkst) ***adj-*** **1** of different kinds: *a bowl of* mixed *nuts.* **2** for or consisting of persons of opposite sex: *a* mixed *class;* mixed *doubles in tennis.* **3** having members or parts of widely different types: *a* mixed *crowd.*

mixed farming ***n-*** the operation of a single farm to produce cash crops, feed crops, and livestock.

mixed metaphor ***n-*** metaphor or comparison that is ridiculous because it consists of parts that contradict one another or obviously do not belong together. Example: His flaming temper dampens all our fun.

mixed number ***n-*** number expressed as an integer plus a proper fraction, such as $3\frac{3}{4}$.

mix·er (mĭk′ sər) ***n-*** **1** device or machine for mixing ingredients: *an electric* mixer; *a cement* mixer. **2** person or thing that combines or associates with others: *He hates crowds, and is a poor* mixer *at parties.*

mix·ture (mĭks′ chər) ***n-*** **1** something made by or resulting from mixing, blending, or combining different things, kinds, qualities, etc.: *to add cream to a* mixture; *a* mixture *of tobacco.* **2** act or process of mixing: *The* mixture *of yellow and blue produces green.* **3** *Chemistry* combination of two or more substances that mingle together to form a whole but do not lose their individual chemical properties (see also *compound*).

mix-up (mĭks′ ŭp′) ***n-*** confused situation; snarl: *a* mix-up *in the train schedule.*

miz·zen (mĭz′ ən) ***n-*** **1** fore-and-aft sail set on the mizzenmast. **2** lowest square sail on the mizzenmast of a full-rigged ship. **3** mizzenmast.

miz·zen·mast (mĭz′ ən măst′, -məst) ***n-*** **1** rear mast in a two-masted or three-masted vessel. **2** the third mast from the bow in a vessel with four or more masts.

mks or **MKS** the system of measurement using the meter, kilogram, and second for length, weight, and time.

ml. or **ml** milliliter or milliliters.

Mlle. mademoiselle.

Mlles. mesdemoiselles.

mm. or **mm** millimeter or millimeters.

MM. messieurs.

Mme. madame.

Mmes. mesdames.

Mn symbol for manganese.

mne·mon·ic (nə mŏn′ ĭk) ***adj-*** **1** serving to help the memory: *Some shorthand symbols are* mnemonic *devices.* **2** of or having to do with memory: *a* mnemonic *skill.*

Mne·mos·y·ne (nə mŏs′ ə nē) ***n-*** in Greek mythology, the goddess of memory and mother of the Muses.

Mo symbol for molybdenum.

mo. month.

Mo. Missouri.

M.O. or **m.o. 1** money order. **2** medical officer.

mo·a (mō′ ə) ***n-*** any of various large, extinct birds of New Zealand, resembling the ostrich.

moan (mōn) ***n-*** low, drawn-out sound of sorrow or pain; hence, any similar sound: *the* moans *of the wounded man; the* moan *of the wind.* ***vi-***: *The sick child* moaned *in his sleep.* ***vt-***: *to* moan *a curse.*

moat (mōt) ***n-*** deep ditch, usually filled with water, surrounding a fortress or castle; also, any similar ditch, such as one surrounding an animal enclosure at a zoo. ***Hom-*** mote.

Moat

mob (mŏb) ***n-*** **1** large, disorderly, or violent crowd of people. **2** *Informal* a criminal gang. **3 the mob** the masses. ***vt-*** [**mobbed, mob·bing**] **1** to attack in a mob. **2** to crowd around and annoy or jostle. **3** to fill (a hall, theatre, etc.) to overflowing: *The lobby was* mobbed.

[1]**mo·bile** (mō′ bəl, -bīl′, -bēl′) ***adj-*** **1** movable; easily moved: *A* mobile *library operates from a truck.* **2** able to change quickly or easily: *an actor's* mobile *features; a*

mobile *mind.* 3 capable of moving from one class or group to another: *a* mobile *society.* —*n-* **mo·bil′i·ty.**

²**mo·bile** (mō′ bēl′) *n-* sculpture or decoration made of bits of colored paper, glass, wood, wire, etc., hung so that it revolves freely.

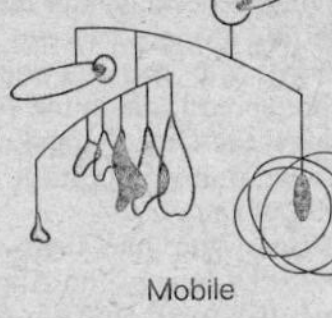
Mobile

mo·bil·ize (mō′ bə līz′) *vt-* [**mo·bi·lized, mo·bil·iz·ing**] to assemble and organize for active service or use: *to* mobilize *an army.* —*n-* **mo′bil·i·za′tion.**

Mö·bi·us strip (mō′bē əs, mφ′-) *n-* a surface studied in topology that, despite its apparent form, has only a single side and edge. It is made by half twisting one end of a paper strip and then fastening it to the other end.

mob·ster (mŏb′ stər) *Slang n-* gangster.

moc·ca·sin (mŏk′ ə sən) *n-* 1 soft, flat-soled leather shoe originally worn by American Indians. 2 water moccasin.

Moccasin

moccasin flower *n-* any of several lady's-slippers common in the United States, usually with a pink flower.

mo·cha (mō′ kə) *n-* fine coffee originally grown in Mocha, Arabia. *adj-* flavored with coffee or with coffee and chocolate: *a cake with* mocha *icing.*

mock (mŏk) *vt-* 1 to ridicule; make fun of: *He* mocked *his opponent's ideas.* 2 to mimic scornfully or teasingly: *to* mock *someone's way of speaking.* 3 to defy or scorn: *to* mock *the law.* *vi-* to express contempt or derision: *He* mocked *at the idea of a peaceful settlement.* *adj-* not real or genuine; make-believe: *a* mock *wedding*; *a* mock *battle.* *n-* something ridiculous or contemptible: *to make a* mock *of justice.* —*n-* **mock′er.** *adv-* **mock′ing·ly.**

mock·er·y (mŏk′ ə rē) *n-* [*pl.* **mock·er·ies**] 1 scornful contempt; derision; ridicule: *The* mockery *in his voice was obvious.* 2 person or thing made fun of. 3 poor or disrespectful imitation: *The trial was a* mockery *of justice.*

mock-he·ro·ic (mŏk′ hĭ rō′ ĭk) *adj-* ridiculing or satirizing heroic action, character, or style: *a* mock-heroic *poem.* —*adv-* **mock′-he·ro′i·cal·ly.**

mock·ing·bird (mŏk′ ĭng bûrd′) *n-* bird of southern United States, about the size of a robin, noted for imitating the calls of other birds.

Mockingbird, 10 1/2 in. long

mock orange *n-* ornamental shrub with fragrant white flowers, related to the lilac; syringa.

mock turtle soup *n-* soup made of meat, seasoned to taste like soup made from the green turtle.

mock-up (mŏk′ ŭp′) *n-* model of an airplane, machine, etc., usually full-sized, for teaching, testing, or display.

mod·al auxiliary (mō′ dəl) *Grammar n-* the term used for those auxiliary verbs such as "can," "do," "may," "will," etc., which combine with infinitives to form finite verb phrases. Examples: *Henry and James* may *arrive tonight. I* should *leave in half an hour.*

mode (mōd) *n-* 1 way, method, or manner of doing something: *a* mode *of speaking*; *a* mode *of travel.* 2 style or fashion in the manner of dress: *Top hats were the* mode *fifty years ago.* 3 *Grammar* mood. 4 *Music* any of various arrangements of the tones of an octave. 5 *Mathematics* score or item that occurs most frequently in a statistical distribution.

mod·el (mŏd′ əl) *n-* 1 person or thing that serves as an example of some desirable quality: *She is a* model *of integrity.* 2 small copy of something: *an airplane* model. 3 figure or copy of something to be reproduced: *a clay* model *for a monument*; *an architect's* model *for a house.* 4 person who poses for a photographer, painter, or sculptor. 5 person who displays or advertises clothes by wearing them: *a fashion* model. 6 style or design of something: *This car is the latest* model. 7 in science, a simplified scheme or structure that corresponds part for part with some complex process, system, or structure and is used to explain its operation. *as modifier*: *a* model *student.* *vt-* 1 to form or mold: *to* model *a head in plaster.* 2 to display by wearing: *to* model *a dress.* 3 to pattern (oneself) after something or someone. *vi-* 1 to shape or fashion: *The sculptor* models *in clay.* 2 to pose, or to wear and display clothes. —*n-* **mod′el·er.**

mod·el·ing (mŏd′ əl ĭng) *n-* 1 the act or profession of a person who models. 2 form produced by or as if by being sculptured: *the* modeling *of her features.*

¹**mod·er·ate** (mŏd′ ər ət) *adj-* 1 midway between extremes; not excessive: *a* moderate *price*; *a* moderate *climate.* 2 not radical or violent; reasonable; mild: *He is a man of* moderate *views.* 3 neither good nor bad; limited: *She had* moderate *success as an actress.* *n-* person who holds views on politics, religion, etc., that are not extreme or violent. —*adv-* **mod′er·ate·ly.**

²**mod·er·ate** (mŏd′ ə rāt′) *vt-* [**mod·er·at·ed, mod·er·at·ing**] 1 to keep within bounds; make less violent, intense, or extreme: *During the argument he* moderated *his views.* 2 to preside over (a discussion, meeting, etc.). *vi-* to become less violent or intense: *The rain* moderated.

mod·er·a·tion (mŏd′ ə rā′ shən) *n-* 1 a moderating; becoming milder or less extreme: *a gradual* moderation *of the climate.* 2 a limiting or restraining, especially of personal behavior; avoidance of overdoing or overindulging: *to eat with* moderation.

in moderation within reasonable bounds; not to excess.

mod·e·ra·to (mŏd′ ə rä′ tō) *Music adj- & adv-* in moderate tempo; slower than allegretto but faster than andante.

mod·er·a·tor (mŏd′ ə rā′ tər) *n-* 1 person or thing that restrains: *Courtesy is a* moderator *of conduct.* 2 presiding officer, especially at a panel discussion.

mod·ern (mŏd′ ərn) *adj-* of or having to do with the present or the recent past: *a* modern *painting.* *n-* 1 person of recent or present times. 2 person with up-to-date views, manners, habits, etc. —*n-* **mod′ern·ness.**

modern history *n-* history of events since about 1500 A.D.

mod·ern·ism (mŏd′ ər nĭz′ əm) *n-* 1 way of thinking or acting characteristic of modern times; any present-day practice, usage, taste, style, or idea. 2 style or theory of modern art, especially of painting, architecture, etc., that breaks with past traditions. —*n-* **mod′ern·ist**: *In architecture he is a* modernist. *adj-* **mod′ern·is′tic.**

mod·ern·i·ty (mə dûr′ nə tē) *n-* condition of being modern.

mod·ern·ize (mŏd′ ər nīz′) *vt-* [**mod·ern·ized, mod·ern·iz·ing**] to make modern or suitable for present needs; to bring up to date: *to* modernize *a house.* —*n-* **mod′ern·i·za′tion.**

mod·est (mŏd′ əst) ***adj-*** **1** not boastful or vain of one's own worth; unassuming. **2** not grand or showy; simple: *a* modest *house*; *the* modest *violet*. **3** not excessive or extreme; moderate: *a* modest *ambition*; *a* modest *price*. **4** having or showing a sense of what is proper or suitable; decent. ***—adv-*** **mod′ est·ly.**

mod·es·ty (mŏd′ ə stē) ***n-*** **1** lack of conceit; freedom from vanity. **2** decency in behavior, dress, etc. **3** simplicity; moderation: *the* modesty *of his needs*.

mod·i·cum (mŏd′ ĭ kəm) ***n-*** small amount: *a* modicum *of success*.

mod·i·fi·ca·tion (mŏd′ ə fə kā′ shən) ***n-*** **1** a modifying; changing. **2** a change; alteration: *Your plans need some* modifications. **3** something that has been modified: *This plan is a* modification *of his first one*.

mod·i·fi·er (mŏd′ ə fī′ ər) ***n-*** **1** someone or something that modifies. **2** *Grammar* word or group of words that modifies another word or word group. A one-word modifier may be an adjective, an adverb, or a noun. Examples:

I like the red *chair*. (adjective limiting a noun)
The house is just *over the hill*. (adverb clarifying a prepositional phrase)
He drove slowly. (adverb limiting a verb)
The train is very *fast*. (adverb strengthening an adjective)
He had a business *conference*. (noun modifier limiting another noun)

mod·i·fy (mŏd′ ə fī′) ***vt-*** **[mod·i·fied, mod·i·fy·ing] 1** to change; alter: *Having learned the facts, he* modified *his opinion*. **2** *Grammar* to limit the meaning of, or describe, a word or group of words in the same part of the sentence. In the following sentences, "red" is a modifier (adjective) modifying "kite": *We had a* red *kite*. *The* red *kite won the prize*. ***—adj-*** **mod′ i·fi′ a·ble.**

mod·ish (mō′ dĭsh) ***adj-*** fashionable; stylish: *a* modish *hat*. ***—adv-*** **mod′ ish·ly.** ***n-*** **mod′ ish·ness.**

mo·diste (mō dēst′) ***n-*** woman who makes fashionable clothes as a business.

Mo·doc (mō′ dŏk′) ***n-*** [*pl.* **Mo·docs,** also **Mo·doc**] member of a tribe of American Indians who lived in California and Oregon and are now in Oklahoma.

mod·u·lar arithmetic (mŏj′ ə lər) ***n-*** any of a group of numeration systems in which numbers are arranged as on a clock's face, so that addition proceeds in a clockwise direction, and subtraction in a counterclockwise direction. In modular arithmetic, starting at the noon position, $3 + 11 = 2$.

mod·u·late (mŏj′ ə lāt′) ***vt-*** **[mod·u·lat·ed, mod·u·lat·ing] 1** to vary the tone, volume, or pitch of: *to* modulate *the voice*. **2** to adjust; regulate. **3** to vary the amplitude, frequency, etc., of (a carrier wave) according to the sound or picture being broadcast. ***vi-*** *Music* to pass from one key to another in a composition or passage.

mod·u·la·tion (mŏj′ ə lā′ shən) ***n-*** **1** a modulating or a being modulated. **2** *Music* a passing from one key to a related key. **3** in electronics, the process in which the amplitude, frequency, or phase of a carrier wave is made to vary in accordance with the signal, sound, etc., being broadcast; also, the result of this process. See also *amplitude modulation* and *frequency modulation*.

mod·u·la·tor (mŏj′ ə lā′ tər, mŏd′ yə-) ***n-*** electronic device for producing modulation.

mod·ule (mŏj′ o͞ol′, mŏd′ yo͞ol′) ***n-*** **1** any standardized unit of measurement. **2** an assembly of parts used as a unit in house construction, furniture, missiles, etc.

mod·u·lus (mŏj′ ə ləs) ***n-*** [*pl.* **mod·u·li** (-lē, -lī)] **1** number that shows the extent to which a substance has a certain property; coefficient. **2** *Mathematics* in a modular arithmetic, the number of numbers.

mo·dus o·pe·ran·di (mō′ dəs ŏp′ ə răn′ dē, -dī′) *Latin* manner in which a person or thing works or operates.

mo·dus vi·ven·di (mō′ dəs və vĕn′ dē) *Latin* manner of living; especially, a practical, often temporary method of getting along.

Mo·gul (mō′ gəl) ***n-*** **1** one of the Mongolian Muslims who conquered India in the 16th century. Each emperor was called the **Great Mogul. 2** a descendant of these people. **3 mogul** any important or powerful person. ***adj-***: *the* Mogul *empire*.

mo·hair (mō′ hâr′) ***n-*** woven fabric or yarn made from the silky hair of the Angora goat.

Mo·ham·med (mō hăm′ əd) ***n-*** Arabian prophet (570?-632) and founder of Islam. Also **Ma·hom′et, Mu·ham′ med.**

Mo·ham·med·an (mō hăm′ ə dən) ***n-*** word often used to mean "Muslim," but disliked by the Muslims. ***adj-*** of or relating to Mohammed or his followers.

Mo·ham·me·dan·ism (mō hăm′ ə də nĭz′ əm) ***n-*** term improperly used for "Islam" and disliked by Muslims.

Mo·hawk (mō′ hȯk′) ***n-*** [*pl.* **Mo·hawks,** also **Mo·hawk**] one of a tribe of Iroquoian Indians who belonged to the Five Nations Confederacy.

Mo·he·gan (mō hē′ gən) ***n-*** [*pl.* **Mo·he·gans,** also **Mo·he·gan**] one of a tribe of Algonquian Indians who formerly lived along the Thames River in Connecticut. ►Should not be confused with MAHICAN.

Mo·hi·can (mō hē′ kən) Mahican.

Mo·ho (mō′ hō′) ***n-*** rock layer of unknown composition, which forms a boundary between the mantle and crust of the earth.

Mo·hole Project (mō′ hōl′) ***n-*** project to drill a hole through the ocean floor and the Moho for the purpose of scientific study of the earth's mantle.

Mohs' scale (mōz) ***n-*** scale for determining the hardness of a mineral according to its ability to scratch or be scratched by any of ten different minerals. Talc is rated the softest of the ten, and diamond the hardest.

moi·e·ty (moi′ ə tē) ***n-*** [*pl.* **moi·e·ties**] **1** a half. **2** portion or share.

moi·ré (mwä rā′) ***adj-*** having a changeable wavy or rippled appearance. ***n-*** fabric, usually of silk or rayon, having such an appearance.

moist (moist) ***adj-*** **1** damp; not dry: *a* moist *cake*. **2** tearful: *her* moist *eyes*. ***—adv-*** **moist′ ly.** ***n-*** **moist′ ness.**

moist·en (mois′ ən) ***vt-*** to make slightly wet or damp: *to* moisten *a stamp*. ***vi-***: *Her eyes* moistened.

mois·ture (mois′ chər) ***n-*** water or other liquid in the air, in a substance, or condensed on a surface.

mol (mōl) [4]mole.

mo·lar (mō′ lər) ***n-*** one of the large teeth in the back of the jaws, used for grinding food. For picture, see *tooth*.

mo·las·ses (mə lăs′ əz) ***n-*** [*pl.* **mo·las·ses**] dark-colored syrup obtained as a by-product in refining cane sugar.

[1]**mold** (mōld) ***n-*** **1** hollow form or container into which something soft or liquid, such as gelatin, molten metal, plaster, etc., is poured to be shaped. **2** something formed in or by such a container: *a* custard *mold*. **3** physical shape; form: *the* mold *of his cheek*. **4** kind; character; type: *a man of honest* mold. ***vt-*** **1** to shape: *to* mold *dough into loaves*. **2** to influence or direct: *to* mold *public opinion*; *to* mold *character*. [from Old French **modle,** "model; shape," from Latin **modus,** "mode."]

[2]**mold** (mōld) ***n-*** fine, soft soil, rich in decayed matter such as leaves. [from Old English **molde.**]

[3]**mold** (mōld) ***n-*** fuzzy fungus growth appearing on the surface of decaying foods, damp leather, wood, etc., and spreading quickly in moist or warm air. ***vi-*** to become covered with such fungus. [of unknown origin.]

mold·board (mōld′ bôrd′) ***n-*** the curved metal plate of a plow that lifts and turns the soil.

[1]mold·er (mōl′ dər) ***vi-*** to crumble to dust by natural decay: *The old walls* moldered. [probably from **[3]mold.**]

[2]mold·er (mōl′ dər) ***n-*** person or thing that molds, shapes, or influences: *a* molder *of public opinion.* [from **[1]mold.**]

mold·ing (mōl′ dĭng) ***n-*** **1** act of shaping by or as if by a mold. **2** a thing so shaped. **3** strip of wood or plaster placed along the wall or ceiling of a room for hanging pictures or for decoration.

mold·y (mōl′ dē) ***adj-*** **[mold·i·er, mold·i·est]** **1** covered with mold: *the* moldy *bread.* **2** damp; musty: *a* moldy *cellar.* **—*n-* mold′ i·ness.**

[1]mole (mōl) ***n-*** dark-colored spot or growth on the skin. [from Old English **māl** of the same meaning.]

[2]mole (mōl) ***n-*** small animal with brownish or grayish velvety fur and tiny, almost sightless eyes. Its large front feet are suited to digging, and it spends most of its life underground. [from Middle English **molle.**]

Mole, about 6 in. long

[3]mole (mōl) ***n-*** **1** solid stone wall or pier built out into the sea to break the force of the waves. **2** harbor formed by such a breakwater. [from French, from Latin **mōlēs,** "mass; heap."]

[4]mole (mōl) *Chemistry* ***n-*** gram molecule. Also **mol.** [from German **mol,** shortened from **molekulargewicht,** "molecular weight."]

mo·lec·u·lar (mə lĕk′ yə lər) ***adj-*** of, having to do with, or produced by molecules.

molecular weight ***n-*** of a molecule, the sum of the atomic weights of its atoms.

mol·e·cule (mŏl′ ə kyōōl′) ***n-*** **1** *Chemistry* the smallest particle of an element or compound that can exist independently and still retain the chemical properties of a larger amount of the element or compound. He, O_2, and H_2O are molecules. **2** any tiny part or thing.

mole·hill (mōl′ hĭl′) ***n-*** mound made by a mole.

mo·lest (mə lĕst′) ***vt-*** **1** to interfere with; annoy; disturb. **2** to annoy in an indecent way. **—*n-* mo′ les·ta′ tion.** ***n-*** **mo·lest′ er.**

moll (mŏl) *Slang* ***n-*** female gangster or female companion of a gangster.

mol·li·fy (mŏl′ ə fī′) ***vt-*** **[mol·li·fied, mol·li·fy·ing]** to soothe; calm; make less violent: *to* mollify *an angry person.* **—*n-* mol′ li·fi·ca′ tion.**

mol·lusk (mŏl′ əsk) ***n-*** any of a large phylum **(Mollusca)** of animals having soft bodies usually enclosed in a hard shell. Snails, oysters, clams, and octopuses are mollusks. Also **mol′ lusc.**

mol·ly·cod·dle (mŏl′ ē kŏd′ əl) ***n-*** coddled or pampered person, especially a man or boy. ***vt-*** **[mol·ly·cod·dled, mol·ly·cod·dling]**: *Don't* mollycoddle *him.*

Mo·loch (mō′ lŏk′, also mŏl′ ək) ***n-*** ancient Semitic deity to whom human sacrifices were offered; hence, anything demanding frightening sacrifices. Also **Mo′ lech.**

molt (mōlt) ***vi-*** to shed a shell, feathers, skin, horns, etc., which are replaced by a new growth. ***vt-***: *The snake* molted *its skin.* ***n-*** the act or process of thus shedding. Also **moult.**

molt·en (mōl′ tən) ***adj-*** made fluid by heat; melted: *a drop of* molten *lead.*

mol·to (mōl′ tō′) *Music* ***adv-*** much; very.

mo·ly (mō′ lē) ***n-*** in ancient legend, and especially in Homer's "Odyssey," an herb with magical powers.

mo·lyb·de·num (mə lĭb′ də nəm) ***n-*** hard, silvery-gray, metal element chiefly used as an alloying metal to harden steel. Symbol Mo, At. No. 42, At. Wt. 95.94.

mom (mŏm) *Informal* ***n-*** mother (used chiefly when addressing or referring to one's own mother).

mo·ment (mō′ mənt) ***n-*** **1** instant; certain point in time: *I waved the* moment *I saw you.* **2** present time: *the hero of the* moment. **3** importance: *news of great* moment.

mo·men·tar·i·ly (mō′ mən tĕr′ ə lē) ***adv-*** **1** at or for the moment; for a short time: *I am* momentarily *out of cash.* **2** in a moment; very soon: *He will be here* momentarily. **3** moment by moment: *He is growing* momentarily *worse.*

mo·men·tar·y (mō′ mən tĕr′ ē) ***adj-*** **1** lasting for a moment: *a* momentary *silence.* **2** happening at any moment: *A spy must expect* momentary *capture.* **—*n-* mo′ men·tar′ i·ness.**

mo·men·tous (mō mĕn′ təs) ***adj-*** very important; of great consequence: *a* momentous *decision.* **—*adv-* mo·men′ tous·ly.** ***n-*** **mo·men′ tous·ness.**

mo·men·tum (mō mĕn′ təm) ***n-*** **1** *Physics* a measure of the amount of force required to stop a moving body within a given time, defined as the product of its mass and velocity. **2** forward motion; impetus.

Mon. Monday.

mo·nad·nock (mə năd′ nŏk′) ***n-*** hill or mass of resistant rock which stands well above the surface of a surrounding plain. Monadnocks are remnants of highlands.

mon·arch (mŏn′ ərk) ***n-*** **1** hereditary ruler of a constitutional monarchy, such as a king or queen; also, the supreme ruler of a kingdom or empire, such as an emperor. **2** the chief of its class or kind: *The lion is the* monarch *of all beasts.* **3** large, orange and black American butterfly. **—*adj-* mon·ar′ chal** (mə när′ kəl): *the king's* monarchal *bearing.*

mo·nar·chic (mə när′ kĭk) or **mo·nar·chi·cal** (-kĭ kəl) ***adj-*** having to do with or characteristic of a monarch or monarchy. **—*adv-* mo·nar′ chi·cal·ly.**

mo·nar·chism (mŏn′ ər kĭz′ əm) ***n-*** **1** belief in or support of monarchy as a form of government. **2** principles or system of government by a monarch.

mon·ar·chist (mŏn′ ər kĭst) ***n-*** person who believes in or supports monarchy as a form of government.

mon·ar·chy (mŏn′ ər kē) ***n-*** [*pl.* **mon·ar·chies**] nation or system of government headed by a monarch. In an **absolute monarchy** the ruler has unlimited power, but in a **constitutional monarchy** his power is limited by law.

mon·as·ter·y (mŏn′ ə stĕr′ ē) ***n-*** [*pl.* **mon·as·ter·ies**] house for persons, especially monks, bound by religious vows, and living and working in seclusion; also, the people living there. **—*adj-* mon′ as·te′ ri·al:** *the* monasterial *quiet of the corridor.*

mo·nas·tic (mə năs′ tĭk) ***adj-*** having to do with or characteristic of monasteries or monks and their manner of life: *a room of* monastic *simplicity*; monastic *discipline.* Also **mo·nas′ ti·cal.** **—*adv-* mo·nas′ ti·cal·ly.**

mo·nas·ti·cism (mə năs′ tə sĭz′ əm) ***n-*** the system, rules, or conditions of life in monasteries.

mon·a·tom·ic (mŏn′ ə tŏn′ ĭk) *Chemistry* ***adj-*** having a single atom in the molecule: *Helium is* monatomic.

mon·au·ral (mŏn′ ŏr′ əl) ***adj-*** **1** of or having to do with a single ear: *a* monaural *hearing aid.* **2** monophonic. **—*adv-* mon′ au′ ral·ly.**

Mon·day (mŭn′ dē, -dā) ***n-*** the second day of the week.

mo·ne·cious (mə nē′ shəs) monoecious.

---

fāte, făt, dâre, bärn; bē, bĕt, mêre; bīte, bĭt; nōte, hŏt, môre, dȯg; fŭn, fûr; tōō, bŏŏk; oil; out; tar; thin; then; hw for wh as in *wh*at; zh for s as in u*s*ual; ə for a, e, i, o, u, as in *a*go, lin*e*n, per*i*l, at*o*m, min*u*s

Mo·nel metal (mō nĕl′) *n-* trademark name of a nickel alloy containing copper, iron, and manganese, used in machine parts because of its high resistance to corrosion.

mon·e·tar·y (mŏn′ ə tĕr′ ē) *adj-* 1 of or having to do with coinage or currency: *The dollar is the* monetary *unit of the United States.* 2 of or having to do with money: *a* monetary *gift*; monetary *theory.*

mon·ey (mŭn′ ē) *n-* [*pl.* **mon·eys** or **mon·ies**] 1 coins or paper currency issued by a government as a medium of exchange, a means of payment, or a measure of value. 2 anything else used this way, such as bank notes, checks, wampum, etc. 3 wealth. 4 **monies** or **moneys** sums of money. *—adj-* **mon′ ey·less.**

in the money *Informal* finishing first, second, or third in a race. **make money** to make a profit or earn a salary or payment.

mon·ey·bag (mŭn′ ē băg′) *n-* 1 bag for holding money. 2 **moneybags** *Slang* (takes singular verb) very rich person.

mon·ey·chang·er (mŭn′ ē chān′ jər) *n-* 1 person whose business is exchanging the money of one country for that of another at an established rate. 2 device that holds and dispenses coins of various denominations.

mon·eyed (mŭn′ ēd) *adj-* 1 having much money; rich. 2 resulting from great wealth: *a* moneyed *elegance.*

mon·ey·lend·er (mŭn′ ē lĕn′ dər) *n-* person whose business is lending money at some rate of interest.

money order *n-* an order for the payment of a stated sum of money; especially, such an order sold by the government at a post office.

Mon·gol (mŏng′ gəl) *n-* 1 a member of any of the native peoples of Mongolia or nearby regions. 2 the language of these people; Mongolian. 3 member of the Mongoloid division of the human species.

Mon·go·li·an (mŏng gō′ lē ən) *adj-* of or pertaining to Mongolia, its people, or their language. *n-* 1 a native of Mongolia; Mongol. 2 the language of the Mongols.

Mongolian idiot *n-* person born with mongolism.

mon·gol·ism (mŏn′ gə lĭz′ əm) *n-* form of congenital mental deficiency in which a child is born with a short, broad skull and slanting eyes.

Mon·go·loid (mŏn′ gə loid′) *adj-* of or relating to a major division of the human species, native to eastern Asia and considered to include most East Asians, the Eskimos, and by some authorities the American Indians. Mongoloid peoples tend to have slightly slanting eyes, yellowish to light brown skin, and straight, black hair.

mon·goose (mŏng′ gōōs′) *n-* [*pl.* **mon·goos·es**] small animal of India, related to the civet. It kills rats, mice, and poisonous snakes.

Indian mongoose, about 16 in. long

mon·grel (mŏng′ grəl, mŭng′-) *n-* 1 animal, especially a dog, of mixed breed. 2 anything of mixed origin, type, etc., (often used to show disfavor). *as modifier*: *a* mongrel *puppy.*

mon·ied (mŭn′ ēd) moneyed.

mon·i·tor (mŏn′ ə tər) *n-* 1 in schools, a student given special duties, such as keeping order and taking attendance. 2 person or thing that warns, reminds, or advises. 3 receiver or screen for checking radio or television transmission. 4 any of various large lizards of Africa, Asia, and Australia. 5 formerly, an armored warship with a low, flat deck and heavy guns mounted on revolving turrets. 6 **Monitor** the first vessel of this type, used by the Union in the Civil War. (See also *Merrimack.*) *vt-* 1 to supervise; oversee: *to* monitor *the halls.* 2 to check (a broadcast) for quality, with or without a special device. 3 to test for radioactivity.

mon·i·tor·y (mŏn′ ə tôr′ ē) *adj-* giving warning or advice; cautioning; admonitory.

monk (mŭngk) *n-* one of a body of men bound by vows to a religious life and usually living in a monastery.

mon·key (mŭng′ kē) *n-* [*pl.* **mon·keys**] 1 animal of the group nearest to man in appearance and intelligence, especially one of the smaller, long-tailed members of this group, differing from the larger apes and baboons. 2 mischievous person (used playfully). *vi-* 1 to play pranks; play the fool. 2 to meddle or tinker (with). *—adj-* **mon′ key·ish.**

Capuchin monkey, about 18 in. long

mon·key·shines (mŭng′ kē-shīnz′) *Slang n- pl.* mischievous pranks; antics.

monkey wrench *n-* wrench with an adjustable jaw. For picture, see *wrench.*

throw a monkey wrench into to spoil or upset (a plan or procedure) by some unexpected action.

monk·ish (mŭng′ kĭsh) *adj-* having to do with, characteristic of, or suitable for a monk. *—adv-* **monk′ ish·ly.**

monks·hood (mŭngks′ hŏŏd′) *n-* plant with spikes of white, purple, or yellow flowers having the upper petal curved like a hood; aconite.

mono- *combining form* one; single: *a* mono*plane*; mono*rail.* Also, before vowels, **mon-**: *a* mon*ocular*; mon*aural.* [from Greek **mono-**, from **monós** meaning "one; alone."]

mon·o·chro·mat·ic (mŏn′ ə krə măt′ ĭk) *adj-* 1 having a single color. 2 consisting of light of a single wavelength or of a very limited range of wavelengths.

mon·o·chrome (mŏn′ ə krōm′) *n-* painting, drawing, or photograph in one color.

mon·o·cle (mŏn′ ə kəl) *n-* eyeglass for one eye. *—adj-* **mon′ o·cled**: *a bearded and* monocled *actor.*

mon·o·cot·y·le·don (mŏn′ ə kŏt′ ə lē′ dən) *n-* any of a large group of plants, including the grasses, lilies, orchids, and palms, having a single cotyledon in the embryo. See also *dicotyledon.* Also **mon′ o·cot′** (mŏn′ ə kŏt′). *—adj-* **mon′ o·cot′ y·le′ don·ous.**

mo·noc·u·lar (mə nŏk′ yə lər) *adj-* 1 of, for, or used with one eye: *a* monocular *microscope.* 2 one-eyed; using one eye. *n-* small telescope using prisms to produce magnification.

mo·noe·cious (mə nē′ shəs) *Biology adj-* having stamens and pistils in separate blossoms on the same plant.

mo·nog·a·mist (mə nŏg′ ə mĭst) *n-* person who practices or believes in monogamy.

mo·nog·a·my (mə nŏg′ ə mē) *n-* marriage with only one husband or wife at the same time. *—adj-* **mo·nog′ a·mous.** *adv-* **mo·nog′ a·mous·ly.**

mon·o·gram (mŏn′ ə grăm′) *n-* group of interlaced or fancifully combined letters, especially the initials of a name, used on stationery, handkerchiefs, silverware, etc. *vt-* [**mon·o·grammed, mon·o·gram·ming**]: *to* monogram *handkerchiefs.*

Monogram of Albrecht Durer

mon·o·graph (mŏn′ ə grăf′) *n-* scholarly paper or treatise on one particular subject.

mon·o·lin·gual (mŏn′ ə lĭng′ gwəl) *adj-* knowing or using only one language.

mon·o·lith (mŏn′ ə lĭth′) *n-* 1 large, single block of stone, often cut to form a monument or column. 2 a massive organization thought to be a uniform whole. *—adj-* **mon′ o·lith′ ic.**

mon·o·logue or **mon·o·log** (mŏn′ ə lŏg′, -lŏg′) ***n-*** a long speech by a single person, especially in a play.

mon·o·ma·ni·a (mŏn′ ə mā′ nē ə) ***n-*** **1** insanity in regard to one single subject or class of subjects. **2** preoccupation with one idea; craze. ***—n-*** **mon′ o·ma′ ni·ac.**

mo·no·mi·al (mŏ nō′ mē əl, mə-) ***n-*** **1** *Mathematics* an expression consisting of a single term. **2** *Biology* a scientific name consisting of a single word. ***adj-***: *a* monomial *term.*

mon·o·phon·ic (mŏn′ ə fŏn′ ĭk) ***adj-*** **1** *Music* having a single melodic line, or one part that predominates over the accompanying parts. See also *polyphonic.* **2** of or having to do with recordings or broadcasts using a single channel; not stereophonic; monaural.

mon·o·plane (mŏn′ ə plān′) ***n-*** airplane with one pair of wings. Most modern airplanes are monoplanes.

mo·nop·o·list (mə nŏp′ ə lĭst′) ***n-*** person, organization, etc., having a monopoly or promoting monopolies. ***—adj-*** **mo·nop′ o·lis′ tic.**

mo·nop·o·lize (mə nŏp′ ə līz′) ***vt-*** **[mo·nop·o·lized, mo·nop·o·liz·ing]** **1** to gain a monopoly of (a product, service, industry, etc.). **2** to take the whole of: *to* monopolize *the attention of another.* ***—n-*** **mo·nop′ o·liz′ er.**

mo·nop·o·ly (mə nŏp′ ə lē) ***n-*** [*pl.* **mo·nop·o·lies**] **1** exclusive control of the use, sale, or distribution of a commodity or service by one person or one group of persons: *One bus company has a* monopoly *of our city's transportation.* **2** a thing controlled in this way: *Coinage is a government* monopoly. **3** organization excercising such control. **4** a monopolizing; exclusive possession.

mon·o·pro·pel·lant (mŏn′ ō prə pĕl′ ənt) ***n-*** a single, usually liquid substance for propelling a rocket.

mon·o·rail (mŏn′ ə rāl′) ***n-*** **1** single rail along which railway cars run, or from which they are suspended. **2** a railway using a single track.

mon·o·syl·lab·ic (mŏn′ ə sə lăb′ ĭk) ***adj-*** **1** having only one syllable. **2** consisting of words of one syllable.

mon·o·syl·la·ble (mŏn′ ə sĭl′ ə bəl) ***n-*** word or other utterance of one syllable.

mon·o·the·ism (mŏn′ ə thē′ ĭz′ əm) ***n-*** belief in only one God. ***—n-*** **mon′ o·the′ ist.** ***adj-*** **mon′ o·the·is′ tic.**

mon·o·tone (mŏn′ ə tōn′) ***n-*** **1** utterance of one syllable after another without change of pitch or key: *to speak in a* monotone. **2** a single color: *illustrations in* monotone. **3** unvarying and tedious style or manner.

mo·not·o·nous (mə nŏt′ ə nəs) ***adj-*** always the same; tiresome because of sameness: *a* monotonous *voice.* ***—adv-*** **mo·not′ o·nous·ly.** ***n-*** **mo·not′ o·nous·ness.**

mo·not·o·ny (mə nŏt′ ə nē) ***n-*** dull sameness; lack of variety; tedious uniformity: *the* monotony *of his stories.*

Mon·o·type (mŏn′ ə tīp′) ***n-*** **1** trademark name for a typesetting machine that casts and sets separate metal pieces of type for each character. See also *Linotype.* **2 monotype** the type produced by such a machine.

mon·o·va·lent (mŏn′ ə vā′ lənt) ***adj-*** having a valence of one.

mo·nox·ide (mə nŏk′ sīd′) *Chemistry* ***n-*** oxide containing only one atom of oxygen in each molecule.

Mon·roe Doctrine (mən rō′) ***n-*** statement of policy made by President Monroe in 1823, expressing the idea that the United States would look with disfavor on any attempt of a European nation to extend its control or influence in the Western Hemisphere.

Mon·sei·gneur or **mon·sei·gneur** (mōⁿ′ sĕ′ nyûr′) ***n-*** [*pl.* **Mes·sei·gneurs** (mā′ sĕ′ nyûr′)] *French* title equivalent to "my lord," given to clergymen of high rank.

mon·sieur (mə syûr′) ***n-*** [*pl.* **mes·sieurs** (mā′ syûr′)] *French* title of courtesy equivalent to "Mr." or "Sir."

Mon·si·gnor or **mon·si·gnor** (mŏn sēn′ yər) ***n-*** [*pl.* **Mon·si·gnors** or **Mon·si·gno·ri** (-yôr′ ē)] a title of honor given by the Pope to deserving clergymen of the Roman Catholic Church.

mon·soon (mŏn sōōn′) ***n-*** **1** wind in the Indian Ocean and Southern Asia which blows from the southwest from April to October, and from the northeast from October to April. **2** rainy season that comes with this wind when it blows from the southwest.

mon·ster (mŏn′ stər) ***n-*** **1** animal or plant that is abnormally misshapen: *A five-legged calf is a* monster. **2** imaginary creature of grotesque form, often combining characteristics of different animals or human and animal characteristics. **3** very wicked or cruel person. **4** something very huge, deformed, or hideous. *as **modifier**: a* monster *whale; a* monster *movie.*

mon·strance (mŏn′ strəns) ***n-*** vessel, usually of gold or silver, in which the consecrated Host is shown in rituals of the Roman Catholic Church.

mon·stros·i·ty (mŏn′ strŏs′ ə tē) ***n-*** [*pl.* **mon·stros·i·ties**] **1** condition of being monstrous. **2** anything unnaturally huge or ugly: *That vase is a* monstrosity.

mon·strous (mŏn′ strəs) ***adj-*** **1** not normal; differing from the natural shape: *a* monstrous *creature with two heads.* **2** huge; enormous; great: *He ate a* monstrous *helping of pie.* **3** shocking; horrible: *a* monstrous *act of cruelty.* ***—adv-*** **mon′ strous·ly.** ***n-*** **mon′ strous·ness.**

Mont. Montana.

mon·tage (mŏn täzh′) ***n-*** picture, especially a photograph, made by combining several pictures or parts of pictures; also, the process of making such a picture.

month (mŭnth) ***n-*** **1** (also **calendar month**) one of the twelve parts, usually a little more than four weeks long, into which the year is divided. **2** period of about four weeks or thirty days. **3** lunar month.

month·ly (mŭnth′ lē) ***adj-*** **1** done, payable, published, or happening once a month: *a* monthly *cleaning;* monthly *bills; a* monthly *magazine.* **2** continuing through a month: *a commuter's* monthly *ticket.* ***adv-*** once a month; every month: *He collects for the paper* monthly. ***n-*** [*pl.* **month·lies**] magazine published once a month.

mon·u·ment (mŏn′ yə mənt) ***n-*** **1** something set up or built in memory of a person or event, such as a statue, column, tomb, etc. **2** work or achievement that is worthy to be remembered: *a* monument *of scientific research.* **3** any fine building, structure, etc., surviving from a past age. **4** natural feature or historical site that is set aside by the government as public property.

mon·u·men·tal (mŏn′ yə mĕn′ təl) ***adj-*** **1** of or serving as a monument: *a* monumental *inscription.* **2** like a monument; enduring; also, notable; important: *a* monumental *speech.* **3** very great; colossal: *Building a bridge is a* monumental *task.* ***—adv-*** **mon′ u·men′ tal·ly.**

moo (mōō) ***n-*** [*pl.* **moos**] the sound made by a cow. ***vi-*** to make the sound of a cow.

mooch (mōōch) *Slang* ***vt-*** to get without paying; obtain by begging or asking for. ***—n-*** **mooch′ er.**

¹**mood** (mōōd) ***n-*** state of mind or feeling; humor; disposition: *in a merry* mood; *in the* mood *to work.* [from Old English **mōd** meaning "spirit; pride; mind."]

²**mood** (mōōd) *Grammar* ***n-*** that feature of a verb or verb phrase which tells whether the utterance is a statement or question, a wish, or a command. Modern English has an indicative and an imperative mood. It also has a

---

fāte, făt, dâre, bärn; bē, bĕt, mêre; bīte, bĭt; nōte, hŏt, môre, dŏg; fŭn, fûr; tōō, bŏŏk; oil; out; tar; thin; then; hw for wh as in what; zh for s as in usual; ə for a, e, i, o, u, as in ago, linen, peril, atom, minus

few verb forms that are remnants of an old subjunctive mood, as in: *I wish he* were *here.* See also *indicative, subjunctive, imperative.* [an altered form of **mode,** from Latin **modus** meaning originally "shape; way."]

mood·y (mōō′dē) ***adj-*** [**mood·i·er, mood·i·est**] **1** having changes in state of mind or temper: *a* moody *disposition.* **2** bad-tempered; gloomy; glum: *Everyone shuns him when he is* moody. **—*adv-* mood′i·ly. *n-* mood′i·ness.**

moon (mōōn) ***n-*** **1** the scarred, airless, celestial body that is the earth's natural satellite. **2** any similar body revolving around another planet. **3** a month. **4** a moon-shaped object, either round or crescent: *The flag of Turkey has a* moon *and star.* **5** moonlight. ***vi-*** to wander or look about in a dreamy, listless way. **—*adj-* moon′-less. *adj-* moon′like′.**

reach for the moon to attempt the impossible.

FIRST QUARTER
FULL MOON
NEW MOON
LAST QUARTER

Phases of the moon

moon·beam (mōōn′bēm′) ***n-*** ray of moonlight.

moon·flow·er (mōōn′flou′ər) ***n-*** any of several climbing vines related to the morning-glory, with fragrant white flowers that bloom at night.

moon·light (mōōn′līt′) ***n-*** the light of the moon, ***as modifier:*** *a* moonlight *walk in the garden.*

moon·light·ing (mōōn′lī′tĭng) *Informal* ***n-*** the practice of holding a second regular job in addition to one's main full-time employment. **—*n-* moon′light′er.**

moon·lit (mōōn′lĭt′) ***adj-*** lighted by the moon: *a* moonlit *landscape.*

moon·scape (mōōn′skāp′) ***n-*** view or appearance of the surface of the moon as seen, photographed, or pictured.

moon·shine (mōōn′shīn′) ***n-*** **1** moonlight. **2** *Informal* foolish or idle talk; nonsense: *His ideas for reform are* moonshine. **3** *Slang* homemade, bootleg whiskey.

moon·shin·er (mōōn′shī′nər) *Slang* ***n-*** person who makes or deals in illegally distilled or smuggled liquor.

moon·stone (mōōn′stōn′) ***n-*** translucent, nearly colorless, semiprecious gem stone with a bluish sheen. It is a variety of feldspar.

moon·struck (mōōn′strŭk′) ***adj-*** **1** mentally deranged, supposedly through the influence of the moon. **2** very romantic or sentimental: *a pair of* moonstruck *lovers.*

moon·y (mōō′nē) ***adj-*** [**moon·i·er, moon·i·est**] **1** *Informal* foolishly absent-minded; silly. **2** moonlike.

¹moor (mōōr) ***n-*** area of open wasteland, especially one in England or Scotland, covered with low plants such as heather. [from Old English **mōr,** "marshy land."]

²moor (mōōr) ***vt-*** to fasten or secure (a ship, aircraft, etc.) in place with cables or anchors; hence, to fasten or secure firmly. ***vi-:*** *The sailboat* moored *in the bay.* [of Germanic origin.]

Moor (mōōr) ***n-*** a Muslim of Arab and Berber ancestry, especially one of the invaders of Spain in the eighth century. **—*adj-* Moor′ish:** *old* Moorish *architecture.*

moor·age (mōōr′ĭj) ***n-*** **1** a mooring or being moored. **2** place for mooring a vessel, aircraft, etc. **3** a charge for mooring.

moor·ing (mōōr′ĭng) ***n-*** **1** act of securing or fastening a vessel, aircraft, etc. **2** long chain, anchored to the bottom and buoyed at the surface, to which boats are tied in a more or less permanent anchorage. **3 moorings** (1) ropes, cables, or anchors used to fasten a vessel, aircraft, etc., in place. (2) place where a vessel, aircraft, etc., is anchored or made fast.

moor·land (mōōr′lănd′) ***n-*** barren land covered with heather or similar plants; moor.

moose (mōōs) ***n-*** [*pl.* **moose**] the largest American deer. It is found in Canada and northern United States, and frequently weighs 1,000 pounds.

Moose, about 6 ft. high at shoulder

moot (mōōt) ***adj-*** open to discussion: *a* moot *question.* ***vt-*** to propose for discussion; also, to argue, discuss, or debate (a question).

mop (mŏp) ***n-*** **1** bundle of coarse yarn, cloth, etc., or a sponge, fastened to a handle and used for washing floors or dishes. **2** any tangled bunch: *a* mop *of hair.* ***vt-*** [**mopped, mop·ping**] to wipe with or as if with such a bundle or sponge: *to* mop *a floor*; *to* mop *one's face.*

mop up 1 to remove or clean up with a mop: *to* mop up *dust.* **2** *Informal* to finish a task. **3** *Military* to clear out remaining enemy forces from captured areas.

mope (mōp) ***vi-*** [**moped, mop·ing**] to be listless and in low spirits: *He* moped *indoors all day.* ***n-*** **1** listless, low-spirited person. **2** spell of gloominess or low spirits.

mo·ped (mō′pĕd) ***n-*** a lightweight motorbike that can be propelled either by its motor or by pedaling.

mo·raine (mə rān′) ***n-*** heap of rocks, gravel, etc., gathered by a glacier and deposited either along its sides or at its lower end.

mor·al (mòr′əl, mŏr′-) ***adj-*** **1** of or having to do with one's conception of what is right or wrong; having to do with the difference between right and wrong; ethical: *a* moral *problem*; moral *sense*; moral *standards.* **2** governed by virtuous conduct; good; just; also, chaste: *a* moral *way of living*; *a* moral *people.* **3** able to understand the difference between right and wrong: *People are* moral *beings.* **4** teaching or expressing standards or right behavior: *a* moral *lecture.* ***n-*** **1** lesson taught by a story, fable, experience, etc. **2 morals** standards of right and wrong; standards of conduct; also, conduct as judged by such standards.

moral certainty *n-* probability so strong as to amount to certainty: *It's a* moral certainty *that we will win.*

mo·rale (mə răl′) ***n-*** state of mind that helps a person keep up hope, courage, good spirits, etc., in the face of danger or discouragement: *The team's* morale *was high.*

mor·al·ist (mòr′ə lĭst′, mŏr′-) ***n-*** person who studies or teaches morals; also, any moralistic person.

mor·a·lis·tic (mòr′ə lĭs′tĭk, mŏr′-) ***adj-*** teaching or concerned with morals, especially in a strict or self-righteous way. **—*adv-* mor′a·lis′ti·cal·ly.**

mo·ral·i·ty (mə răl′ə tē) ***n-*** [*pl.* **mo·ral·i·ties**] **1** the rightness or wrongness of an action. **2** virtue; uprightness; good morals. **3** standards of right and wrong in conduct; morals. **4** system of morals; ethics.

mor·al·ize (mòr′ə līz′, mŏr′-) ***vi-*** [**mor·al·ized, mor·al·iz·ing**] to talk or write at great length about right and wrong, duty, goodness, etc. ***vt-*** to interpret as having a moral; draw a moral from: *He tends to* moralize *everything.* **—*n-* mor′al·i·za′tion. *n-* mor′al·iz′er.**

mor·al·ly (mòr′ə lē, mŏr′-) ***adv-*** **1** in a good or virtuous manner: *Because he lived* morally, *he gained the respect of his neighbors.* **2** according to ideas of right and wrong: *Although he broke no law, his conduct was* morally *questionable.* **3** practically; almost: *I can't prove it, but I'm* morally *certain I've seen her before.*

moral support *n-* encouragement, usually given by taking a person's side.

moral victory ***n-*** a defeat felt to be a victory because of spiritual satisfactions or hopes gained from it.

mo·rass (mə răs′) ***n-*** soft, swampy ground; bog.

mor·a·tor·i·um (mȯr′ ə tôr′ ē əm, mŏr′-) ***n-*** [*pl.* **mor·a·to·ri·ums** or **mor·a·tor·i·a** (-ē ə)] **1** period of time over which payment of a debt may be legally delayed; also, the legal authorization granted in an emergency to make use of such a delay. **2** any temporary ban, suspension, or deferment of action.

mo·ray (môr′ ā′) ***n-*** any of various brightly colored, voracious, eellike, marine fishes with sharp, knifelike teeth, found in all warm seas. Also **moray eel.**

mor·bid (mȯr′ bĭd′, môr′-) ***adj-*** **1** having too much to do with unpleasant and gloomy things; not healthy: *Reading a great many horror stories may show a* morbid *taste.* **2** caused by or having to do with disease: *A cancer is a* morbid *growth in the body.* ***—adv-*** **mor′ bid·ly.** ***n-*** **mor′ bid·ness.**

mor·bid·i·ty (mȯr bĭd′ ə tē) ***n-*** [*pl.* **mor·bid·i·ties**] **1** morbid or gloomy outlook or state of mind. **2** amount of sickness or proportion of sick people in a place.

mor·dant (mȯr′ dənt, môr′-) ***adj-*** biting; keen; sarcastic: *a* mordant *wit.* ***n-*** **1** substance that serves to fix certain colors in dyeing. **2** acid that eats into a metal surface, used in etching. ***—n-*** **mor′ dan·cy.**

Mor·de·cai (mȯr′ də kī′, môr′-) ***n-*** in the Old Testament, the cousin of Esther, who helped her save the Jews from destruction.

more (môr) ***determiner*** (traditionally called adjective or pronoun) a greater amount, degree, or number of: *You have* more *energy and* more *time than I. He wants* more *money and* more *help. He got* more *for his car than he expected.* ***n-*** an additional amount or number of: *Please buy* more *of that cake.* ***adv-*** **1** (used often to form the comparative of adjectives and adverbs) to a greater extent or degree: *This sofa is* more *comfortable than a bench. This sofa seats five men* more *comfortably than that bench.* **2** again: *We shall see her once* more. **3** in addition: *one word* more.

more or less about: *The hat will cost you $15* more or less. **the more** or **all the more** (used adverbially) even more: *That made me like him* the more.

mo·rel (mə rĕl′) ***n-*** any of various small edible mushrooms resembling a sponge.

more·o·ver (môr ō′ vər) ***adv-*** and in addition; besides; also; furthermore: *He is fast;* moreover, *he is tall.*

mo·res (môr′ āz′) ***n-*** *pl.* **1** in anthropology, the customs and the rules for right or wrong behavior that form the basis of a social group: *The* mores *of the tribe forbid marriage between cousins.* **2** customs or special rules or any group or place: *the* mores *of a newspaper office.*

mor·ga·nat·ic (mȯr′ gə năt′ ĭk, môr′-) ***adj-*** relating to the marriage of a man of royal birth or high rank with a woman of lower station. Neither the wife nor children may share the man's rank or inherit his property.

Mor·gan le Fay (mȯr′ gən lə fā′, môr′-) ***n-*** in Arthurian legend, King Arthur's half sister, an enchantress.

morgue (mȯrg, môrg) ***n-*** **1** building or room where dead bodies are temporarily kept until identified or claimed for burial. **2** reference library of a newspaper, where early issues, clippings, etc., are filed.

mor·i·bund (mȯr′ ə bŭnd′, mŏr′-) ***adj-*** dying: *a* moribund *man; a* moribund *civilization.*

Mor·mon (mȯr′ mən, môr′-) ***n-*** a member of the Church of Jesus Christ of Latter-day Saints. ***adj-***: *a* Mormon *doctrine.*

Mor·mon·ism (mȯr′ mə nĭz′ əm, môr′-) ***n-*** the religious doctrine and system of worship of the Church of Jesus Christ of Latter-day Saints.

morn (mȯrn, môrn) ***n-*** morning. ***Hom-*** mourn.

morn·ing (mȯr′ nĭng, môr′-) ***n-*** the first part of the day, from midnight until noon, or from dawn until noon. *as* ***modifier***: *a* morning *walk.* ***Hom-*** mourning.

morning coat ***n-*** a cutaway.

morn·ing-glor·y (mȯr′ nĭng glôr′ ē, môr′-) ***n-*** any of various climbing vines bearing heart-shaped leaves and trumpet-shaped, variously colored blossoms that open in early morning and close in bright sunlight, or in the evening.

morning star ***n-*** bright planet, especially Venus, when it rises after midnight and can be seen in the east before sunrise.

Morning-glory

Mo·ro (môr′ ō) ***n-*** [*pl.* **Mo·ros**] **1** a member of any of the Muslim people of the southern Philippines. **2** their language. ***adj-***: *the* Moro *pottery.*

mo·roc·co (mə rŏk′ ō) ***n-*** [*pl.* **mo·roc·cos**] fine variety of leather made from goatskin, tanned with sumac, and used for bookbinding.

mor·on (môr′ ŏn) ***n-*** **1** person whose mental ability does not develop beyond that of a child between 8 and 12 years old. **2** *Informal* very stupid or foolish person. ***—adj-*** **mo·ron′ ic.** ***adv-*** **mo·ron′ i·cal·ly.**

mo·rose (mə rōs′, môr′ ōs′) ***adj-*** gloomy; sullen. ***—adv-*** **mo·rose′ ly.** ***n-*** **mo·rose′ ness.**

mor·pheme (mȯr′ fēm′, môr′-) ***n-*** in linguistics, a unit of meaning that cannot be divided into smaller units of meaning. Morphemes can be words, or parts of words such as stems, prefixes, suffixes, etc. Examples: "green," "rock," and "has" are morphemes. "Rider" is made up of two morphemes, "ride" and "(e)r," and "cupfuls" is made up of three, "cup," "ful" and "s."

Mor·phe·us (mȯr′ fē əs, môr′-) ***n-*** in Greek mythology, the god of sleep and dreams.

mor·phine (mȯr′ fēn′, môr′-) ***n-*** narcotic drug from opium, used medically to deaden pain or to produce sleep.

mor·phol·o·gy (mȯr fŏl′ ə jē, môr-) ***n-*** **1** branch of biology which deals with the form and structure of plants and animals, without regard to functions or life processes. **2** form and structure of an organism considered as a whole. **3** branch of linguistics which deals with the formation of words, their internal structure, inflections, derivations, etc. ***—adj-*** **mor′ pho·log′ ic** (-fə lŏj′ ĭk) or **mor′ pho·log′ i·cal** (-ĭ kəl).

mor·ris (mŏr′ əs, mȯr′-) ***n-*** old English folk dance.

morris chair ***n-*** large wooden easy chair with an adjustable back and removable cushions.

mor·row (mŏr′ ō, mȯr′-) ***n-*** **1** the day after any particular day. **2** morning: *Good* morrow.

Morse code (mȯrs, môrs) ***n-*** **1** alphabet devised by S. F. B. Morse for sending messages by telegraph and also used for radio telegraphy and signaling by flashing light. Letters are represented by long and short spacing between clicks, or long and short sounds or flashes. **2** a modified form of this alphabet now in prevalent use, the **International Morse Code.**

mor·sel (mȯr′ səl, môr′-) ***n-*** small piece; bit; scrap.

fāte, făt, dâre, bärn; bē, bĕt, mêre; bīte, bĭt; nōte, hŏt, môre, dȯg; fŭn, fûr; to͞o, bo͝ok; oil; out; tar; thin; then; hw for wh as in *wh*at; zh for s as in u*s*ual; ə for a, e, i, o, u, as in *a*go, lin*e*n, per*i*l, at*o*m, min*u*s

mor·tal (mȯr′ təl, môr′-) ***adj-*** **1** subject to death; certain to die: *All living things are* mortal. **2** human: *We all have* mortal *weaknesses.* **3** causing death; fatal: *a* mortal *wound.* **4** associated with the idea of death; extreme; great: *in* mortal *fear.* **5** causing spiritual death: *a* mortal *sin.* **6** implacable; unrelenting: *a* mortal *enemy.* **7** to the death: *a* mortal *combat.* **8** preceding death. **9** *Informal* very long and tedious: *The play ran for three* mortal *hours.* ***n-*** a human being.

mor·tal·i·ty (mȯr tăl′ ə tē) ***n-*** [*pl.* **mor·tal·i·ties**] **1** condition of being mortal or subject to death. **2** loss of life, especially on a large scale: *the* mortality *from war or disease.* **3** number of deaths in a given period in a given area; death rate. **4** human race; mankind. *as* ***modifier*****:** *a high* mortality *rate*; mortality *figures.*

mor·tal·ly (mȯr′ tə lē, môr′-) ***adv-*** **1** in such a manner as to cause death; fatally: *to be* mortally *wounded.* **2** deeply; bitterly; extremely: *to be* mortally *grieved.*

[1]**mor·tar** (mȯr′ tər, môr′-) ***n-*** building material made of lime, cement, sand, and water, used to hold stones or bricks together. [from Middle English **morter,** from Old French **mortier,** from Latin **mortārium** meaning "material pounded in a mixing trough."]

[2]**mor·tar** (mȯr′ tər, môr′-) ***n-*** heavy bowl of glass, earthenware or other material in which drugs, spices, and the like are pounded or ground to powder with a pestle. [from Old English **mortere,** from Latin **mortārium** meaning "a mixing trough."]

Mortar and pestle

[3]**mor·tar** (mȯr′ tər, môr′-) ***n-*** kind of cannon for firing shells in a high curve. [from French **mortier** meaning "a short muzzle-loading cannon; [2]mortar."]

mor·tar·board (mȯr′ tər bôrd′, môr′-) ***n-*** **1** square board with a handle on the underside, for holding mortar. **2** academic cap, with a square, flat, wide top.

mort·gage (mȯr′ gij, môr′-) ***n-*** **1** legal assignment of property, especially real estate, to a creditor as security for the repayment of a loan. **2** contract by which such a transfer is made. **3** title or claim created by such a contract. ***vt-*** **[mort·gaged, mort·gag·ing]** **1** to make over (property) as security for a loan. **2** to pledge: *to* mortgage *one's future for a present advantage.*

mort·ga·gee (mȯr′ gə jē′, môr′-) ***n-*** person, bank, etc., that loans money in return for a mortgage.

mort·gag·or or **mort·gag·er** (mȯr′ gə jər, môr′-) ***n-*** person who mortgages his property as security.

mor·ti·cian (mȯr tĭsh′ ən ***n-*** undertaker.

mor·ti·fi·ca·tion (mȯr′ tə fə kā′ shən, môr′-) ***n-*** **1** shame; humiliation. **2** discipline of oneself by acts of self-denial, such as fasting, penance, etc. **3** a cause of shame or humiliation: *The worn rug was a* mortification *to her.* **4** *Archaic* death or decay of part of the body.

mor·ti·fy (mȯr′ tə fī′, môr′-) ***vt-*** **[mor·ti·fied, mor·ti·fy·ing]** **1** to embarrass; cause shame or humiliation: *It* mortifies *me to forget a name.* **2** to discipline or subdue (the body, passions, etc.) by self-denial, fasting, penance, etc.: *to* mortify *the flesh*; *to* mortify *the appetites.* **—*n-*** **mor′ ti·fi′ er.**

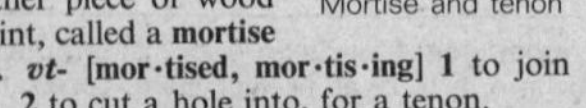

Mortise and tenon

mor·tise or **mor·tice** (mȯr′ təs, môr′-) ***n-*** hole cut in a piece of wood, into which the shaped end (tenon) of another piece of wood fits to form a joint, called a **mortise and tenon joint.** ***vt-*** **[mor·tised, mor·tis·ing]** **1** to join by such a joint. **2** to cut a hole into, for a tenon.

mor·tu·ar·y (mȯr′ chōō ĕr′ ē, môr′-) ***n-*** [*pl.* **mor·tu·ar·ies**] funeral home. ***adj-*** connected with burial of the dead: *solemn* mortuary *rites.*

mos. months.

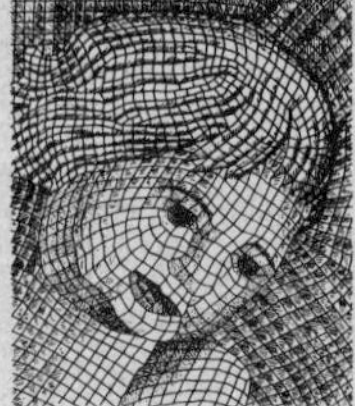
Mosaic

mo·sa·ic (mō zā′ ĭk) ***n-*** **1** picture or design made by fitting together bits of colored glass, stone, or tile. **2** (also **mosaic disease**) any of several virus diseases of plants, marked by wrinkling and mottling of the leaves. *as* ***modifier*****:** *a* mosaic *floor.*

Mo·sa·ic (mō zā′ ĭk) ***adj-*** of or pertaining to Moses, the Hebrew leader and lawgiver, or to laws and writings attributed to him.

Mosaic Law ***n-*** the code of laws contained in the first five books of the Bible and attributed to Moses.

Mo·ses (mō′ zəs) ***n-*** in the Old Testament, the Hebrew prophet and lawgiver who led the Israelites out of Egypt to the Promised Land.

mo·sey (mō′ zē) *Slang* ***vi-*** **1** to go away. **2** to stroll.

Mos·lem (mŏz′ ləm) Muslim.

mosque (mŏsk) ***n-*** a Muslim house of worship.

Mosque

mos·qui·to (mə skē′ tō) ***n-*** [*pl.* **mos·qui·toes** or **mos·qui·tos**] any of various long-legged, two-winged insects, the female of which punctures the skin of men and animals, and feeds on the blood it sucks out. Some mosquitoes carry diseases, including malaria and yellow fever.

mosquito boat ***n-*** PT boat.

mosquito net ***n-*** screen, curtain, or canopy of fine net or gauze placed over windows, beds, etc., for keeping out mosquitoes.

Mosquito

moss (mȯs) ***n-*** **1** a small plant with tiny leaves. Moss grows in thick clusters which form a mat on damp ground, rocks, trees, etc. **2** any of various lichens and other plants resembling this, such as **Iceland moss,** an arctic lichen sometimes used for food and medicine. **—*adj-*** **moss′ like′.**

moss agate ***n-*** agate with markings resembling moss.

moss·back (mȯs′ băk′) ***n-*** **1** old turtle having a growth of moss or seaweed on its back. **2** *Slang* fogy.

moss·y (mȯ′ sē) ***adj-*** **[moss·i·er, moss·i·est]** **1** covered with moss: *a* mossy *stone.* **2** like moss: *a* mossy *coating.*

most (mōst) ***determiner*** (traditionally called adjective or pronoun) greatest in amount, degree, or number: *That is the car with* most *speed and gadgets. The pocketbook with the* most *money is hers.* ***n-*** **1** the majority (of); the larger part or number (of): *I have read* most *of the book.* Most *of his suits were at the cleaner's.* **2** the greatest quantity, amount, or degree; utmost: *This is the* most *I can do for you.* ***adv-*** **1** to the greatest extent or degree: *I like plums* most. **2** very: *a* most *diligent student.* **3** used often to form the superlative of adjectives and adverbs: *He was* most *wise. He replied* most *wisely to all their questions.*

at (or **at the**) **most** not more than; at the very limit: *She will pay only $20* at most. **for the most part** usually;

mostly: *These goods,* for the most part, *are sold at a discount.* **make the most of** use to the best advantage; make the greatest use of: *to* make the most of *time.*

►Do not use MOST for ALMOST unless you want to sound folksy: *He* almost *fell over with surprise.*

-most *suffix* (used to form superlatives from adjectives and adverbs): *fore*most; *upper*most; *top*most.

most·ly (mōst′ lē) ***adv-*** for the most part; chiefly.

mote (mōt) ***n-*** tiny particle, especially of dust. ***Hom-*** moat.

mo·tel (mō tĕl′) ***n-*** roadside hotel or group of cottages for people traveling by car.

moth (mŏth) ***n-*** [*pl.* **moths** (mŏthz, mŏths)] any of a number of downy, four-winged insects of widely different size, resembling the butterflies, usually most active at night. They are generally less brilliantly colored than butterflies and have stouter bodies and pointed or feathered antennae. The larvae of many kinds are destructive of cloth and foliage.

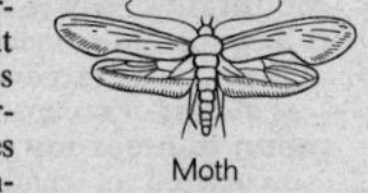
Moth

moth·ball (mŏth′ bŏl′) ***n-*** small ball of camphor or naphthalene used to keep moths out of clothing, especially during storage. ***adj-*** protected against rust, weather, etc., and kept in reserve: *a* mothball *fleet of ships.* ***vt-*** to cover, coat, and otherwise preserve (ships, weapons, etc.) to be kept in reserve.

in mothballs in storage or reserve and protected against rust, weather, etc.: *The ships were* in mothballs.

moth-eat·en (mŏth′ ē′ tən) ***adj-*** **1** eaten by moths; damaged by moths; full of holes. **2** in poor condition because of age; worn out; old.

[1]**moth·er** (mŭth′ ər) ***n-*** **1** female parent. **2** origin; source: *Necessity is the* mother *of invention.* **3 Mother** Mother Superior. *as* ***modifier***: *a clucking* mother *hen*; *the* mother *tongue*; *the* mother *church.* ***vt-*** **1** to care for, fondle, etc., in the manner of a female parent: *to* mother *a hurt child*; *to* mother *all the children in the neighborhood.* **2** to give birth to: *to* mother *an idea.* [from Old English **mōdor.**]

[2]**moth·er** (mŭth′ ər) ***n-*** thick, slimy film of bacteria and yeast cells that forms on the surface of fermenting liquids and is sometimes added to wine or cider to produce vinegar. [from earlier Dutch **modder** meaning originally "dregs; mire," and influenced by [1]**mother.**]

mother country ***n-*** **1** country from which a colony, dominion, etc., was founded. **2** motherland.

moth·er·hood (mŭth′ ər ho͝od′) ***n-*** **1** being a mother: *She took seriously the duties of* motherhood. **2** mothers in general: *to honor the* motherhood *of the country.*

Mother Hub·bard (hŭb′ ərd) ***n-*** **1** character in an old nursery rhyme. **2** long, loose dress for women.

moth·er-in-law (mŭth′ ər ĭn lŏ′) ***n-*** [*pl.* **moth·ers-in-law**] mother of one's husband or wife.

moth·er·land (mŭth′ ər lănd′) ***n-*** **1** one's native land; native country. **2** land of one's ancestors.

moth·er·less (mŭth′ ər ləs) ***adj-*** without a mother.

mother lode ***n-*** principal or very rich vein of ore.

moth·er·ly (mŭth′ ər lē) ***adj-*** **1** of or like that of a mother; maternal: *a* motherly *hug.* **2** like a mother in being concerned for others, giving comfort and guidance, etc.: *a* motherly *woman.* **—*n-*** **moth′ er·li·ness.**

moth·er-of-pearl (mŭth′ ər əv pûrl′) ***n-*** the glossy lining of some shells that shows rainbow colors in changing lights; nacre. ***adj-***: *a* mother-of-pearl *case.*

Mother's Day ***n-*** a holiday to honor all mothers, celebrated on the second Sunday in May.

Mother Superior ***n-*** nun who is at the head of a convent of religious women.

mother tongue ***n-*** **1** one's native language. **2** language from which another language originates.

mother wit ***n-*** natural intelligence or common sense.

moth·y (mŏ′ thē) ***adj-*** [**moth·i·er, moth·i·est**] **1** moth-eaten. **2** infested with moths.

mo·tif (mō tēf′) ***n-*** **1** the subject or main idea of a work of art or literature. **2** something repeated in a design: *wallpaper with a floral* motif. **3** *Music* the shortest recognizable melodic or rhythmic subdivision of a theme; motive.

mo·tile (mō′ tĭl′, -təl) ***adj-*** capable of or demonstrating spontaneous motion, as certain cells and spores do: *a less* motile *strain of bacteria.* **—*n-*** **mo·til′ i·ty.**

mo·tion (mō′ shən) ***n-*** **1** a moving or changing from one place or position to another; also, action or movement: *the* motion *of the planets*; *the ceaseless* motion *of the waves.* **2** a gesture: *a beckoning* motion. **3** formal suggestion or proposal made at a meeting: *a* motion *to adjourn.* ***vt-*** to guide or invite by a gesture: *He* motioned *me in.* ***vi-*** to make a gesture or movement to express meaning: *The host* motioned *for the visitor to be seated.*

mo·tion·less (mō′ shən ləs) ***adj-*** not moving; still: *The hunting dog stood* motionless. **—*adv-*** **mo′ tion·less·ly.**

motion picture ***n-*** **1** succession of continuously moving images projected on a screen from a film moving at a rate no less than 16 photographs or frames per second. **2** a play or story presented by such means. *as* ***modifier*** **(motion-picture):** *the* motion-picture *business.*

mo·ti·vate (mō′ tə vāt′) ***vt-*** [**mo·ti·vat·ed, mo·ti·vat·ing**] to provide a motive or incentive to or for: *What* motivates *him to work so hard?* **—*n-*** **mo′ ti·va′ tion.**

mo·tive (mō′ tĭv) ***n-*** **1** inner reason which causes a person to act as he does under certain circumstances; purpose or incentive for acting in a certain way: *Her* motive *for taking the blame was to shield her brother.* **2** *Music* a motif. ***adj-*** causing motion: *a* motive *force.*

motive power ***n-*** any agent, such as wind, water, steam, or electricity, that produces motion in vehicles or machinery.

mot·ley (mŏt′ lē) ***adj-*** mixed; varied; mottled; made up of different colors or things: *A* motley *crowd filled the street.* ***n-*** a jester's garment of various colors.

Motley

mo·tor (mō′ tər) ***n-*** **1** machine that converts electric power into motion. **2** any engine: *an automobile* motor; *an outboard* motor. **3** *chiefly Brit.* automobile. ***adj-*** **1** driven by an engine: *a* motor *scooter.* **2** for or having to do with engines or electric motors: *a quart of* motor *oil*; *a* motor *housing.* **3** having to do with automobiles: *a* motor *inn*; *a* motor *trip.* **4** causing or controlling motion; especially, relating to nerves that control bodily movement: *a* motor *nerve.* ***vi-*** to travel by automobile.

mo·tor·bike (mō′ tər bīk′) *Informal* ***n-*** **1** bicycle propelled by a small motor. **2** motorcycle.

mo·tor·boat (mō′ tər bōt′) ***n-*** boat whose chief means of propulsion is a motor; powerboat.

mo·tor·cade (mō′ tər kād′) ***n-*** parade of automobiles, especially one in which some important person rides.

mo·tor·car (mō′ tər kär′) ***n-*** automobile.

---

fāte, făt, dâre, bärn; bē, bĕt, mêre; bīte, bĭt; nōte, hŏt, môre, dŏg; fŭn, fûr; to͞o, bo͝ok; oil; out; tar; thin; then; hw for wh as in *wh*at; zh for s as in u*s*ual; ə for a, e, i, o, u, as in *a*go, lin*e*n, per*i*l, at*o*m, min*u*s

motor coach *n-* bus powered by a motor, usually a gasoline engine. Also **mo′ tor·bus′.**

Motorcycle

mo·tor·cy·cle (mō′ tər sī′- kəl) *n-* motor-driven, two-wheeled vehicle, larger and heavier than a bicycle, with one or two riding seats and sometimes with a sidecar attached. *vi-* [**mo·tor·cy·cled, mo·tor·cy·cling**]: *We* motorcycled *to New York.*

mo·tor·cy·clist (mō′ tər sī′ klĭst) *n-* person driving or riding on a motorcycle.

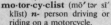

motor generator *n-* an electric motor and a generator with their shafts coupled, used for converting AC to DC or vice-versa, or for transforming voltage.

mo·tor·ist (mō′ tər ĭst) *n-* person who drives or travels in an automobile.

mo·tor·ize (mō′ tə rīz′) *vt-* [**mo·tor·i·zed, mo·tor·iz·ing**] **1** to equip with a motor. **2** to supply with motor vehicles: *We have* motorized *our entire army since World War I.* **—*n-* mo′ tor·i·za′ tion.**

mo·tor·man (mō′ tər mən) *n-* [*pl.* **mo·tor·men**] **1** operator of a streetcar or an electric train. **2** the operator of a motor.

motor nerve *n-* nerve that carries impulses from the central nervous system to a muscle, thus stimulating it to contract.

motor pool *n-* group of government or military vehicles dispatched by a central agency and available for use by authorized personnel.

motor scooter *n-* motor-driven, two-wheeled vehicle similar to a child's scooter but with one or two seats.

mo·tor·ship (mō′ tər shĭp′) *n-* ship propelled by internal-combustion engines, especially Diesel engines.

mot·tle (mŏt′ əl) *vt-* [**mot·tled, mot·tling**] to mark with spots of various colors; dapple; blotch. *n-* **1** a spot; blotch. **2** arrangement of colored spots or blotches, such as those in marble.

mot·tled (mŏt′ əld) *n-* spotted or streaked with different colors: *a* mottled *wallpaper.*

mot·to (mŏt′ ō) *n-* [*pl.* **mot·toes** or **mot·tos**] **1** sentence, phrase, or word used as a guiding rule or principle: *"Early to bed and early to rise" was his* motto. **2** sentence or phrase expressing a principle, slogan, or the like, inscribed on a coin, seal, flag, etc.: *In the United States, the coins all bear the* motto *"In God We Trust."*

mould (mōld) mold.

mould·er (mōl′ dər) molder.

mould·ing (mōl′ dĭng) molding.

mould·y (mōl′ dē) moldy.

moult (mōlt) molt.

mound (mound) *n-* **1** heap or bank of earth, stones, or sand. **2** small hill or knoll. **3** heap or mass of anything: *His foot rested on a* mound *of pillows.* **4** in baseball, a small, raised area from which the pitcher throws.

[1]**mount** (mount) *n-* mountain. [partly from Old English **munt** and partly from Old French **mont,** both of which come from Latin **mons, montis,** "mountain."]

[2]**mount** (mount) *vt-* **1** to climb; ascend: *to* mount *stairs.* **2** to get up on: *to* mount *a horse*; *to* mount *a platform.* **3** to put on, or furnish with, a horse. **4** to set or place on something raised: *to* mount *a house on stilts.* **5** to put in position or set up for use: *to* mount *cannon on a hilltop*; *to* mount *an engine.* **6** to provide a setting, frame, or support for: *to* mount *a jewel*; *to* mount *a picture*; *to* mount *stamps in an album.* **7** to prepare (a specimen, insect, etc.) for examination or display: *to* mount *a specimen on a slide*; *to* mount *an insect.* **8** to provide with scenery, costumes, etc.: *to* mount *a play.* **9** to station; post: *to* mount *guard.* *vi-* **1** to go up; ascend: *to* mount *to the top of the steps.* **2** to go up or rise in amount, degree, etc.; increase: *His debts* mounted *steadily.* **3** to get up on; get on horseback. *n-* **1** something used as a setting, frame, or support, such as a jewelry setting, a microscopic glass slide, etc. **2** horse or other animal for riding. [from Old French **monter,** "to climb," from Latin **mons,** "mountain."]

moun·tain (moun′ tən) *n-* **1** any part of a land mass that rises high above the surrounding area. **2** anything of great size or amount: *a* mountain *of potatoes*; *a* mountain *of work.* *as **modifier**: the* mountain *folk.*

mountain chain *n-* connected row of mountains.

moun·tain·eer (moun′ tə nêr′) *n-* **1** person who lives in a mountain region. **2** person who climbs mountains as a sport or occupation.

moun·tain·eer·ing (moun′ tə nêr′ ĭng) *n-* the sport or occupation of climbing mountains, especially above the timber line with the aid of ropes and other gear.

mountain goat *n-* goatlike antelope of the Rocky Mountains, having shaggy white hair and black horns and hoofs.

mountain laurel *n-* low, gnarled evergreen shrub of eastern North America with white or pink flowers.

mountain lion *n-* a large, tawny cat of western America; catamount; cougar; panther; puma.

Mountain lion, about 8 ft. long

moun·tain·ous (moun′ tə- nəs) *adj-* **1** having many mountains: *a* mountainous *country.* **2** like a mountain; huge; enormous: *The waves were* mountainous *during the gale.* **—*adv-* moun′ tain·ous·ly.** ***n-* moun′ tain·ous·ness.**

mountain range *n-* group of mountains forming a distinct geological or geographical unit.

mountain sheep *n-* any of various wild sheep inhabiting mountains, especially the Rocky Mountain bighorn.

moun·tain·side (moun′ tən sīd′) *n-* slope of a mountain: *We camped on a* mountainside *during our vacation.*

Mountain Standard Time See *standard time.*

moun·tain·top (moun′ tən tŏp′) *n-* top or summit of a mountain.

moun·te·bank (moun′ tĭ băngk′) *n-* person who sells quack medicines, especially from a public platform; hence, any charlatan.

mount·ed (moun′ təd) *adj-* **1** seated or riding on a horse. **2** serving on horseback: *a detachment of* mounted *police.* **3** placed on or in a suitable support, setting, etc.: *a* mounted *photograph.*

mount·ing (moun′ tĭng) *n-* **1** a rising or climbing; also, a getting on horseback. **2** a placing on a suitable support; a preparing for use, study, or observation: *the* mounting *of butterflies in a case.* **3** a support, fixture, or setting: *the* mounting *of a jewel*; *the* mounting *of a gun.*

mourn (môrn) *vi-* to feel or show sorrow or grief; lament; especially, to grieve or be sorrowful for the dead: *The people* mourned *over the death of the king.* *vt-*: *Tommy* mourned *the loss of his pet dog.* ***Hom-*** morn.

mourn·er (môr′ nər) *n-* **1** person who grieves or is sorrowful; especially, person who attends a funeral. **2** at religious revival meetings, person who professes penitence for sin.

mourn·ful (môrn′ fəl) *adj-* sorrowful; sad: *the* mournful *cry of a dove.* **—*adv-* mourn′ ful·ly.** ***n-* mourn′ ful·ness.**

mourn·ing (môr′ nĭng) ***n-*** **1** a grieving. **2** outward expression of sorrow, such as the wearing of black clothes. **3** clothes worn to show grief: *The widow wore* mourning. **4** time during which one mourns. ***Hom-*** morning.

mourning dove ***n-*** any of several North American wild doves with a mournful cry.

mouse (mous) ***n-*** [*pl.* **mice** (mīs)] **1** any of several small gnawing animals with soft gray or brown fur. The common house mouse is gray, has small beady eyes and a long tail, and is most active at night. **2** *Informal* timid or cowardly person. **3** *Slang* a black eye; bruise caused by a blow. ***vi-*** **[moused, mous·ing]** **1** to hunt or catch mice. **2** to prowl and pry.

House mouse, about 7 in. long

mous·er (mouz′ ər) ***n-*** cat that catches mice.

mouse·trap (mous′ trăp′) ***n-*** trap for catching mice; also, stratagem or plot to defeat or destroy someone.

mousse (mo͞os) ***n-*** delicate dessert made of whipped cream, whites of eggs, sugar, etc., flavored and frozen.

mous·tache (mŭs′ tăsh′, mə stăsh′) mustache.

mous·y (mou′ sē) ***adj-*** **[mous·i·er, mous·i·est]** **1** of, relating to, or resembling a mouse: *a* mousy *color.* **2** infested with, or smelling of, mice. **3** quiet; timid; shy: *a* mousy *person.* **—*n-* mous′ i·ness.**

[1]**mouth** (mouth) ***n-*** [*pl.* **mouths** (mouthz, mouths)] **1** opening in the head of a person or animal through which he takes in food and drink. This opening is also used to form sounds. **2** something resembling such an opening in shape or function: *the* mouth *of a cave.* **3** person or animal who needs food: *to have four* mouths *to feed.* **4** place where a river flows into another body of water: *The* mouth *of the Mississippi is near New Orleans.*

down at the mouth downhearted; sad. **with open mouth** amazed; dumbfounded.

[2]**mouth** (mouth) ***vt-*** **1** to utter or speak, especially in an affected or pompous way: *to* mouth *big phrases.* **2** to speak indistinctly; mumble: *The speaker* mouthed *his words.* **—*n-* mouth′ er.**

mouth·ful (mouth′ fo͝ol′) ***n-*** **1** as much as the mouth can usually take in at one time. **2** a small amount: *The sick boy could eat no more than a* mouthful. **3** *Informal* word or phrase that is very long or difficult to articulate.

mouth organ ***n-*** harmonica.

mouth·piece (mouth′ pēs′) ***n-*** **1** the part of a pipe, musical instrument, etc., which a person places against the lips or in the mouth. **2** *Informal* a spokesman.

mouth·wash (mouth′ wŏsh′) ***n-*** antiseptic and scented liquid preparation used to clean and sweeten the mouth.

mov·a·ble (mo͞o′ və bəl) ***adj-*** **1** such as can be moved or carried from one place to another; not fixed. **2** changing from one date to another: *Easter is a* movable *holy day.* ***n-*** **movables** furniture, goods, or any personal property which can be carried from one place to another. Also **move′ a·ble. —*adv-* mov′ a·bly.**

move (mo͞ov) ***vi-*** **[moved, mov·ing]** **1** to change position or place; go from place to place. **2** to change homes, places of business, etc. **3** to go forward; advance; progress: *The work on the new gymnasium* moved *slowly.* **4** to be active; have interests and take part in; live: *to* move *in very important circles.* **5** to be in motion or be set in motion; go: *When you press the button, the wheels of the machine begin to* move. **6** to act; do something; take action: *The police* move *quickly whenever a crime is committed.* **7** to make a formal request: *to* move *for a new trial.* **8** *Informal* to go away; leave (often followed by "on"): *Let's* move *on.* **9** in commerce, to be disposed of by sale: *High-priced goods are usually slow to* move. **10** of the bowels, to evacuate. ***vt-*** **1** to change from one place or position to another: *to* move *a table.* **2** to cause to stir; set in motion: *The breeze* moves *the grass.* **3** to cause to act; impel: *His pride* moved *him to try the high dive. No plea could* move *him to consent.* **4** to arouse or stir up the feelings of: *to* move *an audience to tears.* **5** to propose (in a meeting): *I* move *that we take a vote on the new budget.* **6** to cause (the bowels) to act. ***n-*** **1** a change of place or position: *a* move *to the left.* **2** a motion; movement: *a sharp* move *of the head.* **3** a change of home, place of business, etc. **4** action done for a purpose, step: *What will your next* move *be?* **5** a turn to shift the pieces in games such as chess or checkers: *It's my* move.

on the move moving; busy: *He's always* on the move. **move heaven and earth** to make every effort.

move·ment (mo͞ov′ mənt) ***n-*** **1** a moving; change of position or location; also, a particular instance or manner of such moving: *the* movement *of the planets; graceful* movements *of a dancer.* **2** action; activity: *The detectives watched every* movement *of the gang members.* **3** joint action and effort for a special purpose: *the anti-slavery* movement. **4** the moving parts of a watch, clock, etc. **5** tendency; trend: *a* movement *toward higher taxes.* **6** *Music* (1) tempo; rhythm: *the* movement *of the dance music.* (2) main division or section of a symphony, sonata, etc. **7** in literature, progress of events: *the quick* movement *of the plot.* **8** in painting, sculpture, etc., suggestion of motion or action. **9** an emptying of the bowels; also, the material emptied.

mov·er (mo͞o′ vər) ***n-*** person or thing that moves or causes to move; especially, a person or company that hauls furniture from one house to another.

mov·ie (mo͞o′ vē) ***n-*** **1** a motion picture. **2 movies** (1) a motion-picture showing. (2) the industry producing motion pictures. *as* ***modifier****: a* movie *star.*

mov·ing (mo͞o′ vĭng) ***n-*** the work or business of a furniture mover. *as* ***modifier****: a* moving *company; a* moving *van.* ***adj-*** **1** changing place or position; having movement: *a* moving *wheel.* **2** causing motion or action: *a* moving *force.* **3** stirring the emotions or feelings: *a* moving *story.* **—*adv-* mov′ ing·ly.**

moving picture motion picture.

[1]**mow** (mō) ***vt-*** **[mowed, mowed** or **mown, mow·ing]** **1** to cut down (grass, grain, etc.) with a scythe or machine: *to* mow *grass.* **2** to cut grass or grain from: *The boys* mowed *the lawn.* ***vi-****: The farmers went to the field to* mow. [from Old English **māwan.**]

[2]**mow** (mou) ***n-*** **1** heap of hay or sheaves of grain stored in a barn. **2** place in the barn where hay or sheaves of grain are stored. ***vt-*** to store in such a place. [from Old English **mūga.**]

mow·er (mō′ ər) ***n-*** person or machine that mows: *six* mowers *working in the field; a lawn* mower.

mowing machine ***n-*** farm machine with blades used for cutting grain, hay, etc.

MP (ĕm′ pē′) ***n-*** [*pl.* **MP's** or **MPs**] member of the military police: *He's an* MP. *The* MP's *arrested him.*

M.P. **1** military police. **2** member of Parliament.

mph or **m.p.h.** miles per hour.

Mr. (mĭs′ tər) ***n-*** [*pl.* **Messrs.** (mĕs′ ərz)] Mister; proper title used before a man's name or the name of his position: *my father,* Mr. *Smith;* Mr. *President.*

fāte, făt, dâre, bärn; bē, bĕt, mêre; bīte, bĭt; nōte, hŏt, môre, dóg; fŭn, fûr; to͞o, bo͝ok; oil; out; tar; thin; then; hw for wh as in *wh*at; zh for s as in u*s*ual; ə for a, e, i, o, u, as in *a*go, lin*e*n, per*i*l, at*o*m, min*u*s

Mrs. (mĭs′ əz) *n-* respectful or proper title used before a married woman's name.

Ms. (mĭz) *n-* [*pl.* Ms.es.] respectful or proper title used before a woman's name: Ms. *Wilson.*

MS. or **ms.** [*pl.* MSS. or mss.] manuscript.

M.S. or **M.Cs.** Master of Science.

MST Mountain Standard Time.

Mt. or **mt.** [*pl.* Mts. or mts.] 1 mount. 2 mountain.

much (mŭch) *determiner* (traditionally called adjective or pronoun) 1 great in quantity, extent, degree, or importance: *too* much *noise*; much *money*; much *work.* 2 a great deal; a large amount: *Did that cost* much? *n-* 1 a large part of, usually less than half: *I think that* much *of the book is very funny.* 2 many things of importance: *There is* much *to see in Rome. adv-* 1 to a great degree; greatly: *I'm* much *taller than you.* 2 nearly; almost: *They left the room* much *as they had found it.*

make much of to make a fuss over; to treat or consider as of great importance: *to spoil a pet by* making *too* much of *it.* **much of a (size, height, etc.)** about the same (size, height, etc.) **not much of a** not a very good; a poor: *He's* not much of a *swimmer.* **too much for** 1 more than a match for. 2 more than (one) can bear or stand.

mu·ci·lage (myōō′ sə lĭj) *n-* 1 gummy substance found in certain plants, such as seaweeds, quinces, etc. 2 any watery solution of vegetable gum, glue, etc., used to stick things together.

mu·ci·lag·i·nous (myōō′sə lăj′ ə nəs) *adj-* 1 of, resembling, or producing mucilage. 2 sticky; gummy.

muck (mŭk) *n-* 1 mire or filth. 2 moist manure mixed with decayed vegetable matter, used as a fertilizer. 3 rich, dark soil composed largely of decayed vegetable matter. —*adj-* **muck′y [muck·i·er, muck·i·est].**

muck·rake (mŭk′ rāk′) *vi-* [**muck·racked, muck·rak·ing**] to search for and espose real or alleged corruption, dishonesty, etc., in public life. —*n-* **muck′ rak′er.**

mu·cous (myōō′ kəs) *adj-* having to do with, resembling, or producing mucus. *Hom-* mucus.

mucous membrane *n-* membrane that produces mucus. Mucous membranes line the mouth, nose, throat, and other passages of the body that open directly or indirectly to the outside.

mu·cus (myōō′ kəs) *n-* slimy, sticky fluid produced by the mucous membrane of the nose, throat, etc., which it lubricates, moistens, and protects. *Hom-* mucous.

mud (mŭd) *n-* 1 soft, wet earth. 2 *Informal* slanderous or defamatory remarks: *to throw* mud *at a person.*

mud·dle (mŭd′əl) *vt-* [**mud·dled, mud·dling**] 1 to confuse; stupefy; also, to make slightly drunk. 2 to make a mess of; bungle: *to* muddle *accounts.* 3 to mix; stir: *to* muddle *a drink. vi-* to blunder; act in a haphazard way: *to* muddle *along. n-* state of confusion or disorder; mess; also, mental confusion. —*n-* **mud′ dles.**

mud·dle-head·ed (mŭd′ əl hĕd′ əd) *adj-* mentally confused; stupid; inept: *a* muddle-headed *person.*

mud·dy (mŭd′ē) *adj-* [**mud·di·er, mud·di·est**] 1 full of mud; covered with mud: *a* muddy *road*; muddy *feet.* 2 not clear; dark or cloudy: *a* muddy *color.* 3 obscure; confused: *This composition if full of* muddy *ideas. vt-* [**mud·died, mud·dy·ing**] 1 to soil with mud: *to* muddy *one's hand.* 2 to confuse: *Too many questions* muddied *his mind.* 3 of paint or pigments, to make cloudy; darken. —*adv-* **mud′ di·ly.**

mud puppy *n-* large salamander having a flat tail, weak legs, and purplish-red, external gills, and found in streams and lakes of North America.

mud·sling·er (mŭd′ slĭng′ ər) *n-* person who makes injurious or malicious charges, especially against an opponent in a political campaign. —*n-* **mud′ sling′ing.**

mud turtle *n-* any of various small turtles of North and Central America, that live in muddy lakes and streams.

mu·ez·zin (mōō ĕz′ ən) *n-* Muslim public crier who calls the faithful to prayer.

muff (mŭf) *n-* 1 a tube of padded fur or cloth into which the hands may be placed for warmth. 2 in games such as baseball, a clumsy miss, or a failure to hold a ball when catching it; hence, any bungling or awkward action. *vt-* 1 to fail to hold (a ball). 2 to handle clumsily; bungle: *to* muff *a job. vi-: The pitcher threw him the ball and he* muffed.

Muff

muf·fin (mŭf′ ən) *n-* 1 soft, light, little cake served hot with butter. 2 English muffin.

muf·fle (mŭf′ əl) *vt-* [**muf·fled, muf·fling**] 1 to lessen or deaden (sound): *Closing the window* muffled *the noises from the street outside.* 2 to wrap or cover so as to deaden the sound of: *to* muffle *a bell.* 3 to wrap up closely and warmly: *I* muffled *myself in a warm robe.*

muffle up to wrap oneself in warm clothing.

muf·fler (mŭf′ lər) *n-* 1 scarf worn about the neck. 2 device that muffles noise.

muf·ti (mŭf′ tē) *n-* 1 an interpreter of Muslim law. 2 plain or civilian clothes, when worn by someone who ordinarily wears a uniform: *an officer in* mufti.

[1]**mug** (mŭg) *n-* 1 a large flat-bottomed cup with high straight sides and a large handle. 2 (also **mugful**) amount such a container holds when full. [probably from a Scandinavian language.]

Mug

[2]**mug** (mŭg) *n- Slang* 1 the mouth or face of a person. 2 a thug; criminal. *vt-* [**mugged, mug·ging**] 1 to assault from behind, usually with intent to rob. 2 *Slang* to take a photograph of, especially for police files. *vi- Slang* to make faces; overact, especially to attract the attention of an audience. [of uncertain origin.] —*n-* **mug′ger.**

mug·gy (mŭg′ ē) *adj-* [**mug·gi·er, mug·gi·est**] hot, damp, and stuffy; humid; sultry: *the* muggy *days of August.* —*adv-* **mug′ gi·ly.** *n-* **mug′ gi·ness.**

mug·wump (mŭg′ wŭmp′) *n-* a Republican who, in the presidential election of 1884, refused to support the Republican candidate, James G. Blaine; hence, a person who is not committed to any side, especially in politics.

mu·lat·to (mə lăt′ ō, -lä′ tō) *n-* [*pl.* **mu·lat·toes**] the child of a Negro and a Caucasian.

mul·ber·ry (mŭl′ bĕr′ ē) *n-* [*pl.* **mul·ber·ries**] 1 tree with broad leaves and a sweet, edible, berrylike fruit. Some mulberries are dark purple and some are white. 2 the fruit of any of these trees. 3 a purplish-red color. *adj-*: *a* mulberry *pie*; *a* mulberry *satin.*

mulch (mŭlch) *n-* grass, leaves, straw, etc. spread over the ground around trees and plants. Mulch is used to protect roots from temperature changes, to hold moisture in the soil, and to keep growing strawberries clean. *vt-* to spread or cover with such materials.

mulct (mŭlkt) *vt-* 1 to take something from (a person) by fraud; cheat. 2 to punish with a fine.

[1]**mule** (myōōl) *n-* 1 strong work animal, half horse and half donkey, noted for its stubbornness. 2 machine that spins cotton into yarn and winds it on spools. 3 *Informal* stubborn person. [from Old French **mul,** from Latin **mūlus.**] *Hom-* mewl.

Mule, about 5 ft. high at shoulder

[2]**mule** (myo͞ol) ***n-*** kind of lounging slipper which leaves the heel uncovered. [from French, from Dutch **muil,** from Latin **mulleus,** "slipper."] ***Hom-*** mewl.

mule deer ***n-*** long-eared deer of western United States, having a black tail.

mule skinner *Informal* ***n-*** driver of mules.

mu·le·teer (myo͞o′ lə têr′) ***n-*** driver of mules.

mul·ish (myo͞o′ lĭsh) ***adj-*** like a mule; stubborn. ***—adv-*** **mul′ ish·ly.** ***n-*** **mul′ ish·ness.**

[1]**mull** (mŭl) ***vt-*** to think about deeply; ponder (followed by "over"): *to* mull *a problem over until it's solved.* [from Middle English **mullen,** "to grind," from **mul,** "dust."]

[2]**mull** (mŭl) ***vt-*** to heat, spice, and sweeten (ale, wine, cider, etc.). [perhaps from French **mollir,** "to soften."]

mul·lein or **mul·len** (mŭl′ ən) ***n-*** any of various plants related to the figworts, having coarse, fuzzy leaves and yellow flowers in tall spikes.

mul·let (mŭl′ ət) ***n-*** [*pl.* **mul·let; mul·lets** (kinds of mullet)] any of a number of fresh-water and salt-water fishes, some of which, such as the **striped mullet** and the **gray mullet,** are used as food.

mul·li·gan (mŭl′ ə gən) *Slang* ***n-*** kind of stew made by hoboes from whatever scraps of meat and vegetables they have.

mul·lion (mŭl′ yən) ***n-*** slender upright bar separating the panes of a window, the panels in a door, etc.

multi- *combining form* **1** many; much: multi*cellular*; multi*form.* **2** having more than two: multi*lateral*; multi*colored.* **3** many times over: multi*millionaire.* [from Latin **multi-,** from **multus,** "many; much."]

mul·ti·cel·lu·lar (mŭl′ tĭ sĕl′ yə lər, mŭl′ tī-) ***adj-*** composed of many cells.

mul·ti·col·ored (mŭl′ tĭ kŭl′ ərd) ***adj-*** having many colors.

mul·ti·far·i·ous (mŭl′ tə făr′ ē əs, -fâr′ ē əs) ***adj-*** having much variety; of various kinds; diverse; manifold: *He has* multifarious *interests.* ***—adv-*** **mul′ ti·far′ ious·ly.** ***n-*** **mul′ ti·far′ ious·ness.**

mul·ti·form (mŭl′ tə fòrm′) ***adj-*** having many different forms or shapes: *dark,* multiform *clouds.*

Mul·ti·graph (mŭl′ tə grăf′) ***n-*** trademark name for a rotary typesetting and printing office machine that reproduces typewritten material. ***vt-*** **multigraph:** *to* multigraph *copies of a letter.*

mul·ti·lat·e·ral (mŭl′ tə lăt′ ər əl) ***adj-*** **1** having many sides: *a* multilateral *geometric figure.* **2** involving more than two nations or parties: *a* multilateral *agreement.* ***—adv-*** **mul′ ti·lat′ er·al·ly.**

mul·ti·mil·lion·aire (mŭl′ tĭ mĭl′ yə nâr′, mŭl′ tī-) ***n-*** person having many millions of dollars; very rich person.

mul·ti·ple (mŭl′tə pəl) ***n-*** *Mathematics* of a number, a product of that number and any other number. Example: 5 × 0, 5 × 1, 5 × 2, etc., are multiples of 5. ***adj-*** **1** many times repeated: *We have* multiple *requests for this.* **2** of many parts; made up of many things: *his* multiple *interests.*

multiple sclerosis ***n-*** chronic disease marked by patches of hardened tissue scattered over the brain and spinal chord, and causing such disorders as muscular weakness, tremors, and failure of coordination.

mul·ti·plex (mŭl′ tə plĕks′) ***adj-*** of or having to do with electronic systems that transmit two or more signals or messages over the same line or channel at the same time.

mul·ti·pli·cand (mŭl′ tə plə kănd′) ***n-*** in multiplication, the number that is to be multiplied a specific number of times. In 3 × 4 = 12, 4 is the multiplicand.

mul·ti·pli·ca·tion (mŭl′ tə plə kā′ shən) ***n-*** **1** *Mathematics* the operation through which a number, called the product, is derived from two other numbers. For the natural numbers, multiplication is sometimes thought of as a kind of addition (3 × 4 equals 4 + 4 + 4). Multiplication is the inverse of division, and the symbols used in it are [×] and [·], which are read "times." **2** a multiplying; increasing.

mul·ti·plic·i·ty (mŭl′ tə plĭs′ ə tē) ***n-*** [*pl.* **mul·ti·plic·i·ties**] great number and variety: *a* multiplicity *of details.*

mul·ti·pli·er (mŭl′ tə plī′ ər) ***n-*** in multiplication, the number that indicates how many times another number (the multiplicand) is to be multiplied. In 3 × 4 = 12, 3 is the multiplier.

mul·ti·ply (mŭl′ tə plī′) ***vi-*** [**mul·ti·plied, mul·ti·ply·ing**] **1** *Mathematics* to carry out the operation of multiplication. **2** to increase rapidly in numbers as if by multiplication. ***vt-:*** *to* multiply *4 by 5.*

mul·ti·ra·cial (mŭl′ tĭ rā′ shəl, mŭl′ tī-) ***adj-*** composed of, having to do with, or representing various races: *a* multiracial *society*; *a* multiracial *parliament.*

mul·ti·stage or **mul·ti-stage** (mŭl′ tĭ stāj′) ***adj-*** having or marked by two or more steps or stages in the completion of a process, action, etc.: *a* multistage *booster rocket*; *a* multistage *repair job.*

mul·ti·tude (mŭl′ tə to͞od′, -tyo͞od′) ***n-*** **1** great number; crowd: *a* multitude *of stars.* **2 the multitude** people in general; the common people.

mul·ti·tu·di·nous (mŭl′ tə to͞o′ də nəs, -tyo͞o′ də nəs) ***adj-*** forming a multitude; existing in great numbers; very numerous: *a* multitudinous *people*; *the* multitudinous *noises of the city.* ***—adv-*** **mul′ ti·tu′ di·nous·ly.** ***n-*** **mul′ ti·tu′ di·nous·ness.**

mul·ti·va·lent (mŭl′ tĭ vā′ lənt, mŭl′ tī-) *Chemistry* ***adj-*** having three or more valences. ***—n-*** **mul′ ti·va′ lence.**

[1]**mum** (mŭm) ***adj-*** not saying anything; silent: *to keep* mum *about a surprise party.* [a Middle English word of uncertain origin, perhaps related to **mumble.**]

mum's the word don't say anything; be silent.

[2]**mum** (mŭm) ***n-*** *Informal* chrysanthemum.

mum·ble (mŭm′ bəl) ***vt-*** [**mum·bled, mum·bling**] to speak low and not clearly; mutter: *The old woman* mumbled *something I couldn't understand.* ***vi-:*** *to* mumble *to oneself.* ***n-*** low, muttering sound: *She answered me with a* mumble. ***—n-*** **mum′ bler.** ***adv-*** **mum′ bling·ly′ :** *She answered* mumblingly.

mum·ble·ty·peg (mŭm′ bəl tē pĕg′) ***n-*** game in which the players try to toss a jacknife from various positions so that the blade always sticks in the ground.

mum·mer (mŭm′ ər) ***n-*** **1** person who takes part in masked revels at holidays. **2** actor.

mum·mer·y (mŭm′ ə rē) ***n-*** [*pl.* **mum·mer·ies**] **1** performance by mummers. **2** ridiculous, insincere, or pretentious ceremony.

mum·mi·fy (mŭm′ ə fī′) ***vt-*** [**mum·mi·fied, mum·mi·fy·ing**] to make a mummy of. ***vi-*** to shrivel up; dry. ***—n-*** **mum′ mi·fi·ca′ tion.**

mum·my (mŭm′ ē) ***n-*** [*pl.* **mum·mies**] **1** the body of a human being or animal embalmed in the ancient Egyptian manner. **2** any dead body well preserved by heat, cold, etc.

Upper part of mummy case

mumps (mŭmps) ***n-*** (takes singular verb) contagious virus disease that causes swelling of glands, especially the salivary glands about the jaw.

munch (mŭnch) ***vt-*** to chew noisily and with much working of the jaws: *He* munched *a carrot.* ***vi-***: *The rabbit* munched *in the lettuce patch.* **—*n-* munch′ er.**

mun·dane (mŭn′ dān′) ***adj-*** of or concerned with the everyday world as distinguished from more spiritual or ideal things; worldly: *our* mundane *interests.*

mu·nic·i·pal (myo͞o nĭs′ ə pəl) ***adj-*** of or having to do with a town or city, its government, etc.: *a* municipal *parking lot*; municipal *elections.* **—*adv-* mu·nic′ i·pal·ly.**

mu·nic·i·pal·i·ty (myo͞o nĭs′ ə păl′ ə tē) ***n-*** [*pl.* **mu·nic·i·pal·i·ties**] town, city, or borough that has local self-government.

mu·nif·i·cent (myo͞o nĭf′ ə sənt) ***adj-*** very generous or liberal in giving; bountiful. **—*n-* mu·nif′ i·cence. *adv-* mu·nif′ i·cent·ly.**

mu·ni·tions (myo͞o nĭsh′ ənz) ***n-*** *pl.* ammunition, guns, and similar materials used in war. *as **modifier**: a* munitions *factory.*

mu·ral (myo͞or′ əl) ***n-*** picture painted on a wall. *as **modifier**: a* mural *painter.*

mur·der (mûr′ dər) ***n-*** the unlawful and intentional killing of a person. ***vt-*** **1** to kill (a person) deliberately. **2** *Informal* to spoil or ruin: *to* murder *a song.*

mur·der·er (mûr′ dər ər) ***n-*** person guilty of murder. **—*n-*** *fem.* **mur′ der·ess.**

mur·der·ous (mûr′ dər əs) ***adj-*** **1** able or seemingly able to murder or kill; very dangerous, savage, or bloodthirsty: *a* murderous *bandit*; *a* murderous *glance*; *a* murderous *speed.* **2** of or relating to murder: *a* murderous *plot.* **—*adv-* mur′ der·ous·ly. *n-* mur′ der·ous·ness.**

murk (mûrk) ***n-*** darkness; gloom.

murk·y (mûr′ kē) ***adj-*** **[murk·i·er, murk·i·est] 1** very dark and gloomy: *the* murky *bottom of the lake.* **2** not clear; hazy: *a* murky *fog*; *his* murky *mind.* **—*adv-* murk′ i·ly. *n-* murk′ i·ness.**

mur·mur (mûr′ mər) ***n-*** **1** low, indistinct sound, such as that of voices or of a running stream. **2** low, muttered complaint; grumble: *He paid the fine without a* murmur. ***vi-*** **1** to make a low, indistinct sound: *The wind* murmured *in the trees.* **2** to grumble: *They* murmured *about the work.* ***vt-***: *to* murmur *a protest.* **—*n-* mur′ mur·er.**

mur·rain (mŭr′ ən) ***n-*** a plague, especially a fatal disease among cattle.

mus·cat (mŭs′ kăt′, -kət) ***n-*** any of several light-colored, sweet grapes from which raisins and wine are made.

mus·cle (mŭs′ əl) ***n-*** **1** bodily organ consisting of a bundle of fibers which, by contracting, produce movement in some part of the body. **2** *Informal* great strength or power, especially bodily strength. ***Hom-*** mussel.

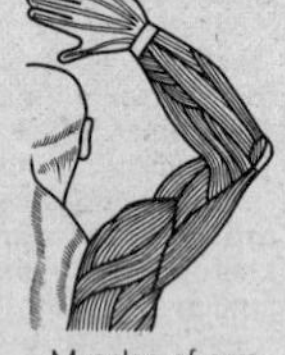

Muscles of arm

mus·cle-bound (mŭs′ əl bound′) ***adj-*** having muscles that are tense and enlarged, and have lost some of their elasticity as a result of too much exercise: *a* muscle-bound *athlete.*

Mus·co·vite (mŭs′ kə vīt′) ***n-*** **1** an inhabitant of Moscow. **2** formerly, a Russian. **3** pale, almost colorless mica. ***adj-*** of or having to do with Muscovy.

Mus·co·vy (mŭs′ kə vē) ***n-*** former name for Russia.

mus·cu·lar (mŭs′ kyə lər) ***adj-*** **1** of or having to do with a muscle: *a* muscular *ache.* **2** having well-developed muscles; strong: *He has* muscular *legs.* **—*n-* mus′ cu·lar′ i·ty** (-lăr′ ə tē). ***adv-*** **mus′ cu·lar·ly.**

muscular dys·tro·phy (dĭs′ trə fē) ***n-*** disease in which the muscles gradually shrink and lose their strength, so that the victim becomes physically helpless.

mus·cu·la·ture (mŭs′ kyə lə chər) ***n-*** system of muscles of an animal, or of a part or organ.

[1]**muse** (myo͞oz) ***vi-*** **[mused, mus·ing]** to think deeply about something; meditate; ponder. [from French **muser** meaning "loiter idly, to gape"; from Old French **muse,** "snout; muzzle."] ***Hom-*** mews. **—*n-* mus′ er.**

[2]**muse** (myo͞oz) ***n-*** **1** a poet's, artist's, or writer's source of inspiration. **2 Muse** in Greek mythology, any one of the nine goddesses who presided over music, poetry, history, astronomy, etc. [from Latin **mūsa,** from Greek **moûsa.**] ***Hom-*** mews.

mu·se·um (myo͞o zē′ əm, myo͞o′ zē-) ***n-*** place where objects of interest, especially of artistic, historical, or scientific interest, are kept and displayed.

[1]**mush** (mŭsh) ***n-*** **1** thick mixture of cornmeal boiled in water or milk. **2** any soft, thick mixture like this. **3** *Informal* silly, sentimental talk or behavior. [apparently a variant of **mash.**]

[2]**mush** (mŭsh) ***vi-*** to travel on foot over snow with a sled and dog team. ***n-*** journey made in this way. ***interj-*** shout urging the dogs pulling a sled to go forward. [American word perhaps from **mush on,** an alteration of French **marchons,** "Let's go."] **—*n-* mush′ er.**

mush·room (mŭsh′ ro͞om′) ***n-*** **1** any rapidly growing, usually umbrella-shaped fungus, especially one that is good to eat. **2** (also **mushroom cloud**) cloud of debris, gas, vapor, etc., that rises from an explosion, especially a nuclear explosion. ***vi-*** **1** to grow or spring up rapidly: *Shopping centers* mushroomed *along the highway.* **2** to appear in a rising cloud with a wide-spreading top: *Dust* mushroomed *in the air.*

Mushrooms

mush·y (mŭsh′ ē) ***adj-*** **[mush·i·er, mush·i·est] 1** like mush; soft and sticky. **2** *Informal* foolishly sentimental: *a* mushy *love story.* **—*adv-* mush′ i·ly. *n-* mush′ i·ness.**

mu·sic (myo͞o′ zĭk) ***n-*** **1** art of combining sounds to form organized, usually harmonious arrangements. **2** a musical composition or compositions; also, the written or printed notes for this. **3** musical compositions collectively: *the* music *of Mozart*; *16th-century* music. **4** any melodious or pleasing sound: *the* music *of the rain.*
face the music to accept the consequences of an action.
set to music to provide music for: *to* set *a poem* to music.

mu·si·cal (myo͞o′ zĭ kəl) ***adj-*** **1** of, having to do with, or producing music: *a* musical *instrument*; *a* musical *program.* **2** melodious: *the* musical *song of a bird.* **3** fond of or skilled in music: *a* musical *family.* ***n-*** (also **musical comedy**) a play with music and singing. **—*adv-* mu′ si·cal·ly.**

mu·si·cale (myo͞o′ zĭ kăl′) ***n-*** private social entertainment featuring a performance of music.

musical instrument ***n-*** device for making music, such as a piano, violin, or trumpet.

music box ***n-*** box containing a mechanical apparatus that produces music, usually when the box lid is opened.

music hall ***n-*** **1** place for holding musical entertainments. **2** *Brit.* a theater for vaudeville.

mu·si·cian (myo͞o zĭsh′ ən) ***n-*** person skilled in music, such as a performer, composer, or conductor.

mu·si·cian·ship (myo͞o zĭsh′ ən shĭp′) ***n-*** art or skill of a musician.

mu·si·col·o·gy (myo͞o′ zə kŏl′ ə jē) ***n-*** the scholarly study of music, as distinguished from performance or composition. **—*n-* mu′ si·col′ o·gist.**

musk (mŭsk) ***n-*** oily substance with a strong odor, obtained from a gland of the male musk deer and used in making perfumes; also, the odor of this substance.
musk deer ***n-*** small, hornless deer, found in the high parts of central Asia.
mus·keg (mŭs′ kĕg′) ***n-*** bog or marsh of the colder regions of North America, especially one in which sphagnum moss grows.
mus·kel·lunge (mŭs′ kə lŭnj′) ***n-*** [*pl.* **mus·kel·lunge**] large pike of North America, a prized game fish.
mus·ket (mŭs′ kət) ***n-*** old-fashioned gun, replaced by the rifle.

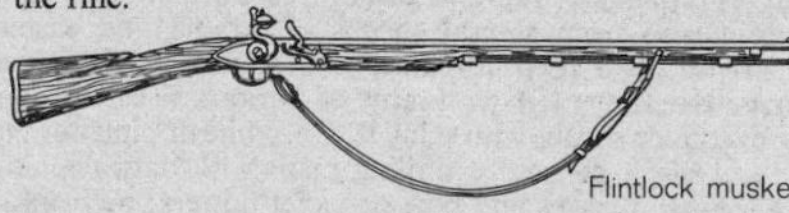

Flintlock musket

mus·ket·eer (mŭs′ kə têr′) ***n-*** foot soldier armed with a musket; especially, one of the royal bodyguard in France during the 17th and 18th centuries.
mus·ket·ry (mŭs′ kə trē) ***n-*** **1** skill of firing guns such as muskets; also, the fire from such guns. **2** muskets collectively.

Musk ox, about 5 ft. high at shoulder

musk·mel·on (mŭsk′ mĕl′ ən) ***n-*** **1** any of various round melons with sweet flesh and a tough rind, such as the cantaloupe. **2** the vine it grows on.
musk ox ***n-*** long-haired animal of Greenland and arctic North America, related to both sheep and cattle.
musk·rat (mŭsk′ răt′) ***n-*** **1** North American water rodent with webbed hind feet and glossy, brown fur. **2** the fur of this animal. *as* ***modifier****: a* muskrat *coat.*

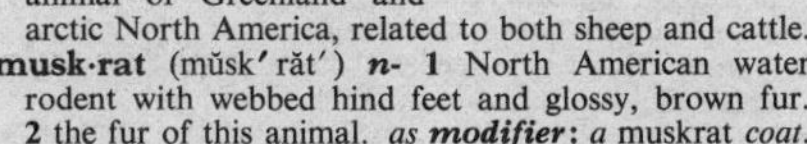

musk·y (mŭs′ kē) ***adj-*** [**musk·i·er, musk·i·est**] having an odor like that of musk. ***—n-*** **musk′ i·ness.**

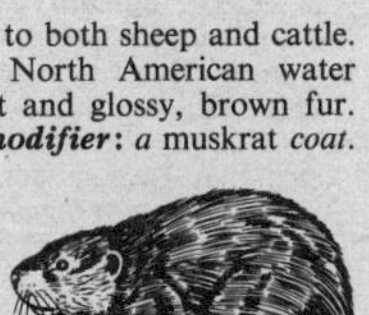

Muskrat, about 2 ft. long including tail

Mus·lim (mŭz′ ləm) ***n-*** a believer in Islam, the religion founded by Mohammed. ***adj-*** of or relating to the followers of Islam or to their customs: *a* Muslim *country.* Also **Moslem.**
mus·lin (mŭz′ lən) ***n-*** any of various sheer or heavy cotton fabrics of plain weave. *as* ***modifier****: a* muslin *sheet.*
muss (mŭs) *Informal* ***vt-*** to make untidy; rumple or soil. ***n-*** state of disorder; mess.
mus·sel (mŭs′ əl) ***n-*** any of several mollusks found in fresh or salt water, especially an edible marine kind with a bluish-black shell. ***Hom-*** muscle.

Mussel, 2-3 in. long

Mus·sul·man (mŭs′ əl mən) *Archaic* ***n-*** a Muslim.
muss·y (mŭs′ ē) *Informal* ***adj-*** [**muss·i·er, muss·i·est**] disarranged; messy. ***—adv-*** **muss′ i·ly.** ***n-*** **muss′ i·ness.**
must (mŭst) ***auxiliary verb*** **1** am, are, or is required or obliged to; have to: *Citizens* must *obey the laws. I* must *go now.* **2** ought to; should: *I* must *try to see her more often.* **3** am, are, or is almost certain to: *This* must *be what he means. Her coat isn't here, so she* must *have gone.* ***n-*** *Informal* something that is necessary, required, or essential: *In winter, warm clothes are a* must.
mus·tache (mŭs′ tăsh′, mə stăsh′) ***n-*** hair that grows on a man's upper lip, especially when left unshaven, but trimmed and groomed. Also **moustache.**
mus·ta·chi·o (mə stăsh′ ē ō) ***n-*** [*pl.* **mus·ta·chi·os**] (usually **mustachios**) mustache, especially a large one.
mus·tang (mŭs′ tăng′) ***n-*** small, sturdy, wild or half-wild horse of western North American plains.
mus·tard (mŭs′ tərd) ***n-*** **1** any of various plants bearing small, four-petaled, yellow flowers and long pods containing peppery seeds. **2** the powdered seeds of this plant, used as a seasoning or mixed with vinegar or water to make a condiment. **3** deep, brownish-yellow color. ***adj-****: a* mustard *flavor; a* mustard *coat.*
mustard gas ***n-*** oily liquid having an odor like that of mustard, and causing severe blistering. It was formerly used in chemical warfare.
mustard plaster ***n-*** a mixture of powdered mustard and other substances, spread on a cloth and placed on a person's chest or back as a treatment for certain ailments.

Mustard

mus·ter (mus′ tər) ***vt-*** **1** to assemble or call up (men or troops) for review, roll call, etc. **2** to summon; gather up: *to* muster *one's courage.* ***n-*** **1** an assembling or gathering, especially of troops, for review. **2** roll or official list of men assembled in a military unit or naval crew.
pass muster to pass review or careful examination.
muster in to enlist (troops, recruits, etc.).
muster out to discharge (troops that have been in service).
must·n't (mŭs′ ənt) must not.
mus·ty (mŭs′ tē) ***adj-*** [**must·i·er, must·i·est**] **1** spoiled with damp or mildew; moldy: *an attic full of* musty *old clothes.* **2** having a stale, moldy odor or taste: *a* musty *attic;* musty *bread.* **3** stale; out of date: *his* musty *ideas.* ***—adv-*** **must′ i·ly.** ***n-*** **must′ i·ness.**
mu·ta·ble (myōō′ tə bəl) ***adj-*** able or likely to change in form, essentials, etc.: *a* mutable *theory;* mutable *plans.* ***—n-*** **mu′ ta·bil′ i·ty.**
mu·tant (myōō′ tənt) ***n-*** plant or animal produced as a result of mutation. ***adj-*** of or resulting from mutation.
mu·tate (myōō′ tāt′) ***vt-*** [**mu·tat·ed, mu·tat·ing**] to cause to undergo mutation, especially by exposure to high-energy radiation. ***vi-*** to undergo mutation.
mu·ta·tion (myōō tā′ shən) ***n-*** **1** change; alteration. **2** *Biology* sudden variation in a plant or animal, which results from a change in the genes and chromosomes and can therefore be inherited. **3** a mutant.
mute (myōōt) ***adj-*** **1** making no sound; silent: *The puppy wagged its tail in* mute *appeal.* **2** lacking the power of speech; dumb. ***n-*** **1** person who cannot speak. **2** device placed in or on a musical instrument to soften or muffle its tone. ***vt-*** [**mut·ed, mut·ing**] to soften or muffle the tone of: *He* muted *his voice.* ***—adv-*** **mute′ ly.** ***n-*** **mute′ ness.**
mu·ti·late (myōō′ tə lāt′) ***vt-*** [**mu·ti·lat·ed, mu·ti·lat·ing**] to damage or destroy by cutting up or cutting off a necessary part. ***—n-*** **mu′ ti·la′ tor.**

---

fāte, făt, dâre, bärn; bē, bĕt, mêre; bīte, bĭt; nōte, hŏt, môre, dôg; fŭn, fûr; tōō, bŏŏk; oil; out; ta*r*; thin; then; hw for wh as in *wh*at; zh for s as in u*s*ual; ə for a, e, i, o, u, as in *a*go, lin*e*n, per*i*l, at*o*m, min*u*s

mu·ti·la·tion (myo͞o′ tə lā′ shən) ***n-*** a mutilating or a being mutilated; also, an instance of this.

mu·ti·neer (myo͞o′ tə nêr′) ***n-*** person who takes part in a mutiny.

mu·ti·nous (myo͞o′ tə nəs) ***adj-*** **1** planning or taking part in a mutiny: *the* mutinous *crew.* **2** rebellious; defiant: *his* mutinous *words.* ***—adv-*** **mu′ ti·nous·ly.** ***n-*** **mu′ ti·nous·ness.**

mu·ti·ny (myo͞o′ tə nē) ***n-*** [*pl.* **mu·ti·nies**] uprising against lawful authority, especially by sailors or soldiers against their commanding officers. ***vi-*** **[mu·ti·nied, mu·ti·ny·ing]:** *The discontented sailors* mutinied.

mutt (mŭt) *Slang* ***n-*** mongrel dog; cur.

mut·ter (mŭt′ ər) ***vi-*** **1** to speak indistinctly in a low voice: *He* muttered *in his sleep.* **2** to make a low, rumbling sound, as thunder does. ***vt-:*** *He* muttered *a reply.* ***n-*** low, indistinct voice or sound: *a* mutter *of discontent*; *the* mutter *of distant thunder,* ***—n-*** **mut′ ter·er.**

mut·ton (mŭt′ ən) ***n-*** flesh of a sheep, used for food. ***—adj-*** **mut′ ton·y.**

mut·ton·chops (mŭt′ ən chŏps′) ***n-*** *pl.* long sideburns that broaden along the lower part of the face. Also **muttonchop whiskers.**

mu·tu·al (myo͞o′ cho͞o əl) ***adj-*** **1** done, felt, or given by each of two toward the other: *The horse and I looked at each other with* mutual *suspicion.* **2** having the same feeling, attitude, etc., toward each other: *They are* mutual *admirers.* **3** having the same relationship to both: *We have a* mutual *friend.* ***—adv-*** **mu′ tu·al·ly.**

mutual fund ***n-*** corporation that invests the pooled capital of its stockholders in other stocks and bonds, and pays dividends when its investments are profitable.

muu·muu (mo͞o′ mo͞o′) ***n-*** loose dress or nightgown with a wide, gathered neckline.

muz·zle (mŭz′ əl) ***n-*** **1** nose and jaws of an animal; snout. **2** arrangement of straps or wire mesh to be placed over an animal's snout to keep it from biting or eating. **3** front end of a gun barrel, cannon, etc. ***vt-*** **[muz·zled, muz·zling]** **1** to put a restraining device over the snout of (an animal). **2** to restrain from free expression of opinion: *to* muzzle *the newspapers.*

Muzzle

muzzle loader ***n-*** gun that is loaded from the muzzle. ***—adj-*** **muz′ zle-load′ ing.**

muzzle velocity ***n-*** speed of a bullet or projectile when it leaves the muzzle of a gun or other firing device.

my (mī) ***determiner*** (possessive case of the pronoun "I," now usually called possessive adjective) **1** of, belonging to, done, or made by me: *I want you to meet* my *mother. This is* my *book.* **2** used in certain forms of address: my *dear Mrs. Smith*; my *lord.* ***interj-*** exclamation of surprise, pleasure, etc.: My! *what a lovely day!*

my·ce·li·um (mī sē′ lē əm) *Botany* ***n-*** [*pl.* **my·ce·li·a** (-ə)] mass of threadlike stalks that form the plant body of certain fungi, such as the common mold.

my·col·o·gist (mī kŏl′ ə jĭst) ***n-*** person who is expert in, and usually occupied in, mycology.

my·col·o·gy (mī kŏl′ ə jē) ***n-*** science or study of fungi.

my·na or **my·nah** (mī′ nə) ***n-*** any of several starlings of Asia, such as the **hill myna** of India, which may be taught to say a few words.

Myn·heer (mīn′ hĕr′) *Dutch* ***n-*** **1** title of courtesy equivalent to "Mr." **2 mynheer** form of address equivalent to "sir."

my·o·pi·a (mī ō′ pē ə) ***n-*** condition affecting the eyesight so that only objects at close range are seen clearly; nearsightedness.

my·op·ic (mī ŏp′ ĭk) ***adj-*** **1** affected by or characteristic of myopia; nearsighted: *a* myopic *stare.* **2** showing lack of foresight; shortsighted. ***—adv-*** **my·op′ i·cal·ly.**

myr·i·ad (mĭr′ ē əd) ***n-*** a vast number. ***adj-*** countless; innumerable: *the* myriad *stars.*

myr·i·a·pod (mĭr′ ē ə pŏd′) ***n-*** a centipede or millipede, formerly classified together as **Myriapoda.**

Myr·mi·don (mûr′ mə dŏn′, -dən) ***n-*** **1** in Greek legend, one of a band of warriors who followed Achilles in the Trojan War. **2 myrmidon** any follower who carries out orders without question.

myrrh (mûr) ***n-*** fragrant, gummy resin with a bitter taste, obtained from several shrubs of Arabia and eastern Africa. It is used in medicines, perfumes, and incense.

myr·tle (mûr′ təl) ***n-*** **1** any of various sweet-smelling evergreen shrubs with shiny leaves, white or pink flowers, and black berries. **2** trailing plant with dark, shining, evergreen leaves and blue or violet flowers; periwinkle.

my·self (mī sĕlf′) ***pron-*** **1** reflexive form of **me**; my own self: *I let* myself *into the house. I am pleased with* myself. **2** my normal or true self: *I don't feel quite* myself *today.* **3** intensive form of I: *I* myself *saw it.* **4** *Irish* I: *Indeed,* myself *will do it.*

by myself **1** alone: *I sat* by myself *in the garden.* **2** without any help: *I cooked this meal* by myself.

mys·te·ri·ous (mĭ stêr′ ē əs) ***adj-*** not understood or explained; of unknown cause or origin; puzzling: *a* mysterious *light in the sky*; *her* mysterious *smile.* ***—adv-*** **mys·te′ ri·ous·ly.** ***n-*** **mys·te′ ri·ous·ness.**

mys·ter·y (mĭs′ tə rē) ***n-*** [*pl.* **mys·ter·ies**] **1** something that is secret, hidden, or unexplained: *The name of the thief is a* mystery. **2** something not known or not understandable: *the* mystery *of the creation of life.* **3** secrecy; obscurity: *a stranger shrouded in* mystery. **4** a religious ritual or sacrament.

mystery play ***n-*** in medieval times, a religious drama based on incidents from the Bible.

mys·tic (mĭs′ tĭk) ***adj-*** **1** of or relating to beliefs, practices, etc., that have hidden or secret meaning: *the* mystic *rites of ancient religions.* **2** of or relating to mysticism. **3** magical or mysterious: *the* mystic *beauty of the night.* ***n-*** person who believes that he can have direct spiritual communication with God.

mys·ti·cal (mĭs′ tĭ kəl) ***adj-*** **1** having a spiritual meaning not explained by reason or logic. **2** of or relating to direct communication with God or absolute truth. ***—adv-*** **mys′ ti·cal·ly.**

mys·ti·cism (mĭs′ tə sĭz′ əm) ***n-*** **1** belief that direct spiritual knowledge of God or absolute truth comes through meditation, inspiration, etc. **2** spiritual qualities of a mystic. **3** vague or illogical thinking.

mys·ti·fy (mĭs′ tə fī′) ***vt-*** **[mys·ti·fied, mys·ti·fy·ing]** to bewilder; baffle; perplex: *His actions* mystify *me.* ***—n-*** **mys′ ti·fi·ca′ tion.**

myth (mĭth) ***n-*** **1** traditional story, often founded on some fact of nature or an event in the early history of a people, and embodying some religious belief of that people. **2** any imaginary person, thing, or event. **3** belief having no sound or logical basis.

myth·i·cal (mĭth′ ĭ kəl) ***adj-*** **1** existing in myths: *Hercules was a* mythical *hero.* **2** imaginary; made-up: *a* mythical *kingdom.* ***—adv-*** **myth′ i·cal·ly.**

myth·o·log·i·cal (mĭth′ ə lŏj′ ĭ kəl) ***adj-*** of, relating to, or existing in mythology: *a* mythological *monster.* ***—adv-*** **myth′ o·log′ i·cal·ly.**

my·thol·o·gy (mĭ thŏl′ ə jē) ***n-*** [*pl.* **my·thol·o·gies**] **1** body of myths in which are recorded a people's beliefs concerning their origin, gods, heroes, etc. **2** study of these stories and beliefs.

N

N, n (ĕn) ***n-*** [*pl.* **N's, n's**] the fourteenth letter of the English alphabet.
n (ĕn) *Mathematics* ***n-*** an indefinite number.
n. **1** noun. **2** noon.
N symbol for nitrogen
N. **1** north. **2** northern.
Na symbol for sodium.
N.A. North America.
NAACP or **N.A.A.C.P.** National Association for the Advancement of Colored People.
nab (năb) *Informal* ***vt-*** [**nabbed, nab·bing**] **1** to seize and arrest: *to* nab *a thief.* **2** to seize suddenly; grab.
na·bob (nā'bŏb') ***n-*** **1** governor of a province in India under the Mogul Empire. **2** any rich and powerful man.
na·celle (nə sĕl') ***n-*** enclosure on an aircraft for an engine, or for the crew.
na·cre (nā'kər) ***n-*** mother-of-pearl.
na·dir (nā'dĭr) ***n-*** **1** that part of the celestial sphere directly beneath the place where one stands, and opposite to the zenith. **2** the lowest point: *the* nadir *of his career.*
[1]**nag** (năg) ***vi-*** [**nagged, nag·ging**] to scold or find fault continually, often about little things. ***vt-*** to torment with tiresome insistence: *He* nagged *his father for a bicycle.* ***n-*** person who constantly scolds or finds fault. [probably from Old Norse **nagga** meaning "nibble; peck; gnaw."]
[2]**nag** (năg) ***n-*** horse, especially one that is old and worn out. [from Middle English **nagge,** of uncertain origin.]
nag·ging (năg'ĭng) ***adj-*** **1** always scolding or finding fault: *a* nagging *brother.* **2** causing constant annoyance or discomfort: *a* nagging *backache.* **—*adv-*** **nag'ging·ly.**
Na·hua·tl (nä'wä'təl) ***n-*** the language of the Aztecs and some Indian peoples of southern Mexico and Central America. ***adj-***: *a* Nahuatl *word.*
nai·ad (nā'ăd', nī'ăd', -əd) ***n-*** [*pl.* **nai·ads** or **nai·a·des** (-ə dēz)] in classical mythology, one of the nymphs who dwelled in fountains, rivers, lakes, etc.
nail (nāl) ***n-*** **1** slender, sharp-pointed, metal spike or pin made to fasten together pieces of wood, leather, etc., by being driven through or into them. **2** horny growth on the upper side of the end of a finger or toe; also, a similar part, such as a claw, on a bird or animal. ***vt-*** **1** to fasten, fix, or secure with or as if with a metal spike or pin: *He* nailed *a shelf to a wall. Panic* nailed *him to his chair.* **2** *Slang* to get or catch: *to* nail *a thief.* **3** *Slang* to hit.

FINISHING
WIRE
HORSESHOE
FINGER
Nails

hit the nail on the head to be exactly to the point, especially in making an observation or criticism.
on the nail with exact accuracy, promptness, etc.
nail down *Informal* to settle finally and in all details.
nail file ***n-*** small metal file for shaping the fingernails.
nail polish ***n-*** lacquer for the fingernails.
nail set ***n-*** punch with a very small tip, used in driving nails flush with, or below, the surface.
nain·sook (nān'sŏŏk') ***n-*** fine, soft muslin with a plain, striped, or checked weave.
na·ïve or **na·ive** (nä ēv') ***adj-*** **1** simple, childlike, and unaffected; artless; unsophisticated: *a* naïve *person;* naive *remarks.* **2** foolishly simple: *a* naive *plan to deceive us.* **—*adv-*** **na·ive'ly.** ***n-*** **na·ive'ness.**
na·ïve·té or **na·ive·té** (nä ē'və tā', -ēv'tā') ***n-*** child-like simplicity; artlessness; also, an act or remark showing this.
na·ked (nā'kəd) ***adj-*** **1** wearing no clothes; nude. **2** bare; without the usual covering: *a* naked *tree; a* naked *sword.* **3** plain; unconcealed: *the* naked *truth.* **—*adv-*** **na'ked·ly.** ***n-*** **na'ked·ness.**
naked eye ***n-*** human eye unassisted by a telescope, microscope, etc.
NAM or **N.A.M.** National Association of Manufacturers.
nam·by-pam·by (năm'bē păm'bē) ***adj-*** foolishly and affectedly sentimental; weak and insipid; wishy-washy. ***n-*** [*pl.* **nam·by-pam·bies**]: *He is a* namby-pamby.
name (nām) ***n-*** **1** term or title by which a person or thing is called or known. **2** character; reputation: *He has a good* name *in his home town.* ***vt-*** [**named, nam·ing**] **1** to give a name to; call: *They* named *the baby "Thomas."* **2** to mention or identify: *He* named *several people involved in the plot.* **3** to choose for a special purpose; appoint; designate: *They* named *her executive director.* **—*n-*** **nam'er.**
call (someone) names to taunt with insulting terms. **in name only** in outward appearance but not in reality. **in the name of** **1** for the sake of: *Avenge yourself* in the name of *your ancestors.* **2** by the authority of: *Go,* in the name of *the king.* **make a name for (oneself)** to establish a reputation; become successful.
name·a·ble ***adj-*** such as can be called by a name or special term. Also **nam'a·ble.**
name day ***n-*** day consecrated to the saint after whom one is named.
name·less (nām'ləs) ***adj-*** **1** unnamed; having no name. **2** unknown: *the* nameless *inventor of the wheel.* **3** not marked or identified with a name: *a* nameless *grave.* **4** impossible to describe or identify: *a* nameless *fear.* **—*adv-*** **name'less·ly.** ***n-*** **name'less·ness.**
name·ly (nām'lē) ***adv-*** specifically; that is to say: *certain fruits,* namely *peaches, pears, and plums.*
name·sake (nām'sāk') ***n-*** person who has been named after another, or has the same name as another.
nan·keen (năn kēn') ***n-*** **1** brownish-yellow cotton cloth, originally made in China. **2** **nankeens** clothing, especially trousers, made of this. Also **nan·kin'** (-kēn').
nan·ny (năn'ē) *Brit.* ***n-*** [*pl.* **nan·nies**] children's nurse.
nanny goat ***n-*** female goat.
Na·o·mi (nā ō'mē) ***n-*** in the Old Testament, the mother-in-law of Ruth. In the CCD Bible, **No·e'mi** (nō ā'mē).
[1]**nap** (năp) ***n-*** short sleep; doze: *to take a* nap *in the afternoon.* [from Old English **hnappian.**]
catch (someone) napping to catch (someone) off guard.
[2]**nap** (năp) ***n-*** surface of short hairs or fibers on some fabrics, such as velvet and many wools; pile. [from Middle English **noppe,** perhaps from Old English **-hnoppa** meaning "tuft."] **—*adj-*** **nap'less.** ***adj-*** **nap'py** [**nap·pi·er, nap·pi·est**].
na·palm (nā'päm', -pälm') ***n-*** a jellylike mixture of gasoline and chemical thickeners, such as oils and fats, used in incendiary bombs.

---

fāte, făt, dâre, bärn; bē, bĕt, mêre; bīte, bĭt; nōte, hŏt, môre, dȯg; fŭn, fûr; to͞o, bo͝ok; oil; out; tar; thin; then; hw for wh as in *wh*at; zh for s as in u*s*ual; ə for a, e, i, o, u, as in *a*go, lin*e*n, per*i*l, at*o*m, min*u*s

nape (nāp) *n-* the back of the neck.

na·per·y (nā′pə rē) *n-* household linen, especially napkins, tablecloths, etc.

naph·tha (năp′thə, năf′-) *n-* clear fluid that will burn easily, made from petroleum and used as fuel and as a solvent.

naph·tha·lene (năp′thə lēn′, năf′-) *n-* white, crystalline compound, obtained by distilling coal tar and used in making mothballs and similar preparations.

nap·kin (năp′kĭn) *n-* small square of cloth or paper used while eating to protect the clothes or for wiping the fingers or lips.

na·po·le·on (nə pō′lē ən) *n-* **1** rich dessert made of several layers of flaky pastry filled with custard or whipped cream. **2** former gold coin of France.

nar·cis·sism (när′sə sĭz′əm) *n-* excessive or abnormal admiration for oneself; self-love.

Narcissus

nar·cis·sus (när sĭs′əs) *n-* [*pl.* **nar·cis·sus·es** or **nar·cis·si** (-ī′, -ē′)] **1** any of various spring-blooming plants that grow from bulbs, with white, cream-colored, or yellow flowers; also, the flower itself. The jonquil and the daffodil are kinds of narcissus. **2 Narcissus** in Greek legend, a beautiful young man who fell in love with his own reflection in the water and was changed into the flower that bears his name.

nar·co·sis (när kō′səs) *n-* deep unconsciousness caused by a drug.

nar·cot·ic (när kŏt′ĭk) *n-* **1** drug that, when used in small doses, causes sleep or relieves pain by dulling the nerves. **2** drug subject to government restrictions imposed on such substances. *adj-*: *a* narcotic *stupor.*

Nar·ra·gan·set (năr′ə găn′sət) *n-* [*pl.* **Nar·ra·gan·sets,** also **Nar·ra·gan·set**] one of a tribe of Algonquian Indians who once occupied most of Rhode Island.

nar·rate (nă rāt′, năr′āt) *vt-* [**nar·rat·ed, nar·rat·ing**] to tell (a story); give an account of (happenings); relate: *The sailor* narrated *his adventures.*

nar·ra·tion (nă rā′shən) *n-* **1** the telling of real or imaginary happenings. **2** story; account.

nar·ra·tive (năr′ə tĭv) *n-* an account of real or imaginary happenings; story; tale. *adj-*: *a* narrative *poem.* —*adv-* **nar′ra·tive·ly.**

nar·ra·tor (năr′ā′tər) *n-* person who narrates; especially, one who recites a spoken account as part of a musical or dramatic performance.

nar·row (năr′ō) *adj-* [**nar·row·er, nar·row·est**] **1** having comparatively small width. **2** limited in amount or size; small; limited. **3** not tolerant; biased: *a very* narrow *mind.* **4** strict; exact: *a* narrow *examination of the facts. vt-* **1** to make less wide; lessen the width of: *We* narrowed *the flower bed.* **2** to limit or restrict (often followed by "down"): *He* narrowed *down the possibilities. vi-*: *The river* narrows *at that point. n-* **narrows** (usually takes plural verb) strait or channel between two wider bodies of water. —*n-* **nar′row·ness.**

narrow escape *n-* an escape by a small margin.

nar·row-gauge (năr′ō gāj′) *adj-* having, or made for, railroad tracks of less than standard gauge.

nar·row·ly (năr′ō lē) *adv-* **1** by a very small margin; barely: *The arrow* narrowly *missed him.* **2** in a narrow manner.

nar·row-mind·ed (năr′ō mīn′dəd) *adj-* having or expressing a limited, biased point of view; intolerant; prejudiced. —*adv-* **nar′row-mind′ed·ly.** *n-* **nar′row-mind′ed·ness.**

nar·whal (när′hwäl′) *n-* sea mammal related to the whale and having a single, long, twisted tusk.

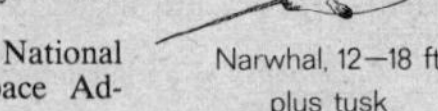
Narwhal, 12—18 ft. plus tusk

nar·y (nâr′ē) **nary a** *Informal* not a single; not one: *We voyaged for days, but* nary a *whale did we see.*

NASA (nă′sə) *n-* National Aeronautics and Space Administration.

na·sal (nā′zəl) *adj-* **1** of or having to do with the nose. **2** pronounced or coming through the nose: *a* nasal *sound*; *a* nasal *voice. n-* **1** a sound produced this way. **2** either of the letters "m" or "n." —*n-* **na·sal′i·ty** (nā zăl′ə tē). *adv-* **na′sal·ly.**

na·sal·ize (nā′zə līz′) *vt-* [**na·sal·ized, na·sal·iz·ing**] to pronounce (a vowel) with resonance through the nose, as in French bon (bō^{n}). *vi-* to speak through the nose.

nas·cent (năs′ənt, nā′sənt) *adj-* beginning to exist or grow; coming into being.

Nasturtium

na·stur·tium (nă stûr′shəm, nə-) *n-* garden plant with showy yellow, orange, or red flowers and nearly circular, edible leaves having a spicy flavor; also, the flower itself.

nas·ty (năs′tē) *adj-* [**nas·ti·er, nas·ti·est**] **1** dirty; filthy. **2** extremely unpleasant; disagreeable: *a* nasty *day*; nasty *disposition* **3** painful and possibly harmful: *a* nasty *fall.* **4** ill-natured; mean: *a* nasty *growl.* —*adv-* **nas′ti·ly.** *n-* **nas′ti·ness.**

na·tal (nā′təl) *adj-* of or having to do with one's birth: *August 10th is his* natal *day.*

Natch·ez (năch′əz) *n-* [*pl.* **Natch·ez**] **1** one of a tribe of Indians who formerly inhabited the lower Mississippi Valley. **2** their language. *adj-*: *the* Natchez *chief.*

na·tion (nā′shən) *n-* **1** the people of an independent country, considered as a unified group: *The President addressed the* nation *in his speech.* **2** an independent country: *to travel from one end of the* nation *to the other.* **3** a people united by the same customs, history, beliefs, etc., but not necessarily living together in one country. **4** tribe or federation, especially of American Indians.

na·tion·al (năsh′ən əl) *adj-* **1** of, relating to, or characteristic of a nation: *the* national *government*; *our* national *customs*; national *pride.* **2** of, affecting, or throughout a nation as a whole: *a* national *problem*; *a* national *election*; national *advertising. n-* citizen or subject: *He is a British* national. —*adv-* **na′tion·al·ly.**

national bank *n-* commercial bank chartered and supervised by the national government.

National Guard *n-* the military forces of a state, supported in part by the Federal government, which become part of the Army or Air Force when called into active service during national emergencies.

na·tion·al·ism (năsh′ən ə lĭz′əm) *n-* ardent belief in the importance of one's nation, its people, customs and language, and its right to independence. This belief sometimes disregards the rights of other countries. —*n-* **na′tion·al·ist.** *adj-* **na′tion·al·is′tic.**

na·tion·al·i·ty (năsh′ə năl′ə tē) *n-* [*pl.* **na·tion·al·i·ties**] **1** legal status as a citizen of a nation; citizenship: *a man of Russian birth and French* nationality. **2** national backgroud or origin: *My grandparents were of Swedish* nationality. **3** group of people united by language, customs, etc., and part of a larger group or nation: *The Kurds are one of the* nationalities *of Iran.*

na·tion·al·ize (năsh′ən ə līz′) *vt-* [**na·tion·al·ized, na·tion·al·iz·ing**] **1** to place (an industry, public service, etc.) under government control: *to* nationalize *the railroads.* **2** to unite into a nation. *—n-* **na′ tion·al·i·za′ tion.** *n-* **na′ tion·al·iz′ er.**

national income *n-* total annual income of a nation, including wages, business profits, rent, interest, etc.

national park *n-* area of natural beauty or special interest set aside and preserved by a government for the enjoyment of all.

na·tion-wide (nā′ shən wīd′) *adj-* including or extending throughout a nation: *a* nation-wide *broadcast.*

na·tive (nā′ tĭv) *adj-* **1** of or relating to one's birth or to the place of one's birth: *one's* native *land.* **2** born, produced in, or belonging to a particular country or place: *a* native *Californian*; native *corn.* **3** inborn; not acquired; natural: *his* native *ability.* **4** produced by nature in nearly pure state: *the* native *copper of Michigan.* *n-* **1** person born in a certain country or place: *a* native *of Ohio.* **2** animal or plant originally found in or growing in a particular place. **3** original inhabitant of a place; aborigine. *—adv-* **na′ tive·ly.** *n-* **na′ tive·ness.**

go native **1** to adopt, often superficially, the customs of a place or country. **2** to live and dress in a simple, often primitive, manner, especially on vacation.

na·tiv·i·ty (nə tĭv′ ə tē) *n-* [*pl.* **na·tiv·i·ties**] **1** birth. **2** the time, place, and circumstances of one's birth. **3 the Nativity** (1) the birth of Christ. (2) painting or sculpture showing Christ as a newborn infant.

NATO (nā′ tō′) *n-* *N*orth *A*tlantic *T*reaty *O*rganization.

nat·ty (năt′ ē) *adj-* [**nat·ti·er, nat·ti·est**] neat; smart; trim: *a* natty *suit.* *—adv-* **nat′ ti·ly.** *n-* **nat′ ti·ness.**

nat·u·ral (năch′ ər əl) *adj-* **1** produced by or occurring in nature; not man-made: *a* natural *gas*; *a* natural *rock formation*; natural *causes.* **2** inborn: *a* natural *talent*; *his* natural *abilities.* **3** of or relating to the world and living things: *the* natural *sciences.* **4** occurring in the usual course of things: *a* natural *result.* **5** characteristic of a person's usual appearance, manner, etc.: *a* natural *portrait.* **6** not artificial or affected: *to speak in a* natural *tone of voice.* **7** *Music* not sharp or flat: *That note is G* natural. *n-* **1** *Music* a sign [♮] placed on a line or space of the staff to remove the effect of a preceding sharp or flat. **2** *Informal* person who seems perfectly suited for something because of certain talents, qualities, etc.: *He's a* natural *for that job.* *—n-* **nat′ u·ral·ness.**

natural gas *n-* combustible gas composed largely of methane and obtained either from natural fissures in the earth or from driven wells. It is used as a fuel.

natural history *n-* the study of plants, minerals, and natural objects in general; especially, the study of animals with relation to their life, habits, etc.

nat·u·ral·ist (năch′ ər ə lĭst′) *n-* person who studies the things of nature, especially plants and animals.

nat·u·ral·is·tic (năch′ ər ə lĭs′ tĭk) *adj-* of art, resembling nature.

nat·u·ral·ize (năch′ ər ə līz′) *vt-* [**nat·u·ral·ized, nat·u·ral·iz·ing**] **1** to give citizenship to (a person born in a foreign country). **2** to adopt (a foreign word, expression, etc.) into a language. **3** to cause (a plant from another region) to grow and become established. *—n-* **nat′ u·ral·i·za′ tion.**

nat·u·ral·ly (năch′ ər ə lē, -ər lē) *adv-* **1** by nature: *Her hair is* naturally *curly.* **2** in a natural or usual way or manner: *He spoke* naturally *on the radio.* **3** as might be expected; of course: *Yes,* naturally, *we will go.*

natural number *n-* *Mathematics* any one of the set of positive integers (1, 2, 3, etc.).

natural resource *n-* anything in nature that man knows how to use, such as water, soil, plants, minerals, etc.

natural rights *n-* rights considered to belong inherently to all human beings, as distinct from legal rights.

natural science *n-* any one of the sciences concerned with the physical universe, such as physics or biology.

natural selection *n-* evolutionary theory that only those living organisms having genetic traits favorable to their survival are able to live, reproduce, and thus transmit these favorable traits to the next generation. In the long run of time, therefore, nature "selects."

na·ture (nā′ chər) *n-* **1** the physical universe as a whole, including what it is and what happens in it. **2** natural scenery; trees, flowers, etc.: *the beauties of* nature. **3** all the qualities of something that make it what it is: *the* nature *of the atom.* **4** kind; sort; type: *books of that* nature. **5** individual character or disposition of a person or animal: *He has a friendly* nature. **6** (often **Nature**) forces or principles thought to govern the universe and living things: *the laws of* nature. **7** uncultivated, primitive, or natural condition: *The garden returned to* nature.

by nature by disposition or make-up: *He is* by nature *a just man.* **of** (or **in**) **the nature of** resembling.

nature study *n-* observation of and learning about the things in nature, especially plants and animals.

naught (nŏt, nŏt) *n-* **1** *Mathematics* zero, written as 0; a cipher. **2** nothing: *All our efforts came to* naught. *Homs-* knot, not.

naugh·ty (nŏ′ tē) *adj-* [**naugh·ti·er, naugh·ti·est**] mischievous; disobedient. *—adv-* **naugh′ ti·ly.** *n-* **naugh′ ti·ness.**

nau·sea (nŏ′ sē ə, -zē ə, nŏ′ shə, -zhə) *n-* **1** sickness of the stomach, with an urge to vomit; queasy feeling. **2** great disgust; loathing.

nau·se·ate (nŏ′ sē āt′, -zē āt′) *vt-* [**nau·se·at·ed, nau·se·at·ing**] to affect with nausea or with a feeling of strong disgust; sicken. *—adv-* **nau′ se·at′ ing·ly.**

nau·seous (nŏ′ shəs, nŏ′ sē əs) *adj-* **1** causing nausea; nauseating; sickening: *a* nauseous *odor.* **2** feeling nausea; nauseated.

►Many people still insist that NAUSEOUS is correct only in sense 1. Unless you are sure you won't be misunderstood, avoid the word in favor of NAUSEATING or NAUSEATED, whichever you mean.

nau·ti·cal (nŏ′ tĭ kəl) *adj-* having to do with ships, sailors, and navigation. *—adv-* **nau′ ti·cal·ly.**

nautical mile See *mile.*

nau·ti·lus (nŏ′tə ləs) *n-* [*pl.* **nau·ti·lus·es** or **nau·ti·li** (-lī′,-lē′)] **1** (also **pearly nautilus** or **chambered nautilus**) mollusk having a pearly, spiral shell divided into narrow compartments. **2** (also **paper nautilus**) related mollusk with a very thin, delicate shell. **3 Nautilus** name of the first atomic submarine.

Shell of pearly nautilus

Nav·a·ho (năv′ ə hō) *n-* [*pl.* **Nav·a·hos** or **Nav·a·hoes,** also **Nav·a·ho**] one of a tribe of American Indians of southwestern United States, now on reservations in Arizona, New Mexico, and Utah. Also **Nav′ a·jo.**

na·val (nā′ vəl) *adj-* of or having to do with a navy or warships. *Hom-* navel. *—adv-* **na′ val·ly.**

nave (nāv) *n-* main, central part of a church, between the side aisles. *Hom-* knave.

na·vel (nā′ vəl) *n-* depression or mark in the center of the abdomen, where the umbilical cord was attached at birth. *Hom-* naval.

navel orange ***n-*** seedless orange with a thick rind and a small mark like a navel at a point opposite the stem.

nav·i·ga·ble (năv′ ə gə bəl) ***adj-*** **1** having depth, width, and currents that permit navigation, especially by commercial ships or boats: *The Mississippi is* navigable *by river boats.* **2** such as can be steered: *a* navigable *raft.* **—*n-*** **nav′ i·ga·bil′ i·ty** or **nav′ i·ga·ble·ness.** ***adv-*** **nav′ i·ga·bly.**

nav·i·gate (năv′ ə gāt′) ***vi-*** **[nav·i·gat·ed, nav·i·gat·ing] 1** to plot a course; direct the course of a ship or an airplane: *He* navigated *around the storm.* **2** *Informal* to move around. ***vt-*** **1** to sail over or through: *to* navigate *a sea.* **2** to plot and direct the course of (a ship or vehicle).

nav·i·ga·tion (năv′ ə gā′ shən) ***n-*** **1** act or process of navigating: *During the winter,* navigation *of the North Sea is dangerous.* **2** science of charting the course for ships, airplanes, and spaceships. **3** science or art of steering or operating ships or aircraft. **4** shipping.

nav·i·ga·tion·al (năv′ ə gā′ shən əl) ***adj-*** of or having to do with navigation.

nav·i·ga·tor (năv′ ə gā′ tər) ***n-*** person skilled in navigation; especially, a person who determines or plots the course of a ship, airplane, or spaceship.

na·vy (nā′ vē) ***n-*** **[*pl.* na·vies] 1** the branch of a nation's military force responsible for warfare at sea. **2** all of the warships belonging to such a force. **3** navy blue. **4 Navy** (1) the navy of the United States. (2) *Informal* the U.S. Naval Academy at Annapolis, Maryland. ***adj-***: *a* Navy *depot*; *a* navy *sweater.*

navy bean ***n-*** small, oval, white bean.

navy blue ***n-*** very dark blue. ***adj-***: *Her dress is* navy blue. Also **navy.**

Navy Cross ***n-*** bronze decoration in the form of a cross, awarded by the U.S. Navy for "extraordinary heroism while in operation against the armed enemy."

navy yard ***n-*** dockyard owned and maintained by the government for building and maintaining warships.

nay (nā) ***adv-*** **1** no. **2** not only that, but also: *I feel,* nay *I'm positive, we'll win.* ***n-*** **1** negative vote; also, a person casting such a vote. **2** a refusal. ***Homs-*** née, neigh.

Naz·a·rene (năz′ ə rēn′) ***n-*** **1** a native or inhabitant of Nazareth. **2 the Nazarene** Jesus Christ. **3** member of a sect of early Christians.

Na·zi (nät′ sē) ***n-*** member of the National Socialist Party that, under the leadership of Adolf Hitler, controlled Germany from 1935 to 1945. ***adj-*** of or relating to this party or its doctrines and principles.

Na·zism (nät′ sĭz′ əm) ***n-*** the social and political doctrines of the National Socialist Party of Germany under the dictatorship of Adolf Hitler. Germany under Nazism was totalitarian, and its industry was state-controlled. Also **Na·zi·ism** (nät′ sē ĭz′ əm).

Nb symbol for niobium.

n.b. or **N.B.** note well. [from Latin **nota bene**].

N.B. New Brunswick.

N.C. North Carolina.

NCO noncommissioned officer.

Nd symbol for neodymium.

N.Dak. North Dakota.

Ne Symbol for neon.

NE or **N.E. 1** northeast. **2** northeastern.

Ne·an·der·thal man (nē ăn′ dər thôl′, -tôl′) ***n-*** extinct species of prehistoric man who lived in caves in Europe, North Africa, and western and central Asia.

Ne·a·pol·i·tan (nē′ ə pŏl′ ə tən) ***n-*** a native or resident of Naples. ***adj-***: *He sang* Neapolitan *songs.*

neap tide (nēp) ***n-*** tide which occurs just after the first and third quarters of the moon, when the difference between high tide and low is the least. Also **neap.**

near (nêr) ***adv-*** **[near·er, near·est] 1** not far off in time, place, or degree; to, at, or within a short distance: *We ran for cover when the storm came* near. **2** *Informal* nearly: *a work of* near *perfect proportions.* ***adj-*** **1** not far in time, place, or degree; close or closer by: *My second shot was a* near *miss. They stood on the* near *side of the lake.* **2** barely avoided: *My first try was a* near *disaster.* **3** associated or related closely: *a* near *and dear relative.* ***prep-*** close to or by: *the house* near *the lake.* ***vt-*** to approach; come or draw close to: *The ship* neared *the dock.* ***vi-***: *The summer* neared. **—*n-*** **near′ ness.**

near·by or **near-by** (nêr′ bī′) ***adj-*** close; near at hand: *a* nearby *farm.*

near·ly (nêr′ lē) ***adv-*** **1** almost: *I tripped and* nearly *fell.* **2** closely: *First cousins are* nearly *related.*

near·sight·ed (nêr′ sī′ təd) ***adj-*** of, related to, or having the condition of eyesight in which only objects at close range are seen clearly; myopic. **—*adv-*** **near′ sight′ ed·ly.** ***n-*** **near′ sight′ ed·ness.**

neat (nēt) ***adj-*** **[neat·er, neat·est] 1** clean and orderly; tidy: *a* neat *desk.* **2** simple and pleasing in appearance: *a* neat *dress.* **3** skillful; clever: *a* neat *job of carpentry.* **4** *Informal* very good. **—*adv-*** **neat′ ly.** ***n-*** **neat′ ness.**

'neath or **neath** (nēth) ***prep-*** beneath.

neat's-foot oil ***n-*** light-yellow oil obtained from the feet and shinbones of cattle, used to condition leather.

Nebr. Nebraska.

Neb·u·chad·nez·zar (nĕb′ yə kəd nĕz′ ər, nĕb′ ə-) ***n-*** king of Babylon (605-562 B.C.) who conquered Jerusalem and enslaved the Jews.

neb·u·la (nĕb′ yə lə) ***n-*** **[*pl.* neb·u·lae** (-lē, -lī) or **neb·u·las] 1** one of the billions of cloudlike masses of gas and dust, often luminous, in the universe. **2** galaxy.

neb·u·lar (nĕb′ yə lər) ***adj-*** of or relating to a nebula or nebulas: *a* nebular *shape.*

►Should not be confused with NEBULOUS.

nebular hypothesis *Astronomy* ***n-*** hypothesis that the solar system was formed from a rotating mass of gas at high temperature.

neb·u·lous (nĕb′ yə ləs) ***adj-*** vague; unclear; cloudy; indistinct. **—*adv-*** **neb′ u·lous·ly.** ***n-*** **neb′ u·lous·ness.**

►Should not be confused with NEBULAR.

nec·es·sar·i·ly (nĕs′ ə sĕr′ ə lē) ***adv-*** as a matter of course: *A forecast of rain does not* necessarily *mean rain.*

nec·es·sar·y (nĕs′ ə sĕr′ ē) ***adj-*** **1** needed; required; essential: *He made the* necessary *adjustments in the controls.* **2** following by necessity; inescapable; unavoidable: *the* necessary *result of his foolishness.* ***n-*** **necessaries** things that cannot be done without; necessities.

nec·es·si·tate (nə sĕs′ ə tāt′) ***vt-*** **[nec·es·si·tat·ed, nec·es·si·tat·ing]** to make necessary; require; demand: *The threat of riot* necessitates *prompt action by the police.*

nec·es·si·ty (nə sĕs′ ə tē) ***n-*** **[*pl.* nec·es·si·ties] 1** something needed; something one cannot get along without: *Water is a* necessity *of life.* **2** situation or occasion that calls for help: *In case of* necessity, *you can call on me.* **3** extreme poverty; lack of things needed for life: *Cruel* necessity *forced him to beg.* **4** a compelling force or need: *the* necessity *of sleep.*

of necessity because of the requirements of a situation.

Neck

neck (nĕk) ***n-*** **1** part of the body between the head and the shoulders; upper or forward end of the spinal column. **2** the part of a garment that fits around this part of the body. **3** narrow part of a bottle, vase, cruet, or other container. **4** point of land extending into water; an isthmus.

neck and neck in a tie.

neck·er·chief (nĕk′ər chĭf) ***n-*** handkerchief or scarf worn around the neck.
neck·lace (nĕk′ləs) ***n-*** string of beads or jewels, or an ornament of metalwork, worn about the neck.
neck·line (nĕk′līn′) ***n-*** the border of a garment, especially a woman's garment, at the neck.
neck·piece (nĕk′pēs′) ***n-*** article of clothing like a scarf, usually of fur, worn around the neck.
neck·tie (nĕk′tī′) ***n-*** narrow band of cloth worn around the neck under the collar and tied in front in a knot or bow; cravat.
neck·wear (nĕk′wâr′) ***n-*** articles of clothing, such as scarves or ties, to be worn around the neck.

Necklace

nec·ro·man·cy (nĕk′rə măn′sē) ***n-*** **1** pretended art of foretelling the future by calling up the spirits of the dead. **2** magic; sorcery. ***—n-*** **nec′ro·man′cer.**
nec·tar (nĕk′tər) ***n-*** **1** sweet liquid found in some flowers: *Bees use* nectar *to make honey.* **2** in Greek mythology, a drink of the gods. **3** any delicious or pleasant drink.
nec·tar·ine (nĕk′tə rēn′) ***n-*** kind of peach having a smooth skin; also, the tree bearing this fruit.
née or **nee** (nā) ***adj-*** born (used only before the maiden name of a married woman to show her maiden name): *Mrs. John Miller,* nee *Brown.* ***Homs-*** nay, neigh.
need (nēd) ***vt-*** to require as a necessity; wish for or have a use for (something lacking): *to* need *a new pair of shoes*; *to* need *rest*; *to* need *to see a doctor.* ***auxiliary verb*** to be required to or obligated to (used with infinitives without "to"): *He* need *not sing.* Need *she come? I* need *hardly tell you that. I* need *not have been so hasty.* ***n-*** **1** a requirement, especially one not yet filled: *a* need *for teachers.* **2** poverty; deprivation. ***Hom-*** knead.
if need be if necessary. **in need** when one is deprived and helpless: *A friend* in need *is a friend indeed.* **in need of** lacking: *They are* in need *of aid and understanding.*
need·ful (nēd′fəl) ***adj-*** required; necessary: *Do whatever is* needful *to help her.* ***—adv-*** **need′ful·ly.**
nee·dle (nē′dəl) ***n-*** **1** sewing tool consisting of a fine, slender, pointed steel wire pierced with a hole, or "eye," to hold a thread. **2** plain slender rod, or a rod with a small hook at the end, used in knitting or crocheting. **3** (also **magnetic needle**) steel bar of a magnetic compass. **4** fine, hollow, pointed wire with an opening at the tip, used for injections. **5** thin, pointed leaf, like that of the pine tree. **6** anything slim and sharp-pointed: *Rocks rise in* needles *near the summit.* ***vt-*** **[nee·dled, nee·dling]** *Informal* to tease; annoy; goad. ***—adj-*** **nee′dle·like′.**

Sewing needle
Compass needle
Crochet needle
Knitting needle

nee·dle-leaf (nē′dəl lēf′) ***adj-*** having sharp, pointed needles such as those of the pines, hemlocks, and similar trees. Also **nee′dle-leaved′**(-lēvd′)
nee·dle·point (nē′dəl point′) ***n-*** embroidery stitch applied to canvas, especially with wool yarn.
need·less (nĕd′ləs) ***adj-*** unnecessary: needless *grumbling annoys people.* ***—adv-*** **need′less·ly.** ***n-*** **need′less·ness.**
needle valve ***n-*** valve in which a slender rod with a cone-shaped end fits into a funnel-shaped opening, used to control the flow of liquids and gases.
nee·dle·work (nē′dəl wûrk′) ***n-*** stitching; sewing; embroidery.
need·n't (nē′dənt) need not.
needs (nēdz) *Archaic* ***adv-*** necessarily; of necessity: *It must* needs *be admitted that this is impossible.*
need·y (nē′dē) ***adj-*** **[need·i·er, need·i·est]** not having enough food, clothing, or other basic wants; very poor. ***—n-*** **need′i·ness.**
ne'er (nâr) never.
ne'er-do-well (nâr′ do͞o wĕl′) ***n-*** worthless, irresponsible person who never amounts to anything.
ne·far·i·ous (nə făr′ē əs, nə fĕr′-) ***adj-*** wicked; sinful; evil: *a dictator's* nefarious *cruelty.* ***adv-*** **ne·far′i·ous·ly.** ***n-*** **ne·far′i·ous·ness.**
ne·gate (nə gāt′) ***vt-*** **[ne·gat·ed, ne·gat·ing]** **1** to deny; contradict: *The facts* negate *what he says.* **2** to nullify; make valueless: *This* negates *all our work.*
ne·ga·tion (nə gā′shən) ***n-*** **1** denial; nullification; a rendering invalid: *a* negation *of the theory.* **2** the opposite or absence of something real or positive: *Dictatorship is a* negation *of freedom.*
neg·a·tive (năg′ə tĭv) ***adj-*** **1** saying "no"; expressing denial or refusal: *a* negative *answer.* **2** tending to oppose or deny: *a* negative *person*; *a* negative *attitude.* **3** in electrochemistry, of or having to do with the cathode. **4** *Mathematics* (1) naming a number or quantity that is to be subtracted; minus. (2) of or having to do with a number whose value is less than zero. (3) on a number line, naming a number on the side of zero that is opposite 1. ***n-*** **1** refusal; denial: *The request received a* negative. **2** word expressing "no"; denial or refusal: *"Never," "nobody," and "nothing" are* negatives. **3** a photographic image having the light and dark reversed; also, the transparent material holding such an image from which a positive can be printed. **4** in debating, the side arguing against the statement. ***—adv-*** **neg′a·tive·ly.**
in the negative with a refusal or denial; saying no.
negative charge *Physics* ***n-*** **1** electrical property or condition of an object that is due to an excess of electrons over protons. By convention, a plastic rod that has been rubbed with fur has a negative charge. **2** property of an elementary particle that causes its path in a magnetic field to be bent in the same direction as an electron's path through the same field. **3** a negative elementary charge. See also *charge* and *positive charge.*
neg·a·tiv·ism (nĕg′ə tə vĭz′əm) ***n-*** habitual tendency to deny or reject ideas, suggestions, etc. ***—n-*** **neg′a·tiv·ist.** ***adj-*** **neg′a·tiv·is′tic.**
ne·glect (nə glĕkt′) ***n-*** failure to do what should be done; lack of care: *The garden, overgrown with weeds, showed* neglect. ***vt-*** **1** to fail to do (what should be done) through carelessness or on purpose: *Don't* neglect *your homework.* **2** to pay too little attention to; fail to care for properly: *He* neglects *his family.* ***—n-*** **ne·glect′er.**
neg·lect·ful (nə glĕct′ fəl) ***adj-*** failing to give proper care or attention; callously indifferent: *a* neglectful *parent.* ***—adv-*** **ne·glect′ful·ly.** ***n-*** **ne·glect′ful·ness.**
►Should not be confused with NEGLIGENT.
neg·li·gee (nĕg′lə zhā′) ***n-*** woman's dressing gown or bathrobe.
neg·li·gence (nĕg′lə jəns) ***n-*** **1** negligent behavior. **2** a negligent act: *Not locking the door was a* negligence. **3** in law, wrongful failure to do what should reasonably and prudently be done to avoid accident, injury, etc.
neg·li·gent (nĕg′lə jənt) ***adj-*** **1** guilty of failing to do what reasonably or properly should be done: *Both*

drivers in the accident were negligent. **2** habitually careless and remiss: *He was a* negligent *man who never paid his bills on time.* **3** casual and easygoing: *a* negligent *way of dressing.* ***—adv-*** **neg′li·gent·ly.**

►Should not be confused with NEGLECTFUL.

neg·li·gi·ble (nĕg′lə jə bəl) ***adj-*** not worth much attention; of little account or value: *a* negligible *loss*; *a* negligible *contribution.* ***—adv-*** **neg′li·gi·bly.**

ne·go·ti·a·ble (nə gō′shə bəl, -shē ə bəl) ***adj-*** **1** in business, such as can be passed from one person to another by endorsement or delivery and serves the purpose of cash: *a* negotiable *bond*; *a* negotiable *check*; *a* negotiable *promissory note.* **2** such as can be settled by negotiation: *Their quarrel did not prove to be* negotiable. ***—n-*** **ne·go′ti·a·bil′i·ty.**

ne·go·ti·ate (nə gō′shē āt′) ***vt-*** [**ne·go·ti·at·ed, ne·go·ti·at·ing**] **1** to discuss and make the arrangements for (a business deal, treaty, loan, etc.): *to* negotiate *a sale of property.* **3** to clear, pass, or surmount (something): *The old car could hardly* negotiate *the hill.* ***vi-*** to discuss or exchange terms, proposals, etc.; parley: *The two sides agreed to* negotiate.

ne·go·ti·a·tion (nə gō′shē ā′shən) ***n-*** act of negotiating; the talking over and settling the terms of a treaty, business agreement, etc.

ne·go·ti·a·tor (nə gō′shē ā tər) ***n-*** person who negotiates.

Ne·gri·to (nə grē′tō) ***n-*** [*pl.* **Ne·gri·tos** or **Ne·gri·toes**] one of a group of small, dark-skinned people living in the Philippines and other parts of southeastern Asia.

Ne·gro (nē′grō) ***n-*** [*pl.* **Ne·groes**] member of the Negroid division of the human species, especially of the peoples of Africa south of the Sahara or their descendants. ***adj-*** *a* Negro *spiritual.*

Ne·groid (nē′groid′) ***adj-*** of or pertaining to a major division of the human species, considered to include peoples of Africa south of the Sahara and of numerous islands in the western Pacific.

Ne·he·mi·ah (nē′hə mī′ə) ***n-*** **1** a Jewish leader of the 5th century B.C. **2** a book of the Old Testament describing the rebuilding of Jerusalem. In the CCD Bible it is called Esdra II.

neigh (nā) ***n-*** the sound that a horse makes; a whinny ***vi-*** to make this sound. ***Homs-*** nay, née.

neigh·bor (nā′bər) ***n-*** **1** person who lives nearby. **2** person, country, or thing that is near another: *Canada is our* neighbor *to the north.* **3** fellow man: *"Love thy* neighbor *as thyself."*

neigh·bor·hood (nā′bər ho͝od′) ***n-*** **1** area or district where a person lives: *Our* neighborhood *has a new shopping center.* **2** the people living nearby or near one another: *The* neighborhood *held a barbecue.*

in the neighborhood of near; not far from: *The town is* in the neighborhood of *the Great Lakes.*

neigh·bor·ing (nā′bər ĭng) ***adj-*** **1** near; nearby: *in a* neighboring *village.* **2** adjoining: *Helene and Evelyn just bought two* neighboring *lots of land.*

neigh·bor·ly (nā′bər lē) ***adj-*** friendly; kindly; proper or suitable for neighbors: *The people here are very* neighborly. ***—n-*** **neigh′bor·li·ness.**

nei·ther (nē′thər, nī′) ***determiner*** (traditionally called adjective or pronoun) not one and not the other: Neither *car is here.* Neither *is here.* ***n-*** not one or the other (of two): *I want* neither *of them.* ***conj-*** **1** (used with "nor" to introduce two negative alternatives): *I have* neither *time nor money.* **2** nor: *You don't want to go?* Neither *do I.*

nem·a·tode (nē′mə tōd′) ***n-*** any of a phylum of slender, parasitic worms (**Nematoda**), including the hookworm, pinworm, and trichina worm.

nem·e·sis (nĕm′ə səs) ***n-*** [*pl.* **nem·e·ses** (-sēz′)] **1** person or thing that afflicts or punishes: *Moby Dick was the* nemesis *of Captain Ahab.* **2** a just punishment for a serious misdeed. **3 Nemesis** in Greek mythology, the goddess of retributive justice or vengeance.

neo- *combining form* new or recent: *a* neo*logism* (new word or meaning); neo*phyte* (beginner; novice). [from Greek **neo-**, from **néos** meaning "new."]

ne·o·dym·i·um (nē′ō dĭ′mē əm) ***n-*** rare-earth metallic element forming rose-colored salts, found associated with cerium. Symbol Nd, At. No. 60, At. Wt. 144.24.

Ne·o·lith·ic (nē′ə lĭth′ĭk) ***adj-*** of or having to do with a period of human culture in which agriculture developed and stone tools were polished not chipped.

ne·ol·o·gism (nē ŏl′ə jĭz′əm) ***n-*** **1** a new word or meaning. **2** the use of such words or meanings.

ne·o·my·cin (nē′ō mī′sən, nē′ə-) ***n-*** antibiotic chemically similar to streptomycin and derived from the same group of soil organisms. It is used especially against skin infections.

ne·on (nē′ŏn) ***n-*** colorless, odorless, inert gaseous element found in the atmosphere in very small amounts. Symbol Ne, At. No. 10, At. Wt. 20.183. ***adj-***: *a* neon *sign.*

neon lamp ***n-*** a small, low-power lamp containing neon, used to monitor the operation of electrical devices.

neon sign ***n-*** advertising sign or other sign using glass tubes containing neon. The neon gives off an intense crimson glow when an electric current passes through it.

ne·o·phyte (nē′ə fīt′) ***n-*** beginner; novice.

ne·o·prene (nē′ə prēn′) ***n-*** a synthetic rubber having high resistance to heat, light, oxidation, and oils.

neph·ew (nĕf′yo͞o′) ***n-*** son of one's brother or brother-in-law, or of one's sister or sister-in-law.

ne·phri·tis (nə frī′təs) ***n-*** inflammation of one or both kidneys. ***—adj-*** **ne·phrit′ic** (nə frĭt′ĭk).

nep·o·tism (nĕp′ə tĭz′əm) ***n-*** too great official favor and preferment shown by a person in power to members of his or her family: *The mayor indulged in* nepotism *by appointing his cousins to the commission.*

Nep·tune (nĕp′to͞on′, tyo͞on′) ***n-*** **1** in Roman mythology, the god of the sea. He is identified with the Greek Poseidon. **2** the fourth largest planet in the solar system, eighth in order of distance from the sun.

nep·tun·i·um (nĕp to͞o′nē əm, nĕp tyo͞o′-) ***n-*** radioactive man-made element produced in a nuclear reactor when plutonium is made. Symbol Np, At. No. 93.

Ne·re·id (nêr′ē əd) ***n-*** [*pl.* **Ne·re·ids,** also **Ne·re·i·des** (nə rē′ə dēz′)] in Greek mythology, one of the fifty sea nymphs, daughters of the sea god **Ne′re·us** (nêr′ē əs), who attended Poseidon.

nerve (nûrv) ***n-*** **1** a bundle of many nerve fibers resembling a rope or cable. Nerves connect all parts of the body with the nervous system by carrying electrochemical nerve impulses. **2** courage; bravery; daring; boldness: *The explorer approached the unknown with* nerves *of steel.* **3** *Informal* brashness; impudence; crust. **4 nerves** (1) the source of self-control, patience, etc: *His* nerves *were bad.* (2) nervousness; jitters; hysteria: *a bad case of* nerves. ***vt-*** [**nerved, nerv·ing**] to give courage or strength to: *he* nerved *himself for a trip to the dentist.*

get on (one's) nerves *Informal* to irritate; vex; exasperate. **strain every nerve** to make a great effort to.

nerve cell See *neuron.*

nerve center ***n-*** **1** region in the brain containing mostly nerve cell bodies having similar or related functions. **2** center from which an operation, mission, etc., is controlled; headquarters.

nerve fiber *n-* a single axon or dendrite.

nerve impulse *n-* the "message" passing along a nerve fiber. It consists of a traveling wave of electrochemical changes associated with the migration of ions across the membrane of a nerve cell.

nerve·less (nûrv′ ləs) *adj-* **1** lacking nerves. **2** *Archaic* weak; paralyzed. *—adv-* **nerve′ less·ly.**

nerve-rack·ing or **nerve-wrack·ing** (nûrv′ răk′ ĭng) *adj-* very upsetting or shocking to the nerves and senses; destroying one's ease and poise: *a* nerve-racking *two hours*; *a* nerve-racking *noise.*

ner·vous (nûr′ vəs) *adj-* **1** of or relating to the nerves: *the* nervous *system.* **2** easily excited; highstrung: *A* nervous *person gets upset often.* **3** fearful; tense; uneasy; restless. *—adv-* **ner′ vous·ly.** *n-* **ner′ vous·ness.**

nervous system *n-* the total system of nerve cells, nerves, brain, spinal cord, and receptors with which an animal responds to external and internal stimuli.

nerv·y (nûr′ vē) *Slang adj-* [**nerv·i·er, nerv·i·est**] audacious; impudent; brash.

-ness *suffix* (used to form nouns from adjectives) condition or quality of being: *hard*ness; *rash*ness; *loveli*ness.

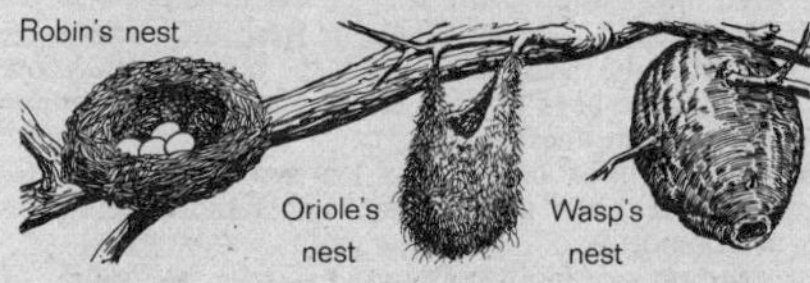

nest (nĕst) *n-* **1** place where a bird lays eggs and cares for its young. **2** place for the same use made by wasps and some other insects. **3** den or burrow, especially the part of it used for sleeping and caring for young: *We found a squirrel's* nest *in the hollow tree.* **4** any warm and cozy place. **5** a group of things fitting neatly into one another: *This* nest *of boxes came from Japan.* *vi-* to build or use a place for laying eggs and caring for young: *Birds* nested *in the maple tree.* *vt-* **1** to place in or as if in such a place: *to* nest *one's head in the pillows.* **2** to fit into one another: *The boys* nested *the cartons to save space.*

nest egg *n-* **1** real or false egg left in a nest to encourage the hen to lay eggs there. **2** money put aside; savings.

nest·er (nĕs′ tər) *n-* formerly, in western United States, a homesteader who settled on open range land (chiefly a contemptuous term used by cattlemen). *Hom-* Nestor.

nes·tle (nĕs′ əl) *vi-* [**nes·tled, nes·tling**] to lie close and snug; snuggle; settle comfortably: *A child* nestles *in its mother's arms.* *vt-* to press closely; cuddle: *The little girl* nestled *her doll in her arms.* *—n-* **nes′ tler.**

nest·ling (nĕst′ lĭng, nĕs′-) *n-* bird too young to fly.

Nes·tor (nĕs′ tər, -tôr′) *n-* **1** in the "Iliad," a wise old Greek king. **2 nestor** any wise old man. *Hom-* nester.

[1]**net** (nĕt) **1** fabric of knotted cords, used in fishing; seine. **2** in sports, any of several pieces of equipment made of such a fabric. A **tennis net** stretches across the court to separate opposing parts. A **basketball net,** with a hoop at the top, is the target for scoring shots. **3** bag of knotted cords with the open end attached to a ring with a handle. It is used to catch butterflies, to land fish, etc. **4** small, circular piece of silk or hair mesh with a drawstring, to keep ladies' hair in place. **5** openwork fabric such as that used for veils. **6** a snare; an entanglement: *He was caught in a* net *of lies.* *vt-* [**net·ted, net·ting**] to catch with or as if with a net. [from Old English **net(t).**]

Butterfly net

[2]**net** (nĕt) *adj-* remaining after all discounts or expenses are subtracted, or similar adjustments made; final; ultimate: *a* net *profit*; *a* net *loss of time*; *a* net *weight.* *n-* profit remaining after expenses are deducted. *vt-* [**net·ted, net·ting**] to earn as clear profit: *The show* netted *$4,000.* [from Old French **net,** "free; clear (of a debt); pure," from Latin **nitidus** meaning "shining (and therefore clean)," and closely related to **neat.**]

neth·er (nĕth′ ər) *adj-* situated below; lying beneath; lower: *the* nether *lip.*

neth·er·most (nĕth′ ər mōst′) *adj-* lowest; farthest down: *the* nethermost *reaches of the mind.*

net·ting (nĕt′ ĭng) *n-* **1** a making of nets. **2** a fabric made of meshes. **3** a texture made from crossed wires, such as a fence. **4** network.

net·tle (nĕt′ əl) *n-* any of several plants which have stems and leaves with hairs or spines that irritate the skin on contact. *vt-* [**net·tled, net·tling**] to vex or annoy: *Joe's questions* nettled *the chairman.*

net·work (nĕt′ wûrk′) *n-* **1** a net. **2** system or arrangement of lines that cross: *a* network *of wires.* **3** a chain of radio or television stations which carry the same programs.

Nettle

neur- or **neuro-** *combining form* nerve: *a* neur*itis*; neuro*logy.* [from Greek **neuron** meaning "sinew."]

neu·ral (no͝or′ əl, nyo͝or′-) *adj-* of or having to do with the nerves or the nervous system. *—adv-* **neu′ ral·ly.**

neu·ral·gia (no͝or ăl′ jə, nyo͝or-) *n-* sharp pain and spasms along the course of a nerve. *—adj-* **neu·ral′ gic.**

neu·ri·tis (no͝or ī′ təs, nyo͝or-) *n-* inflammation of a nerve or nerves.

neu·rol·o·gy (no͝or ŏl′ ə jē, nyo͝or-) *n-* branch of medicine dealing with the nervous system and its diseases. *—adj-* **neu′ ro·log′ i·cal** (no͝or′ ə lŏj′ ĭ kəl, nyo͝or′-).

neu·rol·o·gist (no͝or ŏl′ ə jĭst′, nyo͝or-) *n-* person trained in neurology and engaged in it as a profession.

neu·ron (no͝or′ ŏn′, nyo͝or′-) *n-* basic cell of the nervous system; nerve cell. It consists of a nucleus, cytoplasm, and usually many short, branching dendrites and a single long axon. *—adj-* **neu·ron′ ic.**

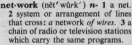

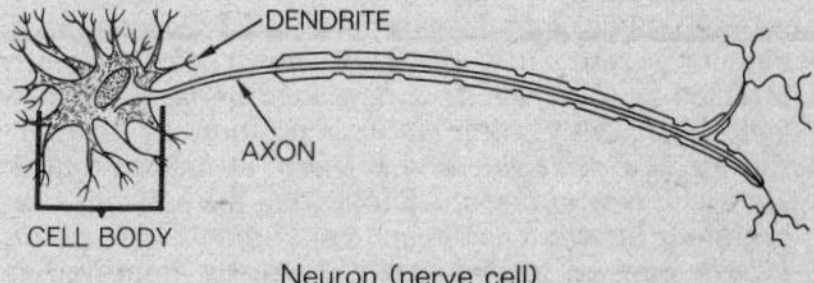

Neuron (nerve cell)

neu·ro·sis (no͝or ō′ səs, nyo͝or-) *n-* [*pl.* **neu·ro·ses** (-sēz′)] any of various emotional disorders marked by anxiety and depression, bodily disturbances, and irresistible impulses to perform certain acts; psychoneurosis.

neu·rot·ic (no͝or ŏt′ ĭk, nyo͝or-) *adj-* having to do with or suffering from neurosis: *a* neurotic *person.* *n-* person suffering from neurosis. *—adv-* **neu·rot′ i·cal·ly.**

neut. neuter.

neu·ter (no͞o′ tər, nyo͞o′-) ***adj-*** **1** *Grammar* gender of adjectives and nouns that corresponds roughly to the class of things having neither male nor female sex. **2** *Biology* having no sex, such as certain plants; without fully developed sex organs: *Worker bees are* neuter. ***n-*** such a word or organism.

neu·tral (no͞o′ trəl, nyo͞o′-) ***adj-*** **1** not taking sides in a war or contest: *During World War II, Switzerland was* neutral. **2** having no special mark or quality: *Gray is a* neutral *color.* **3** *Chemistry* neither acid nor alkaline. **4** in electricity, neither negative nor positive. ***n-*** in automobiles and other machines, the setting of gears in which the engine or other drive is not mechanically connected to what is driven. —***adv-*** **neu′ tral·ly.**

neu·tral·ism (no͞o′ trə lĭz′ əm, nyo͞o′-) ***n-*** **1** policy of, or belief in, not taking sides in a conflict or dispute, especially in international relations. **2** policy of remaining outside the power blocs led by the United States, the Soviet Union, and the People's Republic of China. —***n-*** **neu′ tral·ist.**

neu·tral·i·ty (no͞o trăl′ ə tē, nyo͞o-) ***n-*** refusal to support any side or party, especially in a war.

neu·tral·ize (no͞o′ trə līz′, nyo͞o′-) ***vt-*** **[neu·tral·ized, neu·tral·iz·ing]** **1** to make inactive or without effect: *A defense* neutralized *the attack.* **2** to remove the ability of a country to make war. **3** *Chemistry* to render neutral: *Sodium hydroxide and hydrochloric acid* neutralize *each other.* **4** in electricity, to make (something) inert by counteracting its charge or potential with an opposite charge or potential. —***n-*** **neu′ tral·i·za′ tion.** ***n-*** **neu′ tral·iz′ er.**

neu·tri·no (no͞o trē′ nō, nyo͞o′-) *Physics* ***n-*** [*pl.* **neu·tri·nos**] subatomic particle with a mass near zero and no electric charge.

neu·tron (no͞o′ trŏn, nyo͞o′-) ***n-*** elementary atomic particle having no electric charge. Its mass is slightly greater than that of the proton.

Nev. Nevada.

né·vé (nā vā′) ***n-*** the granular, crystallized snow found on the surface of the upper end of a glacier; also, an area of granular snow.

nev·er (nĕv′ ər) ***adv-*** **1** not ever; not at any time or under any conditions: *You should* never *swim alone.* **2** not even: *He* never *so much as said "Hello."*

nev·er·more (nĕv′ ər môr′) ***adv-*** never again.

nev·er·the·less (nĕv′ ər thə lĕs′) ***conj-*** in spite of that; however; yet; still; nonetheless: *It may rain*; nevertheless, *we will start on our trip.* ***adv-***: *It is raining, but we'll go* nevertheless.

new (no͞o, nyo͞o) ***adj-*** **[new·er, new·est]** **1** recently made, built, or grown: *a* new *car.* **2** not known before; recently invented or discovered: *a* new *kind of motor*; *a* new *land.* **3** recently come into a position or relationship: *a* new *principal*; *a* new *friend.* **4** unaccustomed: *He is still* new *to the job.* **5** following the previous one; beginning afresh: *a* new *year.* **6** not used or worn: *Is the bicycle* new *or second-hand?* **7** greatly improved in health, character, etc.: *After a rest I felt like a* new *man.* **8** modern; different from what went before; not like the old: *a* new *age.* ***adv-*** recently; newly (used only in compound words): *We smelled* new-*mown hay.* ***Hom-*** gnu, knew. —***n-*** **new′ ness.**

new·born (no͞o′ bôrn′, nyo͞o′-) ***adj-*** **1** just born: *a* newborn *baby.* **2** renewed; born anew: *a* newborn *hope.*

new·com·er (no͞o′ kŭm′ ər, nyo͞o′-) ***n-*** someone who has arrived recently; a new arrival.

New Deal ***n-*** the social, economic, and governmental policies of President Franklin D. Roosevelt.

new·el (no͞o′ əl, nyo͞o′-) ***n-*** post which supports the banisters at the head or foot of a stairway.

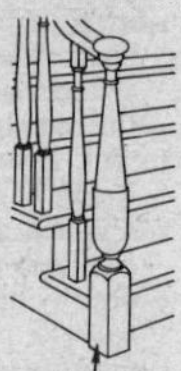

Newel

new·fan·gled (no͞o′ făng′ gəld, nyo͞o′-) ***adj-*** new; recent; different or novel (often used to show disfavor): *a* newfangled *gadget*; newfangled *ideas.*

new-fash·ioned (no͞o′ făsh′ ənd, nyo͞o′-) ***adj-*** **1** having a new fashion or style. **2** up-to-date.

Newfoundland dog ***n-*** very large, shaggy breed of dog, often black, originally from Newfoundland.

New Jerusalem ***n-*** in the New Testament, the city of God; heaven.

new·ly (no͞o′ lē, nyo͞o′-) ***adv-*** recently; lately: *a* newly *married couple.*

new·ly·wed (no͞o′ lē wĕd′, nyo͞o′-) ***n-*** person recently married.

new moon ***n-*** the moon just before or shortly after it enters its first quarter and is barely visible or seen as a slender, growing crescent. For picture, see *moon.*

news (no͞oz, nyo͞oz) ***n-*** (takes singular verb) **1** recent or fresh information: *Have you had any* news *from our old friend Tom?* **2** recent events or fresh information reported in the newspaper or over the radio or television.

break the news to be the first one to tell something surprising or unexpected.

news·boy (no͞oz′ boi′, nyo͞oz′-) ***n-*** newspaper seller.

news·cast (no͞oz′ kăst′, nyo͞oz′-) ***n-*** radio or television news report.

news·cast·er (no͞oz′ kăs′ tər, nyo͞oz′-) ***n-*** radio or television news reporter. —***n-*** **news′ cast′ ing.**

news·deal·er (no͞oz′ dē′ lər, nyo͞oz′-) ***n-*** businessman dealing in newspapers, especially one with a shop or stand where they are for sale.

news·let·ter (no͞oz′ lĕt′ ər, nyo͞oz′-) ***n-*** news report and comment, printed in the form of a letter and usually mailed out periodically to subscribers.

news·pa·per (no͞oz′ pā′ pər, nyo͞oz′-) ***n-*** daily or weekly publication containing current news, editorials, articles, pictures, advertisements, etc., and consisting of unattached sheets of printed paper folded together.

news·pa·per·man (no͞oz′ pā′ pər mən, nyo͞oz′-) ***n-*** [*pl.* **news·pa·per·men**] reporter, editor, or other journalist employed by a newspaper. Also **news′ man′.**

news·print (no͞oz′ prĭnt′, nyo͞oz′-) ***n-*** cheap paper made mainly of wood pulp and used for newspapers.

news·reel (no͞oz′ rēl′, nyo͞oz′-) ***n-*** motion picture of current news events.

news·room (no͞oz′ ro͞om′, nyo͞oz′-) ***n-*** room where news is received, edited, sent out, etc., such as one in a radio or television studio.

news·stand (no͞oz′ stănd′, nyo͞oz′-) ***n-*** stand or store where newspapers and periodicals are sold.

news·wor·thy (no͞oz′ wûr′ thē, nyo͞oz′-) ***adj-*** interesting enough to be printed as news.

news·y (no͞o′ zē, nyo͞o′-) ***adj-*** **[news·i·er, news·i·est]** *Informal* full of news.

newt (no͞ot, nyo͞ot) ***n-*** one of several kinds of small, harmless, insect-eating salamanders that remain amphibious throughout their adult life; eft.

Newt, about 4 in. long

New Testament ***n-*** one of the two main divisions of the Bible, containing accounts of the life and teachings of Jesus, and writings of some of the early Christians.

new·ton (no͞o′ tən, nyo͞o′-) ***n-*** unit of force in the mks system, defined as the amount of force required to give a mass of one kilogram an acceleration of one meter per second per second. It is equal to 100,000 dynes.

New World ***n-*** the Western Hemisphere. *as* ***modifier:*** *a* New World *plant.*

new year ***n-*** **1** the coming year: *In the* new year *we hope to get out of debt.* **2 New Year** (1) (also **New Year's**) the first day of the year; January 1; New Year's Day. (2) Rosh Hashana. (3) the first day of any religious or national calendar: *the Chinese* New Year.

New Year's Day ***n-*** January 1, a legal holiday.

next (nĕkst) ***adj-*** coming immediately after; nearest in time, place, or rank: *the* next *bus*; *the* next *street*; next *month.* ***adv-*** in the time, place, or rank immediately following: *When* next *we meet, smile! My name comes* next *on the list. After Ken, John is the* next *oldest boy.*

next to 1 beside: *Sit* next to *me.* **2** almost: *It's* next to *nothing. It's* next to *impossible.*

next door ***adv-*** in, at, or to a house or other place just beside the place of reference: *Please go* next door. *as* ***modifier*** **(next-door):** *my* next-door *neighbors.*

next door to the nearest thing to: *The act was* next door to *treason.*

next of kin ***n-*** one's nearest relative or relatives, especially when surviving one who has died: *His brother was his* next of kin.

Nez Per·cé (nĕz′ pûrs′, *Fr.* nā′ pĕr sā′) ***n-*** [*pl.* **Nez Per·cés** also **Nez Per·cé**] one of a tribe of American Indians who formerly lived in Idaho, Oregon, and Washington.

Nfld. Newfoundland.

N.G. or **NG** National Guard.

N.H. New Hampshire.

Ni symbol for nickel.

ni·a·cin (nī′ ə sən) ***n-*** nicotinic acid.

nib (nĭb) ***n-*** **1** pen point. **2** sharp tip of anything.

nib·ble (nib′ əl) ***vt-*** [**nib·bled, nib·bling**] to take a small bite of: *The rabbit* nibbled *the lettuce.* ***vi-*** to eat something in small bites or a little at a time (often followed by "at"): *to* nibble *all morning*; *to* nibble *at a carrot.* ***n-*** **1** small bite or piece: *a* nibble *of a cookie.* **2** small or cautious bite at a bait. **—*n-* nib′ bler.**

nib·lick (nĭb′ lĭk′) ***n-*** in golf, a heavy, iron-headed club with a sharply slanting face.

nice (nīs) ***adj-*** [**nic·er, nic·est**] **1** pleasant; agreeable: *What* nice *weather for a picnic!* **2** refined; wellbred: *Children of* nice *families.* **3** discriminating: *a* nice *taste in reading.* **4** precise; very fine: *Artists must make* nice *distinctions between shades of a color.* **5** respectable; virtuous: *a* nice *girl.* **6** well done; very good: *a* nice *job.* **—*adv-* nice′ ly. *n-* nice′ ness. *Hom-*** gneiss.

Ni·cene Creed (nī′ sēn′) ***n-*** Christian creed adopted at the Council of Nicaea in 325 and expanded at the Council of Constantinople in 381.

ni·ce·ty (nī′ sə tē) ***n-*** [*pl.* **ni·ce·ties**] **1** (usually **niceties**) something elegant and refined: *one of the* niceties *of life.* **2** (usually **niceties**) small detail or point; something subtle: *the* niceties *of Japanese etiquette.* **3** careful attention to details; accuracy: *a scene described with great* nicety. **4** subtlety; delicacy: *Diplomatic talks require much* nicety.

niche (nĭch) ***n-*** **1** place hollowed out of a wall to hold a statue, urn, or the like. **2** job or position for which one is best suited: *After graduation, she found her* niche *as a teacher.*

Niche

nick (nĭk) ***n-*** a notch; small cut or chip: *a* nick *in the rim of a glass.* ***vt-*** to make a notch, a small cut, or a chip in: *The bullet* nicked *the tree trunk.*

in the nick of time at the last, crucial moment.

nick·el (nĭk′ əl) ***n-*** **1** hard, silver-white metal element, used chiefly in alloys and for plating. Symbol Ni, At. No. 28, At. Wt. 58.71. **2** in the United States and Canada, a coin of nickel and copper, worth five cents.

nick·el·o·de·on (nĭk′ ə lō′ dē ən) ***n-*** **1** an early type of coin-operated music machine; jukebox. **2** formerly, a motion picture theater charging five cents for admission.

nickel silver ***n-*** lustrous, white alloy of nickel, zinc, and copper; German silver.

nick·nack (nĭk′ năk′) knickknack.

nick·name (nĭk′ nām′) ***n-*** **1** shortened or familiar form of a person's name, such as "Ed" for "Edward" or "Johnny" for "John." **2** substitute for a person's real name, sometimes given in fun, such as "Red" for someone with red hair. ***vt-*** [**nick·named, nick·nam·ing**] to give such a name to.

nic·o·tine (nĭk′ ə tēn′) ***n-*** poisonous, oily alkaloid from tobacco, used as an insecticide and tanning agent.

nic·o·tin·ic acid (nĭk′ ə tĭn′ ĭk, -tē′ nĭk) ***n-*** vitamin of the vitamin B complex, important in metabolism and found in many foods; niacin. Lack of it causes pellagra.

nic·ti·ta·ting membrane (nĭk′ tə tā′ tĭng) ***n-*** thin, translucent tissue found in the eyes of birds and some other vertebrates and functioning as a third eyelid.

niece (nēs) ***n-*** daughter of one's brother or brother-in-law, or of one's sister or sister-in-law.

nif·ty (nĭf′ tē) *Slang* ***adj-*** [**nif·ti·er, nif·ti·est**] excellent; very good.

nig·gard (nĭg′ ərd) ***n-*** miser; stingy person.

nig·gard·ly (nĭg′ ərd lē) ***adj-*** **1** stingy; frugal to excess. **2** very small; scant: *to give* niggardly *aid.* ***adv-*** stingily. **—*n-* nig′ gard·li·ness.**

nigh (nī) *Archaic* ***adj-*** near in time or place: *His hour of triumph is* nigh. ***adv-*** **1** near. **2** almost.

night (nīt) ***n-*** **1** the time from sunset to sunrise, especially the time of darkness between dusk and dawn. **2** the coming of night; nightfall. **3** darkness: *a world wrapped in* night. ***Hom-*** knight.

night blindness ***n-*** vision that is abnormally poor in very faint light.

night·cap (nīt′ kăp′) ***n-*** **1** soft cap or head covering worn in bed. **2** a drink taken before going to bed.

night·clothes (nīt′ klōz′, -klōthz′) ***n-pl.*** garments, such as pajamas or nightgowns, worn to bed; nightdress.

night·club (nīt′ klŭb′) ***n-*** place of entertainment open at night, having food and drink and usually a floor show.

night crawler *Informal* ***n-*** any large earthworm that comes out to the surface of the soil at night.

night·dress (nīt′ drĕs′) ***n-*** **1** nightclothes. **2** nightgown.

night·fall (nīt′ fôl′) ***n-*** the ending of daylight; dusk.

night·gown (nīt′ goun′) ***n-*** loose sleeping garment worn by women and girls; nightdress.

night·hawk (nīt′ hôk′) ***n-*** **1** any of various birds resembling the whippoorwill. **2** person who tends to stay up late at night.

night·in·gale (nī′ tən gāl′, nī′ tĭng-) ***n-*** **1** a small, russet-brown bird related to the thrushes. It is noted for its sweet nocturnal song. **2** person with a fine singing voice.

Nightingale, about 6 in. long

fāte, făt, dâre, bärn; bē, bĕt, mêre; bīte, bĭt; nōte, hŏt, môre, dȯg; fŭn, fûr; to͞o, bo͝ok; oil; out; tar; thin; then; hw for wh as in *wh*at; zh for s as in u*s*ual; ə for a, e, i, o, u, as in *a*go, lin*e*n, per*i*l, at*o*m, min*u*s

night latch ***n-*** latch with a spring-loaded bolt opened from outside by a key and from inside by a knob.
night letter ***n-*** telegram sent at night at a reduced rate and delivered the following morning.
night·long (nīt′ lòng′) ***adj-*** lasting all the night.
night·ly (nīt′ lē) ***adv-*** every night: *The wolf howls* nightly *from the hill.* ***adj-*** happening every night: *the* nightly *howl of the wolf.* ***Hom-*** knightly.
night·mare (nīt′ mâr′) ***n-*** **1** a very bad and frightening dream. **2** terrifying experience: *The train crash was a* nightmare *I shall never forget.*
night owl ***n-*** person who works at night or enjoys staying up late at night.
night rider ***n-*** horseman who rides at night to frighten or punish.
night·shade (nīt′ shād′) ***n-*** any of several plants related to the tomato and potato, including deadly nightshade; especially, a vine with purple flowers and clusters of bright red berries.

Nightshade

night·shirt (nīt′ shûrt′) ***n-*** loose-fitting men's garment like a lengthened shirt, worn in bed.
night·time (nīt′ tīm′) ***n-*** the period between dusk and dawn; night. *as* ***modifier***: *the* nighttime *hours.*
night watch ***n-*** **1** guard kept for protection at night. **2** person or persons on guard at night. **3** period of time during which a night guard is on duty.
ni·hil·ism (nī′ ə lĭz′ əm, nī′ hĭl′ ĭz′ əm) ***n-*** **1** doctrine holding that all present forms of social organization are so evil that they must be destroyed before anything better can be built. **2** violent revolution; anarchism; terrorism. —***n-*** **ni′ hil·ist.** ***adj-*** **ni′ hil·is′ tic.**
Nike (nī′ kē) ***n-*** in Greek mythology, the goddess of victory, usually represented as a winged figure bearing a wreath and palm branch.
nil (nĭl) ***n-*** nothing; nought; zero.
nim·ble (nĭm′ bəl) ***adj-*** **[nim·bler, nim·blest] 1** quick and active; agile: *Squirrels are* nimble *in climbing trees.* **2** quick in thought or reply; clever and alert: *a* nimble *mind.* —***n-*** **nim′ ble·ness.** ***adj-*** **nim′ bly.**
nim·bo·stra·tus (nĭm′ bō strā′ təs, -străt′ əs) ***n-*** in meteorology, a thick, shapeless cloud occurring in dark gray layers at low altitudes and usually accompanied by rain or snow; nimbus.
nim·bus (nĭm′ bəs) ***n-*** [*pl.* **nim·bus·es** or **nim·bi** (-bī, -bē)] **1** the halo or cloud of light represented in pictures as surrounding the heads of divinities, saints, and sovereigns. **2** a feeling or atmosphere of splendor surrounding a person or thing. **3** nimbostratus (for picture, see *cloud*).
Nim·rod (nĭm′ rŏd′) ***n-*** in the Bible, a great-grandson of Noah famed as a mighty hunter.
nin·com·poop (nĭn′ kəm pōōp′) *Informal* ***n-*** silly or stupid person; fool.
nine (nīn) ***n-*** **1** amount or quantity that is one greater than 8; 9. **2** *Mathematics* (1) the cardinal number that is the sum of 8 and 1. (2) a numeral such as 9 that represents this cardinal number. **3** *Informal* baseball team. *as* ***determiner*** (traditionally called adjective or pronoun): *There are* nine *players here and* nine *there.*
nine·fold (nīn′ fōld′) ***adj-*** **1** nine times as many or as much. **2** having nine parts: *a* ninefold *flower.* ***adv-***: *They increased their output* ninefold.
nine·pins (nīn′ pĭnz′) ***n-*** (takes singular verb) game in which one rolls a ball at nine wooden pins set up at one end of a bowling alley.
nine·teen (nīn′ tēn′) ***n-*** **1** amount or quantity that is one greater than 18; 19. **2** *Mathematics* (1) the cardinal number that is the sum of 18 and 1. (2) a numeral such as 19 that represents this cardinal number. *as* ***determiner*** (traditionally called adjective or pronoun): *I see* nineteen *trees here and* nineteen *there.*
nine·teenth (nīn′ tēnth′) ***adj-*** **1** next after eighteenth. **2** the ordinal of 19; 19th. ***n-*** **1** the next after the eighteenth; 19th. **2** one of nineteen equal parts of a whole or group. **3** the last term in the name of a fraction having a denominator of 19: *1/19 is one* nineteenth. ***adv-***: *He finished* nineteenth *in his class.*
nine·ti·eth (nīn′ tē əth) ***adj-*** **1** next after eighty-ninth. **2** the ordinal of 90; 90th. ***n-*** **1** the next after the eighty-ninth; 90th. **2** one of ninety equal parts of a whole or group. **3** the last term in the name of a fraction having a denominator of 90: *1/90 is one* ninetieth. ***adv-***: *He stood* ninetieth *in his class.*
nine·ty (nīn′ tē) ***n-*** [*pl.* **nine·ties**] **1** amount or quantity that is one greater than 89; 90. **2** *Mathematics* (1) the cardinal number that is the sum of 89 and one. (2) a numeral such as 90 that represents this cardinal number. *as* ***determiner*** (traditionally called adjective or pronoun): *There are* ninety *soldiers here and* ninety *there.*
nin·ny (nĭn′ ē) ***n-*** [*pl.* **nin·nies**] foolish person; dunce.
ninth (nīnth) ***adj-*** **1** next after eighth. **2** the ordinal of 9; 9th. ***n-*** **1** the next after the eighth; 9th. **2** one of nine equal parts of a whole or group. **3** the last term in the name of a fraction having a denominator of 9: *1/9 is one* ninth. **4** *Music* (1) an interval of nine tones on the scale counting the extremes, as from C to D in the octave above. (2) The harmonic combination of these tones. ***adv-***: *She finished* ninth *in her class.*
ni·o·bi·um (nī ō′ bē əm) ***n-*** gray or silver-white, hard metal element used in stainless steel and other alloys. Symbol Nb, At. No. 41, At. Wt. 92.906.
[1]nip (nĭp) ***vt-*** **[nipped, nip·ping] 1** to bite, pinch, or squeeze: *My puppy* nips *my ankles playfully.* **2** to clip or pinch off: *to* nip *plant buds.* **3** to sting or hurt, as cold does. **4** to stop the growth of; blight; kill: *A late frost* nipped *the first flowers.* ***vi-*** *chiefly Brit.* to move quickly or briskly. ***n-*** **1** a bite or pinch: *A crab gave my toe a painful* nip. **2** sharp cold: *the* nip *of a fall morning.* [possibly from Dutch **nijpen** or earlier Danish **nippe.**]
nip and tuck very close, as a race.
nip in the bud to stop in the beginning.
[2]nip (nĭp) ***n-*** a small drink, especially of some alcoholic liquor; a swallow. [probably from earlier **nipperkin** meaning "a half-pint measure," probably from Dutch **nippen,** "to sip," and related to **[1]nip.**]
nip·per (nĭp′ ər) ***n-*** **1** anything that pinches or cuts off. **2** large claw of a crab or lobster. **3** horse's front tooth. **4** a small boy. **5 nippers** any of various tools with jaws for gripping or clipping.
nip·ple (nĭp′ əl) ***n-*** **1** small, rounded or pointed protuberance on a breast from which, in females, a baby or young animal draws milk; teat. **2** the mouthpiece of a nursing bottle. **3** a fitting through which grease or oil is put into machinery. **4** short, threaded length of pipe used for making joints.
nip·py (nĭp′ ē) ***adj-*** **[nip·pi·er, nip·pi·est] 1** chilly; very cool: *a* nippy *day*; *a* nippy *wind.* **2** likely to nip.
nir·va·na (nər vä′ nə) ***n-*** in Buddhism, the highest state of religious enlightenment when all desire is extinct and the soul becomes one with its creator.
Ni·sei (nē′ sā′) ***n-*** person born in the United States of parents who immigrated from Japan.
nit (nĭt) ***n-*** egg of a louse or other parasitic insect, or the young insect, especially when attached to body hairs.

ni·ter or **ni·tre** (nī′ tər) ***n-*** potassium nitrate; saltpeter; also, sodium nitrate.

ni·trate (nī′ trāt′) ***n-*** **1** any of the salts or esters of nitric acid. **2** sodium nitrate. **3** potassium nitrate. ***vt-*** **[ni·trat·ed, ni·trat·ing]** to treat, and thus combine with, nitric acid or a nitrate.

ni·tric (nī′ trĭk′) ***adj-*** of a compound, containing nitrogen in its higher valence.

nitric acid ***n-*** strong, corrosive liquid acid (HNO_3) used an an oxidizing agent and in explosives, dyes, etc.

ni·tri·fy (nī′ trə fī′) ***vt-*** **[ni·tri fied, ni·tri·fy·ing]** to combine, saturate, or treat with nitrogen or nitrogen compounds. ***—n-*** **ni′ tri·fi·ca′ tion** (-fĭ kā′ shən).

ni·trite (nī′ trīt′) ***n-*** any salt or ester of nitrous acid.

ni·tro·bac·te·ri·a (nī′ trō băk′ têr′ ē ə) ***n-*** *pl.* various soil bacteria involved in nitrogen fixation.

ni·tro·cel·lu·lose (nī′ trō sĕl′ yə lōs′) ***n-*** cottonlike, flammable compound made by treating cellulose with a mixture of nitric and sulfuric acids; gun cotton; cellulose nitrate. It is used to make explosives, plastics, and solid rocket propellants.

ni·tro·gen (nī′ trə jən) ***n-*** the colorless gaseous element forming four-fifths of the atmosphere. Nitrogen occurs in all living organisms, where it forms an essential part of proteins. Symbol N, At. No. 7, At. Wt. 14.0067.

nitrogen cycle ***n-*** the continuous series of natural processes involving lightning and many living organisms, by which nitrogen is successively a part of the air, the soil, plants, animals, and finally the air again.

nitrogen fixation ***n-*** **1** the binding of free atmospheric nitrogen into nitrates by bacteria living either in the soil or in the roots of such plants as peas and beans. **2** the binding of free nitrogen into such compounds as ammonia and nitrates by industrial means.

ni·trog·e·nous (nī trŏj′ ə nəs) ***adj-*** of, relating to, or containing nitrogen.

ni·tro·glyc·er·in or **ni·tro·glyc·er·ine** (nī′ trō glĭs′ ər ən) ***n-*** highly explosive, oily liquid, made by nitrating glycerin, used in dynamite and as a heart stimulant.

ni·trous (nī′ trəs) ***adj-*** **1** resembling, obtained from, or soaked with saltpeter. **2** of a compound, containing nitrogen in its lower valence.

nitrous acid ***n-*** a compound (HNO_2) of nitrogen that exists only in a water solution as a weak acid.

nitrous oxide ***n-*** colorless gas having a sweet smell and taste; laughing gas. It is used as a general anesthetic.

nit·wit (nĭt′ wĭt′) ***n-*** stupid person.

[1]**nix** (nĭks) ***n-*** water sprite of German mythology, appearing as either a male or female, and sometimes as part fish. [from German.] ***—n-*** *fem.* **nix′ ie** (nĭk′ sē).

[2]**nix** (nĭks) *Slang* ***adv-*** no. ***interj-*** beware; watch out. ***vt-*** to turn down; reject. [from **nicks,** a dialectal variant of German **nichts** meaning "nothing."]

N.J. New Jersey.

NKVD or **N.K.V.D.** People's Commissariat for Internal Affairs (former name of the Soviet secret police) [from Russian **Narodni Kommisariat Vnutrennikh Del].**

N. lat. north latitude.

NLRB National Labor Relations Board.

N. Mex. New Mexico.

NNE north-northeast.

NNW north-northwest.

no (nō) ***adv-*** **1** used to express refusal; nay: *He said* "No, *I won't do it."* **2** not: *Please be at the game* no *later than 3 o'clock.* ***determiner*** (traditionally called adjective) not any: *There will be* no *lights in the hall.* ***n-*** [*pl.* **noes**] **1** refusal; denial: *They would not accept my* no *as an answer.* **2** negative vote: *The* noes *were in the majority.*

no. number.

No symbol for nobelium.

No. 1 north; northern. **2** number.

No·ah (nō′ ə) ***n-*** in the Old Testament, a patriarch who built an ark in which he, his family, and every kind of animal survived the Flood. In the CCD Bible, **No′ e.**

no·be·li·um (nō bē′ lē əm) ***n-*** man-made, radioactive element produced by bombarding curium with carbon nuclei. Symbol No, At. No. 102.

No·bel Prize (nō′ bĕl′, nō′ bĕl′) ***n-*** one of five cash prizes established by Alfred E. Nobel (1833-96) a Swedish inventor, to be awarded annually in the fields of physics, chemistry, physiology or medicine, literature, and the furtherance of peace.

no·bil·i·ty (nō bĭl′ ə tē) ***n-*** **1** greatness of character: *We did not agree with his methods, but admired the* nobility *of his aims.* **2** in some countries, high social position by reason of birth or of title conferred by the ruler. **3 the nobility** persons of noble rank, collectively.

no·ble (nō bəl) ***adj-*** **[no·bler, no·blest] 1** having or showing very high character and great ideals: *a* noble *person*; *a* noble *life*; *a* noble *sacrifice.* **2** in some countries, having a high social position by birth or by title conferred by the ruler: *a* noble *family.* **3** handsome and impressive: *a* noble *building*; *a* noble *brow.* ***n-*** nobleman or noblewoman. ***—n-*** **no′ ble·ness.** ***adv-*** **no′ bly.**

no·ble·man (nō′ bəl mən) ***n-*** [*pl.* **no·ble·men**] man of noble birth or rank; peer. ***—n-*** *fem.* **no′ ble·wom′ an** [*pl.* **no·ble·wom·en**].

no·blesse o·blige (nō′ blĕs′ ō blēzh′) *French* nobility obligates; persons of hereditary wealth and power must be generous and protective towards their inferiors.

no·bod·y (nō′ bŏd′ ē, -bə dē) ***pron-*** no one; no person. ***n-*** [*pl.* **no·bod·ies**] person of no importance or influence: *He felt like a* nobody *in their presence.*

nock (nŏk) ***n-*** notch at the end of an arrow or bow for holding the bowstring. ***vt-*** **1** to put a notch in (an arrow or a bow). **2** to fit (an arrow) to a bowstring. **3** to fit (a bowstring) into the notches at the end of a bow.

noc·tur·nal (nŏk tûr′ nəl) ***adj-*** **1** of the night; happening or done at night: *a* nocturnal *sound*; nocturnal *activity.* **2** active at night: *a* nocturnal *animal.* **3** of plants, having flowers that are open at night and closed in the daytime. ***—adv-*** **noc·tur′ nal·ly.**

noc·turne (nŏk′ tûrn′) ***n-*** **1** picture of a night scene. **2** quiet, melancholy musical piece, especially when written for the piano.

nod (nŏd) ***vt-*** **[nod·ded, nod·ding]** (in senses 1 and 2 considered intransitive when the direct object is implied but not expressed). **1** to bow (the head) and raise it quickly as a greeting or as a sign of assent or agreement: *The boy* nodded *his head when asked if he had lost something.* **2** to express or indicate (agreement, recognition, etc.) by such a motion: *to* nod *a greeting to a friend.* ***vi-*** **1** to let the head droop forward as one drowses. **2** to sway or bend near the top: *Flowers* nod *in the breeze.* ***n-*** quick bending of the head, used as a sign of greeting assent, approval, etc.: *a friendly* nod. ***—n-*** **nod′ der.**

node (nōd) ***n-*** **1** knot, knob, or swelling. **2** the part of a plant stem from which leaves arise. **3** *Astronomy* one of the two points at which the orbit of a celestial body crosses the ecliptic; also, one of two points on the earth's equator where the orbit of an artificial satellite crosses. ***—adj-*** **nod′ al.**

---

nod·ule (nŏj′o͞ol′, nŏd′yo͞ol′) ***n-*** **1** small lump: *a* nodule *of tin ore.* **2** small knot or swelling, especially on the root of a plant or on some part of the body; tubercle. ***—adj-*** **nod′u·lar:** *a* nodular *growth.*

No·el (nō ĕl′) ***n-*** **1** Christmas. **2 noel** a Christmas carol.

nog·gin (nŏg′ən) ***n-*** **1** *Informal* head. **2** small mug or cup. **3** small amount of drink; usually a gill.

no·how (nō′hou′) *Slang* ***adv-*** not in any matter or way; not at all. ***Hom-*** know-how.

noise (noiz) ***n-*** sound, especially if loud, harsh, or confused. ***vt-*** **[noised, nois·ing]** to spread by rumor (followed by "about" or "around"): *He* noised *the story about.*

noise·less (noiz′ləs) ***adj-*** producing no noise, or much less noise than is usual; quiet; silent: *a* noiseless *machine.* ***—adv-*** **noise′less·ly.** ***n-*** **noise′less·ness.**

noi·some (noi′səm) ***adj-*** **1** injurious to health; harmful: *a* noisome *gas.* **2** offensive; disgusting: *a* noisome *odor.* ***—adv-*** **noi′some·ly.** ***n-*** **noi′some·ness.**

nois·y (noi′zē) ***adj-*** **[nois·i·er, nois·i·est]** **1** full of loud, harsh sound: *a* noisy *room.* **2** making noise: *the* noisy *traffic.* ***—adj-*** **nois′i·ly.** ***n-*** **nois′i·ness.**

nom. nominative.

no·mad (nō′măd′) ***n-*** **1** member of a tribe that has no fixed home and wanders from place to place in search of food for itself and its animals. **2** person who moves about aimlessly; wanderer. ***—adj-*** **no·mad′ic.**

no·mad·ism (nō′măd′ĭz′əm) ***n-*** the life, habits, etc., of nomadic tribes or persons.

no-man's-land (nō′mănz′lănd′) ***n-*** **1** in war, land between the lines of opposing armies. **2** any place or area of activity that is wild and dangerous.

nom de plume (nŏm′də plo͞om′) ***n-*** pen name.

no·men·cla·ture (nō′mən klā′chər, *also* nə mĕn′klə-) ***n-*** system of names used in an art or science: *the* nomenclature *of biology is based on Latin.*

nom·i·nal (nŏm′ə nəl) ***n-*** **1** in name but not necessarily in fact; ostensible: *Though the king was the* nominal *ruler, his son governed the country.* **2** very small; hardly worth mentioning; insignificant: *We paid a* nominal *sum of ten dollars for the car.* **3** of or containing a noun. ***—adv-*** **nom′i·nal·ly:** *She is* nominally *the ruler.*

nom·i·nate (nŏm′ə nāt′) ***vt-*** **[nom·i·nat·ed, nom·i·nat·ing]** **1** to propose or select as a candidate for possible election to an office. **2** to appoint: *The governor* nominated *the Commissioner of Education.*

nom·i·na·tion (nŏm′ə nā′shən) ***n-*** **1** a proposing of a candidate for election: *We will now hear the* nominations *for club secretary.* **2** selection by a political party of a single candidate for a public office.

nom·i·na·tive (nŏm′ə nə tĭv′) *Grammar* ***adj-*** of, relating to, or belonging to a case form used chiefly for the subject of the verb. In English, nominative forms are part of the common case of nouns, and make up the subjective case of personal pronouns. See also [1]*case* ***n-*** **1** this case of nouns, pronouns, or adjectives. **2** a word in this case.

nom·i·na·tor (nŏm′ə nā′tər) ***n-*** person who nominates.

nom·i·nee (nŏm′ə nē′) ***n-*** person named as a candidate for an office: *Which* nominee *do you prefer?*

non- *prefix* not; without: *a* non*alcoholic drink;* non*stop.*

non·ac·cept·ance (nŏn′ək sĕp′təns) ***n-*** refusal or failure to accept; especially, refusal to accept a person of another race or group as an equal.

non·a·ge·nar·i·an (nō′nə jə nâr′ē ən) ***n-*** person between the ages of 90 and 100 years. *as* ***modifier:*** *a* nonagenarian *gentleman.*

non·ag·gres·sion (nŏn′ə grĕsh′ən) ***n-*** a refraining from being aggressive or committing aggression. *as* ***modifier:*** *a* nonaggression *agreement between two countries.*

non·a·gon (nō′nə gŏn′, nŏn′ə-) ***n-*** polygon with nine sides and nine angles. For picture, see *polygon.*

non·al·co·hol·ic (nŏn′ăl′kə hŏl′ĭk, -hòl′ĭk) ***adj-*** containing no alcohol: *Root beer is a* nonalcoholic *beverage.*

non·bel·lig·er·ent (nŏn′bə lĭj′ər ənt) ***n-*** **1** country not at war. **2** person who is not fighting or tends not to fight. ***adj-:*** *a* nonbelligerent *nation; a* nonbelligerent *person.*

nonce (nŏns) **for the nonce** for the present occasion

nonce word ***n-*** word that is coined to suit one particular event and is not in general usage, such as the word "pie-thrower" in the following sentence: "The play was pure slapstick; a real pie-thrower."

non·cha·lant (nŏn′shə lənt, nŏn′shə länt′) ***adj-*** calmly unconcerned; cool; indifferent: *John greeted the famous visitors with a* nonchalant *air.* ***—n-*** **non′cha·lance′.** ***adv-*** **non′cha·lant′ly.**

non·com (nŏn′kŏm′) ***n-*** *Informal* noncommissioned officer.

non·com·bat·ant (nŏn′kəm băt′ənt) ***n-*** **1** civilian in wartime. **2** person in the armed forces whose duties do not include fighting, such as a chaplain or nurse.

non·com·mer·cial (nŏn′kə mûr′shəl) ***adj-*** not commercial; especially, not motivated or produced for commercial gain: *a* noncommercial *interest in music.*

non·com·mis·sioned (nŏn′kə mĭsh′ənd) *Military* ***adj-*** of, relating to, or holding an officer's grade that is not conferred by a commission or a warrant: *a* noncommissioned *rank; a* noncommissioned *officer.*

noncommissioned officer *Military* ***n-*** an enlisted person holding a noncommissioned grade. See also *commissioned officer, warrant officer.*

non·com·mit·tal (nŏn′kə mĭt′əl) ***adj-*** not revealing one's opinion or purpose: *His answer was completely* noncommittal. ***—adv-*** **non′com·mit′tal·ly.**

non·com·mu·nist (nŏn′kŏm′yə nĭst) ***adj-*** **1** not communist. **2** (also **non-Communist**) not belonging to or associated with the Communist Party.

Any of these words means non- ("not") plus the meaning of the rest of the word as given in the main text.

non′ab·sorb′ent
non′ac′a·dem′ic
non′ad·her′ence
non′ad·he′sive
non′ad·just′a·ble
non′ad·min′is·tra′tive
non′ad·mis′sion
non′af·fil′i·at′ed
non′ag·gres′sive
non′a·gree′ment
non′ag′ri·cul′tur·al
non′ap·pear′ance
non′a·quat′ic
non′a′que·ous
non′ar′o·mat′ic
non′as′pi·rat′ed
non′as·sess′a·ble
non′as·sim′i·la′tion
non′ath′let′ic
non′at·tend′ance
non′au·thor′i·ta′tive
non′ba′sic
non′be·liev′er
non′be·liev′ing
non′bel·lig′er·en·cy
non′break′able
non′cak′ing
non′cal·car′e·ous
non′ca·non′i·cal
non′cel′lu·lar
non′charge′a·ble
non′cit′i·zen
non′cler′i·cal
non′clot′ting
non′co·he′sive
non′col·lap′si·ble
non′col·lect′i·ble
non′com·bus′ti·ble
non′com·mu′ni·ca·ble
non′com·mu′ni·ca′tion

non·com·pli·ance (nŏn′ kəm plī′ əns) ***n-*** refusal or failure to comply.

non com·pos men·tis (nŏn′ kŏm′ pəs mĕn′ təs) *Latin* not of sound mind; mentally unfit.

non·con·duc·tor (nŏn′ kən dŭk′ tər) ***n-*** material that has the property of preventing the passage of sound, heat, or electricity; insulator: *Glass is a* nonconductor *of electricity.* **—*adj-* non′ con·duct′ ing.**

non·con·form·ist (nŏn′ kən fôr′ mĭst, -fôr′ mĭst) ***n-*** **1** person who does not conform to established beliefs or customs. **2 Nonconformist** one of a group of English Protestants who dissented from the Church of England in the seventeenth century.

non·con·form·i·ty (nŏn′ kən fôr′ mə tē, fôr′ mə tē) ***n-*** failure or refusal to conform.

non·con·sum·a·ble (nŏn′ kən sōō′ mə bəl, -syōō′ mə-bəl) ***adj-*** of natural resources, such as cannot be used up: *Sunshine and air are* nonconsumable *natural resources.*

non·con·ta·gious (nŏn′ kən tā′ jəs) ***adj-*** not contagious: *a* noncontagious *disease.*

non·de·script (nŏn′ də skrĭpt′) ***adj-*** not remarkable in any way; having no special character.

none (nŭn) ***n-*** (takes singular or plural verb) **1** not any; no part or quantity: *He has done* none *of his work.* **2** no one; not one: *I see* none *of them here.* ***Hom-*** nun.
►Since NONE is usually used in a plural compound, the plural verb is generally the most natural: *It is true that* none *of the boys were good.* None *of the people are coming.* It is artificial to use the singular verb: *I know* none *of the boys is there.*

non·en·ti·ty (nŏn ĕn′ tə tē) ***n-*** [*pl.* **non·en·ti·ties**] **1** something that does not exist or exists only in the imagination. **2** person of no importance or influence; a nobody.

non·es·sen·tial (nŏn′ ə sĕn′ chəl) ***adj-*** not essential; of little importance. ***n-***: *We left* nonessentials *behind.*

none·the·less (nŭn′ thə lĕs′) ***adv-*** nevertheless. Also **none the less.**

non·ex·ist·ent (nŏn′ ĭg zĭs′ tənt) ***adj-*** not existing; unreal: *a* nonexistent *place.* **—*n-* non′ ex·ist′ ence.**

non·fer·rous (nŏn′ fĕr′ əs) ***adj-*** not containing or composed of iron; especially, relating to metals other than iron, such as gold, silver, or copper: *a* nonferrous *ore.*

non·fic·tion (nŏn′ fĭk′ shən) ***n-*** essays, biographies, travel books, and other literature that is not fiction.

non·fil·ter·a·ble virus (nŏn′ fĭl′ tər ə bəl) ***n-*** virus that is too big to pass through a porcelain or other filter.

non·fi·nite (nŏn′ fī′ nīt′) ***adj-*** not finite, especially in grammatical function: *a* nonfinite *verb.* See also *finite.*

non·flam·ma·ble (nŏn′ flăm′ ə bəl) ***adj-*** not flammable.
►For usage note see FLAMMABLE.

non·flow·er·ing (nŏn′ flou′ ər ĭng) ***adj-*** of plants, having no flowering stage during their life cycle.

non·in·flam·ma·to·ry (nŏn′ ĭn flăm′ ə tôr′ ē) ***adj-*** not inflammatory, usually as a result of purpose.

non·in·ter·fer·ence (nŏn′ ĭn tər fêr′ əns) ***n-*** policy or habit of not interfering; also, an instance of this.

non·in·ter·ven·tion (nŏn′ ĭn tər vĕn′ shən) ***n-*** refusal to intervene in the affairs of another country; especially, a policy of such refusal.

non·liv·ing (nŏn′ lĭv′ ĭng) ***adj-*** not having life; inanimate.

non·met·al (nŏn′ mĕt′ əl) ***n-*** any of the group of elements lacking the properties of a metal, such as the ability to conduct heat and electricity. **—*adj-* non′ met·al′ lic.**

non·pa·reil (nŏn′ pə rĕl′) ***n-*** **1** person or thing that has no equal in excellence; paragon. **2** small disk of chocolate candy coated on one side with tiny balls of hard

Any of these words means non- ("not") plus the meaning of the rest of the word as given in the main text.

non′ com·pet′ ing
non′ com·pet′ i·tive
non′ com·press′ i·ble
non′ con·clu′ sive
non′ con·cur′ rence
non′ con·cur′ rent
non′ con·duct′ ing
non′ con·duc′ tive
non′ con′ fi·den′ tial
non′ con·form′ ance
non′ con·form′ ing
non′ con·sum′ a·ble
non′ con·tig′ u·ous
non′ con·tin′ u·ous
non′ con′ tra·dic′ to·ry
non′ con·trib′ ut·ing
non′ con·trib′ u·tor′ y
non′ con′ tro·ver′ sial
non′ co·op′ er·a′ tion
non′ co·op′ er·a·tive
non′ cor·rod′ ing
non′ cor·ro′ sive
non′ crim′ i·nal
non′ de·duct′ i·ble
non′ de·fer′ ra·ble
non′ de·liv′ er·y
non′ dem′ o·crat′ ic
non′ de·nom′ i·na′ tion·al
non′ de·rog′ a·to′ ry
non′ de·struc′ tive
non′ det′ o·nat′ ing
non′ di·gest′ i·ble
non′ dis·crim′ i·na·to′ ry
non′ dis·tinc′ tive
non′ dry′ ing
non′ du′ ra·ble
non′ ed′ i·ble
non′ e·lec′ tive
non′ e·lec′ tric
non′ e·lec′ tro·lyte′
non′ en·tan′ gle·ment
non′ e·pis′ co·pal
non′ e·rup′ tive
non′ ex·clu′ sive
non′ ex·empt′
non′ ex·ist′ ence
non′ ex·pend′ a·ble
non′ fac′ tu·al
non′ fat′
non′ fa′ tal
non′ fat′ ten·ing
non′ fic′ tion·al
non′ fil′ ter·a·ble
non′ fis′ sion·a·ble
non′ fly′ ing
non′ fra·ter′ nal
non′ freez′ ing
non′ func′ tion·al
non′ gre·gar′ i·ous
non′ he·red′ i·tar′ y
non′ his·tor′ i·cal
non′ hu′ man
non′ in·duc′ tive
non′ in·dus′ tri·al
non′ in·fec′ tious
non′ in·flam′ ma·ble
non′ in·her′ it·a·ble
non′ in′ sti·tu′ tion·al
non′ in·struc′ tion·al
non′ in′ ter·sect′ ing
non′ in·tox′ i·cat·ing
non′ in·volve′ ment
non′ ju·di′ cial
non′ lin′ e·ar
non′ lu′ mi·nous
non′ mag·net′ ic
non′ mail′ a·ble
non′ ma·lig′ nant
non′ mal′ le·a·ble
non′ mar′ ket·a·ble
non′ ma·te′ ri·al·is′ tic
non′ met′ ri·cal
non′ mil′ i·tar′ y
non′ mo′ tile
non′ ne·go′ ti·a·ble
non′ ob·jec′ tive
non′ ob·serv′ ance
non′ oc·cur′ ence
non′ of·fi′ cial
non′ par′ al·lel′
non′ par′ a·lyt′ ic
non′ par′ a·sit′ ic

fāte, făt, dâre, bärn; bē, bĕt, mêre; bīte, bĭt; nōte, hŏt, môre, dȯg; fŭn, fûr; tōō, bŏŏk; oil; out; tar; thin; then; hw for wh as in *wh*at; zh for s as in u*s*ual; ə for a, e, i, o, u, as in *a*go, lin*e*n, per*i*l, at*o*m, min*us*

white sugar. *—adj-* having no equal in excellence; matchless.

non·par·ti·san (nŏn′ pär′ tə zən) ***adj-*** not partisan; especially, not swayed by or representing any political party.

non·pay·ment (nŏn′ pā′ mənt) ***n-*** failure to pay.

non·per·form·ance (nŏn′ pər fôr′ məns, -fôr′ məns) ***n-*** failure or refusal to carry out responsibilities.

non·plus (nŏn plŭs′, nŏn′-) ***vt-*** [**non·plused** or **non·plussed, non·plus·ing** or **non·pluss·ing**] to bewilder; throw into confusion; bring to a standstill: *Her refusal to decide* nonplused *Hal.*

non·poi·son·ous (nŏn′ poi′ zə nəs) ***adj-*** **1** not poisonous; not toxic. **2** of snakes, insects, etc., having no venom in the bite or sting.

non·pro·duc·tive (nŏn′ prə dŭk′ tĭv) ***adj-*** **1** not productive; unproductive. **2** not directly connected with the production of goods: *a* nonproductive *job.*

non·pro·fit (nŏn′ prŏf′ ĭt) ***adj-*** established or conducted for a purpose other than profit: *a* nonprofit *hospital.*

non·res·i·dent (nŏn′ rĕz′ ə dənt) ***adj-*** not residing at a specific place; especially, not having legal or permanent residence where one works, goes to school, etc. ***n-***: *A* nonresident *may not vote here.* ***—n-*** **non′ res′ i·dence.**

non·re·sist·ance (nŏn′ rĭ zĭs′ təns) ***n-*** a refraining from resistance; especially, the policy or practice of passively submitting to authority, even when it is unjust and tyrannical. ***—adj-*** **non′ re·sist′ ant.**

non·re·stric·tive (nŏn′ rĭ strĭk′ tĭv) ***adj-*** not restrictive.

nonrestrictive clause *Grammar* ***n-*** dependent clause that is used as an adjective to give additional information about a noun or noun phrase: *Henry,* who is taller than I, *opened the window.* Nonrestrictive clauses can usually be omitted without serious damage to the meaning of the sentence. They are set off by commas from the rest of the sentence. See also *restrictive clause.*

non·sched·uled (nŏn′ skĕj′ əld) ***adj-*** **1** not appearing on a schedule: *a* nonscheduled *performance.* **2** (also, *Informal,* **non′ sked′**) of an airline, flying only as passengers or cargo become available.

non·sec·tar·i·an (nŏn′ sĕk târ′ ē ən) ***adj-*** not belonging to, controlled by, or associated with one particular religion or sect: *a* nonsectarian *chapel.*

non·sense (nŏn′ sĕns′) ***n-*** **1** absurd statement, opinion, words, etc.: *Don't talk* nonsense. *"Fee-fi-fo-fum" is* nonsense. **2** foolish or frivolous behavior. **3** thing of little worth; trifles: *Why spend your money for such* nonsense? ***—adj-*** **non′ sen′ si·cal:** *a* nonsensical *remark.* ***adv-*** **non·sen′ si·cal·ly:** *He jabbered* nonsensically.

non se·qui·tur (nŏn′ sĕk′ wə tər) ***n-*** conclusion that does not follow or seem to follow from the information given; inference that is not logical. Example: John is tall, therefore John's father must be tall.

non·skid (nŏn′ skĭd′) ***adj-*** having a tread, coating, or other surface that resists skidding: *a* nonskid *tire.*

non·stan·dard (nŏn′ stăn′ dərd) ***adj-*** **1** not standard. **2** belonging to a level or variety of language not generally used by educated persons: *"He don't" is* nonstandard.

non·stop (nŏn′ stŏp′) ***adj-*** making no stops; express: *a* nonstop *flight from Los Angeles to New York.* ***adv-***: *to fly* nonstop *to Chicago.*

non·sup·port (nŏn′ sə pôrt′) ***n-*** failure to provide for support, especially of a legal dependent.

non·un·ion (nŏn′ yōōn′ yən) ***adj-*** **1** not belong to a trade union: *a* nonunion *electrician.* **2** not recognizing or contracting with trade unions or their members: *a* nonunion *employer.*

non·ver·bal (nŏn′ vûr′ bəl) ***adj-*** not using or expressed in words.

non·vi·o·lence (nŏn′ vī′ ə ləns) ***n-*** belief that only peaceful means should be used to solve problems and defend one's principles. ***—adj-*** **non′ vi′ o·lent:** *a* nonviolent *revolution.*

non·vot·er (nŏn′ vō′ tər) ***n-*** person who is not entitled to vote or does not bother to.

[1]**noo·dle** (nōō′ dəl) ***n-*** narrow strip of dried dough, usually made with egg and eaten in soup or cooked as a casserole. [from German **Nudel.**]

[2]**noo·dle** (nōō′ dəl) ***n-*** **1** silly or stupid person; blockhead. **2** *Informal* the head. [of uncertain origin.]

nook (nŏŏk) ***n-*** **1** small, out-of-the-way place: *I tried to find a quiet* nook *for studying.* **2** corner: *a chimney* nook.

noon (nōōn) ***n-*** midday; 12 o'clock in the middle of the day: *He went home at* noon. *as* ***modifier***: *the* noon *whistle.*

noon·day (nōōn′ dā′) ***adj-*** at noon; occurring at midday: *a* noonday *meal*; *the* noonday *sun.*

no one (nō′ wŭn′) ***pron-*** nobody: *I saw* no one.

noon·time (nōōn′ tīm′) ***n-*** noon. Also, *Archaic,* **noon′ tide′** (nōōn′ tīd′).

Any of these words means non- ("not") plus the meaning of the rest of the word as given in the main text.

non′ par·ti′ ci·pant
non′ par·tic′ i·pat′ ing
non′ par·ti′ ci·pa′ tion
non′ path′ o·gen′ ic
non′ pay′ ing
non′ per′ ish·a·ble
non′ phys′ i·cal
non′ po·lit′ i·cal
non′ por′ ous
non′ pro·duc′ er
non′ pro·fes′ sion·al
non′ pro·pri′ e·tar′ y
non′ pub′ lic
non′ ra′ cial
non′ ra′ di·o·ac′ tive
non′ read′ er
non′ rec′ og·ni′ tion
non′ re·cov′ er·a·ble
non′ re·cur′ rent
non′ re·cur′ ring
non′ re·duc′ ing
non′ re·fill′ a·ble
non′ reg′ is·tered
non′ re·li′ gious
non′ re·new′ a·ble
non′ re·pay′ a·ble
non′ res′ i·den′ tial
non′ res′ o·nant
non′ re·straint′
non′ re·strict′ ed
non′ ret′ ro·ac′ tive
non′ re·turn′ a·ble
non′ re·vers′ i·ble
non′ rig′ id
non′ ro′ tat′ ing
non′ sal′ a·ble
non′ sci′ en·tif′ ic
non′ sea′ son·al
non′ seg′ re·gat′ ed
non′ seg′ re·ga′ tion
non′ se·lec′ tive
non′-self′-gov′ ern·ing
non′ sex′ u·al
non′ smok′ er
non′ smok′ ing
non′ strik′ ing
non′ struc′ tur·al
non′ sub·scrib′ er
non′ sur′ gi·cal
non′ sym·met′ ri·cal
non′ syn′ chro·nous
non′ tar′ nish·a·ble
non′ tax′ a·ble
non′ tech′ ni·cal
non′ ther′ mal
non′ tox′ ic
non′ trans′ fer′ a·ble
non′ ven′ om·ous
non′ vo·ca′ tion·al
non′ vol′ a·tile
non′ vot′ ing
non′ white′
non′ wood′ y

noose (nōōs) ***n-*** **1** loop made with a slipknot, which binds tighter as the cord is drawn through the knot. **2 the noose** execution by hanging.

Noose

Noot·ka (nōōt′ kə) ***n-*** [*pl.* **Noot·kas,** also **Noot·ka**] **1** one of a tribe of North American Indians living in northwestern Washington and on Vancouver Island. **2** the language of these people. ***adj-:*** *some* Nootka *weapons.*

nor (nȯr, nôr) ***conj-*** **1** (used with "neither" to introduce two negative alternatives or with "not" to introduce more than two): *I want neither the gray suit* nor *the brown. He chose not the first* nor *the second* nor *the third, but the fourth.* **2** (used in place of "and . . . not" to introduce a second negative statement): *He hasn't gone,* nor *do I think he will go.*

Nor·dic (nȯr′ dĭk, nôr′-) ***adj-*** of, relating to, or belonging to the Germanic peoples of northern Europe, especially of Scandinavia. ***n-*** member of one of these peoples.

norm (nȯrm, nôrm) ***n-*** **1** average or mean: *The* norm *for daily production is about eight units.* **2** standard or pattern of growth, work, conduct, etc., especially one based on what is normal in experience and observation.

nor·mal (nȯr′ məl, nôr′-) ***adj-*** **1** giving no cause for special concern or alarm; usual; regular; standard: *a* normal *condition; a* normal *temperature.* **2** of average physical or mental development: *a* normal *child of 12 years.* ***n-*** **1** usual condition: *During the flood the river rose five feet above* normal. **2** *Mathematics* a perpendicular. **—*n-* nor·mal′ i·ty** (nȯr măl′ ə tē, nôr-). ***adv-*** **nor′ mal·ly.**

nor·mal·cy (nȯr′ məl sē, nôr′-) ***n-*** ordinary condition of things; normality: *Business returned to* normalcy.

nor·mal·ize (nȯr′ mə līz′, nôr′-) ***vt-*** [**nor·mal·ized, nor·mal·iz·ing**] to make normal; to bring to a usual regular or standard condition: *a plan to* normalize *prices.* **—*n-* nor′ mal·i·za′ tion:** *a* normalization *of diplomatic relations.* ***n-*** **nor′ mal·iz′ er.**

normal school ***n-*** two-year college that prepares people to be teachers.

Nor·man (nȯr′ mən, nôr′-) ***n-*** **1** one of the Viking raiders who conquered and settled Normandy in the tenth century. **2** one of the descendants of these people who, with French allies, conquered England and southern Italy during the 11th and 12th centuries. **3** in architecture, the style that developed in Normandy and England from the Romanesque, and was marked by massive towers and short, heavy columns supporting semicircular arches. ***adj-:*** *churches in the* Norman *style.*

Norman Conquest ***n-*** the conquest of England by William the Conqueror, Duke of Normandy, who won the Battle of Hastings in 1066.

Norse (nȯrs, nôrs) ***adj-*** **1** of or relating to the language, people, or countries of ancient Scandinavia. **2** Norwegian. ***n-*** **1** (also **Old Norse**) the language of ancient Scandinavia. **2 the Norse** (1) the people of ancient Scandinavia. (2) the Norwegians.

Norse·man (nȯrs′ mən, nôrs′-) ***n-*** Scandinavian of ancient times.

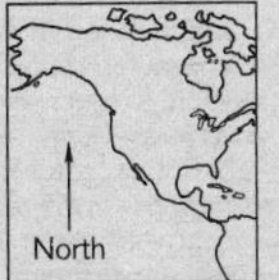

north (nȯrth, nôrth) ***n-*** **1** the direction toward the North Pole; also, the point of the compass indicating this direction; opposite of south. **2** the part of the world, country, or continent in this direction: *the* north *of Europe.* **3 the North** (1) the northern part of the United States, especially the states north of Maryland, the Ohio River, and Missouri. (2) in the Civil War, the States opposed to the Confederacy (the South); the Union. ***adj-*** **1** in or to the north: *the* north *wall.* **2** of winds, from the north. ***adv-*** toward the north: *He walked* north.

North American ***adj-*** of or relating to North America: *We are learning about the* North American *Indians.* ***n-*** person who lives in North America or is of North American descent.

north·bound (nȯrth′ bound′, nôrth′-) ***adj-*** headed north.

north by east ***n-*** the direction halfway between north-northeast and north.

north by west ***n-*** the direction halfway between north and north-northwest.

north·east (nȯrth′ ēst′, nôrth′-) ***n-*** **1** the direction halfway between north and east; also, the point of the compass indicating this direction. **2** the part of any area lying in this direction as seen from the center of the area. **3 the Northeast** the northeastern part of the United States, including New York, New Jersey, Pennsylvania, and New England. ***adj-*** **1** in or to the northeast: *a* northeast *current.* **2** of winds, from the northeast. ***adv-*** toward the northeast: *The wagons moved* northeast.

northeast by east ***n-*** the direction halfway between east-northeast and northeast.

northeast by north ***n-*** the direction halfway between northeast and north-northeast.

north·east·er (nȯr′ ēs′ tər, nȯrth′-, nôrth′-) ***n-*** storm or gale from the northeast.

north·east·er·ly (nȯrth′ ēs′ tər lē, nôrth′-) ***adj-*** **1** generally toward the northeast: *a* northeasterly *route.* **2** of winds, generally from the northeast: *a* northeasterly *breeze.* ***adv-*** generally northeastward: *We sailed* northeasterly *for three days.*

north·east·ern (nȯrth′ ēs′ tərn, nôrth′-) ***adj-*** located in or to the northeast: *the* northeastern *part of the state.*

north·east·ward (nȯrth′ ēst′ wərd, nôrth′-) ***adj-*** toward the northeast: *a* northeastward *route.* ***adv-*** (also **north′ east′ wards**): *We walked* northeastward.

north·er (nȯr′ thər, nôr′-) ***n-*** storm or gale from the north.

north·er·ly (nȯr′ thər lē, nôr′-) ***adj-*** **1** generally toward the north: *a* northerly *route.* **2** of winds, generally from the north: *a* northerly *breeze.* ***adv-*** generally northward: *We sailed* northerly *for three days.*

north·ern (nȯr′ thərn, nôr′-) ***adj-*** **1** located in or to the north: *the* northern *part of the state.* **2** characteristic of, or from the north: *a* northern *custom; a* northern *influence.* **3 Northern** of or relating to the North.

north·ern·er (nȯr′ thər nər, nôr′-) ***n-*** **1** person living in or native to the north. **2 Northerner** person living in or native to the northern part of the United States.

Northern Hemisphere ***n-*** the part of the earth lying north of the equator.

northern lights ***n-*** aurora borealis.

north·ern·most (nȯr′ thərn mōst′, nôr′-) ***adj-*** farthest north.

north·land or **North·land** (nȯrth′ lănd′, nôrth′-) ***n-*** land in the North; the northern part of any country or region. **—*n-* north′ land′ er.**

North·man (nȯrth′ mən, nôrth′-) ***n-*** a Norseman or Norman.

north-north·east (nȯrth′ nȯrth′ ēst′, nôrth′ nôrth′-) ***n-*** the direction halfway between northeast and north.

north-north·west (nôrth′ nôrth′ wĕst′, nôrth′ nôrth′-) ***n-*** the direction halfway between north and northwest.

North Pole ***n-*** **1** northern end of the earth's axis. **2 north pole** the pole of a magnet that points north when a magnet swings freely about a vertical axis.

North Star ***n-*** Polaris.

north·ward (nôrth′ wərd, nôrth′-) ***adv-*** (also **north′ wards**) toward the north: *We traveled* northward. ***adj-***: *a* northward *journey.* ***n-***: *mountains to the* northward.

north·west (nôrth′ wĕst′, nôrth′-) ***n-*** **1** the direction halfway between north and west; also, the point of the compass indicating this direction. **2** the part of any area lying in this direction as seen from the center of the area. **3 the Northwest** (1) the northwestern part of the United States, especially Washington, Oregon, and Idaho, and adjacent Canada. (2) formerly, the territory of the United States lying north of the Ohio River. ***adj-*** **1** in or to the northwest: *a* northwest *current.* **2** of winds, from the northwest. ***adv-*** toward the northwest: *The wagons moved* northwest.

northwest by north ***n-*** the direction halfway between north-northwest and northwest.

northwest by west ***n-*** the direction halfway between northwest and west-northwest.

north·west·er (nôr wĕs′ tər, nôrth′-, nôrth′-) ***n-*** storm or gale from the northwest.

north·west·er·ly (nôrth′ wĕs′ tər lē, nôrth′-) ***adj-*** **1** generally toward the northwest: *a* northwesterly *route.* **2** of winds, generally from the northwest: *a* northwesterly *breeze.* ***adv-*** generally northwestward: *The plane flew* northwesterly.

north·west·ern (nôrth′ wĕs′ tərn, nôrth′-) ***adj-*** located in or to the northwest: *the* northwestern *part of the state.*

Northwest Passage ***n-*** supposed water route between the Atlantic and Pacific oceans north of Canada. It was the goal of early explorers.

north·west·ward (nôrth′ wĕst′ wərd, nôrth′-) ***adj-*** toward the northwest: *a* northwestward *airplane flight.* ***adv-*** (also **north′ west′ wards**): *We drove* northwestward.

Nor·we·gian (nôr wē′ jən) ***n-*** **1** a native or inhabitant of Norway, or one of his descendants. **2** the Germanic language of the Norwegian people. ***adj-***: *We wore* Norwegian *costumes.*

nose (nōz) ***n-*** **1** the part of the face containing the nostrils, through which people and animals breathe and usually smell. **2** snout or muzzle of an animal: *He lightly slapped the puppy on the side of the* nose. **3** front or forward end: *the* nose *of an airplane.* **4** ability to smell: *A bloodhound has a keen* nose. **5** ability to find out as if by scent: *The reporter has a* nose *for news.* ***vt-*** **[nosed, nos·ing] 1** to rub with or as with the nose: *The boat* nosed *the shore. The horse* nosed *my shoulder.* **2** to sniff or smell (something): *The bloodhound* nosed *the grass in search of a trail.* ***vi-*** to advance gently or cautiously: *The ship* nosed *gently through the fog.*

by a nose by a narrow margin: *I missed the train* by a nose. **lead by the nose** to dominate gently but firmly. **look down (one's) nose at** to regard in a superior way. **pay through the nose** to pay an extremely high price. **poke (one's) nose into** (or **in**) to snoop: *I found him* poking his nose into *my diary.* **put (someone's) nose out of joint** to displease (someone), especially by hurting his vanity. **turn up (one's) nose at** to regard in a snobbish or displeasing way: *He* turned up his nose at *our suggestions.* **under (one's) nose** within (one's) immediate view.

nose around (or **about**) to find out as if by scent; to snoop: *I* nosed about *and finally found out their secret.*

nose out to defeat by a narrow margin.

nose·bleed (nōz′ blēd′) ***n-*** a bleeding from the nose.

nose cone ***n-*** cone-shaped front section of a missile or rocket. It is designed to withstand very high heat, and to protect other parts of the vehicle from burning.

nose dive ***n-*** **1** a nose-first plunge by an airplane. **2** any sudden drop: *Stock prices went into a* nose dive. ***vi-*** **(nose-dive) [nose-dived, nose-div·ing]** to take a sudden downward plunge.

nose·gay (nōz′ gā′) ***n-*** small bouquet or bunch of flowers.

nose·piece (nōz′ pēs′) ***n-*** **1** part or piece designed to fit on or protect the nose. **2** frame at the lower end of a microscope that holds the objective lens or lenses.

nos·tal·gia (nŏ stăl′ jə) ***n-*** wistful yearning for things and events of the past: *She had a* nostalgia *for the 1930's.*

nos·tril (nŏs′ trəl) ***n-*** either of the two outer openings of the nose.

nos·trum (nŏs′ trəm) ***n-*** **1** a patent or quack medicine. **2** a favorite remedy or pet scheme for curing.

nos·y or **nos·ey** (nō′ zē) *Informal* ***adj-*** **[nos·i·er, nos·i·est]** prying; inquisitive. **—*adv-* nos′ i·ly.** ***n-*** **nos′ i·ness.**

not (nŏt) ***adv-*** word used to make negative statements: *He is* not *here at the moment.* ***Homs-*** knot, naught.

no·ta·ble (nō′ tə bəl) ***adj-*** worthy of notice or attention; memorable: *a* notable *event in the history of our country.* ***n-*** important or distinguished person. **—*adv-* no′ ta·bly:** *We met some charming people,* notably *Joe's cousin Sally.*

no·ta·rize (nō′ tə rīz′) ***vt-*** **[no·ta·rized, no·ta·riz·ing]** to witness (a document) legally and stamp as legally witnessed, in the capacity of a notary.

no·ta·ry (nō′ tə rē) ***n-*** [*pl.* **no·ta·ries**] public official empowered to witness documents and, by his seal and signature, guarantee that the maker has sworn that they are true and correct. Also **notary public.** **—*adj-* no·tar′ i·al:** *a* notarial *signature.*

no·ta·tion (nō tā′ shən) ***n-*** **1** use of letters, numbers, and other symbols for writing things down more briefly and clearly than they could be written in words. Mathematics, music, chemistry, phonetics, and the ballet are among the fields having special systems of notation. **2** any set of symbols used in such writing or recording. **3** something written; a note: *a* notation *in a margin.*

notch (nŏch) ***n-*** **1** a V-shaped cut in the surface or edge of something. **2** narrow pass with steep sides between two mountains; gap. **3** *Informal* a step, grade, or degree: *The varsity team is a* notch *above the junior varsity team.* ***vt-*** **1** to make a V-shaped cut in; nick. **2** to keep count of by or as if by making such cuts in something.

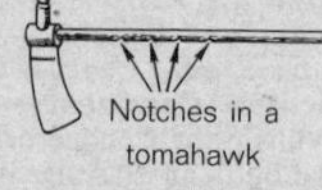
Notches in a tomahawk

note (nōt) ***n-*** **1** short, informal letter: *Send me a* note *when you arrive.* **2** written comment, record, or explanation: *Make a* note *of what we have just discussed. Consult the* notes *at the back of the book.* **3** *Music* (1) single tone made by an instrument or the voice. (2) written sign or character representing the pitch and relative length of such a tone. **4** certain quality; trace; hint: *a* note *of sadness in her voice*; *a* note *of optimism in the report.* **5** notice; attention; heed: *to take* note *of a warning*; *a matter worthy of* note. **6** piece of paper money issued by a government: *a five-pound* note. **7** formal letter from one government to another: *a diplomatic* note. **8** legal paper acknowledging a debt and promising to pay; promissory note. ***vt-*** **[not·ed, not·ing] 1** to make a record or memorandum of: *Please* note *my change of* *address in your files.* **2** to notice; observe: *He* noted *a trace of eagerness in her voice.* **3** to mention specially: *He* noted *that fact in the lecture.*

compare notes to exchange ideas or opinions; discuss: *They* compared notes *on the latest movie.* **of note** important; distinguished: *a writer* of note. **take notes** to write down facts, ideas, etc., to remember.

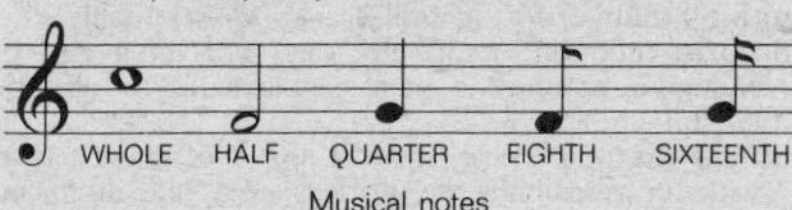

Musical notes

note·book (nōt′bo͝ok′) ***n-*** **1** book with blank pages in which to write notes, reminders, school assignments, observations, etc.

not·ed (nō′təd) ***adj-*** well-known; famous; celebrated: *She is a* noted *musician.*

►Should not be confused with NOTORIOUS.

note·worthy (nōt′wûr′*th*ē) ***adj-*** worthy of attention or notice; outstanding; remarkable: *Her discovery is a* noteworthy *contribution to science.* **—*adv-* note′worth′i·ly.** ***n-*** **note′worth′i·ness.**

noth·ing (nŭth′ĭng) ***pron-*** not anything: *I have* nothing *to tell you.* ***n-*** thing or person of no use, value, or importance: *He felt like a mere* nothing *in the presence of such a great person.* ***adv-*** not at all; by no means; in no way: *That picture looks* nothing *like her.*

for nothing 1 free of charge: *Library books may be borrowed* for nothing. **2** to no purpose; in vain: *All his hard work was* for nothing. **3** for no good reason: *he insulted me* for nothing. **in nothing flat** *Informal* very quickly: *He raced up the stairs* in nothing flat. **nothing doing** *Informal* absolutely not; under no circumstances.

noth·ing·ness (nŭth′ĭng nəs) ***n-*** **1** absence of all things; absolute emptiness; complete void: *The idea of* nothingness *is difficult and frightening.* **2** unconsciousness.

no·tice (nō′tĭs) ***n-*** **1** a taking heed; attention; observation: *He tiptoed quietly into the room to escape* notice. **2** written or printed announcement or description, such as one put up in a public place or published in a newspaper: *I read the* notice *of your marriage in the "Times."* **3** statement or warning of what one intends to do: *I sent him* notice *that I would arrive on Tuesday.* **4** formal notification of something that will happen or be done, usually after a certain interval of time: *He gave two weeks'* notice *before he left his job.* **5** review of a book, play, etc.: *The new movie received good* notices. ***vt-*** **[no·ticed, no·tic·ing] 1** to see; observe: *We* noticed *that he was wearing new shoes.* **2** to give or pay attention to: *people seldom* notice *that sign.*

serve notice to announce; inform; give warning: *He* served notice *that he would stand for no nonsense.* **take notice** give or pay attention; be aware: *Good drivers* take notice *of all traffic regulations.*

no·tice·a·ble (nō′tĭs ə bəl) ***adj-*** easily seen, observed, or detected: *a* noticeable *smudge on his nose; a* noticeable *odor;* noticeable *improvement.* **—*adj-* no′tice·a·bly.**

no·ti·fi·ca·tion (nō′tə fə kā′shən) ***n-*** **1** act or process of notifying: *the* notification *of the authorities in case of accident.* **2** letter or other communication that makes something known: *a* notification *that she had won.*

no·ti·fy (nō′tə fī′) ***vt-*** **[no·ti·fied, no·ti·fy·ing]** to report a fact to; inform: *She* notified *the post office of her change of address. I'll* notify *the police.* **—*n-* no′ti·fi′er.**

no·tion (nō′shən) ***n-*** **1** general idea; conception; understanding: *They didn't have the slightest* notion *of what he was saying.* **2** belief; opinion; view: *He has a strange* notion *that the earth is flat.* **3** a desire; impulse; whim: *She had a* notion *to go swimming.* **4 notions** small, useful articles such as pins, thread, buttons, etc.

no·to·chord (nō′tə kȯrd′, -kôrd′) ***n-*** the elastic, rodlike structure in the adult stage of some primitive vertebrates that serves as the internal skeleton; also, a similar structure occurring in all vertebrate embryos, which is the forerunner of the spinal cord.

no·to·ri·e·ty (nō′tə rī′ə tē) ***n-*** condition of being notorious; unfavorable publicity or reputation: *his* notoriety *as a gambler; to gain* notoriety.

no·to·ri·ous (nō tôr′ē əs) ***adj-*** widely known and disapproved of; famous for some undesirable trait, act, etc.: *a* notorious *pirate; his* notorious *greed.* **—*adv-* no·to′ri·ous·ly.** ***n-*** **no·to′ri·ous·ness.**

►Should not be confused with NOTED.

no-trump (nō′trŭmp′) ***n-*** in card games, a bid calling for or establishing play without any suit as trump. ***adj-***: *a* no-trump *bid; a* no-trump *hand.*

not·with·stand·ing (nŏt′wĭ*th* stăn′dĭng, nŏt′wĭth-) ***prep-*** in spite of: *The property was finally sold,* notwithstanding *its high price.* ***adv-*** still; nevertheless; yet: *Tired as we were, we struggled on* notwithstanding.

nou·gat (no͞o′gət) ***n-*** chewy, sweet candy containing almonds or other nuts, and sometimes candied fruit.

nought (nȯt, nŏt) naught.

noun (noun) *Grammar* ***n-*** word, usually a name, that can fill the subject position in a sentence and also be the chief word of a phrase in the subject position. Most English nouns have a plural formed by adding "-s" or "-es," and many have possessive forms ending in "-'s" or "-s'." A **proper noun** is the name of a particular person, place, or thing and is always capitalized when written. Any other noun is called a **common noun** and is usually not capitalized when written.

noun phrase *Grammar* ***n-*** group of words having a noun as its chief word (nucleus). Examples: the dog; a large dog; sad weeping; a strong muscle. See also *phrase.*

nour·ish (nûr′ĭsh) ***vt-*** **1** to provide (an animal or plant) with food necessary for health and growth: *Water and sunlight* nourish *plants.* **2** to promote the development of; encourage; foster: *Good books* nourish *people's minds.*

nour·ish·ing (nûr′ĭsh ĭng) ***adj-*** providing excellent nourishment; nutritious: *Milk is a* nourishing *food.*

nour·ish·ment (nûr′ĭsh mənt) ***n-*** **1** food, or something like food, that helps to keep up or strengthen the body or mind, promote growth, or improve well-being. **2** act or process of nourishing or of being nourished.

Nov. November.

no·va (nō′və) ***n-*** [*pl.* **no·vae** (-vē) or **no·vas**] star that suddenly explodes, becoming many times brighter and then gradually fading away in a few weeks or months.

[1]**nov·el** (nŏv′əl) ***adj-*** new and unusual: *a* novel *invention; a* novel *experience.* [from Old French **novel** meaning "new," from Latin **novellus,** from **novus,** "new."]

[2]**no·vel** (nŏv′əl) ***n-*** **1** long, narrative story, usually of book length, written about imaginary characters treated as if they were real: *"Treasure Island" is a famous* novel *about pirates and hidden treasure.* [from Italian **novella,** from Latin **novella** meaning literally "new things," and related to [1]**novel.**]

nov·el·ette (nŏv′əl ĕt′) ***n-*** short novel.

nov·el·ist (nŏv′əl ĭst) ***n-*** person who writes novels.

nov·el·ty (nŏv′ əl tē) ***n-*** [*pl.* **nov·el·ties**] **1** new or unusual idea, experience, or thing: *The camel ride at the zoo is a popular* novelty *for small children.* **2** quality of being new or unusual; newness; strangeness: *the* novelty *and excitement of a first plane trip.* **3 novelties** small, attractive, and unusual objects made and sold for a low price: *paper hats, and other* novelties *for New Year's Eve.*

No·vem·ber (nō vĕm′ bər) ***n-*** the eleventh month of the year, having 30 days.

no·ve·na (nō vē′ nə) ***n-*** in the Roman Catholic Church, a devotion consisting of a prayer or service for a special intention, repeated on nine consecutive days.

nov·ice (nŏv′ əs) ***n-*** **1** person without experience in a business, occupation, or activity; beginner. **2** person who is in training to enter a religious order but has not yet taken the vows.

no·vi·ti·ate (nō vĭsh′ ē ət) ***n-*** **1** state or period of being a novice or beginner. **2** period of training and testing for admission to a religious order. **3** part of a religious house where novices live during their training.

No·vo·cain (nō′ və kān′) ***n-*** trademark name of a local anesthetic; procain.

now (nou) ***adv-*** **1** at the present time: *The danger is over* now. **2** at once; immediately: *I must do this* now. *He is leaving* now. **3** next: *We have finished this assignment; what shall we do* now? **4** under these conditions; as things are: *We missed the last bus, so* now *we must spend the night here.* **5** at that point in the course of action or events; then: *They* now *began to climb the hills.* **6** (used without any specific meaning, to give emphasis, introduce an idea, etc.): *Come* now, *you know better than that!* Now *this is our plan of action.* ***conj-*** (often **now that**) since; because: *We'd better start shoveling,* now *that the snow has stopped. I can leave my post,* now *you're here.* ***n-*** the present moment; this time: *You should be finished by* now. ***interj-*** exclamation used to express warning, disbelief, sympathy, etc.: *She said,* "Now, now, *stop that quarreling*!"

just now a moment ago: *He left* just now. **now and then** (or **now and again**) from time to time; occasionally. **now . . . now** alternating one thing, manner, etc., with another: *They continued to argue,* now *in shouts,* now *in whispers.* **now then** tell me: *He shouted,* "now then, *what's for dinner?*"

now·a·days (nou′ ə dāz′) ***adv-*** at the present time; these days: *We do things differently* nowadays.

no·way (nō′ wā′) or **no·ways** (nō′ wāz′) *Informal* ***adv-*** not at all; in no manner; by no means.

no·where (nō′ hwâr′) ***adv-*** not in, to, or at any place: *It is* nowhere *to be found. He worked but got* nowhere.

nowhere near *Informal* not nearly.

no·wise (nō′ wīz′) *Informal* ***adv-*** not at all; in no way.

nox·ious (nŏk′ shəs) ***adj-*** harmful; dangerous; poisonous: *Most paint removers have* noxious *fumes. He is a* noxious *influence.* —***adv-*** **nox′ ious·ly.** ***n-*** **nox′ ious·ness.**

noz·zle (nŏz′ əl) ***n-*** metal spout at the end of a hose, pipe, etc., through which liquids or gases may be released.

Nozzle of hose

Np symbol for neptunium.

N.S. Nova Scotia.

N.T. New Testament.

-n't *suffix* contraction of **not**: *are*n't; *should*n't.

nth (ĕnth) ***adj-*** representing an ordinal number equivalent to "n." Example: 5^n is 5 raised to the nth power.

to the nth degree to the utmost extent.

nt. wt. net weight.

nu·ance (no͞o äns′, nyo͞o-) ***n-*** delicate shade or variation of meaning, expression, feeling, tone, color, etc.

nub (nŭb) ***n-*** **1** small piece, knob, or lump. **2** *Informal* central idea or meaning; gist: *the* nub *of a story.*

nub·bin (nŭb′ ən) ***n-*** **1** imperfectly developed fruit or ear of corn. **2** small knob, bump, or growth.

nub·ble (nŭb′ əl) ***n-*** small lump or knob.

nub·bly (nŭb′ lē) ***adj-*** [**nub·bli·er, nub·bli·est**] having a rough, lumpy surface or texture: *a* nubbly *fabric.*

nub·by (nŭb′ ē) ***adj-*** [**nub·bi·er, nub·bi·est**] nubbly.

nu·bile (no͞o′ bĭl′, nyo͞o′ bĭl′, -bəl) ***adj-*** of a girl, old enough or mature enough to be married. —***n-*** **nu·bil′ i·ty** (-bĭl′ ə tē).

nu·cle·ar (no͞o′ klē ər, nyo͞o′-) ***adj-*** **1** of, having to do with, or resembling the nucleus of a cell, atom, etc. **2** of, having to do with, or using atomic power; *the* nuclear *age*; *a* nuclear *war.*

nuclear energy ***n-*** atomic energy.

nuclear fission ***n-*** the breakdown or disintegration of the nucleus of an atom, with the release of large quantities of energy; atomic fission.

nuclear fusion ***n-*** the combining of the nuclei of two or more atoms to form the nucleus of a heavier atom, resulting in the release of huge amounts of energy; atomic fusion.

nuclear physics ***n-*** branch of physics dealing with the nucleus of the atom.

nuclear reactor ***n-*** structure in which a continuing nuclear fission reaction (chain reaction) takes place and is kept under control; atomic pile; atomic furnace; atomic reactor.

nu·cle·i (no͞o′ klē ī, nyo͞o′) *pl.* of **nucleus.**

nu·cle·ic acid (no͞o klē′ ĭk, nyo͞o-) ***n-*** any of the group of organic acids that direct and control a living organism's metabolism.

nu·cle·o·lus (no͞o klē′ ə ləs, nyo͞o-) ***n-*** [*pl.* **nu·cle·o·li** (-lī)] small, usually rounded structure, rich in RNA, found in the nucleus of a cell.

nu·cle·on (no͞o′ klē ŏn′, nyo͞o′-) ***n-*** proton or neutron in the nucleus of an atom.

nu·cle·on·ics (no͞o′ klē ŏn′ ĭks, nyo͞o′-) ***n-*** (takes singular verb) the study of the practical applications of nuclear physics.

nu·cle·o·plasm (no͞o′ klē ō plăz′ əm, nyo͞o′-) ***n-*** the protoplasm of the nucleus of a cell.

nu·cle·o·pro·tein (no͞o′ klē ō prō′ tēn, nyo͞o′-) ***n-*** any of the large group of compounds consisting of one or more proteins and a nucleic acid.

nu·cle·us (no͞o′ klē əs, nyo͞o′-) ***n-*** [*pl.* **nu·cle·i** (-klē ī) or **nu·cle·us·es**] **1** core or center around which something develops or grows: *Bob, Mary, and Dorothy formed the* nucleus *of the drama group. The* nucleus *of the city consisted of only five square blocks.* **2** *Physics* the positively charged, dense, central part of an atom, which contains almost all its mass. **3** *Biology* the dense round or oval body present in living cells and controlling all chemical functions of the cell. For picture, see *cell.* **4** a nerve center. **5** the main part of a comet that glows when near the sun. **6** *Grammar* the chief or central word in a phrase. In the noun phrase "the big brown bear," the nucleus is "bear." In the verb phrase "should have gone," the nucleus is "gone." See also *phrase.*

nude (no͞od, nyo͞od) ***adj-*** without clothes; naked; bare. ***n-*** painting, sculpture, or photograph of an unclothed human figure. —***adv-*** **nude′ ly.** ***n-*** **nude′ ness** or **nu′di·ty.**

in the nude without clothes; naked.

nudge (nŭj) ***vt-*** [**nudged, nudg·ing**] to push or touch gently: *Henry* nudged *me to get my attention.* ***n-*** gentle push or poke.

nud·ism (no͞o′ dĭz əm, nyo͞o′-) ***n-*** belief in, or practice of, going regularly without clothes. —***n-*** **nud′ ist.**

nug·get (nŭg′ət) ***n-*** 1 lump of precious metal, especially gold, found in the earth. 2 small, valuable bit of anything: *a* nugget *of wisdom.*

nui·sance (no͞o′səns, nyo͞o′-) ***n-*** 1 person, thing, or action that annoys or is troublesome. 2 in law, anything that offends or does injury to an individual or the public.

null (nŭl) ***adj-*** 1 having no force, effect, value, etc. 2 equal to nothing; nonexistent.

null and void without legal force or effect; not binding.

nul·li·fi·ca·tion (nŭl′ə fə kā′shən) ***n-*** 1 the act of nullifying, or the condition of being nullified. 2 doctrine that a State has the right to refuse to obey or enforce an act of Congress or a Federal court decision.

nul·li·fy (nŭl′ə fī′) ***vt-*** [**nul·li·fied, nul·li·fy·ing**] 1 to make of no value; destroy: *to* nullify *the pleasure of going by complaining.* 2 to deprive of effect or legal force; invalidate: *to* nullify *a decision.* **—*n-* nul′li·fi′er.**

nul·li·ty (nŭl′ə tē) ***n-*** [*pl.* **nul·li·ties**] 1 complete absence of value, effect, or importance. 2 law or legal document that is no longer valid.

null set *Mathematics* ***n-*** a set containing no elements; empty set.

Num. Numbers.

numb (nŭm) ***adj-*** [**numb·er, numb·est**] lacking or having lost the power to feel or move: *to be* numb *with cold; to be* numb *with grief.* ***vt-*** to cause to be without feeling; deaden: *The icy wind* numbed *our fingers.* **—*adv-* numb′ly. *n-* numb′ness.**

num·ber (nŭm′bər) ***n-*** 1 *Mathematics* an idea that can answer the question of how many and how much, in regard to a collection of units. A numeral or its equivalent is used to indicate the value of a number, and numbers are categorized according to their kind and function. See also *cardinal number, even number, natural number, odd number, ordinal number, prime number,* and *real number.* 2 a total of persons, things, or units taken together; sum: *the* number *of students in a class; the* number *of eggs in a carton.* 3 word, figure, or numeral that stands for this total: *the* number *12.* 4 figure or numeral that identifies a person or thing: *a locker* number; *a license* number; *a house or apartment* number. 5 one of a series, especially of publications: *the January* number *of a magazine.* 6 musical piece played or sung as part of a performance: *For her next* number, *she will sing a folk song.* 7 *Grammar* form of a word which shows whether it refers to one or more than one: *"Dog" is singular and "dogs" is plural in* number. 8 **numbers** (1) power or force based on size or amount of members, units, etc.: *They were beaten by superior* numbers. (2) arithmetic. (3) poetic meter or form. (4) (also **numbers pool**) kind of lottery in which bets are made that a given number will appear. ***vt-*** 1 to count: *I* number *the people in the group to be 26.* 2 to amount to: *The school's library* numbers *about 5,000 books.* 3 to give a numeral to: *We* numbered *the tickets 1 to 500.* 4 to limit in sum or total: *The days remaining to complete the paper are* numbered. 5 to include: *We* number *him among our closest friends.* **—*n-* num′ber·er.**

a number of many; several: *The sale attracted a number of shoppers.* **beyond** (or **without**) **number** too many to be counted: *Stars* beyond number *appeared in the sky.*

num·ber·less (nŭm′bər ləs) ***adj-*** 1 too many to be counted: *Grains of sand on the beach seem* numberless. 2 not having a number: *a* numberless *page.*

number line *Mathematics* ***n-*** a line on which points are marked off and assigned numbers.

number one *Informal* ***n-*** oneself.

Numbers (nŭm′bərz) ***n-*** (takes singular verb) the fourth book of the Old Testament, in which the census of Israel is recorded.

numb·skull (nŭm′skŭl′) numskull.

nu·mer·a·ble (no͞o′mər ə bəl, nyo͞o′-) ***adj-*** such as can be counted or numbered.

num·er·al (no͞o′mər əl, nyo͞o′-) ***n-*** 1 figure or other symbol that stands for a number. See also *Arabic numerals, Roman numerals.* 2 word that names such a symbol. 3 **numerals** number composed of the last two digits of a student's year of graduation. Official numerals are awarded to and worn by students who have participated in intermural competitive sports.

nu·mer·ate (no͞o′mə rāt′, nyo͞o′-) ***vt-*** [**nu·mer·at·ed, nu·mer·at·ting**] to count or number; enumerate.

nu·mer·a·tion (no͞o′mə rā′shən, nyo͞o′-) ***n-*** 1 the act or process of numbering or counting. 2 the writing or representing of numbers by symbols.

nu·mer·a·tor (no͞o′mə rā′tər, nyo͞o′-) ***n-*** 1 the numeral above the line in a fraction. In the fraction 3/4, 3 is the numerator. 2 the first of two numbers in a ratio. 3 person or device that counts or numbers.

nu·mer·i·cal (no͞o mĕr′ĭ kəl, nyo͞o-) ***adj-*** expressed in, consisting of, or having to do with numbers: *Arithmetic uses* numerical *values. Arrange the numbered sheets in* numerical *order.* **—*adv-* nu·mer′i·cal·ly.**

nu·mer·ous (no͞o′mər əs, nyo͞o′-) ***adj-*** 1 more than a few; many: *I had* numerous *telephone calls this morning.* 2 many in number: *a* numerous *collection of old records.* **—*adv-* nu′mer·ous·ly. *n-* nu′mer·ous·ness.**

nu·mis·mat·ics (no͞o′məz măt′ĭks, nyo͞o′-) ***n-*** (takes singular verb) science of coins or medals; also, the collecting of coins or medals as a hobby or occupation **—*adj-* nu′mis·mat′ic.**

nu·mis·mat·ist (no͞o mĭz′mə tĭst, nyo͞o-) ***n-*** person who collects coins or medals, or is an expert on them.

num·skull (nŭm′skŭl′) ***n-*** stupid person; blockhead.

nun (nŭn) ***n-*** woman who belongs to a religious order. Many nuns do teaching, nursing, charitable work, etc. ***Hom-*** none.

nun·ci·o (nŭn′sē ō′, no͝on′-) ***n-*** [*pl.* **nun·ci·os**] permanent representative or ambassador of the Pope to a foreign government.

nun·ner·y (nŭn′ə rē) ***n-*** [*pl.* **nun·ner·ies**] place where nuns live; convent.

nup·tial (nŭp′shəl) ***adj-*** of or having to do with marriage or a wedding: *the* nuptial *day; a* nuptial *ceremony.* ***n-*** (usually **nuptials**) a marriage or wedding.

nurse (nûrs) ***n-*** 1 person trained to take care of people who are sick or cannot care for themselves, and to assist physicians in their work. 2 one who takes care of a young child or children not her own. ***vt-*** [**nursed, nurs·ing**] 1 to care for or wait on in sickness: *He* nursed *the injured athlete back to health.* 2 to feed (a baby) milk at the breast. 3 to give special care to; tend carefully: *to* nurse *a young plant; to* nurse *a flickering fire.* 4 to keep up; cherish; harbor: *to* nurse *a grudge.* ***vi-*** 1 to care for the sick or infirm. 2 to take milk at the breast; suckle.

nurse·maid (nûrs′mād′) ***n-*** person who takes care of a child or children.

nurs·er·y (nûr′sə rē) ***n-*** [*pl.* **nurs·er·ies**] 1 baby's or child's room. 2 a place where babies or young children are cared for and tended. 3 a place where garden plants, trees, or shrubs are raised, usually for sale.

nurs·er·y·man (nûr′ sə rē mən) ***n-*** [*pl.* **nurs·er·y·men**] man who raises and sells plants, trees, etc.
nursery rhyme ***n-*** short poem in rhyme for young children. "Little Miss Muffet" is a nursery rhyme.
nursery school ***n-*** school for young children, usually between the ages of three and five.
nurs·ing (nûr′ sĭng) ***n-*** profession or work of a nurse. *as* ***modifier***: *a* nursing *school.*
nursing bottle ***n-*** bottle fitted with a rubber nipple and used for feeding babies.
nursing home ***n-*** residence or private hospital where aged, chronically ill, or helpless people are cared for.
nurs·ling (nûrs′ lĭng) ***n-*** **1** baby; infant. **2** person or thing that is lovingly and tenderly cared for.
nur·ture (nûr′ chər) ***vt-*** [**nur·tured, nur·tur·ing**] **1** to feed and care for; promote the growth of; rear. **2** to train; educate; develop: *The music teacher carefully* nurtured *the girl's voice.* ***n-*** **1** food and care; nourishment. **2** training; education; development. **—*n-* nur′ tur·er.**
nut (nŭt) ***n-*** **1** a fruit of certain trees, such as the walnut, pecan, almond, or chestnut, consisting of a kernel or seed enclosed in a hard, woody, or leathery shell. **2** the seed or kernel when removed from the shell. **3** metal block with a threaded hole into which the threaded end of a bolt fits. **4** *Slang* person who behaves in an odd or irrational manner; crazy person. **—*adj-* nut′ like′.**
hard nut to crack **1** problem that is hard to solve. **2** person who is difficult to deal with.

Nut on a bolt

nut·crack·er (nŭt′ krăk′ ər) ***n-*** **1** tool for cracking nuts. **2** bird related to the crow, with a strong, pointed beak able to crack nuts and hard seeds.
nut·hatch (nŭt′ hăch′) ***n-*** any of several small, gray and white birds that creep down the trunks of trees headfirst.
nut·meg (nŭt′ mĕg′) ***n-*** **1** hard, nutlike kernel of the seed of an East Indian tree. It is grated and used as a spice. **2** the tree itself.
nut·pick (nŭt′ pĭk′) ***n-*** sharp tool for removing the kernels from cracked nuts.

Nutcracker

nu·tri·a (nōō′ trē ə, nyōō′-) ***n-*** **1** the coypu. **2** the soft brown fur of the coypu.
nu·tri·ent (nōō′ trē ənt, nyōō′-) ***n-*** substance, especially a food, that promotes growth and nourishes. ***adj-*** promoting growth; nourishing: *a* nutrient *substance.*
nu·tri·ment (nōō′ trə mənt, nyōō′-) ***n-*** anything that provides nourishment; food.
nu·tri·tion (nōō trĭsh′ ən, nyōō-) ***n-*** **1** a nourishing or being nourished with food; especially, the process by which an animal or plant uses food to promote growth. **2** nourishment; food. **—*adj-* nu·tri′ tion·al** (-ən əl): *a* nutritional *deficiency.* ***adv-*** **nu·tri′ tion·al·ly.**
nu·tri·tious (nōō trĭsh′ əs, nyōō-) ***adj-*** promoting growth and good health; nourishing: *a* nutritious *diet.* **—*adv-* nu·tri′ tious·ly.** ***n-*** **nu·tri′ tious·ness.**
nu·tri·tive (nōō′ trə tĭv′, nyōō′-) ***adj-*** of or having to do with nutrition. **—*adv-* nu′ tri·tive·ly.**
nuts (nŭts) *Slang* ***adj-*** **1** crazy. **2** very enthusiastic (about).
nut·shell (nŭt′ shĕl′) ***n-*** hard covering around a nut.
in a nutshell in a few words; briefly.
nut·ting (nŭt′ ĭng) ***n-*** the gathering of nuts.
nut·ty (nŭt′ ē) ***adj-*** [**nut·ti·er, nut·ti·est**] **1** full of nuts; flavored with nuts: *a* nutty *cake.* **2** reminding one of nuts: *a* nutty *flavor.* **3** *Slang* foolish; queer; crazy. **—*n-* nut′ ti·ness.**
nux vom·i·ca (nŭks vŏm′ ĭ kə) ***n-*** **1** poisonous seed of an East Indian tree, from which strychnine and other substances used in medicine are obtained. **2** the tree bearing these seeds.
nuz·zle (nŭz′ əl) ***vt-*** [**nuz·zled, nuz·zling**] to rub or press with the nose: *The puppy* nuzzled *its mother.* ***vi-*** to press or nestle close; snuggle.
NW or **N.W.** **1** northwest. **2** northwestern.
N.W.T. Northwest Territories (Canada).
N.Y. New York.
N.Y.C. New York City.
ny·lon (nī′ lŏn′) ***n-*** **1** any of several synthetic plastic substances from which fibers, cloth, machine parts, etc., are manufactured. **2 nylons** stockings made with fibers of this substance. *as* ***modifier***: *a* nylon *jacket.*
nymph (nĭmf) ***n-*** **1** in Greek and Roman mythology, a minor goddess of nature, living in the mountains, woods, streams, etc.; hence, any beautiful maiden. **2** immature insect, such as a dragonfly or mayfly, in a stage of development that resembles the adult form. **—*adj-* nymph′ like′.**
N.Z. New Zealand.

O

O, o (ō) ***n-*** [*pl.* **O's, o's**] **1** the fifteenth letter of the English alphabet. **2** zero; naught. **3** anything shaped like the letter O.
o ohm.
[1]**O** (ō) ***interj-*** exclamation used in speaking formally to someone: *Hear us,* O *Lord.* ***Homs-*** oh, owe.
[2]**O** symbol for oxygen.
o' (ō, ə) ***prep-*** (now used chiefly in compound words). **1** of the: *four* o'*clock.* **2** of: *will-*o'*-the wisp.*
oaf (ōf) ***n-*** stupid, clumsy fellow.
oaf·ish (ō′ fĭsh) ***adj-*** of or like an oaf; stupid and clumsy. **—*adv-* oaf′ ish·ly.** ***n-*** **oaf′ ish·ness.**
oak (ōk) ***n-*** **1** any of various trees that bear acorns. **2** the hard, durable wood of these trees. *as* ***modifier***: *an* oak *cabinet*; *sturdy* oak *floors.*

WHITE OAK
LIVE OAK
Oaks

oak apple ***n-*** rounded swelling produced on the leaves and twigs of oak trees by certain wasps. Also **oak gall.** For picture, see [3]*gall.*
oak·en (ō′ kən) ***adj-*** made of oak: *an* oaken *bucket.*
oa·kum (ō′ kəm) ***n-*** hemp fiber in loosely twisted strands, treated with tar and used for caulking seams and joints.
oar (ôr) ***n-*** **1** implement with a flat or somewhat curved blade and a long handle, used to row or steer a boat. **2** a rower. ***vt-*** to row. ***Homs-*** o'er, or, ore.
put (one's) oar in to interfere; be meddlesome.

OARLOCK
Oar

oar·lock (ôr′ lŏk′) ***n-*** device consisting of a U-shaped notch mounted on a metal pin, used for holding an oar in place while in use; rowlock. For picture, see *oar.*
oars·man (ôrz′ mən) ***n-*** [*pl.* **oars·men**] person who rows a boat.

O.A.S. Organization of American States.

o·a·sis (ō ā′ səs) ***n-*** [*pl.* **o·a·ses** (-sēz)] the irrigated land near a desert waterhole or river; hence, any place providing refreshment, relief, etc.

Caravan leaving an oasis

oat (ōt) ***n-*** **1** a cereal plant, the seeds of which are used as food or as fodder for horses. **2 oats** the seed or grain of this plant.

feel (one's) oats *Informal* **1** to be lively and frisky, often in a boisterous manner. **2** to feel or act important. **sow (one's) wild oats** of a young man, to live a wild or dissipated life.

Oats

oat·en (ō′ tən) ***adj-*** made of oats, oatmeal, or oat straw.

oath (ōth; *pl.* ōths, ōthz) ***n-*** **1** solemn statement, usually accompanied by an appeal to God as a witness, that one will tell the truth or keep a promise: *He gave his* oath *to tell the whole story.* **2** careless or profane use of the name of God or of anything sacred. **3** curse word: *to shout* oaths *in anger.*

take oath to make a solemn promise or declaration, especially on being installed in office. **under oath** bound by an oath to tell the truth.

oat·meal (ōt′ mēl′) ***n-*** **1** rolled or ground oats. **2** porridge made from this. *as* ***modifier***: *an* oatmeal *cookie.*

O·ba·di·ah (ō′ bə dī′ ə) ***n-*** **1** minor Hebrew prophet of the 6th century B.C. **2** book of the Old Testament containing his prophecies. In the CCD Bible, **Ab′ di·a.**

ob·bli·ga·to (ŏb′ lə gä′ tō) *Music* ***n-*** [*pl.* **ob·bli·ga·tos**] accompaniment or additional part that is essential to a composition: *a flute* obbligato. Also **obligato.**

ob·du·ra·cy (ŏb′ dər ə sē, ŏb′ dyər-) ***n-*** **1** hardness of heart; callousness. **2** stubbornness.

ob·du·rate (ŏb′ dər ət, ŏb′ dyər-) ***adj-*** **1** not to be moved by appeals to the feelings; hardhearted; callous: *an* obdurate *kidnapper.* **2** stubborn; unyielding; obstinate: *an* obdurate *insistence on being heard.* ***—adv-*** **ob′ du·rate·ly.** ***n-*** **ob′ du·rate·ness.**

o·be·di·ence (ō bē′ dē əns) ***n-*** a doing what one is told to do; willingness to obey: *If you are kind and patient, you can teach most dogs* obedience.

o·be·di·ent (ō bē′ dē ənt) ***adj-*** obeying orders, rules, etc.; submitting to the command or will of others: *an* obedient *child.* ***—adv-*** **o·be′ di·ent·ly.**

o·bei·sance (ō bā′ səns, -bē′ səns) ***n-*** **1** a movement or bending of the body that shows obedience or respect; bow or curtsy. **2** respect; homage; deference.

ob·e·lisk (ŏb′ ə lĭsk′) ***n-*** tapering, four-sided column with a tip shaped like a pyramid. Many examples may be found among the monuments of ancient Egypt.

Obelisk

O·ber·on (ō′ bə rŏn′) ***n-*** in medieval folklore, the king of the fairies.

o·bese (ō bēs′) ***adj-*** very fat; corpulent. ***—n-*** **o·bes′ i·ty** or **o·bese′ ness.**

o·bey (ō bā′) ***vt-*** (considered intransitive when the direct object is implied but not expressed) **1** to yield to the authority or commands of: *to* obey *one's parents.* **2** to carry out; comply with: *to* obey *a command.* **3** to act in accordance with; be guided by; follow: *to* obey *one's conscience.*

ob·fus·cate (ŏb′ fəs kāt′) ***vt-*** [**ob·fus·cat·ed, ob·fus·cat·ing**] to make less clear; prevent from being easily understood; confuse. ***—n-*** **ob′ fus·ca′ tion.**

o·bi (ō′ bē) ***n-*** broad sash worn with kimono.

o·bit (ō bĭt′) *Informal* ***n-*** obituary.

o·bit·u·ar·y (ə bĭch′ o͞o ĕr′ ē, ō-) ***n-*** [*pl.* **o·bit·u·ar·ies**] printed announcement of a person's death, often with a brief account of his life. *as* ***modifier***: *the* obituary *page of a newspaper*; *an* obituary *notice.*

obj. **1** object. **2** objection. **3** objective.

[1]**ob·ject** (əb jĕkt′) ***vi-*** **1** to protest; show disapproval: *Mother always* objects *when we leave the turtles in the bathtub.* **2** to be opposed: *The girls* objected *to our plans.* ***vt-*** to offer as an argument, criticism, or opposing reason: *He* objected *that nobody would have time for so much extra work.* ***—n-*** **ob·jec′ tor.**

[2]**ob·ject** (ŏb′ jĭkt) ***n-*** **1** thing that has shape and can be touched or seen: *The only* object *rescued from the fire was an old chair.* **2** purpose; goal; ambition: *the* object *of the meeting*; *one's* object *in life.* **3** person or thing that arouses feeling or action: *an* object *of pity*; *an* object *of praise.* **4** *Grammar* a noun, pronoun, noun phrase, or noun clause which follows a transitive verb or a preposition. Most transitive verbs take only one object, called the **direct object**; but there are a few which take two objects, the first of which is an **indirect object**, and the second the direct object. An object which follows a preposition is called an **object of a preposition.** Examples:

The cat ate the mouse (direct object).
The old woman gave her poor doggie *a bone* (indirect object).
I lent him *my grammar book* (indirect object).
I lent it to the new boy (object of preposition).

ob·jec·tion (əb jĕk′ shən) ***n-*** **1** feeling or expression of opposition, dislike, or disapproval: *The cat showed his* objection *to the stray dog by arching his back.* **2** reason for opposing something: *My only* objection *to the trip is that it will cost too much.*

ob·jec·tion·a·ble (əb jĕk′ shən ə bəl) ***adj-*** likely to be objected to; undesirable; unpleasant: *He uses* objectionable *language.* ***—adv-*** **ob·jec′ tion·a·bly.**

ob·jec·tive (əb jĕk′ tĭv) ***adj-*** **1** not influenced by emotions, prejudices, etc.; unbiased: *an* objective *description of an accident*; *an* objective *point of view.* **2** having actual existence; real; not imaginary: *Space travel is now an* objective *fact.* ***n-*** **1** something one strives to reach or gain; aim; goal: *Our* objective *is to reach the top of the hill.* **2** (also **object glass** or **objective lens**) in a microscope or telescope, the lens or combination of lenses nearest the thing being examined. **3** *Grammar* the objective case; also, a word in the objective case. ***—adv-*** **ob·jec′ tive·ly.**

objective case See [1]*case.*

ob·jec·tiv·i·ty (ŏb′ jək tĭv′ ə tē) ***n-*** lack of bias or prejudice: *Scientific research requires complete* objectivity.

object lesson ***n-*** occurrence or act that teaches, proves, or illustrates a moral principle, general truth, etc.

ob·jet d'art (ŏb'zhä där') *French* ***n-*** [*pl.* **ob·jets d'art** (-zhä där')] thing having artistic merit or value.

ob·late (ŏb'lāt', ō'blāt') ***adj-*** generally circular or spherical but flattened at both ends of a diameter (the two poles). **—*n-* ob'late'ness.**

ob·la·tion (ə blā'shən, ō-) ***n-*** **1** the act of making a religious offering or sacrifice; especially, the offering of the bread and wine of the Communion. **2** anything presented as a religious offering or sacrifice.

ob·li·gate (ŏb'lə gāt') ***vt-*** [**ob·li·gat·ed, ob·li·gat·ing**] to bind by a promise, contract, or sense of duty: *Her desire to succeed* obligates *her to work hard.*

ob·li·ga·tion (ŏb'lə gā'shən) ***n-*** **1** the binding power of a promise, contract, or sense of duty: *The builder was under* obligation *to complete the house by spring.* **2** any duty imposed by law, by social relations, or by good will: *the* obligations *of good citizenship.* **3** debt of gratitude, loyalty, affection,etc.: *I feel an* obligation *to those who help me.* **4** legal debt: *He is careful to meet his* obligations *promptly.*

ob·li·ga·to (ŏb'lə gä'tō) obbligato.

o·blig·a·tor·y (ə blĭg'ə tôr'ē) ***adj-*** required or imposed by duty, rule, law, etc.; compulsory: *Attendance in classes is* obligatory.

o·blige (ə blīj') ***vt-*** [**o·bliged, o·blig·ing**] **1** to place under a duty or obligation; compel: *The law* obliges *us to pay taxes.* **2** (considered intransitive when the direct object is implied but not expressed) to do (someone) a favor: *Will you* oblige *me by lending me your skates? He is always willing to* oblige. **—*n-* o·blig'er.**

be obliged to to be grateful to.

o·blig·ing (ə blī'jĭng) ***adj-*** helpful; willing to help; kindly: *The police in your city are most* obliging *to travelers.* **—*adv-* o·blig'ing·ly. *n-* o·blig'ing·ness.**

o·blique (ō blēk', ə-, *also* ō blīk') ***adj-*** **1** neither vertical nor horizontal; slanting; diagonal: *The wind drove the rain in* oblique *lines.* **2** neither parallel nor perpendicular to a reference line. **3** not direct or straightforward: *an* oblique *answer.* ***n-***: *The line is an* oblique. **—*adv-* o·blique'ly. *n-* o·blique'ness.**

Oblique lines

oblique angle ***n-*** any acute or obtuse angle.

o·bliq·ui·ty (ə blĭk'wə tē) ***n-*** [*pl.* **o·bliq·ui·ties**] **1** condition of being oblique; also, the amount by which something is oblique; obliqueness; slant: *The* obliquity *of the flagpole is 10° from the vertical.* **2** deviation from accepted principles of conduct or ways of thinking.

o·blit·er·ate (ə blĭt'ə rāt') ***vt-*** [**o·blit·er·at·ed, o·blit·er·at·ing**] **1** to destroy completely; wipe out; erase: *The earthquake* obliterated *an entire city.* **2** to cover or hide from view; cause to become invisible: *A cloud* obliterated *the sun.* **— *n-* o·blit'er·a'tion.**

o·bliv·i·on (ə blĭv'ē ən) ***n-*** **1** condition of being forgotten: *A single great work has saved many a writer from* oblivion. **2** unawareness of what is going on; oliviousness; also, unconsciousness.

o·bliv·i·ous (ə blĭv'ē əs) ***adj-*** unaware; inattentive: *He roared down Main Street in his car,* oblivious *of traffic lights.* **—*adv-* o·bliv'i·ous·ly. *n-* o·bliv'i·ous·ness.**

ob·long (ŏb'lȯng') ***n-*** a right-angled figure that is longer than it is wide. ***adj-*** having parallel sides and greater length than width: *an* oblong *shoe box.*

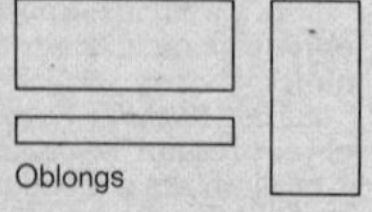

Oblongs

ob·lo·quy (ŏb'lə kwē') ***n-*** [*pl.* **ob·lo·quies**] **1** words spoken in abuse of another or others; violent reproach, accusation, etc. **2** disgrace.

ob·nox·ious (əb nŏk'shəs) ***adj-*** extremely disagreeable; offensive: *an* obnoxious *odor; an* obnoxious *person.* ***adv-*** **ob·nox'ious·ly. *n-* ob·nox'ious·ness.**

o·boe (ō'bō) ***n-*** woodwind instrument with a high, somewhat penetrating tone, played by blowing into a mouthpiece that has a double reed. **—*n-* o'bo·ist.**

Oboe

ob·scene (əb sēn') ***adj-*** extremely and offensively indecent; foul: *an* obscene *joke; an* obscene *gesture.* **—*adv-* ob·scene'ly.**

ob·scen·i·ty (əb sĕn'ə tē) ***n-*** [*pl.* **ob·scen·i·ties**] **1** extreme and offensive indecency in language, behavior, etc. **2** an indecent act, word, etc.

ob·scure (əb skyo͞or') ***adj-*** [**ob·scur·er, ob·scur·est**] **1** dim; dark; shadowy: *an* obscure *corner of the room.* **2** not clear or distinct: *the* obscure *lettering on an old signpost.* **3** hard to understand: *The meaning of that poem is* obscure. **4** out of the way; remote: *an* obscure *village.* **5** unknown; inconspicuous; humble: *to have an* obscure *position in a large company; an* obscure *country doctor.* ***vt-*** [**ob·scured, ob·scur·ing**] **1** to hide from view; darken: *A heavy fog* obscured *the street lamps.* **2** to make less clear or understandable: *All those long words* obscure *his meaning.* **—*adv-* ob·scure'ly. *n-* ob·scure'ness.**

ob·scur·i·ty (əb skyo͞or'ə tē) ***n-*** [*pl.* **ob·scur·i·ties**] **1** lack of clear meaning: *The* obscurity *of the speaker's remarks confused his audience.* **2** condition of being unknown: *Many once famous names have now passed into* obscurity. **3** dimness; indistinctness: *the* obscurity *of the carving on the old monument.*

ob·se·quies (ŏb'sə kwēz') ***n-*** *pl.* funeral ceremonies.

ob·se·qui·ous (əb sē'kwē əs) ***adj-*** too ready or eager to please or obey; fawning: *the* obsequious *courtiers.* **—*adv-* ob·se'qui·ous·ly. *n-* ob·se'qui·ous·ness.**

ob·serv·a·ble (əb zûr'və bəl) ***adj-*** such as can be observed; noticeable: *There is an* observable *improvement in his batting average.* **—*adv-* ob·serv'a·bly.**

ob·serv·ance (əb zûr'vəns) ***n-*** **1** a customary or commemorative celebration: *Birthday parties are annual* observances. **2** the following or keeping of prescribed rules: *strict* observance *of regulations.* **3** observation.

ob·serv·ant (əb zûr'vənt) ***adj-*** **1** quick to notice; watchful: *The baby is very* observant *of everything that goes on.* **2** mindful of duties or authority; attentive: *an* observant *nurse.* **—*adv-* ob·serv'ant·ly.**

ob·ser·va·tion (ŏb'sər vā'shən, ŏb'zər-) ***n-*** **1** act of watching or seeing: *A half-hour's* observation *taught me the game.* **2** ability to see clearly and examine with exactness: *Try to develop your powers of* observation. **3** thing noted by observing: *Write your* observations *of the experiment in your notebook.* **4** a being seen; notice: *Certain birds often escape* observation *because of protective coloring.* **5** a remark or comment that results from observing: *an* observation *about the weather.*

ob·ser·va·tion·al (ŏb'sər vā'shən əl, ŏb'zər-) ***adj-*** of or resulting from observation.

ob·ser·va·tor·y (əb zûr'və tôr'ē) ***n-*** [*pl.* **ob·ser·va·tor·ies**] **1** building or group of buildings fitted with telescopes and other equipment for studying the heavens. **2** tower or place from which there is an extensive view.

ob·serve (əb zûrv') ***vt-*** [**ob·served, ob·serv·ing**] **1** to see; notice; watch carefully: *to observe a flash of lightning; to* observe *the growth of a flower.* **2** to say; remark:

(takes only a clause or quotation as an object): *"A good day for planting," the farmer* observed *as he went outside.* **3** to obey; follow: *Swimmers must* observe *the rules of the pool.* **4** to keep; celebrate: *We* observe *the Fourth of July as a patriotic holiday.* ***vi-*** to act as an observer. ***—adv-*** **ob·serv′ ing·ly.**

ob·serv·er (əb zûr′ vər) ***n-*** **1** one who watches: *He stood apart as an* observer *of the fight.* **2** person who follows or conforms to rules and customs: *a strict* observer *of the Sabbath.* **3** an official delegate at a meeting who takes note of the proceedings but has no part in them.

ob·sess (əb sĕs′, ŏb-) ***vt-*** to rule or trouble the mind of, especially as a fixed idea: *The dream of great riches* obsessed *him.*

ob·ses·sion (əb sĕsh′ ən) ***n-*** fixed idea not easily driven from the mind: *Tidiness is an* obsession *with her.*

ob·ses·sive (əb sĕs′ ĭv) ***adj-*** resulting from or resembling an obsession: *an* obsessive *desire for fame and fortune.* ***—adv-*** **ob·ses′ sive·ly.**

ob·sid·i·an (əb sĭd′ ē ən) ***n-*** dark, glassy rock formed from magma that has been pushed out by volcanic action and has cooled very quickly.

ob·so·les·cent (ŏb′ sə lĕs′ ənt) ***adj-*** passing out of use: *an* obsolescent *word.* ***—n-*** **ob′ so·les′ cence.**

ob·so·lete (ŏb′ sə lēt′) ***adj-*** no longer used or practiced: *an* obsolete *firearm*; *an* obsolete *custom.*

ob·sta·cle (ŏb′ stə kəl) ***n-*** thing that blocks or stands in the way; obstruction; hindrance; impediment.

ob·stet·ric (əb stĕ′ trĭk) ***adj-*** of or having to do with obstetrics: *an* obstetric *instrument.* Also **ob·stet′ ri·cal.** ***—adv-*** **ob·stet′ ri·cal·ly.**

ob·ste·tri·cian (ŏb′ stə trĭsh′ ən) ***n-*** doctor specializing in obstetrics.

ob·stet·rics (əb stĕ′ trĭks) ***n-*** (takes singular verb) the branch of medicine dealing with the birth of children.

ob·sti·na·cy (ŏb′ stə nə sē) ***n-*** stubbornness; determination not to yield: *the* obstinacy *of mules.*

ob·sti·nate (ŏb′ stə nət) ***adj-*** unyielding; not giving in to pressure or reasoning; stubborn: *Once John got an idea, he was so* obstinate *that nobody could argue him out of it.* ***—adv-*** **ob′ sti·nate·ly.** ***n-*** **ob′ sti·nate·ness.**

ob·strep·er·ous (əb strĕp′ ər əs) ***adj-*** clamorous; turbulently noisy; boisterous, especially in resistance to control, advice, etc. ***—adv-*** **ob·strep′ er·ous·ly.** ***n-*** **ob·strep′ er·ous·ness.**

ob·struct (əb strŭkt′) ***vt-*** **1** to block; close: *A fallen tree* obstructed *the road.* **2** to be or get in the way of: *Frost on the windshield* obstructed *the driver's view.* **3** to prevent or slow down the progress of; hinder; impede: *Late snows* obstructed *the building of the tennis court.*

ob·struc·tion (əb strŭk′ shən) ***n-*** **1** something that blocks: *an* obstruction *in the drain.* **2** a blocking: *Heavy snows caused* obstruction *of railroads and highways.*

ob·struc·tion·ism (əb strŭk′ shə nĭz′ əm) ***n-*** act or policy of deliberately hindering work or progress, especially in a legislative body. ***—n-*** **ob·struc′ tion·ist.**

ob·struc·tive (əb strŭk′ tĭv) ***adj-*** tending to block, impede, or hinder: *the* obstructive *tactic of filibustering.* ***—adv-*** **ob·struct′ ive·ly.**

ob·tain (əb tān′) ***vt-*** to get; acquire by effort, purchase, or request: *Practice hard, and you'll* obtain *results.* ***vi-*** to be in use or in fashion; prevail: *Shaking hands is a custom that* obtains *in many countries.* ***—n-*** **ob·tain′able.**

ob·trude (əb trōōd′) ***vt-*** **[ob·trud·ed, ob·trud·ing] 1** to force or thrust (oneself, an opinion, etc.) forward boldly or rudely: *to* obtrude *one's views into a private discussion.* **2** to push (something) out or forward: *He* obtruded *his hand through the opening.* ***vi-*** to intrude: *Do not* obtrude *upon her sorrow.*

ob·tru·sion (əb trōō′ zhən) ***n-*** **1** an obtruding: *He hates the* obtrusion *of new ideas.* **2** something obtruded.

ob·tru·sive (əb trōō′ sĭv, -zĭv) ***adj-*** tending to obtrude; forward: *rude and* obtrusive *behavior.* ***—adv-*** **ob·tru′ sive·ly.** ***n-*** **ob·tru′ sive·ness.**

ob·tuse (əb tōōs′, tyōōs′) ***adj-*** **1** not sensitive; slow to understand; dull: *Sam was* obtuse *in regard to people's feelings.* **2** unpointed; blunt: *an* obtuse *leaf.* ***—adv-*** **ob·tuse′ ly.** ***n-*** **ob·tuse′ ness.**

obtuse angle ***n-*** any angle greater than 90° and less than 180°. For picture, see *angle.*

obtuse triangle ***n-*** any triangle containing an obtuse angle.

ob·verse (ŏb′ vûrs′) ***adj-*** **1** turned toward or facing the observer. **2** in botany, narrower at the base than at the top, as some leaves are. ***n-*** **1** front surface of anything; especially, the side of a coin or medal bearing the main design; opposite of *reverse.* ***—adv-*** **ob·verse′ ly.**

Obverse Reverse

ob·vi·ate (ŏb′ vē āt′) ***vt-*** **[ob·vi·at·ed, ob·vi·at·ing]** to remove or clear away beforehand; forestall; preclude: *These precautions* obviate *any chance of an accident.* ***—n-*** **ob′ vi·a′ tion.**

ob·vi·ous (ŏb′ vē əs) ***adj-*** **1** plain to see; outstandingly clear; evident: *an* obvious *blunder.* **2** not attempting to conceal one's feelings: *He is* obvious *about his dislikes.*

oc·a·ri·na (ŏk′ ə rē′ nə) ***n-*** small wind instrument with a soft tone, often made of terra cotta, with a mouthpiece and finger holes.

Ocarina

oc·ca·sion (ə kā′ zhən) ***n-*** **1** particular time or event: *I remember the* occasion *of our first meeting.* **2** time or event that is special or important: *A girl's first formal dance is a real* occasion. **3** favorable opportunity; chance: *This is the first* occasion *I have had to congratulate him on his graduation.* **4** reason or cause, especially one that directly brings about something not foreseen or intended: *My going into the wrong room was the* occasion *of both laughter and embarrassment.* **5** need: *He never had* occasion *to consult a lawyer.* ***vt-*** to be the direct cause of; bring about, especially something not foreseen or intended: *My mistake* occasioned *a general change in our approach to the project.*

on occasion once in a while; as need or opportunity demands: *He can show great ability* on occasion.

oc·ca·sion·al (ə kā′ zhən əl) ***adj-*** **1** occurring once in a while: *an April day with* occasional *showers.* **2** created or used for a special event: *A poem written for graduation is an* occasional *poem.* **3** of furniture, easily moved and adapted to a wide variety of settings and uses: *an* occasional *chair.*

oc·ca·sion·al·ly (ə kā′ zhən ə lē) ***adv-*** once in a while; now and then: *We swim a lot and* occasionally *go fishing.*

oc·ci·dent (ŏk′ sə dĕnt′, dənt) ***n-*** **1** where the sun sets; the west. **2 the Occident** countries of Europe and the Americas, as distinguished from those of Asia.

oc·ci·den·tal (ŏk′ sə dĕn′ təl) ***adj-*** **1** western. **2** of or pertaining to the countries of the Occident: *our* occidental *food habits.* ***n-*** **Occidental 1** person belonging to or descended from one of the native peoples of the Occident. 2 a Caucasian.

oc·clude (ə klōōd′) ***vt-*** **[oc·clud·ed, oc·clud·ing] 1** to shut up or out. **2** to close. **3** *Chemistry* to adsorb: *Carbon* occludes *nitrogen.* **4** in meteorology, of an advancing cold front, to force (warm air) upwards, and so cut it off from the ground. ***vi-*** of the grinding surfaces of the upper and lower teeth, to meet evenly.

occluded front ***n-*** weather front formed when an advancing mass of cold air forces a warm air mass upwards.

oc·clu·sion (ə klōō′ zhən) ***n-*** an occluding; especially, the fitting together of the upper and lower teeth.

oc·cult (ə kult′, ŏk′ ŭlt′) ***adj-*** **1** hidden and mysterious; secret. **2** relating to supernatural forces.

oc·cul·ta·tion (ŏk′ əl tā′ shən) ***n-*** **1** a hiding or disappearance from view. **2** *Astronomy* the abrupt cutting off of a star's or planet's light when another heavenly body, especially the moon, passes in front of it.

oc·cult·ism (ŏk′ ŭl tĭz′ əm, ə kŭl′-) ***n-*** belief in or investigation of the mysterious, the supernatural, or the magical; also, any practices based on such beliefs.

oc·cu·pan·cy (ŏk′ yə pən sē) ***n-*** [*pl.* **oc·cu·pan·cies**] **1** a taking possession of or holding space in. **2** period during which anything is occupied.

oc·cu·pant (ŏk′ yə pənt) ***n-*** **1** person who lives in or makes use of a building, house, room, etc. **2** person who holds a position.

oc·cu·pa·tion (ŏk′ yə pā′ shən) ***n-*** **1** business, trade, or job: *Selling automobiles is his* occupation. **2** an occupying or being occupied: *Quick* occupation *of these new houses is expected.* **3** seizure and holding: *the* occupation *of an enemy stronghold.* ***as modifier***: *the* occupation *troops*; occupation *currency.*

oc·cu·pa·tion·al (ŏk′ yə pā′ shən əl) ***adj-*** having to do with or resulting from one's work, business, or profession: *an* occupational *disease*; occupational *hazards.*

oc·cu·py (ŏk′ yə pī′) ***vt-*** **[oc·cu·pied, oc·cu·py·ing] 1** to take up; fill up: *The dinner and entertainment* occupied *two hours.* **2** to settle in or live in: *My friend is waiting to* occupy *the new house he just bought.* **3** to take and keep possession of: *The army advanced and* occupied *ten square miles of enemy territory.* **4** to hold; have: *A student council* occupies *an important place in school affairs.* **5** to keep busy. **—*n-* oc′ cu·pi′ er.**

oc·cur (ə kûr′) ***vi-*** **[oc·curred, oc·cur·ring] 1** to take place; happen: *Several accidents have* occurred *at that corner.* **2** to be found; appear; exist: *How many times does the word "the"* occur *in the sentence you are reading?* **occur to** to come into the mind of; suggest itself to.

oc·cur·rence (ə kûr′ əns) ***n-*** **1** something that happens; event: *An eclipse of the sun is a rare* occurrence. **2** a taking place; an occurring.

o·cean (ō′ shən) ***n-*** **1** the vast body of salt water covering three-fourths of the earth's surface. **2** any of the four main divisions of this body: the Atlantic Ocean, the Pacific Ocean, the Indian Ocean, and the Arctic Ocean. ***as modifier***: *an* ocean *voyage*; ocean *currents.*

o·ce·an·ic (ō′ shē ăn′ ĭk) ***adj-*** of, appearing in, or produced by the ocean: *the* oceanic *plant life.*

o·cean·og·ra·phy (ō′ shən ŏg′ rə fē) ***n-*** science that deals with the study of oceans and seas, including their currents, chemical make-up, topography, etc. **—*n-* o′ cean·og′ ra·pher.**

Ocelot, about 4 ft. long

o·ce·lot (ō′ sə lŏt′, ŏs′ ə-) ***n-*** large cat with a spotted yellow or gray coat, of Central and South America.

o·cher or **o·chre** (ō′ kər) ***n-*** **1** variety of clay containing iron ore and ranging in color from yellow to red, used as a pigment in paints. **2** dark-yellow color. ***adj-***: *an* ocher *carpet.*

o'clock (ə klŏk′) ***adv-*** **1** according to the clock: *Let's meet at three* o'clock. **2** in air warfare, position of an attacker, target, etc. as thought of on an imaginary clock face.

Oct. October.

octa- or **octo-** *combining form* eight: *an* octa*gon*; octo*pus* (eight-footed). [from Greek **okto** and **okta,** "eight."]

oc·ta·gon (ŏk′ tə gŏn′) ***n-*** **1** polygon with eight sides and eight angles. **2** (also **regular octagon**) polygon having eight equal sides and eight equal angles.

Octagon

oc·tag·o·nal (ŏk tăg′ ə nəl) ***adj-*** having eight sides. **—*adv-* oc·tag′ o·nal·ly.**

oc·ta·he·dron (ŏk′ tə hē′ drən) ***n-*** geometric solid with eight plane sides.

oc·tane (ŏk′ tān′) ***n-*** any of a small group of oily, liquid hydrocarbons, all having the formula C_8H_{18}, which occur in petroleum.

octane number ***n-*** a number that shows how much a fuel knocks as compared with a specified fuel mixture burned under standard test conditions. A gasoline with an octane number of 75 will knock as much as a mixture of 75 parts of a certain octane and 25 parts of another hydrocarbon. A higher octane number produces less knocking. Also **octane rating.**

oc·tant (ŏk′ tənt) ***n-*** **1** one-eighth of a circle, or an angle of 45°. **2** navigational instrument used to determine the height above the horizon of heavenly bodies. It is similar to the sextant but has an arc of 45°.

oc·tave (ŏk′ təv, *also* -tāv′) ***n-*** **1** *Music* (1) the difference in pitch between a tone and another tone having twice as many vibrations per second or half as many vibrations per second. (2) either of two tones so related in frequency and having the same name. In the drawing, the middle C is an octave of either the lower C or the higher C. (3) two such tones sounded together; also, all the tones between them. **2** any unit of eight parts; especially, an eight-day festival or observance in religion. **3** in poetry, a stanza of eight lines; especially, the first eight lines of a sonnet.

Octaves on piano

oc·ta·vo (ŏk tā′ vō, -tä′ vō) ***n-*** [*pl.* **oc·ta·vos**] **1** in printing, a sheet of paper folded into eight leaves or sixteen pages. **2** book made of such sheets. ***as modifier***: *an* octavo *volume. Abbr.* 8vo.

oc·tet (ŏk tĕt′) ***n-*** **1** *Music* (1) composition for eight voices or instruments. (2) the eight performers of such a composition. **2** any group of eight.

Oc·to·ber ***n-*** the tenth month of the year, having 31 days.

oc·to·ge·nar·i·an (ŏk′ tə jə nâr′ ē ən) ***n-*** person who is eighty to eighty-nine years old. ***as modifier***: *my* octogenarian *grandpa.*

TENTACLES

Octopus, a few inches to 20 ft. spread

oc·to·pus (ŏk′ tə pəs) ***n-*** [*pl.* **oc·to·pus·es**] sea animal living mostly on the sea floor and having a bulb-shaped body from which extend eight long tentacles with sucking disks on the underside for grasping prey.

oc·u·lar (ŏk′ yə lər) ***adj-*** **1** of or relating to the eye or the eyesight: *the* ocular *perception.* **2** depending on or seen by the eye; known from actual sight: *We have* ocular *proof of this fact.*

oc·u·list (ŏk′ yə lĭst) ***n-*** opthalmologist.

O.D. 1 Doctor of Optometry. **2** officer of the day. **3** olive drab. **4** right eye [from Latin **oculus dexter**].

odd (ŏd) ***adj-*** [**odd·er, odd·est**] **1** unusual or strange; peculiar: *It is* odd *that he is so late. The* odd, *old man lives alone.* **2** without the rest of a pair or set: *an* odd *sock*; *an* odd *volume.* **3** plus a few more: *I've 40* odd *dollars in my pocket.* **4** extra: *The* odd *player can keep score or substitute.* **5** occasional: *at* odd *moments*; *an* odd *job.* **6** having a remainder of 1 after being divided by two: *1, 3, 17, and 239 are* odd *numbers.* **—*adv-* odd′ly.** ***n-*** **odd′ ness.**

odd·i·ty (ŏd′ ə tē) ***n-*** [*pl.* **odd·i·ties**] **1** person or thing that is unusual, peculiar, or strange: *Our tame bear was an* oddity *in the neighborhood.* **2** strangeness; peculiarity: *The* oddity *of his behavior made us very curious.*

odd·ment (ŏd′ mənt) ***n-*** scrap, leftover, or miscellaneous object: *some* oddments *left over after packing.*

odd number ***n-*** any whole number that leaves a remainder of 1 when divided by 2.

odds (ŏdz) ***n-*** *pl.* **1** advantages; difference that favors one side against another: *In a tug of war the* odds *are with the heavier team.* **2** chances; probability: *If we have a red sunset, the* odds *are that tomorrow will be fair.* **3** in games and contests, a ratio of probability: *The* odds *are two to one that the Titans will lose.*

at odds in disagreement: *Jack and Pete are always* at odds *as to who bats first.* **by all odds** with great certainty; certainly; surely: *He is* by all odds *the best ball player around.*

odds and ends ***n-*** small articles of little value; things left over.

ode (ōd) ***n-*** lofty and dignified lyric poem, usually in honor of a person or thing.

O·din (ō′ dən) ***n-*** in Germanic mythology, the supreme god and the ruler of all the other gods.

o·di·ous (ō′ dē əs) ***adj-*** hateful or offensive; repulsive; disgusting: *Torture is* odious *to civilized people.* **—*adv-* o′ di·ous·ly.** ***n-*** **o′ di·ous·ness.**

o·di·um (ō′ dē əm) ***n-*** **1** hatred; contempt: *the* odium *we feel for a deliberate liar.* **2** disgrace; stigma: *the* odium *of having been a traitor in wartime.*

o·dom·e·ter (ō dŏm′ ə tər) ***n-*** device for measuring distance traveled, especially of a vehicle.

o·dor (ō′ dər) ***n-*** scent; smell: *a musty* odor; *a pleasant* odor. **—*adj-* o′ dor·less.**

o·dor·if·er·ous (ō′ də rĭf′ ər əs) ***adj-*** having or giving off an odor, especially a pleasant one: *an* odoriferous *blossom.* **—*adv-* o′ dor·if′ er·ous·ly.** ***n-*** **o′ dor·if′ er·ous·ness.**

o·dor·ous (ō′ dər əs) ***adj-*** having or giving off an odor, especially an unpleasant one. **—*adv-* o′ dor·ous·ly.** ***n-*** **o′ dor·ous·ness.**

O·dys·seus (ə dĭs′ ē əs) ***n-*** in Greek legend, king of Ithaca and a leader in the Trojan War; hero of the "Odyssey." Also called **Ulysses.**

Od·ys·sey (ŏd′ ə sē) ***n-*** **1** Greek epic poem, attributed to Homer, describing the wanderings of Odysseus. **2 odyssey** any lone and adventurous journey.

Oed·i·pus (ē′ də pəs, ĕd′ ə-) ***n-*** in Greek legend, a king who unknowingly killed his father and married his mother.

o'er (ôr) *Archaic* over. ***Homs-*** oar, or, ore.

of (ŏv *or* ŭv *when stressed*; əv *when unstressed*) ***prep-*** **1** made with or from: *windows* of *glass*; *ornaments* of *silver*; *carvings* of *wood.* **2** containing: *a box* of *candy*; *a bag* of *oranges.* **3** belonging to: *the roof* of *a house*; *the color* of *violets.* **4** from: *Chicago is west* of *New York.* **5** about; concerning: *a book* of *science*; *news* of *the world*; *pictures* of *a trip.* **6** by: *poems* of *Robert L. Stevenson.* **7** with; having: *a man* of *wealth*; *a girl* of *beauty.* **8** named: *the city* of *Denver.* **9** because of: *dying* of *infection.* **10** so as to be free from: *relieved* of *fear.* **11** directed at or exerted upon: *a love* of *literature*; *the destruction* of *the city.* **12** at, on, or during a particular time: of *late*; of *recent months.* **13** to or before: *We leave at twenty minutes* of *six.* **14** devoted or dedicated to; set aside for: *a day* of *merrymaking.*

off (ôf, ŏf) ***prep-*** **1** so as to be separated or removed from; away from: *Mother took the dishes* off *the table. The boy dived* off *the pier. The island is a mile* off *our course.* **2** seaward from: *They fished* off *Cape Cod.* **3** temporarily free from: *He is* off *duty.* **4** less than or below the usual or standard level of: *ten percent* off *the regular price*; off *one's game.* **5** branching from: *The theater is at 47th Street* off *Broadway.* **6** with the aid or use of; on: *to live* off *one's friends*; *to live* off *fish and rice.* **7** *Informal* abstaining from: *He is* off *cigarettes for life.* ***adv-*** **1** away from a present or understood place or time: *The boy ran* off. *He is* off *to Paris. Vacation is just a week* off. *The station is a mile* off. **2** so as to be no longer working or continuing: *He turned* off *the lights. The switch is* off. **3** so as to be away from work or duty: *He took the summer* off. **4** to less than the usual or standard level: *The price of coffee dropped* off. **5** canceled: *The party is* off *tonight.* ***adj-*** **1** not working or on duty: *one's* off *hours.* **2** not very probable; remote: *an* off *chance.* **3** on the right: *the* off *side.* **4** wrong or mistaken: *He* is off *in his estimate.* **5** below the usual standard or level: *He had an* off *day.* ***interj-*** go away!

off and on not regularly; intermittently. **off with** remove: Off with *his head!* **off with you!** go away!

of·fal (ô′ fəl, ŏf′ əl) ***n-*** **1** discarded remains of a butchered animal. **2** garbage; refuse.

off·beat (ôf′ bēt′, ŏf′-) ***n-*** *Music* any weak or unstressed beat in a measure. ***adj-*** *Informal* departing from convention in fashion, taste, manners, etc.; unusual.

off-col·or (ôf′ kŭl′ ər, ŏf′-) ***adj-*** **1** having faulty coloring: *an* off-color *gem.* **2** indecent; smutty; vulgar.

of·fend (ə fĕnd′) ***vt-*** (in senses 1 and 2 considered intransitive when the direct object is implied but not expressed) **1** to annoy or make angry; insult; hurt the feelings of: *Such a question might* offend *some people.* **2** to be disagreeable to (the senses or sensibilities): *Colors that don't match* offend *the eyes.* ***vi-*** to do wrong; break a law or rule: *Those who* offend *are often punished.*

of·fend·er (ə fĕn′ dər) ***n-*** person or animal that offends; especially, a person who breaks a law or rule of behavior.

of·fense (ə fĕns′) ***n-*** **1** violation of a law or rule: *Stealing is a criminal* offense. **2** act of causing hurt, annoyance, or displeasure: *an* offense *against good taste.* **3** something that causes hurt, annoyance, or displeasure: *The music was an* offense *to his sense of harmony.* **4** (*also* ŏf′ fĕns′) attack; assault; also, an attacking side or team: *A good* offense *makes the best defense.*

give offense to cause a feeling of hurt or annoyance. **take offense** to be annoyed, hurt, or displeased: *Jim* took offense *because his friends were laughing at him.*

---

fāte, făt, dâre, bärn; bē, bĕt, mêre; bīte, bĭt; nōte, hŏt, môre, dȯg; fŭn, fûr; to͞o, bo͝ok; oil; out; tar; thin; then; hw for wh as in *wh*at; zh for s as in u*s*ual; ə for a, e, i, o, u, as in *a*go, lin*e*n, per*i*l, at*o*m, min*u*s

of·fen·sive (ə fĕn′ sĭv) ***adj-*** **1** causing offense or resentment; annoying; disagreeable: *Helen's loud laughter was* offensive *to her quiet friend.* **2** unpleasant to the senses: *Some people think that onions have a very* offensive *smell.* **3** having to do with attack: *to forbid the use of* offensive *weapons; the* offensive *team.* ***n-*** attack: *the enemy's* offensive. **—*adv-*** **of·fen′ sive·ly.** ***n-*** **of·fen′ sive·ness.**

of·fer (ò′ fər, ŏf′ ər) ***n-*** **1** voluntary proposal: *We appreciate your kind* offer *of assistance.* **2** a price bid: *an* offer *of $500 for the old car.* **3** attempt or endeavor: *an* offer *at resistance.* ***vt-*** **1** to volunteer; proffer: *Many strangers* offered *help.* **2** to suggest for acceptance or refusal; propose: *The committee* offered *a plan to the club.* **3** to present as a part of religious worship or sacrifice: *to* offer *a prayer in thanksgiving.* **4** to put up for sale: *We* offered *the house at a fair price.* **5** to attempt: *Will the rebels* offer *any resistance?* ***vi-*** to present itself; arise: *He will travel any time the opportunity* offers.

of·fer·ing (ò′ fər ĭng, ŏf′ ər-) ***n-*** something offered or given; especially, a religious gift, contribution, or sacrifice: *She placed her* offering *in the collection plate.*

of·fer·tor·y (ò′ fər tôr′ ē, ŏf′ ər-) ***n-*** [*pl.* **of·fer·tor·ies**] **1** musical composition performed in church when the collection is made. **2** the collection itself. **3** the part of a Mass or Holy Communion in which the sacramental bread and wine are offered to God before consecration.

off·hand (òf′ hănd′, ŏf′-) ***adv-*** without giving much thought or preparation: *Tell me* offhand, *how many beans are in this jar.* ***adj-*** **1** said or done without preparation: *He made a few* offhand *remarks.* **2** informal; casual: *an* offhand *manner.*

off·hand·ed (òf′ hăn′ dəd, ŏf′-) ***adj-*** offhand. **—*adv-*** **off′ hand′ ed·ly.** ***n-*** **off′ hand′ ed·ness.**

of·fice (ò′ fəs, ŏf′ əs) ***n-*** **1** place where business or professional services are carried on or clerical work is done: *a doctor's* office. **2** position; post: *the* office *of mayor.* **3** duty, charge, or service: *She performs the* office *of hostess very graciously.* **4** branch or department of government: *U.S. Post* Office; *the British Foreign* Office. **5 offices** something done for a person; service: *Through his kind* offices *I received immediate aid.* *as* ***modifier***: *an* office *boy;* office *problems.*

office holder ***n-*** person holding a public office.

of·fi·cer (òf′ ə sər, ŏf′ ə-) ***n-*** **1** person elected or appointed to a position of authority, trust, or responsibility: *class* officers; *company* officers; *police* officer. **2** person who has rank or authority to command in the armed services, especially one who holds a commission or warrant. **3** captain or mates on a commercial ship.

officer of the day ***n-*** officer at a military post who is responsible for security, maintenance of order, performance of the guard, etc., on a given day.

of·fi·cial (ə fĭsh′ əl) ***n-*** person who holds a position of authority: *All the company's* officials *are in a meeting.* ***adj-*** **1** having to do with a position of trust or authority: *The President has many* official *duties to perform.* **2** coming from the proper authority; approved: *The report is considered* official. **—*adv-*** **of·fi′ cial·ly.**
►Should not be confused with OFFICIOUS.

of·fi·cial·dom (ə fĭsh′ əl dəm) ***n-*** officials taken as a class, especially in respect to presumed rigidity, adherence to rules, lack of individual initiative, etc.

of·fi·ci·ate (ə fĭsh′ ē āt′) ***vi-*** [**of·fi·ci·at·ed, of·fi·ci·at·ing**] to perform an official duty or ceremony: *The mayor* officiated *at the Memorial Day Ceremony.*

of·fi·cious (ə fĭsh′ əs) ***adj-*** too forward in offering advice or unwanted services; meddlesome: *an* officious *manner.* **—*adv-*** **of·fi′ cious·ly.** ***n-*** **of·fi′ cious·ness.**
►Should not be confused with OFFICIAL.

off·ing (ò′ fĭng, ŏf′ ĭng) ***n-*** the open sea, visible from shore but beyond anchoring ground; hence, immediate distance or near future.

off·ish (ò′ fĭsh, ŏf′ ĭsh) *Informal* ***adj-*** cool and reserved; distant; aloof.

off-key (òf′ kē′, ŏf′-) ***adj-*** **1** not on pitch: *Her singing was* off-key. **2** not suitable, harmonious, or proper: *an* off-key *chair; an* off-key *joke.* ***adv-***: *She sang* off-key.

[1]**off·set** (òf′ sĕt′, òf′ sĕt′) ***vt-*** [**off·set, off·set·ting**] to make up for; take the place of: *Skill may* offset *weakness.*

[2]**off·set** (òf′ sĕt′) ***n-*** **1** something that makes up for something else; compensation: *Success is an* offset *for failure.* **2** printing process in which a rubber cylinder transfers an inked impression from a plate to a sheet of paper.

off·shoot (òf′ shōōt′, ŏf′-) ***n-*** branch from the main stem of a plant, family, etc.: *French is an* offshoot *of Latin.*

off·shore (òf′ shôr′, ŏf′-) ***adj-*** **1** in a seaward position away from the shore: *an* offshore *light.* **2** of winds, coming from the shore and moving seaward. ***adv-***: *The ship anchored* offshore. *The wind blew* offshore.

off·side (òf′ sīd′, ŏf′-) ***adj-*** **1** in football, illegally ahead of the ball before it is played. **2** in ice hockey, ahead of the puck in the attacking zone. ***adv-***: *The tackle jumped* offside.

off·spring (òf′ sprĭng′, ŏf′-) ***n-*** [*pl.* **off·spring** or **off·springs**] **1** child or children; descendant or descendants of a person or animal. **2** something created: *the* offspring *of a vivid imagination.*

off·stage (òf′ stāj′, ŏf′-) ***adj-*** out of the view of the audience: *The play required many* offstage *sound effects.* ***adv-***: *The actor went* offstage.

oft (òft, ŏft) *Archaic* often.

of·ten (òf′ ən, ŏf′-) ***adv-*** frequently; many times.

of·ten·times (òf′ ən tīmz′, ŏf′-) ***adv-*** often. Also **oft′ times′.**

o·gle (ō′ gəl, ŏ′-) ***vt-*** [**o·gled, o·gling**] to look at with desire; eye amorously. ***n-*** amorous or flirtatious look. **—*n-*** **o′ gler.**

o·gre (ō′ gər) ***n-*** **1** imaginary, man-eating giant. **2** person or thing that is viewed with dread: *the* ogre *of war.*

oh or **Oh** (ō) ***interj-*** exclamation of surprise, wonder, sorrow, etc.: Oh! *how awful!* ***Homs-*** [1]O, owe.

ohm (ōm) ***n-*** unit of electrical resistance in the mks system, equal to the resistance of a conductor through which an electromotive force of 1 volt produces a current of 1 ampere.

ohm·me·ter (ōm′ mē′ tər) ***n-*** instrument for measuring electrical resistance in ohms.

Ohm's law (ōmz) ***n-*** a law first stated by Georg Ohm: in an electrical circuit, the current in amperes is equal to the electromotive force in volts divided by the resistance in ohms.

-oid *suffix* (used to form nouns) that which resembles or has the quality of: *a sphero*id.

oil (oil) ***n-*** **1** any one of many greasy or fatty substances, usually liquid, obtained from animals, plants, or minerals: *whale* oil; *olive* oil. **2** petroleum. **3** oil color. **4** oil painting. *as* ***modifier***: *an* oil *derrick.* ***vt-*** to lubricate: *to* oil *a squeaky hinge.*

burn the midnight oil to study or work until late at night.

oil burner ***n-*** heating element burning oil, such as one in a furnace, stove, etc.

oil·cloth (oil′ klòth′) ***n-*** cloth waterproofed by a coating of oil paint and used for table coverings, shelf linings, etc.

oil color ***n-*** **1** coloring matter used for oil paint. **2** artist's oil paint.

oil field ***n-*** region that is rich in petroleum deposits, especially deposits under development.

oil of vitriol *n-* sulfuric acid.
oil paint *n-* paint made of oil, usually linseed oil, mixed with crushed pigments.
oil painting *n-* **1** picture painted with oil colors. **2** the art of making such paintings.
oil palm *n-* African palm tree bearing fruit that contains oil in both the flesh and the seeds.
oil pan *n-* the lower section of the crankcase of an internal combustion engine, used as a reservoir for lubricating oil.
oil shale *n-* black or brownish-black, compact shale containing petroleum.
oil·skin (oil′ skĭn′) *n-* **1** oiled, waterproof fabric used for clothing and coverings. **2** garment of this cloth.
oil slick *n-* patch of oil floating on water.
oil·stone (oil′ stōn′) *n-* flat block of stone, emery, or other abrasive, used with oil for sharpening blades.
oil well *n-* well from which petroleum is taken.
oil·y (oi′ lē) *adj-* **[oil·i·er, oil·i·est]** **1** like, containing, or covered with oil: *the* oily *feeling of waxed paper*; *a box of* oily *rags.* **2** too smooth in speech or manner; unctuous. ***—adv-*** **oil′ i·ly.** ***n-*** **oil′ i·ness.**
oint·ment (oint′ mənt) *n-* salve, often perfumed or medicated, used to soften the skin or to soothe rashes, burns, etc.
O·jib·wa (ō jĭb′ wā) *n-* [*pl.* **O·jib·was,** also **O·jib·wa**] Chippewa. ***adj-***: *the puckered* Ojibwa *moccasin.*
OK or **o·kay** (ō′ kā′) *Informal* ***adj-*** all right; correct; acceptable: *Everything's* OK. ***adv-*** yes: *He said,* "OK, *I'll do it.*" ***vt-*** **[OK'd** or **o·kayed, OK'ing** or **o·kay·ing]** to approve: *to* OK *a check*; *to* OK *a plan of attack.* ***n-*** [*pl.* **OK's** or **o·kays**]: *He gave the new plan his* OK.
o·ka·pi (ō kä′ pē) *n-* animal of central Africa, related to the giraffe, with short skin-covered horns and horizontal stripes on its legs.

Okapi, about 4 ft high at shoulder

O·kie (ō′ kē) *Informal* ***n-*** in the late 1930's, a migrant harvest worker, so called because many migrant workers were Oklahoma farmers who had been ruined by drought.
Okla. Oklahoma.
o·kra (ō′ krə) *n-* **1** tall plant with yellow blossoms and pointed, sticky seed pods. **2** its young, tender pods, used in soups and eaten as a vegetable.
old (ōld) ***adj-*** **[old·er** or **eld·er, old·est** or **eld·est]** **1** having lived a long time for its kind: *an* old *man of eighty*; *an* old *dog of twelve.* **2** of a certain age: *I am nine years* old. **3** belonging to the remote or historical past; ancient: *an* old *Roman road.* **4** belonging to (one's) past: *my* old *home*; old *haunts.* **5** not new; used; worn: *an* old *suit.* **6** appearing elderly; not youthful: *an* old *face*; *an* old *gait.* **7** known for a long time: *an* old *friend.* **8** of long usage: *an* old *custom*; *an* old *remedy.* ***n-*** former times: *knights of* old. ***—n-*** **old′ ness.**
old country *n-* country, especially a European country, from which a person or his forebears has emigrated.
old·en (ōl′ dən) *Archaic* ***adj-*** long ago; bygone.
Old English *n-* the English language spoken from about 450 until about 1100.
old-fash·ioned (ōld′ făsh′ ənd) *adj-* **1** keeping to old ways; showing a liking for old ideas and customs: *an* old-fashioned *girl.* **2** done or made in the style of a past time: *an* old-fashioned *radio.* **3** out-of-date: *"horseless carriage" is an* old-fashioned *term for "car."*
Old French *n-* language, descended from Latin, that was spoken in France from the ninth century to the fourteenth century.
Old Glory *Informal* ***n-*** the flag of the United States.
Old Guard *n-* **1** imperial guard made up by Napoleon I of his veteran soldiers. **2** any group of conservatives in a community or political party.
old hand *n-* experienced person; veteran: *This man is an* old hand *at diplomacy.*
Old High German *n-* the language spoken in southern Germany from 800 to 1100 A.D.
old·ish (ōl′ dĭsh) *adj-* rather old; somewhat old.
old-line (ōld′ līn′) *adj-* traditional; conservative, especially in following well-established styles, forms, or procedures: *an* old-line *farmer.*
old maid *n-* **1** unmarried woman; spinster. **2** *Informal* prim, fussy, too-precise person. ***—adj-*** **old′-maid′ ish.**
old master *n-* **1** any of the great European painters from about the 15th to the mid-18th century. **2** painting by one of these artists. **3** any veteran artist or workman of great skill.
Old Nick *Informal* ***n-*** the devil; Satan.
Old Norse *n-* language spoken in Norway, Denmark, and Iceland from the eighth century to the fourteenth century. It is related to Old English. Also **Old Icelandic.**
old school *n-* conservative tradition or point of view: *a diplomat of the* old school.
old·ster (ōld′ stər) *Informal* ***n-*** elderly person.
Old Testament *n-* the first part of the Bible, including the history of the Hebrews, the Mosaic Law, and the writings of the prophets. **2** the covenant between God and the Israelites.
old-time (ōld′ tīm′) *adj-* of or relating to former times: *the* old-time *clipper ships.*
old-tim·er (ōld′ tī′ mər) *Informal* ***n-*** **1** person who has been a member of a group for a long time. **2** elderly person.
old wives' tale *n-* superstition; unfounded belief.
Old World *n-* the parts of Europe, Asia, and Africa known before the discovery of America. *as* ***modifier*** **(old-world):** *many* old-world *customs.*
o·le·ag·i·nous (ō′ lē ăj′ ə nəs) *adj-* **1** containing oil: *an* oleaginous *seed.* **2** oily; unctuous: *an* oleaginous *TV commercial.*
o·le·an·der (ō′ lē ăn′ dər) *n-* poisonous evergreen shrub related to dogbane and having scented red or white flowers.
o·le·ic acid (ō lā′ ĭk, -lē′ ĭk) *n-* an unsaturated fatty acid occurring in many animal and vegetable fats and used to make soaps, cosmetics, etc.
o·le·o (ō′ lē ō′) *Informal* ***n-*** oleomargarine.
oleo- *combining form* oil: *an* oleo*margarine.* [from Latin **ole-, oleo-,** from Latin **oleum** meaning "(olive) oil," from Greek **elaia,** "olive tree."]
o·le·o·mar·ga·rine (ō′ lē ō mär′ jə rən, -rēn′) *n-* margarine.
o·le·o·res·in (ō′ lē ō rĕz′ ən) *n-* a naturally occurring mixture of an oil and a resin, such as turpentine.
ol·fac·tion (ōl făk′ shən, ŏl′-) *n-* **1** process or act of smelling. **2** the sense of smell.
ol·fac·to·ry (ōl făk′ tə rē, ŏl-) *adj-* of or relating to smelling: *an* olfactory *nerve.*
ol·i·garch (ŏl′ ə gärk′) *n-* one of the rulers in an oligarchy.

ol·i·gar·chy (ŏl′ə gär′kē) ***n-*** [*pl.* **ol·i·gar·chies**] **1** government in which the supreme power is in the hands of a few. **2** state so governed. **3** the few who rule such a state; oligarchs. **—*adj-* ol′i·gar′chic** or **ol′i·gar′chi·cal.**

Ol·i·go·cene (ŏl′ĭ gō sēn′) ***n-*** the middle epoch of the Tertiary period of geological time, between the Eocene and Miocene; also, a rock from this epoch. In the Oligocene, mammals evolved rapidly and the great apes appeared. ***adj-***: *an* Oligocene *fossil.*

ol·ive (ŏl′ĭv) ***n-*** **1** the small, oval fruit of an evergreen tree which grows in warm regions. Olives are pickled in brine or pressed for their fine oil. **2** the tree itself. **3** the fine wood of this tree, used in making cabinets and ornaments. **4** a greenish-yellow color, like that of unripe olives. ***adj-***: *an* olive *cabinet*; *an* olive *dress.*

Olives

olive branch ***n-*** branch from an olive tree, used as a symbol of peace.

olive drab ***n-*** **1** greenish-brown color. **2** cloth of this color, much used by the military for camouflage and uniforms. **3** uniform made of this cloth.

olive oil ***n-*** oil pressed from ripe olives, used in cooking, for salads, in making soap, etc.

O·lym·pi·ad (ə lĭm′pē ăd′, ō-) ***n-*** **1** in ancient Greece, the period of four years between two successive celebrations of the Olympic games, used as a system of reckoning time. **2** the ancient or modern Olympic games.

O·lym·pi·an (ə lĭm′pē ən, ō-) ***adj-*** **1** of or relating to the gods of Mount Olympus. **2** godlike; majestic. **3** (also **O·lym′pic**) of or relating to the city of Olympia or the Olympic games. ***n-*** **1** one of the gods dwelling on Mount Olympus. **2** participant in the Olympic games. **3** native of Olympia.

O·lym·pic games (ə lĭm′pĭk, ō-) ***n-*** **1** festival of ancient Greece, with contests in athletics, music, and poetry. **2** modern international sports competition held every four years in a different country. Amateur athletes from many countries compete. Also **O·lym′pics.**

O·lym·pus (ə lĭm′pəs, ō-) ***n-*** in Greek legend, a mountain in Thessaly, held to be the home of the gods; hence, any place or condition of serene and remote authority.

o·ma·sum (ō mā′səm) ***n-*** [*pl.* **o·ma·sa** (-sə)] third of the four chambers of the stomach of a cud-chewing animal, in which true digestion begins.

om·buds·man (ăm′bədz mən) ***n-*** [*pl.* **om·buds·men**] **1** government appointee who receives and investigates grievances of citizens against public officials. **2** one who investigates and helps settle complaints from students, consumers, etc.

o·me·ga (ō mē′gə, -mĕg′ə) ***n-*** **1** last letter of the Greek alphabet. Omega is equivalent to the long o (ō) in English. **2** the end.

om·e·let or **om·e·lette** (ŏm′ə lət) ***n-*** eggs beaten with milk, cooked, and folded over, often with chopped ham, cheese, jelly, etc., as a filler.

o·men (ō′mən) ***n-*** sign or happening supposed to foretell good or bad luck; augury; portent.

om·i·nous (ŏm′ə nəs) ***adj-*** like an omen of bad luck; threatening. **—*adv-* om′i·nous·ly.** ***n-*** **om′i·nous·ness.**

o·mis·sion (ō mĭsh′ən) ***n-*** **1** an omitting; a leaving out: *the* omission *of a signature.* **2** thing omitted or left out.

o·mit (ō mĭt′) ***vt-*** [**o·mit·ted, o·mit·ting**] **1** to leave out; fail to include: *Copy the names of the group but* omit *your own.* **2** to fail to do; neglect; leave undone: *Jack* omitted *packing his toothbrush.*

omni- *combining form* all; totally: *an* omni*present element*; *an* omni*potent deity.* [from Latin **omnis,** "all."]

om·ni·bus (ŏm′nə bəs) ***n-*** [*pl.* **om·ni·bus·es**] **1** collection of many different writings: *an* omnibus *of mystery stories.* **2** (*also* **ŏm′nə bŭs′**) a bus. ***adj-*** including many different items: *an* omnibus *bill in Congress.*

om·nip·o·tence (ŏm nĭp′ə təns) ***n-*** **1** infinite or unlimited power. **2 Omnipotence** God, the all-powerful.

om·nip·o·tent (ŏm nĭp′ə tənt) ***adj-*** **1** all-powerful: *The emperor thought himself* omnipotent. **2 the Omnipotent** God; the Almighty. **—*adv-* om·nip′o·tent·ly.**

om·ni·pres·ent (ŏm′nĭ prĕz′ənt) ***adj-*** **1** present everywhere. **2** *Informal* seeming to be present all the time: *the* omnipresent *hecklers.* **—*n-* om′ni·pres′ence.**

om·nis·cient (ŏm nĭsh′ənt) ***adj-*** knowing everything; having unlimited knowledge. **—*n-* om·nis′cience.**

om·niv·o·rous (ŏm nĭv′ər əs) ***adj-*** eating both meat and vegetables. **—*adv-* om·niv′o·rous·ly.** ***n-*** **om·niv′o·rous·ness.**

on (ŏn, ȯn, *also* ən *when unstressed*) ***prep-*** **1** so as to be supported by: *Sit* on *this chair. I'll hang a picture* on *the wall.* **2** located upon: *spots* on *the rug*; *blisters* on *my feet.* **3** situated at or along: *a house* on *the river*; *a town* on *the border.* **4** against: *to hit one's head* on *the floor*; *to trip* on *a board.* **5** covering: *gloves* on *her hands*; *paint* on *the ceiling.* **6** in the process or condition of: *a book* on *order*; *a house* on *sale*; *a union* on *strike.* **7** for the purpose of: *to go* on *vacation*; *to travel* on *business.* **8** subject to the effect and limits of: *to buy* on *credit*; *to live* on *borrowed time*; *to base one's beliefs* on *the evidence.* **9** available by: *water* on *tap*; *a doctor* on *call.* **10** following; keeping to: *to be* on *the trail*; *to stay* on *course.* **11** toward; unto: *Have pity* on *them.* **12** onto; into: *A door opening* on *the garden.* **13** meant for; directed or applied to: *Blessings* on *you.* **14** a member of: *She is* on *the board of directors.* **15** about; concerning: *a talk* on *Alaska*; *to agree* on *a plan.* **16** in the course of; during: *to leave* on *Tuesday.* **17** while or after: *They discovered,* on *opening the box, that it was empty.* **18** at the exact moment or point of: *to arrive* on *time*; *to hit it* on *the right spot.* **19** justified or supported by: *I did it* on *principle. I heard it* on *good authority.* **20** with the aid or use of: *to live* on *fish.* **21** added to: *error* on *error.* **22** *Informal* in the possession of: *I don't have a cent* on *me.* **23** *Informal* pointed toward: *Keep your eyes* on *the road.* **24** *Informal* at the expense of: *The beer is* on *me.* **25** *Informal* taking as medicine, drink, etc.: *The doctor has him* on *penicillin.* ***adv-*** **1** further; more: *Please go* on. *The governor spoke* on. **2** additionally: *to add* on *six*; *to pile it* on. **3** forward; onward: *The army pushed* on. **4** in or at the present place: *to hold* on; *to stay* on. **5** in operation: *The radio is* on. **6** set to start or permit operation: *The switch is* on. **7** *Informal* scheduled: *There is a party* on *tonight. What's* on *at the movies?* **8** *Informal* in progress.

be on to *Informal* to be aware of or alerted to. **on and off** occasionally; not regularly: *I go bowling* on and off. **on and on** for a long time without stopping: *to talk* on and on. **have something on (someone)** *Informal* to have damaging information, evidence, etc., against (someone).

once (wŭns) ***adv-*** **1** at one time; formerly: *We* once *lived in Ohio.* **2** single time: *Sing the song through just* once. **3** at any time; ever: *If he* once *starts talking, he is hard to stop.* ***conj-*** if ever; whenever: *I don't wake easily,* once *I get to sleep.* ***n-*** one time: *I say* once *is enough.*

all at once **1** all at the same time. **2** suddenly. **at once** **1** at the same time. **2** immediately. **once and for all** for the last time; finally. **once in a while** from time to time; occasionally. **once upon a time** a long time ago.

once-o·ver (wŭns′ō′vər) *Slang* ***n-*** quick look or examination.

on·com·ing (ŏn′kŭm′ĭng, ŏn′-) ***adj-*** approaching: *the* oncoming *storm.*

one (wŭn) ***n-*** **1** the first and smallest cardinal number. **2** numeral such as 1 that represents this cardinal number. **3** single person or thing: *If this* one *is right, the other is wrong.* ***determiner*** (traditionally called adjective) **1** a single: *Only* one *person should talk at a time.* **2** a certain: *It happened* one *day last week. The clerk was* one *Miss Hawkins.* **3** some: *I'll call you* one *day next week.* **4** only: *The* one *thing not to do is to lie about it.* ***pron-*** **1** a particular person or thing: *The black puppy is the* one *I want.* **2** any person; a person; you; we: *From here* one *can see the city.* ***Hom-*** won.

all one 1 united; without difference: *We are* all one *in wishing you great success.* **2** of no importance: *It's* all one *to me whether we go now or later.* **at one** in agreement: *We are all* at one *about the plan for the exhibit.* **one another** of a group of three or more, each one (to, with, against, toward, etc.) every other reciprocally: *The committee members should keep* one another *informed as we go along.* (For usage note see *each other.*) **one by one** singly and one after the other.

one-horse (wŭn′hôrs′, -hôrs′) ***adj-*** **1** pulled by or made for one horse: *a* one-horse *shay.* **2** developing one horsepower: *a* one-horse *motor. Informal* unimportant; minor: *a* one-horse *town.*

O·nei·da (ō nī′də) ***n-*** [*pl.* **O·nei·das,** also **O·nei·da**] **1** one of a tribe of Iroquois Indians who belonged to the Five Nations. **2** the language of these Indians. ***adj-:*** *the* Oneida *village.*

one·ness (wŭn′nəs) ***n-*** singleness or sameness; unity: *a* oneness *of purpose.*

on·er·ous (ō′nər əs, ŏn′-) ***adj-*** hanging on one like a heavy weight; burdensome; oppressive: *an* onerous *duty.* **—*adv-*** **on′er·ous·ly.** ***n-*** **on′er·ous·ness.**

one·self (wŭn′sĕlf′) ***pron-*** reflexive form of **one**; one's own self: *To listen to* oneself *on a tape recorder is sometimes fun.* Also **one's self.**

be oneself to act or think according to one's nature, without pretending or straining.

one-sid·ed (wŭn′sī′dəd) ***adj-*** **1** prejudiced; unfair; biased: *a* one-sided *account of an accident.* **2** unequal: *The* one-sided *baseball game ended with a score of 14 to 1.*

one-time (wŭn′tīm′) ***adj-*** former: *a* one-time *friend.*

one-to-one (wŭn′tə wŭn′) ***adj-*** having one thing matched with one other thing.

one-track (wŭn′trăk′) ***adj-*** **1** having one track: *a* one-track *railroad.* **2** *Informal* very limited in action or thought; narrow: *a* one-track *mind.*

one-way (wŭn′wā′) ***adj-*** moving or allowing movment in one direction only: *a* one-way *street.*

on·go·ing (ŏn′gō′ĭng, ŏn′-) ***adj-*** **1** now going on; current: *the* ongoing *projects.* **2** constant and continuing into the future: *our* ongoing *concerns.*

on·ion (ŭn′yən) ***n-*** plant related to the lilies, having long, slender leaves and a rounded bulb with a strong odor and taste. **—*adj-*** **on′ion·like′.**

TOP
BULB
Onion

on·ion·skin (ŭn′yən skĭn′) ***n-*** thin, light, translucent paper, used chiefly for making carbon copies.

on·look·er (ŏn′lo͝ok′ər, ŏn′-) ***n-*** spectator; one who watches but does not take part. **—*adj-*** **on′look′ing:** *the* onlooking *crowd.*

on·ly (ōn′lē) ***adj-*** **1** sole; without others: *our* only *pet; our* only *worry.* **2** most suitable or fit of all: *the* only *person I would trust; the* only *person for the job.* ***adv-*** solely; merely; exclusively: *We play the game for pleasure* only. ***conj-*** but; except that: *I'd go,* only *I have another engagement.*

if only I wish that: *Jack exclaimed,* "If only *I could go swimming!*" **only too** very: *I am* only too *glad to go.*

►The placement of ONLY as a modifier can profoundly affect the meaning of a sentence: Only *I want to please her* (no one but I). *I* only *want to please her* (I want nothing more than). *I want* only *to please her* (I want nothing except). *I want to please* only *her* (I don't want to please anyone else). It is, therefore, important to insure that ONLY modifies solely what you wish it to, whether that be a noun, verb, phrase, or whole sentence. In speaking, you can do this by intonation; in writing, you must do this by proper positioning. It is best to put ONLY next to, and usually just before, what it modifies.

on·o·mat·o·poe·ia (ŏn′ə măt′ə pē′ə) ***n-*** formation or use of a word that imitates a natural sound such as *buzz* or *hiss.*

On·on·da·ga (ŏn′ən dŏ′gə) ***n-*** [*pl.* **On·on·da·gas,** also **On·on·da·ga**] **1** one of a tribe of Iroquois Indians that belonged to the Five Nations. **2** the language of these Indians. ***adj-*** (also **On′on·da′gan**): *the large* Onondaga *reservation.*

on·rush (ŏn′rŭsh′, ŏn′-) ***n-*** strong forward flow or rush: *the* onrush *of the flood.*

on·set (ŏn′sĕt′, ŏn′-) ***n-*** **1** an attack; assault: *the* onset *of our troops.* **2** beginning: *at the* onset *of cold weather.*

on·shore (ŏn′shôr′, ŏn′-) ***adj-*** on or toward the shore: *an* onshore *wind.* ***adv-:*** *The wind blew* onshore.

on·side (ŏn′sīd′, ŏn′-) ***adj-*** in football, hockey, etc., in a legal position to play or receive the ball, puck, etc.

on·slaught (ŏn′slŏt′, ŏn′slŏt′) ***n-*** violent attack or onset: *the* onslaught *of troops; the* onslaught *of a storm.*

Ont. Ontario.

on·to (ŏn′to͞o′, ŏn′-) ***prep-*** **1** to a position on: *Let's get* onto *the boat.* **2** *Informal* aware of: *I'm* onto *your game.*

o·nus (ō′nəs) ***n-*** burden; obligation.

on·ward (ŏn′wərd, ŏn′-) ***adv-*** (also **on′wards**) forward; toward a farther point in time or distance: *to move* onward *into new territory.* ***adj-:*** *the* onward *march.*

on·yx (ŏn′ĭks) ***n-*** kind of quartz in layers of various colors, used as a semiprecious gem.

oo·dles (o͞o′dəlz) *Informal* ***n- pl.*** a great plenty.

[1]**ooze** (o͞oz) ***vi-*** **[oozed, ooz·ing]** to flow out; seep: *The mud* oozed *between the child's squeezing fingers.* ***vt-*** to give out little by little through a small opening or openings: *The hose* oozed *water.* ***n-*** **1** slow flow or leak: *an* ooze *of cream.* **2** something that flows or leaks out slowly. [from Middle English **wosen, wos,** from Old English **wōs** meaning "sap; juice."]

[2]**ooze** (o͞oz) ***n-*** soft, slimy mud, especially at the bottom of a body of water. [from Middle English **wose,** from Old English **wāse** meaning "mud; slime."]

[1]**oo·zy** (o͞o′zē) ***adj-*** **[oo·zi·er, oo·zi·est]** flowing or exuding slowly. [from [1]**ooze.**]

[2]**oo·zy** (o͞o′zē) ***adj-*** **[oo·zi·er, oo·zi·est]** slimy; muddy; mucky. [from [2]**ooze.**] **—*n-*** **oo′zi·ness.**

o·pac·i·ty (ō păs′ə tē) ***n-*** condition of being opaque.

o·pal (ō′pəl) ***n-*** precious stone that displays soft color changes on its smooth surface as it is moved in the light.

o·pal·es·cent (ō′pə lĕs′ənt) ***adj-*** changing color in a soft, rippling way; iridescent. **—*n-*** **o′pal·es′cence.**

o·paque (ō pāk′) ***adj-*** **1** not permitting light to pass through; not transparent: *An* opaque *window shade shuts out the sunlight.* **2** very hard to understand, especially because of poor thought; obscure: *an* opaque *essay.* —***adv-*** **o·paque′ly.** ***n-*** **o·paque′ness.**

op. cit. in the book, article, etc., cited or referred to [from Latin **opere citato.**]

ope (ōp) *Archaic* ***vt-*** **&** ***vi-*** [**oped, op·ing**] to open.

o·pen (ō′ pən) ***adj-*** **1** not closed, covered, sealed, or blocked: *an* open *window; an* open *boat; an* open *book; an* open *drain; an* open *mind; a road* open *to traffic.* **2** *not yet filled or taken; available: The job is still* open. *I have an evening* open *next week.* **3** free or accessible to all; public: *an* open *market; an* open *meeting.* **4** undecided or unsettled; pending: *That murder case is still* open. **5** not hidden or concealed; overt: *a case of* open *hostility;* open *concern.* **6** frank and sincere; straightforward: *an* open *face.* **7** generous: *to give with an* open *hand.* **8** having openings or holes: *an* open *fabric.* **9** exposed; unprotected: *He is* open *to temptation.* **10** *Music* not stopped or not produced by stopping with the finger, a slide, key, etc.: *an* open *string; an* open *tone.* **11** of a syllable, ending in a vowel, as "de-" in "de·pend." ***vt-*** **1** to cause to be no longer closed, covered, etc.: *to* open *a door; to* open *a map; to* open *a road to traffic.* **2** to make an opening in: *to* open *a boil.* **3** to make accessible or available: *Railroads helped* open *the West.* **4** to make receptive to new and different ideas, suggestions, etc.; enlighten: *Traveling to foreign places helps to* open *your mind.* **5** to disclose; lay bare: *to* open *one's heart to a friend.* **6** to begin: *He* opened *the meeting with a reading of the minutes.* **7** to start operating: *to* open *a business; to* open *the new thruway.* ***vi-*** **1** to move or part so as to uncover or create an opening: *The door* opened *quietly. The curtains* opened. **2** to begin: *The program* opened *with a song.* **3** to start operating: *The bridge* opened *last Saturday.* **4** to appear as a gap or other opening: *A huge crack* opened *in the earth.* —***n-*** **o′pen·er.**

the open any wide, clear space, especially the outdoors: *We lived in* the open *all summer.* **open to 1** exposed to: *One side of the shed is* open to *the weather.* **2** subject or liable to: *He is* open to *criticism.* **3** ready to consider: *I am* open to *any interesting offers.*

open (one's) eyes to reveal surprising or unexpected things to (one): *His comments really* opened my eyes *to his true feelings.*

open into (or **onto**) to give access to or a view of: *The kitchen has a door that* opens into *the dining room.*

open up to speak in an honest and straightforward manner, especially after a prolonged silence.

open air ***n-*** outdoors: *We spent the morning in the* open air. *as* ***modifier*** (**open-air**): *an* open-air *concert.*

open door ***n-*** **1** policy of giving all nations equal opportunity to trade in a certain area, as China did in the early twentieth century. **2** free admission to all. *as* ***modifier*** (**open-door**): *the* open-door *policy.*

open-eyed (ō′ pən īd′) ***adj-*** **1** watchful; observant; vigilant. **2** shown by a wide stare of disbelief: *a look of* open-eyed *amazement.*

o·pen-faced (ō′ pən fāst′) ***adj-*** having an honest, frank face.

o·pen-hand·ed (ō′ pən hăn′ dəd) ***adj-*** generous. —***adv-*** **o′pen-hand′ed·ly.** ***n-*** **o′pen-hand′ed·ness.**

o·pen·heart·ed (ō′ pən här′ təd) ***adj-*** **1** frank and honest; candid. **2** generous. —***adv-*** **o′pen·heart′ed·ly.** ***n-*** **o′pen·heart′ed·ness.**

o·pen-hearth (ō′ pən härth′) ***adj-*** **1** of or relating to a process of making steel, in which pig iron and other materials are melted in a furnace with a saucer-shaped hearth, by the heat of burning gases reflected from the roof. **2** of or having to do with the steel so made.

open-heart surgery ***n-*** heart surgery in which the chest is opened and the blood is mechanically recirculated and oxygenated.

open house ***n-*** **1** party or other social event for all who wish to come. **2** period or occasion during which a school, institution, etc., is open to interested observers.

o·pen·ing (ō′ pən ĭng) ***n-*** **1** hole, gap, or space: *an* opening *in the wall; an* opening *in the clouds.* **2** a clearing or open land in woods: *Deer were grazing in an* opening *in the forest.* **3** beginning or formal beginning: *The sound of the guns signaled the* opening *of the battle.* **4** job vacancy: *The Smith Company has an* opening *for an engineer.* **5** favorable opportunity: *He waited for an* opening *in the discussion to offer his plan. as* ***modifier***: *the* opening *guns; the* opening *remarks of a speaker.*

open letter ***n-*** statement of belief, protest, etc., written in the form of a letter and printed in a newspaper or otherwise published for the public to read.

o·pen·ly (ō′ pən lē) ***adv-*** without secrecy; without trying to hide or conceal: *He* openly *admitted the error.*

open market ***n-*** market in which any buyer or seller may trade and compete; free market.

o·pen-mind·ed (ō′ pən mīn′ dəd) ***adj-*** able to consider new facts, ideas, and opinions; unprejudiced; impartial. —***adv-*** **o′pen-mind′ed·ly.** ***n-*** **o′pen-mind′ed·ness.**

o·pen-mouthed (ō′ pən moutht′, -mouthd′) ***adj-*** **1** gaping in wonder or amazement. **2** greedy.

o·pen·ness (ō′ pən nəs) ***n-*** **1** lack of secrecy. **2** open-mindedness. **3** frankness; straightforwardness.

open season ***n-*** period of the year during which hunting or fishing of specified game is not prohibitied.

open sesame ***interj-*** in the "Arabian Nights," a magic saying used to open a secret, locked door.

open shop ***n-*** factory or business where nonunion employees may be hired. See also *closed shop, union shop.*

open syllable ***n-*** spoken syllable that consists of or ends with a vowel or diphthong.

o·pen·work (ō′ pən wûrk′) ***n-*** carving, embroidery, etc., having many small cutouts or openings.

[1]op·er·a (ŏp′ ər ə) ***n-*** musical drama in which all or most of the lines are sung to the accompaniment of an orchestra. Operas are usually more serious in theme and more difficult to sing than operettas and musicals. See also *grand opera, comic opera. as* ***modifier***: *an* opera *singer.* [from Italian, from **opera in musica,** "an effort in music," from Latin **opera,** "effort."]

[2]op·e·ra (ō′ pə rə) *pl.* of **opus.**

op·er·a·ble (ŏp′ ər ə bəl) ***adj-*** **1** such as can be treated by surgery. **2** possible to do or carry out; practicable: *Is the plan* operable?

opera glasses ***n-*** *pl.* small binoculars for use in watching stage performances.

opera house ***n-*** theater for operas.

op·er·ate (ŏp′ ə rāt′) ***vi-*** [**op·er·at·ed, op·er·at·ing**] **1** to go, work, or run; function: *A jet engine should* operate *smoothly.* **2** to have a certain effect or influence: *Some drugs* operate *harmfully on the body.* **3** to perform surgery: *Is Dr. Thomas* operating *today*? **4** to carry on military activity: *The unit will* operate *behind enemy lines.* ***vt-*** **1** to cause to work or run: *Can he* operate *that car?* **2** to be in charge of or manage (a business).

op·er·at·ic (ŏp′ ə răt′ ĭk) ***adj-*** of, in, related to, or suitable for opera: *an* operatic *tenor;* operatic *dialogue.* —***adv-*** **op′er·at′i·cal·ly.**

op·er·a·tion (ŏp′ ə rā′ shən) ***n-*** **1** act or process of working or running; also, the way something works or runs: *Smooth* operation *makes an engine last longer.* **2** surgical treatment: *Removal of the tonsils is usually a simple* operation. **3** move or moves made to carry out a plan of action, especially in warfare; also, the plan itself: *The invasion of France in World War II was a huge* operation. **4** something done by set rules, often as a step in a larger process: *the* operation *of finding a square root.* **5** *Mathematics* something done with mathematical symbols according to set rules: *The* operation *of addition.*

op·er·a·tion·al (ŏp'ə rā'shən əl) ***adj-*** **1** ready to be used or operated: *The plane has been serviced and is now* operational. **2** of or relating to operations, especially military operations: *the division's* operational *plans.* **—*adv-*** **op'er·a'tion·al·ly.**

op·er·a·tive (ŏp'ər ə tĭv') ***adj-*** **1** actively used, enforced, etc.; operating; in force and effect. **2** related to physical or practical work: *one's* operative *skills.* **3** in medicine, related to operations: *post*operative *care.* ***n-*** secret agent or private investigator.

op·er·a·tor (ŏp'ə rā'tər) ***n-*** **1** someone who works or runs a machine, mechanism, etc.: *an X-ray* operator. **2** person who manages a business or other enterprise: *He is a mine* operator. **3** *Informal* person who achieves ends by shrewd means.

op·er·et·ta (ŏp'ə rĕt'ə) ***n-*** light and humorous musical play with much spoken dialogue, usually having a romantic theme and a dancing chorus.

o·phid·i·an (ō fĭd'ē ən) ***n-*** member of the group of reptiles (**Ophidia**) to which all snakes belong; snake. **—*adj-*:** *an* ophidian *reptile*; *an* ophidian *head.*

oph·thal·mi·a (ŏf thăl'mē ə, *also* ŏp-) ***n-*** inflammation of the eye or its membranes or lids.

oph·thal·mol·o·gist (ŏf'thăl mŏl'ə jĭst', *also* ŏp'-) ***n-*** doctor who specializes in ophthalmology.

oph·thal·mol·o·gy (ŏf' thăl mŏl'ə jē, *also* ŏp'-) the branch of medicine dealing with the structure, functions, and diseases of the eye.

o·pi·ate (ō'pē ət, -āt') ***n-*** **1** medicine that contains opium and is used to induce sleep, kill pain, etc. **2** anything that induces sleep, soothes, or relaxes. ***adj-*:** *an* opiate *drug.*

o·pine (ō pīn') *Archaic* ***vt-*** [**o·pined, o·pin·ing**] to have or express as an opinion; suppose (takes only a clause as an object): *He* opined *that it was too late.*

o·pin·ion (ə pĭn'yən) ***n-*** **1** belief or statement based at least partly on one's judgment rather than upon clear or proven fact; notion; view. **2** statement of judgment on a case or point of law: *The Chief Justice wrote the* opinion, *and six justices concurred.*

o·pin·ion·at·ed (ə pĭn'yə nā'təd) ***adj-*** stubbornly attached to one's opinion or belief; dogmatic.

o·pi·um (ō'pē əm) ***n-*** strong, habit-forming narcotic drug made from seed pods of a flower called the **opium poppy.** Opium is the source of morphine, codeine, and other valuable drugs used in medicine.

Opossum, about 2 1/2 ft. long

o·pos·sum (ə pŏs'əm) ***n-*** nocturnal animal of the United States that lives in trees and carries its young in a fur-lined pouch. It falls into a deathlike trance when frightened. Also **possum.**

op·po·nent (ə pō'nənt) ***n-*** person who opposes another in a sport, war, etc.; adversary; rival; antagonist. ***adj-*** acting against each other; antagonistic: *two* opponent *teams.*

op·por·tune (ŏp'ər tōōn', -tyōōn') ***adj-*** **1** well-suited; convenient; fit: *an* opportune *example.* **2** well-timed; timely: *an* opportune *notice.* **—*adv-*** **op'por·tune'ly.** ***n-*** **op'por·tune'ness.**

op·por·tun·ism (ŏp'ər tōō'nĭz əm, -tyōō'nĭz əm) ***n-*** the use of every opportunity to further one's own interests, regardless of right or wrong. **—*n-*** **op'por·tun'ist.** ***adj-*** **op'por·tun·is'tic.**

op·por·tu·ni·ty (ŏp'ər tōō'nə tē, -tyōō'nə tē) ***n-*** [*pl.* **op·por·tu·ni·ties**] **1** time or situation that is apt for a certain purpose; a good chance: *an* opportunity *to be committee chairman*; *an* opportunity *to try the new ice skates.* **2** good chance to better oneself: *That job offers many* opportunities *for an ambitious person.*

op·pos·a·ble (ə pō'zə bəl) ***adj-*** **1** such as can be opposed or resisted: *Such a great force is not* opposable. **2** such as can be used opposite or against something else: *Humans and apes have an* opposable *thumb.* **—*n-*** **op·pos'a·bil'i·ty.**

op·pose (ə pōz') ***vt-*** [**op·posed, op·pos·ing**] **1** to be or struggle against (somebody or something): *to* oppose *a tax*; *to* oppose *a dictator.* **2** to contrast; set against: *to* oppose *light and shadow in a picture.* **—*n-*** **op·pos'er.**

opposed to against: *He seems to be* opposed to *change.*

op·pos·ing (ə pō'zĭng) ***adj-*** on the opposite side; conflicting: *two* opposing *political parties.*

op·po·site (ŏp'ə zĭt) ***adj-*** **1** facing, in front of, or across from: *Who lives in the house* opposite *yours?* **2** contrary: *The whaling ship met a merchant ship traveling in the* opposite *direction.* **3** entirely different; exactly reverse or in marked contrast: *Stop is* opposite *to go.* ***n-*** the reverse; person or thing in marked contrast to another: *Darkness and daylight are* opposites. **—*adv-*** **op'po·site·ly.** ***n-*** **op'po·site·ness.**

►Should not be confused with APPOSITE.

op·po·si·tion (ŏp'ə zĭsh'ən) ***n-*** **1** an opposing or being opposed: *Our governor won praise for her* opposition *to high taxes.* **2** opposing force; resistance: *The enemy attacks met with fierce* opposition. **3** position opposed or opposite to another: *In checkers, the red pieces are placed in* opposition *to the black.* **4** person or persons opposing; especially, a political party not in power: *the leader of the* opposition. **5** *Astronomy* the positioning along a straight line of the sun, earth, and another celestial body, when the earth is in the middle. See also *conjunction.*

op·press (ə prĕs') ***vt-*** **1** to treat harshly and unjustly; rule with a heavy hand; tyrannize: *The king* oppressed *his subjects.* **2** to weigh heavily upon the mind or spirit of: *Alan looks as if all the cares of the world* oppress *him.*

op·pres·sion (ə presh'ən) ***n-*** **1** cruel, unjust treatment; crushing, despotic rule: *political* oppression. **2** sense of being overpowered; feeling of heavy discomfort and depression: *the* oppression *of a hot, muggy day.*

op·pres·sive (ə prĕs'ĭv) ***adj-*** **1** crushing; cruel and unjust: *an* oppressive *law*; *an* oppressive *ruler.* **2** heavy and overpowering; burdensome: *a day of* oppressive *heat.* **—*adv-*** **op·pres'sive·ly.** ***n-*** **op·pres'sive·ness.**

op·pres·sor (ə prĕs'ər) ***n-*** one who oppresses or rules in a harsh, unjust way; tyrant.

op·pro·bri·ous (ə prō'brē əs) ***adj-*** **1** expressing severe reproach; abusive; insulting: *to use* opprobrious *language.* **2** deserving reproach; shameful; disgraceful: *his* opprobrious *conduct.* **—*adv*- op·pro′ bri·ous·ly. *n*- op·pro′ bri·ous·ness.**

op·pro·bri·um (ə prō′ brē əm) ***n*-** disgrace or severe reproach resulting from shameful or infamous conduct; scorn; infamy: *There is great* opprobrium *attached to the name of Benedict Arnold.*

op·tic (ŏp′ tĭk) ***adj*-** relating to the eye or to sight: *the* optic *nerve.* ***n*- optics** (takes singular verb) the science which treats of light, the laws of vision, and the construction of optical instruments.

op·ti·cal (ŏp′ tĭ kəl) ***adj*- 1** relating to optics. **2** of or having to do with the eyesight: *an* optical *illusion.* **3** made to assist sight: *an* optical *instrument.* **—*adv*- op′ ti·cal·ly.**

optical illusion ***n*-** an error in judging the size, shape, distance, etc., of visually perceived objects. Example: the moon appears to be much bigger near the horizon than high in the sky. For picture, see *illusion.*

op·ti·cian (ŏp tĭsh′ ən) ***n*-** one who makes or sells eyeglasses and other optical instruments.

optic nerve ***n*-** nerve connecting the retina of the eye with the part of the brain associated with seeing.

op·ti·mal (ŏp′ tə məl) ***adj*-** best or most favorable for a particular purpose: *the* optimal *conditions for take-off.*

op·ti·mism (ŏp′ tə mĭz′ əm) ***n*- 1** tendency to see only the brighter side of things, or to expect or hope for the best. **2** the belief that everything happens for the best, or that the world is constantly getting better. **—*n*- op′ ti·mist. *adj*- op′ ti·mis′ tic. *adv*- op′ ti·mis′ ti·cal·ly.**

op·ti·mum (ŏp′ tə məm) ***n*-** [*pl.* **op·ti·mums** or **op·ti·ma** (-mə)] the best or most favorable condition, amount, degree, etc.: *Conditions for growth are at an* optimum. ***adj*-** optimal: *an* optimum *temperature for hatching.*

op·tion (ŏp′ shən) ***n*- 1** right or power of choosing; choice; discretion: *You have the* option *to take it or leave it.* **2** the act of choosing: *You can make your decision after his* option. **3** something that is or can be chosen: *I have the* option *of giving an oral report or taking a written exam.* **4** purchased right to buy or sell something at a specified price within a specified time.

op·tion·al (ŏp′ shən əl) ***adj*-** left to one's choice or preference; elective: *an* optional *course of study.* **—*adv*- op′ tion·al·ly.**

op·tom·e·trist (ŏp tŏm′ ə trĭst′) ***n*-** specialist in examining the eyes for visual defects, and in fitting a person with eyeglasses to correct such defects. **—*n*- op·tom′ e·try.**

op·u·lent (ŏp′ yə lənt) ***adj*- 1** very rich; wealthy; affluent: *an* opulent *rajah.* **2** plentiful; abundant; ample: *a full,* opulent *figure.* **—*n*- op′ u·lence.**

o·pus (ō′ pəs) ***n*-** [*pl.* **op·er·a** (ŏ′ pə rə)] a literary or musical work; especially, one of the works of a composer numbered in the order in which they were published.

or (ôr) ***conj*- 1** (used with "either," and often with "whether," to introduce two, and only two, alternatives): *I want either peach pie* or *chocolate ice cream. Whether you go* or *stay is of no concern to me.* **2** (used after a statement to introduce any number of additional alternatives): *I want chocolate* or *strawberry,* or *possibly butter pecan.* **3** else; otherwise: *You'd better go,* or *you'll be sorry.* **4** in other words; namely: *The puma,* or *cougar, is found in the Americas.* ***Homs*-** oar, o'er, ore.

-or *suffix* (used to form nouns) person who or a thing that: *inherit*or; *possess*or.

or·a·cle (ôr′ ə kəl, ŏr′-) ***n*- 1** in ancient Greece and Rome, a priest, a priestess, or other agency believed to receive messages from a god and give them as prophecies to human beings. **2** message so given. **3** place where such messages were given. **4** person whose wisdom and statements are considered beyond question: *Uncle John is the village* oracle.

o·rac·u·lar (ə răk′ yə lər) ***adj*-** of or like an oracle or prophecy; deep and mysterious in meaning; obscure; also, wise: *the* oracular *utterances of a prophet.* **—*adv*- o·rac′ u·lar·ly.**

o·ral (ôr′ əl) ***adj*- 1** spoken, not written: *This year's final examination was* oral. **2** of or having to do with the mouth: *good* oral *hygiene.* **—*adv*- o′ ral·ly.**

►Should not be confused with VERBAL.

or·ange (ŏr′ ĭnj, ôr′-) ***n*- 1** round yellow-red citrus fruit with a juicy pulp. **2** the evergreen tree that bears this fruit and has fragrant white blossoms. **3** (also **or′ ange·wood′**) the wood of this tree. **4** the yellow-red color of this fruit and of pumpkins. Orange is between red and yellow in the spectrum. ***adj*-:** *an* orange *grove; an* orange *ribbon.*

Orange

or·ange·ade (ŏr′ ĭn jād′, ôr′-) ***n*-** drink made of orange juice, sugar, and water.

Or·ange·man (ŏr′ ĭnj mən, ôr′-) ***n*-** [*pl.* **Or·ange·men**] member of a secret society organized in Northern Ireland in 1795 to support Protestantism.

orange pekoe ***n*-** choice black tea of India, Ceylon, and Java, made from the youngest leaves at the tip of the stem. See also *pekoe.*

o·rang-u·tan (ə răng′ ə tăng′) ***n*-** long-armed, tree-dwelling ape of Borneo and Sumatra having reddish-brown hair. Also **o·rang′-u·tang′.**

o·rate (ôr āt′) ***vi*-** **[o·rat·ed, o·rat·ing]** to speak in a grand manner; declaim.

o·ra·tion (ôr ā′ shən) ***n*-** formal public speech, usually given on a special occasion: *a funeral* oration.

or·a·tor (ôr′ ə tər, ŏr′-) ***n*-** public speaker, especially a skillful one.

or·a·tor·i·cal (ôr′ ə tôr′ ĭ kəl, ŏr′ ə tŏr′-) ***adj*-** of or suitable to orators or oratory: *an* oratorical *style.* **—*adv*- or′ a·tor′ i·cal·ly.**

or·a·tor·i·o (ŏr′ ə tôr′ ē ō, ôr′-) ***n*-** [*pl.* **or·a·tor·i·os**] large, dramatic musical work, usually on a sacred theme, sung by solo voices and chorus to orchestral accompaniment, without action, scenery, or costumes.

[1]**or·a·to·ry** (ŏr′ ə tôr′ ē, ôr′-) ***n*- 1** the art of speaking in public. **2** skill and eloquence in public speaking: *Abraham Lincoln's Gettysburg Address is an example of great* oratory. [from Latin **ars ōrātōria** meaning "the oratorical art," from **ōrāre,** "to plead (a case); speak eloquently."]

[2]**or·a·to·ry** (ŏr′ ə tôr′ ē, ôr′-) ***n*-** [*pl.* **or·a·to·ries**] chapel for private prayer. [from Latin **ōrātōrium** meaning "of or for prayer," from **ōrāre,** "to pray; plead."]

orb (ôrb, ŏrb) ***n*- 1** globe; sphere. **2** the sun, moon, or any other heavenly body. **3** the eye. **4** a sphere having an upright cross on top of it, used as a symbol of royal power and justice.

or·bit (ôr′ bĭt, ŏr′-) ***n*- 1** path followed by one heavenly body around another; also, path in which a man-made satellite or spacecraft moves about a heavenly body. **2** circle or range of influence: *Poland is within the Communist* orbit. **3** the bony cavity which contains the eye. ***vt*- 1** to place (a man-

ORBIT
EARTH
SATELLITE

Orbit of a satellite

made satellite or spacecraft) in a path around a heavenly body. **2** to revolve in a path around (a heavenly body): *The earth* orbits *the sun.* ***vi-***: *The spacecraft* orbited *for four days.*

or·bit·al (ôr′ bĭt əl, ôr′-) ***adj-*** **1** of or relating to an orbit. **2** such as can be placed in an orbit: *an* orbital *missile.* ***n-*** **1** the orbit of the skull. **2** *Physics* the probable pattern of movement of the electrons surrounding the nucleus of the atom.

or·chard (ôr′ chərd′, ôr′-) ***n-*** area of land on which fruit trees are cultivated for their fruit; also a group of such fruit trees. **—*n-* or′ chard·man.**

or·ches·tra (ôr′ kə strə, ôr′-) ***n-*** **1** group of musicians who play together on various instruments, usually including stringed instruments. **2** all the instruments played by such a group. **3** sunken section below and in front of the stage of a theater or opera house, where musicians play. **4** main floor of a theater, especially the part near the stage. **5** symphony orchestra.

or·ches·tral (ôr kĕs′ trəl) ***adj-*** of, for, or played by an orchestra: *an* orchestral *suite.*

or·ches·trate (ôr′ kə strāt′, ôr′-) ***vt-*** **[or·ches·trat·ed, or·ches·trat·ing]** to compose, arrange, or adapt (music) for an orchestra. **—*n-* or′ ches·tra′ tion:** *His* orchestration *of the overture stressed the strings and woodwinds.*

or·chid (ôr′ kĭd, ôr′-) ***n-*** **1** any of a large family of plants having variously colored, unusually shaped flowers; also, the flower of any of these plants. **2** pinkish-purple color. ***adj-***: *an* orchid *scarf.*

or·dain (ôr dān′) ***vt-*** **1** to order or decree; establish by law: *to* ordain *a day of Thanksgiving.* **2** to admit to the ministry of a church by means of an official ceremony.

or·deal (ôr dēl′, ôr′ dēl′, ôr′-) ***n-*** severe test or dreadful experience: *the* ordeal *of a hurricane.*

or·der (ôr′ dər, ôr′-) ***n-*** **1** direction to do something; command: *The captain gave the* order *to abandon ship.* **2** direction for the purchase, sale, or supply of goods; also, the goods, purchased, sold, or supplied: *He sent in an* order *for 200 books. Ship this* order *to 21 Midland Avenue.* **3** portion of food for one person: *The chef prepared four* orders *of fried chicken.* **4** arrangement; sequence: *alphabetical* order. **5** condition; state: *My work is in good* order. **6** proper arrangement or condition: *to keep* order *in a closet.* **7** established practice or custom: *the* order *of church worship.* **8** observance of rules and regulations; orderly conduct: *to keep law and* order. **9** class or degree: *His work is usually of a high* order. **10** social, religious, or honorary organization: *Masonic* Order; *Dominican* Order; Order *of the Garter.* **11 orders** holy orders. **12** *Biology* in the classification of plants and animals, a category that is below a class and above a family: *Man belongs to the* order *of primates.* **13** in architecture, a style of column and its entablature; also, any of the classical styles of architecture based on this: *the Doric and Corinthian* orders. ***vt-*** **1** to command: *He* ordered *me to go.* **2** to give a direction for the purchase, sale, or supply of: *to* order *a shipment of oil.* **3** to regulate; manage: *to* order *one's affairs.*

by order of according to the command of: *The troops advanced* by order of *the general.* **call to order 1** to command or request to be still and orderly. **2** to begin (a meeting, conference, etc.). **in order 1** in the right position or arrangement. **2** in good working condition. **3** in keeping with the rules and regulations; permissible: *Nominations for treasurer are now* in order. **in order that** so that. **in order to** for the purpose of: *He's here* in order to *heckle the speaker.* **in short order** quickly. **on order** purchased and to be either delivered or picked up: *two pairs of pants* on order. **on the order of** somewhat like; similar to: *a leader* on the order of *Lincoln.* **out of order** not in order. **take orders** to take holy orders; be ordained. **to order** according to the specifications of the buyer: *a suit made* to order.

ordered pair ***n-*** *Mathematics* any pair of elements or numbers in which one is considered the first, the other is considered the second. The ordered pair (3, 9) on a coordinate system locates the point that is 3 units to the right of the y axis and 9 units above the x axis.

or·der·ly (ôr′ dər lē, ôr′-) ***adj-*** **1** well arranged and tidy: *Mother kept the house clean and* orderly. **2** having regard for order or system; systematic: *An* orderly *person plans his work.* **3** free from trouble or disorder; well managed or behaved; peaceable: *an* orderly *crowd.* ***n-*** [*pl.* **or·der·lies**] **1** soldier assigned to an officer to carry messages and otherwise assist him. **2** attendant in a hospital. **—*n-* or′ der·li·ness.**

Order of the Garter ***n-*** the highest order of knighthood in Great Britain.

or·di·nal or **ordinal number** (ôr′ də nəl, ôr′-) ***n-*** kind of number that shows the position of an object in a series. "First," "1st," "third," "3rd," "tenth," and "10th" are ordinals. See also *cardinal number.*

or·di·nance (ôr′ də nəns, ôr′-) ***n-*** official law, rule, or decree, especially one made by the authorities of a town or city: *Please observe the no smoking* ordinance.
►Should not be confused with ORDNANCE.

or·di·nar·i·ly (ôr′ də nĕr′ ə lē, ôr′-) ***adv-*** usually; normally; customarily: *Our dog* ordinarily *sleeps quietly.*

or·di·nar·y (ôr′ də nĕr′ ē, ôr′-) ***adj-*** **1** usual; customary; normal: *to follow one's* ordinary *routine.* **2** commonplace; mediocre: *It's just an* ordinary *dress.*

in ordinary 1 in regular service: *a painter* in ordinary *to a king.* **2** of a ship, out of commission. **out of the ordinary** unusual; extraordinary.

ordinary seaman ***n-*** seaman who works as a deckhand on a ship, and is subordinate to an able-bodied seaman.

or·di·nate (ôr′ də nət, ôr′-) ***n-*** in plane geometry, the second of two co-ordinates used to locate a point with regard to two axes. The ordinate is customarily the vertical distance of a point from the x axis, measured along a line parallel to the y axis. For picture, see *abscissa.*

or·di·na·tion (ôr′ də nā′ shən, ôr′-) ***n-*** admission to the ministry of a church by means of an official ceremony; also, the ceremony itself.

ord·nance (ôrd′ nəns, ôrd′-) ***n-*** all types of military weapons and ammunition, especially artillery.
►Should not be confused with ORDINANCE.

Or·do·vi·ci·an (ôr′ də vĭsh′ ən, ôr′) ***n-*** the second of the six periods of the Paleozoic era. Primitive fish first appeared during the Ordovician. ***adj-***: *the* Ordovician *period.*

ore (ôr) ***n-*** rock or mineral containing enough of one or more elements, usually metals, to make the mining of it profitable. ***Homs-*** oar, o'er, or.

Oreg. Oregon.

o·reg·a·no (ə rĕg′ ə nō) ***n-*** [*pl.* **o·reg·a·nos**] plant of the mint family, having fragrant leaves and used as an herb in cooking, especially Italian cooking.

Oregon grape ***n-*** **1** small, dark-blue berry of western United States. Its small yellow blossom is the State flower of Oregon. **2** the evergreen shrub on which it grows.

---

or·gan (ȯr′ gən, ôr′-) ***n***- **1** part of an animal or plant, such as the heart, eye, or a leaf, having a particular structure and function. **2** musical instrument played by touching keys which release jets of air into pipes **(pipe organ)** or reeds. **3** similar instrument that produces sound by electronic means. **4** newspaper or magazine that spreads information, especially about the events and views of a specific group or organization.

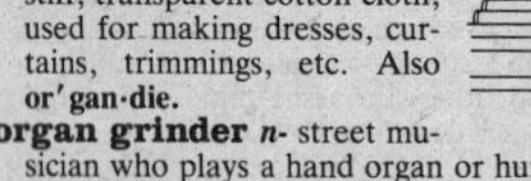
Pipe organ

or·gan·dy (ȯr′ gən dē, ôr′-) ***n***- [*pl.* **or·gan·dies**] very thin, stiff, transparent cotton cloth, used for making dresses, curtains, trimmings, etc. Also **or′ gan·die.**

organ grinder ***n***- street musician who plays a hand organ or hurdy-gurdy.

or·gan·ic (ȯr găn′ ĭk) ***adj***- **1** having to do with the organs of an animal or plant: *an* organic *disease.* **2** relating to or derived from living matter: *Fossils are remains of* organic *bodies.* **3** designating or related to a chemical compound containing carbon: *the study of* organic *chemistry.* **4** made up of related parts: *an* organic *whole.* **5** belonging to, or inherent in, the constitution or organization of something; fundamental: *an* organic *fault.* **—*adv*- or·gan′ i·cal·ly.**

organic chemistry ***n***- branch of chemistry that studies the compounds of carbon.

or·gan·ism (ȯr′ gə nĭz′ əm, ôr′-) ***n***- **1** living plant or animal: *a microscopic* organism. **2** something similar to this; complex, organized whole: *the social* organism.

or·gan·ist (ȯr′ gə nĭst′, ôr′-) ***n***- person who plays the organ.

or·gan·i·za·tion (ȯr′ gə nə zā′ shən) ***n***- **1** a uniting or being united, so that people or things work well together; an organizing or being organized: *the* organization *of a club.* **2** way in which parts of a whole are arranged: *the* organization *of our government.* **3** group of people united to do work: *the Red Cross* organization.

Organization of American States ***n***- association of twenty-two Latin American countries and the United States. It is a regional organization within the framework of the United Nations and provides for economic co-operation and the peaceful settlement of disputes.

or·ga·nize (ȯr′ gə nīz′, ôr′-) ***vt***- [**or·ga·nized, or·ga·niz·ing**] **1** to put together in working order; unite or group so that things or persons work well together: *The coach* organized *a good football team by much drilling and hard work.* **2** to plan and arrange: *Scientists must* organize *their work carefully.* **3** to cause (workers) to join or form a labor union; also, to cause the workers of (a factory, industry, etc.) to join or form a labor union. ***vi***- to form, or join in, an organization: *The workers* organized *for higher wages and shorter hours.* **—*n*- or′ gan·iz′ er.**

or·gan·za (ȯr găn′ zə) ***n***- fine, sheer, crisp fabric used mainly as a stiffening under dresses.

or·gy (ȯr′ jē, ôr′-) ***n***- [*pl.* **or·gies**] **1 orgies** among the ancient Greeks and Romans, secret rites performed as part of the worship of certain gods, especially the god of wine, and accompanied by wild, ecstatic songs and dances, drinking, etc. **2** wild, drunken, or lustful revel; debauch. **3** any spell of uncontrolled or excessive activity: *an* orgy *of eating.*

or·i·el (ôr′ ē əl) ***n***- large bay window projecting from the outside wall of a building.

o·ri·ent (ôr′ ē ĕnt) ***vt***- **1** to place facing the east. **2** to place in the right relation to the points of the compass: *At night I can* orient *myself if I find the North Star.* **3** to adjust or adapt to new or unfamiliar surroundings, ideas, etc.: *It doesn't take very long to* orient *yourself when you move to a new city. I need some time to* orient *my thinking.* ***n***- the east.

Oriel

O·ri·ent (ôr′ ē ĕnt) ***n***- the countries of Asia, especially the Far East and the islands off the coast of Asia; opposite of Occident.

o·ri·en·tal (ôr′ ē ĕn′ təl) ***adj***- **1** eastern. **2** of or pertaining to the countries in the Orient or their people: *an* oriental *language.* ***n***- **Oriental 1** person belonging to or descended from one of the native peoples of the Orient. **2** a Mongolian.

or·i·en·tate (ôr′ ē ən tāt′) ***vi***- [**or·i·en·tat·ed, or·i·en·tat·ing**] to face a specified direction, especially the east. ***vt***- to orient.

o·ri·en·ta·tion (ôr′ ē ən tā′ shən) ***n***- **1** placement or adjustment so as to face a specific direction: *The ship's* orientation *was changed from north to northeast.* **2** direction of attention or emphasis toward a particular goal: *Jack shows a strong* orientation *toward mathematics.* **3** one's sense of direction or participation as a member of society: *the faulty* orientation *of the habitual criminal.* **4** introduction to a new or different situation; also, a period or session during which such an introduction is given: *The new students attended a freshman* orientation. *as* ***modifier:*** *an* orientation *lecture.*

or·i·fice (ôr′ ə fĭs, ŏr′-) ***n***- outlet or opening; vent: *The nostril is the nasal* orifice.

or·i·ga·mi (ôr′ ə gä′ mē) ***n***- Japanese art of paper-folding to produce decorative objects such as birds, animals, and flowers.

or·i·gin (ŏr′ ə jĭn, ȯr′-) ***n***- **1** beginning; start; source: *Nobody knows the* origin *of that rumor.* **2** family background; ancestry: *After he grew famous, he never concealed his humble* origin. **3** *Mathematics* on a set of Cartesian co-ordinates, the point at which the x axis and y axis intersect. For picture, see *abscissa.* **4** in anatomy, that one of the two points of a muscle's attachment that moves relatively little.

o·rig·i·nal (ə rĭj′ ə nəl) ***adj***- **1** first; earliest: *The Indians were the* original *inhabitants of America.* **2** imaginative; producing new ideas; creative: *Your story shows you have an* original *mind.* **3** not copied; new; done for the first time: *Our teacher wrote an* original *Thanksgiving pageant.* ***n***- **1** the first model from which something is copied: *This is a copy of our Constitution, but the* original *is in Washington, D.C.* **2** language in which something is first written: *to read French books in the* original.

o·rig·i·nal·i·ty (ə rĭj′ ə năl′ ə tē) ***n***- [**o·rig·i·nal·i·ties**] **1** novelty; freshness: *That idea has great* originality. **2** ability to create or invent: *Jan's* originality *is seen best in her posters.* **3** any novel or original thing; innovation.

o·rig·i·nal·ly (ə rĭj′ ə nə lē) ***adv***- **1** at first; in the beginning: *The capital of the United States was* originally *Philadelphia.* **2** in a new and fresh way: *The stage decorations were designed very* originally.

o·rig·i·nate (ə rĭj′ ə nāt′) ***vi***- [**o·rig·i·nat·ed, o·rig·i·nat·ing**] to start; begin: *The fire* originated *in the engine room.* ***vt***- to invent; make up: *The Chinese* originated *fireworks.* **—*n*- o·rig′ i·na′ tion.** ***n***- **o·rig′ i·na′ tor:** *the* originator *of a new product.*

o·ri·ole (ôr′ ē ōl′) ***n-*** **1** any of several American songbirds that build hanging nests, especially the black-and-orange Baltimore oriole and the black-and-chestnut orchard oriole. **2** any of several black-and-yellow songbirds of the Old World, related to the crows, that build hanging nests (for picture, see *nest.*).

Baltimore oriole, about 8 in. long

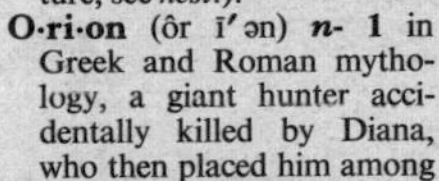

O·ri·on (ô rī′ ən) ***n-*** **1** in Greek and Roman mythology, a giant hunter accidentally killed by Diana, who then placed him among the constellations. **2** large constellation near the celestial equator, named for him.

or·i·son (ôr′ ə sən, ŏr′ ə sən, -zən) *Archaic* ***n-*** a prayer.

Or·lon (ôr′ lŏn, ôr′-) ***n-*** trademark name for a synthetic fiber used in making textiles.

[1]**or·na·ment** (ôr′ nə mənt, ôr′-) ***n-*** **1** object used to decorate or beautify; decoration: *Christmas tree* ornaments. **2** decoration; adornment: *She wore a white dress with blue beads as an* ornament. **3** person who adds grace, dignity, or honor to a group: *She is an* ornament *to the teaching profession.* **4** ornamentation.

[2]**or·na·ment** (ôr′ nə mĕnt′, ôr′-) ***vt-*** to adorn; decorate; beautify: *He* ornamented *the hall with banners and flags.*

or·na·men·tal (ôr′ nə mĕn′ təl, ôr′-) ***adj-*** decorative: *The chest was covered with* ornamental *carvings.* ***—adv-*** **or′ na·men′ tal·ly.**

or·na·men·ta·tion (ôr′ nə mĕn tā′ shən, ôr′-) ***n-*** **1** an ornamenting or being ornamented. **2** ornaments; adornments; decorations.

or·nate (ôr nāt′) ***adj-*** **1** elaborately decorated: *an* ornate *Chinese vase.* **2** florid; highly embellished: *an* ornate *style of writing.* ***—n-*** **or·nate′ ness.**

or·ner·y (ôr′ nə rē, ôr′- *also* ŏn′ ə-) *Informal* ***adj-*** **[or·ner·ier, or·ner·i·est] 1** stubborn and quarrelsome; cantankerous. **2** mean; low. ***—n-*** **or′ ner·i·ness.**

or·ni·tho·log·i·cal (ôr′ nə thə lŏj′ ĭ kəl, ôr′-) ***adj-*** of or relating to ornithology.

or·ni·thol·o·gist (ôr′ nə thŏl′ ə jĭst′, ôr′-) ***n-*** person trained in ornithology and usually engaged in it as a profession.

or·ni·thol·o·gy (ôr′ nə thŏl′ ə jē, ôr′-) ***n-*** branch of zoology that deals with birds.

or·o·tund (ôr′ ə tənd, ŏr′-) ***adj-*** **1** strong, full, and resonant: *an* orotund *voice.* **2** inflated; bombastic: *an* orotund *writing style.*

or·phan (ôr′ fən, ôr′-) ***n-*** child who has lost one or, usually, both parents by death. *as* ***modifier:*** *an* orphan *child; an* orphan *asylum.* ***vt-:*** *Thousands of children were* orphaned *by the last war.*

or·phan·age (ôr′ fə nĭj, ôr-) ***n-*** home or institution for the care of orphans.

Or·phe·us (ôr′ fē əs, ôr′-) ***n-*** in Greek legend, a musician whose music charmed even rocks and trees. When he descended into Hades to seek release of his wife, Eurydice, Pluto permitted him to lead her back provided he would not look at her on the way. He did look, however, and she was forced to return.

or·ris (ôr′ əs, ŏr′-) ***n-*** any of several plants related to the iris and having an aromatic root. Its root, **or′ ris·root,** is dried and ground into a powder for use in perfume, medicine, tooth powder, etc.

ortho- *combining form* **1** upright; straight; vertical: *an* ortho*pterous insect* (having straight fore wings). **2** correct; right: *the* ortho*graphy of a word* (correct writing). **3** corrective: *a specialist in* ortho*dontia* (correction of tooth irregularities). [from Greek **ortho-,** from **orthós** meaning "upright; straight."]

or·tho·don·tia (ôr′ thə dŏn′ chə, ôr′-) ***n-*** branch of dentistry dealing with the correction and prevention of tooth irregularities. Also **or′ tho·don′ tics.**

or·tho·don·tist (ôr′ thə dŏn′ tĭst, ôr′-) ***n-*** dentist specializing in orthodontia.

or·tho·dox (ôr′ thə dŏks, ôr′-) ***adj-*** **1** approved; accepted; also, conventional: *to hold* orthodox *political views.* **2** following accepted teachings or beliefs, especially in religion. **3 Orthodox** (1) of or relating to the Eastern Orthodox Church. (2) of or relating to that branch of Judaism that adheres to the Mosaic Law and strictly observes the dietary laws and other traditions.

Orthodox Church ***n-*** Eastern Orthodox Church.

or·tho·dox·y (ôr′ thə dŏk′ sē, ôr′-) ***n-*** [*pl.* **or·tho·dox·ies**] **1** a holding to accepted beliefs and practices, especially in religion. **2** an orthodox practice or belief.

or·thog·ra·phy (ôr thŏ′ grə fē) ***n-*** [*pl.* **or·thog·ra·phies**] **1** correct spelling in writing. **2** any style or method of representing spoken sounds by written symbols. **3** study of letters and rules of spelling. ***—adj-*** **or′ tho·graph′ ic** (ôr′ thə grăf′ ĭk, ôr′-).

or·tho·pe·dics (ôr′ thə pē′ dĭks, ôr′-) ***n-*** (takes singular verb) branch of medicine and surgery dealing with the prevention and treatment of deformities and diseases of the spine, limbs, or other parts of the skeleton. ***—adj-*** **or′ tho·pe′ dic.**

or·tho·pe·dist (ôr′ thə pē′ dĭst, ôr′-) ***n-*** physician specializing in orthopedics.

or·thop·ter·ous (ôr thŏp′ tə rəs) ***adj-*** of or having to do with an order of insects **(Orthoptera)** that have biting mouth parts, leathery front wings, and membranous hind wings. The cricket, grasshopper, and praying mantis are orthopterous.

-ory *suffix* **1** (used to form adjectives) (1) of or relating to: *sens*ory; *supervis*ory. (2) like; having the nature of: *obligat*ory. **2** (used to form nouns) place or thing for (doing something): *observat*ory; *deposit*ory; *lavat*ory; *cremat*ory.

or·yx (ôr′ ĭks, ŏr′-) ***n-*** [*pl.* **o·ryx·es** or **o·ryx**] a kind of African antelope with long, almost straight horns.

Os symbol for osmium.

O·sage (ō sāj′) ***n-*** [*pl.* **O·sa·ges,** also **O·sage**] one of a tribe of American Indians who formerly inhabited the region between the Missouri and Arkansas rivers and now live in Oklahoma. ***adj-:*** *an* Osage *bow.*

Osage orange ***n-*** **1** ornamental tree related to the mulberry and much used as a hedge. **2** the fruit of this tree, somewhat like an orange in color and size.

os·cil·late (ŏs′ ə lāt′) ***vi-*** **[os·cil·lat·ed, os·cil·lat·ing] 1** to swing back and forth. **2** to pass back and forth from one state to another; waver: *to* oscillate *between two opinions.* **3** *Physics* to cause oscillations.

os·cil·la·tion (ŏs′ ə lā′ shən) ***n-*** **1** an oscillating; a swinging back and forth; also, a wavering. **2** one swing of a pendulum or other object from one extreme position to the other. **3** *Physics* the continuous, regular changing of the value of a quantity, force, etc., back and forth around a midpoint.

os·cil·la·tor (ŏs′ sə lā′ tər) ***n-*** **1** something that oscillates. **2** *Physics* device for producing electric oscillations.

---

fāte, făt, dâre, bärn; bē, bĕt, mêre; bīte, bĭt; nōte, hŏt, môre, dôg; fŭn, fûr; tōō, bŏŏk; oil; out; tar; thin; then; hw for wh as in *wh*at; zh for s as in u*s*ual; ə for a, e, i, o, u, as in *a*go, lin*e*n, per*i*l, at*o*m, min*u*s

os·cil·lo·scope (ə sĭl′ ə skōp′) ***n-*** instrument that makes visible the fluctuations of an electric current on the fluorescent screen of a cathode-ray tube similar to a television picture tube.

os·cu·late (ŏs′ kyə lāt′) ***vi-*** **[os·cu·lat·ed, os·cu·lat·ing]** to kiss. **—*n-* os′ cu·la′ tion.**

1**-ose** *suffix* (used to form adjectives) **1** full of: *verb*ose. **2** like; having the nature of: *grandi*ose; *joc*ose. [from Latin **-osus.**]

2**-ose** *Chemistry suffix* (used to form nouns) sugar or other carbohydrate: *lact*ose; *fruct*ose; *levul*ose. [from **glucose.**]

O·see (ō′ sē, ō sē′) Hosea.

o·sier (ō′ zhər) ***n-*** **1** any of various willows with flexible twigs used in baskets, furniture, etc. **2** twig of this willow. **3** any of various dogwoods, especially the **red-osier dogwood.** *as* ***modifier***: *an* osier *chair*; osier *furniture*.

O·si·ris (ō sī′ rəs) ***n-*** in Egyptian mythology, the god of the underworld; husband and brother of Isis.

-osity *suffix* (used to form nouns from adjectives ending in "-ose"): *joc*osity; *verb*osity; *grandi*osity.

os·mi·um (ŏz′ mē əm) ***n-*** bluish-white metal element that occurs and is used with platinum and iridium in alloys. Symbol Os, At. No. 76, At. Wt. 190.2.

os·mo·sis (ŏs mō′ səs, ŏz-) ***n-*** the migration of a liquid solvent, especially water, through a semipermeable membrane separating solutions of different concentration. In the living cell, water passes through the membrane from the region of higher concentration of water to the region of lesser concentration. **—*adj-* os·mot′ ic** (-mŏt′ ĭk): *the* osmotic *pressure*.

os·mot·ic (ŏs′ mŏt′ ĭk, ŏz′-) ***adj-*** relating to or resulting from osmosis: *an* osmotic *flow*; osmotic *pressure*.

os·prey (ŏs′ prē) ***n-*** [*pl.* **os·preys**] a large fish-eating hawk; fish hawk.

Osprey, about 2 ft. long

os·si·fi·ca·tion (ŏs′ ĭ fə kā′ shən) ***n-*** **1** process of bone formation, in which the flexible cartilage of the skeleton is replaced by bony tissue. **2** something that has become hardened or changed into bone.

os·si·fy (ŏs′ ə fī′) ***vt-*** **[os·si·fied, os·si·fy·ing] 1** to change into bone or bony tissue. **2** to harden; make rigid or unprogressive; *Prejudice* ossifies *the mind.* ***vi-*** **1** to be transformed into bone: *His knee cartilages* ossified *with age.* **2** to become rigid or set in a conventional pattern.

os·ten·si·ble (ə stĕn′ sə bəl) ***adj-*** alleged; professed; apparent: *an* ostensible *reason.* **—*adv-* os·ten′ si·bly:** *He was* ostensibly *friendly, but I doubt his sincerity.*

os·ten·ta·tion (ŏs′ tən tā′ shən) ***n-*** deliberate, unnecessary, and tasteless showiness or display.

os·ten·ta·tious (ŏs′ tən tā′ shəs) ***adj-*** showy; pretentious; done to impress people or to attract attention: *an* ostentatious *show of knowledge*; ostentatious *jewelry.* **—*adv-* os′ ten·ta′ tious·ly. *n-* os′ ten·ta′ tious·ness.**

os·te·o·path (ŏs′ tē ə păth′) ***n-*** one who practices osteopathy.

os·te·op·a·thy (ŏs′ tē ŏp′ ə thē′) ***n-*** a method of treatment which, while recognizing the value of ordinary medical and surgical treatment, holds that many diseases are due chiefly to displacement of body parts, especially the bones, and in healing lays stress on manipulating the displaced parts into place with the hands. **—*adj-* os′ te·o·path′ ic** (-tē ə păth′ ĭk): *an* osteopathic *physician*.

ost·ler (ŏs′ lər) hostler.

ost·mark (ŏst′ märk′) ***n-*** the East German mark.

os·tra·cism (ŏs′ trə siz′ əm) ***n-*** **1** in ancient Greece, temporary banishment by vote of the people. **2** exclusion of someone from favor or privileges by general agreement; social rejection.

os·tra·cize (ŏs′ trə sīz′) ***vt-*** **[os·tra·cized, os·tra·ciz·ing] 1** in ancient Greece, to banish by popular vote. **2** to reject socially; bar or exclude from acceptance or privilege by general consent: *The business community* ostracized *him for his improper dealings.*

os·trich (ŏs′ trĭch′, ŏs′-) ***n-*** the largest of birds. It can run swiftly but cannot fly. Its curly plumes are used for decoration and its skin for leather. *as* ***modifier***: *an* ostrich *plume*.

Ostrich, 6-8 ft. high

O.T. Old Testament.

O·thel·lo (ō thĕl′ ō) ***n-*** in Shakespeare's "Othello," the husband of Desdemona, and hero of the tragedy.

oth·er (ŭth′ ər) ***adj-*** **1** different; not the same: *I have* other *things to worry about.* **2** more; additional: *I have* other *sisters.* **3** designating the remaining one of two or more; also, designating the remaining ones of several: *She lost her* other *shoe. His* other *friends are still in school.* **4** opposite: *the* other *side of the street.* **5** reverse: *the* other *side of the paper.* **6** alternate: *You have no* other *choice.* ***pron-*** a different or additional person or thing: *He felt that he should be doing something or* other. ***n-*** **1** the remaining one of two or more; also, the remaining ones of several: *One laughed, the* other *cried. When shall we tell the* others? **2** a different or additional person or thing: *Each explosion came after the* other. *There will be many* others *here.* **3 others** people beside oneself: *Do good to* others.

each other each the other: *They liked* each other. **every other** every alternate: *We have an art class* every other *day.* **none other than** nobody else but: *Our guest tonight is* none other than *your favorite actor.* **on the other hand** in contrast to this: *I don't want to vote for Jack, but* on the other hand, *I'd hate to hurt his feelings.* **other than 1** except for: *I see no reason for staying indoors* other than *the chance of rain.* **2** different from: *Would you want your best friend to be* other than *what he is?* **someone or other** some unknown person: *Are you sure that* someone or other *will be there to meet you?* **the other day** a few days ago: *I saw your father in town* the other day.

oth·er·wise (ŭth′ ər wīz′) ***adv-*** **1** in a different way; differently: *You seem to think* otherwise. **2** in different conditions or respects: *I know him professionally but not* otherwise. ***conj-*** else: *The story was told to me in confidence,* otherwise *I would tell you.* ***adj-*** different: *The facts were* otherwise.

other world ***n-*** life after death.

oth·er·world·ly (ŭth′ ər wûrld′ lē) ***adj-*** **1** having one's mind on spiritual rather than worldly matters. **2** of or having to do with a spiritual or a future world. **—*n-* oth′ er·world′ li·ness.**

Ot·ta·wa (ŏt′ ə wə) ***n-*** [*pl.* **Ot·ta·was,** also **Ot·ta·wa**] member of an Algonquian people of southern Ontario, who now live along the shores of lakes Superior and Michigan. ***adj-***: *an* Ottawa *canoe*.

ot·ter (ŏt′ər) ***n-*** **1** any of various fish-eating water mammals related to the weasel, valued for their brown fur. **2** the fur of this animal. *as **modifier**: an* otter *hat; an* otter *paw.*

River otter, about 3 1/2 ft. long

Ot·to·man (ŏt′ə mən) ***n-*** [*pl.* **Ot·to·mans**] **1** a Turk. **2 ottoman** (1) a low, cushioned seat. (2) a footstool. (3) a heavy fabric with a plain weave made of wool, silk, or synthetic fiber. ***adj-*** *the* Ottoman *Empire; an* Ottoman *cloth.*

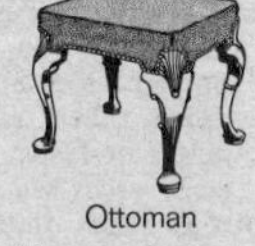
Ottoman

ouch (ouch) ***interj-*** exclamation of sudden pain.

¹ought (ȯt) ***auxiliary verb*** **1** am, is, or are morally bound or obliged (to): *You* ought *to be kind* to *your pets. We* ought *to pay the workmen.* **2** am, is, or are almost certain or expected (to): *The piano* ought *to sound better when it is tuned. This top* ought *to fit the jar.* **3** am, is, or are almost obliged (to): *We* ought *to leave now if we are not going to be late.* [from Old English **āhte,** from **āgan** meaning "to owe."] ***Hom-*** aught.

►For the negative of OUGHT TO, use "ought not to": *He* ought not (to) *go.* Good speakers avoid the expressions "hadn't ought to" or "oughtn't to."

²ought (ȯt) ²aught.

ought·n't (ȯt′ ənt) ought not.

►For usage note see OUGHT.

¹ounce (ouns) ***n-*** **1** in ordinary weight, 1/16 of a pound. **2** in troy weight, for weighing drugs and precious metals, 1/12 of a pound. **3** in liquid measure, 1/16 of a pint or 1/8 of a standard half-pint kitchen measuring cup. [from Old French **unce,** from Latin **uncia** meaning literally "a twelfth part," and very closely related to **inch.**]

²ounce (ouns) ***n-*** snow leopard. [from Old French **once,** from earlier **lonce,** from Latin and Greek **lynx** meaning "lynx."]

our (our, är) ***determiner*** (possessive case of the pronoun "we," now usually called possessive adjective) of, belonging to, done, or made by us: *This is* our *house. We wrote* our *play in three days.* ***Hom-*** hour or are.

Our Father ***n-*** the Lord's Prayer.

Our Lady ***n-*** the Virgin Mary.

ours (ourz, ärz) ***pron-*** (possessive pronoun) thing or things belonging to us: *Those books are* ours.

our·selves (our sĕlvz′, är-) ***pron-*** **1** reflexive form of **us**; our own selves: *We dressed* ourselves. **2** our normal or true selves: *We weren't quite* ourselves *yesterday.* **3** intensive form of **we**: *We* ourselves *saw it.*

by ourselves **1** alone: *We sat* by ourselves *in the garden.* **2** without any help: *We painted the house* by ourselves.

-ous *suffix* (used to form adjectives from nouns) **1** full of; of the nature of; like: *poison*ous; *glamor*ous. **2** *Chemistry* with a valence relatively lower than compounds or ions having an adjective ending in "-ic": *chlor*ous; *sulfur*ous.

oust (oust) ***vt-*** to drive or force out: *The umpire* ousted *him from the game.*

oust·er (ous′ tər) ***n-*** an ousting; also, an instance of this: *The* ouster *of the dictator failed to pacify the country.*

out (out) ***adv-*** **1** away from the center or inside: *to walk* out; *to look* out; *to jut* out. **2** away from a particular or usual place: *We went* out *to dinner. The book is* out. **3** from among others: *to pick* out *a number.* **4** thoroughly; to an extreme degree: *Clean* out *the closet. He is tired* out. **5** into inactivity or extinction: *The tribe died* out. *The light went* out. **6** to the end, conclusion, or outcome: *We heard the speaker* out. *Play the game* out. **7** into existence, view, circulation, etc.: *War broke* out. *The moon came* out. *The magazine is* out *today. The information leaked* out. **8** without restraint or inhibition: *to cry* out. **9** to several or many: *He lends* out *money. The father gave* out *land to his sons.* **10** from a good frame of mind to a bad one: *Missing the train really put me* out. **11** *Informal* into or in a state of unconsciousness: *The woman passed* out. *She was* out *for five minutes.* **12** in baseball, so as to lose the right to continue batting or to run bases: *He struck* out. **13** *Informal* discarded; not considered fashionable: *Long skirts are* out *now.* ***adj-*** **1** pointing, leading, or heading outward: *The* out *sign was painted in green.* **2** outlying; remote: *the* out *country.* ***prep-*** **1** forth by means of: *He went* out *the window.* **2** outward; along: *He drove* out *the old post road.* See also *out of.* ***n-*** **1** person, especially a politician, who is not in power. **2** means of escape or avoidance: *She couldn't find an* out *when asked to attend the meeting.* **3** in baseball, a player who has been ruled out. ***vi-*** to appear; be revealed: *Truth will* out.

all out wholeheartedly; with great effort: *The team went* all out *to win.* **at outs** (or **on the outs**) angry with; in disagreement with: *We are* on the outs *with them.* **out and away** by far: *This boat outclasses the other one* out and away. **out for** with the purpose of: *That country is* out for *conquest.* **out from under** past the point of difficulty: *We are* out from under *our debts.* **out to** fully determined to: *Jack is* out to *win.*

out- *prefix* **1** at a distance away from: *an* out*building,* out*post;* out*lying.* **2** forth; away: *an* out*cry;* out*burst;* out*cast.* **3** greater than; better than: *to* out*do;* out*distance;* out*run.* **4** more than; longer than: *to* out*live;* out*last.*

out-and-out (out′ ənd out′) ***adj-*** outright; thoroughgoing; unqualified; complete: *That's an* out-and-out *lie!*

out·bid (out′ bĭd′) ***vt-*** [**out·bid, out·bid·ding**] to offer to pay more for something than someone else: *He* outbid *all the others at the auction.*

out·board (out′ bôrd′) ***adv-*** **1** outside the hull of a ship. **2** away from the center line of the fuselage of an aircraft. ***adj-*** **1** located on or attached to the outside of a boat: *the* outboard *motor.* **2** located farthest away from the center line of the fuselage of an aircraft: *the* outboard *starboard engine.* **3** of boats, powered by an outboard motor. ***n-*** a boat powered by an outboard motor.

outboard motor ***n-*** gasoline engine complete with shaft and propeller, attached to the outside of the stern of a small boat.

Outboard motor

out·bound (out′ bound′) ***adj-*** outward bound; leaving a port, terminal, airfield, etc.: *An* outbound *plane flew by.*

out·brave (out′ brāv′) ***vt-*** [**out·braved, out·brav·ing**] to face and withstand with courage and defiance; brave out.

out·break (out′ brāk′) ***n-*** **1** an appearance of a disease, riot, or other harmful condition: *an* outbreak *of influenza.* **2** outburst: *The bad news resulted in an* outbreak *of temper.*

out·build·ing (out′ bĭl′ dĭng) ***n-*** small building like a shed, separate from a main building.

out·burst (out′ bûrst′) ***n-*** sudden, violent gush; a bursting forth: *an* outburst *of anger*; *an* outburst *of lava from a volcano.*

out·cast (out′ kăst′) ***n-*** person or animal driven out or rejected by others. ***adj-*** driven out; exiled: *an* outcast *wolf, driven from the pack.*

out·class (out′ klăs′, out′-) ***vt-*** to surpass or excel in quality, skill, etc.: *This model* outclasses *all the competition.*

out·come (out′ kŭm′) ***n-*** result: *His speed made the* outcome *of the race certain.*

out·crop (out′ krŏp′) ***vi-*** **[out·cropped, out·crop·ping]** to come out, especially to the surface of the ground. ***n-*** (also **out′ crop′ ping**) the part of a layer of rock, clay, etc., at the surface of the ground.

out·cry (out′ krī′) ***n-*** [*pl.* **out·cries**] a crying out or shouting; clamor: *The crowd raised an* outcry *at the umpire's decision.*

out·dat·ed (out′ dā′ təd) ***adj-*** old-fashioned; out-of-date; obsolete or obsolescent: *The plant was using* outdated *machinery.*

out·dis·tance (out′ dĭs′ təns) ***vt-*** **[out·dis·tanced, out·dis·tanc·ing]** to leave (something or someone) behind by traveling faster: *The rabbit* outdistanced *the hunting dog.*

out·do (out′ dōō′) ***vt-*** **[out·did, out·done, out·do·ing]** to do better than; surpass: *He can* outdo *me in every subject but science.*

out·door (out′ dôr′) ***adj-*** **1** in the open air: *Football is an* outdoor *game.* **2** fond of the open air: *an* outdoor *man.*

out·doors (out′ dôrz′) ***n-*** (takes singular verb) world outside of buildings; the open air, especially in the country: *Campers can enjoy the* outdoors. ***adv-*** in the open: *It's too nice a day not to go* outdoors.

out·er (ou′ tər) ***adj-*** **1** having to do with the outside: *the* outer *layer of skin.* **2** among the farthest from the center or inside: *Uranus is one of the* outer *planets of our solar system.* **3** among the farthest from the mainland: *the* outer *islands.*

outer ear See [1]*ear.*

out·er·most (ou′ tər mōst′) ***adj-*** farthest out from the center or other place of reference: *the* outermost *planet*; *the* outermost *island of the Hawaiian group.*

outer space ***n-*** **1** the space immediately beyond the earth's atmosphere. **2** interplanetary or interstellar space.

out·face (out′ fās′, out′-) ***vt-*** **[out·faced, out·fac·ing]** to cause (someone) to back down by facing him boldly and defiantly; stare down: *He* outfaced *his accusers.*

out·field (out′ fēld′) ***n-*** **1** part of a baseball field beyond the infield. **2** baseball players who play in the outfield; the outfielders. *as* ***modifier***: *the* outfield *grass.*

out·field·er (out′ fēl′ dər) ***n-*** in baseball, any of the three players, the right fielder, the center fielder, and the left fielder, who play in the outfield.

out·fight (out′ fīt′, out′-) ***vt-*** **[out·fought, out·fight·ing]** to defeat by fighting harder, better, or longer than: *to* outfight *the enemy.*

out·fit (out′ fĭt′) ***n-*** **1** set of equipment used for a special purpose: *a* fishing *outfit*; *a* camping *outfit.* **2** complete costume: *She wore a tweed* outfit. **3** *Informal* group of persons taken as a unit, such as a business firm, army corps, etc.: *This is an excellent* outfit *to work for.* ***vt-*** **[out·fit·ted, out·fit·ting]** to equip for a special purpose: *The Geographic Society will* outfit *an expedition to Antarctica.* **—*n-* out′ fit′ ter.**

out·flank (out′ flăngk′, out′-) ***vt-*** to place (an enemy) in a dangerous or untenable position by passing around his side or wing.

out·flow (out′ flō′) ***n-*** **1** a flowing out; flow (from): *an* outflow *of water from a pipe.* **2** the amount or rate of flow: *We need to measure the* outflow.

out·gen·er·al (out′ jĕn′ ər əl, out′-) ***vt-*** to defeat by superior leadership: *The enemy forces were* outgeneraled *by the allies.*

out·go (out′ gō′) ***n-*** [*pl.* **out·goes**] something expended, especially money.

out·go·ing (out′ gō′ ĭng) ***adj-*** **1** going out: *an* outgoing *ship.* **2** friendly; enthusiastic: *an* outgoing *person.* **3** leaving; retiring: *the* outgoing *chairman.* ***n-*** a going out; departure: *the* outgoing *of ships.*

out·grow (out′ grō′) ***vt-*** **[out·grew, out·grown, out·grow·ing]** **1** to grow too big for: *Those goldfish will* outgrow *that small tank.* **2** to give up or drop as one grows older: *He* outgrew *his shy habits.* **3** to grow larger or faster than: *If you leave your garden without care, weeds will soon* outgrow *the flowers.*

out·growth (out′ grōth′) ***n-*** **1** anything that grows out of something else: *an* outgrowth *of new branches on the tree*; *an* outgrowth *of hair.* **2** condition that grows out of or develops from something; result: *Tom's interest in horses is an* outgrowth *of his visit to his uncle's ranch.*

out·guess (out′ gĕs′, out′-) ***vt-*** to outwit by better guessing or inference.

out·house (out′ hous′) ***n-*** **1** outdoor toilet or privy. **2** building belonging to a house but separate from it.

out·ing (ou′ tĭng) ***n-*** short trip taken for pleasure; excursion: *They had a good* outing *at the beach.*

out·land·er (out′ lăn′ dər) ***n-*** person from an outlying area, distant part, or foreign country.

out·land·ish (out lăn′ dĭsh) ***adj-*** fantastic; bizarre: *The crowd stared at the man's* outlandish *clothes.*

out·last (out′ lăst′, out′-) ***vt-*** **1** to keep on longer than: *On a long hike, he could always* outlast *me.* **2** to wear or remain usable longer than: *Leather shoes usually* outlast *those made of cloth.* **3** to live longer than: *The old man* outlasted *many of his friends.*

out·law (out′ lô′) ***n-*** **1** a declared criminal; a bandit: *Jesse James was a notorious* outlaw. **2** formerly, a person officially declared no longer protected by law; an outcast: *Robin Hood was a famous* outlaw. ***vt-*** to declare outside the law's protection; make unlawful or ban: *The hope of the world is to* outlaw *war.*

out·law·ry (out′ lô′ rē) ***n-*** **1** the act of outlawing. **2** the condition of being an outlaw. **3** reckless or criminal behavior.

out·lay (out′ lā′) ***n-*** **1** a putting forth: *an* outlay *of energy.* **2** total amount expended: *The* outlay *on clothes was $20.*

out·let (out′ lĕt′) ***n-*** **1** an opening or passage to the outside: *the* outlet *of the fish tank.* **2** channel for release of emotions, energy, etc.: *Painting is an* outlet *for emotion.* **3** place in an electrical circuit where an appliance can be plugged in.

out·line (out′ līn′) ***n-*** **1** drawing showing only the outer edge of an object: *Draw an* outline *of Cape Cod.* **2** line which forms such a drawing: *The* outline *of this drawing is scratchy and broken.* **3** short summary; list of main ideas in proper order: *Don wrote an* outline *of his history lesson.* ***vt-*** **[out·lined, out·lin·ing]** **1** to draw the outer line of: *to* outline *the figures in a picture.* **2** to give a summary of: *He quickly* outlined *the methods for the staff.*

Outline target

out·live (out′ lĭv′, out′-) ***vt-*** **[out·lived, out·liv·ing]** **1** to live or last longer than. **2** to live through; survive: *Robinson Crusoe alone* outlived *the shipwreck.*

out·look (out′ lo͝ok′) ***n-*** **1** a view: *The* outlook *from the fire tower includes the lake and the mountains.* **2** way things are expected to happen; prospect: *The business* outlook *for next year is favorable.* **3** point of view; way of thinking: *a narrow* outlook.

out·ly·ing (out′ lī′ ĭng) ***adj-*** located at a distance from the center or main part; remote: *There are still some farms in the* outlying *districts of the city.*

out·ma·neu·ver (out′ mə no͞o′ vər) ***vt-*** to defeat by more skillful maneuvers or management.

out·mod·ed (out′ mō′ dəd) ***adj-*** out of style or fashion; out-of-date: *an* outmoded *idea*; outmoded *furniture.*

out·num·ber (out′ nŭm′ bər) ***vt-*** to be greater in number than; exceed in number.

out of ***prep-*** **1** forth from: *He stepped* out of *the room for a moment.* **2** from among: *One* out of *many.* **3** not in: *His bone is* out of *joint. The chair is* out of *place.* **4** from (a substance or material): *a ring made* out of *gold.* **5** because of: *She cried* out of *sympathy.* **6** lacking; wanting: *The runner was* out of *breath.*

out-of-date (out′ əv dāt′) ***adj-*** **1** old-fashioned: *The old gentleman wore* out-of-date *clothes.* **2** not suited to present conditions: *Gas street lights are* out-of-date *in a modern city.*

out-of-door (out′ əv dôr′) ***adj-*** outdoor.

out-of-doors (out′ əv dôrz′) ***n-*** outdoors.

out-of-the-way (out′ əv thə wā′) ***adj-*** **1** off the beaten track; hard to find or get to. **2** unusual; odd; uncommon.

out·pa·tient (out′ pā′ shənt) ***n-*** person who receives medical or dental care at a clinic or hospital but does not live there during treatment.

out·play (out′ plā′, out′-) ***vt-*** to play better than: *The other team* outplayed *us.*

out·point (out′ point′, out′-) ***vt-*** **1** to score more points than. **2** to sail closer to the wind than (another vessel).

out·post (out′ pōst′) ***n-*** **1** a place manned by soldiers at a distance from the main army and kept to warn of or delay an attack: *Fort Laramie was once an* outpost *of the United States Army.* **2** soldier or soldiers stationed in an outpost. **3** settlement on the frontier or in a distant place.

out·pour·ing (out′ pôr′ ĭng) ***n-*** **1** free outflow. **2** overflow; outburst: *an* outpouring *of enthusiasm.* Also **out′ pour′.**

out·put (out′ po͝ot′) ***n-*** **1** amount made or produced: *The coal mine's daily* output *is 1,000 tons.* **2** the power or energy delivered by a machine or circuit; also, the point at which the power is delivered. **3** the information coming out of a computer.

out·rage (out′ rāj′) ***n-*** **1** any violent, shocking, or shameful act: *A lynching is an* outrage *in a democracy.* **2** resentment at having been injured or insulted: *a sense of* outrage. ***vt-*** **[out·raged, out·rag·ing] 1** to do violence to (a person or thing). **2** to cause shocked resentment: *The daring train robbery and murder* outraged *the citizens.*

out·ra·geous (out rā′ jəs) ***adj-*** shocking; beyond the limits of what is decent and just; atrocious: *an* outrageous *crime*; outrageous *manners.* **—*adv-*** **out·ra′ geous·ly.** ***n-*** **out·ra′ geous·ness.**

out·rank (out′ răngk′, out′-) ***vt-*** to exceed in rank; be the superior of in an organization.

out·reach (out′ rēch′, out′-) ***vt-*** **1** to reach farther than; extend beyond. **2** *Archaic* to delude; outwit.

out·ride (out′ rīd′, out′-) ***vt-*** **[out·rode, out·rid·den, out·riding]** to ride better or faster than: *The scout* outrode *his pursuers.*

out·rid·er (out′ rī′ dər) ***n-*** a horseman who accompanies a carriage.

out·rig·ger (out′ rĭg′ ər) ***n-*** **1** long, narrow float attached to a canoe by a projecting framework and used to keep the canoe from upsetting; also, a canoe so equipped. **2** any projecting board, beam, or framework attached to a boat to act as a means for extending sails, to support an oarlock, etc; also, a boat thus fitted out.

Outrigger

[1]out·right (out′ rīt′) ***adj-*** **1** direct; downright; thorough: *The teacher caught Johnny in an* outright *lie.* **2** complete; entire: *The ruined building was an* outright *loss.*

[2]out·right (out′ rīt′) ***adv-*** **1** openly; straightforwardly; frankly: *He always says* outright *just what he thinks.* **2** at once; immediately: *He responded* outright *to the appeal.* **3** completely; at one time, not in installments: *Father paid for the new car* outright *in cash.*

out·run (out′ rŭn′) ***vt-*** **[out·ran, out·run, out·run·ning] 1** to go or run faster than. **2** to go beyond; exceed: *The scouts' enthusiasm for overnight trips* outran *their counselor's.*

out·sell (out′ sĕl′, out′-) ***vt-*** **[out·sold, out·sell·ing] 1** to surpass (another product) in number of items sold. **2** to sell more items than (another person).

out·set (out′ sĕt′) ***n-*** beginning; start: *It began to rain at the* outset *of our trip.*

out·shine (out′ shīn′, out′-) ***vt-*** **[out·shone, out·shining] 1** to shine more brightly than; surpass in brightness. **2** to surpass in excellence: *to* outshine *the rest of the class in arithmetic.*

out·shoot (out′ sho͞ot′, out′-) ***vt-*** **[out·shot, out·shoot·ing] 1** to shoot beyond; go beyond. **2** to excel or surpass in shooting: *Dick* outshot *John in the contest.*

out·side (out′ sīd′) ***n-*** outer part or side; exterior: *the* outside *of the building.* ***adv-*** outdoors; in the open air: *He went* outside. ***prep-*** beyond; past the limits of: *His trip took him* outside *the country.* ***adj-*** **1** on, or next to the outside: *an* outside *room.* **2** coming from the outside: *Get* outside *help.* **3** besides a person's regular activities: *Golf is one of my father's* outside *interests.* **4** greatest possible: *The* outside *figure given for the cost of the new school* was *$1,000,000.* **5** remote: *an* outside *chance.*

at the outside at the most: *There were twenty-five people there* at the outside. **outside of** besides; except for: *Who will be there* outside of *our friends?*

out·sid·er (out′ sī′ dər) ***n-*** person who does not belong to a particular group or place.

out·size (out′ sīz′) ***adj-*** exceptionally heavy or large. Also **out′ sized′.**

out·skirts (out′ skûrts′) ***n-*** outer edges; outlying parts: *the* outskirts *of a city.*

out·smart (out′ smärt′, out′-) *Informal* ***vt-*** to outwit.

out·spo·ken (out′ spō′ kən) ***adj-*** **1** frank; free of speech. **2** spoken or uttered boldly, freely, or frankly: *an* outspoken *criticism.* **—*adv-*** **out′ spo′ ken·ly.** ***n-*** **out′ spo′ ken·ness.**

out·spread (out′ sprĕd′) ***adj-*** spread out; stretched out; extended: *The dog lay on the floor with* outspread *paws.*

out·stand·ing (out′ stăn′ dĭng, out′-) ***adj-*** **1** standing out; distinguished; excellent: *an* outstanding *general*;

an outstanding *achievement.* **2** unpaid: *an* outstanding *debt of $2,000.* ***—adv-*** **out′ stand′ ing·ly.**

out·stay (out′ stā′, out′-) ***vt-*** **1** to stay longer than or beyond: *to* outstay *one's welcome.* **2** to outlast.

out·stretched (out′ strĕcht′) ***adj-*** spread or stretched out, especially toward someone.

out·strip (out′ strĭp′) ***vt-*** **[out·stripped, out·strip·ping]** **1** to go faster than; leave behind; outrun. **2** to outdo; surpass.

out·ward (out′ wərd) ***adj-*** **1** toward the outside; outbound: *an* outward *flow of traffic.* **2** of or on the outside; outer; external; not inner or essential: *an* outward *appearance*; outward *cheerfulness*; outward *beauty.* ***adv-*** **1** away from a place, especially a shore: *an* outward *bound ship.* **2** (also **out′ wards**) toward the outside: *This door opens* outward.

out·ward·ly (out′ wərd lē) ***adv-*** on the surface; on the outside; in appearance: *to be* outwardly *calm.*

out·wash plain (out′ wŏsh′, -wŏsh′) ***n-*** in geology, a plain formed by deposits of materials washed out from a melting glacier.

out·wear (out′ wâr′, out′-) ***vt-*** **[out·wore, out·worn, out·wear·ing]** to wear longer than; outlast.

out·weigh (out′ wā′) ***vt-*** **1** to be greater in importance, value, etc., than. **2** to be greater in weight than: *The advantages* outweigh *the disadvantages.*

out·wit (out′ wĭt′) ***vt-*** **[out·wit·ted, out·wit·ting]** to get the better of by being more skillful or clever; fool; outsmart: *Jimmy can always* outwit *me at checkers.*

[1]**out·work** (out′ wûrk′) ***vt-*** to outdo; work better or faster than.

[2]**out·work** (out′ wûrk′) ***n-*** a defense or protection built beyond the main body of a fort.

out·worn (out′ wôrn′) ***adj-*** **1** worn out: *an* outworn *nag.* **2** no longer in use; out-of-date: *an* outworn *custom.*

o·va (ō′ və) *pl.* of **ovum.**

o·val (ō′ vəl) ***adj-*** egg-shaped; also, shaped like an ellipse: *A race track is usually* oval. ***n-*** **1** egg-shaped plane figure. **2** ellipse. **3** stadium in the form of an ellipse. ***—adv-*** **o′ val·ly.**

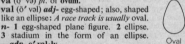

Oval

o·va·ry (ō′ və rē) ***n-*** [*pl.* **o·va·ries**] **1** either of the two organs of the female body in which eggs are formed. **2** the part of a plant in which the seeds are formed.

o·vate (ō′ vāt′) ***adj-*** **1** shaped like an egg. **2** of a leaf, oval.

o·va·tion (ō vā′ shən) ***n-*** **1** very enthusiastic acclaim, usually in the form of hearty and extended applause: *They gave the speaker a standing* ovation. **2** public tribute or welcome for a returning hero.

ov·en (ŭv′ ən) ***n-*** enclosed space for baking, heating, or drying. ***—adj-*** **ov′ en·like′.**

ov·en·bird (ŭv′ ən bûrd′) ***n-*** common American songbird which builds a small, enclosed nest on the ground.

o·ver (ō′ vər) ***prep-*** **1** above in position, authority, dignity, excellence, etc.: *The sky is* over *our heads. A captain is* over *a lieutenant.* **2** from one side to another of; across: *to jump* over *a ditch.* **3** across or along the surface of; upon: *to spill water* over *the floor*; *to drive* over *a new road.* **4** on top of; outside of: *a board* over *a hole*; *a jacket* over *a sweater.* **5** more than: *We spent* over *twenty dollars.* **6** through the period of; during: *to stay* over *the weekend.* **7** on the other side of: *She lives* over *the hill.* **8** throughout: *The news spread* over *the country.* **9** in regard to: *his authority* over *them.* **10** on account of: *to cry* over *a disappointment.* **11** occupied with: *to spend two hours* over *an assignment.* ***adv-*** **1** from a place or person (to another); to a place or person (from another): *to deed property* over *to one's heirs*; *to cross* over *to France*; *to win someone* over; *to go* over *to the enemy.* **2** from beginning to end; through: *to talk the matter* over; *to read it* over. **3** as a remainder: *some sandwiches left* over. **4** so as to bring the under side up: *to turn a coin* over. **5** so as to be no longer upright: *to topple a chair* over. **6** from end to end; throughout: *a landscape dotted* over *with trees.* **7** again; once again: *to do a thing* over. **8** down and outside from the edge, top, or brim: *The water is running* over. **9** at an end: *All is* over. **10** in addition; beyond what was planned: *He stayed five minutes* over.

over again once more: *He played the piece* over again. **over and above** beyond; more than: *We received a second offer* over and above *the original one.* **over and over** again and again: *The boy saw his favorite movie* over and over.

o·ver- *prefix* **1** too; too much; excessively: *an* over*load*; over*tired.* **2** extra; beyond the normal: *an* over*drive*; over*time.* **3** above or across in position, direction, or rank: *an* over*coat*; over*seas.* **4** causing to change to a lower position: *to* over*throw*; over*turn.*

o·ver·a·bun·dant (ō′ vər ə bŭn′ dənt) ***adj-*** too abundant; too profuse or luxuriant; excessive; surplus. ***—n-*** **o′ ver·a·bun′ dance.**

o·ver·act (ōv′ ər ăkt′) ***vi-*** to exaggerate in acting; overplay: *He always* overacts. ***vt-***: *He* overacted *the part.*

o·ver·ac·tive (ōv′ ər ăk′ tĭv) ***adj-*** too active; too lively. ***—adv-*** **o′ ver·ac′ tive·ly.**

[1]**o·ver·age** (ō′ vər āj′) ***adj-*** **1** beyond a specified, usual, or normal age (for doing or being something): *He is* overage *for the little league.* **2** too old to be useful: *some* overage *equipment.* [from **over** plus **age.**]

[2]**o·ver·age** (ō′ vər ĭj) ***n-*** amount in excess of the amount planned or expected. [from **over** plus **-age.**]

o·ver·all (ō′ vər ȯl′) ***adj-*** including everything: *The* overall *cost of our vacation was $300.* ***adv-*** *Informal*: *He was,* overall, *quite pleasant.*

o·ver·alls (ō′ vər ȯlz′) ***n-*** *pl.* loose garment like trousers with an attached chest piece. They are sometimes worn over other clothing to protect it.

Overalls

o·ver·anx·ious (ō′ vər ăngk′ shəs) ***adj-*** **1** too anxious; excessively worried or concerned (about something): *She was* overanxious *about her daughter.* **2** *Informal* over-eager.

o·ver·arch (ō′ vər ärch′) ***vt-*** **1** to form an arch over: *The rainbow* overarched *the mountain.* **2** to cross in an arch: *A bridge* overarched *the river.*

o·ver·awe (ō′ vər ȯ′) ***vt-*** **[o·ver·awed, o·ver·aw·ing]** to inspire (a person) with awe to the point where the person feels subdued or restrained: *The vastness of the cathedral* overawed *the tourists.*

o·ver·bal·ance (ō′ vər băl′ əns) ***vt-*** **[o·ver·bal·anced, o·ver·bal·anc·ing]** **1** to throw off balance. **2** to weigh more than; exceed in importance: *These considerations* overbalance *the others.*

o·ver·bear (ō′ vər bâr′) ***vt-*** **[o·ver·bore, o·ver·borne, o·ver·bear·ing]** to bear down, as by greater physical weight or force; overthrow.

o·ver·bear·ing (ō′ vər bâr′ ĭng) ***adj-*** showing scornful disregard for the rights or feelings of others; self-important; arrogant; dictatorial; insolent. ***—adv-*** **o′ ver·bear′ ing·ly.**

[1]**o·ver·bid** (ō′ vər bĭd′) ***vt-*** **[o·ver·bid, o·ver·bid** or **o·ver·bid·den, o·ver·bid·ding]** **1** to exceed in bidding;

outbid. **2** *to bid beyond the real value of.* ***vi-*** to bid more than the real value. **—*n-* o′ ver·bid′ der.**

[2]**o·ver·bid** (ō′ vər bĭd′) ***n-*** an excessive bid.

o·ver·blown (ō′ vər blōn′) ***adj-*** **1** past blooming: *an* overblown *flower.* **2** exaggerated and bombastic; inflated; pretentious: *an* overblown *piece of oratory.*

o·ver·board (ō′ vər bôrd′) ***adv-*** **1** over the side of a ship or boat and into the water. **2** into the discard: *They threw the plan* overboard.

to go overboard for (or **about**) *Informal* to become wildly enthusiastic about; also, to fall in love with.

o·ver·bold (ō′ vər bōld′) ***adj-*** too bold. **—*adv-* o′ ver·bold′ ly.**

[1]**o·ver·bur·den** (ō′ vər bûr′ dən) ***vt-*** to load with too heavy a weight, such as work, anxiety, etc.: *The President is* overburdened *with responsibilities.*

[2]**o·ver·bur·den** (ō′ vər bûr′ dən) ***n-*** layer of earth and rock lying over a mineral deposit.

o·ver·came (ō′ vər kām′) *p.t.* of **overcome.**

o·ver·cast (ō′ vər kăst′, ō′ vər kăst′) ***adj-*** **1** generally cloudy; clouded over: *an* overcast *sky.* ***n-*** (ō′ vər kăst′ *only*) **1** a cloud cover: *The sun broke through the* overcast. **2** sewing stitch in which the thread passes again and again over the edge of the cloth to prevent raveling. ***vt-*** [**o·ver·cast, o·ver·cast·ing**] **1** to cover over (the sky). **2** to sew (an edge or seam) with long, slanting stitches to prevent raveling.

o·ver·cau·tious (ō′ vər kô′ shəs) ***adj-*** too cautious to be effective.

[1]**o·ver·charge** (ō′ vər chärj′) ***vt-*** [**o·ver·charged, o·ver·charg·ing**] **1** to charge too much: *to* overcharge *a customer*; *to* overcharge *a battery.* **2** to overload; put too great a strain on: *to* overcharge *a gun.*

[2]**o·ver·charge** (ō′ vər chärj′) ***n-*** too great a charge: *an* overcharge *on a dress*; *an* overcharge *on a battery.*

o·ver·cloud (ō′ vər kloud′) ***vt-*** to cover with, or as if with, clouds; darken: *Fog* overclouded *the horizon.*

o·ver·coat (ō′ vər kōt′) ***n-*** man's or boy's outer coat, worn outdoors for warmth.

o·ver·come (ō′ vər kum′) ***vt-*** [**o·ver·came, o·ver·come, o·ver·com·ing**] (in sense 1 considered intransitive when the direct object is implied but not expressed.) **1** to get the better of; conquer: *He* overcame *his fear. We shall* overcome. **2** to render helpless or, especially, unconscious: *The heavy smoke* overcame *two firemen.*

o·ver·con·fi·dent (ō′ vər kŏn′ fĭ dənt) ***adj-*** too confident. **—*n-* o′ ver·con′ fi·dence.**

o·ver·crowd (ō′ vər kroud′) ***vt-*** to fill too full; put too many people or things into: *to* overcrowd *a bus.*

o·ver·de·vel·op (ō′ vər də vĕl′ əp) ***vt-*** to develop too much: *to* overdevelop *a film*; *to* overdevelop *muscles.*

o·ver·do (ō′ vər dōō′) ***vt-*** [**o·ver·did, o·ver·done, o·ver·do·ing**] **1** to carry too far; exaggerate: *You're* overdoing *the story by bringing in so many details.* **2** to cook too long. ***vi-*** to wear oneself out by too much work or activity: *The doctor told him not to* overdo.

[1]**o·ver·dose** (ō′ vər dōs′) ***n-*** too big a dose: *an* overdose *of medicine.*

[2]**o·ver·dose** (ō′ vər dōs′) ***vt-*** [**o·ver·dosed, o·ver·dos·ing**] to give too big or too many doses to.

o·ver·draft (ō′ vər drăft′) ***n-*** **1** a drawing against a bank account by writing a check for a sum greater than the amount on deposit. **2** the amount by which a check exceeds the amount on deposit.

o·ver·draw (ō′ vər drô′) ***vt-*** [**o·ver·drew, o·ver·drawn, o·ver·draw·ing**] **1** to make an overdraft against: *He* overdrew *his account by ten dollars.* **2** to exaggerate: *John greatly* overdrew *the story of the bank robbery.*

o·ver·dress (ō′ vər drĕs′) ***vi-*** to dress in too fancy or showy a manner for the occasion: *She always* overdresses. ***vt-***: *She* overdresses *her children, too.*

o·ver·drive (ō′ vər drīv′) ***n-*** of automobile transmissions, a gear arrangement providing a fourth forward speed.

o·ver·due (ō′ vər dōō′, -dyōō′) ***adj-*** **1** late; not happening at the usual or scheduled time: *The train is 30 minutes* overdue. **2** of a bill, not paid when due.

o·ver·eat (ō′ vər ēt′) ***vi-*** [**o·ver·ate, o·ver·eat·en, o·ver·eat·ing**] to eat too much.

o·ver·em·pha·sis (ō′ vər ĕm′ fə səs) ***n-*** **1** too much emphasis. **2** a placing of too much emphasis (on): *an* overemphasis *on money.*

o·ver·em·pha·size (ō′ vər ĕm′ fə sīz′) ***vt-*** [**o·ver·em·pha·sized, o·ver·em·pha·siz·ing**] to place too much emphasis on.

[1]**o·ver·es·ti·mate** (ō′ vər ĕs′ tə māt′) ***vt-*** [**o·ver·es·ti·mat·ed, o·ver·es·ti·mat·ing**] to estimate at too high a number, force, value, etc.; overvalue: *to* overestimate *one's strength.* **—*n-* o′ ver·es′ ti·ma′ tion.**

[2]**o·ver·es·ti·mate** (ō′ vər ĕs′ tə mət) ***n-*** too high an estimate: *an* overestimate *on building costs.*

o·ver·ex·cite (ō′ vər ĕk sīt′) ***vt-*** [**o·ver·ex·cit·ed, o·ver·ex·cit·ing**] to excite excessively. **—*n-* o′ ver·ex·cite′ ment.**

o·ver·ex·ert (ō′ vər ĕg zûrt′) ***vt-*** to exert (oneself) too much for one's good: *to* overexert *oneself playing tennis.* ***vi-***: *He* overexerted *playing ball.* **—*n-* o′ ver·ex·er′ tion.**

o·ver·ex·pose (ō′ vər ĕk spōz′) ***vt-*** [**o·ver·ex·posed, o·ver·ex·pos·ing**] to expose excessively: *to* overexpose *a film*; *to* overexpose *troops to enemy fire.* **—*n-* o′ ver·ex·po′ sure.**

o·ver·flight (ō′ vər flīt′) ***n-*** a flight over a territory.

[1]**o·ver·flow** (ō′ vər flō′) ***vi-*** [**o·ver·flowed, o·ver·flown, o·ver·flow·ing**] to flow or spread beyond the proper or usual limits: *The sewers* overflowed *after the rainstorm.* ***vt-***: *The river sometimes* overflows *its banks.*

[2]**o·ver·flow** (ō′ vər flō′) ***n-*** **1** a flowing over: *the* overflow *of water at the dam*; *the* overflow *of the audience into the hall.* **2** amount by which something flows over: *The* overflow *of the reservoir is now a million gallons a day.*

o·ver·grow (ō′ vər grō′) ***vt-*** [**o·ver·grew, o·ver·grown, o·ver·grow·ing**] to grow over; spread over with growth: *Every year we kill the weeds that* overgrow *the path.* ***vi-*** to grow too much or too fast.

o·ver·grown (ō′ vər grōn′) ***adj-*** grown beyond normal or usual size: *He acts like an* overgrown *baby.*

o·ver·growth (ō′ vər grōth′) ***n-*** **1** excessive growth: *an* overgrowth *of weeds.* **2** growth on or over something.

o·ver·hand (ō′ vər hănd′) ***n-*** pitch, throw, tennis stroke, etc., with the hand higher than the shoulder and the palm moving or facing downward. ***adj-***: *He pitches with an* overhand *motion.* ***adv-***: *He pitches* overhand.

[1]**o·ver·hang** (ō′ vər hăng′) ***n-*** part, such as the eaves of a house or top of a cliff, that projects above a lower part.

[2]**o·ver·hang** (ō′ vər hăng′) ***vt-*** [**o·ver·hung, o·ver·hang·ing**] **1** to hang, jut, or project over: *Trees* overhang *the brook.* **2** to seem to menace or threaten from above.

Overhang on a house

fāte, făt, dâre, bärn; bē, bĕt, mêre; bīte, bĭt; nōte, hŏt, môre, dóg; fŭn, fûr; tōō, bŏŏk; oil; out; tar; thin; then; hw for wh as in *what*; zh for s as in usual; ə for a, e, i, o, u, as in *ago*, linen, peril, atom, minus

1**o·ver·haul** (ō′ vər hȯl′) ***vt-* 1** to inspect and repair or revise completely: *to* overhaul *a car's engine*; *to* overhaul *the system of taxation.* **2** to catch up with; overtake: *The police car* overhauled *the speeding truck.*

2**o·ver·haul** (ō′ vər hȯl′) ***n-*** thorough examination in order to make repairs, improvements, or changes: *He took his car to the mechanic for a complete* overhaul.

1**o·ver·head** (ō′ vər hĕd′) ***adj-*** located or operating above one's head: *Our room has* overhead *lighting.* ***n-*** general expenses of running a business. Rent, light, heat, etc., are part of overhead.

2**o·ver·head** (ō′ vər hĕd′) ***adv-*** up in the air or sky; above one's head: *Clouds are threatening* overhead.

o·ver·hear (ō′ vər hêr′) ***vt-*** **[o·ver·heard, o·ver·hear·ing]** (considered intransitive when the direct object is implied but not expressed) to hear by accident or by listening to what is said to someone else: *I sometimes* overhear *strange conversations on the bus.*

o·ver·heat (ō′ vər hēt′) ***vt-*** to heat beyond a point of comfort, safety, or efficiency: *The climb up the steep hill* overheated *the car's engine.* ***vi-***: *The engine* overheated.

o·ver·in·dulge (ō′ vər ĭn dŭlj′) ***vi-*** **[o·ver·in·dulged, o·ver·in·dulg·ing]** to eat or drink too much: *I* overindulged *at the party, and I don't feel well.* ***vt-*** to be excessively indulgent toward: *He* overindulges *his son.* **—*n-* o′ ver·in·dul′ gence. *adj-* o′ ver·in·dul′ gent.**

o·ver·joyed (ō′ vər joid′) ***adj-*** filled with joy; made very happy: *Tim was* overjoyed *when he found his lost dog.*

1**o·ver·kill** (ō′ vər kĭl′) ***n-*** ability to inflict greater damage or wider destruction than is necessary to wipe out a military target.

2**o·ver·kill** (ō′ vər kĭl′) ***vt-*** to destroy (a military target) by inflicting greater damage than is necessary.

o·ver·land (ō′ vər lănd′) ***adj-*** across the land, not by sea: *an* overland *route*; *an* overland *trip.* ***adv-***: *The pioneers traveled* overland *in covered wagons.*

1**o·ver·lap** (ō′ vər lăp′) ***vt-*** **[o·ver·lapped, o·ver·lap·ping] 1** to place so as partly to cover (another thing or part): *The carpenter* overlapped *the shingles.* **2** to be partly the same as; partly coincide with: *The treasurer's duties* overlap *those of the secretary. My vacation* overlaps *his.* ***vi-***: *Fish scales* overlap. *Our vacations* overlap.

2**o·ver·lap** (ō′ vər lăp′) ***n-*** an extension of part of one thing over part of another: *The roof shingles have an* overlap *of three inches.*

1**o·ver·lay** (ō′ vər lā′) ***n-* 1** something put or laid on as a covering: *a tissuepaper* overlay *on a drawing.* **2** layer of material, such as fine wood or precious metal, applied to a surface for decoration.

2**o·ver·lay** (ō′ vər lā′) ***vt-*** **[o·ver·laid, o·ver·lay·ing]** to spread or cover with something: *The carpenter will* overlay *the pine table top with a mahogany veneer.*

o·ver·lie (ō′ vər lī′) ***vt-*** **[o·ver·lay, o·ver·lain, o·ver·ly·ing]** to lie over or lie on: *Heavy mist* overlies *the fields.*

o·ver·long (ō′ vər lȯng′) ***adj-*** too long. ***adv-*** for too long a time.

1**o·ver·load** (ō′ vər lōd′) ***n-* 1** too great a load or burden. **2** amount by which a load is too great.

2**o·ver·load** (ō′ vər lōd′) ***vt-* 1** to load or burden too heavily: *to* overload *a car.* **2** to cause to have too much explosive or electric current: *to* overload *a gun*; *to* overload *an electric circuit.*

o·ver·look (ō′ vər lo͝ok′) ***vt-* 1** to fail to see or notice: *to* overlook *a name on a list.* **2** to pass over and excuse; ignore: *I'll* overlook *that mistake if you'll be more careful next time.* **3** to look down on from above; have or give a view over: *The house* overlooks *the harbor.*

o·ver·lord (ō′ vər lôrd′) ***n-*** nobleman ranking above and having power over other lords; hence, supreme ruler.

o·ver·ly (ō′ vər lē) ***adv-*** too; unduly; excessively: *an* overly *sweet pudding*; *an* overly *polite waiter.*

o·ver·mas·ter (ō′ vər măs′ tər) ***vt-*** to overpower; defeat.

o·ver·match (ō′ vər măch′) ***vt-*** to be more than a match for; surpass; outdo: *The visiting team* overmatched *us.*

o·ver·much (ō′ vər mŭch′) ***adv-*** in too great a degree or extent; too much: *He praised her* overmuch. ***adj-*** too great; excessive: *to give* overmuch *praise.*

o·ver·night (ō′ vər nīt′) ***adv-* 1** during the night: *The weather changed* overnight. **2** in a very short time: *Progress is seldom made* overnight. ***adj-* 1** lasting through a night: *an* overnight *trip on the train.* **2** used for or remaining for a night's stay: *an* overnight *bag*; overnight *guests.*

1**o·ver·pass** (ō′ vər păs′) ***n-*** bridge or elevated road over another road, a railway line, etc.

2**o·ver·pass** (ō′ vər păss′) ***vt-*** to pass over.

o·ver·pay (ō′ vər pā′) ***vt-*** **[o·ver·paid, o·ver·pay·ing] 1** to pay (an amount) greater than the required or proper one: *He* overpaid *fifty cents for that cap.* **2** to pay or reward too highly: *to* overpay *an employee.* ***vi-*** to pay too much: *We* overpaid *for dinner.* **—*n-* o′ ver·pay′ ment.**

o·ver·play (ō′ vər plā′) ***vt-* 1** to play (a part) with more feeling and expression than is required; overact; hence, overemphasize. **2** to hit (a golf ball) past the green.

overplay (one's) hand *Informal* to endanger or defeat one's own purposes by being too aggressive.

o·ver·pow·er (ō′ vər pou′ ər) ***vt-* 1** to defeat or subdue with greater force or strength: *The police quickly* overpowered *the thieves.* **2** to affect so strongly as to make helpless: *Grief* overpowered *her.* **3** to provide with too much power: *to* overpower *an aircraft.*

o·ver·price (ō′ vər prīs′) ***vt-*** **[o·ver·priced, o·ver·pric·ing]** to put too high a price on: *to* overprice *a lamp.*

o·ver·pro·duce (ō′ vər prə do͞os′, -dyo͞os′) ***vt-*** **[o·ver·pro·duced, o·ver·pro·duc·ing]** to produce more than can be sold or used profitably.

o·ver·pro·duc·tion (ō′ vər prə dŭk′ shən) ***n-* 1** the producing of more than can be sold or used profitably. **2** the excess or surplus produced.

o·ver·pro·tect (ō′ vər prə tekt′) ***vt-*** to protect or shelter too much, especially from unpleasant things: *That mother* overprotects *her children.* **—*n-* o′ ver·pro·tec′ tion. *adj-* o′ ver·pro·tec′ tive:** *an* overprotective *father.*

o·ver·rate (ō′ vər rāt′) ***vt-*** **[o·ver·rat·ed, o·ver·rat·ing]** to value or estimate too highly: *to* overrate *one's own ability*; *to* overrate *a new movie.*

o·ver·reach (ō′ vər rēch′) ***vt-*** to reach above or beyond. ***vi-*** to reach or go too far.

overreach (oneself) to defeat oneself by reaching too far or attempting too much.

o·ver·ride (ō′ vər rīd′) ***vt-*** **[o·ver·rode, o·ver·rid·den, o·ver·rid·ing] 1** to pass over or set aside, or disregard deliberately: *The committee* overrode *my objections. Congress* overrode *the President's veto.* **2** to be more important or powerful than; prevail over: *The present emergency* overrides *other matters.* **3** to ride over; trample upon. **4** to ride (a horse or other animal) until it is exhausted.

o·ver·rule (ō′ vər ro͞ol′) ***vt-*** **[o·ver·ruled, o·ver·rul·ing] 1** to set aside; declare of no effect: *The superior court* overruled *the judgment of the lower court.* **2** to decide against; veto: *He* overruled *my suggestion.*

1**o·ver·run** (ō′ vər rŭn′) ***vt-*** **[o·ver·ran, o·ver·run, o·ver·run·ning] 1** to spread over or through, often causing harm: *Weeds* overran *the garden. Mice* overran *the attic.* **2** to run or go beyond: *He* overran *first base.* **3** to overwhelm and capture (a military objective).

[2]**o·ver·run** (ō′ vər rŭn′) ***n-*** a running over or beyond what was planned; also, the excess distance, quantity, etc.

o·ver·seas (ō′ vər sēz′) ***adv-*** across or over the sea; abroad: *During the war, many soldiers were sent* overseas. ***adj-*** in a place across the sea; *an* overseas *job*; *the newspaper's* overseas *office*. Also **o′ ver·sea′.**

o·ver·see (ō′ vər sē′) ***vt-*** [**o·ver·saw, o·ver·seen, o·ver·see·ing**] to keep watch over; have charge of; direct; supervise: *to* oversee *work done in a factory.*

o·ver·seer (ō′ vər sêr′) ***n-*** person who has charge of workers and inspects the work they do.

o·ver·shad·ow (ō′ vər shăd′ ō) ***vt-*** **1** to cast a shadow on; darken. **2** to cause to appear less important, as if in a shadow: *His quick temper* overshadowed *his real kindness.* **3** to tower above; be more important than: *His later success* overshadowed *his early failure.*

o·ver·shoe (ō′ vər shōō′) ***n-*** waterproof shoe or boot worn over another shoe to protect against rain, snow, cold, etc.

Overshoe

o·ver·shoot (ō′ vər shōōt′) ***vt-*** [**o·ver·shot, o·ver·shoot·ing**] (considered intransitive when the direct object is implied but not expressed) **1** to shoot over or beyond: *The arrow* overshot *the target.* **2** to go over or beyond: *The plane* overshot *the runway.*

o·ver·shot (ō′ vər shŏt′) ***adj-*** of the upper jaw, protruding over the lower jaw; also, having a protruding upper jaw.

overshot wheel ***n-*** water wheel operated by water flowing over its top.

Overshot wheel

o·ver·sight (ō′ vər sīt′) ***n-*** **1** a slip or mistake caused by carelessness or failure to notice something: *The omission of your name was an* oversight. **2** watchful care; supervision.

o·ver·size (ō′ vər sīz′) ***adj-*** (also **o′ ver·sized′**) larger than is normal or required: *an* oversize *tire.* ***n-*** something of a size larger than normal: *That tire is an* oversize.

o·ver·skirt (ō′ vər skûrt′) ***n-*** skirt worn over and revealing part of another skirt, slacks, or shorts.

o·ver·sleep (ō′ vər slēp′) ***vi-*** [**o·ver·slept, o·ver·sleep·ing**] to sleep longer than intended, or past the usual time for rising: *I* overslept *and was late for school.* ***vt-***: *I* overslept *my first class.*

o·ver·spread (ō′ vər sprĕd′) ***vt-*** [**o·ver·spread, o·ver·spread·ing**] to spread or extend over; cover: *Clouds* overspread *the sky.*

o·ver·state (ō′ vər stāt′) ***vt-*** [**o·ver·stat·ed, o·ver·stat·ing**] to state or express too strongly; exaggerate: *to* overstate *one's case.* **—*n-*** **o′ ver·state′ ment.**

o·ver·stay (ō′ vər stā′) ***vt-*** to stay beyond the time or limits of: *to* overstay *one's welcome.*

o·ver·step (ō′ vər stĕp′) ***vt-*** [**o·ver·stepped, o·ver·step·ping**] to go beyond; exceed: *He* overstepped *his authority.*

[1]**o·ver·stock** (ō′ vər stŏk′) ***vt-*** to provide with too great a supply of merchandise; fill too full: *The grocer* overstocked *his shelves.*

[2]**o·ver·stock** (ō′ vər stŏk′) ***n-*** merchandise in excess of the needed or profitable amount.

o·ver·strung (ō′ vər strŭng′) ***adj-*** strung or stretched too tightly; too tense: *an* overstrung *bow*; overstrung *nerves.*

o·ver·stuff (ō′ vər stŭf′) ***vt-*** to stuff too full.

o·ver·stuffed (ō′ vər stŭft′) ***adj-*** stuffed or padded so as to have a rounded or bulging form: *an* overstuffed *chair.*

o·ver·sub·scribe (ō′ vər səb skrīb′) ***vt-*** [**o·ver·sub·scribed, o·ver·sub·scrib·ing**] to agree to buy in amounts greater than what is offered for sale.

[1]**o·ver·sup·ply** (ō′ vər sə plī′) ***vt-*** [**o·ver·sup·plied, o·ver·sup·ply·ing**] to provide with too great a supply.

[2]**o·ver·sup·ply** (ō′ vər sə plī′) ***n-*** too great a supply.

o·vert (ō vûrt′) ***adj-*** not secret or hidden; openly done or shown: *an* overt *act of war.* **—*adv-*** **o·vert′ ly.**

o·ver·take (ō′ vər tāk′) ***vt-*** [**o·ver·took, o·ver·tak·en, o·ver·tak·ing**] **1** to catch up with; also, to come up to from behind and pass: *With the good lead he has, it will be hard to* overtake *him.* **2** to come upon unexpectedly or inconveniently: *The storm* overtook *the picnickers.*

o·ver·tax (ō′ vər tăks′) ***vt-*** **1** to tax too heavily. **2** to put too great a burden on: *Too much exercise without rest can* overtax *the heart.* **—*n-*** **o′ ver·tax·a′ tion.**

[1]**o·ver·throw** (ō′ vər thrō′) ***vt-*** [**o·ver·threw, o·ver·thrown, o·ver·throw·ing**] **1** to cause to fall or fail; bring down: *The dictator* overthrew *the elected government.* **2** to throw over; overturn: *He stumbled and* overthrew *the chair.* **3** to throw something beyond: *The shortstop* overthrew *first base.*

[2]**o·ver·throw** (ō′ vər thrō′) ***n-*** **1** a bringing down; ruin; defeat: *The revolution ended in the* overthrow *of the dictator.* **2** in sports, a throw beyond where it is aimed.

o·ver·time (ō′ vər tīm′) ***n-*** time worked in addition to regular hours: *He gets paid extra for* overtime. ***adj-***: *to receive* overtime *pay.* ***adv-***: *He worked* overtime.

o·ver·tone (ō′ vər tōn′) ***n-*** **1** *Music* any of various tones that sound along with, but are fainter and higher than, a given basic tone; harmonic. **2** suggestion or hint: *His speech had* overtones *of sarcasm.*

o·ver·top (ō′ vər tŏp′) ***vt-*** [**o·ver·topped, o·ver·top·ping**] **1** to be higher than; rise or tower above: *Huge oaks* overtopped *the surrounding bushes.* **2** to go beyond; excel; surpass: *He* overtopped *his past record.*

o·ver·ture (ō′ vər chər) ***n-*** **1** musical composition for orchestra, played as an introduction to an opera or other large work; also, a concert piece similar to this in style and length. **2** preliminary offer or proposal.

o·ver·turn (ō′ vər tûrn′) ***vt-*** **1** to turn over; upset: *Rough water rocked the canoe but didn't* overturn *it.* **2** to bring to ruin; overthrow: *The rebels* overturned *the government.* ***vi-***: *The car* overturned *after skidding.*

[1]**o·ver·use** (ō′ vər yōōs′) ***n-*** too much use: *His sneakers wore out through* overuse.

[2]**o·ver·use** (ō′ vər yōōz′) ***vt-*** [**o·ver·used, o·ver·us·ing**] to use to excess: *to* overuse *a slang term.*

o·ver·view (ō′ vər vyōō′) ***n-*** broad view; survey.

o·ver·ween·ing (ō′ vər wē′ nĭng) ***adj-*** arrogant and presumptuous: *an* overweening *pride.*

o·ver·weigh (ō′ vər wā′) ***vt-*** **1** to be greater in weight or value than; overbalance; outweigh. **2** to weigh too heavily on; overpower; oppress: *He was* overweighed *by debts.*

[1]**o·ver·weight** (ō′ vər wāt′) ***n-*** weight above a desirable, usual, or permitted amount: *a diet to reduce* overweight; *an* overweight *of luggage.* ***adj-*** (also ō′ vər wāt′) weighing more than is normal: *an* overweight *bulldog.*

[2]**o·ver·weight** (ō′ vər wāt′) ***vt-*** to weigh down; overburden; overload: *to* overweight *a truck.*

o·ver·whelm (ō′ vər hwĕlm′) ***vt-*** **1** to flood or sweep over and make helpless: *A high wave* overwhelmed *the boat. Grief* overwhelmed *her.* **2** to disconcert; embarrass temporarily: *Your kindness* overwhelms *me.* **—*adv-*** **o′ ver·whelm′ ing·ly.**

o·ver·work (ō′ vər wûrk′) ***vt-*** **1** to cause to work too hard; demand too much work from: *The foreman* overworked *his men.* **2** to use (an idea, phrase, joke, etc.) so much that it becomes tiresome. ***vi-*** to work harder or longer than is good for one: *He has* overworked *for months.* ***n-***: *He is sick from* overwork.

o·ver·wrought (ō′ vər ròt′) ***adj-*** **1** too excited; very nervous and tense: *an* overwrought *spectator.* **2** too elaborate: *an* overwrought *style*; overwrought *designs.*

ovi- *combining form* egg: *an* ovi*duct*; ovi*form.* Also **ovo-** [from Latin **ov-**, from **ovum** meaning "egg."]

o·vi·duct (ō′ və dŭkt′) ***n-*** tube in a female animal through which eggs travel from an ovary to the outside of the body, or to an organ having a connection with the outside of the body.

o·vi·form (ō′ və fòrm′, -fôrm′) ***adj-*** shaped like an egg.

o·vip·a·rous (ō vĭp′ ər əs) ***adj-*** producing offspring from eggs that hatch outside the body. Birds and most fish are oviparous. See also *ovoviviparous, viviparous.*

o·vi·pos·i·tor (ō′ və pŏz′ ə tər) ***n-*** organ in the female of certain insects, such as the cricket and the grasshopper, for depositing eggs outside the body. It is located at the extreme end of the abdomen.

o·void (ō′ void′) ***adj-*** having the shape of an egg; egg-shaped. ***n-*** anything shaped like an egg.

o·vo·vi·vip·a·rous (ō′ vō vī′ vĭp′ ər əs) ***adj-*** bringing forth living offspring that develop in eggs or egglike sacs within but not attached to the mother. Certain fishes and snakes, such as the guppy and the copperhead, are ovoviviparous. See also *oviparous, viviparous.*

o·vu·lar (ō′ vyə lər) ***adj-*** of, relating to, or like an ovule.

o·vu·late (ō′ vyə lāt′, *also* ŏv′ yə-) ***vi-*** **[o·vu·lat·ed, o·vu·lat·ing]** to produce eggs or ovules, or to discharge them from an ovary. **—*n-* o′ vu·la′ tion.**

o·vule (ō′ vyōōl′) ***n-*** **1** small part within the ovary of a plant, which develops into a seed when fertilized. **2** small egg, especially one in an early stage of development.

o·vum (ō′ vəm) ***n-*** [*pl.* **o·va** (ō′ və)] female germ cell; egg cell.

owe (ō) ***vt-*** **[owed, ow·ing] 1** to be under obligation to pay or give: *He* owes *two dollars to his brother. We* owe *loyalty to our country. I* owe *you an apology.* **2** to be indebted for: *He* owes *his life to the fireman who saved him.* ***vi-*** to be in debt: *She still* owes *for the groceries.* ***Homs-*** [1]O, oh.

ow·ing (ō′ ĭng) ***adj-*** not paid; due: *bills that are* owing.

owing to because of; as a result of: *The crops are poor,* owing to *the drought.*

►See usage note at DUE TO.

owl (oul) ***n-*** any of a group of birds of prey with flat faces, large eyes, and a short, hooked beak. Owls have a hooting call and a noiseless flight. They usually hunt at night.

owl·et (ou′ lət) ***n-*** young owl.

owl·ish (ou′ lĭsh) ***adj-*** having the appearance or characteristics of an owl; especially, solemn and seemingly wise: *an* owlish *look.*

Horned owl, 18-25 in. long

own (ōn) ***adj-*** (always preceded by a possessive adjective) **1** of or belonging particularly to someone or something: *I have my* own *bicycle. This room is his* own. **2** (intensifier only): *She is my* own *sister. I cooked my* own *dinner.* ***vt-*** **1** to possess; have ownership of: *We used to rent this house but now* own *it.* **2** to admit; acknowledge: *I* own *that I was at fault.*

come into (one's) own to obtain the success or recognition that one deserves. **hold (one's) own** to survive or defend oneself with one's own resources. **of (one's) own 1** belonging to oneself alone: *He has a room* of his own. **2** of that or those belonging to one: *She needed a dress and I gave her one* of my own. **on (one's) own** responsible for one's own work, support, actions, etc. **own up** to admit one's guilt, error, etc.; confess: *He* owned up *to his part in the scheme.*

own·er (ō′ nər) ***n-*** person who owns something; proprietor. **—*adj-* own′ er·less.**

own·er·ship (ō′ nər shĭp′) ***n-*** condition of being an owner; right of possession: *The* ownership *of land carries responsibilities. A deed indicates* ownership *of property.*

ox (ŏks) ***n-*** [*pl.* **ox·en** (ŏk′ sən)] **1** full-grown male of domestic cattle, especially one that has been castrated and trained for hauling, farm work, etc. **2** any of various animals related to domestic cattle, especially the buffaloes and bisons.

ox·al·ic acid (ŏk săl′ ĭk) ***n-*** colorless, poisonous organic acid found in some plants and produced synthetically. It is used in dyeing and bleaching.

ox·a·lis (ŏk săl′ əs) ***n-*** any of several plants with small white, rose-colored, or yellow flowers, and leaves divided into three parts; wood sorrel.

ox·blood (ŏks′ blŭd′) ***n-*** a deep, brownish-red color. ***adj-***: *an* oxblood *vase.*

ox·bow (ŏks′ bō′) ***n-*** **1** U-shaped wooden collar placed under and around the neck of one of a team of oxen. Two oxbows and a crosspiece form a yoke. **2** U-shaped bend in a river.

ox·cart (ŏks′ kärt′) ***n-*** cart drawn by oxen.

ox·eye daisy (ŏk′ sī′) See *daisy.*

ox·ford (ŏks′ fərd) ***n-*** **1** low shoe that laces over the instep. **2** (also **oxford cloth**) cotton fabric with a plain weave, used chiefly for making men's shirts. *as **modifier***: *an* oxford *shirt.*

oxford gray ***n-*** a very dark gray.

ox·i·da·tion (ŏk′ sə dā′ shən) ***n-*** a combining with oxygen, as in all combustion.

ox·ide (ŏk′ sīd′) ***n-*** a compound of oxygen and, usually, one other element.

ox·i·dize (ŏk′ sə dīz′) ***vi-*** **[ox·i·dized, ox·i·diz·ing]** to combine with oxygen; change into oxide: *Iron* oxidizes *quickly in damp weather.* ***vt-*** to cause to combine with oxygen; convert into an oxide.

ox·i·diz·er (ŏk′ sə dī′ zər) *Space* ***n-*** a liquid or solid that chemically combines with fuel to produce the gases that propel a rocket. An oxidizer does not necessarily contain oxygen.

oxidizing agent ***n-*** the atom or ion that takes up electrons during a chemical reaction.

Ox·o·ni·an (ŏk sō′ nē ən) ***adj-*** of or having to do with Oxford University or the town of Oxford, England. ***n-*** student or graduate of Oxford University.

oxy- *combining form* oxygen; containing or combined with oxygen: *an* oxy*acetylene torch*; oxy*hemoglobin.* [from **oxygen.**].

ox·y·a·cet·y·lene torch (ŏk′ sē ə sĕt′ ə lēn) ***n-*** blowtorch using a mixture of oxygen and acetylene to produce a very hot flame. It is used in cutting and welding metals.

ox·y·gen (ŏk′ sə jən) ***n-*** colorless, gaseous element that makes up one-fifth of the atmosphere. Free oxygen is absorbed in respiration, and is essential to almost all living organisms. Symbol O, At. No. 8, At. Wt. 15.9994.

ox·y·gen·ate (ŏk′ sə jə nāt′) ***vt-*** **[ox·y·gen·at·ed, ox·y·gen·at·ing]** to combine or treat with oxygen. **—*n-* ox′ y·gen·a′ tion.**

oxygen mask ***n-*** device that is connected to a supply of pure oxygen and fits closely over the mouth and nose.

oxygen tent ***n-*** tentlike or boxlike enclosure connected to a steady supply of oxygen. It is placed over the head and shoulders of patients who need help in breathing.

ox·y·hem·o·glo·bin (ŏk'sĭ hē'mə glō'bən, -hĕm'ə glō'bən) ***n-*** scarlet compound of oxygen and hemoglobin formed in the red blood cells when the blood passes through the lungs.

o·yez (ō'yā', -yĕz') ***interj-*** cry mean ing "hear ye," usually called thre times to demand attention in a cour room. Also **o'yes'**.

oy·ster (ois'tər) ***n-*** shellfish with a rough, hinged, double shell, found in shallow sea water and valued as food. Some kinds produce pearls. ***—adj-*** **oy'ster·like'**.

Oyster

oyster bed ***n-*** place where oysters breed or are raised.

oyster cracker ***n-*** small, round or six-sided, salted cracker eaten with oysters, soups, etc.

oy·ster·man (ois'tər mən) ***n-*** [*pl.* **oy·ster·men**] person who gathers, raises, or sells oysters.

oyster plant ***n-*** salsify.

oz. ounce or ounces.

o·zone (ō'zōn') ***n-*** the form of oxygen that is a bluish, pungent gas (O_3), each of whose molecules contains three atoms of oxygen. It is a powerful oxidizing agent, and is used as a bleach and disinfectant.

o·zon·o·sphere (ō zō'nə sfêr') ***n-*** region of the stratosphere containing a concentration of ozone that absorbs much of the sun's intense ultraviolet radiation, thereby shielding the earth.

P

P, p (pē) ***n-*** [*pl.* **P's, p's**] the sixteenth letter of the English alphabet.

p. 1 page. 2 participle. 3 [1]piano.

P 1 *Music* [2]piano (softly). 2 (also **p.**) baseball pitcher.

P symbol for phosphorus.

pa (pä, pȯ) *Informal* ***n-*** father.

Pa symbol for protactinium.

PA public-address system.

Pa. Pennsylvania.

pace (pās) ***n-*** **1** a single step: *Walk ten* paces *to the north.* **2** length of a single step, especially when established as a unit of measurement. **3** speed in walking, running, working, etc.; rate of progress.: *He kept a steady* pace. **4** way of walking or running; especially, a horse's gait in which the legs on the same side are lifted and put down together. ***vt-*** [**paced, pac·ing**] **1** to walk back and forth over in anxiety, anger, etc.: *The expectant father* paced *the floor.* **2** to match (a runner) step for step, usually to train him. **3** to cause to act in a desired rhythm. ***vi-*** **1** to walk with long, even steps. **2** of a horse, to move at a gait called a pace.

keep pace with to run or go as fast as; keep up with: *He tried to* keep pace with *us.* **put (someone) through his paces** to have someone demonstrate special skills or accomplishments: *The coach* put the rookie through her paces. **set the pace** (1) to set a speed for others to keep up with. (2) to be an example or model for others to follow: *The forewoman's work* set the pace *for us.*

pace off to measure by even steps: *to* pace off *50 feet.*

pace·mak·er (pās'mā'kər) ***n-*** **1** one who sets the pace in a race or other competition. **2** electrical mechanism implanted in the body to restore the normal rhythm of the heartbeat.

pac·er (pā'sər) ***n-*** one who paces; especially, a horse whose gait is a pace.

pach·y·derm (păk'ĭ dûrm') ***n-*** one of a group of thick-skinned animals, such as the elephant, rhinoceros, or hippopotamus.

pa·cif·ic (pə sĭf'ĭk) ***adj-*** **1** not quarrelsome; peaceable: *the* pacific *words at an international conference*; *a* pacific *people who are not inclined to make war.* **2** calm; tranquil: *rowing on* pacific *waters.* ***—adv-*** **pa·cif'i·cal·ly.**

Pa·cif·ic (pə sĭf'ĭk) ***adj-*** of or pertaining to the Pacific Ocean. ***n-*** the Pacific Ocean.

pac·i·fi·ca·tion (păs'ĭ fə kā'shən) ***n-*** a pacifying or being pacified.

Pacific Standard Time See *standard time.*

pac·i·fi·er (păs'ə fī'ər) ***n-*** **1** person or thing that pacifies. **2** rubber nipple or similar object for a baby to suck on.

pac·i·fism (păs'ə fĭz'əm) ***n-*** principle of opposing war; belief that peaceful methods should be used to settle differences. ***—n-*** **pac'i·fist.**

pac·i·fy (păs'ə fī') ***vt-*** [**pac·i·fied, pac·i·fy·ing**] **1** to calm; quiet; soothe: *to* pacify *a baby.* **2** to bring peace to; end strife between or among: *to* pacify *warring nations.* **3** to subdue (a people) by force or diplomacy. ***—adj-*** **pac'i·fi'a·ble.**

[1]pack (păk) ***n-*** **1** bundle of things tied or wrapped together for carrying, especially on the back of a person or animal. **2** set or number of things arranged or packaged together: *a* pack *of cards.* **3** group, especially of animals, that stays or hunts together: *a* pack *of wolves*; *a* pack *of thieves.* **4** large quantity; mass: *a* pack *of floating ice*; *a* pack *of lies.* **5** method of packaging, canning, etc.: *a loose* pack; *a dry* pack. **6** something applied to or pressed against a part of the body to improve or relieve a troublesome condition. ***vt-*** **1** to place or stow into a bag, box, or other container for storage, travel, etc.: *to* pack *clothes.* **2** to fill (a container or space) entirely: *He* packed *his suitcase. People* packed *the theater.* **3** to press or crowd into a compact mass: *to* pack *earth into a flowerpot*; *to* pack *travelers into a bus.* **4** to fill (a joint, crack, etc.) tightly so as to prevent leaking. **5** *Informal* to carry with or on one: *to* pack *a canteen*; *to* pack *one's lunch on a hike.* **6** *Informal* to be able to give or deliver: *He* packs *a hard punch.* ***vi-*** **1** to put articles into a container or containers for traveling, storage, etc.: *We* packed *last night and are ready to go.* **2** to form or be pressed into a compact mass: *Wet snow* packs *well.* **3** to withstand being pressed or stowed into something: *Ripe fruit doesn't* pack *well.* [from Middle English **pakke,** probably from earlier Dutch **pak.**]

send packing to send away quickly and abruptly.

pack off **1** to send away. **2** to go away hastily.

[2]pack (păk) ***vt-*** to arrange or influence unfairly to suit one's own ends: *to* pack *a jury.* [probably from [1]**pack.**]

pack·age (păk'ĭj) ***n-*** parcel or container of goods: *to mail books in a* package; *to buy a* package *of peanuts.* ***vt-*** [**pack·aged, pack·ag·ing**] to enclose in containers for sale, shipping, or distribution. ***—n-*** **pack'ag·er.**

---

fāte, făt, dâre, bärn; bē, bĕt, mêre; bīte, bĭt; nōte, hŏt, môre, dȯg; fŭn, fûr; to͞o, bo͝ok; oil; out; tar; thin; then; hw for wh as in *wh*at; zh for s as in u*s*ual; ə for a, e, i, o, u, as in *a*go, lin*e*n, per*i*l, at*o*m, min*u*s

package deal *n-* offer or arrangement to sell a number of things as a single unit or as part of a single transaction.
package store *n-* a store that sells alcoholic beverages only in bottles to be taken away from the premises.
pack·ag·ing (păk′ əj ĭng) *n-* **1** process or method of putting goods in containers sold as single units. **2** art of designing and using such containers.
pack animal *n-* any animal that carries goods upon its back, such as a mule, horse, or camel.
pack·er (păk′ ər) *n-* **1** person or machine that packs articles or goods into bags or other containers: *He works as a* packer *at the warehouse. She is a very tidy* packer. **2** person or company whose business is preparing and packaging food: *a meat* packer.
pack·et (păk′ ət) *n-* **1** small bundle or package: *a* packet *of seeds; a* packet *of tea.* **2** a small ship that sails regularly on a fixed route, carrying passengers, mail, and merchandise.
pack·ing (păk′ ĭng) *n-* **1** the work or business of preparing and packaging food for shipment to wholesalers. **2** soft material used to insulate articles from breakage in shipping containers, to fill cracks and joints in pipes, to stop bleeding in a wound, etc.
packing house or **packing plant** *n-* factory where meats, fruits, or vegetables are prepared and packed for shipment to wholesalers.
pack rat *n-* North American rat that collects small articles and places them in its nest; wood rat.
pack·sack (păk′ săk′) *n-* traveling bag of sturdy cloth or other material, usually carried strapped across the back.
pack·sad·dle (păk′ săd′ əl) *n-* saddle shaped for carrying loads and worn by a pack animal.
pack·thread (păk′ thrĕd′) *n-* strong thread or twine used for tying up bundles.
pack train *n-* caravan of pack animals carrying loads.
pact (păkt) *n-* any agreement between people or countries: *a* pact *of friendship; a peace* pact.
[1]**pad** (păd) *n-* **1** cushion or layer of soft resilient material. **2** quantity of writing or drawing paper held together by a strip glued or attached along one edge. **3** ink-soaked cushion used with a marking stamp. **4** the floating leaf of certain water plants, such as the water lily. **5** fleshy cushion on the foot of certain animals, such as the cat or dog. **6** launching pad. *vt-* **[pad·ded, pad·ding] 1** to fill, line, or protect with a cushion or padding. **2** to add padding or additional material to, especially to make seem larger or more impressive: *He* padded *himself to play Santa Claus. He* padded *his story with unnecessary details.* [probably of Germanic origin.]
[2]**pad** (păd) *vi-* **[pad·ded, pad·ding]** to walk softly or stealthily: *She* padded *about her room barefooted.* [probably from Dutch **padder,** "wanderer," and **pad,** "path."]
pad·ding (păd′ ĭng) *n-* **1** material used to fill or form a pad: *The catcher's mitt has thick* padding. **2** words, details, etc., of no value, used to fill up space.
[1]**pad·dle** (păd′ əl) *n-* **1** short oar having a broad blade at one or both ends and used to propel a canoe. **2** implement with a short handle and a broad surface, used to strike the ball in ping-pong and similar games. **3** broad-bladed tool used to stir or mix. **4** one of the wide boards of a paddle wheel or water wheel. *vt-* **[pad·dled, pad·dling] 1** to propel (a boat) with a paddle. **2** to strike or spank with or as if with a paddle. *vi-*: *It's hard to* paddle *against the current.* [of uncertain origin.] *—adj-* **pad′ dle·like′.** *n-* **pad′ dler.**

BLADE
Paddle

[2]**pad·dle** (păd′ əl) *vi-* **[pad·dled, pad·dling] 1** to splash in shallow water: *Children were* paddling *in the mud puddles.* **2** to swim slowly and awkwardly, as some animals do. [probably from earlier German **paddeln** and related to [2]**pad.**]
pad·dle·fish (păd′ əl fĭsh′) *n-* [*pl.* **pad·dle·fish; pad·dle·fish·es** (kinds of paddlefish)] large scaleless fish with a snout shaped like a paddle, found in the Mississippi River and nearby waters.
paddle wheel *n-* a wheel set with projecting paddles, used to propel early steamboats, especially river boats. *as* ***modifier*** **(paddle-wheel):** *a* paddle-wheel *steamer.*
pad·dock (păd′ ək) *n-* **1** small enclosed field used for exercising horses or as a pasture. **2** enclosure at a race track, used to display or saddle horses about to be raced.
pad·dy (păd′ ē) *n-* [*pl.* **pad·dies**] **1** rice in the husk, either growing or gathered. **2** rice field.
pad·lock (păd′ lŏk′) *n-* lock having a curved, movable bar that can be passed through an opening, such as one of the links in a chain or the hasp of a gate, and snapped shut. *vt-*: *to* padlock *a gate.*
pa·dre (pä′ drā′) *n-* **1** father; the Italian, Spanish, and Portuguese title for a priest. **2** a chaplain in the armed forces.

Padlock

pae·an (pē′ ən) *n-* joyful song of praise. ***Hom-*** peon.
pa·gan (pā′ gən) *n-* **1** person who is not a Christian, Jew, or Muslim. The word has been applied to the ancient Romans, Greeks, etc. **2** person who rejects religion. ***adj-***: *ancient* pagan *beliefs;* pagan *customs.*
pa·gan·ism (pā′ gə nĭz′ əm) *n-* **1** condition of being a pagan. **2** beliefs, practices, or customs of pagans.
[1]**page** (pāj) *n-* **1** either side of a leaf of a book, or the written or printed matter on it: *There is a map on* page *72. Read that* page *aloud.* **2** event or period worthy of noting or recording: *an interesting* page *in history.* *vt-* **[paged, pag·ing]** to arrange or number in pages. [from Old French **page,** from Latin **pāgina** meaning "writing; leaf (of a book)."]
[2]**page** (pāj) *n-* **1** in medieval times, a boy in training to become a knight, or serving as an attendant to a person of high rank. **2** person employed to carry messages or do errands in a hotel, large organization, legislative body, etc. *vt-* **[paged, pag·ing]** to call for (a person) by sending a messenger or by announcement over a public address system. [from Old French, from Medieval Latin **pagius** meaning "servant."]
pag·eant (păj′ ənt) *n-* colorful play, procession, or similar display to celebrate a legend or historical event.
pag·eant·ry (păj′ ən trē) *n-* [*pl.* **pag·eant·ries**] **1** brilliant show or display; pomp. **2** pageants collectively. **3** art of creating and staging pageants.
pag·i·na·tion (păj′ ə nā′ shən) *n-* the numbering or arrangement of the pages in a book, manuscript, etc.
pa·go·da (pə gō′ də) *n-* in some Asian countries, a temple or memorial building, often richly decorated, having several stories, each with an overhanging projection.
paid (pād) *p.t. & p.p.* of **pay.**
pail (pāl) *n-* **1** open container with a handle over the top, used for holding or carrying liquids; bucket. **2** pailful. ***Hom-*** pale.
pail·ful (pāl′ fo͝ol′) *n-* amount held by a pail.
pain (pān) *n-* **1** severe soreness or distress of body; ache: *a sharp* pain *in the knee.* **2** distress of mind; sorrow: *to suffer the* pain *of defeat.* *vt-* **1** to

Pagoda

cause bodily soreness to; hurt: *The cut on her arm* pained *her.* **2** to make unhappy or annoyed. ***Hom-*** pane.

on (or **under**) **pain of** at the risk, threat, or penalty of.

take pains be very careful and diligent.

pain·ful (pān′ fəl) ***adj-*** **1** full of or causing a sharp ache or pain: *Bee stings can be very* painful. **2** distressing; unpleasant: *a* painful *duty*; *a* painful *task.* **—*adv-*** **pain′ ful·ly.** ***n-*** **pain′ ful·ness.**

pain·less (pān′ ləs) ***adj-*** without pain; causing no pain: *The* painless *removal of a splinter.* **—*adv-*** **pain′ less·ly.** ***n-*** **pain′ less·ness.**

pains·tak·ing (pānz′ tā′ kĭng) ***adj-*** involving or showing great care and attention to detail: *Embroidery requires* painstaking *skill.* **—*adv-*** **pains′ tak′ ing·ly.**

paint (pānt) ***n-*** **1** coloring matter made of pigment mixed with a liquid such as oil or water. **2** a cosmetic used to add color. *as* ***modifier***: *a* paint *box.* ***vt-*** **1** to coat or cover with paint, medicine, lotion, etc.: *to* paint *a wall*; *to* paint *a cut with iodine.* **2** to use paint to make a picture of: *He* painted *a portrait.* **3** to describe or tell vividly: *He* painted *an exciting story of his travels.* ***vi-*** **1** to practice the art of making pictures with color; be a painter. **2** to use cosmetics on one's face.

paint·brush (pānt′ brŭsh′) ***n-*** a brush for applying paint.

[1]**paint·er** (pān′ tər) ***n-*** **1** person who paints houses, furniture, etc., for a living. **2** person, especially an artist, who paints pictures: *a portrait* painter. [from **paint.**]

[2]**paint·er** (pān′ tər) ***n-*** rope used to tie the front of a boat to something. [from Old French **pentour** meaning "any hanging rope," from Latin **pendere** meaning "to hang."]

[3]**pain·ter** (pān′ tər) *Archaic* ***n-*** puma; cougar. [from an early frontier pronunciation of "panther."]

paint·ing (pān′ tĭng) ***n-*** **1** a picture made with paint: *an oil* painting. **2** the art or work of a painter.

pair (pâr) ***n-*** **1** two things of a kind made to be used together or like each other in some way: *a* pair *of shoes*; *a* pair *of oars*; *a* pair *of pistols.* **2** a single thing composed of two similar parts: *a* pair *of pants*; *a* pair *of scissors.* **3** two individuals working or living together, or usually seen in close association; couple: *a married* pair; *a* pair *of work horses*; *an odd-looking* pair. **4** two legislators of different parties whose votes on a given motion would cancel each other, and who agree that neither will vote. ***vt-*** to join or match in combinations of two: *to* pair *socks before putting them away.* ***vi-***: *Senator Lee and Senator Cohen* paired. ***Homs-*** pare, pear.

pair off to come together as a pair or in pairs.

►Either PAIR or PAIRS may be used as a plural after a cardinal number: *I bought two* pair (or pairs) *of stockings.* PAIRS is the proper plural in all other contexts: *One of the* pairs (of stockings) *is torn. One of this* pair *is defective.* (that is, one stocking of a single pair).

pais·ley (pāz′ lē) ***adj-*** having or consisting of a design with curved, swirling lines and forms, usually of many colors: *a* paisley *shawl.*

Paisley design

Pai·ute (pī′ o͞ot′) ***n-*** [*pl.* **Pai·utes,** also **Pai·ute**] one of a tribe of American Indians of Utah, Arizona, Nevada, and California. ***adj-***: *a* Paiute *hut.*

pa·ja·mas (pə jä′ məz, pə jăm′-) ***n-*** (takes plural verb) garment used for sleeping or informal wear at home, usually consisting of a loose jacket and pants. Also **pyjamas.** *as* ***modifier*** **(pajama):** *a* pajama *top.*

pal (păl) *Informal* ***n-*** close friend; chum. ***vi-*** **[palled, pal·ling]** to have a friendly companionship.

pal·ace (păl′ əs) ***n-*** **1** official home of a ruler or, in some countries, of a bishop. **2** large, splendid house or other building. *as* ***modifier***: *the* palace *wall.*

pal·a·din (păl′ ə dən) ***n-*** any of the knights of Charlemagne; hence, any champion of a cause.

pal·an·quin (păl′ ən kēn′) ***n-*** in the Orient, a covered litter for one person, carried on men's shoulders.

pal·at·a·ble (păl′ ət ə bəl) ***adj-*** **1** having a pleasant taste; enjoyable to eat. **2** agreeable; pleasant to the feelings. **—*n-*** **pal′ at·a·bil′ i·ty.** ***adv-*** **pal′ at·a·bly.**

pal·ate (păl′ ət) ***n-*** **1** the roof of the mouth. The bony front part is the hard palate, and the fleshy back part is the soft palate. **2** sense of taste: *These grapes please my* palate. ***Homs-*** palette, pallet.

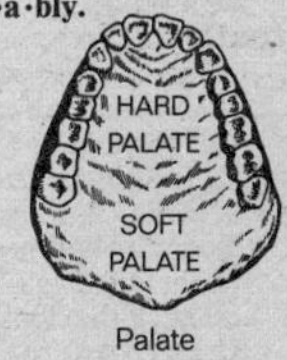

Palate

pa·la·tial (pə lā′ shəl) ***adj-*** of, resembling, or characteristic of a palace; magnificent: *a* palatial *hotel.* **—*adv-*** **pa·la′ tial·ly.**

pal·a·tine (păl′ ə tīn′) ***n-*** in former times, a count, earl, or other nobleman who was given royal privileges within his own domain.

pa·lav·er (pə lăv′ ər) ***n-*** **1** conference or parley, originally between people of primitive culture and Europeans. **2** idle talk. ***vi-*** to talk idly, especially at great length.

[1]**pale** (pāl) ***adj-*** **[pal·er, pal·est] 1** lacking normal color; wan: *Sick people often have* pale *faces.* **2** light in color: *a* pale *pink.* **3** not bright; dim; faint: *the* pale *light of the new moon.* ***vi-*** **[paled, pal·ing]** to lose normal color; turn white: *She* paled *when she heard the bad news.* ***vt-*** to cause to lose color. [from Old French, from Latin **pallidus,** and related to **pallid.**] ***Hom-*** pail. **—*adv-*** **pale′ ly.** ***n-*** **pale′ ness.**

[2]**pale** (pāl) ***n-*** **1** pointed stake or picket in a fence. **2** fence or boundary; limits; bounds: *His acts placed him beyond the* pale *of decent society.* ***vt-*** **[paled, pal·ing]** to enclose or fence with pointed stakes or pickets. [from Old French **pal,** from Latin **palus,** "stake."] ***Hom-*** pail.

Pales

pale·face (pāl′ fās′) ***n-*** light-skinned person; name supposedly given to those of European ancestry by North American Indians.

Pa·le·o·cene (pā′ lē ə sēn′) ***n-*** the earliest of the five epochs of the Tertiary period of geologic time. ***adj-***: *the* Paleocene *epoch.*

Pa·le·o·lith·ic (pā′ lē ə lĭth′ ĭk) ***adj-*** in anthropology, of or relating to a period of early human culture in which chipped or flaked stone tools were made.

pa·le·on·tol·o·gist (pā′ lē ən tŏl′ ə jĭst′) ***n-*** person who is expert in, and usually occupied in, paleontology.

pa·le·on·tol·o·gy (pā′ lē ən tŏl′ ə jē) ***n-*** science dealing with fossils and prehistoric forms of life.

Pa·le·o·zo·ic (pā′ lē ə zō′ ĭk) ***n-*** era of geologic time from about 500 million to about 200 million years ago, during which much land was covered by seas, and life first came onto land. ***adj-***: *the* Paleozoic *era.*

pal·ette (păl′ ət) ***n-*** **1** thin board, usually with a hole at one end for the thumb, and on which a painter mixes colors. **2** mixture and arrangement of colors typical of a certain artist. ***Homs-*** palate, pallet.

pal·frey (pôl′ frē) *Archaic* ***n-*** [*pl.* **pal·freys**] a saddle horse, especially one for a lady.

pal·ing (pā'lĭng) *n-* 1 fence made of narrow, usually pointed, boards or stakes. 2 wood or stake for making such a fence.

pal·i·sade (păl'ə sād') *n-* 1 protective fence of closely set, pointed stakes driven firmly into the ground. 2 **palisades,** line of steep cliffs resembling such a fence, usually along a river. *vt-* [**pal·i·sad·ed, pal·i·sad·ing**] to enclose or fortify with stakes.

Frontier palisade

[1]**pall** (pȯl) *vi-* to become dull or tiresome: *Talk* palled *as we ran out of subjects.* [shortened from **appall.**] ***Homs-*** Paul, pawl.
pall on to have a tiresome effect on.

[2]**pall** (pȯl) *n-* 1 heavy covering of velvet or other cloth, over a coffin. 2 something that covers or overspreads with gloom or darkness: *A* pall *of smoke settled over the city.* [from Old English **pael** from Latin **pallium** meaning "covering cloth; cloak."] ***Homs-*** Paul, pawl.

pal·la·dium (pə lā'dē əm) *n-* silver-white metal element of the platinum group, used in chemical research as a catalyst and in alloys with gold and other precious metals. Symbol Pd, At. No. 46, At. Wt. 106.4.

Pal·las (păl'əs) *n-* in Greek mythology, the goddess of wisdom; Athena. Also **Pallas Athena.** ***Homs-*** palace.

pall·bear·er (pȯl'bâr'ər) *n-* one of the people who help to carry the coffin at a funeral.

pal·let (păl'ət) *n-* small bed or mattress, usually of straw. ***Homs-*** palate, palette.

pal·li·ate (păl'ē āt') *vt-* [**pal·li·at·ed, pal·li·at·ing**] 1 to cause to appear less wrong; excuse: *to* palliate *a fault or a crime.* 2 to ease without curing: *to* palliate *a disease.* **—*n-* pal'li·a'tion.**

pal·li·a·tive (păl'ē ə tĭv') *adj-* serving to palliate: *a* palliative *drug.* *n-*: *This medicine is a* palliative.

pal·lid (păl'ĭd) *adj-* lacking in color; pale: *a* pallid *complexion.*

pal·lor (păl'ər) *n-* lack of color; paleness: *His face had a sickly* pallor.

[1]**palm** (päm, pälm) *n-* the inside of the hand from the wrist to the base of the fingers. *vt-* to hold or conceal in this part of the hand: *The magician* palmed *the coin.* [from Old French **palme,** from Latin **palma,** "palm of hand."]
grease the palm of to bribe.
palm off to get rid of by trickery: *to* palm off *a fake.*

[2]**palm** (päm, pälm) *n-* 1 any of a large group of trees that grow in or near the tropics. Palms usually have an undivided trunk topped with large fan-shaped or plume-shaped leaves. 2 leaf or branches of this tree as a symbol of victory; hence, any prize or honor. [from Old English, from Latin **palma.** It was supposed that the leaf resembled a hand.]
bear (or **carry**) **off the palm** to be the winner.

Date palms

pal·mate (pä'māt', päl'-, păl'-) *adj-* 1 shaped like a hand with fingers spread: *the* palmate *antlers of the moose.* 2 having several leaflets radiating to form a single point: *a* palmate *leaf.*

palm·er (pä'mər, päl'-) *n-* in medieval times, a pilgrim to the Holy Land who brought back a palm branch as a token or sign of the pilgrimage.

pal·met·to (păl mĕt'ō, päl-) *n-* [*pl.* **pal·met·tos** or **pal·met·toes**] any of several kinds of palm trees with fan-shaped leaves, some of which grow in southern United States and the West Indies.

palm·is·try (pä'mĭs'trē, päl'-) *n-* art of supposedly reading character or foretelling the future from the lines and marks of a person's hand. **—*n-* palm'ist.**

palm oil *n-* fatty, buttery substance obtained from the fruits of certain palm trees and used in making soaps, candles, margarine, etc.

Palm Sunday *n-* the Sunday before Easter, commemorating Christ's triumphal entry into Jerusalem, when branches of palm were strewn before him.

palm·y (pä'mē, päl'-) *adj-* [**palm·i·er, palm·i·est**] 1 full of palm trees. 2 prosperous; flourishing: *the* palmy *days of his youth.*

pal·o·min·o (păl'ə mē'nō) *n-* [*pl.* **pal·o·min·os**] tan or cream-colored horse with a white mane and tail, bred chiefly in southwestern United States. [from American Spanish meaning "like a dove; dove-colored," from **paloma,** "dove."]

pal·pa·ble (păl'pə bəl) *adj-* 1 such as can be touched or felt. 2 easily seen; plain; obvious: *a* palpable *error.* **—*n-* pal'pa·bil'i·ty.** ***adv-*** **pal'pa·bly.**

pal·pate (păl'pāt') *vt-* [**pal·pat·ed, pal·pat·ing**] to examine by touch, especially for medical diagnosis. **—*n-* pal'pa'tion.**

pal·pi·tate (păl'pə tāt') *vt-* [**pal·pi·tat·ed, pal·pi·tat·ing**] to beat or throb rapidly; flutter; tremble: *The boy's heart* palpitated *with terror.* **—*n-* pal'pi·ta'tion.**

pal·pus (păl'pəs) *n-* [*pl.* **pal·pi** (păl'pī')] one of the jointed feelers attached to the mouth parts of insects, crustaceans, etc. Also **palp.**

pal·sied (pȯl'zēd') *adj-* affected by palsy; trembling.

pal·sy (pȯl'zē) *n-* [*pl.* **pal·sies**] abnormal condition in which there is a loss of ability to control the movement of part of the body, characterized by paralysis or uncontrollable trembling.

pal·ter (pȯl'tər) *vi-* 1 to deal carelessly or slightingly; trifle: *to* palter *with the truth.* 2 to act deceitfully, especially in bargaining or arguing.

pal·try (pȯl'trē) *adj-* [**pal·tri·er, pal·tri·est**] almost worthless; trifling; petty: *Two dollars is a* paltry *donation for a millionaire to make.* **—*n-* pal'tri·ness.**

pam·pa (păm'pə) *n-* (often **pampas**) vast, grassy, treeless plains of South America.

pam·per (păm'pər) *vt-* to give way to the wishes or desires of; humor; indulge: *to* pamper *a sick child.* **—*n-* pam'per·er.**

pam·phlet (păm'flət) *n-* small book with comparatively few pages and a paper cover.

pam·phlet·eer (păm'flə têr') *n-* writer of pamphlets, especially on controversial subjects.

[1]**pan** (păn) *n-* 1 broad, usually shallow container of metal or glass, used for cooking, baking, and other household uses. 2 any similar container, such as either of the dishes for holding things weighed on scales, or the shallow receptacle for washing out gold from dirt or gravel. *vt-* [**panned, pan·ning**] 1 to cook in a frying pan: *to* pan *fish.* 2 to wash (gravel or dirt) in a vessel to separate out the gold. 3 *Informal* to criticize severely: *The critics* panned *the new play.* [from Old English **panne,** from Medieval Latin **panna.**]
pan out to turn out; result: *The venture* panned out *well.*

Pans

[2]**pan** (păn) *vt-* [**panned, pan·ning**] to move (a motion picture or television camera) from one side to another,

especially to photograph an entire scene. ***vi-*** to use a camera in this way. [shortened from **panorama.**]

Pan (păn) ***n-*** in Greek mythology, a god of forests, flocks, and shepherds, having the legs, hoofs, and horns of a goat. He is identified with the Roman Faunus.

pan- *combining form* **1** all; every; completely: *a* pan*chromatic film* (a film that shows all colors). **2** (usually **Pan-**) including all; applying to all (of a certain group or locality): *a* Pan-*American concern.* [from Greek **pan-**, from **pān** meaning "all."]

pan·a·ce·a (păn′ ə sē′ ə) ***n-*** a remedy for all ills.

pan·a·ma (păn′ ə mä′) ***n-*** lightweight straw hat woven from the leaves of a tree that grows in Middle and South America. Also **Pan′ a·ma′.**

Pan-A·mer·i·can (păn′ ə mĕr′ ĭ kən) ***adj-*** of or relating to the countries of North, Middle, and South America. Also **Pan American.**

Pan-A·mer·i·can·ism (păn′ ə mĕr′ ĭ kə nĭz′ əm) ***n-*** a movement for closer political and economic cooperation among the countries of North, Middle, and South America.

pan·cake (păn′ kāk′) ***n-*** thin cake made of batter and fried in a pan or on a griddle.

pan·chro·mat·ic (păn′ krə măt′ ĭk) ***adj-*** of photographic film, sensitive to light of all colors.

pan·cre·as (păn′ krē əs) ***n-*** large gland near the stomach that secretes a mixture of digestive juices **(pancreatic juice)** through a duct into the small intestine, and insulin into the blood. ***—adj-*** **pan′ cre·at′ ic** (-ăt′ ĭk).

pan·da (păn′ də) ***n-*** either of two Asian animals that feed chiefly on bamboo; the **giant panda** of western China, that resembles a white bear with black markings on the ears, legs, and eyes; and the **lesser panda** of southern China and nearby regions, that looks something like a raccoon with a reddish-brown coat.

Giant panda, about 6 ft. long

pan·de·mo·ni·um (păn′ də mō′ nē əm) ***n-*** **1** place of lawless confusion and disorder. **2** complete confusion; wild uproar: *There was* pandemonium *when we won.*

pan·der (păn′ dər) ***vi-*** to help satisfy the unworthy desires or prejudices of others: *Some writers* pander *to vulgar tastes.* ***n-*** (also **pan′ der·er**) person who helps satisfy the unworthy desires of others; especially, a go-between in an illicit love affair.

pane (pān) ***n-*** piece of thin, flat glass in a window or door. ***Hom-*** pain.

pan·e·gyr·ic (păn′ ə jĭr′ ĭk, -jī′ rĭk) ***n-*** **1** praise formally written or spoken in honor of a person or event. **2** any high praise.

pan·el (păn′ əl) ***n-*** **1** part of a wall, ceiling, or door framed by the surrounding parts or a border. **2** part of a painting or the board on which it is made. **3** group of speakers in an organized discussion: *a* panel *of experts.* **4** list of persons called to serve on a jury. ***vt-*** to furnish or decorate with panels: *to* panel *a room in mahogany.*

panel discussion ***n-*** discussion or debate given by several persons, each of whom contributes his ideas on a given subject.

pan·el·ing (păn′ əl ĭng) ***n-*** set of panels.

pan·el·ist (păn′ ə lĭst) ***n-*** person who takes part in a panel discussion.

pang (păng) ***n-*** **1** sudden, sharp pain: *the* pangs *of hunger.* **2** sudden, strong emotion: *a* pang *of sorrow.*

pan·go·lin (păng gō′ lən) ***n-*** heavily armored ant-eating mammal of Asia, the Malay Archipelago, and Africa.

pan·han·dle (păn′ hăn′ dəl) ***n-*** **1** the handle of a pan. **2** piece of land shaped like this. ***vi-*** *Informal* **[pan·han·dled, pan·han·dling]** to approach a person and beg; ask for a handout of money. ***—n-*** **pan′ han′ dler.**

pan·ic (păn′ ĭk) ***n-*** fear so great as to cause loss of self-control: *The sound of shooting put the crowd into a* panic. ***vi-*** **[pan·icked, pan·ick·ing]** to have such a fear: *The crowd* panicked. ***vt-***: *The shooting* panicked *the crowd.* ***—adj-*** **pan′ ick·y:** *a* panicky *mob.*

pan·i·cle (păn′ ĭ kəl) ***n-*** loose flower cluster with irregularly branching flower stalks.

pan·ic-strick·en (păn′ ĭk strĭk′ ən) ***adj-*** frightened out of one's wits; filled with panic.

pan·nier or **pan·ier** (păn′ yər, -ē ər) ***n-*** **1** basket, especially one of two baskets hung across the back of an animal for carrying market produce. **2** framework of whalebone or steel wire, formerly used to fill out a skirt at the hips.

Panniers

pan·ni·kin (păn′ ĭ kən) ***n-*** small metal pan or cup.

pan·o·ply (păn′ ə plē′) ***n-*** [*pl.* **pan·o·plies**] **1** complete suit of armor. **2** any complete covering, especially for ceremony. ***—adj-*** **pan′ o·plied:** *a* panoplied *knight.*

pan·o·ram·a (păn′ ə răm′ ə, -rä′ mə) ***n-*** **1** wide picture or view of a scene or subject: *the* panorama *of a city as seen from a tall building.* **2** broad view or account of a subject showing its various stages: *a* panorama *of aviation.* ***—adj-*** **pan·o·ram′ ic:** *a* panoramic *view.*

pan·pipe (păn′ pīp′) ***n-*** simple wind instrument made up of hollow reeds of graduated lengths, bound together and played by blowing across the upper edges.

pan·sy (păn′ zē) ***n-*** [*pl.* **pan·sies**] **1** plant of the violet family that bears flowers with large velvety petals of many colors. **2** the flower of this plant.

Pansies

pant (pănt) ***vi-*** to breathe quickly and hard: *The dog* panted *after his long chase.* ***vt-*** to speak in short gasps: *The scout* panted *an urgent message as he rode in.* ***n-*** short, quick gasp.

pan·ta·lets or **pan·ta·lettes** (păn′ tə lĕts′) ***n-*** *pl.* long, frilled drawers, extending below the knees, formerly worn by women and girls.

pan·ta·loon (păn′ tə lo͞on′) ***n-*** **1** clown or foolish character in pantomime. **2 pantaloons** trousers.

pan·the·ism (păn′ thē ĭz′ əm) ***n-*** doctrine that God and universal nature are one, and that God is in everything. ***—n-*** **pan′ the·ist.** ***adj-*** **pan′ the·is′ tic.** ***adv-*** **pan′ the·is′ ti·cal·ly.**

pan·the·on (păn′ thē ŏn′) ***n-*** **1** the gods of a people taken as a whole: *the Greek* pantheon. **2** temple dedicated to all the gods. **3** building where the famous dead of a nation are entombed.

pan·ther (păn′ thər) ***n-*** loosely, any of various large members of the cat family, especially the black leopard or the mountain lion.

pant·ie (păn′ tē) ***n-*** (usually **pant·ies**) short undergarment with an opening for each leg, worn by girls and women. ***as modifier:*** *a* pantie *girdle.* Also **pant′ y.**

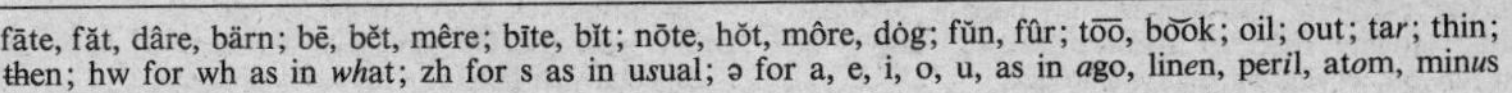

fāte, făt, dâre, bärn; bē, bĕt, mêre; bīte, bĭt; nōte, hŏt, môre, dȯg; fŭn, fûr; to͞o, bo͝ok; oil; out; tar; thin; then; hw for wh as in *wh*at; zh for s as in u*s*ual; ə for a, e, i, o, u, as in *a*go, lin*e*n, per*i*l, at*o*m, min*u*s

pan·to·mime (păn′ tə mīm′) ***n*- 1** actions, gestures, and facial expressions that show meaning without words: *We acted out the story in* pantomime. **2** play acted out without any talking. **—*n*- pan′ to·mim′ ist.**

pan·to·the·nic acid (păn′ tə thē′ nĭk) ***n*-** vitamin of the B-complex, necessary for many metabolic processes. Lack of this vitamin causes disturbances of the nervous system, fatigue, etc.

pan·try (păn′ trē) ***n*-** [*pl.* **pan·tries**] room or closet where food, dishes, etc., are stored.

pants (pănts) ***n*-** (takes plural verb) **1** trousers. **2** panties.

pap (păp) ***n*- 1** soft food for infants. **2** *Slang* fees or favors from official patronage. **3** *Slang* worthless, insipid, and insubstantial matter: *comic books and other* pap.

pa·pa (pä′ pə, *also Brit.*, pə·pä′) ***n*-** father (used chiefly when referring to or addressing one's own father).

pa·pa·cy (pā′ pə sē) ***n*-** [*pl.* **pa·pa·cies**] **1** office, authority, or dignity of the Pope. **2** all the popes since Peter. **3** Roman Catholic system of church government.

pa·pal (pā′ pəl) ***adj*-** of or having to do with the popes or the papacy: *the* papal *crown.*

pa·paw (pȯ′ pȯ′, pə pȯ′) pawpaw.

pa·pa·ya (pə pī′ ə) ***n*- 1** yellow fruit of a tropical American evergreen tree. **2** the tree itself. *as* ***modifier***: *a can of* papaya *juice.* [American word from Spanish **papaya** meaning "fruit," from **papayo,** "tree."]

Papayas

pa·per (pā′ pər) ***n*- 1** material made from wood pulp, rags, straw, etc., usually in the form of a thin sheet: *wrapping* paper. **2** sheet of this material: *Write your address on this* paper. **3** newspaper. **4** written assignment; essay or report: *My history* paper *is due tomorrow.* **5** (usually **papers**) written matter; document: *legal* papers; *official* papers. **6 papers** record that gives information about the person carrying it; identification. **7** small package made of paper: *a* paper *of pins. as* ***modifier***: *a* paper *lantern.* ***vt*-** to cover with wallpaper: *He is* papering *the dining room.* **—*adj*- pa′ per·y**: *a* papery *texture.*

on paper in writing; in a written form: *Let's have that contract* on paper.

pa·per·back (pā′ pər băk′) ***n*-** book having a paper binding, and usually sold more cheaply than the same book bound in leather, cardboard, etc. *as* ***modifier***: *a* paperback *volume.*

paper boy ***n*-** boy who delivers or sells newspapers.

pa·per·hang·er (pā′ pər hăng′ ər) ***n*-** person whose job is to put up wallpaper.

paper knife ***n*-** knife to open envelopes or uncut pages.

paper money ***n*-** notes issued by a government, a bank, etc., and used as currency.

paper profits ***n*-** in finance, a profit that would be realized if a stock were sold.

pa·per·weight (pā′ pər wāt′) ***n*-** any heavy thing, often ornamental, used to hold down loose papers.

paper work ***n*-** work involving the handling of forms, filing, attending to correspondence, etc.

pa·pier-mâché (pā′ pər mə shā′) ***n*-** hard, strong material made of paper pulp mixed with glue, rosin, or other substances, and molded into various shapes. *as* ***modifier***: *a* papier-mâché *mask.*

pa·pil·la (pə pĭl′ ə) ***n*-** [*pl.* **pa·pil·lae** (-ē′)] a minute projection, such as those found on the tongue. **—*adj*- pa′ pil·la′ ry** (păp′ ə lĕr′ ē).

pa·pist (pā′ pĭst) ***n*-** follower of the papacy; Roman Catholic (chiefly used to show disfavor). ***adj*-**: *the* papist *faction*; *having* papist *sympathies.*

pa·poose or **pap·poose** (pă po͞os′) ***n*-** North American Indian baby. [American word from the Algonquian name for "child."]

pap·py (păp′ ē) *Informal* ***n*-** [*pl.* **pap·pies**] daddy; father.

pa·pri·ka (pă prē′ kə, păp′ rə kə) ***n*-** mild, red seasoning made from the pods of various sweet pepper plants.

pa·py·rus (pə pī′ rəs) ***n*-** [*pl.* **pa·py·ri** (-rī′)] **1** reedlike plant from which the ancient Egyptians made a kind of paper. **2** paper made of this or a manuscript written on it.

par (pär) ***n*- 1** normal, usual, or average condition: *With his injured knee, Joe's running is not up to* par. **2** in golf, a standard number of strokes set for a course or hole. **3** in finance, the face value of stocks or bonds when issued, as distinct from the market or actual value.

on a par of equal value.

¹para- *prefix* **1** beside; near; alongside of: *the* para*thyroid glands.* **2** similar to; closely related to: para*typhoid.* [from Greek **para-,** from **para** meaning "beside; alongside of."]

Parabola

²para- *combining form* parachute: *a* para*trooper.* [from **parachute.**]

par·a·ble (păr′ ə bəl) ***n*-** short, simple story that teaches a moral.

pa·rab·o·la (pə răb′ ə lə) ***n*-** set of points, each of which is equally distant from a given fixed point and also from a given fixed line. The curve described by a bullet is a parabola.

par·a·chute (păr′ ə sho͞ot′) ***n*-** umbrella-shaped device made to assure a gentle descent to a person or thing suspended from it, when dropped from a great height. ***vi*-** [**par·a·chut·ed, par·a·chut·ing**] to descend in a parachute: *The troops* parachuted *into the jungle.* ***vt*-**: *They* parachuted *supplies to the besieged outpost.* **—*n*- par′ a·chut′ ist.**

Par·a·clete, the (păr′ ə klēt′) ***n*-** the Holy Spirit as the comforter.

Parachute

pa·rade (pə rād′) ***n*- 1** formal march or procession for display: *a circus* parade; *a military* parade. **2** *Informal* procession of many strollers: *the Easter* parade. **3** group composing such processions. **4** place where soldiers drill or people walk for pleasure: *The mall became a* parade *on Sunday afternoons.* **5** a formal military review or inspection: *evening* parade. **6** vulgar display or showing off: *a* parade *of wealth. as* ***modifier***: *a* parade *uniform.* ***vi*-** [**pa·rad·ed, pa·rad·ing**] to take part in a formal march. ***vt*-** to show off: *Jim liked to* parade *his swimming skill.* **—*n*- pa·rad′ er.**

par·a·digm (păr′ ə dĭm′, pĕr′-) ***n*-** example or model; especially, in grammar, an ordered list of the various forms in the declension or conjugation of a word.

par·a·dise (păr′ ə dīs′, pĕr′-) ***n*- 1** heaven. **2** place or condition of beauty or happiness: *Hawaii has been called an island* paradise. **3 Paradise** the Garden of Eden.

par·a·dox (păr′ ə dŏks′, pĕr′-) ***n*- 1** statement that seems to contradict itself but expresses an element of truth: *"Make haste slowly" is a* paradox. **2** person or thing which seems to show contradictions: *It is a* paradox *that the germ which causes a disease may be used to prevent it.*

par·a·dox·i·cal (păr′ ə dŏk′ sĭ kəl) ***adj*-** seemingly contradictory, but possibly true. **—*adv*- par′ a·dox′ i·cal·ly.**

par·af·fin (păr′ ə fĭn) ***n*-** white or colorless waxy substance made from petroleum and used to make candles, seal preserves, coat wax paper, etc.

par·a·gon (păr′ ə gŏn′, pĕr′-) ***n*-** model of excellence; especially, a person with few weaknesses.

par·a·graph (păr′ ə grăf′, pĕr′-) ***n-*** **1** small section of a piece of writing, usually made up of a number of sentences on one idea or topic. **2** mark (¶) used to indicate where such a section begins. **3** short article or item in a newspaper or magazine. ***vt-*** to divide into paragraphs: *to* paragraph *a speech.*

par·a·keet or **par·ra·keet** (păr′ ə kēt′) ***n-*** small colorful parrot, usually slender-bodied and long-tailed.

Shell parakeet, about 7 1/2 in. long

par·al·lax (păr′ ə lăks′, pĕr′-) ***n-*** the apparent shift in the position of an object when it is viewed from different angles. The parallax of a star viewed from opposite points of the earth's orbit is used to calculate the distance of the star from the earth.

par·al·lel (păr′ ə lĕl, pĕr′-) ***adj-*** **1** everywhere the same distance apart: *Rails of a railroad track are* parallel. **2** similar; alike: *You and I have had* parallel *experiences.* **3** *Mathematics* of or having to do with lines or planes that remain the same distance apart no matter how far extended, and therefore have no common points. **4** in electricity, of or having to do with a type of circuit in which one conductor connects all the positive terminals or electrodes, and another conductor connects the negative ones. ***n-*** **1** similarity throughout; comparison: *a* parallel *in experiences.* **2** (also **parallel of latitude**) any of the east-west lines on a map or globe that mark degrees of latitude: *Philadelphia is on the 40° North* parallel. ***vt-*** **1** to run alongside of and equally distant from: *The road* parallels *the river.* **2** to be similar to: *Your experience* parallels *mine.*

Three sets of parallel lines

par·al·lel·e·pip·ed (păr′ ə lĕl′ ə pī′ pəd, pĕr′-) ***n-*** a six-sided prism with each side a parallelogram.

par·al·lel·ism (păr′ ə lĕl′ĭz′əm, -ləl ĭz′əm, pĕr′-) ***n-*** **1** condition of being parallel. **2** close likeness or similarity in cause and effect, procedure, or development; correspondence. **3** *Grammar* similarity in structure of two or more word groups in a larger expression.

par·al·lel·o·gram (păr′ ə lĕl′ ə grăm′, pĕr′-) ***n-*** a four-sided plane figure whose opposite sides are parallel. For picture, see *polygon.*

pa·ral·y·sis (pə răl′ ə səs) ***n-*** [*pl.* **pa·ral·y·ses** (-sēz′)] **1** loss of ability to move or feel in a part of the body. **2** disease causing such paralysis: *infantile* paralysis. **3** a halting of movement or operation; a standstill.

par·a·lyt·ic (păr′ ə lĭt′ĭk, pĕr′-) ***adj-*** of or relating to paralysis: *a* paralytic *disease.* ***n-*** paralyzed person.

par·a·lyze (păr′ ə līz′, pĕr′-) ***vt-*** [**par·a·lyzed, par·a·lyz·ing**] **1** to cause to lose the ability to move or feel, especially below the waist: *Polio may* paralyze *those who get it.* **2** to stop movement in or of; make unable to do anything: *A flood can* paralyze *transportation.*

par·a·me·ci·um (păr′ ə mē′ sē əm) ***n-*** [*pl.* **par·a·me·ci·a** (-sē, ə, -shē ə)] microscopic one-celled protozoan shaped like a slipper and covered with cilia with which it swims, blunt end forward.

par·a·med·ic (păr′ ə mĕd′ĭk) ***n-*** person who assists a physician or gives emergency medical treatment.

par·a·mount (păr′ ə mount′) ***adj-*** above all others; supreme: *The family was her* paramount *concern.*

par·a·noi·a (păr′ ə noi′ ə, pĕr′-) ***n-*** **1** mental disorder in which a person has delusions of persecution or grandeur. **3** tendency to distrust others without real cause.

par·a·pet (păr′ ə pət, -pĕt′) ***n-*** **1** low wall around a roof or terrace or along a stairway or bridge to keep people from falling off. **2** protective wall on a fortification.

par·a·pher·na·li·a (păr′ə fə năl′ yə, pĕr′-) ***n-*** (takes plural verb) assorted pieces of equipment.

par·a·phrase (păr′ ə frāz′, pĕr′-) ***vt-*** [**par·a·phrased, par·a·phras·ing**] to express the meaning (of a writing or speech) in one's own words. ***n-***: *a* paraphrase *of a poem.*

par·a·ple·gic (păr′ ə plē′ jĭk, pĕr′-) ***n-*** person who is paralyzed below the waist.

par·a·pro·fes·sion·al (păr′ə prə fĕsh′ən əl) ***n-*** a trained aide who works with and helps a professional person. ***adj-***: *a* paraprofessional *occupation.*

par·a·site (păr′ ə sīt′, pĕr′-) ***n-*** **1** plant or animal that lives in or on another of a different species and gains nourishment from it. See also *epiphyte.* **2** person who associates with another to gain some advantage for himself or herself.

par·a·sit·ic (păr′ ə sĭt′ĭk, pĕr′-) ***adj-*** of or having to do with a parasite. **—*adv-*** **par′a·sit′i·cal·ly.**

par·a·sol (păr′ ə sȯl′, pĕr′-) ***n-*** small, light umbrella used for protection against the sun.

par·a·thy·roid glands (păr′ ə thī′ roid′, pĕr′-) ***n-*** either of usually two pairs of small endocrine glands located on or within the thyroid gland. They produce a hormone that regulates the level of calcium in the blood.

par·a·troop·er (păr′ ə tro͞o′pər, pĕr′-) ***n-*** soldier trained to land from the air by parachute.

par·a·troops (păr′ ə tro͞ops′, pĕr′-) ***n-*** *pl.* soldiers trained to parachute from airplanes.

par·a·ty·phoid (păr′ ə tī′ foid′, pĕr′-) ***adj-*** of or having to do with paratyphoid fever. ***n-*** paratyphoid fever.

paratyphoid fever ***n-*** an infectious disease similar to typhoid but less severe, caused by a related bacterium.

par·boil (pär′boil′) ***vt-*** to cook partially by boiling.

par·cel (pär′ səl) ***n-*** **1** package; bundle. **2** group of persons or things of one kind: *a* parcel *of thieves*; *a* parcel *of lies.* **3** piece or section: *a* parcel *of land.* ***vt-*** to divide and distribute (often followed by "out"): *They* parceled *out the food.*

parcel post ***n-*** division of the postal service that carries packages. ***adv-***: *We sent it* parcel post. ***adj-***: *a* parcel post *package.*

parch (pärch) ***vt-*** **1** to dry up: *The desert sun* parched *his throat.* **2** to roast slightly by heating: *to* parch *corn over a fire.* ***vi-***: *The land* parched *under the hot sun.*

parch·ment (pärch′ mənt) ***n-*** **1** writing material prepared from the skin of sheep or goats. **2** manuscript written on this material. **3** heavy paper resembling this material *as modifier*: *a* parchment *scroll.*

par·don (pär′ dən) ***vt-*** **1** to release from penalty: *to* pardon *an offender.* **2** to forgive: *to* pardon *an offense.* **3** to overlook; excuse: *Please* pardon *my mistake.* ***n-*** **1** forgiveness. **2** release from punishment. **3** polite indulgence: *I beg your* pardon. **—*adj-*** **par′don·a·ble:** *a* pardonable *offense.* ***adv-*** **par′don·a·bly.** ***n-*** **par′do·ner.**

pare (pâr) *vt-* [**pared, par·ing**] 1 to cut off the skin or outer part of; peel with a knife: *to* pare *an apple.* 2 to take off (an outer part) by cutting: *to* pare *rind from a melon.* 3 to reduce; cut down: *We must* pare *our expenses until we pay off our debt.* ***Homs-*** pair, pear.

par·e·gor·ic (păr′ ə gôr′ ĭk, -gŏr′ ĭk) ***n-*** a tincture of opium used to ease pain and diarrhea.

pa·ren·chy·ma (pə rĕng′ kə mə) ***n-*** 1 in animals, the functional cells of an organ, as distinguished from the supporting connective tissue. 2 in plants, the commonest simple tissue, making up fruits and flowers and the unspecialized parts of stems and roots.

par·ent (păr′ ənt, pâr′-) ***n-*** 1 father or mother; also, a man or woman who adopts a child or otherwise serves as father or mother. 2 anything regarded as the immediate ancestor of something else. *as* ***modifier***: *a* parent *group*; *a* parent *tree*; *a* parent *organization.*

par·ent·age (pâr′ ən tĭj) ***n-*** birth; family; origin: *of humble* parentage.

pa·ren·tal (pə rĕn′ təl) ***adj-*** of a father or mother; relating to a parent or parents: *an example of* parental *love*; parental *control.* ***—adv-*** **pa·ren′ tal·ly.**

pa·ren·the·sis (pə rĕn′ thə səs) ***n-*** [*pl.* **pa·ren·the·ses** (-sēz′)] 1 explanatory word, phrase, or clause put in a sentence that is grammatically complete without it. 2 **parentheses** the two curved punctuation marks [( )] used to set off such explanatory material.

par·en·thet·ic (păr′ ən thĕt′ ĭk, pĕr′-) ***adj-*** 1 parenthetical: *a* parenthetic *discussion*; *a* parenthetic *remark.* 2 enclosed in parentheses.

par·en·thet·i·cal (păr′ ən thĕt′ ĭk əl, pĕr′-) ***adj-*** as an aside from the main discussion: *a* parenthetical *explanation.* ***—adv-*** **par′ en·thet′ i·cal·ly.**

par·ent·hood (păr′ ənt hŏŏd′, pâr′-) ***n-*** condition of being a parent; motherhood or fatherhood.

Parent-Teacher Association ***n-*** any one of many local, voluntary, community groups belonging to the **National Congress of Parents and Teachers,** a national association of public school teachers and parents of school-age children. *Abbr.* PTA or P.T.A.

pa·re·sis (pə rē′ səs, păr′ ə səs) ***n-*** 1 partial paralysis. 2 an often fatal brain disease caused by syphilis.

par ex·cel·lence (pär′ ĕk′ sə läⁿs′) *French* in the highest degree; preeminently: *scientist* par excellence.

par·fait (pär′ fā′) ***n-*** 1 dessert served cold and made of syrup, fruit, whipped cream, and ice cream in layers. 2 frozen custard made with whipped cream and syrup.

pa·ri·ah (pə rī′ ə) ***n-*** 1 member of one of the lowest castes in southern India. 2 person shunned by others; outcast.

par·ing (pâr′ ĭng) ***n-*** something that has been pared off: *an apple* paring; *a* paring *of cheese.*

Par·is (păr′ əs) ***n-*** in Greek mythology, the son of Priam and Hecuba. He carried Helen off to Troy, thereby causing the Trojan War.

Paris green ***n-*** an emerald-green poisonous powder that is a compound of copper, arsenic, oxygen, and hydrogen. It is used as an insecticide.

par·ish (păr′ ĭsh) ***n-*** 1 church district having its own church and clergyman. 2 the people or members of such a district: *The* parish *voted to enlarge the church.* 3 in Louisiana, a political division corresponding to a county in other States.

pa·rish·ion·er (pə rĭsh′ ən ər) ***n-*** member of a parish.

par·i·ty (păr′ ə tē) ***n-*** [*pl.* **par·i·ties**] 1 equivalence or equality in rank, value, etc. 2 the price or prices a farmer should receive for his products in order to have the same purchasing power as in a chosen earlier period.

park (pärk) ***n-*** 1 area set aside for public recreation. 2 extensive grounds surrounding a big country house. ***vt-*** 1 to place (an auto or other vehicle) in a definite spot outside the stream of traffic: *to* park *a truck.* 2 *Informal* to put or set; place: *He* parked *his coat on a chair.* ***vi-***: *He* parked *near a fire hydrant.*

par·ka (pär′ kə) ***n-*** short coat with a hood.

park·way (pärk′ wā′) ***n-*** wide, landscaped drive or road, often with a center strip of grass or trees.

par·lance (pär′ ləns) ***n-*** way of speaking; kind of talk; language: *legal* parlance; *in the* parlance *of the trade.*

par·lay (pär′ lā′) ***n-*** kind of bet in which an original wager and its winnings are placed on another contest. ***vt-*** 1 to place such a bet. 2 *Informal* to use shrewdly and profitably: *to* parlay *a talent into a fortune.* ***vi-***: *He* parlayed *unsuccessfully all afternoon.*

par·ley (pär′ lē) ***vi-*** to discuss terms with an enemy: *Both groups of soldiers wanted to* parley. ***n-*** [*pl.* **par·leys**] conference or discussion, especially a military conference between representatives of opposing forces.

par·lia·ment (pär′ lə mənt) ***n-*** 1 body of persons appointed or elected as lawmakers of a country. 2 **Parliament** the supreme lawmaking body of Great Britain, including the House of Lords and the House of Commons.

par·lia·men·ta·ri·an (pär′ lə mən târ′ ē ən) ***n-*** one who is versed in parliamentary laws and usages.

par·lia·men·ta·ry (pär′ lə mĕn′ tə rē) ***adj-*** having to do with the customs, rules, or members of a parliament or other public body: *to use* parliamentary *procedure.*

par·lor (pär′ lər) ***n-*** sitting room in a house, hotel, etc., for entertaining guests or for other formal occasions.

parlor car ***n-*** extra-fare railroad passenger car that provides comfortable individual chairs for passengers.

par·lous (pär′ ləs) *Archaic* ***adj-*** hazardous; dangerous; risky. ***—adv-*** **par′ lous·ly.**

Par·nas·sus (pär năs′ əs) ***n-*** 1 mountain in ancient Greece, sacred to Apollo and the Muses. 2 any center of poetic and literary activity.

pa·ro·chi·al (pə rō′ kē əl) ***adj-*** 1 narrow; local; having a limited viewpoint: *He has lived in one place so long that his ideas are* parochial. 2 of or having to do with a parish. ***—adv-*** **pa·ro′ chi·al·ly.**

parochial school ***n-*** school run by a religious group.

par·o·dy (păr′ ə dē) ***n-*** [*pl.* **par·o·dies**] humorous imitation or burlesque of something, such as a work of art. ***vt-*** [**par·o·died, par·o·dy·ing**]: *His play* parodied *unrealistic Western stories.* ***—n-*** **par′ o·dist.**

pa·role (pə rōl′) ***n-*** release, for good conduct, of a criminal from prison before he has finished his full sentence. A person who receives a parole is free, but is under the supervision of a parole officer until the end of the time he has been sentenced to serve. ***vt-*** [**pa·roled, pa·rol·ing**]: *to* parole *a convict.*

pa·rol·ee (păr′ ō lē′, pə rō′-) ***n-*** person who has been paroled from prison.

pa·rot·id glands (pə rŏt′ əd) ***n-*** pair of salivary glands located in front of and below the outer ear.

par·ox·ysm (păr′ ək sĭz′ əm) ***n-*** 1 sudden and violent outburst of emotion; fit: *a* paroxysm *of rage.* 2 spasm of pain or other symptoms of a disease, recurring at intervals. ***—adj-*** **par′ ox·ys′ mal:** *a* paroxysmal *cough.*

par·quet (pär kā′) ***n-*** 1 flooring made of short strips of wood arranged in a pattern. 2 the lower floor of a theater, especially the part extending from the orchestra pit to the parquet circle. *as* ***modifier***: *a* parquet *floor.*

parquet circle ***n-*** part of the lower floor of a theater that extends behind the parquet.

par·quet·ry (pär′ kə trē) ***n-*** patterned wooden inlay work for floors.

par·ra·keet (păr′ ə kēt′) ***n-*** parakeet.

par·ri·cide (păr′ ə sīd′) ***n*-** **1** the murder of a close relative, especially a parent. **2** one who commits such a crime. ***—adj*-** **par′ ri·ci′ dal.**

par·rot (păr′ ət) ***n*-** **1** tropical bird with a hooked beak and bright feathers, often kept as a pet. It may learn to repeat words and phrases. **2** one who repeats ideas rather than originates. ***vt*-** to repeat from memory rather than understanding: *He* parroted *my opinions.*—***adj*-par′rot·like′.**

Green parrot, about 17 in. long

parrot fever ***n*-** psittacosis.

par·ry (păr′ ē) ***vt*-** **[par·ried, par·ry·ing]** to turn aside or deflect: *to* parry *a question; to* parry *a blow.* ***n*-** [*pl.* **par·ries**] **1** in fencing, a defensive move made to ward off or deflect a thrust. **2** any quick turning aside (of a blow, question, etc.).

parse (pärs) ***vt*-** **[parsed, pars·ing]** **1** in grammar, to analyze or describe (a sentence) by stating the parts of speech and their relation to each other. **2** to name the part of speech of (a word) and its position in a sentence. ***vi*-**: *This sentence doesn't* parse *easily.*

Par·see (pär′ sē′) ***n*-** one of a Zoroastrian sect in India, descendants of the Persians who settled there in the 8th century. Also **Par′ si.′**

par·si·mo·ni·ous (pär′ sə mō′ nē əs) ***adj*-** extremely and unnecessarily careful in the handling of money; stingy: *a* parsimonious *old miser.* ***—adv*-** **par′ si·mo′ ni·ous·ly.** ***n*-** **par′ si·mo′ ni·ous·ness.**

par·si·mo·ny (pär′ sə mō′ nē) ***n*-** extreme and unnecessary economy; stinginess.

pars·ley (pär′ slē) ***n*-** plant related to the carrot. Its leaves are used as a garnish and for flavoring.

pars·nip (pär′ snĭp′) ***n*-** **1** plant related to the carrot. **2** the sweet, spicy root of this plant, eaten as a vegetable.

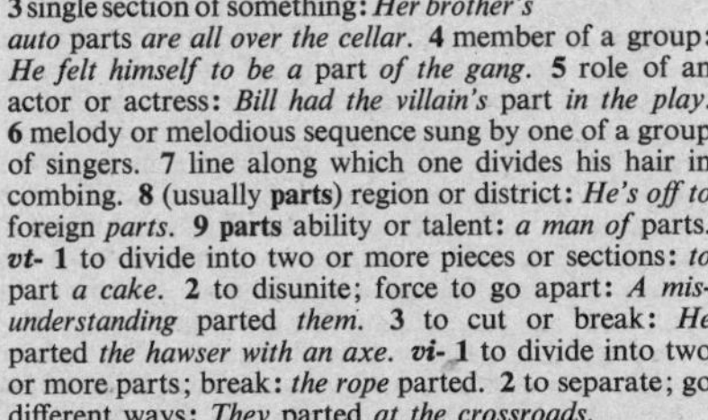

Parsnip

par·son (pär′ sən) ***n*-** **1** clergyman in charge of a parish. **2** *Informal* any clergyman.

par·son·age (pär′ sən ĭj) ***n*-** house provided by a parish for its minister.

part (pärt) ***n*-** **1** anything less than the whole: *Only* part *of that statement was accurate.* **2** share in some job or duty: *The detective's* part *was to find the criminal.* **3** single section of something: *Her brother's auto* parts *are all over the cellar.* **4** member of a group: *He felt himself to be a* part *of the gang.* **5** role of an actor or actress: *Bill had the villain's* part *in the play.* **6** melody or melodious sequence sung by one of a group of singers. **7** line along which one divides his hair in combing. **8** (usually **parts**) region or district: *He's off to* foreign *parts.* **9** **parts** ability or talent: *a man of* parts. ***vt*-** **1** to divide into two or more pieces or sections: *to* part *a cake.* **2** to disunite; force to go apart: *A misunderstanding* parted *them.* **3** to cut or break: *He* parted *the hawser with an axe.* ***vi*-** **1** to divide into two or more parts; break: *the rope* parted. **2** to separate; go different ways: *They* parted *at the crossroads.*

for (one's) part as far as one is concerned: *I don't like candy, and* for my part, *you can take all of it.* **for the most part** mainly; in general. **in good part** good naturedly: *He took the joke* in good part. **in part** partly. **on the part of** on behalf of. **part and parcel** essential part: *The guarantee was* part and parcel *of the bargain.* **take part** to join; participate: *Joan* took part *in every game that year.* **take (someone's) part** to side with someone, especially in an argument.

part company to end a friendship, association, etc.

part from to leave; separate from.

part with to let go of; release: *to* part with *money.*

part. **1** participle. **2** particular.

par·take (pär tāk′) ***vi*-** **[par·took, par·tak·en, par·tak·ing]** to take part; participate: *to* partake *in the activities of the school.* ***—n*-** **par·tak′ er.**

partake of **1** to take some of or share in: *to* partake of *a meal.* **2** to be like; resemble: *Your impatience* partakes of *rudeness.*

Par·the·non (pär′ thə nŏn′) ***n*-** the temple of Athena built on the Acropolis in Athens in the 5th century B.C.

Par·thi·an shot (pär′ thē ən) ***n*-** sharp parting remark. [from the ancient Parthian custom of discharging arrows while seemingly retreating.]

par·tial (pär′ shəl) ***adj*-** **1** incomplete; in part: *I made a* partial *payment on a new radio.* **2** biased: *I can't make a fair judgment because I'm* partial. ***—adv*-** **par′ tial·ly.**

partial to fond of: *She is very* partial to *apple cake.*

par·ti·al·i·ty (pär′ shē ăl′ ə tē) ***n*-** [*pl.* **par·ti·al·i·ties**] **1** fondness or inclination for a person or thing: *John shows a strong* partiality *for mystery books.* **2** favoritism; bias.

par·tic·i·pant (pär tĭs′ ə pənt) ***n*-** person who takes part in some activity: *He was a* participant *in the decision.*

par·tic·i·pate (pär tĭs′ə pāt′) ***vi*-** **[par·tic·i·pat·ed, par·tic·i·pat·ing]** to take part (in); share (in): *He is sick, or he would* participate *in the game.* ***—n*-** **par·tic′ i·pa′ tion.** ***n*-** **par·tic′ i·pa′ tor:** *a* participator *in sports.*

par·ti·cip·i·al (pär′ tə sĭp′ ē əl) *Grammar* ***adj*-** of or having to do with a participle: *a* participial *phrase.* ***—adv*-** **par′ ti·cip′ i·al·ly.**

par·ti·ci·ple (pär′ tə sĭp′ əl) *Grammar* ***n*-** either of two verb forms that are used with the auxiliaries "be" and "have" to form tenses. The **present participle,** which ends in -ing, is used to form the progressive tenses of the verb and is also used as an adjective, noun, or, occasionally, an adverb. The **past participle** may end in -d, -ed, -t, -n, or -en, may sometimes be the same as the infinitive, or may have an entirely different form (swum). It is used to form the passive voice and the perfect tenses of the verb, and is also used as an adjective. Examples:

I am leaving. (present participle used to form the present progressive tense)

He made an agonizing *decision.* (present participle used as an adjective)

Painting *is fun.* (present participle used as a noun)

He was struck *on the hand by the ball.* (past participle used to form the passive)

I have loved. (past participle used to form the present perfect tense)

He has a broken *arm.* (past participle used as an adjective)

par·ti·cle (pär′ tĭ kəl) ***n*-** tiny or minute bit; speck; trace: *There's not a* particle *of truth in that story. I looked at a* particle *of dust under the microscope.* **2** *Physics* one of the extremely small bodies, including the proton, electron, neutron, etc., which make up the atom.

par·ti-col·ored (pär′ tĭ kŭl′ ərd) ***adj*-** having various colors: *a* parti-colored *flower.*

---

fāte, făt, dâre, bärn; bē, bĕt, mêre; bīte, bĭt; nōte, hŏt, môre, dȯg; fŭn, fûr; to͞o, bo͝ok; oil; out; tar; thin; then; hw for wh as in *wh*at; zh for s as in u*s*ual; ə for a, e, i, o, u, as in *a*go, lin*e*n, per*i*l, at*o*m, min*u*s

par·tic·u·lar (pər tĭk′ yə lər) ***adj-*** **1** of or belonging to one person or thing: *His* particular *skill is for tennis.* **2** strict; demanding; fussy: *Edith is most* particular *about her clothes.* **3** special; noteworthy: *to receive a souvenir of* particular *interest.* **4** distinct from others: *a* particular *day of the week.* ***n-*** single thing; detail; item: *In what* particular *did he fail in the chemistry examination?*
in particular **1** especially. **2** in detail.

par·tic·u·lar·i·ty (pər tĭk′ yə lăr′ ə tē, -lĕr′ ə tē) ***n-*** *pl.* **par·tic·u·lar·i·ties**] **1** strict attention to detail; carefulness. **2** particular item. **3** peculiarity or individuality.

par·tic·u·lar·ize (pər tĭk′ yə lə rīz′) ***vt-*** [**par·tic·u·lar·ized, par·tic·u·lar·iz·ing**] to give the details of: *The reporter* particularized *every event leading up to the disaster.* ***vi-***: *He* particularized, *but refused personal comment.* **—*n-* par·tic′ u·lar·i·za′ tion.**

par·tic·u·lar·ly (pər tĭk′ yə lər lē) ***adv-*** unusually; especially: *to be* particularly *careful.*

part·ing (pär′ tĭng) ***n-*** a taking leave; departure; separation: *the* parting *of friends.* ***adj-*** farewell; done on leaving: *The thieves fired a* parting *shot at us.*

par·ti·san (pär′ tə zən) ***n-*** **1** supporter of a person or idea: *He was a* partisan *of the king against the parliament.* **2** (also **par′ ti·zan**) resistance fighter; guerrilla. ***adj-*** one-sided: *She takes a very* partisan *view of that quarrel.*

par·ti·san·ship (pär′ tə zən shĭp′) ***n-*** loyalty, especially unreasonable loyalty to a person or cause.

par·ti·tion (pär tĭsh′ ən) ***n-*** **1** thin wall; dividing panel: *The desks in the office were* separated *by partitions.* **2** a dividing or splitting up of something; division: *the* partition *of disputed territory.* ***vt-*** to divide; split up into parts: *The country was* partitioned *by its conquerors.*

part·ly (pärt′ lē) ***adv-*** in part; not entirely.

part·ner (pärt′ nər) ***n-*** **1** associate in business or other enterprise; especially, a member of a legal partnership. **2** one who shares something with another: *to be* partners *in sorrow.* **3** one who dances with another. **4** someone on the same side as another in a game: *I was his tennis* partner *once a week.* **5** husband or wife: *Grandpa and Grandma were lifelong* partners.

part·ner·ship (pärt′ nər shĭp′) ***n-*** **1** association, especially a legal association, of two or more people in a business or other enterprise: *The salesman and the mechanic formed a* partnership *to sell cars.* **2** association in which two or more share something: *a* partnership *in crime.*

part of speech *Grammar* ***n-*** any of the classes into which the words or word groups of a language are placed according to their ability to fulfill certain functions or fill certain positions in the sentence, clause, or phrase. Traditionally, English has been said to have eight parts of speech: noun, pronoun, adjective, verb, adverb, preposition, conjunction, and interjection. However, modern grammarians have added others, including "determiner" and "intensifier."

par·took (pär to͝ok′) *p.t.* of **partake.**

par·tridge (pär′ trĭj) ***n-*** **1** game bird native to the Old World, having a plump, rounded body and brownish feathers. **2** any of several similar or related birds, such as the bobwhite.

partridge berry ***n-*** **1** American trailing evergreen plant bearing a bright-red berry. **2** the berry itself.

part song *Music* ***n-*** composition for several voice parts, often unaccompanied.

part-time (pärt′ tīm′) ***adj-*** **1** taking up only a part of one's possible working time: *a* part-time *job.* **2** working or serving as such during only a part of one's possible working time: *a* part-time *teacher.* **—*adv-*:** *to work* part-time.

par·tu·ri·tion (pär′ chə rĭsh′ ən, pär′ tyə-) ***n-*** the act of giving birth; labor; childbirth.

par·ty (pär′ tē) ***n-*** [*pl.* **par·ties**] **1** entertainment or social gathering: *a birthday* party. **2** group of people associated or acting together: *A search* party *set out to find the missing boy.* **3** person concerned or interested in some affair, such as a contract or lawsuit: *The injured* party *sued the driver.* **4** political organization: *Each* party *has its candidate.* **5** *Informal* person: *A* party *called you yesterday. as* ***modifier***: *a* party *dress; the* party *decorations; a matter of* party *politics.*

party line ***n-*** **1** (also **party wire**) single telephone circuit linking two or more customers with the exchange. **2** policies or principles of a political group, especially those of the Communist Party.

par value ***n-*** the face value of a stock as distinct from the market value.

par·ve·nu (pär və no͞o′, -nyo͞o′) ***n-*** one who has recently risen, because of his wealth, to a position he is not accustomed to; upstart: *as* ***modifier***: *a* parvenu *family.*

Pasch (păsk) ***n-*** **1** Passover. **2** Easter.

pas·chal (păs′ kəl) ***adj-*** of or having to do with Easter or Passover.

paschal lamb ***n-*** lamb killed and eaten at the Passover.

pa·sha (păsh′ ə, pə shò′) ***n-*** in Turkey, formerly a high military official or provincial governor; also, an honorary title used after a name.

pasque-flow·er (păsk′ flou′ ər) ***n-*** plant of the anemone family with purple or white flowers that bloom in early spring. It is the State flower of South Dakota.

pass (păs) ***vi-*** [**passed, passed** or **past, pass·ing**] **1** to move from place to place, or change from one state to another: *to* pass *down the street; to* pass *from youth to age.* **2** to go by: *Time* passes *quickly.* **3** to make or force one's way: *to* pass *through a crowd.* **4** to go unnoticed, unseen, or unchallenged: *His action* passed *without comment.* **5** to be approved as a bill or law. **6** in cards, to let one's turn go by without playing or bidding. **7** to end: *Old customs* pass *and new ones take their place.* **8** to happen; occur: *to know all that* passed. ***vt-*** (in senses 6 and 11, considered intransitive when the direct object is implied but not expressed) **1** to go by, through, beyond, etc.: *to* pass *the house.* **2** to permit to go past or enter: *The sentry* passed *the returning soldiers.* **3** to give to someone; hand; also, distribute: *Please* pass *the butter.* **4** to go past; overtake: *The second runner* passed *the first at the turn.* **5** to spend (time): *to* pass *the day.* **6** to go through with success or meet the requirements of: *The student* passed *the algebra test.* **7** to exceed: *It* passes *belief.* **8** to give as a judgment: *to* pass *sentence.* **9** to utter or pronounce: *to* pass *an opinion.* **10** to approve or enact (a law): *Congress* passed *the bill without debate.* **11** to throw (a football, basketball, etc.) to another player. ***n-*** **1** gap in a mountain range permitting passage. **2** gesture; motion: *The magician made* passes *over the hat.* **3** note, certificate, or other form that gives one special permission to do something: *a* pass *to inspect a military post.* **4** free ticket. **5** state; situation: *a difficult* pass. **6** throw of the ball from one player to another. **—*n-* pas′ ser.**
a pretty pass a bad or difficult situation: *The explorers were in* a pretty pass *without a compass.* **bring to pass** to cause to come about. **come to pass** to happen.
pass away to go away in time; also, to die.
pass by to reject: *We* passed *the inferior merchandise* by.
pass for to get by as: *That* passed for *a cake.*
pass off to offer or sell as good or genuine; palm off.
pass on **1** to proceed: *Please* pass on *to the next question.* **2** to determine or evaluate the quality of something; judge: *to* pass on *his work.* **3** to pass away; die.

pass out 1 to give out or distribute. 2 *Informal* to faint.
pass over 1 to omit: *If you can't do it,* pass over *it.* 2 to ignore or excuse: *to* pass over *an insult.*
pass through to experience.
pass up to skip; let go by: *He* passed up *dinner.*

pass·a·ble (păs′ ə bəl) ***adj-*** 1 fair; fairly good; not open to great objection: *a book in* passable *condition.* 2 such as can be traveled: *a* passable *road.* **—*adv-*** **pass′ a·bly.**

pas·sage (păs′ ĭj) ***n-*** 1 a passing or moving from one place to another. 2 corridor, aisle, hallway, etc. 3 trip; journey, especially a voyage: *a calm* passage *across the Atlantic.* 4 permission or right to pass through, over, or into: *The government granted the consul* passage *across the country.* 5 verse, sentence, etc., from a writing or speech: *a* passage *from a poem.* 6 approval of a bill, law, etc.: *The* passage *of the bill was certain.* 7 course or progress: *the* passage *of time.* 8 *Archaic* conflict.

pas·sage·way (păs′ ĭj wā′) ***n-*** any way affording passage for persons or things; especially, a hall or corridor.

passbook (păs′ bo͝ok′) ***n-*** book issued by a bank, showing the deposits, withdrawals, and balance in a depositor's account.

pas·sé (pă sā′) ***adj-*** out of date; outmoded.

passed ball ***n-*** in baseball, an error charged against a catcher when he fails to stop a pitch that is within his reach, and thus permits a base runner to advance.

pas·sen·ger (păs′ ən jər) ***n-*** person, not the driver, who rides in a vehicle, ship, plane, etc.

passenger pigeon ***n-*** extinct North American pigeon.

pass·er-by (păs′ ər bī′) ***n-*** [*pl.* **pass·ers-by**] one who goes past or by, especially along a street.

pas·ser·ine (păs′ ə rīn′) ***adj-*** 1 of or having to do with an order of birds that includes all those that sing, as well as many others, ranging widely in size. 2 of or having to do with a sparrow. ***n-***: *a migrating* passerine.

pas·sim (păs′ ĭm) ***adv-*** here and there; in different passages (used as a reference note).

pass·ing (păs′ ĭng) ***adj-*** 1 going by: *the* passing *years.* 2 brief; not lasting: *a* passing *glance*; *a* passing *fashion.* 3 equal to or better than a required standard: *a* passing *grade.* ***n-*** 1 a going by. 2 enactment; the making into law: *the* passing *of an amendment.* 3 death; ending.
in passing incidentally; parenthetically: *Let us say,* in passing, *that. . . .*

pas·sion (păsh′ ən) ***n-*** 1 any strong feeling, such as love, hate, etc. 2 enthusiasm; intense desire: *a* passion *for learning.* 3 object of intense feeling or interest: *Antiques are Mrs. Oldham's* passion. 4 outburst of violent wrath; great rage: *Philip flew into a* passion *when Bob broke his bat.* 5 **Passion** the suffering and death of Christ on the cross; also, the last part of the Gospels relating this.

pas·sion·ate (păsh′ ən ət) ***adj-*** 1 filled with strong feeling or eager desire. 2 hot-tempered; wrathful. 3 intense; overwhelming. **—*adv-*** **pas′ sion·ate·ly.** ***n-*** **pas′ sion·ate·ness.**

passion flower ***n-*** any of several tropical American shrubs or vines with berries and showy flowers.

Passion flower

pas·sion·less (păsh′ ən ləs) ***adj-*** 1 without, or apparently without, anger, intense love, ardor, etc.; tranquil; unmoved. 2 objective; detached.

Passion Play or **passion play** ***n-*** drama dealing with the suffering and death of Christ.

Passion Sunday ***n-*** the fifth Sunday of Lent; two weeks before Easter.

pas·sive (păs′ ĭv) ***adj-*** 1 not acting or taking part: *a* passive *interest in games.* 2 enduring without resistance: *The child listened to the scolding in* passive *silence.* 3 *Grammar* in the passive voice ***n-*** *Grammar* the passive voice; also, a verb phrase in the passive voice. **—*adv-*** **pas′ sive·ly.** ***n-*** **pas′ sive·ness.**

passive resistance ***n-*** policy or technique of resisting a government, law, authority, etc., by means that always stop short of direct and violent defiance, but sometimes drive the ruling powers to acts of force that injure their stability and reputation.

passive voice *Grammar* ***n-*** the form of a transitive verb phrase which shows that the subject is the receiver of the action. Example: *The house* has been sold.

pas·siv·i·ty (pă sĭv′ ə tē) ***n-*** lack of the desire or ability to be active, or especially, to resist or fight back when attacked: *His* passivity *worries me.*

pass·key (păs′ kē′) ***n-*** master key.

Pass·o·ver (păs′ ō′ vər) ***n-*** yearly Jewish holiday celebrated in the spring in memory of the delivering of the Hebrews from slavery in Egypt; Pesach; Pasch.

pass·port (păs′ pôrt′) ***n-*** 1 document or booklet showing citizenship and granting permission to travel in a foreign land. 2 anything that opens the way, usually to something desired: *Her voice is a* passport *to fame.*

pass·word (păs′ wûrd′) ***n-*** secret word or phrase used by members of a group to identify themselves, as in passing a guard.

past (păst) ***n-*** 1 time gone by: *The old men talked of the* past. 2 one's earlier life or history: *The explorer has a colorful* past. ***adj-*** 1 gone by; completed: *a record of* past *events.* 2 just ended: *in the* past *week.* 3 former: *a* past *president*; past *ambitions.* ***prep-*** 1 (considered an adverb when the object is clearly implied but not expressed) so as to pass; by: *We went* past *the post office. The team ran* past. 2 beyond: *It was far* past *Fred's bedtime.*

pas·ta (päs′ tə) *Italian* ***n-*** spaghetti, macaroni, or similar food made from flour paste shaped and dried.

paste (pāst) ***n-*** 1 mixture of flour and water or starch and water, used to stick things together. 2 kind of dough used to make light pie crust. 3 soft, creamy, food preparation of fish, nuts, fruit, etc.: *tomato* paste; *anchovy* paste. 4 material used to make imitation jewels. ***vt-*** [**past·ed, past·ing**] 1 to cover or fasten with a sticky mixture: *Harriet* pasted *the pictures in her scrapbook.* 2 *Slang* to strike or throw very hard.

paste·board (pāst′ bôrd′) ***n-*** stiff material made of pressed pulp or of layers of paper pasted together. *as **modifier***: *a* pasteboard *box.*

pas·tel (păs tĕl′) ***n-*** 1 chalklike crayon used in drawing. 2 picture made with such crayons. 3 any light, soft color. *as **modifier***: *a* pastel *portrait*; pastel *blue.*

pas·tern (păs′ tərn) ***n-*** the part of the foot of a horse and related animals that is between the fetlock and hoof.

pas·teur·ize (păs′ chə rīz′) ***vt-*** [**pas·teur·ized, pas·teur·iz·ing**] to destroy certain harmful bacteria in (milk or other foods) by heating followed by rapid cooling. **—*n-*** **pas′ teur·i·za′ tion.**

pas·tille (pă stēl′) ***n-*** 1 lozenge; troche. 2 small, usually cone-shaped mass of aromatic substances, used to fumigate or scent a room.

pas·time (păs′ tīm′) ***n-*** any game, sport, amusement, or hobby which makes time pass happily.

past master ***n-*** person who has had long and thorough experience in some field; expert.

pas·tor (păs′ tər) ***n-*** Christian minister in charge of a church or congregation.

pas·tor·al (păs′ tə rəl) ***adj-*** **1** having to do with shepherds or country life: *a* pastoral *poem.* **2** full of the rustic charm and simplicity associated with the raising and herding of livestock: *a* pastoral *setting for a play.* **3** having to do with a minister in charge of a church: *to have* pastoral *duties.* ***n-*** **1** any literary or artistic work that depicts country life in an artificial or sentimental manner. **2** letter from a pastor to his congregation or from a bishop to the clergy or people of his diocese.

pas·tor·ate (păs′ tər ət) ***n-*** **1** the office, term of office, or jurisdiction of a pastor. **2** all pastors.

past participle See *participle.*

past perfect tense *Grammar* ***n-*** verb tense formed with the auxiliary verb "had" and indicating an action or condition that occurred before some past action or time. Examples: *When we arrived, he* had gone. *We* had arrived *by 10 o'clock.* Also **past perfect.**

pas·tra·mi (pə strä′ mē) ***n-*** highly seasoned and smoked shoulder cut of beef. *as* ***modifier:*** *a* pastrami *sandwich.*

pas·try (pā′ strē) ***n-*** **1** pies, tarts, or other foods collectively, made of or with a rich crust; also, any sweet baked foods. **2** [*pl.* **pas·tries**] pie, tart, or any piece of pastry: *a Danish* pastry. *as* ***modifier:*** *a* pastry *cook.*

past tense *Grammar* ***n-*** verb tense indicating action or condition at a specific time in the past. Examples: *He* went *home. They* were *sick.*

pas·tur·age (păs′ chər ĭj) ***n-*** **1** land used for grazing animals; pasture land. **2** grass and other plants that cattle eat: *The horses found rich* pasturage *along the river.*

pas·ture (păs′ chər) ***n-*** **1** piece of land on which animals are put to graze. **2** grass and other plants that grazing animals eat: *The rocky hillside had enough* pasture *for sheep.* ***vt-*** **[pas·tured, pas·tur·ing]** to put to graze: *Mr. Wilson* pastured *his cows in the north lot.* ***vi-:*** *The sheep* pastured *on the hillside.*

[1]**past·y** (pās′ tē) ***adj-*** **[past·i·er, past·i·est] 1** like or covered with paste: *a* pasty *liquid; a* pasty *table.* **2** of the skin, pale and unhealthy; pallid: *a* pasty *complexion.* [from **paste.**] ***—n-*** **past′ i·ness.**

[2]**past·y** (păs′ tē) *chiefly Brit.* ***n-*** [*pl.* **past·ies**] pie filled with venison or other meat; meat pie. [from Old French **pastée,** from Late Latin **pasta** meaning "a pastry."]

pat (păt) ***n-*** **1** light, friendly tap. **2** tapping sound; patter: *the* pat *of a child's bare feet.* **3** small, molded portion: *a* pat *of butter.* ***vt-*** **[pat·ted, pat·ting] 1** to touch lightly or affectionately; tap: *to* pat *a dog.* **2** to shape by tapping: *The child* patted *the mud into a cake.* ***adj-*** perfectly suited to the purpose or occasion, and therefore not needing to be changed: *a* pat *answer.*

pat hand in card games, a hand that one wants to hold unchanged. **pat on the back** gesture of approval. **stand pat** to remain firm without shifting. **have down** (or **know**) **pat** to know perfectly.

pat. 1 patent. **2** patented.

patch (păch) ***n-*** **1** small piece of cloth, metal, etc., used to cover a hole or worn spot. **2** piece of cloth, plaster, etc., used to cover an injury or wound: *an eye* patch. **3** small area: *a vegetable* patch. **4** spot differing from the surrounding area: *a* patch *of brown on the black dog.* ***vt-*** **1** to attach or cover with a piece of material in order to repair: *to* patch *a rip; to* patch *a tire.* **2** to make with small pieces of material: *to* patch *quilts.* ***—n-*** **patch′ er.**

patch up 1 to settle; fix; smooth over: *The children* patched up *their quarrel.* **2** to repair; restore in a hasty, makeshift way: *I've* patched up *the leak.*

patch pocket ***n-*** flat pocket sewn to the outside of a garment.

patch test ***n-*** test for allergy, in which a small pad of paper or cloth is soaked in a solution of a suspected substance and applied to the skin.

patch·work (păch′ wûrk′) ***n-*** **1** work consisting of a collection of odds and ends roughly put together; jumble. **2** fabric made of irregular pieces of material sewn together at the edges often used to make quilts. **3** act of making such fabric: *Mother enjoys doing* patchwork. *as* ***modifier:*** *The* patchwork *treaty satisfied nobody.*

patch·y (păch′ ē) ***adj-*** **[patch·i·er, patch·i·est]** like patchwork; uneven; irregular: *a picture filled with* patchy *color; a* patchy *report.* ***—n-*** **patch′ i·ness.**

pate (pāt) ***n-*** the top of the head.

pâ·té (pä tā′) *French* ***n-*** paste made of ground meat.

pa·tel·la (pə tĕl′ ə) ***n-*** kneecap. ***—adj-*** **pa·tel′ lar:** *a* patellar *bruise.*

pat·en (păt′ ən) ***n-*** plate of precious metal for the eucharistic bread. ***Hom-*** patten.

[1]**pat·ent** (păt′ ənt) ***n-*** **1** right granted by the federal government to an inventor, which gives him exclusive control of the manufacture, use, and sale of his invention for a certain length of time; also, the document granting such a right. **2** transfer to a person of title to federal land; also, the official document transferring such title, or the land itself. *as* ***modifier:*** *a* patent *attorney.* ***vt-*** to obtain a patent on. ***—adj-*** **pat′ ent·a·ble.**

[2]**pat·ent** (pā′ tənt, păt′ ənt) ***adj-*** clear to all; obvious; evident: *That is a* patent *lie.* ***—adv-*** **pat′ ent·ly.**

pat·en·tee (păt′ ən tē′) ***n-*** person who holds a patent.

patent leather ***n-*** leather, usually black, with a smooth, shiny surface.

patent medicine ***n-*** medicine that is sold directly to the public without prescription.

Patent Office ***n-*** bureau of the U.S. Department of Commerce where patent claims are examined and patents granted.

pa·ter (pä′ tər, pā′-) *Brit. Informal* ***n-*** father.

pa·ter·nal (pə tûr′ nəl) ***adj-*** **1** of or like a father: *our* paternal *home;* paternal *advice.* **2** related through the father: *a* paternal *grandmother.* ***—adv-*** **pa·ter′ nal·ly.**

pa·ter·nal·ism (pə tûr′ nə lĭz′ əm) ***n-*** system or doctrine of government or business management that combines strong, centralized authority with concern for the welfare of the employees. ***—adj-*** **pa·ter′ nal·ist′ ic.**

pa·ter·ni·ty (pə tûr′ nə tē) ***n-*** **1** fatherhood. **2** male parentage: *to trace the* paternity *of a child.*

pa·ter·nos·ter (păt′ ər nŏs′ tər) ***n-*** **1** *Latin* our father. **2** the Lord's Prayer, which in Latin begins with "Pater Noster . . .". Also **Pa′ ter Nos′ ter.**

path (păth) ***n-*** **1** narrow track worn by human or animal footsteps: *an Indian* path *through the forest.* **2** way made for walking: *a garden* path. **3** course of travel: *the earth's* path *around the sun.* **4** way of conduct: *the* path *of goodness.* ***—adj-*** **path′ less.**

path- or **patho-** *combining form* disease: *a* path*ology laboratory; a* path*ogenic germ.* [from Greek **páthos** meaning "suffering; feeling."]

pa·thet·ic (pə thĕt′ ĭk) ***adj-*** arousing feelings of pity or sympathy; pitiful: *the* pathetic *cries of the wounded.* ***—adv-*** **pa·thet′ i·cal·ly.**

path·find·er (păth′ fīn′ dər) ***n-*** person who finds or leads the way through strange or unknown areas; trailblazer: *a* pathfinder *in the wilderness; a* pathfinder *in science.*

path·o·gen·ic (păth′ ə jĕn′ ĭk) ***adj-*** causing disease: *a* pathogenic *organism.*

path·o·log·i·cal (păth′ ə lŏj′ ĭ kəl) ***adj-*** **1** of or related to pathology: *a* pathological *medical report.* **2** indicating or caused by disease: *a* pathological *liver condition.* Also **path'o·log'ic.**

pa·thol·o·gist (pə thŏl'ə jĭst) ***n-*** doctor who specializes in pathology.

pa·thol·o·gy (pə thŏl'ə jē) ***n-*** **1** the branch of medicine that deals with the nature and causes of disease, especially with the specific changes in tissues and organs that cause or are caused by disease. **2** all the symptoms, processes, and conditions that make up a disease: *the* pathology *of tuberculosis.*

pa·thos (pā'thŏs') ***n-*** quality or condition that arouses feelings of pity or sympathy.

path·way (păth'wā') ***n-*** **1** footpath. **2** any road or course: *the* pathway *to success.*

pa·tience (pā'shəns) ***n-*** **1** endurance of hardship, annoyance, delay, etc., without complaint: *Driving in heavy traffic takes much* patience. **2** perseverance: *the* patience *of a dedicated scientist.*

pa·tient (pā'shənt) ***adj-*** **1** enduring annoyance or hardship without complaining: *a* patient *father*; *the* patient *refugees.* **2** showing patience: *a* patient *smile.* **3** perservering; diligent: *a* patient *scholar.* ***n-*** person under medical care. ***—adv-*** **pa'tient·ly.**

pa·ti·na (păt'ə nə) ***n-*** **1** greenish film that appears on the weathered or treated copper or bronze. **2** surface film or general appearance acquired by something with age and continued use.

pa·ti·o (păt'ē ō) ***n-*** [*pl.* **pa·ti·os**] **1** in Spain and Spanish-American countries, an open courtyard in the center of a building or surrounded by buildings. **2** paved area at the back or side of a home.

Patio

pa·tois (pă'twä') ***n-*** [*pl.* **pa·tois** (-twäz')] dialect spoken by the common or illiterate people of an area; local or provincial speech.

pat. pend. patent pending.

pa·tri·arch (pā'trē ärk') ***n-*** **1** father and ruler of a family, tribe, etc.: *Abraham is one of the great Jewish* patriarchs. **2** old man worthy of honor and respect. **3** title of certain bishops in the Orthodox and Roman Catholic churches. ***—adj-*** **pa'tri·ar'chal.**

pa·tri·cian (pə trĭsh'ən) ***n-*** **1** in ancient Rome, a member of the aristocracy. **2** any aristocrat. **3** person of more than usual refinement; cultivated person. ***adj-*** **1** of or related to the aristocracy, especially of ancient Rome: *a* patrician *villa.* **2** cultivated; refined: *her* patrician *tastes.*

pat·ri·mo·ny (pă'trə mō'nē) ***n-*** [*pl.* **pat·ri·mo·nies**] **1** property inherited from one's father or other ancestor. **2** property held as an endowment by a religious institution. **3** any inheritance; heritage: *a* patrimony *of liberty.* ***—adj-*** **pat'ri·mo'ni·al:** *a* patrimonial *estate.*

pa·tri·ot (pā'trē ət) ***n-*** person who has great love for his or her country and supports it with enthusiasm.

pa·tri·ot·ic (pā'trē ŏt'ĭk) ***adj-*** showing or inspired by patriotism: *a* patriotic *citizen*; *a* patriotic *hymn.* ***—adv-*** **pa'tri·ot'i·cal·ly.**

pa·tri·ot·ism (pā'trē ə tĭz'əm) ***n-*** love of one's country and great devotion to its welfare or interests.

Patriot's Day ***n-*** anniversary of the Battle of Lexington, April 19, 1775; observed as a legal holiday in Maine and Massachusetts.

pa·trol (pə trōl') ***vt-*** [**pa·trolled, pa·trol·ling**] to go the rounds or the length of (a certain area) in order to guard or inspect: *The Coast Guard* patrols *the coast of the United States.* ***vi-***: *The Coast Guard* patrols *day and night.* ***n-*** **1** the act of doing this: *a* patrol *of the* coast. **2** soldiers, ships, etc., engaged in such activity: *The captain sent out a* patrol *of six soldiers.* **3** group of eight boys in a troop of Boy Scouts.

pa·trol·man (pə trōl'mən) ***n-*** [*pl.* **pa·trol·men**] ***n-*** uniformed policeman of the lowest rank, especially one assigned to patrol a certain area.

patrol wagon ***n-*** closed truck used by police to take prisoners to and from a jail.

pa·tron (pā'trən) ***n-*** **1** person who supports or aids a special cause, person, etc.: *Most of the orchestra's expenses are paid by* patrons. **2** regular customer, especially of a restaurant. ***—n- fem.*** **pa'tron·ess.**

pa·tron·age (pā'trə nĭj, pă'-) ***n-*** **1** protection; support; encouragement: *The food bazaar is under the* patronage *of the Arts Club.* **2** the act of buying or spending by a customer: *Thank you for your regular* patronage *of our restaurant.* **3** in politics, power to control appointments to office; also the offices controlled.

pa·tron·ize (pā'trə nīz', pă'-) ***vt-*** [**pa·tron·ized, pa·tron·iz·ing**] **1** to act as a guardian, protector, or supporter of: *to* patronize *the arts.* **2** to treat with a superior air: *The opera star* patronized *the members of the chorus.* **3** to deal with regularly as a customer: *My uncle* patronizes *the grocery store on the corner.*

pa·tron·iz·ing·ly (pā'trə nī'zĭng lē, pă'-) ***adv-*** in a manner showing a feeling of superiority: *They spoke* patronizingly *to the neighbors.*

patron saint ***n-*** saint regarded as the special protector of a person, place, or thing.

pat·ro·nym·ic (pă'trə nĭm'ĭk) ***n-*** family or personal name derived from the name of one's father or paternal ancestor by the addition of a prefix or suffix: *Johnson (son of John) and Macdonald (son of Donald) are* patronymics. ***adj-***: *Johnson and Macdonald are* patronymic *names.*

pa·troon (pə trōōn') ***n-*** during Dutch colonial rule of New York and New Jersey, a person who held a large estate with certain feudal privileges.

pat·ten (păt'ən) ***n-*** **1** formerly a shoe with a wooden sole, mounted on a metal ring to raise the foot above the mire. **2** thick-soled woman's slipper. ***Hom-*** paten.

¹pat·ter (păt'ər) ***vi-*** to move or strike with a quick series of light sounds: *The little girl* pattered *across the room to her father.* ***n-*** quick series of light sounds: *the* patter *of raindrops on the window.* [from **pat.**]

²pat·ter (păt'ər) ***n-*** any rapid talk; especially, the glib, easy speech used by salesmen, magicians, etc. ***vi-*** to speak rapidly and glibly: *The salesman* pattered *on while displaying his wares.* [from **"pater-"** in the Latin phrase **pater noster,** "our father; Lord's Prayer." The meaning arose from the habit of mumbling this prayer.]

pat·tern (păt'ərn) ***n-*** **1** model; example; thing meant to be copied: *The tailor cut the coat according to a* pattern. *The explorer's brave deeds served as a* pattern *for others.* **2** design: *rugs with a rose* pattern; *the frost* pattern *on the window*; *the* pattern *of his life.* ***vt-*** **1** to design after a model: *He* patterned *his life after his father's.* **2** to decorate with a design or figure.

pat·ty (păt'ē) ***n-*** [*pl.* **pat·ties**] **1** small, round cake of fish, meat, or potatoes: *a hamburger* patty. **2** round, flat piece of candy: *mint* patty.

pau·ci·ty (pô'sə tē) ***n-*** scarceness; insufficiency; dearth: *a* paucity *of vital supplies.*

Paul (pól) ***n-*** Roman soldier, originally named Saul, who was converted to Christianity and became a missionary. He was the author of several New Testament epistles. Also **Saint Paul.** ***Homs-*** pall, pawl.

Paul Bun·yan (bŭn′yən) ***n-*** lumberjack hero of American folklore, noted for his superhuman strength.

paunch (pónch) ***n-*** **1** abdomen or belly, especially a large belly. **2** first stomach of a cud-chewing animal; rumen.

paunch·y (pón′chē) ***adj-*** **[paunch·i·er, paunch·i·est]** having a large belly. **—*n-* paunch′i·ness.**

pau·per (pó′pər) ***n-*** very poor person, especially, one living on charity.

pau·per·ize (pó′pə rīz′) **—*vt-*** **[pau·per·ized, pau·per·iz·ing]** to bring to extreme poverty; make very poor: *Bad investments* pauperized *us.* **—*n-* pau′per·i·za′tion.**

pause (póz) ***n-*** **1** brief stop or rest: *Everyone welcomed the* pause *during the long test.* **2** brief stop in speaking, shown in writing by a comma, period, etc. **3** *Music* hold. ***vi-*** **[paused, paus·ing]** to stop or rest for a short time.

pa·vane (pə văn′, -văn′) ***n-*** slow, stately dance of the 16th and 17th centuries; also the music for this dance.

pave (pāv) ***vt-*** **[paved, pav·ing]** to cover with concrete, asphalt, etc.

pave the way to make the way easier, smoother, etc.; prepare the way.

pave·ment (pāv′mənt) ***n-*** hard surface covering a road, sidewalk, or court.

pa·vil·ion (pə vĭl′yən) ***n-*** **1** ornamental shelter in a part garden, etc., open at the sides and used for dancing, or entertainments. **2** large tent, often with a peaked roof. **3** any of the related buildings making up a hospital or sanitarium: *a maternity* pavilion. **4** any of the buildings that house exhibitions or entertainments at a fair or exposition.

Pavilion

pav·ing (pā′vĭng) ***n-*** **1** concrete, asphalt, or other material used for pavement. **2** pavement.

paw (pó) ***n-*** foot of a four-footed animal with claws, especially of a mammal. ***vt-*** **1** to scrape or beat with the front foot: *The horse* pawed *the ground.* **2** to handle or touch roughly or clumsily: *He* pawed *through the stack of exams, looking for his paper.*

pawl (pól) ***n-*** a curved, pivoted device that engages the teeth of a ratchet wheel, and either drives or prevents it from rotating in an undesired direction. For picture, see *ratchet.* ***Homs-*** pall, Paul.

[1]**pawn** (pón) ***vt-*** to leave (something of value) with the lender as security for a loan: *He* pawned *his watch for $20.* ***n-*** thing left to be security for a loan. [from Old French **pan** meaning "pledge; surety," from early Germanic **pand.**]

in pawn in a lender's possession as security for a loan.

[2]**pawn** (pón) ***n-*** **1** the least valuable and the smallest piece in the game of chess. **2** person deliberately used by another; tool: *I was just a* pawn *for his ambitions.* [from Old French **paon, peon,** from Late Latin **pedōn** meaning "foot soldier; flatfoot," from the stem of inflected forms of Latin **pes,** "foot."]

pawn·broker (pón′brō kər) ***n-*** person whose business is lending money at interest on goods left with him as security for the loan.

Paw·nee (pó′nē′) ***n-*** [*pl.* **Paw·nees,** also **Paw·nee**] **1** a member of a tribe of American Indians who formerly lived between the Platte and Arkansas rivers, and now are in Oklahoma. **2** the language of these people. ***adj-*:** *a* Pawnee *artifact.*

pawn·shop (pón′shŏp′) ***n-*** shop of a pawnbroker.

paw·paw (pó′pó, pə pó′) ***n-*** **1** greenish-yellow fruit with a flavor like a banana. **2** the small tree of southern and central United States that bears this fruit. Also **papaw.**

pax vo·bis·cum (păks′wō bĭs′kəm) *Latin* peace be with you.

pay (pā) ***vt-*** **[paid, pay·ing]** (in senses 1, 2, 3, and 4 considered intransitive when the direct object is implied but not expressed.) **1** to give (money) in exchange for goods or services: *to* pay *$5,500 for a car*; *to* pay *the grocer.* **2** to make payment on; settle; discharge: *to* pay *a bill*; *to* pay *income tax.* **3** to be worthwhile or profitable to: *It will* pay *you to follow my advice.* **4** to yield as salary, interest, etc.: *a job that* pays *$250 per week*; *a bond that* pays *7%.* **5** to give (a compliment, attention, etc.): *He* paid *his respects to the host.* ***n-*** money given for work done; wages or salary. ***as modifier:*** *a* pay *day*; *a* pay *telephone*; *a* pay *library.* **—*n-* pay′er.**

in the pay of employed by.

pay as you go **1** to pay debts or expenses as they arise, and not at some later time. **2** relating to a system of income tax payment, in which an employee's tax is deducted regularly from his wages. (see also *withholding tax.*)

pay back to repay: *He* paid back *the loan in a short time.*

pay for **1** to make up or compensate for: *Money will not* pay for *the loss of our home.* **2** to be punished for: *The thief* paid for *his crime with a term in jail.*

pay off **1** to pay in full: *to* pay off *a mortgage in ten years.* **2** to get even with. **3** *Slang* to bribe.

pay out **1** to expend; disburse: *to* pay out *a thousand dollars in wages.* **2** to let out (rope, cable, etc.)

pay up to pay in full.

pay·a·ble (pā′ə bəl) ***adj-*** such as must be paid; due.

pay·check (pā′chĕk′) ***n-*** check given in payment of salary or wages.

pay·day (pā′dā′) ***n-*** day on which salary or wages are paid.

pay dirt ***n-*** **1** earth or rock containing enough metal so that it can be mined profitably; ore. **2** *Slang* anything that yields the desired result.

pay·ee (pā′ē′) ***n-*** person to whom money has been or is to be paid.

pay·load (pā′lōd′) ***n-*** **1** cargo transported for profit in a vehicle, as distinct from the weight of the vehicle. **2** anything an aircraft, rocket, or spacecraft carries that is not essential to the operation of the craft during its flight.

pay·mas·ter (pā′măs′tər) ***n-*** person whose to job is pay out wages.

pay·ment (pā′mənt) ***n-*** **1** a giving of money to pay for something: *The doctor demanded prompt* payment *of the bills.* **2** that which is paid: *monthly* payments *of $10.* **3** reward: *Her thanks was* payment *enough for my work.*

pay·off (pā′óf′, -ŏf′) *Slang* ***n-*** **1** payment, especially of gambling winnings, a bribe, graft, etc. **2** reward or punishment. **3** climax or outcome. **4** decisive factor or situation. ***as modifier:*** *a* payoff *pitch.*

pay·roll (pā′rōl′) ***n-*** **1** list of employees and their salaries. **2** amount paid in salaries for a certain period.

meet the payroll to pay the employees of a company the salaries due them at the time agreed upon.

pay station ***n-*** public telephone that is operated by the insertion of money.

Pb symbol for lead.

pc. piece.

pct. percent.

Pd symbol for palladium.

pd. paid.

P.D. **1** per diem. **2** Police Department.

pea (pē) ***n-*** [*pl.* **peas** or **pease**] **1** plant or vine bearing long, boat-shaped pods that hold several round seeds. **2** the seed, eaten as a vegetable.

peace (pēs) ***n-*** **1** calm; tranquillity: *I need* peace *and quiet in the house.* **2** freedom from war. **3** freedom from disorder, lawlessness, or disturbance: *The strike was marked by riot and other breaches of the* peace. **4** agreement or treaty to end a war. **5** freedom from fear, anxiety, etc.: *my* peace *of mind.* ***Hom-*** piece.

at peace free from war or other strife. **hold** (or **keep**) **(one's) peace** to remain silent.

POD

Pea

peace·a·ble (pē′ sə bəl) ***adj-*** **1** not quarrelsome: *the* peaceable *citizens.* **2** peaceful: *a* peaceable *meeting.* **—*adv-* peace′ a·bly.**

peace·ful (pēs′ fəl) ***adj-*** **1** calm; serene; undisturbed: *a* peaceful *country snow scene.* **2** not given to quarrels or violence; liking peace: *a* peaceful *tribe of Indians.* **—*adv-* peace′ful·ly. *n-* peace′ ful·ness.**

peace·mak·er (pēs′ mā′ kər) ***n-*** one who restores, or tries to restore, peaceful relations between foes.

peace offering ***n-*** offering, such as a gift or promise, that is made to keep or bring about peace.

peace officer ***n-*** officer, such as a policeman or sheriff, whose duty is to preserve law and order.

peace pipe ***n-*** pipe smoked by North American Indians as a rite sealing a peace treaty.

peace·time (pēs′ tīm′) ***n-*** time of peace. *as **modifier**: the* peacetime *use of rockets.*

[1]**peach** (pēch) ***n-*** **1** round fruit with soft, juicy pulp, a single large, rough pit, and fuzzy, usually yellow-pink, skin. **2** the tree bearing this fruit. **3** bright yellow-pink color. ***adj-***: *a* peach *tree*; *a* peach *blouse.* [from Old French **peche,** from Late Latin **persica.**] **—*adj-* peach′ like′.**

[2]**peach** (pēch) *Slang* ***vi-*** to betray an accomplice by turning informer. [from earlier **appeach,** from Middle English **impechen** meaning "to impeach," from Old French **empechier.**]

peach·y (pē′ chē) ***adj-*** [**peach·i·er, peach·i·est**] **1** like a peach. **2** *Informal* very fine; dandy. **—*n-* peach′ i·ness.**

pea·cock (pē′ kŏk′) ***n-*** **1** male of the **pea′fowl′**, a kind of pheasant about the size of a turkey. It is admired for the metallic bronze, blue, green, and gold feathers of its very long tail, which may be spread out like a huge fan. The female is called a **pea′ hen′**. **2** vain person. *as **modifier**: a* peacock *feather.*

Peacock, 7–8 ft., including tail

peacock blue ***n-*** brilliant greenish blue. ***adj-* (peacock-blue):** *a* peacock-blue *dress.*

pea jacket ***n-*** short, heavy woolen jacket, usually worn by seamen. Also **pea′ coat′.**

peak (pēk) ***n-*** **1** sharp tip or point. **2** part of a mountain that rises above surrounding parts; also a single, isolated mountain. **3** highest or greatest point: *the* peak *of traffic.* **4** visor of a cap. ***Homs-*** peek, pique.

Peaks

[1]**peaked** (pēkt) ***adj-*** having a peak or point: *a* peaked *tent.* [from **peak.**]

[2]**peak·ed** (pēk′ əd) ***adj-*** sickly; pale and thin; wan: *a* peaked *face.* [from an archaic verb to **peak** meaning "to be pale; grow thin."]

peal (pēl) ***n-*** **1** loud, rolling sound: *a* peal *of thunder*; *the* peal *of bells*; peals *of laughter.* **2** set of tuned bells. **3** the sound of such bells ringing in certain sequences. ***vi-*** to ring out or sound loudly: *The bells* pealed *gaily.* ***vt-***: *The bells* pealed *a tune of joy.* ***Hom-*** peel.

pea·nut (pē′ nŭt′) ***n-*** **1** the seed pod or the nutlike edible seed of a plant of the pea family. Peanuts are unusual in ripening underground. **2** the plant itself.

peanut butter ***n-*** soft, smooth spread made from ground, roasted peanuts.

pear (pâr) ***n-*** **1** fruit with firm juicy pulp, small hard seeds in a core, and yellow, green, brown, or red skin. **2** the tree that bears this fruit. ***adj-***: *a* pear *preserve.* ***Homs-*** pair, pare. **—*adj-* pear′ like′.**

Pear

pearl (pûrl) ***n-*** **1** smooth, lustrous white or gray precious gem formed in the shells of certain kinds of oysters. **2** something like this in shape, color, or value: *bright* pearls *of dew*; *a* pearl *of a girl.* **3** mother-of-pearl. **4** pearl gray. ***adj-***: *a* pearl *necklace.* ***Hom-*** purl.

pearl gray ***n-*** pale, bluish gray. ***adj-* (pearl-gray):** *a* pearl-gray *cabinet.*

pearl·y (pûr′ lē) ***adj-*** [**pearl·i·er, pearl·i·est**] like pearl or mother-of-pearl: *a* pearly *plastic.* **—*n-* pearl′ i·ness.**

peas·ant (pĕz′ ənt) ***n-*** in Europe, a small farmer or farm laborer. *as **modifier**: a* peasant *dance.*

peas·ant·ry (pĕz′ ən trē) ***n-*** peasants as a social class.

pease (pēz) *Archaic pl.* of **pea.**

peat (pēt) ***n-*** spongy, decayed vegetable matter found in certain swampy places, used in some countries for fuel, but in the United States chiefly as a top dressing for beds of shrubs and flowers. Also **peat moss.**

pea·vey (pē′ vē) ***n-*** [*pl.* **pea·vies**] canthook. Also **pea′ vy.**

peb·ble (pĕb′ əl) ***n-*** **1** small stone worn smooth by water. **2** leather that has a rough, grainy surface; also, such a surface. ***vt-*** [**peb·bled, peb·bling**] **1** to give (leather) a rough, grainy surface. **2** to cover with small stones: *to* pebble *a path.* **—*n-* peb′ ble·like′.**

peb·bly (pĕb′ lē) ***adj-*** [**peb·bli·er, peb·bli·est**] like, covered with, or made up of pebbles: *a* pebbly *beach.*

pe·can (pĭ kän′, -kăn′, pē′ kăn′) ***n-*** **1** smooth, edible, thin-shelled nut grown on a tree of the hickory family in southern United States. **2** the tree.

pec·ca·dil·lo (pĕk′ ə dĭl′ ō) ***n-*** [*pl.* **pec·ca·dil·los, pec·ca·dil·loes**] slight fault; trifling offense.

pec·car·y (pĕk′ ə rē) ***n-*** [*pl.* **pec·car·ies**] American wild pig found from Texas to the middle of South America.

Peccary, about 3 ft. long

[1]**peck** (pĕk) ***n-*** **1** unit of dry measure equal to eight quarts or one quarter of a bushel. **2** *Informal* great deal; lot: *a* peck *of trouble.* [perhaps from Old French **pek,** "a measure for oats."]

[2]**peck** (pĕk) ***vt-*** **1** to strike with the beak, usually with quick jabs or strokes: *The parrot* pecked *my arm.* **2** to cut or chop with the beak or a pointed tool: *To get out of its egg, an unborn chick must* peck *a hole in the shell.* **3** to pick up (grain, feed, etc.) bit by bit with the beak: *The* -

chickens pecked *the corn until it was gone.* ***vi-***: *The rooster* pecked *at the puppy.* ***n-*** **1** jab or stroke made with the beak. **2** *Informal* quick, light kiss. [probably a changed form of [1]**pick.**]

peck at *Informal* to nibble at (food).

pec·tin (pěk′ tĭn) ***n-*** any of a group of related carbohydrates found in fruits and vegetables, which form jellies in the presence of sufficient sugar and acid.

pec·to·ral (pěk′ tər əl) ***adj-*** of, having to do with, or located on the chest.

pec·u·late (pěk′ yə lāt) ***vt-*** **[pec·u·lat·ed, pec·u·lat·ing]** to embezzle. **—*n-* pec′ u·la′ tion.** ***n-*** **pec′ u·la′ tor.**

pe·cul·iar (pə kyōōl′ yər) ***adj-*** **1** odd; queer; strange: *a* peculiar *idea.* **2** special; particular: *This rare orchid will be of* peculiar *interest to a botanist.* **—*adv-* pe·cul′ iar·ly.**

peculiar to possessed exclusively by; characteristic of: *Each person's fingerprints are* peculiar to *himself.*

pe·cu·li·ar·i·ty (pə kyōō′ lē ăr′ ə tē) ***n-*** [*pl.* **pe·cu·li·ar·i·ties**] **1** odd or queer trait or characteristic. **2** distinctive feature or quality: *A keen sense of smell is a* peculiarity *of the bloodhound.* **3** oddness; strangeness: *In New York* peculiarity *attracts less notice than in most places.*

pe·cu·ni·ar·y (pə kyōō′ nē ĕr′ ē) ***adj-*** of or related to money; financial.

ped·a·go·gic (pĕd′ ə gŏj′ ĭk) or **ped·a·go·gi·cal** (-ĭ kəl) ***adj-*** of or related to teaching: *modern* pedagogic *methods.* **—*adv-* ped′ a·go′ gi·cal·ly.**

ped·a·gogue or **ped·a·gog** (pĕd′ ə gŏg′) ***n-*** teacher; especially, a narrow-minded or pedantic teacher.

ped·a·go·gy (pĕd′ ə gŏj′ ē, -gō′ jē) ***n-*** art or science of teaching.

ped·al (pĕd′ əl) ***n-*** foot-controlled lever used to operate a mechanism: *a brake* pedal; *a bicycle* pedal; *a piano* pedal. *as* ***modifier***: *a* pedal *rod.* ***vt-*** to move or operate by using pedals: *to* pedal *a bicycle.* ***vi-***: *He jumped on his bicycle and* pedaled *off.* ***Hom-*** peddle.

Pedal

ped·ant (pĕd′ ənt) ***n-*** learned person, especially a teacher or scholar, who shows a lack of common sense and imagination, a concern with trivial detail, and a rigid adherence to formal rules.

pe·dan·tic (pə dăn′ tĭk) ***adj-*** of or like a pedant or pedantry: *a* pedantic *scholar*; *a* pedantic *book.* **—*adv-* pe·dan′ ti·cal·ly.**

ped·ant·ry (pĕd′ ən trē) ***n-*** the practices, attitudes, or character of a pedant; strict following of rules, concern with trivial detail, etc., in learning.

ped·dle (pĕd′ əl) ***vt-*** **[ped·dled, ped·dling]** **1** to sell (goods carried with one) on the street or from house to house: *He* peddles *fruit in our neighborhood.* **2** to distribute from place to place: *He* peddles *handbills. She loves to* peddle *gossip.* ***vi-***: *He* peddles *for a living.* ***Hom-*** pedal.

ped·dler (pĕd′ lər) ***n-*** **1** (also **ped′ lar**) merchant who sells small articles which he carries from place to place. **2** someone who peddles.

ped·es·tal (pĕd′ əs təl) ***n-*** **1** base or shaft for holding or displaying something: *The bust stood on a* pedestal. **2** the attached base of a tall lamp or vase. **3** place of high regard or admiration: *Mary set her movie hero on a* pedestal.

pe·des·tri·an (pə dĕs′ trē ən) ***n-*** person who goes on foot, especially where vehicles are present. ***adj-*** **1** of or for people on foot: *crowded* pedestrian *traffic*; *a* pedestrian *bridge.* **2** not inspired; dull; plodding: *a* pedestrian *lecture*; *a* pedestrian *performance.*

Pedestal

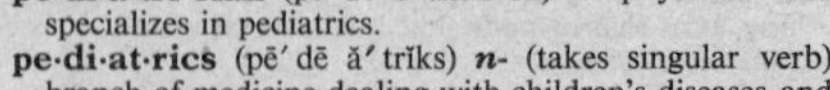

pe·di·a·tri·cian (pē′ dē ə trĭsh′ ən) ***n-*** physician who specializes in pediatrics.

pe·di·at·rics (pē′ dē ă′ trĭks) ***n-*** (takes singular verb) branch of medicine dealing with children's diseases and their treatment.

ped·i·cel (pĕd′ ə səl) ***n-*** the stalk of an individual flower in a cluster.

ped·i·cure (pĕd′ ə kyŏŏr′) ***n-*** beauty treatment of the toenails.

ped·i·gree (pĕd′ ə grē′) ***n-*** **1** systematic list of ancestors; family tree: *Here is my collie's* pedigree. **2** descent; especially, aristocratic descent: *The duke is a man of noble* pedigree.

ped·i·greed (pĕd′ ə grēd′) ***adj-*** having a known pedigree or family tree: *a* pedigreed *wolfhound.*

ped·i·ment (pĕd′ ə mənt) ***n-*** **1** in Greek architecture, a triangular gable over the front of some buildings. **2** any similarly shaped decorative piece over a door, fireplace, bookcase, etc.

Pediment

ped·lar (pĕd′ lər) See *peddler.*

pe·dom·e·ter (pə dŏm′ ə tər) ***n-*** instrument that counts the number of steps taken by the person carrying it and thus measures the distance covered in walking.

pe·dun·cle (pĭ dŭng′ kəl) ***n-*** the stalk of a solitary flower or flower cluster.

peek (pēk) ***vi-*** to look in a cautious or sly way, often through a small or hidden opening; peep: *The hunter* peeked *through the bushes and saw a deer approaching.* ***n-*** cautious or sly look; peep. ***Homs-*** peak, pique.

peel (pēl) ***vt-*** to remove the skin or outer covering from: *to* peel *an orange.* **2** to remove in a layer or strips: *to* peel *the bark from a twig.* ***vi-*** **1** to come off in a layer or in flakes: *Where the paint has* peeled *you can see the bare wood.* **2** to lose the outer layer of skin, bark, etc: *My nose is* peeling *from sunburn.* ***n-*** skin or rind of certain fruits and vegetables: *lemon* peel; *onion* peel; *banana* peel. ***Hom-*** peal.

keep (one's) eyes peeled *Informal* to be watchful.

peel off in aviation, to turn sharply away from a formation in order to dive or land.

peel·ing (pē′ lĭng) ***n-*** fruit rind, bark, skin, etc., that has, or has been, peeled off.

[1]**peep** (pēp) ***vi-*** **1** to look cautiously or slyly, often through a crack or from a hiding place: *The squirrel* peeped *around a branch at me.* **2** to begin to appear; show slightly: *The moon* peeped *from behind a cloud.* ***n-*** quick look; glimpse: *You can get a* peep *at the parade from this window.* [probably a changed form of **peek.**] **—*n-* peep′ er.**

[2]**peep** (pēp) ***n-*** high chirping sound like that made by a young bird; cheep. ***vi-***: *The young robin* peeped *in its nest.* [from Middle English **pepen** meaning "to chirp; pipe," ultimately from Latin **pīpāre,** perhaps an imitation of the sound.]

peep·er (pē′ pər) ***n-*** spring peeper. See also [1]*peep.*

peep·hole (pēp′ hōl′) ***n-*** any opening or aperture through which a person may peep: *a* peephole *in a fence*; *a* peephole *in a door.*

Peeping Tom ***n-*** in English legend, a tailor who was struck blind after peeping at the naked Lady Godiva riding through Coventry; hence, anyone who secretly and illegally watches others from sexual curiosity.

[1]**peer** (pêr) ***n-*** **1** person of equal rank or ability; equal: *tried by a jury of his* peers. **2** member of the nobility, especially in Great Britain. [from Old French **per** from a Latin word **par** meaning "equal."] ***Hom-*** pier.

[2]**peer** (pêr) ***vi-* 1** to look closely, especially out of curiosity: *Please stop* peering *over my shoulder to see what I'm doing.* **2** to peep out; come into sight: *The sun* peered *from behind a cloud.* [from a Germanic language, probably from early Dutch **pieren.**]

peer·age (pêr′ ĭj) ***n-* 1** peers or noblemen as a group; the aristocracy. **2** the rank or dignity of a nobleman. **3** book or list containing the genealogies of peers.

peer·ess (pêr′ əs) ***n-*** woman who is a member of the peerage or nobility, especially in Great Britain.

peer·less (pêr′ ləs) ***adj-*** without equal; matchless: *a princess of* peerless *beauty.*

peeve (pēv) *Informal* ***vt-*** **[peeved, peev·ing]** to vex or irritate. ***n-*** gripe; grudge: *He had several* peeves.

pee·vish (pē′ vĭsh) ***adj-*** annoyed and fretful. ***—adv-* pee′ vish·ly.** ***n-* pee′ vish·ness.**

pee·wee (pē′ wē′) ***n-* 1** pewee. **2** *Informal* someone or something extremely small. *as* ***modifier****: a* peewee *shortstop.*

peg (pĕg) ***n-* 1** short piece of wood, metal, or plastic used to fasten something or to hang something on: *a tent* peg; *a clothes* peg. **2** step, degree, or level, especially of a person's worth, ability, etc.: *His reputation was lowered a* peg *by the rumors.* **3** *Informal* a quick throw: *the shortstop's* peg *to the plate.* ***vt-*** **[pegged, peg·ging]** *Informal* to throw quickly: *The catcher* pegged *the ball to second.*

peg away to work steadily: *to* peg away *at one's work.*

peg out to mark with pegs; stake out.

take down a peg to humble.

Peg·a·sus (pĕg′ ə səs) ***n-* 1** in Greek mythology, a winged horse, the steed of the Muses. **2** a northern constellation.

peg leg *Informal* ***n-* 1** artificial leg, usually attached to the knee. **2** person who wears such a leg.

P.E.I. Prince Edward Island.

Pe·king·ese (pē′ kĭn ēz′, pē′ kĭng-) ***n-*** [*pl.* **Pe·king·ese**] **1** native or inhabitant of Peking. **2** the dialect spoken in Peking. **3** any breed of small, long-haired, flat-faced dogs, first raised in China. Also **Pe′ kin·ese′.**

Pekingese, about 15 in. long

Pe·king man (pē′ kĭng′) ***n-*** genus of apelike man, known from the fossil remains found in the Pleistocene deposits of limestone caves near Peking, China.

pe·koe (pē′ kō) ***n-*** choice black tea of India, Ceylon, and Java, made from leaves near the tip of the stem but older than those used for orange pekoe. ***Hom-*** picot.

pe·lag·ic (pə lăj′ ĭk) ***adj-*** pertaining to or living in the ocean, especially near the surface and far from land.

pelf (pĕlf) ***n-*** money; wealth, especially if improperly acquired.

pel·i·can (pĕl′ ə kən) ***n-*** large water bird with a long bill, the lower part of which has a pouch for storing freshly caught fish.

Pelican, about 5 ft. long

pel·lag·ra (pə lăg′ rə, -lā′ grə) ***n-*** in pathology, a skin disease caused by a vitamin- B deficiency, and occurring frequently in Europe and southern United States. It disturbs the nervous system and often results in melancholia and idiocy. ***—adj-* pel·lag′ rous.**

pel·let (pĕl′ ət) ***n-* 1** little ball, as of paper, food, medicine, etc. **2** small missile; bullet.

pell-mell (pĕl′ mĕl′) ***adv-*** in a disorderly or hurried manner: *The children rushed out onto the playground* pell-mell. ***adj-****: a* pell-mell *existence.*

pel·lu·cid (pə lo͞o′ sĭd) ***adj-* 1** transparent; clear: *a* pellucid *stream.* **2** easily understood: *a* pellucid *language.*

[1]**pelt** (pĕlt) ***n-*** the furry, untanned skin of an animal. [from Middle English **peltry** meaning "skins; fur trading," from Old French **peleterie,** from Latin **pellis,** "an animal skin."]

Pelt

[2]**pelt** (pĕlt) ***vt-* 1** to strike with a number of missiles in rapid succession: *to* pelt *a person with snowballs.* **2** to hurl: *to* pelt *pebbles at a window.* ***vi-*** to beat heavily: *The hail* pelted *down.* ***n-*** blow from something falling or thrown: *the* pelt *of a raindrop.* [probably from Latin **pultāre** meaning "to knock; beat."]

full pelt at top speed.

pel·vis (pĕl′ vəs) ***n-*** [*pl.* **pel·vis·es** or **pel·ves** (-vēz′)] **1** in man's anatomy, the basin-shaped structure of bones which supports the spine and to which the legs are attached. **2** in animals, a similar structure where the backbone and hipbones meet. ***—adj-* pel′ vic:** *a* pelvic *injury.*

ILIUM
PUBIS
ISCHIUM
Human pelvis

pem·mi·can (pĕm′ ĭ kən) ***n-*** an American Indian food made of lean meat, fat, and sometimes fruit, and often dried, pounded, and pressed into cakes. [American word from Cree Indian **pimikkān** meaning "meat with fat added."]

[1]**pen** (pĕn) ***n-*** small enclosure, especially one in which animals are kept: *a* pen *for rabbits.* ***vt-*** **[penned** or **pent, pen·ning]** to shut up in or as if in an enclosure: *to* pen *sheep.* [from Old English **penn.**]

[2]**pen** (pĕn) ***n-* 1** instrument used for writing with ink. **2** in botany, the midrib of a leaf. ***vt-*** **[penned, pen·ning]:** *to* pen *a letter.* [from Latin **penna,** "feather."]

[3]**pen** (pĕn) *Slang* ***n-*** penitentiary.

pen. peninsula.

pe·nal (pē′ nəl) ***adj-* 1** of or pertaining to punishment or to punished persons: *our* penal *laws*; penal *labor*; penal *colony.* **2** warranting punishment: *a* penal *offense.*

pe·nal·ize (pĕn′ ə līz′, pē′ nə-) ***vt-*** **[pe·nal·ized, pe·nal·iz·ing]** to impose a punishment, penalty, or disadvantage on: *The referee* penalized *the team for unnecessary roughness.*

pen·al·ty (pĕn′ əl tē) ***n-*** [*pl.* **pen·al·ties**] **1** punishment for a crime or offense: *The* penalty *for treason is death.* **2** fine, forfeit, or handicap imposed for breaking a law or rule: *Our football team lost five yards as a* penalty *for being offside.*

pen·ance (pĕn′ əns) ***n-* 1** in some Christian churches, a sacramental rite, including contrition, confession to a

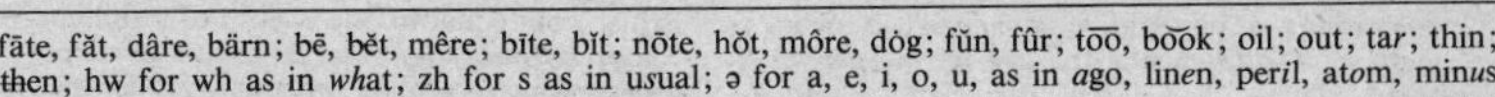

fāte, făt, dâre, bärn; bē, bĕt, mêre; bīte, bĭt; nōte, hŏt, môre, dȯg; fŭn, fûr; to͞o, bo͝ok; oil; out; tar; thin; then; hw for wh as in *wh*at; zh for s as in u*s*ual; ə for a, e, i, o, u, as in *a*go, lin*e*n, per*i*l, at*o*m, min*u*s

priest, and absolution. **2** any suffering or punishment accepted to show repentance for wrongdoing.

do penance to perform an act of penance.

pence (pĕns) *Brit. pl.* of **penny.**

pen·chant (pĕn′ chənt) ***n-*** strong leaning or taste: *She has a* penchant *for music.*

pen·cil (pĕn′ səl) ***n-*** **1** stick of black graphite, colored chalk, etc., usually covered with wood, and used for writing or drawing. **2** small slender implement having a cosmetic or medicinal property or use: *an eyebrow* pencil; *a* styptic *pencil.* ***vt-*** to write or sketch with a pencil: *to* pencil *a note.*

Pendant

pen·dant (pĕn′ dənt) ***n-*** hanging jewel or ornament: *She wore an emerald* pendant *on her necklace. Glass* pendants *decorated the candlestick.* ***Hom-*** pendent.

pen·dent (pĕn′ dənt) ***adj-*** **1** suspended or hanging: *several* pendent *decorations.* **2** jutting out; overhanging: *a* pendent rock. **3** pending. ***Hom-*** pendant. ***—adv-*** **pen′ dent·ly.**

pend·ing (pĕn′ dĭng) ***adj-*** not yet acted on or decided: *The lawsuit between the two companies is still* pending. ***prep-*** until; while awaiting: *We sat in the hotel lobby* pending *Father's return.*

pen·drag·on (pĕn drăg′ ən) ***n-*** in ancient Britain, a leader or chief.

pen·du·lous (pĕn′ dyə ləs) ***adj-*** **1** hanging so as to swing; swaying: *the* pendulous *nest of the oriole.* **2** hanging or drooping: *a* pendulous *branch of a tree.* ***—adv-*** **pen′ du·lous·ly.** ***n-*** **pen′ du·lous·ness.**

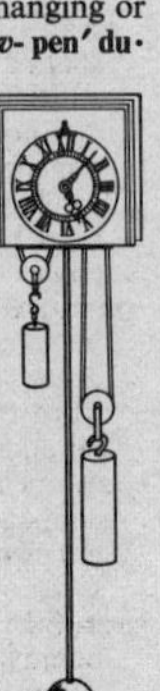
Pendulum

pen·du·lum (pĕn′ dyə ləm) ***n-*** **1** weight suspended from a fixed point by a string or wire, and swinging to and fro under the influence of gravity. **2** such a device used to measure time or regulate a clock. **3** something that alternates between extremes: *the* pendulum *of his opinions.*

Pe·nel·o·pe (pə nĕl′ ə pē) ***n-*** in the "Odyssey," the faithful wife of Odysseus (Ulysses).

pe·ne·plain (pĕn′ ə plān′) ***n-*** land area formerly mountainous but made nearly level by erosion. Also **pe′ ne·plane′.**

pen·e·tra·ble (pĕn′ ə trə bəl) ***adj-*** such as can be entered or pierced: *a* penetrable *fortress.* ***—n-*** **pen′ e·tra·bil′ i·ty.**

pen·e·trate (pĕn′ ə trāt′) ***vt-*** **[pen·e·trat·ed, pen·e·trat·ing]** (in senses 1, 2, and 4, considered intransitive when the direct object is implied but not expressed) **1** to enter into; go through; pierce: *The troops* penetrated *the enemy lines.* **2** to soak through; spread through: *The early morning dampness* penetrated *our clothes.* **3** to find out; understand: *Scientists try to* penetrate *the mysteries of nature.* **4** to affect or move the emotions, feelings, etc., of.

pen·e·trat·ing (pĕn′ ə trā′ tĭng) ***adj-*** **1** piercing; sharp: *a* penetrating *wind.* **2** discerning; knowing: *a* penetrating *remark.* ***—adv-*** **pen′ e·trat′ ing·ly.**

pen·e·tra·tion (pĕn′ ə trā′ shən) ***n-*** **1** a going or entering into; a piercing: *The* penetration *of the jungle was slow and difficult.* **2** keenness or acuteness of mind; insight: *We admired his* penetration *in dealing with the problem.*

pen·e·tra·tive (pĕn′ ə trā′ tĭv) ***adj-*** tending to penetrate; penetrating: *a* penetrative *dampness*; *a* penetrative *question.* ***—adv-*** **pen′ e·tra′ tive·ly.** ***n-*** **pen′ e·tra′ tive·ness.**

pen·guin (pĕng′ gwĭn) ***n-*** any of various related seabirds found near the South Pole. Penguins cannot fly but use their wings to swim.

Emperor penguin, about 3 1/2 ft. long

pen·i·cil·lin (pĕn′ ə sĭl′ ən) ***n-*** any of a group of powerful germ-killing drugs, made from molds and used in treating infectious diseases.

pen·i·cil·li·um (pĕn′ ə sĭl′ ē əm) ***n-*** any of a genus of molds **(Penicillium)** that grow on fruits, cheese, etc. At least two species produce penicillins.

pen·in·su·la (pə nĭn′ sə lə, -syə lə) ***n-*** area of land almost entirely surrounded by water: *Italy is a* peninsula *shaped like a boot.*

pen·in·su·lar (pə nĭn′ sə lər, -syə lər) ***adj-*** of, like, or on a peninsula: *a* peninsular *war.*

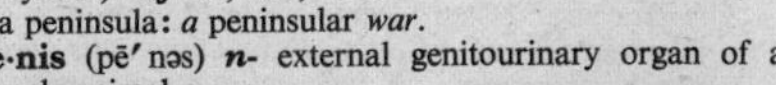

pe·nis (pē′ nəs) ***n-*** external genitourinary organ of a male animal.

Peninsula (Florida)

pen·i·tence (pĕn′ ə təns) ***n-*** repentance; remorse; sorrow for wrongdoing.

pen·i·tent (pĕn′ ə tənt) ***adj-*** sorrowful over one's wrong ways and willing to correct them; repentant. ***n-*** person who is sorry for wrongdoing and is willing to make amends. ***—adv-*** **pen′ i·tent·ly.**

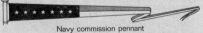

pen·i·ten·tial (pĕn′ ə tĕn′ shəl) ***adj-*** of or pertaining to penitence or to penance: *Lent is a* penitential *season.*

pen·i·ten·tia·ry (pĕn ə tĕn′ chə rē) ***n-*** [*pl.* **pen·i·ten·tia·ries**] prison, especially a state or federal prison, for persons convicted of serious crimes. *as* ***modifier:*** *a* penitentiary *offense.*

pen·knife (pĕn′ nīf′) ***n-*** [*pl.* **pen·knives**] small pocketknife.

pen·man (pĕn′ mən) ***n-*** [*pl.* **pen·men**] **1** person skilled in handwriting. **2** writer; author.

pen·man·ship (pĕn′ mən shĭp′) ***n-*** art or style of handwriting.

pen name ***n-*** fictitious name used by an author; pseudonym; nom de plume.

pen·nant (pĕn′ ənt) ***n-*** **1** long, narrow flag or streamer used on ships. **2** triangular flag used as a decoration or as a school or club flag. **3** flag awarded to a championship team; also, the championship it signifies.

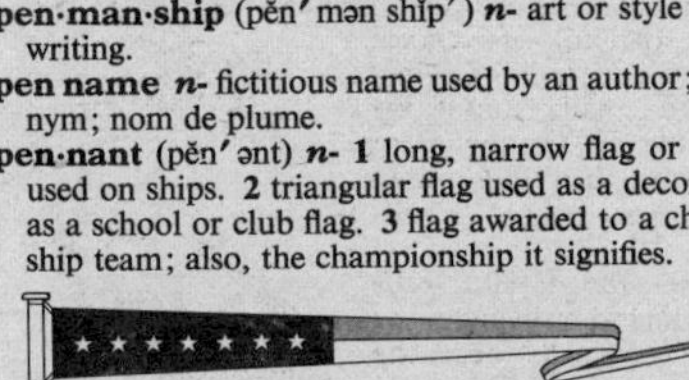
Navy commission pennant

pen·ni·less (pĕn′ ĭ ləs) ***adj-*** without any money; impoverished; very poor.

pen·non (pĕn′ ən) ***n-*** **1** swallow-tailed or triangular flag or streamer, formerly borne on a lance. **2** any flag.

Pennsylvania Dutch ***n-*** **1** descendants of German and Swiss immigrants who settled in Pennsylvania during the eighteenth century. **2** the German dialect spoken by these people. Also **Pennsylvania German.**

pen·ny (pĕn′ ē) ***n-*** [*pl.* **pen·nies**] **1** cent. **2** [*pl.* **pence**] British coin equal to one twelfth of a shilling.

a pretty penny *Informal* large sum of money. **turn an honest penny** to acquire money by proper means.

penny an·te (ăn′ tē) ***n-*** poker game in which the first stake is one cent; also, any low-stakes game. ***adj-*** **(penny-ante):** *a* penny-ante *game.*

penny arcade ***n-*** low-cost amusement center made up largely of coin-operated devices.

pen·ny-pinch (pĕn′ ē pĭnch′) ***vi-*** to give or spend money very reluctantly. ***—n-*** **penny pincher.**

pen·ny·weight (pĕn′ ē wāt′) ***n-*** troy weight equal to 24 grains, or 1/20 of an ounce. *Abbr.* dwt.

pen·ny-wise (pĕn′ ē wīz′) ***adj-*** saving small sums; niggardly; also, wise about trivial matters.

penny-wise and pound-foolish thrifty with small amounts but wasteful with large ones.

pen·ny·worth (pĕn′ ē wûrth′) ***n-*** **1** amount that a penny will buy. **2** fair return for money. **3** small amount.

pe·nol·o·gist (pĭ nŏl′ ə jĭst) ***n-*** expert in penology.

pe·nol·o·gy (pĭ nŏl′ ə jē) ***n-*** the study of prison management and the treatment of prisoners.

[1]**pen·sion** (pĕn′ shən) ***n-*** sum paid regularly by the government or employer to a person after he has been injured and can no longer work or after he has worked for a specified period and retired. ***vt-*** to give a pension to: *He was* pensioned *at age 65.* [from Old French, from Latin **pensiō, -ōnis** meaning "payment," from **pendere,** "to weigh out (in payment)."]

pension off to dismiss or retire with a pension.

[2]**pen·sion** (pä^{n} syō^{n}′) *French* ***n-*** in France and other European countries, a boarding house or boarding school. [from French **pension** of the same meaning, from the same Latin source as [1]**pension.**]

pen·sion·er (pĕn′ shən ər) ***n-*** person who receives a pension.

pen·sive (pĕn′ sĭv) ***adj-*** **1** thoughtful; thinking seriously: *a* pensive *mood.* **2** expressing serious or sad thoughtfulness: *a* pensive *poem.* ***—adv-*** **pen′ sive·ly.** ***n-*** **pen′ sive·ness.**

pen·stock (pĕn′ stŏk′) ***n-*** **1** pipe carrying water to a hydroelectric turbine; also, a trough from a millrace to a water wheel. **2** sluice or floodgate.

pent (pĕnt) *p.t. & p.p.* of [1]**pen.**

pent-up (pĕnt′ ŭp′) ***adj-*** shut in or up; held in: *His* pent-up *rage.*

penta- or **pent-** *combining form* five: *a* penta*gon*; pent*athlon.* [from Greek **penta-,** from **pénte,** "five."]

pen·ta·gon (pĕn′ tə gŏn′) ***n-*** **1** polygon with five sides and five angles. For picture see *polygon.* **2** (also **regular pentagon**) polygon having five equal sides and five equal angles. **3 the Pentagon** five-sided building in Arlington, Virginia, housing the U.S. Defense Department offices; hence, the professional military leadership of the U.S. Armed Forces.

pen·tag·o·nal (pĕn tăg′ ə nəl) ***adj-*** having five sides.

pen·ta·he·dron (pĕn′ tə hē′ drən) ***n-*** geometric solid having five plane faces.

pen·tam·e·ter (pĕn tăm′ ə tər) ***n-*** a line of verse consisting of five stressed syllables; also, verse composed of such lines.

Pen·ta·teuch (pĕn′ tə to͞ok′) ***n-*** the first five books of the Old Testament.

pen·tath·lon (pĕn tăth′ lən) ***n-*** athletic competition in which each contestant performs in five different track and field events.

Pen·te·cost (pĕn′ tə kŏst′, -kŏst′) ***n-*** **1** Christian festival observed on the seventh Sunday after Easter, commemorating the descent of the Holy Spirit on the apostles; Whitsunday. **2** Shabuoth. ***—adj-*** **Pen′ te·cos′ tal:** *the* Pentecostal *feast.*

pent·house (pĕnt′ hous′) ***n-*** apartment or other dwelling on the roof of a building.

pe·nult (pē′ nŭlt′) ***n-*** the next to the last syllable of a word.

pe·nul·ti·mate (pĭ nŭl′ tə mət) ***adj-*** **1** of or pertaining to a penult: *a* penultimate *syllable.* **2** next to the last: *the* penultimate *line in a poem.*

pe·num·bra (pə nŭm′ brə) ***n-*** **1** the outer, lighter portion of a shadow. **2** *Astronomy* (1) the partially illuminated fringe of the shadow of a total eclipse. (2) the lighter fringe surrounding the central part of a sunspot. See also *umbra.*

pe·nu·ri·ous (pə no͝or′ ē əs, -nyo͝or′ ē əs) ***adj-*** **1** stingy or miserly. **2** extremely poor: *the* penurious *conditions of the community.* ***—adv-*** **pe·nu′ ri·ous·ly.** ***n-*** **pe·nu′ ri·ous·ness.**

pen·u·ry (pĕn′ yə rē) ***n-*** extreme poverty.

pe·on (pē′ ŏn′, -ən) ***n-*** **1** in Spanish America, an unskilled laborer who does not own land; hence, a menial drudge. **2** formerly in Spanish America, a landless laborer forced to work for a landowner to pay off debts. ***Hom-*** paean.

pe·on·age (pē′ ə nĭj) ***n-*** **1** condition of being a peon. **2** system of contract labor in which workmen or convicts are leased to employers. **3** system of compulsory servitude for debtors.

pe·o·ny (pē′ ə nē′, *also* pē ō′ nē) ***n-*** [*pl.* **pe·o·nies**] **1** garden plant bearing large, showy, pink or white flowers. **2** flower of this plant.

Peony

peo·ple (pē′ pəl) ***n-*** (takes a plural verb except in the singular of sense 4) **1** persons; men, women, and children: *There were a lot of* people *at the beach.* **2** all persons belonging to a community, race, tribe, or nation: *the American* people. **3 the people** the public, especially the populace or masses. **4** [*pl.* **peo·ples**] tribe or other ethnic group that is distinct from others, especially in language or culture: *a* people *that lives in the Amazon forest.* **5** persons of a particular group, profession, condition, etc.: *farm* people; *rich* people. **6** relatives; family: *I want you to come home with me and meet my* people. ***vt-*** **[peo·pled, peo·pling]** to fill with people; inhabit: *to* people *a new colony.*

pep (pĕp) *Informal* ***n-*** sprightly activity; liveliness; energy; vim: *He's full of* pep.

pep up [pepped up, pep·ping up] **1** to instill with energy and enthusiasm; put life into. **2** to brighten up; feel more cheerful.

pep·lum (pĕp′ ləm) ***n-*** [*pl.* **pep·lums** or **pep·la** (-lə)] flounce or short, fitted overskirt, attached at the waist and extending over the hips.

pep·per (pĕp′ ər) ***n-*** **1** tropical plant bearing small, round berries with a very strong, spicy flavor. **2** the berries of this plant, often ground to a powder with the husks removed **(white pepper)**, or with the husks left on **(black pepper),** and used as a spice or seasoning. **3** any of several plants related to the tomato and potato, having bell-shaped or long, pointed fruits, many of which have a strong flavor and are used as spices. The **sweet** or **bell pepper** has hollow, mildly flavored green or red fruit. **4** fruit of any of these plants. ***vt-*** **1** to season with pepper. **2** to sprinkle

Sweet pepper

with small marks or objects: *She* peppered *her letters with commas. He* peppered *a target with bullets.*

pep·per-and-salt (pěp′ ər ən sôlt′) ***adj-*** having small flecks of black and white mixed together: *a* pepper-and-salt *tweed*; pepper-and-salt *hair.*

pep·per·corn (pěp′ ər kôrn′, -kôrn′) ***n-*** small, dried berry of the pepper plant.

pepper mill ***n-*** small grinder, often used at table, in which peppercorns are ground.

pep·per·mint (pěp′ ər mĭnt′) ***n-*** **1** strong-smelling, cool-tasting plant of the mint family. **2** oil from this plant, used in flavoring. **3** candy flavored with this oil.

pep·per·y (pěp′ ə rē) ***adj-*** **1** containing or suggestive of pepper: *a* peppery *meal.* **2** hot-tempered; spirited or fiery: *a* peppery *quarterback.* **—*n-* pep′ per·i·ness.**

pep·py (pĕp′ ē) *Informal* ***adj-*** **[pep·pi·er, pep·pi·est]** lively; energetic; full of pep. **—*n-* pep′ pi·ness.**

pep·sin (pěp′ sən) ***n-*** **1** enzyme formed by the gastric glands of animals as a natural aid to digestion. **2** preparation from this substance used in medicine.

pep·tic (pěp′ tĭk) ***adj-*** **1** relating to, producing, or containing pepsin. **2** pertaining to digestion.

peptic ulcer ***n-*** an ulcer of the lower end of the esophagus, stomach, or duodenum.

pep·tone (pěp′ tōn′) ***n-*** any of a number of soluble substances into which proteins are changed by the gastric and pancreatic juices.

Pe·quot (pē′ kwŏt′) ***n-*** [*pl.* **Pe·quots,** *also* **Pe·quot**] one of a tribe of American Indians who formerly lived in Connecticut and parts of Rhode Island.

per (pər) ***prep-*** **1** for each: *Melissa earns $10* per *day.* **2** by means of; through: *You will receive a note* per *special delivery.* **3** according to: *We have 300 filters in stock* per *inventory.*

per·ad·ven·ture (pûr′ əd věn′ chər) *Archaic* ***adv-*** perhaps.

per·am·bu·late (pə răm′ byə lāt′) ***vt-*** **[per·am·bu·lat·ed, per·am·bu·lat·ing]** to walk through or over, especially in order to inspect or oversee. ***vi-*** to walk or stroll around. **—*n-* per·am′ bu·la′ tion.**

per·am·bu·la·tor (pə răm′ byə lā′ tər) ***n-*** **1** person who perambulates. **2** *chiefly Brit.* small baby carriage.

per an·num (pər ăn′ əm) *Latin* each year; annually: *He gets a pension of $1,000* per annum.

per·cale (pər kāl′) ***n-*** fine, closely woven cotton fabric.

per cap·i·ta (pər kăp′ ə tə) *Latin* to, for, or by each person: *a* per capita *tax*; per capita *output.*

per·ceive (pər sēv′) ***vt-*** **[per·ceived, per·ceiv·ing]** **1** to become aware of through the senses: *to* perceive *a sound*; *to* perceive *a dim light.* **2** to understand: *I* perceived *that he was about to refuse.*

per·cent or **per cent** (pər sěnt′) ***n-*** **1** one of a hundred parts; hundredth: *Six* percent *of a hundred apples is six apples.* **2** proportion of an original quantity, expressed as a specified number of hundredths: *An increase in speed of five* percent. **3** percentage. *as* ***modifier***: *a six* percent *interest on a loan.* Also **per cen′ tum.**

per·cent·age (pər sěn′ tĭj) ***n-*** **1** portion that can be stated in percent: *A certain* percentage *of his wages is taken in taxes.* **2** *Informal* favorable odds; advantage: *He was a gambler who looked for the* percentage.

►In sense 1, PERCENT is now more common than PERCENTAGE: *Taxes take a large* percent (percentage) *of the profit.*

per·cen·tile (pər sěn′ tīl′) ***n-*** number that indicates a person's relative performance on a test as compared with others. Someone with a percentile of 89 has equaled or exceeded the performance of 89% of the others taking the same test.

per·cep·ti·ble (pər sěp′ tə bəl) ***adj-*** such as can be perceived; noticeable: *a* perceptible *change in the weather.* **—*n-* per·cep′ ti·bil′ i·ty.** ***adv-*** **per·cep′ ti·bly.**

per·cep·tion (pər sěp′ shən) ***n-*** **1** act of perceiving. **2** ability to perceive: *a good* perception *of color*; *a man of keen* perception. **3** something perceived; mental image.

per·cep·tive (pər sěp′ tĭv) ***adj-*** having or showing good perception: *a* perceptive *writer*; *a* perceptive *book.* **—*adv-* per·cep′ tive·ly.** ***n-*** **per·cep′ tive·ness.**

[1]**perch** (pûrch) ***n-*** [*pl.* **perch; perch·es** (kinds of perch)] **1** stout, sharp-finned, yellow-green, fresh-water food fish, growing to a foot in length. **2** a similar salt-water fish. [from Old French **perche,** from Latin **perca,** from Greek **pérkē** meaning literally "spotted."]

[2]**perch** (pûrch) ***n-*** **1** resting place for a bird. **2** any high resting place: *From her* perch *on the high stool, Molly watched the playful kittens.* **3** a cubic measure for wood or stonework, equal to about 25 cubic feet. ***vt-*** to place on or as if on a perch or height: *He* perched *the bird on his hand.* ***vi-***: *Tom* perched *shakily at the edge of the roof.* [from French **perche,** from Latin **pertica,** "pole."]

per·chance (pər chăns′) ***adv-*** perhaps; possibly.

Per·ci·val (pûr′ sə vəl) ***n-*** in Arthurian legend, a knight of the Round Table, who succeeded in the search for the Holy Grail. Also **Per′ ci·vale.**

per·co·late (pûr′ kə lāt′) ***vi-*** **[per·co·lat·ed, per·co·lat·ing]** to drip or seep (through): *Water* percolates *through the soil to form springs.* ***vt-*** **1** to cause (a liquid) to seep through. **2** to prepare (coffee) in a percolator. **—*n-* per′ co·la′ tion.**

per·co·la·tor (pûr′ kə lā′ tər) ***n-*** something that percolates or filters; especially, a coffeepot in which boiling water seeps through ground coffee.

per·cus·sion (pər kŭsh′ ən) ***n-*** **1** a striking of one thing against another: *the* percussion *of ball and bat.* **2** vibration made by one thing striking against another: *the loud* percussion *of a drum.* **3** impression of sound waves on the eardrum. **4** *Medicine* examination of a part of the body by striking it with sharp, light blows so as to determine its condition by the sound produced.

percussion instrument ***n-*** musical instrument that is played by striking it with a hand, stick, hammer, etc.: *Drums and xylophones are* percussion instruments.

per di·em (pər dē′ əm) *Latin* by the day: *He was paid* per diem.

per·di·tion (pər dĭsh′ ən) ***n-*** **1** hell; eternal damnation. **2** *Archaic* total ruin or destruction.

père (pěr) *French* ***n-*** father (often used after the father's name to distinguish him from the son): *Dumas* père.

per·e·gri·na·tion (pěr′ ə grə nā′ shən) ***n-*** a traveling around or wandering from place to place.

per·emp·to·ry (pə rěmp′ tə rē) ***adj-*** **1** positive; final; allowing no discussion: *a* peremptory *command.* **2** dictatorial: *a* peremptory *manner.* **—*adv-* per·emp′ to·ri·ly.** ***n-*** **per·emp′ to·ri·ness.**

pe·ren·ni·al (pə rěn′ ē əl) ***adj-*** **1** lasting the whole year, as evergreen foliage does. **2** growing or blooming for several years without replanting: *a* perennial *plant.* **3** in botany, living from year to year; not dying after a single flowering: *A rose is a* perennial *flower.* **4** continuous; unceasing: *a subject of* perennial *interest.* ***n-*** plant that lives and grows for three or more years. **—*adv-* pe·ren′ ni·al·ly.**

[1]**per·fect** (pûr′ fĭkt) ***adj-*** **1** flawless; without defects; excellent: *a* perfect *gem*; *to enjoy* perfect *weather.* **2** complete; whole: *a* perfect *set of china.* **3** exact: *a* perfect *circle*; *a* perfect *likeness.* **4** utter; entire: *a* perfect *stranger.* ***n-*** *Grammar* perfect tense or a verb in the perfect tense. **—*adv-* per′ fect·ly.** ***n-*** **per′ fect·ness.**

[2]**per·fect** (pər fĕkt′) *vt-* to remove all flaws from: *They have* perfected *a new engine.* **—*n-* per·fect′ er.**

per·fec·ti·ble (pər fĕk′ tə bəl) ***adj-*** such as can be made perfect. **—*n-* per·fect′ i·bil′ ity.**

per·fec·tion (pər fĕk′ shən) ***n-*** **1** quality or condition of completeness, exactness, or freedom from faults: *the sheer* perfection *of his piano playing.* **2** person or thing that has a high degree of excellence: *He is* perfection *at the keyboard.* **3** act or method of perfecting: *the* perfection *of an automotive part.*

to perfection perfectly: *He did his job* to perfection.

per·fec·tion·ism (pər fĕk′ shən ĭz′ əm) ***n-*** **1** a setting of extremely high standards for oneself or others. **2** belief that man can achieve moral perfection or excellence; also, the belief that this achievement is the highest good.

per·fec·tion·ist (pər fĕk′ shən ĭst) ***n-*** one who sets extremely high standards for himself or others. ***adj-*** (*also* **per·fec′ tion·ist′ ic**): *a* perfectionist *attitude toward work.*

perfect participle See *participle.*

perfect tense *Grammar* ***n-*** **1** any of the three verb tenses that indicate that an action or condition has been completed at an unspecified time before the present (see *future perfect tense, present perfect tense, past perfect tense*). **2 the perfect tense** present perfect tense.

per·fid·i·ous (pər fĭd′ ē əs) ***adj-*** treacherous; faithless; disloyal: *a* perfidious *friend.* **—*adv-* per·fid′ i·ous·ly. *n-* per·fid′ i·ous·ness.**

per·fi·dy (pûr′ fə dē) ***n-*** [*pl.* **per·fi·dies**] betrayal of faith or trust; treachery; disloyalty.

per·fo·rate (pûr′ fə rāt′) ***vt-*** **[per·fo·rat·ed, per·fo·rat·ing]** to make a hole or holes in; pierce, especially with a line of small holes to make tearing easy.

per·fo·ra·tion (pûr′ fə rā′ shən) ***n-*** **1** act of perforating or piercing. **2** one of series of holes made in something, especially to making tearing easy: *the* perforations *in a sheet of stamps.*

per·force (pər fôrs′) ***adv-*** of necessity; necessarily: *Being a successful playwright, he* perforce *knows a great deal about the theater.*

per·form (pər fôrm′, -fôrm′) ***vt-*** **1** to do; execute: *The surgeon* performed *an operation.* **2** to carry out; fulfill: *to* perform *a duty.* **3** to act (a part) in a play or other entertainment. ***vi-*** **1** to act in a play or other entertainment: *He is* performing *tonight in "Hamlet."* **2** to carry out one's duties: *He* performs *well on that committee.*

per·form·ance (pər fôr′ məns, -fôr′ məns) ***n-*** **1** a doing or carrying out: *the* performance *of his duty.* **2** that which is done; deed; feat: *The singer's* performance *was brilliant.* **3** public exhibition or presentation, especially on a stage: *There are two* performances *of the play on Saturday.* **4** way in which a person or thing functions or performs: *They were gauging the car's* performance.

per·form·er (pər fôr′ mər, -fôr′ mər) ***n-*** person or animal that performs; especially, an actor, musician, or other entertainer.

[1]**per·fume** (pûr′ fyo͞om′) ***n-*** **1** agreeable fragrance: *The breeze carried the* perfume *of lilacs.* **2** fluid preparation that gives off an agreeable fragrance or scent.

[2]**per·fume** (pər fyo͞om′) ***vt-*** **[per·fumed, per·fum·ing]** to fill with a pleasant odor; scent: *Lilacs* perfumed *the air.*

per·fum·er (pər fyo͞o′ mər) ***n-*** **1** person who makes or sells perfume. **2** person or device that perfumes.

per·fum·er·y (pər fyo͞o′ mə rē) ***n-*** [*pl.* **per·fum·er·ies**] **1** the making of perfume. **2** perfumes collectively. **3** place where perfumes are made.

per·func·to·ry (pər fŭngk′ tə rē) ***adj-*** half-hearted or careless; with the minimum necessary attention: *a* perfunctory *thanks*; perfunctory *work.* **—*adv-* per·func′ to·ri·ly. *n-* per·func′ to·ri·ness.**

per·go·la (pûr′ gə lə, pər gō′-) ***n-*** latticework over a walk or veranda, used as a trellis for climbing plants; arbor.

per·haps (pər hăps′) ***adv-*** maybe; possibly: *If you go,* perhaps *I'll join you.*

pe·ri (pêr′ ē) ***n-*** in Persian mythology, a fairy or elf descended from disobedient angels and barred from paradise until the completion of their penance.

peri- *prefix* **1** around; about; surrounding: *a* peri*meter.* **2** near: *the* peri*gee* (near the earth). [from Greek **peri-**, from **perí** meaning "around."

per·i·anth (pĕr′ ē ănth′) ***n-*** the sepals and petals considered together, especially when indistinguishable or nearly so, as in lilies and tulips.

per·i·car·di·um (pĕr′ ə kär′ dē əm) ***n-*** [*pl.* **per·i·car·di·a** (-de ə)] membrane that encloses and protects the heart.

per·i·carp (pĕr′ ə kärp′) ***n-*** ripened layers that form the wall of a plant ovary and enclose the seeds; seed vessel.

per·i·gee (pĕr′ ə jē′) ***n-*** closest point to the earth in the orbit of the moon or another satellite. See also *apogee.*

per·i·he·lion (pĕr′ ə hēl′ yən) ***n-*** [*pl.* **per·i·he·lia** (-yə)] closest point to the sun in the orbit of a planet or comet.

per·il (pĕr′ əl) ***n-*** **1** very great danger; exposure to loss of life or to great injury; risk: *The sailor adrift at sea was in great* peril. **2** something dangerous; hazard: *Icebergs are a* peril *to ships.* ***vt-*** to expose to danger or risk: *He* periled *his job by lack of attention.*

per·il·ous (pĕr′ ə ləs) ***adj-*** dangerous; risky: *a* perilous *journey.* **—*adv-* per′ il·ous·ly. —*n-* per′ il·ous·ness.**

pe·rim·e·ter (pə rĭm′ ə tər) ***n-*** **1** line, edge, or distance around an area or object: *the* perimeter *of the park.* **2** *Mathematics* (1) the boundary line of a plane figure. (2) the distance around a polygon, or the sum of its sides.

pe·ri·od (pêr′ ē əd) ***n-*** **1** fixed length of time: *Our classes are in 50-minute* periods. **2** indefinite length of time characterized by certain conditions, events, etc.; *a* period *of cold weather*; *the Revolutionary* period. **3** length of time during which something occurs regularly: *A day is divided into* periods *of light and darkness.* **4** punctuation mark [.] used to show the end of a statement or to indicate an abbreviation. **5** division of geological time shorter than an era and longer than an epoch. **6** an occurrence of menstruation. **7** *Physics* the time of one complete oscillation or vibration: *The* period *of a pendulum is one complete back-and-forth movement.* **8** *Astronomy* the time of one complete revolution of a planet or satellite about its primary.

pe·ri·od·ic (pêr′ ē ŏd′ ĭk) ***adj-*** occurring at regular intervals: *the* periodic *changes of the moon*; *the* periodic *drip of a leaking faucet.* **—*adv-* pe′ ri·od′ i·cal·ly.**

pe·ri·od·i·cal (pêr′ ē ŏd′ ĭ kəl) ***adj-*** **1** periodic. **2** of or pertaining to a publication, such as a magazine or journal, appearing at regular intervals. ***n-*** such a publication.

pe·ri·od·ic·i·ty (pêr′ ē ə dĭs′ ə tē) ***n-*** [*pl.* **pe·ri·od·ic·i·ties**] periodic occurrence or activity.

periodic law *Chemistry* ***n-*** statement that when the elements are arranged according to increasing atomic number, their chemical and physical properties tend to recur periodically.

periodic sentence ***n-*** sentence so constructed that the thought and structure are not complete until the end. Example: Last year, while on vacation, I met her.

---

fāte, făt, dâre, bärn; bē, bĕt, mêre; bīte, bĭt; nōte, hŏt, môre, dȯg; fŭn, fûr; to͞o, bo͝ok; oil; out; tar; thin; then; hw for wh as in *wh*at; zh for s as in u*s*ual; ə for a, e, i, o, u, as in *a*go, lin*e*n, per*i*l, at*o*m, min*u*s

PERIODIC TABLE OF THE ELEMENTS

METALS

1 H HYDROGEN 1.00797									
3 Li LITHIUM 6.939	4 Be BERYLLIUM 9.1022								
11 Na SODIUM 22.9898	12 Mg MAGNESIUM 24.312								
19 K POTASSIUM 39.102	20 Ca CALCIUM 40.08	21 Sc SCANDIUM 44.956		22 Ti TITANIUM 47.90	23 V VANADIUM 50.942	24 Cr CHROMIUM 51.996	25 Mn MANGANESE 54.9380	26 Fe IRON 55.847	27 Co COBALT 58.9332
37 Rb RUBIDIUM 85.47	38 Sr STRONTIUM 87.62	39 Y YTTRIUM 88.905		40 Zr ZIRCONIUM 91.22	41 Nb NIOBIUM 92.906	42 Mo MOLYBDENUM 95.94	43 Tc TECHNETIUM [99*]	44 Ru RUTHENIUM 101.07	45 Rh RHODIUM 102.905
55 Cs CESIUM 132.905	56 Ba BARIUM 137.34	57 La LANTHANIUM 138.91	*	72 Hf HAFNIUM 178.49	73 Ta TANTALUM 180.948	74 W TUNGSTEN 183.85	75 Re RHENIUM 186.2	76 Os OSMIUM 190.2	77 Ir IRIDIUM 192.2
87 Fr FRANCIUM [223]	88 Ra RADIUM [226]	89 Ac ACTINIUM [227]	§						

Lanthanide Series *	58 Ce CERIUM 140.92	59 Pr PRASEODYMIUM 140.907	60 Nd NEODYMIUM 144.24	61 Pm PROMETHIUM [147]	62 Sm SAMARIUM 150.35	63 Eu EUROPIUM 151.96
Actinide Series §	90 Th THORIUM 232.038	91 Pa PROTACTINIUM [231]	92 U URANIUM 238.03	93 Np NEPTUNIUM [237]	94 Pu PLUTONIUM [242]	95 Am AMERICIUM [243]

An atomic weight in brackets indicates the isotope of longest known half-life.

periodic table *Chemistry* ***n-*** table in which the elements are arranged according to the periodic law.

per·i·os·te·um (pĕr′ē ŏs′tē əm) ***n-*** [*pl.* **per·i·os·te·a** (tē ə)] tough, fibrous membrane that covers the bones except at the joints. It contains blood vessels that nourish the bone.

per·i·pa·tet·ic (pĕr′ə pə tĕt′ĭk) ***adj-*** walking around; also, done or performed while walking around: *a* peripatetic *discussion.*

pe·riph·e·ral (pə rĭf′ər əl) ***adj-*** of or pertaining to the periphery or outer bounds of anything: *the* peripheral *parts of a city.* **—*adv-*** **pe·riph′e·ral·ly.**

pe·riph·er·y (pə rĭf′ə rē) ***n-*** [*pl.* **pe·riph·er·ies**] outer bounds or limits of anything: *an airport located outside the* periphery *of a city.*

per·i·scope (pĕr′ə skōp′) ***n-*** tube fitted with mirrors and lenses by which a person in a submarine or trench can see what is going on above the surface without exposing himself.

MIRROR

MIRROR

How a periscope works

per·ish (pĕr′ĭsh) ***vi-*** **1** to die. **2** to spoil; decay: *Some fruits* perish *quickly if not properly packed.* **3** to disappear; vanish; become extinct: *Dinosaurs* perished *long ago.*

per·ish·a·ble (pĕr′ĭsh ə bəl) ***adj-*** likely to spoil quickly: *Fresh fruits and vegetables are* perishable *foods.* ***n-*** (usually **perishables**) things that are likely to spoil quickly. **—*n-*** **per′ish·a·bil′i·ty** or **per′ish·a·ble·ness.**

per·i·stal·sis (pĕr′ə stăl′səs, -stòl′səs) ***n-*** the wavelike constrictions of a tubular organ, caused by the successive contraction and relaxation of the circular muscles in the wall of the organ. Food is moved through the intestinal tract by peristalsis.

per·i·to·ne·um (pĕr′ə tə nē′əm) ***n-*** [*pl.* **per·i·to·ne·a** (-nē′ə)] membrane that lines the abdominal walls and covers the abdominal organs. **—*adj-*** **per′i·to·ne′al.**

per·i·to·ni·tis (pĕr′ə tə nī′təs) ***n-*** acute inflammation of the peritoneum.

per·i·wig (pĕr′ə wĭg′) ***n-*** large wig, often powdered and combed in a pompadour, worn in the 18th century.

[1]**per·i·win·kle** (pĕr′ə wĭng′kəl) ***n-*** creeping evergreen plant with shiny leaves and blue or violet flowers; myrtle. [from Old English **pervince,** from Latin **pervinca.**]

[2]**per·i·win·kle** (pĕr′ə wĭng′kəl) ***n-*** any of various snails or their shells. [from Old English **pinewincle.**]

Periwinkle

per·jure (pûr′jər) ***vt-*** [**per·jured, per·jur·ing**] to make (oneself) guilty of swearing falsely or breaking an oath. **—*n-*** **per′jur·er.**

per·jured (pûr′jərd) ***adj-*** guilty of perjury: *a* perjured *witness.*

per·ju·ry (pûr′jə rē) ***n-*** [*pl.* **per·ju·ries**] in law, the willful telling of a lie or the withholding of pertinent information under oath.

perk (pûrk) ***vt-*** to lift in a saucy, brisk way: *The little bird* perked *its head.*

perk up 1 to brighten; regain hope, courage, or enthusiasm: *She* perked up *after his compliment.* **2** to encourage: *His compliment* perked *her* up.

perk·y (pûr′kē) ***adj-*** [**perk·i·er, perk·i·est**] lively; jaunty; self-assured. **—*adv-*** **perk′i·ly.** ***n-*** **perk′i·ness.**

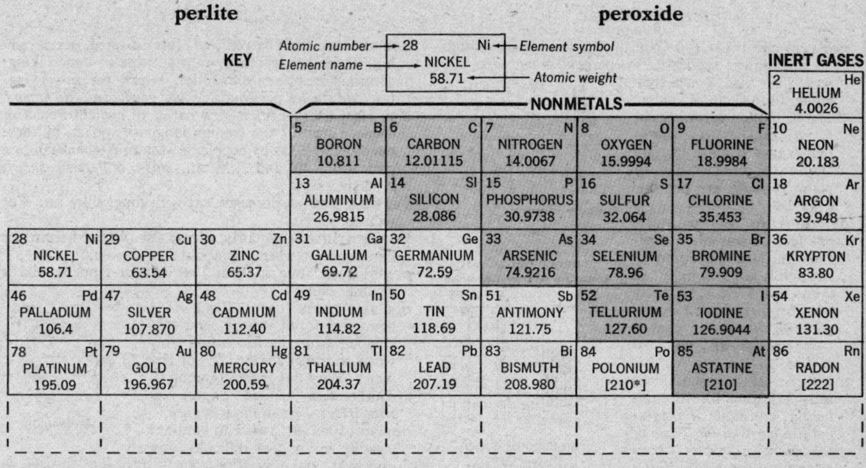

									2 He HELIUM 4.0026
			5 B BORON 10.811	6 C CARBON 12.01115	7 N NITROGEN 14.0067	8 O OXYGEN 15.9994	9 F FLUORINE 18.9984	10 Ne NEON 20.183
			13 Al ALUMINUM 26.9815	14 Si SILICON 28.086	15 P PHOSPHORUS 30.9738	16 S SULFUR 32.064	17 Cl CHLORINE 35.453	18 Ar ARGON 39.948
28 Ni NICKEL 58.71	29 Cu COPPER 63.54	30 Zn ZINC 65.37	31 Ga GALLIUM 69.72	32 Ge GERMANIUM 72.59	33 As ARSENIC 74.9216	34 Se SELENIUM 78.96	35 Br BROMINE 79.909	36 Kr KRYPTON 83.80
46 Pd PALLADIUM 106.4	47 Ag SILVER 107.870	48 Cd CADMIUM 112.40	49 In INDIUM 114.82	50 Sn TIN 118.69	51 Sb ANTIMONY 121.75	52 Te TELLURIUM 127.60	53 I IODINE 126.9044	54 Xe XENON 131.30
78 Pt PLATINUM 195.09	79 Au GOLD 196.967	80 Hg MERCURY 200.59	81 Tl THALLIUM 204.37	82 Pb LEAD 207.19	83 Bi BISMUTH 208.980	84 Po POLONIUM [210*]	85 At ASTATINE [210]	86 Rn RADON [222]

64 Gd GADOLINIUM 157.25	65 Tb TERBIUM 158.924	66 Dy DYSPROSIUM 162.50	67 Ho HOLMIUM 164.930	68 Er ERBIUM 167.26	69 Tm THULIUM 168.934	70 Yb YTTERBIUM 173.04	71 Lu LUTETIUM 174.97
96 Cm CURIUM [247]	97 Bk BERKELIUM [249*]	98 Cf CALIFORNIUM [251*]	99 Es EINSTEINIUM [254]	100 Fm FERMIUM [253]	101 Md MENDELEVIUM [256]	102 No NOBELIUM** [254]	103 Lw LAWRENCIUM [257]

or (marked by an asterisk) a better known one. **Name not officially accepted.

per·lite (pûr′ līt′) ***n-*** glassy rock with a concentric, shell-like structure, occurring as small globules and used as an insulating material.

per·ma·nence (pûr′ mə nəns) ***n-*** quality or state of being permanent; continued existence: *the* permanence *of the universe.* Also **per′ ma·nen·cy.**

per·ma·nent (pûr′ mə nənt) ***adj-*** lasting forever or for a long time: *the* permanent *ice at the poles*; *a* permanent *job.* ***n-*** permanent wave. **—*adv-* per′ ma·nent·ly.**

permanent wave ***n-*** artificially induced wave in the hair that lasts for several months.

per·man·ga·nate (pər măng′ gə nāt′) ***n-*** **1** potassium permanganate. **2** the negative radical (MnO_4^-).

per·me·a·ble (pûr′ mē ə bəl) ***adj-*** having tiny pores that allow the passage of fluids or gases; porous: *a* permeable *membrane.* **—*n-* per′ me·a·bil′ i·ty.**

per·me·ate (pûr′ mē āt′) ***vt-*** **[per·me·at·ed, per·me·at·ing] 1** to pass through the pores or crevices of: *Water* permeates *sand.* **2** to spread itself through; pervade: *The scent* permeated *the house.* **—*n-* per′ me·a′ tion.**

Per·mi·an (pûr′ mē ən) ***n-*** the last of the six periods of the Paleozoic era. In the Permian, reptiles became the dominant animal life. ***adj-***: *a* Permian *fossil.*

per·mis·si·ble (pər mĭs′ ə bəl) ***adj-*** such as can be permitted; allowable: *Stealing bases is* permissible *in a baseball game.* **—*adv-* per·mis′ si·bly.**

per·mis·sion (pər mĭsh′ ən) ***n-*** consent; leave; also, formal authorization: *We need* permission *from the Defense Department to publish the picture of this gun.*

per·mis·sive (pər mĭs′ ĭv) ***adj-*** **1** granting consent or permission: *a* permissive *measure.* **2** not strict; lenient; tolerant: *Jane's* permissive *parents.* **—*adv-* per·mis′ sive·ly. *n-* per·mis′ sive·ness.**

[1]**per·mit** (pər mĭt′) ***vt-*** **[per·mit·ted, per·mit·ting] 1** to give consent to: *The director* permitted *us to watch the rehearsal.* **2** to allow by law; also, to allow by not preventing: *to* permit *parking.* ***vi-*** to offer a chance or opportunity; allow: *If time* permits, *I will discuss it.*

[2]**per·mit** (pûr′ mĭt′) ***n-*** written proof of permission; license: *a hunting* permit.

per·mu·ta·tion (pûr′ myōō tā′ shən, pûr′ myə-) ***n-*** **1** act or process of rearrangement; transformation. **2** *Mathematics* any one of the total number of possible arrangements of a set of elements: *The sequence ACB is one* permutation *of the elements A, B, C.*

per·mute (pər myōōt′) ***vt-*** **[per·mut·ed, per·mut·ing]** to subject to permutation.

per·ni·cious (pər nĭsh′ əs) ***adj-*** very destructive; harmful; ruinous: *the* pernicious *influence of bad companions.* **—*adv-* per·ni′ cious·ly. *n-* per·ni′ cious·ness.**

pernicious anemia ***n-*** anemia caused by the inability to absorb vitamin B_{12} from the intestine, and marked by abnormal red blood cells and low levels of hemoglobin.

per·nick·e·ty (pər nĭk′ ə tē) persnickety.

per·o·ra·tion (pĕr′ ə rā′ shən) ***n-*** concluding part or summing up of a speech or oration.

per·ox·ide (pə rŏk′ sīd′) ***n-*** **1** hydrogen peroxide. **2** oxide containing the highest possible proportion of oxygen. **3** negative ion in which oxygen is bonded to oxygen. ***vt-*** **[per·ox·id·ed, per·ox·id·ing]** to bleach (hair) by applying hydrogen peroxide. *as **modifier***: *a* peroxide *blond.*

per·pen·dic·u·lar (pûr′ pən dĭk′ yə lər) ***adj-*** **1** straight up and down; vertical: *Two* perpendicular *posts supported the roof.* **2** at a right angle to a line or plane: *The* flagpole *is perpendicular to the ground.* ***n-*** *Mathematics* line or plane at right angles to another line or plane. ***—adv-*** **per′ pen·dic′ u·lar·ly.**

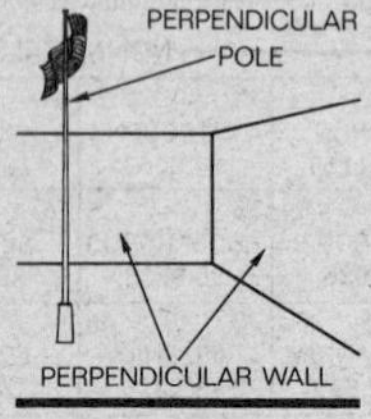

The flagpole is perpendicular to the wall of the building

per·pe·trate (pûr′ pə trāt′) ***vt-*** **[per·pe·trat·ed, per·pe·trat·ing]** to perform (a wrongful act); commit (a crime, error, etc.); be guilty of: *Clive* perpetrated *a cruel joke on his little brother.* ***—n-*** **per′ pe·tra′ tion.** ***n-*** **per′ pe·tra′ tor.**

per·pet·u·al (pər pĕch′ o͞o əl) ***adj-*** **1** lasting forever; unfailing; constant: *A* perpetual *fire burns at the Tomb of the Unknown Soldier.* **2** continuous; unceasing: *to indulge in* perpetual *chatter.* ***—adv-*** **per·pet′ u·al·ly.**

per·pet·u·ate (pər pĕch′ o͞o āt′) ***vt-*** **[per·pet·u·at·ed, per·pet·u·at·ing]** to cause to continue forever or for an indefinitely long time, especially in people's memories: *to* perpetuate *a myth*; *to* perpetuate *the memory of a great man.* ***—n-*** **per·pet′ u·a′ tion.**

per·pe·tu·i·ty (pûr pə to͞o′ ə tē) ***n-*** indefinitely long period of time; eternity.

in perpetuity for a limitless period of time: *He willed his paintings to the museum* in perpetuity.

per·plex (pər plĕks′) ***vt-*** to fill with confusion or uncertainty; puzzle: *His strange silence* perplexes *me.* ***—adv-*** **per·plex′ ing·ly:** *a* perplexingly *difficult problem.*

per·plex·i·ty (pər plĕk′ sə tē) ***n-*** [*pl.* **per·plex·i·ties**] **1** condition of being perplexed; confusion; bewilderment: *I'm in* perplexity *over the meaning of the question.* **2** something that puzzles or confuses.

per·qui·site (pûr′ kwə zət) ***n-*** gain or profit made from one's employment in addition to regular wages or salary. ►Should not be confused with PREREQUISITE.

per se (pər sā′) *Latin* of itself; as such; intrinsically: *Diamonds* per se *are valuable.*

per·se·cute (pûr′ sə kyo͞ot′) ***vt-*** **[per·se·cut·ed, per·se·cut·ing]** **1** to harass or abuse repeatedly or continuously: *He* persecutes *people with continuous faultfinding.* **2** to oppress or put to death on account of religion, politics, or race: *The Roman emperors* persecuted *the early Christians.* ***—n-*** **per′ se·cu′ tor.**

►Should not be confused with PROSECUTE.

per·se·cu·tion (pûr′ sə kyo͞o′ shən) ***n-*** **1** a persecuting or a being persecuted; especially, treatment with injustice or abuse: *He suffered* persecution *for his religion.*

Per·seph·o·ne (pər sĕf′ ə nē) ***n-*** in Greek mythology, a daughter of Zeus and Demeter, who was abducted by Pluto and became queen of the Underworld. She is identified with the Roman Proserpina.

Per·seus (pûr′ sē əs, pûr′ so͞os′) ***n-*** **1** in Greek mythology, a son of Zeus and a mortal, who slew Medusa and saved Andromeda from a sea monster. **2** a northern constellation.

per·se·ver·ance (pûr′ sə vêr′ əns) ***n-*** continued effort in spite of difficulties; steadfastness: *He made his discoveries after years of study and* perseverance.

per·se·vere (pûr′ sə vêr′) ***vi-*** **[per·se·vered, per·se·ver·ing]** to persist steadfastly in a purpose or undertaking; continue in spite of difficulties. ***—adv-*** **per′ se·ver′ ing·ly:** *John studied* perseveringly *and graduated with honors.*

Per·sian (pûr′ zhən) ***n-*** **1** a native of ancient Persia or modern Iran. **2** the Iranian language spoken by these people, as well as by people of western Afghanistan and parts of India and Pakistan. ***adj-***: *a* Persian *shawl*; *a* Persian *word.*

Persian cat ***n-*** domestic cat with long, silky fur. For picture, see *cat.*

Persian lamb ***n-*** curly, glossy fur obtained from the karakul lamb when it is about four days old.

per·si·flage (pûr′ sə fläzh′) ***n-*** light or flippant talk or writing; banter.

per·sim·mon (pər sĭm′ ən) ***n-*** **1** orange-colored, pulpy, smooth-skinned fruit, fit for eating only when thoroughly ripe. **2** tall tree which bears this fruit, common in southeastern United States. *as* ***modifier***: *a* persimmon *branch.*

Persimmon

per·sist (pər sĭst′) ***vi-*** **1** to continue steadily in spite of difficulty, disapproval, or opposition; keep on: *Jim* persists *in mispronouncing my name.* **2** to last for a long period: *We hope the good weather* persists *for our holiday.*

per·sis·tence (pər sĭs′ təns) ***n-*** **1** habit or practice of being persistent; perseverence: *his* persistence *in completing a task.* **2** a persisting or lasting; continuation: *the* persistence *of a disease*; *the* persistence *of fair weather.*

per·sist·ent (pər sĭs′ tənt) ***adj-*** **1** lasting; unceasing: *a month of* persistent *rain.* **2** untiring; undaunted; dogged: *a* persistent *salesman.* ***—adv-*** **per·sist′ ent·ly.**

per·snick·e·ty (pər snĭk′ ə tē) *Informal* ***adj-*** fussily attentive to small details. Also **pernickety.**

per·son (pûr′ sən) ***n-*** **1** human being; man, woman, or child: *She is a very kind* person. **2** body; bodily appearance: *We should keep our* persons *clean.* **3** *Grammar* distinction of pronouns and verbs which marks the difference between the speaker or speakers (first person), the one or ones spoken to (second person), and anyone or anything else (third person). In the sentence "I called John after I called you, but he didn't answer," the pronoun "I" is of the first person, "you" is of the second person, and "he" is of the third person. English verbs now show this distinction only by the -s form of the third person singular of the present tense.

in person in one's own physical form; by or for oneself: *Please send a substitute if you can't come* in person.

per·son·a·ble (pûr′ sə nə bəl) ***adj-*** attractive in appearance or manner: *a* personable *young man.* ***—n-*** **per′ son·able·ness.** ***adv-*** **per′ son·a·bly.**

per·son·age (pûr′ sən ĭj) ***n-*** **1** person of importance or distinction. **2** character in a play or novel.

per·son·al (pûr′ sən əl) ***adj-*** **1** of or about a particular person; private; intimate: *He does not discuss his* personal *business with anyone.* **2** of a person's body or appearance: *her* personal *beauty.* **3** relating to a particular individual, often in an unpleasant way: *I meant nothing* personal, *so do not take my remarks to heart.* **4** done or made in person, and not by an agent: *his* personal *signature*; *a* personal *appearance.* **5** in law, consisting of movable belongings: *Books and furniture are* personal *property.* ***n-*** short announcement or advertisement in a newspaper, directed to a specific person or group.

per·son·al·i·ty (pûr′ sə năl′ ə tē) ***n-*** [*pl.* **per·son·al·i·ties**] **1** combination of traits and qualities which make up an individual: *Every member of that family has a very*

different personality. **2** person, especially an outstanding one; personage: *a leading* personality *of the stage.* **3** attractive qualities or traits: *That girl has no* personality. **4 personalities** offensive remarks about a person: *In their quarrel he would not stoop to* personalities.

per·son·al·ly (pûr′ sə nə lē) ***adj-*** **1** by oneself; without help from another: *Mother attended to all the dinner preparations* personally. **2** in oneself: *I am* personally *opposed to this plan.* **3** as directed toward oneself: *Do not take his remarks* personally. **4** as a person: *I admire his paintings, but he is* personally *unpleasant.*

personal pronoun *Grammar* ***n-*** pronoun which indicates the speaker (I, we, me, us), the person or thing spoken to (you), or the person or persons, or the thing or things spoken about (he, she, it, they, him, her, them). In the sentence "We saw him knock you down," "we," "him," and "you" are personal pronouns. See also *possessive pronoun, possessive adjective.*

per·so·na non gra·ta (pər sō′ nə nŏn grăt′ ə, -grä′ tə) *Latin* person who is not acceptable or welcome, especially as a diplomat, in the judgment of the government to which he is sent.

per·son·i·fi·ca·tion (pər sŏn′ ə fə kā′ shən) ***n-*** **1** figure of speech by which things, qualities, or abstract ideas are represented as having a personal nature or human attributes. Examples: the cruel waves; the giant Despair. **2** a striking example of some quality; also, incarnation: *She is the* personification *of neatness.* **3** a personifying: *a* personification *of the sea as a monster.*

per·son·i·fy (pər sŏn′ ə fī′) ***vt-*** **[per·son·i·fied, per·son·i·fy·ing]** **1** to regard or represent (a thing, quality, or idea) as a person: *The poet* personified *truth as a beautiful maiden.* **2** to represent (an abstract idea, characteristic, etc.) in one's own person: *Caesar* personified *the power of the Roman Empire.*

per·son·nel (pûr′ sə nĕl′) ***n-*** all the people who work in a company, factory, organization, etc.

per·spec·tive (pər spĕk′ tĭv) ***n-*** **1** art of drawing on a flat surface to create an illusion of three dimensions or of true depth. **2** view that includes things in the distance as well as those nearby. **3** way of looking at or considering something; viewpoint. **4** true or proper relation of things to one another: *to consider one's problems in* perspective. *as **modifier**: a* perspective *drawing.*

per·spi·ca·cious (pûr′ spə kā′ shəs) ***adj-*** having or showing the ability to perceive, understand, or judge clearly; discerning; perceptive: *a* perspicacious *mind.* —***adv-*** **per′ spi·ca′ cious·ly.** ***n-*** **per′ spi·ca′ cious·ness.**
►Should not be confused with PERSPICUOUS.

per·spi·cac·i·ty (pûr′ spə kăs′ ə tē) ***n-*** clearness and accuracy of understanding; discernment; perspicaciousness.

per·spi·cu·i·ty (pûr′ spə kyōō′ ə tē) ***n-*** clearness of thought, expression, or style; lucidity; perspicuousness.

per·spic·u·ous (pûr spĭk′ yōō əs) ***adj-*** **1** clear to the understanding; easily understood. —***adv-*** **per·spic′ u·ous·ly.** ***n-*** **per·spic′ u·ous·ness.**
►Should not be confused with PERSPICACIOUS.

per·spi·ra·tion (pûr′ spə rā′ shən) ***n-*** **1** sweat: *Drops of* perspiration *covered his face.* **2** a perspiring: *Exercise causes heavy* perspiration.

per·spire (pər spīər′) ***vi-*** **[per·spired, per·spir·ing]** to sweat: *He* perspired *heavily whenever he played ball.*

per·suade (pər swād′) ***vt-*** **[per·suad·ed, per·suad·ing]** to win over or convince by argument, urging, advice, etc.: *I'm glad you* persuaded *me to change my mind.*

per·sua·sion (pər swā′ zhən) ***n-*** **1** a persuading or a being persuaded: *I am open to* persuasion. **2** tactful argument designed to lead a person to believe or do something: *to use* persuasion *rather than force.* **3** belief, especially religious belief: *They go to different churches because they are of different* persuasions.

per·sua·sive (pər swā′ sĭv, -zĭv) ***adj-*** capable of influencing; convincing: *his* persuasive *arguments.* —***adv-*** **per·sua′ sive·ly.** ***n-*** **per·sua′ sive·ness.**

pert (pûrt) ***adj-*** **1** saucy; bold; impudent: *a* pert *answer.* **2** charming; jaunty; cute: *her* pert *little hat.* —***adv-*** **pert′ ly.** ***n-*** **pert′ ness.**

per·tain (pər tān′) ***vi-*** **1** to refer or relate (to): *Our talk* pertained *to business.* **2** to apply; be relevant; be pertinent: *This does not* pertain *to you.* **3** to belong (to): *the duties that* pertain *to my new job.*

per·ti·na·cious (pûr′ tə nā′ shəs) ***adj-*** holding stubbornly to an opinion, plan, etc.; obstinately persistent: *a* pertinacious *salesman.* —***adv-*** **per′ ti·na·cious′ ly.** ***n-*** **per′ti·na′cious·ness.**

per·ti·nac·i·ty (pûr′ tə năs′ ə tē) ***n-*** firm adherence to a purpose or opinion; unyielding perseverance; stubbornness; pertinaciousness.

per·ti·nent (pûr′ tə nənt) ***adj-*** related to something being considered or discussed; relevant: *a* pertinent *comment.* —***n-*** **per′ ti·nence.** ***adv-*** **per′ ti·nent·ly.**

per·turb (pər tûrb′) ***vt-*** to disturb greatly, especially in the mind; agitate.

per·tur·ba·tion (pûr′ tər bā′ shən) ***n-*** **1** disturbance or agitation, especially of the mind. **2** *Astronomy* of a celestial body, the periodic departures from a simple elliptical orbit caused by gravitational force of neighboring bodies.

pe·ruke (pə rŏŏk′) ***n-*** wig similar to the periwig, but somewhat smaller.

pe·rus·al (pə rōō′ zəl) ***n-*** act of reading carefully; a careful reading: *his daily* perusal *of the newspaper.*

pe·ruse (pə rōōz′) ***vt-*** **[pe·rused, pe·rus·ing]** to read carefully and attentively: *He* perused *the book.*

per·vade (pər vād′) ***vt-*** **[per·vad·ed, per·vad·ing]** to spread throughout; fill every part of: *The smell of fish* pervaded *the cannery. Worries* pervaded *his mind.*

per·va·sion (pər vā′ zhən) ***n-*** a spreading or diffusion throughout every part of something.

per·va·sive (pər vā′ sĭv, -zĭv) ***adj-*** tending to spread or diffuse throughout something: *a* pervasive *odor.* —***adv-*** **per·va′ sive·ly.** ***n-*** **per·va′ sive·ness.**

per·verse (pər vûrs′) ***adj-*** **1** going against what is usual, wanted, or accepted; contrary: *a* perverse *wind; a* perverse *opinion.* **2** stubbornly unreasonable; willful: *The baby is in a* perverse *mood.* **3** morally wrong; corrupt. —***adv-*** **per·verse′ ly.** ***n-*** **per·verse′ ness.**

per·ver·sion (pər vûr′ zhən) ***n-*** **1** a turning from the proper use, purpose, or meaning: *a* perversion *of charitable funds for personal profit.* **2** distortion; biased interpretation: *His report is a* perversion *of the facts.* **3** act or practice that is shockingly abnormal.

per·ver·si·ty (pər vûr′ sə tē) ***n-*** [*pl.* **per·ver·si·ties**] **1** willful refusal to do right. **2** contrariness.

[1]**per·vert** (pər vûrt′) ***vt-*** **1** to turn (something) away from its proper purpose; misuse. **2** to distort or misinterpret, so as to give the wrong meaning: *He* perverted *the facts.* **3** to turn (someone) away from approved conduct or moral standards. —***n-*** **per·vert′ er.**

[2]**per·vert** (pûr′ vûrt′) ***n-*** person whose behavior is shockingly or criminally abnormal.

Pe·sach (pā′ säKH′) ***n-*** Passover.

pes·ky (pĕs′ kē) *Informal* ***adj-*** **[pes·ki·er, pes·ki·est]** annoying; bothersome.

pe·so (pā′ sō) ***n-*** [*pl.* **pe·sos**] **1** the basic unit of money in certain Spanish-American countries and the Philippines. Its value varies in different countries. **2** formerly, a silver coin of Spain; piece of eight.

pes·si·mism (pĕs′ ə mĭz′ əm) ***n-*** **1** tendency to emphasize the dark and gloomy aspects of a situation, especially in a cynical way, or to predict the worst possible outcome for something. **2** belief that the world is essentially evil or that evil is more powerful than good. ***—n-*** **pes′ si·mist.** ***adj-*** **pes′ si·mis′ tic.** ***adv-*** **pes′ si·mis′ ti·cal·ly.**

pest (pĕst) ***n-*** **1** someone or something that annoys or causes trouble; nuisance. **2** something, such as a weed or insect, that causes serious damage. **3** widespread, deadly, contagious disease; plague; pestilence.

pes·ter (pĕs′ tər) ***vt-*** to be a nuisance to; annoy; bother.

pest·hole (pĕst′ hōl′) ***n-*** place in which dangerous contagious diseases are likely to occur and to spread.

pest·house (pĕst′ hous′) ***n-*** a hospital or wing of a hospital for people having contagious diseases.

pest·i·cide (pĕs′ tə sīd′) ***n-*** substance used to destroy harmful or destructive insects, plants, etc.

pes·tif·er·ous (pĕs tĭf′ ər əs) ***adj-*** **1** *Informal* annoying; bothersome. **2** having a harmful effect; especially, carrying an infectious disease. ***—adv-*** **pes·tif′ er·ous·ly.**

pes·ti·lence (pĕs′ tə ləns) ***n-*** deadly, widespread, contagious disease; plague, especially bubonic plague.

pes·ti·lent (pĕs′ tə lənt) ***adj-*** **1** deadly: *a* pestilent *disease*; *a* pestilent *drug.* **2** very bad for health, morals, or society: *the* pestilent *traffic in narcotics.* **3** making mischief; irritable; vexatious: *the* pestilent *barking of a dog.* ***—adv-*** **pes′ ti·lent·ly.**

pes·ti·len·tial (pĕs′ tə lĕn′ shəl) ***adj-*** **1** resembling, caused by, or resulting in pestilence. **2** very harmful.

pes·tle (pĕs′ əl, pĕs′ təl) ***n-*** implement with a blunt, often rounded end, used for pounding and crushing substances, especially in a mortar. For picture, see [2]*mortar.*

[1]**pet** (pĕt) ***n-*** **1** animal of any kind kept for companionship, amusement, etc., rather than for a practical purpose. **2** favorite or especially beloved person or thing. ***as modifier:*** *a* pet *turtle*; *a* pet *idea.* ***vt-*** **[pet·ted, pet·ting] 1** to stroke or smooth as one would a favorite animal; caress. **2** to treat with special kindness and consideration; pamper: *to* pet *a sick child.* ***vi-*** to kiss, embrace, etc., as lovers do. [of uncertain origin, perhaps related to French **petit** meaning "little."]

[2]**pet** (pĕt) ***n-*** peevish state of mind; fit of ill humor. [of unknown origin.]

pet·al (pĕt′ əl) ***n-*** one of the divisions, often brightly colored, forming the corolla of a flower. ***—adv-*** **pet′ aled:** *a many-*petaled *flower.* ***adj-*** **pet′ al·like′.**

Petals

pe·tard (pə tärd′) ***n-*** case filled with explosives, used in former times to knock down a wall or gate.

hoist with (or **by**) **one's own petard** harmed or defeated as a result of one's own actions, scheming, etc.

pet·cock (pĕt′ kŏk′) ***n-*** small faucet or valve, used for releasing steam, air, liquid, etc., from a pipe.

Pe·ter (pē′ tər) ***n-*** **1** one of the twelve apostles; also **St. Peter** or **Simon Peter.** **2** either one of two epistles of the New Testament attributed to him.

pe·ter out (pē′ tər) *Informal* ***vi-*** to grow gradually less and then disappear: *My energy* petered out.

Peter Pan ***n-*** boy who remained a child forever, the hero of a play of the same name by James M. Barrie.

Peter Pan collar ***n-*** turned-down, rounded collar.

pet·i·ole (pĕt′ ē ōl′) ***n-*** the stem of a leaf; leaf stalk.

pe·tite (pə tēt′) ***adj-*** charmingly or daintily small.

pe·tit four (pĕt′ ē fôr′) ***n-*** [*pl.* **petits fours** (pĕt′ ē fôr′) or **petit fours**] small frosted and decorated cake.

pe·ti·tion (pə tĭsh′ ən) ***n-*** **1** an earnest request or prayer. **2** formal request to a superior or official authority: *We sent a* petition *to the mayor asking for a new traffic light.* **3** something asked for in a formal request. ***vt-*** **1** to make a formal request to: *We* petitioned *the mayor for a new traffic light.* **2** to ask for: *to* petition *aid for a worthy cause.* ***—n-*** **pe·ti′ tion·er.**

pe·tit jury (pĕt′ ē) ***n-*** a trial jury as distinguished from a grand jury. ***—n-*** **petit juror.**

pe·tit point (pĕt′ ē) ***n-*** needlework using small, closely placed diagonal stitches, usually done on coarse canvas or similar material.

pet·rel (pĕ′ trəl) ***n-*** small, black-and-white sea bird often seen far from land. ***Hom-*** petrol.

Storm petrel, about 6 in. long

Pe·tri dish (pē′ trē) ***n-*** a small, round, shallow, glass dish, often used to hold bacterial cultures.

pet·ri·fac·tion (pĕ′ trə făk′ shən) ***n-*** **1** a petrifying or being petrified. **2** something petrified. Also **pet′ ri·fi·ca′ tion** (-fə kā′ shən).

pet·ri·fy (pĕ′ trə fī′) ***vt-*** **[pet·ri·fied, pet·ri·fy·ing] 1** to replace animal or vegetable cells with minerals; convert to stone or a stony substance. **2** to make motionless or helpless with fear, amazement, etc.: *The approach of danger* petrified *him.* ***vi-*** to turn to stone.

pet·rol (pĕ′ trəl) *Brit.* ***n-*** gasoline. ***Hom-*** petrel.

pet·ro·lat·um (pĕ′ trə lā′ təm) ***n-*** greasy, jellylike substance obtained from petroleum. Also **petroleum jelly.**

pet·ro·le·um (pə trō′ lē əm) ***n-*** an oily mixture of numerous hydrocarbons found in the earth's crust. Gasoline and motor oils are made from petroleum.

pe·trol·o·gist (pə trŏl′ ə jĭst) ***n-*** person who is expert in, and usually occupied in, petrology.

pe·trol·o·gy (pə trŏl′ ə jē) ***n-*** science that deals with the origin, formation, composition, and structure of rocks.

pet·ti·coat (pĕt′ ĭ kōt′) ***n-*** **1** long, full skirt formerly worn by girls and women. **2** skirt worn under outer clothing; half slip.

pet·ti·fog·ger (pĕt′ ĭ fŏg′ ər) ***n-*** lawyer whose practice is limited to small cases, or who resorts to tricky or disreputable methods; hence, a person who bickers over trifling details. ***—adj-*** **pet′ti·fog′ging.**

pet·tish (pĕt′ ĭsh) ***adj-*** cross; peevish. ***—adv-*** **pet′ tish·ly.** ***—n-*** **pet′ tish·ness.**

pet·ty (pĕt′ ē) ***adj-*** **[pet·ti·er, pet·ti·est] 1** unimportant; trivial: *to argue over* petty *details.* **2** small-minded; mean: *a* petty *person.* **3** having a minor rank or position: *a* petty *official.* ***—adv-*** **pet′ ti·ly.** ***n-*** **pet′ ti·ness.**

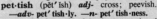

Petunia

petty cash ***n-*** cash kept on hand for small expenses.

petty larceny ***n-*** theft of goods having a relatively small value.

petty officer ***n-*** in the Navy and Coast Guard, a noncommissioned officer.

pet·u·lant (pĕch′ ə lənt) ***adj-*** cross or sulky, especially about a small matter; peevish. ***—n-*** **pet′ u·lance.** ***adv-*** **pet′ u·lant·ly.**

Pews

pe·tu·ni·a (pə tōō′ nē ə, -tōōn′ yə) ***n-*** cultivated plant with trumpet-shaped pink, purple, red, or white flowers.

pew (pyōō) ***n-*** any of the benches in a church.

pe·wee (pē′ wē′) ***n-*** any of several small, insect-eating birds that look somewhat like the phoebe. The bird's call suggests its name. Also **peewee.**

pe·wit (pē′ wĭt′) ***n-*** any of several birds having a high, shrill cry, especially the lapwing.

pew·ter (pyōō′ tər) ***n-*** **1** alloy of tin and other metals, used for dishes, candlesticks, and other utensils. **2** articles made of this alloy. *as* ***modifier:*** *a* pewter *mug.*

Pfc. private first class.

pfd. preferred.

pH (pē′ āch′) *Chemistry* ***n-*** a number assigned to a solution that indicates its relative acidity. Pure water has a pH of 7.0, which is regarded as neutral.

Pha·ë·thon (fā′ ə thŏn′) ***n-*** in Greek mythology, a son of Helios, the sun god. He endangered the safety of the world by trying to drive his father's chariot across the sky, and was slain by a thunderbolt thrown by Zeus.

pha·e·ton (fā′ ə tən) ***n-*** **1** light, four-wheeled, horse-drawn carriage, completely open or open at the sides. **2** automobile having a similar construction.

phag·o·cyte (făg′ ə sīt′) ***n-*** any of the white blood cells that engulf and destroy bacteria and damaged red blood cells.

pha·lanx (fā′ lăngks′) ***n-*** **1** [*pl.* **pha·lanx·es**] in ancient Greece, a company of heavily armed soldiers drawn in close ranks; hence, any similarly massed group of people or things. **2** [*pl.* **pha·lan·ges** (fə lăn′ jēz′)] one of the bones of the fingers or toes.

phan·tasm (făn′ tăz′ əm) ***n-*** **1** imaginary being, such as a ghost or specter; phantom. **2** any deceptive or ghostly image, illusion, etc. ***—adj-*** **phan·tas′ mal:** *a* phantasmal *hallucination.*

phan·ta·sy (făn′ tə zē) fantasy.

phan·tom (făn′ təm) ***n-*** **1** ghost; specter; apparition. **2** anything ghostly or unreal in appearance or effect. *as* ***modifier:*** *We saw* phantom *horses in the night.*

Phar·aoh (fâr′ ō) ***n-*** any of the rulers of ancient Egypt.

Phar·i·see (făr′ ə sē, fĕr′-) ***n-*** **1** one of a former religious sect of Jews who laid strict emphasis on the literal observance of the Law. **2 pharisee** anyone who observes the form rather than the spirit in religion.

phar·ma·ceu·ti·cal (fär′ mə sōō′ tĭ kəl) ***adj-*** of or having to do with pharmacy or prescription drugs. ***n-*** a medicinal product.

phar·ma·cist (fär′ mə sĭst′) ***n-*** person trained in the preparation of medicines; druggist.

phar·ma·col·o·gy (fär′ mə kŏl′ ə jē) ***n-*** the science of the preparation, use, and effects of drugs.

phar·ma·co·poe·ia (fär′ mə kə pē′ ə) ***n-*** **1** book, especially one serving as an official authority, that gives ingredients and formulas for the preparation of drugs and other medicines. **2** collection of drugs.

phar·ma·cy (fär′ mə sē) ***n-*** [*pl.* **phar·ma·cies**] **1** art or profession of preparing medicines. **2** drugstore.

pha·ryn·ge·al (fə rĭn′ jē əl, făr′ ən jē′ əl) ***adj-*** of, having to do with, or produced in the pharynx.

phar·ynx (făr′ ĭngks) ***n-*** [*pl.* **pha·ryn·ges** (fə rĭn′ jēz′) or **phar·ynx·es**] expanded, upper part of the digestive tube, situated between the mouth and nasal cavities and the esophagus.

phase (fāz) ***n-*** **1** stage in the progress or development of a thing: *an early* phase *of airplane flight*; *a* phase *of mitosis.* **2** one side or view of a subject: *The admiral wrote about the naval* phase *of the invasion.* **3** *Astronomy* any of the forms the moon or a planet periodically presents to our view, depending on how much of its surface reflects sunlight. **4** *Chemistry* any of the physical states matter exists in: *One of the* phases *of water is ice.* **5** *Physics* any part of a periodic motion or oscillation, as reckoned from some position arbitrarily chosen as a starting point. ***vt-*** **[phased, phas·ing]** to bring about in stages. ***Hom-*** faze.

phase in (or **out**) to introduce (or get rid of) in stages.

Ph.D. (pē′ āch′ dē′) Doctor of Philosophy.

pheas·ant (fĕz′ ənt) ***n-*** any of various related game birds, usually having a long tail and handsome feathers. Peacocks belong to the same family as pheasants.

Ring-necked pheasant, 34—36 in. long

phe·no·bar·bi·tal (fē′ nō bär′ bə tŏl′) ***n-*** white, crystalline barbiturate used as a sedative.

phe·nol (fē′ nōl′, -nōl′) ***n-*** a colorless, crystalline compound (C_6H_5OH), produced from coal tar and used to make plastics; carbolic acid.

phe·nol·ic resin (fə nōl′ ĭk) ***n-*** any of a large group of synthetic resins and plastics made by combining a phenol with formaldehyde and other similar compounds.

phe·nol·phthal·ein (fē′ nəl thā′ lē ən, -thăl′ ē ən) ***n-*** pale-yellow compound derived from phenol, used as a laxative, and in chemistry as an indicator.

phe·nom·e·nal (fə nŏm′ ə nəl) ***adj-*** unusual; remarkable; extraordinary: *his* phenomenal *memory.* ***—adv-*** **phe·nom′ e·nal·ly:** *He is* phenomenally *brilliant.*

phe·nom·e·non (fə nŏm′ ə nŏn′, -nən) ***n-*** [*pl.* **phe·nom·e·na** (-nə)] **1** thing, fact, occurrence, etc., that can be observed: *The sunrise is a daily* phenomenon. **2** [*pl.* often **phe·nom·e·nons**] unusual or extraordinary occurrence, person, or thing: *His hitting three home runs in a row was a* phenomenon.

►Careful writers and speakers never use the plural PHENOMENA as a singular noun. They also object to the recent plural form, PHENOMENONS.

phi·al (fī′ əl) ***n-*** vial.

phi·lan·der (fə lăn′ dər) ***vi-*** of a man, to flirt or woo in a lighthearted, insincere manner. ***—n-*** **phi·lan′ der·er.**

phil·an·throp·ic (fĭl′ ən thrŏp′ ĭk) or **phil·an·throp·i·cal** (-ĭ kəl) ***adj-*** helping or benefiting others, especially those in need; benevolent; charitable: *a* philanthropic *organization.* ***—adv-*** **phil′ an·throp′ i·cal·ly.**

phi·lan·thro·pist (fə lăn′ thrə pĭst) ***n-*** person whose efforts are devoted to promoting human welfare, often by giving money for hospitals, schools, charities, etc.

phi·lan·thro·py (fə lăn′ thrə pē′) ***n-*** [*pl.* **phi·lan·thro·pies**] **1** love of mankind, especially as expressed by the desire to help people: *The basis of much public charity is* philanthropy. **2** action showing this: *his* many *philanthropies.* **3** organization or institution engaged in promoting human welfare.

phi·lat·e·ly (fə lăt′ ə lē) ***n-*** the collecting and study of postage stamps. ***—n-*** **phi·lat′ e·list.**

-phile *combining form* person especially fond of or devoted to; lover of: *a biblio*phile. [from Greek **-philos,** from **phílos** meaning "loving; fond of."]

Phi·le·mon (fĭl′ ə mən) ***n-*** **1** friend and convert of St. Paul. **2** book of the New Testament consisting of a letter written to him by St. Paul.

phil·har·mon·ic (fĭl′ här′ mŏn′ ĭk) ***adj-*** devoted to or engaged in the performance of music (now used only in the names of orchestras and musical organizations).

Phil·ip (fĭl′ əp) ***n-*** one of the twelve apostles. Also **St. Philip.**

Phi·lip·pi·ans (fə lĭp′ ē ənz) ***n-*** (takes singular verb) book of the New Testament consisting of St. Paul's epistle to the church at Philippi.

Phil·is·tine (fĭl′ ə stēn′) ***n-*** **1** in Biblical times, one of the inhabitants of the southwestern coast of Palestine, who were enemies of the Israelites. **2** (sometimes **philistine**) narrow-minded person who lacks or is indifferent to culture. *as **modifier**: his* Philistine *attitude to the arts.*

phil·o·den·dron (fĭl′ ə dĕn′ drən) ***n-*** trailing plant, cultivated chiefly as a house plant, having glossy leaves.

phi·lol·o·gy (fə lŏl′ ə jē) ***n-*** the study of the origin, relationships, development, etc., of language. See also *linguistics.* **—*adj-*** **phil′ o·log′ i·cal** (fĭl′ ə lŏj′ ĭ kəl): *his* philological *studies.* ***adv-*** **phil′ o·log′ i·cal·ly.**

phi·lol·o·gist (fə lŏl′ ə jĭst) ***n-*** person who is expert in, and usually occupied in, philology.

Phil·o·mel (fĭl′ ə mĕl′) ***n-*** **1** in Greek mythology, an Athenian princess who was changed into a nightingale. **2 philomel** nightingale.

phi·los·o·pher (fə lŏs′ ə fər) ***n-*** **1** founder of a system of philosophy. **2** person who studies philosophy and seeks wisdom. **3** person who calmly and intelligently makes the best of life and events as they happen.

philosopher's stone ***n-*** imaginary stone believed by alchemists to be able to change base metals into gold.

phil·o·soph·ic (fĭl′ ə sŏf′ ĭk) or **phil·o·soph·i·cal** (-ĭ kəl) ***adj-*** **1** of or having to do with philosophy, or with a particular system of philosophy. **2** having or showing ideas, conduct, etc., considered typical of or suitable for a philosopher; wise; patient; thoughtful: *his* philosophic *attitude toward misfortune.* **—*adv-*** **phil′ o·soph′ i·cal·ly.**

phi·los·o·phize (fə lŏs′ ə fīz′) ***vi-*** [**phi·los·o·phized, phi·los·o·phiz·ing**] **1** to reason about or seek to explain the causes or nature of things. **2** to express one's ideas in a thoughtful, often moralistic way.

phi·los·o·phy (fə lŏs′ ə fē) ***n-*** [*pl.* **phi·los·o·phies**] **1** study that aims at understanding the basic principles of the universe, life, morals, etc. **2** system of beliefs about the universe and life, especially those of a particular person or group: *the* philosophy *of Plato.* **3** guiding principles followed in a particular activity or field of knowledge: *a* philosophy *of art. as **modifier**: a* philosophy *course.*

phil·ter or **phil·tre** (fĭl′ tər) ***n-*** any magic potion, especially one supposed to make a person fall in love.

phle·bi·tis (flə bī′ təs) ***n-*** inflammation of a vein, marked by the formation of a clot and by swelling.

phlegm (flĕm) ***n-*** **1** thick, stringy mucus discharged into the throat and mouth, especially when one has a cold or other respiratory ailment. **2** calmness or coolness of disposition, almost lack of emotion.

phleg·mat·ic (flĕg măt′ ĭk) ***adj-*** not easily excited or moved; slow to respond; stolid: *his* phlegmatic *temperament.* **—*adv-*** **phleg·mat′ i·cal·ly.**

phlo·em (flō′ ĕm′) ***n-*** a part of the vascular tissue of a plant, made up of elongated living cells that conduct sap.

phlox (flŏks) ***n-*** any of several plants having clusters or tufts of pink, red, lavender, or white flowers.

Phlox

pho·bi·a (fō′ bē ə) ***n-*** abnormal fear or dread of something: *He had a* phobia *about black cats.*

-phobia *combining form* abnormal fear or dread: *claustro*phobia (fear of a closed space). [from Greek **-phobía** meaning "fear of."]

phoe·be (fē′ bē) ***n-*** small, insect-eating bird with grayish-brown back and wings and a yellowish-white breast, named for its two-note call. It nests near houses.

Phoe·be (fē′ bē) ***n-*** in Greek mythology, Artemis.

Phoe·bus (fē′ bəs) ***n-*** in Greek mythology, Apollo. Also **Phoebus Apollo.**

Phoe·ni·cian (fə nĭsh′ ən) ***adj-*** of or pertaining to ancient Phoenicia, its people, or their language. ***n-*** **1** an inhabitant of Phoenicia. **2** language of these people.

phoe·nix (fē′ nĭks) ***n-*** in ancient legend, a beautiful bird said to live over 500 years and then, after setting fire to itself, to arise, young and beautiful, from its own ashes.

phone (fōn) *Informal* ***n-*** telephone. *as **modifier**: the* phone *company.* ***vt-*** [**phoned, phon·ing**] to telephone: *I* phoned *Jim last night.* ***vi-****: You weren't home when I* phoned.

-phone *combining form* **1** sound: *homo*phone (word with the same sound as another). **2** device or instrument producing a sound: *tele*phone; *xylo*phone. [from Greek **-phōnos,** "sounding," from **phōnē,** "sound; voice."]

pho·neme (fō′ nēm′) ***n-*** smallest structural unit of speech sound which can distinguish one word from another. The phoneme /m/ distinguishes "mat" from "at."

pho·net·ic (fə nĕt′ ĭk) ***adj-*** indicating or having to do with speech sounds. The long mark [¯] and the short mark [˘] over vowels are phonetic symbols to show the difference in pronunciation in words such as "mane" and "man." **—*adv-*** **pho·net′ i·cal·ly.**

phonetic alphabet ***n-*** **1** set of symbols used for writing speech so that for each distinct sound there is one, and only one, symbol. **2** any of various systems for using words in place of letters of the alphabet in voice communication, in order to avoid mistakes. Examples: *alpha, brave, Charlie, delta, echo, foxtrot,* etc.

pho·ne·ti·cian (fō′ nə tĭsh′ ən) ***n-*** specialist in phonetics.

pho·net·ics (fə nĕt′ ĭks) ***n-*** (takes singular verb) science of the sounds of speech and the symbols used to represent them.

phon·ic (fŏn′ ĭk) ***adj-*** of or having to do with the sounds of speech, especially in relation to the teaching of reading.

phon·ics (fŏn′ ĭks) ***n-*** (takes singular verb) method of teaching reading that uses as a base the pronunciation of groups of letters.

phono- *combining form* sound: *a* phono*graph* (instrument for reproducing sound). Also **phon-:** phon*ic.*

pho·no·graph (fō′ nə grăf′) ***n-*** machine for reproducing sound from a disk with grooves in it; record player. *as **modifier**: a* phonograph *needle.*

pho·no·graph·ic (fō′ nə grăf′ ĭk) ***adj-*** of or having to do with a phonograph or the reproduction of sounds by means of a phonograph. **—*adv-*** **pho′ no·graph′ i·cal·ly.**

pho·nol·o·gy (fə nŏl′ ə jē) ***n-*** the analysis of the sound patterns used in particular languages, and in languages in general, focusing on the smallest units which distinguish one word from another.

pho·ny (fō′ nē) *Informal* ***adj-*** [**pho·ni·er, pho·ni·est**] not genuine or sincere; false; counterfeit. ***n-*** [*pl.* **pho·nies**] person or thing that is a fake. Also **pho′ ney.**

phos·phate (fŏs′ fāt′) ***n-*** **1** a salt or ester of phosphoric acid. **2** any of various fertilizers containing such salts. **3** a soft drink made with soda water, syrup, and a few drops of phosphoric acid.

phos·phor bronze (fŏs′ fər) ***n-*** a hard, tough, and elastic alloy of copper, tin, and phosphorus.

phos·pho·res·cence (fŏs′ fə rĕs′ əns) ***n-*** **1** an emission of light not due to the heat of combustion; also, the light so produced. **2** property of many minerals that causes them to glow in the dark after exposure to light. **—*adj-*** **phos′ pho·res′ cent.**

phos·phor·ic acid (fŏs fôr′ ĭk, -fŏr′ ĭk) ***n***- colorless acid or crystalline solid (H_3PO_4), used in fertilizers.

phos·pho·rus (fŏs′ fə rəs) ***n***- a nonmetallic solid element found in nature only in the combined state. Three forms of phosphorus exist, but under ordinary conditions it is a white or yellow waxy solid that is poisonous and phosphorescent. Symbol P, At. No 15, At. Wt. 30.9738.

pho·to (fō′ tō) ***n***- [*pl.* **pho·tos**] *Informal* photograph.

photo- *combining form* **1** light: *a* photo*sensitive film*; photo*synthesis*. **2** photograph; photography: *a* photo*engraving*; photo*copy*. [from Greek **photo-**, from **phôs, phōtos** meaning "light," or sometimes by way of **photography**, as in "photocopy."]

pho·to·chem·i·cal (fō′ tō kĕm′ ĭ kəl) ***adj***- of, having to do with, or produced by, the chemical action of light.

pho·to·cop·y (fō′ tō kŏp′ ē) ***vt***- [**pho·to·cop·ied, pho·to·cop·y·ing**] to make a copy of (a piece of writing or illustration) by means of a photographic device. ***n***- [*pl.* **pho·to·cop·ies**] copy made by such means.

pho·to·e·lec·tric (fō′ tō ə lĕk′ trĭk) ***adj***- of, or having to do with the electronic effects of light.

photoelectric cell ***n***- device in which a certain metal gives off electrons when light strikes it, thus causing a weak electric current; electric eye. Also **pho′ to·cell′**.

pho·to·en·grav·ing (fō′ tō ĭn grā′ vĭng) ***n***- **1** process by which a photograph is reproduced in relief upon a metal plate for printing. **2** the plate itself; also, a picture printed from such a plate.

photo finish ***n***- race so close that a photograph is needed to decide the winner.

pho·to·flood lamp (fō′ tō flŭd′) ***n***- incandescent lamp to illuminate a large area for photographing.

pho·to·gen·ic (fō′ tə jĕn′ ĭk) ***adj***- **1** having such good form or color as to make an effective subject for a photograph: *a* photogenic *face*. **2** *Biology* producing or giving off light, as a firefly does; phosphorescent.

pho·to·graph (fō′ tə grăf′) ***n***- picture made with a camera containing a film or glass plate which is sensitive to light. ***vt***- to take a picture of with a camera. ***vi***- to look or appear a certain way as the subject of such pictures: *Her baby* photographs *well*.

pho·tog·ra·pher (fə tŏg′ rə fər) ***n***- person who takes photographs, especially as an occupation.

pho·to·graph·ic (fō′ tə grăf′ ĭk) ***adj***- **1** having to do with photography: *a* photographic *lens*. **2** able to remember accurately: *a* photographic *mind*. **3** sharp; clear; distinct: *in* photographic *detail*. ***—adv***- **pho′ to·graph′ i·cal·ly.**

pho·tog·ra·phy (fə tŏ′ grə fē) ***n***- the art or process of taking pictures with a camera.

pho·tom·e·ter (fō tŏm′ ə tər) ***n***- any instrument that measures the intensity of light.

pho·to·mi·cro·graph (fō′ tō mī′ krə grăf′) ***n***- photograph of what is seen through a microscope.

pho·ton (fō′ tŏn′) ***n***- a quantum of radiant energy, especially of light.

pho·to·sen·si·tive (fō′ tō sĕn′ sə tĭv′) ***adj***- sensitive or receptive to light or other radiant energy.

pho·to·sphere (fō′ tō sfêr′) ***n***- the shining surface of the sun, as ordinarily seen from the earth.

pho·to·stat (fō′ tə stăt′) ***n***- **1** **Photostat** *Trademark* type of camera used for photographing documents, maps, etc., directly on the surface of prepared paper. **2** photograph made with such a camera. ***vt***- [**pho·to·stat·ed, pho·to·stat·ing**] to photograph with such a camera.

pho·to·syn·the·sis (fō′ tō sĭn′ thə sĭs) ***n***- in living plants, the complex process consisting of many reactions, in which water, inorganic salts, and carbon dioxide are changed into organic compounds by chlorophyll molecules, using some of the energy of sunlight.

pho·tot·ro·pism (fō tŏ′ trə pĭz′ əm) ***n***- *Biology* growth or other involuntary movement toward or away from light. ***—adj***- **pho′ to·trop′ ic** (fō′ tō trŏp′ ĭk): *a* phototropic *response*.

phrase (frāz) ***n***- **1** *Grammar* group of words containing a nucleus and one or more words or groups of words that are subordinate to it. Examples:

I saw a black-and-white kitten. (Noun phrase; the noun "kitten" is the nucleus.)

Jock will have to play *next Saturday*. (Verb phrase; the verb "play" is the nucleus.)

This house is very cold. (Adjectival phrase; the adjective "cold" is the nucleus.)

He ran as fast as possible. (Adverbial phrase; the adverb "fast" is the nucleus.) See also *prepositional phrase*. **2** brief, often forceful, expression. Examples: War on Poverty. Freedom from Want. **3** *Music* group of notes forming a unit that is part of a melody. ***vt***- [**phrased, phras·ing**] **1** to put into words: *to* phrase *an apology*. **2** *Music* to perform or render clearly (the units of a melody).

phra·se·ol·o·gy (frā′ zē ŏl′ ə jē) ***n***- [*pl.* **phra·se·ol·o·gies**] selection and arrangement of words; manner of expression: *legal* phraseology.

phras·ing (frā′ zĭng) ***n***- **1** way of arranging words or phrases in writing or speaking; verbal expression; wording: *the effective* phrasing *of the opening address*. **2** *Music* correct performance of the melodic phrases in a musical composition.

phre·nol·o·gy (frə nŏl′ ə jē) ***n***- system, now scoffed at by anthropologists, that claims to identify character and intelligence by the shape of a person's skull.

phthi·sis (thī′ səs) ***n***- a wasting away of the body, especially from tuberculosis of the lungs; consumption. Also **phthi′ sic** (thĭ′ sĭk, tĭz′ ĭk).

phy·lac·ter·y (fə lăk′ tə rē) ***n***- [*pl.* **phy·lac·ter·ies**] one of two small leather boxes containing a parchment inscribed with texts from Jewish law. One is strapped to the left arm and the other to the forehead by Orthodox Jews during morning prayers.

phy·log·e·ny (fī lŏj′ ə nē) ***n***- [*pl.* **phy·log·e·nies**] evolutionary development or history of a species or other group of animals or plants. Also **phy′ lo·gen′ e·sis** (fī′ lə jĕn′ ə sĭs).

phy·lum (fī′ ləm) ***n***- [*pl.* **phy·la** (-lə)] one of the large primary divisions of the animal or plant kingdom, ranking below a subkingdom and above a class.

phys·ic (fĭz′ ĭk) ***n***- **1** medicine, especially a laxative. **2** *Archaic* science of medicine. ***vt***- [**phys·icked, phys·ick·ing**] *Archaic* to give medicine to; treat with medicine.

phys·i·cal (fĭz′ ĭ kəl) ***adj***- **1** of or related to matter or material objects and forces, as distinct from spiritual, mental, or moral things: *the* physical *world*. **2** having to do with the science of physics: *The change from water to ice is a* physical *change*. **3** having to do with the body: *great* physical *strength*. ***n***- examination of the body by a doctor. ***—adv***- **phys′ i·cal·ly.**

physical education ***n***- education and training in the care, exercise, and development of the body; also, a course or session of a course that gives such instruction.

physical geography ***n***- branch of geography that deals with the natural features of the earth, such as land forms, climate, natural vegetation, etc.

physical science *n-* any science that deals with the properties, structure, etc., of matter that is not living.

physical therapy *n-* treatment of diseases and injuries by physical or external means, rather than by drugs.

phy·si·cian (fə zĭsh′ ən) *n-* person licensed to practice medicine; doctor.

phys·i·cist (fĭz′ ə sĭst) *n-* person who is a specialist in the science of physics and engaged in it as a profession.

phys·ics (fĭz′ ĭks) *n-* (takes singular verb) the science that deals with motion, matter, and energy, and their precise relationships. *as* ***modifier:*** *a* physics *course.*

phys·i·og·no·my (fĭz′ ē og′ nə mē) *n-* [**phys·i·og·no·mies**] 1 the special features or expression of one's face; facial appearance: *a stern* physiognomy. 2 outward appearance or form of anything; contour.

phys·i·og·ra·phy (fĭz′ ē og′ rə fē) *n-* physical geography. —*n-* **phys′i·og·′ra·pher.** *adj-* **phys′i·o·graph′ic** (-ē ə-grăf′ ik).

phys·i·o·log·i·cal (fĭz′ ē ə lŏg′ ĭ kəl) *adj-* of, or having to do with physiology. —*adv-* **phys′i·o·log′i·cal·ly.**

phys·i·ol·o·gist (fĭz′ ē ŏl′ ə jĭst′) *n-* person trained in the science of physiology and engaged in it as a profession.

phys·i·ol·o·gy (fĭz′ ē ŏl′ ə jē) *n-* branch of biology that deals with the processes and functions in living things.

phys·i·o·ther·a·py (fĭz′ ē ō thĕr′ ə pē) *n-* physical therapy.

phy·sique (fĭ zēk′) *n-* structure or appearance of the body: *That football player has a powerful* physique.

pi (pī) *n-* 1 the sixteenth letter of the Greek alphabet. 2 *Mathematics* Greek letter π used to symbolize the ratio of the circumference of a circle to its diameter. Pi is approximately 3.1416 or 3 1/7. ***Hom-*** pie.

P.I. Philippine Islands.

pi·a ma·ter (pī′ ə mā′ tər) *n-* a delicate membrane resembling a cobweb, which is the innermost of three membranes covering the brain and spinal cord.

pi·a·nis·si·mo (pē′ ə nĭs′ ə mō) *Music* ***adj-*** *&* ***adv-*** very soft: *Listen to the* pianissimo *passage. Play the passage* pianissimo. *Abbr.* pp

pi·an·ist (pē ăn′ ĭst, pē′ ə nĭst) *n-* person who plays the piano, especially as a professional musician.

GRAND

UPRIGHT

Pianos

[1]pi·a·no (pē ăn′ ō) *n-* [*pl.* **pi·an·os**] large musical instrument with tuned steel strings that are struck by felt-covered hammers operated by a keyboard. Also **pi·an′o·for′te** (-fôr′ tā, -fôr′ tē, -fôrt′). [shortened from Italian **pianoforte,** from [2]**piano** plus **forte,** meaning "strong."]

[2]pi·a·no (pē ăn′ ō) *Music* ***adj-*** *&* ***adv-*** soft; softly: *to play a* piano *passage; to play a passage* piano. *Abbr.* p [from Italian **piano,** from Latin **plānus** meaning "smooth."]

pi·az·za (pē ăz′ ə) *n-* 1 in Italy, a public square. 2 large porch; veranda.

Piazzas

pi·ca (pī′ kə) *n-* 1 in printing, a unit of measure equal to about 1/6 inch; also, a size of type (12-point) equal to this. 2 similar type size typewriters. *as* ***modifier:*** *a* pica *typewriter.*

pi·ca·dor (pĭk′ ə dôr′) *n-* in a bullfight, a horseman who tires and weakens the bull by pricking it with a lance.

pi·ca·resque (pĭk′ ə rĕsk′) *adj-* having to do with vagabonds and rogues, and their adventures; especially in literature, a series of unrelated adventures: *"The Adventures of Tom Sawyer" is a* picaresque *novel.*

pic·a·yune (pĭk′ ē yōōn′, pĭk′ ə-) *adj-* 1 small-minded; narrow; petty: *a* picayune *concern with details.* 2 of little value or importance; paltry: *a* picayune *sum of money.* *n-* formerly, a Spanish coin of small value used in southern United States; hence, anything of little value or importance.

pic·ca·lil·li (pĭk′ ə lĭl′ ē) *n-* relish made of chopped vegetables and spices.

pic·co·lo (pĭk′ ə lō′) *n-* [*pl.* **pic·co·los**] small flute with a sharp, high tone.

[1]pick (pĭk) *vt-* (in senses, 1, 3, and 8, considered intransitive when the direct object is implied but not expressed) 1 to choose; select: *to* pick *Saturday for the picnic.* 2 to pull off; pluck: *to* pick *a rose from a bush.* 3 to harvest: *to* pick *peaches.* 4 to remove feathers, hulls, etc., from: *to* pick *a chicken.* 5 to clean with a pointed tool: *to* pick *one's teeth.* 6 to break up with a sharp-pointed tool: *to* pick *ice.* 7 to make (a hole) with a sharp instrument. 8 to pluck the strings of with the fingers or a plectrum: *to* pick *a guitar.* 9 to cause deliberately; start: *to* pick *a fight or quarrel.* 10 to open something with a sharp instrument, bit of wire, etc.: *to* pick *a lock.* 11 to steal from by removing stealthily: *to* pick *a pocket.* *n-* 1 choice: *Take your* pick. 2 best of anything: *the* pick *of the crop.* 3 amount of a crop gathered at one time. [from Middle English **picken,** from Old English **pic(i)an,** perhaps influenced by Old Norse **pikka.**]

pick apart (or **to pieces**) 1 to tear or separate into many parts. 2 to examine closely in order to find faults: *Mr. Stanley* picked apart *the report.*

pick at to eat slowly, especially in a dainty or fussy way.

pick flaws to find fault; criticize.

pick off 1 to wound or kill one by one by accurate shooting. 2 in baseball, to put out (a base runner) by catching him off base.

pick on 1 to choose; select. 2 *Informal* to single out for criticism or abuse; annoy; tease: *I could not understand why they* picked on *me.*

pick out 1 to choose; select: *to* pick out *a certain dress from a rack.* 2 to tell apart from the others, or from the surroundings; distinguish. 3 to play note by note, as if from memory: *to* pick out *a tune on a piano.*

pick over to examine one by one, before choosing: *They* picked over *the cherries.*

pick up 1 to lift or raise: *He* picked up *the books that fell down.* 2 to get unexpectedly: *to* pick up *a bargain.* 3 to learn or grasp: *She* picked up *swimming very quickly.* 4 to carry on; continue: *Tom* picked up *where he stopped the day before.* 5 to meet and take along; give a ride to: *He* picked *us* up *on the way to school.*

[2]pick (pĭk) *n-* 1 tool such as a pickax, for breaking up earth. 2 ice pick or similar slim, pointed implement. 3 small, thin piece of metal, horn, or plastic for plucking a guitar, banjo, or similar stringed instrument; plectrum. [from Middle English **pike** meaning "[1]pike; spike."]

pick·a·back (pĭk′ ə băk′) piggyback.

pick·ax or **pick·axe** (pĭk′ ăks′) *n-* digging tool having a slightly curved head with a point at one end and a blade at the other, or with both ends pointed; pick.

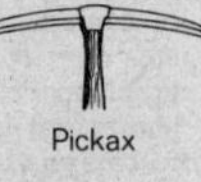

Pickax

pick·er·el (pĭk′ ər əl) *n-* [*pl.* **pick·er·el; pick·er·els** (kinds of pickerel)] any of several slender, mottled, fresh-water food fishes, with a pointed head and large mouth.

pick·et (pĭk′ət) ***n-*** **1** person posted outside a factory, store, government building, etc., to express protest or to persuade others not to enter, especially in a strike by a labor union. **2** pointed post or stake. **3** *Military* guard or lookout posted to give warning of an attack. ***vt-*** to station persons outside of (a factory, store, meeting, court, etc.) in a strike or protest. ***vi-*** to be stationed in this way: *He* picketed *all day yesterday.*

pick·ings (pĭk′ĭngz) ***n-*** *pl.* **1** things left over to be picked or gathered; scraps; gleanings. **2** amount gained for the effort expended: *good* pickings.

pick·le (pĭk′əl) ***n-*** **1** brine, vinegar, or similar solution for preserving foods. **2** cucumber or other vegetable preserved in such a solution. **3** *Informal* difficult or embarrassing situation. **4** an acid, often dilute hydrochloric, or other chemical, in which metals are bathed for cleaning. ***vt-*** **[pick·led, pick·ling]** to preserve or flavor by soaking in brine or vinegar: *to* pickle *herring.*

pick·pock·et (pĭk′pŏk′ət) ***n-*** thief who steals from pockets or handbags.

pick·up (pĭk′ŭp′) ***n-*** **1** collection: *The mail truck makes three* pickups *a day.* **2** acceleration of an automobile. **3** *Informal* increase in activity: *There was a* pickup *in retail sales last month.* **4** *Informal* something that stimulates or cheers: *The letter from home was a* pickup *for the soldier.* **5** in baseball and other sports, a quick, skillful catch or return of a ball immediately after it has struck the ground. **6** device that converts the vibrations of a phonograph's needle into electrical oscillations.

pic·nic (pĭk′nĭk) ***n-*** **1** pleasure trip that includes a meal outdoors: *a family* picnic *at the beach.* **2** any informal outdoor meal. **3** *Slang* pleasant time. *as* ***modifier***: *a* picnic *lunch.* ***vi-*** **[pic·nicked, pic·nick·ing]** to go on or take part in a picnic. **—*n-* pic′nick·er.**

pi·cot (pē′kō′) ***n-*** one of the small, ornamental projecting loops forming the edge of certain laces, ribbons, etc. ***vt-*** **[pi·coted** (-kōd′), **pi·cot·ing** (-kō′ĭng)**]** to finish or edge with such loops. ***Hom-*** pekoe.

pic·ric acid (pĭk′rĭk) ***n-*** yellowish, explosive, and poisonous organic compound used in dyeing, medicine, and explosives.

Pict (pĭkt) ***n-*** one of an ancient, probably non-Celtic people of Britain and the Scottish Highlands, who in the ninth century were united with the Scots.

pic·to·graph (pĭk′tə grăf′) ***n-*** **1** very ancient painting or drawing on a rock wall in a cave, on the side of a cliff, etc. **2** a diagram, chart, or graph using pictures or pictorial forms to present data; also, one of the pictures used in such a diagram.

pic·tor·i·al (pĭk tôr′ē əl) ***adj-*** **1** having to do with, shown by, or containing pictures: *A photograph album is a* pictorial *record of a family.* **2** suitable for or suggesting a picture; graphic. **—*adv-* pic·tor′i·al·ly.**

pic·ture (pĭk′chər) ***n-*** **1** painting, drawing, photograph, or similar visual representation. **2** likeness or embodiment; image: *She is the* picture *of her mother. The old man was a* picture *of health.* **3** the overall situation: *When does atomic power come into the* picture? **4** clear or colorful description: *This book gives a good* picture *of life in Africa.* **5** mental image: *a hazy* picture *of one's childhood days.* **6** image on a television or motion-picture screen. **7** motion picture; movie. ***vt-*** **[pic·tured, pic·tur·ing] 1** to represent in a painting, drawing, photograph, etc.: *The artist* pictured *a country scene.* **2** to describe vividly in words. **3** to imagine: *He liked to* picture *himself as an explorer.*

pic·tur·esque (pĭk′chə rĕsk′) ***adj-*** interesting, colorful, or charming, as a picture might be: *Quebec is a* picturesque *city.* **—*adv-* pic′tur·esque′ly.**

picture tube ***n-*** large, funnel-shaped vacuum tube on which the picture is displayed in a television set.

picture writing ***n-*** kind of writing using pictures.

pid·dling (pĭd′lĭng) ***adj-*** trifling; insignificant; petty.

pid·gin (pĭj′ən) ***n-*** mixed language using the words of more than one language and a simple grammar. *as* ***modifier***: *a* pidgin *English.* ***Hom-*** pigeon.

[1]**pie** (pī) ***n-*** **1** dish of meat, fruit, or other food baked with a single upper or lower crust, or between two crusts. **2** layer cake made with cream, jam, or similar smooth fillings. [of uncertain origin.] ***Hom-*** pi.

Pie

[2]**pie** (pī) ***n-*** magpie. [from Old French, from Latin **pica** meaning "magpie."] ***Hom-*** pi.

pie·bald (pī′bôld′) ***adj-*** having patches of different colors, especially black and white: *a* piebald *horse.* ***n-*** horse or other animal with such coloring.

piece (pēs) ***n-*** **1** part of a whole; bit; fragment: *to tear a sheet to* pieces. **2** single portion or quantity: *a* piece *of leather; a* piece *of land.* **3** fixed amount or size in which something is made or sold: *The toys cost 35 cents a* piece. **4** example or instance: *a* piece *of advice; a* piece *of nonsense.* **5** single object of a set or group: *There are five* pieces *in this set of luggage.* **6** one of the counters used in checkers, dominoes, and similar games. **7** single musical or literary composition: *He played his favorite piano* piece. **8** coin: *a five-cent* piece. **9** gun: *a fowling* piece. ***vt-*** **[pieced, piec·ing] 1** to make by joining sections together: *to* piece *a patchwork quilt; to* piece *together evidence.* **2** to enlarge or mend by adding material: *to* piece *a skirt.* ***Hom-*** peace. **—*n-* piec′er.**

give a piece of (one's) mind to scold or rebuke for a personal injury or insult; reprimand. **go to pieces 1** to fall apart; break up. **2** to fall apart mentally; lose all self-control. **have a piece of** *Slang* to own part of. **of a piece** of the same sort; alike; consistent.

pi·èce de ré·sis·tance (pyĕs′ də rā′zĭs tä^{n}s′) *French* **1** most important item in a group. **2** main dish.

piece·meal (pēs′mēl′) ***adv-*** in portions or parts; by degrees; bit by bit: *to do a job* piecemeal. ***adj-***: *a* piecemeal *task.*

piece of eight ***n-*** old Spanish and Spanish-American silver coin, worth eight reals, or one peso.

piece·work (pēs′wûrk′) ***n-*** work paid for by the piece or job, not by the hour. **—*n-* piece′work′er.**

pied (pīd) ***adj-*** **1** having two or more colors in patches; piebald: *Our black and white cat has a* pied *coat.* **2** wearing many-colored clothing: *the* Pied *Piper of Hamelin.*

pied·mont (pēd′mŏnt′) ***n-*** area at the base of a mountain. *as* ***modifier***: *a* piedmont *valley.*

pie graph ***n-*** a circular graph divided into wedges, each of which is proportional in size to the fraction it represents. Also **pie chart.** For picture, see *graph.*

pie·plant (pī′plănt′) ***n-*** rhubarb.

pier (pêr) ***n-*** **1** landing place for ships that extends over the water; wharf. See also [1]*dock.* **2** supporting pillar, such as one at an end of an arch. **3** the part of a wall between openings. **4** buttress. ***Hom-*** peer.

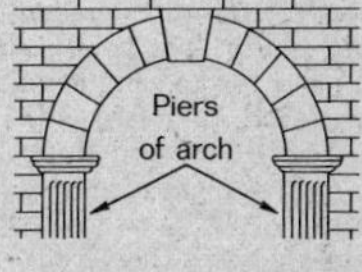

fāte, făt, dâre, bärn; bē, bĕt, mêre; bīte, bĭt; nōte, hŏt, môre, dȯg; fŭn, fûr; to͞o, bo͝ok; oil; out; tar; thin; then; hw for wh as in *wh*at; zh for s as in u*s*ual; ə for a, e, i, o, u, as in *a*go, lin*e*n, per*i*l, at*o*m, min*u*s

pierce (pêrs) ***vt-*** **[pierced, pierc·ing] 1** to puncture: *The rose thorn* pierced *my finger.* **2** to make a hole in; perforate: *The cannonball* pierced *the fortress wall.* **3** to affect deeply or strongly: *The loss of her kitten* pierced *the little girl's heart.* **4** to force a way through; penetrate: *The sun* pierced *the clouds.* **5** to see through; solve: *to* pierce *a mystery.* ***vi-*** to penetrate: *The sun* pierced *through the clouds.*

pierc·ing (pêr′ sĭng) ***adj-*** sharp; cutting; penetrating: *a shrill,* piercing *cry; the* piercing *cold.* ***—adv-*** **pierc′ ing·ly.**

Pi·er·i·an Spring (pī êr′ ē ən) ***n-*** fountain in Pieria, sacred to the Muses and regarded as a source of poetic inspiration.

Pier·rot (pē ə rō′) ***n-*** comic character in French pantomime, usually with a whitened face and wearing loose white pantaloons and jacket.

pi·e·ty (pī′ ə tē) ***n-*** [*pl.* **pi·e·ties**] **1** reverence for God; devotion to religion: *the* piety *of a saint.* **2** loyal devotion to parents, family, country, etc. **3** act of reverence.

pi·e·zo·e·lec·tric (pē ā′ zō ə lĕk′ trĭk) ***adj-*** of or having to do with a property of certain crystals that develop a difference in potential when subjected to mechanical strain. Conversely, when the crystals are subjected to an electric current, they undergo periodic alternations in size.

pif·fle (pĭf′ əl) *Informal* ***n-*** nonsense. ***vi-*** **[pif·fled, pif·fling]** to talk nonsense.

pig (pĭg) ***n-*** **1** four-footed mammal having split hooves and a long snout flattened at the end, raised on farms chiefly for pork, ham, and bacon. **2** pork. **3** *Informal* very greedy or gluttonous person. **4** *Informal* dirty, slovenly person. **5** bar of metal cast from a smelting furnace; also, the mold used to make such a casting.

Pig, about 3 1/2 ft. long

pig in a poke something offered for sale, often dishonestly, without the buyer's being able to see it or determine its true value.

pi·geon (pĭj′ ən) ***n-*** any of various plump birds having great speed of flight and a low, throaty call; especially, the **domestic pigeon** that occurs in great numbers in cities, and is raised for food, racing, and carrying messages. ***Hom-*** pidgin.

Pigeon, about 1 ft. long

pigeon hawk ***n-*** small North American falcon.

pi·geon·hole (pĭj′ ən hōl′) ***n-*** **1** hole in which pigeons nest. **2** boxlike space in a desk, case, etc., for storing letters or other papers. ***vt-*** **[pi·geon·holed, pi·geon·hol·ing] 1** to place (letters, papers, etc.) in such a space. **2** to lay aside and forget.

pi·geon-toed (pĭj′ ən tōd′) ***adj-*** with the feet turned inward toward each other: *a* pigeon-toed *way of running.* ***adv-***: *He walks* pigeon-toed.

pig·ger·y (pĭg′ ə rē) *chiefly Brit.* ***n-*** [*pl.* **pig·ger·ies**] place for keeping or raising pigs.

pig·gish (pĭg′ ĭsh) ***adj-*** **1** very greedy or gluttonous. **2** very dirty and sloppy. **3** like that of a pig: *a* piggish *face.* **4** pigheaded. ***—adv-*** **pig′ gish·ly.** ***n-*** **pig′ gish·ness.**

pig·gy (pĭg′ ē) ***n-*** [*pl.* **pig·gies**] little pig.

pig·gy·back (pĭg′ ē băk′) ***adv-*** **1** (also **pickaback**) on the back or shoulders: *He carried the child* piggyback. **2** in a truck trailer, mounted on a railroad flatcar: *to ship goods* piggyback. ***adj-***: *a* piggyback *shipment.*

piggy bank ***n-*** child's bank for saving coins, made in the shape of a pig.

pig·head·ed (pĭg′ hĕd′ əd) ***adj-*** stubborn; obstinate.

pig iron ***n-*** crude iron as it comes from the blast furnace. It is usually cast into pigs for later refining.

pig·ment (pĭg′ mənt) ***n-*** **1** any substance used to give color to something, especially paints. **2** material that gives color to living things: *the* pigment *in the skin; the* pigment *in plants.* ***—adj-*** **pig′ men·tar′ y** (-mən tĕr′ ē): *a* pigmentary *layer of cells.*

pig·men·ta·tion (pĭg′ mən tā′ shən) ***n-*** the coloring in a plant, animal, or person due to the presence of a pigment in the tissues.

pig·ment·ed (pĭg mĕn′ təd) ***adj-*** colored by a pigment.

pig·my (pĭg′ mē) pygmy.

pig·nut (pĭg′ nŭt′) ***n-*** **1** thin-shelled nut of a certain kind of hickory tree. **2** the tree itself.

pig·pen (pĭg′ pĕn′) ***n-*** **1** place for keeping pigs. **2** very dirty and sloppy place.

pig·skin (pĭg′ skĭn′) ***n-*** **1** the hide of a pig, or the leather made from it. **2** *Informal* a football. *as* ***modifier:*** *a pair of* pigskin *gloves.*

pig·sty (pĭg′ stī′) ***n-*** [*pl.* **pig·sties**] pigpen.

pig·tail (pĭg′ tāl′) ***n-*** **1** braid of hair at the back of the head. **2** long twist of tobacco.

[1]**pike** (pīk) ***n-*** weapon formerly carried by foot soldiers, consisting of a long wooden shaft with a metal spearhead. [from Middle English **pike,** from Old English **píc** meaning "spike," and later applied to the weapon under the influence of French **pique,** "soldier's weapon."] ***—n-*** **pike′ man** [*pl.* **pike·men**].

[2]**pike** (pīk) ***n-*** [*pl.* **pike; pikes** (kinds of pike)] any of several slender fresh-water fishes having long, pointed snouts, especially the **northern pike,** a voracious game fish of northern United States. [from Old English **píc** meaning "a spike," applied to the fish because of the shape of its jaw.]

Pike, 1–4 1/2 ft. long

[3]**pike** (pīk) ***n-*** **1** road on which a charge is usually made for driving; turnpike. **2** any main road [shortened from **turnpike.**]

pik·er (pī′ kər) *Informal* ***n-*** person who tends to be timidly cautious or stingy, especially in business.

pike·staff (pīk′ stăf′) ***n-*** pole with a spike at the end, used by mountain climbers to prevent slipping.

pi·laf or **pi·laff** (pĭ lŏf′) ***n-*** **1** Mediterranean cooked rice. **2** an Oriental dish of meat or fish boiled with pilaf. Also **pi·lau′** (pĭ lou′, -lò′).

pi·las·ter (pə lăs′ tər, pī-) ***n-*** rectangular flat column projecting slightly from a wall.

pil·chard (pĭl′ chərd) ***n-*** **1** very common food fish of European coasts, resembling the herring. **2** any of several herrings or sardines of the United States.

[1]**pile** (pīl) ***n-*** **1** heap; mass; stack: *a* pile *of sand.* **2** *Informal* a large amount or number: *He has a* pile *of money.* **3** *Physics* nuclear reactor. ***vt-*** **[piled, pil·ing] 1** to place or throw in a heap; arrange: *to* pile *bricks.* **2** to fill; load: *to* pile *the wagon with hay.* ***vi-*** to press forward in a mass; crowd: *We* piled *into the bus.* [from Latin **píla** meaning "pillar."]

pile up 1 to accumulate. **2** to amass.

[2]**pile** (pīl) ***n-*** timber or other long, stiff, building column driven into the ground to support a load, especially to support a dock or other structure above water. [from Old English **pil,** "stake," from Latin **pīlum,** "javelin."]

[3]**pile** (pīl) ***n-*** **1** nap of cloth; especially, the furry or velvety surface of velvet, plush, carpets, etc. **2** short, soft hair; down. [from Latin word **pilus,** "a hair."]

pile·driv·er (pīl′ drī′ vər) ***n-*** machine for hammering piles into the ground.

piles (pīlz) ***n-*** *pl.* hemorrhoids.

pil·fer (pĭl′ fər) ***vi-*** to steal in small amounts: *A rat had* pilfered *from the pantry.* ***vt-***: *The thief* pilfered *coins.*

pil·grim (pĭl′ grĭm) ***n-*** **1** traveler to a holy place: *Many* pilgrims *still journey to the Holy Land every year.* **2** traveler; wanderer. **3 Pilgrim** or **Pilgrim Father** one of the Englishmen who landed from the ship "Mayflower" and founded the colony of Plymouth, Massachusetts, in 1620.

pil·grim·age (pĭl′ grə mĭj) ***n-*** journey made because of reverence or affection, especially to a sacred place.

pil·ing (pī′ lĭng) ***n-*** a number of piles driven into position as part of a structure.

pill (pĭl) ***n-*** **1** medicine in the form of a small disk or ball. **2** *Informal* unpleasant or disagreeable person.

a bitter pill to swallow anything hard or unpleasant to bear: *The loss was* a bitter pill to swallow.

pil·lage (pĭl′ ĭj) ***vt-*** **[pil·laged, pil·lag·ing]** to rob or plunder: *The bandits* pillaged *two villages in the west.* ***vi-***: *They* pillaged *through the countryside.* ***n-*** **1** a robbing or plundering. **2** whatever is taken as plunder: *A lot of* pillage *was recovered from the outlaws.* ***—n-*** **pil′ lag·er.**

pil·lar (pĭl′ ər) ***n-*** **1** column used to hold up a floor, or the like, or as a monument or high pedestal. **2** a firm supporter; mainstay: *a* pillar *of society*; *a* pillar *of the church.* ***vt-*** to brace or support with columns (often followed by "up"): *to* pillar *up a floor or roof.* ***—adj-*** **pil′ lared.**

from pillar to post from one place or situation to another, as if driven by circumstances.

Pillar

pill·box (pĭl′ bŏks′) ***n-*** **1** small box for holding or carrying pills. **2** small concrete fort protecting a border, beach, etc. **3** a woman's small round hat.

pil·lion (pĭl′ yən) ***n-*** pad put behind the saddle of a horse, motorcycle, or motor scooter as a second seat.

ride pillion to ride as the second and rear person on a horse, motorcycle, or motor scooter.

pil·lo·ry (pĭl′ ə rē) ***n-*** [*pl.* **pil·lo·ries**] framework with openings for the neck and wrists of a person held up to public shame, used in olden times to punish minor lawbreakers. ***vt-*** **[pil·lo·ried, pil·lo·ry·ing] 1** to punish by this instrument. **2** to expose to public shame: *The newspapers* pillory *dishonest politicians.*

Pillory

pil·low (pĭl′ ō) ***n-*** support for the head in resting or sleeping; cushion. ***vt-*** to rest on or as if on such a support; cushion: *He* pillowed *his head on the sofa.*

pil·low·case (pĭl′ ō kās′) ***n-*** removable cloth cover, open at one end, to hold a pillow. Also **pil′ low·slip′.**

pi·lot (pī′ lət) ***n-*** **1** person who flies a plane or other aircraft: *a bomber* pilot. **2** man who guides a large ship, usually into or out of a harbor. **3** any leader or guide. ***vt-*** **1** to fly (a plane) or guide (a ship). **2** to lead or guide. ***—adj-*** **pi′ lot·less.**

pi·lot·age (pī′ lə tĭj) ***n-*** **1** the guiding of ships in or out of a port, channel, etc. **2** fee paid for such service.

pilot balloon ***n-*** small balloon launched to show the direction and force of the wind.

pilot fish ***n-*** small fish that often accompanies sharks and feeds on scraps left by them.

pi·lot·house (pī′ lət hous′) ***n-*** enclosed space on the bridge of a ship that contains the steering wheel, compass, and other navigational equipment; wheelhouse.

pilot light ***n-*** **1** small flame in a gas stove or hot-water heater that burns continuously and is used to light the main burners. **2** light, usually red, that shows when a machine or appliance is turned on.

pilot project ***n-*** limited organization set up to find the best methods and practices for some full-scale effort. When the project is a factory, it is called a **pilot plant.**

Pilt·down man (pĭlt′ doun′) ***n-*** a type of primitive man supposed to have lived in Europe during the ice age. It was proved to be a hoax.

Pi·ma (pē′ mə) ***n-*** [*pl.* **Pi·mas,** also **Pi·ma**] one of a tribe of American Indians of southern Arizona and northern Mexico. ***—adj-*** **Pi′ man**: *the* Piman *language.*

pi·men·to (pĭ mĕn′ tō) ***n-*** [*pl.* **pi·men·tos**] **1** tree that bears allspice; also, allspice. **2** pimiento.

pi·mien·to (pĭ mĕn′ tō, pĭm yĕn′-) ***n-*** [*pl.* **pi·mien·tos**] a sweet pepper used as a vegetable or garnish.

pim·per·nel (pĭm′ pər nĕl′) ***n-*** plant of the primrose family with white, purple, or scarlet flowers that close in cloudy or rainy weather.

pim·ple (pĭm′ pəl) ***n-*** small, hard, inflamed oil gland in the skin. ***—adj-*** **pim′ pled** or **pim·ply [pim·pli·er, pim·pli·est].**

pin (pĭn) ***n-*** **1** short piece of wire with a sharp point at one end and a round head at the other, used to fasten things together. **2** piece of wood, metal, etc., having a similar use, such as hairpin, safety pin, or clothespin. **3** ornament or badge fitted with a clasp: *a class* pin; *a fraternity* pin. **4** cylinder inserted into a hole as a fastener or anchoring device. **5** in golf, a pole with a small flag which marks the hole on a green. **6** bottle-shaped wooden peg, used as a target in bowling. **7 pins** *Informal* legs. ***vt-*** **[pinned, pin·ning] 1** to fasten with a sharp instrument. **2** to hold firmly in one position: *The fallen tree* pinned *him to the ground.* **3** *Informal* to give a fraternity pin to as a token of becoming engaged. ***—adj-*** **pin′ like′.**

on pins and needles very anxious or uneasy, as if unable to sit or stand still.

pin down to get (a person) to be specific about a course, opinion, etc.: *He couldn't* pin *his boss* down *to a raise in pay.*

pin·a·fore (pĭn′ ə fôr′) ***n-*** loose, sleeveless apron, or covering for a dress.

pi·ña·ta (pēn yä′ tə) ***n-*** container decorated and often shaped like an animal or person, and filled with candies, fruits, etc. In Latin-American countries, it is hung up on holidays, when blindfolded children try to break it with a stick.

Piñata

pin·ball (pĭn′ bôl′) ***n-*** game played with steel balls on a board that slopes downward toward the player. Each ball is propelled by a spring-loaded plunger and rolls downward through a series of channels where it bounces off other springs, drops into a numbered hole, or runs into an alley. ***as modifier***: *a* pinball *machine.*

pince-nez (păns′ nā′) ***n-*** [*pl.* **pince-nez**] pair of eyeglasses kept on the nose by a spring clamp.

pin·cers (pĭn′ sərz) ***n-*** (takes plural verb) **1** tool with jaws hinged like scissors, for holding, pulling, etc. Also **pair of pincers** (takes singular verb). **2** the pinching claws of a crab or lobster. Also **pinch′ers** (pĭn′ chərz).

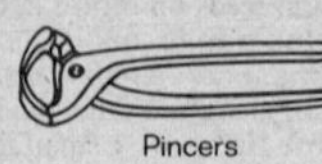
Pincers

pinch (pĭnch) ***vt-*** **1** to squeeze or nip between the thumb and a finger, or between two edges: *Her brother* pinched *her arm. I* pinched *my finger in the door.* **2** to squeeze so as to hurt: *Her shoes* pinch *her toes.* **3** to cause distress or hardship to: *Poverty* pinched *the family for many years.* **4** to cause to become drawn or cramped, as by pain, hunger, etc.: *The biting wind* pinched *the child's face.* **5** *Slang* to arrest; take into police custody. **6** *Slang* to steal. ***vi-*** to economize drastically: *They had to* pinch *when they ran short of money.* ***n-*** **1** a squeeze or nip: *a playful* pinch. **2** painful pressure: *the* pinch *of new shoes.* **3** amount that can be picked up between the thumb and a finger: *a* pinch *of salt.* **4** hardship; distress: *the* pinch *of poverty.* **5** sudden difficulty, necessity, or emergency; tight spot: *Anything will do in a* pinch. **6** *Slang* an arrest. **7** *Slang* a theft. ***—n-*** **pinch′er.**

pinch bar ***n-*** crowbar.

pinch-hit (pĭnch′hĭt′) ***vi-*** [**pinch-hit, pinch-hit·ting**] **1** in baseball, to bat in place of another player. **2** to be a substitute for someone else in any situation. ***vt-***: *He* pinch-hit *a double.* ***n-*** **pinch hit** a base hit made by one player batting for another. ***—n-*** **pinch hitter.**

pin curl ***n-*** hair curl kept in place with a hairpin, bobby pin, etc.

pin·cush·ion (pĭn′ko͝osh′ən) ***n-*** small cushion in which to stick pins and needles not in use.

[1]**pine** (pīn) ***n-*** **1** any of various cone-bearing evergreen trees with needle-shaped leaves growing in clusters of two or more. **2** the wood of these trees. *as* ***modifier:*** *a* pine *forest.* [from Old English **pin,** from Latin **pinus,** "pine; fir."]

White pine

[2]**pine** (pīn) ***vi-*** [**pined, pin·ing**] to become sick gradually from sorrow or loneliness: *The prisoner* pined *away.* [from Old English **pinian,** "to torture; afflict."]
pine for to long intensely for; yearn for.

pi·ne·al body (pĭn′ē əl, pī nē′-) ***n-*** small, cone-shaped body in the vertebrate brain, now believed to regulate the functioning of the sex glands. Also **pineal gland.**

pine·ap·ple (pīn′ăp′əl) ***n-*** **1** tropical fruit shaped like a pine cone, having firm, juicy pulp, a tough, segmented skin, and a tuft of saw-edged leaves at the top. **2** the spiny-leafed plant that bears this fruit. *as* ***modifier:*** *a* pineapple *dessert.*

Pineapple

pine·y (pī′nē) piny.

pin·feath·er (pĭn′fet͟h′ər) ***n-*** small feather just beginning to grow.

ping (pĭng) ***n-*** a slight, sharp, sound, as is made by a bullet hitting an object.

ping-pong (pĭng′pŏng′) ***n-*** game somewhat like tennis, played with solid paddles and a light plastic ball over a low net on a table measuring four-by-eight feet; table tennis. [from **Ping-Pong,** trademark name for table-tennis sets.]

pin·head (pĭn′hĕd′) ***n-*** **1** head of a pin. **2** anything small or insignificant. **3** *Slang* foolish, stupid, or dull-witted person. ***—adj-*** **pin′head′ed.**

pin·hole (pĭn′hōl′) ***n-*** **1** small hole made by a pin or as if by a pin. **2** hole into which a pin or peg fits.

[1]**pin·ion** (pĭn′yən) ***n-*** the wing, or any of the stiff flying feathers, of a bird. ***vt-*** **1** to bind the wings or clip the wing tips of (a bird). **2** to tie or fasten firmly: *to* pinion *a person's arms to his sides.* [from Old French **pignon,** from Latin **penna** meaning "feather."] ***Hom-*** piñon.

[2]**pin·ion** (pĭn′yən) ***n-*** **1** a wheel with cogs that engage those of a larger toothed wheel or rack, so that motion is imparted from one to the other. **2** small gear wheel in a set of gears. For picture, see *gear.* [from French **pignon,** which in Old French meant "battlement" as well as "feather," and related to [1]**pinion.**] ***Hom-*** piñon.

[1]**pink** (pĭngk) ***n-*** **1** very pale red color: *the* pink *and gold of the morning sky.* **2** highest degree; peak: *the* pink *of health*; *the* pink *of perfection.* **3** any of various plants with narrow, pointed leaves and pink, red, or white flowers, especially, a garden plant related to the carnation, with fringed petals and a spicy fragrance; also, the flower of any of these plants. **4** *Informal* person with moderate leftist views in politics. ***adj-*** **1** very pale red in color: *Sunrise turned the sky* pink *in the east.* **2** *Informal* moderately leftist in politics. [from **pink** meaning originally "a flower with pinked (fringed) edges," from [2]**pink.**] ***—adj-*** **pink′ish.**
in the pink in the best of health.

[2]**pink** (pĭngk) ***vt-*** **1** to cut or scallop the edge of (cloth, leather, paper, etc.) in a notched pattern. **2** to prick or pierce with a pointed weapon or instrument. [from Middle English **pynken.**]

pink·eye (pĭngk′ī′) ***n-*** conjunctivitis.

pin·kie (pĭng′kē) *Informal* ***n-*** fourth and smallest finger, not counting the thumb. For picture, see *finger.*

pin money ***n-*** any small sum of money to be used for incidental personal expenses.

pin·nace (pĭn′əs) ***n-*** **1** formerly, a small boat that attended a larger vessel and was used to transport messages, supplies, etc. **2** any boat carried by a ship.

pin·na·cle (pĭn′ə kəl) ***n-*** **1** peak or highest point: *the* pinnacle *of a mountain*; *the* pinnacle *of fame.* **2** high point like a spire: *a* pinnacle *of rock.* **3** small tower or turret above the rest of a building: *the* pinnacle *on the roof of the distant castle.*

pin·nate (pĭn′āt′) ***adj-*** having parts arranged symmetrically along two sides of an axis, as in a feather: *a* pinnate *leaf.* ***—adv-*** **pin′nate·ly.**

pi·noch·le or **pi·noc·le** (pē′nŏk′əl, -nŭk′əl) ***n-*** any of several card games for two to six players, using a pack of 48 cards having two each of the ace, king, jack, ten, and nine of each suit; also, one of the scoring combinations in these games.

pi·ñon (pĭn′yən) ***n-*** pine tree of western United States, having edible seeds; also, the seed itself. ***Hom-*** pinion.

pin·point (pĭn′point′) ***vt-*** **1** to show the exact location of, by or as if by sticking a pin into a map: *The detectives* pinpointed *the criminal's hideout.* **2** to mark, determine, or define precisely: *to* pinpoint *a target*; *to* pinpoint *a cause or influence*; *to* pinpoint *the meaning of a word.* ***n-*** **1** point of a pin. **2** something very small or unimportant. **3** exact or precise location. *as* ***modifier:*** *the* pinpoint *bombing of a target.*

pin·prick (pĭn′prĭk′) ***n-*** **1** tiny puncture made by a pin or other fine point. **2** trivial annoyance or irritation.

pin·stripe (pĭn′strīp′) ***n-*** very thin stripe, as in certain fabrics used for suits.

pint (pīnt) ***n-*** liquid or dry measure equal to half a quart.

pin·to (pĭn′tō) ***adj-*** marked with spots of more than one color; pied; mottled. ***n-*** [*pl.* **pin·tos**] horse or pony with such spots.

pin·wheel (pĭn′hwēl′) ***n-*** **1** toy wheel of different-colored pieces of paper, plastic, etc., pinned to an end of a stick so as to revolve in the wind. **2** kind of firework that revolves when lighted.

pin·worm (pĭn′wûrm′) ***n-*** small, threadlike, parasitic worm that infests the colon and rectum.

pin·y (pī′nē) ***adj-*** **[pin·i·er, pin·i·est]** of or related to pine trees, especially to their scent or resin.

pi·o·neer (pī′ə nêr′) ***n-*** person who is the first or among the first in a new region, new study, new field of work, etc.: *The West was settled by* pioneers. *as* ***modifier:*** *a* pioneer *effort in space.* ***vt-*** to lead the way in some new region, study, etc.: *Walter Reed* pioneered *in finding the cause of yellow fever.* ***vt-*** to take the first steps in; open up: *to* pioneer *the field of weather control.*

pi·ous (pī′əs) ***adj-*** **1** very religious; devout: *a* pious *man.* **2** having to do with religious devotion: *to be put to* pious *uses.* **3** appearing to be religious when one is not: *a* pious *rascal.* ***—adv-*** **pi′ous·ly.** ***n-*** **pi′ous·ness.**

[1]**pip** (pĭp) ***n-*** **1** small seed, as of an apple or orange. **2** *Slang* something very good of its kind: *He's a* pip *at baseball.* [from earlier **pippen,** from Middle English and Old French **pepin** meaning "a seedling apple; seeds from such an apple."]

[2]**pip** (pĭp) ***n-*** **1** one of the marks or spots on a playing card, domino, or on dice. **2** single rootstock of the lily-of-the-valley, or one of its flowers. **3** one of the diamond-shaped sections on a pineapple. [probably from [1]**pip.**]

[3]**pip** (pĭp) ***n-*** disease of poultry, marked by mucus in the mouth and throat and scabs on the tongue. [from earlier Dutch **pippe,** ultimately from Latin **pituita** meaning "phlegm."]

pipe (pīp) ***n-*** **1** tube used to carry liquids, gases, etc., from one place to another. **2** small wooden or clay bowl with a hollow stem, used for smoking tobacco. **3** amount of tobacco used to fill this. **4** any wooden, metal, or reed tube used to make musical sounds, such as a kind of flute or one of the tubes of an organ. **5** high, shrill voice or sound, such as the call of a bird or insect. **6 pipes** (1) bagpipe. (2) panpipe. ***vt-*** **[piped, pip·ing]** **1** to carry through a tube: *to* pipe *oil from the field to the refinery.* **2** to supply with tubes or pipes: *to* pipe *a house for water.* **3** to blow or play on a musical wind instrument: *to pipe a merry tune.* **4** to sound, speak, or utter loudly and shrilly: *The little boy* piped *a tune in his squeaky voice.* **5** to alert, summon, or direct by bagpipes, whistles, or other pipes: *to* pipe *all hands on deck.* **pipe down** *Slang* to be quiet; keep still. **pipe up** to begin to play, sing, or speak.

pipe dream ***n-*** *Informal* any idea or plan that is impractical or unlikely, or seems so at the time.

pipe·fish (pīp′fĭsh′) ***n-*** [*pl.* **pipe·fish; pipe·fish·es** (kinds of pipefish)] any of several long, narrow fishes with bony scales and a tubelike snout.

pipe·line (pīp′līn′) ***n-*** **1** line of pipes for carrying oil, water, gas, etc. **2** means of receiving or distributing information: *He has a* pipeline *to the mayor's office.*

pip·er (pī′pər) ***n-*** person who plays on a pipe, especially the bagpipes.

pay the piper to pay for one's pleasures; accept the consequences of what one does.

pi·pette (pī pĕt′) ***n-*** glass tube used for taking up measured amounts of liquid and putting them onto microscope slides, into laboratory test tubes, etc. ***vt-*** **[pi·pet·ted, pi·pet·ting]** to transfer with such a tube.

pip·ing (pī′pĭng) ***n-*** the pipes of a building, machine, system, etc.: *new* piping *for the engine.* **2** music of the bagpipe, fife, etc. **3** shrill sound, such as the song of a bird. **4** strip of material along a seam or fold, used as a trimming. ***adj-*** **1** shrill: *a* piping *voice.* **2** (also **piping hot**) very hot: *a* piping hot *bowl of soup.*

pip·it (pĭp′ət) ***n-*** any of several small birds resembling sparrows, noted for wagging their tails as they walk.

pip·pin (pĭp′ən) ***n-*** any of several kinds of apples, especially a sweet, yellow or greenish-yellow eating apple.

pip·squeak (pĭp′skwēk′) ***n-*** *Slang* person or thing that is very small or insignificant.

pi·quant (pē′kənt) ***adj-*** **1** agreeably sharp to the taste: a piquant *sauce.* **2** arousing interest; clever; stimulating: *the* piquant *comments of a good critic.* **3** having a lively and attractive charm: *a* piquant *face or manner.* ***—adv-*** **pi′quant·ly.** ***n-*** **pi′quan·cy.**

pique (pēk) ***n-*** slight anger or resentment. ***vt-*** **[piqued, pi·quing]** **1** to wound the pride of; displease: *Their rudeness* piqued her. **2** to stir up; arouse; excite: *to* pique *one's curiosity.* **3** to pride (oneself): *The actor* piqued *himself on his good looks.* ***Homs-*** peak, peek.

pi·qué (pē kā′, pĭ-) ***n-*** firm-textured fabric, usually of cotton, woven with a ribbed effect or with a small, indented diamond or honeycomb pattern.

pi·ra·cy (pī′rə sē) ***n-*** [*pl.* **pi·ra·cies**] **1** armed robbery on the high seas. **2** the use of another's invention, literary work, or the like, without permission.

pi·ra·nha (pĭ rän′yə) ***n-*** small South American freshwater fish that often attacks people and other large animals.

pi·rate (pī′rət) ***n-*** **1** robber on the high seas. **2** person who uses another's invention or creation without permission. ***vt-*** **[pi·rat·ed, pi·rat·ing]** **1** to rob at sea. **2** to use (another's invention or creation) without permission: *The company is being sued for* pirating *an invention.*

pi·rat·i·cal (pī răt′ĭ kəl) ***adj-*** of or like piracy or pirates: *to engage in* piratical *practices.* ***—adv-*** **pi·rat′i·cal·ly.**

pi·rogue (pə rōg′, pē-) ***n-*** **1** canoe made of a hollowed-out log. **2** any boat shaped like a canoe.

pir·ou·ette (pĭr′o͞o ĕt′) ***n-*** a whirling or turning about on the toes. ***vi-*** **[pir·ou·et·ted, pir·ou·et·ting]** to turn on the toes rapidly in one spot.

pis·ca·tor·y (pĭs′kə tôr′ē) ***adj-*** **1** having to do with fishes or with fishing: *articles on* piscatory *subjects.* **2** making a living by fishing: *a* piscatory *people.* Also **pis′ca tor′i·al.**

Pisces (pī′sēz, pĭs′ēz) ***n-*** constellation south of Andromeda, supposed to resemble a pair of fish in outline.

Pisces

pis·ta·chi·o (pĭs tăsh′ē ō) ***n-*** [*pl.* **pis·ta·chi·os**] **1** small tree of southern Europe and Asia, having a greenish, almond flavored nut, the kernel of which is used for flavoring. **2** the nut itself. **3** a very pale green color. ***—adj-:*** *a dish of* pistachio *ice cream; a* pistachio *scarf.*

pis·til (pĭs′təl) ***n-*** the part of the center of a flower that produces the seed. ***Hom-*** pistol.

Pistil

pis·til·late (pĭs′tə lət) ***adj-*** having a pistil or pistils; especially, having a pistil but no stamens.

pis·tol (pĭs′təl) ***n-*** short firearm designed to be held in and fired by one hand. Most modern pistols are of two types, the revolver, which holds cartridges in a revolving cylinder in line with the

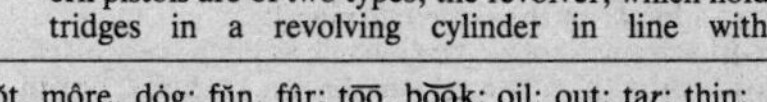

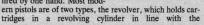

fāte, făt, dâre, bärn; bē, bĕt, mêre; bīte, bĭt; nōte, hŏt, môre, dóg; fŭn, fûr; to͞o, bo͝ok; oil; out; tar; thin; then; hw for wh as in what; zh for s as in usual; ə for a, e, i, o, u, as in ago, linen, peril, atom, minus

barrel, and the **automatic pistol** (or **automatic**), which holds them in a clip that is slid and locked into the handgrip, and is automatically recocked after firing. ***Hom-*** pistil.

pis·ton (pĭs′ tən) ***n-*** **1** in various machines, a close-fitting disk or circular block that slides back and forth in a hollow cylinder. **2** sliding valve in a wind instrument, which changes the pitch of the tones.

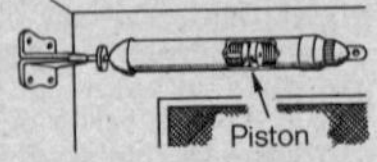
Piston

piston rod ***n-*** in an engine, the rod connecting the piston and crankshaft.

[1]**pit** (pĭt) ***n-*** **1** hole in the ground, either natural or artificial; also, a mine: *a* gravel *pit*; *a* coal *pit.* **2** hollow place on the body: *the* pit *of the stomach.* **3** scar caused by a disease, such as smallpox. **4** low area in front of the stage where the orchestra sits. **5** lowered and enclosed place in which animals are made to fight: *a* pit *for cockfighting.* **6** area on the floor of an exchange, devoted to a particular commodity: *a grain* pit. **7** the abyss; hell. ***vt-*** **[pit·ted, pit·ting] 1** to mark with small scars, dents, etc.: *Smallpox had* pitted *his face.* **2** to set to oppose or fight; match: *to* pit *two wrestlers against each other.* [from Old English **pytt,** from Latin **puteus** meaning "the hole of a well."]

[2]**pit** (pĭt) ***n-*** the seed or stone of certain fruits, such as a cherry or plum. ***vt-*** **[pit·ted, pit·ting]** to remove the seeds or stones of: *to* pit *cherries.* [from Dutch **pit.**]

Pit

pit·a·pat (pĭt′ ə păt′) ***adv-*** with a quick succession of beats, taps, or steps: *Her heart went* pitapat. ***n-*** succession of light, quick sounds. ***vi-*** **[pit·a·pat·ted, pit·a·pat·ting]** to patter; palpitate. Also **pit′ty·pat′** (-ē păt′).

[1]**pitch** (pĭch) ***vt-*** **1** to set up; erect; establish: *to* pitch *camp*; *to* pitch *a tent.* **2** to throw; toss; also, in baseball, to throw (the ball) to a batter: *They* pitched *the hay into the loft. He* pitched *a very fast ball.* **3** to set at a certain level, angle, key, etc.: *He* pitched *the violin a little higher.* **4** to play (a ball game or part of one) in the position of pitcher: *He* pitched *the first two innings.* ***vi-*** **1** to fall headlong: *The painter suddenly* pitched *forward off the ladder.* **2** to plunge up and down in a lengthwise seesaw motion: *The ship* pitched *in the heavy seas.* **3** to slope or slant. **4** in baseball, to act as pitcher: *He* pitched *several seasons for the Yankees.* ***n-*** **1** a plunging forward or down: *a headlong* pitch *from a ladder.* **2** a throwing or tossing; also, in baseball, a throw served to a batter. **3** lengthwise up-and-down motion, as of a ship in a heavy sea. **4** slope downward; slant: *the steep* pitch *of a roof.* **5** point; degree: *the highest* pitch *of excitement.* **6** in music or speech, the lowness or highness of a sound. **7** the distance between two successive threads of a screw, or between the centers of two successive gear teeth. **8** *Slang* a persuasive appeal: *a sales* pitch. [of uncertain origin.]

pitch in *Informal* **1** to start working vigorously. **2** to cooperate.

pitch into *Informal* to attack.

[2]**pitch** (pĭch) ***n-*** **1** thick, sticky, dark-colored substance made from wood, coal, or petroleum. Pitch is used for varnish, roofing paper, street paving, etc. **2** resin from conifers. ***vt-*** to cover with pitch. [from Old English **pic,** from Latin **pix** of the same meaning.]

pitch-black (pĭch′ blăk′) ***adj-*** black as pitch; very black.

pitch·blende (pĭch′ blĕnd′) ***n-*** brown or black ore of uranium that occurs in rounded masses and often contains radium.

pitch-dark (pĭch′ därk′) ***adj-*** extremely dark.

pitched battle ***n-*** intense and close fight between two opposing forces.

[1]**pitch·er** (pĭch′ ər) ***n-*** **1** vessel with a handle on its side and a pouring lip opposite the handle, used to hold and serve liquids. **2** (also **pitcherful**) amount such a container holds when full. [from Old French **pichier,** from Latin **bicārium** meaning "pitcher; beaker."]

Pitcher

[2]**pitch·er** (pĭch′ ər) ***n-*** person who throws or hurls; especially, in baseball, the player who throws the ball to the batter. [from [1]**pitch.**]

pitcher plant ***n-*** any of various insect-eating plants whose leaves are formed in the shape of a pitcher.

pitch·fork (pĭch′ fôrk′) ***n-*** tool with steel tines and a long wooden handle, used to move hay, straw, etc. ***vt-*** to toss with or as if with such a tool.

Pitchfork

pitch·out (pĭch′ out′) ***n-*** **1** in baseball, a pitch deliberately wide of the plate so that the batter cannot hit it, usually made to enable the catcher to check or put out a base runner trying to steal a base. **2** in football, a lateral pass made behind the line of scrimmage.

pitch·o·ver (pĭch′ ō′ vər) *Space* ***n-*** point in the flight of a rocket when it departs from a vertical flight path.

pitch pipe ***n-*** small metal pipe that sounds a single tone. It is used to set the pitch for a singer or instrument.

pitch·y (pĭch′ ē) ***adj-*** **[pitch·i·er, pitch·i·est] 1** full of, or smeared with, pitch or tar. **2** black; extremely dark; pitch-black: *thick* pitchy *smoke.* **—*n-* pitch′ i·ness.**

pit·e·ous (pĭt′ ē əs) ***adj-*** arousing sorrow or pity; pitiful: *An injured animal is a* piteous *sight.* **—*adv-* pit′ e·ous·ly.** ***n-*** **pit′ e·ous·ness.**

pit·fall (pĭt′ fȯl′) ***n-*** **1** hidden pit used as a trap for animals. **2** hidden danger, trap, or unexpected difficulty.

pith (pĭth) ***n-*** **1** soft, spongy tissue forming a central core, especially in the stem of certain plants. **2** important or essential part: *the* pith *of a lecture.*

pit·head (pĭt′ hĕd′) ***n-*** top of a mining shaft; also, grounds or buildings next to a mining shaft.

Pith·e·can·thro·pus (pĭth′ ə kăn′ thrə pəs, -kăn′ thrō′ pəs) ***n-*** Java man.

pith·y (pĭth′ ē) ***adj-*** **[pith·i·er, pith·i·est] 1** like or full of pith. **2** forcible; full of meaning; terse: *Benjamin Franklin is noted for his* pithy *sayings.* **—*adv-* pith′ i·ly.**

pit·i·a·ble (pĭt′ ē ə bəl) ***adj-*** **1** arousing pity or sympathy: *The poor beggar was a* pitiable *sight.* **2** arousing contempt or scorn: *a* pitiable *alibi.* **—*adv-* pit′ i·a·bly.**

pit·i·ful (pĭt′ ə fəl) ***adj-*** **1** arousing pity or sorrow. **2** worthy of contempt; pitiable: *The thief made a* pitiful *attempt to get out of his punishment by lying.* **—*adv-* pit′ i·ful·ly.** ***n-*** **pit′ i·ful·ness.**

pit·i·less (pĭt′ə ləs) ***adj-*** without pity or mercy; merciless: *a* pitiless *tyrant.* **—*adv-* pit′ i·less·ly.** ***n-*** **pit′ i·less·ness.**

pit·tance (pĭt′ əns) ***n-*** small allowance, especially of money; any small quantity

pit·ter-pat·ter (pĭt′ ər păt′ ər) pitapat.

pit·ty·pat (pĭt′ ē păt′) pitapat.

pi·tu·i·tar·y (pĭ to͞o′ ə tĕr′ ē, pĭ tyo͞o′-) ***n-*** [*pl.* **pi·tu·i·tar·ies]** small round gland at the base of the brain. It produces hormones that have an effect on rate of growth, the building up and breaking down of tissues, and the activity of other endocrine glands. ***adj-*** having to do with this gland.

pit viper *n-* any of various poisonous snakes, such as the rattlesnake, copperhead, and the fer-de-lance, having a depression between the eye and the nostril.

pit·y (pĭt′ ē) *n-* [*pl.* **pit·ies**] **1** feeling of sorrow over the suffering of others; mercy. **2** cause for regret or grief: *It is a* pity *that she can't come to our party. vt-* **[pit·ied, pit·y·ing]** to feel sorry for; sympathize with: *I* pity *anybody who is in continual pain.* **—adv- pit′ y·ing·ly.**

have (or **take**) **pity on** to help or forgive because of sympathy and mercy.

piv·ot (pĭv′ ət) *n-* **1** the point on which a thing turns; also, the bar, pin, or other part which forms such a point. **2** a turning movement made as if on such a point. **3** person or thing on which something important depends. *vi-* **1** to turn or depend on: *The argument* pivots *on that point.* **2** to turn on or as if on a point: *Ivan* pivoted on *his toe and faced me. vt-* to supply, or mount on, a pivot.

piv·ot·al (pĭv′ ə təl) *adj-* **1** of, relating to, or acting as a pivot. **2** very important; decisive; crucial: *a* pivotal *State in an election.*

pix·y or **pix·ie** (pĭk′ sē) *n-* [*pl.* **pix·ies**] little fairy; elf.

piz·za (pēt′ sə) *n-* Italian dish resembling a pie, made by baking tomatoes, cheese, etc., on a flat bread dough.

piz·ze·ri·a (pēt′ sə rē′ ə) *n-* place where pizzas are made or sold.

piz·zi·ca·to (pĭt′ sə kä′ tō) *Music adj- & adv-* played on string instruments by plucking the strings with the fingers, rather than played with a bow. *n-* [*pl.* **piz·zi·ca·ti** (-tē)] note or passage played in this manner.

pk. 1 pack. **2** park. **3** peak. **4** peck.

pkg. package.

pl. plural.

plac·ard (plăk′ ärd′) *n-* piece of heavy paper with a public notice or advertisement on it; poster. *vt-* **1** to post such notices on: *to* placard *a wall.* **2** to advertise with such notices: *They* placarded *their show across the country.*

pla·cate (plā′ kāt, plăk′ āt) *vt-* **[pla·cat·ed, pla·cat·ing]** to calm the anger of; appease; pacify: *The mayor's plan for immediate action* placated *the angry crowd.*

place (plās) *n-* **1** particular location: *a* place *to hang a picture.* **2** city, town, village, locality, etc. **3** public square in a city or town; also, a court or street: *Sutton* Place *is a quiet residential street.* **4** building or area used for a special purpose: *a* place *of amusement; a* place *of worship.* **5** a dwelling; house and its grounds: *They have a* place *in town and a* place *in the country.* **6** particular part or spot on the body or a surface: *a sore* place *on the back; a worn* place *in a coat.* **7** rank; position; standing: *to know one's* place; *Shakespeare's* place *in literature.* **8** space or seat, as at a table, in a bus, etc. **9** job; position: *He lost his* place *at the bank.* **10** duty; responsibility: *It's your* place *to look after your guest.* **11** position in order: *in the first* place. **12** in a horse race, second position among the first three winning competitors. **13** *Mathematics* position occupied by a figure in relation to the other figures of a series. *vt-* **[placed, plac·ing] 1** to put in a particular spot, position, or relation: *to* place *dishes on the table*; *to* place *a person in a job.* **2** to identify by connecting with a location, time, circumstance, etc: *I finally* placed *him as an old schoolfellow.* **3** to put: *I* place *trust in him.* **4** to give an order for (a service): *to* place *a telephone call; to* place *an order for a new car. vi-* in a contest, to finish in a certain position; also, to finish among the leaders and thus not be eliminated from further competition: *He* placed *third. I must* place *in this race to stay in the meet.*

in place 1 in a customary, assigned, or proper place: *to put one's books* in place. **2** fitting; proper; timely: *Laughter is not* in place *in church.* **in place of** instead of: *margarine* in place of *butter.* **out of place 1** not in proper place. **2** not fitting. **take place** to happen; occur: *The parade* takes place *tomorrow.* **take the place of** to be a substitute for: *The nurse* takes the place of *the mother.*

pla·ce·bo (plə sē′ bō) *n-* [*pl.* **pla·ce·bos** or **pla·ce·boes**] useless but harmless preparation given to a patient to humor him, especially when his illness is thought to be due to emotional disturbances.

place kick *n-* in football, a kick for a field goal after the ball has been placed on the ground in front of the kicker by another player.

place mat *n-* small table mat serving as an individual table cover.

place·ment (plās′ mənt) *n-* **1** act of placing; especially, the finding of employment for a person or the assignment of a student to a class or course. **2** location or arrangement: *the* placement *of the furniture in a room.* **3** in football, the placing of the ball on the ground for a place kick; also, the kick itself.

pla·cen·ta (plə sĕn′ tə) *n-* the rounded, spongy organ that connects the uterus and the developing embryo and provides the embryo with its nourishment.

plac·er (plăs′ ər) *n-* deposit of loose surface soil or gravel that contains gold or other valuable minerals.

placer mining *n-* mining by washing loose surface deposits so that the lighter matter is carried away and the heavier particles of valuable metal remain. **—n- placer miner.**

plac·id (plăs′ ĭd) *adj-* calm; tranquil: *a* placid *lake*; placid *behavior.* **—adv- plac′ id·ly.** *n-* **plac′ id·ness.**

pla·cid·i·ty (plə sĭd′ ə tē) *n-* calmness; tranquillity.

plack·et (plăk′ ət) *n-* **1** the finished opening or slit, with or without a zipper, in the upper part of a skirt, dress, or blouse, to make it easy to put on. **2** hidden pocket in a woman's skirt.

pla·gia·rism (plā′ jə rĭz′ əm) *n-* **1** a stealing and using, as one's own, of another's ideas, words, etc.; literary theft. **2** the material stolen. **—n- pla′ gia·rist.**

pla·gia·rize (plā′ jə rīz′) *vt-* **[pla·gia·rized, pla·gia·riz·ing]** to steal and use (another's ideas, words, etc.) as one's own. *vi-*: *He deliberately* plagiarized *from earlier novels.* **—n- pla′ gia·riz′ er.**

plague (plāg) *n-* **1** any dangerous disease that spreads quickly; an epidemic, especially of bubonic plague. **2** thing causing misery or great trouble; affliction: *A* plague *of locusts devoured the crops.* **3** *Informal* a nuisance. *vt-* **[plagued, pla·guing] 1** to afflict with disease, evil, or disaster: *A severe unemployment problem* plagued *the nation.* **2** to pester or annoy: *The child* plagued *his uncle with questions.*

plagu·y or **plagu·ey** (plā′ gē) *Informal adj-* annoying; irritating; vexatious.

plaice (plās) *n-* [*pl.* **plaice; plaices** (kinds of plaice)] **1** large European flatfish or flounder. **2** any of various American flatfishes or flounders. ***Hom-*** place.

plaid (plăd) *n-* **1** pattern of weaving made by crossing bands of different colors at right angles; tartan. **2** kind of shawl of such material, worn over one shoulder by a Scottish person. 3 any material with such a pattern. *as **modifier**: a* plaid *blanket*; plaid *wool.*

plain (plān) ***adj-*** **[plain·er, plain·est]** 1 easy to see or hear; distinct: *The printed numbers are very* plain. *His voice was clear and* plain. 2 easy to undersand; clear: *He made his meaning quite* plain. 3 simple; not luxurious: *a* plain *meal;* plain *living.* 4 simple in manners; ordinary: *The politician always said he came from* plain *people.* 5 all of one color; without a pattern or design: *a* plain *yellow dress; a* plain *wallpaper.* 6 without ornament; not elaborate: *dressed in* plain *clothes.* 7 outspoken; frank: *a man of* plain, *blunt speech.* 8 homely: *Many* plain *girls become beautiful.* ***n-*** expanse of land that is fairly flat and level or gradually sloping. ***Hom-*** plane. ***—adv-*** **plain′ly.** ***n-*** **plain′ness.**

plain·clothes·man (plān′klōz′mən) ***n-*** [*pl.* **plain·clothes·men**] police officer wearing ordinary clothes when on duty; especially, a detective.

Plains Indian ***n-*** member of any of the tribes of North American Indians who formerly inhabited the Great Plains of the United States extending from the Mississippi and Missouri rivers to the Rocky Mountains.

plain sailing *Informal* ***n-*** easy progress or an easy part of a task.

plains·man (plānz′ mən) ***n-*** [*pl.* **plains·men**] person who lives on the plains.

plain·song (plān′sȯng′) ***n-*** medieval church music having a single line of vocal melody that is not divided into regular bars and is sung without accompaniment.

plain-spo·ken (plān′ spō′ kən) ***adj-*** frank and direct in speech.

plaint (plānt) ***n-*** 1 *Archaic* lamentation; lament; moaning. 2 a complaint.

plain·tiff (plān′ tĭf) ***n-*** person who brings suit in a court of law; complainant.

plain·tive (plān′ tĭv) ***adj-*** sad; melancholy: *a* plaintive *song.* ***—adv-*** **plain′tive·ly.** ***n-*** **plain′tive·ness.**

plait (plāt) ***n-*** 1 flat fold; pleat. 2 a braid. ***vt-*** 1 to pleat: *Mother* plaited *paper on the edge of the shelf.* 2 to braid: *to* plait *one's hair.* ***Hom-*** plate.

plan (plăn) ***n-*** 1 course of action worked out beforehand; fixed design; scheme: *Paul made* plans *to visit Paris.* 2 arrangement of details: *Here is the* plan *of my story.* 3 drawing showing details of a proposed building, street arrangement, machine, etc. ***vt-*** **[planned, plan·ning]** 1 to arrange; work out: *Ellen* planned *a big party.* 2 to lay out; design: *Engineers will* plan *the new suburb.* 3 to scheme; plot: *The gangsters* planned *to rob a bank.* 4 to have in mind; intend: *They* plan *to go to the beach on Sunday.* ***vi-*** to make arrangements (for) beforehand: *to* plan *for a big crowd.* ***—adj-*** **plan′less.** ***n-*** **plan′er.**

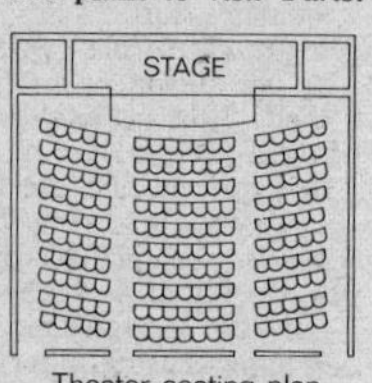

Theater seating plan

pla·nar·i·an (plə năr′ ē ən, plə nĕr′-) ***n-*** any of a class of flatworms that live on moist soil and in water.

[1]**plane** (plān) ***n-*** tool used chiefly in woodworking to smooth materials by shaving off the rough and uneven places. ***vt-*** **[planed, plan·ing]** to make smooth with such a tool: *The carpenter* planed *the board.* ***vi-***: *The carpenter* planed *away at a beam.* [from Latin **plāna,** "tool for flattening," from **plānāre,** "to make flat," from **plānus,** "[2]plane."] ***Hom-*** plain.

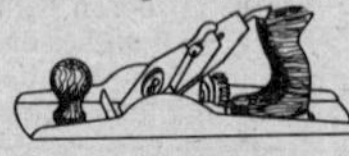
Plane

[2]**plane** (plān) ***n-*** 1 any flat or even surface. 2 a grade or level: *on a high moral* plane; *the* plane *of the discussion.* 3 airplane. 4 one of the flat supporting surfaces of an airplane wing. 5 *Mathematics* set of points such that if any two points are in the plane, then all points of the line containing the two points will also be in the plane. ***adj-*** 1 flat; level; even: *a* plane *surface.* 2 of or having to do with flat surfaces: *to study* plane *figures.* [from Latin **plānus** meaning "flat."] ***Hom-*** plain.

[3]**plane** (plān) or **plane tree** ***n-*** sycamore. [from Latin **platanum,** from Greek **plátanos** meaning literally "having wide leaves."] ***Hom-*** plain.

[4]**plane** (plān) ***vi-*** **[planed, plan·ing]** 1 to glide or soar on outstretched wings, as birds do. 2 of boats, to rise slightly out of the water at high speed. [from French **planer,** from **plan,** "horizontal plane formed by wings of a bird," from Latin **plānus.**] ***Hom-*** plain.

plane geometry ***n-*** branch of geometry that studies the properties and relations between the plane figures, such as circles and triangles.

plan·er (plā′ nər) ***n-*** machine for planing the surface of wood or metal.

plan·et (plăn′ ət) ***n-*** 1 any one of the nine heavenly bodies, such as the Earth and Mars, that revolve around the sun and shine by reflected light. 2 any similar body of any other solar system.

plan·e·tar·i·um (plăn′ ə târ′ ē əm) ***n-*** [*pl.* **plan·e·tar·i·ums** or **plan·e·tar·i·a** (-ē ə)] a theater designed to show the movements of heavenly bodies. It consists of a room with a domed ceiling on which moving points of light show the heavenly bodies in their regular courses.

plan·e·tar·y (plăn′ ə tĕr′ ē) ***adj-*** 1 of or having to do with a planet or the planets: *the* planetary *orbits.* 2 world-wide: *his* planetary *wanderings.*

plan·e·tes·i·mal (plăn′ ə tĕs′ ə məl, -tĕz′ məl) ***adj-*** of or relating to very small planetary bodies. ***n-*** any of these very small bodies.

planetesimal hypothesis *Astronomy* ***n-*** nineteenth-century theory proposing that the solar system was created when gas masses were torn from the sun when a second star passed near the sun at high speed. The gas masses then condensed into planets, asteroids, etc.

plan·e·toid (plăn′ ə toid′) ***n-*** asteroid.

plank (plăngk) ***n-*** 1 long, broad piece of timber; thick board. 2 statement of principle forming a part of the platform of a political party: *a civil rights* plank. 3 gangplank. ***vt-*** 1 to cover or furnish with thick boards. 2 to cook on a board: *to* plank *shad.* 3 *Informal* to lay or put down forcefully: *to* plank *a book on the desk.*

walk the plank to walk blindfold along and off a plank extending from the side of a ship over the water. Pirates used to make their victims do this.

plank down (money) *Informal* to pay in cash.

plank·ing (plăng′ kĭng) ***n-*** 1 layer of planks in or on a floor, deck, wall, or other structure. 2 planks as building materials.

plank·ton (plăngk′ tən) ***n-*** small floating animals and plants, at or near the surface of fresh or salt water.

plant (plănt) ***n-*** 1 any of a kingdom of living organisms including algae, the mosses, trees, etc. Plants typically have rigid cell walls, and synthesize organic compounds through the action of sunlight on chlorophyll. 2 small plant, as opposed to a tree or shrub. 3 a sprout, young shoot, or seedling ready for transplanting: *We bought some tomato* plants *in little pots.* 4 tools, machinery, fixtures, buildings, etc., of a factory or business: *a manufacturing* plant; *an automobile* plant. 5 buildings, grounds, equipment, etc., of an institution: *The school has a fine* plant *but not enough teachers.*

6 *Slang* trick; snare. ***vt-*** **1** to set in the ground in order to cultivate. **2** to provide (an area) with seeds or seedlings; also, to stock (a river, lake, etc.) with fish: *He* planted *a flower garden. They* planted *a lake with trout.* **3** to fix in position; put: *He* planted *his feet and wouldn't move. He* planted *the stake in the ground.* **4** to introduce or instill (an idea, feeling, etc.): *His answer* planted *a doubt in my mind.* **5** to settle; establish: *to* plant *a colony.* **6** *Slang* to place (someone or something) for the purpose of tricking or trapping someone.

[1]**plan·tain** (plăn′ tən) ***n-*** **1** tropical plant bearing a kind of banana. **2** edible fruit of this plant. [from West Indian **prattana,** influenced by Spanish **plátano.**]

[2]**plan·tain** (plăn′ tən) ***n-*** common weed with large leaves that lie on or near the ground. Each plant has slender stalks that become solid spikes of tiny, greenish flowers. [from Old French word that comes from a Latin word **plantāgō,** from **planta,** "sole of the foot."]

Plantain

plan·ta·tion (plăn tā′ shən) ***n-*** **1** farm that is usually large and located in a warm region, and is devoted to the cultivation of a single commercial crop: *a cotton* plantation; *a rubber* plantation. **2** group of plants or trees under cultivation; also, the land on which such plants and trees are planted: *a* plantation *of maple trees.*

plant·er (plăn′ tər) ***n-*** **1** person, machine, or implement that sows or plants. **2** person who owns or manages a plantation. **3** an ornamental container in which plants and flowers are grown.

plant louse ***n-*** aphid.

plan view ***n-*** drawing or photograph picturing something as if seen from directly above it.

plaque (plăk) ***n-*** **1** flat, thin piece of metal, porcelain, or earthenware upon which a picture or design has been enameled or carved, and which is used chiefly as a wall ornament. **2** brooch or similar ornament worn as a badge of an honorary order.

plash (plăsh) ***n-*** splash or splashing sound: *the* plash *of a fountain.* ***vi-*** to splash lightly (against).

-plasm *combining form* the more fluid substance of a cell: *cyto*plasm; *proto*plasm.

plas·ma (plăz′ mə) ***n-*** **1** straw-colored liquid that remains after the blood cells have been removed from whole blood. Plasma contains proteins, salts, water, etc. **2** *Physics* the gaseous mixture of neutral particles, ionized particles, and free electrons that is the form in which most of the matter of the universe occurs. Plasmas occur in fluorescent light bulbs, jet exhausts, and the ionosphere, and in suns, galaxies, etc.

plasma sheath ***n-*** layer of ionized gas enveloping a body moving through an atmosphere at hypersonic speeds. The plasma sheath interrupts radio communication during the reentry of a spacecraft.

plas·ter (plăs′ tər) ***n-*** **1** mixture of lime, sand, and water which hardens as it dries and is used to coat walls. **2** substance spread on a cloth and applied to the body as a remedy: *a mustard* plaster. **3** plaster of Paris. ***vt-*** **1** to cover or repair with building plaster: *to* plaster *a wall; to* plaster *up a hole.* **2** to coat or smear: *They* plastered *the roof of the cabin with mud. She* plastered *greasepaint on her face.* **3** to cover with or attach something to, by pasting: *They* plastered *the wall with posters.* **—*n-*** **plas′ ter·er.**

plas·ter·board (plăs′ tər bôrd′) ***n-*** thin board composed of plaster and paper or felt in alternate layers and covered on both sides with heavy paper, used in building walls, partitions, etc.

plaster cast ***n-*** **1** a copy or cast of a statue or other object made by molding plaster of Paris. **2** hard, molded covering used to keep a broken bone motionless while healing.

plas·ter·ing (plăs′ tər ĭng) ***n-*** **1** a putting on of plaster. **2** a covering of plaster on a wall, ceiling, etc.

plaster of Paris ***n-*** a white powdery substance which, when mixed with water, forms a quick-setting paste. It is used for making casts, moldings, statuettes, etc.

plas·tic (plăs′ tĭk) ***n-*** any of a large group of materials manufactured from organic compounds and other chemicals and made into useful shapes by heat, pressure, etc. Rayon and cellophane are two types of plastics. ***adj-*** **1** made of one or more of these materials: *a* plastic *toy.* **2** having to do with or made by molding or modeling: *We made pottery and clay figures in* plastic *arts class.* **3** such as can be molded: *a* plastic *material.* **—*n-*** **plas·ti′ ci·ty** (plăs tĭs′ ə tē): *This clay has good* plasticity.

plastic surgery ***n-*** surgery for correcting or restoring deformed and mutilated parts of the body. **—*n-*** **plastic surgeon.**

[1]**plat** (plăt) ***vt-*** **[plat·ted, plat·ting]** to braid; plait. ***n-*** a braid. [a variant of **plait.**]

[2]**plat** (plăt) ***n-*** **1** small plot of ground. **2** a chart, plan, or map. ***vt-*** **[plat·ted, plat·ting]** to map. [from Old French, from Medieval Latin **plattus,** from Greek **platys** meaning "wide and flat."]

plate (plāt) ***n-*** **1** shallow, usually round, dish from which food is eaten. **2** the amount of food such a dish will hold: *to eat a* plate *of spaghetti.* **3** food served to one person at a meal: *The banquet cost $25.00 a* plate. **4** dishes and other utensils made of or plated with gold or silver: *She inherited the family* plate. **5** thin, flat piece or sheet of metal or other material. **6** piece of metal on which something is engraved: *a license* plate. **7** print made from an engraved metal surface, woodcut, etc., especially when used in a book; also, the engraved metal surface. **8** thin piece of metal, plastic, etc., fitted to the mouth and holding artificial teeth. **9** thin cut of beef from the lower part of the side. **10** in baseball, home base. **11** in architecture, a horizontal timber on which the lower ends of the rafters are set. **12** in photography, a thin sheet of glass, or transparent plastic, coated with chemicals to make it sensitive to light. **13** in printing, (1) an electrotype or stereotype. (2) full-page illustration. **14** in electronics, the anode of a vacuum tube. ***vt-*** **[plat·ed, plat·ing]** **1** to coat with metal; to cover with sheets of metal. **2** in printing, to make an electrotype or stereotype from. ***Hom-*** plait.

pla·teau (plă tō′) ***n-*** [*pl.* **pla·teaus**] **1** high area of flat land; tableland. **2** relatively stable level in the growth or evolution of something, especially business.

plate·ful (plāte′fo͝ol′) ***n-*** amount held by a plate; hence, a generous portion of food: *He ate a* plateful *of beans.*

plate glass ***n-*** fine kind of glass, rolled in thick plates, ground flat, and polished.

plate·let (plāt′ lət) ***n-*** one of the tiny plate-shaped bodies in the blood that help blood coagulate.

plate tec·ton·ics (tĕk tŏn′ĭks) ***n-*** (takes singular verb) theory that explains volcanic and earthquake activity in terms of the movement of giant rafts of the earth's crust floating on the earth's partially molten interior.

plat·form (plăt′fôrm) ***n-*** **1** flat, horizontal surface, usually raised above the surrounding ground or floor: *a railroad* platform; *a speaker's* platform. **2** statement of a group's beliefs and policies: *a political* platform.

plat·ing (plā′tĭng) ***n-*** **1** a coating of a metal over another metal to add beauty, hardness, corrosion resistance, etc.

plat·i·num (plăt′ə nəm) ***n-*** **1** heavy, silver-white precious metal element. It is very resistant to heat and acids, and used in scientific apparatus and jewelry and as a catalyst. Symbol Pt, At. No. 78, At. Wt. 195.09. **2** a silvery-white color. ***adj-***: *a* platinum *ring.*

plat·i·tude (plăt′ə to͞od′, -tyo͞od′) ***n-*** trite and commonplace remark, usually moralistic; truism.

plat·i·tu·di·nous (plăt′ə to͞o′də nəs, -tyo͞o′də nəs) ***adj-*** **1** having the nature of a platitude; commonplace; trite: *a* platitudinous *remark.* **2** full of or given to platitudes: *a* platitudinous *speaker.*

Pla·ton·ic (plə tŏn′ĭk) ***adj-*** **1** of or relating to the Greek philosopher Plato or to his ideas, doctrines, and maxims. **2 platonic** referring to purely mental or spiritual relationships between two persons: *their* platonic *friendship.*

pla·toon (plə to͞on′) ***n-*** **1** in the Army and Marines, one of the units of a company, usually consisting of four squads and commanded by a lieutenant. **2** in football, a group of players trained specially for offense or defense, who periodically enter and leave the game as a unit. ***vi-*** in sports, to alternate with other players: *One squad* platoons *with the others.* ***vt-***: *The coach* platoons *Joe and Tom at quarterback.*

plat·ter (plăt′ər) ***n-*** **1** large, usually oval, flat dish for serving a main course. **2** *Slang* phonograph record.

Platter

plat·y·pus (plăt′ə pəs) ***n-*** Australian, egg-laying, water-loving, furry mammal with webbed feet and a bill like that of a duck; duckbill; duck-billed platypus.

plau·dit (plô′dĭt) ***n-*** enthusiastic applause or other expression of praise.

Platypus, about 20 in. long

plau·si·ble (plô′zə bəl) ***n-*** **1** seemingly true or reasonable: *a* plausible *excuse.* **2** apparently believable or worthy of confidence: *a* plausible *salesman.* **—*n-* plau′si·bil′i·ty.** ***adv-*** **plau′si·bly.**

play (plā) ***vi-*** **1** to have fun; amuse oneself; take part in recreation. **2** to take part in a game; also to gamble. **3** to act or behave in a certain way: *to* play *false with a friend.* **4** to act in a drama; perform. *He* plays *in summer theater.* **5** to be performed: *"Cleopatra" is* playing *tonight at the theater.* **6** to perform music: *He* plays *in a band. The orchestra* played *with great brilliance.* **7** to move lightly or quickly; flicker: *The moonlight* played *on the water.* **8** to be in constant or repeated action: *fountains* playing *in the sunshine.* ***vt-*** **1** to take part in (a game): *to* play *baseball.* **2** to compete with (in a game or contest): *Our team* played *the high school team.* **3** to act the part of (a character) in a dramatic performance or in real life: *Pat* played *Wendy in "Peter Pan." He always* plays *the hero.* **4** to pretend or imitate in fun: *They* played *store.* **5** to perform; also, to perform music on: *to* play *a comedy*; *to* play *a waltz on the piano*; *to* play *the piano.* **6** to act or give performances in: *The touring company is* playing *San Francisco this week.* **7** to put (something or someone) into action in a game or contest: *He* played *the highest card. The coach* played *Billy in the last half-hour of the game.* **8** to do (something) in fun or to deceive: *He* played *tricks.* **9** to direct in a moving stream or ray: *She* played *a hose on a lawn.* **10** to bet on: *He* plays *the horses.* ***n-*** **1** drama; also, performance of a drama. **2** recreation; fun; sport; game. **3** the playing of a game; also, gambling: *to lose money at* play. **4** way of playing a game: *There is a lot of rough* play *in football.* **5** any act or move in a game; also, a turn: *He made a good* play *at second base. It's Hal's* play *next.* **6** action or use: *All their resources were brought into* play. **7** fun; jest: *She did it in* play. **8** conduct; manner; dealings: *fair* play; *foul* play. **9** movement over a surface: *the* play *of shadows on a wall.* **10** freedom or room for movement or action: *He gives full* play *to his imagination. The piston has* play *within the cylinder.*

in (or **out of**) **play** in (or not in) such a condition or position as to be legitimately in use or motion. **play on words** a pun.

play back to play over or reproduce (a new record or tape) for critical examination.

play down to pay little attention to; attach little importance to; minimize.

play into the hands of to act so as to give an advantage to: *The candidate* played into *his opponent's* hands.

play off **1** to set (a person or thing) against another. **2** to break (a tie) by playing an extra match or game.

play on (or **upon**) to make use of (a person's feelings, good nature, etc.) for one's advantage.

play out **1** to perform to the end; finish: *Let's* play *this game* out. **2** to become or make exhausted: *The ore in that mine has* played out. *The tennis game* played *me out.* **3** to let out (a cable, rope, etc.) little by little.

play up to *Informal* to flatter; try to please by flattery.

play with to trifle with; toy with: *He* played with *the food on his plate. She* played with *the idea of going home.*

pla·ya (plī′ə) ***n-*** shallow lake bed of a desert basin, in which water gathers during the rainy season.

play·a·ble (plā′ə bəl) ***adj-*** such as can be played; suitable for being played or played on: *The actor complained that his part was not* playable. *The old violin is still* playable.

play·act·ing (plā′ăk′tĭng) ***n-*** **1** the acting in plays; dramatic performance. **2** insincere or affected behavior.

play·back (plā′băk′) ***n-*** **1** the playing over or reproducing of a new record or tape for critical examination. **2** part of a recording machine that reproduces sound recordings.

play·bill (plā′bĭl) ***n-*** **1** poster advertising a play. **2** theater program.

play·er (plā′ər) ***n-*** **1** one who plays, especially in a game. **2** actor. **3** performer on a musical instrument. **4** mechanical device for playing a musical instrument or for reproducing music: *a* record *player.*

player piano ***n-*** piano operated by a mechanical playing device.

play·ful (plā′fəl) ***adj-*** **1** lively; frisky: *a* playful *puppy.* **2** joking; merry: *a* playful *remark; a* playful *tap on the back.* **—*adv-* play′ful·ly. *n-* play′ful·ness.**

play·go·er (plā′gō′ər) ***n-*** person who frequently goes to the theater.

play·ground (plā′ground′) ***n-*** ground used for games, especially by children.

play·house (plā′hous′) ***n-*** **1** theater. **2** small house for children to play in.

playing card ***n-*** one of the cards of a pack used for playing games; especially, one of a pack of 52 cards divided into four suits (diamonds, hearts, spades and clubs).

play·let (plā′ lət) ***n-*** a short play.

play·mate (plā′ māt′) ***n-*** one who plays with another person; playfellow.

play·off (plā′ ôf′, -ŏf′) ***n-*** game or match played to break a tie.

play·pen (plā′ pĕn′) ***n-*** small, usually portable, enclosure in which a small child may play safely by himself.

play·thing (plā′ thĭng′) ***n-*** thing to play with; toy.

play·wright (plā′ rīt′) ***n-*** person who writes plays; dramatist.

pla·za (plăz′ ə, plä′ zə) ***n-*** public square or open place in a city or town.

plea (plē) ***n-*** **1** an appeal; entreaty: *a* plea *for help.* **2** explanation; excuse: *Freddy's* plea *was that he had forgotten about the time.* **3** an answer to charges in a law court: *a* plea *of not guilty.*

plead (plēd) ***vi-*** **[plead·ed** or **pled** (plĕd), **plead·ing] 1** to beg earnestly; entreat: *The frightened boy* pleaded *with the others to stop tilting the canoe.* **2** to conduct a case in a court of law: *That lawyer has* pleaded *before many judges.* ***vt-*** **1** to argue for or against something; defend by arguments: *to* plead *a case.* **2** to answer to a charge in a law court: *to* plead *not guilty.* **3** to offer as an excuse or as an apology: *He* pleaded *poverty when caught stealing.* **—*n-* plead′ er.** ***adv-*** **plead′ ing·ly.**

pleas·ant (plĕz′ ənt) ***adj-*** **[pleas·ant·er, pleas·ant·est]** agreeable; delightful; pleasing: *a* pleasant *day; a* pleasant *companion.* **—*adv-* pleas′ ant·ly.** ***n-*** **pleas′ ant·ness.**

pleas·ant·ry (plĕz′ ən trē) ***n-*** [*pl.* **pleas·ant·ries**] **1** humorous or playful remark: *His* pleasantries *were out of place on such a serious occasion.* **2** gaiety; lively talk.

please (plēz) ***vt-*** **[pleased, pleas·ing] 1** to give pleasure or happiness to; be agreeable to: *The good news* pleased *everybody.* **2** to be the will of; suit: *May it* please *Your Highness.* **3** to be kind enough to (usually in the imperative and used to introduce a polite request): *Pass the butter,* please. Please *come in.* ***vi-*** **1** to give satisfaction or enjoyment: *We strive to* please. **2** to choose; prefer: *He always does as he* pleases.

be pleased to to be glad or happy to: *I shall* be pleased *to go.* **if you please** if you like; if you permit.

pleas·ing (plē′ zĭng) ***adj-*** agreeable; enjoyable; delightful. **—*adv-* pleas′ ing·ly.**

pleas·ur·a·ble (plĕzh′ ər ə bəl) ***adj-*** providing pleasure; enjoyable: *a* pleasurable *event.* **—*adv-* pleas′ ur·a·bly.**

pleas·ure (plĕzh′ ər) ***n-*** **1** feeling of delight or satisfaction; enjoyment: *a great deal of* pleasure *from music.* **2** something that gives enjoyment, satisfaction, etc.: *Just being with her is a* pleasure. **3** choice; desire; will: *It is the king's* pleasure. **—*adj-* pleas′ ure·less.**

pleat (plēt) ***n-*** a fold in cloth, paper, etc. ***vt-*** to arrange in folds.

Pleat

plebe (plēb) ***n-*** member of the lowest class in the military academy at West Point or the naval academy at Annapolis.

ple·be·ian (plĭ bē′ ən) ***adj-*** in ancient Rome, of or relating to the common people; hence, common or vulgar: *a person with* plebeian *tastes.* ***n-*** **1** one of the common people of ancient Rome. **2** any person of common breeding.

pleb·i·scite (plĕb′ ə sīt′) ***n-*** direct vote of all the people on some important measure, such as to determine a form of government or to change the constitution.

plec·trum (plĕk′ trəm) ***n-*** [*pl.* **plec·trums** or **plec·tra** (-trə)] small piece of thin ivory, metal, or shell, used to pluck the strings of a lyre, guitar, mandolin, etc.; pick.

pled (plĕd) *p.t. & p.p.* of **plead.**

pledge (plĕj) ***n-*** **1** promise or agreement to do or not to do something. **2** something given or held as security or as a guarantee: *I'm holding his car as a* pledge *for the loan.* **3** possession as security: *Goods held in* pledge. **4** a toast; a drink to one's health. **5** sign of good will, friendship, love, etc.: *We shook hands as a* pledge *of friendship.* **6** person who has promised to join a fraternity but has not been initiated. ***vt-*** **[pledged, pledg·ing] 1** to promise (something) faithfully: *He* pledged *allegiance to the flag.* **2** to bind by a promise: *He* pledged *us to secrecy.* **3** to give as security or guarantee; also, to pawn: *to* pledge *one's honor.* **4** to drink to the health of; toast. **5** to promise to join (a fraternity).

take the pledge to make a promise to abstain from drinking alcoholic beverages.

Ple·ia·des (plē′ ə dēz′) ***n-*** *pl.* [*sing.* **Ple·iad**] **1** in Greek mythology, the seven daughters of Atlas who were transformed into a group of stars. **2** a cluster of small stars in the constellation Taurus.

Pleis·to·cene (plīs′ tə sēn′) ***n-*** the first of the two epochs of the Quaternary period; Ice Age. It was the epoch during which modern man appeared. ***adj-***: *the* Pleistocene *epoch.*

ple·na·ry (plĕn′ ə rē, plē′ nə-) ***adj-*** **1** full; complete; unqualified: *to have* plenary *authority.* **2** completely attended by all qualified members of a legislative body.

plen·i·po·ten·ti·ar·y (plĕn′ ə pō tĕn′ shə rē, -shē ĕr′ ē) ***adj-*** having full power: *a* plenipotentiary *agent.* ***n-*** [*pl.* **plen·i·po·ten·ti·ar·ies**] ambassador or other diplomatic agent to a foreign government, given full powers.

plen·i·tude (plĕn′ ə to͞od′, -tyo͞od′) ***n-*** fullness; abundance: *a* plenitude *of power.*

plen·te·ous (plĕn′ tē əs) ***adj-*** **1** yielding abundantly: *a* plenteous *source of water.* **2** plentiful; abundant. **—*adv-* plen′ te·ous·ly.** ***n-*** **plen′ te·ous·ness.**

plen·ti·ful (plĕn′ tĭ fəl) ***adj-*** **1** existing in great quantity; abundant; copious: *a* plentiful *supply of grain.* **2** yielding abundance; fruitful: *a* plentiful *harvest.* **—*adv-* plen′ ti·ful·ly.** ***n-*** **plen′ ti·ful·ness.**

plen·ty (plĕn′ tē) ***n-*** [*pl.* **plen·ties**] full supply; more than enough; abundance; profusion: *He has* plenty *of money.* ***adv-*** *Informal* quite; sufficiently: *That's* plenty *large.*

ple·si·o·saur (plē′ zē ə sôr′, plē′ sē-) ***n-*** any of various extinct marine reptiles of the Mesozoic era, having a small head, very long neck, and four paddlelike limbs.

pleth·o·ra (plĕth′ ə rə) ***n-*** **1** overabundance; excess. **2** *Medicine* unhealthy condition marked by an excess of blood. **—*adj-* ple·thor′ ic** (plə thôr′ ĭk).

pleu·ra (plo͝or′ ə) ***n-*** a double-walled sac of serous membrane enclosing a lung. The inner layer is attached to the lung, and the outer to the body wall.

pleu·ri·sy (plo͝or′ ə sē) ***n-*** an inflammation of the pleura, marked by chest pain and difficulty in breathing.

Plex·i·glas (plĕk′ sə glăs′) ***n-*** trademark name for a light, transparent plastic, used for airplane windows.

plex·us (plĕk′ səs) ***n-*** [*pl.* **plex·us·es** or **plex·us**] a network of ropelike structures, such as nerves or veins.

pli·a·ble (plī′ ə bəl) ***adj-*** **1** easily bent; flexible: *a thin* pliable *wire.* **2** easily influenced; yielding; docile. **—*n-* pli′ a·bil′ i·ty.** ***adv-*** **pli′ a·bly.**

pli·ant (plī′ ənt) ***adj-*** **1** easily bent without being damaged; supple; pliable: *a* pliant *twig.* **2** readily responsive to influence or changing conditions; adaptable; compliant. **—*n-* pli′ an·cy** or **pli′ ant·ness.** ***adv-*** **pli′ ant·ly.**

plied (plīd) *p.t. & p.p.* of **ply.**

pli·ers (plī′ərz) ***n-*** (takes plural verb) tool of many shapes, with jaws hinged like scissors, for holding, bending, twisting, or pulling. Also **pair of pliers** (takes singular verb).

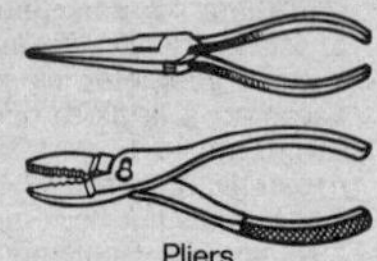
Pliers

plies (plīz) **1** plural of the noun **ply. 2** form of the verb **ply,** used with "he," "she," "it," or singular noun subjects, in the present tense.

[1]**plight** (plīt) ***n-*** unlucky or dangerous situation; sad condition: *Celia wept at the* plight *of the flood refugees.* [from Middle English **plite,** from Old French meaning originally "a fold; pleat," from Latin **plicāta,** "folded."]

[2]**plight** (plīt) ***vt-*** to pledge or promise. [from Old English **plihtan,** "endanger; pledge oneself as ransom."] ►Now used only in reference to love or marriage.

plink (plĭngk) ***n-*** a high, short sound like that of a guitar string being plucked. ***vi-*** to make such a sound: *The banjos* plinked *gaily.* ***vt-***: *He* plinked *a tune on his guitar.*

plinth (plĭnth) ***n-* 1** the lowest, rectangular part of the base of a column or pedestal. **2** square block used as a statue base. **3** row of stones at the base of a wall.

Pli·o·cene (plī′ ə sēn′) ***n-*** the last of the five epochs of the Tertiary period. ***adj-***: *the* Pliocene *epoch.*

Pli·o·film (plī′ ə fĭlm′) ***n-*** trademark name for a tough, flexible, transparent plastic, used as a wrapping and coating for fabric and paper.

plod (plŏd) ***vi-*** **[plod·ded, plod·ding] 1** to walk slowly and with heavy, tired steps: *The prisoners* plodded *past.* **2** to do anything slowly and without skill or talent: *He just* plods *along at his job.* ***n-***: *a long* plod *through the forest.* **—*n-* plod′ der.**

Plover (killdeer), about 10 in. long

plop (plŏp) ***n-*** dull, splashing sound made by something dropping into water, or by a dropped wet mass when it hits: *The towel fell with a* plop. ***vi-*** **[plopped, plop·ping]**: *He* plopped *into the lake.*

plot (plŏt) ***n-* 1** secret plan or scheme; conspiracy: *The rebels formed a* plot *against the government.* **2** small area of ground. **3** main story or plan of a play or novel: *His new play has a very exciting* plot. **4** plan of a piece of land, an estate, etc.; diagram; chart; map. ***vt-*** **[plot·ted, plot·ting] 1** to lay plans for secretly; scheme: *to* plot *a crime.* **2** to make a plan or map of; also, to locate or show on a map or chart: *to* plot *a ship's course.* **3** *Mathematics* to represent a point or set of points through the use of co-ordinates. ***vi-*** to scheme; conspire: *to* plot *against an enemy.* **—*adj-* plot′ less. *n-* plot′ ter.**

plough (plou) plow.

plov·er (plŭv′ ər, plō′ vər) ***n-*** small shore bird with a short bill and tail, long legs, and pointed wings.

plow (plou) ***n-*** farm implement drawn by animals or mechanical power, for turning up or breaking the ground in preparation for planting. ***vt-* 1** to turn up with such an implement; till: *to* plow *a field.* **2** to cut a way through: *The destroyer* plowed *the waves.* ***vi-* 1** to break or turn up soil with a plow. **2** to advance through, or as through, obstructions: *The ship* plowed *through the rough sea.* Also **plough. —*n-* plow′ er.**

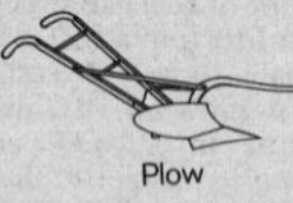
Plow

plow back to reinvest (profits) in a business.

plow under to cover (crop stubble, manure, etc.) by turning the soil over it with a plow.

plow·boy (plou′ boi′) ***n-* 1** boy who guides the plow, or leads the team in plowing. **2** country boy.

plow·man (plou′ mən) ***n-*** [*pl.* **plow·men**] one who operates a plow; hence, a farmer. Also **plough′ man.**

plow·share (plou′ shâr′) ***n-*** the strong, pointed front blade of a plow, which cuts the ground.

pluck (plŭk) ***vt-* 1** to pull off, up, or out; snatch: *to* pluck *weeds*; *to* pluck *a child from a fire.* **2** to pick or gather: *to* pluck *flowers.* **3** to pull or twitch: *to* pluck *the strings of a banjo.* **4** to strip of feathers: *to* pluck *a chicken.* **5** *Slang* to rob; cheat. ***vi-*** to grasp suddenly (at): *The child* plucked *at her mother's skirt.* ***n-* 1** a pull; snatch; tug. **2** courage; bravery: *a man of* pluck.

pluck up to become more cheerful.

pluck up courage to gather or gain courage.

pluck·y (plŭk′ ē) ***adj-*** **[pluck·i·er, pluck·i·est]** brave: *a* plucky *little dog.* **—*adv-* pluck′ i·ly. *n-* pluck′ i·ness.**

plug (plŭg) ***n-* 1** piece of wood or other material used to fill or line a hole or to stop a leak. **2** rubber or metal stopper for a sink or bathtub drain. **3** pronged electrical connection that fits into an electrical outlet. **4** piece of pressed tobacco. **5** spark plug. **6** small wedge cut from a melon to test its ripeness. **7** *Slang* favorable mention or boost for someone or something. ***vt-*** **[plugged, plug·ging] 1** to fill or stop with a piece of wood or other material: *to* plug *a hole*; *to* plug *a leak.* **2** to cut a small wedge from (a melon). **3** *Slang* to advertise or promote. ***vi-*** to work steadily; plod: *to* plug *away at a lesson.* **—*n-* plug′ ger.**

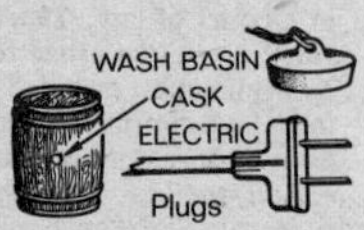

Plugs

plug in to make an electrical connection for by inserting a plug in an outlet: *to* plug in *a toaster.*

plug hat *Slang* ***n-*** top hat.

plum (plŭm) ***n-* 1** round or egg-shaped fruit with soft, juicy pulp, a single hard pit, and smooth, usually red or purple skin. **2** the tree bearing this fruit. **3** dark, reddish-purple color. **4** something very good or desirable, especially a job, prize, etc., for which there is much competition. **5** a raisin in a pudding, cake, etc. ***adj-***: *a jar of* plum *jam*; *a* plum *dress.* ***Hom-*** plumb. **—*adj-* plum′ like′.**

plum·age (plo͞o′ mĭj) ***n-*** feathers of a bird: *The beautiful* plumage *of a peacock.*

plumb (plŭm) ***adj-* 1** exactly perpendicular to the horizontal; vertical. **2** *Informal* out-and-out; absolute: *That's* plumb *nonsense.* ***adv-*** *Informal* completely; entirely: *He's* plumb *crazy.* ***vt-* 1** to check (a structure) with a plumb line to see if it is vertical. **2** to make vertical (often followed by "up"): *to* plumb *up a joist.* **3** to sound (a body of water); also, to probe into: *to* plumb *a mystery.* **4** to reach the very bottom of: *to* plumb *the depths of despair.* ***n-*** plumb bob or plummet. ***Hom-*** plum.

out of (or **off**) **plumb** not vertical.

plumb bob *n-* 1 small pointed weight suspended at the end of a plumb line for indicating a true vertical; plumb. **2** plummet.

plumb·er (plŭm′ ər) ***n-*** workman who supplies, installs, or repairs water and gas pipes, bathroom fixtures, etc.

plumb·ing (plŭm′ ĭng) ***n-* 1** occupation of putting in or repairing pipes, drains, etc. **2** pipes, drains, and the like.

Plumb line and plumb bob

plumb line *n-* 1 cord suspending a weight, used to sound the depth of water or to determine whether something is exactly vertical. **2** an exact vertical line.

plume (plo͞om) ***n-*** 1 fluffy, curly feather or tuft of feathers. 2 fluffy decoration, like a tuft of ostrich feathers: *The horses had* plumes *in their bridles.* ***vt-*** **[plumed, plum·ing]** 1 to smooth (feathers) with the beak. 2 to adorn with or as if with feathers.
plume (oneself) on to show pride in.

Plume

plum·met (plŭm′ət) ***n-*** 1 lead weight attached to the end of a line for measuring depth; plumb. 2 plumb bob. ***vi-*** to fall or plunge straight downward.

[1]**plump** (plŭmp) ***adj-*** **[plump·er, plump·est]** well filled out; well rounded: *a* plump *chicken.* ***vt-*** to cause to become round (often followed by "up" or "out"): plump *up the cushions.* ***vi-***: *Her cheeks plumped out.* [of uncertain orgin.] —***n-*** **plump′ness.**

[2]**plump** (plŭmp) ***vi-*** to fall, sit or drop heavily or suddenly: *She* plumped *into a chair.* ***vt-***: *She* plumped *the bundles on the table.* ***adv-*** heavily and suddenly; also straight down: *He fell* plump *into the water.* ***n-*** sudden heavy fall; also, sound made by such a fall. [from Middle English **plumpen,** possibly an imitation of a sound.]

plum pudding ***n-*** rich steamed pudding made of flour, suet, raisins, currants, and spices.

plum·y (plo͞o′mē) ***adj-*** **[plum·i·er, plum·i·est]** 1 covered or adorned with plumes. 2 like a plume; feathery: *The horse had a* plumy *tail.*

plun·der (plŭn′dər) ***vt-*** to loot, rob, or pillage: *Bandits* plundered *the wagon train.* ***n-*** a pillaging or taking by force; also, that which is taken; loot: *The retreating army left its* plunder *behind.* —***n-*** **plun′der·er.**

plunge (plŭnj) ***vt-*** **[plunged, plung·ing]** 1 to thrust suddenly into a liquid, hole, or any substance that can be penetrated: *He* plunged *his foot into the water.* 2 to place suddenly (into): *to* plunge *a country into war.* ***vi-*** 1 to fall or rush headlong; drive or leap (into) some place or situation: *Ed* plunged *into the pool.* 2 to pitch or move sharply forward or downward: *The ship* plunged *through the waves.* 3 *Informal* to speculate or gamble heavily. ***n-*** 1 sudden dive, leap, or rush: *He took a* plunge *into the cool water.* 2 a swim. 3 *Informal* reckless bet or investment; hazardous speculation.

plung·er (plŭn′jər) ***n-*** 1 person or thing that plunges. 2 *Informal* person who speculates or gambles extravagantly or rashly. 3 any device, such as the piston of a pump, that acts with a plunging motion. 4 suction cup made of rubber and attached to a handle, used to free clogged drains of obstructions.

plunk (plŭngk) ***vt-*** to pluck quickly the (strings of a banjo, guitar, etc.). ***vi-*** 1 to sound with a sharp, vibrating noise; twang. 2 to fall heavily or abruptly. ***n-*** 1 twanging sound. 2 a direct blow, whack; also, its sound.
plunk down to put or fall down quickly and abruptly: *He* plunked *his book down on the desk. He* plunked down *on the sofa.*

plu·per·fect (plo͞o′pûr′fĭkt) *Grammar* ***n-*** past perfect tense.

plur. 1 plural. 2 plurality.

plu·ral (plo͝or′əl) ***adj-*** 1 consisting of or indicating more than one. 2 *Grammar* of or relating to the form of the word that names more than one: *a* plural *noun.* ***n-*** *Grammar* form of a word that shows that more than one is meant. The plural of "cat" is "cats," of "child," "children." —***adv-*** **plu′ral·ly.**

plu·ral·i·ty (plo͝or ăl′ə tē, plə răl′-) ***n-*** [*pl.* **plu·ral·i·ties**] 1 difference between the number of votes cast for the winning candidate and the highest number received by any other candidate. 2 a receiving of more votes than any other candidate, but often less than half of the total votes cast. This can occur when three or more candidates are running. 3 *Grammar* condition of being plural.
►Should not be confused with MAJORITY.

plus (plŭs) ***prep-*** added to or combined with; increased by; and: *Five* plus *three is eight.* ***adj-*** 1 extra; supplemental :*a* plus *value.* 2 and more: *100* plus. 3 indicating addition: *a* plus *sign.* 4 indicating a positive number: *a* plus *three.* ***conj-*** *Informal* and also: *She had talent* plus *a driving ambition to succeed.* ***n-*** [*pl.* **plus·es**] 1 sign [+], showing that the number following is to be added. 2 an extra quantity; an addition; also, a positive quantity or thing, or an advantage.

plush (plŭsh) ***n-*** rich fabric of silk, mohair, synthetic fiber, etc., which has a deeper pile than velvet or velour and is used for clothing or upholstery. ***adj-*** 1 made of this fabric. 2 *Informal* rich; luxurious: *a* plush *hotel.*

Plu·to (plo͞o′tō) ***n-*** 1 in classical mythology, the god of the underworld. 2 the next to the smallest planet of the solar system, and the one farthest from the sun.

plu·toc·ra·cy (plo͞o tŏk′rə sē) ***n-*** [*pl.* **plu·toc·ra·cies**] 1 government by the very rich. 2 wealthy people as a class.

plu·to·crat (plo͞o′tə krăt′) ***n-*** very wealthy person, especially one who has power because of his wealth. —***adj-*** **plu′to·crat′ic.** ***adv-*** **plu′to·crat′i·cal·ly.**

plu·to·ni·um (plo͞o tō′nē əm) ***n-*** radioactive and highly poisonous metal element, made from uranium and used in atomic reactors and bombs. Symbol Pu, At. No. 94.

plu·vi·al (plo͞o′vē′əl) ***adj-*** of or having to do with rain.

[1]**ply** (plī) ***vt-*** **[plied, ply·ing]** 1 to keep supplying (someone) with something in a pressing way: *to* ply *a child with food; to* ply *someone with questions.* 2 to work with; use, especially with diligence: *He* plied *his oars.* 3 to work at steadily: *to* ply *one's trade.* ***vi-*** to go back and forth according to fixed schedule: *This boat* plies *between Philadelphia and Wilmington.* [shortened from **apply,** from Old French **applier,** from Latin **applicāre** meaning "to join to; redouble."]

[2]**ply** (plī) ***n-*** [*pl.* **plies**] 1 thickness or layer of cloth, paper, etc. 2 strand in a cord, rope, etc. [from Old French **pli,** from **plier** meaning "to fold; twist," from Latin **plicāre,** and related to [1]**ply,** [1]**plight,** [1]**plat,** etc.]

ply·wood (plī′wo͝od′) ***n-*** building materials made up of thin layers of wood glued and pressed together.

Pm symbol for promethium.

p.m. or **P.M.** after noon [from Latin **post meridiem**].

pnue·mat·ic (no͞o măt′ĭk, nyo͞o-) ***adj*** 1 of or having to do with air: *under* pneumatic *pressure.* 2 operated by air pressure: *a* pneumatic *drill.* 3 containing air: *a* pneumatic *cushion.* —***adv-*** **pneu·mat′i·cal·ly.**

pneu·mat·ics (no͞o măt′ĭks, nyo͞o-) ***n-*** (takes singular verb) branch of physics that studies the mechanics of gases.

pneu·mo·coc·cus (no͞o′mə kŏk′əs, nyo͞o′-) ***n-*** [*pl.* **pneu·mo·coc·ci** (-kŏk′ī, kŏk′sī)] small, round bacterium that causes one type of pneumonia.

pneu·mo·ni·a (no͞o mōn yə, nyo͞o-) ***n-*** disease characterized by inflammation of the lungs and high fever.

Po symbol for polonium.

P.O. 1 post office. 2 petty officer.

[1]**poach** (pōch) ***vt-*** 1 to cook in a small amount of boiling or simmering water or other liquid. 2 to cook (an egg) whole but without its shell in simmering water or in a container placed above simmering water. [from Old French **pochier,** apparently from **poche** meaning "pocket; bag" and perhaps also "cooking utensil."]

[2]**poach** (pōch) ***vi-*** to hunt or fish illegally, especially on another's property. [from Old French **pocher,** "thrust into (another's land or job)," from Dutch **poken.**]

pock (pŏk) ***n-*** 1 small swelling on the skin filled with pus, as in smallpox. 2 the scar it leaves; pockmark. ***vt-*** to mark with or as if with such swellings or scars.

pock·et (pŏk′ət) ***n-*** 1 small bag sewn in an article of clothing to hold things. 2 any similar hollow, opening, or container: *a* pocket *in a briefcase*; *a* pocket *of ore in a mine.* 3 in airplane travel, a downdraft. *as* ***modifier***: *The book is* pocket *size.* ***vt-*** 1 to put in a pocket, wallet, etc.: *The customer* pocketed *his change.* 2 to suppress; hide: *He* pocketed *his pride.* 3 to take and keep: *to* pocket *the profits.*

in (one's) pocket within one's control; easily managed or influenced. **in pocket** showing a financial gain: *I was* in pocket *a hundred dollars after selling the furniture.* **line (one's) pocket** to make a profit, especially in an illegal or underhanded way. **out of pocket** suffering a loss of money or of a certain amount of money.

pock·et·book (pŏk′ət bo͝ok′) ***n-*** 1 handbag used to carry money and various small personal articles; purse. 2 small, compact case used to carry papers, money, etc. 3 financial condition: *These expenses are too great for our* pocketbook.

pock·et·ful (pŏk′ət fo͝ol′) ***n-*** 1 as much as a pocket can conveniently hold. 2 any large amount.

pock·et·knife (pŏk′ət nīf′) ***n-*** [*pl.* **pock·et·knives**] small knife with blades and sometimes tools that fold into the handle. For picture, see *knife.*

pocket veto ***n-*** veto that takes effect when the chief executive refrains from taking any action on a bill that has been passed by the legislature, and the legislature adjourns before the time at which the bill would automatically become law without the executive's signature.

pock·mark (pŏk′märk′) ***n-*** scar or small pit, such as one left by smallpox. **—*adj-* pock′marked′.**

pod (pŏd) ***n-*** 1 seed container of certain plants, especially the pea and bean (for picture, see *pea*). 2 in an aircraft, a tapering enclosure, usually under a wing, for holding fuel, an engine, etc. (for picture, see *airplane*).

-pod *combining form* animal or thing having a certain number or kind of feet: *a tri*pod (three-footed stand); *a myria*pod (organism with many feet). [from Greek **pous, podos** meaning "foot."]

po·di·a·trist (pō dī′ə trĭst) ***n-*** specialist in the care and treatment of the feet; chiropodist.

po·di·a·try (pō dī′ə trē) ***n-*** branch of medicine which deals with the care and treatment of the feet; chiropody.

po·di·um (pō′dē əm) ***n-*** raised platform from which a conductor leads an orchestra.

po·em (pō′əm) ***n-*** 1 any composition written in poetry. A poem may be from two lines to several volumes in length. 2 any work of art or thing of beauty having the effect of poetry.

po·e·sy (pō′ə sē) *Archaic* ***n-*** 1 poems collectively; poetry. 2 the art of writing poetry.

po·et (pō′ət) ***n-*** 1 person who writes poetry. 2 any artist having the ability to move others by the beauty of his work.

po·et·ic (pō ĕt′ĭk) ***adj-*** 1 of, having to do with, or characteristic of poetry or poets: *Shakespeare's* poetic *language;* poetic *genius.* 2 written in poetry: *Emily Dickinson's* poetic *works.* 3 having qualities or characteristics considered appropriate to poetry or a poet: *her* poetic *description.* Also **po·et′i·cal. —*adv-* po·et′i·cal·ly.**

poetic justice ***n-*** the rewarding of virtue or the punishment of vice in a manner considered especially fitting.

poetic license ***n-*** a violation of the generally accepted rules of language, correct form, etc., considered permissible for poets or other creative artists.

po·et·ics (pō ĕt′ĭks) ***n-*** (takes singular verb) 1 the art, technique, or principles of composing poetry. 2 a written work on such a subject.

poet laureate ***n-*** [*pl.* **poets laureate** or **poet laureates**] in Great Britain, the officially appointed court poet, who composes poems for royal occasions.

po·et·ry (pō′ə trē) ***n-*** 1 spoken or written expression organized into lines and groups of lines by repetition of sounds and rhythms. Poetry differs from prose in organization and in emphasis on form to convey the poet's feelings as a part of his meaning. 2 beauty that is very impressive, especially because of grace and poetic rhythm: *the* poetry *of her dancing.* 3 imagination or feeling, as distinguished from provable fact: *more truth than* poetry.

po·go stick (pō′gō) ***n-*** toy consisting of a pole equipped with footrests, handgrips, and a spring at its base. It is ridden in bouncing bounds.

po·grom (pə grŭm′, pō′grəm) ***n-*** an organized massacre of people belonging to a particular ethnic group, religion, etc.; especially, such a massacre of Jews.

poi (poi) ***n-*** Hawaiian food made from pulverized, cooked, and usually fermented taro root.

poign·ant (poin′yənt) ***adj-*** 1 affecting the feelings deeply; touching: *a* poignant *memory.* 2 deeply painful; piercing: *her* poignant *grief.* 3 sharp; keen: *his* poignant *wit.* **—*n-* poign′an·cy. *adv-* poign′ant·ly.**

poin·set·ti·a (poin sĕt′ə, -sĕt′ē ə) ***n-*** plant whose tiny flowers are surrounded by long, bright-red leaves that look like petals.

point (point) ***n-*** 1 sharp or narrowed end of a thing; tip: *the* point *of a pin*; *a pencil* point; *a* point *of land.* 2 main or important part: *Please keep to the* point *of the discussion.* 3 object or purpose: *There is no* point *in discussing it further.* 4 detail: *The speaker listed each* point *of his plan.* 5 trait: *Everyone has both good and bad* points. 6 certain stage in a process: *He was provoked to the* point *of losing his temper.* 7 place or location on a map or scale: *The freezing* point *of water is 32°F.* 8 written or printed dot: *a decimal* point. 9 one of the thirty-two directions on the compass: *Northwest is a* point *on the compass.* 10 unit of scoring or measuring: *Our team leads by two* points. 11 in printing, a unit of measure equal to about 1/72 inch. Twelve points equal one pica. 12 *Mathematics* (1) member of the set that makes up a curve or geometric figure. (2) a specific location in space, defined by an ordered set of two or three coordinates. (3) any one of the marked positions on a number line, used to represent whole numbers. ***vt-*** 1 to aim; direct: *to* point *a gun at a target*; point *a finger.* 2 to indicate by or as if by extending a finger: *to* point *the way.* 3 to give force or added meaning to; illustrate: *to* point *a moral.* 4 to sharpen the tip of: *to* point *a pencil.* 5 to fill and smooth the joints of (masonry). ***vi-*** 1 to call attention to something by extending one's finger. 2 to be directed; face; tend: *His eyes were* pointed *toward the river.*

at the point of on the verge of: *He is* at the point of *death.* **beside the point** not relevant; unrelated. **in**

point worthy of consideration; relevant: *This is a case* in point. **make a point of** to emphasize or insist upon. **on the point of** just about to do something: *to be* on the point of *leaving.* **strain** (or **stretch) a point** to make an exception.
point off to separate with a decimal point.
point out to direct attention to; show.

point-blank (point′ blăngk′) ***adj-*** **1** aimed directly at a target: *a* point-blank *shot.* **2** so close that missing a target is unlikely or impossible: *to shoot at* point-blank *range.* **3** blunt and direct; forthright: *a* point-blank *question.* ***adv-*** directly: *I asked him* point-blank.

point·ed (poin′ təd) ***adj-*** **1** having a sharp end or apex. **2** directed toward a particular person or thing: *her* pointed *remarks*; *his* pointed *curiosity.* **—*adv-* point′ ed·ly.** ***n-*** **point′ ed·ness.**

point·er (poin′ tər) ***n-*** **1** thing that points to or toward something. **2** slender stick used to point with, used by teachers, lecturers, etc. **3** short-haired hunting dog trained to stand and point with its nose toward game. **4** *Informal* piece of advice.

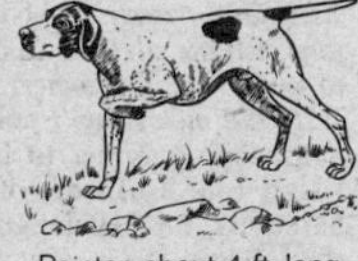

Pointer, about 4 ft. long

point·less (point′ ləs) ***adj-*** **1** without a point; blunt: *a* pointless *pencil.* **2** having no purpose, sense, or worthwhile result: *a* pointless *anecdote*; *a* pointless *attempt.*

point of honor ***n-*** something which closely touches one's honor, reputation, principles, ethical standards, etc.

point of order ***n-*** in parliamentary procedure, a query as to whether business or debate in progress is being properly conducted according to rule.

point of view ***n-*** **1** personal outlook; attitude: *his conservative* point of view. **2** position from which one looks at or considers something.

poise (poiz) ***n-*** **1** calmness and coolness of manner; self-possession: *his* poise *in addressing the audience.* **2** balance; equilibrium: *the* poise *of a tightrope walker.* **3** manner of carrying the head and body; carriage: *the* poise *of a ballet dancer.* ***vi-*** **[poised, pois·ing]** to balance: *The diver* poised *on the edge of the pool.* ***vt-***: *The seal* poised *the ball on its nose.*

poi·son (poi′ zən) ***n-*** **1** substance that can injure or kill when it is taken in or absorbed by a living thing. **2** anything that can corrupt or injure a person's character: *the* poison *of envy.* ***vt-*** **1** to injure or kill with a harmful or deadly substance. **2** to cause to become deadly or harmful by the addition of something: *Sewage* poisoned *the drinking water.* **3** to corrupt; ruin: *Envy* poisoned *their friendship.* **—*n-* poi′ son·er.**

poison ivy ***n-*** bushy or climbing plant having leaves composed of three leaflets, and small, greenish flowers and berries. Touching the plant usually causes a painful rash.

poison oak ***n-*** shrubby plant closely related to and resembling poison ivy.

poi·son·ous (poi′ zən əs) ***adj-*** **1** having properties that may injure or kill; venomous: *a* poisonous *snake.* **2** like a poison; harmful: *a* poisonous *rumor.* **—*adv-* poi′ son·ous·ly.** ***n-*** **poi′ son·ous·ness.**

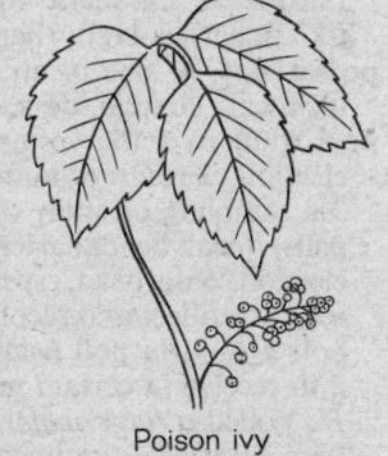

Poison ivy

poison sumac ***n-*** shrub or small tree having compound leaves composed of many pointed leaflets, found chiefly in swampy areas. It produces a very painful rash.

[1]**poke** (pōk) ***vt-*** **[poked, pok·ing] 1** to thrust, jab, or push into or against, especially with a pointed object: *to* poke *a fire*; *to* poke *something with one's finger.* **2** to thrust: *to* poke *one's head out of a doorway*; *to* poke *one's finger into a pie.* **3** to produce by pushing or jabbing: *to* poke *a hole in a screen.* ***vi-*** **1** to make a pushing or jabbing motion: *to* poke *at the fire.* **2** to intrude: *to* poke *into someone else's business.* **3** to move slowly or idly; dawdle. ***n-*** a push or jab. [from Middle English **poken** or **pukken,** from a Germanic word.]

[2]**poke** (pōk) ***n-*** pokeweed. ***as modifier***: *a* poke *salad.* [American word from earlier **puccoon,** from the Algonquian name.]

[3]**poke** (pōk) ***n-*** a bag; sack. [probably from Old Norse **poki** or earlier Dutch **poke** meaning "bag."]

poke·ber·ry (pōk′ bĕr′ ē) ***n-*** [*pl.* **poke·ber·ries] 1** berry of the pokeweed. **2** the plant itself.

poke bonnet ***n-*** bonnet with a deep, projecting brim that shades the face.

[1]**pok·er** (pō′ kər) ***n-*** someone or something that pokes; especially, a metal rod used to stir a fire. [from [1]**poke.**]

[2]**pok·er** (pō′ kər) ***n-*** card game played with money or chips, in which the players bet against each other on the value of their cards. [American word of uncertain origin.]

poker face ***n-*** face held expressionless.

poke·weed (pōk′ wēd′) ***n-*** tall, shrubby plant with pointed clusters of small, greenish-white flowers and dark purple berries; poke; pokeberry. The root and seeds of the plant are poisonous, but the young shoots are eaten as greens.

pok·ey (pō′ kē) *Slang* ***n-*** [*pl.* **pok·eys]** jail.

pok·y (pō′ kē) ***adj-*** **[pok·i·er, pok·i·est] 1** dull and uninteresting; slow: *a* poky *pace.* **2** cramped in space; small and uncomfortable: *a* poky *room.* Also **pokey.**

po·lar (pō′ lər) ***adj-*** **1** of or having to do with the poles of a magnet, sphere, etc. **2** having to do with or near the earth's North and South Poles: *a* polar *exploration.*

polar bear ***n-*** large white bear of the Arctic region.

polar circle ***n-*** either the Arctic or the Antarctic circle.

polar co-ordinates ***n-*** in plane geometry, two co-ordinates which locate one point with respect to another point, called an origin, and a base line passing through the origin. One co-ordinate is the distance from the point to the origin. The other is the angle between the line connecting the point with the origin and the base line.

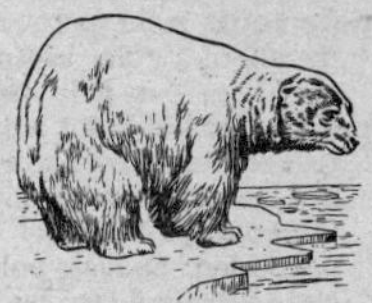

Polar bear, about 9 1/2 ft. long

Po·lar·is (pə lăr′ ĭs) ***n-*** bright star located directly above the North Pole; North Star. Polaris forms the tip of the handle of the Little Dipper.

po·lar·i·ty (pō lăr′ ə tē, pə-) ***n-*** [*pl.* **po·lar·i·ties] 1** a having poles. **2** the having or showing of opposite traits or qualities. **3** of a magnetic body, the possession of two poles whose location and properties are diametrically opposite.

po·lar·ize (pō′ lə rīz′) ***vt-*** **[po·lar·ized, po·lar·iz·ing] 1** to give polarity to. **2** to give a particular direction or meaning to: *to* polarize *public opinion.* **3** to filter (light or other electromagnetic radiation) so that only the

---

fāte, făt, dâre, bärn; bē, bĕt, mêre; bīte, bĭt; nōte, hŏt, môre, dóg; fŭn, fûr; tōō, bŏŏk; oil; out; tar; thin; then; hw for wh as in *wh*at; zh for s as in u*s*ual; ə for a, e, i, o, u, as in *a*go, lin*e*n, per*i*l, at*o*m, min*u*s

part which oscillates in a given direction is allowed through the filter. *—n-* **po′ lar·i·za′ tion.**

polar region *n-* either of the areas of the earth north of the Arctic Circle **(north polar region)** and south of the Antarctic Circle **(south polar region).**

pol·der (pōl′ dər) *n-* land that has been reclaimed from the sea or other body of water by means of dikes.

[1]**pole** (pōl) *n-* **1** long, slender timber, rod, or similar piece of solid material: *a flag* pole; *a fishing* pole. **2** measure of length equal to 5½ yards; rod. *vt-* **[poled, pol·ing]** to push or move with a pole: *to* pole *a boat upstream.* [from Old English **pāl,** from Latin **pālus,** "stake." This word is related to [2]**pale.**] *Hom-* poll. *—n-* **pol′ er.**

[2]**pole** (pōl) *n-* **1** point marking either of the two ends of the axis of a round body such as the earth. The earth's poles are called the North Pole and the South Pole. **2** either of the terminals of an electric battery or a magnet. **3** either of two completely opposed opinions, forces, etc. **4** *Physics* either of two points at which electrical or magnetic forces of opposite character are concentrated. **5** *Biology* either end of an imaginary axis in a cell, with reference to which cell structures are located. [from Old French **pol,** from Greek **pólos** meaning "hinge; pivot."] *Hom-* poll.

Pole (pōl) *n-* a native or inhabitant of Poland, or one of his descendants.

pole·ax (pōl′ ăks′) *n-* battle-ax mounted on a pole, formerly used as a weapon. Also **pole′ axe.**

pole·cat (pōl′ kăt′) *n-* **1** small Old World animal related to the weasel. **2** the North American skunk.

po·lem·ic (pə lĕm′ ĭk) *n-* **1** an argument, dispute, etc., especially a written one, that supports one opinion or body of ideas in opposition to another. **2 polemics** (takes singular verb) the art or practice of dispute, especially in religious matters. *adj-* (also **po·lem′ i·cal**) of, relating to, or consisting of such argument or dispute: *his* polemic *writings. —adv-* **po·lem′ i·cal·ly.**

pole·star (pōl′ stär′) *n-* any star directly above a pole of the earth. In our era, Polaris is the northern polestar, and there is no southern one.

pole vault *n-* in sports, a leap made over a high bar with the aid of a pole. *vi-* **(pole-vault):** *He* pole-vaulted *over the fence. —n-* **pole′-vaul′ ter.**

po·lice (pə lēs′) *n-* **1** a department of government set up to keep order, enforce law, and deal with criminals. **2** (takes plural verb) the persons in such a force. *vi-* **[po·liced, po·lic·ing] 1** to patrol or keep in order as a policeman: *Soldiers* policed *the occupied territory.* **2** to clean up (a military camp, quarters, etc.). *as modifier: a* police *escort; a* police *record.*

police court *n-* a city court having jurisdiction over minor criminal cases and empowered to hold for trial all persons charged with more serious crimes.

police dog *n-* **1** German shepherd. **2** any dog trained to help the police in their work.

po·lice·man (pə lēs′ mən) *n-* [*pl.* **po·lice·men**] member of a police force. *—n- fem.* **po·lice′ wom′ an.**

police state *n-* government that uses a powerful secret police force to control the activities of its citizens.

police station *n-* headquarters used by the police.

[1]**pol·i·cy** (pŏl′ ə sē) *n-* [*pl.* **pol·i·cies**] **1** principles, methods, etc., that determine or influence a course of action, such as that of a government or organization. **2** wisdom in managing affairs; prudence. **3** *Archaic* deceitful craftiness. [from Old French **policie,** from Greek **politéia** meaning "civil government; polity."]

[2]**pol·i·cy** (pŏl′ ə sē) *n-* [*pl.* **pol·i·cies**] **1** written contract between an insurance company and the person or persons insured. **2** gambling lottery in which bets are made on whether a certain number will appear or be chosen. [from French **police,** from Medieval Latin **apódixa,** "voucher," from Greek **apódeixis,** "proof."]

pol·i·cy·hold·er (pŏl′ ə sē hōl′ dər) *n-* person who holds an insurance policy.

po·li·o (pō′ lē ō′) *n-* poliomyelitis. *as modifier: a* polio *injection.*

po·li·o·my·e·li·tis (pō′ lē ō mī′ ə lī′ təs) *n-* acute, infectious, virus disease that destroys nervous tissue and can result in muscle paralysis and, sometimes, death; infantile paralysis. Vaccines have almost eliminated this disease in the United States and Canada.

pol·ish (pŏl′ ĭsh) *n-* **1** paste, liquid, or other preparation used to make something clean and shiny: *a can of shoe* polish; *silver* polish. **2** smooth, glossy finish. **3** refinement or cultivation: *He has acquired* polish *by years of study and travel. vt-* **1** to clean and shine by rubbing: *to* polish *the silver.* **2** to improve the style or elegance of: *to* polish *one's manners. vi-* to be made shining: *This rusty old metal won't* polish. *—n-* **pol′ ish·er.**

polish off *Informal* to finish: *He* polished off *the pie.*

Po·lish (pō′ lĭsh) *adj-* of or relating to Poland, its inhabitants, or their language. *n-* the Slavic language of the Poles.

Pol·it·bu·ro (pə lĭt′ byŏŏr′ ō) *n-* the supreme policy-making committee of the Communist Party of the U.S.S.R., headed by the general secretary.

po·lite (pə līt′) *adj-* **[po·lit·er, po·lit·est] 1** having or showing good manners; courteous: *a* polite *answer.* **2** refined; cultured. *—adv-* **po·lite′ ly.** *n-* **po·lite′ ness.**

pol·i·tic (pŏl′ ə tĭk′) *adj-* showing good judgment or tact; prudent; shrewd: *a* politic *answer. —adv-* **pol′ i·tic′ ly.**

po·lit·i·cal (pə lĭt′ ə kəl) *adj-* **1** of or relating to the science of government or the management of public affairs: *the President's* political *advisers.* **2** of or related to politics: *a* political *club. —adv-* **po·lit′ i·cal·ly.**

political science *n-* branch of social science that deals with the principles, organization, and administration of government.

pol·i·ti·cian (pŏl′ ə tĭsh′ ən) *n-* **1** person who is active in politics, especially as a holder of political office or as a member of a political party. **2** person who is able, shrewd, and tactful in dealing with others.

pol·i·tics (pŏl′ ə tĭks′) *n-* **1** (takes plural verb) activities, principles, etc., that relate to public office or government affairs: *He is active in local* politics. *His* politics *were unpopular.* **2** (takes singular verb) science or theory of government; political science.

pol·i·ty (pŏl′ ə tē) *n-* [*pl.* **pol·i·ties**] **1** organization of the government of a nation, church, etc. **2** any community living under an organized system of government.

pol·ka (pōl′ kə) *n-* **1** lively dance that originated in central Europe. **2** the music for such a dance. *vi-* **[pol·kaed** (-kəd), **pol·ka·ing]:** *They* polkaed *around the room.*

polka dot *n-* one of an arrangement of evenly spaced, identical, circular dots, used as a decorative pattern.

poll (pōl) *n-* **1** the voting and recording of votes in an election. **2** result or number of votes cast in an election. **3** a sampling or study of people's opinions. **4** (usually **polls**) local headquarters where votes are cast in an election. **5** the head, especially the part where hair grows. *vt-* **1** to collect and record the votes and opinions of: *to* poll *a jury; to* poll *housewives on their favorite brands.* **2** to receive (a certain number or proportion of votes): *He* polled *a large majority.* **3** to lop or cut off part of (tree branches, the horns of cattle, etc.). *Hom-* pole.

pol·lack or **pol·lock** (pŏl′ ək) *n-* [*pl.* **pol·lack; pol·lacks** (kinds of pollack)] edible fish of the North Atlantic, related to the cod.

pol·len (pŏl′ən) ***n-*** grains which are the male cells produced by a flower to fertilize egg cells of the same or other flowers.

pol·li·nate (pŏl′ə nāt′) ***vt-*** **[pol·li·nat·ed, pol·li·nat·ing]** to transfer (pollen) from the anther of a flower to the stigma of the same flower or another flower. **—*n-* pol′li·na′tor:** *Bees are* pollinators *of some flowers.*

pol·li·na·tion (pŏl′ə nā′shən) ***n-*** the transfer of pollen from the anthers to the stigmas of flowers, which results in the start of the process by which seeds are formed.

pol·li·wog or **pol·ly·wog** (pŏl′ĭ wŏg′) ***n-*** tadpole.

poll·ster (pōl′stər) ***n-*** person who conducts a poll of public opinion.

poll tax ***n-*** tax of so much per person assessed as a requirement for voting in elections. The 24th Amendment to the United States Constitution prohibits a poll tax in any Federal election.

pol·lu·tant (pə lo͞o′tənt) ***n-*** substance that pollutes.

pol·lute (pə lo͞ot′) ***vt-*** **[pol·lut·ed, pol·lut·ing] 1** to make unclean or impure: *Chemical wastes* polluted *the stream and killed most of the fish.* **2** to destroy the purity of (the mind, morals, etc.); corrupt. **—*n-* pol·lut′er.**

pol·lu·tion (pə lo͞o′shən) ***n-*** a polluting or being polluted; especially, the contamination of air, water, etc., by the discharge of harmful or poisonous substances. ***as modifier:*** *the* pollution *problem in large cities.*

Pol·lux (pŏl′əks) See *Castor and Pollux.*

po·lo (pō′lō) ***n-*** game played on horseback with a wooden ball and long mallets.

po·lo·naise (pŏl′ə nāz′, pō′lə-) ***n-* 1** stately Polish dance. **2** music for this dance, or a composition written in similar style and rhythm. **3** woman's garment, of the 18th century, having a skirt open from below the waist and looped back to show an elaborate underskirt.

po·lo·ni·um (pə lō′nē əm) ***n-*** a radioactive metal element that occurs as one of the stages in the disintegration of radium. Symbol Po, At. No. 84, At. Wt. 210.

Po·lo·ni·us (pə lō′nē əs) ***n-*** in Shakespeare's "Hamlet," the father of Ophelia.

pol·troon (pŏl tro͞on′) *Archaic* ***n-*** coward completely lacking in spirit; dastard.

poly *combining form* many: *a* poly*gon* (many-sided figure). [from Greek **poly-**, from **polys,** "much; many."]

pol·y·an·dry (pŏl′ē ăn′drē) ***n-*** custom or practice of having more than one husband at a time.

pol·y·an·drous (pŏl′ē ăn′drəs) ***adj-* 1** practicing or characterized by polyandry. **2** of a flower, having numerous stamens.

pol·y·chro·mat·ic (pŏl′ē krə măt′ĭk) ***adj-*** having or showing many or changing colors.

pol·y·chrome (pŏl′ē krōm′) ***adj-*** decorated or executed in a variety of colors: *a* polychrome *vase; a* polychrome *painting.* ***n-* 1** a work or article made in this way. **2** a variety of colors: *a painting in* polychrome.

po·lyg·a·mist (pə lĭg′ə mĭst) ***n-*** person who practices polygamy.

po·lyg·a·my (pə lĭg′ə mē) ***n-*** custom or practice of having more than one mate or spouse at the same time. ***adj-* po·lyg′a·mous:** *a* polygamous *society.* ***adv-* po·lyg′a·mous·ly.**

pol·y·glot (pŏl′ĭ glŏt′) ***adj-* 1** speaking and understanding many languages. **2** consisting of or written in several languages: *a* polyglot *edition of the Bible.* ***n-*** person who speaks and understands many languages.

pol·y·gon (pŏl′ĭ gŏn′) ***n-*** a closed plane figure having three or more sides.

po·lyg·y·ny (pə lĭj′ə nē) ***n-*** custom or practice of having more than one wife at a time. **—*adj-* po·lyg′y·nous**

PARALLELOGRAM
PENTAGON
NONAGON

Some polygons

pol·y·he·dron (pŏl′ĭ hē′drən) ***n-*** [*pl.* **pol·y·he·drons** or **pol·y·he·dra** (-drə)] in geometry, a solid figure bounded by plane faces.

pol·y·mer (pŏl′ə mər) ***n-*** any of a very large number of complex chemical compounds that are the result of the stringing together of molecules of simpler compounds. Nylon and cellulose are polymers. **—*adj-* pol′y·mer′ic** (pŏl′ə mĕr′ĭk).

pol·y·mer·ize (pə lĭm′ə rīz′, pŏl′ə mə rīz′) ***vi-*** **[pol·y·mer·ized, pol·y·mer·iz·ing]** to combine into a polymer. ***vt-*** to make (something) into a polymer. **—*n-* pol·y′mer·i·za′tion** or **pol′y·mer·i·za′tion.**

Pol·y·ne·sian (pŏl′ə nē′zhən) ***n-* 1** one of any of the peoples of Polynesia. **2** the languages of these people. ***adj-:*** *a* Polynesian *island.*

pol·y·no·mi·al (pŏl′ĭ nō′mē əl) ***n-*** in mathematics, an expression containing two or more terms. The expression $a(b + c^2)$ is a polynomial. **—*adj-:*** *a* polynomial *expression.*

pol·yp (pŏl′əp) ***n-* 1** small water animal without a backbone, shaped like a flower. Most polyps build skeletons of lime around themselves. For picture, see *coral.* **2** a tumor; especially, a benign tumor.

pol·y·sty·rene (pŏl′ĭ stī′rēn′) ***n-*** a polymer of styrene used to make many plastics.

pol·y·syl·lab·ic (pŏl′ĭ sə lăb′ĭk) ***adj-*** consisting of three or more syllables: *a* polysyllabic *word.*

pol·y·tech·nic (pŏl′ĭ tĕk′nĭk) ***adj-*** of or having to do with many arts or sciences, especially in their practical application: *a* polytechnic *institute.*

pol·y·the·ism (pŏl′ĭ thē′ĭz′əm) ***n-*** belief in the existence of more than one god; also, the worship of such gods. **—*n-* pol′y·the′ist.** ***adj-* pol′y·the·is′tic.**

pol·y·un·sat·u·rat·ed (pŏl′ē ŭn săch′ə rā′təd) ***n-*** of an organic compound, containing more than one pair of carbon-to-carbon double bonds.

po·made (pō măd′) ***n-*** perfumed ointment for the hair. ***vt-*** **[po·mad·ed, po·mad·ing]:** *He* pomaded *his hair.*

pome (pōm) ***n-*** a kind of fruit, consisting of a ripened, fleshy calyx surrounding the ripened ovary. The pear and apple are pomes.

pome·gran·ate (pŭm′grăn′ət, pŏm′-) ***n-* 1** fruit with a thick red skin and many seeds, each surrounded by red, juicy pulp that has a pleasant, acid taste. **2** the tree that bears this fruit. ***as modifier:*** *a* pomegranate *syrup.*

Pomegranate

Pom·e·ra·ni·an (pŏm′ə rā′nē ən) ***n-*** small dog having long, silky hair, a curled-up tail, and a pointed muzzle.

pom·mel (pŭm′əl, pŏm′-) ***n-* 1** the raised front of a saddle. **2** knob on the handle of a sword. ***vt-*** to pummel.

pomp (pŏmp) ***n-*** solemn or showy ceremony, etc.

pom·pa·dour (pŏm′pə dôr′) ***n-*** hair style in which the hair is combed up from the forehead or straight back from the forehead.

pom·pa·no (pŏm′pə nō′) ***n-*** [*pl.* **pom·pa·no; pom·pa·nos** (kinds of pompano)] any of several food fishes of

fāte, făt, dâre, bärn; bē, bĕt, mêre; bīte, bĭt; nōte, hŏt, môre, dóg; fŭn, fûr; to͞o, bo͝ok; oil; out; tar; thin; then; hw for wh as in *wh*at; zh for s as in usual; ə for a, e, i, o, u, as in *a*go, lin*e*n, per*i*l, at*o*m, min*u*s

warm seas, especially one native to the southern Atlantic coast of the United States.

pom·pon (pŏm′ pŏn) ***n-*** **1** ornamental ball-shaped tuft of wool, feathers, etc. **2** a kind of small chrysanthemum.

pom·pos·i·ty (pŏm pŏs′ ə tē) ***n-*** [*pl.* **pom·pos·i·ties**] pompous manner, behavior, language, etc.; also, an instance of this: *a speech full of* pomposities.

pom·pous (pŏm′ pəs) ***adj-*** **1** self-important in a solemn manner; pretentious: *a* pompous *fellow.* **2** using or consisting of elaborate, high-flown language: *a* pompous *orator*; pompous *language.* **—*adv-*** **pom′ pous·ly.** ***n-*** **pom′ pous·ness.**

pon·cho (pŏn′ chō) ***n-*** [*pl.* **pon·chos**] **1** loose cloak consisting of a blanket with a hole in the middle for the head, worn chiefly in Latin America. **2** similar garment of waterproof material, worn as a raincoat. [from American Spanish, from South American Indian **pontho.**]

Boy wearing poncho

pond (pŏnd) ***n-*** small lake or similar still, quiet pool of water.

pon·der (pŏn′ dər) ***vt-*** to think about; think over carefully: *He* pondered *the advantages of joining.* ***vi-***: *He* pondered *over the problem.*

pon·der·ous (pŏn′ dər əs) ***adj-*** **1** weighty and massive; heavy: *The* ponderous *elephants plodded along.* **2** slow, clumsy, or labored: *a* ponderous *style of writing.* **—*adv-*** **pon′ der·ous·ly.** ***n-*** **pon′ der·ous·ness.**

pond lily ***n-*** water lily.

pond scum ***n-*** **1** spirogyra. **2** a tangle of greenish-black algae forming a scum on stagnant ponds.

pond·weed (pŏnd′ wēd′) ***n-*** any of various plants of ponds and streams that grow entirely under water or have leaves that float on the surface.

pone (pōn) ***n-*** bread made of corn meal, with or without milk or eggs; corn pone. [from an Algonquian word.]

pon·gee (pŏn′ jē′) ***n-*** soft, thin, unbleached and undyed silk with an uneven weave, originally from China.

pon·iard (pŏn′ yərd) ***n-*** dagger, especially a small one with a narrow blade.

pon·tiff (pŏn′ tĭf) ***n-*** bishop, especially the Pope.

pon·tif·i·cal (pŏn tĭf′ ĭ kəl) ***adj-*** **1** of or having to do with a pope or bishop. **2** having or showing a proudly authoritative or self-important manner. ***n-*** **pontificals** official robes worn by a bishop. **—*adv-*** **pon·ti′ fi·cal·ly.**

pon·tif·i·cate (pŏn tĭf′ ĭ kāt) ***vi-*** [**pon·tif·i·cat·ed, pon·tif·i·cat·ing**] **1** to speak or act with pompous authority. **2** to perform the duties of a pope or bishop. ***n-*** (*also* pŏn tĭf′ ĭ kət) the rank or term of office of a pope or bishop.

Pon·tius Pi·late (pŏn′ chəs pī′ lət, pŏn′ tē əs) ***n-*** Roman procurator of Judea (26-36 A.D.) under whose authority Christ was crucified.

pon·toon (pŏn to͞on′) ***n-*** **1** flat-bottomed boat or similar craft used in building a bridge supported on floats **(pontoon bridge).** **2** air-filled float, tube, or cylinder, such as one that supports such a bridge or enables a seaplane to land on water.

Pontoons

po·ny (pō′ nē) ***n-*** [*pl.* **po·nies**] **1** any of several breeds of small or dwarf horses, such as the Shetland pony. **2** any small horse. **3** *Slang* literal translation of a text in a foreign language, used by some students to avoid doing assigned work. **4** *Informal* small glass for liquor.

pony express ***n-*** in the pioneer West, a type of postal service carried out by relays of horseback riders.

pooch (po͞och) *Slang* ***n-*** dog, especially a small mongrel.

pood (po͞od) ***n-*** Russian unit of weight equal to 36.1 pounds.

poo·dle (po͞o′ dəl) ***n-*** breed of dog, ranging in size from fairly large to very small, and having thick, curly hair, often trimmed in an elaborate manner.

pooh (po͞o) ***interj-*** exclamation of scorn or disbelief.

pooh-pooh (po͞o′ po͞o′) ***vt-*** to belittle or scoff at scornfully; ridicule: *They* pooh-poohed *the scheme.*

[1]**pool** (po͞ol) ***n-*** **1** small body of still water, such as a pond, a wide place in a stream, or a man-made place or tank for swimming. **2** puddle of any liquid. [from Old English **pōl.**]

[2]**pool** (po͞ol) ***n-*** **1** game played on a special table, with balls that are driven with a cue into pockets at the edge of the table. **2** total amount bet at one time by all the people taking part in a gambling game, lottery, etc. **3** a combination of persons or business corporations, formed to provide a profit to all involved. **4** people participating in a useful service made available to those who need it: *a secretaries'* pool; *a car* pool. ***vt-*** to put to common use; share in common: *Let's* pool *our money and buy a boat.* [from French **poule** meaning "hen," but also "booty; stakes in a game," from Late Latin **pulla**, "pullet."]

pool·room (po͞ol′ ro͝om′) ***n-*** place where the game of pool is played.

poop (po͞op) ***n-*** **1** (also **poop deck)** raised deck in the stern of a vessel. **2** rearmost, upper part of the stern.

Poop deck

poor (po͝or, pôr) ***adj-*** [**poor·er, poor·est**] **1** having little or no money; lacking wealth; needy. **2** inferior in quality, performance, workmanship, condition, etc.: *a* poor *student*; poor *merchandise*; poor *health.* **3** needing affection or sympathy; pathetic: *a* poor, *unhappy kitten.* **4** unworthy: *a* poor *excuse.* ***Homs-*** pore, pour. **—*n-*** **poor′ ness.**

poor·house (po͝or′ hous′, pôr′-) ***n-*** place where poor people are fed and housed at public expense.

poor·ly (po͝or′ lē, pôr′-) ***adv-*** in a poor manner; badly. ***adj-*** *Informal* ill; weak: *The patient is* poorly *today.*

pop (pŏp) ***n-*** **1** short, sharp noise: *The balloon burst with a* pop. **2** carbonated beverage; soda. **3** (also **pop fly**) in baseball, a short, high fly ball that can easily be caught. ***vt-*** [**popped, pop·ping**] **1** to cause to burst open or apart, especially with a sharp sound: *to* pop *a balloon.* **2** to push or thrust suddenly: *She* popped *her head through the doorway.* ***vi-*** **1** to move, come, or go quickly and suddenly; dart: *The rabbit* popped *out of its hole.* **2** to burst suddenly, especially with a sharp sound: *The seed pods* popped *open.* **3** to shoot (at) chiefly for practice. **4** to bulge; protrude: *Her eyes* popped *when she heard the news.* **5** in baseball, to hit a short, high fly ball.

pop off **1** to leave quickly. **2** *Slang* to die.

pop the question *Informal* to propose marriage.

pop up to appear suddenly and unexpectedly.

pop. **1** population. **2** popular; popularly.

pop·corn (pŏp′ kòrn′, -kôrn′) ***n-*** a kind of corn with small, hard grains that explode into fluffy white masses when heated.

Pope or **pope** (pōp) ***n-*** bishop of Rome and the head of the Roman Catholic Church.

pop·gun (pŏp′ gŭn′) ***n-*** harmless toy gun that makes a popping sound.

pop·in·jay (pŏp′ ĭn jā′) ***n-*** vain, conceited fellow who chatters like a parrot.

pop·ish (pō′ pĭsh) ***adj-*** of or having to do with the Roman Catholic Church (used to show disfavor).

pop·lar (pŏp′ lər) *n-* **1** any of various fast-growing trees related to the willows, some of which have slender, upturned branches. The aspen and the cottonwood are poplars. **2** the soft wood of these trees. *as **modifier**: the* poplar *leaves.*

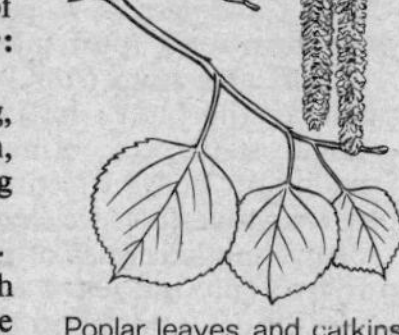
Poplar leaves and catkins

pop·lin (pŏp′ lĭn) *n-* strong, durable cloth of cotton, rayon, silk, or wool, having a fine, crosswise rib.

pop·o·ver (pŏp′ ō′ vər) *n-* light, air-filled muffin which rises over the edge of the muffin pan when baking.

pop·per (pŏp′ ər) *n-* **1** covered metal basket or container for heating popcorn. **2** person or thing that pops.

pop·py (pŏp′ ē) *n-* [*pl.* **pop·pies**] any of several plants with deeply notched leaves, hairy stems, and large-petaled, often scarlet flowers; also, the flower itself. Some kinds of poppy are a source of opium.

Poppy

pop·py·cock (pŏp′ ē kŏk′) *Informal n-* foolish talk; nonsense.

pop·py·seed (pŏp′ ē sēd′) *n-* the small, black seeds of the poppy, used in cooking and baking.

pop·u·lace (pŏp′ yə ləs) *n-* the common people, especially of a particular locality; the masses.

pop·u·lar (pŏp′ yə lər) *adj-* **1** well liked generally or by a group: *a* popular *man.* **2** widespread; common; prevalent; general: *a* popular *myth*; *a* popular *remedy.* **3** of, for, or representing the people: *Democracy is* popular *government.* **4** suited to the average understanding and taste: *a* popular *explanation*; popular *music.* **5** within the means of average persons: *goods at* popular *prices.* **6** springing from or created by the common people: *Folk tales are of* popular *origin.*

popular front *n-* coalition of political parties, usually leftist, labor, and liberal.

pop·u·lar·i·ty (pŏp′ yə lăr′ ə tē, -lĕr′ ə tē) *n-* a being well liked by many people.

pop·u·lar·ize (pŏp′ yə lə rīz′) *vt-* [**pop·u·lar·ized, pop·u·lar·iz·ing**] to make popular. *—n-* **pop′ u·lar·i·za′ tion.** *n-* **pop′ u·lar·i′ zer.**

pop·u·lar·ly (pŏp′ yə lər lē) *adv-* generally; familiarly: *Louis is* popularly *known as* "*Slim.*"

popular vote *n-* total number of votes cast in a national election, as distinguished from the electoral vote.

pop·u·late (pŏp′ yə lāt′) *vt-* [**pop·u·lat·ed, pop·u·lat·ing**] **1** to fill or supply with inhabitants; to people: *to* populate *a frontier region.* **2** to inhabit: *Bands of Gypsies once* populated *this area.*

pop·u·la·tion (pŏp′ yə lā′ shən) *n-* **1** the total number of people living in a city, country, or region. **2** the people themselves or any one group of the people: *the adult* population. **3** the act or process of populating.

Pop·u·list (pŏp′ yə lĭst) *n-* member of a U.S. political party that was formed in 1891 and that advocated government control of utilities, an income tax, and the free coinage of gold and silver.

pop·u·lous (pŏp′ yə ləs) *adj-* having many people; thickly populated: *a* populous *community.* *—n-* **pop′ u·lous·ness.**

por·ce·lain (pôr′ sə lĭn) *n-* **1** fine, white, glazed earthenware so thin that light can be seen through it. **2** dishes, ornaments, or other articles made from this. *as **modifier**: a* porcelain *vase.*

porch (pôrch) *n-* **1** roofed and sometimes partly enclosed extension attached to the outside of a house; veranda. **2** roofed entrance to a building; portico.

por·cine (pòr′ sīn′, pôr′-) *adj-* of, relating to, or typical of a pig: *a* porcine *face.*

por·cu·pine (pòr′ kyə pīn′, pôr′-) *n-* any of various animals covered with stiff, bristly spines that serve as protection against attack. The porcupine is a rodent.

Porcupine, about 30 in. long

[1]pore (pôr) *n-* tiny hole or opening, such as those in the skin or the surface of a leaf, through which water, air, or perspiration can pass. [from French, from Latin **porus** meaning "opening," from Greek **poros.**] ***Homs-*** poor, pour.

[2]pore (pôr) *vi-* [**pored, por·ing**] to study with close attention; ponder; concentrate: *to* pore *over books.* [from Middle English **po(u)ren,** perhaps from Scandinavian **pora,** "to move or work slowly."] ***Homs-*** poor, pour.

por·gy (pòr′ gē, pôr′-) *n-* [*pl.* **porgy; porgies** (kinds of porgy)] any of several salt-water food fishes of Atlantic and Mediterranean waters.

por·i·fer·an (pôr ĭf′ ə rən, pə rĭf′-) *n-* a sponge.

pork (pôrk) *n-* the flesh of pigs, used for food.

pork·er (pôr′ kər) *n-* a pig, especially when fattened for use as food.

por·nog·ra·phy (pòr nŏg′ rə fē) *n-* grossly obscene writing, pictures, etc. ***—adj-*** **por′ no·graph′ ic** (-nə grăf′ ĭk).

por·os·i·ty (pôr ŏs′ ə tē, pə rŏs′-) *n-* [*pl.* **por·os·i·ties**] **1** condition of being porous: *the* porosity *of the soil.* **2** a pore or similar opening.

por·ous (pôr′ əs) *adj-* full of tiny holes through which a liquid may pass or be absorbed: *a* porous *sponge.* ***—adv-*** **por′ ous·ly.** *n-* **por′ ous·ness.**

por·phy·ry (pòr′ fə rē, pôr′-) *n-* [*pl.* **por·phy·ries**] rock consisting of a basic mass, such as granite, in which crystals of feldspar, quartz, etc., are imbedded. ***—adj-*** **por′ phy·rit′ ic** (-rĭt′ ĭk): *a* porphyritic *rock.*

por·poise (pòr′ pəs, pôr′-) *n-* any of various sea animals related to the whales and dolphins, such as the **common** or **harbor porpoise,** which travels in large schools.

Porpoise, 4—6 ft. long

por·ridge (pŏr′ ĭj, pòr′-) *n-* soft, thick food made by boiling oatmeal, lentils, etc., in water or milk.

por·ring·er (pŏr′ ĭn jər, pòr′-) *n-* small bowl, usually of metal, with a single handle, for cereal or other food.

[1]port (pôrt) *n-* **1** place where ships may dock and load or unload. **2** town or city having such a place. [from Old English, from Latin **portus** meaning "a haven."]

[2]port (pôrt) *n-* small window or other opening for a particular purpose. [from Old French **porte,** from Latin **porta,** "doorway; gateway," and related to **portal.**]

[3]port (pôrt) *n-* the left side of a ship as one faces the bow. ***adj-*** of, relating to, or located on this side of a ship: *a* port *cabin.* ***vt-*** to turn (the helm, rudder, etc.) to or toward this side of a ship. [of unknown origin.]

[4]**port** (pôrt) ***n-*** sweet, usually dark-red wine, originally from Portugal. [from **Oporto,** a city in Portugal.]

port·a·ble (pôr′ tə bəl) ***adj-*** such as can be carried conveniently: *a* portable *typewriter.*

por·tage (pôr′ tĭj) ***n-*** **1** the carrying of boats and goods overland from one river or lake to another. **2** the route taken. ***vt-*** **[por·taged, por·tag·ing]** to carry (boats and goods) overland from one river or lake to another: *to* portage *a canoe.* ***vi-***: *We* portaged *from the river to the lake.*

por·tal (pôr′ təl) ***n-*** gate; door; entrance: *the* portal *of the castle.*

portal-to-portal based on or including the whole time one is on the employer's property on a workday, rather than the time one actually works.

port·cul·lis (pôrt kŭl′ əs) ***n-*** heavy grating that can be lowered to close the entrance of a castle or fort.

Portcullis

porte-co·chere (pôrt′ kō shĕr′) ***n-*** **1** large gateway through which a carriage may drive into a courtyard. **2** extension of a porch roof over a driveway to permit carriages to stop under cover.

Porte-cochère

por·tend (pôr tĕnd′) ***n-*** to give warning or sign of; foreshadow: *Ancient sailors believed that a certain bird following their ship would* portend *danger.*

por·tent (pôr′ tĕnt) ***n-*** something that foretells or hints at a coming event; a warning, especially of trouble; omen: *The witchdoctor told of signs and* portents.

por·ten·tous (pôr tĕn′ təs) ***adj-*** **1** foreshadowing evil; threatening: *a* portentous *dream.* **2** remarkable; extraordinary: *a* portentous *event.* ***—adv-*** **por·ten′ tous·ly.** ***n-*** **por·ten′ tous·ness.**

[1]**por·ter** (pôr′ tər) ***n-*** **1** person hired to carry baggage at a depot, airport, or hotel. **2** attendant in the parlor car or sleeping car of a train. [from Old French **port(e)our,** from Latin **portātor,** from **portāre** meaning "to carry."]

[2]**por·ter** (pôr′ tər) ***n-*** doorkeeper. [from Old French **portier,** from Latin **porta** meaning "gate; door."]

[3]**por·ter** (pôr′ tər) *Brit.* ***n-*** heavy, dark-brown beer. [shortened from **porter's ale,** from [2]**porter.** It was once drunk mostly by porters.]

por·ter·house (pôr′ tər hous′) ***n-*** choice cut of beefsteak having considerable tenderloin and a T-shaped bone. Also **porterhouse steak.**

port·fo·li·o (pôrt fō′ lē ō) ***n-*** [*pl.* **port·fo·li·os**] **1** case for carrying loose papers, drawings, etc.; briefcase. **2** office of a minister of the government: *Mr. Allen accepted a* portfolio *in the new administration.* **3** all the stocks, bonds, etc., held by one person or investing institution.

Por·tia (pôr′ shə) ***n-*** in Shakespeare's "Merchant of Venice," the heroine who impersonates a lawyer and contests Shylock's claim.

por·ti·co (pôr′ tə kō′) ***n-*** [*pl.* **por·ti·coes** or **por·ti·cos**] entrance porch having its roof supported by columns.

Portico

por·tiere (pôr tē ĕr′) ***n-*** curtain or drapery hung across a doorway.

por·tion (pôr′ shən) ***n-*** **1** piece or part of something. **2** serving of food; a helping. **3** share of an estate left an heir: *a widow's* portion. ***vt-*** to divide into shares: *Mary* portioned *the candy evenly among us.*

portion out to distribute: *Jack* portioned out *the apples.*

port·ly (pôrt′ lē) ***adj-*** **[port·li·er, port·li·est]** fat; stout: *a* portly *passenger.* ***—n-*** **port′ li·ness.**

port·man·teau (pôrt măn′ tō) ***n-*** [*pl.* **port·man·teaus** or **port·man·teaux** (-tōz)] suitcase; valise.

por·trait (pôr′ trāt′, -trət) ***n-*** **1** painting, drawing, photograph, statue, etc., of a person, especially of the face and upper body. **2** picture in words.

por·trai·ture (pôr′ trə chər, -tyŏŏr′) ***n-*** **1** art or practice of making likenesses of people. **2** portrait or likeness.

por·tray (pôr trā′) ***vt-*** **1** to make a picture, carving, etc., of: *The artist* portrayed *the sunny field in brilliant color.* **2** to describe: *The author* portrayed *the village as a delightful place.* **3** to play (a part) on the stage or screen. ***—n-*** **por·tray′ er.**

por·tray·al (pôr trā′ əl) ***n-*** **1** a portraying: *She is weak in the* portrayal *of tragic roles.* **2** portrait or any representation: *a* portrayal *of life on a dude ranch.*

Por·tu·guese (pôr′ chə gēz′) ***n-*** [*pl.* **Por·tu·guese**] **1** a native or inhabitant of Portugal. **2** the language of Portugal and Brazil. ***adj-***: *a* Portuguese *ship.*

por·tu·la·ca (pôr′ chə lăk′ ə) ***n-*** any of various plants with fleshy leaves, and flowers that open only in sunlight; especially, a hardy, cultivated plant with variously colored, showy flowers.

[1]**pose** (pōz) ***vi-*** **[posed, pos·ing]** **1** to take and hold a certain position of the body and expression of the face, especially so as to be photographed or painted. **2** to put on a false appearance or character: *to* pose *as a detective.* ***vt-*** **1** to cause or present (a difficulty, problem, question, etc.). **2** to place in a certain position or attitude: *He* posed *the model in a chair.* ***n-*** **1** bodily position; posture: *a model's* pose. **2** something done to fool or impress others; deceptive appearance; pretense: *His thoughtfulness is a* pose. [from Old French **poser** meaning "to put into position," partly from Late Latin **pausare,** "pause," and partly from Latin **positus,** "placed; fixed."]

pose as to pretend to be: *He* posed as *a spy.*

[2]**pose** (pōz) ***vt-*** **[posed, pos·ing]** to puzzle or perplex with a difficult question or problem. [shortened from archaic **appose,** "to argue against," influenced by **oppose.**]

Po·sei·don (pə sī′ dən) ***n-*** in Greek mythology, the god of the sea. He is identified with the Roman Neptune.

[1]**pos·er** (pō′ zər) ***n-*** person who poses. [from [1]**pose.**]

[2]**pos·er** (pō′ zər) ***n-*** very baffling question or problem. [from [2]**pose.**]

pos·eur (pō zûr′) ***n-*** person who takes on some manner, appearance, etc., to fool and impress others.

po·si·tion (pə zĭsh′ ən) ***n-*** **1** place where a thing or person stands or is: *I was in a* position *to see the stage.* **2** correct or proper place: *The director told us to take our* positions. **3** posture: *an uncomfortable* position. **4** job; situation: *He has a good* position *at the bank.* **5** social standing or rank: *a high* position *in the community.* **6** way of looking at or thinking about a subject; opinion: *What is your* position *on the question of a longer school year?* ***vt-*** to put or situate in a particular place: *Let's* position *the microphone here.* ***—n-*** **po·si′ tion·er.**

pos·i·tive (pŏz′ ə tĭv) ***adj-*** **1** clearly stated; definite; also, leaving no doubt: *a* positive *assertion of innocence;* positive *proof.* **2** sure; certain: *Are you* positive *that Fred will call?* **3** practical; constructive; real: *He gave us* positive *help.* **4** showing agreement; affirmative: *a* positive *answer to our request.* **5** showing the existence of what is looked for or thought to be present: *a* positive *reaction to the allergy test for eggs.* **6** *Mathematics* of, or having to do with a number that is greater than zero. 7 of, having to do with, or charged with the kind of electricity made by rubbing a glass rod with silk. ***n-*** **1** photographic print made from a negative and showing light and dark in their normal places rather than reversed. **2** *Grammar* (also **positive degree**) the common form of an adjective or adverb before being inflected for the comparative or superlative degree. ***—n-*** **pos′ i·tive·ness.**

positive charge ***n-*** **1** electrical property or condition of an object due to an excess of protons over electrons. By convention, a glass rod rubbed with silk has a positive charge. **2** *Physics* (1) property of an elementary particle that causes the particle's path in a magnetic field to bend in a direction opposite to an electron's path through the same field. (2) a positive elementary charge. See also *charge* and *negative charge*.

pos·i·tive·ly (pŏs′ ə tĭv′ lē) ***adv-*** **1** in a positive manner. **2** (*often* pŏs′ ə tĭv′ lē) utterly and undoubtedly.

pos·i·tron (pŏz′ ə trŏn′) *Physics* ***n-*** the positively charged antiparticle corresponding to the electron.

poss. 1 possessive. **2** possession.

pos·se (pŏs′ ē) ***n-*** **1** group of men authorized by a sheriff to assist in carrying out the law. **2** group of people temporarily organized to carry out a search.

pos·sess (pə zĕs′) ***vt-*** **1** to have; own: *King Midas* possessed *much gold.* **2** to occupy; control: *At one time the Spanish* possessed *Florida.* **3** to influence strongly: *I don't know what* possesses *him to act like that!* ***—n-*** **pos·ses′ sor:** *She is the* possessor *of many jewels.*

pos·sessed (pə zĕst′) ***adj-*** in the complete control of some emotion, desire, or force, especially of a supernatural power: *They screamed as if* possessed.

pos·ses·sion (pə zĕsh′ ən) ***n-*** **1** ownership; control and custody: *The pirate tried to get* possession *of the treasure.* **2** something owned or possessed: *There were few* possessions *she prized as much as the old locket.* **3** control; occupancy: *The new cook took full* possession *of our kitchen.* **4** land under control of a government, but not officially part of that government's national territory: *Guam is a* possession *of the United States.* **5** a controlling by some force, especially a supernatural power.

pos·ses·sive (pə zĕs′ ĭv) ***adj-*** **1** having or relating to a strong desire to own or keep: *a* possessive *man*; *a* possessive *interest in jewelry.* **2** *Grammar* showing possession: *the* possessive *case*; *a* possessive *pronoun.* ***n-*** *Grammar* the possessive case or a word in the possessive case. See [1]*case.* ***—adv-*** **pos·ses′ sive·ly.** ***n-*** **pos·ses′ sive·ness.**

possessive adjective *Grammar* ***n-*** term usually applied to a personal or relative pronoun in the possessive case when the thing possessed is expressed. Examples: *John gave me* his *book. The boy* whose *hat fell off won the race.*

possessive case See [1]*case.*

possessive pronoun *Grammar* ***n-*** any of the pronouns that show possession and can be used in place of noun phrases. They are "mine," "ours," "yours," "his," "hers," "its," "theirs," "whose." Example: *This dog is* yours; *that one is* mine.

pos·si·bil·i·ty (pŏs′ ə bĭl′ ə tē) ***n-*** [*pl.* **pos·si·bil·i·ties**] **1** chance; likelihood: *There's no* possibility *of his coming now.* **2** something that might happen: *Failure is a* possibility. **3** condition of being possible: *Let's not confuse* possibility *with probability.* **4 possibilities** good or desirable results: *Your plan has good* possibilities.

pos·si·ble (pŏs′ ə bəl) ***adj-*** **1** within the limits of what can be done or what can happen: *Specialized work is* possible *only if you have the right training. It is not* possible *to get to our cabin without a car.* **2** worth considering; available among others: *a* possible *candidate*; *a* possible *choice.* ***n-*** *Informal* **1** something that is worth considering: *That idea is a* possible. **2 possibles** small items of necessary equipment for a hunter, trapper, etc. ***—adv-*** **pos′ si·bly:** *We may* possibly *move next April.*

pos·sum (pŏs′ əm) opossum.

play possum to pretend to be helpless or dead.

[1]**post** (pōst) ***n-*** upright piece of timber, metal, stone, etc., used as a marker or support for something: *a sign* post; *a lamp* post; *the starting* post *of a racetrack.* ***vt-*** **1** to display for public notice, especially on a wall or bulletin board: *to* post *the honor roll*; *to* post *an eviction notice.* **2** to provide (money) so as to insure or encourage some special outcome: *to* post *a reward*; *to* post *bail*; *to* post *a bond.* **3** to close (a place) to the public by means of signs or notices. **4** to announce (a name) publicly on or as on a list: *The ship was* posted *as lost.* [from Old English **post,** from Latin **postis** meaning "a prop; something placed or fixed."]

[2]**post** (pōst) ***n-*** **1** the mail or delivery of mail: *It came to me by* post. **2** in earlier times, one of a number of riders placed at regularly spaced stations along a road or route, each of whom carried mail to the next station or stage. ***vt-*** **1** to put (a letter, package, etc.), into the mail: *I* posted *the letter in Boston.* **2** to inform (someone) of the latest news, events, etc.: *I* posted *him yesterday about what had happened.* **3** to write down (figures, accounts, grades, etc.) in a ledger or other record more permanent than the first place of entry. **4** to transfer figures, accounts, grades, etc., into: *to* post *a ledger.* ***vi-*** **1** to travel with speed: *to* post *through the streets.* **2** to rise rhythmically from the saddle according to the motion of a horse, especially when trotting. [from the same French word as [3]**post.** The mail was once forwarded by riders between relay stations or "posts."]

[3]**post** (pōst) ***n-*** **1** place where a person is stationed or assigned for duty. **2** military camp or station: *Most of the officers live off the* post. **3** position of trust: *His grandfather held a* post *in a large bank.* **4** local unit or chapter of a military veteran's organization. **5** trading post. ***vt-*** to station or assign: *The commander* posted *him to duty in Japan.* [from French **poste** meaning "a (military) station or stage in a road," from Latin **pos(i)tum,** meaning literally "placed."]

post- *prefix* after; coming after: *to* post*date*; post*war.*

post·age (pōs′ tĭj) ***n-*** cost of sending something by mail, usually paid by buying an official **postage stamp** and affixing it to the card, letter, or package.

postage meter ***n-*** office machine that prints the amount of postage required on pieces of outgoing mail. It can print only as much postage as has been previously paid for at the post office.

post·al (pōs′ təl) ***adj-*** relating to mail or the mail system.

post·card (pōst′ kärd′) ***n-*** mailing card, often with a picture on one side. Also **postal card.**

post chaise (shāz) ***n-*** in earlier times, a carriage with fast horses, in which mail and passengers were carried along regular routes more quickly than by coach.

post·date (pōst′ dāt′) ***vt-*** [**post·dat·ed, post·dat·ing**] to mark on or assign to (a check, document, etc.,) a date later than the actual date.

post·ed (pōs′ təd) ***adj-*** informed: *Keep us* posted.

post·er (pōs′ tər) ***n-*** **1** placard, sign, etc., by which something is advertised or announced. **2** billposter.

pos·te·ri·or (pŏs têr′ē ər) *adj-* 1 later in time; subsequent (to). 2 towards the rear; hinder. *n-* buttocks.
pos·ter·i·ty (pŏs tĕr′ə tē) *n-* 1 future generations: *If we act wisely,* posterity *will praise us.* 2 all the descendants of a person.
pos·tern (pŏs′tərn, pō′stərn) *n-* back door or gate.
post exchange *Military n-* government store where food and merchandise are sold to members of the armed forces at reduced prices.
post·grad·u·ate (pōst′grăj′o͞o ət) *adj-* having to do with or engaging in studies after graduation from a school or college, especially after having an advanced degree: *Dr. Lansky is taking a* postgraduate *course in pediatrics. n-* person pursuing such studies.
post·haste (pōst′hāst′) *adv-* with great speed; quickly.
post·hole (pōst′hōl′) *n-* hole for a post, especially a fence post.
post·hu·mous (pŏs′chə məs, -tyo͞o məs) *adj-* 1 born after the death of the father: *a* posthumous *child.* 2 published after the death of an author: *a* posthumous *book.* 3 arising or occurring after one's death: *the musician's* posthumous *fame.* —*adv-* **post′hu·mous·ly.**
post·hyp·not·ic (pōst′hĭp nŏt′ĭk) *adj-* of or having to do with the time following a hypnotic trance: *a* posthypnotic *suggestion.*
pos·til·ion or **pos·til·lion** (pō stĭl′yən) *n-* person who rides the left-hand horse of a carriage team to guide it.
post·lude (pōst′lo͞od′) *n-* 1 closing piece of music, especially an organ voluntary after a church service. 2 anything written, spoken, played, or happening at the end, as distinguished from prelude and interlude.
post·man (pōst′mən) *n-* [*pl.* **post·men**] letter carrier.
post·mark (pōst′märk′) *n-* official mark stamped upon mail to cancel stamps and to show the place and date of mailing. *vt-* to stamp with such a mark.
post·mas·ter (pōst′măs′tər) *n-* the director of a post office. *n- fem.* **post′mis′tress** (pōst′mĭs′trəs).
Postmaster General *n-* the title of the person appointed to head the Postal Service.
post·mor·tem (pōst′mör′təm, -môr′təm) *adj-* 1 happening after death. 2 happening after something puzzling, unsuccessful, or unpleasant: *a* postmortem *discussion after a test. n-* 1 postmortem examination. 2 any inquiry into an event that has just taken place.
postmortem examination *n-* a medical examination of a body after death to find the cause of death or to learn more about the disease that caused death; autopsy.
post·na·sal (pōst′nā′zəl) *adj-* situated or happening in the head and throat passages behind the nose.
post office *n-* 1 office for the collection, sorting, and delivery of mail. 2 department responsible for the mails.
post·op·er·a·tive (pōst′ŏp′ər ə tĭv′) *adj-* happening after a surgical operation: *good* postoperative *care.*
post·paid (pōst′pād′) *adj-* having the postage already paid: *a* postpaid *return envelope.*
post·pone (pōst pōn′) *vt-* [**post·poned, post·pon·ing**] to delay; put off to a later time: *The principal* postponed *the school picnic.* —*adj-* **post·pon′a·ble.** *n-* **post·pone′ment:** *the* postponement *of the picnic.*
post road *n-* a road that was built to carry mail.
post·script (pōst′skrĭpt′) *n-* 1 message added to a letter after the signature. *Abbr.* P.S. 2 material added at the end of a book, article, etc.
pos·tu·lant (pŏs′chə lənt) *n-* 1 person who wishes to enter a religious order and is taking the first step before being admitted as a novice. 2 person taking the first step in becoming a candidate for Holy Orders in the Episcopal Church.
pos·tu·late (pŏs′chə lāt′) *vt-* [**pos·tu·lat·ed, pos·tu·lat·ing**] to state or infer (something that is not or cannot be proven); to claim the truth of: *To tell someone to do a thing* postulates *that it can be done. n-* (usually pos′chə lət) something assumed in order to account for or lead to something else; axiom; premise.
pos·ture (pŏs′chər) *n-* 1 way a person holds his body; carriage: *Poor* posture *is unhealthy and unsightly.* 2 position or pose of the body: *to assume an awkward* posture. 3 attitude; frame of mind: *a* posture *of distress. vi-* [**pos·tured, pos·tur·ing**] to take a certain bodily position, especially a ridiculous or affected one. —*adj-* **pos′tur·al:** *a* postural *defect.*
post·voc·al·ic (pōst′vō kăl′ĭk) *adj-* coming immediately after a vowel.
post·war (pōst′wör′) *adj-* coming after a war.
po·sy (pō′zē) *n-* [*pl.* **po·sies**] flower or bunch of flowers.
pot (pŏt) *n-* 1 china or earthenware container: *a flower* pot. 2 metal or earthenware cooking vessel; kettle: *She put the bean* pot *in the oven.* 3 (also **pot′ful′**) the amount a pot will hold: *Ralph made a* pot *of soup.* 4 in poker and other games, the money at stake in any given hand: *to win a large* pot. *vt-* [**pot·ted, pot·ting**] 1 to transplant into a flowerpot. 2 to preserve (meat) in a china or earthenware container or jar.

keep the pot boiling to meet living expenses. **go to pot** to go to ruin: *The store* went to pot.

po·ta·ble (pō′tə bəl) *adj-* drinkable.
po·ta·bles (pō′tə bəlz) *n- pl.* beverages; drinks.
pot·ash (pŏt′ăsh′) *n-* white, alkaline compound of potassium and oxygen, used in making soap, glass, fertilizers, etc.
po·tas·si·um (pə tăs′ē əm) *n-* a soft, silver-white metal element used in making explosives, soap, fertilizer, etc. Symbol K, At. No. 19, At. Wt. 39.102.
potassium nitrate *n-* white, crystalline compound (KNO_3) used in fertilizers, gunpowder, and in medicine; saltpeter.
potassium permanganate *n-* a dark-purple compound ($KMnO_4$) that is a strong oxidizing agent and is used as a bleach, germicide, etc.
po·ta·to (pə tā′tō) *n-* [*pl.* **po·ta·toes**] 1 (also **Irish potato**) rounded tuber growing underground from the roots of a plant native to tropical America, widely used as a vegetable and a source of flour and starch. 2 the plant itself. 3 sweet potato. *as modifier: a* potato *pancake.*

Potato leaf, tuber, and flower

potato beetle or **potato bug** *n-* beetle with black and yellow stripes, that eats the leaves of potatoes and other plants.
potato chip *n-* thin slice of potato that has been immersed in very hot fat or oil and fried crisp.
Pot·a·wot·o·mi (pŏt′ə wŏt′ə mē) *n-* [*pl.* **Pot·a·wot·o·mis,** also **Pot·a·wot·o·mi**] 1 one of a tribe of American Indians who formerly lived along the lower shores of Lake Michigan. 2 the Algonquian language of these Indians. *adj-: the* Potawotomi *cone-shaped lodges.*
pot·bel·ly (pŏt′bĕl′ē) *n-* 1 a protruding belly. 2 person who has such a belly. —*adj-* **pot′bel′lied.**
potbelly stove or **potbellied stove** *n-* upright wood- or coal-burning stove with bulging sides.
pot·boil·er (pŏt′boi′lər) *n-* a literary or artistic work, often inferior, done merely to earn money.

po·tent (pō′tənt) ***adj-*** 1 strong; very effective: *a* potent *medicine.* 2 having authority or power: *a* potent *ruler.* **—*n-* po′ten·cy:** *the* potency *of their political organization.* ***adv-*** **po′tent·ly.**

po·ten·tate (pō′tən tāt′) ***n-*** powerful monarch or ruler.

po·ten·tial (pə tĕn′shəl) ***adj-*** capable of coming into existence or being developed; possible but not actual: *Our mineral deposits are a great source of* potential *wealth.* ***n-*** 1 qualities that can be developed; possibilities; capabilities: *A good student always tries to develop his or her* potential. 2 in electricity, the charge on a body in relation to a reference point or region considered to be at zero potential, such as the earth. **—*adv-* po·ten′tial·ly:** *She is* potentially *a great singer.*

potential energy ***n-*** the stored energy an object has by reason of its position or condition. Water in the reservoir behind a dam has potential energy.

po·ten·ti·al·i·ty (pə tĕn′shē ăl′ə tē) ***n-*** [*pl.* **po·ten·ti·al·i·ties**] 1 possibility of developing, especially successfully. 2 characteristic or condition that may develop in a particular direction: *a* potentiality *for good*; *a* potentiality *for violence.*

po·ten·ti·om·e·ter (pə tĕn′shē ŏm′ə tər) ***n-*** in electricity, a device for measuring electromotive forces.

poth·er (pŏth′ər) ***n-*** confused or noisy excitement; fuss. ***vi-*** to make a stir or fuss. ***vt-*** to worry; bother.

pot·herb (pŏt′ûrb′) ***n-*** 1 any leafy green vegetable, such as spinach, that is cooked and used as food. 2 any herb, such as thyme, that is used to season cooked food.

pot·hole (pŏt′hōl′) ***n-*** 1 deep, round depression in the rock bed of a stream. 2 any deep, round hole or pit, especially one in the surface of a street or road.

pot·hook (pŏt′ho͝ok′) ***n-*** 1 S-shaped iron hook for hanging or carrying pots over an open fire. 2 hooked stroke in handwriting.

po·tion (pō′shən) ***n-*** a drink, especially one with magical powers.

pot·latch (pŏt′lăch′) ***n-*** among various Indian tribes of the Northwest, a ceremony in which property is given away, or sometimes ostentatiously destroyed, as a display of wealth. [American word from Chinook Indian **potshatl** meaning "gift."]

pot·luck (pŏt′lŭk′) ***n-*** whatever meal or food is available for a family or guest without special preparation.

pot·pie (pŏt′pī′) ***n-*** pie made in a deep dish, usually containing meat or fish and vegetables, and having a crust only on the top.

pot·pour·ri (pō po͞o rē′) ***n-*** 1 mixture; medley: *a* potpourri *of songs from musical comedies.* 2 mixture of dried flowers and spices used to perfume a room.

pot roast ***n-*** meat, usually beef, browned in a pot and simmered in a small amount of water until tender.

pot·sherd (pŏt′shûrd′) ***n-*** piece of broken pottery, especially one dug up at an archeological site.

pot·shot (pŏt′shŏt′) ***n-*** 1 shot taken to kill a bird or animal for food, in spite of the rules of sport. 2 any shot fired at easy range and without careful aim: *to take* potshots *at tin cans on the fence.* 3 accusation, criticism, etc., aimed at an opponent: *The candidates took* potshots *at each other.*

pot·tage (pŏt′ĭj) ***n-*** thick soup or broth.

pot·ted (pŏt′əd) ***adj-*** 1 kept in or placed in a pot: *a* potted *plant.* 2 cooked or preserved in a pot: *a* potted *stew;* potted *peach preserves.*

¹pot·ter (pŏt′ər) ***n-*** person who makes pots, dishes, etc., of clay. [from Old English **pottere,** from **pot.**]

²pot·ter (pŏt′ər) ***vi-*** to work lazily or without much purpose: *to* potter *around in the garden.* [from Middle English **poteren,** probably a Dutch word.] **—*n-* pot′ter·er.**

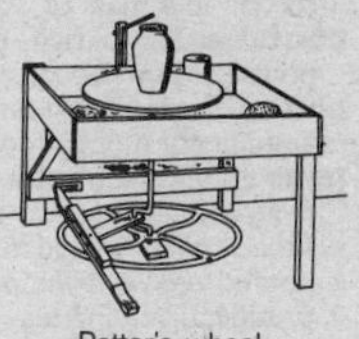

Potter's wheel

potter's field ***n-*** plot of public land used for burying paupers, unidentified persons, and criminals.

potter's wheel ***n-*** horizontal rotating disc, including the spindle and framework that turns and holds it, used by a potter to shape round dishes, vases, etc.

pot·ter·y (pŏt′ə rē) ***n-*** [*pl.* **pot·ter·ies**] 1 pots, dishes, vases, etc., molded from moistened clay and usually hardened in ovens and kilns. 2 place where such things are made. 3 the art of a potter.

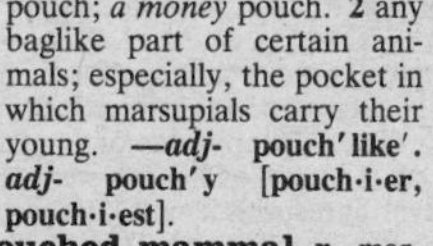

Pottery

pouch (pouch) ***n-*** 1 small bag or sack of any kind: *a mail* pouch; *a money* pouch. 2 any baglike part of certain animals; especially, the pocket in which marsupials carry their young. **—*adj-* pouch′like′.** ***adj-*** **pouch′y** [**pouch·i·er, pouch·i·est**].

pouched mammal ***n-*** marsupial.

poul·tice (pōl′təs) ***n-*** soft, warm, and moist mixture of flour, flaxseed, mustard, etc., put on some part of the body to heal or to relieve pain. ***vt-*** [**poul·ticed, poul·tic·ing**]: *to* poultice *a boil on the neck.*

poul·try (pōl′trē) ***n-*** domestic fowl, such as chickens, turkeys, ducks, and geese. **—*n-* poul′try·man.**

¹pounce (pouns) ***vi-*** [**pounced, pounc·ing**] to spring suddenly or unexpectedly: *The cat* pounced *on the rolling ball of yarn.* ***n-*** sudden, swooping attack. [from an earlier meaning of "the swoop of a hawk; the claws of a hawk," probably from Old French **ponce,** "a fist," ultimately from Latin **punctum,** "a point; pointed tool."]

²pounce (pouns) ***n-*** 1 fine powder, such as powdered cuttlebone, used in earlier times to dry freshly powdered ink. 2 dark powder used to transfer patterns or designs through perforated stencils. [from French **ponce,** from Latin **pumex** meaning "pumice."]

¹pound (pound) ***n-*** 1 in ordinary weight (avoirdupois), a measure equal to 16 ounces. 2 in troy weight, a measure equal to 12 ounces. 3 (also **pound sterling**) the basic unit of money in the United Kingdom. 4 the unit of money in several other countries. [from Old English **pund,** from Latin **pondo,** "by weight."]

²pound (pound) ***n-*** place where animals, especially stray animals, are kept: *a dog* pound. [from Old English **pund,** "an enclosure," and closely related to **pond.**]

³pound (pound) ***vt-*** 1 to beat; strike (something) with force: *to* pound *a nail into the wall.* 2 to crush into small pieces of powder: *to* pound *kernels of grain into meal.* ***vi-*** 1 to deal blows; beat heavily or steadily: *Waves* pounded *against the seashore.* 2 to walk or run heavily: *The cattle* pounded *along the trail.* ***n-*** heavy blow. [from Middle English **pounen,** from Old English **pūnian meaning** "to crush or bruise (especially with a pestle)."]

pound·al (poun′dəl) *n-* unit of force equal to the force that will cause an acceleration of 1 foot per second per second in a mass of 1 pound.

pound cake *n-* rich, plain cake, originally made from a pound each of flour, sugar, and butter, and many eggs.

pound-foolish (pound′fo͞o′lĭsh) *adj-* spending large amounts of money foolishly.

pour (pôr) *vt-* to cause to flow in a stream: *to* pour *milk from a pitcher.* *vi-* 1 to stream: *Water* poured *from the broken pipe.* 2 to go in or out in large numbers: *The pupils* poured *out onto the playground.* 3 to rain heavily. 4 to preside at serving tea, cakes, etc., at a reception or other social occasion. *Homs-* poor, pore. *—n-* **pour′er.**

pour out to tell in detail freely: *to* pour out *a story.*

pout (pout) *vi-* to push out or pucker the lips in sullenness, displeasure, etc. *n-* sullen or sulky expression made in such a way. *—adj-* **pout′y** [**pout·i·er, pout·i·est**]: *a* pouty *expression.*

pout·er (pou′tər) *n-* 1 person who pouts. 2 pigeon that puffs out its crop and stands and walks erectly.

pov·er·ty (pŏv′ər tē) *n-* 1 lack of money or the necessities of life. 2 lack of something needed or wanted; poorness: *the* poverty *of the soil.*

pov·er·ty-strick·en (pŏv′ər tē strĭk′ ən) *adj-* extremely poor; destitute.

pow·der (pou′dər) *n-* 1 any dry material in fine particles; especially, a medicine or beauty preparation in such form: *talcum* powder; *tooth* powder. 2 gunpowder or another finely divided explosive. *vt-* 1 to make into fine particles: *to* powder *sugar.* 2 to cover and sprinkle with or as with fine particles: *to* powder *toast with cinnamon.* 3 to use fine particles on (the face and body). *vi-* to be reduced to very small particles: *Talc* powders *easily.*

take a powder *Slang* to run away; to make a quick getaway.

P.O.W. or **POW** prisoner of war.

powder horn *n-* horn of a cow or other animal, fashioned to carry and funnel gunpowder.

Powder horn

powder puff *n-* soft pad used for applying powder to the skin.

powder room *n-* rest room for women.

pow·der·y (pou′də rē) *adj-* 1 like powder; in the form of powder: *A* powdery *snow is good to ski on.* 2 covered or sprinkled with any kind of powder: *The bee's legs were* powdery *with pollen.* 3 easily crumbled or reduced to powder: *a* powdery *stone.*

pow·er (pou′ər) *n-* 1 strength; vigor: *The pitcher had plenty of* power *but little control. The* power *of her argument won many to her side.* 2 ability to act or do something: *They did everything in their* power *to win the game.* 3 authority to do or have done: *the* powers *of Congress.* 4 control of a government: *in* power; *out of* power. 5 an important or strong person, group, or nation: *At one time the Roman Empire was a world* power. 6 magnifying capacity of a lens: *the* power *of a microscope.* 7 *Physics* rate of doing work, measured by the amount of work that can be done in a given time. 8 *Mathematics* (1) the number of times, indicated by an exponent, that the base of a term is a factor of the term. The power of the term x^4 is 4, which is the number of times that x is a factor of $x^4 (x \times x \times x \times x = x^4)$. (2) number that can be shown by means of a base and exponent. For example, 9 is the second power of 3 because the statement $9 = 3^2$ is a true statement. 9 energy or force that is or can be applied to work: *The house is run by solar* power. *as modifier: a* power *supply; a* power *lawn mower.* *vt-* to provide with mechanical or electrical power.

pow·er·boat (pou′ər bōt′) *n-* motorboat.

power brakes *n- pl.* brakes on a motor vehicle that use engine power to increase the force of the driver's pressure on the brake pedal.

power dive *n-* airplane dive that is accelerated by the power of the engine or engines.

power-driv·en (pou′ər drĭv′ən) *adj-* run by an engine or a motor: *a* power-driven *saw.*

pow·er·ful (pou′ər fəl) *adj-* having great power, strength, or influence: *a* powerful *engine.* *—adv-* **pow′er·ful·ly.**

pow·er·house (pou′ər hous′) *n-* 1 place where power is generated, especially electrical power. 2 *Slang* powerful person.

pow·er·less (pou′ər ləs) *adj-* not having power or ability to act, resist, or help; weak; helpless. *—adv-* **pow′er·less·ly.** *n-* **pow′er·less·ness.**

power of attorney *n-* in law, a written statement authorizing a person to act as the attorney or business agent of someone else.

power pack *n-* compact unit used to provide power for an electrical or electronic device, often by converting one type of electrical energy into another.

power plant *n-* 1 engine or other source of power, along with its installation and accessories. 2 powerhouse.

power politics *n-* international politics based on the threat of military or economic force.

power shovel *n-* excavating machine having a toothed, box-shaped or bucket-shaped digging device at the end of a movable beam.

power steering *n-* steering system of a car, truck, etc., that lessens the driver's effort by taking power from the engine.

power take-off *n-* device on the engine or gear box of a truck, tractor, boat, etc., that permits engine power to be used for driving other machines.

power tool *n-* saw, drill, hammer, or other tool driven by a motor, especially by an electric motor.

Pow·ha·tan (pou hăt′ən) *n-* [*pl.* **Pow·ha·tans,** also **Pow·ha·tan**] 1 a member of a tribe of Algonquian Indians who lived in the tidewater section of Virginia and were led by Chief Powhatan, the father of Pocohontas. 2 a confederacy of thirty tribes of these Indians. *adj- the* Powhatan *village.*

pow·wow (pou′wou′) *n-* 1 ceremonial feast or dance held by North American Indians to gain religious or magical aid for a hunt, war, etc. 2 North American Indian priest or medicine man. 3 *Informal* any meeting or gathering held in order to confer or discuss. *vi-* to hold such a ceremony or discussion.

pox (pŏks) *n-* 1 disease marked by an eruption, or breaking out on the skin. 2 syphilis.

pp pianissimo.

pp. pages.

p.p. past participle.

P.P. 1 parcel post. 2 postpaid.

pr. 1 pair. 2 price.

Pr symbol for praseodymium.

P.R. 1 Puerto Rico. 2 proportional representation.

prac·ti·ca·ble (prăk′tĭ kə bəl) *adj-* such as can be done, practiced, or used: *a* practicable *plan.* *—n-* **prac′ti·ca·bil′i·ty:** *The* practicability *of Jack's plan was questionable.* *adv-* **prac′ti·ca·bly.**

►PRACTICABLE usually refers to plans and procedures and the possibility of carrying them out successfully. PRACTICAL refers to persons who are sensible and realistic, or things, actions, etc., that are sensible and continuously useful: *It is* practical *to put money aside for a rainy day, but many persons do not find this plan to be a* practicable *one.*

prac·ti·cal (prăk′tĭ kəl) ***adj-*** **1** having to do with or gained by experience, action, or use: *a* practical *knowledge of the apparatus.* **2** sensible and realistic: *a* practical *arrangement for dividing the property.* **3** preferring or tending to act or do things rather than to think or daydream about them. ***—n-*** **prac′ti·cal′i·ty.**

►For usage note see PRACTICABLE.

practical joke ***n-*** trick played on someone in fun.

prac·ti·cal·ly (prăk′tĭk ə lē) ***adv-*** **1** in a practical manner; through actual experience or practice: *He knows machinery both* practically *and theoretically.* **2** in fact though not in name; virtually: *He is,* practically, *a dictator.* **3** almost: *It is* practically *impossible to do.*

practical nurse ***n-*** nurse who lacks the training of a registered nurse and is ordinarily not given as much responsibility in caring for the sick.

prac·tice (prăk′tĭs) ***vt-*** **[prac·ticed, prac·tic·ing]** (in senses 3 and 4 considered intransitive when the direct object is implied but not expressed) **1** to put into actual use: *Always* practice *what you preach.* **2** to do as a rule; do regularly: *He* practiced *charity toward all.* **3** to work at as a profession: *to* practice *law.* **4** to perform repeatedly in order to learn: *to* practice *pitching a baseball.* ***n-*** **1** custom; habit: *Being cautious is a good* practice. **2** actual use or performance of something: *He was skilled in theory but not in* practice. **3** repeated performance for the purpose of learning: *After much* practice *he learned to do the card trick.* **4** the exercise of a profession: *the* practice *of law.* **5** the work, list of patients, etc., of a doctor: *He took over a good* practice *from the older doctor.* *as* ***modifier***: *a few* practice *throws; a* practice *session.* ***—n-*** **prac′tic·er.**

prac·ticed or **prac·tised** (prăk′tĭst) ***adj-*** highly experienced: *a* practiced *carpenter.*

prac·tise (prăk′tĭs) ***vt- & vi-*** **[prac·tised, prac·tis·ing]** to practice.

prac·ti·tion·er (prăk tĭsh′ə nər) ***n-*** person engaged in a profession, especially medicine.

prae·tor (prē′tər) ***n-*** in ancient Rome, a magistrate who acted as judge, general, and administrator.

prae·tor·i·an (prē tôr′ē ən) ***adj-*** **1** of or relating to a praetor. **2** of, relating to, or constituting the bodyguard of a Roman emperor.

prag·mat·ic (prăg măt′ĭk) ***adj-*** **1** concerned with practical results rather than with theories, rules, and general ideas: *a* pragmatic *business manager.* **2** of or having to do with the philosophy of pragmatism. Also **prag·mat′i·cal.** ***—adv-*** **prag·mat′i·cal·ly.**

prag·ma·tism (prăg′mə tĭz′əm) ***n-*** **1** philosophy of the 19th and 20th centuries which regards practical results as the only important test of the truth of an idea or belief. **2** tendency to be more concerned with practical results than with theories, rules, and general ideas. ***—n-*** **prag′ma·tist.**

prai·rie (prâr′ē) ***n-*** level or rolling grassland without trees, but in the natural state having thick, tall grass. [American word from French **prairie,** "meadow."]

prairie chicken ***n-*** large brown and white grouse of the prairies of the Mississippi River Valley.

prairie dog ***n-*** burrowing animal that is related to the woodchuck and the ground squirrel and has a whistling bark. Prairie dogs live in "towns" made up of many separate burrows.

Prairie dog 15—17 in. long

prairie schooner ***n-*** covered wagon. For picture, see *covered wagon.*

prairie wolf ***n-*** coyote.

praise (prāz) ***n-*** **1** approval; applause: *She won great* praise *for her acting.* **2** worship of God, especially when expressed in song: *a hymn of* praise. ***vt-*** **[praised, prais·ing] 1** to speak or write favorably of: *Out of politeness I* praised *her singing.* **2** to glorify and worship, especially in song. ***—n-*** **prais′er.**

sing the praises of to laud; extol.

praise·wor·thy (prāz′wûr′thē) ***adj-*** deserving praise or approval: *a* praiseworthy, *charitable organization.* ***—adv-*** **praise′wor′thi·ly.** ***n-*** **praise′wor′thi·ness.**

pra·line (prā′lēn′, prä′-) ***n-*** candy made of nuts and brown or maple sugar.

pram (prăm) ***n-*** *chiefly Brit.* perambulator.

prance (prăns) ***vi-*** **[pranced, pranc·ing] 1** to advance with bounding leaps of the hind legs, as do spirited horses: *Three horses* pranced *around the circus ring.* **2** to caper or skip: *The little boy* pranced *about.* **3** to strut; swagger: *The drum major* pranced *and twirled his baton.* ***vt-*** to cause (a horse) to prance. ***n-*** a caper; skip.

prank (prăngk) ***n-*** piece of mischief; trick.

prank·ish (prăng′kĭsh) ***adj-*** mischievous; playful: *a* prankish *boy.* ***—adv-*** **prank′ish·ly.** ***n-*** **prank′ish·ness.**

pra·se·o·dym·i·um (prā′zē ō dĭm′ē əm) ***n-*** whitish rare-earth metal element whose oxide is used to make a yellow pigment for ceramics. Symbol Pr, At. No. 59, At. Wt. 140.907.

prate (prāt) ***vi-*** **[prat·ed, prat·ing]** to talk idly; prattle. ***vt-*** to speak (idle nonsense or foolishness). ***—n-*** **prat′er.**

prat·tle (prăt′əl) ***vi-*** **[prat·tled, prat·tling]** to talk like a child; babble foolishly; prate. ***vt-*** to tell or speak (something) childishly or foolishly. ***n-***: *the* prattle *of happy tots.* ***—n-*** **prat′tler.**

prau (prou) ***n-*** Malay boat, often equipped with an outrigger and usually without a deck, driven by sails, paddles, or oars. ***Hom-*** prow.

prawn (prȯn) ***n-*** edible shellfish resembling a shrimp but larger, found in either fresh or salt water.

pray (prā) ***vi-*** **1** to speak to God with love, thanks, appeal, etc. **2** to request; beg; implore. ***vt-*** to ask for or of, by means of a prayer or earnest request: *We* pray *Thy forgiveness. They* prayed *the king to free his prisoners.* ***auxiliary verb*** I ask or invite you to; please (used with infinitive without "to"): *Welcome!* Pray *sit down.*

[1]**pray·er** (prā′ər) ***n-*** person who prays.

[2]**prayer** (prâr) ***n-*** **1** a speaking to God with love, thanks, appeal, etc.: *a* prayer *for peace.* **2** an earnest request or appeal: *His entire speech was a* prayer *for justice.* **3** group of words suited for an address to God.

prayer·ful (prâr′fəl) ***adj-*** inclined towards or characterized by prayer: *a* prayerful *community of monks.* ***—adv-*** **prayer′ful·ly.** ***n-*** **prayer′ful·ness.**

praying mantis See *mantis.*

pre- *prefix* before: *a* pre*historic animal; a* pre*paid package.*

preach (prēch) ***vi-*** **1** to talk or teach publicly on a religious subject, especially on a text from the Bible. **2** to give advice and guidance, often when it is not wanted: *He never talks, but always* preaches. ***vt-*** **1** to urge publicly and persistently: *He* preaches *the need for new fire trucks.* **2** to deliver (a sermon, lesson, etc.).

preach·er (prē′chər) ***n-*** **1** person who preaches. **2** *Informal* clergyman.

preach·ment (prēch′mənt) ***n-*** **1** a preaching. **2** sermon or speech, especially a tiresome one.

preach·y (prē′chē) ***adj-*** **[preach·i·er, preach·i·est]** 1 characterized by long and tiresome moralizing: *a* preachy *lecture.* 2 given to preaching: *a* preachy *person.* **—*n-* preach′i·ness.**

pre·am·ble (prē′ăm′bəl) ***n-*** 1 introduction to a statute or law, giving the reason for passing the law: *the* preamble *to the Constitution.* 2 introductory statement or event, especially when it explains what is to follow.

pre·ar·range (prē′ə rānj′) ***vt-*** **[pre·ar·ranged, pre·ar·rang·ing]** to arrange previously or beforehand: *They* prearranged *our meeting.* **—*n-* pre′ar·range′ment.**

Pre·cam·bri·an (prē′kăm′brē ən) ***adj-*** of or having to do with any period of geological time preceding the Cambrian.

pre·car·i·ous (prĭ kâr′ē əs) ***adj-*** uncertain; risky or perilous: *a* precarious *perch in a tree.* **—*adv-* pre·car′i·ous·ly.** ***n-*** **pre·car′i·ous·ness.**

pre·cau·tion (prĭ kô′shən) ***n-*** care taken beforehand to prevent harm, loss, etc.: *the* precautions *against fire.* **—*adj-* pre·cau′tion·ar′y:** *a* precautionary *measure.*

pre·cede (prē sēd′) ***vt-*** **[pre·ced·ed, pre·ced·ing]** to go or happen before in time, place, rank, importance, etc.: *He* preceded *me in line.* ***vi-*** to take precedence.

pre·ced·ence (prĕs′ə dəns) ***n-*** 1 a coming or being before in time, order, rank, or importance. 2 superiority in rank; especially, the right of going before others in ceremonies and formal occasions.

take precedence to be of the greater importance or higher rank; have priority.

prec·e·dent (prĕs′ə dənt) ***n-*** an act or event of the past that can serve as a guide or justification for later actions, decisions, etc.: *a law without* precedent.

pre·cept (prē′sĕpt′) ***n-*** a rule of conduct or moral behavior intended as a guide or example; maxim.

pre·cep·tor (prē sĕp′tər) ***n-*** person who guides or instructs; teacher. **—*n-*** *fem.* **pre·cep′tress.**

pre·ces·sion (prē sĕsh′ən) ***n-*** 1 a going before others; a going foward. 2 the wobbling motion exhibited by any spinning body, such as a gyroscope or the earth, when an external force acts to shift the axis of rotation of the body.

pre·cinct (prē′sĭngkt′) ***n-*** 1 area in a town or city marked off as a police or voting district. 2 space enclosed by walls or boundaries, especially within a church: *the* precinct *of a cathedral.* 3 **precincts** surrounding regions; environs: *the town and its immediate* precincts.

pre·cious (prĕsh′əs) ***adj-*** 1 of great price; costly: *The crown was studded with* precious *stones.* 2 highly valued; much loved: *Freedom is a* precious *right.* 3 affectedly elegant or refined: *a* precious *style of writing*; precious *manners.* 4 (intensifier only): *a* precious *nuisance.* ***adv-*** very; extremely: *He has* precious *little to say for himself.* **—*adv-* pre′cious·ly.** ***n-*** **pre′cious·ness.**

precious stone ***n-*** rare, valuable gem, such as the diamond, emerald, or ruby.

prec·i·pice (prĕs′ə pəs) ***n-*** steep, nearly vertical or overhanging cliff; hence, any potentially disastrous situation.

pre·cip·i·tant (prĭ sĭp′ə tənt) ***adj-*** headlong; abrupt; precipitate. **—*n-* pre·cip′i·tance** or **pre·cip′i·tan·cy.**

[1]**pre·cip·i·tate** (prĭ sĭp′ə tāt′) ***vt-*** **[pre·cip·i·tat·ed, pre·cip·i·tat·ing]** 1 to bring about; hasten the happening of, especially before wanted, needed, or expected: *to* precipitate *a strike.* 2 to cast or hurl down from a height. 3 to condense (water vapor) into moisture that falls as rain, dew, sleet, etc. 4 to separate (a solid) from a liquid solution or suspension: *As the river moves more slowly, it* precipitates *silt.* ***vi-*** to fall in a headlong manner.

[2]**pre·cip·i·tate** (prĭ sĭp′ə tət) ***adj-*** 1 headlong; hasty; rash, especially in violence of motion: *After a warning from a neighbor, he made a* precipitate *flight.* 2 steeply flowing, falling, or rushing. ***n-*** solid that has separated from a solution or suspension: *The crystals were a* precipitate *from the salt solution.* **—*adv-* pre·cip′i·tate·ly.**

pre·cip·i·ta·tion (prĭ sĭp′ə tā′shən) ***n-*** 1 headlong rush, fall, or procedure: *At sight of the hunters, the birds flew away in great* precipitation. 2 rash haste: *She made the decision with* precipitation. 3 moisture, condensed from the water vapor in the air, that falls as rain, snow, or the like: *cold and cloudy with some* precipitation. 4 the measure of moisture that falls in a given time and place: *four inches of* precipitation. 5 process of causing solid matter to separate from a solution or suspension.

pre·cip·i·tous (prĭ sĭp′ə təs) ***adj-*** 1 very steep: *a* precipitous *hillside.* 2 rushing downward rapidly: *a* precipitous *flow.* 3 hasty; rash: *a* precipitous *action.* **—*adv-* pre·cip′i·tous·ly.** ***n-*** **pre·cip′i·tous·ness.**

pré·cis (prā′sē′) ***n-*** [*pl.* **pré·cis** (-sēz′)] brief summary giving the main points of a written work, speech, etc.

pre·cise (prĭ sīs′) ***adj-*** 1 exact; definite; accurate: *a* precise *description*; precise *measurements.* 2 very careful or fussy in following rules or conventions: *a* precise *speaker.* **—*adv-* pre·cise′ly.** ***n-*** **pre·cise′ness.**

pre·ci·sion (prĭ sĭzh′ən) ***n-*** exactness; accuracy: *The* precision *of a clock.* *as* ***modifier***: *a* precision *tool.*

pre·clude (prĭ klōōd′) ***vt-*** **[pre·clu·ded, pre·clud·ing]** to prevent: *Illness* precludes *my joining you at the dance.*

pre·co·cious (prĭ kō′shəs) ***adj-*** showing advanced skill or mental development at an unusually early age: *a* precocious *child.* **—*adv-* pre·co′cious·ly.** ***n-*** **pre·co′cious·ness** or **pre·coc′i·ty** (-kŏs′ə tē).

pre·con·ceive (prē′kən sēv′) ***vt-*** **[pre·con·ceived, pre·con·ceiv·ing]** to form (an idea or opinion) before having actual knowledge.

pre·con·cep·tion (prē′kən sĕp′shən) ***n-*** an idea, concept, or opinion formed by a person before he has actual knowledge.

pre·con·cert·ed (prē′kən sûr′təd) ***adj-*** arranged or agreed upon beforehand: *a* preconcerted *plan.*

pre·cur·sor (prĕ kûr′sər) ***n-*** person or thing that precedes another, and foretells the approach of the other; forerunner: *a* precursor *of disaster.*

pred. predicate.

pre·date (prē′dāt′) ***vt-*** **[pre·dat·ed, pre·dat·ing]** 1 to mark or provide with a date prior to a particular time or event: *to* predate *a check.* 2 to come before in time: *The Civil War* predates *World War I.*

pred·a·tor (prĕd′ə tôr′, -tər) ***n-*** person or animal that preys or plunders.

pred·a·tor·y (prĕd′ə tôr′ē) ***adj-*** 1 living by preying on others: *a* predatory *animal.* 2 characterized by plundering or looting: *a* predatory *attack.* **—*adv-* pred′a·tor′i·ly.** ***n-*** **pred′a·tor′i·ness.**

pre·de·cease (prē′dĭ sēs′) ***vt-*** **[pre·de·ceased, pre·de·ceas·ing]** to die before (someone else).

pred·e·ces·sor (prĕd′ə sĕs′ər) ***n-*** person or thing that comes before another, especially in a job or office.

pre·des·ti·na·tion (prē′dĕs′tə nā′shən) ***n-*** 1 the determining of what is to happen beforehand; destiny; fate. 2 in religion, the doctrine that all things and events have been decreed by God from the very beginning.

pre·des·tine (prē dĕs′tən) ***vt-*** **[pre·des·tined, pre·des·tin·ing]** to decree or determine beforehand.

pre·de·ter·mine (prē′dĭ tûr′mən) ***vt-*** **[pre·de·ter·mined, pre·de·ter·min·ing]** to determine or decide beforehand. **—*n-* pre′de·ter′min·a′tion.**

pre·dic·a·ment (prĭ dĭk′ə mənt) ***n-*** difficult, puzzling, or unpleasant situation; plight.

[1]**pred·i·cate** (prĕd′ ĭ kət) *Grammar* ***n-*** the part of a sentence which remains after the subject and all sentence modifiers have been removed. The predicate consists of a finite verb or verb phrase, which may be accompanied by an object, a complement, or both, and modifiers. Examples:

Marian coughed.
He quickly sketched a horse.
They made Joe president.
She is a good singer.
As a last resort, they jumped in and swam to shore.

[2]**pre·di·cate** (prĕd′ ə kāt′) ***vt-*** **[pre·di·cat·ed, pre·di·cat·ing]** **1** to base or found (a conclusion, argument, proposal, etc.): *He* predicates *his theory on these facts.* **2** to declare (something) to be a property or characteristic of something else: *to* predicate *wetness of water.*

predicate adjective *Grammar* ***n-*** adjective that follows a linking verb and describes the subject of the verb. Examples: *That house is* old. *The grass looks* greener.

predicate nominative *Grammar* ***n-*** **1** subjective complement that is a pronoun. **2** subjective complement that is a noun.

predicate noun *Grammar* ***n-*** a noun that is a subjective complement.

pre·dict (prĭ dĭkt′) ***vt-*** to announce or know about in advance; foresee; prophesy: *I* predict *good weather for the picnic. Who can* predict *the future?* ***—adj-*** **pre·dict′a·ble.** ***adv-*** **pre·dict′a·bly.** ***n-*** **pre·dic′tor.**

pre·dic·tion (prĭ dĭk′ shən) ***n-*** **1** a predicting or foretelling. **2** something predicted; prophecy; forecast.

pre·di·gest (prē′ dĭ jĕst′, -dī jĕst′) ***vt-*** to cause (food) to become partly digested, either by a natural or artificial process, before it is eaten. ***—n-*** **pre′di·ges′tion.**

pre·di·lec·tion (prĕd′ ə lĕk′ shən, prē′ də-) ***n-*** preference; partiality: *a* predilection *for rich food.*

pre·dis·pose (prē′ dĭ spōz′) ***vt-*** **[pre·dis·pos·ed, pre·dis·pos·ing]** **1** to make susceptible, liable, or subject: *Poor nourishment* predisposes *people to illness.* **2** to incline beforehand; influence: *His good manners* predisposed *me to like him.*

pre·dis·po·si·tion (prē′ dĭs′ pə zĭsh′ ən) ***n-*** inclination or tendency toward a person or thing, which is prior to knowledge or personal contact or experience.

pre·dom·i·nant (prĭ dŏm′ ə nənt) ***adj-*** greater in strength, power, number, amount, etc.; prevailing: *a* predominant *influence*; *a* predominant *color.* ***—n-*** **pre·dom′i·nance.** ***adv-*** **pre·dom′i·nant·ly.**

pre·dom·i·nate (prĭ dŏm′ ə nāt′) ***vi-*** **[pre·dom·i·nat·ed, pre·dom·i·nat·ing]** **1** to be greater in numbers, power, influence, etc.: *Roses* predominate *in our garden.* **2** to exert control; prevail: *He* predominated *over his weaker comrades.* ***—n-*** **pre·dom′i·na′tion.**

pre-em·i·nent or **pre·em·i·nent** (prē ĕm′ ĭ nənt) ***adj-*** outstanding or distinguished among others: *a* preeminent *statesman.* ***—n-*** **pre-em′i·nence** or **pre·em′i·nence.** ***adv-*** **pre-em′i·nently** or **pre·em′i·nent·ly.**

pre-empt or **pre·empt** (prē ĕmpt′) ***vt-*** **1** to take possession of before others can: *to* pre-empt *a parking space.* **2** to establish the first claim to (public land). ***—n-*** **pre-emp′tion** or **pre·emp′tion.**

preen (prēn) ***vt-*** **1** to clean and smooth (feathers) with the beak, as a bird does. **2** to dress or adorn (oneself) with care. **3** to express pride or satisfaction in (oneself): *He* preens *himself on his perfect spelling.* ***vi-*** to fuss or take pains over one's appearance; primp: *to* preen *before the mirror.*

pre-ex·ist or **pre·ex·ist** (prē′ ĭg zĭst′) ***vi-*** to have an earlier existence; especially, to exist in a previous life.

pre-ex·is·tent or **pre·ex·is·tent** (prē′ ĭg zĭs′ tənt) ***adj-*** **1** existing before something else: *a* pre-existent *condition.* **2** having existence before the present life. ***—n-*** **pre-′ex·is′tence** or **pre′ex·is′tence.**

pref. 1 preface. **2** prefix. **3** preferred.

pre·fab (prē′făb′) ***n-*** prefabricated thing, especially a house.

pre·fab·ri·cate (prē′ făb′ rə kāt′) ***vt-*** **[pre·fab·ri·cat·ed, pre·fab·ri·cat·ing]** **1** to construct or produce standardized parts of (a house, furniture, etc.) at a factory, so that only the assembling of the units is necessary where they are used. **2** to produce or make up in advance: *to* prefabricate *an excuse.* ***—n-*** **pre′fab′ri·ca′tion.**

pref·ace (prĕf′ əs) ***n-*** introduction to a book, speech, etc., especially in the form of a separate section preceding the main part or parts. ***vt-*** **[pref·aced, pref·ac·ing]** **1** to introduce (a book, speech, etc.) by some act or statement: *She* prefaced *her talk with a cough.* **2** to serve as an introduction to: *A lecture* prefaced *the movie.*

pref·a·tor·y (prĕf′ ə tôr′ ē) ***adj-*** of, resembling, or forming a preface; introductory.

pre·fect (prē′fĕkt′) ***n-*** **1** in the Roman Empire, a military or civil officer of high rank, such as the governor of a province. **2** in France, the administrative head of one of the departments into which the country is divided; also, the chief of the Paris police. **3** in some private or religious schools, the dean; also, the disciplinary head of a dormitory. **4** in some English schools, a senior student appointed as monitor.

pre·fec·ture (prē′ fĕk′ chər) ***n-*** the rank, district, term of office, or residence of a prefect.

pre·fer (prĭ fûr′) ***vt-*** **[pre·ferred, pre·fer·ring]** **1** to like better than something else: *Of the two, I* prefer *this one.* **2** to present for consideration: *She* preferred *charges against the thief.*

pref·er·a·ble (prĕf′ ər ə bəl) ***adj-*** more desirable: *I find summer* preferable *to winter.* ***—n-*** **pref′er·a·bil′i·ty.** ***adv-*** **pref′er·a·bly.**

pref·er·ence (prĕf′ ər əns) ***n-*** **1** the choice or favoring of one thing or person over another: *The employer's son was given* preference. **2** thing that is chosen or favored: *The purple dress is my* preference.

pref·er·en·tial (prĕf′ ə rĕn′ shəl) ***adj-*** showing or resulting from preference; favoring some particular person or thing: *He received* preferential *treatment.* ***—adv-*** **pref′er·en′tial·ly.**

pre·fer·ment (prĭ fûr′ mənt) ***n-*** **1** promotion to higher rank or office: *a political* preferment. **2** the office or position itself, especially a high post of honor or dignity in a church. **3** the presenting of a charge or accusation.

preferred stock ***n-*** stock upon which dividends are payable before any are paid on the common stock.

pre·fig·ure (prē′ fĭg′ yər) ***vt-*** **[pre·fig·ur·ed, pre·fig·ur·ing]** **1** to show or indicate beforehand, especially by some sign or symbol: *A rainbow often* prefigures *the end of a storm.* **2** to imagine or work out in advance: *to* prefigure *the outcome of a contest.* ***—n-*** **pre′fig′ur·a′tion.**

[1]**pre·fix** (prē′fĭks′) ***n-*** syllable or syllables placed at the beginning of a word or word root to qualify its meaning. In the word "unknown," "un" is a prefix.

[2]**pre·fix** (prē′fĭks′) ***vt-*** to place before or at the beginning: *He always* prefixed *"Baron" to his name.*

pre·flight (prē′flīt′) ***adj-*** taking place before flight, especially in an aircraft: *a* preflight *briefing.*

---

preg·nan·cy (prĕg′ nən sē) ***n-*** [*pl.* **preg·nan·cies**] **1** condition of a female carrying unborn young. **2** significance; weightiness: *the* pregnancy *of his remarks.*

preg·nant (prĕg′ nənt) ***adj-*** **1** of a woman or a female animal, carrying unborn young. **2** full of significance or importance: *a* pregnant *statement.* **3** inventive; fruitful; fertile: *his* pregnant *imagination.*

pre·heat (prē′ hēt′) ***vt-*** to heat in advance.

pre·hen·sile (prē hĕn′ səl, -sĭl′) ***adj-*** adapted for grasping or seizing things: *A monkey has a* prehensile *tail.*

pre·his·tor·ic (prē′ hĭs tôr′ ĭk) ***adj-*** of or relating to the time before the existence of written records: *Dinosaurs were* prehistoric *animals.* Also **pre′ his·tor′ i·cal.** ***—adv-*** **pre′ his·tor′ i·cal·ly.**

pre·judge (prē′ jŭj′) ***vt-*** [**pre·judged, pre·judg·ing**] to judge in advance or without waiting to learn all the facts of a case. ***—n-*** **pre′ judg′ ment** or **pre′ judge′ ment.**

prej·u·dice (prĕj′ ə dəs) ***n-*** **1** strong feeling for or against something, formed without any knowledge or logical reason; especially, a general antagonism toward members of other races, religions, etc. **2** injury or harm resulting from hasty or unfair judgment: *to judge a case without* prejudice *to the accused.* ***vt-*** [**pre·ju·diced, prej·u·dic·ing**] **1** to influence or fill with a strong feeling for or against someone or something. **2** to harm by an opinion or act: *to* prejudice *someone's reputation.*

prej·u·di·cial (prĕj′ ə dĭsh′ əl) ***adj-*** tending to cause disfavor; injurious; damaging: *His bad record was* prejudicial. ***—adv-*** **prej′ u·di′ cial·ly.**

prel·a·cy (prĕl′ ə sē) ***n-*** [*pl.* **prel·a·cies**] **1** the position of a clergyman of high rank, such as a bishop. **2** prelates considered as a group. **3** church government by the higher orders of the clergy.

prel·ate (prĕl′ ət) ***n-*** clergyman of high rank, such as a bishop or an archbishop.

pre·lim·i·nar·y (prĭ lĭm′ ə nĕr′ ē) ***adj-*** coming before or preparing for an event or action: *the* preliminary *arrangements.* ***n-*** [*pl.* **pre·lim·i·nar·ies**] something that introduces or prepares for an event or action: *a* preliminary *to the talks.* ***—adv-*** **pre·lim′ i·nar′ i·ly.**

pre·lude (prĕl′ yōōd′, prē′ lōōd′) ***n-*** **1** something that goes before or introduces a larger or more significant thing: *The thunder was a* prelude *to the storm.* **2** piece of music that introduces a larger work or is performed before a church service. ***vt-*** [**pre·lud·ed, pre·lud·ing**] to serve as an introduction to; precede.

pre·ma·ture (prē′ mə chŏŏr′, -tyŏŏr′, -tŏŏr′) ***adj-*** happening or coming before the usual time; too early; untimely: *a* premature *arrival.* ***—adv-*** **pre′ ma·ture′ ly.**

pre·med (prē′ mĕd′) *Informal* ***adj-*** premedical. ***n-*** a premedical student.

pre·med·i·cal (prē′ mĕd′ ĭ kəl) ***adj-*** preparing for studies leading to a medical degree: *a* premedical *student.*

pre·med·i·tate (prĭ mĕd′ ə tāt′) ***vt-*** [**pre·med·i·tat·ed, pre·med·i·tat·ing**] to think over and plan beforehand: *to* premeditate *a crime.* ***—n-*** **pre·med′ i·ta′ tion.**

pre·mier (prēm′ yər, prĭ mêr′, prĕm′ ē ər) ***adj-*** principal; chief; first: *of* premier *importance.* ***n-*** prime minister; chief minister of government.

pre·mière (prĭ myĕr′, -mêr′) ***n-*** first presentation of a movie, play, opera, etc.

prem·ise (prĕm′ əs) ***n-*** **1** statement accepted as true, from which a conclusion is to be drawn; especially, in logic, one of the first two statements of a syllogism. **2 premises** (1) property, such as land or a house, especially when mentioned in a legal document. (2) facts previously stated, especially in a legal document. ***vt-*** [**pre·mised, pre·mis·ing**] to state beforehand as an explanation or as a basis from which to proceed to a conclusion.

pre·mi·um (prē′ mē əm) ***n-*** **1** prize; reward; inducement: *to offer a* premium *to the man with the highest sales.* **2** sum or amount above the usual amount: *to pay a* premium *for a theater ticket.* **3** payment made for an insurance policy. **4** high value or rating: *to place a* premium *on honesty.* ***adj-*** *Informal* of higher than average price or quality.

at a premium **1** in great demand, and therefore valuable or costly. **2** of stocks, at a price above par.

pre·mo·lar (prē′ mō′ lər) ***n-*** bicuspid. ***adj-***: *a* premolar *cavity.*

pre·mo·ni·tion (prē′ mə nĭsh′ ən, prĕm′ ə-) ***n-*** **1** a feeling that something is about to happen; foreboding. **2** advance warning: *no* premonition *of what is to come.*

pre·mon·i·tor·y (prĭ mŏn′ ə tôr′ ē) ***adj-*** serving as or seeming to be a warning of something to come: *a* premonitory *rumble of thunder*; *a* premonitory *shudder.*

pre·na·tal (prē′ nā′ təl) ***adj-*** happening or existing before birth: *a* prenatal *condition*; prenatal *development.*

pre·oc·cu·pa·tion (prē ŏk′ yə pā′ shən) ***n-*** **1** concentration of one's interest or attention on a particular thing or subject; absorption: *his* preoccupation *with his own affairs.* **2** anything that absorbs one's interest.

pre·oc·cu·pied (prē ŏk′ yə pīd′) ***adj-*** lost in thought; engrossed; absorbed: *a* preoccupied *teacher.*

pre·oc·cu·py (prē ŏk′ yə pī′) ***vt-*** [**pre·oc·cu·pied, pre·oc·cu·py·ing**] to fill the mind of; absorb; engross.

pre·or·dain (prē′ ôr′ dān′, -ôr′ dān′) ***vt-*** to decree or determine beforehand.

prep (prĕp) *Informal* ***n-*** **1** (also **prep school**) preparatory school. **2** *Brit.* work or period spent in preparing school assignments. ***vi-*** [**prepped, prep·ping**] to attend a preparatory school. ***vt-*** to prepare; especially, to prepare (a patient) for an examination or operation.

prep. **1** preposition. **2** preparatory.

pre·paid (prē′ pād′) *p.t. & p.p.* of **prepay.**

prep·a·ra·tion (prĕp′ ə rā′ shən) ***n-*** **1** a preparing or being prepared: *the* preparation *of dinner*; preparation *of an assignment*; *his* preparation *for the examination.* **2** thing or action needed to get ready: *Ted took care of the* preparations *for our camping trip.* **3** food, medicine, lotion, etc., made up for a special use: *a* preparation *of sulfur and molasses.*

pre·par·a·to·ry (prĭ păr′ ə tôr′ ē, prĭ pĕr′-) ***adj-*** serving to make ready for something: *to make* preparatory *plans.*

preparatory to as a preparation for.

preparatory school ***n-*** school, especially a private school, that specializes in preparing students for entrance into college.

pre·pare (prĭ pâr′) ***vt-*** [**pre·pared, pre·par·ing**] **1** to make ready or fit for a particular use, purpose, activity; etc.: *to* prepare *an assignment*; *to* prepare *oneself for a journey.* **2** to make or put together from ingredients: *to* prepare *a meal*; *to* prepare *a medicine.* ***vi-*** to get ready: *to* prepare *for a trip*; *to* prepare *for bad news.* ***—n-*** **pre·par′ er.**

pre·par·ed·ness (prĭ pâr′ əd nəs) ***n-*** condition of being prepared for something, especially for war.

pre·pay (prē′ pā′) ***vt-*** [**pre·paid, pre·pay·ing**] to pay or pay for in advance. ***—n-*** **pre′ pay′ ment.**

pre·pon·der·ance (prĭ pŏn′ dər əns) ***n-*** superiority in amount, number, power, or influence: *a* preponderance *of girls on the committee.*

pre·pon·der·ant (prĭ pŏn′ dər ənt) ***adj-*** greater in weight, number, power, etc. ***—adv-*** **pre·pon′ der·ant·ly.**

pre·pon·der·ate (prĭ pŏn′ də rāt′) ***vi-*** [**pre·pon·der·at·ed, pre·pon·der·at·ing**] to exceed others in number, power, influence, etc.; predominate.

prep·o·si·tion (prĕp′ ə zĭsh′ ən) *Grammar* ***n-*** any of a special group of words and phrases, such as "in," "on," "over," "instead of," "owing to," which have nouns, pronouns, noun phrases, or noun clauses as objects.

prep·o·si·tion·al phrase (prĕp′ ə zĭsh′ ən əl) *Grammar* ***n-*** group of words made up of a preposition followed by a noun, pronoun, noun phrase, or noun clause. Examples:
Amy has gone to Chicago. (object a noun)
There is no water in it. (object a pronoun)
The book on the small table *is mine.* (object a noun phrase)
They laughed at what he said. (object a noun clause)

pre·pos·sess (prē′ pə zĕs′) ***vt-*** **1** to fill (the mind) so as to shut out other thoughts. **2** to influence beforehand, especially to a favorable opinion or impression.

pre·pos·sess·ing (prē′ pə zĕs′ ĭng) ***adj-*** making a good impression; pleasing: *his* prepossessing *manner.*

pre·pos·ses·sion (prē′ pə zĕsh′ ən) ***n-*** **1** opinion formed in advance of actual knowledge. **2** preoccupation.

pre·pos·ter·ous (prĭ pŏs′ tər əs) ***adj-*** contrary to what is reasonable; very foolish: *a* preposterous *notion.* ***—adv-*** **pre·pos′ ter·ous·ly.** ***n-*** **pre·pos′ ter·ous·ness.**

prep school ***n-*** preparatory school.

pre·req·ui·site (prĭ rĕk′ wə zət) ***n-*** something that is required before something else can follow: *This course is a* prerequisite *to more advanced studies.* ***adj-***: *a* prerequisite *course in general science.*
►Should not be confused with PERQUISITE.

pre·rog·a·tive (prĭ rŏg′ ə tĭv′) ***n-*** right or privilege belonging to a particular person or group of persons, especially by virtue of rank or position: *a* king's *prerogative*; *a* parent's *prerogative.*

pres. 1 present. **2** president.

Pres. President.

[1]**pres·age** (prĕs′ ĭj) ***n-*** **1** sign or omen foretelling what is about to happen. **2** a feeling about what will happen.

[2]**pre·sage** (prĕs′ ĭj, prĭ sāj′) ***vt-*** **[pre·saged, pre·sag·ing] 1** to give a warning or sign of; portend. **2** to foretell.

pres·by·ter (prĕz′ bə tər, prĕs′ pə-) ***n-*** **1** in the early Christian church, a priest or elder. **2** in various modern churches, a minister or elder.

Pres·by·te·ri·an (prĕz′ bə têr′ ē ən, prĕs′ pə-) ***adj-*** of or relating to various Protestant churches whose members are governed by teaching and ruling elders or presbyters. ***n-*** member of a Presbyterian church.

Pres·by·te·ri·an·ism (prĕz′ bə têr′ ē ə nĭz′ əm, prĕs′ pə-) ***n-*** the faith and doctrine of the Presbyterian Church, including the right of all members to share in its government through their chosen elders or presbyters.

pres·by·ter·y (prĕz′ bə tĕr′ ē, prĕs′ pə-) ***n-*** [*pl.* **pres·by·ter·ies**] **1** in the early Christian Church, a body of elders. **2** in the Presbyterian Church, a court composed of all the ministers and one elder from each congregation in a district. **3** the district itself. **4** the front part of a church, reserved for the clergy. **5** a priest's residence.

pre·school (prē′ sko͞ol′) ***adj-*** of, belonging to, or having to do with the time in a child's life from infancy to the age of five or six, when most children start school.

pre·science (prĕsh′ əns, *also* prē′ shē əns) ***n-*** a knowing of events before they take place; foreknowledge. ***—adj-*** **pre′ scient.** ***adv-*** **pre′ scient·ly.**

pre·scribe (prĭ skrīb′) ***vt-*** **[pre·scribed, pre·scrib·ing] 1** to order or advise (something) as a remedy or cure: *to* prescribe *medicine for a cough*; *to* prescribe *rest for an invalid.* **2** to order or direct, especially officially: *The law* prescribes *these procedures.* ***vi-*** **1** to write or give medical directions. **2** to give laws, rules, or directions.
►Should not be confused with PROSCRIBE.

pre·scrip·tion (prĭ skrĭp′ shən) ***n-*** **1** doctor's written order for the making and use of a medicine, eyeglasses, etc. **2** the medicine ordered by a doctor. **3** any authoritative advice or rule given for the purpose of healing, correcting, or helping. **4** the act or process of prescribing.
►Should not be confused with PROSCRIPTION.

pre·scrip·tive (prĭ skrĭp′ tĭv) ***adj-*** **1** tending to lay down strict rules: *a* prescriptive *teacher*; prescriptive *grammar.* **2** according to prescribed rule: *a* prescriptive *method of teaching.* ***—adv-*** **pre·scrip′ tive·ly.**

pres·ence (prĕz′ əns) ***n-*** **1** a being present in a certain place: *Your* presence *at the meeting is required.* **2** nearness or company of another person or thing: *to swear an oath in the* presence *of witnesses*; *to be calm in the* presence *of danger.* **3** appearance or behavior; bearing: *The young prince had a noble* presence. **4** something that is felt to be near: *an invisible* presence.

presence of mind ***n-*** ability to think and act quickly and calmly in an emergency or other difficult situation.

[1]**pres·ent** (prĕz′ ənt) ***adj-*** **1** here in this place; there in that place; on hand; not absent: *The whole class is* present. *You are* present *in my thoughts.* **2** of concern now; at issue or under consideration now: *his* present *difficulties*; *the* present *quarrel.* ***n-*** **1** *Grammar* the present tense. **2 the present** the time passing now, as distinguished from the past and the future. **3 these presents** this legal or official document: *The diploma reads, "All men to whom* these presents *may come, Greetings."* [from Old French **present,** from Latin **praesens, praesentis** meaning "being in front of."]
at present just now; at this time.

[2]**pre·sent** (prĭ zĕnt′) ***vt-*** **1** to introduce: *The teacher* presented *the visitor to the class.* **2** to put before the public; show; exhibit: *to* present *a new French star*; *to* present *a gay appearance.* **3** to give as a gift. **4** to offer for consideration: *Taking a trip always* presents *the problem of what to do with the pets.* **5** to put (oneself) in another's presence: *He* presented *himself at my office.* **6** to deliver; submit: *to* present *a bill.* [from Old French **presenter,** from Latin **praesentare** meaning "to place before."]
present arms *Military* to salute by holding a rifle in front of one with the muzzle pointing upward.
present with to give, as a gift.

[3]**pres·ent** (prĕz′ ənt) ***n-*** a gift, especially one given on a birthday or holiday. [from [2]**present.**]

pre·sent·a·ble (prĭ zĕn′ tə bəl) ***adj-*** **1** suitable to be presented or offered: *to rewrite a composition in* presentable *form.* **2** suitable or proper in appearance; fit to be seen: *Am I* presentable? ***—adv-*** **pre·sent′ a·bly.**

pres·en·ta·tion (prĕz′ ən tā′ shən, prē′ zĕn′-) ***n-*** **1** the act of giving or offering, especially in a formal manner: *the* presentation *of prizes.* **2** a showing or presenting before the public: *the* presentation *of a school play.* **3** an oral report or demonstration, often accompanied by illustrations; also, the way of presenting the report. **4** formal introduction: *a* presentation *to the queen.*

pres·ent-day (prĕz′ ənt dā′) ***adj-*** of, occurring at, or having to do with the present time; current.

pre·sen·ti·ment (prĭ zĕn′ tə mənt) ***n-*** a feeling that some particular thing is going to happen; foreboding.
►Should not be confused with PRESENTMENT.

pres·ent·ly (prĕz′ ənt lē) ***adv-*** **1** in a little while; soon: *He will be home* presently. **2** at the present time; now: *He is* presently *staying with friends.*

pre·sent·ment (prĭ zĕnt′ mənt) ***n-*** **1** the act of presenting something, especially a bill, note, etc., for acceptance or payment. **2** something that is presented, exhibited, etc. ►Should not be confused with PRESENTIMENT.

present participle See *participle.*

present perfect tense *Grammar* ***n-*** verb tense formed with the auxiliary verb "have" or "has," and indicating an action or condition that began at an unstated time in the past and in some cases is still continuing. Examples: *I* have waited *an hour. He* has taken *my notebook. It* has *just* begun *to rain. I* have gone *there many times.* Also **present perfect.**

present tense *Grammar* ***n-*** verb tense indicating an action or condition now going on or occurring regularly. Examples: *I* feel *uncomfortable. He* walks *three miles to school every day.*

pres·er·va·tion (prĕz′ ər vā′ shən) ***n-*** **1** a rescuing or keeping safe from death, injury, or decay: *the* preservation *of lives in an epidemic*; *the* preservation *of a forest.* **2** a being preserved: *He owes his* preservation *to luck.* **3** freedom from decay or other injury; soundness: *That old house is in an excellent state of* preservation.

pre·serv·a·tive (prĭ zûr′ və tĭv′) ***n-*** substance which tends to prevent deterioration or decay in foods, building materials, etc. ***adj-***: *a* preservative *effect.*

pre·serve (prĭ zûrv′) ***vt-*** **[pre·served, pre·serv·ing] 1** to keep from injury or harm; save: *Heaven* preserve *us!* **2** to maintain; keep up: *He* preserves *a youthful appearance.* **3** to keep from spoiling or decay by canning, pickling, or some other process: *to* preserve *peaches*; *to* preserve *laboratory specimens.* ***n-*** **1** tract of land where animals, trees, etc., are protected. **2** (usually **preserves**) fruit that has been cooked with sugar and stored in sealed containers. **—*n-* pre·serv′ er.**

pre·set (prē′ sĕt′) ***vt-*** **[pre·set, pre·set·ting]** to set in advance: *He* preset *the bomb to explode at 3:00 A.M.*

pre·side (prĭ zīd′) ***vi-*** **[pre·sid·ed, pre·sid·ing] 1** to act as chairman at a meeting. **2** to have direction or control (over): *to* preside *over the affairs of a house.* **3** to have an important or featured position, function, etc.: *Father* presided *at the head of the table.*

pres·i·den·cy (prĕz′ ə dən sē, -dĕn′ sē) ***n-*** [*pl.* **pres·i·den·cies**] **1** office of president. **2** length of time a president holds office.

pres·i·dent (prĕz′ ə dənt, -dĕnt′) ***n-*** **1** the highest officer of a company, bank, college, club, etc. **2** (often **President**) the highest executive officer of a modern republic.

pres·i·dent-e·lect (prĕz′ ə dənt ē′ lĕkt′, prĕz′ ə dĕnt′-) ***n-*** person who has been elected to be president, but who has not yet taken office.

pres·i·den·tial (prĕz′ ə dĕn′ shəl) ***adj-*** of or having to do with a president or his work: *his* presidential *duties.*

pre·sid·i·um (prĭ sĭd′ ē əm, prĭ zĭd′-) ***n-*** **1** in Communist countries, any permanent executive committee selected to act for a larger body. **2 Presidium** formerly, the policy-making committee of the Communist Party of the U.S.S.R., headed by the Party secretary.

¹press (prĕs) ***vt-*** **1** to thrust; push against: *to* press *a button.* **2** to squeeze together; crush: *The meat packer* pressed *the ham into tin cans.* **3** to smooth; iron: *to* press *a shirt.* **4** to clasp; grip: *Bob* pressed *his friend's hand.* **5** to embrace; hug: *The woman* pressed *the baby to her.* **6** to bear down on: *to* press *the pedal of a car brake.* **7** to hasten or urge: *Anxiety* pressed *him on.* **8** to insist upon; urge in a forceful way: *He* pressed *the argument.* **9** to force or thrust upon: *He* presses *unwelcome gifts on me.* **10** to harass, distress, or place in difficulties: *The enemy continued to* press *us.* ***vi-*** **1** to weigh or bear down heavily: *Worries* pressed *on his mind.* **2** to push forward: *The boy* pressed *through the line.* **3** to try or insist too much; be too zealous: *He did well until he began to* press. ***n-*** **1** a crowding or pushing: *the* press *of the crowd.* **2** a crowd. **3** machine made to squeeze, force together,

Printing press and fruit press

stamp, or crush something: *a cider* press; *a printing* press. **4** pressure; urgency: *The* press *of work kept Father late at the office.* **5** newspapers and magazines and those who work for them: *The* press *has great political influence.* [from Old French **presser,** from Latin **pressāre** meaning "to press; squeeze."] **—*n-* press′ er.**

be pressed for to have barely enough: *to* be pressed for *time or money.* **go to press** to begin printing.

press on (or **forward**) to continue with effort or speed; keep going: *The tired hikers* pressed on *toward camp.*

²press (prĕs) ***vt-*** to recruit by force; force into service, especially naval or military service. [altered from **prest money** meaning "money payed in advance for military service," from Old French **prester,** "to advance money," from Latin **praestāre,** "to offer."]

press agent ***n-*** person hired to obtain publicity for a client in newspapers and other publications.

press box ***n-*** group of seats reserved for reporters.

press conference ***n-*** scheduled interview given to news reporters by a public figure.

press·ing (prĕs′ ĭng) ***adj-*** **1** needing immediate attention; urgent: *a* pressing *need.* **2** demanding; insistent: *his* pressing *requests for money.* **—*adv-* press′ ing·ly.**

press·man (prĕs′ mən) ***n-*** [*pl.* **press·men**] **1** person who operates a press, especially a printing press. **2** *Brit.* newspaper reporter.

press release ***n-*** information, usually in written form, given out for publication in a newspaper.

press·room (prĕs′ rōōm′) ***n-*** in a printing plant, the room containing the printing presses.

pres·sure (prĕsh′ ər) ***n-*** **1** a pressing force or weight: *the* pressure *of a clamp*; *the* pressure *of a roller on the road.* **2** force of air, steam, water, etc., against a unit of area: *The air* pressure *in the tire is low.* **3** strong, forceful, and continued attempt to influence: *parental* pressure. **4** urgent and heavy demands: *the* pressure *of business.* **5** burden or stress on a person: *the* pressure *of worries*; *the* pressure *of debts.* ***vt-*** **[pres·sured, pres·sur·ing]** *Informal* to influence forcibly; compel.

pressure cooker ***n-*** heavy container that cooks food under steam pressure.

pressure group ***n-*** group organized to exert great pressure on public officials to follow their ideas.

pressure suit ***n-*** a suit worn by fliers, astronauts, etc., at high altitudes, which is pressurized to counteract decreased atmospheric pressure.

pres·su·rize (prĕsh′ ə rīz′) ***vt-*** **[pres·su·rized, pres·su·riz·ing] 1** to expose to high pressure. **2** to provide a suitable air pressure within (an airplane, spacecraft, pressure suit, etc.) when the air pressure of the environment is less than normal. **—*n-* pres′ su·ri·za′ tion.**

pres·ti·dig·i·ta·tion (prĕs′ tə dĭj′ ə tā′ shən) ***n-*** the skill or actions of a juggler, magician, etc.; sleight of hand. **—*n-* pres′ ti·dig′ i·ta′ tor:** *the* prestidigitator's *tricks.*

pres·tige (prĕs tēzh′, tēj′) ***n-*** influence or reputation gained by achievement, position, etc.: *The old scientist enjoyed great* prestige.

pres·to (prĕs′ tō) ***adv-*** 1 suddenly; in a trice: *The magician waved his hand, and* presto, *the coin vanished!* 2 *Music* very rapidly. ***adj-*** *Music* very rapid: *a* presto *passage.* ***n-*** [*pl.* **pres·tos**] *Music* piece, passage, etc., to be performed very rapidly.

pre·sum·a·ble (prĭ zo͞o′ mə bəl, prĭ zyo͞o′-) ***adj-*** such as may be expected or taken for granted; probable: *a* presumable *outcome.* ***—adv-*** **pre·sum′ a·bly.**

pre·sume (prĭ zo͞om′, -zyo͞om′) ***vt-*** [**pre·sumed, pre·sum·ing**] 1 to take for granted, especially without proof; suppose; assume: *Don't* presume *that he is guilty until he is proven so.* 2 to venture boldly, especially against someone having authority, superior knowledge, etc.; dare: *The young lawyer* presumed *to tell the judge he was wrong.* ***vi-*** to act with improper familiarity or unwarranted boldness; take liberties.

presume on (or **upon**) to make selfish use of; take advantage of: *to* presume on *a friend's hospitality.*

pre·sum·ed·ly (prĭ zo͞o′ məd lē, prĭ zyo͞o′-) ***adv-*** supposedly: *He is* presumedly *innocent of the crime.*

pre·sum·ing (prĭ zo͞o′ mĭng, prĭ zyo͞o′-) ***adj-*** unwarrantedly bold or self-assured; presumptuous.

pre·sump·tion (prĭ zŭmp′ shən) ***n-*** 1 a belief taken for granted, especially when based on something not fully proved; assumption; supposition: *a* presumption *of guilt, based on circumstantial evidence.* 2 unseemly self-assurance or boldness; effrontery; arrogance: *She had the* presumption *to ask for favors after insulting me.*

pre·sump·tive (prĭ zŭmp′ tĭv) ***adj-*** 1 affording reasonable grounds for belief: *the* presumptive *evidence.* 2 based on presumption or likelihood: *the heir* pre*sumptive.* ***—adv-*** **pre·sump′ tive·ly.**

►Should not be confused with PRESUMPTUOUS.

pre·sump·tu·ous (prĭ zŭmp′ cho͞o əs) ***adj-*** unwarrantedly bold or self-assured; impertinent: *a* presumptuous *question*; presumptuous *behavior.* ***—adv-*** **pre·sump′ tu·ous·ly.** ***n-*** **pre·sump′ tu·ous·ness.**

►Should not be confused with PRESUMPTIVE.

pre·sup·pose (prē′ sə pōz′) ***vt-*** [**pre·sup·posed, pre·sup·pos·ing**] 1 to take for granted in advance; assume beforehand. 2 to require as a foregoing condition: *Our plans* presuppose *our having the same vacation.*

pre·sup·po·si·tion (prē′ sŭp′ ə zĭsh′ ən) ***n-*** 1 the forming of a belief in advance of actual knowledge. 2 a belief so formed.

pre·tend (prĭ tĕnd′) ***vt-*** 1 to make believe: *The children* pretended *they were grownups.* 2 to put on an act or false show of; feign: *The acrobat* pretended *to lose his balance. He* pretends *friendship. She* pretended *illness.* 3 to claim falsely or without basis: *He* pretends *to know all the facts.* ***vi-*** 1 to put forward a claim: *to* pretend *to the throne.* 2 to play at make-believe.

pre·tend·ed (prĭ tĕn′ dəd) ***adj-*** not sincere or genuine; feigned; false: *his* pretended *friendship*; pretended *tears.* ***—adv-*** **pre·tend′ ed·ly.**

pre·tend·er (prĭ tĕn′ dər) ***n-*** 1 person who puts forward a claim to something, especially a royal title, right, etc. 2 person who pretends or feigns.

pre·tense (prĭ tĕns′, prē′ tĕns′) ***n-*** 1 a false appearance or action made to deceive: *a* pretense *of innocence.* 2 false reason; excuse; pretext: *to use any* pretense *to avoid work.* 3 false show or display; sham; affectation: *A sincere person is free from* pretense. 4 something imagined or pretended: *His story is all* pretense. Also **pretence.**

pre·ten·sion (prĭ tĕn′ shən) ***n-*** 1 a claim made on either a true or a false basis: *his* pretension *to a royal title*; *her* pretensions *to great knowledge.* 2 false display or affectation: *a man free from* pretension.

pre·ten·tious (prĭ tĕn′ shəs) ***adj-*** 1 showy; ostentatious: *a* pretentious *display of wealth.* 2 making claims to importance, worth, etc.: *a* pretentious *book.* ***—adv-*** **pre·ten′ tious·ly.** ***n-*** **pre·ten′ tious·ness.**

pret·er·it or **pret·er·ite** (prĕt′ ər ĭt) *Grammar* ***n-*** past tense or a verb in that tense. ***adj-***: *the* preterit *tense.*

pre·ter·nat·u·ral (prē′ tər năch′ ər əl) ***adj-*** not in the natural order of things, occurrences, behavior, etc.; extraordinary: *his* preternatural *bravery.* ***—adv-*** **pre′ ter·nat′ u·ral·ly.** ***n-*** **pre′ ter·nat′ u·ral·ness.**

pre·test (prē′ tĕst′) ***n-*** a test designed to get a general impression of something, rather than to arrive at an exact conclusion. ***vt-*** to give such a test to.

pre·text (prē′ tĕkst′) ***n-*** reason, motive, excuse, etc., put forward to conceal the real one.

pret·ty (prĭt′ ē) ***adj-*** [**pret·ti·er, pret·ti·est**] 1 pleasing in a charming or expected way: *a* pretty *girl*; *a* pretty *house.* 2 good, nice, or fine (often used ironically): *a* pretty *wit*; *a* pretty *mess.* 3 *Informal* moderately large: *a* pretty *sum of money.* ***adv-*** *Informal* rather; fairly; moderately: *a* pretty *good performance.* ***—adv-*** **pret′ ti·ly:** *She dresses* prettily. ***n-*** **pret′ ti·ness.**

pretty penny *Informal* ***n-*** fairly large sum of money.

pret·zel (prĕt′ səl) ***n-*** hard, crisp biscuit made from a narrow strip of dough, usually bent into a knot, glazed, and sprinkled with salt.

Pretzel

pre·vail (prĭ vāl′) ***vi-*** 1 to win; triumph: *Good will* prevail *over evil.* 2 to be most common; predominate: *Westerly winds* prevail *in that region.* 3 to be widespread; persist: *Superstition* prevailed *among the natives.*

prevail on (or **upon**) to persuade: *We* prevailed on *the musician to play for us.*

pre·vail·ing (prĭ vā′ lĭng) ***adj-*** 1 most frequent or common: *The islands have* prevailing *winds from the west.* 2 widespread; prevalent; current: *the* prevailing *custom.* ***—adv-*** **pre·vail′ ing·ly.**

prev·a·lence (prĕv′ ə ləns) ***n-*** 1 widespread occurence: *a* prevalence *of colds this winter.* 2 greater influence, effect, etc.; dominance: *the* prevalence *of new methods over the old.*

prev·a·lent (prĕv′ ə lənt) ***adj-*** occurring often; widespread: *Colds are* prevalent *during the winter.* ***—adv-*** **prev′ a·lent·ly.**

pre·var·i·cate (prĭ văr′ ə kāt′) ***vi-*** [**pre·var·i·cat·ed, pre·var·i·cat·ing**] to stray from or misrepresent the truth; lie. ***—n-*** **pre·var′ i·ca′ tion.** ***n-*** **pre·var′ i·ca′ tor:** *A habitual* prevaricator *is rarely believed.*

pre·vent (prĭ vĕnt′) ***vt-*** to keep or stop from happening or doing something; hinder: *to* prevent *an accident by quick thinking*; *to* prevent *him from finishing his work.* ***—adj-*** **pre·vent′ a·ble** or **pre·vent′ i·ble.** ***n-*** **pre·vent′ er.**

pre·ven·tion (prĭ vĕn′ shən) ***n-*** 1 the act of preventing something. 2 something that prevents or hinders: *Take this remedy as a* prevention *against colds.*

pre·ven·tive (prĭ vĕn′ tĭv) ***adj-*** serving, tending, or intended to prevent something, especially something harmful: *to take* preventive *measures against crime*; *to specialize in* preventive *medicine.* ***n-*** something that prevents; especially, something that prevents disease. ***—adv-*** **pre·ven′ tive·ly.** ***n-*** **pre·ven′ tive·ness.**

pre·view (prē′ vyo͞o′) ***n-*** 1 a showing of something, such as a motion picture or an exhibition of paintings, before

---

fāte, făt, dâre, bärn; bē, bĕt, mêre; bīte, bĭt; nōte, hŏt, môre, dòg; fŭn, fûr; to͞o, bo͝ok; oil; out; tar; thin; then; hw for wh as in *wh*at; zh for s as in u*s*ual; ə for a, e, i, o, u, as in *a*go, lin*e*n, per*i*l, at*o*m, min*u*s

it is presented to the general public. **2** (often **previews**) small portions of a motion picture, shown before a scheduled performance as an advertisement. ***vt-*** to see or exhibit ahead of time: *to* preview *spring fashions.*

pre·vi·ous (prē′ vē əs) ***adj-*** earlier; preceeding: *He grew tall since my* previous *visit.* **—*adv-* pre′ vious·ly.**

previous to before: *It happened* previous to *my trip.*

pre·war (prē′ wȯr′) ***adj-*** happening or existing before a war.

prey (prā) ***n-*** **1** animal hunted or killed by another for food. **2** victim: *an easy* prey *for swindlers.* ***Hom-*** pray.

prey on (or **upon**) **1** to hunt or kill for food: *An eagle* preys on *smaller birds.* **2** to plunder or victimize: *The swindler* preyed on *gullible people.* **3** to have a destructive or oppressive effect: *His guilt* preyed on *him.*

Pri·am (prī′ əm) ***n-*** in Greek legend, the king of Troy during the Trojan War, husband of Hecuba and father of Paris, Hector, Cassandra, and many other children.

price (prīs) ***n-*** **1** amount of money something costs: *The* price *of the ball is $2.00.* **2** worth; value: *jewels of great* price. **3** the amount of effort, sacrifice, etc., needed to get something: *the* price *of fame*; *the* price *of victory.* ***vt-*** **[priced, pric·ing] 1** to put a price on: *The car was* priced *too high for our family.* **2** *Informal* to ask the price of: *We* priced *several cars before buying.*

a price on (one's) head money reward offered for a person's capture or killing. **beyond price** priceless.

price·less (prīs′ ləs) ***adj-*** beyond what money can buy; invaluable: *a* priceless *work of art.* **—*n-* price′ less·ness.**

prick (prĭk) ***n-*** **1** small hole made by a sharp point: *The pin left* pricks *in the material.* **2** sharp point: *the* pricks *of a cactus.* **3** sharp pain: *He felt a* prick *when the bee stung him.* ***vt-*** **1** to pierce or wound with a sharp point: *The thorn* pricked *my finger.* **2** to bother; sting: *His conscience* pricked *him after he told the lie.*

prick up the ears 1 to make the ears erect: *The dog* pricked up his ears. **2** to become attentive: *She* pricked up her ears *when she heard his name.*

prick·le (prĭk′ əl) ***n-*** **1** sharp point; especially, a thorn: *This vine is full of* prickles. **2** stinging or tingling feeling: *I feel a* prickle *when I use this lotion on my face.* ***vt-*** **[prick·led, prick·ling]** to give a stinging or tingling feeling to: *The ointment* prickles *my face.* ***vi-***: *This lotion doesn't burn, but it* prickles.

prick·ly (prĭk′ lē) ***adj-*** **[prick·li·er, prick·li·est] 1** full of sharp points or thorns: *A cactus is a* prickly *plant.* **2** tingling or stinging: *a* prickly *feeling from a wool scarf.* **3** quick to take offense; irritable; sensitive: *I'm very* prickly *when I'm tired.* **—*n-* prick′ li·ness.**

prickly heat ***n-*** acute inflammation of the sweat glands, caused by excessive sweating in hot weather and marked by intense itching and burning. Also **heat rash.**

prickly pear ***n-*** **1** any of several cactuses bearing yellow flowers and an edible, often purplish, spiny, pear-shaped fruit. **2** the fruit itself.

Prickly pear, flower and fruit

pride (prīd) ***n-*** **1** excessively high opinion of a person's own ability or importance; conceit: *His* pride *was his downfall.* **2** self-respect; dignity: *His* pride *kept him from asking for money.* **3** feeling of pleasure or satisfaction: *He takes* pride *in his work.* **4** thing or person giving others pleasure or satisfaction: *He was the* pride *of his family.* ***Hom-*** pried.

pride (oneself) on [prid·ed, prid·ing] to be proud of; take pride in.

pride·ful (prīd′ fəl) ***adj-*** full of price or conceit; proud; arrogant; haughty. **—*adv-* pride′ ful·ly.**

pried (prīd) *p.t. & p.p.* of [1]**pry** and [2]**pry.** ***Hom-*** pride.

pries (prīz) form of the verbs [1]**pry** and [2]**pry,** used with "he," "she," "it," or a singular noun subject, in the present tense. ***Hom-*** prize.

priest (prēst) ***n-*** man ordained to perform religious rites; clergyman. **—*n-* *fem.* priest′ ess.**

priest·hood (prēst′ ho͝od′) ***n-*** **1** the office or duties of a priest. **2** priests collectively.

priest·ly (prēst′ lē) ***adj-*** of, like, or befitting a priest: *to carry out* priestly *duties.* **—*n-* priest′ li·ness.**

prig (prĭg) ***n-*** smug, self-righteous person who is highly critical of the morals of others; narrow-minded prude.

prig·gish (prĭg′ ĭsh) ***adj-*** of or like a prig; smug; censorious. **—*adv-* prig′ gish·ly. *n-* prig′ gish·ness.**

prim (prĭm) ***adj-*** **[prim·mer, prim·mest]** very proper and stiff in appearance and conduct; very neat or precise: *the* prim *old maid.* **—*adv-* prim′ ly. *n-* prim′ ness.**

pri·ma ballerina (prē′ mə) ***n-*** leading female dancer of a ballet company.

pri·ma·cy (prī′ mə sē) ***n-*** **1** condition of being foremost in position, importance, or rank: *the* primacy *of a law.* **2** the office or dignity of a high-ranking bishop. **3** in the Roman Catholic Church, the office of the Pope.

pri·ma don·na (prĭm′ ə dŏn′ ə) ***n-*** **1** leading female singer in an opera or concert. **2** *Informal* highly sensitive or temperamental person, especially in the dramatic arts.

pri·mal (prī′ məl) ***adj-*** **1** first; original: *the* primal *source of life.* **2** most important; chief; prime: *the* primal *reason for his success.* **—*adv-* pri′ mal·ly.**

pri·mar·i·ly (prī mĕr′ ə lē, prə-) ***adv-*** above all; principally; chiefly: *He is* primarily *a landscape painter.*

pri·ma·ry (prī′ mĕr′ ē, -mə rē) ***adj-*** **1** major; chief; principal: *the* primary *ingredient*; primary *purpose.* **2** underlying later events, work, etc.; basic; fundamental: *His* primary *discovery occurred in* 1883. **3** elementary: *the* primary *grades of school.* **4** basic; fundamental: *the* primary *colors.* **5** in electricity, relating to a circuit or coil that induces a voltage in a secondary circuit. ***n-*** [*pl.* **pri·ma·ries**] **1** (also **primary election**) election in which members of a political party run against each other in an effort to become the party's candidates in a main election. **2** primary body.

primary accent ***n-*** **1** the stress the voice puts on the strongest syllable of a word. In the word "man′ u·fac′ tur·er," the syllable "fac" has the primary accent. **2** the mark (′) used to show the strongest syllable. Also **primary stress.**

primary body ***n-*** the celestial body around which another body or satellite rotates. The primary body of the earth is the sun.

primary colors ***n-*** the three colors which may be combined to produce all other colors. Primary colors in pigments are red, blue, and yellow. In light they are orange-red, green, and deep blue.

pri·mate (prī′ māt′) ***n-*** **1** any of a large group of mammals including man, apes, monkeys, marmosets, and lemurs. **2** highest prelate of an important church division such as a province or nation.

[1]**prime** (prīm) ***adj-*** **1** chief; major; most important: *His* prime *concern is the welfare of his family.* **2** first in quality; best; choicest: *The* prime *ribs of beef are very expensive.* **3** *Archaic* first in time; original. **4** *Mathematics* of numbers, relating to a natural number whose only factors are 1 and the number itself. ***n-*** the time of a person's life when he is his best in health, mind, beauty, etc. [from Latin **primus,** "first." **—*n-* prime′ness.**

[2]**prime** (prīm) ***vt-*** **[primed, prim·ing] 1** to pour water into (a pump) to soak the pistons so that they expand to fit

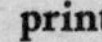

the cylinders. **2** to prepare (a gun, mine, etc.) for firing by supplying it with a primer. **3** to supply beforehand with information, details, etc.; brief; coach: *to* prime *students for an examination.* **4** to prepare (a surface) for painting by providing it with a layer of paint, oil, etc. [probably from [1]**prime.**]

prime factor *Mathematics* ***n-*** factor having only itself and 1 as factors; factor that is a prime number.

prime meridian ***n-*** meridian designated as 0° longitude, in reference to which all other longitude is numbered; especially, the meridian passing through Greenwich, England. For picture, see *longitude.*

prime minister ***n-*** head of an elected government in some countries; chief minister of state; premier.

prime mover ***n-*** **1** original or principal force in any activity or process: *Mr. Allen was the* prime mover *in this campaign.* **2** engine or other machine that provides basic power for a factory, process, train of vehicles, etc.

prime number ***n-*** a natural number that can be divided only by 1 or itself with a zero remainder.

[1]**prim·er** (prĭm′ ər) ***n-*** **1** book used in giving the first lessons in reading. **2** the first instruction book in any subject: *a* primer *in chemistry.* [from a Medieval Latin use of Latin **prīmārius,** "first in rank or time."]

[2]**prim·er** (prī′ mər) ***n-*** **1** small amount of explosive in a cartridge, bomb, etc., used to set off the main charge; detonator. **2** any of various coatings used on wood, steel, plaster, etc., to form a base for the final coat or coats of paint. [from [2]**prime.**]

pri·me·val (prī mē′ vəl) ***adj-*** belonging to the earliest times: *the* primeval *forests.* ***—adv-*** **pri·me′ val·ly.**

prim·ing (prī′ mĭng) ***n-*** **1** primer of an explosive charge. **2** paint or size, applied to a surface before painting.

prim·i·tive (prĭm′ ə tĭv) ***adj-*** **1** original; earliest; of the earliest times: *many relics of* primitive *man.* **2** simple and crude, as in early times: primitive *straw huts.* ***—adv-*** **prim′ i·tive·ly.** ***n-*** **prim′ i·tive·ness.**

pri·mo·gen·i·ture (prī′ mō jĕn′ ə chər) ***n-*** **1** the law or custom by which the eldest child, especially the eldest son, inherits all his father's property or titles; also, the right of such inheritance. **2** the condition of being the first-born child in a family.

pri·mor·di·al (prī môr′ dē əl, -môr′ dē əl) ***adj-*** of the earliest times; original; primeval: *the* primordial *matter of our solar system.* ***—adv-*** **pri·mor′ di·al·ly.**

primp (prĭmp) ***vi-*** to arrange or adorn oneself with great attention to detail and often in a vain manner; prink: *Meg* primped *for an hour.* ***vt-***: *Meg was* primping *her hair.*

prim·rose (prĭm′ rōz′) ***n-*** **1** any of several wild or cultivated plants. Most American kinds spring from a rosette of leaves with a tall flower stalk, and bloom in summer or fall. **2** the blossom of this plant, usually yellow. **3** pale-yellow color. ***adj-***: *a* primrose *dress.*

Evening primrose

primrose path ***n-*** the life or way of pleasure, especially the pleasures of the senses.

Pri·mus stove (prī′ məs) ***n-*** trademark name for a type of stove, especially a portable, kerosene-burning model, used by campers and explorers. Also **primus stove.**

prince (prĭns) ***n-*** **1** male monarch or ruler: *The king appealed to his fellow* princes *for help in repelling the invasion.* **2** male member of a royal family. **3** in Great Britain, the son of a king or queen. **4** in some countries, a nobleman of very high rank. **5** *Informal* very pleasant and good man; good and decent fellow.

prince consort ***n-*** husband of a reigning queen.

prince·ly (prĭns′ lē) ***adj-*** **1** worthy of a prince; generous; lavish: *a* princely *gift.* **2** of or related to a prince; royal; noble: *his* princely *powers.* ***—n-*** **prince′ li·ness.**

Prince of Peace ***n-*** Jesus Christ.

Prince of Wales ***n-*** title given to the oldest male heir to the British throne.

prin·cess (prĭn′ səs, -sĕs′) ***n-*** **1** in Great Britain, the daughter of a reigning monarch, or of a monarch's son. **2** wife or widow of a prince. **3** female member of a royal family.

princess royal ***n-*** eldest daughter of a reigning monarch.

prin·ci·pal (prĭn′ sə pəl) ***adj-*** main; chief; leading; most important: *our* principal *concern; the* principal *cause.* ***n-*** **1** the chief person; leader; head, especially of a school. **2** person who takes a leading part in some activity: *Betty and Bob are* principals *in the play.* **3** sum of money used to earn income or interest. **4** original amount of a loan; also, the amount not yet paid. ***Hom-*** principle. ***—adv-*** **prin′ ci·pal·ly.**

prin·ci·pal·i·ty (prĭn′ sə păl′ ə tē) ***n-*** [*pl.* **prin·ci·pal·i·ties**] the territory ruled by a prince.

principal parts ***n-*** *pl.* the main form and main inflected forms of a verb, from which all other forms are derived. In English, the principal parts are the infinitive, the past tense, and the past participle. Examples: talk, talked, talked; sing, sang, sung; go, went, gone. In this dictionary, the infinitive is shown as the entry word in boldface. The other principal parts, along with the present participle, are shown in brackets after the part-of-speech label: **[sang, sung, sing·ing].** When the past tense and the past participle are the same, only one form is shown: **[raved, rav·ing].** When the past tense and past and present participles are formed regularly (by adding "-ed" and "-ing" directly to the infinitive), they are not shown but should be assumed.

prin·ci·ple (prĭn′ sə pəl) ***n-*** **1** basic fact or rule; law by which something works: *the* principles *of multiplication; a mechanical* principle. **2** rule of conduct: *It is my* principle *to pay bills when they are due.* **3** honesty; integrity: *a man of* principle. ***Hom-*** principal.

in principle according to general law or theory; theoretically: *It works* in principle, *but not in practice.*
on principle because of one's ideas of right and wrong; according to one's morality.

prink (prĭngk) ***vt-*** ***& vi-*** to primp. ***—n-*** **prink′ er.**

print (prĭnt) ***n-*** **1** impressions of letters or other characters, made from inked type, plates, etc.: *The* print *in this book is easy to read.* **2** impression of a picture or design made from an inked woodcut, metal plate, etc.: *a Rembrandt* print. **3** cloth on which a pattern or design has been stamped; also, a dress made of such cloth: *She wore a pretty cotton* print *to the party.* **4** any impression or mark; imprint: *In the sand I saw the* print *of a foot.* **5** photograph made from a negative; positive. **6** copy of a painting, drawing, etc. made on a press: *walls decorated with* prints. **7** fingerprint. ***vt-*** **1** to reproduce by means of inked type, engraved plates, etc.: *to* print *a newspaper.* **2** to publish (a book, story, etc.). **3** to write in letters that resemble those made by type: *Please* print *your name in the upper right-hand corner.* **4** to reproduce (a photograph) from a negative. ***vi-*** **1** to write letters that resemble those made by type: *This child* prints *well.* **2** to reproduce letters, pictures, etc., by the process of printing: *Broken type will* print *poorly.*

in print 1 printed or published: *She finally saw her story* in print. **2** of books, etc., such as can be still purchased from the publisher. **out of print** of books, etc., such as can be no longer purchased from the publisher.

print out to produce as the printed output of a computer: *The machine* printed out *our new schedule.*

print·a·ble (prĭn'tə bəl) ***adj-*** not offensive to a reader; especially, not obscene, shocking, or libelous: *Most of the remarks were* printable.

printed circuit ***n-*** in electronics, a very small, complex circuit made for use in computers, communication equipment, etc., in which the conductive material is deposited on an insulating surface by painting, spraying, electrochemical means, etc.

print·er (prĭn'tər) ***n-*** **1** person whose occupation is printing. **2** (also **printers**) company in the business of printing. **3** machine that prints; especially, a teleprinter.

printer's devil ***n-*** printer's apprentice.

print·ing (prĭn'tĭng) ***n-*** **1** the process or business of reproducing letters, designs, or pictures on paper or other surfaces by means of inked type, plates, or blocks. **2** words, sentences, etc., that have been printed: *The* printing *in this book is very clear.* **3** all the copies of a book, pamphlet, etc., printed at one time. **4** writing that resembles print: *The teacher's* printing *is clear.*

printing press ***n-*** machine for printing letters, pictures, or designs on paper or other surfaces by means of inked type, plates, or blocks.

print-out (prĭnt'out') ***n-*** figures, words, or data forming the output of a computer and printed on an extremely fast typing machine.

[1]**pri·or** (prī' ər) ***adj-*** **1** earlier; previous: *a* prior *invitation.* **2** more important because it came sooner: *the* prior *claim to a reward.*

prior to before: *Our mayor practiced law* prior to her *election.* [from Latin **prior,** "former; previous."]

[2]**pri·or** (prī' ər) ***n-*** the head of a religious house for men, called a priory. [from Old French and Latin **prior,** a special medieval use of [1]**prior.**]

pri·or·ess (prī' ər əs) ***n-*** the head of a religious house for women, called a priory.

pri·or·i·ty (prī ôr' ə tē) ***n-*** [*pl.* **pri·or·i·ties**] the condition or right of being or coming before others; precedence: *the absolute* priority *of a request from the President.*

pri·o·ry (prī' ə rē) ***n-*** [*pl.* **pri·o·ries**] monastery ruled by a prior, or a convent ruled by a prioress. A priory ranks below an abbey and is often under its control.

prism (prĭz'əm) ***n-*** **1** a solid with any number of flat sides and with two flat ends that are parallel and exactly alike in size and shape. **2** transparent solid with triangular ends used to reflect light or separate it into colors.

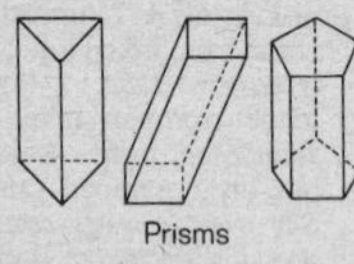
Prisms

pris·mat·ic (prĭz măt'ĭk) ***adj-*** **1** of, relating to, or produced by a prism: *a* prismatic *effect*; prismatic *colors.* **2** many-colored; like the spectrum. ***—adv-*** **pris·mat'i·cal·ly.**

prismatic colors ***n-*** the colors produced when white light is passed through a prism.

prism binoculars ***n- pl.*** binoculars in which the path of the incoming light is made to travel farther by being reflected by several prisms, thus providing an erect image and increased magnification.

pris·on (prĭz'ən) ***n-*** **1** place where convicted criminals serve their sentences of confinement; penitentiary. **2** any place where a person is held against his will: *The office was a* prison *to them on fine spring days.*

pris·on·er (prĭz' ə nər) ***n-*** **1** person who is held in prison. **2** one who is under arrest, or held for a crime: *The* prisoner *pleaded guilty to a charge of reckless driving.* **3** (also **prisoner of war**) soldier captured by the enemy. **4** any person or thing held captive: *The wild bird was a* prisoner *in the cage.*

pris·sy (prĭs'ē) *Informal* ***adj-*** [**pris·si·er, pris·si·est**] overly precise or fussy about matters of dress, conduct, etc.; prim; finicky. ***—adv-*** **pris'si·ly.** ***n-*** **pris'si·ness.**

pris·tine (prĭs'tēn') ***adj-*** **1** pure and unspoiled; uncorrupted: *the* pristine *beauty of a sunset.* **2** of earliest times; original: *the* pristine *state of society.*

prith·ee (prĭth'ē) *Archaic* ***interj-*** I pray thee; please.

pri·va·cy (prī' və sē) ***n-*** [*pl.* **pri·va·cies**] **1** physical separateness from other people; seclusion: *Hard study usually requires* privacy. **2** secrecy: *Sue and her friends studied the treasure map in* privacy. **3** the right to freedom from interference by others: *the* privacy *of citizens.*

pri·vate (prī' vət) ***adj-*** **1** belonging to or intended for a particular person or group; not public or governmental: *a* private *lake*; *a* private *performance*; private *school.* **2** personal; individual: *I have* private *reasons for wanting to stay home.* **3** not official: *in* private *life*; *a* private *citizen.* **4** secret; confidential: *We made* private *arrangements for the surprise party.* ***n-*** **1** in the Army, an enlisted person ranking next below a private first class and next above a recruit. **2** in the Marine Corps, an enlisted person of the lowest rank. ***—adv-*** **pri'vate·ly.** ***n-*** **pri'vate·ness.**

in private secretly: *The thieves met* in private.

private detective ***n-*** person employed by a private citizen or group to investigate crimes, gather evidence, or maintain law and order.

private enterprise ***n-*** free enterprise.

pri·va·teer (prī'və têr') ***n-*** **1** formerly, a privately owned and operated ship given permission by a government to attack and capture enemy ships. **2** commander or one of the crew members of such a ship. ***vi-:*** *During the War of 1812, Decatur* privateered *for the United States.*

private first class ***n-*** **1** in the Army, an enlisted person who ranks next below a corporal and next above a private. **2** in the Marine Corps, an enlisted person who ranks next below a lance corporal and next above a private.

private school ***n-*** school that is owned and operated by a private citizen or group.

pri·va·tion (prī vā' shən) ***n-*** hardship and suffering due to a lack of the necessities of life, especially food, clothing, and shelter.

priv·et (prĭv' ət) ***n-*** shrub of the olive family, having dark leaves and small white flowers, and used for hedges.

priv·i·lege (prĭv' ə lĭj) ***n-*** special right or advantage granted to or enjoyed by a person or group of persons: *the* privilege *of a college education*; *the* privileges *that come with rank and wealth.* ***—adj-*** **priv'i·leged:** *I am* privileged *to know her. A few* privileged *visitors met him.*

priv·i·ly (prĭv' ə lē) *Archaic* ***adv-*** privately; secretly.

priv·y (prĭv'ē) ***adj-*** *Archaic* for private, not public, use; personal. ***n-*** [*pl.* **priv·ies**] enclosed outdoor toilet.

privy to secretly sharing in the knowledge of: *There were only six* privy to *the conspiracy.*

[1]**prize** (prīz) ***n-*** **1** reward offered or won in a contest; award: *to win first* prize. **2** something very valuable or desirable: *This puppy is the* prize *of the litter.* *as* ***modifier:*** *the* prize *painting in the show*; *a* prize *horse.* ***vt-*** [**prized, priz·ing**] to value highly; think highly of:

to prize *someone's friendship.* [from Old French **preisier,** "to value highly," from Late Latin **pretiāre,** "to put a value on." It is related to **price** and **praise.**] ***Hom-*** pries.

[2]**prize** (prīz) ***n-*** something captured in war, especially a ship or its cargo. [from Old French **prise** meaning "a seizing; the thing seized," from **prendre,** from Latin **prehendere,** "to seize; take."] ***Hom-*** pries.

[3]**prize** (prīz) *chiefly Brit.* ***vt-*** **[prized, priz·ing]** to force or raise with a lever; pry: *to* prize *a lid off a box.* [from [2]**prize.**] ***Hom-*** pries.

prize fight ***n-*** match between professional boxers. ***—n-*** **prize fighter.** ***n-*** **prize fighting.**

[1]**pro** (prō) ***adv-*** in favor of; for: *to argue* pro *and con.* ***n-*** [*pl.* **pros**] argument, reason, etc. in favor of something: *to discuss the* pros *and cons of buying a new car.* [from the phrase **pro and con,** from [2]**pro-.**]

[2]**pro** (prō) *Informal* ***n-*** [*pl.* **pros**] **1** person who earns a living in a field or activity usually regarded as a pastime; professional: *a golf* pro. **2** person who is very competent and has long experience in his work: *He's a real* pro. ***adj-:*** *a* pro *ballplayer.* [short for "professional."]

[1]**pro-** *prefix* in front of; before: *a* pro*logue* (introduction to a play, novel, etc.); pro*phase* (first stage in the mitosis of a cell). [from Greek **pro-,** from **pro** meaning "before."]

[2]**pro-** *prefix* **1** on the side of; favoring: *a* pro-*French point of view*; pro-*slavery.* **2** in place of; substituting for: *the* pro*noun*; pro*consul.* [from Latin **pro-,** from **pro** meaning "before; forward; in place of; in favor of."]

prob·a·bil·i·ty (prŏb′ ə bĭl′ ə tē) ***n-*** [*pl.* **prob·a·bil·i·ties**] **1** likelihood; chance: *The* probability *of his making the trip in such a bad snowstorm is very small.* **2** something likely to happen: *His coming this weekend is a* probability. **3** *Mathematics* ratio expressing the relation between the number of chances favoring the occurrence of an event and the total number of ways in which that event could occur. The probability of drawing one of four queens from a pack of 52 cards is 4/52 or 1/13.

prob·a·ble (prŏb′ ə bəl) ***adj-*** very likely to happen or prove true: *When storm clouds gather, rain is* probable. *The rain is the* probable *cause of his lateness.* ***—adv-*** **prob′ a·bly.**

pro·bate (prō′ bāt′) ***n-*** **1** act of legally proving the genuineness of a will. **2** copy of a will so proved. ***adj-:*** *a* probate *court*; *a* probate *judge.* ***vt-*** **[pro·bat·ed, pro·bat·ing]** to prove the genuineness of (a will) legally.

pro·ba·tion (prō bā′ shən) ***n-*** **1** trial or testing of a person's character, ability, etc. **2** legal procedure under which young lawbreakers or first offenders are permitted to go free under strict supervision, instead of being put in prison. **3** the period of trial or supervision.

on probation **1** being watched, tested, and judged: *New employees are* on probation *for three months.* **2** free, but under strict supervision, after being convicted of crime: *The auto thief was* on probation.

pro·ba·tion·ar·y (prō bā′ shən ĕr′ ē) ***adj-*** of, related to, or undergoing probation: *a* probationary *student.*

pro·ba·tion·er (prō bā′ shən ər) ***n-*** person who is undergoing a period of probation.

probation officer ***n-*** officer appointed by a court to supervise and report on an offender who has been placed on probation.

probe (prōb) ***vt-*** **[probed, prob·ing]** **1** to examine or inquire into closely: *to* probe *an area for clues*; *to* probe *one's feelings.* **2** to examine (a wound, cavity, etc.) with a slender surgical instrument. ***vi-:*** *to* probe *for clues*; *to* probe *for a bullet.* ***n-*** **1** searching inquiry or examination. **2** slender surgical instrument for examining a wound, cavity, etc. **3** space probe.

prob·i·ty (prō′ bə tē) ***n-*** honesty and integrity; uprightness: *a man of unquestioned* probity.

prob·lem (prŏb′ ləm) ***n-*** **1** difficult question, issue, set of circumstances, etc., that requires an answer or solution: *the* problems *of our foreign policy*; *the* problem *of housing.* **2** something that causes difficulty or perplexity: *Otto is a* problem *to me. What's your* problem? **3** *Mathematics* statement containing or implying a question that can be answered by mathematical means: *He assigned six algebra* problems. *as* ***modifier:*** *a* problem *child.*

prob·le·mat·ic (prŏb′ lə măt′ ĭk) or **prob·le·mat·i·cal** (-ĭ′ kəl) ***adj-*** like a problem; questionable; uncertain. ***—adv-*** **prob′ le·mat′ i·cal·ly.**

pro·bos·cis (prə bŏs′ əs) ***n-*** **1** trunk of an elephant. **2** insect mouth parts adapted for piercing and sucking or just sucking, such as those of the butterfly.

pro·caine (prō′ kān′) ***n-*** chemical name of Novocain.

pro·ce·dure (prə sē′ jər, prō-) ***n-*** **1** way or system of proceeding to get something done; method: *What* procedure *should I follow in applying for a driver's license?* **2** *Informal* process. ***—adj-*** **pro·ce′ dur·al:** *a* procedural *change.* ***adv-*** **pro·ce′ dur·al·ly.**

pro·ceed (prə sēd′) ***vi-*** to go on or forward, especially after stopping: *to* proceed *on a journey.*

proceed from to result or issue from.

pro·ceed·ing (prə sē′ dĭng) ***n-*** **1** action or course of action: *a strange* proceeding. **2** **proceedings** (1) formal actions of a court, legislature, society, etc. (2) record of such actions; minutes.

pro·ceeds (prō′ sēdz′) ***n-*** *pl.* money received from a business transaction, especially from selling something.

proc·ess (prŏs′ ĕs, -əs, prō′ sĕs′) ***n-*** **1** action or series of actions that bring about a particular result or product: *Training to become a doctor is a lengthy* process. *The company tried out a new* process *for making steel.* **2** in law, (1) the proceedings in a case; action or suit. (2) summons to appear in court. **3** *Biology* (1) projecting or outgrowing part of an organism or any of its structures: *a bony* process. (2) an axon or dendrite. ***vt-*** **1** to make or treat by a special method: *to* process *cheese.* **2** to examine, classify, or attend to, especially by some routine procedure: *to* process *recruits*; process *a loan.*

in process under way; being done or carried out.

pro·ces·sion (prə sĕsh′ ən) ***n-*** **1** formal parade; also, the persons taking part in it: *A military* procession *escorted the President.* **2** movement along a particular course; progression: *the* procession *of the choir.*

pro·ces·sion·al (prə sĕsh′ ən əl) ***n-*** music that accompanies a procession, especially that of a choir entering church. *as* ***modifier:*** *a* processional *hymn.*

pro·claim (prō klām′) ***vt-*** **1** to announce publicly or officially; declare: *to* proclaim *a holiday; to* proclaim *one's ideas to anyone who will listen.* **2** to show plainly; reveal: *His kind acts* proclaimed *a generous heart.*

proc·la·ma·tion (prŏk′ lə mā′ shən) ***n-*** **1** formal or public announcement: *The mayor read the* proclamation. **2** act of proclaiming: *the* proclamation *of a holiday.*

pro·cliv·i·ty (prə klĭv′ ə tē) ***n-*** [*pl.* **pro·cliv·i·ties**] tendency or inclination (to or toward); weakness (for): *a* proclivity *to gossip; a* proclivity *for fine wines.*

pro·con·sul (prō′ kŏn′ səl) ***n-*** **1** in ancient Rome, the governor and military commander of a province. **2** chief administrator of a colony or occupied area.

pro·cras·ti·nate (prə krăs′ tə nāt′) ***vi-*** **[pro·cras·ti·nat·ed, pro·cras·ti·nat·ing]** to put off, often habitually, something that should be done; defer taking necessary action; delay: *While Tom* procrastinated, *Sue prepared for the exam.* **—*n-* pro·cras′ ti·na′ tion.** ***n-*** **pro·cras′ ti·na′ tor:** *A* procrastinator *has ready excuses for delay.*

pro·cre·ate (prō′ krē āt′) ***vi-*** **[pro·cre·at·ed, pro·cre·at·ing]** to reproduce by mating. ***vt-*** to bring forth (offspring); beget. **—*n-* pro′ cre·a′ tion.**

proc·tor (prŏk′ tər) ***n-*** person appointed by a school to supervise students, especially during an examination. ***vt-***: *He* proctored *the examination.*

proc·u·ra·tor (prŏk′ yə rā′ tər) ***n-*** in ancient Rome, an official who was in charge of the financial affairs of a province and sometimes served as the governor of part of a province.

pro·cure (prə kyo͝or′) ***vt-*** **[pro·cured, pro·cur·ing] 1** to get; obtain: *to* procure *the services of a good doctor.* **2** to cause; bring about: *The secret service* procured *the arrest of the spy.* **—*adj-* pro·cur′ a·ble:** *That book is not* procurable; *it is out of print.* ***n-*** **pro·cure′ ment.**

prod (prŏd) ***vt-*** **[prod·ded, prod·ding] 1** to punch or poke with a pointed instrument: *to* prod *cattle.* **2** to urge; goad; rouse: *to* prod *a lazy person.* ***n-* 1** pointed implement, such as a goad, for poking or pricking. **2** poke or dig: *a* prod *in the ribs.* **—*n-* prod′ der.**

prod·i·gal (prŏd′ ə gəl) ***adj-* 1** habitually using and spending in large and wasteful amounts: *Jim is* prodigal *with his allowance.* **2** very generous; lavish: *He is very* prodigal *of compliments.* ***n-*** person who is recklessly extravagant, especially with money; spendthrift. **—*adv-* prod′ i·gal·ly.**

prod·i·gal·i·ty (prŏd′ ə găl′ ə tē) ***n-*** [*pl.* **prod·i·gal·i·ties**] **1** act or habit of being prodigal. **2** great abundance; profuseness: *the* prodigality *of nature.*

pro·di·gious (prə dĭj′ əs) ***adj-* 1** huge; great: vast: *a* prodigious *sum of money.* **2** marvelous; wonderful; amazing: *The Egyptian pyramids are* prodigious *monuments.* **—*adv-* pro·di′ gious·ly.** ***n-*** **pro·di′ gious·ness.**

prod·i·gy (prŏd′ ə jē) ***n-*** [*pl.* **prod·i·gies**] **1** highly gifted or talented person, especially a child. **2** something extraordinary; marvel; wonder: *a* prodigy *of nature.*

[1]**pro·duce** (prə do͞os′, -dyo͞os′) ***vt-*** **[pro·duced, pro·duc·ing] 1** to bring forth or put out; yield: *Boiling water* produces *steam. That oil well* produced *200 barrels yesterday.* **2** to make; especially, to manufacture: *Our company* produces *automobiles.* **3** to bring about; give rise to: *His book* produced *great controversy.* **4** to present for inspection; exhibit; show: *Please* produce *your tickets at the gate.* **5** to present (a play or other entertainment) before the public. ***vi-*** to bring forth something; create; yield: *Tom is not lazy; he* produces!

[2]**pro·duce** (prŏd′ o͞os, prō′ do͞os′) ***n-*** farm products collectively, especially fresh fruit and vegetables.

pro·duc·er (prə do͞o′ sər, -dyo͞o′ sər) ***n-* 1** person or thing that makes or yields something: *Mr. Thompson is a steel* producer. **2** person who supervises the production of a play, motion picture, or other entertainment.

pro·duc·i·ble (prə do͞o′ sə bəl, prə dyo͞o′-) ***adj-* 1** such as can be brought forth; available: *That evidence is not* producible. **2** such as can be made or manufactured: *His product is* producible *on short notice.*

prod·uct (prŏd′ əkt, -ŭkt′) ***n-* 1** anything made or yielded: *farm* products; *a* product *of the imagination.* **2** result; outcome: *His failure was a* product *of laziness.* **3** *Mathematics* the result obtained by multiplying two or more numbers: *The* product *of 4 and 3 is 12.*

pro·duc·tion (prə dŭk′ shen) ***n-* 1** a producing: *the* production *of ball-point pens.* **2** something produced; especially, a play, motion picture, book, or other artistic work. **3** the total amount that is made or produced, especially of a commercial or industrial product.

pro·duc·tive (prə dŭk′ tĭv) ***adj-* 1** having the ability to make or create; creative: *a* productive *inventor.* **2** fertile; rich: *This* productive *soil yields large crops.* **3** yielding a product profitably: *a* productive *oil well; a* productive *idea.* **—*adv-* pro·duc′ tive·ly.** ***n-*** **pro·duc′ tive·ness** or **pro′ duc·tiv′ i·ty** (prŏd′ ək tĭv′ ə tē).

productive of producing, or having the ability to produce; causing: *a man who is* productive of *much good.*

pro·em (prō′ ĕm) ***n-*** introductory statement to a writing or speech; preface.

Prof. or **prof.** professor.

prof·a·na·tion (prŏf′ ə nā′ shən) ***n-* 1** act of profaning; desecration or debasement: *to protect a shrine from* profanation. **2** something that profanes: *Frivolity here is a* profanation.

pro·fane (prō fān′) ***adj-* 1** showing disrespect or contempt for God or sacred things; irreverent: *his* profane *treatment of a shrine.* **2** coarse; vulgar: *using* profane *language.* **3** *Archaic* not concerned with religious matters; secular: *a* profane *history of France.* ***vt-*** **[pro·faned, pro·fan·ing] 1** to treat (something sacred) with disrespect or contempt; be irreverent toward; desecrate: *They* profaned *the temple.* **2** to put to improper or unworthy use; debase. **—*adv-* pro·fane′ ly.** ***n-*** **pro·fane′ ness.**

pro·fan·i·ty (prō făn′ ə tē, prə-) ***n-*** [*pl.* **pro·fan·i·ties**] use of irreverent or vulgar speech; also, an irreverent or vulgar remark: *He uttered a stream of* profanities.

pro·fess (prə fĕs′) ***vt-* 1** to declare openly and freely; affirm: *to* profess *a dislike for playing cards.* **2** to follow or practice as a religion: *to* profess *Buddhism.* **3** to claim; pretend to: *He* professes *a knowledge of music.*

pro·fess·ed·ly (prə fĕs′ əd lē) ***adv-* 1** by open declaration; avowedly: *He is* professedly *in disagreement.* **2** allegedly; ostensibly: *It is* professedly *his own idea.*

pro·fes·sion (prə fĕsh′ ən) ***n-* 1** occupation, such as medicine or law, that requires special education. **2** the group of persons engaged in such an occupation: *the medical* profession. **3** open and free declaration: *a* profession *of faith.*

pro·fes·sion·al (prə fĕsh′ ən əl) ***adj-* 1** having to do with a profession or career: *the* professional *duties of a lawyer.* **2** for pay; not amateur or temporary. ***n-* 1** person who uses his skill in a sport to make money: *She took her ski lessons from a* professional. **2** *Informal* person who is highly skilled and experienced in anything. **—*adv-* pro·fes′ sion·al·ly.**

pro·fes·sor (prə fĕs′ ər) ***n-*** in a college or university, a teacher of the highest rank. This title is also used informally when referring to two lower academic ranks, **associate professor** and **assistant professor.**

pro·fes·sor·i·al (prŏf′ ə sôr′ ē əl) ***adj-*** of, or considered typical of, a professor; academic: *his* professorial *duties; a grave,* professorial *manner.* **—*adv-* pro′ fes·sor′ i·al·ly.**

pro·fes·sor·ship (prə fĕs′ ər shĭp′) ***n-*** the position or duties of a professor.

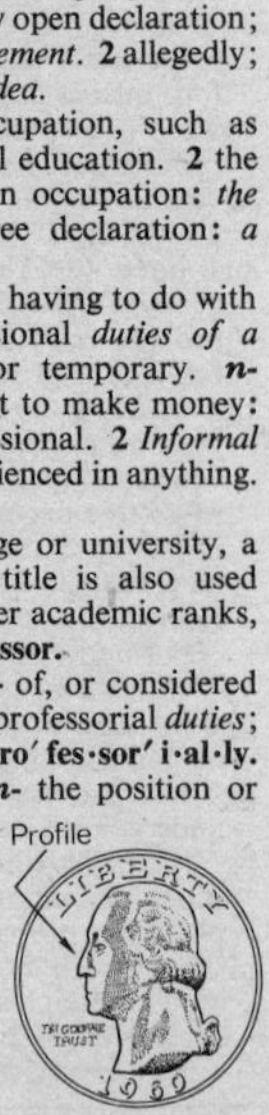

prof·fer (prŏf′ ər) ***vt-*** to offer for acceptance: *to* proffer *a gift.* ***n-*** offer: *a* proffer *of aid.*

pro·fi·cient (prə fĭsh′ ənt) ***adj-*** highly skilled; very competent: *a* proficient *typist.* **—*n-* pro·fi′ cien·cy:** *her* proficiency *at teaching.* ***adv-*** **pro·fi′ cient·ly.**

Profile

pro·file (prō′ fīl′) ***n-* 1** side view, or the outline of a side view, especially of the face: *a handsome* profile; *the* profile *of a sailing ship.* **2** outline: *the* profile *of a mountain range.* **3** brief, vivid biographical sketch. **4** curve that connects the surface elevations or depressions along a chosen line; also, a picture of this. **5** vertical arrangement of soil, rock, or other earth materials at any chosen place; also, a sectional diagram of this. **6** graph or other visual representation of a person's abilities or traits: *a personality* profile.

prof·it (prŏf′ ət) ***n-*** **1** amount gained from a sale or business after deducting all costs or expenses; income minus expenditures. **2** benefit; advantage: *Having such an excellent teacher is to your* profit. ***vt-*** to be of service to; improve; benefit: *It would* profit *you to read better books.* ***vi-***: *He* profited *greatly from his travels abroad.* ***Hom-*** prophet. **—*adj-* prof′ it·less.**

prof·it·a·ble (prŏf′ ĭt ə bəl) ***adj-*** **1** yielding financial gain or profit: *a* profitable *business.* **2** rewarding; beneficial; useful: *It is* profitable *to read good books.* **—*n-* prof′ it·a·ble·ness.** ***adv-*** **prof′ it·a·bly.**

prof·it·eer (prŏf′ ə têr′) ***n-*** person who makes or seeks to make excessive profit during a war or other time of shortage. ***vi-***: *He* profiteered *in coffee.*

prof·li·gate (prŏf′ lə gət) ***adj-*** **1** wholly given up to vice; immoral; dissolute. **2** recklessly extravagant; wasteful. ***n-*** immoral or extravagant person. **—*n-* prof′ li·ga·cy:** *The minister scolded him for the* profligacy *of his life.* ***adv-*** **prof′ li·gate·ly.**

pro·found (prə found′) ***adj-*** **1** having deep meaning or feeling; penetrating: *the* profound *sayings of the Bible*; *a* profound *scholar.* **2** complete; thorough; very great: *a* profound *silence*; profound *knowledge of science*; profound *sorrow.* **3** situated or carried very far down: *a* profound *bow.* **—*adv-* pro·found′ ly.** ***n-*** **pro·found′ ness.**

pro·fun·di·ty (prə fŭn′ də tē) ***n-*** [*pl.* **pro·fun·di·ties**] **1** great depth of meaning or feeling: *the* profundity *of the doctor's theory.* **2** idea, theory, or subject that is deep and complex: *the* profundities *of philosophy.*

pro·fuse (prə fyōōs′) ***adj-*** **1** plentiful; abundant: *a* profuse *display of flowers.* **2** generous; extravagant; lavish: *a* profuse *apology*; profuse *kindness.* **—*adv-* pro·fuse′ly.** ***n-*** **pro·fuse′ ness.**

pro·fu·sion (prə fyōō′ zhən) ***n-*** **1** generous quantity or amount; abundance: *a* profusion *of flowers.* **2** lavishness; extravagance: *She spent money in great* profusion.

pro·gen·i·tor (prə jĕn′ ə tər) ***n-*** **1** direct ancestor; forefather. **2** originator: *Pasteur is one of the* progenitors *of modern germ theory.*

prog·e·ny (prŏj′ ə nē) ***n-*** [*pl.* **prog·e·nies**] children; descendants; offspring.

prog·no·sis (prŏg nō′ səs) ***n-*** **1** *Medicine* the probable course and outcome of a disease. **2** any prediction or forecast of events: *a weather* prognosis.

prog·nos·tic (prŏg nŏs′ tĭk) ***adj-*** of or related to a prognosis; foretelling; predictive: *a* prognostic *report.* ***n-*** **1** omen, token, or other sign of some future happening. **2** prediction or forecast; prophecy.

prog·nos·ti·cate (prŏg nŏs′ tə kāt′) ***vt-*** [**prog·nos·ti·cat·ed, prog·nos·ti·cat·ing**] **1** to foretell; predict; forecast: *The fortuneteller* prognosticated *doom.* **2** to indicate in advance; foreshadow; presage: *The dark clouds* prognosticate *a storm.* **—*n-* prog·nos′ ti·ca′ tion.** ***n-*** **prog·nos′ ti·ca′ tor:** *a* prognosticator *of doom.*

pro·gram (prō′ grăm′) ***n-*** **1** list of the features and participants of an entertainment or ceremony: *a theater* program; *a graduation* program. **2** the entertainment or ceremony itself. **3** radio or television broadcast. **4** plan to be followed: *a* program *for federal aid to education.* **5** in electronics, the complex, specific set of rules by means of which a computer is instructed to carry out a particular operation or series of operations in order to solve a problem. ***vt-*** [**pro·gramed** or **pro·grammed, pro·gram·ing** or **pro·gram·ming**] **1** to schedule; arrange: *to* program *two concerts for the season.* **2** to work out and write a program for (a computer or an operation to be performed by a computer).

[1]**prog·ress** (prŏ′ grĕs′) ***n-*** **1** forward movement; advance: *We made no* progress *through the heavy traffic.* **2** development: *the* progress *of a political campaign.* **3** improvement: *Our record shows continual* progress.

[2]**pro·gress** (prə grĕs′, prō-) ***vi-*** **1** to move forward: *to* progress *on a trip.* **2** to develop: *The new building is* progressing *rapidly.* **3** to improve: *She has* progressed *under the doctor's care.*

pro·gres·sion (prə grĕsh′ ən) ***n-*** **1** a progressing; progress; advance: *the* progression *of events.* **2** *Music* movement from one note or chord to the next; also, a succession of several notes or chords. **3** *Mathematics* a sequence of numbers of which each one after the first is related to the previous number in a constant manner. In an **arithmetical progression,** successive numbers are larger or smaller than preceding ones by a constant amount. In a **geometric progression,** each number after the first is derived by multiplying the preceding number by a fixed number.

pro·gres·sive (prə grĕs′ ĭv) ***adj-*** **1** in favor of progress or reform; advocating new ideas and changes for the sake of improvement: *The* progressive *town council built a new recreation center.* **2** making such progress; advancing; improving: *a* progressive *country.* **3** moving forward steadily or step by step: *The* progressive *stages in growing up.* ***n-*** person who believes in progress or reform, especially in political reform. **—*adv-* pro·gres′ sive·ly.** ***n-*** **pro·gres′ sive·ness.**

progressive tense ***n-*** verb tense that indicates the continuation of an action or condition in the present, past, or future. It is made up of the auxiliary "be" and the present participle. Examples: *I* am writing. *I* was writing. *I* will be writing.

pro·hib·it (prō hĭb′ ĭt) ***vt-*** **1** to refuse to permit; forbid, especially by law: *The police* prohibited *parking on Main Street.* **2** to prevent: *The expenses of the new house* prohibit *a vacation this year.*

pro·hi·bi·tion (prō′ ə bĭsh′ ən) ***n-*** **1** act of forbidding. **2** law, order, or rule that forbids: *Read the* prohibition *against smoking.* **3** the forbidding by law of the manufacture and sale of alcoholic liquors.

pro·hi·bi·tion·ist (prō′ ə bĭsh′ ə nĭst) ***n-*** person who favors the passage of laws prohibiting the manufacture and sale of alcoholic liquors.

pro·hib·i·tive (prō hĭb′ ə tĭv) ***adj-*** forbidding, preventing, or hindering something from being done or used: *a* prohibitive *power*; *a* prohibitive *price.* Also **pro·hib′ i·tor′ y.**

[1]**proj·ect** (prə jĕkt′) ***vt-*** **1** to plan; propose: *to* project *a new school building.* **2** to throw or shoot forward: *to* project *a missile.* **3** to cause (a beam of light, shadow, picture, etc.) to fall on a surface. **4** to cause (one's voice) to be heard clearly at a distance. **5** to visualize or imagine (oneself, an idea, etc.) in another situation or time: *He* projected *his prejudices into the future.* ***vi-*** **1** to jut out or extend: *A balcony* projects *over the sidewalk.* **2** to cause one's voice to be heard clearly at a

distance: *You should* project *when you sing.* **3** in psychology, to see one's own feelings, ideas, etc., in others.

[2]**proj·ect** (prŏj′ ĕkt′) ***n-*** **1** plan; scheme: *a* project *to build a new gymnasium*; Project *Gemini for moon exploration.* **2** special task or problem undertaken by a student or group of students. **3** (also **housing project**) group of dwellings, especially apartment houses, built by the government, a union, company, etc.

pro·jec·tile (prə jĕk′ təl) ***n-*** something thrown or shot forward, especially an artillery shell. ***adj-*** of or relating to the shooting or throwing of missiles: *great* projectile *force.*

pro·jec·tion (prə jĕk′ shən) ***n-*** **1** an extending or jutting out; a projecting. **2** something that extends or juts out: *He disappeared behind a* projection *of rock.* **3** in psychology, the unconscious seeing in other people of one's own feelings, attitudes, prejudices, etc.

pro·jec·tor (prə jĕk′ tər) ***n-*** machine or apparatus for projecting an image on a surface: *a movie* projector.

pro·le·tar·i·an (prō′ lə târ′ ē ən) ***adj-*** of, related to, or considered typical of the proletariat: *a* proletarian *policy*; *a* proletarian *novel.* ***n-*** one of the proletariat.

pro·le·tar·i·at (prō′ lə târ′ ē ət) ***n-*** the working class; especially, the industrial working class.

pro·lif·er·ate (prə lĭf′ ə rāt′) ***vi-*** [**pro·lif·er·at·ed, pro·lif·er·at·ing**] to grow or reproduce rapidly; multiply in quick succession: *Cells* proliferate *during cancer. Rumors* proliferated *within the mob.* ***vt-***: *to* proliferate *buds*; *to* proliferate *new ideas.* **—*n-* pro·lif′ er·a′ tion.**

pro·lif·ic (prə lĭf′ ĭk) ***adj-*** producing much; fertile: *a* prolific *author*; *a* prolific *animal.* **—*adv-* pro·lif′ i·cal·ly.**

pro·lix (prō lĭks′) ***adj-*** tediously wordy; verbose; long-winded: *a* prolix *speech.* **—*n-* pro·lix′ i·ty.**

pro·logue or **pro·log** (prō′ lòg′, -lŏg′) ***n-*** **1** introduction to a literary work or dramatic performance; prelude. **2** any act or event that serves as an introduction or prelude to something else: *a* prologue *to great events.*

pro·long (prə lòng′) ***vt-*** to lengthen, especially the time of; draw out; extend: *to* prolong *a visit.*

pro·lon·ga·tion (prō′ lòng′ gā′ shən) ***n-*** **1** act of prolonging; extension: *the* prolongation *of one's life.* **2** added part that makes something longer: *the* prolongations *of a table.*

prom (prŏm) *Informal* ***n-*** formal school dance.

prom·e·nade (prŏm′ ə nād′, näd′) ***n-*** **1** a walk, especially one taken in public for pleasure, display, or exercise. **2** boulevard, ship's deck, or other place for such a walk. **3** march that begins a dance or is part of a square dance. ***vi-*** [**prom·e·nad·ed, prom·e·nad·ing**] **1** to stroll in public: *to* promenade *along the seashore.* **2** to perform a promenade in a dance: *Jack* promenaded *with his partner.* ***vt-***: *Now* promenade *your partner!*

Pro·me·the·us (prə mē′ thē əs) ***n-*** in Greek mythology, a Titan who stole fire from heaven and taught man how to use it. Zeus punished him with eternal torture.

pro·me·thi·um (prə mē′ thē əm) ***n-*** radioactive, rare-earth element. Symbol Pm, At. No. 61, At. Wt. 147.

prom·i·nence (prŏm′ ə nəns) ***n-*** **1** importance or eminence; esteem: *a place of* prominence *in history.* **2** something that juts up or rises sharply: *Cliff dwellers once lived on this rocky* prominence. **3** solar prominence.

prom·i·nent (prŏm′ ə nənt) ***adj-*** **1** important; well-known; eminent: *a* prominent *citizen.* **2** conspicuous; very noticeable: *a* prominent *place in the newspaper.* **3** standing or jutting out; projecting: *The camel has a* prominent *hump.* **—*adv-* prom′ i·nent·ly.**

pro·mis·cu·i·ty (prŏm′ ĭ skyōō′ ə tē) ***n-*** **1** looseness in sexual relations; profligacy. **2** lack of order and discrimination; confusion: *a* promiscuity *of taste.*

pro·mis·cu·ous (prə mĭs′ kyōō əs) ***adj-*** **1** having sexual relations with more than one person. **2** without distinction or restriction; indiscriminate: *their* promiscuous *hospitality.* **3** mixed together in a confused way; jumbled: *a* promiscuous *gathering.* **—*adv-* pro·mis′ cu·ous·ly.**

prom·ise (prŏm′ ĭs) ***n-*** **1** pledge that one will or will not do something: *Did you keep your* promise *not to eat candy before dinner?* **2** cause or reason to expect something: *the crops gave* promise *of a good harvest.* ***vt-*** [**prom·ised, prom·is·ing**] **1** to pledge; give assurance of: *to* promise *to be on time*; *to* promise *cooperation.* **2** to agree to give or get for someone: *Dad* promised *me a new bicycle for my birthday.* **3** to give reason to expect: *The thunder* promised *rain before the end of our picnic.*

Promised Land ***n-*** **1** in the Bible, the land promised by God to Abraham; Canaan. **2** any longed-for place of happiness; heaven or paradise.

prom·is·ing (prŏm′ əs ĭng) ***adj-*** likely to be successful or satisfactory; likely to turn out well: *a most* promising *offer.* **—*adv-* prom′ is·ing·ly.**

prom·is·sor·y (prŏm′ ə sôr′ ē) ***adj-*** promising to do or not to do something: *a* promissory *agreement.*

promissory note ***n-*** written agreement to pay a certain sum of money on demand or at a fixed date.

prom·on·to·ry (prŏm′ ən tôr′ ē) ***n-*** [*pl.* **prom·on·to·ries**] high point of land jutting into water; headland.

Promontory

pro·mote (prə mōt′) ***vt-*** [**pro·mot·ed, pro·mot·ing**] **1** to help the growth, development, or success of: *a sales campaign to* promote *a new product.* **2** to raise to a higher rank or class: *My father was* promoted *to district manager.* **3** to set in motion; launch: *to* promote *a new business undertaking.*

pro·mot·er (prə mō′ tər) ***n-*** **1** person who encourages or forwards something: *a* promoter *of peace.* **2** person who helps to organize a business venture: *a boxing* promoter.

pro·mo·tion (prə mō′ shən) ***n-*** **1** advancement to a better position or higher class or rank: *to win a* promotion *in the army.* **2** a furthering of any cause or purpose. **—*adj-* pro·mo′ tion·al:** *a* promotional *campaign.*

prompt (prŏmpt) ***adj-*** **1** without delay: *a* prompt *mail service.* **2** ready and quick: *She was* prompt *to show her disapproval.* **3** on time; not tardy: *to be* prompt *in arriving at school.* ***vt-*** **1** to rouse to action; inspire: *His cruelty* prompted *me to scold him.* **2** to supply (someone, especially an actor) with forgotten words. **—*n-* prompt′ er. *adv-* prompt′ ly. *n-* prompt′ ness.**

promp·ti·tude (prŏmp′ tə tōōd′, -tyōōd′) ***n-*** readiness and quickness; promptness.

pro·mul·gate (prŏm′ əl gāt′) ***vt-*** [**pro·mul·gat·ed, pro·mul·gat·ing**] to make known officially and formally; proclaim: *to* promulgate *a decree.* **—*n-* pro′ mul·ga′tion.**

pron. **1** pronoun. **2** pronounced. **3** pronunciation.

prone (prōn) ***adj-*** **1** naturally inclined or disposed (to): *She is* prone *to forget people's names.* **2** lying face downward. **—*n-* prone′ ness.**

Man lying prone

►Should not be confused with SUPINE.

prong (pròng, prŏng) ***n-*** **1** one of the pointed ends of a fork, or other sharp-pointed implement. **2** one of the sharp projections of an antler. **—*adj-* pronged:** *a* pronged *tool*; *a two-*pronged *offensive.*

prong·horn (pròng′ hòrn′, prŏng′-) ***n-*** cud-chewing animal that resembles an antelope and is found on the western plains of North America.

pro·noun (prō′noun′) ***n-*** any of a class of words that regularly replace nouns or noun phrases. *Abbr.* pron or pron. See also *demonstrative, indefinite pronoun, interrogative pronoun, personal pronoun, possessive pronoun, reciprocal pronoun, reflexive pronoun, relative.*

pro·nounce (prə nouns′) ***vt-*** [**pro·nounced, pro·nounc·ing**] **1** to utter or make the sounds of: *to* pronounce *a name correctly.* **2** to declare or announce, especially formally or with authority: *The president* pronounced *the new policy.* ***vi-*** **1** to give a decision or judgment; make a pronouncement: *to* pronounce *on a vital issue.* **2** to utter the sounds of speech; enunciate: *You should* pronounce *carefully.* **—*adj-*** **pro·nounce′a·ble.**

pro·nounced (prə nounst′) ***adj-*** marked; decided: *a* pronounced *change of mood.* **—*adv-*** **pro·nounc′ed·ly.**

pro·nounce·ment (prə nouns′mənt) ***n-*** **1** official declaration; proclamation: *a* pronouncement *on government policy.* **2** formal statement, judgment, or opinion: *the* pronouncements *of critics.*

pron·to (prŏn′tō) *Informal* ***adv-*** quickly; promptly. [from Spanish.]

pro·nun·ci·a·men·to (prō nŭn′sē ə mĕn′tō) ***n-*** [*pl.* **pro·nun·ci·a·men·tos**] official and public declaration.

pro·nun·ci·a·tion (prə nŭn′sē ā′shən) ***n-*** **1** act or manner of uttering the sounds that form words: *American* pronunciation *differs in several ways from British* pronunciation. **2** accepted or standard way of pronouncing a word: *"Rodeo" has two* pronunciations.

proof (prōōf) ***n-*** **1** a proving that something is true: *The burden of* proof *is on him.* **2** something by which another thing is shown to be true or correct: *Give me* proof *of your statement.* **3** in photography, a trial print from a negative. **4** in printing, a trial impression taken from set type for correction: *page* proofs. **5** *Mathematics* (1) demonstration of the logical steps involved in establishing the truth or validity of an argument or statement. (2) process in which new truths are established by reasoning from already accepted principles, such as assumptions, postulates, or axioms.

proof against immune to: *Vaccination made him* proof against *smallpox.* **to the proof** to the test; on trial.

-proof *suffix* resistant to; safe from; protected against: *water*proof; *fire*proof.

proof·read (prōōf′rēd) ***vt-*** [**proof·read, proof·read·ing**] to read and correct errors in (a printer's proof). **—*n-*** **proof′read′er.**

[1]**prop** (prŏp) ***vt-*** [**propped, prop·ping**] (often followed by "up") **1** to hold up by placing something under or against: *They* propped *the roof with steel columns.* **2** to support; sustain: *We* propped *up his low spirits with a bit of good news.* ***n-*** support: *a* prop *for a roof.* [from Middle English **proppe,** perhaps from earlier Dutch **prop(p)e.**]

[2]**prop** (prŏp) *Informal* ***n-*** in the theater, a property. [shortened from **(stage) property.**]

[3]**prop** (prŏp) *Informal* ***n-*** propeller.

prop·a·gan·da (prŏp′ə găn′də) ***n-*** statements, printed material, etc., designed to win the audience over to some point of view. *as* ***modifier:*** *a* propaganda *expert*; propaganda *minister.*

prop·a·gan·dist (prŏp′ə găn′dĭst) ***n-*** person who spreads propaganda. ***adj-:*** *a* propagandist *campaign.*

prop·a·gan·dize (prŏp ə găn′dīz′) ***vt-*** [**prop·a·gan·dized, prop·a·gan·diz·ing**] to subject to propaganda: *to* propagandize *an area.* ***vi-*** to spread propaganda: *The political party* propagandized *on television.*

prop·a·gate (prŏp′ə gāt′) ***vt-*** [**prop·a·gat·ed, prop·a·gat·ing**] to produce offspring: *Rabbits* propagate *rapidly.* ***vt-*** **1** to cause to increase by production of young: *to* propagate *a breed of dogs.* **2** to spread from person to person; disseminate: *to* propagate *an idea.* **—*n-*** **prop′a·ga′tion.**

pro·pel (prə pĕl′) ***vt-*** [**pro·pelled, pro·pel·ling**] **1** to move by pushing or driving: *Ions can* propel *a spacecraft.* **2** to urge onward; impel; motivate: *Ambition* propels *her.*

pro·pel·lant or **pro·pel·lent** (prə pĕl′ənt) ***n-*** **1** fuel used to propel a rocket. **2** the inert, pressurized gas in a spray can that forces out spray.

pro·pel·ler (prə pĕl′ər) ***n-*** device of whirling blades for propelling an airplane, boat, or ship.

BOAT AIRPLANE

Propellers

pro·pen·si·ty (prə pĕn′sə tē) ***n-*** [*pl.* **pro·pen·si·ties**] natural tendency; inclination: *a* propensity *toward colds.*

prop·er (prŏp′ər) ***adj-*** **1** suitable; appropriate: *We wore the* proper *clothes for the sleigh ride and didn't feel the cold.* **2** naturally belonging or peculiar (to): *a climate* proper *to central Africa.* **3** in a narrow or exact sense: *The suburbs are not part of the city* proper. **4** measuring up to standards of good conduct or manners: *Their behavior was* proper.

proper fraction ***n-*** See *fraction.*

prop·er·ly (prŏp′ər lē) ***adv-*** **1** appropriately; suitably: *to be* properly *dressed for skiing.* **2** justifiably; with reason: *quite* properly *afraid of fire.* **3** with accuracy; strictly: Properly *speaking, you were in the wrong.*

proper noun See *noun.*

prop·er·tied (prŏp′ər tēd′) ***adj-*** owning property, especially a great deal of it: *the* propertied *families.*

prop·er·ty (prŏp′ər tē) ***n-*** [*pl.* **prop·er·ties**] **1** thing or things owned by someone; possession: *These books are my* property. **2** land; real estate: *She bought some* property *near the river.* **3** quality or attribute of a thing; feature: *Stickiness is a* property *of glue.* **4** chair, book, or other moveable article, except scenery and costumes, used in a play; prop. **—*adj-*** **prop′er·ty·less.**

property man ***n-*** person in charge of theatrical properties. Also **prop man.**

pro·phase (prō′fāz′) ***n-*** the first of the phases of mitosis, in which the material of the nucleus forms into chromosomes split lengthwise.

proph·e·cy (prŏf′ə sē) ***n-*** [*pl.* **proph·e·cies**] **1** a telling, especially under divine influence, of what is to come; prediction: *a* prophecy *of world peace.* **2** the power of prophesying: *the gift of* prophecy.

proph·e·sy (prŏf′ə sī′) ***vt-*** [**proph·e·sied, proph·e·sy·ing**] to predict (what is going to happen or come); foretell: *to* prophesy *the results.* ***vi-*** to foretell future events: *He likes to* prophesy. **—*n-*** **proph′e·si′er.**

proph·et (prŏf′ət) ***n-*** **1** holy man who warns of or foretells the future; seer. **2** person who predicts events: *I'm no weather* prophet. **3 the Prophets** books in the Old Testament from Joshua to Malachi. **4 the Prophet** Muslim term for Mohammed. ***Hom-*** profit. **—*n-*** *fem.* **proph′et·ess.**

pro·phet·ic (prə fĕt′ĭk) ***adj-*** **1** like or containing a prophecy: *a* prophetic *remark.* **2** like that of a prophet: *his* prophetic *wisdom.* **—*adv-*** **pro·phet′i·cal·ly.**

pro·phy·lac·tic (prōf′ə lăk′tĭk) ***adj-*** tending to guard against or prevent disease: *a* prophylactic *measure against malaria.* ***n-*** **1** something that prevents or helps to prevent disease. **2** any contraceptive device.

pro·pin·qui·ty (prə pĭng′ kwə tē) ***n-*** nearness in time, place, or blood relationship; proximity.

pro·pi·ti·ate (prə pĭsh′ ē āt′) ***vt-*** **[pro·pi·ti·at·ed, pro·pi·ti·at·ing]** to win over (someone who is angry, opposed, etc.); conciliate. ***—n-*** **pro·pi′ ti·a′ tion.** ***n-*** **pro·pi′ ti·a′ tor:** *a* propitiator *of opposing factions.*

pro·pi·tious (prə pĭsh′ əs) ***adj-*** **1** favorable; suitable or appropriate: *to have* propitious *weather; a* propitious *time to ask for a raise.* **2** favorably inclined; gracious. ***—adv-*** **pro·pi′ tious·ly.** ***n-*** **pro·pi′ tious·ness.**

pro·po·nent (prə pō′ nənt) ***n-*** **1** person who supports or favors something specified; advocate: *a* proponent *of the immigration bill.* **2** person who proposes or propounds something: *the first* proponent *of a policy.*

pro·por·tion (prə pôr′ shən) ***n-*** **1** number, size, degree, or amount of a thing or group as compared with another thing or group; ratio: *the* proportion *of men to women in a country*; *the* proportion *of sugar to flour in a cake.* **2** share; part: *a* proportion *of the profits.* **3** *Mathematics* a statement of equality between two ratios: *4/8 = 6/12 is a* proportion. **4 proportions** (1) size; dimensions: *a desert of vast* proportions. (2) dimensions in relation to one another: *the harmonious* proportions *of a room.* ***vt-*** to put (one thing) in proper relation to another: *He* proportions *his rent to his salary.*

in proportion (to or **with)** in proper or pleasing relation: *This building is* in proportion with *its neighbor. These two rooms are* in proportion. **out of proportion (to** or **with)** not in proper or pleasing relation: *Her anger was* out of proportion to *the offense.*

pro·por·tion·al (prə pôr′ shən əl) ***adj-*** **1** having or being in proper relation; proportionate: *All the parts are* proportional. **2** according to proportions: *a* proportional *assignment of duties.* **3** *Mathematics* of terms, varying such that corresponding values make a proportion. ***—adv-*** **pro·por′ tion·al·ly.**

proportional representation ***n-*** method of election in which legislators are seated in very close proportion to the voting strength of their various parties or groups. The system makes possible the representation of relatively small parties and of many parties at once.

pro·por·tion·ate (prə pôr′ shən ət) ***adj-*** having or being in proper relation; commensurate: *success* proportionate *to effort.* ***—adv-*** **pro·por′ tion·ate·ly.**

pro·pos·al (prə pō′ zəl) ***n-*** **1** a presenting or suggesting of a plan: *I was given the task of* proposal. **2** plan or scheme proposed: *a new* proposal. **3** offer of marriage.

pro·pose (prə pōz′) ***vt-*** **[pro·posed, pro·pos·ing] 1** to offer for consideration or discussion; suggest: *to* propose *a plan.* **2** to suggest or present (someone's) name for office; nominate. **3** to intend; plan: *I* propose *to be the first.* ***vi-*** to make an offer of marriage.

prop·o·si·tion (prŏp′ ə zĭsh′ ən) ***n-*** **1** statement offered or taken for discussion, debate, etc.: *Let us examine the mayor's first* proposition. **2** plan; proposal: *His* proposition *was impractical.* **3** *Informal* matter; undertaking: *Blackmail is a dangerous* proposition. **4** *Mathematics* statement of a theorem to be demonstrated or of a problem to be solved. ***vt-*** *Slang* to make a proposal to, often of an improper nature.

pro·pound (prə pound′) ***vt-*** to offer for consideration, discussion, or debate; set forth (a question, problem, etc.). ***—n-*** **pro·pound′ er.**

pro·pri·e·tar·y (prə prī′ ə tĕr′ ē) ***adj-*** **1** of, relating to, or appropriate to ownership or owners: *a* proprietary *interest*; *a* proprietary *attitude*; proprietary *rights.* **2** made and sold by exclusive legal right: *a* proprietary *drug.* ***n-*** [*pl.* **pro·pri·e·tar·ies**] **1** proprietor. **2** person or group to whom the English king granted a colony.

pro·pri·e·tor (prə prī′ ə tər) ***n-*** person who has a legal title to property; owner: *the* proprietor *of a ranch.* ***—n-*** *fem.* **pro·pri′ e·tress.**

pro·pri·e·tor·ship (prə prī′ ə tər shĭp′) ***n-*** legal title to property; ownership.

pro·pri·e·ty (prə prī′ ə tē) ***n-*** [*pl.* **pro·pri·e·ties**] **1** fitness; suitability; correctness: *We question the* propriety *of children's staying out alone after dark.* **2 the proprieties** socially approved manners, conduct, etc., of society.

pro·pul·sion (prə pŭl′ shən) ***n-*** **1** a propelling; a giving of forward motion: *the* propulsion *of blood by the heart.* **2** something that propels; a driving force.

pro·pul·sive (prə pŭl′ sĭv) ***adj-*** having power to propel.

pro ra·ta (prō rā′ tə, -rä′ tə) ***adv-*** on the basis of equal or proper shares: *We divided the expenses* pro rata. ***adj-:*** *the* pro rata *costs.*

pro·rate (prō′ rāt′) ***vt-*** **[pro·rat·ed, pro·rat·ing]** to divide or distribute (something) in equal or proper portions: *We'll* prorate *the expenses among the five of us.*

pro·sa·ic (prō zā′ ĭk) ***adj-*** **1** lacking in imagination and originality; commonplace; dull: *The host bored his guests with* prosaic *jokes.* **2** like prose in being factual and straightforward rather than figurative and imaginative. ***—adv-*** **pro·sa′ i·cal·ly.** ***n-*** **pro·sa′ ic·ness.**

pro·sce·ni·um (prō sē′ nē əm, prə-) ***n-*** [*pl.* **pro·sce·ni·a** (-ə)] **1** in the modern theater, that part of the stage between the curtain and the auditorium. **2** (also **proscenium arch**) the front opening of a stage. **3** in the ancient theater, the stage.

pro·scribe (prō skrīb′) ***vt-*** **[pro·scribed, pro·scrib·ing] 1** to reject or condemn; prohibit: *The government* proscribed *the author's works.* **2** to punish (someone) by outlawing or banishing. ***—n-*** **pro·scrib′ er.**

►Should not be confused with PRESCRIBE.

pro·scrip·tion (prō skrĭp′ shən) ***n-*** **1** a proscribing. **2** condition of being proscribed.

►Should not be confused with PRESCRIPTION.

prose (prōz) ***n-*** **1** ordinary spoken or written language without the rhythm or meter of poetry: *The essay is written in* prose. **2** ordinary or commonplace conversation. *as* ***modifier:*** *the* prose *works of John Milton.*

pros·e·cute (prŏs′ ə kyo͞ot′) ***vt-*** **[pros·e·cut·ed, pros·e·cut·ing] 1** to bring suit against (someone) in a court of law: *The city* prosecuted *the man for stealing.* **2** to bring or conduct (legal action) in a court: *to* prosecute *a claim.* **3** to carry on; follow up; continue: *The detective* prosecuted *the investigation in spite of the difficulties.* ***vi-*** to carry on a lawsuit or conduct a case against a person accused of a crime: *They'll never* prosecute.

►Should not be confused with PERSECUTE.

pros·e·cu·tion (prŏs′ ə kyo͞o′ shən) ***n-*** **1** the bringing or conducting of legal action in a court: *A* prosecution *was begun against the three auto thieves.* **2** the party that begins legal accusation: *The district attorney represented the* prosecution. **3** the following up; carrying on; pursuit: *the* prosecution *of his duties.*

pros·e·cu·tor (prŏs′ ə kyo͞o′ tər) ***n-*** person who prosecutes; especially, a public official whose duty is to present the state's case in a court of law.

pros·e·lyte (prŏs′ ə līt′) ***vi-*** **[pros·e·lyt·ed, pros·e·lyt·ing]** to try to win others over to one's religion, party, or other institution: *Some colleges* proselyte *among high school athletes.* ***vt-*** to try to convince (a person or persons) to join one's religion, party, etc. ***n-*** person who has been persuaded to join some religion, party, etc.

pros·e·ly·tize (prŏs′ ə lə tīz′) ***vt- & vi-*** **[pros·e·ly·tized, pros·e·lyt·iz·ing]** to proselyte.

Pro·ser·pi·na (prō sûr′ pə nə, prə-) or **Pros·er·pine** (prŏs′ ər pīn, prə sûr′ pə nē′) ***n-*** in Roman mythology, daughter of Jupiter and Ceres, who was abducted by Pluto. She is identified with the Greek Persephone.

pros·o·dy (prŏz′ə dē) ***n-*** [*pl.* **pros·o·dies**] **1** science or study of poetic form, especially of meter and rhyme. **2** system of poetic form: *the* prosody *of French poetry.*

pros·pect (prŏs′pĕkt′) ***n-*** **1** broad view or scene: *Below us lay a* prospect *of fertile valleys.* **2** outlook for the future: *The* prospect *for business is good.* **3** hope; expectation: *little* prospect *of arriving on time.* **4** possible customer. **5 prospects** chances for success: *Work should improve your* prospects. ***vt-*** to search or explore (a region) for mineral deposits. ***vi-*** to search or explore: *He had spent most of his life* prospecting *for gold.*

in prospect planned or probable for the future.

pro·spec·tive (prə spĕk′tĭv) ***adj-*** **1** expected; probable; likely to be made or become: *We discussed* prospective *changes.* **2** concerned with the future: *our* prospective *plans.* ***—adv-*** **pro·spec′tive·ly.**

pros·pec·tor (prŏs′pĕk′tər) ***n-*** person who searches or explores a region for gold or other valuable minerals.

pro·spec·tus (prə spĕk′təs) ***n-*** [*pl.* **pro·spec·tus·es**] outline of a proposed undertaking, especially in business.

pros·per (prŏs′pər) ***vi-*** to be successful; thrive; flourish.

pros·per·i·ty (prŏs pĕr′ə tē) ***n-*** success; good fortune; economic well-being: *a period of general* prosperity.

pros·per·ous (prŏs′pər əs) ***adj-*** successful; thriving. ***—adv-*** **pros′per·ous·ly.** ***n-*** **pros′per·ous·ness.**

pros·tate (prŏs′tāt′) ***n-*** the partly muscular gland lying at the neck of the bladder and surrounding the upper part of the urethra in male mammals.. Also **prostate gland.** ***as modifier:*** *a* prostate *operation.* ***—adj-*** **pros·tat′ic** (prŏs tăt′ĭk).

prosthesis (prŏs thē′səs) ***n-*** [*pl.* **pros·the·ses** (-sēz′)] **1** replacement of a missing part of the body by an artificial part. **2** the artificial part, such as an eye or a leg. ***—adj-*** **pros·thet′ic** (-thĕt′ĭk).

pros·ti·tute (prŏs′tə to͞ot′, -tyo͞ot′) ***n-*** person who engages in sex acts for money; whore. ***vt-*** [**pros·ti·tut·ed, pros·ti·tut·ing**] **1** to offer (oneself or another) for sex acts in return for money. **2** to lower (oneself, one's work, etc.) for money or position.

pros·ti·tu·tion (prŏs′tə to͞o′shən, -tyo͞o′shən) ***n-*** **1** an engaging in sex acts for pay. **2** the debasing of one's talent, honor, etc., for money or position.

pros·trate (prŏs′trāt′) ***vt-*** [**pros·trat·ed, pros·trat·ing**] **1** to throw (oneself) down or bow in humility or reverence: *to* prostrate *oneself before the king.* **2** to throw down; flatten: *The storm* prostrated *the birches.* **3** to weaken; make helpless: *An attack of fever completely* prostrated *me.* ***adj-*** **1** lying flat or in a deep bow: *He was found* prostrate *in the street. The worshiper was* prostrate. **2** worn out; exhausted, either emotionally or physically: *to be* prostrate *with grief.* **3** helpless; vanquished: *the* prostrate *victims of war.*

pros·tra·tion (prŏs trā′shən) ***n-*** **1** the act of throwing oneself down, or the condition of lying face down. **2** condition of complete exhaustion or helplessness.

pros·y (prō′zē) ***adj-*** [**pros·i·er, pros·i·est**] **1** of or similar to prose. **2** commonplace; tedious: *a* prosy *lecturer.* ***—n-*** **pros′i·ness.**

Prot. Protestant

pro·tac·tin·i·um (prōt′ăk′tĭn′ē əm) ***n-*** radioactive rare-earth element. Symbol Pa, At. No. 91, At. Wt. 231.

pro·tag·o·nist (prō tăg′ə nĭst, prə-) ***n-*** **1** central character, as in a play or novel. **2** prominent figure in or supporter of a cause, movement, etc.

pro·te·an (prō′tē ən) ***adj-*** readily taking different shapes or forms: *an unstable and* protean *personality.*

pro·tect (prə tĕkt′) ***vt*** **1** to keep safe; guard; defend against danger or injury: *to* protect *one's family*; *an overcoat to* protect *oneself against the cold.* **2** to foster or assist (an industry) by means of protective tariffs. ***—adv-*** **pro·tect′ing·ly.**

pro·tec·tion (prə tĕk′shən) ***n-*** **1** a protecting or being protected. **2** person or thing that protects: *New tires are a* protection *against blowouts.* **3** use of protective tariffs and other restrictions to protect an industry against foreign competition.

pro·tec·tion·ism (prə tĕk′shən ĭz′əm) ***n-*** economic doctrine that advocates protection of a country's industry by protective tariffs and other means. ***—n-*** **pro·tec′tion·ist.**

pro·tec·tive (prə tĕk′tĭv) ***adj-*** giving protection or shelter: *a* protective *coating over a drawing*; *a* protective *cover.* ***—adv-*** **pro·tec′tive·ly.** ***n-*** **pro·tec′tive·ness.**

protective coloring ***n-*** coloring that enables certain animals to blend into their environment or to seem very menacing, and thus protects them from other animals. Also **protective coloration.**

protective tariff ***n-*** tariff intended to protect a domestic industry from foreign competition rather than produce revenue; especially, a tax or duty placed on imported goods so that they cannot be sold more cheaply than domestic products.

pro·tec·tor (prə tĕk′tər) ***n-*** **1** guardian; defender: *He has chosen me as his* protector. **2** something that gives protection: *The umpire wears a chest* protector.

pro·tec·tor·ate (prə tĕk′tər ət) ***n-*** **1** weak country under the control or protection of a strong country. **2** relationship between two such countries.

pro·té·gé (prō′tə zhā′) ***n-*** person who is under the care and guidance of someone who is prominent. ***—n-*** *fem.* **pro′té·gée′.**

pro·te·in (prō′tēn′, -tē ĭn) ***n-*** any of a very large group of complex organic compounds consisting of amino acids bonded together in a chainlike molecule. Plants synthesize proteins directly from the basic chemicals during photosynthesis, but animals can build proteins only from amino acids derived from protein in foods. ***as modifier:*** *a* protein *food.* Also **pro·te·id** (prō′tē əd, prō′tēd′).

pro tem (prō′tĕm′) ***adv-*** for now but not permanently; temporarily: *She is president* pro tem *of the club.*

Prot·er·o·zo·ic (prō′tər ə zō′ĭk) ***n-*** era of geological time between the Paleozoic and Archeozoic in which the basic shape of the continents probably first developed. ***adj-:*** *a* Proterozoic *rock.*

[1]**pro·test** (prō′tĕst′) ***n-*** **1** formal complaint or objection: *The President sent a* protest *to the foreign ambassador.* **2** objection; resistance: *The children went to bed without* protest.

under protest only after expressing objection.

[2]**pro·test** (prə tĕst′, prō-) ***vi-*** to express opposition or dissatisfaction: *We* protested *loudly when he shut the door.* ***vt-*** **1** to object to; express disapproval of: *We* protested *the extra homework.* **2** to assert or maintain strongly in the face of accusation or contradiction: *He* protested *his innocence.* ***—n-*** **pro·test′er.**

Prot·es·tant (prŏt′əs tənt) ***n-*** member of one of the branches of the Christian church that separated from the Roman Catholic Church during the Reformation. ***adj-:*** *a* Protestant *minister*; Protestant *beliefs.*

Protestant Episcopal Church *n-* in the United States, that branch of the western Christian church that is descended from the Church of England but since 1789 has been a separate and independent body. Also **Episcopal Church.**

Prot·es·tan·tism (prŏt′ əs tən tĭz′ əm) *n-* beliefs, practices, etc., of Protestant Christians; also, Protestant churches collectively.

prot·es·ta·tion (prŏt′ əs tā′ shən, prō′ təs-) *n-* a declaring or claiming: *the* protestation *of one's innocence.*

Pro·te·us (prō′ tē əs) *n-* in Greek mythology, a sea god with prophetic powers who could change his shape.

pro·ti·um (prō′ tē əm) *n-* ordinary hydrogen, the nucleus of which contains a single proton.

proto- *combining form* first in time; original; typical: *a* proto*zoan* (first animal); proto*plasm* (first or original life); proto*type.* [from Greek **prōtó-**, from **protos** meaning "first in time or rank."]

pro·to·ac·tin·i·um (prō′ tō ăk′ tĭn′ ē əm) protactinium.

pro·to·col (prō′ tə kȯl′, -kŏl′) *n-* **1** code of proper formal behavior and order of rank in diplomatic affairs and state ceremonies. **2** original copy or record of an official document: *the* protocol *of the treaty.*

pro·ton (prō′ tŏn) *n-* elementary particle of the atomic nucleus, having one unit of positive charge and a mass of about 1.672×10^{-24} grams. The nucleus of any atom has at least one proton.

pro·to·plasm (prō′ tə plăz′ əm) *n-* the transparent, jelly-like substance that makes up the essential living substance of all living cells.

pro·to·type (prō′ tə tīp′) *n-* **1** first or original example of anything: *the* prototype *of a new aircraft.* **2** standard or typical kind: *the* prototype *of the sonata.*

pro·to·zo·an (prō′ tə zō′ ən) *n-* any of a large group of mostly aquatic, microscopic animals **(Protozoa)** that include the ameba and paramecium.

pro·tract (prō trăkt′) *vt-* to draw out or lengthen in time: *to* protract *the meeting.*

pro·trac·tor (prō trăk′ tər) *n-* instrument for measuring or drawing angles by means of a semicircle marked off in degrees.

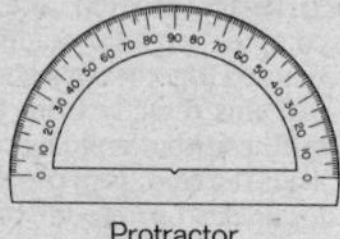
Protractor

pro·trude (prō trōōd′) *vi-* [**pro·trud·ed, pro·trud·ing**] to project; stick out: *A book* protruded *from the man's coat pocket. vt-*: *The turtle* protruded *its head.*

pro·tru·sion (prō trōō′ zhən) *n-* **1** a protruding: *the* protrusion *of his stomach.* **2** something that protrudes.

pro·tu·ber·ance (prə tōō′ bər əns, prə tyōō′-) *n-* **1** a swelling or bulging. **2** a bulge.

pro·tu·ber·ant (prə tōō′ bər ənt, prə tyōō′-) *adj-* bulging. *—adv-* **pro·tu′ ber·ant·ly.**

proud (proud) *adj-* [**proud·er, proud·est**] **1** arrogant; conceited; haughty: *He's too* proud *to play with the rest of us.* **2** dignified; properly self-respecting: *He's just too* proud *to fight over unimportant things.* **3** giving pride and satisfaction: *a* proud *day for the school.* **4** noble; magnificent: *a* proud *display of power. —adv-* **proud′ ly.**

proud of taking great pride in: *We're* proud of *you.*

Prov. 1 Proverbs. **2** Provençal.

prove (prōōv) *vt-* [**proved, proved** or **prov·en, prov·ing**] **1** to show that (someone or something) is true, genuine, valid, etc.: *to* prove *one's friendship*; *to* prove *a claim to property.* **2** to demonstrate by experiment, reasoning, or evidence: *to* prove *the purity of copper*; *to* prove *a theorem in geometry.* **3** to test the quality, workmanship, etc., of: *to* prove *a rifle. vi-* to turn out to be: *The day* proved *warm and sunny. —adj-* **prov′ a·ble.**

Pro·ven·çal (*Fr.* prō vän sal′) *adj-* of or pertaining to Provence, France, its people, or their language. *n-* **1** Romance language of Provence. **2** native of this region.

prov·en·der (prŏv′ ən dər) *n-* dry feed for livestock.

prov·erb (prŏv′ ərb) *n-* short saying, usually traditional, that states some truth or warning, or gives advice about human conduct; maxim; adage. "Half a loaf is better than none" and "Waste not, want not" are proverbs.

pro·ver·bi·al (prə vûr′ bē əl) *adj-* **1** contained in or resembling a proverb: *their* proverbial *wisdom.* **2** widely spoken of; well-known: *Her kindness is* proverbial. *—adv-* **pro·ver′ bi·al·ly.**

Prov·erbs (prŏv′ ərbz) *n-* (takes singular verb) in the Old Testament, a poetical book of moral sayings.

pro·vide (prə vīd′) *vt-* [**pro·vid·ed, pro·vid·ing**] **1** to give or supply: *The earth and sea* provide *food.* **2** to require; stipulate: *The law* provides *that we all pay the tax.*

provide for 1 to support: *to* provide for *a large family.* **2** to take into account and arrange for: *We* provided for *all emergencies.*

provide with to give or supply to.

pro·vid·ed (prə vī′ dəd) or **pro·vid·ing** (prə vī′ dĭng) *conj-* on the condition that; if: *He may go,* provided *he has the money. She'll do it,* providing *you approve.*

prov·i·dence (prŏv′ ə dəns) *n-* **1** thrifty care for the future; prudence: *Because of Father's* providence *we were all able to go to college.* **2** the care and protective guidance of God or nature. **3 Providence** God, thought of as guiding and protecting man.

prov·i·dent (prŏv′ ə dənt) *adj-* **1** showing care in planning for the future; prudent. **2** economical; thrifty: *a* provident *man who wasted nothing. —adv-* **prov′ i·dent·ly.**

►Should not be confused with PROVIDENTIAL.

prov·i·den·tial (prŏv′ ə dĕn′ shəl) *adj-* of or by divine guidance or foresight; hence, fortunate: *a* providential *recovery from illness. —adv-* **prov′ i·den′ tial·ly.**

►Should not be confused with PROVIDENT.

pro·vid·er (prə vī′ dər) *n-* person who provides; especially, a person who supports a family.

prov·ince (prŏv′ ĭns) *n-* **1** division of a country: *Quebec is a* province *of Canada.* **2** certain field of action, study, business, etc.: *All school activities fall in the principal's* province. **3 the provinces** regions that are remote from cultural centers.

pro·vin·cial (prə vĭn′ shəl) *adj-* **1** having to do with a province: *the* provincial *government.* **2** interested only or chiefly in local affairs, opinions, ideas, etc.; hence, narrow-minded or bigoted: *The townspeople were well-meaning but* provincial. **3** crude; awkward; rustic: *his* provincial *manners. n-* person who lives in or comes from a province or typifies the provinces. *—adv-* **pro·vin′ cial·ly.** *n-* **pro·vin′ ci·al′ i·ty.**

pro·vin·cial·ism (prə vĭn′ shəl ĭz′ əm) *n-* **1** narrowness of mind and experience; smug belief that the ideas and customs of one's own place are the best. **2** habit, trait, etc., showing this.

proving ground *n-* place where the performance and efficiency of new weapons, machines, or scientific devices are tested.

proving stand *n-* a stand on which rocket engines are mounted in order to test them.

pro·vi·sion (prə vĭzh′ ən) *n-* **1** a giving or supplying: *the* provision *of grain for the cattle.* **2** condition or clause, as in a law, will, etc.; stipulation: *the* provisions *of the new law.* **3** (often **provisions**) thing or things provided or arranged, especially for some future need or situation: *We made* provision *for a large audience. He changed the* provisions *for his heirs.* **4 provisions** supply of food:

The prospector took three weeks' provisions *with him.* ***vt-*** to supply with food, especially on a large scale.

pro·vi·sion·al (prə vĭsh′ ən əl) ***adj-*** for the time being; temporary: *a* provisional *law.* ***—adv-*** **pro·vi′ sion·al·ly.**

pro·vi·so (prə vī′ zō) ***n-*** [*pl.* **pro·vi·sos** or **pro·vi·soes**] **1** statement in a will, law, or other document that sets down a condition to be met. **2** any condition or stipulation: *You may borrow my car, with one* proviso.

pro·vi·sor·y (prə vī′ zə rē) ***adj-*** **1** having or depending on a proviso. **2** provisional.

prov·o·ca·tion (prŏv′ ə kā′ shən) ***n-*** **1** act of provoking or inciting: *Deliberate* provocation *of a quarrel is a serious matter.* **2** something which arouses anger: *What* provocation *was there for you to hit him?*

pro·voc·a·tive (prə vŏk′ ə tĭv) ***adj-*** **1** tending to arouse anger or resentment. **2** tending to arouse thought; stimulating: *The book has a* provocative *theme.* ***—adv-*** **pro·voc′ a·tive·ly.** ***n-*** **pro·voc′ a·tive·ness.**

pro·voke (prə vōk′) ***vt-*** [**pro·voked, pro·vok·ing**] **1** to annoy or irritate; incite to anger: *Her rude answer* provoked *John.* **2** to arouse; excite; stimulate: *The article against jazz* provoked *much criticism.*

pro·vok·ing·ly (prə vō′ kĭng lē) ***adv-*** so as to annoy.

pro·vost (prō′ vōst′, -vəst) ***n-*** **1** a senior administrative officer of certain universities. **2** head or dean of a group of clergymen at a cathedral. **3** in Scotland, the chief magistrate of a city. **4** provost marshal.

provost marshal ***n-*** military or naval officer who commands the military police of a base or unit.

prow (prou) ***n-*** **1** the forward end of a boat or ship; bow. **2** something resembling a bow, such as the front part of an airplane. ***Hom-*** prau.

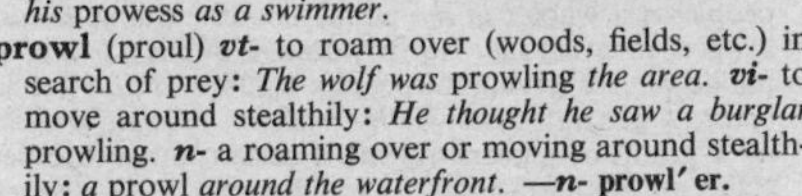

prow·ess (prou′ əs) ***n-*** **1** great bravery; valor: *The troops showed* prowess *in battle.* **2** very great skill or ability: *his* prowess *as a swimmer.*

prowl (proul) ***vt-*** to roam over (woods, fields, etc.) in search of prey: *The wolf was* prowling *the area.* ***vi-*** to move around stealthily: *He thought he saw a burglar* prowling. ***n-*** a roaming over or moving around stealthily: *a* prowl *around the waterfront.* ***—n-*** **prowl′ er.**

on the prowl looking for prey: *a tiger* on the prowl.

prowl car ***n-*** squad car.

prox·im·i·ty (prŏk sĭm′ ə tē) ***n-*** nearness; closeness: *the* proximity *of danger; my* proximity *to my neighbors.*

prox·y (prŏk′ sē) ***n-*** [*pl.* **prox·ies**] **1** person given authority to act for another; agent: *My lawyer acted as my* proxy. **2** authority given to a person to act for another.

prude (pro͞od) ***n-*** person who is excessively or squeamishly proper in dress, speech, or behavior.

pru·dence (pro͞o′ dəns) ***n-*** good sense; caution in practical matters, especially in one's own affairs.

pru·dent (pro͞o′ dənt) ***adj-*** having or showing good judgment in practical affairs; careful; provident: *A* prudent *housewife shops for bargains.* ***—adv-*** **pru′dent·ly.**
►Should not be confused with PRUDISH.

pru·den·tial (pro͞o dĕn′ shəl) ***adj-*** **1** proceeding from or marked by careful thought or judgment: *a* prudential *choice.* **2** using sound judgment: *a* prudential *student.* ***—adv-*** **pru·den′ tial·ly.**

prud·er·y (pro͞o′ də rē) ***n-*** [*pl.* **prud·er·ies**] extreme propriety or modesty in speech or behavior, either genuine or affected; priggishness.

prud·ish (pro͞o′ dĭsh) ***adj-*** excessively proper in speech or behavior; priggish: *a* prudish *disapproval of certain books.* ***—adv-*** **prud′ ish·ly.** ***n-*** **prud′ ish·ness.**
►Should not be confused with PRUDENT.

[1]**prune** (pro͞on) ***n-*** **1** kind of plum that dries without spoiling. **2** dried plum. [from French, from Latin **prūnum** meaning "a plum," from Greek **prounon.**]

[2]**prune** (pro͞on) ***vt-*** [**pruned, prun·ing**] (considered intransitive when the direct object is implied but not expressed) **1** to cut branches, roots, etc., from (a plant) in order to improve it. **2** to cut away unnecessary parts from (anything) in order to improve its quality, appearance, shape, or force: *The author* pruned *his novel.* [from Old French **proignier,** from Late Latin **prōpāginãre,** "to propagate by using grafts," from **prōpāgo,** "a scion; graft."]

pru·ri·ent (pro͝or′ ē ənt) ***adj-*** lewd in thought or desire; libidinous; lascivious; lustful. ***—n-*** **pru′ ri·ence.** ***adv-*** **pru′ ri·ent·ly.**

Prus·sian blue (prŭsh′ ən) ***n-*** any of several deep, vivid blue compounds of iron used as pigments.

prus·sic acid (prŭs′ ĭk) ***n-*** hydrocyanic acid.

[1]**pry** (prī) ***vi-*** [**pried, pry·ing**] to look or inquire closely (into) something, especially in a sly manner: *to* pry *into other people's affairs.* [of unknown origin.] ***—adv-*** **pry′ ing·ly.**

[2]**pry** (prī) ***vt-*** [**pried, pry·ing**] **1** to raise or open (something) with or as if with a lever: *to* pry *the top off the jar.* **2** to move (someone or something) with great difficulty: *to* pry *him from his chair.* ***n-*** lever. [from [2]**prize.**]

P.S. **1** postscript. **2** public school.

psalm (säm, sälm) ***n-*** sacred poem or song.

psalm·ist (sä′ mĭst, säl′-) ***n-*** **1** composer of sacred poems or songs. **2 the Psalmist** David.

Psalms (sämz, sälmz) ***n-*** (takes singular verb) book in the Old Testament, containing 150 sacred songs. Also **Book of Psalms.**

Psal·ter (sȯl′ tər) ***n-*** **1** Psalms. **2** selection or version of Psalms used in church services.

psal·ter·y (sȯl′ tə rē) ***n-*** [*pl.* **psal·ter·ies**] stringed musical instrument resembling the zither.

pseu·do (so͞o′ dō) ***adj-*** false; pretended; not real.

pseudo- *combining form* **1** false; pretended: *a* pseudo*nym* (fictitious name). **2** closely resembling: *a* pseudo*pod* (organic part resembling a foot). Also **pseud-** before vowels. [from Greek **pseudes** meaning "false."]

pseu·do·nym (so͞o′ də nĭm′) ***n-*** fictitious name, especially a pen name; nom de plume.

pseu·do·pod (so͞o′ dō pŏd′) or **pseu·do·po·di·um** (-pō′ dē əm) ***n-*** a temporary extension of the protoplasm of a living cell.

pshaw (shȯ) ***interj-*** expression showing contempt, scorn, or impatience.

p.s.i. or **psi** pounds per square inch.

psit·ta·co·sis (sĭt′ ə kō′ səs) ***n-*** an infectious virus disease of parrots, transmittable to man, in whom it causes a form of pneumonia; parrot fever.

pso·ri·a·sis (sə rī′ ə səs) ***n-*** a usually chronic, but not contagious, skin disease, in which scaly red patches form on the skin.

P.S.T. or **PST** Pacific Standard Time.

psy·che (sī′ kē) ***n-*** **1** human soul; mind; intelligence. **2** in psychoanalysis, the sum total of the attributes of the personality. **3 Psyche** in classical mythology, a beautiful maiden, beloved by Cupid.

psy·chi·at·ric (sī′ kē ă′ trĭk) ***adj-*** having to do with psychiatry. ***—adv-*** **psy′ chi·at′ ri·cal·ly.**

psy·chi·a·trist (sə kī′ ə trĭst) *n-* doctor who specializes in psychiatry.

psy·chi·a·try (sə kī′ ə trē, sī-) *n-* branch of medicine that studies, diagnoses, and treats mental and emotional disorders.

psy·chic (sī′ kĭk) *adj-* (also **psy′ chi·cal**) **1** having to do with the human mind or soul; spiritual: *a poem filled with* psychic *yearnings.* **2** lying outside or beyond the realm of known physical processes; occult: *several* psychic *occurrences.* **3** sensitive to or influenced by things which are apparently independent of the five senses: *You must be* psychic *to know what I'm thinking.* *n-* person who is sensitive to or influenced by such phenomena; medium.

psy·cho (sī′ kō) *Slang n-* [*pl.* **psy·chos**] crazy person. *adj-* crazy.

psycho- or **psych-** *combining form* **1** mind; brain; mental activities: psycho*analysis*; psycho*logy*. **2** combination of mental influences and: psycho*somatic*. [from Greek **psycho-**, from **psyche** meaning "soul; life; breath."]

psy·cho·a·nal·y·sis (sī′ kō ə năl′ ə səs) *n-* system of psychotherapy that treats mental and emotional disorders by revealing the repressed desires that persist in a patient's mind and affect his behavior, thought, etc.

psy·cho·an·a·lyst (sī′ kō ăn′ ə lĭst) *n-* person who practices psychoanalysis.

psy·cho·an·a·lyze (sī′ kō ăn′ ə līz′) *vt-* [**psy·cho·an·a·lyzed, psy·cho·an·a·lyz·ing**] to treat (someone) by psychoanalysis.

psy·cho·chem·i·cal (sī′ kō kĕm′ ĭ kəl) *n-* compound or drug, such as LSD, that acts directly on the mind and influences consciousness and behavior.

psy·cho·dra·ma (sī′ kō dră′ mə, -drä′ mə) *n-* form of treatment for mental or emotional disorders, in which a patient acts out situations involving his problems.

psy·cho·log·i·cal (sī′ kə lŏj′ ĭ kəl) *adj-* **1** having to do with psychology. **2** of, in, or directed toward the mind: *His only cause for alarm was* psychological.

psy·chol·o·gist (sī kŏl′ ə jĭst) *n-* person trained in psychology and usually engaged in it as a profession.

psy·chol·o·gy (sī kŏl′ ə jē) *n-* **1** science that studies the mind, especially the human mind, and its activities. **2** mental, emotional, or behavioral characteristics of an individual, group, period, etc.: *the* psychology *of the poet*; *the* psychology *of the age.*

psy·cho·neu·ro·sis (sī′ kō nŏŏr ō′ səs, -nyŏŏr ō′ səs) *n-* [*pl.* **psy·cho·neu·ro·ses** (-sēz′)] neurosis.

psy·cho·path (sī′ kō păth′) *n-* any person who is mentally ill or unstable. *—adj-* **psy′ cho·path′ ic.**

psy·cho·sis (sī kō′ səs) *n-* [*pl.* **psy·cho·ses** (-sēz′)] severe mental disorder in which a person's sense of reality is impaired or lost.

psy·cho·so·mat·ic (sī′ kō sə măt′ ĭk) *adj-* **1** of or relating to the connections between mental and physical processes, especially to psychological causes of bodily disease. *n-* person who is afflicted with physical symptoms caused by a mental disturbance.

psy·cho·ther·a·py (sī′ kō thĕr′ ə pē) *n-* [*pl.* **psy·cho·ther·a·pies**] treatment of nervous or emotional disorders which is conducted partly or entirely through personal consultation by means of psychoanalysis, hypnosis, etc.

psy·cho·tic (sī kŏt′ ĭk) *n-* person afflicted with a psychosis. *adj-* **1** suffering from psychosis: *a* psychotic *person.* **2** caused by a psychosis: *a* psychotic *symptom.*

psy·chrom·e·ter (sī krŏm′ ə tər) *n-* an instrument for measuring relative humidity of the atmosphere.

Pt symbol for platinum.

pt. **1** pint. **2** point. **3** port. **4** part.

P.T.A. or **PTA** Parent-Teacher Association.

ptar·mi·gan (tär′ mĭ gən) *n-* any of several northern or alpine grouses that change their brown summer plumage to white in winter.

Willow ptarmigan

PT boat *n-* patrol torpedo boat, a small, high-speed vessel armed with torpedoes; mosquito boat.

pter·i·do·phyte (tə rĭd′ ə fīt′) *n-* any of many flowerless and seedless plants such as ferns or club mosses, formerly classified in a single phylum **(Peridophyta).**

pter·o·dac·tyl (tĕr′ ə dăk′ təl) *n-* extinct flying reptile having featherless wing membranes between the body, arm, and the greatly elongated fourth finger.

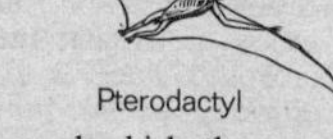
Pterodactyl

Ptol·e·ma·ic system (tŏl′ ə mā′ ĭk) *n-* theory named for the 2nd-century A.D. astronomer Ptolemy, but dating from long before his time, which held that the earth was the center of the universe around which the moon, planets, stars, etc., revolved.

pto·maine or **pto·main** (tō′ mān′) *n-* any of a group of chemicals, often poisonous, produced by the actions of certain bacteria on proteins.

pty·a·lin (tī′ ə lən) *n-* the enzyme in saliva that digests starch.

Pu symbol for plutonium.

pub (pŭb) *Brit. Informal n-* public house.

pu·ber·ty (pyōō′ bər tē) *n-* age, about fourteen for boys and twelve for girls, at which a person is physiologically capable of begetting or bearing a child.

pu·bis (pyōō′ bəs) *n-* [*pl.* **pu·bes** (-bēz′)] either of the bones that make up the forward arch of the pelvis. For picture, see *pelvis.* *—adj-* **pu′ bic.**

pub·lic (pŭb′ lĭk) *adj-* **1** of, for, or having to do with the people as a whole: *in the* public *interest*; public *needs.* **2** open to everyone; not private: *a* public *library*; *a* public *pool.* **3** serving the people: *a* public *utility*; public *office.* **4** generally known: *He made his opinions* public. *n-* **1** group of persons having a certain interest, especially an admiration for a certain person: *the literary* public; *the young violinist's* public. **2 the public** the people as a whole.

in public openly and visibly rather than privately.

public address system *n-* apparatus having one or more microphones, amplifiers, and loudspeakers, used to amplify sound in auditoriums or outdoors; PA.

pub·li·can (pŭb′ lĭ kən) *n-* **1** in England, person who keeps a public house. **2** in ancient Rome, and especially in the Bible, person who collected taxes in return for a part of what he collected.

pub·li·ca·tion (pŭb′ lə kā′ shən) *n-* **1** act or business of publishing. **2** printed and published work, such as a newspaper, magazine, book, etc. **3** a making known to the public: *This fact is not for* publication.

public defender *n-* lawyer appointed by a court to defend an accused person who cannot pay a legal fee.

public domain *n-* **1** government-owned land; land that is open to the public. **2** area of property rights not assigned to any person by copyright, patent, or other means, and hence open to anyone.

public enemy *n-* notorious criminal.

public house *Brit. n-* licensed saloon or tavern.

pub·li·cist (pŭb′ lə sĭst′) *n-* **1** person who writes or comments on international law or on public affairs. **2** press agent.

pub·lic·i·ty (pŭb lĭs′ ə tē) ***n-*** **1** state of being widely known; public attention: *The* publicity *given to a national hero.* **2** means by which someone or something becomes publicly known: *He is in charge of* publicity *for the school play.* *as* ***modifier***: *a* publicity *agent.*

pub·li·cize (pŭb′ lə sīz′) ***vt-*** **[pub·li·cized, pub·li·ciz·ing]** to give publicity to: *to* publicize *a movie star.*

pub·lic·ly (pŭb′ lĭk lē) ***adv-*** in a public manner; openly and visibly.

public opinion ***n-*** opinions, ideas, interests, etc., of the general public: *I think that* public opinion *will force Congress to pass the bill.*

public relations ***n-*** **1** (takes singular verb) occupation of persons who try to establish a favorable public attitude and reception for the business concern, government agency, or other client that hires them. **2** (takes plural verb) feeling or response of the public toward a certain person, institution, etc.

public school ***n-*** **1** school paid for out of taxes and open to all. **2** *Brit.* a private preparatory school.

public servant ***n-*** person who serves the people as a government employee, officeholder, etc.

public speaking ***n-*** act or art of making speeches before an audience; oratory.

pub·lic-spir·it·ed (pŭb′ lĭk spĭr′ ĭ təd) ***adj-*** dedicated to the public welfare: *a* public-spirited *citizen.*

public utility ***n-*** company or industry that supplies such services as electricity, gas, water, transportation, telephone, etc., to a whole community.

public works ***n-*** *pl.* buildings, roads, bridges, sewers, etc., built and cared for by the government for the public.

pub·lish (pŭb′ lĭsh) ***vt-*** **1** to offer to the public (a literary, artistic, or musical work), especially in the form of copies. **2** to make known; especially, to make known formally: *to* publish *a will.* ***—adj-*** **pub′ lish·a·ble.**

pub·lish·er (pŭb′ lĭsh ər) ***n-*** person or company whose business is printing and distributing books, newspapers, magazines, etc.

puce (pyo͞os) ***n-*** color of dark brown or purplish brown. ***adj-***: *a* puce *suit.*

[1]**puck** (pŭk) ***n-*** mischievous sprite; elf. [from Old English **pūca.**]

[2]**puck** (pŭk) ***n-*** hard rubber disk used in ice hockey. [apparently a variant of [1]**poke.**]

puck·er (pŭk′ ər) ***vt-*** to draw up, often in folds or wrinkles: *The green persimmon* puckered *my mouth.* ***vi-*** to become drawn up or wrinkled: *The cloth* puckered *badly after getting wet.* ***n-*** small fold or wrinkle.

puck·ish (pŭk′ ĭsh) ***adj-*** mischievous; impish: *a* puckish *personality.* ***—adv-*** **puck′ ish·ly.**

pud·ding (po͝od′ ĭng) ***n-*** **1** any of various soft foods, usually sweet and often served with a sauce. **2** any of several other soft foods not eaten sweet, such as **blood pudding,** which is a form of sausage.

pud·dle (pŭd′ əl) ***n-*** **1** small pool, usually made up of dirty or muddy water. **2** mixture of clay, sand, and water that becomes waterproof when dry. ***vt-*** **[pud·dled, pud·dling]** **1** to make muddy. **2** to work water into (a mixture of sand and clay). **3** in metallurgy, to subject (pig iron) to the process of puddling. ***—n-*** **pud′ dler.** ***adj-*** **pud′ dly:** *The road was always* puddly *after a rainstorm.*

pud·dling (pŭd′ lĭng) ***n-*** process of converting pig iron into nearly pure wrought iron in a reverberatory furnace lined with iron oxide.

pudg·y (pŭj′ ē) ***adj-*** **[pudg·i·er, pudg·i·est]** **1** short and fat. **2** chubby: *a* pudgy *face.* ***—n-*** **pudg′ i·ness.**

pueb·lo (pwĕb′ lō) ***n-*** [*pl.* **pueb·los**] **1** Indian village of the American Southwest consisting of stone dwellings or adobe houses. **2 Pueblo** member of any of several Indian peoples, such as the Hopi or Zuñi, living in these villages.

pu·er·ile (pyo͝or′ əl, -īl′) ***adj-*** childish; hence, trivial or silly: *a* puerile *argument.* ***—n-*** **pu′ er·il′ i·ty** (pyo͝or ĭl′ ə tē).

puff (pŭf) ***n-*** **1** short, quick blast, as of wind, steam, gas, or breath; also, the accompanying sound: *a* puff *of wind; the* puff *of a locomotive.* **2** soft pad or ball: *a powder* puff. **3** light pastry shell with a filling: *a cream* puff. **4** high praise, as in a newspaper or magazine: *The critic gave the new play quite a* puff. **5** single drawing and blowing out of smoke from a cigarette, cigar, or pipe. ***vi-*** **1** to send out air, smoke, steam, etc.: *The locomotive was* puffing. **2** to breathe quickly and hard, as a runner does. **3** to swell with gas or liquid (usually followed by "up"): *The bruise* puffed *up.* **4** to swell with self-importance (usually followed by "up"). ***vt-*** **1** to send out (air, smoke, etc.). **2** to swell (someone or something) with a fluid or self-importance (usually followed by "up"): *Too much praise* puffed *him up.* **3** to smoke (a cigarette, cigar, or pipe).

puff adder ***n-*** **1** large, heavy African viper that is handsomely marked and poisonous. **2** hognose snake.

puff·ball (pŭf′ bôl′) ***n-*** large, ball-shaped fungus which, when dried and broken open, emits a puff of spores.

puff·er (pŭf′ ər) ***n-*** **1** someone or something that puffs. **2** globefish.

puf·fin (pŭf′ ən) ***n-*** stout-bodied, short-necked northern sea bird with a large bill striped red and yellow.

Puffin, about 13 in. long

puff·y (pŭf′ ē) ***adj-*** **[puff·i·er, puff·i·est]** **1** puffed up; swollen: *to have* puffy *eyelids.* **2** blowing in puffs; breathing hard. ***—n-*** **puff′ i·ness.**

[1]**pug** (pŭg) ***n-*** small, stocky dog with a short, broad nose, wrinkled face, and tightly curled tail. Also **pug dog.** [a variant of [1]**puck.**]

[2]**pug** (pŭg) *Informal* ***n-*** boxer, especially a professional pugilist. [shortened from **pugilist.**]

pu·gil·ism (pyo͞o′ jə lĭz′ əm) ***n-*** practice or sport of fighting with the fists; especially, professional boxing.

pu·gil·ist (pyo͞o′ jə lĭst) ***n-*** person who fights with his fists, especially professionally. ***—adj-*** **pu′ gil·is′ tic.**

pug·mark (pŭg′ märk′) ***n-*** footprint of a wild animal.

pug·na·cious (pŭg nā′ shəs) ***adj-*** quick to fight; quarrelsome. ***—adv-*** **pug·na′ cious·ly.** ***n-*** **pug·na′ cious·ness** or **pug·nac′ i·ty** (-năs′ ə tē).

pug nose ***n-*** turned-up nose, broad at the tip. ***—adj-*** **pug′-nosed′:** *a* pug-nosed *boy.*

pu·is·sance (pwĭs′ əns, pyo͞o′ ə səns) ***n-*** strength to do or achieve; power.

pu·is·sant (pwĭs′ ənt, pyo͞o′ ə sənt) ***adj-*** extremely powerful; mighty: *a* puissant *monarch.* ***—adv-*** **pu′ is·sant·ly.**

puke (pyo͞ok) ***vi-*** **[puked, puking]** to vomit. ***n-*** vomit; also, the act of vomiting.

►Now considered an offensive word by many people.

pul·chri·tude (pŭl′ krĭ to͞od′, -tyo͞od′) ***n-*** beauty of face and figure; especially, female beauty.

pule (pyo͞ol) ***vi-*** **[puled, pul·ing]** to cry weakly; whimper.

pull (po͝ol) ***vt-*** **1** to cause (something) to move by drawing or attracting: *to* pull *a wagon.* **2** to draw out or tear

---

fāte, făt, dâre, bärn; bē, bĕt, mêre; bīte, bĭt; nōte, hŏt, môre, dôg; fŭn, fûr; to͞o, bo͝ok; oil; out; t*a*r; thin; *th*en; hw for wh as in *wh*at; zh for s as in u*s*ual; ə for a, e, i, o, u, as in *a*go, lin*e*n, per*i*l, at*o*m, min*u*s

away: *to* pull *a tooth*; *to* pull *weeds.* **3** to tug at with force: *to* pull *someone's hair.* **4** to tear or rend by tugging: *to* pull *a sheet to pieces.* **5** to strain or injure by wrenching: *to* pull *a tendon.* **6** to draw or attract: *The bill* pulled *six votes in committee.* **7** *Informal* to commit; do: *to* pull *a stupid trick.* **8** to work or stretch (candy) repeatedly while it is cooling. **9** in baseball, golf, etc., to hit (a ball) toward the left (if the hitter is righthanded) or toward the right (if the hitter is lefthanded). ***vi-*** **1** to draw, move, or tug: *He* pulled *at the rope.* **2** to move in any direction: *A car* pulled *into the driveway.* ***n-*** **1** act of drawing, tugging, etc.: *He gave my sleeve a* pull. **2** an attractive force: *the* pull *of a magnet.* **3** continued effort: *It was a long* pull *up the hill.* **4** *Informal* influence or advantage: *His* pull *got him the job.* **5** a deep puff; also, a swallow. **—*n-* pull′ er.**

pull away to increase one's lead over those behind one in a race or other contest.

pull down **1** to raze; demolish: *The houses were* pulled down *in a week.* **2** *Informal* to earn as wages.

pull for to help or lend verbal support: *I'm* pulling for *the Giants this year.*

pull in **1** to arrive: *The train* pulls in *at noon.* **2** to bring to a police station for questioning; apprehend; arrest.

pull off to accomplish in spite of difficulties.

pull (oneself) together to regain one's composure, self-possession, etc.

pull (one's) weight to do one's share.

pull out to leave; depart; withdraw.

pull over to drive a car, truck, etc. to the edge of the road and stop.

pull through to get through a difficult situation; especially, to recover from a serious injury or illness.

pull up to stop; come to a halt.

pull up stakes to leave one's home, job, settled place, etc., for something new.

pull up with to come up even with; overtake.

pul·let (po͝ol′ ət) ***n-*** young hen.

pul·ley (po͝ol′ ē) ***n-*** [*pl.* **pul·leys**] **1** grooved wheel over which a rope may be pulled to raise weights or change the direction of a pull. **2** simple machine consisting of such a wheel, its frame, and ropes.

Pulley

Pull·man (po͝ol′ mən) ***n-*** railroad car with private sleeping rooms or seats that can be made up into berths, or one in which especially comfortable chairs may be reserved. Also **Pullman car.** [from **George M. Pullman,** American who improved sleeping cars.]

pull·out (po͝ol′ out′) ***n-*** **1** a withdrawal; especially, an orderly retreat of troops. **2** a maneuver in which an airplane passes from a dive to horizontal flight.

pull·o·ver (po͝ol′ ō′ vər) ***n-*** a garment, such as a sweater or shirt, that is put on by being drawn over the head. ***as modifier***: *a* pullover *blouse.*

pul·mo·nar·y (po͝ol′ mə nĕr′ ē) ***adj-*** of or having to do with the lungs: *a* pulmonary *disease.*

Pul·mo·tor (po͝ol′ mō′ tər) ***n-*** trademark name for an apparatus that produces artificial breathing by forcing air or oxygen into the lungs where breathing has ceased, as in drowning or suffocation. Also **pulmotor.**

pulp (pŭlp) ***n-*** **1** soft, fleshy part of a fruit or plant stem. **2** inner part of a tooth containing the nerves and blood vessels. **3** any soft, moist mass; especially, a moist mixture of ground-up wood, rags, etc., from which paper is made. **4** (usually **pulps**) magazine printed on cheap paper made of wood pulp, and dealing with sensational material. ***vt-*** to reduce (something) to a soft, moist mass. ***vi-*** to become pulpy.

pul·pit (po͝ol′ pĭt) ***n-*** **1** in some churches, a small elevated balcony from which the priest or minister speaks. **2** the clergy as a group.

pulp·wood (pŭlp′ wo͝od′) ***n-*** wood used for making paper.

pulp·y (pŭl′ pē) ***adj-*** [**pulp·i·er, pulp·i·est**] consisting of or like a soft, moist mass of matter; soft; fleshy. **—*n-* pulp′ i·ness.**

pul·que (po͝ol′ kā) ***n-*** Mexican fermented drink, made from the sweet sap of a century plant.

pul·sate (pŭl′ sāt′) ***vi-*** [**pul·sat·ed, pul·sat·ing**] **1** to throb or beat with a regular rhythm, as the heart does. **2** to quiver; vibrate: *His voice* pulsated *with emotion.*

Pulpit

pul·sa·tion (pəl sā′ shən) ***n-*** **1** a regular beating or throbbing, as of the heart. **2** a single throb or beat.

[1]**pulse** (pŭls) ***n-*** **1** the throbbing or beating in an artery as blood is pumped through it by the heart. **2** any regular stroke or beat: *the* pulse *of the music.* ***vi-*** [**pulsed, puls·ing**] to beat; throb; vibrate. [from French **pou(l)s,** from Latin **pulsus,** "the beating (of the veins)."]

[2]**pulse** (pŭls) ***n-*** the seeds of such plants as peas, beans, and lentils, which are cooked and used as food; also, the plants themselves. [from Old French **pols,** from Latin **puls** meaning "a pottage of beans and meal."]

pulse jet ***n-*** type of jet engine that produces a pulsating thrust by the opening and closing of air valves.

pul·ver·ize (pŭl′ və rīz′) ***vt-*** [**pul·ver·ized, pul·ver·iz·ing**] **1** to grind or pound into a powder or dust. **2** to destroy completely; annihilate: *The air raid* pulverized *the enemy's fortifications.* ***vi-*** to become powder or dust.

pu·ma (pyo͞o′ mə) ***n-*** mountain lion.

pum·ice (pŭm′ əs) ***n-*** light, spongy, volcanic rock, used in polishing and cleaning.

pum·mel (pŭm′ əl) ***vt-*** to beat with the fists; pommel.

[1]**pump** (pŭmp) ***n-*** machine or natural organ for moving liquids or gases by applied pressure or suction. ***vt-*** **1** to move (liquids or gases) by suction or applied pressure: *The heart* pumps *blood.* **2** to raise, draw, or force with a pump: *He* pumped *water from the well.* **3** to use a pump to move a liquid or gas from, into, or through: *We* pumped *the boat dry. He* pumped *up the tire.* **4** to question closely: *The woman* pumped *the child about his father's business.* ***vi-*** **1** to work a pump: *He* pumped *faster.* **2** to function as a pump: *Your heart* pumps *too fast.* [from early German **pumpe.**]

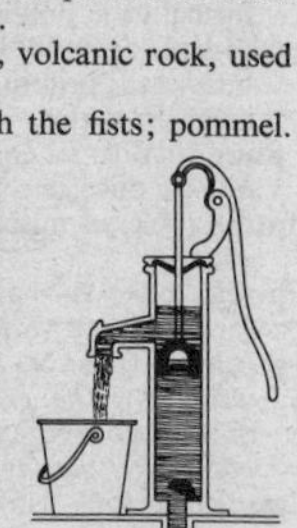

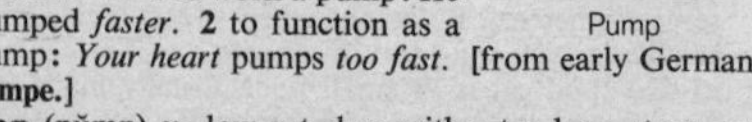

Pump

[2]**pump** (pŭmp) ***n-*** low-cut shoe without a lace, strap, or other fastening. [from Dutch **pampoesje,** from Javanese **pampoes** meaning "slipper," from Persian **pāpirsh.**]

pump·er (pŭm′ pər) ***n-*** **1** person or thing that pumps. **2** fire truck equipped with hoses, a powerful pump, and often a large water tank.

pum·per·nick·el (pŭm′ pər nĭk′ əl) ***n-*** kind of dark bread made of coarse rye flour.

pump·kin (pŭmp′ kĭn, pŭng′-) ***n-*** **1** a large, golden-yellow, usually round fruit of a vine. It is used for pies and as cattle food. **2** the large-leafed vine which bears this fruit.

Pumpkin

pump priming ***n-*** a spending or investment of money by the government to stimulate the economy.

pun (pŭn) ***n-*** a play on words that are the same in sound but different in meaning, or on different meanings of the same word. Example: He went and told the sexton and the sexton tolled the bell. ***vi-*** **[punned, pun·ning]** to make such a play on words: *He is always* punning.

pu·na (po͞o′ nä′) ***n-*** **1** high, cold, arid region in the central Andes. **2** illness marked by weakness, nausea, etc., brought on at high altitudes by lack of oxygen.

[1]punch (pŭnch) ***n-*** **1** tool for making holes. **2** tool to stamp numbers, letters, and the like on metal. **3** a blow with the fist. **4** *Slang* vigor; vitality; force. ***vt-*** **1** to make holes in, emboss, stamp, cut, etc., using a tool: *The conductor* punched *the ticket.* **2** to strike forward with the fist: *The boxer* punched *the punching bag.* **3** *Informal* to drive (cattle). **4** to press the key or keys of (a machine): *to* punch *a typewriter*; *to* punch *a time clock.* ***vi-*** **1** to make a hole, stamp, etc.: *This tool* punches *cleanly.* **2** to hit with the fist: *to* punch *hard.* [from [2]**puncheon.**] **—*n-* punch′ er.**

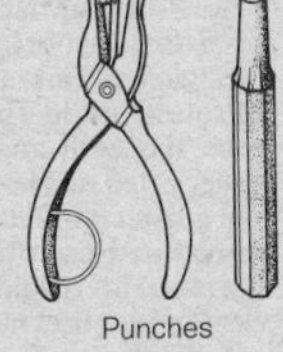
Punches

punch in (or **out**) to punch a time clock to record the time of one's arrival at (or departure from) work.

[2]punch (pŭnch) ***n-*** drink made of a mixture of liquids, usually fruit juices, and often containing alcoholic liquors, spices, and other flavoring. [from Hindi **panch,** from a Sanskrit word meaning "five," from the five ingredients once used in it.]

Punch (pŭnch) ***n-*** the quarreling, hunchbacked hero of a comic puppet show, "Punch and Judy."

[1]pun·cheon (pŭn′ chən) ***n-*** cask of varying capacity (70 to 120 gallons); also, amount such a cask holds when full. [from Middle English **poncion,** from earlier French **ponchon,** of uncertain origin.]

[2]pun·cheon (pŭn′ chən) ***n-*** **1** punch for piercing or stamping. **2** supporting timber, especially one made from a log hewed flat on one side. [from Old French **poinchon,** from Late Latin **punctiō,** from **puncta,** "a point; prick."]

pun·chi·nel·lo (pŭn′ chə nĕl′ ō) ***n-*** [*pl.* **pun·chi·nel·los** or **pun·chi·nel·loes**] buffoon in an Italian puppet show, the forerunner of the English Punch.

punching bag ***n-*** a stuffed or inflated bag, usually suspended, punched for exercise or training in boxing.

punch line ***n-*** last sentence or phrase of a joke, story, or speech that drives home the point.

punc·til·i·o (pŭngk tĭl′ ē ō) ***n-*** [*pl.* **punc·til·i·os**] a small point of etiquette in conduct, manners, or dress; also, formal correctness; formality.

punc·til·i·ous (pŭngk tĭl′ ē əs) ***adj-*** **1** very precise in conduct; paying careful attention to details of dress, speech, or manners. **2** very careful and exact. **—*adv-* punc·til′ i·ous·ly.** ***n-*** **punc·til′ i·ous·ness.**

punc·tu·al (pŭngk′ cho͞o əl) ***adj-*** on time; not late; prompt: *a* punctual *student.* **—*n-* punc′ tu·al′ i·ty** (-cho͞o ăl′ ə tē). ***adv-*** **punc′ tu·al·ly.**

punc·tu·ate (pŭngk′ cho͞o āt′) ***vt-*** **[punc·tu·at·ed, punc·tu·at·ing]** **1** to use periods, commas, and other marks between written words to make the meaning clear: *to* punctuate *a paragraph.* **2** to emphasize: *He* punctuated *his remarks with gestures.* **3** to interrupt from time to time: *Cheers* punctuated *the speaker's words.* ***vi-*** to use punctuation marks: *He* punctuates *badly.*

punc·tu·a·tion (pŭngk′ cho͞o ā′ shən) ***n-*** the use of periods, commas, and other marks between written words to make the meaning clear.

punctuation mark ***n-*** any of the marks used in punctuation. The chief punctuation marks are: the comma [,], semi-colon [;], colon [:], period [.], interrogation mark [?], exclamation mark [!], dash [—], hyphen [-], parentheses [( )], brackets [ ], quotation marks [" . . . . . "], and single quotation marks [' . . . . '].

punc·ture (pŭngk′ chər) ***n-*** **1** small hole or wound made by something pointed: *The nail made a* puncture *in our tire.* **2** a puncturing or perforating. ***vt-*** **[punc·tured, punc·tur·ing]** to make a hole in; pierce; prick: *A nail* punctured *the tire.* **2** to put an end to; deflate.

pun·dit (pŭn′ dĭt) ***n-*** **1** a learned Brahman, especially one versed in the Sanskrit language, the laws of India, the Hindu religion, etc. **2** any man of great learning.

pun·gent (pŭn′ jənt) ***adj-*** **1** sharp or biting: *Mustard has a* pungent *taste.* **2** stinging; piercing; sarcastic: *a* pungent *remark.* **—*n-* pun′ gen·cy.** ***adv-*** **pun′ gent·ly.**

pun·ish (pŭn′ ĭsh) ***vt-*** **1** to cause (a person) to pay a penalty for a fault or crime; chastise: *He was* punished *for stealing.* **2** to impose a penalty for (an offense against the law): *to* punish *manslaughter.* **3** to treat or handle roughly. **—*n-* pun′ ish·er.**

pun·ish·a·ble (pŭn′ ĭsh ə bəl) ***adj-*** liable to or deserving punishment: *In wartime, treason is* punishable *by death.*

pun·ish·ment (pŭn′ ĭsh mənt) ***n-*** **1** penalty imposed for a crime or fault. **2** a punishing or being punished: *harsh* punishment. **3** *Informal* rough treatment.

pu·ni·tive (pyo͞o′ nə tĭv′) ***adj-*** having to do with, or inflicting, punishment: *a* punitive *expedition*; punitive *laws.* **—*adv-* pu′ ni·tive·ly.** ***n-*** **pu′ ni·tive·ness.**

[1]punk (pŭngk) ***n-*** **1** a preparation that burns slowly without flame, often used in sticks to light fireworks. **2** decayed wood used as tinder. [American word from Algonquian Indian.]

[2]punk (pŭngk) *Slang* ***adj-*** poor; worthless; trashy; also not well. ***n-*** a young and inexperienced man; especially, a young hoodlum. [of uncertain origin.]

pun·ster (pŭn′ stər) ***n-*** person who habitually makes puns.

[1]punt (pŭnt) ***n-*** shallow, flat-bottomed boat with square ends. ***vt-*** to drive (a boat) forward by pushing with a pole against a river or lake bottom: *He* punted *the boat along the shallow river.* **2** to transport in such a boat. [from Old English, from Latin **ponto** meaning "a punt; pontoon."] **—*n-* punt′ er.**

[2]punt (pŭnt) ***n-*** **1** in football, a maneuver in which a player on the team having the ball kicks the ball into the territory of the opposing team. The kicker drops the ball from his hands and kicks it before it touches the ground. **2** the kick itself; also, the distance the ball travels. ***vi-***: *Green Bay* punted *on fourth down.* ***vt-***: *He* punted *that ball sixty yards.* [probably from [1]**punt,** from the sense of "propelling."] **—*n-* punt·er.**

pu·ny (pyo͞o′ nē) ***adj-*** **[pu·ni·er, pu·ni·est]** **1** undersized; weak: *a* puny *baby.* **2** half-hearted; feeble: *a* puny *effort.* **—*n-* pu′ ni·ness.**

pup (pŭp) ***n-*** **1** young dog; puppy. **2** the young of foxes, wolves, seals, and several other mammals.

pu·pa (pyo͞o′ pə) ***n-*** [*pl.* **pu·pae** (-pē) or **pu·pas**] stage in the life cycle of insects with a complete metamorphosis, coming between the larva and adult. A pupa

Pupa

usually does not move or feed, but undergoes great changes in form to become like the adult.

[1]**pu·pil** (pyōō′ pəl) ***n-*** person who is learning under the direction of a teacher; student. [from French **pupille,** from Latin **pūpillus** meaning "a ward; orphan," from **pūpus,** "boy."]

[2]**pu·pil** (pyōō′ pəl) ***n-*** the dark, central hole in the iris of the eye through which light enters the eye. In man, the pupil is circular, but in the cat it is slitlike. See also picture at *eye.* [from Latin **pūpilla,** meaning originally "little girl; doll," from the tiny image of oneself seen reflected in another's eyes.]

pup·pet (pŭp′ ət) ***n-*** **1** jointed doll that can be made to move by pulling strings or by movements of a hand inserted in it. **2** person or government who is under the complete control of another: *The king was the* puppet *of his ministers. as* ***modifier:*** *a* puppet *government*; *a* puppet *regime.* **—*adj-* pup′ pet·like′.**

pup·pet·ry (pŭp′ ə trē) ***n-*** puppets in general; performances of puppets; hence, artificial action or display.

pup·py (pŭp′ ē) ***n-*** [*pl.* **pup·pies**] **1** young dog. **2** silly young man.

pup tent ***n-*** shelter tent.

pur·blind (pûr′ blīnd′) ***adj-*** **1** *Archaic* almost without sight; partly blind. **2** slow in understanding; dull; obtuse. **—*adv-* pur′ blind′ ly. *n-* pur′ blind′ ness.**

pur·chase (pûr′ chəs) ***vt-*** [**pur·chased, pur·chas·ing**] to get by paying money or other possession of value; buy. ***n-*** **1** a buying: *the* purchase *of Christmas presents.* **2** something bought: *I brought my* purchase *home to show you.* **3** firm hold or grasp to help one to move something or to keep oneself from slipping: *He got a* purchase *on a rock.* **—*n-* pur′ chas·er.**

pur·chas·a·ble (pûr′ chə sə bəl) ***adj-*** **1** such as can be purchased. **2** ready or willing to be bribed; corrupt.

pure (pyŏŏr) ***adj-*** [**pur·er, pur·est**] **1** free of foreign matter; clean; clear; unmixed: *of* pure *silver*; pure *food.* **2** without guilt or sin; innocent. **3** mere; sheer; nothing but: *to meet by* pure *chance*; *to talk* pure *nonsense.* **4** theoretical: *to study* pure *science.* **—*n-* pure′ ness.**

pure·bred (pyŏŏr′ brĕd′) ***adj-*** of an animal, having ancestors of unmixed breed.

pu·rée (pyŏŏr ā′) ***n-*** **1** boiled or strained pulp of vegetables or fruit. **2** thick soup of such materials.

pure·ly (pyŏŏr′ lē) ***adv-*** **1** merely; only: *I am doing this work* purely *to please you.* **2** completely; entirely: *I have a* purely *unselfish interest in it.* **3** in a pure manner.

pur·ga·tive (pûr′ gə tĭv′) ***adj-*** having the power of cleansing; also, causing bowel movement. ***n-*** medicine for the purpose of causing bowel movement; cathartic.

pur·ga·to·ry (pûr′ gə tôr′ ē) ***n-*** **1** in Roman Catholic belief, an intermediate state or place where the souls of those who die penitent may make full satisfaction for their failings before entering heaven. **2** [*pl.* **pur·ga·to·ries**] any place or state of temporary suffering or misery. **—*adj-* pur′ ga·to′ ri·al.**

purge (pûrj) ***vt-*** [**purged, purg·ing**] **1** to cleanse; remove impurities or foreign matter from; purify. **2** to free from guilt or sin. **3** to rid (a political party, nation, etc.) of persons regarded as undependable or undesirable, especially by forcible or high-handed means. **4** to clear or empty the bowels of with a medicine. ***vi-*** **1** to become pure or clean. **2** to clear the bowels by the use of a medicine. ***n-*** **1** a cleansing by emptying. **2** a removing of persons who are not desirable or loyal. **3** a medicine used to empty the bowels.

pu·ri·fi·ca·tion (pyŏŏr′ ə fə kā′ shən) ***n-*** **1** a cleansing from guilt or sin. **2** removal of impurities or their harmful effects: *the* purification *of water.*

pu·ri·fy (pyŏŏr′ ə fī′) ***vt-*** [**pu·ri·fied, pu·ri·fy·ing**] to make pure; cleanse: *to* purify *the air*; *to* purify *the soul.* ***vi-*** to become pure. **—*n-* pu′ ri·fi′ er.**

Pu·rim (pŏŏr′ ĭm) ***n-*** Jewish feast, usually observed in March, commemorating the rescuing of the Jews from Haman's plot.

pur·ism (pyŏŏr′ ĭz′ əm) ***n-*** excessive observance of, or insistence on, correctness or purity in language, style, etc. **—*n-* pur′ ist. *adj-* pu·ris′ tic.**

pu·ri·tan (pyŏŏr′ ə tən) ***n-*** **1** person who is very strict in religion or morals. **2 Puritan** member of a group of Protestants in England and the American colonies in the sixteenth and seventeenth centuries. The Puritans supported reforms in the Church of England and believed in a strict moral code and simplicity in religious worship.

pu·ri·tan·i·cal (pyŏŏr′ ə tăn′ ĭk əl) ***adj-*** **1** strict and precise in religious duties and moral conduct; also, enforcing strict morality: *rigid,* puritanical *laws.* **2** (often **Puritanical**) of or having to do with the Puritans. **—*adv-* pu′ ri·tan′ i·cal·ly. *n-* pu′ ri·tan′ i·cal·ness.**

pu·ri·tan·ism (pyŏŏr′ ə tən ĭz′ əm) ***n-*** **1** great strictness in matters of religion and morals. **2 Puritanism** the doctrines and practices of the Puritans.

pu·ri·ty (pyŏŏr′ ə tē) ***n-*** **1** freedom from impurities or foreign matter: *Are you certain of the* purity *of this chemical?* **2** freedom from evil or sin; innocence. **3** freedom from the use of words or phrases not sanctioned by good usage; also, accuracy; refined elegance.

[1]**purl** (pûrl) ***n-*** in knitting, a stitch of the type usually found on the wrong side of a garment. ***vi-*** to make such a stitch: *to knit and then* purl. ***vt-:*** *to* purl *a row of stitches.* [from earlier **pirl** meaning "to twist."] ***Hom-*** pearl.

[2]**purl** (pûrl) ***vi-*** **1** to ripple or flow with a gentle murmur. **2** to move in a circular motion; whirl. ***n-*** **1** the continued murmuring sound of a shallow stream. **2** an eddy; small whirlpool. [perhaps from an imitation of the sound of whirling things, especially spinning tops.] ***Hom-*** pearl.

pur·lieu (pûr′ lōō′, -lyōō′) ***n-*** **1** neighboring or outlying district. **2 purlieus** outskirts: *the* purlieus *of a city.*

pur·loin (pər loin′, pûr′ loin′) ***vt-*** to steal; pilfer. **—*n-* pur·loin′ er.**

pur·ple (pûr′ pəl) ***n-*** **1** the color of eggplant rind and grape juice; mixture of red and blue; violet. **2** robe of this color worn by royalty; hence, a symbol of royal power, wealth, or high rank. ***adj-*** **1** of or relating to the color purple. **2** of writing, flowery or very sentimental: *a* purple *passage.* **—*n-* pur′ ple·ness.**

Purple Heart ***n-*** a U.S. military decoration awarded to members of the armed forces or citizens of the United States wounded in action against the enemy.

pur·plish (pûr′ plĭsh) ***adj-*** somewhat purple.

[1]**pur·port** (pər pôrt′) ***vt-*** to appear; to claim, often falsely (takes only an infinitive as object): *The message* purported *to come from the President.*

[2]**pur·port** (pûr′ pôrt′) ***n-*** meaning; significance: *to grasp the* purport *of the note.*

pur·pose (pûr′ pəs) ***n-*** aim; intention; design; desired result. ***vt-*** [**pur·posed, pur·pos·ing**] to intend: *What did he* purpose?

on purpose not by accident; intentionally. **to good purpose** with good result. **to little** (or **no**) **purpose** with little (or no) result.

pur·pose·ful (pûr′ pəs fəl) ***adj-*** **1** having a purpose; determined: *a* purposeful *man.* **2** serving an end; full of meaning; significant: *a* purposeful *life.* —*adv-* **pur′pose·ful·ly.** *n-* **pur′ pose·ful·ness.**

pur·pose·ly (pûr′ pəs lē) *adv-* intentionally; on purpose.

purr (pûr) *n-* **1** the low, murmuring sound made by a cat when it seems to be contented. **2** any similar sound: *the* purr *of a car's motor.* *vi-* to make such a sound. *vt-*: *She* purred *her contentment.*

purse (pûrs) *n-* **1** small bag or case to carry money. **2** woman's handbag. **3** money; funds; treasury: *the public* purse. **4** money offered as a prize, reward, or gift. *vt-* **[pursed, purs·ing]** to wrinkle or pucker: *He* pursed *his lips to whistle.*

purs·er (pûr′ sər) *n-* the officer who has charge of the accounts on board a ship.

purse strings *n-* strings which draw together to close a purse.

hold the purse strings to have charge of the money. **tighten** (or **loosen**) **the purse strings** to reduce (or increase) expenditures.

purs·lane (pûrs′ lən, -lān′) *n-* low-growing, fleshy-leafed plant with tiny yellow flowers.

pur·su·ance (pər sōō′ əns, -syōō′ əns) *n-* a carrying out: *In* pursuance *of her plan, she left by plane.*

pur·su·ant (pər sōō′ ənt, -syōō′ ənt) *adj-* following out; conformable; according.

pursuant to in accordance with; in accord with: *He acted* pursuant to *a plan.*

pur·sue (pər sōō′, -syōō′) *vt-* **[pur·sued, pur·su·ing]** **1** to chase; follow in order to capture: *to* pursue *an escaped convict.* **2** to follow; engage in: *He* pursued *law as a profession.* **3** to follow through; keep up; continue: *She* pursued *her struggle to gain fame.* **4** to seek: *She* pursues *pleasure but she does not seem happy.* **5** to follow (a path, course, etc.). **6** to harass persistently; continue to trouble: *Bad luck* pursued *him.* *vi-* **1** to follow. **2** to continue; go on. —*n-* **pur·su′ er.**

pur·suit (pər sōōt′, -syōōt′) *n-* **1** a chase: *the* pursuit *of a deer.* **2** a seeking; quest: *the* pursuit *of fame.* **3** occupation or pastime: *Singing is one of her many* pursuits.

pu·ru·lent (pyŏŏr′ ə lənt) *adj-* consisting of, discharging, or containing pus. —*n-* **pu′ ru·lence.**

pur·vey (pər vā′) *vt-* to supply (food or other provisions). *vi-* to make a business of supplying provisions to others. —*n-* **pur·vey′ or:** *a* purveyor *of wine.*

pur·vey·ance (pər vā′ əns) *n-* a purveying or supplying.

pus (pŭs) *n-* a yellow-white substance produced by sores, abscesses, etc., and containing dead white blood cells and bacteria.

push (pŏŏsh) *vt-* (in senses 1 through 4 considered intransitive when the direct object is implied but not expressed) **1** to press hard against in order to move: *We* pushed *the desk, but it was too heavy to move.* **2** to open (a way, path, hole, etc.) with effort: *He* pushed *his way in among the crowd.* **3** to urge forward: *We* pushed *him to make a speech. I* pushed *his interests.* **4** to cause a strain on (someone): *It will* push *me to pay you next week.* **5** to make a great effort to sell. *vi-* to move forward with an effort: *The army* pushed *along through the snow.* *n-* **1** a shove or thrust: *Joe gave Tom a playful* push. **2** *Informal* enterprise; energy; drive: *I admire his* push. **3** case or time of pressure or stress; emergency. **4** a lift or help; a boost.

push off *Informal* to leave; depart.
push on to proceed; go on or forward.

push button *n-* a button which, when pushed, turns an electric current on or off: *Our garage door opens and closes by* push button. *as* ***modifier*** **(push-button):** *a* push-button *war; a* push-button *transmission.*

push·cart (pŏŏsh′ kärt′) *n-* small cart pushed by hand.

push·er (pŏŏsh′ ər) *n-* **1** person or thing that pushes. **2** (also **pusher airplane**) airplane with the propeller placed back of the main supporting surfaces.

push·o·ver (pŏŏsh′ ō′ vər) *Slang* *n-* **1** something very simple or easily done. **2** person who is easily defeated, fooled, persuaded, etc.

push·up (pŏŏsh′ ŭp′) *n-* conditioning exercise done by lying face down on the floor and pushing the body up with the arms while holding the spine rigid.

pu·sil·lan·i·mous (pyōō′ sə lăn′ ə məs) *adj-* cowardly; timorous. —*n-* **pu′ sil·la·nim′ i·ty.** *adv-* **pu′ sil·lan′ i·mous·ly.**

[1]**puss** (pōōs) *n-* cat. [of early Germanic origin, perhaps from an imitation of a cat's purring.]

[2]**puss** (pōōs) *Slang* *n-* the face or mouth. [of uncertain origin.]

[1]**puss·y** (pōōs′ ē) *n-* [*pl.* **puss·ies**] a cat. [from [1]**puss.**]

[2]**pus·sy** (pŭs′ ē) *adj-* **[pus·si·er, pus·si·est]** resembling, containing, or secreting pus: *a* pussy *sore.* [from **pus.**]

puss·y·foot (pōōs′ ē fŏŏt′) *vi-* **1** to move as quietly and carefully as a cat. **2** to fail to take a decided stand: *The senator* pussyfooted *on the tax.*

pussy willow *n-* small willow that bears furry, pearl-gray buds early in the spring.

Pussy willow

pus·tule (pŭs′ chŏŏl′) *n-* small elevation of the skin containing pus; also, a pimple or blister.

put (pŏŏt) *vt-* **[put, put·ting]** **1** to set in a certain place or position; place: *to* put *dishes on the table.* **2** to cause to be in a certain condition: *to* put *someone in a temper; to* put *it in order.* **3** to propose or submit for consideration, discussion, etc.: *to* put *a question.* **4** to express; set forth: *to* put *a thought into words.* **5** to set a value on (something); give as an estimate: *He* put *a price on the desk. She* puts *the time at 12 o'clock.* **6** to impose: *to* put *a tax on cigarettes.* **7** to apply; set: *to* put *one's mind to a task.* **8** to assign; ascribe: *to* put *blame on him.* **9** to throw or hurl with an upward and outward motion of the arm: *to* put *a shot.* **10** to adapt; fit: *to* put *words into music.* **11** to bet: *He* put *$50 on a horse.* *vi-* to go; proceed: *The ship* put *to sea at noon.* *n-* a cast or throw.

be hard put to have difficulty: *He* was hard put *to find a reason.* **stay put** *Informal* to remain fixed or in the same place: *My hair won't* stay put.

put about **1** to alter the course of a ship from one tack to another. **2** to change direction.

put across *Informal* **1** to cause to be understood: *to* put across *an idea.* **2** to carry out successfully; also, to deceive; cheat: *to* put across *a scheme.*

put aside (or **away** or **by**) **1** to save; reserve for later use: *to* put *money* aside. **2** to discard; set aside.

put away **1** to put in the proper place: *to* put away *the dishes.* **2** to commit or confine; put in prison or in an asylum: *He was acting so strangely that they finally* put *him* away. **3** to give up; renounce: *to* put away *childish things.* **4** *Informal* to consume (food or drink). **5** *Slang* to kill.

put down **1** to crush; suppress: *to* put down *a rebellion.* **2** to write down; record: *to* put down *an address.* **3** to store: *to* put down *meats in brine.*

---

fāte, făt, dâre, bärn; bē, bĕt, mêre; bīte, bĭt; nōte, hŏt, môre, dȯg; fŭn, fûr; tōō, bŏŏk; oil; out; tar; thin; then; hw for wh as in *wh*at; zh for s as in u*s*ual; ə for a, e, i, o, u, as in *a*go, lin*e*n, per*i*l, at*o*m, min*u*s

put down to to attribute to: *an error* put down to *haste.*
put forth 1 to sprout; grow (shoots, buds, etc.): *to* put forth *leaves.* 2 to exert: *to* put forth *all one's strength.* 3 to propose: *to* put forth *a new theory.* 4 to publish: *to* put forth *a new magazine.* 5 to set out; depart.
put forward to advance; propose; present.
put in 1 to enter a port: *The ship* put in *at Boston.* 2 to insert; interpose: *He* put in *a good word for me.* 3 *Informal* to spend: *to* put in *a day at golf.* 4 to present; submit: *to* put in *a claim.*
put in for to apply for: *He* put in for *a job at the bank.*
put (one) in mind of to remind (one) of.
put off 1 to delay: *He* put off *his departure.* 2 to get rid of for the time being; persuade to wait: *They* put *him* off *with false promises.* 3 to take off; remove.
put on 1 to get into: *He* put on *his clothes in a hurry.* 2 to apply: *to* put on *makeup.* 3 to assume; pretend: *He* put on *a bold front.* 4 to stage: *to* put on *a play.*
put out 1 to extinguish: *to* put out *a light.* 2 to annoy: *I was* put out *by her rudeness.* 3 to disconcert; confuse: *I was* put out *by her giggling.* 4 in baseball, to cause (a batter or runner) to be out. 5 to publish.
put over 1 *Informal* to carry out successfully: *to* put over *a business deal.* 2 to cause to be understood and accepted: *He* put over *his idea.*
put through 1 to cause to be acted on or completed: *I'll* put through *your claim today.* 2 to cause or force to undergo: *They* put *him* through *torture.*
put up 1 to pack or preserve (fruit, vegetables, etc.). 2 to build. 3 to offer for sale: *They* put up *furniture at auction.* 4 to give or occupy lodging: *The tourists* put up *at a motel.* 5 to provide (money); also, to bet. 6 to raise: *to* put up *a flag*; *to* put up *prices.* 7 to nominate; propose for election. 8 to lay aside; put away: *The garden furniture has been* put up *for the winter.* 9 to achieve; carry on: *to* put up *a fight.*
put upon to take advantage of; treat unfairly.
put up to to incite: *Who* put *the boy* up to *that mischief?*
put up with to tolerate; endure.

put-on (pŏŏt′ ŏn′) *adj-* assumed; feigned; pretended: *a* put-on *air of innocence.*

put·out (pŏŏt′ out′) *n-* in baseball, a play causing a batter or a runner to be out.

pu·tre·fac·tion (pyŏŏ′ trə făk′ shən) *n-* 1 decomposition of organic matter by certain bacteria and fungi, resulting in foul-smelling compounds. 2 rottenness.

pu·tre·fy (pyŏŏ′ trə fī′) *vt-* [**pu·tre·fied, pu·tre·fy·ing**] to cause to rot or decay with a foul odor. *vi-* to decay or become rotten.

pu·tres·cent (pyŏŏ trĕs′ ənt) *adj-* becoming rotten; decaying. *—n-* **pu·tres′ cence.**

pu·trid (pyŏŏ′ trĭd) *adj-* 1 rotten; decayed or decaying: *The garbage had become* putrid. 2 foul or fetid as if from rottenness: *a* putrid *odor.* *—n-* **pu·trid′ ·i·ty** or **pu′ trid·ness.** *adv-* **pu′ trid·ly.**

putt (pŭt) *n-* careful stroke on the putting green to play a ball toward or into the hole. *vi-* to make such a stroke: *He* putted *badly today.* *vt-*: *He* putted *the ball too far.*

put·tee (pə tē′, pŭt′ ē) *n-* leg covering made of cloth wrapped spirally from knee to ankle, worn by soldiers or sportsmen; also, a stiff leather legging. *Hom-* putty.

[1]**put·ter** (pŭt′ ər) *n-* 1 in golf, a short club with a flat metal head, used on the putting green. 2 person who putts with such a club. [from **putt.**]

[2]**put·ter** (pŭt′ ər) *vi-* to work lazily or without much purpose; potter: *He* puttered *around the garden all day.* [a variant of **potter.**] *—n-* **put′ ter·er.**

putting green *n-* in golf, the plot of smooth grass around a hole.

put·ty (pŭt′ ē) *n-* soft cement used for filling cracks, holding glass in a window frame, etc. It is usually made of powdered chalk and boiled linseed oil. *vt-* [**put·tied, put·ty·ing**] to apply such a cement to: *to* putty *a window frame.* *Hom-* puttee.

put-up (pŏŏt′ ŭp′) *adj-* planned beforehand in a secret or artful manner: *a* put-up *job.*

put-u·pon (pŏŏt′ ə pŏn′) *adj-* taken advantage of.

puz·zle (pŭz′ əl) *n-* 1 something difficult and confusing to understand: *How he learned the secret is a* puzzle *to me.* 2 toy or game presenting some problem or difficulty which is fun to solve: *a crossword* puzzle; *a jigsaw* puzzle. *vt-* [**puz·zled, puz·zling**] to perplex; confuse; bewilder: *His long silence* puzzles *me.* *vi-* to be perplexed; think about something difficult or confusing: *We* puzzled *three days over the problem.* *—n-* **puz′ zler.**
puzzle out to discover (something perplexing) by careful and persistent thought.

puz·zle·ment (pŭz′ əl mənt) *n-* a being puzzled; perplexity; bewilderment; embarrassment.

Pvt. private.

PX or **P.X.** post exchange.

Pyg·ma·li·on (pĭg māl′ ē ən) *n-* in Greek legend, a sculptor of ancient Cyprus who fell in love with a statue he carved.

pyg·my (pĭg′ mē) *n-* [*pl.* **pyg·mies**] 1 undersized person; a dwarf. 2 **Pygmy** member of an African people whose average height is four feet, eight inches. *adj-* very small; dwarfish. Also **pigmy.**

py·ja·mas (pə jä′ məz, -jăm′ əz) pajamas.

py·lon (pī′ lŏn′) *n-* 1 in architecture, a gateway, especially a monumental gateway to an Egyptian temple in the form of a flat-topped pyramid or two such pyramids. 2 post or tower used as a marker to indicate the course in an air race. 3 high steel tower for holding up high-tension electric power lines.

py·lo·rus (pī lôr′ əs) *n-* [*pl.* **py·lo·ri** (-ī′, -ē′)] the opening between the stomach and the small intestine.

py·or·rhe·a (pī′ ə rē′ ə) *n-* inflammation of the tooth sockets and surrounding gum tissue, resulting in the loosening of the teeth.

pyr- or **pyro-** *combining form* fire; heat: a pyro*meter*; pyro*technic*; pyro*mania.* [from Greek **pyr-, pyro-,** from Greek **pŷr, pyrós** meaning "fire."]

pyr·a·mid (pĭr′ ə mĭd′) *n-* 1 a solid with triangular sides meeting at a point, and a flat base. 2 anything of similar shape. 3 **Pyramids** a group of Egyptian monuments having square bases and triangular sides sloping to an apex, built by the early kings to serve as their tombs. *vt-* to build up layer by layer to a peak: *to* pyramid *stock holdings.* *—adj-* **py·ram′ i·dal** (pə răm′ ə dəl): *the* pyramidal *structures of ancient Egypt.*

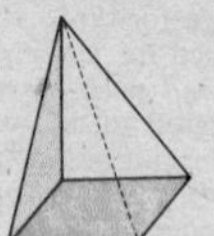
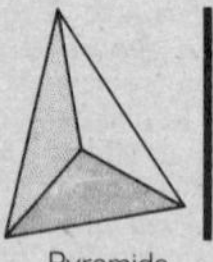

Pyramids

pyre (pīər) *n-* pile of wood for burning a corpse.

py·ret·ic (pī rĕt′ ĭk) *adj-* of, relating to, or affected with fever; feverish; also, causing fever.

py·re·thrum (pī rē′ thrəm, -rĕth′ rəm) *n-* 1 any of various chrysanthemums with long stems and finely cut, often fragrant leaves. Its flowers, when dried and ground into a powder, are used in medicine and as an insecticide. 2 insecticide made of the dried flowers of these plants.

Py·rex (pī′ rĕks′) *n-* trademark name for a heat-resisting glass used in laboratories and for cooking utensils.
pyr·i·dox·ine (pĭr′ ə dŏk′ sēn′) *n-* vitamin B_6.
py·rite (pī′ rīt′) *n-* [*pl.* **py·ri·tes** (pī′ rīts′, pī rī′ tēz′)] **1** native iron disulfide, a common pale-yellow mineral, used as a source of sulfur and in the manufacture of sulfuric acid; fool's gold. **2 pyrites** any of several minerals, chiefly sulfides of iron, copper, or tin.
py·ro·ma·ni·a (pī′ rō mā′ nē ə) *n-* uncontrollable urge to set fire to something. *—n-* **py′ ro·ma′ ni·ac.**
py·rom·e·ter (pī rŏm′ ə tər) *n-* instrument for measuring very high temperatures, such as those of molten metals.
py·ro·tech·nics (pī′ rō tĕk′ nĭks) *n-* **1** (takes singular verb) fireworks or the art of making them. **2** display of fireworks; hence, any brilliant display. *—adj-* **(pyrotechnic):** *a* pyrotechnic *display of oratory.*
py·rox·y·lin (pī rŏk′ sə lĭn) *n-* nitrocellulose.
Pyr·rhic victory (pĭr′ ĭk) *n-* a victory won at a tremendous cost. It was so named after Pyrrhus, whose victory over the Romans in 279 B.C. was ruinous to him.
Py·thag·o·re·an theorem (pə thăg′ ə rē′ ən) *Mathematics n-* theorem stating that in a right triangle, the square of the length of the hypotenuse is equal to the sum of the squares of the lengths of the other two sides.
Pyth·i·as (pĭth′ ē əs) See *Damon and Pythias.*
py·thon (pī′ thŏn′, -thən) *n-* any of a group of non-poisonous snakes related to boas and ranging from 2½ to 33 feet long. Pythons live chiefly in tropical Asia, Africa, and Australia. Like boas, they crush their prey.
pyx (pĭks) *n-* **1** small box or container for carrying the Eucharist to the sick. **2** vessel for the reserved Host in the tabernacle; ciborium.

Q

Q, q (kyo͞o) *n-* [*pl.* **Q's, q's**] the seventeenth letter of the English alphabet.
q. 1 quarter or quarterly. **2** quarto. **3** quetzal. **4** quintal.
Q.E.D. which was to be demonstrated [from Latin **quod erat demonstrandum**].
qt. 1 quantity. **2** [*pl.* **qt.** or **qts.**] quart.
1**quack** (kwăk) *n-* the sound made by a duck. *vi-* to make a sound like a duck. [perhaps from early Dutch **quacken,** probably an imitation of the sound.]
2**quack** (kwăk) *n-* person who dishonestly, or through ignorance, pretends to be skilled in medicine or other science. *as modifier*: *a* quack *doctor; a* quack *medicine.* [shortened from **quacksalver,** from Dutch **kwakzalver,** "one who quacks or boasts of his salves or remedies."]
quack·er·y (kwăk′ ə rē) *n-* [*pl.* **quack·er·ies**] practices, methods, claims, or remedies of a quack.
1**quad** (kwŏd) *Informal n-* quadrangle of a college, prison, or similar group of buildings. [from **quadrangle.**]
2**quad** (kwŏd) *n-* in printing, blank type used for spacing a line. [shortened form of earlier **quadrat** (kwäd′ răt′).]
3**quad** (kwŏd) *n-* fire truck equipped with hoses, pump, ladders, and water tank, and thus able to function both as a pumper and a ladder truck. Also **pumper-ladder.** [from **quadruple.**]
quad·ran·gle (kwŏ′ drăn′ gəl) *n-* **1** in geometry, a plane figure with four angles and four sides. **2** four-sided court or lawn surrounded by buildings, especially on a college campus; also, buildings that surround such a court. *—adj-* **quad·ran′ gu·lar.**
quad·rant (kwŏd′ rənt) *n-* **1** one-fourth of the circumference of a circle; also, the plane area bounded by two perpendicular radii of a circle and the arc subtended by the radii. **2** instrument for measuring the elevation of an object above the horizon. **3** *Mathematics* in a Cartesian coordinate system, any one of the four areas into which a plane is divided by the intersection of the x and y axes. Beginning at the upper right-hand quadrant, the four areas are called, in counterclockwise order, the **first, second, third,** and **fourth quadrants. 4** any object shaped like one quarter of a circular area.
quad·rat·ic (kwə drăt′ ĭk) *adj-* **1** having to do with or resembling a square. **2** having to do with an equation, curve, etc., in which one or more terms is squared. *n-* such an equation.
quad·ren·ni·al (kwə drĕn′ ē əl) *adj-* **1** lasting four years. **2** happening once in four years: *a* quadrennial *election. —adj-* **quad·ren′ ni·al·ly.**
quadri- or **quadru-** *combining form* four: quadri*lateral*; quadru*ped.* Also **quadr-** before vowels: quadr*angular.* [from Latin **quadri-** or **quadru-,** from **quattuor,** "four."]
quad·ri·ceps (kwŏd′ rə sĕps′) *n-* big extensor muscle of the leg that forms the large, fleshy mass covering the front and sides of the thigh bone.
quad·ri·lat·er·al (kwŏd′ rə lăt′ ər əl) *adj-* having four sides. *n-* a four-sided polygon.
qua·drille (kwə drĭl′) *n-* old-fashioned square dance for four couples; also, the music for this dance.
quad·ril·lion (kwə drĭl′ yən) *n-* **1** in the United States, a thousand trillions, or 1×10^{15}. **2** in Great Britain, a million British trillions, or 1×10^{24}.
quad·ri·no·mi·al (kwŏd′ rə nō′ mē əl) *Mathematics n-* algebraic expression with four terms.
quad·ru·ped (kwŏd′ rə pĕd′) *n-* animal with four feet.
quad·ru·ple (kwŏ drŭp′ əl, -dro͞o′ pəl) *adj-* fourfold; multiplied by four; arranged in fours. *vt-* [**quad·ru·pled, quad·ru·pling**] to increase fourfold; to multiply (something) by four: *to* quadruple *one's income. vi-*: *The population* quadrupled *in ten years. n-* number four times as great as another.
quad·ru·plet (kwə drŭp′ lət, -dro͞o′ plət) *n-* **1** any one of four children born at one birth. **2** group or combination of four things.
quaff (kwăf) *vt-* to drink in long, large swallows or gulps: *to* quaff *lemonade. vi-*: *He* quaffed *deeply.*
quag·mire (kwăg′ mīər′, kwŏg′-) *n-* **1** soft, miry ground that yields under the feet; bog. **2** difficult situation.
qua·hog (kō′ hŏg′, kwō′-) *n-* common, almost round clam of the Atlantic coast of North America. [American word from the Algonquian name.]
1**quail** (kwāl) *n-* small, plump game bird. Some kinds are called bobwhite or partridge. [from Old French **quaille,** from Medieval Latin **quaccola,** related to "1quack."]

California quail, 9 1/2—11 in. long

fāte, făt, dâre, bärn; bē, bĕt, mêre; bīte, bĭt; nōte, hŏt, môre, dȯg; fŭn, fûr; to͞o, bo͝ok; oil; out; tar; thin; then; hw for wh as in *wh*at; zh for s as in u*s*ual; ə for a, e, i, o, u, as in *a*go, lin*e*n, per*i*l, at*o*m, min*u*s

²quail (kwāl) ***vi-*** to lose courage; draw back in fear. [from Middle English **quelen,** of uncertain origin.]

quaint (kwānt) ***adj-*** **1** pleasantly old-fashioned: *a* quaint *old hat.* **2** odd but attractive: *a* quaint *old village*; *a* quaint *song.* **—*adv-*** **quaint′ly.** ***n-*** **quaint′ness.**

quake (kwāk) ***vi-*** [**quaked, quak·ing**] **1** to shake from internal shock or convulsion: *the earth* quakes. **2** to tremble or shiver with fear, cold, etc.; quiver: *He* quaked *with cold.* ***n-*** a shaking or trembling; especially, an earthquake.

Quak·er (kwā′kər) ***n-*** member of a religious sect, the Society of Friends (orginally a term of derision). **—*n-*** *fem.* **Quak′er·ess.**

qual·i·fi·ca·tion (kwŏl′ə fə kā′shən) ***n-*** **1** a qualifying or being qualified; also, an instance of this. **2** limitation; modification; reservation: *to praise a performance without any* qualification. **3** (usually **qualifications**) any knowledge, strength, skill, or experience needed for a task or position: *excellent* qualifications *for the job.*

qual·i·fied (kwŏl′ə fīd′) ***adj-*** **1** having done what is required: *a man* qualified *to vote.* **2** having the skills, experience, etc., that are required: *a man* qualified *for a job.* **3** limited; with some reservations: qualified *praise.*

qual·i·fi·er (kwŏl′ə fī′ər) ***n-*** **1** person or thing that qualifies. **2** *Grammar* (1) traditionally, an adjective or adverb. (2) a word such as "very," "quite," or "rather" that comes before and modifies an adjective or adverb, and has no inflected forms. In this dictionary, these words are called adverbs.

qual·i·fy (kwŏl′ə fī′) ***vt-*** [**qual·i·fied, qual·i·fy·ing**] **1** to make fit for any office, occupation, sport, etc.: *Her work* qualifies *her for promotion.* **2** to make less strong or positive; moderate; soften; also, to alter slightly; limit in meaning: *to* qualify *a rebuke*; *to* qualify *a statement.* **3** to give legal authorization to: *The state has* qualified *him to practice medicine.* ***vi-*** to be or become competent or fit for an office, employment, position, etc.: *He* qualified *for the football team.*

qual·i·ta·tive (kwŏl′ə tā′tĭv) ***adj-*** of or relating to quality or kind. **—*adv-*** **qual′i·ta′tive·ly.**

qualitative analysis ***n-*** determination of the chemical components, elements, or radicals of a substance or mixture of substances.

qual·i·ty (kwŏl′ə tē) ***n-*** [*pl.* **qual·i·ties**] **1** that which makes a person or thing different from another; characteristic: *Ability to think is man's outstanding* quality. **2** a certain taste, color, tone, feeling, or other property of anything: *the sad* quality *of a song*; *the acid* quality *of lemons.* **3** degree of excellence; worth; value: *The shop sold goods of both high and low* quality. **4** excellence; high merit: *The restaurant was famous for the* quality *of its food.* **5** *Music* timbre; tone color.

qualm (kwäm, *also* kwälm, kwôm) ***n-*** **1** pang of doubt about one's behavior; twinge of conscience: *I felt* qualms *about neglecting my work.* **2** sudden fear or uneasy feeling; misgiving: *He had* qualms *about climbing the cliff.* **3** sudden feeling of faintness or nausea.

qualm·ish (kwä′mĭsh, *also* kwäl′-) ***adj-*** **1** feeling qualms; nauseated; also, having doubts or misgivings. **2** likely to cause qualms. **—*adv-*** **qualm′ish·ly.** ***n-*** **qualm′ish·ness.**

quan·da·ry (kwŏn′də rē) ***n-*** [*pl.* **quan·da·ries**] condition of hesitation or doubt; dilemma.

quan·ti·ta·tive (kwŏn′tə tā′tĭv) ***adj-*** of or relating to total quantity or value, or to proportionate quantities or values. **—*adv-*** **quan′ti·ta·tive·ly.**

quantitative analysis ***n-*** determination of the amounts or proportions of the chemical components of a substance or mixture of substances.

quan·ti·ty (kwŏn′tə tē) ***n-*** [*pl.* **quan·ti·ties**] **1** amount: *What* quantity *of flour was used in this cake?* **2** any indefinite, usually considerable, amount: *to buy ice in* quantity. **3** the property of things that can be measured with reference to a fixed standard, as of volume, length, weight, etc. **4** in phonetics and prosody, relative time occupied in uttering a sound or syllable. **5** *Music* relative length or duration of a note. **6** *Mathematics* (1) any arithmetic or algebraic expression that has or represents a certain value or magnitude. (2) an amount, value, or number.

quan·tum (kwŏn′təm) ***n-*** [*pl.* **quan·ta** (-tə)] **1** specific amount or quantity. **2** *Physics* according to the quantum theory, the basic or fundamental unit of physical, radiant, or nuclear energy; a fundamental "particle" or "packet" of energy, such as a photon or meson.

quantum theory *Physics* ***n-*** theory proposing that radiant energy is emitted or absorbed only in minute, discrete quanta, each quantum having an energy equal to the product of the frequency of the radiation times a constant.

quar·an·tine (kwŏ′ən tēn′, kwôr′-) ***n-*** **1** legal restrictions on the movement of persons, goods, plants, or animals in or out of a place because of contagious disease. **2** place where such restrictions are enforced. **3** time before a ship docks when passengers are examined for disease. **4** any enforced isolation. ***vt-*** [**quar·an·tined, quar·an·tin·ing**] **1** to keep (a person or thing) away from others. **2** to isolate or cut off from trade, political relations, etc.: *to* quarantine *an unfriendly nation.*

quark (kwôrk) ***n-*** any of the theorized particles believed to be subunits of mesons, protons, and similar heavy subatomic particles.

quar·rel (kwŏr′əl, kwôr′-) ***n-*** **1** an angry dispute, argument, or disagreement. **2** a cause for dispute or disagreement: *He has no* quarrel *with us.* ***vi-*** **1** to have a dispute; fight. **2** to find fault: quarrel *with a proposal.*

quar·rel·some (kwŏr′əl səm, kwôr′-) ***adj-*** inclined to quarrel. **—*adv-*** **quar′rel·some·ly.** ***n-*** **quar′rel·some·ness.**

¹quar·ry (kwŏr′ē, kwôr′-) ***n-*** [*pl.* **quar·ries**] open pit from which marble, slate, or other stone is obtained by cutting or blasting. ***vt-*** [**quar·ried, quar·ry·ing**] to dig or cut from such a pit. [from Old French **quarriere,** from Late Latin **quareria** meaning "place where squared stones are cut."]

²quar·ry (kwŏr′ē, kwôr′-) ***n-*** [*pl.* **quar·ries**] object of pursuit or chase, especially in hunting. [from Old French **cuirée,** from Latin **corium,** "skin." In earlier times a portion of the flesh of a hunted animal was placed on its hide and given to the hounds as a reward.]

quart (kwôrt) ***n-*** **1** a measure, liquid or dry, of two pints or one quarter of a gallon. *as* ***modifier:*** *a* quart *bottle.*

quar·ter (qwôr′tər) ***n-*** **1** one of the four equal parts of a thing; one fourth: *A quart is a* quarter *of a gallon.* **2** the fourth part of a dollar; twenty-five cents; especially, a coin worth this amount. **3** the fourth part of an hour: *The clock just struck the* quarter. **4** fourth part of a year. **5** any one of the four monthly changes of the moon: *The moon was in its last* quarter. **6** part, place, or direction: *to be attacked from all* quarters. **7** district; area: *New Orleans has a quaint French* quarter. **8** any of the four legs of an animal, with the nearby parts: *a* quarter *of beef.* **9** permission to live; mercy: *The enemy showed no* quarter. **12 quarters** place to live; lodging; especially,

Quarters

a military billet. *vt-* **1** to divide into fourths: *Dora* quartered *the apple.* **2** to supply with a place to live: *The colonel* quartered *his men in the town hall.*

at close quarters with nothing in between; very nearby; in actual contact: *to fight* at close quarters.

quar·ter·back (qwȯr′ tər băk′) *n-* in football, member of the backfield who calls the signals and directs the play on the field. His usual position is directly behind the center and near the line of scrimmage.

quar·ter·deck (qwȯr′ tər dĕk′) *n-* the part of a ship's upper deck between the stern and the rearmost mast. In sailing ships the quarterdeck was above the officers' cabins and was reserved for their use.

quar·ter·ly (kwȯr′ tər lē) *adj-* occurring once every three months: *to make* quarterly *payments.* *adv-* every three months: *to publish* quarterly. *n-* [*pl.* **quar·ter·lies**] magazine published every three months.

quar·ter·mas·ter (kwȯr′ tər măs′ tər) *n-* **1** in the Army, officer in charge of stores, equipment, etc. **2** in the Navy, petty officer in charge of steering, signals, etc.

quarter note *n-* note held one fourth as long as a whole note. For picture, see *note.*

quar·ter·saw (qwȯr′ tər sȯ′) *vt-* [**quar·ter·sawed, quar·ter·sawed** or **quar·ter·sawn, quar·ter·saw·ing**] to saw (a log) lengthwise into quarters and then into planks, so as to bring out the long grain on the faces of the planks.

quarter section *n-* 160 acres of land, in the surveying system of the United States and Canada.

quar·ter·staff (kwȯr′ tər stăf′) *n-* sturdy wooden pole from six to eight feet long, formerly used as a weapon.

quar·tet (kwȯr′ tĕt′) *n-* **1** group of four persons or things. **2** musical composition for four singers or instruments. **3** four singers or players who perform together. Also **quar·tette′.**

quar·to (kwȯr′ tō) *n-* [*pl.* **quar·tos**] **1** in printing, a sheet of paper folded into four leaves or eight pages. **2** book made of such sheets. *adj-*: *a* quarto *volume. Abbr.* 4vo.

quartz (kwȯrts) *n-* silicon dioxide, occurring naturally in separate crystals or large masses. Pure quartz is transparent and colorless unless tinted by other minerals. Brightly colored varieties are agates and amethysts. For picture, see *crystal.* *as* ***modifier***: *a* quartz *deposit.*

quartz glass *n-* sheet of glass made from pure quartz. Quartz glass transmits ultraviolet radiation.

quartz·ite (kwȯrt′ sīt′) *n-* metamorphic rock consisting of compressed sandstone.

qua·sar (kwā′ sär′) *Astronomy* *n-* one of a small group of recently discovered, pointlike celestial objects. Quasars emit tremendous quantities of visible light and radio waves, and they are among the most distant objects ever detected. [shortened from *quas*i-stell*ar* radio source.]

[1]**quash** (kwŏsh, kwŏsh) *vt-* to subdue or crush: *The troops* quashed *the rebellion.* [from Old English **cwæscan** meaning "crush out," from Old French **quasser,** from Latin **quassāre** meaning "to shatter; break."]

[2]**quash** (kwŏsh, kwŏsh) *vt-* in law, to cancel or annul (an indictment, lawsuit, etc.). [from Old French **quasser,** from Latin **cassāre,** "to destroy."]

qua·si (kwä′ zē, kwā′ sī′, -zī′) *adj-* similar to but not the same as in every respect: *a* quasi *corporation.* *adv-* (used only with adjectives and adverbs to form hyphenated compounds, and sometimes called a prefix) nearly but not quite; almost: *a* quasi-*historical tale.*

Qua·ter·nar·y (kwŏt′ ər nĕr′ ē) *n-* the last of the two periods of the Cenozoic era. *adj-*: *the* Quaternary *period.*

quat·rain (kwŏ′ trān′) *n-* four-line stanza or poem, in which at least two lines rhyme.

qua·ver (kwā′ vər) *n-* **1** a shaking or trembling. **2** trembling or quivering sound. *vi-* to quiver; tremble; shake. *—adv-* **qua′ ver·ing·ly:** *He spoke* quaveringly *to his captors.* *adj-* **qua′ ver·y.**

quay (kē) *n-* solid, masonry dock or landing for boats and ships. *Hom-* key.

Quay

Que. Quebec.

quea·sy (kwē′ zē) *adj-* [**quea·si·er, quea·si·est**] **1** nauseated; sick at one's stomach; easily upset: *a* queasy *stomach.* **2** squeamish; overly scrupulous: *a* queasy *conscience.* *—adv-* **queas′ i·ly.** *n-* **queas′ i·ness.**

que·bra·cho (kā′ brä′ chō) *n-* any of several South American hardwood trees having a wood rich in tannin. One species produces a red coloring matter used as a dye, and the bark of another is used in medicine.

Quech·u·a (kĕch′ ə wə) *n-* [*pl.* **Quech·u·as,** also **Quech·u·a**] **1** member of a tribe of South American Indians who at one time dominated the Inca Empire. **2** the language of these Indians, still spoken in Peru and Ecuador. *—adj-* **Quech′ u·an:** *a* Quechuan *word.*

queen (kwēn) *n-* **1** wife of a king. **2** female monarch. **3** woman who is a real or honorary ruler in a certain field or activity: *the* queen *of the cherry blossom festival.* **4** town, ship, place, or thing spoken of as first in honor, respect, or value: *the* queen *of a fleet.* **5** ant or bee that lays eggs and is the center of a colony. There is usually only one queen ant or bee in a colony. **6** playing card with the picture of a female monarch on it. **7** in chess, the one piece that can move more than one square in any of the eight directions on the board. *—adj-* **queen′ like′.**

Queen Anne's lace *n-* weed having lacy, flat, whitish flower clusters. It is related to the carrot.

queen consort *n-* wife of a reigning king, as distinguished from a queen who is herself the sovereign.

queen dowager *n-* widow of a king.

queen·ly (kwēn′ lē) *adj-* [**queen·li·er, queen·li·est**] like a queen or fit for a queen. *—n-* **queen′ li·ness.**

queen mother *n-* king's widow who is also mother of a reigning sovereign.

queen post *n-* one of two upright posts placed at equal distances on either side of the center of a roof truss or other truss to tie and support the framework.

queen regent *n-* queen reigning during the childhood, absence, or incapacity of the actual sovereign.

queer (kwêr) *adj-* **1** different from what is normal; odd; peculiar: *He has a* queer *sense of humor.* **2** giddy; dizzy: *I sat down for a moment because I felt* queer. **3** suggestive of deceit and wrongdoing; irregular; dubious: *a* queer *transaction.* *—adv-* **queer′ ly.** *n-* **queer′ ness.**

quell (kwĕl) *vt-* to subdue; put down: *to* quell *a riot.*

quench (kwĕnch) *vt-* **1** to put an end to; slake: *He* quenched *his thirst at the fountain.* **2** to put out: *to* quench *a fire with a bucket of water.* *—adj-* **quench′ a·ble:** *a* quenchable *flame.* *n-* **quench′ er.** *adj-* **quench′less.**

quern (kwûrn) *n-* **1** hand mill used for grinding grain, usually made of two discs of stone. **2** small hand mill for grinding spices.

quer·u·lous (kwĕr′ ə ləs) *adj-* faultfinding; complaining; peevish: *a* querulous *answer.* *—adv-* **quer′ u·lous·ly.** *n-* **quer′ u·lous·ness.**

---

que·ry (kwêr′ē) ***n-*** [*pl.* **que·ries**] a question: *Does anyone have a* query? ***vt-*** [**que·ried, que·ry·ing**] **1** to ask or question: *The reporters* queried *the mayor about his decision.* **2** to question the truth of; feel doubt about.

quest (kwĕst) ***n-*** **1** a search: *a prospector's* quest *for valuable minerals.* **2** in stories of the Middle Ages, a mission; a dedicated search: *Sir Lancelot's* quest *for the Holy Grail.* ***vi-*** to search for; seek: *to* quest *for treasure.*

ques·tion (kwĕs′chən) ***n-*** **1** something asked; a request for information: *Please repeat your* question. **2** objection; doubt: *The new facts raise several* questions. **3** matter to be considered or discussed: *The city council took up the* question *of repairing the streets.* ***vt-*** **1** to inquire of: *The students* questioned *the teacher.* **2** to doubt: *Some* questioned *the truth of the advertisement.* **—*n-* ques′tion·er.** ***adv-*** **ques′tion·ing·ly.**

beyond question absolutely certain: *The general's patriotism is* beyond question. **call in question** to raise doubts about: *This* calls *your honesty* in question. **in question** under consideration: *the matter* in question. **out of the question** not to be considered; impossible: *A trip to Europe is* out of the question *this year.* **without question** certainly: *This is true* without question.

ques·tion·a·ble (kwĕs′chən ə bəl) ***adj-*** **1** open to doubt; not certain: *a* questionable *conclusion.* **2** of a kind to be questioned on moral or practical grounds; dubious: *His actions are highly* questionable. **—*n-* ques′tion·a·ble·ness.** ***adv-*** **ques′tion·a·bly.**

question mark ***n-*** punctuation mark [?] placed at the end of a question; interrogation mark; interrogation point.

ques·tion·naire (kwĕs′chə nâr′) ***n-*** written or printed set of questions to be filled out with answers in order to record opinions, facts, etc.

question signaller *Grammar* ***n-*** word such as "who," "what," or "how," that introduces a question.

Quetzal

quet·zal (kĕt säl′) ***n-*** **1** brilliantly colored bird of Central America, the male of which has a tail of long plumes. It was sacred to the Mayas, whose chiefs alone wore the plumes, and is now the national symbol of Guatemala. **2** the basic unit of money in Guatemala.

Que·tzal·co·a·tl (kĕt säl′kwät′əl) ***n-*** the god of the Aztecs, represented as a plumed serpent.

queue (kyōō) ***n-*** **1** a braid of hair hanging down the back. **2** waiting line of people: *A long* queue *stretched from the ticket-office window.* ***vi-*** [**queued, queu·ing**] *chiefly Brit.* to form a waiting line; also, to stand in such a line (usually followed by "up"). ***Hom-*** cue.

Queue

quib·ble (kwĭb′əl) ***vi-*** [**quib·bled, quib·bling**] to raise trivial objections and questions; cavil, usually in order to prevent defeat in an argument. ***n-*** skillful evasion of the point by advancing a trifling argument or by using words with a double meaning. **—*n-* quib′bler.**

quick (kwĭk) ***adj-*** [**quick·er, quick·est**] **1** done or moving with speed; fast; rapid: *a* quick *decision*; quick *hands.* **2** fast to notice or understand; alert; lively: *a* quick *mind.* **3** easily excited or aroused: *her* quick *temper.* ***adv-*** *Informal* quickly. ***n-*** sensitive flesh, especially under the fingernail. **—*adv-* quick′ly.** ***n-*** **quick′ness.**

to the quick very deeply. **the quick and the dead** the living and the dead.

quick·en (kwĭk′ən) ***vt-*** **1** to cause to move more rapidly; hasten; hurry: *to* quicken *one's steps.* **2** to make keen; give new life to; refresh: *That* quickened *my interest.* **3** to bring to life: *The April rains* quicken *the soil.* ***vi-*** **1** to move more rapidly: *His pace* quickened. **2** to become more lively or eager: *My interest* quickened. **3** to become keener: *My senses* quickened. **4** to begin to show life: *In spring the earth* quickened. **—*n-* quick′en·er.**

quick-freeze (kwĭk′ frēz′) ***vt-*** [**quick-froze, quick-froz·en, quick-freez·ing**] to preserve (food) by very rapid freezing, so that the ice crystals are too small to burst open the cells.

quick·ie (kwĭk′ē) *Informal* ***n-*** something done or made in less than usual time.

quick·lime (kwĭk′ līm′) ***n-*** [1]lime.

quick·sand (kwĭk′sănd′) ***n-*** very fine, wet sand which will not hold up a heavy weight and can engulf a person or animal stepping into it.

quick·sil·ver (kwĭk′ sĭl′ vər) ***n-*** mercury.

quick·step (kwĭk′ stĕp′) ***n-*** rapid marching step; also, a marching tune with a rapid tempo.

quick-tem·pered (kwĭk′ tĕm′ pərd) ***adj-*** easily aroused to anger: *a* quick-tempered *disposition.*

quick time ***n-*** marching pace of 120 thirty-inch steps per minute, the normal pace for military drill.

quick-wit·ted (kwĭk′ wĭt′ əd) ***adj-*** keen; alert; clever: *a* quick-witted *debater.* **—*adv-* quick′wit′ted·ly.**

[1]**quid** (kwĭd) ***n-*** piece of chewing tobacco being chewed or taken for chewing. [a variant of **cud.**]

[2]**quid** (kwĭd) *Brit. Slang* ***n-*** [*pl.* **quid**] a pound sterling or a sovereign. [origin uncertain.]

quid pro quo (kwĭd′prō kwō′) ***n-*** something given or received in return; compensation.

quién sa·be? (kē ĕn′ sä′ bā′) *Spanish* Who knows?

qui·es·cent (kwī ĕs′ ənt, kwē-) ***adj-*** **1** calm; still; tranquil: *a* quiescent *mood.* **2** inactive; not dangerous: *a* quiescent *volcano.* **—*n-* qui·es′cence.** ***adv-*** **qui·es′cent·ly.**

qui·et (kwī′ ət) ***adj-*** [**qui·et·er, qui·et·est**] **1** making little or no sound or disturbance; noiseless; silent: *The baby was* quiet *all night.* **2** motionless; still; calm: *The sea was* quiet, *with hardly any waves.* **3** without activity or excitement; peaceful: *a* quiet *evening.* **4** mild; gentle: *a* quiet *disposition.* **5** not loud or bright; not showy: *Pale blue is a* quiet *color. Mr. Temple favors* quiet *neckties.* ***n-*** **1** stillness; silence: *a sudden* quiet *between claps of thunder.* **2** calmness; peacefulness: *in the* quiet *of the evening.* ***vt-*** to make calm, peaceful, still, or silent: *His calm voice* quieted *the mob.* ***vi-***: *The mob* quieted *when the police arrived.* **—*adv-* qui′et·ly.** ***n-*** **qui′et·ness.**

quiet sun ***n-*** the sun during a period of time when the number of sunspots, solar flares, etc., is observed to be at a minimum. See also *active sun.*

qui·e·tude (kwī′ ə tōōd′, -tyōōd′) ***n-*** tranquillity.

qui·e·tus (kwī ē′ təs) *Archaic* ***n-*** anything which puts an end to action; especially, death.

quill (kwĭl) ***n-*** **1** long, stiff feather. **2** stiff, hollow shaft of a feather. **3** pen made of a feather. **4** a spinelike hair of a porcupine or hedgehog.

Quill

quilt (kwĭlt) ***n-*** bed cover made of two layers of cloth with a layer of wool, down, etc., between them. The layers are held together and the filling kept in place by stitching or by tufting. ***vi-*** to sew or otherwise work on such a bed cover: *The ladies* quilted *as they chatted.* ***vt-*** to sew (a vest, jacket, etc.) with padding between layers of cloth.

quilt·ing (kwĭl′ tĭng) ***n-*** **1** the making of a quilt or of quilted work. **2** the material for such work. **3** the finished work.

quilting bee ***n-*** a gathering at which women make quilts.

quince (kwĭns) ***n-*** **1** hard yellow fruit shaped like a pear, with an acid taste. Quinces are used chiefly in making jellies and preserves. **2** the tree bearing this fruit. ***adj-***: *a* quince *jelly.*

qui·nine (kwī′ nīn′) ***n-*** bitter, white alkaloid extracted from the bark of the cinchona tree. It is used in the treatment of malaria.

quin·quen·ni·al (kwĭn kwĕn′ ē əl) ***adj-*** **1** happening every five years or once in five years. **2** lasting five years. ***n-*** fifth anniversary.

quin·sy (kwĭn′ zē) ***n-*** severe inflammation of the tonsils and throat, accompanied by swelling.

quint (kwĭnt) *Informal* ***n-*** quintuplet.

quin·tal (kwĭn′ təl) ***n-*** **1** hundredweight. **2** in the metric system, 100 kilograms.

quin·tes·sence (kwĭn tĕs′ əns) ***n-*** **1** perfect example of some quality: *He is the* quintessence *of good manners.* **2** pure essence or most refined extract of a substance.

quin·tet (kwĭn tĕt′) ***n-*** **1** any group of five; especially, a group of five musicians. **2** music written for five musical instruments. Also **quin·tette′.**

quin·til·lion (kwĭn tĭl′ yən) ***n-*** **1** in the United States, a thousand quadrillions, or 1×10^{18}. **2** in Great Britain, a million British quadrillions, or 1×10^{30}.

quin·tu·ple (kwĭn tŭp′əl, -tōō′pəl) ***adj-*** fivefold; multiplied by five; arranged in fives. ***vt-*** **[quin·tu·pled, quin·tu·pling]** to multiply (something) by five; increase fivefold: *He* quintupled *his money in ten years.* ***vi-***: *The investment* quintupled *in a short time.* ***n-*** a sum or number five times as great as another.

quin·tup·let (kwĭn tŭp′ lət, -tōō′ plət) ***n-*** **1** any one of five children born at one birth. **2** group or combination of five things; quintet.

quip (kwĭp) ***n-*** **1** sharp or sarcastic remark, joke, or gibe. **2** witty retort. ***vi-*** **[quip·ped, quip·ping]** to make such remarks or retorts.

qui·pu (kē′ pōō) ***n-*** device made of a main cord and smaller cords, knotted and colored, used by the ancient Peruvians for recording and calculating.

quire (kwī′ ər, kwīər) ***n-*** one twentieth of a ream of paper; 24 or 25 sheets of uniform size and quality. ***Hom-*** choir.

quirk (kwûrk) ***n-*** **1** eccentric personal trait, usually a strange or unpleasant one; idiosyncrasy. **2** vagary; twist; turn: *by a strange* quirk *of fate.*

quirt (kwûrt) ***n-*** short-handled riding whip with a lash of braided rawhide.

quis·ling (kwĭz′ lĭng) ***n-*** citizen of a conquered nation who collaborates with the enemy, especially by taking part in a puppet government; traitor.

quit (kwĭt) ***vt-*** **[quit, quit·ting]** **1** to stop; discontinue; cease: *The child* quit *crying.* **2** to leave; depart from: *He* quit *the army.* **3** to give up; relinquish; renounce: *He* quit *his old beliefs.* ***vi-*** **1** to come to a stop: *Let's* quit *and go home.* **2** to depart. **3** *Informal* to resign from a position. ***adj-*** finally free: *I'm* quit *of that debt.*

quit·claim (kwĭt′ klām′) ***n-*** in law, legal paper by which a person gives up claim to, or right in, something. ***vt-*** to give up claim to.

quite (kwīt) ***adv-*** **1** completely; entirely; wholly: *You are* quite *right.* **2** *Informal* to a considerable degree; rather: *It is* quite *cold today.*

quite a (or **an**) *Informal* a remarkable; an outstanding: *He's* quite a *soldier. She's doing* quite a *job.* **quite a few** a large number; many: *to have* quite a few *children.*

quit·rent (kwĭt′ rĕnt′) ***n-*** in law, in feudal times, a rent paid by a freeholder or tenant as a substitute for certain feudal services.

quits (kwĭts) ***adj-*** equal or even with someone, especially after returning or repaying something: *We each did the other a favor, and we're* quits.

be quits with to be even with; neither owing nor being owed by. **call it quits** to give up; have enough of something. **cry quits** to admit that one is ready to cease competing.

quit·tance (kwĭt′ əns) ***n-*** **1** release from a debt or obligation. **2** repayment of a favor or wrong; recompense.

quit·ter (kwĭt′ ər) ***n-*** person who gives up too easily, especially from laziness or cowardice.

[1]**quiv·er** (kwĭv′ ər) ***vi-*** to shake or tremble rapidly: *He* quivered *in the cold. Her voice* quivers *when she sings.* ***n-*** a trembling motion or sound: *I see a* quiver *in the leaves.* [from Old English **cwifer** meaning "moving rapidly or briskly," and probably related to **quaver.**]

[2]**quiv·er** (kwĭv′ ər) ***n-*** case for holding and carrying arrows. [from Old French **cuivre,** perhaps from Old High German **kochar** or Old English **cocer.**]

Quiver

qui vive (kē vēv′) ***n-*** **1** call of a French sentry, corresponding to "Who goes there?" **2** challenge. **3** lookout; alert.

on the qui vive on the alert.

Qui·xo·te (kē hō′ tē, kwĭk′ sət) See *Don Quixote.*

quix·ot·ic (kwĭk sŏt′ ĭk) ***adj-*** rashly and foolishly romantic, idealistic, or chivalrous. ***adv-*** **quix·ot′ i·cal·ly.**

quiz (kwĭz) ***n-*** [*pl.* **quiz·zes**] informal and usually brief examination: *She did very well on the history* quiz. ***vt-*** **[quizzed, quiz·zing]** to question or examine informally: *I* quizzed *him on his studies.* **—*n-* quiz′ zer.**

quiz show or **quiz program** ***n-*** television show or program in which the participants or contestants answer questions, often for a prize in cash or merchandise.

quiz·zi·cal (kwĭz′ ĭ kəl) ***adj-*** **1** puzzled or questioning: *a* quizzical *expression.* **2** likely to banter, chaff, or joke. **3** slightly and humorously odd. **—*adv-* quiz′ zi·cal·ly.**

quoin (koin, *also* kwoin) ***n-*** **1** an outside corner of a building. **2** stone forming such a corner. **3** a wedge-shaped stone in an arch. **4** in printing, a wedge used for locking type into a galley or other frame or holder. ***vt-*** to supply with such wedges. ***Hom-*** coin.

Printer's quoins

quoit (kwoit) ***n-*** iron or rope ring that is tossed over an upright peg in playing the game called **quoits.**

quon·dam (kwŏn′ dăm′, -dəm) ***adj-*** erstwhile; former.

Quon·set hut (kwŏn′ sət) ***n-*** trademark name for a prefabricated metal shelter resembling a half cylinder cut lengthwise.

quo·rum (kwôr′ əm) ***n-*** the number of members of any body, especially legislative, that must be present at its meeting if business is to be transacted legally or officially.

quo·ta (kwō′ tə) ***n-*** portion of something that is due from or allotted to a person, group, or district; share; proportion: *He met the daily* quota *of work.*

quot·a·ble (kwō′ tə bəl) ***adj-*** **1** such as may be repeated: *These remarks are not* quotable. **2** suitable for, or worthy of, quoting: *Mark Twain's very* quotable *remarks.*

quo·ta·tion (kwō tā′ shən) ***n-*** **1** a quoting of someone else's words. **2** the words thus quoted; especially, a passage quoted from a book, poem, etc. **3** statement of a market price: *stock* quotations *in the newspaper*.

quotation marks ***n-*** pair of punctuation marks ("...") placed at the beginning and end of a word or passage to show that it is quoted. Example: "I can't find my hat," he said. A quotation within a quotation is usually enclosed in **single quotation marks** ('...'). Example: He asked, "Did Mary say 'Don't go'?"

quote (kwōt) ***vt-*** **[quot·ed, quot·ing] 1** to repeat the words of another person or a passage from a book, poem, etc. **2** to enclose in quotation marks: *You should* quote *this passage in your composition.* **3** to state (a market price). **4** to refer to as evidence or illustration: *to* quote *a theory*; *to* quote *an incident.* ***n- Informal*** **1** the words or passage repeated. **2** quotation mark. ***interj-*** the quotation begins here: *In Churchill's words,* quote, *It was their finest hour,* unquote. **—*n-* quot′ er.**

quoth (kwōth) *Archaic* ***vt-*** said; spoke.

quo·tient (kwō′ shənt) ***n-*** an answer to a problem in division; result obtained when one number is divided by another: *If* 12 *is divided by 2, the* quotient *is 6.*

q.v. see this; look this up [from Latin **quod vide**].

R

R, r (är) ***n-*** [*pl.* **R's, r's**] the eighteenth letter of the English alphabet.

the three R's reading, writing, and arithmetic as though written "reading, 'riting, and 'rithmetic"; hence, the first essentials of education.

r 1 radius. **2** roentgen.

r. 1 ruble. **2** rupee.

R 1 ratio. **2** in chess, rook.

R. 1 rabbi. **2** Republican. **3** river. **4** road.

[1]**Ra** (rä) ***n-*** in Egyptian mythology, the god of the sun; the supreme deity. Also **Re.**

[2]**Ra** symbol for radium.

rab·bet (răb′ ĭt) ***n-*** **1** groove or slot made in the edge or face of one piece of wood to receive the edge of another piece. **2** joint made this way. ***vt-*** **1** to cut such a groove in. **2** to join this way. ***vi-*** to be joined this way. ***Hom-*** rabbit.

Rabbet joints

rab·bi (răb′ ī′) ***n-*** [*pl.* **rab·bis** or **rab·bies**] **1** in the Jewish religion, a man authorized to teach and interpret law and ritual. **2** minister of a Jewish congregation.

rab·bin·i·cal (rə bĭn′ ĭk əl) ***adj-*** **1** of or relating to rabbis: *a* rabbinical *association*; rabbinical *duties.* **2** of or relating to the traditions, writings, theology, etc., of the rabbis in Judaism.

rab·bit (răb′ ĭt) ***n-*** **1** small burrowing animal related to the hare but having shorter ears and less powerful hind legs. Some hares, such as the jackrabbit, are called rabbits. **2** the fur of this animal. *as **modifier**:* rabbit *earmuffs.* ***Hom-*** rabbet. **—*adj-* rab′ bit·like′.**

Rabbit (eastern cottontail) 11—17 in. long

rabbit fever ***n-*** tularemia.

rab·ble (răb′ əl) ***n-*** **1** an unruly crowd; mob. **2 the rabble** the common people (a term of contempt).

rab·id (răb′ ĭd) ***adj-*** **1** of, related to, or infected with, rabies. **2** fanatical; excessively zealous; extremely unreasonable: *a* rabid *reformer.* **3** furious; raging. **—*adv-* rab′ id·ly. *n-* rab′ id·ness.**

ra·bies (rā′ bēz) ***n-*** virus disease, especially of dogs, foxes, etc., marked by fear of water, inability to swallow, frenzy, and convulsions; hydrophobia. It may be transmitted to man or other animals by a bite.

Raccoon, about 2 ft. long

rac·coon (ră kōōn′) ***n-*** **1** grayish-brown, flesh-eating animal with a bushy, ringed tail and face markings like a black mask. **2** fur of this animal. *as **modifier**: a* raccoon *coat.* Also **racoon.** [American word from the Algonquian **ārāhkunem,** "he scratches with the hands."]

[1]**race** (rās) ***n-*** **1** contest of speed: *a boat* race. **2** contest for a prize, office, etc.: *a* race *for the governorship.* **3** a swift, rushing current: *a* race *of water in a stream.* ***vi-*** **[raced, rac·ing] 1** to participate in a contest of speed. **2** to move with speed; hurry; dash: *to* race *for a bus*; *to* race *after a ball.* **3** of machinery, to turn or run faster than normal or too fast. ***vt-*** **1** to try to outdo in speed: *I'll* race *you to the corner.* **2** to enter or use in a contest of speed: *Will he* race *all three of his cars tomorrow*? **3** to cause (a motor, machinery, etc.) to run or spin faster than usual. [from Old Norse **rās** meaning "a course that is run; a rush."]

[2]**race** (rās) ***n-*** **1** in anthropology, any of several large divisions of the human species having similar physical characteristics and a common ancestry. **2** group of people with similar ancestry or geographical and cultural backgrounds: *the English* race. **3** large division of living creatures: *the cat* race. [from French, from Italian **razza** of the same meaning.]

race course ***n-*** area marked out for contests of speed.

race·horse (rās′ hȯrs′, -hôrs′) ***n-*** horse bred and trained for competing in races, especially those in which a jockey rides the horse.

ra·ceme (rā sēm′, rə-) ***n-*** flower cluster in which the flowers are borne on slender stems at intervals on a flower stalk, as in the lily of the valley.

rac·er (rā′ sər) ***n-*** **1** person or animal trained for or competing in a contest of speed: *That horse is a great* racer. **2** vehicle or boat used or suitable for use in a contest of speed: *His new car is a* racer. **3** any of several swift snakes, especially the American black snake.

race runner ***n-*** swift-moving lizard of North America.

race track ***n-*** a field or course laid out for races.

Ra·chel (rā′ chəl) ***n-*** in the Old Testament, the wife of Jacob and mother of Joseph and Benjamin.

ra·chit·ic (rə kĭt′ ĭk) ***adj-*** of, related to, or afflicted with rickets. ***n-*** person afflicted with rickets.

ra·cial (rā′ shəl) ***adj-*** of or related to race in the human species. **—*adv-* ra′ cial·ly.**

racing form ***n-*** publication giving information about particular racehorses and horse races.

rac·ism (rā′ sĭz′ əm) ***n-*** **1** belief in the inborn superiority of one race, especially a person's own race, over another race of humanity. **2** behavior, politics, etc., based on such a belief. Also **ra′ cial·ism** (rā′ shə lĭz′ əm). **—*n-* ra′ cist** or **ra′ cial·ist.**

[1]**rack** (răk) ***n-*** **1** framework of shelves, bars, or hooks on or in which articles may be hung, stored, or displayed. **2** an old instrument of torture, which stretched and dislocated a victim's joints. **3** in mechanics, a bar

having teeth on one side that engage the teeth of a gear, pinion, etc. ***vt-*** **1** to place in or on a rack: *to* rack *billiard balls.* **2** to torment severely, as if on an instrument of torture: *The disease* racked *the man with pain.*

Towel rack Hay rack Storage rack

[probably from early German or early Dutch **rek,** "a bar; grating of bars."] ***Hom-*** wrack.
on the rack under severe stress.
rack (one's) brains to search intensively in one's mind for a solution.

[2]**rack** (răk) **rack and ruin** widespread and complete destruction. [variant of **wrack,** from Old English **wræc,** "a wreck; that which is driven (ashore)."] ***Hom-*** wrack.

[3]**rack** (răk) ***n-*** rapid gait of a horse in which each foot strikes the ground separately; single-foot. ***vi-*** to move in this gait. [origin uncertain, perhaps a variant of [2]**rock.**"] ***Hom-*** wrack.

[1]**rack·et** (răk′ət) ***n-*** **1** disturbing noise; din; uproar: *The children were causing a* racket. **2** *Informal* dishonest or irregular way of earning a living or making money, often involving extortion, intimidation, or the sale of something forbidden by law. [probably an imitation of a sound.]

[2]**rack·et** (răk′ət) ***n-*** net-covered oval frame ending in a straight handle, used to bat a light ball in certain games. Also **rac′ quet.** [from Old French **raquette,** from an Arabic word **rāhāt** meaning "the palms of the hands; a game, like tennis, in which the ball was hit with the palm."]

Tennis racket

rack·et·eer (răk′ə têr′) ***n-*** person engaged in a criminal racket; gangster.

rack·et·y (răk′ə tē) ***adj-*** causing or making a racket.

rac·on·teur (răk′ ŏn tûr′) ***n-*** teller of stories.

ra·coon (ră ko͞on′) raccoon.

rac·quets (răk′əts) ***n-*** game resembling squash racquets, but played in a larger court. Also **rack′ets.**

rac·y (rā′ sē) ***adj-*** [**rac·i·er, rac·i·est**] **1** rapid and colorful; vivid: *a* racy *manner of talking.* **2** slightly improper; spicy: *a* racy *story.* **—*adv-* rac′ i·ly.** ***n-*** **rac′ i·ness.**

ra·dar (rā′ där′) ***n-*** device that sends out radio waves in a beam that, when reflected back from a distant object, indicates the position, distance, and direction of movement of the object. ***as modifier:*** *a* radar *signal.* [shortened from *ra*dio *d*etecting *a*nd *r*anging.]

ra·di·al (rā′ dē əl) ***adj-*** **1** branching out from a central point; radiating like the spokes of a wheel. **2** of or having to do with a radius. **—*adv-* ra′ di·al·ly.**

radial symmetry ***n-*** symmetry of a body that has its parts equally distributed around a center point or axis. A starfish has radial symmetry.

ra·di·ance (rā′ dē əns) ***n-*** **1** great brightness; luster: *the* radiance *of the sunny sea.* **2** sparkling appearance of well-being, loveliness, or joy. Also **ra′ di·an·cy.**

ra·di·ant (rā′ dē ənt) ***adj-*** **1** giving out rays of heat or light. **2** glowing with brightness, kindness, love, etc.: *a* radiant *expression.* **3** made up of or sent out by radiation: *the sun's* radiant *heat.* **—*adj-* ra′ di·ant·ly.**

radiant energy ***n-*** energy that is transmitted from a source in electromagnetic waves. Various forms are X rays, light, and radio waves.

ra·di·ate (rā′ dē āt′) ***vi-*** [**ra·di·at·ed, ra·di·at·ing**] **1** to give out radiant energy. **2** to reach outward from a center: *Spokes* radiate *from the center of a wheel.* ***vt-*** **1** to emit energy in waves: *The walls* radiated *heat.* **2** to have or show (some feeling) so strongly as to affect others; communicate: *He* radiates *confidence.*

ra·di·a·tion (rā′ dē ā′ shən) ***n-*** **1** the giving off of radiant energy, such as light and radiant heat. **2** radiant energy emitted by a radioactive substance, which is harmful to living tissues; also, X rays.

radiation pressure ***n-*** force exerted on a surface by radiant energy. The radiation pressure of the sun makes a comet's tail point away from the sun.

radiation shield ***n-*** any device used to protect living tissues or instruments from radiation.

radiation sickness ***n-*** disease caused by overexposure to nuclear radiation and marked by nausea, dizziness, the breakdown of tissues, and often death.

ra·di·a·tor (rā′ dē ā′ tər) ***n-*** **1** system of pipes through which hot water or steam is forced to heat a room or building. **2** a honeycomb tank in an automobile where water from the cooling system is cooled by the air. **3** *Physics* any source of radiant energy.

AUTOMOBILE HOUSE
Radiators

rad·i·cal (răd′ĭ kəl) ***adj-*** **1** basic or fundamental; going to the roots: *a* radical *change of policy.* **2** extreme, especially in the support of political positions: *the* radical *wing of a political party.* ***n-*** **1** person holding such extreme opinions. **2** *Chemistry* group of atoms that acts as a unit in chemical reactions. **3** *Mathematics* (1) the indicated root of a number. Example: $\sqrt{9}$. (2) radical sign. ***Hom-*** radicle. **—*adv-* rad′ i·cal·ly.** ***n-*** **rad′ i·cal·ness.**

rad·i·cal·ism (răd′ĭ kə lĭz′ əm) ***n-*** the suggesting and supporting of radical ideas; also, one or more of these ideas.

radical sign *Mathematics* ***n-*** symbol ($\sqrt{\quad}$) that indicates which root of a radicand is to be taken. The index specifies the root, although it is usually omitted for the square root. Example: $\sqrt[3]{\quad}$.

rad·i·cand (răd′ə kănd′) *Mathematics* ***n-*** expression written under the radical sign. In $\sqrt{9}$, 9 is the radicand.

rad·i·cle (răd′ĭ kəl) ***n-*** part of the embryo of a seed plant that becomes the main root of the mature plant. ***Hom-*** radical.

ra·di·i (rā′ dē ī′) *pl.* of **radius.**

ra·di·o (rā′ dē ō′) ***n-*** [*pl.* **ra·di·os**] **1** the sending and receiving of communication signals, especially sound but also television, by means of electromagnetic waves without the use of wires between sender and receiver. **2** instrument for receiving such signals; also, an instrument for sending such signals. **3** system of wireless communication; also, the business of operating it. ***as modifier:*** *a* radio *program.* ***vt-*** [**ra·di·oed, ra·di·o·ing**] to send messages to by means of electromagnetic waves: *We must* radio *the ship that help is coming.* ***vi-*** *The ship* radioed *for help.*

radio- *combining form* **1** radial; radially: *a* radio*larian* (minute sea animal with radial extensions). **2** radio: *a* radio*gram*; radio*telephone.* **3** radioactive: radio*carbon*;

fāte, făt, dâre, bärn; bē, bĕt, mêre; bīte, bĭt; nōte, hŏt, môre, dòg; fŭn, fûr; to͞o, bo͝ok; oil; out; tar; thin; then; hw for wh as in *wh*at; zh for s as in u*s*ual; ə for a, e, i, o, u, as in *a*go, lin*e*n, per*i*l, at*o*m, min*u*s

radio*isotope*. 4 radiation: radio*therapy*; radio*logist*. [from Latin **radius** meaning "ray."]

ra·di·o·ac·tive (rā′ dē ō ăk′ tĭv) ***adj***- having to do with, caused by, or showing radioactivity.

ra·di·o·ac·tiv·i·ty (rā′ dē ō ăk tĭv′ ə tē) ***n***- spontaneous disintegration of an atomic nucleus, accompanied by the emission of a nuclear particle, or of alpha, beta, or gamma rays; also, the radiation so emitted.

radio astronomy ***n***- branch of science that deals with the detection and study of radio waves given off by stars and other celestial objects.

radio beacon ***n***- a stationary radio transmitting station continually sending radio signals that help ships and airplanes to determine their location.

ra·di·o·car·bon (rā′ dē ō kär′ bən) ***n***- carbon 14.

radio frequency ***n***- any electromagnetic wave frequency in the range from 10 kilocycles to 30,000 megacycles, used in the transmission of radio signals.

ra·di·o·gram (rā′ dē ō grăm′) ***n***- message sent by radiotelegraph.

ra·di·o·graph (rā′ dē ō grăf′) ***n***- photograph made by radiation other than light, especially one made by X rays. ***vt***- to produce such a photograph of.

ra·di·o·i·so·tope (rā′ dē ō ī′ sə tōp′) ***n***- isotope of an element that has been made radioactive, usually by artificial means.

ra·di·o·lar·i·an (rā′ dē ō lĕr′ ē ən, -lăr′ ē ən) ***n***- any of an order **(Radiolaria)** of spherical, marine protozoans that resemble the ameba but have a hard, mineral skeleton with projecting, radiating spines.

ra·di·ol·o·gist (rā′ dē ŏl′ ə jĭst) ***n***- doctor specializing in radiology.

ra·di·ol·o·gy (rā′ dē ŏl′ ə jē) ***n***- branch of science dealing with radiant energy, especially its medical applications, such as the use of X rays to diagnose or treat disease.

ra·di·om·e·ter (rā′ dē ŏm′ ə tər) ***n***- instrument that measures intensity of radiant energy.

Radiometer

ra·di·o·phone (rā′ dē ō fōn′) ***n***- **1** any device for producing or transmitting sound by radiant energy. **2** radiotelephone.

ra·di·o·sonde (rā′ dē ō sŏnd′) ***n***- instrument that is carried by a balloon and collects and transmits weather data.

ra·di·o·tel·e·graph (rā′ dē ō tĕl′ ə grăf′) ***n***- telegraph using radio waves rather than cables to transmit and receive impulses.

ra·di·o·tel·e·phone (rā′ dē ō tĕl′ ə fōn′) ***n***- transmitter used for radio communication by voice rather than by Morse code; radiophone.

radio telescope *Astronomy* ***n***- a radio receiver and antenna system that detects and collects radio waves emitted from sources in outer space.

ra·di·o·ther·a·py (rā′ dē ō thĕr′ ə pē) *Medicine* ***n***- treatment of disease by means of X rays or similar radiation from radioactive elements.

radio wave ***n***- an electromagnetic wave of radio frequency.

rad·ish (răd′ ĭsh) ***n***- **1** garden plant related to the mustard and having a pungent root. **2** its red or white root.

ra·di·um (rā′ dē əm) ***n***- radioactive metal element that emits several kinds of very powerful rays, including X rays. It is used in the treatment of cancer and to make materials luminous. Symbol Ra, At. No. 88, At. Wt. 226.

ra·di·us (rā′ dē əs) ***n***- [*pl.* **ra·di·i** (-ē ī′) or **ra·di·us·es**] **1** distance from the center of a circle to its circumference. For picture, see *circle*. **2** a straight line segment showing this distance. **3** area enclosed by a circle of a given radius. **4** the shorter of the two bones of the forearm, on the same side of the arm as the thumb.

ra·dix (rā′ dĭks) ***n***- [*pl.* **ra·di·ces** (răd′ ə sēz′, rā′ də-) or **ra·dix·es**] **1** in botany, the root of a plant. **2** *Mathematics* base of a number system: *The* radix *of the decimal system is 10.*

ra·don (rā′ dŏn′) ***n***- radioactive, gaseous element produced by the disintegration of radium. Symbol Rn, At. No. 86, At. Wt. 222.

Raft

raf·fi·a (răf′ ē ə) ***n***- long, stringy, leaf fiber from the **raffia palm,** a cultivated tree of Madagascar. It is woven into hats, baskets, etc.

raf·fle (răf′ əl) ***n***- lottery in which people buy chances for a small sum to win a prize. ***vt***- **[raf·fled, raf·fling]**: *to* raffle *a television set.*

¹**raft** (răft) ***n***- floating platform made of logs, planks, inflated rubber cells, oil drums, or other buoyant materials. ***vt***- **1** to transport by means of such a platform: *to* raft *supplies to the boat.* **2** to tie (logs) together in floating masses to tow or float them to where used. ***vi***-: *We* rafted *down the river.* [from Middle English, from Old Norse **raftr** and **raptr,** "a spar; rafter."]

²**raft** (răft) *Informal* ***n***- a great many: *a* raft *of children.* [a variant of earlier **raff,** as in **riffraff,** meaning "a heap."]

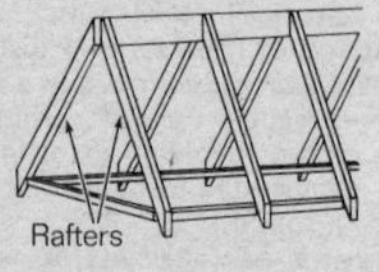
Rafters

raft·er (răf′ tər) ***n***- one of the sloping beams that support a roof.

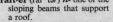

¹**rag** (răg) ***n***- **1** piece of cloth cut or torn from a larger piece; remnant. **2 rags** torn, frayed, worn-out clothing; shreds and tatters: *a beggar's* rags. *as* ***modifier***: *a* rag *doll*; *a* rag *rug*. [probably from Old Norse **rogg,** "shaggy piece."] ***—adj-* rag′ like′.**

²**rag** (răg) *Slang* ***vt***- **[ragged, rag·ging] 1** to scold. **2** to tease or torment. [of uncertain origin.]

³**rag** (răg) ***n***- a tune in ragtime. [from **ragtime.**]

rag·a·muf·fin (răg′ ə mŭf′ ən) ***n***- ragged, dirty child.

rage (rāj) ***n***- **1** intense or violent anger; fury: *a fit of* rage. **2** violent: *the* rage *of the storm.* **3** intense passion: *a* rage *of grief.* **4** *Informal* passing fashion. ***vi***- **[raged, rag·ing] 1** to express violent anger: *He* raged *against war.* **2** to continue with great fury: *The storm* raged.

Raglan sleeve

rag·ged (răg′ əd) ***adj***- **1** torn; tattered; worn out: *a* ragged *coat.* **2** dressed in tattered clothing. **3** shabby; neglected: *a* ragged *garden.* **4** rough; uneven; sharp: *a* ragged *cliff.* ***—adv-* rag′ ged·ly.** ***n***- **rag′ ged·ness.**

rag·ged·y (răg′ ə dē) *Informal* ***adj***- somewhat tattered, disheveled, and torn: *Look at that* raggedy *dress!*

rag·lan (răg′ lən) ***adj***- having sleeves that extend to the collar without a seam from front to back across the shoulder. ***n***- coat with such sleeves.

ra·gout (ră go͞o′) ***n***- highly seasoned stew of meat and vegetables.

rag·time (răg′ tīm′) ***n***- **1** kind of American popular music in vogue from about 1890 to 1920, in which the accent of the melody falls just before the regular beat of the accompaniment; syncopated music. **2** the rhythm of such music.

rag·weed (răg′ wēd′) ***n***- common weed with coarse, deeply notched leaves and yellow-green flowers. The pollen of ragweed is one cause of hay fever.

Ragweed

raid (rād) ***n*-** **1** *Military* sudden surprise thrust or attack, usually by a relatively small and specially trained force that withdraws immediately. **2** in police work, a sudden surprise entering of a place where criminal activity is suspected, for the purpose of confiscating equipment and making arrests. ***vt*-** to make such an attack or surprise entry: *to* raid *the enemy's beach defenses*; *to* raid *a gambling den.*

[1]**rail** (rāl) ***n*-** **1** horizontal bar used in a fence, banister, along the deck of a ship, etc., for separating areas or holding onto. **2** metal or wooden member upon which something runs, usually on wheels: *the* rails *of the railroad.* **3** railroad: *to carry freight by* rail. **4 the rail** fence surrounding a race track. [from Old French **reille,** from Latin **regula** meaning "a straight piece of wood; a ruler."]

Rail fence

[2]**rail** (rāl) ***vi*-** to scold violently; use bitter or angry language at someone (usually followed by "at" or "against"): *It does little good to* rail *at destiny.* [from French **railler** of uncertain origin, perhaps related to [2]**rally.**]

[3]**rail** (rāl) ***n*-** any of several kinds of marsh-dwelling birds having short wings, narrow bodies, and usually long beaks and moderately long legs. [from Old French **rasle** or **raale** of uncertain origin.]

[1]**rail·ing** (rā′ lĭng) ***n*-** a rail and its supports, used either as a fence or as a protective barrier near a dangerous place: *a* railing *around a monument.* [from [1]**rail.**]

Railing

[2]**rail·ing** (rā′ lĭng) ***n*-** scolding; loud and long complaining. [from [2]**rail.**]

rail·ler·y (rā′ lə rē) ***n*-** [*pl.* **rail·ler·ies**] good-natured ridicule or banter.

rail·road (rāl′ rōd′) ***n*-** **1** permanent road with tracks for trains, locomotives, etc. **2** an entire system of transportation, including tracks, trains, buildings, etc. ***vt*-** **1** to ship by rail. **2** to push through rapidly so as to prevent full consideration: *to* railroad *a bill through Congress.* **3** *Slang* to convict or imprison on false charges or flimsy evidence.

rail·way (rāl′ wā′) ***n*-** **1** railroad. **2** any system of tracks on which cars run.

rai·ment (rā′ mənt) *Archaic* ***n*-** clothing.

rain (rān) ***n*-** **1** moisture condensed from the air and falling in drops. **2** a fall or shower of moisture in drops: *The heavy* rains *flooded the land.* **3** shower of anything: *a* rain *of blessings.* **4 rains** rainy season. ***vi*-** to fall in drops of condensed moisture from the air. ***vt*-** to shower; give or offer abundantly: *Friends* rained *presents on them.* ***Homs*-** reign, rein. **—*adj*- rain′ less.**
rained out canceled because of rain: *The baseball game was* rained out.

rain·bow (rān′ bō′) ***n*-** **1** arch of colored light that appears when raindrops, mist, or spray refract, reflect, and disperse the sun's rays. A rainbow shows the colors red, orange, yellow, green, blue, indigo, and violet. **2** any similar display of colors.

rainbow trout ***n*-** kind of trout, common in western North America, that has a red stripe on the side.

rain check ***n*-** **1** stub on the ticket to some outdoor event, entitling the bearer to admission at a future time in case the event is rained out. **2** renewed invitation at a later time: *May I have a* rain check? *I can't come today.*

rain·coat (rān′ kōt′) ***n*-** water-resistant outer coat.

rain·drop (rān′ drŏp′) ***n*-** drop of rain.

rain·fall (rān′ fòl′) ***n*-** **1** shower of rain. **2** quantity of water from rain, snow, etc., falling within a given time and area. Rainfall is measured by the height of a column collected in a rain gauge.

rain forest ***n*-** heavy tropical forest receiving an annual rainfall of at least 100 inches, and made up of tall, broadleaf evergreens whose leaves form a continuous roof.

rain gauge ***n*-** device which measures rainfall by catching, and measuring the depth of, the rain that falls in a certain spot in a certain time.

rain·hat (rān′ hăt′) ***n*-** waterproof or water-resistant hat.

rain·mak·er (rān′ mā′ kər) ***n*-** person who is supposed to be able to bring on a rain. **—*n*- rain′ mak′ ing.**

rain shadow ***n*-** in meteorology, a region of lowered precipitation on the side of a mountain away from the prevailing winds.

rain·spout (rān′ spout′) ***n*-** **1** vertical pipe that drains a roof gutter. **2** waterspout.

rain squall ***n*-** violent windstorm accompanied by rain.

rain·storm (rān′ stórm′, -stôrm′) ***n*-** storm consisting of or accompanied by rain.

rain·wear (rān′ wâr′) ***n*-** garments worn as protection against rain, such as raincoats and overshoes.

rain·y (rā′ nē) ***adj*-** [**rain·i·er, rain·i·est**] **1** showery: *a* rainy *afternoon.* **2** having much rain: *a* rainy *climate.* **—*n*- rain′ i·ness.**

rainy day ***n*-** hard times; time when one is in need: *to save money for a* rainy day.

raise (rāz) ***vt*-** [**raised, rais·ing**] **1** to lift up: *to* raise *a window.* **2** to stir up; bring about: *to* raise *dust*; *to* raise *trouble.* **3** to build; construct: *to* raise *a house.* **4** to cause to develop or gather; collect: *to* raise *an army*; *to* raise *money.* **5** to grow; breed; rear: *to* raise *wheat*; *to* raise *horses*; *to* raise *a family.* **6** to present for consideration; mention: *to* raise *an objection.* **7** to lift up in rank, or position; promote: *They* raised *him to corporal.* **8** to make higher; increase: *to* raise *prices*; *to* raise *the bet.* **9** to reach in order to communicate with: *I can't* raise *him by telephone.* **10** to make rise (with yeast): *to* raise *dough.* **11** to end; abandon: *to* raise *a siege.* **12** to sight on the horizon. **13** to rouse; bring back to life: *That noise is enough to* raise *the dead.* ***n*-** an increase in amount: *a* raise *in pay.* **—*n*- rais′ er.**
raise one's voice against to express opposition to; oppose: *He* raised his voice against *corruption.*
raise the roof to explode with anger.

rai·sin (rā′ zən) ***n*-** dried sweet grape. ***adj*-** made of or containing raisins: *a* raisin *pie.*

rai·son d'ê·tre (rĕ zōⁿ dĕt′ rə) *French* reason for being; excuse for existing.

ra·jah (rä′ jə) ***n*-** king, prince, or chief in some parts of Asia, especially in some states of India.

[1]**rake** (rāk) ***n*-** any of several tools like a large comb with wide spaces between the teeth, joined to a long handle. Rakes are used to collect leaves, sticks, and stones without hurting the grass, to smooth spaded ground, to dig clams, etc. ***vt*-** [**raked, rak·ing**] **1** to use a rake on: *Kenneth* raked *the lawn.* **2** to collect; gather (followed by "up" or "together"): *The reporter* raked *up new evidence of fraud.* **3** to search carefully and

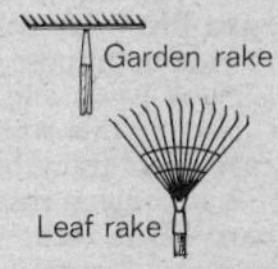

tirelessly: *Bud* raked *the library for material for his story.* **4** to sweep with the eye, with gunfire, etc.: *The young lookout's eyes* raked *the ocean for whales.* [from Old English **raca** of the same meaning.] ***—adj-*** **rake′ like′.**
rake over the coals to scold vigorously.
rake in *Slang* to take in (money, especially in large amounts).

[2]**rake** (rāk) ***n-*** man who promiscuously pursues women. [from Middle English **rakel,** a shortened form of **rakehell,** from Old Norse **reikal** meaning "a vagabond," and from **raka,** "to run about."]

[3]**rake** (rāk) ***n-*** slant or tilt from the horizontal or perpendicular: *the* rake *of a hat*; *the* rake *of a mast.* [from earlier verb **rake,** "to reach; extend," from Scandinavian **raka,** "reach; project"; related to [1]**rake.**]

rake-off (rāk′ ŏf′, -ŏf′) *Informal* ***n-*** commission; share of receipts, especially in an improper transaction.

[1]**rak·ish** (rā′ kĭsh) ***adj-*** jaunty; dashing: *a* rakish *costume.* [from [3]**rake.**] ***—adv-*** **rak′ ish·ly.** ***n-*** **rak′ ish·ness.**

[2]**rak·ish** (rā′ kĭsh) ***adj-*** dissolute; like a rake; having loose morals: *a* rakish *life.* [from [2]**rake.**]

[1]**ral·ly** (răl′ ē) ***vt-*** **[ral·lied, ral·ly·ing] 1** to bring into order again; assemble and reunite: *He* rallied *his troops after the battle.* **2** to bring together for strength and support: *to* rally *one's supporters.* ***vi-*** **1** to recover from disorder: *The troops* rallied *after the retreat.* **2** to regain strength; recover: *to* rally *after a fever.* **3** to come together for strength and support. **4** in sports, to score heavily after having been weak or scoreless earlier: *to* rally *for six runs in the seventh inning.* ***n-*** [*pl.* **ral·lies**] **1** mass meeting in support of something: *a* political *rally.* **2** a return of strength: *a* rally *in prices.* **3** in tennis, an exchange of strokes a number of times before a point is won. **4** in sports, a sudden and heavy scoring after having been weak or scoreless earlier in the contest. **5** competition in careful and precise driving among drivers of sports cars. [from French **railler,** from two Old French forms **re-** meaning "again," and **allier,** "to ally; join," from Latin **alligāre,** "to tie."]

[2]**ral·ly** (răl′ ē) ***vt-*** **[ral·lied, ral·ly·ing]** to make fun of good-naturedly; tease. [from French **railler,** "to tease; rail," and related to [2]**rail.**]

ram (răm) ***n-*** **1** adult male sheep. **2** (also **battering ram**) heavy, iron-tipped pole used to batter a wall or break down a door. **3** an armored projection at the bow of a warship, used for smashing into and sinking other ships. ***vt-*** **[rammed, ram·ming] 1** to strike head-on: *The car* rammed *the wall.* **2** to drive, stuff, or pack with heavy blows: *to* ram *earth into a hole.*

Mutton ram, about 2 ft. high at shoulder

Ra·ma·dan (răm′ ə dän′, -dăn′) ***n-*** the ninth and holiest month of the Muslim year, observed by fasting from dawn to dusk for thirty days.

ram·ble (răm′ bəl) ***vi-*** **[ram·bled, ram·bling.] 1** to stroll without purpose or direction. **2** to flow or meander with many twists and turns: *The river* rambled *along.* **3** to talk or write without thought or sequence. ***n-*** a stroll.

ram·bler (răm′ blər) ***n-*** **1** person or thing that rambles. **2** a climbing rose bearing small flowers in clusters.

ram·bling (răm′ blĭng) ***adj-*** **1** wandering; walking aimlessly. **2** spread out in an irregular way: *a* rambling *castle.* **3** lacking plan or unity: *a* rambling *talk.*

ram·bunc·tious (răm bŭngk′ shəs) *Informal* ***adj-*** unruly and boisterous.

ra·mie (răm′ ē) ***n-*** **1** shrub of the East Indies, China, and Japan, yielding a soft, woody fiber. **2** the fiber of this plant, used for weaving textiles and making cord.

ram·i·fy (răm′ ə fī′) ***vi-*** **[ram·i·fied, ram·i·fying] 1** to divide into branches or divisions; branch out: *Veins* ramify *into many capillaries.* **2** to develop, or prove to have, many connected parts: *The more we examine the problem, the more it* ramifies. ***—n-*** **ram′ i·fi·ca′ tion** (-fə kā′ shən): *the* ramification *of a river into streams.*

ram·jet (răm′ jĕt′) ***n-*** jet engine in which the air for burning is compressed by the force of forward motion rather than by a compressor. See also *turbojet.*

ram·mer (răm′ ər) ***n-*** person or thing that rams; especially, a tool used in building construction for driving stones or piles, or for packing concrete.

[1]**ramp** (rămp) ***n-*** sloping walk or roadway leading from one level to another. [from Old French **ramper,** "[2]ramp," perhaps from an earlier Germanic word.]

Ramp

[2]**ramp** (rămp) ***vi-*** **1** to rush about wildly; storm about; rage. **2** to rear up on the hind legs in a threatening manner: *The bear* ramped *and roared.* [from Old French **ramper** meaning "to clamber; run."]

[1]**ram·page** (răm′ pāj′) ***n-*** fit or period of wild, destructive rage: *The horse went on a* rampage.

[2]**ram·page** (răm pāj′) ***vi-*** **[ram·paged, ram·pag·ing]** to run wildly or in a violent manner; storm; rage: *The flooded river* rampaged *through the countryside.*

ramp·ant (răm′ pənt) ***adj-*** **1** spreading without control; wild; raging. **2** climbing or growing unchecked: *The weeds grew* rampant *in the garden.* **3** in heraldry, standing erect on the hind legs with one foreleg raised above the other, as a lion in a coat of arms. ***—adv-*** **ram′ pant·ly.**

ram·part (răm′ pärt′, -pərt) ***n-*** **1** protective wall or bank of earth around a fort. **2** any protection from danger.

Rampart

ram·rod (răm′ rŏd′) ***n-*** **1** rod used to load a gun through the muzzle, or to clean the barrel of a gun. **2** *Informal* foreman, especially of a ranch. ***vt-*** **[ram·rod·ded, ram·rod·ding]** *Informal* **1** to push through vigorously: *to* ramrod *a bill through a legislature.* **2** *Informal* to act as foreman of.

ram·shack·le (răm′ shăk′ əl) ***adj-*** shaky; rickety.

ran (răn) *p.t.* of **run.**

ranch (rănch) ***n-*** **1** in western United States and Canada, a farm with extensive grazing lands where livestock such as cattle, sheep, and horses are raised. **2** in western United States, any large farm raising a specific crop: *a fruit* ranch. ***vi-*** to own or manage such a farm. [American word from Spanish **rancho,** "a group that eats together; a mess," from Old French **reng,** "[1]rank."]

ranch·er (răn′ chər) ***n-*** person who owns or manages a ranch. Also **ranch′ man** [*pl.* **ranch·men**].

ran·che·ro (răn chĕr′ ō, rän-) ***n-*** [*pl.* **ran·che·ros**] in southwestern United States and Mexico, person who owns, or works on, a cattle ranch.

ranch house ***n-*** **1** main house of a ranch. **2** one-story house with a low-pitched roof and an open floor plan.

ran·cho (răn′ chō, rän′-) ***n-*** [*pl.* **ran·chos**] **1** in Latin America, a hut or group of huts for ranch workers. **2** in southwestern United States, a ranch.

ran·cid (răn′ sĭd) ***adj-*** having the strong smell and taste of spoiled fat or oil: *Butter turns* rancid *when left out in hot weather.* ***—n-*** **ran′ cid·ness** or **ran·cid′ i·ty.**

ran·cor (răng′ kər, -kŏr′) ***n-*** deep hatred; malice.

ran·cor·ous (răng′ kər əs) ***adj-*** full of rancor; showing or marked by rancor: *a* rancorous *tone*; *a* rancorous *attack.* ***—adv-*** **ran′ cor·ous·ly.** ***n-*** **ran′ cor·ous·ness.**

ran·dom (răn′ dəm) ***adj-*** based entirely on chance; without plan or pattern: *a* random *choice*; *a* random *sampling.* ***—adv-*** **ran′ dom·ly.** ***n-*** **ran′ dom·ness.**

at random without plan or pattern; by chance; haphazardly: *to wander* at random *through the streets.*

ra·nee (rän′ ē) rani.

rang (răng) *p.t.* of **ring.**

range (rānj) ***n-*** **1** limits within which someone can do something or something can be done; extent; scope: *beyond the* range *of his vision*; *within the* range *of possibility.* **2** limits within which something varies: *a wide* range *of prices*; *a voice with a* range *of two octaves.* **3** line or row; chain; series: *a* range *of hills or mountains.* **4** tract of land over which cattle graze. **5** large cooking stove. **6** place for target practice: *a rifle* range; *a missile* range. **7** distance to which a gun, cannon, etc., can shoot; also, distance of the target from the gun. **8** maximum distance a ship, plane, etc., can travel without refueling: *a bomber with a* range *of 3000 miles.* **9** area over which a plant or animal may be found in the wild state: *The* range *of the leopard is decreasing.* ***vt-*** **[ranged, rang·ing] 1** to put in a row or in regular order: *to* range *cups on a shelf*; *to* range *books according to height.* **2** to put (oneself) in a certain position with reference to others: *He* ranged *himself with the rebels.* **3** to travel or wander over: *Cattle* ranged *the open prairie.* ***vi-*** **1** to vary within certain limits: *These motors* range *from 50 to 100 horsepower.* **2** to wander; roam. **3** to be found over a certain area: *The magnolia* ranges *northward to Ohio.*

range finder ***n-*** instrument for finding the distance between a target or point and the instrument itself.

rang·er (rān′jər) ***n-*** **1** (also **forest ranger**) officer who patrols a wilderness area, guarding the forest and its wildlife. **2** wanderer. **3 Ranger** (1) Texas Ranger. (2) in the Army, a member of a special commando force.

rang·y (rān′ jē) ***adj-*** **[rang·i·er, rang·i·est] 1** long-legged, lean, and muscular: *a* rangy *racehorse*; *a* rangy *football player.* **2** able to wander far and wide; having a tendency to roam. ***—n-*** **rang′ i·ness.**

ra·ni (rän′ ē) ***n-*** **1** wife of a rajah. **2** Hindu queen or princess. Also **ranee.**

[1]**rank** (răngk) ***n-*** **1** line; row: *a* rank *of soldiers.* **2** position in society or in some official group; grade. **3** high position or station: *a man of* rank *in his state.* **4** merit; degree of worth: *a poet of the first* rank. **5 ranks** (1) an army as a whole. (2) enlisted men as distinguished from officers. ***vt-*** **1** to place in rows; draw up (soldiers) in line. **2** to place in a special order, especially in the order of worth: *He* ranked *the magazines by their story interest.* **3** to be of a higher grade or class than: *A major* ranks *a captain.* ***vi-*** to hold a certain position or grade: *She* ranks *high in her class.* [from Old French **reng** meaning "a row; range," from Germanic **hring.**]

[2]**rank** (răngk) ***adj-*** **1** growing rapidly and unchecked: *Vegetation is* rank *in the tropics.* **2** bad smelling or tasting: *Old bacon becomes* rank. **3** absolute; outright; arrant: *a piece of* rank *nonsense*; *a* rank *insult.* [from Old English **ranc** meaning "strong; bold," from an earlier Germanic word meaning "erect; long and thin."] ***—adv-*** **rank′ ly.** ***n-*** **rank′ ness.**

rank and file ***n-*** (takes singular or plural verb) **1** the ordinary members who form the bulk of an organization or group, as distinguished from the leaders or officers; especially, the ordinary members of a labor union. **2** the common soldiers of an army, including corporals and all ranks below.

rank·ing (răng′ kĭng) ***adj-*** having first, top, or superior rank or standing: *a* ranking *congressman.*

ran·kle (răng′ kəl) ***vi-*** **[ran·kled, ran·kling] 1** to continue to be sore and painful: *His wound* rankled. **2** to be the source of persistent mental pain and irritation: *The insult* rankled *for years.* ***vt-***: *The insult* rankled *him.*

ran·sack (răn′ săk′) ***vt-*** **1** to search thoroughly: *He* ransacked *his desk.* **2** to turn topsy-turvy, as in searching for valuables: *Thieves* ransacked *our apartment.* ***—n-*** **ran′ sack′er.**

ran·som (răn′ səm) ***n-*** **1** payment of a price for the release of a captive: *They kidnaped the girl and held her for* ransom. **2** price demanded for such release: *They demanded a* ransom *of ten thousand dollars.* **3** freedom obtained through payment of a price: *She knew her* ransom *would surely come.* ***vt-*** **1** to set free by paying a demanded price; redeem: *Her father* ransomed *her.* **2** to release after such payment has been made: *The kidnapers* ransomed *her as soon as the money arrived.*

rant (rănt) ***vi-*** to speak loudly and at great length; rave on; bluster: *The speaker* ranted *about the evils of money.* ***n-*** such speaking or raving. ***—n-*** **rant′ er.**

[1]**rap** (răp) ***n-*** **1** quick, sharp blow; tap: *a* rap *on the knuckles.* **2** sound of a sharp blow: *to hear a* rap *on the window.* **3** *Slang* blame; punishment. ***vi-*** **[rapped, rap·ping]** to strike something sharply, often in order to make a noise and gain attention: *The chairman* rapped *for attention.* ***vt-***: *The chairman* rapped *the desk for attention.* [probably from an early Germanic or Scandinavian imitation of a sound.] ***Hom-*** wrap.

[2]**rap** (răp) ***n-*** an old Irish coin of little value. [origin uncertain.] ***Hom-*** wrap.

not give (or **care**) **a rap** *Informal* to have no concern about; be indifferent to: *I don't* care a rap *what you think.*

ra·pa·cious (rə pā′ shəs) ***adj-*** **1** living on prey; seizing by violence; fiercely predatory: *Hawks are* rapacious *birds.* **2** grasping; greedy: *a* rapacious *landlord.* ***—adv-*** **ra·pa′ cious·ly.** ***n-*** **ra·pa′ cious·ness.**

ra·pac·i·ty (rə păs′ ə tē) ***n-*** habit or practice of preying greedily on others: *the* rapacity *of a hungry shark.*

[1]**rape** (rāp) ***vt-*** **[raped, rap·ing]** to force (a woman) to submit to sex acts against her will. ***n-*** **1** act and crime of such forcing. **2** *Archaic* forcible kidnapping or carrying away of a woman or women. [from Old French **rape** or **rapt,** from Latin **raptus,** a form of **rapere** meaning "to seize and take away."]

[2]**rape** (rāp) ***n-*** herb related to mustard and used as food for sheep and hogs. It yields **rape seed,** from which **rape oil** is extracted to be used as a lubricant. [from Latin **rāpa** meaning "a turnip."]

Ra·pha·el (răf′ ē əl, rā′ fē-) ***n-*** one of the seven archangels in Jewish and Christian tradition.

rap·id (răp′ ĭd) ***adj-*** fast; quick; swift: *We walked at a* rapid *pace. There was a* rapid *decline in stock prices.* ***n-*** (usually **rapids**) place in a river or stream where the water flows especially fast because of a steeper slope or narrowing of the channel. ***—adv-*** **rap′ id·ly.**

rap·id-fire (răp′ ĭd fīər′) ***adj-*** **1** able to fire in rapid succession: *a* rapid-fire *rifle.* **2** as quick and insistent as the quick firing of a gun; staccato: *The lawyer directed* rapid-fire *questions at the witness.*

rap·id·i·ty (rə pĭd′ ə tē) ***n-*** speed; swiftness.

---

fāte, făt, dâre, bärn; bē, bĕt, mêre; bīte, bĭt; nōte, hŏt, môre, dȯg; fŭn, fûr; to͞o, bo͝ok; oil; out; tar; thin; then; hw for wh as in *wh*at; zh for s as in u*s*ual; ə for a, e, i, o, u, as in *a*go, lin*e*n, per*i*l, at*o*m, min*u*s

ra·pi·er (rā′ pē ər) ***n-*** sword with a light hand guard and a straight, slender, double-edged blade, used for thrusting.

Rapier

rap·ine (răp′ ĭn) ***n-*** the taking and carrying off of property by force; plunder; pillage.

rap·port (ră pôr′) ***n-*** sympathetic relationship; agreement; harmony: *In a good class there is* rapport *between teacher and students.* [from French.]

rap·proche·ment (ră prōsh mäⁿ′) *French* ***n-*** a coming together in agreement or understanding, after a period of separation; new or renewed harmony: *The United Nations seeks* rapprochement *between East and West.*

rap·scal·lion (răp skăl′ yən) ***n-*** worthless person; rascal; rogue.

rapt (răpt) ***adj-*** carried away with pleasure or delight; enchanted; absorbed: *We listened to the organ in* rapt *silence.* ***Hom-*** wrapt. ***—adv-*** **rapt′ly.** ***n-*** **rapt′ness.**

rap·ture (răp′ chər) ***n-*** extreme delight or pleasure; great joy; bliss; ecstasy.

rap·tur·ous (răp′chə rəs) ***adj-*** feeling, showing, or marked by great joy or delight: *a* rapturous *expression.* ***—adv-*** **rap′tur·ous·ly.** ***n-*** **rap′tur·ous·ness.**

[1]**rare** (râr) ***adj-*** [**rar·er, rar·est**] **1** not common or usual; distinctive; precious: *a* rare *book; a* rare *old lace.* **2** not frequent; seldom occurring: *a* rare *visit to the city.* **3** not thick or dense; thin: *the* rare *atmosphere of high mountains.* [from French, from Latin **rārus** meaning "thin; scattered."] ***—n-*** **rare′ness.**

[2]**rare** (râr) ***adj-*** [**rar·er, rar·est**] lightly cooked; underdone: *a* rare *steak.* [from earlier **rear** meaning "lightly boiled"; from Old English **hrēr** meaning "not thoroughly cooked."] ***—n-*** **rare′ness.**

rare·bit (râr′ bĭt′) ***n-*** Welsh rabbit.

rare-earth element (râr′ ûrth′) ***n-*** any of a group of highly reactive metal elements from atomic number 57 (lanthenum) through 71 (lutetium), which have nearly identical chemical and physical properties.

rar·e·fac·tion (râr′ ə făk′ shən, răr′-) ***n-*** a making or being less dense: *the* rarefaction *of a gas.*

rar·e·fy (râr′ ə fī′, răr′-) ***vt-*** [**rar·e·fied, rar·e·fy·ing**] to cause to become less dense: *Release of pressure* rarefied *the gas in the chamber.* ***vi-***: *The air* rarefies *as one climbs.*

rare·ly (râr′ lē) ***adv-*** **1** seldom; infrequently: *a* rarely *seen bat.* **2** unusually; exceptionally: *a* rarely *beautiful gem.*

rar·i·ty (râr′ ə tē, răr′-) ***n-*** [*pl.* **rar·i·ties**] **1** anything rare and unique: *First editions of Shakespeare are* rarities. **2** infrequency; scarcity; uncommonness: *the* rarity *of true genius.* **3** thinness; lack of density: *the* rarity *of the atmosphere in high altitudes.*

ras·cal (răs′ kəl) ***n-*** **1** bad or mean person; scoundrel. **2** mischievous person, especially a playful child. ***—n-*** **ras·cal′i·ty** (răs kăl′ ə tē).

ras·cal·ly (răs′ kə lē) ***adj-*** dishonest; mean; base: *a* rascally *scheme.*

rase (rāz) raze.

[1]**rash** (răsh) ***n-*** **1** outbreak of red spots on the skin, often accompanied by itching. **2** any general outbreak of unpleasant symptoms or incidents. [from Old French **rasche,** probably from Latin **rāsus,** a form of **rādere** meaning "to scratch."]

[2]**rash** (răsh) ***adj-*** [**rash·er, rash·est**] hasty; reckless: *She regretted her* rash *decision.* [from earlier English **rasch,** probably of Dutch or German origin.] ***—adv-*** **rash′ly.** ***n-*** **rash′ness.**

rash·er (răsh′ ər) ***n-*** thin slice of bacon or ham.

rasp (răsp) ***n-*** **1** coarse file with raised teeth instead of ridges. **2** act of scraping with, or as if with, such a file. **3** rough, harsh sound: *Her voice had an annoying* rasp. ***vt-*** **1** to rub or scrape with such a file: *The blacksmith* rasped *the horse's hoof.* **2** to irritate: *The squeaky door* rasps *my nerves.* ***vi-*** to scrape roughly with a harsh sound. ***—adj-*** **rasp′like′.**

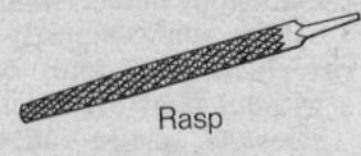
Rasp

rasp·ber·ry (răz′ bĕr′ ē) ***n-*** [*pl.* **rasp·ber·ries**] **1** round, juicy fruit made up of small, closely set globes, usually red, but in some types black, purple, or yellow. **2** bush having leaves in groups of three, and long, prickly stems, which bears this fruit. **3** *Slang* rude, splattering sound made with the tongue and lips and used to show contempt or disfavor.

Raspberry

rasp·y (răs′ pē) ***adj-*** [**rasp·i·er, rasp·i·est**] **1** of sounds, harsh or grating; gravelly: *a* raspy *voice.* **2** rough in texture; irritated or sore; also, crotchety or cranky: *a* raspy *throat; a* raspy *mood.*

rat (răt) ***n-*** **1** gnawing animal, usually gray, black, or brown, with small, beady eyes and a long, hairless tail. Rats look somewhat like large mice. **2** small pad used by women to roll hair over. **3** *Slang* low, worthless, or mean person; especially, an informer or deserter. ***vi-*** [**rat·ted, rat·ting**] **1** to hunt rats. **2** *Slang* to desert. **3** *Slang* to inform (on).

smell a rat to suspect a trick; have a feeling that something is wrong.

Brown rat, about 1 1/2 ft. long

ra·tan (ră tăn′) rattan.

ratch·et (răch′ ət) ***n-*** mechanism consisting of a toothed wheel or bar and one or more fingers (pawls) that pivot so as to fit between two of the teeth and permit motion of the wheel or bar in only one direction. Ratchets are used on the winding stems of clocks, on jacks for hoisting cars, on winches, on wrenches, and on other devices.

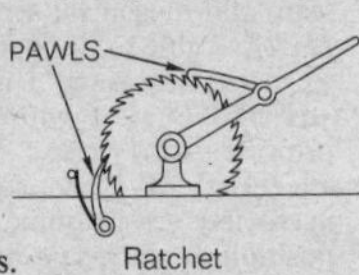

Ratchet

[1]**rate** (rāt) ***n-*** **1** amount or degree of something measured in relation to something else; especially, the number of times something occurs in a given amount of time: *a* rate *of increase;* rate *of consumption.* **2** a speed; pace: *traveling at a fast* rate. **3** set price or charge for goods, service, work, etc.: *a fair* rate *of pay; interest* rates. ***vt-*** [**rat·ed, rat·ing**] **1** to put a value on: *He* rated *her low in reading ability.* **2** to consider; regard: *Many people* rate *baseball as dull to watch.* **3** *Informal* to deserve; merit: *He* rates *a promotion.* ***vi-*** to be ranked or valued: *He* rates *high among the hitters.* [from Old French, from Medieval Latin **rāta,** "fixed; reckoned up."]

at any rate in any case; anyway. **at that** (or **this**) **rate** in that or this case; under such circumstances.

[2]**rate** (rāt) ***vt-*** [**rat·ed, rat·ing**] to scold sharply; chide; berate. [from Old French **reter** meaning "to impute; blame," from Late Latin **reputāre,** "to account (to one's credit)," from earlier meaning "to compute; reckon."]

rath·er (răth′ ər) ***adv-*** **1** to some extent; somewhat: *I'm* rather *tired after our trip.* **2** preferably: *I would* rather *go home now than later.* **3** more correctly; also, on the contrary; instead: *Her dress is red, or* rather, *it's orange-red.* ***interj- Brit.*** I should say so!

raths·kel·ler (rŏt′skĕl′ər, răth′-) ***n-*** restraurant or tavern specializing in beer and German food.

rat·i·fi·ca·tion (răt′ə fə kā′shən) ***n-*** formal approval.

rat·i·fy (răt′ə fī′) ***vt-*** **[rat·i·fied, rat·i·fy·ing]** to approve or confirm: *to* ratify *an amendment.* **—*n-* rat′i·fi′er.**

rat·ing (rā′tĭng) ***n-*** **1** a placing or classifying according to relative value, merit, or standing: *a* rating *of the year's best novels.* **2** standing; rank; class: *a high scholastic* rating; *a low credit* rating. **3** *Military* title showing special training or capability: *He has the* rating *of machinist.* **4** power, limit of operation, etc., of some device: *a fuse with the* rating *of 15 amperes.*

ra·tio (rā′shō′, rā′shē ō′) ***n-*** [*pl.* **ra·tios**] **1** a relationship in quantity, amount, or size between two things, expressed as the quotient of two numbers: *There is a* ratio *of 3 to 1 between the volumes of the two containers.* **2** the indicated quotient of two numbers, expressions, etc., which is written as 3:1, 3/1, 3 ÷ 1, or ³⁄₁.

ra·ti·o·ci·na·tion (răt′ē ō′sə nā′shən) ***n-*** careful and logical thinking; reasoning.

ra·tion (răsh′ən, rā′shən) ***n-*** **1** fixed share or portion; allotment. **2** daily allowance of food for a person or animal. **3 rations** food or supplies, especially when given out in fixed amounts. ***vt-*** to give out in fixed amounts or otherwise limit the use of (something in short supply): *The shipwrecked crew* rationed *their water supply.*

ra·tion·al (răsh′ən əl) ***adj-*** **1** able to reason: *Man is a* rational *being.* **2** guided by or based on reason; logical. **3** *Mathematics* of or having to do with a rational number. **—*adv-* ra′tion·al·ly. *n-* ra′tion·al·ness.**

ra·tion·ale (răsh′ən ăl′) ***n-*** basic principles that justify or explain a theory, belief, policy, line of action, etc.

ra·tion·al·ism (răsh′ən ə lĭz əm) ***n-*** **1** habit of being reasonable and logical: Rationalism *sometimes breaks down under the stress of emotion.* **2** in philosophy, the theory that essential knowledge can be gained by the use of reasoning alone, without experience of the senses, and that such knowledge is superior to any gained by experience. See also *empiricism.* **3** in religion, the tendency to place a high value on reason as compared with divine revelation. **—*n-* ra′tion·al·ist. *adj-* ra′tion·al·is′tic. *adv-* ra′tion·al·is′ti·cal·ly.**

ra·tion·al·i·ty (răsh′ə năl′ə tē) ***n-*** [*pl.* **ra·tion·al·i·ties**] the ability or power to reason; the possession or use of the power of reasoning: *John's* rationality *is in doubt.*

ra·tion·al·ize (răsh′ə nə līz) ***vt-*** **[ra·tion·al·ized, ra·tion·al·iz·ing]** **1** to give a reasonable explanation for (actions, attitudes, etc.) that in fact arise from emotion, selfishness, or prejudice: *They said I merely* rationalized *when I explained my refusal to enter the race.* **2** to explain according to the rules of reason and nature: *to* rationalize *a miracle.* **3** to cause to conform to reason: *to* rationalize *a process.* **—*n-* ra′tion·al·i·za·tion.**

rational number ***n-*** any number that can be expressed as an integer or as a quotient of two integers. Any integer or common fraction is a rational number.

rat·line or **rat·lin** (răt′lən) ***n-*** one of a series of small ropes tied between the shrouds of a ship to form a ladder.

DEADEYE

Ratlines

rat mite ***n-*** mite that sometimes attacks man and is a carrier of epidemic typhus.

rate race ***n- Informal*** life, work, or any activity thought of as frantic, pointless, and endless.

rat·tan or **ra·tan** (ră tăn′) ***n-*** **1** climbin palm of tropical regions, with long, smooth, reedlike stems. **2** these stems, used especially in making wicker furniture. **3** walking stick or cane made of such stems.

rat·ter (răt′ər) ***n-*** **1** person or animal that hunts or catches rats. **2** *Informal* person who deserts, betrays, or informs on his associates or friends.

rat·tle (răt′əl) ***vi-*** **[rat·tled, rat·tling]** **1** to make short, sharp sounds in quick succession: *Hail* rattled *on the roof. The windows* rattled *during the storm.* **2** to move with a clatter: *The wagon* rattled *along the bumpy road.* **3** to talk in a noisy, rapid manner: *They* rattled *on for an hour.* ***vt-*** **1** to cause to make rapid; sharp sounds: *The wind* rattles *the shutters.* **2** to cause to be nervous; confuse; upset: *Interruptions* rattled *the speaker.* ***n-*** **1** series of short, sharp sounds: *The* rattle *of a window.* **2** child's toy that makes a clattering sound when it is shaken. **3** series of horny rings on a rattlesnake's tail that buzz sharply when vibrated. **—*adj-* rat′tly:** *a* rattly *car.*

rattle off to say or do quickly: *He* rattled off *the poem.*

rat·tle·brain (răt′əl brān′) *Informal* ***n-*** stupid, flighty, and prattling person. **—*adj-* rat′tle·brained′.**

rat·tler (răt′əl ər, răt′lər) ***n-*** **1** person or thing that makes a clattering noise, such as a freight train. **2** rattlesnake.

rat·tle·snake (răt′əl snāk′) ***n-*** any of various American poisonous snakes with horny, knoblike rings at the end of the tail. The rings make a rattling sound as the snake vibrates its tail when disturbed.

Diamondback rattlesnake, 4–8 ft. long

rat·tle·trap (răt′əl trăp′) ***n-*** anything very old or wornout, especially an automobile or railroad car.

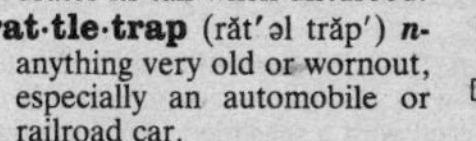

rat·tling (răt′lĭng, răt′əl ĭng) ***n-*** noise made by the clattering together of small hard objects. ***adj-*** **1** making a rapid succession of sharp, noisy sounds. **2** *Informal* quick: *to walk at a* rattling *pace.* **3** *Informal* very good; superior: *They played a* rattling *game.* ***adv- Informal*** (intensifier only): *They saw a* rattling *good movie.*

rat·trap (răt′trăp′) ***n-*** **1** trap for catching rats. **2** hopeless or desperate situation.

rat·ty (răt′ē) ***adj-*** **[rat·ti·er, rat·ti·est]** **1** like a rat. **2** full of rats. **3** *Informal* broken-down; shabby; run-down.

rau·cous (rŏ′kəs) ***adj-*** **1** hoarse; harsh; raspy: *the* raucous *cry of the crow.* **2** mocking and unruly; boisterous: *The* raucous *laughter of the opposition.* **—*adv-* rau′cous·ly. *n-* rau′cous·ness.**

rav·age (răv′ĭj) ***vt-*** **[rav·aged, rav·ag·ing]** **1** to lay waste; devastate; plunder; sack: *Locusts* ravaged *the crops.* **2** to rob of health and vitality: *Poverty and disease* ravaged *half the population.* ***n-*** destructive action, or its result; ruin: *free from* ravage *by flood; the* ravages *of disease.* **—*n-* rav′ag·er.**

rave (rāv) ***vi-*** **[raved, rav·ing]** **1** to talk in a wild and disconnected manner: *The fevered patient* raved *in delirium.* **2** to talk with great enthusiasm: *They* raved *about their vacation.* ***n-*** **1** wild or irrational talk or action. **2** *Slang* person or thing that is the object of enthusiastic approval. **3** *Informal* extravagantly favorable com-

fāte, făt, dâre, bärn; bē, bĕt, mêre; bīte, bĭt; nōte, hŏt, môre, dȯg; fŭn, fûr; to͞o, bo͝ok; oil; out; tar; thin; *th*en; hw for wh as in *wh*at; zh for s as in us*u*al; ə for a, e, i, o, u, as in *a*go, lin*e*n, per*i*l, at*o*m, min*u*s

ment or criticism. *as modifier*: *a* rave *review of a new play.*

rav·el (răv'əl) ***vt-*** to separate the threads of (woven or knitted material) ***vi-*** **1** to come apart or unwoven; fray: *The shirt began to* ravel *at the sleeves.* **2** to entangle or confuse (now rarely used). ***n-*** thread loosened from woven or knitted material. **—*n-* rav'el·er.**

rav·el·ing (răv'əl ĭng) ***n-*** thread that has raveled from woven or knitted material. Also **rav'el·ling.**

[1]ra·ven (rā'vən) ***n-*** large bird related to the crow, having glossy black feathers that are long at the throat. ***adj-*** shiny black: *a girl with* raven *hair. [from Old English* **hræfn**].

Raven, about 2 ft. long

[2]rav·en (răv'ən) ***vt-*** **1** to devour greedily. **2** to seize with force. ***vi-*** to seek and devour prey. [from Middle English **ravine** meaning "booty; robbery," from Old French, from Latin **rapīna** meaning "robbery," from Latin **rapere,** "to seize."]

rav·en·ing (răv'ən ĭng) ***adj-*** hungrily searching for prey: *Wolves are* ravening *animals.*

rav·en·ous (răv'ə nəs) ***adj-*** very eager for food or other satisfaction; wanting much before one is satisfied: *a* ravenous *appetite; to be* ravenous *for riches or fame.* **—*adv-* rav'en·ous·ly.** ***n-*** **rav'en·ous·ness.**

ra·vine (rə vēn') ***n-*** long, deep gully or valley, usually worn by water.

rav·ing (rā'vĭng) ***n-*** wild or furious talk. ***adj-*** **1** talking wildly; delirious. **2** *Informal* very attractive or winning: *The magazine referred to her as a* raving *beauty.* ***adv-*** *Informal* wildly; furiously: *He's* raving *mad.* **—*adv-* rav'ing·ly.**

ra·vi·o·li (răv'ē ō' lē) ***n-*** food dish consisting of small, thin pieces of dough filled with chopped meat, cheese, etc., boiled, and usually served with a seasoned tomato sauce; also, one of the pieces.

rav·ish (răv'ĭsh) ***vt-*** **1** to seize and carry away by force. **2** to rape. **3** to overcome with delight; enchant: *The music* ravished *him.* **—*n-* rav'ish·er.** ***n-*** **rav'ish·ment.**

rav·ish·ing (răv'ĭsh ĭng) ***adj-*** causing great admiration; very charming; enchanting; captivating: *a* ravishing *smile.* **—*adv-* rav'ish·ing·ly.**

raw (rȯ) ***adj-*** **[raw·er, raw·est] 1** in a natural state; unrefined; unprocessed: *One seldom uses* raw *lumber for building.* **2** uncooked. **3** painfully open or exposed: *a* raw *wound.* **4** harsh; crude: *his manners are* raw. **5** not experienced; not trained: *a* raw *beginner.* **6** cold; damp; chilly: *a* raw *wind.* **—*adv-* raw'ly.** ***n-*** **raw'ness.**

raw-boned (rȯ'bōnd) ***adj-*** with little flesh on the bones; thin; gaunt: *a* raw-boned *face.*

raw-hide (rȯ'hīd) ***n-*** **1** hide of cattle or other animals before it is tanned. **2** whip or cord made of this hide.

raw material ***n-*** **1** petroleum, metal ores, coal, wood, and other materials in their natural state, needed to manufacture finished products. **2** person or persons having promising natural ability or talent which needs training: *good* raw material *for the football team.*

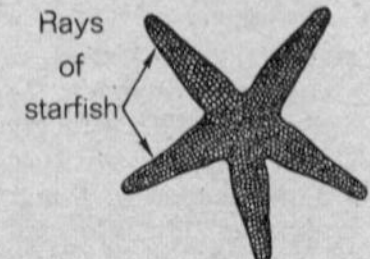

[1]ray (rā) ***n-*** **1** beam of light, heat, electrons, etc.: *The sun's* rays *warm the earth.* **2** one of several parts sticking out from a center: *the* rays *of a starfish;* rays *of a daisy.* **3** *Mathematics* a set of points consisting of any given point on a line and all other points of the line on one side of the given point. **4** slight amount; trace; glimmer; gleam: *The news brought a* ray *of hope.* **5** *Astronomy* one of the many bright streaks seen radiating from craters on the moon's surface, especially when the moon is full. [from Old French **rai,** from Latin **radius,** "a beam."] ***Homs-*** re, [1]Re. **—*adj-* ray·less.**

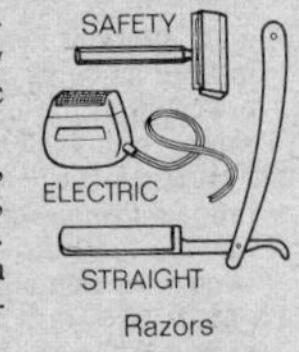
Manta ray, often 20 ft. across

[2]ray (rā) ***n-*** any of several fishes related to the sharks and having a flat, fan-shaped body and a whiplike tail. [from Old French **raie,** from Latin **rāia.**] ***Homs-*** re, [1]Re.

ray·on (rā'ŏn') ***n-*** **1** smooth fiber made from cellulose, obtained from wood pulp and cotton, which is chemically treated and forced through tiny holes. **2** silklike cloth made from such fiber.

raze (rāz) ***vt-*** **[razed, raz·ing]** to tear down; level to the ground; destroy completely: *The fire* razed *the building.* Also **rase.** ***Hom-*** raise.

ra·zor (rā' zər) **1** sharp-edged instrument for shaving off hair, especially mens' beards. **2** close-cutting electric clipper used for the same purpose.

SAFETY
ELECTRIC
STRAIGHT
Razors

ra·zor·back (rā' zər băk') ***n-*** lean, sharp-backed hog with long legs, common in southern United States. **adj-** (often **ra'zor·backed'**) having a long, sharp back: *a small,* razor-backed *dog.*

razz (răz) *Slang* ***vt-*** to make fun of in an annoying way; tease; ridicule; heckle.

Rb symbol for rubidium.

R.C. **1** Red Cross. **2** Roman Catholic.

rd. **1** (also **Rd.**) road. **2** rod or rods. **3** round.

R.D. rural (free) delivery.

[1]re (rā) ***n-*** the second note of a musical scale. [from Italian **re,** the first syllable of Latin **resōnare.**] ***Homs-*** ray, [1]Re.

[2]re (rā, rē) ***prep-*** in the matter of or in the case of (used in business letter writing, law, etc.). [from Latin **rē,** from **rēs** "thing; affair."] ***Homs-*** ray, [1]Re.

[1]Re (rā) [1]Ra. ***Homs-*** ray, re.

[2]Re symbol for rhenium.

re- *prefix* **1** again; once more: *to* re*build;* re*join;* re*write.* **2** back again: *to* re*pay;* re*bound;* re*claim.* [from Latin **re-** maining "again; over (again); back."]

reach (rēch) ***vt-*** **1** to come to; arrive at: *They* reached *home before the rain. The jury finally* reached *a verdict.* **2** to stretch to; extend to: *This road* reaches *the river.* **3** to stretch an arm or hand to touch or grasp: *He is tall and can* reach *the top shelf.* **4** to pass or deliver to another; hand: *Please* reach *me my coat.* **5** to get to; communicate with: *You can* reach *us by calling this phone number.* **6** to affect; influence: *The speaker just couldn't* reach *the audience.* ***vi-*** **1** to extend the hand to touch or grasp something: *He* reached *out to greet us.* **2** to try to get something: *to* reach *for approval or sympathy.* **3** to extend in time, space, amount, etc.: *The damage* reaches *into thousands of dollars. There was sand as far as the eye could* reach. **4** to extend over a desired distance: *This new cord just barely* reaches. ***n-*** **1** distance a person can stretch an arm so as to grasp or touch something: *That boxer has a long* reach. *The ball was out of her* reach. **2** a stretching out to touch something: *a short* reach *from the desk to the telephone.*

3 what one is able to understand, imagine, or do: *Advanced physics is beyond my* reach. 4 (often **reaches**) great distance or expanse: *the far* reaches *of Asia.*

re·act (rē ăkt') *vi-* 1 to respond: *The ear* reacts *to sound. The patient* reacted *favorably to the treatment.* 2 to have an effect upon the person who is acting: *John's bad manners* react *against him.* 3 *Chemistry* to change by the action of two or more substances on each other.

re·ac·tance (rē ăk' təns) *n-* in electricity, the opposition to the flow of an alternating or pulsating current offered either by an induction coil (**inductive reactance**) or by a capacitor (**capacitive reactance**), measured in ohms.

re·ac·tion (rē ăk'shən) *n-* 1 response to an influence: *the ear's* reaction *to sound; a patients's* reaction *to a new medicine*; *the* reaction *of an audience to a speaker.* 2 tendency or wish to return to a former, or opposite, state of affairs: *a* reaction *against new ideas.* 3 *Chemistry* action of two or more substances on each other to form new substances.

re·ac·tion·ar·y (rē ăk'shən ĕr'ē) *n-* [*pl.* **re·ac·tion·ar·ies**] 1 person who favors a return to former conditions. 2 person who seeks to block social or political progress. ***adj-***: *a* reactionary *politician*; *a* reactionary *idea.*

reaction engine *n-* any engine that expels a stream of matter to the rear at very high speed, thus generating a powerful forward thrust.

re·ac·ti·vate (rē ăk'tə vāt', rē'-) *vt-* [**re·ac·ti·vat·ed, re·ac·ti·vat·ing**] to make active again; return to active duty or service: *to* reactivate *an army division; to* reactivate *a naval vessel.* **—*n-* re'ac'ti·va'tion.**

re·ac·tive (rē ăk' tĭv') *adj-* 1 of or relating to reaction or reactance. 2 tending to react: *a readily* reactive *behavior.* **—*n-* re'ac·tiv'i·ty.**

re·ac·tor (rē ăk'tər) *n-* large tank in which controlled nuclear fission takes place. Reactors are used for producing new nuclear fuel, steam for electric power, etc.

read (rēd) *vt-* [**read** (rĕd), **read·ing**] 1 to look at and understand the meaning of (written or printed words or symbols): *to* read *a book; to* read *a thermometer; to* read *music.* 2 to say aloud (written or printed words): *He will* read *the report to the class.* 3 to understand; get the meaning of: *The radio signals were faint, but we* read *them. The riddle was hard to* read. 4 to show; register: *The speedometer* reads *45 miles an hour.* 5 *chiefly Brit.* to study, especially at a university: *he* read *history at Oxford.* *vi-* 1 to be able to understand the meaning of written and printed matter: *half the population cannot* read. 2 to look through and interpret the meaning of written and printed matter: *She* reads *constantly. They seldom* read. 3 to speak aloud something that is written or printed: *he* reads *to the children every day.* 4 of a text, to be as one reads it: *It* reads *thus.* 5 to sound, or impress someone, in a certain way: *This report* reads *well.* ***Hom-*** reed.

read between the lines to find an implied meaning in something written or said.

read into to interpret a certain way; to find more in something written or spoken than was intended.

read out of to expel from a political party, religious organization, or other group.

read·a·ble (rē'də bəl) *adj-* 1 easy to read. 2 pleasant to read; interesting. 3 plainly written; legible. **—*n-* read'a·bil'i·ty** or **read'a·ble·ness.**

read·er (rē'dər) *n-* 1 person who reads or can read: *a slow* reader; *an avid* reader. 2 schoolbook with exercises for learning how to read. 3 person who reads manuscripts for a publisher to determine their merit. 4 professor's assistant who reads students' papers. 5 in some British universities, lecturer or instructor.

read·er·ship (rē'dər shĭp') *n-* the persons, collectively, who read a certain magazine, newspaper, writer, etc.; literary audience: *a magazine with a small* readership.

read·i·ly (rĕd'ə lē) *adv-* 1 willingly and quickly: *She* readily *came to my aid when I needed her.* 2 without difficulty; easily: *The toy is* readily *assembled.*

read·i·ness (rĕd'ē nəs) *n-* 1 condition of being prepared: *Everything is in* readiness *for the arrival of guests.* 2 willingness; favorable desire: *He shows a* readiness *to cooperate.* 3 lack of difficulty; ease: *The* readiness *with which the two substances mix.* 4 the knowledge or experience needed to progress in a learning program: *reading* readiness.

read·ing (rē'dĭng) *n-* 1 a getting of information or amusement from written or printed words. 2 public recital where something is read to the audience: *Our class gave a* reading *of Dickens' "A Christmas Carol."* 3 written or printed words to be read: *There is little* reading *in this picture magazine.* 4 interpretation or manner of interpretation: *various* readings *of the law*; *an actor's* reading *of Hamlet.* 5 record shown by an instrument: *The monthly* reading *on the electric meter.* as **modifier**: *a* reading *textbook*; *a* reading *expert*; *a* reading *room.*

reading glass *n-* large magnifying glass, often having a handle, used for reading fine print.

re·ad·just (rē'ə jŭst') *vt-* to adjust again; set in order again: *The jeweler* readjusted *my watch.* *vt-* to become adjusted again. **—*n-* re'ad·just'ment.**

read·out (rēd'out') *n-* 1 the transmitting of data from a transmitter in a spacecraft upon command from a ground station. 2 printed or displayed results from a computer.

read·y (rĕd'ē) *adj-* [**read·i·er, read·i·est**] 1 prepared, fit, or equipped to do something: *We're packed and* ready *to go on the trip.* 2 prepared for immediate use; finished; complete: *Your dress is* ready. *Dinner is* ready. 3 willing; inclined: *always* ready *to obey;* ready *to criticize.* 4 in the proper condition; also, available: *The peaches are* ready *to be picked.* 5 quick; prompt: *The students gave* ready *answers.* 6 on hand for immediate use; available: *Storekeepers must have* ready *cash.* *vt-* [**read·ied, read·y·ing**] to prepare: *The sailors* readied *the ship for the storm.*

make ready to put in order; prepare.

read·y-made (rĕd'ē mād') *adj-* 1 already prepared; ready for immediate use: *a* ready-made *chicken dinner.* 2 made in quantity from patterns; made in large numbers and many sizes: *Most shirts are* ready-made. 3 commonplace; not original; trite: *full of* ready-made *ideas.*

Any of these words means **re-** ("again") plus the meaning of the rest of the word as given in the main text.

re'ab·sorb'
re'ac·quire'
re'ac'tu·ate'
re'ad·dress'
re'ad·just'a·ble
re'ad·mis'sion
re'ad·mit'
re'ad·mit'tance
re'a·dopt'
re'a·dop'tion

---

fāte, făt, dâre, bärn; bē, bĕt, mêre; bīte, bĭt; nōte, hŏt, môre, dȯg; fŭn, fûr; to͞o, bo͝ok; oil; out; tar; thin; then; hw for wh as in what; zh for s as in usual; ə for a, e, i, o, u, as in ago, linen, peril, atom, minus

read·y-to-wear (rĕd′ ē tə wâr′) ***adj-*** of clothing, having been made from standard patterns and available in retail stores as finished garments; ready-made.

re·a·gent (rē ā′ jənt) *Chemistry* ***n-*** substance known to have a particular reaction under certain conditions, used in the analysis of chemical compounds.

[1]**re·al** (rē′ əl, rēl) ***adj-*** **1** true; genuine: *a* real *friend*; real *diamonds.* **2** actual; not imagined: *Was the figure you saw last night* real *or imaginary?* **3** in law, having to do with land or buildings: *one's* real *property.* ***adv-*** *Informal* really; very: *a* real *good book.* [from Middle English **real,** from Medieval Latin **realis,** "of or relating to things (in law)."] ***Hom-*** reel.

[2]**re·al** (rā äl′) ***n-*** [*pl.* **re·als** or **re·a·les** (rā äl′ ās)] old Spanish and Spanish-American coin, worth 1/8 of a peso (piece of eight). The real was the "bit" on the basis of which the U.S. dollar is said to have eight bits. [from Spanish **real,** "royal," from Latin **regalis.**]

real estate ***n-*** land and anything on it, including buildings, fences, trees, minerals, etc. *as* ***modifier*** **(real-estate):** *a* real-estate *business.*

real image ***n-*** in optics, the inverted image formed by the converging or focusing of light rays. Such an image can be projected on a screen. See also *virtual image.*

re·al·ism (rē′ ə lĭz′ əm) ***n-*** **1** tendency to concern oneself chiefly with facts and practical matters, rather than with ideals. **2** in art and literature, the use of subjects and characters from ordinary life and society, without the adornment of romance. **—*n-* re′ al·ist.**

re·al·is·tic (rē ə lĭs′ tĭk) ***adj-*** **1** tending to be concerned chiefly with facts and practical matters: *He is a* realistic *man, not a dreamer.* **2** of, relating to, or representing realism in literature or art. **—*adv-* re′ al·is′ ti·cal·ly.**

re·al·i·ty (rē ăl′ ə tē) ***n-*** [*pl.* **re·al·i·ties**] **1** existence in fact, as contrasted to existence in imagination, illusion, or mistaken opinion: *the* reality *of nuclear weapons.* **2** something or someone real: *When the boat left the dock, the trip finally became a* reality. **3** the sum total of real things; the actual state of things.
in reality actually; in fact.

re·al·i·za·tion (rē′ əl ə zā′ shən) ***n-*** **1** awareness; understanding: *Full* realization *of what had happened came years later.* **2** the coming or bringing of a hope, dream, fear, etc., into actual existence: *He spent years in the* realization *of his hope for a new hospital.* **3** something that comes or is brought into actual existence: *The new hospital was the* realization *of his hopes.*

re·al·ize (rē′ ə līz′) ***vt-*** **[re·al·ized, re·al·iz·ing] 1** to become fully aware of; understand fully; grasp: *She didn't* realize *that her actions were rude. He* realized *he was making a mistake.* **2** to make real; attain: *He* realized *his ambition.* **3** to get as profit: *Henry* realized *$50 on the sale of the ring.* **—*adj-* re′ al·iz′ a·ble.**

re·al·ly (rē′ ə lē, rē′ lē) ***adv-*** actually; truly; in fact.

realm (rĕlm) ***n-*** **1** kingdom; empire. **2** region or sphere: *the* realm *of fancy.* **3** special field or province: *the* realm *of science.*

real number ***n-*** one of the set of numbers comprising the rational numbers, such as 2, 3, and —1/2, and the irrational numbers, such as pi.

re·al·tor (rē′ əl tər) ***n-*** person whose occupation is buying and selling real estate; especially, a member of the National Association of Real Estate Boards.

re·al·ty (rē′ əl tē) ***n-*** [*pl.* **re·al·ties**] land and buildings; real estate. *as* ***modifier****: a* realty *office.*

[1]**ream** (rēm) ***n-*** **1** amount of paper equal to 20 quires. The ream has been counted as 480, 500, or 516 sheets, and is now usually counted as 500 sheets. **2 reams** *Informal* a large amount: *He wrote* reams *of bad poetry.* [from Old French **raime,** from Spanish **resma,** from Arabic **rismah** meaning "a bundle."]

[2]**ream** (rēm) ***vt-*** **1** to shape, enlarge, or taper (a hole) with a reamer. **2** to clean out by scraping: *to* ream *the bowl of a pipe.* [from Old English **ryman** meaning "to enlarge," from **rum,** "room."]

ream·er (rē′ mər) ***n-*** **1** rotating metal tool, often tapered, for shaping, enlarging, or tapering holes. **2** tool for cleaning a pipe bowl. **3** person who reams. **4** utensil for pressing juice from citrus fruits.

Reamers

re·an·i·mate (rē ăn′ ə māt′, rē′-) ***vt-*** **[re·an·i·mat·ed, re·an·i·mat·ing]** to bring back to life; give new strength to; encourage: *Cheers* reanimated *the losing player.*

reap (rēp) ***vt-*** **1** to cut down and gather in: *to* reap *grain.* **2** to cut a crop from: *to* reap *a field.* **3** to receive the benefit from: *He* reaped *the rewards of hard work.* ***vi-*** to cut and gather grain.

reap·er (rē′ pər) ***n-*** **1** person who cuts grain; mower. **2** machine for mowing grain. **3 the Reaper** (also **the Grim Reaper**) death.

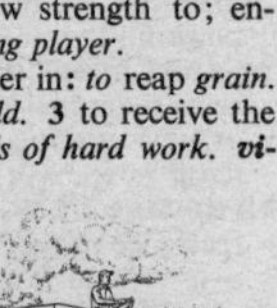

Reaper

re·ap·pear (rē′ ə pêr′) ***vi-*** to come in sight again: *The moon* reappeared *from behind the clouds.* **—*n-* re′ ap·pear′ ance.**

[1]**rear** (rêr) ***n-*** **1** the back part (of anything): *the* rear *of the bus.* **2** the space or position behind: *He was at the* rear *of the building.* **3** back part of an army or fleet: *the enemy in the* rear. ***adj-*** at, in, or near the back: *The* rear *entrance is for deliveries.* [from a shortened form of English **arrear** meaning "that in which one has fallen behind," from Old French **ariere,** from Latin **ad-** meaning "to" and **retrō,** "backward."]
at (or **in**) **the rear of** behind. **bring up the rear** to come last or at the end.

[2]**rear** (rêr) ***vt-*** **1** to bring up and educate, raise: *to* rear *a child.* **2** to grow; breed: *to* rear *animals or plants.* **3** to build; erect: *to* rear *a castle.* **4** to lift; raise up: *He* reared *his head.* ***vi-*** to rise on hind legs: *The horse* reared. [from Old English **ræran,** "to raise."]

rear admiral ***n-*** in the Navy and Coast Guard, a commissioned officer ranking next below a vice admiral and next above a captain.

rear guard ***n-*** the part of a military or naval force that guards the rear.

Any of these words means **re-** ("again") plus the meaning of the rest of the word as given in the main text.

re′ af·firm′
re′ af′ firm·a′ tion
re′ a·lign′
re′ a·lign′ ment
re′ al′ lo·ca′ tion
re′ a·nal′ y·sis
re′ an′ a·lyze′
re′ an′ i·ma′ tion
re′ an·nex′
re′ an′ nex·a′ tion
re′ ap′ pli·ca′ tion
re′ ap·ply′
re′ ap·point′
re′ ap·point′ ment
re′ ap·por′ tion
re′ ap·por′ tion·ment
re′ ap·praise′

re·arm (rē ärm′, rē′-) ***vt-*** to supply again with military arms, especially with newer or improved kinds: *The United States helped* rearm *Britain after Dunkirk.* ***vi-***: *Germany* rearmed *in the 1930's.* **—*n-* re·arm′a·ment** (rē är′ mə mənt): *the* rearmament *of a nation.*

rear·most (rêr′ mōst′) ***adj-*** nearest to or farthest in the rear; last in position: *a ship's* rearmost *mast.*

re·ar·range (rē′ ə rānj′) ***vt-*** **[re·ar·ranged, re·ar·rang·ing]** to arrange again, usually in a different order: *They* rearranged *the seating.* **—*n-* re′ ar·range′ ment.**

rear·view mirror (rêr′ vyōō′) ***n-*** small mirror that enables a driver or pilot to see behind him.

rear·ward (rêr′ wərd) ***adv-*** (also **rear′wards**) at or toward the rear: *A car mirror helps the driver to see* rearward. ***adj-***: *He had a* rearward *position.*

re·as·cend (rē′ ə sĕnd′) ***vt-*** to climb, mount, or rise again: *The firemen* reascended *the ladders to rescue other people.* ***vi-***: *The plane* reascended *through the clouds.*

rea·son (rē′ zən) ***n-*** **1** motive; purpose (for an action). **2** fact or assumption leading someone to a belief, thought, or conclusion: *We have* reasons *for believing that he is still in Mexico.* **3** ability to think; logical and rational faculty. **4** sanity: *He lost his* reason. **5** the realm of common sense or appropriateness: *anything within* reason. ***vi-*** **1** to think or argue logically: *Dr. Brown* reasons *so clearly that anyone can follow him.* **2** to try to use persuasion (with): *It's hard to* reason *with a stubborn child.* ***vt-*** **1** to think or believe on the basis of logic (takes only a clause as object): *He* reasoned *that only John could have done it.* **2** to think over carefully and completely (followed by "through"): *to* reason *through the possible results.* **3** to find or arrive at by means of logic (followed by "out"): *He* reasoned *out a good solution to the problem.* **—*n-* rea′son·er.**

by reason of because of. **in reason** reasonable; sensible. **stand to reason** to seem reasonable or logical: *It* stands to reason *that plants need water and sunshine.* **without rhyme or reason** making no sense at all; having no sensible explanation.

rea·son·a·ble (rē′ zən ə bəl) ***adj-*** **1** in keeping with reason or logic; just; fair; sensible: *a* reasonable *decision.* **2** using or able to use reason; sensible; rational: *He is a* reasonable *man.* **3** within the limits of what is probable: *a* reasonable *guess or conclusion.* **4** not expensive: *Chicken is* reasonable *this week.* **—*adv-* rea′son·a·bly. *n-* rea′son·a·ble·ness.**

rea·son·ing (rē′ zən ĭng) ***n-*** **1** act or process of using thought to reach an answer, form judgments, or come to conclusions; careful and systematic thought; logic: *Jack solved the problem after long* reasoning. **2** presentation of reasons; line of argument: *It was hard to follow the speaker's* reasoning.

re·as·sem·ble (rē′ ə sĕm′ bəl) ***vt-*** **[re·as·sem·bled, re·as·sem·bling]** to put together or bring together again: *to* reassemble *a motor.* ***vi-*** to come together again: *The class* reassembled *after recess.*

re·as·sert (rē′ ə sûrt′) ***vt-*** to state or declare again: *to* reassert *a claim.*

re·as·sume (rē′ ə sōōm′, -syōōm′) ***vt-*** **[re·as·sumed, re·as·sum·ing]** **1** to take on again as a duty, task, responsibility, etc.; undertake again. **2** to take or adopt again: *to* reassume *a position; to* reassume *a belligerent attitude.*

re·as·sur·ance (rē′ ə shŏŏr′ əns) ***n-*** **1** a giving of assurance, confidence, or courage: *With the doctor's* reassurance, *he felt he could walk again.* **2** new assurance, confidence, or courage: *He could face the future with* reassurance *that he was well.*

re·as·sure (rē′ ə shŏŏr′) ***vt-*** **[re·as·sured, re·as·sur·ing]** to give new confidence or courage to comfort: *He* reassured *his mother that he would be careful.*

re·a·wak·en (rē′ ə wā′ kən) ***vt-*** to cause (someone or something) to awaken again: *A fire alarm* reawakened *him after he dozed off. He* reawakened *my interest in skiing.* ***vi-***: *He* rewakened *with a start.*

re·bate (rē′ bāt′) ***n-*** money paid back; discount; refund: *He received a* rebate *from the store for paying cash.* ***vt-*** (*also* rĭ bāt′) **[re·bat·ed, re·bat·ing]** **1** to give back (part of a sum paid). **2** to make a reduction in: *to* rebate *a bill.*

Re·bec·ca (rə bĕk′ ə) ***n-*** in the Old Testament, the wife of Isaac and the mother of Esau and Jacob.

[1]**re·bel** (rĭ bĕl′) ***vi-*** **[re·belled, re·bel·ling]** **1** to oppose or take up arms against the law or government. **2** to oppose or resist any authority: *He* rebels *as a matter of habit.* **3** to react with anger, aversion, disgust, etc. (usually followed by "at" or "against").

[2]**reb·el** (rĕb′ əl) ***n-*** **1** one who opposes or seeks to overthrow the government. **2** one who resists any authority. *as* ***modifier***: *the* rebel *army; his* rebel *spirit.*

re·bel·lion (rĭ bĕl′ yən) ***n-*** **1** a taking up of arms against the government; revolt. **2** defiance of or resistance to any form of authority: *a period of youthful* rebellion.

re·bel·lious (rĭ bĕl′ yəs) ***adj-*** **1** opposing or defying law, government, or lawful authority: *the* rebellious *officers.* **2** resisting control; unruly: *a* rebellious *child.* **—*adv-* re·bel′lious·ly. *n-* re·bel′lious·ness.**

re·bind (rē′ bīnd′) ***vt-*** **[re·bound, re·bind·ing]** to bind or cover again: *to* rebind *a library book.*

re·birth (rē bûrth′, rē′-) ***n-*** return of activity, growth, or life; revival: *a* rebirth *of learning; a spiritual* rebirth; *the* rebirth *of flowers after a long winter.*

re·born (rē′ bôrn′) ***adj-*** born again; taking on new life; renewed: *a* reborn *delight in music.*

[1]**re·bound** (rē′ bound′) ***n-*** **1** a springing or bouncing back: *The sharp* rebound *of the ball took him by surprise.* **2** a ball or puck that has bounced or sprung back: *Bill grabbed the* rebound *and passed.*

on the rebound **1** as it bounces, up or back after hitting: *Try to catch the ball* on the rebound. **2** *Informal* recovering from a bad experience in love, work, etc.: *He was* on the rebound *from a hard first year at college.*

Any of these words means **re-** ("again") plus the meaning of the rest of the word as given in the main text.

re′a·rouse′	**re′as·sign′**	**re′at·tempt′**
re′ar·rest′	**re′as·sign′ment**	**re′au′thor·ize′**
re′as·sail′	**re′as·so′ci·ate′**	**re′a·wake′**
re′as·sem′bly	**re′at·tach′**	**re′bap′tism′**
re′as·ser′tion	**re′at·tach′ment**	**re′bap′tize′**
re′as·sess′	**re′at·tack′**	**re′bid′**
re′as·sess′ment	**re′at·tain′**	**re′bid′da·ble**
	re′at·tain′ment	**re′boil′**

---

[2]**re·bound** (rĭ bound′) *vi-* to spring or bounce back: *The ball* rebounded *off the wall.*

re·broad·cast (rē′ brŏd′ kăst′) *vt-* [**re·broad·cast** or **re·broad·cast·ed, re·broad·cast·ing**] **1** to broadcast (a radio or television program) again from the same station. **2** to broadcast (a program received from another station). *n-* program that is broadcast again.

re·buff (rĭ bŭf′) *n-* **1** sudden or unexpected denial, refusal, or snub: *I met with a* rebuff *when I asked for the car.* **2** a driving back; sudden check; defeat. *vt-* to refuse curtly; repulse; snub: *He* rebuffed *my offer.*

re·build (rē bĭld′, rē′-) *vt-* [**re·built, re·build·ing**] to make again; build anew; reconstruct: *Please* rebuild *the broken steps. vi-* to restore oneself or one's possessions to a former, normal, or improved condition: *The town* rebuilt *after the earthquake.*

re·buke (rĭ byo͞ok′) *vt-* [**re·buked, re·buk·ing**] to speak to in sharp disapproval; scold; reprimand: *The judge* rebuked *the driver for his carelessness. n-* sharp criticism of one's behavior: *He listened to the* rebuke *in silence.*

re·bus (rē′ bəs) *n-* [*pl.* **re·bus·es**] puzzle in which words, phrases, or sentences are represented by signs and pictures of objects. Example: "2 Y's" is a rebus for "too wise."

re·but (rĭ bŭt′) *vt-* [**re·but·ted, re·but·ting**] to oppose or contradict with argument, evidence, or proof, as in a debate. *—n-* **re·but′ tal**: *The affirmative will now begin its* rebuttal.

rec. **1** receipt. **2** received. **3** recipe. **4** record. **5** recorded. **6** recorder. **7** recording.

re·cal·ci·trant (rĭ kăl′ sə trənt) *adj-* refusing to obey or submit; very stubborn or obstinate; unyielding: *a* recalcitrant *horse*; *a* recalcitrant *child. n-* person or animal that refuses to obey or submit. *—n-* **re·cal′ ci·trance**: *The* recalcitrance *of that horse is maddening.*

re·call (rĭ kŏl′) *vt-* **1** to summon or call (somebody) back: *The President* recalled *Senator Baines to Washington.* **2** to bring back to mind: *That chair* recalls *something that I did years ago.* **3** to recreate; restore: *One cannot* recall *the past. n-* **1** a calling back; summoning: *the* recall *of a foreign delegate.* **2** right or procedure by which citizens may petition for a vote to remove an unsatisfactory public official from office. **3** ability to bring back to mind things once known or experienced.

beyond recall with no chance of ever being restored.

re·cant (rĭ kănt′) *vi-* to deny, and acknowledge as error, one's previous statement or belief: *He* recanted *and was forgiven. vt-*: *He publicly* recanted *his unorthodox views. —n-* **re′ can·ta′ tion.**

[1]**re·cap** (rē′ kăp′, *also* rē kăp′) *vt-* [**re·capped, re·cap·ping**] to cement, mold, and vulcanize a strip of rubber on the outer surface of (a worn pneumatic tire). *n-* tire that has been so treated. [from **re-**, "again" and **cap.**]

[2]**re·cap** (rē′ kăp′) *Informal vt-* [**re·capped, re·cap·ping**] to recapitulate: *The reporter* recapped *the news. n-* a recapitulation: *a* recap *of the news.* [from **recapitulate.**]

re·ca·pit·u·late (rē′ kə pĭch′ ə lāt′) *vt-* [**re·ca·pit·u·lat·ed, re·ca·pit·u·lat·ing**] to say again briefly; to sum up the chief points of: *After listening to the speakers, he* recapitulated *their main arguments. vi-* to repeat briefly what had been said at length. *—n-* **re′ ca·pit′ u·la′ tion.**

re·cap·ture (rē kăp′ chər) *vt-* [**re·cap·tured, re·cap·tur·ing**] **1** to take back (something lost) by force; capture again: *The Marines* recaptured *the island yesterday.* **2** to find again (something from one's past): *to* recapture *one's youth. n-*: *the* recapture *of the island.*

re·cast (rē kăst′, rē′-) *vt-* **1** to mold or cast again: *to* recast *a medal.* **2** to plan again or to lay out in a new fashion: *I must* recast *the first chapter.* **3** to provide a new cast for (a play, opera, ballet, etc.).

recd. or **rec'd.** received.

re·cede (rĭ sēd′) *vi-* [**re·ced·ed, re·ced·ing**] **1** to withdraw; move off or away: *The airplane* recedes *in the distance. The waves* recede *from the rocks.* **2** to slope gradually away from: *The beach* receded *from the base of the cliff.*

re·ceipt (rĭ sēt′) *n-* **1** a receiving: *the* receipt *of a letter.* **2** written statement stating that money or goods have been received. **3** a recipe. **4 receipts** money taken in: *the* receipts *of the game. vt-* to sign (a statement or invoice) to indicate that something has been received.

re·ceiv·a·ble (rĭ sē′ və bəl) *adj-* in business, to be collected or received: *the* receivable *bills*; *accounts* receivable.

re·ceive (rĭ sēv′) *vt-* [**re·ceived, re·ceiv·ing**] **1** to get or be given (something): *to* receive *a letter*; *to* receive *a good education.* **2** to take and hold: *a barrel to* receive *rain water.* **3** to take up; support; sustain: *These pillars* receive *the full weight of the roof.* **4** to greet or accept: *The audience* received *the speech with wild applause.* **5** to admit into one's presence; accept; welcome: *The President* received *the new ambassador.* **6** to take (radio and other wave signals) from some medium and change them into sound, speech, pictures, etc. *vi-* to be at home to visitors.

re·ceiv·er (rĭ sē′ vər) *n-* **1** someone who holds, takes, or is given something: *John was the* receiver *of the football award.* **2** receptacle; container: *an ash* receiver. **3** the part of a telephone instrument through which one speaks or listens. **4** radio, television set, or similar device that receives broadcasted signals. **5** person appointed by a court to hold and manage the property and money of a person or firm in receivership. **6** in football, a player who catches a forward pass, kickoff, etc.

re·ceiv·er·ship (rĭ sē′ vər shĭp′) *n-* **1** the office or duty of a receiver appointed by a court. **2** legal and financial condition of a person or company whose assets have been assigned to a receiver.

re·cent (rē′ sənt) *adj-* happening not long ago; occurring lately: *The* recent *storm caused all that damage. —adv-* **re′ cent·ly.** *n-* **re′ cent·ness.**

Re·cent (rē′ sənt) *n-* the second of the two epochs of the Quaternary period. The Recent includes the present geological period. *adj-*: *the* Recent *epoch.*

re·cep·ta·cle (rĭ sĕp′ tĭ kəl) *n-* **1** container; holder. **2** base of a flower where the petals, and sometimes the fruit and seeds, are attached. **3** electrical outlet in a wall or floor of a building.

re·cep·tion (rĭ sĕp′ shən) *n-* **1** a receiving: *Everything is ready for the* reception *of the first shipment.* **2** greeting or welcome: *The team was given a warm* reception. **3** formal entertainment held to greet or introduce someone: *a* reception *for the new club president.* **4** strength and clarity of radio or other broadcast signals received: *poor television* reception.

re·cep·tion·ist (rĭ sĕp′ shən ĭst) *n-* an employee in an office, usually a woman, who receives callers and directs them to the proper person or place.

re·cep·tive (rĭ sĕp′ tĭv) *adj-* willing or eager to receive new ideas, suggestions, etc.: *a* receptive *mind. —adv-* **re·cep′ tive·ly.** *n-* **re·cep′ tive·ness.** *n-* **re′ cep′ tiv′ i·ty.**

re·cep·tor (rĭ sĕp′ tər) *n-* in anatomy, one of the nerve endings involved in receiving stimuli.

Any of these words means **re-** ("again") plus the meaning of the rest of the word as given in the main text.

re′ bur′ i·al **re′ bur′ y** **re′ cal′ cu·late′**

re·cess (rĭ sĕs′, rē′ sĕs′) ***n-*** **1** brief ceasing or adjournment of normal activity: *Congress will be in* recess *until January. The class took a ten-minute* recess. **2** a notch or hollow space between cliffs or in a cliff: *a pool in a rocky* recess. **3** space set back in a wall; a niche: *a bookcase built into the* recess *of a wall.* ***vi-*** to cease or rest from normal activity for a time: *Congress* recessed *till January.* ***vt-*** **1** to put (something) into an alcove or niche: *We* recessed *the statue into the wall.* **2** to make a hollow or niche in. **3** to declare a brief pause in the official activity of: *The judge* recessed *the court at noon.*

re·ces·sion (rĭ sĕsh′ ən) ***n-*** **1** a going back or retiring; withdrawal. **2** mild business depression; moderate but noticeable decline in general economic activity.

re·ces·sion·al (rĭ sĕsh′ ən əl) ***n-*** **1** hymn sung, or music played, at the close of a church service as the clergy and choir leave the chancel. **2** music played when a service, performance, etc., is over and the audience is leaving.

re·ces·sive (rĭ sĕs′ ĭv) ***adj-*** **1** receding; tending to recede or go back. **2** *Biology* of a pair of inherited factors (genes), relating to the one which is suppressed or dominated by the other and therefore appears less often in the offspring (see also *dominant*). ***n-*** *Biology* gene that is suppressed or dominated by another.

re·charge (rē′ chärj′) ***vt-*** **[re·charged, re·charg·ing]** to renew the charge of: *to* recharge *a battery.*

rec·i·pe (rĕs′ ə pē′) ***n-*** **1** directions or formula for preparing a food: *a good* recipe *for a cake.* **2** plan for doing anything: *He offered a* recipe *for world peace.*

re·cip·i·ent (rĭ sĭp′ ē ənt) ***n-*** person or thing that receives something: *He was the* recipient *of the award.* ***adj-*** receiving or ready to receive: *a* recipient *nation.*

re·cip·ro·cal (rĭ sĭp′ rə kəl) ***adj-*** **1** done, given, or offered by each to the other; mutual: *a* reciprocal *promise.* **2** corresponding; equivalent: *a* reciprocal *privilege.* **3** working or operating together: *the* reciprocal *parts of a machine.* **4** *Mathematics* of or having to do with two numbers or expressions whose product is 1. ***n-*** **1** something given or done by each to the other; an equivalent. **2** *Mathematics* number or expression that gives a product of 1 when multiplied by a given number. The reciprocal of 3 is 1/3. The reciprocal of 3/5 is 5/3 since $3/5 \times 5/3 = 1$. ***—adv-*** **re·cip′ ro·cal·ly.**

reciprocal pronoun *Grammar* ***n-*** either of the phrases "each other" or "one another," used to show a mutual or reciprocal relation. Examples: Peter and Ed saw each other last week. We all helped one another.

re·cip·ro·cate (rĭ sĭp′ rə kāt′) ***vt-*** **[re·cip·ro·cat·ed, re·cip·ro·cat·ing]** **1** to give and take in exchange: *They* reciprocate *each other's affection.* **2** to give something in exchange for: *to* reciprocate *a favor.* **3** in mechanics, to cause to move back and forth. ***vi-*** **1** in mechanics, to move back and forth. **2** to make an exchange with one another. **3** to pay back; make a return: *She* reciprocated *with a gift.* ***—n-*** **re·cip′ ro·ca′ tion.**

re·ci·proc·i·ty (rĕs′ ə prŏs′ ə tē) ***n-*** reciprocal arrangement or relationship, especially one between two governments where each grants certain privileges to the subjects of the other.

re·cit·al (rĭ sī′ təl) ***n-*** **1** narration; telling: *They were interested in the* recital *of his adventures.* **2** performance of music or dance, especially one by a learner to show progress: *There was a piano* recital *last night.*

rec·i·ta·tion (rĕs′ ə tā′ shən) ***n-*** **1** the act of repeating (a poem, speech, etc.) from memory. **2** something repeated from memory. **3** oral presentation of a lesson: *a* recitation *in spelling.* **4** a telling; recital.

rec·i·ta·tive (rĕs′ ə tə tēv′) ***n-*** **1** in vocal music, a passage of narration or dialogue sung in a manner resembling that of speech, usually with simple chords as an accompaniment. **2** the vocal style of such a passage. *as* ***modifier***: *a* recitative *opening.*

re·cite (rĭ sīt′) ***vt-*** **[re·cit·ed, re·cit·ing]** **1** to repeat from memory: *He* recited *the poem with fine expression.* **2** to repeat in detail, especially in school: *Mary* recited *the lesson with great ease.* ***vi-***: *Mary* recited *twice last week.* ***—n-*** **re·cit′ er.**

reck (rĕk) *Archaic* ***vt-*** to reckon; heed. ***Hom-*** wreck.

reck·less (rĕk′ ləs) ***adj-*** careless; rash; heedless: *John's* reckless *driving.* ***—adv-*** **reck′ less·ly.** ***n-*** **reck′ less·ness.**

reck·on (rĕk′ ən) ***vt-*** **1** to count; add up: *The cashier* reckoned *my bill.* **2** to judge; consider: *The critics* reckoned *the play a masterpiece.* **3** *Informal* to think; suppose: *I* reckon *that it will rain.* ***vi-*** to make calculations; compute; figure. ***—n-*** **reck′ on·er.**

reckon on (or **upon**) **1** to allow for; consider: *He didn't* reckon on *our strength.* **2** to count on; rely on.

reckon with **1** to take into account: *He's a person to* reckon with. **2** to settle accounts with.

reck·on·ing (rĕk′ ən ĭng) ***n-*** **1** a settling of an account: *a day of* reckoning. **2** a counting or computing: *the* reckoning *of a ship's position.* **3** thinking or planning: *I left that possibility out of my* reckoning. **4** bill for goods or services, especially at a hotel or restaurant.

re·claim (rĭ klām′) ***vt-*** **1** to ask for and get back: *He* reclaimed *his pen at the lost-and-found office.* **2** to bring into use; obtain from waste: *to* reclaim *desert land by irrigation.* ***—adj-*** **re·claim′ able.** ***n-*** **re·claim′ er.**

rec·la·ma·tion (rĕk′ lə mā′ shən) ***n-*** a restoring to useful purpose; especially, the restoring or conversion of wasteland to productive use.

re·cline (rĭ klīn′) ***vi-*** **[re·clined, re·clin·ing]** to lie down; lean back in a restful manner: *She* reclined *on the sofa.* ***vt-***: *He* reclined *his tired body on the cot.*

re·cluse (rĕk′ lo͞os′, -lo͞oz′, rĭ klo͞os′) ***n-*** person who lives alone and shuns the company of others. ***adj-*** (*usually* rĭ klo͞os′) shut off from the world; solitary; secluded: *a* recluse *monastery.*

rec·og·ni·tion (rĕk′ əg nĭsh′ ən) ***n-*** **1** a recognizing. **2** approval; applause; praise.

re·cog·ni·zance (rĭ kŏg′ nə zəns) ***n-*** **1** legal agreement to do, or keep from doing, some particular act. **2** sum of money to be paid or forfeited if an agreement is not kept.

rec·og·nize (rĕk′ əg nīz′) ***vt-*** **[rec·og·nized, rec·og·niz·ing]** **1** to become aware of or perceive something known before; to identify: *He* recognized *his old friend's voice.* **2** to perceive; realize: *I at once* recognized *the conductor's ability.* **3** to accept; admit; acknowledge: *He* recognized *the man's right to argue his point of view.* **4** to greet in an informal way: *She* recognized *him with a wave of the hand.* **5** in a meeting, to acknowledge (someone) as the person entitled to be heard at the time. **6** to set up

---

Any of these words means **re-** ("again") plus the meaning of the rest of the word as given in the main text.

re′ chan′ nel
re′ check′
re′ christ′ en
re′ clas′ si·fi·ca′ tion
re′ clas′ si·fy′
re′ clean′
re′ coal′
re′ cod′ i·fi·ca′ tion
re′ cod′ i·fy′

---

formal relations with (a foreign government): *The United States* recognized *the new African states.* ***—adj-*** **rec'og·niz'a·ble.** ***adv-*** **rec'og·niz'a·bly.**

[1]**re·coil** (rĭ koil') ***vi-*** **1** to shrink back; show distaste or horror: *She* recoiled *at the sight of the accident.* **2** to spring back or rebound: *The rifle* recoiled *powerfully on firing.* **3** to retreat or fall back: *The* enemy *recoiled.* **4** to injure the doer as if by rebounding or backfiring against him (often followed by "on" or "upon"): *His careful plan* recoiled *and he was caught.*

[2]**re·coil** (rē'koil') ***n-*** **1** a shrinking back. **2** a springing back or rebound, especially of a gun when it is fired.

rec·ol·lect (rĕk'ə lĕkt') ***vt-*** to recall; call back to mind; remember: *He* recollected *the days of his childhood.*

re-col·lect (rē'kə lĕkt') ***vt-*** **1** to collect, or gather together again. **2** to compose (one's thoughts) again. **3** rally or summon (one's forces, courage, etc.) again.

rec·ol·lec·tion (rĕk'ə lĕk'shən) ***n-*** **1** the act of calling back to the mind or remembering. **2** person's memory or the period of time over which it extends: *The day you describe is not within my* recollection. **3** memory of something: *It is one of my happiest* recollections.

re·com·bi·nant DNA (rē kăm'bə nənt dē'ēn'a') ***n-*** DNA prepared in the laboratory by dividing and recombining DNA from different species of organisms.

re·com·bine (rē'kəm bīn') ***vt-*** [**re·com·bined, re·com·bin·ing**] to put together again; to cause to combine anew. ***vi-*** to combine again or anew. ***—n-*** **re'com'bin·na'tion.**

rec·om·mend (rĕk'ə mĕnd') ***vt-*** **1** to speak or write favorably of: *to* recommend *a new book.* **2** to advise; counsel: *The doctor* recommended *a long rest.* **3** to make pleasing or worthy of acceptance: *His careful workmanship* recommends *him.* **4** to entrust to someone's care.

rec·om·men·da·tion (rĕk'ə mĕn dā'shən) ***n-*** **1** a recommending; a speaking well of. **2** spoken or written praise: *My* recommendation *helped him to get the job.* **3** advice: *It was the doctor's* recommendation *that I should go to the hospital.*

re·com·mit (rē'kə mĭt') ***vt-*** [**re·com·mit·ted, re·com·mit·ting**] **1** to send or order back: *The judge* recommitted *the man to prison.* **2** to send (a bill or other measure) back to a committee.

rec·om·pense (rĕk'əm pĕns') ***vt-*** [**rec·om·pensed, rec·om·pens·ing**] **1** to reward; repay. **2** to make amends for; atone for: *We will* recompense *your loss.* ***n-*** something given as reward or amends.

re·com·pose (rē'kəm pōz') ***vt-*** [**re·com·posed, re·com·pos·ing**] **1** to compose again. **2** to put into another pattern; rearrange.

rec·on·cile (rĕk'ən sīl') ***vt-*** [**rec·on·ciled, rec·on·cil·ing**] **1** to bring together after a quarrel; make peace between: *We* reconciled *the young couple.* **2** to bring into harmony; settle: *They* reconciled *their differences of opinion.* **3** to bring into agreement (with); make seem consistent: *It is difficult to* reconcile *his promises with what he actually did.* **4** to make (oneself) content with; resign (oneself) to: *He* reconciled *himself to his recent bad luck.* ***—n-*** **rec'on·cil'a·bil'i·ty.** ***adj-*** **rec'on·cil'a·ble:** *I don't think their differences are* reconcilable. ***n-*** **rec'on·cile'ment.** ***n-*** **rec'on·cil'er.**

rec·on·cil·i·a·tion (rĕk'ən sĭl'ē ā'shən) ***n-*** **1** a coming or bringing together on a friendly basis after a quarrel. **2** an adjustment of differences or opinion.

re·con·dense (rē'kən dĕns') ***vt-*** [**re·con·densed, re·con·dens·ing**] **1** to condense again. **2** in distillation, to condense and collect (the evaporated liquid) in a separate container. ***vi-*** to become condensed again.

re·con·dite (rĕk'ən dīt', rĭ kŏn'-) ***adj-*** **1** very hard for the ordinary mind to understand; abstruse: *her* recondite *studies in higher mathematics.* **2** of or having to do with little known matters: *his* recondite *research in the writing of ancient Egypt.* ***—adv-*** **re'con·dite'ly** or **re·con'dite'ly.** ***n-*** **re'con·dite'ness** or **re·con'dite'ness.**

re·con·di·tion (rē'kən dĭsh'ən) ***vt-*** to restore (something) to good condition; overhaul: *She* reconditions *used cars.*

re·con·nais·sance (rĭ kŏn'ə səns) ***n-*** a careful exploring or probing into new territory in order to get information on which to base an expedition, attack, or other effort. *as* ***modifier****: a* reconnaissance *vehicle.*

rec·on·noi·ter or **rec·on·noi·tre** (rē'kə noi'tər, rĕk'ə-) ***vt-*** to make a reconnaissance of or into: *to* reconnoiter *an enemy position.* ***vi-****: The commander decided to* reconnoiter *again.*

re·con·quer (rē'kŏng'kər) ***vt-*** to conquer again; also, to regain by force (a territory that has been lost).

re·con·sid·er (rē'kən sĭd'ər) ***vt-*** to consider again; to think or talk about again: *to* reconsider *a decision.* ***—n-*** **re'con·sid'er·a'tion.**

re·con·sign (rē'kən sīn') ***vt-*** to consign again; especially, to consign (articles in transit) to another person or place.

re·con·sti·tute (rē'kŏn'stə tōōt', -tyōōt') ***vt-*** [**re·con·sti·tut·ed, re·con·sti·tut·ing**] to form or put together again: *to* reconstitute *a defeated political party.*

re·con·struct (rē'kən strŭkt') ***vt-*** **1** to build again: *to* reconstruct *a steeple struck by lightning.* **2** to construct again in exactly the same way; restore to the original form: *Our historical society* reconstructed *a colonial town.* **3** to trace from clues or suggestions.

re·con·struc·tion (rē'kən strŭk'shən) ***n-*** **1** a rebuilding. **2** something restored or rebuilt. **3 Reconstruction** restoration of the former Confederate States to membership in the United States under the **Reconstruction Acts** of 1867.

[1]**re·cord** (rĭ kȯrd', -kôrd') ***vt-*** (in senses 2 and 3 considered intransitive when the direct object is implied but not expressed) **1** to set down officially for the purpose of evidence or historical data: *to* record *the events as they occurred.* **2** to make a tape recording or phonograph

---

Any of these words means **re-** ("again") plus the meaning of the rest of the word as given in the main text.

re'col'o·ni·za'tion
re'col'o·nize'
re'col'or
re'com·mence'
re'com·mence'ment
re'com·mis'sion
re'com·pile'
re'com·pound'
re'com·press'
re'com·pres'sion
re'com'pu·ta'tion
re'com·pute'
re'con·ceive'
re'con'cen·trate'
re'con'cen·tra'tion
re'con·cep'tion
re'con'den·sa'tion
re'con·duct'
re'con·fine'
re'con·firm'
re'con'fir·ma'tion
re'con·nect'
re'con'quest'
re'con'se·crate'
re'con'se·cra'tion
re'con·sign'ment
re'con'sti·tu'tion
re'con·sult'
re'con'sul·ta'tion
re'con'tact'
re'con·tam'i·nate'
re'con·tam'i·na'tion
re'con'tract'
re'con·vene'
re'cook'
re'cop'y

record of: *to* record *the operetta.* **3** to register; tell: *Clocks* record *time.*

²re·cord (rĕk′ərd) ***n*-** **1** body of facts comprising what is known about a person or thing, especially about achievement or failure: *The student had an excellent* record. **2** official document telling of facts or events for future reference: *a congressional* record; *a court* record. **3** disk, cylinder, etc., for reproducing sound on a phonograph. **4** anything that serves as evidence of past events: *the historical* records *of this city.* **5** best or highest performance to date: *He holds the* record *in underwater swimming. as* ***modifier***: *a* record *keeper*; *a* record *player*; *a* record *attendance.*

broken record cracked phonograph record that repeats one short passage over and over again; hence, someone who nags and nags relentlessly. **off the record** not to be quoted or published: *The mayor told three reporters* off the record *about her decision.* **on record** publicly known to have said, done, or committed something.

re·cord·er (rĭ kôr′dər, -kôr′dər) ***n*-** **1** device for recording sound on phonograph records or magnetic tape. **2** any of various devices for making a permanent visual record of something changeable, often by tracing a line on a movable paper tape. **3** a secretary, town clerk, or other person who makes and keeps written records. **4** woodwind musical instrument of the flute type, made in several tonal ranges.

Recorder

re·cord·ing (rĭ kôr′dĭng, -kôr′dĭng) ***n*-** phonograph record or magnetic tape upon which music, speech, or other sound has been recorded; also, the music, speech, etc., so recorded: *a new* recording *of an old song.*

record player ***n*-** phonograph.

¹re·count (rĭ kount′) ***vt*-** to tell or repeat in detail: *She* recounted *her adventures.* [from Old French **reconter** meaning "relate."]

²re·count (rē kount′) ***vt*-** to count again: *He* recounted *his money.* ***n*-** (*also* rē′kount′) a counting again: *a* recount *of the votes.* [from **re-**, "again" plus **¹count.**]

re·coup (rĭ ko͞op′) ***vi*-** to make up for a loss, either by getting back what was lost or by getting something equal to it: *How will he* recoup *after such a disaster*? *Having lost six straight games, the team swore* to recoup. ***vt*-** **1** to regain or recover (something lost): *to* recoup *one's money.* **2** to give or restore something of value to (someone) after a loss; reimburse: *The company will* recoup *you for what you spent.*

re·course (rē′kôrs′) ***n*-** **1** an applying to someone, or a use of something, for aid in difficulties; resort; appeal: *a* recourse *to the law.* **2** person or thing so applied to or used: *Bankruptcy was my only* recourse.

re·cov·er (rĭ kŭv′ər) ***vt*-** **1** to get back; regain: *He* recovered *his health. She* recovered *her sweater.* **2** to make up: *to* recover *lost time.* **3** to obtain by legal judgment: *to* recover *damages for an injury or wrong.* ***vi*-** **1** to return to a healthy or normal state: *Jack quickly* recovered *from his cold.* **2** to win a legal award of damages, compensation, etc. **—*adj*-** **re·cov′er·a·ble.** ***n*-** **re·cov′er·er.**

re-cov·er (rē′kŭv′ər) ***vt*-** to put a new cover on.

re·cov·er·y (rĭ kŭv′ə rē) ***n*-** [*pl.* **re·cov·er·ies**] **1** a return to a healthy or normal state: *a rapid* recovery *from illness.* **2** act of getting back: *the* recovery *of a lost coat.*

recovery room ***n*-** special room in a hospital, for persons who have just undergone surgery or childbirth.

rec·re·ant (rĕk′rē ənt) ***n*-** **1** faithless person; traitor. **2** coward. ***adj*-** cowardly; unfaithful to one's duty or a cause: *a* recreant *knight.* **—*n*-** **rec′re·an·cy.**

re·cre·ate (rē′krē āt′) ***vt*-** [**re-cre·at·ed, re-cre·at·ing**] to make or create again. **—*n*-** **re′-cre·a′tion.**

rec·re·a·tion (rĕk′rē ā′shən) ***n*-** any form of amusement, relaxation, or sport: *Tennis was her favorite* recreation. *as* ***modifier***: *a* recreation *hall.* **—*adj*-** **rec′re·a′tion·al.**

re·crim·i·nate (rĭ krĭm′ə nāt′) ***vi*-** [**re·crim·i·na·ted, re·crim·i·na·ting**] to answer one accusation or charge with another. **—*n*-** **re·crim′i·na′tion.** ***adj*-** **re·crim′i·na·to′ry:** *a* recriminatory *letter.*

re·cruit (rĭ kro͞ot′) ***n*-** **1** in the Army, Air Force, Navy and Coast Guard, an enlisted person of the lowest rank. **2** new member of any organization or group. ***vt*-** **1** to enlist (soldiers, sailors, etc.). **2** to make or build up by getting new members: *We* recruited *a new party in six months.* **3** to build up; restore: *to* recruit *one's strength.* ***vi*-** **1** to obtain fresh supplies of something needed. **2** to recover health and strength. **—*n*-** **re·cruit′er:** *the* recruiter *for the Air Force held interviews at college yesterday.* ***n*-** **re·cruit′ment:** *the* recruitment *of soldiers.*

rec·tal (rĕk′təl) ***adj*-** of, having to do with, or near the rectum.

rec·tan·gle (rĕk′tăng′gəl) ***n*-** parallelogram of which all angles are right angles.

Rectangle

rec·tan·gu·lar (rĕk tăng′gyə lər) ***adj*-** shaped like a rectangle. **—*adv*-** **rec·tan′gu·lar·ly.**

rectangular prism ***n*-** six-sided prism of which opposite sides are parallel and congruent. An ordinary box is a rectangular prism.

rec·ti·fi·er (rĕk′tə fī′ər) ***n*-** something or someone that rectifies; especially, a device that changes alternating current into direct current.

rec·ti·fy (rĕk′tə fī′) ***vt*-** [**rec·ti·fied, rec·ti·fy·ing**] **1** to correct; amend: *to* rectify *a mistake.* **2** to change (an electric current) from alternating to direct. **3** to refine or purify (liquids) by distillation. **—*n*-** **rec′ti·fi·ca′tion.**

rec·ti·lin·e·ar (rĕk′tə lĭn′ē ər) ***adj*-** **1** in a straight line; straight: *a* rectilinear *motion.* **2** made of or bounded by straight lines: *a* rectilinear *pattern*; rectilinear *space.*

rec·ti·tude (rĕk′tə to͞od′, -tyo͞od′) ***n*-** uprightness of moral character; goodness; integrity.

rec·tor (rĕk′tər) ***n*-** **1** clergyman in the Protestant Episcopal Church who has charge of a parish. **2** priest in the Roman Catholic Church who is head of a religious house for men. **3** head of certain universities, colleges, and schools.

rec·to·ry (rĕk′tə rē) ***n*-** [*pl.* **rec·to·ries**] rector's house.

rec·tum (rĕk′təm) ***n*-** lower end of the large intestine that links the colon with the anus. For picture, see *intestine.*

re·cum·bent (rĭ kŭm′bənt) ***adj*-** lying down; reclining; leaning: *a* recumbent *figure.*

re·cu·per·ate (rĭ ko͞o′pə rāt′) ***vi*-** [**re·cu·per·at·ed, re·cu·per·at·ing**] to recover from illness, losses, etc.: *Joe* recuperated *quickly after the accident.* ***vt*-** to regain

---

Any of these words means **re-** ("again") plus the meaning of the rest of the word as given in the main text.
re′cou′ple **re′cross′** **re′crys′tal·li·za′tion**

---

fāte, făt, dâre, bärn; bē, bĕt, mêre; bīte, bĭt; nōte, hŏt, môre, dóg; fŭn, fûr; to͞o, bo͝ok; oil; out; tar; thin; then; hw for wh as in what; zh for s as in usual; ə for a, e, i, o, u, as in ago, linen, peril, atom, minus (one's health). **—*n*- re·cu'per·a'tion.** ***adj*- re·cu'per·a'tive:** *a* recuperative *diet.*

re·cur (rĭ kûr') ***vi*-** **[re·curred, re·cur·ring]** **1** to occur again: *His hay fever* recurs *each autumn.* **2** to return in thought or memory: *One memory often* recurred *to her.* **3** to go back to an earlier subject: *After dinner, we* recurred *to plans for our summer vacation.*

re·cur·rence (rĭ kûr' əns) ***n*-** **1** a recurring; a return; repetition: *the* recurrence *of a disease.*

re·cur·rent (rĭ kûr' ənt) ***adj*-** **1** returning or happening at intervals: *a* recurrent *fever.* **2** turning back in a reverse direction: *a* recurrent *blood vein.* **—*adv*- re·cur' rent·ly.**

re·cycle (rē'sī' kəl) ***vt*-** **[re·cy·cled, re·cy·cling]** **1** to set or establish a different cycle in (a machine, engine, or process). **2** to reset or reestablish a cycle in (a machine, engine, or process). **3** to process or treat metal, glass, etc., for reuse.

red (rĕd) ***n*-** **1** the color of the outermost stripes on the American flag, of the male cardinal bird, and of blood. Red is the lower edge of the rainbow and has the longest wavelength of all visible light. **2** (often **Red**) a Communist. ***adj*-** **[red·der, red·dest]:** *a* red *flower.* **—*n*- red' ness.**

in the red showing a net loss; losing money. **see red** to grow very angry or unreasonably angry.

red alert ***n*-** final warning given to indicate that an attack, especially an air attack, is going to take place immediately.

red·bird (rĕd'bûrd') ***n*-** any of several birds having a red plumage, such as the cardinal, or the scarlet tanager.

red blood cell ***n*-** microscopic solid, occurring naturally in the blood, that contains the red compound hemoglobin. Also **red corpuscle.**

red-blood·ed (rĕd'blŭd'əd) ***adj*-** vigorous.

red·breast (rĕd'brĕst') ***n*-** bird, especially the mature robin, having a reddish breast.

red·cap (rĕd'căp') ***n*-** porter in a railroad station.

red carpet ***n*-** red, plush carpeting rolled out for a distinguished person to walk on; hence, any elaborate and costly treatment of an arriving guest. ***adj*-** **(red-carpet):** *They gave the astronaut the* **red-carpet** *treatment.*

red·coat (rĕd'kōt') ***n*-** soldier of the British army, especially during the Revolutionary War.

Red Cross ***n*-** international organization devoted to caring for the sick and wounded in war and to giving relief in times of calamities such as floods, earthquakes, etc. The **American National Red Cross** is one of more than a hundred affiliates.

red deer ***n*-** the common deer of Europe and Asia, related to the European elk.

red·den (rĕd'ən) ***vi*-** **1** to become red. **2** to blush. ***vt*-** to make red.

red·dish (rĕd'ĭsh) ***adj*-** somewhat red. **—*n*- red'dish·ness.**

re·deem (rĭ dēm') ***vt*-** **1** to buy back; regain possession of (something) by payment in money or action: *to* redeem *a mortgage*; *to* redeem *one's reputation by good actions.* **2** to fulfill; perform: *to* redeem *a promise.* **3** to make up for; compensate: *An apology* redeemed *his rudeness.* **4** to free: *to* redeem *a friend from captivity*; *to* redeem *someone from a sinful life.* **—*adj*- re·deem' a·ble.**

redeem oneself to make atonement for something; to save oneself: *He* redeemed *himself by good works.*

re·deem·er (rĭ dē' mər) ***n*-** **1** person who saves or redeems. **2 the Redeemer** Jesus Christ as the savior.

re·demp·tion (rĭ dĕmp'shən) ***n*-** **1** act of redeeming or buying back. **2** deliverance from sin; salvation.

re·demp·tive (rĭ dĕmp' tĭv) ***adj*-** redeeming, or having the power to redeem: *a* redemptive *act.*

re·de·vel·op (rē'də vĕl' əp) ***vt*-** **1** to develop (something) again; rebuild; renew: *to* redevelop *a slum area.* **2** to make the tones of (a photographic image) stronger by treating it a second time with chemicals. ***vi*-** to develop again. **—*n*- re'de·vel' op·ment.**

red flag ***n*-** anything extremely irritating, as a red cloth is thought to be to a fighting bull.

red-hand·ed (rĕd'hăn'dəd) ***adj*-** in the very act of committing or doing something, especially something wrong: *The thief was caught* red-handed.

red·head (rĕd'hĕd') ***n*-** person who has hair of a reddish color. **—*adj*- red'head'ed:** *a beautiful,* redheaded *girl.*

red heat ***n*-** **1** condition of being red-hot. **2** temperature at which metal turns red-hot.

red herring ***n*-** **1** dried, reddish-brown, smoked herring. **2** something intended to distract attention from an important topic or issue, usually a defensive maneuver.

red-hot (rĕd'hŏt') ***adj*-** **1** red with heat; very hot. **2** inflamed with anger, enthusiasm, hatred, etc. **3** fresh from the source; up-to-the-minute: *a bit of* red-hot *news.*

re·di·rect (rē'də rĕkt') ***vt*-** to give a new direction or course to: *to* redirect *one's efforts.*

re·dis·cov·er (rē'dĭs kŭv' ər) ***vt*-** to find again; discover again.

re·dis·trib·ute (rē'dĭs trĭb'yət') ***vt*-** **[re·dis·trib·u·ted, re·dis·trib·u·ting]** to reassign; distribute again. **—*n*- re·dis'tri·bu'tion.**

re·dis·trict (rē'dĭs'trĭkt) ***vt*-** to rearrange the district boundaries of (a city, state, etc.): *The legislature* redistricted *the state.* ***vi*-:** *The town* redistricted.

red lead ***n*-** bright scarlet powder, an oxide of lead, used as a pigment in glass and as an oxidizing agent.

red-let·ter (rĕd'lĕt' ər) ***adj*-** memorable; lucky or happy: *a* red-letter *day.*

red·line (rĕd'līn) ***vt*-** **[red·lined, red·lin·ing]** to discriminate against neighborhoods considered to be poor economic risks by withholding mortgage loans or insurance funds.

re·do (rē'do͞o') ***vt*-** **[re·did, re·done, re·do·ing]** to do again; especially, to redecorate.

red·o·lent (rĕd'ə lənt) ***adj*-** **1** giving off a pleasing odor; fragrant: *The* redolent *air of the garden.* **2** suggestive: *a scene* redolent *of romance.* **—*n*- red'o·lence.**

re·dou·ble (rē dŭb'əl, rē'-) ***vt*-** **[re·dou·bled, re·dou·bling]** **1** to increase greatly. **2** to double again.

re·doubt (rĭ dout') ***n*-** **1** small enclosed fortification, especially a temporary one. **2** stronghold; citadel.

re·doubt·a·ble (rĭ dou'tə bəl) ***adj*-** arousing fear or respect; valiant; brave: *He is* redoubtable *in the face of danger or hardship.* **—*adv*- re·doubt'a·bly.**

Any of these words means **re-** ("again") plus the meaning of the rest of the word as given in the main text.

re'curved'
re'cut'
re'dec'o·rate'
re'dec'o·ra'tion
re'ded'i·cate'
re'ded'i·ca'tion
re'de·fine'
re'def'i·ni'tion
re'de·liv'er
re'de·liv'er·y
re'de·ploy'
re'de·ploy'ment
re'de·pos'it
re'de·sign'
re'de·ter'mine
re'de·vel'op·er
re'dip'
re'dis·cov'er·y
re'dis·solve'
re'dis·till'
re'dis'til·la'tion
re'do·mes'ti·cate'

re·dound (rĭ dound′) *vi-* to be reflected back, especially in such a way as to add or contribute: *Her actions* redounded *to her success.*

red pepper *n-* cayenne pepper.

re·draft (rē drâft′, rē′-) *vt-* to draft again; to make a new draft or copy of: *The candidate* redrafted *her speech before addressing the group.*

re·dress (rĭ drĕs′) *vt-* to set right; remedy: *to* redress *a wrong. n-* (*also* rē drĕs′) **1** compensation: *no* redress *for a loss of honor.* **2** a redressing: *a* redress *of a wrong.*

re-dress (rē′drĕs′) *vt-* to dress (someone or oneself) again. *vi-* to dress again.

red shift *n-* a Doppler effect shown by the spectral lines of light from distant stars, galaxies, etc., which is proportional to the rate of increase in the distance of the light source.

red·start (rĕd′stärt′) *n-* **1** in America, a black warbler that has bright orange patches on the wings and tail and is notable for its nervous, flitting flight. **2** in Europe, any of severai thrushes notable for the constant twitching motions of their tails.

red tape *n-* excessive attention to details, rules, or forms when carrying on business, especially when this causes delay or inaction: *The museum project was delayed for six months by* red tape.

re·duce (rĭ do͞os′) *vt-* [**re·duced, re·duc·ing**] **1** to make less; decrease: *to* reduce *the price.* **2** to bring from a higher position to a lower position; degrade: *to* reduce *an officer to the ranks. The fire* reduced *the family to poverty.* **3** to conquer; subdue: *The enemy* reduced *the town.* **4** to bring into some particular form or condition, especially a different physical state: *We* reduced *the rocks to pebbles.* **5** *Chemistry* to subject (a compound) to reduction. **6** *Mathematics* to change (an expression) to an equivalent but more elementary or fundamental expression: *It is easy to* reduce *15/25 to 3/5. vi-* to lose weight. **—*n-* re·duc′er.** ***adj-* re·duc′ible.**

reducing agent *Chemistry n-* substance that brings about the reduction of a compound.

re·duc·tion (rĭ dŭk′shən) *n-* **1** a reducing or being reduced. **2** amount by which something is reduced: *a* reduction *of ten dollars.* **3** a copy (of something) that is smaller than the original. **4** *Biology* the stage in meiosis in which the number of chromosomes is reduced to one half of the original number. **5** *Chemistry* the removal of oxygen from a compound. **6** *Mathematics* process of changing an equation or an expression into its lowest terms.

re·dun·dan·cy (rĭ dŭn′dən sē) *n-* [*pl.* **re·dun·dan·cies**] **1** use of more words than are strictly necessary to convey an idea; also, an instance of this. Example: I mean the exact same thing you do. **2** excessive amount; quantity greater than needed. Also **re·dun′dance.**

re·dun·dant (rĭ dŭn′dənt) *adj-* **1** using more words than are necessary; wordy; verbose; tautological. **2** exceeding what is needed or useful. **—*adv-* re·dun′dant·ly.**

re·du·pli·cate (rĭ do͞o′plə kāt′, rĭ dyo͞o′-) *vt-* [**re·du·pli·cated, re·du·pli·cat·ing**] to make again; redouble; multiply. **—*n-* re·du′pli·ca′tion.**

red·wing (rĕd′wĭng′) *n-* **1** (also red-winged blackbird) in America, a blackbird with red patches on the wings of the male. **2** in Europe, a thrush with bright-orange feathers on its side and underwings.

red·wood (rĕd′wo͝od′) *n-* **1** kind of cone-bearing evergreen tree of the Pacific coast. Although these trees grow to giant size, their cones are small. **2** the wood of this tree.

Redwood, cone and twig

re·ech·o or **re-ech·o** (rē ĕk′ō) *vt-* to echo or repeat the sounds of: *The large room* reechoed *our voices. vi-* to echo or repeat again: *My shouts* reechoed *through the cave.*

reed (rēd) *n-* **1** any of various firm-stemmed, jointed grasses growing in or near the water; also, one of their jointed hollow steams. **2** musical pipe made of the hollow stem of a plant. **3** thin, elastic piece of wood, metal, or plastic attached to the mouthpiece of certain musical instruments, such as the clarinet, producing a certain tone when air is blown over it. **4** reed instrument. **5** arrow. **6** part of a loom resembling a comb, that keeps the yarn evenly separated. *as modifier: a* reed *hut; a* reed *ensemble.* ***Hom-*** read. **—*adj-* reed′like′.**

reed instrument *n-* musical wind instrument, such as the clarinet, in which sound is produced by the vibration of one or more reeds.

reed organ *n-* harmonium.

reed·y (rē′dē) *adj-* [**reed·i·er, reed·i·est**] **1** covered with or full of reeds: *a* reedy *swamp.* **2** resembling a reed; especially, having the thinness and fragility of reeds: *the* reedy *legs of a bird;* reedy *arms.* **3** resembling a reed instrument in tone; especially, like certain high, sharp, quavering tones of the clarinet: *piping,* reedy *voices.* **—*n-* reed′i·ness.**

[1]reef (rēf) *n-* sandbar of shelf of rock of coral, at or just below the surface of the water, [from earlier English **riff,** from early Dutch or Old Norse **rif,** "a sandbank or rift in the shoreline."]

Reef in sail

[2]reef (rēf) *vi-* to fold or roll in a sail in order to reduce the area it presents to the wind: *When the wind increased, we had to* reef. *vt-*: *to* reef *a sail. n-* a reducing of the area of a sail. [from earlier English **riff,** from a Sandinavian word meaning "a sandbank; a rib."]

►Should not be confused with FURL.

reef·er (rē fər) *n-* short, tight-fitting, usually double-breasted jacket.

reef knot *n-* square knot.

reek (rēk) *n-* unpleasant smell: *the* reek *of burning rubber. vt-* to give off a disagreeable smell: *The kitchen* reeked *of gas. vt-*: *The kitchen* reeked *burning steak.* ***Hom-*** wreak.

[1]reel (rēl) *n-* **1** spool or similar device on which a length of hose, fishing line, motion-picture film, etc., may be wound for use or storage. **2** amount of motion-picture film wound on a reel. *vi-* to turn or operate a reel: *When the fish struck, I* reeled *furiously. vt-* **1** to wind onto a reel (often followed by "in"): *to* reel *a garden hose.* **2** to pull toward oneself on a line wound on a reel.

Fishing reel

Any of these words means **re-** ("again") plus the meaning of the rest of the word as given in the main test.

re′draw′ **re′draw′er** **re′ed′u·cate′**

---

fāte, făt, dâre, bärn; bē, bĕt, mêre; bīte, bĭt; nōte, hŏt, môre, dôg; fŭn, fûr; to͞o, bo͝ok; oil; out; tar; thin; then; hw for wh as in *wh*at; zh for s as in u*s*ual; ə for a, e, i, o, u, as in *a*go, lin*e*n, per*i*l, at*o*m, min*u*s

(followed by "in" or "into"): *I* reeled *in a three-foot pike. The astronaut grasped the line, and they* reeled *him into the helicopter.* **3** to wind off a spool (followed by "out"): *I* reeled *out 60 feet of rope.* [from Old English **hrēol** meaning "small spindle for winding yarn."] ***Hom-*** [1]real.
reel off to say or tell rapidly: *to* reel off a *list of names.*

[2]**reel** (rēl) ***vi-*** **1** to stagger or sway from a blow or shock; feel dizzy. **2** to seem to rock or whirl: *The room* reeled *before his eyes when he heard the great news.* **3** to walk unsteadily; stagger. [from [1]**reel,** because when people stagger, they tend to move in a circle.] ***Hom-*** [1]real.

[3]**reel** (rēl) ***n-*** **1** a lively folk dance. **2** the music for this dance. [from [1]**reel,** arising from the circular movement of the dance.] ***Hom-*** [1]real.

re·e·lect or **re-e·lect** (rē′ ə lĕkt′) ***vt-*** to elect again. **—*n-* re′ e·lec′ tion** or **re′ -e·lec′ tion.**

re·en·force or **re-en·force** (rē′ ən fôrs′) reinforce.

re·en·list or **re-en·list** (rē′ ən lĭst′) ***vi-*** to enlist again: *The* soldier *reenlisted.* ***vt-*** to enlist (someone or something) again. **—*n-* re′ en·list′ ment** or **re′-en·list′ ment.**

re·en·ter or **re-en·ter** (rē ĕn′ tər) ***vi-*** to enter again. ***vt-*** to enter (someone or something) again.

re·en·trance or **re-en·trance** (rē ĕn′ trəns) ***n-*** a reentering; second or new entry: *an actor's* reentrance.

re·ent·ry or **re-entry** (rē ĕn′ trē) ***n-*** **1** reentrance. **2** *Space* the return of a spacecraft to the earth's atmosphere after travel in space. **3** in law, the retaking possession of a property under a right reserved in a previous transfer of that property, such as when the landlord reclaims an apartment because the tenant has not paid the rent.

re·es·tab·lish or **re-es·tab·lish** (rē′ ə stăb′ lĭsh) ***vt-*** to establish again; restore: *They* reestablished *their theater group after years of inactivity.* **—*n-* re′ es·tab′ lish·ment** or **re′-es·tab′ lish·ment.**

re·ex·am·ine or **re-ex·am·ine** (rē′ ĭg zăm′ ən) ***vt-*** **[re·ex·am·ined** or **re-ex·am·ined, re·ex·am·in·ing** or **re-ex·am·in·ing] 1** to examine again; to scrutinize again. **2** to question (a witness in a legal procedure) again after the cross-examination. **—*n-* re′ ex·am′ i·na′ tion** or **re′ -ex·am′ i·na′ tion.**

re·ex·port (rē′ ĕks′ pôrt′) ***n-*** the shipping of goods out of a country, port, etc., into which they had been brought for such shipping and not for use. ***vt-***: *The shipment was* reexported *to South America.*

re·fash·ion (rē′ făsh′ ən) ***vt-*** to make over, especially in a new or different way: *She* refashioned *the coat.*

re·fec·to·ry (rĭ fĕk′ tə rē) ***n-*** [*pl.* **re·fec·to·ries**] dining hall, especially in a monastery or convent.

re·fer (rĭ fûr′) ***vt-*** **[re·ferred, re·fer·ring] 1** to direct (someone) to a certain place for information or aid: *I* refer *you to the dictionary for correct spelling.* **2** to turn over (to) for settlement or decision: *to* refer *a dispute to a referee.* **3** to explain as due to a certain cause: *The coach* referred *his failure to the sickness of the team.*
refer to 1 to seek information, advice, aid, etc., in: *to* refer to *a dictionary.* **2** to call or direct attention to; cite: *I am* referring to *the talk we had yesterday.*

ref·er·ee (rĕf′ ə rē′) ***n-*** **1** person who settles disputes and whose decision is final. **2** a judge in certain games such as basketball and football; umpire. **3** in law, a person before whom a question in a case is sent by a court to be investigated and decided, or reported to the court. ***vt-*** **[ref·er·eed, ref·er·ee·ing]** to act as an umpire in (a settlement or contest): *to* referee *a football game.* ***vi-***: *Jack* refereed *yesterday.*

ref·er·ence (rĕf′ ər əns) ***n-*** **1** a referring to an authority for information or confirmation: *a* reference *to a dictionary for the spelling of a word.* **2** (also **reference book** or **reference work**) a dictionary, encyclopedia, or other printed work intended chiefly as a source of information. **3** allusion; a mention: *This history contains many* references *to George Washington.* **4** person who may be asked about one's character or ability: *I gave Mr. Lawford as my* reference *when I applied for the job.* **5** written statement answering for someone's character or ability. **6** a passage or note in a book calling attention to some other book or passage. *as* ***modifier***: *a* reference *book.*
in (or **with**) **reference to** in regard to; concerning.

ref·er·en·dum (rĕf′ ə rĕn′ dəm) ***n-*** [*pl.* **ref·er·en·dums** or **ref·er·en·da** (-də)] **1** the submitting of a legislative act to popular vote for approval or rejection. **2** right of the people to vote upon a legislative act. **3** direct popular vote on a proposed measure.

[1]**re·fill** (rē fĭl′, rē′-) ***vt-*** to make full again; fill again.

[2]**re·fill** (rē′ fĭl′) ***n-*** replacement; a new duplicate of something used up: *a* refill *for a ball-point pen.*

re·fill·a·ble (rē fĭl′ ə bəl) ***adj-*** such as can be filled again; especially, designed so as to be refilled or reloaded when something is used up: *a* refillable *pencil.*

re·fi·nance (rē′ fī′ năns′, rē′ fə năns′) ***vt-*** **[re·fi·nanced, re·fi·nanc·ing] 1** to rearrange the terms of (a debt): *to* refinance *a loan.* **2** to alter the financial structure of (a company, stock or bond issue, etc.).

re·fine (rĭ fīn′) ***vt-*** **[re·fined, re·fin·ing] 1** to make pure; rid of all unwanted matter: *to* refine *a metal*; *to* refine *oil.* **2** to free from coarseness, clumsiness, etc.; improve; polish: *She* refined *her table manners.* **—*n-* re·fin′ er.**
refine on (or **upon**) to add refinements to.

re·fined (rĭ fīnd′) ***adj-*** **1** freed from impurities or unwanted matter: *We use* refined *sugar.* **2** having good manners and taste; cultured; free from coarseness: *a* refined *person*; *a* refined *manner.* **3** having or carried out with exactness; subtle: *He took* refined *measurements.*

re·fine·ment (rĭ fīn′ mənt) ***n-*** **1** good manners and taste; freedom from coarseness: *a lady of great* refinement. **2** a change or addition that helps to perfect something; small but important improvement: *My invention needs a few* refinements *before we market it.* **3** a freeing from impurities or unwanted matter: *the* refinement *of sugar.*

re·fin·er·y (rĭ fīn′ ə rē) ***n-*** [*pl.* **re·fin·er·ies**] factory where sugar, ore, oil, etc., is made pure or more usable, or is made into products of several grades and types.

re·fin·ish (rē′ fĭn′ ĭsh) ***vt-*** to give (a car, a piece of furniture, etc.) new coats of paint, varnish, etc.

Any of these words means **re-** ("again") plus the meaning of the rest of the word as given in the main text.

re′ em·bod′ i·ment
re′ em·bod′ y
re′ e·merge′
re′ e·mer′ gence
re′ e·mer′ gent
re′ em′ pha·sis
re′ em′ pha·size′
re′ em·ploy′
re′ en·act′
re′ en·act′ ment
re′ e·quip′
re′ e·val′ u·ate′
re′ e·val′ u·a′ tion
re′ e·vap′ o·ra′ tion
re′ ex·change′
re′ ex′ por·ta′ tion
re′ ex·port′ er
re′ face′
re′ fas′ ten
re′ fight′
re′ fig′ ure
re′ film′
re′ fil′ ter
re′ find′
re′ fin′ ish·er

[1]**re·fit** (rē fĭt′, rē′-) *vt-* **[re·fit·ted, re·fit·ting]** to make ready for use again; repair or equip with supplies again: *to* refit *a ship.* *vi-*: *We'll* refit *in Singapore.*

[2]**re·fit** (rē′ fĭt′) *n-* a making ready for renewed use.

re·flect (rĭ flĕkt′) *vt-* **1** to throw back (rays of light, heat, sound, etc.). **2** to give back an image of, as does a mirror or clear water. **3** to give back as a result: *His act* reflects *honor upon him.* *vi-* **1** to think about someone or something carefully; meditate: *The old man* reflected *about his youthful days.* **2** to think aloud.

reflect on to cast discredit on; cast doubt on: *Much of what he said* reflected on *his truthfulness.*

re·flec·tion (rĭ flĕk′ shən) *n-* **1** image of anything in a mirror or in still water: *the* reflection *of the mountains in the lake.* **2** a throwing back: *An echo is caused by the* reflection *of a sound.* **3** serious thought; meditation: *A week's* reflection *led to a new plan.* **4** statement or observation resulting from serious thought: *Einstein's* reflections *on the universe.* **5** *Physics* the turning or bouncing back of radiant energy, such as light or heat, from a surface.

Reflection in water

reflection on a casting of discredit or reproach on: *Your remarks are a* reflection on *my truthfulness.*

re·flec·tive (rĭ flĕk′ tĭv) *adj-* **1** reflecting sound or images: *the* reflective *surface of a pond.* **2** thoughtful; meditative: *a* reflective *mind.* —*adv-* **re·flec′ tive·ly.**

re·flec·tiv·i·ty (rē′ flĕk′ tĭv′ ə tē) *n-* [*pl.* **re·flec·tiv·i·ties**] **1** property or ability to throw back rays of light or other forms of radiant energy. **2** *Physics* ratio of the radiant energy reflected from a surface to the total radiant energy falling on the surface.

re·flec·tor (rĭ flĕk′ tər) *n-* **1** surface, often polished, that reflects light, heat, nuclear radiation, or other radiation. **2** any object, surface, or device that reflects or redirects radio frequency waves or sound waves. **3** telescope that uses a large mirror to reflect and focus light rays. **4** in photography, an adjustable movable screen used to reflect and control the lighting on an object.

re·flex (rē′ flĕks′) *n-* **1** in physiology, an involuntary movement or function, such as the contraction of a muscle or secretion by a gland. **2** reflection of radiant energy or sound. **3** light reflected to a shaded surface.

re·flex·ive (rĭ flĕk′ sĭv) *Grammar* *adj-* referring back to the subject of the construction. —*adv-* **re·flex′ ive·ly.**

reflexive pronoun *n-* pronoun which, although used as the object of a verb, invariably refers back to the subject. Example: *He hurt* himself *accidentally.*

re·for·est (rē fŏr′ əst, -fŏr′ əst) *vt-* to replant (deforested land) with trees. —*n-* **re′ for·es·ta′ tion:** *the* reforestation *of land by the lumber company.*

re·form (rĭ fŏrm′, -fôrm′) *vt-* to correct what is wrong with, especially by removing some evil or abuse: *The judge promised to* reform *the courts if elected.* *vi-* to give up evil ways. *n-* a change for the better; improvement: *The* reform *in the school system was long overdue.* *adj-* **1** having to do with correction: *a reform* bill; *a reform* movement. **2 Reform** of or having to do with that branch of Judaism that believes each generation has the right to accept or reject the traditions of the old, and places less importance on ritual than Orthodox Judaism. —*adj-* **re·form′ a·ble.**

re-form (rē′ fŏrm′, -fôrm′) *vt-* to reshape or reorganize: *They* re-formed *the club under a new name.* *vi-*: *After the defeat the army had to* re-form *for another attack.*

ref·or·ma·tion (rĕf′ ər mā′ shən) *n-* **1** a changing for the better; improvement in social, political, or religious affairs. **2 Reformation** religious movement in the 16th century begun by Martin Luther, which resulted in the establishment of various Protestant churches.

re·form·a·to·ry (rĭ fŏr′ mə tŏr′ ē, rĭ fôr′-) *n-* [*pl.* **re·form·a·to·ries**] school or institution for the special training of young offenders against the law and for the betterment of their character and conduct.

re·form·er (rĭ fŏr′ mər, rĭ fôr′-) *n-* person who speaks for, or attempts to carry out, improvements or reforms.

reform school *n-* reformatory.

re·fract (rĭ frăkt′) *vt-* to cause (light or other radiation) to undergo refraction.

re·frac·tion (rĭ frăk′ shən) *Physics* *n-* the bending of, or change of direction in, a ray of light or other radiation as it passes from one medium to another that has a different density, or through a medium whose density is not uniform.

Refraction

re·frac·tor (rĭ frăk′ tər) *n-* telescope whose main optical elements are a converging objective lens and an eyepiece.

re·frac·to·ry (rĭ frăk′ tə rē) *adj-* **1** disobedient; stubborn; unmanageable: *a* refractory *boy.* **2** not yielding to treatment: *a* refractory *disease.* **3** resisting heat; hard to fuse: *a* refractory *ore.* *n-* [*pl.* **re·frac·to·ries**] substance that resists heat or is hard to fuse, especially brick or clay that is resistant to heat.

[1]**re·frain** (rĭ frān′) *n-* phrase or verse repeated at regular intervals in a poem or song; chorus; also, the musical setting for these words. [from French of the same spelling, from Latin **refringere,** "to refract," literally, "to break back."]

[2]**re·frain** (rĭ frān′) *vi-* to hold oneself back; restrain oneself: *Please* refrain *from interrupting me.* [from Old French **refrener** meaning "to bridle," from Latin **frēnum,** "a bridle" and **refrēnāre,** "to bridle."]

re·fresh (rĭ frĕsh′) *vt-* **1** to make fresh again; restore; renew after fatigue, usually with food or rest: *A nap will* refresh *you.* **2** to quicken; stimulate: *His words* refreshed *my memory.* **3** to make fresh, by wetting, cooling, etc.: *The rain* refreshed *the scorched lawn.* **4** to fill again or replenish with or as if with new supplies.

re·fresh·er (rĭ frĕsh′ ər) *n-* **1** something that refreshes; also, a reminder. **2** a review of material previously studied; especially, additional instruction designed to update one's professional background: *He is taking a* refresher *in physics.* *as* **modifier:** *a* refresher *course.*

re·fresh·ing (rĭ frĕsh′ ĭng) *adj-* **1** reviving; invigorating; restoring; renewing: *a* refreshing *rain.* **2** unexpectedly

---

Any of these words means **re-** ("again") plus the meaning of the rest of the word as given in the main text.

re′ fix′	**re′ fo′ cus**	**re′ for′ ti·fy′**
re′ float′	**re′ fold′**	**re′ found′**
re′ flow′ er	**re′ forge′**	**re′ frame′**
	re′ for′ mu·late′	**re′ freeze′**

---

fāte, făt, dâre, bärn; bē, bĕt, mêre; bīte, bĭt; nōte, hŏt, môre, dȯg; fŭn, fûr; to͞o, bo͝ok; oil; out; tar; thin; then; hw for wh as in *wh*at; zh for s as in u*s*ual; ə for a, e, i, o, u, as in *a*go, lin*e*n, per*i*l, at*o*m, min*u*s

pleasing; pleasingly new, unusual, fresh, etc.: *her* refreshing *frankness.* **—*adv*- re·fresh' ing·ly.**

re·fresh·ment (rĭ frĕsh' mənt) ***n*- 1** a refreshing or being refreshed: *the* refreshment *of a shower bath.* **2** something that refreshes or revives. **3 refreshments** food, drink, or both, served at a party, meeting, etc.

re·frig·er·ant (rĭ frĭj' ər ənt) ***n*- 1** any substance, such as ice, Dry Ice, or various gases, used for refrigeration. **2** *Medicine* a drink, evaporating lotion, or other remedy used to relieve fever and thirst. ***adj*-**: *a* refrigerant *gas.*

re·frig·er·ate (rĭ frĭj' ə rāt') ***vt*- [re·frig·er·at·ed, re·frig·er·at·ing]** to make or keep cold; especially, to chill or freeze (food) for the purpose of preserving. **—*n*- re·frig' er·a' tion.**

re·frig·er·a·tor (rĭ frĭj' ə rā' tər) ***n*-** a box, cabinet, or room where food or other perishables are kept at a low temperature by means of ice or a cooling system.

reft (rĕft) ***adj*-** taken away by force.

re·fu·el (rē fyōō' əl, rē'-) ***vt*-** to put in a fresh supply of fuel: *The attendant* refueled *the buses.* ***vi*-**: *The truck* refueled *at the gas station.*

re·fuge (rĕf' yōōj') ***n*- 1** safety or shelter: *He sought* refuge *from the storm in a nearby barn.* **2** a place of safety or shelter: *The barn was a* refuge. **3** anyone or anything offering peace or rest: *Music was his* refuge *from his many cares.*

ref·u·gee (rĕf' yōō jē') ***n*-** person who flees from danger; especially, one forced to leave his own country in time of war or because of political or religious persecution.

re·ful·gent (rĭ fōōl' jənt, -fŭl' jənt) ***adj*-** casting a brilliant light; shining; radiant: *a* refulgent *diamond.* **—*n*- re·ful' gence** or **re·ful' gen·cy.** ***adv*- re·ful' gent·ly.**

¹re·fund (rĭ fŭnd') ***vt*-** to give back (money previously paid): *Please* refund *my payment on the camera.* **—*adj*- re·fund' a·ble**: *The first payment is* refundable *within thirty days if you decide not to buy.*

²re·fund (rē' fŭnd') ***n*-** a repayment; also, money paid back or to be paid back.

re·fur·bish (rē fûr' bĭsh) ***vt*-** to furbish again; renovate or improve; brighten up: *to* refurbish *a room.*

re·fus·al (rĭ fyōō' zəl) ***n*- 1** a refusing or denying; rejection or denial of anything offered or asked: *His plans met with a* refusal. **2** the right to accept or reject something before others have the opportunity: *She was to have first* refusal *if the property was offered for sale.*

¹re·fuse (rĭ fyōōz') ***vt*- [re·fused, re·fus·ing] 1** to decline to accept; reject: *to* refuse *an invitation*; *to* refuse *an offer*; *to* refuse *a bribe.* **2** to decline to give; deny: *to* refuse *permission*; *to* refuse *food.* ***vi*-** to decline to do something: *I asked him to leave but he* refused.

²ref·use (rĕf' yōōs', -yōōz') ***n*-** waste matter; garbage.

re·fute (rĭ fyōōt') ***vt*- [re·fut·ed, re·fut·ing]** to prove false: *It was easy to* refute *his argument.* **—*adj*- re·fut' a·ble**: *His argument is easily* refutable. ***n*- ref' u·ta' tion**: *the* refutation *of a statement.* ***n*- re·fut' er.**

re·gain (rĭ gān') ***vt*- 1** to get back; recover: *to* regain *leadership.* **2** to reach again; return to: *The driver* regained *the main road after a detour.*

re·gal (rē' gəl) ***adj*- 1** of or having to do with a king; royal: *the* regal *power*; regal *descent.* **2** fit for a king; splendid: *a* regal *feast.* **—*n*- re·gal' i·ty** (rĭ găl' ə tē). ***adv*- re' gal·ly.**

re·gale (rĭ gāl') ***vt*- [re·galed, re·gal·ing] 1** to entertain or amuse; delight: *They* regaled *their friends with music and a banquet.* **2** to feed sumptuously: *The girls* regaled *themselves on wild strawberries.* ***vi*-** to feast: *The boys* regaled *on apples.* **—*n*- re·gale' ment.**

re·ga·li·a (rĭ gāl' yə) ***n*- *pl.* 1** signs or emblems of royalty, such as the crown and scepter. **2** insignia of a special group such as a fraternal order. **3** clothes for a special occasion; finery.

re·gard (rĭ gärd') ***vt*- 1** to look at closely; scrutinize: *Peter* regarded *the beggar suspiciously.* **2** to consider: *Do you* regard *him as fit for the job?* **3** to pay attention to; heed: *Now* regard *what I have to say.* **4** to concern: *My decision* regards *your happiness.* **5** to admire or esteem: *She* regards *scholarship highly.* ***n*- 1** consideration; care: *to feel* regard *for one's safety.* **2** esteem; respect: *a high* regard *for truth.* **3** a look; gaze. **4 regards** best wishes: *Please give them my* regards.

in (or **with**) **regard to** in reference to; with respect to: *John spoke* in regard to *the meeting.* **in this** (or **that**) **regard** regarding a particular point or matter.

re·gard·ful (rĭ gärd' fəl) ***adj*- 1** taking notice; heedful; attentive. **2** respectful. **—*adv*- re·gard' ful·ly.** ***n*- re·gard' ful·ness.**

re·gard·ing (rĭ gär' dĭng) ***prep*-** concerning; about; in respect to.

re·gard·less (rĭ gärd' ləs) ***adj*-** heedless; showing no consideration for; unmindful: *He continued to nag,* regardless *of her feelings.* ***adv*- *Informal*** anyway: *I am going out tonight,* regardless. **—*adv*- re·gard' less·ly.**

re·gat·ta (rĭ gä' tə, -găt' ə) ***n*-** boat race or races.

re·gen·cy (rē' jən sē) ***n*- [*pl.* re·gen·cies] 1** office, powers, or government of a regent or body of regents. **2** body of regents ruling a country. **3** period of government of, or territory governed by, a regent or body of regents. **4 Regency** in English history, the period from 1811-1820 during the rule of George, Prince of Wales, later George IV. ***adj*- Regency** of or having to do with the furniture and dress of the period in English history from 1811-1820.

¹re·gen·er·ate (rĭ jĕn' ə rāt') ***vt*- [re·gen·er·at·ed, re·gen·er·at·ing] 1** to cause to be spiritually reborn or morally improved. **2** to put new vitality and energy into; vitalize again; revive: *His discovery* regenerated *a whole field of study.* **3** *Biology* to grow (new tissue, a new limb or organ, etc.) in place of something lost or damaged. **4** in certain radio circuits, to amplify (a current, output, signal, etc.) by feeding a part of the output back into the input. ***vi*- 1** to form again: *The lizard's tail* regenerated. **2** to become healthy and vital again: *The tissue* regenerated *in six days.* **3** to be spiritually reborn or morally improved. **—*n*- re·gen' er·a' tion.** ***adj*- re·gen' er·a' tive.**

²re·gen·er·ate (rĭ jĕn' ər ət) ***adj*- 1** completely renewed and improved, as if born anew: *a* regenerate *city.* **2** undergoing regeneration: *a* regenerate *corporation.*

re·gent (rē' jənt) ***n*- 1** person appointed to govern when a ruler is under age or incapable. **2** member of the governing board in some state universities.

reg·i·cide (rĕj' ə sīd') ***n*- 1** the killing of a king. **2** person who kills or assists in killing a king.

re·gime or **ré·gime** (rĭ zhēm', rā-') ***n*- 1** a system of government; method of ruling; also, period of rule of a system of government: *a* communist *regime*; *during the* regime *of Napoleon.* **2** orderly way of living to improve health, treat an illness, etc.; regimen.

reg·i·men (rĕj' ə mən) ***n*- 1** a system of diet, exercise, sleep, and daily routine, prescribed for some special purpose. **2** government; control.

Any of these words means **re-** ("again") plus the meaning of the rest of the word as given in the main text.

re' front'
re' fur' nish
re' gath' er
re' gen' er·a' tor
re' gild'

[1]**reg·i·ment** (rĕj′ ə mənt) ***n-* 1** group of battalions under the command of a colonel. **2** any large number of persons; multitude. [from Old French **regiment** meaning a military division, from the same Latin sources as [2]**regiment.**]

[2]**reg·i·ment** (rĕj′ ə mĕnt′) ***vt-* 1** to organize into a rigid pattern or system for the sake of discipline and control: *The dictator* regimented *even the children.* **2** to require the same rigid pattern of behavior from all: *That school is very strict and* regiments *the boys.* [from Late Latin **regimentum,** from Latin **regere,** "to rule; govern."]

reg·i·men·tal (rĕj′ ə mĕn′ təl) ***adj-*** of or having to do with a regiment: *a* regimental *uniform.*

reg·i·men·tals (rĕj′ ə mĕn′ təlz) ***n- pl.* 1** uniform of a regiment. **2** any military uniform.

reg·i·men·ta·tion (rĕj′ ə mən tā′ shən) ***n-*** a regimenting or bringing into line with a plan or system; an organizing into uniform groups: *the* regimentation *of workers.*

re·gion (rē′ jən) ***n-* 1** a part of the earth having at least one unifying trait throughout its area, which sets it apart from surrounding areas: *an industrial* region; *the Rocky Mountain* region; *tropical* regions. **2** any part of the land, sea, air, or space: *the upper* regions *of the atmosphere.* **3** area or sphere of thought or action: *the* region *of politics*; *in the* region *of science.* **4** division or part of the body: *the* region *of the liver.*

re·gion·al (rē′ jə nəl) ***adj-* 1** of or relating to a whole region, especially a geographical one: *the* regional *distribution of rainfall.* **2** of or having to do with a particular region; sectional; local: *a* regional *election.* **—*adv-* re′ gion·al·ly.**

re·gion·al·ism (rē′ jə nə lĭz′ əm) ***n-* 1** special attention or devotion to a particular region. **2** expression, manner of dress, custom, or other characteristic of a particular region. **—*adj-* re′ gion·al·ist′ ic.**

reg·is·ter (rĕj′ ĭs tər) ***n-* 1** official written record; also, a book for keeping such records, or an entry in it: *a* register *of births and deaths.* **2** mechanical device that records: *a cash* register. **3** person who keeps a record; registrar: *He is* register *of deeds.* **4** registration; registry. **5** in a heating system, device that regulates the passage of air. **6** *Music* (1) set of organ pipes controlled by one stop. (2) range or a specific part of the range of a human voice or instrument: *the alto* register. **7** in printing, (1) exact alignment or correspondence of the lines, margins, columns, etc., on both sides of a sheet. (2) correct or exact placing of one color upon another. ***vt-* 1** to enter in a record; record officially: *to* register *a birth*; *to* register *securities.* **2** to enroll: *to* register *students.* **3** to show on an instrument or scale: *Yesterday the thermometer* registered *97°.* **4** to show (a response or reaction) through movement of the face or body: *He* registered *surprise.* **5** to protect (mail) from possible loss by paying a fee at the post office to have it specially recorded. **6** in printing, to adjust so as to obtain correct alignment. ***vi-* 1** to enter one's name in a record or list: *They* registered *for voting.* **2** *Informal* to make an impression. **3** in printing, to be in correct alignment.

registered nurse ***n-*** nurse who has successfully completed two to four years of formal training and has been licensed by a state authority to administer but not prescribe medicines or treatment, to assist surgeons, etc.

reg·is·trar (rĕj′ ĭs trär′) ***n-*** official who keeps records: *a* registrar *in a college or university.*

reg·is·tra·tion (rĕj′ ĭs trā′ shən) ***n-* 1** a registering or entering of names, facts, etc., in a register. **2** entry in a register. **3** number of persons registered; total enrollment. **4** document showing a registering: *an* automobile *registration.*

reg·is·try (rĕj′ ĭs trē′) ***n-*** [*pl.* **reg·is·tries**] **1** a registering; registration. **2** a ship's nationality as evidenced by its registration. **3** written account or record of births, marriages, deaths, etc. **4** place where such a record is kept.

[1]**re·gress** (rĭ grĕs′) ***vi-*** to go back; return, especially to an earlier condition: *The project* regressed *to the level of six months ago.* **—*adj-* re·gres′ sive:** *a* regressive *fashion.*

[2]**re·gress** (rē′ grĕs′) ***n-* 1** passage back; way of return: *A place which offers no* regress. **2** power or privilege of returning: *the right of free egress and* regress. **3** retrogression.

re·gres·sion (rĭ grĕsh′ ən) ***n-* 1** a going back in movement or development. **2** *Biology* the return to an earlier, more primitive or more general form. **3** *Medicine* a lessening of the symptoms of a disease. **4** in psychiatry, a partial return to earlier and immature patterns of thought and behavior, usually as a means of escaping stress and responsibility.

re·gret (rĭ grĕt′) ***vt-*** **[re·gret·ted, re·gret·ting] 1** to be sorry about: *to* regret *a mistake.* **2** to remember with a sense of loss: *to* regret *the years gone by.* ***n-* 1** distress of mind over some past event, with the wish that it had been otherwise: *He expressed* regret *for his harsh words.* **2** sadness; disappointment: *I hear with* regret *that you will not come.* **3 regrets** courteous reply declining an invitation: *to send one's* regrets.

re·gret·ful (rĭ grĕt′ fəl) ***adj-*** feeling or showing regret; remembering with sorrow. **—*adv-* re·gret′ ful·ly. *n-* re·gret′ ful·ness.**

re·gret·ta·ble (rĭ grĕt′ ə bəl) ***adj-*** to be regretted; lamentable; deplorable. **—*adv-* re·gret′ ta·bly.**

re·group (rē gro͞op′, rē′-) ***vt-*** to form into new groups: *The coach* regrouped *the players into teams of equal ability.* ***vi-*:** *The troops fell back and* regrouped.

Regt. 1 regent. **2** regiment.

reg·u·lar (rĕg′ yə lər) ***adj-* 1** usual; habitual; customary: *a* regular *seat in school.* **2** habitual or consistent in action; orderly: *a* regular *routine*; *a* regular *life.* **3** happening at even intervals of time: *the* regular *tick of a clock*; *the* regular *beating of the heart.* **4** happening again and again at fixed times: *the* regular *holiday of Thanksgiving*; regular *meals.* **5** even in form, arrangement, etc.; symmetrical: *Ann's features are very* regular. **6** *Informal* thorough; complete: *a* regular *rascal.* **7** conforming to established rules, customs, party platform, etc.; orthodox: *a* regular *Republican.* **8** belonging to a religious order; bound by religious rule: *the* regular *clergy.* **9** *Military* belonging to or making up a permanent armed force: *a* regular *Navy officer*; regular *Army.* **10** *Grammar* following the usual rules of declension, conjugation, or comparison: *a* regular *verb.* **11** *Mathematics* (1) of a polygon, having all sides and all angles equal. (2) of a polyhedron, having faces all of which are congruent regular polygons, and having all the angles congruent where these faces join. **—*adv-* reg′ u·lar·ly.**

Any of these words means **re-** ("again") plus the meaning of the rest of the word as given in the main text.

re′ glaze′	**re′ grade′**	**re′ grow′**
re′ glue′	**re′ grind′**	**re′ growth′**

---

fate, făt, dâre, bärn; bē, bĕt, mêre; bīte, bĭt; nōte, hŏt, môre, dŏg; fŭn, fûr; to͞o, bo͝ok; oil; out; tar; thin; then; hw for wh as in *wh*at; zh for s as in u*s*ual; ə for a, e, i, o, u, as in *a*go, lin*e*n, per*i*l, at*o*m, min*u*s

regular army *n-* permanent army kept up in peace as well as in war; standing army.

reg·u·lar·i·ty (rĕg'yə lĕr' ə tē, -lăr' ə tē) *n-* the condition of being regular; evenness; balance.

reg·u·late (rĕg' yə lāt') *vt-* **[reg·u·lat·ed, reg·u·lat·ing] 1** to govern or correct according to rule or custom: *to* regulate *a person's own habits.* **2** to put into working order; adjust: *He* regulated *the furnace.* **3** to make regular or even; control: *to* regulate *the temperature of a room.* **4** to put or keep in proper order: *to* regulate *a household.* **—*adj-* reg' u·la' tive** or **reg' u·la·to' ry** (-yə lə tôr' ē): *a* regulative *device on a furnace; a* regulatory *agency of the government.*

reg·u·la·tion (rĕg'yə lā' shən) *n-* **1** a regulating or being regulated: *the* regulation *of temperatures; foreign trade dwindling from too much* regulation. **2** a rule, direction, or law: *hospital* regulations. ***adj-*** conforming to a regular style, method, or rule: *a* regulation *uniform.*

reg·u·la·tor (rĕg' yə lā'tər) *n-* person or thing that regulates; especially, any of various devices that automatically control all or part of a machine or system.

re·gur·gi·tate (rĭ gûr' jə tāt') *vt-* **[re·gur·gi·tat·ed, re·gur·gi·tat·ing]** to cause to surge or rush back; especially, to cast out again from the stomach. ***vi-*** to vomit. **—*n-* re·gur' gi·ta' tion.**

re·ha·bil·i·tate (rē'hə bĭl' ə tāt') *vt-* **[re·ha·bil·i·tat·ed, re·ha·bil·i·tat·ing] 1** to bring back to a healthy condition or to a state of useful activity through treatment, training, etc.: *The doctors are trying to* rehabilitate *the invalid.* **2** to restore to a good condition: *to* rehabilitate *an old house.* **3** to restore to a former state, rank, or privilege; reinstate. **—*n-* re' ha·bil' i·ta' tion.**

re·hash (rē' hăsh') *vt-* to use or go over again; work into a new form, especially without real change or improvement: *The writer* rehashed *an old plot.* ***n-*** **1** a going over again: *a* rehash *of the argument.* **2** something made over into a new form: *Her book is* a rehash *of old stories.*

re·hear·ing (rē' hêr' ĭng) *n-* in law, a new hearing or consideration of a case by the court in which the case was originally tried.

re·hears·al (rĭ hûr' səl) *n-* **1** a practice performance, especially of a play, opera, etc., in preparation for a public performance. **2** a telling over: *a* rehearsal *of his summer experiences in Europe.*

re·hearse (rĭ hûrs') *vt-* **[re·hearsed, re·hears·ing] 1** to practice in preparation for a public performance; also, to train by rehearsal: *They* rehearsed *the play. The conductor* rehearsed *the soprano.* **2** to give an account of; tell: *He* rehearsed *the story of his life.* **3** to repeat; tell over; recite from beginning to end: *She* rehearsed *in detail the old story.* ***vi-*** to practice or take part in a private performance: *The actors* rehearsed *daily.*

re·house (rē houz') *vt-* **[re·housed, re·hous·ing]** to provide with, or place in, other housing.

reign (rān) *n-* **1** supreme rule; royal power. **2** period of rule, as of a king: *the* reign *of George III.* ***vi-*** **1** to rule as a monarch. **2** to hold sway; prevail: *Terror* reigned *in the village.* ***Homs-*** rain, rein.

re·im·burse (rē'ĭm bûrs') *vt-* **[re·im·bursed, re·im·burs·ing]** to pay back; repay (a person): *The company* reimbursed *the woman for her expenses on the trip.* **—*n-* re' im·burse' ment.**

rein (rān) *n-* **1** one of the two long straps attached to the bit of a horse to guide and control it. **2** (often **reins**) any means of restraint or control: *a tight* rein *on one's temper; the* reins *of government.* ***vt-*** **1** to hold in, direct, or stop by means of control straps: *to* rein *a horse.* **2** to control; check: *to* rein *one's anger.* ***Homs-*** rain, reign.

draw rein to stop. **give free rein to** to give complete freedom to.

rein in (or **up**) to stop a horse by means of reins.

Reins

re·in·car·na·tion (rē'ĭn'kär'nā' shən) *n-* new embodiment or incarnation; especially, in certain cults and religions, the rebirth of the soul in another body.

rein·deer (rān' dêr') *n-* [*pl.* **rein·deer** or **rein·deers**] a northern deer with large, branching antlers, related to the caribou. It is easily tamed, and is valued as a draft animal and for its milk, meat, and hide.

Reindeer, about 6 ft. long

re·in·force (rē'ĭn fôrs') *vt-* **[re·in·forced, re·in·forc·ing]** to add to for strength: *to* reinforce *an army platoon; to* reinforce *a sleeve.*

reinforced concrete *n-* concrete containing metal bars or mesh for strength.

re·in·force·ment (rē'ĭn fôrs' mənt) *n-* **1** a strengthening or a being strengthened by addition of something. **2** person or thing added in order to strengthen. **3 reinforcements** fresh troops, supplies, ships, etc., sent to an area of combat.

re·in·state (rē'ĭn stāt') *vt-* **[re·in·stat·ed, re·in·stat·ing]** to put back into a former position or condition: *They* reinstated *him as chairman.* **—*n-* re' in·state' ment.**

re·in·sure (rē'ĭn shoor') *vt-* **[re·in·sured, re·in·sur·ing]** of an insurance company, to share (the risk involved in an insurance contract) with another company.

re·in·ter·pret (rē'ĭn tûr' prət) *vt-* to interpret in a new or different manner.

re·in·vest (rē'ĭn vĕst') *vt-* to invest (money) again; especially, to invest (income from other investments).

re·in·vig·o·rate (rē'ĭn vĭg' ə rāt') *vt-* **[re·in·vig·o·rat·ed, re·in·vig·o·rat·ing]** to impart new vigor to.

re·is·sue (rē ĭsh' ōō) *n-* a publishing again of something previously published and allowed to go out of print; also, a copy of the thing published: *This book is a* reissue. ***vt-*** **[re·is·sued, re·is·su·ing]** to issue again.

re·it·er·ate (rē ĭt' ə rāt') *vt-* **[re·it·er·at·ed, re·it·er·at·ing]** to say or do again or several times: *to* reiterate *a complaint.* **—*n-* re·it' er·a' tion. *adj-* re·it' er·a' tive.**

¹re·ject (rĭ jĕkt') *vt-* **1** to turn down; refuse to take, believe, use, etc.: *He* rejected *my offer of assistance.* **2** to throw away as worthless; discard: *They* rejected *all imperfect specimens.* **—*n-* re·jec' tion.**

²re·ject (rē' jĕkt') *n-* rejected person or thing.

re·joice (rĭ jois') *vi-* **[re·joiced, re·joic·ing]** to feel or express joy or happiness: *I* rejoice *to hear of your good*

Any of these words means **re-** ("again") plus the meaning of the rest of the word as given in the main text.

re' ham' mer
re' han' dle
re' hear'
re' heat'
re' im·pose'
re' im' po·si' tion
re' in·car' nate'
re' in·cor' po·rate'
re' in·fec' tion
re' in·sert'
re' in·ser' tion
re' in' tro·duce'
re' in' tro·duc' tion

luck. ***vt-*** to gladden; delight: *The sight of her gifts* rejoiced *Mary greatly.*

[1]**re·join** (rĭ join′) ***vi-*** to answer; reply to: *"I don't need any help, thank you," Mary* rejoined *to her brother's offer*

[2]**re·join** (rē′ join′) ***vt-*** **1** to join together again. **2** to return to after separation: *Frank will* rejoin *us soon.*

re·join·der (rĭ join′ dər) ***n-*** a reply or retort, especially an answer to a reply.

re·ju·ve·nate (rĭ jo͞o′ və nāt′) ***vt-*** **[re·ju·ve·nat·ed, re·ju·ve·nat·ing]** to make young again; to cause to feel young again. **—*n-* re·ju′ ve·na′ tion.**

re·kin·dle (rē kĭn′ dəl, rē′-) ***vt-*** **[re·kin·dled, re·kin·dling]** to set fire to again; also, to arouse (hope, enthusiasm, etc.) again: *to* rekindle *hope.* ***vi-***: *His hopes* rekindled.

re·lapse (rĭ lăps′) ***vi-*** **[re·lapsed, re·laps·ing] 1** to fall back into a former state, practice, habit, etc.; especially, to fall back into wrongdoing; backslide: *He* relapsed *into silence. The tribe* relapsed *into paganism.* **2** to fall back into illness after a state of partial recovery. ***n-*** *(also* rē′ lăps′) a return to a former condition or habit; especially, a setback in recovery from a disease.

re·late (rĭ lāt′) ***vt-*** **[re·lat·ed, re·lat·ing] 1** to tell; narrate. **2** to connect; associate: *The detective tried to* relate *the two clues.* ***vi-*** to be connected or associated; refer or allude (to): *The letter* relates *to his success.*

re·lat·ed (rĭ lā′ təd) ***adj-*** **1** connected by blood or marriage. **2** connected in some way. **—*n-* re·lat′ ed·ness**

re·la·tion (rĭ lā′ shən) ***n-*** **1** a telling or narrating: *We heard his* relation *of what had happened.* **2** a connection between two or more things; relevance of one to another; position with respect to each other; relationship: *the* relation *of poverty to crime*; *the* relation *of climate to agriculture.* **3** family connection, especially by birth: *She's of no* relation *to me.* **4** *Informal* a relative: *He's one of my* relations. **5** *Mathematics* a set of ordered pairs. **6 relations** dealings; affairs: *business* relations.

in (or **with**) **relation to** in regard to; concerning.

re·la·tion·ship (rĭ lā′ shən shĭp′) ***n-*** **1** connection. **2** tie of blood, marriage, or affection between people.

re·l·a·tive (rĕl′ ə tĭv) ***adj-*** **1** measured by comparison; comparative: *the* relative *speeds of a car and a bicycle.* **2** having meaning only as related to something else: *More, less, small, and large are* relative *words.* ***n-*** **1** person connected by blood or marriage. **2** *Grammar* (traditionally called **relative pronoun**) word that introduces a subordinate clause that modifies a preceding noun, pronoun, noun phrase, or noun clause, called the antecedent of the relative. The relatives are "who," "whose," "whom," "that," "which," "when," and "where." Examples:

The boy who *just entered is class president.* (relative as subject)

Where is the gyroscope that *was on the table?* (relative as subject)

There's the man whom *I met last night.* (relative as object of a verb)

There's the girl of whom *I was speaking.* (relative as object of a preposition.)

There's the boy whose *wallet I found.* (relative as determiner)

This is the place where *he was shot.* (relative as adverb)

This is the time when *he should arrive.* (relative as adverb)

relative clause ***n-*** subordinate clause introduced by one of the relatives.

relative humidity ***n-*** the ratio, in percent, of the actual amount of water vapor in the air to the amount that would be present if the air were saturated at the same temperature and pressure.

rel·a·tive·ly (rĕl′ ə tĭv lē) ***adv-*** in comparison with other persons or things: *In his town, Mr. Jackson was considered* relatively *rich.*

rel·a·tiv·ism (rĕl′ ə tə vĭz′ əm) ***n-*** the assigning of worth and importance to things on the basis of their relation to other things, and therefore giving nothing a fixed and absolute value. **—*n-* rel′ a·tiv·ist′.**

rel·a·tiv·i·ty (rĕl′ ə tĭv′ ə tē) ***n-*** **1** condition of being relative; relation: *the* relativity *among several ideas.* **2** *Physics* (1) theory of **special relativity** formulated by Albert Einstein, according to which (a) the laws of physics are the same for any two systems that move uniformly with respect to each other; (b) all motion is described relative to something, and the idea of absolute motion is meaningless; (c) nothing in the universe can travel faster than the speed of light; (d) the speed of light in a uniform medium is constant in all directions, in spite of any motion of the light source; and (e) mass and energy are equivalent, and their relation is stated in the equation $E = mc^2$. (2) theory of **general relativity** also formulated by Albert Einstein, which applies the principles of special relativity to the law of gravitation and the motion of celestial objects.

re·lax (rĭ lăks′) ***vt-*** **1** to make less tight or tense; slacken: *to* relax *one's grip.* **2** to make less strict, severe, or harsh: *to* relax *the rules.* **3** to ease; relieve from strain: *Playing folk songs on the banjo* relaxes *me.* ***vi-*** **1** to become less tense; to rest in mind and body: *After work John* relaxed *with a mystery novel.* **2** to become less tight, firm, or severe: *His grip* relaxed.

re·lax·ant (rĭ lăk′ sənt) *Medicine* ***n-*** any medication that relieves tension; especially, a drug that relieves muscular spasms. ***adj-***: *a* relaxant *drug.*

re·lax·a·tion (rē′ lăk′ sā′ shən) ***n-*** **1** a relaxing or being relaxed: *a* relaxation *of the rules*; relaxation *of the muscles.* **2** a resting; a seeking of amusement: *He plays tennis for* relaxation. **3** thing that provides rest and amusement; recreation: *My* relaxation *is tennis.*

re·lay (rē′ lā′) ***n-*** **1** team, shift, or other similar group that relieves another such group on a job or in a game or race: *They worked in* relays. *I was in the second* relay. **2** in electricity, a switch of the solenoid type, usually operating at a low voltage. **3** (also **relays**) in sports, a race among teams, in which each person covers a certain distance and starts the next person on the team by touching or by passing on a rod or other token. *as* ***modifier***: *a* relay *circuit*; relay *race.* ***vt-*** (*also* rĭ lā′) to pass (something) along: *I will* relay *the news to her.*

re-lay (rē′ lā′) ***vt-*** **[re-laid, re-lay·ing]** to lay again: *We* re-laid *the tiles on the kitchen floor.*

relay race ***n-*** running race between teams, in which each member of a team runs part of the course.

re·lease (rĭ lēs′) ***vt-*** **[re·leased, re·leas·ing] 1** to let go; unlock: *He* released *the brakes of the car.* **2** to set free: *to* release *a prisoner.* **3** to free from obligation or penalty: *to* release *a person from a promise.* **4** in law, to give up title to; surrender: *Mr. Right* released *his summer home*

Any of these words means **re-** ("again") plus the meaning of the rest of the word as given in the main text.

re′ judge′ **re′ knit′** **re′ learn′**

---

to the bank. **5** to permit publication, use, etc.: *to* release *a news item or motion picture.* ***n-*** **1** act or process of setting free; also, the result of this: *the* release *of a prisoner*; *a* release *from duty*; *a* release *from pain*; *a* release *from a debt.* **2** an order to set free; written discharge: *The prisoner's* release *arrived today.* **3** publication; a making public: *the* release *of a new movie.* **4** something published or placed before the public: *a press* release. **5** any device for unlocking. **6** in law, document stating that someone has surrendered a claim to something; quitclaim.

re-lease (rē′ lēs′) ***vt-*** **[re-leased, re-leas·ing]** to lease again: *We* re-leased *the apartment for two more years.*

rel·e·gate (rĕl′ ə gāt′) ***vt-*** **[rel·e·gat·ed, rel·e·gat·ing]** **1** to send away; exile; hence, to remove, usually to a worse or less desirable place or position: *We* relegated *the old furniture to the attic.* **2** to turn over (a task, duty, etc.) to someone else. **—*n-* rel′ e·ga′ tion.**

re·lent (rĭ lĕnt′) ***vi-*** to become less harsh, cruel, or severe; yield to pity or to earnest entreaty.

re·lent·less (rĭ lĕnt′ ləs) ***adj-*** unyielding; without letup; without pity or mercy: *a* relentless *drive for power.* **—*adv-* re·lent′ less·ly. *n-* re·lent′ less·ness.**

rel·e·vant (rĕl′ ə vənt) ***adj-*** having to do with; having some bearing on; related: *The judge ruled that the evidence was* relevant *to the case.* **—*n-* rel′ e·vance** or **rel′ e·van·cy. *adv-* rel′ e·vant·ly.**

re·li·a·bil·i·ty (rĭ lī′ ə bĭl′ ə tē) ***n-*** habit or trait of being reliable; trustworthiness; dependability.

re·li·a·ble (rĭ lī′ ə bəl) ***adj-*** such as can be trusted or relied upon; trustworthy: *a* reliable *source of information*; *a* reliable *person.* **—*adv-* re·li′ a·bly.**

re·li·ance (rĭ lī′ əns) ***n-*** **1** trust; confidence: *The little girl had complete* reliance *in her parents.* **2** dependence: *As she grew older, she had less* reliance *on her family.* **3** person or thing depended on; mainstay: *The widow's son was her chief* reliance.

re·li·ant (rĭ lī′ ənt) ***adj-*** having confidence; depending upon a person or thing: *Grandma is* reliant *on our care.*

rel·ic (rĕl′ ĭk) ***n-*** **1** object or idea from the past that no longer has a practical use; a trace or memorial of a custom, period, people, etc.: *The suit of armor is a* relic *from the days of knighthood.* **2** object cherished for its age or associations; keepsake; souvenir. **3** the body or part of the body of a martyr or saint; also, an object held sacred for having belonged to a holy person.

re·lief (rĭ lēf′) ***n-*** **1** a lessening of pain, worry, fear, or the like: *It is a* relief *to know that you are safe.* **2** anything that lessens worry, pain, tenseness, etc.: *The warm sun was a* relief *after days of rain.* **3** a release from a job or duty: *the* relief *of a sentinel by another.* **4** one who takes over the duties of another: *My* relief *is late.* **5** aid; help; assistance: *The Red Cross sent* relief *to the flood victims.* **6** fresh supplies of men, food, etc.; especially, fresh troops coming to take the place of those tired out in action. **7** sharpness of outline, due to contrast: *a tower in bold* relief *against the sky.* **8** sculpture in which the figures stand out from a surface. **9** in painting, the effect of elevation obtained by shadings, colors, etc. **10** the amount by which landforms differ in height; also, all the differences in height of land in a given area.

Relief on Mount Rushmore

in relief carved or molded so as to stand out from a flat surface. **on relief** totally or partially supported by payments from government funds.

relief map ***n-*** map on which the differences in height of mountains, valleys, plains, etc., are given by contour lines, color, shading, or by molding solid material.

re·lieve (rĭ lēv′) ***vt-*** **[re·lieved, re·liev·ing]** **1** to free from pain, anxiety, distress. **2** to bring help or succor: *Red Cross nurses helped to* relieve *the town after the flood.* **3** to remove or lessen; alleviate: *to* relieve *the pressure.* **4** to release from a post; take the place of: *He* relieved *the guard at midnight.* **5** to lessen the monotony of.

re·li·gion (rĭ lĭj′ ən) ***n-*** **1** belief in and worship of God or the supernatural. **2** particular system of faith and worship: *the Christian* religion; *the Buddhist* religion. **3** a way of living based on moral beliefs; a philosophy. **4** something of great importance in a person's life: *The stage was her* religion.

re·li·gious (rĭ lĭj′ əs) ***adj-*** **1** of or having to do with religion: *a* religious *book.* **2** devout; pious. **3** extremely careful; strict: *a* religious *attention to work.* **4** bound by monastic vows; belonging to a religious order. ***n-*** person who has taken the vows of a religious community. **—*adv-* re·li′ gious·ly. *n-* re·li′ gious·ness.**

re·line (rē′ līn′) ***vt-*** **[re·lined, re·lin·ing]** **1** to make new lines on. **2** to put a new lining in.

re·lin·quish (rĭ lĭng′ kwĭsh) ***vt-*** **1** to retire from; leave; abandon: *He* relinquished *his position.* **2** to give up; surrender: *to* relinquish *a right.* **3** to let go of: *They* relinquished *their hold on me.* **—*n-* re·lin′ quish·ment.**

rel·ish (rĕl′ ĭsh) ***n-*** **1** taste or preference; fondness; also, enjoyment: *a* relish *for excitement*; *to eat with great* relish. **2** the quality that makes a thing pleasurable: *Dangers add* relish *to an adventure.* **3** food eaten with other food to add flavor to sharpen the appetite, such as olives, chopped pickles, or a highly seasoned sauce. ***vt-*** to enjoy: *He didn't* relish *the idea of losing his car.*

re·live (rē′ lĭv′) ***vt-*** **[re·lived, re·liv·ing]** to live over again; experience again (a sensation, emotion, etc.), especially in imagination: *to* relive *a childhood.* ***vi-*** to live again.

re·load (rē lōd′, rē′-) ***vt-*** (considered intransitive when the direct object is implied but not expressed) **1** to fill again: *Will you* reload *the wagon?* **2** to put ammunition in (a gun) again.

re·lo·cate (rē lō′ kāt′, rē′ lō-) ***vt-*** **[re·lo·cat·ed, re·lo·cat·ing]** to move (a person or thing) to a new location: *to* relocate *a factory.* ***vi-***: *The downtown store* relocated *in the suburbs.* **—*n-* re·lo′ ca′ tion.**

re·luc·tance (rĭ lŭk′ təns) ***n-*** lack of eagerness; unwillingness; hesitation: *The students returned to school with* reluctance. Also **re·luc′ tan·cy.**

re·luc·tant (rĭ lŭk′ tənt) ***adj-*** **1** unwilling: *I was* reluctant *to spend more money.* **2** marked by unwillingness: *a* reluctant *acceptance.* **—*adv-* re·luc′ tant·ly.**

re·ly (rĭ lī′) **[re·lied, re·ly·ing] rely on** or **upon** to depend on; trust: *You can always* rely upon *Jane to do her best.*

re·main (rĭ mān′) ***vi-*** **1** to stay behind after others go: *Will you* remain *after the dance and help clean up?* **2** to be left: *So much work* remains *to be done! One side of the house* remained *after the tornado.* **3** to continue to be as before: *He* remained *my friend.*

re·main·der (rĭ mān′ dər) ***n-*** **1** portion left after part has been taken away, used, or destroyed. **2** *Mathematics*

Any of these words means **re-** ("again") plus the meaning of the rest of the word as given in the main text.

re′ let′ **re′ let′ ter** **re′ light′** **re′ load′ er**

number left over after one number has been subtracted from another: *5 subtracted from 8 leaves a* remainder *of 3.* 3 *Mathematics* number left over after a number has been divided by another: *5 divided by 2 gives 2 and a* remainder *of 1. 4 divided by 2 gives 2 and a* remainder *of 0.*

re·mains (rĭ mānz′) ***n-*** *pl.* **1** part or parts left; remnants: *the* remains *of a meal.* **2** ruins, especially of ancient times: *the* remains *of ancient Rome.* **3** a dead body.

[1]**re·make** (rē māk′, rē′-) ***vt-*** **[re·made, re·mak·ing]** to make again: *After her nap, she* remade *the bed.*

[2]**re·make** (rē′ māk′) ***n-*** something remade: *a* remake *of an old motion picture.*

re·mand (rĭ mănd′) ***vt-*** **1** to send or order back; especially, to send a prisoner to jail to await trial, or to send back a case to a lower court for reconsideration. ***n-***: *The judge ordered the* remand *of the prisoner to jail.*

re·mark (rĭ märk′) ***n-*** **1** a brief comment or observation: *Did he make a* remark *about my lateness?* **2** notice or comment: *an object of* remark. **3 remarks** conversation in general: *His* remarks *were interesting.* ***vt-*** **1** to say or write briefly and casually as a comment; mention: *He* remarked *that he would be in New York today.* **2** to take note of; notice; observe: *We* remarked *his worried look.* ***vi-*** to comment (often followed by "on" or "upon"): *He* remarked *upon the subject.*

re·mark·a·ble (rĭ mär′ kə bəl) ***adj-*** worthy of notice; extraordinary: *He has a* remarkable *memory.* ***—n-*** **re·mark′ a·ble·ness.** ***adv-*** **re·mark′ a·bly.**

re·mar·ry (rē măr′ ē, rē′-) ***vt-*** **[re·mar·ried, re·mar·ry·ing]** to marry (a former spouse) again. ***vi-***: to marry again after being widowed or divorced: *Two years later she* remarried. ***—n-*** **re·mar′ riage.**

re·me·di·a·ble (rĭ mē′ dē ə bəl) ***adj-*** such as can be corrected or cured; curable: *a* remediable *disease*; *a* remediable *fault.* ***—adv-*** **re·me′ di·a·bly.**

re·med·i·al (rĭ mē′ dē əl) ***adj-*** for the purpose of correcting; providing a remedy: *After her accident,* remedial *exercises helped her walk.* ***—adv-*** **re·med′ i·al·ly.**

rem·e·dy (rĕm′ ə dē) ***n-*** [*pl.* **rem·e·dies**] **1** anything to cure or relieve illness: *a headache* remedy. **2** action or method to right wrongs: *Your only* remedy *is to go to court.* ***vt-*** **[rem·e·died, rem·e·dy·ing] 1** to cure, or cause to improve, with medicine: *to* remedy *a cough.* **2** to repair; make right; correct (evils, defects, faults, etc.).

re·mem·ber (rĭ mĕm′ bər) ***vt-*** **1** to bring back to the mind; think again of; recall: *She suddenly* remembered *an unpleasant experience. He can't* remember *her name.* **2** to retain or keep in the mind: *I* remember *the poem very well.* **3** to give a present to; tip: *Will you* remember *the elevator man at Christmas?* **4** to carry greetings for: *Please* remember *me to your family.* ***vi-*** to have or use the faculty of memory: *He learned to* remember.

re·mem·brance (rĭ mĕm′ brəns) ***n-*** **1** a remembering; a recalling to mind: *The* remembrance *of that day gave Jean pleasure.* **2** object or objects that call to mind persons or events: *The blue ribbon was a* remembrance *of Paul's first horse show.* **3** gift or token: *The pin was a* remembrance *from her father.* **4** the length of time over which one's memories extend; total memory: *the most remarkable event in my* remembrance. **6 remembrances** greetings: *Give her my* remembrances.

re·mind (rĭ mīnd′) ***vt-*** to bring to mind; cause to remember: *Please* remind *me to return that book tomorrow.*

re·mind·er (rĭ mīn′ dər) ***n-*** anything that helps a person to remember.

rem·i·nisce (rĕm′ ə nĭs′) ***vi-*** **[rem·i·nisced, rem·i·nisc·ing]** to think or talk about past experiences.

rem·i·nis·cence (rĕm′ ə nĭs′ əns) ***n-*** **1** the recollection of past experiences; remembrance. **2 reminiscences** written or spoken account of one's past experiences.

rem·i·nis·cent (rĕm′ ə nĭs′ ənt) ***adj-*** **1** given to recalling the past; dwelling on the past: *a* reminiscent *letter.* **2** reminding or suggestive (of): *a poem* reminiscent *of the style of Burns.* ***—adv-*** **rem′ i·nis′ cent·ly.**

re·miss (rĭ mĭs′) ***adj-*** **1** careless in matters of duty, business, etc.; neglectful; lax: *He is* remiss *in keeping appointments.* **2** marked by carelessness or negligence: *The service in this restaurant is very* remiss. ***—adv-*** **re·miss′ ly.** ***n-*** **re·miss′ ness.**

re·mis·sion (rĭ mĭsh′ ən) ***n-*** **1** a canceling, discharging, or annulling: *the* remission *of a debt.* **2** forgiveness; pardon: *the* remission *of a sin.* **3** temporary lessening: *a* remission *of pain.*

re·mit (rĭ mĭt′) ***vt-*** **[re·mit·ted, re·mit·ting] 1** to submit in payment: *Please* remit *the money you owe.* **2** to forgive or pardon: *to* remit *sins.* **3** to refrain from demanding or insisting upon: *He* remitted *the fine.* **4** to make less; relax: *He* remitted *his efforts.* **5** to submit (a matter) for consideration, action, etc.: *He* remitted *the question to the advisory committee.* **6** in law, to send back (a case) to a lower court. ***vi-*** **1** to become less severe; lessen in force: *Her fever* remitted. **2** to send money: *Please* remit *by return mail.* ***—n-*** **re·mit′ ter.**

re·mit·tance (rĭ mĭt′ əns) ***n-*** **1** a sending of money, especially to someone far away. **2** the money sent.

rem·nant (rĕm′ nənt) ***n-*** **1** small piece or part left over; fragment; scrap: *the scattered* remnants *of an army.* **2** piece of fabric left from a large piece and sold cheap.

re·mod·el (rē mŏd′ əl, rē′-) ***vt-*** to make over in a new pattern: *The tailor* remodeled *the suit.*

re·mon·strance (rĭ mŏn′ strəns) ***n-*** strong protest: *a* remonstrance *against prejudice.*

re·mon·strate (rĭ mŏn′ strāt′) ***vi-*** **[re·mon·strat·ed, re·mon·strat·ing]** to plead strongly in protest: *They* remonstrated *against higher taxes.*

re·morse (rĭ mórs′, -môrs′) ***n-*** painful regret or anguish caused by a feeling of guilt: *The driver felt* remorse *when he hit the puppy.* ***—adj-*** **re·morse′ ful.** ***adv-*** **re·morse′ ful·ly.** ***n-*** **re·morse′ ful·ness.**

re·morse·less (rĭ mórs′ ləs, -môrs′ ləs) ***adj-*** merciless; pitiless: *a* remorseless *person.* ***—adv-*** **re·morse′ less·ly.** ***n-*** **re·morse′ less·ness.**

re·mote (rĭ mōt′) ***adj-*** **[re·mot·er, re·mot·est] 1** far-off; distant in time: *the* remote *past.* **2** far away; distant in space: *a* remote *land.* **3** set apart; secluded: *a house* remote *from the village.* **4** only distantly related or connected: *a* remote *relative*; *a* remote *bearing on a question.* **5** slight: *I haven't a* remote *idea of what you mean.* ***—adv-*** **re·mote′ ly.** ***n-*** **re·mote′ ness.**

remote control ***n-*** the control of a machine or device from a distance, especially by radio signals. *as* ***modifier*** **(remote-control)**: *a* remote-control *system.*

Any of these words means **re-** ("again") plus the meaning of the rest of the word as given in the main text.

re′ man′
re′ man′ u·fac′ ture
re′ melt′
re′ mi′ grate′
re′ mi·gra′ tion
re′ mil′ i·ta·ri·za′ tion
re′ mix′
re′ mold′

---

[1]**re·mount** (rē mount′) ***vt-*** **1** to go up on again: *The fireman* remounted *the ladder.* **2** to put (a photograph, jewel, etc.) on a new mount. ***vi-*** to mount a horse again.

[2]**re·mount** (rē′ mount′) ***n-*** fresh horse to replace one killed, disabled, or fatigued.

re·mov·al (rĭ mōō′ vəl) ***n-*** **1** a removing or being removed: *The* removal *of the junkyard pleased us.* **2** a moving to a new place: *the* removal *of furniture to a new house.* **3** a dismissing from an official position.

re·move (rĭ mōōv′) ***vt-*** **[re·moved, re·mov·ing] 1** to take away, or off, or out: *He* removed *the dishes from the table. She* removed *her hat.* **2** to get rid of; put an end to: *I* removed *a cause of worry by paying the debt.* **3** to dismiss from an official position. ***vi-*** to move from one place to another; change residence. ***n-*** interval of distance; step: *many* removes *from his former way of life.* ***—adj-*** **re·mov′ a·ble:** *a* removable *filter.* ***n-*** **re·mov′ er.**

re·moved (rĭ mōōvd′) ***adj-*** **1** existing apart; distant: *Their house was far* removed *from the village.* **2** separated by a degree in relationship: *A first cousin once* removed *is the child of that first cousin.*

re·mu·ner·ate (rĭ myōō′ nə rāt′) ***vt-*** **[re·mu·ner·at·ed, re·mu·ner·at·ing] 1** to make an equivalent payment to (a person) in return for a service, loss, expense, etc.; compensate; repay: *They* remunerated *him for his trouble.* **2** to pay for. ***—n-*** **re·mu′ ner·a′ tion.**

re·mu·ner·a·tive (rĭ myōō′ nə rā′ tĭv) ***adj-*** profitable.

Re·mus (rē′ məs) ***n-*** in Roman legend, the twin brother of Romulus, by whom he was slain.

Ren·ais·sance (rĕn′ ə säns′, -zäns′) ***n-*** **1** period of a great revival of learning and classical art in Europe, from the fourteenth to the seventeenth centuries, beginning in Italy and spreading through other countries. **2** the style of art and architecture characteristic of this period. **3 renaissance** a new birth; a revival of interest and activity in artistic and intellectual pursuits. ***adj-*:** *They studied* Renaissance *painting.*

re·nal (rē′ nəl) ***adj-*** of or near the kidneys.

re·nas·cence (rĭ năs′ əns, rĭ nā′ səns) ***n-*** **1** a new birth; a revival of interest and activity in artistic and intellectual pursuits. **2 Renascence** Renaissance.

re·nas·cent (rĭ năs′ ənt, rĭ nā′ sənt) ***adj-*** being born again; rising again into vigor: *a* renascent *interest.*

rend (rĕnd) ***vt-*** **[rent** or **rend·ed, rend·ing] 1** to tear apart violently: *We watched the wind* rend *the sails to tatters.* **2** to tear away: *to* rend *power from a King.*

ren·der (rĕn′ dər) ***vt-*** **1** to cause to be or become; make: *Surprise* rendered *him speechless.* **2** to give in return; pay back: *He* rendered *blow for blow.* **3** to pay as something owed or due: *to* render *homage.* **4** to present or submit for payment, consideration, etc.: *to* render *a bill.* **5** to give up; yield; surrender: *He* rendered *his life.* **6** to deliver or state: *to* render *a decision.* **7** to furnish; give: *They* rendered *aid to the poor.* **8** to translate: *We* rendered *French into English.* **9** to perform; interpret; depict: *He* rendered *the role of Hamlet.* **10** to extract and purify by melting: *to* render *lard.*

ren·dez·vous (rän′ də vōō′) ***n-*** [*pl.* **ren·dez·vous** (-vōōz′)] **1** a meeting by arrangement. **2** place of meeting. ***vi-*** **[ren·dez·voused** (-vōōd′), **ren·dez·vous·ing** (-vōō′ ĭng)] to meet by arrangement: *We will* rendezvous *at the ranger's cabin.* ***vt-*** to cause to meet by arrangement: *to* rendezvous *spacecraft as part of a space program.*

ren·di·tion (rĕn dĭsh′ ən) ***n-*** **1** a rendering; a giving out or forth: *the* rendition *of the verdict.* **2** a version or translation. **3** a giving over, especially of a person: *the* rendition *of the fugitives by their lawyer.* **4** the performance of a dramatic role, piece of music, etc.; also, the particular interpretation given it: *the* rendition *of a symphony.*

ren·e·gade (rĕn′ ə gād′) ***n-*** a person who deserts his own people, political party, etc.; traitor. *as* ***modifier*:** *a* renegade *officer.*

re·nege (rĭ nĭg′, -nĕg′) ***vi-*** **[re·neged, re·neg·ing] 1** in a card game, to violate the rules by not following a suit of cards when able to do so. **2** *Informal* to fail to live up to a promise.

re·ne·go·ti·ate (rē′ nə gō′ shē āt′) ***vt-*** **[re·ne·go·ti·at·ed, re·ne·go·ti·at·ing]** to negotiate again, especially in order to make a fairer arrangement.

re·new (rĭ nōō′, -nyōō′) ***vt-*** **1** to make new again; revive: *Encouragement* renewed *his enthusiasm.* **2** to take up again; resume: *to* renew *one's efforts*; *to* renew *a friendship.* **3** to continue under a new agreement, payment, etc.: *to* renew *a loan*; *to* renew *a subscription.* **4** to replace; replenish; also, to fill again: *We must* renew *our stock of goods. He* renewed *the water in the tank.* **5** to rebuild; renovate. ***—adj-*** **re·new′ a·ble:** *a* renewable *loan.* ***n-*** **re·new′ al:** *the* renewal *of a subscription.*

ren·net (rĕn′ ət) ***n-*** substance prepared from the stomach lining of a calf, and used for curdling milk, making cheese, etc.

ren·nin (rĕn′ ən) ***n-*** enzyme found in rennet.

re·nounce (rĭ nouns′) ***vt-*** **[re·nounced, re·nounc·ing] 1** to cast off; disown; refuse to have to do with: *to* renounce *an heir.* **2** to give up; abandon; surrender: *The princess* renounced *her right to the throne.* ***—n-*** **re·nounce′ ment.**

ren·o·vate (rĕn′ ə vāt′) ***vt-*** **[ren·o·vat·ed, ren·o·vat·ing]** to make like new; restore: *They* renovated *the entire house.* ***—n-*** **ren′ o·va′ tion:** *the* renovation *of the house.* ***n-*** **ren′ o·va′ tor:** *He is a* renovator *of old houses.*

re·nown (rĭ noun′) ***n-*** fame; reputation: *a novelist of* renown. ***—adj-*** **re·nowned′:** *a* renowned *composer.*

[1]**rent** (rĕnt) ***n-*** sum of money paid or charged for the use of something: *The* rent *for the room was ten dollars a week.* ***vt-*** to pay or charge a sum of money periodically for the use of (something); hire; lease: *We* rented *a cottage at the lake. The owner* rented *it to us for a reasonable price.* ***vi-*:** *This room* rents *for ten dollars a day.* [from French **rente,** from Late Latin **rendita** meaning "something paid in," from Latin **reddita,** "something given back."] ***—adj-*** **rent′ able.**

for rent available for use by the payment of rent.

[2]**rent** (rĕnt) *p.t. & p.p.* of **rend.** ***n-*** **1** torn place: *a* rent *in a dress.* **2** division; split: *a* rent *in a political party.*

rent·al (rĕn′ təl) ***n-*** **1** amount paid or received as rent; income from rents. **2** a schedule or list of rents. **3** property offered for rent. **4** the act of renting.

rent·er (rĕn′ tər) ***n-*** person who rents something; especially, a tenant.

re·nun·ci·a·tion (rĭ nŭn′ sē ā′ shən) ***n-*** a renouncing: *the author's* renunciation *of his earlier views.*

re·o·pen (rē′ ō′ pən) ***vt-*** **1** to open again: *to* reopen *the shop after the holiday.* **2** to begin again; renew: *I do not want to* reopen *the argument.* ***vi-*:** *The wound* reopened.

re·or·der (rē′ ȯr′ dər, -ôr′ dər) ***vt-*** **1** to order (something) again: *to* reorder *coffee.* **2** to put in proper order again: *to* reorder *the files.* **3** to arrange or organize in a different way. ***n-*** something ordered again: *a* reorder *of coffee.*

re·or·gan·ize (rē′ ȯr′ gə nīz, rē′ ôr′-) ***vt-*** **[re·or·gan·ized, re·or·gan·iz·ing]** to organize anew; change (a system):

Any of these words means **re-** ("again") plus the meaning of the rest of the word as given in the main text.

re′ name′ | **re′ nom′ i·nate′** | **re′ oc′ cu·py′**
re′ num′ ber | **re′ oc·cur′ rence**

The new owner completely reorganized *the firm.* ***vi-***: *The company* reorganized. ***—n-*** **re′ or·gan·i·za′ tion.**

[1]**rep** (rĕp) ***n-*** silk, wool, cotton, or rayon fabric with a finely corded surface. *as* ***modifier***: *a* rep *tie.* [from French **reps,** from English **ribs.**]

[2]**rep** (rĕp) ***n-*** unit of ionizing nuclear radiation. [shortened from *r*oentgen *e*quivalent *p*hysical.]

Rep. **1** Republican. **2** Representative. **3** Republic.

re·paid (rĭ pād′) *p.t. & p.p.* of **repay.**

[1]**re·pair** (rĭ pâr′) ***vt-*** **1** to restore to good condition or proper working order: *to* repair *a fence*; *to* repair *a car.* **2** to fix (something) that is torn, cracked, etc.: *to* repair *a page*; *to* repair *a pipe.* **3** to make up for; remedy; set right: *to* repair *a wrong.* ***n-*** **1** a restoring to sound condition or proper working order; also, a fixing of something broken, torn, etc. **2** condition of something compared with a new or perfect specimen of the same thing: *My car is in bad* repair. *My house is in good* repair. [from Old French **reparer,** from Latin **reparāre** meaning "to recover; prepare anew."] ***—adj-*** **re·pair′ a·ble.** ***n-*** **re·pair′ er.** ***n-*** **re·pair′ man.**

[2]**re·pair** (rĭ pâr′) ***vi-*** to go: *to* repair *to the living room after dinner.* ***n-*** **1** place; locale; den: *The café was a favorite* repair *of artists and writers.* **2** a going or journeying: *his* repair *to the country.* [from Old French **repairer** meaning "to return," from Latin **repatriāre,** "to return to one's country."]

rep·a·ra·ble (rĕp′ər ə bəl) ***adj-*** such as can be repaired; repairable: *The damage is* reparable.

rep·a·ra·tion (rĕp′ ə rā′ shən) ***n-*** **1** a making good for a mistake, wrong, or injury; compensation: *They sent a check in* reparation *for the damage they caused.* **2** something done or given by way of compensation: *The check was adequate* reparation. **3 reparations** money or goods paid in compensation, especially that paid by a defeated nation for the cost and damage it has inflicted on a victorious nation.

rep·ar·tee (rĕp′ är tē′, -tā′) ***n-*** quick-witted, clever reply; also, conversation full of such replies.

re·pass (rē păs′, rē′-) ***vt-*** **1** to pass (someone or something) again: *They* repassed *the house on their way back to town.* **2** to adopt or put into effect again.

re·past (rĭ păst′) ***n-*** a meal; food.

[1]**re·pa·tri·ate** (rĭ pā′ trē āt′) ***vt-*** [**re·pa·tri·at·ed, re·pa·tri·at·ing**] to return (someone) to his country of birth or citizenship: *We* repatriated *our prisoners after the war.* ***—n-*** **re·pa′ tri·a′ tion.**

[2]**re·pa·tri·ate** (rĭ pā′ trē ət) ***n-*** person who has been returned to his country of birth or citizenship.

re·pay (rĭ pā′) ***vt-*** [**re·paid, re·pay·ing**] **1** to pay back: *He* repayed *the loan. I want to* repay *her for her kindness.* **2** to make return for: *to* repay *a favor.* ***—adj-*** **re·pay′ a·ble**: *The loan is* repayable *on demand.* ***n-*** **re·pay′ ment.**

re·peal (rĭ pēl′) ***vt-*** to do away with; annul; revoke: *to* repeal *a law.* ***n-*** a doing away with; annulment; revocation: *the* repeal *of a law.* ***—adj-*** **re·peal′ a·ble.**

re·peat (rĭ pēt′) ***vt-*** **1** to do or say again: *to* repeat *the first part of the song*; *to* repeat *a blunder.* **2** to tell what one has heard: *to* repeat *the news.* **3** to recite from memory: *to* repeat *a poem.* **4** to say exactly what someone else has said: *Please* repeat *these words after me.* ***n-*** **1** a doing or saying again; also, what is done or said: *a* repeat *of last week's show.* **2** *Music* part or section that is to be played again: *The pianist omitted the* repeats. *as* ***modifier***: *a* repeat *performance.*

repeat (oneself) to say the same thing again.

re·peat·ed (rĭ pē′ təd) ***adj-*** done, said, or sounded again or over and over: *The* repeated *words became tedious.* ***—adv-*** **re·peat′ ed·ly.**

re·peat·er (rĭ pē′ tər) ***n-*** **1** person or thing which repeats. **2** gun that fires several shots without having to be reloaded. **3** a watch that strikes the current hours, and sometimes the parts of the hour, when a spring is pressed. **4** person who has been arrested several times for criminal acts.

repeating decimal *Mathematics* ***n-*** decimal fraction in which a set of one or more digits is repeated indefinitely. Examples: .3333 . . . $(=\frac{1}{3})$; .121212 . . . $(=\frac{4}{33})$; .142857142857 . . . $(=\frac{1}{7})$.

re·pel (rĭ pĕl′) ***vt-*** [**re·pelled, re·pel·ling**] **1** to drive back; repulse: *They* repelled *the invaders.* **2** to push back or away: *The corresponding poles of two magnets* repel *each other.* **3** to refuse to accept or consider; reject: *He* repelled *the offer of a bribe.* **4** to cause a feeling of dislike in; disgust: *The violence of the scene* repelled *me.*

re·pel·lent (rĭ pĕl′ ənt) ***adj-*** **1** driving or forcing back: *a* repellent *thrust by the army.* **2** causing disgust or loathing; repulsive: *a* repellent *sight*; *a* repellent *manner.* ***n-*** something that repels; especially, a substance that drives away insects.

re·pent (rĭ pĕnt′) ***vi-*** to feel regret or contrition for something done or left undone, usually with a promise to behave better: *He taught his followers to* repent. ***vt-*** to feel regret or sorrow for (a deed, word, etc.): *He* repented *the sale of the house.* ***—n-*** **re·pent′ er.**

repent of to regret; change one's mind about.

re·pent·ance (rĭ pĕn′ təns) ***n-*** regret or sorrow for one's wrongdoing, with desire to mend one's ways.

re·pent·ant (rĭ pĕn′ tənt) ***adj-*** feeling or showing regret and sorrow for wrongdoing; contrite; penitent: *She was* repentant *for her rudeness.* ***—adv-*** **re·pent′ ant·ly.**

re·per·cus·sion (rē′ pər kŭsh′ ən) ***n-*** **1** echo and reverberation of a loud noise: *The* repercussion *of gunfire could be heard for miles.* **2** effect or result of some act, occurrence, etc.: *the* repercussions *of his decision.*

rep·er·toire (rĕp′ ər twär′) ***n-*** all the plays, operas, musical pieces, or parts that a company, musician, or actor is prepared to perform; repertory.

rep·er·to·ry (rĕp′ ər tôr′ ē) ***n-*** [*pl.* **rep·er·to·ries**] **1** repertoire. **2** a collection, especially of information, facts, etc. ***adj-*** of or having to do with repertory theater.

repertory theater ***n-*** form or organization of the theater in which a permanent group of performers (a **repertory company**) appears in various roles in several productions repeated during the season.

rep·e·ti·tion (rĕp′ ə tĭsh′ ən) ***n-*** **1** a doing or saying something more than once; a repeating: *There was a great deal of unnecessary* repetition *in his letter.* **2** something that is said or done over again: *This lesson is a* repetition *of one we did earlier.*

rep·e·ti·tious (rĕp′ ə tĭsh′ əs) ***adj-*** containing unnecessary repetition; tending to repeat unnecessarily: *a*

Any of these words means **re-** ("again") plus the meaning of the rest of the word as given in the main text.

re′ or′ gan·iz′ er
re′ o′ ri·ent
re′ o′ ri·en·tate′
re′ o′ ri·en·ta′ tion
re′ pack′
re′ pack′ age
re′ paint′
re′ peo′ ple

---

fāte, făt, dâre, bärn; bē, bĕt, mêre; bīte, bĭt; nōte, hŏt, môre, dóg; fŭn, fûr; to͞o, bo͝ok; oil; out; ta*r*; thin; then; hw for wh as in *wh*at; zh for s as in u*s*ual; ə for a, e, i, o, u, as in *a*go, lin*e*n, per*i*l, at*o*m, min*u*s

repetitious *story; an absent-minded,* repetitious *man.* **—*adv-* rep′ e·ti′ tious·ly.** ***n-*** **rep′ e·ti′ tious·ness.**
►Should not be confused with REPETITIVE.

re·pet·i·tive (rə pĕt′ ə tĭv′) ***adj-*** occurring over and over again: *the* repetitive *motion of the pendulum.*
►Should not be confused with REPETITIOUS.

re·phrase (rē frāz′, rē′-) ***vt-*** **[re·phrased, re·phras·ing]** to say or write in a different way: *to* rephrase *a letter.*

re·pine (rĭ pīn′) ***vi-*** **[re·pined, re·pin·ing]** to fret; complain; feel discontent.

re·place (rĭ plās′) ***vt-*** **[re·placed, re·plac·ing] 1** to put or place back; restore to the original place or position: *She* replaced *the book on the shelf.* **2** to take or fill the place of; supersede: *The new car* replaces *the old.* **3** to supply an equivalent in place of: *to* replace *a broken doll.*

re·place·ment (rĭ plās′ mənt) ***n-*** **1** person or thing that takes the place of another; especially, a soldier assigned to a military unit to make up for battle and other losses. **2** a replacing or being replaced: *a* replacement *of parts.*

replacement set *Mathematics* ***n-*** the set of elements, numbers, things, etc., from which the replacement for a variable in an open sentence is chosen.

re·plant (rē plănt′, rē′-) ***vt-*** (considered intransitive when the direct object is implied but not expressed) **1** to plant with new crops, trees, etc.: *to* replant *a field; to* replant *a forest area.* **2** to plant again in new soil: *She* replanted *her geraniums.*

re·plen·ish (rĭ plĕn′ ĭsh) ***vt-*** to fill up again; restock: *to* replenish *food supplies.* **—*n-*** **re·plen′ ish·er.** ***n-*** **re·plen′ ish·ment.**

re·plete (rĭ plēt′) ***adj-*** **1** completely or abundantly filled or provided (with): *The room is* replete *with vases.* **2** sated with food or drink; gorged: *I am* replete.

re·ple·tion (rĭ plē′ shən) ***n-*** **1** condition of being abundantly or excessively full: *to eat to* repletion. **2** fulfillment of a craving, desire, etc.

rep·li·ca (rĕp′ lĭ kə) ***n-*** **1** exact copy; duplicate: *This portrait is a* replica *of the original.* **2** any close copy.

rep·li·cate (rĕp′ lə kāt′) ***vi-*** **[rep·li·cat·ed, rep·li·cat·ing]** of a DNA molecule, to duplicate itself exactly.

rep·li·ca·tion (rĕp′ lə kā′ shən) ***n-*** **1** the making of a replica; a reproducing. **2** exact copy; replica; reproduction. **3** an answer; reply. **4** *Biology* process occurring during mitosis in which the DNA molecules in the nuclei of living cells form exact duplicates of themselves. As the two strands that make up the double helix of the molecule unwind, each reconstitutes the other, thus forming two identical but separate molecules of DNA.

re·ply (rĭ plī′) ***vi-*** **[re·plied, re·ply·ing]** to say, write, or do something in answer; respond: *When he inquired, I* replied. *The enemy* replied *quickly to our attack.* ***vt-*** to offer as an answer (takes only a clause as object): *He* replied *that he could not do it.* ***n-*** **[*pl.* re·plies]** something said, written, or done in answer. **—*n-*** **re·pli′ er.**

re·port (rĭ pôrt′) ***vt-*** **1** to give a written or oral account of; relate: *He* reported *the results of the investigation.* **2** to complain about or make a charge against (someone): *to* report *a man to the police.* ***vi-*** **1** to give an account of one's work or experiences. **2** to present oneself: *Did he* report *for work on time?* ***n-*** **1** written or oral statement or account, often formal or official: *a government* report; *a school* report. **2** general talk; rumor; hence, reputation or fame: *a man of good* report. **3** sound of an explosion: *a rifle* report. *as* ***modifier***: *a* report *card.*

re·port·er (rĭ pôr′ tər) ***n-*** **1** person employed by a newspaper or magazine to gather information and write factual articles. **2** (also **court reporter**) person who takes down what is said and done in a court trial, and prepares the record for official publication. **3** anyone who reports.

¹re·pose (rĭ pōz′) ***n-*** **1** quiet rest; sleep: *a night's* repose. **2** calmness, composure, or tranquillity: *Her manner was one of* repose. **3** peace and quiet: *the* repose *of the countryside.* ***vi-*** **[re·posed, re·pos·ing] 1** to lie at rest; hence, to sleep: *The child* reposed *on the couch.* **2** to lie or rest on a support: *The statue* reposes *on a pedestal.* [from French, from Late Latin **repausāre,** "to rest."]

²re·pose (rĭ pōz′) ***vt-*** **[re·posed, re·pos·ing]** to place (trust and confidence): *He* reposed *great trust in his son.* [from Latin **repositus** and **repōnere** meaning "to store; lay up."]

re·po·si·tion (rē′ pə zĭsh′ ən) ***vt-*** to alter the position of: *Shall I* reposition *my desk?*

re·pos·i·to·ry (rĭ pŏz′ ə tôr′ ē) ***n-*** **[*pl.* re·pos·i·to·ries]** place, such as a bank or warehouse, for the storing and safekeeping of goods.

re·pos·sess (rē′ pə zĕs′) ***vt-*** to recover possession of; especially, to take back (something bought on installments or credit) because the buyer has not made the proper payments. **—*n-*** **re′ pos·ses′ sion.**

rep·re·hend (rĕp′ rĭ hĕnd′) ***vt-*** to show or express disapproval of; censure: *I must* reprehend *your hastiness.* **—*n-*** **rep′ re·hen′ sion.**

rep·re·hen·si·ble (rĕp′ rĭ hĕn′ sə bəl) ***adj-*** deserving reproof or rebuke; blamable: *Some of his acts were* reprehensible. **—*adv-*** **rep′ re·hen′ si·bly.**

rep·re·sent (rĕp′ rĭ zĕnt′) ***vt-*** **1** to produce a likeness of; portray in art or describe in writing: *This statue* represents *Lincoln as a young man.* **2** to point out; set forth: *This book* represents *very clearly the dangers facing the nation.* **3** to act for (another person or group): *He will* represent *us ably in the Senate.* **4** to correspond to; stand for; symbolize: *The letters of the alphabet* represent *sounds.* **5** to stand as a type or specimen of; typify: *Bach* represents *the baroque period in music.* **6** to be a case or instance of: *This law* represents *a new attitude.*

rep·re·sen·ta·tion (rĕp′ rĭ zən tā′ shən) ***n-*** **1** fact of being represented; means of being heard and taking part. **2** picture, statue, etc., that represents: *The statue is a* representation *of a sleeping tiger.* **3** symbol; sign; emblem. **4** word picture; account: *His* representation *of her part in the accident was untrue.* **5 representations** arguments and pleadings in favor of a point of view or an action. **—*adj-*** **rep′ re·sen·ta′ tion·al.**

rep·re·sent·a·tive (rĕp′ rĭ zĕn′ tə tĭv) ***n-*** **1** person who has authority to act for others; delegate; agent: *our* representative *at the United Nations.* **2** example; specimen: *a poor* representative *of its type.* **3 Representative** elected member of the lower house in Congress or in some State legislatures. ***adj-*** **1** serving to represent; portraying. **2** acting or holding the power to act for others: *a* representative *government.* **3** typical; characteristic: *That was a* representative *sample of his wit.*

re·press (rĭ prĕs′) ***vt-*** **1** to keep back or down; check; restrain: *He might have been a great actor, but his family* repressed *his talent.* **2** to put down; suppress: *The ship's captain sternly* repressed *the mutiny.* **3** to keep (a feeling, desire, etc.,) from emerging into one's conscious mind from one's unconscious mind. **—*n-*** **re·press′ er.** ***adj-*** **re·pres′ sive.**

re·pres·sion (rĭ prĕsh′ ən) ***n-*** a repressing; a holding down of desire, ability, etc.; also, an instance of this.

re·prieve (rĭ prēv′) ***n-*** **1** temporary delay in carrying out the sentence of a judge. **2** temporary relief from pain or

---

Any of these words means **re-** ("again") plus the meaning of the rest of the word as given in the main text.

re′ pho′ to·graph′ **re′ play′** **re′ pur′ chase**

escape from danger. *vt-* **[re·prieved, re·priev·ing]** 1 to grant a delay in the execution of: *to* reprieve *a condemned prisoner.* 2 to free for a time from pain or danger.

rep·ri·mand (rĕp′ rə mănd′) *n-* severe reproof or formal rebuke; censure. *vt-* to rebuke severely for some fault.

[1]**re·print** (rē prĭnt′, rē′-) *vt-* to print again; print a new copy or edition of: *to* reprint *a book.*

[2]**re·print** (rē′ prĭnt′) *n-* new edition of a printed work.

re·pris·al (rĭ prī′ zəl) *n-* in war, injury or loss inflicted upon an enemy in return for an injury or loss suffered; hence, any repayment of injury with injury.

re·proach (rĭ prōch′) *vt-* to charge with something wrong or disgraceful; blame or rebuke: *He* reproached *the clerk for carelessness. n-* 1 blame; censure; also, the words that express this: *John well deserved his mother's* reproach. 2 cause or occasion of blame, scorn, or shame: *The slums of the city are a* reproach *to the citizens.*

re·proach·ful (rĭ prōch′ fəl) *adj-* expressing blame or rebuke; full of reproach: *a* reproachful *look. —adv-* **re·proach′ ful·ly.**

rep·ro·bate (rĕp′ rə bāt′) *adj-* given to immorality; depraved; sinful: *a* reprobate *life. n-* immoral or depraved person. *vt-* **[rep·ro·bat·ed, rep·ro·bat·ing]** to disapprove of strongly; condemn.

rep·ro·ba·tion (rĕp′ rə bā′ shən) *n-* strong disapproval; condemnation; censure.

re·pro·duce (rē′ prə do͞os′, -dyo͞os′) *vt-* **[re·pro·duced, re·pro·duc·ing]** 1 to cause to appear or sound again by means of a recording process: *This record* reproduces *the trumpets well. This photo* reproduces *her expression exactly.* 2 to create an exact copy of; duplicate: *Please* reproduce *these three letters.* 3 to imitate successfully: *The actors* reproduced *a frontier atmosphere.* 4 of plants or animals, to bring forth new members of (the species). *vi-* 1 to appear or sound after having been photographed, printed, recorded, etc.: *This scene will* reproduce *well in color.* 2 to produce offspring: *Mules cannot* reproduce. *—n-* **re′ pro·duc′ er.**

re·pro·duc·i·ble (rē′ prə do͞o′ sə bəl, -dyo͞o′ sə bəl) *adj-* such as can be reproduced by a recording, printing, or photographic process or device.

re·pro·duc·tion (rē′ prə dŭk′ shən) *n-* 1 a causing to appear or sound again by means of a recording or printing process or by exact imitation: *the* reproduction *of a symphony; the* reproduction *of a frontier atmosphere.* 2 the producing, by living things, of further individuals of their own biological species. 3 a close or exact copy. *as* ***modifier****: a* reproduction *process.*

re·pro·duc·tive (rē′ prə dŭk′ tĭv) *adj-* having to do with or employed in biological reproduction. *—adv-* **re′ pro·duc′ tive·ly.** *n-* **re′ pro·duc′ tive·ness.**

reproductive system *n-* the group of organs, parts, or structures in any particular organism that are concerned with reproduction.

re·proof (rĭ pro͞of′) *n-* 1 a reproving; rebuking; censure: *She deserves* reproof *for her rudeness.* 2 a rebuke; reprimand: *He got a stiff* reproof *from the judge.*

re·prove (rĭ pro͞ov′) *vt-* **[re·proved, re·prov·ing]** to rebuke; censure; reprimand; blame: *She* reproved *me for my actions. —n-* **re·prov′ er.** *adv-* **re·prov′ ing·ly.**

rep·tile (rĕp′ tĭl) *n-* 1 any of a group of cold-blooded animals **(Reptilia)** that comprises the snakes, lizards, turtles, alligators and crocodiles, and many extinct forms including the dinosaurs. 2 person who is cold-blooded, insidious, and dangerous as a snake is supposed to be. *as* ***modifier****: the* reptile *house at the zoo.*

rep·til·i·an (rĕp tĭl′ yən, -tĭl′ ē ən) *adj-* 1 of or relating to reptiles: *the* reptilian *population.* 2 resembling a reptile or some part or feature of a reptile: *a chilly,* reptilian *man; a* reptilian *head. n-* reptile.

Repub. 1 Republic. 2 Republican.

re·pub·lic (rĭ pŭb′ lĭk) *n-* 1 country in which the supreme power of government rests with the voting public, which elects executive officers and representatives to govern the country: *The United States is a* republic. 2 form of government in which those who govern hold office through the vote of the people. 3 group of persons working in the same field, for the same cause, etc.: *the* republic *of letters.*

►Should not be confused with DEMOCRACY.

re·pub·li·can (rĭ pŭb′ lĭ kən) *adj-* 1 of or relating to a republic or the form of government a republic uses. 2 favoring a republic: *She had* republican *sentiments.* 3 **Republican** having to do with the Republican Party: *a* Republican *rally. n-* 1 person who favors a republic: *At heart he was a* republican. 2 **Republican** member of the Republican Party in the United States.

Republican Party *n-* one of two chief political parties in the United States.

re·pub·li·can·ism (rĭ pŭb′ lĭ kən ĭz′ əm) *n-* 1 system or principle of government used by republics. 2 advocacy of or belief in such principles: *His speech was an honest expression of his* republicanism. 3 **Republicanism** in the United States, the principles and doctrines of the Republican Party.

re·pub·lish (rē′ pŭb′ lĭsh) *vt-* to publish (a book, story, essay, etc.) again. *—n-* **re′ pub′ li·ca′ tion.**

re·pu·di·ate (rĭ pyo͞o′ dē āt′) *vt-* **[re·pu·di·at·ed, re·pu·di·at·ing]** 1 to refuse to accept as valid; reject as unjust or untrue: *to* repudiate *a statement.* 2 to refuse to have anything to do with; disown: *He* repudiated *his family.* 3 to refuse to pay (a debt). *—n-* **re·pu′ di·a′ tion.**

re·pug·nance (rĭ pŭg′ nəns) *n-* extreme dislike; disgust.

re·pug·nant (rĭ pŭg′ nənt) *adj-* 1 extremely distasteful or disagreeable: *a* repugnant *chore.* 2 contrary or opposed (to): *a course* repugnant *to one's principles.*

re·pulse (rĭ pŭls′) *vt-* **[re·pulsed, re·puls·ing]** 1 to drive back; repel: *The army* repulsed *the advance of the enemy.* 2 to reject by coldness, lack of sympathy, or the like: *She* repulsed *his flattery. n-* 1 a driving back or repelling; defeat or setback: *The army met with a* repulse. 2 refusal or rejection: *His request was answered with a* repulse.

re·pul·sion (rĭ pŭl′ shən) *n-* 1 a driving back or away; a repelling: *the* repulsion *of a pole of a magnet by the like pole of another.* 2 extreme dislike; disgust or aversion; repugnance: *The sight made him feel a strong* repulsion.

re·pul·sive (rĭ pŭl′ sĭv) *adj-* 1 causing a feeling of strong dislike; disgusting: *Rotten eggs have a* repulsive *odor.* 2 tending to repel: *to exert a* repulsive *force. —adv-* **re·pul′ sive·ly.** *n-* **re·pul′ sive·ness.**

rep·u·ta·ble (rĕp′ yə tə bəl) *adj-* having a good name; of good reputation; respected: *It pays to buy from a* reputable *firm. —adv-* **rep′ u·ta·bly.**

rep·u·ta·tion (rĕp′ yə tā′ shən) *n-* 1 worth or quality of a person or thing as judged and reported by others: *He had a poor* reputation *as a lawyer.* 2 good name; honor.

re·pute (rĭ pyo͞ot′) *n-* popular estimate of worth or ability; reputation: *a man of good* repute. *vt-* **[re·put·ed, re·put·ing]** to regard; consider: *We* repute *him honest.*
by repute by report or gossip.

re·put·ed (rĭ pyo͞o′ təd) *adj-* supposed; generally considered: *the house's* reputed *worth. —adv-* **re·put′ ed·ly.**

re·quest (rĭ kwĕst′) *vt-* **1** to ask: *She* requested *me to leave her a book. She* requested *that I leave her a book.* **2** to ask for: *She* requested *a book.* *n-* **1** act of asking for something: *I heard a* request *for a book.* **2** something asked for: *I thought one book was a small enough* request. **3** condition of being sought after or asked for; demand: *He appears by* request. *I'll give it to you on* request.

re·qui·em (rĕk′ wē əm) *n-* **1** any hymn or solemn musical service in honor of the dead. **2 Requiem** (1) in the Roman Catholic Church, a Mass sung for the repose of the souls of the dead. (2) music for such a Mass.

re·quire (rĭ kwīər′) *vt-* **[re·quired, re·quir·ing] 1** to need: *I* require *seven hours sleep a night.* **2** to demand; order; compel: *Good taste* requires *that he make an apology immediately. The government* required *him to testify.*

re·quire·ment (rĭ kwīər′ mənt) *n-* **1** something required; a demand; necessary condition: *That school has several* requirements *for admission.* **2** a need; necessity: *the body's* requirement *of food and rest.* **3** quantity needed.

req·ui·site (rĕk′ wə zĭt) *n-* a necessary thing; an essential: *A library card is a* requisite *for taking out a book.* *adj-* necessary; indispensable: *a* requisite *amount of food.*

req·ui·si·tion (rĕk′ wə zĭsh′ ən) *vt-* to make an official order or request for (food, supplies, etc.): *to* requisition *a toaster for the clubhouse.* *n-* official order or demand, especially in writing: *I have a* requisition *for paper.*

re·quite (rĭ kwīt′) *vt-* **[re·quit·ed, re·quit·ing] 1** to repay (someone) for something; compensate: *to* requite *a person for a kindness.* **2** to repay (something); reciprocate: *He* requites *kindness with ingratitude.* **—*n-* re·quit′ al:** *He met with a just* requital *for his act.*

re·route (rē′ ro͞ot′, -rout′) *vt-* **[re·rout·ed, re·rout·ing]** to send by a different route; change the routing of.

[1]re·run (rē rŭn′, rē′-) *vt-* **[re·ran, re·run, re·run·ning] 1** to show (a motion picture, TV film, etc.) again after its initial run is over. **2** to run again: *They* reran *the race.*

[2]re·run (rē′ rŭn′) *n-* a rerunning; also, a motion picture, TV film, etc., that is run again: *the* rerun *of a movie.*

re·sale (rē′ sāl′) *n-* a selling of something one has bought: *If you buy this car,* resale *will be easy.*

re·scind (rĭ sĭnd′) *vt-* to repeal; annul or cancel: *to* rescind *a law.*

res·cue (rĕs′ kyo͞o′) *vt-* **[res·cued, res·cu·ing]** to save from danger, harm, or imprisonment: *They* rescued *the child from the burning building.* *n-* such a saving: *The lifeguard made a daring* rescue. **—*n-* res′ cu·er.**

re·search (rē′ sûrch′, rĭ-) *n-* **1** careful and orderly study for the purpose of finding or proving facts: *I am doing* research *for my report. He is doing* research *for his new book.* **2** scientific experimentation for the purpose of explaining something: *the latest* research *on arthritis.* ***as modifier***: *a* research *laboratory;* research *funds; a* research *project.* *vt- Informal* **1** to make a study of or investigation into: *to* research *heart disease.* **2** to study or investigate for: *I must* research *my report carefully.* **—*n-* re′ search′ er** or **re·search′ er.**

re·seed (rē′ sēd′) *vt-* **1** to seed again: *It was time to* reseed *the lawn.* **2** of a plant, to propagate (itself) by dropping or otherwise sowing its own seeds.

re·sem·blance (rĭ zĕm′ bləns) *n-* likeness; similarity.

re·sem·ble (rĭ zĕm′ bəl) *vt-* **[re·sem·bled, re·sem·bling]** to be like or similar to: *Her dress* resembles *mine.*

re·sent (rĭ zĕnt′) *vt-* to feel angry or indignant at (someone or something that injures one's self-esteem or seems unfair): *He* resents *any prying into his personal affairs.*

re·sent·ful (rĭ zĕnt′ fəl) *adj-* feeling or showing resentment. **—*adv-* re·sent′ ful·ly.** ***n-* re·sent′ ful·ness.**

re·sent·ment (rĭ zĕnt′ mənt) *n-* feeling of having been badly treated or insulted; anger; indignation; ill will: *I feel* resentment *when I am treated unfairly.*

res·er·va·tion (rĕz′ ər vā′ shən) *n-* **1** arrangement by which something is reserved: *You must have a* reservation *to eat there.* **2** a reserved seat, place, etc.: *Our* reservations *are in the fifth row.* **3** limitation; qualification: *I accept it with no* reservations. **4** land set aside by the government for a particular purpose: *an Indian* reservation.

re·serve (rĭ zûrv′) *vt-* **[re·served, re·serv·ing] 1** to hold back for later use: *to* reserve *some money for an emergency.* **2** to keep for the special use of: *The hotel* reserved *a room for us.* **3** to set apart for a special purpose: *We* reserve *Saturday evenings for entertaining friends.* **4** to keep as one's own; maintain control of: *He* reserves *all rights in his inventions.* **5** to postpone; hold over until later: *The judge* reserved *his decision.* *n-* **1** something stored or kept back for later use: *a* reserve *of food; bank* reserves. **2** tract of land set aside for a special purpose: *a game* reserve; *a forest* reserve. **3** tendency or habit of keeping one's ideas and feelings to oneself; restraint: *It is difficult to break through Mary's* reserve. **4** (often **reserves**) trained naval or military force or personnel not on active duty but subject to quick call. ***as modifier***: *a* reserve *supply;* reserve *funds; a* reserve *unit in the navy.*
in reserve kept back for special use; not expended or committed except in real need: *some cash* in reserve.

re·served (rĭ zûrvd′) *adj-* **1** arranged for in advance: *This seat is* reserved. **2** quiet in manner; restrained in speech and behavior; self-contained: *She is* reserved *with strangers but very gay with friends.* **3** held back, or restricted to certain people: *a* reserved *right.*

re·serv·ed·ly (rĭ zûr′ vəd lē) *adv-* in a restrained and dignified manner; also, cautiously.

re·serv·ist (rĭ zûr′ vĭst) *n-* member of a military or naval reserve.

re·ser·voir (rĕz′ ər vwär′) *n-* **1** lake or pond, often man-made, where water is collected and stored for a city, for irrigation, for generating electricity, etc. **2** part of a machine or any apparatus that holds liquid: *an ink* reservoir *in a fountain pen.* **3** a supply or store of facts, knowledge, feeling, etc.: *a* reservoir *of experience.*

re·set (rē sĕt′, rē′-) *vt-* **[re·set, re·set·ting] 1** to place in position again: *Please* reset *the stakes that were knocked down.* **2** to place in a different position: *He* reset *all the boundary markers.* **3** to set in type again.

re·set·tle (rē′ sĕt′ əl) *vt-* **[re·set·tled, re·set·tling] 1** to settle (a person, group, etc.) in a new place: *They* resettled *the refugees on good farms.* **2** to settle (land, a region, etc.) with new people. *vi-* to settle again after moving: *The family left Maine and* resettled *in Ohio.*

re·shape (rē shāp′, rē′-) *vt-* **[re·shaped, re·shap·ing]** to give a different shape to; hence, to alter (an idea).

Any of these words means **re-** ("again") plus the meaning of the rest of the word as given in the main text.

re′ ra′ di·ate′
re′ read′
re′ re·cord′
re′ roll′
re′ roll′ er
re′ sail′
re′ sal′ a·ble
re′ saw′
re′ say′
re′ scale′
re′ score′
re′ screen′
re′ seal′
re′ seat′
re′ sell′
re′ send′
re′ sen′ si·tize′
re′ set′ tle·ment

---

re·ship (rē′ shĭp′) ***vt-*** **[re·shipped, re·ship·ping]** to ship again; especially, to transfer to another ship. ***vi-*** to embark on a ship again, especially as a crew member.

re·shuf·fle (rē′ shŭf′ əl) ***vt-*** **[re·shuf·fled, re·shuf·fling]** **1** to shuffle again: *He* reshuffled *the cards.* **2** to reorganize: *to* reshuffle *a team.*

re·side (rĭ zīd′) ***vi-*** **[re·sid·ed, re·sid·ing]** **1** to live in or at a place, especially for a considerable time: *Our family has* resided *in this town for generations.* **2** to have a certain location or source: *The choice* resides *with you.*

res·i·dence (rĕz′ ə dəns) ***n-*** **1** home; dwelling: *The White House is the* residence *of the President.* **2** fact of residing at a certain place; legal domicile; occupancy: *Proof of* residence *is required for voting.* **3** period of time in which one lives in a place: *her three years'* residence *in Italy.*
in residence actually living and available at a place where one has some official connection: *The school has a doctor* in residence *at all times.*

res·i·dent (rĕz′ ə dənt) ***n-*** **1** person who lives in a place; especially, one who has legal residence: *She is a* resident *of New York.* **2** a physician who undergoes advanced training in a medical specialty while in residence at a hospital. ***adj-*** living in a place: *a* resident *New Yorker.*

res·i·den·tial (rĕz′ ə dĕn′ shəl) ***adj-*** **1** having to do with residence: *There are certain* residential *requirements for voting in this city.* **2** made up of or suitable for homes or apartments: *the* residential *section of a city.*

re·sid·u·al (rĭ zĭj′ o͞o əl) ***adj-*** remaining as a residue after some process or event: *He had some* residual *cash after paying his debts.* ***n-*** remainder; residue; residuum.

res·i·due (rĕz′ ə do͞o′, -dyo͞o′) ***n-*** **1** what remains after part has been taken away: *There was a* residue *of ash after the fire.* **2** in law, that part of an estate remaining after payment of all debts, charges, and particular bequests.

re·sid·u·um (rə zĭj′ o͞o əm) ***n-*** [*pl.* **re·sid·u·a** (-ə)] residue.

re·sign (rĭ zīn′) ***vt-*** to give up (a position, office, etc.) voluntarily: *He* resigned *his position on the school board.* ***vi-***: *The president of the club has just* resigned.
resign (oneself) to to submit to; accept without complaint: *He* resigned himself to *his fate.*

res·ig·na·tion (rĕz′ ĭg nā′ shən) ***n-*** **1** voluntary giving up of a job, office, etc. **2** formal statement of this: *The boss read John's* resignation. **3** acceptance of what must come; submission: *his* resignation *in the face of disaster.*

re·signed (rĭ zīnd′) ***adj-*** accepting calmly and without complaint; submitting patiently: *his* resigned *obedience.* —***adv-*** **re·sign′ ed·ly.**

re·sil·i·ence (rĭ zĭl′ ē əns) ***n-*** power of being resilient. Also **re·sil′ i·en·cy.**

re·sil·i·ent (rĭ zĭl′ ē ənt) ***adj-*** **1** having the property of springing back and returning to a former shape after having been pushed, struck, bent, etc.: *Springs are made of* resilient *metal.* **2** recovering strength or good humor quickly; buoyant; cheerful: *to have a* resilient *nature.* —***adv-*** **re·sil′i·ent·ly.**

res·in (rĕz′ ən) ***n-*** **1** sticky substance found in certain trees, especially firs and pines. It turns yellow or brown when hard, and is used in varnish and some medicines. **2** any of various similar synthetic substances, especially those used as plastics or adhesive cements.

re·sist (rĭ zĭst′) ***vt-*** **1** to fight back against; prevent the advance of; repel: *The regiment successfully* resisted *the attack.* **2** to withstand; try not to yield to: *to* resist *temptation.* **3** to be only slightly or not at all affected by (force, heat, corrosion, etc.): *This material* resists *crushing. The alloy* resists *rust.* ***vi-*** to offer opposition; refuse to agree or obey: *He continues to* resist *against all reason.*

re·sis·tance (rĭ zĭs′ təns) ***n-*** **1** a resisting; opposition: *His* resistance *spoiled our plans. They offered no* resistance *to the invasion.* **2** organization of patriots in an occupied or oppressed country who fight back by underground and guerrilla means: *the* resistance *in Holland.* **3** ability of the body to combat disease: *Fatigue lowered his* resistance, *and he caught a cold.* **4** anything, especially gravity, friction, or inertia, that opposes movement or change in the rate of movement. **5** in electricity, the opposition that a material offers to the flow of current through it. Resistance is measured in ohms.

re·sist·ant (rĭ zĭs′ tənt) ***adj-*** tending to or able to resist: *He had a* resistant *nature.* ***n-*** person or thing that resists.

re·sist·er (rĭ zĭs′ tər) ***n-*** person who resists, or is a member of an organized resistance. ***Hom-*** resistor.

re·sis·tive (rĭ zĭs′ tĭv) ***adj-*** inclined to oppose; opposing; obstructing. —***adv-*** **re·sis′ tive·ly.** ***n-*** **re·sis′ tive·ness.**

re·sis·tiv·i·ty (rē′ zĭs′ tĭv′ ə tē) ***n-*** the power of an object or body to resist the transmission of heat, electricity, etc.

re·sist·less (rĭ zĭst′ ləs) ***adj-*** **1** not to be withstood; irresistible: *a* resistless *urge to travel.* **2** not offering resistance: *a* resistless *acceptance of fate.* —***adv-*** **re·sist′ less·ly.** ***n-*** **re·sist′ less·ness.**

re·sis·tor (rĭ zĭs′ tər) ***n-*** in electricity and electronics, any of various devices used to introduce resistance into a circuit or vary the resistance of a circuit. ***Hom-*** resister.

res·o·lute (rĕz′ ə lo͞ot′) ***adj-*** determined; firm: *a* resolute *effort.* —***adv-*** **res′ o·lute′ ly.** ***n-*** **res′ o·lute′ ness.**

res·o·lu·tion (rĕz′ ə lo͞o′ shən) ***n-*** **1** firmness of will, belief, and action; determination. **2** firm pledge or vow; solemn commitment: *a New Year's* resolution. **3** formal proposition to be debated and voted upon by some group acting officially: *a joint* resolution *of Congress; the club's* resolution *expressing its concern.* **4** final explanation or unraveling; final solving of problems and answering of questions: *the* resolution *of a mystery; the* resolution *of a play.* **5** *Music* the move from a dissonant note or chord to a harmonious (consonant) note or chord. **6** resolving power.

re·solve (rĭ zŏlv′) ***vt-*** **[re·solved, re·solv·ing]** **1** to decide firmly and solemnly; vow; swear (takes only a clause or an infinitive as object): *He* resolved *that he would win.* **2** to cause or find a solution of: *to* resolve *a conflict; to* resolve *a mystery.* **3** to separate; divide; analyze: *He* resolved *the main topic into four subtopics.* **4** to declare formally by vote (takes only a clause or an infinitive as object): *The club* resolved *that a letter of thanks be sent to the mayor.* **5** in optics, to detect or reproduce (points, lines, etc., that are or appear to be very close together) as separate images. ***vi-*** to be separable or divisible: *The question* resolves *into three parts.* ***n-*** **1** firmness of purpose; resolution: *a man of great* resolve. **2** something decided on or determined; resolution: *to keep one's* resolve *to work hard.* —***adj-*** **re·solv′ a·ble.**

Any of these words means **re-** ("again") plus the meaning of the rest of the word as given in the main text.

re′ sew′
re′ show′
re′ sil′ ver
re′ sit′ ting
re′ smooth′

---

re·solved (rĭ zŏlvd′) ***adj-*** firmly purposeful; determined: *a* resolved *person.* **—*adv-* re·solv′ ed·ly.**
resolved, that it is formally stated that (a certain fact is true, a certain course should be taken, etc.).

resolving power ***n-*** the ability of an optical system, such as a telescope or spectroscope, to produce separate images of closely spaced points, lines, objects, etc.

res·o·nance (rĕz′ ə nəns) ***n-*** **1** richness and volume of sound, especially when this is produced by a cavity or chamber that amplifies the sound and improves its quality: *a voice of great* resonance; *the* resonance *of a guitar.* **2** ability of a cavity or chamber to produce this: *the* resonance *of the room.* **3** *Physics* the condition of a vibrating system under which the intensity of vibrations increases greatly when relatively weak vibrations of the same frequency are superimposed, either from outside the system or by feedback.

res·o·nant (rĕz′ ə nənt) ***adj-*** **1** echoing; resounding: *the* resonant *walls of the cave.* **2** having a full, rich sound: *a* resonant *voice.* **3** *Physics* of, having to do with, or exhibiting resonance. **—*adv-* res′ o·nant·ly.**

res·o·nate (rĕz′ ə nāt′) ***vi-*** **[res·o·nat·ed, res·o·nat·ing]** to be resonant; reach or exhibit resonance.

res·o·na·tor (rĕz′ ə nā′ tər) ***n-*** something that resonates or promotes resonance, especially in a musical instrument or an electronic apparatus.

re·sort (rĭ zȯrt′, -zôrt′) ***n-*** **1** place where people go on vacations and holidays for rest, sport, etc.: *a winter* resort *in New Hampshire*; *a gambling* resort. **2** person or thing applied to or appealed to for help; recourse: *Your best* resort *in this case is a lawyer.* **3** place where people meet, hang about, drink, etc.: *That barroom is a* resort *of criminals.* ***vi-*** **1** to apply or appeal for help: *I* resorted *to the dictionary. Where will I* resort *in my need?* **2** to go (to) for pleasure, relaxation, companionship, etc.: *I often* resort *to the movies in the evenings.*

re·sound (rĭ zound′) ***vi-*** **1** to echo and reecho; reverberate: *The hills* resounded *with their shouts. His fame* resounded *far and wide.* **2** to make a loud sound: *The trumpet* resounded *through the auditorium.*

re·sound·ing (rĭ zoun′ dĭng) ***adj-*** **1** resonant; echoing. **2** leaving no doubt; emphatic: *a* resounding *failure.* **—*adv-* re·sound′ ing·ly.**

re·source (rĭ sôrs′, -zôrs′, rē′ sôrs′) ***n-*** **1** person or thing a person turns to in an emergency; resort: *With his supplies gone, his only* resource *was his knowledge of the woods.* **2** stock or supply of anything useful: *Power is a necessary* resource *for industry.* **3 resources** all the wealth of an individual, company, or country: *a country of unlimited* resources; *natural* resources. **4** ability to handle a difficult or dangerous situation; resourcefulness: *a man of* resource.

re·source·ful (rĭ sôrs′fəl, rĭ zôrs′-) ***adj-*** capable of handling a difficult situation: *He was always very* resourceful *in emergencies.* **—*adv-* re·source′ ful·ly. *n-* re·source′ ful·ness.**

re·spect (rĭ spĕkt′) ***vt-*** **1** to show esteem for; honor: *He* respected *the man's honesty.* **2** to pay attention to; show consideration; heed: *to* respect *the advice of parents*; *to* respect *someone's wishes.* **3** to be mindful of; avoid breaking or violating: *to* respect *his privacy*; *to* respect *the law.* **4** to have relation to; concern: *The matter* respects *our welfare.* ***n-*** **1** honor; esteem: *He won the* respect *of the community.* **2** manner or deportment that indicates courtesy, consideration, duty, etc.: *her* respect *for her parents*; respect *for the law.* **3 respects** good wishes; regards or greetings: *to pay one's* respects. **4** condition of being honored or esteemed: *The community held him in* respect. **5** special point or particular; detail: *In certain* respects *the concerto is similar to Beethoven's.* **—*n-* re·spec′ ter.**
in respect to (or **of**) or **with respect to** in reference to; about; concerning.

re·spect·a·ble (rĭ spĕk′ tə bəl) ***adj-*** **1** deserving respect; having a good reputation: *a* respectable *man.* **2** of a kind considered proper or good enough: *to wear* respectable *clothes*; respectable *behavior.* **3** fairly large or good: *a* respectable *number*; respectable *talents.* **—*n-* re·spect′ a·ble·ness. *adv-* re·spect′ a·bly.**

re·spect·a·bil·i·ty (rĭ spĕk′ tə bĭl′ ə tē) ***n-*** [*pl.* **re·spect·a·bil·i·ties**] **1** condition of having a good reputation; good name: *His* respectability *was most important to him.* **2 respectabilities** certain customs, conventions, etc., that are considered socially proper.

re·spect·ful (rĭ spĕkt′ fəl) ***adj-*** showing proper respect or courtesy; polite. **—*adv-* re·spect′ ful·ly. *n-* re·spect′ ful·ness.**
►Should not be confused with RESPECTIVE.

re·spect·ing (rĭ spĕk′ tĭng) ***prep-*** regarding; concerning; about: *an argument* respecting *the merits of the case.*

re·spect·ive (rĭ spĕk′ tĭv) ***adj-*** belonging or proper to each; particular; individual: *The students were graded according to their* respective *efforts.*
►Should not be confused with RESPECTFUL.

re·spec·tive·ly (rĭ spĕk′ tĭv lē) ***adv-*** each in the order named: *Andy, Helen, and Ralph won the first, second, and third prizes* respectively.

re·spell (rē′ spĕl′) ***vt-*** **1** to spell again. **2** to represent (a word, speech sound, etc.) with letters or symbols that differ from those of its ordinary spelling, in order to show pronunciation; spell phonetically.

res·pi·ra·tion (rĕs′ pə rā′ shən) ***n-*** **1** the inhaling and exhaling of air; breathing. **2** *Biology* any of various processes by which living organisms take in oxygen, use it in metabolism, and expel carbon dioxide and other wastes of metabolism.

res·pi·ra·tor (rĕs′ pə rā′ tər) ***n-*** **1** device worn over the mouth and nose to prevent the breathing of harmful substances. **2** automatic device, such as a Pulmotor, for applying artificial respiration.

res·pi·ra·to·ry (rĕs′ pə rə tôr′ ē) ***adj-*** of, relating to, or affecting respiration: *a* respiratory *disease.*

respiratory system ***n-*** the group of organs, parts, or structures in any particular organism that are concerned with respiration.

re·spire (rĭ spīər′) ***vi-*** **[re·spired, re·spir·ing]** to inhale and exhale air; breathe.

res·pite (rĕs′ pĭt) ***n-*** **1** short period of rest or relief: *a* respite *from worry.* **2** short postponement of a penalty, such as a sentence of death; reprieve. ***vt-*** **[res·pit·ed, res·pit·ing]** to grant relief or a delay to (someone).

re·splen·dent (rĭ splĕn′ dənt) ***adj-*** shining brilliantly; splendid; dazzling: *The birthday cake was* resplendent *with candles.* **—*adv-* re·splen′ dent·ly. *n-* re·splen′-dence:** *the* resplendence *of the sunset.*

re·spond (rĭ spŏnd′) ***vi-*** **1** to reply; answer: *to* respond *to a letter.* **2** to react; show the effects of: *to* respond *to kindness*; respond *to medical treatment.*

re·sponse (rĭ spŏns′) ***n-*** **1** act of responding; answer; reply: *Her* response *to my question was very intelligent. My letter to her brought no* response. **2** reaction: *He was disappointed by the lack of* response *to his jokes.* **3** reaction of muscles, glands, etc., to a stimulus. **4** in church, the words spoken or sung by the people in reply to the priest or minister.

re·spon·si·bil·i·ty (rĭ spŏn′ sə bĭl′ ə tē) ***n-*** [*pl.* **re·spon·si·bil·i·ties**] **1** condition or fact of being responsible: *He refuses to accept any* responsibility *for the accident.*

2 something for which one is responsible; duty: *A family is a great* responsibility. *The President has many* responsibilities. 3 capability; reliability: *His* responsibility *in the matter was reassuring.*

re·spon·si·ble (rĭ spŏn′ sə bəl) ***adj-*** 1 able to assume or carry out a duty; reliable; trustworthy: *A* responsible *boy should be chosen to collect the club dues.* 2 liable to blame for loss, damage, etc.; in a position where one can be held to blame; accountable: *The students are* responsible *for any books lent them. A bus driver is* responsible *for the safety of the passengers.* 3 operating as the cause or reason; causative: *What is* responsible *for the shortage of water?* 4 requiring a person to take charge of important matters: *a* responsible *job.* **—*n-* re·spon′ si·ble·ness. *adv-* re·spon′ si·bly.**

re·spon·sive (rĭ spŏn′ sĭv) ***adj-*** 1 answering or replying: *He showed his support by a* responsive *wink.* 2 responding readily; sympathetic: *a* responsive *nature*; *a* responsive *audience.* **—*adv-* re·spon′ sive·ly. *n-* re·spon′ sive·ness.**

[1]**rest** (rĕst) ***vi-*** 1 to be still; stop working; relax: *to* rest *a bit before going back to work.* 2 to lie down; sleep: *He went upstairs to* rest. 3 to lie dead; be buried: *The old man now* rests *with his forefathers.* 4 to escape and be free from excitement, anxiety, etc.; be calm or tranquil: *He often* rested *in the country.* 5 to be supported by; stand, lean, or lie upon: *The house* rests *upon its foundation. She* rested *against the arm of the sofa.* 6 to be based or founded (usually followed by "on" or "upon"): *His theory* rested *on few facts.* 7 to rely or depend (usually followed by "on" or "upon"): *Success or failure* rests *on your efforts.* 8 in law, to finish the presentation of a case in court: *The defense* rests. ***vt-*** 1 to give or permit (someone or something) a relief from working: *to* rest *a horse*; *to* rest *one's eyes.* 2 to place on a support; lean or lay: *to* rest *the statue on a pedestal.* 3 to base; found: *I* rest *my conclusion on three facts.* 4 in law, to finish presenting (a case) in court: *The prosecutor* rested *his case.* ***n-*** 1 ease and relaxation after work; ceasing of effort; also, lack of motion: *to need* rest; *a week of* rest. 2 death, thought of as freeing one from work and trouble: *He went to his* rest *calmly, after a hard life.* 3 something that supports; a stand: *an arm* rest. 4 place of shelter or lodging: *a sailors'* rest. 5 *Military* in drill, condition under which soldiers in ranks may talk and move, but must keep one foot in

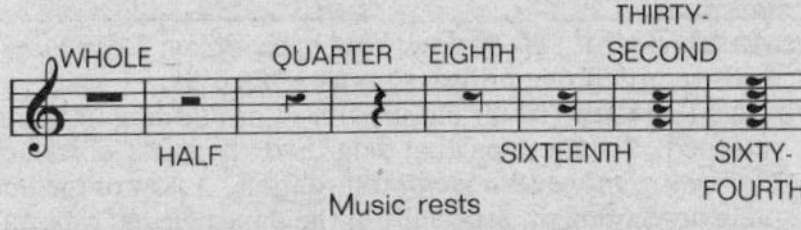

Music rests

place. 6 *Music* silence or pause of definite and indicated length; also, any of several signs for this. ***as modifier:*** *a* rest *camp*; *a* rest *stop*; *a* rest *home.* [from Old English **rest** of the same meaning.] ***Hom-*** wrest.

at rest 1 lying still; having no motion: *Nothing was* at rest *on the tossing boat.* 2 dead and buried: *He lies* at rest *in the churchyard.* **come to rest** to stop moving: *The falling rock* came to rest *near my tent.* **lay (someone) to rest** to bury (a dead person).

[2]**rest** (rĕst) ***n-*** whoever or whatever remains; residue: *Some of us stayed; the* rest *went home.* [from French, from Latin **restāre** meaning "to stop or stay back or behind."] ***Hom-*** wrest.

re·start (rē′ stärt′) ***vt-*** 1 to start again. 2 to undertake again after an interruption; resume: *to* restart *production.* ***vi-***: *The factory* restarted *after seven days.*

re·state (rē stāt′, rē′-) ***vt-*** **[re·stat·ed, re·stat·ing]** to state or express again, or in a different way. **—*n-* re·state′ ment.**

res·tau·rant (rĕs′ tə rənt, -ränt′) ***n-*** public dining room where meals are served to customers. ***as modifier:*** *the* restaurant *business*; restaurant *food.*

res·tau·ra·teur (rĕs′ tə rə tûr′) ***n-*** keeper or proprietor of a restaurant.

rest·ful (rĕst′ fəl) ***adj-*** 1 giving rest: *a* restful *sleep.* 2 giving a sense of peace or tranquillity: *a* restful *scene.* **—*adv-* rest′ ful·ly. —*n-* rest′ ful·ness.**

resting stage ***n-*** *Biology* interphase.

res·ti·tu·tion (rĕs′ tə to͞o′ shən, -tyo͞o′ shən) ***n-*** 1 act of giving back to the rightful owner something that has been taken away or lost; restoration. 2 act of making good any loss, injury, or damage; reparation.

res·tive (rĕs′ tĭv) ***adj-*** 1 constantly moving or looking about; too impatient to be still; restless: *The children soon became* restive. 2 tending to resist control: *a* restive *horse.* **—*adv-* res′ tive·ly. *n-* res′ tive·ness.**

rest·less (rĕst′ ləs) ***adj-*** 1 unable to be still; nervous and impatient: *The tired children became very* restless. *The* restless *spirit of adventure drives me.* 2 giving no rest: *a troubled and* restless *sleep.* **—*adv-* rest′ less·ly. *n-* rest′ less·ness.**

re·stock (rē stŏk′, rē′-) ***vt-*** 1 to fill or supply again with goods, provisions, etc.: *to* restock *the kitchen with food after the holiday*; *to* restock *the store after a sale.* 2 to stock (a lake, river, etc.) again with fish. ***vi-*** to get provisions or supplies again: *The expedition* restocked *and climbed on.*

res·to·ra·tion (rĕs′ tə rā′ shən) ***n-*** 1 a restoring or being restored: *the* restoration *of an old building*; *his* restoration *to health*; *the* restoration *of a child to its parents.* 2 something restored to a former or original condition: *This antique chair is a good* restoration. 3 **Restoration** in British history, the return of monarchy with Charles II in 1660 after the period of Puritan rule; also, the twenty-five year period following this return.

re·stor·a·tive (rĭ stôr′ ə tĭv) ***adj-*** 1 having power to restore: *a* restorative *medicine.* 2 of or relating to restoration: *the* restorative *work on the church.* ***n-*** something which has power to restore; especially, medicine used to bring back health or to restore consciousness.

re·store (rĭ stôr′) ***vt-*** **[re·stored, re·stor·ing]** 1 to bring back to a former or original condition: *to* restore *an old building*; *to* restore *health.* 2 to put back into a former position or place: *to* restore *a person to office*; *to* restore *a book to the shelf.* 3 to give back or return to the owner: *to* restore *stolen money*; *to* restore *a lost pet.* 4 to cause to exist again; reestablish: *to* restore *order.* **—*adj-* re·stor′ able. *n-* re·stor′ er.**

re·strain (rĭ strān′) ***vt-*** 1 to check; hold back; suppress; keep within reasonable limits: *I could not* restrain *my*

Any of these words means **re-** ("again") plus the meaning of the rest of the word as given in the main text.

re′ sow′
re′ spring′
re′ staff′
re′ stage′
re′ stim′ u·late′
re′ straight′ en

fāte, făt, dâre, bärn; bē, bĕt, mêre; bīte, bĭt; nōte, hŏt, môre, dȯg; fŭn, fûr; to͞o, bo͝ok; oil; out; tar; thin; then; hw for wh as in *wh*at; zh for s as in u*s*ual; ə for a, e, i, o, u, as in *a*go, lin*e*n, per*i*l, at*o*m, min*u*s

enthusiasm. Please restrain *yourself.* **2** to tie up or otherwise confine: *The police had to* restrain *the drunken man.* **—*adj-* re·strain'a·ble. *n-* re·strain'er.**

re·strain·ed·ly (rĭ strān'əd lē) ***adv-*** in a restrained manner; without excess; with restraint or discipline.

re·straint (rĭ strānt') ***n-*** **1** a restraining; a limiting of freedom; a keeping in check: *He kept his angry feeling under* restraint. **2** confinement, especially in a strait jacket or in bonds: *The prisoner was kept in* restraint. **3** something that restrains or holds back: *The harsh law was a* restraint *to freedom.* **4** self-control; reserve.

restraint of trade ***n-*** artificial setting of prices, the creation of a monopoly, or any similar practice that hinders the free exchange of goods and services and interferes with fair competition.

re·strict (rĭ strĭkt') ***vt-*** to keep within a certain limit; confine: *He* restricted *himself to two meals a day.*

re·strict·ed (rĭ strĭk'təd) ***adj-*** **1** confined; limited. **2** not available to the general public; not for release or circulation; also, limited to a certain group: *a* restricted *publication;* restricted *information.*

re·stric·tion (rĭ strĭk'shən) ***n-*** **1** a limiting or confining: *We are permitted to use the library without* restriction. **2** something that restricts: *He resents all* restrictions.

re·stric·tive (rĭ strĭk'tĭv) ***adj-*** serving or tending to restrict. **—*adv-* re·stric'tive·ly. *n-* re·stric'tive·ness.**

restrictive clause *Grammar* ***n-*** dependent clause that is used as an adjective to restrict or specify the identity of the noun or pronoun. Example: *People* who don't pay their bills *have poor credit.* (Without the restrictive clause, the preceding sentence would be a foolish statement.) Restrictive clauses cannot be omitted without seriously damaging the meaning of the sentence. They are not set off by commas from the word or phrase they modify. See also *nonrestrictive clause.*

rest room ***n-*** room in a public building equipped with washing and toilet facilities.

re·sult (rĭ zŭlt') ***n-*** that which follows a cause, series of causes, or process; consequence; outcome: *All this damage is the* result *of the wind storm.* ***vi-*** to happen or occur from a cause: *A flood* resulted *from the heavy rain.*
result in to end in: *Your efforts should* result in *success.*

re·sult·ant (rĭ zŭl'tənt) ***adj-*** following as a consequence: *the* resultant *damage to the crops.* ***n-*** **1** result. **2** *Physics* a single force or velocity that represents the combined effect of two or more forces or velocities; especially, a vector that represents the algebraic sum of several vectors.

re·sume (rĭ zōōm', -zyōōm') ***vt-*** **[re·sumed, re·sum·ing] 1** to begin again after an interruption: *Class will* resume *work after the holiday.* **2** to occupy again: *Please* resume *your seats.* ***vi-*** to continue; begin again.

ré·su·mé (rĕz'ə mā') ***n*** **1** brief account of one's career, qualifications, and employment record. **2** synopsis or summary: *a* résumé *of a book.*

re·sump·tion (rĭ zŭmp'shən) ***n-*** a resuming; a beginning again after an interruption.

re·sur·gence (rĭ sûr'jəns) ***n-*** a rising again: *a* resurgence *of business activity.* **—*adj-* re·sur'gent.**

res·ur·rect (rĕz'ə rĕkt') ***vt-*** **1** to bring to life again; raise from the dead. **2** to bring back to attention or into use again: *to* resurrect *a forgotten opera.*

res·ur·rec·tion (rĕz'ə rĕk'shən) ***n-*** **1** a return to life after death. **2** a bringing back into use; revival: *the* resurrection *of forgotten style.* **3 the Resurrection** Christ's rising from the dead, celerated at Easter.

re·sus·ci·tate (rĭ sŭs'ə tāt') ***vt-*** **[re·sus·ci·tat·ed, re·sus·i·tat·ing]** to bring back to life from apparent death; revive from unconsciousness. **—*n-* re·sus'ci·ta'tion. *adj-* re·sus'ci·ta'tive.**

ret (rĕt) ***vt-*** **[ret·ted, ret·ting]** to soak (flax, hemp, timber, etc.) to decompose the woody matter around the bast.

re·tail (rē'tāl') ***adj-*** **1** of or relating to the selling of goods directly to the user or consumer, as distinguished from wholesale selling: *the* retail *price;* retail *sales.* **2** engaged in such selling: *a* retail *store.* ***adv-*** (also **at retail**) within the prices, quantities, and methods appropriate to selling directly to the user or consumer: *He buys wholesale and sells* retail. ***n-*** such selling: *the* retail *of food.* ***vt-*** **1** to sell in this way: *My father* retails *shoes.* **2** (also rē'tāl') to tell in detail; pass along to others: *to* retail *gossip.* ***vi-*** to be sold directly to the user or consumer: *The shirt* retails *for $25.*

re·tail·er (rē'tā'lər) ***n-*** person who sells goods retail.

re·tail·ing (rē'tā'lĭng) ***n-*** the selling of goods at retail; also, the specialized study and management of such selling. *as* ***modifier*: *a* retailing *expert.*

re·tain (rĭ tān') ***vt-*** **1** to keep; preserve; continue to have: *I tried to* retain *my sense of humor. This paint* retains *its luster.* **2** to keep in a fixed place or condition; hold: *We built a wall to* retain *the earth behind our house. Some stones* retain *heat for a long time.* **3** to remember: *to* retain *facts.* **4** to engage the services of, usually by payment of a fee: *to* retain *a lawyer.*

re·tain·er (rĭ tā'nər) ***n-*** **1** fee paid in advance, as to a lawyer. **2** formerly, the servant of a person of high rank. **3** metal wire used to help hold the teeth in place. **4** person who retains or keeps possession.

[1]re·take (rē tāk', rē'-) ***vt-*** **[re·took, re·tak·en, re·tak·ing] 1** to take or receive again; also, to recapture: *to* retake *a town.* **2** to photograph again; especially, to film (part of a motion picture) over in order to improve it.

[2]re·take (rē'tāk') ***n-*** another filming or recording of a motion-picture or television scene, a part of a musical piece, etc., in order to make improvements.

re·tal·i·ate (rĭ tăl'ē āt') ***vi-*** **[re·tal·i·at·ed, re·tal·i·at·ing]** to reply to an action or utterance by a similar one; to pay back an injury or insult; return like for like: *It is only natural to* retaliate *when you are injured or insulted.* **—*n-* re·tal'i·a'tion. *adj-* re·tal'i·a·to'ry** (-ē ə tôr'ē): *a* retaliatory *attack.*

re·tard (rĭ tärd') ***vt-*** to slow; hold back; delay: *Deep snowdrifts* retarded *our progress.* **—*n-* re·tard'er.**

re·tar·da·tion (rē'tär dā'shən) ***n-*** **1** a retarding or being retarded. **2** something that retards or hinders; obstacle: *Our lack of money is a major* retardation. **3** slow or incomplete development, especially of the mind: *mental* retardation.

retch (rĕch) ***vi-*** to try to vomit.

re·tell (rē tĕl', rē'-) ***vt-*** **[re·told, re·tell·ing]** to relate again: *to* retell *a story.*

re·ten·tion (rĭ tĕn'shən) ***n-*** **1** a retaining or being retained. **2** the power to retain; especially, the power of keeping things in mind; memory.

re·ten·tive (rĭ tĕn'tĭv) ***adj-*** tending, or having the power, to retain: *a* retentive *memory* **—*adv-* re·ten'tive·ly. *n-* re·ten'tive·ness.**

Any of these words means **re-** ("again") plus the meaning of the rest of the word as given in the main text.

re'strength'en
re'string'
re'struc'ture
re'stud'y
re'stuff'
re'style'
re'sub·mis'sion
re'sub·mit'
re'sum'mon
re'sur'face
re'sur'vey'

ret·i·cence (rĕt′ ə səns) ***n-*** caution or hesitation, especially in speaking; habitual reserve: *My* reticence *is due to lack of knowledge, not to shyness.*

ret·i·cent (rĕt′ ə sənt) ***adj-*** inclined to reticence; behaving with reticence. ***—adv-* ret′ i·cent·ly.**

re·tic·u·lat·ed (rĭ tĭk′ yə lā′ təd) ***adj-* 1** having a pattern like a network: *a* reticulated *decoration on a vase.* **2** woven in a network: *a bag of* reticulated *string.*

ret·i·na (rĕt′ ə nə) ***n-*** [*pl.* **ret·i·nas** or **ret·i·nae** (-nē)] inner lining of the eyeball, made up of several layers of specialized cells and nerve fibers and forming the outer end of the optic nerve. Images fall on the retina through the lens, and pass along the optic nerve to the brain. For picture, see *eye.*

ret·i·nue (rĕt′ ə nōō′, -nyōō′) ***n-*** group of servants, assistants, aides, etc., accompanying a person of rank or importance.

re·tire (rĭ tīər′) ***vi-*** [**re·tired, re·tir·ing**] **1** to give up one's work or position, usually after long service and because of age or poor health: *He will receive a pension when he* retires. **2** to withdraw; go away: *He has* retired *to the country for a rest.* **3** to go to bed: *to* retire *at ten o'clock.* **4** to retreat: *Heavy attacks caused the enemy to* retire. ***vt-* 1** to remove from work or position, usually after long service: *The company* retires *its employees at 65.* **2** to withdraw; especially, to take (money, bonds, etc.) out of circulation. **3** in baseball, to put out (a batter, side, etc.): *Three putouts* retire *a side in baseball.*

re·tired (rĭ tīərd′) ***adj-* 1** withdrawn from activity; secluded: *Widow Brown lives a* retired *life.* **2** no longer actively doing one's lifework: *a* retired *doctor.*

re·tire·ment (rĭ tīər′ mənt) ***n-* 1** a retiring or being retired. **2** period after being retired: *During his* retirement *he spent much time reading.* as **modifier**: *a* retirement *plan*; retirement *benefits offered by the company.*

re·tir·ing (rĭ tīər′ ĭng) ***adj-*** avoiding society or publicity; shy; modest: *He has a* retiring *nature.*

re·tool (rē′ tōōl′) ***vi-* 1** to make or get the machines, tools, dies, etc., needed for a new manufacturing project or process: *The plant will* retool *for next year's model.* **2** to make changes for a new kind of work, new conditions, etc.: *Under new management the whole company* retooled. ***vt-***: *We have six months to* retool *the factory.*

[1]**re·tort** (rĭ tŏrt′, -tôrt′) ***vi-*** to answer back or reply sharply: *He* retorted *quickly when they made fun of him.* ***n-*** quick, witty, sharp, or angry answer. [from Latin **retortus** and **retorquere,** "to twist back violently."]

[2]**re·tort** (rē′ tŏrt′, -tŏrt′) ***n-*** piece of apparatus, usually of glass and having a long, tapering spout. Retorts are used for distilling or decomposing substances with heat. [from Medieval Latin **retorta,** "[1]retort."]

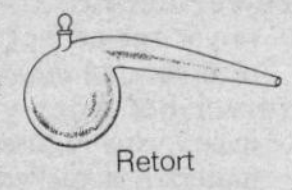
Retort

re·touch (rē′ tŭch′) ***vt-*** to touch up; improve by going over with a fine brush, airbrush, etc.: *to* retouch *a painting*; *to* retouch *a negative.*

re·trace (rĭ trās′) ***vt-*** [**re·traced, re·trac·ing**] **1** to go back over: *to* retrace *one's steps.* **2** to trace back to an origin or source: *to* retrace *one's family line.* **3** (*also* rē′ trās′) to trace over again: *He carefully* retraced *the map.*

re·tract (rĭ trăkt′) ***vt-* 1** (considered intransitive when the direct object is implied but not expressed) to take back (a statement, opinion, or promise); renounce; disown: *I will not* retract *what I said about him.* **2** to pull back or in: *Cats can* retract *their claws.* ***—adj-* re·tract′ a·ble.**

re·trac·tile (rĭ trăk′ təl, -tīl′) ***adj-*** such as can be drawn back or drawn in: *the* retractile *claws of a cat.*

re·trac·tion (rĭ trăk′ shən) ***n-*** a retracting or being retracted; a drawing in or back: *a retraction of a claim.*

re·trac·tor (rĭ trăk′ tər) ***n-* 1** *Medicine* surgical instrument for drawing back the edges of a wound or incision. **2** *Biology* any muscle that draws back or draws in a retractile organ or part.

[1]**re·tread** (rē′ trĕd′) ***n-*** a tire furnished with a new tread.

[2]**re·tread** (rē trĕd′, rē′-) ***vt-*** to put a new tread on (the stripped casing of a tire).

re·tread (rē′ trĕd′) ***vt-*** [**re·trod, re·trod·den, re·tread·ing**] to tread again: *I* re-trod *the old path.*

re·treat (rĭ trēt′) ***vi-* 1** to fall back; withdraw from action; retire: *The troops* retreated. **2** to go for privacy or rest: *He* retreats *to the country on weekends.* ***n-* 1** a falling back; withdrawal; especially, the retiring of troops before an enemy. **2** *Military* (1) a signal for withdrawal: *The trumpets sounded* retreat. (2) bugle call sounded at a flag-lowering ceremony at sunset. **3** place for quiet, rest, or refuge: *He goes to his mountain* retreat *every Saturday.* **4** withdrawal to a place of seclusion for meditation, prayer, religious instruction, etc.; also, time spent in such a place.

beat a retreat to signal for retreat by beating a drum; hence, to retreat.

re·trench (rĭ trĕnch′) ***vt-* 1** to reduce: *to* retrench *expenses.* **2** to take away; remove: *to* retrench *certain rights.* ***vi-*** to cut down expenses. ***—n-* re·trench′ ment.**

re·tri·al (rē′ trī′ əl) ***n-*** second or further trying of a case in court: *The hung jury caused a* retrial.

ret·ri·bu·tion (rĕ′ trə byōō′ shən) ***n-*** punishment for evil done; especially, loss or suffering inflicted as a just punishment.

re·trib·u·tive (rĭ trĭb′ yə tĭv′) or **re·trib·u·to·ry** (-tôr ē) ***adj-*** of or relating to retribution; coming as retribution; inflicted or given as punishment for bad actions: *the power of* retributive *justice.* ***—adv-* re·trib′ u·tive·ly.**

re·trieve (rĭ trēv′) ***vt-*** [**re·trieved, re·triev·ing**] **1** to get back; regain; recover: *He* retrieved *the ball from the river. You may* retrieve *your lost fortune.* **2** to make good; put right again; make amends for: *to* retrieve *a mistake.* **3** of dogs, to find and bring back (wounded or dead game). ***vi-*** to find and bring in dead or wounded game: *He trained his dog to* retrieve.

re·triev·er (rĭ trē′ vər) ***n-*** dog trained to go after and bring back game shot by a hunter.

Retriever, about 4 ft. long

retro- *prefix* back; backward: *a* retro*rocket*; retro*grade.*

ret·ro·ac·tive (rĕ′ trō ăk′ tĭv) ***adj-*** having the power to influence, alter, or affect what has been done in the past: *a* retroactive *law.*

ret·ro·flex (rĕ′ trō flĕks′) ***adj-*** bent abruptly backward.

ret·ro·grade (rĕ′ trə grād′) ***adj-* 1** moving backward; retreating; reversed: *a* retrograde *motion.* **2** going from a better to a worse state or character: *a* retrograde

---

Any of these words means **re-** ("again") plus the meaning of the rest of the word as given in the main text.

re′ test′ | **re′ train′** | **re′ trans′ mit′**
re′ think′ | **re′ trans′ mis′ sion** | **re′ trav·erse′**

---

people. 3 *Astronomy* of or relating to an apparent backward motion of a planet, from west to east, or to any other motion that is contrary to the general motion. ***vi-*** **[ret·ro·grad·ed, ret·ro·grad·ing]** 1 to go, or appear to go, backward. 2 to go from better to worse; decline.

ret·ro·gress (rĕ′ trə grĕs′) ***vi-*** to move or go backward; especially, to go back to a less advanced state; decline.

ret·ro·gres·sion (rĕ′ trə grĕsh′ ən) ***n-*** 1 a retrogressing or moving backward; a going back to a less advanced stage. 2 *Biology* a return by an animal or plant to a simpler, more primitive state. **—*adj-*** **ret′ ro·gres′ sive.** ***adv-*** **ret′ ro·gres′ sive·ly.**

ret·ro·rock·et (rĕ′ trō rŏk′ ət) *Space* ***n-*** a braking rocket that produces thrust opposite to the direction in which a spacecraft moves.

ret·ro·spect (rĕ′ trə spĕkt′) ***n-*** a review of the past.

ret·ro·spec·tion (rĕ′ trə spĕk′ shən) ***n-*** 1 a meditating upon things past. 2 a reviewing of the past.

ret·ro·spec·tive (rĕ′ trə spĕk′ tĭv) ***adj-*** 1 looking back, or given to looking back, on things past: *a* retrospective *mood.* 2 applying to the past; retroactive. **—*adv-*** **ret′ ro·spec′ tive·ly.**

re·try (rē trī′, rē′-) ***vt-*** **[re·tried, re·try·ing]** to try, or put on trial, again: *to* retry *a prisoner.*

re·turn (rĭ tûrn′) ***vi-*** 1 to come or go back to a place, person, or condition: *to* return *to one's home.* 2 to begin or appear again: *Spring* returns. 3 to come or go back in thought: *to* return *to the subject.* ***vt-*** 1 to bring, send, carry, or put back; restore: *to* return *a borrowed book.* 2 to give, pay, or send back in the same manner: *They* returned *the enemy's fire. I* returned *his call.* 3 to yield: *Her investment will* return *a profit.* 4 to report, state, or describe officially: *to* return *a verdict.* 5 to throw back; reflect (light, sound, etc.). ***n-*** 1 a coming or going back to or from a place, condition, etc.: *a* return *from a vacation*; *a* return *to health.* 2 a restoring or giving back: *the* return *of books to the library.* 3 something restored or given back. 4 profit or yield: *a good* return *on his investment.* 5 an official report or account: *an income tax* return. 6 in certain games, the striking or carrying back of the ball toward the opponent's area: *the* return *of a serve*; *the* return *of a kickoff.* 7 **returns** (1) results: *election* returns. (2) proceeds: *the* returns *from a sale.* *as* ***modifier***: *a* return *journey*; *a* return *ticket*; *a* return *engagement.*

in return as repayment; in exchange.

re·turn·a·ble (rĭ tûr′ nə bəl) ***adj-*** 1 such as can be returned: *The items on sale are not* returnable. 2 due at a certain time or place: *The order blank is* returnable *in three weeks.*

re·uni·fi·ca·tion (rē′ yo͞o′ nə fə kā′ shən) ***n-*** a reunifying.

re·un·i·fy (rē yo͞o′ nə fī′) ***vt-*** **[re·un·i·fied, re·un·i·fy·ing]** to restore unity to; make one or single again: *to* reunify *a country after a civil war.*

re·un·ion (rē yo͞on′ yən) ***n-*** 1 a reuniting or being reunited: *The* reunion *of the two friends.* 2 a bringing or coming together again of friends, relatives, or groups: *a family* reunion; *a class* reunion.

re·u·nite (rē′ yo͞o nīt′) ***vt-*** **[re·u·nit·ed, re·u·nit·ing]** to bring together again; join (persons or things) after a separation: *The wedding* reunited *all the members of the family.* ***vi-***: *The former enemies* reunited *by treaty.*

re·us·a·ble (rē yo͞o′ zə bəl) ***adj-*** such as can be used again or repeatedly: *a* reusable *bottle.*

[1]**re·use** (rē yo͞oz′, rē′-) ***vt-*** **[re·used, re·us·ing]** to use again.

[2]**re·use** (rē′ yo͞os′) ***n-*** a using again; further use: *Scrap iron is fused for* reuse.

rev (rĕv) *Informal* ***n-*** a single revolution of an engine. ***vt-*** **[revved, rev·ving]** to increase the number of revolutions per minute of (usually followed by "up"): *to* rev *up an engine.* ***vi-***: *The airplane* revved *up before taking off.*

rev. 1 revenue. 2 reverse; reversed. 3 review; reviewed. 4 revise; revised; revision. 5 revolution.

Rev. 1 Revelation. 2 Reverend.

re·val·ue (rē văl′ yo͞o′) ***vt-*** **[re·val·ued, re·val·u·ing]** to estimate or set the value of again: *to* revalue *property.*

re·vamp (rē vămp′) ***vt-*** to supply (a shoe) with a new vamp or upper; hence, to patch up; make over; revise: *to* revamp *a play.*

re·veal (rĭ vēl′) ***vt-*** 1 to make known; disclose; divulge: *You must never* reveal *our secrets.* 2 to show; expose.

rev·eil·le (rĕv′ ə lē) *Military* ***n-*** early morning bugle call to wake up the troops and begin the day.

rev·el (rĕv′ əl) ***vi-*** to make merry; be gay and noisy: *They* reveled *all night long.* ***n-*** a merry celebration. **—*n-*** **rev′ el·er** or **rev′ el·ler.**

revel in to take pleasure in; take delight in; enjoy thoroughly: *They* reveled in *their good fortune.*

rev·e·la·tion (rĕv′ ə lā′ shən) ***n-*** 1 a revealing or disclosing, especially of something secret or private: *His* revelation *of the secret was quite a surprise.* 2 something revealed or made known. 3 *Theology* communication of divine truth, especially by supernatural means; also, an instance of this. 4 **Revelation** the last book of the New Testament. It is ascribed to the apostle St. John, and contains symbolic prophecies.

rev·el·ry (rĕv′ əl rē) ***n-*** [*pl.* **rev·el·ries**] boisterous, gay merrymaking: *The sound of their* revelry *kept me awake.*

re·venge (rĭ vĕnj′) ***vt-*** **[re·venged, re·veng·ing]** 1 to pay back (a wrong or injury); do something to get satisfaction for (a wrong or injury); avenge: *to* revenge *an insult.* 2 to pay back a wrong or injury done to (oneself, some other person, one's country, etc.): *We will* revenge *ourselves. They hurt my brother, but I* revenged *him.* ***n-*** 1 the returning of injury for injury. 2 a chance to obtain satisfaction: *to give a loser at cards his* revenge.

re·venge·ful (rĭ vĕnj′ fəl) ***adj-*** showing or feeling a desire for revenge. **—*adv-*** **re·venge′ ful·ly.** ***n-*** **re·venge′ ful·ness.**

rev·e·nue (rĕv′ ə no͞o′, -nyo͞o′) ***n-*** 1 money yielded by an investment; income from any property. 2 general income of a government from taxes, customs, and other sources. *as* ***modifier***: *the* revenue *figures*; revenue *agent*; revenue *office.*

revenue stamp ***n-*** stamp placed on an article showing that the tax on it has been paid.

re·ver·ber·ate (rĭ vûr′ bə rāt′) ***vi-*** **[re·ver·ber·at·ed, re·ver·ber·at·ing]** to echo back; resound: *The thunder* reverberated *through the house.* **—*n-*** **re·ver′ ber·a′ tion.**

re·ver·ber·a·tor·y furnace (rĭ vûr′ bə rə tôr′ ē) ***n-*** furnace, usually used to process metals, in which the material is melted when the heat of burning gases is deflected downward from the roof of the furnace.

re·vere (rĭ vêr′) ***vt-*** **[re·vered, re·ver·ing]** to feel deep respect toward; respect and love: *The whole family* revered *Grandfather.*

rev·er·ence (rĕv′ ər əns) ***n-*** 1 deep respect mingled with wonder; veneration. 2 an act or sign of respect; a bow or curtsy. 3 **Reverence** title given to certain high-ranking clergymen, often preceded by "His," "Your," etc. ***vt-*** **[rev·er·enced, rev·er·enc·ing]** to feel deep respect for: *He* reverences *his country's traditions.*

rev·er·end (rĕv′ ər ənd) ***adj-*** 1 worthy of deep respect or reverence, especially because of clerical office: *three* reverend *gentlemen.* 2 **Reverend** a title for clergymen and church officials: *the* Reverend *Mr. Jones*; Reverend *Mother Agnes.* ***n-*** *Informal* clergyman, especially a Protestant minister.

rev·er·ent (rĕv′ ər ənt) ***adj-*** **1** feeling and showing deep respect: *He was* reverent *toward the law.* **2** feeling and showing love and respect for God or sacred things. Also **rev′ er·en′ tial.** ***—adv-*** **rev′ er·ent·ly.**

rev·er·ie or **rev·er·y** (rĕv′ ə rē) ***n-*** [*pl.* **rev·er·ies**] deep musing or dreaminess; a daydream.

re·ver·sal (rĭ vûr′ səl) ***n-*** a reversing or being reversed; also, an instance of this: *the* reversal *of a rotating wheel.*

re·verse (rĭ vûrs′) ***adj-*** **1** turned the opposite way round; turned backward; having the opposite position or direction: *the* reverse *side of a page*; *a* reverse *movement*; *in* reverse *order.* **2** causing an opposite motion: *the* reverse *gear in an automobile.* ***n-*** **1** the opposite; the contrary: *He did the* reverse *of what he was asked to do.* **2** the back or less important side of anything: *the* reverse *of a coin.* For picture, see *obverse.* **3** machine gear that causes the machine to go backwards. **4** a change from good to bad; loss or defeat; reversal: *He had a business* reverse. ***vt-*** [**re·versed, re·vers·ing**] **1** to turn the other way round; turn inside out; turn upside down. **2** to cause to move in an opposite direction. **3** to transpose; exchange: *to* reverse *positions.* **4** to change to the contrary: *to* reverse *an opinion.* **5** to set aside; revoke: *The judge* reversed *the original sentence.* ***vi-*** to whirl and move in the opposite direction: *A good waltzer* reverses *with great ease.* ***—n-*** **re·vers′ er.** ***adv-*** **re·verse′ ly.**

re·vers·i·ble (rĭ vûr′ sə bəl) ***adj-*** **1** such as can be reversed; such as can go either backward or forward. **2** such as can be used with either side out; also, finished on both sides: *a* reversible *coat*; *a* reversible *cloth.* **3** such as can be set aside or anulled: *a* reversible *judgment.* ***—n-*** **re·vers′ i·bil′ i·ty.** ***adv-*** **re·vers′ i·bly.**

re·ver·sion (rĭ vûr′ zhən) ***n-*** **1** a reversing or being reversed; a turning in an opposite direction: *an abrupt* reversion *of the breeze.* **2** a reverting or being reverted; a return to a former condition, state, practice, belief, etc. **3** in law, the return of an estate to the grantor or his heirs after the term of the grant has ended; also, an estate so returned. **4** right to future possession: *the* reversion *of a title.* **5** *Biology* atavism.

re·vert (rĭ vûrt′) ***vi-*** **1** to return or go back to a former habit, condition, idea, belief, or practice: *Many tamed animals* revert *to a wild state when set free.* **2** in law, to return to the original owner or his heirs. **3** *Biology* to return to an earlier type.

rev·er·y (rĕv′ ə rē) reverie.

re·view (rĭ vyōō′) ***n-*** **1** a going over; a looking back at: *a* review *of what one has learned*; *a* review *of past events.* **2** a brief lesson covering the same material as a prior lesson. **3** a general survey: *a* review *of the news.* **4** a critical account of a new book, play, etc. **5** magazine which contains articles on current events, essays in criticism, etc. **6** official inspection of naval or military forces. **7** revue. **8** in law, examination by a higher court of a decision of a lower court. ***vt-*** **1** to go over, study, or examine again: *They* reviewed *their lessons for the test.* **2** to look back on; think about: *We* reviewed *the events of the past.* **3** to go over in order to make corrections; revise; examine critically; also, to write a critical account of: *to* review *a book*; *to* review *a concert.* **4** to inspect officially: *The general* reviewed *the troops.* **5** in law, to reexamine (a decision of a lower court). ***vi-*** to write criticisms of books, plays, works of art, etc.

re·view·er (rĭ vyōō′ ər) ***n-*** person who reviews; especially, one whose business is to write critical reviews of books, plays, movies, etc.

re·vile (rĭ vīl′) ***vt-*** [**re·viled, re·vil·ing**] to address with abusive language; swear at; call bad names: *He* reviled *his enemies.* ***vi-*** to use abusive language. ***—n-*** **re·vile′ ment.** ***n-*** **re·vil′ er.**

re·vise (rĭ vīz′) ***vt-*** [**re·vised, re·vis·ing**] **1** to change; correct; alter: *to* revise *one's opinion of someone.* **2** to go over carefully and correct, improve, or bring up-to-date: *to* revise *a manuscript*; *to* revise *a textbook.* ***n-*** in printing, proof containing the corrections made in a former proof. ***—n-*** **re·vis′ er.**

re·vi·sion (rĭ vĭzh′ ən) ***n-*** **1** a revising or being revised: *the* revision *of a manuscript.* **2** a revised form or version; a new and amended edition: *a third* revision *of a play.*

re·vi·so·ry (rĭ vī′ zə rē) ***adj-*** engaged in or intended to make revision: *a* revisory *committee.*

re·viv·al (rĭ vī′ vəl) ***n-*** **1** a reviving or being revived: *the* revival *of flagging spirits*; *a* revival *of trade.* **2** new performance of a play, opera, motion picture, etc., some time after its original performance or showing. **3** religious awakening or reawakening of a community. **4** (also **revival meeting**) meeting to arouse interest in religion.

re·viv·al·ist (rĭ vī′ və lĭst) ***n-*** preacher who holds revival meetings.

re·vive (rĭ vīv′) ***vt-*** [**re·vived, re·viv·ing**] **1** to bring back to life or consciousness: *to* revive *a patient whose heart had stopped*; *to* revive *memories of childhood.* **2** to give new strength or vigor to; refresh: *Coffee often* revives *a tired person.* **3** to bring back from a state of neglect; make current again; also, to present again: *to* revive *old customs*; *to* revive *a classical play.* ***vi-*** **1** to come back to life or return to consciousness. **2** to return to vigor or activity, especially from a state of neglect, oblivion, etc.: *Flowers* revive *in water.* ***—n-*** **re·viv′ er.**

rev·o·ca·ble (rĕv′ ə kə bəl) ***n-*** such as can be revoked, canceled, or repealed: *a* revocable *privilege.*

rev·o·ca·tion (rĕv′ ə kā′ shən) ***n-*** a revoking or being revoked; reversal; repeal: *the* revocation *of a license.*

re·voke (rĭ vōk′) ***vt-*** [**re·voked, re·vok·ing**] to cancel; repeal; annul: *to* revoke *a driver's license.* ***vi-*** in card playing, to fail to follow suit when one could and should. ***n-*** in card playing, failure to follow suit when one could and should.

re·volt (rĭ vōlt′) ***n-*** an uprising against authority; rebellion. ***vi-*** **1** to rise up against authority; rebel: *Charlotte* revolted *against her family's discipline.* **2** to turn or be turned away in disgust: *Human nature* revolts *at the mistreatment of children.* ***vt-*** to disgust: *Cruelty* revolts *decent people.*

re·volt·ing (rĭ vōl′ tĭng) ***adj-*** **1** disgusting; loathsome; nauseating. **2** rebelling. ***—adv-*** **re·volt′ ing·ly.**

rev·o·lu·tion (rĕv′ ə lōō′ shən) ***n-*** **1** the overthrow of one form of government and the setting up of another; also, a sudden change in the government of a country. **2** any far-reaching change in habits of thought, methods of labor, manner of life, etc. **3** a revolving; especially, a single complete turn of a shaft, wheel, etc.: *The propeller shaft makes 3,000* revolutions *a minute.* **4** *Astronomy* movement of a heavenly body or artificial satellite around another body, especially the movement of a

---

Any of these words means **re-** ("again") plus the meaning of the rest of the word as given in the main text.

re′ ver′ i·fi·ca′ tion **re′ ver′ i·fy′**

---

planet about the sun; also, one complete trip of one body around another.

rev·o·lu·tion·ar·y (rĕv′ ə lo͞o′shən ĕr′ ē) ***adj-*** **1** of, relating to, or working for a thorough and sometimes violent change in the government of a country: *a* revolutionary *period*; *a* revolutionary *leader*. **2** causing or likely to cause a great change in ideas, methods, etc.: *a* revolutionary *invention*. ***n-*** [*pl.* **rev·o·lu·tion·ar·ies**] revolutionist.

Revolutionary War ***n-*** the American Revolution.

rev·o·lu·tion·ist (rĕv′ ə lo͞o′ shən ĭst) ***n-*** **1** person who helps cause, or takes part in, a revolution. **2** person who believes in and preaches radical change, especially in government.

rev·o·lu·tion·ize (rĕv′ ə lo͞o′ shən īz′) ***vt-*** [**rev·o·lu·tion·ized, rev·o·lu·tion·iz·ing**] to cause an entire change in the government, affairs, or character of: *Electricity* revolutionized *all kinds of industry*.

re·volve (rĭ vŏlv′) ***vi-*** [**re·volved, re·volv·ing**] **1** to turn around on an axis; rotate: *Wheels* revolve *on their axles*. **2** to move in a curved path around a center: *The moon* revolves *around the earth*. **3** to occur regularly; come round again and again: *The seasons* revolve. ***vt-*** **1** to turn over and over in the mind; consider: *Anne* revolved *the problem in her mind all night*. **2** to cause to turn: *He* revolved *the wheel*. **3** to cause to move in a curved path around a center.

Revolver

re·volv·er (rĭ vŏl′ vər) ***n-*** pistol that carries a supply of cartridges in a cylinder, so that the cartridges are lined up one by one with the firing mechanism and the barrel. It may be fired several times without reloading.

re·vue (rĭ vyo͞o′) ***n-*** musical show consisting of songs, dances, and skits that satirize events, people, etc.

re·vul·sion (rĭ vŭl′ shən, -vo͝ol′ shən) ***n-*** **1** deep disgust and hatred: *When I saw that, I could not hide my* revulsion. **2** a strong turning away or drawing back from something: *the* revulsion *of capital from an industry*.

re·ward (rĭ wôrd′) ***n-*** **1** something given in return for service or performance: *The soldier got a medal as a* reward *for valor in battle*. **2** something given for the return of a lost object: *He offered a* reward *for his missing wallet*. **3** money given for information or capture of a criminal: *There is a $1,000* reward *for the capture of the bank robber*. *as* ***modifier***: *a* reward *notice showing the picture of a criminal*; reward *money*. ***vt-*** **1** to give something to (someone) as an award or payment. **2** to give something as an award or payment for: *She* rewarded *my loyalty*.

in reward in return.

re·ward·ing (rĭ wôr′ dĭng) ***adj-*** profitable; beneficial.

[1]**re·wind** (rē wīnd′, rē′-) ***vt-*** [**re·wound, re·wind·ing**] **1** to wind again; especially, to wind (a film) back onto the original reel. **2** to replace the windings of: *to* rewind *an armature*.

[2]**re·wind** (rē′ wīnd′) ***n-*** **1** a winding again. **2** device for rewinding something; especially a device on a motion-picture projector or tape recorder. *as* ***modifier***: *a* rewind *mechanism*.

re·wire (rē wīər′, rē′-) ***vt-*** [**re·wired, re·wir·ing**] to wire again or anew: *to* rewire *an old house*.

re·word (rē wûrd′, rē′-) ***vt-*** to state in different words.

re·work (rē′ wûrk′) ***vt-*** **1** to work again: *to* rework *an algebra problem*. **2** to make corrections and changes in (something already done); revise: *He took the time to* rework *his essay*.

[1]**re·write** (rē rīt′, rē′-) ***vt-*** [**re·wrote, re·writ·ten, re·writ·ing**] **1** to write (something) again; write in different words. **2** in journalism, to put (a story or news submitted by a reporter) into a form suitable for publication.

[2]**re·write** (rē′ rīt′) ***n-*** **1** thoroughly revised version of something written: *This is the fourth* rewrite *of his novel*. **2** in journalism, the job of writing news stories from facts telephoned to the office by reporters. *as* ***modifier***: *a* rewrite *man*.

rey·nard (rā′ nərd, rā närd′) ***n-*** a name for a fox, used chiefly in medieval fables.

r.f. or **RF** **1** radio frequency. **2** rapid-fire.

R.F.D. or **RFD** rural free delivery.

Rh symbol for rhodium. See also *Rh factor*.

RH or **r.h.** **1** relative humidity. **2** right hand.

rhap·sod·ic (răp sŏd′ ĭk) or **rhap·sod·i·cal** (-ĭ kəl) ***adj-*** **1** too enthusiastic; gushing: *a* rhapsodic *book review*. **2** of a music composition, extravagant; emotional and disconnected. ***—adv-*** **rhap·sod′ i·cal·ly**.

rhap·so·dize (răp′ sə dīz′) ***vi-*** [**rhap·so·dized, rhap·so·diz·ing**] to write, speak, or compose in a rapturous and disconnected way: *to* rhapsodize *on a new play*.

rhap·so·dy (răp′ sə dē) ***n-*** [*pl.* **rhap·so·dies**] **1** speech or writing expressing extravagant feelings; also, any rapturous utterance. **2** *Music* type of instrumental composition that is emotional in tone and irregular in form.

rhe·a (rē′ə) ***n-*** any of various three-toed South American birds that resemble the African ostrich but are smaller and have less valuable plumage.

Rhen·ish (rĕn′ ĭsh) ***adj-*** of or relating to the river Rhine or to the country nearby. ***n-*** wine from the vineyards bordering the Rhine.

rhe·ni·um (rē′ nē əm) ***n-*** hard, gray, metal element used to make thermocouples. Symbol Re, At. No. 75, At. Wt. 186.2.

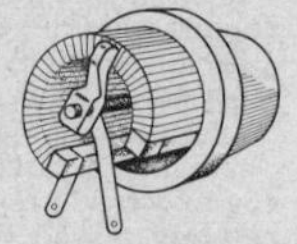
Rheostat

rhe·o·stat (rē′ ə stăt′) ***n-*** a variable resistor used to regulate the flow of electric current in a circuit.

rhe·sus monkey (rē′ səs) ***n-*** small, pale-brown, short-tailed monkey of India, widely used in medical experiments.

rhet·o·ric (rĕt′ ə rĭk) ***n-*** **1** the art of correct, forceful, and elegant use of language, written or spoken, with special emphasis on figures of speech and on devices for swaying and persuading the audience. **2** the use of artificially ornamented language to make a fine show. **3** language without conviction or feeling: *His plea was mere* rhetoric. *as* ***modifier***: *a* rhetoric *teacher*.

rhe·tor·i·cal (rə tôr′ ĭ kəl) ***adj-*** **1** of or relating to rhetoric: *a* rhetorical *style of writing*. **2** showy in language; flowery; also, designed to produce an emotional effect: *a* rhetorical *speech*. ***—adv-*** **rhe·tor′ i·cal·ly**.

rhetorical question ***n-*** a question asked only for emphasis or effect, and with no wish for the reader's or listener's answer.

rhet·o·ri·cian (rĕt′ ə rĭsh′ ən) ***n-*** **1** teacher of or expert in rhetoric. **2** showy or eloquent writer or speaker.

Any of these words means **re-** ("again") plus the meaning of the rest of the word as given in the main text.

re′ vote′	**re′ wa′ ter**	**re′ weigh′**
re′ warm′	**re′ weave′**	**re′ weigh′ er**
re′ wash′	**re′ wed′**	**re′ weld′**

rheum (rōōm) ***n-*** **1** a watery discharge from mucous membranes of the eyes or nose. **2** a cold, or inflammation of the nasal tissues. ***Hom-*** room.

rheu·mat·ic (rōō măt' ĭk) ***adj-*** relating to, having, or caused by rheumatism. ***n-*** person with rheumatism.

rheumatic fever ***n-*** an infectious disease, especially of the young, marked by fever and swelling of the joints and often followed by serious heart disease.

rheu·ma·tism (rōō' mə tĭz' əm) ***n-*** **1** an acute, infectious disease, marked by fever and inflammation, swelling, stiffness, and pain in the joints. **2** any of various conditions marked by pains in the muscles, joints, etc. **3** rheumatic fever.

Rh factor (är' āch') ***n-*** any of several antigens transmitted by genes and occurring on the surface of the red blood cells in most people. People with these antigens are termed **Rh positive,** and those without, **Rh negative.** When Rh-positive and Rh-negative bloods come into contact, severe and usually fatal reactions occur.

rhine·stone (rīn' stōn') ***n-*** colorless paste gem made to imitate a diamond and used in costume jewelry. *as* ***modifier****: a* rhinestone *brooch.*

Rhine wine (rīn) ***n-*** **1** any of several light, dry, still white wines produced from grapes grown along or near the Rhine. **2** any similar wine produced elsewhere.

rhi·no (rī' nō) ***n-*** [*pl.* **rhi·nos**] rhinoceros.

rhi·noc·er·os (rī nŏs' ər əs) ***n-*** any of several massive, plant-eating mammals of Africa and Asia, having a thick skin and three toes on each foot. The African rhinos have two horns on the nose, and the main Asian varieties have one.

African rhinoceros, up to 15 ft. long

rhi·zome (rī' zōm') ***n-*** an underground, rootlike stem that grows horizontally and is often thickened with stored food.

Rho·de·si·an man (rō dēzh' ən) ***n-*** a kind of Neanderthal man, known from fossil remains found in 1921 in Northern Rhodesia (now Zambia).

rho·di·um (rō' dē əm) ***n-*** a hard, grayish-white metal element similar to platinum, and used to electroplate silver and jewelry. Symbol Rh, At. No. 45, At. Wt. 102.905.

rho·do·den·dron (rō' də dĕn' drən) ***n-*** any of various shrubs with glossy, evergreen leaves and large clusters of brilliantly colored flowers.

Rhododendron

rhom·boid (rŏm' boid') ***n-*** a parallelogram with oblique angles whose adjacent sides are of unequal lengths.

rhom·bus (rŏm' bəs) ***n-*** parallelogram with oblique angles and all sides of equal length.

Rhombus

rhu·barb (rōō' bärb') ***n-*** **1** plant related to the buckwheats, with large green leaves and long, fleshy, reddish stems or stalks. **2** the stalks of this plant, used for sauce and for pie filling. **3** a medicine made from the roots of certain varieties of rhubarb. **4** *Slang* quarrel, especially one among players in a ball game.

rhum·ba (rŭm' bə) rumba.

rhyme (rīm) ***n-*** **1** in poetry, repetition of the sound of the final stressed vowels and of any consonants or unstressed syllables following those vowels. Examples: b*ird* and h*erd,* n*ever* and cl*ever,* s*anity* and v*anity.* **2** one of two or more words that have such similarity of sound: *"Bird" and "heard" are* rhymes. *"Third" is a* rhyme *for "heard."* **3** verse or poetry in which the last words of some of the lines correspond in sound. ***vi-*** **[rhymed, rhym·ing] 1** to accord in sound; also, to end in similar sounds: *"June" and "moon"* rhyme. **2** to make verses. ***vt-*** **1** to use as a rhyme: *to* rhyme *"never" with "clever."* **2** to express in verse. Also **rime.** ***Hom-*** rime. **—*n-* rhym' er.**

without rhyme or reason without meaning.

rhyme·ster (rīm' stər) ***n-*** one who fancies himself a poet; writer of poor verse. Also **rime' ster.**

rhythm (rĭth' əm) ***n-*** **1** regular repetition of sound, beat, movement, etc., usually in a measured or harmonious pattern: *the* rhythm *of the pulse.* **2** in poetry, patterns of stressed and unstressed syllables, more or less regularly repeated; also, a particular form of this: *iambic* rhythm. **3** *Music* the ebb and flow of sound in measured intervals of time set off by beats; also, a particular form of this: *waltz* rhythm. *as* ***modifier****: a* rhythm *band.*

rhyth·mi·cal (rĭth' mĭ kəl) or **rhyth·mic** (rĭth' mĭk) ***adj-*** of, relating to, or having rhythm. **—*adv-* rhyth' mi·cal·ly.**

R.I. Rhode Island.

ri·al·to (rē ăl' tō) ***n-*** [*pl.* **ri·al·tos**] **1** an exchange or market. **2** theater district of a town.

[1]**rib** (rĭb) ***n-*** **1** one of the bones curving forward from the spine and enclosing the chest cavity. **2** something that resembles such a bone in appearance or function: *the* ribs *of an umbrella*; ribs *of a ship's frame*; *the* rib *of a leaf.* **3** a cut of meat including one or more of such bones. **4** a ridge in fabrics or knitted work. ***vt-*** **[ribbed, rib·bing]** to enclose, strengthen, or mark with or as if with ribs: *to* rib *a ship; to* rib *an umbrella.* [from Old English **ribb** of the same meaning.]

[2]**rib** (rĭb) *Informal* ***vt-*** **[ribbed, rib·bing]** to kid; make fun of. [probably from tickling people in the ribs.]

rib·ald (rĭb' əld, -ŏld') ***adj-*** **1** given to coarse, vulgar jesting. **2** humorous in a coarse and often offensive manner: *a* ribald *song.*

rib·ald·ry (rĭb' əl drē) ***n-*** [*pl.* **rib·ald·ries**] coarse and offensive jesting; ribald language.

rib·bon (rĭb' ən) ***n-*** **1** woven strip of fabric, used for decoration. **2** fabric strip used for a special purpose: *a typewriter* ribbon. **3** a colored strip or piece of cloth worn as a symbol of a military decoration, membership in an order, etc. **4 ribbons** shreds; tatters: *torn to* ribbons. **—*adj-* rib' boned:** *a* ribboned *parasol.* ***adj-*** **rib' bon·like'.**

ri·bo·fla·vin (rī' bō flā' vən) See *vitamin B complex.*

ri·bo·nu·cle·ic acid (rī' bō nōō' klē' ĭk) ***n-*** any of various nucleic acids found in the cytoplasm and nuclei of cells and involved in the synthesis of proteins; RNA.

ri·bo·some (rī' bə sōm') ***n-*** one of a class of tiny, dense granules found in the cytoplasm of cells. Ribosomes are composed of a combination of proteins and a type of ribonucleic acid, and are the site of protein synthesis.

rice (rīs) ***n-*** **1** plant of the grass family, usually grown in flooded fields. It yields a grain which is a staple food in many parts of the world. **2** the grain of this plant. *as* ***modifier****: fine* rice *paper*; rice *cakes.* ***vt-*** **[riced, ric·ing]** to press (food) through a ricer.

rice·bird (rīs'bûrd') *n-* bobolink.

rice paper *n-* 1 thin paper made from rice straw. 2 a delicate paper made in China from the pith of a shrub.

ric·er (rī'sər) *n-* utensil with small holes through which cooked potatoes and other soft foods are forced.

rich (rĭch) *adj-* [**rich·er, rich·est**] 1 having much money, land, etc.; wealthy. 2 luxurious; expensive: *a* rich *fabric.* 3 abundant or rewarding: *a* rich *harvest.* 4 productive; fertile: *a* rich *soil.* 5 heavily spiced or seasoned; made with large quantities of butter, eggs, sugar, etc.: *a* rich *pudding.* 6 of colors, deep and glowing. 7 of sound, full-toned; sonorous: *a* rich *voice.* 8 *Informal* highly humorous or entertaining: *a* rich *situation.* 9 having a high proportion of fuel to air: *a* rich *fuel mixture.* **—adv- rich'ly.** ***n-*** **rich'ness.**

rich in (or **with**) fully or abundantly supplied with.

rich·es (rĭch'əz) *n- pl.* 1 wealth; abundance. 2 valuable possessions or qualities: *the* riches *of contentment.*

Rich·ter scale (rĭk'ter) *n-* system of using numbers to designate the force of earthquakes.

rick (rĭk) *n-* outdoor stack of hay or straw. *vt-* to pile or heap into a stack.

rick·ets (rĭk'əts) *n-* disease occurring in infants and young children, caused chiefly by a deficiency of vitamin D in the diet or from lack of sunlight, and marked by a softening of the bones and consequent deformity.

rick·et·tsi·a (rĭ kĕt'sē ə) *n-* [*pl.* **rick·et·tsi·ae** (-sē ē) or **rick·et·tsi·as**] any of a group of parasitic, true bacteria that are slightly larger than viruses, and can grow only in living cells. They cause typhus, Rocky Mountain spotted fever, etc.

rick·et·y (rĭk'ə tē) *adj-* 1 feeble; shaky: *a* rickety *old table.* 2 having rickets; rachitic. **—n- rick'et·i·ness.**

rick·sha or **rick·shaw** (rĭk'shó') *n-* jinrikisha.

ric·o·chet (rĭk'ə shā') *vi-* [**ric·o·cheted** (-shād'), **ric·o·chet·ing** (-shā'ĭng)] to rebound or skip away after touching the ground or the surface of the water, as a bullet or a flat stone does; bounce off at a slant. *vt-* to cause to rebound or skip. *n-* the skipping away or rebound of an object from a flat surface.

rid (rĭd) *vt-* [**rid** or **rid·ded, rid·ding**] to free of something not wanted: *He wants to* rid *himself of debt.*

be (or **get**) **rid of** to be freed of: *to* get rid of *a cold.*

rid·dance (rĭd'əns) *n-* a ridding or freeing.

good riddance an exclamation of relief that something or someone disagreeable has been removed.

rid·den (rĭd'ən) *p.p.* of **ride.**

[1]**rid·dle** (rĭd'əl) *n-* 1 puzzling question or problem. 2 person or thing difficult to understand; mystery. *vt-* [**riddled, rid·dling**] to explain; solve: *Please,* riddle *me this. vi-* to speak in a puzzling and cryptic way so that what one says must be guessed at. [from Middle English **redels,** from Old English **rǣdels** and **rǣdan** meaning "to guess; explain" and related to **read.**]

speak in riddles to speak in a puzzling way.

[2]**rid·dle** (rĭd'əl) *vt-* [**rid·dled, rid·dling**] 1 to pierce with holes in many places: *They* riddled *the target.* 2 to sift through a coarse sieve. 3 to disprove; refute successfully: *to* riddle *evidence.* *n-* 1 coarse sieve for separating chaff from corn or for sifting sand, coal, etc. 2 device consisting of pins set upright, used in straightening wire. [from Middle English **ridil,** from Old English **hriddel** meaning "sieve for winnowing grain."]

ride (rīd) *vi-* [**rode** (rōd), **rid·den** (rĭd'ən), **rid·ing**] 1 to be carried on the back of a horse or other animal; especially, to sit on and manage a moving horse: *do you* ride *well?* 2 to be carried or travel in or on a vehicle or any kind of conveyance: *We* rode *in the car as Tim drove.* 3 to be carried or supported along: *The ship proudly* rides *over the waves. The train* rides *on rails.* 4 to float or seem to float in space: *The moon is* riding *high.* 5 to rest or turn on something as a wheel does on an axle. 6 to be determined by or depend on something: *All their chances seem to* ride *on his being elected.* 7 to move in a particular way: *This car* rides *smoothly.* 8 *Slang* to go on as is. *vt-* 1 to sit on and manage or cause to move: *Do you* ride *a bicycle or a horse?* 2 to be carried on: *The ship* rides *the waves.* 3 to compete in (a horse race). 4 to carry (someone) as if on horseback: *He* rode *the baby on his back.* 5 to drive (someone): *The foreman* rode *the workers.* 6 *Informal* to harass by teasing or criticism. *n-* 1 a journey on an animal or in a vehicle, boat, etc.: *her first airplane* ride. 2 roller coaster, merry-go-round, or similar moving mechanical device for riding at amusement parks. 3 *Informal* means of transportation: *he wants a* ride *to Boston.*

take (someone) for a ride *Slang* 1 to swindle or cheat (someone) 2 to murder (someone) in gangster style.

ride at anchor of ships, to rest at anchor.

ride down 1 to knock down by riding against. 2 to overtake by riding; also, to overcome.

ride out to survive through (a storm, trouble, etc.).

ride up to move upward out of place; climb up.

rid·er (rī'dər) *n-* 1 person or thing that rides, especially a horseman. 2 an addition to a document; especially, a clause attached to a piece of legislation so that it might be passed because its opponents are not willing to vote against the entire bill. **—adj- rid'er·less.**

ridge (rĭj) *n-* 1 long hill or mountain: *the* ridges *of western Pennsylvania.* 2 part of a hill or mountain that rises more or less gently in profile toward the summit, but has steeper slopes on each side of this rising line: *the north* ridge *of Mount Everest.* 3 raised line or strip: *A washboard has* ridges. 4 the backbone of an animal. 5 raised part between furrows in a field. 6 top line where two sloping sides meet: *the* ridge *of a roof.* 7 in meteorology, a band of high pressure on a weather map. *vt-* [**ridged, ridg·ing**] to mark with raised lines or ridges: *I* ridged *the edge of the garden path with pebbles.* *vi-* of a hill, to form a ridge. **—adj- ridg'y:** *a* ridgy *beach.*

ridge·pole (rĭj'pōl') *n-* the timber at the top of a sloping roof. The upper ends of the rafters are fastened to it.

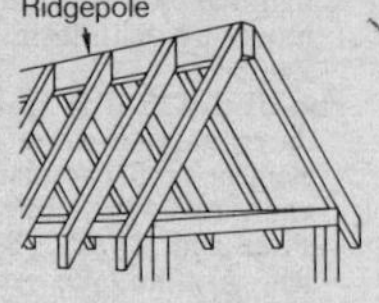

rid·i·cule (rĭd'ə kyo͞ol') *vt-* [**rid·i·culed, rid·i·cul·ing**] to laugh at; make fun of; cause (somebody or something) to appear foolish: *to* ridicule *an idea or suggestion.* *n-* words or acts intended to make fun of someone or to make something seem absurd; mockery; derision.

ri·dic·u·lous (rĭ dĭk'yə ləs) *adj-* deserving or causing scornful laughter; absurd: *a* ridiculous *costume.* **—adv- ri·dic'u·lous·ly.** ***n-*** **ri·dic'u·lous·ness.**

rife (rīf) *adj-* widespread: *Gossip is* rife *in the town.*

rife with full of: *The village was* rife with *rumors.*

Riff (rĭf) *n-* a native of the mountainous regions of northern Morocco.

rif·fle (rĭf'əl) *n-* 1 natural obstruction or very shallow place in a stream. 2 stretch of rippling, choppy, or broken water caused by rocks close to the surface or by a shoal; rapid. 3 wavelet or succession of wavelets; ripple. 4 a shuffling of playing cards. *vt-* [**rif·fled, rif·fling**] 1 to cause wavelets in; ruffle slightly; ripple: *The breeze* riffled *the pond.* 2 to thumb or leaf through; examine quickly or hastily: *to* riffle *the pages of a book.* 3 to shuffle (playing cards) by bending up the corners of the adjacent halves of a deck and forcing the cards to intermix as they flip down one upon the other. ***vi-***: *The lake* riffled *in the wind. He* riffled *through his files.*

riff·raff (rĭf′ răf′) ***n-*** **1** the rabble. **2** trash; rubbish.

[1]**ri·fle** (rī′ fəl) ***n-*** **1** gun with spiral grooves inside the barrel to give the bullet spin for greater accuracy; especially, such a gun that is designed to be fired from the shoulder. **2 rifles** a group of soldiers armed with such guns. ***vt-*** **[ri·fled, ri·fling] 1** to groove (a gun barrel) spirally. **2** to throw (a ball) very fast and straight. [shortened from **rifled gun,** "gun with a grooved barrel," from French **rifler,** "to groove," from earlier Germanic **rifeln** "to rifle; to furrow."]

[2]**ri·fle** (rī′ fəl) ***vt-*** **[ri·fled, ri·fling]** to plunder and strip bare of; to search in order to steal: *The thieves* rifled *the safe.* [from Old French **rifler,** "steal," from Old Norse **rifa,** "to catch; grasp."] ***—n-*** **ri′ fler.**

ri·fle·man (rī′ fəl mən) ***n-*** [*pl.* **ri·fle·men**] soldier or other person armed with, or skilled in the use of, a rifle.

ri·fling (rī′ flĭng) ***n-*** spiral grooves inside the barrel of a gun, designed to give the bullet spin for greater accuracy.

rift (rĭft) ***n-*** **1** an opening made by splitting; fissure; cleft; crevice: *a* rift *in a rock.* **2** any break; breach: *a* rift *in their friendship.* ***vi-*** to burst open; split: *The rock* rifted *over the years.* ***vt-***: *The earthquake* rifted *the rock.*

[1]**rig** (rĭg) ***vt-*** **[rigged, rig·ging] 1** to equip (a ship) with ropes, sails, spars, etc. **2** to furnish with special equipment; fit out; equip: *Paul* rigged *his jeep to plow snow.* **3** to set up; make or prepare (often followed by "up"): *My brother* rigged *up a raft out of boards and four old barrels.* ***n-*** **1** arrangement of sails, masts, etc., on a ship. **2** special equipment or gear; tackle; *a drilling* rig; *fishing* rig. **3** *Informal* vehicle drawn by a horse or horses. **4** *Informal* unusual clothes: *Ed was dressed in his clown's* rig. [from Middle English **riggen,** probably from Norwegian **riggat** meaning "to bind; wrap up."]
rig out *Informal* to dress: *He was* rigged out *as a clown.*

[2]**rig** (rĭg) ***vt-*** **[rigged, rig·ging]** to arrange by fraud; manipulate dishonestly: *They* rigged *the prices.* [from [1]**rig.**]

rig·ger (rĭg′ ər) ***n-*** **1** person skilled in the use of tackles and other hoisting equipment used in cranes, derricks, etc. **2** person who rigs anything. ***Hom-*** rigor.

rig·ging (rĭg′ ĭng) ***n-*** **1** ropes and cables that support a ship's masts and sails. **2** any gear or tackle; especially, equipment used in drilling for oil or working on the outside of tall buildings.

right (rīt) ***n-*** **1** anything correct, just, or honorable; opposite of wrong. **2** side at which one finishes reading the lines of a page of English; the opposite of left. **3** direction to this side: *to turn to the* right. **4** (often **rights**) a moral or legal claim: *the* right *to vote*; *the film* rights *of the musical comedy.* **5** boxer's punch with the right hand. **6 Right** in politics, the right wing. **7 rights** (1) natural rights. (2) civil rights. ***adj-*** **1** just; good: *Telling the truth was the* right *thing to do.* **2** exact; as desired; suitable: *the* right *man for the job.* **3** correct; true: *He was* right *in his opinions.* **4** on or to the side opposite left: *the* right *hand*; *a* right *turn.* **7** straight: *a* right *line.* **8** having its axis perpendicular to the base: *a* right *cone*; *a* right *prism.* **9** having the surface that is meant to be seen: *Place the tablecloth with the* right *side up.* **10** in politics, conservative. ***adv-*** **1** correctly: *John guessed* right. **2** in the correct manner; properly: *I did the job* right *the first time.* **3** straight on; directly: *He looked* right *at the target.* **4** precisely; exactly; immediately: *He stood* right *behind me.* **5** *Informal* very: *Jack is a* right *nice fellow.* **6 Right** used with certain titles: *the* Right *Reverend Monsignor*; *the* Right *Honorable Mayor.* **7** in the direction of the right side: *Turn* right *at the corner.* **8** completely; all the way: *The curtains hung* right *to the floor.* **9** so as to be in good order or condition: *We'll soon put it* right. ***vt-*** **1** to make (something) good, just, or correct: *to* right *an injustice.* **2** to put in proper order: *She* righted *the bedspread. We* righted *the capsized boat.* **3** to make straight or upright: *They* righted *the flagpole.* ***vi-*** to go back to a natural, generally an upright, position: *The boat slowly* righted. ***Homs-*** rite, wright, write. ***—n-*** **right′ ness.**
by rights in keeping with justice; if things had happened in the proper manner. **in the right** correct factually or morally: *I am* in the right *this time.* **put to rights** to put in proper condition. **right about!** turn to the right so as to face the opposite direction. **right along** coming shortly: *I'll be* right along. **right away** or **right off** immediately: *You must come* right away.

right angle ***n-*** an angle of 90 degrees formed by two straight lines perpendicular to each other. For picture, see *angle.*

right·eous (rī′ chəs) ***adj-*** **1** doing what is right; virtuous. **2** justified. ***—adv-*** **right′ eous·ly.** ***n-*** **right′ eous·ness.**

right field ***n-*** in baseball, the section of the outfield to the right of second base; also, the position of the player who covers this section. ***—n-*** **right fielder.**

right·ful (rīt′ fəl) ***adj-*** **1** belonging to one legally: *his* rightful *property.* **2** having legal claim to: *a* rightful *heir.* **3** just; by rights: *his* rightful *position as leader of the team.* ***—adv-*** **right′ ful·ly.** ***n-*** **right′ ful·ness.**

right-hand (rīt′ hănd′) ***adj-*** **1** situated on the right: *a* right-hand *turn.* **2** having to do with the right hand.

right-hand·ed (rīt′ hăn′dəd) ***adj-*** **1** using the right hand more skillfully than the left. **2** used or done with the right hand: *a* right-handed *pitch.* **3** made to be used by a right-handed person: *a* right-handed *golf club.* **4** turning from left to right; clockwise: *a* right-handed *screw.* **5** in baseball, standing on the left side of the plate while batting. ***adv-***: *Johnny writes* right-handed. ***—adv-*** **right′-hand′ ed·ly.** ***n-*** **right′-hand′ ed·ness.**

right·hand·er (rīt′ hăn′ dər) ***n-*** right-handed person; especially, a right-handed baseball pitcher.

right-hand man ***n-*** valuable helper; a chief helper.

right·ist (rī′ tĭst) ***n-*** person who advocates conservative or reactionary policies. ***adj-***: *his* rightist *views.*

right·ly (rīt′ lē) ***adv-*** **1** honestly; justly: *a duty* rightly *performed.* **2** properly; suitably: *He is* rightly *called our benefactor.* **3** correctly: *You are* rightly *informed.*

right-mind·ed (rīt′ mīn′ dəd) ***adj-*** devoted to principles considered to be moral or correct.

right of asylum ***n-*** right of a sovereign state or its embassies, legations, and consulates to grant full protection to refugees in times of disorder or persecution.

right of way ***n-*** **1** the right of traffic to cross in front of other traffic. **2** legal right of a person to pass over another's property; also, the path used. **3** strip of land used by a railroad, public highway, or any public utility. Also **right-of-way.**

right triangle ***n-*** triangle of which an interior angle is a right angle.

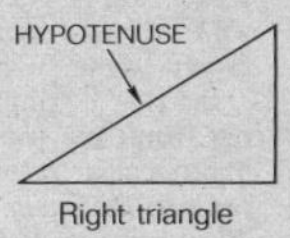

Right triangle

right whale ***n-*** any of various whales with baleen.

right wing ***n-*** **1** all the political parties or groups that advocate conservative or reactionary policies in government, economics, etc. **2** any faction within a group whose views are more conservative or reactionary than those of the group as a whole. ***adj-* (right-wing):** *a* right-wing *faction.* ***—n-* right'-wing' er.**

rig·id (rĭj' ĭd) ***adj-*** **1** not to be bent; stiff; hard: *He used a* rigid *stick to poke the fire.* **2** inflexible; strict; severe: *a* rigid *discipline*; *a* rigid *schoolmaster.* ***—n-* ri·gid' i·ty** (rĭ jĭd' ə tē) or **rig' id·ness.** ***adv-* rig' id·ly.**

rig·ma·role (rĭg' ə mə rōl', rĭg' mə-) ***n-*** **1** foolish, disconnected talk; nonsense. **2** complicated procedure.

rig·or (rĭg' ər) ***n-*** **1** strictness and severity; harsh or severe action: *The traffic laws were enforced with* rigor. **2** preciseness; exactness: *the* rigor *of a geometry course.* **3** hardship; also, severity of climate. **4** violent chill or shivering caused by cold or shock. ***Hom-*** rigger.

rigor mor·tis (môr' təs, môr' təs) ***n-*** a stiffening of the muscles occurring shortly after death.

rig·or·ous (rĭg' ər əs) ***adj-*** **1** strict; exact; precise: *The scientist insisted on* rigorous *accuracy in his assistants.* **2** harsh; severe: *a* rigorous *climate.* ***—adv-* rig' or·ous·ly.**

rile (rīl) *Informal* ***vt-*** **[riled, ril·ing] 1** to make (a liquid) cloudy or muddy by stirring. **2** to vex; anger.

rill (rĭl) ***n-*** **1** small brook or stream. **2** long, narrow trench or valley on the surface of the moon.

rim (rĭm) ***n-*** **1** border, margin, or edge, especially when round or raised: *the* rim *of a plate*; *the horn* rims *of his glasses.* **2** outer edge of a wheel, usually connected to the hub by spokes. ***vt-*** **[rimmed, rim·ming] 1** to put or form a border or edge around: *Ice* rimmed *the pond.* **2** in sports, to go around the edge of: *The basketball* rimmed *the hoop several times.* ***—adj-* rim' less.**

[1]**rime** (rīm) ***n-*** white, icy covering of frozen dew found on grass, leaves, etc.; hoarfrost. ***vt-*** **[rimed, rim·ing]** to coat with or as if with hoarfrost. [from Old English **hrim**]. ***Hom-*** rhyme. ***—adj-* rim' y [rim·i·er, rim·i·est].**

[2]**rime** (rīm) rhyme. [from Old French **rime,** probably from a blend of earlier Germanic **rim,** "row; number," and Latin **rhythmus,** "rhythm; meter."] ***—n-* rim' er.**

rind (rīnd) ***n-*** **1** outer skin or covering: *the* rind *of a melon.* **2** the bark of a tree.

rin·der·pest (rĭn' dər pĕst') ***n-*** acute, usually fatal, intestinal virus disease of cattle, sheep, and goats, marked by fever, dysentery, and inflammation of the mucous membrane.

[1]**ring** (rĭng) ***n-*** **1** circular band, usually of precious metal and often ornamented, for wearing on the finger. **2** any object of circular form: *John put a tag on his key* ring. **3** a circle, especially a circle around something: *We saw a* ring *of toadstools.* **4** a place for showing animals, holding exhibitions, conducting sporting events, and the like: *Bareback riders performed in the circus* ring. **5** group of people using underhand methods for gain. **6** one of the concentric layers produced yearly in the trunks of certain trees. **7** *Chemistry* closed chain of atoms so united that they may be graphically represented by a polygon: *the benzene* ring. ***vt-*** **1** to put a ring around: *He* ringed *the horse in an enclosure.* **2** to toss a ring or curved object over: *Tony* ringed *the stake with his last horseshoe.* [from Old English **hring.**] ***Hom-*** wring. ***—adj-* ring' like'.**

Finger ring

the ring boxing: *Joe takes an interest in* the ring.

[2]**ring** (rĭng) ***vi-*** **[rang** (răng), **rung** (rŭng), **ring·ing] 1** to make a clear resonant sound: *The blacksmith's hammer* rang *on the anvil.* **2** to cause a bell or buzzer to sound: *They* rang *but they got no answer.* **3** to sound loudly and clearly: *Her voice* rang *with anger. His voice* rang *out.* **4** to be filled with sound; resound; echo; hence, to be filled with report or talk: *The schoolyard* rang *with children's voices.* **5** to appear to be; seem: *His excuse* rings *false.* **6** to have a sensation of a buzzing sound: *My ears* ring. ***vt-*** **1** to cause (a buzzer, bell, or other metal object) to sound: *He* rang *a bell. They* rang *the silver coins.* **2** to announce by or as if by a bell: *to* ring *the hours.* **3** to utter again and again or proclaim aloud. **4** to telephone. ***n-*** **1** a clear and resonant sound made by a blow on metal; also, any similar sound: *the* ring *of a hammer on iron*; *the* ring *of fine glass*; *the* ring *of a telephone.* **2** particular quality or tone: *The general's voice had the* ring *of authority.* **3** telephone call. **4** any repeated sound: *the* ring *of applause.* **5** act of sounding a bell. [from Old English **hringan.**] ***Hom-*** wring.

ring for to summon by a bell: *She* rang for *the maid.*
ring in to greet or usher in, especially in a festive way.
ring off to end a telephone call.

ring·bolt (rĭng' bōlt') ***n-*** a bolt having an eye at one end, linked to a ring.

[1]**ring·er** (rĭng' ər) ***n-*** horseshoe or quoit that falls around one of the pins. [from [1]**ring.**]

[2]**ring·er** (rĭng' ər) ***n-*** **1** person or thing that rings a bell, chime, etc. **2** *Slang* athlete, horse, etc., illegally entered in a sporting event under false identity or information about age, record, etc. **3** *Slang* person who bears a strong resemblance to another. [from [2]**ring.**]

ring·lead·er (rĭng' lē' dər) ***n-*** person who leads others in a mutiny, riot, crime, etc.; leader in any sort of mischief.

ring·let (rĭng' lət) ***n-*** lock of hair; curl.

ring·mas·ter (rĭng' măs' tər) ***n-*** person who introduces the acts at a circus performance.

ring·neck (rĭng' nĕk') ***n-*** animal having a ring of color around its neck. ***—adj-* ring' necked'.**

ring·side (rĭng' sīd') ***n-*** space immediately surrounding the ring at a boxing match, circus, etc.

ringside seat ***n-*** place with a close view of something.

ring-tailed (rĭng' tāld') ***adj-*** having a tail marked with rings of different colors.

ring·worm (rĭng' wûrm') ***n-*** any of various contagious skin diseases caused by varieties of fungus.

rink (rĭngk) ***n-*** area of ice for ice-skating; also, a floor used for roller-skating.

rinse (rĭns) ***vt-*** **[rinsed, rins·ing] 1** to wash lightly. **2** to use clear water for removing soap after cleansing. **3** to treat (hair) with a liquid preparation that conditions or tints. ***n-*** **1** water used for removing soap after cleansing. **2** a light washing. **3** liquid preparation that slightly tints and brings out the highlights of or conditions the hair.

ri·ot (rī' ət) ***n-*** **1** a severe outbreak of disorder by a group of persons: *The fans of the singing group started a* riot. **2** in law, tumultuous disturbance of the peace by three or more persons acting together to terrorize the people. **3** bright, luxuriant display: *The fields were a* riot *of color.* **4** *Slang* extremely amusing person or thing. ***vi-*** to join in rebellious disorder. ***—n-* ri' ot·er.**

read the riot act to warn or scold sternly. **run riot 1** to act without restraint. **2** of plants, to grow wildly and luxuriantly.

ri·ot·ous (rī' ət əs) ***adj-*** **1** marked by violent or noisy disturbance of the peace: *The police brought the* riotous *crowd to order.* **2** running wild; unrestrained: *He indulged in* riotous *living.* ***—adv-* ri' ot·ous·ly.** ***n-* ri' ot·ous·ness.**

[1]**rip** (rĭp) ***vt-*** **[ripped, rip·ping] 1** to tear; rend: *The nail* ripped *my coat.* **2** to divide or open by tearing or cutting: *Mary* ripped *open the package. She* ripped *out the seams of the dress.* **3** to saw (wood) along the grain. ***vi-*** to become torn apart. ***n-*** a tear; torn place. [from Scandinavian **rīpa** meaning "to scratch; tear apart," perhaps from Old French **riper,** "to scratch."] ***—n-* rip' per.**

rip into *Informal* to attack vigorously.

[2]**rip** (rĭp) ***n-*** **1** rough stretch of water in a river. **2** (also **tide rip**) rough, turbulent water caused by a tide or current flowing against another tide. [from [1]**rip.**]

R.I.P. May he rest in peace (frequently used on tombstones). [from Latin **requiescat in pace.**]

rip cord ***n-*** cord on a parachute which releases a small parachute, which in turn pulls out the parachute.

ripe (rīp) ***adj-*** **[rip·er, rip·est] 1** ready to be gathered; ready to use as food: *The apples are* ripe. **2** fully developed; mature: *My uncle has* ripe *experience in these matters.* **3** prepared; ready for action: *The infantry company was* ripe *for the assault.* **4** advanced in years: *He reached the* ripe *age of 80.* **5** opportune; suitable: *The time is* ripe. **—*adv-* ripe′ ly.** ***n-*** **ripe′ ness.**

rip·en (rī′ pən) ***vi-*** to grow to the stage of full development; mature: *The grapes* ripened *on the vine.* ***vt-***: *The bright sun* ripened *the tomatoes.*

ri·poste (rĭ pōst′) ***n-*** **1** in fencing, the quick return thrust given after a parry. **2** quick, clever reply. ***vi-*** **[ri·post·ed, ri·post·ing]** to make a quick return thrust or reply.

rip·ple (rĭp′ əl) ***n-*** **1** tiny wave on the surface of water. **2** wave or a wavelike surface in any soft material. **3** sound similar to that of small waves: *a* ripple *of laughter.* ***vt-*** **[rip·pled, rip·pling]** to make tiny waves on or in; also, to give a wavy appearance to: *The breeze* rippled *the surface of the pond, He flexed and* rippled *his arm muscles.* ***vi-*** **1** to become waved or ruffled on the surface; also, to flow in tiny waves: *The brook* rippled *over the stones.* **2** to sound like running water.

rip·ply (rĭp′ lē) ***adj-*** **1** having ripples. **2** sounding like running water.

rip·rap (rĭp′ răp′) ***n-*** **1** layer of stones loosely thrown together in deep water or against a sustaining wall to prevent erosion, or to form a foundation or bedding. **2** stones so used. ***vt-*** **[rip·rapped, rip·rap·ping]** to make such a layer in or upon.

rip-roar·ing (rĭp′ rôr′ ĭng) *Slang* ***adj-*** extremely funny.

rip·saw (rĭp′ sò′) ***n-*** a saw with coarse teeth, used for cutting wood with the grain.

rip·tide (rĭp′ tīd′) ***n-*** strong, narrow current flowing rapidly outwards from a shore or surf.

Rip Van Win·kle (rĭp′ văn′ wĭng′ kəl) ***n-*** in Washington Irving's "Sketch Book," a Dutch villager in colonial times, who after sleeping for twenty years awakens to find everything changed and himself forgotten.

rise (rīz) ***vi-*** **[rose** (rōz), **ris·en, ris·ing] 1** to get up from a sitting, lying, or kneeling position: *We all* rose *when the flag went by.* **2** to go from a lower to a higher place; mount; ascend. **3** to get out of bed: *Arlene* rises *late Saturday mornings.* **4** to revolt; rebel: *The slaves* rose *against their masters.* **5** to extend upward; reach or attain; also, to slope upward: *The building* rises *to a height of 80 feet. The ground* rises *gently.* **6** to come into view: *The mountain* rose *before us on the horizon.* **7** to swell; increase in size: *Bread dough* rises. **8** to increase in value, force, intensity, quantity, etc.: *The stock market* rose. **9** to achieve promotion or higher rank: *You will* rise *in the company if you have ability.* **10** to have its origin or source: *The Nile* rises *near the equator.* **11** to return to life; be resurrected: *to* rise *from death.* ***n-*** **1** a going up from a lower to a higher position; ascent or climb: *a sudden* rise *to power; a* rise *in food prices.* **2** distance from one level to another higher level. **3** small hill or incline. **4** *Slang* reaction; response.

give rise to to be the cause of; start.

rise to to be able to deal with effectively; to be equal to.

riser (rī′ zər) ***n-*** **1** person who rises, especially from bed: *We are late* risers. **2** upright part of a step or stair.

ris·i·bil·i·ty (rĭz′ ə bĭl′ ə tē) ***n-*** [*pl.* **ris·i·bil·i·ties**] **1** readiness to laugh. **2** (usually **risibilities**) sensitiveness to the ridiculous.

ris·i·ble (rĭz′ ə bəl) ***adj-*** **1** laughable; ridiculous. **2** able to laugh: *Man is a* risible *animal.* **3** relating to, or used in laughing: *the* risible *muscles.*

risk (rĭsk) ***vt-*** to take a chance on loss or danger: *Tom* risked *his life to save the child.* ***n-*** chance of loss; danger; peril; also, a person on whom a chance is taken.

run (or **take**) **a risk** to take a chance.

risk·y (rĭs′ kē) ***adj-*** **[risk·i·er, risk·i·est]** dangerous; hazardous. **—*n-* risk′ i·ness.**

ris·qué (rĭ skā′) ***adj-*** improper; daring: *a* risqué *joke.*

rit. or **ritard.** ritardando.

ri·tar·dan·do (rĭ′ tär′ dän′ dō, rē′-) *Music* ***adj- & adv-*** gradually decreasing in tempo.

rite (rīt) ***n-*** **1** customary form used in a solemn ceremony; also, the ceremony itself: *the* rite *of baptism; funeral* rites. **2** branch of the Christian church that uses a special set of ceremonies: *the Latin* rite.

rit·u·al (rĭch′ o͞o əl) ***n-*** **1** set form or way of conducting a ceremony, service, etc.; also, a set of ceremonies used in any church or order. **2** routine faithfully followed: *His daily game of tennis has become a* ritual *with him.* ***adj-*** or or relating to solemn ceremonies: *a* ritual *dance.*

rit·u·al·ism (rĭch′ o͞o ə lĭz′ əm) ***n-*** insistance upon the strict observance of ritual, especially in church services. **—*n-* rit′ u·al·ist.** ***adj-*** **rit′ u·al·ist′ ic.** ***adv-*** **rit′ u·al·ist′ i·cal·ly.**

ritz·y (rĭt′ sē) *Slang* ***adj-*** **[ritz·i·er, ritz·i·est]** elegant; fashionable.

ri·val (rī′ vəl) ***n-*** **1** person trying to achieve the same particular goal as another; competitor: *John was my* rival *in the race.* **2** person or thing that matches another: *In intelligence, John was a* rival *to his brother.* ***vt-*** **1** to try to do as well as or better than; compete with: *The stores* rivaled *one another in special sales.* **2** to be a match for: *She* rivaled *her sister in beauty.* ***adj-*** acting as a competitor or competitors: *the* rival *stores.*

ri·val·ry (rī′ vəl rē) ***n-*** [*pl.* **ri·val·ries**] an attempting to do as well or better; competition.

rive (rīv) ***vt-*** **[rived, rived** or **riv·en, riv·ing]** to split or tear apart; cleave: *to* rive *a tree stump.* ***vi-*** to become split.

riv·er (rĭv′ ər) ***n-*** **1** large stream of water that flows in a natural channel and empties into a lake, ocean, sea, or another river. **2** any great stream or flow: *a* river *of tears.* *as* ***modifier***: *a* river *basin.*

send up the river *Slang* to send to prison (Sing Sing Prison being up the Hudson River from New York City).

riv·er·bank (rĭv′ ər băngk′) ***n-*** bank of a river.

river basin ***n-*** the land which a river drains.

riv·er·bed (rĭv′ ər bĕd′) ***n-*** the channel or what was formerly the channel of a river.

riv·er·head (rĭv′ ər hĕd′) ***n-*** the source of a river.

river horse ***n-*** hippopotamus.

riv·er·side (rĭv′ ər sīd′) ***n-*** bank of a river. *as* ***modifier***: *a* riverside *trail.*

riv·et (rĭv′ ət) ***n-*** kind of bolt without threads, one end of which is flattened after the bolt is in place thus making a head on each end. ***vt-*** to fasten with or as if with rivets: *Fear* riveted *his feet to the floor.* **—*n-* riv′ et·er.**

Rivets

riv·u·let (rĭv′ yə lət) ***n-*** small or tiny stream.

rm. 1 ream. **2** room.

Rn symbol for radon.

R.N. 1 registered nurse. 2 Royal Navy.

RNA ribonucleic acid.

[1]**roach** (rōch) cockroach. [shortened from **cockroach,** American word from Spanish **cucaracha.**]

[2]**roach** (rōch) ***n-*** [*pl.* **roach**; **roach·es** (kinds of roach)] **1** silvery-white European fresh-water fish with a greenish back, related to the carp. **2** any of various fish resembling it. [from Old French **roche.**]

road (rōd) ***n-*** **1** public way for foot travel or vehicles between two or more places. **2** means by which anything is reached: *There is no simple* road *to success.* **3** railroad. **4** (usually **roads**) roadstead. ***Hom-*** rode.
  on the road **1** on tour: *The theatrical company is* on the road. **2** traveling, especially as a salesman.

road agent ***n-*** in the old West, a stage or train robber.

road·bed (rōd′ bĕd′) ***n-*** **1** bed or foundation for the rails and ties of a railroad. **2** stone and gravel base for a paved road; also, the surface of such a road.

road·block (rōd′ blŏk′) ***n-*** arrangement of men or materials to block traffic on a road; hence, any obstruction in a course of action.

road hog ***n-*** driver who uses more than one lane of a road or who drives near the middle of the road, making it difficult for other drivers to pass.

road·house (rōd′ hous′) ***n-*** cabaret or restaurant at the side of a road outside city limits.

road runner ***n-*** long-tailed ground cuckoo, found in southwestern United States and noted for running fast.

road·side (rōd′ sīd′) ***n-*** land along a road or highway. *as* ***modifier****: a* roadside *store.*

road·stead (rōd′ stĕd′) ***n-*** anchorage for ships offshore, less sheltered than a harbor.

road·ster (rōd′ stər) ***n-*** small, open automobile, usually seating only two people.

road test ***n-*** **1** test of a car, especially a new model, under actual driving conditions. **2** test in which an applicant for a driver's license is required to show his skill in the actual handling of a car, truck, motorcycle, etc. ***vt-*** **(road-test)** to test under actual driving conditions.

road·way (rōd′ wā′) ***n-*** **1** road. **2** the part of a street or highway used by vehicles.

road·work (rōd′ wûrk′) ***n-*** physical exercise or conditioning, consisting of long outdoor runs.

roam (rōm) ***vi-*** to ramble; wander without purpose: *I like to* roam *over the countryside on weekends.* ***vt-****: He* roamed *the mountains.* ***Hom-*** Rome. **—*n-*** **roam′ er.**

roan (rōn) ***adj-*** of animals, reddish-brown, chestnut, or black, thickly sprinkled with gray or white. ***n-*** **1** such a color. **2** animal of this color.

roar (rôr) ***n-*** any loud, deep, hoarse sound or noise made by people, animals, waves, etc.: *the* roar *of a lion*; *the* roar *of traffic*; *a* roar *of laughter.* ***vi-*** to make such a loud, deep, hoarse sound or noise: *The lion* roared. ***vt-*** to utter boisterously; cry aloud. **—*n-*** **roar′ er.**

roast (rōst) ***vt-*** **1** to cook meat or other food before or over an open fire or in an oven: *We* roasted *corn.* **2** to dry and parch under the action of heat; *to* roast *peanuts.* **3** to heat (an ore) with air in a furnace to cause oxidation, remove sulphur or other impurities, etc. **4** *Informal* to criticize or ridicule harshly. ***vi-*** **1** to be cooked by heat: *A turkey* roasted *in the oven.* **2** to be uncomfortably warm: *We* roasted *in this summer heat.* ***n-*** **1** large piece of meat cooked, or suitable for cooking, over a fire or in an oven. **2** picnic at which food is cooked over an open fire, coals, or embers. *as* ***modifier****: a* roast *chicken.*

roast·er (rōs′ tər) ***n-*** **1** person or thing that roasts, especially a pan or oven suitable for roasting. **2** animal suitable for roasting, especially a pig or large chicken.

rob (rŏb) ***vt-*** **[robbed, rob·bing]** **1** to take unlawfully and forcibly from: *to* rob *a bank.* **2** to deprive in an unjust way: *Slander* robbed *him of honor.* ***vi-*** to commit robbery.

rob·ber (rŏb′ ər) ***n-*** person who robs.

rob·ber·y (rŏb′ ə rē) ***n-*** [*pl.* **rob·ber·ies**] the unlawful and forcible taking of another's money or possessions.

robe (rōb) ***n-*** **1** any long covering garment, especially one replacing ordinary street clothes with informal wear: *a lounging* robe; *a bath*robe. **2** (also **robes**) long, loose, outer garment worn on official or ceremonial occasions as a mark of office or rank: *the judge's* robe; *the priest's* robes. **3** blanket for covering the legs for extra warmth. ***vi-*** **[robed, rob·ing]** to put on a garment, especially one worn on official or ceremonial occasions. ***vt-*** **1** to dress, especially in a garment worn on official or ceremonial occasions. **2** to cover or conceal with, or as with, a large cloth: *Fog* robed *the city in white.*

rob·in (rŏb′ ən) ***n-*** **1** American bird related to the thrush, having a dark back and a reddish breast. **2** somewhat smaller, more colorful European bird.

American robin, about 10 in. long

Rob·in Good·fel·low (rŏb′ ən go͝od′ fĕl′ ō) ***n-*** in English folklore, a mischievous, good-natured goblin.

Rob·in Hood (rŏb′ ən ho͝od′) ***n-*** in English legend, the merry bandit of Sherwood Forest, who robbed the rich to help the poor.

Rob·in·son Cru·soe (rŏb′ ən sən kro͞o′ sō) ***n-*** a shipwrecked sailor in Defoe's novel "Robinson Crusoe."

ro·bot (rō′ bət, -bŏt′) ***n-*** **1** machine made to look and act somewhat like a human being; hence, person who behaves or works like a machine. **2** any mechanism or device that operates without human assistance or is guided by remote controls. *as* ***modifier****: a* robot *plane.*

robot bomb ***n-*** buzz bomb.

ro·bust (rō′ bəst, rō bŭst′) ***adj-*** **1** strong and healthy: *Tom was so* robust *that he never caught cold.* **2** requiring strength: *a* robust *exercise.* **3** rough; unpolished: *his* robust *manners.* **—*adv-*** **ro·bust′ ly.** ***n-*** **ro·bust′ ness.**

roc (rŏk) ***n-*** in Arabian and Persian legend, a bird of prey of gigantic size. ***Hom-*** rock.

[1]**rock** (rŏk) ***n-*** **1** in geology, the consolidated, naturally formed mass of mineral matter constituting the earth's crust; also, a particular variety of such matter. **2** stony mass rising steeply above the level of the earth or sea to form a cliff or crag. **3** detached, single piece of stone. **4** firm foundation or support. *as* ***modifier****: a* rock *wall*; rock *wool.* [from Old French **roque**, from Medieval Latin **rocca.**] ***Hom-*** roc. **—*adj-*** **rock′ like′.**
  on the rocks *Informal* **1** of beverages, served over ice cubes. **2** without money; ruined; bankrupt.

[2]**rock** (rŏk) ***vt-*** **1** to move (a person or thing) back and forth or from side to side: *We* rocked *the cradle.* **2** to cause to shake or sway violently: *The earthquake* rocked *many houses.* ***vi-*** **1** to move backward and forward: *She* rocked *gently in her chair.* **2** to shake or sway violently. ***n-*** a movement backward and forward. [from Old English **roccian,** "pull or push."] ***Hom-*** roc.

rock bottom ***n-*** lowest level possible; the very bottom: *Food prices hit* rock bottom. *as* ***modifier*** **(rock-bottom):** *The store sells at* rock-bottom *prices.*

rock candy ***n-*** chunks of crystallized sugar.

rock crystal ***n-*** transparent, usually colorless, quartz.

rock·er (rŏk′ ər) ***n-*** **1** one of the curved wooden pieces on the legs of a chair or the bottom of a cradle, which enables it to move with a swaying motion. **2** rocking chair. **3** in certain machines, a part with a rocking movement.

rock·et (rŏk′ət) ***n-*** **1** missile consisting of a cylinder filled with a fuel that produces gases which escape through a vent in the rear, thus driving their container forward. Rockets are used as fireworks, signals, or weapons. **2** a space vehicle using such propulsion. ***vi-*** to move quickly; speed: *The car* rocketed *by us.* *as* ***modifier***: *the* rocket *engine.*

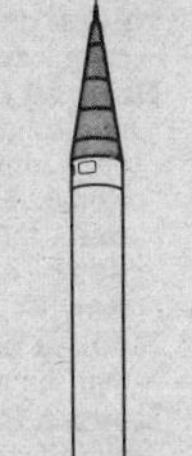
Military rocket

rock·et·eer (rŏk′ə têr′) ***n-*** **1** person who pilots or launches a rocket. **2** person who designs or studies rockets.

rocket launcher ***n-*** device consisting of a tube or cluster of tubes for firing rockets.

rock·et·ry (rŏk′ə trē) ***n-*** branch of science which deals with the building and firing of rockets.

rocket ship ***n-*** space vehicle driven by rocket propulsion.

rock garden ***n-*** garden with many stones and planted with special flowers and plants that thrive this way.

rocking chair ***n-*** chair with legs set on curved pieces of wood; rocker.

rocking horse ***n-*** child's toy horse set on rockers or springs.

rock lobster ***n-*** spiny lobster.

rock maple ***n-*** sugar maple.

rock 'n' roll ***n-*** form of popular music derived from blues and folk music, marked by much repetition of a simple melody and a strong, persistent beat, and often performed with exaggerated mannerisms. *as* ***modifier***: *a* rock 'n'roll *singer.* Also **rock and roll.**

Rockers of a rocking chair

rock·oon (rŏ ko͞on′) ***n-*** small rocket equipped with various meteorological recording instruments and fired from a high-altitude aircraft.

rock·ribbed (rŏk′rĭbd′) ***adj-*** **1** rocky. **2** inflexible.

rock salt ***n-*** common salt found in solid, rocklike state.

rock·weed ***n-*** any of various seaweeds growing on rocks.

rock wool ***n-*** a glassy, fibrous insulating material made by mixing rock or stone with molten slag and then forcing steam through the mixture.

[1]**rock·y** (rŏk′ē) ***adj-*** **[rock·i·er, rock·i·est] 1** full of rocks. **2** hard; unyielding. [from [1]**rock.**] **—*n-* rock′i·ness.**

[2]**rock·y** (rŏk′ē) ***adj-*** **[rock·i·er, rock·i·est] 1** not firm; shaky; wobbly. **2** *Informal* weak; dizzy. [from [2]**rock.**]

Rocky Mountain spotted fever ***n-*** acute, infectious disease characterized by pain in the joints and muscles, fever, and skin eruptions. It is caused by rickettsia.

ro·co·co (rə kō′kō, rō′kə kō′) ***n-*** ornate style of decoration, popular in the 18th century, marked by designs representing shells, leaves, scrolls, and other similar forms often without symmetry. ***adj-*** relating to this style; in this style: *a* rococo *palace;* rococo *architecture.*

rod (rŏd) ***n-*** **1** thin, straight, usually cylindrical stick made of wood, metal, etc.: *a fishing* rod; *a curtain* rod. **2** stick or switch used to punish or correct children; hence, correction; discipline: *Spare the* rod *and spoil the child.* **3** staff, wand, or scepter carried as a badge of office; hence, power; authority. **4** measure of length equal to 5½ yards. **5** stick or bar used to measure something. **6** *Slang* revolver; pistol. **7** any of the straight, slender, somewhat cylindrical cells found in the retina of the eye and sensitive to dim light. **—*adj-* rod′like′.**

rode (rōd) *p.t.* of **ride.** ***Hom-*** road.

ro·dent (rō′dənt) ***n-*** any member of a large order of gnawing mammals **(Rodentia)** with a single pair of strong upper incisors. Rats, mice, squirrels, and beavers are all rodents. *as* ***modifier***: *Mice have* rodent *teeth.*

ro·de·o (rō′dē ō′, *also* rō dā′ō) ***n-*** [*pl.* **ro·de·os**] **1** a show where cowboys compete in horseback riding, roping cattle, etc. **2** a roundup of cattle.

[1]**roe** (rō) ***n-*** eggs of fish, especially when enclosed in an ovarian membrane. [from Middle English **rowne,** from Old Norse **hrogn.**] ***Homs-*** [1]row, [2]row.

[2]**roe** (rō) ***n-*** [*pl.* **roe** or **roes**] small deer found in Europe and western Asia. Also **roe deer.** [from Old English **rā,** "spotted," from earlier **rāha.**] ***Homs-*** [1]row, [2]row.

roe·buck (rō′bŭk′) ***n-*** [*pl.* **roe·buck** or **roe·bucks**] male roe deer.

roent·gen (rĕnt′gən, rŭnt′jən) *Physics* ***n-*** unit of X-ray radiation or gamma radiation.

Roentgen ray ***n-*** X ray.

rog·er (rŏj′ər) ***interj-*** message received and understood.

rogue (rōg) ***n-*** **1** dishonest person; cheat. **2** one who plays pranks or teases; mischievous one. **3** solitary, often vicious animal living apart from the herd. *as* ***modifier***: *a* rogue *trick; a* rogue *elephant.*

ro·guer·y (rō′gə rē) ***n-*** [*pl.* **ro·guer·ies**] **1** dishonest practices; cheating. **2** playfully mischievous behavior.

rogues' gallery ***n-*** collection of the photographs of persons arrested as criminals, kept by the police.

ro·guish (rō′gĭsh) ***adj-*** **1** mischievous; playful: *a* roguish *smile.* **2** *Archaic* dishonest; rascally. **—*adv-* ro′guish·ly. *n-* ro′guish·ness.**

roil (roil) ***vt-*** **1** to stir up sediment in water or other liquids. **2** to irritate; vex.

roil·y (roi′lē) ***adj-*** **[roil·i·er, roil·i·est]** full of sediment; muddy: *the* roily *waters of the lake.*

roi·ster (roi′stər) ***vi-*** to act in a noisy or boisterous manner; carouse. **—*n-* roist′er·er.**

Ro·land (rō′lənd) ***n-*** in French romance, nephew of Charlemagne, hero of the wars against the Saracens.

role or **rôle** (rōl) ***n-*** **1** part or character taken by an actor: *the* role *of Romeo.* **2** duty or function: *his* role *as president; the* role *of hormones in the body.* ***Hom-*** roll.

roll (rōl) ***vi-*** **1** to move by turning over and over: *The ball* rolled *down the hill.* **2** to move on wheels or rollers: *The carriage* rolled *down the street.* **3** to form, when being wound, the shape of a ball or cylinder: *The cloth* rolls *easily.* **4** to extend or move in gentle rises and falls: *The hills* roll *to the sea. The ocean* rolled *toward shore.* **5** to pass; go by (often followed by "on" or "by"): *The seasons* roll *on.* **6** to tilt or sway to one side, or alternately from one side to the other: *The ship* rolled *heavily in the waves.* **7** to flatten under some kind of roller: *The dough* rolls *easily.* **8** to make a long echoing sound: *The thunder* rolled. ***vt-*** **1** to cause to move onward by turning over and over: *The boy* rolled *the hoop.* **2** to move or push along on wheels or rollers: *Ed* rolled *the scooter down the street.* **3** to wrap (something) upon itself or on some other object: *The movers* rolled *the rug.* **4** to wrap up: *He* rolled *himself in a blanket.* **5** to cause a tilt to one side, or an alternate tilting from one side to the other: *The giant waves* rolled *the ship.* **6** to impel or cause to move onward with a sweeping motion: *The ocean* rolls *its waves against the reefs.* **7** to turn around or partly turn around: *She* rolled *her eyes.* **8** to utter or express with a deep, vibrating sound: *The organ* rolls *forth its music.* **9** to pronounce with a trill: *He* rolls *his r's.* **10** to level with a heavy revolving cylinder: *he* rolled *the lawn.* **11** to beat rapid sounds on: *The soldier* rolled *the drum.* **12** to throw (dice). **13** *Slang* to rob (a sleeping or helpless person). ***n-*** **1** list of names, especially an official one: *The teacher called the* roll. **2** anything wound into the shape of a tube or ball: *a* roll *of yarn*; *a* roll *of wallpaper.* **3** small cake of bread or pastry. **4** food made in the shape of a tube: *an egg* roll. **5** roller. **6** *Slang* money; especially, a wad of paper bills. **7** gentle rising and falling: *the* roll *of hills*; *the* roll *of the ocean.* **8** a tilting to one side, or alternately from one side to the other: *the alarming* roll *of the ship.* **9** long echoing sound: *the* roll *of thunder.* **10** rapid series of short sounds: *the* roll *of a drum.* **11** a toss of dice. **12** maneuver in which an airplane in flight performs a complete rotation around its longitudinal axis. **13** rapid movement of an aircraft on the ground after landing or before taking off. ***Hom-*** role.

roll in to accumulate; arrive in large quantities.

roll out to unwind from a roll: *He* rolled out *the map.*

roll up **1** to wind into a tube or ball: *We* rolled up *the carpet.* **2** to accumulate; pile up in large quantities.

roll bar ***n-*** strong metal bar in the roof of an automobile to protect occupants if the automobile overturns.

roll call ***n-*** a calling of a list of names to determine who is present; also, the time when this is done.

roll·er (rō′lər) ***n-*** **1** cylinder that rolls, smooths, or crushes. **2** small wheel: *Walter oiled the* rollers *of his skates.* **3** rod on which something is rolled up: *Oliver tacked the window shade to its* roller. **4** one of the round bars placed under heavy objects to make pushing them easy: *Workmen moved the heavy box on* rollers. **5** one of the metal cylinders in a roller bearing. **6** large wave: *Heavy* rollers *make swimming difficult.* **7** canary with a trilling song.

Road roller

roller bearing ***n-*** a bearing in which the shaft turns inside rollers arranged lengthwise in a ringlike casing. It is used to reduce friction. For picture, see *bearing.*

roller coaster ***n-*** amusement railway, in which small cars on wheels run along sharply inclined tracks.

roller skate ***n-*** skate with small wheels instead of a blade. ***vi-*** **(roller-skate)** [**roll·er-skat·ed, roll·er-skat·ing**]: *He* roller-skated *all morning with his friends.*

Roller skate

rol·lick (rŏl′ĭk) ***vi-*** to frolic or sport in a joyous, carefree manner.

rol·lick·ing (rŏl′ĭk ĭng) ***adj-*** very jovial and gay; carefree: *a* rollicking *song;* rollicking *fun.*

roll·ing (rō′lĭng) ***adj-*** **1** moving along by turning over and over. **2** rising and falling gentle slopes: *the* rolling *plains.* **3** moving on wheels: *a* rolling *coffee table.* **4** turned back or down on itself: *a* rolling *hat rim.* **5** moving from side to side: rolling *eyes.* **6** resounding: *the* rolling *thunder.* **7** trilling: *a* rolling *high note.* ***n-*** act of a person or thing that rolls or is rolled.

rolling mill ***n-*** **1** factory where metal is rolled into sheets, bars, etc. **2** machine used for doing this.

rolling pin ***n-*** cylinder for rolling out dough.

rolling stock ***n-*** wheeled equipment used by a railroad, trucking company, etc.

roll-top desk (rōl′tŏp′) ***n-*** desk with a flexible sliding cover that may be pushed back into the frame.

ro·ly-po·ly (rō′lē pō′lē) ***n-*** [*pl.* **ro·ly-po·lies**] short and plump person or thing. ***adj-*** short and plump; dumpy.

ro·maine (rō′mān) ***n-*** type of lettuce with long, narrow, crisp leaves.

Ro·man (rō′mən) ***adj-*** **1** of or relating to ancient or modern Rome or its people. **2** pertaining to the Roman Catholic Church. ***n-*** **1** a native or citizen of ancient or modern Rome. **2 Romans** (takes singular verb) in the New Testament, the epistle written by St. Paul to the Christians at Rome. **3 roman** upright type used in ordinary print. This sentence is printed in roman.

Roman candle ***n-*** kind of firework consisting of a tube that sends out balls of varicolored fire.

Roman Catholic ***adj-*** of or relating to the Roman Catholic Church, its doctrines and its liturgy. ***n-*** a member of the Roman Catholic Church.

Roman Catholic Church ***n-*** that body of the Christian church that recognizes the Pope at Rome as its supreme head. Also **Catholic Church.**

ro·mance (rō măns′, rō′măns′) ***n-*** **1** love affair. **2** ideal of love, excitement, adventure, etc., as it is found in some old stories: *an air of* romance. **3** story of unusual adventures or love in an exotic setting: *a* romance *of the South Seas.* **4** medieval tale of heroic adventure: *The story of King Arthur is a* romance. ***vi-*** [**ro·manced, ro·manc·ing**] **1** to think or talk about romantic things or in a romantic manner. **2** to invent adventures: *That child is always* romancing. **3** *Informal* to court; to woo. ***vt-*** *Informal* to court someone. **—*n-* ro·manc′er.**

Romance languages ***n-*** *pl.* languages, such as French, Spanish, and Italian, which developed from Latin.

Roman Empire ***n-*** ancient empire which was founded in 27 B.C. and at one time included much of Europe and parts of Africa and Asia, all ruled from the city of Rome. It lasted until 395 A.D. when it was divided into the **Eastern Roman Empire** and the **Western Roman Empire.**

Ro·man·esque (rō′mə nĕsk′) ***adj-*** **1** of or referring to the style of architecture developed in Italy and western Europe from the fifth to the tenth century A.D., characterized in its later stages by rounded arches and massive walls. **2** of or relating to the art of that period.

Ro·ma·ni·an (rŏ mā′nē ən) Rumanian.

Roman numeral ***n-*** any of the letters used instead of figures in ancient Rome. They are used today mainly in inscriptions and the like.

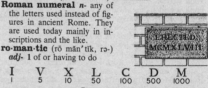

ERECTED MCMXLVIII

I	V	X	L	C	D	M
1	5	10	50	100	500	1000

Roman numerals

ro·man·tic (rō măn′tĭk, rə-) ***adj-*** **1** of or having to do with high adventure, chivalry, courtly love, far-off places, etc.: *a* romantic *story of the Orient.* **2** affected by ideas of romance and adventure; impractical; unreal; visionary: *The young couple had a* romantic *idea of married life.* **3** appealing to the imagination; picturesque: *a* romantic *inn in the Alps.* **4** of or having to do with romanticism in art, music, or literature. **5** of or having to do with love. **—*adv-* ro·man′ti·cal·ly.**

ro·man·ti·cism (rō măn′tə sĭz′əm, rə-) ***n-*** movement in art, literature, and music that began in the late 18th century in Europe and was characterized by freedom of form and subject matter, with emphasis on feeling, imagination, and natural beauty, as opposed to the strict requirements of classicism. **—*n-* ro·man′ti·cist.**

ro·man·ti·cize *vt-* [**ro·man·ti·cized, ro·man·ti·ciz·ing**] to make, or represent as, romantic: *He likes to* romanticize *his trips to the Orient.* *vi-*: *When he writes about his trips, he refuses to* romanticize.

Ro·ma·ny (rō′ mə nē, rŏm′ ə-) *n-* [*pl.* **Ro·ma·nies**] **1** the basic language of the Gypsies. **2** a Gypsy.

Ro·me·o (rō′ mē ō′) *n-* the hero of Shakespeare's "Romeo and Juliet."

romp (rŏmp) *vi-* **1** to play or frolic in a lively or noisy way: *The children* romped *all over the house.* **2** to run quickly and easily: *The horse* romped *to the finish line.* *n-* lively or noisy play. —*n-* **romp′ er.**

romp·ers (rŏm′ pərz) *n- pl.* one-piece outer garment worn by small children; jumpers.

Rom·u·lus (rŏm′ yə ləs) *n-* in Roman mythology, a son of Mars and founder of Rome, who together with his twin brother Remus was reared by a she-wolf.

ron·do (rŏn′ dō) *Music n-* [*pl.* **ron·dos**] instrumental composition having one principal theme repeated at intervals, with contrasting episodes between repetitions.

rönt·gen (rĕnt′ gən, rŭnt′ jən) roentgen.

rood (rōōd) *n-* **1** cross or crucifix; especially, a large crucifix over an altar. **2** *Brit.* measure of length varying locally between six and eight yards. **3** land measure equal to ¼ of an acre, or 40 square rods. ***Hom-*** rude.

roof (rōōf, rŏŏf) *n-* **1** top covering of a house or other building; hence, a home or house. **2** any similar top covering: *the* roof *of a car; the* roof *of the mouth.* *vt-* to cover with a roof: *to* roof *a house.* —*adj-* **roofed:** *a* roofed *pavilion.* *n-* **roof′ er.** *adj-* **roof′ like.**

roof garden *n-* **1** garden on the flat roof of a building. **2** top floor or roof having a garden.

roof·ing (rōōf′ ĭng, rŏŏf′-) *n-* **1** materials for constructing a roof. **2** a roof or other covering.

roof·less (rōōf′ ləs, rŏŏf′-) *adj-* **1** having no roof: *a* roofless *shack; the* roofless *vault of the heavens.* **2** having no home or shelter; homeless: *a* roofless *wanderer.*

roof·tree (rōōf′ trē, rŏŏf′-) *n-* large timber along the top of a roof, to which rafters are attached; ridgepole.

[1]**rook** (rŏŏk) *n-* **1** European bird that looks like a small crow and lives in large flocks. **2** a cheat, especially at dice or cards. *vt-* to cheat; defraud. [from Old English **hrōc.**]

Rook, about 1 1/2 ft. long

[2]**rook** (rŏŏk) *n-* one of a pair of chessmen that may move parallel to the sides of the board; castle. [from Old French **roc,** from Spanish **roque,** from Persian **rokh.**]

rook·er·y (rŏŏk′ ə rē) *n-* [*pl.* **rook·er·ies**] **1** place where rooks gather and build their nests; also, a colony of these birds. **2** colony or breeding place of gulls, seals, etc. **3** *Archaic* old tenement or group of tenements in a slum.

rook·ie (rŏŏk′ ē) *Informal n-* raw recruit; also, any novice.

room (rōōm, rŏŏm) *n-* **1** area separated by walls or partitions from the rest of the structure in which it is located: *a dining* room. **2** space: *This table takes up too much* room. *Is there* room *for me in the back seat?* **3** space within which something may happen; scope; opportunity: *some* room *for improvement.* **4** people in a room. **5 rooms** lodgings; apartment. *vi-* to have living quarters (at): *Jack* rooms *at a Y.M.C.A.* ***Hom-*** rheum.

room·er (rōō′ mər) *n-* person who rents a room; lodger.

room·ful (rōōm′ fəl, rŏŏm′-) *n-* **1** as much or as many as a room can contain. **2** all the people or things in a room.

rooming house *n-* house with furnished rooms for rent.

room·mate (rōōm′ māt′, rŏŏm′-) *n-* one who shares a room or rooms with one or more persons.

room·y (rōō′ mē) *adj-* [**room·i·er, room·i·est**] having plenty of room; ample; large. —*n-* **room′ i·ness.**

roost (rōōst) *n-* **1** branch or perch on which birds rest at night. **2** shelter in which birds can stay at night. **3** any resting place, especially a temporary one. *vi-* **1** to sit or sleep upon a perch or pole. **2** *Informal* to settle, especially for the night; lodge.

come home to roost to recoil to harm the author; boomerang. **rule the roost** to be master.

roost·er (rōōs′ tər) *n-* male barnyard fowl; cock.

[1]**root** (rōōt, rŏŏt) *n-* **1** that part of a plant, usually growing downward into the soil, which holds the plant in place, absorbs water and minerals, and stores food. **2** underground part of a plant; especially, a large part suitable for food, such as a beet or turnip; tuber; bulb. **3** anything looking like a root in use or position: *the* roots *of his hair.* **4** basic part: *to get to the* root *of the matter.* **5** source; origin; cause: *The* root *of Ellen's difficulties is her lack of money.* **6** word from which other words are formed; usually, a basic vocabulary word consisting of only one syllable: *"Love" is the* root *of "lovable."* **7** *Mathematics* (1) number, quantity, or dimension which, when used as a factor a specified number of times, will produce a given expression. Example: 3 is the square root of 9 ($3 \times 3 = 9$). (2) a value which, if substituted for the unknown quantity in an equation, will satisfy the equation. **8** *Music* the first or lowest member of a common chord or triad. *vt-* **1** to implant or fix by or as if by the roots: *Fear* rooted *him to the spot.* **2** of ideas, principles, etc., to implant deeply; establish firmly: *His beliefs were* rooted *in prejudice.* *vi-* to begin to grow; also, to become firmly or permanently established: *The bulbs began to* root *in February.* [from Middle English **rote.**] ***Hom-*** route. —*adj-* **root′ less.**

Plymouth Rock rooster about 9 1/2 pounds

take root to begin growing by putting forth roots; hence, to become firmly or permanently established.

[2]**root** (rōōt, rŏŏt) *vi-* **1** to turn over or dig up soil with the snout, as a pig does. **2** to search for something; rummage. [from Old English **wrōtan,** "root up" and **wrōt,** "swine's snout."] ***Hom-*** route. —*n-* **root′ er.**

root out (or **up**) **1** to dig out; destroy. **2** to discover by rummaging: *We* rooted out *their secret.*

[3]**root** (rōōt) *vi-* to give support to or cheer for a team, contestant, etc. [probably from Scottish **rout,** "to make a loud noise," from Old English **wrūtan.**] ***Hom-*** route. —*n-* **root′ er.**

root beer *n-* carbonated soft drink flavored with extracts of the roots of sarsaparilla, sassafras, etc.

root crop *n-* crop such as carrots, sweet potatoes, or turnips grown for its usually edible roots.

root hair *n-* in botany, one of the fine tubular outgrowths found near the tip of the root of a plant.

root·let (rōōt′ lət rŏŏt′-) *n-* little root; especially, a secondary root thrown out by a climbing plant.

root·stock (rōōt′ stŏk′, rōōt′-) ***n-*** **1** in botany, a rhizome. **2** source or origin.

rope (rōp) ***n-*** **1** large, strong cord made of twisted, smaller cords. **2** collection of things braided or twined together in a line or string; also, a festoon: *a* rope *of pearls*; ropes *of laurel.* **3** slimy or stringy thread formed in a liquid. **4** execution or death by hanging. **5** lasso; lariat. ***vt-*** **[roped, rop·ing] 1** to fasten, bind, or tie with, or as if with, a rope: *We* roped *and tied his feet so he couldn't escape.* **2** to mark off or enclose by means of a rope: *to* rope *off a street.* **3** to lasso: *to* rope *a calf.* ***vi-*** to form stringy threads, as syrup does. **—*n-* rop′ er.**

Rope

give (someone) rope to give someone freedom of action in the expectation that he will defeat himself by overdoing matters. **know the ropes** *Informal* **1** to know all the details of a job or procedure. **2** to be sophisticated or worldly-wise. **the end of one's rope** the point at which one reaches the end of one's resources or strength. **rope in** *Informal* to involve or persuade by trickery, enticement, etc.; take in; deceive.

rop·y (rō′ pē) ***adj-*** **[rop·i·er, rop·i·est] 1** forming slimy threads; stringy: *a* ropy *paint*; ropy *syrup.* **2** like cords or rope. **—*n-* rop′ i·ness.**

Roque·fort (rōk′ fərt) ***n-*** blue-veined cheese from ewe's milk, ripened in caves near Roquefort, France.

ror·qual (rȯr′ kwəl, rôr′-) ***n-*** finback whale.

Ror·schach test (rȯr′ shäk′, rôr′-) ***n-*** in psychology, a personality test in which a person is shown ten standardized ink blots and asked to tell what they suggest to him.

ro·sa·ry (rō′ zə rē) ***n-*** [*pl.* **ro·sa·ries**] **1** string of beads for counting and reciting a series of prayers. **2** series of prayers thus recited.

[1]**rose** (rōz) ***n-*** **1** any of various thorny shrubs or plants bearing fragrant flowers of many colors. **2** the flower of this plant. **3** delicate pink color. **4** something shaped like a rose, such as certain cuts of gems. ***adj-***: *a* rose *satin.* [from Old English **rose,** from Latin **rosa.**] **—*adj-* rose′ like′.**

Wild and garden roses

[2]**rose** (rōz) *p.t.* of **rise.**

ro·se·ate (rō′ zē ət) ***adj-*** **1** like a rose, especially in color. **2** optimistic: *a* roseate *view of the world.*

rose·bud (rōz′ bŭd′) ***n-*** bud of a rose.

rose·bush (rōz′ bo͝osh′) ***n-*** shrub or vine bearing roses.

rose fever ***n-*** form of hay fever appearing early in summer and believed to be caused by rose pollen.

rose geranium ***n-*** any of several geraniums with clusters of small, pink or purplish flowers.

rose·mar·y (rōz′ mĕr′ ē) ***n-*** [*pl.* **rose·mar·ies**] fragrant evergreen shrub of the mint family. The leaves are used as a seasoning and in making perfume.

rose of Sharon ***n-*** **1** unidentified flower mentioned in the Bible, perhaps the autumn crocus. **2** garden shrub related to the mallows.

Ro·set·ta stone (rō zĕt′ ə) ***n-*** tablet found near Rosetta, Egypt, in 1799, bearing inscriptions in both Egyptian hieroglyphics and Greek alphabet. It provided the key for deciphering the ancient Egyptian writings.

Rosette

ro·sette (rō zĕt′) ***n-*** **1** rose-shaped ornament made of loops of ribbon gathered at the center, or of a piece of cloth drawn in around a center. **2** any ornament of a similar shape. **3** circle of lines, leaves, or the like, stretching from a central point: *a* rosette *of flat leaves.*

rose window ***n-*** circular stained-glass window with divisions radiating from, or arranged around, its center.

rose·wood (rōz′ wo͝od′) ***n-*** **1** valuable, hard, dark-colored wood yielded by various tropical trees and used for fine furniture. **2** any tree that yields such wood.

Rose window

Rosh Ha·sha·na (rōsh′ hä shä′ nə, -shȯ′ nə) ***n-*** Jewish New Year, occurring in the early autumn.

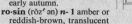

ro·sin (rŏz′ ən) ***n-*** **1** amber or reddish-brown, translucent residue remaining after distillation of the oil of turpentine from crude turpentine. It is used to make varnish and soap, and to prevent slipping on violin bows and ballet slippers. **2** resin.

ros·ter (rŏs′ tər) ***n-*** list of military and naval officers and men enrolled for duty; hence, any list of names.

ros·trum (rŏs′ trəm) ***n-*** **1** pulpit, platform, or stage for public speaking. **2** in ancient Rome, prow or beak of a war galley used for ramming. **3** *Biology* any structure resembling a bird's beak.

ros·y (rō′ zē) ***adj-*** **[ros·i·er, ros·i·est] 1** pinkish or reddish: *cheeks* rosy *with cold.* **2** hopeful; full of promise: *his* rosy *prospects.* **—*adv-* ros′ i·ly. *n-* ros′ i·ness.**

rot (rŏt) ***vi-*** **[rot·ted, rot·ting] 1** to spoil; decay: *The fruit will* rot *on the ground.* **2** to become morally degraded; degenerate. ***vt-*** to cause to decay: *Dampness* rots *most woods.* ***n-*** **1** a decaying or being decayed: *Dry* rot *had set in the old timbers.* **2** something that is decayed or decaying: *a mass of crumbling* rot. **3** certain diseases of plants or animals. **4** *Informal* nonsense. ***interj-*** nonsense!

ro·ta·ry (rō′ tə rē) ***adj-*** **1** turning or rotating, as does a wheel on an axis. **2** having parts that turn around: *a* rotary *engine.* **3** consisting of movement around an axis: *swift* rotary *motion.* ***n-*** traffic circle.

rotary engine ***n-*** **1** any engine in which a rotating motion is produced directly, as in a steam turbine. **2** an internal combustion engine having cylinders radially arranged and rotating around a stationary crankshaft.

ro·tate (rō′ tāt′) ***vi-*** **[ro·tat·ed, ro·tat·ing] 1** to turn around on a center point or line: *A wheel* rotates *on its axle. The earth* rotates *on its axis.* **2** to take turns: *The men* rotated *in office.* ***vt-***: *to* rotate *a wheel*; *to* rotate *men in office.* **—*adj-* ro′ tat·a·ble:** *a* rotatable *shaft.*

ro·ta·tion (rō tā′ shən) ***n-*** **1** a rotating around a center or axis: *the* earth's *rotation.* **2** periodic changing or occurence: *the* rotation *of men in office.* **3** system of varying the crops grown in the same field to keep up the fertility of the soil.

ro·ta·tor (rō′ tā′ tər) ***n-*** **1** person or thing that rotates or causes rotation. **2** a muscle that causes a part of the body to revolve on its axis.

ro·ta·tor·y (rō′ tə tôr′ ē) ***adj-*** having, relating to, or causing rotation: *a* rotatory *muscle.*

R.O.T.C. or **ROTC** Reserve Officers' Training Corps.

rote (rōt) ***n-*** set, mechanical way of doing something; mere routine. ***as modifier***: *a* rote *performance*; rote *learning.* ***Hom-*** wrote.

by rote by memory without understanding.

ro·ti·fer (rō′ tə fər) ***n-*** any of a group of microscopic water animals that feed by means of the rows of cilia resembling revolving wheels that are located at one end.

ro·tis·ser·ie (rō tĭs′ ə rē) ***n-*** electrical appliance with a rotating spit for roasting meat.

ro·to·gra·vure (rō′ tə grə vyŏŏr′) *n-* 1 printing process in which an impression is made from an engraved cylindrical plate on a revolving press. 2 picture printed by this process. 3 newspaper section with such pictures.

ro·tor (rō′ tər) *n-* 1 part that revolves in or around a stationary part, such as the rotating part of a dynamo or motor. 2 system of horizontally rotating wings: *the* rotor *of a helicopter*.

rot·ten (rŏt′ ən) *adj-* 1 decayed; spoiled: *a* rotten *egg*. 2 not sound; in danger of breaking: *a* rotten *beam*. 3 bad; disagreeable; contemptible: *That was a* rotten *trick*. 4 corrupt; dishonest. *—adv-* **rot′ ten·ly.** *n-* **rot′ ten·ness.**

rot·ten·stone (rŏt′ ən stōn′) *n-* an easily crumbled, gray to olive-colored stone, consisting of the oxides of aluminum, silicon, and iron, that are residues from the weathering of ancient limestone. It is used as an abrasive in metal and wood finishing.

ro·tund (rō′ tŭnd′) *adj-* 1 round; plump. 2 full-toned; deep: *a* rotund *phrase*. *—n-* **ro·tun′ di·ty** or **ro·tund′- ness.** *adv-* **ro·tund′ ly.**

ro·tun·da (rō tŭn′ də) *n-* large circular building or room, especially one with a dome.

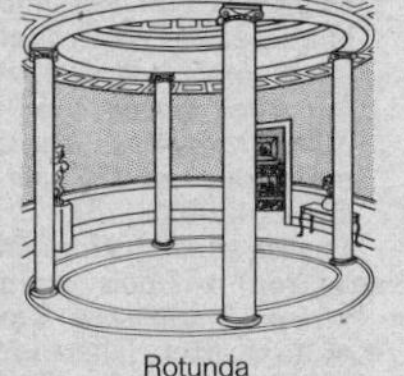

Rotunda

rou·ble (rōō′ bəl) ruble.

rouge (rōōzh) *n-* 1 pink or red cosmetic for coloring the cheeks. 2 finely powdered, reddish iron oxide used for polishing glass, metal, and gems. *vt-* **[rouged, roug·ing]:** *to* rouge *the cheeks*.

rough (rŭf) *adj-* **[rough·er, rough·est]** 1 having an uneven surface; not smooth: *a* rough *cloth*. 2 marked by boisterous or vigorous action: *in* rough *games*; rough *sports*. 3 stormy; tempestuous: *a* rough *sea*; rough *weather*. 4 not polished: *a* rough *gem*. 5 incomplete; unfinished: *a* rough *sketch*. 6 vulgar; without refinement: *his* rough *manners*. 7 harsh to the ear; jarring: *a* rough *tone*; *a* rough *voice*. 8 unpleasant; difficult: *a* rough *day*. 9 approximate; not thought out: *a* rough *guess*. 10 lacking in comfort or luxury: *a* rough *life in the jungle*. 11 rude; uncivil: *a* rough *reply*; rough *words*. *n-* 1 coarse, violent person; rowdy. 2 on a golf course, area of grass and weeds not tended. *vt-* 1 to produce an uneven surface on; destroy the smoothness of; roughen: *The bird* roughed *its feathers*. 2 to treat with unnecessary and intentional violence, especially in football. *Hom-* ruff. *—adv-* **rough′ ly.** *n-* **rough′ ness.**

in the rough in an unfinished condition.

rough in (or **out**) to sketch or outline in a general way.

rough it to do without comforts, as on a camping trip.

rough up *Informal* to treat in a rough way; manhandle.

rough·age (rŭf′ ĭj) *n-* 1 material in a rough or crude state. 2 any rough, largely indigestible substance, such as bran, that stimulates the peristalsis of the digestive tract.

rough-and-tum·ble (rŭf′ ən tŭm′ bəl) *n-* violent fight or struggle with little regard for rules of fair play. *as modifier*: *a* rough-and-tumble *fight*.

rough·en (rŭf′ ən) *vt-* to make rough: *The wind* roughened *her skin*. *vi-*: *Her skin* roughened *with age*.

rough-hew (rŭf′ hyōō′) *vt-* **[rough-hewed, rough-hewed** or **rough-hewn, rough-hew·ing]** 1 to hew or cut (timber) without smoothing. 2 to shape in a crude, coarse way.

rough·house (rŭf′ hous′) *Informal n-* noisy, rowdy, or violent game, especially indoors; horseplay. *vt-* **[rough·housed, rough·hous·ing]** to treat roughly; rough up without harming: *to* roughhouse *a friend*. *vi-*: *The boys* roughhoused *in the basement*.

rough·neck (rŭf′ nĕk′) *Slang n-* rough person; tough.

rough·rid·er (rŭf′ rī′ dər) *n-* 1 person who breaks horses for riding or who is a skilled rider of untrained horses. 2 **Roughrider** in the Spanish-American War of 1898, a member of the First U.S. Volunteer Cavalry commanded by Theodore Roosevelt.

rough·shod (rŭf′ shŏd′) *adj-* shod with horseshoes having calks to prevent slipping.

ride roughshod over to domineer or prevail over in a harsh and arrogant manner; override.

rou·lette (rōō lĕt′) *n-* 1 game of chance played with a revolving wheel, **roulette wheel,** marked off in 37 or 38 compartments. The players bet on which compartment a small ivory ball spun in the wheel will come to rest. 2 instrument with a toothed wheel used for making dotted lines or perforations.

Rou·ma·ni·an (rōō mā′ nē ən) Rumanian.

round (round) *adj-* **[round·er, round·est]** 1 shaped like a ball, circle, or tube: *a* round *yellow apple*; *a* round *plate*; *a* round *pencil*. 2 having a curved contour or surface; also, plump; chubby: *a* round *cheek*. 3 full; whole; complete: *a* round *dozen*. 4 large; ample: *a good* round *sum*. 5 moving in a circle: *a* round *dance*. 6 full in sound; not jarring: *the* round *tones of a voice*. 7 easy and brisk: *a good* round *trot*. 8 outspoken; frank: *a* round *scolding*. 9 in architecture, semicircular: *a* round *arch*. 10 in phonetics, made with the lips formed into a circle, as a long "o" [ō]. *n-* 1 anything that is circular or cylindrical in shape, such as a circle or a rung of a ladder; also, a curved part. 2 (often **rounds**) fixed course or route; beat: *The police officer made his* rounds. 3 series of events or acts; also, routine: *a* round *of parties*; *the daily* round *of duties*. 4 division of a sport or game; also, one complete game or set of games: *the sixth* round *of a fight*; *a* round *of golf*. 5 some action in which a number of persons take part at one time: *a* round *of applause*; *a* round *of cheers*. 6 simultaneous volley of shots, each soldier firing once; also, ammunition needed for such a volley, or enough for a single shot. 7 portion of drink served to each of the members of a group: *a* round *of drinks*. 8 round dance. 9 *Music* song sung by two or more people, each one singing the same thing, starting at intervals one after another. 10 a cut of beef between the rump and the leg: *a* round *of beef*. *vt-* 1 to make circular or curved: *to* round *the lips*; *to* round *the corners of a table*. 2 to travel or pass around: *He* rounded *the curve*. *The ship* rounded *the cape*. 3 to pronounce with the lips formed into a circle: *to* round *a vowel*. 4 to make plump: *Age* rounded *her girlish figure*. *vi-* to become round, shapely, plump, etc. *prep- & adv-* around. *—adj-* **round′ ish.** *n-* **round′ ness.**

in the round 1 of sculpture, carved out or modeled fully on all sides; not done in relief. 2 in a theater with a central stage surrounded by seats.

round off 1 to finish; bring to perfection. 2 to express in round numbers.

round out 1 to make or become fuller or plumper. 2 to make complete: *Your visit* rounds out *my day*.

round up to gather together: *to* round up *cattle*.

round·a·bout (round′ ə bout′) *adj-* not direct; not straightforward: *a* roundabout *route*. *adv-* all around: *the country* roundabout.

round dance *n-* 1 folk dance in which the dancers move in a circle. 2 ballroom dance with a circular motion.

roun·del (roun′ dəl) ***n***- poem with three groups of three lines each, and a refrain after the first and the third.

roun·de·lay (roun′ də lā′) ***n***- **1** simple tune. **2** song with a simple melody in which a phrase or line is often repeated. **3** folk dance performed in a circle; round dance.

Round·head (round′ hĕd′) ***n***- in 17th-century England, a derisive name applied, during the English civil war, to the Puritans or supporters of the Parliament, many of whom adopted a cropped haircut.

round·house (round′ hous′) ***n***- **1** cabin on the after part of a ship's quarterdeck. **2** circular building for storing and repairing locomotives in stalls entered by means of a turntable. **3** in baseball, a pitch in which the ball makes a wide curve. **4** *Informal* punch or blow delivered with a wide swing of the arm.

round·ly (round′ lē) ***adv***- **1** with vigor; bluntly; in plain language: *to scold* roundly. **2** fully; thoroughly: *He was* roundly *snubbed by her friends.*

round number ***n***- number expressed to the nearest unit of ten, hundred, thousand, etc. Also **round figure.**

round robin ***n***- **1** tournament in which every player is matched with every other player. **2** letter sent around to the members of a group, each of whom signs it and usually adds a comment. **3** document bearing signatures written in a circle so as not to show who signed it first.

round-shoul·dered (round′ shōl′ dərd) ***adj***- having shoulders that bend forward; not erect.

round steak ***n***- cut of steak from the whole round of beef.

round table ***n***- **1** group of persons seated at, or as if at, a circular table for discussion of a given topic; also, such a meeting. *as* ***modifier*** **(round-table):** *a* round-table *conference.* **2 Round Table** (1) in medieval legend, a table at which King Arthur and his knights sat. (2) King Arthur and his knights.

round trip ***n***- journey to a place and then back again to the starting point. *as* ***modifier*** **(round-trip):** *a* round-trip *bus ticket.*

round·up (round′ ŭp′) ***n***- **1** a herding together of cattle for branding or inspection. **2** men and horses that herd the cattle together. **3** *Informal* a gathering together of things or people: *a* roundup *of opinions.*

round·worm (round′ wûrm′) ***n***- red or yellow nematode pointed at both ends, and eight to twelve inches long. It is a common intestinal parasite.

rouse (rouz) ***vt***- **[roused, rous·ing] 1** to awaken from sleep: *The fire alarm* roused *the household.* **2** to excite; stir up to anger or strong action. ***vi***- **1** to awake from sleep. **2** to show signs of activity. **—*n*- rous′ er.**

rous·ing (rou′ zĭng) ***adj***- **1** stirring; exciting; inspiring: *a* rousing *song.* **2** brisk; lively; very active: *a* rousing *trade.* **3** *Informal* very great; outrageous: *a* rousing *fib.*

roust·a·bout (roust′ ə bout′) ***n***- **1** laborer, especially on a river boat or wharf, in the oil fields, or in a circus. **2** man who tramps around the country doing odd jobs for a living, especially on cattle ranches. Also **rous′ ter.**

[1]**rout** (rout) ***n***- **1** complete defeat followed by a disorderly flight: *The army's retreat turned into a* rout. **2** disorderly mob; rabble. ***vt***- to defeat so completely that the enemy is in hopeless disorder. [from Old French **route,** "a throng; a defeat," from Latin **rupta,** "a path broken through the woods; a dispersed troop."] ***Hom***- route.

[2]**rout** (rout) ***vt***- **1** to scoop or dig out with, or as if with, a gouging tool. **2** to drag by force; drive out. ***vi***- to rummage. [from [2]**root.**] ***Hom***- route.

rout out to turn up; bring to view; discover.

route (ro͞ot, rout) ***n***- **1** certain road, way, or course: *sea* routes; *U.S.* Route *1.* **2** job of supplying customers in a certain district with a particular thing; also, set of customers regularly supplied with something: *a newspaper* route. ***vt***- **[rout·ed, rout·ing]** to send or forward by a certain road or way. ***Hom***- root or rout.

rou·tine (ro͞o tēn′) ***n***- usual or regular way of doing things: *the daily* routine *of classes and homework.* ***adj***- (*also* ro͞o′ tēn′) regular or usual; ordinary; customary.

rove (rōv) ***vi***- **[roved, rov·ing]** to wander; go from place to place and not settle down: *to* rove *all over the world.* ***vt***-: *to* rove *the plains.*

rov·er (rō′ vər) ***n***- **1** person who wanders. **2** pirate.

[1]**row** (rō) ***n***- **1** series of persons or things in a line, especially a straight line: *a* row *of beets; a* row *of seats.* **2** line of houses side by side on a street; also, the street. **3** street or neighborhood marked by one type of business or occupancy: *cannery* row; *publishers'* row. [from Old English **rōw** or **rǣw** meaning "a line; series."] ***Hom***- roe.

hard row to hoe hard task.

[2]**row** (rō) ***vt***- **1** to propel by means of oars. **2** to take or carry in a boat with oars: *The boatman* rowed *us up the river.* **3** of a boat, to use (a specific number of oars): *The barge* rowed *ten oars.* **4** to use (oars or rowers), especially in a race: *The crew* rowed *five new men.* **5** to participate in, or compete against, with oars: *to* row *a race; to* row *last year's winning crew.* ***vi***- **1** to move a boat by means of oars: *John has learned to* row. **2** to be moved by means of oars: *The boat* rows *easily.* ***n***- act of moving a boat by oars; also, a ride in a rowboat. [from Old English **rōwan.**] ***Hom***- roe. **—*n*- row′ er.**

[3]**row** (rou) ***n***- **1** noisy argument or quarrel: *to have a* row *with one's neighbors.* **2** loud noise; disturbance; uproar. ***vi***- to quarrel. [altered from **rouse,** of uncertain origin.]

row·an (rou′ ən) ***n***- **1** tree bearing large clusters of orange or red berries. **2** the berry of this tree.

row·boat (rō′ bōt′) ***n***- small boat moved in water by means of oars.

Rowboat

row·dy (rou′ dē) ***adj***- **[row·di·er, row·di·est]** noisy, rough, and disorderly: *a* rowdy *audience;* rowdy *behavior.* ***n***- *[pl.* **row·dies]** rude and disorderly person. **—*adv*- row′ di·ly. *n*- row′ di·ness. *adj*- row′ dy·ish.**

row·dy·ism (rou′ dē ĭz′ əm) ***n***- disorderly conduct.

row·el (rou′ əl) ***n***- the small wheel of a spur. ***vt***- to prick (a horse) with this.

Rowel

roy·al (roi′ əl) ***adj***- **1** of or having to do with kings or queens: *the* royal *family.* **2** like a king; regal: *He behaved with* royal *dignity.* **3** of or having to do with the government of a king or queen: *the* royal *navy.* **4** fit for a king; splendid: *a* royal *welcome.* ***n***- small sail above the topgallant sail and under the skysail. **—*adv*- roy′ al·ly.**

roy·al·ist (roi′ ə lĭst′) ***n***- **1** believer in, and supporter of, government by a king. **2 Royalist** (1) Cavalier. (2) Tory. ***adj***-: *a* royalist *party.*

royal jelly ***n***- white, concentrated food paste produced from pollen by the salivary glands of the worker honeybee and fed to larvae. Larvae that are fed royal jelly throughout their development become queen bees.

royal palm ***n***- any of several tall, ornamental American palm trees, widely planted in tropical regions.

roy·al·ty (roi′ əl tē) ***n***- *[pl.* **roy·al·ties] 1** kings, queens, and their families: *a play performed before* royalty. **2** position, power, or duties of kings or queens: *Crowns and scepters are symbols of* royalty. **3** kingly nature or quality. **4** payment made to the owner of a copyright or patent: *Publishers pay a* royalty *to an author on the copies of his books they sell.* **5** tax paid to the crown, such as a percentage of gold mined or minted.

r.p.m. revolutions per minute.
R.R. **1** railroad. **2** rural route.
R.S.F.S.R. or **RSFSR** Russian Soviet Federated Socialist Republic.
R.S.V.P. please reply [from French **Répondez s'il vous plaît**].
rte. route.
Ru symbol for ruthenium.
rub (rŭb) ***vt-*** **[rubbed, rub·bing] 1** to move (something) up and down or backwards and forwards against another: *to* rub *a cloth over a mirror.* **2** to move (two things) against each other in this way: *to* rub *sticks to make a fire.* **3** to clean, polish, dry, etc., with such a motion: *to* rub *a table with linseed oil*; *to* rub *oneself with a towel.* **4** to spread or apply with a rubbing motion: *to* rub *suntan lotion on one's back.* **5** to cause to become sore, frayed, chafed, etc., from friction: *The tight collar* rubs *his neck.* **6** to touch with a scraping or brushing movement: *The wheel* rubbed *her dress.* ***vi-*** to move along a surface with pressure; scrape: *The wheels are* rubbing *together.* ***n-*** **1** the use of friction and pressure upon a surface. **2** something that causes trouble; difficulty; hindrance: *"There's the* rub." **3** something that is harsh to the feelings, such as a gibe or sarcasm.
rub down 1 to massage. **2** to polish by rubbing.
rub elbows with to be friendly with; come into contact with: *The prince* rubbed elbows with *the people.*
rub it in *Informal* to keep mentioning a failure, mistake, etc., in order to irritate someone.
rub off to remove; erase.
rub the wrong way to annoy; irritate.
[1]**rub·ber** (rŭb'ər) ***n-*** **1** elastic material coagulated from natural latex or manufactured synthetically. **2** article made of this material, such as an eraser. **3** an overshoe made of rubber, especially one that stops short of the ankle. **4** person or thing that rubs, polishes, erases, etc. *as* ***modifier****: a pair of* rubber *gloves.* **—*adj-* rub'ber·like'** or **rub'ber·y.** [from **rub** meaning "erase."]
[2]**rub·ber** (rŭb'ər) ***n-*** **1** in bridge, whist, etc., the two or three games played until one side has won two; also, the third decisive game played after each side has won one. **2** any game that breaks a tie. *as* ***modifier****: a* rubber *match.* [from an alteration of earlier **a rubbers** meaning "the deciding game in any series."]
rubber band ***n-*** elastic band made of rubber.
rubber cement ***n-*** waterproof glue consisting of a solution of latex in a chemical solvent.
rub·ber·ize (rŭb'ə rīz') ***vt-*** **[rub·ber·ized, rub·ber·iz·ing]** to coat, fill, or treat with rubber or with a rubber preparation: *to* rubberize *canvas.*
rubber stamp ***n-*** **1** stamp made of rubber for printing. **2** *Informal* person who approves or endorses something as a matter of routine. ***vt-*** **(rubber-stamp):** *to* rubber-stamp *one's address*; *to* rubber-stamp *a proposal.*
rub·bing (rŭb'ĭng) ***n-*** reproduction of an indented, raised, or sculptured surface made by placing paper over it and rubbing with a pencil, crayon, etc.
rubbing alcohol ***n-*** solution of water and denatured alcohol for external use only, especially to rub down.
rub·bish (rŭb'ĭsh) ***n-*** **1** waste; trash; junk. **2** nonsense.
rub·ble (rŭb'əl) ***n-*** **1** rough, broken pieces of stone; also, masonry built of them. **2** ruins of buildings after a bombing, earthquake, or other disaster; debris.
rub·down (rŭb'doun') ***n-*** a massage.
ru·bel·la (ro͞o bĕl'ə) ***n-*** German measles.
ru·be·o·la (ro͞o bē'ə lə) ***n-*** measles.
Ru·bi·con (ro͞o'bə kŏn') ***n-*** river in northern Italy forming the boundary between Caesar's province of Gaul and ancient Italy, the crossing of which by Caesar in 49 B.C. led to civil war with Pompey.
cross the Rubicon to take a decisive step.
ru·bi·cund (ro͞o'bə kŭnd') ***adj-*** reddish; ruddy; flushed. **—*n-* ru'bi·cun'di·ty.**
ru·bid·i·um (ro͞o bĭd'ē əm) ***n-*** soft, reactive metal element resembling sodium or potassium. Symbol Rb, At. No. 37, At. Wt. 85.47.
ru·ble (ro͞o'bəl) ***n-*** **1** basic unit of money in Soviet Russia. **2** coin or paper money representing it.
ru·bric (ro͞o'brĭk) ***n-*** **1** part of an old book or manuscript that was printed in red or some special type, such as titles, directions, or initial letters. **2** title or heading of a law, chapter, etc. **3** in a prayer book, directions for a religious service, formerly printed in red. **4** any direction or rule of conduct.
ru·by (ro͞o'bē) ***n-*** [*pl.* **ru·bies**] **1** deep-red, transparent corundum, valued as a precious stone; also, a gem or bearing from this material. **2** a deep-red color. ***adj-****: a* ruby *ring*; ruby *lips*; ruby *wine.*
ruck·sack (rŭk'săk') ***n-*** knapsack.
ruck·us (rŭk'əs) *Informal* ***n-*** noisy fight; uproar.
ruc·tion (rŭk'shən) *Informal* ***n-*** **1** noisy fight; free-for-all; row. **2** disturbance; uproar; commotion.
rud·der (rŭd'ər) ***n-*** **1** broad, flat piece of wood or metal hinged vertically to the stern of a boat or ship and used to steer it. **2** a similar surface on the tail of an aircraft (for picture, see *airplane*). **—*adj-* rud'der·less.**

Rudder

rud·dy (rŭd'ē) ***adj-*** **[rud·di·er, rud·di·est] 1** rosy; red or reddish: *a* ruddy *apple.* **2** having the color and glow of good health: *a* ruddy *complexion.* **—*n-* rud'di·ness.**
rude (ro͞od) ***adj-*** **[rud·er, rud·est] 1** not polite; discourteous: *a* rude *reply*; *a* rude *person.* **2** roughly made; crude: *a* rude *carving*; rude *verses.* **3** primitive; not civilized: *a* rude *people.* **4** rough; violent: *a* rude *shock.* ***Hom-*** rood. **—*adv-* rude'ly.** ***n-*** **rude'ness.**
ru·di·ment (ro͞o'də mənt) ***n-*** **1** (often **rudiments**) a first or beginning step; one of the basic rules and principles (of any skill, art, or science). **2** *Biology* (1) organ or structure that is incompletely developed and functionless in the adult individual; vestige: *The appendix is a* rudiment. (2) organ or structure seen in its incomplete, embryonic stage of development.
ru·di·men·ta·ry (ro͞o'də mĕn'tə rē) ***adj-*** **1** beginning; elementary: *Alan had only a* rudimentary *knowledge of science.* **2** *Biology* remaining undeveloped or without function: *the* rudimentary *antlers of some deer.*
[1]**rue** (ro͞o) ***vt-*** **[rued, ru·ing]** to look at with shame and sorrow; be sorry for; regret. ***n-*** regret. [from Old English **hreowan,** related to **ruthless.**]
[2]**rue** (ro͞o) ***n-*** yellow-flowered plant with a strong odor and bitter taste, formerly used in medicine. [from Old French, from Latin **rūta.**]
rue·ful (ro͞o'fəl) ***adj-*** **1** filled with regret; sadly disappointed; mournful; doleful: *a* rueful *smile.* **2** causing pity or grief: *She was a* rueful *sight.* **—*adv-* rue'ful·ly.** ***n-*** **rue'ful·ness.**

Ruff

ruff (rŭf) ***n-*** **1** high collar formed by vertical folds of starched cloth, worn by men and women in the

fāte, făt, dâre, bärn; bē, bĕt, mêre; bīte, bĭt; nōte, hŏt, môre, dȯg; fŭn, fûr; to͞o, bo͝ok; oil; out; tar; thin; then; hw for wh as in *wh*at; zh for s as in u*s*ual; ə for a, e, i, o, u, as in *a*go, lin*e*n, per*i*l, at*o*m, min*u*s

16th and 17th centuries. **2** ring or roll of feathers or fur which makes a standing collar around the neck of a bird or other animal. **3** Old World sandpiper, the male of which has in breeding season an enormous frill of feathers about his neck. ***Hom-*** rough. ***—adj-*** **ruffed:** *a* ruffed *bird.*

ruffed grouse ***n-*** North American grouse with brownish feathers and a fan-shaped tail. For picture, see *grouse.*

ruf·fi·an (rŭf′ ē ən) ***n-*** brutal, lawless fellow; bully. ***adj-:*** *a* ruffian *manner.*

ruf·fi·an·ly (rŭf′ ē ən lē) ***adj-*** of or like a ruffian; coarse; rough; brutal: *a* ruffianly *appearance*; *a* ruffianly *person.*

[1]**ruf·fle** (rŭf′ əl) ***vt-*** **[ruf·fled, ruf·fling] 1** to make rough; cause to lose the flatness or evenness of: *A bird* ruffles *its feathers. The wind* ruffled *the pond.* **2** to disturb; annoy; disquiet: *Our late arrival* ruffled *our hostess.* **3** to draw into folds or pleats: *to* ruffle *a skirt.* **4** to shuffle (cards); riffle. ***vi-*** **1** to become vexed or annoyed. **2** to form folds or ripples; flutter: *The tarpaulin* ruffled *in the breeze.* ***n-*** pleated or gathered strip of material used as a trimming; frill: *a* ruffle *of lace.* [from Middle English **ruffelen** meaning "to disorder; entangle," from early Germanic **ruffelen,** "to wrinkle; pleat."]

[2]**ruf·fle** (rŭf′ əl) ***n-*** low, continuous drumbeat. [perhaps from Middle English **ruffelen** with the meaning "to make noise or turbulence."]

rug (rŭg) ***n-*** **1** heavy woven, braided, or hooked mat used to cover part of a floor; carpet woven in a single piece. **2** covering made of animal skin: *a leopard* rug. **3** *chiefly Brit.* thick, warm piece of cloth used as a blanket.

Rug·by (rŭg′ bē) ***n-*** in England, a form of football from which the American game developed. Also **Rugby football.**

rug·ged (rŭg′ əd) ***adj-*** **1** rough and uneven; steep and rocky: *Our hike took us through very* rugged *country.* **2** strongly marked: *He has* rugged *features.* **3** harsh; severe: *a* rugged *winter.* **4** sturdy; robust; vigorous: *a* rugged *man.* ***—adv-*** **rug′ ged·ly.** ***n-*** **rug′ ged·ness.**

ru·in (rōō′ ĭn) ***n-*** **1** destruction; severe damage: *the* ruin *of hope.* **2** the cause of destruction or of someone's downfall: *Gambling was his* ruin. **3** something that has fallen into pieces or decay: *The old castle is now only a* ruin. **4 ruins** remains of a building, city, etc: *the* ruins *of an Egyptian temple.* ***vt-*** **1** to damage or spoil entirely; destroy: *Locusts* ruined *the crops.* **2** to make bankrupt or impoverished: *The market crash* ruined *him.*

ru·in·a·tion (rōō′ ə nā′ shən) ***n-*** **1** destruction; downfall. **2** something that ruins: *Gambling was his* ruination.

ru·in·ous (rōō′ ə nəs) ***adj-*** leading to or being in a state of downfall or collapse: *a* ruinous *war*; *a barn in a* ruinous *state.* ***—adv-*** **ru′ in·ous·ly.** ***n-*** **ru′ in·ous·ness.**

rule (rōōl) ***n-*** **1** principle made to guide and control action or behavior; standard; regulation; also, an established usage or law: *the Golden* Rule; *the* rules *of a game.* **2** regulations governing the conduct of members of a given order: *the Franciscan* rule. **3** usual or expected course of action: *It is his* rule *to go to bed early. Scholarship is the* rule *in a university.* **4** government; authority; also, period of such government; reign: *a country under foreign* rule; *during the* rule *of Henry VIII.* **5** piece of wood, metal, etc., used as a measuring device; ruler. **6** in law, an order or decision from a judge or a court of law with reference to some specific point. **7** in printing, a thin strip of metal for printing lines. ***vt-*** **[ruled, rul·ing] 1** to have power over; govern: *The king* ruled *his country wisely.* **2** to guide; influence or control: *He was* ruled *by hatred.* **3** to establish by a decision; order: *The court* ruled *the genuineness of the will.* **4** to restrain; curb: *You should learn how to* rule *your temper.* **5** to make straight lines on, with a ruler or other straight edge. ***vi-*** **1** to exercise authority (over): *He* ruled *over the country for ten years.* **2** in law, to decide a point.

as a rule usually: *Cats,* as a rule, *don't like water.*

rule out to exclude; reject: *to* rule out *compromise.*

rule of thumb ***n-*** **1** rule or opinion based on practice or experience. **2** rough measurement.

rul·er (rōō′ lər) ***n-*** **1** person who governs or reigns. **2** strip of wood, metal, etc., that is often marked with inches or the like and is used to draw or measure straight lines.

rul·ing (rōō′ lĭng) ***n-*** decision made by an authority: *the* ruling *of the court.* ***adj-*** **1** governing; having authority: *the* ruling *classes.* **2** most widely held: *The* ruling *sentiment of the town is in favor of the new mayor.*

[1]**rum** (rŭm) ***n-*** **1** alcoholic drink made from sugar cane, molasses, etc. **2** loosely, any alcoholic liquor. [shortened from earlier **rumbullion,** of uncertain origin.]

[2]**rum** (rŭm) *Brit. Slang* ***adj-*** odd; queer. [perhaps from Romany **rom** meaning "a Gypsy."]

Ru·ma·ni·an (rōō mān′ ē ən, rō-) ***adj-*** of or relating to Rumania, its people, or their language. ***n-*** **1** a native or inhabitant of Rumania. **2** the Romance language of Rumania. Also **Romanian.**

rum·ba (rŭm′ bə) ***n-*** **1** dance of Cuban origin. **2** modern ballroom dance resembling this; also, the music for this dance.

rum·ble (rŭm′bəl) ***n-*** **1** dull, heavy, rolling sound: *the* rumble *of thunder*; *the* rumble *of city traffic.* **2** *Slang* fight between gangs. ***vi-*** **[rum·bled, rum·bling]** to make, or move with, a heavy, rolling sound: *His stomach* rumbled *from lack of food. The truck* rumbled *down the street.* ***vt-*** to utter with such a sound: *to* rumble *a reply.*

rumble seat ***n-*** folding outside seat at the back of an automobile, especially a coupé.

ru·men (rōō′ mən) ***n-*** first of the four pouches of the stomach of a cud-chewing animal, in which the cud is stored.

ru·mi·nant (rōō′ mə nənt) ***n-*** any of a group of mammals that have a stomach with four divisions. Animals that chew cud, such as the sheep, goat, cow, deer, and camel, are ruminants. ***adj-:*** *a* ruminant *mammal.*

ru·mi·nate (rōō′ mə nāt′) ***vi-*** **[ru·mi·nat·ed, ru·mi·nat·ing] 1** to chew the cud. **2** to muse or meditate (usually followed by "over"): *He* ruminated *over the message.* ***—n-*** **ru′ mi·na′ tion.** ***adj-*** **ru′ mi·na′ tive.**

rum·mage (rŭm′ ĭj) ***n-*** thorough search made by turning things over in a disorderly way. ***vt-*** **[rum·maged, rum·mag·ing]** to search thoroughly by turning over the contents of; ransack: *to* rummage *a box.* ***vi-:*** *He* rummaged *in a closet.*

rummage up (or **out**) to find or discover by rummaging.

rummage sale ***n-*** **1** sale of odds and ends, unwanted articles, or old clothes to raise money for charity. **2** sale of unclaimed articles, or a sale for clearance.

rum·my (rŭm′ ē) ***n-*** card game in which the object is to get groups of three or more cards that make a set.

ru·mor (rōō′ mər) ***n-*** talk, story, or report that is passed from person to person before the actual facts are known or without regard for its truthfulness; also, idle talk; gossip; hearsay. ***vt-*** to declare or imply by unproven talk or report: *He is* rumored *to be very ill.*

rump (rŭmp) ***n-*** **1** hind quarters of an animal. **2** cut of meat from this region. **3** the last and inferior part; remnant. **4** legislative body having only a trace of its former membership because of the departure or expulsion of a large number of its members, and therefore regarded as unrepresentative.

rum·ple (rŭm′ pəl) ***vt-*** **[rum·pled, rum·pling]** to wrinkle and crease; crumple; also, to muss; tousle: *to* rumple *clothes*; *to* rumple *hair.* ***vi-***: *My clothes* rumpled.

rum·pus (rŭm′ pəs) *Informal* ***n-*** noisy disturbance; row.

rumpus room ***n-*** room, usually in the basement of a house, for games, informal parties, etc.

run (rŭn) ***vi-*** **[ran** (răn), **run, run·ning] 1** to move faster than at a walking speed. **2** to hurry; rush; hasten: *George* ran *carelessly through his homework.* **3** to depart suddenly; flee: *He* ran *away from home.* **4** to travel; move: *The train* runs *60 miles an hour.* **5** to make regular trips or follow a regular route: *The train* runs *between Boston and New York.* **6** to make a short trip: *We* ran *up to the country to visit a friend.* **7** to compete in a race; be a candidate: *He* ran *for office in the election.* **8** to finish a contest or race in a certain position or manner: *Our horse* ran *first in the race.* **9** to move about freely; also, to go or pass swiftly, easily, etc.: *He let his dog* run *loose. The rope* ran *through the pulley.* **10** to work; function: *This car won't* run. **11** to flow; also, to melt and flow: *Tears* ran *down her cheeks. The butter* ran. **12** to discharge a fluid: *His nose* ran. **13** to continue; extend; keep on going: *This road* runs *to the river. His play* ran *for a year. Her family line* runs *back to the Pilgrims.* **14** to climb or creep: *The ivy* ran *along the wall.* **15** to spread to parts where it does not belong: *Will the color* run *in this cloth?* **16** to become; pass into a specified condition: *The river* ran *dry. The ship* ran *aground.* **17** to be present; occur: *The idea* ran *through my mind.* **18** to be written, expressed or related: *That is how the story* runs. **19** to lose stitches; become unraveled: *Her stocking* ran. **20** to incline; tend: *Her taste* runs *to classical music.* **21** to vary in price, size, etc.: *The tickets* run *from $1.50 to $5.00.* **22** of fish, to travel in schools; especially, to go up a river to spawn. ***vt-*** **1** to go along, pass over, perform, or do by or as if by going at a pace faster than walking: *They* ran *a race. The actress* ran *the whole range of emotions.* **2** to cause to move in a certain direction or in a certain place: *She* ran *her fingers through her hair. I* ran *my eyes over the page.* **3** to operate: *I* ran *the business.* **4** to cause to flow: *We* ran *the water.* **5** to flow with: *My eyes* ran *tears.* **6** to enter (a person or thing) in a race or as a candidate: *They agreed to* run *Mr. Ade for mayor.* **7** to expose oneself to: *I* ran *a risk.* **8** to cause to extend: *They* ran *the cable down the mountain.* **9** to pierce; thrust: *I* ran *a splinter into my toe.* **10** to publish: *We* ran *the ad.* **11** in a game, to make a series of (points, strokes, etc.,) without a miss. **12** to sew or stitch (a series of short, even stitches). **13** to chase after; hunt: *to* run *a deer.* **14** to cause to move at a gallop: *to* run *a horse.* **15** to drive forcibly: *He* ran *his head against the wall.* **16** to cast; mold: *to* run *bullets.* **17** to slip through or past: *They* ran *a blockade.* **18** to smuggle. **19** to mark on or draw: *I* ran *a red line across the page.* ***n-*** **1** a pace faster than a walk. **2** distance traveled: *The train's* run *from St. Louis to Chicago is over 300 miles.* **3** trip or journey: *The bus makes two* runs *daily. The boat made its usual* run. **4** a flowing, or that which flows: *a* run *of maple sap.* **5** school of fish moving together: *a* run *of tuna.* **6** place passed over frequently by animals; also, an enclosed place for animals: *a* chicken *run.* **7** steep hill or course suitable for skiing, sledding, etc. **8** continuous extent or length of something: *a* run *of rope*; *a* run *of trees.* **9** succession; repetition: *a* run *of good luck.* **10** period of operation; also, number of performances: *The mill had a long* run *this season. The play had a short* run. **11** trend; tendency: *the* run *of the market.* **12** average sort: *The* run *of people you meet believe in fair play.* **13** a losing of stitches; an unraveling: *a* run *in a stocking.* **14** sudden and pressing demand: *a* run *on a bank.* **15** free use: *the* run *of a friend's house.* **16** *Music* succession of notes sung or played rapidly. **17** in a game, a series of points, strokes, etc., made without a miss. **18** in baseball, scoring of a point by a player's reaching home base after having touched the other three bases safely; also, the point so scored.

a run for (one's) money 1 satisfaction or enjoyment for money or effort spent: *The show gave me* a run for my money. **2** hard competition: *My opponent gave me* a run for my money. **in the long run** eventually: *We won* in the long run. **on the run 1** busy. **2** running or running away.

run across to meet or come upon accidentally.

run after 1 to chase after; also, to seek the company of: *He* ran after *the thief. At 15 he started* running after *the girls.* **2** to follow: *to* run after *every new fad.*

run against 1 to meet with: *We* ran against *opposition.* **2** to be in opposition: *His beliefs* ran against *mine.*

run along to leave: *I have to* run along *now.*

run a temperature (or **a fever**) to have a fever.

run away with to outdo greatly all others in; also, to get (a prize, award, etc.) in such a way.

run down 1 of machinery, to stop operating: *My watch* ran down. **2** to knock down. **3** to speak against: *He cruelly* ran down *his best friend.* **4** to capture: *He* ran down *the criminal.* **5** to find by investigating: *I* ran down *the location of her new address.* **6** to cause to be in poor physical condition: *overwork* ran *him* down.

run for it to get out of the way quickly; escape.

run foul of 1 to smash into. **2** to have trouble with.

run in 1 to insert: *I* ran in *some footnotes in my term paper.* **2** *Slang* to arrest. **3** in printing, to print without a break or paragraph.

run into 1 to collide with or meet accidentally: *He* ran into *a tree. I* ran into *an old friend.* **2** to be likely to fall into: *If John buys the boat, he will* run into *debt.*

run off 1 to print, typewrite, etc.; make copies of: *I* ran off *a letter on the typewriter. We* ran off *10,000 posters on the press.* **2** to decide the winner of (a tied game or race) by another game, race, etc. **3** to leave.

run on 1 to continue; especially, in printing, to continue without a break or paragraph. **2** to talk excessively.

run out to come to an end: *His money* ran out.

run out of to reach the end of: *We* ran out of *milk.*

run out on *Informal* to abandon.

run over 1 to overflow: *The rain barrel* ran over. **2** to review; go over again: *Let's* run over *the script again.* **3** to knock down with a vehicle and often to drive over: *Jack* ran over *a box in the middle of the road.*

run ragged to exhaust; wear out.

run rings around to show obvious superiority to; outdo.

run riot 1 to act without restraint. **2** of plants, to grow wildly and luxuriantly.

run short (or **low**) **of** to become insufficient.

run through 1 to pierce: *A splinter* ran through *my toe.* **2** to spend: *I* ran through *the money in one day.* **3** to examine or rehearse quickly.

run up 1 to make quickly: *We* ran up *a new batch of punch.* **2** to permit to mount up: *He* ran up *a bill.*

run upon to meet; come across.

run·a·bout (rŭn′ ə bout′) ***n-*** **1** light, open automobile or wagon. **2** light motorboat. **3** person who wanders about.

run·a·round (rŭn′ ə round′) ***n-*** **1** *Slang* evasive excuse, answer, etc., especially in response to a request or question. **2** in printing, column of type set narrower than usual to fit around an illustration.

run·a·way (rŭn′ ə wā′) ***n-*** **1** person who runs away; a fugitive: *a* runaway *from home.* **2** a horse out of control. ***adj-*** **1** running away; out of control: *a* runaway *horse; his* runaway *spending.* **2** brought about by running away or eloping: *a* runaway *marriage.* **3** *Informal* won by a wide margin: *a* runaway *victory.*

run·down (rŭn′ doun′) ***n-*** summary: *a news* rundown.

run-down (rŭn′ doun′) ***adj-*** **1** weakened in health: *Joan has felt* run-down *ever since her operation.* **2** in a bad state of repair: *a* run-down *house.* **3** unwound: *a* run-down *clock.*

rune (ro͞on) ***n-*** **1** any of the characters of an early Germanic alphabet, dating from the third century and used especially by the Scandinavians. **2** magic mark or mysterious saying or verse. **—*adj-* ru′ nic.**

[1]**rung** (rŭng) *p.t. & p.p.* of [2]**ring.** ***Hom-*** wrung.

[2]**rung** (rŭng) ***n-*** rodlike step of a ladder, or a rod joining the legs of a chair. [from Old English **hrung** meaning "staff; rod; spar."] ***Hom-*** wrung.

run-in (rŭn′ ĭn′) ***n-*** argument; quarrel.

run·nel (rŭn′ əl) or **run·let** (rŭn′ lət) ***n-*** small stream; rivulet.

run·ner (rŭn′ ər) ***n-*** **1** person or thing that runs: *a* runner *in a race.* **2** messenger: *a bank* runner. **3** one of the long, narrow pieces on which a sled or ice skate moves. **4** piece of long, narrow cloth used to cover a table, chest of drawers, etc. **5** long, thin rug. **6** a stem that runs along the ground, putting down roots at intervals, or a plant with this stem, such as the strawberry.

run·ner-up (rŭn′ ər ŭp′, -ŭp′) ***n-*** in a race or other contest, person or team that finishes second.

run·ning (rŭn′ ĭng) ***adj-*** of measurements, in a straight line: *the cost per* running *foot.* ***adv-*** *Informal* in succession: *for three days* running.

in the running having a chance of winning a contest.

out of the running having no chance of winning a contest.

running board ***n-*** narrow footboard along the sides of a vehicle, especially an automobile.

running gear ***n-*** **1** the working parts of a machine, especially the wheels and axles of a vehicle such as a car or a locomotive, as distinguished from the body. **2** system of ropes and wires on a ship or boat, used to raise, lower, or trim the sails.

running knot ***n-*** slipknot. For picture, see *knot.*

running light ***n-*** one of a pair of lights, red on the port side and green on the starboard side, shown by a ship or airplane after sunset; sidelight.

running mate ***n-*** candidate for a lesser office, such as the vice-presidency, who is paired on the same ticket with his party's candidate for the higher office.

running stitch ***n-*** series of short, even stitches.

run·off (rŭn′ ŏf′, -ôf′) ***n-*** **1** rain not absorbed by the soil but drained off in streams. **2** deciding final contest held to break a tie.

run-of-the-mill (rŭn′ əv thə mĭl′) ***adj-*** having no special merit or value; ordinary; average.

run-on (rŭn′ ŏn′) ***n-*** dictionary entry added at the end of a definition. It is derived from the word being defined by the addition of a suffix, and its meaning can be inferred from the meaning of the main word.

runt (rŭnt) ***n-*** undersized animal or person: *the* runt *in a litter of puppies.* **—*adj-* runt′ y [runt·i·er, runt·i·est].**

run-through (rŭn′ thro͞o′) ***n-*** summary or rehearsal.

run·way (rŭn′ wā) ***n-*** **1** beaten path or way along which animals pass. **2** a paved or cleared strip where planes take off and land. **3** fenced place: *a* runway *for dogs.* **4** ramp which serves as an extension to a stage or platform; also, ramp which is built over stairs for the passage of wheeled vehicles.

Runway

ru·pee (ro͞o′ pē) ***n-*** **1** unit of money in India, Pakistan, and Ceylon. **2** the coin representing this unit.

rupture (rŭp′ chər) ***n-*** **1** a bursting or breaking apart: *a* rupture *of the appendix.* **2** a breaking off or interruption of friendly relations. **3** hernia. ***vt-*** **[rup·tured, rup·tur·ing] 1** to burst or break apart. **2** to cause a hernia in. **3** to bring about a breach of (friendship). ***vi-*** to suffer a breach or break.

ru·ral (ro͝or′ əl) ***adj-*** of or having to do with the country, country life, or agriculture. **—*adv-* ru′ ral·ly.**

rural free delivery or **rural delivery** ***n-*** free mail delivery in country districts.

ruse (ro͞oz, ro͞os) ***n-*** a trick or plan intended to deceive.

[1]**rush** (rŭsh) ***vi-*** **1** to move with speed; hurry: *The doctor* rushed *to his patient.* **2** to act quickly, often without enough thought: *They* rushed *into the new project.* ***vt-*** **1** to cause to move or act with great speed: *Please* rush *this package to the post office. They* rushed *troops to the battlefield.* **2** to do something quickly, often without enough care: *He* rushed *the job.* **3** to attack swiftly and in force: *The troops* rushed *the enemy's outpost.* **4** in fraternities and sororities, to entertain (a prospective member) in order to persuade him or her to join. **5** *Informal* to pay marked attention to; court. **6** in football, to advance (the ball) by carrying it. ***n-*** **1** a driving forward with eagerness and haste; sudden forward motion: *a* rush *of wind; the* rush *of a flood.* **2** hurry; bustle and excitement: *the* rush *of life in a big city.* **3** sudden movement of people; state of unusual activity: *the gold* rush *to California in 1849; the Christmas shopping* rush. **4** an attack; charge. **5** an unusual demand: *a* rush *on bonds.* **6** a rough-and-tumble contest between students from different classes. **7** in football, a play in which the ball is carried toward the goal. **8 rushes** in motion pictures, the first prints of uncut and unedited film. ***adj-*** done with or requiring haste: *a* rush *job; a* rush *order.* [from Old English **hryscan.**] **—*n-* rush′ er.**

[2]**rush** (rŭsh) ***n-*** any of certain marsh plants having hollow stems. The stems are often dried and used for making baskets, hats, chair seats, etc. [from Old English **rysc.**] **—*adj-* rush′ like′.**

rush hour ***n-*** time of day when traffic or business is at its peak.

rush·y (rŭsh′ ē) ***adj-*** **[rush·i·er, rush·i·est] 1** full of or covered with rushes: *a* rushy *pond.* **2** like rushes.

Russ. **1** Russia. **2** Russian.

rus·set (rŭs′ ət) ***n-*** **1** reddish-brown color. **2** homespun cloth of this color. **3** kind of winter apple with a rough, reddish-brown skin. ***adj-***: *a* russet *leaf.*

Rus·sian (rŭsh′ ən) ***n-*** **1** member of the dominant Slavic-speaking peoples of Russia or one of his descendants. **2** one of the Slavic languages of the Soviet Union, now the official language. ***adj-***: *The* Russian *winters are long.*

Russian dressing ***n-*** mayonnaise to which chili sauce, pimientos, and chopped pickles have been added.

Russian Orthodox Church *n-* a self-governing branch of the Eastern Orthodox Church in the Soviet Union under the spiritual leadership of the patriarch of Moscow.

Russian wolfhound *n-* a breed of long-haired dogs resembling the greyhound.

rust (rŭst) *n-* **1** reddish coating of iron oxide formed by oxidation of iron when it is exposed to air and moisture. **2** any coating formed on the surface of a metal by oxidation or corrosion. **3** in botany, any of a large group of diseases due to parasitic fungi and marked by the formation of spots on the leaves and stems; also, any of the fungi causing such a disease. **4** reddish-brown color. *vi-* to become covered with a reddish-brown coating caused by oxidation: *The rake* rusted *when it was left out in the rain.* *vt-* **1** to cause to be covered with rust: *Damp air* rusts *iron.* **2** of a plant, to cause to be affected with a parasitic fungus. *as* ***modifier***: *a* rust *fungus*; *a* rust *brown.*

rus·tic (rŭs′ tĭk) *adj-* relating to the country; hence, simple and unsophisticated: *his* rustic *manners*; rustic *furniture.* *n-* person from the country, especially an unsophisticated one. —*adv-* **rus′ ti·cal·ly.** *n-* **rus·tic′ i·ty** (rŭs′ tĭs′ ə tē): *the* rusticity *of the landscape.*

rus·ti·cate (rŭs′ tə kāt′) *vi-* [**rus·ti·cat·ed, rus·ti·cat·ing**] to live temporarily in the country. *vt- chiefly Brit.* to suspend from college. —*n-* **rus′ ti·ca′ tion.**

rus·tle (rŭs′ əl) *vt-* [**rus·tled, rus·tling**] **1** to cause to make a soft sound by stirring or fluttering (something): *The wind* rustled *the dry leaves.* **2** *Informal* to move, handle, or get by energetic or vigorous action. **3** *Informal* to steal (cattle). *vi-* **1** to make a stirring or fluttering sound: *Her long skirt* rustled *on the grass.* **2** *Informal* to move quickly and energetically. **3** *Informal* to steal cattle. *n-* soft, crackling sound or a succession of such sounds: *the* rustle *of dry leaves*; *the* rustle *of a taffeta skirt.*

rus·tler (rŭs′ lər) *n-* a cattle thief.

rust·proof (rŭst′ prōōf′) *adj-* of such a nature, or treated in such a way, as to remain free from rust: *made of* rustproof *steel.* *vt-*: *to* rustproof *an iron grill.*

rus·ty (rŭs′ tē) *adj-* [**rus·ti·er, rus·ti·est**] **1** covered with rust: *a* rusty *tool.* **2** imperfect because of lack of practice: *My Latin is* rusty. **3** faded or discolored by age or wear: *a* rusty *gray.* **4** having the color of rust. —*adv-* **rus′ ti·ly.** *n-* **rus′ ti·ness.**

[1]**rut** (rŭt) *n-* **1** track or groove made by a wheel or by continuous use. **2** fixed or mechanical way of living; boring routine: *Some people get into a* rut *and never get out.* *vt-* [**rut·ted, rut·ting**] to make tracks or grooves in: *The wagons* rutted *the plains.* [from Middle English **rute,** from the same sources as [1]**rout.**] —*adj-* **rut′ ty.**

[2]**rut** (rŭt) *n-* sexual excitement in male mammals, such as the deer, moose, or elephant. *vi-* [**rut·ted, rut·ting**] of male mammals, to feel sexual excitement. [from Old French **ru(i)t** meaning "noise of beasts," from Late Latin **rūgītus,** "roaring," from Latin **rugire,** "to roar; rumble."] —*adj-* **rut′ tish.**

ru·ta·ba·ga (rōō′ tə bā′ gə, rōō′-) *n-* large, yellow turnip,

Ruth (rōōth) *n-* **1** in the Bible, a widow who left her own land and accompanied her mother-in-law Naomi to Bethlehem. Ruth was the great-grandmother of David. **2** a book of the Old Testament which contains this story.

ru·the·ni·um (rōō thē′ nē əm) *n-* hard, brittle, silvery metal element of the platinum group. It occurs in platinum ores. Symbol Ru, At. No. 44, At. Wt. 101.07.

ruth·less (rōōth′ ləs) *adj-* showing no mercy; cruel: *a* ruthless *enemy.* —*adv-* **ruth′ less·ly.** *n-* **ruth′ less·ness.**

R.V. Revised Version of the Bible.

Ry. or **Rwy.** railway.

-ry *suffix* See *-ery.*

rye (rī) *n-* **1** cereal plant closely related to wheat and having a grain used as food. **2** the grain of this plant. **3** whiskey made from this grain. *as* ***modifier***: *a* delicious *rye bread.* ***Hom-*** wry.

S

S, s (ĕs) *n-* [*pl.* **S's, s's**] the nineteenth letter of the English alphabet.

S symbol for sulfur.

-s or **-es** *word ending* **1** used to form the plural of nouns: *two hats*; *nine dresses.* **2** used to form the third person singular of verbs, indicating that he, she, or it is doing an action at the present time: *He works. She fixes.*

[1]**'s** *word ending* used to form the possessive of singular nouns and of plural nouns not ending in "-s": *the man's hat. Jane's book.* For plurals that end in "-s" or "-es," the possessive is formed by adding an apostrophe to the noun: *the boys' dormitory*; *the churches' windows.*

[2]**'s** **1** is: *It's Tuesday.* **2** has: *He's gone.* **3** us: *Let's go.*

s. **1** second. **2** shilling. **3** south. **4** southern. **5** singular.

S. **1** south. **2** southern. **3** saint. **4** senate. **5** signor.

Sa symbol for samarium.

S.A. **1** Salvation Army. **2** Sociedad Anónima (Spanish for corporation). **3** Société Anonyme. (French for corporation). **4** South Africa. **5** South America. **6** South Australia.

Sab·bath (săb′ əth) *n-* day of rest and religious worship. The Sabbath is Sunday for most Christians. It is Saturday for Jews and some groups of Christians.

sab·bat·i·cal (sə băt′ ĭ kəl) *adj-* **1** of, having to do with, or resembling the Sabbath. **2** bringing a period of rest that occurs at regular intervals: *a* sabbatical *trip.*

sabbatical leave or **sabbatical year** *n-* a year or half year off, awarded usually to a teacher every seven years.

sa·ber (sā′ bər) *n-* **1** cavalry sword with a long, one-edged, slightly curved blade. **2** light sword for fencing. *vt-* to cut, kill, or strike with a cavalry sword. Also **sabre.**

Saber

saber rattling *n-* threatening display of military might.

saber saw *n-* portable electric saw with the blade fixed and powered only at one end.

sa·ber·tooth (sā′ bər tōōth′) *n-* any of various large prehistoric cats that had long, curved, upper canine teeth. Also **saber-toothed cat, saber-toothed tiger.**

Sa·bine (sā′ bīn′) *n-* **1** one of an ancient people of central Italy who were conquered and absorbed by the Romans in 290 B.C. **2** their language. *adj-*: *the* Sabine *women.*

sa·ble (sā′ bəl) *n-* **1** small, dark-brown mammal of northern Europe and Asia, related to the weasels. **2** the valuable fur of these animals. **3** the American

---

marten (for picture, see *marten*). 4 the color black. 5 (usually **sables**) mourning dress. ***adj*-:** *a* sable *coat*; *a* sable *velvet cloth*; sable *night*.

sa·bot (să bō′) ***n*- 1** wooden shoe worn by European peasants. **2** shoe with a leather top and wooden sole.

sab·o·tage (săb′ ə täzh′) ***n*- 1** deliberate destruction of an employer's property by workmen during labor troubles. **2** damage to a nation's property such as bridges, railroads, etc., by enemy agents in time of war. ***vt*- [sab·o·taged, sab·o·tag·ing]** to damage deliberately.

sab·o·teur (săb′ ə tûr′) ***n*-** person who sabotages.

sa·bra (săb′ rə) ***n*-** a native-born Israeli.

sab·re (sā′ bər) saber.

sac (săk) *Biology* ***n*-** bag or structure resembling a pouch, usually filled with liquid. ***Hom*- sack.** **—*adj*- sac′ like′.**

Sac (săk) Sauk.

sac·cha·rin (săk′ ər ən) ***n*-** white, crystalline compound that is 300 to 500 times as sweet as cane sugar and is used as a calorie-free sweetening agent.

sac·cha·rine (săk′ ər ən) ***adj*- 1** of, having to do with, or producing sugar: *a* saccharine *taste; a* saccharine *fluid.* **2** too sweet: *a* saccharine *voice.* **—*adv*- sac′ cha·rine·ly.**

sac·cha·rose (săk′ ə rōs′) ***n*-** sucrose.

sac·er·do·tal (săs′ ər dō′ təl, săk′-) ***adj*-** of or relating to a priest or the priesthood; priestly: *long,* sacerdotal *robes.* **—*adv*- sac′ er·do′ tal·ly.**

sa·chem (sā′ chəm) ***n*-** American Indian chief. [American word from the Algonquian name.]

sa·chet (să shā′) ***n*-** small bag containing a fragrant substance, used to scent linen closets, etc. ***Hom*-** sashay.

[1]**sack** (săk) ***n*- 1** a bag, especially one of rough cloth: *a potato* sack. **2** any cloth or paper bag. **3** (also **sackful**) the amount a bag holds when full. **4** loose jacket, especially for women and children; also, a woman's loose-fitting dress. **5** *Slang* bed. **6 the sack** *Slang* dismissal from a job. ***vt*- 1** to put into a bag: *They* sacked *the wheat.* **2** to dismiss: *He* sacked *two incompetents.* [from Old English **sacc** from Latin **saccus,** from Greek **sakkoos** from Hebrew **saq** meaning "sackcloth; grain sack."] ***Homs*-** sac, sacque.

hit the sack *Slang* to go to bed. **hold the sack** *Informal* to take the blame.

sack out *Slang* to go to bed.

[2]**sack** (săk) ***vt*-** to break into and steal from; rob or plunder. ***n*-** the robbing and looting of a town or city that has been taken by the enemy during a war. [from French **sac** meaning [1]**sack,** from Medieval Latin **saccāre,** "put in a sack; plunder." (A sack was used in carrying off booty.)] ***Homs*-** sac, sacque. **—*n*- sack′ er.**

[3]**sack** (săk) ***n*-** strong, dry white wine from southern Europe. [from French (vin) **sec** meaning "dry (wine)," from Latin **siccus.**] ***Homs*-** sac, sacque.

sack·but (săk′ bŭt′) ***n*-** a medieval trombone.

sack·cloth (săk′ klòth′) ***n*- 1** coarse material used in making bags; sacking. **2** coarse, rough cloth worn as a symbol of mourning or penance.

sack coat ***n*-** a loose-fitting man's jacket.

sack·ing (săk′ ĭng) ***n*-** coarse material, such as burlap, used for making sacks or bags.

sacque (săk) ***n*-** short, loose-fitting jacket worn by women and children. ***Homs*-** sac, sack.

sac·ra·ment (săk′ rə mənt) ***n*- 1** act or ceremony of worship considered a sign or symbol of a deep spiritual reality; especially, one of the seven Christian rites or acts instituted by Jesus Christ. **2 the Sacrament** the Eucharist.

sac·ra·men·tal (săk′ rə mĕn′ təl) ***adj*- 1** of, relating to, or used in a sacrament: *a chalice for* sacramental *wine*; sacramental *rites.* **2** solemnly binding: *a* sacramental *obligation.* ***n*-** any of the rites, actions, or sacred objects instituted by some Christian churches as forms of worship. **—*adv*- sac′ ra·men′ tal·ly.**

sa·cred (sā′ krəd) ***n*- 1** holy; belonging to God: *Jehovah is the* sacred *name in the Old Testament.* **2** set apart for religious use; having to do with religion: *a* sacred *book.* **3** worthy of great respect; deserving reverence: *a* sacred *promise.* **—*adv*- sa′ cred·ly.** ***n*- sa′ cred·ness.**

sacred cow ***n*-** anything supposedly above criticism.

sac·ri·fice (săk′ rə fīs′) ***n*- 1** the making of an offering, especially of a human or animal life, to a deity as an act of worship; also, person, animal, or thing offered. **2** a giving up of something for someone or something else; also, what is given up. **3** loss of profit; price below cost: *The house was sold at a* sacrifice. **4** in baseball, a sacrifice hit. ***vt*- [sac·ri·ficed, sac·ri·fic·ing] 1** to offer (something) to a deity as an act of worship. **2** to give up (something) for the sake of someone or something else: *She* sacrificed *her leisure to work for the hospital.* **3** to sell at a loss. **4** in baseball, to advance (a player) by means of a sacrifice hit. ***vi*- 1** to make an offering to a deity as an act of worship. **2** to make a sacrifice hit.

sacrifice fly ***n*-** fly ball that is caught by a fielder but allows a runner at third base time to score.

sacrifice hit ***n*-** in baseball, a bunt which permits a runner to advance a base, but on which the batter is put out unless an error is committed.

sac·ri·fi·cial (săk′ rə fĭsh′ əl) ***adj*-** relating to, used in, or offering a sacrifice: *the* sacrificial *wine*; sacrificial *rites.* **—*adv*- sac′ ri·fic′ ial·ly.**

sac·ri·lege (săk′ rə lĭj) ***n*-** act of violence or disrespect toward sacred things or persons.

sac·ri·le·gious (săk′ rə lĭj′ əs, -lē′ jəs) ***adj*-** showing insult, violence, or disrespect to sacred persons or things. **—*adv*- sac′ ri·le′ gious·ly.** ***n*- sac′ ri·le′ gious·ness.**

sac·ris·tan (săk′ rə stən) ***n*- 1** church official in charge of a sacristy. **2** a sexton.

sac·ris·ty (săk′ rə stē) ***n*- [*pl.* sac·ris·ties]** room in a church for sacred vessels and vestments; vestry.

sac·ro·il·i·ac (săk′ rō ĭl′ ē ăk′) ***adj*-** of or having to do with the sacrum and the ilium, especially of the joint between these two bones. ***n*- 1** the region of the joint between the sacrum and ilium. **2** *Informal* painful inflammation in and around this joint.

sac·ro·sanct (săk′ rə săngkt′) ***adj*-** most sacred; inviolable. **—*n*- sac′ ro·sanc′ ti·ty.**

sa·crum (săk′ rəm, sā′ krəm) ***n*- [*pl.* sac·ra (-rə)]** broad, thick, slightly curved triangular bone situated at the lower end of the spinal column.

sad (săd) ***adj*- [sad·der, sad·dest] 1** unhappy; sorrowful. **2** causing unhappiness or grief: *the* sad *news.* **3** pathetic; pitiful: *a* sad *attempt at humor.* **—*adv*- sad′ ly.** ***n*- sad′ ness.**

sad·den (săd′ ən) ***vt*-** to make sad: *Her troubles* sadden *me.* ***vi*-:** *She* saddened *at the news.*

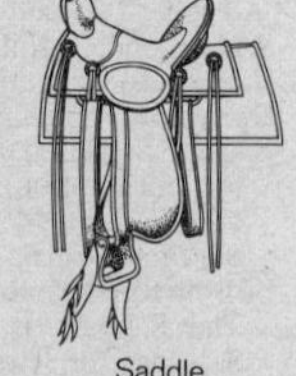
Saddle

sad·dle (săd′ əl) ***n*- 1** padded leather seat for a rider, strapped on the back of an animal; also, the seat of a bicycle, motorcycle, etc. **2** padded part of a harness which rests on the horse's back and supports the shafts. **3** cut of meat consisting of the unsplit back of an animal including the two loins: *a* saddle *of mutton.* **4** ridge joining two hilltops. ***vt*- [sad·dled, sad·dling] 1** to equip with a seat for a rider.

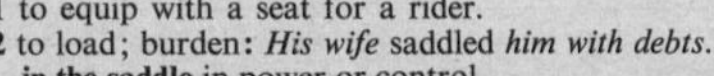

2 to load; burden: *His wife* saddled *him with debts.*

in the saddle in power or control.

sad·dle·bag (săd′ əl băg′) ***n-*** pouch or bags attached to a saddle for carrying small articles.
saddle blanket or **sad·dle·cloth** (săd′ əl klȯth′) ***n-*** thick cloth placed on an animal under a saddle.
sad·dle·bow (săd′ əl bō′) ***n-*** the arched front part of a saddle.
sad·dler (săd′ lər) ***n-*** person who makes, repairs, or sells saddles, harnesses, etc.
sad·dler·y (săd′ lə rē) ***n-*** [*pl.* **sad·dler·ies**] **1** business or shop of a saddler. **2** articles made by a saddler.
saddle shoes ***n-*** light-colored sport shoes with a band or saddle of dark leather across the instep.
saddle soap ***n-*** a mild soap, usually containing neat's-foot oil, used to clean, soften, and preserve leather.
Sad·du·cee (săj′ ə sē′, săd′ yo͞o sē′) ***n-*** member of an ancient aristocratic Jewish sect that followed only the Mosaic law and rejected all other doctrines. They were directly opposed to the Pharisees in politics.
sad·i·ron (săd′ ī′ ərn) ***n-*** flatiron with two pointed ends and a removable handle.
sa·dism (sā′ dĭz′ əm, săd′ ĭz′ əm) ***n-*** tendency of a person to get pleasure from hurting others. **—*n-* sad′ ist.**
sa·dis·tic (sə dĭs′ tĭk) ***adj-*** of, having to do with, or marked by sadism. **—*adv-* sa·dis′ ti·cal·ly.**
sa·fa·ri (sə fä′ rē, -făr′ ē) ***n-*** hunting trip or expedition, especially in Africa.
safe (sāf) ***adj-*** **[saf·er, saf·est] 1** free from danger or harm; secure: *to be* safe *indoors in a storm.* **2** not involving risk or loss; certain to be successful: *a* safe *bet*; *a* safe *investment.* **3** not injured: *He came home* safe *after the war.* **4** cautious; prudent: *a* safe *player.* **5** securely held: *The thief is* safe *in prison.* ***n-*** metal cabinet or chest to protect things of value, such as money and jewelry, from fire and theft. **—*adv-* safe′ ly. *n-* safe′ ness.**
safe-con·duct (sāf′ kŏn′ dŭkt′) ***n-*** **1** safe passage through a military or occupied zone, or an enemy's country in wartime. **2** pass guaranteeing safe passage.
safe cracker ***n-*** person who breaks open safes to rob them.
safe-de·pos·it box (sāf′ də pŏz′ ət) ***n-*** fireproof box in the vault of a bank, rented to a person for storing securities, jewelry, and other valuables.
safe·guard (sāf′ gärd′) ***vt-*** to keep safe; keep from harm or danger; protect. ***n-*** person or thing that guards or protects; protection: *A dike is a* safeguard *against floods.*
safe·keep·ing (sāf′ kē′ pĭng) ***n-*** a keeping or being kept safe; protection: *Put it in the file for* safekeeping.
safe·ty (sāf′ tē) ***n-*** [*pl.* **safe·ties**] **1** freedom from danger, injury, or damage; security; protection. **2** device or catch for preventing accidents, as in a gun or machine. **3** in football (1) a two-point score made by the defensive team when a player of the offensive team, who is carrying the ball, is tackled on or behind his own goal line. (2) a defensive player who takes the position nearest to his own goal line. *as* ***modifier***: *a* safety *pin*; *a* safety *valve.*
safety belt ***n-*** **1** strong belt or harness that fastens a person to a fixed object and prevents him from slipping and falling. **2** seat belt.
safety glass ***n-*** shatterproof glass made of two sheets of glass separated by a layer of transparent plastic.
safety match ***n-*** a match that will not light unless struck upon a special surface.
safety pin ***n-*** pin bent back on itself to form a spring, with its point held behind a guard.
safety razor ***n-*** razor with a replaceable blade and a guard to prevent serious cuts. For picture, see *razor.*
safety valve ***n-*** valve which permits some steam to escape from a boiler when the pressure is so high that an explosion might result. **2** outlet for repressed emotion.
saf·flow·er (săf′ lou′ ər) ***n-*** **1** Asiatic plant resembling the thistle, having yellowish-red flower heads and seeds that yield an edible oil. **2** the dried flower heads of this plant, used in medicine or as a red dye.

Safflower

saf·fron (săf′ rən) ***n-*** **1** a variety of crocus that blooms in the fall. **2** bright orange-yellow dye or flavoring obtained from this flower. **3** (also **saffron yellow**) orange yellow. ***adj-***: *a dish of* saffron *rice*; saffron *satin.*
S. Afr. 1 South Africa. **2** South African.
sag (săg) ***vi-*** **[sagged, sag·ging] 1** to bend or sink downward in the middle from pressure, weight, or lack of tension: *The clothesline* sagged. **2** to become weak; lose firmness; droop: *His spirits* sagged. **3** to lean to one side; become lopsided: *The door* sags. **4** to decline: *Stock prices* sagged. *Automobile production* sagged *because of the strike.* ***n-*** a drooping; a settling; also, the extent of drooping or sinking under weight or pressure.
sa·ga (sä′ gə) ***n-*** **1** medieval Norse legend or history of heroes or their families. **2** any tale of heroic deeds.
sa·ga·cious (sə gā′ shəs) ***adj-*** of keen intelligence; shrewd; having sound judgment: *a* sagacious *ruler.* **—*adv-* sa·ga′ cious·ly. *n-* sa·ga′ cious·ness.**
sa·gac·i·ty (sə găs′ ə tē) ***n-*** sound judgment; shrewdness.
sag·a·more (săg′ ə môr′) ***n-*** an Algonquian Indian chief, usually ranking below a sachem.
[1]**sage** (sāj) ***adj-*** **[sag·er, sag·est] 1** wise; having good judgment; learned: *a* sage *magistrate.* **2** showing wisdom or keen judgment: *a* sage *reply*; sage *advice.* ***n-*** wise and venerable man. [from Old French, from Latin **sapiens,** from **sapere,** "to know."] **—*adv-* sage′ ly. *n-* sage′ ness.**
[2]**sage** (sāj) ***n-*** **1** plant related to the mints, with gray-green leaves used for flavoring foods. **2** sagebrush. [from Old French **sauge,** from Latin **salvia,** "well; healthy." (The plant was once thought to heal.)]

Sagebrush

sage·brush (sāj′ brŭsh′) ***n-*** low, woody shrub of the dry plains of western United States.
sage hen ***n-*** large grouse found on the dry plains of western United States.
Sag·it·tar·i·us (săj′ ə târ′ ē əs,) ***n-*** constellation thought to outline the figure of an archer.
sa·go (sā′ gō′) ***n-*** powdered starch obtained from the pith of East Indian palms **(sago palms).** It thickens puddings, soups, etc.
sa·gua·ro (sə gwär′ ō, -wär′ ō) ***n-*** [*pl.* **sa·gua·ros**] giant desert cactus of Mexico and southwestern United States, bearing white flowers and an edible fruit. [American word from American Spanish, of American Indian origin.]

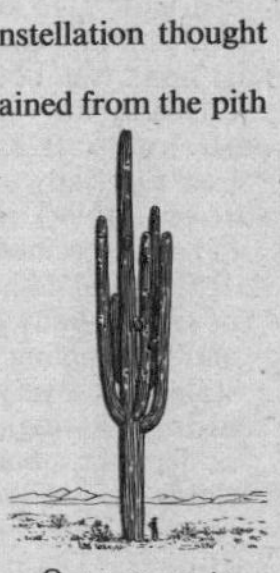
Saguaro, up to 50 ft. high

sa·hib (sä′ ĭb′, -hĭb′) ***n-*** Indian and Pakistani title or form of address for people of rank and, formerly, for Europeans, equivalent to "Master," "Mr.," or "sir."
said (sĕd) *p.t.* & *p.p.* of **say.**

---

fāte, făt, dâre, bärn; bē, bĕt, mêre; bīte, bĭt; nōte, hŏt, môre, dȯg; fŭn, fûr; to͞o, bo͝ok; oil; out; tar; thin; then; hw for wh as in *wh*at; zh for s as in u*s*ual; ə for a, e, i, o, u, as in *a*go, lin*e*n, per*i*l, at*o*m, min*u*s

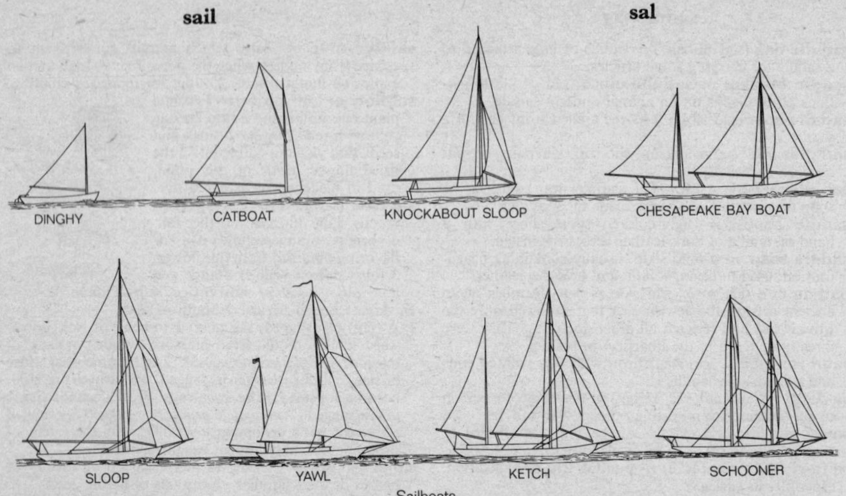

Sailboats

sail (sāl) ***n-*** **1** canvas or other material rigged to the masts and spars of a vessel to catch the wind and propel the vessel. **2** such pieces of canvas collectively: *under full* sail. **3** voyage in a boat, especially a sailboat. **4** anything resembling a sail in form or use, such as the arm of a windmill. **4** [*pl.* **sail**] any sailboat: *There are 30* sail *in the fleet.* ***vi-*** **1** to be driven or propelled by the force of the wind upon spread canvas. **2** to travel on a ship: *We* sailed *to England on the "Queen Mary."* **3** to begin a voyage: *The ship* sailed *at noon.* **4** to move or glide smoothly: *The eagle* sailed *through the air.* **5** to direct or navigate a ship, especially with sails. **6** *Informal* to pass by quickly: *My vacation* sailed *by.* ***vt-*** **1** to cross on or as if on a ship: *They* sailed *the Pacific on a raft.* **2** to navigate or steer (a ship). ***Hom-*** sale.

make sail 1 to spread or unfurl a sail or sails; hence, to begin a voyage. **set sail** to begin a voyage. **under full sail** having all sails set in place. **under sail** moving under the power of sails.

sail into 1 to begin with vigor or enthusiasm. **2** to attack or criticize severely.

sail·boat (sāl′ bōt′) ***n-*** boat with sails, designed to be driven by the wind.

sail·cloth (sāl′ klòth′) ***n-*** very strong cotton canvas, used especially for sails and tents.

sail·er (sā′ lər) ***n-*** sailing vessel considered as sailing in some specified manner: *a swift* sailer. ***Hom-*** sailor.

sail·fish (sāl′ fĭsh′) ***n-*** [*pl.* **sail·fish; sail·fish·es** (kinds of sailfish)] any of various large ocean fishes related to and resembling the swordfish, but with teeth and scales and a very large dorsal fin resembling a sail.

sail·ing (sā′ lĭng) ***n-*** **1** art or skill of managing, steering, or directing a boat, ship, etc. **2** the sport of managing or riding in a sailboat. **3** departure of a ship: *The ship's* sailing *is at noon.*

sail·or (sā′ lər) ***n-*** **1** member of a ship's crew; seaman. **2** straw hat with a flat brim and a low, flat crown. ***Hom-*** sailer. ***—adj-*** **sail′ or·like′.**

a good sailor person who does not get seasick easily.

saint (sānt) ***n-*** **1** holy and godly person. **2** in some churches, an exceptionally godly person who after death is officially declared worthy of reverence. **3** person who is very patient, unselfish, pious, etc. **4 Saint** Latter-Day Saint; Mormon. ***vt-*** to canonize; declare to be a saint.

Saint Ber·nard (sānt′ bər närd′) ***n-*** a breed of large, powerful dogs that were originally trained and used for mountain rescue work in Switzerland.

Saint Bernard, about 2 1/2 ft. at shoulder

saint·ed (sān′ təd) ***adj-*** **1** canonized. **2** having to do with or worthy of a saint. **3** pious; saintly.

Saint Elmo's fire (ĕl′ mōz′) ***n-*** discharge of electricity in the atmosphere that sometimes appears as a flamelike light on ships' masts, aircraft wings, etc., during storms.

saint·hood (sānt′ hŏŏd′) ***n-*** **1** the state or quality of being a saint. **2** saints collectively.

saint·ly (sānt′ lē) ***adj-*** [**saint·li·er, saint·li·est**] **1** like a saint; very good: *a* saintly *person.* **2** worthy of a saint: *a* saintly *work.* ***—n-*** **saint′ li·ness.**

Saint Patrick's Day (pă′ trĭks) ***n-*** March 17, celebrated by the Irish to honor their patron saint.

Saint Valentine's Day (văl′ ən tīnz′) ***n-*** February 14, a day on which valentines are exchanged, and St. Valentine, a third-century bishop, is honored.

Saint Vi·tus' dance (vī′ təs, vī′ təs əz) ***n-*** chorea. Also **Saint Vitus's dance.**

saith (sĕth, sā′ əth) *Archaic* form of **says** used with "he," "she," "it," or singular noun subjects in the present tense.

[1]**sake** (sāk) ***n-*** **1** purpose; motive; end: *for the* sake *of argument.* **2** benefit; welfare: *The soldier fights for his country's* sake. [from Middle English **sake,** "cause; purpose," from Old English **sacu,** "(law)suit; strife."]

for old time's sake because of, or in memory of, former days or old friendship.

[2]**sa·ke** or **sa·ki** (sä′ kē) ***n-*** Japanese fermented liquor made from rice and usually served hot. [from Japanese.]

sal (săl) ***n-*** salt.

sa·laam (sə läm′) ***n-* 1** Oriental greeting which means "Peace." **2** low bow with the palm of the hand placed on the forehead. ***vi-*** to make a low, formal bow or salaam. ***vt-*** to greet with such a bow.

sal·a·ble (sā′ lə bəl) ***adj-*** such as can be sold: *a* salable *product.* **—*n-* sal′ a·ble·ness** or **sal′ a·bil′ i·ty.**

sa·la·cious (sə lā′ shəs) ***adj-* 1** lustful; lewd. **2** obscene; indecent: *a* salacious *remark.* **—*adv-* sa·la′ cious·ly. *n-* sa·la′ cious·ness.**

sal·ad (săl′ əd) ***n-*** cold preparation of lettuce or other vegetables, meat, fish, fruit, etc., usually served with a dressing. *as* ***modifier***: *a* salad *bowl*; *a* salad *dressing.*

salad days ***n-*** days of youth and inexperience.

sal·a·man·der (săl′ ə măn′- dər) ***n-* 1** amphibian with a smooth skin that looks much like a lizard and lives part or all of its life in water. Those on land hide in damp places. **2** mythical creature able to live in fire; hence, anything that can bear intense heat.

Salamander (mud puppy), about 12 in. long

sa·la·mi (sə lä′ mē) ***n-*** sausage made of cooked, highly spiced pork or beef, or a mixture of the two.

sal ammoniac (săl′ ə mō′ nē ăk′) ***n-*** white crystalline chloride of ammonia (NH_4Cl) used in dyeing, tanning, etc.

sal·a·ried (săl′ ə rēd′) ***adj-* 1** getting a salary: *a* salaried *accountant.* **2** yielding a salary: *a* salaried *position.*

sal·a·ry (săl′ ə rē) ***n-*** [*pl.* **sal·a·ries**] fixed sum of money paid at regular intervals for work.

sale (sāl) ***n-* 1** exchange of goods or property for money: *the* sale *of a house.* **2** an offering of goods at a reduced price: *a big January* sale. **3** chance to sell; market: *There is almost no* sale *for ice skates in the summer.* **5 sales** (1) amount sold. (2) business of selling.

on sale offered at a reduced price.

sale·a·ble (sā′ lə bəl) salable.

sales·clerk (sālz′ klûrk′) ***n-*** person who sells goods in a store. If this person is a young woman, she is called a **salesgirl**; if she is older, she is called a **saleslady.**

sales·man (sālz′ mən) ***n-*** [*pl.* **sales·men**] person who sells; especially, one who visits prospective customers as representative of a firm.

sales·man·ship (sālz′ mən shĭp′) ***n-*** skill or ability in selling.

sales tax ***n-*** tax which is calculated as a fixed percentage of the money received from sales of goods and services.

sales·wom·an (sālz′ wo͝om′ ən) ***n-*** [*pl.* **sales·wom·en**] woman who sells; especially, one who sells merchandise in a store; saleslady.

sal·i·cyl·ate (sə lĭs′ ə lāt′) ***n-*** any salt or ester of salicylic acid.

sal·i·cyl·ic acid (săl′ ə sĭl′ ĭk) ***n-*** white, crystalline organic acid used as a food preservative and mild antiseptic and to make aspirin.

sa·li·ent (sā′ lē ənt, sāl′ yənt) ***adj-* 1** outstanding; notable: *the* salient *feature of a face*; *the* salient *point of an argument.* **2** projecting outward: *a* salient *angle.* **3** leaping; moving by jumps: *a* salient *fish.* **4** gushing; jetting up: *a* salient *fountain.* ***n-*** the part of a fortification, trench system, or battle line that projects farthest toward the enemy. **—*adv-* sa′ lient·ly.**

sa·line (sā′ lĭn′, -lēn′) ***adj-*** of or having to do with salt or sodium chloride; salty. ***n-* 1** solution containing a relatively large amount of sodium chloride and used extensively in medicine, biological experiments, etc. **2** any of the metallic salts.

sa·lin·i·ty (sə lĭn′ ə tē) ***n-* 1** saltiness. **2** the measure of salt concentration in one liter of saline solution.

Salis·bur·y steak (sălz′ bûr′ ē, sôlz′-) ***n-*** finely ground beef to which cream, eggs, and bread crumbs are added before being shaped into patties for frying.

sa·li·va (sə lī′ və) ***n-*** colorless, watery fluid secreted by the salivary glands of the mouth. It contains an enzyme, ptyalin, which begins the digestion of starchy foods.

sal·i·var·y (săl′ ə vĕr′ ē) ***adj-*** of or producing saliva.

salivary gland ***n-*** any one of the three pairs of glands which secrete saliva into the mouth cavity.

sal·i·vate (săl′ ə vāt′) ***vi-*** [**sal·i·vat·ed, sal·i·vat·ing**] to secrete saliva. **—*n-* sal′ i·va′ tion.**

sal·low (săl′ ō) ***adj-*** of a pale, sickly, greenish-yellow color or complexion. **—*n-* sal′ low·ness. *adj-* sal′ low·ish.**

sal·ly (săl′ ē) ***n-*** [*pl.* **sal·lies**] **1** a sudden rushing forth; especially, a sortie of troops from a fortified place to attack the enemy. **2** bold verbal attack or outburst, especially a clever or witty one: *The two lawyers traded* sallies. *We enjoyed his impudent* sallies. **3** short trip; excursion. ***vi-*** [**sal·lied, sal·ly·ing**] **1** to rush out suddenly. **2** to go (forth or out); set out.

salm·on (săm′ ən) ***n-*** [*pl.* **salm·on**; **salm·ons** (kinds of salmon)] **1** any of various salt-water or fresh-water food fishes with silver scales and yellowish-pink flesh. **2** (also **salmon pink**) orange-pink color. ***adj-***: *a* salmon *mousse*; *a dress of* salmon *velvet.*

Chinook salmon, 25 pounds or over

Sa·lo·me (sə lō′ mē) ***n-*** in the New Testament, the stepdaughter of Herod Antipas. She demanded and got the head of John the Baptist as a reward for her dancing.

sa·lon (sə lŏn′, *Fr.* să lōⁿ′) ***n-* 1** large room for receiving and entertaining guests. **2** periodic gathering of noted persons, usually at the home of a distinguished woman. **3** an art gallery; also, an exhibition at such a gallery. **4** a small, stylish shop or store. **5** a beauty parlor.

sa·loon (sə lo͞on′) ***n-* 1** place where alcoholic drinks are sold; bar; tavern. **2** large room or hall, especially on a passenger ship, where people gather.

sal·si·fy (săl′ sə fē′) ***n-*** plant grown for its root, which tastes like an oyster and is used as a vegetable; oyster plant.

sal soda (săl) ***n-*** sodium carbonate; washing soda.

salt (sôlt) ***n-* 1** white substance, sodium chloride, found in sea water and mineral deposits and used to season and preserve food. **2** *Chemistry* any of a very large group of compounds formed when acids and bases react with each other. **3** anything which, like sodium chloride, gives flavor or character; savor; zest. **4** sharp wit; dry humor. **5** *Informal* sailor. **6 salts** (1) Epsom salts. (2) smelling salts. ***adj-* 1** flavored with, seasoned with, or containing sodium chloride: *a* salt *pork*; *pan of* salt *water.* **2** growing in water containing sodium chloride: *a* salt *plant.* **3** sharp; bitter. ***vt-* 1** to season or preserve with sodium chloride: *Did you* salt *the potatoes?* **2** to flavor or add zest to. **3** to place a mineral, such as gold, throughout (a mine), in order to deceive someone.

salt of the earth those people thought to lead good and useful lives and to be models for others. **with a grain of salt** with doubt or reserve; with allowance for exaggeration. **worth one's salt** to be worthwhile or useful.

salt away (or **down**) **1** to preserve in brine: *to* salt down *meat.* **2** to store or keep; to save.

fāte, făt, dâre, bärn; bē, bĕt, mêre; bīte, bĭt; nōte, hŏt, môre, dȯg; fŭn, fûr; to͞o, bo͝ok; oil; out; tar; thin; then; hw for wh as in what; zh for s as in usual; ə for a, e, i, o, u, as in ago, linen, peril, atom, minus

salt·cel·lar (sȯlt′ sĕl′ ər) ***n-*** a dish or shaker for salt.
salt grass ***n-*** any of several grasses that grow on wet brackish areas or alkaline ground.
sal·tine (sȯl′ tēn′) ***n-*** crisp cracker sprinkled with salt.
salt lick ***n-*** natural deposit of salt which animals lick.
salt·pe·ter or **salt·pe·tre** (sȯlt′ pē′ tər) ***n-*** **1** potassium nitrate. **2** (usually **Chile saltpeter**) sodium nitrate.
salt water ***n-*** **1** ocean water. **2** water containing salt. ***adj-*** **(salt-water):** *a* salt-water *fish*; *a* salt-water *lake*.
salt·y (sȯl′ tē) ***adj-*** **[salt·i·er, salt·i·est] 1** full of or tasting of salt. **2** suggesting the sea: *a* salty *smell*. **3** witty; sharp. ***—adv-*** **salt′ i·ly.** ***n-*** **salt′ i·ness.**
sa·lu·bri·ous (sə lo͞o′ brē əs) ***adj-*** promoting health; healthful: *a* salubrious *climate*. ***—adv-*** **sa·lu′ bri·ous·ly.** ***n-*** **sa·lu′ bri·ous·ness.**
sal·u·tar·y (săl′ yə tĕr′ ē) ***adj-*** **1** good for the health: *the* salutary *mountain air*. **2** bringing a good effect; beneficial: *some* salutary *advice*.
sal·u·ta·tion (săl′ yə tā′ shən) ***n-*** **1** a saluting or greeting; also, the words or the gestures used: *He waved his hand in* salutation *as we passed him*. **2** the opening words of a letter. Example: Dear Sir.
sal·u·ta·to·ri·an (sə lo͞o′ tə tôr′ ē ən) ***n-*** student, usually ranking second in the graduating class, who delivers the salutatory oration at the commencement exercises.
sa·lu·ta·to·ry (sə lo͞o′ tə tôr′ ē) ***adj-*** of, relating to, or expressing a greeting or salutation. ***n-*** [*pl.* **sa·lu·ta·to·ries**] the opening address at the commencement exercises.
sa·lute (sə lo͞ot′) ***n-*** **1** act of respect or recognition; greeting: *He waved his good-morning* salute. **2** formal act of respect done in a set way, such as the raising of fingers to the forehead, the discharge of guns, or the lowering and raising again of a flag. ***vt-*** **[sa·lut·ed, sa·lut·ing] 1** to greet with words or gestures. **2** to honor with a set act of respect. ***vi-*** to make a gesture of respect; especially, to raise one's fingers to the forehead.

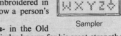

Salute

sal·vage (săl′ vĭj) ***n-*** **1** rescue of a ship or cargo from wreck, fire, etc.; also, the rescue of any property from destruction. **2** the saved ship or property. **3** payment made to those who rescued the property. ***vt-*** **[sal·vaged, sal·vag·ing]** to save or rescue from destruction: *The ship sank but they* salvaged *the cargo*.
sal·va·tion (săl vā′ shən) ***n-*** **1** a saving or rescue, especially from evil, danger, or sin. **2** something that saves or rescues: *Her care was my* salvation *when I was sick*. **3** in various religions, a soul's acceptance by God and the receiving of a soul into heaven; redemption. ***—adj-*** **sal·va′ tion·al:** *a* salvational *procedure*.
Salvation Army ***n-*** a worldwide religious and charitable body founded by General William Booth in England in 1865.
[1]**salve** (săv, säv) ***n-*** **1** soft greasy substance or ointment used on sores or wounds to heal or lessen pain. **2** something that calms and soothes: *The trip was a* salve *for his nervousness*. ***vt-*** **[salved, salv·ing]** to soothe: *Nothing could* salve *his grief*. [from Old English **sealf** or **salb.**]
[2]**salve** (sălv) ***vt-*** **[salved, salv·ing]** to salvage. [from Old French **salvage,** from Medieval Latin **salvatium,** from Latin **salvere** meaning "to save."]
[3]**sal·ve** (săl′ vā) *Latin* hail. [from Late Latin **salvere** meaning "to be safe or healthy."]
sal·ver (săl′ vər) ***n-*** a serving tray, usually made of metal.
sal·vi·a (săl′ vē ə) ***n-*** any of several plants related to the mints; especially, a sage with scarlet blossoms.
sal·vo (săl′ vō) ***n-*** [*pl.* **sal·vos** or **sal·voes**] **1** a discharge of cannon, rockets, bombs, or other firearms at the same time or in regular succession; also, a simultaneous throwing of things: *a* salvo *of bombs*. **2** any salute or simultaneous outburst: *a* salvo *of applause*.
Sam. Samuel I and II.
S. Am. 1 South America. **2** South American.
Sa·mar·i·tan (sə măr′ ə tən, sə mĕr′-) ***n-*** a native or inhabitant of Samaria, with whom, during the time of Christ, the Jews were not allowed to associate. ***adj-:*** *the* Samaritan *woman at the well*. See also *Good Samaritan*.
sa·mar·i·um (sə mĕr′ ē əm, sə măr′-) ***n-*** rare, hard, brittle, pale-gray element. Symbol Sm, At. No. 62, At. Wt. 150.35.
sam·ba (săm′ bə) ***n-*** Brazilian dance marked by bouncy steps; also, the music for this dance.
Sam Browne belt ***n-*** leather belt with a strap fastened diagonally over the right shoulder.
same (sām) ***adj-*** identical; not different in any way: *We left at the* same *time. Others have made the* same *suggestion. These two are the* same. ***n-*** identical thing previously encountered or mentioned (always preceded by "the"): *Please give me more of the* same. *The* same *is true today*. ***pron-*** in archaic and legal use, person or thing previously mentioned: *He gave me the hammer, and I took* same *and hit the nail*.
all (or **just**) **the same** nevertheless: *He was frightened, but he jumped* all the same. **same here** *Informal* ditto. **the same** (used as an adverb) in a similar or identical way, degree, etc.: *She and I feel* the same *about it*.
same·ness (sām′ nəs) ***n-*** **1** likeness in nature or character; identity; similarity. **2** monotony.
sam·i·sen (săm′ ə sĕn′) ***n-*** musical instrument of Japan that has three strings and resembles the banjo.
sam·ite (săm′ īt′, sā′ mīt′) ***n-*** rich, silk fabric of medieval times, generally interwoven with gold or silver. *as* ***modifier:*** *a* samite *gown*.
Sa·mo·an (sə mō′ ən) ***adj-*** of or relating to the islands of Samoa, or to their inhabitants. ***n-*** **1** a native of Samoa. **2** the language of these people.

Samovar

sam·o·var (săm′ ə vär′) ***n-*** metal urn with a heating tube, used especially in Russia to heat water for making tea.
samp (sămp) ***n-*** coarsely ground hominy; also, a porridge of this. [American word from the Algonquian name.]
sam·pan (săm′ păn′) ***n-*** light, flat-bottomed boat with one sail, rowed from the stern, used along the coasts and on the rivers of China and Japan.

Sampan

sam·ple (săm′ pəl) ***n-*** a part that shows what the whole is like; an example; a specimen: *a* sample *of the artist's work. as* ***modifier:*** *a* sample *copy of a book*. ***vt-*** **[sam·pled, sam·pling]** to test or judge by taking a small piece or amount: *I* sampled *the stew*.
sam·pler (săm′ plər) ***n-*** **1** person who judges what a whole is like from a small amount or sample. **2** a piece of cloth embroidered in various designs to show a person's skill with the needle.

Sampler

Sam·son (săm′ sən) ***n-*** in the Old Testament, a Hebrew judge known for his great strength; hence, any very strong man.

Sam·u·el (săm′ yōō əl) ***n-*** **1** in the Bible, a Hebrew priest, prophet, judge, and military commander. **2** either of two Old Testament books, Samuel I and II, giving his history.

sam·u·rai (săm′ yə rī′) ***n-*** [*pl.* **sam·u·rai**] **1** under the ancient feudal system of Japan, the military class of the lesser nobility, who acted as military retainers to the feudal lords. **2** member of this group.

-san *Japanese* suffix meaning "Mr.," "Mrs.," "Miss," or "sir," used after the last name.

San (sän, *English* săn) *Spanish & Italian* Saint (used only before men's names): San *Francisco*; San *Pietro*.

san·a·to·ri·um (săn′ ə tôr′ ē əm) ***n-*** [*pl.* **san·a·to·ri·ums** or **san·a·to·ri·a** (-ē ə)] ***n-*** **1** institution for the care and treatment of invalids and convalescents. **2** health resort.

San·cho Pan·za (săn′ chō păn′ zə) ***n-*** the squire of Don Quixote in Cervantes' novel, "Don Quixote."

sanc·ti·fi·ca·tion (săngk′ tĭ fə kā′ shən) ***n-*** a sanctifying or being sanctified.

sanc·ti·fy (sănkg′ tə fī′) ***vt-*** [**sanc·ti·fied, sanc·ti·fy·ing**] **1** to make pure and holy; consecrate. **2** to cause to be considered sacred: *Tradition* sanctifies *many customs.*

sanc·ti·mo·ni·ous (săngk′ tə mō′ nē əs) ***adj-*** having the appearance of or making a show of piety or holiness; also, hypocritically devout or holy. ***—adv-*** **sanc′ ti·mo′ ni·ous·ly.** ***n-*** **sanc′ ti·mo′ ni·ous·ness.**

sanc·tion (săngk′ shən) ***n-*** **1** approval or permission from the authorities. **2 sanctions** in law, measures adopted by a group of nations against another nation considered to have violated international law. ***vt-*** to give permission for; approve. ***—n-*** **sanc′ tion·er.**

sanc·ti·ty (sănkg′ tə tē) ***n-*** [*pl.* **sanc·ti·ties**] **1** piety of life and character; godliness. **2** sacredness; holiness: *the* sanctity *of a shrine.* **3** privacy of place or person that must not be violated; inviolability: *the* sanctity *of the home.* **4 sanctities** sacred objects, rites, duties, etc.

sanc·tu·ar·y (săngk′ chōō ĕr′ ē) ***n-*** [*pl.* **sanc·tu·ar·ies**] **1** holy place; temple; church. **2** most sacred part of a church or temple: *In a Christian church the altar is in the* sanctuary. **3** place of refuge or protection. **4** refuge and protection: *The exile sought* sanctuary *in our country.*

sanc·tum (săngk′ təm) ***n-*** [*pl.* **sanc·tums** or **sanc·ta** (-tə)] **1** sacred place. **2** private room or study.

sanctum sanc·to·rum (săngk tôr′ əm) ***n-*** **1** most sacred of all sacred places or things. **2** very private place.

Sanc·tus (săngk′ təs, săngk′ tōōs′) ***n-*** **1** an ancient Christian hymn of praise preceding the most sacred part of the Mass, beginning with "Sanctus, sanctus, sanctus" or "Holy, holy, holy." **2** musical setting for this.

sand (sănd) ***n-*** **1** loose material consisting of fine grains of worn or crushed rock, found on the seashore, in deserts, etc. **2 sands** minutes and hours, as if measured by a sandglass; alotted time: *The* sands *of life run fast.* ***vt-*** **1** to smooth down or polish (something) by rubbing with sandpaper: *to* sand *the floor.* **2** to sprinkle or cover with sand: *to* sand *a road after an ice storm.*

san·dal (săn′ dəl) ***n-*** **1** topless shoe held to the foot by leather cords or straps. **2** modern light shoe with an openwork top. ***—adj-*** **san′ daled.**

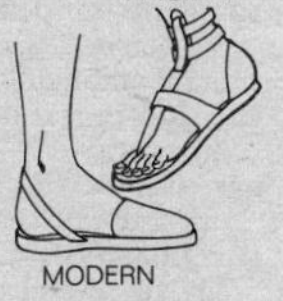

Sandals

san·dal·wood (săn′ dəl wŏŏd′) ***n-*** **1** aromatic heartwood of several evergreen trees of southern Asia, used in carving and yielding an oil for perfume; also, the tree itself. **2** any of several other Asian trees, some of which yield dyes.

sand·bag (sănd′ băg′) ***n-*** **1** bag filled with sand and used for ballast, for the parapets of trenches, for dikes, etc. **2** bag partly filled with sand and swung as a weapon. ***vt-*** [**sand·bagged, sand·bag·ging**] **1** to ballast or build up with such bags. **2** to strike or stun with such a bag.

sand·bank (sănd′ băngk′) ***n-*** ridge of sand on a hillside, shoal, etc.

sand·bar (sănd′ bär′) ***n-*** bar or ridge of sand formed by water action in a riverbed at the mouth of a harbor or river, or along the shore.

sand·blast (sănd′ blăst′) ***n-*** **1** sand driven by a blast of air and used to cut, polish, or engrave glass and other hard substances or to clean walls, castings, etc. **2** machine used in this work. ***vt-*** to cut, polish, etc., with such a machine.

sand·box (sănd′ bŏks′) ***n-*** **1** box on a locomotive, containing sand for sprinkling over slippery rails. **2** low box on the ground, with sand for children to play in.

sand dollar ***n-*** any of several small, flat, disk-shaped sea urchins found on sandy bottoms.

Sand dollar

sand·er (săn′ dər) ***n-*** person or device that sands; especially, a machine used for sandpapering.

sand flea ***n-*** **1** sand-dwelling flea, such as a chigoe. **2** tiny crustacean of seashores that leaps like a flea.

sand fly ***n-*** any of various small double-winged flies found near the seashore.

sand·glass (sănd′ glăs′) ***n-*** hourglass, especially one that measures an interval of time shorter than an hour.

sand·hog (sănd′ hŏg′, -hŏg′) ***n-*** construction worker who excavates in a caisson under high atmospheric pressure.

sand·lot (sănd′ lŏt′) ***n-*** vacant lot, especially one used for amateur ball games. *as* ***modifier***: *a* sandlot *game.*

sand·man (sănd′ măn′) ***n-*** imaginary person supposed to make children sleepy by sprinkling sand in their eyes.

sand painting ***n-*** design made by American Indians, chiefly the Navahos, in which variously colored sands are trickled on a flat base of sand or buckskin; also, the art of making such designs.

sand·pa·per (sănd′ pā′ pər) ***n-*** strong, heavy paper with a coating of sand or other abrasive material, used in wearing down, smoothing, or polishing surfaces. ***vt-*** to smooth or polish with such material.

sand·pile (sănd′ pīl′) ***n-*** pile of sand, especially one in which children play.

sand·pip·er (sănd′ pī′ pər) ***n-*** any of several small shore birds having sharp bills, rather long legs, and an odd, mincing walk.

Spotted sandpiper, 7—9 in. long

sand·stone (sănd′ stōn′) ***n-*** kind of sedimentary rock usually made up of quartz sand held together by silica, lime, or some other natural cement.

sand·storm (sănd′ stôrm′, -stôrm′) ***n-*** storm of wind in which sand is blown around in clouds.

sand table ***n-*** table with a shallow sandbox on top, for play or for terrain and architectural models.

sand trap ***n-*** in golf, a sunken area of sand placed so as to increase the difficulty of playing.

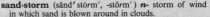

sand·wich (sănd′ wĭch) ***n-*** two or more slices of bread with a layer of meat, cheese, or other food placed between them. *as modifier*: *a* sandwich *shop*; sandwich *spread*. *vt-* to fit tightly or squeeze between two others: *We* sandwiched *our store between two buildings.*

sandwich man *n-* **1** *Informal* person who carries two attached boards, one slung before him and the other behind, to advertise or picket a place of business. **2** person who makes or sells sandwiches.

sand·wort (sănd′ wərt) *n-* any of several low herbs, usually tufted, that grow in sandy terrain.

sand·y (săn′ dē) *adj-* **[sand·i·er, sand·i·est] 1** made of, filled with, or like sand. **2** reddish yellow: *His* sandy *hair is too light to be called red.* *—n-* **sand′i·ness.**

sane (sān) *adj-* **[san·er, san·est] 1** sound and healthy in mind. **2** sensible; rational: *a* sane *approach to a problem.* *Hom-* seine. *—adv-* **sane′ly.** *n-* **sane′ness.**

sang (săng) *p.t.* of **sing.**

sang-froid (säⁿ frwä′) *French n-* calmness under trying circumstances; composure.

san·gui·nar·y (săng′ gwə nĕr′ ē) *adj-* **1** attended with or accompanied by bloodshed: *a* sanguinary *battle.* **2** cruel; bloodthirsty: *a* sanguinary *pirate.*

san·guine (săng′ gwən) *adj-* **1** having an active blood circulation; hence, full of vitality; vivacious: *a* sanguine *disposition.* **2** ardent; hopeful; confident: *His outlook is* sanguine. **3** having somewhat the color of blood; ruddy: *a* sanguine *complexion.* *—adv-* **san′guine·ly.**

san·guin·i·ty (săng gwĭn′ ə tē) *n-* condition of being sanguine.

San·he·drin (săn hĕd′ rən, -hē′ drən) *n-* in the time of Christ, the supreme council and judicial court of the Jews, presided over by the high priest.

san·i·tar·i·an (săn′ ə târ′ ē ən) *n-* person whose occupation is sanitation and public health.

san·i·tar·i·um (săn′ ə târ′ ē əm) *n-* sanatorium.

san·i·tar·y (săn′ ə tĕr′ ē) *adj-* **1** having to do with health; hygienic: *effective* sanitary *laws.* **2** free from dirt and disease: *a* sanitary *kitchen.* *—adv-* **san′i·tar′i·ly.**

san·i·ta·tion (săn′ ə tā′ shən) *n-* method and practice of bringing about sanitary conditions that protect health; hygiene. *as modifier*: *a* sanitation *engineer.*

san·i·tize (săn′ ə tīz′) *vt-* **[san·i·tized, san·i·tiz·ing]** to make (something) sanitary: *to* sanitize *a hospital room.*

san·i·ty (săn′ ə tē) *n-* **1** soundness of mind; mental balance or health: *Did he lose his* sanity? **2** sensibleness; reasonableness: *His decision displays* sanity.

San Jo·se scale (hō zā′) *n-* scale insect that is very injurious to various fruit trees.

sank (săngk) *p.t.* of **sink.**

sans (sănz, *Fr.* säⁿ) *prep-* without.

San·skrit (săn′ skrĭt′) *n-* the ancient sacred language of the Hindus of India. It is the oldest Indo-European language of which written records exist. *adj-*: *a* Sanskrit *scholar.* Also **San′scrit.**

sans sou·ci (säⁿ sōō sē′) *French* gay and easy; carefree.

San·ta (săn′ tə, săn′ tə) *Italian, Spanish, & Portuguese* female saint.

San·ta Claus (săn′ tə klȯz′) *n-* the jolly white-bearded old man in a red suit who personifies the spirit of Christmas. Often identified with St. Nicholas.

Santa Ger·tru·dis (gər trōō′ dəs) *n-* breed of cherry-red beef cattle developed in southern United States by cross-breeding cattle from India (for heat tolerance and resistance to disease) with shorthorn cattle (for good beef and the ability to put on flesh).

¹sap (săp) *n-* **1** juice that circulates through the tissues of trees and plants and keeps them alive. **2** any vital or health-promoting liquid constituent of an organism; hence, vigor or vitality. **3** *Slang* stupid or foolish person. [from Old English **sæp.**]

²sap (săp) *vt-* **[sapped, sap·ping] 1** to weaken gradually: *His brother's cruel teasing* sapped *his confidence in himself.* **2** to undermine; dig under: *Floods* sapped *the foundations.* [from French **saper,** "to undermine," from Old French **sappe,** "spade," from Italian **zappe.**]

sap·head (săp′ hĕd′) *Slang n-* simple-minded person; sap. *—adj-* **sap′head′ed.**

sa·pi·ence (sā′ pē əns) *n-* wisdom.

sa·pi·ent (sā′ pē ənt) *adj-* intelligent; wise: *a* sapient *adviser*; sapient *guidance.* *—adv-* **sa′pi·ent·ly.**

sap·less (săp′ ləs) *adj-* **1** without sap; dry. **2** lacking energy or vitality; uninteresting; dull; insipid: *a* sapless *play.* *—n-* **sap′less·ness**

sap·ling (săp′ lĭng) *n-* young tree.

sap·o·dil·la (săp′ ə dĭl′ ə) *n-* evergreen tree of the West Indies and tropical America; also, the edible fruit of this tree, which is a source of chicle.

sap·on·i·fi·ca·tion (sə pŏn′ ə fə kā′ shən) *n-* a making or changing into soap.

sap·on·i·fy (sə pŏn′ ə fī′) *vt-* **[sap·on·i·fied, sap·on·i·fy·ing]** to change (a fat) into soap by combining it chemically with an alkali. *vi-* to undergo this change.

sap·per (săp′ ər) *Military n-* soldier of the engineering corps who makes field fortifications, lays and detects land mines, etc. *as modifier*: *a* sapper *lieutenant.*

sap·phire (săf′ īər′) *n-* **1** deep-blue variety of transparent corrundum, valued as a precious stone; also, a gem or bearing from this material. **2** a bright, hard, deep-blue color. *adj-*: *the* sapphire *sky.*

sap·py (săp′ ē) *adj-* **[sap·pi·er, sap·pi·est] 1** full of sap or juice. **2** *Slang* foolish. *—adv-* **sap′pi·ly.** *n-* **sap′pi·ness.**

sap·ro·phyte (săp′ rə fīt′) *n-* plant which lacks chlorophyll and lives on dead plants and animals. Saprophytes include the fungi, some mosses, and orchids.

sap·suck·er (săp′ sŭk′ ər) *n-* any of several small American woodpeckers that feed partly on tree sap.

sap·wood (săp′ wŏŏd′) *n-* soft living wood between the bark and the hard inner wood of most trees.

Sar·a·cen (săr′ ə sən) *n-* **1** in ancient times, an Arab. **2** in the Middle Ages, any Muslim who fought against the Crusaders. *adj-*: *a* Saracen *camp.*

Sar·ah (săr′ ə, sâr′-) *n-* in the Old Testament, the wife of Abraham.

sa·ra·pe (sə rä′ pē) serape.

sar·casm (sär′ kăz′ əm) *n-* **1** bitter, taunting way of talking or writing; strong and scornful irony: *His* sarcasm *lost him friends.* **2** sneering, taunting remark.

sar·cas·tic (sär kăs′ tĭk) *adj-* bitterly scornful or sneering; mocking; contemptuous. *—adv-* **sar·cas′ti·cal·ly.**

sar·co·ma (sär kō′ mə) *n-* a kind of malignant tumor made up of cells resembling those of embryonic connective tissue.

sar·coph·agus (sär kŏf′ ə gəs) *n-* [*pl.* **sar·coph·a·gi** (-gī′, -jī′)] stone tomb.

sard (särd) *n-* reddish-yellow or brownish-yellow chalcedony, used as a gem.

sar·dine (sär dēn′) *n-* small fish related to the herring. Sardines are often preserved in oil and tightly packed in cans.

sar·don·ic (sär dŏn′ ĭk) *adj-* bitter; mocking; derisive. *—adv-* **sar·don′i·cal·ly.**

sar·don·yx (sär dŏn′ ĭks) *n-* variety of onyx, usually reddish brown and white.

sar·gas·so (sär găs′ ō) *n-* [*pl.* **sar·gas·sos**] any of several coarse, floating seaweeds with round air sacs, found in the Gulf Stream and among the West Indies.

Woman wearing sari

sa·ri (sä′ rē) *n-* [*pl.* **sa·ris**] long garment of cotton or silk worn by the women of India and Pakistan.

sa·rong (sə ròng′) ***n-*** style of skirt with the hem pulled up at the front, worn by men and women of the Malay Archipelago and other islands of the Pacific.

sar·sa·pa·ri·la (săs′ pə rĭl′ ə, sär′ sə pə-) ***n-*** **1** any of various tropical American plants, the roots of which are used as medicine or for flavoring. **2** soda water flavored with extract of sarsaparilla.

sar·tor·i·al (sär tôr′ ē əl) ***adj-*** of or relating to tailoring or to men's clothes: *his* sartorial *elegance.* ***—adv-*** **sar·tor′ i·al·ly.**

[1]**sash** (săsh) ***n-*** broad band of cloth or ribbon worn around the waist, or often across one shoulder as part of a uniform or as a decoration. [from Old English **shash,** from Arabic **shāsh,** "a length of muslim cloth."]

[2]**sash** (săsh) ***n-*** the framework which holds the glass in a window. [from earlier English **sashes,** from French **chassis,** from Old French **chasse,** "casket for relics; chest; [2]case."]

Sash

sa·shay (să shā′) *Informal* ***vi-*** **1** to go or go about in a vigorous and showy way. **2** to move rapidly sideways in dancing, with the same foot always leading. [American word from French **chassé** meaning "a gliding dance step."] ***Hom-*** sachet.

Sask. Saskatchewan.

sas·sa·fras (săs′ ə frăs′) ***n-*** **1** tree related to the laurels and having aromatic roots, leaves, and flowers. **2** root bark of this tree, used in medicine and for flavoring. [American word from Spanish **sasafras.**]

sas·sy (săs′ ē) *Informal* ***adj-*** [**sas·si·er, sas·si·est**] saucy.

sat (săt) *p.t.* and *p.p.* of **sit.**

Sat. Saturday.

Sa·tan (sā′ tən) ***n-*** the Devil.

sa·tan·ic (sā tăn′ ĭk) ***adj-*** having to do with Satan; hence, devilish; evil: *a* satanic *plot.* ***—adv-*** **sa·tan′ i·cal·ly.**

satch·el (săch′ əl) ***n-*** a small suitcase or briefcase.

sate (sāt) ***vt-*** [**sat·ed, sat·ing**] to satiate.

sa·teen (să tēn′) ***n-*** cotton or woolen fabric with a glossy finish similar to that of satin.

sat·el·lite (săt′ ə līt′) ***n-*** **1** a moon, planet of the solar system, or other heavenly body that moves in an orbit about a body more massive than itself. **2** man-made device sent by rocket into an orbit about the earth or some other body. **3** country that is officially independent but actually under the control or very strong influence of another. **4** member of a retinue; steady attendant: *the actress and her* satellites.

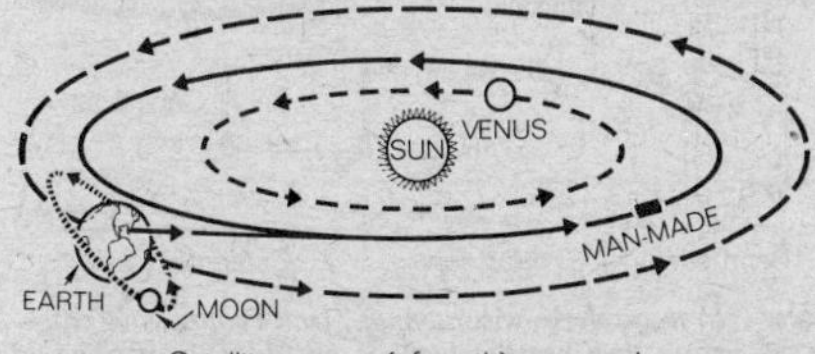

Satellites: moon (of earth); man-made, Earth, and Venus (of Sun)

sa·ti·a·ble (sā′ shə bəl) ***adj-*** such as can be satisfied: *His appetite was easily* satiable.

sa·ti·ate (sā′ shē āt′) ***vt-*** [**sa·ti·at·ed, sa·ti·at·ing**] to gratify fully; especially, to gratify to excess; sate. ***—n-*** **sa′ti·a′tion.**

sa·ti·e·ty (sə tī′ ə tē) ***n-*** condition of having got as much as or more than one wants; repletion.

sat·in (săt′ ən) ***n-*** closely woven silk or rayon material with a glossy surface. ***adj-*** made of or resembling satin; glossy; very smooth: *a* satin *dress*; *a* satin *skin.*

sat·in·wood (săt′ ən wo͝od′) ***n-*** **1** satiny, yellow-brown wood of an East Indian tree of the mahogany family; also, the tree itself. **2** similar wood of a Brazilian tree; also, the tree itself. **3** hard, satiny, durable orange-brown wood of the Near Eastern acacia tree that yields gum arabic.

sat·in·y (săt′ ən ē) ***adj-*** smooth or glossy; like satin.

sat·ire (să′ tīər′) ***n-*** **1** biting sarcasm, ridicule, or irony directed toward falseness, pompousness, hypocrisy, etc., in individuals or institutions. **2** a literary work of this sort. ***—adj-*** **sa·tir′ ic** (sə tĭr′ ĭk) or **sa·tir′ i·cal.** ***adv-*** **sa·tir′ i·cal·ly.**

sat·i·rist (săt′ ər ĭst) ***n-*** person who satirizes; especially, one who writes satire.

sat·i·rize (săt′ ə rīz′) ***vt-*** [**sat·i·rized, sat·i·riz·ing**] to subject to satire: *He* satirized *Victorian values.*

sat·is·fac·tion (săt′ ĭs făk′ shən) ***n-*** **1** condition of being pleased; contentment: *The cat purred with* satisfaction *over its bowl of milk.* **2** source of pleasure or contentment. **3** compensation or getting even; reparation.

sat·is·fac·to·ry (săt′ ĭs făk′ tə rē) ***adj-*** meeting needs, hopes, or requirements; sufficient; adequate. ***—adv-*** **sat′ is·fac′ to·ri·ly.** ***n-*** **sat′ is·fac′ to·ri·ness.**

sat·is·fy (săt′ ĭs fī′) ***vt-*** [**sat·is·fied, sat·is·fy·ing**] **1** to meet (a desire or need); to content; gratify: *That* satisfied *my hunger.* **2** to convince: *We* satisfied *the police that we had nothing to do with the accident.* **3** to fulfill. **4** to pay in full; make good: *to* satisfy *a claim.* ***vi-*** to give satisfaction or gratification. ***—adv-*** **sat′ is·fy′ ing·ly.**

sa·trap (să′ trăp′, sā′-) ***n-*** governor of a province in ancient Persia; hence, any secondary ruler or chief, especially a tyrannical one.

sa·trap·y (să′ trə pē, sā′-) ***n-*** [*pl.* **sa·trap·ies**] office or jurisdiction of a satrap.

sat·u·rate (săch′ ə rāt′) ***vt-*** [**sat·u·rat·ed, sat·u·rat·ing**] **1** to soak through and through: *The rain* saturated *my clothing.* **2** to fill or cover completely: *They* saturated *the market with the product.* **3** *Chemistry* to concentrate (a solution) until no more of the solute can be dissolved.

sat·u·rat·ed (săch′ ə rā′ təd) *Chemistry* ***adj-*** **1** of a solution, containing all of a certain substance that can be dissolved in the solvent. **2** of an organic compound, having most or all the valence bonds of its carbon atoms attached to other atoms, and hence not available for further combination.

sat·u·ra·tion (săch′ ə rā′ shən) ***n-*** **1** condition of being saturated: *The sugar solution is near* saturation. **2** act or process of saturating: *the* saturation *of the market.* ***as modifier***: *a* saturation *test*; saturation *bombing.*

saturation point ***n-*** **1** point in any process of taking in, accepting, going into solution, etc., where saturation is reached. **2** dew point.

Sat·ur·day (săt′ ər dē, -dā′) ***n-*** the seventh day of the week.

Sat·urn (săt′ ərn) ***n-*** **1** second largest planet in the solar system, sixth in order of distance from the sun. **2** Roman god of agriculture.

sat·ur·na·li·a (săt′ ər nā′ lē ə) ***n-*** **1** period of riotous merrymaking. **2 Saturnalia** in ancient Rome, the annual feast of Saturn, popularly celebrated as a kind of carnival. ***—adj-*** **sat′ ur·na′ li·an:** *a* saturnalian *party.*

sat·ur·nine (săt′ər nīn′) *adj-* gloomy; dismal: *a* saturnine *disposition.* **—*adv-* sat′ur·nine′ly.**

sat·yr (sā′tər, săt′ər) *n-* **1** in ancient Greece, one of a group of woodland gods, part man and part goat, given to wild revels. **2** any wanton or lustful man.

sauce (sȯs) *n-* **1** liquid preparation served with food to add spice or flavor: *spaghetti* sauce. **2** stewed fruit: *plum* sauce. **3** *Informal* impertinence.

sauce·pan (sȯs′păn′) *n-* cooking pot with a handle.

sau·cer (sȯs′ər) *n-* shallow dish with slightly raised edges, used to hold a cup. **—*adj-* sau′cer·like′.**

sau·cy (sȯ′sē) *adj-* **[sau·ci·er, sau·ci·est] 1** pert; rude; impudent: *a* saucy *answer.* **2** roguish; sprightly. **—*adv-* sau′ci·ly.** ***n-*** **sau′ci·ness.**

sauer·kraut (sou′ər krout′) *n-* finely sliced cabbage, fermented in a brine made of its own juice.

Sauk (sȯk) *n-* [*pl.* **Sauks,** also **Sauk**] one of a tribe of Algonquian Indians who originally lived in Michigan, and are now on reservations in Oklahoma, Iowa, and Kansas. Also **Sac.** ***adj-*:** *the* Sauk *lodges.*

Saul (sȯl) *n-* **1** in the Old Testament, the first king of Israel. **2** the Hebrew name of the apostle Paul, who changed his name after his conversion.

sau·na (sȯ′nə) *n-* **1** steam bath with steam provided by water thrown on hot stones. **2** room or building in which to take such a bath.

saun·ter (sȯn′tər) *vi-* to stroll idly: *to* saunter *in the park.* ***n-*** leisurely walk; stroll. **—*n-* saun′ter·er.**

sau·sage (sȯ′sĭj) *n-* ground, seasoned meat, usually enclosed in a thin, tubelike casing.

sau·té (sȯ tā′) *vt-* **[sau·téed** or **sau·téd, sau·té·ing]** to fry quickly so as to brown (meat or vegetables) lightly in a little fat. ***n-*:** *a veal* sauté. ***adj-*** (also **sau·téed**): *The* sauté *onions were delicious.*

sau·terne (sȯ tûrn′) *n-* slightly sweet, white French wine.

sav·age (săv′ĭj) *n-* **1** member of a primitive tribe. **2** uncultivated person. **3** cruel, fierce person. ***adj-*** **1** uncivilized; barbaric: savage *rites.* **2** fierce; vicious: *a* savage *animal*; *a* savage *reply.* **3** wild, rugged: savage *scenery.* **—*adv-* sav′age·ly.** ***n-*** **sav′age·ness.**

sav·age·ry (săv′ĭj rē) *n-* [*pl.* **sav·age·ries**] **1** condition of being uncivilized or uncultivated. **2** fierceness; cruelty: *the* savagery *of wolverines*; *the* savagery *of his sudden verbal attack.*

sa·van·na or **sa·van·nah** (sə văn′ə) *n-* open grassland with scattered trees.

sa·vant (să vänt′, săv′ənt) *n-* learned person; scholar.

[1]**save** (sāv) *vt-* **[saved, sav·ing] 1** to free from danger or disaster; rescue: *to* save *a drowning man.* **2** to keep from wear or decay: *to* save *a dress by wearing an apron.* **3** to avoid the waste of: *to* save *time, labor, and trouble.* **4** to lay away; keep; refrain from spending: *to* save *money.* **5** to preserve from sin and its consequences: *to* save *souls.* ***n-*** in sports, a play or effort that keeps the opponents from scoring or from winnng: *The goalkeeper made ten* saves. [from Old French **salver,** from Latin **salvāre,** from **salvus** meaning "safe; whole."] **—*adj-* save′a·ble** or **sav′a·ble.** ***n-*** **sav′er.**

save the day to do something that prevents disaster; to bring a good end to a bad situation: *We were afraid we'd be late, but Ed* saved the day *with his car.*

[2]**save** (sāv) *prep-* except; not including: *Jack attended every meeting* save *one.* [from Old French **sauf** meaning "making exception of."]

[1]**sav·ing** (sā′vĭng) *adj-* **1** redeeming: *Her only* saving *trait was a sense of humor.* **2** frugal; economical; thrifty: *a* saving *wife.* ***n-*** **1** act of rescuing; delivery from danger: *the* saving *of lives.* **2** act of putting aside money for later need. **3** amount of money, time, effort, etc., one need not expend; an economy: *a* saving *of over $3;* a saving *of two hours.* **4 *savings*** money saved, especially such money in a bank account. [from [1]**save.**]

[2]**saving** (sā′vĭng) *prep-* **1** with the exception of; save: *I like them all,* saving *this one.* **2** *Archaic* without disrespect to. [from [2]**save.**]

saving grace *n-* redeeming feature.

savings account *n-* bank account, which pays interest, for the purpose of saving money.

savings bank *n-* bank that specializes in receiving and paying interest on money deposited in savings accounts.

sav·ior or **sav·iour** (săv′yər) *n-* **1** person who rescues or saves. **2 Savior** or **Saviour** Jesus Christ.

sa·voir-faire (săv′wär′fĕr′) *French n-* knowledge of the proper thing to do and when to do it; tact.

sa·vor (sā′vər) *n-* **1** a taste or odor: *The salad had a* savor *of garlic.* **2** pleasing or lively elements: *a dull play entirely without* savor. ***vt-*** **1** to taste, smell, or consider with pleasure; enjoy; relish: *to* savor *the odor of cooking.* **2** to flavor or season. **—*n-* sa′vor·er.** ***adj-*** **sa′vor·less.**

savor of to contain a suggestion or hint of.

[1]**sa·vor·y** (sā′və rē) *adj-* pleasing or agreeable, usually in taste or smell. [from Old French **savo(u)ré,** from Latin **sapor** meaning "scent; taste," from **sapere,** "to taste."]

[2]**sa·vor·y** (sā′və rē) *n-* [*pl.* **sa·vor·ies**] herb related to mint, and used in cooking. [from Old French **savoreie** and **sarrie,** from Latin **satureia.**]

Sa·voy·ard (să′voi ärd′, sə voi′ärd′) *n-* actor, producer, or admirer of Gilbert and Sullivan's comic operas. Many were first produced in the Savoy Theatre in London.

sav·vy (săv′ē) *Slang vi-* **[sav·vied, sav·vy·ing]** to understand: *Do you* savvy? ***n-*** **1** good sense; practicality; shrewdness. **2** knowledge; know-how. [American word partly from Spanish **sage** meaning "do you know," and partly from French **savez** of the same meaning.]

[1]**saw** (sȯ) *n-* any of various cutting tools having teeth along the edge of a thin, flat blade; also, a cutting machine having one or more such blades. ***vt-*** **[sawed, sawed** or **sawn, saw·ing] 1** to cut with such a tool: *to* saw *wood.* **2** to form or fashion with such a tool: *He* sawed *logs for the fireplace. I* sawed *a square end.* ***vi-*** **1** to use such a tool: *He will* saw *for an hour.* **2** to be cut with such a tool: *Hardwood* saws *with difficulty.* [from Old English **sagu** meaning "a cutter."]

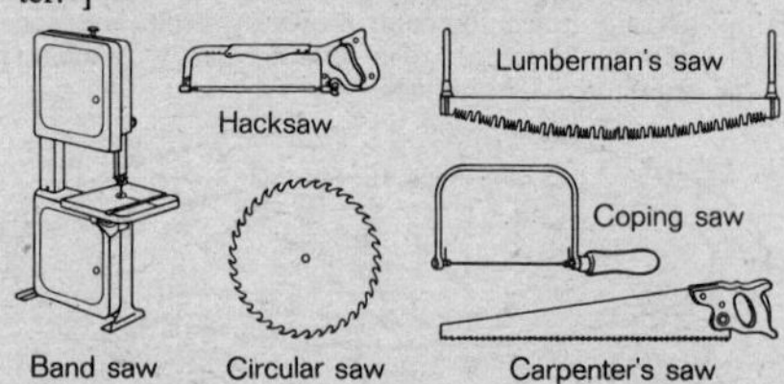

[2]**saw** (sȯ) *n-* proverb; wise saying: *"Don't count your chickens before they are hatched" is an old* saw. [from Old English **sagu,** "a saying," and related to **say.**]

[3]**saw** (sȯ) *p.t.* of [1]**see.**

saw·buck (sȯ′bŭk′) *n-* **1** sawhorse having an X-shaped frame at each end and chiefly used for sawing logs. **2** *Slang* ten-dollar bill.

saw·dust (sȯ′dŭst) *n-* fine particles that fall when wood is sawed.

sawed-off (sȯd′ŏf′) *adj-* **1** having one end cut off or shortened: *a* sawed-off *shotgun.* **2** *Slang* short; of less than average height.

saw·fish (sȯ′ fĭsh′) ***n-*** any of various large fishes related to the rays and having a long, flat snout with toothlike spines on each edge.

saw·horse (sȯ′ hȯrs′, -hôrs′) ***n-*** frame for supporting wood for sawing, usually consisting of a horizontal bar with two spreading legs at each end.

saw·mill (sȯ′ mĭl′) ***n-*** place where logs are sawed into lumber by machine.

sawn (sȯn) *p.p.* of [1]**saw.**

saw·yer (sȯ′ yər) ***n-*** person whose occupation is the sawing of logs or timber.

sax (săks) ***n-*** *Informal* saxophone.

sax·horn (săks′ hȯrn′, -hôrn′) ***n-*** any of a group of brass musical wind instruments with valves.

sax·i·frage (săk′ sə frĭj, -frāj′) ***n-*** any of a genus of low-growing plants with white, red, or yellow flowers.

Sax·on (săk′ sən) ***n-*** **1** member of a Germanic people who inhabited northern Germany and, together with the Angles and Jutes, invaded and conquered England in the fifth and sixth centuries A.D. **2** native of Saxony; also, the dialect of German spoken in Saxony. ***adj-*** **1** of or relating to the Germanic people who invaded England in the fifth and sixth centuries A.D. **2** of or relating to modern Saxony, its inhabitants, or its dialect.

sax·o·phone (săk′ sə fōn′) ***n-*** wind instrument consisting of a sharply bent metal tube with keys, and a reed mouthpiece. **—*n-* sax′ o·phon′ ist.**

Saxophone

say (sā) ***vt-*** **[said,** (sĕd), **say·ing]** **1** to utter; speak: *He* said *only six words.* **2** to assert; declare (takes only a clause as object): *I* say *that you are wrong.* **3** to repeat; recite: *Claire* said *her prayers.* **4** to estimate; assume: *I would* say *he's worth a million dollars.* **5** to mean; communicate (takes only a clause as object): *These tracks* say *that a bear has passed by here.* ***n-*** **1** chance or right to express an opinion: *Give him his* say. ***interj-*** **1** used to attract attention, express surprise, etc: "Say! *Look at that!*" **2** meaning "I offer as an example (or estimate or assumption)": *He's worth,* say, *half a million dollars.* **—*n-* say′ er.**

goes without saying is too obvious to need mention. **that is to say** in other words.

say·ing (sā′ ĭng) ***n-*** **1** something said: *one of Mark Twain's famous* sayings. **2** proverb: *an old* saying *of my aunt.*

says (sĕz) form of **say** used with "he," "she," "it," or singular noun subjects, in the present tense.

say-so (sā′ sō′) *Informal* ***n-*** **1** bare statement: *That's just his* say-so. **2** authority to make a decision.

Sb symbol for antimony.

S.B. Bachelor of Science.

Sc symbol for scandium.

sc. scene.

S.C. **1** South Carolina. **2** Supreme Court. **3** Security Council.

scab (skăb) ***n-*** **1** crust of dried blood and serum that forms over a sore or wound while it heals. **2** *Informal* worker who accepts a lower wage than a union worker; also, one who takes a striker's job.

scab·bard (skăb′ ərd) ***n-*** sheath or case for a sword, dagger, or bayonet. ***vt-*** to put into such a case.

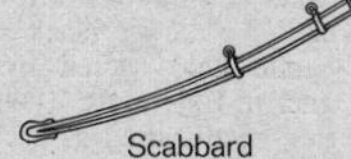

Scabbard

scab·by (skăb′ ē) ***adj-*** **[scab·bi·er, scab·bi·est]** **1** covered with a scab or scabs. **2** resembling a scab. **3** afflicted with scabies. **4** *Informal* mean or contemptible. **—*n-* scab′ bi·ness.**

sca·bies (skā′ bēz) ***n-*** severe itch and inflammation caused by tiny mites that burrow into the skin.

scads (skădz) *Informal* ***n-*** *pl.* an abundant supply; great quantity: *just* scads *of money.*

scaf·fold (skăf′ əld, -ōld′) ***n-*** **1** temporary platform on which workmen may stand while building, painting, etc. **2** platform on which criminals are put to death.

Scaffold

scaf·fold·ing (skăf′ əl dĭng) ***n-*** scaffold or series of scaffolds; also, the materials used in erecting a scaffold.

scal·a·wag or **scal·la·wag** (skăl′ ə wăg′) ***n-*** **1** originally, a stunted, inferior animal; hence, a worthless person; rascal. **2** during the Reconstruction period, a white Southerner who favored the Republican Party.

scald (skȯld) ***vt-*** **1** to burn with hot liquid or steam. **2** to rinse or dip in boiling-hot water: *to* scald *dishes*; *to* scald *tomatoes before peeling them.* **3** to heat almost to the boiling point: *to* scald *milk.* ***n-*** **1** act or instance of scalding. **2** burn or injury from hot water or steam. ***Hom-*** skald.

[1]**scale** (skāl) ***n-*** **1** any machine or device for weighing. **2** one of the pans or dishes of a balance. **3** (usually **scales**) the balance itself. ***vi-*** **[scaled, scal·ing]** to weigh: *This piece* scales *ten pounds.* [perhaps from Old French **escale,** from Old Norse **skāl,** "bowl." The plural came to mean a weighing balance.]

Scales

tip the scales to cause or lead to a definite choice where things had been in balance or nearly equal. **tip the scales at** to have a specified weight.

[2]**scale** (skāl) ***n-*** **1** one of the thin, horny plates that form the covering of most fishes, reptiles, etc. **2** any thin, dry, flaky plate or piece resembling this: *The paint came off in* scales. ***vt-*** **[scaled, scal·ing]** to scrape off such a covering, as from a fish. ***vi-*** to break or peel off in small bits: *The paint is* scaling *from the wall.* [from Old French **escale** meaning "a husk; (egg)shell; flake," from earlier German **skala.**] **—*adj-* scale′ less.** ***adj-*** **scale′ like′.**

[3]**scale** (skāl) ***n-*** **1** series of marks made at certain distances for measuring; graduated markings: *the* scale *on a thermometer*; *the* scale *on a slide rule.* **2** arrangement in order from low to high or high to low; hierarchy: *a wage* scale; *the social* scale; scales *of performance.* **3** relation between the actual size of something and its representation on a drawing, map, set of plans, etc.; ratio of represented size to actual size: *a map with a* scale *of one inch to a mile.* **4** *Music* any of various fixed and inclusive sets of tones having certain intervals between them. See also *chromatic scale, diatonic scale, major scale, minor scale.* **5** *Mathematics* the numbers of a system having a certain base. For example, all the numbers of the binary number system make up the binary scale. ***vt-*** **[scaled, scal·ing]** **1** to climb; mount: *He* scaled *the mountain in six days.* **2** to adjust or control with respect to something else: *Try to* scale *your spending to your income.* **3** to change the size or amount of (followed by "up" or "down"): *He* scaled *up his request*

for funds. **4** to get the exact proportions of, in order to get a good fit or true representation: *The editor* scaled *the drawings for engraving and printing. I* scaled *the statue carefully before I copied it.* [from Italian, from Latin **scāla** meaning "a ladder; a gradation."]

on a (large, small, vast, modest, etc.) scale at a (specified) level of size, ambitiousness, or complexity.

scale insect ***n-*** any of a large group of tiny insects that at one stage are covered with a waxy or scaly substance. They are serious pests to plants and trees.

sca·lene triangle (skā′ lēn′) ***n-*** triangle in which each side has a different length.

scal·lion (skăl′ yən) ***n-*** kind of onion with a long, thick stem and a very small bulb.

scal·lop (skăl′ əp, skŏl′-) ***n-*** **1** one of a series of shell-shaped curves or semicircles used to ornament the edge of lace, shelf paper, and the like. **2** a shellfish with a roundish, hinged, double shell marked with fanlike grooves and an indented edge. **3** the muscle of this shellfish, used as food. ***vt-*** **1** to bake (oysters, potatoes, etc.) in layers with milk, butter, flour, or crumbs, and seasoning; escallop. **2** to make shell-shaped curves in or on: *Lois* scalloped *the paper.* Also **scollop.**

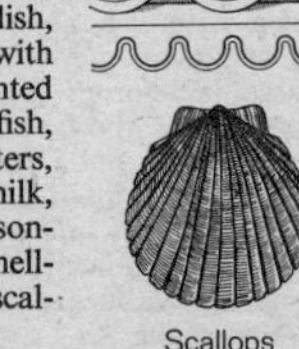
Scallops

scal·lo·pi·ni (skŏl′ ə pē′ nē) ***n-*** thin slices of meat, usually veal, covered with flour and fried.

scalp (skălp) ***n-*** **1** the skin at the top of the head, usually covered by hair. ***vt-*** **1** to cut off or tear off the scalp or part of it. **2** *Informal* to buy (theater tickets or the like) and then sell at exorbitant prices. **—*n-* scalp′ er.**

scal·pel (skăl′ pəl) ***n-*** small, thin, pointed knife used for surgery or dissection.

scalp lock ***n-*** long lock of hair on the crown of the otherwise shaved heads of some American Indians.

scal·y (skā′ lē) ***adj-*** **[scal·i·er, scal·i·est] 1** having thin, horny plates; covered with scales: *Snakes have a* scaly *skin.* **2** flaky; peeling: *The walls are* scaly. **3** resembling scales: *a patch of* scaly *skin on his hand.* **—*n-* scal′ i·ness.**

¹scamp (skămp) ***n-*** **1** rogue; rascal. **2** person, especially a young person, who is playfully mischievous. [from Old French **escamper** meaning "to flee; decamp," from Latin **ex-**, "out" and **campus,** "battlefield."]

²scamp (skămp) ***vt-*** to perform (work, a job, etc.) carelessly, hastily, or with poor materials; scant. [perhaps from earlier Dutch **schamp** meaning "playing; joke."]

scam·per (skăm′ pər) ***vi-*** to run, frolic, or move around merrily. ***n-*** such a run or frolic.

scan (skăn) ***vt-*** **[scanned, scan·ning] 1** to examine closely; scrutinize: *She* scanned *his face.* **2** to look through hastily: *I* scanned *his new book.* **3** to search, especially with a sweeping, back-and-forth motion: *The general* scanned *the battlefield. The radar* scanned *the sky.* **4** to show or mark the metrical pattern of: *Please* scan *this line of poetry.* **5** of an electron beam or light beam, to sweep line by line across (the fluorescent screen of a television tube, a photograph in a wirephoto apparatus, etc.) in order to produce differences of light and shade that correspond to differences among electrical pulses.

Scand. 1 Scandinavia. **2** Scandinavian.

scan·dal (skăn′ dəl) ***n-*** **1** something shameful or causing public indignation: *The slums in this city are a* scandal. **2** malicious gossip: *Mother loves a bit of* scandal. **3** outcry, anger, or indignation caused by a violation or supposed violation of public trust, morality, etc.

scan·dal·ize (skăn′ də līz′) ***vt-*** **[scan·dal·ized, scan·dal·iz·ing]** to shock or offend by misbehaving; jar (someone) by acting against his ideas of what is proper: *Max* scandalized *his aunt by his behavior.*

scan·dal·mong·er (mŏng′ gər, mŭng′-) ***n-*** person who listens to and repeats gossip.

scan·dal·ous (skăn′ də ləs) ***adj-*** **1** disgraceful; shocking: *a* scandalous *act.* **2** tending to harm the reputation of someone: *What* scandalous *gossip!* **—*adv-* scan′ dal·ous·ly. *n-* scan′ dal·ous·ness.**

Scan·di·na·vi·an (skăn′ də nā′ vē ən) ***n-*** **1** native or citizen of Norway, Sweden, or Denmark, and, less strictly, of Iceland or Finland; also, a descendant of such a person. **2** group of Germanic languages that includes Norwegian, Swedish, Danish, and Icelandic. ***adj-***: *a* Scandinavian *custom*; *a* Scandinavian *word.*

scan·di·um (skăn′ dē əm) ***n-*** a rare metal element. Symbol Sc, At. No. 21, At. Wt. 44.956.

scan·ner (skăn′ ər) ***n-*** person or thing that scans; especially, a device, circuit, etc., for scanning in a television system, wirephoto system, or the like.

scan·sion (skăn′ shən) ***n-*** act or art of dividing verses into the metrical elements of which they are composed.

scant (skănt) ***adj-*** hardly enough; insufficient; small: *a* scant *supply of cookies.* ***vt-*** **1** to provide a meager supply of; stint: *They didn't* scant *the food.* **2** to do or deal with inadequately: *to* scant *a job.* **—*adv-* scant′ ly.**

scant·ling (skănt′ lĭng) ***n-*** **1** piece of lumber of small size, especially one used as an upright in a partition of a building. **2 scantlings** the dimensions of timber or other building material.

scant·y (skăn′ tē) ***adj-*** **[scant·i·er, scant·i·est] 1** not enough; too small: *a* scanty *jacket.* **2** barely enough: *a* scanty *portion.* **—*adv-* scant′ i·ly. *n-* scant′ i·ness.**

-scape *combining form* picture or view of an outdoor scene: *land*scape; *sea*scape, *cloud*scape. [from **landscape,** from Dutch **landskip.**]

scape·goat (skāp′ gōt′) ***n-*** **1** person or group wrongfully blamed and punished for the mistakes and failures of others. **2** in ancient times and among primitive peoples, a person or animal chosen to bear the sins of the entire group, and to be punished by death or banishment.

scape·grace (skāp′ grās′) ***n-*** irresponsible, unprincipled person.

scap·u·la (skăp′ yə lə) ***n-*** [*pl.* **scap·u·lae** (-lē) or **scap·u·las**] shoulder blade.

scap·u·lar (skăp′ yə lər) ***adj-*** of or relating to a shoulder blade. ***n-*** **1** monk's or nun's outer garment consisting of two long, narrow pieces of cloth worn over the shoulders and falling in front of and behind the shoulders. **2** pair of small cloth squares bearing religious figures, worn one in front and one in back on two narrow ribbons passing over the shoulders.

scar (skär) ***n-*** **1** mark or blemish left on the skin after the healing of a wound or burn. **2** any mark resembling this, as on a damaged table or on a stem where a leaf has fallen. **3** lasting impression made on someone by grief or other emotional troubles: *the* scars *of one's childhood.* ***vt-*** **[scarred, scar·ring]**: *Several wounds* scarred *his face.*

scar·ab (skăr′ əb) ***n-*** **1** (also **scarab beetle**) any of a large group of beetles, many of which feed upon dung and other rotting material; especially, a large, black dung beetle held sacred by the ancient Egyptians. **2** gem or ornament cut in the form of this beetle, used as a charm by the ancient Egyptians. *as* ***modifier***: *a* scarab *bracelet*; scarab *brooch.*

Scarab gem Scarab beetle

scarce (skârs) ***adj-*** **[scarc·er, scarc·est] 1** not available in large quantity; scanty; hard to get: *Strawberries are very* scarce *this year.* 2 seldom seen or found; rare: *a* scarce *old phonograph record.* **—*n*- scarce′ ness.**

make (oneself) scarce *Informal* to go or stay away.

scarce·ly (skârs′ lē) ***adv*-** 1 almost not; hardly: *There is* scarcely *any sugar.* 2 only just; barely: *I* scarcely *saw him.* 3 surely not: *I could* scarcely *interrupt.*

scar·ci·ty (skâr′ sə tē) ***n*-** [*pl.* **scar·ci·ties**] insufficient supply; deficiency; lack: *a* scarcity *of fresh fruit.*

scare (skâr) ***vt*-** [**scared, scar·ing**] to frighten; fill with sudden fear: *A crash* scared *me.* ***vi*-**: *I don't* scare *easily.* ***n*-** panicky, and often groundless, fear: *a war* scare.

scare up *Informal* to get or make quickly.

scare·crow (skâr′ krō′) ***n*-** 1 figure, usually made of sticks dressed in old clothes, set up in a field; hence, something that frightens without harming. 2 thin, ragged person.

[1]**scarf** (skärf) ***n*-** [*pl.* **scarfs** or **scarves** (skärvz)] 1 long piece of cloth worn about the shoulders or neck, or over the head, for warmth or decoration. 2 long strip of cloth used to cover tables, dressers, or other furniture. [from Old French **escarpe,** from Old Norse **skreppa** of the same meaning.]

[2]**scarf** (skärf) ***n*-** [*pl.* **scarves**] 1 (also **scarf joint**) joint by which two pieces of wood are connected lengthwise to make one piece, the ends being cut or grooved so as to fit into each other. 2 the cut or grooved end of a piece of wood used to form such a joint. ***vt*-** 1 to unite with such a joint. 2 to groove (wood) for such a joint.

Scarf joints

scarf·pin (skärf′ pĭn′) ***n*-** ornamental pin on a scarf.

scar·i·fi·ca·tion (skăr′ ə fə kā′ shən) ***n*-** 1 act of scarifying or scratching. 2 scratch or scratches: *the* scarifications *on a rock surface.*

scar·i·fy (skăr′ ə fī′) ***vt*-** [**scar·i·fied, scar·i·fy·ing**] 1 to scratch or make slight cuts in. 2 to criticize harshly; lacerate; flay. 3 to loosen or break up the surface of: *to* scarify *a roadbed.* 4 to cut or soften the coating of (a seed) in order to hasten sprouting.

scar·la·ti·na (skär′ lə tē′ nə) ***n*-** scarlet fever, especially a mild form of it.

scar·let (skär′ lət) ***n*-** vivid red color. ***adj*-**: *a* scarlet *dress.*

scarlet fever ***n*-** acute, contagious streptococcus disease, whose symptoms are vomiting, sore throat, high fever, and a bright-red skin rash.

scarp (skärp) ***n*-** 1 steep slope or cliff; escarpment. 2 steep wall or ditch around a fortification. ***vt*-** to cause to slope steeply: *The waves* scarped *the cliffs.*

scarves (skärvz) *pl.* of **scarf.**

scar·y (skâr′ ē) *Informal* ***adj*-** [**scar·i·er, scar·i·est**] 1 causing fear; frightening: *a* scary *movie.* 2 easily scared; timid: *a* scary *pony.*

scat (skăt) *Informal* ***interj*-** go away quickly!

scath·ing (skā′ thĭng) ***adj*-** bitterly adverse; denunciatory: *a* scathing *criticism.* **—*adv*- scath′ ing·ly.**

scat·ter (skăt′ ər) ***vt*-** 1 to fling about in all directions; throw here and there: *to* scatter *rubbish all over a picnic ground.* 2 to drive in different directions; disperse: *The police* scattered *the mob.* ***vi*-** to go in different directions: *The crowd* scattered. ***n*-** a scattering. **—*n*- scat′ ter·er.**

scat·ter·brain (skăt′ ər brān′) ***n*-** person incapable of serious or concentrated thinking; giddy, heedless person. **—*adj*- scat′ ter·brained′**: *a* scatterbrained *scheme.*

scat·ter·ing (skăt′ ər ĭng) ***n*-** 1 small, scattered number of persons or things; sparse group: *a* scattering *of voters.* 2 *Physics* irregular or diffuse reflection, refraction, or dispersion of waves or particles, caused by collisions with other particles or waves.

scaup duck (skȯp) ***n*-** either of two kinds of American duck, the **greater scaup duck** or the **lesser scaup duck,** that have black head and chest, black tail, and a long white stripe along the rear of the wings.

scav·en·ger (skăv′ ən jər) ***n*-** any of various animals, such as hyenas, crabs, and vultures, that eat waste matter and spoiled food.

sce·nar·i·o (sə nĕr′ ē ō′, -năr′ ē ō′) ***n*-** [*pl.* **sce·nar·i·os**] 1 plot summary of a play. 2 the script for a motion picture, including dialogue, acting and camera directions; shooting script.

sce·nar·ist (sə nĕr′ ĭst, -năr′ ĭst) ***n*-** writer of movie scenarios.

scene (sēn) ***n*-** 1 place of an action or event; locale: *the* scene *of heavy fighting.* 2 setting of a play, opera, or story: *The* scene *of the novel is prewar Poland.* 3 division of an act in a dramatic work: *Act II,* scene *3 of "Hamlet."* 4 episode or incident in a play, opera, or story: *the storm* scene *in "King Lear."* 5 landscape: *a lush tropical* scene. 6 display of anger or other strong feeling: *to make a* scene *in a restaurant.* ***Hom*-** seen.

behind the scenes not directly in front of a theater audience; hence, out of public view; in private. **come on the scene** to arrive; begin to take part in something.

scen·er·y (sē′ nə rē) ***n*-** 1 general view of a landscape: *The* scenery *in the Alps is beautiful.* 2 the backdrops, platforms, canvas-covered frames, etc., that make up the setting of a stage performance.

sce·nic (sē′ nĭk, sĕn′ ĭk) ***adj*-** 1 of or related to natural scenery; picturesque: *the* scenic *delights of the mountain trail.* 2 having to do with stage effects or stage scenery.

scent (sĕnt) ***n*-** 1 odor; smell: *These roses have a delightful* scent. 2 odor left by an animal: *The hounds picked up the* scent *of the fox.* 3 sense of smell: *Hounds hunt by their keen* scent. 4 hint or clue by which something is recognized or followed: *the* scent *of danger.* 5 perfume: *a bottle of* scent. ***vt*-** 1 to recognize by smelling: *The hounds* scented *a fox.* 2 to get a hint of; become aware of: *The reporter* scented *a story.* 3 to fill with an odor; perfume: *Lilacs* scent *the air.* ***Homs*-** cent, sent. **—*adj*- scent′less.**

scep·ter (sĕp′ tər) ***n*-** 1 ornamental rod or staff held in ceremonies by a ruler as a sign of authority and power. 2 royal rank or power. Also **scep′ tre.**

scep·tic (skĕp′ tĭk) ***n*-** skeptic. **—*adj*- scep′ ti·cal.** ***n*-** **scep′ ti·cism′.**

sched·ule (skĕj′ o͞ol, -əl) ***n*-** 1 list of events or procedures arranged in chronological order: *a radio* schedule; *a factory's production* schedule. 2 any ordered list or catalogue: *a* schedule *of shipping rates.* 3 transportation timetable: *a train* schedule. 4 group of things to be done; agenda: *a doctor with a very heavy* schedule. ***vt*-** [**sched·uled, sched·ul·ing**] 1 to enter in a schedule: *The bus line* scheduled *a new time of departure.* 2 to plan, for a particular time: *He* scheduled *the meeting for today.*

on schedule at the planned or proper time; on time.

Sche·her·a·zade (shə hĕr′ ə zäd′) ***n*-** in the "Arabian Nights," the Sultan's bride whose life was spared because of her unequaled art of storytelling.

sche·ma (skē′ mə) ***n*-** [*pl.* **sche·ma·ta** (-mə tə)] outline or diagram showing something broadly or generally, without details.

sche·mat·ic (skĭ măt′ ĭk) ***adj*-** showing something in outline or plan, and not as it appears really or finally: *a*

---

fāte, făt, dâre, bärn; bē, bĕt, mêre; bīte, bĭt; nōte, hŏt, môre, dȯg; fŭn, fûr; to͞o, bo͝ok; oil; out; tar; thin; then; hw for wh as in *wh*at; zh for s as in u*s*ual; ə for a, e, i, o, u, as in *a*go, lin*e*n, per*i*l, at*o*m, min*u*s

schematic *drawing*. ***n-*** diagram showing the parts, values, and connections of an electric or electronic device by the use of accepted symbols. ***—adv-* sche·mat′ i·cal·ly.**

scheme (skēm) ***n-*** **1** a plan, design, or system to be followed in doing something: *a* scheme *for building a new highway.* **2** underhanded plot: *a* scheme *to overthrow the government.* **3** outline sketch or diagram; schema: *the* scheme *of a missile's electrical system.* **4** arrangement or design; layout: *the* scheme *of a living room.* ***vt-*** **[schemed, schem·ing]** to plan, especially in an underhanded manner; plot: *to* scheme *a way to escape.* ***vi-*:** *He* schemed *for many years.* ***—n-* schem′ er.**

scher·zo (skĕrt′ sō) *Music* ***n-*** [*pl.* **scher·zos** or **scher·zi** (-sē)] lively part, usually the third movement, of many symphonic and chamber works.

Schick Test (shĭk) ***n-*** skin test that shows whether a person is immune to diphtheria. If the skin is inflamed after injection of a small amount of toxin, the person is not immune.

schism (skĭz′ əm) ***n-*** **1** division or split within a religious group; also, the offense of causing such a division. **2** group or sect formed by such a division.

schis·mat·ic (skĭz măt′ ĭk) ***adj-*** of, related to, or causing a schism: *a* schismatic *faction.* ***n-*** person who advocates or takes part in a schism.

schist (shĭst) ***n-*** type of metamorphic rock that contains layers of mica, graphite, hornblende, or other minerals.

schis·to·some (shĭs′ tə sōm′, skĭs′-) ***n-*** any of a large group of parasitic flatworms that are the cause of many diseases of the liver, intestines, blood, and bladder.

schiz·oid (skĭt′ soid′) ***adj-*** **1** resembling schizophrenia: *a* schizoid *disorder.* **2** showing a tendency toward schizophrenia: *a* schizoid *personality.* ***n-*** person who shows a tendency toward schizophrenia.

schiz·o·phre·ni·a (skĭt′ sə frē′ nē ə, -frēn′ yə) ***n-*** any of a group of severe mental diseases marked by withdrawal into a stupor, splitting of the personality, hallucinations and delusions, lack of contact with reality, etc.

schiz·o·phren·ic (skĭt′ sə frĕn′ ĭk) ***adj-*** of or having to do with schizophrenia: *a* schizophrenic *symptom.* ***n-*** person suffering from schizophrenia.

schmaltz (shmälts) *Slang* ***n-*** excessive sentimentality or ornateness, especially in music or art.

schnapps or **schnaps** (shnäps) ***n-*** any strong alcoholic liquor, especially Dutch or German.

schol·ar (skŏl′ ər) ***n-*** **1** person having thorough and expert knowledge in one or more fields of learning, especially in the humanities; also, one doing careful research in such a field: *a Shakespeare* scholar. **2** person going to school; student; pupil. **3** person holding a grant to allow him to continue his studies.

schol·ar·ly (skŏl′ ər lē) ***adj-*** **1** of, related to, or containing the work of a learned, careful, and thorough expert or experts: *a* scholarly *paper.* **2** learned; studious; erudite: *a* scholarly *newspaper man.* ***—n-* schol′ ar·li·ness.**

schol·ar·ship (skŏl′ ər shĭp) ***n-*** **1** knowledge gained through long study, especially by a person with thorough and expert knowledge in some field of learning. **2** thorough research and careful methods by such a learned person. **3** money or aid given to a deserving student or scholar to allow him to continue his studies.

scho·las·tic (skə lăs′ tĭk) ***adj-*** **1** having to do with schools, teachers, studies, or students; academic: *the high* scholastic *standing of our school.* **2** of or related to scholasticism. ***n-*** in the Middle Ages, philosopher or theologian whose teachings were based on the doctrines of scholasticism; schoolman. ***—adv-* scho·las′ ti·cal·ly.**

scho·las·ti·cism (skə lăs′ tə sĭz′ əm) ***n-*** system of philosophy that developed in Europe during the Middle Ages as a means of reconciling Greek philosophy, especially that of Aristotle, with the teachings of the church fathers.

[1]school (skōōl) ***n-*** **1** any institution for learning, especially below the level of college. **2** the building or buildings of such an institution. **3** group of pupils at one place of learning: *The entire* school *will go to the track meet.* **4** time or session of instruction: *to have no* school *because of the snowstorm.* **5** group of persons influenced by the same teacher or body of ideas; also, the doctrines or practices of such a group: *the impressionist* school *of painting.* **6** division of a university given over to one branch of learning: *Does your university have a law* school? *as* ***modifier*:** *a* school *cafeteria.* ***vt-*** **1** to educate; teach: *to* school *someone in biology.* **2** to discipline: *to* school *yourself in self-control.* [from Old English **scōl,** from Latin **schola,** from Greek **scholé.**]

[2]school (skōōl) ***n-*** large group of fish that swims or feeds together; shoal. [from a earlier Dutch word of the same spelling, and related to [2]**shoal.**]

school age ***n-*** age, often fixed by law, at which a child begins to attend school; also, the period of life when a child is attending school or is required to do so. *as* ***modifier*** **(school-age):** *a* school-age *child.*

school·bag (skōōl′ băg′) ***n-*** bag or case for carrying a student's books and supplies.

school board ***n-*** group of persons in charge of a local public school system; board of education.

school·book (skōōl′ bŏŏk′) ***n-*** textbook used in grade schools or high schools.

school·boy (skōōl′ boi′) ***n-*** boy who attends school.

school·fel·low (skōōl′ fĕl′ ō) ***n-*** schoolmate.

school·girl (skōōl′ gûrl′) ***n-*** girl who attends school.

school·house (skōōl′ hous′) ***n-*** building, especially a one-room or other small building, where school is held.

school·ing (skōō′ lĭng) ***n-*** training and instruction, especially in school; education.

school·man (skōōl′ mən) ***n-*** [*pl.* **school·men**] a scholastic of the Middle Ages.

school·mas·ter (skōōl′ măs′ tər) *chiefly Brit.* ***n-*** man who teaches in a school. ***n-*** *fem.* **school′ mis′ tress.**

school·mate (skōōl′ māt′) ***n-*** companion at school.

school·room (skōōl′ rōōm′) ***n-*** room where students are taught; classroom.

school·teach·er (skōōl′ tē′ chər) ***n-*** person who teaches in school, especially below the college level.

school·work (skōōl′ wûrk′) ***n-*** lesson or lessons assigned to a student.

school·yard (skōōl′ yärd′) ***n-*** playground of a school.

school year ***n-*** that part of the year, from about September to about June, when school is in session.

schoon·er (skōō′ nər) ***n-*** **1** sailing vessel having two or more masts and a fore-and-aft rig. In a two-masted schooner the foremast is always the shorter. For picture, see *sailboat.* **2** *Informal* large beer glass.

schot·tische (shŏt′ ĭsh) ***n-*** round dance similar to the polka; also, the music for this dance.

schuss (shŏŏs) ***n-*** in skiing, a high-speed run down a straight, steep course; also, the course itself. ***vi-*:** *They all* schussed *for home.* ***vt-*:** *to* schuss *a slope.*

schwa (shwä) ***n-*** **1** phonetic symbol [ə] for various indistinct vowel sounds that occur in many unstressed syllables in English, such as the sound of *a* in *about, e* in *spoken, i* in *pencil, o* in *atom, u* in *circus.* **2** any of these sounds.

sci. **1** science. **2** scientific.

sci·at·ic (sī ăt′ ĭk) ***adj-*** **1** of or relating to the sciatic nerve. **2** of or relating to the hipbone.

sci·at·i·ca (sī ăt′ ĭ kə) ***n-*** pain along the sciatic nerve, caused by injury or inflammation.

sciatic nerve *n-* large nerve that, with its branches, extends from the lower back through the hip and back of the thigh and down the back of the leg to the foot.

sci·ence (sī′ əns) *n-* **1** the study of the physical universe and all things in it, pursued chiefly because of a desire or need to explain them and conducted according to the scientific method. **2** any branch of such study: *the* science *of physics*; *the* science *of anthropology.* **3** any systematic study: *the* science *of theology.* **4** knowledge and skill in any subject, sport, etc.: *the* science *of boxing.* *as* ***modifier***: *a* science *course.*

science fiction *n-* type of fiction, often set in the future or on another world, that deals chiefly with the effect of a highly developed science and technology on man.

sci·en·tif·ic (sī′ ən tĭf′ ĭk) *adj-* **1** of or relating to science or the methods of science: *a* scientific *instrument.* **2** based on facts or logical ideas developed from facts: *a* scientific *attitude.* **—*adv-* sci′ en·tif′ i·cal·ly.**

scientific method *n-* method of obtaining knowledge, based on careful observation, analytical thinking, and controlled experimentation. In general, it follows this pattern: a) the gathering of pertinent information on a specific problem, b) the formulation of a tentative hypothesis concerning the problem, c) the testing of the hypothesis through controlled experimentation, and d) the rejection of the hypothesis and the formulation and testing of a new one, or the acceptance of the hypothesis as a tentative conclusion.

scientific notation *n-* **1** the recording of scientific data by means of systems of symbols that are briefer and more precise than words and can be used by scientists of all nations. **2** any such system, such as the notation used in astronomy.

sci·en·tist (sī′ ən tĭst) *n-* **1** person trained or skilled in some branch of science and engaged in it as a profession. **2 Scientist** Christian Scientist.

scim·i·tar (sĭm′ ə tər) *n-* Oriental sword with a curved blade formerly used by soldiers of the Middle East.

Scimitar

scin·til·la (sĭn tĭl′ ə) *n-* scarcely detectable amount; particle; trace: *not a* scintilla *of evidence.*

scin·til·late (sĭn′ tə lāt′) *vi-* **[scin·til·lat·ed, scin·til·lat·ing]** to sparkle or glitter; flash: *The sword* scintillated *in the sun. His speech* scintillates *with humor.* ***vt-***: *That novel* scintillates *wit on almost every page.*

scin·til·la·tion (sĭn′ tə lā′ shən) *n-* **1** a scintillating: *the* scintillation *of the stars.* **2** a spark or flash of light.

scintillation counter *Physics n-* device for measuring the intensity of ionizing radiation by counting the scintillations caused when an ionizing particle strikes a phosphorescent material in the instrument. Also **scintillation detector.**

sci·on (sī′ ən) *n-* **1** shoot or branch cut from a plant for rooting or grafting; cutting. **2** descendant or heir, especially of a wealthy or noble family.

scis·sor (sĭz′ ər) *vt-* to cut with scissors.

scis·sors (sĭz′ ərz) *n-* (takes plural verb) cutting tool with pivoted double blades that slip tightly beside one another in closing and cut with a shearing action; shears. Also **pair of scissors** (takes singular verb).

Scissors

scissors kick *n-* swimming kick performed usually with the side stroke, in which one leg is bent back at the knee, the other is thrust forward and kept straight, then both are brought together sharply.

scle·ra (sklĭr′ ə) *n-* the tough, opaque, white, outer covering of the eyeball.

scle·ro·sis (sklə rō′ səs) *n-* abnormal hardening of tissues, especially in the nervous system or artery walls.

scle·rot·ic (sklə rŏt′ ĭk) *adj-* of, relating to, or affected by sclerosis.

scoff (skŏf, skȯf) *vi-* to express scorn or contempt; mock or jeer (at): *Many people* scoffed *at Fulton's steamboat.* *n-* expression of scorn or contempt; jeer: *the* scoffs *of the mob.* **—*n-* scoff′ er. *adv-* scoff′ ing·ly.**

scoff·law (skŏf′ lȯ′, skȯf-) *n-* person who treats the law with disdain; especially, a person who habitually flouts traffic laws by ignoring summonses.

scold (skōld) *vt-* to speak sharply to; rebuke; chide; reprove: *to* scold *someone for being late.* ***vi-*** to chatter angrily: *The frightened monkeys began to* scold. *n-* quarrelsome woman; shrew. **—*n-* scold′er.**

scol·lop (skăl′ əp, skŏl′-) scallop.

sconce (skŏns) *n-* ornamental wall bracket for holding a candle or electric light.

Sconce

scone (skōn, skŏn) *n-* **1** Scottish batter cake of oatmeal, barley, or wheat, baked on a griddle. **2** rich baking-powder biscuit.

scoop (sko͞op) *n-* **1** any of various shovellike tools that are used to take up flour, sugar, coal, or other loose material. **2** the bucket of a dredge or power shovel. **3** (also **scoop′ ful′**) amount held by such a tool or bucket. **4** dipping movement: *Harvey caught the minnow with a* scoop *of the hand.* **5** *Informal* a news story published first, before rival newspapers carry it. ***vt-* 1** to take up with or as if with a shovel: *to* scoop *fish into a net.* **2** to dig or hollow out with or as if with a shovel: *to* scoop *holes in the sand.* **3** *Informal* to beat (a rival newspaper, reporter, etc.) in publishing a story.

Scoop

scoot (sko͞ot) *Informal vi-* to run or walk swiftly; dart quickly, especially in getting away from someone or something: *He* scooted *away when he saw me coming.*

scoot·er (sko͞o′ tər) *n-* **1** toy vehicle consisting of a board slung between two aligned wheels and equipped with an upright steering bar. **2** motor scooter.

Scooter

¹scope (skōp) *n-* **1** range of understanding, outlook, or ability: *a task in my* scope. **2** area covered; extent: *The* scope *of his travels includes Europe and America.* **3** freedom or opportunity: *He has been given enough* scope *in his work to do as he pleases.* [from Italian **scopo** meaning "goal; purpose," from Latin **scopus,** from Greek **skopos,** "watcher."]

²scope (skōp) *Informal n-* any of various optical or viewing instruments, such as a telescope, microscope, or oscilloscope. *as* ***modifier***: *a* scope *reading.* [from **-scope.**]

-scope *combining form* instrument for viewing or examining: *tele*scope (device for viewing things at a distance). [from Greek **-skopeion,** "apparatus for viewing."]

fāte, făt, dâre, bärn; bē, bĕt, mêre; bīte, bĭt; nōte, hŏt, môre, dȯg; fŭn, fûr; to͞o, bo͝ok; oil; out; ta*r*; thin; ~~th~~en; hw for wh as in *wh*at; zh for s as in u*s*ual; ə for a, e, i, o, u, as in *a*go, lin*e*n, per*i*l, at*o*m, min*u*s

sco·pol·a·mine (skə pŏl′ ə mēn′) ***n-*** drug extracted from several plants related to the potato and used as a sedative and truth serum.

scor·bu·tic (skôr byo͞o′ tĭk) ***adj-*** of, related to, or having scurvy: *a* scorbutic *symptom.*

scorch (skôrch, skôrch) ***vt-*** **1** to burn the surface of; discolor by burning: *I* scorched *a shirt when I ironed it.* **2** to wither or dry up by heat: *The sun* scorched *the grass.* **3** to critize harshly. ***n-*** slight burn.

scorch·er (skôr′ chər, skôr′-) *Informal* ***n-*** very hot day.

scorch·ing (skôr′ chĭng, skôr′-) ***adj-*** **1** very hot; burning: *a* scorching *day.* **2** severely critical; caustic; biting: *a* scorching *remark.* ***—adv-*** **scorch′ ing·ly.**

score (skôr) ***n-*** **1** record of points won in a game: *What was the final* score *in the football game?* **2** grade in a test; rating. **3** written copy of music; also, the music as distinct from the words of an opera or musical comedy. **4** obligation; debt; injury; grudge: *to settle a* score. **5** set of twenty: *a* score *of years.* **6 scores** large unspecified number: *There were* scores *of people.* *as* ***determiner*** (always preceded by another determiner): *There are two* score *deer here but many* score *there.* ***vt-*** [**scored, scor·ing**] **1** to cut notches in. **2** to mark down the points in (a game); keep account of by marking down. **3** to arrange (music) in a certain way; orchestrate; compose: *to* score *a piece for three violins.* **4** to win (points) in a game: *I* scored *five points over my opponent.* **5** *Informal* to criticize harshly; excoriate; scourge: *The candidate* scored *his opponent.* **6** in baseball, to cause (a base runner) to reach home plate safely: *His hit* scored *the runner from second.* ***vi-*** **1** to win points in a game. **2** to achieve a success or advantage: *to* score *in an argument.* ***—adj-*** **score′ less.** ***n-*** **scor′ er.**

keep score to keep a record of points won in a game. **know the score** *Slang* to be aware of what is happening about one; be in the know. **on that score** regarding that matter. **on the score that** on account of; because.

score·board (skôr′ bôrd′) ***n-*** in sports, a large board that shows the score of a game and other information.

score·card (skôr′ kärd′) ***n-*** in sports, a card for recording the score of a game.

score·keep·er (skôr′ kē′ pər) ***n-*** person, usually an official, who keeps score during a game.

sco·ri·a (skôr′ ē ə) ***n-*** **1** rough and glassy basalt rock having bubbles and holes and formed when lava cools very quickly. **2** slag from the smelting of ore.

scorn (skôrn, skôrn) ***n-*** **1** feeling that a person or thing is mean or worthy of contempt; disdain: *to have* scorn *for a coward.* **2** object of contempt: *He was the* scorn *of the neighborhood.* ***vt-*** to treat or reject with contempt; disdain: *She* scorned *his small gift.* ***—n-*** **scorn′ er.**

scorn·ful (skôrn fəl, skôrn′-) ***adj-*** feeling or showing great disapproval, contempt, or disdain: *She was* scornful *of us.* ***—adv-*** **scorn′ ful·ly.** ***n-*** **scorn′ ful·ness.**

Scor·pi·o (skôr′ pē ō, skôr′-) ***n-*** southern constellation thought to outline the figure of a scorpion.

scor·pi·on (skôr′ pē ən, skôr′-) ***n-*** animal related to the spiders, having a slender body, pincers, and a sting at the end of its tail.

Scorpion, 1–8 in. long

Scot (skŏt) ***n-*** **1** native or inhabitant of Scotland, or a descendant of such a person. **2** member of a Gaelic people of northern Ireland who settled in Scotland.

Scot. 1 Scotch. 2 Scotland. 3 Scottish.

scotch (skŏch) ***vt-*** **1** to stamp out, suppress, or hinder; crush: *to* scotch *a revolution*; *to* scotch *a rumor.* **2** to wound or injure so as render harmless: *to* scotch *a snake.*

Scotch (skŏch) ***n-*** **1** (also **Scotch whiskey**) whiskey made in Scotland from malted barley. **2 the Scotch** (takes plural verb) the Scottish. ***—adj-*** Scottish.

►The Scottish dislike the term Scotch when applied to themselves.

Scotch-Irish (skŏch′ ī′ rĭsh) ***n-*** **1** the people of northern Ireland, descended from Scottish settlers. **2** people of such stock who emigrated to the United States before 1846, and their descendants. ***adj-***: *the* Scotch-Irish *settlers of the Cumberlands.*

Scotch·man (skŏch′ mən) ***n-*** [*pl.* **Scotch·men**] Scot.

Scotch terrier or **Scottish terrier** ***n-*** any of a breed of terrier that originated in Scotland, with short legs, square muzzle, and rough, wiry hair; scottie.

sco·ter (skō′ tər) ***n-*** any of several large sea ducks found in the north; coot.

scot-free (skŏt′ frē′) ***adj-*** free from punishment or loss; safe: *The defendant went* scot-free.

Scotland Yard ***n-*** headquarters of the London police, and especially of the detective force (Criminal Investigation Division).

Scots (skŏts) ***adj-*** Scottish. ***n-*** (takes singular verb) the English language as spoken and written by the Scottish.

Scots·man (skŏts′ mən) ***n-*** [*pl.* **Scots·men**] Scot.

Scot·ti·cism (skŏt′ ə sĭz′ əm) ***n-*** Scottish word or idiom.

scot·tie (skŏt′ ē) *Informal* ***n-*** Scotch terrier.

Scot·tish (skŏt′ ĭsh) ***adj-*** of or relating to the Scots, their language, customs, land, etc.; Scots: *the* Scottish *highlands.* ***n-*** **1** the English language as spoken and written by the people of Scotland; Scots. **2 the Scottish** (takes plural verb) the people of Scotland collectively.

Scottish Gaelic ***n-*** the Gaelic dialects of Scotland. ***adj-*** **(Scottish-Gaelic)**: *a* Scottish-Gaelic *poem.* Also **Scots Gaelic.**

scoun·drel (skoun′ drəl) ***n-*** person of bad character; rascal; rogue.

scoun·drel·ly (skoun′ drə lē) ***adj-*** **1** having the character of a scoundrel: *a* scoundrelly *man.* **2** typical of a scoundrel: *a* scoundrelly *deed.*

[1]**scour** (skour) ***vt-*** **1** to clean by rubbing hard: *to* scour *a pot with steel wool.* **2** to wear away by rubbing: *The stream* scoured *a new bed during the rains.* ***n-*** a cleaning by hard rubbing: *I gave the kitchen floor a good* scour. [from Medieval Dutch **schuren,** from Old French **escurer** meaning "scour; clean," from Latin **excūrāre,** "take good care of; clean off."] ***—n-*** **scour′ er.**

[2]**scour** (skour) ***vt-*** to look over carefully and minutely; search thoroughly: *to* scour *the woods for a lost child.* [from Old French **escourre,** from Latin **excurrere,** "to run out; make a (military) excursion; sally."]

scourge (skûrj) ***n-*** **1** a whip. **2** person or thing that causes pain, torment, or trouble: *war, the* scourge *of man.* ***vt-*** [**scourged, scourg·ing**] **1** to whip. **2** to devastate; afflict: *a plague that* scourges *a country.* **3** to criticize severely; lash: *to* scourge *a writer for his poor taste.*

[1]**scout** (skout) ***n-*** **1** person sent out to get information, especially during a war. **2** person engaged in discovering new talent, especially in entertainment or sports. **3** (also **Scout**) member of the Boy Scouts or of the Girl Scouts. **4** *Informal* (also **good scout**) good fellow; friend; nice guy. ***vt-*** to go out to gather information about: *One squad* scouted *the area.* ***vi-*** **1** to take part in the activities of the Boy Scouts or Girl Scouts. **2** to go in search of something: *You'd better* scout *for wood before dark.* [from Old French **escoute,** "spy; listener," from **escouter,** "to listen," from Late Latin **ascultāre.**]

[2]**scout** (skout) ***vt-*** to scoff at; dismiss with contempt: *He* scouted *any objection to his plan.* [from Old Norse **skūta** meaning "taunts; shot out," related to **shoot.**]

scout·ing (skou′tĭng) ***n-*** the activities of scouts, especially of the Boy Scouts or of the Girl Scouts.

scout·mas·ter (skout′măs′-tər) ***n-*** man who leads a troop of Boy Scouts.

Scow

scow (skou) ***n-*** boat with a flat bottom and square ends, used for carrying garbage, gravel, or other heavy loads.

scowl (skoul) ***n-*** a wrinkling of the forehead in anger or displeasure. ***vi-***: *Jesse* scowled *at his bad grade.* ***vt-***: *to* scowl *displeasure.* **—*n-* scowl′er.**

Scowl

scrab·ble (skrăb′əl) ***vi-*** **[scrab·bled, scrab·bling]** **1** to work hard against heavy odds or in very unpromising conditions: *The pioneers had to* scrabble *for a living.* **2** to scratch, scrape, or claw about: *The chickens* scrabbled *in the dirt.* **3** to scrawl; scribble: *She* scrabbled *on the paper.*

scrag·gly (skrăg′lē) ***adj-*** **[scrag·gli·er, scrag·gli·est]** **1** unkempt; shaggy: *a* scraggly *beard.* **2** jagged; irregular: *a* scraggly *cliff.*

scrag·gy (skrăg′ē) ***adj-*** **[scrag·gi·er, scrag·gi·est]** **1** lean and bony; scrawny. **2** jagged; rough.

scram (skrăm) *Slang* ***interj-*** get out of here at once! ***vi-*** **[scrammed, scram·ming]** to leave quickly.

scram·ble (skrăm′bəl) ***vi-*** **[scram·bled, scram·bling]** **1** to force one's way by the use of hands and feet; crawl: *to* scramble *up a rock*; *to* scramble *through the underbrush.* **2** to struggle or fight to get something: *They* scrambled *for pennies in the street.* **3** *Slang* to take off quickly in fighter planes in order to intercept an enemy air attack. ***vt-*** **1** to mix (the whites and yolks of eggs) and fry. **2** to mix up: *He* scrambled *the letters.* **3** in communications, to distort (speech sounds) by electrical means in order to produce a signal that cannot be understood. ***n-*** **1** hard climb: *It was a* scramble *to reach the top of the hill.* **2** confused struggle: *There was a* scramble *at the store during the bargain day sale.*

[1]**scrap** (skrăp) ***n-*** **1** small piece; bit: *a* scrap *of lace*; *a* scrap *of evidence.* **2** broken, worn-out, or useless material; junk: *The foundry bought a ton of* scrap. **3 scraps** rejected or leftover food. *as* ***modifier***: scrap *metal*; scrap *paper.* ***vt-*** **[scrapped, scrap·ping]** to discard; throw away: *to* scrap *worn-out shoes.* [from Old Norse **skrap** meaning "scrapings."]

[2]**scrap** (skrăp) *Slang* ***n-*** fight; quarrel. ***vi-*** **[scrapped, scrap·ping]** to fight or quarrel. [a variant of **scrape.**] **—*n-* scrap′per.**

scrap·book (skrăp′bo͝ok′) ***n-*** book with blank pages in which clippings, photographs, etc., may be pasted.

scrape (skrāp) ***vt-*** **[scraped, scrap·ing]** **1** to push or strip away (paint, dirt, rust, etc.) by forcing a blade or other tool edgewise across a surface. **2** to remove something from in this way: *to* scrape *walls.* **3** to grind or graze harshly against: *The board* scraped *my skin.* ***vi-*** **1** to make, or move with, a scratching sound: *The chair* scraped *along the floor.* **2** to pass or squeeze (by or through) with difficulty: *The two cars managed to* scrape *by without touching. He barely* scraped *through the examination.* ***n-*** **1** mark left by scraping or scratching something. **2** harsh or grating sound: *the* scrape *of her fingernail on glass.* **3** difficult or embarrassing situation.

scrape along to manage to live, but with difficulty.
scrape up (or **together**) to gather; accumulate.

scrap·er (skrā′pər) ***n-*** person or thing that scrapes; especially, any of various tools or machines used to remove paint, varnish, or similar covering.

WALL
FLOOR
Scrapers

scrap heap ***n-*** heap of scrap or junk; place where used or unwanted things are thrown; junk pile.

scrap·ple (skrăp′əl) ***n-*** dish of pork scraps boiled together with corn meal or flour, allowed to set, and sliced and fried.

[1]**scrap·py** (skrăp′ē) ***adj-*** **[scrap·pi·er, scrap·pi·est]** made up of scraps or bits; not coherent and complete: *a* scrappy *report.* [from [1]**scrap.**]

[2]**scrap·py** (skrăp′ē) *Slang* ***adj-*** **[scrap·pi·er, scrap·pi·est]** **1** full of fighting spirit; aggressive. **2** given to fighting or quarreling; quarrelsome. [from [2]**scrap.**]

scratch (skrăch) ***vt-*** **1** to mark or tear the surface of with something rough or pointed: *to* scratch *the polished table.* **2** to mark or write with a sharp instrument: *Bob* scratched *his name on the wall.* **3** to dig or scrape with claws or nails: *He* scratched *his ear.* **4** *Informal* to cancel: *The weather caused them to* scratch *the flight.* ***vi-*** **1** to dig or scrape with claws or nails. **2** relieve itching by scraping the skin: *That dog is always* scratching. **3** to become marked or scraped: *That surface* scratches *easily.* **4** to make a scraping sound: *Chalk* scratches *on the blackboard.* ***n-*** **1** mark left by scraping or tearing something: *a* scratch *on furniture*; *a* scratch *on one's cheek.* **2** harsh, scraping sound: *the* scratch *of a pen.* **—*n-* scratch′er.**

from scratch **1** from the beginning. **2** from nothing.
up to scratch *Informal* at the normal or standard level.

scratch line ***n-*** the take-off line that may not be crossed by a contestant in the broad jump, javelin throw, etc.

scratch pad ***n-*** pad containing blank **scratch paper** for jotting down memos and similar notes.

scratch sheet ***n-*** daily racing publication that provides information about horses scheduled to compete that day, including past performances, jockeys, odds, etc.

scratch test ***n-*** **1** *Medicine* (1) test made to determine allergic sensitivity by introducing various allergens into scratches in the skin. (2) test for the presence of tuberculosis, glanders, leprosy, tinea, or certain other diseases, made by introducing the toxin in a scratch in the skin. **2** test of the hardness of a material, made by scratching it with other minerals of known hardness under controlled pressure.

scratch·y (skrăch′ē) ***adj-*** **[scratch·i·er, scratch·i·est]** **1** irritating; itchy: *a* scratchy *sweater.* **2** making a harsh, scraping sound; grating: *a* scratchy *phonograph record.* **—*adv-* scratch′i·ly.** ***n-*** **scratch′i·ness.**

scrawl (skrôl) ***vt-*** to write or draw hastily, carelessly, or awkwardly: *to* scrawl *one's name on a wall.* ***n-***: *I can hardly read his* scrawl. **—*n-* scrawl′er.** ***adj-*** **scrawl′y [scrawl·i·er, scrawl·i·est]**: *a* scrawly *handwriting.*

scraw·ny (skrô′nē) ***adj-*** **[scraw·ni·er, scraw·ni·est]** lean; skinny.

scream (skrēm) ***vi-*** to give a loud, shrill, piercing cry, especially from fear or pain: *He* screamed *when he saw the tiger.* ***vt-***: *She* screamed *her name.* ***n-*** **1** loud, shrill, piercing cry: *to utter a* scream. **2** *Informal* person, thing, or situation that provokes laughter or ridicule.

scream·er (skrē′ mər) ***n-*** **1** person who screams. **2** any of various large South American birds related to the ducks and having a raucous cry.

scream·ing (skrē′ mĭng) ***adj-*** **1** uttering screams: *a* screaming *baby.* **2** sensational; startling: *a* screaming *headline.* **—*adv-*** **scream′ ing·ly.**

screech (skrēch) ***n-*** harsh, piercing cry or sound: *the* screech *of brakes.* ***vi-*** to utter a piercing cry: *An owl* screeched. ***vt-***: *He* screeched *a reply.* **—*n-*** **screech′ er.**

screech owl ***n-*** any of various owls of North America, with hornlike tufts of feathers and a shrill cry.

screech·y (skrē′ chē) ***adj-*** **[screech·i·er, screech·i·est]** harsh and piercing; shrill: *a* screechy *voice.*

screen (skrēn) ***n-*** **1** frame covered with fine net or mesh of wire or plastic, used in doors and windows to keep out insects. **2** something that hides or conceals: *a* screen *of trees*; *a smoke* screen. **3** partition or frame of folding panels. **4** a surface on which motion pictures or slides are shown; also, the surface of a television set or radar upon which images appear. **5 the screen** (also **the silver screen**) motion pictures as an art and industry: *a play adapted for* the screen. **6** coarse wire mesh set in a frame, used in sifting or grading. ***vt-*** **1** to shelter; shield: *to* screen *one's eyes with an eyeshade.* **2** to sift. **3** to show (a motion picture). **4** to examine in order to classify or choose: *to* screen *applicants for a job.* **—*n-*** **screen′ er.**

Window screen

Television screen

Japanese screen

screen·ing (skrē′ nĭng) ***n-*** **1** examination in order to classify or choose: *a* screening *for a job.* **2** showing of a motion picture, to a select audience. **3** use of a screen to sift out particles of a certain size.

screen·ings (skrē′ nĭngz) ***n-*** *pl.* material separated out by a sieve or screen.

screen·play (skrēn′ plā′) ***n-*** story created for a movie.

screen test ***n-*** motion-picture scene or scenes made to test a person being considered for a role.

screw (skrōō) ***n-*** **1** device used chiefly for fastening objects and consisting of a slender cylinder with a spiral thread and, often, a slotted head. It is forced into place by twisting. **2** simple machine consisting of an inclined plane wound on a cylinder. **3** screw propeller. ***vt-*** **1** to fasten by the use of screws: *I* screwed *the planks to the crossbeams.* **2** to turn (something with threads) in order to tighten, loosen, fix into place, etc.: *to* screw *a lid on.* **3** to contort: *He* screwed *his face into a frown.* **—*adj-*** **screw′ like′.**

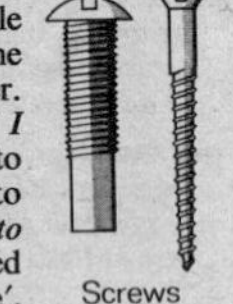
Screws

have a screw loose *Slang* to be crazy or eccentric.
put the screws on *Slang* to put pressure or force on in order to get something.

screw·ball (skrōō′ bôl′) ***n-*** **1** in baseball, a pitch thrown by a right-handed pitcher that curves toward a right-handed batter, or one delivered with the left hand that curves toward a left-handed batter. **2** *Slang* eccentric or odd person.

screw·driv·er (skrōō′ drī′ vər) ***n-*** tool with a tip that fits into the slot or head of a screw and is used to turn it.

screw·eye (skrōō′ ī′) ***n-*** ring with a projecting screw for fixing it solidly in place.

screw pine ***n-*** any of various tropical plants with stiltlike roots and narrow, spirally arranged leaves.

screw propeller ***n-*** device consisting of two or more thin and usually rounded blades set or molded on a hub at such an angle that a thrust is produced when the propeller turns, used underwater to drive boats.

screw thread ***n-*** spiral ridge running around a cylinder to form a screw.

scrib·ble (skrĭb′ əl) ***vt-*** **[scrib·bled, scrib·bling]** to write hastily and carelessly: *She* scribbled *her name.* ***vi-***: *He* scribbled *on a pad.* ***n-*** hasty, careless piece of writing.

scrib·bler (skrĭb′ lər) ***n-*** **1** person who scribbles. **2** petty, untalented writer.

scribe (skrīb) ***n-*** **1** person who copied manuscripts before the invention of printing presses. **2** formerly, a clerk or secretary. **3** among the ancient Jews, a teacher of the law. ***vt-*** **[scribed, scrib·ing] 1** to score (a line, mark, etc.) with a scriber. **2** to mark (metal, wood, etc.) with a scriber.

scrib·er (skrī′ bər) ***n-*** sharp tool for scribing.

scrim (skrĭm) ***n-*** loosely woven fabric of cotton or linen.

scrim·mage (skrĭm′ ĭj) ***n-*** **1** rough and confused struggle; tussle: *a* scrimmage *over the ball.* **2** in football, the action that takes place after the ball is put into play by snapping it back; also, a practice game between members of the same team or between rival teams. ***vi-*** **[scrim·maged, scrim·mag·ing]** to engage in a football scrimmage: *We'll* scrimmage *on Saturday.*

scrimp (skrĭmp) ***vi-*** to be very economical or frugal; skimp; stint: *He* scrimps *on food.* ***vt-***: *to* scrimp *cloth.*

scrimp·y (skrĭm′ pē) ***adj-*** **[scrimp·i·er, scrimp·i·est]** scanty; skimpy. **—*adv-*** **scrimp′ i·ly.** ***n-*** **scrimp′ i·ness.**

scrim·shaw (skrĭm′ shô′) ***n-*** **1** carved or engraved ornamental articles of bone, ivory, shell, etc.; especially, such articles made from whalebone by American whalers in the 19th century. **2** the art and practice of carving whalebone and making such articles. ***vt-***: *He* scrimshaws *ivory.* ***vi-***: *He* scrimshaws *on long voyages.*

scrip (skrĭp) ***n-*** **1** any of various certificates, often issued in place of money, indicating that the bearer is entitled to receive goods or services. **2** certificate for a part of a share of stock or a bond.

script (skrĭpt) ***n-*** **1** letters or figures written by hand. **2** style of writing: *old-fashioned* script. **3** printing type that resembles handwriting. **4** text of a play or movie that is used by the actors and members of the production staff. *as* ***modifier***: *a* script *change during rehearsals.*

Scrip·tur·al or **scrip·tur·al** (skrĭp′ chər əl) ***adj-*** of or relating to the Scriptures. **—*adv-*** **scrip′ tur·al·ly.**

Scrip·ture (skrĭp′ chər) ***n-*** **1** (also **the Scriptures** or **the Holy Scriptures**) the books of the Old and New Testament, and often the Apocrypha. **2 scriptures** any sacred writing.

scriv·e·ner (skrĭv′ ə nər) *Archaic* ***n-*** clerk; scribe.

scrod (skrŏd) ***n-*** young cod, especially one split to cook.

scrof·u·la (skrŏf′ yə lə) ***n-*** tubercular infection of the lymph glands, and sometimes of the bones and joints, producing abscesses and fistulas. **—*adj-*** **scrof′ u·lous**: *a* scrofulous *skin.*

Scrolls

scroll (skrōl) ***n-*** **1** book handwritten on a long strip of paper or parchment that a reader may roll up as he reads. **2** curved ornament. **—*adj-*** **scroll′-like′.**

scroll saw ***n-*** saw with a narrow blade for cutting thin wood in intricate, ornamental patterns.

scroll·work (skrōl′ wûrk′) ***n-*** ornamental work of scroll-like patterns; especially, such work made with a scroll saw.

Scrooge (skrōōj) ***n-*** the miserly old man in Dickens' "A Christmas Carol"; hence, any miser,

scro·tum (skrō′ təm) ***n-*** [*pl.* **scro·ta** (-tə) or **scro·tums**] in male mammals, the pouch containing the testes and their accessory organs.

scrounge (skrounj) *Slang* ***vt- & vi-*** [**scrounged, scroung·ing**] **1** to hunt up; scare up; forage (usually followed by "around" or "up"). **2** to beg; mooch. ***n-*** person who mooches; sponge.

¹**scrub** (skrŭb) ***vt-*** [**scrubbed, scrub·bing**] **1** to wash or clean by hard rubbing or brushing: *to* scrub *a floor.* **2** *Slang* to cancel: *The weather caused them to* scrub *the flight.* **3** to cleanse impurities from (a gas). ***vi-*** to clean oneself thoroughly with soap and a brush; especially, among surgeons, to cleanse the hands and arms before an operation. ***n-***: *She gave the floor a* scrub. [from Middle English **scrobben,** probably of Scandinavian origin.]

²**scrub** (skrŭb) ***n-*** **1** any animal or plant that is undersized or inferior in growth or quality. **2** player on a second or inferior team: *The varsity practiced against the* scrubs. **3** stunted shrubs, bushes, or trees: *The rabbit ran into the* scrub. *as* ***modifier***: *a member of the* scrub *team*; *a thick cover of* scrub *growth.* [probably from Danish **skrub** meaning "brushwood," and related to **shrub.**]

scrub·ber (skrŭb′ ər) ***n-*** person or thing that scrubs; especially, an apparatus for freeing gas of impurities.

scrub·by (skrŭb′ ē) ***adj-*** [**scrub·bi·er, scrub·bi·est**] **1** covered with scrub or brushwood: *a* scrubby *field.* **2** stunted: *a* scrubby *tree.* **3** shabby; paltry.

scruff (skrŭf) ***n-*** back of the neck; nape.

scrump·tious (skrŭmp′ shəs) *Slang* ***adj-*** splendid; excellent; delightful; delicious.

scrunch (skrŭnch) ***vt-*** to crush or crumple; crunch. ***vi-*** to make, or walk with, a crunching sound: *He* scrunched *through the deep snow.* ***n-*** crunching sound.

scru·ple (skrōō′ pəl) ***n-*** feeling of uneasiness, doubt, or uncertainty arising from one's conscience: *I had* scruples *about missing class.* ***vi-*** [**scru·pled, scru·pling**] to hesitate or be stopped by conscience or unwillingness (always in the negative, and usually followed by an infinitive or "about"): *He did not* scruple *to take his sister's share of the money. They did not* scruple *about abandoning us.*

scru·pu·lous (skrōōp′ yə ləs) ***adj-*** strict; conscientious: *He has a* scrupulous *regard for the truth.* ***—adv-*** **scru′ pu·lous·ly.** ***n-*** **scru′ pu·lous·ness.**

scru·ti·nize (skrōō′ tə nīz′) ***vt-*** [**scru·ti·nized, scru·ti·niz·ing**] to examine closely or minutely: *The police* scrutinized *the fingerprints.* ***—n-*** **scru′ ti·niz′ er.**

scru·ti·ny (skrōō′ tə nē) ***n-*** [*pl.* **scru·ti·nies**] close examination: *Will your work bear close* scrutiny?

scu·ba (skōō′ bə, skyōō′-) ***adj-*** **1** of or relating to a breathing device allowing a diver to carry his own air supply and swim freely underwater with no connections to the surface. A scuba outfit consists of one or more tanks of compressed air worn on the back, and a regulator that permits a diver to breathe this air at the same pressure as the surrounding water. **2** of or relating to the entire operation of undersea swimming with such a device: *a* scuba *handbook*; *a* scuba *tank*; *a* scuba *diver.* [from *s*elf-*c*ontained *u*nderwater *b*reathing *a*pparatus.]

scud (skŭd) ***vi-*** [**scud·ded, scud·ding**] to run or move swiftly; skim along: *The boat* scudded *before the rising gale.* ***n-*** **1** clouds, spray, or rain driven by the wind. **2** a skimming along: *the* scud *of the clouds.*

scuff (skŭf) ***vt-*** to make rough or scratched by wear: *He* scuffed *his shoes.* ***vi-*** **1** to shuffle: *to* scuff *along, kicking up the fallen leaves.* **2** to become roughened or scratched: *These shoes* scuff *easily.* ***n-*** **1** worn or rough spot. **2** flat woman's slipper that is open at the heel.

scuf·fle (skŭf′ əl) ***n-*** **1** confused, often playful, fight or struggle: *There was a* scuffle *over the football.* **2** the sound of shuffling. ***vi-*** [**scuf·fled, scuf·fling**] **1** to fight or struggle in a disorderly manner. **2** to walk with dragging feet; shuffle. ***—n-*** **scuf′ fler.**

Boy sculling a boat

scull (skŭl) ***n-*** **1** kind of short oar. **2** light racing boat. ***vt-*** to row with a scull or sculls, especially to row with a single oar at the stern of a boat: *We'll have to* scull *the boat.* ***vi-*** **1** to row a boat with a scull or sculls: *We* sculled *for miles.* **2** to move oneself through the water, usually lying on one's back, by moving the hands in figure eights. ***Hom-*** skull. ***—n-*** **scul′ ler.**

scul·ler·y (skŭl′ ə rē) *chiefly Brit.* ***n-*** [*pl.* **scul·ler·ies**] the part of a kitchen where the rough, dirty work is done, and where utensils are cleaned and stored. *as* ***modifier***: *a* scullery *maid.*

scul·lion (skŭl′ yən) *Archaic* ***n-*** **1** servant who does rough work in a kitchen. **2** base fellow; wretch.

scul·pin (skŭl′ pən) ***n-*** [*pl.* **scul·pin**; **scul·pins** (kinds of sculpin)] any of various spiny fish of fresh and salt waters, with a broad mouth and large head.

sculpt (skŭlpt) *Informal* ***vt-*** to sculpture: *to* sculpt *a head.* ***vi-***: *to* sculpt *for a living.*

sculp·tor (skŭlp′ tər) ***n-*** artist who carves or models sculpture. ***—n-*** *fem.* **sculp′ tress.**

sculp·tur·al (skŭlp′ chər əl) ***adj-*** having to do with or like sculpture. ***—adv-*** **sculp′ tur·al·ly.**

sculp·ture (skŭlp′ chər) ***n-*** **1** the art of carving, modeling, or casting figures or designs in various materials, such as stone, wood, or clay. **2** figure or design formed in this way. ***vt-*** [**sculp·tured, sculp·tur·ing**]: *to* sculpture *a bust.* ***vi-***: *to* sculpture *for a living.*

scum (skŭm) ***n-*** **1** thin layer of matter on the surface of a liquid or body of water: *A green* scum *often forms on still ponds.* **2** worthless people: *the* scum *of the earth.*

scum·my (skŭm′ ē) ***adj-*** [**scum·mi·er, scum·mi·est**] **1** covered with, containing, or like scum: *a* scummy *lake.* **2** mean and worthless; contemptible.

scup (skŭp) ***n-*** [*pl.* **scup**] marine food fish related to the porgy and found along the eastern coast of the United States.

scup·per (skŭp′ ər) ***n-*** opening in the side of a ship to carry off water from the deck.

scup·per·nong (skŭp′ ər nŏng′) ***n-*** **1** yellowish-green grape grown in southern United States. **2** white wine made from this grape.

scurf (skûrf) ***n-*** **1** flaky scales on the skin; especially, dandruff. **2** any scaly matter sticking to a surface.

scurf·y (skûr′ fē) ***adj-*** [**scurf·i·er, scurf·i·est**] covered with or like scurf: *a* scurfy *scalp.*

scur·ril·ous (skûr′ ə ləs) ***adj-*** indecent and abusive; coarse; vulgar: *a* scurrilous *writer.* ***—adv-*** **scur′ ril·ous·ly.** ***n-*** **scur′ ril·ous·ness** or **scur·ril′ i·ty** (skə rĭl′ ə tē).

scur·ry (skûr′ē) ***vi-*** **[scur·ried, scur·ry·ing]** to run quickly; hurry; scamper: *The mice* scurried *into a hole.* ***n-*** [*pl.* **scur·ries**] hasty running; scamper: *a* scurry *of feet.*
scur·vy (skûr′ vē) ***n-*** disease resulting from a deficiency of vitamin C in the diet. Its symptoms are weakness, loss of weight, and bleeding gums. ***adj-*** **[scur·vi·er, scur·vi·est]** mean; contemptible. **—*adv-* scur′ vi·ly.**
scut (skŭt) ***n-*** short tail, especially of a rabbit or deer.
scutch·eon (skŭch′ ən) escutcheon.
[1]**scut·tle** (skŭt′ əl) ***vi-*** **[scut·tled, scut·tling]** to scurry; scamper: *to* scuttle *down a hatch.* ***n-*** scurry. [from a variant of earlier English **scuddle,** related to **scut.**]
[2]**scut·tle** (skŭt′ əl) ***n-*** kind of pail with a projecting lip, used for carrying coal to a stove or fireplace; hod. [from Old English **scutel,** "shallow container; dish," from Latin **scūtella,** "small dish; tray."]

Scuttle

[3]**scut·tle** (skŭt′ əl) ***n-*** **1** small opening with a lid in the roof of a house or in the deck, side, or bottom of a ship. **2** the lid for such an opening. ***vt-*** **[scut·tled, scut·tling]** to sink (a ship) by opening holes in its bottom or sides, usually by opening valves that let water in. [from Old French **escoutille,** from Spanish **escotilla,** from **escotar,** "to cut neck and shoulder holes of a garment."]
scut·tle·butt (skŭt′ əl bŭt′) *Informal* ***n-*** gossip; rumor.
Scyl·la (sĭl′ ə) ***n-*** in Greek mythology, a hideous sea monster who lived on a headland of the Italian peninsula on the Strait of Messina. Opposite it was the whirlpool, **Charybdis,** near the coast of Sicily.
between Scylla and Charybdis between two dangerous or hazardous alternatives.
scythe (sīth) ***n-*** mowing tool consisting of a long curved blade on a long, bent handle.
S. Dak. South Dakota.
Se symbol for selenium.
SE or **S.E.** , **1** southeast. **2** southeastern.
sea (sē) ***n-*** **1** the body of salt water that covers most of the earth's surface; ocean. **2** any large part of this that is partly enclosed by land: *the Caribbean* Sea. **3** large inland body of water, either salt or fresh: *the Caspian* Sea; *the* Sea *of Galilee.* **4** the surface condition of the ocean: *a calm* sea. **5** high wave; ocean swell. **6** anything like the ocean in vastness: *a* sea *of trouble.* *as* ***modifier:*** *a* sea *bird.* ***Homs-*** see, [1]si.

Scythe

at sea 1 sailing on the ocean. **2** confused; lost. **follow the sea** to earn a living by working as a sailor. **go to sea** to become a sailor. **put to sea** to sail from land.
sea anchor ***n-*** large, usually conical, canvas-covered frame used as a floating drag to prevent a vessel from drifting or to keep its head to the wind.
sea anemone ***n-*** any of various stationary marine animals with tentacles at their mouths, which give them the appearance of flowers.
sea bass ***n-*** **1** any of various salt-water fishes common along the Atlantic coast, many species of which are valuable as food, especially the **black sea bass** or blackfish. **2** any of various similar fishes common along the Pacific coast, especially the **giant sea bass** and the **white sea bass.**

Sea anemone

Sea·bee (sē′ bē′) ***n-*** any member of the *C*onstruction *B*attalions of the U.S. Navy.
sea biscuit ***n-*** hardtack.
sea·board (sē′ bôrd′) ***n-*** land along a sea or ocean; coastline; shore: *the Atlantic* seaboard. *as* ***modifier:*** *a* seaboard *city.*
sea·coast (sē′ kōst′) ***n-*** land bordering a sea or ocean.
sea cow ***n-*** dugong.
sea cucumber ***n-*** any of various cucumber-shaped sea animals with a spiny skin and a mouth surrounded by tentacles.
sea dog ***n-*** old, experienced sailor.
sea elephant ***n-*** large seal found chiefly in the Southern Hemisphere. Adult males have a short, trunklike snout.
sea·far·er (sē′ fâr′ ər) ***n-*** sailor; mariner.
sea·far·ing (sē′ fâr′ ĭng) ***adj-*** **1** traveling on the sea or ocean: *a* seafaring *ship.* **2** making a living as a sailor: *a* seafaring *man.* ***n-*** the work of a sailor.
sea·food (sē′ fōōd′) ***n-*** fish or shellfish used as food.
sea·girt (sē′ gûrt′) ***adj-*** surrounded by the sea: *a* seagirt *city.*
sea·go·ing (sē′ gō′ ĭng) ***adj-*** **1** seafaring. **2** suitable or fitted for use on the open sea: *a* seagoing *yacht.*

Sea horse, 4—12 in. long

sea gull ***n-*** gull.
sea horse ***n-*** [*pl.* **sea horse; sea horses** (kinds of sea horse)] **1** any of various small fishes with a head like that of a horse. **2** mythical beast, half horse, half fish.
[1]**seal** (sēl) ***n-*** **1** sea animal with a round head, long body, and flippers instead of feet. Some kinds are valuable for their fur. **2** skin or fur of these animals; sealskin. *as* ***modifier:*** *a* seal *coat.* ***vi-*** to hunt such animals. [from Old English **seolh** of the same meaning.]

Fur seal, 4—6 ft. long

[2]**seal** (sēl) ***n-*** **1** engraved stamp, ring, or die used to make an impression in wax or some similar substance; also, the impression itself. **2** paper wafer, wax or embossed impression, or the word "seal," used to prove the genuineness of a document or prevent its alteration: *The notary put his* seal *upon the paper.* **3** design or mark used in place of a signature or to guarantee a signature: *given under my hand and* seal. **4** something that fastens firmly or closes completely: *a* seal *on an envelope.* **5** anything that secures or guarantees; pledge: *a* seal *of silence on his lips.* **6** gummed, ornamental stamp: *a Christmas* seal. **7** any of several devices, such as the small amount of water left standing in the trap of a drainage pipe, preventing the entrance of gas from below. ***vt-*** **1** to fasten or close with, or as with, a seal: *to* seal *a letter*; *to* seal *a jar.* **2** to set or affix a seal to (a document) to prove its authenticity: *The notary* sealed *the deed.* **3** to ratify; confirm; settle once and for all: *They* sealed *a bargain. The edict* sealed *his fate.* **4** to enclose tightly: *He* sealed *the document in a tube.* [from Old French **seel,** from Latin **sigillum** meaning "a little image," and related to **signum,** "a mark; a sign."] **—*adj-* seal′ a·ble.**

United States seal

sea legs ***n-*** *pl.* ability to adapt oneself to the pitching and rolling motion of a ship.

[1]**seal·er** (sē′ lər) ***n-*** sailor or ship engaged in the trade of hunting seals. [from [1]**seal.**]

[2]**seal·er** (sē′ lər) ***n-*** **1** person, device, or material that closes, seals, packages, makes watertight or airtight, etc. **2** paint applied to unfinished surfaces to prevent subsequent coats of paint, varnish, etc., from sinking in or being absorbed unevenly. **3** official who certifies that certain standards have been met. [from [2]**seal.**]

sea level ***n-*** position of the surface of the ocean when it is halfway between high tide and low tide. The positions of all other land on the earth, including the bottoms of seas, are measured above or below sea level. For picture, see *elevation.*

sealing wax ***n-*** kind of wax that softens when heated and hardens quickly on cooling and is used for sealing letters, packages, etc.

sea lion ***n-*** large seal that lives in the Pacific Ocean.

seal·skin (sēl′ skĭn′) ***n-*** **1** skin or fur of a fur seal. **2** garment made of it. *as* ***modifier:*** *a* sealskin *coat.*

seam (sēm) ***n-*** **1** line made when two pieces of material are sewn, welded, or otherwise joined together. **2** wrinkle, welt, scar, or furrow: *The* seam *of an old cut crossed his cheek.* **3** layer of mineral in the earth: *A* seam *of quartz runs through the cliff.* ***vt-*** **1** to join together, especially by sewing: *to* seam *a dress.* **2** to mark with scars and furrows: *Wind and water had* seamed *the old seaman's face.* ***Hom-*** seem. **—*adj-*** **seam′ less.**

sea·man (sē′ mən) ***n-*** [*pl.* **sea·men**] **1** sailor. **2** in the Navy and Coast Guard, an enlisted man who ranks below a petty officer and above a recruit. ***Hom-*** semen. **—*adj-*** **sea′ man·like′.**

sea·man·ship (sē′ mən shĭp′) ***n-*** skill in sailing.

sea mew ***n-*** gull; especially, one of the common European gulls.

sea·mount (sē′ mount′) ***n-*** in geology, an isolated, undersea mountain that does not reach sea level.

seam·stress (sēm′ strəs) ***n-*** woman who sews for a living.

seam·y (sē′ mē) ***adj-*** [**seam·i·er, seam·i·est**] **1** having seams. **2** showing the rough, inner sides of seams. **—*n-*** **seam′ i·ness.**

the seamy side the worst, roughest side.

sé·ance (sā′ äns′) ***n-*** meeting of persons to receive spiritualistic messages.

sea otter ***n-*** large, nearly extinct otter having a valuable dark-brown fur and found along the North Pacific.

sea·plane (sē′ plān′) ***n-*** airplane designed to land on and take off from water; hydroplane.

sea·port (sē′ pôrt′) ***n-*** **1** port or harbor for ocean vessels. **2** town or city containing such a port or harbor.

sea power ***n-*** **1** nation having a powerful navy. **2** naval strength.

sear (sêr) ***vt-*** **1** to dry up; wither: *A hot summer has* seared *the crops this year.* **2** to burn the surface of; scorch: *to* sear *a steak.* **3** to damage and leave a scar: *The tragedy had* seared *his mind.* ***adj-*** *Archaic* withered; dried up. ***n-*** mark made by burning. ***Homs-*** seer, sere.

search (sûrch) ***vt-*** **1** to examine carefully for something hidden or concealed: *They* searched *the room. He* searched *the prisoner for weapons.* **2** to look deeply into; probe: *to* search *one's heart.* ***n-*** a seeking or looking for a person or thing; investigation. **—*n-*** **search′ er.**

in search of looking for; trying to find.

search out to find or learn by searching.

search·ing (sûr′ chĭng) ***adj-*** sharply penetrating; scrutinizing: *a* searching *look.* **—*adv-*** **search′ ing·ly.**

search·light (sûrch′ līt′) ***n-*** large, powerful electric light, the beam of which may be turned in any direction.

search warrant ***n-*** written order giving a peace officer the authority to search for stolen goods, suspected lawbreakers, concealed weapons, etc.

sea room ***n-*** space at sea needed for maneuvering or changing the position of a ship.

sea rover ***n-*** a pirate; also, a pirate ship.

sea·scape (sē′ skāp′) ***n-*** **1** any picture showing a scene at sea. **2** view of the sea or ocean.

sea serpent ***n-*** snakelike monster reported to live in the ocean but never proved to exist.

sea·shell (sē′ shĕl′) ***n-*** the shell of any sea mollusk.

sea·shore (sē′ shôr′) ***n-*** land bordering the sea; seacoast.

sea·sick (sē′ sĭk′) ***adj-*** suffering from illness or nausea caused by the motion of a ship. **—*n-*** **sea′ sick′ ness.**

sea·side (sē′ sīd′) ***n-*** land bordering the sea; seashore. *as* ***modifier:*** *a* seaside *cottage.*

sea snake ***n-*** any of several venomous, fish-eating snakes related to the cobras and found in warm parts of the Indian and Pacific oceans.

sea·son (sē′ zən) ***n-*** **1** any of the four divisions of the year (spring, summer, autumn, winter). **2** appropriate or proper time: *There is a* season *for everything.* **3** time of year associated with a special activity: *the opera* season. ***vt-*** **1** to make tasty by adding seasoning. **2** to bring to the best state for use or survival; toughen; mature: *to* season *timber*; *to* season *troops by hardship.* **3** to make agreeable; add interest to: *to* season *a lecture with pleasant anecdotes.* ***vi-*** to become fit for use: *Timber* seasons *well in the open air.* **—*n-*** **sea′ son·er.**

for a season for a while. **in good season** in good time for something; early enough. **in season 1** available and fresh for use as food: *Oysters are* in season *now.* **2** legally subject to be hunted or caught: *Pheasants are* in season *for another month.* **3** at the proper or right time. **in and out of season** at all times. **out of season** not in season.

sea·son·a·ble (sē′ zə nə bəl) ***adj-*** **1** occurring or coming in good time: *his* seasonable *advice.* **2** in keeping with the season: *the* seasonable *weather.* **—*n-*** **sea′ son·a·ble·ness.** ***adv-*** **sea′ son·a·bly.**

►Should not be confused with SEASONAL.

sea·son·al (sē′ zə nəl) ***adj-*** relating to or influenced by certain periods of the year: *a* seasonal *disease*; seasonal *rates*; seasonal *labor.* **—*adv-*** **sea′ son·al·ly.**

►Should not be confused with SEASONABLE.

sea·son·ing (sē′ zən ĭng) ***n-*** **1** ingredient or ingredients, such as salt, pepper, and spices or herbs, added to food to flavor it. **2** anything that adds interest, variety, etc.

sea squirt ***n-*** any of various small sea animals having a leathery covering that contracts its soft body and causes it to squirt out jets of water.

seat (sēt) ***n-*** **1** place to sit, such as a chair, stool, or bench. **2** the part of a chair, stool, or bench on which one sits. **3** the part of the body on which one sits, or the part of a garment covering it: *the* seat *of one's trousers.* **4** place where anything is situated: *the* seat *of government.* **5** mansion or estate, especially in the country. **6** the position and rights of a member; membership: *a* seat *in Congress*; *a* seat *on the stock exchange.* **7** chair or space on a bench for a spectator: *three* seats *for a play.* **8** manner of sitting, as in riding a horse. **9** part or surface supporting another part or surface: *a valve* seat.

---

fāte, făt, dâre, bärn; bē, bĕt, mêre; bīte, bĭt; nōte, hŏt, môre, dôg; fŭn, fûr; tōō, bŏŏk; oil; out; tar; thin; then; hw for wh as in *wh*at; zh for s as in u*s*ual; ə for a, e, i, o, u, as in *a*go, lin*e*n, per*i*l, at*o*m, min*u*s

vt- **1** to assign or conduct to a place to sit: *The usher* seated *them in the fifth row center.* **2** to furnish with places to sit: *The theater* seats *two thousand persons.* **3** to restore or repair the seat or bottom of; put a seat on: *to* seat *a chair.* **4** to adjust on a seat: *to* seat *a valve.*

be seated **1** to sit down; also, to be sitting. **2** to be located.

seat belt *n-* strap that fastens a person to the seat of an airplane, automobile, etc., to protect him from being tossed about by bumps or jolts; safety belt.

sea trout *n-* **1** any of several trouts that live in the sea but ascend rivers to spawn. **2** any of several weakfishes.

sea urchin *n-* any of various small, round sea animals that have a thin shell covered with movable spines.

Sea urchin

sea wall *n-* wall or embankment to break the force of the waves or prevent erosion of the seashore.

sea·ward (sē′ wərd) *adj-* going toward, or situated in the direction of, the sea: *the* seaward *course of the explorers.* *adv-* (also **sea′ wards**) toward the sea: *The river flowed* seaward.

sea·way (sē′ wā′) *n-* **1** inland route to the sea for ocean shipping: *St. Lawrence* Seaway. **2** lane for travel on the sea. **3** forward motion of a ship; headway.

sea·weed (sē′ wēd′) *n-* any plant or plants, such as kelp or dulse, growing in the sea.

sea·wor·thy (sē′ wûr′ thē) *adj-* fit for a voyage on the open sea: *a* seaworthy *boat.* *—n-* **sea′ wor′ thi·ness.**

se·ba·ceous (sə bā′ shəs) *adj-* **1** of or having to do with fat. **2** secreting fat or oil.

sebaceous gland *n-* gland of the skin that secretes oil.

SEC or **S.E.C.** Securities and Exchange Commission.

sec. **1** second. **2** seconds.

se·cant (sē′ kănt′, -kənt) *Mathematics n-* **1** a straight line that intersects a curve in at least two points; especially, such a line that intersects a circle. **2** of an acute angle in a right triangle, the ratio of the hypotenuse to the side adjacent to the acute angle; the reciprocal of the cosine of the angle.

se·cede (sĭ sēd′) *vi-* [**se·ced·ed, se·ced·ing**] to withdraw formally from a union or association, especially from a political or religious body. *—n-* **se·ced′ er.**

se·ces·sion (sĭ sĕsh′ ən) *n-* **1** deliberate and formal withdrawal from a group, union, or organization. **2 Secession** the withdrawal of the Southern States from the Federal Union in 1860-1861.

se·ces·sion·ist (sĭ sĕsh′ ən ĭst) *n-* person who believes in or promotes secession. *adj-*: *a* secessionist *speech.*

se·clude (sĭ klo͞od′) *vt-* [**se·clud·ed, se·clud·ing**] to keep apart from others; shut off; isolate: *He* secluded *himself from society. The dense forest* secluded *the cabin.*

se·clud·ed (sĭ klo͞o′ dəd) *adj-* shut off from others; isolated: *a* secluded *life.* *—adv-* **se·clud′ ed·ly.**

se·clu·sion (sĭ klo͞o′ zhən) *n-* secluded or isolated way of life; solitude: *He sought* seclusion *in the desert.*

se·clu·sive (sĭ klo͞o′ sĭv, -zĭv) *adj-* keeping or living apart from others; fond of seclusion: *a* seclusive *country squire.* *—adv-* **se·clu′ sive·ly.** *n-* **se·clu′ sive·ness.**

¹sec·ond (sĕk′ ənd) *n-* **1** amount of time equal to 1/60 of a minute. **2** *Informal* very short time: *I'll be finished in just a* second. **3** 1/60 of a minute of an angle or circle, or 1/360 of a degree. [from French, from Medieval Latin **secunda minuta** meaning "second minute," that is, a further division beyond a minute.]

²sec·ond (sĕk′ ənd) *adj-* **1** next after first: *She was our* second *choice.* **2** the ordinal of 2; 2nd: *He lives on* Second *Avenue.* **3** another of the same class or group; additional: *They called him a* second *Lincoln.* **4** *Music* playing or singing a part that is lower in pitch: *the* second *violin*; *a* second *tenor.* *n-* **1** the next after the first; 2nd: *He was the* second *in command.* **2** person who assists another, as in a duel or prize fight. **3** the next higher forward gear after first. **4** *Music* an interval of two tones on the scale counting the extremes, as from C to D, and the harmonic combination of these tones. **5** article of goods having a defect in manufacture. *vt-* **1** to back up, assist, or promote: *He* seconded *his son's desire to become an actor.* **2** in parliamentary practice, to support (a motion, resolution, nomination, etc.) put forth by another. *adv-*: *He mentioned you* second. [from Old French, from Latin **secundus** meaning "following; second," from **sequi**, "to follow."] *—n-* **sec′ ond·er.**

sec·on·dar·i·ly (sĕk′ ən dĕr′ ə lē) *adv-* in the second or other place after the first; not primarily.

sec·on·dar·y (sĕk′ ən dĕr′ ē) *adj-* **1** next in order in place, time, importance, etc. **2** higher than elementary. **3** in electricity, relating to a coil or circuit in which a voltage is induced from a primary circuit. *n-* [*pl.* **sec·on·dar·ies**] in football, the defensive players stationed behind the defensive line.

secondary accent *n-* **1** in a word with two or more accented syllables, any stress that is somewhat weaker than the primary accent. In the word "man′ u·fac′ tur·er," the syllable "man" has the secondary accent. **2** the mark (′) used to show the somewhat weaker syllable.

secondary colors *n-* the three colors obtained by mixing equal amounts of any two primary colors. Secondary colors in pigments are green, orange, and purple. In light they are magenta, blue-green, and yellow.

secondary school *n-* high school, or any other school ranking between elementary school and college.

second childhood *n-* feeble-mindedness of old age.

second class *n-* **1** the class, rank, type, or group next below the highest or the best. **2** class of cabin, seating, service, etc., on a ship, train, or airplane just below the most expensive or first class. **3** mail consisting of newspapers, magazines, etc. *adj-* (**second-class**): *a* second-class *cabin.* *adv-* (**second-class**): *to travel* second-class.

second fiddle *n-* second violin.

be (or **play**) **second fiddle** to be of secondary importance; fill a subordinate role or function.

second hand *n-* on a clock or watch, the hand that marks the seconds.

sec·ond-hand (sĕk′ ənd hănd′) *adj-* **1** not new; having had a former owner: *a* second-hand *coat.* **2** dealing in used goods: *a* second-hand *furniture store.* **3** taken from someone else: *a* second-hand *piece of news.*

second lieutenant See *lieutenant.*

sec·ond·ly (sĕk′ ənd lē) *adv-* as second in a series.

second nature *n-* deeply fixed acquired habits.

second person *Grammar n-* **1** the form of the personal or possessive pronoun which stands for or refers to the one or the ones addressed. In English these forms are "you," "your," "yours." **2** the form of the verb used with "you," such as "dance" in "you dance," or "are" in "you are."

sec·ond-rate (sĕk′ ənd rāt′) *adj-* of inferior or mediocre quality or importance; second-class: *a* second-rate *hotel.*

second sight *n-* the supposed power to foresee future events; clairvoyance.

second-story man *Slang n-* burglar, especially one who breaks into a house through an upstairs window.

second violin *n-* violinist who plays the lower-pitched of two violin parts in an orchestra, string quartet, etc.; also, the part played. *—n-* **second violinist.**

se·cre·cy (sē′ krə sē) *n-* **1** condition of keeping or being kept secret: *the* secrecy *of his plans*; *sworn to* secrecy.

2 the ability to keep a secret: *I am relying on your* secrecy *in this matter.*

in secrecy not openly; secretly.

se·cret (sē′ krət) ***adj-*** **1** kept from the knowledge or sight of others: *a* secret *pocket*; *a* secret *treaty*; *a* secret *drawer.* **2** working or acting without others' knowledge: *a* secret *agent*; secret *society.* **3** remote; secluded: *a* secret *retreat.* **4** mysterious; unknown: *the* secret *operations of nature.* ***n-*** **1** something hidden or concealed: *She can't keep a* secret. **2** hidden cause or true explanation: *The* secret *of Bill's success was hard work.* **3** something not widely known: *the* secrets *of science.* **—*adv-*** **se′ cret·ly.**

in secret without the knowledge of others; secretly.

sec·re·tar·i·at (sĕk′ rə tĕr′ ē ət) ***n-*** **1** the official position of a secretary. **2** office where a secretary carries on his business, preserves records, etc. **3** secretarial staff. **4** government department headed by a secretary.

sec·re·tar·y (sĕk′ rə tĕr′ ē) ***n-*** [*pl.* **sec·re·tar·ies**] **1** someone who writes letters and keeps records for a person, company, etc. **2** government official in charge of a department and usually belonging to the chief executive's cabinet: *the* Secretary *of Labor.* **3** writing desk with an upper section for books. **—*adj-*** **sec′ re·tar′ i·al.**

secretary bird ***n-*** large, long-legged, South African bird that feeds on snakes and other reptiles and has long feathers suggesting pens stuck behind the ear.

Secretary bird

sec·re·tar·y-gen·er·al (sĕk′ rə tĕr′ ē jĕn′ ər əl) ***n-*** [*pl.* **sec·re·tar·ies-gen·er·al**] chief administrative or executive officer.

sec·re·tar·y·ship (sĕk′ rə tĕr′ ē shĭp′) ***n-*** term of office, position, or work of a secretary.

se·crete (sĭ krēt′) ***vt-*** [**se·cret·ed, se·cret·ing**] **1** of living things, to produce and give off (a secretion): *Glands* secrete *hormones. Flowers* secrete *nectar.* **2** to hide; put in a secret place: *Squirrels* secrete *nuts and acorns.*

se·cre·tion (sĭ krē′ shən) ***n-*** **1** the process of producing and giving off substances by a plant or animal organ, especially substances that are useful to the organism. **2** substance secreted: *Bile is a* secretion *of the liver.*

se·cre·tive (sē′ krə tĭv′, sĭ krē′-) ***adj-*** **1** inclined to secrecy; not frank or open: *a* secretive *man.* **2** relating to or causing secretion. **—*adv-*** **se·cre′ tive·ly.** ***n-*** **se·cre′ tive·ness.**

se·cre·to·ry (sĭ krē′ tə rē) ***adj-*** of, relating to, or producing a secretion.

secret service ***n-*** **1** government service or branch charged with secret investigation. **2** espionage service or work. **3 Secret Service** branch of the Department of Treasury charged with the discovery and arrest of counterfeiters, the protection of the President, etc.

sect (sĕkt) ***n-*** group, especially a religious group, having the same principles, beliefs, or opinions.

sec·tar·i·an (sĕk târ′ ē ən) ***n-*** **1** relating or belonging to a particular religious sect or denomination: *a* sectarian *school*; sectarian *education.* **2** having or showing bias toward the principles of one sect; hence, narrow-minded. ***n-*** person biased toward the ideas of a sect.

sec·tar·i·an·ism (sĕk târ′ ē ə nĭz′ əm) ***n-*** excessive or narrow-minded attachment to the principles of a religious denomination, political party, or school; sectarian spirit: *his* sectarianism *in politics.*

sec·tion (sĕk′ shən) ***n-*** **1** part; division; one of a group of units: *New England is a* section *of the United States.* **2** a cutting, especially a cutting across the grain; also, a view of such a cutting. **3** printing symbol [§] indicating a subdivision of a chapter or used as a reference mark. **4** area of land equal to one square mile. It is also one of the 36 subdivisions of a township. **5** *Mathematics* figure that is formed by the intersection of a solid and a plane. ***vt-*** to cut or divide into parts.

sec·tion·al (sĕk′ shən əl) ***adj-*** **1** of or relating to a certain section, district, or part of a country; local; regional: *a* sectional *problem*; sectional *strife.* **2** consisting of parts: *a* sectional *bookcase.* ***n-*** large sofa made up of several units. **—*adv-*** **sec′ tion·al·ly.**

sec·tion·al·ism (sĕk′ shən ə lĭz′ əm) ***n-*** devotion to local interests above the interests of the country at large.

sec·tor (sĕk′ tər) ***n-*** **1** *Mathematics* of a circle, an area bounded by two radii and the arc they intercept. **2** military area for which a commander is responsible. **3** specific part or section: *the industrial* sector.

sec·u·lar (sĕk′ yə lər) ***adj-*** **1** having to do with this world and its affairs; not religious or spiritual: *a* secular *education in the public schools.* **2** of the state as opposed to the church; civil: *a* secular *court.* **3** not bound by monastic vows or living in monastic communities: *A priest of the* secular *clergy.* **—*adv-*** **sec′ u·lar·ly.**

sec·u·lar·ism (sĕk′ yə lə rĭz′ əm) ***n-*** the view that public education and civil affairs should remain free from religious elements or influences. **—*n-*** **sec′ u·lar·ist.**

sec·u·lar·ize (sĕk′ yə lə rīz′) ***vt-*** [**sec·u·lar·ized, sec·u·lar·iz·ing**] **1** to transfer from church to state control: *to* secularize *church property*; *to* secularize *education.* **2** to make worldly: *to* secularize *the Sabbath.* **—*n-*** **sec′ u·lar·i·za′ tion.**

se·cure (sə kyo͝or′) ***adj-*** **1** free from fear, care, or worry: *She felt* secure *because her parents were home.* **2** safe; affording safety; protected against attack, loss, etc.: *The cellar is a* secure *hiding place.* **3** firmly fixed, fastened, or closed; fast: *a* secure *knot*; *a* secure *foundation.* **4** sure and certain: *Victory is* secure. **5** in safekeeping: *The prisoner is* secure *in his cell.* ***vt-*** [**se·cured, se·cur·ing**] **1** to make safe; protect: *The new levee* secured *the city against floods.* **2** to make certain or sure; ensure: *Our Constitution* secures *freedom of speech, press, and religion.* **3** to get; obtain: *We* secured *the reading list from our librarian.* **4** to tie or fasten firmly; latch or lock: *He* secured *the door.* **5** to lock up: *They* secured *the prisoner in his cell.* **6** to guarantee repayment of: *He gave a mortgage to* secure *the loan.* ***vi-*** to put all in order so as to be safe: *Let's* secure *for the night.* **—*adv-*** **se·cure′ ly.** ***n-*** **se·cure′ ness.**

se·cure·ment (sə kyo͝or′ mənt) ***n-*** **1** a making secure: *the* securement *of the ship.* **2** procurement.

se·cu·ri·ty (sə kyo͝or′ ə tē) ***n-*** [*pl.* **se·cu·ri·ties**] **1** freedom from fear, danger, or anxiety; safety or a feeling of safety: *She enjoyed the cozy* security *of her room.* **2** means of safety or protection; also, protection: *The watchman was hired for* security. **3** something given as a pledge that a person will pay his debt: *the* security *for the loan.* **4** person who becomes responsible for another; surety. **5** measures taken for ensuring secrecy or safety against enemy espionage or sabotage: *The Army Intelligence was concerned with* security. **6 securities** bonds or stocks.

secy. or **sec'y.** secretary.

se·dan (sə dăn′) ***n-*** **1** closed automobile with a front and back seat for four to six passengers. **2** sedan chair.

---

sedan chair ***n-*** enclosed traveling chair for one person, carried about on poles by two men.

se·date (sə dāt′) ***adj-*** calm; composed; grave. ***—adv-*** **se·date′ly.** ***n-*** **se·date′ness.**

Sedan chair

se·da·tion (sə dā′ shən) ***n-*** a reducing of excitement, irritation, or pain, especially by the use of sedatives.

sed·a·tive (sĕd′ ə tĭv′) ***adj-*** having the property of reducing excitement, irritation, or pain. ***n-*** medicine that has a calming effect.

sed·en·tar·y (sĕd′ ən tĕr′ ē) ***adj-*** **1** accustomed to much sitting: *a* sedentary *scholar.* **2** requiring much sitting: *a* sedentary *job.* **3** remaining in one place; not migratory: *a* sedentary *tribe*; *a* sedentary *bird.* **4** not very busy or productive; inactive: *a* sedentary *life.* **5** resulting from too much sitting or inactivity: *a* sedentary *ailment.* ***—adv-*** **sed′en·tar′i·ly.** ***n-*** **sed′en·tar′i·ness.**

Se·der (sā′ dər) ***n-*** ceremonial feast held in Jewish homes at Passover, in memory of the Exodus.

sedge (sĕj) ***n-*** any of many grasslike herbs or plants with solid stems, growing in wet places.

sedg·y (sĕj′ ē) ***adj-*** **[sedg·i·er, sedg·i·est] 1** covered or bordered with sedge: *a* sedgy *marsh.* **2** of or like sedge.

sed·i·ment (sĕd′ ə mənt) ***n-*** **1** solid matter that settles to the bottom of a body of water or other liquid: *ocean* sediment. **2** in geology, matter deposited, usually by water but sometimes by wind and ice.

sed·i·men·ta·ry (sĕd′ ə mĕn′ tə rē) ***adj-*** formed from a sediment: *Sandstone is a* sedimentary *rock.*

sed·i·men·ta·tion (sĕd′ ə mən tā′ shən, sĕd′ ə mĕn′-) ***n-*** precipitation or accumulation of sediment.

se·di·tion (sə dĭsh′ ən) ***n-*** **1** a stirring up of discontent or rebellion against a government, just short of insurrection or treason. **2** language or action promoting rebellion.

se·di·tious (sə dĭsh′ əs) ***adj-*** promoting, inspired by, or engaged in sedition: *a* seditious *speech*; seditious *behavior.* ***—adv-*** **se·di′tious·ly.** ***n-*** **se·di′tious·ness.**

se·duce (sə do͞os′, -dyo͞os′) ***vt-*** **[se·duced, se·duc·ing] 1** to persuade to do wrong; tempt; entice: *They* seduced *him with a bribe to lose the game.* **2** to induce to engage in sex acts, especially for the first time. ***—n-*** **se·duc′er.**

se·duc·tion (sə dŭk′ shən) ***n-*** **1** a tempting or leading astray. **2** something that may lead astray; temptation.

se·duc·tive (sə dŭk′ tĭv) ***adj-*** tending to seduce or charm; alluring; enticing: *a* seductive *woman*; *a* seductive *offer.* ***—adv-*** **se·duc′tive·ly.** ***n-*** **se·duc′tive·ness.**

sed·u·lous (sĕj′ ə ləs) ***adj-*** steadily industrious; hardworking; diligent; tireless. ***—adv-*** **sed′u·lous·ly.** ***n-*** **sed′u·lous·ness.**

[1]**see** (sē) ***vt-*** **[saw** (sȯ, sŏ), **seen** (sēn), **see·ing] 1** to perceive with the eyes; look at. **2** to discern mentally; understand; grasp: *Do you* see *what I mean? I* see *your point.* **3** to escort; accompany: *He* saw *the visitor to the door.* **4** to find out; discover: *Will you please* see *who is at the door?* **5** to know; experience: *That old man had* seen *better days.* **6** to make sure (takes a clause as object): *Please* see *that you finish your work.* **7** to call on or talk with: *We went to* see *her. I'll* see *her tomorrow.* **8** to admit to one's presence; receive: *She refused to* see *us.* **9** to attend as a spectator: *He went to* see *a show.* **10** to imagine; visualize: *I can't* see *him as chairman of the board.* **11** to regard; judge; deem: *He didn't* see *the question my way.* **12** in card games, to meet (a bet) or equal the bet of (a player) by staking an equal sum. ***vi-*** **1** to have or use the power of sight: *The old dog could hardly* see. **2** to understand; perceive mentally: *to* see *into the heart of things.* **3** to consider; reflect: *Will you do it? I will* see. **4** to come to know through observation, experience, etc.: *We'll soon* see *if we are right.* [from Old English **sēon** of the same meaning.] ***Homs-*** sea, [1]si.

see about 1 to inquire into. **2** to take care of.

see off to accompany (someone) to the place of his departure.

see out to wait till the end of; continue with to the end.

see through 1 to understand the actual character or purpose of: *She* saw through *his scheme.* **2** to stay or continue with to the end of.

see to to take care of: *Please* see *to dinner.*

[2]**see** (sē) ***n-*** district in which a bishop has authority. [from Old French **sie(d),** from Latin **sēdēs,** "a seat."] ***Homs-*** sea, [1]si.

seed (sēd) ***n-*** **1** small object produced by a flowering plant and containing an egg cell which can grow into a young plant. **2** milt; semen. **3** offspring; descendants: *"the* seed *of Abraham."* **4** the beginning or origin of anything: *The* seeds *of discontent grew rapidly into open revolt.* **5** young clams or oysters of a size for transplanting. ***vt-*** **1** to sow with seed: *I helped my next door neighbor* seed *his lawn.* **2** to remove seeds from: *She* seeded *the grapefruit and the oranges.* **3** in sports (1) to arrange (a tournament) so that the more skilled contestants will not meet in the early rounds. (2) to rank (a contestant, player, etc.) for this purpose. **4** to treat (a cloud) with certain chemicals in an attempt to produce rain. **5** to transplant young clams or oysters to (a new area).

seed·bed (sēd′ bĕd′) ***n-*** bed of fine soil, usually covered with glass, for growing plants from seed for transplanting.

seed·case (sēd′ kās′) ***n-*** hollow container, such as the pod of a pea or a milkweed, containing seeds.

seed·coat (sēd′ kōt) ***n-*** outer covering of a seed.

seed·er (sē′ dər) ***n-*** **1** person or machine that sows seeds. **2** device for removing seeds. ***Hom-*** cedar.

seed leaf ***n-*** cotyledon.

seed·ling (sēd′ lĭng) ***n-*** **1** plant grown from seed, as distinct from that grown by grafting or cutting. **2** young plant or tree.

seed pearl ***n-*** very small pearl.

seed plant ***n-*** any plant bearing seeds.

seeds·man (sēdz′ mən) ***n-*** [*pl.* **seeds·men**] **1** person who sells seeds. **2** person who sows seeds.

seed vessel ***n-*** pericarp.

seed·y (sē′ dē) ***adj-*** **[seed·i·er, seed·i·est] 1** full of seeds: *a* seedy *orange.* **2** having small air bubbles or similar inclusions, such as glass. **3** *Informal* shabby; threadbare: *old,* seedy *clothes.* **4** *Informal* out of sorts; low; wretched: *to feel* seedy. ***—adv-*** **seed′i·ly.** ***n-*** **seed′i·ness.**

see·ing (sē′ ĭng) ***n-*** power of sight; vision. ***conj-*** in view of the fact; since: *He said,* "Seeing *that you are going, I shall go too."*

seek (sēk) ***vt-*** **[sought** (sȯt, sŏt), **seek·ing] 1** to go in search of; look for; try to find: *to* seek *a lost child.* **2** to aim at; try to obtain: *to* seek *wealth.* **3** to ask or appeal for: *to* seek *aid.* **4** to resort to; go to: *He* sought *the theater for recreation.* **5** to attempt or try (takes only an infinitive as object): *For years men* sought *to climb Mount Everest.* ***vi-*** to make search; inquire: *to* seek *in vain.* ***—n-*** **seek′er.**

seem (sēm) ***vi-*** **1** to appear to be; give the impression of being: *Things are not always as they* seem. **2** to appear in the mind or imagination (to be): *I* seemed *to be floating in space.* ***Hom-*** seam.

can't seem to *Informal* can't, even with effort or persistance: *I* can't seem to *understand his motives.*

it seems that *Informal* it is reported that.

seem·ing (sē′ mĭng) ***adj-*** having an appearance which may or may not be true; apparent: *her* seeming *indignation*; seeming *neglect*. ***n-*** appearance; show; especially, false show. **—*adv-* seem′ ing·ly.**

seem·ly (sēm′ lē) ***adj-*** **[seem·li·er, seem·li·est]** fit or becoming to the circumstances; decent; proper: *her* seemly *behavior*. **—*n-* seem′ li·ness.**

seen (sēn) *p.p.* of **see.** ***Hom-*** scene.

seep (sēp) ***vi-*** to leak slowly through small openings; ooze: *Water* seeps *into our cellar*. ***n-*** small spring, or a place where water, oil, or other liquid oozes from the ground.

seep·age (sē′ pĭj) ***n-*** **1** a slow leaking through; ooze; percolation. **2** fluid or the amount of fluid that oozes.

seer (sêr) ***n-*** person supposed to have prophetic sight into the future. ***Homs-*** sear, sere. **—*n-*** *fem.* **seer′ ess.**

seer·suck·er (sêr′ sŭk′ ər) ***n-*** thin fabric of cotton, linen, nylon, rayon, etc., usually having alternating stripes and a crinkled or puckered surface.

see·saw (sē′ sȯ′) ***n-*** **1** board balanced on a central support, the ends of which alternately rise and fall as riders on the ends shift their weight. **2** pastime enjoyed on such a board. **3** any up-and-down or to-and-fro movement. *as* ***modifier***: *a* seesaw *motion*. ***vi-*** **1** to ride a seesaw. **2** to fluctuate: *The game* seesawed *back and forth until the home team won.*

Seesaw

seethe (sēth) ***vi-*** **[seethed, seeth·ing] 1** to move with a boiling, bubbling motion: *The flood* seethed *through town.* **2** to be violently moved or agitated: *I* seethed *with anger.*

Segment of a line

Segment

seg·ment (sĕg′ mənt) ***n-*** **1** any of the structurally similar parts into which an object naturally separates or is divided: *a* segment *of an orange*; *the* segments *of a worm*; *the last* segment *of a plot*. **2** *Mathematics* (1) a line segment. (2) part of a circle bound by an arc and a chord. (3) solid formed when two parallel planes cut through a sphere. ***vt-*** to divide into parts.

Segment of a circle

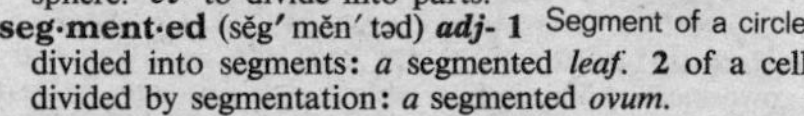

seg·ment·ed (sĕg′ mĕn′ təd) ***adj-*** **1** divided into segments: *a* segmented *leaf*. **2** of a cell, divided by segmentation: *a* segmented *ovum*.

seg·men·ta·tion (sĕg′ mən tā′ shən) ***n-*** **1** a dividing or being divided into segments. **2** *Biology* division of a fertilized egg cell into a number of cells.

se·go (sē′ gō) ***n-*** [*pl.* **se·gos**] bulb of the sego lily.

sego lily ***n-*** plant of the lily family, having white, trumpet-shaped flowers. It is common in western United States. [American word from the Ute Indian language.]

Sego lily

seg·re·gate (sĕg′ rə gāt′) ***vt-*** **[seg·re·gat·ed, seg·ra·gat·ing] 1** to separate from others; isolate; set apart: *to* segregate *people who have been exposed to a disease.* **2** to set apart because of race or color.

seg·re·gat·ed (sĕg′ rə gā′ təd) ***adj-*** of or relating to segregation, especially of races: *a* segregated *school*.

seg·re·ga·tion (sĕg′ rə gā′ shən) ***n-*** **1** a separation from others; a setting apart: *The doctor ordered the* segregation *of unvaccinated students.* **2** a separation of one race from other races, especially in public places.

seg·re·ga·tion·ist (sĕg′ rə gā′ shən ĭst) ***n-*** person who practices or is in favor of racial segregation.

sei·gneur (sā nyôr′ *Fr.* sā nyûr′) ***n-*** **1** lord; noble. **2** formerly, feudal lord; lord of a manor. **3** title of respect equivalent to "Sir." Also **sei′ gnior.**

sei·gnior·y (sēn′ yə rē) ***n-*** [*pl.* **sei·gnior·ies**] authority or rights of a feudal lord; also, territory under his rule.

seine (sān) ***n-*** large net used by fishermen. Weighted on one edge, it has floats on the other, so that it hangs straight down in the water. ***vt-*** **[seined, sein·ing]**: *to* seine *fish*. ***vi-***: *to* seine *off the coast.* ***Hom-*** sane. **—*n-* sein′ er.**

seis·mic (sīz′ mĭk) ***adj-*** of, related to, or produced by an earthquake: *a* seismic *tremor*.

seis·mo·graph (sīz′ mə grăf′) ***n-*** instrument used to record the time, duration, and intensity of an earthquake.

seis·mol·o·gist (sīz mŏl′ ə jĭst′) ***n-*** person trained or skilled in seismology and engaged in it as a profession.

seis·mol·o·gy (sīz mŏl′ ə jē) ***n-*** the scientific study of earthquakes and artificially produced vibrations in the earth. **—*adj-* seis′ mo·log′ i·cal.** ***adv-*** **seis′ mo·log′ i·cal·ly.**

seize (sēz) ***vt-*** **[seized, seiz·ing] 1** to lay hold of violently; grip suddenly: *She* seized *his arm.* **2** to take possession of by force or legal authority; also, to arrest; capture: *The sheriff* seized *the outlaw's house and lands.* **3** to grasp with the mind: *He was quick to* seize *the suggestion.* **4** to avail oneself of; take advantage of: *to* seize *an opportunity.* **5** to attack suddenly; have a sudden effect upon; strike: *Panic* seized *the retreating army.* **6** to fasten with several lashings of cord: *to* seize *ropes together.*

seize on (or **upon**) **1** to grasp and make use of, especially in a crisis: *The drowning man* seized on *the rope. She'll* seize upon *any excuse.* **2** to take possession of.

seiz·ing (sē′ zĭng) ***n-*** **1** a fastening or lashing together of things with rope; also, the rope used. **2** the fastening made in this way.

sei·zure (sē′ zhər) ***n-*** **1** sudden possession by force; capture: *the* seizure *of the town by the enemy.* **2** sudden attack, as of a disease; fit: *a* seizure *of cramps.*

sel·dom (sĕl′ dəm) ***adv-*** hardly ever; rarely.

se·lect (sĭ lĕkt′) ***vt-*** to pick out; choose: *I* selected *two books from our reading list.* ***vi-***: *to* select *carefully.* ***adj-*** **1** carefully or specially chosen; choice: *a* select *brand of canned goods.* **2** of great excellence; choicest or best: *a volume of* select *poems.* **3** not open to all; made up of chosen persons: *a* select *club*; *a* select *group.*

se·lec·tion (sĭ lĕk′ shən) ***n-*** **1** a selecting or choosing: *The* selection *of a house requires much thought.* **2** person or thing chosen; choice: *Jack is a fine* selection *for captain of the team.* **3** *Biology* natural selection.

se·lec·tive (sĭ lĕk′ tĭv) ***adj-*** **1** of or relating to selection. **2** having the power of selecting; tending to select: *He is an avid and* selective *reader.* **—*adv-* se·lec′ tive·ly.** ***n-*** **se·lec′ tiv′ i·ty.**

selective service ***n-*** required military service according to age, physical fitness, etc.

se·lect·man (sĭ lĕkt′ mən) ***n-*** [*pl.* **se·lect·men**] one of a board of officials chosen annually in most New England towns to carry on the public business of the town.

fāte, făt, dâre, bärn; bē, bĕt, mêre; bīte, bĭt; nōte, hŏt, môre, dȯg; fŭn, fûr; to͞o, bo͝ok; oil; out; tar; thin; then; hw for wh as in *wh*at; zh for s as in u*s*ual; ə for a, e, i, o, u, as in *a*go, lin*e*n, per*i*l, at*o*m, min*u*s

se·lec·tor (sə lĕk′ tər) *n-* **1** person who selects or chooses. **2** dial, switch, or similar device for selecting or controlling: *a TV* selector.

se·le·ni·um (sə lē′ nē əm) *n-* nonmetallic element of the sulfur group, whose electrical conductivity varies with the intensity of the light falling on it. It is used in photoelectric cells. Symbol Se, At. No. 34, At. Wt. 78.96.

self (sĕlf) *n-* [*pl.* **selves**] **1** the entire personality that makes one person different from another; one's own person: *His whole* self *revolted at the idea.* **2** particular side or aspect of a person's character: *I lost my temper and showed my worst* self. **3** personal interest and advantage: *He has no thought of* self. *adj-* **1** in clothing and draperies, made of the same material as the rest of the article: *a* self *lining. pron- Informal* myself; himself or herself; yourself: *theater tickets for* self *and wife.*

self- *combining form* **1** of the self (the object of the action named by the second word): self-*reproach*; self-*worship.* **2** by oneself or itself (the subject of the action named by the second word): self-*educated.* **3** to, for, in, on, with, or toward oneself: self-*addressed*; self-*indulgence.* **4** automatic or automatically: self-*recording.*

self-act·ing (sĕlf′ ăk′ tĭng) *adj-* having the power to act or move of itself; automatic. —*n-* **self′-ac′ tion.**

self-ad·dressed (sĕlf′ ə drĕst′) *adj-* addressed to oneself; bearing one's own name and address.

self-as·ser·tion (sĕlf′ ə sûr′ shən) *n-* insistence on one's own opinions, rights, or claims; personal boldness.

self-as·ser·tive (sĕlf′ ə sûr′ tĭv) *adj-* inclined to put oneself forward or to insist on one's own opinions or rights; bold; aggressive. —*adv-* **self′-as·ser′ tive·ly.** *n-* **self′-as·ser′ tive·ness.**

self-as·sur·ance (sĕlf′ ə shŏŏr′ əns) *n-* confidence in one's own ability or talent; self-confidence. —*adj-* **self′-as·sured′**: *a* self-assured *singer.*

self-cen·tered (sĕlf′ sĕn′ tərd) *adj-* concerned chiefly with one's own interests; selfish; egocentric. —*adv-* **self′-cen′ tered·ly.** *n-* **self′-cen′ tered·ness.**

self-com·mand (sĕlf′ kə mănd′) *n-* control of one's actions and emotions; self-control; self-possession.

self-com·pla·cent (sĕlf′ kəm plā′ sənt) *adj-* pleased with oneself; self-satisfied. —*n-* **self′-com·pla′ cen·cy.** *adv-* **self′-com·pla′ cent·ly.**

self-con·ceit (sĕlf′ kən sēt′) *n-* too high an opinion of one's own abilities or qualities; vanity. —*adj-* **self′-con·ceit′ ed.**

self-con·fi·dence (sĕlf′ kŏn′ fə dəns) *n-* trust and belief in one's self and ability. —*adj-* **self′-con′ fi·dent.** *adv-* **self′-con′ fi·dent·ly.**

self-con·scious (self′ kŏn′ shəs) *adj-* **1** uncomfortably aware of one's appearance or actions in the presence of others; embarrassed; ill at ease; shy: *He was* self-conscious *at his first dance.* **2** aware of one's own existence. —*adv-* **self′-con′ scious·ly.** *n-* **self′-con′ scious·ness.**

self-con·tained (sĕlf′ kən tānd′) *adj-* **1** cautious in expressing oneself; reserved; not inclined to talk. **2** in full control of one's words and actions; self-controlled. **3** sufficient or complete in itself: *a* self-contained *community*; *a* self-contained *machine.*

self-con·tra·dic·tion (sĕlf′ kŏn′ trə dĭk′ shən) *n-* **1** contradiction of oneself or itself. **2** statement or idea that contains elements or parts contradicting one another. —*adj-* **self′-con′ tra·dic′ to·ry.**

self-con·trol (sĕlf′ kən trōl′) *n-* command over one's own actions and feelings. —*adj-* **self′-con·trolled′.**

self-cor·rect·ing (sĕlf′ kə rĕk′ tĭng) *adj-* automatically correcting, adjusting, or compensating for its own errors, deficiencies, etc.: *a* self-correcting *mechanism.*

self-de·cep·tion (sĕlf′ dĭ sĕp′ shən) *n-* a deceiving of oneself or a being deceived by oneself.

self-de·fense (sĕlf′ dĭ fĕns′) *n-* protection of one's own person, property, or good name from attack or injury.

self-de·ni·al (sĕlf′ dĭ nī′ əl) *n-* a setting aside of one's own desires for the sake of others; self-sacrifice. —*adj-* **self′-de·ny′ ing.** *adv-* **self′-de·ny′ ing·ly.**

self-de·ter·min·a·tion (sĕlf′ dĭ tûr′ mə nā′ shən) *n-* **1** a making of one's own decisions without help from others. **2** the right of a people to choose the type of government that will rule them.

self-dis·ci·pline (sĕlf′ dĭs′ ə plĭn′) *n-* the discipline or control of oneself, often for improvement.

self-ed·u·cat·ed (sĕlf′ ĕj′ ə kā′ təd, -ĕd′ yŏŏ kā′ təd) *adj-* educated by one's own efforts without the aid of teachers; self-taught.

self-ef·fac·ing (sĕlf′ ə fās′ ĭng) *adj-* staying in the background through modesty, shyness, tact, or policy. —*n-* **self′-ef·face′ ment.** *adv-* **self′-ef·fac′ ing·ly.**

self-em·ployed (sĕlf′ ĕm ploid′) *adj-* earning income from one's own profession, trade, or business; not working for an employer.

self-es·teem (sĕlf′ ə stēm′) *n-* **1** proper respect for oneself; self-respect. **2** too high an opinion of oneself.

self-ev·i·dent (sĕlf′ ĕv′ ə dənt) *adj-* entirely clear or evident; without need of explanation or proof: *a* self-evident *truth.* —*adv-* **self′-ev′ i·dent·ly.**

self-ex·plan·a·to·ry (sĕlf′ ĕk splăn′ ə tôr′ ē) *adj-* entirely clear; without need of explanation or proof.

self-ex·pres·sion (sĕlf′ ĕk sprĕsh′ ən) *n-* expression of one's own feelings, ideas, etc.

self-gov·erned (sĕlf′ gŭv′ ərnd) *adj-* governed by its own people; independent: *a* self-governed *country.* Also **self′-gov′ ern·ing.**

self-gov·ern·ment (sĕlf′ gŭv′ ərn mənt) *n-* government of a nation by its own people; independence.

self-help (sĕlf′ hĕlp′) *n-* a taking care of oneself without the aid of others; self-reliance.

self-im·por·tant (sĕlf′ ĭm pôr′ tənt, -pôr′ tənt) *adj-* having an exaggerated sense of one's own value. —*n-* **self′-im·por′ tance.** *adv-* **self′-im·por′ tant·ly.**

self-im·posed (sĕlf′ ĭm pōzd′) *adj-* imposed on oneself; self-inflicted: *a* self-imposed *sacrifice.*

self-im·prove·ment (sĕlf′ ĭm prōōv′ mənt) *n-* improvement of oneself by one's own efforts.

self-in·duc·tion (sĕlf′ ĭn dŭk′ shən) *Physics n-* process in which an electromotive force is induced in a circuit as a result of a changing current in the same circuit.

self-in·dul·gent (sĕlf′ ĭn dŭl′ jənt) *adj-* gratifying one's own inclinations, desires, whims, etc., especially without self-control or at the expense of others. —*n-* **self′-in·dul′ gence.** *adv-* **self′-in·dul′ gent·ly.**

self-in·flict·ed (sĕlf′ ĭn flĭk′ təd) *adj-* inflicted on oneself: *a* self-inflicted *punishment.*

self-in·ter·est (sĕlf′ ĭn′ trəst, -ĭn′ tə rĕst′) *n-* **1** personal interest or advantage. **2** undue regard for one's own interest, regardless of the rights of others.

self·ish (sĕl′ fĭsh) *adj-* **1** putting one's own wishes or needs ahead of other people's. **2** showing or arising from an undue regard for oneself: *a* selfish *deed*; *a* selfish *thought.* —*adv-* **self′ ish·ly.** *n-* **self′ ish·ness.**

self·less (sĕlf′ ləs) *adj-* having no thought for oneself: *a* selfless *heroism.* —*adv-* **self′ less·ly.** *n-* **self′ less·ness.**

self-love (sĕlf′ lŭv′) *n-* fondness of oneself; tendency to put one's own happiness or desires first.

self-made (sĕlf′ mād′) *adj-* having risen to wealth, power, etc., by one's own efforts: *a* self-made *man.*

self-pit·y (sĕlf′ pĭt′ ē) *n-* lingering pity for one's own sorrows and misfortunes; a feeling sorry for oneself.

self-pol·li·na·tion (sĕlf′ pŏl′ ə nā′ shən) ***n-*** transfer of pollen from anthers to pistils of the same flower.

self-pos·sessed (sĕlf′ pə zĕst′) ***adj-*** having self-possession; calm; poised. ***—adv-*** **self′-pos·ses′ sed·ly.**

self-pos·ses·sion (sĕlf′ pə zĕsh′ ən) ***n-*** control over one's feelings; composure; calmness; poise.

self-praise (sĕlf′ prāz′) ***n-*** praise of oneself.

self-pres·er·va·tion (sĕlf′ prĕz′ ər vā′ shən) ***n-*** **1** a keeping of oneself from harm or danger. **2** the urge, regarded as an instinct, to protect oneself when danger threatens.

self-pride (sĕlf′ prīd′) ***n-*** pride in oneself.

self-pro·pelled (sĕlf′ prə pĕld′) ***adj-*** **1** containing within itself its own means of propulsion; propelled by itself: *a* self-propelled *missile.* **2** of artillery, mounted on and fired from a truck or tractor.

self-pro·tec·tion (sĕlf′ prə tĕk′ shən) ***n-*** self-defense.

self-re·cord·ing (sĕlf′ rĭ kȯr′ dĭng, -kôr′ dĭng) ***adj-*** making an automatic record; self-registering.

self-reg·is·ter·ing (sĕlf′ rĕj′ ĭs tər ĭng) ***adj-*** registering or recording automatically: *a* self-registering *thermometer.*

self-reg·u·lat·ing (sĕlf′ rĕg′ yə lā′ tĭng) ***adj-*** regulating or correcting itself: *a* self-regulating *guidance system.*

self-re·li·ance (sĕlf′ rĭ lī′ əns) ***n-*** dependence on or confidence in one's own resources, ability, or judgment. ***—adj-*** **self′-re·li′ ant.** ***adv-*** **self′-re·li′ ant·ly.**

self-re·proach (sĕlf′ rĭ prōch′) ***n-*** reproach, blame, or accusation of oneself. ***—adj-*** **self′-re·proach′ ing.** ***adv-*** **self′-re·proach′ ing·ly.**

self-re·spect (sĕlf′ rĭ spĕkt′) ***n-*** proper regard for oneself; self-esteem: *He had too much* self-respect *to tell a lie.* ***—adj-*** **self′-re·spect′ ing.**

self-re·straint (sĕlf′ rĭ strānt′) ***n-*** control of one's impulses or desires by force of will; self-control. ***—adj-*** **self′-re·strained′.**

self-right·eous (sĕlf′ rī′ chəs) ***adj-*** convinced of the superiority of one's morals; morally vain: *a* self-righteous *prude.* ***—adv-*** **self′-right′ eous·ly.** ***n-*** **self′-right′ eous·ness.**

self-ris·ing (sĕlf′ rī′ zĭng) ***adj-*** rising by itself; especially, rising without the addition of baking powder, leaven, etc.: *a* self-rising *batter.*

self-sac·ri·fice (sĕlf′ săk′ rə fīs′) ***n-*** sacrifice or subordination of one's personal interests or welfare for the sake of duty, another's happiness, etc. ***—adj-*** **self′-sac′ ri·fic′ ing.** ***adv-*** **self′-sac′ ri·fic′ ing·ly.**

self-same (sĕlf′ sām′) ***adj-*** the very same; identical.

self-sat·is·fac·tion (sĕlf′ săt′ ĭs făk′ shən) ***n-*** excessive satisfaction with oneself and one's actions, position, etc.

self-sat·is·fied (sĕlf′ săt′ ĭs fīd′) ***adj-*** entirely pleased with oneself and one's actions; complacent.

self-seek·ing (sĕlf′ sē′ kĭng) ***n-*** a looking out for one's own interests; selfishness. ***adj-***: *He is a* self-seeking *hypocrite.* ***—n-*** **self′-seek′ er.**

self-ser·vice (sĕlf′ sûr′ vəs) ***n-*** a serving of oneself in a restaurant, store, etc. ***adj-***: *That is a* self-service *store.*

self-start·er (sĕlf′ stär′ tər) ***n-*** automatic or partly automatic device, such as an electric motor, for starting an internal-combustion engine.

self-styled (sĕlf′ stīld′) ***adj-*** given a specific name or designation by oneself alone: *a* self-styled *cook.*

self-suf·fi·cient (sĕlf′ sə fĭsh′ ənt) ***adj-*** **1** needing no help from others: *a* self-sufficient *community.* **2** having undue confidence in oneself; self-confident. ***—n-*** **self′-suf·fi′ cien·cy.** ***adv-*** **self′-suf·fi′ cient·ly.**

self-sup·port (sĕlf′ sə pôrt′) ***n-*** financial support of oneself or itself without outside help. ***—adj-*** **self′-sup·port′ ing:** *a* self-supporting *institution.*

self-sus·tain·ing (sĕlf′ sə stā′ nĭng) ***adj-*** maintaining oneself or itself without outside help; self-supporting.

self-taught (sĕlf′ tȯt′) ***adj-*** self-educated.

self-treat·ment (sĕlf′ trēt′ mənt) ***n-*** treatment of one's own disease or injury without medical supervision.

self-un·der·stand·ing (sĕlf′ ŭn′ dər stăn′ dĭng) ***n-*** knowledge of one's own character, abilities, etc.

self-will (sĕlf′ wĭl′) ***n-*** insistence on having one's own way; stubbornness; obstinacy. ***—adj-*** **self′-willed′.**

self-wor·ship (sĕlf′ wûr′ shĭp) ***n-*** worship or admiration of oneself. ***—n-*** **self′-wor′ ship·er.**

self-wind·ing (sĕlf′ wīn′ dĭng) ***adj-*** winding itself automatically: *a* self-winding *clock.*

sell (sĕl) ***vt-*** **[sold** (sōld), **sell·ing] 1** to give in exchange for money: *She* sells *flowers.* **2** to deal in: *We* sell *only shoes in this shop.* **3** to give up, especially in violation of duty or trust; betray for a reward: *He* sold *his country for money.* **4** to promote or help the sale of: *Newspaper ads* sell *many products.* **5** *Informal* to cause to be accepted or approved: *He couldn't* sell *his ideas to the board of directors.* **6** *Informal* to persuade to accept, approve, or adopt something (usually followed by "on"): *to* sell *the public on an idea.* ***vi-*** **1** to engage in selling; work as a salesman: *He* sells *in the garment center.* **2** to be for sale; be sold: *This cloth* sells *at $5 a yard.* **3** to find purchasers or a market: *Umbrellas* sell *best on a rainy day.* **4** *Informal* to be approved, accepted, or adopted. ***n-*** *Informal* sales appeal. ***Hom-*** cell.

sell off to dispose of by sale.

sell out 1 to get rid of one's business by selling it. **2** *Informal* to betray by a secret deal.

sell·er (sĕl′ ər) ***n-*** **1** person who sells; salesman. **2** something that has a (good, bad, etc.) sale.

sell·ing (sĕl′ ĭng) ***n-*** the work or business of a salesman, especially one who works on commission or within a specific area; sales. *as* ***modifier***: *a good* selling *point.*

sell·out (sĕl′ out′) ***n-*** **1** performance for which all tickets have been sold. **2** betrayal of one's cause or associates.

selt·zer (sĕlt′ sər) ***n-*** carbonated water. Also **Seltzer, Seltzer water.**

sel·va (sĕl′ və) ***n-*** tropical rain forest.

sel·vage (sĕl′ vĭj) ***n-*** the edge of fabric woven so as to prevent raveling. Also **sel′ vedge.**

selves (sĕlvz) *pl.* of **self.**

se·man·tic (sə măn′ tĭk) ***adj-*** **1** of or relating to meaning: *a* semantic *difference.* **2** of or relating to semantics. ***—adv-*** **se·man′ ti·cal·ly.**

se·man·ti·cist (sə măn′ tə sĭst) ***n-*** person who is expert in semantics.

se·man·tics (sə măn′ tĭks) ***n-*** (takes singular verb) the branch of linguistics that deals with word meanings and their historical development.

sem·a·phore (sĕm′ ə fôr′) ***n-*** **1** signaling system that uses different positions of arms, bars, or flags to transmit messages. **2** apparatus, such as a lantern or flags, for signaling in such a manner. ***vi-*** **[sem·a·phored, sem·a·phor·ing]** to reply by semaphore: *to* semaphore *with flags.* ***vt-***: *The sailor* semaphored *a message.*

Semaphore

fāte, făt, dâre, bärn; bē, bĕt, mêre; bīte, bĭt; nōte, hŏt, môre, dȯg; fŭn, fûr; to͞o, bo͝ok; oil; out; tar; thin; then; hw for wh as in *wh*at; zh for s as in u*s*ual; ə for a, e, i, o, u, as in *a*go, lin*e*n, per*i*l, at*o*m, min*u*s

sem·blance (sĕm′ bləns) ***n-*** **1** outward appearance: *a* semblance *of wealth.* **2** appearance that is false or put on; pretense. **3** likeness; resemblance.

se·men (sē′ mən) ***n-*** the fluid in a male animal that contains the male reproductive cells. ***Hom-*** seaman.

se·mes·ter (sə mĕs′ tər) ***n-*** one of the terms that make up the school year in high school or college.

sem·i (sĕm′ ī′) *Informal* ***n-*** semitrailer.

semi- *prefix* **1** half: *a* semi*circle.* **2** partly: *a* semi*formal dance.* **3** happening twice in a specified period: *a* semi*annual event.* [from Latin **semi-**, "half (of)."]
►For usage note see BI-.

sem·i·an·nu·al (sĕm′ ē ăn′ yo͞o əl) ***adj-*** occurring twice a year: *a* semiannual *visit.* ***—adv-*** **sem′ i·an′ nu·al·ly.**

sem·i·ar·id (sĕm′ ē ăr′ ĭd) ***adj-*** having light rainfall; having an annual rainfall of 10 to 20 inches.

sem·i·cir·cle (sĕm′ ĭ sûr′ kəl) ***n-*** half circle.

sem·i·cir·cu·lar (sĕm′ ĭ sûr′ kyə lər) ***adj-*** having the shape of a semicircle: *a* semicircular *stone.*

semicircular canal ***n-*** one of three curved channels in the inner ear of higher vertebrates. They are filled with a fluid and form part of the sense organ that maintains balance. For picture, see *ear.*

sem·i·co·lon (sĕm′ ĭ kō′ lən) ***n-*** punctuation mark [;] used chiefly to show a greater separation of the parts of a sentence than that indicated by a comma.

sem·i·con·duc·tor (sĕm′ ē kən dŭk′ tər, sĕm′ ī-) ***n-*** **1** substance, such as silicon, whose electrical conductivity is between that of metals and insulators, and at sufficiently high temperatures increases with temperature. **2** electronic component made of this material.

sem·i·con·scious (sĕm′ ē kŏn′ shəs, sĕm′ ī-) ***adj-*** in a stunned or fainting condition; only partly conscious. ***—adv-*** **sem′ i·con′ scious·ly.** ***n-*** **sem′ i·con′ scious·ness.**

sem·i·dark·ness (sĕm′ ē därk′ nəs, sĕm′ ī-) ***n-*** partial darkness; twilight.

sem·i·des·ert (sĕm′ ē dĕz′ ərt, sĕm′ ī-) ***n-*** area having some of the characteristics of a desert and usually lying between a desert and a grassland.

sem·i·fi·nal (sĕm′ ē fī′ nəl, sĕm′ ī-) ***n-*** game, contest, round, etc., before the final one in a match, tournament, or the like. ***adj-*** or of having to do with such a game, contest, round, etc.

sem·i·for·mal (sĕm′ ē fôr′ məl, sĕm′ ī-, -fôr′ məl) ***n-*** event, such as a party or dance, at which formal dress may be worn but is not required. ***adj-***: *It's a* semiformal *dance.*

sem·i·month·ly (sĕm′ ē mŭnth′ lē, sĕm′ ī-) ***adj-*** occurring twice a month: *a* semimonthly *inspection.* ***n-*** a publication issued twice a month.

sem·i·nal (sĕm′ ĭ nəl) ***adj-*** **1** of, having to do with, or containing seed or semen. **2** forming or providing an original or major source for further developments, ideas, research, etc.: *a* seminal *theory*; *a* seminal *thinker.*

sem·i·nar (sĕm′ ə när′) ***n-*** **1** group of advanced students taking an advanced course that usually requires independent research and writing, under the guidance of an expert in the special field; also, the course itself. **2** meeting of such a group. *as* ***modifier***: *a* seminar *room*; *a* seminar *paper.*

sem·i·nar·i·an (sĕm′ ə nâr′ ē ən) ***n-*** seminary student.

sem·i·nar·y (sĕm′ ə nĕr′ ē) ***n-*** [*pl.* **sem·i·nar·ies**] **1** (also **theological seminary**) school that prepares its students to be clergymen. **2** *Archaic* private school of high school level. *as* ***modifier***: *a* seminary *student.*

Sem·i·nole (sĕm′ ə nōl′) ***n-*** [*pl.* **Sem·i·noles,** also **Sem·i·nole**] one of a tribe of American Indians now living mostly in Oklahoma and partly in the swamps of Florida. The Seminoles were the last tribe to submit to the United States, the final treaty being signed in 1934. ***adj-***: *the* Seminole *chief.*

sem·i·of·fi·cial (sĕm′ ē ə fĭsh′ əl, sĕm′ ī-) ***adj-*** having some, but not complete, official authority.

sem·i·per·me·a·ble (sĕm′ ē pûr′ mē ə bəl, sĕm′ ī-) ***adj-*** permeable to some substances, but not to all; separating a solvent from the dissolved substance: *a* semipermeable *membrane.*

sem·i·pre·cious (sĕm′ ē prĕsh′ əs, sĕm′ ī-) ***adj-*** of or having to do with gems, such as opals and amethysts, that are not as valuable as precious stones.

sem·i·pri·vate (sĕm′ ē prī′ vət, sĕm′ ī-) ***adj-*** not for one person, nor for many, but for two or three.

sem·i·skilled (sĕm′ ē skĭld′, sĕm′ ī-) ***adj-*** having or requiring a certain amount of skill but not a long apprenticeship or training: *a* semiskilled *job.*

Sem·ite (sĕm′ īt′) ***n-*** person whose present or ancestral language is one of the Semitic family of languages; especially, a Jew or an Arab.

Se·mit·ic (sə mĭt′ ĭk) ***adj-*** **1** of, relating to, or belonging to the Semites. **2** of or relating to a family of languages chiefly represented by Arabic and Hebrew.

sem·i·tone (sĕm′ ē tōn′) *Music* ***n-*** tone at an interval of half a step from a given tone; half step.

sem·i·trail·er (sĕm′ ē trā′ lər, sĕm′ ī-) ***n-*** large highway trailer that rides on rear wheels only, the front end being mounted over the rear wheels of a tractor; semi.

sem·i·trop·i·cal (sĕm′ ē trŏp′ ĭ kəl, sĕm′ ī-) ***adj-*** partly tropical.

sem·i·week·ly (sĕm′ ē wēk′ lē, sĕm′ ī-) ***adj-*** occurring twice a week: *a* semiweekly *paper.* ***adv-***: *The paper came out* semiweekly.

sem·o·li·na (sĕm′ ə lē′ nə) ***n-*** the large, hard grains of flour remaining after the finer grains have been sifted out. It is used in making such foods as macaroni and spaghetti. *as* ***modifier***: *a* semolina *dough.*

Sen. or **sen. 1** senate. **2** senator. **3** senior.

sen·ate (sĕn′ ət) ***n-*** **1** council or lawmaking group made up of senior persons, such as the senior faculty in many universities. **2 Senate** (1) the upper house of Congress in the United States, to which members are elected, two from each State, for a six-year term. (2) the upper house of many State legislatures. (3) the upper legislative house in Canada, Australia, France, and other countries. (4) the governing council of ancient Rome, especially of the Republic. *as* ***modifier***: *the* senate *house*; *a* Senate *committee.*

sen·a·tor (sĕn′ ə tər) ***n-*** member of a senate.

sen·a·tor·i·al (sĕn′ ə tôr′ ē əl) ***adj-*** relating to or befitting a senator or a senate: *his* senatorial *dignity.*

send (sĕnd) ***vt-*** **[sent, send·ing] 1** to cause, make, or order to go: *He* sent *a messenger.* **2** to cause to be carried or transmitted: *I* sent *a telegram.* **3** to force to go; cast; throw: *His answer* sent *me into a temper. He* sent *the ball into the stands.* **4** to transmit. ***—n-*** **send′ er.**

send around (or **round**) to circulate; distribute.
send away for to order by mail.
send flying 1 to smash violently. **2** to force to leave.
send for 1 to request someone to come; summon. **2** to ask that something be sent; place an order for.
send forth to make appear; produce.
send off 1 to mail or dispatch. **2** to give a send-off to.
send on to send ahead of the sender.
send out to give off; emit.
send packing to dismiss abruptly or forcefully.
send up *Informal* to sentence to a term in prison.

send-off (sĕnd′ ôf′) ***n-*** act of helping someone to leave on a journey or to begin a new effort or project; especially, a festivity wishing such a person success.

Sen·e·ca (sĕn′ ə kə) ***n-*** [*pl.* **Sen·e·cas,** also **Sen·e·ca**] one of the largest Iroquoian tribes that formed the Five Nations confederacy. ***adj-***: *the* Seneca *clans.*

sen·es·chal (sĕn′ ə shəl) ***n-*** official in medieval times who managed the castle of a lord.

se·nile (sĕn′ īl′, sē′ nīl′) ***adj-*** in a state of or showing senility: *a* senile *man*; senile *forgetfulness.*

se·nil·i·ty (sĭ nĭl′ ə tē) ***n-*** state of infirmity, usually mental, associated with old age; dotage.

sen·ior (sēn′ yər) ***n-*** **1** person who is older or higher in rank. **2** student in his last year of high school or college. ***adj-*** **1** older or oldest (used after the name of a father when the father and son have the same name). *Abbr.* Sr.: *Thomas Cox,* Sr. **2** higher in rank or position; longer in office: *the* senior *senator from Utah.* **3** having to do with the final year in high school or college.

senior high school ***n-*** school comprising the last three years of high school.

se·nior·i·ty (sēn yôr′ ə tē, sēn yŏr′-) ***n-*** priority because of age, rank, or length of service.

sen·na (sĕn′ ə) ***n-*** **1** any of several related plants, some of which have leaves and pods used in making medicine. **2** the medicine from these plants, used as a laxative.

se·ñor (sān yôr′) *Spanish* **1** title of courtesy equivalent to "Mr." or "sir." **2** a gentleman.

se·ño·ra (sān yôr′ ə) *Spanish* **1** title of courtesy equivalent to "Mrs." or "Madam." **2** a lady.

se·ño·ri·ta (sān′ yôr ē′ tə) *Spanish* **1** title of courtesy equivalent to "Miss." **2** a young lady.

sen·sa·tion (sĕn sā′ shən) ***n-*** **1** a feeling through the senses: *a* sensation *of hearing*; *a* sensation *of cold.* **2** a mental or emotional feeling: *a* sensation *of dread.* **3** an arousing or exciting of the senses or feelings: *It was a great* sensation *to see the Grand Canyon.* **4** general excitement and interest: *His play created a* sensation.

sen·sa·tion·al (sĕn sā′ shən əl) ***adj-*** **1** having to do with the senses. **2** thrilling; startling; extraordinary. **3** causing intense feeling, shock, thrill, etc.: *a* sensational *movie.* **—*adv-*** **sen·sa′ tion·al·ly.**

sen·sa·tion·al·ism (sĕn sā′ shən ə lĭz′ əm) ***n-*** sensational writing or language intended to please vulgar taste. **—*n-*** **sen·sa′ tion·al·ist.**

sense (sĕns) ***n-*** **1** any one of the physical powers by which an individual perceives the outside world or his own bodily changes. The five senses generally recognized are hearing, sight, smell, taste, and touch. **2** bodily feeling; sensation: *a* sense *of cold*; *a* sense *of pain.* **3** understanding; judgment; practical intelligence or wisdom: *He shows a great deal of* sense. **4** keen awareness; appreciation: *a* sense *of humor.* **5** meaning of a word or statement: *I don't intend it in that* sense. **6** (often **senses**) clear or sound mental faculties or mind; normal ability to think: *He came to his* senses. **7** that which is wise, sound, intelligent, or sensible: *to talk* sense. *as* ***modifier***: *a* sense *organ*; sense *perception.* ***vt-*** [**sensed, sens·ing**] **1** to feel or be conscious of: *I* sensed *the danger.* **2** *Informal* to understand.

in a sense from one aspect; looking at it one way: *What he says, is,* in a sense, *true.* **make sense** to be logical; to have a meaning that can be understood.

sense·less (sĕns′ ləs) ***adj-*** **1** without the power of feeling; unconscious: *The ball hit him and knocked him* senseless. **2** without meaning or sense; stupid; foolish: *a* senseless *argument.* **—*adv-*** **sense′ less·ly.** ***n-*** **sense′ less·ness.**

sense of humor ***n-*** ability to see and enjoy the absurd or amusing: *He has no* sense of humor.

sense organ ***n-*** any organ or structure specialized to perceive a particular class of stimuli. The eyes, nose, ears, tongue, and skin are sense organs.

sen·si·bil·i·ty (sĕn′ sə bĭl′ ə tē) ***n-*** [*pl.* **sen·si·bil·i·ties**] **1** capacity to feel: *the body's* sensibility *to cold.* **2** sensitiveness in feeling and perception: *an artistic* sensibility.

sen·si·ble (sĕn′ sə bəl) ***adj-*** **1** full of good sense; reasonable: *You're a* sensible *person.* **2** large enough to be felt; considerable: *a* sensible *change in the weather.* **3** aware; conscious. **—*adv-*** **sen′ si·bly.** ***n-*** **sen′ si·ble·ness.**

sen·si·tive (sĕn′ sə tĭv) ***adj-*** **1** quick to be affected by external objects or conditions: *a* sensitive *skin.* **2** responding to or recording slight shades or changes of sound, light, touch, etc.: *a* sensitive *photographic film*; sensitive *fingers.* **3** having or showing sensitivity to other people, their problems, or their work: *a* sensitive *teacher.* **—*adv-*** **sen′ si·tive·ly.** ***n-*** **sen′ si·tive·ness.**

sensitive to readily affected by or responsive to.

sensitive plant ***n-*** **1** any of several tropical mimosas having leaves that fold or droop when touched. **2** (also **wild sensitive plant**) a cassia of the United States having leaves that open and close. **3** sensitive person.

sen·si·tiv·i·ty (sĕn′ sə tĭv′ ə tē) ***n-*** [*pl.* **sen·si·tiv·i·ties**] **1** condition of being sensitive. **2** *Biology* (1) ability of an organism or sense organ to respond to a stimulus. (2) degree of responsiveness to stimulation. **3** in electricity, degree to which a receiving set reacts to incoming radio waves. **4** in photography, degree to which a photographic plate, film, etc., responds to light.

sen·si·tize (sĕn′ sə tīz′) ***vt-*** [**sen·si·tized, sen·si·tiz·ing**] **1** to make sensitive or responsive. **2** of a photographic plate or film, to make susceptible to the action of light, X rays, etc. **3** to make (the cells of the body) hypersensitive to some foreign substance, so that its presence will cause a typical reaction. **—*n-*** **sen′ si·tiz′ er.**

sen·sor (sĕn′ sôr′, -sər) ***n-*** instrument or device, such as a photoelectric cell, designed to receive and respond to a physical stimulus and transmit a resulting impulse for interpretation or measurement or for operating a control.

sen·so·ry (sĕn′ sə rē) ***adj-*** **1** of or relating to the senses or sensation: *a* sensory *impression.* **2** conveying sense impulses: *a* sensory *nerve.*

sensory nerve ***n-*** nerve that conveys impulses from the sense organs to the spinal cord or brain.

sen·su·al (sĕn′ sho͞o əl) ***adj-*** **1** having to do with or associated with the pleasures of the body; not mental or spiritual: *a* sensual *life.* **2** indulging in the pleasures of the body, especially sexual pleasure. **3** appealing to sexual pleasure; voluptuous; fleshy. **4** sensuous. **—*adv-*** **sen′ su·al·ly.** ***n-*** **sen′ su·al′ i·ty.**

►Both SENSUAL and SENSUOUS refer to the senses. SENSUAL suggests something gross or excessive or lewd. SENSUOUS suggests something more delicate and refined.

sen·su·al·ist (sĕn′ sho͞o ə lĭst) ***n-*** person who indulges in sensual pleasure.

sen·su·ous (sĕn′ sho͞o əs) ***adj-*** **1** having to do with or appealing to the senses: *his* sensuous *music.* **2** resembling sensation or sense imagery: *her* sensuous *narration of the poem.* **3** readily responding to sense impression or the pleasures to be received through the senses. **—*adv-*** **sen′ su·ous·ly.** ***n-*** **sen′ su·ous·ness.**

►For usage note see SENSUAL.

sent (sĕnt) *p.t.* and *p.p.* of **send.** ***Homs-*** cent, scent.

sentence (sĕn′ təns) ***n-*** **1** *Grammar* group of words that is separate from any other grammatical construction, consists of at least one subject with its predicate, and must contain a finite verb or verb phrase. See also *simple sentence, complex sentence, compound sentence.* 2 *Mathematics* expression that uses numerals and symbols to show the relationships between numbers. The assertion that the difference between two numbers is 9, and the lesser number is 5, can be written as n — 5 = 9. *as* ***modifier***: *good* sentence *structure.*

sentence modifier ***n-*** word or phrase that modifies a complete statement, rather than any particular word or phrase within the statement. Examples: Surely *you are not going to go now.* To be certain, *I'll ask him.*

sen·ten·tious (sĕn tĕn′ shəs) ***adj-*** 1 short and energetic in expression; pithy. 2 containing, using, or likely to use pompous or moralizing language: *a* sententious *speech.* ***—adv-*** **sen·ten′ tious·ly.** ***n-*** **sen·ten′ tious·ness.**

sen·tient (sĕn′ chənt) ***adj-*** having the power of sense or sense impression; having the ability to feel or to perceive: *Stones are not* sentient. ***—adv-*** **sen′ tient·ly.**

sen·ti·ment (sĕn′ tə mənt) ***n-*** 1 feeling; emotion: *a painting that shows deep* sentiment; *a novel full of mushy* sentiment. 2 (often **sentiments**) conviction; belief; opinion: *We must find out the* sentiment *of the people.* 3 thought or meaning as distinct from form or expression: *This is an ugly card, but I appreciate the* sentiment.

sen·ti·men·tal (sĕn′ tə mĕn′ təl) ***adj-*** 1 easily moved and touched by emotions; tender in feeling: *a* sentimental *person.* 2 appealing deliberately and chiefly to the emotions rather than to reason: *The play was far too sweet and* sentimental. 3 of or caused by sentiment or nostalgia. ***—adv-*** **sen′ ti·men′ tal·ly.**

sen·ti·men·tal·ism (sĕn′ tə mĕn′ tə lĭz′ əm) ***n-*** 1 tendency to be guided by feelings rather than reason; emotionalism; sentimentality. 2 behavior of one guided by feeling rather than reason. ***—n-*** **sen′ ti·men′ tal·ist.**

sen·ti·men·tal·i·ty (sĕn′ tə mən tăl′ ə tē) ***n-*** condition of being sentimental, especially excessively sentimental.

sen·ti·men·tal·ize (sĕn′ tə mĕn′ tə līz′) ***vt-*** [**sen·ti·men·tal·ized, sen·ti·men·tal·iz·ing**] to treat with excessive sentiment; give a weakly sentimental character to: *The author* sentimentalized *the hero.* ***vi-*** to behave in, or to regard in, an excessively sentimental manner. ***—n-*** **sen′ ti·men′ tal·i·za′ tion.**

sen·ti·nel (sĕn′ tə nəl) ***n-*** person, trained animal, fort, etc., that guards and keeps watch; sentry.

sen·try (sĕn′ trē) ***n-*** [*pl.* **sen·tries**] person, especially in the armed forces, stationed to prevent illegal passing or to warn of approaching danger; guard.

se·pal (sē′ pəl) ***n-*** one of the divisions of the calyx of a flower, usually small and leaflike, but sometimes brightly colored and like a petal. For picture, see *flower.*

sep·a·ra·ble (sĕp′ ər ə bəl) ***adj-*** such as can be separated. ***—n-*** **sep′ a·ra·bil′ i·ty.** ***adv-*** **sep′ a·ra·bly.**

[1]**sep·a·rate** (sĕp′ ə rāt′) ***vt-*** [**sep·a·rat·ed, sep·a·rat·ing**] 1 to divide: *A river* separates *the two parts of the city.* 2 to set apart; place in or as if in groups: *He* separated *truth from fiction.* 3 to take away from or out of: *Mom* separated *the cream from the milk.* ***vi-*** 1 to withdraw from an association: *After five years of marriage the couple* separated. 2 to become divided; branch; spread apart: *The trunk* separated *into branches.*

[2]**sep·a·rate** (sĕp′ ər ət) ***adj-*** 1 branching; different: *to go* separate *ways.* 2 taken one by one; individual: *Let's question each* separate *child.* 3 distinct; individual; apart; not joined: *The children have* separate *rooms.* ***n-*** **separates** pieces of clothing sold individually, but designed to be worn with certain other articles of clothing. ***—adv-*** **sep′ a·rate·ly.**

sep·a·ra·tion (sĕp′ ə rā′ shən) ***n-*** 1 a separating or being separated. 2 a line, boundary, or gap: *the large* separation *between his front teeth.* 3 an official parting of a husband and wife without divorce.

sep·a·ra·tism (sĕp′ ər ə tĭz′ əm) ***n-*** a belief in, or the upholding of, a policy of separation or secession.

sep·a·ra·tist (sĕp′ ə rə tĭst) ***n-*** 1 person who advocates separation or secession. 2 **Separatist** person belonging to a religious movement of the seventeenth century, the members of which separated completely from the Church of England. The Pilgrims were Separatists.

sep·a·ra·tive (sĕp′ ər ə tĭv) ***adj-*** having to do with, tending to cause, or causing separation.

sep·a·ra·tor (sĕp′ ə rā′ tər) ***n-*** 1 person or thing that divides or separates. 2 mechanical device used to separate one thing from another: *a cream* separator.

se·pi·a (sē′ pē ə) ***n-*** 1 dark-brown pigment made from the inky secretion of the cuttlefish. 2 color of this pigment. ***adj-***: *rich* sepia *tones in a painting.*

se·poy (sē′ poi′) ***n-*** native of India serving as a soldier for the British or other foreign government.

sep·sis (sĕp′ səs) ***n-*** blood poisoning caused by disease germs and their toxins in the blood; septicemia.

Sept. September.

Sep·tem·ber (sĕp tĕm′ bər) ***n-*** the ninth month of the year. September has 30 days.

sep·tet (sĕp tĕt′) ***n-*** 1 any group of seven. 2 *Music* composition for seven instruments or seven voices; also, this group of seven musicians. Also **sep·tette′.**

sep·tic (sĕp′ tĭk) ***adj-*** 1 having to do with poisoning or decay of animal tissue by germs. 2 infected by germs.

sep·ti·ce·mi·a (sĕp′ tə sē′ mē ə) ***n-*** sepsis.

septic tank ***n-*** tank for sewage in which bacteria destroy the refuse and kill harmful germs.

sep·tu·a·ge·nar·i·an (sĕp′ to͞o ə jə nâr′ ē ən) ***n-*** person who is seventy to seventy-nine years old. *as* ***modifier***: *my* septuagenarian *grandparents.*

Sep·tu·a·gint (sĕp to͞o′ ə jĭnt) ***n-*** Greek version of the Old Testament made in Alexandria between 280 and 130 B.C. and used by the early Christian church.

sep·tum (sĕp′ təm) *Biology* ***n-*** [*pl.* **sep·ta** (-tə)] 1 The partition between the two channels of the nose. 2 any dividing wall or partition between two cavities or masses of softer tissue.

sep·ul·cher or **sep·ul·chre** (sĕp′ əl kər) ***n-*** 1 tomb or grave. 2 receptacle for religious relics, especially one that is built into an altar; repository.

se·pul·chral (sə pŭl′ krəl) ***adj-*** 1 of or relating to a tomb or burial. 2 gloomy; funereal: *He spoke in a* sepulchral *voice.*

sep·ul·ture (sĕp′ əl cho͝or′) ***n-*** burial.

se·quel (sē′ kwəl) ***n-*** 1 something that follows or comes after: *Winter is the* sequel *of fall.* 2 result or consequence: *Anger was the* sequel *of their argument.* 3 literary work that further develops the story of a previous work.

se·quence (sē′ kwəns) ***n-*** 1 the coming of one thing after another; a succession; also, the order in which things occur or are arranged: *the* sequence *of words in a sentence.* 2 a number of things following one another; continuous or connected series: *a* sequence *of plays in a game*; *a sonnet* sequence. 3 *Mathematics* an ordered set of elements or quantities, arranged so that there is a first element or term, a second, a third, etc. Example: 1, 1/2, 1/3, 1/4, 1/5, ... 4 *Music* repetition of a musical phrase at a higher or lower pitch than the original. 5 in card games, a set of three or more cards of the same suit immediately following one another in value, such as the jack, queen, and king.

se·quent (sē′ kwənt) ***adj-*** following in order; succeeding.

se·quen·tial (sĭ kwĕn′ shəl) ***adj-*** 1 of or relating to a sequence. 2 sequent. ***—adv-*** **se·quen′ tial·ly.**

se·ques·ter (sĭ kwĕs′ tər) *vt-* **1** to withdraw; seclude; isolate; separate: *He sequestered himself in order to study.* **2** to seize (property) until some claim is satisfied.

se·ques·tra·tion (sē′ kwə strā′ shən, sē′ kwĕs′-) *n-* a sequestering or being sequestered: *He protested against the* sequestration *of the shipment by the government.*

se·quin (sē′ kwən) *n-* **1** in former times, a gold coin of Italy and Turkey. **2** spangle decoration on clothing.

se·quoi·a (sĭ kwoi′ ə) *n-* **1** the redwood. **2** the big tree. [American word from the name of the Cherokee chief, **Sikwayi,** who invented the Cherokee system of writing.]

se·ra (sêr′ ə) *pl.* of **serum.**

se·ragl·io (sə răl′ yō, -räl′ yō) *n-* harem.

se·ra·pe (sə rä′ pē) *n-* wool blanket, often in bright colors, worn by Mexican men around the shoulders; sarape. [American word from Mexican Spanish.]

ser·aph (sĕr′ əf) *n-* [*pl.* **ser·aphs** or **ser·a·phim** (-ə fĭm′)] one of the highest order of angels.

se·raph·ic (sə răf′ ĭk) *adj-* **1** of or having to do with a seraph. **2** angelic; heavenly. ***—adv-* se·raph′ i·cal·ly.**

sere (sêr) *adj-* withered; dried up: *the* sere *leaves of autumn.* ***Homs-*** sear, seer.

ser·e·nade (sĕr′ ə nād′) *n-* **1** music sung or played at night, usually beneath a lady's window and in her honor. **2** musical composition for small orchestra, resembling a suite. **3** a singing or playing of such music. *vt-* [**ser·e·nad·ed, ser·e·nad·ing**] to sing or play such music to: *Let's go* serenade *the girls.* ***—n-* ser′ e·nad′ er.**

ser·en·dip·i·ty (sĕr′ ən dĭp′ ə tē) *n-* **1** lucky knack of finding important things by accident. **2** an instance of such a knack or discovery. ***—adj-* ser′ en·dip′ i·tous.**

se·rene (sə rēn′) *adj-* **1** calm; peaceful: *a* serene *sea*; *a* serene *disposition.* **2 Serene** title for certain rulers, preceded by "His": *His* Serene *Highness.* ***—adv-* se·rene′ly.**

se·ren·i·ty (sə rĕn′ ə tē) *n-* calmness; peacefulness; also, composure: *The noise did not disturb her* serenity.

serf (sûrf) *n-* **1** in the Middle Ages, a person who could not leave the land he worked on and who was usually sold with it. **2** a slave. ***Hom-*** surf.

serf·dom (sûrf′ dəm) *n-* **1** condition of being a serf. **2** condition of servitude; slavery.

serge (sûrj) *n-* woolen material woven with slanting ribs, used for clothing. *as **modifier**: a pair of* serge *trousers.* ***Hom-*** surge.

ser·geant (sär′ jənt) *n-* **1** in the Army and Marine Corps, a noncommissioned officer who ranks below a warrant officer and above a corporal. **2** in the Air Force, a noncommissioned officer who ranks below a warrant officer and above an airman. **3** officer ranking below a lieutenant in a police department, fire department, etc.

sergeant at arms *n-* [*pl.* **sergeants at arms**] officer of a legislative or other official group, who is responsible for keeping order at meetings.

sergeant major *n-* in the Army and Marine Corps, a noncommissioned officer who ranks below a warrant officer but above all other noncommissioned officers.

se·ri·al (sêr′ ē əl) *n-* story told in one installment after another in a magazine, on television, etc. *adj-* **1** of, having to do with, or arranged in a series, rank, or order. **2** occurring or happening in installments: *a* serial *motion picture.* ***Hom-*** cereal. ***—adv-* se′ ri·al·ly.**

se·ri·al·ize (sêr′ ē ə līz′) *vt-* [**se·ri·al·ized, se·ri·al·iz·ing**] to arrange, publish, or show in a serial form.

serial number *n-* number that corresponds to and identifies a particular individual in a numbered series of persons, machines, etc.

ser·i·cul·ture (sĕr′ ə kŭl′ chər) *n-* the breeding of silkworms for the production of raw silk.

se·ries (sêr′ ēz) *n-* [*pl.* **se·ries**] **1** a number of things or events following one another in regular order or succession: *a* series *of games.* **2** *Mathematics* the indicated sum of a sequence. Example: $1 + \frac{1}{2} + \frac{1}{3} + \frac{1}{4} + \frac{1}{5} + \ldots$ **3** in electricity, an arrangement of the elements in an electric circuit so that the positive electrode of any given element is connected to the negative electrode of another element.

se·ries-wound (sêr′ ēz wound′) *adj-* of a motor or generator, having a winding in which the field-magnet coil and the armature coil are connected in series.

se·ri·o·com·ic (sêr′ ē ō kŏm′ ĭk) *adj-* having a mixture of seriousness and humor. ***—adv-* se′ri·o·com′i·cal·ly.**

se·ri·ous (sêr′ ē əs) *adj-* **1** thoughtful; grave; solemn: *That young man has a* serious *manner for his age.* **2** not frivolous or trifling; in earnest: *A good worker is* serious *about his job.* **3** demanding thought and attention: *a* serious *book.* **4** important because of possible danger: *a* serious *illness.* ***—adv-* se′ ri·ous·ly.** ***n-* se′ ri·ous·ness.**

se·ri·ous-mind·ed (sêr′ ē əs mīn′ dəd) *adj-* **1** having a serious personality. **2** occupied with serious thoughts.

ser·mon (sûr′ mən) *n-* **1** public talk on religion or morals, usually delivered as part of a religious service by a clergyman. **2** any serious talk on morals, behavior, duty, etc.

ser·mon·ize (sûr′ mə nīz′) *vi-* [**ser·mon·ized, ser·mon·iz·ing**] **1** to compose or write a sermon. **2** to preach. ***—n-* ser′ mon·iz′ er.**

Sermon on the Mount *n-* in the New Testament, the discourse of Jesus, as recorded in Matthew and Luke, that presents the principles of Christian conduct.

se·rol·o·gy (sə rŏl′ ə jē) *n-* science dealing with serums and their use in treating disease. ***—n-* se·rol′ o·gist.**

se·rous (sêr′ əs) *adj-* **1** of, relating to, or like serum; also, containing or producing serum. **2** thin and watery.

ser·pent (sûr′ pənt) *n-* **1** snake or dragon. **2** the devil. **3** sly, deceitful person.

ser·pen·tine (sûr′ pən tēn′, -tīn′) *adj-* **1** having to do with or resembling a snake. **2** curving in and out; winding; sinuous: *a* serpentine *road.* **3** sly and crafty; cunning; diabolic. *n-* **1** something that moves or winds in and out. **2** spotted green mineral resembling marble, used in making asbestos and for decorative stonework.

ser·rate (sĕr′ āt′, sĕr′ ət) *adj-* **1** having notches along the edge, like a saw: *a* serrate *leaf.* **2** notched: *a* serrate *edge.* Also **ser′ rat·ed.**

ser·ra·tion (sĕr′ ā′ shən, sə rā′-) *n-* **1** condition of having notches along the edge, like a saw. **2** one of the projections or teeth on a serrate edge.

ser·ried (sĕr′ ēd) *adj-* close together; crowded together; compact: *the* serried *ranks of soldiers.*

se·rum (sêr′ əm) *n-* [*pl.* **se·rums** or **se·ra** (-rə)] **1** yellowish, clear, watery fluid that remains after blood has clotted. **2** such a fluid, taken from the blood of an animal that has been rendered immune to some disease by inoculation, and used to fight the same disease in other animals or human beings. **3** any serous secretion, such as chyle or lymph.

ser·val (sûr′ vəl) *n-* black-spotted African wildcat with long legs and a ringed tail.

ser·vant (sûr′ vənt) *n-* **1** person who works as a maid, butler, footman, chauffeur, etc., for wages. **2** person who dedicates himself or offers his services to a belief, cause, government, etc.: *a* servant *of God*; *a public* servant.

serve (sûrv) ***vt-*** **[served, serv·ing] 1** to provide (food, a meal, etc.): *Mrs. Allen* served *fried chicken.* **2** to wait upon (persons) at a table or in a shop: *The waiter* served *us quickly.* **3** to obey and honor: *to* serve *God.* **4** to take an interest in the welfare of; make a contribution to: *He* served *the cause of science.* **5** be useful to: *The old car* served *me all summer.* **6** to be sufficient for: *This cake* serves *eight people.* **7** to go through the time or period of: *to* serve *three terms in the legislature*; *to* serve *a sentence.* **8** to deliver: *I* served *a summons on him.* **9** to supply (customers) at regular or stated times. **10** to work for, especially as a servant or underling. **11** in games, such as tennis, to put (the ball or shuttlecock) into play. ***vi-*** **1** to discharge a duty of office or position: *He* served *as president.* **2** to be a soldier, sailor, airman, etc.: *I* served *in the navy.* **3** to act as a substitute; be sufficient: *The sleeping bag* served *as a bed.* **4** to be favorable; be correct: *when the occasion* serves. **5** in games, such as tennis, to start the ball or shuttlecock going by sending it to an opponent as the first stroke. ***n-*** in games, such as tennis, the sending of a ball or shuttlecock into play; also, the ball so sent and the turn for sending: *It's your* serve.

serve (one) right to be exactly what one deserves.

serv·er (sûr′ vər) ***n-*** **1** person who serves. **2** tray for dishes. **3** one who assists the priest at church services.

ser·vice (sûr′ vəs) ***n-*** **1** employment: *ten years in the* service *of this company.* **2** devotion of one's time, energy, etc., over a period of time: *He was rewarded for outstanding* service. **3** period of time one serves in the armed forces: *a veteran of ten years'* service. **4** a providing of something useful, especially to the public and for pay; also, that which is provided: *laundry* service; *telephone* service; *postal* service. **5** manner of providing food and help: *The* service *here is very good.* **6** set of articles for use in giving food or drink: *a silver tea* service. **7** religious ceremony: *the wedding* service; *the ten o'clock* service. **8** in the armed forces, a branch, such as the medical or quartermaster department, whose duty is to provide materiel or aid rather than to fight. **9** the serving of the ball in tennis. **10** care and repair: *The dealer handles both sales and* service. **11** efficiency and dependability in operation: *This machine has given me good* service. **12** official delivery: *the* service *of a subpoena.* **13 the service** the armed forces: *Have you been in* the service? **14 services** (1) professional attention; skillful aid: *You need the* services *of a doctor.* (2) economic activities other than manufacturing. *as* ***modifier***: *the* service *manager*; *his* service *uniform.* ***vt-*** **[ser·viced, ser·vic·ing]** to repair and maintain.

at (someone's) service available for use: *The car is at your* service. **in service 1** operating. **2** *Brit.* working as a servant. **of service** helpful; useful.

ser·vice·a·ble (sûr′ vĭs ə bəl) ***adj-*** **1** useful. **2** capable of withstanding long use or wear: *an overcoat of* serviceable *material.* **—*n-* ser′ vice·a·bil′ i·ty.** ***adv-*** **ser′ vice·a·bly.**

ser·vice·man (sûr′ vəs mən) ***n-*** [*pl.* **ser·vice·men**] **1** male member of the armed forces. **2** man who services or maintains equipment. **—*n-* *fem.* ser′ vice·wo′ man.**

service station ***n-*** filling station.

ser·vi·ette (sər vyĕt′) *chiefly Brit.* ***n-*** table napkin.

ser·vile (sûr′ vĭl′, -vəl) ***adj-*** **1** behaving like a slave; lacking self-respect; extremely obsequious: *his* servile *temperament.* **2** relating to or consisting of slaves: *the* servile *laws of Rome*; servile *labor.* **—*adv-* ser′ vile·ly.** ***n-*** **ser·vil′ i·ty** (sər vĭl′ ə tē).

ser·vi·tor (sûr′ və tər) ***n-*** male servant.

ser·vi·tude (sûr′ və to͞od′, -tyo͞od′) ***n-*** **1** lack of freedom; slavery; bondage. **2** work enforced as a punishment.

ser·vo·mech·a·nism (sûr′ vō mĕk′ ə nĭz′ əm) ***n-*** any of various devices that automatically control and regulate machinery, in response to a system of electrical signals.

ses·a·me (sĕs′ ə mē) ***n-*** East Indian plant that yields **sesame seed,** used in making oil and as a flavoring.

ses·qui·cen·ten·ni·al (sĕs′ kwĭ sĕn′ tĕn′ ē əl) ***n-*** 150th anniversary, or its celebration.

ses·sile (sĕs′ ĭl′) ***adj-*** **1** attached directly at its base; having no stalk: *a* sessile *leaf.* **2** permanently attached to a base of support, such as oysters, sponges, or certain crustaceans.

ses·sion (sĕsh′ ən) ***n-*** **1** a meeting of a court, council, lawmaking body, or the like. **2** series of such meetings, and the time covered by them: *a* session *of Congress.*

in session now meeting: *School is* in session.

ses·tet (sĕs tĕt′) ***n-*** last six lines of a sonnet; also, a stanza or poem of six lines.

[1]**set** (sĕt) ***vt-*** **[set, set·ting] 1** to place or fix in position; put: *He* set *the baby in the chair.* **2** to put in order; make ready for use; regulate: *Please* set *the clock. He* set *the dial. I will* set *the trap.* **3** to place permanently; cause to be solid or firm: *He* set *the brick with cement.* **4** to make (something, such as a color) permanent or fast. **5** to put (someone or something) into a specified condition: *They* set *the field on fire. He will* set *the prisoner free.* **6** to start: *He* set *the men to work. I* set *him on his way.* **7** to plan or arrange: *He* set *his arrival for noon. She* set *the schedule.* **8** to assign: *He* set *a guard at the post.* **9** to prepare (a table) for eating. **10** to mount or place (something, such as a gem) in a setting. **11** to adorn with; decorate: *He* set *the crown with jewels.* **12** to arrange (hair) in a special way, usually with some kind of lotion. **13** to put (a broken bone) into a position to knit. **14** in printing, to arrange (type) in words, lines, etc.; also, to put (copy, manuscript, etc.) into type; compose. **15** to adapt (words) to music: *In this song the composer* set *a poem by Robert Frost.* **16** to put forth; pose: *He* set *an interesting question. Don't* set *a bad example.* ***vi-*** **1** to sink below the horizon: *The moon* sets *early at this time of the month.* **2** to become firm or rigid: *The cement* set *overnight.* **3** to fit or hang: *This coat* sets *well.* **4** to flow; tend: *The current* sets *north.* **5** of a broken bone, to mend. **6** of a fowl, to sit upon a nest of eggs. ***adj-*** **1** fixed; established; firm; rigid: *a* set *time for a play; a* set *opinion; the* set *smile on his face.* **2** formed; built: *a heavy-*set *man.* **3** prepared to begin immediately: *On your mark! Get* set! *Go!* ***n-*** **1** a setting or being set. **2** complete scenic unit used in the theater, motion pictures, or television: *The opera had a complex* set *in the first act.* **3** the sinking of something below the horizon: *the* set *of the moon.* **4** flow or direction of a wind or current. **5** posture; arrangement: *the* set *of her head.* **6** way something fits or hangs: *the* set *of his coat.* **7** permanent change of form, as of a metal, due to excessive stress or a chemical change. [from old English **settan,** from **sittan** meaning "to sit; cause to sit."]

all set ready: *I'm all* set.

set about to start (a task).

set against 1 to compare with for the purpose of judging. **2** to cause to be hostile toward.

set apart 1 to distinguish (from). **2** in religion, to choose for a special purpose.

set a record to surpass previous achievements.

set aside 1 to place to one side for a purpose; save. **2** to discard or dismiss. **3** in law, to declare null and void.

set back 1 to hinder or retard the progress of: *The mistake* set *me* back *for a long time.* **2** *Informal* to cost.

set down 1 to put in writing or print. **2** to consider; judge. **3** to attribute: *I'll* set *that* down *to ignorance.*

set eyes on to see: *I first* set eyes on *her last week.*
set foot in to enter.
set forth 1 to publish. 2 to declare or express in words. 3 to start out on a journey.
set in 1 to enter, or cause to be in, a particular condition: *Summer seemed to* set in *early this year. He* set *the machine* in *motion.* 2 of a wind, tide, or current, to blow or flow toward the shore.
set off 1 to explode: *We* set off *the fireworks.* 2 to make more striking by contrast; enhance: *The gray suit* set off *his bright tie.* 3 to start; begin.
set on (or **upon**) to attack or urge to attack.
set out 1 to start, especially on a journey or a career: *He* set out *for Europe.* 2 to display or exhibit. 3 to lay out; arrange: *They* set out *the boundary of the town.* 4 to have the intention of: *He* set out *to win.*
set to 1 to start: *The children* set to *work.* 2 to start fighting. 3 to start eating.
set up 1 to put or place in an upright position. 2 to put or place in a position of authority: *We* set *him* up *as leader of the committee.* 3 to put the parts together, or to put in working order: *He* set up *the train set.* 4 to provide with the means of establishing something: *He* set up *his son in a new apartment.* 5 to plan carefully.
►For usage note see SIT.

[2]**set** (sĕt) ***n-*** 1 a group of things that belong together and are used together: *a chemistry* set; set *of golf clubs;* set *of dishes.* 2 group of people united by a common interest: *the jazz* set. 3 in tennis, a group of games in which one side wins at least six games and leads the other side by two or more games. 4 an electrical apparatus that receives radio signals: *a television* set. 5 the number of couples needed in a square dance; also, their arrangement. 6 *Mathematics* collection of elements (objects, quantities, etc.) having a certain characteristic or property that distinguishes the elements within the collection from all other elements in the universe. [from Old French **sette,** from Latin **secta,** "a group; cut off."]

Set (sĕt) ***n-*** in Egyptian mythology, the god of evil and darkness, usually represented with a strange animal head.

se·ta (sē′ tə) ***n-*** [*pl.* **se·tae** (-tē′)] 1 in zoology, a bristly organ or part of an animal, such as the hairlike processes on the underside of an earthworm. 2 in botany, a fine, slender stalk or bristle.

set·back (sĕt′ băk′) ***n-*** 1 a stop; check to progress or advancement: *Money troubles caused a temporary* setback *in his education.* 2 distance that something is set back from anything: *a ten-foot* setback *from the curb.*

Seth (sĕth) ***n-*** in the Old Testament, Adam's third son.

set screw ***n-*** screw designed to be screwed through one part and to jam tightly upon another so as to bind the parts together.

set·tee (sĕ tē′) ***n-*** long seat or short sofa with a back and arms.

set·ter (sĕt′ ər) ***n-*** kind of bird dog with long, silky black-and-white or red hair. Setters are trained to stand rigid and point with the muzzle when they scent game.

Irish setter, about 27 in. at shoulder

set·ting (sĕt′ ĭng) ***n-*** 1 the surroundings, environment, and background of anything: *The novel has an ancient Grecian* setting. 2 framework in which a jewel is securely held: *Mother's diamond ring has a gold* setting. 3 music that is composed for a special story or poem. 4 scenery, costumes, and background for a play or opera. 5 eggs on which a brooding hen sets.

[1]**set·tle** (sĕt′ əl) ***vt-*** [**set·tled, set·tling**] 1 to put in order. 2 to put (something) firmly or evenly in place. 3 to relieve discomfort or tension in: *Knitting* settled *her nerves.* 4 to cause to sink or subside: *The rain* settled *the dust.* 5 to make impurities or dregs sink: *He* settled *the coffee.* 6 to adjust or decide finally; agree upon: *He* settled *the argument. We* settled *the price.* 7 to pay. 8 to populate; colonize. ***vi-*** 1 to sink gradually: *Dust* settled *on the piano.* 2 to sink slightly so as to become more firmly or evenly based: *A new house* settles *after a few years.* 3 to come to rest: *The parakeet* settled *on my finger.* 4 to make one's home: *We* settled *in a distant town.* 5 to compose oneself; make oneself comfortable: *Dad* settled *in his easy chair.* 6 to pay a bill (often followed by "up"). [from Old English **setlan** meaning "to fix; take a seat," from **setl,** "[2]**settle,"** and **sahtlian,** "to reconcile."]
settle down 1 to settle in a specific place or in a fixed way of life. 2 to begin to act or work in an orderly fashion.
settle on (or **upon**) in law, to give someone possession of money or property.

[2]**set·tle** (sĕt′ əl) ***n-*** old-fashioned, long, wooden seat with arms and a high, straight back. [from Old English **setl** meaning "a seat," and related to **sit** and [1]**set.**]

set·tle·ment (sĕt′ əl mənt) ***n-*** 1 group of dwellings; town, village: *a* settlement *on the banks of the river.* 2 the deciding of a disagreement or legal conflict, especially about money or property: *The two parties reached a* settlement. *We made a* settlement *out of court.* 3 a settling of a new region: *They encourage the* settlement *of the Yukon.* 4 property or money given as a legal gift: *a large marriage* settlement. 5 settlement house.

settlement house ***n-*** community house, often in the poorer section of a city, which gives instruction, recreation, and advice to people in the section.

set·tler (sĕt′ lər) ***n-*** person who makes his home in a new, or newly developed, country; colonist.

set-to (sĕt′ to͞o′) ***n-*** [*pl.* **set-tos**] quarrel; fight.

set·up (sĕt′ ŭp′) ***n-*** 1 structure or plan of an organization. 2 state of things; situation: *He explained the* setup *to us before we attacked.* 3 silverware, napkin, etc., arranged for serving a meal to one person. 4 a glass, ice, soda water, etc., to which whiskey or other liquor is added to make a drink. 5 *Informal* fight, contest, etc., which one side is certain to lose; also, the losing side or person.

sev·en (sĕv′ ən) ***n-*** 1 amount or quantity that is one greater than 6. 2 *Mathematics* (1) the cardinal number that is the sum of 6 and 1. (2) numeral such as 7 that represents this cardinal number. *as* ***determiner*** (traditionally called adjective or pronoun): *There are* seven *sticks here and* seven *there.*

sev·en·fold (sĕv′ ən fōld′) ***adj-*** 1 seven times as many or as much. 2 having seven parts. ***adv-***: *The machine increased production* sevenfold.

Seven Seas ***n-*** *pl.* the oceans of the world: the North Atlantic, South Atlantic, North Pacific, South Pacific, Indian, Arctic, and (formerly) the Antarctic.

sev·en·teen (sĕv′ ən tēn′) ***n-*** 1 amount or quantity that is one greater than 16. 2 *Mathematics* (1) the cardinal number that is the sum of 16 and 1. (2) a numeral such as 17 that represents this cardinal number. *as* ***determiner*** (traditionally called adjective or pronoun): *There are* seventeen *trees here and* seventeen *there.*

sev·en·teenth (sĕv′ən tēnth′) ***adj-*** **1** next after sixteenth. **2** the ordinal of 17; 17th. ***n-*** **1** the next after the sixteenth; 17th. **2** one of seventeen equal parts of a whole or group. **3** the last term in the name of a fraction having a denominator of 17: *1/17 is one* seventeenth.

sev·enth (sĕv′ənth) ***adj-*** **1** next after sixth. **2** the ordinal of 7; 7th. ***n-*** **1** the next after the sixth; 7th. **2** one of seven equal parts of a whole or group. **3** the last term in the name of a fraction having a denominator of 7: *1/7 is one* seventh. **4** *Music* an interval of seven tones on the scale counting the extremes, as from C to B; also, the harmonic combination of these tones. ***adv-***: *He spoke of him* seventh.

Seventh-Day Adventist ***n-*** a member of a Protestant denomination in the United States that emphasizes preparation for the second coming of Christ, and has Saturday as its chief day of rest instead of Sunday.

seventh heaven ***n-*** in ancient astronomy and some theologies, the seventh and highest of the heavens; hence, extreme or perfect happiness.

sev·en·ti·eth (sĕv′ən tē əth) ***adj-*** **1** next after sixty-ninth. **2** the ordinal of 70; 70th. ***n-*** **1** the next after the sixty-ninth; 70th. **2** one of seventy equal parts of a whole or group. **3** the last term in the name of a fraction having a denominator of 70: *1/70 is one* seventieth.

sev·en·ty (sĕv′ən tē) ***n-*** [*pl.* **sev·en·ties**] **1** amount or quantity that is one greater than 69. **2** *Mathematics* (1) the cardinal number that is the sum of 69 and 1. (2) a numeral such as 70 that represents this number. *as* ***determiner*** (traditionally called adjective or pronoun): *There are* seventy *eggs here and* seventy *there.*

sev·er (sĕv′ər) ***vt-*** **1** to cut off; divide; cut in two: *to* sever *the limb of a tree.* **2** to break off (a relationship). ***vi-*** to be torn apart. **—*adj-*** **sev′er·a·ble.**

sev·er·al (sĕv′ər əl) ***determiner*** (traditionally called adjective or pronoun) three or more, but not many: *There are* several *new people in this room, and* several *in the other.* ***n-***: *In that village,* several *of the houses are white.* ***adj-*** separate; respective.

sev·er·al·ly (sĕv′ər ə lē) ***adv-*** individually; singly.

sev·er·ance (sĕv′ər əns) ***n-*** **1** a severing. **2** the condition of being severed; separation. **3** termination of employment. *as* ***modifier***: *a* severance *payment.*

se·vere (sə vêr′) ***adj-*** [**se·ver·er, se·ver·est**] **1** strict; grave; stern: *a* severe *schoolmaster.* **2** simple; very plain: *a* severe *dress.* **3** sharp; extreme: *a* severe *pain*; *a* severe *cold.* **4** hard; difficult: *a* severe *exam.* **5** extreme and very serious: *a* severe *drought.* **—*adv-*** **se·vere′ly.** ***n-*** **se·ver′i·ty** (sə vĕr′ə tē) or **se·vere′ness.**

sew (sō) ***vt-*** [**sewed, sewed** or **sewn, sew·ing**] to make, fasten, or mend with stitches, using a needle and thread or a sewing machine: *She* sewed *a dress.* ***vi-***: *She* sews *beautifully.* ***Homs-*** so, [2]sow.

sew up 1 to close with stitches. **2** *Informal* to complete successfully; make sure of: *He* sewed up *the deal.*

sew·age (sōō′ĭj) ***n-*** waste matter carried off by sewers. Also **sew′er·age** (sōō′ər ĭj).

[1]**sew·er** (sōō′ər) ***n-*** underground pipe or drain that carries off waste matter and water from buildings, streets, towns, etc. *as* ***modifier***: *a* sewer *system.* [from Old French **se(u)wiere,** "drainage sluice," from Late Latin **exaquāria,** from **ex-,** "out" and **aqua,** "water."]

[2]**sew·er** (sō′ər) ***n-*** person who sews. [from **sew.**]

sew·ing (sō′ĭng) ***n-*** **1** a making of stitches. **2** anything to be sewed; needlework. **3** work of someone who sews.

sewing machine ***n-*** any of various machines that sew.

sewn (sōn) *p.p.* of **sew.**

sex (sĕks) ***n-*** **1** one of two groups into which human beings and most animals are divided: *Men and boys belong to the male* sex. *Women and girls belong to the female* sex. **2** all of the characteristics which make the difference between male and female; especially, the characteristics related to reproduction. **3** *Informal* sexual practices. *as* ***modifier***: *a* sex *lecture.*

sex·a·ge·nar·i·an (sĕk′sə jə nâr′ē ən) ***n-*** person who is sixty to sixty-nine years old.

sex chromosome *Biology* ***n-*** one of two types of chromosomes, called the **X chromosome** and the **Y chromosome,** that determine the sex of an offspring. In fertilization, females are produced by the pairing of an X chromosome with another X (XX), while males are produced by the pairing of an X and a Y chromosome (XY).

sex·ism (sĕks′ĭz′əm) ***n-*** prejudice or discrimination based on a person's sex, especially against the female sex. **—*n-*** **sex′ist.** ***adj-*** **sex′ist.**

sex·less (sĕks′ləs) ***adj-*** having no sex; neuter. **—*adv-*** **sex′less·ly.** ***n-*** **sex′less·ness.**

sex·tant (sĕks′tənt) ***n-*** instrument used by a navigator to measure the angle between the horizon and the sun or a star. With these measurements he can find his position (latitude and longitude).

Sextant

sex·tet (sĕks tĕt′) ***n-*** **1** *Music* composition for six voices or instruments; also, the six performers of such a composition. **2** any group of six. Also **sex·tette′.**

sex·ton (sĕks′tən) ***n-*** man employed by a parish to take care of the church and attend to various other duties such as arranging for burials.

sex·u·al (sĕk′shōō əl) ***adj-*** of, relating to, or depending upon sex or sexuality. **—*adv-*** **sex′u·al·ly.**

sex·u·al·i·ty (sĕk′shōō ăl′ə tē) ***n-*** **1** condition of having sex. **2** interest in sex. **3** strength or importance of sexual interest, drive, function, etc.

sex·y (sĕk′sē) *Slang* ***adj-*** [**sex·i·er, sex·i·est**] strongly or overly suggestive of sex. **—*adv-*** **sex′i·ly.**

S.F.S.R. or **SFSR** Soviet Federated Socialist Republic.

Sgt. sergeant.

shab·by (shăb′ē) ***adj-*** [**shab·bi·er, shab·bi·est**] **1** worn out; much used; frayed; old: *a* shabby *coat.* **2** poorly dressed; ragged: *a* shabby *beggar.* **3** mean; unfair: *a* shabby *trick.* **—*adv-*** **shab′bi·ly.** ***n-*** **shab′bi·ness.**

Sha·bu·oth (shə vōō′ōt, -əs) ***n-*** Jewish festival observed in the spring, commemorating the giving of the Ten Commandments on Mt. Sinai. It was originally a harvest festival.

shack (shăk) ***n-*** *Informal* very poor, small house; hut.

shack·le (shăk′əl) ***n-*** **1** iron ring joined by a chain to another ring, used for fastening a prisoner's ankles or wrists; handcuff. **2** any of various devices for securing something; especially, a clevis. **3 shackles** anything that prevents free action. ***vt-*** [**shack·led, shack·ling**] **1** to bind or fasten with a device such as handcuffs. **2** to hinder; restrain. **—*n-*** **shack′ler.**

shad (shăd) ***n-*** [*pl.* **shad; shads** (kinds of shad)] any of several fishes related to the herrings, especially the **American shad,** that lives in the Atlantic and Pacific oceans, swims up fresh-water streams to spawn, and is highly valued as food.

shad·bush (shăd′bŏŏsh′) ***n-*** tall shrub or small tree bearing white flowers, and a purple, edible, berrylike fruit called **shad′ber′ry.**

shade (shād) ***n-*** **1** reduced light or partial darkness caused by blocking off or screening rays of light;

especially, a place not exposed to the direct rays of the sun: *The tree gave wonderful* shade. **2** something that reduces the glare of direct light: *a lamp* shade. **3** degree of darkness of a color; a variation of a color: *Olive is a* shade *of green.* **4** dark part of a picture, drawing, or engraving. **5** slight difference; nuance: *a* shade *of meaning.* **6** ghost; hence, any unreal thing or semblance. **7 shades** in ancient times, place where spirits were thought to go after death; Hades. ***vt-*** **[shad·ed, shad·ing] 1** to come between (something) and a light source. **2** to protect or shield from glare. **3** to darken or make gloomy; overcast; cloud. **4** to hide or protect from something, such as harm or injury; shelter. **5** to cause to blend, soften, or change by slight degrees. **6** in the graphic arts, to show varying degrees of light and darkness by using dark tones to make the lighter tones stand out, thereby creating a natural perspective. **7** *Informal* in sports, to defeat (an opponent) by a small margin. ***vi-*** to change from one thing to another) by slight degrees. ***—adj-*** **shade′less.**

in the shade in an obscure position in comparison with another's.

shad·ing (shā′dĭng) ***n-*** in the graphic arts, varying degrees of lightness and darkness used to give a rounded or other three-dimensional effect.

shad·ow (shăd′ō) ***n-*** **1** darkened image caused by something that blocks light, especially when the image is clearly outlined and has the shape of the figure that blocks the light. **2** poor likeness. **3** a reflecting image. **4** the shading of a picture. **5** close follower or companion: *Tom was his brother's* shadow. **6** person who trails someone to keep track of his movements. **7** slight trace. **8** a ghost; phantom. **9** sadness; gloom. **10 shadows** darkness. **11** *Archaic* protection: *under God's* shadow. ***vt-*** **1** to shade; darken; cloud. **2** to make gloomy. **3** to keep under observation; follow: *The spy* shadowed *him.* **4** to represent with a faint image or outline.

under (or **in**) **the shadow of 1** very close to. **2** under the influence or power of.

shad·ow·box·ing (shăd′ō bŏk′sĭng) ***n-*** boxing with an imaginary opponent as a form of exercise or training.

shad·ow·graph (shăd′ō grăf′) ***n-*** **1** a play that uses shadows from hands or puppets to illustrate the characters and the action. Also **shadow play. 2** photograph taken by an X ray.

shad·ow·y (shăd′ō ē) ***adj-*** **[shad·ow·i·er, shad·ow·i·est] 1** shady; filled with shadows: *a* shadowy *lane.* **2** faint; dim; ghostly: *a* shadowy *figure in the mist.* **3** impossible to explain or account for: *a* shadowy *fear.*

shad·y (shā′dē) ***adj-*** **[shad·i·er, shad·i·est] 1** sheltered from the sun; dusky. **2** *Informal* of doubtful or questionable character. ***—adv-*** **shad′i·ly.** ***n-*** **shad′i·ness.**

on the shady side 1 legally or morally questionable; also, slightly in violation (of the law). **2** of an age in excess of (a specified age).

shaft (shăft) ***n-*** **1** straight rod or bar; especially, the handle or long, slender part of any of a number of tools, machine parts, or items of athletic equipment: *Lyle broke the* shaft *of his golf club.* **2** arrow or spear. **3** vertical well or passage: *a mine* shaft. **4** ray or beam: *a* shaft *of light.* **5** either of the two long bars by which a vehicle is drawn by a horse harnessed between them. **6** the part of a column between its base and its capital. **7** well-aimed critical remark: *a* shaft *of ridicule.*

shag (shăg) ***n-*** **1** coarse variety of cut tobacco. **2** coarse, rough, wooly hair. **3** coarse nap on cloth; also, cloth having such a nap. ***vt-*** **[shagged, shag·ging] 1** to make hairy or shaggy; roughen. **2** *Informal* to catch or retrieve balls hit during batting practice.

shag·bark (shăg′bärk′) ***n-*** any of several kinds of white hickory bearing edible nuts; also, the wood of this tree.

shag·gy (shăg′ē) ***adj-*** **[shag·gi·er, shag·gi·est] 1** having long, rough, and uneven hair or threads: *The sheep had a* shaggy *coat.* **2** not properly groomed; unkempt: *a* shaggy *beard.* ***—adv-*** **shag′gi·ly.** ***n-*** **shag′gi·ness.**

Shah (shä) ***n-*** traditional title of the ruler of Iran, formerly Persia.

shake (shāk) ***vt-*** **[shook** (sho͞ok), **shak·en, shak·ing] 1** to move (something) quickly back and forth; also, to dislodge with such a motion: *Please* shake *the snow from your shoes.* **2** to cause to move, quiver, or tremble: *The wind* shook *the window panes.* **3** to weaken; unnerve: *The thunderstorm* shook *the puppy.* **4** to wave; brandish: *He* shook *his fist in victory.* **5** to clasp (another person's hand) in greeting or as a sign of goodwill, respect, congratulation, agreement, farewell, etc.: *It was an honor to* shake *the hand of the great poet. They* shook *hands and left.* **6** to get away from or get rid of: *He* shook *his pursuers.* ***vi-*** to tremble or quiver; jerk. ***n-*** **1** agitation or vibration; jolt: *a* shake *of the head.* **2 the shakes** a violent trembling from fear or a chill.

a fair shake *Informal* fair treatment. **no great shakes** *Informal* nothing much; not too important.

shake a leg *Informal* to hurry.

shake down 1 to cause to settle or fall, especially by agitating or vibrating. **2** to settle down to smooth operation. **3** *Slang* to extort money from.

shake off to escape or get rid of.

shake out to agitate something, such as a cloth or rug, especially to remove wrinkles, dust, etc.

shake up to agitate the feelings of; jar.

shake·down (shāk′doun′) ***adj-*** intended as a test under operating conditions: *a* shakedown *cruise.* ***n-*** **1** period of gaining experience and efficiency. **2** *Slang* extortion.

shak·er (shā′kər) ***n-*** **1** person or thing that shakes. **2** container used for shaking: *a cocktail* shaker; *a salt* shaker.

Shak·er (shā′kər) ***n-*** member of a religious celibate sect that lives in community settlements in the United States. The name derives from the motions of their religious dances.

Shake·spear·e·an (shāks pêr′ē ən) ***adj-*** of or relating to Shakespeare or his works. ***n-*** expert on Shakespeare or his writings and times. Also **Shake·spear′i·an.**

shake-up (shāk′ŭp′) ***n-*** thorough reorganization.

shak·o (shā′kō, shăk′ō) ***n-*** **[*pl.* shak·os]** high, stiff military cap, usually cylindrical and having an upright plume or tuft.

shak·y (shā′kē) ***adj-*** **[shak·i·er, shak·i·est] 1** not firm or secure; ready to fall: *The table was too* shaky *to use.* **2** trembling; shaking; weak: *We were still* shaky *from the explosion.* **3** not convincing or sound; questionable: *a* shaky *excuse.* ***—adv-*** **shak′i·ly.** ***n-*** **shak′i·ness.**

shale (shāl) ***n-*** rock formed by the hardening of clay and found in layers that are easily split.

shall (shăl) **auxiliary verb 1** am, is, or are going to: *I* shall *be leaving tomorrow. We* shall *eat soon.* **2** am, is, or are bound to: *You* shall *do this, whether you want to or not.* **3** am, is, or are determined to: *I* shall *return.*

►Traditionally SHALL with "I" and "we" was used to express a simple future idea, and WILL to mean obligation or determination. *I* shall *leave tomorrow. I* will *leave whether you like it or not.* The reverse was true for the other pronouns. *He* will *leave tomorrow. They* shall *not stop him.* This distinction in usage between "I" and "we" and all other pronouns has generally broken down, and most people use WILL for simple future with all pronouns, and SHALL for determination.

shal·lop (shăl′ əp) ***n-*** small, open boat with sails, oars, or both.

shal·lot (shə lŏt′) ***n-*** **1** kind of small, onionlike vegetable similar to garlic but of milder flavor. **2** green onion.

shal·low (shăl′ ō) ***adj-*** **[shal·low·er, shal·low·est] 1** not deep: *a* shallow *stream.* **2** lacking in depth of thought or emotion; superficial: *a* shallow *review of a book.* ***n-*** (usually **shallows**) place or places where the water is not deep. ***—adv-*** **shal′ low·ly.** ***n-*** **shal′ low·ness.**

sha·lom (shă lŏm′) *Hebrew* Peace.

shalom a·lei·chem (ə lā′ KHəm) *Hebrew* Peace be with you.

shalt (shălt) *Archaic* form of **shall** used with "thou."

sham (shăm) ***n-*** **1** a pretense or show intended to deceive; false appearance: *His anger is a* sham. **2** person who uses such pretenses and deceits; poseur. ***adj-*** **1** intended to deceive; false; affected: *a* sham *sympathy.* **2** imitating or substituting for something genuine: *a bottle of* sham *perfume.* ***vt-*** **[shammed, sham·ming]**: *to* sham *a concern for justice.* ***vi-***: *She was* shamming *when she said she was sick.*

sha·man (shăm′ ən) ***n-*** tribal medicine man.

sham battle ***n-*** a bloodless imitation of an actual battle for training, entertainment, deception, etc.

sham·ble (shăm′ bəl) ***vi-*** **[sham·bled, sham·bling]** to walk awkwardly; shuffle. ***n-*** an awkward, shuffling gait.

sham·bles (shăm′ bəlz) ***n-*** (takes singular verb) **1** state of disorder or destruction. **2** slaughterhouse.

shame (shām) ***n-*** **1** painful feeling caused by a sense of awkwardness, wrongdoing, or improper behavior: *He was filled with* shame *when caught in the lie.* **2** disgrace; dishonor. **3** something to be ashamed of: *Our air pollution is a* shame *and a disgrace.* **4** cause for being sorry; pity. ***vt-*** **[shamed, sham·ing] 1** to cause to feel shame. **2** to force or drive by a feeling of shame or guilt.

for shame! shame on you! **put to shame** to show someone up by excelling him.

shame·faced (shām′ fāst′) ***adj-*** **1** bashful; shy. **2** showing embarrassment or shame: *a* shamefaced *apology.* ***—adv-*** **shame′ fac′ ed·ly.** ***n-*** **shame′ fac′ed·ness.**

shame·ful (shām′ fəl) ***adj-*** causing shame; disgraceful. ***—adv-*** **shame′ ful·ly.** ***n-*** **shame′ ful·ness.**

shame·less (shām′ ləs) ***adj-*** showing no sense of shame, decency, or modesty: *a* shameless *lie.* ***—adv-*** **shame′ less·ly.** ***n-*** **shame′ less·ness.**

sham·poo (shăm pōō′) ***n-*** **1** preparation used in washing the hair. **2** a washing of the hair with such a preparation. ***vt-***: *to* shampoo *one's hair.* ***—n-*** **sham·poo′ er.**

sham·rock (shăm′ rŏk′) ***n-*** clover or sorrel plant with a leaf that has three lobes, used as the Irish national emblem.

Shamrocks

shang·hai (shăng′ hī′) ***vt-*** **[shang·haied, shang·hai·ing]** to drug and kidnap for service as a sailor; hence, to make (someone) do anything by force or trickery.

shank (shăngk) ***n-*** **1** leg; especially, the part of the leg between ankle and knee in man and some animals. **2** the straight, slender part of an implement: *the* shank *of a spoon*; shank *of a fishhook.* **3** cut of beef from the upper part of the foreleg. **4** narrow part of a shoe's sole.

shan·tung (shăn′ tŭng′) ***n-*** silk textile resembling pongee and having a nubby surface, originally of wild silk, now rayon and cotton. *as* ***modifier***: *a* shantung *dress.*

shan·ty (shăn′ tē) ***n-*** [*pl.* **shan·ties**] flimsy, poorly made, small house; shack; hovel. ***Hom-*** chantey.

shape (shāp) ***n-*** **1** outward appearance or form of a person or thing; contour; outline: *the* shape *of one's head*; *the* shape *of a box.* **2** real or imaginary figure; body: *a dark* shape *in the mist*; *a picture filled with strange* shapes. **3** appearance assumed by a person or thing; guise: *a prince in the* shape *of a beast.* **4** condition: *Swimming keeps a person in good* shape. **5** pattern; mold: *a milliner's* shape. **6** definite form; orderly arrangement: *to put one's plans into* shape. **7** kind or type; sort: *opportunities of every* shape. ***vt-*** **[shaped, shap·ing] 1** to give form to; mold: *to* shape *a sculptured head*; *to* shape *one's character.* **2** to adapt; regulate; adjust: *to* shape *one's ideas to the times.* **3** to plan or devise; contrive: *to* shape *a practical scheme.* **4** to direct; conduct: *to* shape *the course of events.* ***vi-*** to take form; develop: *His ideas are* shaping *as we thought they would.* ***n-*** **shap′ er.**

take shape to assume a definite form.

shape up *Informal* **1** to take shape. **2** to become disciplined to a particular method of behavior.

shape·less (shāp′ ləs) ***adj-*** without definite form or shape: *a* shapeless *dress*; *a* shapeless *lump of clay.* ***—adv-*** **shape′ less·ly.** ***n-*** **shape′ less·ness.**

shape·ly (shāp′ lē) ***adj-*** **[shape·li·er, shape·li·est]** having a pleasing shape; well-formed. ***—n-*** **shape′ li·ness.**

shape-up (shāp′ ŭp′) ***n-*** method of hiring longshoremen for a shift by having the workers gather daily for selection by a hiring boss.

shard (shärd) ***n-*** fragment of thin, brittle material, especially of pottery; sherd.

1**share** (shâr) ***vt-*** **[shared, shar·ing] 1** to use, enjoy, or endure with someone: *to* share *a burden*; *to* share *the cost*; *to* share *a room.* **2** to divide; apportion (usually followed by "out"): *to* share *out portions equally.* ***vi-*** to take part; join: *to* share *in a friend's joy*; *to* share *in the expense.* ***n-*** **1** portion or part of something received, owned, done, etc.; allotment: *his* share *of the profits*; *her* share *of the work.* **2** each of the equal parts into which the capital of a business is divided. [from Old English **scearu,** "a division," from **sceran,** "to cut; shear."]

go shares to take part equally. **on shares** taking part equally in profits and risks.

2**share** (shâr) ***n-*** plowshare. [from Old English **scear** of the same meaning, from **sceran,** "to cut; shear."]

share·crop (shâr′ krŏp′) ***vi-*** **[share·cropped, share·crop·ping]** to farm as a sharecropper. ***vt-***: *to* sharecrop *land.*

share·crop·per (shâr′ krŏp′ ər) ***n-*** tenant farmer who gives part of his crop as rent to his landlord; cropper.

share·hold·er (shâr′ hōl′ dər) ***n-*** person who owns a share or shares of stock in a company; stockholder.

sha·rif (shə rēf′) sherif.

Hammerhead shark, 15 ft. long, and blue shark, 22 ft. long

1**shark** (shärk) ***n-*** any of several large, sharp-toothed fish, found mostly in warm seas. Some species are dangerous to swimmers. ***—adj-*** **shark′ like′.** [probably from 2**shark.**]

2**shark** (shärk) ***n-*** **1** grasping person; swindler; cheat. **2** *Slang* person having unusual skill in a particular field.

[of uncertain origin, perhaps from Old French **cherquier,** "to prowl; search," or from German **Schurke,** "rascal."]

shark·skin (shärk′ skĭn′) ***n*-** **1** hide of a shark. **2** crisp, smooth fabric of wool or synthetic fibers, used widely in men's suits. *as* ***modifier*:** *a* sharkskin *suit.*

sharp (shärp) ***adj*-** **[sharp·er, sharp·est] 1** having a thin, fine cutting edge or point: *a* sharp *knife*; *a* sharp *needle.* **2** having a point or edge; not rounded: *a* sharp *nose*; sharp *features*; *a* sharp *ridge.* **3** of sound, piercing; shrill: *a* sharp *whistle*; *a* sharp *cry of distress.* **4** quickly aware of things; observant; keen: *a* sharp *eye*; sharp *ears*; sharp *wits.* **5** having a nipping or biting taste: *a* sharp *cheese.* **6** cutting; harsh: *a* sharp *remark*; *a* sharp *scolding.* **7** abrupt and sudden: *a* sharp *curve in the road.* **8** of feeling, piercing; keen: *a* sharp *pain.* **9** clear; distinct: *a* sharp *outline.* **10** keen with regard to one's advantage; shrewd: *a* sharp *bargain*; *a* sharp *gambler.* **11** fierce; violent: *a* sharp *contest.* **12** *Slang* well-dressed or well-groomed. **13** *Music* (1) above the true pitch: *a* sharp *note.* (2) raised by a half step: *C* sharp. ***n*-** the musical sign [#], to show that a note is raised half a tone. ***adv*-** **1** promptly; punctually: *The game begins at two o'clock* sharp. **2** above the true pitch: *She always sings* sharp. ***vt*-** to raise in pitch: *to* sharp *a note.* ***vi*-**: *The soprano* sharped. **—*adv*- sharp′ ly.** ***n*-** **sharp′ ness.**

sharp·en (shär′ pən) ***vt*-** **1** to give a sharp edge or point to: *to* sharpen *the pencils.* **2** to make quick and keen: *This puzzle should* sharpen *your wits.* ***vi*-**: *This knife* sharpens *easily.* **—*n*- sharp′ en·er.**

sharp·er (shär′ pər) ***n*-** swindler or cheat: *a card* sharper.

sharp·ie (shär′ pē) ***n*-** **1** long, pointed, flat-bottomed boat having a centerboard and usually two masts, each carrying a triangular sail. **2** *Slang* unusually alert, keen person.

sharp·shoot·er (shärp′ sho͞o′ tər) ***n*-** excellent marksman, especially with a rifle.

sharp-sight·ed (shärp′ sī′ təd) ***adj*-** **1** having keen vision. **2** sharp-witted.

sharp-wit·ted (shärp′ wĭt′ əd) ***adj*-** having a keen, astute, or agile mind; acute: *a* sharp-witted *lawyer.*

shat·ter (shăt′ ər) ***vt*-** **1** to break or smash suddenly into small pieces, as by a blow or fall: *to* shatter *a window.* **2** to ruin; destroy: *to* shatter *hope.* ***vi*-**: *A glass* shattered.

shat·ter·proof (shăt′ ər pro͞of′) ***adj*-** made so as not to shatter: *a* shatterproof *glass.*

shave (shāv) ***vt*-** **[shaved, shaved** or **shav·en, shav·ing] 1** to cut off (hair) with a razor; also, to cut off hair from (the face, etc.) with a razor. **2** to cut thin slices from: *to* shave *a ham.* **3** to pass very close to; graze. ***vi*-** to remove hair with a razor: *He* shaves *twice a day.* ***n*-** **1** a cutting off of hair with a razor. **2** (usually **close shave**) a grazing or passing very close; also, a narrow escape.

shav·er (shā′ vər) ***n*-** **1** person or thing that shaves: *an electric* shaver. **2** *Informal* young fellow; youth.

shav·ing (shā′ vĭng) ***n*-** very thin slice of wood, metal, etc., cut off by a plane or similar tool; paring.

shawl (shȯl) ***n*-** large piece of cloth worn over the shoulders or head, especially by women.

Shaw·nee (shȯ′ nē) ***n*-** [*pl.* **Shaw·nees,** also **Shaw·nee]** one of a tribe of Algonquian Indians, who formerly lived in the Cumberland River basin and now live in Oklahoma. ***adj*-**: *a* Shawnee *arrow.*

shay (shā) ***n*-** light, horse-drawn carriage; chaise.

she (shē) ***pron*-** (used as a singular subject in the third person) **1** female person or animal, that has been named or is being pointed out: *Where is Jane?* She *is upstairs. And what is* she *doing on the front porch?* **2** thing, thought of as a female: *Being a strong ship,* she *rode out the hurricane.* **3** any female (often followed by "who" or "that"): *They said that* she *who is chosen queen will have a screen test.* ***n*-** a female: *Is that rabbit a* she *or a he?* *as* ***modifier*:** *a* she-*rabbit.*

sheaf (shēf) ***n*-** [*pl.* **sheaves** (shēvz)] **1** bundle of cut grain tied in the middle. **2** bundle of things: *a* sheaf *of arrows.*

Sheaf

shear (shêr) ***vt*-** **[sheared, sheared** or **shorn** (shôrn), **shear·ing] 1** to clip off (wool, hair, etc.) with shears or clippers: *to* shear *wool.* **2** to remove wool or hair from, with shears or clippers: *to* shear *a lamb.* **3** to slice (often followed by "off"): *It* sheared *off a wall.* ***vi*-** to break in a crosswise direction. ***n*-** *Physics* of a solid body under stress, displacement of two or more sections of it in opposite, crosswise directions by equal and opposite forces, as when rivets break crosswise in the failure of a riveted joint. ***Hom*-** sheer. **—*n*- shear′ er.**

shears (shêrz) ***n*-** (takes plural verb) any of various kinds of large scissors for shearing sheep or cutting cloth, sheet metal, etc. Also **pair of shears** (takes singular verb).

sheath (shēth) ***n*-** [*pl.* **sheaths** (shēthz, shēths)] **1** protective covering or envelope: *The caterpillar wound a silken* sheath *about itself.* **2** close-fitting case for a sword or dagger; scabbard. ***vt*-** to sheathe.

sheathe (shēth) ***vt*-** **[sheathed, sheath·ing] 1** to put into a scabbard or sheath: *to* sheathe *a sword.* **2** to enclose or cover fo protection: *to* sheathe *a roof with tin.*

Sheath

sheath·ing (shē′ thĭng, -thĭng) ***n*-** something that encases, covers, or protects, such as the copper casing on a ship's hull or the protective boarding on the outside of a frame house; also, the material used.

sheath knife ***n*-** knife with a fixed blade, designed to be worn on a belt in a sheath.

[1]**sheave** (shēv) ***vt*-** **[sheaved, sheav·ing]** to gather and bind into bundles or sheaves: *to* sheave *wheat.* [from **sheaf,** from Old English **sceaf,** and related to **shove.**]

[2]**sheave** (shĭv, shēv) ***n*-** grooved wheel turning in a frame and used with a rope for raising weights; pulley. [variant form of **shive,** from Middle English **schēve.**]

sheaves (shēvz) *pl.* of **sheaf.**

She·ba (shē′ bə), **Queen of** ***n*-** in the Old Testament, a queen who visited King Solomon to find out for herself about his reputed wisdom.

she·bang (shə băng′) *Slang* ***n*-** business; concern; affair.

[1]**shed** (shĕd) ***vt*-** **[shed, shed·ding] 1** to pour out; let fall: *to* shed *tears.* **2** to cause to flow: *The war* shed *the blood of thousands.* **3** to pour forth; spread about: *The moon* shed *its light on us.* **4** to throw off; get rid of: *He* shed *his troubles as a duck* sheds *water.* **5** to cast away; let fall: *Our snake* shed *its skin.* ***vi*-** to give off a covering: *The cat is starting to* shed. [from Old English **sc(e)ādan** meaning "to separate; cut apart."]

shed blood to kill or wound as a hostile act.

shed light on to clarify: *to* shed light on *a problem.*

[2]**shed** (shĕd) ***n*-** small building, usually of one story and sometimes with open sides, used for storage, shelter, etc.: *a tool* shed; *a cow* shed. [from an earlier meaning of **shade.** A shed would afford shade for cattle.]

she'd (shēd) **1** she had. **2** she would.

sheen (shēn) ***n*-** brightness or shine, especially from a surface that reflects light; luster: *the* sheen *of her hair.*

sheep (shēp) ***n-*** [*pl.* **sheep**] **1** animal related to the goat, with a thick coat of curly wool. It is raised for meat, wool, and hide. **2** timid person. ***—adj-*** **sheep′ like′.**

as well be hanged for a sheep as a lamb (or a goat) as well commit a big crime as a small one (since the punishment will be severe in any case). **make sheep's eyes** to flirt; make longing, amorous glances.

Wool sheep

sheep·cote (shēp′ kōt′, -kŏt′) ***n-*** sheepfold.

sheep dog ***n-*** any one of several breeds of dogs, such as the collie, the Old English sheep dog, and the German shepherd dog, that are trained to help shepherds.

sheep·fold (shēp′ fōld′) ***n-*** pen for sheep; sheepcote.

sheep·herd·er (shēp′ hûr′ dər) ***n-*** person who tends flocks of sheep.

sheep·ish (shē′ pĭsh) ***adj-*** embarrassed and feeling somewhat silly. ***—adv-*** **sheep′ ish·ly.** ***n-*** **sheep′ ish·ness.**

sheep·man (shēp′ mən, -măn′) ***n-*** [*pl.* **sheep·men**] person who raises sheep.

sheep·shank (shēp′ shăngk′) ***n-*** knot for shortening a rope.

sheeps·head (shēps′ hĕd′) ***n-*** common and valuable food fish of the Atlantic coast.

sheep·skin (shēp′ skĭn′) ***n-*** **1** skin of a sheep, usually with the wool left on, often used for making clothing. **2** leather or parchment made from the skin of sheep. **3** *Informal* graduation diploma.

[1]**sheer** (shêr) ***adj-*** [**sheer·er, sheer·est**] **1** unmixed; utter; complete: *It was* sheer *madness.* **2** very thin or fine; transparent: *The sunlight streamed through the* sheer *curtains.* **3** straight; steep; perpendicular: *a* sheer *drop of 1,000 feet to the valley below.* [from Middle English **schere** meaning "brightly shining; clear; unbroken; unbroken drop," from Old Norse.] ***Hom-*** shear. ***—adv-*** **sheer′ ly.** ***n-*** **sheer′ ness.**

[2]**sheer** (shêr) ***vi-*** to turn from a course; swerve: *The car* sheered *away from the animal in the road.* [from Dutch **scheren,** "draw away; cut; shear."] ***Hom-*** shear.

[1]**sheet** (shēt) ***n-*** **1** broad, thin piece of cloth, glass, metal, etc. **2** piece of cloth used to cover a bed: *to cover the* sheets *with a blanket.* **3** single piece of paper: *The letter went on to a second* sheet. **4** broad expanse or surface: *a* sheet *of water or snow.* **5** sheet metal. *as* ***modifier:*** *some* sheet *copper.* [from Old English **scēte** and **sciēte,** "corner (of a sail); a projection" related to **shoot.**]

[2]**sheet** (shēt) ***n-*** rope attached to the lower corner of a sail to hold and regulate it. [from Old English **scēatline** meaning "a line or rope tied to the lower corner of a sail," from **scēat** meaning [1]**sheet.**]

sheet erosion ***n-*** type of erosion in which water washes away exposed topsoil evenly on a slope.

sheet·ing (shē′ tĭng) ***n-*** material for bed sheets.

sheet lightning ***n-*** reflection by clouds of distant flashes of lightning.

sheet metal ***n-*** metal prepared or processed in sheets. *as* ***modifier*** **(sheet-metal):** *a* sheet-metal *roof.*

sheet music ***n-*** music printed on unbound sheets of paper, especially popular music.

sheik (shēk) ***n-*** **1** in Islam, a venerable man or high priest. **2** head of an Arab family, tribe, or clan. Also **sheikh.**

shek·el (shĕk′ əl) ***n-*** ancient Hebrew unit of weight, equal to about a half ounce; also, a unit of money based on, or a coin equal to, this weight.

shel·drake (shĕl′ drāk′) ***n-*** fish-eating, wild duck of the Old World that resembles the goose.

shelf (shĕlf) ***n-*** [*pl.* **shelves** (shĕlvz)] **1** flat, narrow piece of wood, metal, etc., fastened to or set into a wall for holding things. **2** something resembling this, such as a slab of rock that sticks out. ***—adj-*** **shelf′ like′.**

on the shelf put aside; no longer used.

shelf ice ***n-*** glacial ice that extends from land into the sea. It may be several hundred feet thick.

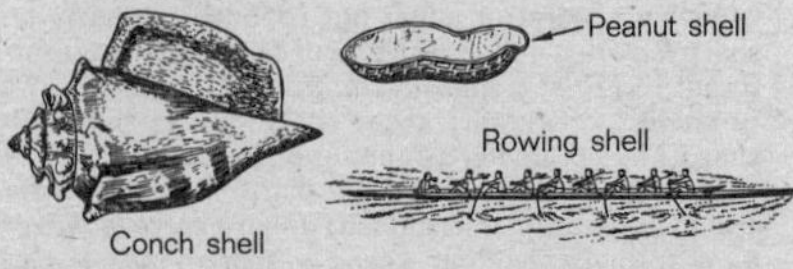

shell (shĕl) ***n-*** **1** the hard protective covering of a nut, seed, egg, crab, or the like. **2** hollow structure somewhat like a shell: *a* pastry *shell.* **3** the outer walls and roof of a building: *After the fire the building was a mere* shell. **4** the horny material covering a turtle. **5** explosive missile fired from a cannon. **6** cartridge for a rifle or shotgun. **7** light racing boat propelled by rowing. **8** *Physics* (1) any one of the separate regions around the nucleus of an atom in which electrons of approximately the same energy move. Each shell corresponds to a certain amount of energy. (2) within the nucleus, a region occupied by a definite number (the mass number) of protons or neutrons. ***vt-*** **1** to bombard: *to* shell *a fort.* **2** to remove from a shell, husk, or cob. ***—n-*** **shell′ er.**

come out of (one's) shell to become less shy and communicate with people. **retire into one's shell** to become shy and withdrawn.

shell out *Slang* to spend or pay out money.

she'll (shēl) **1** she will. **2** she shall.

shel·lac (shə lăk′) ***n-*** sticky substance made from lac, and used to give a clear and shiny finish to wood or as a filler and base for varnish, paint, waxes, etc. ***vt-*** [**shel·lacked, shel·lack·ing**] **1** to coat with this material. **2** *Slang* to defeat utterly; clobber.

shel·lack·ing (shə lăk′ ĭng) *Slang* ***n-*** thorough defeat.

shell·fire (shĕl′ fīər′) ***n-*** a firing or shooting of artillery shells; bombardment.

shell·fish (shĕl′ fĭsh′) ***n-*** [*pl.* **shell·fish**] water animal having a shell, such as an oyster, lobster, or crab.

shell game ***n-*** swindling game in which spectators bet on the location of a pea supposedly concealed under one of three inverted shells or cups that have been shuffled by the exhibitor.

shell·proof (shĕl′ pro͞of′) ***adj-*** designed to withstand bombardment: *a* shellproof *fort.*

shell shock ***n-*** combat fatigue. ***—adj-*** **shell′ shocked′.**

shel·ter (shĕl′ tər) ***n-*** **1** anything that protects, covers, or shields; refuge: *We run for any* shelter *in a storm.* **2** protection from weather or other danger or inconvenience: *to seek* shelter. ***vt-*** to protect; defend: *The roof* sheltered *us from rain.* ***vi-*** to take cover or find refuge: *We* sheltered *in a cave.* ***—adj-*** **shel′ ter·less.**

shelter tent ***n-*** small tent made of two pieces, each called a **shelter half,** that are arranged to button or tie together; pup tent.

shelve (shĕlv) ***vt-*** [**shelved, shelv·ing**] **1** to put on a shelf. **2** to dismiss from the mind; postpone indefinitely: *to* shelve *a problem.* **3** to slope gradually.

shelves (shĕlvz) *pl.* of **shelf.**

shelv·ing (shĕl′ vĭng) ***n-*** shelves or the material for making them.

Shem (shĕm) ***n-*** in the Old Testament, Noah's eldest son.

she·nan·i·gans (shə năn′ ĭ gənz) *Informal* ***n-pl.*** **1** pranks; high jinks. **2** questionable or devious conduct.

She·ol (shē'ōl', shē ōl') *n-* in the Old Testament, the abode of departed spirits in the depths of the earth; the underworld or Hades.

shep·herd (shĕp'ərd) *n-* 1 person who takes care of sheep. 2 minister, priest or other religious leader. *vt-* to take care of; guide; lead: *to* shepherd *students through a museum. n- fem.* **shep'herd·ess.**

sher·bet (shûr'bət) *n-* frozen dessert made of fruit juices with water, milk, gelatin, etc.

sherd (shärd, *also* shûrd) shard.

she·rif (shə rēf') *n-* a descendant of Mohammed through Fatima, his daughter; hence, a person of aristocratic birth in the Muslim world. Also **she·reef', sha·rif'.**

sher·iff (shĕr'ĭf) *n-* chief law-enforcing officer of a county.

Sher·lock Holmes (shûr'lŏk'hōlmz) *n-* fictional detective created by Sir Arthur Conan Doyle.

sher·ry (shĕr'ē) *n-* [*pl.* **sher·ries**] strong wine, light yellow to brown in color, originally made in Spain.

she's (shēz) 1 she is. 2 she has (auxiliary verb only).

Shet·land pony (shĕt'lənd) *n-* one of a breed of small, shaggy ponies, originally from the Shetland Islands.

Shetland wool *n-* fine, loosely twisted yarn spun from the undercoat of Shetland sheep.

shew (shō) *Archaic* show.

shib·bo·leth (shĭb'ə ləth) *n-* 1 custom or usage considered to identify members of a certain group. 2 party slogan or watchword.

shied (shīd) *p.t. & pp.* of **shy.**

MEDIEVAL
GREEK
ROMAN
Shields

shield (shēld) *n-* 1 leather- or metal-covered protective piece of armor once carried on the arm by soldiers. 2 anything that, or anyone who, protects: *Vaccination is a* shield *against smallpox.* 3 thing shaped like a soldier's shield. 4 movable barrier which protects miners or tunnel workers from a cave-in. 5 safety screen, as for moving machine parts. 6 plastic-lined cloth cover for the inside of the armhole of a garment to prevent soiling by perspiration. 7 in geology, a large portion of the earth's crust that has not been severely folded or distorted, but only gently warped. 8 in physics and electronics, any device or structure used to exclude or hold in unwanted radiations. A shield can be a metal box, a woven outer covering on a wire, a large and thick wall of lead, etc. *vt-* 1 to protect: *This tent will* shield *you against wind.* 2 to provide with a device that excludes or holds in unwanted radiation.

shi·er (shī'ər) *compar.* of **shy.**

shies (shīz) form of the verb **shy** used with "he," "she," "it," or singular noun subjects in the present tense.

shi·est (shī'əst) *superl.* of **shy.**

shift (shĭft) *vt-* to move from one person, place, or position to another: *to* shift *the blame*; *to* shift *a bundle from one hand to the other. vi-* 1 to change position or direction: *The load* shifted. 2 to change gears in a car. *n-* 1 a move from one person, place, position, to another; change: *a* shift *in jobs*; *a* shift *in ideas*; *a* shift *in the weather.* 2 group of people working at one time; also, the time during which the group works: *a night* shift *in a factory.* 3 trick; indirect method; expedient: *Tom tried every* shift *he could think of to avoid work.* 4 woman's dress, loosely fitted and with straight lines; also, formerly, a woman's undergarment. 5 gearshift. *—n-* **shift'er.**

make shift to make do (with) what is available.

shift for oneself to make one's own way.

shift·less (shĭft'ləs) *adj-* without motivation or initiative; lazy; worthless. *—adv-* **shift'less·ly.** *n-* **shift'less·ness.**

shift·y (shĭf'tē) *adj-* [**shift·i·er, shift·i·est**] 1 evasive; tricky; sly: *a* shifty *reply.* 2 capable; resourceful. *—adv-* **shift'i·ly.** *n-* **shift'i·ness.**

shi·kar (shĭk är') *n-* in India, a wild-animal hunt.

shi·ka·ri (shĭk är'ē) *n-* in India, a professional big-game hunter or guide.

shil·le·lagh or **shil·la·lah** (shə lā'lē) *Irish n-* strong cudgel or club.

shil·ling (shĭl'ĭng) *n-* former unit of money in Great Britain, equal to twelve pence or one twentieth of a pound; also, a silver coin of this value.

shil·ly-shal·ly (shĭl'ē shăl'ē) *vi-* [**shil·ly-shal·lied, shil·ly-shal·ly·ing**] to hesitate; be indecisive; vacillate.

shim (shĭm) *n-* thin piece of metal, stone, or other material, used to adjust the fit of a machine part or structural member in a building.

shim·mer (shĭm'ər) *vi-* to shine with a wavering light; glimmer: *Moonlight* shimmers *on the lake. n-* wavering light; sheen: *the* shimmer *of satin. —adj-* **shim'mer·y.**

shim·my (shĭm'ē) *n-* [*pl.* **shim·mies**] 1 a wiggling or shaking back and forth: *a* shimmy *in the front wheel.* 2 dance in which the body is moved in such a manner. *vi-* [**shim·mied, shim·my·ing**]: *The wheel* shimmied.

shin (shĭn) *n-* the forepart of the leg between the ankle and the knee. *vi-* [**shinned, shin·ning**] to climb with alternate grips of knees and hands: *Percy* shinned *up the tree. vt-: to* shin *a tree.*

Shin

shin bone (shĭn'bōn') *n-* tibia.

shin·dig (shĭn'dĭg') *Slang n-* noisy party.

shine (shīn) *vi-* [**shone** (shōn) or **shined, shin·ing**] 1 to give off or reflect light or radiance; gleam: *The sun* shone. *His face* shone *with joy.* 2 to be best; excel: *Jenny* shines *in foreign languages. vt-* to cause to give forth a glow or luster; polish: *to* shine *silverware*; *to* shine *shoes. n-* 1 glow; radiance; luster: *the* shine *of new money.* 2 a polishing; especially, a polishing of shoes. 3 sunshine: *come rain or* shine.

take a shine to *Slang* to develop a liking for.

shine up to *Slang* to make friends with.

shin·er (shī'nər) *n-* 1 person or thing that shines or polishes. 2 *Slang* black eye. 3 any of various small, silvery, fresh-water fishes related to the minnows.

[1]**shin·gle** (shĭng'gəl) *n-* 1 one of the thin, wedge-shaped boards placed on buildings in overlapping rows. 2 small signboard hung outside the office of a doctor, lawyer, etc. *vt-* [**shin·gled, shin·gling**] 1 to place shingles on (a building). 2 to cut (a woman's hair) short from the back of the head downward. [from Middle English **shindle,** from Latin **scindula** from **scindere,** "to split."]

Shingles

hang out (one's) shingle to establish oneself in a business or profession.

[2]**shin·gle** (shĭng'gəl) *n-* rounded seashore pebbles. coarser than ordinary gravel; also, a beach or other area covered with such pebbles. [from Norwegian **singla,** "make a ringing sound," from **singa,** "sing." The meaning arises from the sound of walking or riding on gravel.]

shin·gles (shĭng'gəlz) *n-* (takes singular or plural verb) painful skin disease caused by a virus and marked by small sores and blisters along the path of a nerve.

shin·ing (shī′nĭng) ***adj-*** **1** gleaming; glittering: *the* shining *coins.* **2** outstanding; illustrious.

shin·ny (shĭn′ē) ***n-*** [*pl.* **shin·nies**] **1** kind of hockey played by boys. **2** stick used in playing this game.

Shin·to (shĭn′tō) ***n-*** a religion of Japan marked by a great reverence of nature, ancestors, and emperors. Also **Shin′to·ism.** —***n-*** **Shin′to·ist.**

shin·y (shī′nē) ***adj-*** [**shin·i·er, shin·i·est**] **1** bright and clear; shining: *a* shiny *day.* **2** glossy. —***n-*** **shin′i·ness.**

ship (shĭp) ***n-*** **1** large vessel built for ocean or other deep-water travel. **2** entire company of such a vessel: *The rumor raced through the* ship. **3** airplane, airship, or spacecraft. ***vt-*** [**shipped, ship·ping**] **1** to send or transport by ship, rail, truck, etc.: *to* ship *a package.* **2** to take (water) in over the sides of a vessel. **3** to place (oars) inside a boat. ***vi-*** **1** to take a job on a vessel: *He* shipped *as a steward.* **2** of perishable foods, to withstand the rigors of transportation: *Oranges* ship *well.*
when one's ship comes in when one's fortune is made.

-ship *suffix* (used to form nouns) **1** condition or quality of: *friend*ship; *hard*ship. **2** position or rank of: *king*ship. **3** art or skill of: *leader*ship; *horseman*ship.

ship biscuit ***n-*** coarse, hard biscuit made for use on shipboard; hardtack.

ship·board (shĭp′bôrd′) **on shipboard** aboard a ship. *as* ***modifier***: *a* shipboard *party*; shipboard *friends.*

ship·build·ing (shĭp′bĭl′dĭng) ***n-*** **1** act or process of building a ship. **2** business or trade of building ships. —***n-*** **ship′build′er.**

ship·fit·ter (shĭp′fĭt′ər) ***n-*** **1** worker who fits structural parts of a ship together before riveting or welding. **2** in the navy, an enlisted man who serves as shipboard plumber and who works in sheet metal.

ship·load (shĭp′lōd′) ***n-*** amount of cargo or number of passengers that a ship carries when loaded.

ship·mas·ter (shĭp′măs′tər) ***n-*** captain of a merchant ship.

ship·mate (shĭp′māt′) ***n-*** fellow sailor on the same ship.

ship·ment (shĭp′mənt) ***n-*** **1** transportation of goods: *to prepare goods for* shipment. **2** goods sent at one time.

ship of the line ***n-*** a warship large enough to be placed in the battle line.

ship·per (shĭp′ər) ***n-*** person or company that sends goods by any means of transportation.

ship·ping (shĭp′ĭng) ***n-*** **1** business of transporting goods: *Jack's father wanted him to go into* shipping. **2** all of the ships of a port, nation, company, etc.; also, their tonnage. *as* ***modifier***: *a* shipping *firm*; shipping *costs.*

shipping clerk ***n-*** worker engaged in shipping and receiving goods.

ship·shape (shĭp′shāp′) ***adj-*** in good order; neat.

ship·worm (shĭp′wûrm′) ***n-*** any of several wormlike mollusks that bore into ship timbers, wharf piles, etc.

ship·wreck (shĭp′rĕk′) ***n-*** **1** destruction or loss of a ship: *The whole crew survived the* shipwreck. **2** ship that has been wrecked. **3** utter destruction; ruin: *the* shipwreck *of plans.* ***vt-***: *A storm* shipwrecked *the vessel.*

ship·yard (shĭp′yärd′) ***n-*** place where ships are built or repaired.

shire (shīər) *chiefly Brit.* ***n-*** district or county.

shirk (shûrk) ***vt-*** to neglect or shun deliberately: *to* shirk *one's work*; *to* shirk *a responsibility.* —***n-*** **shirk′er.**

shirr (shûr) ***vt-*** **1** to gather (cloth) along parallel rows of stitching. **2** to bake (eggs) in a buttered dish. ***n-*** a gathering of cloth along parallel rows of stitching.

shirt (shûrt) ***n-*** garment, usually with a collar and sleeves, for the upper part of the body. —***adj-*** **shirt′less.**
keep (one's) shirt on *Slang* to remain calm or patient.
lose (one's) shirt *Slang* to lose all of one's money.

shirt·ing (shûr′tĭng) ***n-*** cloth used to make shirts.

shirt·waist (shûrt′wāst′) ***n-*** **1** woman's blouse or shirt with collar and cuffs, usually worn tucked in under a skirt or trousers. **2** tailored dress with a bodice that resembles such a blouse. *as* ***modifier***: *a* shirtwaist *style.*

shish ke·bab (shĭsh′kə bŏb′) ***n-*** small pieces of seasoned meat roasted on a skewer; kabob; kebab; kebob.

Shi·va (shē′və) ***n-*** in Hinduism, the god of destruction and reproduction, forming with Brahma and Vishnu the supreme triad. Also **Si′va.**

shiv·a·ree (shĭv′ə rē′) ***n-*** noisy mock serenade to a couple on their wedding night. [from French **charivari** of the same meaning.]

[1]**shiv·er** (shĭv′ər) ***vi-*** to tremble, shake, or quiver, as from cold or fear: *He* shivered *under his blanket.* ***n-***: *Cold* shivers *ran up and down his spine.* [partly from Middle English **chiveren,** "to shake," and partly from Old English **cwifer,** "a quivering."] —***n-*** **shiv′er·er.**

[2]**shiv·er** (shĭv′ər) ***vt-*** to cause to break into small pieces or splinters; shatter: *He* shivered *the glass with a single blow.* ***vi-***: *The glass* shivered *at a single blow.* ***n-*** small piece or fragment; sliver. [probably from **shive,** a variant of [2]**sheave.**]

shiv·er·y (shĭv′ə rē) ***adj-*** **1** shivering or quivering; trembling: *to be* shivery *from the cold.* **2** causing shivers or quivers: *a* shivery *horror movie.*

[1]**shoal** (shōl) ***n-*** **1** shallow place in any body of water. **2** sandbank or sandbar that is exposed at low tide. ***adj-*** shallow: *to sail in* shoal *water.* ***vi-*** to become shallow: *where the river* shoaled. [from Middle English **shold,** from Old English **sceald** meaning "shallow."]

[2]**shoal** (shōl) ***n-*** **1** large group, number, or mass. **2** school of fish. ***vi-*** of fish, to gather in a school: *Salmon* shoal *in large numbers.* [from Old English **scolu** meaning "a crowd," and related to [2]**school.**]

shoat (shōt) ***n-*** young hog that has been weaned.

[1]**shock** (shŏk) ***n-*** **1** sudden or violent blow; impact, jar, or concussion: *The* shock *of the explosion was felt for miles around.* **2** violent disturbance of the mind or emotions as a result of fear, pain, grief, etc. **3** effect of electric current on the body. **4** *Medicine* a state of bodily collapse associated with an acute drop in the volume and pressure of the blood, as from wounds, burns, etc. It is marked by apathy, clamminess and grayness of the skin, nausea, and often unconsciousness. ***vt-*** to surprise, horrify, or disgust: *His crime* shocked *the nation.* [from Old French **choq** meaning "a collision," and **choquer,** "to collide," from earlier German **scoc.**]

[2]**shock** (shŏk) ***n-*** thick, bushy mass of hair. [from **shag** meaning "coarse or rough hair."]

[3]**shock** (shŏk) ***n-*** sheaves of grain stacked upright in a field to dry. ***vt-*** to gather and stack (grain) in sheaves. [from Middle English **schokke,** from a word of Germanic origin meaning "corn shock," and probably related to [1]**shock.**] —***n-*** **shock′er.**

shock absorber ***n-*** any of various devices that take up the impact of sudden starts, stops, or bumps by means of springs, a hydraulic or pneumatic piston, etc.

shock·er (shŏk′ər) *Informal* ***n-*** anything, especially a story or movie, that is shocking or horrifying.

shock-head·ed (shŏk′hĕd′əd) ***adj-*** having hair that is thick and bushy.

shock·ing (shŏk′ĭng) ***adj-*** **1** very offensive or disgusting; revolting: *a* shocking *novel.* **2** causing great horror and surprise: *a piece of* shocking *news.* —***adv-*** **shock′ing·ly.**

shock therapy ***n-*** treatment of certain mental diseases in which convulsions and usually unconsciousness are induced in the patient by electricity or drugs.

shock troops ***n-*** troops trained for leading an assault.

shock wave *Physics* ***n-*** wave produced by a sudden and powerful compression of the air or other medium and traveling faster than sound. Explosions and high-speed projectiles produce shock waves in the air, and earthquakes produce them in the rocky material of the earth.

shod (shŏd) *p.t. & p.p.* of **shoe.**

shod·dy (shŏd′ ē) ***n-*** [*pl.* **shod·dies**] woolen cloth made by reweaving woolen waste, raveled rags, etc. ***adj-*** **[shod·di·er, shod·di·est]** of poor quality: *a* shoddy *product.* **—*adv-*** **shod′ di·ly.** ***n-*** **shod′ di·ness.**

shoe (sho͞o) ***n-*** **1** outer covering for the foot, usually of leather and generally consisting of a stiff bottom layer or sole and a soft upper part. **2** horseshoe. **3** the sliding contact plate of a subway or other electrical train by which current is picked up from the third rail. **4** the outer casing of a pneumatic tire. **5** the part of the brake that presses against the wheel or drum to stop its motion. **6** metal band attached to the runner of a sled. **7** metal band or socket to protect the end of a pole or staff. *as* ***modifier***: *a* shoe *box*; shoe *tree.* ***vt-*** **[shod** (shŏd), **shoe·ing]** to furnish or protect with a shoe: *to* shoe *a horse*; *to* shoe *a flagpole with an iron tip.* ***Hom-*** shoo. **—*adj-*** **shoe′ less.**

fill someone's shoes to take someone's place. **in another's shoes** in another's place or situation. **where the shoe pinches** where the real source of difficulty is.

shoe·horn (sho͞o′ hôrn′, -hôrn′) ***n-*** curved implement of horn, wood, or metal, used to help slip on a shoe.

shoe·lace (sho͞o′ lās′) ***n-*** length of string, cord, or leather used to fasten or lace a shoe.

shoe·mak·er (sho͞o′ mā′ kər) ***n-*** person who makes or repairs shoes; cobbler. **—*n-*** **shoe′ mak′ ing.**

shoe·string (sho͞o′ strĭng′) ***n-*** shoelace.

on a shoestring with very little money.

shoe tree ***n-*** form placed into a shoe to stretch it or help keep its shape.

sho·far (shō′ fər, -fär′) ***n-*** [*pl.* **shof·roth** (shō frōth′)] in Judaism, a ram's horn formerly blown in battle, and still sounded in the synagogue on the holidays of Rosh Hashana and Yom Kippur.

sho·gun (shō′ gən, -go͞on′) ***n-*** any of the hereditary military rulers who governed Japan from the 12th to the 19th century.

shone (shōn) *p.t. & p.p.* of **shine.** ***Hom-*** shown.

shoo (sho͞o) ***vt-*** to scare or drive away (animals or birds): *Tod* shooed *the chickens.* ***interj-*** be off! ***Hom-*** shoe.

[1]**shook** (sho͝ok) *p.t.* of **shake.**

[2]**shook** (sho͝ok) ***n-*** **1** set of the parts of a barrel, box, etc., ready to be assembled. **2** stack of sheaves; shock. [probably a variant of [3]**shock.]**

shoot (sho͞ot) ***vt-*** **[shot, shoot·ing] 1** to hit, wound, or kill with a bullet, arrow, or other missile: *to* shoot *a lion.* **2** to discharge or fire (a gun, arrow, or the like). **3** to send forth like a bullet or arrow: *to* shoot *questions*; *to* shoot *a look.* **4** to streak with different colors: *The sun* shot *the sky with crimson.* **5** to move (a bolt) in or out of place: *to* shoot *the bolt of a barn door.* **6** to pass over or through rapidly: *to* shoot *the rapids.* **7** to cause to grow (forth): *The trees* shot *forth buds.* **8** to cause to move swiftly; dart; also, to throw, discharge, or dump quickly and with force: *The snake* shot *out its tongue. Bob* shot *coal through the basement window.* **9** to photograph: *to* shoot *a picture.* **10** in sports (1) to throw or cast: *to* shoot *dice*; *to* shoot *marbles.* (2) to make (a score or points): *He* shot *two under par in the golf tournament.* (3) to play (golf, pool, or craps). ***vi-*** **1** to discharge or fire a gun, arrow, etc., at a target: *He* shoots *well.* **2** to grow or thrust upward or out: *Plants* shoot *up in the spring.* **3** to jut (out); protrude: *The cape* shoots *out into the sea.* **4** to move or flash swiftly; dart: *The meteor* shot *through the sky. A sharp pain* shot *up her arm.* ***n-*** **1** a shooting match; hunt: *a turkey* shoot. **2** young and tender branch or stem of a plant. **3** swift or sudden thrusting movement: *an outward* shoot *of the arm.* **4** sharp twinge. **—*n-*** **shoot′ er.**

shooting gallery ***n-*** place, especially in an amusement area, for shooting guns at targets.

shooting star ***n-*** meteor.

shop (shŏp) ***n-*** **1** place where merchandise is sold at retail; store. **2** place where a particular kind of work is done: *a carpenter's* shop. ***vi-*** **[shopped, shop·ping]** to visit stores to look at or purchase merchandise.

set up shop to start a business. **shut up shop 1** to close business. **2** to go out of business. **talk shop** to talk about one's business or profession.

shop·keep·er (shŏp′ kē′ pər) ***n-*** person who carries on business in a shop; retailer.

shop·lift·er (shŏp′ lĭf′ tər) ***n-*** person who steals exposed goods in a store. **—*n-*** **shop′ lift′ ing.**

shop·per (shŏp′ ər) ***n-*** **1** person who shops in a retail store; customer. **2** (also **comparative shopper)** person who is engaged by a store to compare the quality and price of a competitor's merchandise.

shop·ping (shŏp′ ĭng) ***n-*** a looking at or purchasing of merchandise. *as* ***modifier***: *a* shopping *cart.*

shop·talk (shŏp′ tòk′) ***n-*** talk restricted to one's work.

shop·worn (shŏp′ wôrn′) ***adj-*** **1** soiled or worn from being handled or displayed in a store for a long time. **2** no longer original or fresh; stale: *a* shopworn *idea.*

sho·ran (shôr′ ăn′) ***n-*** system of navigation in which radar beams sent out by an airplane are returned to it by ground stations of known location, and thus fix its position by the intersection of two beams. [shortened from *sho*rt *ra*nge *n*avigation.]

[1]**shore** (shôr) ***n-*** land that borders on a body of water. [from Old English **scor(e),** related to **shear.]**

[2]**shore** (shôr) ***vt-*** **[shored, shor·ing]** to prop, steady, or hold up with timbers: *We* shored *up the walls.* ***n-*** timber used as a prop. [from Dutch **schoor,** "a prop."]

shore dinner ***n-*** dinner consisting mainly of seafood.

shore·line (shôr′ līn′) ***n-*** outline of the shore where it meets the water.

shore patrol ***n-*** the military police of the United States Navy, Coast Guard, or Marine Corps.

shore·ward (shôr′ wərd) ***adv-*** (also **shore′ wards)** toward the shore: *to sail* shoreward. ***adj-***: *a* shoreward *breeze.*

shor·ing (shôr′ ĭng) ***n-*** **1** a propping with or as if with shores. **2** timbers used to prop or shore up something.

shorn (shôrn) *p.p.* of **shear.**

[1]**short** (shôrt, shôrt) ***adj-*** **[short·er, short·est] 1** not tall or long: *a* short *man*; short *pair of pants.* **2** curt: *a* short *"No."* **3** brief in time: *a* short *visit.* **4** insufficient or scarce: *to have a* short *supply of food.* **5** having, including, or showing less than is proper or expected: *I am ten bushels* short. *His accounts are* short *five dollars.* **6** of vowels, having the sound of the *a* in "hat," the *e* in "net," the *i* in "hit," the *o* in "not," the *u* in "nut," and the *oo* in "took." **7** of pastry or cake, crisp or crumbling; rich. **8** in finance, not owning the stocks or commodities one is selling. ***adv-*** **1** suddenly: *to stop* short. **2** in finance, without owning the stocks or commodities one is selling: *to sell* short. [from Old English

---

fāte, făt, dâre, bärn; bē, bĕt, mêre; bīte, bĭt; nōte, hŏt, môre, dòg; fŭn, fûr; to͞o, bo͝ok; oil; out; tar; thin; then; hw for wh as in *wh*at; zh for s as in u*s*ual; ə for a, e, i, o, u, as in *a*go, lin*e*n, per*i*l, at*o*m, min*u*s

sc(e)ot meaning "lacking; cut off," and related to **skirt** and **shirt.**] **—n- short′ ness.**

cut short to bring to an immediate close; stop: *The chairman* cut *the speaker* short. **fall short** to fail to come up to expectations, promise, etc.: *The play* fell short *of what we expected.* **for short** as a shorter form: *We call Thomas Tom* for short. **in short** briefly; in a few words. **run short** 1 to use up all (of): *I* ran short *of patience.* 2 to be used up: *The ice cream* ran short *at the picnic.* **short for** being a shortened form of; being a nickname for: *Tom is* short for *Thomas.* **short of 1** not having enough of; lacking. 2 less than; below.

[2]**short** (shôrt, shôrt) *Informal* **n-** short circuit. **vt-** to cause a short circuit in. **vi-**: *The generator* shorted *out.* [from **short circuit.**]

short·age (shôr′ tĭj, shôr′-) **n-** 1 amount lacking to complete anything: *There is a* shortage *of $50 in his bank account.* 2 too small a quantity to satisfy a need.

short·bread (shôrt′ brĕd′, shôrt′-) **n-** rich, crumbly cake or flat cookie made with much shortening.

short·cake (shôrt′ kāk′, shôrt′-) **n-** slightly sweetened biscuit or sponge cake, usually served with crushed berries as a dessert.

short-change (shôrt′ chānj′, shôrt′-) *Informal* **vt-** [**short-changed, short-chang·ing**] 1 to give less change than is due to (someone). 2 to fail to give what is rightfully due; cheat: *A lax teacher may* short-change *his students.*

short circuit n- electrical circuit, usually made by accident, in which the current flows to the ground or to the negative side of the source without passing through a resistance, motor, appliance, etc. Short circuits cause sparks and fire, and they damage equipment. **vt-** (**short-circuit**): *Too much power* short-circuited *the transformer.* **vi-**: *The whole power system* short-circuited.

short·com·ing (shôrt′ kŭm′ ĭng, shôrt′-) **n-** defect or deficiency; fault.

short cut n- route or method shorter than the regular one: *a* short cut *across the field*; *a* short cut *to success.*

short·en (shôr′ tən, shôr′-) **vt-** 1 to make shorter: *Mother* shortened *her coat.* 2 to add shortening to (cake or pastry dough). **vi-** to become shorter.

short·en·ing (shôr′ tən ĭng, shôr′-) **n-** 1 a making short: *the* shortening *of a skirt.* 2 butter, lard, or other fat added to bread, cake, or pastry dough to make it crisp or crumbly.

short-haired (shôrt′ hârd′, shôrt′-) **adj-** having short hair or fur: *a* short-haired *dog.*

short·hand (shôrt′ hănd′, shôrt′-) **n-** any system of rapid writing in which strokes, symbols, or abbreviations are used instead of letters, words, and phrases.

short·hand·ed (shôrt′ hăn′ dəd, shôrt′-) **adj-** lacking the usual or needed amount of workers or helpers.

short·horn (shôrt′ hôrn′, shôrt′-) **n-** one of a large, heavy breed of beef cattle with short horns.

short-lived (shôrt′ lĭvd′, shôrt′-) **adj-** living or lasting only a short time: *a* short-lived *reform.*

short·ly (shôrt′ lē, shôrt′-) **adv-** 1 very soon; presently: *The plane leaves* shortly. 2 briefly; concisely: *Speak* shortly *and to the point.*

shorts (shôrts, shôrts) **n-** (takes plural verb) 1 short trousers. 2 men's or boys' underpants.

short shrift n- little delay or mercy in dealing with a person or situation.

make short shrift of or **give short shrift** to deal with quickly; make short work of.

short-sight·ed (shôrt′ sī′ təd, shôrt′-) **adj-** 1 considering only the present; lacking foresight. 2 nearsighted; unable to see distant objects clearly. **—adv- short′-sight′ ed·ly. n- short′-sight′ ed·ness.**

short·stop (shôrt′ stŏp′, shôrt′-) **n-** in baseball, the infielder between second and third base; also, the position occupied by this player.

short story n- a fictional prose narrative shorter than a novel or novelette.

short-tem·pered (shôrt′ tĕm′ pərd, shôrt′-) **adj-** easily angered; quick-tempered.

short-term (shôrt′ tûrm′, shôrt′-) **adj-** 1 lasting for a short time: *a* short-term *project.* 2 of a loan, bond, etc., payable within a short time, usually less than a year.

short ton See *ton.*

short wave n- radio wave of 60 meters or less, which is short compared with the waves used in ordinary AM radio. *as* **modifier** (**short-wave**): *a* short-wave *set.*

short-wind·ed (shôrt′ wĭn′ dəd, shôrt′-) **adj-** having difficulty in breathing, especially after exercise.

Sho·sho·ni or **Sho·sho·ne** (shə shō′ nē) **n-** [*pl.* **Sho·sho·nis,** also **Sho·sho·ni**] member of a tribe of American Indians who formerly lived on the Snake River plateau and in the adjoining mountains of Idaho, Montana, Nevada, Utah, and Wyoming. Today they live on reservations in these states. **adj-**: *a* Shoshoni *moccasin.*

[1]**shot** (shŏt) **n-** 1 discharge of a firearm or the sound made by it: *The* shot *echoed through the woods.* 2 [*pl.* **shot**] pellet fired from a gun, especially a shotgun; also, any quantity of such pellets. 3 distance which is or can be covered by a missile, sound, etc. 4 *Informal* the launching of a rocket or spacecraft toward a specific target: *a moon* shot; *a Mars* shot. 5 person who shoots; marksman: *Sylvia is a good* shot. 6 throw; cast: *The basketball player made a long* shot. 7 *Informal* injection of medicine into the body; hypodermic: *Have you had your polio* shot? 8 try; attempt. 9 photograph; snapshot: *a* shot *of the baby.* 10 heavy metal ball thrown in the shot-put event. 11 *Slang* drink of alcoholic liquor. 12 in motion pictures and television, the film or tape record of a scene; also, process of photographing it. [from Old English **sceot** and **sceotan,** "to shoot."]

[2]**shot** (shŏt) *p.t. & p.p.* of **shoot.**

shot·gun (shŏt′ gŭn′) **n-** smoothbore firearm for shooting a spreading charge of shot at short range.

Shotgun

shot-put (shŏt′ po͝ot′) **n-** 1 athletic field event in which contestants attempt to throw a shot or heavy metal ball as far as they can. 2 single throw of the shot in this event. **—n- shot′ put′ ter.**

should (sho͝od) **auxiliary verb** 1 am, is, or are almost obliged to; ought to: *He* should *telephone his parents before he leaves town. I really* should *go now.* 2 am, is, or are almost certain or expected to: *The plane* should *be landing at noon. This book* should *give you the answer.* 3 happen or happens to; were to (used only in clauses expressing what might or might not happen): *If it* should *rain, close the windows. If he* should *try it, he must face the consequences.* [**should** was originally a past tense of **shall,** but is now rarely used in the same sense.]

►Both SHOULD and WOULD imply uncertainty or hesitancy. You may use either in a sentence like "*I* should (would) *be happy to see you again.*"

shoul·der (shōl′ dər) **n-** 1 the part of the human body between the neck and the arm, or the part between the neck and the foreleg of most animals. 2 **shoulders** the two shoulders and the part of the back between them. 3 section of a garment intended to cover this part. 4 cut of meat consisting of the upper joint of the foreleg and the parts near it: *a* shoulder *of mutton.* **5** anything resembling this part of the body: *the* shoulder *of a vase*; *the* shoulder *of a hill.* **6** edge of a road or highway: *This road has soft* shoulders. ***vt-*** **1** to push aside or force with or as if with one's shoulder: *He* shouldered *his way through the crowd.* **2** to place upon this part of the body: *He* shouldered *the gun.* **3** to take on; assume: *to* shoulder *responsibilities.* ***vi-*** to push through a crowd; jostle.

put one's shoulder to the wheel to work with utmost effort; set to work vigorously. **shoulder to shoulder 1** side by side and close together. **2** working together for a common goal; united. **straight from the shoulder** frankly and honestly; straightforwardly. **turn** (or **give**) **a cold shoulder to 1** to treat with contempt or scorn; show disdain for. **2** to ignore or avoid; shun.

shoulder arms to place one's rifle almost upright on either the right or left shoulder with the butt supported by the hand on the same side.

shoulder blade ***n-*** flat, triangular bone behind each shoulder, containing the socket of the shoulder joint; scapula.

shoulder patch ***n-*** cloth insignia or badge worn on the upper part of the sleeve of one's uniform.

shoulder strap ***n-*** **1** one of a pair of buttoned-down shoulder flaps on some uniforms, often bearing an insignia of rank or other identifying mark. **2** strap worn over the shoulder to support an article of clothing.

should·n't (shŏŏd′ənt) should not.

shout (shout) ***vi-*** to cry, call, or talk loudly: *The children* shouted *with joy.* ***vt-***: *He* shouted *her name.* ***n-*** loud cry or call. **—*n-* shout′ er.**

shout down to silence by shouting.

shove (shŭv) ***vt-*** **[shoved, shov·ing] 1** to push: *Jack* shoved *the paper across the table to me.* **2** to push roughly; jostle: *The big, surly man* shoved *the boy.* ***vi-*** **1** to exert oneself to move something. **2** to push one's way: *He* shoved *through the crowd.* **3** *Informal* to move reluctantly or with difficulty: *Let's* shove *out.* ***n-*** a push.

shove off 1 to push (a boat) away from shore. **2** *Informal* to leave; depart.

shov·el (shŭv′əl) ***n-*** **1** tool with a long handle and a broad blade, used for digging or scooping coal, snow, earth, etc. **2** (also **shov′ el·ful**) amount this tool holds: *He put a* shovel *of coal in the furnace.* **3** power shovel. ***vt-*** **1** to dig or throw with, or as if with, a shovel: *Omar* shoveled *the snow from the steps.* **2** to clear with a shovel: *to* shovel *a path.* ***vi-***: *to* shovel *rapidly.*

Shovels

shov·el·er (shŭv′ ə lər) ***n-*** **1** person who shovels. **2** any of several river ducks with broad bills.

show (shō) ***vt-*** **[showed, shown** or **showed, show·ing] 1** to place in sight; display; exhibit: *to* show *goods in a shop.* **2** to reveal; make known: *to* show *one's feelings.* **3** to explain, describe, or demonstrate: *Let me* show *just what I mean. He* showed *me how to skate.* **4** to prove; establish: *I shall* show *that he is wrong.* **5** to disclose; reveal: *This* shows *who did it.* **6** to direct; guide; lead: *to* show *a person to his seat.* **7** to record; register: *A calendar* shows *the date.* **8** to give; grant; bestow: *to* show *kindness.* ***vi-*** **1** to be visible or noticeable: *Her embarrassment* showed *when she blushed.* **2** in a horse race, to finish third. ***n-*** **1** any kind of public performance, exhibition, or display: *a horse* show. **2** appearance: *a* show *of health in her rosy cheeks.* **3** pretense; deceitful appearance: *His boasting was only a* show *of courage.* **4** in a horse race, the third position at the finish. **5** *Informal* any undertaking, business, or affair: *He runs the whole* show.

for show for display or effect. **show of hands** display of raised hands expressing the vote of a group.

show off to make a display to impress.

show up 1 to reveal truth about; expose: *to* show up *an imposter.* **2** to appear: *He didn't* show up *for class.*

show·boat (shō′ bōt′) ***n-*** river steamboat, especially an old paddle-wheel steamer on the Mississippi, carrying actors and a theater for giving shows at riverside towns.

show·case (shō′ kās′) ***n-*** glass case, such as one in a store or museum, for displaying and protecting articles.

show·er (shou′ ər) ***n-*** **1** short fall of rain. **2** shower bath. **3** great outburst or flow: *a* shower *of abuse.* **4** party, especially for a bride-to-be, at which presents are given. *as **modifier**: a* shower *curtain.* ***vt-*** **1** to spray or sprinkle with a liquid. **2** to give (someone) a lavish amount of something: *to* shower *a winner with praise.* ***vi-*** **1** to take a shower bath. **2** to rain for a short time. **—*adj-* show′ er·y.**

shower bath ***n-*** bath in which water is sprayed on the person from an overhead or side nozzle; also, an apparatus or room used for such a bath.

show·ing (shō′ ĭng) ***n-*** **1** presentation or display; exhibition: *a* showing *of spring fashions.* **2** performance in a test or contest: *He made a poor* showing *in the race.*

show·man (shō′ mən) ***n-*** [*pl.* **show·men**] **1** person who puts on shows or other entertainment. **2** person who presents anything in a dramatic or vivid manner.

show·man·ship (shō′ mən shĭp′) ***n-*** skill as a showman.

shown (shōn) *p.p.* of **show. *Hom-*** shone.

show-off (shō′ ȯf′) *Informal* ***n-*** **1** person who shows off. **2** a showing off; display to impress.

show·piece (shō′ pēs′) ***n-*** outstanding example or model; exemplar.

show·place (shō′ plās′) ***n-*** place that is highly regarded for its beauty, historic value, etc.

show·room (shō′ rōōm′) ***n-*** room or place in which merchandise is displayed to prospective buyers.

show·y (shō′ ē) ***adj-*** **[show·i·er, show·i·est] 1** making a brilliant display; attracting attention: *a* showy *corsage*; showy *flowers.* **2** flashy and not in good taste; gaudy; ostentatious. **—*adv-* show′ i·ly. *n-* show′ i·ness.**

shrank (shrăngk) *p.t.* of **shrink.**

►For usage note see SHRINK.

shrap·nel (shrăp′ nəl) ***n-*** [*pl.* **shrap·nel**] **1** a type of artillery shell filled with a powder charge and a number of metal balls that are scattered by a mid-air explosion. **2** jagged steel fragments hurled by an exploding shell.

shred (shrĕd) ***n-*** small piece cut or torn off something; hence, any small piece; fragment: *to tear a letter into* shreds; *not a* shred *of evidence.* ***vt-*** **[shred·ded** or **shred, shred·ding]** to cut or tear into strips or fragments: *to* shred *cabbage for a salad.*

shrew (shrōō) ***n-*** **1** quarrelsome, scolding woman. **2** any of several small animals resembling mice, with soft brown fur, a long, pointed nose, and tiny eyes.

Short-tailed shrew, about 4 1/2 in. long

shrewd (shrōōd) ***adj-*** **[shrewd·er, shrewd·est]** clever and keen in practical matters: *a* shrewd *gambler*; *a* shrewd *deal.* **—*adv-* shrewd′ ly. *n-* shrewd′ ness.**

shrew·ish (shrōō′ ĭsh) ***adj-*** bad-tempered; scolding; nagging. **—*adv-* shrew′ ish·ly. *n-* shrew′ ish·ness.**

fāte, făt, dâre, bärn; bē, bĕt, mêre; bīte, bĭt; nōte, hŏt, môre, dȯg; fŭn, fûr; tōō, bŏŏk; oil; out; ta*r*; thin; *th*en; hw for wh as in *wh*at; zh for s as in u*s*ual; ə for a, e, i, o, u, as in *a*go, lin*e*n, per*i*l, at*o*m, min*u*s

shriek (shrēk) ***n-*** loud, sharp cry; outcry. ***vi-:*** *to* shriek *with laughter.* ***vt-:*** *to* shriek *an oath.*

shrift (shrĭft) *Archaic* ***n-*** confession to a priest and the absolution granted by him.

shrike (shrīk) ***n-*** any of various birds with a hooked bill, which feed chiefly on insects but sometimes kill smaller birds, mice, etc.

shrill (shrĭl) ***adj-*** [**shrill·er, shrill·est**] high and sharp in sound: *the* shrill *cry of a hyena; a* shrill *whistle.* ***vi-*** to make a high, piercing sound or cry: *Katydids* shrilled *in the tree.* ***vt-:*** *The bird* shrilled *a cry.* **—*n-*** **shrill′ness.** ***adv-*** **shril′ly.**

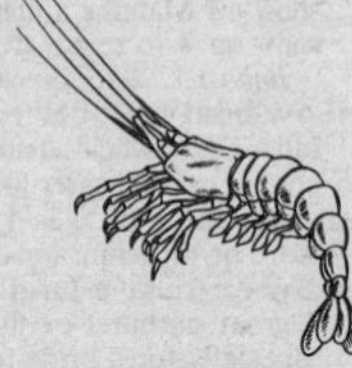
Shrimp, 2—3 in. long

shrimp (shrĭmp) ***n-*** **1** any of various small, long-tailed crustaceans, used for food. **2** *Slang* small or unimportant person. *as* ***modifier:*** *a* shrimp *salad.*

shrine (shrīn) ***n-*** **1** holy place; sacred building or city: *Mecca is a Muslim* shrine. **2** place of prayer or meditation, often containing a sacred statue. **3** box containing sacred relics. **4** the tomb of a saint. **5** any place held in reverence for historic or other reasons: *The Lincoln Memorial is a national* shrine.

shrink (shrĭngk) ***vi-*** [**shrank** (shrăngk) or **shrunk** (shrŭngk), **shrunk, shrink·ing**] **1** to become smaller: *The sweater* shrank *when it was washed in hot water.* **2** to withdraw or move away (from) something dangerous or unpleasant: *He* shrank *from a hard task.* ***vt-*** to make smaller; cause to contract: *to* shrink *a shirt by washing.* **—*adj-*** **shrink′a·ble.** ***n-*** **shrink′er.**

►The principal forms of SHRINK are either SHRINK, SHRANK, SHRUNK, or SHRINK, SHRUNK, SHRUNKEN. The first series is now preferred, although SHRUNKEN is frequently used as the adjective: *He wore a* shrunken, *faded jacket.*

shrink·age (shrĭngk′ĭj) ***n-*** **1** a reducing in size or quantity; contraction; decrease: *the* shrinkage *of woolen goods;* shrinkage *of dollar value.* **2** amount anything shrinks: *allowance for a* shrinkage *of one inch.*

shrinking violet *Informal* ***n-*** retiring or bashful person.

shrive (shrīv) *Archaic* ***vt-*** [**shrove** (shrōv) or **shrived, shriv·en** (shrĭv′ən) or **shrived, shriv·ing**] to hear the confession of and give absolution to. ***vi-*** to confess one's sins to a priest.

shriv·el (shrĭv′əl) ***vt-*** to dry or curl up; wither; wrinkle: *The hot sun* shriveled *the leaves.* ***vi-:*** *The leaves* shriveled.

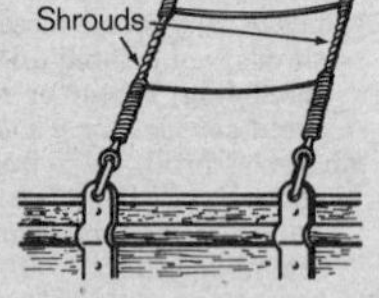

shroud (shroud) ***n-*** **1** garment or covering in which a dead person is buried. **2** something that covers or conceals: *a* shroud *of mist; a* shroud *of mystery.* **3 shrouds** (1) the ropes or cables extending from the mast to the side of the ship, serving as a support for the mast. (2) the cords of a parachute that suspend the harness from the canopy. ***vt-*** to cover or veil: *Fog* shrouded *the airport.*

shrove (shrōv) *p.t.* of **shrive.**

Shrove Tuesday ***n-*** the day before Ash Wednesday.

shrub (shrŭb) ***n-*** woody plant, such as a rosebush, that is smaller than a tree, and usually has many separate stems starting from near the ground.

shrub·ber·y (shrŭb′ə rē) ***n-*** [*pl.* **shrub·ber·ies**] **1** group of shrubs; bushes. **2** place planted with shrubs.

shrub·by (shrŭb′ē) ***adj-*** [**shrub·bi·er, shrub·bi·est**] of, like, or covered with shrubs: *a* shrubby *tract of land.*

shrug (shrŭg) ***vi-*** [**shrugged, shrug·ging**] to raise the shoulders in doubt, indifference, impatience, etc.: *Tom* shrugged *when asked his opinion.* ***vt-:*** *She* shrugged *her shoulders.* ***n-:*** *He turned away with a* shrug.

shrunk (shrŭngk) *p.t. & p.p.* of **shrink.**

►For usage note see SHRINK.

shrunk·en (shrŭngk′ən) *Archaic p.p.* of **shrink.** ***adj-*** made smaller; contracted; reduced: *a* shrunken *shirt.*

shuck (shŭk) ***n-*** outer covering; shell; husk. ***vt-*** **1** to take off an outer covering from; shell; husk: *He* shucked *a basket of corn for the picnic.* **2** *Informal* to take or cast off: *He* shucked *his jacket.* **—*n-*** **shuck′er.**

shud·der (shŭd′ər) ***vi-*** to tremble; shake; quiver: *He* shuddered *in the chill wind.* ***n-*** a trembling; shiver; tremor: *He thought of the horror movie with a* shudder.

shuf·fle (shŭf′əl) ***vt-*** [**shuf·fled, shuf·fling**] **1** to pass or shift from one person or place to another: *We* shuffled *the money from hand to hand.* **2** to mix up or rearrange: *He* shuffled *the deck of cards.* **3** to trail (the feet) in walking or dancing. ***vi-*** **1** to shift things from one position to another. **2** to walk with a scuffling or dragging step. **3** to do something in a careless, clumsy manner: *He* shuffled *through his work.* **—*n-*** **1** dragging step. **2** a rearranging or mixing up. **—*n-*** **shuf′fler.**

shuffle off to get rid of hastily or carelessly.

shuf·fle·board (shŭf′əl bôrd′) ***n-*** game in which disks are slid with a stick along a flat surface to numbered squares; also, the surface on which the game is played.

shun (shŭn) ***vt-*** [**shunned, shun·ning**] to avoid; keep away from: *He* shunned *their company.* **—*n-*** **shun′ner.**

shunt (shŭnt) ***vt-*** **1** to turn off or switch to one side: *They* shunted *the train from the main track.* **2** to move or cause to go repeatedly from side to side or place to place: *He* shunted *me from office to office.* **3** to provide (an electrical circuit) with a connection that provides another parallel path and reduces the power to the rest of the circuit. **4** to reduce the power to (a piece of electrical equipment) by means of such a connection. **5** to divert (part of the power in an electrical circuit) by means of such a connection. ***vi-:*** *The train* shunted *off the main track.* ***n-*** **1** a moving to the side or from side to side. **2** electrical connection that provides another parallel path in a circuit and reduces the power to the rest of the circuit. **—*n-*** **shunt′er.**

shush (shŭsh) *Informal* ***interj-*** be silent! ***vt-*** *Slang* to silence.

shut (shŭt) ***vt-*** [**shut, shut·ting**] **1** to close: *Please* shut *the door.* **2** to fold up: *to* shut *a screen and put it away.* ***vi-*** to become closed: *The gate* shut *in the wind.*

shut down to stop working or operating.

shut in to confine: *She* shut *the horse* in *the barn.*

shut off to turn off; stop from working.

shut out **1** to prevent from entering. **2** in baseball, to prevent (the opposing team) from scoring.

shut up **1** to confine; enclose. **2** to discontinue; close. **3** to stop talking, or cause to stop talking.

shut-down (shŭt′doun′) ***n-*** a closing down of a factory, mine, etc.

shut-in (shŭt′ĭn) ***n-*** person who is too ill to leave his or her home. ***adj-:*** *a* shut-in *student.*

Shutters

shut·out (shŭt′out′) ***n-*** **1** in baseball, a game in which a team is defeated without having scored. **2** lockout.

shut·ter (shŭt′ər) ***n-*** **1** screen or panel to cover the outside of a window. **2** device that covers a camera lens and opens briefly to expose the film or plate. ***vt-*** **1** to cover (a window or door) with shutters. **2** to supply with shutters.

shut·tle (shŭt′əl) ***n-*** **1** in weaving, an instrument in the shape of a cigar that carries the thread from side to side. **2** sewing machine device that holds thread and carries it back and forth to an upper thread to make a stitch. **3** anything that moves back and forth in a similar way; especially, a transport system that makes short trips back and forth between two points. ***vt-*** **[shut·tled, shut·tling]** to move back and forth frequently: *They* shuttled *Jim from job to job.* ***vi-***: *He* shuttled *between jobs.*

shut·tle·cock (shŭt′əl kŏk′) ***n-*** small cork ball with feathers or plastic imitation feathers, used in badminton.

Shuttlecock

[1]shy (shī) ***adj-*** **[shi·er** or **shy·er, shi·est** or **shy·est] 1** timid; bashful; self-conscious. **2** *Informal* having a shortage of; short. ***vi-*** **[shied, shy·ing]** to jump; start; draw back quickly: *The horse* shied *at the car.* [from Old English **scēoh.**] **—*adv-*** **shy′ly.** ***n-*** **shy′ness.**

fight shy of to avoid; evade.

[2]shy (shī) ***vt-*** **[shied, shy·ing]** to throw with a sudden movement; to fling: *He* shied *a stone into the water.* ***n-*** [*pl.* **shies]** sudden throw; fling. [of uncertain origin.]

Shy·lock (shī′lŏk′) ***n-*** in Shakespeare's "Merchant of Venice," a revengeful moneylender who requires a pound of flesh as a pledge for a loan to his enemy, Antonio.

shy·ster (shī′stər) *Slang* ***n-*** sly and unscrupulous person in the practice of a profession, especially law.

[1]si (sē) *Music* ***n-*** the seventh note of a musical scale. Also **ti.** [from Italian **si,** from the first letters of Latin **Sancte Ioannes,** "Saint John."] ***Homs-*** sea, see.

[2]si (sē) ***adv-*** word for "yes" in Spanish, Italian, and sometimes French.

Si symbol for silicon.

Si·a·mese (sī′ə mēz′) ***n-*** native or inhabitant of Siam (now Thailand), its people, or their language. ***adj-***: *in* Siamese *history.*

Siamese cat ***n-*** short-haired, blue-eyed cat with a fawn-colored body that is darker at the tips of the tail, feet, ears, and face. For picture, see *cat.*

Siamese twins ***n-*** *pl.* twins born joined together.

sib·i·lant (sĭb′ə lənt) ***n-*** **1** consonant made by producing a hissing sound. **2** symbol for this consonant, such as "s," or "z." ***adj-*** **1** of or relating to such consonants. **2** hissing: *the* sibilant *sounds of a snake.* **—*n-*** **sib′i·lance.**

sib·ling (sĭb′lĭng) ***n-*** **1** brother or sister. **2 siblings** brothers and sisters.

sib·yl (sĭb′əl) ***n-*** **1** in ancient Greece and Rome, a woman who could foretell the future. **2** any prophetess.

[1]sic (sĭk) *Latin* thus; so, placed in brackets after a quoted statement to show that, in spite of an obvious error, it is reproduced exactly. Example: "a yung [sic] man." ***Hom-*** sick.

[2]sic (sĭk) ***vt-*** **[sicked, sick·ing] 1** to attack (used as a command to a dog). **2** to urge to attack. Also **sick.** [variant of **seek.**]

sick (sĭk) ***adj-*** **[sick·er, sick·est] 1** ill; in poor health: *He's in bed,* sick. **2** vomiting or feeling as if one is going to vomit; nauseated: *Bus rides make him* sick. **3** greatly troubled or annoyed; disgusted: *It makes me* sick *to think of what he has done.* **4** annoyed and tired (of): *I'm* sick *of this weather.* **5** mentally ill or emotionally unbalanced; also, morbid; gruesome; macabre: *a* sick *mind*; *a* sick *joke*; sick *humor.* ***Hom-*** sic.

sick bay ***n-*** the hospital on a ship.

sick·bed (sĭk′bĕd′) ***n-*** bed to which a sick person is confined.

sick·en (sĭk′ən) ***vt-*** to make ill; also, to make disgusted: *The odor* sickened *him.* ***vi-***: *She* sickened *at the thought.*

sick·en·ing (sĭk′ən ĭng) ***adj-*** causing nausea or disgust; revolting: *a* sickening *odor.* **—*adv-*** **sick′en·ing·ly.**

sick·ish (sĭk′ĭsh) ***adj-*** **1** somewhat ill, especially with nausea: *I feel* sickish. **2** somewhat sickening; nauseating: *a* sickish *smell.* **—*adv-*** **sick′ish·ly.** ***n-*** **sick′ish·ness.**

sick·le (sĭk′əl) ***n-*** tool consisting of a curved blade on a short handle, used for cutting grain, grass, etc.

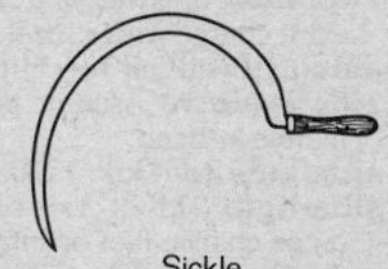
Sickle

sickle-cell anemia ***n-*** an inherited blood disease that occurs especially among black people. Red blood cells containing abnormal hemoglobin become sickle-shaped from a lack of oxygen. Oxygen supply to the tissues is inadequate.

sick·ly (sĭk′lē) ***adj-*** **[sick·li·er, sick·li·est] 1** weak; frail; unhealthy: *a* sickly *child.* **2** having to do with or caused by illness: *His face had a* sickly *color.* **3** likely to cause illness: *a* sickly *climate.* **4** weak; dim: *a* sickly *light.* **5** lacking spirit: *a* sickly *smile.* **6** sickening: *a* sickly *odor.* ***adv-*** in a sick manner. **—*n-*** **sick′li·ness.**

sick·ness (sĭk′nəs) ***n-*** **1** illness; poor health. **2** a particular disease; malady: *sleeping* sickness. **3** nausea.

sick·room (sĭk′ro͞om′) ***n-*** room to which a sick person is confined.

sid·dur (sĭd′o͞or′, -ər) ***n-*** [*pl.* **sid·dur·im** (-əm)] in Judaism, a prayer book for weekdays and the Sabbath.

side (sīd) ***n-*** **1** any of the lines or surfaces that bound a geometric figure: *A cube has six* sides. **2** one of the two longer lines or surfaces of an object as distinguished from the top, bottom, or the ends: *the two* sides *of a rectangle.* **3** either of the two usually vertical surfaces of a building or other structure that are not the front or back; also, the area near this surface: *the* side *of a house.* **4** either of the two surfaces of any object thought of as having no appreciable thickness: *the finished* side *of a garment.* **5** the right or left part of the body of a person or animal; also, the space beside these parts: *to lie on one's* side. **6** position to the right or left of a central point or line: *the left* side *of a stage.* **7** either of two hemispheres: *the dark* side *of the moon.* **8** the slope or face of a hill, ridge, mountain, etc. **9** group of partisans, contestants, etc., in opposition to another group: *the losing* side *in a baseball game.* **10** any opposing position, version, point of view, etc.: *two* sides *to an argument.* **11** aspect; quality; part: *to look on the bright* side. **12** line of descent through the father or mother: *my grandfather on my mother's* side. ***as modifier:*** *a* side *ache*; *a* side *door*; *a* side *glance.* ***vi-*** **[sid·ed, sid·ing]** to think or act in favor of one party in a dispute.

on the side *Informal* **1** in addition to one's full-time job. **2** in addition to what is regularly included in a meal ordered in a restaurant: *a salad* on the side. **split one's sides** to laugh uproariously; howl with laughter. **take sides** to favor one side in a dispute.

side·arm (sīd′ärm′) ***adj-*** in baseball, thrown with a sideways motion: *a* sidearm *pitch.* ***adv-***: *to pitch* sidearm.

---

side arm ***n-*** weapon, especially a revolver or automatic pistol, worn at one's side.
side·board (sīd′ bôrd′) ***n-*** piece of dining-room furniture with cupboards and drawers for table linen and silver.
side·burns (sīd′ bûrnz′) ***n-*** *pl.* hair allowed to grow down on the sides of a man's face in front of the ears, when the rest of the beard is shaved off.
side·car (sīd′ kär′) ***n-*** one-wheeled passenger car attached to the side of a motorcycle.
sid·ed (sī′ dəd) ***adj-*** having sides of a certain number or kind: *a six*-sided *box*; *a plastic*-sided *container.*
side dish or **side order** ***n-*** portion of food served at extra charge with a meal ordered in a restaurant.
side·hill (sīd′ hĭl′) ***n-*** hillside.
side issue ***n-*** issue or point that is not essential to the matter at hand.
side·kick (sīd′ kĭk′) *Slang* ***n-*** close companion; buddy.
side·light (sīd′ līt′) ***n-*** **1** a light from the side. **2** incidental or chance fact or information.
side line or **side·line** (sīd′ līn′) ***n-*** **1** line bordering and limiting an area: *The spectators sit behind the* side lines *at a tennis match.* **2** branch from a main line: *A* side line *of pipe runs from the house to the garage.* **3** trade or occupation followed in addition to a main one: *The artist had a* side line *of cabinet making.* **4** goods carried by a merchant in addition to his main stock: *The florist carried a* side line *of candy.* ***vt-*** **sideline** **[side·lined, side·lin·ing]** to prevent (someone) from taking part in an activity.
on the sidelines in the role of a spectator.
side·long (sīd′ lòng′) ***adj-*** **1** directed to or along a side: *a* sidelong *look.* **2** indirect or surreptitious; not straightforward: *a* sidelong *approach to a person.* ***adv-***: *to move* sidelong.
si·de·re·al (sī dêr′ ē əl) ***adj-*** of, related to, or measured by the stars: *a* sidereal *year.*
sidereal day ***n-*** the time of one complete rotation of the earth with respect to the vernal equinox, equal to 23 hours, 56 minutes, 4.09 seconds.
sidereal year ***n-*** time during which the earth makes one complete revolution around the sun with respect to the fixed stars, equal to 365 days, 6 hours, 9 minutes, and 9.54 seconds.
sid·er·ite (sĭd′ ə rīt′) ***n-*** natural iron carbonate that is an important iron ore.
side·sad·dle (sīd′ săd′ əl) ***n-*** woman's saddle having one stirrup for the left foot and a horn over which to hook the right knee, so that both feet of the rider rest on the same side of the horse. ***adv-***: *to* ride *sidesaddle.*
side show ***n-*** minor show accompanying a main one.
side·slip (sīd′ slĭp′) ***n-*** **1** sideward slip or skid. **2** downward, sideways movement of an airplane. ***vi-*** **[side·slipped, side·slip·ping]**: *The car* sideslipped *on the road.*
side·split·ting (sīd′ splĭt′ ĭng) ***adj-*** causing great laughter; hilarious: *a* sidesplitting *comedy.*
side step ***n-*** step taken to one side.
side·step or **side-step** (sīd′ stĕp′) ***vt-*** **[side·stepped** or **side-stepped, side·step·ping** or **side-step·ping]** to avoid by, or as if by, stepping to the side; evade: *He* sidestepped *all unpleasant issues.* ***vi-***: *He* sidesteps *when he should confront issues.* **—*n-* side′ step′ per.**
side·stroke (sīd′ strōk′) ***n-*** in swimming, a stroke in which the swimmer lies on the side while his arms thrust forward alternately and his legs perform a scissors kick.
side·swipe (sīd′ swīp′) ***vt-*** **[side·swiped, side·swip·ing]** to strike with a sweeping blow with or along the side: *to* sideswipe *an auto.* ***n-*** such a blow.
side·track (sīd′ trăk′) ***vt-*** **1** to switch (a train) to a siding or off the main track. **2** to turn from a main course; divert: *He* sidetracked *the argument from the real issues.* ***n-*** railroad spur.
side·walk (sīd′ wòk′) ***n-*** footpath at the side of a road.
side wall ***n-*** the outer surface of a tire between the tread and the rim of the wheel.
side·ward (sīd′ wərd) ***adj-*** toward the side: *a* sideward *glance.* ***adv-*** (also **side′ wards**): *He ran* sideward.
side·ways (sīd′ wāz′) ***adv-*** **1** from or toward a side; sidewise: *to look at a thing* sideways. **2** with the side or edge foremost: *to move* sideways; *to carry a table through a door* sideways. ***adj-***: *a* sideways *movement.*
side·wheel·er (sīd′ hwē′ lər) ***n-*** steamboat with a paddle wheel on each side.
[1]**side·wind·er** (sīd′ wīn′ dər) ***n-*** small rattlesnake that moves by throwing loops of the body forward, found in the deserts of southwestern United States.
[2]**side·wind·er** (sīd′ wīn′ dər) ***n-*** heavy, swinging blow with a fist, delivered from the side.
side·wise (sīd′ wīz′) ***adv-*** sideways: *to glance* sidewise. ***adj-***: *a* sidewise *glance.*
sid·ing (sī′ dĭng) ***n-*** **1** short railroad track to which trains may be switched from a main track. **2** clapboards, shingles, etc., forming the outer walls of a frame house.
si·dle (sī′ dəl) ***vi-*** **[si·dled, si·dling]** to move sideways, especially in a shy or stealthy manner.
siege (sēj) ***n-*** **1** the surrounding of a place by an army in order to cut off its supplies and weaken its ability to resist assault. **2** condition of being surrounded in this way; also, the time covered by this. **3** long, distressing period: *a* siege *of illness.*
lay siege to **1** to besiege. **2** to attempt to gain, capture, or win by long and persistent effort.
Sieg·fried (sēg′ frēd, sĭg′-) ***n-*** hero of several Germanic legends with many different versions, and a principal character in some of Richard Wagner's operas.
si·en·na (sē ĕn′ ə) ***n-*** a brownish-yellow or reddish-brown clay used as a coloring matter or pigment. In its natural state it is called **raw sienna.** When it is burned, it becomes richer and brighter in color and is called **burnt sienna.** ***adj-***: *the* sienna *tones of the painting.*
si·er·ra (sē ĕr′ ə) ***n-*** chain or range of mountains rising in irregular peaks that resemble the teeth of a saw.
si·es·ta (sē′ ĕs tə) ***n-*** a nap or rest at noon or after the midday meal, customary in Spain, Portugal, and Latin American countries.
sieve (sĭv) ***n-*** utensil with a perforated or screened bottom for draining or sifting, or for separating solid materials from a liquid.

Sieve

sift (sĭft) ***vt-*** **1** to separate the finer from the coarser parts of, especially by using a sieve: *to* sift *sand.* **2** to sprinkle with a sieve: *to* sift *flour over meat.* **3** to examine closely; study; scrutinize: *to* sift *the facts.* ***vi-***: *The snow* sifted *through the cracks.* **—*n-* sift′ er.**
sigh (sī) ***vi-*** **1** to let out a deep, audible breath expressing fatigue, sorrow, relief, etc.: *The old woman* sighed *with regret.* **2** to make a sound similar to this: *The wind* sighed *through the trees.* **3** to long; grieve: *She* sighed *for her lost youth.* ***vt-***: *He* sighed *his relief at seeing the children safe.* ***n-*** **1** a deep, audible breath expressing fatigue, sorrow, relief, etc. **2** a sound similar to this: *the* sigh *of the wind.* **—*n-* sigh′ er.** ***adv-*** **sigh′ ing·ly.**
sight (sīt) ***n-*** **1** power of seeing; vision. **2** view or visual perception of something; setting of eyes on something: *my first* sight *of the sea*; *love at first* sight. **3** something seen; view; spectacle: *The rainbow was a glorious* sight. **4** *Informal* something unattractive or unpleasant to be seen: *The room was a* sight *after the party.* **5** attention

with the eyes; gaze: *He fixed his* sight *upon the lighthouse.* **6** the limit or range within which a person can see or an object can be seen; visibility: *The plane flew out of* sight. **7** manner of looking at or considering something; opinion: *In her* sight, *the boy did very well.* **8** examination; inspection: *This report is for the* sight *of the committee only.* **9** device on a gun or optical instrument to help in guiding the aim or eye. **10** careful aim or observation by means of such a device: *to take a* sight *with a sextant.* **11 sights** things worth seeing; interesting places: *all the* sights *at the fair.* ***vt-*** **1** to see with the eye or a device to aid the eye: *to* sight *land in the distance*; *to* sight *a target from a plane.* **2** to aim: *to* sight *a gun.* **3** to test and adjust the gunsight of (a rifle). ***vi-*** to look carefully: *I'll* sight *around to find it.* ***Homs-*** cite, site.

a sight *Informal* (used as an adverb) very much; a lot. **at sight 1** as soon as seen: *He recognized the queen* at sight. **2** upon presentation: *Certain notes are payable* at sight. **by sight** by appearance, without personal acquaintance: *He knows the mayor only* by sight. **not by a long sight** not at all; by no means. **on sight** as soon as seen. **sight unseen** without seeing the thing in question beforehand: *I'll buy it* sight unseen.

sight·ed (sī′ təd) ***adj-*** able to see; not blind.

sight·less (sīt′ ləs) ***adj-*** unable to see; blind. **—*n-* sight′ less·ness.**

sight·ly (sīt′ lē) ***adj-*** **[sight·li·er, sight·li·est]** pleasing to the eye; attractive. **—*n-* sight′ li·ness.**

sight·see·ing (sīt′ sē′ ĭng) ***n-*** a visiting of places of interest: *I love* sightseeing *in Paris. as* ***modifier***: *a* sightseeing *trip.* **—*n-* sight′ se′ er.**

sign (sīn) ***n-*** **1** a lettered board or plate giving the name of a business, information, etc.: *a shoemaker's* sign; *a road* sign. **2** a mark or character that stands for a thing or an idea; symbol: *The Cross is the* sign *of the Christian religion.* **3** something by which something else is made known; indication or indicator: *His gift was a* sign *of his love. This skin rash is a* sign *of an allergy.* **4** motion or gesture used instead of words to express some wish, thought, or command: *The policeman gave a* sign *to the driver to stop.* **5** omen; portent. **6** anything left by an animal showing where it was; trail; trace; scent: *There were deer* signs *in the woods.* **7** one of the 12 equal divisions of the zodiac, or its symbol. **8** *Mathematics* (1) symbol used to indicate a mathematical operation such as addition or multiplication, as [+] or [×]. (2) symbol that represents a certain relation between two or more quantities, as [<] (less than) or [>] (greater than). (3) one of two symbols [+] (plus) or [—] (minus) that precedes a numeral or a variable and indicates, respectively, a positive or a negative value. ***vt-*** **1** to write (one's name) as a signature. **2** to write one's name at the end of: *to* sign *a letter.* **3** to hire by getting the signature of: *The foreman* signed *another carpenter.* **4** to guarantee to be genuine by putting one's signature, initials, or mark on: *to* sign *a check*; *to* sign *a work of art.* ***vi-*** **1** to write one's signature: *He* signed *on the dotted line.* **2** to motion; signal: *He* signed *for them to approach.* **3** to agree to the terms of a contract by putting one's signature to it: *The ballplayer* signed *for the next season.* ***Hom-*** sine. **—*n-* sign′ er.**

sign away to waive or renounce (a right, claim, etc.) by or as if by putting one's signature on a document.

sign off to announce the end of a radio or television program and stop broadcasting for the day.

sign on to agree to work for someone.

sign over to transfer (a right to property) by putting one's signature to a document.

sign up 1 to enlist for military service. **2** to enroll.

sig·nal (sĭg′ nəl) ***n-*** **1** sign agreed upon for sending information, instructions, notice of danger, etc.: *a train* signal; *a fire* signal; *a* signal *of distress.* **2** something that brings about action: *The shout of "Fire!" was a* signal *for panic.* **3** in radio, television, radar, etc., the modulation of an electromagnetic wave or electric current that transmits a sound, image, or message; also, the wave or current itself. **4 signals** in football, numbers called out by the quarterback in announcing the play or as an indication of the instant it should start. *as* ***modifier***: *a* signal *light.* ***adj-*** remarkable; extraordinary; memorable: *The affair was a* signal *success.* ***vt-*** to communicate with, inform, or notify by signs: *The captain* signaled *us to come to.* ***vi-***: *I* signaled *for help.*

signal flag ***n-*** flag of special design that represents a letter of the alphabet, a numeral, or a message; also, a flag used for signaling by waving or holding it in certain positions.

sig·nal·ize (sĭg′ nə līz′) ***vt-*** **[sig·nal·ized, sig·nal·iz·ing]** to make noteworthy or prominent; mark; distinguish; characterize: *Poets* signalized *the reign of Elizabeth I.*

sig·nal·ly (sĭg′ nə lē) ***adv-*** in a remarkable or striking manner; notably: *The meeting hall was* signally *quiet.*

sig·na·tor·y (sĭg′ nə tôr′ ē) ***n-*** [*pl.* **sig·na·tor·ies**] person or nation that has signed an official document such as a treaty, charter, etc. ***adj-*** having to do with or bound by the terms of such a document: *the* signatory *powers.*

sig·na·ture (sĭg′ nə chər) ***n-*** **1** person's name written by his or her own hand in an individual way which is the same time after time; autograph. **2** *Music* (1) (also **key signature**) symbols placed at the beginning of the staff, or whenever a change is indicated, to show the key in which the music is to be played or sung. (2) (also **time signature**) a fraction placed at the beginning of the staff, or wherever a change is indicated, to show the number of beats in the measure (top number) and the note that is the unit of measurement (bottom number). **3** in a book or magazine, a set of consecutive pages, now usually 32, 48, or 64, that forms a unit for binding.

sign·board (sīn′ bôrd′) ***n-*** board with a sign, advertisement, or notice on it.

sig·net (sĭg′ nət) ***n-*** a seal; official stamp.

signet ring ***n-*** finger ring bearing a signet, formerly used for sealing letters and other documents.

sig·nif·i·cance (sĭg nĭf′ ə kəns) ***n-*** **1** meaning; sense: *I don't understand the* significance *of your remark.* **2** importance: *an event of great* significance *in history.*

sig·nif·i·cant (sĭg nĭf′ ə kənt) ***adj-*** **1** important; notable: *a* significant *improvement.* **2** having a special meaning; expressive; suggestive. **—*adv-* sig·nif′ i·cant·ly.**

significant digit *Mathematics* ***n-*** in an approximate number, all digits of the numeral except the zeros used to locate the decimal point. Example: In the number 92,000,000 the 9 and 2 are significant digits. The decimal point to the right of the last zero is normally not shown.

sig·nif·i·ca·tion (sĭg′ nə fə kā′ shən) ***n-*** **1** a signifying or symbolizing: *the* signification *of speech sounds by written letters.* **2** import; significance.

sig·ni·fy (sĭg′ nə fī′) ***vt-*** **[sig·ni·fied, sig·ni·fy·ing] 1** to make known by actions, words, or signs; declare: *Nodding his head* signifies *his agreement.* **2** to mean; represent; denote: *The letter "A"* signifies *"excellent" on a test paper.* ***vi-*** to be of importance; matter; count.

sign language ***n-*** system of gestures with the hands and body by which persons who do not speak the same language can communicate, or by which one can communicate with deaf persons.

si·gnor (sēn′ yôr′) *Italian* ***n-*** [*pl.* **si·gno·ri** (-ē)] form of **signore** used before names or other titles, and usually the equivalent of "Mr."

si·gno·ra (sēn yôr′ ä) *Italian* ***n-*** [*pl.* **si·gno·re** (-ā)] **1** title or form of address, equivalent to "Mrs." or "Madam." **2** a lady or noblewoman.

si·gno·re (sēn yôr′ ā) *Italian* ***n-*** [*pl.* **si·gno·ri** (-rē)] **1** form of respectful address, equivalent to "Sir," and used without the person's name. **2** gentleman; lord.

si·gno·ri·na (sēn′ yə rē′ nä) *Italian* ***n-*** [*pl.* **si·gno·ri·ne** (-nā)] **1** title or form of address, equivalent to "Miss." **2** young lady.

si·gno·ri·no (sēn′ yə rē′ nō) *Italian* ***n-*** [*pl.* **si·gno·ri·ni** (-nē)] **1** title or form of address, equivalent to "Master." **2** young gentleman.

sign·post (sīn′ pōst′) ***n-*** **1** post having a notice or direction on it. **2** anything serving as an indication.

Sikh (sēk) ***n-*** follower of a religion that originated in India during the 16th century and is related both to Hinduism and Islam.

si·lage (sī′ lĭj) ***n-*** green fodder cut up fine and stored in a silo to ferment; ensilage.

si·lence (sī′ ləns) ***n-*** **1** absence of sound or noise; stillness; quiet. **2** refusal or reluctance to speak; a holding of one's tongue: *Your* silence *will be interpreted as approval.* **3** lack of mention or notice: *They passed over the subject in* silence. ***vt-*** **[si·lenced, si·lenc·ing]** **1** to cause to be still: *to* silence *barking dogs.* **2** to put to rest; quiet: *to* silence *one's conscience.* **3** to force (guns) to cease firing. ***interj-*** keep quiet; be still!

si·lenc·er (sī′ lən sər) ***n-*** **1** person or thing that dulls or muffles sound or noises. **2** tubelike device attached to the muzzle of a gun to reduce its sound when fired.

si·lent (sī′ lənt) ***adj-*** **1** saying nothing; making no sound; mute: *He was* silent *during the meeting.* **2** free from sound or noise; quiet; still: *It was a* silent *evening.* **3** not expressed by sound; not spoken: *a* silent *approval*; *a* silent *command.* **4** not active or in operation; dormant: *a* silent *volcano.* **5** written but not pronounced: *The "b" in dumb is* silent. ***—adv-*** **si′ lent·ly.**

silent butler ***n-*** dish with a handle and hinged cover, used for collecting cigarette butts, ashes, etc.

Silent butler

silent movie ***n-*** motion picture without accompanying sound on a sound track; especially, such a motion picture made before about 1928.

silent partner ***n-*** partner who has a share in a business but takes no active part in its management.

Si·le·nus (sī lē′ nəs) ***n-*** in Greek mythology, the foster father of Bacchus, usually represented as a fat, jolly old satyr riding on a donkey.

sil·hou·ette (sĭl′ ōō ĕt′) ***n-*** **1** outline drawing filled in with a solid color, usually black; especially, such a drawing of a human profile. **2** an outline of a figure seen in front of, or as if in front of, a bright light. ***vt-*** **[sil·hou·et·ted, sil·hou·et·ting]** to show as an outline filled in with a solid color.

Silhouette

sil·i·ca (sĭl′ ĭ kə) ***n-*** silicon dioxide.

sil·i·cate (sĭl′ ĭ kət, -kāt′) ***n-*** any one of a number of salts, especially complex metal salts, of silicon.

si·li·ceous (sə lĭsh′ əs) ***adj-*** containing silica or silicates.

sil·i·con (sĭl′ ə kən, -kŏn′) ***n-*** nonmetallic element, the second commonest element in the earth's crust, where it occurs in silicon dioxide and many silicates. When pure it has two forms, a dark-gray crystalline solid and a brown powder. It is used in alloys and materials that resist acid. Symbol Si, At. No. 14, At. Wt. 28.086.

silicon dioxide ***n-*** colorless, transparent, crystalline compound (SiO_2) that occurs naturally in several forms, including sand and quartz; silica. It is the main ingredient in glass.

sil·i·cone (sĭl′ ə kōn′) ***n-*** any of a large group of polymers in which some carbon atoms have been replaced by silicon atoms. Silicones have great resistance to moisture and extremes of temperature.

sil·i·co·sis (sĭl′ ə kō′ səs) ***n-*** serious lung disease due to the inhalation of silica dusts.

silk (sĭlk) ***n-*** **1** soft, shiny fiber obtained from the cocoons of silkworms. **2** similar fiber spun by spiders and some insects. **3** thread made from the cocoon fibers of silkworms. **4** fabric made from this thread. **5** anything having the softness or appearance of this thread: *corn* silk. **6 silks** jockey's costume of colors that show the owner of the horse he rides. *as* ***modifier:*** *a* silk *curtain.* ***—adj-*** **silk′ like′.**

silk·en (sĭl′ kən) ***adj-*** **1** made of silk. **2** like silk; soft, smooth, and shiny: *a* silken *texture.* **3** luxurious; elegant: *a queen in her* silken *chamber.* **4** well-spoken and suave: *a salesman with a* silken *manner.*

silk-stock·ing (sĭlk′ stŏk′ ĭng) ***adj-*** having to do with wealthy persons; elegant; aristocratic: *the* silk-stocking *district of a city.*

silk·worm (sĭlk′ wûrm′) ***n-*** larva of the **silkworm moth,** native to Asia but raised in the United States and Europe as well. The cocoon yields silk fiber.

silk·y (sĭl′ kē) ***adj-*** **[silk·i·er, silk·i·est]** **1** soft and smooth like silk. **2** covered with fine, soft, and shiny hairs, as certain leaves. ***—adv-*** **silk′ i·ly.** ***n-*** **silk′ i·ness.**

sill (sĭl) ***n-*** **1** piece or bar of wood, stone, etc., forming the bottom of a door or window frame. **2** lowest beam in the frame of a building, forming its foundation. **3** layer of igneous rock produced by a lava flow which forces its way between two layers of other rock.

sil·ly (sĭl′ ē) ***adj-*** **[sil·li·er, sil·li·est]** **1** having little judgment; stupid: *You are* silly *to believe such a liar.* **2** not sensible; absurd. **3** *Informal* dazed. ***n-*** [*pl.* **sil·lies**] *Informal* foolish person. ***—n-*** **sil′li·ness.**

si·lo (sī′ lō) ***n-*** [*pl.* **si·los**] **1** airtight and waterproof cylindrical building for storing green fodder, cornstalks, or the like to be used as cattle feed. **2** underground structure for storing a guided missile that is ready to fire.

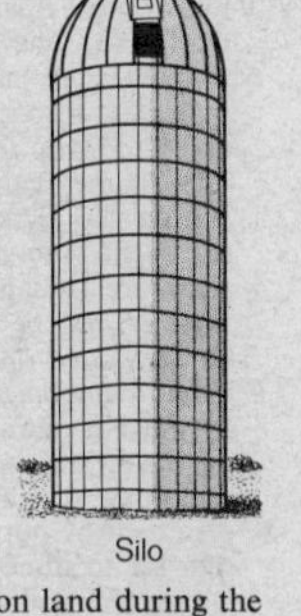
Silo

silt (sĭlt) ***n-*** fine particles of earth or sand suspended in or carried by water and left as sediment. ***vt-*** to fill or block up by such a deposit: *Heavy erosion* silted *the channel.* ***vi-***: *The channel* silted *up.*

silt·y (sĭl′ tē) ***adj-*** **[silt·i·er, silt·i·est]** of, like, or filled with silt: *a* silty *deposit*; *a* silty *stream.*

Si·lu·ri·an (sə lŏŏr′ ē ən) ***n-*** the third of the six periods of the Paleozoic era. Plants first appeared on land during the Silurian. ***adj-***: *a* Silurian *fossil.*

sil·van (sĭl′ vən) sylvan.

sil·ver (sĭl′ vər) ***n-*** **1** a soft, white, shining metal element, classed as a precious metal. It is often used for ornamental purposes and is the best conductor of heat and electricity known. Symbol Ag, At. No. 47, At. Wt. 107.87. **2** anything made of silver, such as silverware. **3** any kind of coin: *loose* silver *jingling in his pockets.* ***vt-*** to cover with silver or something resembling silver: *to* silver *a mirror with mercury.* ***vi-*** to turn shiny white or gray: *Her hair* silvered *at a very early age.* ***adj-*** **1** made of or looking like silver: *a* silver *spoon*; silver *dew.* **2** clear and pure: *her* silver *tones.* **—*adj-* sil′ ver·like′.**

silver bromide ***n-*** yellowish crystalline compound (AgBr) used in photography because, after exposure to light, the silver can be liberated by a developer.

silver certificate ***n-*** U.S. banknote representing the deposit of a stated value of silver in the Treasury, and valid as legal tender.

silver chloride *Chemistry* ***n-*** white salt of silver (AgCl) used in photography because it acts like silver bromide.

sil·ver·fish (sĭl′ vər fĭsh′) ***n-*** [*pl.* **sil·ver·fish**] **1** tarpon. **2** bristletail.

Silverfish, about 1/2 in. long

silver fox ***n-*** **1** common red fox having black fur tipped with white. Such foxes can be bred to produce others of this coloration. **2** its fur.

silver nitrate *Chemistry* ***n-*** white, crystalline, poisonous compound ($AgNO_3$) formed by the action of nitric acid on metallic silver. It is used in silver plating, photography, and medicine.

silver plate ***n-*** **1** metal tableware and utensils plated with silver. **2** such articles made entirely of silver. **3** a plating of silver. **4** a plate made of silver.

sil·ver·smith (sĭl′ vər smĭth′) ***n-*** person who makes articles of silver.

silver standard ***n-*** use of silver as the standard of value for the money of a country. The basic unit of money is declared to be equal to and exchangeable for a certain quantity of silver.

sil·ver-tongued (sĭl′ vər tŭngd′) ***adj-*** having fluent, graceful, and persuasive speech; eloquent.

sil·ver·ware (sĭl′ vər wâr′) ***n-*** tableware made of or plated with silver.

silver wedding ***n-*** twenty-fifth wedding anniversary.

sil·ver·y (sĭl′ və rē) ***adj-*** **1** silver in appearance: *the* silvery *moonlight.* **2** clear and sweetly ringing: *the* silvery *tone of a bell.* **—*n-* sil′ ver·i·ness.**

sim·i·an (sĭm′ ē ən) ***adj-*** having to do with or like an ape or monkey. ***n-*** ape or monkey.

sim·i·lar (sĭm′ ə lər) ***adj-*** alike without being the same: *Pink and rose are* similar *colors.* **—*adv-* sim′ i·lar·ly.**

sim·i·lar·i·ty (sĭm′ ə lăr′ ə tē) ***n-*** [*pl.* **sim·i·lar·i·ties**] likeness; resemblance: *a* similarity *between pink and red.*

similar triangles ***n-*** triangles whose corresponding angles are equal and whose corresponding sides are proportional.

sim·i·le (sĭm′ ə lē) ***n-*** figure of speech in which two different things having some likeness are compared by the use of "like" or "as." Examples: The ice is like glass.

si·mil·i·tude (sə mĭl′ ə to͞od′, -tyo͞od′) ***n-*** likeness.

sim·mer (sĭm′ ər) ***vt-*** **1** to cook or boil gently. **2** to cook in liquid at or just below the boiling point: *She* simmered *the meat for three hours.* ***vi-*** **1** to cook in water kept at or just below the boiling point: *The meat* simmered *for three hours.* **2** to make a low, gentle, murmuring sound when boiling gently. **3** to be on the verge of breaking out with emotion: *He* simmered *with rage while the policeman gave him a ticket.* ***n-*** **1** a gentle boiling: *to cook the soup at a* simmer. **2** state of tense, suppressed emotion. **simmer down 1** to make less by boiling down slowly. **2** *Informal* to calm down; quiet down.

Si·mon Le·gree (sī′ mən lə grē′) ***n-*** in Harriet Beecher Stowe's "Uncle Tom's Cabin," a villainous overseer.

Simon Peter See *Peter.*

si·mon-pure (sī′ mən pyo͝or′) *Informal* ***adj-*** true; real.

sim·o·ny (sī′ mə nē) ***n-*** a buying or selling of church offices or positions of honor; dealing in sacred things.

si·moom (sə mo͞om′, sī-) or **si·moon** (-mo͞on′) ***n-*** hot, suffocating, dust-laden wind that blows from the deserts of Arabia or from the Sahara.

sim·pa·ti·co (sĭm păt′ ĭ kō) ***adj-*** pleasant and agreeable; sympathetic; compatible. [from Italian and Spanish.]

sim·per (sĭm′ pər) ***vi-*** to smile in a silly, self-conscious, or affected way; smirk. ***n-*** such a smile or smirk. **—*n-* sim′ per·er. *adv-* sim′ per·ing·ly.**

sim·ple (sĭm′ pəl) ***adj-*** [**sim·pler, sim·plest**] **1** easy to understand or do; not complicated: *a* simple *problem*; *a* simple *task*; simple *directions.* **2** not fancy; plain: *a* simple *meal*; *a* simple *dress.* **3** without qualification; mere: *a* simple *fact*; *the* simple *truth.* **4** not affected; straightforward; sincere: *a* simple *manner.* **5** of low social rank; ordinary; humble: *His parents are* simple *people.* **6** of low or weak intelligence; stupid; foolish. **7** uneducated. ***n-*** *Archaic* plant from which medicine is made; also, the medicine itself. **—*n-* sim′ ple·ness.**

simple fraction ***n-*** common fraction.

sim·ple-heart·ed (sĭm′ pəl här′ təd) ***adj-*** having an open, unaffected, sincere nature or disposition. **—*adv-* sim′ ple-heart′ ed·ly. *n-* sim′ ple-heart′ ed·ness.**

simple interest ***n-*** interest computed only on the principal, not on principal plus accumulated interest.

simple machine ***n-*** one of the six basic mechanical devices used to multiply force or speed in doing work. They are the lever, the pulley, the wheel and axle, the inclined plane, the screw, and the wedge.

sim·ple-mind·ed (sĭm′ pəl mīn′ dəd) ***adj-*** **1** ignorant; naive. **2** foolish; stupid. **3** weak of mind; feeble-minded. **—*adv-* sim′ ple-mind′ ed·ly. *n-* sim′ ple-mind′ ed·ness.**

simple polygon *Mathematics* ***n-*** polygon with sides that do not cross one another.

simple sentence *Grammar* ***n-*** a sentence that includes only one independent clause and no dependent clauses.

sim·ple·ton (sĭm′ pəl tən) ***n-*** person who is foolish, silly, or easily fooled.

sim·pli·ci·ty (sĭm plĭs′ ə tē) ***n-*** [*pl.* **sim·pli·ci·ties**] **1** lack of confusing parts, connections, etc.; understandable at once. **2** naturalness; artlessness: *the very charming* simplicity *of a child.* **3** lack of showiness: *the neat* simplicity *of her dress.* **4** lack of cunning; sincerity; directness: *his* simplicity *of dealing.* **5** lack of common sense; foolishness.

sim·pli·fi·ca·tion (sĭm′ plə fə kā′ shən) ***n-*** **1** a making clearer, plainer, or easier. **2** anything made simpler.

sim·pli·fy (sĭm′ plə fī′) ***vt-*** [**sim·pli·fied, sim·pli·fy·ing**] to make clearer, plainer, or easier. **—*n-* sim′ pli·fi′ er.**

sim·ply (sĭm′ plē) ***adv-*** **1** in a clear and plain way: *Dr. Barnes presented his talk very* simply. **2** without show or adornment: *Ann dresses* simply. **3** just; merely; only: *His reply was* simply *one of ignorance.* **4** *Informal* absolutely; quite: *The painting is* simply *beautiful.*

sim·u·late (sĭm′ yə lāt′) ***vt-*** [**sim·u·lat·ed, sim·u·lat·ing**] **1** to take the appearance or form of; imitate: *Some plastics* simulate *leather. Certain moths* simulate *leaves.* **2** to produce many of the conditions and problems of (some process or event): *The machine* simulates *the flight of a jet transport.* **3** to make a show or pretense of: *to* simulate *sorrow.* **—*n*- sim′u·la′tion.**

sim·u·la·tive (sĭm′yə lā′tĭv) ***adj*-** **1** tending to or able to simulate: *a* simulative *device.* **2** not genuine.

sim·u·la·tor (sĭm′yə lā′tər) ***n*-** person or thing that simulates; especially, a complicated device that simulates the operation of an airplane, submarine, etc., for research or training.

si·mul·cast (sī′məl kăst) ***vt*-** **[si·mul·cast** or **si·mul·cast·ed, si·mul·cast·ing]** to broadcast a program by radio and television simultaneously. ***n*-:** *We enjoyed the* simulcast *of "Tosca" last night.*

si·mul·ta·ne·ous (sī′məl tā′nē əs) ***adj*-** happening, existing, or done at the same time: *Their responses were* simultaneous. **—*adv*- si′mul·ta′ne·ous·ly.**

sin (sĭn) ***n*-** **1** the breaking or violation of God's laws in act or thought. **2** any instance of this, such as stealing, telling a lie, or thinking of harming someone. **3** any serious fault, error, or offense. ***vi*-** **[sinned, sin·ning]** **1** to break God's laws in any way. **2** to commit evil deeds.

sin sine (abbreviation).

since (sĭns) ***prep*-** (considered an adverb when the object is clearly implied but not expressed) from the time of; during the time after: *We haven't been home* since *last Sunday. We haven't been home* since. ***adv*-** at some time after a past event and before now: *They lived here during the war but have* since *moved away.* ***conj*-** **1** from and after a time when: *I have not seen her* since *then.* **2** seeing that; because: *I'll do it,* since *he can't.*

long since for a long period of time before now.

►If the part of the sentence introduced by SINCE refers to cause or reason, the present tense is most common. Since *he is here, we can go.* Here SINCE means "because." If SINCE refers only to a time sequence, a past tense should be used. *I have been unhappy* since *you went away.*

sin·cere (sĭn sêr′) ***adj*-** **[sin·cer·er, sin·cer·est]** really meaning what one says or does; honest; truthful; genuine: *His praise was* sincere. **—*adv*- sin·cere′ly.**

sin·cer·i·ty (sĭn sĕr′ə tē) ***n*-** freedom from pretense; truthfulness; genuineness of character; honesty.

Sind·bad the Sailor (sĭn′băd′) ***n*-** in the "Arabian Nights," a wealthy merchant of Baghdad who relates marvelous tales of his travels on the Seven Seas.

sine (sīn) ***n*-** of an acute angle in a right triangle, the ratio between the side opposite the angle and the hypotenuse. *Abbr.* sin ***Hom*-** sign.

si·ne·cure (sī′nə kyo͞or′, sĭn′ə-) ***n*-** **1** position or office that pays a salary but requires little work or responsibility.

sine curve ***n*-** curve that represents the trigonometric function y = sin x, and describes, for example, the motion of a system in simple harmonic vibration.

si·ne di·e (sĭn′ā dē′ā, sī′nē dī′ē) *Latin* without setting a time for reassembling: *The meeting adjourned* sine die.

si·ne qua non (sĭn′ə kwä′nōn′, sī′nē kwā′ nŏn′) *Latin* an absolute necessity; indispensable condition.

sin·ew (sĭn′yo͞o) ***n*-** **1** tendon. **2** strength or power, or the means of supplying it: *Imagination, courage, and discipline are the* sinews *of success.*

sin·ew·y (sĭn′yo͞o ē) ***adj*-** **1** having many sinews; tough; stringy: *a piece of* sinewy *meat.* **2** strong and vigorous; muscular: *a blacksmith's* sinewy *arms.* **—*n*- sin′ew·i·ness.** ***adj*-** **sin′ew·less.**

sin·ful (sĭn′fəl) ***adj*-** **1** guilty of many sins: *a* sinful *man.* **2** wicked; wrong: *Murder is* sinful. **—*adv*- sin′ful·ly.** ***n*-** **sin′ful·ness.**

sing (sĭng) ***vi*-** **[sang** (săng), **sung** (sŭng), **sing·ing]** **1** to use the voice to make musical sounds: *We* sang *as we rode along. Birds* sing *in the treetops.* **2** to make a humming or whistling sound: *Arrows* sang *around us. The kettle* sings. **3** to ring with a humming or buzzing sound: *When he has a cold, his ears* sing. **4** to tell in song or poetry (of): *Homer* sang *of the Trojan war.* **5** *Slang* to confess to a crime and inform on others. ***vt*-** **1** to utter with musical tones of the voice: *to* sing *a song.* **2** to chant; intone. **3** to quiet by making musical sounds with the voice: *to* sing *a child to sleep.* ***n*-** *Informal* a gathering of people for making vocal music together.

sing out to call loudly; shout: *to* sing out *commands.*

sing (someone's or **something's) praises** to praise loudly or lavishly: *The lover* sings his sweetheart's praises.

sing. singular.

singe (sĭnj) ***vt*-** **[singed, singe·ing]** **1** to burn slightly; scorch: *The hot iron* singed *my dress.* **2** to burn away feathers, bristle, or down from: *to* singe *a duck before cooking it.* **3** to burn the tips of: *to* singe *hair.* ***n*-** slight burn on the outside or surface.

sing·er (sĭng′ər) ***n*-** person or bird that sings.

Sing·ha·lese (sĭng′gə lēz′, -lēs′) Sinhalese.

sin·gle (sĭng′gəl) ***adj*-** **1** one and no more; individual: *a* single *page; a* single *ticket to the theater.* **2** not married: *a* single *man.* **3** for the use of one person only: *a* single *bed; a* single *room.* **4** of flowers, having only one row of petals, as a wild rose or a tulip. ***n*-** **1** theater ticket, hotel room, etc., for one person. **2** golf game between two players. **3** **singles** game, such as tennis, handball, or ping-pong, when it is played with only one player on a side. **4** in baseball, a base hit that allows the hitter to reach first base, but no further base, safely. ***vi*-** **[sin·gled, sin·gling]** in baseball, to make such a base hit.

single out to choose from among others.

sin·gle-breast·ed (sĭng′gəl bres′təd) ***adj*-** having the two front edges of a coat, jacket, vest, etc., meet with little overlap, and fasten by a single row of buttons.

single combat ***n*-** fight between two persons, especially knights or swordsmen.

single file ***n*-** line of persons one behind the other.

sin·gle-foot (sĭng′gəl fo͝ot′) ***n*-** horse's gait in which each foot hits the ground singly at regular intervals, in this order: right hind, right fore, left hind, left fore. ***vi*-** to travel with this gait.

sin·gle-hand·ed (sĭng′gəl hăn′dəd) ***adj*-** without help from others; done by one person: *The officer made a* single-handed *arrest.* **—*adv*- sin·gle-hand′ed·ly.**

sin·gle-heart·ed (sĭng′gəl här′təd) ***adj*-** **1** free from deceitfulness; straightforward; sincere. **2** having only one purpose. **—*adv*- sin′gle-heart′ed·ly.** ***n*-** **sin′gle-heart′ed·ness.**

sin·gle-mind·ed (sĭng′gəl mīn′dəd) ***adj*-** having only one purpose or aim: *a* single-minded *dedication.* **—*adv*- sin′gle-mind′ed·ly.** ***n*-** **sin′gle-mind′ed·ness.**

sin·gle·ness (sĭng′gəl nəs) ***n*-** **1** condition of being alone or separate; especially, being unmarried. **2** of a feeling or aim, the condition of being unmixed, direct, and wholehearted: *the* singleness *of his devotion.*

sin·gle·ton (sĭng′gəl tən) ***n*-** **1** in certain card games, the only card of a suit held by a player at a deal. **2** single or separate person or thing.

sin·gle-track (sĭng′gəl trăk′) ***adj*-** **1** having only one track or pair of rails: *a* single-track *railroad.* **2** able to act or think in only one way; narrow; limited.

sin·gly (sĭng′glē) ***adv*-** **1** one by one; one at a time; separately; individually: *Let's take up the matters* singly. **2** without help from others; alone; solely.

sing·song (sĭng′sòng′) ***n*-** **1** song or verse having a monotonous rhythm. **2** monotonous tone. ***adj*-** monotonous in tone or rhythm: *a* singsong *voice.*

sin·gu·lar (sĭng′ gyə lər) ***adj-*** **1** unusual; rare; noteworthy; exceptional: *a* singular *example of courage.* **2** odd; peculiar; eccentric: *a person of* singular *habits.* **3** *Grammar* of or relating to the form of the word that names a single person or thing. ***n-*** *Grammar* form of a word that names a single person or thing, as distinguished from the plural. **—*adv-* sin′ gu·lar·ly.**

sin·gu·lar·i·ty (sĭng′ gyə lăr′ ə tē, -lĕr′ ə tē) ***n-*** [*pl.* **sin·gu·lar·i·ties**] **1** condition of being singular: *the* singularity *of his opinions.* **2** something singular.

Sin·ha·lese (sĭn′ hə lēz′) ***n-*** **1** member of a people who form a majority in Ceylon. **2** the language of these people, related to Hindi and Dravidian. ***adj-***: *the* Sinhalese *children.* Also **Singhalese.**

sin·is·ter (sĭn′ ə stər) ***adj-*** **1** showing ill will; expressing evil intentions: *a* sinister *look*; *a* sinister *scheme.* **2** evil and menacing, especially secretly. **3** in heraldry, having to do with the side of a shield toward the left of the bearer. **—*adv-* sin′ is·ter·ly.** ***n-*** **sin′ is·ter·ness.**

sink (sĭngk) ***vi-*** **[sank** (săngk) or **sunk** (sŭngk), **sunk, sink·ing] 1** to go partly or completely beneath the surface of water, snow, quicksand, etc.; submerge. **2** to become lower little by little; descend gradually: *The sun* sank *in the west. The land* sinks *to the sea.* **3** to decrease in intensity or value: *His spirits* sank. *The stocks* sank *to a new low.* **4** to descend gradually from a normal level of consciousness, health, morality, etc.: *to* sink *into sleep.* **5** to enter deeply; make a lasting impression: *The danger slowly* sank *into their minds.* ***vt-*** **1** to cause to go into, under, or to the bottom: *The submarine* sank *the ship.* **2** to make by digging downward: *to* sink *a well.* **3** to place in an excavation thus made: *to* sink *a pipe or a shaft.* **4** to invest: *He* sank *all his savings in stocks.* **5** in basketball, to score (a shot). **6** in golf, to hit (a ball) into a cup. ***n-*** **1** basin of porcelain, metal, etc., with a drain, used for washing. **2** slight hollow of land with little or no outlet for water. **—*adj-* sink′ a·ble.**

sink·age (sĭng′ kĭj) ***n-*** a sinking or lowering of level.

sink·er (sĭng′ kər) ***n-*** **1** a weight attached to a fishing line to make the bait and hook sink. **2** in baseball, a pitch that curves downward as it reaches the plate. **3** *Slang* doughnut.

sink·hole (sĭngk′ hōl′) ***n-*** in geology, any hole worn by water through rock and serving to drain surface water.

sinking fund ***n-*** money set aside regularly for the purpose of paying a debt.

sin·less (sĭn′ ləs) ***adj-*** without sin; blameless; innocent: *a* sinless *life.* **—*adv-* sin′ less·ly.** ***n-*** **sin′ less·ness.**

sin·ner (sĭn′ ər) ***n-*** person who sins; offender; wrongdoer.

Sino- *combining form* Chinese; China.

sin·u·ous (sĭn′ yōō əs) ***adj-*** curving in and out; winding; twisting: *a* sinuous *motion.* **—*adv-* sin′ u·ous·ly.** ***n-*** **sin′ u·os′ i·ty** (sĭn′ yōō ŏs′ ə tē) or **sin′ u·ous·ness.**

si·nus (sī′ nəs) ***n-*** [*pl.* **si·nus·es**] **1** a hollow in a bone or soft tissue, especially one of several such hollows occurring in the bones of the skull and connecting with the nose. **2** a space in which pus collects before breaking out to the surface.

si·nus·i·tis (sī′ nə sī′ təs) ***n-*** inflammation of the sinus.

Si·on (sī′ ən) Zion.

-sion See *-ion.*

Siou·an (sōō′ ən) ***n-*** [*pl.* **Siou·ans,** also **Siou·an**] **1** a major family of North American Indian languages, formerly spoken from the west banks of the Mississippi to the Rocky Mountains. **2** large group of Indian peoples speaking these languages. ***adj-***: *the* Siouan *councils.*

Sioux (sōō) ***n-*** [*pl.* **Sioux** (sōōz, *also* sōō)] **1** name commonly used to designate a confederacy of Siouan-speaking Indian tribes. **2** member of any of these tribes. **3** any of the Siouan languages.

sip (sĭp) ***vt-*** **[sipped, sip·ping]** to drink a very little at a time; drink little by little: *to* sip *tea.* ***n-*** **1** small quantity of liquid; a little taste. **2** act of drinking a little at a time.

si·phon (sī′ fən) ***n-*** **1** bent tube or pipe by which a liquid can be carried up out of a container and down to a lower level by atmospheric pressure alone. **2** a closed pipe that carries water from a canal through a valley to another lower canal on the other side of the valley. **3** bottle from which a stream of liquid may be forced by the pressure of a gas. ***vt-*** to draw off or conduct with a siphon.

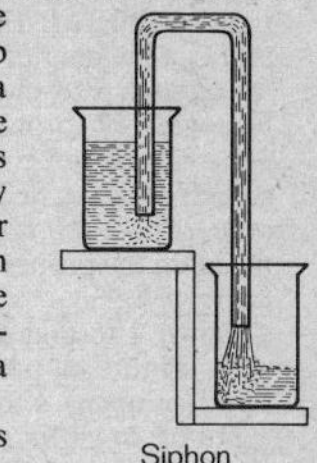
Siphon

sir (sûr) ***n-*** **1** polite form of address for a stranger, friend, or equal, or as a term of respect to a superior. **2 Sir** *Brit.* title used before the given name of a knight or baronet.

sir·dar (sûr′ där′) ***n-*** a chief or military leader in India and certain other Oriental countries.

sire (sīər) ***n-*** **1** father or male ancestor. **2** male parent of animals. **3 Sire** title of respect used when addressing a king or ruler. ***vt-*** **[sired, sir·ing]** to be the father of: *to* sire *five sons.*

si·ren (sī′ rən) ***n-*** **1** device that makes a very loud and high sound by the spinning of a hollow rotor: *a police* siren. **2** in Greek mythology, one of a group of beautiful women who lured sailors to their destruction on the rocks by singing. **3** bewitching or captivating woman. ***adj-*** dangerously fascinating; bewitching: *a* siren *voice.*

Sir·i·us (sĭr′ ē əs) ***n-*** brightest star in the sky; Dog Star.

sir·loin (sûr′ loin′) ***n-*** choice cut of beef taken from the upper part of the loin.

si·roc·co (sə rŏk′ ō) ***n-*** [*pl.* **si·roc·cos**] hot, moist or dusty wind that blows across the Mediterranean from Africa to southern Europe.

sir·rah (sĭr′ ə) *Archaic* ***n-*** sir; fellow (used to express annoyance, anger, or contempt toward a person regarded as inferior).

sir·up (sûr′ əp, sĭr′) syrup.

si·sal (sī′ səl, sĭs′ əl) ***n-*** **1** strong, white fiber of a plant resembling cactus, used for making cord or rope. **2** plant from which this fiber comes. Also **sisal hemp.**

sis·sy (sĭs′ ē) ***n-*** [*pl.* **sis·sies**] boy or man who lacks masculine traits, especially courage; effeminate boy or man.

sis·ter (sĭs′ tər) ***n-*** **1** girl or woman having the same parents as another person. **2** female fellow member of a club or other organization. **3** nun. **4** one of several ships, languages, colleges, or other things thought of as female. **5** *Brit.* chief nurse in a hospital. *as* ***modifier:*** *English and German are* sister *languages.*

sis·ter·hood (sĭs′ tər hŏŏd′) ***n-*** **1** condition of being a sister. **2** group or association of things regarded as sisters: *a* sisterhood *of churches.* **3** number of women united by a common interest; especially, an organization of the women of a parish or congregation.

sis·ter-in-law (sĭs′ tər ĭn lô′) ***n-*** [*pl.* **sis·ters-in-law**] **1** wife of one's brother. **2** sister of one's husband or wife.

sis·ter·ly (sĭs′ tər lē) ***adj-*** of or like a sister; affectionate: *a* sisterly *concern for her classmates.* **—*n-* sis′ ter·li·ness.**

---

fāte, făt, dâre, bärn; bē, bĕt, mêre; bīte, bĭt; nōte, hŏt, môre, dòg; fŭn, fûr; tōō, bŏŏk; oil; out; tar; thin; then; hw for wh as in *wh*at; zh for s as in u*s*ual; ə for a, e, i, o, u, as in *a*go, lin*e*n, per*i*l, at*o*m, min*u*s

Sis·y·phus (sĭs′ə fəs) ***n-*** in Greek mythology, a greedy king of Corinth who in Hades was condemned forever to roll uphill a huge stone that always rolled back down.

sit (sĭt) ***vi-*** [**sat** (săt), **sit·ting**] **1** to rest one's weight on the lower part of the body; be seated: *He* sits *in an easy chair after supper.* **2** to perch or roost, as a bird does. **3** to cover eggs to be hatched, as a hen does. **4** to have place or position; be situated: *The trunk* sits *on the floor.* **5** to occupy a seat as a member of a council or assembly: *to* sit *in the state legislature.* **6** to meet or be in session: *The court will* sit *next week.* **7** to press or weigh: *His duties* sat *heavily on him.* **8** to pose or model: *to* sit *for a portrait.* **9** to fit or suit: *Her jacket doesn't* sit *well in the shoulders.* ***vt-*** **1** to seat: *He* sat *the boy down and gave him a lecture.* **2** to maintain the proper position on (a riding animal): *He* sits *a horse well.*

sit down 1 to take a seat. **2** to begin a siege.

sit in on to take part in; participate in.

sit on (or **upon**) **1** to meet in judgment on. **2** to be a member of: *to* sit *on a jury or committee.*

sit out 1 to remain seated during: *to* sit out *a dance.* **2** to wait through; endure: *to* sit out *a storm.*

sit up 1 to raise the body to an upright sitting position: *to* sit up *in bed.* **2** to pay attention: *His great speed made the other players* sit up *and watch.* **3** to stay up past one's usual bedtime.

►The principal forms of SIT are SIT, SAT, SAT. *We* sat *for a long time. She* sat *her baby on the sofa.* Do not confuse this with SET, which has a different meaning.

sit·com (sĭt′kŏm) *Informal* ***n-*** television or radio comedy series [shortened from ***situation comedy.***]

sit-down strike (sĭt′doun′strīk′) ***n-*** strike during which workers remain in their place of employment until an agreement is reached.

site (sīt) ***n-*** **1** place where something is or was situated: *the* site *of the battle.* **2** area set aside for a particular purpose: *the building* site. ***Homs-*** cite, sight.

sit-in (sĭt′ĭn′) ***n-*** a protest demonstration in which people sit down in a public place and refuse to leave.

sit·ter (sĭt′ər) ***n-*** **1** person who sits, especially in a seat or for a portrait. **2** baby sitter. **3** hen that sits on eggs to hatch them.

sit·ting (sĭt′ĭng) ***n-*** **1** session or meeting of a court, legislature, etc. **2** period of posing or act of posing: *a* sitting *for a portrait.* **3** group of eggs for hatching.

at one sitting at one time; without a break.

sitting duck *Informal* ***n-*** any easy target, like a duck sitting still on the water.

sit·u·ate (sĭch′o͞o āt′) ***vt-*** [**sit·u·at·ed, sit·u·at·ing**] to place in a location; locate: *Where will you* situate *the new factory?*

sit·u·at·ed (sĭch′o͞o ā′təd) ***adj-*** **1** placed; located: *a properly* situated *fort.* **2** living in a certain condition or at a certain level with respect to wealth, social standing, etc.: *He is comfortably* situated *financially.*

sit·u·a·tion (sĭch′o͞o ā′shən) ***n-*** **1** place; location. **2** circumstances; state of affairs: *an amusing* situation. **3** job; position. **—*adj-* sit′u·a′tion·al.**

situation comedy ***n-*** comedy in which the characters are placed in amusing or ridiculous predicaments, often highly improbable.

sit-up (sĭt′ŭp′) ***n-*** conditioning exercise done by lying flat on the back and raising the head and trunk to an upright position repeatedly.

Si·va (sē′və, shē′-) Shiva.

six (sĭks) ***n-*** **1** amount or quantity that is one greater than 5. **2** *Mathematics* (1) the cardinal number that is the sum of 5 and 1. (2) a numeral such as 6 that represents this cardinal number. *as* ***determiner*** (traditionally called adjective or pronoun): *There are* six *insects here and* six *there.*

at sixes and sevens 1 in confusion. **2** in disagreement.

six·fold (sĭks′fōld′) ***adj-*** **1** six times as many or as much. **2** having six parts. ***adv-***: *to increase the output* sixfold.

Six Nations ***n-*** the Five Nations of the Iroquois, plus the Tuscaroras who joined them later.

six·pence (sĭks′pəns) ***n-*** former British silver coin worth half a shilling.

six-shoot·er (sĭks′sho͞o′tər) *Informal* ***n-*** revolver that can fire six bullets without reloading.

six·teen (sĭks′tēn′) ***n-*** **1** amount or quantity that is one greater than 15. **2** *Mathematics* (1) the cardinal number that is the sum of 15 and 1. (2) a numeral such as 16 that represents this cardinal number. *as* ***determiner*** (traditionally called adjective or pronoun): *There are* sixteen *persons here and* sixteen *there.*

six·teenth (sĭks′tēnth′) ***adj-*** **1** next after fifteenth. **2** the ordinal of 16; 16th. ***n-*** **1** the next after the fifteenth; 16th. **2** one of sixteen equal parts of a whole or group. **3** the last term in the name of a fraction having a denominator of 16: *1/16 is one* sixteenth.

sixteenth note *Music* ***n-*** note held one sixteenth as long as a whole note. For picture, see *note.*

sixth (sĭksth) ***adj-*** **1** next after fifth. **2** the ordinal of 6; 6th. ***n-*** **1** the next after the fifth; 6th. **2** one of six equal parts of a whole or group. **3** the last term in the name of a fraction having a denominator of 6: *1/6 is one* sixth. **4** *Music* an interval of six tones on the scale counting the extremes, as from C to A, and the harmonic combination of these tones. ***adv-***: *He called my name* sixth.

sixth·ly (sĭksth′lē) ***adv-*** as sixth in a series.

sixth sense ***n-*** acute power of perception, regarded as a sense independent of the five senses; intuition: *His* sixth sense *told him the situation was dangerous.*

six·ti·eth (sĭks′tē əth) ***adj-*** **1** next after fifty-ninth. **2** the ordinal of 60; 60th. ***n-*** **1** the next after the fifty-ninth; 60th. **2** one of sixty equal parts of a whole or group. **3** the last term in the name of a fraction having a denominator of 60: *1/60 is one* sixtieth.

six·ty (sĭks′tē) ***n-*** [*pl.* **six·ties**] **1** amount or quantity that is one greater than 59. **2** *Mathematics* (1) the cardinal number that is the sum of 59 and 1. (2) a numeral such as 60 that represents this cardinal number. *as* ***determiner*** (traditionally called adjective or pronoun): *There are* sixty *boxes here and* sixty *there.*

like sixty *Informal* very fast: *He ran* like sixty.

siz·a·ble or **size·a·ble** (sī′zə bəl) ***adj-*** of considerable size, amount, or quantity; fairly large: *a* sizable *business*; *a* sizable *profit.* **—*adv-* siz′a·bly** or **size′a·bly.** ***n-*** **siz′a·ble·ness** or **size′a·ble·ness.**

[1]size (sīz) ***n-*** **1** amount of height, width, or thickness of a thing; dimensions: *the* size *of a hat, room, or tire.* **2** largeness or smallness; bulk: *Notice the* size *of that spider.* **3** a measure showing how large something is: *What* size *is that dress?* **4** *Informal* actual fact; truth: *That's the* size *of it.* ***vt-*** [**sized, siz·ing**] **1** to arrange in order of bulk, height, volume, or extent. **2** to make or shape to certain dimensions. [from a shortened form of Middle English **assize** meaning "that which is fixed," from Late Latin **assisa,** "an assembly or sitting; judges."]

of a size of the same size.

size up 1 to form an opinion of; estimate; judge: *She* sized *him* up *carefully.* **2** to meet certain standards.

►For usage note see SIZED.

[2]size (sīz) ***n-*** (also **siz′ing**] any of various thin pastes or glues used to glaze paper, cloth, walls, etc., or make them heavier. ***vt-*** [**sized, siz·ing**] to cover or treat with this type of paste or glue. [from Old French **sise,** from **assise,** or from earlier Italian **siza.**]

sized (sīzd) ***adj-*** having a certain size (used only in compound modifiers): *an oversized box*; *a giant-sized shoe.* ►Either SIZED or SIZE is in general use, as in *a king-size container, a small-sized boy.* In formal writing, it is best to avoid both and let a well-chosen adjective do all the work. *He was a small boy. He had a severe* (not *a king-sized*) *headache.*

siz·zle (sĭz′ əl) ***vi-*** **[siz·zled, siz·zling]** **1** to make a hissing sound, as grease in a very hot frying pan. **2** to be very hot: *The streets* sizzled *in the heat.* ***n-*** a hissing sound.

siz·zler (sĭz′ ə lər) ***n-*** **1** person or thing that sizzles. **2** a very hot day: *Yesterday was a real* sizzler.

skald (skȯld) ***n-*** ancient Scandinavian poet or ballad singer; bard. ***Hom-*** scald.

[1]**skate** (skāt) ***n-*** **1** ice skate. **2** roller skate. ***vi-*** **[skat·ed, skat·ing]** to move about on such devices: *Can you* skate? *She* skates *often.* [from Dutch **schaats,** from Old French **escache,** "shank; leg."] **—*n-* skat′er.**

[2]**skate** (skāt) ***n-*** any of various ocean fishes having a flat body in the shape of a fan and a whiplike tail. [from Old Norse **skata.**]

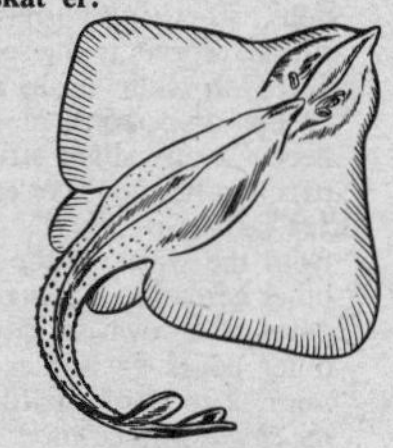

Barndoor skate, about 5 ft. long

skate·board (skāt′ bôrd) ***n-*** short, narrow board with two pairs of wheels attached to the bottom for gliding on a hard surface. ***vi-*** *We* skateboarded *to school.*

ske·dad·dle (skĭ dăd′ əl) *Informal* ***vi-*** **[ske·dad·dled, ske·dad·dling]** to run away in haste.

skeet (skēt) ***n-*** kind of trapshooting in which the shooter moves from station to station along a semicircle and attempts to break clay pigeons launched from each end of the semicircle.

skein (skān) ***n-*** **1** quantity of thread or yarn wound in a loose coil. **2** continuous line or thread: *I lost the* skein *of his story.*

skel·e·tal (skĕl′ ə təl) ***adj-*** of or relating to a skeleton: *the* skeletal *muscles.*

skel·e·ton (skĕl′ ə tən) ***n-*** **1** body framework of an animal, especially an animal with a backbone; also the bones fitted together after the flesh has decayed away or been removed: *a dinosaur* skeleton. For picture, see *spine.* **2** the midrib and veins of a leaf. **3** supporting framework for a building or ship. **4** very thin, lean person or animal. **5** first outline or idea for something: *a* skeleton *for a play.*

skeleton key ***n-*** key with part of the bit filed away so that it will open a number of locks.

skep·tic (skĕp′ tĭk) ***n-*** **1** person who is generally doubtful concerning the truth of what he hears, reads, etc. **2** person who doubts the truth of any theory or belief, and questions the possibility of human knowledge of anything.

skep·ti·cal (skĕp′ tĭ kəl) ***adj-*** doubting or questioning: *a* skeptical *look.* **—*adv-* skep′ti·cal·ly.**

skep·ti·cism (skĕp′ tə sĭz′ əm) ***n-*** **1** a doubting state of mind. **2** in philosophy, the doctrine that ultimate truth or absolute knowledge is unattainable by man.

sketch (skĕch) ***n-*** **1** simple, quickly made drawing. **2** short, brief description or account of something; outline. **3** short, simple piece of literature or music; also, short scene or act in a revue, variety show, etc. **4** *Informal* an amusing person. ***vt-*** to draw or describe quickly: *to* sketch *a kitten*; *to* sketch *the plot of a play.* ***vi-*** to make simple, quick drawings: *She* sketched *quickly.* **—*n-* sketch′er.**

sketch·book (skĕch′ bo͝ok′) ***n-*** **1** book of or for drawings. **2** book of notes or outlines, as of stories to be written.

sketch·y (skĕch′ ē) ***adj-*** **[sketch·i·er, sketch·i·est]** done roughly and without care or detail; incomplete: *a* sketchy *plan.* **—*adv-* sketch′i·ly.** ***n-*** **sketch′i·ness.**

skew (skyo͞o) ***n-*** deviation from a straight line; a turn, twist, or slant. ***adj-***: *his* skew *reasoning*; *a* skew *bridge.* ***vt-*** **1** to give an oblique direction or position to; turn or place at an angle. **2** to give a bias to; distort: *He* skewed *his report to prove his point.* ***vi-*** to take a slanting course; twist; swerve: *The road* skews *to the left.*

skew·er (skyo͞o′ ər) ***n-*** pin of wood or metal for keeping meat in shape while roasting; also, a spit. ***vt-*** to fasten or run through with or as if with a spit or pin.

skew lines ***n-*** two lines that do not intersect and are not parallel.

ski (skē) ***n-*** [*pl.* **skis** or **ski**] one of a pair of long, narrow strips of wood, metal, or plastic, strapped to the boots for traveling or sliding over snow. *as* ***modifier*** : *a* ski *trail.* ***vi-*** **[skied, ski·ing]**: *He* skied *all morning.* ***vt-***: *I have* skied *that slope.* **—*n-* ski′er.**

ski boot ***n-*** heavy shoe that covers the ankles and is made to fasten securely to the ski bindings.

skid (skĭd) ***n-*** **1** wedge or drag used to check the motion of a wheel. **2** rail, often one of a pair and sometimes greased, on which heavy weights may be slid. **3** piece of timber on which something rests: *a boat on* skids. **4** runner in the landing gear of an airplane or helicopter. **5** a slipping or sliding sideways: *a* skid *on ice.* ***vi-*** **[skid·ded, skid·ding]** **1** to slip or slide sideways while moving: *The car* skidded. **2** of a wheel, to slide without turning. ***vt-*** **1** to check or brake with a drag or wedge. **2** to place, slide, drag, or haul on a pair or set of rails or logs. **—*n-* skid′der.**

on the skids *Informal* rapidly losing prestige or influence, or one's respectable position.

skid road ***n-*** **1** road, often made of logs, along which logs are skidded. **2** *Slang* skid row.

skid row *Slang* ***n-*** run-down section made up chiefly of saloons, cheap hotels, etc., and inhabited by vagrants.

skies (skīz) *pl.* of **sky.**

skiff (skĭf) ***n-*** small, light boat, usually for a single rower.

ski jump ***n-*** long jump made by a skier; also, a specially prepared course or track for making such jumps.

ski lift ***n-*** device, usually a cable with attached chairs or bars, used to transport skiers up a hill or slope.

skill (skĭl) ***n-*** **1** ability to do something well and expertly as a result of training, practice, or experience: *his* skill *in fencing.* **2** an art; accomplishment.

skilled (skĭld) ***adj-*** **1** experienced; trained; expert; possessing or showing skill: *an example of* skilled *work*; *a* skilled *worker.* **2** requiring skill: *a* skilled *job.*

skil·let (skĭl′ ət) ***n-*** shallow cooking vessel with a projecting handle, used for frying; frying pan.

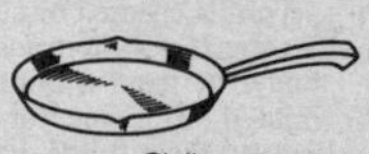

Skillet

skill·ful (skĭl′ fəl) ***adj-*** having or showing the ability to do something well; adept. Also, *chiefly Brit.,* **skil′ful.** **—*adv-* skill′ful·ly.** ***n-*** **skill′ful·ness.**

skim (skĭm) ***vt-*** **[skimmed, skim·ming]** **1** to remove from the surface of a liquid: *to* skim *the cream off milk.* **2** to remove something from the surface of: *to* skim

fāte, făt, dâre, bärn; bē, bĕt, mêre; bīte, bĭt; nōte, hŏt, môre, dȯg; fŭn, fûr; to͞o, bo͝ok; oil; out; tar; thin; then; hw for wh as in *wh*at; zh for s as in u*s*ual; ə for a, e, i, o, u, as in *a*go, lin*e*n, per*i*l, at*o*m, min*u*s

soup. **3** to move swiftly and lightly over (a surface) barely touching: *A gull* skimmed *the water.* **4** to read or look through quickly or carelessly; skip: *to* skim *a book.* ***vi-***: *The birds* skimmed *over the lake. He* skimmed *through the book.*

skim·mer (skĭm′ ər) ***n-*** **1** person or thing that skims; especially, a shallow, perforated spoon or ladle for skimming. **2** any of several long-winged sea birds related to the terns, that fly close to the water with the large, lower mandible immersed for skimming up fish.

Skimmer

skim milk ***n-*** milk from which the cream has been removed.

skimp (skĭmp) ***vt-*** **1** to perform (work) carelessly, hastily, and with poor material. **2** to be overly sparing with: *to* skimp *cloth.*. ***vi-*** to be miserly; save: *They* skimped *on the budget.*

skimp·y (skĭm′ pē) ***adj-*** **[skimp·i·er, skimp·i·est]** scanty; inadequate: *I had a very* skimpy *breakfast.* **—*adv-* skimp′ i·ly.** ***n-*** **skimp′ i·ness.**

skin (skĭn) ***n-*** **1** outer covering of the body in man and animals. **2** pelt or hide of an animal after it is removed from the body: *a rug made of the* skin *of a tiger.* **3** rind of a fruit: *orange* skin; *banana* skin. **4** any thin covering that surrounds completely: *the* skin *of a frankfurter.* **5** container made of skin for liquids such as wine or water. *as* ***modifier***: *a* skin *disease.* ***vt-*** **[skinned, skin·ning] 1** to remove the covering of (an animal or bird): *to* skin *a rabbit.* **2** to scrape: *to* skin *a knee in a fall.* **3** *Slang* to defraud. **—*adj-* skin′ less.**

EPIDERMIS PAPILLA DERMIS SWEAT GLAND HAIR FOLLICLE BLOOD VESSEL

Human skin, cross section

have a thick skin to be insensitive; be difficult to hurt by rebuke, criticism, or unkindness. **have a thin skin** to be sensitive; be easily hurt by rebuke, unkindness, or criticism. **mere skin and bones** extremely thin or skinny. **save one's skin** to escape with one's life. **the skin of one's teeth** a narrow margin.

skin-deep (skĭn′ dēp′) ***adj-*** **1** on the surface of the skin: *a* skin-deep *cut.* **2** superficial: *Her beauty is* skin-deep.

skin dive ***vi-*** to practice skin diving. **—*n-* skin diver.**

skin diving ***n-*** sport in which a person swims underwater for exploration, spear fishing, etc., usually equipped with goggles, foot fins, and a snorkel, and sometimes with a portable breathing device.

skin·flint (skĭn′ flĭnt′) ***n-*** person who hates to part with his money; miser.

skin·ful (skĭn′ fo͝ol′) ***n-*** **1** amount a skin container holds when full. **2** *Slang* large amount of liquor drunk.

skin game *Informal* ***n-*** any trick or game in which a person is cheated or swindled.

skin graft ***n-*** the transfer of skin from one part of the body, or from a donor, to an area where the skin is injured or missing, for the purpose of growing new skin.

skinned (skĭnd) ***adj-*** having a skin of a stated kind, texture, etc.: *a thin-*skinned *orange*; *a tough-*skinned *animal.*

skin·ner (skĭn′ ər) ***n-*** **1** person who removes the hides of animals. **2** *Slang* driver of draft animals, especially mules.

skin·ny (skĭn′ ē) ***adj-*** **[skin·ni·er, skin·ni·est]** very thin; without much flesh. **—*n-* skin′ ni·ness.**

skin-tight (skĭn′ tīt′) ***adj-*** closely fitting: *a pair of* skin-tight *gloves.*

skip (skĭp) ***vi-*** **[skipped, skip·ping] 1** to leap or bound lightly; move with light trips and hops: *He* skipped *away.* **2** to pass along rapidly; hurry along omitting portions: *He* skipped *through the book.* **3** *Informal* to leave hurriedly: *He* skipped *with the money.* ***vt-*** **1** to jump lightly over: *to* skip *rope.* **2** to make bounce; cause to skim: *He liked to* skip *flat stones across the pond.* **3** to leave out; pass over; omit: *He always* skips *a book's preface.* **4** *Informal* to run away from; escape: *He* skipped *town.* ***n-*** **1** gay, light walk with hops on alternate feet. **2** a passing over; omission.

ski pole ***n-*** pole with a metal point on the bottom, an encircling disk set just above this point, and a strap at the top, used as an aid by skiers.

¹skip·per (skĭp′ ər) ***n-*** captain of a ship. [from earlier Dutch **schipper** meaning "a sailor," from **schip,** "a ship."]

²skip·per (skĭp′ ər) ***n-*** **1** person or thing that skips. **2** any of various butterflies having small but stout bodies and a swift, jerky flight. [from **skip.**]

skirl (skûrl) ***vi-*** to produce a shrill sound as the bagpipe does. ***vt-*** to play (music) on the bagpipe. ***n-*** a shrill sound, especially the sound of the bagpipe.

skir·mish (skûr′ mĭsh) ***n-*** **1** a brief fight between small groups of persons, or small detachments of armies or fleets. **2** any slight struggle or encounter. ***vi-*** to take part in a brief fight or encounter. **—*n-* skir′ mish·er.**

skirt (skûrt) ***n-*** **1** girl's or woman's garment that hangs from the waist. **2** the lower part of a dress, coat, or other garment. **3** *Slang* girl or woman. **4 skirts** outlying parts of a town or city; outskirts. ***vt-*** **1** to form the outer edges or border of: *That community* skirts *the town.* **2** to border (with something): *The sunset* skirted *the clouds with crimson.* **3** to run or pass along or around the edge of; also, to avoid (an issue, problem, etc.): *We* skirted *the town. The mayor* skirted *the issue.* ***vi-*** to move along or be near the edge of something.

ski run ***n-*** slope or trail used by skiers.

skit (skĭt) ***n-*** short piece of humor, especially a short play.

skit·ter (skĭt′ ər) ***vi-*** to glide lightly; skim a surface.

skit·tish (skĭt′ ĭsh) ***adj-*** **1** easily frightened; quick to shy: *a* skittish *horse.* **2** coyly playful; lively; also, capricious or fickle: *a* skittish *woman.* **—*adv-* skit′ tish·ly.** ***n-*** **skit′ tish·ness.**

skit·tles (skĭt′ əlz) ***n-*** (takes singular verb) game resembling ninepins.

skoal (skōl) ***interj-*** "to your good health," a toast used especially by Scandinavians.

sku·a (skyo͞o′ ə) ***n-*** any of several large, fierce birds that resemble gulls.

skul·dug·ger·y (skŭl dŭg′ ə rē) *Informal* ***n-*** sneaky, unscrupulous behavior; underhandedness.

skulk (skŭlk) ***vi-*** **1** to hide or stay out of sight through cowardice or to avoid duties or dangers: *Tom* skulked *in the barn to avoid punishment.* **2** to move stealthily; to sneak about. ***n-*** person who is idle and stealthy. **—*n-* skulk′ er.** ***adv-*** **skulk′ ing·ly.**

skull (skŭl) ***n-*** **1** bony covering enclosing the brain, together with the upper jaw and sometimes including the lower jaw. **2** *Informal* the head as the seat of intelligence: *Can't you get that through your* skull? ***Hom-*** scull.

skull and crossbones ***n-*** representation of the human skull over two crossed bones, used as an emblem of piracy or to warn of danger.

skull·cap (skŭl′ kăp′) ***n-*** a soft, close-fitting cap without a brim.

skunk (skŭngk) ***n-*** **1** black and white, striped or spotted animal with a bushy tail. A skunk protects itself with a spray of strong, choking scent. **2** the fur of this animal. **3** *Informal* a contempt-

Skunk, about 3 ft. long

ible person. ***vt-*** *Informal* to beat (an opponent) so badly that he makes no score.

skunk cabbage ***n-*** swamp plant related to the arums, having a hooded spathe that appears in early spring and emits a fetid odor similar to that of a skunk.

sky (skī) ***n-*** [*pl.* **skies**] **1** the upper air or heavens; space above the earth; the arch that seems to be above the world and on clear days has a light-blue color because the sun's light passes through the air. **2** (often **skies**) atmospheric conditions; weather: *They predicted cloudy* skies *for tomorrow.* **3** the celestial regions; heaven.

out of a clear sky suddenly; unexpectedly. **to the skies** enthusiastically; without reserve.

sky blue ***n-*** color of a clear sky; azure. ***adj-*** **(sky-blue):** *a* sky-blue *flower*; sky-blue *walls.*

sky-high (skī′ hī′) ***adj-*** extremely high: *a* sky-high *peak*; sky-high *prices.* ***adv-*** **1** highly: *He was praised* sky-high. **2** in pieces or to pieces; apart: *His theories were blown* sky-high.

sky·lark (skī′ lärk′) ***n-*** **1** small European bird that nests on the ground and is noted for its sweet, continuous song as it flies up into the sky. ***vi-*** to frolic: *The children* skylarked *on Halloween.*

sky·light (skī′ līt′) ***n-*** window in a roof or ceiling.

Skylight

sky·line (skī′ līn′) ***n-*** **1** line where the sky appears to meet land or water; horizon. **2** outline of buildings, trees, etc., against the sky.

sky pilot *Slang* ***n-*** clergyman; especially, a chaplain in the armed forces.

sky·rock·et (skī′ rŏk′ ət) ***n-*** small rocket that explodes high in the air with a shower of colored sparks, stars, etc. ***vi-*** to rise with great speed: *She* skyrocketed *to fame.*

sky·sail (skī′ sāl′) ***n-*** the sail at the top of a mast, above the royal.

sky·scrap·er (skī′ skrā′ pər) ***n-*** very tall building.

sky·ward (skī′ wərd) ***adv-*** (also **sky′ wards**) toward the sky. ***adj-***: *a* skyward *look.*

sky·way (skī′ wā′) ***n-*** **1** travel route for airplanes; air lane. **2** elevated highway.

sky·writ·ing (skī′ rī′ tĭng) ***n-*** the tracing of words or messages in the sky by means of smoke or vapor released from an airplane; also, the message left in this way. **—*n-* sky′ writ′ er.**

slab (slăb) ***n-*** **1** thick, flat piece: *a* slab *of stone*; *a* slab *of bread.* **2** outside piece, with or without the bark, cut from a log when it is sawed into boards.

[1]**slack** (slăk) ***adj-*** [**slack·er, slack·est**] **1** loose; relaxed; not tight: *a* slack *rope.* **2** slow: *a* slack *current in a stream.* **3** not busy; dull; inactive: *a* slack *time of day.* **4** careless; slipshod: *a* slack *student.* ***n-*** **1** that part of something that is not stretched tight: *the* slack *in a rope.* **2** slow or dull season, as in business. ***vt-*** **1** to slacken. **2** to slake (lime). ***vi-*** to be or become sluggish; slacken. [from Old English **slæc.**] **—*adv-* slack′ ly. *n-* slack′ ness.**

slack off to slacken.

[2]**slack** (slăk) ***n-*** coal in many small pieces; also, a mixture of small pieces of coal and dirt resulting from the screening of coal. [probably from early Dutch **slak** or early German **slacke.**]

slack·en (slăk′ ən) ***vt-*** **1** to make slower: *to* slacken *speed at a crossroads.* **2** to loosen: *to* slacken *a taut rope.* ***vi-*** **1** to become loose; relax: *The wire* slackened *under its own weight.* **2** to lessen: *My energy* slackens *in the afternoon.*

slack·er (slăk′ ər) ***n-*** person who shirks his duties; especially, one who evades military service in time of war.

slacks (slăks) ***n-*** (takes plural verb) trousers for casual wear. Also **pair of slacks** (takes singular verb).

slag (slăg) ***n-*** **1** waste rock left over from the smelting of an ore. The slag is taken from the furnace as a liquid and allowed to cool and harden. **2** volcanic scoria.

slain (slān) *p.p.* of **slay.**

slake (slāk) ***vt-*** [**slaked, slak·ing**] **1** to relieve; quench; satisfy: *to* slake *thirst.* **2** to mix (lime) with water.

[1]**slam** (slăm) ***vt-*** [**slammed, slam·ming**] **1** to shut with violence and noise: *to* slam *a door.* **2** to hit or throw with violence and noise: *He* slammed *the book down on the desk.* **3** *Slang* to criticize severely. ***vi-*** to close with a bang: *The gate* slammed *in the wind.* ***n-*** **1** noisy blow; a bang: *I heard a* slam *and thought someone had come in the house.* **2** a banging or shutting noisily: *the* slam *of the door.* **3** *Slang* severe criticism. [probably from Old Norse **slamra,** from the imitation of the sound.]

[2]**slam** (slăm) ***n-*** in bridge, the winning of all the tricks in a round of play **(grand slam)** or the winning of all but one **(little slam).** [from [1]**slam.**]

slan·der (slăn′ dər) ***n-*** false oral statement made with malice to hurt a person's reputation; also, the utterance of such a statement: *The* slander *almost ruined the politician's career.* ***vt-*** to make a false report that damages a person's character or reputation: *They* slandered *him when they accused him wrongly of theft.* See also *libel.* **—*n-* slan′ der·er.**

slan·der·ous (slăn′ dər əs) ***adj-*** **1** given to uttering false statements about people. **2** characterized by or containing false, malicious statements. **—*adv-* slan′ der·ous·ly. *n-* slan′ der·ous·ness.**

slang (slăng) ***n-*** special words or phrases (or special meanings of standard expressions) which are in common use in one or more particular groups such as musicians, soldiers, sailors, or the underworld, but are not accepted as standard spoken English by most educated people. Some slang spreads beyond its original groups, but remains slang as long as it is consciously used by outsiders only for humorous, folksy, satirical, socially defiant, or contemptuous expression. ***adj-***: *a* slang *word.*

slang·y (slăng′ ē) ***adj-*** [**slang·i·er, slang·i·est**] **1** having to do with slang. **2** given to the use of slang.

slant (slănt) ***n-*** **1** a turning from the level; an angle; a tilt; a slope: *The roof has a slight* slant. **2** attitude; point of view; bias: *We need a new* slant *on this problem.* ***vt-*** **1** to put on a slope or at an angle: *to* slant *a board to make a slide.* **2** to present from a certain point of view; bias; also, to gear toward a certain group, organization, etc.: *This magazine* slants *news.* ***vi-*** to slope or tilt.

slant·wise (slănt′ wīz′) ***adv-*** obliquely; slantingly. Also **slant′ ways′** (-wāz′).

slap (slăp) ***n-*** **1** a blow, particularly with the open hand. **2** an insult. ***vt-*** [**slapped, slap·ping**] **1** to hit, especially with the open hand. **2** to throw or place noisily or carelessly: *He* slapped *the books down on the desk. She* slapped *her papers together hurriedly.* ***adv-*** *Informal* **1** suddently; abruptly. **2** directly: *He ran* slap *into me.*

slap down 1 to prohibit from acting in a specified way; crush; squelch. **2** to suppress.

slap·dash (slăp′ dăsh′) ***adj-*** acting or done in a dashing, haphazard manner; careless; sloppy: *a* slapdash *job.* ***adv-***: *He did it* slapdash. ***n-*** something done carelessly or hurriedly; also, carelessness; sloppiness: *His work is mere* slapdash.

slap·jack (slăp′jăk′) *n-* **1** griddlecake. **2** card game.
slap·stick (slăp′stĭk′) *n-* **1** a form of comedy that uses exaggerated movements, the throwing of pies, etc. *adj-* having to do with this kind of comedy: *a* slapstick *movie.*
slash (slăsh) *vt-* **1** to cut with a sweeping motion: *He* slashed *the tall weeds with a scythe.* **2** to cut slits in (a garment) to expose the material beneath. **3** to lash with a whip. **4** to criticize severely: *The critics* slashed *the novel unmercifully.* **5** to reduce in a drastic manner: *The council* slashed *the mayor's budget. vi-* to lash out wildly with or as if with a knife or sword: *The pirates* slashed *at each other. n-* **1** sweeping stroke. **2** long cut; gash. **3** slit in a garment showing the cloth beneath. **4** drastic reduction: *a* slash *in prices.* —*n-* **slash′er.**
slat (slăt) *n-* thin, narrow strip of wood or metal.
slate (slāt) *n-* **1** hard, blue-gray rock that splits into thin, smooth layers. **2** thin layer of this rock, used for roofing, blackboards, etc. **3** dark blue-gray color. **4** list of candidates for election. *vt-* **[slat·ed, slat·ing] 1** to cover with hard, blue-gray rock: *to* slate *a roof.* **2** to choose; assign to a job or position: *He was* slated *for the office.* **3** to schedule: *The government* slated *the elections for November. adj-: a* slate *fabric.* —*adv-* **slate′like′.**
a clean slate a record without a bad mark or blemish.
slath·er (slăth′ər) *Informal vt-* to spread thickly or lavishly: *He* slathered *jam on the toast. They* slathered *the walls with paint. n-* **slathers** a great quantity.
slat·tern (slăt′ərn) *n-* untidy, slovenly woman.
slat·tern·ly (slăt′ərn lē) *adj-* of or relating to a slattern; slovenly; untidy. *adv-* in a slovenly manner.
slat·y (slā′tē) *adj-* **[slat·i·er, slat·i·est] 1** of, similar to, or made of slate. **2** having the bluish-gray color of slate.
slaugh·ter (slô′tər) *n-* **1** the killing of an animal for food. **2** brutal, violent killing; massacre. *vt-* **1** to kill for food. **2** to kill brutally or violently, often in large numbers. —*n-* **slaugh′ter·er.**
slaugh·ter·house (slô′tər hous′) *n-* place where animals are butchered for the market.
Slav (släv, slăv) *n-* member of any of the Slavic-speaking peoples of eastern and southeastern Europe.
slave (slāv) *n-* **1** person who is owned by or completely under the control of someone else. **2** person who is under the control of some impelling influence: *a* slave *to fashion; a* slave *to a habit.* **3** someone who works hard and long; drudge. *as* ***modifier****: a* slave *market. vi-* **[slaved, slav·ing]** to work hard and long.
slave driver *n-* **1** person who is in charge of slaves at work. **2** any exacting employer.
slave·hold·er (slāv′hōl′dər) *n-* person who owns or keeps slaves. —*n-* **slave′hold′ing.**
[1]**slav·er** (slā′vər) *n-* vessel or person engaged in the slave trade. [from **slave.**]
[2]**slav·er** (slā′vər, slăv′ər) *vi-* to let saliva run from the mouth; drool. *vt-* to cover or dribble with saliva. *n-* saliva running from the mouth. [from Old Norse **slafr** and **slafra** meaning "to slobber."]
slav·er·y (slā′və rē) *n-* **1** condition or state of being a slave; bondage: *He was sold into* slavery. **2** the practice of buying, selling, and owning slaves. **3** long, hard work that is poorly paid; drudgery. **4** condition of being under some control or influence: *her* slavery *to fashion.*
slave state *n-* **1** before the American Civil War, a State in which slavery was legal. **2** nation that is ruled by a despot.
slave trade *n-* traffic in slaves, especially the kidnaping of African Negroes for sale as slaves, now universally outlawed.
slav·ey (slā′vē) *Brit. Informal n-* [*pl.* **slav·eys**] female domestic servant, especially one who does menial work.

Slav·ic (slä′vĭk, slăv′ĭk) *n-* a major subfamily of the Indo-European family of languages. *adj-* of or relating to the Slavs or their languages.
slav·ish (slā′vĭsh) *adj-* **1** befitting a slave; mean; base: *a* slavish *job.* **2** not original; imitating blindly: *a* slavish *imitation.* —*adj-* **slav′ish·ly.** *n-* **slav′ish·ness.**
slaw (slô) *n-* shredded raw cabbage mixed with a dressing and served as a relish or salad; cole slaw.
slay (slā) *vt-* **[slew** (slo͞o), **slain** (slān), **slay·ing]** to kill by violent means. *Hom-* sleigh. —*n-* **slay′er.**
slea·zy (slē′zē) *adj-* **[slea·zi·er, slea·zi·est] 1** lacking firmness; thin, as some silk. **2** marked by cheapness and disrepair: *a* sleazy *rooming house.* **3** carelessly made or made of inferior materials: *a* sleazy *new building.* —*adv-* **slea′zi·ly.** *n-* **slea′zi·ness.**

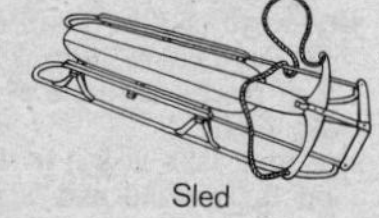
Sled

sled (slĕd) *n-* vehicle on low runners, either for coasting or for moving heavy loads on snow or ice. *vi-* **[sled·ded, sled·ding]** to travel or be carried on such a vehicle: *We* sledded *across the pack ice. vt-: They* sledded *the heavy boxes over the frozen lake.*
sled·ding (slĕd′ĭng) *n-* **1** condition of the snow which admits of the use of sleds. **2** use of a sled.
hard sledding difficult situations, times, etc., as they affect work or progress.
[1]**sledge** (slĕj) *n-* sled; sleigh. *vi-* **[sledged, sledg·ing]** to travel or be carried on such a vehicle. *vt-* to transport on a sled or sleigh. [from earlier Dutch **sleedsa,** and related to **sled** and **slide.**]
[2]**sledge** (slĕj) *n-* sledge hammer. [from Old English **slecg** of the same meaning, and related to **slay.**]

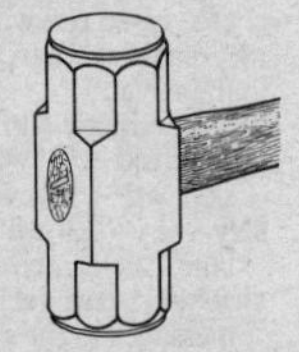
Sledge hammer

sledge hammer *n-* hammer weighing four to sixteen pounds, used for driving posts, breaking up pavement, etc. *as* ***modifier*** **(sledge-hammer):** *a* sledge-hammer *blow.*
sleek (slēk) *adj-* **[sleek·er, sleek·est] 1** smooth; glossy: *her* sleek *hair.* **2** well-fed; well-groomed: *a* sleek *cat. vt-* to make smooth or glossy. —*adv-* **sleek′ly.** *n-* **sleek′ness.**
sleep (slēp) *n-* **1** rest of mind and body; state of not being awake. **2** state like this: *the* sleep *of death. vi-* **[slept** (slĕpt), **sleep·ing] 1** to have the ordinary activity of the body and mind at rest; be or fall asleep: *A baby* sleeps *most of the time.* **2** to be in a very quiet state; remain inactive: *The town* slept. *vt-* to provide with a bed or beds.
sleep away 1 to waste, pass, or spend in sleeping or in doing nothing: *On awaking that evening, Jane discovered she had* slept away *the whole day.* **2** to get rid of by sleeping: *He* slept away *his problems.*
sleep in to live or sleep at the place where one is employed as a household servant: *Her* cook *sleeps in.*
sleep off to get rid of by sleep: *to* sleep off *a cold.*
sleep on to postpone (a decision) to think about it: *Before you act on this,* sleep on *it for a night or two.*
sleep·er (slē′pər) *n-* **1** person who sleeps: *I'm a light* sleeper. **2** (also **sleeping car**) railroad car with accommodations for sleeping: *to take the* sleeper *for Chicago.* **3** heavy beam that supports the rails on a railroad, the floor joists of a building, etc. **4** *Informal* something unimportant or unnoticed that suddenly becomes popular or valuable, such as a stock, racehorse, play, movie, or book.
sleeping bag *n-* large, warmly lined bag, usually waterproof, for sleeping outdoors.

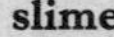

sleeping porch ***n-*** porch or veranda, often on an upper story, that is open to the air on one or more sides and arranged to permit sleeping.

sleeping sickness ***n-*** disease of the central nervous system characterized by dizziness and often death. It is caused by a trypanosome and is transmitted by the bite of the tsetse fly, common in tropical Africa.

sleep·less (slēp′ ləs) ***adj-*** **1** without sleep: *a* sleepless *night.* **2** constantly active; restless: *the* sleepless *sea.* ***—adv-*** **sleep′ less·ly.** ***n-*** **sleep′ less·ness.**

sleep·walk·er (slēp′ wȯ′ kər) ***n-*** person who walks in his sleep; somnambulist. ***—n-*** **sleep′ walk′ ing.**

sleep·y (slē′ pē) ***adj-*** **[sleep·i·er, sleep·i·est] 1** drowsy; ready for sleep. **2** inactive: *a* sleepy *village.* ***—adv-*** **sleep′ i·ly.** ***n-*** **sleep′ i·ness.**

sleep·y·head (slē′ pē hĕd′) ***n-*** sleepy person.

sleet (slēt) ***n-*** frozen or partially frozen rain. ***vi-*** to fall from the air as frozen or partially frozen rain. ***—adj-*** **sleet′ y.** ***n-*** **sleet′ i·ness.**

sleeve (slēv) ***n-*** **1** that part of a garment which covers the arm. **2** tubular part of a machine, designed to fit over another part. ***—adj-*** **sleeved.** ***adj-*** **sleeve′ less.**

up one's sleeve ready for use when needed.

sleigh (slā) ***n-*** vehicle on runners, used on snow or ice. ***vi-*** to travel by or ride in such a vehicle. ***Hom-*** slay.

sleigh·ing (slā′ ĭng) ***n-*** **1** a riding or traveling in a sleigh. **2** condition of the snow or ice which admits of the use of sleighs.

Sleigh

sleight (slīt) ***n-*** **1** dexterity or skill. **2** artful trick; especially, a trick done so expertly and quickly as to deceive the eye. ***Hom-*** slight.

sleight of hand ***n-*** tricks or skill of a juggler or magician; legerdemain.

slen·der (slĕn′ dər) ***adj-*** **[slen·der·er, slen·der·est] 1** slim; thin: *a* slender *figure.* **2** weak; slight: *a* slender *possibility.* ***—adv-*** **slen′ der·ly.** ***n-*** **slen′ der·ness.**

slen·der·ize (slĕn′ də rīz′) ***vt-*** **[slen·der·ized, slen·der·iz·ing]** to make slender: *a diet to* slenderize *the figure.*

slept (slĕpt) *p.t. & p.p.* of **sleep.**

sleuth (slo͞oth) ***n-*** detective. ***vi-*** to act as a detective.

sleuth·hound (slo͞oth′ hound′) ***n-*** bloodhound.

¹slew (slo͞o) *p.t.* of **slay.**

²slew (slo͞o) *Informal* ***n-*** a great number; a lot of. [American word probably from Irish **sluagh,** "a crowd."]

³slew (slo͞o) ¹slue. [of uncertain origin.]

slice (slīs) ***n-*** **1** flat section cut from something: *a* slice *of bread.* **2** in golf, a ball's path of flight curving to the right away from a right-handed player; also, stroke that causes this. **3** *chiefly Brit.* a flat-bladed food server. ***vt-*** **[sliced, slic·ing] 1** to cut into thin, flat pieces; also, to cut with or as if with a knife: *He* sliced *the roast. The destroyer* sliced *the waves.* **2** to cut (a thin, flat piece) from a big piece: *He* sliced *off a piece of meat.* **3** of a right-handed golfer, to hit (a ball) so that it curves to the right. ***vi-*** in golf, to make such a stroke. ***—n-*** **slic′ er.**

slick (slĭk) ***adj-*** **[slick·er, slick·est] 1** smooth and glossy: *a* slick *paper.* **2** smooth and silky in speech and manner; tricky; also, ingenious; cleverly done, said, or devised; skillful: *a* slick *salesman.* **3** slippery. **4** *Slang* excellent; very good. ***n-*** **1** smooth place or spot, especially an oil-covered area on a surface of water. **2** a magazine printed on glossy paper. ***vt-*** to smooth down; make glossy. ***—adv-*** **slick′ ly.** ***n-*** **slick′ ness.**

slick up *Informal* to make smart or neat; spruce up.

slick·er (slĭk′ ər) ***n-*** **1** long, loose waterproof coat made of oiled or varnished cloth. **2** *Informal* clever, devious person.

slide (slīd) ***vi-*** **[slid** (slĭd), **slid** or **slid·den** (slĭd′ ən), **slid·ing] 1** to move smoothly along on a surface. **2** to move quietly or without being seen: *The cat* slid *back into the room.* **3** to lose one's foothold; shift from a position; slip: *The plate* slid *from her hands.* **4** to pass gradually: *The days* slid *by during vacation.* **5** to backslide. ***vt-*** to cause to move smoothly: *to* slide *a drawer into a chest.* ***n-*** **1** smooth move; glide. **2** any smooth surface, either flat or sloping, on which a person or thing may move: *a* slide *in a playground.* **3** piece of glass on which one puts objects to examine them under a microscope. **4** transparent picture that can be projected on a screen or wall. **5** mass of earth, rock, snow, etc., that falls down a steep slope; avalanche: *a rock* slide.

let slide to let go by; postpone.

slide over to pass over quickly.

slide fastener ***n-*** zipper.

slide projector ***n-*** device that projects photographic slides on a screen or wall.

slid·er (slī′ dər) ***n-*** **1** person who slides; also, sliding thing. **2** any of several North American terrapins.

slide rule ***n-*** instrument for quick mathematical computation, consisting of a ruler with a sliding central part, both marked with logarithmic scales.

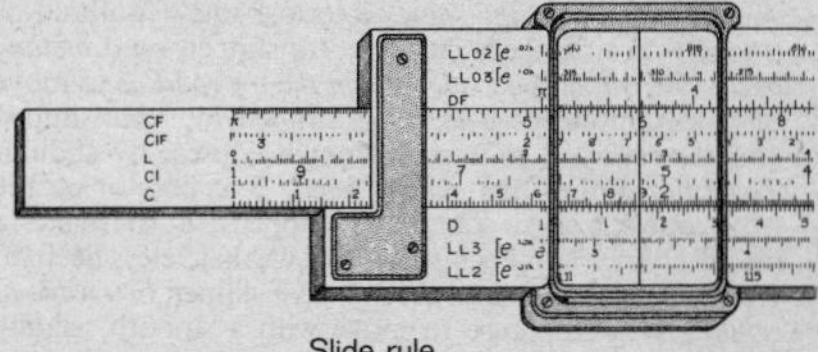

Slide rule

slid·ing (slī′ dĭng) ***adj-*** **1** moving in or as if in a groove: *a* sliding *door.* **2** varying with changing conditions: *a* sliding *scale of wages.*

slight (slīt) ***adj-*** **[slight·er, slight·est] 1** slender; thin. **2** not important: *a* slight *error.* **3** small in amount or degree: *a* slight *hope; a* slight *trace of gas.* ***n-*** a show of disrespect or neglect; snub. ***vt-*** **1** to insult: *They* slighted *Dotty by not inviting her.* **2** to pay little attention to: *Jack's football practice caused him to* slight *his studies.* ***Hom-*** sleight. ***—n-*** **slight′ ness.**

slight·ing (slī′ tĭng) ***adj-*** showing indifference or discourtesy; disparaging: *to speak in* slighting *terms; a* slighting *remark.* ***—adv-*** **slight′ ing·ly.**

slight·ly (slīt′ lē) ***adv-*** **1** to a small or unimportant degree: *I am* slightly *ill.* **2** slenderly: *She is very* slightly *built.*

sli·ly (slī′ lē) ***adv-*** in a sly manner; slyly.

slim (slĭm) ***adj-*** **[slim·mer, slim·mest] 1** slender; thin: *a* slim *figure.* **2** slight or scant; also, insufficient: *a* slim *excuse.* ***vt-*** **[slimmed, slim·ming]** to make slender: *Her new dress* slims *her waist.* ***vi-*** (often followed by "down") to become slimmer: *She ought to* slim *down.* ***—adv-*** **slim′ ly.** ***n-*** **slim′ ness.**

slime (slīm) ***n-*** **1** soft, slippery mud. **2** any sticky, slippery, or unpleasant substance; filth. **3** sticky substance given off by certain animals, such as snails.

---

fāte, făt, dâre, bärn; bē, bĕt, mêre; bīte, bĭt; nōte, hŏt, môre, dȯg; fŭn, fûr; to͞o, bo͝ok; oil; out; tar; thin; then; hw for wh as in *wh*at; zh for s as in u*s*ual; ə for a, e, i, o, u, as in *a*go, lin*e*n, per*i*l, at*o*m, min*u*s

slim·y (slī′ mē) ***adj-*** **[slim·i·er, slim·i·est] 1** sticky; slippery; covered with or oozing slime. **2** unpleasant; foul. ***—adv-*** **slim′ i·ly.** ***n-*** **slim′ i·ness.**

sling (slĭng) ***n-*** **1** device of ropes and hooks for raising and lowering heavy objects. **2** strap for suspending a gun, pack, or the like, from the shoulder. **3** bandage to support an injured arm. **4** piece of leather between two thongs, from which a stone may be thrown. **5** a hurling or flinging; sudden throw. ***vt-*** **[slung** (slŭng), **sling·ing] 1** to throw with a swinging motion of the arm; hurl; fling: *Amos* slung *a stone over the wall.* **2** to put or place with a swinging motion: *Albert* slung *the rifle over his shoulder.* **3** to place or suspend in a device for hoisting or lowering; also, to raise or lower by such means. **4** to hang (a hammock) so that it will swing.

sling·shot (slĭng′ shŏt′) ***n-*** stick in the shape of a "Y" with a rubber band tied to its pointed ends, for shooting stones and other small objects.

slink (slĭngk) ***vi-*** **[slunk** (slŭngk), **slink·ing]** to go furtively; sneak: *The tiger* slinks *silently through the tall grass.*

slink·y (slĭng′ kē) ***adj-*** **[slink·i·er, slink·i·est] 1** sneaky or furtive. **2** *Slang* sinuous or sleek in movement or form: *a* slinky *dress.* ***—n-*** **slink′ i·ness.**

¹**slip** (slĭp) ***vi-*** **[slipped** or **slipt, slip·ping] 1** to slide or glide smoothly: *The drawers* slip *in and out easily. The sleigh* slipped *along over the snow.* **2** to lose one's foothold or traction on a slippery surface: *He* slipped *on a banana peel. The car* slipped *sidewise on the icy road.* **3** to move or pass unnoticed: *The hours* slipped *by. She* slipped *into the room.* **4** to escape from a control by sliding: *The knife* slipped *and cut my hand.* **5** to pass or escape from one's grasp: *The glass* slipped. **6** to make a mistake; err. **7** to become worse, weaker, etc.; decline: *His memory is* slipping. *Stock prices* slipped *in a wave of selling.* ***vt-*** **1** to cause to move with a smooth, sliding motion; cause to slide or glide: *He* slipped *the key into the lock.* **2** to put (on or off) with ease: *She* slipped *on a ring. He* slipped *off his coat.* **3** to free oneself from; get out of: *The horse* slipped *his bridle.* **4** to escape from; also, to elude; get away from: *It* slipped *my mind. The prisoner* slipped *his guards.* **5** to pass, put, or convey quickly, slyly, or secretly: *She* slipped *a note into his pocket.* ***n-*** **1** a sliding or missing of one's foothold; sudden slide; also, a decline: *a* slip *on the icy pavement; a* slip *in prices.* **2** an involuntary small error; also, a mishap. **3** woman's undergarment similar to a dress. **4** pillow case. **5** a place between wharves for a ship to enter. [from Middle English **slippen.**]

give the slip to escape from: *The thief* gave *the police* the slip. **let slip** to tell or say without meaning to.
slip one over on to cheat; deceive; trick.
slip up to make a mistake.

²**slip** (slĭp) ***n-*** **1** small piece; strip: *a* slip *of paper.* **2** printed form: *a sales* slip; *a laundry* slip. **3** a plant cutting intended for planting or grafting. ***vt-*** **[slipped, slip·ping]** to cut a part from (a plant) for planting. [from earlier Dutch **slippe** and **slippen,** "to cut away."]

³**slip** (slĭp) ***n-*** liquid clay used by potters for coating rough surfaces or for decorating. [from Old English **slypa** meaning "paste; slime."]

slip·cov·er (slĭp′ kŭv′ ər) ***n-*** fitted cloth cover which can be easily slipped on or off a chair, sofa, etc.

slip·knot (slĭp′ nŏt′) ***n-*** knot which slips along the cord around which it is formed; running knot.

slip noose ***n-*** noose that has a slipknot.

slip-on (slĭp′ ŏn′) ***n-*** article of clothing, such as a shoe, glove, or sweater, that slips on or off easily. *as* ***modifier:*** *a* slip-on *blouse;* slip-on *shoes.*

slip·o·ver (slĭp′ ō′ vər) ***n-*** garment that is easily put on by being drawn over the head. *as* ***modifier:*** *a* slipover *shirt.*

slipped disk ***n-*** protrusion of one of the pads of connective tissue between the vertebrae, so that the pad presses on neighboring nerves and causes pain.

slip·per (slĭp′ ər) ***n-*** light, low shoe that slips on or off easily. ***—adj-*** **slip′ pered:** *her* slippered *feet.*

slip·per·y (slĭp′ ə rē) ***adj-*** **[slip·per·i·er, slip·per·iest] 1** difficult to hold or stand on because of smoothness, grease, or slime: *as* slippery *as an eel; a* slippery *sidewalk.* **2** skillful at getting out of trouble. **3** tricky; not trustworthy: *a* slippery *criminal.* ***—n-*** **slip′ per·i·ness.**

slippery elm ***n-*** **1** North American elm having a sticky inner bark. **2** its bark.

slip ring ***n-*** one of two or more rings on the armature of an electric generator which transmit the current through carbon brushes to the outside circuit.

slip·shod (slĭp′ shŏd′) ***adj-*** careless; sloppy; slovenly: *a* slipshod *way of dressing;* slipshod *work.*

slipt (slĭpt) *p.t.* of ¹**slip.**

slip-up (slĭp′ ŭp′) *Informal* ***n-*** error; mistake.

slit (slĭt) ***n-*** long, narrow cut or opening: *The cat's eyes narrowed into* slits. ***vt-*** **[slit, slit·ting]** to make a straight, narrow cut or slot in: *to* slit *cloth to make a fringe; to* slit *a box cover.* ***—adj-*** **slit′ like′.** ***n-*** **slit′ ter.**

slith·er (slĭth′ ər) ***vi-*** **1** to slide. **2** to move like a snake. ***—adj-*** **slith′ er·y:** *a* slithery *sidewalk;* slithery *motion.*

sliv·er (slĭv′ ər) ***n-*** small, slender, sharp-pointed piece of wood, glass, etc.; a splinter. ***vt-*** to split into slender fragments: *Lightning* slivered *the sturdy old oak.* ***vi-:*** *The dead tree* slivered *when it fell.*

slob (slŏb) *Informal* ***n-*** careless, crude, or sloppy person.

slob·ber (slŏb′ ər) ***vi-*** **1** to let saliva or some other liquid dribble from the mouth; drool. **2** *Slang* to show or express feeling gushingly. ***vt-*** to wet with saliva that dribbles from the mouth. ***n-*** saliva dribbling from the mouth. ***—adj-*** **slob′ ber·y.**

sloe (slō) ***n-*** **1** a purplish, oval fruit similar to the plum. **2** the thorny bush bearing this fruit. **3** any of various wild plums. *as* ***modifier:*** *a jar of* sloe *jam.* ***Hom-*** slow.

slog (slŏg) ***vt-*** **[slog·ged, slog·ging] 1** to make (one's way) with great effort. **2** to slug. ***vi-*** to plod heavily; also, work hard: *He* slogged *away at his business.* ***n-*** journey or course of action involving slow, hard work: *a* slog *through the snow.*

slo·gan (slō′ gən) ***n-*** **1** motto, phrase, jingle, or the like, intended by frequent repetition to impress the hearer or reader: *"All the news that's fit to print," is a famous newspaper* slogan. **2** any rallying or battle cry.

sloop (slo͞op) ***n-*** sailing ship with a single mast, a fore-and-aft mainsail, a jib, and often one or more auxiliary sails. For picture, see *sailboat.*

slop (slŏp) ***vi-*** **[slopped, slop·ping] 1** to spill in splashes: *Milk* slopped *from Roy's pail as he walked along.* **2** to walk with splashes through water or mud: *We* slopped *through the rain.* ***vt-*** to splash or spill: *The baby* slopped *milk on the floor.* ***n-*** **1** soft, watery mush; slush; also, water or other liquid carelessly spilled. **2** unappetizing drink or watery food: *The meals were* slop. **3 slops** household wastes; especially, waste food fed to animals.

slop over 1 to overflow or splash. **2** to talk or behave in a silly, gushy way.

slope (slōp) ***n-*** **1** any line or surface that slants upward or downward. **2** degree of slant: *The land rises in a gentle* slope. **3** *Mathematics* (1) of a straight line, the ratio of the difference, or change, in y-coordinates to the corresponding difference in x-coordinates. For example, if (x_1, y_1) and (x_2, y_2) are any two distinct points on the line, then the slope is $\frac{y_2-y_1}{x_2-x_1}$. (2) of a plane curve at a point, the slope of the line that is tangent to the curve at that point.

slop·py (slŏp′ ē) ***adj-*** **[slop·pi·er, slop·pi·est] 1** wet; rainy: *the* sloppy *weather this spring.* **2** muddy; filled with slush: *the* sloppy *sidewalks.* **3** careless or slovenly: *a piece of* sloppy *work.* **4** *Informal* weakly sentimental. **—*adv-* slop′ pi·ly. *n-* slop′ pi·ness.**

slosh (slŏsh) ***vi-*** to splash about; flounder; wallow: *We* sloshed *through the mud.* ***vt-*** to throw or splash around.

slot (slŏt) ***n-* 1** straight, narrow opening or channel; slit. **2** hole designed to receive a door bolt or machine part; hence, any suitable opening. ***vt-*** **[slot·ted, slot·ting]** to cut a slit or slits in.

sloth (slòth, slŏth, slōth) ***n-*** **1** extreme laziness; dislike of effort. **2** any of various slow-moving mammals of South and Central America that live in trees and cling upside down to the branches.

Two-toed sloth, about 2 ft. long

sloth bear ***n-*** black bear of Ceylon and India that feeds chiefly on fruit and honey.

sloth·ful (slòth′ fəl, slŏth′-, slōth′-) ***adj-*** very lazy; slow to act. **—*adv-* sloth′ ful·ly. *n-* sloth′ ful·ness.**

slot machine ***n-* 1** gambling machine worked by inserting a coin into a slot. **2** vending machine.

slouch (slouch) ***vi-* 1** to act with slow, loose-jointed movements; shamble: *Leon* slouched *lazily to school.* **2** to stand or sit with the back curved and the shoulders drooping: *Marie* slouched *in her chair.* ***n-* 1** drooping, loose-jointed posture: *to walk with a* slouch. **2** person who habitually acts in this manner.

no slouch (at) very good (at).

slouch hat ***n-*** soft hat, usually made of felt, with a brim that can be turned down.

slouch·y (slouch′ ē) ***adj-*** **[slouch·i·er, slouch·i·est]** slouching. **—*adv-* slouch′ i·ly. *n-* slouch′ i·ness.**

[1]**slough** (slo͞o, *also* slou) ***n-* 1** place full of deep mud; any miry place; mudhole. **2** (*usually* slo͞o) swamp; also, an inlet from a river; backwater; slue. **3** (*usually* slou) state of gloom or depression into which one sinks and from which it is difficult to free oneself: *the* slough *of despair.* [from Old English **slōh** meaning "a swamp; bog."]

[2]**slough** or **sluff** (slŭf) ***n-* 1** castoff skin of a snake or other animal. **2** anything that can be or has been cast off, such as dead tissue, a bad habit, or the like: *to cast off the* slough *of ignorance.* ***vi-* 1** to come off or be shed: *The skin of a snake* sloughs *every year.* **2** to cast off one's skin: *A snake* sloughs *every year.* ***vt-*** to shed; cast off: *The snake* sloughed *its skin.* [from Middle English, probably from a Germanic source.]

slough off to discard.

Slo·vak (slō′ väk′, -văk′) ***n-*** one of a Slavic-speaking people who live in central Europe and are now mainly centered in southeastern Czechoslovakia. ***adj-***: *the* Slovak *territory.* Also **Slo·vak′ i·an** (slə vä′ kē ən).

slov·en (slŭv′ ən) ***n-*** person who is untidy or slipshod.

Slo·vene (slō′ vēn′) or **Slo·ve·ni·an** (slō vē′ nē ən) ***n-*** **1** member of a southern Slavic people living in Yugoslavia. **2** the language of these people. ***adj-*** of or relating to these people or to their language.

slov·en·ly (slŭv′ ən lē) ***adj-*** **[slov·en·li·er, slov·en·li·est]** slipshod; sloppy; untidy; not neat. **—*n-* slov′ en·li·ness.**

slow (slō) ***adj-*** **[slow·er, slow·est] 1** not quick; moving, acting, or progressing with little speed; sluggish: *the* slow *passing of the hours; the* slow *progress of a snail.* **2** not up to normal speed: *a moving picture in* slow *motion.* **3** behind time: *The clock is ten minutes* slow. **4** not quick to understand: *a* slow *pupil.* **5** tending to hinder rapid motion: *a* slow *track.* **6** not active or lively; dull; tedious: *The stock market was* slow *today.* ***adv-*** slowly. ***Hom-*** sloe. **—*adv-* slow′ ly. *n-* slow′ ness.**

slow down (or **up**) to reduce speed.

►Either SLOW or SLOWLY is used to modify certain verbs, especially in an imperative sense. *Drive* slow. *Drive* slowly. However, most good writers would now write: *He walked* slowly. *He drank* slowly.

slow·down (slō′ doun′) ***n-*** intentional slowing of the rate of production by workers or management.

slow match ***n-*** fuse that burns slowly, used for firing a blast, mine, etc.

slow motion ***n-*** movement in a motion picture that appears to happen at a much slower speed than the actual movement. *as* ***modifier*** **(slow-motion)**: *a* slow-motion *sequence.*

slow·poke (slō′ pōk′) *Informal* ***n-*** person who moves, works, etc., at an extremely slow pace.

slow-wit·ted (slō′ wĭt′ əd) ***adj-*** slow in understanding; dull-witted or stupid.

sludge (slŭj) ***n-* 1** slush; mire; sticky mud. **2** anything resembling slush, such as the refuse from the treatment of sewage. **3** half-formed or broken floating ice. **—*adj-* sludg′ y [sludg·i·er, sludg·i·est].**

[1]**slue** (slo͞o) ***vt-*** **[slued, slu·ing]** to cause to turn around a fixed point or pivot. ***vi-*** to slide around; to twist or turn about: *The boat* slued *around.* [variant of [3]**slew,** of uncertain origin.]

[2]**slue** (slo͞o) ***n-*** swamp; slough. [variant of [1]**slough.**]

sluff (slŭf) ***n-*** [2]slough.

[1]**slug** (slŭg) ***n-* 1** any of various gastropods related to the snail, but with a more elongated, less twisted body, and a rudimentary shell or no shell. **2** caterpillar or larva that looks like this. [from Middle English **slugge,** "a slow or clumsy person."]

Slug, 2—4 in. long

[2]**slug** (slŭg) ***n-* 1** small, unshaped piece of metal; especially, a kind of rough, small bullet. **2** counterfeit metal disk used in place of a coin in slot machines, dial telephones, etc. **3** piece of metal used for spacing printing type; also, thick piece of metal of the same height as type, used by printers as a marker. **4** line of type produced by the Linotype machine. [probably from an early Dutch or early Germanic word meaning "to slay; strike."]

[3]**slug** (slŭg) ***vt-*** **[slugged, slug·ging]** to strike heavily with the fist, a blunt weapon, or an implement such as a baseball bat: *He* slugged *the ball out of the park.* ***n-*** hard blow with the fist or a weapon. [perhaps from Old English **slēan** meaning "to strike; slay."] **—*n-* slug′ ger.**

[4]**slug** (slŭg) ***n-*** unit of mass equal to the mass that is accelerated at the rate of one foot per second per second when acted on by a force of one pound. [from [2]**slug.**]

slug·gard (slŭg′ ərd) ***n-*** person who is habitually lazy and listless; one who thinks or acts slowly and unwillingly; idler. ***adj-*** lazy; slothful.

slug·gish (slŭg′ ĭsh) ***adj-*** **1** slow-moving: *a* sluggish *river.* **2** slow in thought or action; indolent: *a* sluggish *brain.* **3** not working with normal efficiency: *a* sluggish *motor; a* sluggish *sink.* **—*adv-* slug′ gish·ly.** ***n-*** **slug′ gish·ness.**

sluice (slo͞os) ***n-*** **1** channel or trough for directing the flow of water. **2** an overflow channel. **3** dam and water gate, or the gate alone, for regulating the flow of water. **4** inclined trough with water flowing through it, for washing gold ore, carrying down logs, etc. ***vt-*** **[sluiced, sluic·ing] 1** to draw off (water) by a channel or water gate. **2** to throw water on; drench. **3** to wash in or with running water: *to* sluice *gold.* **4** to transport (logs) by water in a channel or trough.

Sluice and sluice gate of irrigation canal

slum (slŭm) ***n-*** (often **slums**) poor, run-down, crowded section of a city or town. ***vi-*** **[slummed, slum·ming]** to visit such a section for snobbish curiosity or pleasure.

slum·ber (slŭm′ bər) ***n-*** **1** light sleep. **2** rest, calm, or inactivity: *The city lay in* slumber. ***vi-*** **1** to sleep lightly. **2** to be quiet, calm, or inactive: *Main street* slumbered *under the August sun.* **—*n-* slum′ ber·er.**

slum·ber·ous (slŭm′ bər əs) or **slum·brous** (-brəs) ***adj-*** **1** slumbering; dormant; inactive: *a* slumberous *mood.* **2** bringing on sleep or sleepiness; soporific; drowsy: *strains of* slumberous *music.*

slump (slŭmp) ***vi-*** **1** to sink or fall heavily or suddenly: *Maude* slumped *to the floor in a faint. Sales* slumped *during the summer.* **2** to have a stooping posture; slouch: *She always* slumps. ***n-*** **1** a falling, sagging, or dropping: *a* slump *to the floor.* **2** period of poor business or performance.

slung (slŭng) *p.t. & p.p.* of **sling.**

slunk (slŭngk) *p.t. & p.p.* of **slink.**

slur (slûr) ***vt-*** **[slurred, slur·ring] 1** to pass over rapidly or lightly: *The congressman* slurred *over the facts to make his point.* **2** to pronounce indistinctly: *He* slurred *"won't you," so that it sounded like "woncha."* **3** to insult; slight: *to* slur *the family name.* ***n-*** **1** indistinct pronunciation: *to speak with a* slur. **2** anything harmful to a person's reputation; discredit; insult: *His remark was a* slur *on my family name.* **3** *Music* curved line connecting notes that are to be sung or played without a break.

slurp (slûrp) *Slang* ***vt-*** to drink or eat noisily: *to* slurp *one's soup.* ***vi-***: *You shouldn't* slurp *while eating.*

slush (slŭsh) ***n-*** **1** partly melted snow or ice. **2** greasy mixture for oiling machinery. **3** *Slang* silly, emotional talk or writing; gush. ***vt-*** **1** to oil (machinery) with a greasy mixture. **2** to fill in (the cracks in masonry) with cement or mortar.

slush fund ***n-*** money put aside for bribes, graft, etc.

slush·y (slŭsh′ ē) ***adj-*** **[slush·i·er, slush·i·est]** like or full of slush: *a* slushy *path.* **—*n-* slush′ i·ness.**

slut (slŭt) ***n-*** **1** untidy, dirty woman. **2** *Archaic* female dog.

slut·tish (slŭt′ ĭsh) ***adj-*** dirty; messy; untidy: *a* sluttish *housekeeper.* **—*adv-* slut′ tish·ly.** ***n-*** **slut′ tish·ness.**

sly (slī) ***adj-*** **[sli·er** or **sly·er, sli·est** or **sly·est] 1** cunning and tricky: *a* sly *old fox.* **2** mischievous in a playful way: *a* sly *wink.* **—*adv-* sly′ ly** or **sli′ ly.** ***n-*** **sly′ ness.**

on the sly in a secret way; stealthily.

Sm symbol for samarium.

[1]**smack** (smăk) ***n-*** **1** slight taste or flavor: *a* smack *of garlic in the meat.* **2** suggestion; trace: *a* smack *of the Orient.* [from Old English **smæc,** "a taste."]

smack of to suggest; have a trace of.

[2]**smack** (smăk) ***n-*** **1** sharp blow made with or as if with the flat of the hand. **2** quick, sharp noise made by such a blow. **3** loud, resounding kiss. ***vt-*** **1** to hit sharply and quickly with or as if with the flat of the hand; slap: *Dad* smacked *Paul for talking back.* **2** to open (lips) with a sharp, clapping noise: *He* smacked *his lips with pleasure.* ***vi-*** to strike something with force: *He* smacked *against the pole with his bike.* ***adv-*** *Informal* fully and directly; squarely: *He ran* smack *into an old friend.* [from a Germanic source, probably the imitation of a sound.]

[3]**smack** (smăk) ***n-*** small sailing vessel or sloop with one sail. [from Dutch **smak.**]

smack·ing (smăk′ ĭng) ***adj-*** lively; brisk.

small (smȯl) ***adj-*** **[small·er, small·est] 1** not big or large; little in size, amount, or degree: *An ounce is a* small *weight. The mouse is a* small *animal.* **2** unimportant; insignificant; petty: *Don't bother me with these* small *matters.* **3** mean; not generous: *It was* small *of him to refuse to pay.* **4** doing business in a limited manner: *a* small *farmer.* **—*adj-* small′ ish.** ***n-*** **small′ ness.**

small arms ***n- pl.*** light, usually portable firearms of small caliber, such as pistols, rifles, and machine guns.

small capital ***n-*** capital letter made about the size of the lowercase letters of a particular size of type. THIS SENTENCE IS IN SMALL CAPITALS. Also **small cap.**

small change ***n-*** **1** coins of small value; loose change. **2** *Informal* person or thing of small importance or value.

small fry ***n-*** (takes plural verb) **1** young children; youngsters. **2** unimportant persons or things.

small hours ***n-*** hours between midnight and dawn.

small intestine See *intestine.*

small letter ***n-*** letter that is not capitalized.

small-mind·ed (smȯl′ mīn′ dəd) ***adj-*** narrow-minded or shallow; petty; prejudiced: *a* small-minded *attitude.* **—*adv-* small′-mind′ ed·ly.** ***n-*** **small′-mind′ ed·ness.**

small·mouth (smȯl′ mouth′) ***n-*** black bass, valued for food and game.

small·pox (smȯl′ pŏks′) ***n-*** very contagious viral disease marked by fever and sores, which often leave pitted scars. *as* ***modifier***: *a* smallpox *vaccination.*

small talk ***n-*** light conversation about everyday things.

smart (smärt) ***adj-*** **[smart·er, smart·est] 1** brisk; fresh: *They ran at a* smart *pace.* **2** bright; quick; clever: *He was very* smart *in mathematics.* **3** neat; trim: *The captain presented a very* smart *picture in his uniform.* **4** fashionable: *She is always* smart *in her Paris clothes.* ***vi-*** **1** to feel or cause a sharp, stinging pain: *The extreme cold made my face* smart. *Ouch! That alcohol* smarts. **2** to feel injury or distress: *He* smarted *from the rebuke.* ***n-*** sharp, stinging pain; also, an acute feeling of distress. **—*adv-* smart′ ly.** ***n-*** **smart′ ness.**

smart al·eck (ăl′ ək) *Informal* ***n-*** person who is obnoxiously conceited and cocky. **—*adj-* smart′-al′ eck** or **smart′-al′ eck·y.**

smart·en (smär′ tən) ***vt-*** **1** to make smart or spruce; spruce up. **2** to make more intelligent, alert, or clever.

smash (smăsh) ***vt-*** **1** to break into pieces with violence: *He* smashed *the window with a rock.* **2** to destroy; shatter: *The depression* smashed *his business.* **3** to strike violently: *He* smashed *his bat against the ground.* ***vi-*** **1** to be broken: *The glass* smashed *on the floor.* **2** to collide or crash violently: *The car* smashed *into the wall.* ***n-*** **1** sound of breaking or crashing: *The* smash *of glass startled me.* **2** violent collision: *the* smash *of two cars.* **3** (also **smash hit**) *Slang* popular and successful show.

go to smash to collapse.

smash·ing (smăsh′ ĭng) ***adj-*** **1** crashing; crushing: *We heard a* smashing *noise.* **2** *Informal* outstandingly impressive, effective, or successful.

smash·up (smăsh′ŭp′) ***n-*** **1** violent collision. **2** a complete wreck or collapse.

smat·ter·ing (smăt′ər ĭng) or **smat·ter** (smăt′ər) ***n-*** slight knowledge of anything: *a* smattering *of French.*

smear (smêr) ***vt-*** **1** to cover, spread, or streak with anything dirty, greasy, or sticky: *The baby* smeared *the walls with jam.* **2** to harm or injure the reputation of, by hints or accusations of wrongdoing: *The politician* smeared *his opponent.* ***n-*** **1** stain; smudge; streak: *a* smear *of jam on the baby's face.* **2** a libel or slander. **3** small quantity of something such as blood or pus, placed on a slide for microscopic examination. *as* ***modifier:*** *his* smear *tactics.* **—*n-* smear′er.**

smear·y (smêr′ē) ***adj-*** **[smear·i·er, smear·i·est] 1** covered or streaked with anything dirty, greasy, or sticky. **2** likely to cause such soiling: *a* smeary *paint.*

smell (smĕl) ***vt-*** **[smelled** or **smelt** (smĕlt), **smell·ing] 1** to recognize or detect by inhaling its odor: *I* smell *burning rags.* **2** to test by this method; sniff: *He* smelled *the meat to see if it was fresh.* **3** to detect or sense; be aware of: *We* smelled *trouble.* ***vi-*** **1** to give off an odor: *The garden* smells *of lilacs.* **2** to give off an unpleasant odor; stink: *The garbage can* smells. ***n*** **1** act of sniffing: *With one* smell *the dog picked up the scent.* **2** odor; aroma.
smell up to fill with a bad odor; stink up.

smelling salts ***n- pl.*** aromatic, often scented, preparation that gives off ammonia and is used to relieve faintness or headache.

smell·y (smĕl′ē) ***adj-*** **[smell·i·er, smell·i·est] 1** having a strong odor. **2** disgusting: *a* smelly *situation.*

[1]smelt (smĕlt) ***vt-*** **1** to melt (ore) in order to separate metal from rock. **2** to refine or extract (metal) by this process. [from earlier Dutch **smelten** meaning "to smelt; melt."]

[2]smelt (smĕlt) ***n-*** [*pl.* **smelt; smelts** (kinds of smelt)] any of various small, silvery food fishes found in northern waters. [from Old English **smelt** of the same meaning.]

[3]smelt (smĕlt) *p.t. & p.p.* of **smell.**

smelt·er (smĕl′tər) ***n-*** **1** person who smelts ore. **2** furnace or place for smelting ore.

smid·gen or **smid·geon** (smĭj′ən) *Informal* ***n-*** little bit.

smi·lax (smī′lăks) ***n-*** **1** delicate, trailing green plant of the lily family, much used for decoration. **2** any one of several related prickly vines or herbs.

smile (smīl) ***n-*** upward movement of the corners of the mouth, showing pleasure, happiness, etc.: *a pleasant* smile. ***vi-*** **[smiled, smil·ing] 1** to show a smile: *Let's all* smile *for the camera.* **2** to present a cheerful attitude: *to* smile *at misfortune.* **—*adv-* smil′ing·ly.**
smile on to favor; approve: *Fortune* smiled on *us.*

smirch (smûrch) ***vt-*** **1** to smear, soil, or stain. **2** to bring disgrace upon; besmirch: *to* smirch *one's reputation.* ***n-:*** *a* smirch *on the window; a* smirch *on his record.*

smirk (smûrk) ***n-*** smile that indicates feelings of self-satisfaction or of knowing something unknown to others. ***vi-:*** *She* smirked *as she gave the answer.*

smite (smīt) ***vt-*** **[smote** (smōt), **smit·ten** (smĭt′ən) or **smit** (smĭt) or **smote, smit·ing] 1** to strike with the hand or a weapon. **2** to affect with any strong feeling. **3** to come upon as a sudden blow. **—*n-* smit′er.**

smith (smĭth) ***n-*** person who shapes or makes things out of metal; blacksmith.

smith·er·eens (smĭth′ə rēnz′) *Informal* ***n- pl.*** little pieces; bits; fragments.

smith·y (smĭth′ē, smĭth′-) ***n-*** [*pl.* **smith·ies**] workshop of a blacksmith; forge.

smit·ten (smĭt′ən) *p.p.* of **smite.** ***adj-*** *Informal* completely in love.

smock (smŏk) ***n-*** long, loose, shirtlike garment with sleeves gathered into cuffs, worn to protect the clothing. ***vt-*** to decorate with smocking.

smock·ing (smŏk′ĭng) ***n-*** ornamental needlework used to hold gathers in place and create a honeycomb texture.

smog (smŏg) ***n-*** combination of smoke and fog in the air: *Automobile exhaust fumes cause* smog *in our city.* [shortened from *smoke* and *fog.*] **—*adj-* smog′gy.**

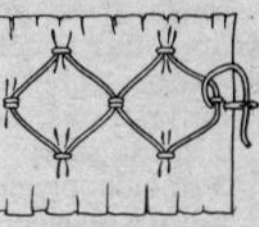
Smocking

smoke (smōk) ***n-*** **1** cloud of gas and solid particles given off when something is burned. **2** anything like smoke. **3** the act of breathing tobacco smoke for pleasure: *to take a* smoke. ***vi-*** **[smoked, smok·ing] 1** to give off smoke, especially more smoke than wanted, or in a wrong place: *The fireplace* smokes. **2** to breath the fumes of burning tobacco. ***vt-*** **1** to use (a cigar, pipe, etc.). **2** to preserve or flavor (food) by exposing to wood smoke.
go up in smoke 1 burn up. **2** vanish as if by burning.
smoke out 1 to drive out by smoke: *to* smoke *bees* out *of a tree.* **2** to drive (a criminal) out of hiding.

smoke·house (smōk′hous′) ***n-*** building where meat, fish, hides, etc., are cured by smoking.

smoke·less (smōk′ləs) ***adj-*** burning with little or no smoke: *a* smokeless *gunpowder.*

smok·er (smō′kər) ***n-*** **1** person who smokes tobacoo. **2** railway car, or section of one, where smoking is allowed. **3** *Informal* social function for men.

smoke screen ***n-*** dense smoke laid down to hide troops, ships, etc., from enemy observation.

smoke·stack (smōk′stăk′) ***n-*** tall chimney on a factory, steam locomotive, steamship, etc.

smok·y (smō′kē) ***adj-*** **[smok·i·er, smok·i·est] 1** giving off smoke: *The* smoky *fire made me cough.* **2** like smoke in taste, smell, or color: *the* smoky *flavor of ham; eyes of a* smoky *blue.* **3** filled with smoke: *a* smoky *room.* **—*adv-* smok′i·ly. *n-* smok′i·ness.**

smol·der (smōl′dər) ***vi-*** **1** to burn and smoke without flame. **2** to exist beneath the surface; remain pent up: *His rage* smoldered *at the insult.* Also **smoulder.**

smooth (smo͞oth) ***adj-*** **[smooth·er, smooth·est] 1** not rough; even in texture or surface: *as* smooth *as silk.* **2** steady in motion; not jerky or jarring: *The airplane made a* smooth *landing.* **3** calm; pleasant; serene: *a* smooth *disposition.* **4** easy and flattering in speech or manner; ingratiating: *a* smooth *talker.* ***vt-*** **1** to remove roughness from; make flat or even: *to* smooth *the sheets on a bed.* **2** to calm or soothe: *to* smooth *a person's feelings.* **3** to make easy: *to* smooth *a person's way.* **4** to remove: *to* smooth *the rough spots.* **5** to polish; refine. **—*n-* smooth′er. *adv-* smooth′ly. *n-* smooth′ness.**
smooth down to calm; soothe.
smooth over to make less unpleasant or serious; soften.

smooth·bore (smo͞oth′bôr′) ***adj-*** of firearms, having a smooth, ungrooved bore. ***n-*** firearm with such a bore.

smooth-faced (smo͞oth′fāst′) ***adj-*** without a beard or mustache: *a* smooth-faced *youth.*

smooth-spo·ken (smo͞oth′spō′kən) ***adj-*** speaking easily and fluently: *a* smooth-spoken *orator.*

smooth-tongued (smo͞oth′tŭngd′) ***adj-*** having the ability to flatter, ingratiate, and persuade with speech.

smooth·y or **smooth·ie** (smo͞o′thē) *Informal* ***n-*** [*pl.* **smooth·ies**] poised, suave, ingratiating person; especially, a man who flatters women.

smor·gas·bord (smôr′ gəs bôrd′, smôr′ gəs bôrd′) ***n-*** buffet containing many different kinds of hot or cold dishes. *as **modifier**: a* smorgasbord *dinner.*

smote (smōt) *p.t. & p.p.* of **smite.**

smoth·er (smŭth′ ər) ***vt-*** **1** to kill by depriving of air; stifle; suffocate. **2** to put out (a fire) by keeping out air. **3** to suppress or conceal: *He* smothered *his resentment.* **4** in cooking, to cover, as with onions, and cook in a covered dish. ***vi-*** to die from lack of breath. ***—n-*** **smoth′ er·er.** ***adj-*** **smoth′ er·y:** *black,* smothery *fumes.*

smoul·der (smōl′ dər) smolder.

smudge (smŭj) ***vt-*** **[smudged, smudg·ing]** to mark with dirty streaks; smear; blur: *to* smudge *a drawing.* ***n-*** **1** stain; smear: *The child had a* smudge *on his face.* **2** smoldering, smoky fire, usually made in a container called a **smudge pot,** for protecting fruit trees from frost or for keeping off insects. ***—adj-*** **smudg′ y.**

smug (smŭg) ***adj-*** **[smug·ger, smug·gest]** highly pleased with oneself; self-satisfied; complacent: *a* smug *air of accomplishment.* ***—adv-*** **smug′ ly.** ***n-*** **smug′ ness.**

smug·gle (smŭg′ əl) ***vt-*** **[smug·gled, smug·gling]** to bring into or out of a place secretly and illegally: *to* smuggle *goods into a country.* ***vi-***: *It is illegal to* smuggle.

smug·gler (smŭg′ lər) ***n-*** person who takes into or out of a country, county, etc., something that is prohibited or for which the tax has not been paid: *a gold* smuggler.

smut (smŭt) ***n-*** **1** language, book, picture, etc., that is foul and indecent; obscenity. **2** spot or stain made by soot or dirt; also, the soot or dirt itself. **3** any of various fungi that have black spores and attack grain.

smut·ty (smŭt′ ē) ***adj-*** **[smut·ti·er, smut·ti·est]** **1** indecent; vulgar; obscene: *a* smutty *novel.* **2** soiled with soot or dirt. **3** affected with the smut fungus.

Sn symbol for tin.

snack (snăk) ***n-*** light meal usually eaten between meals.

snaf·fle (snăf′ əl) ***n-*** horse's bit that is jointed in the middle. ***vt-*** **[snaf·fled, snaf·fling]** to provide with, or control by means of, such a bit.

sna·fu (snă fo͞o′) *Slang* ***n-*** confused and chaotic situation.

snag (snăg) ***n-*** **1** sharp or jagged projecting part: *the* snags *in a bramble patch*; *the* snags *on barbed wire.* **2** stump or branch held fast in a riverbed or lake bed, dangerous to boats. **3** any unexpected obstacle. **4** part that has been caught or torn: *a* snag *in the cloth.* ***vt-*** **[snagged, snag·ging]** to catch or tear on a sharp or rough projection: *I* snagged *my stocking.* ***—adj-*** **snag′ gy.**

snaggle-tooth (snăg′ əl to͞oth′) ***n-*** tooth that is broken or projecting beyond the rest. ***—adj-*** **snag′ gle-toothed′.**

snail (snāl) ***n-*** **1** small, slow-moving mollusk with a soft body, spiral shell, and eyes on long stalks. **2** sluggish or lazy person.

Land snail, about 2 in. long

snake (snāk) ***n-*** **1** any of various limbless, scaled reptiles with long, slender, and tapering bodies. Some inject or infuse venom when biting, but most are nonpoisonous. **2** deceitful, treacherous person. **3** flexible wire or rod used to clear clogged drainage pipes. ***vi-*** **[snaked, snak·ing]** **1** to crawl close to the ground. **2** to follow a winding course. ***vt-*** *Informal* to drag forcibly; jerk: *to* snake *a log out of a swamp.* ***—adv-*** **snake′ like′.**

Snake (snāk) ***n-*** Shoshoni Indian. ***adj-***: *a* Snake *lodge.*

snake dance ***n-*** **1** procession that moves in a snakelike manner, as in celebration of an athletic victory. **2** ritual dance of the Hopi Indians in which live rattlesnakes are held in the dancers' mouths.

snake·root (snāk′ ro͞ot′, -ro͝ot′) ***n-*** **1** any of various plants supposed to cure the bite of a snake. **2** the root of any of these plants.

snake·skin (snāk′ skĭn′) ***n-*** **1** the skin or hide of a snake. **2** leather made from this. *as **modifier**: a* snakeskin *bag.*

snak·y (snā′ kē) ***adj-*** **[snak·i·er, snak·iest]** **1** resembling or reminding one of a snake: *a* snaky *walk.* **2** infested with snakes. **3** deceitful; treacherous; cunning. ***—adv-*** **snak′ i·ly.** ***n-*** **snak′ i·ness.**

snap (snăp) ***vi-*** **[snapped, snap·ping]** **1** to break with a sharp, sudden sound: *The branch* snapped *in the strong wind.* **2** to make a sudden, sharp sound: *The wood* snapped *and crackled in the fireplace.* **3** to give way under strain: *After hours of waiting, his patience* snapped. **4** to make a quick bite, snatch, or grasp (at): *The dog* snapped *at the bone. John* snapped *at the opportunity.* **5** to speak harshly or irritably; bark: *She* snapped *at her unruly students.* **6** to fasten, close, strike, etc., with a sudden, sharp sound: *The door* snapped *shut.* **7** to move quickly: *The sentry* snapped *to attention.* ***vt-*** **1** to break or cut with a sudden, sharp sound: *to* snap *a wire.* **2** to utter quickly or sharply (often followed by "out"): *to* snap *a command.* **3** to fasten, close, strike, etc., with a sudden, sharp sound: *to* snap *a lock*; *to* snap *a lid shut*; *to* snap *one's fingers.* **4** to take (a photograph) with a still camera; also, to photograph (a subject). ***n-*** **1** a sudden cracking or breaking off, as of something stiff or tense: *the* snap *of a twig.* **2** sudden, sharp sound: *The twig broke with a* snap. **3** sudden snatch or bite: *The fish caught the bait with a* snap. **4** kind of thin, crisp cookie: *ginger*snap. **5** clasp or fastening. **6** *Informal* anything easily done or had. **7** sudden, short period of cold or warm weather. ***adj-*** **1** quick and without much thought; impulsive; offhand: *a* snap *decision.* **2** *Informal* calling for little effort; easy: *a* snap *course in college.*

snap one's fingers at to show contempt or disinterest.

snap out of it *Informal* to come or cause to come out of melancholy state, a trance, mischief, etc.

snap up **1** to seize and swallow quickly: *The fish* snapped up *the bait.* **2** to grab and keep: *to* snap up *the profits.*

snap·drag·on (snăp′ drăg′ ən) ***n-*** flowering plant with bag-shaped flowers of white, purple, red, or yellow, that open like a mouth when squeezed.

snap·per (snăp′ ər) ***n-*** **1** person or thing that snaps. **2** large food fish of warm seas; especially, the **red snapper** of the Gulf of Mexico. **3** snapping turtle.

snapping turtle ***n-*** any of several large turtles of American rivers and lakes, with very strong jaws.

snap·pish (snăp′ ĭsh) ***adj-*** **1** apt to bite or snap. **2** curt and sharp in speech or manner; irritable; peevish. ***—adv-*** **snap′ pish·ly.** ***n-*** **snap′ pish·ness.**

snap·py (snăp′ ē) ***adj-*** **[snap·pi·er, snap·pi·est]** **1** *Informal* quick; lively; brisk: *The soldiers marched with a* snappy *step.* **2** irritable; short-tempered. ***—adv-*** **snap′ pi·ly.**

snap·shot (snăp′ shŏt′) ***n-*** small, informal photograph.

[1]snare (snâr) ***n-*** **1** kind of trap that catches game in a noose. **2** anything that entraps or entangles: *His flattery proved a* snare. ***vt-*** **[snared, snar·ing]**: *to* snare *a rabbit*; *to* snare *a criminal.* [probably from Old Norse **snara** meaning "a cord; noose."]

Snare

[2]snare (snâr) ***n-*** **1** catgut strings or wires fastened across a snare-drum head in order to give the drum's tone a rattling effect. **2** snare drum. [probably partly from **[1]snare,** and partly from an earlier Dutch or Germanic word.]

snare drum ***n-*** small drum the lower head of which has catgut strings that rattle when the upper head is struck.

[1]**snarl** (snärl) ***n-*** **1** angry or vicious growl with the teeth exposed. **2** angry, rough tone of voice. ***vi-*** **1** to show the teeth and make a growling noise: *Rover* snarled *at the strangers.* **2** to speak in a rough, angry tone of voice: *Mr. Jones* snarled *at the noisy children.* ***vt-*** to utter in a rough, angry way; growl out: *He* snarled *commands.* [from earlier English **snar**, probably from a Germanic imitation of the sound.] **—*n-* snarl′ er. *adv-* snarl′ ing·ly.**

[2]**snarl** (snärl) ***n-*** **1** tangle; knot: *a* snarl *in one's hair.* **2** any disordered, chaotic condition: *Traffic here is in a continual* snarl. ***vt-*** to tangle or entangle: *The kitten* snarled *the ball of wool. Unexpected visitors* snarled *our plans.* ***vi-***: *The wool* snarled. [probably from [1]**snare.**]

[1]**snarl·y** (snär′ lē) ***adj-*** **[snarl·i·er, snarl·i·est]** ill-tempered; growly. [from [1]**snarl.**]

[2]**snarl·y** (snär′ lē) ***adj-*** **[snarl·i·er, snarl·i·est]** full of snarls. [from [2]**snarl.**]

snatch (snăch) ***vt-*** to grab or try to grab suddenly or rudely; seize: *to* snatch *a purse*; *to* snatch *victory from defeat.* ***n-*** **1** quick, grabbing motion: *to make a* snatch *at a rope.* **2** small piece, bit, or period of time: *a* snatch *of music*; *to sleep in* snatches. **—*n-* snatch′ er.**

snatch at to make a quick, grasping motion toward.

snatch·y (snăch′ ē) ***adj-*** **[snatch·i·er, snatch·i·est]** not continuous; interrupted; irregular.

sneak (snēk) ***vi-*** **1** to move or go in a secret or sly way; slink: *She* sneaked *into the house after everyone was asleep.* **2** to act in a sly or furtive way: *Why do you* sneak *instead of acting openly?* ***vt-*** to take in a furtive way; steal. ***n-*** **1** sly, underhanded person. **2** a stealthy and surreptitious movement. *as* ***modifier***: *a* sneak *attack.*

sneak·ers (snē′ kərz) *Informal* ***n-*** *pl.* canvas shoes with rubber soles, used for sports.

sneak·ing (snē′ kĭng) ***adj-*** **1** sly and underhanded; furtive: *a* sneaking *glance.* **2** not openly acknowledged; unavowed; secret: *a* sneaking *ambition to act*; *a* sneaking *suspicion that he is right.* **—*adv-* sneak′ ing·ly.**

sneak thief ***n-*** petty thief who steals without using force.

sneak·y (snē′ kē) ***adj-*** **[sneak·i·er, sneak·i·est]** sly, stealthy and furtive; also, underhanded. **—*adv-* sneak′ i·ly. *n-* sneak′ i·ness.**

sneer (snêr) ***n-*** **1** look of contempt or scorn made by slightly curling the upper lip. **2** contemptuous or scornful remark: *I have had enough of his* sneers. ***vi-***: *She* sneered *at his offer to help.* ***vt-***: *He* sneered *his disfavor.* **—*n-* sneer′ er. *adv-* sneer′ ing·ly.**

sneeze (snēz) ***n-*** sudden, explosive burst of breath through the mouth and nostrils. ***vi-*** **[sneezed, sneez·ing]**: *The dust made her* sneeze. **—*n-* sneez′ er.**

not to be sneezed at *Informal* not to be scorned.

snell (snĕl) ***n-*** short piece of leader whipped on a fishhook to attach it to a line. **—*adj-* snelled.**

snick·er (snĭk′ ər) ***n-*** sly laugh indicating scorn, disrespect, or amusement; giggle; titter. ***vi-***: *Tom* snickered *at Fred's clumsy movements.* Also **snigger.**

snide (snīd) ***adj-*** **[snid·er, snid·est]** slyly malicious or disparaging; nasty. **—*adv-* snide′ ly. *n-* snide′ ness.**

sniff (snĭf) ***vi-*** **1** to draw air through the nostrils in short breaths that can be heard: *I* sniffed *but couldn't smell a thing.* **2** to express contempt by, or as by, such a breath: *She* sniffed *at my attempt to be funny.* ***vt-*** **1** to breathe in; inhale: *He* sniffed *the morning air.* **2** to test by means of odor; smell: *to* sniff *expensive perfume.* **3** to detect or recognize; perceive: *to* sniff *danger*; *to* sniff *a revolt.* ***n-*** **1** short intake of air that can be heard; also, the sound made by this. **2** act of smelling: *a* sniff *of perfume.*

snif·fle (snĭf′ əl) ***vi-*** **[snif·fled, snif·fling]** to breathe heavily and noisily, as from a cold or crying; snuffle. ***n-*** **1** sound made by this. **2** *Informal* **the sniffles** slight cold. **—*n-* snif′ fler.**

snig·ger (snĭg′ ər) snicker.

snip (snĭp) ***vt-*** **[snipped, snip·ping]** to cut with short, quick clips: *to* snip *a piece of paper.* ***vi-***: *to* snip *along the dotted line.* ***n-*** **1** small piece; bit: *a* snip *of cloth.* **2 snips** scissors or shears.

snipe (snīp) ***n-*** brown-and-white marsh bird with short legs and a long bill. ***vi-*** **[sniped, snip·ing]** **1** to hunt such birds. **2** to shoot (at) individuals from an ambush.

Snipe, about 1 ft. long

snip·er (snī′ pər) ***n-*** one who shoots at from ambush.

snip·pet (snĭp′ ət) ***n-*** small piece; bit; scrap.

snip·py (snĭp′ ē) ***adj-*** **[snip·pi·er, snip·pi·est]** *Informal* **1** short and curt in speaking; snappy. **2** saucy and impertinent. Also **snip′ pet·y. —*n-* snip′ pi·ness.**

snitch (snĭch) *Informal* ***vt-*** to steal; swipe. ***vi-*** to tattle or inform (on) someone.

sniv·el (snĭv′ əl) ***vi-*** **1** to complain in a weak, tearful manner. **2** to run at the nose; snuffle. **—*n-* sniv′ el·er.**

snob (snŏb) ***n-*** **1** person who values wealth and social position above all else, and scorns or patronizes those who do not have them. **2** someone who thinks himself better than others in some way: *an intellectual* snob.

snob·ber·y (snŏb′ ə rē) ***n-*** conduct of a snob.

snob·bish (snŏb′ ĭsh) ***adj-*** of or like a snob. **—*adv-* snob′ bish·ly. *n-* snob′ bish·ness.**

snood (sno͞od) ***n-*** coarse net for holding a woman's hair.

snook (sno͝ok) ***n-*** [*pl.* **snook; snooks** (kinds of snook)] large game and food fish of warm seas.

snoop (sno͞op) ***vi-*** to search in a sneaky way; pry: *He* snooped *through my desk when I wasn't home.* ***n-*** *Informal* (also **snoop′ er**) person who pries.

snoot·y (sno͞o′ tē) *Informal* ***adj-*** **[snoot·i·er, snoot·i·est]** haughty; snobbish. **—*adv-* snoot′ i·ly. *n-* snoot′ i·ness.**

snooze (sno͞oz) *Informal* ***vi-*** **[snoozed, snooz·ing]** to doze; take a nap. ***n-*** nap; doze.

snore (snôr) ***vi-*** **[snored, snor·ing]** to breathe with a hoarse noise while sleeping. ***n-*** noisy, hoarse breathing of a sleeping person. **—*n-* snor′ er.**

snor·kel (snôr′ kəl, snôr′-) ***n-*** **1** on submarines, a system of tubes to take air in and out while the submarine is submerged. **2** J-shaped tube, worn by swimmers to permit breathing while the face is under water. ***vi-*** to swim with such a tube to observe marine life.

snort (snôrt, snôrt) ***n-*** harsh noise made by forcing air out through the nostrils. ***vi-*** **1** to make such a noise. **2** to express anger or contempt by a harsh nasal sound: *He* snorted *with rage.* ***vt-*** to utter with a harsh nasal sound: *He* snorted *his answer to me.* **—*n-* snort′ er.**

snout (snout) ***n-*** **1** projecting nose, and sometimes mouth and jaws, of an animal; muzzle: *a pig's* snout. **2** something, such as a nozzle, that resembles this.

snow (snō) ***n-*** **1** groups of ice crystals matted together to form flattened, feathery flakes as a result of slow crystallization of water vapor at a temperature less than 32°. **2** such flakes while still falling, or an accumulation of them lying on the ground. **3** a fall of snow, or a

---

fāte, făt, dâre, bärn; bē, bĕt, mêre; bīte, bĭt; nōte, hŏt, môre, dȯg; fŭn, fûr; to͞o, bo͝ok; oil; out; tar; thin; then; hw for wh as in *wh*at; zh for s as in u*s*ual; ə for a, e, i, o, u, as in *a*go, lin*e*n, per*i*l, at*o*m, min*u*s

shower resembling this: *the heavy* snows *last winter*; *a* snow *of confetti. as* ***modifier***: *a* snow *shovel.* ***vi-*** **1** to become snow and fall to earth. **2** to fall or shower like snow: *Streamers* snowed *down.*

snow in to shut in with snow.

snow under to overwhelm, especially with work.

snow·ball (snō′ bôl′) ***n-*** **1** snow packed together into a ball. **2** shrub of the honeysuckle family with large clusters of white flowers. ***vi-*** to grow rapidly, as a rolling ball of snow: *The rumor* snowballed.

snow·bank (snō′ băngk′) ***n-*** large drift or heap of snow.

snow·ber·ry (snō′ bĕr′ ē) ***n-*** [*pl.* **snow·ber·ries**] bushy North American shrub bearing white berries.

snow·bird (snō′ bûrd′) ***n-*** **1** junco. **2** snow bunting.

snow-blind (snō′ blīnd′) ***adj-*** affected with an inflammation of the eyes and temporary, although sometimes permanent, blindness, caused by the reflection of ultraviolet light from snow fields to the unprotected eyes. **—*n-* snow-blindness.**

snow·bound (snō′ bound′) ***adj-*** shut in by snow.

snow bunting ***n-*** black and white finch of North America.

snow·cap (snō′ kăp′) ***n-*** cap or crest of snow, especially on a mountain peak. **—*adj-* snow′ capped′.**

snow·drift (snō′ drĭft′) ***n-*** heap of snow piled up by the wind.

snow·drop (snō′ drŏp′) ***n-*** **1** plant with white flowers that blooms in early spring. **2** flower of this plant.

snow·fall (snō′ fôl′) ***n-*** **1** a falling of snow. **2** amount of snow that falls during one period of time or in one area.

snow·flake (snō′ flāk′) ***n-*** form in which snow falls, consisting of a tiny, feathery, six-sided crystal or mass of such crystals.

snow leopard ***n-*** large, spotted cat of central Asia, with long, heavy fur that is almost white in winter; ounce.

snow line ***n-*** lower edge of a permanent field of snow on a mountain.

snow·man (snō′ măn′) ***n-*** [*pl.* **snow·men**] mass of packed snow shaped to resemble the figure of a man.

snow·mo·bile (snō′ mō bēl′) ***n-*** vehicle, often equipped with caterpillar treads and runners, used for traveling over snow and ice.

snow·plow (snō′ plou′) ***n-*** device for clearing snow from roads and tracks.

snow·shed (snō′ shĕd′) ***n-*** shelter erected, as over a railroad track, to protect against snowslides.

snow·shoe (snō′ sho͞o′) ***n-*** one of a pair of racket-shaped wooden frames strung with rawhide cords and tied to the feet for walking on deep snow.

Snowshoes

snow·slide (snō′ slīd′) ***n-*** avalanche of snow.

snow·storm (snō′ stôrm′, -stôrm′) ***n-*** heavy snowfall with strong winds.

snow·suit (snō′ so͞ot′) ***n-*** heavy, one- or two-piece garment worn by children in cold weather.

snow tire ***n-*** tire with a deep tread designed to give additional traction on ice or snow.

snow train ***n-*** special train that carries people to a resort for winter sports, especially skiing.

snow-white (snō′ hwīt′) ***adj-*** white as snow.

snow·y (snō′ ē) ***adj-*** [**snow·i·er, snow·i·est**] **1** having or covered with snow: *a* snowy *winter*; snowy *mountain peaks.* **2** white or clean like fresh snow: *a* snowy *sheet.* **—*adv-* snow′ i·ly. *n-* snow′ i·ness.**

snub (snŭb) ***vt-*** [**snubbed, snub·bing**] **1** to treat rudely or with deliberate show of indifference: *Mary* snubbed *some of the girls by not inviting them to her party.* **2** to check or stop abruptly by means of a cable or rope. ***n-*** **1** rude treatment or deliberate show of indifference. **2** check or restraint by means of a cable or rope. **—*n-* snub′ ber.**

snub·by (snŭb′ ē) ***adj-*** [**snub·bi·er, snub·bi·est**] short and slightly turned up, as a nose. **—*n-* snub′ bi·ness.**

snub nose ***n-*** a short, turned-up nose; pug nose. **—*adj-* (snub-nose** or **snub-nosed) 1** having a snub nose. **2** of revolvers, having a very short barrel.

[1]**snuff** (snŭf) ***vi-*** to smell; sniff; inhale. ***n-*** fine tobacco powder that is sniffed in through the nose. [from early Dutch **snuffen,** "clear the nose," from Dutch **snuf,** "snuff tobacco," and related to **sniff.**] **—*n-* snuff′ er.**

up to snuff *Informal* up to a usual standard.

[2]**snuff** (snŭf) ***vt-*** to put out (a candle), as by pinching the wick. ***n-*** charred portion of a candlewick. [from Middle English **snuffen,** "put out a candle."]

snuff out 1 to put out; extinguish. **2** to destroy.

snuff·box (snŭf′ bŏks′) ***n-*** small container for snuff.

snuff·er (snŭf′ ər) ***n-*** **1** person who snuffs out candles. **2** small metal cone or cup with a handle, used to snuff out candles. **3 snuffers** small scissors used for cropping charred candlewicks.

snuf·fle (snŭf′ əl) ***vi-*** [**snuf·fled, snuf·fling**] to speak or breathe noisily through the nose, especially when it is obstructed; sniffle. ***vt-*** to utter through the nose: *The old man* snuffled *a reply.* ***n-*** **1** a snuffling or the sound made by it. **2 the snuffles** *Informal* slight head cold; sniffles. **—*n-* snuf′ fler.**

snug (snŭg) ***adj-*** [**snug·ger, snug·gest**] **1** comfortable; cozy: *a* snug *corner by the hearth.* **2** tight in fit; close-fitting: *a* snug *dress.* **—*adv-* snug′ ly. *n-* snug′ ness.**

snug·gle (snŭg′ əl) ***vi-*** [**snug·gled, snug·gling**] to cuddle; press close; nestle: *The child* snuggled *in his mother's arms.* ***vt-***: *Mother* snuggled *the baby.*

[1]**so** (sō) ***adv-*** **1** just as shown, stated, understood, etc.: *Now that I've shown you, make the bed* so. **2** to such a degree: *It was* so *hot that we went swimming.* **3** also; likewise: *The Smiths were present and* so *were the Farleys.* **4** *Informal* too: *I can* so *climb trees!* **5** according to the truth: *That statement just isn't* so. **6** approximately as many or as much as already expressed; thereabouts: *Visit us a week or* so. **7** *Informal* apparently; it seems that: *And* so *you don't like him!* **8** *Informal* to an exceptional degree; very much (used as intensifier): *That problem was* so *hard. My sprained ankle hurts* so. ***pron-*** **1** what has already been said or named: *He was always a poor player and will always remain* so. **2** more or less: *a dollar or* so. ***conj-*** **1** with the purpose that; in order that: *We came early* so *we could see him.* **2** and therefore: *The children were bad,* so *their mother punished them.* ***interj-*** exclamation expressing surprise, doubt, etc.: *They exclaimed,* "So, *he is the guilty one!*" [from Old English **swā.**] ***Homs-*** sew, [2]sow.

and so (on) in a similar manner. **and so forth** in a similar manner. **so as** in order to. **so . . . as** word combination used after "not" in sentences to make a comparison: *He is not* so *big* as *I am.* **so that** in order that: *We all left* so that *he could rest.*

►Many people prefer so in place of the first AS in a negative statement or question that expresses or implies a comparison. *I hope it will not be* so *hot tomorrow (as it was yesterday).* So is often used in conversation for "in order that," but in writing, the full form SO THAT should be used. *I want the money* so (that) *I can go to the opera.*

²so (sō) *Music* ***n-*** sol. [altered by an Italian, G. B. Doni, from earlier **sol.**] ***Homs-*** sew, ²sow.

s.o. or **so** 1 struck out. 2 strike-out.

So. 1 south. 2 southern.

soak (sōk) ***vt-*** 1 to wet through and through: *The rain* soaked *the ground.* 2 to let lie in water or other liquid: *Mother* soaked *the beans in water before cooking.* 3 *Slang* to overcharge. ***vi-*** 1 to lie in water or other liquid; steep: *The clothes* soaked *for two hours.* 2 to penetrate (in, into, or through) something: *to* soak *into the ground.* ***n-*** a thorough wetting: *a* soak *in the rain.*

soak up to absorb: *He* soaks up *learning.*

so-and-so (sō′ ən sō′) *Informal* ***n-*** person whom one does not like. ***pron-*** unspecified person.

soap (sōp) ***n-*** cleansing substance used in washing. Soap is made of boiled fats and oils mixed with alkalis. *as* ***modifier***: *a* soap *dish.* ***vt-*** to cover or wash with soap. **—*adv-*** **soap′less**: *a* soapless *lather.*

soap·ber·ry (sōp′ bĕr′ ē) ***n-*** [*pl.* **soap·ber·ries**] 1 any of several tropical trees bearing fruit rich in suds-producing material. 2 the fruit of this tree, used for washing.

soap·box (sōp′ bŏks′) ***n-*** box used as a platform by street speakers. *as* ***modifier***: *a* soapbox *oratory.*

soapbox derby ***n-*** car race in which boys race unpowered model racing cars down a steep slope.

soap bubble ***n-*** 1 inflated, thin, irridescent sphere that consists of a very thin film of soapy water. 2 anything of a charming but fragile and insubstantial nature.

soap opera ***n-*** sentimental and emotional radio or television serial.

soap·stone (sōp′ stōn′) ***n-*** soft, grayish stone with a smooth surface that feels like soap.

soap·suds (sōp′ sŭdz′) ***n-*** (takes plural verb) foam made with soap and water.

soap·y (sō′ pē) ***adj-*** [**soap·i·er, soap·i·est**] 1 filled or covered with soap. 2 like soap. **—*n-*** **soap′i·ness.**

soar (sôr) ***vi-*** 1 to fly or glide high: *The eagle* soared *through the air.* 2 to rise rapidly: *The cost of living has* soared *in the last ten years.* 3 to rise above the ordinary or commonplace: *His ambitions* soared. ***Hom-*** sore.

sob (sŏb) ***vi-*** [**sobbed, sob·bing**] to weep with gasping, short breaths. ***n-*** tearful, choking sound.

sob out to tell while crying: *to* sob out *one's troubles.*

so·ber (sō′ bər) ***adj-*** [**so·ber·er, so·ber·est**] 1 sedate; staid; not gay or frivolous: *The Pilgrims were noted for their* sober *lives.* 2 quiet; not showy: *Gray is a* sober *color.* 3 serious; solemn: *From his* sober *expression, I feared bad news.* 4 reasonable; serious: *Father gave us some* sober *advice about spending money.* 5 not drunk. ***vt-*** to make serious: *The news of the accident* sobered *the gay party.* ***vi-***: *The party* sobered *after hearing the news.* **—*adv-*** **so′ber·ly.** ***n-*** **so′ber·ness.**

sober down to make or become calm or serious.

sober up 1 to recover from intoxication. 2 to sober down.

so·ber-mind·ed (sō′ bər mīn′ dəd) ***adj-*** serious and well-balanced in outlook: *a* sober-minded *realist.*

so·bri·e·ty (sə brī′ ə tē) ***n-*** 1 seriousness, calmness, or moderation; gravity. 2 temperance in the use of liquor.

so·bri·quet (sō′ brə kā′) ***n-*** nickname. Also **soubriquet.**

sob story *Slang* ***n-*** sad story about personal misfortunes, told to gain sympathy.

so-called (sō′ kôld′) ***adj-*** named so, but not correctly called: *This* so-called *butter is really margarine.*

soc·cer (sŏk′ ər) ***n-*** form of football in which the ball may be hit with any part of the body except the arms.

so·cia·ble (sō′ shə bəl) ***adj-*** 1 friendly and liking company. 2 giving or affording opportunity for conversation and companionship: *a pleasant,* sociable *evening with friends.* ***n-*** informal party or social gathering; social. **—*n-*** **so′cia·bil′i·ty.** ***adv-*** **so′cia·bly.**

so·cial (sō′ shəl) ***adj-*** 1 of or having to do with human beings in a group: *Slums are an urgent* social *problem.* 2 inclined to live in association with others: *Human beings are* social *creatures.* 3 of or having to do with the activities of the rich and fashionable: *the* social *whirl; a* social *climber.* 4 of, for, or in the company of others: *a* social *club; a* social *evening.* 5 liking the company of others; sociable. 6 of animals, living together in colonies or communities. ***n-*** informal party.

social democrat ***n-*** member of a political party supporting a shift from capitalism to socialism by peaceful, gradual, and democratic means.

social disease ***n-*** 1 venereal disease. 2 disease, such as tuberculosis, related to social and economic conditions.

so·cial·ism (sō′ shə lĭz′ əm) ***n-*** 1 doctrine or system by which the means of producing and distributing food and goods are owned by the people as a whole and operated by the government. 2 political movement that seeks to bring about such a system.

so·cial·ist (sō′ shə lĭst) ***n-*** 1 person who advocates socialism. 2 **Socialist** member of the Socialist Party. ***adj-*** 1 of or relating to socialism. 2 **Socialist** of or relating to the Socialist Party.

so·cial·is·tic (sō′ shə lĭs′ tĭk) ***adj-*** 1 socialist. 2 inclining toward or resembling socialism: *He thought my ideas were* socialistic. **—*adv-*** **so′cial·is′ti·cal·ly.**

Socialist Party ***n-*** U.S. political party based on democratic socialism, founded in 1901 by E. V. Debs.

so·cial·ite (sō′ shə līt′) *Informal* ***n-*** member of fashionable society.

so·cial·ize (sō′ shə līz′) ***vt-*** [**so·cial·ized, so·cial·iz·ing**] 1 to place under government or group control, especially in accordance with the principles of socialism. 2 to help (someone) toward attitudes of friendliness, cooperation, and sociability. 3 to make suitable for the needs of society as a whole. ***vi-*** to take part in social activity.

socialized medicine ***n-*** system of tax-supported medical care under which doctors are employed by the government, and treatment, services, etc., are provided for a relatively low fee or no fee at all.

so·cial·ly (sō′ shə lē) ***adv-*** 1 in a social manner: *to be* socially *successful.* 2 as part of society: *to be* socially *deprived.* 3 from or by society.

so·cial-mind·ed (sō′ shəl mīn′ dəd) ***adj-*** having one's mind on the betterment of society; public-spirited.

social sciences ***n-*** those branches of learning that deal with man as a member of society, social groups, and social institutions.

social security ***n-*** 1 any system that provides economic and other forms of assistance for needy members. 2 Federal program of old age insurance, public assistance to dependents such as widows and blind persons, and contribution to state unemployment insurance, established under the **Social Security Act** of 1935.

social studies ***n-*** the study of man in relation to society and his physical environment, encompassing history, geography, economics, anthropology, etc.

social work ***n-*** 1 organized effort aimed at the betterment of the community in such areas as housing, health, recreation, etc. 2 profession specializing in such effort. **—*n-*** **social worker.**

so·ci·e·ty (sə sī′ ə tē) ***n-*** [*pl.* **so·ci·e·ties**] **1** community of people living together at a particular time and place; also, all people collectively: *The police exist to protect* society. **2** persons joined together for a common aim. **3** class of people of wealth and fashion; also, their activities: *She reports on* society *for the newspaper.* **4** company; companionship: *We missed his* society *after he moved away.* *as* ***modifier***: *a* society *column.*

Society of Friends ***n-*** dissenting Christian sect founded in England by George Fox around 1650. It stresses "Inner Light," rejects outer rites and ceremonies, and opposes war. Also known as **Quakers.**

Society of Jesus ***n-*** the Roman Catholic religious order of Jesuits founded by St. Ignatius of Loyola in 1534.

so·ci·o-e·co·nom·ic (sō′ sē ō ĕk′ ə nŏm′ ĭk, sō′ shē ō-) ***adj-*** of or having to do with a combination of social and economic matters: *Poverty is a* socio-economic *problem.*

so·ci·ol·o·gist (sō′ sē ŏl′ ə jĭst, so′ shē-) ***n-*** person trained in sociology and engaged in it as a profession.

so·ci·ol·o·gy (sō′ sē ŏl′ ə jē, sō′ shē-) ***n-*** the social science that deals with human society, including its development, forms, and relationships. ***—adj-*** **so′ ci·o·log′ i·cal** (-ə lŏj′ ĭ kəl). ***adv-*** **so′ ci·o·log′ i·cal·ly.**

[1]**sock** (sŏk) ***n-*** short stocking reaching above the ankle but below the knee. [from Old English **socc,** from Latin **soccus** meaning "light shoe; comedian's buskin."]

[2]**sock** (sŏk) *Slang* ***vt-*** to hit or strike with the fist; punch. ***n-*** a blow with the fist; punch. [of uncertain origin.]

sock·et (sŏk′ ət) ***n-*** a hollow into which something is fitted, fastened, or secured: *the* socket *of the eye.*

Sockets

So·crat·ic (sə krăt′ ĭk) ***adj-*** of or relating to Socrates or to his method of teaching. ***n-*** follower of Socrates.

sod (sŏd) ***n-*** **1** layer of soil containing grass and its roots; turf. **2** piece of this, usually cut square. ***vt-*** [**sod·ded, sod·ding**] to cover with sod: *to* sod *a path.*

so·da (sō′ də) ***n-*** **1** sodium carbonate. **2** sodium bicarbonate. **3** sodium hydroxide. **4** soda water.

soda biscuit ***n-*** **1** biscuit made with sodium bicarbonate and sour milk or buttermilk. **2** soda cracker.

soda cracker ***n-*** cracker made with sodium bicarbonate and cream of tartar.

soda fountain ***n-*** **1** counter, often in a drug store, at which soda water, soft drinks, ice cream, sandwiches, etc., are prepared and sold. **2** apparatus with faucets for dispensing soda water.

so·dal·i·ty (sō dăl′ ə tē) ***n-*** [*pl.* **so·dal·i·ties**] a society; especially, a lay group with religious or charitable aims.

soda water ***n-*** water that contains dissolved carbon dioxide under pressure. It bubbles and fizzes when pressure is released, and when flavored and sweetened, it may be called **soda pop.**

sod·den (sŏd′ ən) ***adj-*** **1** very damp and heavy with moisture; soggy: *My shoes are still* sodden *from crossing the stream.* **2** stupid from fatigue or drunkenness. ***—adv-*** **sod′ den·ly.** ***n-*** **sod′ den·ness.**

so·di·um (sō′ dē əm) ***n-*** soft, silver-white metal element that reacts violently with water, producing sodium hydroxide and hydrogen. Symbol Na, At. No. 11, At. Wt. 22.9898.

sodium benzoate ***n-*** poisonous, white, crystalline salt of benzoic acid, widely used as a preservative.

sodium bicarbonate ***n-*** white, slightly alkaline powder ($NaHCO_3$), used in baking powder and fire extinguishers, and as an antacid; baking soda; bicarbonate of soda.

sodium carbonate ***n-*** sodium salt (Na_2CO_3) of carbonic acid.

sodium chloride ***n-*** common salt (NaCl), a white chrystalline compound, found in salt water, mineral springs, subterranean beds, etc., and used especially to season and preserve food.

sodium fluoride ***n-*** white, solid compound (NaF), the sodium salt of hydrofluoric acid, used for etching glass and in rat and roach poisons.

sodium hydroxide ***n-*** white, crystalline compound (NaOH), that is a strong and caustic base. It is used in making soap, paper, and other products in the chemical industry; caustic soda; lye.

sodium nitrate ***n-*** white, solid compound ($NaNO_3$) used in the manufacture of other nitrates, nitric acid, and fertilizers; Chile saltpeter.

sodium silicate ***n-*** water glass.

sodium thi·o·sul·fate (thī′ ə sŭl fāt′) ***n-*** white, crystalline compound ($Na_2S_2O_3$), used especially in photography for fixing negatives, and as a bleach; hypo.

Sod·om and Go·mor·rah (sŏd′ əm ən gə mŏr′ ə) ***n-*** two cities lying near the Dead Sea, which, according to the Bible, were destroyed for people's wickedness.

so·fa (sō′ fə) ***n-*** long, upholstered seat or couch.

soft (sȯft) ***adj-*** [**soft·er, soft·est**] **1** not hard; easily yielding to touch or pressure; readily shaped or worked: *a* soft *pillow*; soft *clay.* **2** quiet and gentle; low and mild: *a* soft *voice.* **3** smooth; pleasing to the touch: *a* soft *skin.* **4** weak; lacking strength; flabby: *His muscles were* soft *from lack of exercise.* **5** pronounced with the sound of (g) in "gentle" or (c) in "cease," not hard like the (g) in "got" or (c) in "cow." ***—adv-*** **soft′ ly.** ***n-*** **soft′ ness.**

soft·ball (sȯft′ bȯl′) ***n-*** **1** game similar to baseball but played on a smaller field with a softer ball, and a lighter bat. **2** ball used in this game.

soft coal ***n-*** coal that burns with more smoke and leaves more ash than hard coal; bituminous coal.

soft drink ***n-*** carbonated beverage with no alcohol.

soft·en (sȯf′ ən, sŏf′-) ***vt-*** to make less hard, loud, glaring, severe, etc.: *Awnings* soften *the light. The judge* softened *the punishment.* ***vi-***: *The butter* softened *in the heat. He* softened *toward his enemies.* ***—n-*** **soft′ en·er.**

soft-heart·ed (sȯft′ här′ təd) ***adj-*** sympathetic; tender; kind. ***—adv-*** **soft′ -heart′ ed·ly.** ***n-*** **soft′ -heart′ ed·ness.**

soft palate ***n-*** the soft back part of the roof of the mouth. For picture, see *palate.*

soft pedal ***n-*** pedal of a piano that is pressed with the foot to reduce the volume of the sound.

soft-pedal (sȯft′ pĕd′ əl) ***vt-*** **1** to mute (a musical passage, certain notes, etc.) by using the soft pedal. **2** *Informal* to make less emphatic or conspicuous; play down; tone down: *to* soft-pedal *one's achievements.*

soft sell *Informal* ***n-*** salesmanship using subtle suggestion rather than intense pressure to influence buying.

soft soap ***n-*** **1** soap in a fluid or partly fluid state. **2** *Informal* flattery.

soft-soap (sȯft′ sōp′) *Informal* ***vt-*** to flatter or cajole: *Don't* soft-soap *me into letting you go!* ***—n-*** **soft′-soap′er.**

soft-spo·ken (sȯft′ spō′ kən) ***adj-*** speaking in a gentle or soft tone of voice; mild: *a* soft-spoken *young man.*

soft water ***n-*** water in which soap lathers readily. It is free of certain salts of magnesium and calcium.

soft·wood (sȯft′ wŏŏd′) ***n-*** any cone-bearing tree; also, the wood of such a tree, whether hard or soft.

soft·y (sȯf′ tē) *Slang* ***n-*** [*pl.* **soft·ies**] very sentimental or sympathetic person.

sog·gy (sŏg′ ē) ***adj-*** [**sog·gi·er, sog·gi·est**] wet and heavy; soaked; sodden. ***—adv-*** **sog′ gi·ly.** ***n-*** **sog′ gi·ness.**

[1]soil (soil) ***n-*** **1** deposit of fine particles on the earth's top layer, composed of rock ground up by erosion, usually together with organic substances from the decay of plant and animal materials. **2** land; country: *his native* soil. *as* ***modifier***: *Prevent* soil *erosion!* [from Old French **soile,** from Late Latin **solea,** from Latin **solum** meaning "ground," and **solium,** "a seat."]

[2]soil (soil) ***vt-*** **1** to make dirty: *He* soiled *his hands working in the garden.* **2** to defame; sully; tarnish: *A false rumor may* soil *a reputation.* [from Old French **soillier,** from Latin **suillus,** "piglike," from **sūs,** "pig."]

soi·ree or **soi·rée** (swä rā') ***n-*** an evening party.

so·journ (sō' jûrn', sō jûrn') ***vi-*** to stay for a time; dwell: *This winter he plans to* sojourn *in Florida.* ***n-*** short stay or outing: *a* sojourn *in the country.* **—*n-* so'journ'er.**

sol (sōl) *Music* ***n-*** the fifth note of the scale; so.

Sol (sŏl) ***n-*** **1** the sun. **2** the sun god of the ancient Romans.

sol·ace (sŏl' əs) ***n-*** comfort; consolation, especially in sorrow or disappointment: *He found* solace *for his loss in helping others.* ***vt-*** **[sol·aced, sol·ac·ing]**: *He* solaced *himself with reading the Bible.*

so·lar (sō' lər) ***adj-*** of or having to do with the sun: *a* solar *eclipse*; solar *time*; solar *energy.*

solar battery ***n-*** device for producing an electric current directly from sunlight.

solar collector ***n-*** device for collecting heat from the rays of the sun.

solar eclipse ***n-*** the complete or partial obscuring of the sun's disk by the moon when it passes directly between the earth and the sun.

solar energy ***n-*** radiant energy from the sun.

solar flare ***n-*** sudden discharge of an unusually bright cloud of high energy particles near a sunspot, which causes radio disturbances on earth.

so·lar·i·um (sō lĕr' ē əm, sō lăr'-, sə-) ***n-*** [*pl.* **so·lar·i·ums** or **so·lar·i·a** (-ē ə)] porch or room especially built with glass walls and large windows to admit sunlight.

solar plexus ***n-*** a mass of nerve tissue at the top of the abdomen just behind the stomach, that helps to regulate functions not controlled voluntarily, such as heartbeat.

solar prominence *Astronomy* ***n-*** one of the giant outbursts of gas observed to shoot out from one point to another on the sun's surface.

solar system ***n-*** **1** the sun together with the planets, their satellites, asteroids, and all other bodies under the gravitational influence of the sun and moving as a unit through space. **2** any similar group of heavenly bodies revolving around a sun.

solar wind ***n-*** stream of highly charged particles emitted from the sun.

solar year ***n-*** length of time it takes the earth to revolve once around the sun, equal to 12 months, or 365 days, 5 hours, 48 minutes, and 46 seconds.

sold (sōld) *p.t. & p.p.* of **sell.**

sol·der (sŏd' ər) ***n-*** any of various alloys that melt at a fairly low temperature and are used to join metal surfaces. ***vt-*** to attach or join with this metal: *to* solder *wires.* ***vi-***: *Copper* solders *well.* **—*n-* sol'der·er.**

sol·dier (sōl' jər) ***n-*** **1** person serving in an army, especially a private. **2** man who is experienced and skilled in warfare: *Washington was a great* soldier. ***vi-*** to serve in an army: *He* soldiered *in Burma and India.*

sol·dier·ly (sōl' jər lē) ***adj-*** like or relating to a soldier or soldiers; military: *his* soldierly *bearing.*

soldier of fortune ***n-*** **1** man who will serve in any army for money or adventure. **2** adventurer.

sol·dier·y (sōl' jə rē) ***n-*** **1** soldiers collectively; military troops. **2** military knowledge or training.

[1]sole (sōl) ***adj-*** **1** one and only; single: *the* sole *occupant of an apartment*; *the* sole *reason for going.* **2** belonging or relating to one group or individual: *He had* sole *rights to the book.* [from Old French **sol,** from Latin **sōlus** meaning "alone."] ***Hom-*** soul.

[2]sole (sōl) ***n-*** **1** underside of the foot, especially the part forward of the heel. **2** bottom of a shoe, boot, or slipper. ***vt-*** **[soled, sol·ing]** to put a new bottom on (a shoe, boot, or slipper). [from Old English **sole,** from Latin **solea,** "sole of a shoe."] ***Hom-*** soul.

[3]sole (sōl) ***n-*** [*pl.* **sole; soles** (kinds of sole)] **1** any of various flatfishes of American and European waters. **2** its flesh, prized as food. [from Old French, from Latin **solea,** "sole of a shoe."] ***Hom-*** soul.

European sole, 1–1 1/2 ft. long

sol·e·cism (sŏl' ə sĭz' əm, sō' lə-) ***n-*** **1** mistake in the use of words or in the structure of a sentence; error in grammar. **2** rude or absurd breach of manners.

sole·ly (sōl' lē, sō' lē) ***adv-*** **1** by oneself; singly: *He is* solely *responsible.* **2** exclusively; only; simply: *We ski* solely *for pleasure.*

sol·emn (sŏl' əm) ***adj-*** **1** carried out with sacred rites or ceremonies: *the* solemn *festivals of the church.* **2** causing awe: *a* solemn *hall.* **3** very earnest and serious: *a* solemn *pledge.* **4** grave; sober: *The judge has a* solemn *face.* **—*adv-* sol'emn·ly. *n-* sol'emn·ness.**

so·lem·ni·ty (sə lĕm' nə tē) ***n-*** [*pl.* **so·lem·ni·ties**] **1** great seriousness; gravity. **2** formal ceremony.

sol·em·nize (sŏl' əm nīz') ***vt-*** **[sol·em·nized, sol·em·niz·ing]** **1** to perform (a rite, especially a marriage) in a ceremonious or a legally formal manner. **2** to celebrate formally: *to* solemnize *a festival.* **—*n-* sol'em·ni·za'tion.**

so·le·noid (sō' lə noid') ***n-*** cylindrical wire coil that produces a magnetic field when a current is passed through it, used in electromagnets.

so·li·cit (sə lĭs' ĭt) ***vt-*** **1** to ask (someone) earnestly or repeatedly for something; entreat or beg (someone) for something: *She* solicited *her friends for campaign contributions.* **2** to seek (orders, support, votes, etc.). **—*n-* so·lic'i·ta'tion.**

so·lic·i·tor (sə lĭs' ĭ tər) ***n-*** **1** one who seeks trade, votes, etc. **2** *chiefly Brit.* attorney or lawyer. **3** civil law officer of some cities, government departments, etc.

so·lic·it·ous (sə lĭs' ĭ təs) ***adj-*** **1** concerned, especially in a sympathetic way: *He was* solicitous *about my health.* **2** eager. **—*adv-* so·lic'i·tous·ly. *n-* so·lic'i·tous·ness.**

so·lic·i·tude (sə lĭs' ə tōōd', -tyōōd') ***n-*** concern; care; sympathetic apprehension: *his* solicitude *for my health.*

sol·id (sŏl' ĭd) ***n-*** **1** any substance in the solid state under the general conditions of temperature and pressure existing on earth. —**2** *Mathematics* any geometric figure having length, width, and height. ***adj-*** **[sol·id·er, sol·id·est]** **1** able to support weight or resist pressure; hard; firm: *the* solid *ground*; *a* solid *muscle.* **2** without space inside; not hollow: *a* solid *bar of iron.* **3** unmixed throughout; pure: *of* solid *silver or gold*; *a* solid *color.* **4** firmly built; strong: *a* solid *building.* **5** of sound character; reliable; trustworthy: *a* solid *man.* **6** with a strong financial position: *a* solid *business.* **7** whole; uninterrupted; continuous: *We waited a* solid *week.* **8** showing firm agreement among a great majority: *a* solid *vote for the mayor.* **9** *Mathematics* having to do with three dimensions (length, width, and height). ***—adv-*** **sol′ id·ly.** ***n-*** **sol′ id·ness.**

sol·i·dar·i·ty (sŏl′ ə dăr′ ə tē, -dĕr′ ə tē) ***n-*** agreement and unity in opinion, interests, and efforts.

solid fuel ***n-*** **1** any solid used for fuel, such as wood and coal. **2** solid propellant.

solid geometry ***n-*** geometry of three-dimensional figures.

so·lid·i·fi·ca·tion (sə lĭd′ ə fə kā′ shən) ***n-*** a solidifying or being solidified, as the freezing of water.

so·lid·i·fy (sə lĭd′ ə fī′) ***vt-*** **[so·lid·i·fied, so·lid·i·fy·ing]** **1** to make solid or more solid; especially, to change from a fluid to a solid state: *Cold* solidifies *water into ice.* **2** to unite firmly: *to* solidify *a friendship.* ***vi-***: *The paste has* solidified. *Their friendship* solidifies *yearly.*

so·lid·i·ty (sə lĭd′ ə tē) ***n-*** [*pl.* **so·lid·i·ties**] **1** solid state or condition; hardness. **2** firmness and stability: *the* solidity *of their friendship.* **3** moral, intellectual, or financial soundness.

solid propellant ***n-*** propellant developed for use in rockets, containing a fuel combined with an oxidizer in a solid form.

solid state ***n-*** one of the three physical states of matter, in which a substance has a definite volume and a definite shape. Solids cannot be easily compressed. See also *gaseous state* and *liquid state.* *as* ***modifier*** **(solid-state):** *a* solid-state *physicist.*

so·lil·o·quize (sə lĭl′ ə kwīz′) ***vi-*** **[so·lil·o·quized, so·lil·o·quiz·ing]** to talk to oneself; converse with oneself; also, to deliver a soliloquy. ***—n-*** **so·lil′ o·quiz′ er.**

so·lil·o·quy (sə lĭl′ ə kwē) ***n-*** [*pl.* **so·lil·o·quies**] a talking to oneself; especially, a monologue in a play.

sol·i·taire (sŏl′ ə târ′) ***n-*** **1** any of various card games played by one person. **2** gem, especially a diamond, that is mounted alone.

sol·i·tar·y (sŏl′ ə tĕr′ ē) ***adj-*** **1** alone; without companions: *a* solitary *monk*; *a* solitary *traveler.* **2** seldom visited; secluded: *a* solitary *village.* **3** spent or done alone: *a* solitary *walk.* **4** single: *Not a* solitary *boat was in the bay.* ***n-*** [*pl.* **sol·i·tar·ies**] a hermit. ***—adv-*** **sol′ i·tar·i·ly.** ***n-*** **sol′ i·tar′ i·ness.**

solitary confinement ***n-*** punishment in which a prisoner is kept in complete isolation.

sol·i·tude (sŏl′ ə to͞od′, -tyo͞od′) ***n-*** **1** a being or living alone; seclusion. **2** remoteness; loneliness: *the* solitude *of the mountains.* **3** lonely and remote place.

so·lo (sō′ lō) ***n-*** [*pl.* **so·los** or **so·li** (-lē)] **1** piece of music to be played or sung by a single performer: *a violin* solo. **2** any performance by one person: *a dance* solo. ***adj-*** **1** done or performed by one person: *a* solo *dance*; *a* solo *flight.* **2** performing alone: *a* solo *dancer*; *a* solo *violinist.* ***adv-***: *He flew* solo *today.* ***vi-*** **1** to perform by oneself. **2** to fly an airplane alone immediately after training.

so·lo·ist (sō′ lō ĭst) ***n-*** person who performs a solo.

Sol·o·mon (sŏl′ ə mən) ***n-*** in the Bible, the king of Israel and son of David. Noted for his wisdom, he built the first temple in Jerusalem, 10th century B.C.

Sol·o·mon's-seal (sŏl′ ə mənz sēl′) ***n-*** any of various plants of the lily family, having marks on the stem that resemble a six-pointed star, and blue-black berries.

so·lon (sō′ lŏn′, -lən) ***n-*** wise man; especially, any wise lawmaker.

so long (sō′ lông′) *Informal* ***interj-*** good-by; farewell.

sol·stice (sŏl′ stəs, sōl′-) ***n-*** **1** one of the two times of the year when the sun is directly over some point on the tropic of Cancer or tropic of Capricorn. The **summer solstice,** when the sun is directly above the tropic of Cancer, occurs about June 22, and the **winter solstice,** when the sun is directly above the tropic of Capricorn, about December 22. **2** *Astronomy* one of the two points on the ecliptic where the sun is farthest from the celestial equator.

sol·sti·tial (sōl stĭsh′ əl, sŏl-) ***adj-*** of or having to do with a solstice.

sol·u·bil·i·ty (sŏl′ yə bĭl′ ə tē) ***n-*** the ability of one substance to dissolve in another.

sol·u·ble (sŏl′ yə bəl) ***adj-*** **1** such as can be dissolved: *Sugar is* soluble *in water.* **2** solvable. ***—adv-*** **sol′ u·bly.**
►Something SOLUBLE can be dissolved in something specific. *Sugar is* soluble *in water.* Something SOLVABLE can be solved. *This problem is hard, but* solvable.

sol·ute (sŏl′ yo͞ot′) ***n-*** substance dissolved in something else: *In a salt solution, salt is the* solute.

so·lu·tion (sə lo͞o′ shən) ***n-*** **1** a solving: *The* solution *of the problem took him ten minutes.* **2** correct answer; explanation: *He found the* solution *of the problem in ten minutes.* **3** a mixing of two or more substances so that single molecules or ions of one are evenly dispersed through the others; a dissolving. **4** such a mixture: *a sugar-and-water* solution. **5** *Mathematics* (1) a number or value that satisfies an equation or, in general, makes a sentence true when its numeral replaces the variable in the sentence. (2) a method or procedure for determining such a number.

solution set *Mathematics* ***n-*** the set of all solutions for a number sentence. The elements of the solution set of $p + 3 < 7$ are 0, 1, 2, and 3, when p is a whole number.

solv·a·ble (sŏl′ və bəl) ***adj-*** of a nature that allows being solved or explained. ***—n-*** **solv′ a·bil′ i·ty.**
►For usage note see SOLUBLE.

solve (sŏlv) ***vt-*** **[solved, sol·ving]** **1** to find the answer to (a problem or puzzle). **2** to find the way out of (a difficulty). **3** *Mathematics* (1) to find the solution set of (an equation). (2) to find the unknown parts of (a triangle) from known parts such as angles and sides. ***—n-*** **solv′ er.**

sol·ven·cy (sŏl′ vən sē) ***n-*** ability to pay one's debts.

sol·vent (sŏl′ vənt) ***n-*** the dissolving substance of a solution, usually considered to be the liquid if the solution consists of a solid and a liquid or a gas and a liquid.

so·ma (sō′ mə) ***n-*** [*pl.* **so·ma·ta** (-mə tə)] all parts of an organism except for its germ or reproductive cells.

so·mat·ic (sə măt′ ĭk) ***adj-*** **1** of or having to do with the body; not spiritual; corporeal. **2** in anatomy, of or having to do with the body, especially the partitions of the body as distinguished from the organs.

somatic cell ***n-*** cell of any part of the body, except the reproductive cells.

som·ber or **som·bre** (sŏm′ bər) ***adj-*** **1** dark; dull: *a* somber *sky.* **2** gloomy; dismal. ***—adv-*** **som′ ber·ly** or **som′ bre·ly.** ***n-*** **som′ ber·ness** or **som′ bre·ness.**

som·brer·o (sŏm brâr′ ō) ***n-*** [*pl.* **som·brer·os**] hat with a broad brim and high crown, popular in Latin America and southwestern United States. [American word from Spanish, from Latin **sub-** meaning "under," and **umbra,** "shade."]

Sombrero

some (sŭm) ***determiner*** (traditionally called adjective or pronoun) **1** a certain or a particular, but not known or named: *I heard* some *woman scream.* **2** of an indefinite number or quantity; a few; a little: *You must get* some *new clothes. Do you want* some? *There were* some *who came very late.* **3** *Informal* of a considerable amount, number, degree, or quantity: *It took* some *courage to* *break the bad news to John.* ***n-*** indefinite number or quantity: *He spilled* some *of the water.* ***adv-*** approximately; about: *There were* some *20 persons.* ***Hom-*** sum.

1**-some** *suffix* (used to form adjectives) 1 showing a tendency to: *venture*some; *tire*some. 2 rather or somewhat: *blithe*some; *light*some. [from Old English **-sum,** and related to **some** and **same.**]

2**-some** *suffix* (used to form nouns) specific group of: *a four*some. [from **some.**]

3**-some** (sōm) *combining form* body: *chromo*some. [from Greek **sōma** meaning "body."]

some·bod·y (sŭm′ bŏd′ ē, -bŭd′ ē) ***pron-*** some person; someone: *I think* somebody *has borrowed my umbrella.* ***n-*** [*pl.* **some·bod·ies**] an important person: *Having that new car makes her think she is* somebody.

some·day (sŭm′ dā′) ***adv-*** on some future day; also, at some future time: *We will talk* someday *soon.*

some·how (sŭm′ hou′) ***adv-*** 1 in one way or another; in some way: *We'll get home* somehow. 2 for some reason or other: *I* somehow *don't like the candidate.*

some·one (sŭm′ wŭn′) ***pron-*** some person; somebody.

som·er·sault (sŭm′ ər sȯlt′) ***vi-*** to leap, roll, or dive and turn head over heels. ***n-*** such a leap, roll, or dive. Also **som′ er·set′** (-sĕt′).

some·thing (sŭm′ thĭng′) ***pron-*** 1 particular thing not specified: *The baby wants* something *to play with.* 2 thing not definitely known or understood: *There is* something *strange about that house.* ***n-*** a person or thing of importance: *It's* something *to own property.* ***adv-*** somewhat; rather: *You look* something *like him.*

something of somewhat of.

some·time (sŭm′ tīm′) ***adv-*** at a time or date not known or exactly indicated: *The trains stopped running* sometime *last year.* ***adj-*** former: *a* sometime *football star.*

some·times (sŭm′ tīmz′) ***adv-*** now and then; from time to time; once in a while: *We go there* sometimes.

some·way or **some way** (sŭm′ wā′) ***adv-*** in an unspecified manner; somehow: *I'll get there* someway.

some·what (sŭm′ hwăt′, -hwət′) ***adv-*** to some extent; in some degree; rather: *She is* somewhat *lazy.* ***pron-*** *Archaic* something.

somewhat of having some of the characteristics of: *It was* somewhat of *a surprise to see him.*

some·where (sŭm′ hwâr′) ***adv-*** 1 in, at, or to some place not known or named: *I've left my gloves* somewhere. 2 sometime: *I'll be there* somewhere *around nine.*

som·nam·bu·lism (sŏm năm′ byə lĭz′ əm) ***n-*** active behavior, resembling many of the activities of the waking state, carried on by a sleeping person; sleepwalking. —***n-*** **som′ nam′ bu·list.**

som·no·lence (sŏm′ nə ləns) ***n-*** sleepiness; drowsiness.

som·no·lent (sŏm′ nə lənt) ***adj-*** 1 sleepy; drowsy; heavy with sleep. 2 tending to cause sleep; also, marked by quiet, lazy peace: *the* somnolent *drone of the engines.*

son (sŭn) ***n-*** 1 boy or man in relation to his parents. 2 male descendant: *the* sons *of Jacob.* 3 male who is representative of or closely related to a nation, cause, etc.: *a true* son *of France.* 4 **the Son** Jesus Christ.

so·nar (sō′ när′) ***n-*** device that detects and locates objects under water by means of sound waves reflected back from them. *as* ***modifier****: a* sonar *reading.* [shortened from *so*und *na*vigation and *r*anging.]

so·na·ta (sə nä′ tə) *Music* ***n-*** composition in three or four movements, usually for one or two instruments.

song (sȯng) ***n-*** 1 music produced by the human voice. 2 particular set of words sung to a melody; also, the melody itself. 3 series of tuneful sounds uttered vocally, such as the call of a bird: *the* song *of a canary.* 4 poem that can be set to music. 5 a singing: *to break into* song.

for a song cheaply: *He sold it* for a song. **song and dance** *Informal* explanation that offers an alibi or an excuse: *His speech was the same old* song and dance.

song·bird (sȯng′ bûrd′) ***n-*** bird that sings, such as a canary, thrush, or nightingale.

song·book (sȯng′ bo͝ok′) ***n-*** book of songs.

song·less (sȯng′ ləs) ***adj-*** 1 unable to sing: *a* songless *bird.* 2 devoid of song; without singing.

Song of Solomon or **Song of Songs** ***n-*** twenty-second book of the Old Testament. In the CCD Bible, the **Canticle of Canticles.**

song sparrow ***n-*** singing sparrow of eastern United States, having a streaked breast with one large spot.

song·ster (sȯng′ stər) ***n-*** 1 singing bird. 2 man who sings. 3 writer of songs or poetry. —***n-*** *fem.* **song′ stress.**

son·ic (sŏn′ ĭk) ***adj-*** 1 of, having to do with, or caused by sound: *a* sonic *vibration.* 2 at or near the speed of sound: *a* sonic *airplane flight.*

sonic barrier ***n-*** sudden increase in drag on an aircraft as it approaches the speed of sound; sound barrier.

sonic boom ***n-*** noise caused by a convergence of shock waves from an airplane traveling at or above the speed of sound.

son-in-law (sŭn′ ĭn lȯ′) ***n-*** [*pl.* **sons-in-law**] husband of one's daughter.

son·net (sŏn′ ət) ***n-*** fourteen-line poem usually having ten-syllable lines, and consisting of either three quatrains and a couplet **(Shakespearean sonnet)** or an octave and a sestet **(Italian sonnet).**

son·net·eer (sŏn′ ə têr′) ***n-*** person who writes sonnets.

son·ny (sŭn′ ē) *Informal* ***n-*** little boy (used as a form of address). ***Hom-*** sunny.

so·nor·i·ty (sə nôr′ ə tē, sə nŏr′-) ***n-*** [*pl.* **so·nor·i·ties**] 1 depth, fullness, and richness of tone: *the* sonority *of the bass section; the* sonority *of his verse.* 2 word or phrase rendered in such tones: *a speech full of* sonorities.

so·no·rous (sə nôr′ əs, sŏn′ ər əs) ***adj-*** having sonority: *a* sonorous *voice.* —***adv-*** **so·nor′ ous·ly** or **son′ or·ous·ly.**

soon (so͞on) ***adv-*** **[soon·er, soon·est]** 1 in a short time from now; before long: *We shall* soon *be having snow.* 2 shortly; quickly: *They left* soon *after five o'clock.* 3 at a time earlier than expected: *You came so* soon!

as soon as willingly; as readily: *I'd* as soon *leave as not.*

soot (so͝ot, sŭt, so͞ot) ***n-*** black powder, mostly of carbon, that forms when organic material is burned. ***vt-*** to cover or smear with such a powder. ***Hom-*** suit.

sooth (so͞oth) *Archaic* ***n-*** truth. ***adj-*** true; real. —***adv-*** **sooth′ ly.**

soothe (so͞oth) ***vt-*** **[soothed, sooth·ing]** 1 to make quiet and calm; to comfort: *to* soothe *a restless patient.* 2 to make less painful; relieve: *The salve* soothed *Eric's earache.* —***n-*** **sooth′ er.** ***adv-*** **sooth′ ing·ly.**

sooth·say·er (so͞oth′ sā′ ər) ***n-*** person who claims to have the power of foretelling the future; fortuneteller. —***n-*** **sooth′ say′ ing.**

soot·y (so͝ot′ ē, sŭt′ ē, so͞o′ tē) ***adj-*** **[soot·i·er, soot·i·est]** 1 relating to or covered with soot. 2 dusky; black: *a* sooty *sky.* —***adv-*** **soot′ i·ly.** ***n-*** **soot′ i·ness.**

sop (sŏp) ***n-*** 1 anything soaked, dipped, or softened in a liquid, such as bread in broth. 2 something given to pacify: *a* sop *to injured feelings.* ***vt-*** **[sopped, sop·ping]** 1 to dip or soak. 2 to wet; make soaking wet: *The rain* sopped *him.* 3 to soak up.

---

soph·ism (sŏf′ĭz′əm) *n-* bit of unsound reasoning.

soph·ist (sŏf′ĭst) *n-* 1 one who argues with sophisms. 2 learned person. *—adj-* **so·phis′tic** (sə fĭs′tĭk) or **so·phis′ti·cal.** *adv-* **so·phis′ti·cal·ly.**

[1]**so·phis·ti·cate** (sə fĭs′tə kāt′) *vt-* [**so·phis·ti·cat·ed, so·phis·ti·cat·ing**] 1 to deprive of naturalness and simplicity; to make worldly-wise. 2 to complicate and refine (a mechanism, system, device, etc.): *They have* sophisticated *the storage units of computers. vi-* to argue in sophisms. *—n-* **so·phis′ti·ca′tion.**

[2]**so·phis·ti·cate** (sə fĭs′tĭ kət, -kāt) *n-* person who is worldly-wise and cultivated.

so·phis·ti·cat·ed (sə fĭs′tə kā′təd) *adj-* 1 formed by or showing worldly experience, cultivation, education, etc.: *a* sophisticated *taste in food*; *a* sophisticated *audience.* 2 artificial; not natural or simple: sophisticated *chatter.* 3 developed to a highly complex and detailed level: *a* sophisticated *missile guidance system. —adv-* **so·phis′ti·cat′ed·ly.**

soph·ist·ry (sŏf′ə strē) *n-* [*pl.* **soph·ist·ries**] 1 clever but unsound reasoning. 2 sophism.

soph·o·more (sŏf′ə môr′) *n-* student in the second year at an American university or college, or one in the tenth grade of a high school.

soph·o·mor·ic (sŏf′ə môr′ĭk) *adj-* having less knowledge and understanding than one confidently thinks one has; showing immature intellectual conceit.

Soph·o·ni·as (sŭf′ə nī′əs) Zephaniah.

so·po·rif·ic (sŏp′ə rĭf′ĭk) *adj-* 1 causing or tending to induce sleep: *a* soporific *climate.* 2 drowsy. *n-* medicine, drug, plant, etc., that causes sleep.

sop·ping (sŏp′ĭng) *adj-* wet through; drenched.

sop·py (sŏp′ē) *adj-* [**sop·pi·er, sop·pi·est**] very wet.

so·pra·no (sə prăn′ō) *Music n-* [*pl.* **so·pra·nos**] musical range of the highest female or boy's singing voice; also, a singer having this range, or musical part written for it. *adj-* having this or a similar range: *a* soprano *voice.*

sor·cer·er (sôr′sə rər, sôr′-) *n-* person who practices sorcery; magician; wizard. *—n- fem.* **sor·cer·ess.**

sor·cer·y (sôr′sə rē, sôr′-) *n-* [*pl.* **sor·cer·ies**] employment of evil powers; witchcraft; magic.

sor·did (sôr′dĭd, sôr′-) *adj-* 1 dirty and squalid. 2 mean and base; contemptible: *a* sordid *quarrel. —adv-* **sor′did·ly.** *n-* **sor′did·ness.**

sore (sôr) *adj-* [**sor·er, sor·est**] 1 painful and tender; hurting when touched: *a* sore *knee.* 2 filled with sorrow; sad; grieved: *Her heart was* sore *after the loss of her son.* 3 *Informal* resentful; offended. 4 grievous; severe: *The boy is in* sore *need of rest. n-* 1 ulcer or lesion, usually painful, on the skin or mucous membrane. 2 *Archaic* wound. 3 any cause of distress. *Hom-* soar. *—n-* **sore′ness.**

sore·head (sôr′hĕd′) *Slang n-* person who angers easily and harbors resentment.

sore·ly (sôr′lē) *adv-* 1 severely; in a grievous way: *The remark* sorely *hurt him.* 2 very much; to a great extent: *to be* sorely *tempted.*

sor·ghum (sôr′gəm, sôr′-) *n-* 1 any of various grasses with a jointed stalk somewhat like Indian corn, grown for grain, fodder, and syrup. 2 syrup made from its juice.

Sorghum

so·ror·i·ty (sə rôr′ə tē, sə rŏr′-) *n-* [*pl.* **so·ror·i·ties**] 1 society or group of women or girls joined by a common interest, especially such an organization in a school. 2 sisterhood.

[1]**sor·rel** (sôr′əl, sŏr′-) *n-* any of several common edible plants with sour leaves and juice. [from Old French **sorele,** from **sur,** from earlier German **sūr,** "sour." The leaves have a pleasantly acid taste.]

[2]**sor·rel** (sôr′əl, sŏr′-) *n-* 1 reddish-brown color. 2 reddish-brown horse. *adj-*: *a* sorrel *horse*; *a* sorrel *mane.* [from Old French **sorel** of the same meaning.]

sor·row (sŏr′ō, sôr′-) *n-* 1 distress of mind caused by loss, suffering, disappointment, etc.; grief; deep sadness: *the* sorrow *caused by the death of a friend.* 2 cause of grief, sadness, etc.: *Bob's laziness was a* sorrow *to his parents. vi-* to feel or express grief, sadness, etc.: *He* sorrowed *over a lost chance. —n-* **sor′row·er.**

sor·row·ful (sŏr′ō fəl, sôr′-) *adj-* 1 sad; unhappy; melancholy: *a* sorrowful *occasion.* 2 expressing sadness or grief: *a* sorrowful *song.* 3 causing distress or unhappiness: *The train wreck was a* sorrowful *sight. —adv-* **sor′row·ful·ly.** *n-* **sor′row·ful·ness.**

sor·ry (sŏr′ē, sôr′-) *adj-* [**sor·ri·er, sor·ri·est**] 1 feeling regret, repentance, or pity: *I'm* sorry *I can't meet you. I'm* sorry *I told a lie. Agnes was* sorry *for her sick friend.* 2 sad; miserable: *It was a* sorry *day when our team lost.* 3 poor; worthless: *This old wreck is a* sorry *excuse for a piano. —adv-* **sor′ri·ly.** *n-* **sor′ri·ness.**

sort (sôrt, sôrt) *n-* 1 kind; type: *This* sort *of weather is good for the farmer.* 2 thing bearing some, but very slight, resemblance to something: *The cold war is a* sort *of peace.* 3 *Informal* particular kind of person: *He is a good* sort. *vt-* to classify; put into groups: *to* sort *laundry. —n-* **sort′er.**

of sorts of some, but not great, ability. **out of sorts** out of humor; in bad temper: also, not feeling well; slightly ill. **sort of** somewhat: *I'm* sort of *hungry.*
sort out to separate one kind from the others.

sor·tie (sôr′tē, sôr′-) *Military n-* 1 sudden attack of troops from a besieged position upon the besiegers. 2 a single round trip of an airplane on a military mission.

SOS (ĕs′ō′ĕs′) *n-* the international signal of distress, usually sent by radio on the high seas; a call for help.

so-so (sō′sō′) *Informal adj-* neither very good nor very bad; passable; tolerable: *The movie was* so-so.

sot (sŏt) *n-* habitual drunkard.

sot·tish (sŏt′ĭsh) *adj-* 1 like a drunkard; stupid; foolish. 2 given to excessive drinking. *—adv-* **sot′tish·ly.** *n-* **sot′tish·ness.**

sot·to vo·ce (sŏt′ō vō′chā) *Italian* in an undertone; aside; privately: *He spoke to me* sotto voce.

sou·brette (sōō brĕt′) *n-* 1 pert, scheming lady's maid or a coquettish young woman in comedies. 2 actress who plays such parts.

sou·bri·quet (sō′brə kā′) sobriquet.

souf·flé (sōō flā′) *n-* light, delicate dish of eggs, milk, and a principal ingredient, such as cheese, ham, or mushrooms.

sough (sou, sŭf) *n-* hollow murmuring or sighing sound, like that made by the wind blowing gently through trees. *vi-* to make such a sound.

sought (sôt) *p.t. & p.p.* of **seek.**

soul (sōl) *n-* 1 spiritual part of a person, which many believe immortal; vital principle. 2 moral or emotional nature of a human being: *a man with a great* soul. 3 vital part; quality that gives life or energy: *The* soul *of the music was lost through careless playing.* 4 person who leads and inspires: *The leader was the* soul *of the expedition.* 5 person who is an example of some quality: *the* soul *of honesty.* 6 person: *not a* soul *there.* 7 among Black Americans, their feeling of racial pride and cultural solidarity. *as* ***modifier***: soul *music. **Hom-*** sole.

soul·ful (sōl′ fəl) ***adj-*** full of feeling; appealing to the deeper emotions: *her* soulful *eyes*; soulful *music.* ***—adv-*** **soul′ ful·ly.** ***n-*** **soul′ ful·ness.**

soul·less (sōl′ ləs) ***adj-*** **1** without a soul. **2** lacking nobility: *a* soulless *wretch.* **3** spiritless; dull: *a* soulless *verse.* ***—adv-*** **soul′ less·ly.** ***n-*** **soul′ less·ness.**

soul-search·ing (sōl′ sûr′ chĭng) ***n-*** careful examination of one's own motives, convictions, values, etc.

[1]**sound** (sound) ***n-*** **1** waves caused by the mechanical vibration of a suitable gas, liquid, or solid medium. The human ear can perceive sound waves of frequencies as low as 20 cycles per second and up to 20,000 cycles. **2** that which is heard; sensation produced by sound waves in a surrounding medium such as air or water and picked up by the ear: *the* sound *of bells.* **3** meaning attached to what is heard; implication: *I don't like the* sound *of what you say.* **4** distance to which a sound is audible; earshot: *within* sound *of the bell.* **5** noise of the vocal organs: *the "ch"* sound *in "church."* **6** meaningless noise: *the* sound *of unrest.* ***vt-*** **1** to cause to vibrate audibly: *to* sound *a bell.* **2** to utter, play, etc.: *to* sound *a high note.* **3** to examine or test by rapping: *to* sound *the walls of a house.* **4** to order or announce by sound: *to* sound *an alarm.* ***vi-*** to make a noise or sound: *Running feet* sounded *through the halls.* **2** to give a certain impression when heard; seem: *Her voice* sounds *sad.* [alteration of Middle English **soun,** from French **son,** from Latin **sonus** meaning "a sound."] ***—n-*** **sound′ er.**

[2]**sound** (sound) ***adj-*** **[sound·er, sound·est] 1** free from illness, injury, decay, or defect: *a* sound *floor*; sound *lungs.* **2** safe; prudent; dependable: *a* sound *business*; sound *advice.* **3** founded on truth, or valid reasoning. **4** legal; valid: *a* sound *title to property.* **5** thorough: *a* sound *whipping.* **6** deep: *a* sound *sleep.* [from Old English **(ge)sund,** "strong; healthy."] ***—n-*** **sound′ ness.**

[3]**sound** (sound) ***vt-*** **1** to measure the depth of (water) by means of a weight attached to a line; fathom. **2** to try to discover (a person's) opinions or feelings, usually in an indirect way (often followed by "out"): *Mr. Jones* sounded *out the members of the committee.* ***vi-*** **1** to measure the depth of water: *He* sounded *with a plummet.* **2** to dive deeply, as whales do. [from French **sonder,** from Latin **subūndāre,** from **sub-** meaning "under," and **unda** meaning "wave."] ***—n-*** **sound′ er.**

[4]**sound** (sound) ***n-*** long, narrow stretch of water, wider than a strait, connecting two large bodies of water, or lying between an island and the mainland. [from Old English **sund,** "a strait that could be swum."]

sound barrier ***n-*** sonic barrier.

sound·board (sound′ bôrd′) ***n-*** on certain keyboard instruments, a wooden board that causes the volume of sound to be amplified when the strings are struck.

[1]**sound·ing** (soun′ dĭng) ***n-*** **1** a measuring of the depth of water by letting down a weighted line, called a **sounding line,** from the surface, or more recently by the use of sonar. **2** result or measurement thus obtained. **3** a sampling of opinions; inquiry. **4 soundings** place where the water is shallow enough to permit depth measurements to be taken by a hand line. [from [3]**sound.**]

[2]**sound·ing** (soun′ dĭng) ***adj-*** resounding, resonant, or ringing: *the* sounding *brass.* [from [1]**sound.**]

sounding board ***n-*** **1** frame behind or above a pulpit or podium, which causes the volume of the speaker's voice to be amplified. **2** soundboard. **3** any device or means that gives force to or helps spread opinions, speeches, etc.: *The senator uses the press as his* sounding board.

sound·less (sound′ ləs) ***adj-*** silent: *a* soundless *prayer.* ***—adv-*** **sound′ less·ly.**

sound·ly (sound′ lē) ***adv-*** **1** thoroughly: *He was* soundly *beaten.* **2** deeply: *He sleeps* soundly. **3** well and wisely: *That is* soundly *reasoned.* **4** firmly; securely.

sound·proof (sound′ pro͞of′) ***adj-*** not letting sound in or out. ***vt-*** to insulate so that sound cannot pass through.

sound track ***n-*** the continuous strip along one side of a motion picture film that carries the sound recording.

soup (so͞op) ***n-*** **1** liquid food prepared by boiling meat, vegetables, or fish in a fluid. **2** *Slang* thick fog. **3** *Slang* nitroglycerin. ***vt-*** *Slang* to increase the power of; speed up (often followed by "up").

in the soup *Slang* in trouble.

soup·çon (so͞op sōⁿ′) ***n-*** *French* minute amount; a trace: *a* soupçon *of garlic in the stew.*

soup kitchen ***n-*** place where the needy are given free food, especially soup and bread.

soup·y (so͞o′ pē) ***adj-*** **[soup·i·er, soup·i·est] 1** relating to soup. **2** relating to thick fog: *the* soupy *weather.*

sour (sou′ ər) ***adj-*** **[sour·er, sour·est] 1** having an acid taste, like vinegar or green fruit. **2** fermented: *a dish of* sour *cream.* **3** unpleasant; disagreeable: *Despite his* sour *face, he is a nice person.* **4** acid in reaction: *a* sour *soil.* ***vt-*** **1** to cause to become acid: *Hot weather will* sour *milk.* **2** to make peevish or disagreeable: *Many years of hardship have* soured *her temper.* ***vi-*** **1** to turn to acid: *The milk* soured *overnight.* **2** to become peeved or disagreeable: *She has* soured *in the past months.* ***n-*** something acid or distasteful. ***—adv-*** **sour′ ly.** ***n-*** **sour′ ness.**

source (sôrs) ***n-*** **1** beginning of a stream or river. **2** place or thing from which something comes or is obtained: *Brazil is a* source *of coffee. Potatoes are a* source *of starch.* **3** origin of any act or effect; also, originator: *The* source *of the argument was political.* **4** person, book, or article from which information is obtained.

sour·dough (sour′ dō′) ***n-*** **1** fermented dough used as leaven in baking bread in order to avoid the need for fresh yeast. **2** formerly, a prospector or pioneer.

souse (sous) ***n-*** **1** a plunging into liquid, or a steeping in brine. **2** anything soaked or preserved in pickle, such as pigs' feet. **3** pickling fluid; brine. **4** *Slang* drunkard. ***vt-*** **[soused, sous·ing] 1** to steep or soak in brine or vinegar; pickle. **2** to dip or plunge into any liquid; drench: *to* souse *linen in soapsuds.* **3** to pour or dash; splash: *He* soused *water on the fire.* **4** *Slang* to make drunk. ***vi-*** **1** to soak oneself. **2** *Slang* to get drunk.

south (south) ***n-*** **1** the direction toward the South Pole; also, the point of the compass indicating this direction; opposite of *north.* **2** the part of the world, country, or continent in this direction: *the* south *of France.* **3 the South** (1) the part of the United States lying generally south of the Ohio River and Pennsylvania. (2) in the Civil War, the States opposed to the Union (the North); the Confederacy. ***adj-*** **1** in or to the south. **2** of winds, from the south. ***adv-*** toward the south: *He turned* south.

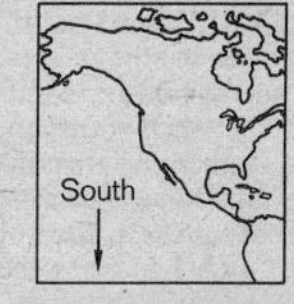

South American ***adj-*** of or relating to South America: *We are drinking* South American *coffee.* ***n-*** person who lives in South America or is of South American descent.

south·bound (south′ bound′) ***adj-*** headed south.

south by east ***n-*** the direction halfway between south-southeast and south.

south by west ***n-*** the direction halfway between south and south-southwest.

south·east (south′ēst′) ***n-*** **1** the direction halfway between south and east; also, the point of the compass indicating this direction. **2** the part of any area lying in this direction as seen from the center of the area. **3 the Southeast** the southeastern part of the United States. ***adj-*** **1** in or to the southeast. **2** of winds, from the southeast. ***adv-*** toward the southeast: *We marched* southeast.

southeast by east ***n-*** the direction halfway between east-southeast and southeast.

southeast by south ***n-*** the direction halfway between southeast and south-southeast.

south·east·er (south′ ēs′ tər, sou ēs′-) ***n-*** storm or gale from the southeast.

south·eas·ter·ly (south′ ēs′ tər lē, sou ēs′-) ***adj-*** **1** generally toward the southeast: *a* southeasterly *route.* **2** of winds, generally from the southeast: *a* southeasterly *breeze.* ***adv-*** generally southeastward.

south·east·ern (south′ ēs′ tərn) ***adj-*** located in or to the southeast: *a* southeastern *state.*

south·east·ward (south′ ēst′ wərd) ***adj-*** toward the southeast: *a* southeastward *route.* ***adv-*** (also **south′ east′ wards**): *We walked* southeastward.

south·er·ly (sŭth′ ər lē) ***adj-*** **1** generally toward the south: *a* southerly *direction.* **2** of winds, generally from the south: *a* southerly *breeze.* ***adv-*** generally southward.

south·ern (sŭth′ ərn) ***adj-*** **1** located in or to the south: *the* southern *part of the state.* **2** characteristic of or from the south. **3 Southern** of or relating to the South.

Southern Cross ***n-*** constellation in the Southern Hemisphere, with four bright stars forming a cross.

south·ern·er (sŭth′ ər nər) ***n-*** **1** person living in or native to a southern region. **2 Southerner** person living in or native to the southern part of the United States.

Southern Hemisphere ***n-*** the part of the earth lying south of the equator.

southern lights ***n-*** aurora australis.

south·ern·most (sŭth′ ərn mōst′) ***adj-*** farthest south.

south·land or **Southland** (south′ lănd′, -lənd) ***n-*** land in the South; the southern part of any region.

south·paw (south′ pô′) *Slang* ***n-*** left-handed person.

South Pole ***n-*** **1** southern end of the earth's axis. **2 south pole** pole of a magnet opposite the north pole.

south-south·east (south′ south′ ēst′, sou′ sou′-) ***n-*** the direction halfway between southeast and south.

south-south·west (south′ south′ wĕst′, sou′ sou′-) ***n-*** the direction halfway between south and southwest.

south·ward (south′ wərd) ***adv-*** (also **south′ wards**) toward the south: *to sail* southward. ***adj-***: *a* southward *cruise.*

south·west (south′ wĕst′) ***n-*** **1** the direction halfway between south and west; also, the point of the compass indicating this direction. **2** the part of any area lying in this direction as seen from the center of the area. **3 the Southwest** the southwestern part of the United States. ***adj-*** **1** in or to the southwest: *a* southwest *current.* **2** of winds, from the southwest. ***adv-*** toward the southwest: *The car turned* southwest.

southwest by south ***n-*** the direction halfway between south-southwest and southwest.

southwest by west ***n-*** the direction halfway between southwest and west-southwest.

south·west·er (south′ wĕs′ tər, sou wĕs′-) or **sou'-west·er** ***n-*** **1** storm or gale from the southwest. **2** waterproof hat of which the brim is widest at the back to keep the neck dry.

Southwester

south·west·er·ly (south′ wĕs′ tər lē, sou wĕs′-) ***adj-*** **1** generally toward the southwest: *a* southwesterly *direction.* **2** of winds, generally from the southwest: *a* southwesterly *breeze.* ***adv-*** generally southwestward.

south·west·ern (south′ wĕs′ tərn) ***adj-*** located in or to the southwest: *the* southwestern *part of the state.*

South·west·ern·er (south′ wĕs′ tər nər) ***n-*** native or inhabitant of the southwestern part of the United States.

south·west·ward (south′ wĕst′ wərd) ***adj-*** toward the southwest: *a* southwestward *flight of birds.* ***adv-*** (also **south′ west′ wards**): *We walked* southwestward.

sou·ve·nir (so͞o′ və nêr′) ***n-*** something kept as a reminder of a person, place, or event; keepsake.

sou'west·er (sou wĕs′ tər) southwester.

sov·er·eign (sŏv′ rən) ***n-*** **1** a ruler or supreme power, such as a king, emperor, or other monarch; also, a governing body or state having supreme authority. **2** British gold coin equal to one pound sterling but no longer in use. ***adj-*** **1** supreme; highest: *A king holds* sovereign *power in a monarchy.* **2** having independent power; free: *a* sovereign *state.* **3** most effective; greatest; best: *a* sovereign *remedy.*

sov·er·eign·ty (sŏv′ rən tē, sŭv′-) ***n-*** [*pl.* **sov·er·eign·ties**] **1** supreme power: *In a monarchy* sovereignty *rests with the king, but in a democracy it rests with the people.* **2** independent political power; power or right of self-government. **3** sovereign state or nation.

so·viet (sō′ vē ĕt′, sŏv′ ē ət) ***n-*** **1** (often **Soviet**) any of various councils or governing bodies of the U.S.S.R. which are elected by the people, and which send delegates to the higher congresses. **2 Supreme Soviet** the highest legislative body of the Soviet Union. **3 Soviets** the people of the U.S.S.R. or its political and military leaders. ***adj-*** of or relating to the U.S.S.R.

so·vi·et·ize (sō′ vē ə tīz′, sŏv′ ē-) ***vt-*** [**so·vi·et·ized, so·vi·et·iz·ing**] to spread communist principles in; also, to bring within the Soviet orbit. **—*n-* so′ vi·et·i·za′ tion.**

[1]**sow** (sou) ***n-*** full-grown female pig. [from Old English **sū** and **sugu** of the same meaning.]

[2]**sow** (sō) ***vt-*** [**sowed, sown** or **sowed, sow·ing**] **1** to spread or scatter seeds for growth; plant: *They* sowed *corn in the spring.* **2** to plant with seeds: *He* sowed *the lawn.* **3** to plant in the mind; spread: *She* sowed *hatred with her bitter words.* ***vi-*** to scatter seed for growing. [from Old English **sāwan.**] ***Homs-*** sew, so. **—*n-* sow′ er.**

sow bug ***n-*** any of various small, terrestrial crustaceans often found in damp places; wood louse.

sox (sŏks) *Informal* socks.

soy (soi) ***n-*** **1** Asian sauce made from soybeans. **2** soybean.

soy·bean (soi′ bēn′) or **soy·a** (soi′ ə) ***n-*** **1** Asiatic plant related to the beans, grown for food and fodder. Its seed is used in the making of many plastics and oil products, flour, etc. **2** the seed or bean of this plant.

spa (spä) ***n-*** **1** a mineral spring. **2** resort or locality with mineral springs.

space (spās) ***n-*** **1** expanse without limits in which the universe exists. **2** space science. **3** definite distance or area: *the* space *between houses*; *the* space *for a desk.* **4** interval of time: *She worked for the* space *of one hour.* **5** in written music, the open places between the lines of the staff. **6** in writing or printing, the open places separating letters or words. *as* ***modifier***: *a* space *hazard.* ***vt-*** [**spaced, spac·ing**] to arrange with open gaps in between: *She* spaced *the letters far apart.*

space capsule ***n-*** the part of a spacecraft that contains the astronaut after the major propelling sections have dropped off.

space·craft (spās′ krăft′) ***n-*** [*pl.* **space·craft**] any device, manned or unmanned, designed for space travel.

space heater *n-* small, often portable heater designed to heat a room or a portion of a room.

space·man (spās′măn′, -mən) *n-* [*pl.* **space·men**] a man trained for travel in a spacecraft or one who has already made such a trip; astronaut.

space medicine *n-* the branch of medicine concerned with the health of spacemen.

space·port (spās′pôrt′) *n-* installation for testing and launching rockets, missiles, and spacecraft.

space probe *n-* spacecraft carrying instruments to gather and radio back information about the upper atmosphere or beyond it, or about another celestial body.

space science *n-* scientific study of the physical universe outside the earth's atmosphere.

space ship *n-* vehicle for carrying man through space beyond the earth's atmosphere.

space shuttle *n-* spacecraft designed as transportation between earth and an orbiting space station.

space station *n-* manned artificial satellite made to orbit the earth and used for observation or as a launching site for travel in outer space.

space suit *n-* suit that completely covers the body and provides for an air supply, temperature and pressure control, etc., for existence in space.

space-time (spās′tīm′) *n-* a set of four dimensions in which a physical object or event can be exactly located. Three of these dimensions are spatial and the fourth is time. Also **space-time continuum.**

spac·ing (spā′sĭng) *n-* 1 an arranging of persons or things with respect to the space between them: *the* spacing *of the furniture.* 2 space between things, especially between letters and words.

spa·cious (spā′shəs) *adj-* 1 roomy; ample; not narrow: *a* spacious *house.* 2 vast; expansive: *a* spacious *tract.* —*adv-* **spa′cious·ly.** *n-* **spa′cious·ness.**

spade (spād) *n-* 1 digging tool consisting of a broad, flat blade of iron with a long handle; shovel. 2 **spades** any one of a suit of playing cards marked with a black figure [♠] resembling such a tool. *vt-* [**spad·ed, spad·ing**] to dig or work (ground) with a shovel: *to* spade *a flower bed.*

Spades

spa·dix (spā′dĭks) *n-* [*pl.* **spa·di·ces** (-də sēz′)] long flower head bearing numerous tiny flowers shaped like spikes and often enclosed in a spathe. For picture, see *jack-in-the-pulpit.*

spa·ghet·ti (spə gĕt′ē) *n-* food made of wheat paste shaped into stringlike pieces thinner than macaroni.

spake (spāk) *Archaic p.t.* of **speak.**

[1]span (spăn) *n-* 1 distance measured from the outstretched thumb to the tip of the little finger, equal to nine inches when used as a measure. 2 period of time: *a* span *of years.* 3 distance between two definite bounds: *the* span *of a river.* 4 distance between the supports of an arch, bridge, etc.; also, the section of a girder, beam, etc., between two supports. *vt-* [**spanned, span·ning**] 1 to measure by the extended thumb and fingers. 2 to extend across: *His memory* spans *many decades.* [from Old English **spann** meaning "a measure," from **spannan,** "to extend; connect; bind," and related to **[2]span.**]

[2]span (spăn) *n-* pair of horses or other draft animals driven together in harness. [American word from Dutch or German **spannen** meaning "to yoke horses or animals to a team," and related to **[1]span.**]

span·gle (spăng′gəl) *n-* 1 tiny disk of shining metal or plastic used for decoration. 2 any small, glittering object. *vt-* [**span·gled, span·gling**] to cover or decorate with or as if with small, brilliant objects.

Span·iard (spăn′yərd) *n-* citizen of Spain; person of Spanish descent.

span·iel (spăn′yəl) *n-* one of several kinds of small to medium-size hunting or pet dogs, all of which have long, silky hair, hanging ears, and short legs.

English springer spaniel, 18 in. high

Span·ish (spăn′ĭsh) *adj-* of or pertaining to Spain, its people, language, or culture. *n-* 1 the Romance language spoken in Spain, Spanish America, and the Philippine Islands. 2 **the Spanish** (takes a plural verb) the people of Spain collectively.

Spanish American *n-* 1 a native or inhabitant of the Spanish-speaking countries of the Americas, especially one of Spanish descent. 2 a resident of the United States whose language and background are Spanish. —*adj-* (**Spanish-American**): *the* Spanish-American *settlers.*

Spanish-American War *n-* war between the United States and Spain, fought in 1898.

Spanish Armada *n-* fleet sent to attack England in 1588, destroyed by storms and the English navy.

Spanish Main *n-* 1 originally, the mainland of Spanish America, especially the northeastern coast. 2 loosely, the Caribbean Sea and the coastline of the West Indies.

Spanish moss *n-* grayish-green plant that grows on certain trees, from which it hangs in streamers.

spank (spăngk) *vt-* to punish by slapping on the bottom; strike; smack. *n-* slap, especially on the buttocks.

spank·er (spăng′kər) *n-* a fore-and-aft sail attached to the mast nearest the stern of a square-rigged vessel or four-masted schooner. *as modifier*: *a* spanker *boom.*

spank·ing (spăngk′ĭng) *n-* as punishment, a number of slaps with the open hand. *adj-* brisk; moving swiftly.

span·ner (spăn′ər) *n-* 1 measuring worm. 2 *Brit.* a wrench for bolts and nuts.

[1]spar (spär) *n-* yard, boom, mast, etc., used to support and stretch out a ship's sails. [from Middle English and Old English **sparre.**]

[2]spar (spär) *vt-* [**sparred, spar·ring**] 1 to engage in boxing, especially for practice or conditioning. 2 to wrangle or quarrel in a restrained way, watching for an advantage. [from Old French **esparer** used in cockfighting and meaning "to strike with spurs," from Italian **sparare,** "to kick; discharge."]

[3]spar (spär) *n-* any of various nonmetallic minerals that have luster and a tendency to cleavage. [from Old English **spær-(stān)** meaning "spar (-stone)."]

spare (spâr) *vt-* [**spared, spar·ing**] 1 to avoid injuring, harming or destroying; show mercy to: *The victors* spared *their prisoners.* 2 to show consideration for; deal gently with: *He* spared *the boy's feelings.* 3 to do without: *Can you* spare *this book?* 4 to withhold or refrain from; omit (used only in the negative): *to* spare *no effort.* 5 to afford to give: *I can* spare *the time.* *adj-* [**spar·er, spar·est**] 1 held in reserve; extra: *a* spare *tire.* 2 thin; lean; having little flesh: *a tall,* spare *man.* *n-* 1 an extra part or thing. 2 in bowling, the knocking over of all the pins in two attempts; also, the score for this. —*adv-* **spare′ly.** *n-* **spare′ness.**

spare·ribs (spâr′ rĭbz′) ***n-*** *pl.* ends of pork ribs, with the meat that joins them.

spar·ing (spâr′ ĭng) ***adj-*** **1** careful; frugal: *a* sparing *housewife.* **2** not generous; stingy: *He was* sparing *with his praise.* ***—adv-*** **spar′ ing·ly.** ***n-*** **spar′ ing·ness.**

[1]**spark** (spärk) ***n-*** **1** tiny, hot, glowing particle thrown off from something burning, produced by striking hard stone and metal, etc. **2** heat and light produced by an electric charge when leaping a gap; especially, the discharge in a spark plug. **3** any bright, small flash; hence, any sudden flash: *the* spark *of a firefly*; *the* spark *of genius.* **4** small trace or bit: *He showed a* spark *of interest.* [from Old English **spearca,** "something sprinkled or shot out," and related to [2]**spark.**]

[2]**spark** (spärk) *Archaic* ***n-*** gay, dashing young man; beau; gallant. [from Old Norse **sparkr** meaning "lively," and related to [1]**spark.**]

spark coil ***n-*** an induction coil having a spark gap; especially, such a coil used to provide a high voltage to the spark plugs of an engine.

spark gap ***n-*** in spark plugs, a break in the electrical circuit across which sparks are made to pass in order to ignite the combustible mixture.

spar·kle (spär′ kəl) ***vi-*** **[spar·kled, spar·kling] 1** to send forth sparks of light; glitter; glisten: *Her eyes* sparkled *with amusement. The diamond* sparkles *in the light.* **2** to be brilliant; witty: *His conversation* sparkles. **3** to bubble, as ginger ale. ***n-***: *the* sparkle *of fireworks*; *the* sparkle *of his wit.* ***—adv-*** **spar′ kling·ly.**

spar·kler (spär′ klər) ***n-*** **1** piece of fireworks consisting of a wire coated with material that sparkles brightly when burned. **2** *Slang* a gem, especially a diamond.

spark plug ***n-*** device fitted into the cylinder head of an internal-combustion engine for the purpose of igniting the mixture of gases in the combustion chamber by means of an electric spark.

sparring partner ***n-*** person with whom a boxer spars while training for a fight.

spar·row (spăr′ ō) ***n-*** any of a large group of brownish-gray birds, often having striped wings. They are found in most parts of the world and especially in cities.

sparrow hawk ***n-*** small North American falcon which feeds on insects, grasshoppers, small birds, etc.

sparse (spärs) ***adj-*** **[spars·er, spars·est]** thinly scattered; meager; not dense or thick: *a* sparse *population*; *a* sparse *growth of trees.* ***—adv-*** **sparse′ ly.** ***n-*** **sparse′ ness** or **spar′ si·ty.**

Spar·tan (spär′ tən) ***n-*** **1** a native or inhabitant of ancient Sparta. **2** person of stern discipline and unflinching courage. ***adj-*** **1** of or relating to Sparta or its people. **2** like that of ancient Sparta: *his* Spartan *courage*; Spartan *self-denial.*

spasm (spăz′ əm) ***n-*** **1** involuntary and convulsive contraction of a muscle or a group of muscles. **2** sudden violent seizure: *a* spasm *of pain*; spasm *of fear.* **3** sudden brief spell of activity or energy: *a* spasm *of work.*

spas·mod·ic (spăz mŏd′ ĭk) ***adj-*** **1** of or like spasms; convulsive: *a* spasmodic *cough.* **2** in fits and starts; occurring irregularly: *He took only* spasmodic *interest in his stamp collection.* ***—adv-*** **spas·mod′ i·cal·ly.**

spas·tic (spăs′ tĭk) ***adj-*** **1** of or relating to a spasm. **2** relating to or suffering from a form of paralysis in which there is prolonged muscular contraction: *a* spastic *child.* ***n-***: *The crippled man is a* spastic. ***—adv-*** **spas′ ti·cal·ly.**

[1]**spat** (spăt) *Informal* ***n-*** **1** slight or petty quarrel. **2** a spatter, as of rain. ***vi-*** **[spat·ted, spat·ting]** to engage in a petty quarrel: *to* spat *over trifles.* [probably from the imitation of a sound.]

[2]**spat** (spăt) *p.t. & p.p.* of **spit.**

[3]**spat** (spăt) ***n-*** (usually **spats**) cloth covering for the ankle and upper part of a shoe. [from a shortened form of earlier **spatter-dash,** "a gaiter; a covering for the leg."]

[4]**spat** (spăt) ***n-*** the eggs or spawn of shellfish, especially oysters; also, young oysters. ***vi-*** **[spat·ted, spat·ting]** of shellfish, to spawn. [of uncertain origin, but probably related to **spatter** and **spit.**]

spate (spāt) ***n-*** a sudden or strong outpouring, as of words, emotion, etc.; overflow: *a* spate *of anger.*

spathe (spāth) ***n-*** a modified leaf that encloses a flower cluster (spadix) and grows from the same stem. For picture, see *jack-in-the-pulpit.*

spa·tial (spā′ shəl) ***adj-*** pertaining to, occupying, or of the nature of space. Also **spa′ cial.** ***—adv-*** **spa′ tial·ly.**

spat·ter (spăt′ ər) ***vt-*** to dash against or strike upon in spots, drops, or clusters: *Grease* spatters *the wall. Rain* spatters *the window. Bullets* spatter *the target.* ***vi-***: *Bullets* spattered *all around him.* ***n-***: *a* spatter *of mud.*

spat·u·la (spăch′ ə lə) ***n-*** flexible, broad-bladed, dull-edged, knifelike implement for use in cooking or for spreading pastes or the like.

Kitchen spatula

spat·u·late (spăch′ ə lət) ***adj-*** shaped like a spatula; broad and flat: *my* spatulate *fingers.*

spav·in (spăv′ən) ***n-*** bony enlargement of the hock of a horse, causing lameness. ***—adj-*** **spav′ ined.**

spawn (spȯn) ***n-*** **1** eggs, or the newly hatched young, of fishes, frogs, oysters, and other aquatic animals. **2** product or offspring: *The book produced a* spawn *of new ideas.* ***vi-*** of aquatic animals, to lay eggs: *Salmon* spawn *in fresh water.* ***vt-*** to give birth to; produce.

spay (spā) ***vt-*** to remove the ovaries of (a living animal).

S.P.C.A. Society for the Prevention of Cruelty to Animals.

S.P.C.C. Society for the Prevention of Cruelty to Children.

speak (spēk) ***vi-*** **[spoke** (spōk), **spok·en, speak·ing] 1** to utter words; talk. **2** to make an address: *to* speak *to an audience.* **3** to convey information, ideas, opinions, etc., orally: *He* spoke *about his favorite subject.* ***vt-*** **1** to utter as a word; pronounce. **2** to express in words: *to* speak *the truth.* **3** to use or be able to use (a language) for vocal communication: *I* speak *Spanish.*

so to speak in a way that is not literally true, but nevertheless meaningful: *He was,* so to speak, *an idiot.*

speak for 1 to speak in behalf of. **2** to ask for.

speak one's mind to say exactly what one thinks.

speak out to speak loudly and clearly.

speak up to give one's opinions without fear.

speak volumes to say a lot; be significant.

speak well for to be evidence in favor of; give a favorable idea of: *It* spoke well for *the boy that he apologized.*

speak well of to say favorable things about.

speak·er (spē′ kər) ***n-*** **1** person who speaks, especially in public. **2 Speaker** officer who presides over an assembly or lawmaking body: *the* Speaker *of the House of Representatives.* **3** loudspeaker.

speak·er·ship (spē′ kər shĭp′) ***n-*** position of presiding officer in a legislative body.

speak·ing (spē′ kĭng) ***n-*** the use of speech, especially in public speaking; oratory. *as* ***modifier***: *a fine* speaking *voice*; speaking *aids.*

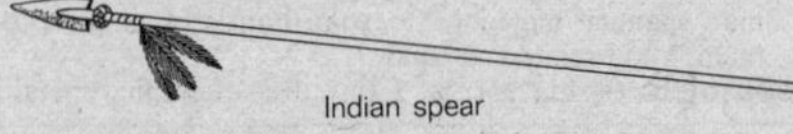

Indian spear

[1]**spear** (spêr) ***n-*** **1** weapon having a long, slender shaft and a sharp-pointed head, for throwing or thrusting.

2 instrument with barbed prongs for catching fish. ***vt-*** to thrust or pierce with or as if with a spear: *to* spear *fish.* [from Old English **spere.**] **—*n-* spear′ er.**

[2]**spear** (spêr) ***n-*** blade or sprout of a plant: *a* spear *of grass.* [altered from [1]**spire** by influence of [1]**spear.**]

spear·fish (spêr′ fĭsh′) ***n-*** [*pl.* **spear·fish; spear·fish·es** (kinds of spearfish)] either of two kinds of ocean fishes related to marlins and having slender, sharp bills.

spear·head (spêr′ hĕd′) ***n-* 1** point of a spear. **2** leading person or group in an endeavor, especially in a military attack. ***vt-*** to take the lead in (an attack, campaign, etc.): *George* spearheaded *the drive for a new library.*

spear·man (spêr′ mən) ***n-*** [*pl.* **spear·men**] person, especially a soldier, armed with a spear.

spear·mint (spêr′ mĭnt′) ***n-*** common garden mint, with leaves shaped like a spearhead.

spe·cial (spĕsh′ əl) ***adj-* 1** distinct from all others; unique as a group: *Surgery requires* special *skills.* **2** designed for a particular purpose: *a* special *course of study.* **3** out of the ordinary; unusual: *a* special *holiday*; *a* special *favor.* **4** highly esteemed: *a* special *friend.* ***n-*** *Informal* something not of the ordinary kind, especially something made, sold, or published. **—*adv-* spe′ cial·ly.**

special delivery ***n-*** the delivery of mail by special messenger in advance of regular delivery for an extra fee; also, a piece of mail delivered this way. ***adv-***: *Send it* special delivery.

spe·cial·ist (spĕsh′ əl ĭst) ***n-*** person who devotes himself to a particular branch of study, business, etc.; especially, a doctor who devotes himself to one field of medicine.

spe·ci·al·i·ty (spĕsh′ ē ăl′ ə tē) ***n-*** [*pl.* **spe·ci·al·i·ties**] **1** way or respect in which something is special. **2** specialty.

spe·cial·ize (spĕsh′ ə līz′) ***vi-*** [**spe·cial·ized, spe·cial·iz·ing**] **1** to concentrate on a particular action or course of study: *The doctor* specializes *in surgery.* **2** *Biology* to become adapted to a special environment or for some special function; evolve in a special way. ***vt-*** to apply, modify, or adapt for a specific use or purpose: *He* specialized *his studies.* **—*n-* spe′ cial·i·za′ tion.**

spe·cial·ty (spĕsh′ əl tē) ***n-*** [*pl.* **spe·cial·ties**] **1** line of study or work to which a person particularly devotes himself: *His* specialty *is physics.* **2** service, article, or line of goods mainly or exclusively dealt in: *The* specialty *of the shop is rare books.* **3** craft or product at which a person or business firm excels. **4** speciality.

spe·cie (spē′ shē, -sē) ***n-*** coin, usually of gold or silver, as distinguished from paper money.

spe·cies (spē′ shēz′, -sēz′) ***n-*** [*pl.* **spe·cies**] **1** group of plants or animals exhibiting the same characteristics and freely interbreeding. **2** kind; variety: *Teasing is often a* species *of cruelty.*

spec·i·fi·a·ble (spĕs′ ə fī′ ə bəl) ***adj-*** such as can be specified: *a* specifiable *disease.*

spe·cif·ic (spə sĭf′ ĭk) ***adj-* 1** definite; precise; clear; particular: *He had* specific *orders to wait.* **2** of or relating to a species; characteristic; typical: *the* specific *features of the wood louse.* **3** having a distinctive, usually curative, influence upon a particular thing: *Quinine is a* specific *remedy for malaria.* ***n-* 1** anything suited to a particular use or purpose; especially, a remedy for a certain disease. **2 specifics** *Informal* particular facts; exact and relevant data: *the* specifics *of a case.* **—*n-* spe·cif′ ic·ness.**

spe·cif·i·cal·ly (spə sĭf′ ĭ kə lē) ***adv-*** in a specific manner; clearly and directly; in particular.

spec·i·fi·ca·tion (spĕs′ ə fə kā′ shən) ***n-* 1** act of specifying; a laying down of details or particulars: *the* specification *of necessary changes.* **2** something that is specified, as in a contract, plan, etc. **3 specifications** detailed statement of requirements for carrying out some work or project: *the* specifications *for a building.*

specific gravity ***n-*** ratio of the density of a substance to the density of a standard (water for solids and liquids, and air for gases).

specific heat ***n-*** ratio of the amount of heat needed to raise the temperature of one gram of a substance one degree centigrade to the amount required to raise one gram of water one degree.

specific impulse ***n-*** a measure of the efficiency of a rocket engine, found by multiplying thrust by burning time and dividing by the weight of the propellant.

spec·i·fy (spĕs′ ə fī′) ***vt-*** [**spec·i·fied, spec·i·fy·ing**] **1** to mention or name definitely; state exactly and clearly: *to* specify *a time and a place for a meeting.* **2** to require; prescribe: *This recipe* specifies *brown sugar.*

spec·i·men (spĕs′ ə mən) ***n-*** sample of something, or one of a group of things, which can be studied as an example of the whole: *a* specimen *of iron ore.*

spe·cious (spē′ shəs) ***adj-*** appearing to be honest, just, or fair, but not really so; plausible but not genuine: *a* specious *claim.* **—*adv-* spe′ cious·ly. *n-* spe′ cious·ness.**

speck (spĕk) ***n-* 1** small spot or stain; blemish. **2** tiny bit; particle: *a* speck *of dust.* ***vt-*** to speckle.

speck·le (spĕk′ əl) ***vt-*** [**speck·led, speck·ling**] to mark with small spots or specks. ***n-*** small spot; speck.

speckled trout ***n-*** brook trout.

[1]**specs** (spĕks) *Informal* ***n-*** *pl.* eyeglasses; spectacles. [from **spectacles.**]

[2]**specs** (spĕks) *Informal* ***n-*** *pl.* specifications: *What are the* specs *for this new building?* [from **specifications.**]

spec·ta·cle (spĕk′ tə kəl) ***n-* 1** grand, unusual, and impressive sight: *Travelers are awed by the* spectacle *of the Alps.* **2** play, opera, or other performance done on a grand scale with a large cast, imposing scenery, etc. **3** something unusual that attracts attention: *The debate was quite a* spectacle. **4 spectacles** eyeglasses.

spec·ta·cled (spĕk′ tə kəld) ***adj-* 1** having or wearing eyeglasses. **2** having markings suggesting eyeglasses.

spec·tac·u·lar (spĕk tăk′ yə lər) ***adj-*** of, relating to, or constituting a spectacle; striking; sensational: *a* spectacular *celebration*; *a* spectacular *rescue.* ***n-*** *Informal* a performance done in a lavish and grand manner, especially on television. **—*adv-* spec·tac′ u·lar·ly.**

spec·ta·tor (spĕk′ tā′ tər, spĕk tā′-) ***n-*** person who looks on, as at a parade, without taking part; observer.

spectator sport ***n-*** game or other athletic event regarded as interesting to watch. Baseball, football, and basketball are popular spectator sports.

spec·ter or **spec·tre** (spĕk′ tər) ***n-*** ghost.

spec·tra (spĕk′ trə) *pl.* of **spectrum.**

spec·tral (spĕk′ trəl) ***adj-* 1** pertaining to or like a ghost; ghostly. **2** of or caused by a spectrum. **—*adv-* spec′ tral·ly.**

spec·tro·graph (spĕk′ trə grăf′) ***n-*** instrument for producing a spectrum. **—*adj-* spec′ tro·graph′ ic. *adv-* spec′ tro·graph′ i·cal·ly.**

spec·tro·he·li·o·graph (spĕk′ trō hē′ lē ə grăf′) ***n-*** instrument that records the spectra of the radiations given off by the sun.

spec·trom·e·ter (spĕk trŏm′ ə tər) ***n-* 1** instrument that measures the index of refraction of a substance. **2** spectroscope that measures the wavelengths in the spectra recorded by it.

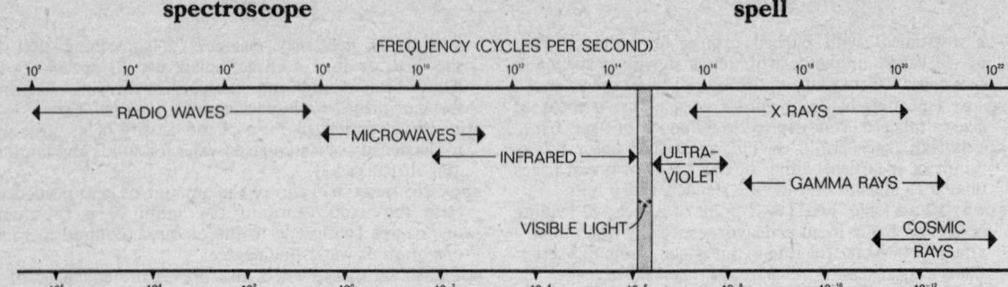

Electromagnetic spectrum

spec·tro·scope (spĕk′ trə skōp′) ***n-*** optical instrument used to produce a spectrum by passing a light beam through a system of prisms or a diffraction grating. ***—adj-*** **spec′ tro·scop′ ic** (-skŏp′ ĭk). ***adv-*** **spec′ tro·scop′ i·cal·ly.**

spec·tros·co·py (spĕk trŏs′ kə pē) ***n-*** the study of spectra by means of a spectroscope.

spec·trum (spĕk′ trəm) ***n-*** [*pl.* **spec·tra** (-trə) or **spec·trums**] a band of radiations, usually of light, arranged in order by wavelengths, such as the band of colors formed when white light is passed through a prism.

spec·u·late (spĕk′ yə lāt′) ***vi-*** [**spec·u·lat·ed, spec·u·lat·ing**] **1** to ask and answer questions about what might be or might happen; guess without having complete knowledge; wonder: *to* speculate *on the existence of life on other planets.* **2** to assume a business risk with the hope of profiting from a change of prices.

spec·u·la·tion (spĕk′ yə lā′ shən) ***n-*** **1** a speculating about causes, results, the future, etc.: *a plan based on* speculation. **2** something based on such speculating: *He explained his* speculations *to me.* **3** the buying or selling of shares of stock, goods, etc., with the hope of profiting from a change in prices.

spec·u·la·tive (spĕk′ yə lā′ tĭv, -lə tĭv) ***adj-*** **1** marked by questioning curiosity; reflective; meditative: *He has a* speculative *turn of mind.* **2** theoretical rather than practical: *a* speculative *conclusion.* **3** of or relating to financial transactions involving considerable risk and the hope of great or quick profits. ***—adv-*** **spec′ u·la′ tive·ly.** ***n-*** **spec′ u·la′ tive·ness.**

spec·u·la·tor (spĕk′ yə lā′ tər) ***n-*** person who speculates.

sped (spĕd) *p.t. & p.p.* of **speed.**

speech (spēch) ***n-*** **1** power of expressing and communicating thoughts by speaking. **2** act or way of speaking: *I could tell by her* speech *that she was angry.* **3** something spoken before an audience as part of a formal occasion; address: *a* speech *at a banquet.* **4** lines spoken in a play, pageant, etc.: *His part has only two* speeches. **5** school or college subject that covers public speaking, phonetics, the correction of faults in speaking, etc.: *He majored in* speech. **6** language; dialect; tongue. *as* ***modifier***: *a* speech *teacher*; *a* speech *lesson.*

speech community ***n-*** all the persons who use the same language or dialect in communicating with each other.

speech correction ***n-*** the correcting of speech defects, especially by experts on the causes and remedies.

speech defect ***n-*** a fault or irregularity, such as stammering, stuttering, or lisping, that makes one's speech hard to understand.

speech·less (spēch′ ləs) ***adj-*** **1** unable to speak because of shock, amazement, anger, etc. **2** silent; not speaking: *He remained* speechless *all evening.* ***—adv-*** **speech′ less·ly.** ***n-*** **speech′ less·ness.**

speed (spēd) ***n-*** **1** swiftness of motion; rapidity. **2** rate of motion; velocity: *a* speed *of five miles an hour*; *a typing* speed *of forty words per minute.* **3** gear setting in a car, truck, etc.: *This car has four forward* speeds. **4** *Archaic* luck; success: *He wished him good* speed. ***vt-*** [**sped** (spĕd) or **speed·ed, speed·ing**] **1** to cause to move faster: *to* speed *a car*; *to* speed *a job to completion.* **2** *Archaic* to help to succeed; aid: *May God* speed *you!* ***vi-*** **1** to move quickly: *The car* sped *towards him.* **2** to drive a vehicle faster than is legal or safe.

speed·boat (spēd′ bōt′) ***n-*** a fast motorboat.

speed·er (spē′ dər) ***n-*** person or thing that speeds; especially, a motorist who drives too fast.

speed limit ***n-*** rate of speed above which, or sometimes below which, it is illegal to drive a car, boat, etc., in a certain place.

speed·om·e·ter (spē dŏm′ ə tər) ***n-*** device for measuring the speed at which a wheeled vehicle goes and the number of miles that it travels. *as* ***modifier***: *a* speedometer *reading*; speedometer *dial*; speedometer *cable.*

speed·ster (spēd′ stər) ***n-*** **1** very fast vehicle. **2** speeder.

speed trap *Informal* ***n-*** place where the speed limit lowers abruptly, so that the traffic police can arrest a great many drivers for speeding.

speed-up (spēd′ ŭp′) ***n-*** an increase in speed, movement, work, etc.

speed·way (spēd′ wā′) ***n-*** a track for automobile races; hence, a highway where drivers travel at high speed.

speed·well (spēd′ wĕl′) ***n-*** herb which bears small blue, white, pink, or purple flowers.

speed·y (spē′ dē) ***adj-*** [**speed·i·er, speed·i·est**] swift; prompt. ***—adv-*** **speed′ i·ly.** ***n-*** **speed′ i·ness.**

spe·le·ol·o·gist (spē′ lē ŏl′ ə jĭst) ***n-*** person who scientifically studies caves and related geological features.

spe·le·ol·o·gy (spē′ lē ŏl′ ə jē) ***n-*** the scientific study or exploration of caves and related geological features.

[1]**spell** (spĕl) ***vi-*** [**spelled** (spĕld or spĕlt), also *chiefly Brit.* **spelt** (spĕlt), **spell·ing**] to form words with letters: *to learn how to* spell. ***vt-*** **1** to give in proper order the letters of (a word). **2** to make up or form (a word): *The letters d-o-g* spell *"dog."* **3** to mean; signify: *The signal* spells *danger.* [from Old French **espeller,** perhaps from a Germanic source, or from Latin **expellere** meaning "drive or pursue to the end."]

spell down to defeat in a spelling contest.

spell out **1** to read or make out with difficulty. **2** *Informal* to explain in complete detail.

[2]**spell** (spĕl) ***n-*** **1** word or words supposed to have magic power. **2** magic influence; fascination: *The music cast a* spell *over us.* [from Old English **spell,** "story; saying."]

[3]spell (spĕl) ***n-*** **1** any period of time: *a hot* spell; *a dry* spell. **2** a turn at work to relieve another: *He took a* spell *at the wheel.* **3** attack of bodily or mental disorder: *a fainting* spell. ***vt-*** [**spelled, spell·ing**] to take the place of someone; alternate with: *Let me* spell *you at the oars.* [From Old English **spelian,** "act for another."]
spell·bind (spĕl′bīnd′) ***vt-*** [**spell·bound, spell·bind·ing**] to hold as by a spell; fascinate. **—*n-* spell′bind′er.**
spell·bound (spĕl′bound′) ***adj-*** held as if by a spell.
spell·er (spĕl′ər) ***n-*** **1** person who spells: *He is a poor* speller. **2** book for teaching students how to spell.
spell·ing (spĕl′ĭng) ***n-*** **1** the act of forming words with letters. **2** the way in which a particular word is spelled. *as modifier: a* spelling *book*; *a* spelling *lesson.*
spelling bee ***n-*** contest in spelling.
spelt (spĕlt) *chiefly Brit. p.t. & p.p.* of **[1]spell.**
spe·lunk·ing (spĭ lŭngk′ĭng) ***n-*** practice or hobby of exploring and mapping caves. ***n-*** **spe′lunk·er** [from Latin **spelunca** meaning "cave."]
spend (spĕnd) ***vt-*** [**spent, spend·ing**] **1** to pay out or expend: *to* spend *money.* **2** to use up; wear out; exhaust; squander: *He* spent *his energy working on wild schemes.* **3** to pass (time): *He* spent *the summer at the beach.* ***vi-*** to expend money or other possessions: *He loves to* spend. **—*n-* spend′er.**
spend·ing (spĕn′dĭng) ***n-*** the paying out of money, especially by a government or public agency.
spend·thrift (spĕnd′thrĭft′) ***n-*** person who spends money carelessly; squanderer. ***adj-*** wasteful.
spent (spĕnt) *p.t. & p.p.* of **spend.** ***adj-*** **1** exhausted; worn-out. **2** without force: *a* spent *arrow.*
sperm (spûrm) ***n-*** **1** male fertilizing fluid; semen. **2** male reproductive cell; spermatozoön.
sper·ma·ce·ti (spûr′mə sĕt′ē) ***n-*** fatty substance found in the head of sperm whales and used in making candles and ointments.
sper·ma·to·phyte (spər măt′ə fīt′) ***n-*** any seed plant, such as a conifer or a flowering plant, all of which were formerly classified together in a single major group (**Spermatophyta**).
sper·ma·to·zo·ön (spər măt′ə zō′ən, spûr′mə tə-) ***n-*** [*pl.* **sper·ma·to·zo·a** (-zō′ə)] in animals, the male reproductive cell, usually having independent movement by means of a long tail.
sperm oil ***n-*** oil from the blubber of the sperm whale.
sperm whale ***n-*** whale that secretes spermaceti in a large cavity in the head.
spew (spyo͞o) ***vi-*** **1** to come out in a flow or gush: *Oil* spewed *all over the ground.* **2** to vomit. ***vt-*** to cast forth; eject; emit: *The volcano* spews *lava.* **—*n-* spew′er.**
sp. gr. specific gravity.
sphag·num (sfăg′nəm) ***n-*** any of a group of pale-gray plants related to the mosses, found in bogs, and used widely for potting plants.
sphere (sfêr) ***n-*** **1** geometric solid with a surface that is everywhere the same distance from a center point; ball; globe. **2** place, field, or extent of a person's knowledge, activity, etc.: *When he talks about music, he is outside his* sphere. **3** *Astronomy* the celestial sphere. **4** celestial body, such as a planet. **5** in ancient astronomy, any of the revolving, spherical, crystalline shells in which the heavenly bodies were supposed to be set.
spher·i·cal (sfêr′ĭ kəl, sfĕr′-) ***adj-*** **1** having the shape of a sphere. **2** of or relating to a sphere or spheres: *She is studying* spherical *geometry.* **—*adv-* spher′i·cal·ly.**
sphe·ric·i·ty (sfêr ĭs′ə tē) ***n-*** [*pl.* **sphe·ric·i·ties**] condition of being spherical or nearly spherical; roundness.
sphe·roid (sfêr′oid′, sfĕr′-) ***n-*** a solid similar to a sphere but not having the same diameter in all directions.
sphinc·ter (sfĭngk′tər) ***n-*** circular muscle that closes off a passage or opening in the body when contracted.
sphinx (sfĭngks) ***n-*** [*pl.* **sphinx·es**] **1** in Egyptian and Greek legend, a monster with a human head and a lion's body. **2** statue of such a monster. **3 the Sphinx** such a statue at Giza, Egypt. **4** secretive, mysterious person.

The sphinx at Giza

sphyg·mo·ma·nom·e·ter (sfĭg′mō′mə nŏm′ə tər) ***n-*** instrument for measuring the blood pressure.
spice (spīs) ***n-*** **1** aromatic vegetable substance such as ginger, cinnamon, nutmeg, pepper, used to flavor food. **2** that which gives added interest or zest: *His wit added* spice *to the conversation.* **3** pungent or fragrant odor. *as modifier: a* spice *merchant*; *the* spice *trade*; spice *shelf.* ***vt-*** [**spiced, spic·ing**] to season or flavor.
spice·bush (spīs′bo͝osh′) ***n-*** aromatic shrub related to the laurel and bearing small, clustered yellow flowers.
spick-and-span (spĭk′ən spăn′) ***adj-*** neat and clean.
spic·ule (spĭk′yo͞ol′) ***n-*** **1** small, pointed, hard body, needlelike or branched, such as those in the skeletons of many sponges. **2** in astronomy, one of the various small jets of hot gas in the chromosphere of the sun, which leap outward and last for only a brief period of time.
spic·y (spī′sē) ***adj-*** [**spic·i·er, spic·i·est**] **1** containing, flavored with, or fragrant with spice. **2** like spice: *a* spicy *taste.* **3** spirited; witty: *a* spicy *conversation.* **4** somewhat scandalous. **—*adv-* spic′i·ly.** ***n-*** **spic′i·ness.**
spi·der (spī′dər) ***n-*** any of many kinds of small, eight-legged animals, most of which can spin silken threads for egg-cases and webs, and many of which secrete venom for paralyzing or killing their prey. **—*adj-* spi′der·y.** ***adj-*** **spi′der·like′.**
spi·der·web (spī′dər wĕb′) ***n-*** silken web spun by a spider to catch insects.

Garden spider, 1/2—3/4 in. across

spied (spīd) *p.t. & p.p.* of **spy.**
spiel (spēl) *Slang* ***n-*** noisy talk; speech; harangue.
spig·ot (spĭg′ət) ***n-*** **1** small plug or peg used to stop the vent in a barrel, cask, etc. **2** faucet.
[1]spike (spīk) ***n-*** **1** long, heavy nail. **2** pointed piece of metal, such as the sharp point fixed to the soles of some sports shoes, or at the top of an iron fence. **3** any slender, pointed object, such as the single antler of a young deer. ***vt-*** [**spiked, spik·ing**] **1** to fasten or equip with large nails or sharp points. **2** to mark, pierce, cut, etc., with a sharp point. **3** to thwart, block, or frustrate: *to* spike *a piece of malicious gossip.* [from Old Norse **spīk** or **spikr,** "nail," and related to **[1]spoke.**] **—*adj-* spike′like′.**

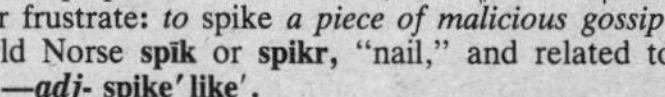
Spike of wheat
Railroad spike

spike a gun to put an old-fashioned cannon out of action by driving a heavy nail solidly into its touchhole.

fāte, făt, dâre, bärn; bē, bĕt, mêre; bīte, bĭt; nōte, hŏt, môre, dȯg; fŭn, fûr; to͞o, bo͝ok; oil; out; tar; thin; then; hw for wh as in *wh*at; zh for s as in u*s*ual; ə for a, e, i, o, u, as in *a*go, lin*e*n, per*i*l, at*o*m, min*u*s

²**spike** (spīk) *n-* 1 ear or head of grain. 2 slender, pointed flower cluster, in which the flowers grow along the sides of the stalk, as on the hyacinth. [from Latin **spica** meaning "ear of grain."]

spike·let (spīk′lət) *n-* a small spike, as in a flower cluster.

spike·nard (spīk′närd′) *n-* 1 fragrant ointment used in ancient times; also, the East Indian aromatic plant from which it may have been derived. 2 North American plant with whitish flowers and an aromatic root.

spik·y (spī′kē) *adj-* [**spik·i·er, spik·i·est**] 1 having spikes; sharp and pointed: *a* spiky *thorn.* 2 resembling a spike; spikelike: *a* spiky *projection.*

spile (spīl) *n-* 1 large timber driven into the ground as part of a foundation; pile. 2 wooden plug used to stop the vent of a cask. 3 spout driven into a tree to drain off the sap. *vt-* [**spiled, spil·ing**] to drive a spile into.

¹**spill** (spĭl) *vt-* [**spilled** (spĭld, spĭlt) *also* **spilt** (spĭlt), **spill·ing**] 1 to let, or cause to, run over or pour out: *Don't* spill *the water.* 2 to cause to be scattered, wasted, or lost. *vi-*: *The milk* spilled *all over the table. n-* 1 an act or instance of overflowing; overflow: *a* spill *of population into the suburbs.* 2 *Informal* a fall, especially from a horse or motorcycle. [from Middle English **spillen,** from Old English **spillan,** "destroy."]

²**spill** (spĭl) *n-* 1 thin strip of wood or small roll of paper for lighting a fire. 2 slender, rigid object, such as a splinter, wooden pin, metal rod, etc. [altered from Middle English **speld** meaning "a splinter."]

spill·way (spĭl′wā′) *n-* channel for overflow water to escape from a reservoir, usually over or around a dam.

spin (spĭn) *vt-* [**spun** (spŭn), **spin·ning**] 1 to draw out and twist fibers of (silk, cotton, flax, etc.) into thread. 2 to produce (threads) as do silkworms, spiders, etc. 3 to cause to whirl rapidly: *to* spin *a top. vi-* 1 to engage in twisting fibers into threads, or in making thread as a spider does. 2 to whirl; twirl; turn around quickly and rapidly: *The man* spun *around.* 3 to seem to be whirling, as from dizziness: *My head* spins. 4 *Informal* of a vehicle, to move swiftly: *to* spin *along on a bicycle. n-* 1 a rapid whirling: *the* spin *of a wheel.* 2 *Informal* a drive or ride, especially for pleasure. 3 a maneuver in which an airplane descends nose first and turns on its vertical axis.
spin out to prolong (a task, story, etc.). *—n-* **spin′ner.**

spin·ach (spĭn′əch) *n-* common garden vegetable, the leaves of which are cooked and eaten.

spi·nal (spī′nəl) *adj-* 1 of or relating to the spine. 2 introduced into the spine: *a* spinal *anesthetic.*

spinal column *n-* series of bones, the vertebrae, that enclose and protect the spinal cord and provide for support in the back of vertebrate animals.

spinal cord *n-* long cord of nerve tissue that begins in the brain and passes down through the spinal column.

spinal nerve *n-* any one of the various paired nerves that come off the spinal cord and supply the muscles of the trunk and limbs.

spin·dle (spĭn′dəl) *n-* 1 slender rod, often cigar-shaped, that draws out and twists the thread in hand spinning. 2 any slender rod, such as a spike for holding papers or a slender axle. 3 *Biology* any of a group of fibers found in cells during the stage of mitosis or meiosis preceding cell division. The chromosomes appear to be attached to and move along these fibers.

spin·dle-leg·ged (spĭn′dəl lĕg′əd) *adj-* having long, slender legs: *a* spindle-legged *table.*

spin·dle·shanks (spĭn′dəl shăngks′) *n-* 1 (takes plural verb) long, thin legs. 2 (takes singular verb) tall person with such legs. *—adj-* **spin′dle-shanked′.**

spin·dling (spĭnd′lĭng) *adj-* tall and slim; especially, too thin in proportion to height: *a* spindling *plant.*

spin·dly (spĭnd′lē) *adj-* [**spind·li·er, spind·li·est**] spindling.

spin·drift (spĭn′drĭft′) *n-* foam or spray blown up from a rough sea. Also **spoondrift.**

spine (spīn) *n* 1 the backbone, or spinal column. 2 anything that resembles or functions as a backbone, such as the back of a book. 3 stiff, thorn-shaped out-growth on a plant or animal. *—adj-* **spined.**

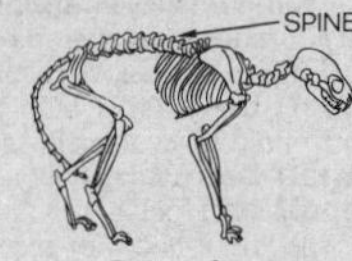

Spine of a cat

spine·less (spīn′ləs) *n-* 1 having no backbone; invertebrate. 2 without thorns or pointed outgrowths: *a* spineless *cactus.* 3 without courage; lacking spirit or resolution. *—adv-* **spine′less·ly.** *n-* **spine′less·ness.**

spin·et (spĭn′ət) *n-* 1 any of various small harpsichords, especially one like a virginal. 2 small upright piano.

spin·na·ker (spĭn′ə kər) *n-* large sail, triangular in shape and having a deep belly, used chiefly by racing boats running before the wind. *as* ***modifier***: *the* spinnaker *sheet*; spinnaker *halyard.*

spin·ner·et (spĭn′ə rĕt′) *n-* 1 organ of spiders and larvae of certain insects through which a liquid protein is extruded to congeal into silk. 2 a plate with fine holes through which artificial fibers are extruded into the hardening agent.

spinning jenny *n-* machine with many spindles so that a number of threads can be spun at a time.

spinning reel *n-* reel for casting a fishing line, so arranged that the line comes off in coils without snarling.

spinning wheel *n-* machine consisting of a spindle turned by a large wheel, used formerly for spinning fibers of cotton, linen, or wool into thread or yarn.

Spinning wheel

spin-off (spĭn′ŏf′, -ôf′) *n-* product that results indirectly from work on a program or another product: *This plastic was a* spin-off *from the space program.*

spi·nose (spī′nōs′) *adj* full of, or covered with, prickles; spiny. *—adv-* **spi′nose′ly.**

spin·ster (spĭn′stər) *n-* woman who has not married. *as* ***modifier***: *a* spinster *aunt.*

spin·y (spī′nē) *adj-* [**spin·i·er, spin·i·est**] 1 full of, or covered with thorny prongs or points; prickly. 2 shaped like a spine: *a* spiny *outgrowth.* *—n-* **spin′i·ness.**

spiny lobster *n-* any of a group of sea crustaceans similar to the common lobster but lacking the large claws; crayfish; rock lobster.

spi·ra·cle (spĭr′ĭ kəl, spī′rĭ-) *n-* an opening for breathing; especially, any of the paired openings in the abdomens of insects, or the blowhole of a whale.

spi·ral (spī′rəl) *n-* 1 plane curve described around a point and having a continously increasing radius. 2 helix. 3 something that has either of these forms: *A snail shell is a* spiral. 4 any course or path that rises gradually as if it were a helix: *the* spiral *of rising costs. adj-*: *the* spiral *shape of the shell*; *a* spiral *path. vi-* 1 to take a spiral form or course. 2 to go up or down gradually as if in a helical path: *Prices* spiraled. *vt-*: *The breeze* spiraled *the leaves to the ground.*

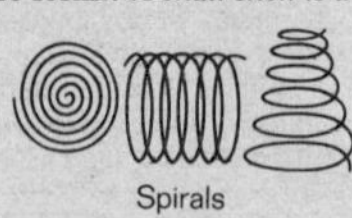
Spirals

spiral galaxy ***n-*** galaxy in the shape of a spiral. Also **spiral nebula.**

[1]**spire** (spīər) ***n-*** **1** pointed roof surmounting a tower or steeple. **2** anything that tapers to a point, such as a mountain peak. **3** slender blade or stalk, as of grass. [from Old English **spīr** meaning "spike; stalk."]

[2]**spire** (spīər) ***n-*** **1** spiral, or single turn of a spiral; coil. **2** the upper part of a spiral shell. [from Old French, from Latin, from Greek **speira** meaning "a coil."]

spi·re·a or **spi·rae·a** (spī rē′ ə) ***n-*** any of a group of shrubs bearing clusters of small white or pink flowers.

spi·ril·lum (spī rĭl′ əm) ***n-*** [*pl.* **spi·ril·la** (-lə)] any of a genus **(Spirillum)** of long, curved bacteria with tails.

spir·it (spĭr′ ĭt) ***n-*** **1** the immortal, nonphysical part of man; soul. **2** supernatural being, such as a ghost, sprite, fairy, etc. **3** an individual's mind and character: *He had a great* spirit. **4** a person, thought of as the sum of mental and moral qualities: *She was a noble* spirit. **5** courage; vigor; energy: *to fight with* spirit; *to break an opponent's* spirit. **6** general mood and motive: *a* spirit *of fun*; *the* spirit *of scientific inquiry*. **7** intention; real meaning: *the* spirit *of the law*. **8** loyalty; special devotion: *school* spirit; *local* spirit. **9** **spirits** (1) state of mind; mood: *He is in high* spirits *today*. (2) any strong, distilled liquor. (3) an alcoholic solution of certain volatile drugs. ***vt-*** to carry off or away suddenly or mysteriously.

spir·it·ed (spĭr′ ə təd) ***adj-*** full of life or vigor; animated; lively. ***—adv-*** **spir′ it·ed·ly.** ***n-*** **spir′ it·ed·ness.**

spir·it·less (spĭr′ ĭt ləs) ***adj-*** without spirit; dejected; depressed; lacking animation. ***—adv-*** **spir′ it·less·ly.**

spirit level ***n-*** an instrument for testing whether a surface is horizontal or vertical. It consists of closed tubes containing a liquid and an air bubble which comes to rest in the middle when the tube is horizontal.

spir·it·u·al (spĭr′ ə chōō əl) ***adj-*** **1** having to do with the spirit or mind rather than with material things. **2** pertaining to the soul or higher nature of man. **3** pertaining to sacred or religious things; pure; holy. ***n-*** hymn or sacred song, especially one created by the Negroes of the South. ***—adv-*** **spir′ it·u·al·ly.**

spir·it·u·al·ism (spĭr′ ə chə lĭz′ əm, -chōō ə lĭz′ əm) ***n-*** **1** belief that the spirits of the dead communicate with the living, especially through a person with the gifts of a medium. **2** insistence on the spiritual side of things; idealism. ***—n-*** **spir′ it·u·al·ist′.** ***adj-*** **spir′ it·u·al·is′ tic.**

spir·it·u·al·i·ty (spĭr′ ə chōō ăl′ ə tē) ***n-*** **1** devotion to or concern with spiritual values. **2** trait of a person who seems less concerned with the everyday world than with the realm of the spirit: *an aura of* spirituality *about him.*

spir·it·u·ous (spĭr′ ə chōō əs) ***adj-*** containing alcohol.

spi·ro·chete (spī′ rə kēt′) ***n-*** any of various bacteria with a spiral shape and a flexible, undulating body.

spi·ro·gy·ra (spī′ rə jī′ rə) ***n-*** green, fresh-water algae containing chloroplasts with a spiral shape.

spir·y (spī′ rē) ***adj-*** shaped like a spire; tall and tapering.

[1]**spit** (spĭt) **1** rod or bar on which meat is roasted over an open fire. **2** narrow cape or point of land extending into a body of water. ***vt-*** **[spit·ted, spit·ting]** to pierce with a rod; also, to impale on anything sharp. [from Old English **spitu** meaning "a sharp-pointed stick."]

[2]**spit** (spĭt) ***n-*** saliva. ***vt-*** **[spat** (spăt) or **spit, spit·ting]** **1** to eject (saliva or other matter) from the mouth; expectorate. **2** to eject or expel with sudden force: *The cannon* spat *fire*. ***vi-*** **1** to expel saliva from the mouth. **2** to make an angry, hissing sound. [from Old English **spittan,** "to spit."] ***—n-*** **spit′ ter.**

spit·ball (spĭt′ bòl′) ***n-*** **1** small lump of chewed paper. **2** in baseball, an illegal pitch delivered after the ball has been moistened with saliva.

spite (spīt) ***n-*** malice; ill will; desire to injure: *He stayed away out of* spite. ***vt-*** **[spit·ed, spit·ing]** to show ill will or malice toward; seek to hurt: *He did it only to* spite *his brother.*

in spite of regardless of; despite.

spite·ful (spīt′ fəl) ***adj-*** full of ill will; malicious; having a desire to hurt. ***—adv-*** **spite′ ful·ly.** ***n-*** **spite′ ful·ness.**

spit·fire (spĭt′ fīər′) ***n-*** highly emotional, quick- tempered person.

spit·tle (spĭt′ əl) ***n-*** saliva; spit.

spit·toon (spĭ tōōn′) ***n-*** receptable for spit; cuspidor.

spitz (spĭts) ***n-*** small dog with a sharp muzzle, long, silky hair, and a bushy tail.

splash (splăsh) ***vt-*** **1** to scatter (a liquid) and set it flying. **2** to slop, toss, or throw (a liquid): *to* splash *water on a campfire*. **3** to soil with water, mud, etc.; also, to decorate with scattered dots: *Mud* splashed *our car*. ***vi-*** **1** to dash a liquid about: *Please, don't* splash. **2** to paddle vigorously or romp in the water; also, to fall or move with a dash or splatter. **3** to fall or fly about in drops: *The paint* splashed *over the floor*. ***n-*** **1** violent scattering and flying about of a liquid, caused by a stroke, plunge, or slop: *The diver made a great* splash *when he hit the water*. **2** sound of this: *a loud* splash. **3** blotch, spot, or patch: *a* splash *of crimson*. ***—n-*** **splash′ er.**

make a splash *Informal* to attract wide attention by a sudden and sensational feat or success.

splash·y (splăsh′ ē) ***adj-*** **[splash·i·er, splash·i·est]** **1** making a splash: *the* splashy *raindrops on the window sill.* **2** full of irregular marks or streaks: *a* splashy *print*. **3** *Informal* showy; loud: *a* splashy *car*.

splat·ter (splăt′ ər) ***vt-*** to spatter; splash: *to* splatter *water*. ***vi-***: *Water* splattered *everywhere*. ***n-***: *He was drenched with a* splatter *of water.*

splay (splā) ***adj-*** spread out; broad and flat: *to have* splay *feet*. ***n-*** **1** in architecture, a beveled or sloped surface, especially at the sides of a door or window. **2** enlargement; spread. ***vt-*** **1** to slope or slant (the side of a door or window frame). **2** to spread out; extend.

splay·foot (splā′ fŏŏt′) ***n-*** [*pl.* **splay·feet**] **1** foot that is flat and widely spread out. **2** deformed foot in which the heel turns outward. ***—adj-*** **splay′ foot′ ed.**

spleen (splēn) ***n-*** **1** oval, pulpy organ located near the stomach in most vertebrates. Its chief function in human beings is the production of white blood cells, but it also destroys worn out red blood cells. **2** spite; ill temper; bitterness; malice; anger.

splen·did (splĕn′ dĭd) ***adj-*** **1** magnificent; spectacular: *the* splendid *procession*. **2** excellent; fine; praiseworthy: *a* splendid *effort*. ***—adv-*** **splen′ did·ly.** ***n-*** **splen′ did·ness.**

splen·dif·er·ous (splĕn dĭf′ ər əs) *Informal* ***adj-*** magnificent; grand; glorious. ***—adv-*** **splen·dif′ er·ous·ly.** ***n-*** **splen·dif′ er·ous·ness.**

splen·dor (splĕn′ dər) ***n-*** **1** great brightness; brilliance: *the* splendor *of a summer sunset*. **2** great show; pomp; magnificence: *the* splendor *of the royal court*.

sple·net·ic (splə nĕt′ ĭk) ***adj-*** **1** of or related to the spleen. **2** ill-tempered; spiteful. ***—adv-*** **sple·net′ i·cal·ly.**

splice (splīs) ***vt-*** **[spliced, splic·ing] 1** to join (ropes) by weaving together the ends. **2** to join (timbers) by overlapping. **3** to join (strips of film or magnetic tape) by gluing. ***n-*** a joining of ropes, strips of film, etc., in this way; also, the junction or place of union. **—*n-* splic′ er.**

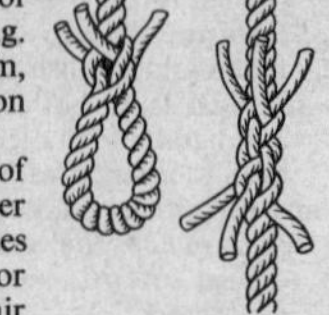

Rope splices

splint (splĭnt) ***n-*** **1** device made of wood strips, plaster, or other material, used to hold broken bones in place. **2** thin strip of wood or cane used in making baskets, chair seats, etc. **3** a splinter. ***vt-*** to immobilize, support, or brace with or as if with a splint.

splin·ter (splĭn′ tər) ***n-*** thin, sharp, broken piece of wood, bone, glass, etc.; sliver. ***vt-*** to break into sharp, thin pieces, or slivers: *Lightning* splintered *the tree.* ***vi-***: *The tree* splintered *under his ax.* **—*adj-* splin′ ter·y.**

split (splĭt) ***vt-*** **[split, split·ting] 1** to divide or cut lengthwise or in layers: *The farmer* split *the logs for firewood.* **2** to tear or burst apart: *The extreme cold* split *the rocks.* **3** to divide or separate into portions: *Please* split *the ice cream among the four of us.* **4** to cause fission in: *to* split *a cell*; *to* split *an atom.* **5** to issue two or more shares of (a stock) for each share outstanding. ***vi-***: *The warped plank* split. *The cell* split *into two cells.* ***n-*** **1** crack or cleft; fissure: *a* split *in the rock.* **2** division of a political party or other group: *There was a* split *on the tax issue.* **3** stock split. **4 splits** acrobatic trick in which a person jumps up and lands with the legs spread out horizontally, one in front and one behind. ***adj-*** **1** cracked or broken apart, especially lengthwise; cleft: *a* split *board*; split *lip.* **2** of or relating to a stock of which two or more shares have been issued for each share outstanding. **—*n-* split′ ter.**

split hairs to make overly precise or petty distinctions.

split (one's) vote to vote for political candidates of more than one party.

split infinitive *Grammar* ***n-*** infinitive in which "to" is separated from the verb. Examples: to *truly* believe; to *never really* know.

►The best simple rule is to trust your instinct. If it sounds natural to place an adverb between "to" and its verb, it is better to do so rather than to write an awkward or ambiguous sentence. But beware of splitting infinitives with whole phrases or clauses.

split second *Informal* ***n-*** instant; flash.

split ticket ***n-*** ballot cast for political candidates of more than one party. See also *straight ticket.*

split·ting (splĭt′ ĭng) ***adj-*** very severe: *a* splitting *pain.*

splotch (splŏch) ***n-*** irregular spot; smear; blotch. ***vt-***: *to* splotch *paint on a wall.* **—*adj-* splotch′ y.**

splurge (splûrj) *Informal* ***vi-*** **[splurged, splurg·ing]** to spend money in an extravagant or wasteful manner: *He* splurged *and bought three suits.* ***n-*** spending spree.

splut·ter (splŭt′ ər) ***vi-*** **1** to speak in a hasty or confused manner, as in excitement or embarrassment. **2** to make sharp, popping sounds; sputter. ***vt-*** to utter in a hasty or confused manner: *He could only* splutter *his name in all that excitement.* ***n-*** **1** noisy or confused talk; commotion. **2** sputtering or splashing sounds: *the* splutter *of frying meat.* **—*n-* splut′ ter·er.** ***adj-*** **splut′ ter·y.**

spoil (spoil) ***vt-*** **[spoiled** or **spoilt, spoil·ing] 1** to damage or injure; ruin: *You* spoil *milk by not keeping it cool.* **2** to cause to become lazy, expect too much from others, etc., by pampering: *The mother* spoiled *the child.* ***vi-*** to become unfit for use: *The milk* spoiled. ***n-*** **spoils** (1) things won or taken by force; loot. (2) public offices gained by a successful political party in an election.

spoil·age (spoi′ lĭj) ***n-*** **1** process of spoiling; especially, the decay of food. **2** something, especially food, that has spoiled. **3** amount that has spoiled; also, its cost.

spoil·er (spoil′ ər) ***n-*** **1** person or thing that spoils. **2** long, narrow panel on the upper surface of an airplane wing that raises to decrease lift and increase drag.

spoil·sport (spoil′ spôrt′) ***n-*** person who ruins the fun of others.

spoils system ***n-*** the practice of rewarding supporters of a successful political party with appointive public offices.

[1]**spoke** (spōk) ***n-*** **1** bar connecting the hub of a wheel and its rim. **2** ladder rung. [from Old English **spāca.**]

Spoke

[2]**spoke** (spōk) *p.t.* of **speak.**

spo·ken (spō′ kən) *p.p.* of **speak.**

spoke·shave (spōk′ shāv′) ***n-*** wood-working tool having a handle on both ends of a blade, useful for planing curved surfaces.

spokes·man (spōks′ mən) ***n-*** [*pl.* **spokes·men**] man who speaks for another or others: *a* spokesman *for labor.* **—*n-* *fem.* spokes′ wom′ an.**

spo·li·a·tion (spō′ lē ā′ shən) ***n-*** a plundering or despoiling, especially of neutral ships in time of war; robbery; pillage. **—*n-* spo′ li·a′ tor.**

sponge (spŭnj) ***n-*** **1** any of a phylum of immobile, aquatic animals **(Porifera)**, having porous skeletons. Sponges are of many sizes, shapes, and colors. **2** a light, dried, highly absorbent skeleton of one of these animals, used as an absorbent or for bathing, cleaning, etc.; also, any porous implement similarly used. **3** any light substance with many pores, such as porous rubber. **4** *Informal* a parasitic person. **5** pad of gauze used in medicine and surgery to remove blood, apply medicine, etc. *as* ***modifier***: *some* sponge *rubber.* ***vt-*** **[sponged, spong·ing] 1** to bathe, clean, or wet with anything that soaks up much water: *He* sponged *the car.* **2** to absorb (liquid). **3** *Informal* to get, by imposing on another or others: *He* sponged *a meal off his friend.* ***vi-*** **1** *Informal* to live or get something by imposing on others: *He* sponges *off me all the time.* **2** to be absorbent: *This cloth* sponges *well.* **3** to gather sponges from the sea. **—*adj-* sponge′ like′.**

Two kinds of sponge

throw in the sponge *Informal* to admit defeat; give up.

sponge bath ***n-*** bath taken by washing with a sponge or cloth outside of a bathtub or shower.

sponge·cake (spŭnj′ kāk′) ***n-*** light, spongy cake made of flour, eggs, sugar, etc., but no shortening.

spong·er (spŭn′ jər) ***n-*** **1** *Informal* person who lives off others; parasite. **2** person or ship that gathers sponges. **3** person or thing that sponges.

spon·gy (spŭn′ jē) ***adj-*** **[spon·gi·er, spon·gi·est]** like a sponge; full of small holes, easily compressed, and absorbent. **—*n-* spon′ gi·ness.**

spon·son (spŏn′ sən) ***n-*** **1** projection from the side of a ship or tank to protect or support some part, such as a platform for a gun. **2** curved projection on either side of the hull of a vessel or seaplane to increase its stability in the water. **3** air-filled compartment on either side of a canoe to keep it from upsetting or sinking.

spon·sor (spŏn′ sər) ***n-*** **1** person who lends support to, or is responsible for, another person or thing: *a* sponsor *for one's application to college.* **2** business firm or other organization that pays the cost of a radio or TV program in return for the advertisement of its goods or services. 3 godfather; godmother. ***vt-*** **1** to endorse, support, or be responsible for: *to* sponsor *a bill in Congress.* **2** to assume the costs of production of.

spon·sor·ship (spŏn′ sər shĭp′) ***n-*** the position, functions, or duties of a sponsor.

spon·ta·ne·ous (spŏn tā′ nē əs) ***adj-*** **1** arising or acting from a natural impulse: *a* spontaneous *burst of applause.* **2** produced by internal forces rather than by an external cause: *a* spontaneous *growth*; spontaneous *combustion.* ***—adv-*** **spon·ta′ ne·ous·ly.** ***n-*** **spon·ta′ ne·ous·ness** or **spon′ ta·ne′ i·ty** (spŏn′ tən ē′ ə tē, -ā′ ə tē).

spontaneous combustion ***n-*** a burning or ignition without the application of external heat. It results from the accumulation of heat by slow oxidation.

spoof (spo͞of) *Informal* ***vt-*** to treat or mimic in a humorous and satirical manner; parody; burlesque. ***n-*** parody of a person or thing; take-off. ***—n-*** **spoof′ er.**

spook (spo͞ok) ***n-*** ghost; spirit; specter. ***vt-*** *Informal* to frighten; startle; scare: *The falling leaf* spooked *my horse.*

spook·y (spo͞o′ kē) *Informal* ***adj-*** **[spook·i·er, spook·i·est] 1** of, having to do with, or suggesting spooks: *a* spooky *castle.* **2** nervous: *a* spooky *herd.* ***—n-*** **spook′ i·ness.**

spool (spo͞ol) ***n-*** **1** cylindrical piece of wood with flaring ends on which thread may be wound. **2** anything in the shape of a cylinder that is used in a like way; reel: *a* spool *of motion picture film.* **3** quantity of thread, wire, etc., held by such a cylinder; also, the cylinder and the material upon it. ***vt-*** to wind (thread, wire, etc.) on a cylinder.

Spool

spoon (spo͞on) ***n-*** **1** a utensil with a small shallow bowl at the end of a handle, used in preparing, serving, or eating food. **2** (also **spoon′ ful**) amount such a utensil will hold when full. **3** something resembling this utensil, such as an oar with a curved blade or a metal fishing lure. **4** golf club with a wooden head that gives more lift than a brassie. ***vt-*** to take up with or as if with a spoon. ***vi-*** *Informal* to kiss, embrace, etc., as lovers do.

spoon·bill (spo͞on′ bĭl′) ***n-*** any of various wading birds related to the ibises, with long legs and a broad bill.

spoon bread ***n-*** soft bread, made from milk, eggs, shortening, and cornmeal, and served with a spoon.

spoon·drift (spo͞on′ drĭft′) ***n-*** spindrift.

spoon·er·ism (spo͞o′ nə rĭz′ əm) ***n-*** accidental interchange of sounds, usually the first, in two or more words. Example: *"She* kissed *like an angry* hat," for *"She* hissed *like an angry* cat." [from Reverend W. A. **Spooner.**]

spoon-feed (spo͞on′ fēd′) ***vt-*** **[spoon-fed, spoon-feed·ing] 1** to feed with a spoon. **2** to spoil; pamper. **3** to teach or give out information in such a way as to leave no room for independent thought or action.

spoor (spo͝or) ***n-*** a track, scent, or trail, especially of a wild animal. ***vt-*** to track: *The hunters* spoored *the boar through the woods.* ***vi-***: *The pup can* spoor *well already.*

spo·rad·ic (spə răd′ ĭk) ***adj-*** **1** appearing or happening from time to time; occasional: *a few* sporadic *outbreaks of violence.* **2** appearing singly; widely separated from others: *the* sporadic *occurrence of a plant.* **3** of a disease, occurring in a few cases only; not epidemic. ***—adv-*** **spo·rad′ i·cal·ly.**

spo·ran·gi·um (spə răn′ jē əm) ***n-*** [*pl.* **spo·ran·gi·a** (-ə)] sac in which asexual spores are produced in algae, ferns, fungi, etc. Also **spore case.**

spore (spôr) ***n-*** **1** in plants, a very small reproductive body. **2** in bacteria, a kind of inactive cell that is extremely resistant to heat, strong chemicals, etc., and becomes active again under suitable conditions.

spo·ro·phyll or **spo·ro·phyl** (spôr′ ə fĭl′) ***n-*** leaf that bears sporangia.

spo·ro·phyte (spôr′ ə fīt′) ***n-*** in the life cycle of plants, the phase that produces spores. See also *gametophyte.*

spor·ran (spòr′ ən, spŏr′-) ***n-*** large purse or pouch worn in front of a Highland man's kilt.

sport (spôrt) ***n-*** **1** game, pastime, or contest that requires a reasonable amount of physical activity along with individual skill: *Skiing, tennis, and billiards are all* sports. **2** amusement; fun: *Mother teased us in* sport. **3** *Informal* unselfish companion. **4** *Informal* person who plays fair and is a good loser. **5** *Informal* person interested in sporting events, especially to bet on them. **6** *Biology* animal or plant which exhibits a spontaneous variation from the usual or normal type. ***vi-*** **1** to play or frolic; trifle. **2** to participate in a sporting event. **3** *Biology* to exhibit suddenly or spontaneously a variation from the normal type; mutate. ***vt-*** to show off in public; wear: *Bob* sported *a new hat on Sunday.* ***as modifier*** (also **sports**): *a* sport *shirt*; *a* sport *jacket*; sports *page.*

make sport of to make fun of; ridicule.

sport·ing (spôr′ tĭng) ***adj-*** **1** engaged or interested in sports: *The athlete belonged to a* sporting *crowd.* **2** playing fair and willing to be a good loser: *The children were taught to be* sporting *in their games.* **3** having to do with sports. **4** risky but offering a reasonable chance for success: *a* sporting *chance.* ***—adv-*** **sport′ ing·ly.**

spor·tive (spôr′ tĭv) ***adj-*** frolicsome; playful: *his* sportive *humor.* ***—adv-*** **spor′ tive·ly.** ***n-*** **spor′ tive·ness.**

sports car or **sport car** ***n-*** small, low automobile, usually a two-seat convertible, built for high speeds.

sports·cast (spôrts′ kăst′) ***n-*** radio or television broadcast of a sports event.

sports·man (spôrts′ mən) ***n-*** [*pl.* **sports·men**] **1** person who takes part in sports, such as hunting and fishing, etc. **2** person who plays fair or is honorable. ***—n-*** ***fem.*** **sports′ wom′ an.** ***adj-*** **sports′ man·like′.**

sports·man·ship (spôrts′ mən shĭp′) ***n-*** **1** behavior expected of a sportsman, such as fair play or good grace in defeat. **2** skill in or liking for sports.

sports·wear (spôrts′ wâr′) ***n-*** casual clothes.

sports·writ·er (spôrts′ rī′ tər) ***n-*** person who writes about sports for a magazine or newspaper.

sport·y (spôr′ tē) *Informal* ***adj-*** **[sport·i·er, sport·i·est] 1** relating to or characteristic of a sport or sportsman. **2** loud; showy; flashy: *a* sporty *suit.* ***—adv-*** **sport′ i·ly.** ***n-*** **sport′ i·ness.**

spot (spŏt) ***n-*** **1** a blot or mark; discolored place or stain; patch: *a grease* spot; *a* spot *of white on the black dog.* **2** a blemish: *a* spot *on the family name.* **3** locality, place, or area: *We can picnic in this* spot. **4** *Informal* particular position or situation: *They have a good* spot *on the program.* **5** *Brit.* small amount: *a* spot *of tea.* ***vt-*** **[spot·ted, spot·ting] 1** to cause to become marked or stained; discolor; stain. **2** to disgrace; mar; blemish. **3** to place at a designated location: *to* spot *a billiard ball.* **4** *Informal* to recognize; detect: *He* spotted *the guilty man.* ***vi-*** to become marked or stained.

hit the spot *Informal* to be just what was needed or desired. **in a spot** *Informal* in trouble; in a bad situation. **on the spot 1** at once; immediately. **2** on or at the place mentioned. **3** *Informal* in trouble; in a bad situation. **4** *Informal* in a position where a true answer, explanation, or effective solution must be given.

---

spot cash *Informal* ***n-*** money paid at delivery.
spot check ***n-*** examination or inspection of a few items or places selected at random. ***vt-*** **(spot-check):** *They* spot-checked *the income tax returns.*
spot·less (spŏt′ ləs) ***adj-*** without a mark or stain; immaculate. —***adv-*** **spot′ less·ly.** ***n-*** **spot′ less·ness.**
spot·light (spŏt′ līt′) ***n-*** **1** lamp or apparatus, usually movable, that projects a strong, focused beam of light. **2** strong beam of light projected by such a lamp. **3** *Informal* public attention; notoriety.
spot pass ***n-*** in goal games such as football and hockey, a pass to a predetermined spot where a player is supposed to arrive and receive the pass.
spot·ted (spŏt′ əd) ***adj-*** marked with spots or stains: *a* spotted *dog*; *a* spotted *tie.*
spotted fever ***n-*** any of a widespread group of diseases caused by rickettsiae and carried by ticks. Rocky Mountain spotted fever is the best known.
spot·ter (spŏt′ ər) ***n-*** **1** *Informal* a person who keeps watch; especially, a detective who checks on the honesty of employees. **2** person who watches for enemy aircraft. **3** in dry cleaning, a worker who removes spots.
spot·ty (spŏt′ ē) ***adj-*** **[spot·ti·er, spot·ti·est] 1** marked with spots. **2** not steady; irregular: *His attendance in class was* spotty. —***adv-*** **spot′ ti·ly.** ***n-*** **spot′ ti·ness.**
spouse (spous, spouz) ***n-*** one's husband or wife.
spout (spout) ***n-*** **1** projection, such as a tube or nozzle, with an opening from which a liquid flows or is poured: *the* spout *of a teapot.* **2** a gush of liquid: *a* spout *of oil.* ***vt-*** **1** to spurt (liquid): *The leaking pipe* spouted *oil.* **2** *Informal* to utter in a self-important, pompous way: *He* spouts *his opinions at every opportunity.* ***vi-*** **1** to spurt a jet of liquid or vapor: *A fountain* spouts. *A whale* spouts. **2** to come forth in a jet or stream: *Blood* spouted *from the wound.* **3** *Informal* to speak pompously. —***n-*** **spout′ er.**
sprag (sprăg) ***n-*** small log or steel bar used to prevent a wheeled vehicle from slipping backward on an incline.
sprain (sprān) ***n-*** injury caused by a bad twist to the muscles or ligaments around a joint. ***vt-*** to twist the muscles or ligaments around a joint.
sprang (sprăng) *p.t.* of **spring.**
sprat (sprăt) ***n-*** [*pl.* **sprat; sprats** (kinds of sprat)] **1** small fish, similar to the herring, found in shoals along the European Atlantic coast and used as food. **2** any of several other similar fish, such as a young herring.
sprawl (sprȯl) ***vi-*** **1** to sit or lie in a careless or awkward position with the limbs stretched out: *He* sprawled *on the sofa.* **2** to move along awkwardly, using the arms and legs; scramble: *The baby* sprawled *across the floor.* **3** to spread out in an irregular way: *The branches* sprawled *across the path.* ***vt-*** to cause to spread awkwardly or irregularly. ***n-*** awkward or spreading movement or position: *We found him asleep in a* sprawl *across the bed.*
[1]**spray** (sprā) ***n-*** **1** fine drops or a mist of water driven by the wind, as from waves breaking on the shore or a boat cutting through the water. **2** anything like these fine drops: *a* spray *of sand.* **3** a device that scatters a fine liquid mist: *a garden* spray. **4** a liquid used in such a device: *a* spray *for mosquitoes.* ***vt-*** **1** to apply in fine drops or mist: *She* sprayed *perfume on her handkerchief.* **2** to cover (something) with a fine mist of anything: *He* sprayed *the walls with paint.* ***vi-*** to scatter a liquid in fine drops or a mist: *The hose* sprayed *gently across the lawn.* [probably from early Dutch **sprāyen** meaning "drizzle."] —***n-*** **spray′ er.**
[2]**spray** (sprā) ***n-*** **1** small branch or shoot of a plant with its leaves and flowers or berries. **2** jewelry, decorative pattern, etc., resembling a small branch: *a* spray *of diamonds.* [perhaps from Old English **spræg,** "sprig."]
spray gun ***n-*** device for spraying insecticides or paint.
spread (sprĕd) ***vt-*** **[spread, spread·ing] 1** to put as a covering on: *He* spread *butter on the toast.* **2** to cover the surface of: *He* spread *the toast with butter.* **3** to unfold; unroll; open out: *She* spread *the blanket on the bed.* **4** to stretch out; also, to extend over a period of time: *The bird* spread *its wings.* **5** to distribute; scatter: *We* spread *the pamphlets through the town.* **6** to make known; communicate or carry from person to person: *to* spread *news*; *to* spread *disease.* **7** to push or force apart: *He* spread *the desks.* **8** to set (a table); also, to place food upon: *She* spread *the table.* ***vi-*** **1** to extend over an area: *Fire* spread *through the building.* **2** to be dispersed, scattered, or distributed; also, to permit being distributed: *Rumors* spread *quickly. Jam* spreads *easily.* **3** to become or be forced apart: *During the summer the rails* spread. ***n-*** **1** a stretching out or extension: *the* spread *of an eagle's wings.* **2** the extent something stretches; width: *the* spread *of a man's hand.* **3** growth or expansion: *the* spread *of knowledge.* **4** the covering on a bed, table, etc. **5** *Informal* meal set out on a table; feast. **6** jam, peanut butter, or similar food meant to be put on bread or crackers. **7** two facing pages of a magazine or newspaper printed with related material; also, the printed matter occupying these pages or several columns. **8** *Informal* a ranch: *a cattle* spread. **9** distance between two points or the difference between two prices: *a wide* spread *between reality and myth.* —***n-*** **spread′ er.**
spread-ea·gle (sprĕd′ ē′ gəl) ***adj-*** **1** having or resembling the figure of an eagle with wings and legs spread out. **2** *Informal* exaggerated or boastful, especially in a display of patriotism. ***vi-*** **[spread-ea·gled, spread-ea·gling]** to stand or lie spread out in the form of an eagle with outspread wings: *The children* spread-eagled *in the snow.* ***vt-*** to force (someone) into such a position.
spree (sprē) ***n-*** **1** lively frolic; merry time. **2** unrestrained indulgence in some activity: *a buying* spree.
sprig (sprĭg) ***n-*** **1** small twig, shoot, or branch. **2** ornament having a similar form. **3** headless nail or brad. ***vt-*** **[sprigged, sprig·ging]** to secure or fasten with brads.
spright·ly (sprīt′ lē) ***adj-*** **[spright·li·er, spright·li·est]** lively; gay. —***n-*** **spright′ li·ness.**
spring (sprĭng) ***n-*** **1** metal spiral, set of clamped plates, or a strip of elastic material used to move, drive, or cushion something: *an automobile* spring. **2** a place where water comes to the surface of the ground; natural well. **3** a source or beginning; origin; wellspring. **4** bounce; elasticity: *the* spring *in his step.* **5** a leap; jump; bound: *The dog made a* spring *toward us.* **6** the season of the year between winter and summer; in the northern hemisphere usually from March 21 to June 21. *as* ***modifier:*** *a* spring *flower*; spring *rains.* ***vi-*** **[sprang** or **sprung, sprung, spring·ing] 1** to leap; jump; bound: *The dog* sprang *at me.* **2** to move by or as if by an elastic force: *The trap* sprang *shut.* **3** to arise suddenly; grow: *Flowers* sprang *out of the earth.* **4** to become warped, split, bent, etc.: *Because of the damp weather, the door* sprang. ***vt-*** **1** to reveal or produce with unexpected suddenness: *He* sprang *a surprise.* **2** to release the catch of: *to* spring *a trap.* **3** to split, warp, crack open, etc.: *The blow* sprang *the tennis racket.*

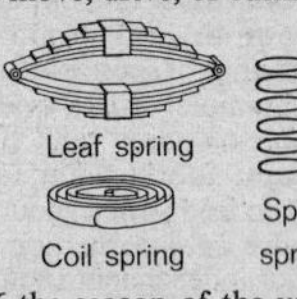

spring a leak to develop a leak suddenly.
spring back to rebound; recoil.
spring from to come from; result from.
spring up to arise suddenly; come into being.

spring beauty ***n-*** any of several delicate wild plants related to the purslane, having white or pink flowers.

spring·board (sprĭng′ bôrd′) ***n-*** **1** a flexible board that gives added height or spring to a jump; diving board. **2** something that gives a good start.

spring·bok (sprĭng′ bŏk′) ***n-*** small South African animal resembling the gazelle, noted for its grace.

springer spaniel ***n-*** any of various medium-sized, spotted spaniels. For picture, see *spaniel.*

spring fever ***n-*** the feeling of laziness or restlessness that people have during the first warm sunny spring days.

spring·house (sprĭng′ hous′) ***n-*** small building located over a cold-water spring and used for storing food.

spring-load·ed (sprĭng′ lō′ dəd) ***adj-*** loaded or having force applied to by means of a spring.

spring peeper ***n-*** small tree toad that breeds in ponds and produces a chirping sound on spring evenings.

spring·tide (sprĭng′ tīd′) ***n-*** springtime.

spring tide ***n-*** very high tide that occurs near the full moon and the new moon.

spring·time (sprĭng′ tīm′) ***n-*** season of spring.

spring wheat ***n-*** wheat that is planted in the spring and ripens the same summer.

spring·y (sprĭng′ ē) ***adj-*** **[spring·i·er, spring·i·est]** able to spring back; elastic; flexible; full of spring. ***—adv-*** **spring′ i·ly.** ***n-*** **spring′ i·ness.**

sprin·kle (sprĭng′ kəl) ***vt-*** **[sprin·kled, sprin·kling] 1** to spray with small drops of water: *You'll have to* sprinkle *the garden today.* **2** to scatter in small drops or particles: *The child* sprinkled *sand on the floor.* ***vt-*** to rain lightly. ***n-*** **1** a light rain. **2** small amount of something.

sprin·kler (sprĭng′ klər) ***n-*** **1** any of various devices for sprinkling lawns, roads, etc., with water or other fluids. **2** one of the outlets of a sprinkler system.

sprinkler system ***n-*** **1** automatic system for putting out fires inside a building. **2** arrangement of pipes and outlets for watering a lawn, garden, or similar area.

sprink·ling (sprĭngk′ lĭng) ***n-*** **1** small, scattered quantity. **2** a light rain. **3** a scattering of drops of liquid.

sprint (sprĭnt) ***vi-*** to run a rather short distance at full speed. ***n-*** a short race at full speed. ***—n-*** **sprint′ er.**

sprit (sprĭt) ***n-*** small spar running diagonally from the bottom of the mast to the top of the fore-and-aft sail.

sprite (sprīt) ***n-*** fairy, elf, or goblin.

sprit·sail (sprĭt′ səl, -sāl′) ***n-*** fore-and-aft sail extended by a sprit.

sprock·et (sprŏk′ ət) ***n-*** **1** any of the teeth on a chain-driven cogwheel. **2** (also **sprocket wheel**) the wheel itself.

SPROCKETS
Sprocket wheel

sprout (sprout) ***vi-*** **1** to start to grow; to put forth buds or shoots: *The cabbages* sprouted. **2** to grow quickly; shoot up: *Gas stations* sprouted *along the new highway.* ***vt-***: *The rain and warm weather* sprouted *the flowers.* ***n-*** **1** a beginning growth; a bud; a shoot. **2 sprouts** brussels sprouts.

[1]**spruce** (sproo͞s) ***n-*** **1** any of various pointed evergreen trees related to the pines and bearing cones and short, thick needles. **2** the wood of this tree, used for lumber and paper pulp. **3** any of various related trees, such as the hemlock. ***as modifier:*** *a* spruce *log.* [from a shortened form of earlier **sprucefir** meaning "a fir from Spruce." "Spruce" was an English misspelling of Old French **Pruce,** "Prussia."]

Red spruce, twig and cone

[2]**spruce** (sproo͞s) ***adj-*** **[spruc·er, spruc·est]** neat; tidy; trim. ***vt-*** **[spruced, spruc·ing]** to make neat and tidy (usually followed by "up"): *She* spruced *up the room.* ***vi-*** to make oneself neat (usually followed by "up"): *She will* spruce *up before going home.* [from earlier **spruce leather** meaning "Prussian leather," and related to [1]**spruce.**] ***—adv-*** **spruce′ ly.** ***n-*** **spruce′ ness.**

sprung (sprŭng) *p.t. & p.p. of* **spring.**

spry (sprī) ***adj-*** **[spry·er** or **spri·er, spry·est** or **spri·est]** active and nimble: *The old lady is very* spry *for her age.* ***—adv-*** **spry′ ly.** ***n-*** **spry′ ness.**

spud (spŭd) ***n-*** **1** sharp, narrow spade, especially for digging up weeds with large roots. **2** *Informal* potato. ***vt-*** **[spud·ded, spud·ding]** to dig with such a spade. ***vi-*** to begin the drilling of an oil well; cut through the soft upper strata with a special bit.

spume (spyoo͞m) ***n-*** foam; froth; scum. ***vi-*** **[spumed, spum·ing]** to foam; froth. ***—adj-*** **spum′ y.**

spu·mo·ni or **spu·mo·ne** (spə mō′ nē) ***n-*** Italian frozen dessert resembling a mousse, usually made with ice cream arranged in layers of different colors or flavors and often containing dried fruits and nuts.

spun (spŭn) *p.t. & p.p.* of **spin.**

spun glass ***n-*** Fiberglas.

spunk (spŭngk) *Informal* ***n-*** courage; spirit.

spunk·y (spŭng′ kē) ***adj-*** **[spunk·i·er, spunk·i·est]** courageous; spirited. ***—adv-*** **spunk′ i·ly.** ***n-*** **spunk′ i·ness.**

spur (spûr) ***n-*** **1** metal frame with pricking point or points, fitted to a rider's boot heel, with which to urge on his horse; hence, anything that urges to action; incentive: *He offered a prize as a* spur *to good work.* **2** sharp, horny spine on a rooster's leg; also, anything of similar shape. **3** ridge of hills at an angle with a main ridge. **4** short railroad line connected with the main line at only one end. ***vt-*** **[spurred, spur·ring]** to urge (a horse) on with a special pricking device; hence, to urge; goad: *Fear* spurred *him.* ***vi-*** to goad a horse or oneself to special effort (usually followed by "on").

Spur

on the spur of the moment without any planning; on impulse. **win one's spurs** to gain distinction or honor.

spu·ri·ous (spyoo͝r′ ē əs, spoo͝r′-) ***adj-*** not genuine; false. ***—adv-*** **spu′ ri·ous·ly.** ***n-*** **spu′ ri·ous·ness.**

spurn (spûrn) ***vt-*** **1** to push away, as with the foot. **2** to turn down with scorn.

spurred (spûrd) ***adj-*** wearing or having a spur or spurs.

spurt (spûrt) ***n-*** **1** sudden gush of liquid. **2** sudden increase: *a* spurt *of activity; a* spurt *of speed.* ***vi-*** **1** to gush forth suddenly in streams: *Blood* spurted *from the open wound.* **2** to have a short burst of energy or activity; increase greatly: *Sales* spurted *greatly before Christmas.* ***vt-*** to throw or force out in a stream; squirt: *The wound* spurted *blood.* Also **spirt.**

sput·ter (spŭt′ ər) ***n-*** **1** noise like spitting or spluttering: *The engine gave a final* sputter *and died.* **2** confused, rapid speech. ***vi-*** **1** to make a noise like spitting or spluttering. **2** to throw off particles of saliva in excited speech. **3** to talk in a disconnected and explosive manner. ***vt-*** to utter in an excited or confused way: *He* sputtered *his message.* ***—n-*** **sput′ ter·er.**

spu·tum (spyoo͞′ təm) ***n-*** saliva; spit; spittle.

spy (spī) ***n-*** [*pl.* **spies**] **1** secret agent employed by a government to get information about another government. **2** person who watches others secretly. ***as modifier***: *a* spy *novel*; *a* spy *plane.* ***vi-*** **[spied, spy·ing] 1** to act as a secret agent; watch secretly. **2** to make a close examination or investigation (usually followed by "into"). ***vt-*** **1** to notice at a distance; catch sight of: *She* spied *a friend in the crowd.* **2** to examine carefully.
spy out to examine closely or secretly.

spy·glass (spī' glăs') ***n-*** small telescope.

sq. square.

squab (skwŏb) ***n-*** young pigeon about four weeks old.

squab·ble (skwŏb' əl) ***n-*** noisy, petty quarrel. ***vi-*** **[squab·bled, squab·bling]**: *The children have been* squabbling *all morning.* **—*n-* squab' bler.**

squad (skwŏd) ***n-*** **1** in the Army and the Marines, the smallest unit, consisting usually of eleven men and commanded by a sergeant or corporal. **2** small group of people gathered together for a common enterprise: *a traffic* squad; *a football* squad.

squad car ***n-*** police patrol car equipped with a two-way radio for communicating with headquarters.

squad·ron (skwŏd' rən) ***n-*** **1** in the Air Force, a unit that usually consists of eight or more planes and their personnel. **2** in the Navy, a unit consisting of a group of warships of a similar type on a special mission. **3** formerly, a cavalry unit corresponding to a company. **4** any group organized for work.

squal·id (skwŏl' ĭd) ***adj-*** **1** dirty; unclean. **2** wretched; miserable; sordid: *a* squalid *existence.* **—*adv-* squal' id·ly.** ***n-*** **squal' id·ness.**

[1]**squall** (skwȯl) ***n-*** **1** sudden, violent, brief wind storm. It may be accompanied by rain. **2** *Informal* brief trouble or commotion. ***vi-*** to storm briefly. [from [2]**squall,** from the imitation of the noise of the wind.]

[2]**squall** (skwȯl) ***n-*** harsh, loud cry or scream, as of a baby. ***vi-*** to cry or scream violently and harshly. [from Old Norse **skvala,** "to squeal; gush out."] ***n-*** **squall' er.**

squall line ***n-*** line of thunderstorms, often hundreds of miles long and up to fifty miles wide, occurring in the warm area in advance of a cold front.

squall·y (skwȯ' lē) ***adj-*** **[squall·i·er, squall·i·est] 1** gusty; stormy. **2** *Informal* promising or threatening trouble.

squal·or (skwŏl' ər, skwā' lər) ***n-*** wretched and filthy condition; poverty and dirt.

squan·der (skwŏn' dər) ***vt-*** to spend in a wasteful manner; waste foolishly: *to* squander *money.*

square (skwâr) ***n-*** **1** plane figure having four equal sides and four right angles; equilateral rectangle. **2** something resembling this figure: *a* square *of cake.* **3** tool shaped like an L or T for checking or marking right angles. **4** *Mathematics* the product that results when a number is multiplied by itself once. The square of 3 is 9 ($3 \times 3 = 9$). **5** city block; area enclosed by two pairs of parallel streets. **6** the length of the side of a city block: *Go three* squares *east.* **7** public place, often a park, surrounded by streets. **8** place where several streets come together. ***adj-*** **1** in the form of an equilateral rectangle: *a* square *design.* **2** having or making right angles and straight sides: *his* square *shoulders*; square *angle*; square *room.* **3** honest; fair: *We respect* square *dealings.* **4** full; complete; satisfying: *a* square *meal.* **5** stated in terms of square measure: *A* square *foot has 144* square *inches.* **6** having credit balanced; in order; settled: *a* square *account.* **7** even in score, especially in golf; tied. ***vt-*** **[squared, squar·ing] 1** to form with four equal sides and four right angles. **2** to cut to a right angle; also, shape roughly to a right angle. **3** to mark with or divide into shapes that have four equal sides and four right angles. **4** to put in order; adjust: *He* squared *his account. He* squared *his conduct.* **5** to check (an edge) for straightness, or (an angle) for accuracy. **6** *Mathematics* to multiply (a number) by itself once. **7** *Informal* to arrange, fix, or balance, especially by illegal means. ***vi-*** **1** to be cut or placed so as to be at right angles (with). **2** to agree; fit in: *That doesn't* square *with what you said last night.* **—*adv-* square' ly.** ***n-*** **square' ness.**

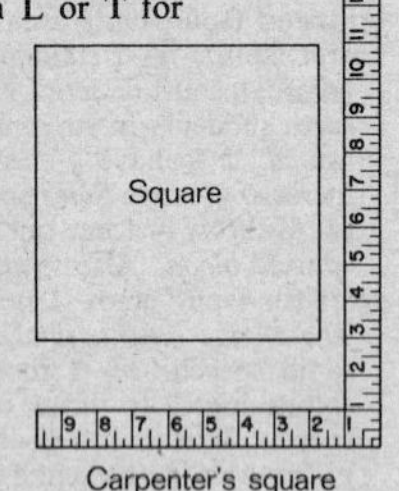

Carpenter's square

on the square 1 at right angles. **2** in a fair or honest way; honestly. **out of square 1** not at right angles; oblique. **2** *Informal* not in agreement; incorrect.
square away 1 to square up. **2** to set sail, make the ship trim, etc., for a long voyage.
square off to put oneself into a position for fighting.
square oneself *Informal* to make up for a wrong.
square the circle 1 to make a square equal in area to a given circle. This cannot be done with ruler and compass alone. **2** to attempt something that seems impossible.
square up 1 to adjust; settle; balance: *He* squared up *his account.* **2** to prepare for a fight or argument.

square dance ***n-*** old-fashioned dance consisting of a series of set steps for a number of couples arranged in a square. ***vi-*** **square-dance [square-danced, square-danc·ing]** to perform such a dance.

square deal ***n-*** honest and just treatment.

square foot ***n-*** unit of area equal to that of a square one foot long and one foot wide.

square inch ***n-*** unit of area equal to that of a square one inch long and one inch wide.

square knot ***n-*** knot used for joining the ends of ropes, cords, etc., and consisting of two loops intertwined so that each passes around, and tightens down on, the two strands forming the other; reef knot. For picture, see *knot.*

square meal ***n-*** a full or satisfying meal.

square measure ***n-*** system for measuring area in two-dimensional units such as square inches, square feet, square centimeters, square meters, etc.

square-rigged (skwâr' rĭgd') ***adj-*** having square or rectangular sails as the main sails. They are hung crosswise to the length of the ship, not lengthwise.

square-rig·ger (skwâr' rĭg' ər) ***n-*** square-rigged ship.

square root ***n-*** of a number, a number that when multiplied by itself produces the given number. For example, 3 is a square root of 9 ($3 \times 3 = 9$).

square shooter *Informal* ***n-*** fair and honest person.

[1]**squash** (skwŏsh) ***vt-*** **1** to crush; mash into a pulp: *Tim* squashed *the berries.* **2** to suppress; put an end to: *They* squashed *the uprising.* ***vi-*** **1** to be crushed or smashed. **2** to make sounds by tramping through slush or soft mud. ***n-*** **1** a crushed object or mass. **2** the sound made by the fall of something soft and heavy. **3** the sound made by tramping through slush or soft mud. **4** either of two games similar to tennis and played with rackets and a rubber ball in a walled court. In **squash racquets** or **rackets** a small, black, firm ball is used; in **squash tennis** an inflated, green ball the size of a tennis ball, covered with tight webbing. [from Old French **esquasser,** from Latin **exquassāre,** from **ex-** meaning "very," and **quassus,** "shaken."] **—*n-* squash' er.**

[2]squash (skwŏsh) ***n-*** **1** any of various vines related to gourds, bearing a fleshy fruit. **2** fruit of this plant used as a vegetable. [American word from Algonquian **askut-asquash** meaning "vegetables eaten green."]

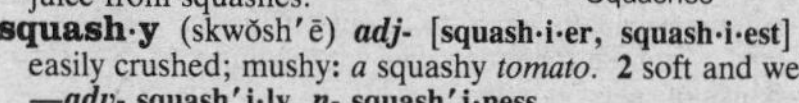
Squashes

squash bug ***n-*** large, dark-brown insect that sucks the juice from squashes.
squash·y (skwŏsh'ē) ***adj-*** [**squash·i·er, squash·i·est**] **1** easily crushed; mushy: *a* squashy *tomato.* **2** soft and wet. ***—adv-*** **squash'i·ly.** ***n-*** **squash'i·ness.**
squat (skwŏt) ***vi-*** [**squat·ted, squat·ting**] **1** to crouch on one's heels; also, to sit on the ground or floor with the legs drawn up closely to the body: *The boy* squatted *to pick up the pencil.* **2** to settle on land without the right to do so. **3** to settle on government land in order to get title to it. ***adj-*** [**squat·ter, squat·test**] **1** crouching. **2** short and stocky: *a* squat *figure.* ***n-*** a crouching on one's heels; also, a crouching position.
squat·ter (skwŏt'ər) ***n-*** **1** person who settles on land without legal right. **2** person who settles on public land to acquire ownership. **3** person or thing that sqauts.
squat·ty (skwŏt'ē) ***adj-*** [**squat·ti·er, squat·ti·est**] short and thick; stocky; dumpy; squat.
squaw (skwȯ) ***n-*** American Indian woman or wife (now considered an offensive term). [American word from Algonquian.]
squaw·fish (skwȯ'fĭsh') ***n-*** [*pl.* **squaw·fish; squaw·fish·es** (kinds of squawfish)] any of various large food fishes related to the minnows, common in rivers of the northern Pacific coast.
squawk (skwȯk) ***n-*** **1** loud, harsh cry. **2** *Slang* noisy, loud complaint or protest. ***vi-*** **1** to utter a loud, harsh cry: *The ducks* squawked *and the hens cackled.* **2** *Slang* to complain or protest loudly. ***—n-*** **squawk'er.**
squeak (skwēk) ***n-*** **1** weak, thin, shrill noise, like that of a mouse. **2** *Informal* escape; squeeze: *a tight* squeak. ***vi-*** **1** to make a weak, shrill noise: *Mice* squeak. **2** *Slang* to turn informer; squeal. **3** to pass or succeed by the narrowest margin: *He* squeaked *by the final exams.* ***vt-*** to utter in a weak, shrill tone: *The young children* squeaked *their lines.*
squeak·y (skwē'kē) ***adj-*** [**squeak·i·er, squeak·i·est**] making weak, thin, shrill sounds. ***—adv-*** **squeak'i·ly** ***n-*** **squeak'i·ness.**
squeal (skwēl) ***vi-*** **1** to utter a shrill, prolonged cry: *The pigs* squealed *at the intruder.* **2** *Slang* to tattle on another. ***vt-*** to utter with a shrill tone: *The child* squealed *the answer.* ***n-*** shrill, prolonged cry. ***—n-*** **squeal'er.**
squeam·ish (skwē'mĭsh) ***adj-*** **1** easily nauseated. **2** prudish; easily shocked. **3** too fussy about trifles; fastidious. ***—adv-*** **squeam'ish·ly.** ***n-*** **squeam'ish·ness.**
squee·gee (skwē'jē') ***n-*** **1** tool with a handle and a crosspiece that is fitted with a rubber edge or plate, for removing excess water in cleaning floors, windows, etc. **2** in photography, similar but smaller implement, or a device with a roller, used for wiping off excess moisture, for pressing a print close to the mount, etc. ***vt-*** [**squee·geed, squee·gee·ing**] to use a squeegee on.
squeeze (skwēz) ***vt-*** [**squeezed, squeez·ing**] **1** to put pressure on from the outside; press; also, to compress so as to extract juice: *He* squeezed *her hand. She* squeezed *oranges.* **2** to extract by or as if by pressure: *to* squeeze *juice from a lemon.* **3** to force by pressure; also, to crowd into a small space; cram: *She* squeezed *the papers into the small envelope. They* squeezed *the people into the hall.* **4** to oppress: *The feudal lord* squeezed *the peasants with heavy taxes.* **5** to narrow the margin of; reduce the amount of: *The tax increase* squeezes *our profits.* ***vi-*** **1** to make one's way by force; push; press: *He* squeezed *through the crowd.* **2** to give way or yield to pressure: *A down pillow* squeezes *easily.* **3** to ease into another traffic lane, especially before the pavement narrows. ***n-*** **1** a pressure: *Tom gave Bill's arm a* squeeze. **2** a hug; embrace. **3** a crowding together; crush; jam. **3** financial pressure. ***—n-*** **squeez'er.** ***adj-*** **squeez'a·ble.**
  a tight (or **close** or **narrow**) **squeeze** situation from which escape is difficult; predicament.
squeeze play ***n-*** baseball play in which the batter bunts the ball into fair territory, giving a runner on third base time to reach home plate safely and score a run.
squelch (skwĕlch) ***n-*** **1** *Informal* a crushing, silencing argument or reply. **2** a squashing sound: *the* squelch *of his boots in the slush.* ***vt-*** **1** *Informal* to silence by a crushing rebuke; subdue or suppress completely: *She* squelched *the rude audience.* **2** to crush down, smash, or squash. ***vi-*** to make a sound as if walking in wet shoes or through slush. ***—n-*** **squelch'er.**
squib (skwĭb) ***n-*** **1** a ball filled with gunpowder, or a firecracker, meant to explode in midair like a rocket. **2** broken firecracker that burns with a hissing, spitting sound instead of a loud bang. **3** sarcastic speech or article; lampoon.
squid (skwĭd) ***n-*** any of various sea animals having a cigar-shaped body with a fin on each side, ten arms of which two are much longer than the others, and a bony internal plate. Squids are mollusks.

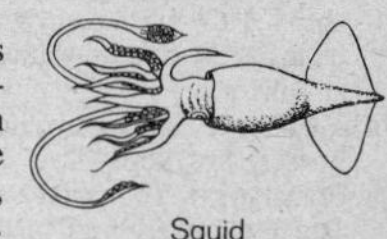
Squid

squint (skwĭnt) ***vi-*** **1** to close the eyes partly. **2** to look sideways. **3** to be cross-eyed. ***n-*** **1** partial closing of the eyes. **2** sidelong glance: *He eyed me with an angry* squint. **3** condition of being cross-eyed. ***—n-*** **squint'er.** ***adj-*** **squint'y.**
squire (skwīər) ***n-*** **1** formerly, young man who attended a knight, bore his shield or armor, and usually sought knighthood himself. **2** *chiefly Brit.* owner of a country estate; country gentleman. ***vt-*** [**squired, squir·ing**] to escort (a lady).
squirm (skwûrm) ***vi-*** to twist about; writhe; wriggle: *The little boy* squirmed *in embarrassment.* ***n-*** a twist; a wriggle. ***—adj-*** **squirm'y.**
squir·rel (skwûr'əl) ***n-*** **1** any of various small rodents, usually reddish or gray, with a bushy tail. Squirrels live mostly in trees and feed principally on grain and nuts. **2** fur of this animal. *as* ***modifier:*** *a* squirrel *cape.* ***adj-*** **squir'rel·like'.**

Gray squirrel, about 18 in. long

squirt (skwûrt) ***vi-*** **1** to gush from a small opening in a fine jet or stream; spurt; spray: *The lemon juice* squirted *in my eye.* ***vt-*** to force out in a fine jet or stream: *He* squirted *water from the hose.* ***n-*** **1** a small stream or jet spurted out: *a* squirt *of perfume.* **2** instrument used for spurting or spraying, such as a syringe. **3** *Slang* impudent young person. ***—n-*** **squirt'er.**

squish·y (skwĭsh′ ē) *Informal adj-* [**squish·i·er, squish·i·est**] **1** easily squashed; mushy. **2** soft and wet.

Sr symbol for strontium.

Sr. 1 senior. **2** sister. **3** señor.

SS or **S.S.** steamship.

SSE or **S.S.E.** south-southeast.

SSR or **S.S.R.** Soviet Socialist Republic.

SSW or **S.S.W.** south-southwest.

St. 1 saint. **2** street. **3** strait.

stab (stăb) *vt-* [**stabbed, stab·bing**] **1** to pierce with any pointed instrument or weapon. **2** to hurt the feelings of, by treachery, harsh words, or the like: *The children's jeers* stabbed *Tony to the heart.* *vi-* **1** to make a jabbing motion. **2** to wound a person's feelings. *n-* **1** piercing wound made by something pointed. **2** jabbing motion; jab; thrust. *—n-* **stab′ ber.**

have (or **make**) **a stab at** to make an effort at; try.

Sta·bat Ma·ter (stä′ bät′ mä′tər, -mā′tər) *n-* **1** thirteenth-century Latin hymn recounting the suffering of the Virgin Mary at the Crucifixion. **2** any of several musical settings to this narrative.

sta·bil·i·ty (stə bĭl′ ə tē) *n-* condition of being stable.

sta·bi·lize (stā′ bə līz′) *vt-* [**sta·bi·lized, sta·bi·liz·ing**] to make or keep stable. *—n-* **sta′ bi·li·za′ tion.**

sta·bi·liz·er (stā′ bə līz′ ər) *n-* **1** the fixed crosswise airfoil at the tail of an airplane, to which the elevators are attached. **2** any of various devices, consisting of or controlled by a gyroscope, that reduce the rolling of a ship. **3** *Chemistry* substance used to prevent unwanted changes in a compound. **4** any person or thing that stabilizes.

¹sta·ble (stā′ bəl) *n-* **1** building in which animals, especially horses, are kept. **2** a group of horses under a single ownership: *The prince had a large racing* stable. *vt-* [**sta·bled, sta·bling**] to put or keep in such a building: *We* stable *our horses here.* [from Old French **estable,** from Latin **stabulum** meaning "a standing place for animals," from **stāre,** "to stand (firm)."]

²sta·ble (stā′ bəl) *adj-* **1** not likely to change; durable. **2** not shaky or shifting: *a* stable *platform*; *a* stable *foundation.* **3** regular and predictable in behavior; not erratic; steady: *a* stable *personality.* **4** *Chemistry* of chemical compounds, not easily decomposed. **5** *Physics* of an atom or nucleus, not capable of spontaneous change. [from Latin **stabilis** meaning "firm; steady," from **stāre,** "to stand (firm)."] *—adv-* **sta′ bly.**

sta·ble·man (stā′ bəl mən, -măn′) *n-* [*pl.* **sta·ble·men**] person who works in a stable; hostler; groom. If this person is a boy, he is called a **stableboy.**

stac·ca·to (stə kä′ tō′) *adj- & adv-* **1** *Music* performed or to be performed in an abrupt, clear-cut manner with each note detached from the note that precedes or follows it. **2** abrupt; disconnected: *a* staccato *remark.* *n-* [*pl.* **stac·ca·tos**] note or passage performed in this manner.

Stacks of guns

stack (stăk) *n-* **1** a large, round pile: *a* stack *of straw.* **2** neat, orderly pile: *a* stack *of magazines.* **3** tall chimney; smokestack. **4** set of open bookshelves. **5 stacks** part of a library where most books are stored on shelves. **6** conical stand of three or more rifles with their muzzles together. **7** *Informal* (often **stacks**) large amount or number. *vt-* **1** to pile neatly; heap up. **2** *Slang* to arrange dishonestly.

sta·di·a (stā′ dē ə) *n-* in surveying, a method for determining the distance between two points by sighting through a telescope placed at one point, to a rod held vertically at the other point. The distance is proportional to the number of one-inch (or one-centimeter) intervals on the rod that can be seen between two horizontal lines in the telescope. *as* ***modifier****: a* stadia *rod.*

sta·di·um (stā′ dē əm) *n-* [*pl.* **sta·di·ums** or **sta·di·a** (-dē ə)] **1** field for athletic contests, surrounded or partially surrounded by permanent tiers of seats. **2** in ancient Greece, a unit of measurement usually equal to about 607 feet; also, a course for foot races with sloping banks of seats on both sides.

Staff

staff (stăf) *n-* [*pl.* **staffs** or **staves** (stāvz)] **1** long cane or stick, used for walking or defense: *a shepherd's* staff. **2** a rod as a sign of authority: *a bishop's* staff. **3** long, slender pole serving as a support or handle: *a flag* staff; *the* staff *of a spear.* **4** a prop; support: *Bread is the* staff *of life.* **5** [*pl.* **staffs**] (1) group of persons working as a unit: *The museum* staff *is made up of the director and his assistants.* (2) group of assistants working under a head: *the editor and his* staff. (3) in the armed forces, group of officers without combat duties or command but assisting a commander in his executive and administrative duties. **6** *Music* [*pl.* **staffs**] set of five lines and the spaces between them on which music is written. *vt-* to provide with or hire workers.

Stag, about 6 ft. high at shoulder

stag (stăg) *n-* **1** the full-grown male of some kinds of deer. **2** man who attends a social function unaccompanied by a woman. **3** social gathering where only men are present. *as* ***modifier****: a* stag *party.*

go stag to attend a social function unaccompanied by a woman.

stage (stāj) *n-* **1** raised platform or other part of a theater on which a play or other performance is acted. **2 the stage** profession of acting. **3** place or field of action; scene: *Europe has been the* stage *for many important battles.* **4** degree, phase, or period of development, growth, advancement, etc.: *He has reached an important* stage *in his career.* **5** stagecoach. *as* ***modifier****: a* stage *career.* *vt-* [**staged, stag·ing**] to prepare or produce for theatrical performance: *to* stage *an opera.*

stage·coach (stāj′ kōch′) *n-* in former times, a closed, horse-drawn coach that ran on a regular schedule and carried passengers, mail, and baggage.

Stagecoach

stage·craft (stāj′ krăft′) *n-* art or skill of creating or preparing works for performance in the theater.

stage fright *n-* feeling of fear or panic sometimes experienced by a person who is about to face an audience.

stage·hand (stāj′ hănd′) *n-* worker in a theater who moves scenery, operates lights, raises the curtain, etc.

stage-struck (stāj′ strŭk′) *adj-* fascinated by the life of the theater; especially, very eager to become an actor.

stage whisper *n-* loud whisper by an actor that is supposed to be overheard by the audience; hence, any loud whisper intended to be heard by others.

stag·ger (stăg′ ər) *vi-* **1** to move in an unsteady, swaying manner; reel; totter: *The wounded man* staggered *across the room.* **2** to be shocked, dazed, or stunned: *Our imagination* staggers *at the destruction caused by the earthquake.* *vt-* **1** to cause to sway, totter, or reel: *The heavy blows* staggered *the boxer.* **2** to cause to lose confidence or assurance; overwhelm; shock: *The loss of his fortune* staggered *him.* **3** to place in alternately arranged rows, series, etc.: *to* stagger *theater seats.* **4** to fix or set at different times: *to* stagger *traffic lights.* *n-* **1** unsteady or reeling motion. **2 staggers** or **blind staggers** (takes singular verb) disease of the nervous system that affects horses, sheep, cattle, etc., causing them to stagger and fall. *—n-* **stag′ger·er.** *adv-* **stag′ger·ing·ly:** *a* staggeringly *heavy blow.*

stag·ing (stā′ jĭng) *n-* **1** temporary structure of boards for support. **2** art or process of putting on a play.

stag·nant (stăg′ nənt) *adj-* **1** not flowing or moving; especially, stale from being motionless: *a* stagnant *pond; smoky,* stagnant *air.* **2** not active or brisk; sluggish: *a* stagnant *mind.* *—n-* **stag′nan·cy.** *adv-* **stag′nant·ly.**

stag·nate (stăg′ nāt′) *vi-* **[stag·nat·ed, stag·nat·ing]** to become motionless, stale, or sluggish; grow stagnant: *The water* stagnated *in the pond.* *—n-* **stag·na′ tion.**

stag·y (stā′ jē) *adj-* **[stag·i·er, stag·i·est]** suggestive of a theatrical performance; exaggerated and unnatural: *a* stagy *manner.* *—adv-* **stag′i·ly.** *n-* **stag′i·ness.**

staid (stād) *adj-* quiet and dignified; sedate: *a* staid *house;* staid *behavior.* *—adv-* **staid′ly.** *n-* **staid′ness.**

stain (stān) *vt-* **1** to spot, soil, or discolor, especially with a substance that soaks in: *He* stained *his tie with gravy.* **2** to color with a penetrating pigment: *He* stained *the wood a deep mahogany color.* **3** to dye (plant or animal tissue) with a special substance that produces a darker color in the parts or structures one wishes to examine under a microscope. **4** to harm or taint (someone's reputation, character, etc.); sully. *vi-* to become spotted, discolored, or dyed: *This cloth* stains *easily.* *n-* **1** soiled or discolored spot. **2** penetrating dye or pigment. **3** taint of guilt, wrongdoing, etc.: *a* stain *on his reputation.* *—adj-* **stain′a·ble.** *n-* **stain′er.** *adj-* **stain′less.**

stained glass *n-* glass that has been stained or colored by various methods, used widely for church windows.

stainless steel *n-* steel alloy that contains chromium and, often, nickel and is highly resistant to corrosion.

stair (stâr) *n-* **1** one of the steps in a flight of steps: *She tripped on the top* stair. **2** (usually **stairs**) flight of steps or a series of several flights of steps. *Hom-* stare.

below stairs *Brit.* the basement or lower part of a house, especially the part in which servants live.

stair·case (stâr′ kās′) *n-* flight or series of flights of stairs, together with banisters and supports; stairway.

stair·way (stâr′ wā′) *n-* flight of stairs or steps.

stake (stāk) *n-* **1** strong stick or post pointed at one end and fixed in the ground or in a solid surface as a marker or support. **2 the stake** in former times, the post to which a person condemned to death by burning was fastened; hence, death by this method of execution. **3** something of value risked, bet, or competed for. **4** interest or share, especially in a business venture. *vt-* **[staked, stak·ing] 1** to mark the limits of with sticks or posts: *to* stake *a plot of ground.* **2** to support with, or fasten to, a stick or post: *to* stake *tomato plants; to* stake *a horse.* **3** to wager; risk. **4** to provide with necessary funds, provisions, etc., especially for a business enterprise. *Hom-* steak.

at stake in jeopardy or hazard; risked. **pull up stakes** *Informal* to leave permanently; move on.

stake a claim to give notice of ownership by marking with, or as if with, a stake.

stake·hold·er (stāk′ hōl′ dər) *n-* person who holds the stakes of bettors until the final outcome is determined.

sta·lac·tite (stə lăk′ tīt′) *n-* stone formation resembling an icicle, hanging from the roof of a cave and formed by water seeping through and dissolving small amounts of limestone or similar rock.

sta·lag·mite (stə lăg′ mīt′) *n-* cone-shaped stone formation on the floor of a cave, formed by the dissolved minerals in water dripping from a stalactite.

stale (stāl) *adj-* **[stal·er, stal·est] 1** lacking former freshness, flavor, or strength: *a piece of* stale *bread; a glass of* stale *soda.* **2** worn out by repetition; no longer interesting or novel: *a* stale *joke.* **3** in poor condition as a result of lack of activity or training: *a* stale *athlete.* *vi-* **[staled, stal·ing]:** *The bread* staled *in the cupboard. A story* stales *after much repetition.* *vt-:* *Inactivity* staled *his skill.* *—adv-* **stale′ly.** *n-* **stale′ness.**

stale·mate (stāl′ māt′) *n-* **1** a deadlock; standstill. **2** in chess, a draw that results when any move that a player makes will place his king in check. *vt-* **[stale·mat·ed, stale·mat·ing]** to bring to a deadlock or standstill: *Sharp differences among us* stalemated *the talks.*

[1]**stalk** (stȯk, stŏk) *n-* **1** main stem of a nonwoody plant, or a stemlike part supporting a plant part, such as a leaf, blossom, etc. **2** any slender, rod-shaped structure, such as that on which the eye of a lobster is supported. [from Old English **stealc,** "high."] *Hom-* stock. *—adj-* **stalked.** *adj-* **stalk′less.**

Stalks

[2]**stalk** (stȯk, stŏk) *vt-* **1** to approach stealthily: *to* stalk *a deer.* **2** to move through silently and threateningly: *Fear* stalked *the city.* *vi-* to walk in a stiff, haughty manner: *The angry man* stalked *from the room.* *—n-* act of pursuing cautiously. [from a shortened form of Old English **(be)stealcian,** "to walk carefully," from **stealc,** "high." You step high when walking warily.] *Hom-* stock.

stalk·ing-horse (stȯ′ kĭng hȯrs′, -hôrs′) *n-* horse or figure of a horse behind which a hunter hides in stalking game; hence, anything used to hide one's real purpose.

[1]**stall** (stȯl) *n-* **1** enclosed space for an animal in a stable or barn. **2** booth or small enclosure in which merchandise is displayed or sold. **3** partly enclosed seat in a church. **4** *Brit.* orchestra seat near the front of a theater. **5** protective covering for a finger. **6** sudden, unintended stop of

Stalls in a stable

a vehicle, engine, etc.; also, of an airplane, a loss of speed and sudden drop in altitude. ***vt-*** **1** to place or keep in an individual enclosure: *to* stall *a horse for the night.* **2** to cause an unintended stop of: *I* stalled *the car on the hill.* ***vi-*** *His car* stalls *in cold weather.* [from Old English **st(e)all** meaning "standing place; stall."]

[2]**stall** (stôl) *Informal* ***vt-*** to delay, put off, or keep waiting by means of excuses, postponements, etc.: *to* stall *one's creditors because of lack of cash.* ***vi-***: *Stop* stalling *and pay up!* ***n-*** excuse or pretext intended to prevent or delay an action or outcome. [from a variant of earlier **stale** meaning "decoy," from Old French **estale.**]

stal·lion (stăl′ yən) ***n-*** male horse that has not been castrated.

stal·wart (stôl′ wərt) ***adj-*** **1** strong and sturdy. **2** courageous and steady: *a* stalwart *fighter for liberty.* ***n-*** **1** strong or brave person. **2** firm, loyal supporter or partisan. ***—adv-*** **stal′ wart·ly.** ***n-*** **stal′ wart·ness.**

sta·men (stā′ mən) ***n-*** pollen-bearing organ of a flower, consisting of an anther supported by a filament. For picture, see *flower.*

stam·i·na (stăm′ ə nə) ***n-*** power of endurance; strength.

stam·i·nate (stăm′ ə nət, stā′ mə nət, -nāt′) ***adj-*** having stamens; especially, having stamens but not pistils.

stam·mer (stăm′ ər) ***vi-*** to hesitate, falter, or repeat sounds or syllables in speaking: *He* stammers *when he is embarrased.* ***vt-***: *He* stammered *an apology.* ***n-***: *He speaks with a* stammer. ***—n-*** **stam′ mer·er.** ***adv-*** **stam′ mer·ing·ly**: *He speaks* stammeringly.

stamp (stămp) ***n-*** **1** object, such as a die, carved block, or piece of rubber, that is pressed against something to make a mark. **2** mark made by pressing such an object into or against a surface. **3** small piece of paper sold by the government and stuck on a letter, package, document, etc., to show that a fee or tax has been paid: *a postage* stamp; *a revenue* stamp. **4** downward blow with the sole of the foot, a die, or a marker. **5** characteristic mark or impression: *His manners show the* stamp *of breeding.* **6** special quality: *Men of his* stamp *are rare.* ***vt-*** **1** to mark with a design or impression by, or as if by, means of a die or other device that is pressed against something: *He* stamped *the paper with a seal.* **2** to put a postage stamp or similar official paper on: *to* stamp *a letter.* **3** to set (one's foot, hoof, etc.) down heavily and sharply. **4** to strike or trample with the bottom of the foot: *to* stamp *the ground impatiently.* **5** to mark; indicate: *His manners* stamp *him as a man of good breeding.* **6** to shape or cut by pressure of a die or similar device: *to* stamp *automobile parts.* **7** to crush or grind (ore, rock, etc.) into powder. ***vi-*** **1** to set down the foot with a heavy, forceful motion: *He* stamped *on the ground.* **2** to walk with heavy, noisy steps.

stamp out **1** to put out (a fire) by trampling it. **2** to put an end to by forceful action: *to* stamp out *crime.*

stam·pede (stăm pēd′) ***n-*** **1** sudden, wild running away, as of a herd of animals. **2** any sudden rush or movement of a crowd: *a* stampede *for the exit.* ***vt-*** **[stam·ped·ed, stam·ped·ing]** to cause to panic and run wildly: *to* stampede *a crowd.* ***vi-***: *The crowd* stampeded.

stance (stăns) ***n-*** **1** manner of standing; posture. **2** in baseball or golf, the position taken by a player as he prepares to strike the ball.

[1]**stanch** (stônch, stănch) ***vt-*** **1** to stop the flow of: *to* stanch *blood from a wound.* **2** to stop the flow of blood from: *to* stanch *a wound.* [from Old French **estanchier,** from Late Latin **stancāre,** from Latin **stagnāre** meaning "cease to flow."] ***—n-*** **stanch′ er.**

[2]**stanch** (stônch, stănch) ***adj-*** **[stanch·er, stanch·est]** staunch. [from [1]**stanch,** "not leaky."] ***—adv-*** **stanch·ly.**

stan·chion (stăn′ chən) ***n-*** **1** upright post or support, as in a window. **2** framework placed around an animal's neck to confine it in a stall. ***vt-***: *to* stanchion *a window; to* stanchion *a cow.*

stand (stănd) ***vi-*** **[stood** (sto͝od), **stand·ing]** **1** to rest on the feet, or on other supporting part or parts, in an upright position: *We* stood *in the sun all day. The broom* stood *in a corner.* **2** to rise to such a position: *Please* stand *when I call your name.* **3** to be situated: *Our house* stands *on the top of the hill.* **4** to remain in one place or position: *The pile of rubbish* stood *in the yard for days.* **5** to be in a certain position, condition, or attitude: *to* stand *acquitted of a crime; to* stand *prepared for action.* **6** to occupy a place or position relative to others: *to* stand *first in line; to* stand *high in one's class.* **7** to remain firm or in force: *The rule* stands. **8** to take a position in defense or support of someone or something: *to* stand *behind a candidate; to* stand *for law and order.* ***vt-*** **1** to set in an upright position: *to* stand *books on a shelf.* **2** to bear; endure; tolerate: *She cannot* stand *the cold. I can't* stand *that noise!* **3** to remain firm against; withstand: *Flimsy materials cannot* stand *heavy pressure.* **4** to be subjected to; undergo: *to* stand *a heavy penalty; to* stand *trial.* **5** to pay for: *to* stand *the expenses of a party.* ***n-*** **1** stop or halt, especially to maintain a position or offer resistance: *The retreating army made a* stand *at the river.* **2** place or post in which one remains erect. **3** a position or attitude in regard to something: *What is your* stand *on this question?* **4** rack, pedestal, or small table for holding or supporting something: *a music* stand; *a* plant *stand.* **5** booth or counter from which something is sold: *a fruit* stand; *a cigar* stand. **6** platform or similar raised structure for a special purpose: *the witness* stand *in a courtroom.* **7** group of upright growing plants: *a* stand *of maples; a* stand *of wheat.* **8 stands** outdoor seats in tiers; grandstand.

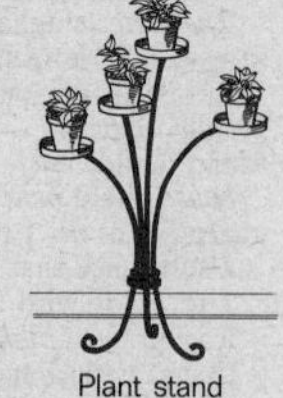
Plant stand

stand a chance to be likely to succeed.

stand by **1** to give support to; aid. **2** to wait in readiness.

stand for **1** to take the place of; represent; symbolize: *"U.S."* stands for *"United States."* **2** to put up with; tolerate: *I won't* stand for *such nonsense!*

stand in for to take the place of, or be ready to take the place of: *to* stand in for *a sick actor.*

stand off to repel (an attack, enemy, etc.).

stand on **1** to be based on. **2** to insist firmly on.

stand out **1** to project; protrude: *figures that* stand out *from a background.* **2** to be outstanding or noticeable.

stand over to stand near in order to watch closely.

stand up **1** to withstand wear, stress, etc. **2** *Slang* to fail deliberately to keep an appointment or date with.

stand up for to be firm or loyal in support of.

stand up to to face or fight with courage.

stan·dard (stăn′ dərd) ***n-*** **1** generally accepted level or example of excellence, considered as a basis of comparison. **2** established measure of weight, length, value, etc. **3** flag, banner, or figure used as an emblem: *a naval* standard. **4** upright support: *a lamp on a tall* standard. ***adj-*** **1** conforming to or serving as a basis or model for measurement, value, comparison, etc.: *a* standard *mile;* standard *time.* **2** of recognized excellence or authority: *a* standard *reference work.* **3** widely used or practiced, and considered generally acceptable by those whose judgment is regarded as authoritative: *to speak* standard *English.*

standard conditions ***n-*** a temperature of 0°C **(standard temperature)** and a pressure of 760 mm **(standard pressure)**, used for making many scientific measurements.

stan·dard·ize (stăn′ dər dīz′) ***vt-*** **[stan·dard·ized, stan·dard·iz·ing]** **1** to make uniform or standard in size, quality, etc.: *to* standardize *automobile parts.* **2** to regulate or test by a standard: *to* standardize *a pressure gauge.* **—*n-* stan′ dard·i·za′ tion.**

standard of living ***n-*** degree to which the economic needs or wants of a person or group are satisfied. A country has a **high standard of living** when the amount of goods per person is comparatively high, and a **low standard of living** when this amount is low.

standard time ***n-*** system of keeping time in 24 time zones, east and west, around the earth. All clocks in one time zone are set one hour ahead of the next time zone to the west. The seven time zones used throughout the United States are (from east to west): Eastern, Central, Mountain, Pacific, **Yukon, Alaska** (same as **Hawaii**), and **Bering.**

stand·by (stănd′ bī′) ***n-*** [*pl.* **stand·bys**] person or thing ready to be called on or used in an emergency.

stand·ee (stăn′ dē′) ***n-*** person who must stand on a bus, at a play, etc., because he hasn't a seat.

stand-in (stănd′ ĭn′) ***n-*** in motion pictures and television, a person who takes the place of an actor while equipment is being adjusted or during hazardous scenes; hence, anyone who substitutes for another.

stand·ing (stăn′ dĭng) ***n-*** **1** relative position or rank: *What is his* standing *in his high school class?* **2** repute; good name: *a man of* standing *in his profession.* **3** duration: *a habit of long* standing.

standing army ***n-*** army that is permanently prepared for action, especially during times of peace.

standing room ***n-*** room or space available for standees.

stand·off (stănd′ ôf′, -ŏf′) ***n-*** **1** deadlock; tie. **2** condition in which one set of circumstances, facts, etc., counterbalances or offsets another. **3** cold, distant behavior.

stand·off·ish (stănd′ ôf′ ĭsh, -ŏf′ ĭsh) ***adj-*** coldly distant; reserved; aloof. **—*n-* stand′ off′ ish·ness.**

stand·pipe (stănd′ pīp′) ***n-*** vertical pipe or high tower into which water is pumped to provide pressure in the water system of an apartment house, factory, etc.

stand·point (stănd′ point′) ***n-*** basis or standard from which things are considered or judged; point of view.

stand·still (stănd′ stĭl′) ***n-*** stop; halt.

stank (stăngk) *p.t.* of **stink.**

stan·nic (stăn′ ĭk) ***adj-*** of or containing tin, especially in compounds where it has a valence of four.

stan·nous (stăn′ əs) ***adj-*** of or containing tin, especially in compounds where it has a valence of two.

stan·za (stăn′ zə) ***n-*** part of a poem consisting of an organized group of lines, often having the same rhyme scheme and meter as the other parts of the same poem.

staph·y·lo·coc·cus (stăf′ ə lō kŏk′ əs) ***n-*** [*pl.* **staph·y·lo·coc·ci** (-kŏk′ sī′, -kŏk′ sē)] any of various spherical bacteria that usually form irregularly shaped clusters.

¹sta·ple (stā′ pəl) ***n-*** **1** small, U-shaped piece of metal driven into wood or similar material to fasten wires, a hook, bolt, etc. **2** thin, bracket-shaped piece of wire pressed into papers, cloth, leather, etc., as a fastening device. ***vt-*** **[sta·pled, sta·pling]:** *Please* staple *the card to the large sheet.* [from Old English **stapol** meaning "pillar; post; a step."]

for WOOD
for PAPER
Staples

²sta·ple (stā′ pəl) ***n-*** **1** principal product of a place. **2** very important or major element: *The election was the* staple *of conversation.* **3** raw material for manufacture. **4** fiber of cotton, wool, flax, etc., before it is spun or twisted into thread. **5** something produced regularly and in large amounts because of constant need or demand: *Sugar is a* staple. *as* ***modifier:*** *a* staple *product; a* staple *topic.* [from Old French **estaple,** from early Dutch **stapel** meaning "a post; support."]

sta·pler (stā′ plər) ***n-*** device used to press staples into paper, cardboard, cloth, etc.

star (stär) ***n-*** **1** any heavenly body visible from the earth as an apparently fixed point of light in the clear night sky. **2** *Astronomy* any of the gaseous heavenly bodies of great mass that shine by their own light, as distinguished from comets, meteors, nebulae, plants, and satellites. The stars are at such a distance from the earth that they appear as points of light, and most can be seen only with the aid of a telescope. **3** figure, usually with five or six points, that represents or resembles one of these bodies. **4** asterisk. **5** any of the heavenly bodies supposedly having an influence on human events; hence, fate; destiny: *It was not in our* stars *to win today.* **6** any person who is outstanding in his field; especially, a leading actor or actress. *as* ***modifier:*** *a* star *shape; a* star *performer.* ***vi-*** **[starred, star·ring]** to appear in a leading role: *My favorite actor* stars *in that play.* ***vt-*** **1** to mark or adorn with a star or stars. **2** to present or feature in a leading role. **—*adj-* star′ less.** ***adj-*** **star′ like′.**

Stars

star·board (stär′ bərd) ***n-*** the right side of a ship or boat as one faces the bow (for picture, see *aft*). ***adj-*** on or moving toward this side: *a* starboard *cabin; a* starboard *breeze.* ***adv-:*** *Move* starboard *a little.*

starch (stärch) ***n-*** **1** white, odorless, tasteless carbohydrate that is an important source of nourishment. It is present in most plants and is especially plentiful in grain and potatoes. **2** commercial preparation of this substance, used to stiffen cloth. **3** *Informal* energy; vigor; stamina. ***vt-*** to stiffen with commercial starch: *to* starch *a shirt.*

starch·y (stär′ chē) ***adj-*** **[starch·i·er, starch·i·est]** **1** containing much starch: *Potatoes are a* starchy *food.* **2** stiffened with starch: *a* starchy *collar.* **3** stiff and formal in manner; not friendly. **—*n-* starch′ i·ness.**

stare (stâr) ***vi-*** **[stared, star·ing]** **1** to look or gaze intently or fixedly with wide open eyes, because of surprise, curiosity, etc.: *to* stare *at a strange sight.* **2** to show brightly or conspicuously; glare: *Bright colors* stared *from the gaudy paintings.* ***vt-*** to affect in some way with a fixed, intent look: *She* stared *him into silence.* ***n-*** fixed gaze with wide-open eyes. ***Hom-*** stair. **—*n-* star′ er.**

stare down (or **out of countenance**) to make uneasy by staring.

stare (one) in the face to be right in front of one's eyes; be perfectly plain and clear.

star·fish (stär′ fĭsh′) ***n-*** [*pl.* **star·fish; star·fish·es** (kinds of starfish)] any of various star-shaped sea animals with five or more arms.

Starfish, 3—5 in. across

star·gaze (stär′ gāz′) ***vi-*** **[star·gazed, star·gaz·ing]** **1** to gaze or look at the stars, especially because one is interested in astronomy or astrology. **2** to daydream. **—*n-* star′ gaz′ er.**

fāte, făt, dâre, bärn; bē, bĕt, mêre; bīte, bĭt; nōte, hŏt, môre, dȯg; fŭn, fûr; to͞o, bo͝ok; oil; out; tar; thin; then; hw for wh as in *wh*at; zh for s as in u*s*ual; ə for a, e, i, o, u, as in *a*go, lin*e*n, per*i*l, at*o*m, min*u*s

stark (stärk) *adj-* [**stark·er, stark·est**] **1** unadorned; bare. **2** bleak; desolate; barren: *a* stark *scene.* **3** sheer; utter; absolute: *She was speechless with* stark *terror.* **4** rigid: *to be* stark *with cold.* ***adv-*** completely; totally: *He is* stark *blind.* **—*adv-* stark′ ly.** ***n-*** **stark′ ness.**

star·let (stär′ lət) *Informal* ***n-*** young motion-picture actress who has small roles but receives much publicity.

star·light (stär′ līt′) ***n-*** light given by the stars.

star·ling (stär′ lĭng) ***n-*** any of various birds with dark, glossy, iridescent feathers that are speckled in winter.

Starling, about 8 1/2 in. long

star·lit (stär′ lĭt′) ***adj-*** lighted by the stars: *a* starlit *evening.*

star-of-Beth·le·hem (stär′ əv bĕth′ lĭ hĕm′) ***n-*** plant related to the lilies, with clusters of star-shaped white flowers and narrow leaves.

star of Bethlehem ***n-*** large star which, according to the New Testament, guided the Magi to the manger of Jesus in Bethlehem.

Star of David ***n-*** six-pointed star, used as the symbol of Judaism and Israel.

star·ry (stär′ ē) ***adj-*** [**star·ri·er, star·ri·est**] **1** showing or having many stars: *a* starry *sky*; *a* starry *night.* **2** shining like stars; sparkling; bright: *her* starry *eyes.* **3** shaped like a star. **—*n-* star′ ri·ness.**

star·ry-eyed (stär′ ē īd′) ***adj-*** looking on the bright side of things; naively trusting and optimistic.

Stars and Bars ***n-*** (takes singular or plural verb) first flag of the Confederacy, having three bars of alternating red and white and a blue field with white stars in a circle, each star representing a seceded State.

Stars and Stripes ***n-*** (takes singular or plural verb) the flag of the United States, with thirteen alternating red and white stripes representing the original colonies and, in the upper left corner, a blue field covered with white stars representing each State.

Star-Span·gled Banner (stär spăng′ gəld) ***n-*** **1** the Stars and Stripes. **2** the national anthem of the United States, the words of which were written by Francis Scott Key in 1814.

start (stärt) ***vi-*** **1** to begin to go somewhere or do something; set out: *to* start *on a journey*; *to* start *in a new business.* **2** to have a beginning; commence: *Classes* start *at nine o'clock.* **3** to make a sudden, involuntary movement of surprise, pain, shock, etc.: *He* started *at a loud noise.* **4** to spring or leap forth suddenly: *The rabbit* started *from the underbrush.* **5** of a nail, screw, etc., to become loosened. ***vt-*** **1** to put into operation or action; set going: *to* start *a clock.* **2** to bring into being; originate: *to* start *a rumor*; *to* start *an argument.* **3** to begin; commence: *to* start *a course in French.* **4** to cause or help to begin an enterprise or activity: *to* start *a friend in business*; *to* start *a traveler on the right road.* **5** to enter in a contest, game, etc.: *to* start *a horse in a race.* **6** to rouse into motion, especially from a place of concealment; flush: *to* start *a rabbit from its burrow.* **7** to cause (a nail, screw, etc.) to loosen. ***n-*** **1** beginning. **2** sudden involuntary movement: *a* start *of surprise*; *to wake with a* start. **3** lead or advantage: *He has a* start *of two miles over the others.* **4** assistance or opportunity in beginning an activity or enterprise: *to give someone a* start *in a new career.* **5** brief spurt of motion or activity.

to start with as a beginning; in the first place.

start·er (stär′ tər) ***n-*** **1** person or thing that starts an activity or undertaking: *He was a slow* starter, *but he soon caught up with the others.* **2** device that sets a machine or engine in operation; self-starter. **3** person who gives the signal for the start of a race. **4** person who dispatches buses, taxicabs, etc., according to a schedule.

starting point ***n-*** place from which something or someone starts out: *the* starting point *of a journey.*

star·tle (stär′ təl) ***vt-*** [**star·tled, star·tling**] **1** to cause to move suddenly in surprise, alarm, etc.: *That loud noise* startled *me.* **2** to fill with surprise or alarm; shock: *Her boldness* startles *me.* ***vi-***: *She* startles *easily.*

star·tling (stärt′ lĭng) ***adj-*** causing alarm or surprise; shocking; astonishing: *a* startling *discovery.* **—*adv-* star′ tling·ly**: *a* startlingly *loud noise.*

star·va·tion (stär vā′ shən) ***n-*** a starving or being starved.

starve (stärv) ***vi-*** [**starved, starv·ing**] **1** to die or suffer from lack of food. **2** *Informal* to be very hungry: *I ate a light lunch, and now I'm* starving! ***vt-*** to cause to die, suffer, weaken, etc., from lack of food: *to* starve *a prisoner to death*; *to* starve *the enemy into submission.*

starve for to have great need for; long for; hunger.

starve·ling (stärv′ lĭng) ***n-*** person, animal, or plant that is thin or weak from lack of nourishment. *as* ***modifier***: *a* starveling *poet.*

state (stāt) ***n-*** **1** condition of a person or thing: *a* state *of good health*; *a* state *of confusion.* **2** *Informal* excited mental or emotional condition: *She is in such a* state *today!* **3** body of people united under one government; commonwealth; nation. **4** powers, organization, government, or territory of such a body of people: *to defend one's* state; *to surround a* state. **5** (often **State**) one of the main political and geographical subdivisions of the United States and certain other nations. **6** dignity and great ceremony; pomp: *to receive an ambassador in* state. *as* ***modifier***: *a* state *document*; *a* state *dinner.* ***vt-*** [**stat·ed, stat·ing**] to express in words; declare; set forth: *to* state *an opinion.*

lie in state of a distinguished person, to be on public and formal display before burial.

state bank ***n-*** **1** bank owned or operated by a sovereign state. **2** (often **State Bank**) bank chartered and regulated by the State in which it is located. See also *national bank.*

state·craft (stāt′ krăft′) ***n-*** art or skill of managing the political affairs of a nation; statesmanship.

stat·ed (stā′ təd) ***adj-*** **1** fixed; regular: *a* stated *amount.* **2** announced; declared: *his* stated *motives.*

state·hood (stāt′ hŏŏd′) ***n-*** condition of being a state; especially, official standing as one of the States of the United States of America: *Alaska was admitted to* statehood *in 1959.*

State·house or **state·house** (stāt′ hous′) ***n-*** building in which the business of a State legislature is conducted; State capitol. Also **State House.**

state·less (stāt′ ləs) ***adj-*** having no officially recognized nationality; lacking citizenship in any country: *a* stateless *immigrant.* **—*n-* state′ less·ness.**

state·ly (stāt′ lē) ***adj-*** [**state·li·er, state·li·est**] having a grand manner or appearance; impressive; dignified: *a* stately *walk*; *a* stately *palace.* **—*n-* state′ li·ness.**

state·ment (stāt′ mənt) ***n-*** **1** act of stating or declaring something; declaration: *his* statement *of the facts.* **2** something stated in speech or writing: *All these* statements *are correct.* **3** organized report or summary, especially on financial matters: *a* bank *statement.*

State police ***n-*** **1** police force under the jurisdiction of a State rather than that of a city or local municipality. **2** national police force of a totalitarian government.

state·room (stāt′ rōōm′) ***n-*** luxurious bedroom or private suite on a passenger ship or railroad car.

state·side (stāt′ sīd′) *Informal* ***adj-*** of, located in, or directed toward the continental United States, as contrasted with distant or overseas places: *The airline's* stateside *offices are in San Francisco.* ***adv-***: *He will return* stateside *in a month.*

states·man (stāts′ mən) ***n-*** [*pl.* **states·men**] person skilled and usually active in government and public affairs. —***adj-*** **states′ man·like′.** ***n- fem.*** **states′ wom′ an.**

states·man·ship (stāts′ mən shĭp′) ***n-*** skill of a statesman in managing public affairs.

state socialism ***n-*** limited form of socialism that may include government control or regulation of key industries, socialized medicine, state support of the aged and disabled, etc.

states' rights ***n-*** the rights and powers not specifically assigned by the Constitution of the United States to the Federal government nor denied by it to the individual States; especially, these rights interpreted as giving the greatest possible powers to the States' governments.

state-wide (stāt′ wīd′) ***adj-*** occurring in or affecting an entire State: *a* state-wide *housing shortage.*

stat·ic (stăt′ ĭk) ***adj-*** **1** not moving or changing; remaining the same; inactive: *a* static *condition.* **2** of or relating to statics. **3** produced by weight alone, not by motion: *the* static *pressure of a liquid.* **4** in electricity, of or relating to electrical charges at rest, as distinguished from an electric current. ***n-*** interference or noises produced in a radio or television receiver by electrical discharges such as lightning or those resulting from the operation of electrical equipment; also, the electrical discharges or disturbances producing these interferences or noises. —***adv-*** **stat′i·cal·ly.**

static electricity ***n-*** **1** electric charge on an object, resulting from the addition, subtraction, or dislocation of electrons. **2** sudden movement of electrons from one object to another, often as a spark or a lightning flash.

stat·ics (stăt′ ĭks) ***n-*** (takes singular verb) branch of physics that deals with forces in equilibrium on bodies at rest, or within structures.

sta·tion (stā′ shən) ***n-*** **1** place or position, especially an assigned or customary one, in which a person or thing stands or remains: *the guard's* station *at the gate.* **2** official place for those performing a particular service or duty; headquarters: *a police* station; *an overseas military* station. **3** building or spot used as a regular stopping place for railroad trains, buses, etc.; terminal; depot. **4** the equipment or place used for broadcasting radio or television programs. **5** rank or standing in life or society: *a man of high* station. **6** in Australia or New Zealand, a ranch or farm on which sheep or cattle are raised and kept. ***vt-*** to place in or assign to a certain position: *to* station *a guard at the gate.*

station agent ***n-*** person having official duties at a railroad station, bus depot, etc.

sta·tion·ar·y (stā′ shən ĕr′ ē) ***adj-*** **1** not moving; motionless: *The traffic was* stationary *during the parade.* **2** not movable; fixed: *a* stationary *bookcase.* **3** not changing in size, numbers, conditions, etc. ***Hom-*** stationery.

stationary front ***n-*** in meteorology, a front formed when two air masses of different kinds meet, and each blocks the normal movement of the other.

stationary orbit ***n-*** orbit of an earth satellite moving in such a direction and at such speed that its position above a point on the earth's surface remains the same.

station break ***n-*** in radio and television, a pause during which the name of the station is announced.

sta·tion·er (stā′ shən ər) ***n-*** person who deals in stationery and similar merchandise.

sta·tion·er·y (stā′ shən ĕr′ ē) ***n-*** **1** paper and envelopes, especially those used for writing letters. **2** materials used in writing, school work, office work, etc., such as paper, notebooks, pencils, and pens. ***Hom-*** stationary.

station house ***n-*** police station.

sta·tion·mas·ter (stā′ shən măs′ tər) ***n-*** person in charge of a railroad station.

station wagon ***n-*** automobile having one or more folding or removable rear seats for carrying additional baggage or passengers.

sta·tis·tic (stə tĭs′ tĭk) ***n-*** single statistical item.

sta·tis·ti·cal (stə tĭs′ tĭ kəl) ***adj-*** of or having to do with statistics. —***adv-*** **sta·tis′ ti·cal·ly.**

stat·is·ti·cian (stăt′ əs tĭsh′ ən) ***n-*** person trained or skilled in the science of statistics and engaged in it as a profession.

sta·tis·tics (stə tĭs′ tĭks) ***n-*** **1** (takes plural verb) facts and figures gathered to give information about a particular subject: *traffic* statistics. **2** (takes singular verb) science of gathering and interpreting facts and figures.

stat·u·ar·y (stăch′ ōō ĕr′ ē) ***n-*** [*pl.* **stat·u·ar·ies**] **1** statues collectively; also, a collection of statues. **2** the art of sculpturing statues.

stat·ue (stăch′ ōō) ***n-*** three-dimensional representation of a person or thing sculptured, modeled, or cast.

Statue of Liberty ***n-*** huge figure of a woman holding aloft a torch in her hand, located in the Harbor of New York City on Liberty Island. It was presented as a gift by the French people to the United States in 1884.

stat·u·esque (stăch′ ōō ĕsk′) ***adj-*** having the beauty, proportions, or formal dignity of a statue: *a* statuesque *queen.* —***adv-*** **stat′ u·esque′ ly.** ***n-*** **stat′ u·esque′ ness.**

stat·u·ette (stăch′ ōō ĕt′) ***n-*** little statue.

stat·ure (stăch′ ər) ***n-*** **1** height of a person in a standing position: *a man of average* stature. **2** standing or achievement resulting from development, effort, or natural qualities: *a man of great moral* stature.

sta·tus (stā′ təs, stăt′ əs) ***n-*** **1** position or rank of a person or group in relation to others; standing: *his high* status *in the community*; *the team's low* status *in the league.* **2** general state, condition, or stage of development: *What is the present* status *of the negotiations?* **3** desirable position or rank: *He tried to achieve* status *by making money.* *as* **modifier**: *Fred's car is his* status *symbol.*

status quo (kwō′) ***n-*** condition or situation now existing.

stat·ute (stăch′ ōōt′) ***n-*** law or ordinance enacted by a lawmaking body; official decree or rule.

statute book ***n-*** the record or collection of all the statutes enacted by a city, State, etc.

statute mile ***n-*** mile having a length of 5,280 feet, used as an established measure of land distance in the United States. See also *mile.*

stat·u·tor·y (stăch′ ə tôr′ ē) ***adj-*** **1** of, relating to, or constituting a statute or law: *a* statutory *decree.* **2** defined, enacted, or regulated by statute or law.

staunch (stónch) ***adj-*** [**staunch·er, staunch·est**] **1** loyal and steadfast; dependable: *a* staunch *friend.* **2** resolute and vigorous: *to put up a* staunch *defense.* **3** well and sturdily built; sound: *a* staunch *ship.* —***adv-*** **staunch′ ly.** ***n-*** **staunch′ ness.**

stave (stāv) ***n-*** **1** one of the flat, curved, flexible strips of wood forming the sides of a barrel, cask, or bucket. **2** heavy stick; staff; cudgel. **3** stanza or verse. **4** *Music* staff. ***vt-*** [**staved** or **stove** (stōv), **stav·ing**] to smash or knock (a hole, break, etc.) in something: *The heavy waves* stove *a hole in the side of the ship.*

stave in to break by forcing inward; crush; smash.

stave off to keep back or drive away; ward off: *to* stave off *defeat*; *to* stave off *disease*.

staves (stāvz) *pl.* of **staff.**

[1]**stay** (stā) ***vi-*** **1** to remain in one place; wait: *He* stayed *after the others left.* **2** to continue in a specific condition; keep on being: *The weather* stayed *hot. She* stayed *in good health.* **3** to dwell for a time; be a temporary resident or guest: *to* stay *at a hotel.* **4** to keep going; endure: *to* stay *through the course of the entire race.* ***vt-*** **1** to hold or keep back: *to* stay *one's hunger.* **2** to postpone; delay; put off: *to* stay *a sentence of execution.* **3** to last or keep going through: *to* stay *the course of a race.* ***n-*** **1** period of temporary residence or visit: *a short* stay *in France.* **2** postponement; delay: *a* stay *of execution.* [from Old French **ester,** from Latin **stāre** meaning "to stand."] **—*n-* stay′ er.**

[2]**stay** (stā) ***n-*** **1** something that supports; prop. **2** thin strip of metal, plastic, or, formerly, whalebone, used for stiffening corsets, shirt collars, etc. **3 stays** *chiefly Brit.* firm, stiff corset or similar garment. ***vt-*** to give support to; hold up; steady: *to* stay *someone in low spirits.* [from Old French **estai** meaning "a prop," probably from a Germanic word related to [3]**stay.**]

[3]**stay** (stā) ***n-*** rope or strong wire used as a brace or support, especially for a ship's mast or spar. ***vt-*** to brace or support with such a rope or wire. [from Old English **stæg** meaning "a rope for supporting the mast."]

staying power ***n-*** strength to endure; stamina.

stay·sail (stā′ səl, -sāl′) ***n-*** any three-sided sail attached to a stay.

stead (stĕd) ***n-*** usual or expected place: *My sister went in my* stead.

stand (one) in good stead to be useful to one.

stead·fast (stĕd′ făst′) ***adj-*** **1** firmly fixed; not moving or shifting: *a* steadfast *gaze.* **2** not fickle or changing; constant; loyal: *his* steadfast *faith.* **—*adv-* stead′ fast′ ly. *n-* stead′ fast′ ness.**

stead·y (stĕd′ ē) ***adj-*** [**stead·i·er, stead·i·est**] **1** firmly fixed or supported; secure; stable: *That table is not* steady. **2** continuing without a break or change; uniform; constant: *a* steady *gain.* **3** not easily excited or agitated; calm: *a* steady *temperament*; steady *nerves.* **4** serious and dependable in one's work, conduct, etc.; reliable: *a* steady *young man.* ***vt-*** [**stead·ied, stead·y·ing**]: *I'll* steady *the ladder. Having this responsibility may* steady *the men.* ***vi-***: *The wheel* steadied *in his hands.* **—*adv-* stead′ i·ly. *n-* stead′ i·ness.**

go steady *Informal* of a young man and woman, to have dates with each other only.

steady-state theory ***n-*** theory that new matter is being continuously created throughout the universe, so that as the universe expands its average density remains the same. See also *expanding universe.*

steak (stāk) ***n-*** slice of beef, game, or fish for broiling or frying; also, a large patty of chopped beef to broil or fry. ***Hom-*** stake.

steal (stēl) ***vt-*** [**stole** (stōl), **stol·en** (stō′ lən), **steal·ing**] (in sense 3 considered intransitive when the direct object is implied but not expressed) **1** to take by theft; take without right or permission: *to* steal *a car.* **2** to take or get for oneself by secret, sly, or artful means: *to* steal *a glance.* **3** in baseball, to advance to (second base, third base, or home) by running when the ball has not been hit or is not otherwise in play. ***vi-*** **1** to engage in theft: *to lie, cheat, and* steal. **2** to move secretly or very quietly: *She* stole *about on tiptoe. A gentle breeze* stole *through the grass.* ***n-*** **1** the act of taking something unrightfully or by stealth. **2** *Informal* something obtained at an extremely low price; great bargain. ***Hom-*** steel.

stealth (stĕlth) ***n-*** secret or sly means or action.

stealth·y (stĕl′ thē) ***adj-*** [**stealth·i·er, stealth·i·est**] secret, sly, or very quiet in action or manner; furtive: *the cat's* stealthy *approach*; *a* stealthy *glance.* **—*adv-* stealth′ i·ly. *n-* stealth′ i·ness.**

steam (stēm) ***n-*** **1** hot, invisible vapor formed by water heated to its boiling point. It is used under pressure as a source of power for engines and other machinery. **2** visible mass of tiny water drops formed when this vapor cools: *A cloud of* steam *rose from the spout of the kettle.* **3** power generated by the vapor produced by boiling water. **4** *Informal* any effort or energy that produces motion or effective results: *We got there under our own* steam. *as* ***modifier***: *a* steam *engine*; steam *power.* ***vi-*** **1** to give off visible vapor: *The kettle* steamed. **2** to rise or pass off as visible vapor: *Moisture* steamed *from the ground.* **3** to procede by means of, or as if by means of, a steam engine: *The ship* steamed *away.* **4** *Informal* to be furious or annoyed; fume. ***vt-*** to treat or prepare by exposure to heated water vapor: *to* steam *a wrinkled coat*; *to* steam *vegetables.*

full steam ahead with great speed or energy. **let** (or **blow**) **off steam** to express or relieve strong, pent-up feelings. **steamed up** *Informal* angry; annoyed.

steam up (or **over**) to become covered with condensed water vapor: *The kitchen windows* steamed up.

steam·boat (stēm′ bōt′) ***n-*** steamship.

steam engine ***n-*** engine driven by the pressure of hot steam, especially on a piston that moves back and forth in a cylinder.

steam·er (stē′ mər) ***n-*** **1** steamship. **2** engine, vehicle, etc., driven by steam. **3** container in which things are cooked by steam. **4** clam with a thin, narrow shell, usually cooked by steaming.

steamer rug ***n-*** warm, sturdy blanket used especially by passengers who sit in chairs on the open ship deck.

steam·fit·ter (stēm′ fĭt′ ər) ***n-*** person who installs or repairs steam pipes or similar equipment.

steam·rol·ler (stēm′ rō′ lər) ***n-*** **1** steam-driven mechanical device with a large, cylindrical roller, used to press down and level the surface of roads and other paved areas. **2** *Informal* any power used to crush opposition. ***vt-***: *to* steamroller *a road*; *to* steamroller *opposition.*

steam·ship (stēm′ shĭp′) ***n-*** ship driven by steam power; steamboat; steamer.

steam shovel ***n-*** **1** power shovel using steam power. **2** any power shovel.

steam turbine ***n-*** an engine in which the steam drives an enclosed wheel having fan blades mounted on it.

steam·y (stē′ mē) ***adj-*** [**steam·i·er, steam·i·est**] of, filled with, or resembling steam. **—*n-* steam′ i·ness.**

ste·ap·sin (stē ăp′ sən) ***n-*** enzyme in pancreatic juice that breaks up fat in the process of digestion.

stear·ic acid (stêr′ ĭk) ***n-*** white, crystalline, fatty acid ($C_{17}H_{35}COOH$), found in most animal and vegetable fats and oils.

stea·rin (stêr′ ən) ***n-*** **1** white, crystalline ester of glycerol and stearic acid, found in many animal and vegetable fats and oils. **2** stearic acid, especially as used in making candles, soaps, etc. **3** the solid portion of a fat.

sted·fast (stĕd′ făst′) steadfast.

steed (stēd) *Archaic* ***n-*** horse, especially a spirited horse.

steel (stēl) ***n-*** **1** iron that contains carbon and, usually, other substances in varying small amounts. Steel is stronger and more flexible than cast iron. **2** weapon or implement made of this substance, such as a sword, a knife sharpener, or a piece of metal formerly used for striking sparks from flint to start a fire. 3 tough, unyielding nature or quality: *He has nerves of* steel. *as* ***modifier***: *a* steel *blade.* ***vt-*** to make firm or ready; toughen: *to* steel *oneself for shock.* ***Hom-*** steal.

steel·head (stēl′ hĕd′) ***n-*** large, silvery trout of western North America, which migrates between the ocean and fresh-water streams.

steel wool ***n-*** mass of fine threads of steel, used to clean and polish metal and other surfaces.

steel·work (stēl′ wûrk′) ***n-*** 1 part or structure made of steel. 2 **steelworks** (takes singular or plural verb) industrial plant where steel is produced. —***n-*** **steel′ work′ er.**

steel·y (stē′ lē) ***adj-*** [**steel·i·er, steel·i·est**] 1 made of steel. 2 like steel in color, appearance, or hardness: *eyes of* steely *blue*; *his* steely *grip.* —***n-*** **steel′ i·ness.**

steel·yard (stēl′ yärd′) ***n-*** weighing device, usually hung from a support, having a horizontal bar marked in units of weight, with hooks at one end for holding objects to be weighed, and a counterweight that slides toward the other end of the bar and balances it when the correct weight is shown.

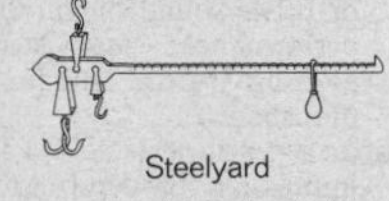
Steelyard

1**steep** (stēp) ***adj-*** [**steep·er, steep·est**] 1 having a sharp slope or a nearly vertical face: *a* steep *hill*; *a* steep *flight of stairs*; *a* steep *cliff.* 2 *Informal* excessively high; exorbitant: *a* steep *price.* [from Old English **steap,** "tall," "prominent."] —***adv-*** **steep′ ly.** ***n-*** **steep′ ness.**

2**steep** (stēp) ***vt-*** 1 to soak in a liquid: *to* steep *tea leaves.* 2 to cause (oneself) to become completely absorbed: *to* steep *oneself in scientific studies.* ***vi-*** to be soaked in a liquid: *The tea should* steep *thoroughly.* [from earlier English **stēpan,** from **steap** meaning "a vessel," probably from Old Norse **steypa,** "to pour."] —***n-*** **steep′ er.**

steeped in fully engaged in or devoted to.

steep·en (stē′ pən) ***vt-*** to make steeper: *to* steepen *a trench.* ***vi-***: *The mountain* steepens *sharply near the top.*

stee·ple (stē′ pəl) ***n-*** high, tapering tower above the roof of a building, especially a church; spire.

stee·ple·chase (stē′ pəl chās′) ***n-*** cross-country race on horseback over a course obstructed by artificial obstacles, such as hurdles and hedges.

stee·ple·jack (stē′ pəl jăk′) ***n-*** workman who climbs high structures such as steeples or smokestacks, to make repairs.

1**steer** (stêr) ***vt-*** (considered intransitive when the direct object is implied but not expressed) 1 to direct or guide by, or as if by, means of a wheel, rudder, or similar device: *to* steer *a ship toward shore*; *to* steer *carefully.* 2 to set and follow (a course): *to* steer *a course to the west*; *to* steer *homeward.* ***vi-*** to be guided by the motion of a wheel, rudder, etc.: *This car doesn't* steer *easily.* ***n-*** *Slang* piece of information or advice; tip. [from Old English **stēoran** of the same meaning.]

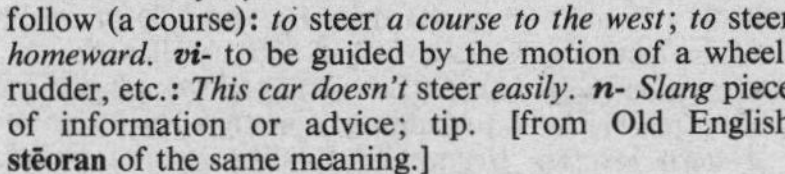
Steeple

steer clear of to avoid: *to* steer clear of *trouble.*

2**steer** (stêr) ***n-*** young, castrated male of domestic cattle, especially when raised for beef. [from Old English **stēor** meaning "heavy" as applied to beasts.]

steer·age (stêr′ ĭj) ***n-*** formerly, the part of a ship set aside for passengers paying the lowest rates.

steer·age·way (stêr′ ĭj wā′) ***n-*** minimum forward speed to permit a boat to be steered.

steering committee ***n-*** legislative committee that determines the order in which bills will be considered.

steering wheel ***n-*** wheel for steering a car, ship, etc.

steg·o·sau·rus (stĕg′ ə sȯr′ əs) ***n-*** [*pl.* **steg·o·sau·rus·es** or **steg·o·sau·ri** (-rī)] large dinosaur of the Jurassic period, having a small head and a double row of pointed bony plates along its back. For picture, see *dinosaur.*

stein (stīn) ***n-*** 1 large beer mug. 2 amount held by it.

ste·la (stē′ lə) or **ste·le** (stē′ lē) ***n-*** [*pl.* **ste·lae** (-lē)] upright stone slab, often carved and used in ancient times as a grave marker or monument.

stel·lar (stĕl′ ər) ***adj-*** 1 of, relating to, or consisting of stars: *the* stellar *system.* 2 chief; starring; prominent.

stel·la·ra·tor (stĕl′ ə rā′ tər) *Physics* ***n-*** experimental thermonuclear device consisting of a doughnut-shaped tube surrounded by magnetizing coils in which a plasma may be confined and heated to temperatures of about 100 million degrees C.

1**stem** (stĕm) ***n-*** 1 main stalk of a plant. 2 any stalk or slender part that supports or connects a leaf, flower, fruit, etc. 3 any comparatively slender shaft, support, or connecting part. 4 on a boat or a ship, the central support to which the sides are joined at the front; prow or bow. 5 *Grammar* main part of a word to which prefixes, suffixes, inflectional endings, etc., may be added. 6 *Music* the line or stroke extending up or down from the rounded part of a written note. ***vt-*** [**stemmed, stem·ming**] to remove the stalk or stalks from: *to* stem *cherries.* [from Old English **stemn,** from **stæfn** meaning "stem of a tree."] —***adj-*** **stem′ like′.** ***adj-*** **stem′ less.**

Stems

from stem to stern from one end to the other.

stem from 1 to branch out from. 2 to be directly connected with (a source, origin, ancestry, etc.).

2**stem** (stĕm) ***vt-*** [**stemmed, stem·ming**] 1 to stop; check; dam up: *He* stemmed *the flow of water.* 2 to make progress or headway against: *They* stemmed *the heavy gale. He* stemmed *the opposition.* [probably from Old Norse **stemma,** "to stop," and related to **stammer.**]

stemmed (stĕmd) ***adj-*** having a stem or a particular kind of stem: *a* stemmed *wineglass*; *a long-*stemmed *rose.*

stench (stĕnch) ***n-*** extremely unpleasant smell; stink.

sten·cil (stĕn′ səl) ***n-*** 1 thin sheet of metal, paper, plastic, etc., into which an open design, pattern, or letters are cut. When it is placed on a surface and ink or color is applied over it, the design or letters appear on the surface beneath. 2 design made this way. ***vt-***: *to* stencil *a sign.*

ste·nog·ra·pher (stə nŏg′ rə fər) ***n-*** person employed to take dictation in shorthand and later transcribe it.

sten·o·graph·ic (stĕn′ ə grăf′ ĭk) ***adj-*** of, related to, or written in shorthand. —***adv-*** **sten′ o·graph′ i·cal·ly.**

ste·nog·ra·phy (stə nŏg′ rə fē) ***n-*** 1 rapid, abbreviated method of writing; shorthand. 2 process of taking dictation in shorthand and later transcribing it.

sten·tor·i·an (stĕn tôr′ ē ən) ***adj-*** extremely loud and powerful: *a* stentorian *voice.* [from **Stentor,** a herald in the "Iliad" famous for his loud voice.]

step (stĕp) ***n-*** **1** movement made by raising a foot and placing it in a new position; pace. **2** distance covered by, or as if by, such a movement: *Our house is a few* steps *from the corner.* **3** definite pattern of foot and body movements, such as those made in dancing: *a waltz* step. **4** manner of walking; gait: *a light, rhythmic* step. **5** sound made in walking or running; footstep: *I heard his* step *in the hall.* **6** footprint: *We followed his* steps *in the snow.* **7** tread in a stairway or a rung of a ladder. **8** stage in rank, progress, etc.: *one* step *nearer fame.* **9** one of a series of actions or measures taken toward a goal: *the first* step *in an undertaking.* **10** *Music* interval between two successive notes in a scale. **11** block or frame with a socket in which the base of a mast is placed. ***vi-*** [**stepped step·ping**] **1** to move in any direction by raising a foot and placing it in a new position, or by making a series of such motions: *to* step *forward.* **2** to walk a short distance: *to* step *across the street.* **3** to place the foot (on) or (in) something: *to* step *on a tack*; *to* step *in a puddle.* **4** *Informal* to move briskly or energetically. ***vt-*** **1** to measure by strides or lengths of one's foot (usually followed by "off"): *to* step *the distance between two points.* **2** to place (a mast) in an upright position with its base resting in a socket. ***Hom-*** steppe. **—*n-*** **step′ per.**

in step **1** with the same pace or rhythm as that of another person or thing. **2** in accord. **keep step with** to keep one's steps, actions, or ideas in harmony with. **out of step** **1** progressing or moving at a different pace or in a different rhythm. **2** not in accord with usual or accepted ways and customs. **take steps** to do something decisive to achieve an aim or purpose. **watch (one's) step** to proceed with caution.

step down **1** to resign from a high position or official post. **2** to decrease (a voltage).

step into to gain or take possession of without effort.

step on it *Informal* to hurry.

step out **1** to leave for a short time. **2** *Informal* to go out for an enjoyable social activity.

step up **1** to increase the rate of; speed up: *to* step up *production in a factory.* **2** to increase (a voltage).

step·broth·er (stĕp′ brŭth′ ər) ***n-*** son of one's stepfather or stepmother.

step·child (stĕp′ chīld′) ***n-*** child of one's husband or wife by a previous marriage.

step·daugh·ter (stĕp′ dô′ tər) ***n-*** daughter of one's husband or wife by a previous marriage.

step-down (stĕp′ doun′) ***adj-*** of an electrical transformer, producing an output voltage that is less than the input voltage.

step·fa·ther (stĕp′ fä′ thər) ***n-*** husband of one's mother following the death or divorce of one's father.

step·lad·der (stĕp′ lăd′ ər) ***n-*** short, portable set of steps supported at the back by a hinged prop that may be folded flat for convenience in carrying or storage.

Stepladder

step·moth·er (stĕp′ mŭth′ ər) ***n-*** wife of one's father following the death or divorce of one's mother.

step·par·ent (stĕp′ pâr′ ənt) ***n-*** stepfather or stepmother.

steppe (stĕp) ***n-*** dry, level or rolling grassland without trees, but in the natural state having a cover of short grass. [from Russian **step.**] ***Hom-*** step.

stepping stone ***n-*** **1** stone that projects above the surface of a stream, swampy ground, etc., and provides a footing for someone going across. **2** any aid in making progress: *Education is a* stepping stone *to success.*

step·sis·ter (stĕp′ sĭs′ tər) ***n-*** daughter of one's stepfather or stepmother.

step·son (stĕp′ sŭn′) ***n-*** son of one's husband or wife by a previous marriage.

step-up (stĕp′ ŭp′) ***n-*** increase in rate of production, activity, etc.: *a* step-up *in sales.* ***adj-*** of an electrical transformer, producing an output voltage that is greater than the input voltage.

ster·e·o (stĕr′ ē ō) ***n-*** phonograph, radio, etc., that transmits stereophonic sound. *as* ***modifier***: *a* stereo *broadcast.*

stereo- *combining form* having or giving the effect of three dimensions: *a* stereo*scope*; stereo*phonic.* [from Greek **stereo-**, from **stereos** meaning "solid; hard."]

ster·e·o·phon·ic (stĕr′ ē ə fŏn′ ĭk) ***adj-*** of, relating to, or produced by a system of sound reproduction that uses two or more independent microphones, channels, and speakers to give the illusion that one is hearing the music or other sound binaurally, as one would at an actual performance. **—*adv-*** **ster′ e·o·phon′ i·cal·ly.**

ster·e·op·ti·con (stĕr′ ē ŏp′ tĭ kən) ***n-*** projector for film slides.

ster·e·o·scope (stĕr′ ē ə skōp′) ***n-*** device for giving the impression of depth to a picture, by the use of two lenses for viewing a pair of photographs or drawings showing the same scene from slightly different angles.

ster·e·o·scop·ic (stĕr′ ē ə skŏp′ ĭk) ***adj-*** **1** of, relating to, or producing the impression of depth in vision by the simultaneous viewing of the same scene from two slightly separated points, such as the two eyes: *a* stereoscopic *camera*; stereoscopic *vision.* **2** done by means of a stereoscope: *the* stereoscopic *examination of aerial photographs.* **—*adv-*** **ster′ e·o·scop′ i·cal·ly.**

ster·e·o·type (stĕr′ ē ə tīp′) ***n-*** **1** in printing, plate made by pouring metal into a mold made from the original type; also, the process of making such a plate. **2** conventional, oversimplified, and often false representation of a person, thing, or idea: *The strong, silent hero of Western movies is a Hollywood* stereotype. *as* ***modifier***: *the* stereotype *process of making printing plates.* ***vt-*** [**ster·e·o·typed, ster·e·o·typ·ing**] **1** to make a plate of by the stereotype process. **2** to form an oversimplified opinion about: *He* stereotyped *all actors as shiftless creatures.* **—*n-*** **ster′ e·o·typ′ er.**

ster·e·o·typed (stĕr′ ē ə tīpt′) ***adj-*** **1** oversimplified; commonplace; trite. **2** made from a stereotype plate.

ster·ile (stĕr′ ĭl) ***adj-*** **1** not fertile; unable to produce young; barren: *a* sterile *piece of land*; *the* sterile *old mare.* **2** free from living germs or microbes: *a* sterile *bandage.* **3** intellectually or spiritually barren; unimaginative; dull: *a* sterile *lecture.* **—*adv-*** **ster′ ile·ly.** ***n-*** **ste·ril′ i·ty.**

ster·i·lize (stĕr′ ə līz′) ***vt-*** [**ster·i·lized, ster·i·liz·ing**] to make sterile: *to* sterilize *forceps.* **—*n-*** **ster′ i·li·za′ tion.**

ster·i·liz·er (stĕr′ ə lī′ zər) ***n-*** apparatus used for sterilizing food, medical or dental equipment, etc.

ster·ling (stûr′ lĭng) ***n-*** **1** in Great Britain, the standard of metallic purity for coins. **2** (also **sterling silver**) silver that is 92.5 percent pure, used widely in making knives, forks, and similar items. ***adj-*** **1** of British coins, made of metal of standard purity. **2** made of sterling silver: *a* sterling *fruit bowl.* **3** of high excellence.

[1]**stern** (stûrn) ***adj-*** **1** severe or strict: *Mr. Parnell gave us a* stern *talking to.* **2** forbidding: *a* stern *look.* **3** resolute: *a* stern *resolve.* [from Old English **styrne.**] **—*adv-*** **stern′ ly.** ***n-*** **stern′ ness.**

[2]**stern** (stûrn) ***n-*** aft, or rear, end of a ship or boat. *as* ***modifier***: *the* stern *deck.* [from Old Norse **stjörn** meaning "a steering; helm," and related to [1]**steer.**]

ster·num (stûr′ nəm) ***n-*** [*pl.* **ster·na** (-nə) or **ster·nums**] long, bony plate that runs down the center of the upper chest and joins the upper ribs; breastbone.

stern·wheel·er (stûrn′ hwē′ lər) ***n-*** steamboat driven by a paddle wheel at the stern.

stet (stĕt) ***n-*** in printing, "let it stand," a direction to restore a word, phrase, etc., that has been deleted or altered. It is indicated in the margin of a manuscript or proof by the word "stet" and in the text by a row of dots under the matter to be restored. ***vt-*** [**stet·ted, stet·ting**] to mark (a word, etc.) with such a direction.

steth·o·scope (stĕth′ ə skōp′) ***n-*** medical instrument consisting of a small diaphragm or hollow cone connected by a rubber tube to two metal tubes that fit into the ears. It is used for listening to heartbeats and other internal body sounds. ***—adj-*** **steth′ o·scop′ ic** (-skŏp′ ĭk).

ste·ve·dore (stē′ və dôr′) ***n-*** person hired to load and unload the cargoes of ships.

stew (sto͞o, styo͞o) ***n-*** **1** dish made of small pieces of meat or fish and vegetables cooked slowly in a liquid. **2** *Informal* worry: *I'm in a* stew *as to my future.* ***vi-*** **1** to cook slowly in a liquid: *The lamb* stewed *for an hour.* **2** *Informal* to worry; fret. ***vt-***: *Mother* stewed *the meat.*
stew in one's own juice to worry or suffer over a situation brought on by oneself.

stew·ard (sto͞o′ ərd, styo͞o′-) ***n-*** **1** man in charge of another's property. **2** man in charge of the food and table service in a ship, club, dining car, etc. **3** on passenger ships, an attendant. ***—n-*** *fem.* **stew′ ard·ess.**

stew·ard·ship (sto͞o′ ərd shĭp′, styo͞o′-) ***n-*** **1** office, duties, or term of a steward. **2** the responsibility for managing, especially as affecting life and property.

[1]**stick** (stĭk) ***n-*** **1** long, narrow piece of wood. **2** anything shaped like this: *a candy* stick; *a walking* stick. **3** *Informal* stiff or dull person. **4 the sticks** *Informal* rustic area lying far from the city; backwoods or country. [from Old English **sticca** meaning "stick," "peg."]

[2]**stick** (stĭk) ***vt-*** [**stuck, stick·ing**] **1** to push something pointed or jagged into: *I* stuck *myself with the needle.* **2** to penetrate; pierce: *The nail* stuck *me in the foot.* **3** to cause (something) to stay on or adhere to something else. **4** to cause (separate things) to stay together and in contact: *to* stick *pieces of wood together with glue.* **5** *Informal* to place: *Please* stick *these in the corner.* **6** *Slang* to force or appoint (someone) to do an unwanted job: *They* stuck *him with the fund-raising.* **7** *Slang* to sell something to (someone) for too high a price; also, to cheat by such a sale. ***vi-*** **1** to become tightly set in place; be unable to move or operate: *The car* stuck *in the mud.* **2** to stay or hold together; adhere: *This glue* sticks *well.* **3** to have the point or points embedded: *The rake* stuck *in his foot.* **4** *Informal* to stay; remain firmly: *We must all* stick *together.* [from Old English **stician** meaning "to stab; pierce; cling to a thing."]
stick around *Informal* to remain in a certain place.
stick at to be firmly resolved against; refuse to do; balk at: *He* stuck at *wading through the mud.*
stick by *Informal* to be loyal or faithful to; stick to.
stick it out *Informal* to continue in spite of difficulty; persevere; endure.
stick out 1 to protrude: *She* stuck out *her tongue.* **2** to be obvious or conspicuous.
stick to 1 to keep on with; continue with: *He* stuck to *the job until it was finished.* **2** to be faithful to; keep.
stick up *Informal* to rob someone at gun point.
stick up for to stand up for; take sides for.

stick·ball (stĭk′ bòl′) ***n-*** game that is loosely similar to baseball, played with a rubber ball and a broomstick.

stick·er (stĭk′ ər) ***n-*** small gummed label or sign.

stick·le (stĭk′ əl) *Archaic* ***vi-*** [**stick·led, stick·ling**] to argue or hesitate over trivial matters; haggle.

stick·le·back (stĭk′ əl băk′) ***n-*** any of several small, scaleless fishes with sharp spines on their backs, notable for their nests that are built and guarded by the males.

stick·ler (stĭk′ lər) ***n-*** **1** person who insists upon thoroughness and exactness (usually followed by "for"): *He's a* stickler *for detail.* **2** *Informal* something that baffles.

stick·pin (stĭk′ pĭn′) ***n-*** tiepin.

stick·tight (stĭk′ tīt′) ***n-*** any of a genus of coarse herbs whose small, dry seed pods stick to clothing.

stick·up (stĭk′ ŭp′) ***n-*** *Informal* holdup or robbery, usually at gun point.

stick·y (stĭk′ ē) ***adj-*** [**stick·i·er, stick·i·est**] **1** tending to stick or cling; adhesive; tacky: *a* sticky *coat of drying paint.* **2** hot and humid: *the* sticky *weather of the tropics.* ***—adv-*** **stick′ i·ly.** ***n-*** **stick′ i·ness.**

sticky fingers *Informal* ***n-*** *pl.* tendency to steal. ***adj-*** (**stick′ y-fin′ gered**): *a* sticky-fingered *customer.*

sties (stīz) *plural* of **sty.**

stiff (stĭf) ***adj-*** [**stiff·er, stiff·est**] **1** not easily bent; firm: *a* stiff *collar.* **2** hard to move or operate: *a* stiff *lock*; *a* stiff *crank.* **3** not able to move with ease and freedom: *a* stiff *neck.* **4** formal: *The butler gave us a* stiff *bow.* **5** difficult; hard: *a* stiff *chemistry test*; *a* stiff *climb.* **6** harsh; severe: *a* stiff *punishment.* **7** strong and steady: *a* stiff *breeze.* **8** not liquid or fluid: *to beat egg whites until* stiff. **9** hard to pay; high: *a* stiff *price.* ***n-*** *Slang* **1** dead body. **2** dull, formal, unresponsive person. ***—adv-*** **stiff′ ly.** ***n-*** **stiff′ ness.**

stiff·en (stĭf′ ən) ***vt-*** to make stiff or rigid: *She* stiffened *the shirt with starch.* ***vi-***: *His limbs* stiffened *with age.* ***—n-*** **stiff′ en·er.**

stiff·en·ing (stĭf′ ən ĭng) ***n-*** starch, glue, or a similar substance used to stiffen fabric.

stiff-necked (stĭf′ nĕckt′) ***adj-*** stubborn; obstinate: *his* stiff-necked *pride.*

sti·fle (stī′ fəl) ***vt-*** [**sti·fled, sti·fling**] **1** to make breathing more difficult for; suffocate; smother: *The heat in the room* stifled *us.* **2** to extinguish: *We* stifled *the campfire with sand.* **3** to hold back; discourage or deter: *to* stifle *a yawn*; *to* stifle *freedom.* ***vi-***: *He'll* stifle *in that room.*

sti·fling (stī′ flĭng) ***adj-*** **1** suffocating; choking: *a* stifling *apartment.* **2** tending to discourage or suppress; suppressive: *a* stifling *set of rules.* ***—adv-*** **sti′ fling·ly.**

stig·ma (stĭg′ mə) ***n-*** [**stig·mas** or **stig·ma·ta** (stĭg mä′ tə, stĭg′ mə-)] **1** any defect in one's life or reputation; token of shame; burden of dishonor: *He lived under the* stigma *of having been in prison.* **2** in flowers, the part of the pistil that receives pollen. **3** *Medicine* a sign or symptom of disease. **4 stigmata** marks resembling the wounds on the body of the crucified Christ.

stig·ma·tize (stĭg′ mə tīz′) ***vt-*** [**stig·ma·tized, stig·ma·tiz·ing**] to hold up to disgrace or dishonor: *to* stigmatize *a man as a traitor.* ***—n-*** **stig′ ma·ti·za′ tion.**

stile (stīl) ***n-*** **1** set of steps leading over a fence or wall. **2** turnstile. ***Hom-*** style.

Stile

sti·let·to (stə lĕt′ ō) ***n-*** [*pl.* **sti·let·tos, sti·let·toes**] **1** small, sharp dagger with a slender blade. **2** pointed instrument used in needlework for making holes for eyelets.

[1]**still** (stĭl) ***adj-*** **[still·er, still·est]** **1** without movement; motionless: *Please stand* still. **2** quiet; silent: *Please be* still *while she is talking.* **3** calm or tranquil: *a* still *night.* ***vt-*** to make quiet; calm: *Andrew* stilled *the baby by giving her a toy.* ***adv-*** **1** in spite of that; nevertheless: *Tim's toothache grew worse;* still *he didn't complain.* **2** even; yet: *You may be tall but your brother is* still *taller.* **3** continuance of action or condition: *The weather is* still *cool.* ***n-*** **1** stillness; tranquility: *in the* still *of the night.* **2** still photograph. [from Old English **stille** meaning "quiet" as in a stall, and related to **stall.**]

[2]**still** (stĭl) ***n-*** **1** any of various apparatus for distilling liquids by evaporation and condensation, used especially for making strong alcoholic liquors. **2** distillery. [from earlier **still** meaning "to distill," from Latin **stillare,** "to drop or drip," from **stilla,** "a drop."]

still·birth (stĭl′bûrth′) ***n-*** birth of a dead child; also, the dead child.

still·born (stĭl′bôrn′) ***adj-*** dead at the time of birth.

still life ***n-*** painting or photograph of inanimate objects.

still·ness (stĭl′nəs) ***n-*** absence of sound or motion; calm: *the* stillness *of the sea; the* stillness *of the night.*

still photograph ***n-*** single photograph; especially, a photograph taken by a **still camera,** designed to take pictures one at a time and not rapidly enough to produce a series of photographs for a motion picture.

stilt (stĭlt) ***n-*** **1** one of a pair of long poles, each with a block on which a person may stand and walk at a distance above the ground. **2** one of the posts used to support a house, dock, or other structure above land or water. **—*adj-*** **stilt′like′.**

Stilts

stilt·ed (stĭl′təd) ***adj-*** **1** stiffly formal; pompous: *a play with* stilted *dialogue.* **2** supported by slender props.

stim·u·lant (stĭm′yə lənt) ***n-*** **1** drug, beverage, etc., that arouses, quickens, or intensifies the senses or bodily functions. **2** anything that urges or spurs one on; stimulus: *Fame was his major* stimulant.

stim·u·late (stĭm′yə lāt′) ***vt-*** **[stim·u·lat·ed, stim·u·lat·ing]** **1** to quicken; arouse to greater activity: *Brisk walking* stimulates *the circulation.* **2** to excite; stir up: *This book has* stimulated *my interest.* **3** to act as a stimulus to (a sense organ, nerve, certain pattern of behavior, etc.): *Light* stimulates *the retina.* **—*n-*** **stim′u·la′tion.** ***n-*** **stim′u·la′tor:** *Walking is a good* stimulator *of the circulation.*

stim·u·lus (stĭm′yə ləs) ***n-*** [*pl.* **stim·u·li** (-lī, -lē)] anything that stimulates; especially, anything that causes a response in the nervous system, sensory system, feelings, etc., of a person or other organism.

sting (stĭng) ***vi-*** **[stung** (stŭng), **sting·ing]** **1** of certain animals and plants, to prick with a sharp organ that injects poison: *Bees, scorpions, and sting rays can* sting. **2** to cause a sharp pain or hurt, either to the body or the feelings: *Alcohol* stings *when put on a wound. His harsh words* stung. **3** to be sharply painful; smart: *This finger* stings. *Our eyes* stung. ***vt-*** **1** of certain animals and plants, to inject poison into by means of a sharp organ: *A hornet* stung *my brother.* **2** to incite to action by taunts: *The harsh speech* stung *them.* ***n-*** **1** the organ used by some animals or plants to inject poison. **2** act of wounding with such an organ; also, such a wound. **3** sharp, burning pain, either of the body or the feelings; smart. **4** a taunt, reproach, etc., that incites one to action. **—*adv-*** **sting′ing·ly.** ***adj-*** **sting′less.**

sting·a·ree (stĭng′ə rē′) ***n-*** sting ray.

sting·er (stĭng′ər) ***n-*** **1** person, animal, or thing that stings. **2** the organ of a bee, scorpion, etc., that stings. **3** *Informal* sharp, stinging remark or blow.

sting ray ***n-*** any of several large tropical fish having a broad, flat body and a tail armed with bony spines that can inflict severe wounds. Also **sting′ray′.**

stin·gy (stĭn′jē) ***adj-*** **[stin·gi·er, stin·gi·est]** **1** reluctant to give, lend, or spend. **2** scanty; skimpy: *a* stingy *helping of food.* **—*adv-*** **stin′gi·ly.** ***n-*** **stin′gi·ness.**

stink (stĭngk) ***vi-*** **[stank** (stăngk) or **stunk** (stŭngk), **stunk, stink·ing]** **1** to give off a disgusting odor: *Garbage* stinks. **2** *Slang* to be extremely bad in character, worth, or quality. ***n-*** **1** disgusting odor: *the* stink *of spoiled fish.* **2** *Slang* moral outrage; scandal.

stink·bug (stĭnk′bŭg′) ***n-*** any of various broad, flat bugs that emit an unpleasant odor.

stink·er (stĭng′kər) ***n-*** **1** any of several large sea birds that emit an offensive odor. **2** *Slang* person or thing that is extremely offensive or irritating.

stink·weed (stĭngk′wēd′) ***n-*** any of various plants such as the jimson weed, having a strong, offensive scent.

stink·y (stĭng′kē) *Informal* ***adj-*** **[stink·i·er, stink·i·est]** **1** having a bad smell; smelly. **2** hateful, offensive. **3** of inferior quality.

stint (stĭnt) ***vt-*** to be frugal or sparing with; skimp: *to* stint *an allowance.* ***vi-***: *Don't* stint *during your vacation.* ***n-*** chore; task assigned: *My* stint *is washing dishes.*

without stint without sparing: *to give* without stint.

stipe (stīp) ***n-*** in botany, a stem or support, especially one supporting a pistil or one of the fronds of a fern.

sti·pend (stī′pənd) ***n-*** fixed pay or allowance; especially, the amount paid to a scholarship student.

stip·ple (stĭp′əl) ***vt-*** **[stip·pled, stip·pling]** to draw, paint, or engrave by means of dots or light touches rather than lines. ***n-*** art or method of drawing, painting, or engraving in such a way; also, the effect so produced.

stip·u·late (stĭp′yə lāt′) ***vt-*** **[stip·u·lat·ed, stip·u·lat·ing]** to arrange or settle definitely; specify as part of an agreement: *She* stipulated *that he be paid in advance.*

stip·u·la·tion (stĭp′yə lā′shən) ***n-*** specific condition or requirement in a contract or agreement.

stip·ule (stĭp′yo͞ol′) ***n-*** in some plants, either of two small appendages at the base of the leaf or petiole. **—*adj-*** **stip′uled′.**

stir (stûr) ***vt-*** **[stirred, stir·ring]** **1** to set in motion; move: *A light breeze* stirred *the leaves.* **2** to mix or rearrange with a moving implement: *to* stir *one's coffee.* **3** to rouse or excite; provoke; incite (often followed by "up"): *to* stir *men to action;* stir *one's heart; to* stir *up trouble.* ***vi-*** **1** to move: *He would not* stir *from his chair.* **2** to be mixed by a moving implement: *This cake* stirs *easily.* **3** to be roused or excited: *Pity* stirred *in his heart.* **4** to be active or begin to show signs of activity: *Is anything* stirring *in town?* ***n-*** **1** slight movement: *There was a* stir *in the woods.* **2** a mixing: *Give the soup a* stir. **3** excitement; commotion. **—*n-*** **stir′rer.**

stir·ring (stûr′ĭng) ***adj-*** rousing; exciting; thrilling. **—*adv-*** **stir′ring·ly.**

stir·rup (stûr′əp) ***n-*** **1** one of a pair of metal or wooden loops hung from the side of a saddle to hold a rider's foot. **2** (also **stirrup bone**) the inner one of the three tiny, sound-transmitting bones of the middle ear (for picture, see [1]*ear*).

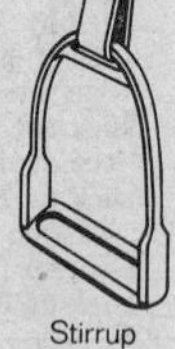
Stirrup

stirrup cup ***n-*** **1** cup of liquor given to a rider about to depart. **2** any farewell drink.

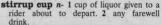

stitch (stĭch) ***n-*** **1** complete movement of a threaded needle in and out of material; also, a similar movement of a knitting needle or crochet hook. **2** loop of thread or yarn made with such a movement of a needle or crochet hook. **3** sudden sharp pain: *a* stitch *in the side.* **4** *Informal* the smallest article of clothing: *I haven't a* stitch *to wear.* ***vt-*** to sew: *to* stitch *a sock.* ***vi-***: *She* stitches *on a sewing machine.* **—*n-* stitch′ er.**

in stitches in a state of uproarious laughter.

stitch·ing (stĭch′ ĭng) ***n-*** series or arrangement of stitches.

stoat (stōt) ***n-*** the ermine, especially in its summer coat of reddish brown.

stock (stŏk) ***n-*** **1** a supply; store: *Jones' store has a large* stock *of goods.* **2** livestock. **3** raw or basic material: *A ham bone is* stock *for soup.* **4** liquid in which meat, and sometimes vegetables, has been cooked. It is often used as the basis for various soups. **5** trunk or stump of a tree, or stem of a plant. **6** ancestry. **7** an ethnic group; race. **8** shares in a business: *Mr. White owns most of the company's* stock. **9** shoulder piece of a firearm or crossbow. **10** repertoire of a stock company. **11** garden plant with single or double sweet-scented flowers growing along the stalk. **12 the stocks** formerly, a frame for holding a seated prisoner's ankles while he was held up to public scorn. ***vt-*** **1** to furnish with; supply: *They* stocked *the freezer.* **2** to keep a supply of for sale. ***Hom-*** stalk.

Stocks

in stock available for use or sale; on hand. **out of stock** not available for use or sale; lacking. **take stock** **1** to take an inventory of goods on hand. **2** to estimate value, as of a business. **take stock in** **1** to invest money by buying shares in. **2** to have confidence in.

stock up (on) to lay in an ample supply (of).

stock·ade (stŏk ād′) ***n-*** **1** strong defensive fence made of tall, closely set posts with sharpened tops, much used around frontier forts and animal pens; palisade. **2** the area or buildings enclosed by such a fence. **3** in the Army, Marines, and Air Force, a prison for service personnel. ***vt-*** **[stock·ad·ed, stock·ad·ing]** to surround or defend with a stockade.

Stockade

stock·bro·ker (stŏk′ brō′ kər) ***n-*** person who buys and sells stocks or securities for others.

stock car ***n-*** standard automobile adjusted for racing.

stock clerk ***n-*** person who is responsible for supplies in a stockroom.

stock company ***n-*** **1** corporation whose capital is divided into shares of stock. **2** theatrical company that is more or less permanently associated with one management and presents a repertoire of plays.

stock exchange ***n-*** **1** place where stocks and bonds are bought and sold. **2** association of stockbrokers engaged in the business of buying and selling stocks.

stock·hold·er (stŏk′ hōl′ dər) ***n-*** person who owns stock or shares in a company; shareholder.

stock·ing (stŏk′ ĭng) ***n-*** close-fitting woven or knit covering for the foot and leg.

stocking cap ***n-*** long, tapered knitted cap with a tassel or pompon at the end, usually worn in winter.

stock in trade ***n-*** **1** merchandise that a store has ready for sale. **2** most effective skill or quality; resources: *The quick joke was his* stock in trade.

stock·man (stŏk′ mən) ***n-*** [*pl.* **stock·men**] person who owns, raises, or is in charge of livestock.

stock market ***n-*** **1** trade in stocks and bonds; also, the prices at which these are selling. **2** stock exchange.

stock·pile (stŏk′ pīl′) ***n-*** reserve supply of materials, food, etc., to be used during a shortage. ***vt-*** **[stock·piled, stock·pil·ing]** to store a reserve supply of.

stock·room (stŏk′ rōōm′) ***n-*** place where a business stores its supplies.

stock split ***n-*** the exchange by a business of two shares of its stock for each share held by a stockholder.

stock-still (stŏk′ stĭl′) ***adj-*** completely motionless.

stock·y (stŏk′ ē) ***adj-*** **[stock·i·er, stock·i·est]** short, solid, and sturdy in build. **—*adv-* stock′ i·ly.** ***n-*** **stock′ i·ness.**

stock·yard (stŏk′ yärd′) ***n-*** enclosure with pens and sheds where livestock is kept before being shipped or slaughtered.

stodg·y (stŏj′ ē) ***adj-*** **[stodg·i·er, stodg·i·est]** **1** commonplace; dull: *a* stodgy *movie.* **2** old-fashioned and stuffy: *a* stodgy *opponent of progress.* **3** of food, thick or heavy; indigestible. **—*adv-* stodg′ i·ly.** ***n-*** **stodg′ i·ness.**

sto·gie or **sto·gy** (stō′ gē) ***n-*** [*pl.* **sto·gies**] long, coarse, inexpensive cigar.

sto·ic (stō′ ĭk) ***n-*** **1** person who practices great self-control and is largely indifferent to pleasure and pain: *She was a* stoic *throughout her illness.* **2 Stoic** member of a school of philosophy founded by Zeno around 300 B.C., holding that a wise man should be governed by reason, overcome his passions, and resign himself to natural law or the divine will. ***adj-*** **1** self-controlled; restrained; uncomplaining. **2 Stoic** having to do with the Stoics or their philosophy.

sto·i·cal (stō′ ĭ kəl) ***adj-*** like a stoic; self-controlled; impassive. **—*adv-* sto′ i·cal·ly.**

sto·i·cism (stō′ ə sĭz′ əm) ***n-*** **1** great self-control and restraint; indifference to pleasure or pain. **2 Stoicism** philosophy of the Stoics.

stoke (stōk) ***vt-*** **[stoked, stok·ing]** to tend (a fire or furnace), especially by adding fuel.

stoke·hold (stōk′ hōld′) ***n-*** the room containing the boilers in a steamship.

stoke·hole (stōk′ hōl′) ***n-*** **1** opening to the grate of a furnace through which the fire is tended. **2** stokehold.

stok·er (stō′ kər) ***n-*** person or device that supplies fuel to a furnace; especially, the man who tends the furnace on a steamship.

[1]**stole** (stōl) ***n-*** **1** long scarf of cloth or fur worn over the shoulders with the ends hanging down in front. **2** long, narrow band worn over the shoulders during services by priests and bishops, over the left shoulder by deacons.

[2]**stole** (stōl) *p.t.* of **steal.**

sto·len (stō′ lən) *p.p.* of **steal.** ***Hom-*** stolon.

stol·id (stŏl′ ĭd) ***adj-*** not easily aroused or excited; impassive. **—*n-* sto·lid′ i·ty.** ***adv-*** **stol′ id·ly.**

sto·lon (stō′ lən, -lŏn′) ***n-*** **1** in botany, a trailing branch, as of the strawberry plant, that takes root at the tip or at a node and forms a new plant. **2** in zoology, a prolongation of the body wall, as of the coral polyp, from which reproductive buds develop. ***Hom-*** stolen.

sto·ma (stō′ mə) ***n-*** [*pl.* **sto·ma·ta** (stō′ mə tə)] in botany, one of the many tiny holes in the surfaces of leaves,

---

fāte, făt, dâre, bärn; bē, bĕt, mêre; bīte, bĭt; nōte, hŏt, môre, dòg; fŭn, fûr; tōō, bŏŏk; oil; out; tar; thin; then; hw for wh as in *wh*at; zh for s as in u*s*ual; ə for a, e, i, o, u, as in *a*go, lin*e*n, per*i*l, at*o*m, min*u*s

which by opening and closing regulate the movement of water vapor and other gases into and out of the leaf.

stom·ach (stŭm′ək) ***n-*** **1** pouchlike part of the alimentary canal, between the esophagus and the duodenum in man and other vertebrates, that secretes the gastric juices and has an important digestive function. For picture, see *intestine.* **2** ability to endure or enjoy: *She has no* stomach *for a quarrel.* ***vt-*** to endure; tolerate: *I could not* stomach *his rudeness.*

stom·ach·er (stŭm′ə kər) ***n-*** formerly, the part of a woman's dress covering the stomach and chest.

stomp (stŏmp) ***vt-*** to tread heavily upon; stamp: *to* stomp *the ground.* ***vi-***: *He* stomped *hard on the floor.* ***n-*** jazz dance featuring a lively, heavy step.

stone (stōn) ***n-*** **1** hard mineral body; rock. **2** mineral matter which makes up such bodies of any size. **3** precious stone; gem. **4** something like a stone in looks or hardness: *a cherry* stone; *a gall*stone; *a kidney* stone. ***vt-*** **[stoned, ston·ing] 1** to remove stones from: *to* stone *cherries.* **2** to throw stones at; especially, to put to death by throwing stones at. ***adj-*** **1** made of rock: *a* stone *house.* **2** made of stoneware.

Stone Age ***n-*** the earliest known period in human culture, in which implements were made of stone.

stone-blind (stōn′ blīnd′) ***adj-*** completely blind.

stone·cut·ter (stōn′ kŭt′ ər) ***n-*** person or machine that cuts stone or prepares it for use.

stone-deaf (stōn′ dĕf′) ***adj-*** completely deaf.

Stone·henge (stōn′ hĕnj′) ***n-*** prehistoric monument in southern England, north of Salisbury, consisting of a group of thirty huge, rough-cut stones dating back approximately to 1848 B.C.

stone·ma·son (stōn′ mā′ sən) ***n-*** person whose work is to cut, prepare, and lay stones for walls, buildings, etc.

stone·ware (stōn′ wâr′) ***n-*** coarse, glazed pottery containing clay, sand, and flint.

stone·work (stōn′ wûrk′) ***n-*** **1** stone structure or part of it; masonry. **2** process of working in stone. **—*n-*** **stone′ work′ er.**

ston·y (stō′ nē) ***adj-*** **[ston·i·er, ston·i·est] 1** covered with stones: *a* stony *beach.* **2** like stone; cold, hard, or rigid: *a* stony *look.* **—*adv-*** **ston′ i·ly.** ***n-*** **ston′ i·ness.**

stood (sto͝od) *p.t. & p.p.* of **stand.**

stooge (sto͞oj) *Informal* ***n-*** **1** actor who is the foil for a comedian. **2** person who unquestioningly carries out the wishes of another.

stool (sto͞ol) ***n-*** **1** seat on a long leg or legs, sometimes with a low back. **2** backless and armless seat with short legs: *a milking* stool. **3** low rest for the feet. **4** feces.

Stools

stool pigeon ***n-*** **1** pigeon used as a decoy to help trap other pigeons. **2** *Slang* person who informs on criminals for the police.

¹stoop (sto͞op) ***vi-*** **1** to lean down with back and shoulders bent: *He had to* stoop *to pick up the box.* **2** to stand or walk in this way: *He* stooped *when he was tired.* **3** to degrade or lower oneself: *She would not* stoop *to gossip.* **4** to pounce or swoop down, as a bird on prey. ***n-*** **1** a leaning down. **2** bent posture: *He stood with a* stoop. [from Old English **stupian.**] ***Hom-*** stoup.

²stoop (sto͞op) ***n-*** porch, platform, or stairway at the entrance of a house. [American word from Dutch **stoep** meaning "a high step at the door."] ***Hom-*** stoup.

stop (stŏp) ***vt-*** **[stopped, stop·ping] 1** to halt the motion, action, or progress of: *to* stop *a car*; *to* stop *a rumor*; *to* stop *a revolt.* **2** to hold back; hinder; restrain (often followed by "from"): *to* stop *him from leaving.* **3** to close up; fill in: *to* stop *a bottle*; *to* stop *a wound.* **4** to obstruct; block (often followed by "up"): *to* stop *up a channel.* **5** *Informal* in boxing, to defeat, especially by a knockout. **6** *Music* to press (a string) or close (a finger hole) so as to produce the desired pitch. ***vi-*** **1** to halt or cease: *The car* stopped *at the gas station. He* stopped *in the middle of his speech.* **2** to stay: *We are* stopping *at my sister's house overnight.* ***n-*** **1** halt or pause: *He came to a* stop *when he saw the sign.* **2** halting place: *a subway* stop. **3** short visit: *We made a* stop *at the museum.* **4** block, peg, plug, etc., to regulate or check motion or to keep a movable part in place: *a window* stop. **5** *Music* any means or device for regulating pitch; also, in an organ, a set of pipes producing tones of the same quality.
stop off (or **over**) to stop at a place for a short time while traveling.

stop·cock (stŏp′ kŏk′) ***n-*** faucet or tap having a valve to regulate the flow of a liquid or gas.

stop·gap (stŏp′ găp′) ***n-*** something that closes an opening; hence, a temporary substitute. *as* ***modifier***: *a* stopgap *job.*

stop·light (stŏp′ līt′) ***n-*** **1** traffic light **2** light on the rear of a car or truck, that lights when the driver brakes.

stop·o·ver (stŏp′ ō′ vər) ***n-*** brief stay in a place, in the course of a journey; also, a place used as a waiting point.

stop·page (stŏp′ ĭj) ***n-*** **1** act of stopping; stop; halt: *a work* stoppage. **2** obstruction; block: *a* stoppage *in the nasal passages.*

stop·per (stŏp′ ər) ***n-*** **1** plug or cork used to close an opening in a bottle, sink, etc. **2** person or thing that stops or deters some action or movement; check. ***vt-***: *He* stoppered *the bottle tightly.*

stop·ple (stŏp′ əl) ***n-*** plug; stopper, ***vt-*** **[stop·pled, stop·pling]** to close with, or as if with, a stopper.

stop·watch (stŏp′ wŏch′) ***n-*** watch with a hand that indicates fractions of a second and can be started or stopped instantly by pressing a button.

stor·age (stôr′ ĭj) ***n-*** **1** a keeping or reserving of goods in a safe place: *the* storage *of furniture in a warehouse.* **2** place for storing or state of being stored: *My piano is in* storage. **3** the cost of keeping goods in a warehouse or other place for storing: *Can you pay the* storage *on your piano?* **4** part of an electronic computer that stores information; memory. *as* ***modifier***: *a* storage *bin.*

storage battery ***n-*** set of electrical cells that can change chemical energy into direct-current electrical energy and vice versa.

store (stôr) ***n-*** **1** place where goods are kept and sold: *a grocery* store; *a department* store. **2** supply gathered together; fund: *a* store *of acorns*; *a* store *of wisdom.* **3 stores** supplies kept for future use; reserves. ***vt-*** **[stored, stor·ing] 1** to put aside for future use or for safekeeping: *I have* stored *my furniture in a warehouse.* **2** to fill with; furnish: *I* stored *my mind with information.*
in store set aside; waiting. **set store by** to value.

store·house (stôr′ hous′) ***n-*** **1** place where goods are kept for future use; warehouse. **2** any abundant source or supply: *He is a* storehouse *of information.*

store·keep·er (stôr′ kē′ pər) ***n-*** person who owns or operates a retail store; shopkeeper.

store·room (stôr′ ro͞om′) ***n-*** room in which goods or supplies are stored.

stor·ey (stôr′ ē) *chiefly Brit.* ***n-*** [*pl.* **stor·eys**] ¹story.

¹stor·ied (stôr′ ēd) ***adj-*** having floors or stories: *a three-*storied *building.*

²stor·ied (stôr′ ēd) ***adj-*** **1** celebrated in story, history, or legend: *a* storied *personality.* **2** decorated with historical or legendary scenes: *a* storied *frieze.*

stork (stôrk, stòrk) ***n-*** long-legged, sharp-beaked bird related to the heron. **—*adj-* stork′ like′.**

Stork, about 3 ft. high

storm (stòrm, stôrm) ***n-* 1** any disturbed condition of the atmosphere, especially when marked by high winds and rain, hail, or snow. **2** outburst of passion or excitement; any violent commotion: *a* storm *of tears. as **modifier***: *a* storm *warning.* ***vi-* 1** to blow violently; rain, hail, snow, etc.: *It* stormed *all night.* **2** to speak or act in rage: *He* stormed *out.* ***vt-*** to attack with force: *to* storm *a fort.*
take by storm to capture by violent attack.

storm·bound (stòrm′ bound′, stôrm′-) ***adj-*** detained, confined, or cut off from the outside by a storm.

storm cellar ***n-*** cyclone cellar.

storm center ***n-* 1** the center of a cyclonic storm, a point of low atmospheric pressure and relative calm. **2** place at which, or issue around which, a debate or conflict is most violent.

storm door ***n-*** outer door that affords protection against storms and other severe weather.

storm petrel ***n-*** small sea bird of the North Atlantic and the Mediterranean, believed to signify an impending storm. Also **stormy petrel.** For picture, see *petrel.*

storm window ***n-*** protective window attached to a regular window and used for heat insulation and as protection against storms.

storm·y (stòr′ mē, stôr′-) ***adj-*** **[storm·i·er, storm·i·est] 1** having to do with storms: *a season of* stormy *weather.* **2** having to do with violent emotions; agitated: *a* stormy *meeting.* **—*adv-* storm′ i·ly.** ***n-*** **storm′ i·ness.**

[1]**sto·ry** (stôr′ ē) ***n-*** [*pl.* **sto·ries**] any level of a building: *Dot lives on the third* story. Also, *chiefly Brit.*, **storey.** [from [2]**story** in a special use that grew out of its earlier meaning of "a row of painted windows that told or illustrated a story."]

[2]**sto·ry** (stôr′ ē) ***n-*** [*pl.* **sto·ries**] **1** account, oral or written, of something that has happened: *a newspaper* story *of an accident.* **2** tale of fiction. **3** *Informal* a lie. [from Old French **(e)storie,** from Latin **historia,** "narrative."]

stor·y·tell·er (stôr′ ē tĕl′ ər) ***n-*** **1** person who tells stories. **2** *Informal* person who exaggerates or lies. **—*n-* stor′ y·tell′ ing.**

stoup (sto͞op) ***n-*** **1** *Archaic* drinking vessel. **2** basin for holy water at the entrance of a church. ***Hom-*** stoop.

stout (stout) ***adj-*** **[stout·er, stout·est] 1** fat and bulky; thickset. **2** strong: *bound with* stout *cords.* **3** brave; courageous: *the* stout *self-confidence of the pioneers.* ***n-*** strong, dark porter. **—*adv-* stout′ ly.** ***n-*** **stout′ ness.**

stout-heart·ed (stout′ här′ təd) ***adj-*** brave; courageous; undaunted: *a* stout-hearted *settler.* **—*adv-* stout′-heart′ ed′ ly.** ***n-*** **stout′-heart′ ed·ness.**

Early American stove

[1]**stove** (stōv) ***n-*** any of various heating or cooking devices that use coal, wood, oil, gas, or electricity as a fuel. [from Old English **stofa,** "a room for a warm bath."]

[2]**stove** (stōv) *p.t. & p.p.* of **stave.**

stove·pipe (stōv′ pīp′) ***n-*** **1** metal pipe for carrying off smoke and gases from a stove. **2** *Informal* tall top hat.

stow (stō) ***vt-*** to put away; store: *to* stow *cargo.*
stow away 1 to put in a safe place; conceal. **2** to be a stowaway.

stow·a·way (stō′ ə wā′) ***n-*** person who hides on a ship in order to get free passage.

strad·dle (străd′ əl) ***vt-*** **[strad·dled, strad·dling] 1** to sit or stand with one leg on each side of: *to* straddle *a horse or a chair.* **2** *Informal* to support or seem to support both sides of (an argument, issue, etc.). **—*n-* strad′dler.**

Strad·i·va·ri·us (străd′ ə vâr′ ē əs) ***n-*** any one of the world-famous violins or other stringed instruments made by Antonio Stradivari (1644-1737) in Cremona, Italy.

strafe (strāf) ***vt-*** **[strafed, straf·ing]** to attack with gunfire, especially with machine guns from low-flying airplanes: *We* strafed *the road.* ***vi-***: *The planes* strafed *without letup.* **—*n-* straf′ er.**

strag·gle (străg′ əl) ***vi-*** **[strag·gled, strag·gling] 1** to wander in a rambling manner; stray: *The children* straggled *in one by one.* **2** to spread or grow in a ragged, uneven fashion: *Vines* straggled *over the fence.* **3** to lag (behind or after). **—*n-* strag′ gler.** ***adj-*** **strag′ gly.**

straight (strāt) ***adj-*** **[straight·er, straight·est] 1** without bend or curve: *a* straight *road.* **2** perpendicular; erect: *Is the pole* straight? **3** properly placed or arranged; also, level: *Is my hat* straight? **4** in good order; tidy: *to keep a room* straight; *to keep records* straight. **5** honest; sincere: *a* straight *answer.* **6** not deviating at any time: *a* straight *path*; *a* straight *Democrat.* ***adv-* 1** in a direct line: *to shoot* straight. **2** by a direct route: *to go* straight *home.* **3** without delay: *Please go* straight *in to see the doctor.* **4** undeviatingly: *to vote* straight *Republican.* ***n-*** in poker, five cards in sequence. ***Hom-*** strait. **—*adv-* straight′ ly.** ***n-*** **straight′ ness.**
straight away (or **off**) at once; straightway. **straight from the shoulder** in an honest manner; frankly and directly: *Dave spoke* straight from the shoulder.

straight angle *Mathematics* ***n-*** an angle of 180°.

straight·a·way (strāt′ ə wā′) ***adj-*** without turns or curves. ***n-*** straight course; especially, the straight part, or stretch, of a race course. ***adv-*** straightway.

straight·edge (strāt′ ĕj′) ***n-*** strip or bar having a perfectly straight edge with which to test lines or surfaces or to draw straight lines.

straight·en (strā′ tən) ***vt-*** **1** to make straight and even: *to* straighten *a path.* **2** to make neat or tidy: *to* straighten *a drawer.* ***vi-*** to become straight. ***Hom-*** straiten. **—*n-* straight′ en·er.**
straighten out 1 to put in order: *She finally* straightened out *her room.* **2** *Informal* to make or become a mature, responsible person: *He'll* straighten out *soon.*

straight face ***n-*** face that shows no emotion. **—*adj-* straight′-faced′**: *a* straight-faced *lie.*

straight·for·ward (strāt′ fòr′ wərd, -fôr′ wərd) ***adj-*** honest; frank; direct: *a* straightforward *answer.* **—*adv-* straight′ for′ ward·ly.** ***n-*** **straight′ for′ ward·ness.**

straight ticket ***n-*** vote cast for all the candidates of a particular party. See also *split ticket.*

straight·way (strāt′ wā′) ***adv-*** at once; immediately.

[1]**strain** (strān) ***n-*** **1** stock or breed: *a horse of the Arabian* strain. **2** inherited trait or quality: *There was a* strain *of madness in that family.* **3** manner of expression; tone; style: *a* strain *of sadness in her voice.* **4** melody or tune. [probably from Old English **strēon,** "offspring."]

---

fāte, făt, dâre, bärn; bē, bĕt, mêre; bīte, bĭt; nōte, hŏt, môre, dòg; fŭn, fûr; to͞o, bo͝ok; oil; out; t*a*r; thin; *th*en; hw for wh as in *wh*at; zh for s as in u*s*ual; ə for a, e, i, o, u, as in *a*go, lin*e*n, per*i*l, at*o*m, min*u*s

[2]**strain** (strān) ***vt-*** **1** to stretch or pull with great force: *The weight of the piano* strained *the ropes almost to breaking.* **2** to exert to the utmost: *She* strained *her ears to overhear the conversation.* **3** to weaken or injure by too much exertion; sprain: *Bill* strained *his back lifting the carton.* **4** to pass through a strainer or sieve: *to* strain *tea.* **5** to stretch or force beyond what is usual or normal: *Jack* strained *the truth to justify himself.* ***vi-*** **1** to make strenuous effort; strive: *to* strain *for victory.* **2** to pass through a strainer: *a liquid that* strains *well.* ***n-*** **1** extreme pressure, force, or pull: *The cable snapped under the* strain. **2** severe physical or mental exertion or tension; also, an injury or illness resulting from this: *a muscle* strain; *heart* strain; *nervous* strain. **3** the distortion produced in an elastic material, such as a spring, by a stress. [from Old French **estraindre,** from Latin **stringere** meaning "to draw tightly."]

strained (strānd) ***adj-*** **1** put through a sieve: *a glass of* strained *orange juice.* **2** showing the effects of great effort: *a* strained *expression.* **3** injured: *a* strained *muscle.* **4** forced or unnatural: *a* strained *laugh.*

strain·er (strā′ nər) ***n-*** any of various devices or utensils, such as a sieve or colander, for separating liquid from solid matter.

Strainer

strait (strāt) ***n-*** **1** narrow channel connecting two larger bodies of water. **2 straits** difficulties; desperate circumstances: *He is always in financial* straits, *since he spends more than he earns.* ***adj-*** *Archaic* **1** narrow; confined. **2** strict; scrupulous: *the* strait *and narrow.* ***Hom-*** straight. **—*adv-* strait′ ly.** ***n-*** **strait′ ness.**

strait·en (strā′ tən) *Archaic* ***vt-*** **1** to narrow; contract. **2** to cause to be in need of money. ***Hom-*** straighten.

in straitened circumstances in great need of money.

strait jacket ***n-*** tight, narrow canvas coat put on violent mental patients to confine their arms.

strait-laced (strāt′ lāst′) ***adj-*** morally strict; prudish.

[1]**strand** (strănd) ***n-*** beach or shore of an ocean. ***vi-*** to run aground: *The skiff* stranded *on a reef.* ***vt-*** to place or leave (a boat) aground; hence, to place or leave in a helpless position: *The loss of our money* stranded *us in Singapore.* [from Old English **strand.**]

[2]**strand** (strănd) ***n-*** **1** one of several bundles of thread, wire, etc., twisted together to form a rope or cable. **2** something resembling this; thread or rope: *a* strand *of hair*; *a* strand *of beads.* [from Old French **estran** of the same meaning, from earlier Germanic **streno** meaning "a skein."]

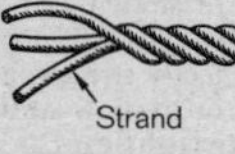
Strand

strange (strānj) ***adj-*** **[strang·er, strang·est] 1** unusual; odd; peculiar: *That was a* strange *thing to say.* **2** not previously experienced, met, or seen; unfamiliar: *a* strange *country.* **3** out of place; uneasy: *In Bombay I felt* strange. **—*adv-* strange′ ly.** ***n-*** **strange′ ness.**

stran·ger (strān′ jər) ***n-*** **1** person one does not know. **2** somebody from another place.

stranger to person who is unfamiliar with: *He is a* stranger to *our customs.*

stran·gle (străng′ gəl) ***vt-*** **[stran·gled, stran·gling] 1** to kill or attempt to kill by squeezing the throat; throttle; choke. **2** to suppress or stifle: *He* strangled *the impulse to answer.* ***vi-***: *He* strangled *on a bone.* **—*n-* stran′ gler.**

stran·gle·hold (străng′ gəl hōld′) ***n-*** in wrestling, an illegal hold by which one wrestler chokes another; hence, any force that makes someone helpless.

stran·gu·late (străng′ gyə lāt′) ***vt-*** **[stran·gu·lat·ed, stran·gu·lat·ing]** *Medicine* to constrict or obstruct (a tube or duct) so as to stop circulation.

stran·gu·la·tion (străng′ gyə lā′ shən) ***n-*** **1** act of strangling or choking someone: *death by* strangulation. **2** *Medicine* construction or obstruction of a tube or duct so as to stop circulation.

strap (străp) ***n-*** narrow strip of leather or other material, used to hold things together or keep something in place: *a watch* strap. ***vt-*** **[strapped, strap·ping] 1** to fasten with a strap: *to* strap *the luggage to the car.* **2** to cause to be short of money: *That vacation really* strapped *him.*

strap·hang·er (străp′ hăng′ ər) *Informal* ***n-*** person who stands on a subway or bus and, usually, holds onto an overhead handgrip; standee.

strap·less (străp′ ləs) ***adj-*** having no strap; especially, without shoulder straps: *a* strapless *evening gown.*

strap·ping (străp′ ĭng) ***adj-*** tall and robust; burly.

stra·ta (strā′ tə, străt′ ə) *pl.* of **stratum.**

strat·a·gem (străt′ ə jəm) ***n-*** any trick to deceive an enemy or gain an advantage; deception.

stra·te·gic (strə tē′ jĭk) ***adj-*** **1** having to do with military strategy: *Gibraltar is of* strategic *importance in defending the Mediterranean.* **2** skillfully adapted to a purpose: *By several* strategic *moves he gained control of the business.* **—*adv-* stra·te′ gi·cal·ly.**

strat·e·gist (străt′ ə jĭst) ***n-*** person who is skilled in strategy: *a military* strategist; *a political* strategist.

strat·e·gy (străt′ ə jē) ***n-*** [*pl.* **strat·e·gies**] **1** the art or science of maneuvering military forces on a large scale. **2** skill in managing any affair: *The team succeeded more by* strategy *than by brute force.* See also *tactic.*

strat·i·fi·ca·tion (străt′ ə fə kā′ shən) ***n-*** **1** an arranging in levels or layers: *the* stratification *of rocks*; *the* stratification *of society.* **2** something arranged in layers.

strat·i·fied (străt′ ə fīd′) ***adj-*** **1** arranged in levels or layers. **2** deposited in layers: *a* stratified *rock.*

strat·i·fy (străt′ ə fī′) ***vt-*** **[strat·i·fied, strat·i·fy·ing]** to arrange in layers or levels: *Wealth tends to* stratify *certain societies.* ***vi-***: *Certain societies* stratify *according to family descent.*

strato- *combining form* stratus: strato*cumulus*; strato*sphere.* [from modern Latin **strato-,** from Latin **strati-,** from **stratus** or **strata** meaning "(thing) spread out; spread out level," as in **street.**]

strat·o·cum·u·lus (străt′ ō kyōōm′ yə ləs) ***n-*** [*pl.* **strat·o·cum·u·li** (-lī)] mass of puffy, soft, low clouds arranged in a dappled pattern with open spaces between.

strat·o·sphere (străt′ ə sfêr′) ***n-*** layer of the earth's atmosphere from about 7 to about 20 miles above sea level. **—*adj-* strat′ o·spher′ ic** (-sfêr′ ĭk, -sfĕr′ ĭk).

stra·tum (strā′ təm, străt′ əm) ***n-*** [*pl.* **stra·ta** (-tə), also **stra·tums**] **1** layer of a material lying above or below another layer of different composition; especially, a layer of rock or soil: *an igneous* stratum *in a ridge.* **2** level or class of anything structured from top to bottom: *the middle* stratum *of wage earners.*

Rock strata

stra·tus (străt′ əs, strā′ təs) ***n-*** [*pl.* **stra·ti** (-tī)] any of several types of clouds that form in gray, usually unbroken, layers; especially, the lowest of these. For picture, see *cloud.*

straw (strò) ***n-*** **1** stalk of grain after it has been cut and threshed. **2** bunch or pack of such stalks: *a bed of* straw. **3** slender tube used for sipping liquids. *as* ***modifier***: *a* straw *basket*; *a* straw *hat.*

not worth a straw worthless. **catch at a straw** to try desperately any means that offers a solution or escape.

straw·ber·ry (strô′ bĕr′ ē) ***n-*** [*pl.* **straw·ber·ries**] **1** red oval fruit with tiny seeds like dots on its surface. **2** the plant that bears this fruit.

Strawberry

straw boss *Informal* ***n-*** person who assists a foreman in supervising the workers.

straw man ***n-*** in debate, editorials, etc., the opponent as deliberately misrepresented to make him an easy target for one's own logic.

straw vote ***n-*** an unofficial sampling of voter's wishes, intentions, etc., before an election.

stray (strā) ***vi-*** **1** to lose one's way; straggle; wander: *We* strayed *off our path in the dark woods.* **2** to digress; ramble: *His argument was forever* straying. ***adj-*** **1** lost and wandering; also, homeless: *a* stray *dog.* **2** isolated; occasional: *a* stray *taxi at night.* **3** casual; incidental: *a* stray *remark.* ***n-*** lost person or animal. **—*n-* stray′ er.**

streak (strēk) ***n-*** **1** long, often uneven mark or line: *a* streak *of paint.* **2** trait of character; trace: *a* streak *of cruelty.* ***vi-*** **1** to form a streak: *Lightning* streaked *in the sky.* **2** to move very rapidly; rush: *A train* streaked *by.* ***vt-***: *Clowns* streak *their faces with paint.*

streak·y (strē′ kē) ***adj-*** [**streak·i·er, streak·i·est**] **1** marked with streaks: *a* streaky *face.* **2** inconsistent: *a* streaky *nature.* **—*adv-* streak′ i·ly.** ***n-*** **streak′ i·ness.**

stream (strēm) ***n-*** **1** flow of water, such as a creek or small river. **2** steady flow: *a* stream *of light*; *a* stream *of cars.* ***vi-*** **1** to move or flow continuously: *The crowd* streamed *out of the stadium.* **2** to pour or flow (with): *to* stream *with sweat.* **3** wave: *Flags* streamed *in the wind.*

stream·er (strē′ mər) ***n-*** **1** long, narrow ribbon or flag. **2** shaft of light, such as sometimes occurs in auroras. **3** newspaper headline that runs across the page.

stream·let (strēm′ lət) ***n-*** little stream or brook.

stream·line (strēm′ līn′) ***vt-*** [**stream·lined, stream·lin·ing**] **1** to design or change (a vehicle or other solid object) so as to offer less resistance to the passage of air or water around it. **2** to simplify or otherwise improve the efficiency of (an organization, process, etc.).

stream·lined (strēm′ līnd′) ***adj-*** designed to offer the least resistance to air or water: *a* streamlined *train.*

street (strēt) ***n-*** road or way in a city or town, usually lined with buildings; also, the part of this way that extends between the sidewalks and is used for vehicles. *as* ***modifier***: *the* street *noises.*

street·car (strēt′ kär′) ***n-*** trolley car.

strength (strĕngth, strĕngkth) ***n-*** **1** power or force; toughness: *the* strength *of an athlete*; strength *of will*; strength *of a rope.* **2** effectiveness; potency: *the* strength *of a drug.* **3** intensity: *the* strength *of her love.* **4** force in numbers: *The squadron is at full* strength. **5** source of power; support: *Knowledge is his* strength.

on the strength of depending or relying on.

strength·en (strĕngk′ thən, strĕng′-) ***vt-*** **1** to make strong or stronger: *to* strengthen *a muscle.* **2** to encourage; inspire; hearten. **—*n-* strength′ en·er.**

stren·u·ous (strĕn′ yo͞o əs) ***adj-*** **1** vigorous; energetic; zealous: *a* strenuous *campaigner.* **2** requiring great effort or exertion: *a* strenuous *schedule.* **—*adv-* stren′ u·ous·ly.** ***n-*** **stren′ u·ous·ness.**

strep (strĕp) *Informal* ***n-*** streptococcus; also, an infection caused by a streptococcus. *as* ***modifier***: *a* strep *throat.*

strep·to·coc·cus (strĕp′ tə kŏk′ əs) ***n-*** [*pl.* **strep·to·coc·ci** (-kŏk′ sī, -kŏk′ sē)] any of a large group of spherical bacteria tending to form chains, some kinds of which cause severe sore throat, scarlet fever, rheumatic fever, and other diseases.

strep·to·my·cin (strĕp′ tə mī′ sən) ***n-*** an antibiotic drug derived from a mold that grows in the soil. It is used against many diseases, especially tuberculosis.

stress (strĕs) ***n-*** **1** applied force or pressure: *the* stress *of wind on tall buildings.* **2** overload on emotions, nerves, self-control, etc.: *a period of national* stress; *a disease related to* stress. **3** emphasis; importance: *This school puts* stress *on discipline.* **4** emphasis given to a syllable in a word. In the word "bicycle" the stress is on the first syllable. (See also *primary accent* and *secondary accent.*) ***vt-*** **1** to insist upon; emphasize: *The mayor* stressed *the need for reform.* **2** to accent (the syllable of a word). **3** to apply a force to (an elastic material).

stretch (strĕch) ***vt-*** **1** to draw out in length or width; draw taut: *to* stretch *a rubber band*; *to* stretch *canvas over a frame.* **2** to extend (often followed by "out"): *I* stretched *out my hand. We* stretched *ourselves full-length on the ground.* **3** to strain; exert to the utmost: *She* stretched *every effort to join us.* **4** to exaggerate: *to* stretch *the truth*; *to* stretch *a story.* **5** to make the most of; use completely or as much as possible: *We must* stretch *every dollar.* ***vi-*** **1** to spread; reach: *The rope* stretched *across the sidewalk.* **2** to be elastic; be capable of extension: *This cloth* stretches. **3** to strain the body so as to pull the muscles out full-length, when one is stiff or tired. ***n-*** **1** act of straining or extending: *He gave the rope a good* stretch. *I could not understand by any* stretch *of my imagination.* **2** continuous space or time: *a* stretch *of six years*; *a* stretch *of eighteen miles.* **3** elasticity: *The rubber lost its* stretch. **4** act of pulling the muscles out full length by bending and twisting the body: *We all stood up and had a good* stretch. **—*n-* stretch′ a·ble.**

stretch·er (strĕch′ ər) ***n-*** **1** a frame or expanding instrument by which something may be given shape or made larger: *a curtain* stretcher; *a glove* stretcher. **2** portable cot or mattress on which a sick or injured person may be carried or moved while lying at full length.

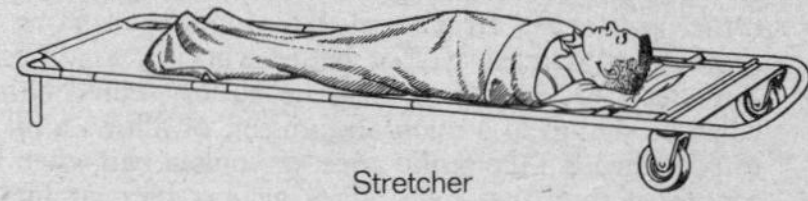
Stretcher

strew (stro͞o) ***vt-*** [**strewed, strewed** or **strewn, strew·ing**] **1** to scatter or let fall in a careless way: *He* strewed *his clothes about.* **2** to cover with something scattered.

stri·at·ed (strī′ ā′ təd) ***adj-*** **1** having narrow stripes, streaks, or lines, whether of structure or color. **2** having fine ridges or grooves, especially a series of parallel grooves or stripes.

striated muscle ***n-*** muscle whose fibers have encircling light and dark bands. Such muscles are under the conscious control of the organism.

stri·a·tion (strī ā′ shən) ***n-*** **1** condition of being striated: *We noticed the* striation *of the rocks.* **2** long, thin marking or scratch: *the* striations *on the rock.*

strick·en (strĭk′ ən) *p.p.* of **strike.** ***adj-*** struck or attacked suddenly by sickness, troubles, etc.

strict (strĭkt) ***adj-*** [**strict·er, strict·est**] **1** severe; stern: *Father is* strict *but fair.* **2** rigid; not changing: *a* strict *rule.* **3** absolute; entire: *in* strict *privacy*; *in* strict *confidence.* **—*adv-* strict′ ly.** ***n-*** **strict′ ness.**

stric·ture (strĭk′ chər) ***n-*** **1** severe criticism or blame; censure: *I resent this* stricture *on my conduct.* **2** thing that limits, confines, or restricts; restraint. **3** abnormal narrowing of a passage; constriction.

stride (strīd) ***vi-*** [**strode** (strōd), **strid·den** (strĭd′ ən), **strid·ing**] to walk with long steps: *to* stride *along the beach.* ***vt-*** to sit or stand with one leg on either side of something; straddle; bestride: *to* stride *a horse.* ***n-*** long step or steps: *a steady* stride. **—*n-* strid′ er.**

hit one's stride to reach one's peak of performance.

take in stride to deal with or handle without great fuss.

stri·den·cy (strī′ dən sē) ***n-*** shrill and penetrating quality: *a* stridency *of tone.* Also **stri′ dence.**

stri·dent (strī′ dənt) ***adj-*** harsh; grating; shrill: *a* strident *tone.* **—*adv-* stri′ dent·ly.**

strife (strīf) ***n-*** **1** a conflict; struggle: *the* strife *of battle.* **2** discord; contention: *the* strife *over a will.*

strike (strīk) ***vt-*** [**struck** (strŭk), **struck** or **strick·en** (strĭk′ ən), **strik·ing**] **1** to hit: *The ball* struck *the ground.* **2** to deliver a blow against: *to* strike *the floor with one's foot.* **3** to afflict or affect by disease, emotion, etc.: *An epidemic* struck *the town.* **4** to make an impression on: *The idea* struck *us as absurd.* **5** to produce by stamping or printing: *to* strike *a gold medal.* **6** to make burn by friction: *to* strike *a match.* **7** to sound: *The clock is* striking *the hour.* **8** to discover luckily or in a sudden manner: *The miner* struck *gold.* **9** to reach; make; conclude: *The shopkeeper* struck *a bargain with the customer.* **10** to cross out; cancel: *to* strike *a word from the minutes of the meeting.* **11** to stop work at (a factory, shop, etc.) in order to get more pay, better working conditions, etc. **12** of a venomous snake, to bite (someone or something) with a violent lunge: *The cobra* struck *him on the ankle.* **13** to take down and pack: *to* strike *a tent*; *to* strike *camp.* ***vi-*** **1** to deal a quick blow or thrust; make an attack: *The army* struck *in two places at once.* **2** to hit; collide; become stranded: *The ship* struck *on the reef.* **3** to proceed: *They* struck *into the woods.* **4** to sound, as a bell or clock. **5** to cease working in order to gain better pay, working conditions, etc. **6** of a venomous snake, to bite with a violent lunge: *The rattler coiled and* struck. ***n-*** **1** a stopping of work in order to gain more pay or better working conditions. **2** in baseball, a tally against the batter, scored either when he swings at a pitch and misses, or allows a pitch to pass through the strike zone, or fouls a ball when he has fewer than two such tallies against him, or hits a foul tip which the catcher holds, when he already has two such tallies against him. **3** a lucky discovery, especially of oil or ore; hence, any sudden success: *a gold* strike; *a lucky* strike. **4** in fishing, a hard bite.

on strike not working, because of a stoppage called in order to improve pay, working conditions, etc.

strike home to deliver a well-aimed and effective blow.

strike it rich to earn or produce wealth suddenly.

strike off to make (something) quickly but well.

strike out **1** in baseball, of a batter, to have three strikes recorded against him, and therefore be called out. **2** of a baseball pitcher, to cause a batter to strike out.

strike up to begin: *We* struck up *a friendship.*

strike·bound (strīk′ bound′) ***adj-*** closed by a strike.

strike·break·er (strīk′ brā′ kər) ***n-*** worker hired to take the place of one out on strike.

strike·out (strīk′ out′) ***n-*** in baseball, an out caused by three strikes charged against the batter. *as* ***modifier***: *the league's* strikeout *record.*

strik·er (strī′ kər) ***n-*** **1** worker who ceases working as a protest against existing wages and working conditions or as a means of securing improvements in them. **2** person or thing that strikes. **3** in the U.S. Navy, a seaman training for a petty officer's rating.

strike zone ***n-*** in baseball, the rectangular area above home plate, as wide as the plate itself and as high as the distance between the batter's knees and armpits, through which a pitch must pass to be called a strike, if the batter does not swing.

strik·ing (strī′ kĭng) ***adj-*** very noticeable; claiming attention; attractive: *a* striking *example of efficiency*; *a* striking *dress.* **—*adv-* strik′ ing·ly.**

string (strĭng) ***n-*** **1** thin cord or twine. **2** anything used to tie something: *an apron* string. **3** set of things arranged on a cord: *a* string *of beads.* **4** series or line of something: *a* string *of lanterns*; *a* string *of cars.* **5** wire or catgut cord for a musical instrument. **6** *Informal* team or part of a team: *I was on the first* string *in football.* **7 strings** (1) section of an orchestra composed of stringed instruments. (2) *Informal* accompanying conditions: *The grant had a great many* strings *attached.* ***vt-*** [**strung** (strŭng), **string·ing**] **1** to put on a cord: *to* string *beads for a necklace.* **2** to furnish with cords: *to* string *a racket*; *to* string *a guitar.* **3** to pull the tough fibers off the edges of (vegetables). **—*adj-* string′ less. *adj-* string′ like′.**

have two strings to (one's) bow to have more than one possibility of action or response. **pull strings** to use special influence in order to get something done.

string along with to cooperate with; play along with.

string out **1** to extend. **2** to space out in a line.

string up **1** to hang. **2** *Informal* to execute by hanging.

string bean ***n-*** **1** kind of bean grown for its edible pods. **2** the pod itself. **3** *Slang* very tall and thin person.

stringed instrument ***n-*** musical instrument fitted with strings, such as a guitar, violin, or harp.

strin·gent (strĭn′ jənt) ***adj-*** strict; rigid; severe in requirements; exacting, as a law: *a* stringent *standard*; *a* stringent *rule.* **—*n-* strin′ gen·cy. *adv-* strin′ gent·ly.**

string·er (strĭng′ ər) ***n-*** **1** person or thing that strings. **2** in a building, airplane, boat, bridge, etc., a long timber or member connecting uprights or crosspieces.

string·y (strĭng′ ē) ***adj-*** [**string·i·er, string·i·est**] **1** like string. **2** full of fibers: *a* stringy *piece of meat.* **—*n-* string′ i·ness.**

[1]strip (strĭp) ***vt-*** [**stripped, strip·ping**] **1** to remove (a covering); peel: *to* strip *wallpaper from a wall.* **2** to rob: *The invaders* stripped *the country of its treasures.* ***vi-*** to undress: *The boys* stripped *and went swimming.* [from Old English **(be)strypan,** "to plunder."] **—*n-* strip′ per.**

[2]strip (strĭp) ***n-*** **1** long, narrow, flat piece. **2** place for airplanes to land and take off; also, a road or street. **3** comic strip. [from **[1]strip,** and influenced by **stripe.**]

strip cropping ***n-*** planting crops in strips that alternate with strips of grass or hay and run across the slope of the land, to reduce erosion.

stripe (strīp) ***n-*** **1** band or streak: *a tiger's* stripes; *a suit with a narrow black* stripe. **2** *Military Informal* a chevron. **3** sort or kind: *They are persons of the same* stripe. **4** blow with a whip or rod: *They gave the thief ten* stripes. **5 stripes** prison uniform having broad horizontal bands, usually of black and white. ***vt-*** [**striped, strip·ing**] to mark with bands or streaks.

striped (strīpt, *also* strī′ pəd) ***adj-*** marked with or made in stripes: *a small,* striped *snake.*

striped bass ***n-*** large sea bass with horizontal stripes on the sides and valued as food and game. Also **strip′ er.**

strip·ling (strĭp′ lĭng) ***n-*** boy between youth and manhood.

strive (strīv) ***vi-*** [**strove** (strōv), **striv·en** (strĭv′ ən), **striv·ing**] **1** to try hard; make an effort: *You must* strive *for better marks.* **2** to struggle; battle: *to* strive *against a gale.*

stro·bo·scope (strō′ bə skōp′) ***n-*** any of various devices that permit something in rapid motion to be seen or photographed as if it were standing still. Most stroboscopes use a rapidly flashing light synchronized with the motion of the subject.

strode (strōd) *p.t.* of **stride.**

[1]**stroke** (strōk) ***vt-*** **[stroked, stro·king]** to move the hand gently along a surface of: *to* stroke *a kitten.* ***n-*** a gentle, repeated movement of the hand, etc., in the same direction across something. [from Old English **strāc** and **strācian,** related to **strike.**] **—*n-* strok′ er.**

[2]**stroke** (strōk) ***n-*** **1** act of striking a blow, or the blow itself: *The lumberjack lopped off the branch with one* stroke *of his ax.* **2** anything resembling a blow: *a* stroke *of lightning.* **3** one of a series of complete movements or actions: *a* stroke *of a swimmer*; *a* stroke *of an oar.* **4** the sound of a striking clock and the time marked: *on the* stroke *of midnight.* **5** movement or mark made by a pen, pencil, brush, etc.: *The painter completed the picture with a few* strokes. **6** any sudden attack of illness, especially of apoplexy, in which a blood vessel supplying the brain ruptures or becomes obstructed. **7** single effort, or its result: *We passed the summer without a* stroke *of work.* **8** the rower who sets the pace for a rowing crew. ***vi-*** **[stroked, stroking]**: *The swimmer* stroked *to shore. A good oarsman* strokes *smoothly.* [from Old English **strac,** and related to [1]**stroke.**] **—*n-* strok′ er.**

stroke of luck sudden good fortune.

stroll (strōl) ***n-*** quiet, slow walk; saunter: *We went for a* stroll *after dinner.* ***vi-*** **1** to go for a slow, easy walk. **2** to wander on foot from place to place.

stroll·er (strō′ lər) ***n-*** **1** person who strolls. **2** baby carriage in the form of a chair.

strong (strȯng) ***adj-*** **[strong·er, strong·est] 1** physically powerful: *a* strong *wrestler*; *a* strong *horse.* **2** healthy; sound: *a* strong *constitution*; *to feel* strong *again.* **3** determined; firm: *a* strong *character*; *a* strong *will.* **4** hearty; ardent; passionate: *a man of* strong *affections and* strong *dislikes.* **5** intellectually powerful; vigorous: *a* strong *mind*; *the* strong *arguments in his favor.* **6** affecting one of the senses powerfully: *a* strong *light*; *a* strong *odor*; *a* strong *flavor.* **7** not easily broken or destroyed; durable: *a* strong *fortress.* **8** firmly held and not easily changed: *his* strong *religious beliefs.* **9** in strength of numbers: *an army 20,000* strong. **—*adv-* strong′ ly.**

strong-arm (strȯng′ ärm′) ***adj-*** using force, violence, or physical coercion: *his* strong-arm *tactics.* ***vt-*** to use force against: *His thugs* strong-arm *any opponents.*

strong·box (strȯng′ bŏks′) ***n-*** very strong box or chest equipped with a lock, used for storing money, jewelry, and other valuables; safe.

strong·hold (strȯng′ hōld′) ***n-*** **1** a place, such as a fortress, that is safe from attack or danger. **2** place where a certain idea or cause is especially strong.

strong-mind·ed (strȯng′ mīn′ dəd) ***adj-*** firmly independent in judgment; having a mind of one's own. **—*adv-* strong′-mind′ ed·ly. *n-* strong′-mind′ ed·ness.**

strong suit ***n-*** **1** in card games, a long suit with high cards. **2** something that a person is very good at.

strong verb *Grammar* ***n-*** verb which forms its past tense or past participle, or both, by internal vowel change, either with or without other change. Examples: sing, sang, sung; draw, drew, drawn. See also *weak verb.*

stron·ti·um (strŏn′ chəm, strŏn′ tē əm) ***n-*** soft, silver-white metal element that burns with a red flame. Symbol Sr, At. No. 38. At. Wt. 87.62.

strontium 90 ***n-*** radioactive isotope of strontium, atomic weight 90, produced by a thermonuclear explosion. It is dangerous because it accumulates in the bones when taken in food or drink.

strop (strŏp) ***n-*** strap on which a razor is sharpened. ***vt-*** **[stropped, strop·ping]** to sharpen on such a strap.

stro·phe (strō′ fē) ***n-*** **1** in ancient Greek drama, part of an ode sung by the chorus as it danced in one direction. **2** stanza. **—*adj-* stro′ phic.**

strove (strōv) *p.t.* of **strive.**

struck (strŭk) *p.t. & p.p.* of **strike.**

struc·tur·al (strŭk′ chər əl) ***adj-*** **1** of or relating to structure or structures. **2** used to bear weight or provide strength in a structure: *These beams are* structural, *not ornamental.* **3** in geology, having to do with structure rather than materials. **—*adv-* struc′ tur·al·ly.**

structural formula *Chemistry* ***n-*** formula that shows the arrangement of atoms and bonds in a molecule.

struc·ture (strŭk′ chər) ***n-*** **1** way in which something is put together, or in which things go together to form more complex things: *the* structure *of the human body.* **2** a building: *the large* structure *across the street.* **3** in various sciences, a separate feature or item. An arm is a structure in anatomy; a mountain is a structure in geology. ***vt-*** **[struc·tured, struc·tur·ing]** to organize carefully for a special purpose; shape; arrange: *to* structure *a conference*; *to* structure *a program.*

stru·del (stro͞o′ dəl, shtro͞o′-) ***n-*** pastry made of a thin sheet of dough in which fruit, nuts, etc., are rolled.

strug·gle (strŭg′ əl) ***vi-*** **[strug·gled, strug·gling] 1** to make a strong effort; strive: *He* struggled *to get an education.* **2** to fight; compete: *The two men* struggled *for years.* ***n-*** **1** very great effort or attempt: *It was a* struggle *to learn to spell.* **2** a contest; fight. **—*n-* strug′ gler.**

strum (strŭm) ***vt-*** **[strummed, strum·ming]** to pluck the strings of (a musical instrument): *to* strum *a guitar.* ***vi-***: *She* strummed *and sang.* ***n-***: *I heard a* strum *on a banjo.* **—*n-* strum′ mer.**

strum·pet (strŭm′ pət) ***n-*** prostitute; harlot.

strung (strŭng) *p.t. & p.p.* of **string.**

[1]**strut** (strŭt) ***vi-*** **[strut·ted, strut·ting]** to walk with vain, showy, self-important steps: *The peacock* strutted *and spread his tail.* ***n-*** such a vain walk. [from Old English **strūtian** meaning "to walk holding oneself at a stiff angle," and related to [2]**strut.**] **—*n-* strut′ ter.**

[2]**strut** (strŭt) ***n-*** piece of timber or metal placed at an angle to something for a support. [from earlier Germanic **strutt** meaning "stiff; rigid," or from Old Norse **strūtr,** "stiff projection."]

Struts

strych·nine (strĭk′ nīn′, -nən) ***n-*** poisonous alkaloid derived from the seeds of nux vomica and related plants.

Stu·art (sto͞o′ ərt, styo͞o′) ***n-*** name of the family that ruled Scotland from 1371 to 1603, and Great Britain from 1603 to 1649, 1660 to 1689, and 1702 to 1714. ***as modifier:*** *the* Stuart *dynasty*; *a* Stuart *king.*

stub (stŭb) ***n-*** **1** short remaining end of anything, such as a cigar, pencil, etc. **2** part of a check, bill, ticket, etc., kept after the rest has been torn off. ***vt-*** **[stubbed, stub·bing]** to strike against some fixed object: *to* stub *one's toe.*

stub·ble (stŭb′ əl) ***n-*** **1** short stalks of grain left standing in the field after the harvest. **2** anything looking like this, such as a short growth of beard. **—*adj-* stub′ bly.**

stub·born (stŭb′ ərn) ***adj-*** **1** fixed in an opinion, way, etc.; not willing to change; obstinate: *The* stubborn *child refused to wear mittens.* **2** done in a determined, persistent way: *The settlers made a* stubborn *effort to clear the forests.* **3** difficult or hard to manage, handle, or treat: *a* stubborn *cold.* **—*adv-* stub′ born·ly.** ***n-*** **stub′ born·ness.**

stub·by (stŭb′ ē) ***adj-*** **[stub·bi·er, stub·bi·est] 1** like a stub; short and thick: *a* stubby *beard*; stubby *fingers.* **2** covered with stubble: *a* stubby *field.* **—*n-* stub′ bi·ness.**

stuc·co (stŭk′ ō) ***n-*** [*pl.* **stuc·coes** or **stuc·cos**] a kind of plaster or cement used to cover walls, moldings, etc. *as* ***modifier***: *a* stucco *house.* ***vt-*** to cover with stucco.

stuck (stŭk) *p.t. & p.p.* of *stick.*

stuck-up (stŭk′ ŭp′) *Informal* ***adj-*** vain; conceited.

[1]**stud** (stŭd) ***n-*** **1** small knob, button, etc., used as a fastener or for decoration. **2** upright timber in a wall to which horizontal boards or laths may be nailed. ***vt-*** **[stud·ded, stud·ding] 1** to set or decorate with projecting objects: *The jeweler* studded *the bracelet with diamonds.* **2** to cover in great number: *Stars* studded *the midnight sky.* [from Old English **studu** meaning "post; prop; rivet nail; the head (of these)."]

[2]**stud** (stŭd) ***n-*** **1** any male animal, especially a horse, kept for breeding purposes. **2** collection of horses for racing, hunting, or breeding, or the place where they are kept. *as* ***modifier***: *a* stud *farm.* [from Old English **stōd** meaning a "herd of horses," and related to [1]**stud.** These animals were kept in corrals enclosed by posts.]

stud·ding (stŭd′ ĭng) ***n-*** **1** upright timbers in a wall. **2** lumber from which such timbers are cut.

stu·dent (stōō′ dənt, styōō′) ***n-*** **1** person who attends an educational institution or who receives other instruction. **2** person who is devoted to books and learning: *a* student *of history.* *as* ***modifier***: *a* student *meeting.*

stud·ied (stŭd′ ēd) ***adj-*** deliberate; showing thought and effort: *The courtier made a* studied *effort to praise the king.* **—*adv-* stud′ ied·ly.** ***n-*** **stud′ ied·ness.**

stu·di·o (stōō′ dē ō, styōō′-) ***n-*** [*pl.* **stu·di·os**] **1** room where an artist works. **2** place set up to broadcast radio or TV programs or to film motion pictures.

studio couch ***n-*** couch, usually backless, that converts into a double bed by sliding a spring from beneath it.

stu·di·ous (stōō′ dē əs, styōō′-) ***adj-*** **1** given to or fond of study. **2** thoughtful; painstaking: *a* studious *attention to detail.* **—*adv-* stu′ di·ous·ly.** ***n-*** **stu′ di·ous·ness.**

stud·y (stŭd′ ē) ***n-*** [*pl.* **stud·ies**] **1** an effort to gain knowledge by using the mind: *to devote much time to* study. **2** branch of learning: *Claude did better in science than in English* studies. **3** investigation; report: *The city prepared a* study *on the slum problem.* **4** deep thought; reflection: *He was in deep* study *and didn't hear a thing.* **5** room in a house set aside for reading and writing. **6** sketch in preparation for a painting: *The artist made several* studies *of his subject before he began the portrait.* **7** picture: *He was a* study *of gloom.* **8 studies** school or college work; schooling. *as* ***modifier***: *my* study *habits*; study *group.* ***vi-*** **[stud·ied, stud·y·ing]** to make an effort to gain knowledge by using the mind: *I have to* study *for two hours.* ***vt-*** **1** to make a mental effort to learn (something): *to* study *arithmetic.* **2** to think about carefully; examine: *to* study *a map.* **3** to examine carefully; investigate: *a commission to* study *foreign trade.*

stuff (stŭf) ***vt-*** **1** to fill very full; pack closely; cram: *to* stuff *oneself at the table*; *to* stuff *a trunk.* **2** to fill the inside of (something): *Mother* stuffed *the turkey. The upholsterer* stuffed *the cushions with feathers.* ***n-*** **1** *Informal* things; belongings: *Put all your* stuff *away.* **2** essential element; material. **3** cloth.

stuff and nonsense foolishness.

stuffed shirt ***n-*** formal and pompous individual.

stuff·ing (stŭf′ ĭng) ***n-*** **1** material with which something is filled or packed: *mattress* stuffing; *the* stuffing *of a sofa.* **2** mixture of bread, chopped meat, seasonings, etc., used to fill a turkey, green pepper, etc.

stuff·y (stŭf′ ē) ***adj-*** **[stuf·fi·er, stuf·fi·est] 1** without fresh air; close. **2** boring; dull: *a* stuffy *conversation.* **3** smug and self-important; priggish and solemn. **—*adv-* stuf′ fi·ly.** ***n-*** **stuf′ fi·ness.**

stul·ti·fi·ca·tion (stŭl′ tə fə kā′ shən) ***n-*** a stultifying.

stul·ti·fy (stŭl′ tə fī′, stōōl′-) ***vt-*** **[stul·ti·fied, stul·ti·fy·ing]** to weaken; hinder; repress: *to* stultify *progress.*

stum·ble (stŭm′ bəl) ***vi-*** **[stum·bled, stum·bling] 1** to fall or trip while walking: *I* stumbled *over a log in the path.* **2** to make a mistake; falter; blunder: *Everyone* stumbled *over his lines in the play.* ***n-*** **1** a fall or trip while walking. **2** a mistake; error: *Joseph made several* stumbles *while reciting the poem.* **—*n-* stumb′ ler.** ***adv-*** **stumb′ ling·ly.**

stumble on (or **across**) to come upon by chance.

stumbling block ***n-*** something that stops or slows progress; impediment; obstacle.

stump (stŭmp) ***n-*** **1** the base of a tree or plant left after most of the trunk has been cut down. **2** what remains after the main part has been removed; stub: *That puppy has only a* stump *of tail.* **3** a place or platform used by a political speaker. ***vt-*** **1** to defeat; baffle: *Your question* stumps *me and I can't answer it.* **2** to travel over (an area) making political speeches: *He* stumped *the whole country before the election.* ***vi-*** to walk stiffly with noisy steps: *He* stumped *into the house.* **—*n-* stump′ like′.**

take the stump to give a public speech or series of speeches: *He* took the stump *in favor of prohibition.*

stump·y (stŭm′ pē) ***adj-*** **[stump·i·er, stump·i·est]** of or resembling a stump; short and stunted. **—*adv-* stump′i·ly.** ***n-*** **stump′ i·ness.**

stun (stŭn) ***vt-*** **[stunned, stun·ning] 1** to make unconscious; daze: *A blow on the head* stunned *him.* **2** to shock; overwhelm: *The bad news* stunned *everyone.*

stung (stŭng) *p.t. & p.p.* of **sting.**

stunk (stŭngk) *p.t. & p.p.* of **stink.**

stun·ner (stŭn′ ər) *Informal* ***n-*** person or thing that is very striking, especially in beauty or excellence.

stun·ning (stŭn′ ĭng) *Informal* ***adj-*** striking; very handsome: *a* stunning *girl.* **—*adv-* stun′ ning·ly.**

[1]**stunt** (stŭnt) ***vt-*** to check the growth or development of; retard: *The dry weather* stunted *the tomato plants.* [from Old English **stunt** meaning "short (in physical or mental growth); foolish."]

[2]**stunt** (stŭnt) ***n-*** **1** a show or display of skill or daring: *a* stunt *on a high trapeze.* **2** act or trick: *That was a stupid* stunt. [perhaps from German **Stunde,** "lesson."]

stunt flyer ***n-*** pilot who is expert at flying his airplane through difficult maneuvers. Also **stunt pilot.**

stunt man ***n-*** man who replaces an actor in a motion picture, television show, etc., when something dangerous like a fall or crash is to be filmed.

stu·pe·fac·tion (stōō′ pə făk′ shən, styōō′-) ***n-*** **1** act of stupefying. **2** stupefied condition.

stu·pe·fy (stōō′ pə fī′, styōō′-) ***vt-*** **[stu·pe·fied, stu·pe·fy·ing] 1** to put into a stupor; dull the senses of: *The heat and noise* stupefied *us.* **2** to amaze; stun: *The sudden attack* stupefied *the soldiers.* **—*n-* stu′ pe·fi·er.**

stu·pen·dous (stōō pĕn′ dəs, styōō-) ***adj-*** amazing, particularly because of great size; tremendous; marvelous; immense: *The Grand Canyon is* stupendous. **—*adv-* stu·pen′ dous·ly.** ***n-*** **stu·pen′ dous·ness.**

stu·pid (stōō′ pĭd, styōō′-) ***adj-*** **1** not intelligent; dull: *a* stupid *person.* **2** boring; uninteresting: *a* stupid *conversation.* **—*adv-* stu′ pid·ly.** ***n-*** **stu′ pid·ness.**

stu·pid·i·ty (stōō pĭd′ ə tē, styōō-) ***n-*** [*pl.* **stu·pid·i·ties**] **1** lack of intelligence. **2** stupid act or remark.

stu·por (stōō′ pər, styōō′-) ***n-*** dazed or stunned condition; daze: *I had so little sleep that I was in a* stupor.

stur·dy (stûr′ dē) ***adj-*** [**stur·di·er, stur·di·est**] **1** strong; robust. **2** firm; resolute: *a* sturdy *resolve.* **—*adv-*** **stur′ di·ly.** ***n-*** **stur′ di·ness.**

stur·geon (stûr′ jən) ***n-*** [*pl.* **stur·geon; stur·geons** (kinds of sturgeon)] any of various large ocean and fresh-water fishes having bony plates along their sides. Smoked roe of sturgeon is considered a great delicacy.

Atlantic sturgeon, about 15 ft. long

stut·ter (stŭt′ ər) ***vi-*** to speak with pauses, repeating the beginning sounds of words; stammer. ***vt-:*** *to* stutter *a reply.* ***n-*** hesitant speech with a repetition of the beginning sounds of words; a stammer: *to speak with a* stutter. ***n-*** **stut′ ter·er.** ***adv-*** **stut′ ter·ing·ly.**

St. Vi·tus's dance (sānt′ vī′ təs dăns′) ***n-*** chorea. Also **St. Vitus dance.**

¹sty (stī) ***n-*** [*pl.* **sties**] **1** pen for pigs. **2** filthy place. [from Old English **stig** meaning "enclosure; farm buildings."]

²sty (stī) ***n-*** [*pl.* **sties**] sore and swollen sebaceous gland on an eyelid. [from Middle English **styanye,** from Old English ***stīgend*** meaning "a rising; pustule," from **stigan,** "to rise," and **ye,** "eye."]

Styg·i·an (stĭj′ ē ən) ***adj-*** **1** of or referring to the mythological river Styx in Hades over which the shades of the dead were ferried by the boatman Charon. **2** (also **styg′ i·an**) infernal; dark and gloomy: *a* stygian *cave.*

style (stīl) ***n-*** **1** particular or personal manner of doing or making something, such as writing, speaking, acting, building, etc.: *a graceful* style *of dancing; the Gothic* style *of architecture.* **2** polish, grace, and distinction in the execution of something, in manner, or in appearance: *The diplomat conducted herself with* style. **3** the current mode or fashion: *His clothes are always in* style. **4** elegance or luxury: *to live in* style *in a mansion.* **5** sort or kind: *What* style *of man is he?* **6** stylus. **7** plan of punctuation, spelling, typography, etc., chosen for printed matter. **8** in botany, the middle portion of the pistil of a flower, between the ovary and the stigma. ***vt-*** [**styled, styl·ing**] **1** to call; name: *Washington was* styled *"the Father of our Country."* **2** to design according to some particular fashion: *to* style *hats.* ***Homs-*** stile.

styl·ish (stī′ lĭsh) ***adj-*** fashionable; up to date; elegant: *a* stylish *dress.* **—*adv-*** **styl′ ish·ly.** ***n-*** **styl′ ish·ness.**

styl·ist (stī′ lĭst) ***n-*** **1** person who creates or is expert in a style: *prose* stylist. **2** designer, especially of automobiles.

sty·lis·tic (stī lĭs′ tĭk) ***adj-*** of or relating to style, especially literary style: *for* stylistic *reasons.* **—*adv-*** **sty′ lis′ ti·cal·ly.**

styl·ize (stī′ līz′) ***vt-*** [**styl·ized, styl·iz·ing**] to draw or represent in a conventional and usually simplified and schematic way.

sty·lus (stī′ ləs) ***n-*** [*pl.* **styl·us·es** or **styl·i** (-lī′)] **1** writing instrument of antiquity for use on wax tablets. **2** instrument with a point for marking or engraving on stencils, carbons, etc. **3** needle of a phonograph. **4** pen of a seismograph or other recording instrument.

sty·mie (stī′ mē) ***n-*** in golf, the position of a ball on the putting green when it lies directly between the hole and the ball of the person who must putt next. ***vt-*** [**sty·mied, sty·my·ing**] to obstruct; to block so that one is unable to move.

styp·tic (stĭp′ tĭk) ***adj-*** able to stop or check bleeding especially by contracting the opened blood vessels. ***n-:*** *Alum is a* styptic.

sty·rene (stī′ rēn′) ***n-*** an organic compound (C_8H_8) that is a constituent of one kind of synthetic rubber.

Sty·ro·foam (stī′ rə fōm′) ***n-*** trademark name for a lightweight, rigid plastic foam used to make cups, coolers, etc., and as an insulating material in buildings. Also **styrofoam.**

Styx (stĭks) ***n-*** Greek mythology, the principal river of the underworld.

sua·sion (swā′ zhən) ***n-*** persuasion. **—*adj-*** **sua′ sive.** ***adv-*** **sua′ sive·ly.** ***n-*** **sua′ sive·ness.**

suave (swäv) ***adj-*** [**suav·er, sauv·est**] bland, smooth, and winningly pleasant in manner. **—*adj-*** **suave′ ly.** ***n-*** **suav′ i·ty** or **suave′ ness.**

sub (sŭb) *Informal* ***n-*** **1** submarine. **2** substitute. **3** subordinate. **4** subaltern.

sub- *prefix* **1** under; below; beneath: *a* sub*way;* sub*marine;* sub*soil;* sub*entry.* **2** less than; near but not quite: *a* sub*tropical climate.*

sub·ac·id (sŭb ăs′ ĭd) ***adj-*** somewhat or slightly acid or sour: *a* subacid *flavor.* **—*adv-*** **sub·a′ cid·ly.**

sub·a·gent (sŭb′ ā′ jənt) ***n-*** person who works for an agent and is subordinate to him.

sub·al·tern (sŭb′ ôl′ tərn) ***n-*** **1** *Brit.* any army officer who ranks below a captain. **2** a subordinate.

sub·arc·tic (sŭb är′ tĭk, -ärk′ tĭk) ***adj-*** of or having to do with the region just outside the Arctic Circle.

sub·a·tom·ic (sŭb′ ə tŏm′ ĭk) ***adj-*** inside of or smaller than the atom: *a* subatomic *field; a* subatomic *particle.*

sub·com·mit·tee (sŭb′ kə mĭt′ ē) ***n-*** committee which is part of a larger committee and subject to it.

sub·con·scious (sŭb kŏn′ shəs, sŭb′ kŏn′-) ***adj-*** not felt, thought, or experienced in the consciousness, although present in another part of the mind: *a* subconscious *desire,* subconscious *impulse.* ***n-*** the sum of the wishes, memories, etc., that are present in the mind but not in the consciousness, and are believed to affect conscious judgment and action. **—*adv-*** **sub·con′ scious·ly.** ***n-*** **sub·con′ scious·ness.**

sub·con·tract (sŭb′ kŏn′ trăkt′) ***n-*** contract made after and subordinate to another contract. ***vt-*** to make such a contract: *He* subcontracted *to install the plumbing.* ***vt-:*** *We* subcontracted *the plumbing.*

sub·con·trac·tor (sŭb′ kŏn′ trăk′ tər) ***n-*** person who subcontracts to do work specified in a contract.

sub·cu·ta·ne·ous (sŭb′ kyōō tā′ nē əs) ***adj-*** beneath the surface of the skin: *a* subcutaneous *inflammation.* **—*adv-*** **sub′ cu·ta′ ne·ous·ly:** *to* inject *subcutaneously.*

sub·dea·con (sŭb′ dē′ kən) ***n-*** member of the clergy next in rank below a deacon.

sub·di·vide (sŭb′ də vīd′) ***vt-*** [**sub·di·vid·ed, sub·di·vid·ing**] to divide or separate again into smaller parts; especially, to divide (an area of land) into lots or other parcels for sale: *The buyer* subdivided *the farm into acre lots.* ***vi-:*** *This book* subdivides *into six short chapters.*

sub·di·vi·sion (sŭb′ də vĭzh′ ən) ***n-*** **1** division of parts into smaller parts. **2** a smaller part produced by subdividing something larger. **3** an area or tract that has been subdivided for building.

sub·due (səb do͞o′, -dyo͞o′) ***vt-*** [**sub·dued, sub·du·ing**] **1** to conquer; overcome: *The army* subdued *the enemy and captured the town.* **2** to control; calm: *to* subdue *one's temper.* **3** to tone down or soften: *The heavy drapes* subdued *the noise from the street.* **—*n-*** **sub·du′ er.**

sub·en·try (sŭb′ ĕn′ trē) ***n-*** [*pl.* **sub·en·tries**] entry occurring below, and as part of, another entry.

sub·fam·i·ly (sŭb′ făm′ ə lē, -făm′ lē) ***n-*** [*pl.* **sub·fam·i·lies**] any of the divisions of a group called a family that rank in size, importance, etc., next below the main group itself: *a* subfamily *of plants*; *a* subfamily *of languages.*

sub·floor·ing (sŭb′ flôr′ ĭng) ***n-*** flooring laid below another flooring; especially, a layer of rough boards laid directly on the floor joists.

sub·group (sŭb′ gro͞op′) ***n-*** any of the divisions of a group, especially one that ranks next below the group itself in size, importance, etc.

sub·head (sŭb′ hĕd′) ***n-*** **1** (also **sub′ head′ ing**) secondary title under a main title, covering a division of a book, article, etc. **2** newspaper headline printed beneath another headline and in smaller type. ***vt-*** to give such a title or headline to: *We* subheaded *the section "Ideas."*

sub·hu·man (sŭb′ hyo͞o′ mən) ***adj-*** **1** inferior to what is human. **2** bestial.

subj. **1** subjunctive. **2** subject. **3** subjective.

[1]**sub·ject** (sŭb′ jĭkt) ***n-*** **1** topic treated in writing, conversation, painting, etc.; theme: *What* subject *is under discussion?* **2** course of study: *Art is one* subject *he is taking at school.* **3** person or thing that is submitted to an experiment or treatment: *The* subject *of the experiment reported drowsiness.* **4** person owing loyalty and obedience to a sovereign. **5** *Grammar* one of the two chief parts of a sentence, consisting of the noun, pronoun, noun phrase, or noun clause, that usually precedes the main verb. In some questions the subject comes after an auxiliary verb, as in: *How did* he *know that?* ***adj-*** under the power or control of another: *a* subject *people.*

subject to **1** under the control of: *He is* subject to *his father's will.* **2** liable to; likely to have: *He is* subject to *moodiness.* **3** on the condition of; dependent on.

[2]**sub·ject** (səb jĕkt′) ***vt-*** (always followed by "to") **1** to bring under control: *to* subject *a people to conquest.* **2** to expose; to make undergo: *to* subject *a witness to questioning.* **3** to submit; make liable; predispose.

sub·jec·tion (səb jĕk′ shən) ***n-*** **1** a bringing under the rule of another: *Pizarro accomplished the* subjection *of the Incas.* **2** condition of being under the power or control of another: *They lived in complete* subjection.

sub·jec·tive (səb jĕk′ tĭv) ***adj-*** **1** existing in the mind; belonging to the thoughts and feelings rather than to outward objects; inner; private and personal; opposite of objective: *a* subjective *view of life.* **2** in literature and art, dealing with thoughts and feelings rather than with action and things in the world outside: *a* subjective *painting.* **3** *Grammar* of, relating to, or in the subjective case. **—*adv-*** **sub·jec′ tive·ly.** ***n-*** **sub·jec′ tive·ness** or **sub′ jec·tiv′ i·ty** (sŭb′ jĭk tĭv′ ə tē).

subjective case See [1]*case.*

subjective complement *Grammar* ***n-*** **1** (also **subject complement**) noun, pronoun, or noun phrase that follows a linking verb and is equivalent in meaning to the subject. Examples: *Mr. Allen is* a policeman. *It is* I. *His health became* a very large problem. **2** predicate adjective or phrase whose chief word is an adjective. Examples: *The house is* red. *The house is* very large indeed.

subject matter ***n-*** subject under consideration, as in a textbook, college course, speech, etc.

sub·ju·gate (sŭb′ jə gāt′) ***vt-*** [**sub·ju·gat·ed, sub·ju·gat·ing**] to conquer and impose one's rule over: *to* subjugate *a neighboring people.* **—*n-*** **sub′ ju·ga′ tion.** ***n-*** **sub′ ju·ga′ tor:** *a* subjugator *of small, weak nations.*

sub·junc·tive (səb jŭngk′ tĭv) *Grammar* ***adj-*** of, relating to, or in the subjunctive mood. ***n-*** the subjunctive mood.

subjunctive mood *Grammar* a term showing that the verb or verb phrase in a sentence expresses a wish, a doubt, or a condition which does not exist. Modern English does not have a subjunctive mood except in a few cases left over from an earlier form of the language, as in: *If I were you, I wouldn't do that.*

sub·king·dom (sŭb′ kĭng′ dəm) *Biology* ***n-*** any of the main divisions of the animal or vegetable kingdom; phylum.

sub·lease (sŭb′ lēs′) ***n-*** lease given to a third party by a tenant who holds a lease from the landlord. ***vt-*** *(also* sŭb′ lēs′) [**sub·leased, sub·leas·ing**] to lease (property already rented from another): *They* subleased *their apartment for a year while they traveled.*

[1]**sub·let** (sŭb′ lĕt′) ***vt-*** [**sub·let, sub·let·ting**] to sublease.

[2]**sub·let** (sŭb′ lĕt′) ***n-*** dwelling or property held under a sublease.

sub·li·mate (sŭb′ lə māt′) ***vt-*** [**sub·li·mat·ed, sub·li·mat·ing**] **1** to use the energy of (an impulse or desire one disapproves of or fears) in more acceptable behavior. **2** to sublime (a substance). ***vi-*** to use or undergo one of these processes. ***n-*** crystal or other product made by subliming. **—*n-*** **sub′ li·ma′ tion.**

sub·lime (sə blīm′) ***adj-*** **1** inspiring awe, reverence, and wonder: *to hear* sublime *music.* **2** out of the ordinary; supreme: *a* sublime *conceit;* sublime *ignorance.* **3** something that is lofty or noble: *from the* sublime *to the ridiculous.* ***vt-*** [**sub·limed, sub·lim·ing**] to cause (a substance) to vaporize by heating and then to go directly back into solid form; sublimate. **—*n-*** **sub·lim′ i·ty** (sə blĭm′ ə tē). ***adv-*** **sub·lime′ ly.**

sub·ma·chine gun (sŭb′ mə shēn′) ***n-*** lightweight machine gun designed to be fired from the shoulder or hip.

Submachine gun

sub·mar·gin·al (sŭb′ mär′ jə nəl) ***adj-*** **1** below a necessary standard or minimum in worth or productivity.

sub·ma·rine (sŭb′ mə rēn′, -rēn′) ***adj-*** being, living, or growing beneath the sea; undersea: *a* submarine *plant.* ***n-*** boat that can travel on or beneath the surface of the water. *as* ***modifier:*** *a* submarine *task force.*

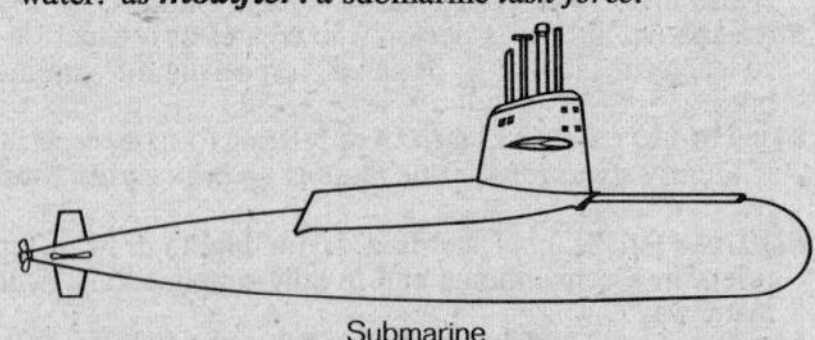
Submarine

submarine chaser ***n-*** naval vessel equipped to detect, pursue, and destroy submarines.

sub·max·il·lar·y (sŭb′ măk′ sə lĕr′ ē) ***adj-*** **1** beneath the jawbone. **2** of or relating to the lower jaw.

sub·merge (səb mûrj′) ***vt-*** [**sub·merged, sub·merg·ing**] to cover with water or liquid: *Water* submerges *the*

small island at high tide. ***vi-*** to sink or plunge under water: *The submarine* submerged.
sub·mer·gence (səb mûr′ jəns) ***n-*** a submerging.
sub·merse (səb mûrs′) ***vt-*** **[sub·mersed, sub·mers·ing]** to put under water; submerge; immerse.
sub·mers·i·ble (səb mûr′ sə bəl) ***adj-*** such as can be placed under water. ***n-*** a submarine.
sub·mer·sion (səb mûr′ zhən) ***n-*** a putting or being put under water; immersion.
sub·mis·sion (səb mĭsh′ ən) ***n-*** a giving in to the power and authority of another; a surrender.
sub·mis·sive (səb mĭs′ ĭv) ***adj-*** obedient; humble; docile: *The* submissive *child obeyed without question.* ***—adv-*** **sub·mis′ sive·ly.** ***n-*** **sub·mis′ sive·ness.**
sub·mit (səb mĭt′) ***vi-*** **[sub·mit·ted, sub·mit·ting]** to give way or yield to the power or authority of another; surrender: *The team* submitted *to the umpire's decision.* ***vt-*** **1** to refer or present for criticism, judgment, or decision: *The artist* submitted *his drawings for approval.* **2** to surrender (oneself): *He* submitted *himself to the authority of the state.* **3** to subject to a certain influence or process: *to* submit *steel to heat.*
sub·nor·mal (sŭb′ nôr′ məl, -nôr′ məl) ***adj-*** below or less than normal: *of* subnormal *intelligence.* ***n-*** person who is below normal in intelligence.
sub·or·der (sŭb′ ôr′ dər, -ôr′ dər) *Biology* ***n-*** any of the main divisions of an order of plants or animals.
[1]**sub·or·di·nate** (sə bôr′ də nət, sə bôr′-) ***adj-*** **1** of lower rank; inferior in rank (to): *In the army, a captain is* subordinate *to a major.* **2** dependent upon; subject (to): *The army's movements were* subordinate *to the plans of the general.* ***n-*** one who is below another in rank, power, etc.: *He expected loyalty from his* subordinates. ***—adv-*** **sub·or′ di·nate·ly.** ***n-*** **sub·or′ di·nate·ness.**
[2]**sub·or·di·nate** (sə bôr′ də nāt′, sə bôr′-) ***vt-*** **[sub·or·di·nat·ed, sub·or·di·nat·ing]** to make obedient or subject; make secondary: *The children* subordinated *their wishes to those of their parents.* ***—n-*** **sub·or′ di·na′ tion.**
sub·orn (sə bôrn′, -bôrn′) ***vt-*** **1** to persuade (someone) to commit perjury; also, to get perjured information under oath from. **2** to persuade secretly to commit an unlawful act. ***—n-*** **sub′ or·na′ tion** (sŭb′ ər nā′ shən).
sub·poe·na or **sub·pe·na** (sə pē′ nə) ***n-*** written order commanding a person to appear in court or at some other official session. ***vt-*** **[sub·poe·naed** or **sub·pe·naed, sub·poe·na·ing** or **sub·pe·na·ing]** to serve or summon with such a written order.
sub ro·sa (sŭb′ rō′ zə) ***adv-*** secretly; privately; in strict confidence: *He told it to me* sub rosa. ***adj-*** **(sub-rosa):** *our* sub-rosa *meetings.*
sub·scribe (səb skrīb′) ***vi-*** **[sub·scribed, sub·scrib·ing]** **1** to arrange to receive a certain magazine, newspaper, etc., by mail for a certain period; also, to arrange to receive a book or set of books, usually by mail, at a later date. **2** to give approval or consent (to something); show agreement: *I cannot* subscribe *to those ideas.* ***vt-*** to give or promise to give (a sum of money or something else) to some cause: *I* subscribe *$100 to the Red Cross each year.* ***—n-*** **sub·scrib′ er.**
sub·script (sŭb′ skrĭpt′) ***n-*** something written below the line: *In* X_2, *2 is the* subscript. *as* ***modifier***: *a* subscript *number.*
sub·scrip·tion (səb skrĭp′ shən) ***n-*** **1** an order for a certain number of issues of a magazine or newspaper; also, an order for a number of books, to be paid for on delivery. **2** sum of money given for a cause.
sub·sec·tion (sŭb′ sĕk′ shən) ***n-*** section of another section: *a* subsection *of this article.*
sub·se·quent (sŭb′ sə kwənt) ***adj-*** coming after; following: *We made plans, but* subsequent *developments changed them.* ***—adv-*** **sub′ se·quent·ly.**
sub·serve (sŭb′ sûrv′) ***vt-*** **[sub·served, sub·serv·ing]** to serve; advance; promote: *to* subserve *his interests.*
sub·ser·vi·ence (səb sûr′ vē əns) or **sub·ser·vi·en·cy** (-vē ən sē) ***n-*** subjection to or complete submission to the will or rule of another person, country, etc.
sub·ser·vi·ent (səb sûr′ vē ənt) ***adj-*** subject to, or inclined to submit to, the will or rule of others: *a* subservient *streak in his character.* ***—adv-*** **sub·ser′ vi·ent·ly.**
sub·set (sŭb′ sĕt′) *Mathematics* ***n-*** any set that is wholly contained within another set.
sub·side (səb sīd′) ***vi-*** **[sub·sid·ed, sub·sid·ing]** **1** to sink to a lower level; fall: *The flood waters will* subside *when the rain stops.* **2** to become quiet, calm, or less violent; diminish; grow less: *Tom's fever* subsided.
sub·sid·ence (səb sī′ dəns) ***n-*** a subsiding; especially, a sinking of land.
sub·sid·i·ar·y (səb sĭd′ ē ĕr′ ē) ***adj-*** **1** helping or supporting the main effort, person, etc.; auxiliary: *He has a* subsidiary *role in the project.* **2** owned or controlled by another company. **3** of or relating to a subsidy. ***n-*** [*pl.* **sub·sid·i·ar·ies**] corporation owned or controlled by another corporation.
sub·si·dize (sŭb′ sə dīz′) ***vt-*** **[sub·si·dized, sub·si·dizing]** to aid with money; to furnish financial aid to: *to* subsidize *a bankrupt railroad.* ***—n-*** **sub′ si·di·za′ tion. sub′ si·diz′ er.**
sub·si·dy (sŭb′ sə dē) ***n-*** [*pl.* **sub·si·dies**] a money grant, especially as assistance to a project or organization serving the public.
sub·sist (səb sĭst′) ***vi-*** **1** to maintain life; live, especially at a minimum level: *We cannot* subsist *without food.* **2** to continue to be; exist: *Ancient festivals still* subsist.
sub·sist·ence (səb sĭs′ təns) ***n-*** **1** a subsisting. **2** means of supporting life: *Eskimos used to depend on hunting and fishing for their* subsistence. *as* ***modifier***: *a* subsistence *wage; to eat at the* subsistence *level.*
sub·soil (sŭb′ soil′) ***n-*** layer of earth lying just below the topsoil.
sub·son·ic (sŭb′ sŏn′ ĭk) ***adj-*** below the speed of sound.
sub·spe·cies (sŭb′ spē′ sēz′, -shēz′) ***n-*** [*pl.* **sub·spe·cies**] **1** *Biology* any of the significantly different types of plants or animals that occur within one species. **2** any division of a type.
sub·stance (sŭb′ stəns) ***n-*** **1** matter; material: *Wood is a solid* substance. **2** stuff of which something is made: *A soft limestone is the* substance *of chalk.* **3** essential part or meaning; essence: *Tell me the* substance *of last night's speech.* **4** body; denseness: *A vegetable soup has more* substance *than a broth.* **5** property; money.
sub·stand·ard (sŭb′ stăn′ dərd) ***adj-*** below standard.
sub·stan·tial (səb stăn′ shəl) ***adj-*** **1** made or built in a solid or strong manner: *a* substantial *bridge; a* substantial *house.* **2** ample: *a* substantial *meal.* **3** wealthy; important; prosperous: *a* substantial *business.* **4** essential; reasonable: *The witnesses were in* substantial *agreement.* ***—adv-*** **sub·stan′ tial·ly.** ***n-*** **sub·stan′ ti·al′ i·ty** (səb stăn′ shē ăl′ ə tē).
sub·stan·ti·ate (səb stăn′ shē āt′) ***vt-*** **[sub·stan·ti·at·ed, sub·stan·ti·a·ting]** to establish the truth of (a claim, rumor, theory, etc.,) by proof or evidence; prove or verify. ***—n-*** **sub·stan′ ti·a′ tion.**

sub·stan·tive (sŭb′ stən tĭv′) *adj-* **1** having independent and permanent substance or reality. **2** *Grammar* used as or functioning as a noun: *a* substantive *clause.* **3** substantial. *n-* noun or group of words used as a noun. *—adv-* **sub′ stan·tive·ly.**

sub·sta·tion (sŭb′ stā′ shən) *n-* station which is subsidiary to a main one, especially in an electrical power system.

sub·sti·tute (sŭb′ stə to͞ot′, -tyo͞ot′) *n-* **1** person replacing another; one acting instead of another: *You will be my* substitute *for three days.* **2** thing that is used instead of something else. *vt-* **[sub·sti·tut·ed, sub·sti·tut·ing]** to use in place of something: *Let's* substitute *sugar for honey in the recipe. vi-: Do you think sugar will* substitute *for honey?*

sub·sti·tu·tion (sŭb′ stə to͞o′ shən, -tyo͞o′ shən) *n-* the putting of a person or thing in the place of another: *the* substitution *of honey for sugar in a recipe. as* ***modifier****: Do you know the new* substitution *rules?*

sub·stra·tum (sŭb′ strā′ təm, -străt′ əm) *n-* [*pl.* **sub·stra·ta**] **1** an underlying layer: *sand on a* substratum *of gravel.* **2** thing that forms the groundwork or support of some other structure; foundation: *Education is the* substratum *of culture.*

sub·struc·ture (sŭb′ strŭk′ chər) *n-* **1** structure, such as a building foundation, which supports another structure. **2** bed of soil, gravel, etc., that supports railroad tracks.

sub·ter·fuge (sŭb′ tər fyo͞oj′) *n-* scheme, excuse, or trick by which one seeks to escape from a difficulty.

sub·ter·ra·ne·an (sŭb′ tə rā′ nē ən) *adj-* **1** below the surface of the earth; underground: *a* subterranean *river.* **2** hidden; out of sight; secret: *a* subterranean *maneuver.*

sub·tile (sŭt′ əl, sŭb′ təl) *adj-* **[sub·til·er, sub·til·est] 1** of fluids, extremely thin and tenuous; delicate and rarefied; lacking density: *This antifreeze is very* subtile, *and easily leaks out.* **2** subtle. ***Hom-*** subtle.

sub·ti·tle (sŭb′ tī′ təl) *n-* **1** second title under a main title of a book, essay, poem, etc. **2** translation of words spoken in a motion picture, printed at the bottom of the frames for persons who do not know the language being spoken. *vt-* **[sub·ti·tled, sub·ti·tling]**: *I* subtitled *my story "How to Avoid Leaping Crocodiles."*

sub·tle (sŭt′ əl) *adj-* **[sub·tler, sub·tlest] 1** delicate; fine: *to make a* subtle *distinction*; *the* subtle *difference in two shades of blue.* **2** difficult to understand the meaning of; elusive: *It was hard to tell from her* subtle *smile what she meant.* **3** able to understand or make fine differences of meaning; discerning: *a* subtle *mind*; *a* subtle *wit.* **4** underhanded; crafty; sly: *a* subtle *trick to outwit another.* ***Hom-*** subtile. *—n-* **sub′ tle·ness.** *adv-* **sub′ tly.**

sub·tle·ty (sŭt′ əl tē) *n-* [*pl.* **sub·tle·ties**] **1** quality of being subtle; discernment; keenness or delicacy of mind. **2** something subtle; especially, a finely drawn distinction: *I cannot follow the* subtleties *of your argument.*

sub·top·ic (sŭb′ tŏp′ ĭk) *n-* a division of the subject under the main topic.

sub·tract (səb trăkt′) *vt-* to deduct (one number or quantity) from another: *If you* subtract *3 from 6, you have 3. vi-: to learn to* subtract. *—n-* **sub·tract′ er.**

sub·trac·tion (səb trăk′ shən) *n-* **1** *Mathematics* operation that is the opposite of addition; also, operation or process of computing the difference between two numbers. **2** a taking away or deducting. **3** something subtracted.

sub·trac·tive (səb trăk′ tĭv) *adj-* of, relating to, or involving subtraction.

sub·tra·hend (sŭb′ trə hĕnd′) *Mathematics n-* the number that is subtracted from another given number. Example: In 8 — 6 = 2, the subtrahend is 6. See also *minuend.*

sub·trop·i·cal (sŭb trŏp′ ĭ kəl) *adj-* having to do with a region bordering on the tropics. Also **sub′ trop′ ic.**

sub·trop·ics (sŭb′ trŏp′ ĭks) *n-pl.* the subtropical regions.

sub·urb (sŭb′ ûrb′) *n-* **1** residential district that lies close to a large city: *to live in a* suburb *and work in the city.* **2 the suburbs** (1) all of the residential districts near a city: *to live in* the suburbs *near Chicago.* (2) such districts in general, regarded as a type of society: *the average income of* the suburbs.

sub·ur·ban (sə bûr′ bən) *adj-* of or having to do with a suburb: *a* suburban *community.*

sub·ur·ban·ite (sə bûr′ bə nīt′) *n-* person who lives in the suburbs.

sub·urb·i·a (sə bûr′ bē ə) *n-* suburbs and suburbanites, collectively; also, the special habits, viewpoints, interests, etc., of suburbs and suburbanites.

sub·ver·sion (səb vûr′ zhən) *n-* **1** a gradual undermining and destroying of something: *Your ideas will bring about the* subversion *of all we have worked for.* **2** activity aimed at such ends: *to combat* subversion *in government.*

sub·ver·sive (səb vûr′ sĭv, -zĭv) *adj-* having the aim or effect of subverting something: *a* subversive *doctrine. n-* person who subverts. *—adv-* **sub·ver′ sive·ly.** *n-* **sub·ver′ sive·ness.**

sub·vert (səb vûrt′) *vt-* to undermine or overthrow, especially in a gradual or insidious way: *to* subvert *a government*; *to* subvert *a principle. —n-* **sub·vert′ er.**

sub·way (sŭb′ wā′) *n-* **1** underground electric railway. **2** underground passage: *a* subway *under the street. as* ***modifier****: a* subway *train*; *a* subway *conductor.*

suc·ceed (sək sēd′) *vi-* **1** to gain or accomplish one's aim or purpose; to do extremely well: *Jim is a person who is bound to* succeed *in life.* **2** to be the heir or follow next in line (to an office, title, or property): *Queen Elizabeth* succeeded *to the throne when her father died. vt-* to come directly after: *Dawn* succeeded *night.*

suc·cess (sək sĕs′) *n-* **1** favorable result; good outcome; triumph: *Hard work is often the surest means of* success. **2** person or thing that succeeds. **3** degree of achievement (in gaining a desired result): *What* success *did you have in persuading him?* **4** gain of wealth, fame, etc.

suc·cess·ful (sək sĕs′ fəl) *adj-* **1** having or meeting with success; gaining what is desired or aimed at; turning out favorably. **2** fortunate and prosperous: *Dick's father is a* successful *lawyer. —adv-* **suc·cess′ ful·ly.**

suc·ces·sion (sək sĕsh′ ən) *n-* **1** the coming of one after another in unbroken order; series; sequence: *a long* succession *of happy days.* **2** the taking over of another's office, title, or property through legal right or inheritance: *the* succession *to the throne.* **3** system by which rank, an office, etc., changes hands. **4** series of descendants; heirs.

in succession one after another.

suc·ces·sive (sək sĕs′ ĭv) *adj-* following one after the other without interruption; consecutive: *Last spring our baseball team won six* successive *games. —adv-* **suc·ces′ sive·ly.**

suc·ces·sor (sək sĕs′ ər) *n-* person or thing that succeeds another; especially, a person who succeeds to an office, rank or property.

suc·cinct (sək sĭngkt′) *adj-* clearly expressed in a very few words; concise; terse; exactly to the point. *—adv-* **suc·cinct′ ly.** *n-* **suc·cinct′ ness.**

suc·cor (sŭk′ ər) *vt-* to give needed help; aid. *n-* aid or relief given. ***Hom-*** sucker.

suc·co·tash (sŭk′ ə tăsh′) *n-* corn and beans, usually lima beans, cooked together.

suc·cu·lent (sŭk′ yə lənt) *adj-* full of juice, as fruit; juicy: *a* succulent *pear. —n-* **suc′ cu·lence.**

suc·cumb (sə kŭm′) ***vi-*** **1** to give way (to) or surrender (to) after a struggle: *Father* succumbed *to our persuasion.* **2** to die: *When she was 94, she quietly* succumbed.

such (sŭch) ***determiner*** (traditionally called adjective or sometimes pronoun) **1** of the same kind, quality, or degree: *In her pockets were pens, pencils and* such *things; in his were marbles, stones, and* such. **2** of that sort or kind already mentioned or meant; the same: *My mother would never repeat* such *gossip.* **3** so very: *He did* such *good work that he took honors.*

as such 1 as being what is meant or suggested: *A policeman,* as such, *works against crime.* **2** in or by itself: *Beauty,* as such, *is only skin deep.* **such a** in so great a degree; so: *He felt* such *a terrible pain. It was* such a *weak rope that it broke.* **such as 1** for example: *fruits,* such as *strawberries.* **2** of the same general kind; similar to: *a flour* such as *I have always used.* **such-and-such 1** not named; not specified: *I met* such-and-such *a man.* **2** something deliberately not named or specified: *If he says* such-and-such, *I'll deny it.*

suck (sŭk) ***vt-*** **1** to draw into, or hold in, the mouth by action of the lips and tongue: *The baby* sucked *the milk from his bottle. He* sucked *the lollipop.* **2** to draw or drain the liquid from: *to* suck *oranges.* **3** to take in; absorb; engulf: *Plants* suck *moisture from the ground.* ***vi-*** to draw milk from the breast or udder; suckle. ***n-*** a sucking into the mouth: *a* suck *of lemon.*

suck·er (sŭk′ ər) ***n-*** **1** person or animal that sucks. **2** [*pl.* **suck·er; suck·ers** (kinds of sucker)] any of several kinds of soft-lipped, fresh-water fishes that suck up their food. **3** one of the organs on the arm of an octopus by which it holds its prey, or a like organ on certain other animals. **4** shoot from the root of a plant or tree. **5** lollipop. **6** *Slang* person easily deceived; dupe. ***Hom-*** succor.

White sucker, about 20 in. long

suck·le (sŭk′ əl) ***vt-*** [**suck·led, suck·ling**] to nurse; also, to draw milk from the breast or udder of: *The mother* suckled *her baby. The calf* suckled *its mother.* ***vi-*** to take the breast or udder: *They* suckle *three times a day.*

suck·ling (sŭk′ lĭng) ***n-*** infant or young mammal that suckles. *as **modifier**: a* suckling *lamb;* suckling *pig.*

su·crose (sōō′ krōs′) ***n-*** the kind of sugar ($C_{12}H_{22}O_{11}$) found naturally in most plants, especially beets and sugar cane; saccharose.

suc·tion (sŭk′ shən) ***n-*** **1** act or process of sucking. **2** the movement of a fluid into a space that is under a lower pressure than a surrounding space. **3** the apparent pulling force that seems to be exerted by a space from which air has been withdrawn, but is actually the pushing force of the surrounding air toward the evacuated space. *as **modifier**: a* suction *pump.*

suction pump ***n-*** a pump for the transferring of gases or liquids by means of suction.

sud·den (sŭd′ ən) ***adj-*** **1** unexpected; unforeseen: *a* sudden *turn in the path.* **2** happening quickly and without warning: *a* sudden *escape.* **3** quickly done; hasty: *a* sudden *decision.* **—*adv-* sud′ den·ly.** ***n-*** **sud′ den·ness.**

all of a sudden *Informal* in a sudden manner; suddenly.

sudden death ***n-*** procedure in hockey, polo, basketball, etc., by which the winner of a tie game is decided by the first score in a special overtime period.

suds (sŭdz) ***n-*** *pl.* **1** froth and lather that form when a soap or detergent dissolves in water; soapsuds. **2** *Slang* beer.

sue (sōō) ***vt-*** [**sued, su·ing**] to take legal steps against in order to collect payment for damages; lodge a lawsuit against: *He is going to* sue *the newspaper for libel.* ***vi-*** **1** to beg or plead (for): *They* sued *for peace. He* sued *for her hand in marriage.* **2** to begin a lawsuit. **—*adj-* su′ a·ble.** ***n-*** **su′ er.**

suede (swād) ***n-*** **1** soft leather with a dull surface and a slightly raised nap. **2** cloth material which resembles this. *as **modifier**: a* suede *skirt.* Also **suède.**

su·et (sōō′ ət) ***n-*** hard fat that comes from the loins and around the kidneys of sheep and beef.

suf·fer (sŭf′ ər) ***vi-*** **1** to bear physical or mental pain or distress: *He* suffers *during the hay-fever season.* **2** to be damaged, harmed, or injured: *His work* suffered *from his lack of attention in class.* ***vt-*** **1** to feel or endure (pain, hardship, grief, etc.). **2** to allow; permit; tolerate: *I will not* suffer *his nonsense.* **3** to experience; undergo: *The patient* suffered *a relapse.* **—*n-* suf′ fer·er.**

suf·fer·ance (sŭf′ ər əns) ***n-*** **1** consent or permission implied by not forbidding or hindering; *He remained in the house on* sufferance *only. He is here by the* sufferance *of his parents.* **2** *Archaic* ability to endure; endurance.

suf·fer·ing (sŭf ər ĭng) ***n-*** physical or mental pain.

suf·fice (sə fīs′) ***vi-*** [**suf·ficed, suf·fic·ing**] to be enough or sufficient: *This money will not* suffice *for my needs.* ***vt-*** to be sufficient for; satisfy: *The money* sufficed *him.*

suffice it to say that obviously and in short.

suf·fi·cien·cy (sə fĭsh′ ən sē) ***n-*** [*pl.* **suf·fi·cien·cies**] **1** enough of anything; supply equal to demand; adequacy: *a* sufficiency *of food.* **2** ability or capacity for the task at hand: *a* sufficiency *far greater than their competitors.*

suf·fi·cient (sə fĭsh′ ənt) ***adj-*** equal to the need; enough: *a* sufficient *supply of food.* **—*adv-* suf·fi′ cient·ly.**

suf·fix (sŭf′ ĭks) *Grammar* ***n-*** **1** syllable or syllables added to the end of a word to form another word, sometimes with a change in spelling of the original word. Most suffixes signal a change in part of speech. Examples: *suit*able; *suit*ably; *suit*ableness.. **2** word ending. ***vt-*** to add a syllable or syllables to the end of (a word).

suf·fo·cate (sŭf′ ə kāt′) ***vt-*** [**suf·fo·cat·ed, suf·fo·cat·ing**] **1** to kill by stopping the breath of; stifle. **2** to cut the supply of air from; extinguish: *to* suffocate *a fire.* ***vi-*** to be smothered or choked: *I thought I would* suffocate *in the crowded theater.* **—*adv-* suf′ fo·cat′ ing·ly.** ***n-*** **suf′ fo·ca′ tion.**

suf·fra·gan (sŭf′ rə gən) ***n-*** assistant bishop who aids a bishop in the administration of a diocese. *as **modifier**: a* suffragan *bishop.*

suf·frage (sŭf′ rĭj) ***n-*** **1** right of voting; franchise: *women's* suffrage. **2** approval by vote; also, a vote.

suf·fra·gette (sŭf′ rə jĕt′) ***n-*** woman who advocates the right of women to vote.

suf·fra·gist (sŭf′ rə jĭst) ***n-*** person who advocates the right to vote, especially for women.

suf·fuse (sə fyōōz′) ***vt-*** [**suf·fused, suf·fus·ing**] of a fluid, color, etc., to spread over: *Tears* suffused *her eyes. A blush* suffused *her cheeks.* **—*n-* suf·fu′ sion.**

sug·ar (shŏŏg′ ər) ***n-*** any of various sweet natural compounds obtained from sugar beets, sugar cane, maple trees, fruits, etc. Sugars are carbohydrates. ***vt-*** **1** to sweeten with sugar or sprinkle sugar on: *Do you want me to* sugar *your berries?* **2** to make pleasant or less disagreeable: *to* sugar *criticism with flattery.*

sugar off 1 to make maple syrup or sugar by boiling down the maple sap. **2** to tap a maple tree for sap.

sugar beet *n-* kind of beet with a white root and high sugar content, grown as a source of sugar.

sugar cane *n-* tall, jointed, tropical grass that is grown for the sugar in its stems.

Sugar cane

sug·ar-coat (shŏŏg′ ər kōt′) *vt-* **1** to cover with sugar. **2** to make to seem attractive or pleasant: *He* sugar-coated *the episode.* *—n-* **sug′ ar coat′ ing.**

sugar loaf *n-* **1** cone-shaped mass of hard, refined sugar. **2** something shaped like this. *as* ***modifier*** **(sugar-loaf):** *a* sugar-loaf *mountain.*

sugar maple *n-* a maple tree of eastern United States, valued for its hard wood and sap from which maple syrup and maple sugar are made; rock maple.

sugar pine *n-* very tall Pacific coast pine with large cones. It is valuable for lumber.

sugar plum *n-* small ball or disk of candy; bonbon.

sug·ar·y (shŏŏg′ ə rē) *adj-* **1** like, made of, or containing sugar; sweet. **2** sweetly flattering. *—n-* **sug′ ar·i·ness.**

sug·gest (səg jĕst′) *vt-* **1** to offer (a plan, idea, etc.) for consideration; to propose: *She* suggests *that we meet at the station.* **2** to call to mind through a natural connection or relationship: *This weather* suggests *spring.* **3** to hint at; imply: *His look* suggested *a hard life.*

sug·gest·i·ble (səg jĕs′ tə bəl) *adj-* **1** easily influenced by suggestion, such as hypnotic suggestion. **2** such as can be suggested. *—n-* **sug′ gest·i·bil′ i·ty.**

sug·ges·tion (səg jĕs′ chən) *n-* **1** a suggesting: *We joined his party at his* suggestion. **2** thing suggested: *We accepted his* suggestion *and changed route.* **3** hint; trace: *a* suggestion *of a French accent in his speech.* **4** idea brought to mind because of its association with something else: *The smell of burning leaves carries a* suggestion *of autumn.* **5** hints, associations, or other indirect means of influencing ideas or behavior. **6** direct instruction given to a person who is hypnotized or drugged.

sug·ges·tive (səg jĕs′ tĭv) *adj-* **1** tending to bring to mind ideas, images, etc.: *This painting is* suggestive *of the hills of upper New York.* **2** tending to bring something improper or indecent to mind: *a* suggestive *movie.* *—adv-* **sug·ges′ tive·ly.** *n-* **sug·ges′ tive·ness.**

su·i·cid·al (sōō′ ə sī′ dəl) *adj-* **1** inclining or urging one to suicide: *a* suicidal *impulse.* **2** fatal to one's own interests: *Those plans are* suicidal. *—adv-* **su′ i·cid′ al·ly.**

su·i·cide (sōō′ ə sīd′) *n-* **1** intentional killing of oneself; self-destruction. **2** person who intentionally takes his own life. **3** ruin of one's own political, social, or commercial interests: *Not selling those bonds is* suicide. *as* ***modifier:*** *the* suicide *rate*; *a* suicide *note.*

suit (sōōt) *n-* **1** set of clothes to be worn together, such as a jacket and either trousers or a skirt. **2** lawsuit. **3** set or number of things used together; outfit; suite: *a* suit *of sails*; *a* suit *of armor.* **4** one of the four sets of cards into which a pack is divided: *The four* suits *are spades, hearts, clubs, and diamonds.* **5** courtship; courting: *She rejected his* suit. *vt-* **1** to be suitable for; fit: *These decorations* suit *the Christmas season.* **2** to look well on; become: *That dress* suits *you.* **3** to please; satisfy: *We cannot* suit *every taste.* ***Hom-*** soot.

bring suit to sue; lodge a lawsuit. **follow suit 1** to do as the person before has done: *If you contribute a dollar I will* follow suit. **2** to play a card of the same suit as has just been played.

suit oneself to follow one's own wishes.

suit·a·ble (sōō′ tə bəl) *adj-* fitting; appropriate: *That dress is not* suitable *for the dance.* *—n-* **suit′ a·ble·ness** or **suit′ a·bil′ i·ty.** *adv-* **suit′ a·bly.**

suit·case (sōōt′ kās′) *n-* flat, rectangular traveling bag for carrying clothes; valise.

suite (swēt) *n-* **1** a number of things making up a set, series, etc.: *a* suite *of furniture*; *a* suite *of rooms.* **2** group of servants; staff; retinue: *The king never traveled without his* suite. **3** *Music* instrumental piece in several movements, originally named after and representing various dances. ***Hom-*** sweet.

suit·ing (sōō′ tĭng) *n-* cloth for making suits of clothes.

suit·or (sōō′ tər) *n-* **1** man who courts or woos a woman. **2** person who brings a case into a court of law. **3** someone who makes a request or petition.

su·ki·ya·ki (skē ä′ kē) *n-* Japanese dish made by briefly simmering thin strips of beef, bean sprouts, spinach, onions, etc., in soy sauce and fat or oil.

Suk·koth (sōōk′ əth, -əs) *n-* Feast of Tabernacles, a Jewish festival originally celebrated at the end of the harvest season, commemorating the temporary shelter of the Jews during their wandering. Also **Suc·coth.**

sul·fa drug (sŭl′ fə) *n-* any of a group of drugs containing sulfur and used in the treatment of bacterial diseases.

sul·fate (sŭl′ fāt′, sōōl′-) *n-* the negative ion, SO_4, found in sulfuric acid, (H_2SO_4) and many salts, such as copper sulfate, ($CuSO_4$).

sul·fide or **sul·phide** (sŭl′ fīd′, sōōl′-) *n-* compound containing two elements of which one is sulfur.

sul·fite (sŭl′ fīt′, sōōl′-) *n-* a salt or ester of sulfurous acid.

sul·fur or **sulp·hur** (sŭl′ fər, sōōl′-) *n-* a nonmetallic chemical element usually occurring as a yellow solid. It is used to make many important chemicals including sulfuric acid, sulfur dioxide, and the sulfa drugs. Symbol S, At. No. 16, At. Wt. 32.064.

sulfur dioxide *n-* an irritating, choking gas (SO_2), produced by the burning of sulfur.

sul·fu·ric or **sul·phu·ric** (səl fyōōr′ ĭk) *adj-* of, having to do with, or containing sulfur, especially in its higher valence, as in sulfuric acid.

sulfuric acid *n-* strong, oily, colorless liquid acid (H_2SO_4), that is a powerful oxidizing and dehydrating agent and is used in many manufacturing processes; oil of vitriol; vitriol.

sul·fur·ous or **sul·phu·rous** (sŭl′ fər əs, sōōl′-) *adj-* **1** of or pertaining to the fires of Hell; hellish; infernal: *to burn in the* sulfurous *depths.* **2** marked by profanity: *his* sulfurous *language.* **3** (*usually* səl fyōōr′ əs) of, having to do with, or containing sulfur, especially in its lower valence, as in sulfurous acid (H_2SO_3).

sulk (sŭlk, sōōlk) *vi-* to pout; show bad humor; be sullen. *n-* **1** fit of pouting; sullen mood. **2 the sulks** such a fit or mood when prolonged or habitual.

¹sulk·y (sŭl′ kē, sōōl′-) *adj-* **[sulk·i·er, sulk·i·est]** in a sullen mood: *He becomes* sulky *when he is disappointed.* [perhaps from earlier **sulke,** "slow; sluggish," from Old English **āsolcan.**] *—adv-* **sulk′ i·ly.** *n-* **sulk′ i·ness.**

²sulk·y (sŭl′ kē, sōōl′-) *n-* [*pl.* **sulk·ies**] very light, horse-drawn, two-wheeled vehicle for one person, used in harness racing. [probably from **¹sulky.**]

Racing sulky

sul·len (sŭl′ ən, sōōl′-) *adj-* **1** showing bad humor; silent because of resentfulness; sulky; glum: *a* sullen *look.* **2** gloomy; dismal: *the* sullen *winter skies.* *—adv-* **sul′ len·ly.** *n-* **sul′ len·ness.**

sul·ly (sŭl′ ē, so͝ol′-) ***vt-*** **[sul·lied, sul·ly·ing]** to tarnish or soil; dirty or stain: *He* sullied *my reputation.*

sul·phate (sŭl′ fāt′, so͝ol′-) sulfate.

sul·phide (sŭl′ fīd′, so͝ol′-) sulfide.

sul·phur (sŭl′ fər, so͝ol′-) sulfur.

sul·tan or **Sul·tan** (sŭl′ tən, so͝ol′-) ***n-*** in certain Muslim countries, the ruler or governor.

sul·tan·a (səl tăn′ ə) ***n-*** **1** wife, daughter, mother, or sister of a sultan. **2** variety of seedless grapes valued for raisins and wine.

sul·tan·ate (sŭl′ tə nāt′, so͝ol′-) ***n-*** rule, rank, or territory of a sultan.

sul·try (sŭl′ trē, so͝ol′-) ***adj-*** **[sul·tri·er, sul·tri·est]** hot, close, and moist; oppressive: *The jungle has a* sultry *climate.* ***—adv-*** **sul′ tri·ly.** ***n-*** **sul′ tri·ness.**

sum (sŭm) ***n-*** **1** total of two or more numbers, things, or quantities; whole: *The grocer adds the prices of items sold to find the* sum *the customer must pay.* **2** result obtained by addition: *He added 2 and 3 and 4 to get the* sum *of 9.* **3** *chiefly Brit.* problem in arithmetic. **4** amount of money: *the* sum *of five dollars.* **5** summary; essence; substance: *That book contains the* sum *of 50 years of thought.* ***vi-*** **[summed, sum·ming]** *chiefly Brit.* to do simple arithmetic. ***Hom-*** some.

sum up 1 to add into one amount: *He* summed up *the figures.* **2** to state in a brief form; summarize: *The boss* summed up *the talk.*

su·mac or **su·mach** (so͞o′ măk′, sho͞o′-) ***n-*** **1** any of various shrubs, trees or vines with divided green leaves that turn to a vivid red in the fall, and with clusters of flowers followed by red or white berries. See also *poison sumac.* **2** dried leaves and roots of this plant, used in tanning and dyeing.

Staghorn sumac

Su·me·ri·an (so͞o mĕr′ ē ən) ***n-*** **1** one of an ancient people who lived in the lower part of Mesopotamia (Iraq) before 3000 B.C. **2** language of these people, written and preserved on rocks and clay tablets. ***adj-***: *large* Sumerian *settlements.*

sum·ma cum lau·de (so͝om′ ə ko͝om lou′ də) *Latin* with highest praise (used on diplomas to indicate that the recipient has received the highest academic honors): *He graduated* summa cum laude.

sum·ma·ri·ly (sə mĕr′ ə lē, sŭm′ ər ə lē) ***adv-*** in a brief or instant manner: *He was punished* summarily.

sum·ma·rize (sŭm′ ə rīz′) ***vt-*** **[sum·ma·rized, sum·ma·riz·ing]** to sum up briefly the main points of (a fuller statement): *Mary was asked to* summarize *the book.*

sum·ma·ry (sŭm′ ə rē) ***n-*** [*pl.* **sum·ma·ries**] brief statement giving only the main points: *He gave a five-point* summary *of the last session of Congress.* ***adj-*** **1** brief; condensed: *a* summary *account of the accident on the radio program.* **2** done without delay or formality; prompt and direct: *a* summary *court martial*; summary *action against traffic violators.* ***Hom-*** summery.

sum·ma·tion (sə mā′ shən) ***n-*** **1** addition. **2** summary.

sum·mer (sŭm′ ər) ***n-*** hottest season of the year, between spring and autumn; in the northern hemisphere the season between June 21 and September 22. *as **modifier**: the* summer *resorts.* ***vi-*** to spend the summer: *He always.*summers *abroad.*

sum·mer·house (sŭm′ ər hous′) ***n-*** small, open, rustic house in a park or garden, used for sitting.

sum·mer·time (sŭm′ ər tīm′) ***n-*** season of summer. *as **modifier**: a* summertime *activity.*

sum·mer·y (sŭm′ ə rē) ***adj-*** suitable for or typical of the summer: *light,* summery *clothes.* ***Hom-*** summary.

sum·mit (sŭm′ ĭt) ***n-*** top; highest point or degree: *the* summit *of the mountain*; *the* summit *of our hopes.*

summit conference ***n-*** meeting between heads of government, rather than between diplomats, for the conduct of foreign relations. Also **summit meeting.**

sum·mon (sŭm′ ən) ***vt-*** **1** to call; send for: *We* summoned *the doctor in the middle of the night.* **2** to require the presence of by a summons: *The court* summoned *him to appear for trial.* **3** to arouse; stir to activity; gather together: *He* summoned *all his courage.*

sum·mons (sŭm′ ənz) ***n-*** [*pl.* **sum·mons·es**] **1** in law, a document ordering a sheriff to order a defendant to appear in court at a certain time. **2** signal or command to appear: *a military* summons *for active duty.*

sump (sŭmp) ***n-*** **1** natural pit, such as a marsh with a mud bottom. **2** pit for the collection of sewage or industrial wastes. **3** in metallurgy, a round pit for the collection of fused metal. **4** in mining, an excavation ahead of, or below, the main working level, into which water drains.

sump pump ***n-*** a pump that removes excess water from a sump dug to collect seepage, as in a cellar.

sump·tu·ar·y law (sŭmp′ cho͞o ĕr′ ē) ***n-*** a statute that restricts extravagant spending or showiness in dress, decoration, diet, etc.

sump·tu·ous (sŭmp′ cho͞o əs) ***adj-*** costly, lavish; luxurious; magnificent: *a* sumptuous *entertainment.* ***—adv-*** **sump′ tu·ous·ly.** ***n-*** **sump′ tu·ous·ness.**

sun (sŭn) ***n-*** **1** star which is the central body of our solar system and around which the earth and other planets revolve. It is our source of light and heat. **2** sunshine: *Dragonflies flitted about in the* sun. ***vt-*** **[sunned, sun·ning]** to expose to sunlight: *Alex* sunned *himself.* ***Hom-*** son.

Sun. Sunday.

sun bath ***n-*** exposure of the body to sunlight or a sunlamp.

sun·bathe (sŭn′ bāth′) ***vi-*** **[sun·bathed, sun·bath·ing]** to take a sun bath: *She* sunbathes *several hours a day.*

sun·beam (sŭn′ bēm′) ***n-*** ray of sunlight.

sun·bon·net (sŭn′ bŏn′ ət) ***n-*** woman's or child's hat with a wide brim surrounding the face and a panel covering the neck.

Sunbonnet

sun·burn (sŭn′ bûrn′) ***n-*** painful reddening or blistering of the skin, caused by overexposure to sunlight or a sunlamp. ***vi-*** **[sun·burned** or **sun·burnt, sun·burn·ing]** to have the skin burned by the rays of the sun or a sunlamp: *He* sunburns *easily.* ***vt-***: *The noon sun* sunburned *his back.*

sun·burst (sŭn′ bûrst′) ***n-*** **1** sudden shining through of sunlight, as during a cloud break. **2** jewelry or other decoration in the form of a central disk with rays spreading out from it.

sun·dae (sŭn′ dē) ***n-*** serving of ice cream topped with syrup, fruit, nuts, whipped cream, etc. ***Hom-*** Sunday.

Sun·day (sŭn′ dā, -dē) ***n-*** first day of the week; Christian Sabbath or Lord's Day. ***Hom-*** sundae.

Sunday school ***n-*** classes held by churches on Sunday for the study of religion and the Bible.

sun·der (sŭn′ dər) ***vt-*** to divide; separate; part: *They* sundered *connections.* ***vi-***: *We will never* sunder.

sun·di·al (sŭn′ dī′ əl) ***n-*** device showing the time of day by the position of the shadow cast by a pointer on a dial.

Sundial

sun·down (sŭn′ doun′) ***n-*** the time at which the sun disappears below the horizon; sunset.

sun·dry (sŭn′ drē) ***adj-*** various; several: *the* sundry *items for a church bazaar.* ***n-*** *pl.* **sundries** odds and ends; items too small or numerous to be mentioned.

sun·fish (sŭn′ fĭsh′) ***n-*** [*pl.* **sun·fish**; **sun·fish·es** (kinds of sunfish)] **1** any of a large group of small fresh-water fishes having very deep, flat bodies. **2** (also **ocean sunfish**) large ocean fish of similar shape that can weigh as much as a ton.

sun·flow·er (sŭn′ flou′ ər) ***n-*** any of various tall plants that bear yellow and brown flowers and have edible seeds that yield a useful oil.

Garden sunflower

sung (sŭng) *p.p.* of **sing.**

sun·glass·es (sŭn′ glăs′ əz) ***n-*** *pl.* eyeglasses with colored lenses to protect the eyes from glare.

sunk (sŭngk) *p.p.* of **sink.**

sunk·en (sŭngk′ ən) ***adj-*** **1** situated below the surface of the water or the ground: *the* sunken *gardens*; sunken *rocks.* **2** fallen in; hollow: *the invalid's* sunken *cheeks.*

sun lamp ***n-*** lamp that gives off ultraviolet radiations and is used for imitating the tanning effect of natural sunlight and for medical treatments.

sun·less (sŭn′ ləs) ***adj-*** without sunlight.

sun·light (sŭn′ līt′) ***n-*** the light of the sun, especially when it falls directly, without being interrupted by anything that casts a shadow; sunshine: *The* sunlight *makes the room more cheerful.*

sun·lit (sŭn′ lĭt′) ***adj-*** in sunlight; receiving sunlight.

sun·ny (sŭn′ ē) ***adj-*** [**sun·ni·er, sun·ni·est**] **1** filled, warmed, or lighted by sunlight. **2** cheerful; bright: *a* sunny *disposition.* **—*adv-*** **sun′ ni·ly.** ***n-*** **sun′ ni·ness.**

sun porch ***n-*** porch or room having large windows or glass walls for the purpose of admitting sunlight. Also **sun parlor, sun room.**

sun·rise (sŭn′ rīz′) ***n-*** **1** morning rising of the sun from below the horizon; sunup. **2** time when the sun rises. **3** appearance of the sky when the sun rises: *the colorful* sunrises *in the tropics.*

sun·set (sŭn′ sĕt′) ***n-*** **1** disappearance of the sun below the horizon. **2** time at which the sun disappears below the horizon; sundown. **3** appearance of the sky when the sun sets: *The* sunset *was a brilliant orange.*

sun·shade (sŭn′ shād′) ***n-*** anything used as a protection against the sun, such as an awning, hat brim, tube fitted to a camera lens, etc.

sun·shine (sŭn′ shīn′) ***n-*** **1** light rays from the sun. **2** place where rays of the sun fall: *Stand in the* sunshine *and you will feel warmer.* **3** brightness; cheer: *His smile is always full of* sunshine. **—*n-*** **sun′ shin′ y.**

sun·spot (sŭn′ spŏt′) ***n-*** one of the dark spots periodically observed on the sun's surface. Sunspots are usually visible only through a very dark filter.

sun·stroke (sŭn′ strōk′) ***n-*** a sickness due to excessive exposure to sunlight and marked by convulsions, coma, and high skin temperature.

sun·tan (sŭn′ tăn′) ***n-*** a browning of the skin, by the sun.

sun·up (sŭn′ ŭp′) ***n-*** the time when the sun rises; sunrise.

[1]**sup** (sŭp) ***vt-*** [**supped, sup·ping**] to take liquid in small mouthfuls; sip. ***n-*** small mouthful of liquid. [from Old English **sūpan** of the same meaning, and related to **sip.**]

[2]**sup** (sŭp) ***vi-*** [**supped, sup·ping.**] to eat the evening meal; have supper. [from **supper,** or from Old French **soper** meaning "to take supper."]

su·per (so͞o′ pər) *Slang* ***n-*** **1** superintendent. **2** theatrical supernumerary. ***adj-*** especially good or fine.

super- *prefix* **1** above; over: *a* super*script.* **2** going beyond; more than: *a* super*human effort*; super*natural.* **3** unusually large; in excess: *a* super*market.*

su·per·a·bun·dant (so͞o′ pər ə bŭn′ dənt) ***adj-*** much more than is sufficient; excessive: *America has a* superabundant *wheat supply.* **—*n-*** **su′ per·a·bun′ dance.**

su·per·an·nu·at·ed (so͞o′ pər ăn′ yo͞o ā′ təd) ***adj-*** **1** unfit for work or use because of old age. **2** pensioned because of old age or infirmity: *a* superannuated *man.* **—*n-*** **su′ per·an′ nu·a′ tion.**

su·perb (so͞o pûrb′) ***adj-*** **1** grand; majestic: *The view from the hill was* superb. **2** unusually elegant, beautiful, or rich: *The bride's gown is* superb. **3** very fine; excellent: *a* superb *performance.* **—*adv-*** **su·perb′ ly.**

su·per·car·go (so͞o′ pər kär′ gō) ***n-*** [*pl.* **su·per·car·goes** or **su·per·car·gos**] officer on a merchant ship who is in charge of its cargo and business during the voyage.

su·per·charge (so͞o′ pər chärj′) ***vt-*** [**su·per·charged, su·per·charg·ing**] to increase the power of (an internal-combustion engine) by using a supercharger.

su·per·char·ger (so͞o′ pər chär′ jər) ***n-*** blower or pump used to increase the intake of air in an internal-combustion engine and thereby increase the power of the engine or overcome the effect of reduced atmospheric pressure.

su·per·cil·i·ous (so͞o′ pər sĭl′ ē əs) ***adj-*** haughty; overbearing; proud: *a* supercilious *student.* **—*adv-*** **su′ per·cil′ i·ous·ly.** ***n-*** **su′ per·cil′ i·ous·ness.**

su·per·con·duc·tive (so͞o′ pər kən dŭk′ tĭv) ***adj-*** having no electrical resistance after being cooled to nearly absolute zero.

su·per·con·duc·tiv·i·ty (so͞o′ pər kŏn′ dək tĭv′ ə tē) ***n-*** the sudden disappearance of all resistance to the passage of an electric current in a metal, alloy, etc., cooled to near absolute zero.

su·per·cool (so͞o′ pər ko͞ol′) ***vt-*** to cool (something) below the freezing point without solidifying it.

su·per·er·o·ga·tion (so͞o′ pər ĕr′ ə gā′ shən) ***n-*** a doing more than necessary, or more than is required; superfluity: *About half his effort is* supererogation. **—*adj-*** **su′ per·er·og′ a·tor′ y** (so͞o′ pər ə rŏg′ ə tôr′ ē).

su·per·fi·cial (so͞o′ pər fĭsh′ əl) ***adj-*** **1** on the surface only; not deep: *His wound was only* superficial. **2** slight; not thorough: *a* superficial *understanding of art.* **3** lacking depth of feeling and understanding; shallow: *a* superficial *person.* **—*adv-*** **su′ per·fi′ cial·ly.**

su·per·fi·ci·al·i·ty (so͞o′ pər fĭsh′ ē ăl′ ə tē) ***n-*** [*pl.* **su·per·fi·ci·al·i·ties**] **1** condition of being superficial. **2** something superficial.

su·per·fine (so͞o′ pər fīn′) ***adj-*** **1** having the choicest quality: *That is* superfine *beef.* **2** extremely subtle or refined; overly nice: *a* superfine *distinction.* **3** having very tiny grains or particles: *a* superfine *powder.*

su·per·flu·i·ty (so͞o′ pər flo͞o′ ə tē) ***n-*** superabundance; excess.

su·per·flu·ous (so͞o pûr′ flo͞o əs) ***adj-*** beyond what is needed or desired; excessive: *a* superfluous *phrase.* **—*adv-*** **su·per′ flu·ous·ly.** ***n-*** **su·per′ flu·ous·ness.**

su·per·heat (so͞o′ pər hēt′) ***vt-*** **1** *Physics* to heat (a vapor) above the temperature required to maintain the gaseous condition 2 *Physics* to heat (a liquid) above the normal boiling point, under pressure. 3 to overheat.

su·per·high·way (sōō'pər hī'wā') ***n-*** public highway designed for high-speed travel, having four or more lanes and a barrier between lanes going in opposite directions.

su·per·hu·man (sōō'pər hyōō'mən) ***adj-*** 1 beyond human limits: superhuman *strength.* 2 supernatural; divine: *a* superhuman *inspiration.* **—*adv-* su'per·hu'man·ly.** ***n-*** **su'per·hu'man·ness.**

su·per·im·pose (sōō'pər ĭm pōz') ***vt-*** **[su·per·im·posed, su·per·im·pos·ing]** to place or lay (something) over something: *He* superimposed *a coat of yellow on blue.*

su·per·in·tend (sōō pər ĭn tĕnd', sōō'prĭn tĕnd') ***vt-*** to have charge of; supervise, manage, or direct.

su·per·in·tend·ence (sōō'prĭn tĕn'dəns) ***n-*** supervision; management; direction

su·per·in·tend·en·cy (sōō'prĭn tĕn'dən sē) ***n-*** 1 office and position of a superintendent. 2 superintendence.

su·per·in·tend·ent (sōō'prĭn tĕn'dənt) ***n-*** 1 person who supervises or directs: *the* superintendent *of schools.* 2 person in charge of maintenance of a building.

su·pe·ri·or (sə pêr'ē ər, sōō-) ***adj-*** 1 above the average in quality or excellence; exceptional: *She has a* superior *mind.* 2 higher in rank, position, office, etc.: *a* superior *officer.* 3 greater in quantity or number: *The* superior *strength of the opposing army caused our defeat.* 4 snobbish; disdainful: *Paul's* superior *attitude lost him friends.* 5 placed or located above; upper: *Mark your footnotes with* superior *figures or letters.* ***n-*** one who is higher in rank or position: *Captain Jones is my* superior.

superior to 1 above; not stooping or yielding to: *He is* superior *to petty jealousies.* 2 better or greater than.

su·pe·ri·or·i·ty (sə pêr ē ŏr'ə tē, -ŏr'ə tē) ***n-*** 1 excellence, worth, value, etc., greater than that of something or someone else: *We are proud of the* superiority *of our product.* 2 snobbish or disdainful view of other persons: *We all resented his offensive* superiority.

su·per·la·tive (sōō pûr'lə tĭv) ***adj-*** 1 best or greatest in degree, kind, etc.; supreme: *a woman of* superlative *intelligence.* 2 *Grammar* of, relating to, or representing the highest degree of comparison in adjectives and adverbs. ***n-*** *Grammar* the form of an adjective that normally fits the pattern: The ______ of all the tables. Most superlatives are formed by adding the ending -est to the adjective or its root: tallest, largest. Some, however, are completely different from their adjectives: good, best. Many adjectives do not have superlatives, but are compared by adding "most": He is the most intelligent man I know. Some adverbs also have superlatives: well, best. **—*adj-* su·per'la·tive·ly.** ***n-*** **su·per'la·tive·ness.**

su·per·man (sōō'pər măn') ***n-*** [*pl.* **su·per·men**] man of unusual strength or ability. **—*n-*** ***fem.*** **su'per·wom'an.**

su·per·mar·ket (sōō'pər mär'kət) ***n-*** large store where food and other goods are so arranged that customers can wait on themselves. *as* ***modifier:*** *a* supermarket *manager;* supermarket *selling.*

su·per·nal sōō pûr'nəl) ***adj-*** relating to, or living in the heavens: *the* supernal *gods.* **—*adj-* su·per'nal·ly.**

su·per·nat·u·ral (sōō'pər năch'ər əl) ***adj-*** outside or beyond what is natural; not explained by the laws of nature: *ghosts and other* supernatural *beings.* ***n-*** **the supernatural** something outside of nature: *an act of* the supernatural. **—*adv-* su'per·nat'u·ral·ly.**

su·per·nat·u·ral·ism (sōō'pər năch'ər ə lĭz'əm) ***n-*** 1 supernatural quality. 2 belief in the supernatural.

su·per·nu·mer·ar·y (sōō'pər nōō'mə rĕr'ē) ***n-*** [*pl.* **su·per·nu·mer·ar·ies**] 1 person or thing beyond the stated number, or beyond what is necessary or usual. 2 actor employed merely to appear in a performance, as one of a crowd, with no speaking part. ***adj-*** more than the desired or usual number: *a* supernumerary *quantity.*

su·per·pow·er (sōō'pər pou'ər) ***n-*** an extremely dominant or powerful nation: *The United States and the Soviet Union are* superpowers.

su·per·sat·u·rate (sōō'pər săch'ə rāt') ***vt-*** **[su·per·sat·u·rat·ed, su·per·sat·u·rat·ing]** to cause (a solution or solvent) to hold more of a solute than required for saturation, usually by warming the solvent and then allowing it to cool.

su·per·script (sōō'pər skrĭpt') ***n-*** something written above the line: *In* x^2, *2 is the* superscript. *as* ***modifier:*** *a* superscript *number.*

su·per·scrip·tion (sōō'pər skrĭp'shən) ***n-*** a writing or engraving on the outside or top of something; also, that which is so written, such as the address on a letter.

su·per·sede (sōō'pər sēd') ***vt-*** **[su·per·sed·ed, su·per·sed·ing]** 1 to take the place of; supplant: *Automobiles* superseded *the horse and carriage.* 2 to remove and put another in the place of: *The judge* superseded *the original sentence.* **—*n-* su'per·sed'er.**

su·per·sen·si·tive (sōō'pər sĕn'sə tĭv) **adv-** oversensitive. **—*adv-* su'per·sen'si·tive·ly.** ***n-*** **su'per·sen'si·tive·ness** or **su'per·sen'si·tiv'i·ty.**

su·per·son·ic (sōō'pər sŏn'ĭk) ***adj-*** 1 able to travel faster than the speed of sound: *a* supersonic *flight*; supersonic *travel.*

su·per·sti·tion (sōō'pər stĭsh'ən) ***n-*** 1 belief in, fear of, or reverence for the unknown or mysterious. 2 beliefs or practices, often of a religious character, based on fear of the unknown; any belief in the power of omens or charms.

su·per·sti·tious (sōō'pər stĭsh'əs) ***adj-*** having to do with or caused by superstition; full of superstitions. **—*adv-* su'per·sti'tious·ly,** ***n-*** **su'per·sti'tious·ness.**

su·per·struc·ture (sōō'pər strŭk'chər) ***n-*** any structure built on or above a foundation: *the* superstructure *of a building*; *the* superstructure *of his theory.*

su·per·vene (sōō'pər vēn') ***vi-*** **[su·per·vened, su·per·ven·ing]** to happen unexpectedly so as to change the course of events: *He would have won easily, but his illness* supervened. **—*n-* su'per·ven'tion** (-vĕn'chən).

su·per·vise (sōō'pər vīz') ***vt-*** **[su·per·vised, su·per·vis·ing]** to watch over and control the work of; direct; superintend; manage: *She* supervised *the display.*

su·per·vi·sion (sōō'pər vĭzh'ən) ***n-*** direction; management: *The playground is under my* supervision.

su·per·vi·sor (sōō'pər vī'zər) ***n-*** person who supervises. **—*adj-* su'per·vi'sor·y:** *in a* supervisory *position.*

su·pine (sōō'pīn') ***adj-*** 1 lying on the back with the face upward. 2 careless; indifferent; listless: *a* supine *attitude.* 3 vanquished; cowed; submissive.

Man lying supine

►Should not be confused with PRONE.

sup·per (sŭp'ər) ***n-*** evening meal when dinner is eaten at midday; last meal of the day. *as* ***modifier:*** *the* supper *table; the* supper *dishes.* **—*adj-* sup'per·less.**

sup·plant (sə plănt') ***vt-*** 1 to take the place of; displace: *Machines have* supplanted *persons in many jobs.* 2 to take the place of by unfair means: *The prince tried to* supplant *his father on the throne.*

fāte, făt, dâre, bärn; bē, bĕt, mêre; bīte, bĭt; nōte, hŏt, môre, dȯg; fŭn, fûr; tōō, bŏŏk; oil; out; tar; thin; then; hw for wh as in what; zh for s as in usual; ə for a, e, i, o, u, as in ago, linen, peril, atom, minus

sup·ple (sŭp′ əl) ***adj-*** **[sup·pler, sup·plest] 1** bending without breaking; flexible; pliant:. *The* supple *young trees withstood the storm.* **2** adaptable to other persons or changing circumstances; elastic: *a* supple *mind.* **—*adv-* sup′ple·ly. *n-* sup′ple·ness.**

sup·ple·ment (sŭp′ lə mənt) ***n-*** something added to complete a thing, such as an extra section of a newspaper or an addition to a book. ***vt-*** to make additions to; complete: *He* supplemented *the evidence by producing the gun.* **—*adj-* sup′ple·men′tal:** *the* supplemental *income from overtime work.*

sup·ple·men·ta·ry (sŭp′ lə mĕn′ tə rē) ***adj-*** additional; added to supply some lack: *the* supplementary *evidence.*

supplementary angles ***n-*** two angles whose combined value is 180°.

sup·pli·ant (sŭp′ lē ənt) ***n-*** person who supplicates. ***adj-*** beseeching; asking humbly: *a* suppliant *request.* **—*adv-* sup′pli·ant·ly.**

sup·pli·cant (sŭp′ lĭ kənt) ***n-*** person who entreats humbly; suppliant. ***adj-*:** *He sent a* supplicant *letter.*

sup·pli·cate (sŭp′ lə kāt′) ***vi-*** **[sup·pli·cat·ed, sup·pli·cat·ing]** to plead humbly; beg: *I have asked; must I now* supplicate? ***vt-*** **1** to plead of: *They* supplicated *him for mercy.* **2** to plead for: *They* supplicated *mercy.* **—*adv-* sup′pli·cat′ing·ly. *n-* sup′pli·ca′tor. *adj-* sup′pli·ca·tor′y** (-plĭ kə tôr′ ē): *She gave him a* supplicatory *look.*

sup·pli·ca·tion (sŭp′ lə kā′ shən) ***n-*** humble request; entreaty; prayer: *an earnest* supplication *for forgiveness.*

[1]sup·ply (sə plī′) ***vt-*** **[sup·plied, sup·ply·ing] 1** to furnish; provide: *The farmer* supplied *shelter for the hikers.* **2** to fill; satisfy: *Can you* supply *the demand for coffee?* ***n-*** [*pl.* **sup·plies**] **1** amount needed: *a winter's* supply *of fuel.* **2** the providing of what is needed: *Who handles the* supply *of fuel?* **3 supplies** stocks of things needed, especially of food and other things that are consumed; provisions: *The expedition ran out of* supplies. *as* ***modifier*:** *a* supply *train.* [from Old French **suppleier,** from Latin **supplēre** meaning "to fill up."] **—*n-* sup·pli′er.**

[2]sup·ply (sŭp′ lē) ***adv-*** supplely. [from **supple.**]

sup·port (sə pôrt′) ***vt-*** **1** to bear or hold up; prop: *Buttresses* support *the walls of the church.* **2** to put up with; endure: *She could not* support *the children's rudeness.* **3** to provide for; maintain: *The widow* supported *her three children.* **4** to aid; comfort: *Her kindness always* supports *me in time of trouble.* **5** to uphold: *to* support *a plan.* **6** to show the truth of; make valid; verify: *These papers* support *his claim to the property.* ***n-*** **1** thing that bears or holds up something: *Cables are the* support *for a suspension bridge.* **2** provision for food and shelter. **3** approval; backing: *We must all give our* support *to the president's decision.* **4** something that helps to verify: *Your evidence is a* support *to my theory.*

sup·port·a·ble (sə pôr′ tə bəl) ***adj-*** such as can be supported: *a* supportable *idea.* **—*adv-* sup·port′a·bly.**

sup·port·er (sə pôr′ tər) ***n-*** **1** person or thing that supports something. **2** person who upholds or backs something; partisan: *a* supporter *of town planning.*

sup·pose (sə pōz′) ***vt-*** **[sup·posed, sup·pos·ing] 1** to assume; take for granted: *I* suppose *I'll see you at the party?* **2** to imagine; believe: *Just* suppose *you were a king.* ***vi-*** to think; imagine. **—*adj-* sup·pos′a·ble.**

sup·posed (sə pōzd′) ***adj-*** thought to be; assumed: *He is the* supposed *author of the anonymous book.* **—*adv-* sup·pos′ed·ly.**

by supposed to *Informal* to have an obligation to.

sup·po·si·tion (sŭp′ ə zĭsh′ ən) ***n-*** **1** a supposing; guessing or estimating with little factual support: *His whole explanation is only* supposition. **2** something supposed; assumption: *a* supposition *of innocence.*

sup·pos·i·to·ry (sə pŏz′ ə tôr′ ē) ***n-*** solid, medicated preparation, designed for insertion into a cavity or passage of the body, such as the rectum.

sup·press (sə prĕs′) ***vt-*** **1** to put down by force; crush; subdue: *The police* suppressed *the riot.* **2** to restrain; hold back: *He tried to* suppress *his laughter.* **3** to stop or prevent publication of: *The censors* suppressed *the essay.* **—*adj-* sup·pres′sive:** *a* suppressive *law.*

sup·pres·sion (sə prĕsh′ ən) ***n-*** a suppressing.

sup·pres·sor (sə prĕs′ ər) ***n-*** **1** person, group, etc., that suppresses: *They soon became* suppressors *of the freedom they had fought for.* **2** something that suppresses; especially, a device that keeps the noise from electric sparks from causing static in a radio or other electronic system. Also **sup·press′er.**

sup·pu·rate (sŭp′ yə rāt′) ***vi-*** **[sup·pu·rat·ed, sup·pu·rat·ing]** to form pus; fester: *His wound will* suppurate *if not drained.* **—*n-* sup′pu·ra′tion.**

su·pra·re·nal glands (sōō′ prə rē′ nəl) ***n-*** adrenal glands.

su·prem·a·cy (sə prĕm′ ə sē) ***n-*** [*pl.* **su·prem·a·cies**] **1** condition of being supreme: *Shakespeare's* supremacy *among poets.* **2** highest authority or power.

su·preme (sə prēm′, sōō-) ***adj-*** **1** most powerful; highest in authority. **2** of highest degree: *an act of* supreme *courage.* **3** most important or intense; greatest; ultimate: *the* supreme *moment of the opera.* **—*adv-* su·preme′ly.**

Supreme Being ***n-*** God; the Deity.

Supreme Court ***n-*** **1** federal court that is the highest in the United States. It determines the constitutionality of federal, State, and local laws. **2** similar court in some States and in other countries. **3** civil and criminal trial court in New York State.

Supt. or **supt.** superintendent.

sur- *prefix* over; beyond: *a* sur*coat*; sur*charge.*

sur·cease (sûr′ sēs′) *Archaic* ***n-*** final end; stop.

sur·charge (sûr′ chärj′) ***n-*** excessive or added charge, load, or burden. ***vt-*** **[sur·charged, sur·charg·ing]** to overcharge, overload, or overburden.

sur·cin·gle (sûr′ sĭng′ gəl) ***n-*** belt passed around the body of a horse to hold a blanket in place.

sur·coat (sûr′ kōt′) ***n-*** outer coat; especially, the long, loose cloak worn by a knight over his armor.

surd (sûrd) ***n-*** **1** *Mathematics* irrational number that is the root of a positive integer or fraction, such as the square root of two or the square root of two-thirds. **2** in phonetics, a voiceless consonant. ***adj-*** **1** *Mathematics* irrational. **2** voiceless.

sure (shŏŏr) ***adj-*** **[sur·er, sur·est] 1** confident: *I am* sure *you will succeed.* **2** certain: *You are* sure *to find what you are looking for in that book.* **3** safe; reliable; trustworthy: *a* sure *bet.* **4** firm; sound: *a* sure *foothold.* ***adv-*** *Informal* surely; certainly. **—*n-* sure′ness.**

for sure *Informal* certainly. **make sure** assure oneself; be certain; confirm: *Please* make sure *the door is locked.* **to be sure** no doubt: *He is,* to be sure, *a good worker.*

sure-fire (shŏŏr′ fīər′) *Informal* ***adj-*** certain to be successful: *a* sure-fire *plan.*

sure·foot·ed (shŏŏr′ fŏŏt′ əd) ***adj-*** not likely to fall or stumble: *Mountain goats are* sure-footed. **—*adv-* sure′-foot′ed·ly. *n-* sure′-foot′ed·ness.**

sure·ly (shŏŏr′ lē) ***adv-*** **1** with skill; in a deft manner; without a slip: *The expert skier glided* surely *down the slope.* **2** certainly; undoubtedly: *You* surely *can't be serious.* **3** without fail: *Slowly but* surely *fall returns.*

sur·e·ty (shŏŏr′ ē tē) ***n-*** **[sur·e·ties] 1** sureness; certainty. **2** guarantee against damage, loss, etc.: *The government gave the farmers* surety *for their crops.* **3** person who assumes responsibility, usually for debts, for another.

surf (sûrf) ***n-*** waves of the sea as they break in foam upon the shore. ***vi-*** to ride a surfboard. ***Hom-*** serf.

sur·face (sûr′ fəs) ***n-*** **1** the face or outside of anything: *the gleaming* surface *of the furniture.* **2** outward appearance. ***adj-*** **1** relating to the top or outside of anything: *the underground and* surface *transportation of the city.* **2** insincere; superficial: *Garry showed only a* surface *interest in the subject.* ***vt-*** **[sur·faced, sur·fac·ing]** to give a surface to; to smooth: *I* surfaced *this table with three coats of varnish.* ***vi-*** to come to the surface from below: *The whale* surfaced *to port.* **—*n-* sur′ fac·er.**

surface tension ***n-*** tendency of the free surface on a liquid to contract as if the liquid had a thin, elastic surface film. It is caused by the unbalanced molecular force at the surface and can be seen in the spherical beading of water on a waxed surface.

sur·fac·ing (sûr′ fəs ĭng) ***n-*** substance or material used for an applied surface on something.

surf·board (sûrf′ bôrd′) ***n-*** long, flat board, rounded at the ends and having a tiny fixed rudder at the rear, used for riding waves in toward a beach. **—*n-* surf′ board′ ing.**

surf·boat (sûrf′ bōt′) ***n-*** strong, buoyant boat for riding through the surf. **—*n-* surf′ boat′ ing.**

surf casting ***n-*** fishing by casting a bait or lure from a beach into the surf. **—*n-* surf caster.**

sur·feit (sûr′ fət) ***n-*** **1** indulgence to excess, especially in eating or drinking. **2** fullness or sickness caused by such excess. **3** an overabundance or excess of anything; plethora. ***vt-*** to feed to excess; cloy; satiate.

surf·er (sûr fər) ***n-*** person who rides waves on a surfboard.

surge (sûrj) ***n-*** **1** large wave, swell, or billow of water. **2** great, rolling motion; rush: *the* surge *of a mob.* **3** sudden and great onset or increase. ***vi-*** **[surged, surg·ing]** **1** to rush, sweep, or push forth like a rolling or swelling wave: *The crowd* surged *past the line of police.* **2** to begin or increase violently. ***Hom-*** serge.

sur·geon (sûr′ jən) ***n-*** doctor who has additional and specialized training in surgery.

surgeon general ***n-*** **1** chief medical officer of the United States Army, with the rank of major general. **2** chief of the U.S. Public Health Service, with the rank of brigadier general.

sur·ger·y (sûr′ jə rē) ***n-*** [*pl.* **sur·ger·ies**] **1** branch of medicine dealing with the treatment of illness by operation, such as removing diseased parts of the body, repairing injuries, correcting deformities, etc. **2** the work of a doctor who operates on people or animals; operation. **3** room in which operations are performed.

sur·gi·cal (sûr′ jĭ kəl) ***adj-*** **1** used in or for surgery: *a* surgical *ward*; surgical *procedures.* **2** by means of surgery: *a* surgical *treatment.* **3** specialized in surgery: *a* surgical *nurse*; surgical *training.* **—*adv-* sur′ gi·cal·ly.**

sur·ly (sûr′ lē) ***adj-*** **[sur·li·er, sur·li·est]** bad-tempered; rude; sullen: *a* surly *mood.* **—*n-* sur′ li·ness.**

sur·mise (sər mīz′) ***vt-*** **[sur·mised, sur·mis·ing]** to form an opinion about with very little evidence; guess; suppose; conjecture: *He* surmised *that we were absent because of illness.* ***vi-*** to make a guess. ***n-*** (*also* sûr′ mīz′) a thought or supposition based upon little evidence; conjecture; guess: *His* surmise *proved correct.*

sur·mount (sər mount′) ***vt-*** **1** to overcome; conquer: *He* surmounted *his difficulties by working harder.* **2** to be situated at the top of: *The castle* surmounts *the hill.* **3** to rise or tower above: *The mountain* surmounts *the village.* **4** to mount upon and cross over: *The troops* surmounted *the hill.*

sur·mount·a·ble (sər moun′ tə bəl) ***adj-*** such as can be surmounted or overcome: *a* surmountable *handicap.*

sur·name (sûr′ nām′) ***n-*** **1** last or family name: *"Dickens" is Charles Dickens'* surname. **2** in former times, name added to a first or given name to indicate some characteristic or trait; nickname. Example: "*Charles* the Fat." ***vt-*** **[sur·named, sur·nam·ing]** to give an additional name to: *They* surnamed *him "the Brave."*

sur·pass (sər păs′) ***vt-*** **1** to be better, stronger, etc., than (something); exceed: *The results* surpassed *my highest hopes.* **2** to go beyond the reach, power, or limit of (something): *Their difficulties* surpassed *their endurance.* **—*adj-* sur·pass′ able. —*adv-* sur·pass′ ing·ly.**

sur·plice (sûr′ pləs) ***n-*** loose, white, outer garment with wide sleeves, worn in some churches by the clergy and the choir.

sur·plus (sûr′ plŭs′) ***n-*** **1** amount or quantity over and above what is used or needed; excess: *The farmer stored enough corn for his livestock and sold the* surplus. **2** in a business, profit left over after debts are paid and all other obligations are met. *as* ***modifier*** (*also* sûr′ pləs): *a* surplus *store*; surplus *wheat.*

sur·prise (sər prīz′) ***vt-*** **[sur·prised, sur·pris·ing]** **1** to come upon unexpectedly: *He* surprised *us by his visit.* **2** to attack without warning; take unawares: *The patrol's night raid* surprised *the enemy.* **3** to cause to feel wonder or astonishment: *The old car's speed* surprised *us.* **4** to hurry (someone) into doing something unintended: *The police* surprised *the thief into confessing.* ***n-*** **1** a coming upon unexpectedly; a catching unawares: *The watchman caught them by* surprise. **2** something sudden or unexpected: *The new toaster was a* surprise *for mother.* **3** feeling caused by something sudden or unexpected; astonishment. *as* ***modifier***: *a* surprise *party.*

take by surprise **1** to come upon suddenly or without warning. **2** to astonish; amaze.

sur·pris·ing (sər prī′ zĭng) ***adj-*** causing surprise, wonder, or astonishment: *His decision not to play was* surprising. **—*adv-* sur·pris′ ing·ly.**

sur·re·al·ism (sə rē′ ə lĭz′ əm) ***n-*** a style of art characterized by dreamlike rearrangements or distortions of objects painted in sharp outlines and carefully shaded shapes. **—*n-* sur·re′ al·ist. *adj-* sur·re′ al·is′ tic. *adv-* sur·re′ al·is′ ti·cal·ly.**

sur·ren·der (sə rĕn′ dər) ***vt-*** **1** to give up under pressure to the power or authority of another; yield: *The army* surrendered *its guns to the enemy.* **2** to give up or relinquish: *to* surrender *a claim*; *to* surrender *a title.* **3** to yield (oneself) to an influence or emotion: *He* surrendered *himself to the beautiful music.* ***vi-*** to yield; give up the struggle: *The outlaw* surrendered *to the sheriff.* ***n-*** a giving up or yielding.

sur·rep·ti·tious (sûr′ əp tĭsh′ əs) ***adj-*** done by secret or improper means; stealthy; clandestine: *a* surreptitious *whisper*; *a* surreptitious *meeting.* **—*adv-* sur′ rep·ti′ tious·ly. *n-* sur′ rep·ti′ tious·ness.**

sur·rey (sûr′ ē) ***n-*** [*pl.* **sur·reys**] light carriage with four wheels and two seats.

Surrey

sur·ro·gate (sûr′ ə gāt′, -gət) ***n-*** **1** person appointed to act for another; deputy; a substitute, either a person or thing. **2** in certain States, a court officer who deals with the probating of wills and the administration of estates.

sur·round (sə round′) *vt-* to shut in on all sides; enclose; encircle: *The army* surrounded *the fort.*

sur·round·ings (sə roun′ dĭngz) *n- pl.* conditions, people, things, etc., that surround one; environment.

sur·tax (sûr′ tăks′) *n-* additional tax over and above another tax; especially, graduated income tax in addition to the normal income tax, imposed on the amount by which net income exceeds a specified sum. *vt-* to impose an additional tax upon.

sur·veil·lance (sər vā′ ləns) *n-* close watch; inspection: *to be under police* surveillance.

[1]**sur·vey** (sər vā′) *vt-* **1** to examine generally; take a broad view of: *We* surveyed *the scene from the hill.* **2** to examine closely with regard to condition or value: *Dad* surveyed *the used car carefully before he bought it.* **3** to locate and establish points on (land or property) for the purpose of fixing boundaries, building a highway, locating a canal, etc. **4** to locate and fix the points of (a boundary, highway, canal, etc.).

[2]**sur·vey** (sûr′ vā′) *n-* **1** act of examining: *a* survey *of goods on sale.* **2** examination made by gathering information such as statistics: *a* survey *of the drivers in the town.* **3** a locating of points on the land of or for: *We are making a* survey *for a new road.* **4** general review or examination: *a* survey *of English literature.*

sur·vey·ing (sər vā′ ĭng) *n-* act, science, or occupation of measuring, determining, and recording points and lines on land.

sur·vey·or (sər vā′ ər) *n-* **1** person who surveys; especially, a person who surveys land. **2** a customs inspector in charge of the duties levied on imported goods.

sur·vi·val (sər vī′ vəl) *n-* **1** act or fact of surviving: *the* survival *of the buffalo.* **2** person or thing that has survived: *Superstitions are* survivals *of former times.*

sur·vive (sər vīv′) *vi-* [**sur·vived, sur·viv·ing**] **1** to continue to live or be: *The pyramids have* survived *through the centuries.* *vt-* **1** to live or last through; endure: *The great oak* survived *the hurricane.* **2** to live longer than; outlive; outlast: *The old woman* survived *her husband.*

sur·vi·vor (sər vī′ vər) *n-* person or thing left after others have died or disappeared.

Su·san·na (so͞o zăn′ ə) *n-* the Old Testament Apocrypha book telling the story of Susanna, a chaste Jewish captive who was falsely accused of adultery.

sus·cep·ti·bil·i·ty (sə sĕp′ tə bĭl′ ə tē) *n-* [*pl.* **sus·cep·ti·bil·i·ties**] **1** condition of being susceptible. **2 susceptibilities** sensitive feelings. **3** *Physics* the property of a substance that allows it to be magnetized when placed in a magnetic field.

sus·cep·ti·ble (sə sĕp′ tə bəl) *adj-* easily influenced or affected; sensitive: *He is a* susceptible *child, quick to respond to kindness.* **—*adv-* sus·cep′ ti·bly.**

susceptible of capable of; allowing: *The poem is* susceptible of *several interpretations.* **susceptible to** easily affected by: *He is* susceptible *to flattery.*

[1]**sus·pect** (sə spĕkt′) *vt-* **1** to consider (someone) possibly guilty without proof: *I* suspect *him of cheating.* **2** to think likely (takes only a clause as object): *I* suspect *you are correct.* **3** to view with suspicion; doubt; question: *I* suspect *his motives.* *vi-* to be suspicious.

[2]**sus·pect** (sŭs′ pĕkt′) *n-* person under suspicion, especially of having committed a crime: *After the robbery, the police arrested several* suspects. *adj-* (*also* sə spĕkt′) viewed with suspicion; questionable; dubious: *The miser's sudden generosity was* suspect.

sus·pend (sə spĕnd′) *vt-* **1** to attach to and allow to hang down (from): *We* suspended *a sprig of mistletoe from the ceiling.* **2** to cause to hang: *The balloons appeared to be* suspended *in midair.* **3** to delay; withhold: *to* suspend *judgment.* **4** to cause to cease for a time; stop temporarily; also, to set aside temporarily; disregard for a time: *to* suspend *a rule.* **5** to keep out, for a while, from some privilege, office, or the like.

sus·pend·ers (sə spĕn′ dərz) *n-* (takes plural verb) straps worn over the shoulders to hold up the trousers. Also **pair of suspenders** (takes singular verb).

sus·pense (sə spĕns′) *n-* state of doubt or uncertainty, accompanied by anxiety: *the* suspense *of waiting.*

sus·pen·sion (sə spĕn′ shən) *n-* **1** a suspending or being suspended: *a* suspension *of judgment*; *a* suspension *of work.* **2** mixture in which particles of a solid or liquid are dispersed throughout another liquid but not dissolved (see also *emulsion*).

suspension bridge *n-* bridge hung on cables stretched across a river, canyon, etc. For picture, see *bridge.*

sus·pen·so·ry (sə spĕn′ sə rē) *adj-* **1** fitted or serving to suspend or support: *a* suspensory *ligament*; *a* suspensory *bandage.* **2** temporarily stopping; causing delay: *a* suspensory *veto.* *n-* [*pl.* **sus·pen·so·ries**] something that supports, such as a bandage.

sus·pi·cion (sə spĭsh′ ən) *n-* **1** a believing that something is wrong, with little or no evidence: *A* suspicion *of foul play made the police investigate.* **2** feeling; impression; notion: *Robert had a* suspicion *that he was being followed.* **3** trace; hint: *a* suspicion *of garlic in the salad.*

under suspicion suspected of being guilty, wrong, etc., on little evidence: *He was* under suspicion *for the theft.*

sus·pi·cious (sə spĭsh′ əs) *adj-* **1** inclined to doubt or distrust: *I am* suspicious *of a politician's promise.* **2** open to doubt or distrust: *His actions were* suspicious *enough to make the police watch him.* **3** showing or suggesting suspicion: *a* suspicious *question*; *a* suspicious *glance.* **—*adv-* sus·pi′ cious·ly.** ***n-* sus·pi′ cious·ness.**

sus·tain (sə stān′) *vt-* **1** to nourish and support: *enough air to* sustain *life.* **2** to bear up; hold up: *Stone arches* sustain *the weight of the dome.* **3** to uphold: *The Supreme Court* sustained *the decision of the lower courts.* **4** to undergo; suffer: *to* sustain *a loss*; *to* sustain *a broken leg.* **5** to hold; continue; keep going: *to* sustain *a high note*; *to* sustain *a discussion.* **6** to bear out; confirm. **—*adj-* sus·tain′ a·ble.** ***n-* sus·tain′ er.**

sustaining program *n-* radio or television program supported by a station without sponsors.

sus·te·nance (sŭs′ tə nəns) *n-* **1** something that supports or sustains life, such as food and water. **2** a supporting or sustaining with food, drink, or other necessities.

sut·ler (sŭt′ lər) *n-* person who follows an army to sell food, liquor, etc., to soldiers.

su·ture (so͞o′ chər) *n-* **1** the drawing together of the edges of a cut or wound by stitches; also, the thread used. **2** line or seam where bones are united, as in the skull. *vt-* [**su·tured, su·tur·ing**] to draw together or join by stitches: *to* suture *a cut.*

su·ze·rain (so͞o′ zə rən, -rān′) *n-* **1** in feudal times, a lord with authority over vassals who owed him loyalty and service in return for the use of land. **2** state holding sovereign power over a semi-independent, internally self-governing state. **—*n-* su′ ze·rain·ty.**

svelte (svĕlt) *adj-* slender; slim; lithe.

SW or **S.W.** **1** southwest. **2** southwestern.

swab (swŏb) *n-* **1** a mop for cleaning decks, floors, etc. **2** bit of sponge or cotton fastened to the end of a stick, used to clean or apply medicine to the mouth, throat, ears, etc. **3** a brush for cleaning the barrel of a gun. *vt-* [**swabbed, swab·bing**] to clean with any of these devices; also, to apply medicine to with cotton. **—*n-* swab′ ber.**

swad·dle (swŏd′ əl) *vt-* [**swad·dled, swad·dling**] to wrap (a baby) with strips of cloth. *n-* cloth used for this.

swaddling clothes ***n-*** strips of cloth formerly used to wrap around a newborn baby, to prevent it from moving too much.

swag (swăg) *Slang* ***n-*** stolen goods or money; loot.

swag·ger (swăg′ ər) ***vi-*** **1** to strut about and act in a showy or overbearing manner. **2** to boast noisily; bluster. ***n-*** **1** an overbearing walk or way of acting. **2** noisy boasting; bluster. **—*n-* swag′ger·er.** ***adv-*** **swag′ ger·ing·ly:** *He moved* swaggeringly *down the street.*

swagger stick ***n-*** light cane carried by army officers.

Swa·hi·li (swä hē′ lē) ***n-*** a Bantu language with some Arabic elements, used widely in commerce and in government circles of East Africa and in the Congo.

swain (swān) ***n-*** **1** *Archaic* country youth. **2** young male lover (used humorously).

[1]**swal·low** (swŏl′ ō) ***vt-*** **1** to transfer (food, drink, etc.) from the mouth to the stomach through the throat: *to* swallow *a piece of bread.* **2** to take in; absorb: *Expenses* swallowed *the profits.* **3** to take up completely and make disappear; engulf: *Darkness* swallowed *the fugitives.* **4** to believe or accept without question: *to* swallow *a story.* **5** to hold back; refrain from expressing: *to* swallow *one's pride*; *to* swallow *anger.* **6** to accept without protest; endure: *to* swallow *an insult.* **7** to take back; retract: *to* swallow *one's words.* ***vi-*** to perform the act of taking down food or liquid: *He had a sore throat and couldn't* swallow. ***n-*** **1** act of transferring food, drink, etc., from the mouth to the stomach through the throat. **2** amount so transferred at one time: *a* swallow *of water.* **3** space between the grooved edge of the wheel and the frame of a pulley, through which the rope passes. [from Old English **swelgan** meaning "to swallow; engulf."] **—*n-* swal′ low·er.**

[2]**swal·low** (swŏl′ ō) ***n-*** any of various slender, migratory birds with a long, forked tail and pointed wings, admired for swift, graceful flight. [from Old English **swalwe.**]

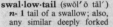

Barn swallow, about 5 in. long

swal·low·tail (swŏl′ ō tāl′) ***n-*** **1** tail of a swallow; also, any similar deeply forked tail. **2** any of various large butterflies having the hind wing extended so as to suggest a tail. **3** (also **swallow-tailed coat**) *Informal* tails; tailcoat.

swam (swăm) *p.t.* of **swim.**

swa·mi (swä′ mē) ***n-*** [*pl.* **swa·mis**] **1** Hindu title of respect, equivalent to "Master," "lord." **2** Hindu teacher, especially of religion; pundit.

swamp (swŏmp) ***n-*** low, spongy land soaked with water, often having a growth of trees, but unfit for cultivation; marsh; bog. *as* ***modifier:*** *a* swamp *boat*; swamp *fever.* ***vt-*** **1** to fill with water or cause to sink by flooding: *The big wave* swamped *the boat.* **2** to overwhelm: *Christmas mail* swamped *the post office.* ***vi-*** to tip so as to be flooded: *The boat* swamped. **—*adj-* swamp′ ish.**

swamp·y (swŏm′ pē) ***adj-*** [**swamp·i·er, swamp·i·est**] like a swamp; muddy; marshy; also, filled with swamps.

swan (swŏn) ***n-*** any of various large, usually white, swimming birds having very long, curved necks, admired for their grace on the water. See also *cygnet.* *as* ***modifier:*** *a* swan *feather.* **—*adj-* swan′ like′.**

Swan, about 5 ft. long

swan dive ***n-*** long forward dive with the back arched, the legs held straight, and arms held out sideways until near the water, when they are brought rapidly together and extended straight ahead in line with the body.

swank (swăngk) *Informal* ***adj-*** fashionable or stylish in a showy way: *a* swank *limousine*; *a* swank *hotel.* ***n-*** **1** action or manner that is ostentatious or arrogant; swagger; pretentiousness. **2** smartness; style.

swank·y (swăng′ kē) *Informal* ***adj-*** [**swank·i·er, swank·i·est**] fashionable or stylish in a showy way; pretentious; ostentatious: *a* swanky *nightclub.* **—*adv-* swank′ i·ly.**

swans·down (swŏnz′ doun′) ***n-*** **1** soft feathers of the swan, often used for trimming, powder puffs, etc. **2** soft, thick, woolen or cotton cloth resembling down.

swan song ***n-*** **1** mythical beautiful song, once believed to be sung by a swan before its death. **2** last work, performance, etc., before a person's death or retirement.

swap (swŏp) *Informal* ***vt-*** [**swapped, swap·ping**] to exchange for something other than money; trade; barter: *Stephen* swapped *his knife for a baseball.* ***vi-*** to make an exchange; barter. ***n-:*** *We made an even* swap.

sward (swȯrd) ***n-*** a stretch of land covered with cropped grass; turf.

swarm (swȯrm) ***n-*** **1** mass or large number of moving animals or people. **2** a mass of bees that is led by a queen bee, which flies off from a hive to form a new colony. **3** colony of bees settled in a hive permanently. ***vi-*** **1** of bees, to leave a hive in a mass to form a new colony. **2** to move in great numbers: *Europeans* swarmed *to America.* **3** to be crowded: *The beach* swarmed *with people.* ***vt-*** to throng: *People* swarmed *the streets.*

swart (swȯrt) swarthy. **—*n-* swart′ ness.**

swarth·y (swȯr′ thē) ***adj-*** [**swarth·i·er, swarth·i·est**] of a dusky color; having a dark skin: *a* swarthy *complexion*; *a* swarthy *person.* **—*adv-* swarth′ i·ly.** ***n-*** **swarth′ i·ness.**

swash (swŏsh, swȯsh) ***vi-*** to dash or wash with a splashing sound: *The waves* swashed *against the boat.* ***vt-*** to splash (water) about. ***n-*** a dashing of water, as against rocks.

swash·buck·ler (swŏsh′ bŭk′ lər, swȯsh′-) ***n-*** a swaggering soldier or adventurer. **—*adj-* swash′ buck′ ling.**

swas·ti·ka or **swas·ti·ca** (swŏs′ tĭ kə) ***n-*** a crosslike symbol, used in the Old World and in America since ancient times. It was adopted as the national symbol of Nazi Germany.

American Indian swastika

swat (swŏt) ***vt-*** [**swat·ted, swat·ting**] to hit with a sharp, quick blow: *to* swat *a fly.* ***n-*** sharp, quick blow. **—*n-* swat′ ter.**

swatch (swŏch) ***n-*** sample piece of cloth.

swath (swȯth, swŏth) ***n-*** **1** line or row of cut grain or grass. **2** the whole reach of a mowing machine or scythe; also, the space cleared in one continuous cut.

cut a wide swath to make a showy appearance.

swathe (swāth) ***vt-*** [**swathed, swath·ing**] **1** to bind with a band or bandage. **2** to wrap; envelop: *to* swathe *oneself in furs.* ***n-*** a band or bandage.

sway (swā) ***vi-*** **1** to move from side to side or backward and forward: *The boat* swayed *with the movement of the waves.* **2** to lean or go to one side; veer: *The tightrope walker* swayed *and fell. The bus* swayed *to the left.* **3** to incline in opinion, judgment, etc.: *Public opinion* swayed *to their cause.* ***vt-*** **1** to cause to move from side to side or backward and forward: *The wind* sways *the branches.* **2** to move or influence: *The politician knew how to* sway *people to his side.* **3** to cause to change one's mind; make waver: *No one could* sway *the stubborn old*

fāte, făt, dâre, bärn; bē, bĕt, mêre; bīte, bĭt; nōte, hŏt, môre, dȯg; fŭn, fûr; to͞o, bo͝ok; oil; out; tar; thin; then; hw for wh as in *wh*at; zh for s as in u*s*ual; ə for a, e, i, o, u, as in *a*go, lin*e*n, per*i*l, at*o*m, min*u*s

man. 4 to govern; rule over: *He* sways *the nation.* ***n-*** a moving from side to side or backward and forward. 2 control, rule, or influence: *the* sway *of public opinion.*

sway-backed (swā′ băkt′) ***adj-*** having an abnormally sagging back, especially from overwork: *a* sway-backed *horse.* Also **sway′-back′.**

swear (swâr) ***vi-*** [**swore** (swôr), **sworn** (swôrn), **swear·ing**] 1 to declare that what one says is true, with an appeal to God or to some sacred object: *In a court, you must* swear *before you can testify.* 2 to make a solemn vow or promise: *You must not* swear *if you do not mean it.* 3 to use bad words or profane language; curse. ***vt-*** 1 to declare solemnly, with an appeal to God or to some sacred object: *He* swore *that he would tell the truth. They* swore *an oath.* 2 to promise or vow solemnly: *He* swore *eternal friendship.* 3 to bind by a solemn promise or vow; obtain a solemn promise from: *He* swore *me to secrecy.* 4 to cause (a person) to take an oath: *to* swear *a witness.* **—*n-* swear′ er.**

swear by to have great confidence in; recommend highly.
swear in to administer an oath of office or duty to.
swear off *Informal* to promise to give up: *to* swear off *smoking.*
swear out to get by making a charge under oath.
swear to to affirm by or as if by taking an oath.

sweat (swĕt) ***vi-*** [**sweat·ed** or **sweat, sweat·ing**] 1 to give forth moisture through or as if through the pores of the skin; perspire. 2 to form moisture on the outside; become damp: *A glass of ice water* sweats *in a humid room.* 3 *Informal* to work hard: *They* sweated *to repair the car in time for their trip.* ***vt-*** 1 to cause to perspire freely: *The hard gallop* sweated *the pony.* 2 *Informal* to force to work very hard. 3 to cause to give off moisture, especially by applying heat. 4 to get rid of by perspiring (often followed with "out" or "off"): *He* sweated *off three pounds in the steam room.* 5 to cause to ferment (tobacco or hides). 6 to remove particles of metal from (coins) by shaking in a bag. 7 to melt and apply (solder) between two surfaces that are to be joined. ***n-*** 1 moisture given off through the pores of the skin; perspiration. 2 moisture given off by any substance.

by the sweat of one's brow by hard work. **in a cold sweat** badly frightened and having a chilly feeling. **in a sweat** 1 covered with sweat; wet with perspiration. 2 very eager, anxious, or impatient.
sweat out *Slang* to wait long or anxiously for a result.

sweat·er (swĕt′ ər) ***n-*** knitted or crocheted garment, with or without sleeves, for the upper part of the body.

sweat gland ***n-*** any of the tiny, coiled, tubelike glands in the skin that secrete sweat through the pores.

sweat shirt ***n-*** thick, long-sleeved pullover, often lined with fleece, worn by athletes.

sweat·shop (swĕt′ shŏp′) ***n-*** place where people work long hours for very low wages, often under conditions dangerous to health.

sweat·y (swĕt′ ē) ***adj-*** [**sweat·i·er, sweat·i·est**] 1 covered with sweat; sweating: *Nervous people often have* sweaty *hands.* 2 causing sweat; laborious: *Digging ditches is* sweaty *work.* **—*adv-* sweat′ i·ly. *n-* sweat′ i·ness.**

Swede (swēd) ***n-*** a native of Sweden or a person of Swedish descent.

Swed·ish (swē′ dĭsh) ***adj-*** of or relating to Sweden, its people, or its language. ***n-*** language of the Swedish people.

sweep (swēp) ***vt-*** [**swept** (swĕpt), **sweep·ing**] 1 to clean or brush with a broom, brush, etc.: *She* swept *the floor.* 2 to move or remove with a brush: *to* sweep *up the fallen leaves.* 3 to move quickly on or over with great force: *Waves* swept *the deck. A hurricane* swept *the coast.* 4 to displace or remove suddenly by violent action: *Flood waters* swept *the pier away. The waves* swept *them off the raft.* 5 to win every game or contest in; win decisively: *to* sweep *a tournament*; *to* sweep *an election.* 6 to pass lightly over or across: *to* sweep *the strings of a guitar.* 7 to move or pass over swiftly as if searching; scan: *The searchlight* swept *the sky. The lookout* swept *the seas.* ***vi-*** 1 to clean or clear away dirt with a broom, brush, etc.: *She helps by* sweeping *up after dinner.* 2 to move or stretch over a long, curving course: *The current* sweeps *along the coast.* 3 to move or pass with speed and force. 4 to move in a quick but very stately manner: *The bride* swept *down the aisle.* 5 to touch in passing; trail: *Her gown* swept *along the floor.* ***n-*** 1 act of cleaning away, clearing out, or getting rid of. 2 a swift, curving motion: *with a* sweep *of one's arm.* 3 the range of such a motion; also, reach; compass; scope: *the* sweep *of a telescope.* 4 long, gradual curve or curving line: *the* sweep *of an arch*; *the* sweep *of his forehead.* 5 wide expanse: *the* sweep *of land.* 6 a winning of every game or contest in a tournament, meet, series, etc.: *The ball team made a* sweep *of the series.* 7 single or steady stroke: *the* sweep *of an oar.* 8 long oar for moving or steering a boat. 9 long pole for raising or lowering a bucket in a well. 10 person whose job is sweeping: *a chimney* sweep. 11 *Informal* sweepstakes.

make a clean sweep to get rid of old things or of old ways of doing things.
sweep all before (one) to have great success at doing something.
sweep off (one's) feet to overcome or carry away by power of persuasion or fascination.

sweep·er (swē′ pər) ***n-*** person or thing that sweeps: *a street* sweeper; *a carpet* sweeper; *a mine* sweeper.

sweep·ing (swē′ pĭng) ***n-*** 1 a cleaning or brushing with a broom or brush, etc. 2 **sweepings** rubbish, dust, or refuse swept together for disposal: *Put the* sweepings *in the dust can.* ***adj-*** 1 moving or extending in a wide curve: *a* sweeping *gesture.* 2 of great scope or covering a wide range: *a* sweeping *reform.* **—*adv-* sweep′ ing·ly.**

sweep·stakes (swēp′ stāks′) ***n-*** 1 horse race in which the purse is made up by the owners of the horses, the winner taking all. 2 form of gambling, as on a horse race, in which persons buy tickets and the money paid in is distributed among certain ticket holders whose numbers are chosen by lot. Also **sweep′ stake.**

sweet (swēt) ***adj-*** [**sweet·er, sweet·est**] 1 having the taste or flavor of sugar or honey. 2 not stale, sour, or salty: *the taste of* sweet *milk*; sweet *butter or cream.* 3 having a pleasant fragrance or aroma: *the* sweet *scent of lilacs*; sweet *herbs.* 4 having a pleasant, melodious, or soothing sound: *a* sweet *voice*; *a* sweet *song.* 5 kind; gentle; mild: *a* sweet *disposition or personality.* 6 charming in appearance or manner: *a* sweet *little girl.* 7 containing sugar; not dry or hard: *a bottle of* sweet *wine*; sweet *cider.* 8 free from excessive acid: *a* sweet *soil.* ***n-*** 1 pie, pudding, tart, etc.; dessert. 2 **sweets** chocolate, candy, etc.; confectionery. 3 dearly beloved person; darling. ***Hom-*** suite. **—*adv-* sweet′ ly. *n-* sweet′ ness.**

sweet a·lys·sum (ə lĭs′ əm) ***n-*** low-growing garden plant related to the mustard, having clusters of small, white, fragrant flowers.

sweet bay ***n-*** 1 ornamental shrub related to the magnolia, with thick leaves and very fragrant, white flowers. 2 the laurel.

sweet·bread (swēt′ brĕd′) ***n-*** pancreas or thymus of a calf or lamb, used for food.

sweet·bri·er or **sweet·bri·ar** (swēt′ brī′ ər) ***n-*** wild rose with fragrant pink flowers and thorns; eglantine.

sweet corn *n-* kind of corn with a sweetish flavor, usually eaten when it is young and tender; green corn.

sweet·en (swē′ tən) *vt-* **1** to make sweet to the taste with sugar, honey, etc.: *He likes to* sweeten *his tea.* **2** to make more pleasant or agreeable: *A friend's kindness* sweetened *his convalescence.* *vi-*: *The old lady's disposition* sweetened *with her advancing years.* —*n-* **sweet′ en·er.**

sweet·en·ing (swē′ tən ĭng) *n-* **1** something used to make sweet: *to use honey as* sweetening. **2** a making sweet.

sweet flag *n-* marsh plant with long, slender leaves and an aromatic root used in medicine; calamus.

sweet·heart (swēt′härt′) *n-* person who is beloved; lover.

sweet·ish (swē′ tĭsh) *adj-* rather sweet.

sweet marjoram *n-* fragrant herb of the mint family, used as a flavoring in cooking; marjoram.

sweet·meats (swēt′ mēts′) *n- pl.* small pieces of fruit or nuts preserved in sugar; candy.

sweet pea *n-* **1** garden plant related to the peas, having slender, climbing stems and fragrant flowers of many colors. **2** flower of this plant.

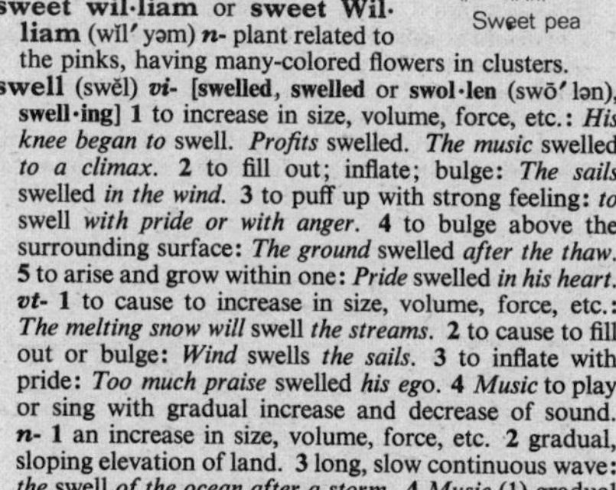
Sweet pea

sweet potato *n-* **1** trailing plant with a sweetish, starchy root. **2** this root cooked and eaten as a vegetable. **3** *Slang* ocarina.

sweet tooth *Informal n-* great liking for candy or other sweet foods.

sweet wil·liam or **sweet Wil·liam** (wĭl′ yəm) *n-* plant related to the pinks, having many-colored flowers in clusters.

swell (swĕl) *vi-* [**swelled, swelled** or **swol·len** (swō′ lən), **swell·ing**] **1** to increase in size, volume, force, etc.: *His knee began to* swell. *Profits* swelled. *The music* swelled *to a climax.* **2** to fill out; inflate; bulge: *The sails* swelled *in the wind.* **3** to puff up with strong feeling: *to* swell *with pride or with anger.* **4** to bulge above the surrounding surface: *The ground* swelled *after the thaw.* **5** to arise and grow within one: *Pride* swelled *in his heart.* *vt-* **1** to cause to increase in size, volume, force, etc.: *The melting snow will* swell *the streams.* **2** to cause to fill out or bulge: *Wind* swells *the sails.* **3** to inflate with pride: *Too much praise* swelled *his ego.* **4** *Music* to play or sing with gradual increase and decrease of sound. *n-* **1** an increase in size, volume, force, etc. **2** gradual, sloping elevation of land. **3** long, slow continuous wave: *the* swell *of the ocean after a storm.* **4** *Music* (1) gradual increase and decrease of sound; also, the sign [> <] indicating this. (2) device in wind instruments, such as an organ, for controlling the loudness of the tones. **5** *Informal* person of high society; also, fashionably dressed person. *adj-* *Informal* **1** first-rate. **2** stylish.

swell·ing (swĕl′ ĭng) *n-* **1** an increase in size; enlargement. **2** swollen place or lump on the body.

swel·ter (swĕl′ tər) *vi-* to suffer from the heat; sweat a great deal. *n-* very uncomfortable heat.

swel·ter·ing (swĕl′ tər′ ĭng) *adj-* **1** oppressively hot; sultry: *a* sweltering *day.* **2** very uncomfortable because of heat. —*adv-* **swel′ ter·ing·ly.**

swept (swĕpt) *p.t. & p.p.* of **sweep.**

swept-back (swĕpt′ băk′) *adj-* of airplane wings, having the leading edge inclined backward to form an acute angle with the fuselage.

swerve (swûrv) *vi-* [**swerved, swerv·ing**] **2** to turn aside from a straight or direct course: *The car* swerved *on the icy pavement.* *vt-*: *He* swerved *his car to avoid hitting the dog.* *n-* a sudden turning aside.

swift (swĭft) *adj-* [**swift·er, swift·est**] **1** moving or able to move rapidly; fast: *the* swift *runner.* **2** coming, happening, or done quickly or without delay: *a* swift *reply to a letter.* *n-* **1** bird resembling the swallow, noted for the speed of its flight. **2** any of various fast-running lizards common in western United States. —*adv-* **swift′ ly.** *n-* **swift′ ness.**

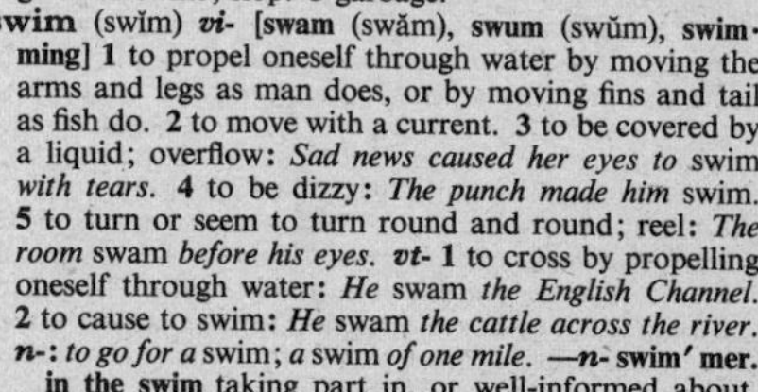
Chimney swift, about 5 in. long

swig (swĭg) *Informal vt-* [**swigged, swig·ging**] to drink in large gulps. *n-* large gulp of a liquid.

swill (swĭl) *vt-* to drink or gulp greedily in large quantities: *The pirates* swilled *the brandy from the captured ship.* *n-* **1** drink taken in large quantities. **2** liquid food for animals, especially household wastes given to swine; slop. **3** garbage.

swim (swĭm) *vi-* [**swam** (swăm), **swum** (swŭm), **swim·ming**] **1** to propel oneself through water by moving the arms and legs as man does, or by moving fins and tail as fish do. **2** to move with a current. **3** to be covered by a liquid; overflow: *Sad news caused her eyes to* swim *with tears.* **4** to be dizzy: *The punch made him* swim. **5** to turn or seem to turn round and round; reel: *The room* swam *before his eyes.* *vt-* **1** to cross by propelling oneself through water: *He* swam *the English Channel.* **2** to cause to swim: *He* swam *the cattle across the river.* *n-*: *to go for a* swim; *a* swim *of one mile.* —*n-* **swim′ mer.**
in the swim taking part in, or well-informed about, what is current or fashionable.

swim bladder *n-* air bladder of a fish.

swim·ming·ly (swĭm′ ĭng lē) *adv-* easily and smoothly.

swin·dle (swĭn′ dəl) *vt-* [**swin·dled, swin·dling**] to get money or property from (someone) under false pretenses; cheat; defraud: *Mr Krook* swindled *the old lady out of her fortune.* *n-* a cheating; dishonest scheme: *He was jailed for the* swindle. —*n-* **swind′ ler** (swĭnd′ lər).

swine (swīn) *n-* [*pl.* **swine**] **1** animal of the hog family with bristly skin and a long snout; pig. **2** crude or vicious person.

swine·herd (swīn′ hûrd′) *n-* person who tends pigs.

swing (swĭng) *vi-* [**swung, swing·ing**] **1** to move back and forth in regular motion, as a pendulum does. **2** to turn on or as if on a hinge or axis: *The wind made the door* swing *open.* **3** to be suspended and swaying back and forth. **4** to ride back and forth on a suspended seat. **5** to turn or wheel round; veer: *The wind* swung *to the east.* **6** to move with a loose, free motion: *The carefree boys* swung *along the street.* **7** *Slang* to be hanged in execution. **8** to strike (at) with a sweeping motion: *He* swung *at the pitch.* *vt-* **1** to cause to move back and forth: *to* swing *a child in a hammock.* **2** to move or wave back and forth: *The policeman walked,* swinging *his stick.* **3** to direct in a sweeping curve: *The player* swung *the bat at the ball and missed.* **4** to lift with a sweeping motion: *He* swung *his pack onto his shoulder.* **5** to cause to turn or wheel about: *He* swung *the car into the driveway.* **6** to put up so as to hang freely or on hinges: *to* swing *a hammock*; *to* swing *a gate.* **7** to manage or handle successfully: *He* swung *a loan at the bank.* *n-* **1** a swaying motion or sweeping stroke; also, distance through which an object sways: *the* swing *of a pendulum*; *the* swing *of a bat.* **2** a seat suspended on ropes or chains. **3** course or movement of a practice, career, business, event, etc.: *to catch the* swing *of affairs.*

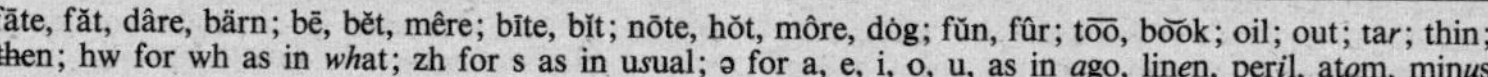
fāte, făt, dâre, bärn; bē, bĕt, mêre; bīte, bĭt; nōte, hŏt, môre, dȯg; fŭn, fûr; to͞o, bo͝ok; oil; out; tar; thin; then; hw for wh as in *wh*at; zh for s as in u*s*ual; ə for a, e, i, o, u, as in *a*go, lin*e*n, per*i*l, at*o*m, min*u*s

4 a loose, free gait. 5 free scope to exercise ability: *He gave his son full* swing *in the family business.* 6 strong, steady beat or rhythm, as in poetry or music. 7 *Music* (1) (also **swing music**) development in jazz after about 1935, marked by large bands, a variety of instruments, and an insistent beat, with variations of the original melody freely interpreted and improvised on by the individual players. (2) the particular rhythmic element of such music, characterized by its crispness. *as modifier*: *a* swing *band*; swing *musician.*

in full swing at the height of activity.

swing on *Informal* to try to hit (someone) with a fist.

swin·ish (swī′nĭsh) ***adj***- like swine or fit for swine; coarse; beastly: *a cruel and* swinish *action*; swinish *habits.* **—*adv*- swin′ish·ly. *n*- swin′ish·ness.**

swipe (swīp) ***n***- powerful, sweeping blow: *One* swipe *of the bear's paw knocked down the dog.* ***vt***- **[swiped, swip·ing]** 1 to hit with such a blow. 2 *Slang* to steal.

swirl (swûrl) ***vi***- 1 to move with a twisting, whirling motion: *The snowflakes* swirled *through the air.* 2 to be dizzy; swim: *The noise made her head* swirl. ***vt***- to cause to whirl: *The cheerleaders* swirled *their skirts.* ***n***- 1 a circular motion of water, falling snow, or the like, such as a whirlpool. 2 spiral twist. **—*adj*- swirl′y.**

swish (swĭsh) ***n***- rustling or hissing sound or the movement that makes it: *the* swish *of the actress' petticoats as she came on stage.* ***vi***- to move with a rustling or hissing sound: *The snake* swished *through the dry leaves.* ***vt***- to move briskly back and forth; switch: *He* swished *his cane to and fro.*

Swiss (swĭs) ***n***- [*pl.* **Swiss**] 1 a native of Switzerland or a person of Swiss descent. 2 **the Swiss** the people of Switzerland collectively. ***adj***-: *He owns a* Swiss *watch.*

Swiss cheese ***n***- a pale-yellow, hard cheese with many large holes, originally made only in Switzerland.

switch (swĭch) ***n***- 1 thin, flexible shoot of a tree, often used as a light whip. 2 blow with such a shoot or whip. 3 on a railroad, a set of movable rails for connecting one track with another. 4 device for making, breaking, or shifting electric circuits. 5 sudden change: *a* switch *in plans.* 6 an exchange: *a* switch *of seats at a movie.* 7 tress of long hair to be added to a woman's own hair. ***vt***- 1 to whip lightly: *to* switch *the grass with a stick.* 2 to brush with a whipping motion; flick; whisk: *The horse* switched *the flies with its tail.* 3 to make a whipping motion; lash: *The horse* switched *its tail.* 4 to shift (cars) to another track. 5 to make, break, or shift (an electric circuit). 6 to change: *The wind* switched *direction.* 7 to exchange: *They* switched *seats at the movie.* ***vi***-: *The train* switched *to the outside track.* **—*n*- switch′er.**

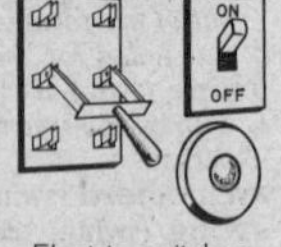

Electric switches

switch·back (swĭch′băk′) ***n***- railway up a steep incline. The tracks are laid in a series of zigzag curves to offset the steepness of the grade.

switch·blade (swĭch′blād′) ***n***- pocketknife with a spring mechanism that bares the blade when a button is pressed.

switch·board (swĭch′bôrd′) ***n***- panel or panels with switches and plugs for connecting electrical lines.

switch hitter ***n***- baseball player who can bat both right-handed and left-handed.

switch·man (swĭch′mən) ***n***- [*pl.* **switch·men**] worker in charge of operating railroad switches.

swi·vel (swĭv′əl) ***n***- 1 pair of links or other mechanical parts, connected by a bolt or rivet on which one of them can turn. 2 anything consisting of a part which turns on a fixed part: *the* swivel *of a revolving stool.* ***vi***- to turn or swing with a circular motion: *Mr. Brown* swiveled *around and faced me.* ***vt***-: *He* swiveled *his eyes around and glared at her.*

swivel chair ***n***- chair with a seat that can turn on a swivel.

swob (swŏb) swab. **—*n*- swob′ber.**

swol·len (swōl′ən) *p.p.* of **swell.** ***adj***-: enlarged by swelling: *a* swollen *ankle*; swollen *glands.*

swoon (swo͞on) ***vi***- to faint: *She* swooned *in fright.* ***n***- a fainting spell: *to fall into a* swoon. **—*n*- swoon′er.**

swoop (swo͞op) ***vi***- to descend swiftly and suddenly with a sweeping motion: *The hawk* swooped *toward the rabbit.* ***vt***- to fall upon and seize (often followed by "up"): *The eagle* swooped *up its prey.* ***n***- sudden downward sweep, as of a bird of prey or an airplane. **—*n*- swoop′er.**

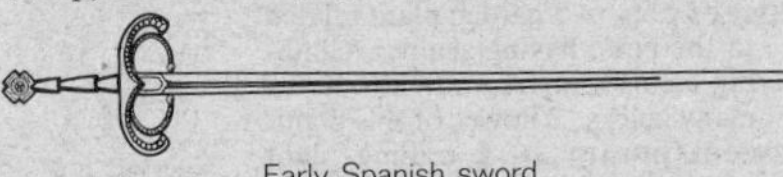
Early Spanish sword

sword (sôrd) ***n***- 1 weapon with a long, pointed blade having one or two sharp edges and set in a handle or hilt. 2 **the sword** this weapon as a symbol of war, military power, or aggressive force: *"The pen is mightier than the* sword." **—*adj*- sword′like′.**

at sword's point ready to fight or quarrel; hostile.

cross swords to fight or quarrel.

sword cane ***n***- hollow walking cane with a sword or dagger concealed in it.

sword·fish (sôrd′fĭsh′) ***n***- [*pl.* **sword·fish; sword·fish·es** (kinds of swordfish)] large, edible sea fish, whose upper jaw ends in a long, slender, bony blade.

Swordfish, about 15 ft. long

sword·play (sôrd′plā′) ***n***- act or art of using a sword.

swords·man (sôrdz′mən) ***n***- [*pl.* **swords·men**] 1 person who fights with a sword. 2 person skilled in the use of a foil; fencer.

swore (swôr) *p.t.* of **swear.**

sworn (swôrn) *p.p.* of **swear.** ***adj***- declared with an oath; bound by an oath: *a* sworn *statement*; sworn *enemies.*

swum (swŭm) *p.p.* of **swim.**

swung (swŭng) *p.t. & p.p.* of **swing.**

syb·a·rite (sĭb′ə rīt′) ***n***- person who devotes himself to pleasure and luxury. **—*adj*- syb′a·rit′ic** (-rĭt′ĭk). ***adv*- syb′a·rit′i·cal·ly.**

syc·a·more (sĭk′ə môr′) ***n***- large tree with bark that peels off in patches, leaves similar to those of the maple, and round, bristly seed cases; buttonwood; plane tree.

syc·o·phan·cy (sĭk′ə fən sē) ***n***- [*pl.* **syc·o·phan·cies**] character or practices of a sycophant.

syc·o·phant (sĭk′ə fənt) ***n***- person who seeks favor by flattering people of wealth or authority; toady. **—*adj*- syc′o·phan′tic. *adv*- syc′o·phan′ti·cal·ly.**

syl·lab·ic (sə lăb′ĭk) ***adj***- of, relating to, or consisting of a syllable or syllables. **—*adv*- syl·lab′i·cal·ly.**

syl·lab·i·cate (sə lăb′ ə kāt′) ***vt-*** [**syl·lab·i·cat·ed, syl·lab·i·cat·ing**] to separate or divide into syllables. ***—n-*** **syl·lab′ i·ca′ tion.**

syl·lab·i·fy (sə lăb′ ə fī′) ***vt-*** [**syl·lab·i·fied, syl·lab·i·fy·ing**] to syllabicate. ***—n-*** **syl·lab′ i·fi·ca′ tion** (-fə kā′ shən).

syl·la·ble (sĭl′ ə bəl) ***n-*** **1** unit of pronunciation consisting of a vowel sound, or a vowel sound grouped with one or more consonant sounds, pronounced by a single impulse of the voice, and forming either a complete word or one of the units that together make a word. Example: "dog" is the first syllable of "dog·mat·ic." **2** group of letters corresponding, though not always exactly, to such a unit as pronounced.

syl·la·bus (sĭl′ ə bəs) ***n-*** [*pl.* **syl·la·bus·es** or **syl·la·bi** (-bī′)] brief summary of a book, subject, etc.

syl·lo·gism (sĭl′ ə jĭz′ əm) ***n-*** logical form of reasoning, consisting of a major premise, a minor premise, and a conclusion. Example: All dogs can bark (major premise). Pal is a dog (minor premise). Therefore, Pal can bark (conclusion).

sylph (sĭlf) ***n-*** **1** imaginary being supposed to live in the air. **2** slender, graceful young woman. ***—adj-*** **sylph′like′.**

syl·van (sĭl′ vən) ***adj-*** **1** of or having to do with woods or forests: *a* sylvan *god.* **2** full of woods or trees; wooded; rustic: *a* sylvan *scene*; sylvan *surroundings.* ***n-*** god or spirit of the woods. Also **silvan.**

sym·bi·o·sis (sĭm′ bē ō′ səs, sĭm′ bī-) ***n-*** mutually beneficial association of two different organisms, such as that between the termite and its intestinal protozoa, which digest the wood eaten by the termite. ***—adj-*** **sym′ bi·ot′ ic** (-ŏt′ ĭk).

sym·bol (sĭm′ bəl) ***n-*** **1** anything used as a sign for something else: *Our flag is our nation's* symbol. *A word is a* symbol *for a thing.* **2** in writing and printing, a mark or letter that takes the place of or indicates a word, phrase, or thing: *O is the* symbol *of oxygen. $ is the* symbol *for dollar.* ***Hom-*** cymbal. ***—adj-*** **sym·bol′ ic** or **sym·bol′ i·cal.** ***adv-*** **sym·bol′ i·cal·ly.**

sym·bol·ism (sĭm′ bə lĭz′ əm) ***n-*** use of symbols to express ideas, especially in art and literature.

sym·bol·ize (sĭm′ bə līz′) ***vt-*** [**sym·bol·ized, sym·bol·ing**] **1** to stand for; represent: *The skull and crossbones* symbolize *piracy.* **2** to represent by a symbol: *The artist* symbolized *famine by a child with hollow cheeks.* ***vi-*** to use symbols. ***—n-*** **sym′ bol·i·za′ tion.**

sym·met·ri·cal (sĭ mĕ′ trĭ kəl) ***adj-*** having or relating to symmetry. ***—adv-*** **sym·met′ ri·cal·ly.**

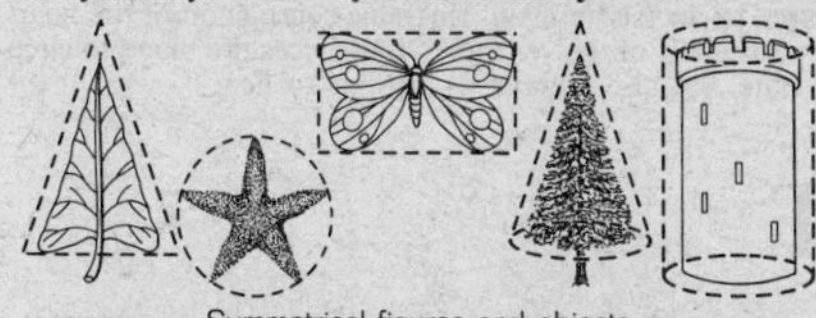

Symmetrical figures and objects

sym·me·try (sĭm′ ə trē) ***n-*** [*pl* **sym·me·tries**] **1** correspondence of parts. There are two kinds of symmetry, one a balance of halves on opposite sides of a line or plane, and the other a balance of parts around a central point. **2** balanced proportion; orderly arrangement of parts: *A face with regular features has* symmetry *but it is not always interesting.* See also *bilateral symmetry* and *radial symmetry.*

sym·pa·thet·ic (sĭm′ pə thĕt′ ĭk) ***adj-*** **1** feeling or showing sympathy. **2** inclined toward; in agreement with; favorable to: *I am* sympathetic *to your ideas for our vacation.* **3** understanding or sharing the same feelings; congenial: *a* sympathetic *friend.* **4** of or relating to part of the autonomic nervous system. ***—adv-*** **sym′ pa·thet′ i·cal·ly.**

sym·pa·thize (sĭm′ pə thīz′) ***vi-*** [**sym·pa·thized, sym·pa·thiz·ing**] **1** to feel compassion for another's troubles. **2** to share in another's feelings; be in agreement: *Many Englishmen* sympathized *with our cause in the Revolution.* ***—n-*** **sym′ pa·thiz′ er.** ***adv-*** **sym′ pa·thiz′ ing·ly.**

sym·pa·thy (sĭm′ pə thē) ***n-*** [*pl.* **sym·pa·thies**] **1** a sharing of another's feelings, etc.: *Nell's* sympathy *soothed Joan in her grief.* **2** fellow feeling; harmony of interests: *The group of actors was united in a bond of* sympathy. **3** compassion: *We feel* sympathy *for the flood victims.* **4** general agreement: *I am in* sympathy *with your plan.*

sym·phon·ic (sĭm fŏn′ ĭk) ***adj-*** **1** of, having to do with, or like a symphony. **2** agreeing in sound; harmonious. ***—adv-*** **sym·phon′ i·cal·ly.**

sym·pho·ny (sĭm′ fə nē) ***n-*** [*pl.* **sym·pho·nies**] **1** *Music* long and elaborate composition, usually consisting of three or four movements, for a full orchestra. **2** symphony orchestra. **3** pleasing blend of sound, colors, or the like; harmony.

symphony orchestra ***n-*** large orchestra for playing symphonies and other similar compositions, usually composed of string, brass, wind, and percussion sections.

sym·po·si·um (sĭm pō′ zē əm) ***n-*** [*pl.* **sym·po·si·ums** or **sym·po·si·a** (-zē ə)] **1** conference or meeting for discussion of a particular subject. **2** collection of opinions or brief essays on the same subject.

symp·tom (sĭmp′ təm) ***n-*** **1** sign of illness: *Chills and fever are* symptoms *of the flu.* **2** indication of something: *I saw* symptoms *of unrest in the crowd.*

symp·to·mat·ic (sĭmp′ tə măt′ ĭk) ***adj-*** **1** serving as a sign or indication of: *Fever is* symptomatic *of illness.* **2** of or having to do with symptoms; also, according to symptoms: *a* symptomatic *treatment.*

syn- *prefix* **1** with; along with; together: syn*thesis* (the assembling of separate parts into a whole). **2** the same: syn*onymous* (having the same meaning). [from Greek **syn-**, from **syn** meaning "with."]

syn. **1** synonym. **2** synonymous.

syn·a·gogue (sĭn′ ə gŏg′, -gôg′) ***n-*** **1** a Jewish religious congregation. **2** Jewish house of worship.

syn·apse (sĭn′ ăps′) ***n-*** the junction area that transfers nerve impulses between two or more neurons.

syn·chro·nize (sĭng′ krə nīz′) ***vt-*** [**syn·chro·nized, syn·chro·niz·ing**] to cause (events, processes, machines, etc.) to happen or operate in unison: *They* synchronized *movements.* ***vi-***: *The music and the action* synchronized *perfectly.* ***—n-*** **syn′ chro·niz′ er.** ***n-*** **syn′ chro·ni·za′ tion.**

syn·chro·nous (sĭn′ krə nəs) ***adj-*** **1** occurring at the same time; simultaneous: *two* synchronous *events.* **2** happening at the same rate: *the* synchronous *drum beats.* **3** *Physics* having an identical period or rate of vibration. ***—adv-*** **syn′ chro·nous·ly.**

synchronous satellite *Space* ***n-*** artificial satellite that orbits the earth in an equatorial path from west to east once every 24 hours, and is always above a particular point on the earth's surface.

syn·chro·tron (sĭn′ krə trŏn′) ***n-*** a particle accelerator in which the strength of the magnetic field that accelerates the particles is changed as the particles gain speed.

fāte, făt, dâre, bärn; bē, bĕt, mêre; bīte, bĭt; nōte, hŏt, môre, dôg; fŭn, fûr; to͞o, bo͝ok; oil; out; tar; thin; then; hw for wh as in *wh*at; zh for s as in u*s*ual; ə for a, e, i, o, u, as in *a*go, lin*e*n, per*i*l, at*o*m, min*u*s

syn·cline (sĭn'klīn') *n-* folded layers of rock that are arched downward. See also *anticline.* **—*adj-* syn'clin'al.**

syn·co·pate (sĭn'kə pāt') *vt-* [**syn·co·pa·ted, syn·co·pa·ting**] **1** *Music* to alter the expected pattern of accent, rhythm, or meter of, in order to surprise the listener in a pleasing way. **2** *Grammar* to shorten (a word) by omitting a letter or letters from the middle, as in "e'er" for "ever." **—*n-* syn'co·pa'tion.**

[1]**syn·di·cate** (sĭn'də kāt') *vt-* [**syn·di·cat·ed, syn·di·cat·ing**] **1** to manage as or combine into a syndicate: *to* syndicate *a group of newspapers.* **2** to publish in a number of newspapers or magazines at the same time: *to* syndicate *a comic strip.* **—*n-* syn'di·ca'tion.**

[2]**syn·di·cate** (sĭn'dĭ kət) *n-* combination of companies or persons formed to pursue a business enterprise.

syn·drome (sĭn'drōm) *n-* an aggregate of symptoms that characterizes a particular disease or abnormality.

syn·er·gism (sĭn'ər jĭz'əm) *n-* **1** the simultaneous action of two agents whose working together creates an effect greater than the sum of their individual effects. **2** the action of different parts of the body working in correlation with each other, for example, the muscles. **—*adj-* syn'er·gis'tic. *adv-* syn'er·gis'ti·cal·ly.**

syn·fuel (sĭn'fyōō'əl) *n-* fuel produced chemically from coal or other substances.

syn·od (sĭ'nəd) *n-* **1** church council or meeting. **2** any assembly or council. **—*adj-* syn'od·al.**

syn·o·nym (sĭn'ə nĭm') *n-* word or phrase having the same or almost the same meaning as another word or phrase. A synonym for "happy" is "glad."

syn·on·y·mous (sə nŏn'ə məs) *adj-* similar or nearly similar in meaning. **—*adv-* syn·on'y·mous·ly.**

syn·op·sis (sĭ nŏp'səs) *n-* [*pl.* **syn·op·ses** (-sēz')] condensed statement of a book, speech, or similar work; summary: *a one-page* synopsis *of a novel.*

syn·op·tic (sĭ nŏp'tĭk) *adj-* in a condensed form.

syn·tac·tic (sĭn tăk'tĭk) or **syn·tac·ti·cal** (-tĭ kəl) *Grammar adj-* of or relating to syntax: *a* syntactic *rule.* **—*adv-* syn·tac'ti·cal·ly.**

syn·tax (sĭn'tăks') *Grammar n-* the relationship or arrangement of words into larger constructions, such as phrases, clauses, and sentences; also, the part of grammar that treats of this.

syn·the·sis (sĭn'thə səs) *n-* [*pl.* **syn·the·ses** (-sēz')] **1** a combining of separate elements or parts to make a new form or whole. **2** a whole made of parts or elements combined. **3** *Chemistry* the production of a compound by the union of two or more elements, radicals, or simpler compounds, especially by industrial or laboratory methods: *the* synthesis *of a new drug.*

syn·the·size (sĭn'thə sīz') *vt-* [**syn·the·sized, syn·the·siz·ing**] to combine into a new form or whole; also, to make by combining separate parts or elements.

syn·thet·ic (sĭn thĕt'ĭk) *adj-* **1** of, relating to, or using synthesis: *a* synthetic *manufacturing process.* **2** made by a combination of chemicals similar to those of which a natural product is composed; man-made: *nylon, rayon, and other* synthetic *fibers*; synthetic *rubber.* **3** not spontaneous; artificial. *n-* man-made substance formed by combining chemicals. **—*adv-* syn·thet'i·cal·ly.**

syph·i·lis (sĭf'ə ləs) *n-* contagious venereal disease, usually affecting first the genitals, second the skin, and third the bones, viscera, brain, and spinal cord.

syph·i·lit·ic (sĭf'ə lĭt'ĭk) *adj-* relating to or affected with syphilis. *n-* person affected with syphilis.

sy·phon (sī'fən) siphon.

sy·ringe (sə rĭnj', sĭr'ĭnj) *n-* **1** narrow tube with a rubber bulb or plunger at one end for drawing in and discharging liquid. It is used for injecting fluid into the body, cleaning wounds, etc. **2** hypodermic syringe. **—*vt-* [sy·ringed, sy·ring·ing]** to cleanse with a syringe.

syr·inx (sĭr'ĭngks') *n-* [**sy·rin·ges** (-ĭn jēz') or **sy·rinx·es**] **1** the song organ of birds, located at the lower end of the windpipe. **2** in anatomy, Eustachian tube. **3** panpipe.

syr·up (sûr'əp, sĭr'-) *n-* any of various thick, sweet liquids. Also **sirup. —*adj-* syr'up·like'** or **syr'up·y.**

sys·tem (sĭs'təm) *n-* **1** a group or combination of parts or units functioning together as a whole according to some common law or purpose: *the solar* system; *a railroad* system. **2** in physiology, a combination of parts of the body that work together and are dependent on one another: *the digestive* system. **3** set of facts, rules, laws, etc., organized so as to make up a body of knowledge or a way of doing something: *a* system *of education.* **4** orderly method of doing things; routine: *Hugh has a* system *for his day's work.* **5** bodily and mental makeup: *One's* system *can stand just so much.*

sys·tem·at·ic (sĭs'tə măt'ĭk) or **sys·tem·at·i·cal** (-ĭ kəl) *adj-* **1** arranged or carried on according to a system: *a* systematic *survey of population growth.* **2** careful and orderly in one's work or habits; methodical: *a* systematic *worker.* **—*adv-* sys'tem·at'i·cal·ly.**

sys·tem·a·tize (sĭs'tə mə tīz') *vt-* [**sys·tem·a·tized, sys·tem·a·tiz·ing**] to arrange or organize according to a regular method. **—*n-* sys'tem·a·ti·za'tion. *n-* sys'tem·a·tiz'er.**

sys·tem·ic (sĭ stĕm'ĭk) *Medicine adj-* of, relating to, or affecting the body as a whole: *a* systemic *infection.* **—*adv-* sys·tem'i·cal·ly.**

sys·to·le (sĭs'tə lē) *n-* rhythmic contraction of the heart, especially of the ventricles, that forces the blood to circulate. See also *diastole.* **—*adj-* sys·to'lic.**

T

T, t (tē) *n-* [*pl.* **T's, t's**] the twentieth letter of the English alphabet.

to a T perfectly; with precision.

T temperature (on the Kelvin scale.)

Ta symbol for tantalum

tab (tăb) *n-* **1** small projection on a file card or on the edge of a page for indexing purposes; also, any device used to bring special attention to something. **2** little loop or tag on a garment for lifting or hanging it, or on a package for pulling it open or closing it. **3** small, usually ornamental, flap or strip attached to something such as a garment: *a shoulder* tab *on an army shirt.* **4** small auxiliary airfoil that helps control an airplane. **5** *Informal* bill; check: *He picked up the* tab. *vt-* [**tab·bed, tab·bing**] **1** to mark with a tab. **2** *Informal* to pick out from a group; choose specially: *The reporter* tabbed *Jim as the best player on the team.*

keep tab (or **tabs**) **on** to watch closely.

tab·ard (tăb'ərd) *n-* loose garment worn by a knight over armor and decorated with his coat of arms; a similar coat worn by a herald, decorated with the arms of his lord.

tab·by (tăb′ ē) ***n-*** [*pl.* **tab·bies**] **1** gray or tawny domestic cat with dark stripes. **2** any domestic cat, especially a female.

tab·er·nac·le (tăb′ ər năk′ əl) ***n-*** **1** place of worship; especially, a large and imposing church. **2** in some churches, a locked boxlike enclosure resting on the altar and containing the sacred Host. **3 the Tabernacle** structure carried by the Jews on their journey from Egypt to Palestine for use as a place of worship.

ta·ble (tā′ bəl) ***n-*** **1** piece of furniture having a flat top supported by legs and used for eating meals, writing, playing games, etc. **2** people seated at such a piece of furniture: *His conversation amused the whole* table. **3** food served at a certain place: *a hotel noted for its good* table. **4** orderly and convenient arrangement of facts, figures, etc.; tabulation; list: *the multiplication* table; *the* table *of contents in a book.* **5** tableland. **6** flat piece of wood, stone, or metal used as a writing or carving surface; tablet: *Moses received the Ten Commandments on* tables *of stone.* **7** water table. *as* ***modifier***: *a* table *leg*; table *saw.* ***vt-*** [**ta·bled, ta·bling**] to lay aside (a bill, proposal, etc.) for future consideration.

on the table laid aside for future consideration. **set a good table** to serve food of high quality or in abundance. **turn the tables** to reverse a situation. **under the table 1** very drunk. **2** surreptitiously, and often illegally.

tab·leau (tă blō′, tăb′ lō′) ***n-*** [*pl.* **tab·leaux** (-lōz′) or **tab·leaus**] **1** striking and vivid representation or description: *The novel is a* tableau *of Civil War life.* **2** dramatic representation, usually of a historical event, posed by silent and motionless persons or wax figures.

ta·ble·cloth (tā′ bəl klŏth′) ***n-*** cloth to cover a table.

table d'hôte (tä′ bəl dōt′, tăb′ əl-) *French* complete meal of several courses served at a fixed price. See also *à la carte.*

table fork ***n-*** fork used for eating. For picture, see *fork.*

ta·ble·land (tā′ bəl lănd′) ***n-*** area of fairly level land that stands above the surrounding land; mesa.

ta·ble·spoon (tā′ bəl spōōn′) ***n-*** **1** large spoon used in preparing and serving food. **2** (also **ta′ ble·spoon′ ful**) amount a tablespoon will hold. **3** cooking measure, equal to three teaspoons or half a fluid ounce.

tab·let (tăb′ lət) ***n-*** **1** book or pad of writing or drawing paper. **2** small, flat, compressed cake of material, such as medicine or soap. **3** stone slab or metal plate bearing an inscription. **4** formerly, a thin sheet or several joined sheets of hard material, used for writing, drawing, or painting.

Tablets

table tennis ***n-*** ping-pong.

ta·ble·ware (tā′ bəl wâr′) ***n-*** articles, such as dishes and forks, placed on a table for use at meals.

tab·loid (tăb′ loid′) ***n-*** newspaper whose dimensions are approximately 10 in. x 14 in. (half the standard page size), and often contains many photographs and brief articles of a sensational nature. *as* ***modifier***: *a* tabloid *newspaper.*

ta·boo (tă bōō′, tə-) ***n-*** [*pl.* **ta·boos**] practice among primitive peoples, in which certain things are held sacred and dangerous and are generally forbidden; hence, any ban or prohibition based on social custom or convention. ***vt-*** to place under a ban; forbid; prohibit. ***adj-*** **1** untouchable or sacred. **2** prohibited by social custom. Also **ta·bu′.**

ta·bor (tā′ bər) ***n-*** in former times, a small drum beaten with one hand by a piper to accompany himself.

tab·u·lar (tăb′ yə lər) ***adj-*** **1** arranged in a table, list, or column: *a* tabular *report.* **2** having a broad, flat top: *a* tabular *region.* **—*adv-*** **tab′ u·lar·ly.**

tab·u·late (tăb′ yə lāt′) ***vt-*** [**tab·u·lat·ed, tab·u·lat·ing**] to arrange in a table, list, or other systematic outline: *to* tabulate *election returns.* **—*n-*** **tab′ u·la′ tion.**

tab·u·la·tor (tăb′ yə lā′ tər) ***n-*** **1** typewriter device that automatically shifts the carriage to preset positions. **2** any of various office machines used for tabulating data.

ta·chis·to·scope (tə kĭs′ tə skōp′) ***n-*** an instrument that displays visual images on a screen very briefly. It is used to study perception and attention and also to improve reading speed.

ta·chom·e·ter (tă kŏm′ ə tər, tə-) ***n-*** an instrument for measuring the speed of rotation of an engine shaft.

tac·it (tăs′ ĭt) ***adj-*** not spoken or written down, but nevertheless implied: *a* tacit *agreement.* **—*adv-*** **tac′ it·ly.**

tac·i·turn (tăs′ ə tûrn′) ***adj-*** silent or reserved; not inclined to talk: *a* taciturn *scholar.* **—*n-*** **tac′ i·turn′ i·ty.** ***adv-*** **tac′ i·turn′ ly.**

tack (tăk) ***n-*** **1** small, sharp-pointed nail with a broad, flat head. **2** in sailing ships, (1) a rope for lashing down the lower forward corner of certain sails; also, the corner of the sail so held down. (2) the direction of a ship as determined by the position of her sails. (3) change in a ship's direction to take advantage of side winds. **3** one's course of action: *His thoughts went off on a new* tack. **4** a simple stitch, often used as a temporary fastening. ***vt-*** **1** to fasten with tacks: *to* tack *a carpet*; *to* tack *a bow to a dress.* **2** to attach: *to* tack *a note to a report.* **3** to change the direction of (a sailboat) by turning into and across the wind in order to go indirectly toward one's destination; also, to navigate (a sailboat) in a zig-zag course toward one's destination, because the wind is against one. ***vi-*** **1** to sail in a zig-zag course. **2** to suddenly change one's course of action or attitude; veer. **—*n-*** **tack′ er.**

Tacks

tack·le (tăk′ əl) ***n-*** **1** any act of seizing violently, usually with intent to subdue. **2** in football, (1) an attempt to seize and stop and, usually, throw to the ground an opponent who is running with the ball. (2) one of the two players in the line position between guard and end; also, the position itself. **3** the special equipment or gear for a job or sport: *fishing* tackle. **4** system of pulleys and ropes used for lifting and lowering weights; especially, on a boat or ship, the pulleys and ropes for managing sails and spars, taking on cargo, etc. **5** in soccer, the act of kicking, or attempting to kick, a ball away from an opponent. ***vt-*** [**tack·led, tack·ling**] **1** to seize and throw down violently: *The policeman* tackled *the suspect.* **2** to contend with; undertake energetically: *to* tackle *a problem.* **—*n-*** **tack′ ler.**

Single and double tackles

[1]**tack·y** (tăk′ ē) ***adj-*** [**tack·i·er, tack·i·est**] slightly sticky: *the* tacky *surface of a freshly painted wall.* [from **tack.**]

[2]**tack·y** (tăk′ ē) *Informal* ***adj-*** [**tack·i·er, tack·i·est**] **1** shabby; seedy. **2** cheap and showy; gaudy. [American word of uncertain origin.]

tac·o·nite (tăk′ ə nīt′) ***n-*** a low-grade iron ore.

tact (tăkt) ***n-*** sharp sense of the right thing to do or say to avoid giving offense or to win good will, especially in difficult situations; diplomatic handling.

tact·ful (tăkt′fəl) ***adj-*** having or showing tact; diplomatic. ***—adv-*** **tact′ful·ly.** ***n-*** **tact′ful·ness.**

tac·tic (tăk′tĭk) ***n-*** maneuver used by a military force in combat; also, any maneuver or device to gain an end.

tac·ti·cal (tăk′tĭ kəl) ***adj-*** of or relating to tactics: *a* tactical *retreat*; *a* tactical *evasion.* ***—adv-*** **tac′ti·cal·ly.**

tac·ti·cian (tăk tĭsh′ən) ***n-*** one skilled in tactics.

tac·tics (tăk′tĭks) ***n-*** **1** (takes singular verb) the science and art of maneuvering military forces in combat. **2** (takes plural verb) any maneuvers to gain an end.

tac·tile (tăk′təl, -tĭl′) ***adj-*** of, relating to, or perceived by the sense of touch. ***—n-*** **tac·til′i·ty** (-tĭl′ə tē).

tact·less (tăkt′ləs) ***adj-*** lacking in tact; not diplomatic. ***—adv-*** **tact′less·ly.** ***n-*** **tact′less·ness.**

tac·tu·al (tăk′chōō əl) ***adj-*** tactile. ***—adv-*** **tac′tu·al·ly.**

How a tadpole grows

tad·pole (tăd′pōl′) ***n-*** the larval form of a frog or toad, having a tail and gills that later disappear.

taf·fe·ta (tăf′ə tə) ***n-*** fine, shiny, slightly stiff fabric of silk or synthetic fibers. *as* ***modifier***: *a* taffeta *dress.*

taff·rail (tăf′rāl′) ***n-*** **1** rail around the deck of a ship's stern. **2** upper part of a ship's stern.

taf·fy (tăf′ē) ***n-*** [*pl.* **taf·fies**] chewy candy made of boiled brown sugar or molasses, often with butter added.

[1]**tag** (tăg) ***n-*** **1** identifying card or label attached to something: *a price* tag. **2** anything loosely attached to something; appendage. **3** *Informal* licence plate. **4** stiff binding at the end of a shoelace. **5** saying or quotation, especially one that is commonplace; cliché. **6** closing line or lines of a verse, song, or actor's speech. ***vt-*** [**tagged, tag·ging**] **1** to fix an identifying card or label to: *to* tag *a trunk.* **2** *Informal* to single out; designate; tab. ***vi-*** to follow closely. [of uncertain origin.]

[2]**tag** (tăg) ***n-*** **1** children's game in which the player called "it" runs after the other players until he touches someone, who then becomes "it." **2** in baseball, the act of putting out a runner by touching him with the ball. ***vt-*** [**tagged, tag·ging**] **1** to touch with the hand, as in the game of tag. **2** in baseball, to put out (a runner) by touching him with the ball. **3** *Informal* to hit with great force: *to* tag *a ball for a home run.* [of uncertain origin.]

Ta·ga·log (tə gä′lŏg′) ***n-*** **1** member of one of the chief native tribes of the Philippines, especially of Luzon. **2** the language used by these people; since 1940, the official language of the Philippines.

Ta·hi·tian (tə hē′shən, -hē′tē ən) ***n-*** **1** one of a native people of Tahiti. **2** the Polynesian language of these people. ***adj-***: *a* Tahitian *paradise.*

tai·ga (tī′gə) ***n-*** any of the far northern coniferous forests of Siberia, North America, and Europe, that extend to the northern limit of trees.

tail (tāl) ***n-*** **1** hindmost part of an animal, especially the extension of an animal's backbone beyond its body; hence, something resembling this in position or shape: *the* tail *of a comet*; *kite* tail; *shirt* tail. **2** (often **tails**) the reverse side of a coin from the head. **3** the rear assembly of an airplane. ***vt-*** [**tailed, tail·ing**] *Informal* to follow closely and secretly. ***Hom-*** tale. ***—adj-*** **tail′less.**

turn tail to flee from danger or trouble. **with (one's) tail between (one's) legs** in fear or humiliation, like a frightened dog.

tail·board (tāl′bôrd′) ***n-*** tailgate.

tail·coat (tail′kōt′) ***n-*** man's swallow-tailed coat, worn as part of a full-dress suit; tails.

tailed (tāld) ***adj-*** having a tail, usually of a specified length or kind: *a* tailed *ape*; *a bushy-*tailed *deer.*

tail·first (tāl′fûrst′) or **tail·fore·most** (tāl′fôr′mōst′) ***adv-*** with the rear end first.

tail·gate (tāl′gāt′) ***n-*** panel at the rear end of a truck, station wagon, or cart, hinged at the bottom and let down for loading and unloading. ***vi-*** [**tail·gat·ed, tail·gat·ing**] *Informal* to drive dangerously close to the rear of another vehicle.

tail gun ***n-*** defensive machine gun mounted in the tail of a bomber or other military aircraft. ***—n-*** **tail′gun′ner.**

tail light ***n-*** warning light, usually red, that is mounted at the rear of a vehicle.

tai·lor (tā′lər) ***n-*** person who repairs or alters clothing; also, a person who makes clothing, especially to order. ***vt-*** **1** to repair, alter, or make (clothing): *to* tailor *a suit.* **2** to make, design, or adapt for a special purpose: *to* tailor *a law to the needs of society.*

tai·lor·ing (tā′lər ĭng) ***n-*** **1** the occupation or business of a tailor; also, the workmanship of a tailor: *a suit that shows fine* tailoring. **2** a making, designing, or adapting of something for a special purpose.

tai·lor-made (tā′lər mād′) ***adj-*** **1** made by a tailor. **2** made or fitted to one's particular needs or circumstances; made-to-order: *a* tailor-made *apartment.*

tail·piece (tāl′pēs′) ***n-*** **1** something added at the end. **2** flat piece of wood at the wider end of a violin or similar instrument, to which the strings are attached.

tail pipe ***n-*** exhaust pipe of a gasoline engine.

tail·race (tāl′rās′) ***n-*** channel for carrying used water away from a water wheel.

tails (tālz) ***n-*** *pl.* **1** man's swallow-tailed coat; tailcoat. **2** the full-dress suit of which it is part.

tail·spin (tāl′spĭn′) ***n-*** downward spiral movement of an airplane performing a stunt or out of control, in which the tail forms a wider circle than the nose.

tail wind ***n-*** wind blowing in the same general direction as that of a moving airplane or ship.

taint (tānt) ***vt-*** **1** to cause to spoil or infect; contaminate; pollute: *One bad apple can* taint *a whole barrel.* **2** to stain or blemish. ***n-*** blemish: *a* taint *on his character.*

take (tāk) ***vt-*** [**took** (tŏŏk), **tak·en, tak·ing**] **1** to get hold of; grasp: *He* took *the child's hand.* **2** seize by force; capture: *The Indians* took *the fort.* **3** to get or obtain: *We* took *the apartment. Our team* took *first prize.* **4** to subscribe to: *We* take *two morning papers.* **5** to accept: *Please* take *this gift. Jack* took *the bad news calmly.* **6** to remove or subtract (usually followed by "away"): *Mom* took *away the dishes.* **7** to select; choose: *You may* take *any hat.* **8** to eat, drink, or inhale: *Jack* took *the medicine.* **9** to lead: *This road* takes *you to town.* **10** to carry or convey: *I will* take *your trunk to the attic.* **11** to require; need. **12** to attract: *Your hat* takes *my fancy.* **13** to travel by means of: *Mary* took *a plane to Boston.* **14** to make (an image or recording): *Frank* took *my picture.* **15** to feel; experience: *I* take *pride in my work.* **16** to engage in doing or making: *I* took *a walk.* **17** to conduct; escort: *I* took *my aunt to lunch.* **18** to consider; regard: *We* took *him to be intelligent.* **19** to react to or accept in the proper way: *The silk* took *the dye.* **20** to come upon: *I* took *him by surprise.* **21** *Grammar* to require as part of the construction or usage: *The verb* takes *an object.* **22** to determine by means of examination or a measuring instrument: *The nurse* took *my temperature.* **23** in baseball, of a batter, to allow (a pitch) to pass by without swinging at it. **24** *Informal* to cheat; deceive. ***vi-*** **1** to develop or work effectively: *My* *vaccination didn't* take *the first time. The seeds* took. **2** to catch on; start: *The fire* took *with only one match.* ***n-*** **1** amount or quantity of game, especially fish, caught at one time; catch. **2** a recording, or a filmed or televised scene, made without stopping the recording device or camera. **3** *Slang* amount of money collected. **4** *Slang* share; part. **—*n-* tak′ er.**

take advantage of to make unfair use of for one's own advantage.

take after **1** to resemble: *Mary* takes after *her mother.* **2** to follow as an example: *Why don't you* take after *your brother?* **3** to run after: *He* took after *his ball.*

take amiss to be offended by.

take back to withdraw: *Ed would not* take back *the insult.*

take care to be careful.

take care of **1** to give care to. **2** to attend to.

take down **1** to tear down. **2** to take apart; dismantle. **3** *Informal* to make less proud; humble.

take effect to become effective.

take for to mistake for: *I* took *him* for *an actor.*

take ill to become sick.

take in **1** to include: *The survey* takes in *all the colleges.* **2** to understand; consider. **3** to make smaller: *I am going to* take in *the waist on my skirt.* **4** *Informal* to cheat; deceive. **5** *Informal* to go to see: *I* took in *a movie.* **6** to receive or admit, and care for.

take in vain to use the name of (a deity) profanely or blasphemously.

take issue (with) to disagree (with).

take it **1** to assume. **2** to endure hardship, pain, or grief.

take it out on *Informal* to relieve one's anger or disappointment by abusing (another person or thing).

take off **1** to remove: *We* took off *our coats.* **2** to release: *First* take off *the emergency brake.* **3** *Informal* to depart: *She* took off *for California.* **4** to leave the ground: *The airplane* took off. **5** *Informal* to mimic.

take on **1** to hire. **2** to undertake.

take over to gain control of: *to* take over *a nation.*

take out **1** to obtain: *I* took out *a loan from the bank.* **2** to escort: *I* took *Nancy* out *to lunch.*

take part to join; participate.

take place to happen.

take to **1** to like or enjoy instinctively: *I* took to *the stranger at once. The baby* took to *the water.* **2** to go to, usually in escape: *We* took to *the mountains.*

take up **1** to lift; pull up: *Please* take up *the curtain.* **2** to make smaller or shorter: *She* took up *the hem of her skirt.* **3** to begin; start. **4** to support. **5** agree to: *I* took up *the bet.*

take up with *Informal* to become friendly with.

►For usage note see BRING.

take-off (tāk′ ôf′, -ŏf′) ***n-*** **1** a leaving the ground to begin flight, especially by an airplane. **2** *Informal* parody; burlesque. *as* ***modifier****: an airplane's* take-off *speed.*

tak·ing (tā′ kĭng) ***adj-*** attractive; captivating; winning: *His manners are very* taking. ***n-*** **takings** the money taken or received; receipts.

talc (tălk) ***n-*** soft, white or variously colored magnesium silicate, slippery to the touch, used in making talcum powder, soap, paper, and other products. Also **talcum.**

tal·cum powder (tăl′kəm) ***n-*** fine powder made from white talc, usually perfumed, and used to powder the face and body.

tale (tāl) ***n-*** **1** story: *a good* tale *to tell by an open fire.* **2** falsehood; lie. ***Hom-*** tail.

tell tales to tattle or gossip.

tale·bear·er (tāl′ bâr′ ər) ***n-*** one who delights in spreading gossip or scandal; gossip. **—*n-* tale′ bear′ ing.**

tal·ent (tăl′ ənt) ***n-*** **1** unusual ability or skill in a particular field of work or other activity: *musical* talent; *a* talent *for tennis.* **2** persons of such ability collectively: *the* talent *of the stage.* **3** ancient coin or weight of Palestine, Syria, Greece, and other states. **—*adj-* tal′ ent·ed.**

tal·is·man (tăl′ ĭz mən, -ĭs mən) ***n-*** engraved ring, stone, or other object supposed to bring good luck and to protect against evil; hence, anything regarded as having miraculous powers; charm.

talk (tòk) ***vi-*** **1** to express ideas or feelings by speech; speak; converse: *We* talked *all night.* **2** to confer; consult: *to* talk *with the doctor.* **3** to express oneself by means other than speech: *to* talk *by gestures*; *eyes that* talk. **4** to speak in an idle, aimless manner; chatter: *His wife just* talks *and* talks. **5** *Informal* to disclose secrets or betray someone: *One convict* talked *and the escape was foiled.* ***vt-*** **1** *Informal* to speak of; discuss: *to* talk *business.* **2** to use in one's speech: *to* talk *French.* **3** to persuade by speech: *We* talked *him out of leaving.* ***n-*** **1** speech; conversation: *an evening of friendly* talk. **2** subject of discussion: *the* talk *of the town.* **3** mention or rumor; also, gossip: *There is* talk *of a strike.* **4** meaningless speech; prattle: *That's just a lot of* talk! **5** conference. **6** lecture or address, usually informal.

talk back to answer rudely or defiantly.

talk down **1** to overwhelm with words; silence. **2** to direct the landing of (an airplane) in bad weather by radioed instructions to the pilot.

talk down to to speak to as if to an inferior; condescend to; patronize.

talk over to discuss.

talk up to speak loudly or brashly.

talk·a·tive (tò′ kə tĭv) ***adj-*** fond of talking a great deal. **—*adv-* talk′ a·tive·ly. *n-* talk′ a·tive·ness.**

talk·er (tò′ kər) ***n-*** person who talks, or talks a lot.

talking book ***n-*** phonograph record of a reading of a book or magazine, used chiefly by the blind.

talk·ing-to (tò′ kĭng too′) ***n-*** *Informal* a scolding.

talk·y (tò′ kē) ***adj-*** **[talk·i·er, talk·i·est]** **1** talkative. **2** containing much useless or irrelevant talk: *a* talky *play.*

tall (tòl) ***adj-*** **[tall·er, tall·est]** **1** of more than average height: *a* tall *man*; *a* tall *building.* **2** of a specific height: *He is six feet* tall. **3** exaggerated; unbelievable: *a* tall *story.* **4** unusually large: *a* tall *sum.* **—*adj-* tall′ ish. *n-* tall′ ness.**

tal·lith or **tal·lit** (tä′ ləs, tä′ lət, tăl′ əs) ***n-*** shawl worn by Jewish men while praying.

tal·low (tăl′ ō) ***n-*** fat from certain animals, melted and used to make candles and soap. **—*adj-* tal′ low·y.**

tal·ly (tăl′ ē) ***n-*** [*pl.* **tal·lies**] score of a game or contest; also, any reckoning or account. ***vt-*** **[tal·lied, tal·ly·ing]** **1** to keep score of; count; reckon. **2** to make correspond or agree: *to* tally *one's stories.* ***vi-*** to correspond; agree.

tal·ly·ho (tăl′ ē hō′) ***interj-*** the huntsman's cry to urge on the hounds.

Tal·mud (tăl′ mood′, -məd) ***n-*** the collection of Jewish civil and religious law, including commentaries on it, not included in the Pentateuch. **—*adj-* Tal·mud′ ic.**

tal·on (tăl′ ən) ***n-*** claw of a bird, especially of a hawk, eagle, or other bird of prey.

Talon

fāte, făt, dâre, bärn; bē, bĕt, mêre; bīte, bĭt; nōte, hŏt, môre, dòg; fŭn, fûr; too, book; oil; out; tar; thin; then; hw for wh as in *wh*at; zh for s as in u*s*ual; ə for a, e, i, o, u, as in *a*go, lin*e*n, per*i*l, at*o*m, min*u*s

¹ta·lus (tā′ ləs) ***n-*** [*pl.* **ta·li** (-lī′)] bone of the ankle; also, the entire ankle joint. [from Latin **tālus** of the same meaning.]

²ta·lus (tā′ ləs) ***n-*** [*pl.* **ta·li** (-lī′)] **1** slope. **2** in geology, a sloping heap of rocks at the foot of a cliff. [from Old French **talu,** probably from Latin **talutium** meaning "slope at the mouth of a mine."]

tam (tăm) ***n-*** tam-o'-shanter.

tam·a·ble or **tame·a·ble** (tā′ mə bəl) ***adj-*** such as can be tamed: *a* tamable *beast.*

ta·ma·le (tə mä′ lē) ***n-*** Mexican dish made of chopped meat, red peppers, and corn meal, wrapped in corn husks and cooked. [American word from American Spanish **tamales,** from Nahuatl Indian **tamalli.**]

tam·a·rack (tăm′ ə răk′) ***n-*** American larch tree or its wood. [American word from Algonquian.]

tam·a·rind (tăm′ ə rĭnd′, -rənd) ***n-*** **1** tall, tropical tree having yellow flowers striped with red. **2** its fruit, the acid pulp of which is used in drinks, food, and medicine.

tam·a·risk (tăm′ ə rĭsk′) ***n-*** any of a number of tropical shrubs or small trees with slender, feathery branches.

tam·bou·rine (tăm′ bə rēn′) ***n-*** musical instrument consisting of a drumhead stretched over a shallow metal hoop in which are set tinkling metal disks.

Tambourine

tame (tām) ***adj-*** **[tam·er, tam·est]** **1** made useful, obedient, or friendly to man after having been wild; also, domesticated: *a* tame *elephant.* **2** gentle: *a* tame *horse.* **3** tedious; dull: *a* tame *debate.* ***vt-*** **[tamed, tam·ing]** **1** to change from a wild to a tame condition: *to* tame *an elephant.* **2** to crush the spirit or courage of; subdue: *to* tame *a rebel.* ***—adv-*** **tame′ly.** ***n-*** **tame′ ness.** ***n-*** **tam′ er.**

Tam·il (tăm′ əl) ***n-*** **1** one of the Dravidian people inhabiting southern India and northern Ceylon. **2** the language of these people.

Tam·ma·ny (tăm′ ə nē) ***n-*** formerly, a patriotic and fraternal society in New York City; later, an influential organization within the Democratic Party of New York City. ***as modifier:*** *a* Tammany *candidate.*

tam-o'-shan·ter (tăm′ ə shăn′ tər) ***n-*** Scottish cap with a tight headband and a loose, flat top, often with a pompon in the center.

Tam-o'-shanter

tamp (tămp) ***vt-*** **1** to fill in (a hole containing a blasting charge) with clay, earth, or similar material. **2** to drive in or down by repeated light strokes: *to* tamp *down sod.*

tam·per (tăm′ pər) ***vi-*** **1** to meddle (with) so as to injure or alter anything: *He* tampered *with the car and now it won't run.* **2** to attempt to influence by bribery or coercion: *The lawyer* tampered *with the jury.* ***—n-*** **tam′ per·er.**

tam·pon (tăm′ pŏn′) *Medicine* ***n-*** plug, usually of cotton, placed into a wound or a cavity to stop bleeding or absorb secretions.

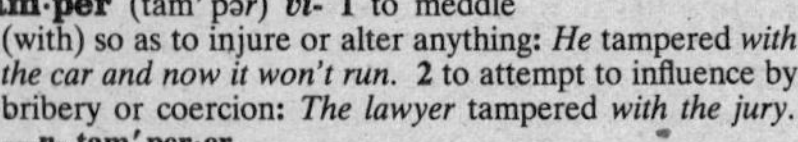

tan (tăn) ***vt-*** **[tanned, tan·ning]** **1** to turn (hide or skin) into leather by soaking it in tannin. **2** to make (the skin) brown by exposing it to the sun. **3** *Informal* to whip thoroughly. ***vi-:*** *Good leather takes time to* tan. *I* tan *easily.* ***n-*** **1** light yellowish-brown color. **2** tannin. **3** tanbark. ***adj-*** **[tan·ner, tan·nest]:** *a* tan *horse.*

tan. tangent.

tan·a·ger (tăn′ ə jər) ***n-*** any of a large group of birds, chiefly of Central and South America, many of which have red plumage and colorful markings. One, the **scarlet tanager,** the males of which are bright red with black wings and tail, is found in eastern United States.

tan·bark (tăn′ bärk′) ***n-*** any of various barks rich in tannic acid, which, after the acid has been removed, is used in making soft surfaces, as in circus rings.

tan·dem (tăn′ dəm) ***adv-*** one behind another. ***adj-*** arranged in this way: *a pair of* tandem *bicycle seats.* ***n-*** **1** bicycle for two or more persons with seats placed one behind the other. **2** pair of horses harnessed one behind the other; also, a two-wheeled carriage pulled by such a file of horses.

tang (tăng) ***n-*** **1** strong, sharp taste, smell, or flavor: *a* tang *of ginger.* **2** faint suggestion; tinge. **3** the part of a knife, sword, fork, etc., that goes into the handle.

tan·gent (tăn′ jənt) ***n-*** **1** *Mathematics* straight line that touches a curve at only one point. For picture, see *circle.* **2** *Mathematics* of an acute angle in a right triangle, the ratio of the side opposite to the acute angle and the side adjacent to it. **3** an abrupt and unplanned change of course in thought or discussion; digression: *He tried to concentrate, but his mind kept flying off on a* tangent. ***adj-*** **1** touching a curve or surface at only one point and not intersecting the curve or surface: *a* tangent *line.* **2** touching at one point but not intersecting: *two* tangent *circles.*

tan·gen·tial (tăn jĕn′ shəl) ***adj-*** **1** *Mathematics* of, related to, or in the direction of a tangent. **2** only slightly related or relevant to a subject: *a* tangential *comment.* ***—adj-*** **tan·gen′ tial·ly.**

tan·ge·rine (tăn′ jə rēn′) ***n-*** **1** small, reddish-yellow, sweet orange with a loose skin somewhat thinner than that of an orange. **2** reddish-orange color. ***adj-:*** *some* tangerine *juice; a* tangerine *scarf.*

tan·gi·ble (tăn′ jə bəl) ***adj-*** **1** such as can be touched or felt by the touch: *a* tangible *object, not an illusion.* **2** real; definite: *Tom's visit was* tangible *proof of his friendship.* **3** in economics, having physical or material substance; also, such as can be accurately appraised: *A house is* tangible *property.* ***n-*** **tangibles** material assets.

tan·gle (tăng′ gəl) ***vt-*** **[tan·gled, tan·gling]** to knot or twist so as to make difficult to unravel; entangle: *to* tangle *strands of yarn.* ***vi-*** **1** to become entangled: *The ropes* tangled *around the beams.* **2** *Informal* to argue or fight: *They* tangled *over political differences.* ***n-*** **1** knotted or twisted mass; hence, any confused condition: *a* tangle *of opposing stories.* **2** *Informal* argument or fight.

tan·gly (tăng′ glē) ***adj-*** **[tan·gli·er, tan·gli·est]** full of tangles; entangled; snarled.

tan·go (tăng′ gō) ***n-*** [*pl.* **tan·gos**] ballroom dance of Latin-American origin, with gliding steps and deliberate poses; also, the music for this dance.

tan·gy (tăng′ ē) ***adj-*** **[tang·i·er, tang·i·est]** having a strong, sharp taste or smell; pungent.

Army tank with water tank in background

tank (tăngk) ***n-*** **1** any large container for liquids or gas: *a water* tank; *an oil* tank. **2** (often **tank′ ful′**) amount that fills a tank; amount held by a tank. **3** large armored combat vehicle carrying guns and moving on caterpillar treads. ***vt-*** to put, store, or process in a tank.

tank·ard (tăngk′ərd) ***n-*** **1** tall mug with a handle and, often, a hinged cover. **2** amount held by a tankard.

tank·er (tăng′kər) ***n-*** ship, truck, or airplane fitted with tanks for carrying oil or other liquids as cargo.

tank farm ***n-*** area that has many oil storage tanks.

tank town *Informal* ***n-*** town where trains formerly stopped only to refill from a water tank; hence, a small, unimportant town.

tan·ner (tăn′ər) ***n-*** worker who makes leather by tanning hides.

tan·ner·y (tăn′ə rē) ***n-*** [*pl.* **tan·ner·ies**] place where leather is made by tanning hides.

Tankard

tan·nic acid (tăn′ĭk) ***n-*** tannin.

tan·nin (tăn′ən) ***n-*** a group of organic substances found in the bark and wood of many plants, and used for tanning, dyeing, ink manufacture, etc.

tan·ning (tăn′ĭng) ***n-*** **1** process or business of making hides into leather. **2** *Informal* a whipping.

tan·sy (tăn′zē) ***n-*** [*pl.* **tan·sies**] any of various strong-smelling herbs with small clusters of yellow flowers.

tan·ta·lize (tăn′tə līz′) ***vt-*** [**tan·ta·lized, tan·ta·liz·ing**] to tease or torment by being out of reach or showing something that is out of reach. ***—n-*** **tan′ta·liz′er.** ***adv-*** **tan′ta·liz′ing·ly.**

tan·ta·lum (tăn′tə ləm) ***n-*** bluish metal element, used as a substitute for platinum in chemical apparatus, and in the surgical repair of injured bone. Symbol Ta, At. No. 73, At. Wt. 180.948.

Tan·ta·lus (tăn′tə ləs) ***n-*** in Greek mythology, a son of Zeus who was punished in Hades by being placed in water up to his neck and under fruit-laden trees. Both receded when he tried to obtain them.

tan·ta·mount (tăn′tə mount′) **tantamount to** having the same effect or importance as; equivalent to.

tan·trum (tăn′trəm) ***n-*** an uncontrolled outburst of temper.

Tao·ism (tou′ĭz′əm) ***n-*** Chinese religious system founded in the sixth century B.C. by Lao-tze, who prescribed a life of harmony and natural simplicity.

Tao·ist (tou′ĭst) ***n-*** follower of Taoism or of Lao-tze. ***adj-***: *the* Taoist *philosophy.*

Taos (tous) ***n-*** [*pl.* **Taos**] one of a group of American Pueblo Indians living in and around Taos, New Mexico.

[1]tap (tăp) ***vt-*** [**tapped, tap·ping**] **1** to strike or touch lightly; pat: *He* tapped *my shoulder.* **2** to cause to hit or strike lightly: *We* tapped *our feet to the music.* **3** to make or produce by a series of strikes or blows: *The woodpecker* tapped *a hole in the pole.* **4** to place a new walking surface on the toe or heel of (a shoe or boot). ***vi-*** to strike lightly: *to* tap *in tune to the music.* ***n-*** **1** light blow or touch; pat: *Give him a* tap *so that he will wake up.* **2** metal plate on the toe or heel of a shoe; also, any new walking surface on the toe or heel of a shoe or boot. [from Old French **taper,** from earlier Germanic **tappen,** "grope."]

[2]tap (tăp) ***n-*** **1** faucet; spigot. **2** tool used for cutting internal screw threads. **3** a point in an electric circuit where a connection may be made. ***vt-*** [**tapped, tap·ping**] **1** to draw or let out (liquid). **2** to pierce in order to let out liquid: *to* tap *a cask.* **3** to provide with a faucet or spigot. **4** to make a connection with (a fuel or water supply or electrical circuit) in order to draw off part of the supply; also, to make such a connection with (a telephone line) in order to listen in on conversations. **5** to make a screw thread on the inner surface of: *to* tap *a nut.* [from Old English **tæppa.**]

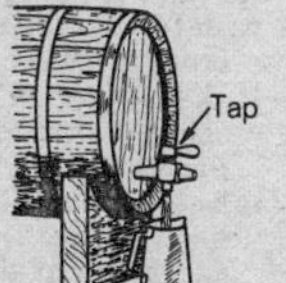

on tap of beer, drawn from a faucet or spigot.

ta·pa (tä′pə, tă′-) ***n-*** **1** inner bark of an Asiatic mulberry tree, used in making a kind of cloth. **2** (also **tapa cloth**) the cloth made from this bark.

tap dance ***n-*** fast dance, usually solo, in which the dancer emphasizes the sound and the rhythm of his steps by means of large metal plates attached to the heels and toes of his shoes. ***—n-*** **tap dancer.**

tap-dance (tăp′dăns′) ***vi-*** [**tap-danced, tap-danc·ing**] to perform a tap dance.

tape (tāp) ***n-*** **1** long, narrow strip used to tie or bind something; also, any long, narrow strip: *ticker* tape. **2** long strip of magnetic tape wound on a reel and used in a tape recorder. **3** line or rope stretched chest-high across a track to mark the finish of a race. **4** tape measure. ***vt-*** [**taped, tap·ing**] **1** to fix, fasten, or bind with a long band or strip. **2** to measure with a tape measure. **3** to record on magnetic tape. ***—adj-*** **tape′like′.**

tape deck ***n-*** device for playing or recording sounds on magnetic tape.

tape measure ***n-*** long, narrow strip that is marked off like a ruler, for measuring length.

ta·per (tā′pər) ***n-*** **1** long, slender candle. **2** long waxed wick, used for lighting candles, stoves, or fires. **3** gradual decrease of thickness toward a point: *the* taper *of a pyramid.* ***vt-*** to make gradually smaller or narrower toward one end: *to* taper *a flagpole*; *to* taper *a pair of pants.* ***vi-***: *The flagpole* tapers *to a point.* ***Hom-*** tapir.

taper off 1 to narrow toward one end. **2** to lessen or diminish gradually.

tape recorder ***n-*** machine used to record and play back sound by means of a magnetic tape.

tape recording ***n-*** recording made on magnetic tape.

tap·es·try (tăp′ə strē) ***n-*** [*pl.* **tap·es·tries**] fabric that is woven with pictures or designs and usually hung on walls. ***—adj-*** **tap′es·tried:** *a* tapestried *wall.*

tape·worm (tāp′wûrm′) ***n-*** any of several kinds of tapelike worms that live as parasites in the intestines.

tap·i·o·ca (tăp′ē ō′kə) ***n-*** grainy starch made from the roots of the cassava and used chiefly for puddings.

ta·pir (tā′pər) ***n-*** any of several large, hoofed mammals with a long, flexible snout, found throughout South and Central America and the Malay Peninsula. ***Hom-*** taper.

tap·room (tăp′ro͞om′, -ro͝om′) ***n-*** barroom.

Tapir, 6—8 ft. long

tap·root (tăp′ro͞ot′, -ro͝ot′) ***n-*** main root of a plant, growing downward and having smaller roots branching from it.

aps (tăps) ***n-*** (takes singular or plural verb) military bugle or drum signal to order lights out at night. Taps is also played at military funerals and memorial sevices.

ır (tär) ***n-*** thick, black, sticky substance obtained from wood, petroleum, etc. ***vt-*** [**tarred, tar·ring**] to cover or treat with tar: *to* tar *a roof.* ***as modifier***: *a* tar *roof.* [from Old English **tēoru,** "the resin of the fir tree."]

[2]**tar** (tär) *Informal* ***n-*** sailor. [from **tarpaulin.**]

tar·an·tel·la (tăr′ ən tĕl′ ə) ***n-*** lively Italian dance, once thought to cure the bite of the tarantula; also, the music for this dance.

ta·ran·tu·la (tə răn′ chə lə) ***n-*** [*pl.* **ta·ran·tu·las** or **ta·ran·tu·lae** (-lē)] any of various large, hairy spiders found throughout tropical and semitropical areas of America and Europe. Tarantulas have a painful, but not dangerous, bite.

Tarantula, body about 3 1/2 in. long

Ta·ras·can (tä rä skän′) ***n-*** [*pl.* **Ta·ras·cans,** also **Ta·ras·can**] one of an important Mexican Indian people of southwestern Mexico. ***adj-***: *the* Tarascan *empire.*

tar·dy (tär′ dē) ***adj-*** [**tar·di·er, tar·di·est**] **1** not on time; late: *the* tardy *arrival of the train.* **2** slow: *a* tardy *growth of plants.* **—*adv-* tar′ di·ly.** ***n-*** **tar′ di·ness.**

[1]**tare** (târ) ***n-*** **1** vetch. **2** the seed of this plant. **3** in the Bible, a harmful weed that grows among wheat. [from a shortened form of earlier **tare-etch,** from Middle English **tare** meaning "the darnel."] ***Hom-*** [2]tear.

[2]**tare** (târ) ***n-*** allowance of weight made to the purchaser by deducting the weight of the container. ***vt-*** [**tared, tar·ing**] to weigh (a container) in order to determine the weight to be deducted. [from French **tare,** "a loss in value," from Spanish **tara,** "an allowance in weight," from Arabic **tarha,** "thing thrown away."] ***Hom-*** [2]tear.

tar·get (tär′ gət) ***n-*** **1** something to be shot at or attacked, such as a series of painted circles one within the other, aimed at in archery, or the objective of a bombing raid. **2** something to work or strive for; goal; aim. **3** any object of insult, ridicule, or similar treatment: *A man in public life is always a* target *for criticism.* *as* ***modifier***: *a* target *date*; target *practice.*

Target

tar·iff (tăr′ ĭf) ***n-*** **1** list of duties or taxes placed by a government on goods entering or leaving a country. **2** the tax or duty levied according to such a list or schedule: *There is a* tariff *on Swiss watches.* **3** any list or scale of rates or charges. *as* ***modifier***: *new* tariff *laws.*

tar·mac (tär′ măk′) *chiefly Brit. & Canadian* ***n-*** **1** tarmacadam road or runway. **2 Tarmac** *Trademark* special preparation used for tarmacadam pavement.

tar·mac·ad·am (tär′ mə kăd′ əm) ***n-*** pavement consisting largely of pebbles held together by various tars; also, a mixture of such tars that is ready to use.

tarn (tärn) ***n-*** small mountain lake or pool.

tar·nish (tär′ nĭsh) ***vi-*** to lose brightness; become dull: *Silver* tarnishes *rapidly in this climate.* ***vt-*** to stain: *Egg yolk* tarnishes *silver. Slander* tarnished *his reputation.* ***n-*** **1** loss of brightness; dullness. **2** a stain; blemish. **3** a film of oxide or sulfide that stains some metal substances.

tar·nish·a·ble (tär′ nĭsh ə bəl) ***adj-*** such as can be tarnished or easily tarnished: *a* tarnishable *silver bowl.*

ta·ro (tăr′ ō) ***n-*** [*pl.* **ta·ros**] any of several tropical plants cultivated for their edible starchy roots; also, the root of such a plant. *as* ***modifier***: *a* taro *farm.*

tar·pau·lin (tär pô′ lən) ***n-*** heavy, waterproofed canvas or cloth, used as a protective covering. Also **tarp.**

tar·pon (tär′ pən) ***n-*** large, silvery game fish found throughout the Caribbean Sea and slightly north.

tar·ra·gon (tăr′ ə gən, -gŏn′) ***n-*** plant related to the wormwood, with aromatic leaves that are used as a seasoning; also, its leaves.

[1]**tar·ry** (tăr′ ē) ***vi-*** [**tar·ried, tar·ry·ing**] **1** to stay or live in a place for a short time: *We* tarried *in Italy longer than we had planned.* **2** to linger or delay: *He is always late because he* tarries *on his way to work.* [from Old English **tergan,** "hinder, delay," from Old French **targer,** from Late Latin **tardicāre,** "delay," from **tardus** "tardy."]

[2]**tar·ry** (tär′ ē) ***adj-*** [**tar·ri·er, tar·ri·est**] of, covered with, or like tar: *some* tarry *footprints.* [from [1]**tar.**]

tar·sal (tär′ səl) ***adj-*** of or relating to the ankle.

tar·sus (tär′ səs) ***n-*** [*pl.* **tar·si** (sē′)] **1** the ankle; also, in man, the group of seven bones which form the ankle. **2** in birds, the shank of the leg.

[1]**tart** (tärt) ***adj-*** [**tart·er, tart·est**] **1** sour; acid: *a* tart *apple.* **2** sharp; somewhat biting; caustic: *his* tart *reply.* [from Old English **teart,** "sharp; rough."] **—*adv-* tart′ly.**

[2]**tart** (tärt) ***n-*** small pastry shell filled with fruit or jam, without a top crust. [from Old French **tarte,** related to Latin **torta,** "twisted."]

tar·tan (tär′ tən) ***n-*** **1** woolen cloth, woven with plaid patterns, worn in the Scottish Highlands. **2** any of the designs of such a plaid; called by the name of the clan it belongs to: *the Campbell* tartan. ***adj-***: *a* tartan *skirt.*

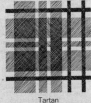

Tartan

[1]**tartar** (tär′ tər) ***n-*** **1** a hard yellowish deposit on the teeth consisting mostly of calcium salts precipitated from the saliva. **2** a crust formed in wine casks. [from Middle English **tartre,** "wine sediment."]

[2]**tar·tar** (tär′ tər) ***n-*** intractable or savage person: *George is a real* tartar *when he loses his temper.* [from **Tartar.**]

Tar·tar (tär′ tər) ***n-*** **1** member of any of the nomadic peoples of central Asia, who in the Middle Ages invaded western Asia and eastern Europe and whose descendants are now found mainly in the north Caucasus, Crimea, and parts of Siberia. **2** the language of these people. ***adj-***: *the* Tartar *invasions.* Also **Tatar.**

tar·tar·ic (tär tär′ ĭk, -tăr′ ĭk) ***adj-*** relating to or derived from tartar or tartaric acid.

tartaric acid ***n-*** an organic acid ($H_2C_4H_4O_6$) found in fruits. Its potassium salt is cream of tartar.

tartar sauce ***n-*** sauce made of mayonnaise, chopped cucumber pickles, and often olives, capers, and parsley, and served with fish or shellfish.

Tar·ta·rus (tär′ tər əs) ***n-*** in Greek mythology, the deep abyss below Hades into which Zeus hurled the Titans who had rebelled against his authority; later, any place of punishment for sinners.

task (tăsk) ***n-*** piece of work to be done; chore; duty. ***vt-*** to burden; put a strain on.

take to task to scold; find fault with.

task force *Military* ***n-*** group of units or of parts of units brought together for a specific mission.

task·mas·ter (tăsk′ măs′ tər) ***n-*** man who assigns work, especially exacting labor, and rigorously supervises its completion.

tas·sel (tăs′ əl) ***n-*** **1** tuft of threads, or cords of silk, wool, etc., loose at one end and gathered into a ball at the other, used as a hanging ornament. **2** hanging flower cluster of certain plants, such as corn. ***vi-*** [**tas·seled, tas·sel·ing**] of plants, to put forth hanging, flowery clusters. ***vt-*** to trim with, or make into, tassels.

Curtain tassel

taste (tāst) ***n-*** **1** sense by which flavor is perceived. **2** flavor as perceived by the tongue and palate. **3** a sample: *At the farm, we had a* taste *of country life.* **4** judgment of what is good or bad in art, decoration, etc., or of what is proper and suitable in speech, manners, etc. **5** personal preference; predilection: *I have no* taste *for that game. There's no accounting for* taste. ***vt-*** **[tast·ed, tast·ing] 1** to perceive or know by the tongue or palate: *I* taste *vanilla in the yogurt.* **2** to sample: *Let me* taste *your fried chicken.* **3** to experience: *a country that has* tasted *freedom.* ***vi-*** to have a certain flavor: *the butter* tastes *fishy.* ***—n-*** **tast′ er.**

taste bud ***n-*** any one of the small groups of cells that are the organs of taste. They are located chiefly on the tongue.

taste·ful (tāst′ fəl) ***n-*** showing good judgment and appreciation of beauty: *a talent for* tasteful *flower decoration.* ***—adv-*** **taste′ ful·ly.** ***n-*** **taste′ ful·ness.**

taste·less (tāst′ ləs) ***adj-*** **1** without flavor; flat: *This cake is simply* tasteless. **2** dull; not attractive. **3** lacking good judgment in art, manners, etc.: *a* tasteless *display of goods in a store.* ***—adv-*** **taste′ less·ly.** ***n-*** **taste′ less·ness.**

tast·y (tās′ tē) ***adj-*** **[tast·i·er, tast·i·est]** having a good flavor; pleasing to the taste: *a* tasty *dinner.* ***—adv-*** **tast′ i·ly.** ***n-*** **tast′ i·ness.**

tat (tăt) ***vt-*** **[tat·ted, tat·ting]** to make (trimming or lace) by looping and knotting thread wound on a shuttle. ***vi-***: *She likes to* tat *in the evenings.*

Ta·tar (tä′ tər) Tartar.

tat·ter (tăt′ ər) ***n-*** **1** torn and hanging part; rag; shred. **2 tatters** torn and ragged clothing: *The beggar was dressed in* tatters. ***vt-*** to tear or wear to pieces: *The boys* tattered *their clothes playing football.*

tat·ter·de·mal·ion (tăt′ ər dĭ mā′ lē ən, -māl′ yən) ***n-*** ragged fellow; ragamuffin.

tat·tered (tăt′ ərd) ***adj-*** torn in shreds; ragged.

tat·ting (tăt′ ĭng) ***n-*** kind of narrow lace or edging made by a person who tats.

tat·tle (tăt′ əl) ***vi-*** **[tat·tled, tat·tling]** to tell secrets; gossip; chatter: *If nobody* tattles, *the other team can't learn our plans.* ***vt-***: *He* tattled *our secret.* ***n-*** foolish, indiscreet talk; chatter. ***—n-*** **tat′ tler.**

tat·tle·tale (tăt′ əl tāl′) ***n-*** person who tattles.

[1]**tat·too** (tă to͞o′) ***n-*** [*pl.* **tat·toos**] **1** *Military* (1) drum or bugle signals calling soldiers or sailors to their quarters at night. (2) display of troops for entertainment. **2** continuous beating or tapping: *John was beating a* tattoo *with his fingers against the windowpane.* [from Dutch **taptoe** meaning "shut the tap" since a drum roll was the signal for the night closing of taverns.]

[2]**tat·too** (tă to͞o′) ***n-*** [*pl.* **tat·toos**] picture or design pricked into the skin with indelible dye. ***vt-*** to make (such a design): *The man* tattooed *a ship on the sailor's chest.* [from Tahitian **tatu,** "mark."] ***—n-*** **tat′ too′ er.**

Tattoos

taught (tót, tŏt) *p.p. & p.t.* of **teach.** ***Hom-*** taut or tot.

taunt (tónt) ***vt-*** to ridicule with bitter, sarcastic, or insulting language; jeer at: *The bully* taunted *him for refusing to fight.* ***n-*** a stinging remark; gibe.

taupe (tōp) ***n-*** dark-gray color with a tinge of dull yellow. ***adj-***: *a* taupe *dress.* ***Hom-*** tope.

Tau·rus (tór′ əs) ***n-*** constellation of stars thought to outline the figure of a bull.

taut (tót, tŏt) ***adj-*** **[taut·er, taut·est] 1** tightly stretched; tense: *a* taut *rope; a* taut *muscle.* **2** in good condition; neat: *a* taut *ship.* ***—adv-*** **taut′ ly.** ***n-*** **taut′ ness.** ***Hom-*** taught or tot.

tau·tog (tó tóg′, tó′ tóg′) ***n-*** fairly large game fish of the Atlantic Coast; blackfish.

tau·tol·o·gy (tó tŏl′ ə jē) ***n-*** [*pl.* **tau·tol·o·gies**] **1** useless repetition of an idea. **2** an instance of such repetition. Example: to descend down. ***—adj-*** **tau′ to·log′ i·cal** (tó′ tə lŏj′ ĭ kəl). ***adv-*** **tau′ to·log′ i·cal·ly.**

tav·ern (tăv′ ərn) ***n-*** **1** place where beer, wine, or other alcoholic beverages are sold and drunk. **2** inn.

taw (tó) ***n-*** **1** marble with which a player shoots. **2** mark or line from which players shoot in the game of marbles.

taw·dry (tó′ drē) ***adj-*** **[taw·dri·er, taw·dri·est]** showy but cheap; gaudy. ***—n-*** **taw′ dri·ness.**

taw·ny (tó′ nē) ***adj-*** **[taw·ni·er, taw·ni·est]** having a brownish-yellow color: *her* tawny *eyes; a* tawny *lion.* ***—n-*** **taw′ ni·ness.**

tax (tăks) ***n-*** **1** money paid by citizens to the government for public purposes. **2** a burden; strain: *a* tax *on the heart.* ***vt-*** **1** to impose a charge upon, especially for the support of the government: *The city* taxes *property.* **2** to put a heavy burden on; strain: *Climbing the mountain in the heavy snowstorm* taxed *the strength of the rangers.* **3** to find fault with; accuse: *to* tax *a person with bribery.* *as* ***modifier***: *a* tax *collector; yearly* tax *bill;* tax *exemption.* ***—n-*** **tax′ er.** ***adj-*** **tax′ less.**

tax·a·ble (tăk′ sə bəl) ***adj-*** subject or liable to tax.

tax·a·tion (tăk sā′ shən) ***n-*** the raising of money by taxes: *Unjust* taxation *angered the American colonists.* *as* ***modifier***: *a* taxation *expert; a* taxation *policy.*

tax-ex·empt (tăks′ ĕg zĕmpt′) ***adj-*** not subject to being taxed: *Certain kinds of income are* tax-exempt.

tax·i (tăk′ sē) ***n-*** [*pl.* **tax·is**] taxicab. *as* ***modifier***: *a* taxi *driver;* taxi *fare.* ***vi-*** **[tax·ied, tax·i·ing] 1** to ride in a taxicab. **2** of an airplane, to move under its own power on the ground or on water.

tax·i·cab (tăk′ sĭ kăb′) ***n-*** automobile for public hire, usually for short distances, having a taximeter that registers the fare to be paid; taxi.

tax·i·der·mist (tăk′ sə dûr′ mĭst) ***n-*** person whose work is taxidermy.

tax·i·der·my (tăk′ sə dûr′ mē) ***n-*** art of preparing, stuffing, and mounting the skins of animals.

tax·i·me·ter (tăk′ sĭ mē′ tər) ***n-*** automatic meter of a taxicab for computing the fare.

tax·o·nom·ic (tăk′ sə nŏm′ ĭk) ***adj-*** relating to taxonomy. ***—adv-*** **tax′ o·nom′ i·cal·ly.**

tax·on·o·my (tăk sŏn′ ə mē) ***n-*** **1** the classification of plants or of animals according to their natural relationships. **2** the study of the general principles of scientific classification.

tax·pay·er (tăks′ pā′ ər) ***n-*** person who is subject to or pays a tax.

Tb symbol for terbium.

TB or **T.B.** tuberculosis. Also **t.b.**

T-bar (tē′ bär′) ***n-*** T-shaped bar hung top down from the cable of a ski lift so that two skiers can be carried up the slope by leaning back against the crosspiece. *as* ***modifier***: *a* T-bar *lift; a* T-bar *tow.*

tbs. or **tbsp.** tablespoon; tablespoons.

Tc symbol for technetium.

Te symbol for tellurium.

tea (tē) ***n-*** **1** shrub with pointed leaves and white flowers, grown mainly in Asia and Af. **2** the dried leaves of this shrub. **3** drink made from soaking these leaves in hot water. **4** similar drink made from leaves or meat extract: *sage* tea; *beef* tea. **5** late afternoon meal or party at which hot tea is served. ***as modifier:*** *a* tea *merchant.* ***Homs-*** tee, ti.

Tea

tea bag ***n-*** porous sack of tea leaves on a string, dipped into hot water to brew a small amount of tea.

teach (tēch) ***vt-*** **[taught** (tȯt, tŏt), **teach·ing]** **1** to instruct; educate: *to* teach *a pupil.* **2** to give instruction in: *Mr. Bean* teaches *kindergarten.* **3** to help to learn: *Experience* taught *me to work carefully.* ***vi-*** to give instruction: *She* taught *for many years.*
►Avoid using LEARN when you mean TEACH: *The teacher* teaches. *The learner* learns. Do not say: *He* learned *his son a lesson.* Say instead: *He* taught *his son a lesson.*

teach·a·ble (tē′ chə bəl) ***adj-*** **1** such as can learn by being taught: *a* teachable *child.* **2** such as can be taught. ***—n-*** **teach′a·ble·ness** or **teach′a·bil′i·ty.**

teach·er (tē′chər) ***n-*** person who teaches; especially, a person whose profession is teaching.

teach·ing (tē′chĭng) ***n-*** **1** work of one who teaches; profession of a teacher. **2** something which is taught.

tea·cup (tē′kŭp′) ***n-*** **1** cup in which tea is served. **2** (also **tea′cup·ful′**) amount that such a cup holds.

tea·house (tē′hous′) ***n-*** in the Orient, a public place that serves tea and light meals; also, in Japan, a small garden house where tea is served with great ceremony.

teak (tēk) ***n-*** **1** tall East Indian tree, the leaves of which yield a red dye. **2** hard, durable timber of this tree, used in the making of ships and furniture. ***as modifier:*** *a* teak *table*; teak *decks.* Also **teak′wood′.**

tea·ket·tle (tē′kĕt′əl) ***n-*** covered kettle with a spout in which water is boiled.

teal (tēl) ***n-*** any of several kinds of small river or marsh ducks of central and eastern United States and Canada.

Blue-winged teal, about 16 in. long

team (tēm) ***n-*** **1** group of people who make up one side in an athletic game or other contest; also, group of people who work together for any purpose: *a* team *of architects.* **2** two or more horses, oxen, or other animals harnessed together to a plow, carriage, etc. ***as modifier:*** *a* team *effort*; *good* team *spirit.* ***vi-*** to join in a group: *Bill* teamed *with his friends.* ***vt-*** **1** to join (animals) together: *to* team *horses.* **2** to transport with animals: *to* team *logs.* ***Hom-*** teem.

team·mate (tēm′māt′) ***n-*** fellow member of a team.

team·ster (tēm′stər) ***n-*** **1** driver of a team of animals. **2** truck driver.

team·work (tēm′wûrk′) ***n-*** common effort of a group of people working together; cooperation.

Teapot

tea·pot (tē′pŏt′) ***n-*** covered vessel with a spout and handle, for brewing and serving tea.

[1]**tear** (têr) ***n-*** drop of salty fluid from the eye, especially while crying. [from Old English **tēar.**] ***Hom-*** [1]**tier.**
in tears crying; weeping: *The audience left* in tears.

[2]**tear** (târ) ***vt-*** **[tore, torn, tear·ing]** **1** to rend by pulling; rip: *The hungry dog* tore *the meat with its teeth.* **2** to cut deeply; gash: *The loose nail* tore *a jagged gash in his leg.* **3** to remove by force: *The wind* tore *the awning from the wall.* **4** to cause great pain or sadness: *It* tore *his heart to leave his children.* ***vi-*** **1** to become ripped: *Her dress* tore *on a nail.* **2** to come apart on being pulled or roughly handled: *Cloth* tears *easily.* **3** to rush; move at great speed: *The car* tore *past us.* ***n-*** hole or gash made by ripping or pulling apart: *a* tear *in my coat.* [from Old English **teran** meaning "to destroy."] ***Hom-*** tare.
tear down **1** to dismantle or raze (a building). **2** to disprove (an argument).
tear into *Informal* to attack vigorously.
tear up to rip into many pieces.

tear·drop (têr′drŏp′) ***n-*** **1** a tear falling from the eye. **2** anything shaped like a dropping tear. ***as modifier:*** *a* teardrop *pendant.*

tear·ful (têr′fəl) ***adj-*** **1** shedding tears; weeping. **2** causing tears. ***—adv-*** **tear′ful·ly.** ***n-*** **tear′ful·ness.**

tear gas (têr) ***n-*** gas which causes severe stinging and watering of the eyes and temporary blindness.

tear·less (têr′ləs) ***adj-*** without tears; dry-eyed: *a* tearless *child.* ***—adv-*** **tear′less·ly.**

tea·room (tē′ro͞om′) ***n-*** small restaurant which serves light meals in a quiet, genteel atmosphere.

tear·y (têr′ē) ***adj-*** **[tear·i·er, tear·i·est]** accompanied by weeping; tearful: *a* teary *farewell.*

tease (tēz) ***vt-*** **[teased, teas·ing]** **1** to taunt or annoy in fun or with malicious intent, especially by offering something and then taking it away: *Joe* teased *his cat with a ball of string.* **2** to beg repeatedly; pester: *Rob* teased *his father for a new bat.* **3** to separate the fibers of (wool, flax, hair, etc.). **4** to roughen the surface of: *to* tease *cloth.* ***n-*** person who annoys someone for fun. ***—adv-*** **teas′ing·ly.** ***n-*** **teas′er.**

tea·sel or **tea·zel** (tē′zəl) ***n-*** **1** herb bearing stiff, hooked spines and white or purplish flowers in dense, long heads. **2** its dried flower head used to raise the nap on woolen cloth; also, any device similarly used.

tea service ***n-*** serving set consisting of a teapot, cream pitcher, sugar bowl, and often cups, saucers, plates, and a tray. Also **tea set.**

tea·spoon (tē′spo͞on′) ***n-*** **1** small spoon for general table use. **2** (also **tea′spoon·ful′**) amount a teaspoon will hold when full; also, a measure used in cooking, equal to one third of a tablespoon.

teat (tĭt, tēt) ***n-*** nipple on the breast or udder of female animals, through which milk passes. ***Hom-*** tit.

tea wagon ***n-*** tray or light table on wheels, for serving or transporting food indoors.

tech. **1** technology. **2** technical.

tech·ne·ti·um (tĕk nē′shē əm) ***n-*** a radioactive element, produced by nuclear fission and related processes in the laboratory and not known to occur naturally. Symbol Tc, At. No. 43, At. Wt. 99.

tech·ni·cal (tĕk′nĭ kəl) ***adj-*** **1** having to do with the industrial or mechanical arts and sciences: *An architect must have a long* technical *training.* **2** having to do with the methods of an occupation, art, or science: *A surgeon must have both knowledge and* technical *skill.* **3** having to do with technique: *She has mastered the* technical *details of poetry.* **4** according to formal or legal fact rather than to the practical realities of a case or situation: *That's true, if you want to be* technical. ***—adv-*** **tech′ni·cal·ly.**

tech·ni·cal·i·ty (tĕk′nə kăl′ə tē) ***n-*** [*pl.* **tech·ni·cal·i·ties]** **1** point of law or formal procedure that may be minor and easily overlooked, but can affect larger issues: *The contract was cancelled because of a legal* technicality. **2** technical complexity: *The* technicality *of the book frightened me.*

technical knockout ***n-*** in boxing, a knockout scored by one boxer when the referee stops the fight because the other boxer is injured or helpless, although not lying down.

tech·ni·cian (tĕk nĭsh′ ən) ***n-*** **1** person who is skilled in technique: *That painter is a good* technician. **2** skilled assistant to a doctor, scientist, engineer, etc.: *a* laboratory *technician.* **3** person having great technical knowledge.

tech·nics (tĕk′ nĭks) ***n-*** *pl.* **1** methodology; technique. **2** (takes singular verb) technology.

tech·nique (tĕk nēk′) ***n-*** method used in carrying out a mechanical, artistic, or scientific work; technical skill: *the* technique *of heart surgery*; technique *at the piano.*

tech·no·log·i·cal (tĕk′ nə lŏj′ ĭ kəl) ***adj-*** of or relating to technology: *recent* technological *advances.* Also **tech′ no·log′ ic.** ***—adv-*** **tech′ no·log′ i·cal·ly.**

tech·nol·o·gist (tĕk nŏl′ ə jĭst′) ***n-*** person who specializes in technology.

tech·nol·o·gy (tĕk nŏl′ ə jē) ***n-*** **1** the practical application of scientific research and discovery; engineering. **2** [*pl.* **tech·nol·o·gies**] such application in a particular field.

ted (tĕd) ***vt-*** [**ted·ded, ted·ding**] to turn or spread for drying: *to* ted *hay.* ***—n-*** **ted′ der.**

ted·dy bear (tĕd′ ē) ***n-*** stuffed doll in the shape of a chubby bear. [named for Theodore (Teddy) Roosevelt.]

Te De·um (tā dā′ əm, tē dē′-) ***n-*** **1** ancient Christian hymn beginning "Te Deum laudamus" ("We praise thee, Lord"). **2** musical setting for this hymn. **3** any religious service of praise in which this hymn is sung.

te·di·ous (tē′ dē əs, tē′ jəs) ***adj-*** wearisome; tiresome; boring: *a* tedious *job*; *a* tedious *conversation.* ***—adv-*** **te′ di·ous·ly.** ***n-*** **te′ di·ous·ness.**

te·di·um (tē′ dē əm) ***n-*** tediousness; tiresomeness; monotony: *the* tedium *of the long hours of work.*

¹tee (tē) ***n-*** **1** the letter T. **2** anything shaped like this. [from Middle English.] ***Homs-*** tea, ti.

²tee (tē) ***n-*** **1** in golf, the place at each hole from which the ball is first driven. **2** small pin of wood, metal, or rubber with a slightly cupped head, or a small mound of earth, on which a golf ball is placed for driving off at the beginning of each hole. **3** (also **kicking tee**) triangular rest that holds a football for the kickoff. ***vt-*** [**teed, tee·ing**] to place (the ball) on a tee. [probably from earlier Scottish **teaz.**] ***Homs-*** tea, ti.
tee off to drive a golf ball off the tee.

¹teem (tēm) ***vi-*** **1** to be crowded to overflowing; swarm: *On holidays the beaches* teem *with bathers.* **2** to be full, productive, fertile, etc.: *The plains* teem *with wild animals. His brain* teems *with ideas.* [from Old English **tieman,** related to **team.**] ***Hom-*** team.

²teem (tēm) ***vi-*** of rain, to fall very heavily. [from Middle English **temen,** from Old Norse **tœma.**] ***Hom-*** team.

teen-age (tēn′ āj′) ***adj-*** of or relating to teen-agers.

teen-ag·er (tēn′ ā′ jər) ***n-*** person older than 12 and younger than 20 years of age.

teens (tēnz) ***n-*** *pl.* years of age from 13 to 19.

tee·ny (tē′ nē) *Informal* ***adj-*** [**tee·ni·er, tee·ni·est**] tiny.

tee·pee (tē′ pē) tepee.

tee shirt ***n-*** T-shirt.

tee·ter (tē′ tər) ***vi-*** **1** to move unsteadily from side to side: *The boys* teetered *on the fence.* **2** to seesaw.

tee·ter-tot·ter (tē′ tər tŏt′ ər) ***n-*** seesaw. Also **tee′ ter·board′.**

teeth (tēth) ***n-*** *pl.* of **tooth.**

teethe (tēth) ***vi-*** [**teethed, teeth·ing**] to cut, grow, or develop teeth: *The infant is just beginning to* teethe.

tee·to·tal (tē′ tō′ təl) ***adj-*** **1** entire; total. **2** relating to total abstinence from alcoholic beverages.

tee·to·tal·er (tē′ tō′ tə lər) ***n-*** person who advocates total abstinence from alcoholic beverages.

teg·u·ment (tĕg′ yə mənt) ***n-*** natural outer covering, such as the human skin or animal hide or shell. ***—adj-*** **teg′ u·men′ ta·ry** (-mĕn′ tə rē): *a* tegumentary *layer.*

tel. **1** telephone. **2** telegram. **3** telegraph.

tele- *combining form* at a distance; afar: *a* tele*vision set*; tele*phone.* [from Greek **tele-**, from **tēle,** "far off."]

tel·e·cast (tĕl′ ə kăst′) ***vt-*** [**tel·e·cast** or **tel·e·cast·ed, tel·e·cast·ing**] to broadcast by television. ***n-*** television broadcast. ***—n-*** **tel′ e·cast′ er.**

tel·e·gram (tĕl′ ə grăm′) ***n-*** message sent by telegraph.

telegraph (tĕl′ ə grăf′) ***n-*** **1** instrument for sending and receiving messages over electric wires by rapidly interrupting the circuit. **2** teletypewriter. *as* ***modifier:*** *a* telegraph *key.* ***vt-*** to send or communicate with by means of either of these instruments: *She* telegraphed *the good news to me.* ***vi-:*** *He* telegraphed *all over the world.*

te·leg·ra·pher (tə lĕg′ rə fər) ***n-*** person who operates a telegraph.

te·leg·ra·phy (tə lĕg′ rə fē) ***n-*** science, art, or process of using the telegraph to transmit messages.

Te·lem·a·chus (tə lĕm′ ə kəs) ***n-*** in Homer's "Odyssey," the son of Odysseus (Ulysses) and Penelope, who helped his father slay his mother's suitors.

tel·e·me·ter (tə lĕm′ ə tər) ***n-*** automatic instrument or system of instruments used to measure conditions at a distance, such as in outer space, and to radio the measurements back to a receiver. ***vt-*** to measure or send by telemeter.

te·lem·e·try (tə lĕm′ ə trē) ***n-*** the use of telemetering instruments and the interpretation of the signals.

te·lep·a·thy (tə lĕp′ ə thē) ***n-*** communication of thought from one person to another without the use of words or signs. ***—adj-*** **tel′ e·path′ ic** (tĕl′ ə păth′ ĭk): *in* telepathic *communication.* ***adv-*** **tel′ e·path′ i·cal·ly.**

tel·e·phone (tĕl′ ə fōn′) ***n-*** instrument or system for sending and receiving speech over electric wires. *as* ***modifier:*** *the* telephone *company*; *a* telephone *operator.* ***vt-*** [**tel·e·phoned, tel·e·phon·ing**] **1** to call (someone) with this instrument: *Please* telephone *him today.* **2** to give or convey by this instrument: *Please* telephone *the news to me tomorrow.* ***vi-:*** *He is always* telephoning. ***—adj-*** **tel′ e·phon′ ic** (-fŏn′ ĭk).

te·leph·o·ny (tə lĕf′ ə nē) ***n-*** science, art, or process of using telephones to transmit messages.

tel·e·pho·to·graph (tĕl′ ə fō′ tə grăf′) ***n-*** a photograph made at a great distance through a magnifying lens.

tel·e·pho·tog·ra·phy (tĕl′ ə fə tŏg′ rə fē) ***n-*** the use of instruments that take telephotographs.

tel·e·pho·to lens (tĕl′ ə fō′ tō) ***n-*** any of various special camera lenses that are used in telephotography.

tel·e·print·er (tĕl′ ə prĭn′ tər) ***n-*** teletypewriter.

tel·e·scope (tĕl′ ə skōp′) ***n-*** instrument for making distant things appear larger; especially, a large instrument of this kind for studying heavenly bodies. ***vt-*** [**tel·e·scoped, tel·e·scop·ing**] **1** to fit a smaller into a larger simi-

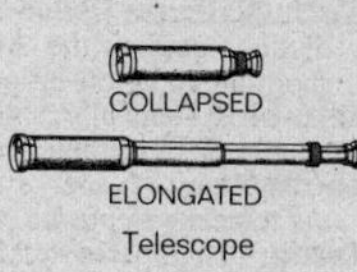

Telescope

lar object; nest: *Let us* telescope *these boxes to save space.* **2** to cause to collapse like the sections of a field telescope. ***vi-*** to collapse in this manner.

tel·e·scop·ic (tĕl′ə skŏp′ĭk) ***adj-*** **1** through a telescope: *a* telescopic *view.* **2** used as or functioning like a telescope: *a* telescopic *lens.* **3** visible only by means of the telescope: *some* telescopic *stars.* **4** farseeing: *That's very* telescopic *vision.* **5** collapsible in tubular sections: *a* telescopic *handle.* **—*adv-*** **tel′e·scop′i·cal·ly.**

Tel·e·type (tĕl′ə tīp′) ***n-*** **1** trademark name for a kind of teletypewriter. **2 teletype** message sent by teletypewriter. ***vt-*** **teletype [tel·e·typed, tel·e·typ·ing]** to send (a message) by teletypewriter.

tel·e·type·writ·er (tĕl′ə tīp′rī′tər) ***n-*** telegraphic system in which a typewriter at one end automatically reproduces a message typed at the other end; teleprinter.

tel·e·view·er (tĕl′ə vyōō′ər) ***n-*** person who watches television.

tel·e·vise (tĕl′ə vīz′) ***vt-*** **[tel·e·vised, tel·e·vis·ing]** to broadcast by television: *They* televised *the parade.*

tel·e·vi·sion (tĕl′ə vĭzh′ən) ***n-*** **1** the sending and receiving of moving pictures by shortwave radio signals. **2** a television receiver: *Our* television *is out of order.* **3** the industry or medium of television broadcasting. *as* ***modifier:*** *a* television *program.*

Tel·ex or **tel·ex** (tĕl′ĕks) ***n-*** system of communication based on the use of teletypewriters both to send and receive messages. **—*vt-*** **tel′ex.**

tell (tĕl) ***vt-*** **[told** (tōld), **tell·ing]** **1** to relate; narrate; utter; say: *to* tell *the truth; to* tell *a story.* **2** to reveal; make known: *Your actions* tell *more than your words.* **3** to recognize; be sure; see: *I can't* tell *what is best to do. I can't* tell *who it is at this distance.* **4** to order; command: *Don't* tell *me what to do.* **5** identify by contrast; distinguish: *I can't* tell *one twin from the other.* **6** *Archaic* to count: *The clock* tells *the hours.* ***vi-*** **1** to give an account (usually followed by "of"): *He* told *of days gone by.* **2** to be very important or decisive: *Courage* tells, *in the end.* **—*adj-*** **tell′able.**

tell apart to distinguish between.

tell off *Informal* to scold harshly.

tell on **1** to inform on. **2** to have a marked effect on.

tell·er (tĕl′ər) ***n-*** **1** person who tells a story; narrator. **2** clerk in a bank who pays out and receives money. **3** person who counts the votes in a meeting, etc.

tell·ing (tĕl′ĭng) ***adj-*** **1** striking; impressive: *His words had a* telling *effect.* **2** effective: *a* telling *blow.* **—*adv-*** **tell′ing·ly.**

tell·tale (tĕl′tāl′) ***n-*** **1** person who reveals secrets; one who tattles. **2** device that gives information or warning, such as a small piece of cloth or flag that flaps freely in the wind and thereby tells the wind's direction. ***adj-*** giving information about something supposed to be secret; betraying: *a* telltale *smile.*

tel·lu·ri·um (tə lŏŏr′ē əm) ***n-*** a brittle, silvery-white element with some metallic properties, found in several metal ores and used in certain hard steel alloys. Symbol Te, At. No. 52, At. Wt. 127.60.

Tell, William (tĕl) ***n-*** legendary Swiss hero who because of disrespect to the Austrian governor was ordered to shoot an apple off his son's head with his crossbow.

tem·blor (tĕm′blər, -blôr′) ***n-*** earthquake. [from Spanish **temblar,** "to tremble," from Latin, **tremulare.**]

te·mer·i·ty (tə mĕr′ə tē) ***n-*** boldness; rashness: *He had the* temerity *to push a police officer.*

temp. **1** temperature. **2** temporary.

tem·per (tĕm′pər) ***n-*** **1** disposition; mood: *an even* temper. **2** tendency to anger: *He has a violent* temper. **3** rage: *She flies into a* temper *when she's contradicted.* **4** control of anger: *Don't lose your* temper. **5** the degree of hardness, toughness, etc., in a substance: *the* temper *of the steel in a blade.* ***vt-*** **1** to make less extreme; to moderate: *He* tempered *his impulse with reason.* **2** to change the toughness or hardness of (metal).

tem·per·a (tĕm′pər ə) ***n-*** **1** any of various painting mediums for use with powder pigments; especially, egg yolk thinned with water. **2** paint made with such a medium. **3** technique of painting with such paints.

tem·per·a·ment (tĕm′pər ə mənt, tĕm′prə-) ***n-*** person's disposition; mental and emotional makeup.

tem·per·a·men·tal (tĕm′pər ə mĕn′təl, tĕm′prə-) ***adj-*** **1** arising from or relating to one's mental or emotional makeup: *He has a* temperamental *aptitude for the life of a hermit.* **2** subject to sudden changes of mood, especially to fits of displeasure. **—*adv-*** **tem′per·a·men′tal·ly.**

tem·per·ance (tĕm′pər əns) ***n-*** **1** avoidance of extremes, especially in eating and drinking; moderation. **2** complete abstinence from alcoholic drink. *as* ***modifier:*** *a* temperance *crusader; the* temperance *movement.*

tem·per·ate (tĕm′pər ət) ***adj-*** **1** moderate; restrained; controlled, especially in the use of alcoholic drink: *a man of* temperate *habits.* **2** neither hot nor cold; moderate in temperature: *a* temperate *climate.* **—*adv-*** **tem′per·ate·ly.** ***n-*** **tem′per·ate·ness.**

Temperate Zone ***n-*** area between 23° 27′ and 66° 33′ North Latitude or the corresponding area south of the Equator.

tem·per·a·ture (tĕm′pər ə chər, tĕm′prə-) ***n-*** **1** heat or cold, as measured by a thermometer and corresponding to the amount of excitation of the molecules of a substance. The **normal temperature** of a well person is about 98.6°F. See *Fahrenheit; Celsius scale; Kelvin.* **2** *Informal* body temperature above normal; fever.

tem·pered (tĕm′pərd) ***adj-*** having a certain temper or disposition: *a good-*tempered *man.*

tem·pest (tĕm′pəst) ***n-*** **1** violent windstorm, usually accompanied by rain, hail, etc. **2** any violent outburst.

tempest in a teapot big fuss over something small.

tem·pes·tu·ous (tĕm pĕs′chōō əs) ***adj-*** stormy; violent; agitated: *a* tempestuous *wind; a* tempestuous *rage.* **—*adv-*** **tem·pes′tu·ous·ly.** ***n-*** **tem·pes′tu·ous·ness.**

Tem·plar (tĕm′plər) ***n-*** knight of a military-religious order founded in 1119 in Jerusalem to protect pilgrims and the holy places in Jerusalem. Also **Knight Templar.**

tem·plate or **tem·plet** (tĕm′plĭt) ***n-*** **1** mold or pattern used as a guide for producing an accurate copy of a shape or object. **2** *Biology* molecule in a biological system, which carries the genetic code for another molecule.

[1]**tem·ple** (tĕm′pəl) ***n-*** **1** building dedicated to the worship of a god or gods: *the* temple *of Apollo.* **2** place for worship; church; synagogue, especially a Reform Jewish house of worship. **3 Temple** (1) any of the three temples built by the Jews at various times in ancient Jerusalem. (2) any of the houses of the Templars. [from Latin **templum,** "area marked off for worship."]

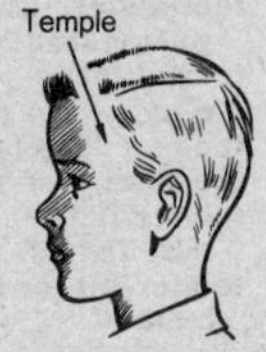

[2]**tem·ple** (tĕm′pəl) ***n-*** flat place on either side of the forehead between the eye and the upper part of the ear. [from Old French **temples,** from Latin **tempora** meaning "the temples of the head."]

tem·po (tĕm′pō) ***n-*** [*pl.* **tem·pos** or **tem·pi** (-pē)] **1** *Music* rate of speed at which a composition is, or should be, rendered. **2** rate of speed; pace: *the* tempo *of city life.*

[1]tem·po·ral (tĕm′ pər əl) ***adj-*** **1** limited in time: *a* temporal *phase.* **2** relating to the world; earthly: *a* temporal *concern.* **3** *Grammar* expressing time: *a* temporal *clause.* [from Middle English, from Latin **temporalis,** from **tempor-,** and **tempus,** "time."]

[2]tem·por·al (tĕm′ pər əl) ***adj-*** pertaining to parts of the head behind the eyes at the sides, either external or internal, such as the bones at the sides and base of the skull, and muscles and blood vessels in this region. [from Late Latin **temporalis,** from Latin **tempora** meaning "the temples (of the head)."]

tem·po·rar·y (tĕm′ pə rĕr′ ē) ***adj-*** continuing for or meant for a limited time only; not permanent; *a* temporary *job.* ***—adv-*** **tem′po·rar′i·ly.** ***n-*** **tem′po·rar′i·ness.**

temporary star nova.

tem·po·rize (tĕm′ pə rīz′) ***vi-*** **[tem·po·rized, tem·po·riz·ing] 1** to yield temporarily to current public opinion or circumstances: *The candidate* temporized *about several issues.* **2** to adopt a policy of delay; also, be evasive to gain time. ***—n-*** **tem′ po·ri·za′ tion.** ***n-*** **tem′ po·riz′ er.**

tempt (tĕmpt) ***vt-*** **1** to persuade or try to persuade to do something, especially something wrong or evil: *Hunger* tempts *some to steal.* **2** to lure; entice: *The bargains at the sale* tempted *her.* **3** to provoke or defy: *to* tempt *fate.*

temp·ta·tion (tĕmp tā′ shən) ***n-*** **1** a tempting: *the* temptation *of a weak person by bad companions.* **2** condition of being tempted: *I try to avoid* temptation. **3** something that tempts: *That candy's a* temptation.

tempt·er (tĕmp′ tər) ***n-*** **1** person who tempts. **2 the Tempter** Satan; the Devil ***—n-*** *fem.* **tempt′ ress.**

tempt·ing (tĕmp′ tĭng) ***adj-*** alluring; attractive; seductive: *a* tempting *idea.* ***—adv-*** **tempt′ ing·ly.**

ten (tĕn) ***n-*** **1** amount or quantity that is one greater than 9. **2** *Mathematics* (1) the cardinal number that is the sum of 9 and 1. (2) numeral such as 10 that represents this cardinal number. *as* ***determiner*** (traditionally called adjective or pronoun): *There are* ten *books here and* ten *there.*

ten·a·ble (tĕn′ ə bəl) ***adj-*** such as can be held, defended, etc.: *a* tenable *viewpoint*; *a* tenable *fortress.* ***—n-*** **ten′ a·bil′ i·ty.** ***adv-*** **ten′ a·bly.**

te·na·cious (tə nā′ shəs) ***adj-*** **1** tight and unyielding: *a* tenacious *grip on the rope*; *a* tenacious *hold on life.* **2** holding or keeping hold very tightly: *He has a* tenacious *memory. He is as* tenacious *as a bulldog when he gets an idea.* ***—adv-*** **te·na′ cious·ly.** ***n-*** **te·na′ cious·ness.**

te·nac·i·ty (tə năs′ ə tē) ***n-*** condition of being tenacious.

ten·an·cy (tĕn′ ən sē) ***n-*** [*pl.* **ten·an·cies**] occupancy or use of land or buildings on the payment of rent to the owner; also, the length of such use or occupancy.

ten·ant (tĕn′ ənt) ***n-*** **1** person who pays rent for the use of property. **2** any occupant or inhabitant: *The deer and fox are* tenants *of the woods.* **3** tenant farmer. ***vt-*** to occupy; inhabit. ***—adj-*** **ten′ ant·less.**

tenant farmer ***n-*** farmer who rents, works, and usually lives on land belonging to someone else; especially, a sharecropper.

ten·ant·ry (tĕn′ ən trē) ***n-*** [*pl.* **ten·ant·ries**] **1** condition of being a tenant. **2** the entire group of tenants occupying land and houses on one estate.

Ten Commandments ***n-*** in the Bible, the ten laws given to Moses by God.

[1]tend (tĕnd) ***vi-*** **1** to be inclined in action or thought: *He* tends *to follow the ideas of his parents.* **2** to be likely to have a certain result: *Ill health* tends *to make some people grumpy.* **3** to move or take a direction toward: *Our course* tends *eastward.* [from Old French **tendre,** from Latin **tendere,** "stretch toward; aim at; extend."]

[2]tend (tĕnd) ***vt-*** **1** to care for; watch over: *The shepherd* tends *his flock.* **2** to take charge of; manage: *to* tend *a machine.* [from **attend.**]

tend·en·cy (tĕn′ dən sē) ***n-*** [*pl.* **tend·en·cies**] **1** trend or movement in some direction: *All governments have a* tendency *to increase taxes.* **2** natural bent; inclination: *Her hobbies show artistic* tendencies.

ten·den·tious (tĕn dĕn′ shəs) ***adj-*** written or spoken with the purpose of supporting a doctrine or point of view; amounting to propaganda; partisan: *a* tendentious *book.* ***—adv-*** **ten·den′ tious·ly.** ***n-*** **ten·den′ tious·ness.**

[1]ten·der (tĕn′ dər) ***adj-*** **[ten·der·er, ten·der·est] 1** not tough; soft: *a* tender *steak*; *a baby's* tender *skin.* **2** not hardy; delicate: *These* tender *plants must be protected against strong wind.* **3** painfully sensitive to touch, movement, reference, etc.: *His leg was still* tender *in the place where he was kicked.* **4** gentle; loving: *the* tender *touch of his hand*; *a* tender *glance*; *a* tender *smile.* **5** young; immature: *a child's* tender *years.* [from French **tendre,** from Latin **tener** meaning "soft; delicate."] ***—adv-*** **ten′ der·ly.** ***n-*** **ten′ der·ness.**

[2]ten·der (tĕn′ dər) ***vt-*** **1** to offer for acceptance: *to* tender *a resignation.* **2** in law, to offer money in payment of a debt. ***n-*** **1** offer, bid, or proposal: *a* tender *of gratitude.* **2** the thing offered. [from **[1]tend.**] ***—n-*** **ten′ der·er.**

[3]tend·er (tĕn′ dər) ***n-*** **1** person who takes charge of or attends to: *A nurse is a* tender *of children.* **2** railroad car attached to a steam locomotive, to carry fuel and water for the boiler. **3** small boat supplying a larger one with provisions, fuel, etc., or used to land passengers from a larger boat. [from **[2]tend.**]

ten·der·foot (tĕn′ dər fo͝ot′) ***n-*** [*pl.* **ten·der·foots**] **1** inexperienced person, especially one unused to hardships or rough living; greenhorn or newcomer to pioneer life in western United States. **2** beginning rank of the Boy Scouts; also, a boy of this rank.

ten·der·heart·ed (tĕn′ dər här′ təd) ***adj-*** readily touched by the pain, grief, or love of others; compassionate; sympathetic.

ten·der·ize (tĕn′ də rīz′) ***vt-*** **[ten·der·ized, ten·der·iz·ing]** to make (meat) softer and easier to chew, by pounding, marinating, or treating with enzymes.

ten·der·iz·er (tĕn′ də rī′ zər) ***n-*** liquid or powder, usually containing an enzyme from papaya juice, sprinkled on meat before cooking in order to tenderize it.

ten·der·loin (tĕn′ dər loin′) ***n-*** **1** the tender part of the loin in beef, pork, etc. **2** *Archaic Slang* the part of a city where vice is more or less openly practiced.

ten·don (tĕn′ dən) ***n-*** tough cord or band of tissue that attaches a muscle to a bone, another muscle, or an organ of the body; sinew.

ten·dril (tĕn′ drəl) ***n-*** **1** slender stem of certain climbing plants, which twines about any support. **2** a curling, threadlike part: *a* tendril *of hair.*

Tendril

ten·e·ment (tĕn′ ə mənt) ***n-*** **1** tenement house. **2** any dwelling house, especially a rented one. **3** in law, any kind of permanent property that is rented.

tenement house ***n-*** apartment building containing many sets of rooms and usually crowded, located in a slum, and occupied by poor people.

ten·et (tĕn′ ət) ***n-*** creed, principle, or belief maintained as true by an individual or organization.

ten·fold (tĕn′ fōld′) ***adj-*** **1** ten times as many or as much. **2** having ten parts. ***adv-***: *Our output increased* tenfold.

Tenn. Tennessee.

ten·nis (tĕn′ əs) ***n-*** **1** game for two or two pairs of players, in which a light ball is hit back and forth across a net with a **tennis racket** in the middle of a marked area called a **tennis court**; lawn tennis. **2** (also **court tennis**) a similar, more complicated, indoor game in which the walls and slanting roof are also employed.

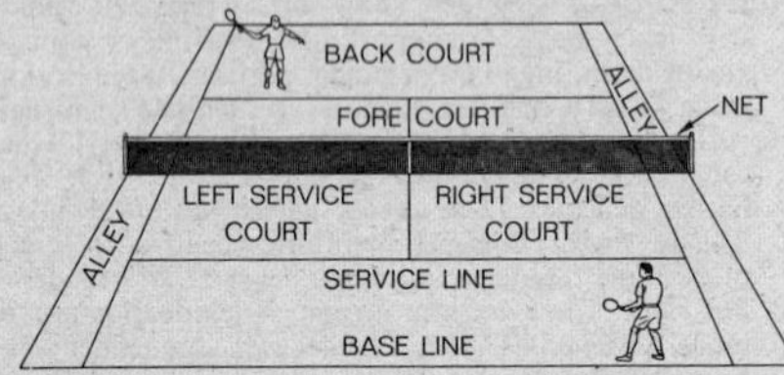

Tennis court

ten·on (tĕn′ ən) ***n-*** projection cut at the end of a piece of wood to fit into a hole in another piece of wood. For picture, see *mortise*. ***vt-*** **1** to cut such a projection at the end of (a timber). **2** to join (two timbers) with a mortise and tenon joint.

ten·or (tĕn′ ər) ***n-*** **1** *Music* (1) range of the highest natural male singing voice. (2) singer having such a voice. (3) part written for such a voice. (4) similar range covered by certain instruments such as recorders and saxophones. **2** general settled course or direction: *the quiet* tenor *of a monk's life.* **3** general meaning or effect: *the* tenor *of his sermon.* ***adj-***: *a* tenor *saxophone.*

ten·pins (tĕn′ pĭnz′) ***n-*** (takes singular verb) **1** bowling game played with ten large pins set up at one end of a bowling alley, and bowled at with a ball; bowling. **2** similar game played anywhere with ten smaller pins.

[1]**tense** (tĕns) ***adj-*** **[tens·er, tens·est] 1** stretched taut; rigid: *His muscles were* tense *from exercise.* **2** having to do with or showing mental or emotional strain: *It was a* tense *moment when the car almost hit us.* ***vt-*** **[tensed, tens·ing]** to make taut; tighten: *Andy proudly* tensed *the muscles of his arm.* ***vi-*** to become taut: *He* tensed *during the trial.* [from Latin **tensus** and **tendere** meaning "to stretch."] ***—adv-*** **tense′ ly.** ***n-*** **tense′ ness.**

[2]**tense** (tĕns) *Grammar* ***n-*** any of various forms of a verb or verb phrase that show the time when an event occurs. English verbs have only two such forms — the present tense and the past tense — and all other English tenses are verb phrases. Examples:

Joe plays *football.* (verb, present tense)
Jack played *football.* (verb, past tense)
Henry will play *football tomorow.* (verb phrase, future tense)
Alex had played *football before yesterday.* (verb phrase, past perfect tense)

[from Old French **tens,** from **temps,** from Latin **tempus** meaning "time."]

ten·sile (tĕn′ səl, -sĭl′) ***adj-*** relating to stretching or pulling: *the* tensile *strength of a wire*; *a* tensile *force.*

tensile strength ***n-*** the greatest stretching force that can be applied to a material without breaking it. It is expressed in pounds per square inch.

ten·sion (tĕn′ shən) ***n-*** **1** a stretching, straining, or pulling taut. **2** condition of being stretched or pulled taut. **3** mental or emotional strain: *He was under great* tension. **4** friction or ill will between people: *Since the quarrel over the car, there is* tension *between Ralph and his brother.* **5** *Physics* stress caused by a pulling force; also, the condition of a body due to such a force.

ten·sor (tĕn′ sər, -sôr) ***n-*** a muscle that stretches an organ or holds it under tension.

tent (tĕnt) ***n-*** portable shelter, usually made of waterproof canvas supported by poles and guyed by ropes attached to pegs in the ground. *as* ***modifier***: *a* tent *pole.* ***vi-*** to camp in such a shelter. ***—adj-*** **tent′ like′.**

Wall tent — Pup tent — Squad tent

ten·ta·cle (tĕn′ tə kəl) ***n-*** **1** one of the slender, flexible organs growing from the heads or around the mouths of certain animals and used for holding, feeling, etc. For picture, see *octopus*. **2** hairlike growth on some leaves.

ten·ta·tive (tĕn′ tə tĭv) ***adj-*** made or done as a trial; not final; provisional: *a* tentative *schedule*; *a* tentative *offer.* ***—adv-*** **ten′ ta·tive·ly.** ***n-*** **ten′ ta·tive·ness.**

ten·ter (tĕn′ tər) ***n-*** frame on which to stretch cloth to prevent shrinkage in drying. ***vt-*** to hang or stretch on such a frame.

ten·ter·hook (tĕn′ tər ho͝ok′) ***n-*** one of the sharp, hooked nails set on a tenter for stretching cloth.

on tenterhooks in an anxious or suspenseful state.

tenth (tĕnth) ***adj-*** **1** next after ninth. **2** the ordinal of 10; 10th. ***n-*** **1** the next after the ninth; 10th. **2** one of ten equal parts of a whole or group. **3** the last term in the name of a common fraction having a denominator of 10 or of the corresponding decimal fraction: *1/10 and .1 are each one* tenth. **4** *Music* an interval of ten tones on the scale, counting the extremes, as from C to E, and the harmonic combination of these tones. ***adv-***: *He spoke of you* tenth.

ten·u·ous (tĕn′ yo͞o əs) ***adj-*** **1** slender; thin; weak: *a* tenuous *thread*; *a* tenuous *grip on life.* **2** delicate; insubstantial: *a* tenuous *outline in the fog.* ***—adv-*** **ten′ u·ous·ly.** ***n-*** **ten′ u·ous·ness.**

ten·ure (tĕn′ yər) ***n-*** **1** a holding of something, especially of position, office, or property. **2** period during which an office or position is held. **3** the status of a teacher who has fulfilled certain requirements and cannot be dismissed except for misconduct.

te·pee or **tee·pee** (tē′ pē) ***n-*** a cone-shaped tent used by the Plains Indians. [from Sioux **tipi** meaning "used for dwelling."]

tep·id (tĕp′ ĭd) ***adj-*** slightly warm; lukewarm. ***—adv-*** **tep′ id·ly.** ***n-*** **tep′ id·ness.**

ter·bi·um (tûr′ bē əm) ***n-*** a rare-earth metal element. Symbol Tb, At. No. 65, At. Wt. 159.924.

Tepee

term (tûrm) ***n-*** **1** expression or word, especially one with a special meaning in some profession, science, art, etc.: *I don't understand the legal* terms *in this document.* **2** period of time set for a purpose; fixed, limited period of time: *the spring* term *at school.* **3** the time during which something is in effect; duration: *I am bound through the* term *of the contract.* **4** the end or limit of a period of time: *The contract is approaching its* term. **5** *Mathematics* (1) algebraic expression, or numerical expression, that consists only of a single constant or variable, or the product or quotient of constants and variables; monomial. (2) numerator or denominator of a fraction. **6 terms** conditions offered for acceptance in an agreement: *the* terms *of surrender.*

bring to terms to force to give in or agree. **come to terms** to arrive at an agreement. **in terms of** with reference to. **not on speaking terms** not friendly with one another. **on good** (or **bad**) **terms** of two or more people, to be friendly (or unfriendly).

ter·ma·gant (tûr′mə gənt) ***n-*** noisy, shrewish, quarrelsome woman. *as **modifier**: her* termagant *shrieking.*

ter·mi·na·ble (tûr′mə nə bəl) ***adj-*** such as can be terminated: *a* terminable *contract.* **—*n-* ter′mi·na·bil′i·ty** or **ter′mi·na·ble·ness.**

ter·mi·nal (tûr′mə nəl) ***adj-*** **1** forming the end or being at the end of something: *a* terminal *examination at the close of school*; *a* terminal *bud.* **2** ending in death: *a* terminal *illness.* ***n-*** **1** station at the end of a railway, bus line, or air line. **2** metal connection on an electric wire, battery, etc. **3** device such as a teletypewriter which enables a person to communicate with a computer. **—*adv-* ter′mi·nal·ly.**

ter·mi·nate (tûr′mə nāt′) ***vt-*** **[ter·mi·nat·ed, ter·mi·nat·ing]** **1** to put an end to; finish; conclude: *to* terminate *a friendship.* **2** to mark the end of; bound: *The river* terminates *our farm.* ***vi-*** to come to an end: *Our lease* terminates *in June.* **—*n-* ter′mi·na′tion.**

ter·mi·nol·o·gy (tûr′mə nŏl′ə jē) ***n-*** [*pl.* **ter·mi·nol·o·gies**] words or expressions, especially those belonging to a particular art, science, business, etc.: *the* terminology *of physics*; *medical* terminology. **—*adj-* ter′mi·no·log′i·cal** (-nə lŏj′ĭ kəl). ***adv-* ter′mi·no·log′i·cal·ly.**

term insurance ***n-*** insurance which is in effect for a specified period only and has a fixed premium.

ter·mi·nus (tûr′mə nəs) ***n-*** [*pl.* **ter·mi·ni** (-nī) or **ter·mi·nus·es**] **1** an end; limit. **2** station or town at the end of a railway line, bus line, etc. **3** boundary or border.

ter·mite (tûr′mīt′) ***n-*** any of various insects that live in social colonies like the ants and bees and feed on wood. Some kinds damage houses and trees.

Termite

tern (tûrn) ***n-*** any of various sea birds that resemble gulls, but are usually smaller and have sharper bills. Most terns have forked tails. ***Hom-*** turn.

terp·si·cho·re·an (tûrp′sə kôr′ē ən) ***adj-*** of or having to do with dancing.

terr. territory.

ter·race (tĕr′əs) ***n-*** **1** balcony or porch, used for dancing, dining, etc. **2** raised and level platform of earth, either paved or grown with grass and having sloping sides. **3** level strip along the side of a hill or mountain, used for farming. ***vt-*** **[ter·raced, ter·rac·ing]** to make such platforms on: *The Incas* terraced *the mountainsides in Peru.*

Terraces

ter·ra cot·ta (tĕr′ə kŏt′ə) ***n-*** **1** reddish-brown clay that is hard and durable when fired and is widely used in pottery, tiles, building material, etc. **2** the orange-brown color of this clay. **3** a statue of this material. **—*adj-* (terra-cotta):** *a* terra-cotta *vase.*

ter·ra fir·ma (tĕr′ə fûr′mə) ***n-*** solid earth; dry land.

ter·rain (tĕr′ān′, tə rān′) ***n-*** land, especially in respect to its contours and its suitability for a particular purpose.

ter·ra·pin (tĕr′ə pĭn) ***n-*** **1** any of various kinds of web-footed turtles of North and Central America having shells covered with horny shields. **2** the flesh of some such turtles, prized as food.

Diamondback terrapin, 7—8 in. long

ter·rar·i·um (tə râr′ē əm) ***n-*** [*pl.* **ter·rar·i·ums** or **ter·rar·i·a** (-ē ə)] an enclosure like a dry aquarium for growing plants indoors or keeping small land animals such as toads or lizards.

ter·res·tri·al (tə rĕs′trē əl) ***adj-*** **1** of or relating to the planet Earth: *Satellites have helped scientists study* terrestrial *weather patterns.* **2** consisting of land; not water or air: *the* terrestrial *surface of the earth.* **3** living on or in the ground. **—*adv-* ter·res′tri·al·ly.**

ter·ri·ble (tĕr′ə bəl) ***adj-*** **1** causing terror; dreadful; awful: *a* terrible *hurricane.* **2** distressing; causing sorrow: *a* terrible *accident.* **3** severe; causing extreme discomfort: *The heat was* terrible *last week.* **4** very bad; unpleasant: *a* terrible *book.* **—*adv-* ter′ri·bly.**

ter·ri·er (tĕr′ē ər) ***n-*** any of several kinds of small, active, intelligent dogs, such as the Airedale, Scotch, or Welsh terriers, once used to hunt small game.

Airedale terrier, 23 in. high

ter·ri·fic (tə rĭf′ĭk) ***adj-*** **1** arousing great fear or dread; terrible; appalling; alarming: *A* terrific *tornado almost destroyed the town.* **2** excessive; great: *The Presidency places a man under a* terrific *strain.* **3** *Slang* wonderful; marvelous; extremely good. **—*adv-* ter·rif′i·cal·ly.**

ter·ri·fy (tĕr′ə fī′) ***vt-*** **[ter·ri·fied, ter·ri·fy·ing]** to cause great alarm to; frighten: *The fire in the barn* terrified *the horses.* **—*adv-* ter′ri·fy′ing·ly:** *The slope was* terrifyingly *steep.*

ter·ri·tor·i·al (tĕr′ə tôr′ē əl) ***adj-*** of or having to do with a territory. **—*adv-* ter′ri·tor′i·al·ly.**

ter·ri·to·ry (tĕr′ə tôr′ē) ***n-*** [*pl.* **ter·ri·to·ries**] **1** large area of land; district or region. **2** an extent of land and water under the jurisdiction of a government or sovereign state: *The Northwest Territories is a* territory *of Canada.* **3** district alloted to a salesman or agent: *Tom's* territory *is outside Boston.* **4** land or space regarded by a person or animal as its special domain.

ter·ror (tĕr′ər) ***n-*** **1** overwhelming fear; fright: *He has a* terror *of heights.* **2** person or thing which terrifies or fills with fear or dread: *My cat is a* terror *to the dog next door.* **3** *Informal* annoying or mischievous person.

ter·ror·ism (tĕr′ə rĭz′əm) ***n-*** the committing of violent and terrifying acts for political purposes or to frighten a population into submission.

ter·ror·ist (tĕr′ər ĭst) ***n-*** person who believes in or practices terrorism. **—*adj-* ter′ror·is′tic.**

ter·ror·i·za·tion (tĕr′ər ə zā′shən) ***n-*** a terrorizing.

ter·ror·ize (tĕr′ə rīz′) ***vt-*** **[ter·ror·ized, ter·ror·iz·ing]** **1** to fill with terror by threats or acts of cruelty; terrify. **2** to control or dominate by terroristic means.

ter·ror-strick·en (tĕr′ər strĭk′ən) ***adj-*** in a state of extreme fright or intimidation.

ter·ry cloth (tĕr′ē) ***n-*** cotton fabric woven with a deep pile with the loops uncut. ***adj-*** **(terry-cloth):** *a* terry-cloth *robe.*

terse (tûrs) ***adj-*** [**ters·er, ters·est**] brief, concise, and to the point: *The witness gave a* terse *account of the event.* ***—adv-*** **terse′ly.** ***n-*** **terse′ness.**

ter·tian (tûr′shən) *Medicine* ***adj-*** recurring every other day, as attacks of certain fevers. ***n-*** fever which recurs every other day.

ter·ti·ar·y (tûr′shē ĕr′ē) ***adj-*** third in order of importance, value, rank, etc.

Ter·ti·ar·y (tûr′shē ĕr′ē) ***n-*** the first of the two periods of the Cenozoic era of geologic time. The Tertiary is marked by the appearance and development of mammals. ***adj-***: *the* Tertiary *period.*

test (tĕst) ***n-*** **1** examination; trial; critical evaluation: *a driver's* test. **2** questions and exercises to judge the skill, knowledge, and intelligence of a student: *The English* test is *tomorrow morning.* **3** something which tries or measures a person or thing: *Misfortune is often a* test *of a man's character.* **4** a chemical reaction or other procedure carried out to identify a substance, condition, etc.: *a* test *for copper in ore*; *a skin* test. ***vt-*** **1** to prove the quality, strength, etc., of a person or thing; try: *Misfortunes* test *a person's character.* **2** to examine in order to identify the presence of particular substances or conditions: *to* test *someone for allergies.* ***vi-***: *That alloy* tests *40% copper.* ***—adj-*** **test′a·ble.**

test out to try out: *The new process was* tested out.

Test. Testament.

tes·ta (tĕs′tə) ***n-*** [*pl.* **tes·tae** (-tē′)] the outer covering of a seed.

tes·ta·ment (tĕs′tə mənt) ***n-*** **1** written document in which a person provides for the disposal of his property after his death; will. **2** in the Bible, a dispensation or covenant; also, statement of faith or conviction. **3 Testament** either one of the two main parts of the Bible, the Old Testament or the New Testament.

tes·ta·men·ta·ry (tĕs′tə mĕn′tə rē) ***adj-*** **1** of or relating to a will or to the administration or settlement of a will: *the letters* testamentary. **2** given or bequeathed by a will. **3** done according to, or provided by, a will.

tes·tate (tĕs′tāt′) ***adj-*** in law, having made and left a will.

tes·ta·tor (tĕs′tā′tər) ***n-*** in law, a person who leaves a valid will at his death. ***—n-*** *fem.* **tes·ta′trix.**

[1]**test·er** (tĕs′tər) ***n-*** person or thing that tests; especially, a device for checking electrical parts. [from **test.**]

[2]**test·er** (tēs′tər) ***n-*** canopy over a four-poster bed, a tomb or a pulpit. [from Middle English **testere,** "headpiece," from Old French **testiere,** from **teste,** "head," from Late Latin **testa,** "skull," from Latin **testa,** "shell."]

tes·ti·cle (tĕs′tĭ kəl) ***n-*** either of the two testes of mammals.

tes·ti·fy (tĕs′tə fī′) ***vi-*** [**tes·ti·fied, tes·ti·fy·ing**] **1** to give testimony under oath in court: *He* testified *against the accused.* **2** to make a formal declaration: *The mayor* testified *in favor of the law.* **3** to bear witness: *Her work* testifies *to her ability.* ***vt-*** **1** to state or maintain under oath: *He* testified *his innocence. She* testified *that she did not see the robbery.* **2** to bear witness to: *Their smiles* testify *to their happiness.* ***—n-*** **tes′ti·fi′er.**

tes·ti·mo·ni·al (tĕs′tə mō′nē əl) ***n-*** **1** formal expression of esteem, such as a statement. **2** acknowledgement in writing of the value of something such as a new product or service; letter of recommendation. *as* ***modifier***: *a* testimonial *banquet*; *a* testimonial *plaque.*

tes·ti·mo·ny (tĕs′tə mō′nē) ***n-*** [*pl.* **tes·ti·mo·nies**] **1** statement made to establish a fact; especially, a statement given under oath in a court of law. **2** evidence; proof: *Her kind words were* testimony *of her compassion.*

tes·tis (tĕs′təs) ***n-*** [*pl.* **tes·tes** (-tēz′)] organ in animals that produces the male reproductive cells.

test pilot ***n-*** flier who tests newly designed aircraft.

test tube ***n-*** slender, hollow glass cylinder, closed at one end, used in chemical and biological laboratories.

tes·ty (tĕs′tē) ***adj-*** [**tes·ti·er, tes·ti·est**] irritable; cross: *a* testy *old man.* ***—adv-*** **tes′ti·ly.** ***n-*** **tes′ti·ness.**

tet·a·nus (tĕt′ə nəs) ***n-*** serious disease causing contraction of the muscles until they are rigid; lockjaw. It is caused by a germ that gets into the body through an open wound.

tête-à-tête (tāt′ə tāt′, *Fr.* tĕt′ä′tĕt′) ***n-*** private conversation between two persons, intimate chat.

Test tube

teth·er (tĕth′ər) ***n-*** rope or chain by which an animal is tied. ***vt-*** to tie (an animal) with a tether.

at the end of (one's) tether at the limit of (one's) endurance.

tet·ra·he·dron (tĕt′rə hē′drən) ***n-*** geometric solid having four plane sides of which all are triangles.

Teu·ton (to͞o′tən, tyo͞o′-) ***n-*** **1** one of an ancient Germanic people. **2** member of any Germanic nation.

Teu·ton·ic (to͞o tŏn′ĭk, tyo͞o-) ***adj-*** **1** of or relating to Germanic people. **2** Germanic.

Tex. Texas.

Tex·as leaguer (tĕk′səs) ***n-*** in baseball, a short fly ball that falls safely between the infield and outfield.

Texas Ranger ***n-*** member of the State police of Texas.

text (tĕkst) ***n-*** **1** the main body of writing in a book or on a printed page, as distinguished from the notes and illustrations. **2** a passage of the Bible taken as the theme of a sermon. **3** theme; subject: *the* text *of a speech.* **4** textbook. **5** printed or written version of something: *Which* text *of Shakespeare do you use?*

text·book (tĕkst′bo͝ok′) ***n-*** book written for the teaching of a certain subject.

tex·tile (tĕks′təl, -tīl′) ***n-*** woven or knit material; cloth. *as* ***modifier***: *the* textile *industry*; textile *fibers.*

tex·tu·al (tĕks′cho͞o′əl) ***adj-*** of or relating to a text or texts: *a* textual *error.* ***—adv-*** **tex′tu·al·ly.**

tex·ture (tĕks′chər) ***n-*** **1** kind or quality of surface: *Tweed has a rough* texture. **2** structure or arrangement of parts; composition: *This cake has a very spongy* texture.

tex·tured (tĕks′chərd) ***adj-*** having a rough or otherwise distinctive surface; not smooth and even: *a* textured *wallpaper*; *a* textured *masonry wall.*

Th symbol for thorium.

-th or **-eth** *suffix* used to form ordinal numbers: *four*th; *twenti*eth.

Thai (tī) ***n-*** **1** a native or inhabitant of Thailand, or one of his descendants. **2** the official language of Thailand. ***Hom-*** tie.

thal·a·mus (thăl′ə məs) ***n-*** [*pl.* **thal·a·mi** (-mī, -mē)] a part of the brain of vertebrates, located beneath the cerebrum, which is a receiving and relaying center for sensory impulses and for the feeling of pain, and is thought to be the site of consciousness.

thal·li·um (thăl′ē əm) ***n-*** a bluish-gray, soft, metal element found in certain ores of iron and zinc. Its compounds are poisonous and are used as rat poisons and insecticides. Symbol Tl, At. No. 81, At. Wt. 204.37.

thal·lo·phyte (thăl′ə fīt′) ***n-*** any of the fungi or algae, formerly classified as one phylum **(Thallophyta).**

thal·lus (thăl′əs) ***n-*** [*pl.* **thal·li** (-lī, -lē)] a simple plant body, such as occurs in fungi and algae, which is not differentiated into root, stem, or leaf.

than (t͟hăn, t͟hən) ***conj-*** in comparison with: *You read faster* than *Helen.*

other than with the exception of.

thane (thān) ***n-*** in the Middle Ages, a Scottish lord.

thank (thăngk) ***vt-*** to say that one is grateful to; express or show gratitude to: *I will* thank *him myself for the book.*
have (oneself) to thank to be solely to blame.
thank·ful (thăngk′ fəl) ***adj-*** feeling or showing gratitude or thanks; grateful: *I am* thankful *for this good weather.* ***—adv-*** **thank′ ful·ly.** ***n-*** **thank′ ful·ness.**
thank·less (thăngk′ ləs) ***adj-*** 1 not appreciated; unrewarding: *a* thankless *task.* 2 showing no appreciation; ungrateful. ***—adv-*** **thank′ less·ly.** ***n-*** **thank′ less·ness.**
thanks (thăngks) ***interj-*** thank you. ***n-*** *pl.* gratitude or an expression of gratitude.
thanks to owing or due to; because of: *It was* thanks to *him that things went so well.*
thanks·giv·ing (thăngks′ gĭv′ ĭng) ***n-*** expression of gratitude or thanks; a prayer expressing thanks. *as* ***modifier***: *a* thanksgiving *prayer.*
Thanks·giv·ing (thăngks′ gĭv′ ĭng) or **Thanksgiving Day** ***n-*** in the United States, the fourth Thursday in November, a day set apart for giving thanks to God. Thanksgiving was first celebrated by the Pilgrims at Plymouth in 1621. *as* ***modifier***: *his* Thanksgiving *dinner.*
that (t͟hăt) ***determiner*** (traditionally called demonstrative adjective or demonstrative pronoun) [*pl.* **those** t͟hōz)] 1 thing or person at a distance: *This is the house I was talking about, not* that *one.* 2 indicating a thing or person at a distance or already mentioned: *Give the papers to* that *boy over there.* 3 something already mentioned or pointed out: *Do I have to tell you* that *again?* 4 the other, as in contrast with this: *This is a nicer ring than* that *(ring).* 5 indicating the degree or amount previously mentioned or pointed out: *She lost the race by* that *much. She can walk* that *far.* ***pron-*** (relative pronoun) 1 who; whom; which: *the book* that *was here.* 2 in, on, or at which: *the years* that *he was gone.* 3 for which: *the reason* that *he came.* ***conj-*** 1 used to introduce clauses that can function as subjects, objects, and modifiers: *He said,* "That *I must go is certain." I know* that *he is there. We are sure* that *it is true. I'll look everywhere* that *I can.* 2 used to introduce clauses of purpose: *Work hard,* that *you may prosper.* 3 used to introduce subordinate clauses of result: *I am so sleepy* that *I can hardly see.* 4 used to introduce an expression of desire: *Oh,* that *what you say were true!*
at that at a given moment: *And,* at that, *she left.*
in that 1 as far as a certain thing is concerned: *He said it was pink, and* in that *he was right.* 2 since; because: *He cannot,* in that *he has not the tools.*
thatch (thăch) ***n-*** 1 straw, reeds or the like, used to cover a roof. 2 roof of such material: *Mice made their nests in the* thatch. 3 something that looks like thatch, such as thick, ragged hair. ***vt-*** to put thatch on.

Thatched cottage

that's (t͟hăts) 1 that is. 2 that has.
thaw (thȯ) ***vi-*** 1 to melt: *The ice* thawed *in the warm room.* 2 to become friendlier or less formal: *The guests* thawed *when the birthday party got under way.* ***vt-*** to cause to melt; also, to bring to a temperature above the freezing point: *The sun will* thaw *the snow.* Thaw *the turkey before you cook it.* ***n-*** a melting of ice; also, weather warm enough to melt ice: *The* thaw *came late this spring.*
the (t͟hə; t͟hē *before vowels)* ***definite article*** 1 pointing out a specific or known person or thing: *There's* the *man I told you about. The boy in* the *back row has* the *book.* 2 (t͟hē) emphasizing a person or thing as the best known, the greatest, etc.: *Our Christmas dance is* the *dance of the school year.* 3 making a noun general: The *horse is a useful animal.* 4 replacing a possessive adjective: *a pain in* the *back.* 5 (often considered a preposition) a; per; each: *three dollars* the *gallon.*
the·a·ter or **the·a·tre** (thē′ ə tər, thĭ′-) ***n-*** 1 place built or used for dramatic or musical performances, showing motion pictures, etc. 2 the drama and the activities connected with it; the writing and acting of plays: *He is writing a book on the modern American* theater. 3 scene, play, idea, etc., regarded as drama or dramatic material: *The chariot race in "Ben Hur" is good* theater. 4 area of action; arena: *General Eisenhower commanded the European* theater *in World War II. as* ***modifier***: *a* theater *design;* theater *critic;* theater *tickets.*
the·at·ri·cal (thē ă′ trĭ kəl) ***adj-*** 1 having to do with the theater or actors: *the* theatrical *profession; a* theatrical *tradition in the family.* 2 more appropriate for the theater than for real life; not natural; exaggerated; designed for effect: *She always does things in the most* theatrical *way.* ***—adv-*** **the·at′ ri·cal·ly.**
the·at·ri·cals (thē ă′ trĭ kəlz) *Informal* ***n-*** plays, skits, and other performances, usually amateur.
the·at·rics (thē ă′ trĭks) ***n-*** *pl.* highly dramatic behavior and effects.
thee (t͟hē) ***pron-*** objective case of **thou,** used mainly in religion and poetry, and used also by some Quakers as a subject pronoun.
theft (thĕft) ***n-*** act of stealing; robbery: *The* theft *was committed last week.*
their (t͟hâr) ***determiner*** (possessive case of the pronoun "they," now usually called possessive adjective) 1 of or belonging to them: *First prize was given to* their *class project.* 2 made or done by them: *The artists displayed* their *work.* 3 inhabited by them: *They went into* their *tent.* ***Homs-*** there, they're.
theirs (t͟hârz) ***pron-*** (possessive pronoun) thing or things belonging to them: *The book is* theirs *but you may borrow it. That car of* theirs *is worn out.* ***Hom-*** there's.
the·ism (thē′ ĭz′ əm) ***n-*** 1 belief in the existence of a god or gods. 2 belief in a personal God as the creator and supreme ruler of the universe. ***—n-*** **the′ ist.** ***adj-*** **the·is′ tic.**
them (t͟hĕm) ***pron-*** objective case of **they**: *I heard* them *singing. Put* them *on the shelf. Pass* them *the cookies. I waved to* them. *We went with* them.
the·mat·ic (thē mă′ tĭk) ***adj-*** of, relating to, or being a theme: *Loneliness is* thematic *in all his writing.* ***—adv-*** **the′ mat′ i·cal·ly.**
theme (thēm) ***n-*** 1 subject written or talked about; topic: *the* theme *of a discussion.* 2 short essay: *Students write* themes *at school.* 3 *Music* a short melody that occurs again and again in various forms in a composition.
them·selves (t͟həm sĕlvz′) ***pron-*** 1 reflexive form of **their**; their own selves: *They hid* themselves *quickly. They are proud of* themselves. 2 their normal or true selves: *After a fit of rage, they came to* themselves. 3 intensive form of *they*: *They* themselves *will come.*
by themselves 1 alone: *The two boys went hunting* by themselves. 2 without any help: *The children planned the party* by themselves.
then (t͟hĕn) ***adv-*** 1 at that time: *We were working* then, *but now we are resting.* 2 after that: *Eat dinner and* then *go to bed.* 3 therefore; in that case: *If you are sure you*

can climb it, then *do it! You won't go,* then? ***pron-*** that time; a time mentioned: *By* then *I will be ready.*

but then however; on the other hand: *I like my school,* but then *it is so far from home.* **now and then** once in a while. **now then** and now: *She said,* "Now then, *let's begin."* **then and there** at once; immediately.

thence (thĕns) ***adv-*** **1** from that place: *First she went to Paris, and* thence *to Rome.* **2** from or after that time: *a week* thence. **3** from that source, cause, or fact; therefore: *It* thence *appeared that he was entirely wrong.*

thence·forth (thĕns′fôrth′, thĕns′fôrth′) ***adv-*** from that time on; thereafter; also, from that place on: *They quarreled and* thenceforth *never spoke again.*

thence·for·ward (thĕns′fôr′wərd, -fôr′wərd) ***adv-*** thenceforth. Also **thence·for′wards.**

the·oc·ra·cy (thē ŏk′rə sē) ***n-*** [*pl.* **the·oc·ra·cies**] government by religious authorities; hence, government thought to be headed by gods or God.

the·oc·ra·tic (thē′ə krăt′ĭk) ***adj-*** **1** of or relating to a theocracy: *a* theocratic *ruler.* **2** based on theocracy: *a* theocratic *constitution.*

the·od·o·lite (thē ŏd′ə līt′) ***n-*** surveyor's transit.

the·o·lo·gi·an (thē′ə lō′jən) ***n-*** person who is expert in theology; especially, a person who writes theological essays, books, etc.

the·o·log·i·cal (thē′ə lŏj′ĭ kəl) ***adj-*** **1** of or relating to theology. **2** related to or engaged in preparation for religious ministry: *to complete one's* theological *studies*; *a* theological *student.* **—*adv-*** **the′o·log′i·cal·ly.**

theological virtues ***n-*** *pl.* faith, hope, and charity (or love), which provide spiritual completion for the four cardinal virtues. See *cardinal virtues.*

the·ol·o·gy (thē ŏl′ə jē) ***n-*** the systematic study of God or of the relation of man and the universe to God; the study of divinity: *Though very religious, my father had no interest in* theology. *as* ***modifier***: *a* theology *textbook.*

the·o·rem (thē′ər əm, thêr′əm) ***n-*** **1** a statement that can be logically proved from other statements. **2** *Mathematics* a statement or proposition that has been proved or can be proved on the basis of certain assumptions, undefined terms, and definitions.

the·o·ret·i·cal (thē′ə rĕt′ĭ kəl) ***adj-*** **1** relating to or depending on abstract principles or theories: *a* theoretical *solution*; *a* theoretical *essay.* **2** based on ideas rather than on fact or experience: *I have only a* theoretical *knowledge of business.* **—*adv-*** **the·o·ret′i·cal·ly.**

the·o·rist (thē′ə rĭst, thêr′ĭst) ***n-*** person who theorizes; one who draws conclusions from abstract principles or theories. Also **the′o·re·ti′cian** (thē′ər ə tĭsh′ən).

the·o·rize (thē′ə rīz′, thêr′īz′) ***vi-*** [**the·o·rized, the·o·riz·ing**] to form theories; speculate: *to* theorize *about the universe.* **—*n-*** **the′o·ri·za′tion.** ***n-*** **the′o·riz′er.**

the·o·ry (thē′ə rē, thêr′ē) ***n-*** [*pl.* **the·o·ries**] **1** the principles as distinguished from the practice of an art or science: *Although he did not draw well, he had studied art* theory. **2** in science, a general statement that logically accounts for everything that is definitely known about a phenomenon, but is not accepted as a final explanation because it also implies or depends upon specific statements that are not yet proven or tested. See also *hypothesis.* **3** a guess based upon observation and supported by some evidence: *After the first chapter, I had a* theory *about the outcome.* **4** abstract thought; speculation.

ther·a·peu·tic (thĕr′ə pyōō′tĭk) ***adj-*** **1** of or relating to therapy. **2** helpful for healing; curative; restorative: *His week in the country was very* therapeutic. **—*adv-*** **ther′a·peu′ti·cal·ly.**

ther·a·peu·tics (thĕr′ə pyōō′tĭks) ***n-*** *pl.* (takes singular verb) medical science and practice of therapy.

ther·a·pist (thĕr′ə pĭst) ***n-*** person who gives therapy.

ther·a·py (thĕr′ə pē) ***n-*** [*pl.* **ther·a·pies**] the treatment of physical or mental disease or injury; also, a particular treatment or kind of treatment.

there (thêr) ***adv-*** **1** in that or at that place: *Put it* there, *not here.* **2** to or toward that place; thither: *I can walk* there *in an hour.* **3** on that point; in that matter: *I disagree with you* there. ***pron-*** **1** that place or point: *I just came from* there. *Please read up to* there. **2** word of no meaning used to introduce a statement that something exists or is true: *I told him that* there *were two solutions.* There *is a new car outside.* **3** used as a vague intensifying substitute for a person's name or for "you": *Hello,* there! *Stop talking,* there! ***interj-*** exclamation of defiance, joy, sympathy, etc.: *I won't do it, so* there! There, *you did it!* There, there, *don't cry.* ***Homs-*** their, they're.

all there normally intelligent; sane: *He's not* all there.

►For usage note see HERE.

there·a·bouts (thâr′ə bouts′) ***adv-*** close to that time, place, degree, etc.: *We will come at six or* thereabouts. *They lived in Boston or* thereabouts. *He earned five thousand a year or* thereabouts. Also **there′a·bout′.**

there·af·ter (thâr ăf′tər) ***adv-*** from that time or place on; after that; afterwards: *For the first few days they came on time, but not* thereafter.

there·at (thâr′ăt′) ***adv-*** **1** for that reason; therefore: *He was not invited, and was sad* thereat. **2** at that point; thereupon: *She made a bow, and* thereat *left.*

there·by (thâr′bī′) ***adv-*** by that means: *She gave the dog a bone,* thereby *stopping his barking.*

there·for (thâr′fôr′, -fôr′) ***adv-*** for that, this, or it: *They gave money for a hospital and the equipment* therefor. ***Hom-*** therefore.

there·fore (thâr′fôr′) ***adv-*** for that reason; on account of that; hence: *He was sick and* therefore *missed three days.* ***Hom-*** therefor.

there·from (thâr′frŭm′, -frŏm′) ***adv-*** from this; from that; from it: *The project was financed by investment and the income* therefrom.

there·in (thâr ĭn′) ***adv-*** **1** in this or that place; in it: *The house and all the furniture* therein *are for sale.* **2** in that respect: *I thought him honest,* but therein *I was wrong.*

there·of (thâr′ŭv′, -ŏv′) ***adv-*** **1** of this; of that: *When he saw the wine, he drank* thereof. **2** from this or that cause: *He gobbled up the green fruit and became sick* thereof.

there·on (thâr ŏn′, -ôn′) ***adv-*** on that place or thing: *the table and all the silver* thereon.

there's (thârz) there is. ***Hom-*** theirs.

there·to (thâr tōō′) ***adv-*** **1** to it; to that: *He locked the box and lost the key* thereto. **2** *Archaic* moreover; also.

there·un·der (thâr′ŭn′dər) ***adv-*** under that, it, or them.

there·un·to (thâr ŭn′tōō) ***adv-*** thereto.

there·up·on (thâr′ə pŏn′, -pôn′) ***adv-*** **1** upon that; at once; immediately after: *The teacher said, "Ready," and* thereupon *Matilda began to read.* **2** thereon.

there·with (thâr′wĭth′, -wĭth′) ***adv-*** **1** with it; with that; with this: *He received a diploma and all the privileges connected* therewith. **2** thereupon: *Our host said, "Good-by," and* therewith *we left.*

there·with·al (thâr′wĭth ôl′) *Archaic* ***adv-*** **1** therewith; with that, it, or them. **2** at the same time; forthwith. **3** over and above; in addition.

therm- or **thermo-** *combining form* heat: *a* therm*ionic radio tube*; *a* thermo*meter.* [from Greek **thérmē** meaning "heat," and from **thermos,** "hot."]

ther·mal (thûr′məl) ***adj-*** **1** of or relating to heat: *a* thermal *unit.* **2** hot or warm: *a* thermal *bath.* ***n-*** a current of air moving upward because it is warmer than surrounding air.

thermal spring ***n-*** spring that produces hot water.
therm·i·on (thûr′ mī′ ən, -mē ən) ***n-*** a charged particle emitted by an incandescent body.
therm·i·on·ic (thûr′ mī ŏn′ ĭk, -mē ŏn′ ĭk) ***adj-*** relating to thermions or the emission of them.
ther·mo·coup·le (thûr′ mō kŭp′ əl) ***n-*** an accurate, sensitive thermometer consisting of a junction of two wires or bars of different metals, alloys, or semiconductors, whose other ends are connected to a voltmeter, galvanometer, etc. A temperature difference between the junction and the ends of the wires causes a weak electric current proportional to the temperature difference.
ther·mo·dy·nam·ic (thûr′ mō dī năm′ ĭk) ***adj-*** relating to the conversion of heat to mechanical forms of energy.
ther·mo·dy·nam·ics (thûr′ mō dī năm′ ĭks) ***n-*** (takes singular verb) branch of physics that deals with the quantitative relationships between heat and other forms of energy.
ther·mo·e·lec·tric (thûr′ mō ə lĕk′ trĭk) ***adj-*** relating to the relationship between temperature and electrical phenomena in metals, semiconductors, etc.
ther·mo·graph (thûr′ mə grăf′) ***n-*** instrument that records temperature readings on a graph.
ther·mom·e·ter (thər mŏm′ ə tər) ***n-*** instrument for indicating temperature, usually by the expansion and contraction of a material according to temperature. The commonest form is a tube containing mercury or colored alcohol, set against a Fahrenheit or centigrade scale. Other forms use a gas or metal as an indicating agent.

Centigrade and Fahrenheit thermometers

ther·mo·nu·cle·ar (thûr′ mō nōō′ klē ər) ***adj-*** **1** of, relating to, or involving nuclear fusion. **2** armed with or based on the hydrogen bomb.
ther·mo·plas·tic (thûr′ mō plăs′ tĭk) ***n-*** a plastic that is softened by heat and can be molded under pressure. ***adj-***: *a* thermoplastic *toy.*
Ther·mos bottle (thûr′ məs) ***n-*** **1** trademark name for a kind of vacuum bottle. **2 thermos bottle** vacuum bottle.
ther·mo·set·ting (thûr′ mō sĕt′ ĭng) ***adj-*** of a plastic, keeping its shape after being heated under pressure.
ther·mo·stat (thûr′ mə stăt′) ***n-*** instrument that automatically controls furnaces, air conditioners, refrigerators, etc., according to the readings of a thermometer contained in it. **—*adj-* ther′ mo·stat′ ic:** *a* thermostatic *control.* ***adv-*** **ther′ mo·stat′ i·cal·ly.**
the·sau·rus (thĭ sôr′ əs) ***n-*** [*pl.* **the·sau·rus·es** or **the·sau·ri** (-sôr′ ī, -sôr′ ē)] **1** book that lists synonyms and antonyms of its entry words, or lists all the words relating to a general idea, without making fine distinctions among their meanings. **2** storehouse or treasury.
these (thēz) ***determiner*** (traditionally called demonstrative adjective or demonstrative pronoun) *pl.* of **this:** *I know* these *people. Are* these *the ones you mean?*
The·se·us (thē′ sē əs, thē′ sōōs′) ***n-*** in Greek mythology, the great hero of Attica, famed for slaying the Minotaur in Crete and carrying off Ariadne, the king's daughter.
the·sis (thē′ səs) ***n-*** [*pl.* **the·ses** (-sēz)] **1** something stated or proclaimed, especially by a person who plans to support it by argument. **2** main point or argument contained in an essay, play, etc.; theme. **3** long essay, based on original research, offered by a candidate for an advanced degree at a college or university.
thes·pi·an (thĕs′ pē ən) ***n-*** an actor or actress. ***adj-*** **1** of or relating to drama; dramatic. **2 Thespian** of or relating to Thespis, a Greek poet of the sixth century B.C., who is credited with the invention of tragedy.
Thes·sa·lo·ni·ans (thĕs′ ə lō′ nē ənz) ***n-*** *pl.* (takes singular verb) either of two books of the New Testament consisting of letters written by the apostle Paul to the young church at Thessalonica.
The·tis (thē′ tĭs) ***n-*** in Greek mythology, a Nereid who was the mother of Achilles.
thews (thyōōz) ***n-*** *pl.* muscles; sinews.
they (thā) ***pron-*** (used as a plural subject in the third person) **1** the people, animals, or things named before: *The boys and girls met, and then* they *went to the art show.* **2** people in general: *What do* they *say?*
they'd (thād) **1** they would: *I think* they'd *be better off at home.* **2** they had: *They thought* they'd *come too early.*
they'll (thāl) **1** they will: *If they don't study,* they'll *regret it.* **2** they shall: *If I insist,* they'll *do it.*
they're (thâr) they are: *Do you think* they're *ready?* ***Homs-*** their, there.
they've (thāv) they have: *It seems that* they've *vanished.*
T.H.I. temperature-humidity index.
thi·a·mine (thī′ ə mən, -mēn′) or **thi·a·min** (-mən) See *vitamin* B_1.
thick (thĭk) ***adj-*** **[thick·er, thick·est] 1** large in diameter, or large between the broad surfaces; not thin: *a* thick *branch; a* thick *slice of bread.* **2** of a liquid, heavy; not watery: *a* thick *syrup;* thick *condensed milk.* **3** dense; close together: *the* thick *woods;* thick *hair.* **4** in distance through; in distance between opposite sides: *a board two inches* thick. **5** foggy; not clear: *The weather was* thick *and drizzly.* **6** hoarse; muffled: *a* thick *voice.* **7** stupid; dull. **8** *Informal* friendly: *The two were very* thick *for a while.* ***n-*** **1** the thickest part of anything: *the* thick *of the thumb.* **2** the most intense moment; center of action: *the* thick *of the battle.* **—*adv-* thick′ ly.** ***n-*** **thick′ ness.**
thick and fast many and rapidly. **through thick and thin** through fortune and misfortune; under all conditions.
thick·en (thĭk′ ən) ***vt-*** to make thick or thicker: *Mother* thickened *the gravy with flour.* ***vi-*** **1** to become thicker: *The woods* thickened *as we pushed into them.* **2** to become more complicated or intricate: *The plot* thickened.
thick·en·er (thĭk′ ən ər) ***n-*** **1** something added to a substance to make it thicker; thickening: *Put some* thickener *in that soup.* **2** person that thickens.
thick·en·ing (thĭk′ ən ĭng) ***n-*** **1** substance added to a liquid to thicken it. **2** a thickened place or part.
thick·et (thĭk′ ət) ***n-*** clump of dense and tangled underbrush. **—*adj-* thick′ et·ed:** *a* thicketed *hillside.*
thick-head·ed (thĭk′ hĕd′ əd) ***adj-*** **1** *Informal* stupid; dense. **2** having a thick head: *a* thick-headed *stalk.* **—*n-* thick′ head′ ed·ness.**
thick·set (thĭk′ sĕt′) ***adj-*** **1** stocky; husky; burly: *a* thickset *body.* **2** growing closely: *the* thickset *branches.*
thick-skinned (thĭk′ skĭnd′) ***adj-*** **1** having a thick skin. **2** insensitive, especially to hints or unpleasant treatment.
thick-wit·ted (thĭk′ wĭt′ əd) ***adj-*** stupid; dull.
thief (thēf) ***n-*** [*pl.* **thieves**] person who steals; especially, one who steals secretly rather than by force.

thieve (thēv) ***vi-*** **[thieved, thiev·ing]** to commit theft: *He* thieves *for a living.* ***vt-***: *The bird* thieved *a piece of string for its nest.*

thiev·er·y (thē′ və rē) ***n-*** [*pl.* **thiev·er·ies**] act or habit of stealing: *They were punished for their* thievery.

thieves (thēvz) *pl.* of **thief.**

thiev·ish (thē′ vĭsh) ***adj-*** **1** given or addicted to stealing. **2** typical or characteristic of a thief: *his* thievish *habits.* **—*adv-*** **thiev′ ish·ly.** ***n-*** **thiev′ ish·ness.**

thigh (thī) ***n-*** muscular part of the leg between the knee and the trunk; especially, the upper part.

thigh·bone (thī′ bōn′) ***n-*** femur.

thim·ble (thĭm′ bəl) ***n-*** **1** metal or plastic cap for the finger, used to push a needle in sewing. **2** metal lining used inside a fixed loop at the end of a rope or cable to reduce wear.

Thimble

thim·ble·ful (thĭm′ bəl fo͝ol′) ***n-*** a very small quantity of something.

Nautical thimble

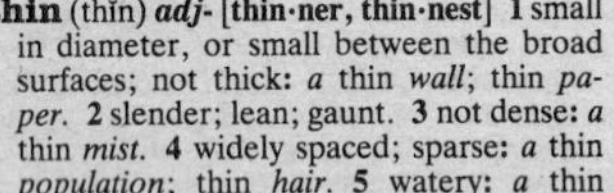

thin (thĭn) ***adj-*** **[thin·ner, thin·nest]** **1** small in diameter, or small between the broad surfaces; not thick: *a* thin *wall*; thin *paper.* **2** slender; lean; gaunt. **3** not dense: *a* thin *mist.* **4** widely spaced; sparse: *a* thin *population*; thin *hair.* **5** watery: *a* thin *soup.* **6** weak; not deep or strong: *The singers had* thin *voices.* **7** easy to see through; flimsy: *a* thin *excuse.* ***vt-*** **[thinned, thin·ning]** **1** to make less fat, thick, or dense: *They* thinned *out the woods.* **2** to reduce in numbers: *Drought had* thinned *the corn crop.* ***vi-*** to become less fat, dense, or numerous: *He has* thinned *down in recent months.* **—*adv-*** **thin′ ly.** ***n-*** **thin′ ness.**

thine (thīn) *Archaic* ***determiner*** variant of **thy** used before words beginning with a vowel. ***pron-*** (possessive pronoun) thing or things belonging to you: *Are these words* thine?

thing (thĭng) ***n-*** **1** any separate object that can be known through the senses, thought or spoken of, or imagined; entity. **2** act; affair: *What a* thing *to do! This* thing *is none of your concern.* **3** person or animal (spoken of with affection, contempt, pity, etc.): *The poor* thing *broke its leg.* **4 things** (1) personal belongings: *I can get all my* things *into one suitcase.* (2) state of affairs; situation: *Are* things *getting better or worse?* **5 the thing** something in fashion: *Boots are* the thing *this year.*

think (thĭngk) ***vi-*** **[thought, think·ing]** **1** to use the mind in order to come to decisions, form ideas, opinions, judgments, etc.: *Always* think *before you speak. Do animals* think? **2** to consider; meditate; muse. **3** to have in mind, or call to mind, a thought, idea, or image (of) something: *to* think *of a picture.* **4** to judge the value (of) someone or something: *I* think *highly of people like him.* **5** to plan or intend: *I* thought *of going tomorrow.* ***vt-*** **1** to occupy the mind with; imagine: *to* think *no evil.* **2** to believe; hold as an opinion (often takes a clause as object): *I* think *that you are wrong.* **—*adj-*** **think′ a·ble.** ***n-*** **think′ er.**

think better of to reconsider; change one's mind about.
think nothing of to consider of slight value; ignore.
think over to consider: *Before you quit* think *it* over.
think through to reason (something) out in the mind.
think twice to consider very carefully.
think up to conceive or devise in the mind.

thin·ner (thĭn′ ər) ***n-*** something used to thin a substance, especially paint, varnish or shellac.

thin-skinned (thĭn′ skĭnd′) ***adj-*** very sensititive to slights, insults, reproaches, etc.; easily hurt.

third (thûrd) ***adj-*** **1** next after second: *She was* third *in her class.* **2** ordinal of 3; 3rd: *He lives on* Third *Avenue.* ***n-*** **1** the next after the second; 3rd: *She was the* third *in line.* **2** one of three equal parts of a whole or a group: *He ate a third of the pie.* **3** the last term in the name of a common fraction having a denominator of 3: *1/3 is one* third. **4** the forward gear above second gear in a motor vehicle. **5** *Music* an interval of three tones on the scale counting the extremes, as from C to E, and the harmonic combination of these tones. **6** in baseball, third base: *He was out at* third. ***adv-***: *He spoke of you* third.

third class ***n-*** **1** in U.S. postage, the class of mail that includes advertising and other printed matter, but not newspapers and magazines. **2** class of accommodations on trains, ships, etc., that is usually the least expensive and least comfortable. **—*adj-*** **(third-class):** *a* third-class *letter.* ***adv-*** **(third-class):** *to travel* third-class.

third degree ***n-*** *Informal* police interrogation of a prisoner which resorts to brutality in extracting a confession. *as* ***modifier*** **(third-degree):** *The detective used* third-degree *methods in questioning.*

third estate ***n-*** in former times, the common people, as distinguished from the nobility and the clergy.

third·ly (thûrd′ lē) ***adv-*** as third in a series.

third party ***n-*** **1** person other than the two main persons involved in a particular situation. **2** political party existing in addition to the major parties normally functioning in a two-party system.

third person *Grammar* ***n-*** **1** the form of the personal or possessive pronoun which stands for or refers to the person or persons, or the thing or things, spoken of. In English these forms are "he," "him," "his," "she," "her," "hers," "it," "its," "they," "them," "their," "theirs." **2** the form of the verb used with "he," "she," or "it," as "he sits," or with "they," as "they are."

third rail ***n-*** rail which runs parallel to the tracks of an electric railway and carries the electric current.

third-rate (thûrd′ rāt′) ***adj-*** **1** third in quality or rank. **2** very poor; quite inferior.

Third World or **third world** ***n-*** group of countries aligned with neither the noncommunist nor communist blocs. *as* ***modifier***: Third World *countries.*

thirst (thûrst) ***n-*** **1** dry feeling in the mouth and throat caused by the need for something to drink. **2** strong desire; craving: *a* thirst *for praise.* ***vi-*** **1** to desire something to drink; to be thirsty. **2** to have a strong desire; have a craving: *to* thirst *for knowledge.*

thirst·y (thûr′ stē) ***adj-*** **1** feeling thirst. **2** without moisture; parched: *the* thirsty *garden.* **3** wanting something very much. **4** *Informal* producing thirst: *Digging is* thirsty *work.* **—*adv-*** **thirst′ i·ly.** ***n-*** **thirst′ i·ness.**

thir·teen (thûr′ tēn′) ***n-*** **1** amount or quantity that is one greater than 12. **2** *Mathematics* (1) the cardinal number that is the sum of 12 and 1. (2) a numeral such as 13 that represents this cardinal number. *as* ***determiner*** (traditionally called adjective or pronoun): *There are* thirteen *shirts here and* thirteen *there.*

thir·teenth (thûr′ tēnth′) ***adj-*** **1** next after twelfth. **2** the ordinal of 13; 13th. ***n-*** **1** the next after the twelfth; 13th. **2** one of thirteen equal parts of a whole or group. **3** the last term in the name of a fraction having a denominator of 13: *1/13 is one* thirteenth.

thir·ti·eth (thûr′ tē əth) ***adj-*** **1** next after twenty-ninth. **2** the ordinal of 30; 30th. ***n-*** **1** the next after the twenty-ninth; 30th. **2** one of thirty equal parts of a whole or group. **3** the last term in the name of a fraction having a denominator of 30: *1/30 is one* thirtieth.

thir·ty (thûr′ tē) ***n-*** [*pl.* **thir·ties**] **1** amount or quantity that is one greater than 29. **2** *Mathematics* (1) the cardinal number that is the sum of 29 and 1. (2) a numeral such as 30 that represents this cardinal number. *as **determiner*** (traditionally called adjective or pronoun): *There were* thirty *swans here and* thirty *there.*

thir·ty-sec·ond note (thûr′ tē sĕk′ ənd) *Music* ***n-*** note held 1/32nd as long as a whole note. For picture, see *note.*

this (t͟hĭs) ***determiner-*** (traditionally called demonstrative adjective or demonstrative pronoun) [*pl.* **these** (t͟hēz)] **1** thing or person near at hand or just mentioned: *I think* this *is the picture I wanted you to see.* **2** indicating a thing or person near at hand or just mentioned: *John, I want you to meet* this *man.* **3** fact or idea about to be mentioned or pointed out: *What I mean is* this. **4** thing or person contrasted with another thing or person: *You will agree that* this *is a better house than that.* **5** referring to a thing or person contrasted with another thing or person: *I can tell that* this *painting is finer than that one.* **6** indicating the degree or amount previously mentioned or now pointed out: *She can walk* this *far.*

this·tle (thĭs′ əl) ***n-*** **1** any of several plants with spiny, deeply cut leaves, a spiny stem, and handsome, usually purple, flowers. **2** flower of this plant. The purple thistle is the national flower of Scotland **—*adj-* this′ tly.**

Thistle

this·tle·down (thĭs′ əl doun′) ***n-*** the soft down on ripe thistle seeds.

thith·er (thĭt͟h′ ər, t͟hĭt͟h′-) *Archaic* ***adv-*** to or toward that place; in that direction.

tho or **tho’** (t͟hō) though.

thole (thōl) ***n-*** upright rod, often one of a pair, set into the side of a boat to keep the oar in place. Also **thole′ pin′** (thōl′ pĭn′).

thong (thŏng, thòng) ***n-*** **1** narrow strip of leather, especially one used as a fastening. **2** lash of a whip.

Tholepins

Thor (thòr, thôr) ***n-*** in Norse mythology, the god of war, thunder, and strength.

tho·rac·ic (thə răs′ ĭk) ***adj-*** of or relating to the thorax or the chest: *to perform* thoracic *surgery.*

tho·rax (thôr′ ăks) ***n-*** [*pl.* **tho·rax·es** or **tho·ra·ces** (thə rā′ sēz′)] **1** the part of the human body between the neck and the abdomen, containing the cavity framed by the ribs and the breastbone in which the lungs, heart, and other organs are situated. For picture, see *abdomen.* **2** a corresponding part in the body of higher vertebrates. **3** in insects, the middle of the three main sections of the body, bearing the organs of locomotion.

thor·i·um (thôr′ ē əm) ***n-*** rare, dark-gray, radioactive metal element. Symbol Th, At. No. 90, At. Wt. 232.038.

thorn (thòrn, thôrn) ***n-*** **1** sharp, slender spike growing on certain trees, shrubs, and vines. **2** in animals, a similar projection; spine. **3** any of various trees or shrubs bearing thorns. **—*n-* thorn′ less.**

thorn in (one’s) side anything that annoys; source of worry.

thorn apple ***n-*** **1** the fruit of the hawthorn; haw. **2** jimson weed.

thorn·y (thòr′ nē, thôr′-) ***adj-*** [**thorn·i·er, thorn·i·est**] **1** covered with thorns; spiny. **2** annoying; difficult; perplexing: *a* thorny *problem.* **—*n-* thorn′ i·ness.**

thor·ough (thûr′ ō) ***adj-*** **1** complete; to the fullest degree: *a* thorough *success.* **2** accurate; careful; exhaustive: *a* thorough *job of research.* **3** absolute; in every way. **—*adv-* thor′ ough·ly.** ***n-*** **thor′ ough·ness.**

thor·ough·bred (thûr′ ə brĕd′) ***n-*** **1** an animal of pure breed: *That dog is a* thoroughbred. **2** person or thing thought to have the grace, refinement, spirit, etc., of a splendid racehorse. **3 Thoroughbred** a horse descended from one of three sires whose offspring are recorded in the English Stud Book. ***adj-***: *a* thoroughbred *horse.*

thor·ough·fare (thûr′ ə fâr′) ***n-*** street, road, or passage open at both ends.

thor·ough·go·ing (thûr′ ō gō′ ĭng) ***adj-*** leaving nothing undone; complete; thorough.

those (t͟hōz) ***determiner*** (traditionally called demonstrative adjective or demonstrative pronoun) *pl.* of **that**: *I know* those *people. Are* those *the ones you mean?*

thou (t͟hou) ***pron-*** old, poetic, or religious form of “you” (used always as a subject).

though (t͟hō) ***conj-*** **1** in spite of the fact that: *He kept on working,* though *he was tired.* **2** but; yet: *He is intelligent,* though *not as quick as his brother.* ***adv-*** however; nevertheless: *You can’t trust him,* though.

as though *Informal* as if. **even though** in spite of the fact that; even if: *I’ll go,* even though *it’s raining.*

[1]**thought** (thòt) ***n-*** **1** process of thinking; reasoning and imagining; mental activity; reflection; meditation: *I found him deep in* thought. **2** something that the mind conceives, considers, remembers, or imagines; idea; opinion; belief: *He recorded his* thoughts *in a diary.* **3** care; consideration; concern: *Give some* thought *to the future.* **4** way of thinking characteristic of a particular period, group, etc.: *modern* thought; *scientific* thought. *as **modifier***: *my* thought *processes*; thought *patterns.* [from Middle English **thoght,** from Old English **(ge)thōht,** “a thing thought of.”]

[2]**thought** (thòt) *p.t. & p.p.* of **think.**

thought·ful (thòt′ fəl) ***adj-*** **1** full of thought; thinking; serious: *a* thoughtful *expression.* **2** kind; considerate of others. **—*adv-* thought′ ful·ly.** ***n-*** **thought′ ful·ness.**

thought·less (thòt′ ləs) ***adj-*** **1** not thinking; reckless; rash: *The* thoughtless *student forgot his book.* **2** lacking concern for others; inconsiderate: *a* thoughtless *host.* **—*adv-* thought′ less·ly.** ***n-*** **thought′ less·ness.**

thou·sand (thou′ zənd) ***n-*** amount or quantity that is one greater than 999; 1,000. *as **determiner*** (always preceded by another determiner): *a* thousand *cars here and a* thousand *there.*

thou·sand·fold (thou′ zənd fōld′) ***n-*** a thousand times: *larger by a* thousandfold. ***adj-*** amounting to a thousand times: *a* thousandfold *increase in production.*

thous·andth (thou′ zəndth) ***adj-*** **1** next after 999th. **2** the ordinal of 1,000; 1,000th. ***n-*** **1** the next after the 999th; 1,000th. **2** one of a thousand equal parts of a whole or group. **3** the last term in the name of a common fraction having a denominator of 1,000 or of the corresponding decimal fraction: *1/1000 and .001 are each one* thousandth.

thrall (thròl) ***n-*** **1** slave or serf; hence, person who has lost his freedom to some dominating power: *a helpless* thrall *to alcohol.* **2** slavery; serfdom; servitude.

thral·dom or **thrall·dom** (thròl′ dəm) ***n-*** servitude; slavery; bondage.

---

fāte, făt, dâre, bärn; bē, bĕt, mêre; bīte, bĭt; nōte, hŏt, môre, dòg; fŭn, fûr; to͞o, bo͝ok; oil; out; tar; thin; t͟hen; hw for wh as in *wh*at; zh for s as in u*s*ual; ə for a, e, i, o, u, as in *a*go, lin*e*n, per*i*l, at*o*m, min*u*s

thrash (thrăsh) ***vt-*** **1** to beat or flog. **2** to thresh.
thrash about to move or toss restlessly or violently.
thrash out to discuss thoroughly.
thrash over to go over again and again: *She* thrashed *the matter* over *in her mind.*

thrash·er (thrăsh′ ər) ***n-*** **1** person who thrashes. **2** brown thrasher. **3** thresher.

thrash·ing (thrăsh′ ĭng) ***n-*** **1** beating; flogging. **2** threshing.

thread (thrĕd) ***n-*** **1** thin, twisted strand of silk, cotton, wool, etc., from which cloth is woven or with which things are sewed. **2** any similar fiber or filament: *the* threads *of a spiderweb.* **3** something running through and connecting the parts of anything: *I can't follow the* thread *of his story.* **4** the spiral ridge of a screw or nut. ***vt-*** **1** to put a thread through: *to* thread *a needle*; *to* thread *beads.* **2** to provide with, or as with, a spiral ridge: *to* thread *a screw.* **3** to pass through (something difficult or perplexing): *They* threaded *their way through narrow streets.* **—*adj-*** **thread′ like′.** ***n-*** **thread′ er.**

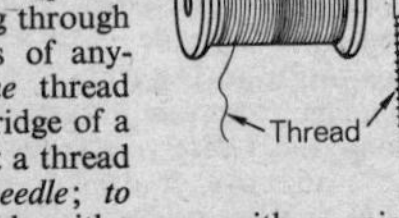

thread (one's) way to go with care and difficulty: *We* threaded our way *through the reefs.*

thread·bare (thrĕd′ bâr′) ***adj-*** **1** worn down to the threads; shabby: *a* threadbare *carpet*; *a* threadbare *suit.* **2** worn out; trite: *a* threadbare *joke.*

thread·y (thrĕd′ ē) ***adj-*** **[thread·i·er, thread·i·est] 1** consisting of or covered with fibers or filaments: *a* thready *root.* **2** of liquids, forming threads; viscid. **3** resembling a thread in thinness or weakness: *a* thready *voice*; *a* thready *pulse.* **—*n-*** **thread′ i·ness.**

threat (thrĕt) ***n-*** **1** expression of an intention to hurt or punish: *I took his statement as a* threat. **2** a warning of unpleasantness or evil to come: *the* threat *of war.*

threat·en (thrĕt′ ən) ***vt-*** **1** to offer a threat to: *He* threatened *me.* **2** to announce as a threat; make a threat of: *They* threaten *war.* **3** to be a warning of: *The sky* threatens *rain.* ***vi-*** to give warning of itself; be about to happen: *A storm* threatens. *Disaster* threatens. **—*n-*** **threat′ en·er.** ***adv-*** **threat′ en·ing·ly.**

three (thrē) ***n-*** **1** amount or quantity that is one greater than two; 3. **2** *Mathematics* (1) the cardinal number that is the sum of 2 and 1. (2) a numeral such as 3 that represents this cardinal number. *as* ***determiner*** (traditionally called adjective or pronoun): *There are* three *coats here and* three *there.*

three-base hit ***n-*** in baseball, a triple. Also **three′-bag′ ger** (thrē′ băg′ ər).

three-di·men·sion·al (thrē′ də mĕn′ shən əl) ***adj-*** **1** of, having, or relating to the three dimensions of space. **2** giving an illusion of depth and perspective: *a method of taking* three-dimensional *photographs.*

three·fold (thrē′ fōld′) ***adj-*** **1** three times as many or as much. **2** having three parts: *Our trip served a* threefold *purpose.* ***adv-***: *He increased his earnings* threefold.

three·pence (thrĭp′ əns) ***n-*** small British coin equal to three British pennies.

three·pen·ny (thrĭp′ ə nē) *Brit.* ***adj-*** **1** costing or worth threepence. **2** of little value; poor.

Three R's ***n-*** *pl.* reading, writing, and arithmetic.

three·score (thrē′ skôr′) ***determiner-*** (traditionally called adjective) three times twenty; sixty: *He lived* threescore *years.*

three·some (thrē′ səm) ***n-*** **1** group of three persons or things. **2** golf match in which two players, using one ball and taking turns hole by hole, compete with a single player.

thren·o·dy (thrĕn′ ə dē) ***n-*** [*pl.* **thren·o·dies**] song of lamentation or sorrow; dirge.

thresh (thrĕsh) ***vt-*** to separate (grain) from stalks, husks, etc.; also, to separate grain from (a harvest of ripened plants). ***vi-*** to toss or move about wildly; thrash.

thresh·er (thrĕsh′ ər) ***n-*** **1** person who threshes. **2** threshing machine. **3** thresher shark.

thresher shark ***n-*** large shark having a long tail with which it threshes the water to herd food fish together.

threshing machine ***n-*** large machine used on farms for threshing; thresher.

thresh·old (thrĕsh′ ōld′ *also* thrĕsh′ əld) ***n-*** **1** the stone or piece of wood under a door; sill of a doorway. **2** point of entering; beginning point: *the* threshold *of a new era.* **3** in psychology and physiology, the point or degree of intensity at which a stimulus becomes just barely perceptible or produces a response: *the* threshold *of pain.*

threw (thro͞o) *p.t.* of **throw.** ***Hom-*** through.

thrice (thrīs) ***adv-*** **1** three times. **2** in a threefold manner or degree; greatly: *He was* thrice *blessed.*

thrift (thrĭft) ***n-*** careful management of money and possessions; economy; habit of saving.

thrift·less (thrĭft′ ləs) ***adj-*** extravagant; wasteful. **—*adv-*** **thrift′ less·ly.** ***n-*** **thrift′ less·ness.**

thrifty (thrĭf′ tē) ***adj-*** **[thrift·i·er, thrift·i·est] 1** not extravagant; saving; economical: *a* thrifty *housewife.* **2** thriving; prosperous; flourishing: *a* thrifty *plant.* **—*adv-*** **thrift′ i·ly.** ***n-*** **thrift′ i·ness.**

thrill (thrĭl) ***n-*** feeling or quiver of joy, excitement, fear, etc.: *the* thrill *of a first plane ride.* ***vt-*** to fill with intense emotion; stir deeply: *She* thrilled *the audience with her singing.* ***vi-*** **1** to feel excitement or a strong wave of emotion: *She* thrilled *at the idea.* **2** to quiver; tremble: *to* thrill *with terror.* **—*adv-*** **thrill′ ing·ly.**

thrill·er (thrĭl′ ər) ***n-*** **1** motion picture, play, book, etc., that arouses terror and excitement. **2** event or experience that arouses such feelings.

thrive (thrīv) ***vi-*** **[thrived** or **throve** (thrōv), **thrived** or **thriv·en** (thrĭv′ ən), **thriv·ing] 1** to flourish; prosper; increase in wealth or property; succeed: *The business* thrived *under new management.* **2** to grow vigorously; improve physically: *He* thrives *in this climate.*

throat (thrōt) ***n-*** **1** muscular sac connecting the back of the mouth with the esophagus; pharynx. **2** front of the neck between the collarbone and the chin. **3** any narrow entrance or passage: *the* throat *of a bottle.* *as* ***modifier***: *a* throat *muscle*; *a* throat *lozenge.*

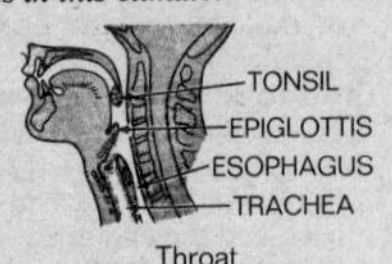

Throat

a lump in the throat a tight feeling in the throat, as when one tries not to cry.

throat·ed (thrō′ təd) ***adj-*** **1** having a certain kind of throat: *a yellow-*throated *bird.* **2** in or having a certain kind or tone of voice: *a deep-*throated *roar.*

throat·latch (thrōt′ lăch′) ***n-*** the strap of a horse's bridle or halter which passes under the throat.

throat·y (thrō′ tē) ***adj-*** **[throat·i·er, throat·i·est]** uttered from the throat or as if from the throat; guttural: *a* throaty *voice.* **—*adv-*** **throat′ i·ly.** ***n-*** **throat′ i·ness.**

throb (thrŏb) ***vi-*** **[throbbed, throb·bing]** to beat, pulsate, or vibrate rhythmically and powerfully: *My heart* throbbed. *The drums* throbbed *in the night.* ***n-***: *I heard the* throb *of an engine.*

throes (thrōz) ***n-*** *pl.* spasms or convulsions of agony: *in the* throes *of disease*; *the* throes *of civil war.*

throm·bo·sis (thrŏm bō′ səs) *Medicine* ***n-*** [*pl.* **throm·bo·ses** (sēz′)] the formation of a blood clot in the heart or in a blood vessel, causing a local obstruction to the flow of blood.

throm·bus (thrŏm′ bəs) ***n-*** [*pl.* **throm·bi** (-bī′, -bē)] blood clot formed in thrombosis.

throne (thrōn) ***n-*** **1** the chair of state of a king, bishop, or other high dignitary. **2** royal power or authority; sovereignty: *The* throne *commands obedience.* ***vt-*** [**throned, thron·ing**] to enthrone. ***Hom-*** thrown.

throng (thrŏng, thrὸng) ***n-*** large gathering of people; crowd. ***vt-*** to crowd into; fill: *Soldiers* thronged *the streets.* ***vi-***: *People* thronged *towards the platform.*

throt·tle (thrŏt′ əl) ***vt-*** [**throt·tled, throt·tling**] **1** to choke by pressing on the windpipe; strangle. **2** to hold down or back; suppress: *He* throttled *his feelings. The dictator* throttled *all opposition.* ***n-*** **1** valve to control the flow of fuel. **2** the handle or pedal that controls this valve.

throttle down (or **back**) to reduce the speed of an engine or vehicle by giving it less fuel.

through (thrōō) ***prep-*** (in senses 1 and 2 considered an adverb when the object is clearly implied but not expressed) **1** from the beginning to the end of: *We stayed* through *the winter. I read* through *the book.* **2** in one side or end and out the other side or end of: *to bore* through *a plank; to drive* through *a city.* **3** here and there in; around and about in: *The dogs ran* through *the streets. I strolled* through *the fields.* **4** by means of: *I reached her* through *a friend.* **5** as a result of: *He succeeded* through *hard work.* ***adv-*** **1** in a thorough way; entirely: *The meat is cooked* through. **2** to the end or to a destination or conclusion: *to get a message* through; *to see a job* through. ***adj-*** **1** going all the way; not closed or partial: *a* through *passage.* **2** going to the end without stop or change: *a* through *plane.* ***Hom-*** threw.

be through to be finished: *Are you* through *with your work?* **through and through** completely; thoroughly.

through·out (thrōō out′) ***prep-*** **1** in every part of: *There was smoke* throughout *the house.* **2** during the whole of: *It stormed* throughout *the night.* ***adv-*** **1** everywhere; in every part: *The jewelry is gold* throughout. **2** from beginning to end: *He remained loyal* throughout.

through·way (thrōō′ wā′) ***n-*** expressway.

throve (thrōv) *p.t.* of **thrive.**

throw (thrō) ***vt-*** [**threw, thrown, throw·ing**] **1** to fling or hurl with the arm; pitch; toss: *to* throw *a ball.* **2** to give forth or cast (a glance, shadow, etc.): *She* threw *him a glance.* **3** to upset; make someone fall. **4** to put or place in a certain condition or position: *The fire* threw *the people into confusion.* **5** to move (a switch or lever) to connect or disconnect. **6** in ceramics, to shape on a potter's wheel. **7** *Informal* to give or have (a party, dance, etc.). **8** *Slang* to amaze or disconcert (someone) extremely. ***vi-*** to cast or hurl something: *He* throws *with his left hand.* ***n-*** **1** the act of hurling, casting, or flinging. **2** a cast of dice. **—*n-* throw′ er.**

a stone's throw a short distance.

throw away to waste (an opportunity).

throw back to repulse: *We* threw back *the enemy.*

throw cold water on to discourage.

throw in *Slang* to add as an extra; include.

throw in the towel (or **sponge**) *Slang* to give up; quit.

throw off to avoid or repel successfully.

throw on to put on hastily or carelessly.

throw (oneself) at to make a great effort to gain the affection or attention of someone.

throw open **1** to open suddenly and widely. **2** to remove restrictions from.

throw out **1** to discard; dispose of. **2** *Informal* to eject or evict. **3** to put forth: *to* throw out *a suggestion.* **4** in baseball, to put out (a base runner) by throwing the ball to a teammate covering a base.

throw over to abandon; leave; jilt.

throw together *Informal* to put together in a hurry.

throw up to vomit.

throw·back (thrō′ băk′) ***n-*** something that is patterned or modeled after an earlier type or condition: *The new styles were a* throwback *to another era.*

thrown (thrōn) *p.p.* of **throw.** ***Hom-*** throne.

thru (thrōō) through.

thrum (thrŭm) ***vt-*** [**thrummed, thrum·ming**] to play idly or listlessly on (a stringed musical instrument); strum: *to* thrum *a guitar.* ***vi-*** **1** to speak droningly and tiresomely. **2** to make a low, humming sound: *The wires* thrummed *in the wind.* ***n-*** low strumming or similar sound.

[1]**thrush** (thrŭsh) ***n-*** any of a large, nearly world-wide group of small or medium-sized songbirds, most often of plain color, but sometimes with spotted throat and breast. [from Middle English **thrusche** and **thrusch,** from Old English **thrysce.**]

Wood thrush, 7—8 in. long

[2]**thrush** (thrŭsh) *Medicine* ***n-*** mouth disease, especially of infants, caused by a fungus and marked by small, white patches. [probably of Scandinavian origin, perhaps from Danish **trøske.**]

thrust (thrŭst) ***vt-*** [**thrust, thrust·ing**] **1** to push or shove with sudden force: *She* thrust *the money into his hand.* **2** to stab or pierce. ***vi-*** **1** to attack with a pointed weapon; stab or lunge at something: *to* thrust *with a dagger.* **2** to push against something or to force one's way, such as through a crowd. ***n-*** **1** a violent or sudden push or shove. **2** a stab: *the* thrust *of a sword.* **3** the force of reaction that propels a jet plane or a rocket in the forward direction, and is due to the force exerted in the opposite direction by gases expelled from rear jet nozzles. **4** in mechanics, a stress tending to push a part out of position: *the* thrust *of rafters on the walls.*

thru·way (thrōō′ wā′) ***n-*** throughway.

thud (thŭd) ***n-*** **1** heavy, dull sound. **2** blow; thump. ***vi-*** [**thud·ded, thud·ding**] to fall or hit with a dull sound.

thug (thŭg) ***n-*** violent criminal; gangster; assassin.

Thu·le (thōō′ lē) ***n-*** in ancient geography, the part of the world regarded as furthest north, thought now to have been either Iceland, Norway, or the Shetland and Orkney islands; hence, any mysterious or remote region.

thu·li·um (thōō′ lē əm) ***n-*** rare-earth metal element. Symbol Tm, At. No. 69, At. Wt. 168.934.

thumb (thŭm) ***n-*** **1** in man and other primates, the short, thick first finger of the hand, which can be used opposite the other fingers for grasping and manipulating. For picture see *finger.* **2** the part of a mitten or glove that covers this finger. ***vt-*** **1** to feel, rub, or handle with this finger, especially in order to read or consult (a book). **2** *Informal* to ask for or obtain (a ride) or make (one's way) by signaling with this finger. ***vi-*** *Informal* to hitchhike. **—*adj-* thumb′ like′.**

all thumbs clumsy. **thumbs down** *Informal* sign of rejection or disapproval. **thumbs up** sign of acceptance or approval. **under the thumb of** under the power of.

thumb through to go through (a book, magazine, etc.) hastily, reading here and there.

---

fāte, făt, dâre, bärn; bē, bĕt, mêre; bīte, bĭt; nōte, hŏt, môre, dὸg; fŭn, fûr; tōō, bŏŏk; oil; out; tar; thin; th̶en; hw for wh as in *wh*at; zh for s as in u*s*ual; ə for a, e, i, o, u, as in *a*go, lin*e*n, per*i*l, at*o*m, min*u*s

thumb index ***n-*** in dictionaries and other reference books, a series of indentations cut into the outside edge of the pages, which show the various sections one might wish to consult directly.

thumb·nail (thŭm′ nāl′) ***n-*** the nail of the thumb.

thumbnail sketch ***n-*** concise summary.

thumb·print (thŭm′ prĭnt′) ***n-*** fingerprint of a thumb.

thumb·screw (thŭm′ skrōō′) ***n-*** **1** screw having a flattened, upright head, often oval or shaped like a pair of wings, that can be grasped between the thumb and forefinger for turning. **2** formerly, an instrument of torture used for crushing the thumb.

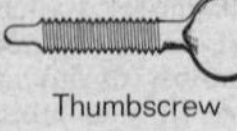
Thumbscrew

thumb·tack (thŭm′ tăk′) ***n-*** tack, usually having a very broad, circular head, which can be pressed into wood, cardboard, etc., with the thumb. ***vt-***: *He* thumbtacked *the notice onto the bulletin board.*

thump (thŭmp) ***n-*** **1** a hard, heavy blow. **2** the sound made by such a blow: *It fell with a* thump. ***vt-*** to pound, strike, or beat with dull, heavy blows: *He* thumped *the wall with his fists.* ***vi-***: *His heart* thumped *with excitement.* **—*n-* thump′ er.**

thump·ing (thŭm′ pĭng) *Informal* ***adj-*** large; great.

thun·der (thŭn′ dər) ***n-*** **1** rumbling or crashing sound caused by the passage of lightning through the air. **2** any noise resembling such a sound: *the* thunder *of guns.* ***vi-*** to make a loud, crashing noise: *First it* thundered, *then it started to rain. The cannon* thundered. ***vt-*** to shout with a roar: *He* thundered *commands from the deck of the ship.* **—*n-* thun′ der·er.**

steal (someone's) thunder to use ideas or methods that someone else was intending to use, before he can.

thun·der·bird (thŭn′ dər bûrd′) ***n-*** in the folklore of certain North American Indian tribes, a huge bird believed to produce thunder, lightning, and rain.

thun·der·bolt (thŭn′ dər bōlt′) ***n-*** **1** flash of lightning followed by a clap of thunder. **2** anything, especially bad news, that is sudden, unexpected, and terrible.

thun·der·clap (thŭn′ dər klăp′) ***n-*** **1** loud crash of thunder. **2** something sharp, loud, or sudden that resembles this: *a* thunderclap *of applause.*

thun·der·cloud (thŭn′ dər kloud′) ***n-*** dark, heavy cloud charged with electricity and producing lightning and thunder; cumulonimbus.

thun·der·head (thŭn′ dər hĕd′) ***n-*** round mass of cumulus clouds, usually dark with shining white edges, often seen before a thunderstorm.

thun·der·ous (thŭn′ der əs) ***adj-*** full of or like thunder: *a* thunderous *applause.* **—*adv-* thun′ der·ous·ly.**

thun·der·show·er (thŭn′ dər shou′ ər) ***n-*** brief fall of rain, accompanied by thunder and lightning.

thun·der·storm (thŭn′ dər stôrm′, -stôrm′) ***n-*** storm of lightning, thunder, and usually rain.

thun·der·struck (thŭn′ dər strŭk′) ***adj-*** amazed; astonished; stunned: *I was* thunderstruck *by his death.*

Thurs. or **Thur.** Thursday.

Thurs·day (thûrz′ dā, -dē) ***n-*** the fifth day of the week.

thus (thŭs) ***adv-*** **1** in this or that manner; in the following way: *Do the outline* thus. **2** to this degree or extent; so: *We have had no news* thus *far.* **3** therefore; consequently: *He is out of town and* thus *unable to attend.*

thwack (thwăk) ***vt-*** to strike with something flat; whack. ***n-***: *a* thwack *with a paddle.*

thwart (thwôrt) ***vt-*** to hinder or frustrate by opposing; cross; block: *My next move* thwarted *him. We* thwarted *the enemy's scheme.* ***n-*** plank or other support placed crosswise between the gunwales of a boat or canoe and used chiefly as a seat or rest.

thy (thī) ***determiner*** (possessive case of the pronoun "thou," now usually called possessive adjective) old, poetic, or religious form of **your.**

thyme (tīm) ***n-*** small herb with fragrant leaves, used for seasoning. ***Hom-*** time.

thy·mus (thī′ məs) ***n-*** [*pl.* **thy·mus·es**] **1** ductless gland that produces lymphocytes and is believed to have a major influence on the development of immunity. It is found in the chest of infants, beneath the breastbone, but gradually wastes away. **2** similar organ present in the young of vertebrates. Also **thymus gland.**

thy·roid (thī′ roid) ***n-*** **1** (also **thyroid gland**) ductless gland lying on either side of the windpipe in the neck below the pharynx, consisting of two lobes and secreting a hormone, thyroxin, which regulates body growth and the level of bodily metabolism. **2** thyroid cartilage. **3** medicine prepared from animal thyroid glands, used to help people whose own thyroids do not work properly. ***adj-*** **1** of or relating to the thyroid gland or the thyroid cartilage. **2** shield-shaped.

thyroid cartilage ***n-*** in anatomy, the chief cartilage of the larynx, forming its outer wall or Adam's apple.

thy·rox·in (thī rŏk′ sən) ***n-*** a colorless, crystalline hormone secreted by the thyroid gland. Thyroxin is now manufactured synthetically.

thy·self (thī sĕlf′) ***pron-*** poetic, old, or religious form of **yourself.**

ti (tē) *Music* the seventh note of a musical scale. ***Homs-*** tea, tee.

Ti symbol for titanium.

ti·ar·a (tē ăr′ ə, -är′ ə, tī âr′ ə) ***n-*** **1** head ornament like a small crown, worn by women. **2** the Pope's crown, consisting of three separate crowns, one above the other.

Woman wearing tiara

Ti·bet·an (tĭ bĕt′ ən) ***adj-*** of or relating to Tibet, its inhabitants, or its culture. ***n-*** **1** chief language of Tibet. **2** an inhabitant of Tibet.

tib·i·a (tĭb′ ē ə) ***n-*** [*pl.* **tib·i·ae** (tĭb′ ē ē, -ē ī) or **tib·ias**] the inner and larger of the two bones of the leg or hind limb, extending from the knee to the ankle; shinbone. **—*adj-* tib′ i·al:** *a* tibial *fracture.*

tic (tĭk) ***n-*** a twitching of the muscles, especially of the face. ***Hom-*** tick.

[1]**tick** (tĭk) ***vi-*** **1** to make a slight clicking or tapping sound which is regularly repeated: *A watch* ticks. **2** *Informal* to operate; function; run: *The machine won't* tick. ***vt-*** to mark or note with check marks, dots, etc. ***n-*** **1** light, regular clicking or tapping sound, as that made by a clock. **2** a mark like a check or dot. [from an imitation of the sound of a watch.] ***Hom-*** tic.

make (someone or **something) tick** *Informal* to be the cause or source of behavior: *What* makes *him* tick?

tick off **1** to count or measure by ticking: *The clock* ticked off *ten seconds.* **2** *Informal* to mark with a check or tick; also, to present in a series of statements. **3** *Informal* to reprimand.

[2]**tick** (tĭk) ***n-*** **1** any of various tiny animals related to the spiders, that attack the skin of man and other warm-blooded animals and are often carriers of disease. **2** any of various small insects that are related to the fly and suck blood and live on the bodies of certain animals. [from earlier English **tike** and **teke.**] ***Hom-*** tic.

Sheep tick

Dog tick

[3]**tick** (tĭk) ***n-*** **1** cloth case for pillows, mattresses, etc., which contains the filling. **2** ticking. [from Latin **thēca,** from Greek **thḗke** meaning "a case; chest."] ***Hom-*** tic.

⁴tick (tĭk) *Brit. Informal* ***n-*** credit: *He has* tick *at the tobacconist's.* [contracted from **ticket.**] ***Hom-*** tic.

tick·er (tĭk′ ər) ***n-*** **1** something that ticks. **2** telegraphic instrument that prints stock quotations or news on a paper tape. **3** *Informal* the heart.

ticker tape ***n-*** paper tape on which a telegraphic ticker records information.

ticker-tape parade ***n-*** procession in honor of some hero or distinguished person, who rides in an open car and is showered with ticker tape and torn paper.

tick·et (tĭk′ ĭt) ***n-*** **1** slip of paper or card that allows the holder certain privileges, such as transportation, entrance to amusements, etc. **2** small tag or label stating the price, size, etc., of goods. **3** list of candidates offered by a particular party, group, or faction, to be voted upon by the public: *the* Liberal *ticket*; *the* Democratic *ticket.* **4** summons issued to a person alleged to have violated a traffic law: *a* ticket *for speeding. as* ***modifier***: *the* ticket *booth at a theater.* ***vt-*** **1** to mark or identify with a tag or label. **2** to issue a traffic summons to.

tick fever ***n-*** any of several diseases that are transmitted by the bite of a tick.

tick·ing (tĭk′ ĭng) ***n-*** strong, closely woven cloth, usually striped, used to cover mattresses and pillows; tick.

tick·le (tĭk′ əl) ***vt-*** **[tick·led, tick·ling] 1** to touch in a light way, producing a tingling sensation and usually causing laughter. **2** to please or amuse; delight: *The idea* tickled *me.* ***vi-*** to feel a tingling sensation: *My nose* tickles. ***n-*** a tingling or itching, or the touch causing this sensation.

tick·ler (tĭk′lər) ***n-*** **1** person or thing that tickles. **2** card index, memorandum book, or any other automatic reminder to bring matters to timely attention.

tick·lish (tĭk′ lĭsh) ***adj-*** **1** easily aroused to laughter, squirming, etc., by light touches on the skin. **2** delicate or risky to handle: *a* ticklish *problem.* **3** easily upset or irritated; sensitive: *She is* ticklish *on the subject of waste.* ***—adv-*** **tick′ lish·ly.** ***n-*** **tick′ lish·ness.**

tick-tack-toe (tĭk′ tăk′ tō′) ***n-*** game in which two players alternately put crosses or circles in a block of nine squares, trying to get three of the same marks in a line before the opponent does.

tid·al (tī′ dəl) ***adj-*** **1** of, relating to, or resembling a tide or tides: *the* tidal *rhythm*; *a* tidal *movement of the earth's crust.* **2** holding water that is moved by the tides: *a* tidal *river.* **3** caused by a tide or tides: *a* tidal *current.*

tidal wave ***n-*** **1** one of a series of enormous and usually destructive ocean waves produced by undersea earthquakes or oceanic volcanic explosions; tsunami. **2** any widespread movement or exhibition of strong emotion, opinion, feeling, etc.: *a* tidal wave *of popular opposition.*

tid·bit (tĭd′ bĭt′) ***n-*** small, choice bit of anything: *a* tidbit *of cake*; *a* tidbit *of gossip.* Also **titbit.**

tid·dly·winks (tĭd′ lē wĭngks′) ***n-*** game in which players try to snap small disks into a cup by pressing their edges with larger disks.

tide (tīd) ***n-*** **1** rhythmic rising and falling of ocean waters, with high water occurring about every twelve hours at any given place, caused by the gravitational pull of the moon and sun. Much less noticeable tides occur in seas and large lakes. **2** anything that rises and falls or ebbs and floods in a similar way: *a* tide *of immigrants.* **3** *Archaic* time. *as* ***modifier***: *a* tide *gauge*; tide *table*; tide *chart.* ***Hom-*** tied. ***—adj-*** **tide′ less.**

turn the tide to change to the opposite condition.

tide over to enable (one or someone) to manage.

tide·land (tīd′ lănd′, -lənd) ***n-*** land that is flooded during high tide.

tide·wa·ter (tīd′ wô′ tər, -wŏ′ tər) ***n-*** **1** water affected by the rise and fall of the tide, such as in streams along a seacoast. **2** lowlands along a seacoast.

ti·dings (tī′ dĭngz) ***n-*** *pl.* news; information; message.

ti·dy (tī′ dē) ***adj-*** **[ti·di·er, ti·di·est] 1** neat; orderly; trim: *a* tidy *room.* **2** *Informal* considerable: *He saved a* tidy *sum.* ***vt-*** **[ti·died, ti·dy·ing]** to make neat; put in order (often followed by "up"): *to* tidy *up a room.* ***vi-***: *They* tidied *up before their guests arrived.* ***n-*** any of various articles for keeping things clean, such as a small cover for the back of a chair. ***—adv-*** **ti′ di·ly.** ***n-*** **ti′ di·ness.**

tie (tī) ***vt-*** **[tied, ty·ing] 1** to attach, fasten, or bind (something) with a string, rope, etc., by bringing the ends together and knotting: *to* tie *a tag to a box*; *to* tie *one's shoelaces.* **2** to make a knot or bow in: *to* tie *a scarf.* **3** to form (a knot, bow, etc.): *Show me how to* tie *a bowline.* **4** to equal in score: *to* tie *a record*; *to* tie *another team.* **5** to cause the scores in (a game, contest, etc.) to be equal for all teams or players: *His run* tied *the game.* **6** *Music* to connect (two notes of the same pitch) with a curved line showing that they are to be played or sung as one sustained note with the combined time values. **7** to make (an artificial fly for fishing). ***vi-*** **1** to be designed for a knot: *This sash* ties *at the back.* **2** to make the same score: *Two teams* tied. ***n-*** **1** necktie. **2** condition in which scores, number of votes, etc., are equal for all participants: *The election ended in a* tie. **3** crosswise timber to which railroad tracks are fastened. **4** bond or connection: *a family* tie; *business* ties; *a strong* tie *between two schools.* **5** cord or rope used to fasten or secure: *The* ties *are attached to the flap of the tent.* **6** *Music* curved line connecting two notes of the same pitch to show that they are to be played or sung as one sustained note with the combined time values. ***Hom-*** Thai.

fit to be tied extremely angry or upset.

tie down to restrict; limit: *His business* ties *him* down.

tie in to have a connection or association: *This* ties in *with what I told you yesterday.*

tie the knot to marry.

tie the score to cause the scores of competing teams to be equal.

tie up 1 to halt the activity of: *The strike* tied up *the East Coast.* **2** to place (property, money, etc.) in such a condition that it cannot be freely used: *He* tied *his money* up *in real estate.* **3** to be unavailable because busy or in use: *He's* tied up *in a meeting. The telephone is* tied up.

tie-in (tī′ ĭn′) ***n-*** **1** necessary connection. **2** something that relates to something else.

tie·pin (tī′ pĭn′) ***n-*** ornamental pin for holding down a necktie; stickpin.

¹tier (têr) ***n-*** row, rank, or layer; especially, one of the seating levels above the lowest in a theater, baseball park, etc. ***Hom-*** ¹tear. [from Middle English **tire,** from Old French.]

²ti·er (tī′ ər) ***n-*** person or thing that ties. [from **tie.**]

tierce (têrs) ***n-*** **1** former liquid measure equivalent to 42 gallons. **2** sequence of three playing cards in the same suit. **3** third position in fencing. **4** *Music* interval of a third.

tie-up (tī′ ŭp′) ***n-*** **1** a stopping of work or action because of a strike, accident, etc.: *a* tie-up *in transportation.* **2** *Informal* connection or relation.

tiff (tĭf) ***n-*** slight quarrel; show of anger; spat.

ti·ger (tī′ gər) ***n***- largest of the cats, found in India, Siberia, China, Malaya, and Indonesia. It has tawny yellow fur with black stripes. *as* ***modifier***: *a* tiger *hunt*; tiger *cub*; tiger *cage*. ***—adj***- **ti′ ger·like′.**

Tiger, about 10 ft. long

tiger beetle ***n***- any of various beetles that live in dry or sandy places and feed on other insects.
tiger cat ***n***- **1** domestic cat with striped markings somewhat like those of a tiger. **2** any of several wildcats somewhat resembling tigers, such as the ocelot and the serval. **3** any of several small pouched mammals of Australia and Tasmania, with spotted markings, that somewhat resemble cats.
ti·ger·eye (tī′ gər ī′) ***n***- semiprecious yellow-brown stone having a changeable color like the eyes of a tiger. Also **ti′ ger's-eye′.**
ti·ger·ish (tī′ gər ĭsh) ***adj***- **1** tigerlike. **2** bloodthirsty; fiercely cruel.
tiger lily ***n***- orange-colored lily spotted with black.
tiger moth ***n***- any of a group of moths with broad striped or spotted wings and stout bodies.
tiger shark ***n***- large, brownish-gray, usually striped shark that is dangerous to swimmers and divers.
tight (tīt) ***adj***- **[tight·er, tight·est] 1** not loose; fastened or applied firmly: *The tiles aren't* tight. *These bolts are* tight. **2** having a close texture or fit that will not allow the passage of water, air, etc., in or out: *a* tight *pot lid*; *a* tight *faucet*. **3** taut or stretched: *a* tight *wire*. **4** fitting close to a part of the body, usually too close for comfort: *a* tight *belt*; tight *shoes*. **5** leaving no room to spare; very close: *a* tight *fit*; *a* tight *squeeze*; tight *quarters*. **6** having no loose ends or sloppy place; neat: *a* tight *argument*. **7** not easily obtained; scarce: *Money is* tight. **8** *Informal* difficult to handle or manage: *to be in a* tight *situation*. **9** strict; stringent: *a* tight *control over a business*. **10** *Informal* close: *a* tight *game*. **11** *Informal* stingy. **12** *Slang* intoxicated. ***adv***- firmly; securely. ***—adv***- **tight′ ly.** ***n***- **tight′ ness.**
sit tight *Informal* to refuse to move or change. **sleep tight** to sleep deeply and restfully. **tight squeeze** difficult passage or situation that one barely gets through.
tight·en (tī′ tən) ***vt***- to draw or make tight: *to* tighten *a screw*. ***vi***-: *The rope* tightened.
tight-fist·ed (tīt′ fĭs′ təd) *Informal* ***adj***- stingy.
tight-lipped (tīt′ lĭpt′) ***adj***- **1** having the lips closed tightly. **2** silent; secretive.
tight·rope (tīt′ rōp′) ***n***- tightly stretched rope or cable on which acrobats walk and balance themselves while performing; highwire. *as* ***modifier***: *a* tightrope *act*; tightrope *walker*. Also **tight′ wire′** (tīt′ wīər′).
tights (tīts) ***n***- (takes singular verb) garment that fits tightly over the legs and lower part of the body and is worn by circus performers, dancers, etc.
tight·wad (tīt′ wŏd′) *Slang* ***n***- a stingy person; miser.
ti·gress (tī′ grəs) ***n***- female tiger.
tike (tīk) tyke.
til·de (tĭl′ də) ***n***- **1** in Spanish, an accent mark [~] placed over the letter "n" to indicate that it is followed by a /y/ sound before the next vowel. Spanish "cañon" is pronounced (kän yōn′) and appears in English as "canyon." **2** in Portuguese, a similar mark placed over a vowel to indicate a nasal sound, as in "lã" which is pronounced (lă^{n}).
tile (tīl) ***n***- **1** piece of terra cotta or cement, used for roofing. **2** any of various flat pieces of glazed earthenware or porcelain, cemented together to make a watertight covering on floors, walls, etc.; also, a linoleum or plastic square used chiefly to surface floors. **3** tiling: *a roof of* tile. **4** earthenware or cement pipe used as a drain. *as* ***modifier***: *a* tile *floor*; *a* tile *roof*. ***vt***- **[tiled, til·ing]** to cover with tiles.
til·ing (tī′ lĭng) ***n***- **1** a surface of tiles. **2** tiles collectively.
[1]till (tĭl) ***prep***- to the time of; until: *Wait* till *one o'clock*. ***conj***- **1** until; to the time when: *Wait* till *I return*. **2** before or unless: *He won't come* till *you call him*. [from Old English **til** meaning "to," from Old Norse **til.**]
[2]till (tĭl) ***vt***- to plow and prepare (land, soil, a field, etc.) for raising crops; cultivate. [from Old English **tillan** meaning "to till land; strive after."] ***—adj***- **till′ a·ble.**
[3]till (tĭl) ***n***- drawer or other container in which money is kept, especially in a store. [from Middle English **tillen** meaning "to draw; pull," from Old English **-tyllan.**]
[4]till (tĭl) ***n***- in geology, mass of clay, pebbles, boulders, etc., carried and deposited by a glacier but not arranged in strata. [origin uncertain.]
till·age (tĭl′ ĭj) ***n***- **1** a tilling of land: *the* tillage *of 100 acres*. **2** land under cultivation. Also **tilth.**
[1]till·er (tĭl′ ər) ***n***- the handle of a rudder by which a boat is steered. [from Middle English **tillen** meaning "something to pull by," and related to **[3]till.**]

Tiller

[2]till·er (tĭl′ ər) ***n***- person who tills land. [from **[2]till.**]
til·ler·man (tĭl′ ər mən) ***n***- [*pl.* **til·ler·men**] **1** person who steers a boat with a tiller. **2** fireman who steers the rear end of a ladder truck.

Knights tilting

tilt (tĭlt) ***vi***- **1** to slope; slant: *The land* tilts *toward the sea*. **2** in a medieval tournament, to fight with lances on horseback. **3** to rush (at) as if with a lance: *He* tilted *at all his critics*. ***vt***- to cause to slope or slant; tip: *Don't* tilt *the table*. ***n***- **1** a sloping or slanting position: *the* tilt *of her head*; *the* tilt *of a roof*. **2** a duel with lances on horseback; a joust.
full tilt at full speed: *I ran* full tilt *against a fence*. **tilt at windmills** to attack imaginary enemies.
tilth (tĭlth) ***n***- tillage.
tim·ber (tĭm′ bər) ***n***- **1** trees suitable for, or planted for, cutting into lumber. **2** lumber. **3** a beam or other relatively heavy piece of lumber: *He needed* timbers *and planks for building his barn*. ***vt***- **1** to cut trees from (land) for sawing into lumber: *They* timbered *the hillside*. **2** to use or put in place (large wooden beams) for building: *to* timber *a barn*. ***vi***- to cut down and saw trees as a business or occupation; lumber. ***Hom***- timbre.
tim·bered (tĭm′ bərd) ***adj***- **1** covered with trees; wooded. **2** built with exposed timbers and having the space between filled with plaster: *a* timbered *cottage*.
tim·ber hitch ***n***- hitch used for tying a rope to a log or spar when the pull will be in the direction of the length of the log or spar.
tim·ber·ing (tĭm′ bər ĭng) ***n***- **1** lumbering. **2** timber or timbers when in place as part of a building, ship, etc.
tim·ber·land (tĭm′ bər lănd′) ***n***- forest land.

timber line *n-* line on mountains and in arctic regions beyond which trees will not grow because of the cold.
timber wolf *n-* the large, gray wolf of North America.
tim·bre (tăm′ bər, tĭm′-) *n-* the special quality given to a sound by its overtones, and by which voices, musical instruments, etc., can be distinguished from each other even though they have the same pitch. ***Hom-*** timber.
tim·brel (tĭm′ brəl) *n-* small drum or tambourine.
time (tīm) *n-* **1** past, present, and future, taken separately or as a whole: *until the end of* time. **2** amount of; duration; number of seconds, minutes, hours, etc.: *How much* time *do you need?* **3** instant, minute, etc., when something happens: *Nobody was around at the* time *of the explosion.* **4** regular, planned, or appropriate moment or period for something to happen: *It is* time *to go home.* **5** hour, minutes, seconds, by the clock: *What* time *is it?* **6** period associated with certain historical happenings; epoch or age: *in Washington's* time. **7** part of the year associated with special activity; season: *harvest* time; *carnival* time. **8** *Music* the grouping of rhythmic beats; tempo. **9** system of measuring the passage of hours, days, etc.: *daylight saving* time; *standard* time. **10** single occasion or instance: *Do that exercise five* times. **11** an experience extending over a certain period: *a hard* time *leaving.* **12** the rate of speed at which something is done: *to run in double-quick* time. **13** period that an employee works; also, the pay received: *He earns double* time *on holidays.* **14 times** a period or era regarded as good or bad for the persons involved: *Those were good* times. *We had hard* times *for a while.* ***vt-*** **[timed, tim·ing] 1** to choose the moment for: *He* timed *his visit to suit my convenience.* **2** to measure the speed of: *to* time *a runner.* **3** to regulate (a machine that operates in cycles). ***Hom-*** thyme.

against time trying to finish before a certain time. **at the same time** however; nevertheless. **at times** once in a while; now and then. **at one time 1** together. **2** earlier. **beat time** to tap one's foot, finger, etc., in the rhythm of music one is playing, singing, or hearing. **behind the times** not up to date on current events, ideas, etc. **for the time being** for now; for the present. **from time to time** now and then. **gain time 1** to go at too fast a rate: *Our clock* gains time. **2** to save time. **in good time 1** soon; quickly. **2** at the right time. **in no time** in very little time: *I'll have this finished* in no time. **in time 1** eventually; in the end. **2** before it is too late. **3** keeping the tempo in music, marching, dancing, etc.: *Please sing* in time. **keep time 1** to record the hours worked by employees. **2** to march, sing, play, etc., in the proper rhythm. **3** to beat time. **lose time** to go at too slow a rate. **make time** to work, travel, etc., at a rapid pace. **on time 1** not late. **2** to be paid for in installments: *They bought the furniture* on time. **out of time** not in the right rhythm, tempo, etc. **take (one's) time** to use as much time as is needed for a certain act; work or behave deliberately: *He* took his time *and did a thorough job.* **time after time** or **time and again** repeatedly; again and again. **time out** period of rest, recess, etc., in a game or other regulated activity. **time out of mind** longer than anyone can remember.
time and a half *n-* one and a half times one's usual wage, paid for overtime work.
time bomb *n-* bomb prepared to go off at a set time.
time capsule *n-* container for preserving records and objects of the life of its period, deposited for discovery by men of the future.
time·card (tīm′ kärd′) *n-* card for recording the hours worked, usually by stamping in a time clock.
time clock *n-* clock equipped for automatically recording something, especially the times of arrival and departure on the timecards of employees.
time con·sum·ing (tīm′ kən sōō′ mĭng, -syōō′ mĭng) ***adj-*** taking up a lot of time: *a* time-consuming *job.*
time exposure *n-* in photography, a long exposure not made automatically by the shutter of the camera; also, a picture made by such an exposure.
time fuse *n-* fuse that can be set to explode a charge after a certain interval.
time-hon·ored (tīm′ ŏn′ ərd) ***adj-*** honored or respected over a long period of time, and now partly because of its age; old and venerable: *a* time-honored *custom.*
time·keep·er (tīm′ kē′ pər) *n-* person or mechanism that keeps or records time in a game or at a factory.
time·less (tīm′ ləs) ***adj-*** **1** having no beginning or end; eternal. **2** unaffected by time; ageless: *a* timeless *masterpiece.* **—*adv-* time′ less·ly.** ***n-*** **time′ less·ness.**
time·ly (tīm′ lē) ***adj-*** **[time·li·er, time·li·est]** occurring at the right time: *a* timely *remark.* **—*n-* time′ li·ness.**
time·piece (tīm′ pēs′) *n-* a watch, clock, or other instrument for recording time.
tim·er (tī′ mər) *n-* **1** person or device that keeps track of time and time intervals: *the* timer *at a race track.* **2** device that can be set to signal when a certain time has passed. **3** device that regulates a machine that operates in cycles: *the* timer *on a washing machine.*
times (tīmz) ***prep-*** multiplied by: *Five* times *two equals ten.*
time·table (tīm′ tā′ bəl) *n-* systematically arranged list of the arrival and departure times of trains, planes, boats, etc.; hence, any time schedule.
time·worn (tīm′ wôrn′) ***adj-*** **1** showing the effects of time; deteriorated. **2** stale; hackneyed; overused: *a* timeworn *phrase.*
time zone *n-* one of the 24 divisions of the earth's surface, roughly corresponding to 15° of longitude each, for determining standard time. They are measured through 180° both east and west of the meridian of Greenwich, England, and each zone is equivalent to an additional hour ahead of (eastward) or behind (westward) standard Greenwich time. See also *standard time.*
tim·id (tĭm′ ĭd) ***adj-*** lacking in courage, nerve, etc.; shy; easily frightened. **—*adv-* tim′ id·ly.** ***n-*** **tim′ id·ness.**
ti·mid·i·ty (tĭ mĭd′ ə tē) *n-* shyness; lack of courage.
tim·ing (tī′ mĭng) *n-* **1** judgment of the best time to do something, and the ability to do it then: *The dancer's* timing *was perfect.* **2** a recording of the time or rate of doing something. **3** regulation of a machine that operates in cycles: *the* timing *of the engine.*
tim·or·ous (tĭm′ ər əs) ***adj-*** **1** fearful of danger; lacking in courage. **2** expressing or suggesting fear: *a* timorous *look.* **—*adv-* tim′ or·ous·ly.** ***n-*** **tim′ or·ous·ness.**
tim·o·thy (tĭm′ ə thē) *n-* a coarse grass with long spikes, grown for fodder. [American word named after **Timothy Hanson,** a U.S. farmer, who is said to have introduced the grass in the Carolinas.]
Tim·o·thy (tĭm′ ə thē) *n-* in the New Testament, either of two epistles written by St. Paul to Timothy, his companion and follower. Also **First and Second Timothy.**
tim·pa·ni (tĭm′ pə nē) tympani. **—*n-* tim′ pa·nist.**
tin (tĭn) *n-* **1** a soft, silver-white metal element. It is used to coat the inside of food containers made of other metals and also in many alloys. Symbol Sn, At. No. 50, At. Wt.

118.69. 2 thin plates of iron or steel covered with this metal; tin plate. 3 *chiefly Brit.* container made of this metal or of aluminum; a can. 4 *Informal* any metal considered inferior: *This wrench is made of* tin. *as* ***modifier***: *a* tin *plate*; tin *mine*. ***vt-*** **[tinned, tin·ning] 1** to coat with tin. 2 *chiefly Brit.* to can (food, soup, etc.). 3 to coat (the tip of a soldering iron) with solder.

tin can *Slang* ***n-*** naval destroyer.

tinc·ture (tĭngk′ chər) ***n-*** **1** a solution, usually in alcohol, of a medicinal substance: *a drop of* tincture *of iodine.* 2 small amount; trace; touch: *a* tincture *of hope.* 3 a tinge of color; tint. ***vt-*** **[tinc·tured, tinc·tur·ing]** to color slightly; tinge: *His words were* tinctured *with irony.*

tin·der (tĭn′ dər) ***n-*** any easily inflammable material, especially when used to kindle a fire from a spark.

tin·der·box (tĭn′ dər bŏks′) ***n-*** **1** formerly, a metal box for holding tinder, flint, and steel for kindling a fire. 2 any highly inflammable structure. 3 situation likely to erupt into conflict.

tine (tīn) ***n-*** sharp projecting spike or prong: *the* tine *of a fork.* ***—adj-*** **tined**: *a* tined *antler.*

tin·e·a (tĭ nē′ ə) ***n-*** any of various skin diseases caused by a fungus; especially, ringworm.

tin·foil (tĭn′ foil′) ***n-*** very thin sheet of tin alloy or aluminum, used to wrap cigarettes, candy, etc.

ting (tĭng) ***n-*** a light, ringing sound, such as that of a small bell. ***vi-***: *A bell* tinged. ***vt-***: *She* tinged *the bell.*

tinge (tĭnj) ***vt-*** **[tinged, tinge·ing] 1** to tint or stain slightly; color. 2 to give a trace, touch, flavor, etc., to: *Sadness* tinged *the joy of their reunion.* ***n-*** **1** slight degree of some color: *a* tinge *of red.* 2 a touch; trace: *a* tinge *of humor.*

tin·gle (tĭng′ gəl) ***vi-*** **[tin·gled, tin·gling] 1** to have a slight prickling or stinging feeling, as from cold, a sharp slap, etc. 2 to thrill; be roused or stirred: *The audience* tingled *with excitement.* ***n-*** **1** a stinging feeling. 2 an emotional feeling of excitement, expectancy, etc.

tin·ker (tĭng′ kər) ***n-*** **1** person who makes minor repairs in metal, such as mending leaks in pots and pans. 2 clumsy or unskillful workman. 3 any of various small fishes prized as food, such as the mackerel. ***vi-*** to work or busy oneself aimlessly. ***—n-*** **tink′ er·er.**

tin·kle (tĭng′ kəl) ***n-*** short, light, clinking sounds, such as those made by a small bell. ***vt-*** **[tin·kled, tin·kling]** to cause to make such sounds: *He* tinkled *the bell.* ***vi-***: *Ice* tinkled *in the glasses.* ***—adj-*** **tin′ kly.**

tin·ny (tĭn′ ē) ***adj-*** **[tin·ni·er, tin·ni·est] 1** of, relating to, or containing tin: *a* tinny *substance.* 2 having a flat, metallic taste or sound: *a* tinny *piano.* ***—adv-*** **tin′ ni·ly.** ***n-*** **tin′ ni·ness.**

Tin Pan Alley ***n-*** the musicians, composers, and publishers of popular music; also, the industry.

tin plate ***n-*** thin sheet of iron or steel that has been coated with tin. ***vt-*** **tin-plate [tin-plat·ed, tin-plat·ing]**: *to* tin-plate *steel.* ***—adj-*** **tin′-plat′ ed.**

tin·sel (tĭn′ səl) ***n-*** **1** fabric covered or woven with gold or silver threads. 2 threads, foil, or spangles of glittering metallic substance, used for decoration, especially on Christmas trees; hence, anything showy or gaudy but of little value. *as* ***modifier***: *a* tinsel *ornament.* ***vt-*** to decorate with tinsel: *He* tinseled *the tree as the final touch.* ***—adj-*** **tin′ sel·ly.**

tin·smith (tĭn′ smĭth′) ***n-*** person who works with tin; maker of tinware.

tint (tĭnt) ***n-*** **1** slight coloring; tinge: *just a* tint *of gold in the hair.* 2 delicate or pale color, or a pale tinge of a color: *There are different* tints *of blue. Pink is a* tint *of red.* ***vt-*** to give a slight coloring to: *She* tinted *her hair.*

tin·tin·nab·u·la·tion (tĭn′ tə năb′ yə lā′ shən) ***n-*** a tinkling or ringing of bells.

tin·type (tĭn′ tīp′) ***n-*** photograph made on a sensitized metal plate.

tin·ware (tĭn′ wâr′) ***n-*** articles made of tin plate.

ti·ny (tī′ nē) ***adj-*** **[ti·ni·er, ti·ni·est]** very small; wee.

-tion See *-ion, -ation, -ition.*

[1]**tip** (tĭp) ***n-*** **1** point or end of anything: *the* tip *of my finger.* 2 small piece or part attached to the end of a thing: *Shoelaces have metal* tips. 3 foul tip. ***vt-*** **[tipped, tip·ping] 1** to place a point on: *to* tip *an arrow with steel.* 2 in baseball, to hit (the ball) with a glancing blow. [probably from Germanic **tip,** probably related to [1]**tap.**]

[2]**tip** (tĭp) ***vt-*** **[tipped, tip·ping] 1** to slant or tilt; raise at one end or side: *to* tip *a table.* 2 to raise (one's hat) in greeting. ***vi-*** to assume a slant or tilt: *His chair* tipped *dangerously.* [probably altered from [1]**tip** having the original special sense of "pushing the tip over."]

tip over to overturn: *to* tip over *a vase.*

[3]**tip** (tĭp) ***n-*** **1** sum of money given to a waiter, cab driver, etc., for services. 2 bit of private, helpful information: *a* tip *on the stock market.* ***vt-*** **[tipped, tip·ping]** to give a small fee to for services: *He* tipped *the waiter.* ***vi-***: *He* tips *generously.* [of unknown origin.] ***—n-*** **tip′ per.**

tip off *Informal* to give private, helpful information to: *He* tipped *me* off *on the coming sale.*

ti·pi (tē′ pē′) tepee.

tip-off (tĭp′ ôf′, -ŏf′) *Informal* ***n-*** **1** warning or hint. 2 unplanned disclosure of one's secret purpose.

[1]**tipped** (tĭpt) ***adj-*** having a tip or point: *a* tipped *pole.* [from [1]**tip.**]

[2]**tipped** (tĭpt) ***adj-*** tilted. [from [2]**tip.**]

tip·pet (tĭp′ ət) ***n-*** **1** neck scarf or shoulder cape that hangs down in front. 2 in the Anglican communion, a long scarf worn by the clergy.

tip·ple (tĭp′ əl) ***vt-*** **[tip·pled, tip·pling]** to drink (liquor) habitually but in small amounts. ***vi-***: *They are* tippling *at the tavern.* ***—n-*** **tip′ pler.**

tip·ster (tĭp′ stər) ***n-*** person who gives or sells tips, especially for betting on horse races.

tip·sy (tĭp′ sē) ***adj-*** **[tip·si·er, tip·si·est]** slightly drunk. ***—adv-*** **tip′ si·ly.** ***n-*** **tip′ si·ness.**

tip·toe (tĭp′ tō′) ***vi-*** **[tip·toed, tip·toe·ing]** to walk or stand on the tips of one's toes; hence, to walk softly.

on tiptoe 1 on the tips of one's toes. 2 cautiously; softly. 3 eagerly; expectantly: *She waited* on tiptoe.

tip·top (tĭp′ tŏp′) ***n-*** highest point: *At the* tiptop *of the crag was an eagle's nest.* ***adj-*** *Informal* very fine; excellent; first-rate: *The snow was* tiptop *for skiing.*

ti·rade (tī′ rād′, tə rād′) ***n-*** long, violent, usually abusive speech; harangue.

[1]**tire** (tīər) ***vt-*** **[tired, tir·ing]** to fatigue in body, mind, or spirit: *The work quickly* tired *me.* ***vi-***: *He* tires *easily.* [from Old English **teorian.**]

[2]**tire** (tīər) ***n-*** band of metal or rubber, or a circular, air-filled rubber tube, around the rim of a wheel. [from Middle English, a shortened form of **attire,** "the covering (of a wheel)".] ***—adj-*** **tired**: *a rubber-*tired wheel.

tired (tīərd) ***adj-*** exhausted; weary; fatigued. ***—adv-*** **tired′ ly.** ***n-*** **tired′ ness.**

tire·less (tīər′ ləs) ***adj-*** not easily fatigued; untiring: *a* tireless *worker.* ***—adv-*** **tire′ less·ly.** ***n-*** **tire′ less·ness.**

tire·some (tīər′ səm) ***adj-*** boring; wearying; tedious: *a* tiresome *day.* ***—adv-*** **tire′ some·ly.** ***n-*** **tire′ some·ness.**

ti·ro (tī′ rō) tyro.

'tis (tĭz) *Archaic* it is.

tis·sue (tĭsh′ o͞o) ***n-*** **1** the cells and connecting parts that make up any part of an animal or plant: *muscle* tissue. 2 thin, gauzy cloth. 3 soft, thin paper used chiefly as a handkerchief. 4 web or network: *a* tissue *of lies.* *as* ***modifier***: *extensive* tissue *damage*; tissue *paper.*

tissue paper ***n-*** thin, soft paper used for wrapping.

[1]**tit** (tĭt) ***n-*** any of various small birds, especially the titmouse. [from Old Norse **tittr.**] ***Hom-*** teat.

[2]**tit** (tĭt) ***n-*** teat. [from Old English **tit(t),** a variant of **teat.**]

Ti·tan (tī′ tən) ***n-*** **1** in Greek mythology, one of a family of giants who fought against the Olympian gods and were overthrown. **2 titan** man of great strength.

Ti·ta·ni·a (tī tān′ ē ə, tī-) ***n-*** in Shakespeare's "A Midsummer Night's Dream," the queen of the fairies.

ti·tan·ic (tī tăn′ ĭk) ***adj-*** **1** of great size or power; enormous: *a* titanic *issue.* **2** *Chemistry* of or having to do with titanium, especially when of higher valence.

ti·ta·ni·um (tī tā′ nē əm) ***n-*** a white, metal element that is light in weight, strong, and highly resistant to corrosion. Symbol Ti, At. No. 22, At. Wt. 47.90.

titanium white ***n-*** titanium dioxide (TiO_2), an intensely white pigment used in paints, glass, and rubber.

tit·bit (tĭt′ bĭt′) tidbit.

tit for tat ***n-*** injury given for an injury received.

tithe (tīth) ***n-*** **1** the tenth part of anything; especially, one tenth of a person's income, given toward the support of his church or for charitable purposes. **2** *Informal* any small part. ***vi-*** **[tithed, tith·ing]** to pay a tenth part of one's income. ***vt-*** to impose a tax of such an amount on. **—*n-* tith′ er.**

tith·ing (tī′ thĭng) ***n-*** **1** a paying or taking of tithes. **2** amount that is taken or set apart as a tithe.

ti·tian (tĭsh′ ən) ***n-*** golden-red color. ***adj-***: *a* titian *wig.*

tit·il·late (tĭt′ ə lāt′) ***vt-*** **[tit·il·lat·ed, tit·il·lat·ing]** to arouse or excite in a pleasurable way: *to* titillate *one's fancy.* **—*n-* tit′ il·la′ tion.**

tit·i·vate (tĭt′ ə vāt′) *Informal* ***vt-*** **[tit·i·vat·ed, tit·i·vat·ing]** to dress up; spruce up. **—*n-* tit′ i·va′ tion.**

tit·lark (tĭt′ lärk′) ***n-*** small songbird that resembles a lark; pipit.

ti·tle (tī′ təl) ***n-*** **1** name of a book, painting, etc. **2** name showing the office, rank, status, etc., of a person, generally used before a person's name or as a mark of respect: *Judge, Lord, and Mr. are* titles. **3** in law, right of ownership: *Mr. White holds* title *to his house.* **4** championship: *He held the golf* title. ***vt-*** **[ti·tled, ti·tling]** to give a name to; entitle.

ti·tled (tī′ təld) ***adj-*** having a title of nobility.

title page ***n-*** page of a book containing the title of the work, the names of the author and the publisher, etc.

title role ***n-*** the role or part for which the play is named.

tit·mouse (tĭt′ mous′) ***n-*** [*pl.* **tit·mice**] any of various small songbirds, such as the chickadee; tit.

tit·ter (tĭt′ ər) ***vi-*** to laugh with slight, restrained sounds, as in ridiculing someone or from shyness; snicker: *She* tittered *at his clumsiness.* ***n-***: *the* titters *of an audience.*

tit·tle (tĭt′ əl) ***n-*** diacritical mark over a letter, such as the dot over the j; hence, any very small part.

tit·tle-tat·tle (tĭt′əl tăt′əl) ***n-*** trifling talk; senseless chatter. ***vi-*** **[tit·tle-tat·tled, tit·tle-tat·tling]** to chatter.

tit·u·lar (tĭt′ yə lər) ***adj-*** **1** having the name or title of an office, but without the accompanying duties or powers; existing in name only; nominal: *the* titular *head of a nation.* **2** of or related to a title: *the* titular *character in a play.* **—*adv-* tit′ u·lar·ly.**

Ti·tus (tī′ təs) ***n-*** in the New Testament, an epistle written by St. Paul to Titus, his companion and disciple.

tiz·zy (tĭz′ ē) *Slang* ***n-*** [*pl.* **tiz·zies**] frenzy; dither.

Tlin·git (tlĭng′ gĭt) ***n-*** [*pl.* **Tlin·gits,** also **Tlin·git**] one of a group of American Indians who still inhabit the Alexander Archipelago of southeastern Alaska.

TNT ***n-*** trinitrotoluene.

to (to͞o, tə) ***prep-*** **1** toward; in the direction of: *on my way* to *school; from right* to *left.* **2** as far as: *going* to *Boston; generous* to *a fault.* **3** for: *a key* to *the door; the door* to *the oven; a room* to *himself.* **4** into the possession of: *a present given* to *father.* **5** opposite: *face* to *face.* **6** on; upon; against: *Please fasten the notice* to *the bulletin board.* **7** before; until; till: *It is five minutes* to *six.* **8** in agreement or harmony with: *words set* to *music;* to *my way of thinking.* **9** included in: 12 *eggs* to *a dozen.* **10** used for introducing infinitives in various positions: *I don't want* to *go. I don't want* to. To *err is human.* ***adv-*** **1** into a closed position: *Wind blew the door* to. **2** into a normal condition: *She soon came* to. ***Homs-*** too, two.

American toad, 2—4 in. long

toad (tōd) ***n-*** any of various small, tailless amphibians that resemble frogs. Toads are hatched in water and go through a tadpole stage, then live on land. They are valuable destroyers of insect pests. ***Hom-*** toed.

toad·stool (tōd′ sto͞ol′) ***n-*** mushroom; especially, a poisonous mushroom.

Toadstools

toad·y (tō′ dē) ***n-*** [*pl.* **toad·ies**] person who caters to or flatters someone for the sake of gain. ***vi-*** **[toad·ied, toad·y·ing]**: *He* toadied *to his superiors.*

to and fro ***adv-*** back and forth: *The gate swung* to and fro. **—*adj-* (to-and-fro)**: *a* to-and-fro *movement.*

[1]**toast** (tōst) ***vt-*** **1** to brown by heating: *to* toast *a muffin.* **2** to warm or heat thoroughly: *We* toasted *our hands before the open fire.* ***vi-***: *The bread* toasts *well.* ***n-*** sliced bread browned by heat. [from Old French **toster,** "to roast," from Latin **tosta,** from **torrēre,** "to parch."]

[2]**toast** (tōst) ***vt-*** to drink in honor of, or to the health of: *We* toasted *the royal guests.* ***n-*** **1** act of drinking for such a purpose: *We raised our glasses in a* toast. **2** person who is very famous or admired: *She was the* toast *of Broadway.* [from [1]**toast.** The meaning arises from an old habit of putting bits of toast in wine which was drunk at parting, or in honor of a lady.]

toast·er (tōs′ tər) ***n-*** electrical device for toasting bread.

toast·mas·ter (tōst′ măs′ tər) ***n-*** person who proposes the toasts and introduces the speakers at a public dinner.

to·bac·co (tə băk′ ō) ***n-*** [*pl.* **to·bac·cos** or **to·bac·coes**] **1** any of various plants of the nightshade family of North America, having large leaves with pink or white flowers. **2** the dried leaves of this plant, prepared in various ways for smoking, chewing, or as snuff. **3** cigars, cigarettes, or other products prepared from these leaves.

Drying tobacco

to·bac·co·nist (tə băk′ ə nĭst) ***n-*** one who sells tobacco.

To·bit (tō′ bĭt) ***n-*** book in the Old Testament Apocrypha, relating the story of the devout Jew, Tobit. In the CCD Bible, **To·bi′ a** (tə bī′ ə).

to·bog·gan (tə bŏg′ ən) ***n-*** long, flat sled without runners and with a curved end. ***vi-***: *to* toboggan *downhill.*

toc·sin (tŏk′ sən) ***n-*** bell or other signal for sounding an alarm. ***Hom-*** toxin.

Toboggan

to·day or **to-day** (tə dā′) ***n-*** the present day: *the menu for* today; *the writers of* today. ***adv-*** **1** on the present day: *We will go to the movies* today. **2** in these times; in this particular age: *Many people have television* today.

tod·dle (tŏd′ əl) ***vi-*** [**tod·dled, tod·dling**] to walk with short, uncertain steps, as a baby does.

tod·dler (tŏd′ lər) *Informal* ***n-*** young child; baby.

tod·dy (tŏd′ ē) ***n-*** [*pl.* **tod·dies**] **1** drink made of the sap of certain palm trees of East India; also, the sap of such palms. **2** drink made of liquor, hot water, and sugar.

to-do (tə dōō′) *Informal* ***n-*** bustle or stir; fuss: *a great* to-do *about nothing.*

toe (tō) ***n-*** **1** one of the separate digits or divisions of the foot. **2** the fore part of the foot or of any foot covering: *the* toe *of his shoe.* **3** any of various things resembling a toe: *the* toe *of Italy.* ***vt-*** [**toed, toe·ing**] **1** to provide with a toe: *She* toed *the socks.* **2** to drive at a slant, such as a nail; also, to attach by nails driven slantwise: *to* toe *a beam.* ***vi-*** to hold the toes in a given way: *to* toe *in or out.* ***Hom-*** tow.

on (one's) toes physically or mentally alert.

to toe the line (or **the mark**) **1** to put the tip of the foot on the starting line of a race. **2** to conform to the rules.

toed (tōd) ***adj-*** having a certain type or number of toes: *pigeon-*toed; *three-*toed *sloth.* ***Hom-*** toad.

toe·nail (tō′ nāl′) ***n-*** **1** nail growing on a toe. **2** nail driven slantwise. ***vt-*** to fasten by such nails.

tof·fee (tòf′ ē, tŏf′-) ***n-*** candy made of sugar and butter, boiled until it thickens, and then poured into a dish to cool and harden. Also **tof′fy.**

tog (tŏg) *Informal* ***vt-*** [**togged, tog·ging**] to dress, especially in one's finery (often followed by "out" or "up"): *He* togged *himself out for dinner.*

to·ga (tō′ gə) ***n-*** **1** in ancient Rome, a loose outer garment consisting of an elaborately draped piece of woolen cloth with the wearer's rank shown by the color of its border. **2** robe or gown characteristic of certain professions: *academic* toga.

Toga

to·geth·er (tōō gĕth′ ər, tə-) ***adv-*** **1** in one gathering, company, or association; with each other: *We live* together *in one house.* **2** in or into contact or union: *to mix flour and water* together; *to come* together. **3** without a break; continuously: *We marched for three days* together. **4** at the same time; simultaneously: *All the cannon went off* together. **5** in or into agreement: *Let's get* together *on a plan.*

together with as well as; in addition to.

tog·ger·y (tŏg′ ə rē) *Informal* ***n-*** clothing.

tog·gle (tŏg′ əl) ***n-*** **1** oblong button for a coat, usually inserted through a loop instead of a buttonhole. **2** any crosspiece, such as a bolt or rod, that is attached to a rope or chain and used for fastening or tightening. ***vt-*** [**tog·gled, tog·gling**] to fasten or furnish with a toggle.

toggle bolt ***n-*** bolt with a pivoted, winglike anchor that closes parallel to the bolt when entering a hole in a wall, and then opens up behind the wall to anchor the bolt.

toggle switch ***n-*** electric switch having a projecting lever whose movement through a small arc opens or closes a circuit.

togs (tŏgz) *Informal* ***n-*** *pl.* clothes: *ski* togs.

[1]**toil** (toil) ***vi-*** **1** to work long or hard; labor: *The farmer* toiled *in the field.* **2** to move with difficulty; plod; trudge. ***n-*** exhausting work or effort: *After years of* toil, *he owned the farm.* [from Old French **toillier,** from Latin **tudiculāre,** "to stir about."] **—*n-* toil′ er.**

[2]**toil** (toil) ***n-*** **1** *Archaic* net; trap. **2 toils** snare; grip: *caught in the* toils *of crime.* [from Old French **toile,** from Latin **tēla** meaning "woven material; a web."]

toile (twäl) ***n-*** **1** sheer linen fabric. **2** cretonne with scenic designs printed in one color.

toi·let (toi′ lət) ***n-*** **1** bathroom or lavatory, especially one equipped with a water closet; also, the water closet. **2** a washing, dressing, and grooming of oneself. *as* ***modifier***: *one's* toilet *articles*; toilet *paper.*

make (one's) toilet to wash, dress, and groom (oneself).

toi·let·ry (toi′ lə trē) ***n-*** [*pl.* **toi·let·ries**] any of various articles, such as soap, toothpaste, or deodorant, used in washing or grooming oneself.

toilet water ***n-*** fragrant liquid that is milder than perfume and is used in the bath or on the skin.

toil·some (toil′ səm) ***adj-*** laborious; tiresome.

toil·worn (toil′ wôrn′) ***adj-*** fatigued or worn out by hard work.

to·ken (tō′ kən) ***n-*** **1** sign, mark, or symbol: *A four-leaf clover is a* token *of good luck.* **2** keepsake; remembrance: *The pin was a* token *from my uncle.* **3** piece of metal resembling a coin and used in place of money, especially to operate a tollgate, telephone, or other machine. **4** something partial or incomplete; inadequate portion: *What we got was a mere* token *of what we deserved.* ***adj-*** of no real value or effect; minimal: *a* token *resistance.* ►The phrase "BY THE SAME TOKEN" is often loosely used as a meaningless connector or transition in speech, and it should be avoided unless used to mean "on the same evidence; for the same reason; therefore."

token payment ***n-*** part payment of a debt that shows a debtor's intent to pay it all.

told (tōld) *p.t. & p.p.* of **tell.**

all told counting all: *There were 26 people there* all told.

tol·er·a·ble (tŏl′ ər ə bəl) ***adj-*** **1** such as can be suffered or endured: *The pain was bad, but it was* tolerable. **2** fairly good; not bad; acceptable: *His drawing was only* tolerable. **—*n-* tol′ er·a·bil′ i·ty. *adv-* tol′ er·a·bly.**

tol·er·ance (tŏl′ ər əns) ***n-*** **1** willingness to allow other people to hold opinions or follow customs that differ from one's own; freedom from prejudice or bigotry: *his great* tolerance *for my opinions.* **2** ability to resist the harmful effects of a drug or poison. **3** allowable variation from a standard or specified size, especially in machine parts or coins.

tol·er·ant (tŏl′ ər ənt) ***adj-*** **1** not opposing or interfering with the beliefs and actions of others. **2** *Medicine* able to resist the harmful effects of a drug or poison. **—*adv-* tol′ er·ant·ly.**

tol·er·ate (tŏl′ ə rāt′) ***vt-*** [**tol·er·at·ed, tol·er·at·ing**] **1** to permit to exist without interference; put up with; endure: *Lateness will not be* tolerated. *We must* tolerate *other people's ideas.* **2** to be able to resist the harmful effects of (a drug, extreme weather conditions, etc.).

tol·er·a·tion (tŏl′ ə rā′ shən) ***n-*** a permitting to exist or continue without interference; especially, the recognition of the right of an individual to his own opinions and practices: *religious* toleration.

[1]**toll** (tōl) ***n-*** **1** tax or fee paid for some special privilege, or for the right to use something: *We paid a* toll *to use the new highway.* **2** charge for a long-distance telephone call. **3** loss in number or value: *a heavy* toll *of lives.* [from Old English, ultimately from Greek **télos,** "tax."]

[2]**toll** (tōl) ***vt-*** to cause (a bell) to sound with regular and continuous strokes. ***vi-***: *The church bells* toll *every Sunday.* ***n-*** the sound made by the regular striking of a bell. [from Middle English **tollen** meaning "to sound a bell by pulling; pull."]

toll·booth (tōl′ bo͞oth′) ***n-*** booth where tolls are paid.

toll·gate (tōl′ gāt′) ***n-*** gate on a bridge or road, at which tolls are paid.

toll·house (tōl′ hous′) ***n-*** booth where tolls are paid.

toll·keep·er (tōl′ kē′ pər) ***n-*** person who collects tolls at a tollgate.

Tol·tec (tōl′tĕk′, tŏl′-) ***n-*** [*pl.* **Tol·tecs,** also **Tol·tec**] member of a highly civilized Indian people of central Mexico, between 900 and 1200 A.D., who influenced both the Aztecs and the Mayans. ***adj-*** (also **Tol·tec′ an**): *the* Toltec *ruins.*

tol·u·ene (tŏl′ yo͞o ēn′) ***n-*** hydrocarbon ($C_6H_5CH_3$) related to benzene, obtained from coal tars, and used in the manufacture of dyes and explosives.

tom or **Tom** (tŏm) ***n-*** the male of certain animals, especially cats and birds.

tom·a·hawk (tŏm′ ə hòk′) ***n-*** American Indian ax that was used as a weapon and a tool. ***vt-*** to strike or kill with such an ax. [American word from Algonquian.]

Tomahawk

to·ma·to (tə mā′ tō, -mä′ tō) ***n-*** [*pl.* **to·ma·toes**] **1** red or yellow juicy fruit of a garden plant of the nightshade family, widely eaten as a vegetable. **2** the plant bearing this fruit. [American word from American Spanish **tomate,** from Nahuatl Indian **tomatl.**]

tomb (to͞om) ***n-*** grave or vault for the dead.

tom·boy (tŏm′ boi′) ***n-*** lively, noisy girl who behaves like a boy.

tomb·stone (to͞om′ stōn′) ***n-*** stone placed over or at the head of a grave, usually bearing the dead person's name and dates of birth and death; gravestone; headstone.

tom·cat (tŏm′ kăt′) ***n-*** male cat.

tome (tōm) ***n-*** large, heavy, and usually scholarly book.

tom·fool·er·y (tŏm fo͞o′ lə rē) ***n-*** [*pl.* **tom·fool·er·ies**] foolish conduct; nonsense; silliness.

tom·my·rot (tŏm′ ē rŏt′) *Informal* ***n-*** utter nonsense.

to·mor·row (tə mŏr′ ō, -mòr′ ō) ***n-*** **1** the day after today: *Is* tomorrow *a holiday?* **2** the future: *space systems of* tomorrow. ***adv-*** on the day after today: *My mother will roast a turkey* tomorrow.

Tom Thumb ***n-*** in English fables, a dwarf who was no bigger than his father's thumb.

tom-tom (tŏm′ tŏm′) ***n-*** kind of drum, usually beaten with the hands. *as* ***modifier***: *a* tom-tom *beat.*

ton (tŭn) ***n-*** **1** unit of weight; specifically, the **short ton** of 2,000 pounds, of the United States and Canada; the **long ton** of 2,240 pounds, of Great Britain; or the **metric ton** of 2,204.6 pounds. **2** unit of measure of the displacement of a ship, equal to 35 cubic feet, the amount of sea water that weighs about 2,240 pounds. **3** unit of measure for ship's cargo, equal to 40 cubic feet. **4** unit of measure of the internal capacity of ships, equal to 100 cubic feet. ***Hom-*** tun.

ton·al (tō′ nəl) ***adj-*** of or relating to tone or tonality.

to·nal·i·ty (tə năl′ ə tē) ***n-*** [*pl.* **to·nal·i·ties**] **1** *Music* melodic and harmonic relationships in a composition; also, the principle of key relationship between scales. **2** the scheme of hues or shades of color in a painting.

tone (tōn) ***n-*** **1** vocal or musical sound; also, its quality: *the quiet* tones *of a harp.* **2** one of the intervals or notes in a musical scale: *to sing the* tone *of G.* **3** style or manner of speaking or writing: *a pleading* tone. **4** spirit; general character; quality: *The* tone *of the meeting was set by the president's friendly welcoming speech.* **5** normal, healthy condition of the body: *An athlete keeps his body in* tone. **6** in painting, the general effect of combined colors. **7** tint or shade of a particular color: *a gray* tone. ***vt-*** **[toned, ton·ing] 1** to bring to a required shade or color: *to* tone *a photographic print.* **2** to bring (the body or a part of it) to a more healthy and active condition. ***vi-*** to harmonize in color: *The wallpaper* tones *with the curtains.*

tone down to make less harsh, vivid or loud.

tone up to make or become stronger, brighter, or more intense: *to* tone up *a print*; *to* tone up *the body.*

tone arm ***n-*** the part of a phonograph that contains the needle and pickup.

tong (tŏng, tòng) ***n-*** formerly, any of various Chinese secret societies active in the United States.

tongs (tŏngz, tòngz) ***n-*** (takes plural verb) tool with two arms joined by a hinge, used for handling ice, embers, etc. Also **pair of tongs.**

Ice tongs

Fire tongs

tongue (tŭng) ***n-*** **1** the muscular, movable organ in the mouth, used for tasting and swallowing, and in man also for speech. **2** animal's tongue used as food. **3** language: *His native* tongue *is English.* **4** power or manner of speech: *He has a sharp* tongue. **5** anything resembling an animal's tongue in shape, position, or use, such as the clapper of a bell or the strip of leather under the lacing of a shoe. **6** in carpentry, the projection on the edge of one board that fits into a groove on the edge of another board.

hold (one's) tongue to be silent. **on the tip of (one's) tongue** almost or about to be remembered. **tongue in cheek** with a sarcastic or humorous intention.

tongue-lash (tŭng′ lăsh′) *Informal* ***vt-*** to scold severely.

tongue-tied (tŭng′ tīd′) ***adj-*** **1** unable to speak distinctly because of an abnormally short connecting membrane under the tongue. **2** unable to speak freely because of shyness, shock, surprise, etc.

tongue twister ***n-*** word, phrase, or sentence difficult to say. Example: Shelly sells shells by the seashore.

ton·ic (tŏn′ ĭk) ***n-*** **1** something that strengthens; especially, a medicine that braces or stimulates. **2** liquid preparation for the hair or scalp. **3** carbonated water containing quinine, used as a mixture in cocktails: *gin and* tonic. **4** in New England, carbonated beverage; soda pop. **5** *Music* the keynote of a scale or composition. ***adj-*** **1** bracing; stimulating: *the* tonic *effect of a cold shower.* **2** relating to sounds or tones. **3** *Music* relating to the keynote: *a* tonic *chord.*

to·nic·i·ty (tə nĭs′ ə tē) ***n-*** the condition of slight continuous contraction normal to a healthy muscle; tonus.

to·night (tə nīt′) ***n-*** the night of this present day: *He said that* tonight *is the night of the party.* ***adv-*** on or during this night: *The weatherman predicts snow* tonight.

ton·nage (tŭn′ ĭj) ***n-*** **1** displacement or carrying capacity of a ship, fleet of ships, etc., as measured in one of the marine tons. **2** toll or other charge paid by ships on the basis of displacement or capacity. **3** weight in tons of goods that are shipped, mined, produced, etc.

ton·sil (tŏn′ səl) ***n-*** one of a pair of oval lumps of spongy tissue on each side of the interior wall of the throat.

ton·sil·lec·to·my (tŏn′ sə lĕk′ tə mē) *Medicine* ***n-*** [*pl.* **ton·sil·lec·to·mies**] operation to remove tonsils.
ton·sil·li·tis (tŏn′ sə lī′ təs) ***n-*** inflammation of the tonsils.
ton·so·ri·al (tŏn sôr′ ē əl) ***adj-*** relating to a barber or his trade (often used humorously).
ton·sure (tŏn′ shər) ***n-*** **1** a shaving of the head or the crown of the head of persons entering the priesthood or a monastic order. **2** the part of the head left bare by such shaving. ***vt-*** [**ton·sured, ton·sur·ing**] to shave the crown of the head of: *to* tonsure *a monk.*
to·nus (tō′ nəs) ***n-*** tonicity.
too (to͞o) ***adv-*** **1** also; in addition; besides: *The school band was invited, and the glee club,* too. **2** more than enough: *This dress is* too *long.* **3** *Informal* very; exceedingly: *I am not* too *happy to hear it.* **4** (intensifier only): *He will* too *rake the lawn!* ***Homs-*** to, two.
►Reserve TOO to mean "greatly in excess," usually in respect to a related fact or a purpose: *He's* too *sick to work.* Avoid TOO in the sense of VERY: *I'm not* too *sick.*
took (to͝ok) *p.t.* of **take.**
tool (to͞ol) ***n-*** **1** instrument used in doing work, especially with the hands, such as a chisel, hammer, knife, or saw. **2** anything used in one's vocation, such as books, money, etc.: *Books are the scholar's* tools. **3** person used as an agent of another; dupe: *The general was a* tool *of the dictator's scheme.* ***vt-*** to shape or mark with a tool: *to* tool *leather.* ***Hom-*** tulle.
tool up to equip a plant or industry with the tools and machinery necessary for a certain type or amount of production: *The auto company* tooled up *its plant.*
toot (to͞ot) ***vt-*** to cause (a horn, whistle, etc.) to sound, especially with short, quick blasts. ***vi-*** to make such or similar sounds: *He* tooted *on his horn.*

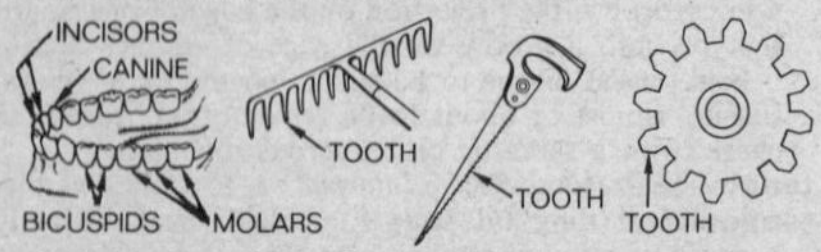

Teeth of a man, of a rake, of a saw, and of a gear

tooth (to͞oth) ***n-*** [*pl.* **teeth** (tēth)] **1** one of the hard, bony structures set in the jaws, used for biting and chewing and sometimes for attacking and defending. **2** any projection resembling a tooth, such as that on a gear wheel, comb, rake, or saw. ***vt-*** **1** to indent or make jagged: *to* tooth *an edge.* **2** to supply with projections or teeth: *to* tooth *a saw.*
armed to the teeth fully or heavily armed. **by the skin of (one's) teeth** narrowly; barely. **fight tooth and nail** to fight with every bit of strength. **in the teeth of** directly against; opposed to.

CROWN
NECK
ROOT
Tooth

tooth·ache (to͞oth′ āk′) ***n-*** pain in a tooth or in the teeth.
tooth·brush (to͞oth′ brŭsh′) ***n-*** small brush for cleaning the teeth.
toothed (to͞otht) ***adj-*** **1** having teeth: *a sharp-*toothed *fish.* **2** having notches; jagged: *a bird with a* toothed *bill.*
tooth·less (to͞oth′ ləs) ***adj-*** without teeth.
tooth·paste (to͞oth′ pāst′) ***n-*** paste for cleaning teeth.
tooth·pick (to͞oth′ pĭk′) ***n-*** sliver of wood, metal, plastic, etc., for removing bits of food from between the teeth.
tooth powder ***n-*** powder used for cleaning the teeth.
tooth·some (to͞oth′ səm) ***adj-*** **1** pleasant to the taste: *a* toothsome *bit of food.* **2** *Archaic* very attractive.
tooth·y (to͞o′ thē) ***adj-*** [**tooth·i·er, tooth·i·est**] having or showing teeth that are large and prominent.
[1]**top** (tŏp) ***n-*** **1** highest part; summit; peak: *the* top *of a mountain*; *the* top *of a building.* **2** upper side or surface of anything: *the* top *of a car*; *the* top *of a table.* **3** cover or lid for a box, jar, etc. **4** the part of a plant above ground, especially a plant with edible roots, such as a carrot or radish. **5** person who ranks highest; also, the highest rank, position, degree, etc.: *at the* top *of his class*; *at the* top *of her powers.* ***vt-*** [**topped, top·ping**] **1** to put a lid on: *to* top *a jar.* **2** to be at the head of: *He* tops *his history class.* **3** to surpass; exceed: *to* top *last year's record.* **4** to go over the summit of; surmount: *We* topped *the hill.* **5** to cut off the upper part of (a plant). *as* ***modifier***: *the* top *shelf*; *at* top *speed*; *the* top *half of his class*; *the* top *price.* [from an Old English word of the same spelling, and related to [1]**tip.**]
on top 1 successful. **2** in a position of control.
top off to finish: *to* top off *a meal with a mint.*
[2]**top** (tŏp) ***n-*** child's toy that is shaped like a cone and has a point on which it is spun by means of a string or spring. [from Old English **top.**]
sleep like a top to sleep very deeply.
to·paz (tō′ păz′) ***n-*** **1** mineral whose crystals vary in color from yellow to blue or green, of which the yellow variety is prized as a gem. **2** any of various gems or stones that resemble the topaz in color, such as the yellow sapphire. *as* ***modifier***: *a* topaz *bracelet.*
top boot ***n-*** high boot that often has a light-colored leather band around the top.
top·coat (tŏp′ kōt′) ***n-*** lightweight overcoat.
tope (tōp) ***vi-*** [**toped, top·ing**] to drink alcoholic liquor frequently through the day. ***Hom-*** taupe. **—*n-* top′ er.**
top·flight (tŏp′ flīt′) *Informal* ***adj-*** excellent; superior.
top·gal·lant (tə găl′ ənt, tŏp-) ***adj-*** relating to or naming the spars, sails, and rigging of a ship that are next above the topmasts and topsails, and are usually the highest.
top hat ***n-*** man's black or gray hat having a tall, roundish crown, worn on formal occasions. Also **high hat.**
top-heav·y (tŏp′ hĕv′ ē) ***adj-*** heavier at the top than at the bottom; improperly balanced.
top·ic (tŏp′ ĭk) ***n-*** subject of a discussion, speech, argument, composition, etc.
top·i·cal (tŏp′ ĭ kəl) ***adj-*** **1** relating to current interest: *articles on* topical *subjects.* **2** relating to a topic or subject. **3** arranged according to topics: *a* topical *reference book.* **4** *Medicine* applied locally: *a* topical *remedy.* **—*adv-* top′ i·cal·ly.**
topic sentence ***n-*** sentence, usually near the beginning of a paragraph or chapter, that states the main thought.
top kick *Slang* ***n-*** first sergeant.
top·knot (tŏp′ nŏt′) ***n-*** **1** tuft of hair on the top of the head, or a crest of feathers on the head of a bird. **2** decorative knot or bow worn on the top of the head by women.
top·less (tŏp′ ləs) ***adj-*** without a top.
top·loft·y (tŏp′ lôf′ tē, -lŏf′ tē) *Informal* ***adj-*** [**top·loft·i·er, top·loft·i·est**] haughty and pompous; snobbish.
top·mast (tŏp′ măst′, -məst) ***n-*** in sailing ships, the second mast above the deck.
top·most (tŏp′ mōst′) ***adj-*** the very highest; uppermost.
top-notch (tŏp′ nŏch′) *Informal* ***adj-*** excellent; first rate.
to·pog·ra·pher (tə pŏg′ rə fər) ***n-*** person trained or skilled in the art of topography and engaged in it as a profession.
top·o·graph·ic (tŏp′ ə grăf′ ĭk) ***adj-*** of, relating to, or showing topography: *a* topographic *map.* **—*adj-* top′ o·graph′ i·cal.** ***adv-*** **top′ o·graph′ i·cal·ly.**
to·pog·ra·phy (tə pŏg′ rə fē) ***n-*** **1** all the natural and man-made surface features of a given area of land, such

as mountains, valleys, roads, and bridges. **2** the art or practice of representing such features on a map.

to·pol·o·gy (tə pŏl′ ə jē) ***n-*** branch of mathematics that studies those properties of geometric figures that do not change when the figures are stretched, twisted, or otherwise distorted without cutting or folding.

top·ping (tŏp′ ĭng) ***n-*** anything that forms a top; especially, whipped cream placed on the top of cake or dessert.

top·ple (tŏp′ əl) ***vi-*** **[top·pled, top·pling] 1** to fall headlong; tumble: *The tree* toppled. **2** to collapse; be overthrown: *The government* toppled. ***vt-***: *to* topple *a tower.*

tops (tŏps) *Informal* ***adj-*** top-notch; excellent; first-rate.

top·sail (tŏp′ səl, -sāl′) ***n-*** **1** the second and third sails above the deck of a full square-rigged vessel. **2** the sail above the upper gaff of a fore-and-aft rigged vessel. *as* ***modifier***: *a* topsail *yard.*

top-se·cret (tŏp′ sē′ krət) ***adj-*** secret to all but the highest officials: *a* top-secret *missile program.*

top sergeant *Informal* ***n-*** first sergeant.

top·side (tŏp′ sīd′) ***adv-*** on deck: *He's stationed* topside. Also **top′ sides′**.

top·soil (tŏp′ soil′) ***n-*** top or upper part of the soil; especially, the fertile surface layer of soil.

top·sy-tur·vy (tŏp′ sē tûr′ vē) ***adj-*** **1** upside down. **2** confused and disordered: *a* topsy-turvy *situation.* ***adv-***: *The boat turned* topsy-turvy.

toque (tōk) ***n-*** woman's close-fitting, small hat without a brim.

tor·ah (tôr′ ə) ***n-*** **1** in Judaism, the whole body of religious thought and literature. **2 Torah** the first five books of the Old Testament; Pentateuch. **3** leather or parchment scroll containing this.

torch (tòrch, tôrch) ***n-*** **1** flaming light consisting of a stick of resinous wood, bundle of rushes, etc., burning at one end. **2** any of various devices that give off a hot flame: *a plumber's* torch. **3** anything that inspires, enlightens, etc.: *the* torch *of science.* **4** *chiefly Brit.* flashlight.

carry a torch for to continue to love.

Torch of liberty

torch bearer ***n-*** **1** person who carries a torch. **2** person who gives inspiration.

torch·light (tòrch′ līt′, tôrch′-) ***n-*** light given by torches. *as* ***modifier***: *a* torchlight *assembly.*

torch singer ***n-*** person who sings sad songs of unrequited love or yearning, called **torch songs.**

tore (tôr) *p.t.* of **tear.**

tor·e·a·dor (tôr′ ē ə dôr′, -dòr′) *Informal* ***n-*** a bullfighter.

to·re·ro (tō rā′ rō) *Spanish* ***n-*** [*pl.* **to·re·ros**] bullfighter, especially one fighting on foot.

to·ri·i (tôr′ ē ē) ***n-*** the gateway of a Japanese Shinto temple or shrine, consisting of two upright posts supporting a concave lintel with a straight crossbeam below it.

Torii

[1]**tor·ment** (tòr mĕnt′) ***vt-*** **1** to inflict severe physical or mental pain on; torture: *to* torment *a captive.* **2** to annoy or harass; vex: *He* tormented *her with complaints.*

[2]**tor·ment** (tòr′ mĕnt′, tôr′-) ***n-*** **1** extreme mental or physical suffering; great pain; agony: *suffering the* torments *of jealous rage.* **2** something that causes suffering or pain: *His reckless driving was her* torment.

tor·men·tor or **tor·men·ter** (tòr mĕn′ tər) ***n-*** person or thing that torments; torturer.

torn (tôrn) *p.p.* of **tear.**

tor·na·do (tòr nā′ dō) ***n-*** [*pl.* **tor·na·does** or **tor·na·dos**] violent, whirling wind that travels rapidly in a narrow path, usually over land, and is seen as a twisting, dark cloud shaped like a funnel; twister.

tor·pe·do (tòr pē′ dō) ***n-*** [*pl.* **tor·pe·does**] **1** underwater, self-driven explosive missile used to blow up enemy ships. **2** kind of firework that explodes by being thrown against a hard surface. **3** noise-making explosive charge placed on a railroad track as a signal. ***vt-*** **[tor·pe·doed, tor·pe·do·ing]** to hit or sink (a ship) with a torpedo.

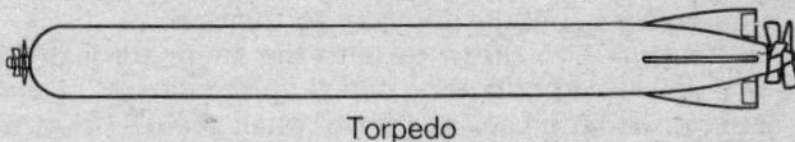

Torpedo

torpedo boat ***n-*** small, fast warship equipped with tubes for firing torpedos.

torpedo tube ***n-*** tube in a submarine or other warship through which torpedos are fired.

tor·pid (tòr′ pĭd, tôr′-) ***adj-*** **1** inactive; sluggish; dull: *a* torpid *mind.* **2** temporarily inactive; dormant: *Bears live in a* torpid *state during the winter.* **—*n-*** **tor·pid′ i·ty.** ***adv-*** **tor′ pid·ly.**

tor·por (tòr′ pər, tôr′-) ***n-*** **1** temporary loss of feeling or of the power of motion; dormancy; stupor. **2** dullness; apathy; sluggishness.

torque (tòrk, tôrk) ***n-*** the force that causes a thing to rotate or twist.

tor·rent (tòr′ ənt, tŏr′-) ***n-*** **1** violent, rapidly flowing stream of water. **2** any similar flow: *a* torrent *of words.*

tor·ren·tial (tə rĕn′ shəl) ***adj-*** caused by or resembling a torrent: *a* torrential *flood.* **—*adv-*** **tor·ren′ tial·ly.**

tor·rid (tòr′ ĭd, tŏr′-) ***adj-*** **1** extremely hot or burning, especially from the heat of the sun; scorching: *a* torrid *climate.* **2** passionate; inflamed: *a* torrid *romance.* **—*adv-*** **tor′ rid·ly.** ***n-*** **tor′ rid·ness** or **tor·rid′ i·ty.**

Torrid Zone ***n-*** former term for the tropics.

tor·so (tòr′ sō, tôr′-) ***n-*** [*pl.* **tor·sos**] **1** the trunk of the human body. **2** statue of this.

tort (tòrt, tôrt) ***n-*** in law, any wrong, injury, or damage, other than a breach of contract, for which the injured party may sue for damages in a civil action. Slander and trespassing are examples of torts.

tor·til·la (tòr tē′ yə) ***n-*** thin, unleavened cake made from cornmeal and baked on a plate of iron or a flat stone. It is a staple food in Mexico. [from Spanish, from Latin **torta,** "a round cake," and related to [2]**tart.**]

tor·toise (tòr′ təs, tôr′-) ***n-*** a land turtle.

tortoise shell ***n-*** **1** the mottled yellow-and-brown shell of certain turtles, widely used in the making of combs and ornaments. **2** any of several butterflies with black and yellow markings. ***adj-*** **(tortoise-shell)** made of or marked like tortoise shell.

Gopher tortoise, about 1 ft. long

tor·tu·ous (tòr′ chōō əs, tôr′-) ***adj-*** **1** winding; twisting: *a* tortuous *channel.* **2** not straightforward; crooked: *a* tortuous *scheme.* **—*adv-*** **tor′ tu·ous·ly.** ***n-*** **tor′ tu·ous·ness.**

tor·ture (tòr′ chər, tôr′-) ***vt-*** **[tor·tured, tor·tur·ing] 1** to inflict severe pain upon, especially to gain information or for revenge: *to* torture *a prisoner.* **2** to cause severe pain;

torment; agonize: *His toothache* tortured *him.* 3 to twist out of shape; distort: *He* tortured *my words when he reported them to the others.* ***n-*** 1 an inflicting of severe pain: *The rack used to be a form of* torture. 2 extreme pain of mind or body; agony: *to suffer* torture *from a toothache.* 3 cause of extreme pain or agony: *That work is* torture! —***n-*** **tor′tur·er.**

Tor·y (tôr′ ē) ***n-*** [*pl.* **Tor·ies**] 1 formerly, a member of an English political party that favored royal power and the established church. After 1832, it became known as the Conservative Party. 2 in the American Revolution, one who favored continued loyalty to England.

toss (tòs) ***vt-*** 1 to throw up into the air or through the air; throw without using much force: *to* toss *a ball.* 2 to cause to roll back and forth; pitch about: *The waves* tossed *the small boat.* 3 to lift quietly; jerk: *She* tossed *her head and walked away.* 4 to mix (a salad). 5 to flip a (coin) to determine a choice or settle a dispute. ***vi-*** 1 to be restless; roll from side to side: *I couldn't sleep and I* tossed *all night.* 2 to be flung back and forth; be buffeted: *The balloons* tossed *about in the wind.* 3 to flip a coin. ***n-*** 1 pitch; throw: *a* toss *of a ball.* 2 quick, abrupt lift; jerk: *a* toss *of the head.* 3 flip of a coin.
toss off 1 to perform an action casually or effortlessly. 2 to finish (a drink) in one long gulp.

toss-up (tòs′ ŭp′) ***n-*** 1 *Informal* even chance. 2 a flipping of a coin to make a choice, settle a dispute, etc.

tot (tŏt) ***n-*** 1 small child; toddler. 2 *chiefly Brit.* small amount (of alcoholic liquor).

to·tal (tō′ təl) ***adj-*** 1 whole; entire: *This is our* total *supply for the year.* 2 complete; utter; absolute: *in* total *confusion.* ***n-*** whole sum or amount: *When you finish adding, please give me the* total. ***vt-*** to find the sum of; add up. ***vi-*** to amount to. —***adv-*** **to′tal·ly.**

to·tal·i·tar·i·an (tō tăl′ ə târ′ ē ən) ***adj-*** of or relating to a form of government in which one political party exercises absolute control over all phases of the people's lives, often by the use of force and violence. ***n-*** person who supports or advocates such a government.

to·tal·i·tar·i·an·ism (tō tăl′ ə târ′ ē ə nĭz′ əm) ***n-*** totalitarian beliefs, practices, or form of government.

to·tal·i·ty (tō tăl′ ə tē) ***n-*** [*pl.* **to·tal·i·ties**] 1 the total amount; sum: *the* totality *of voters in an area.* 2 wholeness or completeness; entirety: *a* totality *of interest.* 3 *Astronomy* phase of an eclipse where the light of the sun or moon is completely cut off.

tote (tōt) *Informal* ***vt-*** [**tot·ed, tot·ing**] to carry or convey, especially on one's back or in one's arms; haul: *to* tote *wood.*

to·tem (tō′ təm) ***n-*** animal, plant, or natural object that is associated with a clan or smaller group of a tribe, and is regarded by the members of the group as a protector or sacred ancestor. The name of the group is often derived from the totem. [from Ojibwa **ototeman** meaning "his totem; his relation."]

to·tem·ism (tō′ tə mĭz′ əm) ***n-*** all the customs and beliefs that bind social groups to their totems.

totem pole ***n-*** among the Indians of the northern Pacific Coast, a tall memorial post that is carved and painted with representations of stories and events concerning the dead person's totem.

Totem pole

tot·ter (tŏt′ ər) ***vi-*** 1 to walk with weak, unsteady steps. 2 to shake or wobble as if about to fall: *The cup* tottered *on the edge of the table.* 3 to be on the verge of collapse or downfall. —***n-*** **tot′ter·er.** ***adj-*** **tot′ter·y.**

tou·can (to͞o′ kăn′) ***n-*** any of various fruit-eating birds of Central and South America, with very large beaks and bright plumage.

Toucan

touch (tŭch) ***vt-*** 1 to cause to be in contact with; bring into contact with: *He* touched *the stick to the ground.* 2 to feel with the fingers: *Don't* touch *the wet paint.* 3 to strike lightly; tap: *He* touched *the piano keys.* 4 to eat; drink; taste: *Mary didn't* touch *her food. Ed won't* touch *wine.* 5 to refer to; mention: *I didn't dare* touch *that subject.* 6 to compare with; equal: *My ability can't* touch *yours.* 7 to have to do with; concern: *Our conversation doesn't* touch *you.* 8 to affect the feelings or emotions of; cause sympathy or gratitude in; move: *Your kindness* touches *me.* 9 to be in contact with; adjoin: *The two estates* touch *each other.* 10 to mark or affect slightly: *That saw can't* touch *iron.* 11 to reach: *I* touched *my goal.* 12 *Slang* to borrow from. ***vi-*** 1 to be or come in contact: *The two benches* touch. 2 to make a brief stop at a port (usually followed by "at"): *The ship* touched *at several villages.* ***n-*** 1 in physiology, the special sense responsive to contact, located at or near the surface of an organism. 2 small amount; trace: *a* touch *of pepper; a* touch *of humor.* 3 a mild attack (of a disease): *a* touch *of flu.* 4 special way of doing something; style: *You can see his* touch *in all these paintings.* 5 a single delicate stroke on a painting, drawing, etc.; also, the result produced by such a stroke. 6 manner of action of the fingers or hands on a keyboard machine or instrument, such as a piano or typewriter: *a light* touch. 7 the ease with which the keys on a keyboard machine or instrument move: *That typewriter has a firm* touch. 8 *Slang* a successful attempt to borrow money; also, the lender. —***adj-*** **touch′a·ble.** ***n-*** **touch′er.**
in touch (with) in communication (with); in contact (with). **out of touch (with)** not in contact (with).
touch down in air travel, to stop briefly at a place and then go on; also, to land on an airfield.
touch off 1 to cause to start or happen; also, to motivate. 2 to cause to explode; fire.
touch on (or **upon**) to refer to or concern briefly.
touch up to improve (something) by making slight changes: *He* touched up *the photograph.*

touch and go ***n-*** risky, uncertain, or precarious condition or situation. ***adj-*** **(touch-and-go):** *The second half of the game was* touch-and-go.

touch·back (tŭch′ băk′) ***n-*** in football, the grounding of the ball by a player behind his own goal line, provided that it was put there by an opponent.

touch-down (tŭch′ doun′) ***n-*** 1 in football, the major scoring play, counting six points, in which a player grounds the ball on or over the opponent's goal line; also, the score made by so doing. 2 of an airplane, a touching the ground with the landing gear; also, the moment when this happens.

touched (tŭcht) ***adj-*** 1 affected by a feeling of gratitude, sympathy, pity, etc.; emotionally stirred; moved. 2 *Informal* somewhat mentally unbalanced.

touch football ***n-*** game resembling football, in which the ball carrier is tagged rather than tackled and physical contact is avoided for the most part.

touch·hole (tŭch′ hōl′) ***n-*** hole at the breech of an old-fashioned firearm through which the powder was ignited.

touch·ing (tŭch′ ĭng) ***adj-*** causing feelings of sympathy or gratitude; moving: *Your concern for my happiness is* touching. ***prep-*** with regard to; concerning: *The teacher said nothing* touching *a holiday.* **—*adv-* touch′ ing·ly.**

touch-me-not (tŭch′ mē nŏt′) ***n-*** jewelweed.

touch·stone (tŭch′stōn′) ***n-* 1** piece of black stone used for a quick test for gold and silver. The color of the streak left on the stone when it is rubbed with the metal roughly indicates the purity of the metal. **2** standard or test by which the value of something is determined.

touch·y (tŭch′ ē) ***adj-*** **[touch·i·er, touch·i·est 1** easily offended; irritable; peevish. **2** extremely sensitive to touch or pressure: *a* touchy *bruise.* **3** requiring careful consideration or handling; delicate: *a* touchy *subject.* **—*adv-* touch′ i·ly. *n-* touch′ i·ness.**

tough (tŭf) ***adj-*** **[tough·er, tough·est] 1** strong and pliant: *a baseball glove of* tough *cowhide.* **2** not easily broken, split, etc.; also, hard to cut or chew: *a* tough *wood*; *a* tough *steak.* **3** able to endure hardship or strain; strong; robust; hardy: *a* tough *body*; *a* tough *boxer.* **4** hard to change; stubborn: *a* tough *will.* **5** rough; disorderly: *a* tough *neighborhood.* **6** difficult: *a* tough *lesson.* **7** without softness or sentimentality; also, harshly realistic; firmly determined: *His novels have a very* tough *style.* **8** *Informal* unfortunate; bad. ***n-*** a hardened person. **—*adv-* tough′ ly. *n-* tough′ ness. *Hom-*** tuff.

tough·en (tŭf′ ən) ***vt-*** to make tough: *He* toughened *himself by exercise.* ***vi-***: *They* toughened *in combat.*

tou·pee (to͞o pā′) ***n-*** small wig to cover a bald spot.

tour (to͝or) ***n-* 1** a journey in which a traveler makes a short stop at a number of places and returns to the place from which he started; a sightseeing trip: *a* tour *through Europe.* **2** a passing through or going around from place to place to give performances or inspect: *the* tour *of the ballet company*; *a* tour *of the museum.* **3** a shift or period: *a* tour *of duty.* ***vt-*** to travel through: *We* toured *Europe.* ***vi-***: *They* toured *along the Rhine.*

on tour going from place to place giving performances.

tour de force (to͝or′ də fôrs′) ***n-*** [*pl.* **tours de force**] feat of extraordinary skill or strength.

tour·ism (to͝or′ ĭz′ əm) ***n-* 1** travel for pleasure; touring. **2** the management and conducting of parties of tourists as a business or a government function.

tour·ist (to͝or′ ĭst) ***n-*** person who travels for pleasure. *as **modifier***: *a* tourist *agency*; *a* tourist *guide.*

tourist class *n-* 1 on a passenger ship, class of accomodations next below cabin class. **2** on an airplane, class of accomodations next below first class.

tourist court *n-* motel.

tour·ma·line (to͝or′ mə lən, -lēn′) ***n-*** mineral that contains boron and aluminum and is usually black but sometimes red, blue, green, or, rarely, colorless. Some varieties are gems. *as **modifier***: *a* tourmaline *ring.*

tour·na·ment (tûr′ nə mənt, to͝or′-) ***n-* 1** a series of contests in skill among many players to determine a championship. **2** a medieval contest with blunt weapons by knights on horseback; also, a complete series of such contests.

tour·ney (tûr′ nē) ***n-*** [*pl.* **tour·neys**] tournament.

tour·ni·quet (tûr′ nə kət, to͝or′-) ***n-*** device for compressing a blood vessel to stop bleeding or control the flow of blood, consisting of a bandage twisted tight by a stick, an elastic rubber bandage, etc.

Tourniquet

tou·sle (tou′ zəl) ***vt-*** **[tou·sled, tou·sling]** to put into disorder; ruffle; muss: *to* tousle *the hair.* ***n-*** a disordered or tumbled mass, especially of hair.

tout (tout) *Informal* ***vi-* 1** to solicit or canvass for customers, votes, etc.; seek patronage. **2** *chiefly Brit.* to spy on race horses in training, in order to give betting tips. ***vt-*** to solicit in an importunate manner; also, to praise or recommend excessively. ***n-* 1** person who looks out for customers or solicits patronage. **2** person who sells tips on race horses. **—*n-* tout′ er.**

¹tow (tō) ***vt-*** to pull by a rope or chain: *We* towed *the canoe up to the dock.* ***n-* 1** condition of being pulled: *a car in* tow. **2** something pulled: *The tugboat couldn't manage its large* tow. **3** rope or chain used in pulling. *as **modifier***: *a* tow *truck.* [from Old English **togian** meaning "drag; pull; tug."] ***Hom-*** toe.

have (or **take**) **in tow** to have or take under one's influence or charge.

²tow (tō) ***n-*** short, coarse fibers of hemp or flax, ready for spinning. [from Old English **tow-**.] ***Hom-*** toe.

to·ward (tôrd, tə wȯrdz′) ***prep-*** (also **towards**) **1** in the direction of: *We sailed* toward *China.* **2** close upon; near: *We camped* toward *sundown.* **3** about; regarding: *What is your attitude* toward *the candidates?* **4** with a view to; for the purpose of: *to save* toward *one's old age.* ***adj-*** (tôrd *only*) **1** going on; being done: *What's* toward? **2** *Archaic* ready to learn; promising: *a* toward *child.*

tow·boat (tō′ bōt′) ***n-*** tugboat.

tow·el (tou′ əl) ***n-*** piece of cloth or paper for drying something wet. *as **modifier***: *a* towel *rack.* ***vt-*** to wipe or dry with a piece of cloth or paper.

tow·el·ing or **tow·el·ling** (tou′ əl ĭng) ***n-*** material used for towels.

tow·er (tou′ ər) ***n-* 1** high structure, or part of a building rising higher than the rest of it: *a water* tower; *church* tower. **2** stronghold; fortress. **3** anything superior to others: *a* tower *of strength; a* tower *of wisdom.* *as **modifier***: *a* tower *clock.* ***vi-*** to rise high: *The mountain* towers *to the sky.*

Bell tower

tow·er·ing (tou′ ər ĭng) ***adj-* 1** very high; tall: *a* towering *mountain.* **2** intense; violent: *a* towering *rage.*

tow·head (tō′ hĕd′) ***n-*** head of very light-blond hair; also, person with such hair. **—*adj-* tow′ head′ ed.**

tow·hee (tō′ ē) ***n-*** any of various American finches, especially a black, white, and rust bird; chewink.

tow·line (tō′ līn′) ***n-*** line used for towing; towrope.

town (toun) ***n-* 1** group of houses and buildings, larger than a village but smaller than a city. **2** the city as opposed to the country. **3** the people of a community. **4** township. **5** business or shopping district: *She went to* town. *as **modifier***: *a* town *hall*; town *clerk.*

go to town *Slang* to do anything exuberantly and well.

on the town *Slang* out for an enjoyable evening.

town clerk *n-* public officer who keeps the town records.

town crier *n-* formerly, an officer who made public announcements in the streets of a town or village.

town hall *n-* building where public meetings are held and town offices are located.

town meeting *n-* 1 under a form of direct democratic government now used chiefly in parts of New England, a meeting of the qualified voters of a town for the transacting of all public business not delegated to town officials. 2 general meeting of the people of a town.

towns·folk (tounz'fōk') *n-* townspeople.

town·ship (toun'shĭp') *n-* 1 subdivision of a county, consisting of a village or group of villages having certain powers of self-government. 2 in U.S. surveys of public lands, a unit of area six miles square, divided into 36 sections of one mile square each.

towns·man (tounz'mən) *n-* [*pl.* **towns·men**] inhabitant or citizen of a town or city; also, fellow citizen.

towns·peo·ple (tounz'pē'pəl) *n-pl.* 1 people who live in a town or city; townsfolk; townsmen. 2 people who live in a town or city, as distinguished from those living in the country.

tow·path (tō'păth') *n-* path beside a canal or river, along which men or animals walk when towing boats.

tow·rope (tō'rōp') *n-* towline.

tox·e·mi·a or **tox·ae·mi·a** (tŏk sē' mē ə) *n-* a general poisoning of the body due to bacterial toxins conveyed by the blood. *—adj-* **tox·e'mic** or **tox·ae'mic.**

tox·ic (tŏk'sĭk) *adj-* 1 poisonous: *a* toxic *drug.* 2 relating to or caused by poison: *acute* toxic *symptoms.* *—n-* **tox·ic'i·ty** (tŏk sĭs'ə tē).

tox·i·col·o·gy (tŏk'sə kŏl'ə jē) *n-* the science of poisons and their sources, effects, tests, and antidotes.

tox·in (tŏk'sən) *n-* a poison of plant, animal, or bacterial origin, especially one that stimulates the body to produce a neutralizing antitoxin. ***Hom-*** tocsin.

tox·in-an·ti·tox·in (tŏk'sən ăn'tĭ tŏk'sən) *n-* mixture of diphtheria toxin with its antitoxin, used to produce immunity.

tox·oid (tŏk'soid') *n-* toxin treated so that it loses its poisonous qualities but it is still able to stimulate the production of antibodies.

toy (toi) *n-* 1 child's plaything. 2 something of no real value; trinket. 3 something, especially a dog, that is very small. *as* ***modifier***: *a* toy *radio*; *a* toy *poodle.*

toy with 1 to handle carelessly or in an absent-minded way: *He* toyed with *his pencil.* 2 to amuse oneself with; to play with (an idea, object, etc.).

Tr symbol for terbium.

[1]**trace** (trās) *n-* 1 a mark or sign left by something that has passed or happened: *We found* traces *of an old civilization. We saw* traces *of snow on the road.* 2 slight evidence: *a* trace *of sorrow.* 3 small quantity or amount: *a* trace *of yellow.* 4 in psychology, a change in certain cells of the nervous system believed to result from stimuli and considered the physiological basis of memory. 5 mark or indication made by a recording instrument: *The* trace *of a cardiogram.* *vt-* [**traced, trac·ing**] 1 to draw on transparent paper by following lines underneath it. 2 to draw (letters, figures, etc.) carefully. 3 to sketch; outline: *The commander* traced *the plan of attack.* 4 to follow the tracks or signs of: *She* traced *the deer through the forest. He* traced *his family back to the "Mayflower."* 5 to make a graphic record of: *The cardiogram* traced *her heartbeat.* *vi-* to follow a trail. [from Old French **tracier,** from Latin **tractus,** from **trahere,** "to draw."]

[2]**trace** (trās) *n-* either of the two straps of a harness by which a vehicle is pulled. [from Old French **trais** meaning "traces," from Latin **tractus,** "a dragging."]

kick over the traces *Informal* to show independence or insubordination.

trace·a·ble (trā'sə bəl) *adj-* 1 such as can be traced: *a characteristic* traceable *through many generations*; *a* traceable *inscription.* 2 attributable: *His weakness was* traceable *to a lack of vitamins.* *—adv-* **trace'a·bly.**

trace element *n-* chemical element considered essential to the proper functioning of an organism but required only in very small amounts.

trac·er (trā'sər) *n-* 1 person or thing that traces; especially, a person who traces missing persons or objects, or an instrument used in copying pictures. 2 inquiry sent out for the recovery of letters, packages, etc., which have been lost in transit. 3 ammunition having a small firework that burns continuously so that it reveals the path of the projectile to which it is attached. 4 *Biology* radioactive isotope of an element that can be introduced into the body and followed in its course to obtain information about chemical processes taking place.

trac·er·y (trā'sə rē) *n-* [*pl.* **trac·er·ies**] graceful, delicate design; especially, openwork carved in stone.

tra·che·a (trā'kē ə) *n-* air tube leading from the back of the mouth to the lungs; windpipe. For picture, see *lungs.* *—adj-* **tra'che·al.**

tra·cho·ma (trə kō'mə) *n-* an infectious virus disease of the conjunctiva, resulting in redness, swelling, pain, and excessive sensitivity to light.

trac·ing (trā'sĭng) *n-* 1 a copy of a picture, inscription, etc., made on transparent paper placed over the original. 2 graph or record made by a self-registering or self-recording instrument.

track (trăk) *n-* 1 a print left by a foot, tire, etc. 2 a trail of footprints, wheel marks, sparks, etc., left by a moving object: *We followed the* track *of the deer.* 3 course along which something moves; path; road: *A wagon* track *leads across the field.* 4 a specially prepared course used for races: *a race* track; *a cinder* track. 5 a rail or rails for directing the course of something: *railroad* tracks. 6 track and field. *vt-* 1 to follow by sight or scent: *The lion* tracked *the zebra.* 2 to observe or note the moving path of (missiles, satellites, etc.) 3 to leave marks or footprints on or with: *Boys* tracked *the fresh cement. as* ***modifier***: *a* track *official*; track *damage*; *a* track *man.* *—n-* **track'er.**

keep track of to keep informed about; keep in touch with: *He* kept track of *old school friends.* **lose track of** to fail to keep informed about; be out of touch with. **make tracks** to leave quickly; hurry. **off the track** 1 in error; wrong. 2 leading a project, discussion, etc., away from its proper course or objective. **on the track** 1 correct; right. 2 keeping a project, discussion, etc., on its proper course or objective. **stop in (one's) tracks** to stop abruptly or in such a way that there is no further movement: *My scream* stopped *Mary* in her tracks.

track down to find by following tracks or evidence.

track and field *n-* the competitive sports of foot-racing, jumping, vaulting, hurdling, and weight throwing, collectively. *as* ***modifier*** (**track-and-field**): *a* track-and-field *champion.*

tracking station *n-* an installation located in a favorable position to follow the path of a space vehicle or man-made satellite by telemetry.

track·less (trăk'ləs) *adj-* 1 without human roads or trails; pathless: *a* trackless *forest.* 2 not running on tracks: *a* trackless *trolley.*

track meet *n-* track-and-field athletic contest.

[1]**tract** (trăkt) *n-* pamphlet, especially one upon a religious or political subject. [from earlier **tractate,** "pamphlet," from Latin **tractātus,** from **tractāre,** "to handle."]

[2]**tract** (trăkt) *n-* 1 unbroken expanse or area: *a* tract *of land*; *a vast* tract *of ocean.* 2 a part of the body that has a specialized function and occupies an extended space: *a nerve* tract; *the* digestive *tract.* [from Latin **tractus,** "a stretch of land," from **trahere,** "to stretch."]

trac·ta·ble (trăk'tə bəl) *adj-* 1 easily managed or led; docile. 2 easily handled or worked; malleable: *Gold is* tractable. *—n-* **trac'ta·bil'i·ty.** *adv-* **tract'a·bly.**

trac·tion (trăk′ shən) ***n-*** **1** a drawing or pulling anything. **2** the power used in pulling: *electric* traction. **3** friction that prevents a powered wheel from sliding on the surface along which it moves; also, the friction between a drive belt and its pulleys. **4** *Medicine* a continuous pulling of the muscles of a leg, arm, etc., by means of a system of weights and pulleys, in order to bring fractured or dislocated bones into place or for the realignment of the spine. *as* ***modifier***: *a* traction *engine*; traction *force*.

trac·tor (trăk′ tər) ***n-*** **1** heavy motor vehicle for pulling farm machinery, heavy loads, etc. **2** heavy truck with a driver's cab and no body, used to haul trailers. *as* ***modifier***: *a* tractor *tread*.

Tractor

trade (trād) ***n-*** **1** a buying and selling; commerce: *an increase in foreign* trade. **2** exchange of goods for other goods; barter: *a* trade *of candy for a top*. **3** work one does for a living; especially, skilled work done with the hands; craft: *the carpenter's* trade. **4** people in the same business considered as a group: *the building* trade. **5** customers: *The new clerk was popular with the* trade. **6 the trades** trade winds. *as* ***modifier***: *a* trade *magazine*; trade *name*; trade *union*. ***vi-*** **[trad·ed, trad·ing] 1** to buy and sell goods: *He* trades *in furs*. **2** to make an exchange. ***vt-*** **1** to buy and sell. **2** to exchange; swap.
trade in to give (something) in exchange as part payment for something else.
trade off to dispose of by exchanging or trading.
trade on to take unfair advantage of.

trade-in (trād′ ĭn′) ***n-*** something given or taken in payment or part payment of a purchase.

trade·mark (trād′ märk′) ***n-*** a mark, word, picture, etc., registered with the government by a manufacturer to identify his product. *as* ***modifier***: *a* trademark *name*. ***vt-*** **1** to label (a product) with a trademark. **2** to register (a name, symbol, etc.) as a trademark.

trade name ***n-*** **1** name given by a merchant or manufacturer to an article to distinguish it from other articles of the same class. A trade name may be used and protected as a trademark. **2** name by which an article is known in the industry that uses it.

trad·er (trā′ dər) ***n-*** **1** person who trades. **2** a ship used in trade; especially, a small ship visiting islands.

trade school ***n-*** school that trains students for a trade.

trades·man (trādz′ mən) ***n-*** [*pl.* **trades·men**] shopkeeper or any of his employees.

trades·peo·ple (trādz′ pē′ pəl) ***n-*** *pl.* tradesmen.

trade union or **trades union** ***n-*** labor union.

trade unionism ***n-*** principles and practices of a trade union. **—*n-*** **trade unionist.**

trade wind ***n-*** steady wind found in either of two belts about 25° wide just north and south of the equator. The northeast trade winds, blowing from northeast to southwest, are found in the northern belt; and the southeast trade winds, blowing from southeast to northwest, in the southern.

trading post (trā′ dĭng) ***n-*** frontier store.

tra·di·tion (trə dĭsh′ ən) ***n-*** **1** the handing down of tales, beliefs, customs, etc., from generation to generation: *Many legends are preserved by* tradition. **2** something handed down in this way.

tra·di·tion·al (trə dĭsh′ ən əl) ***adj-*** **1** having to do with tales, beliefs, customs, etc., handed down from generation to generation. **2** established by long usage; customary. **—*adv-*** **tra·di′ tion·al·ly.**

tra·duce (trə do͞os′, -dyo͞os′) ***vt-*** **[tra·duced, tra·duc·ing]** to harm the good name of. **—*n-*** **tra·duc′ er.**

traf·fic (trăf′ ĭk) ***n-*** **1** movement of people, goods, and vehicles from place to place: *The* traffic *on city streets is a problem*. **2** the transportation business done by a railway, steamship line, etc., carrying persons or goods. **3** trade; business: *the* traffic *in stolen goods*. *as* ***modifier***: *a* traffic *jam*. ***vi-*** **[traf·ficked, traf·fick·ing]** to trade or deal: *to* traffic *in cotton*. **—*n-*** **traf′ fick·er.**

traffic circle ***n-*** circular intersection around which all traffic flows counterclockwise.

traffic light ***n-*** signal light that, by showing various colors, directs the flow of traffic.

trag·a·canth (trăg′ ə kănth) ***n-*** gum tragacanth.

tra·ge·di·an (trə jē′ dē ən) ***n-*** **1** writer of tragedies. **2** actor who plays tragic parts. **—*n-*** *fem.* **tra·ge′ di·enne′** (-də ĕn′).

trag·e·dy (trăj′ ə dē) ***n-*** [*pl.* **trag·e·dies**] **1** sad event, especially one that involves death; disaster. **2** in dramatic literature, a serious play with an unhappy ending, arousing pity or terror by the misfortunes that befall the principal characters. **3** such plays as a group.

trag·ic (trăj′ ĭk) ***adj-*** **1** very sad; disastrous: *a* tragic *accident*. **2** of or having to do with tragedy: *a* tragic *drama*. Also **trag′ i·cal.** **—*adv-*** **trag′ i·cal·ly.**

trag·i·com·e·dy (trăj′ ĭ kŏm′ ə dē) ***n-*** [*pl.* **trag·i·com·e·dies**] **1** a play containing both tragic and comic scenes, especially one that has generally gloomy or tragic events but ends happily for the main characters. **2** a situation or event blending tragic and comic elements. **—*adj-*** **trag′ i·com′ ic** (-kŏm′ ĭk): *a* tragicomic *scene*.

trail (trāl) ***n-*** **1** path through woods or wild country: *After the blizzard we couldn't find the* trail. **2** scent or footprints left by a moving person or animal; track: *The dog followed the* trail *of the rabbit*. **3** a stream of people, dust, rubbish, etc., behind something moving: *The train left a* trail *of smoke*. ***vt-*** **1** to follow the path or footprints of. **2** to pull along or behind: *to* trail *a wagon*. **3** to bring along as a burden or hindrance: *I* trailed *my younger brothers with me*. ***vi-*** **1** to fall or hang down so as to sweep along the ground: *Her dress* trailed *in the mud*. **2** to move in a long and straggling line: *They* trailed *home one by one*. **3** to lag behind; be last. **4** to grow to some length: *The bush* trailed *along the fence*.

trail·blaz·er (trāl′ blā′ zər) ***n-*** **1** person who marks a trail for others. **2** a leader in new ventures; pioneer.

trail·er (trā′ lər) ***n-*** **1** person, animal, or thing that follows behind. **2** van for carrying loads, which is hooked to any vehicle. **3** vehicle with living quarters that can be hauled from place to place by a car. **4** a trailing plant or vine. **5** short film with scenes from a coming picture, used to advertise. *as* ***modifier***: *a* trailer *camp*.

train (trān) ***n-*** **1** a connected line of railroad cars with or without an engine attached. **2** a group of people or things traveling together: *wagon* train. **3** a connected series of ideas, events, etc.: *a* train *of thought*. **4** group of attendants; retinue. **5** an extension of a lady's skirt that trails behind her. **6** a

Train

fāte, făt, dâre, bärn; bē, bĕt, mêre; bīte, bĭt; nōte, hŏt, môre, dȯg; fŭn, fûr; to͞o, bo͝ok; oil; out; tar; thin; then; hw for wh as in *wh*at; zh for s as in u*s*ual; ə for a, e, i, o, u, as in *a*go, lin*e*n, per*i*l, at*o*m, min*u*s

line of gunpowder laid to fire a charge. **7** a connected series of wheels, gears, etc., transmitting motion: *a gear* train. *as* ***modifier***: *a* train *inspector*; *a* train *schedule*. ***vt-*** **1** to educate; bring up; rear: *He* trained *the children to be polite*. **2** to teach so as to make skillful; instruct systematically: *He* trained *the dog to do tricks*. **3** to aim; point: *The officer* trained *his guns on the fort*. **4** to cause to grow in a certain way: *to* train *vines to climb up a wall*. ***vi-*** to prepare for by practice: *to* train *for a race*. ***—adj-*** **train′a·ble.**

train·ee (trā′ nē′) ***n-*** person who is being trained. *as* ***modifier***: *a* trainee *program*.

train·er (trā′ nər) ***n-*** person who trains athletes for sports contests, horses for racing, animals for the circus, etc.

train·ing (trā′ nĭng) ***n-*** **1** instruction for some occupation: *Have you had* training *as a nurse?* **2** course of exercise, diet, etc., for an athlete. **3** good condition maintained by following such a course: *I am out of* training. *as* ***modifier***: *a* training *school*; *a* training *ship*.

train·load (trān′ lōd′) ***n-*** total amount of passengers or total amount of freight a train can hold.

train·man (trān′ mən) ***n-*** [*pl.* **train·men**] person who works on a train and assists the conductor; especially, a brakeman.

train oil ***n-*** oil obtained from the blubber of whales and other sea animals.

traipse (trāps) *Informal* ***vi-*** **[traipsed, traips·ing]** to walk about idly or aimlessly; ramble.

trait (trāt) ***n-*** feature or characteristic, especially of personality: *Kindness and generosity are fine* traits.

trai·tor (trā′ tər) ***n-*** person who betrays his country, a cause, a friend, etc. ***—n-*** *fem.* **trai′tress.**

trai·tor·ous (trā′ tər əs) ***adj-*** **1** of or like a traitor; treacherous. **2** of or having to do with treason: *a* traitorous *act*. ***—adv-*** **trai′tor·ous·ly.**

tra·jec·to·ry (trə jĕk′ tə rē) ***n-*** path of an object moving through space, such as the path of a bullet.

tram (trăm) ***n-*** **1** kind of coal wagon used in mines. **2** *chiefly Brit.* streetcar.

tram·mel (trăm′ əl) ***n-*** **1** net used for catching birds, fish, etc. **2** a shackle or fetter for teaching a horse to amble. **3 trammels** anything that hinders progress, action, or freedom. **4** an S-shaped hook from which pots are hung in a fireplace. ***vt-*** **1** to hamper or hinder; shackle. **2** to catch in a net.

tramp (trămp) ***n-*** **1** the sound of heavy steps: *I heard the* tramp *of soldiers*. **2** a walk or hike: *a* tramp *through the woods*. **3** man who goes about on foot doing odd jobs or begging; vagabond. **4** freight steamer that has no regular schedule but picks up cargo wherever it can. *as* ***modifier***: *a* tramp *ship*; *a* tramp *dog*. ***vi-*** **1** to walk with heavy steps; trudge: *He* tramped *upstairs. He* tramped *home, tired after a day's hike*. **2** to travel or wander about as a vagabond. ***vt-*** **1** to step on heavily and repeatedly; tread: *The peasants* tramp *the grapes in making wine*. **2** to walk over; roam about. ***—n-*** **tramp′er.**

tram·ple (trăm′ pəl) ***vt-*** **[tram·pled, tram·pling]** to tramp on; stamp on; crush: *The cows* trampled *my flower bed*. ***vi-*** to walk with heavy steps; stamp. ***n-*** the sound of tramping or stamping. ***—n-*** **tram′pler.**

tram·po·lin or **tram·po·line** (trăm′ pə lēn′, -lən) ***n-*** sheet of canvas or other strong material stretched tightly on a frame, used by acrobats as a springboard.

tram·way (trăm′ wā′) ***n-*** **1** *chiefly Brit.* streetcar line; also, streetcar. **2** road or track for heavy hauling; especially, a railway in a mine.

trance (trăns) ***n-*** **1** an unconscious state like sleep. **2** a daze; daydream: *The music put him in a* trance. **3** a state produced by hypnotism, in which a person cannot govern his actions but is governed by outside suggestion. ***—adj-*** **trance′like′.**

tran·quil (trăng′ kwəl) ***adj-*** **1** free from mental tension or strain; serene: *a* tranquil *mind*. **2** free from disturbance or tumult: *a* tranquil *country scene*; tranquil *waters*.

tran·quil·ize (trăng′ kwə līz′) ***vt-*** **[tran·quil·ized, tran·quil·iz·ing]** to make tranquil; especially, to reduce anxiety in (a patient) by use of drugs.

tran·quil·iz·er (trăng′ kwə lī′ zər) ***n-*** any of a group of drugs that tend to make a person calm and relaxed.

tran·quil·li·ty or **tran·quil·i·ty** (trăng′ kwĭl′ ə tē) ***n-*** a being tranquil; calmness; peacefulness; serenity.

trans- *prefix* **1** across; over; beyond: trans*atlantic*. **2** above and beyond: trans*sonic*; trans*uranium*. **3** with a complete change: trans*form*.

trans. 1 transitive. **2** transpose. **3** translated. **4** translator. **5** translation. **6** transportation. **7** transverse.

trans·act (trăn′ săkt′, -zăkt′) ***vt-*** to carry on; perform; complete (business, negotiations, etc.): *to* transact *a deal*. ***—n-*** **trans·ac′tor**: *a* transactor *of shady business*.

trans·ac·tion (trăn′ săk′ shən, -zăk′ shən) ***n-*** **1** the management of any business or affair. **2** business deal: *This* transaction *involves a lot of money*. **3 transactions** report, especially the published report, of the proceedings of a meeting of a society, organization, etc.

trans·at·lan·tic (trănz′ ət lăn′ tĭk, trăns′-) ***adj-*** **1** going across the Atlantic: *a* transatlantic *flight*. **2** on the other side of the Atlantic.

tran·scend (trăn′ sĕnd′) ***vt-*** **1** to rise above or go beyond; exceed: *Miracles* transcend *human knowledge*. **2** to excel; surpass: *His ability* transcends *mine*.

tran·scend·ent (trăn′ sĕn′ dənt) ***adj-*** **1** surpassing or rising above the usual; extraordinary: *the* transcendent *joys of childhood*. **2** transcendental. ***—adv-*** **tran·scend′ent·ly.**

tran·scen·den·tal (trăn′ sən dĕn′ təl) ***adj-*** of or relating to eternity, infinity, absolute love, perfect joy, and other matters outside the world of ordinary sense experience; also, relating to philosophers or a philosophy dealing chiefly with such matters. ***—adv-*** **tran′scen·den′tal·ly.**

trans·con·ti·nen·tal (trăns′ kŏn tə nĕn′ təl) ***n-*** **1** going across a continent: *a* transcontinental *flight from New York to Los Angeles*. **2** on the other side of a continent.

tran·scribe (trăn′ scrīb′) ***vt-*** **[tran·scribed, tran·scrib·ing]** **1** to copy in writing: *The medieval monks* transcribed *many ancient manuscripts*. **2** to make a copy of (shorthand notes, dictation, etc.) on a typewriter or in longhand. **3** to record (a radio program, commercial, etc.) for broadcast at a later date. **4** *Music* to arrange or adapt (music) for an instrument or voice other than that for which it was originally intended. ***—n-*** **tran·scrib′er.**

tran·script (trăn′ scrĭpt′) ***n-*** **1** written, typewritten, or printed copy. **2** an exact official copy, especially of a student's academic record.

tran·scrip·tion (trăn′ scrĭp′ shən) ***n-*** **1** a transcribing or copying. **2** written copy; transcript. **3** *Music* arrangement or adaptation of a composition to suit a voice or instrument other than that for which it was written. **4** (also **electrical transcription**) a recording of a radio program, performance, etc., made for broadcast later.

trans·duc·er (trăns′ dōō′ sər, -dyōō′ sər) ***n-*** device that transforms one form of energy into another.

tran·sept (trăn′ sĕpt′) ***n-*** in churches that have the shape of a cross, the section that forms the transverse crosspiece; also, either of the two projecting ends of this part.

[1]**trans·fer** (trăns′ fûr′) ***vt-*** **[trans·ferred, trans·fer·ring]** **1** to carry or remove from one person or place to another. **2** to give ownership of (something) to another: *to* transfer *a piece of land*. **3** to imprint on one surface

from another: *He* transfers *the designs by a stencil.* ***vi-*** **1** to change from one place, position, school, etc., to another. **2** to change from one streetcar, bus, etc., to another.

[2]**trans·fer** (trăns′ fər) ***n-*** **1** a passing or carrying from one person or place to another: *the* transfer *of luggage at the airport.* **2** person or thing that is passed, carried, or moved to another place; especially, a picture or design that is removed from one surface and placed on another. **3** a ticket allowing passage from one public vehicle to another; also, the place where this change takes place. **4** in law, the handing over of a title, right, property, etc., to another person. *as* ***modifier***: *a* transfer *point.*

trans·fer·a·ble (trăns′ fûr′ ə bəl, trănz′-) ***adj-*** such as can be transferred: *a* transferable *mortgage.*

trans·fer·ence (trăns′ fûr′ əns, trăns′ fər-) ***n-*** **1** a transfering; transfer. **2** in psychoanalysis, the transfer of the patient's love, hatred, etc., from one person to another, especially to the psychoanalyst himself.

transfer orbit *Space* ***n-*** elliptical path followed by a space vehicle in transferring from the orbit of the earth to that of another planet.

trans·fig·u·ra·tion (trăns′ fĭg′ yə rā′ shən) ***n-*** **1** a change in outward form or appearance, especially to a glorified or exalted condition. **2 the Transfiguration** the supernatural change in the appearance of Jesus Christ on Mount Tabor; also, the church festival on August 6, celebrating this event.

trans·fig·ure (trăns′ fĭg′ yər) ***vt-*** **[trans·fig·ured, trans·fig·ur·ing]** **1** to change the form or appearance of. **2** to make glow or shine; illumine; make seem glorious.

trans·fix (trăns′ fĭks′) ***vt-*** **1** to pierce with a pointed weapon. **2** to make motionless: *Fear* transfixed *him.*

trans·form (trăns′ fôrm′, -fôrm′) ***vt-*** **1** to change the nature or appearance of; change into something else: *Cinderella's fairy godmother* transformed *mice into coachmen.* **2** to change the character or personality of: *Loving care* transformed *the child.* **3** *Physics* (1) to change (an electric current) to a higher or lower voltage, or from alternating to direct current or vice-versa. (2) to change (one form of energy) into another.

trans·for·ma·tion (trăns′ fər mā′ shən) ***n-*** **1** a transforming or being transformed, in appearance, nature, or the like: *the* transformation *of a tadpole into a frog.* **2** *Grammar* statement that shows the relationship between a sentence and a set of simple structures which underlie the sentence.

trans·for·ma·tion·al grammar (trăns′ fər mā′ shən əl) ***n-*** theory of grammar which states that certain processes, called transformations, exist in language and can automatically specify the relationships between sentences and their underlying simple structures.

trans·form·er (trăns′ fôr′ mər, -fôr′ mər) ***n-*** **1** person or thing that transforms. **2** *Physics* device used to increase or decrease AC voltage by electromagnetic induction.

trans·fuse (trăns′ fyo͞oz′) ***vt-*** **[trans·fused, trans·fus·ing]** **1** to transfer (blood) from one person or animal to another. **2** to pass (something) through or into.

trans·fu·sion (trăns′ fyo͞o′ zhən) ***n-*** a transfer of liquid from one vessel to another; especially, a transfer of blood from one person to another.

trans·gress (trăns′ grĕs′, trănz′-) ***vi-*** to break a law, rule, etc.; sin. ***vt-*** **1** to break, sin against, or violate: *He* transgressed *an important rule.* **2** to go beyond (any limit or bounds): *His behavior* transgressed *all boundaries of good conduct.* **—*n-* trans·gres′ sor.**

trans·gres·sion (trăns′ grĕsh′ ən, trănz′-) ***n-*** a transgressing; violation of a law, rule, boundary, etc.; especially, a sin.

tran·ship (trăn′ shĭp′) ***vt-*** **[tran·shipped, tran·ship·ping]** to transship. **—*n-* tran·ship′ ment.**

tran·sient (trăn′ shənt) ***adj-*** **1** not permanent; brief; passing: *Her joy was* transient. **2** stopping for a short time: *a* transient *guest at the hotel.* ***n-*** visitor or boarder who remains only for a short time: *a hotel for* transients. **—*n-* tran′ sience** (-shəns) or **tran′ sien·cy** (-shən sē): *the* transiency *of life.* ***adv-*** **trans′ ient·ly.**

tran·sis·tor (trăn′ zĭs′ tər, -sĭs′ tər) ***n-*** small electronic device made of semiconductors such as germanium or silicon and used as a substitute for a vacuum tube in controlling or amplifying an electric current. *as* ***modifier***: *a* transistor *radio*; *a* transistor *circuit.*

tran·sit (trăn′ sĭt, -zĭt) ***n-*** **1** a passing through or over; passage: *a rapid* transit. **2** a carrying from one point to another: *The tomatoes were spoiled in* transit. **3** public system of transportation including buses, subways, etc. **4** transition; change. **5** surveyor's instrument consisting of a telescope, a leveling device, and two scales for measuring horizontal and vertical angles; theodolite. **6** *Astronomy* (1) passage of a celestial body across a meridian. (2) passage of one celestial body in front of another as seen from the earth. ***vt-*** to pass through or over. *as* ***modifier***: *the* transit *system*; *a* transit *strike.*

tran·si·tion (trăn′ zĭsh′ ən) ***n-*** **1** the passing from one place, period, state, subject, or the like, to another; change: *the* transition *from boyhood to manhood*; *the* transition *to the next paragraph.* **2** *Music* (1) abrupt change from one key to another. (2) passage serving to join two themes or sections more important than itself.

tran·si·tion·al (trăn′ zĭsh′ ən əl) ***adj-*** of or having to do with transition; intermediate: *a* transitional *period in history.* **—*adv-* tran·si′ tion·al·ly.**

tran·si·tive (trăn′ sə tĭv, -zə tĭv) *Grammar* ***adj-*** of verbs, having an object. Examples: *John* rode *his bicycle down the street.* ("His bicycle" is the object of the verb "rode.") *I* hope *that you will come.* ("That you will come" is the object of the verb "hope.") ***n-***: *That verb is a* transitive. **—*adv-* tran′ si·tive·ly. *n-* tran′ si·tive·ness.**

tran·si·tor·y (trăn′ sə tôr′ ē, trăn′ zə-) ***adj-*** lasting but a short time; brief; quickly passing. **—*n-* tran′si·to′ri·ness.**

trans·late (trăns′ lāt′, tranz′ lāt′) ***vt-*** **[trans·lat·ed, trans·lat·ing]** **1** to change from one language into another. **2** to put into different words or express in a different manner: *He* translated *the theory of atomic power into language I could understand.* **3** to move from one place, condition, or position to another. ***vi-*** **1** to be adaptable for translation: *His novels* translate *easily.* **2** to act as a translator: *He* translates *for the French Embassy.* **—*adj-* trans·lat′ a·ble.**

trans·la·tion (trăns′ lā′ shən, trănz′-) ***n-*** **1** the changing of something written or spoken from one language to another; a translating: *The United Nations has a large staff for* translation. **2** result of translating: *three* translations *of a book.* **3** in mechanics, the movement of a body in one direction without rotation.

trans·la·tor (trăns′ lā′ tər, trănz′-) ***n-*** person who translates from one language into another; interpreter.

trans·lu·cence (trăns′ lo͞o′ səns, trănz′-) or **trans·lu·cen·cy** (-sən sē) ***n-*** the quality of being translucent.

trans·lu·cent (trăns′ lo͞o′ sənt, trănz′-) ***adj-*** letting light pass through, but not allowing images to be clearly seen on the other side. **—*adv-* trans·lu′ cent·ly.**

---

fāte, făt, dâre, bärn; bē, bĕt, mêre; bīte, bĭt; nōte, hŏt, môre, dȯg; fŭn, fûr; to͞o, bo͝ok; oil; out; tar; thin; then; hw for wh as in *wh*at; zh for s as in u*s*ual; ə for a, e, i, o, u, as in *a*go, lin*e*n, per*i*l, at*o*m, min*u*s

trans·lu·nar (trăns′ lōō′ nər, trănz′-) ***adj-*** beyond the moon.

trans·mi·grate (trăns′ mī′ grāt, trănz′-) ***vi-*** **[trans·mi·grat·ed, trans·mi·grat·ing]** of a soul, to pass at death into another body.

trans·mi·gra·tion (trăns′ mī grā′ shən, trănz′-) ***n-*** **1** the passing of a soul at death from one body to another; metempsychosis. **2** migration.

trans·mis·si·ble (trăns′ mĭs′ ə bəl, trănz′-) ***adj-*** such as can be transmitted. **—*n-* trans·mis′ si·bil′ i·ty.**

trans·mis·sion (trăns′ mĭsh′ ən, trănz′-) ***n-*** **1** a passing from one person or place to another; communication: *the* transmission *of electric power, disease, etc.* **2** in an automobile or similar vehicle, the part of the mechanism that connects two drive shafts by means of gears, hydraulic devices, etc., and changes the ratio of the speeds between them. **3** the passing of radio waves through the air.

trans·mit (trăns′ mĭt′, trănz′-) ***vt-*** **[trans·mit·ted, trans·mit·ting]** **1** to send from one person or place to another; to pass on; transfer: *to* transmit *information.* **2** to pass on by inheritance or as by heredity. **3** to conduct: *Copper wires* transmit *electricity. Glass* transmits *light.* **4** *Physics* to cause (light, heat, etc.) to pass through a medium. **5** to pass along (a force, movement, etc.) from one mechanical part to another. **6** to send out (signals) by electromagnetic waves. **—*adj-* trans′ mit′ ta·ble.**

trans·mit·tal (trăns′ mĭt′ əl, trănz′-) ***n-*** a transmitting.

trans·mit·ter (trăns′ mĭt′ ər, trănz′-) ***n-*** **1** person or thing through which something is sent or carried. **2** mouthpiece of a telephone, including the mechanism that picks up sound waves and converts them to electromagnetic impulses. **3** apparatus that sends out electromagnetic waves such as radio signals, radar pulses, etc.

trans·mute (trăns′ myōōt′, trănz′-) ***vt-*** **[trans·mut·ed, trans·mut·ing]** to change in form, appearance, nature, etc.; transform; convert: *The decline in exports* transmuted *the economic life of the country.* **2** *Physics* to convert (one element) into another by nuclear bombardment: *to* transmute *nitrogen into oxygen.* **—*n-* trans·mut′ er.**

trans·mu·ta·tion (trăns′ myōō tā′ shən, trănz′-) ***n-*** **1** a transmuting or condition of being transmuted. **2** *Chemistry* the conversion of one element into another.

trans·o·ce·an·ic (trănz′ ō′ shē ăn′ ĭk, trăns′-) ***adj-*** **1** across or beyond the ocean. **2** crossing the ocean: *the* transoceanic *telephone cables.*

Transom

tran·som (trăn′ səm) ***n-*** **1** hinged window above a door, or a movable section of a large window. **2** crosspiece to which such a window is hinged.

tran·son·ic (trăn′ sŏn′ ĭk) ***adj-*** **1** of, relating to, or capable of moving at speeds between 600 to 900 miles per hour: *a* transonic *flight.* **2** of or relating to conditions encountered when crossing the sound barrier.

trans·pa·cif·ic (trăns′ pə sĭf′ ĭk, trănz′-) ***adj-*** **1** going across the Pacific: *a* transpacific *flight.* **2** on the other side of the Pacific.

trans·par·ence (trăns′ păr′ əns, pĕr′ əns) ***n-*** the quality of being transparent.

trans·par·en·cy (trăns′ păr′ ən sē, trăns′ pĕr′-) ***n-*** [*pl.* **trans·par·en·cies**] **1** transparence. **2** something transparent; especially, a picture or inscription on transparent glass, film, etc.

trans·par·ent (trăns′ păr′ ənt, -pĕr′ ənt) ***adj-*** **1** clear enough or thin enough to be easily seen through; sheer: *a* transparent *glass*; transparent *gauze.* **2** easy to detect, understand, etc.: *a* transparent *lie.* **—*adv-* trans′ par′ ent·ly. *n-* trans′ par′ ent·ness.**

tran·spi·ra·tion (trăn′ spə rā′ shən) ***n-*** the passing off of water vapor or other waste in vapor form.

tran·spire (trăn′ spīər′) ***vi-*** **[tran·spired, tran·spir·ing]** **1** to pass off water or waste products as vapor. **2** *Informal* to happen; occur. ***vt-*** to pass off (water or waste products) as vapor; exhale.

trans·plant (trăns′ plănt′) ***vt-*** **1** to remove and plant (any plant) again in another place. **2** to move to another place: *After the war whole populations were* transplanted *to other countries.* **3** to transfer (a section of tissue) from one part of the body to another, or from one person's body to another's: *to* transplant *a kidney.* ***vi-*** to admit of being removed and placed again in another place: *These shrubs* transplant *easily.* ***n-*** **1** something that is moved or transferred from one place to another: *This rose is a* transplant. **2** a removing and placing again in another place: *The surgeon performed the* transplant *of the kidney with great skill.* **—*adj-* trans′ plant′ a·ble. *n-* trans′ plant′ er.**

trans·po·lar (trăns′ pō′ lər) ***adj-*** across or beyond either of the polar regions: *a* transpolar *flight.*

[1]**trans·port** (trăns′ pôrt′) ***vt-*** **1** to carry from one place to another: *Large vans* transported *the elephants.* **2** to carry away emotionally by passion, pleasure, etc.: *A good play* transports *him.* **3** to deport (criminals) from a country. **—*adj-* trans′ port′ a·ble. *n-* trans′ port′ er.**

[2]**trans·port** (trăns′ pôrt) ***n-*** **1** a carrying, as of goods or soldiers. **2** ship, plane, or other vehicle that moves troops, supplies, passengers, mail, or the like. **3** system of transportation; transit. **4** sudden burst of emotion: *in a* transport *of fury.* *as* ***modifier***: *a* transport *plane.*

trans·por·ta·tion (trăns′ pər tā′ shən) ***n-*** **1** a carrying or being carried from one place to another: *All* transportation *came to a standstill during the blizzard.* **2** means of carrying or being transported. **3** cost of travel. **4** the banishing of a criminal to another country. *as* ***modifier***: *a* transportation *system.*

trans·pose (trăns′ pōz′) ***vt-*** **[trans·posed, trans·pos·ing]** **1** to change the relative position of; change the natural order of: *I* transposed *the sentence "Up he went," to "Up went he."* **2** *Music* to rewrite or play (a musical composition) in a key other than the original. ***vi-*** to rewrite or play music in a key different from the original. **—*adj-* trans′ pos′ a·ble. *n-* trans′ pos′ er.**

trans·po·si·tion (trăns′ pə zĭsh′ ən) ***n-*** **1** a transposing or being transposed: *the* transposition *of the letters in a word.* **2** something that has been transposed.

trans·ship (trăn′ shĭp′) ***vt-*** **[trans·shipped, trans·ship·ping]** to transfer from one carrier, such as a ship or truck, to another for further shipment. **—*n-* trans′ ship′ ment.**

trans·son·ic (trăn′ sŏn′ ĭk) transonic.

tran·sub·stan·ti·a·tion (trăn′ səb stăn′ shē ā′ shən) ***n-*** **1** the changing of any substance into something essentially different. **2** doctrine that the bread and wine of the Eucharist are converted into the true presence of Christ, although their appearance remains the same.

trans·u·ra·ni·um (trănz′ yə rā′ nē əm, trăns′-) ***adj-*** of or pertaining to those man-made elements that have an atomic number greater than that of uranium.

trans·verse (trănz′ vûrs′, trăns′-) ***adj-*** lying across or crosswise: *the* transverse *beams*; *a* transverse *muscle.* ***n-*** anything that lies crosswise. **—*adv-* trans′ verse′ ly. *n-* trans′ verse′ ness.**

[1]**trap** (trăp) ***n-*** fine-grained, dark, igneous rock, often found in seams through other rocks. [from Swedish **trappa**

meaning "a stair; set of steps." The meaning arose from the layered appearance of the rock.]

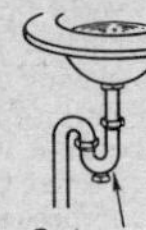
Sink trap

[2]**trap** (trăp) ***n-*** **1** any device for catching and holding animals or persons; snare; pitfall. **2** situation from which a person cannot escape, brought about by tricky questioning, clever arguments, etc.: *He laid a clever* trap *for the witness.* **3** S-shaped or U-shaped bend for sealing a drainpipe with water against the return of sewer gas. **4** in golf, sand trap. **5** trap door. **6** machine for hurling clay disks as rifle targets. **7** a light, horse-drawn carriage with two wheels. **8 traps** drums, cymbals, etc., in a band. ***vt-*** **[trapped, trap·ping] 1** to catch in a snare or trap: *He* trapped *mink.* **2** to hold back; seal off; stop: *The rocks* trapped *the water.* **3** to ambush or ensnare: *They* trapped *the enemy.* **4** to prove (someone) to be lying, wrong, etc., by tricky questioning, clever arguments, or the like: *My arguments* trapped *him into admitting his error.* ***vi-*** to set snares or traps for animals: *Jacques* traps *for a living.* [from Old English **træppe** meaning "a step; trap (worked by stepping on some part of it)."]

trap door ***n-*** a hinged or sliding door that covers an opening in a floor, ceiling, or roof.

trap-door spider ***n-*** any of various ground spiders that dig tubular nests and cover them with a hinged lid.

tra·peze (tră pēz′) ***n-*** swinging horizontal bar hung on ropes, used by acrobats and gymnasts.

tra·pez·i·um (tră pē′ zē əm) ***n-*** [*pl.* **tra·pe·zi·a** (-zē ə) or **tra·pe·zi·ums**] a quadrilateral with no parallel sides.

apezium

trap·e·zoid (trăp′ ə zoid′) ***n-*** a quadrilateral with one pair of parallel sides.

Trapezoid

trap·per (trăp′ ər) ***n-*** person who traps animals for their furs.

trap·pings (trăp′ ĭngz) ***n-*** **1** decorative covering or harness for a horse. **2** any ornamental dress; decorations.

Trap·pist (trăp′ ĭst) ***n-*** member of an order of monks, branch of the Cistercians, known for strict discipline.

trap·shoot·ing (trăp′ shōō′ tĭng) ***n-*** sport in which clay disks are thrown from a spring trap and shot at with shotguns. **—*n-* trap′ shoot′ er.**

trash (trăsh) ***n-*** **1** worthless, useless things; rubbish; refuse. **2** worthless person or persons. **3** parts broken off, such as leaves, twigs, or husks.

trash·y (trăsh′ ē) ***adj-*** **[trash·i·er, trash·i·est]** resembling trash; worthless: *a* trashy *novel.* **—*n-* trash′ i·ness.**

trau·ma (trou′ mə, trȯ′ mə) ***n-*** **1** a physical wound or injury. **2** a psychic shock with lasting effects. **—*adj-* trau·mat′ ic** (trə măt′ ĭk).

trav·ail (trə vāl′, trăv′ āl′) ***n-*** **1** exhausting labor; toil. **2** physical or mental agony. **3** the labor and pain of childbirth. ***vi-*** to toil; work hard and painfully.

trav·el (trăv′ əl) ***vi-*** **1** to go from place to place for pleasure, recreation, or adventure; take a trip: *We* traveled *around England.* **2** to journey from place to place on business: *That salesman* travels *for a paint firm.* **3** to move: *Light* travels *much faster than sound.* ***vt-*** to journey over or through: *The car* traveled *a hard road. He* traveled *the South from end to end.* ***n-*** **1** the going from place to place: *I* like *travel.* **2** number of persons, vehicles, etc., on a road; traffic: *heavy* travel. **3** movement or progression of any kind. **4** in mechanics, movement or stroke, as of a piston; also, the length of the stroke. *as* ***modifier:*** *a* travel *agent.* **5 travels** (1) journey; trip. (2) a written account of a person's journey.

trav·el·er (trăv′ əl ər) ***n-*** person who travels.

trav·eled (trăv′ əld) ***adj-*** **1** having traveled widely. **2** used by many travelers: *a heavily* traveled *road.*

trav·e·logue or **trav·e·log** (trăv′ ə lȯg′, -lŏg′) ***n-*** **1** a lecture about a journey, usually illustrated by films, slides, or pictures. **2** motion picture of a region.

trav·erse (trăv′ ərs) ***n-*** **1** something lying across something else, such as a crossbar or a rung of a ladder. **2** a crossing; also, route or path across. **3** zigzag course made by a sailing ship due to contrary winds, or by a skier on a steep slope. **3** communicating gallery across a building. **4** mound of earth, bags, etc., that protects a trench. **5** in surveying, a single line established across a plot of ground. ***vt-*** (*also* trə vûrs′) **[trav·ersed, trav·ers·ing] 1** to pass over, across, or through: *They* traversed *the swamp safely.* **2** to move forward and backward over; cross and recross: *The beams of the* searchlight *traversed the sky.* **3** to lie or extend across: *A bridge* traverses *the stream.* ***vi-*** **1** to walk or move across; move back and forth or in a zigzag manner: *The skier* traversed *down the mountain.* **2** to turn; swivel. **—*adj-* trav′ ers·a·ble.** ***n-*** **trav′ ers·er.**

traverse rod (trăv′ ərs) ***n-*** metal rod or track for curtains or draperies, having a pulley mechanism for drawing them.

trav·es·ty (trăv′ ə stē) ***n-*** [*pl.* **trav·es·ties**] **1** any deliberate imitation with intent to ridicule; burlesque; parody **2** any likeness that is fantastic or ridiculous. ***vt-*** **[trav es·tied, trav·es·ty·ing]** to burlesque or parody.

Horse pulling a travois

tra·vois (trə voi′, trăv′ oi′) ***n-*** [*pl.* **tra·vois** (-voiz′) or **tra·vois·es** (-voiz′ əz)] primitive sled formerly used by Plains Indians and consisting of a platform or netting supported by two long poles, the forward ends of which are fastened to a horse or dog, while the rear ends trail along the ground. Also **tra·voise′** (-voiz′). [from Canadian French, from **travail**, "a brake."]

trawl (trȯl) ***n-*** **1** large baglike net dragged behind a boat in catching fish. **2** long fishing line to which are attached many short lines with hooks. *as* ***modifier:*** *a* trawl *net*; trawl *line.* ***vi-*** to fish with a trawl.

trawl·er (trȯ′ lər) ***n-*** **1** person who fishes with a trawl. **2** boat used in trawling.

tray (trā) ***n-*** flat receptacle of wood, metal, etc., with a raised edge or rim, used for carrying, holding, or displaying articles. *as* ***modifier:*** *a* tray *shop.* ***Hom-*** trey.

treach·er·ous (trĕch′ ər əs) ***adj-*** **1** betraying a trust; traitorous; disloyal: *The* treacherous *servant spied on his employer.* **2** not to be trusted in spite of appearances; deceptive; unreliable: *a* treacherous *current in a quiet river.* **—*adv-* treach′ er·ous·ly.** ***n-*** **treach′ er·ous·ness.**

treach·er·y (trĕch′ ə rē) ***n-*** [*pl.* **treach·er·ies**] betrayal of faith or confidence; disloyal conduct.

trea·cle (trē′ kəl) *Brit.* ***n-*** molasses.

tread (trĕd) ***vt-*** **[trod, trod·den** or **trod, tread·ing] 1** to walk on, over, or along: *He* trod *the moors all night.* **2** to press beneath the foot. **3** to make by walking or trampling: *to* tread *a path through the woods.* ***vi-*** **1** to step or walk: *You should* tread *carefully here.* **2** to step

fāte, făt, dâre, bärn; bē, bĕt, mêre; bīte, bĭt; nōte, hŏt, môre, dȯg; fŭn, fûr; tōō, bŏŏk; oil; out; tar; thin; then; hw for wh as in *wh*at; zh for s as in u*s*ual; ə for a, e, i, o, u, as in *a*go, li*n*en, per*i*l, at*o*m, min*u*s

(on) or (in) something: *He* trod *on the dog's tail.* ***n-*** **1** a walking or marching; also, the manner or sound of this: *the* tread *of troops; a heavy* tread. **2** horizontal part of a step or stair. **3** part of a wheel, tire, or sole that makes contact with a surface. **—*n-* tread′ er.**

tread on air to be extremely gay or happy.

tread on (one's) toes to offend by encroaching on another's rights or feelings.

tread underfoot to crush forcibly; oppress.

tread water to maintain one's head above water while in an upright position by moving the feet up and down.

trea·dle (trĕd′ əl) ***n-*** lever or pedal worked by the foot to operate a lathe, sewing machine, etc. ***vi-*** **[trea·dled, trea·dling]** to operate a machine with such a device.

tread·mill (trĕd′ mĭl′) ***n-*** **1** mill worked by animals or persons walking on the moving steps of a wheel, or treading an endless sloping belt. **2** monotonous or tiring activity in which one seems to get nowhere.

treas. **1** treasurer. **2** treasury.

trea·son (trē′ zən) ***n-*** betrayal of one's own country by waging war against it or by consciously and purposely acting to aid its enemies.

trea·son·a·ble (trē′ zən ə bəl) ***adj-*** of, related to, or involving treason: *a* treasonable *act.* **—*n-* trea′ son·a·ble·ness. *adv-* trea′ son·a·bly.**

trea·son·ous (trē′ zən əs) ***adj-*** treasonable. **—*adv-* trea′ son·ous·ly.**

treas·ure (trĕzh′ ər) ***n-*** **1** hoard of money, precious stones, etc.: *a pirate* treasure. **2** any valued thing or person: *The faded photographs were the old lady's* treasures. ***vt-*** **[treas·ured, treas·ur·ing]** to value highly; cherish: *He* treasured *the memory of his school days.*

treasure up to collect or retain in one's memory.

treas·ur·er (trĕzh′ ər ər) ***n-*** person in charge of the funds or finances of a business, government, club, etc.

treas·ure-trove (trĕzh′ ər trōv′) ***n-*** in law, money, jewels, or other valuables found in the earth or in any secret hiding place and not claimed by its owner; hence, any valuable discovery.

treas·ur·y (trĕzh′ ə rē) ***n-*** [*pl.* **treas·ur·ies**] **1** place where funds or revenues of a company, government, etc., are kept; also, such funds or revenues. **2** any collection of valuable objects: *a* treasury *of art.* **3 the Treasury** (also **Department of the Treasury**) branch of the U.S. government that administers public finances.

treat (trēt) ***vt-*** **1** to deal with; handle: *The lecturer* treated *his subject in great detail.* **2** to behave or act toward: *She* treated *her guests with the utmost courtesy.* **3** to help toward a cure: *Has a doctor* treated *your cold?* **4** to regard; consider: *He* treated *the matter far too seriously.* **5** to subject to some process for a particular result: *to* treat *a metal with acid.* **6** to entertain at one's own expense; also, to give, especially as a friendly or sociable gesture: *His father* treated *him to the movies.* ***n-*** act of paying for entertainment or food for someone; also, the entertainment or food so given. **2** something that gives great pleasure: *The party was a real* treat. **—*n-* treat′ er.**

treat of to discuss: *a book that* treats of *politics.*

trea·tise (trē′ təs) ***n-*** formal book or essay on a particular subject: *a* treatise *on whaling.*

treat·ment (trēt′ mənt) ***n-*** **1** the act or manner of dealing with someone or something: *the captain's excellent* treatment *of his crew; the writer's* treatment *of his theme.* **2** medical or surgical care: *a new* treatment *for polio.*

trea·ty (trē′ tē) ***n-*** [*pl.* **trea·ties**] formal agreement between nations; also, the document containing such an agreement: *a peace* treaty.

tre·ble (trĕb′ əl) ***vt-*** **[tre·bled, tre·bling]** to make three times as great or as many; triple: *to* treble *a score.* ***adj-*** **1** threefold; triple. **2** *Music* of or for the highest vocal or instrumental part; soprano. ***n-*** **1** *Music* the highest part in music; also, the instrument or voice playing or singing this part; soprano. **2** high-pitched or shrill sound.

treble clef *Music* ***n-*** symbol, originally a letter G, centered on the second line of a musical staff to indicate the position of G above middle C; G clef.

Treble clef

treb·ly (trĕb′ lē) ***adv-*** in three ways or threefold: *He was* trebly *tormented: by illness, poverty, and a nagging wife.*

tree (trē) ***n-*** **1** large plant with a woody trunk that has branches bearing leaves. **2** shrub or bush resembling a tree: *a rose* tree. **3** piece of wood used for a particular purpose: *a shoe* tree; *a hat* tree. ***vt-*** **[treed, tree·ing]** to chase up a tree. **—*adj-* tree′ less. *adj-* tree′ like′.**

Cross-section of tree trunk

up a tree *Informal* in a situation from which there is no apparent escape; also, in an embarrassing position.

tree farm ***n-*** forest area managed for the commercial production of trees.

tree fern ***n-*** large tropical fern with a woody stem.

tree toad ***n-*** any of various amphibians that are related to toads and frogs and live in trees. Also **tree frog.**

tree·top (trē′ tŏp′) ***n-*** highest part of a tree; also, the part of the tree near the top.

tre·foil (trĕf′ oil′, trē′ foil′) ***n-*** **1** any three-leafed plant, such as clover. **2** ornament resembling a cloverleaf.

trek (trĕk) ***vi-*** **[trekked, trek·king]** among the early Boers of South Africa, to make a journey by ox wagon; hence, to travel slowly and with great difficulty: *The Boers* trekked *across the veldt.* ***n-*** journey; also, a migration: *the* trek *to the West.* **—*n-* trek′ ker.**

trel·lis (trĕl′ əs) ***n-*** ornamental framework, used as support for vines or other creeping plants. It is usually made of small wood strips, crossed and widely spaced. ***vt-*** to fasten or support on a trellis: *to* trellis *a climbing rose.*

Trellis

trem·a·tode (trĕm′ ə tōd′) ***n-*** a parasitic flatworm or fluke, such as the liver flukes and blood flukes.

trem·ble (trem′ bəl) ***vi-*** **[trem·bled, trem·bling]** **1** to shake or shiver, as from fear or cold; shudder. **2** to quaver, as a voice. ***n-*** involuntary shaking; shudder. **—*n-* trem′ bler. *adv-* trem′ bling·ly.**

trem·bly (trĕm′ blē) ***adj-*** trembling; shaking.

tre·men·dous (trə mĕn′ dəs) ***adj-*** **1** huge; vast; enormous. **2** of enormous value or importance; extraordinary: *a* tremendous *idea.* **3** *Informal* wonderful. **—*adv-* tre·men′ dous·ly. *n-* tre·men′ dous·ness.**

trem·o·lo (trĕm′ ə lō) *Music* ***n-*** [*pl.* **trem·o·los**] **1** rapid repetition of a tone or tones by a vocalist or instrumentalist in order to produce a tremulous effect. **2** vibrato.

tre·mor (trĕm′ ər, trē′ mər) ***n-*** **1** a shaking; quivering. **2** thrill of emotion; shiver: *a* tremor *of anxiety.*

trem·u·lous (trĕm′ yə ləs) ***adj-*** **1** quivering, shaking, or trembling: *a voice* tremulous *with fear.* **2** nervous or fearful; timid: *The young actress was* tremulous *as the curtain went up.* **—*adv-* trem′ u·lous·ly. *n-* trem′ u·lous·ness.**

trench (trĕnch) ***n-*** **1** long, narrow furrow in the earth. **2** deep ditch used as a protection for troops in combat. ***vt-*** to dig ditches in: *to* trench *a field for drainage.*

trench·ant (trĕn′chənt) ***adj-*** sharp and forceful; keen; also, biting or caustic: *a* trenchant *remark.* **—*n-* trench′an·cy.** ***adv-*** **trench′ant·ly.**

trench coat ***n-*** loose, belted, double-breasted raincoat.

[1]**trench·er** (trĕn′chər) ***n-*** in former times, a wooden plate or platter on which food was carved or served. [from Old French **trencheor,** "something to cut with."]

[2]**trench·er** (trĕn′chər) ***n-*** person who digs trenches or ditches. [from **trench.**]

trench·er·man (trĕn′chər mən) ***n-*** [*pl.* **trench·er·men**] person who has a hearty appetite.

trench mouth ***n-*** Vincent's infection.

trend (trĕnd) ***n-*** general tendency or course; drift: *the* trend *of business.* ***vi-***: *The river* trends *eastward.*

trep·i·da·tion (trĕp′ə dā′shən) ***n-*** **1** feeling of nervous alarm; fear mingled with uncertainty: *He approached us with* trepidation. **2** *Archaic* a trembling or vibration.

tres·pass (trĕs′pəs) ***vi-*** **1** in law, to commit an illegal act; especially, to enter property illegally: *We* trespassed *in the neighboring woods.* **2** to intrude; encroach (on or upon): *Are we* trespassing *on your time?* **3** to sin. ***n-*** **1** offense; sin. **2** in law, an illegal act; especially, illegal entry. **—*n-* tres′pass·er.**

tress·es (trĕs′əz) ***n-*** *pl.* loose feminine hair.

tres·tle (trĕs′əl) ***n-*** **1** metal or timber framework used as a bridge. **2** frame, such as a carpenter's horse, used to support a platform.

Trestle

tres·tle·work (trĕs′əl wûrk′) ***n-*** system of connected trestles built to support a railroad or road.

trey (trā) ***n-*** card, or the side of a die or domino, that has three spots. ***Hom-*** tray.

tri- *prefix* **1** three; threefold: tri*color*; tri*angle.* **2** once in three; happening every third: tri*weekly.* **3** three times; into three parts: tri*sect.* [from Latin **tri-,** from **tres,** "three," or from Greek **tri-,** from **treis,** "three."]

tri·ad (trī′ăd′) ***n-*** **1** set or group of three, especially of three closely related persons or things. **2** *Music* three-note chord consisting of a particular note plus the third and fifth notes above it.

tri·al (trī′əl) ***n-*** **1** a hearing and deciding of a case in a court of law: *His* trial *for theft started yesterday.* **2** test of something to determine its efficiency, flaws, etc.: *the* trial *of a new ship.* **3** hardship, temptation, etc., that tries one's endurance: *The long winter was a* trial *for the pioneers.* **4** person or thing that tries one's patience, faith, or love: *He was a* trial *to his family.* *as* ***modifier***: *a* trial *run of a car.*
 on trial being tried.

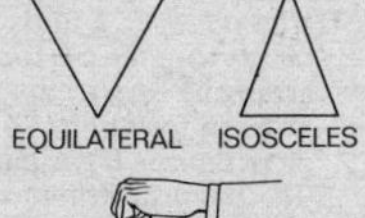

trial jury See *jury.*

tri·an·gle (trī′ăng′gəl) ***n-*** **1** any closed figure formed by three straight lines. **2** anything shaped like a triangle. **3** musical instrument, consisting of a steel rod bent in the form of a triangle, open at one corner and sounded with a light metal rod. **4** flat, usually transparent, triangular drafting instrument for ruling lines, drawing right angles, etc. **5** romantic situation in which two persons of one sex are involved with one of the opposite.

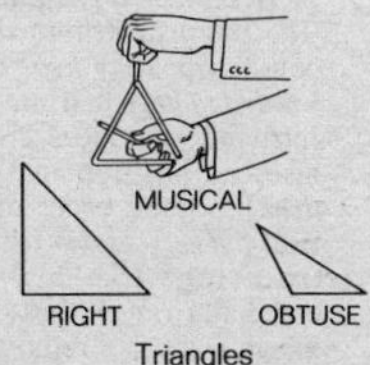

Triangles

tri·an·gu·lar (trī ăng′gyə lər) ***adj-*** **1** shaped like a triangle; having three sides and three angles: *a* triangular *frame.* **2** concerned with or made up of three persons or things: *a* triangular *treaty.* **—*n-* tri·an′gu·lar′i·ty** (-lăr′ə tē, -lĕr′ə tē). ***adv-*** **tri·an′gu·lar·ly.**

tri·an·gu·late (trī ăng′gyə lāt′) ***vt-*** [**tri·an·gu·lat·ed, tri·an·gu·lat·ing**] **1** to divide into triangles. **2** to determine or survey by triangulation.

tri·an·gu·la·tion (trī ăng′gyə lā′shən) ***n-*** the application of trigonometry to measuring distances, locating points in navigation, determining areas, etc.

Tri·as·sic (trī ăs′ĭk) ***n-*** the first of the three periods of the Mesozoic era. During the Triassic, small dinosaurs became common and primitive mammals first appeared. ***adj-***: *a* Triassic *fossil.*

trib·al (trī′bəl) ***adj-*** having to do with a tribe: *a* tribal *dance*; *a* tribal *custom.* **—*adv-* tri′bal·ly.**

tribe (trīb) ***n-*** **1** group of people, especially primitive people, having a common ancestor and forming a community under a common leader: *Several Indian* tribes *once roamed these prairies.* **2** group of people united by a common interest, occupation, etc.: *a* tribe *of thieves.* **3** group or class of plants or animals.

tribes·man (trībz′mən) ***n-*** [*pl.* **tribes·men**] member of a tribe.

trib·u·la·tion (trĭb′yə lā′shən) ***n-*** great distress or sorrow; affliction; trial; also, anything that causes this.

tri·bu·nal (trī byo͞o′nəl, trĭ-) ***n-*** **1** court of justice; also, the seat of a judge. **2** any final authority: *the* tribunal *of conscience.*

tri·bune (trĭ′byo͞on′) ***n-*** in ancient times, a Roman magistrate elected by the people to protect their liberties; hence, any person who champions people's rights.

trib·u·tar·y (trĭb′yə tĕr′ē) ***n-*** [*pl.* **trib·u·tar·ies**] **1** stream or river flowing into a larger stream, river, or lake. **2** state or government that pays taxes to, or is under the control of, a superior government. ***adj-*** **1** flowing into another: *a* tributary *stream.* **2** paying tribute, such as taxes: *a* tributary *country.* **3** paid or due as a tribute.

trib·ute (trĭb′yo͞ot′, -yət) ***n-*** **1** stated sum of money or amount of goods paid by one government or ruler to another to obtain protection, insure peace, or fulfill the terms of a treaty. **2** any money exacted for safety or protection: *The gangsters collected* tribute *from the timid merchant.* **3** acknowledgment of worth, service rendered, etc.; praise: *to pay* tribute *to a hero.*

trice (trīs) ***vt-*** [**triced, tric·ing**] to pull and tie with a small rope (usually followed by "up"): *to* trice *up a sail.*
 in a trice in a very short space of time; in an instant.

tri·ceps (trī′sĕps′) ***n-*** the large muscle along the back of the upper arm, the function of which is to extend the forearm.

tri·cer·a·tops (trī′sĕr′ə tŏps′) ***n-*** large, plant-eating dinosaur of the Cretaceous period, with two large horns attached to an immense bony plate that extends backward from the head and protects the neck. For picture, see *dinosaur.*

tri·chi·na (trĭ kī′nə) ***n-*** [*pl.* **tri·chi·nae** (-nē)] microscopic worm that is parasitic in the muscles of human beings, swine, and other animals and causes trichinosis. **—*adj-* trich′i·nous:** *a* trichinous *pig.*

tri·chi·no·sis (trĭk′ə nō′səs) ***n-*** disease caused by the presence of trichinae in the muscles and intestines.

trick (trĭk) ***n-*** **1** something done in order to deceive or cheat: *His illness was only a* trick *to avoid school.* **2** prank; practical joke: *He played a* trick *on his mother.* **3** foolish or mean act: *the* trick *of putting salt in the sugar bowl.* **4** show of skill in order to amuse: *a* trick *in balancing*; *a card* trick. **5** particular skill; knack: *The cook knew all the* tricks *of pleasing hungry boys.* **6** peculiarity of manner; habit: *He had an annoying* trick *of cracking his knuckles.* **7** in card games, the cards played in one round of a game: *She took the* trick *with her king. as* ***modifier***: *a* trick *cigar.* ***vt-*** to deceive or cheat.

do the trick *Slang* to bring about a successful result.

trick out to dress, especially in an outlandish way.

trick·er·y (trĭk′ ə rē) ***n-*** [*pl.* **trick·er·ies**] the use of tricks; deception; fraud; cheating.

trick·le (trĭk′ əl) ***vi-*** [**trick·led, trick·ling**] to flow slowly in a thin or broken stream: *Rain* trickles *from the trees.* ***vt-***: *He* trickled *sand through his fingers.* ***n-*** thin, slow flow or stream: *a* trickle *of blood*; *a* trickle *of people.*

trick·ster (trĭk′ stər) ***n-*** cunning cheat or deceiver.

trick·y (trĭk′ ē) ***adj-*** [**trick·i·er, trick·i·est**] **1** likely to play tricks; deceitful: *a* tricky *card player.* **2** complicated; unpredictable: *a* tricky *horse*; *a* tricky *problem.* ***—adv-*** **trick′ i·ly.** ***n-*** **trick′ i·ness.**

tri·col·or (trī′ kŭl′ ər) ***adj-*** (also **tri′ col′ ored**) having three colors: *a* tricolor *banner.* ***n-*** flag having three large areas of color; especially, the flag of France, which is blue, white, and red.

tri·cot (trē′ kō) ***n-*** **1** material of wool, silk, or cotton that resembles a knitted fabric. **2** ribbed dress goods.

tri·cus·pid (trī′ kŭs′ pĭd) ***adj-*** of the teeth of mammals, having three projections on their grinding surfaces. ***n-*** any of the molars.

tri·cy·cle (trī′ sĭk′ əl) ***n-*** three-wheeled vehicle, usually worked by pedals; especially, one made for children.

tri·dent (trī′ dənt) ***n-*** spear with three prongs; especially, in classical mythology, the spear carried by Neptune.

Trident

tried (trīd) *p.t. & p.p.* of **try.**

tri·en·ni·al (trī ĕn′ ē əl) ***adj-*** **1** lasting three years: *a* triennial *plague.* **2** occurring every three years: *They called a* triennial *meeting.* ***n-*** **1** event occurring every three years. **2** third anniversary of an event. ***—adv-*** **tri·en′ ni·al·ly.**

tri·er (trī′ ər) ***n-*** person or thing that tries.

tries (trīz) **1** plural of the noun **try.** **2** form of the verb **try** used with "he," "she," "it," or singular noun subjects, in the present tense.

tri·fle (trī′ fəl) ***n-*** **1** anything of little value or importance. **2** dessert of alternate layers of cake and fruit filling, covered with custard and meringue or whipped cream. ***vt-*** [**tri·fled, tri·fling**] to spend foolishly (usually followed by "away"): *He* trifled *away his talent.* ***vi-*** **1** to deal with something in a light and flippant manner: *This work is not to be* trifled *with.* **2** to play or toy (with). **3** to waste time: *She was always* trifling. ***—n-*** **tri′ fler.**

a trifle slightly: *I'll be* a trifle *late.*

tri·fling (trī′ flĭng) ***adj-*** of slight value or importance; trivial; frivolous: *a* trifling *sum.* ***—adv-*** **tri′ fling·ly.**

trig. **1** trigonometric. **2** trigonometry.

trig·ger (trĭg′ ər) ***n-*** **1** small lever on a firearm that is squeezed by the finger to fire it. **2** catch that springs a trap. ***vt-*** to set going; start: *The battle* triggered *the revolution.*

Trigger

quick on the trigger *Informal* quick to shoot; hence, quick to react or respond; sharp-witted.

trig·o·no·met·ric (trĭg′ ə nə mĕ′ trĭk) ***adj-*** having to do with trigonometry. ***—adv-*** **trig′ o·no·met′ ri·cal·ly.**

trigonometric function ***n-*** any of various functions of an angle, or its subtended arc, that consists of a variable ratio between two sides of a right triangle which contains the angle as an acute angle. The ratio varies with the size of the angle. The most commonly used trigonometric functions are the sine, cosine, and tangent.

trig·o·nom·e·try (trĭg′ ə nŏm′ ə trē) ***n-*** branch of mathematics that is based on the relations between the sides and angles of triangles.

tri·graph (trī′ grăf′) ***n-*** group of three letters representing one sound, such as "eau" in "beauty."

tri·lat·er·al (trī′ lăt′ ər əl) ***adj-*** **1** participated in by three sides or parties: *a* trilateral *agreement.* **2** three-sided.

tri·lin·gual (trī′ lĭng′ gwəl) ***adj-*** **1** written or expressed in three languages: *a* trilingual *edition.* **2** fluent in three languages: *a* trilingual *person.*

trill (trĭl) ***n-*** **1** *Music* trembling sound made by a rapid alternation of notes that are a tone or half-tone apart. **2** similar sound, such as the warble of a bird. ***vt-*** to sing, play, or speak with a trill: *to* trill *a musical passage*; *to* trill *an "r."* ***vi-***: *The birds* trilled *gaily.*

tril·lion (trĭl′ yən) ***n-*** in the United States, a thousand billion (1,000,000,000,000); in Great Britain, a million million million (1,000,000,000,000,000,000).

tril·lionth (trĭl′ yənth) ***adj-*** **1** last in a series of a trillion. **2** ordinal of 1,000,000,000,000. ***n-*** **1** last in a series of a trillion. **2** one of a trillion equal parts of a whole or group. **3** last term in the name of a common fraction having a denominator of 1,000,000,000,000, or of the corresponding decimal fraction, .000000000001.

tril·li·um (trĭl′ ē əm) ***n-*** any of various plants of the lily family, having three leaves with one large flower in the middle.

Trillium

tri·lo·bate (trī′ lō′ bāt′) ***adj-*** having three lobes: *a* trilobate *leaf.*

tri·lo·bite (trī′ lə bīt′) ***n-*** any of a class of extinct arthropods that were abundant in the Cambrian period and died out at the close of the Paleozoic era. Their nearest living relative is the horseshoe crab.

tril·o·gy (trĭl′ ə jē) ***n-*** [*pl.* **tril·o·gies**] series of three dramas, novels, or musical compositions, each complete in itself but forming a unified whole by reason of theme, subject matter, or treatment.

trim (trĭm) ***vt-*** [**trimmed, trim·ming**] **1** to make orderly, neat, and tidy by cutting, clipping, etc.: *to* trim *hair*; *to* trim *a hedge.* **2** to decorate; adorn: *to* trim *a coat with fur*; *to* trim *the Christmas tree.* **3** to balance (a vessel) by arranging cargo, etc.; also, to adjust (sails and yards) in position for sailing. **4** *Informal* to defeat; also, to cheat or victimize: *We* trimmed *our opponents by a good score. The salesman* trimmed *the tourist.* ***n-*** **1** order; proper condition: *They kept the business in* trim. *The old man wanted to keep in* trim. **2** woodwork of a building around the windows, doors, etc. **3** of a vessel, fitness for sailing; also, its position in the water. ***adj-*** [**trim·mer, trim·mest**] in good order or condition; neat: *a* trim *lawn*; *a* trim *figure.* ***—adv-*** **trim′ ly.** ***n-*** **trim′ mer.** ***n-*** **trim′ ness.**

trim·ming (trĭm′ ĭng) ***n-*** **1** decoration or ornament, especially on clothes: *the* trimming *on a hat.* **2** **trimmings** (1) parts removed by cutting off the edges: *the* trimmings *of meat.* (2) the side dishes of a meal: *roast goose with its* trimmings. **3** *Informal* severe beating.

tri·month·ly (trī′ mŭnth′ lē) ***adj-*** occurring every three months: *a* trimonthly *meeting.* ***adv-***: *to meet* trimonthly.

tri·ni·tro·tol·u·ene (trī′ nī′ trō tŏl′ yo͞o ēn′) a very unstable compound ($C_6H_2CH_3(NO_2)_3$), used chiefly as a high explosive; TNT. Also **tri′ ni′ tro·tol′ u·ol.**

Trin·i·ty (trĭn′ ə tē) ***n-*** **1** *Theology* the union of the Father, Son, and Holy Spirit in one divine being. **2 trinity** [*pl.* **trin·i·ties**] any union of three in one; triad.

trin·ket (trĭng′ kət) ***n-*** **1** small ornament or jewel. **2** toy.

tri·no·mi·al (trī′ nō′ mē əl) *Mathematics* ***n-*** polynomial having three terms. Example: x − 2xy − y^2. *as* ***modifier***: *a* trinomial *expression.*

tri·o (trē′ ō) ***n-*** [*pl.* **tri·os**] **1** *Music* composition for three voices or three instruments. **2** group of three singers or musicians. **3** any group of three: *a* trio *of brothers.*

tri·ode (trī′ ōd′) ***n-*** vacuum tube with three electrodes (anode, cathode, and grid).

trip (trĭp) ***n-*** **1** journey; voyage: *He took a flying* trip *to Brazil.* **2** stumble: *a* trip *on the stairs.* **3** slip; mistake or error. ***vi-*** **[tripped, trip·ping] 1** to stumble: *He* tripped *on the dais.* **2** to make a mistake; err: *He* tripped *on the arithmetic test.* ***vt-*** **1** to cause to stumble (often followed by "up"): *The toy on the floor* tripped *him up.* **2** to catch in an error, falsehood, etc. (often followed by "up"): *He* tripped *him up with that question.* **3** to release, as by pulling a catch or trigger: *to* trip *an animal trap.*

tri·par·tite (trī pär′ tĭt′, trī′-) ***adj-*** **1** in three parts, such as a three-leaf clover; also, having three similar parts or copies. **2** made or existing among three persons or groups: *a* tripartite *agreement.*

tripe (trīp) ***n-*** **1** part of the stomach of an ox or cow, used for food. **2** *Informal* anything worthless or foolish.

trip hammer ***n-*** large power hammer that is hoisted into the air and then suddenly allowed to drop by a tripping device, delivering regular and heavy blows.

tri·ple (trĭp′ əl) ***adj-*** **1** having three parts; threefold: *a* triple *picture frame.* **2** three times as much or as many: *to charge a* triple *price.* ***n-*** **1** an amount three times as much or as many: *In that shop you pay* triple *for everything you buy.* **2** in baseball, a hit on which the batter reaches third base; three-base hit. ***vt-*** **[tri·pled, tri·pling]** to make or cause to be three times as much or as many: *to* triple *the output of work*; *to* triple *the value of the property.* ***vi-*** **1** to become three times as much as or as many. **2** in baseball, to get a three-base hit.

triple play ***n-*** in baseball, a play in which three outs are made.

tri·plet (trĭp′ lət) ***n-*** any one of three children born at one birth; also, any set of three things.

triple threat ***n-*** in football, a player who is good at running, kicking, and passing. *as* ***modifier***: *a* triple-threat *back.*

[1]**trip·li·cate** (trĭp′ lĭ kət) ***adj-*** threefold; made in sets of three: *a* triplicate *record.* ***n-*** something identical with two others; also, three identical things.

[2]**trip·li·cate** (trĭp′ lĭ kāt′) ***vt-*** **[trip·li·cat·ed, trip·li·cat·ing]** to reproduce three identical copies of: *to* triplicate *the letter.*

trip·ly (trĭp′ lē) ***adv-*** in a triple amount or degree; trebly.

tri·pod (trī′ pŏd′) ***n-*** **1** support or stand with three legs, as for a camera or gun. **2** any article with three legs, such as a stool.

trip·per (trĭp′ ər) ***n-*** releasing device or mechanism, such as one for operating a railroad signal.

Tripod

trip·ping (trĭp′ ĭng) ***adj-*** light and graceful; nimble: *a* tripping *gait.* ***—adv-*** **trip′ ping·ly.**

trip·tych (trĭp′ tĭk′) ***n-*** **1** picture, design, or carving on three hinged panels, often depicting a religious scene and serving as an altarpiece. **2** in ancient Greece and Rome, three writing tablets joined together.

tri·sect (trī′ sĕkt′) ***vt-*** to cut or divide into three parts; especially, in geometry, to divide into three equal parts. ***—n-*** **tri′sec′ tion.**

tri·syl·la·ble (trī′ sĭl′ ə bəl) ***n-*** word made up of three syllables. ***—adj-*** **tri′ syl·lab′ ic.**

trite (trīt) ***adj-*** stale from too frequent use; commonplace: *such a* trite *expression.* ***—adv-*** **trite′ ly.** ***n-*** **trite′ ness.**

trit·i·um (trĭt′ ē əm, trĭsh′-) ***n-*** isotope of hydrogen containing two neutrons in addition to the proton in the atomic nucleus.

tri·ton (trī′ tən) ***n-*** **1** any of various large sea snails with long, spiraled shells. **2 Triton** in Greek mythology, a demigod of the sea, son of Poseidon, generally pictured as part man and part dolphin and blowing a shell trumpet to calm the sea.

tri·umph (trī′ əmf) ***n-*** **1** victory; conquest; achievement; success: *the* triumph *of knowledge.* **2** in ancient Rome, a spectacular parade and celebration in honor of a returning victorious general and his army. **3** joy or acclaim over success, victory, etc. (often preceded by "in"): *There were shouts of* triumph. *He sat in* triumph. ***vi-*** **1** to be victorious or successful: *to* triumph *over great odds.* **2** to exult about victory or success: *to* triumph *over one's captives.*

tri·um·phal (trī ŭm′ fəl) ***adj-*** done or made in celebration or memory of a victory or triumph: *a* triumphal *feast*; *a* triumphal *arch.*

tri·um·phant (trī ŭm′ fənt) ***adj-*** **1** victorious: *a* triumphant *army.* **2** rejoicing or showing elation over having been successful or victorious: *a* triumphant *march.* ***—adv-*** **tri·um′ phant·ly.**

tri·um·vir (trī ŭm′ vər) ***n-*** [*pl.* **tri·um·virs** or **tri·um·vi·ri** (-və rē)] one of three persons who together govern a state; especially, in ancient Rome, one of the three ruling magistrates of the republic.

tri·um·vi·rate (trī ŭm′ və rāt′, -rət) ***n-*** **1** government by triumvirs. **2** group or association of three: *a* triumvirate *of friends.*

triv·et (trĭv′ ət) ***n-*** **1** three-legged stand for holding a kettle near or over an open fire. **2** short-legged metal plate on which to set hot dishes.

triv·i·a (trĭv′ ē ə) ***n-*** *pl.* (takes singular or plural verb) petty matters; trifles: *preoccupied with* trivia.

triv·i·al (trĭv′ ē əl) ***adj-*** **1** insignificant; unimportant; of little value; paltry: *a* trivial *remark.* **2** ordinary; commonplace: *the* trivial *tasks of everyday life.* **3** occupied or concerned with trifles: *He was a* trivial *person.* ***—adv-*** **triv′ i·al·ly.**

triv·i·al·i·ty (trĭv′ ē ăl′ ə tē) ***n-*** [*pl.* **triv·i·al·i·ties**] **1** insignificance; pettiness. **2** insignificant matter.

tri·week·ly (trī′ wēk′ lē) ***adj-*** **1** done or occurring three times a week. **2** done or occurring every third week: *a* triweekly *magazine.* ***adv-***: *They published it* triweekly. ***n-*** publication that appears three times a week or every third week.

-trix *suffix* (used to form feminine nouns from masculine nouns ending in **-tor**): *avia*trix.

tro·che (trō′ kē) ***n-*** medicated lozenge. ***Hom-*** trochee.

tro·chee (trō′ kē) ***n-*** **1** measure or foot in poetry, made up of one accented syllable followed by one unaccented

---

fāte, făt, dâre, bärn; bē, bĕt, mêre; bīte, bĭt; nōte, hŏt, môre, dòg; fŭn, fûr; to͞o, bo͝ok; oil; out; ta*r*; thin; then; hw for wh as in *wh*at; zh for s as in u*s*ual; ə for a, e, i, o, u, as in *a*go, lin*e*n, per*i*l, at*o*m, min*u*s

syllable. **2** line in poetry made up of such measures. Example: "Tell′ me/not′ in/mourn′ ful/num′bers." ***Hom-*** troche. ***—adj-* tro·cha′ ic** (trō kā′ ĭk): *a* trochaic *stanza.*

trod (trŏd) *p.t. & p.p.* of **tread.**

trod·den (trŏd′ ən) *p.p.* of **tread.**

trog·lo·dyte (trŏg′ lə dīt′) ***n-*** **1** dweller in a cave; especially, a prehistoric caveman. **2** recluse; hermit.

troi·ka (troi′ kə) ***n-*** Russian carriage drawn by three horses abreast; also, the horses.

Troi·lus (troi′ ləs) ***n-*** **1** in Greek mythology, a son of Priam, slain by Achilles. **2** in medieval legend, the lover of the faithless Cressida.

Tro·jan (trō′ jən) ***n-*** **1** inhabitant of ancient Troy. **2** fearless and industrious person. ***adj-*** of or relating to ancient Troy: *the* Trojan *women.*

Trojan horse ***n-*** **1** huge wooden horse built by the Greeks and filled with Greek warriors, which the Trojans were tricked into taking within Troy's walls. **2** any treacherous person, group, or plot that destroys from within.

Trojan War ***n-*** the ten-year conflict between the Greeks and the Trojans, caused by the abduction of Helen.

[1]**troll** (trōl) ***vi-*** to fish by dragging the line through the water from a moving boat: *to* troll *for striped bass.* ***vt-*** *Music* to sing the parts of in succession, with different parts sung by different voices, as in a round: *They* trolled *"Three Blind Mice."* [from Old French **troller** meaning "to ramble; run without plan; run around in circles," from earlier **trauler,** probably Germanic.]

[2]**troll** (trōl) ***n-*** in Scandinavian folklore, an ugly giant or, in later tales, an impish dwarf who was supposed to live in caves, hills, and such places. [probably Old Norse.]

trol·ley (trŏl′ ē) ***n-*** [*pl.* **trol·leys**] **1** grooved wheel at the end of a pole on a streetcar, which makes contact with an overhead electric wire. **2** trolley car. **3** wheeled carriage, basket, etc., that runs suspended from an overhead track. *as* ***modifier****: a* trolley *wire.*

Electric trolley

trolley bus ***n-*** bus that is propelled electrically by current picked up from an overhead wire by a trolley.

trolley car ***n-*** electric streetcar that gets its power through a trolley.

trol·lop (trŏl′ əp) ***n-*** prostitute.

trom·bone (trŏm′ bōn′, trŏm bōn′) ***n-*** brass instrument of the trumpet family. A **slide trombone** changes tone by means of the U-shaped tube; a **valve trombone** changes tone by means of valves. ***—n-* trom·bon′ ist.**

Trombone

troop (tro͞op) ***n-*** **1** large number, group, company, or collection of people or animals: *a* troop *of tourists.* **2 troops** soldiers. **3** formerly, a cavalry unit corresponding to an infantry company. **4** in the Boy Scouts and Girl Scouts, a group consisting of from two to four patrols (from 16 to 32 scouts). ***vi-*** to gather or move in large numbers: *Crowds* trooped *out of the gate.* ***Hom-*** troupe.

troop·er (tro͞o′ pər) ***n-*** **1** member of a troop of mounted or motorized police. **2** State policeman. **3** formerly, a member of a cavalry unit.

troop·ship (tro͞op′ shĭp′) ***n-*** ship that carries troops; military transport.

tro·phy (trō′ fē) ***n-*** [*pl.* **tro·phies**] **1** something captured in battle and kept as a token of victory, such as a gun or flag. **2** any token of achievement; prize: *a tennis* trophy.

trop·ic (trŏp′ ĭk) ***n-*** **1** the tropic of Cancer or the tropic of Capricorn. **2 the tropics** or **the Tropics** the region between the tropic of Cancer and the tropic of Capricorn.

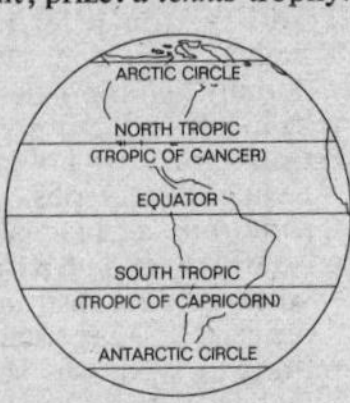

North and South Tropics

trop·i·cal (trŏp′ ĭ kəl) ***adj-*** of or like the tropics: *a* tropical *climate*; *a* tropical *plant.* ***—adv-* trop′ i·cal·ly.**

tropical year ***n-*** the interval of time between consecutive passages of the sun through the vernal equinox, containing 365 days, 5 hours, 48 minutes, and 46 seconds; astronomical year.

tropic of Cancer ***n-*** the parallel of latitude around the earth at about 23½ °N, the northernmost parallel at which the sun is ever directly overhead.

tropic of Capricorn ***n-*** the parallel of latitude around the earth at about 23½ °S, the southernmost parallel at which the sun is ever directly overhead.

tro·pism (trō′ pĭz əm, trŏp′ ĭz-) ***n-*** growth movements in plants, or reflex movements in some simple animals, in response to an outside stimulus.

trop·o·pause (trō′ pə pôz′) ***n-*** the boundary layer of the earth's atmosphere between the troposphere and the stratosphere.

tro·po·sphere (trō′ pə sfêr′, trŏp′ ə-) ***n-*** the layer of the atmosphere nearest the earth, extending to a height of about seven miles and having air currents, varying temperatures, and clouds.

trot (trŏt) ***n-*** **1** jogging gait of a horse when the right front foot and the left hind foot are raised first, and then the other two feet. A trot is faster than a walk but slower than a canter or gallop. **2** a jogging run: *The children came at a* trot. ***vi-*** **[trot·ted, trot·ting] 1** to move with a jogging gait or run: *The horses* trotted *to the fence. The boy* trotted *to his mother's side.* ***vt-****: He* trotted *his horse.*
trot out *Informal* to exhibit for approval or inspection.

troth (trôth, trōth) *Archaic* ***n-*** faith, loyalty, or truth.
plight one's troth to pledge one's word to marry.

trot·ter (trŏt′ ər) ***n-*** person or horse that trots.

trou·ba·dour (tro͞o′ bə dôr′) ***n-*** one of a number of lyric poets who flourished from the 11th through the 13th centuries in southern France and northern Italy; hence, any singer of love songs.

trou·ble (trŭb′ əl) ***n-*** **1** disturbance; commotion: *The police rushed to the scene of* trouble. **2** distress; worry: *He is having money* troubles. **3** inconvenience; effort; bother: *Please don't go to any* trouble *for me.* **4** difficulty: *the* trouble *with your plan*; *in* trouble *at home.* **5** ailment: *heart* trouble; *stomach* trouble. ***vt-*** **[trou·bled, trou·bling] 1** to worry or distress: *His debts* troubled *him.* **2** to inconvenience; bother: *May I* trouble *you for a loan?* ***vi-*** to take pains; bother: *Don't* trouble *to apologize.*

trou·ble·mak·er (trŭb′ əl mā′ kər) ***n-*** person who constantly causes trouble, usually intentionally.

trou·ble-shoot·er (trŭb′ əl sho͞o′ tər) ***n-*** **1** person who seeks out difficulties or failures in industrial equipment and repairs them. **2** person adept at resolving disputes, such as those in labor-management relations.

trou·ble·some (trŭb′ əl səm) ***adj-*** **1** causing trouble; annoying: *a* troublesome *child.* **2** hard to handle or solve; difficult: *a* troublesome *problem.* ***—adv-* trou′ ble·some·ly.** ***n-*** **trou′ ble·some·ness.**

trou·blous (trŭb′ ləs) ***adj-*** full of or bringing trouble and distress: *these* troublous *times.*

trough (trôf, trŏf, *also* trôth) ***n-*** **1** long, narrow container to hold water or food for animals. **2** similar container for kneading dough or washing ore. **3** uncovered gutter for draining water. **4** hollow or depression, such as between waves or hills: *gulls floating in the* troughs *of the sea.* **5** in meteorology, a region of low atmospheric pressure between two regions of higher pressure.

trounce (trouns) ***vt-*** **[trounced, trounc·ing] 1** to whip severely: *His father* trounced *him for lying.* **2** *Informal* to defeat thoroughly: *She* trounced *him in tennis.*

troupe (tro͞op) ***n-*** group of people, especially of performers: *a* troupe *of actors*; *a* troupe *of acrobats.* ***vi-*** **[trouped, troup·ing]** to travel or perform with such a group: *The amateur drama group* trouped *500 miles.* ***Hom-*** troop. **—*n-* troup′ er.**

trou·sers (trou′ zərz) ***n-*** (takes plural verb) two-legged outer garment worn from the waist to the ankles.

trous·seau (tro͞o′ sō′) ***n-*** bride's personal outfit of clothes, linens, etc.

trout (trout) ***n-*** [*pl.* **trout; trouts** (kinds of trout)] any of a group of food or game fishes of the salmon family, such as the brook trout or rainbow trout, found chiefly in cold, fresh waters.

Brook trout, about 1 ft. long

trout lily ***n-*** the dogtooth violet.

trove (trōv) ***n-*** something that has been found: *a treasure* trove.

trow (trō) *Archaic* ***vi-*** to suppose; believe; think.

trow·el (trou′ əl) ***n-*** small, short-handled tool, used by masons, plasterers, and gardeners.

GARDEN
MASON'S
Trowels

troy weight ***n-*** system of weights for precious metals and gems, in which twelve ounces equal one pound.

tru·ant (tro͞o′ ənt) ***n-*** person who shirks his work or duty; especially, a boy or girl who stays away from school without permission. ***adj-*** idle; errant: *a* truant *worker.* **—*n-* tru′ an·cy.**

play truant to stay away from school or work.

truant officer ***n-*** official of a public school system who investigates cases of truancy.

truce (tro͞os) ***n-*** temporary lull or rest; especially, a temporary suspension of fighting, brought about by mutual agreement during a war.

[1]**truck** (trŭk) ***vt-*** *Archaic* to barter or trade. ***n-*** **1** garden vegetables raised for market. **2** *Informal* trash; rubbish. [from Old French **troquer** meaning "to barter."]

have no truck with *Informal* to have no dealings with.

[2]**truck** (trŭk) ***n-*** **1** large vehicle for carrying heavy loads: *an oil* truck. **2** small vehicle operated by hand or motor and used for carrying loads in a factory, on a wharf, etc. **3** group of wheels and their frame at each end of a railroad car. ***vt-*** to move or carry by truck: *He* trucked *the goods to Chicago.* ***vi-*** to drive a truck or otherwise work at trucking. [from Latin **trochus** meaning "iron hoop; wheel."]

Hand truck

truck·er (trŭk′ ər) ***n-*** person who transports goods by truck; also, one who supplies trucks. Also **truck′ man.**

truck farm ***n-*** farm that grows vegetables for market.

truck·ing (trŭk′ ĭng) ***n-*** business of transporting goods by truck.

truck·le (trŭk′ əl) ***vi-*** **[truck·led, truck·ling] 1** to yield without opposition (to) the will of another; be subservient (to). **2** to roll on casters. ***vt-*** to cause to move on casters. **—*n-* truck′ ler.**

truc·u·lent (trŭk′ yə lənt, tro͞o′ kyə-) ***adj-*** **1** ready to attack; fierce or savage; ferocious; belligerent: *a* truculent *warrior.* **2** harsh; scathing: *a* truculent *satire.* **—*n-* truc′ u·lence** or **truc′ u·len·cy.** ***adv-*** **truc′ u·lent·ly.**

trudge (trŭj) ***vi-*** **[trudged, trudg·ing]** to walk steadily and wearily: *He* trudged *home after the day's work.* ***n-*** **1** long, tiring walk: *a* trudge *to the station.* **—*n-* trudg′ er.**

true (tro͞o) ***adj-*** **[tru·er, tru·est] 1** according to fact; not false: *She gives a* true *account of what happened.* **2** loyal; faithful: *to be* true *to one's word.* **3** real; genuine: *a* true *gentleman*; true *gold.* **4** corresponding to a standard or type; correct; exact: *a* true *color*; *a* true *copy.* **5** rightful; legitimate: *the* true *heir to the throne.* ***adv-*** **1** truly; truthfully: *He spoke* true. **2** accurately: *The arrow sped* true *to the mark.* ***vt-*** **[trued, tru·ing** or **true·ing]** to make accurate; adjust: *to* true *a door frame.*

come true to become a realized fact.

true bill ***n-*** in law, an indictment endorsed by a grand jury as being supported by enough evidence to justify prosecution.

true-blue (tro͞o′ blo͞o′) ***adj-*** faithful; loyal.

true north ***n-*** direction toward the North Pole. See also *magnetic north.*

truf·fle (trŭf′ əl) ***n-*** any of various potato-shaped fungi that grow underground and are highly prized as food.

tru·ism (tro͞o′ ĭz′ əm) ***n-*** obvious and self-evident truth; commonplace: *"You can only die once" is a* truism.

tru·ly (tro͞o′ lē) ***adv-*** **1** in a true manner; faithfully: *Please answer* truly. **2** really; indeed: *I am* truly *sorry.*

[1]**trump** (trŭmp) *Archaic* ***n-*** trumpet. [from Old French **trompe,** from earlier German **trumpa.**]

[2]**trump** (trŭmp) ***n-*** **1** in cards, a card of a suit that temporarily outranks any other suit. **2** (usually **trumps**) the suit itself. ***vt-*** to take with such a card: *to* trump *a trick.* ***vi-***: *If he plays that card, I will* trump. [from **triumph.**]

trump up to devise or invent fraudulently; fabricate: *to* trump up *an excuse.*

trumped-up (trŭmpt′ ŭp′) ***adj-*** invented deceitfully or fraudulently; concocted: *a* trumped-up *charge of treason.*

trump·er·y (trŭm′ pə rē) ***n-*** [*pl.* **trump·er·ies**] worthless finery; hence, any useless stuff; rubbish; nonsense.

trum·pet (trŭm′ pət) ***n-*** **1** brass wind instrument with a looped tube, keys, and a flaring bell. **2** a sound made by this instrument; also, any similar sound: *the elephant's* trumpet. **3** something shaped like this instrument: *a speaking* trumpet. ***vt-*** to announce widely as if by trumpet; proclaim: *He* trumpeted *his woes to all who would listen.* ***vi-*** **1** to sound such an instrument. **2** to utter a similar sound. **—*n-* trum′ pet·er.** ***adj-*** **trum′ pet·like′.**

Trumpet

trumpet creeper ***n-*** perennial vine of North America, bearing large, red blossoms that resemble trumpets. Also **trumpet vine.**

trumpeter swan ***n-*** any of several large North American wild swans with a loud, sonorous call.

trun·cate (trŭng′ kāt′) *vt-* **[trun·cat·ed, trun·cat·ing]** to shorten by cutting off the top or end: *to* truncate *a plant.* *adj-* having a flat top or broad end as if cut off evenly: *a* truncate *leaf.* *—n-* **trun·ca′ tion.**

trun·cheon (trŭn′ chən) *n-* **1** *chiefly Brit.* policeman's club. **2** baton or staff indicating power or authority. **3** *Archaic* club or cudgel. *vt- Archaic* to beat with a club; cudgel.

trun·dle (trŭn′ dəl) *vt-* **[trun·dled, trun·dling]** to roll along: *Hector* trundled *his wagon behind him wherever he went.* *vi-*: *The empty cart* trundled *down the hill with a clatter.* *n-* small wheel or roller; caster.

trundle bed *n-* low bed on casters, that may be rolled under another bed when not in use.

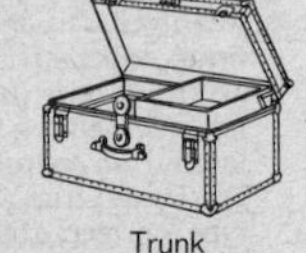
Trunk

trunk (trŭngk) *n-* **1** the main stem of a tree. **2** box with a hinged cover for storing or moving goods. **3** all the body except the limbs and head. **4** the long nose of an elephant. **5** main line or part of a railroad, highway system, nervous system, etc. **6 trunks** men's shorts that reach about halfway to the knee and are worn chiefly for sports and swimming. *as **modifier**: a* trunk *railroad.*

trunk line *n-* **1** main line or route of a railroad, airline, or other transportation system. **2** telephone line between two telephone exchanges.

Bridge truss

truss (trŭs) *n-* **1** in engineering, a supporting framework composed of joined triangles. **2** bundle; pack. **3** belt used to support a hernia. **4** *chiefly Brit.* weighed measure, or bundle of hay or straw. *vt-* **1** to tie securely: *The robbers* trussed *up their victim.* **2** to bind or fasten with skewers and string: *to* truss *a turkey.* **3** to support with a brace, framework, etc.

trust (trŭst) *n-* **1** firm belief in the honesty, justice, and reliability of someone or something: *We place our* trust *in God.* **2** expectation; hope: *a* trust *that all will be well.* **3** credit granted because of the belief in one's ability or intention to pay at some future time: *to sell goods on* trust. **4** responsibility for something entrusted to someone's care; charge; also, care or custody: *The child was committed to her* trust. **5** in law, property or an interest in property, held and managed by a person, called the trustee, for the benefit of another, called the beneficiary. **6** any company or group of companies that have the power to fix prices and restrict competition in a particular market; monopoly. *vt-* **1** to place confidence in; rely on: *to* trust *one's own opinion.* **2** to entrust: *to* trust *a secret to someone.* **3** to expect with confidence; hope: *I* trust *you'll come again.* **4** to give business credit to. *vi-* to have confidence or faith. *—n-* **trust′ er.**

in trust in custody or keeping for another.

trust company *n-* company or corporation whose main purpose is to act as a trustee, but which also carries on banking and other financial activities.

trus·tee (trŭs′ tē′) *n-* **1** person or firm to whom the property or affairs of another person, company, or institution is entrusted: *the* trustees *of a college.* **2** country that supervises a trust territory.

trus·tee·ship (trŭs′ tē′ shĭp′) *n-* **1** the position or function of a trustee. **2** administration of a trust territory; also, the trust territory itself.

trust·ful (trŭst′ fəl) *adj-* ready to believe in others; trusting. *—adv-* **trust′ ful·ly.** *n-* **trust′ ful·ness.**

trust fund *n-* person's money or other property that is held and managed for his benefit by another.

trust·ing (trŭs′ tĭng) *adj-* not suspicious; ready to believe in others; trustful. *—adv-* **trust′ ing·ly.**

trust territory *n-* colony or other dependent territory that has been placed under the administrative authority of a country by the United Nations.

trust·wor·thy (trŭst′ wûr′ thē) *adj-* reliable; dependable: *a* trustworthy *assistant.* *—n-* **trust′ wor′ thi·ness.**

trust·y (trŭs′ tē) *adj-* **[trust·i·er, trust·i·est]** reliable; faithful; trustworthy: *His* trusty *servant had been with him for 20 years.* *n-* [*pl.* **trust·ies**] person to be trusted; especially, a prisoner who has special privileges because of good behavior.

truth (trōōth) *n-* [*pl.* **truths** (trōōths, trōōthz)] **1** accordance with fact or actuality; veracity: *His story has a ring of* truth. **2** honesty or sincerity of speech and action: *There is no* truth *in him.* **3** generally accepted or proven statement, fact, or principle: *scientific* truths.

in truth in fact; actually.

truth·ful (trōōth′ fəl) *adj-* **1** telling the truth; honest: *a* truthful *witness.* **2** according to the facts; true: *a* truthful *report.* *—adv-* **truth′ ful·ly.** *n-* **truth′ ful·ness.**

truth serum *n-* any of several drugs that are said to induce a person to talk freely.

try (trī) *vt-* **[tried, try·ing] 1** to attempt to do, use, etc.: *He* tried *a harder problem. She* tried *every way to please him.* **2** to put to a trial or experiment; test: *to* try *a car before buying.* **3** to subject to trouble, affliction, or annoyance: *Light* tries *my eyes.* **4** to decide by argument or contest: *to* try *an issue by war.* **5** to extract by heating; melt or refine (usually followed by "out"): *to* try *out silver.* **6** in law, to examine in a court: *to* try *a case*; *to* try *the accused.* *vi-* to make an effort; attempt: *Do* try *to come.* *n-* [*pl.* **tries**] *Informal* attempt; effort: *Have a* try *at fixing this.*

try for to attempt to make or reach: *to* try for *a field goal.*

try on to test the appearance or fit of (something) by putting it on: *to* try on *new shoes.*

try out to test thoroughly: *to* try out *a new car.*

try out for to attempt to qualify for.

►Avoid the informal TRY AND when you mean TRY TO: Try to *(not* try and) *finish before dark.* Although widely used, TRY AND in this sense is often ambiguous.

try·ing (trī′ ĭng) *adj-* annoying; tiresome; distressing: *a* trying *climate*; *a* trying *child.* *—adv-* **try′ ing·ly.**

try·out (trī′ out′) *Informal n-* any test or performance to determine fitness or effectiveness: *a* tryout *for a role.*

tryp·a·no·some (trĭ păn′ ə sōm′) *n-* any of a group of one-celled microscopic animals **(Trypanosoma)** that infect the blood of higher animals and man and cause serious disease. Many are transmitted by insect bites.

tryp·sin (trĭp′ sən) *n-* an enzyme found in the pancreatic juice. Trypsin digests proteins.

try·sail (trī′ sāl′, -səl) *n-* small fore-and-aft sail set with or without a gaff on the foremast or mainmast, and used during bad weather. *as **modifier**: a* trysail *mast.*

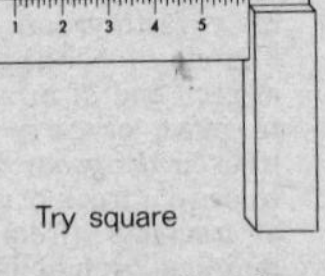

Try square

try·square (trī′ skwâr′) *n-* carpenter's tool consisting of two straight edges that are fastened at right angles. It is used for laying off and testing right angles.

tryst (trĭst) *n-* **1** agreement to meet at a certain place and time: *a lover's* tryst. **2** prearranged meeting. **3** (also **trysting place**) meeting place.

tsar (tsär, zär) *n-* title of any of the former Russian emperors; czar.

tsa·ri·na (tsä rē′ nə, zä-) czarina.
tset·se fly (tsĕt′ sē, tĕt′-) ***n-*** any of several kinds of bloodsucking flies of southern Africa, one of which is a carrier of the germs of sleeping sickness. Others transmit animal diseases. Also **tset′ se.**
T-shirt (tē′ shûrt′) ***n-*** light, collarless, short-sleeved sport shirt or undershirt.
tsp. teaspoon.
T square (tē′ skwâr′) ***n-*** ruler with a cross bar at one end that slides along the edge of a drawing board.

T square

tsu·na·mi (so͞o näm′ ē, tso͞o-) *Japanese* ***n-*** tidal wave.
Tu. Tuesday.
tub (tŭb) ***n-*** **1** large, round vessel used to hold water for washing clothes, bathing, etc. **2** bathtub. **3** *chiefly Brit.* bath. **4** container for holding butter, lard, etc. **5** the amount a tub holds: *a large* tub *of butter.* **6** *Informal* unwieldy or run-down ship. ***vi-*** **[tubbed, tub·bing]** to take a bath.

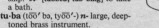

Tub

tu·ba (to͞o′ bə, tyo͞o′-) ***n-*** large, deep-toned brass instrument.
tub·by (tŭb′ ē) ***adj-*** **[tub·bier, tub·biest] 1** short and fat. **2** dull or flat in sound. **—*n-* tub′ bi·ness.**
tube (to͞ob, tyo͞ob) ***n-*** **1** hollow cylinder that is longer than it is wide, used for holding or conveying various substances, especially liquids and gases; also, a similar structure in animals and plants: *the bronchial* tubes. **2** soft container for toothpaste, glue, etc., from which the contents are removed by squeezing. **3** tunnel for an electric railroad. **4** electron tube. **5** inner tube. **—*adj-* tube′ less. *adj-* tube′ like′.**

Tuba

tu·ber (to͞o′ bər, tyo͞o′-) ***n-*** **1** thick, often edible, part of an underground stem, such as the potato, bearing small eyes. **2** *Medicine* rounded swelling; tubercle.
tu·ber·cle (to͞o′ bər kəl, tyo͞o′-) ***n-*** small swelling or lump found on plant or animal organs.
tubercle bacillus ***n-*** the bacterium that causes tuberculosis.
tu·ber·cu·lar (to͞o bûr′ kyə lər) ***adj-*** **1** tuberculous. **2** of, related to, or having tubercles.
tu·ber·cu·lin (to͞o bûr′ kyə lĭn′) ***n-*** a filtrate of cultures of the tuberculosis bacillus, used as a test for the disease.
tu·ber·cu·lo·sis (to͞o bûr′ kyə lō′ səs) ***n-*** contagious disease affecting the lungs and other parts of the body.
tu·ber·cu·lous (to͞o bûr′ kyə ləs) ***adj-*** of, related to, or affected with tuberculosis: *a* tuberculous *lung.*
tube·rose (to͞ob′ rōz′, tyo͞ob′-) ***n-*** Mexican plant with a bulbous root, cultivated for its spike of white flowers.
tu·ber·ous (to͞o′ bər əs, tyo͞o′-) ***adj-*** **1** covered with knoblike swellings. **2** of, like, or bearing tubers.
tub·ing (to͞o′ bĭng, tyo͞o′-) ***n-*** **1** piece of tube. **2** material used for tubes: *rubber* tubing. **3** set or series of tubes.
tu·bu·lar (to͞o′ byə lər, tyo͞o′-) ***adj-*** **1** tube-shaped: *a* tubular *pipe.* **2** made up of tubes: *a* tubular *construction.*
tu·bule (to͞ob′ yo͞ol′, tyo͞ob′-) ***n-*** very small tube.

tuck (tŭk) ***vt-*** **1** to roll or gather into folds: *Your sleeves will get wet unless you* tuck *them up.* **2** to put the edges of into place: *Before you go,* tuck *your shirt in.* **3** to cover or wrap snugly: *She* tucked *the baby into the crib.* **4** to fit or press into a small space: *Alice* tucked *her handbag into her suitcase.* **5** to make or sew a fold or folds in: *to* tuck *a skirt.* ***n-*** stitched fold in a garment.
[1]**tuck·er** (tŭk′ ər) ***n-*** **1** person or device that makes tucks or folds. **2** formerly, a piece of lace, linen, or other fine material worn around the top part of a woman's dress. [from **tuck.**]
[2]**tuck·er** (tŭk′ ər) *Informal* ***vt-*** to exhaust; tire (usually followed by "out"): *The long march* tuckered *him out.* [origin uncertain.]
Tu·dor (to͞o′ dər) ***adj-*** **1** of or relating to an English royal house from 1485 to 1603, whose reigning members included Henry VIII, Mary, and Elizabeth. **2** of or relating to English architecture developed during this period. ***n-***: *Henry VII was the first* Tudor *to reign.*
Tues. Tuesday.
Tues·day (to͞oz′ dā, tyo͞oz′ dā, -dē) ***n-*** third day of the week.
tu·fa (to͞o′ fə, tyo͞o′-) ***n-*** **1** tuff. **2** form of porous limestone deposited by water.
tuff (tŭf) ***n-*** porous rock, usually stratified, that is formed from volcanic dust and ash. ***Hom-*** tough.
tuft (tŭft) ***n-*** **1** bunch of feathers, grass, etc., growing or held together at the base: *a* tuft *of hair.* **2** clump of bushes or trees. **3** fringed threads or a button at the end of a cord, drawn through a mattress or cushion to hold the filling in place. ***vt-*** to decorate or supply with such tufts: *to* tuft *a quilt.* **—*n-* tuft′ er. *adj-* tuft′ like′.**
tug (tŭg) ***vt-*** **[tugged, tug·ging] 1** to pull hard; haul or drag: *He* tugged *the stuck drawer.* **2** to tow with a tugboat. ***vi-*** to pull hard: *He* tugged *at my hand.* ***n-*** **1** hard pull: *a* tug *at a rope.* **2** tugboat. **3** trace on a harness.

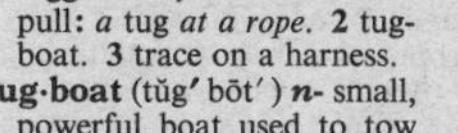

Tugboat

tug·boat (tŭg′ bōt′) ***n-*** small, powerful boat used to tow or push heavier vessels; tug; towboat.
tug of war ***n-*** contest of strength in which two teams pull on a rope against each other in an attempt to draw one team across a central mark.
tu·i·tion (to͞o ĭsh′ ən, tyo͞o-) ***n-*** **1** fee paid to a school for instruction. **2** instruction; teaching.
tu·la·re·mi·a (to͞o′ lə rē′ mē ə, tyo͞o′-) ***n-*** an infectious disease of rabbits and rodents caused by a bacillus and transmitted to man by insect bites and the handling of infected animals.
tu·lip (to͞o′ lĭp, tyo͞o′-) ***n-*** any of a number of plants of the lily family, bearing brilliantly colored, cup-shaped flowers; also, the bulb or flower of one of these plants.
tulip tree ***n-*** magnolia tree of North America, with greenish-yellow, tulip-shaped flowers and wood used for furniture.
tulle (to͞ol) ***n-*** delicate netting of silk or synthetic material, used for veils, scarfs, etc. ***Hom-*** tool.
tum·ble (tŭm′ bəl) ***vi-*** **[tum·bled, tum·bling] 1** to fall suddenly and

Tulip

fāte, făt, dâre, bärn; bē, bĕt, mêre; bīte, bĭt; nōte, hŏt, môre, dòg; fŭn, fûr; to͞o, bo͝ok; oil; out; tar; thin; then; hw for wh as in *wh*at; zh for s as in u*s*ual; ə for a, e, i, o, u, as in *a*go, lin*e*n, per*i*l, at*o*m, min*u*s

heavily: *He* tumbled *downstairs. Water* tumbled *over the dam.* 2 to roll about: *The children* tumbled *in the grass.* 3 to perform somersaults or other acrobatic feats. 4 to move in an awkward, hasty manner: *He* tumbled *into the room.* ***vt-*** **1** to cause to fall; throw down: *The truck driver* tumbled *the barrels out of the van.* **2** to rumple: *to* tumble *a heap of clothes.* ***n-*** **1** fall: *He took a* tumble. **2** acrobatic feat, such as a somersault. **3** confusion; disorder: *a* tumble *of papers and books.*

tum·ble·bug (tŭm′ bəl bŭg′) ***n-*** any of several beetles that roll up balls of dung and lay their eggs in them.

tum·ble-down (tŭm′ bəl doun′) ***adj-*** falling apart; rickety; dilapidated: *a* tumble-down *shack.*

tum·ble·weed (tŭm′ bəl wēd′) ***n-*** any of various weeds of western North America, which break off from their root in autumn and blow about in the wind.

tum·bler (tŭm′ blər) ***n-*** **1** stemless drinking glass. **2** the amount such a glass will hold: *a* tumbler *of milk.* **3** acrobat who performs somersaults, leaps, balancing, and similar feats. **4** part of a lock that must be turned to a certain point by a key before the lock will open. **5** (also **tumbling box**) revolving box in which articles, such as castings, are polished by being tumbled about with an abrasive substance.

tum·brel or **tum·bril** (tŭm′ brəl) ***n-*** cart used by farmers for carrying and dumping manure. Tumbrels were used in the French Revolution to take condemned prisoners to the guillotine.

tu·mes·cent (tōō mĕs′ ənt, tyōō-) ***adj-*** swelling; somewhat tumid. ***—n-*** **tu·mes′ cence.**

tu·mid (tōō′ mĭd, tyōō′-) ***adj-*** **1** swollen and enlarged; bulging: *a* tumid *stomach.* **2** full of high-sounding words: *a* tumid *speech.* ***—n-*** **tu·mid′i·ty.** ***adv-*** **tu′mid·ly.**

tu·mor (tōō′ mər, tyōō′-) ***n-*** an abnormal enlargement of plant or animal tissue. ***—adj-*** **tu′ mor·ous.**

tu·mult (tōō′ mŭlt′, tyōō′-) ***n-*** **1** the noise and confusion of a crowd; uproar: *The rally ended in utter* tumult. **2** violent agitation, as of the mind.

tu·mul·tu·ous (tōō mŭl′ chōō əs, tyōō-) ***adj-*** **1** noisy; excited: *a* tumultuous *crowd.* **2** stormy; tempestuous: *a* tumultuous *sea.* ***—adv-*** **tu·mul′ tu·ous·ly.**

tu·mu·lus (tōōm′ yə ləs, tyōōm′-) ***n-*** [*pl.* **tu·mul·lus·es, tu·mu·li** (-lī, -lē)] artificial hill or mound; especially, a burial mound or barrow.

tun (tŭn) ***n-*** **1** large cask, used especially for wine. **2** measure of capacity for wine (252 gallons). ***Hom-*** ton.

tu·na (tōō′ nə) ***n-*** [*pl.* **tu·na; tu·nas** (kinds of tuna)] **1** any of various large food and game fishes of the mackerel family, found in warm seas. **2** any of various related smaller fishes, such as the bonito. **3** tuna fish.

tuna fish ***n-*** the flesh of tuna, especially when canned.

tun·dra (tŭn′ drə) ***n-*** area of grass, moss, flowering plants, and a few stunted trees, found mostly in high latitudes.

tune (tōōn, tyōōn) ***n-*** **1** *Music* (1) series of musical tones having rhythm and melody and forming a complete theme; air or melody. (2) musical setting, as for a hymn or ballad. (3) a giving forth tones in the proper pitch: *to be in* tune. (4) proper adjustment in respect to musical tone sounds: *The piano and the violin are in* tune. **2** harmonious adjustment; fitting mood: *to be in* tune *with one's surroundings.* ***vt-*** **[tuned, tuning] 1** to cause (a voice or musical instrument) to produce the proper sounds; adjust to the correct musical pitch. **2** to put into harmony with something. **3** to put into proper working condition: *to* tune *a motor.*

to the tune of *Informal* to the extent or sum of.

tune in (or **in on**) **1** to adjust a radio or television to receive a particular station or signal. **2** *Informal* to listen intently and often unobtrusively to: *I* tuned in on *their conversation.*

tune out to adjust a radio or television to exclude (a particular station or signal).

tune·ful (tōōn′ fəl, tyōōn′-) ***adj-*** harmonious; melodious: *a* tuneful *opera.* ***—adv-*** **tune′ ful·ly.** ***n-*** **tune′ ful·ness.**

tune·less (tōōn′ ləs, tyōōn′-) ***adj-*** **1** without harmony or melody. **2** not producing music; silent. ***—adv-*** **tune′ less·ly:** *He whistled* tunelessly.

tun·er (tōō′ nər, tyōō′-) ***n-*** **1** person who repairs and adjusts musical instruments to their proper pitch: *a piano* tuner. **2** the part of a radio receiver that selects the desired radio signals and converts them into electrical impulses that can be amplified.

Policeman's tunic

tung·sten (tŭng′ stən) ***n-*** a brittle, hard, silvery-gray metallic element, used in hard alloy steels for cutting tools, and in lamp filaments; wolfram. Symbol W, At. No. 74, At. Wt. 183.85.

tung tree (tŭng) ***n-*** tropical broadleaf tree grown mostly in China, whose seeds produce a yellow oil, called **tung oil,** that is used in paints, varnishes, and waterproofing materials.

tu·nic (tōō′ nĭk, tyōō′-) ***n-*** **1** in ancient Greece and Rome, a shirtlike garment worn by both men and women. **2** woman's loose blouse reaching to the hips. **3** of some military and police uniforms, a close-fitting, short coat.

tuning fork ***n-*** fork-shaped steel device that sounds a certain fixed note when struck, used to find the right pitch in singing and in tuning instruments.

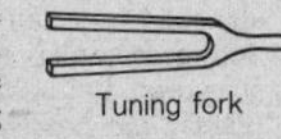
Tuning fork

tun·nel (tŭn′ əl) ***n-*** **1** underground passageway for trains, cars, etc. **2** hole dug by a burrowing animal. ***vt-*** to dig underground passageways in: *to* tunnel *a mine.* ***vi-***: *Rats* tunneled *under the eaves.* ***—n-*** **tun′ nel·er.**

tun·ny (tŭn′ ē) ***n-*** [*pl.* **tun·nies**] tuna.

tu·pe·lo (tōō′ pə lō, tyōō′-) ***n-*** [*pl.* **tu·pe·los**] any of various North American trees with blue-black berries and close-grained wood; also, the wood of this tree. *as* ***modifier***: *a* tupelo *leaf.* [from American Indian.]

tup·pence (tŭp′ əns) ***n-*** twopence.

tur·ban (tûr′ bən) ***n-*** **1** Eastern headdress for men, consisting of a scarf wound about the head or about a cap. **2** bandanna, towel, etc., worn in a similar manner. **3** woman's close-fitting, brimless hat; toque. ***—adj-*** **tur′ baned.**

Turban

tur·bid (tûr′ bĭd) ***adj-*** **1** muddy or cloudy; thick; dense: *the* turbid *waters of a river.* **2** confused; muddled: *a* turbid *mind.* ***—adv-*** **tur′ bid·ly.** ***n-*** **tur·bid′ i·ty** or **tur′ bid·ness.**

tur·bi·nate (tûr′ bə nāt′, -nət) ***adj-*** shaped like a spiral; whorled: *a* turbinate *shell.* ***n-*** any of the three curved bones within the upper cavity of the nose of higher vertebrates.

tur·bine (tûr′ bīn′, -bən) ***n-*** engine driven by the pressure of water, steam, or other heated gases against curved vanes or cups on the rim of a wheel.

turbo- *combining form* turbine: *a* turbo*jet.* [from Latin **turbo** meaning "any whirling object."]

tur·bo·gen·er·a·tor (tûr′ bō jĕn′ ə rā′ tər) ***n-*** an electric generator driven by a turbine coupled to it.

tur·bo·jet (tûr′ bō jĕt′) ***n-*** **1** jet engine in which the air taken in at the front is compressed by a fan driven by a turbine. The turbine is driven by hot gases passing through it at the rear of the engine. See also *ramjet.* **2** plane driven by such engines.

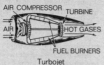

AIR COMPRESSOR
TURBINE
AIR
HOT GASES
FUEL BURNERS
Turbojet

tur·bo·prop (tûr′ bō prŏp′) ***n-*** **1** jet engine in which part of the power of the burning fuel drives a turbine hooked up to a propeller. **2** an airplane using such engines.

tur·bot (tûr′ bət) ***n-*** [*pl.* **tur·bot; tur·bots** (kinds of turbot)] large European flatfish prized as food; also, any of similar flatfishes.

tur·bu·lence (tûr′ byə ləns) ***n-*** **1** *Physics* rapid, disordered movement of particles of a gas or liquid, often occurring as swirls or eddies that change shape continuously, as in the wake of a ship or aircraft. **2** (also **tur′ bu·len·cy**) condition of being turbulent.

tur·bu·lent (tûr′ byə lənt) ***adj-*** **1** not easily controlled; disorderly; unruly: *a* turbulent *crowd.* **2** disturbed; agitated; stormy: *a* turbulent *sea.* ***—adv-*** **tur′ bu·lent·ly.**

tu·reen (tə rēn′) ***n-*** large, deep dish with a lid, for serving soup.

Tureen

turf (tûrf) ***n-*** **1** surface layer of ground, containing plant debris and matted grass roots; sod; also, a piece of sod. **2** peat. **3 the turf** (1) track for horse racing. (2) the sport of horse racing. ***vt-*** to cover with grassy sod.

tur·gid (tûr′ jĭd) ***adj-*** **1** swollen; puffed up; bloated. **2** bombastic; pompous: *his* turgid *prose.* ***—n-*** **tur·gid′ i·ty** (tər jĭd′ ə tē) or **tur′ gid·ness.**

tur·gor (tûr′ gər, -gȯr′) ***n-*** **1** distended condition of plant or animal cells that have been filled with fluid. **2** firmness of plant parts resulting from this condition.

Turk (tûrk) ***n-*** **1** native or inhabitant of Turkey. **2** any member of numerous Asian peoples who speak the Turkic languages.

tur·key (tûr′ kē) ***n-*** **1** large native American bird that still occurs wild but has been domesticated and is bred in large flocks for the market. **2** flesh of this bird used as food. *as* ***modifier***: *a* turkey *leg.* ***—adj-*** **tur′ key·like′.**

talk turkey *Informal* to talk frankly and openly.

Domestic turkey, about 4 ft. long

turkey buzzard ***n-*** large black vulture with a bald, red head and neck. For picture, see *buzzard.*

Turk·ic languages (tûr′ kĭk) ***n-*** *pl.* languages belonging to a group of peoples that include the Turks, the Turkomans, and other Tartar tribes of the U.S.S.R.

Turk·ish (tûr′ kĭsh) ***adj-*** of or relating to Turkey or the Turks. ***n-*** the Turkic language of Turkey.

Turkish bath ***n-*** bath in which one is made to perspire freely in a steam-heated room, and is then showered and given a rubdown; also, an establishment having such a bath.

turkish towel ***n-*** thick cotton terry-cloth towel.

Tur·ko·man (tûr′ kə mən) ***n-*** [*pl.* **Tur·ko·mans**] **1** member of various Turkish tribes, chiefly nomadic, living mainly in south central Asia. **2** the Turkic language of these people.

tur·mer·ic (tûr′ mər ĭk) ***n-*** **1** East Indian plant of the ginger family; also, its aromatic root, used as a yellow dye and as a condiment, particularly in curry powder. **2** any of several similar plants.

tur·moil (tûr′ moil′) ***n-*** disturbance or commotion; uproar; tumult: *She was in a* turmoil *over his absence.*

turn (tûrn) ***vt-*** **1** to cause to go around; make rotate: *to* turn *a wheel*; *to* turn *a key.* **2** to change the position or direction of: *to* turn *a page*; *to* turn *soil.* **3** to unsettle or upset (the stomach). **4** to twist or wrench: *to* turn *one's ankle.* **5** to change from one shape, form, color, etc., to another: *to* turn *failure into success*; *to* turn *cream into butter*; *to* turn *leaves red.* **6** to cause to go; send: *She* turned *the beggar from the door.* **7** to move to the other side of; go around: *to* turn *a corner.* **8** to invert; reverse: *to* turn *a collar.* **9** to spoil or sour: *The hot weather* turned *the cream.* **10** to shape by rotating in a lathe: *to* turn *a table leg.* **11** to translate: *to* turn *English into French.* **12** to cause to become: *The sight* turned *him ill.* **13** to gain: *He* turned *a thousand dollars on the deal.* ***vi-*** **1** to move around; rotate; revolve: *The earth* turns *on its axis.* **2** to change one's form, direction, position, or attitude: *He* turned *into a tyrant. She* turned *around. He* turned *against his friends.* **3** to seem to whirl or spin; reel: *My head is* turning. **4** to change in condition, color, etc.: *The milk* turned *sour. She* turned *pale. The dog* turned *friendly.* ***n-*** **1** revolving; rotation: *the* turn *of the wheel.* **2** change of direction; also, a curve or bend: *a* turn *in the road.* **3** short ride or walk: *to take a* turn *around the park.* **4** deed or act: *You did me a good* turn. **5** time or opportunity to do something after someone else: *It's your* turn *to stand guard.* **6** change in condition. **7** *Informal* shock: *That shriek in the night gave me quite a* turn. **8** ability or tendency; bent: *He is of a mechanical* turn. **9** short piece or act on the stage. **10** *Music* embellishment consisting of four notes played or sung rapidly in the following order: the major or minor tone above a given tone, the main tone, the tone immediately below, and the main tone. **11** loop of a rope. ***Hom-*** tern.

at every turn on every occasion; constantly. **in turn** in succession; in proper order: *Get on the bus* in turn. **out of turn 1** not in succession; not in proper order. **2** with impudence; rashly: *He spoke* out of turn. **take turns** to do something in the proper order or one after the other. **to a turn** just right; perfectly: *The roast was done* to a turn. **turn about** or **turn and turn about** one by one in regular order.

turn down 1 to reject; refuse. **2** to fold back or over: *to* turn down *a bed*; *to* turn down *a card.* **3** to decrease volume, brightness, etc.: *Please* turn down *the radio.*

turn in 1 *Informal* to go to bed. **2** to return (equipment) to the person responsible for it. **3** to exchange: *to* turn in *an old car for a new one.* **4** to point (toes) inward. **5** to turn and enter: *We* turn in *here.*

turn off 1 to cause to stop working; shut off; put out. **2** to leave (a road).

turn on 1 to cause to start working; put on; switch on: *to* turn on *the lights and the radio.* **2** to depend on.

turn out 1 to shut off; put out: *to* turn off *the lights.* **2** to produce or make by work: *He* turns out *a new book every year.* **3** to prove finally to be: *It* turned out *worthless.* **4** to come out for a meeting, duty, etc.: *A few* turned out *to greet him.* **5** to put outside:

Please, turn out *the dog.* **6** *Informal* to get out of bed. **7** to dress; equip. **8** to point outward.

turn over 1 to hand over; transfer. **2** to think about; ponder: *She* turned *the question* over *in her mind.* **3** to roll over; invert: *The doctor asked the patient to* turn over. *Please* turn over *the mattress.* **5** to do business that amounts to: *to* turn over *$50,000.* **6** to overturn; upset: *He* turned over *the milk bottle.*

turn tail *Informal* to turn the back to; also, to run away.

turn to 1 to open a book to a specific place: *Please* turn to *page 90.* **2** to start to work; busy oneself: *He* turned to *the task at hand.* **3** to seek advice, assistance, etc., from; apply to: *He* turned to *me for solace.*

turn up 1 to arrive; appear; be found. **2** to shorten the hem of: *to* turn up *a skirt or drape.* **3** to plow; dig: *to* turn up *the soil.* **4** to increase the volume, brightness, etc. **5** to turn and ascend.

turn·buck·le (tûrn′ bŭk′ əl) ***n-*** a threaded coupling between two rods, one having a right-hand thread and the other a left-hand thread, so that turning the coupling lengthens or shortens the whole assembly.

Turnbuckle

turn·coat (tûrn′ kōt′) ***n-*** person who abandons his comrades, principles, etc., and joins the enemy; traitor; renegade.

turn·down (tûrn′ doun′) ***adj-*** folded down or over: *a* turndown *collar.*

turn·er (tûr′ nər) ***n-* 1** person or device that turns something: *a pancake* turner. **2** person who shapes articles with a lathe.

turning point ***n-*** crucial, decisive change or event; also, the specific time at which it takes place.

tur·nip (tûr′ nəp) ***n-* 1** the fleshy, rounded, edible root, white or yellow, of a plant of the mustard family, the leaves of which may also be cooked and eaten. **2** the plant itself.

Turnips

turn·key (tûrn′ kē′) ***n-*** [*pl.* **turn·keys**] person who has charge of the keys of a prison; jailer; warder.

turn·off (tûrn′ ôf′, -ŏf′) ***n-*** place where one may turn off a main road.

turn·out (tûrn′ out′) ***n-* 1** gathering or crowd of people; attendance: *There was a large* turnout *for the play.* **2** a turning out. **3** yield; output. **4** railroad siding; also, any similar area of a highway where vehicles can park or pass each other.

turn·o·ver (tûrn′ ō′ vər) ***n-* 1** a turning over; upset. **2** pie or tart made by turning half the crust over the other half, with filling in between. **3** number or quantity of people or things gone and replaced: *the* turnover *of guests in a hotel*; *the fast* turnover *of merchandise.*

turn·pike (tûrn′ pīk′) ***n-* 1** road, especially a main highway, on which tolls are collected. **2** station where tolls are collected; tollgate.

turn·spit (tûrn′ spĭt′) ***n-*** mechanical device that turns a spit; also, a spit so turned.

turn·stile (tûrn′ stīl′) ***n-* 1** in rural areas, a gate of revolving crossed bars pivoted on a post, that permits people, but not cattle, to pass through. **2** similar device at any entrance, that admits persons one at a time, often after depositing a coin or token, and counts them as they enter.

Turnstile

turn·ta·ble (tûrn′ tā′ bəl) ***n-* 1** in railroads, a circular rotating platform with a track, used for turning locomotives and cars around. **2** the rotating disk of a phonograph upon which a record turns; also, the disk together with its driving mechanism.

tur·pen·tine (tûr′ pən tīn′) ***n-* 1** a light-yellow oil obtained from the sap of certain trees, including the pine and fir, and used in paint, varnish, and certain medicines. **2** the sap from which this oil is obtained.

tur·pi·tude (tûr′ pə to͞od′, -tyo͞od′) ***n-*** shameful wickedness; baseness; depravity: *moral* turpitude.

tur·quoise (tûr′ kwoiz′) ***n-* 1** blue or blue-green precious stone. **2** the color of this stone; blue-green. ***adj-***: *a* turquoise *sky.*

tur·ret (tûr′ ət) ***n-* 1** small tower built into the corner of a building or larger tower. **2** low, round, rotating structure on a ship or in a fort, from which big guns are fired. **3** any similar structure on bombers or tanks, which affords protection to a gun or gunner. **4** on certain lathes, a tool holder that can hold several different cutting bits and can be quickly pivoted so as to bring them to bear as needed. ***—adj-* tur′ ret·ed.**

Turrets

tur·tle (tûr′ təl) ***n-* 1** any of numerous reptiles having the body encased in a horny round or oval shell into which its head and legs may be drawn for protection. **2** such a reptile living mostly in salt water.

turn turtle to capsize.

Spotted turtle, about 5 in. long

tur·tle·dove (tûr′ təl dŭv′) ***n-*** small Old World wild dove noted for its long tail and soft cooing.

tur·tle·neck (tûr′ təl nĕk′) ***n-*** high collar that fits close around the neck; also, a sweater or blouse with such a collar. *as* ***modifier***: *a* turtleneck *sweater.*

Tus·can (tŭs′ kən) ***n-* 1** native or inhabitant of Tuscany, Italy. **2** the standard literary language of Italy, considered the purest form of Italian. ***adj-*** of or relating to Tuscany, its language, or its specific type of architecture.

Tus·ca·ro·ra (tŭs′ kə rôr′ ə) ***n-*** [*pl.* **Tus·ca·ro·ras,** also **Tus·ca·ro·ra**] **1** one of a tribe of Iroquois Indians, who moved from North Carolina to join the confederacy of the Iroquois around 1722, and now live in New York and Ontario. **2** the language of these Indians.

¹tush (tŭsh) ***interj-*** exclamation expressing disapproval, contempt, restraint, or reproof.

²tush (tŭsh) ***n-* 1** tusk. **2** one of the horse's four canine teeth. [from Old English **tusc,** "tusk."]

tusk (tŭsk) ***n-* 1** one of a pair of long, pointed teeth of certain animals such as the elephant or wild boar, used in digging and defense. **2** any abnormally long tooth or toothlike part. ***vt-*** to dig up or pierce with tusks. ***—adj-* tusked.** ***adj-*** **tusk′ like′.**

Tusks

tusk·er (tŭs′ kər) ***n-*** male animal that has tusks.

tus·sah (tŭs′ ə, -ŏ′) ***n-*** Asian silkworm that spins a strong, coarse, brownish silk; also, silk or fabric from it.

tus·sle (tŭs′ əl) ***vi-*** [**tus·sled, tus·sling**] to struggle; wrestle: *The two children* tussled *over the rag doll.* ***n-* 1** rough fight or struggle; scuffle. **2** any rough argument or conflict: *a* tussle *over political issues.*

tus·sock (tŭs′ ək) ***n-*** tuft of grass, feathers, etc.

tut (tŭt) ***interj-*** exclamation of annoyance, rebuke, impatience, or disapproval.

tu·te·lage (to͞o′ tə lĭj, tyo͞o′-) ***n-*** **1** a teaching; instruction: *under his able* tutelage. **2** position or function of a guardian; guardianship. **3** care of a tutor or guardian.

tu·te·lar·y (to͞o′ tə lĕr′ ē, tyo͞o′-) or **tu·te·lar** (-lər) ***adj-*** **1** acting as a guardian; protecting: *a* tutelary *deity.* **2** of or relating to a guardian: *his* tutelary *responsibility.*

tu·tor (to͞o′ tər, tyo͞o′-) ***n-*** **1** private teacher. **2** in some colleges, a teacher ranking below an instructor. **3** *Brit.* college official who guides undergraduate students in their studies and has general supervision over them. ***vt-*** to teach privately; train: *to* tutor *a slow student.* ***vi-*** **1** to work as a private teacher. **2** *Informal* to be taught privately: *to* tutor *in Latin.* **—*n-*** *fem.* **tu′ tor·ess.**

tu·to·ri·al (to͞o tôr′ ē əl, tyo͞o-) ***adj-*** of or relating to a private instructor. ***n-*** class or session with a tutor.

tut·ti-frut·ti (to͞o′ tē fro͞o′ tē) ***n-*** ice cream, gum, etc., made with various kinds of candied fruits or fruit flavorings. *as **modifier**: a* tutti-frutti *flavor.*

tux (tŭks) *Informal* ***n-*** tuxedo.

tux·e·do or **Tux·e·do** (tŭk sē′ dō) ***n-*** [*pl.* **tux·e·dos**] man's semiformal evening wear, consisting of a black or dark-blue coat, trousers, and bow tie. [American word from Tuxedo Park, N.Y.]

TV television.

T.V.A. or **TVA** Tennessee Valley Authority.

twad·dle (twŏd′ əl) ***n-*** silly talk; prattle. ***vi-*** **[twad·dled, twad·dling]**: *She* twaddles *endlessly.* **—*n-*** **twad′ dler.**

twain (twān) *Archaic* ***adj-*** two. ***n-*** **1** pair; two. **2** term formerly used by river navigators to indicate a depth of two fathoms.

twang (twăng) ***n-*** **1** sharp, vibrating sound produced by, or as by, plucking a stringed instrument. **2** nasal tone of voice: *He spoke with a* twang. ***vt-*** to cause to make this sound: *to* twang *a banjo.* ***vi-***: *The string* twanged.

tweak (twēk) ***vt-*** to pinch; twist. ***n-***: *a* tweak *of his nose.*

tweed (twēd) ***n-*** **1** soft, woolen twilled cloth with a rough surface, woven from yarns of different colors to give it a mottled appearance. **2 tweeds** clothes made from this fabric. *as **modifier**: a* tweed *suit.*

twee·dle·dum and twee·dle·dee (twē′ dəl dŭm′ ən twē′ dəl dē′) ***n-*** **1** two things between which there is little or no difference. **2 Tweedledum and Tweedledee** two almost identical twins in Lewis Carroll's "Through The Looking-Glass."

tweet (twēt) ***n-*** thin, low, chirping note of a bird. ***vi-***: *The robin* tweeted *in the branches.*

tweet·er (twē′ tər) ***n-*** radio or phonograph loudspeaker designed to reproduce sounds of high frequency.

tweez·ers (twē′ zərz) ***n-*** (takes plural verb) small instrument for grasping or pulling out something tiny, such as hair; pincers: *eyebrow* tweezers. Also **pair of tweezers** (takes singular verb).

twelfth (twĕlfth) ***adj-*** **1** next after eleventh. **2** the ordinal of 12; 12th. ***n-*** **1** the next after the eleventh; 12th. **2** one of twelve equal parts of a whole or group. **3** the last term in the name of a fraction having a denominator of 12: *1/12 is one* twelfth.

Twelfth-night (twĕlfth′ nīt′) ***n-*** the evening before Epiphany, the twelfth day after Christmas.

twelve (twĕlv) ***n-*** **1** amount or quantity that is one greater than eleven. **2** *Mathematics* (1) the cardinal number that is the sum of 11 and 1. (2) numeral, such as 12 or XII, that represents this cardinal number. **3 the Twelve** the twelve apostles of Jesus. *as **determiner*** (traditionally called adjective or pronoun): *There are* twelve *students here and* twelve *there.*

twelve·month (twĕlv′ mŭnth′) ***n-*** period of twelve months; year.

twen·ti·eth (twĕn′ tē əth) ***adj-*** **1** next after nineteenth. **2** the ordinal of 20; 20th. ***n-*** **1** the next after the nineteenth; 20th. **2** one of twenty equal parts of a whole or group. **3** the last term in the name of a fraction having a denominator of 20: *1/20 is one* twentieth.

twen·ty (twĕn′ tē) ***n-*** [*pl.* **twen·ties**] **1** the amount or quantity that is one greater than 19. **2** *Mathematics* (1) the cardinal number that is the sum of 19 and 1. (2) numeral, such as 20, that represents this cardinal number. *as **determiner*** (traditionally called adjective or pronoun): *I see* twenty *men here and* twenty *there.*

twen·ty-one (twĕn′ tē wŭn′) ***n-*** **1** amount or quantity that is one greater than 20. **2** *Mathematics* (1) the cardinal number that is the sum of 20 and 1. (2) numeral, such as 21, that represents this cardinal number. **3** gambling game with cards, whose object is to obtain exactly 21 points with one's hand; blackjack. *as **determiner*** (traditionally called adjective or pronoun): *There are* twenty-one *gold ingots here and* twenty-one *there.*

twen·ty-two (twĕn′ tē to͞o′) ***n-*** **1** amount or quantity that is one greater than 21. **2** *Mathematics* (1) the cardinal number that is the sum of 21 and 1. (2) numeral, such as 22, that represents this cardinal number. **3** .22-caliber bullet; also, any rifle or pistol that fires such a bullet. *as **determiner*** (traditionally called adjective or pronoun): *There are* twenty-two *cannon here and* twenty-two *there.*

twice (twīs) ***adv-*** two times: *He visited me* twice.

twice-told tale ***n-*** tale that has become stale and trite from being told so often.

twid·dle (twĭd′ əl) ***vt-*** **[twid·dled, twid·dling]** to turn or twirl idly round and round: *sitting around and* twiddling *my thumbs.* ***vi-*** to play or trifle; fool: *He* twiddled *away the day.* ***n-*** a twirling motion, as of the thumbs.

twig (twĭg) ***n-*** small branch or shoot of a tree or plant.

twi·light (twī′ līt′) ***n-*** **1** the diffused light from the sky just after sunset and before darkness; also, this period of time. **2** period of time marking the dying out or end of something: *the* twilight *of his life.* *as **modifier**: a* twilight *baseball game; his* twilight *years.*

twill (twĭl) ***n-*** **1** a weave of cloth that shows diagonal lines or ribs on the surface. **2** fabric woven with such ribs. *as **modifier**: a* twill *cloth; pair of* twill *trousers.* ***vt-*** to weave (cloth) so as to show diagonal lines or ribs.

twin (twĭn) ***n-*** **1** either of two children or animals born at one birth. **2** one of two persons or things that are very much alike: *This vase is the* twin *of that one.* ***adj-*** **1** born at the same time: *The girls are* twin *sisters.* **2** forming or being one of a closely connected pair: *a* twin *peak.* ***vi-*** **[twinned, twin·ning]** to give birth to twins.

twine (twīn) ***n-*** **1** strong, twisted string or thread made up of two or more strands. **2** a twist or tangle. ***vt-*** **[twined, twin·ing]** **1** to twist together; wind: *to* twine *flowers into a garland.* **2** to make by twisting or coiling: *to* twine *a garland.* **3** to encircle: *to* twine *ribbons around a pole.* ***vi-***: *The vine* twines *over the porch.*

twinge (twĭnj) ***n-*** sudden, sharp pain of body or mind: *a muscular* twinge; *a* twinge *of conscience.* ***vi-*** **[twinged, twing·ing]** to feel a sudden, sharp pain.

twin·kle (twĭng′ kəl) ***vi-*** **[twin·kled, twin·kling]** **1** to shine with a light that comes and goes in flashes; flicker: *The stars* twinkled *above.* **2** to sparkle: *Her eyes* twinkled *with delight.* **3** to move quickly and lightly: *The dancer's feet* twinkled *to and fro.* ***n-*** **1** a flicker of light; sparkle. **2** time occupied by a wink; moment; flash; twinkling.

twin·kling (twĭngk′ lĭng) ***n-*** very brief time; moment.

twirl (twûrl) ***vt-*** to turn around rapidly; spin; whirl: *to* twirl *a cane or a baton.* ***vi-***: *Autumn leaves* twirled *in the wind.* ***n-*** a twist, spin, or whirl. —***n-*** **twirl′ er.**

twist (twĭst) ***vt-*** **1** to wind about or wind together; subject to torsion: *to* twist *strands to make a rope*; *to* twist *a wire until it breaks.* **2** to form (a rope or twine) in this way. **3** to sprain or wrench by turning: *He* twisted *his leg playing football.* **4** to change the shape of: *He* twisted *his lips wryly.* **5** to change the meaning of by false emphasis or interpretation; distort: *The reporter* twisted *the speaker's words.* ***vi-*** **1** to become joined by winding. **2** to loop and tangle: *This silk is* twisting *badly.* **3** to become sprained or wrenched; turn: *His ankle* twisted *as he fell.* **4** to turn or wind in a curve: *The stream* twists *around the bend.* ***n-*** **1** a turn: *a* twist *of a steering wheel.* **2** shape or condition produced by winding: *a* twist *of bread.* **3** a sprain or wrench: *a* twist *of the neck or ankle.* **4** variation: *Putting the engine behind was a new* twist. **5** dance in which the hips are strongly and repeatedly rotated.

twist·er (twĭs′ tər) *Informal* ***n-*** tornado.

twit (twĭt) ***vt-*** **[twit·ted, twit·ting]** to tease in a good-natured way, especially by reminding of a mistake.

twitch (twĭch) ***vt-*** **1** to move in a quick, jerky manner: *He nervously* twitched *his fingers.* **2** to pull at suddenly; jerk: *Impatiently she* twitched *the cloth from the table.* ***vi-***: *Her face* twitched. ***n-*** **1** brief, involuntary spasm of a muscle: *a facial* twitch. **2** short pull or jerk.

twit·ter (twĭt′ ər) ***vi-*** to make a series of short, sharp sounds; chirp: *The canary* twittered *in its cage.* ***n-*** **1** rapid series of short, sharp sounds; a chirping. **2** state of restless, nervous excitement; flutter.

two (to͞o) ***n-*** [*pl.* **twos**] **1** amount or quantity that is one greater than 1. **2** *Mathematics* (1) the cardinal number that is the sum of 1 and 1. (2) a numeral such as 2 that represents this cardinal number. *as* ***determiner*** (traditionally called adjective or pronoun): *There are* two *dogs here and* two *there.* ***Homs-*** to, too.

in two in two pieces or parts. **put two and two together** to come to the obvious conclusion.

two-base hit ***n-*** in baseball, a hit which allows the batter to reach second base but no further. Also **two′-bag′ ger** (to͞o′ băg′ ər).

two-by-four (to͞o′ bī fôr′) ***n-*** length of lumber two inches thick and four inches wide when rough or, after planing, 1⅝ inches thick and 3⅝ inches wide. ***adj-*** **1** measuring two units by four units. **2** *Informal* very small or narrow; unimportant; petty.

two-edged (to͞o′ ĕjd′) ***adj-*** **1** having two edges: *a* two-edged *sword.* **2** having two meanings, implications, or effects; ambiguous: *a* two-edged *compliment.*

two-faced (to͞o′ fāst′) ***adj-*** **1** having both sides decorated, engraved, finished, etc. **2** deceitful; hypocritical.

two-fist·ed (to͞o′ fĭs′ təd) *Informal* ***adj-*** powerful and vigorous; manly and aggressive; virile.

two·fold (to͞o′ fōld′) ***adj-*** **1** two times as many or as much. **2** having two parts; double: *a* twofold *answer to his question.* ***adv-***: *He increased his earnings* twofold.

two-hand·ed (to͞o′ hăn′ dəd) ***adj-*** **1** having two hands. **2** used or done with two hands: *a* two-handed *sword*; *a* two-handed *shot in basketball.* **3** intended for use by two persons: *a* two-handed *saw.*

two·pence (tŭp′ əns) ***n-*** **1** in Great Britain, the sum of two pennies. **2** former British coin of this value. Also **tuppence.**

two·pen·ny (tŭp′ ə nē) *Brit.* ***adj-*** **1** having the value of twopence. **2** commonplace; trifling; cheap.

two-ply (to͞o′ plī′) ***adj-*** **1** made of two strands or layers of material. **2** of cloth, made of two separate webs woven into each other: *a* two-ply *carpet.*

two·score (to͞o′ skôr′) ***determiner*** (traditionally called adjective or pronoun) two times twenty; forty.

two·seat·er (to͞o′ sē′ tər) ***n-*** airplane, car, etc., having seats for two passengers.

two·some (to͞o′ səm) ***n-*** **1** two persons together. **2** game, dance, etc., by or for two persons.

two-star (to͞o′ stär′) ***adj-*** having the two stars of a major general or rear admiral as insignia of rank.

two-step (to͞o′ stĕp′) ***n-*** **1** ballroom dance in march or polka tempo performed with sliding steps. **2** music for such a dance.

two-time (to͞o′ tīm′) ***vt-*** **[two-timed, two-tim·ing]** *Slang* to deceive; be unfaithful to. —***n-*** **two′-tim′ er.**

two-way (to͞o′ wā′) ***adj-*** **1** having or allowing movement in two directions: *a* two-way *street.* **2** able to transmit and receive: *a* two-way *radio.*

1-ty *suffix* (used to form nouns) state, condition, or quality: *loyal*ty; *royal*ty. [ultimately from Latin **-tas** and **-tatis.**]

2-ty *suffix* (used to form some cardinal numerals) multiplied by ten: *six*ty; *nine*ty. [from Old English **-tig.**]

ty·coon (tī′ ko͞on′) *Informal* ***n-*** rich and powerful industrialist or financier.

ty·ing (tī′ ĭng) *pres. p.* of **tie.**

tyke (tīk) ***n-*** **1** *Informal* a child, especially a mischievous one. **2** mongrel dog; cur.

tym·pa·ni (tĭm′ pə nē) ***n-*** *pl.* kettledrums, especially those in a symphony orchestra. —***n-*** **tym′ pa·nist.**

tym·pan·ic (tĭm′ păn′ ĭk) ***adj-*** **1** like a drum or drumhead. **2** having to do with the eardrum.

tympanic membrane ***n-*** membrane between the outer and middle ear, often called the eardrum.

tym·pa·num (tĭm′ pə nəm) ***n-*** [*pl.* **tym·pa·na** (-nə) or **tym·pa·nums**] middle ear; also, less correctly, eardrum.

type (tīp) ***n-*** **1** person or thing having the features that set apart a group or class; typical example: *Charles Dickens's characters are* types *of middle-class English life.* **2** group of persons or things that share common traits; kind; sort: *Men of that* type *like fast cars.* **3** *Biology* group or division of animals or plants having a common structure or form. **4** piece of metal with a raised letter or figure on one surface, used in printing or as part of a typewriter. **5** impression made from such pieces: *a line of italic* type. *as* ***modifier***: *a* type *size*; *a* type *face.* ***vt-*** **[typed, typ·ing]** **1** to write on a typewriter: *to* type *a letter.* **2** to classify: *The director* typed *the actor for comic parts.* ***vi-***: *She* types *at the rate of 60 words a minute.*

Type and type faces

►TYPE generally means "kind," and careful writers and speakers do not use TYPE as a modifier unless referring to printing type. Avoid saying: *this* type *airplane*; *that* type *person.* It is correct to say: *this* type *of airplane*; *that* type *of person.*

type metal ***n-*** an alloy of lead, tin, and antimony, used for casting printing type.

type·script (tīp′ skrĭpt′) ***n-*** manuscript prepared by typewriter.

type·set·ter (tīp′ sĕt′ ər) ***n-*** person or machine that arranges type for printing. —***n-*** **type′ set′ ting.**

type·write (tīp′ rīt′) ***vt-*** [**type·wrote, type·writ·ten, type·writ·ing**] to write with a typewriter. ***vi-*** to use a typewriter.

type·writ·er (tīp′ rī′ tər) ***n-*** machine that prints letters, numbers, punctuation, etc., on a sheet of paper when keys are struck by the operator's fingers.

ty·phoid (tī′ foid′) ***n-*** typhoid fever. ***adj-*** **1** of or related to typhoid fever. **2** resembling typhus.

typhoid fever ***n-*** infectious bacterial disease transmitted by water, milk, food, flies, and human carriers, and marked by severe digestive disturbances, fever, etc.

ty·phoon (tī fo͞on′) ***n-*** hurricane occuring over the western Pacific.

ty·phus (tī′ fəs) ***n-*** disease caused by rickettsia, transmitted by rat fleas and the body louse, and marked by fever, nausea, chills, and a rash. Also **typhus fever.**

typ·i·cal (tĭp′ ĭ kəl) ***adj-*** **1** having the traits of its kind but no other notable features; representing a whole group: *a* typical *high school library*; *a* typical *suburban community.* **2** such as can be expected from knowing the type or group; characteristic: *He gave one of his* typical *answers.* **—*adv-*** **typ′ i·cal·ly.** ***n-*** **typ′ i·cal·ness.**

typ·i·fy (tĭp′ ə fī′) ***vt-*** [**typ·i·fied, typ·i·fy·ing**] **1** to be typical of; represent: *The cat* typifies *a family of animals.* **2** to symbolize: *The lamb* typifies *meekness.*

typ·ist (tī′ pĭst) ***n-*** person who knows how to operate a typewriter; especially, one employed to do so.

ty·po·graph·ic (tī′ pə grăf′ ĭk) or **ty·po·graph·i·cal** (-ĭ kəl) ***adj-*** of or relating to printing. **—*adv-*** **ty′ po·graph′ i·cal·ly.**

ty·pog·ra·phy (tī pŏg′ rə fē) ***n-*** [*pl.* **ty·pog·ra·phies**] **1** the art of printing, especially letterpress printing. **2** the arrangement or appearance of printed matter. **—*n-*** **ty·pog′ ra·pher.**

ty·ran·ni·cal (tĭ răn′ ĭ kəl) ***adj-*** of or like a tyrant; unjustly severe; cruel; despotic: *a* tyrannical *ruler.* Also **ty·ran′ nic. —*adv-*** **ty·ran′ ni·cal·ly.**

tyr·an·nize (tĭr′ ə nīz′) ***vi-*** [**tyr·an·nized, tyr·an·niz·ing**] to be a tyrant. ***vt-*** to act like a tyrant toward; rule severely and cruelly: *The father* tyrannized *his children.*

ty·ran·no·sau·rus (tĭ răn′ ə sôr′ əs) ***n-*** giant, predatory, carnivorous dinosaur of North America during the Cretaceous period, with powerfully developed hind legs and erect posture. For picture, see *dinosaur.*

tyr·an·nous (tĭr′ ə nəs) ***adj-*** unjustly severe and cruel; tyrannical **—*adv-*** **tyr′ an·nous·ly.**

tyr·an·ny (tĭr′ ə nē) ***n-*** [*pl.* **tyr·an·nies**] **1** oppression; despotism: *To deny us that right is* tyranny. **2** any oppressive and absolute rule or government: *The fascist state was a* tyranny.

ty·rant (tī′ rənt) ***n-*** **1** ruler or master who uses his power to oppress those under him. **2** an absolute monarch; despot.

Tyr·i·an purple (tĭr′ ē ən) ***n-*** a dye of deep, purplish red obtained in the ancient world from a fluid secreted by certain mollusks, and now made synthetically.

ty·ro (tī′ rō) ***n-*** [*pl.* **ty·ros**] beginner in doing or learning anything. *as* ***modifier***: *a* tyro *skier.* Also **tiro.**

tzar (tsär, zär) czar.

tza·ri·na (tsä rē′ nə, zä-) czarina.

U

U or **u** (yo͞o) ***n-*** [*pl.* **U's, u's**] **1** the 21st letter of the English alphabet. **2** anything shaped like this letter.

U symbol for uranium.

u·biq·ui·tous (yo͞o bĭk′ wĭ təs) ***adj-*** being, or seeming to be, everywhere at the same time. **—*adv-*** **u·biq′ ui·tous·ly.** ***n-*** **u·biq′ ui·tous·ness** or **u·biq′ ui·ty.**

U-boat (yo͞o′ bōt′) ***n-*** German submarine. *as* ***modifier***: *a* U-boat *attack*; U-boat *fleet.*

ud·der (ŭd′ ər) ***n-*** sac that hangs down between the hind legs of a cow, ewe, she-goat, etc., and holds one or more milk-producing glands, each with its own teat.

UFO or **ufo** unidentified flying object.

ugh (o͝o, ŭ, ŭg, UKH, or various other grunts) ***interj-*** exclamation of distaste or sound made when one is hit.

ugly (ŭg′ lē) ***adj-*** [**ug·li·er, ug·li·est**] **1** very unpleasant to the sight: *an* ugly *face.* **2** disagreeable: *an* ugly *task.* **3** threatening; dangerous: *an* ugly *sky.* **4** cross; quarrelsome: *an* ugly *mood.* **5** morally repulsive: *an* ugly *deed.***—*n-*** **ug′ li·ness.**

UHF or **uhf** ultrahigh frequency.

U.K. United Kingdom.

u·kase (yo͞o kās′, o͞o kās′, -kāz′) ***n-*** **1** in Russia under the czars, an imperial decree taking effect as law. **2** any official ruling or decree.

u·ku·le·le (yo͞o′ kə lā′ lē) ***n-*** any of several kinds of small, four-stringed musical instruments of the guitar type. [American word from Hawaiian.]

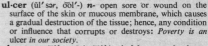

Ukulele

ul·cer (ŭl′ sər, o͞ol′-) ***n-*** open sore or wound on the surface of the skin or mucous membrane, which causes a gradual destruction of the tissue; hence, any condition or influence that corrupts or destroys: *Poverty is an* ulcer *in our society.*

ul·cer·ate (ŭl′ sə rāt′, o͞ol′-) ***vi-*** [**ul·cer·at·ed, ul·cer·at·ing**] to form an ulcer; become ulcerous: *His stomach lining* ulcerated. **—*n-*** **ul′ cer·a′ tion.**

ul·cer·ous (ŭl′ sər əs, o͞ol′-) ***adj-*** **1** marked or affected by an ulcer or ulcers: *an* ulcerous *area of skin.* **2** ulcerated: *an* ulcerous *sore.*

ul·na (ŭl′ nə, o͞ol′-) ***n-*** [*pl.* **ul·nae** (-nē)] the inner and larger of the two bones of the forearm. **—*adj-*** **ul′ nar:** *an* ulnar *fracture.*

ul·ster (ŭl′ stər, o͞ol′-) ***n-*** long, loose overcoat, often with a belt.

ult. **1** ultimate. **2** ultimately. **3** ultimo.

ul·te·ri·or (ŭl′ têr′ ē ər, o͞ol′-) ***adj-*** **1** beyond what is expressed or admitted; deliberately not mentioned: *an* ulterior *motive.* **2** farther off; more remote: *the* ulterior *regions of the country.* **—*adv-*** **ul′ te′ ri·or·ly.**

ul·ti·ma (ŭl′ tə mə, o͞ol′-) ***n-*** last syllable of a word.

ul·ti·mate (ŭl′ tə mət, o͞ol′-) ***adj-*** **1** final; last: *his* ultimate *goal; the* ultimate *result of one's actions.* **2** basic; fundamental: *some* ultimate *truths.* **3** farthest known or imagined in time past or future: *his* ultimate *ancestors.* ***n-*** the final or last state or degree: *the* ultimate *in style.*

ul·ti·mate·ly (ŭl′ tə mət lē, o͞ol-) ***adv-*** at the beginning or end.

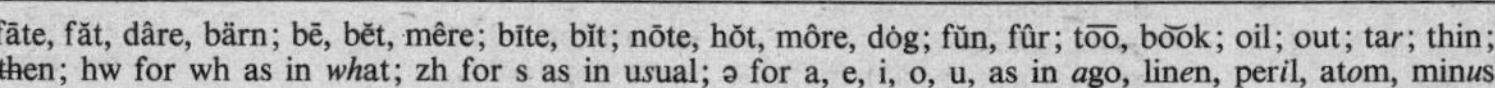
fāte, făt, dâre, bärn; bē, bĕt, mêre; bīte, bĭt; nōte, hŏt, môre, dȯg; fŭn, fûr; to͞o, bo͝ok; oil; out; tar; thin; then; hw for wh as in *wh*at; zh for s as in u*s*ual; ə for a, e, i, o, u, as in *a*go, lin*e*n, per*i*l, at*o*m, min*u*s

ul·ti·ma·tum (ŭl′ tə mā′ təm, o͝ol′-) ***n-*** [*pl.* **ul·ti·ma·tums** or **ul·ti·ma·ta** (-tə)] **1** statement of a final demand or offer. **2** in diplomatic relations, a last offer of conditions, the rejection of which may cause a break in negotiations.

ul·ti·mo (ŭl′ tə mō′, o͝ol′-) *Archaic* ***adj-*** of the month preceding the present month: *I wrote on the 16th* ultimo.

ul·tra (ŭl′ trə, o͝ol′-) ***adj-*** going beyond what is usual, ordinary, or average; extreme: *His views are very* ultra. ***n-*** person with extreme opinions.

ultra- *prefix* **1** beyond: *an* ultra*sonic speed.* **2** extremely; excessively: *an* ultra*modern tendency.* [from Late Latin **ultra-**, from Latin **ultrā** meaning "beyond."]

ul·tra·high frequency (ŭl′ trə hī′, o͝ol′-) ***n-*** any radio frequency between 300 and 3,000 megacycles per second.

ul·tra·ma·rine (ŭl′ trə mə rēn′, o͝ol′-) ***n-*** **1** blue coloring matter made from the gem lapis lazuli. **2** a bright, deep-blue color. ***adj-***: *Ask for an* ultramarine *dye.*

ul·tra·mod·ern (ŭl′ trə mŏd′ ərn, o͝ol′-) ***adj-*** extremely modern: *an* ultramodern *structure*; ultramodern *tastes.*

ul·tra·son·ic (ŭl′ trə sŏn′ ĭk, o͝ol′-) ***adj-*** of sound, beyond the range of normal human hearing, usually above 20,000 cycles per second: *an* ultrasonic *dog whistle.*

ul·tra·vi·o·let (ŭl′ trə vī′ ə lət, o͝ol′-) ***adj-*** of or related to electromagnetic radiation, called **ultraviolet rays,** lying beyond the violet end of the visible spectrum and having wavelengths that range between about 40 and 4,000 angstroms.

ul·u·la·tion (yo͞ol′ yə lā′ shən, ŭl′-) ***n-*** a howling; howl.

U·lys·ses (yo͞o lĭs′ ēz′) ***n-*** Latin name for Odysseus.

um·bel (ŭm′ bəl) ***n-*** flower cluster with stalks of about equal length radiating from a point at the top of the stem.

Umbel

um·ber (ŭm′ bər) ***n-*** **1** a dark, yellowish-brown earth used as a coloring matter. In its natural state, it is called **raw umber.** When heated and made powdery, it becomes darker and more reddish, and is called **burnt umber. 2** a rich, dark-brown color. ***adj-***: *He wants an* umber *pigment.*

um·bil·i·cal cord (əm bĭl′ ĭ kəl) ***n-*** **1** tubelike structure extending from the navel of a fetus to the placenta of the mother. It carries food and oxygen to, and removes wastes from, a fetus. **2** any of the lines that carry electricity, fuel, etc., to a spacecraft on a launching pad.

um·bil·i·cus (əm bĭl′ ĭ kəs) ***n-*** [*pl.* **um·bil·i·ci** (-ĭ sī′)] **1** the navel. **2** the rootlike attachment of a lichen to the substratum. **3** the hilum of a seed. **4** the opening at either end of the hollow stem of a bird's flight feather.

um·bra (ŭm′ brə) ***n-*** [*pl.* **um·brae** (-brē, -brī) or **um·bras**] **1** shadow or dark spot. **2** *Astronomy* (1) the cone of complete shadow cast by the earth or moon, or by another planet or satellite, in the direction away from the sun. (2) the dark, central portion of a sunspot. **3** *Physics* the central portion of a shadow from which all direct light is excluded. See also *penumbra.*

um·brage (ŭm′ brĭj) ***n-*** feeling that one has been slighted in some way; resentment.
take umbrage to feel offended.

um·brel·la (ŭm brĕl′ ə) ***n-*** **1** circular, waterproof cloth cover spread on metal ribs attached to the end of a long handle, used as a protection against sun or rain. **2** any protective covering.

umbrella tree ***n-*** an American magnolia tree having leaves so arranged as to suggest an open umbrella.

u·mi·ak (o͞o′ mē ăk′) ***n-*** a long, open, Eskimo boat made of skins stretched on a frame.

Umiak

um·pire (ŭm′ pīər′) ***n-*** **1** an official in certain sports who supervises play, enforces the rules, and decides disputed points. **2** person chosen to settle a controversy by hearing both sides and coming to a decision: *an* umpire *in a labor-management dispute.* ***vt-*** [**um·pired, um·pir·ing**] to supervise or enforce the rules of (a game) or settle (a dispute): *Who* umpired *the game?* ***vi-***: *Who* umpired *yesterday?*

¹un- *prefix* **1** not; the opposite of; lack of: *to be* un*accustomed to joy.* **2** the opposite of; lack of: un*lovely*; un*importance.* [from Old English **un-** and **on-** of the same meaning.]

²un- *prefix* **1** do the opposite of; reverse the action of: *to* un*bar*; un*bend.* **2** take away: *to* un*frock*; un*mask.* **3** release from: *to* un*hand.* **4** take out of: *to* un*bosom*; un*earth.* **5** cause to be no longer: *to* un*man.* **6** completely; entirely: *to* un*loose.* [from Old English **un-** meaning "back; against."]

U.N. or **UN** United Nations.

un·a·bashed (ŭn′ ə băsht′) ***adj-*** not embarrassed, ashamed, or confused. ***—adv-*** **un′ a·bash′ ed·ly.**

un·a·ble (ŭn′ ā′ bəl) ***adj-*** not able; lacking ability or power: *to be* unable *to walk*; unable *to attend.*

un·a·bridged (ŭn′ ə brĭjd′) ***adj-*** not shortened or condensed: *an* unabridged *novel.*

un·ac·cent·ed (ŭn′ ăk sĕn′ təd, ŭn′ ăk′ sĕn′-) ***adj-*** not accented or stressed: *an* unaccented *syllable.*

un·ac·com·pa·nied (ŭn′ ə kŭm′ pə nēd) ***adj-*** **1** without another person or thing: *an* unaccompanied *guest.* **2** *Music* performed without accompaniment.

un·ac·count·a·ble (ŭn′ ə koun′ tə bəl) ***adj-*** **1** impossible to account for or explain; strange; odd: *an* unaccountable *delay.* **2** not responsible: *The poor fellow is* unaccountable *for his acts.* ***—adv-*** **un′ ac·count′ a·bly.**

un·ac·cus·tomed (ŭn′ ə kŭs′ təmd) ***adj-*** **1** not accustomed; unused (to): *He is* unaccustomed *to heavy work.* **2** not customary: *his* unaccustomed *interest.*

un·ad·vised (ŭn′ əd vīzd′) ***adj-*** **1** not careful or prudent; too bold; rash: *an* unadvised *action or decision.* **2** without having received advice. ***—adv-*** **un′ ad·vis′ ed·ly.**

¹un·af·fect·ed (ŭn′ ə fĕk′ təd) ***adj-*** not influenced: *an* unaffected *audience.* [from **¹affect.**]

²un·af·fect·ed (ŭn′ ə fĕk′ təd) ***adj-*** natural and sincere in manner; unassuming; straightforward: *Although he was the best player, he remained* unaffected. ***—adv-*** **un′ af·fect′ ed·ly.** ***n-*** **un′ af·fect′ ed·ness.** [from **²affect.**]

Any of these words means un- ("not") plus the meaning of the rest of the word as given in the main text.

un′ a·bat′ ed
un′ ab·bre′ vi·at′ ed
un′ ab·solved′
un′ ab·sorbed′
un′ ac′ a·dem′ ic
un′ ac·cen′ tu·at′ ed
un′ ac·cept′ a·ble
un′ ac·cept′ ed
un′ ac′ cli·mat′ ed
un′ ac·cli′ ma·tized′
un′ ac·com′ mo·dat′ ed
un′ ac·com′ mo·dat′ ing
un′ ac·com′ plished
un′ ac·count′ a·bil′ i·ty
un′ ac·count′ ed
un′ ac·cred′ it·ed
un′ ac·knowl′ edged
un′ ac·quaint′ ed
un′ act′ ed
un′ a·dapt′ a·ble
un′ a·dapt′ ed
un′ ad·just′ ed
un′ ad′ mi·ra·ble
un′ a·dorned′
un′ adul′ ter·at′ ed
un′ ad·ven′ tur·ous
un′ ad′ ver·tised′
un′ ad·vis′ a·ble
un′ aes·thet′ ic

un·aid·ed (ŭn′ ā′ dəd) ***adj-*** not aided; without help.

un·al·ter·a·ble (ŭn′ ôl′ tər ə bəl) ***adj-*** such as cannot be altered or changed. **—*adv-* un′ al′ ter·a·bly.**

un·al·tered (ŭn′ ôl′ tərd) ***adj-*** not altered or changed: *an* unaltered *policy.*

un-A·mer·i·can (ŭn′ ə mĕr′ ĭ kən) ***adj-*** not American in beliefs, actions, or attitudes; especially, not loyal to the American government or ideals.

u·na·nim·i·ty (yōō′ nə nĭm′ ə tē) ***n-*** complete agreement in opinion.

u·nan·i·mous (yōō năn′ ə məs) ***adj-* 1** united in a single opinion; agreeing: *We were* unanimous *in our approval.* **2** showing complete agreement: *a* unanimous *vote.* **—*adv-* u·nan′ i·mous·ly. *n-* u·nan′ i·mous·ness.**

un·an·swer·a·ble (ŭn′ ăn′ sər ə bəl) ***adj-*** such as cannot be answered or disproved: *an* unanswerable *letter.*

un·ap·pe·tiz·ing (ŭn′ ăp′ ə tī′ zĭng) ***adj-*** not appetizing, especially to the taste.

un·ap·proach·a·ble (ŭn′ ə prō′ chə bəl) ***adj-* 1** such as cannot be approached or reached: *The mountain peak is* unapproachable *in winter.* **2** not easy to know or deal with; unfriendly; cool: *The principal seemed to be* unapproachable. **—*adv-* un′ ap·proach′ a·bly. *n-* un′ ap·proach′ a·ble·ness.**

un·armed (ŭn′ ärmd′) ***adj-*** not armed; lacking weapons; defenseless.

un·as·sail·a·ble (ŭn′ ə sā′ lə bəl) ***adj-*** such as cannot be assailed, attacked, or disputed: *an* unassailable *defense*; *an* unassailable *reputation.* **—*adv-* un′ as·sail′ a·bly.**

un·as·sum·ing (ŭn′ ə sōō′ mĭng) ***adj-*** modest; retiring; not given to pushing oneself forward. **—*adv-* un′ as·sum′ ing·ly. *n-* un′ as·sum′ ing·ness.**

un·at·tached (ŭn′ ə tăcht′) ***adj-* 1** not attached or connected: *an* unattached *house.* **2** not married or engaged to be married. **3** *Military* not assigned to a company or regiment. **4** in track meets, competing on one's own, not as a member of any athletic organization. **5** in law, not taken or held under legal process.

un·at·tend·ed (ŭn′ ə tĕn′ dəd) ***adj-* 1** without an escort; alone: *Mrs. Roberts is going to the concert* unattended. **2** receiving no attention or care; without supervision.

un·a·vail·ing (ŭn′ ə vā′ lĭng) ***adj-*** without result or effect; useless; futile: *Her calls for help were* unavailing. **—*adv-* un′ a·vail′ ing·ly.**

un·a·void·a·ble (ŭn′ ə voi′ də bəl) ***adj-*** such as cannot be avoided; inevitable: *an* unavoidable *delay.* **—*adv-* un′ a·void′ a·bly. *n-* un′ a·void′ a·ble·ness.**

un·a·ware (ŭn′ ə wâr′) ***adj-*** not aware or conscious: *They were* unaware *of danger.*

un·a·wares (ŭn′ ə wârz′) ***adv-* 1** without being aware: *He walked into the surprise party* unawares. **2** by surprise: *You came upon me* unawares.

un·bal·anced (ŭn′ băl′ ənst) ***adj-* 1** not in balance; out of equilibrium: *The scales were* unbalanced. **2** not adjusted as to be even in credit and debit: *an* unbalanced *account*; *an* unbalanced *budget.* **3** not sound mentally; partly insane: *an* unbalanced *mind.* **4** in football, having more players on one side of the center than on the other: *an* unbalanced *line.*

un·bar (ŭn′ bär′) ***vt-*** **[un·barred, un·bar·ring]** to remove a bar or bars from; open; unlock: *to* unbar *a door.*

un·bear·a·ble (ŭn′ bâr′ ə bəl) ***adj-*** such as cannot be borne; impossible to endure; intolerable: *an* unbearable *pain*; unbearable *suspense.* **—*adv-* un′ bear′ a·bly.**

un·beat·a·ble (ŭn′ bē′ tə bəl) ***adj-*** such as cannot be surpassed or defeated; invincible: *an* unbeatable *team.*

un·beat·en (ŭn′ bē′ tən) ***adj-* 1** never beaten or surpassed: *an* unbeaten *team or player*; *an* unbeaten *record.* **2** never walked over; untrodden: *an* unbeaten *path.*

un·be·com·ing (ŭn′ bĭ kŭm′ ĭng) ***adj-* 1** not suitable or fit; improper; unworthy: *their* unbecoming *conduct.* **2** not suited to one's appearance; not flattering: *an* unbecoming *hat.* **—*adv-* un′ be·com′ ing·ly.**

un·be·known (ŭn′ bĭ nōn′) or **un·be·knownst** (ŭn′ bĭ nōnst′) ***adj-*** unknown; not known of: *an* unbeknown *poet.* ***adv-*** in an unknown or unnoticed way; unknown (to): *He stole into the room* unbeknownst *to us.*

un·be·lief (ŭn′ bĭ lēf′) ***n-*** lack of positive belief or faith; especially, refusal to accept the teachings of religion.

un·be·liev·a·ble (ŭn′ bĭ lē′ və bəl) ***adj-*** such as cannot be believed; incredible: *an* unbelievable *story*; unbelievable *cruelty.* **—*adv-* un′ be·liev′ a·bly.**

un·be·liev·er (ŭn′ bĭ lē′ vər) ***n-* 1** person who lacks faith; doubter. **2** person who refuses to accept the teachings of any religion.

un·be·liev·ing (ŭn′ bĭ lē′ vĭng) ***adj-* 1** not believing; doubting; incredulous. **2** not accepting religious teachings. **—*adv-* un′ be·liev′ ing·ly.**

un·bend (ŭn′ bĕnd′) ***vt-*** **[un·bent, un·bend·ing] 1** to straighten: *to* unbend *a crooked nail*; *to* unbend *one's legs after a long ride.* **2** to unfasten (a sail) from a spar. **3** to free from strain; relax: *to* unbend *the mind.* ***vi-* 1** to become straight. **2** to become less formal or stiff; relax: *After a little while, he* unbent *and joined the party.*

Any of these words means un- ("not") plus the meaning of the rest of the word as given in the main text.

un′ af·fil′ i·at′ ed
un′ a·fraid′
un′ aged′
un′ ag·gres′ sive
un′ aimed′
un′ aired′
un′ al′ ien·a·ble
un′ a·ligned′
un′ a·like′
un′ al·lied′
un′ al·low′ a·ble
un′ al·loyed′
un′ al′ ter·a·bil′ i·ty
un′ am·big′ u·ous
un′ am·bi′ tious
un′ a′ mi·a·ble
un′ an′ chor
un′ an′ i·mat′ ed
un′ an·nounced′
un′ an′ swered
un′ an·tic′ i·pat′ ed
un′ a·pol′ o·get′ ic
un′ ap·palled′
un′ ap·par′ ent
un′ ap·peal′ a·ble
un′ ap·peal′ ing
un′ ap·peas′ a·ble
un′ ap·peased′
un′ ap·pre′ ci·at′ ed
un′ ap·pre′ ci·a·tive
un′ ap·proached′
un′ ap·pro′ pri·at′ ed
un′ ap·proved′
un′ arm′
un′ ar′ mored
un′ ar·rest′ ed
un′ ar·tis′ tic
un′ a·shamed′
un′ asked′
un′ as′ pi·rat′ ed
un′ as·pir′ ing
un′ as·sailed′
un′ as·ser′ tive
un′ as·sist′ ed
un′ as·so′ ci·at′ ed
un′ at·tain′ a·ble
un′ at·tempt′ ed
un′ at·test′ ed
un′ at·trac′ tive
un′ aus·pi′ cious
un′ au·then′ tic
un′ au·then′ ti·cat′ ed
un′ au′ thor·ized′
un′ a·vail′ a·ble
un′ a·vowed′
un′ a·wak′ened
un′ awed′
un′ backed′
un′ baked′
un′ bal′ ance
un′ bal′ last·ed
un′ band′ age
un′ bap·tized′
un′ barred′
un′ beau′ ti·ful
un′ be·fit′ ting

---

un·bend·ing (ŭn′ bĕn′ dĭng) ***adj-*** **1** stiff; rigid; inflexible. **2** unyielding; stubborn: *an* unbending *attitude or policy;* unbending *determination.* **—*adv-*** **un′ bend′ ing·ly.**

un·bi·ased or **un·bi·assed** (ŭn′ bī′ əst) ***adj-*** not biased; not taking sides; free from prejudice; impartial: *Judges are expected to give* unbiased *opinions.*

un·bid·den (ŭn′ bĭd′ ən) ***adj-*** **1** not asked; not invited: *He came* unbidden *to our party.* **2** not ordered; not commanded.

un·bind (ŭn′ bīnd′) ***vt-*** **[un·bound, un·bind·ing] 1** to untie; unfasten: *to* unbind *a bandage.* **2** to set free; release: *They* unbound *the prisoner.*

un·bleached (ŭn′ blēcht′) ***adj-*** not bleached: *a yard of* unbleached *muslin; a sack of* unbleached *flour.*

un·blem·ished (ŭn′ blĕm′ ĭsht) ***adj-*** without a blemish, spot, or stain; spotless; pure: *an* unblemished *life.*

un·blush·ing (ŭn′ blŭsh′ ĭng) ***adj-*** **1** not blushing; not embarrassed. **2** not ashamed or timid; bold: *an* unblushing *offer of a bribe.* **—*adv-*** **un′ blush′ ing·ly.**

un·bolt (ŭn′ bōlt′) ***vt-*** to unlock (a door, gate, etc.) by pulling back the bolt; unbar.

un·born (ŭn′ bôrn′) ***adj-*** not yet born; still to come; future: *Generations of* unborn *children will hear of him.*

un·bos·om (ŭn′ bo͝oz′ əm) ***vt-*** to bring out (something one knows or feels but has not revealed); reveal: *to* unbosom *a secret.* ***vi-*** to free one's mind by telling one's thoughts.

unbosom (oneself) to tell (one's) thoughts, feelings, or secrets.

un·bound (ŭn′ bound′) ***adj-*** **1** not tied; free: *The* unbound *pony galloped across the field.* **2** not confined or limited: *a man* unbound *by custom.* **3** having pages not fastened together or not bound between covers.

un·bound·ed (ŭn′ boun′ dəd) ***adj-*** without limits; boundless; measureless: *a universe of* unbounded *space.*

un·bowed (ŭn′ boud′) ***adj-*** **1** not bowed or bent: *The old man was dignified and* unbowed. **2** not conquered; still erect and proud, though defeated.

un·bri·dled (ŭn′ brī′ dəld) ***adj-*** **1** not fastened with a bridle. **2** not restrained: *an* unbridled *tongue.*

un·bro·ken (ŭn′ brō′ kən) ***adj-*** **1** not broken; not damaged: *an* unbroken *toy.* **2** without interruption: *an* unbroken *dry spell.* **3** not tamed or trained: *an* unbroken *colt.* **4** not beaten or surpassed: *an* unbroken *record.*

un·buck·le (ŭn′ bŭk′ əl) ***vt-*** **[un·buck·led, un·buck·ling]** to undo or unfasten the buckle of: *to* unbuckle *a belt.*

un·bur·den (ŭn′ bûr′ dən) ***vt-*** **1** to rid of a load; ease: *He* unburdened *his horse after the long ride.* **2** to relieve of a burden: *He* unburdened *himself of a secret.*

un·but·ton (ŭn′ bŭt′ ən) ***vt-*** to unfasten the button or buttons of; open: *to* unbutton *a coat.*

un·called-for (ŭn′ kòld′ fòr′, -fôr′) ***adj-*** not needed; out of place; improper: *an* uncalled-for *remark.*

un·can·ny (ŭn′ kăn′ ē) ***adj-*** **[un·can·nier, un·can·ni·est] 1** not to be explained by reason: *his* uncanny *knowledge of my past.* **2** mysterious; strange; weird: *an* uncanny *atmosphere.* **—*adv-*** **un′ can′ ni·ly.** ***n-*** **un′ can′ ni·ness.**

un·cap (ŭn′ kăp′) ***vt-*** **[un·capped, un·cap·ping]** to remove the cap, covering, or lid from: *to* uncap *a bottle.*

un·ceas·ing (ŭn′ sē′ sĭng) ***adj-*** without a stop; continuous: *an* unceasing *din.* **—*adv-*** **un′ ceas′ ing·ly.**

un·cer·e·mo·ni·ous (ŭn′ sĕr′ ə mō′ nē əs) ***adj-*** **1** without any formality; informal: *an* unceremonious *visit; an* unceremonious *conference.* **2** without the usual courtesy; abrupt: *an* unceremonious *dismissal.* **—*adv-*** **un′ cer′ e·mo′ ni·ous·ly.** ***n-*** **un′ cer′ e·mo′ ni·ous·ness.**

un·cer·tain (ŭn′ sûr′ tən) ***adj-*** **1** not certain; not sure; doubtful: *to be* uncertain *of the answer to a question; butter of* uncertain *quality.* **2** not regular, dependable, or predictable: *the* uncertain *weather of early spring.* **3** not steady or firm: *an* uncertain *support or step.* **4** changing; fluctuating; variable: *the* uncertain *tide;* uncertain *prices.* **—*adv-*** **un′ cer′ tain·ly.** ***n-*** **un′ cer′ tain·ness.**

un·cer·tain·ty (ŭn′ sûr′ tən tē) ***n-*** [*pl.* **un·cer·tain·ties**] **1** lack of certainty; doubt: *There was some* uncertainty *about the date.* **2** uncertain or doubtful matter.

un·chain (ŭn′ chān′) ***vt-*** to unfasten the chain of; let loose; set free: *to* unchain *a door;* unchain *a dog.*

un·change·a·ble (ŭn′ chān′ jə bəl) ***adj-*** such as cannot be changed; unlikely to change or be changed: *His honesty is* unchangeable. **—*adv-*** **un′ change′ a·bly.** ***n-*** **un′ change′ a·ble·ness.**

un·char·i·ta·ble (ŭn′ chăr′ ə tə bəl) ***adj-*** **1** not charitable or generous to persons in need. **2** not kind in judging others or in dealing with others; harsh: *an* uncharitable *remark;* uncharitable *criticism.* **—*adv-*** **un′ char′ i·ta·bly.** ***n-*** **un′ char′ i·ta·ble·ness.**

un·chart·ed (ŭn′ chär′ təd) ***adj-*** **1** not covered by a map or chart; not mapped: *miles of* uncharted *wilderness.* **2** not shown on a map or chart: *an* uncharted *reef.* **3** not shown on a graph or other chart.

un·chaste (ŭn′ chāst′) ***adj-*** not chaste or morally pure; not virtuous; lewd: *her* unchaste *behavior; an* unchaste *remark.* **—*adv-*** **un′ chaste′ ly.** ***n-*** **un′ chaste′ ness.**

un·checked (ŭn′ chĕkt′) ***adj-*** not held back, or controlled; not restrained: *an* unchecked *flood.*

un·chris·tian (ŭn′ krĭs′ chən) ***adj-*** **1** not of the Christian religion. **2** not in keeping with the Christian religion: *an* unchristian *custom or practice.* **3** not kind or charitable: *an* unchristian *act or remark.*

un·ci·al (ŭn′ chəl) ***adj-*** having to do with characters or letters found in manuscripts from the fourth to about the ninth century, which resembled modern capital letters but were more rounded. ***n-*** **1** character or letter of this kind. **2** manuscript written in such characters or letters.

un·civ·il (ŭn′ sĭv′ əl) ***adj-*** not civil or courteous; impolite; rude: *an* uncivil *letter.* **—*adv-*** **un′ civ′ il·ly.**

un·civ·i·lized (ŭn′ sĭv′ ə līzd′) ***adj-*** not civilized; barbaric: *an* uncivilized *manner;* uncivilized *tribes.*

un·clad (ŭn′ klăd′) ***adj-*** without clothes; naked.

Any of these words means un- ("not") plus the meaning of the rest of the word as given in the main text.

un′ blam′ a·ble
un′ blamed′
un′ blink′ ing
un′ bolt′ ed
un′ bor′ rowed
un′ bought′
un′ braid′
un′ branched′
un′ brand′ ed
un′ break′ a·ble
un′ bridge′ a·ble
un′ bridged′
un′ bri′ dle
un′ broth′ er·ly
un′ bruised′
un′ brushed′
un′ budg′ ing
un′ built′
un′ bur′ dened
un′ bur′ ied
un′ burn′ a·ble
un′ burned′
un′ bur′ nished
un′ burnt′
un′ but′ toned
un′ cage′
un′ called′
un′ can′ celed
un′ cap′ i·tal·ized′
un′ cared′-for′
un′ car′ ing
un′ cas′ trat·ed
un′ cat′ a·logued′
un′ caught′
un′ caused′
un′ cen′ sored
un′ cen′ sured
un′ chal′ lenged
un′ chang′ ing
un′ chap′ er·oned′
un′ char′ ac·ter·is′ tic
un′ charged′
un′ chast′ ened
un′ chiv′ al·rous
un′ chris′ tened
un′ cir′ cum·cised′

un·clasp (ŭn′ klăsp′) ***vt-*** **1** to undo the clasp of: *to* unclasp *a brooch.* **2** to let go of; release: *to* unclasp *one's hold.* ***vi-*** to come open: *The buckle of my boot* unclasped.

un·cle (ŭng′ kəl) ***n-*** **1** brother of one's father or mother. **2** husband of one's aunt.

say (or **cry**) **uncle** *Informal* to surrender; give in.

un·clean (ŭn′ klēn′) ***adj-*** **1** not clean; dirty: *hands* unclean *from work.* **2** impure; sinful: *an* unclean *mind.* **—*adv-*** **un′ clean′ ly.** ***n-*** **un′ clean′ ness.**

un·clean·ly (ŭn′ klĕn′ lē) ***adj-*** **1** not cleanly; habitually dirty; unclean. **2** unchaste; impure; sinful. **—*n-*** **un′ clean′ li·ness.**

Uncle Sam ***n-*** *Informal* **1** the United States of America represented as a tall, slender, old man with long, white hair and a goatee, and dressed in the national colors. **2** the United States Government.

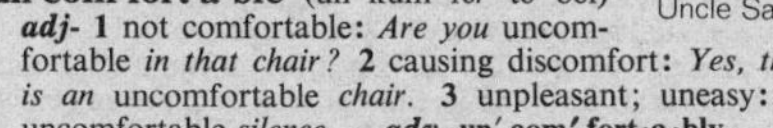

Uncle Sam

un·coil (ŭn′ koil′) ***vt-*** to unwind: *to* uncoil *a spool of wire.* ***vi-***: *The snake* uncoiled.

un·com·fort·a·ble (ŭn′ kŭm′ fər tə bəl) ***adj-*** **1** not comfortable: *Are you* uncomfortable *in that chair?* **2** causing discomfort: *Yes, this is an* uncomfortable *chair.* **3** unpleasant; uneasy: *an* uncomfortable *silence.* **—*adv-*** **un′ com′ fort·a·bly.**

un·com·mon (ŭn′ kŏm′ ən) ***adj-*** not common; unusual; rare; extraordinary. **—*adv-*** **un′ com′ mon·ly.** ***n-*** **un′ com′ mon·ness.**

un·com·pli·men·ta·ry (ŭn′ kŏm′ plə mĕn′ tə rē) ***adj-*** not complimentary or flattering; derogatory.

un·com·pro·mis·ing (ŭn′ kŏm′ prə mī′ zĭng) ***adj-*** not willing to compromise; unyielding; firm: *an* uncompromising *honesty.* **—*adv-*** **un′ com′ pro·mis′ ing·ly.**

un·con·cern (ŭn′ kən sûrn′) ***n-*** **1** lack of worry or anxiety: *She showed an amazing* unconcern *when her purse was stolen.* **2** lack of interest; indifference: *He was worried over his son's* unconcern *about school.*

un·con·cerned (ŭn′ kən sûrnd′) ***adj-*** not concerned; indifferent. **—*adv-*** **un′ con·cern′ ed·ly.**

un·con·di·tion·al (ŭn′ kən dĭsh′ ən əl) ***adj-*** without conditions or limitations; absolute: *an* unconditional *surrender.* **—*adv-*** **un′ con·di′ tion·al·ly.**

un·con·quer·a·ble (ŭn′ kŏng′ kər ə bəl) ***adj-*** not conquerable; invincible. **—*adv-*** **un′ con′ quer·a·bly.**

un·con·scion·a·ble (ŭn′ kŏn′ shən ə bəl) ***adj-*** such as cannot be approved by the conscience; indefensible; outrageous: *an* unconscionable *lie*; *an* unconscionable *price.* **—*adv-*** **un′ con′ scion·a·bly.**

un·con·scious (ŭn′ kŏn′ shəs) ***adj-*** **1** not conscious: *to be* unconscious *after a bad accident.* **2** without realization; not aware: *to be* unconscious *of having done or said the wrong thing.* **3** not deliberate; accidental: *an* unconscious *slip of the tongue.* ***n-*** the subconscious, especially the part of it that is the site of wishes, memories, etc., that have been repressed from consciousness. **—*adv-*** **un′ con′ scious·ly.**

un·con·scious·ness (ŭn′ kŏn′ shəs nəs) ***n-*** the condition of being unconscious.

un·con·sti·tu·tion·al (ŭn′ kŏn′ stə to͞o′ shən əl, -tyo͞o′ shən əl) ***adj-*** not authorized by, or in keeping with, the constitution of a country or State, especially with the Constitution of the United States. **—*adv-*** **un′ con′ sti·tu′ tion·al·ly.** ***n-*** **un′ con′ sti·tu′ tion·al′ i·ty** (-ăl′ ə tē).

un·con·trol·la·ble (ŭn′ kən trō′ lə bəl) ***adj-*** such as cannot be controlled; impossible to check or restrain: *He had an* uncontrollable *impulse to laugh.* **—*n-*** **un′ con·trol′ a·bil′ i·ty.** ***adv-*** **un′ con·trol′ la·bly.**

un·con·trolled (ŭn′ kən trōld′) ***adj-*** not controlled, checked, or restrained.

un·con·ven·tion·al (ŭn′ kən vĕn′ shən əl) ***adj-*** not bound by convention, custom, or fixed rules: *an* unconventional *procedure.* **—*n-*** **un′ con·ven′ tion·al′ i·ty** (-ăl′ ə tē). ***adv-*** **un′ con·ven′ tion·al·ly.**

un·cork (ŭn′ kȯrk′, -kôrk′) ***vt-*** **1** to open by removing the cork from: *to* uncork *a wine bottle.* **2** *Informal* to let fly; let loose: *to* uncork *a wild pitch.*

un·count·ed (ŭn′ koun′ təd) ***adj-*** **1** not counted. **2** too many to be counted; innumerable.

un·cou·ple (ŭn′ kŭp′ əl) ***vt-*** **[un·cou·pled, un·cou·pling]** **1** to unloose from a coupling; disconnect; detach: *to* uncouple *a locomotive.* **2** to set free; unleash.

un·couth (ŭn′ ko͞oth′) ***adj-*** **1** rude; vulgar: *to behave in an* uncouth *way.* **2** lacking grace and polish in behavior or appearance: *an* uncouth *backwoodsman*; *an* uncouth *hut in the forest.* **—*adv-*** **un′ couth′ ly.** ***n-*** **un′ couth′ ness.**

un·cov·er (ŭn′ kŭv′ ər) ***vt-*** **1** to remove the cover or covering from: *to* uncover *a sleeping person.* **2** to make known; disclose; reveal; expose: *The police* uncovered *the plot.* **3** to take the hat or cap from: *to* uncover *one's head.* ***vi-*** to remove one's hat or cap as a sign of respect or greeting: *to* uncover *for a passing funeral.*

un·cross (ŭn′ krȯs′) ***vt-*** to change from a position of being crossed: *to* uncross *one's legs.*

un·crowned (ŭn′ kround′) ***adj-*** not crowned; especially, not officially recognized as king or queen.

Any of these words means un- ("not") plus the meaning of the rest of the word as given in the main text.

un′ claimed′
un′ clas′ si·fi′ a·ble
un′ clas′ si·fied′
un′ cleaned′
un′ clear′
un′ cloak′
un′ clothe′
un′ clothed′
un′ cloud′ ed
un′ clut′ tered
un′ coat′ ed
un′ cocked′
un′ coiled′
un′ coined′
un′ col·lect′ ed
un′ col·lect′ i·ble
un′ col′ ored
un′ combed′
un′ come′ ly
un′ com′ fort·ed
un′ com·mit′ ted
un′ com·mu′ ni·ca′ tive
un′ com·pan′ ion·a·ble
un′ com′ pen·sat′ ed
un′ com·plain′ ing
un′ com·plet′ ed
un′ com′ pli·cat′ ed
un′ com′ pre·hend′ ing
un′ com′ pre·hen′ si·ble
un′ con·cealed′
un′ con·fined′
un′ con·firmed′
un′ con·gealed′
un′ con·gen′ ial
un′ con·nect′ ed
un′ con′ quered
un′ con′ sci·en′ tious
un′ con′ se·crat′ ed
un′ con·sid′ ered
un′ con·sol′ i·dat′ ed
un′ con·strained′
un′ con·sumed′
un′ con·tam′ i·nat′ ed
un′ con·test′ ed
un′ con′ tra·dict′ ed
un′ con·vinced′
un′ con·vinc′ ing
un′ cooked′
un′ co·op′ er·a·tive
un′ co·or′ di·nat′ ed
un′ cor′ dial
un′ corked′
un′ cor·rect′ ed
un′ cor·rob′ o·rat′ ed
un′ cor·rupt′ ed
un′ count′ a·ble
un′ cour′ te·ous
un′ cov′ered
un′ cre·at′ ed
un′ cred′ it·ed
un′ crip′ pled
un′ crit′ i·cal
un′ cropped′
un′ crossed′
un′ crowd′ ed
un′ crys′ tal·lized′

---

fāte, făt, dâre, bärn; bē, bĕt, mêre; bīte, bĭt; nōte, hŏt, môre, dȯg; fŭn, fûr; to͞o, bo͝ok; oil; out; tar; thin; then; hw for wh as in what; zh for s as in usual; ə for a, e, i, o, u, as in ago, linen, peril, atom, minus

unc·tion (ŭngk′ shən) *n-* **1** act of anointing as a rite of consecration. **2** an ointment; hence, anything soothing. **3** excessive and insincere courtesy; a smooth, oily manner. See also *extreme unction.*

unc·tu·ous (ŭng′ choo͞ əs) *adj-* **1** oily; smooth. **2** insincerely courteous or suave: *an* unctuous *manner.* —*adv-* **unc′ tu·ous·ly.** *n-* **unc′ tu·ous·ness.**

un·cul·ti·vat·ed (ŭn′ kŭl′ tə vā′ təd) *adj-* **1** not tilled; not cultivated for production of food. **2** not developed; not practiced; neglected: *an* uncultivated *talent for art.* **3** uncivilized; not refined by education.

un·curl (ŭn′ kûrl′) *vt-* to straighten out: *The rain* uncurled *her hair. vi-*: *Her hair* uncurled *in the rain.*

un·cut (ŭn′ kŭt′) *adj-* **1** not cut down, cut off, or cut apart: *an* uncut *forest*; uncut *flowers*; *an* uncut *ham.* **2** not shortened or reduced in size, length, etc.: *an* uncut *novel or motion picture.* **3** having the edges untrimmed, so that the pages cannot be turned one at a time until they are slit apart. **4** unchanged by cutting, polishing, etc.: *an* uncut *diamond.*

un·daunt·ed (ŭn′ dȯn′ təd) *adj-* not afraid or fearful; bold. —*adv-* **un′ daunt′ ed·ly.**

un·de·ceive (ŭn′ dĭ sēv′) *vt-* [**un·de·ceived, un·de·ceiv·ing**] to free from error or a mistaken idea or belief: *I thought it was a diamond, until the jeweler* undeceived *me.*

un·de·cid·ed (ŭn′ dĭ sī′ dəd) *adj-* **1** not yet decided or settled: *The question of moving to the country is still* undecided. **2** not having made up one's mind; wavering; vacillating: *We are* undecided *about what to do.* —*adv-* **un′ de·cid′ ed·ly.**

un·de·filed (ŭn′ dĭ fīld′) *adj-* **1** not soiled or contaminated. **2** not dishonored: *his* undefiled *name.*

un·de·mon·stra·tive (ŭn′ dĭ mŏn′ strə tĭv) *adj-* reserved in showing one's feelings. —*adv-* **un′ de·mon′ stra·tive·ly.** *n-* **un′ de·mon′ stra·tive·ness.**

un·de·ni·a·ble (ŭn′ dĭ nī′ ə bəl) *adj-* not to be denied; true or real beyond doubt; obvious: *You may not like him but his good looks are* undeniable.

un·de·ni·a·bly (ŭn′ dĭ nī′ ə blē) *adv-* without doubt; truly; certainly.

un·der (ŭn′ dər) *prep-* **1** in, to, or at a place or position directly below or beneath the surface of: *slippers* under *the bed*; *a picnic* under *the trees.* **2** concealed by; behind: *flowers* under *the leaves of a tree*; *to live* under *an assumed name.* **3** lower than (another) in rank, importance, value, etc.: *a rank* under *that of captain.* **4** less than (another) in amount, size, age, weight, etc.: *a price* under *two dollars*; *children* under *ten years of age.* **5** subject to the action or effect of: *to be* under *another's influence*; under *treatment by a doctor.* **6** subjected to; dominated by: *They suffer* under *a tyrant. He is* under *great strain.* **7** guided by; directed by: *He learned* under *great teachers.* **8** because of: *He refused* under *the circumstances.* **9** in conformity with; bound by: *to live* under *the laws of the land*; under *oath.* **10** during the time or rule of: *England* under *Queen Elizabeth. adv-* beneath or inside a surface: *The current sucked him* under. *She turned the hem* under. *adj-* **1** situated beneath something or on a lower surface: *the* under *surface of a leaf.* **2** lower in rank: *an* under *officer.*

go under to meet defeat or downfall; fail; be ruined.

under- *prefix* **1** beneath; below: under*ground*; under*line.* **2** not sufficiently; inadequately: under*cooked*; under*valued.* **3** lower in rank, importance, etc.: *an* under*secretary.*

un·der·age (ŭn′ dər āj′) *adj-* below the required age.

un·der·arm (ŭn′ dər ärm′) *adj-* **1** placed or situated under the arm, especially in the armpit. **2** in baseball, tennis, etc., underhand: *an* underarm *throw of the ball. adv-*: *to throw* underarm. *n-* the armpit.

[1]**un·der·bid** (ŭn′ dər bĭd′) *vt-* [**un·der·bid, un·der·bid·ding**] (considered intransitive when the direct object is implied but not expressed) **1** to make a bid lower than that of (a competing bidder), especially in offering to sell or do something at a lower price. **2** in card games, especially bridge, to bid too low to indicate the true value of (one's hand). —*n-* **un′ der·bid′ der.**

[2]**un·der·bid** (ŭn′ dər bĭd′) *n-* **1** a bid lower than that of a competitor. **2** in card games, a bid so low that it does not show the true value of one's hand.

un·der·brush (ŭn′ dər brŭsh′) *n-* bushes, shrubs, small trees, etc., growing thickly under large trees in a forest.

un·der·car·riage (ŭn′ dər kăr′ ĭj) *n-* **1** framework that supports an automobile, railroad train, etc., from below. **2** the landing gear of an airplane.

[1]**un·der·charge** (ŭn′ dər chärj′) *vt-* [**un·der·charged, un·der·charg·ing**] to charge (someone) too low a price.

[2]**un·der·charge** (ŭn′ dər chärj′) *n-* a charge that is below the usual or proper amount.

un·der·clothes (ŭn′ dər klōz′) *n- pl.* clothes worn under outer clothing; underwear.

un·der·cloth·ing (ŭn′ dər klō′ thĭng) *n-* underclothes.

un·der·cov·er (ŭn′ dər kŭv′ ər) *adj-* working or done in secret: *an* undercover *agent for the FBI.*

un·der·cur·rent (ŭn′ dər kûr′ ənt) *n-* **1** current of water, air, etc., flowing below the surface or below another current. **2** hidden trend of opinion, feeling, etc.

[1]**un·der·cut** (ŭn′ dər kŭt′) *vt-* [**un·der·cut, un·der·cut·ting**] **1** to cut material from beneath or from the lower part of (something). **2** to compete with (a rival) by doing work, selling merchandise, etc., at lower rates. **3** in sports, to strike (a ball) with a slanting, downward motion so as to give it backspin or lift.

[2]**un·der·cut** (un′ dər kŭt′) *n-* **1** mark, opening, etc., made by cutting into or below the lower part of something. **2** the lower of the two cuts made in a tree for felling, one on each side. The tree falls toward this cut.

un·der·de·vel·oped (ŭn′ dər dĭ vĕl′ əpt) *adj-* **1** not fully or sufficiently developed: *an* underdeveloped *physique.* **2** showing little or slow progress in economic development: *a remote,* underdeveloped *region.*

un·der·dog (ŭn′ dər dȯg′) *n-* **1** the losing dog in a dogfight. **2** person or group expected to be defeated.

un·der·done (ŭn′ dər dŭn′) *adj-* not thoroughly or completely cooked: *an* underdone *steak.*

[1]**un·der·es·ti·mate** (ŭn′ dər ĕs′ tə māt′) *vt-* [**un·der·es·ti·mat·ed, un·der·es·ti·mat·ing**] to rate or judge (someone or something) too low in value, amount, ability, etc.: *He* underestimated *his yearly earnings. He* underestimated *his power.* —*n-* **un′ der·es′ ti·ma′ tion.**

[2]**un·der·es·ti·mate** (ŭn′ dər ĕs′ tə mət) *n-* an estimate that is too low.

Any of these words means un- ("not") plus the meaning of the rest of the word as given in the main text.

un′ cul′ tured
un′ curbed′
un′ cured′
un′ cu′ ri·ous
un′ cur′ tained
un′ dam′ aged
un′ damped′
un′ dat′ ed
un′ daz′ zled
un′ de·ci′ pher·a·ble
un′ decked′
un′ de·clin′ a·ble
un′ dec′ o·rat′ ed
un′ de·feat′ ed
un′ de·fend′ ed
un′ de·fin′ a·ble
un′ de·fined′
un′ de·layed′
un′ de·liv′ er·a·ble
un′ de·mand′ ing
un′ dem′ o·crat′ ic
un′ de·nom′ i·na′ tion·al
un′ de·pend′ a·ble

un·der·ex·pose (ŭn'dər ĕk spōz') *vt-* [**un·der·ex·posed, un·der·ex·pos·ing**] to expose (a photographic film, plate, etc.) to light for less than the usual or required amount of time. *—n-* **un'der·ex·po'sure.**
un·der·feed (ŭn'dər fēd') *vt-* [**un·der·fed, un·der·feed·ing**] to give insufficient nourishment to.
un·der·foot (ŭn'dər fo͝ot') *adv-* 1 beneath the feet; on the ground. 2 in the way; in danger of being stepped on.
un·der·gar·ment (ŭn'dər gär'mənt) *n-* garment worn under one's outer clothing.
un·der·go (ŭn'dər gō') *vt-* [**un·der·went, un·der·gone, un·der·go·ing**] to be subjected to; go through; experience: *to* undergo *changes*; *to* undergo *hardships.*
un·der·grad·u·ate (ŭn'dər grăj'o͞o ət) *n-* college or university student who has not yet received a bachelor's degree. *as* ***modifier:*** *an* undergraduate *student.*
un·der·ground (ŭn'dər ground') *adj-* 1 situated, operating, or done beneath the surface of the earth: *an* underground *passage.* 2 acting or carried on in secret: *an* underground *system of spying.* *adv-* (*also* ŭn'dər ground') 1 beneath the surface of the earth. 2 in a secret place or by means of secret methods: *The spies worked* underground. *n-* 1 something situated under the ground, such as a space or passage. 2 secret group working against established authority. 3 *Brit.* subway.
Underground Railroad *n-* a pre-Civil War system by which abolitionists helped fugitive slaves escape to the free states or to Canada.
un·der·grown (ŭn'dər grōn') *adj-* below normal size.
un·der·growth (ŭn'dər grōth') *n-* plants, bushes, vines, etc., growing thickly under trees or taller plants.
un·der·hand (ŭn'dər hănd') *adj-* 1 not open or honest; secret and deceitful. 2 in baseball, tennis, etc., done with or using a motion in which the hand and elbow are moved forward and are kept lower than the level of the shoulder: *an* underhand *pitch.* *adv-*: *to throw* underhand.
un·der·hand·ed (ŭn'dər hăn'dəd) *adj-* not open and aboveboard; deceptive and unfair; underhand. *—adv-* **un'der·hand'ed·ly.** *n-* **un'der·hand'ed·ness.**
un·der·lie (ŭn'dər lī') *vt-* [**un·der·lay, un·der·lain, un·der·ly·ing**] 1 to lie or be under (something). 2 to be at the bottom of: *What motives* underlie *his actions?*
[1]**un·der·line** (ŭn'dər līn') *vt-* [**un·der·lined, un·der·lin·ing**] 1 to draw a line under. 2 to emphasize.
[2]**un·der·line** (ŭn'dər līn') *n-* line placed under a word, phrase, etc., especially for emphasis.
un·der·ling (ŭn'dər lĭng) *n-* person having an inferior rank or position; subordinate.
un·der·lin·ing (ŭn'dər lī'nĭng) *n-* lines drawn under words, usually for emphasis.
un·der·ly·ing (ŭn'dər lī'ĭng) *adj-* 1 lying beneath another layer, surface, etc.: *The* underlying *soil is rocky.* 2 basic; essential: *the* underlying *causes.*
un·der·mine (ŭn'dər mīn') *vt-* [**un·der·mined, un·der·min·ing**] 1 to dig a hollow or tunnel under; dig beneath. 2 to weaken by wearing away the base of: *The flood* undermined *our house.* 3 to work secretly against; injure by underhand methods: *to* undermine *a person's authority.* 4 to destroy gradually; weaken; impair.
un·der·most (ŭn'dər mōst') *adj-* lowest in place or position: *the* undermost *layer.*
un·der·neath (ŭn'dər nēth') *prep-* (considered an adverb when the object is clearly implied but not expressed) under; beneath; below: *plants* underneath *the snow*; *to hide something* underneath *a pile of papers.*
un·der·nour·ished (ŭn'dər nûr'ĭsht) *adj-* not nourished sufficiently to maintain good health or normal growth.
un·der·pants (un'dər pănts') *n- pl.* drawers.
un·der·pass (ŭn'dər păs) *n-* road or passage that goes under a highway, bridge, etc.
un·der·pay (ŭn'dər pā') *vt-* [**un·der·paid, un·der·pay·ing**] to give insufficient pay to: *He* underpays *his workers.*
un·der·pin·ning (ŭn'dər pĭn'ĭng) *n-* part or structure that supports a building or wall from below; hence, any support or prop.
un·der·priv·i·leged (ŭn'dər prĭv'ə lĭjd) *adj-* lacking opportunities or advantages because of poverty, poor education, poor health, neglect, etc.
un·der·pro·duc·tion (ŭn'dər prə dŭk'shən) *n-* production that falls short of what is normal or required.
un·der·rate (ŭn'dər rāt') *vt-* [**un·der·rat·ed, un·der·rat·ing**] to place too low an estimate or value upon.
[1]**un·der·score** (ŭn'dər skôr') *vt-* [**un·der·scored, un·der·scor·ing**] 1 to draw a line under; underline. 2 to give emphasis to.
[2]**un·der·score** (ŭn'dər skôr') *n-* an underline.
[1]**un·der·sea** (ŭn'dər sē') *adj-* existing or taking place beneath the surface of the sea: *an* undersea *exploration.*
[2]**un·der·sea** (ŭn'dər sē') or **un·der·seas** (-sēz') *adv-* beneath the surface of the sea.
un·der·sec·re·tar·y (ŭn'dər sĕk'rə tĕr'ē) *n-* [*pl.* **un·der·sec·re·tar·ies**] government official who ranks next below a secretary: *an* Undersecretary *of State.*
un·der·sell (ŭn'dər sĕl') *vt-* [**un·der·sold, un·der·sel·ling**] to sell at a lower price than (a competitor).
un·der·shirt (ŭn'dər shûrt') *n-* close-fitting undergarment for the upper part of the body.
un·der·shoot (ŭn'dər sho͞ot') *vt-* [**un·der·shot, un·der·shoot·ing**] 1 to miss (a target) by shooting short of it. 2 of an airplane, to land short of (the runway, field, etc.).
un·der·shot (ŭn'dər shŏt') *adj-* of the lower jaw, projecting beyond the upper jaw; also, having such a jaw.
undershot wheel *n-* water wheel driven by water passing beneath it.

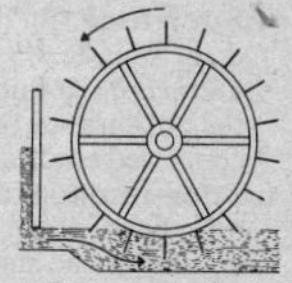
Undershot wheel

un·der·side (ŭn'dər sīd') *n-* the lower side or surface of something: *the* underside *of a leaf.*
un·der·signed (ŭn'dər sīnd') *adj-* signed at the end of a document, letter, etc.: *the* undersigned *names.* *n-* **the undersigned** person or persons who have signed a document.
un·der·sized (ŭn'dər sīzd') *adj-* smaller than the usual or normal size: *an* undersized *portion of cake.*
un·der·skirt (ŭn'dər skûrt') *n-* skirt worn under an outer skirt and sometimes showing beneath it.
un·der·slung (ŭn'dər slŭng') *adj-* of an automobile, having the supporting springs of the chassis attached to the underside of the axle.
un·der·stand (ŭn'dər stănd') *vt-* [**un·der·stood, un·der·stand·ing**] (in senses 1 and 5 considered intransitive when the direct object is implied but not expressed) 1 to know or grasp the meaning of; comprehend: *They* understand *that.* 2 to have thorough knowledge of; be familiar with: *She* understands *French.* 3 to perceive clearly; recognize: *to* understand *the consequences of one's actions.* 4 to accept as a fact; have been told; believe: *I* understand *he will come tomorrow.* 5 to have a sympathetic attitude toward: *My friend* understands *me.*

un·der·stand·a·ble (ŭn' dər stăn' də bəl) ***adj-*** **1** such as can be understood. **2** such as can be explained, excused, or sympathized with: *Your lateness is* understandable *under the circumstances.* **—*adv-*** **un' der·stand' a·bly.**

un·der·stand·ing (ŭn' dər stăn' dĭng) ***n-*** **1** a grasping by the mind; knowledge; comprehension: *his* understanding *of the subject.* **2** ability to comprehend; intelligence: *His superior* understanding *makes him a quick learner.* **3** agreement about what another wants and means. ***adj-*** sympathetic in an intelligent way: *She is a very* understanding *person.* **—*adv-*** **un' der·stand' ing·ly.**

un·der·state (ŭn' dər stāt') ***vt-*** **[un·der·stat·ed, un·der·stat·ing]** to state inadequately or with deliberate lack of emphasis: *to* understate *the evidence in a lawsuit.* **—*n-*** **un' der·state' ment.**

un·der·stood (ŭn' dər stŏŏd') *p.t. & p.p.* of **understand.** ***adj-*** **1** agreed; taken for granted: *several* understood *conditions.* **2** unexpressed but implied by context, as "talk" omitted from the end of the following sentence: "I'll talk if he will."

un·der·stud·y (ŭn' dər stŭd' ē) ***n-*** [*pl.* **un·der·stud·ies**] actor who is prepared to act a role if the actor who usually plays it cannot appear; hence, any person who stands ready to replace another when necessary. ***vt-*** **[un·der·stud·ied, un·der·stud·y·ing]** **1** to learn (another person's part, duties, etc.) in order to take his place if necessary: *He* understudied *the lead in the play.* **2** to act as understudy to (another): *She* understudies *the star.*

un·der·take (ŭn' dər tāk') ***vt-*** **[un·der·took, un·der·tak·en, un·der·tak·ing]** **1** to take upon oneself; attempt: *She* undertook *a big task.* **2** to contract to do; promise; guarantee: *He* undertakes *to do it by winter.*

un·der·tak·er (ŭn' dər tā' kər) ***n-*** person who makes a business of preparing the dead for burial, and of making arrangements for funerals; mortician.

un·der·tak·ing (ŭn' dər tā' kĭng) ***n-*** **1** the taking upon oneself of a task or responsibility. **2** something attempted or entered upon; task; enterprise. **3** (ŭn' dər tā' kĭng) the work or business of an undertaker.

un·der·tone (ŭn' dər tōn') ***n-*** **1** low tone of voice or subdued sound: *We talked in an* undertone *to avoid being overheard.* **2** faint color that shows through or affects the appearance of another color. **3** suppressed or partly concealed emotion or thought: *an* undertone *of bitterness.*

un·der·tow (ŭn' dər tō') ***n-*** current below the surface of a body of water, moving in a direction opposite to the current at the surface.

un·der·val·ue (ŭn' dər văl' yōō) ***vt-*** **[un·der·val·ued, un·der·val·u·ing]** to put too low a value on; underrate; underestimate. **—*n-*** **un' der·val' u·a' tion.**

un·der·wa·ter (ŭn' dər wô' tər) ***adj-*** situated, happening, growing, or used beneath the surface of the water: *a record for* underwater *swimming*; *an* underwater *plant.*

un·der·wear (ŭn' dər wâr') ***n-*** clothing worn close to the body and underneath outer clothes.

un·der·weight (ŭn' dər wāt') ***adj-*** weighing less than the normal or desirable amount. ***n-*** weight below what is considered normal or desirable.

un·der·went (ŭn' dər wĕnt') *p.t.* of **undergo.**

un·der·world (ŭn' dər wûrld') ***n-*** **1** in certain mythologies, such as that of the Greeks and Romans, the underground dwelling place of the dead; Hades. **2** criminals and their associates, regarded as a separate class of society; especially, those engaged in organized crime.

un·der·write (ŭn' dər rīt') ***vt-*** **[un·der·wrote, un·der·writ·ten, un·der·writ·ing]** **1** to write underneath or below (something). **2** to assume (an insurance risk), guaranteeing payment in event of loss, damage, etc. **3** to subscribe to or provide funds for (a project requiring capital); finance. **4** to agree to buy, on a given date and at a specified price (the whole issue of stock or bonds of a corporation to be sold to the public); also, to agree to buy any portion of (a given issue of stocks or bonds, not bought by others before a certain date). ***vi-*** to act as an underwriter.

un·der·writ·er (ŭn' dər rī' tər) ***n-*** person or organization that guarantees payment on or for something; especially, one that issues insurance policies and guarantees payment on them.

un·de·served (ŭn' də zûrvd') ***adj-*** not deserved; not earned: *an* undeserved *honor.* **—*adv-*** **un' de·serv' ed·ly.**

un·de·sir·a·ble (ŭn' dĭ zī' rə bəl) ***adj-*** not desirable; objectionable. ***n-*** person considered to be objectionable or obnoxious. **—*adv-*** **un' de·sir' a·bly.**

un·de·vel·oped (ŭn' dĭ vĕl' əpt) ***adj-*** **1** not developed: *an* undeveloped *film*; undeveloped *resources.* **2** not fully or completely developed: *an* undeveloped *fruit.*

un·did (ŭn' dĭd') *p.t.* of **undo.**

un·dies (ŭn' dēz') *Informal* ***n-*** *pl.* women's underwear.

un·dig·ni·fied (ŭn' dĭg' nə fīd') ***adj-*** lacking dignity.

un·dis·ci·plined (ŭn' dĭs' ə plĭnd') ***adj-*** not subjected to discipline; not under control.

un·dis·guised (ŭn' dĭs gīzd') ***adj-*** not disguised or concealed; open: *her* undisguised *jealousy.*

un·dis·put·ed (ŭn' dĭs pyōō' təd) ***adj-*** not disputed; not questioned or doubted; accepted: *an* undisputed *right*; *an* undisputed *fact.* **—*adv-*** **un' dis·put' ed·ly.**

un·dis·tin·guished (ŭn' dĭs tĭng' gwĭsht) ***adj-*** not distinguished; not unusual or outstanding.

un·dis·turbed (ŭn' dĭs tûrbd') ***adj-*** not disturbed; peaceful; calm: *the* undisturbed *quiet of the evening.*

un·di·vid·ed (ŭn' dĭ vī' dəd) ***adj-*** not divided; entire: *an* undivided *tract of land*; *your* undivided *attention.*

un·do (ŭn' dōō') ***vt-*** **[un·did, un·done, un·do·ing]** **1** to loosen; unfasten; open: *Please* undo *this package. He* undid *the knot.* **2** to do away with the result or effect of: *We can't* undo *the damage now.* **3** to bring to ruin: *His recklessness will* undo *him.* **—*n-*** **un' do' er.**

un·do·ing (ŭn' dōō' ĭng) ***n-*** **1** a reversing or canceling out what has been done: *There is no* undoing *the injury done to him.* **2** destruction; ruin: *the* undoing *of all our plans.* **3** cause of ruin or downfall: *Pride was his* undoing.

un·done (ŭn' dŭn') *p.p.* of **undo.** ***adj-*** **1** not performed or completed: *his* undone *chores.* **2** ruined; defeated: *We are* undone! **3** unfastened: *My shoelaces are* undone.

un·doubt·ed (ŭn' dou' təd) ***adj-*** not doubted or questioned; assured; certain: *his* undoubted *ability*; *an* undoubted *fact.* **—*adv-*** **un' doubt' ed·ly.**

Any of these words means un- ("not") plus the meaning of the rest of the word as given in the main text.

un' de·serv' ing
un' de·sign' ing
un' de·sir' a·bil' i·ty
un' de·sired'
un' de·tach' a·ble
un' de·tect' ed
un' de·ter' mi·na·ble
un' de·ter' mined
un' de·terred'
un' de' vi·at' ing
un' dif' fer·en' ti·at' ed
un' di·gest' ed
un' di·lut' ed
un' di·min' ished
un' dimmed'
un' dip' lo·mat' ic
un' di·rect' ed
un' dis·cern' ing
un' dis·charged'
un' dis·closed'
un' dis·cov' ered
un' dis·crim' i·nat' ing
un' dis·mayed'
un' dis·so' ci·at' ed
un' dis·solved'
un' dis·trib' ut·ed
un' di·ver' si·fied'
un' di·vulged'
un' do·mes' ti·cat' ed
un' doub' led
un' doubt' ing

un·dreamed-of (ŭn′ drēmd′ ŏv′, -ŭv′) ***adj-*** not imagined or considered possible: *an* undreamed-of *opportunity.* Also **un′ dreamt′ -of′** (ŭn′ drĕmt′-).

[1]**un·dress** (ŭn′ drĕs′) ***vi-*** to take off one's clothes. ***vt-*** to remove the clothing of: *to* undress *a doll.* ***n-* 1** casual or informal clothing. **2** a being incompletely clothed: *in a state of* undress.

[2]**un·dress** (ŭn′ drĕs′) ***adj-*** not intended for formal wear: *an* undress *uniform.*

un·due (ŭn′ dōō′, -dyōō′) ***adj-* 1** more than necessary; excessive: *He pays* undue *attention to trifles.* **2** not right or proper: *an* undue *disregard for authority.*

un·du·lant fever (ŭn′ dyə lənt) ***n-*** disease characterized by recurring attacks of fever, swelling of the joints, and general bodily pain. It is caused by certain bacteria, and is transmitted to human beings chiefly through the milk of animals infected with the disease.

un·du·late (ŭn′ dyə lāt′) ***vi-*** **[un·du·lat·ed, un·du·lat·ing] 1** to move in waves, or in a wavelike, curving way; also, to form waves; have a rippling surface or appearance: *The wheat field* undulated *in the breeze.* ***vt-*** to cause to form waves or move with a wavelike motion. ***—n-* un′ du·la′ tion.** ***adj-* un′ du·la·tor′ y** (-lə tôr′ ē).

un·du·ly (ŭn′ dōō′ lē, -dyōō′ lē) ***adv-*** in an undue manner; unnecessarily: *He is* unduly *nervous.*

un·dy·ing (ŭn′ dī′ ĭng) ***adj-*** lasting or supposedly lasting forever; everlasting; eternal: *his* undying *devotion.*

un·earned (ŭn′ ûrnd′) ***adj-* 1** not earned by effort or labor: *an* unearned *income.* **2** not deserved or merited: *an* unearned *scolding.*

un·earth (ŭn′ ûrth′) ***vt-* 1** to take or dig up from or as if from the earth: *They* unearthed *the buried treasure.* **2** to bring to light; discover: *He* unearthed *evidence.*

un·earth·ly (ŭn′ ûrth′ lē) ***adj-* 1** not of this world; unlike what occurs in nature: *an* unearthly *being from outer space.* **2** eerie; weird; uncanny: *strange,* unearthly *cries.* **3** *Informal* very odd; inconvenient; unseemly: *He called at an* unearthly *hour.* ***—n-* un′ earth′ li·ness.**

un·eas·y (ŭn′ ē′ zē) ***adj-*** **[un·eas·i·er, un·eas·i·est] 1** not easy or relaxed in manner; awkward: *He felt* uneasy *before such a large audience.* **2** anxious; restless; worried: *The storm made everyone* uneasy. **3** disturbing; upsetting: *an* uneasy *suspicion.* ***—adv-* un′ eas′ i·ly.** ***n-* un′ eas′ i·ness.**

un·ed·u·cat·ed (ŭn′ ĕj′ ə kā′ təd, ŭn′ ĕd′ yōō-) ***adj-*** not educated; especially, lacking formal education.

un·em·ploy·a·ble (ŭn′ ĭm ploi′ ə bəl) ***adj-*** unable to hold a job because of poor health, bad habits, irresponsibility, etc. ***n-:*** *He is considered an* unemployable.

un·em·ployed (ŭn′ ĭm ploid′) ***adj-* 1** not being put to use: *his* unemployed *skills*; unemployed *funds.* **2** lacking employment; out of work. ***n-*** **the unemployed** people out of work.

un·em·ploy·ment (ŭn′ ĭm ploi′ mənt) ***n-*** lack of employment; condition of being jobless.

un·end·ing (ŭn′ ĕn′ dĭng) ***adj-*** having or seeming to have no end; endless. ***—adv-* un′ end′ ing·ly.**

un·e·qual (ŭn′ ē′ kwəl) ***adj-* 1** not of the same amount, size, degree, etc.: *lines of* unequal *length.* **2** not equal or comparable in rank, excellence, ability, etc.: *a competition between* unequal *teams.* **3** unfair or unbalanced because of ill-matched competition: *an* unequal *contest.* **4** not uniform; uneven. ***—adv-* un′ e′ qual·ly.**

unequal to lacking sufficient strength, skill, intelligence, etc., for a particular activity: *He was* unequal to *the task.*

un·e·qualed or **un·e·qualled** (ŭn′ ē′ kwəld) ***adj-*** not equaled or surpassed: *an* unequaled *achievement.*

un·e·quiv·o·cal (ŭn′ ĭ kwĭv′ ə kəl) ***adj-*** not equivocal; unmistakably clear as to meaning or intent: *an* unequivocal *refusal.* ***—adv-* un′ e·quiv′ o·cal·ly.** ***n-* un′ e·quiv′ o·cal·ness.**

un·er·ring (ŭn′ ĕr′ ĭng, -ûr′ ĭng) ***adj-* 1** making no mistakes; unfailing: *He is* unerring *in the performance of his duties.* **2** not deviating; accurate: *the* unerring *flight of the arrow to the target.* ***—adv-* un′ er′ ring·ly.**

UNESCO or **U·nes·co** (yōō nĕs′ kō) ***n-*** United Nations Educational, Scientific and Cultural Organization.

un·es·sen·tial (ŭn′ ə sĕn′ chəl) ***adj-*** not essential; not necessary or of major importance.

un·e·ven (ŭn′ ē′ vən) ***adj-* 1** not smooth or flat; not level: *an* uneven *floor.* **2** not of the same size, shape, etc.; irregular: *an* uneven *border of rocks along the path.* **3** not uniform or balanced. **4** of numbers, not even; odd. ***—adv-* un·e′ ven·ly.** ***n-* un·e′ ven·ness.**

un·e·vent·ful (ŭn′ ĭ vĕnt′ fəl) ***adj-*** not eventful; lacking unusual occurrences or activities; quiet: *an* uneventful *day.* ***—adv-* un′ e·vent′ ful·ly.** ***n-* un′ e·vent′ ful·ness.**

un·ex·am·pled (ŭn′ ĕg zăm′ pəld) ***adj-*** so unusual as to have no comparable example or instance; unparalleled: *a person of* unexampled *kindness.*

un·ex·celled (ŭn′ ĕk sĕld′) ***adj-*** unsurpassed; supreme.

un·ex·cep·tion·a·ble (ŭn′ ĕk sĕp′ shən ə bəl) ***adj-*** not open to blame or criticism; beyond reproach: *an* unexceptionable *man.* ***—adv-* un′ ex·cep′ tion·a·bly.**

►Should not be confused with UNEXCEPTIONAL.

un·ex·cep·tion·al (ŭn′ ĕk sĕp′ shən əl) ***adj-*** not exceptional; not unusual in any way: *an* unexceptional *record.* ***—adv-* un′ ex·cep′ tion·al·ly.**

►Should not be confused with UNEXCEPTIONABLE.

un·ex·pect·ed (ŭn′ ĕk spĕk′ təd) ***adj-*** not expected; unforeseen: *an* unexpected *thing to say*; *an* unexpected *pleasure.* ***—adv-* un′ ex·pect′ ed·ly.** ***n-* un′ ex·pect′ ed·ness.**

Any of these words means un- ("not") plus the meaning of the rest of the word as given in the main text.

un′ drained′
un′ dra·mat′ ic
un′ drape′
un′ draw′
un′ dreamed′
un′ dreamt′
un′ drink′ a·ble
un′ dulled′
un′ du′ ti·ful
un′ dyed′
un′ ea′ ger
un·ease′
un′ eat′ a·ble
un′ eat′ en
un′ ec′ o·nom′ ic
un′ ed′ i·fy′ ing
un·ed′ u·ca·ble
un′ em·bar′ rassed
un′ em·bel′ lished
un′ e·mo′ tion·al
un′ en·closed′
un′ en·cum′ bered
un′ en·dorsed′
un′ en·dur′ a·ble
un′ en·dur′ ing
un′ en·force′ a·ble
un′ en·forced′
un′ en·gaged′
un′ en·joy′ a·ble
un′ en·larged′
un′ en·light′ ened
un′ en·rolled′
un′ en′ ter·pris′ ing
un′ en′ ter·tain′ ing
un′ en·thu′ si·as′ tic
un′ en′ vi·a·ble
un′ en′ vied
un′ en′ vi·ous
un′ e·quipped′
un′ es·cap′ a·ble
un·eth′ i·cal
un′ ex·ag′ ger·at′ ed
un′ ex·am′ ined
un′ ex·cit′ ed
un′ ex·cit′ ing
un·ex′ e·cut′ ed
un′ ex·haust′ ed
un′ ex·pand′ ed
un′ ex·pend′ ed

---

fāte, făt, dâre, bärn; bē, bĕt, mêre; bīte, bĭt; nōte, hŏt, môre, dòg; fŭn, fûr; tōō, bŏŏk; oil; out; tar; thin; then; hw for wh as in *wh*at; zh for s as in u*s*ual; ə for a, e, i, o, u, as in *a*go, lin*e*n, per*i*l, at*o*m, min*u*s

un·fail·ing (ŭn′ fā′ lĭng) ***adj-*** **1** not failing or likely to fail; inexhaustible: *an* unfailing *water supply.* **2** constant; reliable: *an* unfailing *friend.* **—*adv-* un′ fail′ ing·ly.**

un·fair (ŭn′ fâr′) ***adj-*** **1** not fair; unjust: *an* unfair *wage.* **2** not fairly matched or balanced: *an* unfair *contest.* **—*adv-* un′ fair′ ly. *n-* un′ fair′ ness.**

un·faith·ful (ŭn′ fāth′ fəl) ***adj-*** **1** not faithful; false to a promise or duty; disloyal: *an* unfaithful *friend.* **2** not accurate or reliable: *an* unfaithful *version of the facts.* **—*adv-* un′ faith′ ful·ly. *n-* un′ faith′ ful·ness.**

un·fal·ter·ing (ŭn′ fòl′ tər ĭng) ***adj-*** not faltering; steady; steadfast. **—*adv-* un′ fal′ ter·ing·ly.**

un·fa·mil·iar (ŭn′ fə mĭl′ yər) ***adj-*** **1** not familiar; not well known: *an* unfamiliar *face.* **2** not acquainted: *to be* unfamiliar *with a language.* **—*n-* un′ fa·mil′ i·ar′ i·ty** (-mĭl′ ē ăr′ ə te, -ĕr′ ə tē). ***adv-* un′ fa·mil′ iar·ly.**

un·fas·ten (ŭn′ făs′ ən) ***vt-*** to undo the fastening of; untie; loosen: *He* unfastened *the chain.* ***vi-***: *This chain* unfastens *easily.*

un·fath·om·a·ble (ŭn′ făth′ əm ə bəl) ***adj-*** **1** too deep to measure. **2** impossible to understand or explain.

un·fath·omed (ŭn′ făth′ əmd) ***adj-*** **1** not fathomed; not measured for depth: *the* unfathomed *waters.* **2** not understood or explained: *an* unfathomed *secret.*

un·fa·vor·a·ble (ŭn′ fā′ vər ə bəl) ***adj-*** **1** not favorable; not helpful in producing good results: *They work under* unfavorable *conditions.* **2** disapproving; opposing; adverse: *an* unfavorable *opinion.* **—*n-* un′ fa′ vor·a·ble·ness. *adv-* un′ fa′ vor·a·bly.**

un·feel·ing (ŭn′ fē′ lĭng) ***adj-*** **1** pitiless; hard-hearted; cruel: *an* unfeeling *person.* **2** lacking feeling or sensation. **—*adv-* un′ feel′ ing·ly. *n-* un′ feel′ ing·ness.**

un·feigned (ŭn′ fānd′) ***adj-*** not feigned; sincere; genuine: *his* unfeigned *enthusiasm.* **—*adv-* un′ feign′ ed·ly.**

un·fet·ter (ŭn′ fĕt′ ər) ***vt-*** to set free.

un·fin·ished (ŭn′ fĭn′ ĭsht) ***adj-*** **1** not finished; not complete: *an* unfinished *story*; unfinished *business.* **2** left in the rough state; not smoothed, varnished, or painted: *an* unfinished *piece of furniture.* **3** of fabrics, not processed after weaving: *an* unfinished *woolen cloth.*

un·fit (ŭn′ fĭt′) ***adj-*** **1** lacking fitness; not suitable because of some lack or shortcoming: *clothes* unfit *for this climate*; *a man* unfit *for high office.* **2** in poor physical or emotional condition. ***vt-*** to make unsuitable; disqualify: *His bad record* unfits *him for the job.* **—*n-* un′ fit′ ness.**

un·flag·ging (ŭn′ flăg′ ĭng) ***adj-*** not flagging; untiring: *his* unflagging *enthusiasm.* **—*adv-* un′ flag′ ging·ly.**

un·fledged (ŭn′ flĕjd′) ***adj-*** **1** of a young bird, lacking feathers needed for flight. **2** lacking experience.

un·flinch·ing (ŭn′ flĭn′ chĭng) ***adj-*** not flinching; unyielding in the face of danger, pain, or disagreeable duty; steadfast; resolute. **—*adv-* un′ flinch′ ing·ly.**

un·fold (ŭn′ fōld′) ***vt-*** **1** to open the folds of; spread open: *She* unfolded *the towel.* **2** to reveal by degrees: *The spy* unfolded *the details of his plan.* ***vi-*** **1** to become open, as the petals of a flower do. **2** to develop so as to be seen or known: *The plot of the story* unfolded *gradually.*

un·fore·seen (ŭn′ fôr sēn′) ***adj-*** not foreseen; not counted on or provided for; unexpected.

un·for·get·ta·ble (ŭn′ fər gĕt′ ə bəl) ***adj-*** not likely to be forgotten; memorable. **—*adv-* un′ for·get′ ta·bly.**

un·formed (ŭn′ fòrmd′) ***adj-*** **1** not formed; not given definite shape: *an* unformed *mass of clay.* **2** not fully developed: *an* unformed *mind*; unformed *plans.*

un·for·tu·nate (ŭn′ fôr′ chə nət, ŭn′ fôr′-) ***adj-*** **1** lacking good fortune; unlucky: *an* unfortunate *person.* **2** unsuccessful; disastrous: *an* unfortunate *business venture.* **3** badly chosen; unsuitable; regrettable: *an* unfortunate *remark.* ***n-*** unlucky and unhappy person. **—*adv-* un′ for′ tu·nate·ly.**

un·found·ed (ŭn′ foun′ dəd) ***adj-*** lacking a sound basis; not backed by facts or evidence: *an* unfounded *hope.*

un·friend·ly (ŭn′ frĕnd′ lē) ***adj-*** [**un·friend·li·er, un·friend·li·est**] **1** not friendly; hostile. **2** not favorable; not pleasant: *an* unfriendly *climate.* **—*n-* un′ friend′ li·ness.**

un·frock (ŭn′ frŏk′) ***vt-*** to expel (a priest) from the clergy by official authority.

un·fruit·ful (ŭn′ fro͞ot′ fəl) ***adj-*** **1** not fruitful; not producing fruit or offspring; barren. **2** not producing wanted results; fruitless. **—*adv-* un·fruit′ ful·ly.**

un·furl (ŭn′ fûrl′) ***vt-*** to unroll; spread out: *to* unfurl *sails.* ***vi-***: *The flag* unfurled *in the breeze.*

un·fur·nished (ŭn′ fûr′ nĭsht) ***adj-*** not furnished; without furniture: *an* unfurnished *apartment.*

un·gain·ly (ŭn′ gān′ lē) ***adj-*** [**un·gain·li·er, un·gain·li·est**] awkward; clumsy. **—*n-* un′ gain′ li·ness.**

un·gen·er·ous (ŭn′ jĕn′ ər əs) ***adj-*** **1** not generous; not bountiful; stingy. **2** lacking kindness or sympathy; unfeeling; mean. **—*n-* un′ gen′ er·ous·ness.**

un·god·ly (ŭn′ gŏd′ lē) ***adj-*** [**un·god·li·er, un·god·li·est**] **1** lacking reverence for God or established religion; impious. **2** unholy; sinful; wicked. **3** *Informal* highly unsuitable; outrageous. **—*n-* un′ god′ li·ness.**

un·gov·ern·a·ble (ŭn′ gŭv′ ər nə bəl) ***adj-*** such as cannot be governed or restrained; uncontrollable; unruly: *an* ungovernable *temper.* **—*adv-* un′ gov′ ern·a·bly.**

un·grace·ful (ŭn′ grās′ fəl) ***adj-*** lacking grace; clumsy; awkward. **—*adv-* un′ grace′ ful·ly. *n-* un′ grace′ ful·ness.**

un·gra·cious (ŭn′ grā′ shəs) ***adj-*** lacking graciousness; rude. **—*adv-* un′ gra′ cious·ly. *n-* un′ gra′ cious·ness.**

un·grate·ful (ŭn′ grāt′ fəl) ***adj-*** **1** lacking gratitude; not thankful or appreciative. **2** causing discomfort or displeasure; disagreeable: *an* ungrateful *task.* **—*adv-* un′ grate′ ful·ly. *n-* un′ grate′ ful·ness.**

un·ground·ed (ŭn′ groun′ dəd) ***adj-*** **1** having no sound basis; unfounded: *his* ungrounded *fears.* **2** lacking instruction or information; untaught: *He is* ungrounded

Any of these words means un- ("not") plus the meaning of the rest of the word as given in the main text.

un′ ex·pired′
un′ ex·plain′ a·ble
un′ ex·plained′
un′ ex·plod′ ed
un′ ex·plored′
un′ ex·posed′
un′ ex·pressed′
un′ ex·pres′ sive
un·ex′ pur·gat′ ed
un′ ex·tend′ ed
un′ ex·tin′ guished
un′ fad′ ing
un′ fash′ ion·a·ble
un′ fas′ tened
un′ fea′ si·ble
un′ fed′
un′ fem′ i·nine
un′ fenced′
un′ fer·ment′ ed
un′ fer′ til·ized′
un′ filled′
un′ fired′
un′ fit′ ted
un′ fit′ ting
un′ fix′
un′ flat′ ter·ing
un′ fla′ vored
un′ flexed′
un′ forced′
un′ fore′ see′ a·ble
un′ for·giv′ a·ble
un′ for·giv′ ing
un′ for′ mu·lat′ ed
un′ for′ ti·fied′
un′ framed′
un′ free′
un′ fre′ quent·ed
un′ fro′ zen
un′ ful·filled′
un′ gal′ lant
un′ gar′ nished
un′ gath′ ered
un′ gen′ tle
un′ gift′ ed
un′ gird′
un′ girt′
un′ glazed′
un′ gov′ erned
un′ grad′ ed
un′ gram·mat′ i·cal

in the arts. 3 not having an electrical connection with the ground: *an* ungrounded *wire.*

un·grudg·ing (ŭn′ grŭj′ ĭng) ***adj-*** not grudging; free from ill will, selfishness, envy, etc.; wholehearted: *his* ungrudging *admiration.* **—*adv-* un′ grudg′ ing·ly.**

un·guard·ed (ŭn′ gär′ dəd) ***adj-*** 1 not guarded; not watched over or protected: *an* unguarded *gateway.* 2 thoughtless; careless: *She revealed the secret in an* unguarded *moment.* **—*adv-* un′ guard′ ed·ly.**

un·guent (ŭng′ gwənt, ŭn′ jənt) ***n-*** soothing salve or ointment.

un·gu·late (ŭng′ gyə lət) ***n-*** member of an order of mammals **(Ungulata),** which includes hoofed animals such as horses, cattle, pigs, rhinoceroses, and others. ***adj-*** 1 of or belonging to this order. 2 having hoofs.

un·hal·lowed (ŭn′ hăl′ ōd′) ***adj-*** 1 not hallowed; not blessed or set aside for religious purposes: *He was buried in* unhallowed *ground.* 2 unholy; sinful.

un·hand (ŭn′ hănd′) *Archaic* ***vt-*** to let go of.

un·hand·y (ŭn′ hăn′ dē) ***adj-*** **[un·hand·i·er, un·hand·i·est]** 1 hard to handle; cumbersome: *an* unhandy *tool.* 2 clumsy; awkward: *an* unhandy *janitor.*

un·hap·py (ŭn′ hăp′ ē) ***adj-*** **[un·hap·pi·er, un·hap·pi·est]** 1 lacking happiness; sad; sorrowful: *an* unhappy *child*; *an* unhappy *life.* 2 unlucky; unfortunate: *an* unhappy *result.* 3 not right for the occasion or circumstances. **—*adv-* un′ hap′ pi·ly. *n-* un′ hap′ pi·ness.**

un·harmed (ŭn′ härmd′) ***adj-*** not harmed; not hurt or injured in any way; safe; undamaged.

un·har·ness (ŭn′ här′ nəs) ***vt-*** 1 to remove a harness from: *to* unharness *a horse.* 2 to strip of armor or similar heavy or confining gear.

un·health·ful (ŭn′ hĕlth′ fəl) ***adj-*** not healthful; harmful to good health: *He avoids eating* unhealthful *foods.* **—*adv-* un′ health′ ful·ly. *n-* un′ health′ ful·ness.**

un·health·y (ŭn′ hĕl′ thē) ***adj-*** **[un·health·i·er, un·health·i·est]** 1 not in good physical or mental health; sickly: *an* unhealthy *person.* 2 indicating poor physical or mental health: *an* unhealthy *appearance*; unhealthy *ideas.* 3 harmful to health: *an* unhealthy *climate.* 4 morally harmful; unwholesome: *an* unhealthy *influence.* **—*adv-* un′ health′ i·ly. *n-* un′ health′ i·ness.**

un·heard (ŭn′ hûrd′) ***adj-*** 1 not heard; not perceived by the sense of hearing: *an* unheard *cry.* 2 not given a hearing: *an* unheard *plea for justice.*

un·heard-of (ŭn′ hûrd′ ŏv′, -ŭv′) ***adj-*** 1 not heard of before; unknown previously; unprecedented: *an* unheard-of *improvement in transportation.* 2 strange; outlandish: *such* unheard-of *behavior.*

un·heed·ed (ŭn′ hē′ dəd) ***adj-*** not heeded; not paid attention to; disregarded.

un·heed·ing (ŭn′ hē′ dĭng) ***adj-*** not paying attention; disregarding warnings, precautions, pleas, etc. **—*adv-* un′ heed′ ing·ly.**

un·hes·i·tat·ing (ŭn′ hĕz′ ə tā′ tĭng) ***adj-*** done or acting without hesitation, doubt, or delay: *his* unhesitating *advance*; unhesitating *steps.* **—*adv-* un′ hes′ i·tat′ ing·ly.**

un·hinge (ŭn′ hĭnj′) ***vt-*** **[un·hinged, un·hing·ing]** 1 to remove from hinges. 2 to put in a state of confusion; upset; unsettle: *The train crash* unhinged *his mind.*

un·hitch (ŭn′ hĭch′) ***vt-*** to set free from being hitched; untie; set loose: *He* unhitched *the horse from the wagon.*

un·ho·ly (ŭn′ hō′ lē) ***adj-*** **[un·ho·li·er, un·ho·li·est]** 1 not holy or sacred; unhallowed. 2 wicked; sinful. 3 *Informal* very bad; dreadful: *such an* unholy *mess!* **—*n-* un′ ho′ li·ness.**

un·hon·ored (ŭn′ ŏn′ ərd) ***adj-*** 1 not honored; not given respect or recognition. 2 not accepted for payment or as a pledge: *an* unhonored *check*; *an* unhonored *signature.*

un·hook (ŭn′ ho͝ok′) ***vt-*** 1 to open or loosen by unfastening a hook: *Please* unhook *the latch. Can you* unhook *this collar?* 2 to free from something that has hooked or caught. ***vi-***: *This clasp* unhooks *easily.*

un·horse (ŭn′ hôrs′, -hôrs′) ***vt-*** **[un·horsed, un·hors·ing]** to throw or force (a rider) from the back of a horse.

un·hur·ried (ŭn′ hûr′ ēd) ***adj-*** not hurried; leisurely. **—*adv-* un′ hur′ ried·ly.**

un·hurt (ŭn′ hûrt′) ***adj-*** not hurt; not injured or damaged.

uni- *prefix* one; single: *a* unicorn (animal with a single horn). [from Latin **uni-**, from **unus**, "one; alone."]

U·ni·at Church (yo͞o′ nē ăt′) ***n-*** group of Eastern Christian churches that acknowledge the Pope of Rome as their supreme head.

u·ni·cam·er·al (yo͞o′ nə kăm′ ər əl) ***adj-*** consisting of a single legislative chamber: *a* unicameral *legislature.*

UNICEF (yo͞o′ nə sĕf′) United Nations Children's Fund. Also **U′ ni·cef′.**

u·ni·cel·lu·lar (yo͞o′ nə sĕl′ yə lər) ***adj-*** consisting of a single cell: *The ameba is a* unicellular *organism.*

u·ni·corn (yo͞o′ nə kôrn′, -kôrn′) ***n-*** legendary animal somewhat resembling a horse, usually represented as having one long horn on its forehead, the hind legs of an antelope, and the tail of a lion.

Unicorn

u·ni·fi·ca·tion (yo͞o′ nə fə kā′ shən) ***n-*** a unifying or being unified.

u·ni·form (yo͞o′ nə fôrm′, -fôrm′) ***adj-*** 1 the same in form, degree, size, or quality; not varying or changing: *a* uniform *temperature.* 2 the same as or corresponding to another or others: *The two cities have* uniform *traffic laws.* ***n-*** special clothing worn by members of the same group or profession, or people working at the same kind of job: *a nurse's* uniform. ***vt-*** to provide with or dress in such clothing. **—*adv-* u′ ni·form′ ly. *n-* u′ ni·form′ ness.**

u·ni·form·i·ty (yo͞o′ nə fôr′ mə tē, -fôr′ mə tē) ***n-*** [*pl.* **u·ni·form·i·ties]** 1 condition of being the same or alike: *a* uniformity *in customs*; uniformity *in dress.* 2 continuous sameness; monotony: *the* uniformity *of a dull job.*

u·ni·fy (yo͞o′ nə fī′) ***vt-*** **[u·ni·fied, u·ni·fy·ing]** to form into or cause to act as a single unit; unite: *Resistance to British rule* unified *the American colonies.* ***vi-***: *The colonies* unified *to form a nation.* **—*n-* u′ ni·fi′ er.**

Any of these words means un- ("not") plus the meaning of the rest of the word as given in the main text.

un′ guid′ ed	**un′ hard′ ened**	**un′ heat′ ed**	**un′ hin′ dered**
un′ ham′ pered	**un′ har·mo′ ni·ous**	**un′ heed′ ful**	**un′ his·tor′ i·cal**
un′ hand′ i·capped′	**un′ har′ nessed**	**un′ help′ ful**	**un′ hoped′-for′**
un′ hand′ i·ness	**un′ har′rowed**	**un′ her′ ald·ed**	**un′ housed′**
un′ hand′ some	**un′ har′vest·ed**	**un′ he·ro′ ic**	**un′ hy′ gi·en′ ic**
un′ hanged′	**un′ hatched′**	**un′ he·ro′ i·cal·ly**	**un′ i·den′ ti·fied′**
un′ har′ assed	**un′ healed′**	**un′ hewn′**	**un′ id′ i·o·mat′ ic**

u·ni·lat·er·al (yo͞o′ nə lăt′ ər əl) ***adj-*** **1** of or undertaken by one party or person only: *a* unilateral *decision.* **2** *Biology* affecting but one side of an animal, organ, etc. ***—adv-*** **u′ ni·lat′ er·al·ly.**

un·im·ag·i·na·ble (ŭn′ ĭ măj′ ə nə bəl) ***adj-*** such as cannot be imagined; inconceivable: *an* unimaginable *distance.* ***—adv-*** **un′ im·ag′ i·na·bly.**

un·im·ag·i·na·tive (ŭn′ ĭ măj′ ə nə tĭv′) ***adj-*** lacking imagination; prosaic. ***—adv-*** **un′ im·ag′ i·na·tive′ ly.**

un·im·peach·a·ble (ŭn′ ĭm pēch′ ə bəl) ***adj-*** too good and honest to be reasonably doubted: *a man of* unimpeachable *character.* ***—adv-*** **un′ im·peach′ a·bly.**

un·in·hab·it·ed (ŭn′ ĭn hăb′ ə təd) ***adj-*** not inhabited; having no inhabitants: *an* uninhabited *island.*

un·in·hib·it·ed (ŭn′ ĭn hĭb′ ə təd) ***adj-*** lacking inhibitions; free and relaxed in behavior, often more so than is socially acceptable. ***—adv-*** **un′ in·hib′ it·ed·ly.**

un·in·jured (ŭn′ ĭn′ jərd) ***adj-*** not injured; unharmed.

un·in·spired (ŭn′ ĭn spīrd′) ***adj-*** lacking inspiration or creative originality; dull.

un·in·tel·li·gent (ŭn′ ĭn tĕl′ ə jənt) ***adj-*** lacking intelligence; unwise; stupid. ***—adv-*** **un′ in·tel′ li·gent·ly.**

un·in·tel·li·gi·ble (ŭn′ ĭn tĕl′ ə jə bəl) ***adj-*** not intelligible; impossible to understand or make out: *an* unintelligible *scrawl.* ***—adv-*** **un′ in·tel′ li·gib·ly.**

un·in·ter·est·ed (ŭn′ ĭn′ tə rĕs′ təd) ***adj-*** not interested or curious; indifferent.

►For usage note see DISINTERESTED.

un·in·ter·rupt·ed (ŭn′ ĭn′ tə rŭp′ təd) ***adj-*** having no interruption; continuous. ***—adv-*** **un′ in′ ter·rup′ ted·ly.**

un·in·vit·ed (ŭn′ ĭn vī′ təd) ***adj-*** not invited.

un·ion (yo͞on′ yən) ***n-*** **1** a uniting or being united; combination: *the* union *of church and state.* **2 the Union** (1) the United States of America. (2) those States that remained under the Federal government during the Civil War. **3** league or association formed to protect or promote a common interest: *a labor* union. **4** partnership or association in marriage: *a long and happy* union. **5** harmony; agreement: *a* union *of like minds.* **6** coupling device for connecting pipes or rods. **7** part of a flag that stands for the joining of states or parts, and that appears in the upper corner near the flagstaff. A blue square covered with stars forms the union of the U.S. flag. **8** *Mathematics* set made up of all the elements of a pair of sets, without duplication of any element belonging to both of them. *as* ***modifier***: *the* Union *forces*; *a* union *member.*

un·ion·ism (yo͞on′ yə nĭz′ əm) ***n-*** policies or beliefs that favor the formation of a union or membership in a union, especially a labor union. ***—n-*** **un′ ion·ist.**

un·ion·ize (yo͞on′ yə nīz′) ***vt-*** **[un·ion·ized, un·ion·iz·ing]** to organize into or cause to join a labor union. ***—n-*** **un′ ion·i·za′ tion.**

union jack ***n-*** **1** flag consisting of the union from a national flag. **2 Union Jack** the national flag of Great Britain.

union shop ***n-*** factory or other business in which all workers must be or become union members.

u·nique (yo͞o nēk′) ***adj-*** **1** alone of its kind; different from all others: *The platypus is* unique *among animals.* **2** odd; rare; unusual; singular: *a* unique *bit of china.* ***—adv-*** **u·nique′ ly.** ***n-*** **u·nique′ ness.**

►If something is UNIQUE, it is the only one of its kind, and careful writers avoid using the word to mean "unusual" or "outstanding." Thus, the following should be avoided: *It is a most* unique *experience.* If the experience is UNIQUE, the word "most" is unnecessary.

u·ni·son (yo͞o′ nə sən) ***n-*** **1** *Music* a playing or singing together of the same note or melody, not necessarily in the same octave. **2** exact agreement in all aspects.

in unison 1 all together; with exactly the same timing: *to dance* in unison; *to recite* in unison. **2** *Music* sounding the same note or melody together, but not necessarily in the same octave: *The chorus sang the hymn* in unison.

u·nit (yo͞o′ nĭt) ***n-*** **1** one person or thing of a group; also, a single group in an association of groups: *a* unit *of the Army.* **2** fixed amount, quantity, distance, etc., taken as a standard of measurement: *A degree is a* unit *of temperature.* **3** part of a mechanism or apparatus having a specific function: *the power* unit *of a rocket.* **4** *Mathematics* a term whose value is 1.

U·ni·ta·ri·an (yo͞o′ nə târ′ ē ən) ***n-*** member of a religious denomination originally founded on the rejection of the Christian Trinity, and stressing freedom, tolerance, and reason. The Unitarians are now officially affiliated with the Universalists. ***adj-***: *a* Unitarian *minister.*

U·ni·ta·ri·an·ism (yo͞o′ nə târ′ ē ə nĭz′ əm) ***n-*** the beliefs and practices of the Unitarians.

u·ni·tar·y (yo͞o′ nə tĕr′ ē) ***adj-*** **1** relating to a unit or to unity. **2** like a unit; undivided: *a* unitary *structure.*

u·nite (yo͞o nīt′) ***vt-*** **[u·nit·ed, u·nit·ing]** **1** to join together; combine so as to make one: *to* unite *states into a nation.* **2** to bring into close association; ally: *Churches* unite *people in fellowship.* ***vi-***: *The two clubs decided to* unite. ***—n-*** **u·nit′ er.**

u·nit·ed (yo͞o nī′ təd) ***adj-*** **1** joined; allied. **2** in agreement or harmony. ***—adv-*** **u·nit′ ed·ly.**

United Nations ***n-*** an international organization that was founded in 1946 for the purpose of maintaining peace and security, to develop friendly relations among nations, and to cooperate in solving international economic and social problems. Its headquarters are in New York City. *as* ***modifier***: *a* United Nations *official.*

u·ni·ty (yo͞o′ nə tē) ***n-*** [*pl.* **u·ni·ties**] **1** oneness; singleness. **2** an arrangement of parts to form a complete whole: *A work of art should have* unity. **3** harmony; agreement: *to live together in* unity. **4** *Mathematics* the number one.

u·ni·valve (yo͞o′ nə vălv′) ***n-*** **1** mollusk having a one-piece shell; especially, a gastropod. **2** shell having only one piece. ***adj-***: *a* univalve *mollusk.*

u·ni·ver·sal (yo͞o′ nə vûr′ səl) ***adj-*** **1** embracing or including all or the whole of something; prevailing everywhere: *a* universal *joy*; universal *peace.* **2** relating to the entire universe: *the* universal *law of gravitation.* **3** in logic, including all within a given class; such as can be stated of all the members of a class. "All languages have vowels and consonants" is a universal proposition. ***n-*** **1** in logic, a proposition which is an absolute; concept, idea, or rule which corresponds to reality. **2** universal joint. ***—adv-*** **u′ ni·ver′ sal·ly.**

Any of these words means un- ("not") plus the meaning of the rest of the word as given in the main text.

un′ il·lu′ mi·nat′ ed
un′ im·paired′
un′ im·pas′ sioned
un′ im·ped′ ed
un′ im·por′ tance
un′ im·por′ tant
un′ im·pos′ ing
un′ im·pres′ sion·a·ble
un′ im·pres′ sive
un′ im·proved′
un′ in·cor′ po·rat′ ed
un′ in·fect′ ed
un′ in·flect′ ed
un′ in′ flu·enced
un′ in·formed′
un′ in·hab′ it·a·ble
un′ in·i′ ti·at′ ed
un′ in·spir′ ing
un′ in·struct′ ed
un′ in′ su·lat′ ed
un′ in·tel′ li·gi·bil′ i·ty
un′ in·tend′ ed
un′ in·ten′ tion·al
un′ in′ ter·est·ing
un′ in·vest′ ed
un′ in·vit′ ing

U·ni·ver·sal·ism (yōō'nə vûr'sə lĭz'əm) ***n-*** the beliefs and practices of the Universalists.

U·ni·ver·sal·ist (yōō'nə vûr'sə lĭst) ***n-*** member of a religious denomination that stresses the salvation of all souls and the complete triumph of good over evil. The Universalists are now officially affiliated with the Unitarians. ***adj-***: *a* Universalist *congregation.*

u·ni·ver·sal·i·ty (yōō'nə vûr'săl'ə tē) ***n-*** [*pl.* **u·ni·ver·sal·i·ties**] universal presence, application, or truth: *the* universality *of the custom of marriage.*

universal joint ***n-*** in an engine, a joint or coupling between two shafts that allows torque to be transmitted when the shafts are not in line.

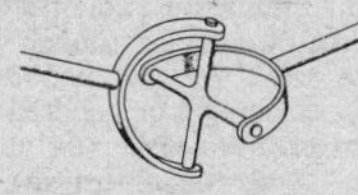

Universal joint

universal time mean time.

u·ni·verse (yōō'nə vûrs') ***n-*** **1** the whole system of existing material things; all creation; the cosmos. **2** humankind: *I proclaim my views to the whole* universe. **3** in logic, all objects, collectively, that are under consideration at one time.

u·ni·ver·si·ty (yōō'nə vûr'sə tē) ***n-*** [*pl.* **u·ni·ver·si·ties**] institution for higher learning which offers advanced degrees and usually has a liberal arts college, a graduate school, and colleges of education, law, medicine, engineering, etc. *as* ***modifier***: *the* university *bookstore.*

un·just (ŭn'jŭst') ***adj-*** not just; unfair. ***—adv-*** **un'just'ly.** ***n-*** **un'just'ness.**

un·jus·ti·fi·a·ble (ŭn'jŭs'tə fī'ə bəl) ***adj-*** such as cannot be justified. ***—adv-*** **un'jus'ti·fi'a·bly.**

un·kempt (ŭn'kĕmpt') ***adj-*** **1** not combed: *to have* unkempt *hair.* **2** sloppy; untidy. **3** unpolished; rough.

un·kind (ŭn'kīnd') ***adj-*** [**un·kind·er, un·kind·est**] not kind or sympathetic; harsh; cruel. ***—adv-*** **un'kind'ly.** ***n-*** **un'kind'ness.**

un·know·a·ble (ŭn'nō'ə bəl) ***adj-*** such as cannot be known.

un·know·ing (ŭn'nō'ĭng) ***adj-*** not knowing: *an* unknowing *accomplice in a crime.* ***—adv-*** **un'know'ing·ly.**

un·known (ŭn'nōn') ***adj-*** **1** strange; unfamiliar; not in one's knowledge: *The book you speak of is* unknown *to me.* **2** not discovered: *He was shipwrecked on an* unknown *island.* ***n-*** person or thing not known.

un·lace (ŭn'lās') ***vt-*** [**un·laced, un·lac·ing**] to unfasten; loosen (something held together with laces).

un·latch (ŭn'lăch') ***vt-*** to open the latch of.

un·law·ful (ŭn'ló'fəl) ***adj-*** **1** against the law; illegal: *Driving above the speed limit is* unlawful. **2** breaking moral law; wrongful; sinful: *It is* unlawful *to hate.* ***—adv-*** **un'law'ful·ly.** ***n-*** **un'law'ful·ness.**

un·lead·ed (ŭn lĕd'əd) ***adj-*** not containing lead or lead compounds: unleaded *fuel*; unleaded *paint.*

un·learn (ŭn'lûrn') ***vt-*** to forget or not do (something which one has previously learned): *to* unlearn *a habit.*

¹un·learn·ed (ŭn'lûr'nəd) ***adj-*** **1** not educated; ignorant; without schooling. **2** betraying lack of knowledge: *an* unlearned *comment.*

²un·learned (ŭn'lûrnd') ***adj-*** not learned by experience or study: *Blinking is an* unlearned *reflex.*

un·leash (ŭn'lēsh') ***vt-*** **1** to remove the leash from: *Don't* unleash *the dog.* **2** to release (something destructive) as if from a leash: *The storm* unleashed *its fury.*

un·leav·ened (ŭn'lĕv'ənd) ***adj-*** not leavened; especially, made without yeast.

un·less (ŭn lĕs') ***conj-*** in all cases except that; except if: *The snow will melt* unless *the weather gets colder.* ►Should not be confused with WITHOUT.

un·let·tered (ŭn'lĕt'ərd) ***adj-*** not able to read or write.

un·like (ŭn'līk') ***adj-*** having no resemblance; different: *They contributed* unlike *amounts.* ***prep-*** **1** not typical or characteristic of: *How* unlike *Jack to forget to lock up!* **2** in a manner different from; not becoming: *behavior* unlike *a soldier.* ***—n-*** **un'like'ness.**

un·like·ly (ŭn'līk'lē) ***adj-*** [**un·like·li·er, un·like·li·est**] **1** not likely; not believable; not probable: *a most* unlikely *story*; *an* unlikely *event.* **2** not likely to succeed: *Jack is* unlikely *material for the team.* ***—n-*** **un'like'li·ness.**

un·lim·ber (ŭn'lĭm'bər) ***vt-*** **1** to detach (the limber) from a cannon. **2** to prepare for action or use. ***vi-***: *We* unlimbered *before the first shots were fired.*

un·lim·it·ed (ŭn'lĭm'ə təd) ***adj-*** **1** without limits; having no bounds; vast: *the* unlimited *expanse of the sky.* **2** very great; unrestricted: *to have* unlimited *power.*

un·load (ŭn'lōd') ***vt-*** **1** to remove (a load, cargo, etc.): *to* unload *trunks from a car.* **2** to remove a load or cargo from: *They* unloaded *the three freight cars.* **3** to remove ammunition from: *to* unload *a gun.* **4** to rid oneself of: pass off: *He* unloaded *his troubles onto his father.* **5** *Informal* to get rid of in large quantities: *to* unload *stocks.* ***vi-*** to discharge cargo. ***—n-*** **un'load'er.**

un·lock (ŭn'lŏk') ***vt-*** **1** to open the lock of: *to* unlock *the door.* **2** to release; unloose: *He* unlocked *his grip on the railing.* **3** to make clear; reveal: *to* unlock *a mystery.*

un·looked-for (ŭn'lŏŏkt'fòr', -fôr') ***adj-*** not expected: *an* unlooked-for *happiness.*

un·loose (ŭn'lōōs') ***vt-*** [**un·loosed, un·loos·ing**] **1** to let go; unfasten: *She unloosed her grip on the branch.* **2** to set free; release. Also **un'loos'en.**

un·love·ly (ŭn'lŭv'lē) ***adj-*** [**un·love·li·er, un·love·li·est**] **1** not attractive or pleasing to the eye: *an* unlovely *color.* **2** unpleasant; disagreeable: *an* unlovely *episode.* ***—n-*** **un'love'li·ness.**

un·luck·y (ŭn'lŭk'ē) ***adj-*** [**un·luck·i·er, un·luck·i·est**] **1** not lucky; not fortunate: *an* unlucky *gambler*; *an* unlucky *choice.* **2** bringing bad luck: *Many people consider 13 an* unlucky *number.* **3** bringing trouble: *an* unlucky *day.* ***—adv-*** **un'luck'i·ly.** ***n-*** **un'luck'i·ness.**

un·made (ŭn'mād') ***adj-*** not made up or put in order.

un·man (ŭn'măn') ***vt-*** [**un·manned, un·man·ning**] **1** to rob of courage, virility, or strength.

Any of these words means un- ("not") plus the meaning of the rest of the word as given in the main text.

un'joint'ed	**un'la'dy·like'**	**un'lined'**	**un'lov'ing**
un'jus'ti·fied'	**un'laid'**	**un'link'**	**un'mag'ni·fied'**
un'kept'	**un'lam·en'ted**	**un'list'ed**	**un'mail'a·ble**
un'kind'li·ness	**un'lead'ed**	**un'lit'**	**un'mal'le·a·ble**
un'kind'ly	**un'li'censed**	**un'liv'a·ble**	**un'man'age·a·ble**
un'knowl'edge·a·ble	**un'light'ed**	**un'lobed'**	**un'man'ful**
un'la'bored	**un'lik'a·ble**	**un'lov'a·ble**	**un'man'gled**
	un'like'li·hood'	**un'loved'**	**un'ma·nip'u·lat'ed**

---

fāte, făt, dâre, bärn; bē, bĕt, mêre; bīte, bĭt; nōte, hŏt, môre, dóg; fŭn, fûr; tōō, bŏŏk; oil; out; tar; thin; then; hw for wh as in *wh*at; zh for s as in u*s*ual; ə for a, e, i, o, u, as in *a*go, lin*e*n, per*i*l, at*o*m, min*u*s

un·man·ly (ŭn′ măn′ lē) ***adj-*** **[un·man·li·er, un·man·li·est]** 1 not manly; lacking courage. 2 like a woman; effeminate. ***—n-*** **un′ man′ li·ness.**

un·man·ner·ly (ŭn′ măn′ ər lē) ***adj-*** impolite; rude. ***adv-*** impolitely; rudely. ***—n-*** **un′ man′ ner·li·ness.**

un·mar·ried (ŭn′ măr′ ēd) ***adj-*** not married; single.

un·mask (ŭn′ măsk′) ***vt-*** 1 to remove a mask or disguise from: *to* unmask *a traitor.* 2 to show the true nature of: *to* unmask *a plot.* ***vi-*** to remove a mask or disguise.

un·mean·ing (ŭn′ mē′ nĭng) ***adj-*** senseless; without significance: *such* unmeaning *chatter.*

un·meet (ŭn′ mēt′) ***adj-*** not proper or fitting.

un·men·tion·a·ble (ŭn′ mĕn′ shən ə bəl) ***adj-*** not fit to be spoken about; embarrassing: *an* unmentionable *topic.*

un·mer·ci·ful (ŭn′ mûr′ sə fəl) ***adj-*** 1 without pity or mercy; cruel. 2 unreasonable; extreme: *an* unmerciful *delay.* ***—adv-*** **un′ mer′ ci·ful·ly.** ***n-*** **un′ mer′ ci·ful·ness.**

un·mind·ful (ŭn′ mīnd′ fəl) ***adj-*** heedless; careless; forgetful: *We started out* unmindful *of the weather.* ***—adv-*** **un′ mind′ ful·ly.**

un·mis·tak·a·ble (ŭn′ mĭs tā′ kə bəl) ***adj-*** such as cannot be mistaken; clear; certain; obvious: *an* unmistakable *symptom.* ***—adv-*** **un′ mis·tak′ a·bly.**

un·mit·i·gat·ed (ŭn′ mĭt′ ə gā′ təd) ***adj-*** 1 not lessened; not softened: *an* unmitigated *fury.* 2 very bad; absolute: *an* unmitigated *liar.* ***—adv-*** **un′ mit′ i·gat·ed·ly.**

un·mixed (ŭn′ mĭkst′) ***adj-*** not mixed with anything else; uniform in character throughout.

un·mo·lest·ed (ŭn′ mə lĕs′ təd) ***adj-*** not harmed or disturbed; left in peace.

un·moor (ŭn′ mo͞or′) ***vt-*** to cast off the moorings of: *They* unmoored *the ships at dawn.* ***vi-***: *They* unmoored *yesterday.*

un·mor·al (ŭn′ mȯr′ əl, -mŏr′ əl) ***adj-*** having no sense of right or wrong; neither moral nor immoral; not involving a question of morality. ***—adv-*** **un′ mor′ al·ly.**

un·moved (ŭn′ mo͞ovd′) ***adj-*** 1 not moved; in the same place. 2 not swayed by feelings, thoughts, or ideas: *He was* unmoved *by his friend's argument.*

un·muz·zle (ŭn′ mŭz′ əl) ***vt-*** **[un·muz·zled, un·muz·zling]** to take the muzzle off of: *He* unmuzzled *his dog.*

un·nat·u·ral (ŭn′ năch′ ə rəl) ***adj-*** 1 not like or true to nature; abnormal; artificial: *an* unnatural *way of speaking*; *an* unnatural *color for a dog.* 2 lacking ordinary human goodness or moderation; vicious; perverted: *an* unnatural *streak of cruelty*; *an* unnatural *desire for fame.* ***—adv-*** **un′ nat′ u·ral·ly.** ***n-*** **un′ nat′ u·ral·ness.**

un·nec·es·sar·y (ŭn′ nĕs′ ə sĕr′ ē) ***adj-*** not necessary; not needed; needless: *It was an* unnecessary *error.* ***—adv-*** **un′ nec′ es·sar′ i·ly.**

un·nerve (ŭn′ nûrv′) ***vt-*** **[un·nerved, un·nerv·ing]** to deprive of courage, nerve, or self-control: *The sight of the disaster* unnerved *him.*

un·no·ticed (ŭn′ nō′ tĭst) ***adj-*** not seen or noticed: *He let the matter pass* unnoticed.

un·num·bered (ŭn′ nŭm′ bərd) ***adj-*** 1 not counted. 2 without numbers: *a series of* unnumbered *paragraphs.* 3 numerous; countless: *the* unnumbered *stars.*

un·ob·served (ŭn′ əb zûrvd′) ***adj-*** 1 not noticed; not seen: *He was* unobserved *when he came in.* 2 not celebrated or honored: *The holiday went* unobserved.

un·ob·tru·sive (ŭn′ əb tro͞o′ sĭv) ***adj-*** not obtrusive. ***—adv-*** **un′ ob·tru′ sive·ly.**

un·oc·cu·pied (ŭn′ ŏk′ yə pīd′) ***adj-*** 1 vacant; without an occupant: *an* unoccupied *house.* 2 having no occupation troops: *Part of France remained* unoccupied *during World War II.* 3 not at work or busy; idle.

un·of·fi·cial (ŭn′ ə fĭsh′ əl) ***adj-*** not official: *an* unofficial *report.* ***—adv-*** **un′ of·fi′ cial·ly.**

un·o·pened (ŭn′ ō′ pənd) ***adj-*** not yet opened.

un·or·gan·ized (ŭn′ ȯr′ gə nīzd′, ŭn′ ôr′-) ***adj-*** 1 not organized or arranged in systematic order. 2 not organized into trade unions: *some* unorganized *workers.*

un·or·tho·dox (ŭn′ ȯr′ thə dŏks′, ŭn′ ôr′-) ***adj-*** 1 not orthodox. 2 differing from the standard; peculiar.

un·pack (ŭn′ păk′) ***vt-*** 1 to open and take away the contents of: *to* unpack *a trunk.* 2 to take out (goods) from a receptacle: *to* unpack *groceries.* 3 to remove the load from (a pack animal); disburden: *They* unpacked *the horses.* ***vi-***: *They* unpacked *after the trip.*

un·paid (ŭn′ pād′) ***adj-*** 1 not paid: *to leave a bill* unpaid. 2 without pay: *an* unpaid *volunteer.*

un·pal·a·ta·ble (ŭn′ păl′ ə tə bəl) ***adj-*** not palatable; not tasty.

un·par·al·leled (ŭn′ păr′ ə lĕld′) ***adj-*** having no equal; unrivaled: *an* unparalled *achievement.*

un·par·lia·men·ta·ry (ŭn′ pär′ lə mĕn′ tə rē) ***adj-*** not parliamentary; not conforming to parliamentary rules.

un·pin (ŭn′ pĭn′) ***vt-*** **[un·pinned, un·pin·ning]** to unfasten by removing pins.

un·pleas·ant (ŭn′ plĕz′ ənt) ***adj-*** not pleasant; disagreeable. ***—adv-*** **un′ pleas′ ant·ly.** ***n-*** **un′ pleas′ ant·ness.**

un·plumbed (ŭn′ plŭmbd′) ***adj-*** 1 not plumbed; unfathomed. 2 not measured by a plumb.

Any of these words means un- ("not") plus the meaning of the rest of the word as given in the main text.

un′ manned′
un′ man′ nered
un′ man′ ner·li·ness
un′ man′ u·fac′ tured
un′ marked′
un′ mar′ ket·a·ble
un′ mas′ tered
un′ matched′
un′ meant′
un′ meas′ ur·a·ble
un′ meas′ ured
un′ me·chan′ i·cal
un′ med′ i·tat′ ed
un′ me·lo′ di·ous
un′ melt′ ed
un′ men′ tioned
un′ mer′ it·ed
un′ me·thod′ i·cal
un′ met′ ri·cal
un′ mil′ i·tar′ y
un′ milled′
un′ min′ gled
un′ mod′ i·fied′
un′ mod′ u·lat′ ed
un′ mort′ gaged
un′ mo′ ti·vat′ ed
un′ mount′ ed
un′ mov′ a·ble
un′ mov′ ing
un′ muf′ fle
un′ mu′ si·cal
un′ name′ a·ble
un′ named′
un′ nat′ u·ral·ized′
un′ nav′ i·ga·ble
un′ neigh′ bor·ly
un′ no′ tice·a·ble
un′ ob·jec′ tion·a·ble
un′ o·blig′ ing
un′ ob·scured′
un′ ob·ser′ vant
un′ ob·serv′ ing
un′ ob·struct′ ed
un′ ob·tain′ a·ble
un′ o′ pen
un′ op·posed′
un′ or′ dered
un′ o·rig′ i·nal
un′ os′ ten·ta′ tious
un′ owned′
un′ ox′ y·gen·at′ ed
un′ paired′
un′ par′ don·a·ble
un′ par′ doned
un′ par·ti′ tioned
un′ pas′ teur·ized′
un′ pas′ tor·al
un′ pa′ tient
un′ pa′ tri·ot′ ic
un′ paved′
un′ ped′ i·greed
un′ per·ceived′
un′ per·ceiv′ ing
un′ per·cep′ tive
un′ per·formed′
un′ per·suad′ a·ble
un′ per·sua′ sive
un′ per·turbed′
un′ phil′ o·soph′ ic
un′ phil′ o·soph′ i·cal
un′ pit′ ied
un′ pit′ y·ing
un′ placed′
un′ planned′
un′ plant′ ed
un′ play′ a·ble
un′ pleas′ ing
un′ pledged′
un′ plowed′

un·pop·u·lar (ŭn′ pŏp′ yə lər) ***adj-*** not generally liked. **—*n-* un′ pop′ u·lar′ i·ty. *adv-* un′ pop′ u·lar·ly.**

un·prac·ticed or **un·prac·tised** (ŭn′ prăk′ tĭst) ***adj-*** **1** not practiced; not put into practice. **2** unskilled; not expert: *an* unpracticed *beginner.*

un·prec·e·dent·ed (ŭn′ prĕs′ ə dĕn′ təd) ***adj-*** not done before; having no precedent: *an* unprecedented *voyage.* **—*adv-* un′ prec′ e·dent′ ed·ly.**

un·pre·dict·a·ble (ŭn′ prĭ dĭk′ tə bəl) ***adj-*** not predictable. **—*adv-* un′ pre·dict′ a·bly.**

un·prej·u·diced (ŭn′ prĕj′ ə dĭst) ***adj-*** not prejudiced; not biased; fair.

un·pre·med·i·tat·ed (ŭn′ prĭ mĕd′ ə tā′ təd) ***adj-*** not premeditated; not planned.

un·pre·pared (ŭn′ prĭ pârd′) ***adj-*** **1** not prepared: *an* unprepared *pupil.* **2** done without preparation; not arranged beforehand. **3** not equipped; not ready: *He was* unprepared *for college.*

un·pre·ten·tious (ŭn′ prĭ tĕn′ shəs) ***adj-*** not pretentious; not showy. **—*adv-* un′ pre·ten′ tious·ly. *n-* un′ pre·ten′ tious·ness.**

un·prin·ci·pled (ŭn′ prĭn′ sə pəld) ***adj-*** without moral principles; unscrupulous.

un·print·a·ble (ŭn′ prĭn′ tə bəl) ***adj-*** not suited for publication: *That story is* unprintable.

un·pro·fes·sion·al (ŭn′ prə fĕsh′ ən əl) ***adj-*** **1** not consistent with the rules or standards of a profession: *his* unprofessional *conduct.* **2** spoken or done by one outside a profession. **—*adv-* un′ pro·fes′ sion·al·ly.**

un·prof·it·a·ble (ŭn′ prŏf′ ə tə bəl) ***adj-*** not profitable; useless. **—*adv-* un′ prof′ it·a·bly.**

un·qual·i·fied (ŭn′ kwŏl′ ə fīd′) ***adj-*** **1** lacking the proper qualifications; unfit: *She is* unqualified *for the job.* **2** lacking legal authority; not legally suited: *He is* unqualified *to vote.* **3** absolute. **—*adv-* un′ qual′ i·fied′ ly.**

un·quench·a·ble (ŭn′ kwĕn′ chə bəl) ***adj-*** not quenchable: *my* unquenchable *thirst.*

un·ques·tion·a·ble (ŭn′ kwĕs′ chən ə bəl) ***adj-*** beyond question; indisputable. **—*adv-* un′ ques′ tion·a·bly.**

un·ques·tioned (ŭn′ kwĕs′ chənd) ***adj-*** not questioned; indisputable: *his* unquestioned *loyalty.*

un·ques·tion·ing (ŭn′ kwĕs′ chən ĭng) ***adj-*** not questioning; without any doubt or reservation: *his* unquestioning *love.*

un·qui·et (ŭn′ kwī′ ət) ***adj-*** **1** disturbed, especially by fear or anxiety: *an* unquiet *mind.* **2** restless, turbulent, or stormy. **—*adv-* un′ qui′ et·ly. *n-* un′ qui′ et·ness.**

un·quote (ŭn′ kwōt′) ***interj-*** the quotation ends here.

un·rav·el (ŭn′ răv′ əl) ***vt-*** **1** to undo; separate a thread or threads from: *Mother* unraveled *the sweater and used the wool for something else.* **2** to untangle: *I* unraveled *the ball of yarn.* **3** to solve: *to* unravel *a mystery.* ***vi-***: *The sock* unraveled *at the heel.*

un·read (ŭn′ rĕd′) ***adj-*** **1** not read: *an* unread *script.* **2** uneducated: *an* unread *man.*

un·read·y (ŭn′ rĕd′ ē) ***adj-*** not ready; not prepared. **—*n-* un′ read′ i·ness.**

un·re·al (ŭn′ rē′ əl, -rēl′) ***adj-*** not real; imaginary; fantastic; artificial. ***Hom-*** unreel. **—*n-* un′ re·al′ i·ty.**

un·rea·son·a·ble (ŭn′ rē′ zən ə bəl) ***adj-*** **1** not rational or reasonable; without good sense or sound judgment: *an* unreasonable *person*; *an* unreasonable *request.* **2** excessive; exorbitant: *an* unreasonable *price.* **—*n-* un′ rea′ son·a·ble·ness. *adv-* un′ rea′ son·a·bly.**

►Should not be confused with UNREASONING.

un·rea·son·ing (ŭn′ rē′ zən ĭng) ***adj-*** without reason: *his* unreasoning *hate.* **—*adv-* un′ rea′ son·ing·ly.**

►Should not be confused with UNREASONABLE.

un·reel (ŭn′ rēl′) ***vt-*** to unwind: *He* unreeled *a yard of line.* ***vi-***: *The line* unreeled *slowly.* ***Hom-*** unreal.

un·re·gen·er·ate (ŭn′ rĭ jĕn′ ər ət) ***adj-*** not reformed morally or spiritually; also, not wanting to change or improve one's conduct. **—*n-* un′ re·gen′ er·ate·ness.**

un·re·lent·ing (ŭn′ rĭ lĕn′ tĭng) ***adj-*** **1** not relenting; inflexible: *an* unrelenting *attitude.* **2** not relaxing the pace, effort, etc.: *an* unrelenting *worker.* **—*adv-* un′ re·lent′ ing·ly. *n-* un′ re·lent′ ing·ness.**

un·re·li·a·ble (ŭn′ rĭ lī′ ə bəl) ***adj-*** such as cannot be relied on or trusted. **—*n-* un′ re·li′ a·bil′ i·ty.**

un·re·mit·ting (ŭn′ rĭ mĭt′ ĭng) ***adj-*** without stopping; unceasing; persistent; not slackening or giving up: *to require* unremitting *toil.* **—*adv-* un′ re·mit′ ting·ly.**

Any of these words means un- ("not") plus the meaning of the rest of the word as given in the main text.

un′ po·et′ ic
un′ po·et′ i·cal
un′ point′ ed
un′ po′ lar·ized′
un′ pol′ ished
un′ polled′
un′ pol·lut′ ed
un′ po′ lym·er·ized′
un′ posed′
un′ pos·sess′ ing
un′ pow′ ered
un′ pre·dict′ a·bil′ i·ty
un′ pre′ pos·sess′ ing
un′ pre·scribed′
un′ pre·sent′ a·ble
un′ pressed′
un′ pre·tend′ ing
un′ pret′ ty
un′ pre·vent′ a·ble
un′ print′ ed
un′ priv′ i·leged
un′ proc′ essed
un′ pro·duc′ tive
un′ pro·fessed′
un′ pro·gres′ sive
un′ pro·hib′ it·ed
un′ prom′ is·ing
un′ prompt′ ed
un′ pro·nounce′ a·ble
un′ pro·nounced′
un′ pro·pi′ tious
un′ pro·por′ tion·ate
un′ pro·por′ tioned
un′ pros′ per·ous
un′ pro·tect′ ed
un′ pro·test′ ing
un′ proved′
un′ prov′ en
un′ pro·vid′ ed
un′ pro·voked′
un′ pruned′
un′ pub′ lished
un′ punc′ tu·al
un′ pun′ ished
un′ quenched′
un′ ques′ tion·ing·ly
un′ raised′
un′ ran′ somed
un′ rat′ i·fied′
un′ rav′ ished
un′ read′ a·ble
un′ re′ al·is′ tic
un′ re′ al·is′ ti·cal·ly
un′ re′ al·iz′ a·ble
un′ re′ al·ized′
un′ rea′ son
un′ rea′ soned
un′ rec′ og·nized′
un′ rec′ om·pensed′
un′ rec′ on·ciled′
un′ re′ con·struct′ ed
un′ re·cord′ ed
un′ re·deemed′
un′ re·fined′
un′ re·flect′ ing
un′ re·flec′ tive
un′ re·formed′
un′ re·gard′ ed
un′ reg′ i·ment·ed
un′ reg′ is·tered
un′ reg′ u·lat′ ed
un′ re·hearsed′
un′ re·lat′ ed
un′ re·laxed′
un′ re·lax′ ing
un′ re·lieved′
un′ re·mark′ a·ble
un′ re·mem′ bered
un′ re·mit′ ted
un′ re·mu′ ner·a′ tive
un′ re·nowned′
un′ re·paid′
un′ re·paired′
un′ re·pealed′
un′ re·pen′ tant
un′ re·port′ ed
un′ rep′ re·sent′ ed
un′ re·pressed′
un′ re·proved′
un′ re·quit′ ed

---

fāte, făt, dâre, bärn; bē, bĕt, mêre; bīte, bĭt; nōte, hŏt, môre, dȯg; fŭn, fûr; tōō, bŏŏk; oil; out; tar; thin; then; hw for wh as in *wh*at; zh for s as in u*s*ual; ə for a, e, i, o, u, as in *a*go, lin*e*n, per*i*l, at*o*m, min*u*s

un·re·served (ŭn′rĭ zûrvd′) *adj*- 1 not held in reserve. 2 frank; outspoken. *—adv*- **un′re·serv′ed·ly.**

un·rest (ŭn′rĕst′) *n*- restlessness; anxiety; dissatisfaction: *Injustice and poverty cause social* unrest.

un·re·strained (ŭn′rĭ strānd′) *adj*- not restrained; not held back; unchecked: *Our joy was* unrestrained. *—adv*- **un′re·strain′ed·ly.**

un·right·eous (ŭn′rī′chəs) *adj*- 1 not righteous; not just. 2 wicked; sinful. *—adv*- **un′right′eous·ly.** *n*- **un′right′eous·ness.**

un·ripe (ŭn′rīp′) *adj*- 1 not ripe; immature. 2 not ready or prepared: *He was* unripe *for promotion.*

un·ri·valed or **un·ri·valled** (ŭn′rī′vəld) *adj*- having no rival; unequaled: *an* unrivaled *reputation.*

un·roll (ŭn′rōl′) *vt*- 1 to unfold and spread out: *to* unroll *a carpet.* 2 to make known; display; reveal: *The book* unrolled *the story of Captain Cook's voyages. vi*-: *The carpet* unrolled. *We listened intently as the story* unrolled.

un·ruf·fled (ŭn′rŭf′əld) *adj*- 1 smooth: *an* unruffled *pond.* 2 not disturbed or upset: *his* unruffled *calm.*

un·ruled (ŭn′ro͞old′) *adj*- 1 having no ruled lines; entirely blank: *a sheet of* unruled *paper.* 2 ungoverned.

un·ru·ly (ŭn′ro͞o′lē) *adj*- [**un·ru·li·er, un·ru·li·est**] not obeying; difficult to control: *an* unruly *child*; *an* unruly *disposition.* *—n*- **un′ru′li·ness.**

un·sad·dle (ŭn′săd′əl) *vt*- [**un·sad·dled, un·sad·dling**] 1 to remove the saddle from (a horse, etc.). 2 to cause to fall out of a saddle; unhorse.

un·safe (ŭn′sāf′) *adj*- not safe; dangerous; insecure: *an* unsafe *bridge.*

un·said (ŭn′sĕd′) *adj*- not said or spoken; thought but not expressed: *Some things are better left* unsaid.

un·san·i·tar·y (ŭn′săn′ə tĕr′ē) *adj*- not sanitary; unclean; unhealthy. *—adv*- **un·san′i·tar′i·ly.** *n*- **un′san′i·tar′i·ness.**

►Should not be confused with INSANITARY.

un·sat·is·fac·to·ry (ŭn′săt′ĭs făk′tə rē) *adj*- not satisfactory; not satisfying or fulfilling a requirement; disappointing: *an* unsatisfactory *answer to a question*; *an* unsatisfactory *experience.* *—adv*- **un′sat′is·fac′to·ri·ly.**

un·sat·is·fied (ŭn′săt′ĭs fīd′) *adj*- not satisfied, fulfilled, or relieved: *an* unsatisfied *hunger.*

un·sat·u·rat·ed (ŭn′săch′ə rā′təd) *adj*- not saturated. See *saturated.*

unsaturated fat *n*- a fat in which one pair of carbon atoms possesses a double bond.

un·sa·vor·y (ŭn′sā′və rē) *adj*- 1 lacking taste or seasoning. 2 disagreeable to taste or smell. 3 morally bad. Also, *Brit.*, **un′sa′vour·y.** *—n*- **un′sa′vor·i·ness.**

un·say (ŭn′sā′) *vt*- [**un·said, un·say·ing**] to cancel or retract (something that has been said).

un·scathed (ŭn′skāthd′) *adj*- uninjured; not hurt.

un·sci·en·tif·ic (ŭn′sī′ ən tĭf′ĭk) *adj*- not done in a scientific way or supported by good evidence: *an* unscientific *inquiry.* *—adv*- **un′sci′en·tif′i·cal·ly.**

un·scram·ble (ŭn′skrăm′bəl) *vt*- [**un·scram·bled, un·scram·bling**] 1 to make clear; resolve. 2 to untangle; put in order. 3 to put (a scrambled message) back into plain language.

un·screw (ŭn′skro͞o′) *vt*- 1 to take out or remove the screw or screws from: *to* unscrew *the hinges of a door.* 2 to remove by turning on threads: *to* unscrew *the top of a jar. vi*-: *The top of the jar* unscrews *easily.*

un·scru·pu·lous (ŭn′skro͞o′pyə ləs) *adj*- without moral principles; unprincipled: *an* unscrupulous *scoundrel.* *—adv*- **un′scru′pu·lous·ly.** *n*- **un′scru′pu·lous·ness.**

un·seal (ŭn′sēl′) *vt*- 1 to remove or break the seal of. 2 to open (something that has been tightly shut).

un·search·a·ble (ŭn′sûr′chə bəl) *adj*- such as cannot be found by searching; hidden; mysterious.

un·sea·son·a·ble (ŭn′sē′zən ə bəl) *adj*- 1 out of season. 2 coming at an ill-chosen time; untimely: *an* unseasonable *request.* *—n*- **un′sea′son·a·ble·ness.** *adv*- **un′sea′son·a·bly.**

un·seat (ŭn′sēt′) *vt*- 1 to throw or remove (someone) from a seat; unhorse: *The horse* unseated *his rider.* 2 to remove (someone) from an official position; depose.

un·seem·ly (ŭn′sēm′lē) *adj*- [**un·seem·li·er, un·seem·li·est**] not proper; unfitting: *It is* unseemly *to gossip about one's neighbors.* *—n*- **un′seem′li·ness.**

un·seen (ŭn′sēn′) *adj*- 1 unnoticed: *He entered* unseen. 2 invisible: *an* unseen *presence in the room.*

un·self·ish (ŭn′sĕl′fĭsh) *adj*- not selfish; generous: *her* unselfish *attention to the patients in the hospital.* *—adv*- **un′self′ish·ly.** *n*- **un′self′ish·ness.**

un·set·tle (ŭn′sĕt′əl) *vt*- [**un·set·tled, un·set·tling**] 1 to disturb; upset; make restless or nervous: *The news* unsettled *him.* 2 to move; loosen; displace.

un·set·tled (ŭn′sĕt′əld) *adj*- 1 not decided or determined: *an* unsettled *question.* 2 without order or stability; disturbed: *The country was in an* unsettled *condition for many months after the revolution.* 3 not paid or disposed of: *an* unsettled *debt.* 4 not populated or inhabited: *an* unsettled *land.* 5 uncertain; changeable: *an* unsettled *temper*; unsettled *weather.*

un·shack·le (ŭn′shăk′əl) *vt*- [**un·shack·led, un·shack·ling**] 1 to release by opening a shackle. 2 to set free; unfetter: *They* unshackled *the rescued prisoners.*

un·shak·a·ble (ŭn′shā′kə bəl) *adj*- firm; determined.

Any of these words means un- ("not") plus the meaning of the rest of the word as given in the main text.

un′re·serve′
un′re·sist′ed
un′re·sist′ing
un′re·solved′
un′re·spon′sive
un′rest′ful
un′re·straint′
un′re·strict′ed
un′re·tract′ed
un′re·turn′a·ble
un′re·turned′
un′re·vealed′
un′re·venged′
un′re·voked′
un′re·ward′ed
un′re·ward′ing
un′rhymed′
un′rhyth′mic
un′rhyth′mi·cal
un′rig′
un′right′ful
un′rinsed′
un′rip′ened
un′ro·man′tic
un′roofed′
un′saint′ly
un′sal′a·ble
un′sal′a·ried
un′salt′ed
un′sanc′ti·fied′
un′sanc′tioned
un′sa·pon′i·fied′
un′sat′ed
un′sa′ti·at′ed
un′sat′is·fy′ing
un′saved′
un′scaled′
un′scanned′
un′scarred′
un′scent′ed
un′sched′uled
un′schol′ar·ly
un′schooled′
un′scorched′
un′screened′
un′sealed′
un′sea′soned
un′sea′wor′thy
un′sec′ond·ed
un′se·cured′
un′seed′ed
un′see′ing
un′seg′ment′ed
un′seg′re·gat′ed
un′se·lect′ed
un′self′con′scious
un′sen′si·tive
un′sen′ti·men′tal
un′sep′a·rat′ed
un′served′
un′ser′vice·a·ble
un′set′
un′set′tle·ment
un′sex′
un′shad′ed
un′shad′owed

un·shak·en (ŭn′ shā′ kən) ***adj-*** **1** firm; unyielding: *an* unshaken *belief.* **2** not confused; strong while under stress. ***—adv-*** **un′ shak′ en·ly.**

un·shaped (ŭn′ shāpt′) ***adj-*** not shaped; not in final form; amorphous: *certain* unshaped *concepts.*

un·sheathe (ŭn′ shēth′) ***vt-*** **[un·sheathed, un·sheath·ing]** to remove from a sheath: *to* unsheathe *a sword.*

un·shod (ŭn′ shŏd′) ***adj-*** without shoes; barefoot.

un·sight·ly (ŭn′ sīt′ lē) ***adj-*** not attractive or appealing to the eye; ugly. ***—n-*** **un′ sight′ li·ness.**

un·skilled (ŭn′ skĭld′) ***adj-*** **1** without training or skill for a specific kind of work. **2** not needing skill: *an* unskilled *job.* **3** lacking skill: *She's an* unskilled *sailor.*

un·skill·ful (ŭn′ skĭl′ fəl) ***adj-*** without skill; awkward. ***—adv-*** **un′ skill′ ful·ly.** ***n-*** **un′ skill′ ful·ness.**

un·snap (ŭn′ snăp′) ***vt-*** **[un·snapped, un·snap·ping]** to undo the snap or snaps of; unfasten.

un·snarl (ŭn′ snärl′) ***vt-*** to remove the tangles from.

un·so·cia·ble (ŭn′ sō′ shə bəl) ***adj-*** not disposed to seek companions; not friendly; stand-offish.

un·so·phis·ti·cat·ed (ŭn′ sə fĭs′ tə kā′ təd) ***adj-*** **1** not sophisticated; without knowledge or experience in the ways of the world. **2** simple; artless. ***—adv-*** **un′ so· phis′ ti·cat′ ed·ly.** ***n-*** **un′ so·phis′ ti·ca′ tion.**

un·sought (ŭn′ sȯt′) ***adj-*** not sought; not requested.

un·sound (ŭn′ sound′) ***adj-*** **1** not strong or solid; weak; unsafe: *The bridge has two* unsound *arches.* **2** not based on provable facts and good reasoning. **3** not reliable: *an* unsound *investment.* **4** unhealthy; infirm. ***—adv-*** **un′ sound′ ly.** ***n-*** **un′ sound′ ness.**

un·spar·ing (ŭn′ spâr′ ĭng) ***adj-*** **1** not sparing; liberal; extravagant. **2** unmerciful. ***—adv-*** **un′ spar′ ing·ly.**

un·speak·a·ble (ŭn′ spē′ kə bəl) ***adj-*** **1** such as cannot be expressed in words; beyond description: *an* unspeakable *happiness.* **2** evil or bad beyond words: *his* unspeakable *treachery.* ***—adv-*** **un′ speak′ a·bly.**

un·spot·ted (ŭn′ spŏt′ əd) ***adj-*** **1** not spotted. **2** having no moral fault or blemish: *an* unspotted *reputation.*

un·sta·ble (ŭn′ stā′ bəl) ***adj-*** **1** not fixed, secure, or steady: *an* unstable *friendship*; *an* unstable *ladder.* **2** of chemical compounds, easily decomposed. **3** *Physics* of an atom or nucleus, capable of spontaneous change. ***—n-*** **un′ sta′ ble·ness.** ***adv-*** **un′ sta′ bly.**

un·stained (ŭn′ stānd′) ***adj-*** **1** not stained. **2** having no moral fault or blemish: *an* unstained *character.*

un·stead·y (ŭn′ stĕd′ ē) ***adj-*** **[un·stead·i·er, un·stead·i·est]** **1** not steady; shaky. **2** not stable and reliable: *an* unsteady *life.* ***—adv-*** **un′ stead′ i·ly.** ***n-*** **un′ stead′ i·ness.**

un·step (ŭn′ stĕp′) ***vt-*** **[un·stepped, un·step·ping]** to remove (a mast) from a boat or ship.

un·strap (ŭn′ străp′) ***vt-*** **[un·strapped, un·strap·ping]** to take off, undo, or loosen the straps of.

un·stressed (ŭn′ strĕst′) ***adj-*** not stressed or accented: *The word "ebony" has two* unstressed *syllables.*

un·string (ŭn′ strĭng′) ***vt-*** **[un·strung, un·string·ing]** **1** to take off or loosen a string from: *to* unstring *a violin.* **2** to take off from a string: *to* unstring *beads.* **3** to unnerve; make nervous and helpless: *The accident* unstrung *me.*

un·strung (ŭn′ strŭng′) ***adj-*** **1** having the strings loose or missing: *an* unstrung *harp.* **2** nervously upset; unnerved: *an* unstrung *mother.*

un·stud·ied (ŭn′ stŭd′ ēd) ***adj-*** not premeditated; spontaneous; natural: *her* unstudied *grace.*

un·sub·stan·tial (ŭn′ səb stăn′ shəl) ***adj-*** **1** not strong; not firmly put together. **2** without material form or body; fanciful; imaginary. ***—adv-*** **un′ sub·stan′ tial·ly.** ►Should not be confused with INSUBSTANTIAL.

un·suc·cess·ful (ŭn′ sək sĕs′ fəl) ***adj-*** not successful; without success. ***—adv-*** **un′ suc·cess′ ful·ly.**

un·suit·a·ble (ŭn′ sōō′ tə bəl, ŭn′ syōō′-) ***adj-*** not suitable; not proper for the circumstances: *A bathing suit is* unsuitable *in a classroom.* ***—adv-*** **un′ suit′ a·bly.**

un·suit·ed (ŭn′ sōō′ təd, ŭn′ syōō′-) ***adj-*** not fit or appropriate: *Our methods are* unsuited *to new conditions.*

un·sul·lied (ŭn′ sŭl′ ēd) ***adj-*** not soiled or tainted; pure.

un·sung (ŭn′ sŭng′) ***adj-*** **1** not sung. **2** not praised or celebrated, especially in song or poetry: *the* unsung *heroes who fought for their country.*

un·sus·pect·ed (ŭn′ sə spĕk′ təd) ***adj-*** **1** not regarded as possible or likely: *an* unsuspected *source of wealth.* **2** not under suspicion: *The real thief was* unsuspected.

un·sus·pect·ing (ŭn′ sə spĕk′ tĭng) ***adj-*** not suspecting; having no suspicion. ***—adv-*** **un′ sus·pect′ ing·ly.**

un·sym·met·ri·cal (ŭn′ sə mĕ′ trĭ kəl) ***adj-*** not symmetrical; lacking balance. ***—adv-*** **un′ sym·met′ ri·cal·ly.**

un·tamed (ŭn′ tāmd′) ***adj-*** not tamed; wild.

Any of these words means un- ("not") plus the meaning of the rest of the word as given in the main text.

un′ shape′ ly
un′ shap′ en
un′ shared′
un′ shaved′
un′ shed′
un′ shel′ tered
un′ shield′ ed
un′ ship′
un′ shorn′
un′ shrink′ a·ble
un′ shrink′ ing
un′ shut′
un′ sift′ ed
un′ signed′
un′ sing′ a·ble
un′ sink′ a·ble
un′ sized′
un′ slaked′
un′ sling′
un′ smil′ ing
un′ so′ cia·bil′ i·ty
un′ so′ cial
un′ so′ cial·ly
un′ soiled′
un′ sold′
un′ sol′ dier·ly
un′ so·lic′ it·ed
un′ so·lic′ i·tous
un′ solv′ a·ble
un′ solved′
un′ sort′ ed
un′ sound′
un′ sour′ ed
un′ sown′
un′ spe′ cial·ized′
un′ spe·cif′ ic
un′ spec′ i·fied′
un′ spent′
un′ spir′ i·tu·al
un′ split′
un′ spoiled′
un′ spo′ ken
un′ sports′ man·like′
un′ spun′
un′ squared′
un′ states′ man·like′
un′ ster′ il·ized
un′ stick′
un′ stint′ ing
un′ stop′
un′ stopped′
un′ strained′
un′ strat′ i·fied′
un′ striped′
un′ struc′ tured
un′ stuck′
un′ sub·dued′
un′ sub·stan′ ti·at′ ed
un′ sup·port′ a·ble
un′ sup·port′ ed
un′ sup·pressed′
un′ sure′
un′ sur·pass′ a·ble
un′ sur·passed′
un′ sus·cep′ ti·ble
un′ sus·pi′ cious
un′ sus·tained′
un′ swathe′
un′ swayed′
un′ sweet′ ened
un′ swerv′ ing
un′ sworn′
un′ sym′ pa·thet′ ic
un′ sym′ pa·thiz′ ing
un′ sys′ tem·at′ ic
un′ sys′ tem·a·tized′
un′ tact′ ful
un′ taint′ ed
un′ tal′ ent·ed
un′ talked′-of′
un′ tam′ a·ble

---

un·tan·gle (ŭn′ tăng′ gəl) ***vt-*** [**un·tan·gled, un·tan·gling**] **1** to take out knots or snarls from: *to* untangle *yarn.* **2** clear up; explain: *to* untangle *a mystery.*

un·taught (ŭn′ tôt′) ***adj-*** **1** not taught or educated; ignorant: *an* untaught *backwoodsman.* **2** learned without instruction; natural: *an* untaught *skill in drawing.*

un·think·ing (ŭn′ thĭngk′ ĭng) ***adj-*** **1** not thinking; careless; inconsiderate. **2** without the power of thought. —***adv-*** **un′ think′ ing·ly.**

un·thought-of (ŭn′ thôt′ ŭv, -ŏv′) ***adj-*** not thought of; not conceived of; unimagined.

un·thread·ed (ŭn′ thrĕd′ əd) ***adj-*** **1** not threaded. **2** not having threads.

un·ti·dy (ŭn′ tī′ dē) ***adj-*** [**un·ti·di·er, un·ti·di·est**] not tidy; sloppy. —***adv-*** **un′ ti′ di·ly.** ***n-*** **un′ ti′ di·ness.**

un·tie (ŭn′ tī′) ***vt-*** [**un·tied, un·ty·ing**] **1** to undo or loosen (something that has been tied); open (a knot or bow): *He* untied *his shoelaces and removed his shoes.* **2** to set loose: *He* untied *the horse and let it wander.* ***vi-*** to become unfastened: *His laces* untied.

un·til (ən tĭl′) ***prep-*** **1** up to the time of: *We shall wait for you* until *ten o'clock.* **2** before (used after a negative): *He did not go* until *dawn.* ***conj-*** **1** up to the time that: *We shall wait* until *you arrive.* **2** up to the place, or degree, that: *He talked* until *he was hoarse.* **3** before (used after a negative): *Don't leave* until *noon.*

un·time·ly (ŭn′ tīm′ lē) ***adj-*** **1** happening at an unsuitable time: *an* untimely *request for a favor.* **2** happening too soon or before the usual time: *An early snow put an* untimely *end to autumn.* ***adv-*** inopportunely; too soon. —***n-*** **un′ time′ li·ness.**

un·tir·ing (ŭn′ tīər′ ĭng) ***adj-*** not growing tired or weary; tireless: *her* untiring *efforts.* —***adv-*** **un′ tir′ ing·ly.**

un·to (ŭn′ too͞) *Archaic* ***prep-*** to: *Give* unto *each his due.*

un·told (ŭn′ tōld′) ***adj-*** **1** not told; not revealed: *an* untold *story.* **2** countless; innumerable: *the* untold *stars in the sky.*

un·touch·a·ble (ŭn′ tŭch′ ə bəl) ***adj-*** **1** such as cannot be touched, reached, or affected. **2** such as must not be touched. **3** disgusting or defiling to the touch. ***n-*** In India, a member of the lowest hereditary caste of Hindu belief, thought to defile or contaminate members of the higher castes even by touch. Distinctions and disabilities based on caste are now illegal.

un·touched (ŭn′ tŭcht′) ***adj-*** not having been touched or affected: *a sleepy old town* untouched *by modern life.*

un·toward (ŭn′ tôrd′) ***adj-*** **1** inconvenient; unfortunate: *an* untoward *meeting.* **2** unbecoming; uncouth: *We disliked his* untoward *rudeness to the stranger.* **3** hard to manage; stubborn; wayward: *an* untoward *child.* —***adv-*** **un′ toward′ ly.** ***n-*** **un′ toward′ ness.**

un·trained (ŭn′ trānd′) ***adj-*** not trained; without discipline, education, or preparation: *an* untrained *horse.*

un·tram·meled or **un·tram·melled** (ŭn′ trăm′ əld) ***adj-*** free from ties and restraint: *We were young and* untrammeled.

un·tried (ŭn′ trīd′) ***adj-*** **1** not tried; not tested: *Mother has many* untried *recipes.* **2** without a court trial.

un·trod (ŭn′ trŏd′) ***adj-*** not having been trodden or walked upon; hence, unfrequented: *an* untrod *path.*

un·true (ŭn′ troo͞′) ***adj-*** **1** not true; false: *All his stories about hunting elephants were* untrue. **2** not faithful; not loyal: *She was* untrue *to her promise.* **3** varying from a standard, such as lines, angles, etc. —***adv-*** **un′ tru′ ly.**

un·truth (ŭn′ troo͞th′) ***n-*** **1** lack of truth; falseness: *We proved the* untruth *of all his claims.* **2** lie; false statement: *She has told many* untruths.

un·truth·ful (ŭn′ troo͞th′ fəl) ***adj-*** **1** not truthful; false. **2** not telling the truth; lying. —***adv-*** **un′ truth′ ful·ly.** ***n-*** **un′ truth′ ful·ness.**

un·tu·tored (ŭn′ too͞′ tərd, -tyoo͞′ tərd) ***adj-*** having little learning; not taught.

un·twine (ŭn′ twīn′) ***vt-*** [**un·twined, un·twin·ing**] to undo something twined or twisted: *He* untwined *the rope end.* ***vi-***: *The cheap hemp* untwined *easily.*

un·twist (ŭn′ twĭst′) ***vt-*** to loosen or separate by turning in the reverse direction; untwine.

un·used (ŭn′ yoo͞zd′) ***adj-*** not having been used; not put to use: *Lucie returned the* unused *dishes to the store.*
unused to not accustomed to: *I am* unused to *city life.*

un·u·su·al (ŭn′ yoo͞′ zho͞o əl) ***adj-*** not usual; out of the ordinary; uncommon; rare: *It is* unusual *for him to be late.* —***adv-*** **un′ u′ su·al·ly.** ***n-*** **un′ u′ su·al·ness.**

un·ut·ter·a·ble (ŭn′ ŭt′ ər ə bəl) ***adj-*** such as cannot be put into words; unspeakable: *our* unutterable *joy.* —***adv-*** **un′ ut′ ter·a·bly.**

un·var·nished (ŭn′ vär′ nĭsht) ***adj-*** **1** not varnished. **2** without embellishment; plain: *the* unvarnished *truth.*

un·veil (ŭn′ vāl′) ***vt-*** to remove a veil or covering from; reveal: *The artist* unveiled *his monument.* ***vi-*** to take off one's veil: *The mysterious stranger* unveiled.

un·voiced (ŭn′ voist′) ***adj-*** **1** not expressed: *an* unvoiced *opinion.* **2** in phonetics, uttered without vibration of the vocal cords; voiceless. In English, p, t, k, and f are among the unvoiced consonants.

un·war·rant·a·ble (ŭn′ wăr′ ən tə bəl) ***adj-*** such as cannot be warranted or justified: *an* unwarrantable *expense.* —***adv-*** **un′ war′ rant·a·bly.**

un·war·y (ŭn′ wâr′ ē) ***adj-*** not cautious; careless; heedless: *He is* unwary *of the dangers around him.* —***adv-*** **un′ war′ i·ly.** ***n-*** **un′ war′ i·ness.**

Any of these words means un- ("not") plus the meaning of the rest of the word as given in the main text.

un′ tanned′
un′ tapped′
un′ tar′ nished
un′ taxed′
un′ teach′ a·ble
un′ tech′ ni·cal
un′ tem′ pered
un′ ten′ a·ble
un′ ten′ ant·ed
un′ tend′ ed
un′ ter′ ri·fied′
un′ test′ ed
un′ teth′ er
un′ thanked′
un′ thank′ ful
un′ thatched′
un′ thawed′
un′ the·at′ ri·cal
un′ think′
un′ think′ a·ble
un′ thought′ ful
un′ thread′
un′ thrift′ y
un′ till′ a·ble
un′ tilled′
un′ tired′
un′ ti′ tled
un′ touch′ a·bil′ i·ty
un′ trace′ a·ble
un′ tracked′
un′ trans′ lat′ a·ble
un′ trans′ lat′ ed
un′ trav′ eled
un′ trav·ersed′
un′ treat′ ed
un′ trimmed′
un′ trod′ den
un′ troub′ led
un′ trust′ wor·thy
un′ tuft′ ed
un′ twist′ ed
un′ typ′ i·cal
un′ us′ a·ble
un′ ut′ tered
un′ val′ ued
un′ var′ ied
un′ var′ y·ing
un′ veiled′
un′ ven′ ti·lat′ ed
un′ ve·ra′ cious
un′ ver′ i·fi′ a·ble
un′ ver′ i·fied′
un′ versed′
un′ vexed′
un′ vis′ it·ed
un′ vul′ can·ized′
un′ walled′
un′ want′ ed
un′ war′ like′
un′ war′ rant·ed
un′ washed′
un′ watched′

un·wea·ried (ŭn′ wêr′ ēd) ***adj-*** **1** not weary; not tired: *He was* unwearied *despite the trip.* **2** tireless; untiring.

un·wel·come (ŭn′ wĕl′ kəm) ***adj-*** not welcome; not received with pleasure; not desired: *an* unwelcome *guest.*

un·well (ŭn′ wĕl′) ***adj-*** not well; sick; ill.

un·wept (ŭn′ wĕpt′) ***adj-*** **1** not mourned for, as a dead person. **2** not shed, as tears.

un·whole·some (ŭn′ hōl′ səm) ***adj-*** **1** not good for the mind or body; unhealthy: *an* unwholesome *food.* **2** morally harmful: *his* unwholesome *companions.* **3** appearing unhealthy: *an* unwholesome *complexion.* **—*adv-* un′ whole′ some·ly. *n-* un′ whole′ some·ness.**

un·wield·y (ŭn′ wēl′ dē) ***adj-*** **[un·wield·i·er, un·wield·i·est]** hard to handle or manage; bulky; clumsy: *an* unwieldy *sofa.* **—*n-* un′ wield′ i·ness.**

un·will·ing (ŭn′ wĭl′ ĭng) ***adj-*** not willing; reluctant: *The taxi driver was an* unwilling *accomplice in the bank robbery.* **—*adv-* un′ will′ ing·ly. *n-* un′ will′ ing·ness.**

un·wind (ŭn′ wīnd′) ***vt-*** **[un·wound, un·wind·ing]** **1** to wind (rope, ribbon, wire, etc.) off a reel or coil: *He* unwound *ten feet of cable.* **2** to straighten: *He* unwound *the twisted wire.* ***vi-*** **1** to uncoil: *The cable* unwound *from the reel.* **2** to become free from anxiety, tension, etc.; relax: *He needs a vacation to* unwind. **3** to be revealed little by little: *The tale* unwound.

un·wise (ŭn′ wīz′) ***adj-*** not wise; not sensible; foolish: *an* unwise *decision.* **—*adv-* un′ wise′ ly.**

un·wit·ting (ŭn′ wĭt′ ĭng) ***adj-*** not conscious or intentional: *an* unwitting *insult.* **—*adv-* un′ wit′ ting·ly.**

un·wont·ed (ŭn′ wŭn′ təd, -wōn′ təd) ***adj-*** not usual; infrequent; not customary: *His* unwonted *gaiety surprised us all.* **—*adv-* un′ wont′ ed·ly. *n-* un′ wont′ ed·ness.**

un·work·a·ble (ŭn′ wûr′ kə bəl) ***adj-*** **1** such as cannot be successfully applied or effected; impracticable: *an* unworkable *scheme.* **2** inoperable: *an* unworkable *switch.* **3** unsolvable: *an* unworkable *chess problem.*

un·world·ly (ŭn′ wûrld′ lē) ***adj-*** **1** free from worldly or material interests; spiritually minded: *He was a solitary,* unworldly *man.* **2** not of the world; unearthly: *an* unworldly *melody.* **—*n-* un′ world′ li·ness.**

un·wor·thy (ŭn′ wûr′ thē) ***adj-*** **[un·wor·thi·er, un·wor·thi·est]** **1** not worthy; not deserving; lacking merit (usually followed by "of"): *This is* unworthy *of you.* **2** not deserving respect; not suitable: *his* unworthy *conduct.* **—*adv-* un′ wor′ thi·ly. *n-* un′ wor′ thi·ness.**

un·wound (ŭn′ wound′) *p.t. & p.p.* of **unwind.**

un·wrap (ŭn′ răp′) ***vt-*** **[un·wrapped, un·wrap·ping]** to take the covering or wrapper off: *to* unwrap *a package.* ***vi-***: *The parcel* unwrapped *in the mail.*

un·writ·ten (ŭn′ rĭt′ ən) ***adj-*** not expressed in writing; well known and understood, but not written down: *the* unwritten *legends of the tribe*; *an* unwritten *law.*

unwritten law ***n-*** **1** common law as distinguished from written or statute law. **2** rule of conduct based on public sentiment or custom, but not recognized legally.

un·yield·ing (ŭn′ yēl′ dĭng) ***adj-*** firm; resolute; not yielding or giving way. **—*adv-* un′ yield′ ing·ly.**

un·yoke (ŭn′ yōk′) ***vt-*** **[un·yoked, un·yok·ing]** **1** to free from a yoke: *to* unyoke *oxen.* **2** to separate (things held together by or as if by a yoke): *to* unyoke *two ideas.*

un·zip (ŭn′ zĭp′) ***vt-*** **[un·zipped, un·zip·ping]** to open by means of a zipper: *to* unzip *a valise.*

up (ŭp) ***adv-*** **1** from a lower to a higher place, position, etc.; away from the center of the earth: *to go* up *in an elevator*; *to throw a ball* up. **2** at a higher place: *He put it* up *on the shelf.* **3** from less to more; to a higher degree or to a higher position on a scale: *Prices go* up. *He climbed* up *on the social ladder.* **4** in an erect position; on one's feet: *He sat* up. *Please stand* up. **5** out of bed: *He isn't* up *yet.* **6** entirely; thoroughly: *Eat* up *your dinner. He broke the toy* up. **7** into being or action; into notice or consideration: *I must bring* up *an unpleasant subject.* **8** in or into a condition of equality; even: *He doesn't come* up *to her in skill. He can't catch* up. *The score is now 10* up. **9** away; aside; in reserve: *We stored* up *all we could.* **10** in the sky; above the horizon: *The sun is* up. **11** comparatively high; higher than the average: *The river is* up *today. Our spirits were* up. **12** of time, at an end; finished: *The hour is* up. **13** especially keen and well prepared: *He is* up *in algebra. The singers were all* up *for that performance.* **14** ahead of an opponent: *Our team is now five* up *in the game.* **15** in baseball, at bat: *The catcher is* up. ***adj-*** leading, moving, or sloping toward a higher place or position: *the* up *escalator*; *the* up *curve.* ***prep-*** **1** from a lower to a higher place on or in: *We walked* up *the hill. They pushed it* up *the tube.* **2** to, toward, at, or near the top of: *I climbed* up *the tree.* **3** along: *He walked* up *the road toward the next farm.* **4** of streams, toward the source: *They paddled* up *the river.* **5** toward the north on, or along: *They sailed* up *the coast.* ***vt-*** **[upped, up·ping]** *Informal* to increase or cause to increase: *They* upped *their prices.* ***n-*** *Informal* an increase: *an* up *in prices.*

all up with the end or finish of, especially the final defeat of. **on the up and up** sincere; honest: *The offer was* on the up and up. **up against** having to fight or contend with. **up against it** in a difficult situation: *When the car stalled we were really* up against it. **up for** **1** being voted on or considered for: *He is* up for *governor.* **2** on trial for. **up on** well-informed on: *He is* up on *world politics.* **ups and downs** alternate good and bad luck, spirits, condition, etc. **up to** **1** doing; engaged in: *What's he* up to? **2** depending on the will or action of: *What we do is* up to *you.*

up-and-com·ing (ŭp′ ən kŭm′ ĭng) ***adj-*** doing well and likely to succeed; promising.

up-and-down (ŭp′ ən doun′) ***adj-*** **1** having an alternate rising and falling rhythm. **2** perpendicular; vertical.

up·beat (ŭp′ bēt′) ***n-*** **1** *Music* (1) an unaccented beat in a measure, especially the final beat. (2) note or several notes preceding the first accent of a piece of music. ***adj-*** *Slang* cheerful; joyous; optimistic.

up·braid (ŭp′ brād′) ***vt-*** to scold severely; blame: *She* upbraided *him for rudeness.* **—*adv-* up′ braid′ ing·ly.**

Any of these words means un- ("not") plus the meaning of the rest of the word as given in the main text.

un′ wa′ tered	**un′ wed′ ded**	**un′ wished′**	**un′ worn′**
un′ wa′ ver·ing	**un′ weed′ ed**	**un′ wit′ nessed**	**un′ wor′ ried**
un′ weaned′	**un′ weld′ ed**	**un′ wom′ an·ly**	**un′ wound′ ed**
un′ wear′ a·ble	**un′ wife′ ly**	**un′ won′**	**un′ wo′ ven**
un′ wea′ ry·ing	**un′ willed′**	**un′ wood′ ed**	**un′ wreathe′**
un′ weath′ ered	**un′ wink′ ing**	**un′ worked′**	**un′ wrin′ kled**
un′ wed′	**un′ wis′ dom**	**un′ work′ man·like′**	**un′ wrought′**

---

up·bring·ing (ŭp′ brĭng′ ĭng) ***n-*** training during childhood and youth; way a person is raised; rearing.

up-coun·try (ŭp′ kŭn′ trē) *Informal* ***n-*** the interior or remote parts of a country. ***adj-***: *an* up-country *town*; *an* up-country *boy*. ***adv-***: *They traveled* up-country.

up·date (ŭp′ dāt′) ***vt-*** [**up·dat·ed, up·dat·ing**] to bring up to date by adding new material or revising to accord with recent events: *to* update *a dictionary*.

up·draft (ŭp′ drăft′) ***n-*** upward movement of air or some other gas.

up·end (ŭp′ ĕnd′) ***vt-*** to set or place on end: *The collision* upended *one car*. ***vi-***: *The car* upended.

up·grade (ŭp′ grād′) ***n-*** an upward slope, especially in a road or railroad. ***vt-*** [**up·grad·ed, up·grad·ing**] to raise or improve in rank, quality, status, etc.: *to* upgrade *an employee*; *to* upgrade *a product*.

on the upgrade improving.

up·heav·al (ŭp′ hē′ vəl) ***n-*** **1** sudden great and violent change in conditions: *The revolution caused a great* upheaval *in Cuba*. **2** great pushing upward or heaving from below: *an* upheaval *of the earth's crust*.

up·hill (ŭp′ hĭl′) ***adv-*** upward on a slope; toward the top of a hill: *They ran* uphill. ***adj-*** **1** sloping upward; going up a hill: *an* uphill *path*. **2** difficult; arduous.

up·hold (ŭp′ hōld′) ***vt-*** [**up·held, up·hold·ing**] **1** to give support to; back: *She* upheld *his opinions*. **2** to hold up; support: *Marble columns* uphold *the roof*. **3** to refuse to set aside; confirm. **—*n-*** **up′ hold′ er.**

up·hol·ster (ŭp′ hōl′ stər) ***vt-*** to supply (the frames of chairs, sofas, and other seats) with webbing, stuffing, fabric, etc. **—*n-*** **up′ hol′ ster·er.**

up·hol·ster·y (ŭp′ hōl′ stə rē) ***n-*** **1** materials used for upholstering. **2** art or business of upholstering. *as* ***modifier***: *an* upholstery *shop*; upholstery *tools*.

up·keep (ŭp′ kēp′) ***n-*** the work and cost of keeping something in good order and repair; maintenance: *I am in charge of* upkeep. *The* upkeep *of the park is too high*.

up·land (ŭp′ lənd, -lănd′) ***n-*** (also **up′ lands′**) any region that is moderately higher than the land around it. ***adj-***: *an* upland *farm*. See also *highland*.

1**up·lift** (ŭp′ lĭft′) ***vt-*** **1** to raise; elevate. **2** to improve the condition of, especially socially or morally.

2**up·lift** (ŭp′ lĭft′) ***n-*** **1** a raising: *a mountain chain formed by the* uplift *of a plain*. **2** moral or spiritual improvement: *books devoted to* uplift. **3** something raised.

up·most (ŭp′ mōst′) ***adj-*** uppermost.

up·on (ə pŏn′, -pȯn′) ***prep-*** on.

up·per (ŭp′ ər) ***adj-*** **1** higher or above in place or position: *the* upper *floor*; *the* upper *grades*. **2** northern; farther north: *the* upper *counties of the State*. **3** lying upstream: *the* upper *river*. ***n-*** top part of a shoe.

on one's uppers poor; destitute. **the upper hand** the stronger and controlling position; the advantage.

upper·case (ŭp′ ər kās′) ***n-*** in printing, the capital letters. ***adj-***: *Use* uppercase *letters*.

upper class ***n-*** **1** social group regarded as superior to the middle class because of wealth or family background. **2** the junior or senior class in a high school or college. **—*adj-*** **(upper-class)**: *an* upper-class *neighborhood*; *an* upper-class *activity*.

up·per·class·man (ŭp′ ər klăs′ mən) ***n-*** [*pl.* **up·per·class·men**] junior or senior in high school or college.

upper crust *Informal* ***n-*** the wealthy and socially exclusive group in a society.

up·per·cut (ŭp′ ər kŭt′) ***n-*** in boxing, a punch directed upward. ***vt-*** [**up·per·cut, up·per·cut·ting**] to hit with such a blow: *Zeke* uppercut *Caleb*.

Upper House ***n-*** the smaller and usually less directly representative house of a bicameral legislature; Senate.

up·per·most (ŭp′ ər mōst′) ***adj-*** **1** highest: *the* uppermost *pinnacle*. **2** most important; most urgent: *It is* uppermost *in my thoughts*. ***adv-***: *Keep this part* uppermost. *Put it* uppermost *in your mind*.

up·pi·ty (ŭp′ ə tē) *Informal* ***adj-*** insolent; pretentious; snobbish. Also **up′ pish** (ŭp′ ĭsh). **—*n-*** **up′ pi·ty·ness.**

up·raise (ŭp′ rāz′) ***vt-*** [**up·raised, up·rais·ing**] to lift up.

up·rear (ŭp′ rêr′) ***vt-*** **1** upraise. **2** to bring up (children, animals, etc.).

up·right (ŭp′ rīt′) ***adj-*** **1** straight up; vertical; erect: *He has an* upright *posture*. **2** just; honorable: *an* upright *character*. ***n-*** something set or standing straight up. **—*adv-*** **up′ right′ ly.** ***n-*** **up′ right′ ness.**

upright piano ***n-*** piano of compact size, with the strings arranged vertically. For picture, see *piano*.

up·rise (ŭp′ rīz′) *Archaic* ***vi-*** [**up·rose, up·ris·en, up·ris·ing**] to mount; rise up, as the sun above the horizon.

up·ris·ing (ŭp′ rī′ zĭng, ŭp′ rī′-) ***n-*** insurrection; rebellion; mutiny.

up·roar (ŭp′ rôr′) ***n-*** noisy, violent disturbance; tumult.

up·roar·i·ous (ŭp′ rôr′ ē əs) ***adj-*** **1** making or accompanied by noise and disturbance. **2** extremely funny. **—*adv-*** **up′ roar′ i·ous·ly.** ***n-*** **up′ roar′ i·ous·ness.**

up·root (ŭp′ ro͞ot′, -ro͝ot′) ***vt-*** **1** to tear out by the roots: *to* uproot *a plant*. **2** to remove completely and forcibly: *Wars* uproot *many families*.

1**up·set** (ŭp′ sĕt′) ***vt-*** [**up·set, up·set·ting**] **1** to knock over; overturn: *The baby* upset *the teapot*. **2** to throw out of order; interfere with: *The holiday crowds* upset *the train schedule*. **3** to disturb mentally or physically: *The news of the shipwreck* upset *the captain's wife*. *Too much lobster* upset *Malcolm's stomach*. **4** to defeat (an opponent, team, candidate, etc., that was expected to win). ***adj-*** **1** mentally or emotionally disturbed; ill at ease: *She felt* upset *in those surroundings*. **2** overturned: *an* upset *car*. **3** thrown out of order: *our* upset *schedule*.

2**up·set** (ŭp′ sĕt′) ***n-*** **1** an interfering with or disturbing: *the* upset *of our plans*. **2** defeat of a favored opponent.

up·shot (ŭp′ shŏt′) ***n-*** result; conclusion: *The* upshot *of all our planning was a trip to the mountains*.

up·side (ŭp′ sīd′) ***n-*** upper side or top part.

up·side-down (ŭp′ sīd′ doun′) ***adj-*** having the top side or part down; reversed in position; topsy-turvy; hence, disordered: *It was an* upside-down *day*. ***adv-***: *He turned the table* upside-down.

1**up·stage** (ŭp′ stāj′) ***adj-*** **1** having to do with the rear of a stage. **2** *Informal* proud or haughty. ***adv-*** (*often* ŭp′ stāj′) toward or at the rear of a stage.

2**up·stage** (ŭp′ stāj′) ***vt-*** [**up·staged, up·stag·ing**] **1** to move toward the rear of a stage, thereby forcing (another actor) to turn his back on the audience; hence, steal a scene from. **2** *Informal* to treat in a proud, snobbish way: *They really* upstaged *him*.

1**up·stairs** (ŭp′ stârz′) ***adv-*** in, to, or toward an upper floor: *They live* upstairs. *Let's go* upstairs.

kick (someone) upstairs to promote (someone) in order to get a better person for the job he held.

2**up·stairs** (ŭp′ stârz′) ***n-*** upper floor or floors of a building. *as* ***modifier***: *an* upstairs *sitting room*.

up·stand·ing (ŭp′ stăn′ dĭng) ***adj-*** upright; honorable: *He is a fine,* upstanding *member of the community*.

up·start (ŭp′ stärt′) ***n-*** person who has suddenly risen to wealth or high position; especially, one who takes liberties or is arrogant because of success. ***adj-***: *He's an impudent,* upstart *boy*.

up·state (ŭp′ stāt′) ***adj-*** in or having to do with the part of a State that lies outside and usually north of a big city: *a town in* upstate *New York*. ***adv-*** toward such a region: *They traveled* upstate.

up·stream (ŭp′strēm′) ***adv-*** toward the source of a stream; against the current. ***adj-:*** *an* upstream *village.*

[1]**up·surge** (ŭp′sûrj′) ***n-*** a sudden rise or rising.

[2]**up·surge** (ŭp′sûrj′) ***vi-*** [**up·surged, up·surg·ing**] to rise up suddenly.

up·swing (ŭp′swĭng′) ***n-*** **1** a swinging upward: *the* upswing *of a golf club.* **2** rise; increase.

up·take (ŭp′tāk′) ***n-*** a taking up or into; intake.

on the uptake *Informal* with regard to understanding or catching an idea: *George is very quick* on the uptake.

up·thrust (ŭp′thrŭst′) ***n-*** **1** a thrusting upward. **2** in geology, an upward lift, usually violent, of part of the earth's crust.

up-to-date (ŭp′tə dāt′) ***adj-*** **1** up to the present in records, information, etc.: *an* up-to-date *medical book.* **2** in the current fashion: *an* up-to-date *hair style.*

up·town (ŭp′toun′) ***adj-*** having to do with the northern or more northern part of a town or city: *an* uptown *resident.* ***adv-*** (*often* ŭp′ town′) in or toward that part of town: *Are you going* uptown?

up·trend (ŭp′trĕnd′) ***n-*** a rising trend; especially, an improvement in economic matters.

up·turn (ŭp′tûrn′) ***n-*** an upward turn; especially, a change for the better: *an* upturn *in one's fortunes.*

up·ward (ŭp′wərd) ***adj-*** moving from a lower to a higher level: *the* upward *flight of a bird.* ***adv-*** (also **up′wards′**) from a lower to a higher level or condition: *The climbers struggled* upward.

upward (or upwards) of in total over; more than.

up·wind (ŭp′wĭnd′) ***adv-*** in the direction from which the wind blows; into the wind: *to stand* upwind *from a fire*; *to shout* upwind. ***adj-:*** *an* upwind *position.*

ur·a·ni·um (yo͞or ā′ nē əm) ***n-*** white metal element that is the heaviest natural element, with three naturally occurring isotopes and a number of artificial ones, used in atomic reactors and bombs. Compounds are used in coloring glazes and porcelains. Symbol U, At. No. 92, At. Wt. 238.03.

uranium 235 ***n-*** the naturally occurring isotope of uranium which emits neutrons and thus can start a chain reaction.

uranium 238 ***n-*** the most abundant naturally occurring isotope of uranium.

U·ra·nus (yo͞or ā′nəs) ***n-*** **1** in Greek mythology, the father of the Titans and the Cyclopes. **2** the third largest planet in the solar system, seventh in order of distance from the sun.

ur·ban (ûr′bən) ***adj-*** having to do with, living in, or located in a city or town; not rural: *an* urban *resident.*

ur·bane (ər bān′) ***adj-*** courteous and refined in manner. **—*adv-*** **ur·bane′ly.** ***n-*** **ur·ban′i·ty** (ər băn′ə tē).

ur·ban·ize (ûr′bə nīz′) ***vi-*** [**ur·ban·ized, ur·ban·iz·ing**] to become urban or more urban: *American society continues to* urbanize. ***vt-:*** *Machines are* urbanizing *our population.* **—*n-*** **ur′ban·i·za′tion.**

urban renewal ***n-*** program to improve urban areas by replacing or restoring substandard buildings or slums. ***as modifier:*** *an* urban renewal *project.*

ur·chin (ûr′chĭn) ***n-*** **1** impudent or mischievous child, especially an impish city child. **2** sea urchin.

Ur·du (ûr′do͞o′) ***n-*** language related to Hindi and Sanskrit and spoken by the Muslims of Pakistan and India. Urdu is the official language of Pakistan.

-ure *suffix* (used to form nouns from verbs) action; state; result: *seizure*; *mixture*.

u·re·a (yo͞or ē′ə) ***n-*** white, highly soluble, crystalline compound [CO $(NH_2)_2$], found in the urine of mammals and also produced synthetically. It is used in fertilizers and medicine, and in the making of plastics.

u·re·mi·a (yo͞or ē′mē ə) ***n-*** poisoned condition of the blood resulting from the presence of waste products that should be eliminated in the urine. **—*adj-*** **u·re′mic.**

u·re·ter (yo͞or ē′tər) ***n-*** one of a pair of tubes in animals through which the urine passes from a kidney to the bladder or cloaca.

u·re·thra (yo͞or ē′thrə) ***n-*** the duct or canal through which urine is discharged from the bladder. **—*adj-*** **u·re′thral.**

urge (ûrj) ***vt-*** [**urged, urg·ing**] **1** to plead with; persuade: *His friends* urged *him to accept the job.* **2** to encourage, drive, or force onward: *The jockey* urged *her horse forward.* **3** to speak earnestly for; recommend strongly: *She* urged *exercise to maintain good health.* ***n-*** strong impulse: *He felt the* urge *to travel.*

ur·gen·cy (ûr′jən sē) ***n-*** [*pl.* **ur·gen·cies**] condition of being urgent: *the* urgency *of our need.*

ur·gent (ûr′jənt) ***adj-*** **1** calling for immediate action or attention; pressing: *There was an* urgent *message waiting for her at her office.* **2** insistent; desperate: *an* urgent *plea.* **—*adv-*** **ur′gent·ly.**

u·ric (yo͞or′ĭk) ***adj-*** of, relating to, or derived from urine.

uric acid ***n-*** white, odorless, almost insoluble compound found in small quantities in the urine of mammals; the chief constituent of the urine of birds and reptiles.

u·ri·nal (yo͞or′ə nəl) ***n-*** **1** room or enclosure with facilities for urinating; also, an upright wall fixture used for this purpose. **2** glass receptacle for urine.

u·ri·nal·y·sis (yo͞or′ə năl′ə səs) *Medicine* ***n-*** [*pl.* **u·ri·nal·y·ses** (-sēz′)] chemical analysis of the urine.

u·ri·nar·y (yo͞or′ə nĕr′ē) ***adj-*** of or relating to urine, or to the organs concerned with urine.

u·ri·nate (yo͞or′ə nāt′) ***vi-*** [**u·ri·nat·ed, u·ri·nat·ing**] to pass urine. **—*n-*** **u′ri·na′tion.**

u·rine (yo͞or′ĭn) ***n-*** fluid given off by the kidneys and discharged from the bladder as waste.

urn (ûrn) ***n-*** **1** vase, especially one with a foot or a pedestal. **2** such a container, or one of another shape, used for the ashes of cremated persons. **3** large container for holding and serving a warm beverage. ***Hom-*** earn.

Decorative urn

Ur·sa Ma·jor (ûr′sə mā′jər) ***n-*** constellation thought to outline the figure of a bear; Great Bear. Ursa Major is one of the brightest constellations in the northern sky and contains the Big Dipper.

Ur·sa Mi·nor (ûr′sə mī′nər) ***n-*** northern constellation of eight stars thought to outline the figure of a bear; Little Bear. Because the seven brightest stars in Ursa Minor form the Little Dipper, the two are often confused.

Coffee urn

us (ŭs) ***pron-*** objective case of **we.**

U.S. or **US** United States.

U.S.A. or **USA** United States of America.

us·a·ble (yo͞o′zə bəl) ***adj-*** such as can be used; fit to be used: *a* usable *tool.* **—*n-*** **us′a·bil′i·ty** or **us′a·ble·ness.**

USAF or **U.S.A.F.** United States Air Force.

us·age (yo͞o′sĭj) ***n-*** **1** all the ways in which the words, grammatical forms and combinations, etc., of a language

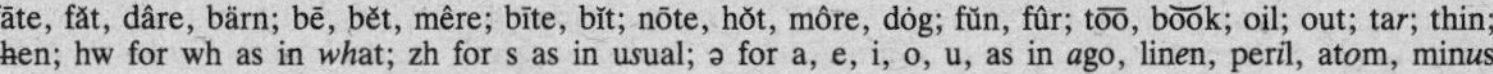
fāte, făt, dâre, bärn; bē, bĕt, mêre; bīte, bĭt; nōte, hŏt, môre, dóg; fŭn, fûr; to͞o, bo͝ok; oil; out; tar; thin; then; hw for wh as in *wh*at; zh for s as in u*s*ual; ə for a, e, i, o, u, as in *a*go, lin*e*n, per*i*l, at*o*m, min*u*s

are used in speech and writing, either by habit or by choice: *modern American* usage; *a very formal level of* usage. This dictionary indicates certain levels and styles of usage by labels, and gives advice on preferred usage in notes preceded by a special symbol [►]. **2** any particular case or instance of such use: *To say "I live in Baker Street" instead of "on Baker Street" is a British* usage. **3** way of using something; treatment; wear: *I give my clothing hard* usage. **4** habitual and common practice; custom: *the* usages *of a rural community. as* ***modifier***: *to consult* usage *notes.*

USCG or **U.S.C.G.** United States Coast Guard.

[1]**use** (yōōz) ***vt-*** **[used, us·ing] 1** to put into service; employ; utilize: *Do you* use *the library? You should* use *sharp tools very carefully.* **2** to make a habit of employing: *She* uses *a lot of garlic in her salads.* **3** to act or behave toward; treat: *The foreman* used *his workers in an inconsiderate manner.* **—*n*- us′ er.**

used to 1 accustomed to; familiar with: *We are* used to *sleeping in a cold room.* **2** formerly did: *Mary* used to *scream when she saw a mouse.*

use up to consume completely: *I* used up *all the eggs.*

►Don't write USE TO for USED TO even though they sound the same. Note carefully the two opposite meanings of USED TO.

[2]**use** (yōōs) ***n*- 1** an employing: *The* use *of fireworks is forbidden in the city.* **2** ability or opportunity to use: *He has the* use *of his arm. I have the* use *of my brother's car whenever I need it.* **3** way of using: *He learned the proper* use *of woodworking equipment.*

be of use to have practical value; be useful: *That tool* is of *no* use *to me.* Was *your recent experience* of use? **have no use for** to be contemptuous of: *He* had no use for *that sort of thing.* **in use** now employed or occupied: *The telephone is* in use. *Is this room* in use? **make use of** to have occasion to employ: *Did they* make use of *the facilities?* **put to use** to find a purpose for.

use·ful (yōōs′ fəl) ***adj*-** helpful; serviceable: *To earn her allowance, Betty made herself* useful *around the house.* **—*adv*- use′ ful·ly. *n*- use′ ful·ness.**

use·less (yōōs′ ləs) ***adj*- 1** worthless; having no use: *These old clothes may be* useless *to you but someone can use them.* **2** producing no worthwhile results; vain; futile: *It is* useless *to tell him to stop biting his nails.* **—*adv*- use′ less·ly. *n*- use′ less·ness.**

ush·er (ŭsh′ ər) ***n*-** person who directs people to their seats in a church, theater, concert hall, etc. ***vt*-** to escort; conduct; bring in: *He* ushered *me to my seat.*

USMC or **U.S.M.C.** United States Marine Corps.

USN or U.S.N. United States Navy.

U.S.S. 1 United States Ship. **2** United States Senate.

U.S.S.R. or **USSR** Union of Soviet Socialist Republics.

u·su·al (yōō′ zhōō əl, -zhəl) ***adj*-** ordinary; customary; commonplace; routine: *It is* usual *for him to swim before breakfast.* **—*adv*- u′ su·al·ly. *n*- u′ su·al·ness.**

as usual in the ordinary or expected way.

u·sur·er (yōō′ zhər ər) ***n*-** person who lends money at a very high rate of interest; loan shark.

u·su·ri·ous (yōō zhōōr′ ē əs) ***adj*- 1** suited to a usurer: *a* usurious *rate of interest.* **2** engaged in usury: *a* usurious *scoundrel.* **—*adv*- u·su′ ri·ous·ly. *n*- u·su′ ri·ous·ness.**

u·surp (yōō sûrp′, -zûrp′) ***vt*-** to take possession of (power, position, or authority) without right, or by force: *to* usurp *power.* **—*n*- u′ sur·pa′ tion. *n*- u′ surp′ er.**

u·su·ry (yōō′ zhə rē) ***n*-** [*pl.* **u·su·ries**] **1** the lending of money at a very high rate of interest. **2** exorbitant rate of interest: *to charge* usury *for a loan.*

Ute (yōōt) ***n*-** [*pl.* **Utes,** also **Ute**] **1** one of a group of American Indians who formerly lived in parts of Colorado, Utah, and New Mexico, and are now on reservations in Utah and Colorado. **2** their language.

u·ten·sil (yōō tĕn′ səl) ***n*-** implement, tool, dish, etc., used in making or doing something: *kitchen* utensils.

u·ter·ine (yōō′ tər ən, -tə rīn′) ***adj*- 1** of or relating to the uterus or womb. **2** born of the same mother, but by a different father: *two* uterine *brothers.*

u·ter·us (yōō′ tər əs) ***n*-** [*pl.* **u·ter·i** (-tər ē, -ī)] **1** hollow, pear-shaped organ of a female mammal, in which the young are carried and nourished before birth; womb. **2** in zoology, a corresponding part in various animals other than mammals, which serves as a resting place for the eggs or young during all or part of their development.

U·ther (yōō′ thər) ***n*-** legendary king of Britain; father of King Arthur. Also **U′ ther Pen′ drag′ on** (pĕn′ drăg′ ən).

u·til·i·tar·i·an (yōō tĭl′ ə târ′ ē ən) ***adj*- 1** useful and practical; having utility: *The new building is* utilitarian, *but rather ugly.* **2** of or relating to utilitarianism: *a* utilitarian *view of economics.* ***n*-** person who tends toward or is an advocate of utilitarianism.

u·til·i·tar·i·an·ism (yōō tĭl′ ə târ′ ē ə nĭz′ əm) ***n*-** philosophical doctrine that an act or thing is good insofar as it is useful and effects the greatest happiness of the greatest number.

u·til·i·ty (yōō tĭl′ ə tē) ***n*-** [*pl.* **u·til·i·ties**] **1** usefulness. **2** useful object: *A kitchen cabinet is a* utility. **3** public utility. **4 utilities** the stocks of public utilities. *as* ***modifier***: *a side of* utility *beef.*

u·til·ize (yōō′ tə līz′) ***vt*-** [**u·til·ized, u·til·iz·ing**] to put to profitable use; employ; take advantage of: *We must* utilize *every bit of space we have.* **—*adj*- u′ til·iz′ a·ble. *n*- u′ til·iz′ er. *n*- u′ til·i·za′ tion.**

►UTILIZE, when USE is meant, is often pretentious and unnecessary. UTILIZE implies using an object for a new, temporary, or emergency purpose: *He needed a doorstop and* utilized *the dictionary.*

ut·most (ŭt′ mōst′) ***adj*-** greatest; extreme; farthest: *the* utmost *confidence*; utmost *poverty*; utmost *borders of the country.* ***n*-** greatest possible extent or effort.

u·to·pi·a (yōō tō′ pē ə) ***n*- 1** place where everything is perfect and everyone is happy; paradise. **2** social and political ideal of creating such a place. **3 Utopia** imaginary island described by Sir Thomas More, where perfect social and political life existed.

u·to·pi·an (yōō tō′ pē ən) ***adj*- 1** of or relating to a utopia. **2** intended to be a utopia: *a* utopian *community in Ohio.* **3** based on a belief in perfect human conduct and an ideal society; hence, visionary: *a* utopian *scheme.* **4 Utopian** of, relating to, or like Utopia. ***n*-** person who believes in, proposes, or works for a utopia.

u·to·pi·an·ism or **U·to·pi·an·ism** (yōō tō′ pē ən ĭz′əm) ***n*-** tendency toward or belief in utopian ideas.

[1]**ut·ter** (ŭt′ ər) ***vt*- 1** to say; speak: *Muriel* uttered *the new word slowly.* **2** to sound: *to* utter *a scream of terror*; *to* utter *a vowel sound.* [from Old English **uttera** and **ūtera**, comparative form of **ūt** meaning "out."]

[2]**ut·ter** (ŭt′ ər) ***adj*-** entire; absolute; complete: *This is* utter *nonsense.* **—*adv*- ut′ ter·ly.** [from [1]**utter.**]

ut·ter·ance (ŭt′ ər əns) ***n*- 1** something uttered: *I wrote down every* utterance *of the witness.* **2** manner of speaking: *Her* utterance *was hoarse and thick.* **3** act of saying: *John's continued* utterance *of proverbs became tiresome.*

ut·ter·most (ŭt′ ər mōst′) utmost.

u·vu·la (yōōv′ yə lə) ***n*-** [*pl.* **u·vu·las** or **u·vu·lae** (-lē, -lī)] small, fleshy projection hanging from the soft palate above the back part of the tongue. **—*adj*- u′ vu·lar.**

ux·o·ri·ous (ək sôr′ ē əs, əg zôr′-) ***adj*-** excessively or foolishly attentive to one's wife. **—*adv*- ux·o′ ri·ous·ly. *n*- ux·o′ ri·ous·ness.**

V

V, v (vē) ***n-*** [*pl.* **V's, v's**] **1** the 22nd letter of the English alphabet. **2** Roman numeral for five.

v volt; voltage.

V symbol for vanadium.

v. **1** verb. **2** verse. **3** versus. **4** vice-. **5** volt; voltage.

V-1 (vē′ wŭn′) ***n-*** buzz bomb.

V-2 (vē′ to͞o′) ***n-*** rocket-propelled guided missile used by Germany in World War II; rocket bomb.

VA or **V.A.** **1** Veterans Administration. **2** vice admiral.

Va. Virginia.

va·can·cy (vā′ kən sē) ***n-*** [*pl.* **va·can·cies**] **1** unoccupied place or position: *a* vacancy *in the new office building.* **2** empty space; void. **3** condition of being empty or unoccupied: *the* vacancy *of his mind.*

va·cant (vā′ kənt) ***adj-*** **1** empty; unoccupied: *a* vacant *building lot*; *a* vacant *job*; *a* vacant *house.* **2** showing lack of understanding or unawareness of surroundings: *a* vacant *stare.* —***adv-*** **va′ cant·ly.** ***n-*** **va′ cant·ness.**

va·cate (vā′ kāt′) ***vt-*** [**va·cat·ed, va·cat·ing**] **1** to make empty; move out of (a house, apartment, etc.). **2** to give up (an office, position, etc.).

va·ca·tion (vā kā′ shən) ***n-*** **1** period of time granted to an employee in which he can rest, travel, etc. **2** period of time in which school courses are suspended: *Their* vacation *was from July to September.* **3** pleasure trip or visit. *as **modifier**: a* vacation *trip out West.* ***vi-*** to spend a period of rest and recreation: *We* vacationed *in the mountains.* —***n-*** **va·ca′ tion·er** or **va·ca′ tion·ist.**

vac·ci·nate (văk′ sə nāt′) ***vt-*** [**vac·ci·nat·ed, vac·ci·nat·ing**] to introduce vaccine into (a person or animal) to prevent certain diseases, such as smallpox or polio.

vac·ci·na·tion (văk′ sə nā′ shən) ***n-*** **1** act or process of vaccinating. **2** sore or scar caused by vaccinating.

vac·cine (văk sēn′, văk′ sēn′) ***n-*** preparation containing killed or weakened germs of a disease, introduced into the body to make it resistant to attacks of that disease.

vac·il·late (văs′ ə lāt′) ***vi-*** [**vac·il·lat·ed, vac·il·lat·ing**] to waver back and forth in forming an opinion or making a decision: *He* vacillated *until we lost all interest in his opinion.* —***n-*** **vac′ il·la′ tion.**

va·cu·i·ty (vă kyo͞o′ ə tē, və-) ***n-*** [*pl.* **va·cu·i·ties**] **1** condition of being vacuous. **2** something vacuous.

vac·u·ole (văk′ yo͞o ōl′) *Biology* ***n-*** **1** one of the spaces scattered through the cytoplasm of a cell and containing a watery fluid. For picture, see *cell.* **2** very small cavity in the tissues of an organism, containing fluid or air.

vac·u·ous (văk′ yo͞o əs) ***adj-*** **1** completely empty; void; vacant. **2** stupid; imbecilic: *a* vacuous *look*; *a* vacuous *mind.* **3** silly; inane: *a* vacuous *remark.*

vac·u·um (văk′ yo͞o əm, văk′ yo͞om′) ***n-*** **1** partial or complete absence of air and all other matter in a space; especially, such emptiness in a container from which air has been pumped out. **2** ignorance or lack of concern about facts, events, other people, etc.: *An artist should not live in a* vacuum. **3** vacuum cleaner. *as **modifier**: a* vacuum *pump.* ***vt-*** to use a vacuum cleaner on.

vacuum bottle ***n-*** **1** glass container made of two bottles, one inside the other, with a vacuum between them. **2** such a container and a metal or plastic covering, used to keep substances hot or cold; Thermos bottle.

vacuum cleaner ***n-*** electrical appliance for cleaning by means of suction which draws dirt into a bag.

vacuum tube ***n-*** electron tube.

vag·a·bond (văg′ ə bŏnd′) ***n-*** person who travels idly from place to place with no settled home; wanderer. ***adj-*** of, related to, or resembling such a person; roving.

va·gar·y (vā′ gə rē, və gâr′ ē) ***n-*** [*pl.* **va·gar·ies**] wild or extravagant notion or act; eccentricity; whim: *the* vagaries *of his conduct.*

va·gi·na (və jī′ nə) ***n-*** [*pl.* **va·gi·nas** or **va·gi·nae** (-nē)] **1** in female mammals, the curved canal that leads downward and forward from the uterus to the external genital organs. **2** in some invertebrates, the outside opening of the oviduct. **3** a sheath or a covering shaped like a sheath; especially, a sheath formed by certain leaves around a stem. —***adj-*** **vag′ i·nal** (văj′ ə nəl).

vag·i·nate (văj′ ə nāt′) ***adj-*** resembling a sheath; also, having a sheath.

va·gran·cy (vā′ grən sē) ***n-*** [*pl.* **va·gran·cies**] **1** condition of being a vagrant. **2** legal offense of being a vagrant.

va·grant (vā′ grənt) ***n-*** **1** idle, homeless wanderer; tramp; hobo. **2** anyone who is given to wandering or roaming. ***adj-*** **1** wandering or acting unlawfully. **2** having an inconsistent quality; capricious: *a meandering book filled with* vagrant *thoughts.* —***adv-*** **va′ grant·ly.**

vague (vāg) ***adj-*** [**vagu·er, vagu·est**] lacking clarity and distinctness; lacking sharpness of outline: *a* vague *shape in the mist.* —***adv-*** **vague′ ly.** ***n-*** **vague′ ness.**

va·gus (vā′gəs) ***n-*** [*pl.* **va·gi** (-gī, -jī)] either of a pair of cranial nerves that arise in the medulla oblongata and have branches to the heart, lungs, stomach, and most of the abdominal organs.

vain (vān) ***adj-*** **1** proud of oneself; self-satisfied; conceited. **2** useless; unavailing; futile: *a* vain *effort.* **3** worthless; idle; without force: *a* vain *threat.* ***Homs-*** vane, vein. —***n-*** **vain′ ness.**

in vain without success: *to resist* in vain.

vain·glo·ri·ous (vān′ glôr′ ē əs) ***adj-*** excessively proud or vain; extremely boastful: *his* vainglorious *manner.* —***adv-*** **vain′ glo′ ri·ous·ly.** ***n-*** **vain′ glo′ ri·ous·ness.**

vain·glo·ry (vān′ glôr′ ē) ***n-*** excessive and boastful pride.

vain·ly (vān′ lē) ***adv-*** **1** in a conceited or self-satisfied manner: *She* vainly *paraded before her mirror.* **2** without success; fruitlessly; in vain.

val·ance (văl′ əns) ***n-*** **1** short drapery hung around or on the framework or canopy of a bed. **2** short drapery, or wood or metal frame, hung at the top of a window.

Valance

vale (vāl) *Archaic* ***n-*** valley. ***Hom-*** veil.

val·e·dic·tor·i·an (văl′ ə dĭk′ tôr′ ē ən) ***n-*** person who makes a farewell address; especially, a member of a graduating class in school or college who is usually chosen because he is highest in academic standing.

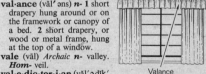

val·e·dic·to·ry (văl′ ə dĭk′ tə rē) ***n-*** [*pl.* **val·e·dic·to·ries**] farewell address; especially, a farewell address at a school or college commencement. ***adj-*** of, relating to or serving as a farewell: *his* valedictory *remarks.*

va·lence (vā′ ləns) ***n-*** combining power of an element or radical, measured by the number of hydrogen atoms with which the radical or one atom of the element will combine or which it will replace in a chemical reaction. Example: In water (H_2O) hydrogen has a valence of one, and oxygen has a valence of two.

val·en·tine (văl′ən tīn′) ***n-*** **1** card or gift sent on St. Valentine's Day, usually to a member of the opposite sex, as a token of affection. **2** sweetheart.

Valentine's Day ***n-*** February 14, the day on which valentines and gifts are sent. Also **St. Valentine's Day.**

va·le·ri·an (və lêr′ē ən) ***n-*** **1** herb with small pink or white flowers and a pungent odor. **2** drug obtained from the dried root of this plant.

val·et (vă lā′, văl′ət) ***n-*** **1** man who acts as a personal servant to another, taking care of his clothes and other personal items. **2** hotel employee who performs various services for guests.

val·e·tu·di·nar·i·an (văl′ə to͞o′də nĕr′ē ən, văl′ə tyo͞o′-) ***n-*** person who is in chronic bad health; especially, one who is preoccupied with his condition. ***adj-*** having to do with such a person.

Val·hal·la (văl hăl′ə) ***n-*** in Norse mythology, the great hall of Odin, into which heroes slain in battle were brought by the Valkyries.

val·iant (văl′ yənt) ***adj-*** showing great bravery; courageous; heroic: *a* valiant *knight*; *a* valiant *act.* —***adv-*** **val′ iant·ly.** ***n-*** **val′ iant·ness.**

val·id (văl′ ĭd) ***adj-*** **1** based on facts; legitimate; acceptable: *He had a* valid *excuse for missing the meeting.* **2** acceptable in a court of law; binding: *The judge said the rumor was not* valid *evidence.* —***n-*** **va·lid′ i·ty** (və lĭd′ ə tē). ***adv-*** **val′ id·ly.**

val·i·date (văl′ə dāt′) ***vt-*** **[val·i·dat·ed, val·i·dat·ing]** to ratify; make valid; confirm.

va·lise (və lēs′) ***n-*** traveling case used for carrying clothes or other personal possessions; suitcase.

Val·ky·rie (văl kêr′ē) ***n-*** in Norse mythology, one of Odin's warlike maidens who chose the fallen heroes from the battlefield and carried them to Valhalla.

val·ley (văl′ē) ***n-*** **1** lowland area between mountains or hills. **2** all the land drained by a river system: *the Tennessee* Valley.

val·or (văl′ər) ***n-*** great courage, especially in battle.

val·or·ous (văl′ər əs) ***adj-*** brave; fearless; courageous. —***adv-*** **val′ or·ous·ly.**

valse (vȯls) ***n-*** a waltz, especially one for the concert hall.

val·u·a·ble (văl′ yo͞o ə bəl, -yə bəl) ***adj-*** **1** highly prized; held in esteem; very useful: *Joe was a* valuable *member of the team.* **2** costing much money; worth a great deal: *Her diamonds were very* valuable. ***n-*** **valuables** possessions having special value, especially jewelry, money, securities, precious heirlooms, etc. —***adv-*** **val′ u·a·bly.**

val·u·a·tion (văl′ yo͞o ā′ shən) ***n-*** **1** act of estimating the worth of something. **2** estimated worth or price.

val·ue (văl′ yo͞o) ***n-*** **1** quality that makes a thing worth having: *The ring has a sentimental* value. **2** amount something is worth in money or other things; price: *The* value *of that necklace is $50.* **3** fair or adequate return in goods, services, or money: *to receive* value *for money spent.* **4** estimated worth: *He puts a high* value *on his ability.* **5** importance; worth: *His report was of* value *to the governor.* **6** exact meaning: *the* value *of a word.* **7** *Music* the relative duration of a tone or silence as indicated by a note or rest. **8** *Mathematics* the number or numerical magnitude represented by a numeral or an algebraic symbol or expression. **9** in phonetics, the quality of a sound represented by a letter or letters: *the sound* value *of the letter "a."* **10 values** principles, ideas, customs, etc., regarded as important by a person, group of people, etc. ***vt-*** **[val·ued, val·u·ing]** **1** to estimate the worth of; put a price on: *He* valued *the car at $300.* **2** to consider to have worth or importance; hold dear: *The cowboy* values *his horse.* —***n-*** **val′ u·er.**

val·ued (văl′ yo͞od′) ***adj-*** having worth; highly esteemed.

val·ue·less (văl′ yo͞o ləs) ***adj-*** worthless.

valve (vălv) ***n-*** **1** any of various mechanical devices for opening and closing a pipe, and thus regulating or directing the movement of a substance through it. **2** any of various membranous structures in the heart and blood vessels that allow blood to flow in one direction only. **3** either of the two pieces of the shell of a clam, oyster, etc. **4** *Brit.* electron tube. **5** *Music* device in certain brass wind instruments for changing the length and direction of the column of air and thus varying the pitch of the instrument's scale. **6** in botany, one of the parts into which a ripe seed capsule splits.

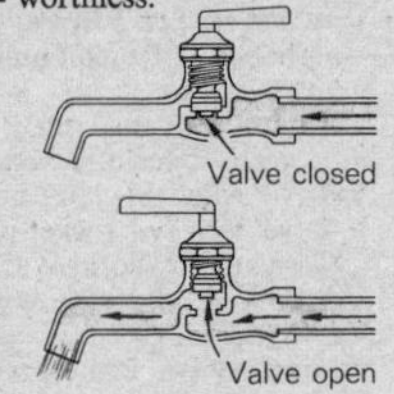

val·vu·lar (văl′ vyə lər) ***adj-*** of or relating to a valve.

va·moose (vă mo͞os′) *Slang* ***vi-*** **[va·moosed, va·moos·ing]** to run away; leave quickly. [American word from Spanish **vamos** meaning "let's go."]

[1]**vamp** (vămp) ***n-*** **1** the part of a shoe or boot just above the sole, that covers the toes and extends to the sides. **2** new part added to something old in order to give it a new appearance. **3** *Music* improvised introduction or accompaniment. ***vt-*** **1** to provide (a shoe or boot) with a vamp. **2** to add a new part to (often followed by "up"): *The producer* vamped *up the old show.* **3** *Music* to provide an improvised accompaniment to. [from Middle English **vampe,** from Old French **avantpié,** from **avant,** "before," and **pied,** "the foot."]

[2]**vamp** (vămp) *Informal* ***n-*** woman who uses her charms and tricks to tempt and seduce men for her own profit; vampire. ***vt-*** to tempt and seduce (a man). [shortened from **vampire.**]

vam·pire (văm′ pīər′) ***n-*** **1** corpse that is superstitiously believed to rise from its grave at night and suck the blood of sleeping persons. **2** person who insidiously preys on others; especially, a vamp. **3** vampire bat.

vampire bat ***n-*** any of several kinds of tropical American bats that feed on fresh blood sucked from animals.

[1]**van** (văn) ***n-*** front part of an army, fleet, etc.; hence, the position of those who lead a movement, cause, etc.: *He was in the* van *of all reform.* [from **vanguard,** from French **avant garde.**]

[2]**van** (văn) ***n-*** large, covered truck. [from **caravan,** from Persian **kārwān.**]

va·na·di·um (və nā′ dē əm) ***n-*** silvery-white metal element used in special steel alloys for hardness and toughness. Symbol V, At. No. 23, At. Wt. 50.942.

Van Al·len radiation belts (văn′ ăl′ ən) ***n-*** a region of intense radiation from charged particles circling the earth in a belt along the lines of force of the earth's magnetic field to an altitude of about 40,000 miles.

van·dal (văn′ dəl) ***n-*** **1** person who, with malice, destroys property, especially beautiful or valuable property: *The police caught the* vandal *who broke the statues.* **2 Vandal** one of a Germanic people who ravaged Gaul, Spain, northern Africa, and Rome in the fourth and fifth centuries. ***adj-*** **Vandal** of or pertaining to this people.

van·dal·ism (văn′ də lĭz′ əm) ***n-*** malicious destruction of property, especially, beautiful or valuable property. —***adj-*** **van′ dal·is′ tic.**

Van de Graaff generator (văn′ də grăf′) ***n-*** an electrostatic generator capable of producing high voltages, and consisting of a large metal sphere and a moving charged belt that picks up electrostatic charges and transfers them to the sphere.

Van·dyke (văn′ dīk′) ***n-*** beard trimmed to a point.

vane (vān) ***n-*** **1** movable device fastened to an elevated object to show which way the wind blows; weathercock. **2** one of the blades of an electric fan, windmill, etc. **3** the flat, spreading part of a feather. ***Homs-*** vain, vein.

Vane

van·guard (văn′ gärd′) ***n-*** **1** leading section of a moving army or other organized march. **2** the leaders of a political or social movement or the leading position in such a movement.

va·nil·la (və nĭl′ ə) ***n-*** **1** tropical American climbing plant related to the orchids. **2** (usually **vanilla bean**) the pod or bean of this plant, used to make a flavoring extract. **3** the flavoring so obtained. ***adj-***: *a* vanilla *cooky.*

va·nil·lin (văn′ ə lən, və nĭl′-) ***n-*** the essential oil ($C_8H_8O_3$), extracted from the vanilla bean, and used for flavoring and in perfumes.

van·ish (văn′ ĭsh) ***vi-*** **1** to be removed from sight; disappear from view: *The ship* vanished *in the fog as we watched.* **2** to cease to be; depart forever: *Dinosaurs have* vanished. *All hope* vanished. ***—n-*** **van′ ish·er.**

vanishing cream ***n-*** face cream, less oily than cold cream, used as a softener or a makeup foundation.

vanishing point ***n-*** **1** in perspective, the point where receding parallel lines seem to meet. **2** point at which something disappears.

van·i·ty (văn′ ə tē) ***n-*** [*pl.* **van·i·ties**] **1** excessive pride in one's appearance or abilities; conceit. **2** a lack of usefulness, worth, or effect: *the* vanity *of trying to reason with him.* **3** dressing table. **4** vanity case.

vanity case ***n-*** **1** small, flat case containing a mirror, face powder, etc.; compact. **2** small suitcase or handbag for carrying cosmetics.

van·quish (văng′ kwĭsh) ***vt-*** to defeat thoroughly; conquer. ***—n-*** **van′ quish·er.**

van·tage (văn′ tĭj) ***n-*** **1** superior position; advantage. **2** in tennis, first point scored after deuce; advantage.

vantage ground ***n-*** favorable position.

vantage point ***n-*** position giving advantage.

vap·id (văp′ ĭd) ***adj-*** **1** lacking flavor, taste, etc.; flat; stale: *a* vapid *drink*; vapid *beer.* **2** lacking life or spirit; dull; insipid: *a* vapid *smile*; vapid *talk.* ***—adv-*** **vap′ id·ly.** ***n-*** **vap′ id·ness** or **va·pid′ i·ty** (və pĭd′ ə tē).

va·por (vā′ pər) ***n-*** **1** gaseous form of a substance that is usually liquid or solid: *water* vapor; *mercury* vapor. **2** cloud of tiny drops or particles suspended in the air; smoke; fog or mist. **3 the vapors** *Archaic* depression of spirits; melancholy.

va·por·ish (vā′ pər ĭsh) ***adj-*** **1** full of or like vapor. **2** *Archaic* easily depressed; also, inclined to hysteria.

va·por·ize (vā′ pə rīz′) ***vt-*** [**va·por·ized, va·por·iz·ing**] to change into vapor: *to* vaporize *water.* ***vi-***: *Alcohol* vaporizes *easily.* ***—adj-*** **va′ por·iz′ a·ble:** *a* vaporizable *liquid.* ***n-*** **va′ por·i·za′ tion.**

va·por·iz·er (vā′ pə rīz′ ər) ***n-*** a device for vaporizing liquids, especially medicated liquids.

va·por·ous (vā′ pər əs) ***adj-*** **1** full of or like vapor; foggy; misty. **2** without substance; unreal. ***—adv-*** **va′ por·ous·ly.** ***n-*** **va′ por·ous·ness.**

vapor trail ***n-*** trail of water droplets behind high-flying aircraft.

va·por·y (vā′ pə rē) ***adj-*** vaporous.

va·que·ro (vä kē′ rō) ***n-*** [*pl.* **va·que·ros**] in southwestern United States and Spanish America, a cowboy. [from American Spanish, from Latin **vacca,** "cow."]

vari- or **vario-** *prefix* varied; different; diverse: vari*form*; vari*colored.* [from Latin **vari-,** from **varius.**]

var·i·a·ble (vâr′ ē ə bəl, văr′-) ***adj-*** **1** likely to change; changing: *the* variable *climate.* **2** fickle; fitful; inconstant: *her* variable *temper.* ***n-*** **1** something that varies. **2** *Mathematics* a symbol for which different numbers may be substituted under given conditions. ***—n-*** **var′ i·a·bil′ i·ty** or **var′ i·a·ble·ness.** ***adv-*** **var′ i·a·bly.**

variable star ***n-*** star that grows brighter and dimmer over a period of time, thus seeming to pulsate; Cepheid.

var·i·ance (vâr′ ē əns, văr′-) ***n-*** **1** disagreement; difference: *There is a large* variance *in our opinions of him.* **2** variation; change: *a* variance *in temperature.*
at variance not agreeing; differing.

var·i·ant (vâr′ ē ənt, văr′-) ***adj-*** having or showing variation; differing from another or others of the same kind or class: *a* variant *spelling of a word.* ***n-*** something that differs from another thing in form, though both are essentially the same: *"Rime" is a* variant *of "rhyme."*

var·i·a·tion (vâr′ ē ā′ shən, văr′-) ***n-*** **1** a varying or change; also, the amount of such change: *We can expect a* variation *of 10 degrees in temperature tonight.* **2** difference: *a* variation *in color between two napkins*; *a* variation *of several dollars in price.* **3** form or version (of something) that differs from the original version: *a new* variation *of an old song.* **4** *Music* the repeating of a single tune or theme with changes that vary, and often elaborate it.

var·i·col·ored (vâr′ ə kŭl′ ərd, văr′-) ***adj-*** spotted, streaked, or marked with various colors.

var·i·cose (văr′ ə kōs′) ***adj-*** abnormally or irregularly swollen or dilated: *a* varicose *vein.*

var·ied (vâr′ ēd, văr′-) ***adj-*** **1** having different shapes, forms, colors, sizes, etc.: *The town has houses of* varied *appearance.* **2** of many sorts or kinds; full of variety: *a* varied *collection of pictures*; *a* varied *career.* **3** altered.

var·i·e·gate (vâr′ ē ə gāt′, văr′-) ***vt-*** [**var·i·e·gat·ed var·i·e·gat·ing**] **1** to change the appearance of, by marking with different colors; streak; spot. **2** to give variety to; make varied. ***—n-*** **var′ i·e·ga′ tion.**

var·i·e·gat·ed (vâr′ ē ə gā′ təd, văr′-) ***adj-*** **1** having marks, streaks, or patches of different colors: *a* variegated *marble.* **2** marked by variety; diversified.

va·ri·e·ty (və rī′ ə tē) ***n-*** [*pl.* **va·ri·e·ties**] **1** lack of sameness or monotony; change; diversity: *She had great* variety *in her daily activities.* **2** assortment of many different kinds: *a large* variety *of candy.* **3** kind; type; sort: *a new* variety *of popular song.* **4** *Biology* subdivision of species; group which distinctly differs from a typical member of a species; subspecies; also, a variation of any kind within a species.

variety show ***n-*** theatrical performance consisting of many short and different acts or numbers.

variety store ***n-*** store that sells assorted merchandise.

var·i·form (vâr′ ə fôrm′, văr′-) ***adj-*** having various forms: *many* variform *corals.*

var·i·ous (vâr′ ē əs, văr′-) ***adj-*** **1** of different kinds: *Beverly received* various *gifts on her birthday.* **2** several; many and different: *Roses are of* various *colors.* ***—adv-*** **var′ i·ous·ly.** ***n-*** **var′ i·ous·ness.**

►VARIOUS refers to things that are individual and separate, without commenting on the degree of likeness among them: *The* various *reports all agreed that the fight began when John hit George.* DIFFERENT refers to the lack of likeness between individual things: *The reports were* different; *some said John hit George first, while others said George hit John first.*

var·let (vär′ lət) *Archaic* ***n-*** scoundrel.

var·mint (vär′ mĭnt′) *Informal* ***n-*** harmful or offensive animal; hence, a troublesome or objectionable person.

var·nish (vär′ nĭsh) ***n-* 1** liquid made from resins. It is transparent and can be spread like paint to give, when dry, a hard, smooth, glossy finish to wood, metal, plastics, etc. **2** surface made by such a liquid. **3** outer show; superficial polish: *His fine manners are mere* varnish. *as* ***modifier:*** *a* varnish *remover.* ***vt-* 1** to cover with varnish. **2** to cover up (defects); gloss over: *He* varnishes *his ignorance with platitudes.* **—*n-* var′ nish·er.**

var·si·ty (vär′ sə tē) ***n-*** [*pl.* **var·si·ties**] team that represents a school or college in interscholastic activities. *as* ***modifier:*** *the* varsity *teams.*

var·y (vâr′ ē, văr′ ē) ***vi-*** [**var·ied, var·y·ing**] **1** to change; be or become different: *Weather* varies *from day to day.* **2** *Mathematics* of one term, to assume different values under different conditions. ***vt-*** to cause to alter: *She* varies *the appearance of the room by rearranging the furniture.* **—*adv-* var′ y·ing·ly.**

vas·cu·lar (văs′ kyə lər) ***adj-*** pertaining to or consisting of plant or animal systems that transport fluids, such as the vessels of plants which carry water, and the blood and lymph vessels of animals.

vase (vās, vāz, väz) ***n-*** ornamental container of glass, pottery, etc., often used as a flower holder. **—*adj-* vase′ like′.**

Vase

Vas·e·line (văs′ ə lēn′) ***n-*** trademark name for petroleum jelly and certain other pharmaceutical preparations. Also **vaseline.**

vas·sal (văs′ el) ***n-* 1** in the feudal system, person who placed himself under the protection of a lord or master, and in return rendered homage and service; person who held land under feudal tenure. **2** a servant; retainer. *as* ***modifier:*** *a* vassal *state.*

vas·sal·age (văs′ əl ĭj) ***n-* 1** the condition of being a vassal. **2** services, homage, duties, etc., due from a vassal. **3** slavery; servitude. **4** land held by a vassal; fief.

vast (văst) ***adj-*** very great in size, extent, amount, or the like; huge; enormous. **—*adv-* vast′ ly. *n-* vast′ ness.**

vat (văt) ***n-*** large tank, tub, or vessel, especially one for holding liquors, dyes, etc., in process of manufacture.

Vat·i·can (văt′ ĭ kən) ***n-* 1** palace of the Pope at Rome. **2** headquarters in Rome of the Roman Catholic Church.

vau·de·ville (vòd′ ə vĭl′, vòd′ vĭl′, vōd′ vĭl) ***n-*** theatrical performance consisting of a series of variety acts, such as songs, dances, acrobatic feats, and short dramatic sketches. *as* ***modifier:*** *a* vaudeville *performer.*

Bank vault entrance

[1]**vault** (vòlt) ***n-* 1** arched roof or ceiling. **2** any arched covering; especially, the arch of the sky. **3** storage cellar. **4** room in a bank where valuables may be kept. **5** tomb. *as* ***modifier:*** *the* vault *door.* ***vt-*** to put such an arched roof over. [from Old French **volte** from Latin **volūtus,** from **volvere,** "to turn about."]

[2]**vault** (vòlt) ***n-*** a leap over something, made with the aid of the hands or a pole. ***vi-*** to make such a leap. ***vt-:*** *Benton* vaulted *the wall.* [from [1]**vault** in a special sense, arising from the fact that in leaping one moves in a curve that is like an arch.] **—*n-* vault′ er.**

vault·ed (vòl′ təd) ***adj-* 1** covered with a vault. **2** shaped like a vault; arched.

vault·ing (vòl′ tĭng) ***adj-* 1** leaping up or over; hence, reaching too far; exaggerated: *a* vaulting *ambition.* **2** used in leaping over: *a* vaulting *pole.*

vaunt (vònt) ***vi-*** to brag. ***vt-*** to boast of; display boastfully: *to* vaunt *one's courage.* ***n-*** a boast; brag; vain display. **—*adv-* vaunt′ ing·ly.**

veal (vēl) ***n-*** flesh of a calf, used as food. *as* ***modifier:*** *a* veal *cutlet.*

vec·tor (vĕk′ tər) ***n-* 1** *Physics* a force, velocity, or other physical phenomenon, having both magnitude and direction and usually represented by a line segment with an arrowhead to show direction. The length of the segment corresponds to the magnitude, and the arrowhead indicates the direction of the vector. **2** *Medicine* an organism that carries disease.

veer (vêr) ***vi-*** to change direction; shift: *The north wind* veered *to the east.* ***vt-:*** *Bob* veered *the car to avoid the hole.* ***n-*** a change of direction.

Ve·ga (vē′ gə, vā′-) ***n-*** brightest star in the constellation Lyra.

veg·e·ta·ble (vĕj′ tə bəl, vĕj′ ə tə-) ***n-* 1** a plant or part of a plant (root, blossom, leaves, etc.) used for food. Carrots, potatoes, cauliflower, and cabbage are vegetables. Tomatoes, peas, and beans are also commonly called vegetables, although by botanical classification they are fruits. **2** any plant. ***adj-* 1** made from plants or parts of plants. **2** having to do with plants. **3** dull; monotonous: *a* vegetable *existence.*

vegetable ivory *n-* hard seed of a South American palm, resembling ivory, used for buttons, trinkets, etc.

veg·e·tar·i·an (vĕj′ ə târ′ ē ən) ***n-*** person who eats only vegetables or vegetable products, and avoids eating animal flesh. *as* ***modifier:*** *a* vegetarian *diet.*

veg·e·tar·i·an·ism (vĕj′ ə târ′ ē ə nĭz′ əm) ***n-*** beliefs or practices of vegetarians.

veg·e·tate (vĕj′ ə tāt′) ***vi-*** [**veg·e·tat·ed, veg·e·tat·ing**] **1** to grow as a plant does; hence, to lead an idle, unthinking existence. **2** of a wart, pimple, etc., to grow abnormally.

veg·e·ta·tion (vĕj′ ə tā′ shən) ***n-* 1** plants of any kind: *the thick* vegetation *on the hillside.* **2** act or process of vegetating. **3** *Medicine* an abnormal growth of tissue.

veg·e·ta·tive (vĕj′ ə tā′ tĭv) ***adj-* 1** of or pertaining to vegetation or vegetating. **2** *Biology* of or having to do with growth or other life processes of plants, exclusive of sexual reproduction.

ve·he·mence (vē′ ə məns) ***n-* 1** great feeling; fervor; passion: *He spoke with* vehemence. **2** violence; fury.

ve·he·ment (vē′ ə mənt) ***adj-* 1** forceful; fiery; fervent: *a* vehement *demand for better housing.* **2** violent; wild; furious: *a* vehement *wind.* **—*adv-* ve′ he·ment·ly.**

ve·hi·cle (vē′ ĭ kəl) ***n-* 1** any device for carrying passengers or goods, especially one traveling on land, such as a car, bicycle, or sleigh. **2** a means of conveying thoughts, information, etc.: *Books are* vehicles *for authors' thoughts.* **3** liquid in which pigments, drugs, etc. are dissolved: *Water is the* vehicle *for water colors.*

ve·hic·u·lar (vĭ hĭk′ yə lər) ***adj-* 1** of, relating to, or for vehicles, especially motor vehicles: *a* vehicular *bridge*; vehicular *traffic.* **2** serving as a vehicle.

veil (vāl) ***n-* 1** piece of cloth, often wide-meshed and transparent, used to hide or protect the face, or for ornament. **2** the part of a nun's or bride's headdress that covers the head and falls over the shoulders, on each side of the face. **3** anything that hides like a curtain: *a* veil *of secrecy*; *a* veil *of mist*. ***vt-* 1** to hide or cover with a thin, gauzy piece of cloth. **2** to hide partially: *He* veiled *his dislike*. ***Hom-*** vale.

take the veil to become a nun.

veil·ing (vā′ lĭng) ***n-* 1** thin, gauzy material used for veils. **2** a veil.

vein (vān) ***n-* 1** blood vessel in which blood flows toward the heart. **2** one of the vascular ribs in a leaf, which also acts as a support. **3** one of the branching supports of an insect's wing. **4** in geology, strip of color or of ore in a rock. **5** a strain; streak: *A* vein *of humor ran through the book*. ***Homs-*** vain, vane. **—*adj-* veined.** ***adj-* vein′ less.** ***adj-* vein′ like′.**

vein·ing (vā′ nĭng) ***n-*** system or pattern of veins.

veld or **veldt** (vĕlt, fĕlt) ***n-*** in South Africa, open pasture land or thinly wooded country.

vel·lum (vĕl′ əm) ***n-* 1** thin, smooth, tanned skin, usually of a calf, once used as writing paper but now used for covers of expensive books; fine parchment. **2** writing paper imitating this. *as* ***modifier***: *a* vellum *binding*.

ve·loc·i·pede (və lŏs′ ə pēd′) ***n-* 1** a child's tricycle. **2** an early form of the bicycle or tricycle.

ve·loc·i·ty (və lŏs′ ə tē) *Physics* ***n-*** [*pl.* **ve·loc·i·ties**] **1** rate of change of position in a given direction; the distance a moving object travels with respect to time. Velocity is a vector quantity having both magnitude (speed) and direction. **2** speed.

ve·lour or **ve·lours** (və lo͝or′, -lo͝orz′) ***n-*** [*pl.* **ve·lours**], soft, smooth, closely woven cotton or woolen fabric having a short, thick pile like that of velvet. *as* ***modifier***: *a* velour *shirt*; velour *pillows*.

ve·lum (vē′ ləm) ***n-*** [*pl.* **ve·la** (-lə)] **1** *Biology* a thin membranous covering or partition. **2** the soft palate.

vel·vet (vĕl′ vət) ***n-* 1** fine, closely woven fabric of silk, cotton, rayon, etc., with either a silk or cotton backing and a short, thick, soft nap or pile. **2** anything resembling the feel and softness of such a fabric. **3** the fuzzy, thin skin on the growing antler of a deer. *as* ***modifier***: *a* velvet *evening gown*; *the* velvet *darkness of a summer sky*.

vel·vet·een (vĕl′ və tēn′) ***n-*** cotton material with a short pile like velvet. *as* ***modifier***: *a* velveteen *dress*.

vel·vet·y (vĕl′ və tē) ***adj-* 1** of a texture like velvet to the touch. **2** soft and mellow to sight, hearing, or taste.

ve·nal (vē′ nəl) ***adj-* 1** ready or willing to be bribed: *a* venal *judge*. **2** obtained or influenced by a bribe; corrupt: *his* venal *services*. **—*adv-* ve′ nal·ly.**

ve·nal·i·ty (vĭ năl′ ə tē) ***n-*** [*pl.* **ve·nal·i·ties**] willingness to cheapen one's talents or services for gain.

ve·na·tion (və nā′ shən, vē-) ***n-*** system or pattern of veins: *the* venation *of an insect's wing*.

vend (vĕnd) ***vt-*** to sell, offer for sale; peddle.

ven·det·ta (vĕn dĕt′ ə) ***n-*** feud between two families, carried on by murder for vengeance.

vending machine ***n-*** machine operated by the insertion of a coin into a slot, used for selling merchandise.

ven·dor or **vend·er** (vĕn′ dər) ***n-*** seller of goods.

ve·neer (və nêr′) ***n-* 1** thin layer of fine wood used to overlay the surface of furniture. **2** thin layer of tile or brick, covering a coarser building material: *a building with a brick* veneer. **3** any of the thin sheets of wood glued together to form plywood. **4** a disguise for something that is coarse or inferior. ***vt-* 1** to apply a thin layer of fine wood to. **2** to glue (thin sheets of wood) together to form plywood. **3** to cover or conceal (something coarse or inferior) with an attractive surface.

ven·er·a·ble (vĕn′ ər ə bəl) ***adj-* 1** deserving of respect and honor by reason of age, dignity, character, and reputation: *a* venerable *scholar*. **2** of buildings or places, sacred because of historic, religious, or ancient associations: *a* venerable *church*. **3 Venerable** a title for an archdeacon in Anglican churches. **—*n-* ven′ er·a·bil′ i·ty.** ***adv-* ven′ er·a·bly.**

ven·er·ate (vĕn′ ə rāt′) ***vt-*** [**ven·er·at·ed, ven·er·at·ing**] to regard with feelings of the highest respect and honor; to revere: *The old man's students* venerate *him*.

ven·er·a·tion (vĕn′ ə rā′ shən) ***n-* 1** a venerating or being venerated; worship: *the* veneration *of martyrs*. **2** deep respect and reverence.

ve·ne·re·al (və nêr′ ē əl) ***adj-*** of, having to do with, or resulting from sex acts: *a* venereal *disease*.

ve·ne·tian blind (və nē′ shən) ***n-*** a shade of movable slats hung on tapes. The slats may be tilted, or the shade raised, by cords.

Venetian blind

venge·ance (vĕn′ jəns) ***n-*** act of causing harm to another in payment for harm suffered at his hands; revenge.

with a vengeance with great energy or violence.

venge·ful (vĕnj′ fəl) ***adj-*** filled with a desire for vengeance; vindictive. **—*adv-* venge′ ful·ly.** ***n-* venge′-ful·ness.**

ve·ni·al (vē′ nē əl) ***adj-*** such as can be easily pardoned; not beyond forgiveness: *a* venial *sin*. **—*adv-* ve′ ni·al·ly.** ***n-* ve′ ni·al′ i·ty** (-ăl′ ə tē) or **ve′ ni·al·ness.**

ve·ni·re (və nī′ rē, -nêr′ ē) ***n-*** in law, a legal writ to a sheriff for the summoning of a jury to a court trial.

ve·ni·re·man (və nī′ rē mən, -nêr′ ē mən) ***n-*** person who has been summoned to serve on a jury by a venire.

ven·i·son (vĕn′ ə sən, -zən) ***n-*** the flesh of a deer, used as food. *as* ***modifier***: *a* venison *stew*.

Venn diagram (vĕn) *Mathematics* ***n-*** diagram in which regions, usually circular, are used to represent relations and operations in the algebra of sets.

ven·om (vĕn′ əm) ***n-* 1** the poisonous fluid injected by the bite of some snakes or by the sting or bite of scorpions and some insects. **2** spite; ill will; malice: *Her comment had a trace of* venom. **—*adj-* ven′ om·less.**

ven·om·ous (vĕn′ əm əs) ***adj-* 1** secreting venom; also, capable of giving a poisonous bite or sting; poisonous: *a* venomous *snake*. **2** full of spite or malice: *a* venomous *tongue*. **—*adv-* ven′ om·ous·ly.** ***n-* ven′ om·ous·ness.**

ve·nous (vē′ nəs) ***adj-* 1** having to do with a blood vein. **2** of blood, bluish and poor in oxygen.

[1]**vent** (vĕnt) ***n-* 1** hole, opening, or outlet that serves as a passage for air, gas, liquid, etc.: *steam from the* vent *of a radiator*. **2** an outlet; a means of escape: *to find* vent *in tears*. ***vt-* 1** to give expression to; pour out: *He* vented *his anger on a dog*. **2** to make a small hole or opening in. **3** to allow to escape through a small opening. [partly from Old French **fente,** "[2]**vent,**" and partly from **vent,** "wind," from Latin **ventus,** "wind."]

[2]**vent** (vĕnt) ***n-*** slash or slit in a garment, especially at the back of a coat. [from Old French **fente** meaning "a hole; slit," from **fendre,** "to cleave," from Latin **findere.**]

fāte, făt, dâre, bärn; bē, bĕt, mêre; bīte, bĭt; nōte, hŏt, môre, dȯg; fŭn, fûr; to͞o, bo͝ok; oil; out; tar; thin; then; hw for wh as in *wh*at; zh for s as in u*s*ual; ə for a, e, i, o, u, as in *a*go, lin*e*n, per*i*l, at*o*m, min*u*s

ven·ti·late (vĕn′ tə lāt′) ***vt-*** [**ven·ti·lat·ed, ven·ti·lat·ing**] **1** to bring fresh air into and drive stale air out of; to air: *Open the windows and* ventilate *the room.* **2** to bring out (a subject) for public examination and discussion: *The plans for the new park were* ventilated *in the newspapers.* **3** to supply with an escape for air, gas, etc.

ven·ti·la·tion (vĕn′ tə lā′ shən) ***n-*** a ventilating; especially, the supplying and circulation of fresh air: *the* ventilation *in a room. as* ***modifier****: a* ventilation *system.*

ven·ti·la·tor (vĕn′ tə lā′ tər) ***n-*** any device for admitting, exhausting, or circulating air, such as an opening, a fan, or an air-conditioning unit.

ven·tral (vĕn′ trəl) ***adj-*** relating to, or situated on or near, the belly of an animal: *the* ventral *fins of a fish.*

ven·tri·cle (vĕn′ trĭ kəl) ***n-*** either of the two lower chambers of the heart which receive blood from the auricles and transmit it to the arteries. For picture, see *heart.*

ven·tril·o·quism (vĕn trĭl′ ə kwĭz′ əm) ***n-*** the art of producing voice sounds so that they seem to come from another person or a distance. ***—n-*** **ven·tril′ o·quist.**

ven·ture (vĕn′ chər) ***n-*** course of action or undertaking that contains some risk: *a* venture *into a wilderness*; *a mining* venture; *a new business* venture. ***vt-*** [**ven·tured, ven·tur·ing**]. **1** to hazard; dare to say or do: *She* ventured *an opinion on the candidate.* **2** to risk; stake. ***vi-*** to take a risk; dare. ***—n-*** **ven′ tur·er.**

at a venture without any particular aim or purpose; at hazard; offhand.

ven·ture·some (vĕn′ chər səm) ***adj-*** **1** willing to take risks; daring: *The* venturesome *boy was rescued from the mountain.* **2** involving risk, hazard, danger, etc.: *a* venturesome *experiment.* ***—adv-*** **ven′ ture·some·ly.** ***n-*** **ven′ ture·some·ness.**

Ven·tu·ri tube (vĕn to͝or′ ē) ***n-*** short tube having a constriction in the middle, used for measuring the rate of flow of fluids. It can be used to measure airspeed.

ven·tur·ous (vĕn′ chər əs) ***adj-*** venturesome. ***—adv-*** **ven′ tur·ous·ly.** ***n-*** **ven′ tur·ous·ness.**

ven·ue (vĕn′ yo͞o′) ***n-*** in law, the place where the alleged events occurred that caused the lawsuit; also, the place from which the jury must be drawn and where the case must be tried.

Ve·nus (vē′ nəs) ***n-*** **1** the most brilliant planet in our solar system, as seen from the earth, second in order of distance from the sun. **2** in Roman mythology, goddess of beauty and love, identified with Greek Aphrodite.

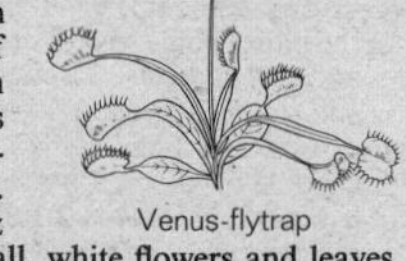

Venus-flytrap

Ve·nus's-fly·trap (vē′ nə səz flī′ trăp′) ***n-*** plant with small, white flowers and leaves tipped with bristly extensions that can close together and trap insects.

ve·ra·cious (və rā′ shəs) ***adj-*** **1** habitually telling the truth; truthful. **2** true; reliable: *a* veracious *report.* ***Hom-*** voracious. ***—adv-*** **ve·ra′ cious·ly.** ***n-*** **ve·ra′ cious·ness.**

Veranda

ve·rac·i·ty (və răs′ ə tē) ***n-*** [*pl.* **ve·rac·i·ties**] **1** truthfulness; honesty. **2** accuracy; exactness: *the* veracity *of a news report.* **3** something true; truth. ***Hom-*** voracity.

ve·ran·da or **ve·ran·dah** (və răn′ də) ***n-*** porch, especially a covered one of some length.

verb (vûrb) *Grammar* ***n-*** word which may occupy the predicate position in a sentence or be the chief word of a phrase in that position. Verbs in Enlgish are further identified by having three finite forms ("give," "gives," "gave") and three nonfinite forms preceded by "to," an auxiliary verb, or both ("to give," "has given," "to have given.")

ver·bal (vûr′ bəl) ***adj-*** **1** having to do with words; also, consisting merely of words: *The thief's penitence was only* verbal. **2** relating to or concerned with words only rather than meaning, facts, etc.: *a* verbal *exercise.* **3** spoken rather than written; oral: *a* verbal *agreement.* **4** of or having to do with a verb: *a* verbal *prefix*; *a* verbal *phrase.* **5** word for word; literal: *This is a* verbal *translation of the Latin proverb.* ***n-*** word or phrase that occupies the position of a verb. Examples:

He walks *to work every day.*
He must walk *to work every day.*
He has been walking *to work every day.*

—adv- **ver′ bal·ly.**

ver·bal·ize (vûr′ bə līz′) ***vt-*** [**ver·bal·ized, ver·bal·iz·ing**] **1** to express (something) in words: *The young boy* verbalized *his fear.* **2** to change into a verb. ***vi-*** to use many words; be verbose. ***—n-*** **ver′ bal·i·za′ tion.**

ver·ba·tim (vər bā′ təm) ***adv-*** in the same words; word for word: *He reported the speech* verbatim. ***adj-****: a* verbatim *report.*

ver·be·na (vər bē′ nə) ***n-*** any of several garden plants of spicy fragrance with flat clusters of flowers of various colors.

Verbena

ver·bi·age (vûr′ bē ĭj) ***n-*** the use of more words than necessary; wordiness.

ver·bose (vər bōs′) ***adj-*** using more words than necessary; wordy. ***—adv-*** **ver·bose′ ly.** ***n-*** **ver·bose′ ness** or **ver·bos′ i·ty** (vər bŏs′ ə tē).

verb phrase *Grammar* ***n-*** a phrase whose nucleus or chief word is a verb. Verb phrases may be finite, as in the following example: *The leader of the pack* will be given *a gold key,* or nonfinite, as in the following example: *The astronauts were the first* to be awarded *that honorary degree.*

ver·dant (vûr′ dənt) ***adj-*** **1** covered with fresh green grass or foliage; fresh; green: *a* verdant *landscape.* **2** unsophisticated: *a* verdant *lad.* ***—adv-*** **ver′ dant·ly**

ver·dict (vûr′ dĭkt) ***n-*** decision or judgment, especially one made by a jury in a court trial.

ver·di·gris (vûr′ də grēs′, -grĭs′) ***n-*** **1** greenish patina or crust that collects on the surface of copper or brass after long exposure to air. **2** green or bluish-green poisonous pigment produced by the action of acetic acid on copper.

ver·dure (vûr′ jər) ***n-*** **1** greenness or freshness, especially of grass and growing plants. **2** green vegetation; foliage. ***Hom-*** verger. ***—adj-*** **ver′ dured:** *these* verdured *hills.*

[1]**verge** (vûrj) ***n-*** **1** edge; border; brink: *on the* verge *of the woods*; *on the* verge *of starvation.* **2** rod or staff carried before a bishop, dean, etc., as a sign of authority or of office. ***vi-*** [**verged, verg·ing**] to border on; adjoin; approach (usually followed by "on"): *Her remarks* verge *on rudeness.* [from Old French, from Latin **virga,** "pliant twig; rod; hoop; border."]

[2]**verge** (vûrj) ***vi-*** [**verged, verg·ing**] to tend; incline (usually followed by "to" or "toward"): *He was a tall man,* verging *toward obesity.* [from Latin **vergere.**]

verg·er (vûr′ jər) ***n-*** **1** officer who carries a rod or a staff before a bishop, dean, canon, etc., as a sign of authority or of office. **2** *chiefly Brit.* sexton. ***Hom-*** verdure.

ver·i·fi·a·ble (vĕr′ ə fī′ ə bəl) ***adj-*** such as can be verified: *This is* verifiable *evidence.* ***—adv-*** **ver′ i·fi′ a·bly.**

ver·i·fi·ca·tion (vĕr′ ə fə kā′ shən) ***n-*** a verifying or being verified: *the* verification *of a statement.*

ver·i·fy (vĕr′ ə fī′) *vt-* [**ver·i·fied, ver·i·fy·ing**] **1** to check or test the correctness or accuracy of: *Science* verifies *its theories by experiments.* **2** to check the truth of; confirm: *to* verify *a statement.* **—*n-* ver′ i·fi′ er.**

ver·i·ly (vĕr′ ə lē) *Archaic* ***adv-*** truly; really; in fact.

ver·i·si·mil·i·tude (vĕr′ ə sə mĭl′ ə tōōd′, -tyōōd′) ***n-*** closeness or similarity to truth.

ver·i·ta·ble (vĕr′ ə tə bəl) ***adj-*** true; genuine: *a* veritable *genius.* **—*adv-* ver′ i·ta·bly. *n-* ver′ i·ta·ble·ness.**

ver·i·ty (vĕr′ ə tē) ***n-*** [*pl.* **ver·i·ties**] **1** truth and accuracy: *the* verity *of her version of the story.* **2** something true; truth; fact: *the student's search for* verities. **3** honesty.

ver·mi·cel·li (vûr′ mə chĕl′ ē, -sĕl′ ē) ***n-*** food similar to spaghetti but with thinner strands.

ver·mi·cide (vûr′ mə sīd′) ***n-*** substance that kills worms; especially, a drug for killing intestinal worms.

ver·mic·u·lite (vər mĭk′ yə līt′) ***n-*** mineral similar to mica, occurring in masses easily split into thin plates, and used in insulating materials.

ver·mi·form (vûr′ mə fòrm′, -fôrm′) ***adj-*** worm-shaped.

vermiform appendix ***n-*** appendix.

ver·mil·ion (vər mĭl′ yən) ***n-*** **1** bright-red pigment, especially one consisting of mercuric sulfide. **2** bright-red color. ***adj-***: *a* vermilion *dye.* Also **vermillion.**

ver·min (vûr′ mĭn) ***n-*** [*pl.* **ver·min**] unpleasant or harmful insects and small animals: *The house was overrun with* vermin. **—*adj-* ver′ min·ous:** *a* verminous *hovel.*

ver·mouth (vûr′ mōōth′) ***n-*** kind of alcoholic liquor made from white wine flavored with herbs.

ver·nac·u·lar (vər năk′ yə lər) ***n-*** **1** native language of a particular country, region, etc., that is used in common everyday speech. **2** fashion of speech among the people of a particular business or profession; jargon: *the* vernacular *of the stage.* ***adj-*** **1** of or relating to the language of a particular country, region, etc., that is naturally spoken by the people: *the* vernacular *speech of the Georgia Sea Islands.* **2** using the informal spoken language of a particular place; colloquial rather than literary: *a* vernacular *poet.* **3** of or relating to a common term or name rather than a scientific one.

ver·nal (vûr′ nəl) ***adj-*** **1** having to do with or appearing in the spring: *the* vernal *breezes.* **2** like the spring; hence, youthful.

vernal equinox ***n-*** **1** the point at which the center of the sun crosses the celestial equator from south to north. **2** the time at which this occurs, about March 21, when day and night are of equal length.

ver·ni·er (vûr′ nē ər) ***n-*** **1** small, auxiliary scale made to slide along a main scale, by which tenths of the smallest subdivision of the fixed scale can be read. **2** device designed to make very fine adjustments in the setting of an instrument.

[1]**ve·ron·i·ca** (və rŏn′ ĭ kə) ***n-*** speedwell. [from modern Latin used in scientific writing, and related to [2]**veronica.**]

[2]**ve·ron·i·ca** (və rŏn′ ĭ kə) ***n-*** **1** a picture of Jesus Christ's face said to have been miraculously impressed on a cloth handed to him by Saint Veronica to wipe the perspiration from his face on his way to Calvary; also, the cloth having this picture. **2** any cloth or handkerchief having a representation of Christ's face. [from the name of a Medieval Latin saint, from Late Latin **veraiconica** meaning "characterized by the true image," from **vera,** "true," and **ikon (icon),** "image."]

ver·sa·tile (vûr′ sə təl) ***adj-*** able to do many things; having many abilities: *The* versatile *actor could play any role.* **—*adv-* ver′ sa·tile·ly. *n-* ver′ sa·til′ i·ty.**

[1]**verse** (vûrs) ***n-*** **1** poetry; poem; a rhythmic composition, usually in rhyme. **2** section of a poem or song; stanza. **3** short, numbered division of a chapter of the Bible. **4** single line of poetry. *as* ***modifier***: *a* verse *drama.* [from Old English **vers,** from Latin **vertere,** "to turn."]

[2]**verse** (vûrs) ***vt-*** [**versed, vers·ing**] to familiarize (oneself) with something by study or experience: *He* versed *himself in French during his stay in France.* [from **versed,** from Latin **versatus** meaning "made at ease in; turning often or easily," from **vertere,** "to turn."]

versed in experienced or skilled in.

ver·si·fi·ca·tion (vûr′ sə fə kā′ shən) ***n-*** **1** the art or practice of composing verses. **2** poetic structure.

ver·si·fy (vûr′ sə fī′) ***vi-*** [**ver·si·fied, ver·si·fy·ing**] to make verses. ***vt-*** to express in verse; to change (prose) into verse. **—*n-* ver′ si·fi′ er.**

ver·sion (vûr′ zhən) ***n-*** **1** account or description from one point of view: *This is his* version *of the accident.* **2** a particular translation or edition (of a written work): *the King James* version *of the Bible.* **3** an adaptation (of a literary work): *a film* version *of a play.*

ver·sus (vûr′ səs) *Latin* **1** against: *Harvard* versus *Yale.* **2** as the alternative of: *democracy* versus *dictatorship.*

ver·te·bra (vûr′ tə brə) ***n-*** [*pl.* **ver·te·brae** (-brē, -brā) or **ver·te·bras**] any one of the individual bones making up the spinal column.

ver·te·bral (vûr′ tə brəl) ***adj-*** having to do with, resembling, or composed of vertebrae.

ver·te·brate (vûr′ tə brāt′, -brət) ***n-*** any of a group of animals **(Vertebrata)** having a backbone or notochord. The vertebrates comprise the fishes, amphibia, reptiles, birds, and mammals. ***adj-*** characterized by or having a spinal column: *a* vertebrate *structure.*

ver·tex (vûr′ tĕks′) ***n-*** [*pl.* **ver·ti·ces** (vûr′ tə sēz′) or **ver·tex·es**] **1** highest point; top; apex: *the* vertex *of a pyramid.* **2** in anatomy, the top of the head. **3** *Mathematics* (1) the point where the sides of an angle meet. (2) point on the axis of a parabola that is half way between the focus and fixed line.

ver·ti·cal (vûr′ tĭ kəl) ***adj-*** **1** straight up and down on a line through the center of the earth; erect: *The flagpole is* vertical. **2** of a line or plane, perpendicular to a horizontal line or plane: *a* vertical *wall.* **3** of an angle, in a plane that is perpendicular to a horizontal plane. ***n-*** a line that is perpendicular to the horizontal. **—*adv-* ver′ ti·cal·ly.**

Vertical

ver·ti·go (vûr′ tə gō′) ***n-*** [*pl.* **ver·ti·goes**] sensation of whirling or falling; dizziness.

verve (vûrv) ***n-*** enthusiasm, energy, or vigor, especially in literary or artistic work.

ver·y (vĕr′ ē) ***adv-*** **1** in a high degree; extremely: *She does* very *good work. The book was* very *dull.* **2** absolutely; truly: *This is the* very *last thing I'll do for you.* ***adj-*** [**ver·i·er, ver·i·est**] **1** identical; the same: *That is the* very *dress.* **2** mere: *The* very *thought of an accident frightens me.* **3** (intensifier only): *The* very *act is risky.* ►For usage note see TOO.

very high frequency ***n-*** in radio broadcasting, the band of frequencies (30 to 300 megacycles). *Abbr.* VHF.

ves·i·cle (vĕs′ ĭ kəl) ***n-*** any small sac or cavity resembling a bladder and filled with fluid or gas.

ve·sic·u·lar (və sĭk′ yə lər) ***adj-*** of, having to do with, or resembling a vesicle.

ves·per (vĕs′ pər) ***n-*** **1** bell that calls to vespers; also, an evening prayer service. **2 Vesper** evening star or Hesperus; especially, the planet Venus as the evening star. *as* ***modifier:*** *a* vesper *service*; vesper *hymns.*

ves·pers or **Ves·pers** (vĕs′ pərz) ***n-*** *pl.* the sixth of the canonical hours; a late-afternoon religious service.

ves·sel (vĕs′ əl) ***n-*** **1** hollow container for holding something, especially a liquid. **2** boat larger than a rowboat; ship. **3** tube or canal that transports or contains a body fluid, such as the blood or lymph. **4** tube that transports water in a plant.

vest (vĕst) ***n-*** **1** man's sleeveless jacket worn over a shirt and under a coat, reaching usually to the waist in back and below it in front; waistcoat. **2** an undershirt. ***vt-*** **1** to clothe or endow (with authority, power, or the like): *The church* vests *its bishops with certain powers.* **2** to put into the care of: *They* vest *the authority in their president.* **3** to robe or clothe. ***vi-*** **1** to rest or reside (in) or devolve (upon) some person, group, etc.: *In this country, executive power* vests *in the president.* **2** to robe oneself for a ceremony. **—*adj-*** **vest′ less.**

Ves·ta (vĕs′ tə) ***n-*** in Roman mythology, the goddess of the hearth and the hearth fire.

ves·tal (vĕs′ təl) ***adj-*** **1** of or having to do with the Roman goddess Vesta, or to the virgins who served in her temple; hence, suitable to a virgin or nun; chaste. ***n-*** **1** (also **vestal virgin**) one of the six virgin priestesses who tended the sacred fire in the temple of Vesta. **2** a virgin; also, a nun.

vest·ed (vĕs′ təd) ***adj-*** **1** dressed, especially in priestly or other ceremonial garments. **2** in law, marked by rights established by law; not subject to contingency or suspension; fixed: *his* vested *interests.*

vest·ee (vĕs tē′) ***n-*** small vest or a piece of material forming a V-shaped front, worn with a dress or jacket.

ves·ti·bule (vĕs′ tə byōōl′) ***n-*** **1** small entrance hall to a building or room. **2** enclosed platform of a railway passenger car.

ves·tige (vĕs′ tĭj) ***n-*** **1** trace, sign, or mark left of something: *Not a* vestige *of the original paint was to be seen.* **2** *Biology* a structure or organ reduced and simplified in the course of evolution from a larger and functional ancestral form, until it has lost its original function.

ves·ti·gi·al (vĕ stĭj′ ē əl) ***adj-*** having the nature of a vestige. **—*adv-*** **ves·ti·gi′ al·ly.**

vest·ment (vĕst′ mənt) ***n-*** robe; gown; garment, especially an official or ceremonial garment, or one worn by a clergyman performing religious rites.

vest-pock·et (vĕst′ pŏk′ ət) ***adj-*** suitable for or able to fit into a vest pocket; hence, small; compact.

ves·try (vĕs′ trē) ***n-*** [*pl.* **ves·tries**] **1** room in a church where the clergy put on their vestments or where such vestments and other sacred articles are kept. **2** room in a church used for Sunday school, a chapel, etc. **3** in the Anglican and Protestant Episcopal churches, a body of men who direct the affairs of a parish. **—*n-*** **ves′ try·man.**

ves·ture (vĕs′ chər) ***n-*** **1** clothing; garments. **2** a covering.

[1]**vet** (vĕt) *Informal* ***n-*** veterinarian.

[2]**vet** (vĕt) *Informal* ***n-*** veteran.

vetch (vĕch) ***n-*** any of various climbing vines related to the peas, often used as fodder.

vet·er·an (vĕt′ ər ən) ***n-*** **1** person who has done active military service: *His father is a* veteran *of both World Wars.* **2** one who is experienced from long practice and service: a veteran *of the stage.* *as* ***modifier:*** *a* veteran *society*; veteran *benefits*; veteran *troops*; *a* veteran *actor.*

Veteran's Day ***n-*** November 11, originally a holiday to celebrate the Armistice of World War I, now a holiday in honor of the veterans of the Armed Forces. Also **Armistice Day.**

vet·er·i·nar·i·an (vĕt′ ər ə nâr′ ē ən) ***n-*** doctor who treats sick or injured animals; veterinary.

vet·er·i·nar·y (vĕt′ ər ə nĕr′ ē) ***adj-*** having to do with surgical or medical care of animals: *a* veterinary *hospital.* ***n-*** [*pl.* **vet·er·i·nar·ies**] veterinarian.

ve·to (vē′ tō) ***n-*** [*pl.* **ve·toes**] **1** right or power of a president, governor, etc., to prevent or delay bills from becoming law: *the Presidential* veto. **2** power of one of the five permanent members of the United Nations Security Council to forbid a proposed action of the Security Council. **3** the exercise of such right: *The bill met with a* veto. ***vt-*** [**ve·toed, ve·to·ing**] to forbid with authority; refuse to consent to: *The governor* vetoed *a bill to make gambling legal.* **—*n-*** **ve′ to·er.**

vex (vĕks) ***vt-*** to annoy; make cross; disturb: *My friend* vexed *me by being late.* **—*adv-*** **vex′ ed·ly.**

vex·a·tion (vĕk sā′ shən) ***n-*** **1** annoyance; irritation: *The captain's face showed* vexation *at the delay.* **2** something that annoys or distresses: *That dull knife is a* vexation.

vex·a·tious (vĕk sā′ shəs) ***adj-*** causing vexation; annoying; irritating: *a* vexatious *delay.* **—*adv-*** **vex·a′ tious·ly.**

VHF or **vhf** very high frequency.

v.i. intransitive verb.

V.I. Virgin Islands.

vi·a (vī′ ə) ***prep-*** by way of: *We drove there* via *Reno.*

vi·a·ble (vī′ ə bəl) ***adj-*** **1** of a normal, newly born infant, such as can live; physically fit to live. **2** such as can grow; *a* viable *seed*; viable *plant.* **3** workable; practicable: *a* viable *plan.* **—*n-*** **vi′ a·bil′ i·ty.**

vi·a·duct (vī′ ə dŭkt′) ***n-*** long bridge of many short spans, built to carry a road or railway over a valley, marsh, etc.; also, an elevated roadway over city traffic.

vi·al (vī′ əl) ***n-*** small glass or plastic bottle, often ornamental, for perfume or medicine. ***Hom-*** viol.

vi·and (vī′ ənd) ***n-*** **1** article of food, especially meat. **2 viands** food, especially delicacies.

vi·at·i·cum (vī ăt′ ĭ kəm) ***n-*** [*pl.* **vi·at·i·ca** (-kə) or **vi·at·i·cums**] Holy Communion given to a dying person or a person in danger of death.

vi·brant (vī′ brənt) ***adj-*** **1** vibrating, as with life, energy, enthusiasm, etc.: *a* vibrant *personality.* **2** rich in sound; resonant: *Her* vibrant *soprano voice thrilled the audience.* **—*n-*** **vi′ bran·cy.** ***adv-*** **vi′ brant·ly.**

vi·bra·phone (vī′ brə fōn′) ***n-*** musical instrument that resembles the xylophone, but has electrically operated resonators that give a vibrating sound to the tone. **—*n-*** **vi′ bra·phon′ ist.**

vi·brate (vī′ brāt′) ***vi-*** [**vi·brat·ed, vi·brat·ing**] **1** to move back and forth very rapidly, often making a sound; also, to swing back and forth like a pendulum: *The windows* vibrated *with every passing truck.* **2** to thrill; be stirred: *to* vibrate *with happiness.* **3** to make a tremulous sound; quiver: *His voice* vibrated *with anger.* ***vt-*** to cause to quiver or move back and forth.

vi·bra·tion (vī brā′ shən) ***n-*** **1** *Physics* (1) periodic back-and-forth motion of an elastic solid or a fluid medium influenced by such a solid. (2) any periodic physical process such as a cyclic variation in the intensity of a magnetic field. (3) one complete oscillation. **2** any rapid back-and-forth motion, especially one that produces a sound; shaking: *the* vibration *of the loose window.* **—*adj-*** **vi·bra′ tion·less.**

vi·bra·to (vĭ brä′tō) *Music n-* [*pl.* **vi·bra·tos**] pulsating effect imparted to a tone by rapid and regular fluctuations in pitch.

vi·bra·tor (vī′brā′tər) *n-* **1** person or thing that vibrates or causes vibration. **2** electric massager. **3** in electricity, a device that converts direct current into alternating current or pulsating direct current; oscillator.

vi·bra·tor·y (vī′brə tôr′ē) *adj-* of or marked by vibration; also, able to cause, or causing, vibration.

vi·bur·num (vī bûr′nəm) *n-* any of various shrubs with simple leaves and white or pink flowers.

vic·ar (vĭk′ər) *n-* **1** person who acts in place of another, especially in church affairs. **2** in the Episcopal churches, clergyman who is the head of a chapel or division of a parish; also, a bishop's representative in charge of a church. **3** in the Roman Catholic Church, a higher ranking clergyman.

vic·ar·age (vĭk′ər ĭj) *n-* office, position, or residence of a vicar.

vi·car·i·ous (vī kâr′ē əs) *adj-* **1** representing or acting for another. **2** done or endured in place of another: *a* vicarious *punishment.* **3** felt or experienced as a result of imagined participation in the actions or emotions of another: vicarious *pleasure.* —*adv-* **vi·car′i·ous·ly.** *n-* **vi·car′i·ous·ness.**

vice (vīs) *n-* **1** bad habit or fault: *Drunkenness is a* vice. **2** wickedness; corruption. *Hom-* vise.

vice- *combining form* subordinate or substitute; deputy: a vice-*president*; vice-*principal.* [from Latin **vice-**, from **vice** meaning "in place of; by turn."]

vice admiral (vīs′ăd′mər əl) *n-* in the Navy and Coast Guard, an officer ranking above a rear admiral and below an admiral.

vice-pres·i·den·cy (vīs′prĕz′ə dən sē, -dĕn′sē) *n-* the office or position of a vice-president.

vice-pres·i·dent (vīs′prĕz′ə dənt) *n-* officer next in rank below a president, who, under certain circumstances, takes the president's place. —*adj-* **vice′pres′i·den′tial.**

vice-prin·ci·pal (vīs′prĭn′sə pəl) *n-* school official who is next in charge below a principal.

vice·re·gal (vīs′rē′gəl) *adj-* of or relating to a viceroy.

vice·roy (vīs′roi′) *n-* **1** person who rules a colony, province, or country as a representative of a king or queen. **2** butterfly with red-and-black marks and white spots.

vice·roy·al·ty (vīs′roi′əl tē) *n-* the office, position, or tenure of a viceroy.

vi·ce ver·sa (vīs′vûr′sə, vīs′ə-) *adv-* the same is true, but in the reversed order; conversely: *Emily has great respect for Victor, and* vice versa.

vi·chys·soise (vĭsh′ē swäz′, vē′shē-) *n-* soup made of puree of potatoes and cream, usually served cold.

vi·cin·i·ty (vī sĭn′ə tē) *n-* [*pl.* **vi·cin·i·ties**] surrounding area; neighborhood: *There is no park in our* vicinity.

in the vicinity of close to; near: *a village* in the vicinity of *Paris*; in the vicinity of *$5,000.*

vi·cious (vĭsh′əs) *adj-* **1** bad-tempered; unruly and dangerous: *a* vicious *dog*; *a* vicious *criminal.* **2** full of malice; spiteful: *a* vicious *retort*; vicious *gossip.* **3** corrupt; depraved; wicked: *a* vicious *life.* **4** *Informal* severe; intense. —*adv-* **vi′cious·ly.** *n-* **vi′cious·ness.**

vicious circle *n-* situation that arises when the solution to a problem causes a new problem whose solution reproduces the original problem.

vi·cis·si·tude (vĭ sĭs′ə tōōd′, -tyōōd′) *n-* (usually **vicissitudes**) unexpected change or variation: *the* vicissitudes *of war.*

vic·tim (vĭk′təm) *n-* **1** one who is injured or killed by another, by a disease, or by an act of nature: *the* victims *of an earthquake.* **2** one who is misused, cheated, or tormented by another: *the* victim *of a practical joke.*

vic·tim·ize (vĭk′tə mīz′) *vt-* [**vic·tim·ized, vic·tim·iz·ing**] to make a victim of, especially by swindling or cheating. —*n-* **vic′tim·i·za′tion.**

vic·tor (vĭk′tər) *n-* person who triumphs; winner.

vic·tor·i·a (vĭk tôr′ē ə) *n-* **1** low, four-wheeled carriage with a top that may be lowered and a high seat in front for the coachman. **2** old model touring car with a canvas top that could be raised or lowered over the back seat. **3** any of a number of South American water lilies, with huge leaves and rose-white flowers.

Vic·tor·i·an (vĭk tôr′ē ən) *adj-* **1** of or relating to Queen Victoria of England or to her reign. **2** of or characteristic of the arts, letters, standard of morality, or taste typical of that period. *n-* **1** person, especially a writer, active during Victoria's reign. **2** anyone who is prudish.

Vic·to·ri·an·ism (vĭk tôr′ē ə nĭz′əm) *n-* **1** the thought, morals, and tendencies common during the reign of Queen Victoria. **2** prudery.

vic·to·ri·ous (vĭk tôr′ē əs) *adj-* having conquered in battle or some kind of contest; triumphant. —*adv-* **vic·to′ri·ous·ly.** *n-* **vic·to′ri·ous·ness.**

vic·to·ry (vĭk′tə rē) *n-* [*pl.* **vic·to·ries**] **1** defeat of an enemy or opponent. **2** any successful achievement; triumph: *a* victory *over fear.* *as* ***modifier:*** *a* victory *celebration.*

Vic·tro·la (vĭk trō′lə) *n-* **1** trademark name of a phonograph. **2 victrola** any phonograph.

vict·uals (vĭt′əlz) *n-* food (often used humorously).

vi·cu·ña (vī kōōn′yə) *n-* **1** cud-chewing animal of the Andes, related to the alpaca and llama, and furnishing a very soft, reddish wool. **2** cloth made from this wool.

vid·e·o (vĭd′ē ō) *adj-* of or relating to the transmission or reception of images by television. *n-* television.

video disc *n-* plastic disk on which information is recorded as indentations in grooves for playback on a television set.

vid·e·o·tape (vĭd′ē ō tāp′) *n-* tape on which information can be recorded magnetically for playback on a television set. *vt-* [**vid·e·o·taped, vid·e·o·tap·ing**] to make a recording on videotape.

vie (vī) *vi-* [**vied, vy·ing**] to strive for victory or success; contend; compete: *Sue* vied *with Jim for class honors.*

view (vyōō) *n-* **1** the act of seeing; survey: *Our first* view *of the ocean was in March.* **2** scene; prospect: *The* view *from the tower is magnificent.* **3** pictorial representation. **4** range of vision: *The ship was soon beyond our* view. *The train came into* view. **5** way of regarding something; opinion; judgment: *We have different* views *on the matter.* **6** goal; aim: *He had a* view *of being a writer.* *vt-* **1** to see; look at: *to* view *paintings in an art gallery.* **2** to examine critically; form an opinion of; judge: *He* viewed *the plan from every angle.* —*adj-* **view′less.**

in view 1 within the range of vision. **2** under consideration. **3** as an aim. **in view of** in consideration of. **on view** on display for the public: *The drawings will be* on view *all week.* **with a view to** with the hope or purpose of.

view·er (vyōō′ər) *n-* **1** person who views; especially, a person who watches television. **2** any of several small optical instruments used especially in viewing photographic slides.

---

fāte, făt, dâre, bärn; bē, bĕt, mêre; bīte, bĭt; nōte, hŏt, môre, dȯg; fŭn, fûr; tōō, bŏŏk; oil; out; tar; thin; then; hw for wh as in *wh*at; zh for s as in u*s*ual; ə for a, e, i, o, u, as in *a*go, lin*e*n, per*i*l, at*o*m, min*u*s

view·point (vyōō′point′) ***n-*** way of looking at things; point of view; standpoint.

vi·ges·i·mal (vī jĕs′ ə məl) ***adj-*** **1** twentieth. **2** of or having to do with twenty. **3** progressing by twenties: *a* vigesimal *system of counting.*

vig·il (vĭj′ əl) ***n-*** **1** a keeping awake for the purpose of watching or protecting: *to keep* vigil *over a sick person.* **2 vigils** (1) religious devotions in the evening or nighttime. (2) devotional watch kept on the eve of a feast day. (3) the eve of a feast, especially an eve that is a fast.

vig·i·lance (vĭj′ ə ləns) ***n-*** watchfulness; alertness: *Through his* vigilance *we avoided a trap.*

vigilance committee ***n-*** formerly, an unauthorized and self-appointed group organized to prevent and punish crime where law enforcement is absent.

vig·i·lant (vĭj′ ə lənt) ***adj-*** watchful; alert: *a* vigilant *sentry.* **—*adv-*** **vig′ i·lant·ly.**

vig·i·lan·te (vĭj′ ə lăn′ tē) ***n-*** member of a vigilance committee.

vi·gnette (vĭn yĕt′) ***n-*** **1** brief, subtle literary description; sketch: *a* vignette *of country life.* **2** design of leaves and tendrils around a capital letter in a manuscript. **3** any ornamental design decorating a blank space, such as at the end of a chapter. **4** any picture or photograph whose background shades off gradually at the edge. ***vt-*** [**vi·gnet·ted, vi·gnet·ting**] to cause (a picture or photograph) to shade off gradually at the edge.

vig·or (vĭg′ ər) ***n-*** **1** physical or mental strength and energy; stamina; vitality. **2** force; power; intensity: *the* vigor *of his reply.* **3** active, healthy growth.

vig·or·ous (vĭg′ ər əs) ***adj-*** full of vigor; energetic or forceful: *a* vigorous *youth*; *a* vigorous *campaign.* **—*adv-*** **vig′ or·ous·ly.** ***n-*** **vig′ or·ous·ness.**

Vi·king or **vi·king** (vī′ kĭng) ***n-*** one of the Scandinavian sea rovers who terrorized the coastal towns of Europe from the 8th to the 10th centuries.

vile (vīl) ***adj-*** [**vil·er, vil·est**] **1** morally low; base: *a* vile *coward.* **2** disgusting; loathsome; foul: *a* vile *odor.* **3** wretched; unpleasant. **—*adv-*** **vile′ ly.** ***n-*** **vile′ ness.**

vil·i·fy (vĭl′ ə fī′) ***vt-*** [**vil·i·fied, vil·i·fying**] to speak evil of; slander; defame: *to* vilify *a man's good name.* **—*n-*** **vil′ i·fi′ er.** ***n-*** **vil′ i·fi·ca′ tion.**

vil·la (vĭl′ ə) ***n-*** large, often luxurious country home, found chiefly along the Mediterranean.

vil·lage (vĭl′ ĭj) ***n-*** **1** group of houses that usually is larger than a hamlet and smaller than a town. **2** the people who live in a village: *The whole* village *went to the band concert.* *as* ***modifier***: *the* village *postmaster.*

vil·lag·er (vĭl′ ə jər) ***n-*** person who lives in a village.

vil·lain (vĭl′ ən) ***n-*** **1** wicked person; scoundrel. **2** in a play or novel, the character who opposes the hero. **3** villein. ***Hom-*** villein.

vil·lain·ous (vĭl′ ən əs) ***adj-*** **1** wicked; base: *a* villainous *deed.* **2** wretched; vile: *I have a* villainous *cold.* **—*adv-*** **vil′ lain·ous·ly.** ***n-*** **vil′ lain·ous·ness.**

vil·lain·y (vĭl′ ə nē) ***n-*** [*pl.* **vil·lain·ies**] **1** wickedness. **2** wicked deed; crime: *That is only one of his* villainies.

vil·lein (vĭl′ ən, -ān′) ***n-*** under the feudal system, a serf who was bound to his lord as a slave but was legally free in his relations with other people. ***Hom-*** villain.

vil·lus (vĭl′ əs) ***n-*** [*pl.* **vil·li** (vĭl′ ī′)] **1** in anatomy, one of the short, threadlike projections on some membranes, especially the mucous membrane on the inside of the small intestine. **2** in botany, one of the straight, fine, soft hairs on the surface of fruit, flowers, etc.

vim (vĭm) ***n-*** vigor; energy; spirit.

Vincent's infection ***n-*** highly infectious bacterial disease characterized by sores in the mouth, throat, and gums; trench mouth. Also **Vincent's angina.**

vin·di·cate (vĭn′ də kāt′) ***vt-*** [**vin·di·cat·ed, vin·di·cat·ing**] **1** to clear of suspected guilt or wrongdoing; absolve: *to* vindicate *someone under arrest.* **2** to show to be true or right against opposition; uphold: *to* vindicate *an action.* **3** to justify: *His brave acts* vindicated *their faith in him.* **—*n-*** **vin′ di·ca′ tion.** ***n-*** **vin′ di·ca′ tor.**

vin·dic·tive (vĭn dĭk′ tĭv) ***adj-*** filled with a desire for revenge; spiteful and malicious: *a* vindictive *attack.* **—*adv-*** **vin·dic′ tive·ly.** ***n-*** **vin·dic′ tive·ness.**

vine (vīn) ***n-*** **1** any plant, such as ivy or honeysuckle, with a long stem that trails along the ground or climbs upward by fastening its tendrils to a support. **2** the stem of such a plant.

vin·e·gar (vĭn′ ə gər) ***n-*** sour liquid, consisting largely of acetic acid produced by the fermentation of wine, cider, etc., used to flavor or preserve food. **—*adj-*** **vin′ e·gar·y.**

vinegar eel ***n-*** minute worm commonly found in vinegar or other fermenting liquids.

vine·yard (vĭn′ yərd) ***n-*** land used for the cultivation of grapes.

vin·tage (vĭn′ tĭj) ***n-*** **1** wine made from the grapes of a particular region in a particular year. **2** group or crop of anything: *That's a play of an old* vintage. ***adj-*** **1** of high quality; choice: *a* vintage *crop.* **2** out-of-date.

vint·ner (vĭnt′ nər) ***n-*** wine merchant.

vin·y (vī′ nē) ***adj-*** [**vin·i·er, vin·i·est**] **1** of, relating to, or like vines: *a* viny *plant.* **2** covered with vines.

vi·nyl (vī′ nəl) ***n-*** a monovalent radical that is the ethylene molecule minus one atom of hydrogen. Various vinyl compounds are used in plastics, resins, and synthetic fibers. *as* ***modifier***: *a* vinyl *floor.*

Vi·nyl·ite (vī′ nə līt′) ***n-*** trademark name for a synthetic, thermoplastic substance used to make phonograph records, protective coatings, etc. Also **vinylite.**

vinyl resin or **vinyl plastic** ***n-*** any of various durable resins or plastics obtained by the polymerization of vinyl compounds.

vi·ol (vī′ əl) ***n-*** **1** any of various stringed instruments played with the bow that were used mainly in the 16th and 17th centuries, after which time they were replaced by the violin family. **2** bass viol; double bass. ***Hom-*** vial.

¹vi·o·la (vē ō′ lə) ***n-*** stringed instrument of the violin family, somewhat larger and deeper in tone than the violin. [from Italian and Spanish **viola** and **viol.**]

²vi·o·la (vī ō′ lə, vī′ ə lə) ***n-*** johnny jump-up. [from Latin **violet.**]

vi·o·late (vī′ ə lāt′) ***vt-*** [**vi·o·lat·ed, vi·o·lat·ing**] **1** to disregard; break: *to* violate *a treaty*; *to* violate *a law.* **2** to disturb: *to* violate *silence.* **3** to profane: *to* violate *a shrine.* **4** to rape. **—*n-*** **vi′ o·la′ tor.**

vi·o·la·tion (vī′ ə lā′ shən) ***n-*** **1** a breaking of a law, treaty, promise, etc.; infringement. **2** interruption or disturbance: *a* violation *of privacy.* **3** a profaning; desecration: *a* violation *of the court's dignity.* **4** rape.

vi·o·lence (vī′ ə ləns) ***n-*** **1** physical force, usually resulting in harm: *an act of* violence; *the* violence *of a storm.* **2** intensity; passion: *the* violence *of his rage.* **3** damage; outrage: *The deer did* violence *to my garden by tramping through it.*

vi·o·lent (vī′ ə lənt) ***adj-*** **1** marked by or resulting from the use of physical force: *a* violent *blow on the head*; *a* violent *death.* **2** having or showing strong feeling; passionate; intense: *his* violent *temper.* **3** extreme or severe: *a* violent *storm.* **—*adv-*** **vi′ o·lent·ly.**

Common violet

vi·o·let (vī′ ə lət) ***n-*** **1** small, low-growing spring plant with purple, yellow, or white flowers; also, the flower of this plant. **2** bluish-purple color. Violet is at the higher edge of the rainbow and has the shortest wavelength of all visible light. ***adj*-:** *a* violet *dress.*

vi·o·lin (vī′ ə lĭn′) ***n*- 1** the smallest and highest in tone of the modern four-stringed instruments played with a bow. **2** violin player in an orchestra: *the first* violin. *as* ***modifier*:** *a* violin *maker.* **—*n*- vi′ o·lin′ ist.**

vi·o·list (vē ō′ lĭst) ***n*-** person who plays the viola.

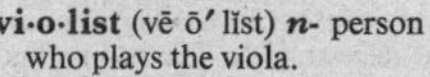

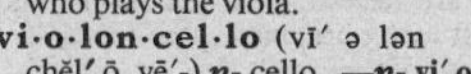

Girl playing violin

vi·o·lon·cel·lo (vī′ ə lən chĕl′ ō, vē′-) ***n*-** cello. **—*n*- vi′ o·lon·cel′ list.**

vi·os·te·rol (vī ŏs′ tə rōl′) ***n*-** See *vitamin D.*

VIP or **V.I.P.** very important person.

vi·per (vī′ pər) ***n*- 1** any of a group of Old World poisonous snakes with hollow front fangs and, usually, heavy bodies. **2** pit viper. **3** evil, treacherous person.

vi·per·ine (vī′ pə rēn′) ***n*- 1** belonging to the viper family. **2** resembling a viper in being swiftly venomous.

vi·per·ous (vī′ pər əs) ***adj*- 1** of or relating to vipers. **2** malignant; venomous; viperine. **—*adv*- vi′ per·ous·ly.**

vi·ra·go (və rä′ gō′, vĭr′ ə gō′) ***n*-** [*pl.* **vi·ra·gos, vi·ra·goes**] quarrelsome, ill-tempered woman; scold.

vi·ral (vī′ rəl) ***adj*-** of, related to, or caused by a virus.

vir·e·o (vĭr′ ē ō′) ***n*-** [*pl.* **vir·e·os**] any of a family of small, insect-eating songbirds of North America, that are olive or gray in color.

vir·gin (vûr′ jən) ***n*- 1** young girl or woman who is unmarried; also, an unmarried woman in a religious order. **2** person or animal that has not been mated. ***adj*- 1** pure; undefiled: *the* virgin *snow.* **2** untouched; unused: *a* virgin *forest.* **3** unmixed; unadulterated: *the* virgin *oil of olives.* **4** of or befitting a virgin: *a* virgin *blush.*

Vir·gin (vûr′ jĭn) or **Virgin Mary** ***n*-** the mother of Jesus. Also **the Blessed Virgin.**

vir·gin·al (vûr′ jĭ nəl) ***adj*-** of, relating to, or fitting for a virgin. ***n*-** small harpischord with no legs, popular in the 16th and 17th centuries.

Vir·gin·i·a creeper (vər jĭn′ yə) ***n*-** common North American climbing vine, with divided leaves and bluish-black berries; woodbine.

Virginia reel ***n*-** country dance in which the partners face each other in two lines and perform various steps.

Virginia creeper

vir·gin·i·ty (vər jĭn′ ə tē) ***n*-** [*pl.* **vir·gin·i·ties**] condition of being a virgin; maidenhood.

Vir·go (vûr′ gō) ***n*-** constellation thought to outline the figure of a woman.

vir·ile (vĭr′ əl) ***adj*- 1** of or like a man; masculine; forceful. **2** capable of begetting children; potent. **—*n*- vi·ril′ i·ty.**

vir·tu·al (vûr′ chōō əl) ***adj*-** real in effect or for practical purposes, but not in name or fact: *The expression on her face was a* virtual *admission of guilt.* **—*adv*- vir′ tu·al·ly.**

virtual image ***n*-** the image produced by a mirror or lens that can be seen by an observer but that cannot be projected on a screen. The erect image produced by a plane mirror is a virtual image.

vir·tue (vûr′ chōō) ***n*- 1** moral excellence; goodness; rectitude. **2** particular moral excellence: *the* virtue *of charity.* **3** excellence; merit; value. **4** effectiveness or

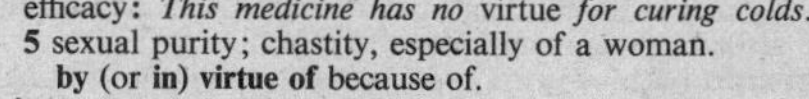

efficacy: *This medicine has no* virtue *for curing colds.* **5** sexual purity; chastity, especially of a woman.

by (or **in**) **virtue of** because of.

vir·tu·o·so (vûr′ chōō ō′ sō) ***n*-** [*pl.* **vir·to·o·sos, vir·tu·o·si** (-sē)] **1** person who is skilled in the technique of an art; especially, a person skilled in a musical art, such as playing the violin. **2** person who has a cultivated taste for, or knowledge of, artistic excellence; connoisseur. **—*n*- vir′ tu·os′ i·ty** (-ŏs′ ə tē): *his* musical *virtuosity.*

vir·tu·ous (vûr′ chōō əs) ***adj*- 1** having moral excellence. **2** chaste. **—*adv*- vir′ tu·ous·ly.** ***n*- vir′ tu·ous·ness.**

vir·u·lent (vĭr′ ə lənt, -yə lənt) ***adj*- 1** poisonous; deadly: *a* virulent *disease.* **2** extremely hostile: *a* virulent *child.* **3** malicious; intensely bitter: *his* virulent *abuse.* **—*n*- vir′ u·lence.** ***adv*- vir′ u·lent·ly.**

vi·rus (vī′ rəs) ***n*-** [*pl.* **vi·rus·es**] **1** a form of matter that is smaller than bacteria but larger than molecules, and consists of a protein coat surrounding a core of either RNA or DNA. Viruses reproduce themselves only in living cells, and cause measles, mumps, smallpox, etc. **2** anything poisonous to the mind or spirit: *the* virus *of hate.* **3** venom. *as* ***modifier*:** *a* virus *infection.*

vi·sa (vē′ zə) ***n*-** official endorsement made on a passport of one country by an authority of another country, to permit the bearer to enter the country from which the endorsement was obtained. ***vt*-** [**vi·saed, vi·sa·ing**] to mark (a passport) with a visa.

vis·age (vĭz′ ĭj) ***n*- 1** the face. **2** appearance; aspect.

vis·cer·a (vĭs′ ər ə) ***n*- *pl.*** [*sing.* **vis·cus** (vĭs′kəs)] the organs, such as the stomach, liver, and intestines, found in the large cavity of the body of an animal. **—*adj*- vis′ cer·al.** ***adv*- vis′ cer·al·ly.**

vis·cid (vĭs′ ĭd) ***adj*- 1** sticky; gluelike. **2** of certain leaves, covered with a sticky substance.

vis·cose (vĭs′ kōs′) ***n*-** substance produced by treating cellulose with caustic soda and other chemicals, and used in making rayon, cellophane, etc.

vis·cos·i·ty (vĭs kŏs′ ə tē) ***n*- 1** quality of being viscous; stickiness. **2** *Physics* property of a fluid that causes it to offer resistance to flow because of forces that hold together its molecules; the internal friction of a fluid.

vis·count (vī′ kount′) ***n*-** nobleman of a rank below an earl or count and above a baron.

vis·count·ess (vī′ koun′ təs) ***n*- 1** wife or widow of a viscount. **2** woman who has the rank of viscount.

vis·cous (vĭs′ kəs) ***adj*- 1** thick and sticky; gluelike. **2** having relatively high viscosity.

vise (vīs) ***n*-** any of various devices with two jaws that are tightened by turning a screw, used to hold objects firmly while work is being done to them. ***Hom*-** vice.

Vish·nu (vĭsh′ nōō′) ***n*-** Hindu deity, the second member of the Hindu trinity, associated with Brahma and Shiva.

Vises

vis·i·bil·i·ty (vĭz′ ə bĭl′ ə tē) ***n*- 1** the degree to which something is visible: *poor* visibility. **2** the distance at which things can be seen under given conditions: *The* visibility *from this tower is forty miles on a clear day.*

vis·i·ble (vĭz′ ə bəl) ***adj*- 1** such as can be seen: *In the fog my hand was not* visible *before my face.* **2** clear; apparent; perceptible: *He has no* visible *income.* **—*adv*- vis′ i·bly.**

Vis·i·goth (vĭz′ ə gŏth′) ***n*-** one of the western Goths, an ancient Teutonic race that overran the Roman

Empire in the fifth and sixth centuries A.D. and finally settled in Spain and southern France.

vi·sion (vĭzh′ ən) ***n-*** **1** sense of sight; ability to see: *His* vision *was affected by the heavy smoke.* **2** beautiful sight: *She was a* vision *of loveliness.* **3** foresight; imagination; broad understanding: *the* vision *of a great scientist.* **4** mental image: *her* vision *of the way the new house would look.* ***vt-*** *Archaic* to imagine; envisage.

vi·sion·ar·y (vĭzh′ ə nĕr′ ē) ***n-*** [*pl.* **vi·sion·ar·ies**] **1** person of great imagination; especially, one with impractical ideas or schemes; dreamer: *He was a poet and a* visionary. **2** person who sees visions. ***adj-*** **1** of or seen in a vision: *The* visionary *form beckoned her to follow.* **2** like a dream or vision; not practical; dreamy: *a* visionary *scheme.*

vis·it (vĭz′ ət) ***vt-*** **1** to come or go to see; pay a call on: *We* visit *our grandparents every Christmas.* **2** to stay at or in for a time: *to* visit *New York.* **3** to be a guest of: *I am* visiting *Thelma for two weeks.* **4** to afflict; come upon: *Many towns in the Middle Ages were* visited *by the plague.* ***vi-*** **1** *Informal* to converse with someone in a casual manner; chat. **2** to stay for a time: *to* visit *in New York.* ***n-*** brief call or stay: *a doctor's* visit.

visit with to go to see socially.

vis·i·tant (vĭz′ ə tənt) ***n-*** **1** visitor, especially one regarded as coming from a strange or supernatural place. **2** migratory bird that appears in an area at intervals for a time.

vis·it·a·tion (vĭz′ ə tā′ shən) ***n-*** **1** visit. **2** reward or punishment from God, especially, a severe affliction. **3 Visitation** in the New Testament, the visit of Mary to her cousin, Elizabeth, before the birth of the latter's son, John the Baptist; also, the holy day, July 2, commemorating this visit.

visiting card ***n-*** small card bearing a person's name, used when making a visit. Also **calling card.**

visiting fireman *Informal* ***n-*** visitor to a large city, who makes incidental calls on friends there.

visiting teacher ***n-*** officer of a public school system who visits the homes of students in order to instruct sick students, enforce attendance, and attempt to solve various emotional and social problems affecting a student's work.

vis·i·tor (vĭz′ ə tər) ***n-*** person who visits; guest.

vi·sor (vī′ zər) ***n-*** **1** in former times, the movable part of a helmet that protected the face. **2** the projecting portion of a cap that serves to shade the eyes; also, a projection above the windshield in a vehicle. ***—adj-*** **vi′sored:** *a* visored *helmet.* ***adj-*** **vi′sor·less.**

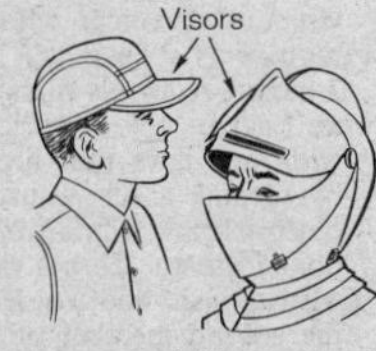

vis·ta (vĭs′ tə) ***n-*** **1** view or outlook; prospect: *a* vista *of rolling green hills.* **2** mental view of events in the past or future: *a* vista *of happiness.*

vis·u·al (vĭzh′ o͞o əl) ***adj-*** **1** of, related to, or used in sight: *The eye is a* visual *organ.* **2** perceptible by the eye or the mind; visible: *a* visual *object.* **3** produced in the mind by sight: *a* visual *impression.* ***—adv-*** **vis′u·al·ly.**

visual aid ***n-*** educational device or method that instructs by visual means, such as motion pictures or slides.

vis·u·al·ize (vĭzh′ o͞o əl īz′) ***vt-*** [**vis·u·al·ized, vis·u·al·iz·ing**] to form a mental picture of; imagine: *to* visualize *a house from sketches.* ***—n-*** **vis′u·al·i·za′tion.**

vi·tal (vī′ təl) ***adj-*** **1** of, related to, or necessary for life: *the* vital *functions*; vital *energy.* **2** full of life and energy; lively: *a* vital *youth.* **3** of great importance; essential: *Your help is* vital *if we are to get this work done.* **4** causing death or ruin; fatal: *a* vital *wound*; *to strike a* vital *blow.* **5 vitals** organs of the body essential for life, such as the heart, liver, and lungs. ***—adv-*** **vi′tal·ly.**

vi·tal·i·ty (vī tăl′ ə tē) ***n-*** [*pl.* **vi·tal·i·ties**] **1** strength; liveliness; energy. **2** ability to keep on living or existing: *the* vitality *of our nation.*

vi·tal·ize (vī′ tə līz′) ***vt-*** [**vi·tal·ized, vi·tal·iz·ing**] to fill with life or vigor. ***—n-*** **vi′tal·i·za′tion.**

vital statistics ***n-pl.*** statistics of births, deaths, and other factors concerning population increase and decrease.

vi·ta·min (vī′ tə mən) ***n-*** any of a class of complex organic compounds that are present in foods in minute quantities and which are necessary to the health and normal growth of most living organisms. ***as modifier:*** *a* vitamin *deficiency*; vitamin *pill.*

vitamin A ***n-*** any of a small group of fat-soluble vitamins made by animal cells from the carotene of plants. Vitamin A is also found in fish-liver oils and dairy products. Lack of this vitamin causes night blindness.

vitamin B ***n-*** original name for the vitamin B complex, before it was known to contain many different vitamins.

vitamin B_1 ***n-*** vitamin that is essential to the normal functioning of the nervous system; thiamine. It is found in the outer covering of various grains, in milk, in liver, and in kidneys. Lack of this vitamin causes beriberi.

vitamin B_2 ***n-*** vitamin that is essential to the normal functioning of the body cells; riboflavin. It is found in milk, meats, etc., and lack of it causes abnormalities of the skin and eyes.

vitamin B_6 ***n-*** vitamin that is important in metabolism; pyridoxine. It is found in meat and the husks of some grains. Lack of it causes dermatitis and convulsions.

vitamin B_{12} ***n-*** vitamin that is important in the synthesis of nucleic acid. It is found in liver, and lack of it causes pernicious anemia.

vitamin B complex ***n-*** group of water-soluble vitamins found together in foodstuffs such as yeast and liver. Biotin, vitamin B_1, vitamin B_2, vitamin B_6, vitamin B_{12}, nicotinic acid, and pantothenic acid are parts of the vitamin B complex.

vitamin C ***n-*** vitamin that is found in most fruits, especially citrus fruits, and vegetables; ascorbic acid. Lack of it causes scurvy.

vitamin D ***n-*** vitamin found in fish-liver oils, fish, eggs, and specially prepared milk; viosterol. Lack of it causes rickets.

vitamin E ***n-*** vitamin that prevents sterility and muscular dystrophy in experimental animals, and is found in wheat germ and leafy vegetables.

vitamin G ***n-*** vitamin B_2.

vitamin H ***n-*** biotin.

vitamin K ***n-*** any of a small group of vitamins that are vital to the clotting of blood. They are present in green, leafy vegetables and in tomatoes.

vitamin P ***n-*** group of substances, no longer considered vitamins, that help to keep the capillaries healthy.

vi·ti·ate (vĭsh′ ē āt′) ***vt-*** [**vi·ti·at·ed, vi·ti·at·ing**] **1** to make worthless; invalidate: *to* vitiate *a ballot.* **2** to impair the quality of; debase; contaminate: *The escaping gas* vitiated *the air.* ***—n-*** **vi′ti·a′tion.**

vit·re·ous (vĭ′ trē əs) ***adj-*** **1** of, like, or obtained from glass: *a* vitreous *rock.* **2** of or related to the vitreous humor.

vitreous humor ***n-*** jellylike, transparent substance that fills the space between the lens and the retina of the eye.

vit·ri·fy (vĭ′ trə fī′) ***vt-*** [**vit·ri·fied, vit·ri·fy·ing**] to change into glass or a glassy substance by the action of heat: *The nuclear explosion* vitrified *the sand.* ***vi-*** *The sand* vitrified. ***—n-*** **vit′ri·fi·ca′tion** (vĭ′ trə fə kā′ shən).

vit·ri·ol (vĭ′ trē əl) ***n-*** **1** sulfuric acid; oil of vitriol. **2** any of various sulfates of metals, such as **blue vitriol** (copper sulfate), **green vitriol** (iron sulfate), and **white vitriol** (zinc sulfate). **3** anything sharp or biting: *His sarcasm was sheer* vitriol. ***—adj-*** **vit′ ri·ol′ ic** (vĭ′trē ŏl′ ĭk).

vi·tu·per·ate (vī to͞o′ pə rāt′, vī tyo͞o′-) ***vt-*** **[vi·tu·per·at·ed, vi·tu·per·at·ing]** to heap abuse upon; berate. ***—n-*** **vi·tu′ per·a′ tion.**

vi·tu·per·a·tive (vī to͞o′ pər ə tĭv′, vī tyo͞o′-) ***adj-*** full of or given to vituperation; abusive: *his* vituperative *language.* ***—adv-*** **vi·tu′ per·a′ tive·ly.**

vi·va (vē′ və) *Italian, Portuguese, & Spanish* long live! (used as a shout of acclaim).

vi·va·cious (vĭ vā′shəs, vī-) ***adj-*** lively; gay; high-spirited. ***—adv-*** **vi·va′ cious·ly.** ***n-*** **vi·va′ cious·ness.**

vi·vac·i·ty (vĭ văs′ ə tē, vī-) ***n-*** gaiety; liveliness; high spirits; vivaciousness.

vi·var·i·um (vī vâr′ ē əm, vī vĕr′-) ***n-*** [*pl.* **vi·var·i·a** (-ə) or **vi·var·i·ums**] place, such as a zoo or aquarium, for duplicating natural habitats for live animals.

vive (vēv) *French* long live! (used as a shout of acclaim).

viv·id (vĭv′ ĭd) ***adj-*** **1** bright; intense: *a* vivid *red.* **2** lifelike; convincing: *a* vivid *description of a circus.* **3** lively; active: *a* vivid *imagination.* **4** sharp and clear; distinct: *a* vivid *recollection.* ***—adv-*** **viv′ id·ly.** ***n-*** **viv′ id·ness.**

viv·i·fy (vĭv′ ə fī′) ***vt-*** **[viv·i·fied, viv·i·fying]** **1** to fill with life; animate; liven: *Joe's records* vivified *the party.* **2** to make vivid. ***—n-*** **viv′ i·fi·ca′ tion.**

vi·vip·a·rous (vī vĭp′ ər əs, vĭ-) ***adj-*** bringing forth living young instead of eggs. All but a few mammals, and many reptiles and fishes, are viviparous. See also *oviparous, ovoviviparous.*

viv·i·sec·tion (vĭv′ ə sĕk′ shən) ***n-*** operation, dissection, or experimentation on a living animal for the purpose of scientific investigation. ***—n-*** **viv′ i·sec′ tion·ist.**

vix·en (vĭk′ sən) ***n-*** **1** female fox. **2** sharp-tempered, quarrelsome woman; shrew.

vix·en·ish (vĭk′ sə nĭsh) ***adj-*** short tempered and quarrelsome; shrewish. ***—adv-*** **vix′ en·ish·ly.**

viz. (vĭz) namely; that is [from Latin **videlicet.**]

vi·zier (vĭ zêr′) ***n-*** in various Muslim countries, a high official, especially a minister or councilor. Also **vi·zir′**.

vi·zor (vī′ zər) visor.

vo·cab·u·lar·y (vō kăb′ yə lĕr′ ē) ***n-*** [*pl.* **vo·cab·u·lar·ies**] **1** all the words in a language. **2** all the words used by a profession, group, or individual: *He had a very limited* vocabulary. **3** alphabetical list of words, often with translations or definitions; lexicon; glossary.

vocabulary entry ***n-*** **1** any word or phrase listed in a word list, glossary, vocabulary, etc. **2** in a dictionary, any word or phrase whose meaning is explained either directly by a definition, or indirectly by being listed as a derived form of a word or phrase that has a definition. In this dictionary, the vocabulary entries are in boldface.

vo·cal (vō′ kəl) ***adj-*** **1** of or having to do with the voice; oral: *the* vocal *cords.* **2** inclined to speak freely or insistently: *a loudly* vocal *person.* **3** produced by or intended for the voice: *a* vocal *protest.* ***—adv-*** **vo′ cal·ly.**

vocal cords ***n-*** two bands of tough, elastic tissue in the larynx that vibrate when air from the lungs is pushed between them, thus producing the sound of the voice.

vo·cal·ic (vō kăl′ ĭk) ***adj-*** **1** relating to vowels. **2** pronounced as a vowel. The *"r"* in this dictionary is vocalic and represents that used in several parts of the country. **3** having many vowels: *Hawaiian is a* vocalic *language.*

vo·cal·ist (vō′ kə lĭst) ***n-*** singer of popular songs.

vo·cal·ize (vō′ kə līz′) ***vt-*** **[vo·cal·ized, vo·cal·iz·ing]** **1** to utter with the voice; make vocal; utter or sing. **2** to make or change (a consonant) into a vowel: *to* vocalize *"r" at the end of a word.* ***vi-*** to produce sound with the voice; speak or sing. ***—n-*** **vo′ cal·i·za′ tion.**

vo·ca·tion (vō kā′ shən) ***n-*** **1** person's occupation, trade, or profession. **2** work that a person feels called to do.

vo·ca·tion·al (vō kā′ shən əl) ***adj-*** of, relating to, or being instructed for a vocation or occupation: *a* vocational *school.* ***—adv-*** **vo·ca′ tion·al·ly.**

vo·cif·er·ous (vō sĭf′ ər əs) ***adj-*** making a loud outcry; clamorous; noisy: *a* vociferous *audience.* ***—adv-*** **vo·cif′ er·ous·ly.** ***n-*** **vo·cif′ er·ous·ness.**

vod·ka (vŏd′ kə) ***n-*** alcoholic liquor, originally made in Russia, distilled from fermenting rye, potatoes, or corn.

vogue (vōg) ***n-*** popularity: *His play has a great* vogue *now.*
in vogue in fashion; fashionable: *Big hats are in* vogue.

voice (vois) ***n-*** **1** sound that proceeds from the mouth, especially the human mouth. **2** quality of vocal sounds: *She has a soft* voice. **3** power of producing speech: *The singer lost his* voice. **4** expression of thought, feeling, or opinion. **5** anything resembling or likened to human speech or sound: *the* voice *of the wind*; *the* voice *of conscience.* **6** right to make or help make a decision; opinion; choice: *He had no* voice *in the matter.* **7** in phonetics, the sound produced when the vocal cords vibrate, as in pronouncing most vowels and certain consonants, such as "b," "d," and "g." **8** *Grammar* form of a transitive verb or verb phrase, that shows that the subject is performing the action (active voice) or receiving the action (passive voice). ***vt-*** **[voiced, voic·ing]** to give expression to; declare: *He* voiced *his feelings.* **2** in phonetics, to produce with a vibration of the vocal cords: *You* voice "*b,*" *but do not* voice "*p.*"
in voice in proper condition for singing. **with one voice** unanimously: *They chose him* with one voice.

voice box ***n-*** larynx.

voiced (voist) ***adj-*** **1** having a voice; also, expressed by the voice: *a* voiced *protest.* **2** made entirely or partly by the vibration of the vocal cords: *All vowels in English are* voiced. *The consonant "d" is a* voiced *consonant.*

voice·less (vois′ ləs) ***adj-*** **1** having no voice; mute; silent: *his* voiceless *anger.* **2** made without vibration of the vocal cords: *"P," "t," and "k" are* voiceless *consonants.* ***—adv-*** **voice′ less·ly.**

Voice of America ***n-*** international U.S. government radio service that broadcasts programs in English and in foreign languages in order to acquaint other peoples with U.S. activities, goals, and policy.

void (void) ***adj-*** **1** in law, not having any force; not valid: *The will was declared* void *by the court.* **2** *Archaic* empty. **3** *Archaic* without effect; useless. ***n-*** **1** empty space; vacuum: *to fill a* void. **2** feeling of emptiness or loss: *His death left a* void *in our hearts.* ***vt-*** **1** in law, to cancel or annul; invalidate: *to* void *a contract.* **2** to empty; discharge. ***—adv-*** **void′ a·ble.** ***n-*** **void′ er.**
void of lacking in; devoid of: *He is* void of *humor.*

voile (voil) ***n-*** sheer fabric made of cotton, silk, wool, or synthetics, used for summer dresses or for curtains.

vol. volume.

vol·a·tile (vŏl′ ə təl) ***adj-*** **1** easy or quick to evaporate; readily turning into vapor at a relatively low temperature: *Gasoline is a* volatile *liquid.* **2** changeable; fickle; lively; lighthearted: *a* volatile *disposition.* **3** unstable; shaky; explosive: *a* volatile *political situation.* ***—n-*** **vol′ a·til′ i·ty** (-ə tĭl′ ə tē).

vol·can·ic (vŏl kăn′ ĭk) ***adj-*** **1** of, like, or produced by a volcano: *high* volcanic *peaks.* **2** violent; explosive.

vol·can·ism (vŏl′ kə nĭz′ əm) ***n-*** the phenomena of volcanoes and volcanic action. Also **vulcanism.**

vol·ca·no (vŏl kā′ nō) ***n-*** [*pl.* **vol·ca·noes** or **vol·ca·nos**] **1** an opening in the earth's crust, which is generally surrounded by a mass of ejected material forming a hill or mountain, and from which molten rock, ashes, steam are or have been expelled. **2** the hill or mountain so formed, called "active" when in eruption, "dormant" during a long cessation of activity, or "extinct" when eruptions are believed to have ceased permanently.

Alaskan volcano

vol·ca·nol·o·gy (vŏl′ kə nŏl′ ə jē) ***n-*** the scientific study of volcanoes and volcanic phenomena. ***—adj-*** **vol′ can·o·log′ i·cal** (vŏl′ kə nə lŏj′ ĭ kəl) ***n-*** **vol′ ca·nol′ o·gist.**

vole (vōl) ***n-*** any of various rodents similar to rats and mice but usually having shorter tails.

Vole

vo·li·tion (və lĭsh′ ən) ***n-*** act of willingly or freely choosing something; also, one's power of willing: *He came of his own* volition. ***—adj-*** **vo·li′ tion·al.** ***adv-*** **vo·li′ tion·al·ly.**

vol·ley (vŏl′ ē) ***n-*** [*pl.* **vol·leys**] **1** flight or discharge of many bullets or other missiles at the same time: *a* volley *of arrows.* **2** any burst of a number of things at once. **3** in tennis, a return of the ball before it touches the ground. **4** in soccer, a kick at a ball before it touches the ground. ***vi-*** [**vol·leyed, vol·ley·ing**] **1** to be discharged all at once: *Guns* volleyed *to his left.* **2** in tennis, soccer, and badminton, to return the ball or shuttlecock before it touches the ground.

vol·ley·ball (vŏl′ ē bȯl′) ***n-*** **1** game in which two teams attempt to bat a large ball back and forth across a high net with their hands without letting the ball touch the ground. **2** the ball used in this game.

volt (vōlt) ***n-*** unit for measuring the force that causes electrons to move in an electric circuit. One volt causes one coulomb of electricity per second to flow through a circuit with a resistance of one ohm.

volt·age (vōl′ tĭj) ***n-*** the value of an electromotive force, measured in volts.

voltage divider ***n-*** in electronics, a resistor having several terminals, each of which delivers a different fraction of the original voltage.

vol·ta·ic cell (vōl tā′ ĭk) ***n-*** an electrical device that consists of two electrodes of different materials immersed in an electrolyte, and generates a current by chemical action.

volt·me·ter (vōlt′ mē′ tər) ***n-*** instrument for measuring the voltage between two points in an electrical circuit.

vol·u·ble (vŏl′ yə bəl) ***adj-*** speaking with an easy flow of words; talkative; fluent; glib: *a* voluble *speaker.* ***—n-*** **vol′ u·bil′ i·ty.** ***adv-*** **vol′ u·bly.**

vol·ume (vŏl′ yəm) ***n-*** **1** a book. **2** one of a set of books making up a single work: *an encyclopedia of 20* volumes. **3** all of the periodic issues of a newspaper or magazine that come out during a year, and are often bound into a book. **4** the amount of space occupied by a body in three dimensions, as measured by cubic units: *the* volume *of water in a tank.* **5** amount; quantity: *a large* volume *of business*; *a small* volume *of sales.* **6** loudness: *to adjust the* volume *of the radio.* **7** the quality of a sound of low or medium pitch that makes it seem to fill space.

speak volumes to be full of meaning or significance.

vol·u·met·ric (vŏl′ yə mĕ′ trĭk) ***adj-*** of or relating to measurement by volume.

vo·lu·mi·nous (və lo͞o′ mə nəs) ***adj-*** large in quantity, bulk, or output: *a* voluminous *flow of water.* ***—adv-*** **vo·lu′ mi·nous·ly.** ***n-*** **vo·lu′ mi·nous·ness.**

vol·un·tar·y (vŏl′ ən tĕr′ ē) ***adj-*** **1** done or made of one's own free choice, without force or compulsion: *a* voluntary *confession.* **2** acting of one's own free choice, and often without payment: *a* voluntary *worker.* **3** in law, done intentionally; not accidental. **4** controlled by the will: *Some arm muscles are* voluntary. ***n-*** [*pl.* **vol·un·tar·ies**] *Music* improvised organ solo played before, during, or after church service. ***—adv-*** **vol′ un·tar′ i·ly.**

vol·un·teer (vŏl′ ən têr′) ***n-*** person who offers to do something, or enters into a service, especially one of the armed services, of his own free will: *The sergeant called for* volunteers *for the dangerous patrol.* *as* ***modifier***: *a* volunteer *regiment*; *a* volunteer *nurse.* ***vt-*** to offer of one's own accord: *He* volunteered *the information.* ***vi-***: *He* volunteered *for a dangerous mission.*

vo·lup·tu·ar·y (və lŭp′ cho͞o ĕr′ ē) ***n-*** [*pl.* **vo·lup·tu·ar·ies**] person who is devoted to luxury and sensuous pleasures. ***adj-***: *their* voluptuary *tastes.*

vo·lup·tu·ous (və lŭp′ cho͞o əs) ***adj-*** **1** of, related to, or giving sensual pleasure; sensuous: *a* voluptuous *joy.* **2** beautiful and shapely in form: *a* voluptuous *woman.* ***—adv-*** **vo·lup′ tu·ous·ly.** ***n-*** **vo·lup′ tu·ous·ness.**

vo·lute (və lo͞ot′) ***n-*** **1** in architecture, a spiral, scroll-shaped ornament, especially one found on the Ionic capital. **2** any of various mollusks with a whorled shell, which are found chiefly in tropical waters and prized for their beauty. **3** single turn of a spiral shell. ***adj-*** shaped like a spiral shell; rolled up: *a* volute *spring.*

vom·it (vŏm′ ĭt) ***vi-*** **1** to discharge the contents of the stomach through the mouth; throw up. **2** to be discharged with violence: *Lava* vomited *out.* ***vt-***: *He* vomited *his food.* ***n-*** matter thrown up by the stomach.

voo·doo (vo͞o′ do͞o) ***n-*** form of religious worship mixed with sorcery, of West African origin, but now practiced chiefly in Haiti. **2** person who worships or practices voodoo. **3** charm or fetish used in voodoo. *as* ***modifier***: *a* voodoo *witch-doctor.* ***vt-*** to cast a spell on.

voo·doo·ism (vo͞o′ do͞o ĭz′ əm) ***n-*** the beliefs and practices of voodoo. ***—adj-*** **voo′ doo·is′ tic.**

vo·ra·cious (vôr ā′ shəs, və rā′ -) ***adj-*** **1** greedy in eating; craving huge amounts of food; ravenous: *a* voracious *animal*; *a* voracious *appetite.* **2** eager in some pursuit; devouring; insatiable: *a* voracious *reader.* ***Hom-*** veracious. ***—adv-*** **vo·ra′ cious·ly.** ***n-*** **vo·ra′ cious·ness.**

vo·rac·i·ty (vôr ăs′ ə tē, və răs′-) ***n-*** **1** greediness in eating. **2** eagerness. ***Hom-*** veracity.

vor·tex (vȯr′ tĕks, vôr′ -) ***n-*** [*pl.* **vor·tex·es** or **vor·ti·ces** (-tə sēz′)] **1** mass of gas or liquid with a rotary motion tending to suck bodies caught in it into a depression or vacuum at the center; eddy; whirlpool. **2** any violent situation or activity that seems to swallow up everything exposed to it: *the* vortex *of war.*

vor·ti·cel·la (vȯr′ tə sĕl′ ə, vôr′ -) ***n-*** [*pl.* **vor·ti·cel·lae** (-sĕl′ ē) or **vor·ti·cel·las**] goblet-shaped, one-celled animal having a circle of cilia at the top and an elastic stem by which it attaches itself to other objects.

vo·ta·ry (vō′ tə rē) ***n-*** [*pl.* **vo·ta·ries**] **1** person bound by a vow or promise to some service: *A nun is a* votary *of the church.* **2** person devoted to any pursuit: *a* votary *of music.* Also **vo′ ta·rist.** ***—n-*** *fem.* **vo′ ta·ress.**

vote (vōt) ***n-*** **1** formal expression of the choice, judgment, or wish of a person or group: *Our President is elected by the* vote *of the people.* **2** the right to express such choice: *Women were given the* vote *shortly after World*

War I. **3** the entire number of such expression, usually classified by preference: *The* vote *was 500 to 495.* **4** the expressed preferences of a particular group taken as a whole: *the farm* vote. ***vt-*** **[vot·ed, vot·ing] 1** to cast a ballot for (a particular party): *He* voted *Republican.* **2** to declare, authorize, or establish by ballot: *to* vote *funds.* **3** to declare by consent: *We* voted *it a failure.* ***vi-*** to cast a ballot: *I* voted *for you.*

vote down to defeat in an election.

vote in to elect.

vot·er (vō′ tər) ***n-*** person who votes or has a legal right to vote in an election.

voting machine ***n-*** machine for recording and counting votes cast in an election.

vo·tive (vō′ tĭv) ***adj-*** given, offered, or performed in consecration or fulfillment of a vow: *a* votive *sacrifice.* ***—adj-*** **vo′ tive·ly.**

vouch (vouch) ***vt-*** to guarantee.

vouch for 1 to be a witness for. **2** to be responsible for; answer for: *I will* vouch for *his attendance.*

vouch·er (vou′ chər) ***n-* 1** receipt for payment. **2** (also **voucher check**) check that bears on its face or stub the items covered by it.

vouch·safe (vouch′ sāf′) ***vt-*** **[vouch·safed, vouch·saf·ing]** to be kind or gracious enough to give or grant; deign: *to* vouchsafe *someone a reply*; *to* vouchsafe *an opinion.*

vow (vou) ***n-*** solemn promise or pledge: *a* vow *of secrecy; their marriage* vows. ***vt-*** to promise or assert solemnly; swear: *to* vow *secrecy.* ***vi-***: *He* vowed *to be faithful.*

take vows to enter a religious order.

vow·el (vou′ əl) ***n-* 1** voiced speech sound that is made without contact of the tongue or lips and allows the expelled air to pass freely out of the mouth without audible friction. **2** letter representing this sound, such as "a," "e," "i," "o," "u." *as* ***modifier***: *a* vowel *sound.*

vox po·pu·li (vŏks pŏp′ yə lī′) *Latin* the voice of the people.

voy·age (voi′ ĭj) ***n-*** journey, especially by ship and usually to a distant place: *a* voyage *to the Philippine Islands*; *a* voyage *up the Amazon.* ***vi-*** **[voy·aged, voy·ag·ing]**: to take a journey by sea. ***—n-*** **voy′ ag·er.**

voy·ag·eur (vwä′ yä zhûr′) ***n-*** formerly in Canada, an employee of a fur company who furnished transportation for men and goods to and from remote places.

V.P. or **VP** vice-president.

vs. versus.

Vt. Vermont.

v.t. verb transitive.

Vul·can (vŭl′ kən, vo͝ol′-) ***n-*** in Roman mythology, god of fire and metalworking, a son of Jupiter and Juno.

vul·can·ism (vŭl′ kə nĭz′ əm, vo͝ol′-) volcanism.

vul·can·ite (vŭl′ kə nīt′, vo͝ol′-) ***n-*** ebonite.

vul·can·ize (vŭl′ kə nīz′, vo͝ol′-) ***vt-*** **[vul·can·ized, vul·can·iz·ing]** to toughen (rubber) by treatment with sulfur or other chemicals under heat and pressure. ***—n-*** **vul′ can·i·za′ tion.** ***n-*** **vul′ can·iz′ er.**

vul·ca·nol·o·gy (vŭl′ kə nŏl′ ə jē, vo͝ol′-) volcanology.

Vulg. Vulgate.

vul·gar (vŭl′ gər, vo͝ol′-) ***adj-* 1** showing bad taste; crude; coarse: *a* vulgar *person*; *a* vulgar *joke.* **2** of the common people: *the* vulgar *tongue.* ***—adv-*** **vul′ gar·ly.**

vul·gar·i·an (vəl gâr′ ē ən) ***n-*** vulgar person.

vul·gar·ism (vŭl′ gə rĭz′ əm, vo͝ol′-) ***n-* 1** word or expression used chiefly by uneducated persons, and not considered part of the formal or informal standard vocabulary. **2** vulgarity.

vul·gar·i·ty (vəl găr′ ə tē, -gĕr′ ə tē) ***n-*** [*pl.* **vul·gar·i·ties**] behavior or speech showing a lack of refinement, delicacy, or good taste.

vul·gar·ize (vŭl′ gə rīz′, vo͝ol′-) ***vt-*** **[vul·gar·ized, vul·gar·iz·ing] 1** to make coarse, cheap, or low. **2** to make (a difficult and specialized study, book, etc.) easy and simple enough for general understanding: *This author skillfully* vulgarizes *nuclear physics.* ***—n-*** **vul′ gar·iz·er.**

vul·gar·i·za·tion (vŭl′ gə rə zā′ shən, vo͝ol′-) ***n-* 1** a vulgarizing: *the* vulgarization *of manners*; *the* vulgarization *of a philosophical treatise.* **2** something vulgarized.

Vul·gate (vŭl′ gāt′, vo͝ol′-) ***n-* 1** the authorized Latin version of the Bible used in the Roman Catholic Church. **2 vulgate** (1) the common or accepted version of any writing. (2) the ordinary language of the masses, partly made up of slang and vulgarisms; vernacular.

vul·ner·a·ble (vŭl′ nər ə bəl, vo͝ol′-) ***adj-* 1** open to or not safe against attack and ruin; not invincible: *a* vulnerable *outpost*; *a* vulnerable *reputation.* **2** such as can easily be wounded or hurt: *His feelings are very* vulnerable. ***—n-*** **vul′ ner·a·bil′ i·ty.** ***adv-*** **vul′ ner·a·bly.**

vulnerable to easily hurt or conquered by; open to: *He is* vulnerable to *ridicule.*

vul·pine (vŭl′ pīn′, vo͝ol′-) ***adj-* 1** of or relating to a fox or foxes. **2** crafty; cunning; sly; foxy.

Vulture (California condor), about 4 ft. long

vul·ture (vŭl′ chər, vo͝ol′-) ***n-* 1** any of various large, bald-headed birds of prey, related to the hawks and eagles, that feed chiefly on dead and decaying flesh. **2** grasping and merciless person who profits from misfortunes and disasters of other persons.

vul·va (vŭl′ və, vo͝ol′-) ***n-*** the external parts of the female sex organs.

vy·ing (vī′ ĭng) *pres. p.* of **vie.**

W

W, w (dŭb′ əl yo͞o′) ***n-*** [*pl.* **W's, w's**] the 23rd letter of the English alphabet.

W symbol for tungsten.

W or **w 1** watt; watts. **2** west; western.

w. 1 width; wide. **2** week. **3** with. **4** weight. **5** west; western. **6** *Physics* work.

W. 1 Wednesday. **2** Wales; Welsh. **3** west; western.

wab·ble (wŏb′ əl) wobble. ***—adj-*** **wab′ bly.**

WAC or **W.A.C.** (wăk) Women's Army Corps.

wack·y (wăk′ ē) *Slang* ***adj-*** **[wack·i·er, wack·i·est]** slightly insane in an amusing way. ***—adv-*** **wack′ i·ly.** ***n-*** **wack′ i·ness.**

wad (wŏd) ***n-* 1** tight mass of soft material, especially one squeezed into an opening. **2** *Slang* fat roll of paper money; also, a large amount of money. ***vt-*** **[wad·ded, wad·ding] 1** to pack or squeeze into a tight mass: *to* wad *a cloth.* **2** to plug with such a mass: *to* wad *one's ears with cotton.*

wad·ding (wŏd′ ĭng) ***n-*** a wad; also, material used as a wad.

wad·dle (wŏd′ əl) ***vi-*** **[wad·dled, wad·dling]** to walk with short, clumsy steps in a rocking and swaying motion from side to side: *The duck* waddled *back to the pond.* ***n-*** clumsy, rocking gait. **—*n-* wad′ dler.**

wade (wād) ***vi-*** **[wad·ed, wad·ing] 1** to walk through something that hinders one's progress; especially, to walk through or walk about in water: *The man* waded *to the middle of the stream.* **2** to proceed slowly and with difficulty: *to* wade *through a tedious lesson.* ***vt-*** to cross by walking through water, mud, etc.: *to* wade *a stream.*

wade into to go at (something) with vigor.

wad·er (wā′ dər) ***n-*** **1** person who wades. **2** any long-legged bird, such as the sandpiper, snipe, crane, or heron, that wades in shallow water while hunting for food. **3 waders** (1) waterproof boots reaching to the hips. (2) pair of pants having such boots as legs and used chiefly by fishermen.

wa·di (wŏ′ dē) ***n-*** in North Africa and southwestern Asia, a dry valley or ravine that becomes a river or stream during the rainy season; also, the stream itself.

WAF or **W.A.F.** (wăf) Women in the Air Force.

wa·fer (wā′ fər) ***n-*** **1** very thin biscuit or cake. **2** small, round piece of unleavened bread used in the communion service in certain churches. **3** small colored disk of sticky paper or dried paste used for sealing documents, letters, etc. ***vt-*** to seal or hold together with such a disk.

waf·fle (wŏf′ əl) ***n-*** flat, crisp, batter cake having a pattern of square-shaped impressions made by the **waffle iron** in which it is baked.

waft (wăft, wäft) ***vt-*** to carry lightly through the air or over the water: *The breeze* wafted *the scent of roses in from the garden.* ***vi-***: *A scent of roses* wafted *through the window.* ***n-*** a gust or puff, as of wind: *a* waft *of smoke; a* waft *of cooking smells.*

[1]**wag** (wăg) ***vt-*** **[wagged, wag·ging]** to swing or turn repeatedly from side to side, up and down, or forwards and backwards: *The dog* wagged *his tail.* ***vi-***: *The dog's tail* wagged. *Her tongue* wagged *in gossip all over town.* ***n-***: *the* wag *of a dog's tail.* [from Old Norse **vagga.**]

[2]**wag** (wăg) ***n-*** person fond of making jokes; a wit. [shortened form of earlier **wag-halter** meaning "person who deserves hanging."]

wage (wāj) ***vt-*** **[waged, wag·ing]** to engage in; carry on: *to* wage *a war; to* wage *a campaign against mosquitoes.* ***n-*** (also **wages**) payment made or received for work or services: *a weekly* wage; *summer* wages *earned by students. as* ***modifier***: *new* wage *demands by a labor union.* **—*adj-* wage′ less**: *The unemployed are* wageless.

wage earner ***n-*** person employed for a salary or wages.

wa·ger (wā′ jər) ***n-*** a bet: *He made a* wager *at the race track.* ***vt-*** to bet: *He* wagered *ten dollars.* ***vi-*** to make bets; gamble: *He promised not to* wager. **—*n-* wa′ ger·er.**

wage scale ***n-*** set of wage levels, arranged according to the type of work, the seniority of the worker, etc.

wag·ger·y (wăg′ ə rē) ***n-*** [*pl.* **wag·ger·ies**] **1** joking, especially practical joking. **2** merrymaking, especially of a humorous or mischievous kind: *The children's* waggery *amused their parents.* **3** a joke or jest; quip.

wag·gish (wăg′ ĭsh) ***adj-*** **1** fond of playing jokes; mischievous. **2** lightly humorous or jesting; roguish: *a* waggish *remark.* **—*adv-* wag′ gish·ly.** ***n-*** **wag′ gish·ness.**

wag·gle (wăg′ əl) ***vt-*** **[wag·gled, wag·gling]** to wag in short, quick jerks; wiggle: *The teacher* waggled *her finger at the noisy class.* ***vi-***: *His tongue* waggles *day and night.* ***n-***: *I noticed a* waggle *of the dog's tail.*

wag·on (wăg′ ən) ***n-*** **1** four-wheeled vehicle that is drawn by a horse and used to carry loads. **2** light motor truck for house-to-house delivery: *a milk* wagon; *a bread* wagon. **3** hand cart for indoor use: *a tea* wagon. **4** (also **express wagon**) child's four-wheeled toy cart. Also, *Brit.,* **wag′ gon.** *as* ***modifier***: *a* wagon *wheel.*

Wagon

on the wagon (or **water wagon**) no longer drinking alcoholic beverages.

wag·on·er (wăg′ ən ər) ***n-*** person who drives a wagon or carries goods in a wagon.

wagon train ***n-*** line of wagons, especially those driven by early American settlers through undeveloped regions.

waif (wāf) ***n-*** homeless wanderer; lost person or animal, especially a lost child.

wail (wāl) ***vi-*** **1** to cry or moan in grief or pain: *The sick child* wailed *all day.* **2** to make a mournful sound: *The wind* wailed *in the pine branches.* ***n-*** a sound of pain or misery. ***Hom-*** wale. **—*n-* wail′ er.**

wain (wān) *Archaic* ***n-*** open wagon with four wheels, used to carry heavy loads. ***Hom-*** wane.

wain·scot (wān′ skət, -skōt′) ***n-*** in carpentry, the wooden lining, often paneled, of the lower part of an interior wall. ***vt-*** to apply such a lining to.

wain·scot·ing (wāns′ kō′ tĭng, kŏt′ ĭng) ***n-*** material used for a wainscot; also, a wainscot. Also **wain′ scot′ ting.**

waist (wāst) ***n-*** **1** the part of the body between the ribs and the hips. **2** part of an object which is narrower than the rest of it: *the* waist *of a violin.* **3** section of a ship between the forecastle and the quarterdeck. **4** midsection of an airplane. ***Hom-*** waste.

waist·band (wāst′ bănd′) ***n-*** band that is part of a skirt or pair of trousers and encircles the waist.

waist·coat (wĕs′ kət, wāst′ kōt′) *chiefly Brit.* ***n-*** a man's vest.

waist·line (wāst′ līn′) ***n-*** **1** the line of the waist between the ribs and the hips. **2** the part of a piece of clothing which falls at the waist, or above or below it, as the fashion changes: *This year* waistlines *are higher.*

wait (wāt) ***vi-*** to pass the time until some expected event, arrival, etc. (often followed by "for"): *We* waited *for the train. I can't* wait. ***vt-*** **1** to refrain from taking or doing before the proper time: *They* waited *their turn.* **2** to pass the time watchfully until: *I* waited *my chance.* **3** *Informal* to delay: *She* waited *supper for us.* ***n-*** length of time one passes until some expected event, arrival, etc.: *a long* wait *for morning.* ***Hom-*** weight.

lie in wait to remain in hiding in order to attack.

wait on (or **upon**) **1** to serve (people) in a shop, restaurant, etc.: *Marcel* waited on *us.* **2** to call on formally: *The duke* waited on *the king.*

wait table to serve people in a restaurant or dining room.

►If you mean WAIT FOR, meaning to await, don't use WAIT ON, which means to serve: *We* waited for *the waiter to* wait on *us.*

wait·er (wā′ tər) ***n-*** **1** man who serves food or drinks to people at a table or counter. **2** person who waits. **3** a serving tray for dishes.

wait·ing (wā′ tĭng) ***n-*** the skill and work of a restaurant waiter.

in waiting in attendance: *a lady* in waiting *at court.*

waiting game ***n-*** watchful refusal to act or move before one's opponent does or before the time is right.

waiting list ***n-*** list of persons waiting for some chance, admission, privilege, etc., usually in the order that they applied: *a* waiting list *for the new apartments.*

waiting room ***n-*** a room for those who are waiting.

wait·ress (wā′ trəs) ***n-*** woman who serves food or drinks to people at a table or counter.

waive (wāv) ***vt-*** **[waived, waiv·ing] 1** to give up a claim to; refrain from pressing; relinquish: *to* waive *a jury.* **2** to postpone; put aside: *to* waive *a question.* ***Hom-*** wave.

waiv·er (wā′ vər) ***n-*** **1** the voluntary giving up of a right, especially a legal right. **2** a document affirming this act.

[1]**wake** (wāk) ***vi-*** **[woke** (wōk) or **waked, waked, wak·ing] 1** to stop sleeping: *I* wake *at seven o'clock.* **2** to become alert or awake: *They* woke *to their danger.* ***vt-*** to cause (a sleeper) to stop sleeping; rouse: *Don't* wake *the dog.* ***n-*** vigil; especially, a watch over a dead body before burial. [from Middle English **waken** and **wakien,** partly from Old English **wacan** meaning "to arise," and partly from **wacian,** "to wake (someone) up to watch."]

[2]**wake** (wāk) ***n-*** track left behind a moving ship. [probably from Old Norse **vok** meaning "an opening in the ice."]
in the wake of following close behind; after.

wake·ful (wāk′fəl) ***adj-*** **1** unable to sleep; free from sleep: *The baby spent a* wakeful *night.* **2** alert; keen; watchful. ***—adv-*** **wake′ful·ly.** ***n-*** **wake′ful·ness.**

wak·en (wā′ kən) ***vi-*** to wake: *He* wakened *to the smell of coffee.* ***vt-***: *The noise* wakened *Kathy.*

wake-rob·in (wāk′ rŏb′ ən) ***n-*** any of a group of related plants, including jack-in-the-pulpit and trillium.

wale (wāl) ***n-*** **1** rib which forms part of a series of ribs in the texture of a fabric: *This corduroy has four* wales *to the inch.* **2** a ridge or mark produced on flesh by flogging; weal; welt. **3** one of several extra-heavy planks formerly used at intervals in the sides of a wooden ship. **4** a timber fastened to a row of piles to hold them in position. **5** in basketry, a protecting or strengthening ridge made of interwoven rods. ***vt-*** **[waled, wal·ing] 1** to mark with a ridge or welt. **2** to secure or protect with a heavy plank or timber. ***Hom-*** wail.

walk (wòk) ***vi-*** **1** to go on foot at a moderate pace: *It is better to* walk *across the street than run.* **2** to ramble or take a stroll for exercise or pleasure: *I like to* walk *in the park.* **3** to live in a regular manner; to behave: *He* walked *justly all his days.* **4** in baseball, to move to first base because four balls have been pitched. **5** to move or creep: *The vibration made the fan* walk *off the edge of the table.* ***vt-*** **1** to go over on foot: *I've* walked *this path before.* **2** to accompany (a person or animal) on foot: *Please* walk *the visitor to the gate. He* walked *the dog before bedtime.* **3** to cause (a horse, etc.) to go at the slowest gait: *to* walk *a horse uphill.* **4** in baseball, to allow (a batter) to go to first base by pitching four balls. ***n-*** **1** a going somewhere on foot; a stroll: *a pleasant* walk *through the woods.* **2** distance which may be covered on foot: *It is a long* walk *to the store.* **3** path along which people may go on foot. **4** manner of walking: *He had a* walk *like a duck.* **5** in baseball, the putting of a batter on first base by the pitching of four balls.
walk into to get into a certain situation, bad or good, without expecting or being aware of it.
walk off with to win easily and by a good margin.
walk out 1 to go on strike: *The electricians* walked out. **2** to depart or quit as a strong sign of disagreement.
walk out on to desert: *His partner* walked out on *him.*
walk over to defeat easily: *Our team* walked over *theirs.*
walk the plank to be put to death by being forced to walk off a plank into the sea while tied up.
walk through to practice or rehearse a dance, football play, etc., at less than the actual rate of speed.

walk·a·way (wòk′ ə wā′) ***n-*** contest that is easily won.

walk·er (wò′ kər) ***n-*** **1** person who walks. **2** wheeled frame which carries the weight of a person learning to walk. **3** shoe suitable for wearing on long walks.

walk·ie-talk·ie (wò′ kē tò′ kē) ***n-*** a sending and receiving radio which is light enough to be carried by one person; especially, a military set carried on the back.

walk-in (wòk′ ĭn′) ***adj-*** large enough to be entered, or so laid out as to be walked into directly: *a* walk-in *closet.* ***n-*** **1** cold-storage room that can be walked into. **2** an election victory that is easily won.

walk of life ***n-*** **1** profession or occupation. **2** social position or class.

walking stick ***n-*** **1** cane or stick that may be leaned on when walking. **2** any of a group of wingless insects whose long bodies resemble twigs.

walk-on (wòk′ ŏn′, -òn′) ***n-*** very minor role in a play; also, the actor or actress having such a role.

walk·out (wòk′ out′) ***n-*** **1** labor strike. **2** departure or desertion intended as a strong sign of disagreement.

walk·o·ver (wòk′ ō′ vər) **1** any easy and decisive victory. **2** in horse racing, the action of a lone horse going around the track and being called the winner of a race.

walk-up (wòk′ ŭp′) ***n-*** **1** apartment, room, or office in a building without an elevator. **2** the building itself.

wall (wòl) ***n-*** **1** solid, upright structure that encloses an area, separates one space from another, or supports a roof or ceiling. **2** side; lining: *the* wall *of the stomach.* **3** anything that acts as a barrier: *a* wall *of silence.* ***vt-*** to build a solid, upright structure or barrier around.
drive (or **push) to the wall** to put in a desperate situation; be about to defeat or destroy. **go to the wall** to be ruined or destroyed, or nearly so.

wal·la·by (wŏl′ ə bē) ***n-*** [*pl.* **wal·la·bies**] any of several kinds of pouched mammals of Australia and nearby islands, related to the kangaroos but generally smaller.

wall·board (wòl′ bôrd′) ***n-*** a building material made of wood pulp, plastic, gypsum, etc., formed in sheets and used instead of plaster or wood for interior walls.

wal·let (wŏl′ ət) ***n-*** small, flat, folding case, usually made of leather, to hold money and papers.

wall·eye (wòl′ ī′) ***n-*** **1** an outward turning eye. **2** eye that shows more white than is normal. **3** large, fiercely staring eye. **4** (also **wall′eyed′ pike**) fresh-water game fish of northern North America, related to the perches. ***—adj-*** **wall′eyed′.** ***n-*** **wall′eyed′ness.**

wall·flow·er (wòl′ flou′ ər) ***n-*** **1** *Informal* at a dance, a person, especially a woman or girl, who sits at the side of the room for lack of a partner. **2** plant of the mustard family with sweet yellow, orange, or red flowers.

Wal·loon (wŏ lo͞on′) ***n-*** **1** Belgian whose language is French. **2** the French language of such Belgians.

wal·lop (wŏl′ əp) *Informal* ***vt-*** **1** to hit hard; beat; thrash: *The boxer* walloped *his opponent on the head.* **2** to defeat thoroughly: *Our team* walloped *the other side.* ***n-*** a very hard blow.

wal·lop·ing (wŏl′ əp ĭng) *Informal* ***adj-*** tremendous; whopping: *a* walloping *bill for the repairs.* ***adv-***: *a* walloping *big whale.*

wal·low (wŏl′ ō) ***vi-*** **1** to roll around in something: *Pigs* wallow *in mud.* **2** to live and revel in: *She* wallows *in luxury.* ***n-*** **1** a rolling around: *The elephants had a good* wallow *in the mud.* **2** place where animals habitually roll around in mud, dust, etc.

wall·pa·per (wòl′ pā′ pər) ***n-*** paper used to decorate the inside walls of houses. ***vt-***: *She* wallpapered *her room.*

---

fāte, făt, dâre, bärn; bē, bĕt, mêre; bīte, bĭt; nōte, hŏt, môre, dòg; fŭn, fûr; to͞o, bo͝ok; oil; out; tar; thin; then; hw for wh as in *wh*at; zh for s as in u*s*ual; ə for a, e, i, o, u, as in *a*go, lin*e*n, per*i*l, at*o*m, min*u*s

Wall Street ***n-*** **1** street in downtown New York that is the site of banks, stock exchanges, and other financial institutions. **2** U.S. banking and finance in general.

wal·nut (wôl′ nŭt′) ***n-*** **1** any of the hard-shelled, edible nuts of a widespread group of trees; especially, the black walnut and the **English walnut,** which has a pale beige shell and is native to the Middle East but is grown in Europe and North America. **2** any of the trees bearing these nuts. **3** the wood of several of these trees, valued for furniture and other fine woodwork. **4** reddish-brown color. ***adj-***: *a* walnut *flavor*; *a* walnut *table*; walnut *dye*.

Walrus, about 10 1/2 ft. long

wal·rus (wôl′ rəs, wŏl′-) ***n-*** [*pl.* **wal·rus** or **wal·rus·es**] large ocean mammal of arctic regions, related to the seals. Walruses are valued for their blubber, oil, hides, and the ivory of their long tusks.

waltz (wôlts) ***n-*** **1** gliding and whirling dance for a couple. **2** music for this dance, having three beats to the measure with the first beat accented. ***vi-*** **1** to dance this dance. **2** to move confidently and sweepingly: *She* waltzed *into the room like a queen.* **—*n-*** **waltz′ er.**

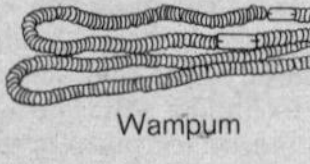

Wampum

wam·pum (wŏm′ pəm) ***n-*** **1** strands, belts, and sashes made of polished shells, and formerly used by American Indians as money. **2** *Slang* money. [American word from Algonquian.]

wan (wŏn) ***adj-*** [**wan·ner, wan·nest**] **1** pale; pallid: *The sick child's face was drawn and* wan. **2** weak; sickly: *a* wan *smile.* **—*adv-*** **wan′ ly.** ***n-*** **wan′ ness.**

wand (wŏnd) ***n-*** **1** a slender rod: *a magician's* wand; *an orchestra leader's* wand. **2** rod which indicates the rank or status of the bearer: *the* wand *of office.*

wan·der (wŏn′ dər) ***vi-*** **1** to roam without a particular purpose. **2** to get lost; stray: *The child had* wandered *from camp.* **3** to ramble in speech or thought: *The speaker began to* wander *from the subject.* **4** to meander or proceed in an irregular course: *The river* wandered *through a meadow.* **5** to move from place to place at random or aimlessly: *His hands* wandered *over the piano keys.* **—*n-*** **wan′ der·er.**

wan·der·lust (wŏn′ dər lŭst′) ***n-*** strong impulse or craving to wander.

wane (wān) ***vi-*** [**waned, wan·ing**] **1** to become smaller or less; decrease: *The moon* wanes *after it is full.* **2** to decline; weaken. ***n-*** **1** a decreasing. **2** time from the full moon to the new moon. ***Hom-*** wain.

on the wane decreasing in size, amount, strength, etc.

wan·gle (wăng′ gəl) *Informal* ***vt-*** [**wan·gled, wan·gling**] to get by tricky and indirect methods: *He* wangled *an appointment with the mayor.* ***vi-*** to use tricky and indirect methods in getting and arranging things.

want (wŏnt, wônt) ***vt-*** **1** to wish for or desire: *All I* want *is a little quiet!* **2** to need; require: *This soup* wants *a little salt.* **3** to be without; lack: *My friend sings well, but she* wants *confidence.* ***vi-*** to be in poverty. ***n-*** **1** state or condition of being without; lack; scarcity: *There is a* want *of scholarship in this region.* **2** state or condition of being without necessities; hence, poverty: *a family in* want. **3** thing needed or greatly desired; a necessity: *My* wants *are few.* ***Hom-*** wont.

want for to lack; be in need of: *I* want for *nothing.*

want ad ***n-*** small advertisement that offers things for sale or rent, describes a job that is open, etc.

want·ing (wŏn′ tĭng, wôn′ tĭng) ***adj-*** **1** lacking; missing; absent: *Directions for assembling this toy are* wanting. **2** deficient; inadequate: *He was* wanting *in ability.*

wan·ton (wŏn′ tən) ***adj-*** **1** not limited or checked by concern for what is right; utterly thoughtless; immoderate: *his* wanton *cruelty.* **2** having or showing loose morals. ***n-*** an immoral person, especially a woman. **—*adj-*** **wan′ ton·ly.** ***n-*** **wan′ ton·ness.**

wap·i·ti (wŏp′ ə tē) ***n-*** [*pl.* **wa·pi·tis** or **wa·pi·ti**] large North American deer related to the European red deer; elk.

war (wôr) ***n-*** **1** armed combat between definite and usually large groups, such as the armies of nations, the warriors of tribes, rebel troops and loyal troops within a nation, etc. **2** any organized struggle on a large scale: *a* war *on poverty.* **3** science and practice of organized combat, strategy, tactics, etc.: *an expert in* war. ***as modifier***: *a* war *loan*; war *conditions.* ***vi-*** [**warred, war·ring**]: *The two tribes* warred *for years.*

at war in a condition of organized combat: *a nation* at war. **go to war** to enter into organized combat.

War between the States ***n-*** term preferred in the former Confederate States for the U.S. Civil War.

war·ble (wôr′ bəl) ***vi-*** [**war·bled, war·bling**] **1** to trill; sing with trills: *The canary* warbled *in the window.* **2** to make such a trilling or melodious sound: *The brook* warbled *as it crossed the rocks.* ***vt-*** **1** to sing (a song), especially with trills: *Alice* warbled *a song.* **2** to sound in such a manner: *The saxophones* warbled *the melody.* ***n-*** any trilling sound; especially, the call of certain birds.

war·bler (wôr′ blər) ***n-*** **1** person or bird that warbles. **2** any of a large group of European songbirds related to the thrushes. **3** (also **wood warbler**) any of a large group of small and often brightly colored American songbirds.

war bonnet ***n-*** feathered ceremonial headdress of certain North American Plains Indians.

war cry ***n-*** **1** customary words or sounds shouted in battle to rally and incite warriors. **2** slogan of a political party in an election campaign.

ward (wôrd) ***n-*** **1** section of a hospital containing a number of beds, and often devoted to the treatment of a special disease, condition, or group: *a children's* ward; *a surgical* ward. **2** one of the sections into which some cities are divided for purposes of government. **3** person under the care of a guardian: *The orphan was a* ward *of the court.* **4** the act of guarding: *to keep watch and* ward. **5** projection or ridge in a lock to block any but the proper key; also, the notch made in the key to correspond with this. **6** division of a prison.

ward off to turn aside; avert: *to* ward off *danger.*

-ward or **-wards** *suffix* in the direction of; toward: *east*ward; *home*wards.

ward·en (wôr′ dən) ***n-*** **1** the governing officer of a prison. **2** officer empowered to enforce certain laws: *a game* warden; *an air-raid* warden.

ward·er (wôr′ dər) ***n-*** watchman; guard.

ward heel·er (hē′ lər) *Slang* ***n-*** flunky of a local political boss.

ward·robe (wôr′ drōb′) ***n-*** **1** all of one's clothes. **2** closet or cabinet in which clothing is kept.

ward·room (wôrd′ rōōm′) ***n-*** **1** commissioned officers' dining and recreation room on a warship. **2** a warship's officers, collectively.

ware (wâr) ***n-*** **1** kind of article manufactured for sale: *porcelain and other fine* ware; *glass*ware; *silver*ware. **2 wares** articles for sale. ***Homs-*** wear, where.

ware·house (wâr′ hous′) ***n-*** building where goods are stored, especially by a manufacturer or a wholesale seller; storehouse. ***vt-*** (*also* wâr′ houz′) [**ware·housed,**

ware·hous·ing] to store (goods) in such a building. **—*n-* ware′ house′ man.**

war·fare (wòr′ fâr′) ***n-*** the waging of war; especially, fighting between armed forces.

war hawk ***n-*** warmonger; especially, an American of about 1812 who demanded war with Great Britain.

war·head (wòr′ hĕd′) ***n-*** front part of a guided missile or torpedo, containing the explosive charge.

war·horse (wòr′ hòrs′, -hôrs′) ***n-*** **1** horse used in battle; charger. **2** *Informal* person who is deeply experienced and very dependable; veteran.

war·i·ly (wâr′ ə lē) ***adv-*** in a very cautious manner.

war·i·ness (wâr′ ē nəs) ***n-*** caution; distrust; suspicion.

war·like (wòr′ līk′) ***adj-*** **1** fond of fighting; quick to fight: *a* warlike *people.* **2** hostile; threatening war: *The chief sent a* warlike *challenge to the neighboring tribe.* **3** of or relating to war; military.

war·lock (wòr′ lŏk′) ***n-*** sorcerer; wizard.

war·lord (wòr′ lòrd′, -lôrd′) ***n-*** powerful military chief who rules a region despotically.

warm (wòrm) ***adj-*** **[warm·er, warm·est] 1** having or giving off a moderate degree of heat; more hot than cold: *Hawaii has a* warm *climate. I drink* warm *milk at bedtime.* **2** keeping the heat in: *a* warm *blanket.* **3** affectionate; enthusiastic: *a* warm *greeting.* **4** excited; heated; brisk: *The debate aroused* warm *interest.* **5** of colors, suggesting warmth, as red, orange, or yellow: *Her dress was a* warm *shade of brown.* **6** *Informal* near something being looked for or guessed at: *That's not it, but you're* warm. ***vt-*** **1** to make slightly hot (often followed by "up"): *Mother* warmed *the milk.* **2** to make eager, excited, friendly, etc.: *The thought of seeing the family again* warmed *my heart.* ***vi-*** **1** to become slightly hot: *The rolls* warmed *in the oven.* **2** to become friendly or approving (to or toward) some person or thing. **—*adv-* warm′ ly. *n-* warm′ ness.**

warm up 1 to run a gasoline engine or other device until it is at operating temperature. **2** to exercise or practice briefly before entering a game, contest, etc.: *The new pitcher is* warming up. **3** to make or become more friendly, interested, etc.

warm-blood·ed (wòrm′ blŭd′ əd) ***adj-*** **1** having warm blood and a steady body temperature not depending greatly on the temperature of the environment: *Mammals are* warm-blooded. **2** very affectionate or excitable.

warm·er (wòr′ mər) ***n-*** appliance or container used for warming something.

warm front ***n-*** the forward edge of an advancing mass of warm air.

warm-heart·ed (wòrm′ här′ təd) ***adj-*** **1** affectionate; friendly; kind. **2** ardent; eager; enthusiastic. **—*n-* warm′ -heart′ ed·ness.**

warming pan ***n-*** large, long-handled, covered pan for holding live coals, formerly used to warm beds by passing it between the sheets.

war·mon·ger (wòr′ mŏng′ gər, -mŭng′ ər) ***n-*** person or group which favors or tries to provoke war; war hawk.

warmth (wòrmth) ***n-*** condition of being warm.

warm-up (wòrm′ ŭp′) ***n-*** **1** act of practicing or exercising to get one's body, voice, etc., ready for activity or performance. **2** act of running an engine or other device up to operating temperature. **3** act of entertaining and relaxing a studio audience before a television program. *as* ***modifier:*** *a few* warm-up *pitches.*

warn (wòrn) ***vt-*** **1** to put on guard against danger or evil; alert; caution: *The Coast Guard* warned *all ships of the hurricane.* **2** to give advance notice; to inform. **3** to admonish; counsel; advise: *I* warned *you not to swim out that far.* **4** to notify; signal: *Her look* warned *us it was time to leave.* **—*n-* warn′ er. *adv-* warn′ ing·ly.**

war·ning (wòr′ nĭng) ***n-*** **1** notice of danger or unpleasantness: *He had plenty of* warning. **2** act or thing that gives such notice: *This letter is a* warning.

War of 1812 ***n-*** the war between the United States and Great Britain from 1812 to 1815.

War of Independence ***n-*** the American Revolution.

warp (wòrp) ***n-*** **1** the lengthwise threads of a woven cloth through which woof threads are woven. **2** bend; twist: *Dampness gave the board a bad* warp. **3** mental twist: *Worry had given his mind a strange* warp. **4** heavy rope or cable used for hauling ships to or from a dock or mooring. ***vt-*** **1** to twist or bend: *The hot sun had* warped *the shingles.* **2** to twist mentally: *Bias* warped *the man's thinking.* **3** to haul (a ship) to or from a dock or mooring. ***vi-*** to become twisted or bent: *The planks* warped.

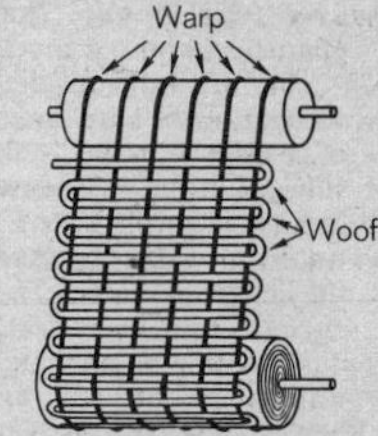

war paint ***n-*** **1** paint applied to the face and body by American Indians as a ceremonial decoration before going to war. **2** *Slang* a woman's makeup.

war·path (wòr′ păth′) ***n-*** route taken by American Indians on a warlike expedition.

on the warpath 1 at war or ready for war. **2** angry; ready for a fight.

war·plane (wòr′ plān′) ***n-*** airplane designed for military use, especially for combat.

war·rant (wŏr′ ənt, wòr′-) ***n-*** **1** official paper or writ that gives authority to do something, especially, to make an arrest or to search or seize property; legal authorization. **2** that which gives a right; justification: *What* warrant *have you to say such a thing?* **3** certificate of appointment issued to a warrant officer. ***vt-*** **1** to justify; give sufficient grounds for: *The crime* warranted *a severe punishment.* **2** to guarantee; promise: *The manufacturer* warranted *the product as genuine.* **3** to authorize; empower, especially legally. **4** to state with confidence: *I* warrant *that he will come.*

war·rant·a·ble (wŏr′ ən tə bəl, wòr′-) ***adj-*** such as can be warranted: *a* warrantable *product.* **—*n-* war′ rant·a·ble·ness. *adv-* war′ rant·a·bly.**

warrant officer ***n-*** in the Army, Air Force, Navy, Marine Corps, and Coast Guard, an officer who ranks between the highest noncommissioned officer and the lowest commissioned officer, and whose authority is granted by a warrant.

war·ran·tor (wŏr′ ən tər′, wòr′-) ***n-*** in law, person who gives or makes a warranty to another.

war·ran·ty (wŏr′ ən tē, wòr′-) ***n-*** [*pl.* **war·ran·ties**] **1** a guarantee. **2** authorization; warrant.

war·ren (wŏr′ ən, wòr′-) ***n-*** **1** a place in which small animals, especially rabbits, breed or are numerous. **2** game enclosure for small animals. **3** slum.

war·ri·or (wòr′ ē ər) ***n-*** man experienced in fighting; soldier.

war·ship (wòr′ shĭp′) ***n-*** ship built and armed for war.

wart (wòrt) ***n-*** a small, usually hard lump on the skin or on a plant, caused by a virus infection.

wart hog *n-* wild hog of Africa, with two pairs of warty growths on the face, and large tusks.

Wart hog

war·time (wŏr′tīm′) *n-* a time or period when a war is taking place. *as* ***modifier***: *a* wartime *precaution.*

war·ty (wŏr′ tē) *adj-* **[wart·i·er, wart·i·est]** having or resembling warts.

war whoop *n-* American Indian battle cry.

war·y (wâr′ ē) *adj-* **[war·i·er, war·i·est] 1** on one's guard; cautious. **2** marked by caution; guarded.

wary of suspicious of: *He is always* wary of *flattery.*

was (wəz, *when unstressed*; wŏz, wŭz, *when stressed*) form of **be** used with "he," "she," and "it," and singular noun subjects in the past tense.

wash (wŏsh, wŏsh) *vt-* **1** to clean with a liquid, usually water: *to* wash *the dishes.* **2** to push or carry away by the action of water: *The flood* washed *the bridge downstream.* **3** to make wet; cover with water; flow over. **4** in painting or drawing, to cover with a thin coating of watercolor, ink, etc. *vi-* **1** to clean oneself, especially one's hands, with soap and water: *to* wash *before dinner.* **2** to clean clothes, linens, etc., in water: *She* washes *on Monday.* **3** to be removed by cleaning, as with water: *That stain will* wash *out easily.* **4** to undergo cleaning by water without damage: *This sweater* washes *beautifully.* **5** to swirl and splash: *The waves* washed *at the cliff.* *n-* **1** clothes, bed linen, etc., that are being laundered, will be laundered, or have been laundered: *I'll hang out the* wash. **2** a cleaning with a liquid, especially with soap and water. **3** the motion, action, and sound of moving water: *the* wash *of waves on the beach.* **4** disturbed water left by a passing ship; also, the turbulent flow of air behind the propellers of an airplane. **5** liquid used for rinsing: *a mouth*wash. **6** in painting and drawing, a thin coating of watercolor, ink, etc.

wash down 1 to clean thoroughly from top to bottom. **2** to follow (food, a meal, etc.) by a drink.

wash (one's) hands of to refuse to take responsibility for; refuse to be involved in: *I* wash my hands of *it.*

wash out 1 to clean the inside of. **2** *Informal* to fail, or cause to fail, a course and be dropped. **3** of water, to destroy or carry away (a bridge, road, etc.).

wash up 1 to clean oneself, especially the face and hands. **2** *Slang* to ruin (a person, plan, etc.). **3** *Brit.* to clean the dishes after a meal.

Wash. Washington (the State).

wash·a·ble (wŏsh′ ə bəl, wŏsh′-) *adj-* such as can be washed without damage. **—*n-* wash′ a·bil′ i·ty.**

wash·ba·sin (wŏsh′ bā′ sən, wŏsh′-) *n-* bathroom fixture with faucets and drain, used for washing hands and face, shaving, etc.

wash·board (wŏsh′ bôrd′, wŏsh′-) *n-* frame holding a ridged surface on which clothes are rubbed while being washed.

wash·bowl (wŏsh′ bōl′, wŏsh′-) *n-* bowl or basin for use in washing one's hands and face, etc.

wash·cloth (wŏsh′ clŏth′, wŏsh′-) *n-* small cloth used in washing the face or body; washrag.

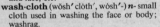

Washboard

wash·day (wŏsh′ dā′, wŏsh′-) *n-* day on which it is customary to do laundry: *Monday is my* washday.

washed out (wŏsht′ out′, wŏsht′-) *adj-* **1** of color, faded. **2** exhausted; drained of energy and vitality.

washed-up (wŏsht′ ŭp′, wŏsht′-) *adj-* **1** *Slang* finished; through; no longer popular, successful, etc. **2** *Informal* tired; ready to give up.

wash·er (wŏsh′ ər, wŏsh′-) *n-* **1** person who washes something: *window* washer; *a car* washer. **2** washing machine. **3** disk of metal, leather, fiber, or rubber used to give a larger bearing surface to a nut or bolt, lock a nut or bolt in place, or make a watertight closure.

METAL FAUCET

Washers

wash·er·wom·an (wŏsh′ ər wo͝om′ ən, wŏsh′-) *n-* [*pl.* **wash·er·wom·en**] woman who works as a laundress.

wash·ing (wŏsh′ ĭng, wŏsh′-) *n-* **1** clothes washed or to be washed. **2** thin coating: *a* washing *of brown ink.*

washing machine *n-* household machine that washes, rinses, and partially dries laundry.

washing soda *n-* sodium carbonate, used in washing as a water softener and bleach.

wash·out (wŏsh′ out′, wŏsh′-) *n-* **1** the carrying away of a road, a bridge, earth, rocks, etc., by rushing water. **2** place where this has happened. **3** *Slang* a failure.

wash·rag (wŏsh′ răg′, wŏsh′-) *n-* washcloth.

wash·room (wŏsh′ ro͞om′, wŏsh′-) *n-* lavatory.

wash·stand (wŏsh′ stănd′, wŏsh′-) *n-* **1** a stand holding a basin for washing hands and face. **2** washbasin.

wash·tub (wŏsh′ tŭb′, wŏsh′-) *n-* tub for washing clothes, often fitted with water faucets and a drain.

wash·wom·an (wŏsh′ wo͝om′ ən, wŏsh′-) washerwoman.

was·n't (wŏz′ ənt, wŭz′-) was not.

wasp (wŏsp, wŏsp) *n-* any of a large group of insects related to the ants and bees, having slender waists, venomous stings, and a wide range of living and nesting habits. The most familiar type is a social insect that builds a papery nest out of chewed-up wood and leaves.

Mud wasp, about 1 in. long

wasp·ish (wŏs′ pĭsh, wŏs′-) *adj-* acting like an angry wasp or having a disposition like one; snappish; peevish; irritable. **—*adv-* wasp′ ish·ly. *n-* wasp′ ish·ness.**

wasp waist *n-* a very slender waist, like that of a wasp.

was·sail (wŏs′ əl) *n-* **1** in early English times, an expression of good will uttered on a solemn or festive occasion when drinking a health. **2** the liquor, especially a spiced ale, in which healths were drunk on such occasions. **3** festive celebration; drinking bout. *vi-* to take part in such merrymaking; carouse.

was·sail·er (wŏs′ ə lər) *n-* person who takes part in a wassail; merrymaker.

wast (wŏst) *Archaic* form of **be** used with "thou" in the past tense.

wast·age (wās′ tĭj) *n-* **1** a wasting or wasting away. **2** something lost through this.

waste (wāst) *vt-* **[was·ted, was·ting] 1** to squander; use without profit: *My brother* wastes *his allowance.* **2** to destroy; spoil; ruin: *The forest fire* wasted *many acres of timber.* **3** to wear away (a person's body, energy, vitality, etc.): *The disease* wasted *him for months. Worry* wasted *his spirits and strength.* *vi-* **1** to lose vigor, substance, or strength gradually: *She* wasted *day by day as the disease progressed.* **2** to become less little by little: *Our supplies slowly* wasted. **3** of time, to pass. *n-* **1** neglectful and profitless use or expenditure; wastage. **2** discarded materials; refuse; something left over: *Factory* waste *pollutes our rivers.* **3** wilderness; desert: *Nothing grows in these desolate* wastes. **4** a wearing down gradually; slow decay, especially when caused by disease. *as* ***modifier***: *a program of* waste *control*; waste *space*; *a* waste *container.* ***Hom-*** waist. **—*n-* wast′ er.**

go to waste to be unused; be thrown away in spite of

being valuable: *His training* went to waste. **lay waste** to turn into a desolate wilderness; destroy; ruin; ravage.

waste·bas·ket (wāst′ bās′ kət) *n-* basket or box for wastepaper or other discarded material.

waste·ful (wāst′ fəl) *adj-* using or spending more than necessary; extravagant: *He is* wasteful *with his parents' money.* —*adv-* **waste′ ful·ly.** *n-* **waste′ ful·ness.**

waste·land (wāst′ lănd′, -lənd) *n-* desolate, unproductive region; desert.

waste·pa·per (wāst′ pā′ pər) *n-* paper thrown away.

waste pipe *n-* pipe which drains off waste material.

wast·rel (wās′ trəl) *n-* person who wastes goods, money, etc., that others provide or earn; lazy spendthrift.

watch (wŏch, wȯch) *vi-* **1** to look carefully; be attentive; be on the lookout: *If you* watch, *you may see how I do this trick.* **2** to be or keep awake; be on vigil: *to* watch *at night at the bedside of a sick person.* **3** to keep guard. *vt-* **1** to tend; guard: *The shepherd* watches *his flock.* **2** to keep in sight; observe; look at: *to* watch *a parade.* **3** to wait for expectantly: *Please,* watch *your turn.* *n-* **1** wakefulness for the purpose of guarding or protecting; vigil. **2** close observation or a being attentive: *If you keep careful* watch, *you may see a falling star.* **3** person or group on guard: *The* watch *reported a ship on the horizon.* **4** the time a guard is on duty; also, any one of the periods into which a day is divided and during which a given part of a ship's crew is on duty. **5** timepiece worn on the wrist or carried in the pocket. *as modifier*: *a* watch *hand*; *a* watch *chain*; *a* watch *fire*.

on the watch on the lookout.

watch for to look in order to see; wait for.

watch out to be alert or careful.

watch·band (wŏch′ bănd′, wȯch′-) *n-* strap or bracelet for a wristwatch.

watch·dog (wŏch′ dȯg′, wȯch′-) *n-* **1** dog kept or trained to guard property. **2** person or organization acting as a guardian against loss, theft, inefficiency, etc.

watch·er (wŏch′ ər, wȯ′ chər) *n-* person who watches.

watch fire *n-* fire kept burning as a signal or for the use of a guard or watcher.

watch·ful (wŏch′ fəl, wȯch′-) *adj-* wide-awake; vigilant; on the watch. —*adv-* **watch′ ful·ly.** *n-* **watch′ ful·ness.**

watch·mak·er (wŏch′ mā′ kər) *n-* person who makes or repairs watches. —*n-* **watch′ mak′ ing.**

watch·man (wŏch′ mən, wȯch′-) *n-* [*pl.* **watch·men**] person whose duty it is to watch and guard; especially, a person hired to guard property at night.

watch·tow·er (wŏch′ tou′ ər, wȯch′-) *n-* tower from which a guard or sentinel keeps watch.

watch·word (wŏch′ wûrd′, wȯch′-) *n-* **1** a rallying cry; slogan: *The* watchword *is Liberty.* **2** password.

wa·ter (wȯ′ tər, wŏt′ ər) *n-* **1** colorless, tasteless, odorless liquid compound of hydrogen and oxygen (H_2O) that freezes at 32 degrees F. or 0 degrees C. and boils at 212 degrees F. or 100 degrees C. under standard pressure. **2** lake, river, ocean, or other body of this liquid: *We crossed the* water *by ferry.* **3** any liquid containing or resembling water: *soda* water; *toilet* water. **4** kind of wavy, shiny pattern given to some fabrics or metals. *as modifier*: *a* water *pipe*; water *sports.* *vt-* **1** to moisten, sprinkle, or cover with water: *to* water *the lawn.* **2** to provide with a supply of water: *to* water *an oil tanker.* **3** to irrigate: *The Columbia River* waters *a large valley.* **4** to give drinking water to (an animal): *to* water *horses.* **5** to dilute with water: *to* water *wine.* **6** in finance, to issue (shares of stock) without a corresponding increase in assets. **7** to give a shiny, wavy pattern to: *to* water *silk.* *vi-* **1** to secrete tears: *His eyes* watered *in the smog.* **2** to salivate. **3** of animals, to drink water: *The elephants* water *at the river.* —*n-* **wa′ ter·er.** *adj-* **wa′ ter·less.**

above water out of trouble. **by water** by ship: *to travel* by water. **hold water** **1** to be true, valid, and logical: *Your theory doesn't* hold water. **2** to stop or steady a small boat by holding the oars or paddles steady in the water. **in hot water** in trouble: *He's* in hot water *with his parents.* **keep (one's) head above water** to stay in control of a situation. **of the first water** of the first class.

water bag *n-* **1** bag for holding water. **2** the second stomach of a camel or a related animal.

water beetle *n-* any of several fresh-water beetles with fringed legs for swimming.

water bird *n-* bird that swims in or lives near water.

water blister *n-* blister filled with lymph.

wa·ter-borne (wȯ′ tər bôrn′, wŏt′ ər-) *adj-* **1** floating on water. **2** carried by water; transported by ship.

wa·ter·buck (wȯ′ tər bŭk′, wŏt′ ər-) *n-* [*pl.* **wa·ter·buck** or **wa·ter·bucks**] either of two large African antelopes, found near water.

water buffalo *n-* common, wide-horned buffalo of Asia, often domesticated for its milk and used as a draft animal; water ox; carabao.

water bug *n-* **1** Croton bug. **2** any of various bugs that propel themselves through the water with their legs.

water chestnut *n-* **1** water plant with an edible nutlike fruit. **2** the fruit of this plant.

water closet *n-* toilet; bathroom.

water color *n-* **1** paint that is mixed with water instead of oil. **2** painting done with this kind of paint or pigment. **3** art of painting with water colors. *as modifier* **(water-color)**: *a* water-color *portrait.*

water cooler *n-* device that cools and dispenses water.

wa·ter·course (wȯ′ tər kôrs′, wŏt′ ər-) *n-* **1** stream of water, such as a brook or river. **2** channel for water.

wa·ter·craft (wȯ′ tər krăft′, wŏt′ ər-) *n-* [*pl.* **wa·ter·craft**] any boat or ship; also, ships or boats collectively.

wa·ter·cress (wȯ′ tər krĕs′, wŏt′ ər-) *n-* green water plant of the mustard family with crisp leaves, used in salads.

water cure *n-* **1** the treatment of diseases by use of water, either as baths or internally. **2** *Informal* method of torturing by forcing water down someone's throat.

water cycle *n-* the continuous process by which water moves from the earth to the atmosphere by evaporation and then returns to the earth by precipitation.

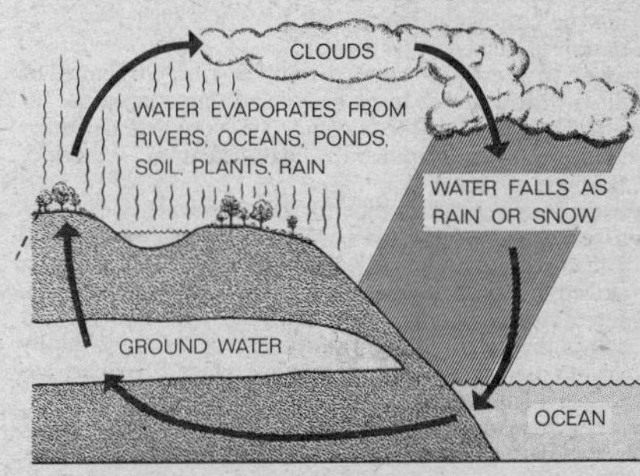

Water cycle

fāte, făt, dâre, bärn; bē, bĕt, mêre; bīte, bĭt; nōte, hŏt, môre, dȯg; fŭn, fûr; to͞o, bo͝ok; oil; out; tar; thin; then; hw for wh as in *wh*at; zh for s as in u*s*ual; ə for a, e, i, o, u, as in *a*go, lin*e*n, per*i*l, at*o*m, min*us*

wa·ter·fall (wȯ′ tər fȯl′, wŏt′ ər-) ***n-*** stream of water falling over a cliff or ledge; cataract; cascade.
water flea ***n-*** daphnia.
wa·ter·fowl (wȯ′ tər foul′, wŏt′ ər-) ***n-*** [*pl.* **wa·ter·fowl**] **1** bird that lives on or near water; especially, a swimming game bird. **2** such birds collectively.
wa·ter·front (wȯ′ tər frŭnt′, wŏt′ ər-) ***n-*** **1** real property bounded by or overlooking a natural body of water. **2** the part of a town that fronts on a body of water; especially, the wharf section of a port. *as* ***modifier***: *a* waterfront *café.*
water gap ***n-*** gorge or ravine in a mountain, through which a stream runs.
water gas ***n-*** poisonous, flammable mixture of hydrogen and carbon monoxide, produced by forcing steam through hot coke, and used for heating and giving light.
water glass ***n-*** **1** glass for holding drinking water. **2** water solution of sodium silicate (Na_2SiO_3), used chiefly as a fireproofing material and for preserving eggs. **3** tube or box with a glass bottom, used for observing objects under water.
water hammer ***n-*** **1** the concussion caused by the sudden stoppage of water flowing through a pipe; also, the sound of such a concussion. **2** hammering sound caused by live steam entering a radiator filled with water.
water hole ***n-*** place where water collects, as in a hollow or dry river bed, especially one where animals drink.
water hyacinth ***n-*** floating water plant of tropical America, with bluish-violet or white flowers. It often impedes navigation and clogs pipes.
watering place ***n-*** **1** place for getting water. **2** *chiefly Brit.* fashionable pleasure resort, noted either for mineral springs or for bathing beaches.
water jacket ***n-*** casing filled with flowing water that surrounds and cools a mechanism.
water level ***n-*** **1** height of the surface of any body of still water. **2** ship's water line.
water lily ***n-*** **1** any of various related water plants having round, flat, floating leaves and a fragrant, beautiful flower. **2** flower of this plant.

Water lily

water line ***n-*** **1** any of several lines or watermarks on the sides of a vessel, which show the water level at various weights of load. **2** line marking, or corresponding to, a past or predicted water level.
wa·ter·logged (wȯ′ tər lŏgd′, wŏt′ ər-) ***adj-*** so soaked or filled with water as to be heavy and unmanageable.
wa·ter·loo (wȯ′ tər lo͞o′, wŏt′ ər-) ***n-*** complete defeat or failure. [from Napoleon's final defeat at Waterloo, Belgium in 1815.]
water main ***n-*** main pipe for carrying water.
wa·ter·man (wȯ′ tər mən, wŏt′ ər-) ***n-*** [*pl.* **wa·ter·men**] **1** man who operates or works a boat for hire. **2** person skilled in handling small boats.
wa·ter·mark (wȯ′ tər märk′, wŏt′ ər-) ***n-*** **1** mark that shows the height or limit of the rise of water. **2** faintly visible marking or design in some kinds of paper. ***vt-*** to mark (something) with such a design.
wa·ter·mel·on (wȯ′ tər mĕl′ ən, wŏt′ ər-) ***n-*** **1** large, edible fruit of a trailing plant related to the cucumbers, having a green rind and sweet, juicy, pink or red pulp. **2** the plant bearing this fruit. *as* ***modifier***: *a jar of* watermelon *preserves.*
water meter ***n-*** device for measuring and recording the amount of water flowing through a pipe.
water mill ***n-*** mill run by waterpower.
water moccasin ***n-*** poisonous swamp pit viper of southeastern United States, closely related to the copperhead; cottonmouth.
water of crystallization ***n-*** water in chemical combination with another substance in a crystal. When the water is removed from such a substance, the crystals break up into powder. Also **water of hydration.**
water ou·zel (o͞o′ zəl) ***n-*** any of various birds related to the wrens, having the habit of diving into streams and walking under the water in search of food.
water polo ***n-*** game played in the water by teams of swimmers with a ball like that used in soccer.
wa·ter·pow·er (wȯ′ tər pou′ ər, wŏt′ ər-) ***n-*** power produced by the flow or fall of water, used to generate electricity, run machinery, etc.
wa·ter·proof (wȯ′ tər pro͞of′, wŏt′ ər-) ***adj-*** completely resistant to penetration by water: *a* waterproof *raincoat*; *a* waterproof *paint.* ***n-*** **1** any material treated to shed water. **2** *chiefly Brit.* raincoat. ***vt-***: *to* waterproof *cloth.*
water rat ***n-*** **1** any of several rodents that live near water. **2** *Slang* waterfront thief or loafer.
wa·ter·shed (wȯ′ tər shĕd′, wŏt′ ər-) ***n-*** **1** the land area from which water drains into a river system, lake, city water supply, etc. **2** the divide between two such areas; drainage divide.
water ski ***n-*** either of two skis worn to skim across water while being towed by a line attached to a motorboat. *as* ***modifier*** **(water-ski)**: *a* water-ski *championship.*
wa·ter-ski (wȯ′ tər skē′, wŏt′ ər-) ***vi-*** [**wa·ter·skied, wa·ter·ski·ing**] to skim across water on water skis.
water snake ***n-*** any of various harmless snakes that live in or near fresh water.
water softener ***n-*** any of a group of chemicals or synthetic resins used to soften water.
wa·ter·spout (wȯ′ tər spout′, wŏt′ ər-) ***n-*** **1** rapidly whirling column of mist and spray raised by a tornado moving over a large body of water. **2** rainspout.
water table ***n-*** level below which the ground is saturated with water.
wa·ter·tight (wȯ′ tər tīt′, wŏt′ ər-) ***adj-*** **1** made in such a way that water cannot enter; without a leak: *The ship's bottom was* watertight. **2** so clear and sound that it cannot be misunderstood or disturbed; without fault.
water tower ***n-*** **1** tower serving as a reservoir or tank for holding water. **2** fire-fighting apparatus provided with a pipe which may be raised to deliver a jet of water at high pressure into the upper stories of high buildings.
water vapor ***n-*** water in its gaseous state, especially when below the boiling point, as in the air.
wa·ter·way (wȯ′ tər wā′, wŏt′ ər-) ***n-*** **1** body of water that is navigable. **2** channel through which water flows.
water wheel ***n-*** wheel turned by flowing or falling water. For picture, see *overshot wheel* and *undershot wheel.*
water wings ***n-*** air-filled device, shaped somewhat like a pair of wings, sometimes worn when learning to swim.
wa·ter·works (wȯ′ tər wûrks′, wŏt′ ər-) ***n-*** *pl.* system for supplying water to a city, town, etc.; also, a pumping station.
wa·ter·worn (wȯ′ tər wôrn′, wŏt′ ər-) ***adj-*** worn away or worn smooth by running or falling water.
wa·ter·y (wȯ′ tə rē, wŏt′ ə-) ***adj-*** **1** of or like water: *a* watery *soup.* **2** soggy: *the* watery *ground.* **3** full of or discharging water: *the* watery *skies*; watery *eyes.*
watt (wŏt) ***n-*** unit of electric power equal to the energy needed to do one joule of work per second. One watt equals 1/746 horsepower. ***Hom-*** what.
watt·age (wŏt′ ĭj) ***n-*** amount of electric power, expressed in watts.

watt-hour (wŏt′ ou′ ər) ***n-*** work unit of electrical energy, equal to one watt of power acting for one hour.

wat·tle (wŏt′ əl) ***n-*** **1** twig or rod easily bent; also, a framework of pliant rods. **2** material made of pliant twigs twisted together and used for walls, fences, etc. **3 wattles** rods used in a roof to support thatch made of straw. **4** fold of loose red flesh under the throat of certain birds or reptiles. ***vt-*** **[wat·tled, wat·tling]** **1** to twist or interweave (twigs or rods) into a framework, fence, etc. **2** to cover or fence in with rods.

wat·tled (wŏt′ əld) ***adj-*** **1** made or built with wattles. **2** of a bird, snake, etc., having a wattle.

wave (wāv) ***n-*** **1** rise and swell on the surface of a body of water: *an ocean* wave. **2** something resembling this in shape or movement. **3** increase or surge of something: *a* wave *of anger*; *a heat* wave. **4** *Physics* (1) any periodic or cyclic vibration produced in and propagated through a medium. (2) an electromagnetic wave. ***vi-*** **[wave, wav·ing]** **1** to move up and down or back and forth: *The flag* waved *in the breeze.* **2** to signal by such motion: *He* waved *to us.* **3** to form into ripples: *Her hair* waves *easily.* ***vt-***: *to* wave *a flag*; *to* wave *good-by*; *to* wave *one's hair.* ***Hom-*** waive. **—*adj-* wave′ like′.**

wave·length (wāv′ lĕngth′) *Physics* ***n-*** distance between any two corresponding points on a wave, measured along the line of travel of the wave.

wa·ver (wā′ vər) ***vi-*** **1** to hestitate; be undecided: *She* wavered *over choosing the present.* **2** to flicker; tremble. **3** to sway back and forth. **4** to fail or begin to give way: *The sick man's mind* wavered. ***n-*** a flickering, trembling, or shaking. **—*n-* wa′ ver·er.** ***adv-*** **wa′ ver·ing·ly.**

WAVES or **W.A.V.E.S.** (wāvz) corps of women in the U.S. Navy, including all women except nurses. Officially, **Women in the U.S. Navy.** [from the former name, *W*omen *A*ppointed for *V*oluntary *E*mergency *S*ervice.]

wav·y (wā′ vē) ***adj-*** **[wav·i·er, wav·i·est]** **1** moving to and fro in waves or swells. **2** full of waves or curves. **—*adv-* wav′ i·ly.** ***n-*** **wav′ i·ness.**

Wavy lines

[1]**wax** (wăks) ***n-*** **1** sticky, yellowish substance made by bees, from which the honeycomb is built; beeswax. **2** any of several substances somewhat resembling this: *a sealing* wax; *paraffin* wax. **3** compound containing wax for giving a luster to floors, furniture, etc. ***vt-*** to polish or coat with this. *as **modifier***: *a* wax *fruit.* [from Old English **weax,** "beeswax."] **—*adj-* wax′ like′.**

[2]**wax** (wăks) ***vi-*** **1** to increase in apparent size, power, degree, etc., as the moon does as it approaches fullness. **2** to grow; become increasingly: *He* waxed *talkative after dinner.* [from Old English **weaxan,** "to grow."]

wax bean ***n-*** yellow string bean.

wax·en (wăk′ sən) ***adj-*** **1** made of wax. **2** like wax in appearance, consistency, etc.; soft; plastic. **3** pallid.

wax myrtle ***n-*** any of several slender, evergreen shrubs or trees of eastern United States that bear wax-covered berries from which candle wax is obtained; bayberry.

wax paper ***n-*** paper coated with wax that repels water, grease, etc.

wax·wing (wăks′ wĭng′) ***n-*** crested gray and brown bird with a yellow tail band and hard, red, waxy tips on some of its wing feathers; cedarbird; cedar waxwing.

Cedar waxwing

wax·work (wăks′ wûrk′) ***n-*** **1** modeled work in wax. **2 waxworks** collection of wax figures of persons, usually life-size representations of historical characters .

wax·y (wăk′ sē) ***adj-*** **[wax·i·er, wax·i·est]** **1** resembling wax. **2** made of, or coated with, wax. **—*n-* wax′ i·ness.**

[1]**way** (wā) ***n-*** **1** path, road, course, or any passage; also, room or space for passing: *The* way *was muddy after the* rain. *Make* way *for the parade.* **2** the route from one place to another: *the* way *to Boston*; *the* way *home.* **3** direction: *Everyone face this* way! **4** distance: *She lives a long* way *from here.* **5** progress; advance; headway: *We pushed our* way *through the crowd. He made his* way *in business.* **6** manner toward others: *The child has winning* ways. **7** means or method: *Sailors know many* ways *of tying a knot.* **8** habit; customary manner. **9** course of action that one wishes, or decides, to follow; also, a wish; will; desire: *She goes her* way *through life. Have your own* way *about it.* **10** characteristic; respect; feature: *In many* ways *she is like her father.* **11** *Informal* condition: *The old dog is in a bad* way. **12** *Informal* neighborhood: *out my* way. **13** in law, a right of way. **14 ways** structure of timbers on which a ship is built and down which it slides when being launched. [from Old English **wæg**] ***Homs-*** weigh, whey.

by the way incidentally. **by way of** **1** by a route that includes: *He traveled* by way of *Chicago.* **2** as a substitute for; as a means or method for: *He said that* by way of *apology.* **give way** **1** to collapse: *The bridge* gave way *in the flood.* **2** to surrender: *She* gave way *to my persuasion.* **go out of the** (or **one's**) **way** to do something that one would not normally do; to do something inconvenient. **in the way** in one's path; in a position to hinder, hamper, obstruct, etc.: *The children's skates are always* in the way. **make (one's) way** to make progress on a course; procede: *He* made his way *along the river road.* **out of the way** **1** not obstructing; not underfoot. **2** secluded; off the main road: *a cabin that is* out of the way. **3** not on the right or usual course. **4** improper; wrong. **5** *Informal* dead. **pave the way** to make things easy; serve as an introduction: *He* paved the way *for my request.* **under way** in motion and making progress: *a ship* under way *at full steam*; *a project already well* under way. **ways and means** methods and resources for accomplishing an end, especially for meeting expenses in a government.

►We sometimes hear WAYS used for WAY in a sentence like the following one: *He was a long* way (*not* ways) from home. The added "-s" is unnecessary and meaningless and generally considered incorrect. Save WAYS only for the plural.

[2]**way** (wā) ***adv-*** *Informal* away. [a shortened form of **away.**] ***Homs-*** weigh, whey.

►WAY, like AWAY, refers to distance: *He is* way *over there.* Avoid using it to mean "unusually large size, degree, or difference," as in the following sentence: *His father is* way (much) *richer than mine.*

way·bill (wā′ bĭl′) ***n-*** paper containing shipping instructions for goods carried by train or steamer.

way·far·er (wā′ fâr′ ər) ***n-*** traveler, especially one who travels on foot.

way·far·ing (wā′ fâr′ ĭng) ***n-*** traveling, especially on foot. *as **modifier***: *a* wayfaring *man.*

way·lay (wā′ lā′) ***vt-*** **[way·laid, way·lay·ing]** **1** to lie in wait for and attack; ambush. **2** to wait for and stop (a person) by surprise: *The fans* waylaid *the actress to ask for her autograph.* **—*n-* way′ lay′ er.**

---

fāte, făt, dâre, bärn; bē, bĕt, mêre; bīte, bĭt; nōte, hŏt, môre, dȯg; fŭn, fûr; to͞o, bo͝ok; oil; out; ta*r*; thin; t͟hen; hw for wh as in *wh*at; zh for s as in u*s*ual; ə for a, e, i, o, u, as in *a*go, lin*e*n, per*i*l, at*o*m, min*u*s

-ways *suffix* (used to form adverbs) indicating position, direction, manner, etc.: *length*ways; *side*ways.

way·side (wā′ sīd′) ***n-*** edge of a road: *They stopped by the* wayside. *as* ***modifier***: *a* wayside *fruit stand.*

way station ***n-*** small station between larger ones on a railroad.

way·ward (wā′ wərd) ***adj-*** **1** disobedient; willful: *a* wayward *child.* **2** not steady; unpredictable: *a* wayward *wind.* **—*adv-* way′ ward·ly. *n-* way′ ward·ness.**

we (wē) ***pron-*** (used as a plural subject in the first person) **1** persons who are speaking or writing. **2** one person speaking or writing officially, such as a sovereign, author, judge, etc. ***Hom-*** wee.

weak (wēk) ***adj-*** **[weak·er, weak·est] 1** lacking in strength of body or in endurance: *to be* weak *from hunger*; weak *eyes.* **2** liable to break, collapse, etc., under pressure or strain: *a* weak *bridge*; *a* weak *rope*; *a* weak *link in a chain.* **3** lacking in ability; below standard: *He is* weak *in many subjects at school.* **4** lacking in mental or moral strength; easily influenced: *a* weak *will.* **5** lacking in force, power, or effectiveness: *a* weak *leader.* **6** faint in sound; feeble: *a* weak *cry.* **7** thin and watery; diluted: *this* weak *coffee.* **8** not based on sound reasoning or logic: *a* weak *argument.* ***Hom-*** week.

weak·en (wē′ kən) ***vt-*** to make weak or weaker: *Sickness* weakened *her.* ***vi-*** to become weak or weaker: *His eyes* weakened *as he grew older.*

weak·fish (wēk′ fĭsh′) ***n-*** any of several food and game fishes with a tender mouth, found along the coastal waters of eastern United States.

weak-kneed (wēk′ nēd′) ***adj-*** **1** weak in the knees. **2** easily intimidated; without courage; spineless.

weak·ling (wēk′ lĭng) ***n-*** person lacking strength of body or character. *as* ***modifier***: *a* weakling *child.*

weak·ly (wēk′ lē) ***adj-*** **[weak·li·er, weak·li·est]** not robust; sickly: *a* weakly *child.* ***adv-*** in a weak or faint way: *She answered* weakly. ***Hom-*** weekly.

weak-mind·ed (wēk′ mīn′ dəd) ***adj-*** **1** not strong-willed; indecisive: *a* weak-minded *decision.* **2** feeble-minded.

weak·ness (wēk′ nəs) ***n-*** **1** lack of strength, power, or force: *He suffered* weakness *after the accident.* **2** weak point; fault: *the* weakness *in your argument.* **3** a liking; special fondness: *That girl has a* weakness *for chocolates.*

weak verb *Grammar* ***n-*** in English, a verb that forms its past tense or past participle, or both, by adding the word ending -ed. Verbs that end in -e drop the e before adding the -ed. Examples: call, called, called; dance, danced, danced. See also *strong verb.*

[1]**weal** (wēl) ***n-*** happiness; welfare; prosperity: *public* weal. [from Old English **wela.**] ***Homs-*** we'll, wheel.

[2]**weal** (wēl) ***n-*** ridge or mark made on the skin by flogging; welt; wale; wheal. [variant of **wale.**] ***Homs-*** we'll, wheel.

wealth (wĕlth) ***n-*** **1** large amounts of money or possessions; riches. **2** abundance of anything: *a* wealth *of ideas*; *a* wealth *of words.* **3** everything that can be valued in money: *a nation's* wealth.

wealth·y (wĕl′ thē) ***adj-*** **[wealth·i·er, wealth·i·est]** rich; marked by abundance: *a* wealthy *man.*

wean (wēn) ***vt-*** **1** to accustom (a child or a young animal) to take food other than its mother's milk. **2** to draw (someone) away from a habit or interest. ***Hom-*** ween.

weap·on (wĕp′ ən) ***n-*** **1** any implement used for fighting or defense: *Cave men made* weapons *of stone.* **2** any means of contest: *His tongue was his best* weapon. **—*adj-* weap′ on·less.**

wear (wâr) ***vt-*** **[wore, worn, wear·ing] 1** to have on or about the body: *She* wore *furs, a corsage, and pearls.* **2** to display; bear or maintain about one: *He* wore *a broad grin.* **3** to diminish by friction; rub: *The swift stream* wore *the stones smooth.* **4** to use up; injure or destroy by use or action: *The rough streets* wore *the soles of my shoes.* **5** to bring about by use, friction, etc.: *to* wear *a hole in a rug.* ***vi-*** **1** to last: *This cloth* wears *well.* **2** to pass gradually: *Time* wore *on, day by day.* **3** to reach gradually a specified state: *His patience* wore *thin.* ***n-*** **1** articles of clothing: *men's* wear. **2** endurance; service; lasting quality: *material famous for its long* wear. **3** damage, injury, etc., from use or age: *The machine showed signs of* wear. **4** a using or being used: *These shoes have seen a lot of* wear. ***Homs-*** ware, where. **—*adj-* wear′ a·ble. *n-* wear′ er.**

wear and tear loss or damage from time and use.

wear down 1 to damage by use or wear. **2** to reduce or overcome by constant effort; weaken.

wear off to lose effect gradually: *The pain* wore off.

wear out 1 to wear until no longer fit for use. **2** to tire out; weary; to make or become exhausted.

wear·ing (wâr′ ĭng) ***adj-*** **1** having to do with or made for wear: *That store deals in* wearing *apparel.* **2** tiring; fatiguing: *a* wearing *journey.* **3** subjected to wear: *the* wearing *surface of a tool.*

wea·ri·some (wêr′ ĭ səm) ***adj-*** wearying; fatiguing; tedious: *a* wearisome *lecture.* **—*adv-* wea′ ri·some·ly.**

wea·ry (wêr′ ē) ***adj-*** **[wea·ri·er, wea·ri·est] 1** tired; fatigued: *to be* weary *after work.* **2** exhausted, as in patience, by continuance of something tiresome, boring, etc.: *I'm* weary *of that old tune.* **3** characteristic of, or showing, fatigue: *a* weary *sigh.* **4** causing, or accompanied by fatigue: *to walk many* weary *miles*; *a* weary *round of duties.* ***vt-*** **[wea·ried, wea·ry·ing]** to wear out or make tired: *The long argument* wearied *me.* ***vi-*** to become tired. **—*adv-* wea′ ri·ly. *n-* wea′ ri·ness.**

wea·sel (wē′ zəl) ***n-*** **1** small, active animal related to the minks and skunks and having a pointed face and a long, thin body. It is destructive to poultry. **2** sneaky, dangerous person. ***vi-*** *Informal* to act or speak evasively.

weasel out *Informal* to avoid doing something promised.

weath·er (wĕth′ ər) ***n-*** **1** the atmospheric conditions at any place at a particular time: *The* weather *in Chicago today is cool, dry, and sunny.* **2** stormy condition: *We have just passed through a spell of* weather. *as* ***modifier***: *a* weather *map*; weather *report.* ***vt-*** **1** to endure, resist, withstand: *to* weather *a storm*; *to* weather *a crisis.* **2** to expose to the elements; also, to wear away, bleach, toughen, dry, etc., by exposure to the sun, wind, and rain: *Wind* weathers *rocks.* **3** to sail or pass to the windward of. ***vi-*** to become bleached, dried, etc., by the action of the sun, wind, rain, and frost, etc.: *The shingles* weathered *to a gray.* ***Homs-*** wether, whether.

under the weather *Informal* **1** not feeling well; sick; ill. **2** slightly intoxicated.

weath·er-beat·en (wĕth′ ər bē′ tĕn) ***adj-*** **1** worn by the weather: *a* weather-beaten *shack.* **2** toughened by exposure to the weather: *his* weather-beaten *face.*

weath·er·board (wĕth′ ər bôrd′) ***n-*** clapboard.

Weather Bureau ***n-*** bureau of the U.S. Department of Commerce that gathers information in order to predict the weather and issue warnings of storms, floods, etc. It has about 300 offices at various cities and airports.

weath·er·cock (wĕth′ ər kŏk′) ***n-*** weather vane, the pointer of which is shaped like a rooster.

Weathercock

weath·er·glass (wĕth′ ər glăs′) ***n-*** any of several instruments, such as a barometer, for predicting the weather, usually by indicating changes in atmospheric pressure.

weath·er·ing (wĕth′ ər ĭng) ***n-*** **1** in geology, the physical and chemical process by which surface rock is broken down into fragments by the action of rain, snow, carbon dioxide, and other atmospheric agents. **2** similar process by which any object exposed to the weather undergoes changes in color, texture, or form.

weath·er·man (wĕth′ ər măn′) ***n-*** [*pl.* **weath·er·men**] **1** person who forecasts the weather. **2** person who works for the Weather Bureau.

weather map ***n-*** map showing various weather conditions at a particular time, usually over a wide area.

weath·er·proof (wĕth′ ər pro͞of′) ***adj-*** such as can withstand exposure to weather. ***vt-*** to make capable of withstanding exposure to weather.

weather ship ***n-*** ship that acts as a weather station.

weather station ***n-*** place where meteorological observations are taken and recorded.

weather strip ***n-*** strip of felt, copper, or other material placed along the joints or edges of a window or door to keep out drafts, rain, etc.

weather vane ***n-*** movable pointer, often shaped like an arrow, horse, ship, etc., fastened to an elevated object to show which way the wind blows.

weave (wēv) ***vt-*** [**wove** (wōv) or **weaved, woven** (wō′ vən) or **wove, weav·ing**] **1** to interlace (threads, wires, etc.), to make cloth, screens, etc.: *Polly* wove *rushes into a mat.* **2** to form by interlacing: *to* weave *cloth on a loom.* **3** to spin: *A spider* weaves *a silken web.* **4** to wind (one's way) in and out: *Waldo* weaved *his way through the crowd.* **5** to gather deeds, events, etc., into a story; compose: *The author* wove *an exciting tale of pirates.* ***vi-*** **1** to make cloth on a loom. **2** to become twisted together or interlaced. **3** to wind in and out. ***n-*** style of weaving. ***Hom-*** we've.
►The standard past tense of WEAVE [WOVE] is acceptable for all meanings and is preferred when referring to the making of a fabric: *They* wove *cloth. They* wove *a tale.* However, many people prefer WEAVED in the sense "wound or threaded (one's way) in and out."

Weave

weav·er (wē′ vər) ***n-*** person who weaves or whose trade is weaving.

weav·er·bird (wē′ vər bûrd′) ***n-*** any of various Old World birds that resemble the finches and make their nests by interlacing twigs, grass, etc.

web (wĕb) ***n-*** **1** something made of interwoven fibers, strips, or strands; especially, the structure of delicate threads spun by a spider; cobweb. **2** something that entangles or traps; snare: *caught in a* web *of lies.* **3** any complex network: *a* web *of turnpikes.* **4** large roll of paper, especially newsprint, used in a rotary printing press. **5** *Biology* (1) the skin joining the toes of ducks, beavers, and certain other aquatic animals. (2) the parts of a feather on either side of the shaft. **6** thin plate connecting the frames, ribs, or other heavier sections of a structure or machine. **7** in architecture, the section between the ribs of a ribbed vault. **—*adj-* web′ like′.**

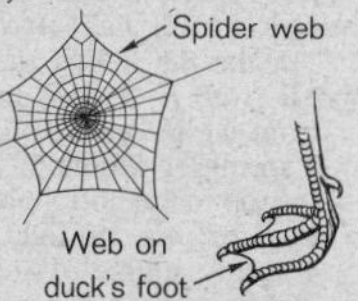

webbed (wĕbd) ***adj-*** **1** having a web: *the* webbed *seat of a chair.* **2** joined by a membrane, as are a duck's toes.

web·bing (wĕb′ ĭng) ***n-*** **1** heavy woven strip of cotton or linen, used for safety belts, in upholstery, etc. **2** anything that forms a web.

web·foot (wĕb′ fo͝ot′) ***n-*** [*pl.* **web·feet**] **1** foot with webbed toes. **2** any animal with this kind of feet.

web-foot·ed (wĕb′ fo͝ot′ əd) ***adj-*** having toes that are joined by webs: *Swans are* web-footed.

web-toed (wĕb′ tōd′) ***adj-*** web-footed.

wed (wĕd) ***vt-*** [**wed·ded, wed·ded** or **wed, wed·ding**] **1** to marry; unite in wedlock. **2** to unite; join: *to* wed *skill with hard work.* ***vi-*** to enter into marriage; marry.

we'd (wēd) **1** we had. **2** we would; we should. ***Hom-*** weed.

Wed. Wednesday.

wed·ded (wĕd′ əd) ***adj-*** united in marriage.
wedded to firmly devoted to: *to be* wedded *to a job.*

wed·ding (wĕd′ ĭng) ***n-*** **1** marriage ceremony; also, the festivities. **2** anniversary of a marriage: *a silver* wedding. *as* ***modifier:*** *a* wedding *ring*; wedding *march.*

wedge (wĕj) ***n-*** **1** triangular block of metal or wood, used for splitting wood, rocks, etc. **2** anything used like such a block to force an entrance: *Jake used his father's permission as a* wedge *for greater demands.* **3** anything of a similar shape used as a brace, prop, filler, etc. ***vt-*** **[wedged, wedg·ing] 1** to split with a wedge. **2** to fasten with a wedge. **3** to pack tightly; press or crowd in: *He* wedged *us into the car.* ***vi-*** to enter sideways by means of pressure: *He* wedged *into the elevator.*

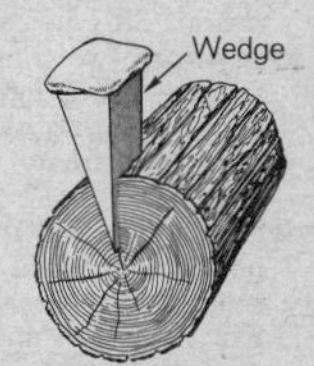

wed·lock (wĕd′ lŏk′) ***n-*** the married state; matrimony.

Wednes·day (wĕnz′ dā, -dē) ***n-*** the fourth day of the week.

wee (wē) ***adj-*** **[we·er, we·est] 1** small; tiny; very little. **2** very early: *in the* wee *hours of the morning.* ***Hom-*** we.

[1]**weed** (wēd) ***n-*** **1** any wild, uncultivated, useless plant: *The* weeds *have ruined our lawn.* **2** anything useless or troublesome; especially, a weak, lanky horse. **3 the weed** tobacco; also, cigar or cigarette. ***vt-*** to remove undesirable plants from: *to* weed *the flower beds.* ***vi-*** to take out such plants or anything obnoxious. [from Old English **wēod.**] ***Hom-*** we'd.
weed out to remove what is useless, harmful, inferior, and not wanted: *to* weed out *bad apples from a bushel.*

[2]**weed** (wēd) ***n-*** **1** *Archaic* any garment. **2 weeds** mourning garments. [from Old English **wæd.**] ***Hom-*** we'd.

weed·er (wē′ dər) ***n-*** **1** person who weeds. **2** device used for weeding.

weed·y (wē′ dē) ***adj-*** **[weed·i·er, weed·i·est] 1** overgrown with weeds: *a* weedy *path.* **2** of, relating to, or resembling weeds: *a* weedy *growth.* **3** of persons or animals, long or tall, thin, and ungainly: *a* weedy *colt.*

week (wēk) ***n-*** **1** period of seven successive days, usually beginning with midnight on Saturday and lasting until midnight on the following Saturday. **2** the working days or working period of the week; also, the five school days of the week: *We live in town all* week *but spend weekends in the country.* ***Hom-*** weak.

week·day (wēk′ dā′) ***n-*** any day of the week except Sunday. *as* ***modifier:*** *a* weekday *interest.*

week·end (wēk′ ĕnd′) ***n-*** **1** the time from Friday night or Saturday to Monday morning, usually used for rest

---

fāte, făt, dâre, bärn; bē, bĕt, mêre; bīte, bĭt; nōte, hŏt, môre, dȯg; fŭn fûr; to͞o, bo͝ok; oil; out; tar; thin; then; hw for wh as in *wh*at; zh for s as in u*s*ual; ə for a, e, i, o, u, as in *a*go, lin*e*n, per*i*l, at*o*m, min*u*s

or recreation. **2** visit, holiday, or house party during this period: *a* weekend *at the beach.* *as **modifier**: a* weekend *trip.* ***vi-*** to spend this time at some place: *He* weekended *in Boston.* ***adv-*** **weekends** on every weekend; on any weekend: *He works* weekends.

week·end·er (wēk′ĕn′dər) ***n-*** person who vacations or visits for a weekend.

week·ly (wēk′lē) ***adj-*** **1** of or for a week: *the student's* weekly *assignment.* **2** performed, happening, appearing, payable, etc., regularly each week or once a week: *a* weekly *letter*; *a* weekly *wage.* ***adv-*** once a week. ***n-*** [*pl.* **week·lies**] newspaper or magazine published once a week. ***Hom-*** weakly.

ween (wēn) *Archaic* ***vt- & vi-*** to think or suppose. ***Hom-*** wean.

wee·ny (wē′nē) *Informal* ***adj-*** [**wee·ni·er, wee·ni·est**] very small; minute.

weep (wēp) ***vi-*** [**wept** (wĕpt), **weep·ing**] **1** to express sorrow, grief, anguish, or some other deep emotion by tears; cry: *Susan* wept *when the kitten was injured.* **2** to give forth moisture: *The skies* wept. ***vt-*** **1** to shed (tears). **2** to mourn or lament. ***—n-*** **weep′er.**

weep·ing (wē′pĭng) ***adj-*** **1** of certain trees, having slender, drooping branches: *a* weeping *cypress.* **2** in tears; crying: *a* weeping *child.*

weeping willow ***n-*** willow having slender, drooping branches.

wee·vil (wē′vəl) ***n-*** any of several beetles with hard shells and long snouts. Weevils are very destructive to cotton and grain. ***—adj-*** **wee′vil·y** or **wee′vil·ly.**

Cotton-boll weevil

weft (wĕft) ***n-*** **1** in weaving, the yarn or threads that are carried by the shuttle back and forth across the warp; woof. **2** something woven.

weigh (wā) ***vt-*** **1** to find out the heaviness of (something) by means of a scale or balance, or by balancing in the hand: *to* weigh *a parcel.* **2** to turn over in the mind; ponder: *to* weigh *the advantages of a scholarship.* **3** to bear down by weight; bend: *Fruit* weighed *down the plum tree.* ***vi-*** **1** to have a certain weight: *Those bricks* weigh *over a ton. He* weighs *150 pounds.* **2** to have importance: *His opinion doesn't* weigh *with me at all.* ***Homs-*** way, whey. ***—n-*** **weigh′er.**

weigh anchor to raise an anchor from the water; hence, to start a voyage.

weigh in **1** of a boxer, jockey, etc., to be weighed before or after a fight, race, etc. **2** to find out the weight of luggage before a flight.

weigh on to be a burden; press: *His lie* weighed on *him.*

weigh (one's) words to choose (one's) words carefully.

weigh out to measure or dole out in set amounts.

weight (wāt) ***n-*** **1** amount that a person or thing weighs on earth: *His* weight *is 150 pounds.* **2** *Physics* the force of gravity exerted by the earth, another planet, or a satellite on an object near it. **3** object of specific heaviness used to balance a scale: *a set of* weights *from one ounce to five pounds.* **4** system of units used in determining weight: *troy* weight. **5** something used for its heaviness: *a paper* weight; *the* weights *in a grandfather clock.* **6** burden of care, responsibility, etc.; load; pressure: *Dennis found being club treasurer quite a* weight *on his mind.* **7** importance; value; influence: *a man of potential* weight *in the future government.* ***vt-*** **1** to load down: *He sank the boat by* weighting *it.* **2** to burden: *He is* weighted *with cares.* ***Hom-*** wait.

pull (one's) weight to do one's part or share of anything. **put on weight** to grow fat; become heavier.

weight·less (wāt′ləs) ***adj-*** **1** *Physics* of any system in space, lacking any acceleration that can be detected by an observer within the system. **2** seeming to have little or no weight: *a* weightless *burden.* ***—n-*** **weight′less·ness.**

weight·y (wā′tē) ***adj-*** [**weight·i·er, weight·i·est**] **1** of great weight; heavy: *a* weighty *body.* **2** crushing; burdensome: *his* weighty *responsibilities.* **3** influential; important: *a* weighty *argument.* **4** serious in aspect; solemn. ***—adv-*** **weight′i·ly.** ***n-*** **weight′i·ness.**

weir (wêr) ***n-*** **1** dam in a stream to stop and raise the water, in order to lead it into a mill or into ditches for irrigation. **2** fence of brush or stakes set in a stream to catch fish. **3** notch in a plank set into a dam, used to measure the volume of water flowing through it. ***Hom-*** we're.

weird (wêrd) ***adj-*** **1** very strange; mysterious; uncanny; eerie: *a* weird *noise in the attic.* **2** curious in appearance or nature; odd: *a* weird *hat*; *a* weird *character.* ***—adv-*** **weird′ly.** ***n-*** **weird′ness.**

Weird Sisters ***n-*** *pl.* **1** the Fates. **2** in Shakespeare's "Macbeth," the three witches.

welch (wĕlch) ***vi-*** to welsh.

wel·come (wĕl′kəm) ***vt-*** [**wel·comed, wel·com·ing**] to greet kindly and gladly; receive with hospitality: *She* welcomed *her guests at the front door.* ***n-*** hospitable greeting: *a hearty* welcome. ***adj-*** **1** giving pleasure and joy: *a* welcome *letter.* **2** received with gladness or hospitality: *a* welcome *guest.* ***—n-*** **wel′com·er.**

be welcome to to be gladly permitted to; to be given a right to: *You* are welcome to *any book.* **you are** (or **you're) welcome** you are under no obligation (used as a conventional response to thanks).

weld (wĕld) ***vt-*** **1** to join (pieces of metal) by heating the edges to the melting point and pressing or hammering them together, or until the melted edges flow together: *The plumber* welded *the broken pipe.* **2** to unite closely: *Deep affection and respect* welded *the family together.* ***vi-***: *Some metals* weld *easily.* ***n-*** welded joint.

wel·fare (wĕl′fâr′) ***n-*** **1** good health, happiness, and prosperity. **2** system of government aid to private citizens who cannot otherwise maintain themselves. *as **modifier**: a* welfare *office*; *a* welfare *worker.*

welfare state ***n-*** state, nation, or form of government in which the social welfare of the citizens is the accepted responsibility of the government, as through unemployment insurance, social security, medical care, etc.

welfare work ***n-*** the work of volunteers or government employees to help needy people in the community.

wel·kin (wĕl′kən) *Archaic* ***n-*** the vault of heaven; sky.

make the welkin ring to make a very loud sound.

[1]**well** (wĕl) ***n-*** **1** deep hole or shaft sunk into the earth, from which water, oil, gas, and the like are obtained. **2** spring or fountain. **3** enclosed space extending from the top to the bottom of a building, such as a shaft for an elevator, air, or light, or inside a winding staircase. **4** steady source of supply: *The encyclopedia is a* well *of information.* **5** a container for a liquid: *an ink*well; *a platter with a* well *for gravy.* ***vi-*** to flow, or gush forth: *Water* welled *from the ground.* [from Old English **wella,** "a spring," related to **wiellan,** "boil up."]

[2]**well** (wĕl) ***adv-*** [**bet·ter, best**] **1** in a right, just, or praiseworthy manner: *The work was done* well. **2** satisfactorily or suitably: *to dine* well; *to sleep* well. **3** with reason; justifiably: *He may* well *question the verdict.* **4** fortunately; favorably: *The house is* well *situated in a large valley.* **5** to a considerable extent or degree: *a man* well *over sixty.* **6** clearly: definitely: *You know* well *what I mean.* **7** intimately: *Do you know him* well?

8 wholly; thoroughly: *He should be* well *rewarded for this.* 9 at some distance; far: *He stayed* well *behind us.* ***adj-*** 1 in good health or condition: *I'm perfectly* well *now. All's* well *in Boston.* 2 good; for the best; most appropriate or fitting: *It was* well *you left just then.* ***interj-*** exclamation of surprise, wonder, relief, etc.; also, introduction to something further to be said: Well, *that's over.* Well, *I'm here at last.* [from Old English **wel** meaning "at one's pleasure."]

as well 1 in addition: *He went* as well. 2 equally.
as well as 1 also; in addition to. 2 to the same extent or degree as.

►For usage note see GOOD.

we'll (wēl) we shall; we will. ***Homs-*** weal, wheel.

well-ad·vised (wĕl′ əd vīzd′) ***adj-*** 1 acting with wisdom; judicious; prudent: *She would be* well-advised *to follow the instructions.* 2 showing careful planning; based upon wise counsel: *a* well-advised *action.*

well-ap·point·ed (wĕl′ ə poin′ təd) ***adj-*** properly equipped or furnished: *a* well-appointed *ship.*

well·a·way (wĕl′ ə wā′) or **well·a·day** (wĕl′ ə dā′) *Archaic* ***interj-*** exclamation of grief or sorrow; alas.

well-bal·anced (wĕl′ băl′ ənst) ***adj-*** 1 balanced evenly; properly regulated or adjusted: *a* well-balanced *budget.* 2 having good judgment; sensible; reasonable; sound.

well-be·ing (wĕl′ bē′ ĭng) ***n-*** general health and happiness; welfare.

well·born (wĕl′ bôrn′) ***adj-*** 1 born into a good family. 2 in former times, of noble birth.

well-bred (wĕl′ brĕd′) ***adj-*** 1 having or showing good breeding; of good family; having good manners. 2 of animals, bred of good stock: *a* well-bred *spaniel.*

well-con·tent (wĕl′ kən tĕnt′) ***adj-*** completely happy or pleased.

well-dis·posed (wĕl′ dĭ spōzd′) ***adj-*** 1 inclined to be friendly, kind, etc. 2 receptive to an idea, plan, etc.

well-done (wĕl′ dŭn′) ***adj-*** 1 done with skill and thoroughness. 2 cooked thoroughly, as meat.

well-fa·vored (wĕl′ fā′ vərd) ***adj-*** handsome; pretty.

well-fixed (wĕl′ fĭkst′) *Informal* ***adj-*** having lots of money; wealthy.

well-found (wĕl′ found′) ***adj-*** well equipped or provided; well-appointed: *a* well-found *ship.*

well-found·ed (wĕl′ foun′ dəd) ***adj-*** founded on good reasoning or on facts: *a* well-founded *suspicion.*

well-groomed (wĕl′ grōōmd′) ***adj-*** 1 carefully dressed; neat and tidy. 2 carefully cared for; curried and combed.

well-ground·ed (wĕl′ groun′ dəd) ***adj-*** 1 well instructed in fundamental principles. 2 well-founded.

well-hand·led (wĕl′ hăn′ dəld) ***adj-*** managed with capability and efficiency.

well·head (wĕl′ hĕd′) ***n-*** fountainhead; source.

well-heeled (wĕl′ hēld′) *Informal* ***adj-*** having a good amount of money; rich.

well-in·formed (wĕl′ ĭn fôrmd′, -fôrmd′) ***adj-*** 1 having complete knowledge of one subject. 2 having considerable knowledge of many subjects, especially current events.

well-in·ten·tioned (wĕl′ ĭn tĕn′ shənd) ***adj-*** having good intentions; well-meaning.

well-knit (wĕl′ nĭt′) ***adj-*** strongly and firmly jointed, constructed, formed, etc.: *a* well-knit *argument.*

well-known (wĕl′ nōn′) ***adj-*** generally recognized; widely known; famous: *a* well-known *actor.*

well-man·nered (wĕl′ măn′ ərd) ***adj-*** having or displaying good manners; polite.

well-mean·ing (wĕl′ mē′ nĭng) ***adj-*** showing or having good intentions; intending well.

well-nigh (wĕl′ nī′) ***adv-*** very nearly; almost: *He was* well-nigh *exhausted.*

well-off (wĕl′ ŏf′, -ŏf′) ***adj-*** in a favorable condition; especially, wealthy; prosperous.

well-or·dered (wĕl′ ôr′ dərd, -ôr′ dərd) ***adj-*** arranged or set up so as to run smoothly; carefully ordered.

well-pre·served (wĕl′ prĭ zûrvd′) ***adj-*** in good condition or having a good appearance in spite of age: *a* well-preserved *monument; a* well-preserved *woman.*

well-read (wĕl′ rĕd′) ***adj-*** having read many books on many subjects; having read much.

well-set (wĕl′ sĕt′) ***adj-*** 1 properly built; firmly set up. 2 strongly built: *a* well-set *person.*

well-spo·ken (wĕl′ spō′ kən) ***adj-*** 1 skillfully said. 2 accustomed to speak with accuracy and refinement.

well·spring (wĕl′ sprĭng′) ***n-*** 1 a flow of water issuing from the earth; spring. 2 source of a never-failing supply: *He is a* wellspring *of ideas.*

well-thought-of (wĕl′ thŏt′ əv, -ŏv′) ***adj-*** having a good reputation; esteemed.

well-timed (wĕl′ tīmd′) ***adj-*** done or said at the right time; timely.

well-to-do (wĕl′ tə dōō′) ***adj-*** moderately rich.

well-wish·er (wĕl′ wĭsh′ ər) ***n-*** person who has kind feelings for another person, a cause, etc.

well-worn (wĕl′ wôrn′) ***adj-*** 1 showing much wear or use: *a* well-worn *rug.* 2 trite; banal: *a* well-worn *joke.*

welsh (wĕlsh) *Slang* ***vi-*** 1 to cheat by avoiding payment of a bet or other debt (usually followed by "on"). 2 to fail to fulfill an obligation; go back on (usually followed by "on"). Also **welch.** ***—n-*** **welsh′ er.**

Welsh (wĕlsh) ***adj-*** of or relating to Wales, its people, or their language. ***n-*** 1 the language spoken in Wales. 2 **the Welsh** the people of Wales, collectively.

Welsh·man (wĕlsh′ mən) ***n-*** [*pl.* **Welsh·men**] a native or citizen of Wales. ***—n-*** *fem.* **Welsh′ wom′ an.**

Welsh rabbit ***n-*** a dish of melted, seasoned cheese cooked with milk and ale or beer, served on toast or crackers. Erroneously called **Welsh rarebit.**

Welsh terrier ***n-*** one of a breed of black-and-tan terriers that resemble Airedales but are smaller. They were developed for hunting in Wales.

welt (wĕlt) ***n-*** 1 narrow strip of leather joining the sole and upper part of a shoe; also, a strip of cloth stitched to a seam, border, or edge in order to reinforce or trim it. 2 swelling on the skin caused by a blow. ***vt-*** to secure with a strip of leather or cloth.

wel·ter (wĕl′ tər) ***vi-*** 1 to tumble around or lie soaked in something wet, such as mud or slush; wallow. 2 to rise and fall with violent tossing, as waves do during a storm. ***n-*** 1 a violent tossing. 2 state of confusion.

wel·ter·weight (wĕl′ tər wāt′) ***n-*** boxer or wrestler whose fighting weight is usually 136 to 147 pounds.

wen (wĕn) ***n-*** a benign tumor consisting of a cyst filled with fatty secretions from the skin. ***Hom-*** when.

wench (wĕnch) ***n-*** 1 girl or young woman (used humorously). 2 *Archaic* young peasant woman; also, a maid.

wend (wĕnd) ***vt-*** to go or proceed on (one's way): *The caravan* wended *its way across the desert.*

went (wĕnt) *p.t.* of **go.**

wept (wĕpt) *p.t. & p.p.* of **weep.**

were (wûr) form of **be** used with "you," "we," "they," and plural noun subjects in the past tense. ***Hom-*** whir.

as it were as if it were so; so to speak.

---

fāte, făt, dâre, bärn; bē, bĕt, mêre; bīte, bĭt; nōte, hŏt, môre, dóg; fŭn, fûr; tōō, bŏŏk; oil; out; tar; thin; then; hw for wh as in *wh*at; zh for s as in u*s*ual; ə for a, e, i, o, u, as in *a*go, lin*e*n, per*i*l, at*o*m, min*u*s

we're (wêr) we are. ***Hom-*** weir.
were·n't (wûr′ ənt) were not.
were·wolf (wêr′ wŏŏlf′, wûr′-, wâr′-) ***n-*** [*pl.* **were·wolves**] in folklore, person who could assume the form of a wolf at will and often committed murderous acts.
west (wĕst) ***n-*** **1** the direction halfway between north and south and generally toward the setting sun; also, the point of the compass indicating this direction; opposite of *east.* **2** the region or part of a country or continent in this direction: *the* west *of England.* **3 the West** (1) Europe and North and South America, as distinct from Asia; the Occident. (2) the western part of the United States, especially the area west of the Mississippi River. (3) the United States and its allies, as distinct from the Soviet Union and its allies. ***adj-*** **1** in or to the west: *the* west *side of town.* **2** of winds, from the west. ***adv-*** toward the west: *We drove* west.

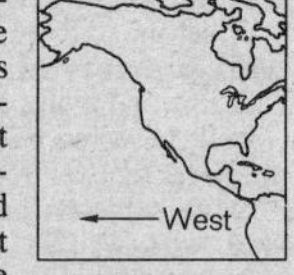

west·bound (wĕst′ bound′) ***adj-*** headed toward the west: *a* westbound *truck.*
west by north ***n-*** the direction halfway between west and west-northwest.
west by south ***n-*** the direction halfway between west and west-southwest.
west·er·ly (wĕs′ tər lē) ***adj-*** **1** generally toward the west: *a* westerly *direction.* **2** of winds, generally from the west: *a* westerly *breeze.* ***adv-*** generally westward: *a wagon moving* westerly. ***n-*** [*pl.* **west·er·lies**] wind from the west.
west·ern (wĕs′ tərn) ***adj-*** **1** in or toward the west: *the* western *part of town.* **2** characteristic of or from the west: *a* western *custom*; *a shipment of* western *apples arrived.* **3 Western** (1) of or relating to the western part of the United States. (2) of or relating to the Christian churches of the western Roman Empire. (3) of or relating to Europe and the Americas. ***n-*** (often **Western**) story, motion picture, or television show about cowboy or pioneer life in the western United States.
Western Church ***n-*** **1** the medieval church of the western Roman Empire, as distinguished from the church of the eastern empire. **2** that part of the Catholic Church that acknowledges the Pope as its spiritual head.
West·ern·er (wĕs′ tər nər) ***n-*** person who lives in or comes from the western part of the United States.
Western Hemisphere ***n-*** the half of the earth that extends from pole to pole and includes North and South America and the surrounding oceans.
west·ern·ize (wĕs′ tər nīz′) ***vt-*** [**west·ern·ized, west·ern·iz·ing**] to cause to be like Europe and the Americas in respect to methods, ideas, or customs: *Heavy industry* westernized *that country.* **—*n-* west′ern·i·za′tion.**
west·ern·most (wĕs′ tərn mōst′) ***adj-*** farthest west.
West Indian ***n-*** native or inhabitant of the West Indies. ***adj-***: *We imported* West Indian *birch.*
west-north·west (wĕst′ nôrth′ wĕst′, -nôrth′ wĕst′) ***n-*** the direction halfway between west and northwest.
west-south·west (wĕst′ south′ wĕst′) ***n-*** the direction halfway between west and southwest.
west·ward (wĕst′ wərd) ***adv-*** (also **westwards**) to or toward the west: *The wagons traveled* westward. ***adj-***: *a* westward *trek.* ***n-***: *mountains to the* westward.
wet (wĕt) ***adj-*** [**wet·ter, wet·test**] **1** covered or soaked with water or other liquid; moist; damp: *to change* wet *clothes.* **2** not yet dry: *Be careful of the* wet *paint.* **3** rainy; misty: *a* wet *season.* **4** *Informal* permitting the manufacture and sale of alcoholic beverages: *a* wet *town.* ***n-*** **1** moisture; wetness; rain: *Let's seek shelter from the* wet. **2** *Informal* person who opposes prohibition of alcohol liquor. ***vt-*** [**wet** or **wet·ted, wet·ting**] to moisten or soak with water or some other liquid: *to* wet *the lawn.* ***Hom-*** whet. **—*n-* wet′ness.**
wet·back (wĕt′ băk′) *Informal* ***n-*** Mexican, especially a laborer, who enters the United States illegally.
wet blanket *Informal* ***n-*** person who discourages fun.
wet cell ***n-*** electrical cell in which the electrolyte between the electrodes is liquid.
weth·er (wĕth′ ər) ***n-*** castrated ram. ***Homs-*** weather, whether.
wet nurse ***n-*** woman who suckles the child of another.
wet suit ***n-*** close-fitting rubber suit worn by surfers, skin divers, etc.
wetting agent ***n-*** a substance that reduces the surface tension of a liquid and makes it spread more easily over a solid surface.
we've (wēv) we have. ***Hom-*** weave.
whack (hwăk) *Informal* ***n-*** sharp, resounding slap or blow; also, the sound of this. ***vt-***: *to* whack *a ball.*
  have a whack at *Slang* to take an attempt or turn at; try.
  out of whack *Slang* not working properly.
whack·ing (hwăk′ ĭng) *chiefly Brit. Informal* ***adj-*** extremely large; whopping.

Blue whale, 80—100 ft. long

[1]**whale** (hwāl) ***n-*** any of several large sea mammals that live in herds. Some whales are hunted for their oil and bone. ***as modifier***: *a barrel of* whale *oil.* ***vi-*** [**whaled, whal·ing**] to hunt whales. [from Old English **hwæl.**] ***Homs-*** wail, wale.
  a whale of *Informal* a very large or good example of.
[2]**whale** (hwāl) *Informal* ***vt-*** [**whaled, whal·ing**] to hit very hard: *to* whale *a ball out of the park.* [perhaps a variant of **wale.**] ***Homs-*** wail, wale.
whale·back (hwāl′ băk′) ***n-*** long, low freight steamer with an upper deck shaped like a whale's back, used for carrying ore, coal, and grain on the Great Lakes.
whale·boat (hwāl′ bōt′) ***n-*** long, narrow rowboat that is sharp and slanted at both ends, first used by whale fishermen but now used as a lifeboat on ships.
whale·bone (hwāl′ bōn′) ***n-*** long, springy plates in the mouths of toothless whales, used in straining plankton from the water; baleen.
whal·er (hwā′ lər) ***n-*** person or vessel that goes whaling.
whale shark ***n-*** large shark that feeds on small fish.
whal·ing (hwā′ lĭng) ***n-*** occupation or industry of hunting and processing whales for oil, bone, and other products. ***as modifier***: *the* whaling *industry.*
wharf (hwôrf) ***n-*** [*pl.* **wharves** (hwôrvs) or **wharfs**] structure built at the water's edge and used for the mooring, loading, and unloading of ships; pier.
wharf·age (hwôr′ fĭj) ***n-*** **1** use of, or accommodation at, a wharf. **2** fee for using a wharf. **3** wharves collectively.
what (hwŏt, hwŭt) ***pron-*** **1** (interrogative pronoun) which thing or things, action, etc.: What *do you want?* What *is wrong?* **2** the thing that; that which: *A good scolding is* what *he needs.* **3** in exclamations, what things: What *he has suffered!* ***determiner*** (traditionally called adjective) **1** which; also, how much: *To* what *school do you go?* What *bus should I take?* What *good will that do?* **2** used as an exclamation to express an extreme degree or amount: What *talent!* What *riches he has!* What *a game!* **3** what-

ever: What *food we couldn't eat was given away.* ***adv-*** in what way; to what extent; how: What *does it help to cry?* What *does it profit a man?* ***conj-*** that (used only in negative sentences): *I don't know but* what *it is true.* ***interj-*** used as an exclamation to express surprise: What! *More rain?* ***Hom-*** watt.

and what not and all sorts of other things; et cetera. **what for** why: What *did you do that* for? **and what have you** and similar things; et cetera: *He likes magazines, books,* and what have you. **what if** suppose: What if *we leave early and go home?* **what about** what is thought of or about: What about *the new boy helping me?* **what though** even granting that; even though: What though *we failed today, all is not lost.* **what's what** *Informal* the actual state of affairs. **what with** partly as a result of.

what·ev·er (hwŏt ĕv′ər, hwŭt-) ***pron-*** **1** all that; anything that: *Give* whatever *you can.* **2** no matter what: *Don't give up,* whatever *you do.* **3** *Informal* what (strong form of "what" used only to introduce questions): *Tell me,* whatever *did you do?* ***determiner*** (traditionally called adjective) no matter what: Whatever *course I take, I'll fail.* ***adv-*** (also **what′ so·ev′ er**) of any kind at all: *He owns no property* whatever.

what·not (hwŏt′ nŏt′, hwŭt′-) ***n-*** set of shelves for holding bric-a-brac, curios, and similar items.

what's (hwŏts, hwŭts) **1** what is. **2** what has.

wheal (wēl) [2]weal.

wheat (hwēt) ***n-*** **1** a kind of grass-like grain. **2** the plant bearing this grain, with spikes that sometimes have bristles (**bearded wheat**) and sometimes do not (**beardless wheat**). **3** the seeds of this plant, used especially to make flour. *as* ***modifier***: *a* wheat *field.*

WITHOUT BEARD WITH BEARD
Wheat

wheat cake ***n-*** pancake.

wheat·en (hwē′ tən) ***adj-*** made of wheat: *a* wheaten *bread.*

wheat germ ***n-*** embryo of a wheat kernel, used especially as a source of vitamins.

whee·dle (hwē′ dəl) ***vt-*** **[whee·dled, whee·dling] 1** to influence by flattery or an ingratiating manner; coax: *Guy* wheedled *his father into giving him a bigger allowance.* **2** to get by coaxing: *Ann* wheedled *a new dress from her mother.* ***vi-***: *He is always* wheedling. **—*n-* wheed′ ler.** ***adv-*** **wheed′ ling·ly.**

wheel (hwēl) ***n-*** **1** round frame supported by spokes or a disk, on which a vehicle rolls. **2** round, movable part of certain machines, such as a steering wheel or cogwheel. **3** something resembling this in shape or motion, such as circular, revolving fireworks. **4** revolving or turning movement: *a* wheel *in the opposite direction.* **5** machine of which a wheel is the main part: *a potter's* wheel. **6 wheels** workings of something: *the* wheels *of government.* ***vt-*** **1** to move by means of wheels: *to* wheel *a cart. He* wheeled *the cart away.* **2** to change the direction of: *He* wheeled *his horse about.* ***vi-*** **1** to rotate or revolve; move in circles: *Gulls* wheeled *overhead.* **2** to change direction or course: *He* wheeled *about.* **3** to move or travel on wheels. ***Homs-*** weal, we'll.

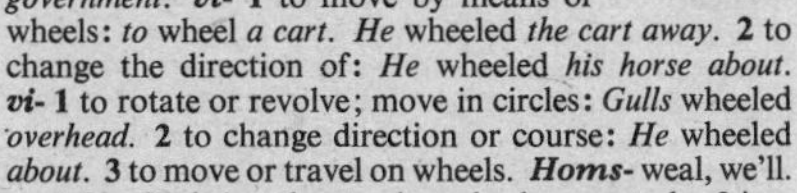

Wheel

at the wheel 1 at the steering wheel or controls. **2** in a position of command; in control. **wheels within wheels** complicated series of motives, influences, or other factors that affect one another.

wheel and axle ***n-*** a simple machine consisting of a wheel concentric with and firmly attached to a narrower cylinder, the axle, so that the two turn together. When a rotating force is applied to the rim of the wheel, the axle exerts a proportionally greater force on a rope or belt wound around it. The force so developed is proportional to the two diameters and the circular distance traveled by the rims.

wheel·bar·row (hwēl′ băr′ ō) ***n-*** vehicle with a wheel at one end and two straight handles at the other, used to push about small loads.

Wheelbarrow

wheel·base (hwēl′ bās′) ***n-*** distance from the front axle to the rear axle of an automobile or truck.

wheel·chair (hwēl′ châr′) ***n-*** mobile chair mounted on wheels, used by invalids.

wheeled (hwēld) ***adj-*** having wheels: *a* wheeled *vehicle.*

wheel·er (hwē′ lər) ***n-*** **1** something having wheels: *That bicycle is a three-*wheeler. **2** wheelhorse.

wheel·horse (hwēl′ hȯrs′, hôrs′) ***n-*** horse in a team that is nearest the front of a carriage or wagon; hence, a person who bears the most work or responsibility.

wheel·house (hwēl′ hous′) ***n-*** pilothouse.

wheel·wright (hwēl′ rīt′) ***n-*** person who makes or repairs wheels and wheeled vehicles.

wheeze (hwēz) ***vi-*** **[wheezed, wheez·ing]** to breathe with, or make, a sighing, whistling sound: *The old man* wheezed *and coughed. The tugboat* wheezed. ***n-***: *the* wheeze *of a sick man; the* wheeze *of Pete's old car.*

wheez·y (hwē′ zē) ***adj-*** **[wheez·i·er, wheez·i·est]** making a sighing, whistling sound: *a* wheezy *old horse.* **—*adv-* wheez′ i·ly.** ***n-*** **wheez′ i·ness.**

whelk (hwĕlk) ***n-*** any of several large sea snails with cone-shaped spiral shells, especially one used as food.

whelm (hwĕlm) *Archaic* ***vt-*** to cover, flood, or submerge with, or as if with, water; hence, to overwhelm.

whelp (hwĕlp) ***n-*** **1** young flesh-eating animal, such as a puppy or cub. **2** boy or girl (used humorously). **3** worthless or hated person. ***vi-*** to give birth to puppies or cubs.

when (hwĕn) ***adv-*** **1** at or during which time: *the day* when *the war started.* **2** at what time: *He asked,* "When *are you coming?*" ***conj-*** **1** at or after the time that: *It was too late* when *he came home.* **2** at whatever time; whenever: *He doesn't speak* when *I meet him.* **3** as soon as: *You may leave* when *dinner is over.* **4** in spite of the fact that; whereas; although: *He brought me oatmeal* when *I had asked for cornflakes.* **5** in the event that; at such time as; if: *How can I read,* when *you are shouting? Ask your teacher* when *in doubt.* ***pron-*** what or which time: *Since* when *have you been here?* ***n-*** time in which something occurs: *I don't know the why or* when *of it.* ***Hom-*** wen.

whence (hwĕns) ***adv-*** from where; from which place.

whence·so·ev·er (hwĕns′ sō ĕv′ ər) *Archaic* whence.

when·ev·er (hwĕn ĕv′ ər) ***conj-*** **1** every time that: *He telephones* whenever *he's in town.* **2** (also **when′ so·ev′ er**) at any time that: *He comes* whenever *he can.* ***adv-*** when (strong form of "when" used only to introduce questions): Whenever *did you arrive?*

where (hwâr) ***adv-*** **1** at or in what place or point: Where *do they live?* Where *am I wrong?* **2** to what place: Where *are you going?* **3** from what source or place: Where *did* *you get that?* ***pron-*** **1** the place at, in, or to which: *That is* where *I was born.* **2** which place: Where *do you come from?* ***n-*** place; location: *the* where *and when of the matter.* ***conj-*** **1** in, at, or to the place in which: *He lives* where *I lived.* **2** whereas: *He did much,* where *we expected little.* **3** under conditions or circumstances in which: *He played well* where *skill was concerned.* ***Homs-*** ware, wear.

where·a·bouts (hwâr′ ə bouts′) ***n-*** place where a person or thing is. ***adv-*** about where; near where.

where·as (hwâr ăz′) ***conj-*** **1** considering that; since: *The judge said,* "Whereas *the court declares the defendant guilty, he is ordered to pay the fine.*" **2** while on the contrary: *He is fat,* whereas *she is thin.*

where·at (hwâr ăt′) ***conj-*** whereupon: *The king came to the balcony,* whereat *the crowd cheered.*

where·by (hwâr′ bī′) ***adv-*** by which; by means of which: *the stars* whereby *the ship is steered.*

where·fore (hwâr′ fôr′) *Archaic* ***adv-*** why: *Now* wherefore *should we worry?* ***conj-*** for which reason; therefore.

where·from (hwâr′ frŭm′, -frŏm′) ***adv-*** from which or where.

where·in (hwâr′ ĭn′) ***adv-*** **1** in which: *a government* wherein *we can put our trust.* **2** in what; in what way: *My friend,* wherein *have I deceived you?*

where·of (hwâr ŏv′, -ŭv′) ***adv-*** of what; of which; of whom: *to know* whereof *one speaks.*

where·on (hwâr′ ŏn′, -ȯn′) *Archaic* ***adv-*** on which; on what: *the ground* whereon *he stood.*

where·to (hwâr′ to͞o′) ***adv-*** toward what place, purpose, or end: *The minister asked,* "Whereto *do we yearn?*" ***conj-*** *Archaic* toward which or whom.

where·un·to (hwâr ŭn′ to͞o′) *Archaic* whereto.

where·up·on (hwâr′ ə pŏn′, -pȯn′) ***conj-*** following which; upon which: *The child fell asleep,* whereupon *the mother went downstairs.* ***adv-*** on what grounds.

wher·ev·er (hwâr ĕv′ ər) ***conj-*** (also **where′ so·ev′ er**) in any place that or circumstance in which: *He does well* wherever *he goes.* Wherever *he can contribute, he does.* ***adv-*** where (strong form of "where" used only to introduce questions): Wherever *have I put my hat?*

where·with (hwâr′ wĭth′, -wĭth′) ***conj-*** with which.

where·with·al (hwâr′ wĭth ȯl′) ***n-*** necessary means or resources; especially, money.

wher·ry (hwĕr′ ē) ***n-*** [*pl.* **wher·ries**] **1** light rowboat. **2** racing scull for one person. **3** *Brit.* large, light barge.

whet (hwĕt) ***vt-*** **[whet·ted, whet·ting]** **1** to put a keen edge on by rubbing or grinding; sharpen: *to* whet *a knife.* **2** to stimulate or excite; make eager: *What I have read of his book* whets *my appetite for more.* ***Hom-*** wet.

wheth·er (hwĕth′ ər) ***conj-*** **1** if it is the case that; if: *I do not know* whether *you are telling the truth.* **2** no matter if: *The race is beginning,* whether *you are ready or not.* **3** (used to introduce the first of two alternatives, the second of which is introduced by "or"): *It doesn't matter* whether *he comes or not.* ***Homs-*** weather, wether.

whether or no in any case; no matter what happens.

►For usage note see IF.

whet·stone (hwĕt′ stōn′) ***n-*** stone for sharpening tools.

whew (hwyo͞o′) ***interj-*** exclamation of relief, surprise, disgust, dismay, etc.

whey (hwā) ***n-*** thin, watery part of milk that separates from the thicker part after coagulation. ***Homs-*** way, weigh.

which (hwĭch) ***determiner*** (traditionally called adjective or pronoun) **1** what one or ones of several: Which *house is yours?* Which *is your book?* **2** the one or ones that; whatever: *Point out* which *hat is yours and* which *is his.* **3** being the thing just mentioned: *After a month, during* which *time he did nothing, he had to submit a progress report.* ***pron-*** **1** (relative pronoun) that: *the books* which *we have read.* **2** (relative pronoun) *Archaic* who or whom: *"Our Father* which *art in heaven."* **3** whichever: *Take* which *of these books you please.* **4** thing or fact that: *He is washing the car*—which *reminds me—tell him to buy some gasoline.* ***Hom-*** witch.

►For usage note see WHOSE.

which·ev·er (hwĭch ĕv′ ər) ***determiner*** (traditionally called adjective or pronoun) **1** any one or ones that: *Read* whichever *book looks most interesting. Buy* whichever *pleases you most.* **2** no matter which: *It's all the same* whichever *day you come.* Also **which′ so·ev′ er** (-sō ĕ′ vər).

whiff (hwĭf) ***n-*** **1** light gust or puff; breath: *a* whiff *of smoke; a* whiff *of fresh air.* **2** slight odor or smell: *the* whiff *of burning leaves.* ***vt-*** **1** to inhale or exhale: *to* whiff *the sea breeze.* **2** to smell or sniff: *to* whiff *smoke.*

whif·fle·tree (hwĭf′ əl trē′) ***n-*** on a horse-drawn carriage or wagon, the pivoted horizontal crossbar to which the traces of the harness are fastened; whippletree.

Whig (hwĭg) ***n-*** **1** in England (17th-19th centuries), a member of a political party that opposed royal power and favored increased parliamentary control and social reform, later named the Liberal Party. **2** in the United States (1834-1855), a member of a political party that opposed the policies of the Democrats and was succeeded in 1856 by the Republican Party. **3** in the American Revolution, a colonist who favored independence from Great Britain. ***adj-***: *a* Whig *candidate.* ***Hom-*** wig.

while (hwīl) ***n-*** **1** period of time; especially, a brief period of time: *He came and stayed with us a* while. **2 the while** at the same time: *She sewed and hummed* the while. ***conj-*** **1** during the time that; at the same time that: *John was busy studying* while *the other children played outside.* **2** although; whereas: *Alex is tall* while *his parents are short.* ***vt-*** **[whiled, whil·ing]** to spend (time) leisurely and pleasantly (followed by "away"): *Tom* whiled *the hours away with his toys.* ***Hom-*** wile.

worth (one's) while worth (one's) time or effort.

whi·lom (hwī′ ləm) *Archaic* ***adj-*** former. ***adv-*** formerly.

whilst (hwīlst) *chiefly Brit.* ***conj-*** while.

whim (hwĭm) ***n-*** sudden or passing fancy; caprice.

whim·per (hwĭm′ pər) ***vi-*** **1** to cry with feeble, whining, broken sounds: *The sick puppy* whimpered. **2** to complain with such sounds; whine: *He* whimpered *about his hard life.* ***vt-*** to utter with such sounds: *to* whimper *a weak protest.* ***n-***: *She answered with a* whimper. —***n-*** **whim′ per·er.** ***adv-*** **whim′ per·ing·ly:** *He spoke* whimperingly.

whim·si·cal (hwĭm′ zĭ kəl) ***adj-*** **1** full of odd or fanciful notions; capricious. **2** odd; quaint: *a* whimsical *look.* —***n-*** **whim′ si·cal′ i·ty** (-zə kăl′ ə tē). ***adv-*** **whim′ si·cal·ly.**

whim·sy (hwĭm′ zē) ***n-*** [*pl.* **whim·sies**] **1** odd fancy or whim. **2** odd or quaint humor. Also **whim′ sey.**

whine (hwīn) ***vi-*** **[whined, whin·ing]** **1** to make a high-pitched complaining cry or sound: *The dog* whines *when he is cold.* **2** to complain or coax in a peevish, childish way: *He* whined *to be taken to the movies.* ***vt-*** to utter peevishly: *to* whine *complaints.* ***n-***: *the puppy's* whines. ***Hom-*** wine. —***n-*** **whin′ er.** ***adv-*** **whin′ ing·ly.**

whin·ny (hwĭn′ ē) ***n-*** [*pl.* **whin·nies**] neigh of a horse, especially, a low and gentle neigh. ***vi-*** **[whin·nied, whin·ny·ing]**: *The horse* whinnied *as the boy stroked its mane.*

whip (hwĭp) ***vt-*** **[whipped** or **whipt, whip·ping]** **1** to strike with, or as if with, a lash, often to punish: *to* whip *a horse;* whip *the grass with a cane.* **2** to drive or urge forward with, or as if with, a lash (often followed by "on"): *Desperation* whipped *him on.* **3** to draw or pull suddenly (often followed by "off" or "out"): *to* whip *off a belt*; whip *out a gun.* **4** to beat to a froth: *to* whip *eggs for an omelet.* **5** *Informal* to defeat decisively. ***vi-* 1** to move suddenly; dart about: *to* whip *around a corner.* **2** to flap or thrash about: *The flag* whipped *in the breeze.* ***n-* 1** flexible rod or a rod ending in a lash, used to drive animals onward or to deliver punishment. **2** member of a legislative body who is chosen by his political party to maintain discipline and regular attendance among party members; hence, any person who urges on or encourages others. **3** dessert made of whipped cream or egg white, often containing fruit: *a* prune *whip.* **—*adj-* whip′ like′. *n-* whip′ per.**

whip up 1 to prepare in a hurry. **2** to stir the emotions of; excite: *The speaker* whipped up *the crowd.*

whip·cord (hwĭp′ kȯrd′, -kôrd′) ***n-* 1** sturdy, tightly twisted cord, often used for whiplashes. **2** cord of catgut. **3** closely woven worsted fabric with diagonal ribs.

whip graft ***n-*** type of plant graft made by fitting part of a twig to a slit that has been cut in the stock.

whip hand ***n-*** the hand that holds the whip in riding or driving; hence, advantage; control.

whip·lash (hwĭp′ lăsh′) ***n-* 1** the striking part, or lash, of a whip. **2** injury of the spinal cord in the area of the neck and lower part of the brain, caused by a violent snapping, as in an automobile collision.

whipped cream ***n-*** cream beaten into a froth.

whip·per-snap·per (hwĭp′ ər snăp′ ər) ***n-*** insolent and arrogant person, especially a young person.

whip·pet (hwĭp′ ət) ***n-*** small, fleet dog resembling a greyhound, used especially for racing.

whip·ping (hwĭp′ ĭng) ***n-* 1** a beating. **2** a cord binding at the end of a rope.

whipping boy ***n-*** formerly, a person who served as companion to a nobleman and was punished for the latter's misdeeds; hence, anyone blamed for another.

whipping post ***n-*** post to which persons to be punished by flogging are tied.

whip·ple·tree (hwĭp′ əl trē′) ***n-*** whiffletree.

whip·poor·will (hwĭp′ ər wĭl′) ***n-*** small North American bird related to the goatsuckers and active at night. It gained its name from its whistling call.

Whippoorwill, about 10 in. long

whip·saw (hwĭp′ sȯ′) ***n-*** narrow, tapering saw about six feet long, set in a frame and operated by one or two persons. ***vt-*** **[whip·sawed, whip·sawed** or **whip·sawn, whip·saw·ing]**: *to* whipsaw *wood.*

whip·stock (hwĭp′ stŏk′) ***n-*** handle of a whip.

whir (hwûr) ***vi-*** **[whirred, whir·ring]** to revolve or move rapidly with a whizzing or buzzing sound: *The helicopter* whirred. ***n-*** such a sound. Also, *Brit.*, **whirr.** ***Hom-*** were.

whirl (hwûrl) ***vi-* 1** to turn around and around rapidly; spin. **2** to move swiftly: *She* whirled *angrily out of the room.* ***vt-*** to give a spinning motion to: *The wind* whirled *people's hats away.* ***n-* 1** spinning movement: *the* whirl *of a falling leaf.* **2** bewilderment; confusion of mind. **3** hectic, bustling activity. ***Hom-*** whorl. **—*n-* whirl′ er.**

whirl·i·gig (hwûr′ lə gĭg′) ***n-* 1** child's toy that spins or whirls. **2** merry-go-round. **3** anything that turns or whirls around rapidly; also, a whirling motion.

whirl·pool (hwûrl′ po͞ol′) ***n-*** swift, circling current of water, with a central depression into which floating objects are drawn; vortex.

whirl·wind (hwûrl′ wĭnd′) ***n-* 1** violent windstorm with a whirling, spiral motion. **2** sudden, violent rush or activity: *a* whirlwind *of preparations.* *as* ***modifier***: *a* whirlwind *courtship.*

whirl·y (hwûr′ lē) ***adj-*** whirling; spinning.

whisk (hwĭsk) ***vt-* 1** to brush with a quick, sweeping motion: *The horse* whisked *the flies away with his tail.* **2** to cause to move suddenly or rapidly. **3** to beat into a froth: *to* whisk *eggs.* ***vi-*** to move rapidly and nimbly: *The squirrel* whisked *up the tree.* ***n-* 1** sudden, light, quick movement: *a few* whisks *of his paint brush.* **2** (also **whisk broom**) small broom or brush with a short handle. **3** wire kitchen utensil for whipping foods.

whisk·er (hwĭs′ kər) ***n-* 1** long, bristly hair on each side of the mouth of some animals, such as cats or rats. **2 whiskers** hair growing on a man's face; beard. **—*adj-* whisk′ ered. *adj-* whisk′ er·like′.**

whis·ker·y (hwĭs′ kə rē) ***adj-* 1** having whiskers; whiskered. **2** like whiskers; whiskerlike.

whis·key (hwĭs′ kē) ***n-*** [*pl.* **whis·keys** or **whis·kies**] strong alcoholic drink made of grain. Also **whis′ ky.**

whis·per (hwĭs′ pər) ***n-* 1** soft, low, spoken sound: *We spoke in* whispers *because it was late.* **2** faint, rustling sound; murmur: *the* whisper *of rustling leaves.* **3** hint; suggestion. ***vi-* 1** to speak very softly; also, to speak cautiously or secretly: *Tom* whispered *in order not to be overheard.* **2** to make a faint, rustling or hissing sound: *The leaves* whispered *in the wind.* ***vt-*** to say softly: *She* whispered *the words to him.* **—*n-* whis′ per·er.**

whispering campaign ***n-*** campaign in which malicious rumors and gossip are deliberately spread in an attempt to discredit a person, especially a candidate.

whist (hwĭst) ***n-*** card game for four players in partnerships of two and two, from which the modern game of bridge has been developed. ***Hom-*** wist.

whis·tle (hwĭs′ əl) ***vi-*** **[whis·tled, whis·tling] 1** to make a shrill sound by forcing the breath between the teeth or puckered lips, or by forcing air or steam through a small opening, such as a valve. **2** to make any similar shrill sound: *The birds* whistled *in the trees. The wind* whistled *through the wires.* **3** to go or pass swiftly with or as if with a shrill sound: *Bullets* whistled *by us.* ***vt-* 1** to produce (a melody, tune, etc.) by forcing the breath between the teeth or puckered lips. **2** to call or signal in such a way: *He* whistled *us to a stop.* **3** to cause to move with a shrill sound: *They* whistled *arrows toward the target.* ***n-* 1** any of various devices that produce a shrill, piercing sound by the passage of breath, air, or steam through it: *a policeman's* whistle. **2** shrill sound: *the* whistle *of the radiator.* **—*n-* whis′ tler.**

Whistles

wet one's whistle *Informal* to take a drink, especially to relieve a great thirst.

whistle for *Informal* to try for in vain.

whistle stop *Informal* ***n-* 1** town so small that trains stop there only on signal; hence, any small town. **2** brief appearance or speech made by a political candidate at a small town, often from the rear platform of a train. *as* ***modifier*** **(whistle-stop)**: *a* whistle-stop *tour.* ***vi-*** **whistle-stop [whistle-stopped, whis·tle-stop·ping]** of political candidates, to make brief appearances in small towns: *to* whistle-stop *through the West.*

whit (hwĭt) ***n-*** the least bit: *It doesn't make a* whit *of difference.* ***Hom-*** wit.

white (hwīt) ***n-* 1** the lightest of all colors, that of snow and teeth. It is not strictly a color, but the total presence

fāte, făt, dâre, bärn; bē, bĕt, mêre; bīte, bĭt; nōte, hŏt, môre, dȯg; fŭn, fûr; to͞o, bo͝ok; oil; out; tar; thin; then; hw for wh as in *wh*at; zh for s as in u*s*ual; ə for a, e, i, o, u, as in *a*go, lin*e*n, per*i*l, at*o*m, min*u*s

or reflection of color or light. 2 clothing of this color: *Nurses wear* white. 3 part that has this color, especially the albumen of an egg or the light-colored part of the eyeball. 4 a Caucasian. ***adj-*** **[whit·er, whit·est]** 1 having the color of snow: *a* white *wedding dress.* 2 pale from fear or some other strong emotion. 3 of or having to do with the Caucasian race. 4 having silvery hair because of age: *He grew* white *with age.* ***vt-*** **[whit·ed, whit·ing]** *Informal* to whiten; bleach. ***Hom-*** wight. **—*n-* white′ ness.**

white out to cover with white paint in order to erase.

white ant ***n-*** termite.

white blood cell ***n-*** any of five types of colorless blood cells; leucocyte. Three types engulf and destroy bacteria and damaged red blood cells.

white·cap (hwīt′ kăp′) ***n-*** crest of a wave as it breaks.

white-col·lar (hwīt′ kŏl′ ər) ***adj-*** having to do with clerical or professional work: *a* white-collar *job.*

white dwarf *Astronomy* ***n-*** dwarf star that is extremely dense and very hot, but not as bright as most stars.

white elephant ***n-*** 1 rare variety of Asian elephant, regarded as sacred in India, Burma, and Ceylon. 2 possession that requires much care or expense while yielding little value.

white feather ***n-*** emblem of cowardice.

show the white feather to behave as a coward.

white·fish (hwīt′ fĭsh′) ***n-*** [*pl.* **white·fish; white·fish·es** (kinds of whitefish)] any of various North American fresh-water fishes of the salmon family having silvery sides and small mouths.

white flag ***n-*** flag of truce or surrender.

white-footed mouse ***n-*** deer mouse.

white gasoline ***n-*** gasoline with no lead compounds.

white gold ***n-*** alloy of gold with platinum, nickel, or another white metal.

White·hall (hwīt′ hȯl′) ***n-*** 1 street in London on which are situated the principal administrative offices of the British Government; hence, the government itself. 2 former royal palace near Westminster Abbey.

white-head·ed (hwīt′ hĕd′ əd) ***adj-*** having white hair, feathers, or fur, on the head; also, very blond.

white heat ***n-*** 1 temperature at which anything becomes incandescent. 2 condition of great excitement, emotion, or activity. **—*adj-* white′-hot′**: *a rod of* white-hot *metal.*

White House ***n-*** 1 official residence of the President of the United States, in Washington, D.C.; officially called the Executive Mansion. 2 *Informal* the resident and his personal staff: *Is the* White House *behind it?*

white lead ***n-*** any of various white, poisonous lead compounds, especially lead carbonate, used as pigment.

white lie ***n-*** lie or fib, especially one told for the sake of politeness or kindness.

white-liv·ered (hwīt′ lĭv′ ərd) ***adj-*** cowardly.

white matter ***n-*** in the brain and spinal cord, a whitish tissue composed of nerve fibers and their fatty sheaths. See also *grey matter.*

white metal ***n-*** any one of a number of white metallic alloys, such as pewter and Babbit metal.

whit·en (hwī′ tən) ***vt-*** to make white or whiter: *The bleach* whitened *the sheets.* ***vi-***: *The shirts* whitened.

white noise ***n-*** a sound that contains all audible frequencies at nearly equal intensities, usually produced electronically. Also **white sound.**

white oak ***n-*** 1 any of various oaks; especially, an oak of eastern North America, highly valued for its strong, durable wood. 2 the wood of any of these oaks.

white paper ***n-*** government report on any subject.

white pine ***n-*** 1 tall pine tree of Canada and northeastern United States, with long, slender needles growing in clusters of five. 2 the soft, light wood of this tree, widely used in carpentry.

White Russian ***adj-*** of or relating to the people and language of the Byelorussian S.S.R. ***n-*** Byelorussian member or sympathizer of a faction that fought the Bolsheviks in the Russian civil war.

white sale ***n-*** sale of towels, sheets, and other such goods at reduced prices.

white sauce ***n-*** sauce made mainly of milk, butter, and flour, and used for vegetables, fish, or meat.

white·wash (hwīt′ wȯsh′, -wŏsh′) ***n-*** mixture of lime and water used to whiten walls, fences, and other surfaces. ***vt-*** 1 to coat with such a mixture. 2 to cover up or hide the faults or mistakes of; gloss over: *to* whitewash *a political administration.*

white water ***n-*** foaming and turbulent water in rapids and breakers.

whith·er (hwĭth′ ər) ***adv-*** to what place; where.

whith·er·so·ev·er (hwĭth′ ər sō ĕv′ ər) *Archaic* ***adv-*** to whatever place.

white whale ***n-*** large, white dolphin of Arctic seas; beluga.

[1]**whit·ing** (hwī′ tĭng) ***n-*** any of several food fishes found along the Atlantic and Gulf coasts. [from Old English **hwītling,** from **hwīt** meaning "white."]

[2]**whit·ing** (hwī′ tĭng) ***n-*** powdered chalk used in whitewashing, the manufacture of putty, and for polishing. [from **white.**]

whit·ish (hwī′ tĭsh) ***adj-*** somewhat white.

Whit·sun·day (hwĭt′ sŭn′ dē) ***n-*** the Christian Pentecost.

Whit·sun·tide (hwĭt′ sən tīd′) ***n-*** the week following Whitsunday, especially the first three days.

whit·tle (hwĭt′ əl) ***vt-*** **[whit·tled, whit·tling]** 1 to trim or shape bit by bit with a knife: *to* whittle *a branch.* 2 to make in this way; carve: *to* whittle *wooden spoons.* ***vi-*** to carve wood, usually in an aimless manner: *He was sitting around* whittling. **—*n-* whit′ tler.**

whittle down (or **away**) to reduce or diminish little by little: *They* whittled down *the lengthy report.*

whiz (hwĭz) ***vi-*** **[whizzed, whiz·zing]** to speed with a buzzing or hissing sound: *The motorcycle* whizzed *by in a cloud of dust.* ***vt-*** to cause to move with such a sound: *He* whizzed *the magazine across the room.* ***n-*** [*pl.* **whiz·zes**] 1 buzzing or hissing noise: *the* whiz *of the airplane overhead.* 2 *Slang* person endowed with extraordinary ability: *He's a* whiz *at chess.* Also **whizz.**

who (ho͞o) ***pron-*** (interrogative pronoun) 1 what or which person or persons: Who *was there with you? I don't know* who *he was.* 2 (relative pronoun) the one or ones that: *Mr. Smith,* who *owns this land, is the mayor.* 3 whoever: Who *steals my purse, steals trash.*

who's who pertinent facts or information about each of a group of persons.

whoa (wō, hwō) ***interj-*** stop! stand still! (used especially in halting horses).

who'd (ho͞od) 1 who would. 2 who had. ***Hom-*** [2]hood.

who·dun·it (ho͞o′ dŭn′ ĭt) *Informal* ***n-*** mystery story, movie, or play in which the reader or viewer tries to guess who the guilty party is.

who·ev·er (ho͞o ĕv′ ər) ***pron-*** 1 anyone or everyone who: *The coach said,* whoever *wants to play should be on the field.* 2 no matter who: *Don't open the door,* whoever *it may be.* 3 who (strong form of "who" used only to introduce questions): Whoever *did it?*

whole (hōl) ***adj-*** 1 with no part left out; complete; entire: *the* whole *world*; *the* whole *school*; *the* whole *job.* 2 in one piece; not broken; uninjured: *The cup fell, but it's still* whole. 3 not divided into parts; with nothing removed; entire: *a box of* whole *cloves*; *a* whole *loaf of bread.* **4** having the same father and mother: *a* whole *brother or sister.* ***n-*** **1** all the parts of something taken together; total: *The* whole *is equal to the sum of its parts.* **2** complete system; unity: *Animals are organic* wholes. ***Hom-*** hole. **—*n-* whole′ ness.**

as a whole as a complete thing or unit; completely; altogether. **on the whole** all things considered; generally. **out of whole cloth** completely false or made up; fictitious.

whole·heart·ed (hōl′ här′ təd) ***adj-*** completely earnest; sincere; hearty: *You have my* wholehearted *approval.* **—*adv-* whole′ heart′ ed·ly. *n-* whole′ heart′ ed·ness.**

whole note *Music* ***n-*** note taking up a whole measure in common time. For picture, see *note.*

whole number *Mathematics* ***n-*** any of the numbers 0, 1, 2, 3, etc.; any non-negative integer.

whole rest *Music* ***n-*** rest that takes up as much time as a whole note. For picture, see *rest.*

whole·sale (hōl′ sāl′) ***adj-*** **1** of or relating to the selling of goods to dealers, stores, and other retail outlets, either by the producer directly or by specialized merchants: *the* wholesale *price*; wholesale *selling.* **2** engaged in such selling: *a* wholesale *distributor.* **3** on a large scale; widespread; indiscriminate: *the* wholesale *slaughter of wildlife.* ***adv-*** (also **at wholesale**) within the prices, quantities, and methods appropriate to the selling of goods to dealers, stores, etc.: *He buys* wholesale *and sells retail.* ***n-*** such selling: *the* wholesale *of leather goods.* ***vt-*** **[whole·saled, whole·sal·ing]** to sell (goods) in this way: *Mr. Lyman* wholesales *plumbing supplies.* ***vi-***: *These books* wholesale *at $2.19.*

whole·sal·er (hōl′ sā′ lər) ***n-*** person or company that sells goods wholesale.

whole·some (hōl′ səm) ***adj-*** **1** healthful for body, mind, or morals: *a* wholesome *diet*; wholesome *exercise.* **2** indicating good health: *a* wholesome *complexion.* **—*adv-* whole′ some·ly. *n-* whole′ some·ness.**

whole step or **whole tone** *Music* ***n-*** interval between two tones on the diatonic scale.

whole-wheat (hōl′ hwēt′) ***adj-*** made of entire wheat kernels, ground: *a* whole-wheat *roll*

who'll (hōōl) **1** who will. **2** who shall.

whol·ly (hōl′ lē, hō′ lē) ***adv-*** completely; entirely: *I am* wholly *satisfied with our new house.* ***Hom-*** holy.

whom (hōōm) ***pron-*** (objective case of the pronoun "who"): *To* whom *am I speaking? This is the man* whom *I mentioned yesterday.*

whom·ev·er (hōō mĕv′ ər) ***pron-*** objective case of **whoever.**

whom·so·ev·er (hōōm′ sō ĕv′ ər) ***pron-*** whomever.

whoop (hwōōp, hōōp, hwŏŏp, hŏŏp) ***vi-*** **1** to shout loudly: *to* whoop *for joy.* **2** to gasp loudly, while coughing or in whooping cough. ***vt-*** to call, drive, or urge with loud shouts or cries. ***n-*** **1** loud shout or cry. **2** loud gasp, as after an attack of coughing. ***Hom-*** hoop.

whoop it up *Slang* **1** to make a lot of noise in celebrating, carousing, etc. **2** to give enthusiastic support.

whooping cough ***n-*** contagious respiratory disease marked by severe spasms of coughing and gasping.

whooping crane ***n-*** large American crane having a red face and black wing tips. Whooping cranes are almost extinct. For picture, see *crane.*

whop·per (hwŏp′ ər) *Informal* ***n-*** **1** something that is unusually large. **2** a big lie; tall tale.

whop·ping (hwŏp′ ĭng) *Informal* ***adj-*** unusually large; great: *a* whopping *lie.* ***adv-***: *a* whopping *big dog.*

whore (hôr, hŏŏr) ***n-*** prostitute. ***Hom-*** hoar.

whorl (hwôrl, hwûrl) ***n-*** **1** in botany, a circular arrangement of flowers or leaves around the stem of a plant. **2** one of the turns of a spiral seashell. **3** one of the curved ridges of a fingerprint. ***Hom-*** whirl. **—*adj-* whorled:** *a* whorled *plant.*

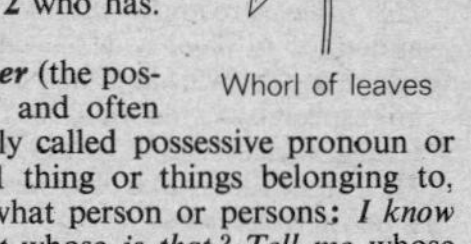
Whorl of leaves

whor·tle·ber·ry (hwûr′ təl bĕr′ ē, hwôr′-) ***n-*** [*pl.* **whor·tle·ber·ries**] **1** European and Asian type of blueberry. **2** its black berry.

who's (hōōz) **1** who is. **2** who has. ***Hom-*** whose.

whose (hōōz) ***determiner*** (the possessive case of "who," and often of "which," traditionally called possessive pronoun or possessive adjective). **1** thing or things belonging to, done by, or made by what person or persons: *I know* whose *house this is, but* whose *is that? Tell me* whose *is best.* **2** of which: *Name the city* whose *area is greatest.* ***Hom-*** who's.

►WHOSE is no longer restricted to persons, but is standard English in the meaning "of which": *the birds* whose *nest was robbed*; *the wheel* whose *spoke is broken.*

who·so·ev·er (hōō′ sō ĕv′ ər) ***pron-*** **1** anyone or everyone who. **2** no matter who.

why (hwī) ***adv-*** **1** for what reason: *He wondered* why *you smiled.* **2** for which; on account of which: *the reason* why. ***n-*** [*pl.* **whys**] the cause; reason: *Men still puzzle over the* why *of the universe.* ***interj-*** **1** (as an exclamation showing surprise or pleasure): *She said,* "Why! *It couldn't be easier.*" **2** (used for emphasis in various ways): Why, *it's only about a mile from here.*

W.I. 1 West Indian. **2** West Indies.

wick (wĭk) ***n-*** cord or tape of loosely woven, absorbent fibers in a candle or lamp, that draws up the melted wax or the kerosene or other oil to be burned.

Wick

wick·ed (wĭk′ əd) ***adj-*** **1** bad; evil; sinful: *a* wicked *deed*; *a* wicked *rascal.* **2** mischievous; naughty: *a* wicked *grin.* **3** severe; dangerous: *a* wicked *blow*; *a* wicked *weapon.* **—*adv-* wick′ ed·ly.**

wick·ed·ness (wĭk′ əd nəs) ***n-*** **1** condition of being wicked; wrongfulness; sinfulness: *a sermon on the* wickedness *of greed.* **2** something wicked; sin; iniquity.

wick·er (wĭk′ ər) ***n-*** flexible twigs, especially of willow, that can be woven to make baskets, etc. *as* ***modifier***: *a* wicker *basket*; *a* wicker *chair.*

wick·er·work (wĭk′ ər wûrk′) ***n-*** **1** the weaving of wicker into baskets, furniture, parts of furniture, etc.: *He is skilled at* wickerwork. **2** things woven of wicker. *as* ***modifier***: *a* wickerwork *sofa*; wickerwork *mats.*

wick·et (wĭk′ ət) ***n-*** **1** small door or gate, especially one in a larger door or gate. **2** an opening like a window, especially one with a grill or grate in a ticket office. **3** in croquet, an arch through which the ball is driven. **4** in cricket, either of the two frames at which the ball is bowled.

wick·ing (wĭk′ ĭng) ***n-*** material for making candle or lamp wicks.

wick·i·up (wĭk′ ē ŭp′) ***n-*** hut made of brush, woven reed mats, etc., used by some American Indians of western and southwestern United States. Also **wikiup.**

wide (wīd) ***adj-*** **[wid·er, wid·est] 1** extending some distance from side to side or edge to edge; broad: *a* wide *road*; *a* wide *piece of cloth.* **2** having a certain measure from side to side; in width: *a sheet of paper eight inches* wide. **3** of great extent; including much: *a* wide *range of friends*; *a person of* wide *experience.* **4** fully opened: *Her eyes were* wide *with surprise and wonder.* ***adv-*** **1** to the full extent; fully: *to open a door* wide; *a door that is* wide *open.* **2** to a considerable distance or extent: *The ranch stretches far and* wide. *His fame spread far and* wide. **3** far from the mark aimed at: *to shoot* wide. **—*adv-* wide′ ly. *n-* wide′ ness.**

wide-an·gle (wīd′ ăng′ gəl) ***adj-*** in photography, having an especially wide field of view: *a* wide-angle *lens.*

wide-a·wake (wīd′ ə wāk′) ***adj-*** **1** fully awake. **2** alert: *He's a* wide-awake *boy with many interests.* **—*n-* wide′-a·wake′ ness.**

wide-eyed (wīd′ īd′) ***adj-*** with eyes open wide, as if in surprise, wonder, etc.: *We were* wide-eyed *at his feats.*

wide·mouthed (wīd′ moutht′) ***adj-*** having a wide mouth: *a* widemouthed *bottle.*

wid·en (wī′ dən) ***vt-*** to make wider; broaden: *The county* widened *the two main roads. Reading* widens *our understanding.* ***vi-***: *The stream* widens *as it goes along.*

wide-o·pen (wīd′ ō′ pən) ***adj-*** **1** open wide. **2** very lax about law enforcement, especially concerning liquor laws, gambling, or vice: *a* wide-open *town.*

wide·spread (wīd′ sprĕd′) ***adj-*** **1** found over a large area or among many people; extensive: *a* widespread *drought*; *a* widespread *agreement on a subject.* **2** spread out wide; opened up: *his* widespread *hand.*

wid·geon (wĭj′ ən) ***n-*** either of two types of marsh duck: a gray European duck with a reddish-brown head, or a brown American duck with a white crown.

wid·ow (wĭd′ ō) ***n-*** woman whose husband has died and who has not remarried. **—*adj-* wid′ owed.**

wid·ow·er (wĭd′ ō ər) ***n-*** man whose wife has died and who has not remarried.

wid·ow·hood (wĭd′ ō hŏŏd′) ***n-*** condition of being a widow.

width (wĭdth) ***n-*** size or measurement from side to side; breadth: *The* width *of this is 54 inches. The porch runs the* width *of the house.*

wield (wēld) ***vt-*** **1** to use with the hands: *to* wield *a brush*; *to* wield *a sword.* **2** to exercise (power, influence, authority, etc.). **—*n-* wield′ er.**

Wig

wie·ner (wē′ nər) ***n-*** frankfurter. Also **wie′ nie** (-nē).

wife (wīf) ***n-*** [*pl.* **wives** (wīvz)] woman to whom a man is married; female spouse. **—*adj-* wife′ less.**

take to wife to marry (a certain woman).

wife·hood (wīf′ hŏŏd′) ***n-*** condition of being a wife.

wife·ly (wīf′ lē) ***adj-*** **[wife·li·er, wife·li·est]** of or relating to a wife; suitable to a wife: *her* wifely *duties.* **—*n-* wife′ li·ness.**

wig (wĭg) ***n-*** a head covering of human or other hair, used to hide baldness, for adornment, or as a part of an official uniform. **—*adj-* wigged.**

wig·gle (wĭg′ əl) ***vt-*** **[wig·gled, wig·gling]** to move or jerk about with short, quick, nervous movements; squirm; wriggle: *to* wiggle *one's toes.* ***vi-***: *to* wiggle *about in a chair.* ***n-*** movement of this kind.

wig·gler (wĭg′ lər) ***n-*** **1** person or thing that wiggles. **2** larva of the mosquito; wriggler.

wig·gly (wĭg′ lē) ***adj-*** **[wig·gli·er, wig·gli·est] 1** tending to wiggle. **2** wavy: *a* wiggly *line.*

wight (wīt) *Archaic* ***n-*** creature; person. ***Hom-*** white.

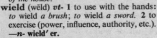

wig·wag (wĭg′ wăg′) ***vt-*** **[wig·wagged, wig·wag·ging]** to signal by moving flags, flashing lights, etc., in a code: *to* wigwag *a message for help.* ***vi-***: *to* wigwag *for help.* ***n-*** a signaling with flags, lights, etc. **—*n-* wig′ wag′ ger.**

DOT DASH

Wigwag

wig·wam (wĭg′ wŏm′, -wôm′) ***n-*** hut made of poles tied together and covered with bark, hides, or other material, usually in the shape of a dome. The wigwam was used by some of the eastern American Indians.

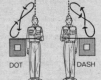

Wigwam

wil·co (wĭl′ kō′) *Military* ***interj-*** will comply; will do as you ask or order.

wild (wīld) ***adj-*** **[wild·er, wild·est] 1** living in a natural state; not captured or tamed: *a* wild *horse.* **2** living or growing without the care and effort of man; not domesticated or cultivated: *a* wild *dog*; *a* wild *rose.* **3** not civilized; savage: *the* wild *tribes of Borneo.* **4** with few or no inhabitants; remote: *the* wild *north woods.* **5** not controlled or disciplined; unruly: *a* wild *temper*; *a* wild *party.* **6** not kept in order; disarranged: *The boy's hair looked* wild. **7** unreasonable; rash; fantastic: *a* wild *scheme or claim.* **8** very disturbed or agitated: *to be* wild *with rage*; *a* wild *sea or storm.* **9** *Informal* very eager; keen; enthusiastic: *They are* wild *to start on the trip.* **10** wide of the mark: *a* wild *throw to first base*; *to make a* wild *guess.* **11** given the same value as another card: *to play deuces* wild *in poker.* ***adv-*** without control; wildly: *to play* wild; *to throw* wild. ***n-* wilds** region not inhabited or cultivated by human beings; wilderness; desert: *to explore the* wilds *of Africa.* **—*adv-* wild′ ly. *n-* wild′ ness.**

wild about *Informal* **1** very enthusiastic about or appreciative of: *to be* wild about *sports.* **2** to be very fond of; be in love with: *She's* wild about *a boy in her class.* **run wild** to live or grow without control.

wild boar ***n-*** any of several types of wild hogs found in Europe, Africa, Asia, and the United States, from which the domestic pigs have derived.

wild·cat (wīld′ kăt′) ***n-*** **1** any of several types of small, undomesticated cat, including the lynx, the bobcat, and a similar cat of Africa and southern Asia. **2** very risky business venture or investment; especially, an oil well drilled where no oil has yet been found. **3** *Informal* fierce, quick-tempered woman. *as* ***modifier***: *a* wildcat *well*; wildcat *bank.*

American wildcat, about 3 ft. long

wildcat strike ***n-*** labor strike not authorized by the strikers' union.

wil·de·beest (wĭl′ də bēst′) ***n-*** gnu.

wil·der·ness (wĭl′ dər nəs) ***n-*** **1** any wild, uninhabited region, especially one that is forbidding and desolate. **2** any tangled and confusing place or mass: *a* wilderness *of old cars. as* ***modifier***: *a* wilderness *retreat.*

wilderness area ***n-*** tract of forest land, prairie, or any other uninhabited area, set aside for preservation by the U.S. Government.

wild-eyed (wīld′ īd′) ***adj-*** staring wildly, as if from fear, anger, or other intense emotion: *a* wild-eyed *mob.*
wild·fire (wīld′ fīər′) ***n-*** fire that spreads very rapidly and is difficult to extinguish.
wild flower ***n-*** **1** the flower of any uncultivated plant found in fields, woods, etc. **2** the plant itself.
wild fowl ***n-*** wild birds hunted as game, such as wild geese and ducks, partridges, pheasants, and quail.
wild-goose chase (wīld′ go͞os′) ***n-*** useless pursuit or fruitless attempt.
wild·ing (wīl′ dĭng) ***n-*** wild plant or its fruit; especially, a wild apple or crab apple. *as* ***modifier****: a* wilding *tree.*
wild·life (wīld′ līf′) ***n-*** wild living things; especially, wild animals. *as* ***modifier****: a* wildlife *preserve.*
wild oat ***n-*** a tall grass that grows like a weed in fields and resembles the cultivated oat.
sow (one's) wild oats to do foolish or socially unacceptable things as a youth, before settling down.
wild pitch ***n-*** in baseball, an error charged against the pitcher when he throws a ball that the catcher cannot reach, and allows one or more base runners to advance.
wild rice ***n-*** the grain of a North American water grass, regarded as superior to rice and served as a delicacy.
Wild West ***n-*** western United States in the late 19th century, the land of cowboys and Indians. This period and its adventures were formerly celebrated in the traveling **Wild West show,** a spectacle like a circus.
wild·wood (wīld′ wo͝od′) ***n-*** forest in its natural state. *as* ***modifier****: a* wildwood *scene*; wildwood *flower.*
wile (wīl) ***n-*** clever or crafty trick or words, intended to deceive or lure: *She used her* wiles *to get him to do as she wanted.* ***vt-*** **[wiled, wil·ing]** to obtain by trickery: *She* wiled *the secret from him.* ***Hom-*** while.
wil·i·ness (wī′ lē nəs) ***n-*** craftiness; slyness; foxiness.
[1]**will** (wĭl) ***n-*** **1** act of choosing or ability to choose: *to do something by one's own free* will. **2** control over one's impulses or appetites: *to have the* will *to stop smoking.* **3** strong purpose; determination: *Where there's a* will *there's a way. The sick man lost the* will *to live.* **4** a wish; choice; intention: *It is his* will *that we come. Thy* will *be done.* **5** attitude toward others: *a person of good* will. **6** person's written instructions telling what is to be done with his property after his death, or who is to be his executor. ***vt-*** **1** to have as a wish or purpose: *He* willed *success for his children.* **2** to compel or influence by mental power: *The boy* willed *himself to stay awake.* **3** to give by terms of a legal paper disposing of one's property after death: *His grandfather* willed *him the farm.* [from Old English **willa** meaning "a wish; a determination," from **willan.**]
at will as one wishes or sees fit. **with a will** with energy or enthusiasm: *He went to work* with a will.
[2]**will** (wĭl) ***auxiliary verb*** **1** am, is, or are going to: *They* will *like this new game.* **2** am, is, or are determined to: *I* will *go even if I am punished for it.* **3** want or wants to; wish or wishes to: *Ask him if he* will *have some cake.* **4** am, is, or are bound or are able to: *This radio* will *receive only three stations.* [from Old English **willan** meaning "to wish," and related to [1]**will.**]
►For usage note see SHALL.
willed (wĭld) ***adj-*** having a certain kind of will (used in compound words): *a strong-*willed *man.*
will·ful (wĭl′ fəl) ***adj-*** **1** determined to have one's own way; stubborn: *The* willful *boy will not obey.* **2** deliberate; intentional: *a* willful *waste of food*; willful *destruction.* Also **wil′ ful.** **—*adv-*** **will′ ful·ly.** ***n-*** **will′ ful·ness.**

wil·lies (wĭl′ ēz) *Slang* ***n-*** *pl.* nervous feelings; jitters.
will·ing (wĭl′ ĭng) ***adj-*** **1** ready to do what is necessary or requested; favorably disposed: *to be* willing *to work hard*; *to be* willing *to help others.* **2** cheerfully ready: *a* willing *worker.* **3** given or done freely and gladly: *his* willing *assistance.* **—*adv-*** **will′ ing·ly.** ***n-*** **will′ ing·ness.**
will-o'-the-wisp (wĭl′ ə *th*ə wĭsp′) ***n-*** **1** phosphorescent lights that appear to flit above marshy ground at night. **2** anything that is misleading or elusive.
wil·low (wĭl′ ō) ***n-*** **1** tree or shrub with slender leaves and tough, flexible branches, usually growing in watery ground. **2** the wood and branches of this tree, used for furniture, baskets, etc. *as* ***modifier****: a* willow *branch*; willow *wand.*

Weeping willow

wil·low·y (wĭl′ ō ē) ***adj-*** **1** full of willows; covered with willows. **2** like a willow; slender; lithe; graceful: *the* willowy *figure of a dancer.*
will power ***n-*** ability to control one's acts and desires by one's will; strength of mind or character; determination; resolve: *It takes* will power *to give up a bad habit.*
wil·ly-nil·ly (wĭl′ ē nĭl′ ē) ***adv-*** whether one likes it or not; willingly or unwillingly: *He must accept the decision,* willy-nilly. ***adj-*** uncertain; indecisive; wavering: *a* willy-nilly *policy.*
[1]**wilt** (wĭlt) ***vi-*** **1** to droop or fade; become limp: *The leaves* wilted *in the hot sun.* **2** to become weak or faint; lose strength or courage: *The mob* wilted *when the police came.* ***vt-****: The hot sun* wilted *the geraniums.* ***n-*** **1** plant disease that causes leaves to soften and droop. **2** a cause of drooping or weakening: *Nothing was a* wilt *to his joy.* [from earlier **welk** meaning "to wither."]
[2]**wilt** (wĭlt) *Archaic* form of [2]**will** used with "thou" in the present tense. [from [2]**will.**]
wil·y (wī′ lē) ***adj-*** **[wil·i·er, wil·i·est]** sly; cunning; crafty: *a* wily *fox*; *a* wily *maneuver.*
wim·ble (wĭm′ bəl) ***n-*** tool for boring, such as an auger or a gimlet. ***vt-*** **[wim·bled, wim·bling]** to bore with such a tool.
wim·ple (wĭm′ pəl) ***n-*** a covering of cloth for the head, neck, and chin, worn by women generally in medieval times, and still part of the dress of some orders of nuns. ***vt-*** **[wim·pled, wim·pling]** **1** to clothe with such a covering. **2** to lay in folds. ***vi-*** **1** to lie in folds. **2** to ripple, as a stream does.

Woman wearing wimple

win (wĭn) ***vt-*** **[won, win·ning]** **1** to come off best in: *to* win *a battle.* **2** to gain by effort, charm, or persuasion: *to* win *honors*; *to* win *friends*; *to* win *support.* ***vi-*** to gain a victory; come off best. ***n-*** *Informal* victory; success: *Ten* wins *and three defeats.*
win out to succeed over all others.
win over to persuade; induce.
wince (wĭns) ***n-*** a sudden tensing of the muscles, or a spasmodic drawing away, as one reacts to pain. ***vi-*** **[winced, winc·ing]**: *I* winced *when he hit my hand.*
winch (wĭnch) ***n-*** machine for lifting or pulling consisting of a roller that is turned by a crank or engine and on which a rope, cable, chain, etc., is wound. For picture, see *windlass.*

[1]**wind** (wĭnd) ***n-*** 1 movement, current, or blast of air, especially a strong natural movement. 2 ability to breathe without difficulty; breath: *A man out of training soon loses his* wind. 3 air-borne scent: *The cat caught* wind *of the food.* 4 gas formed in the digestive organs. **5 winds** wind instruments in an orchestra. *as **modifier**: a* wind *gauge*; wind *speed.* ***vt-*** 1 to cause to be out of breath: *The steep climb* winded *the mountaineers.* 2 to get or follow the scent of: *The fox* winded *the rabbit.* 3 to allow to rest to recover one's breath: *to* wind *a horse.* [from Old English **wind.**]

before the wind with the wind: *to sail* before the wind. **down the wind** moving or situated in the direction the wind is blowing. **get the** (or **one's**) **wind up** to become nervous, excited, or irritated. **get wind of** to know or hear about; get news of: *He* got wind of *a good job.* **in the wind** about to happen; being discussed. **off the wind** with the wind blowing from behind. **how** (or **the way**) **the wind blows** the trend of events, opinions, etc., especially in politics or intrigue: *We won't act until we see* how the wind blows. **take the wind out of (one's) sails** to take away someone's advantage in an unexpected way. **under the wind** in a place protected from the wind. **up the wind** (upwind).

[2]**wind** (wīnd) ***vt-*** [**wound** (wound), **wind·ing**] 1 to twist; twine; wrap: *to* wind *a string around one's finger*; *to* wind *a bandage on one's ankle.* 2 to cover; enwrap: *to* wind *an electrical splice with friction tape.* 3 to twist together: *to* wind *the strands of a rope.* 4 to tighten the driving spring of: *to* wind *a clock.* 5 to make (one's way): *He* wound *his course through the hills.* ***vi-*** 1 to follow a twisting course: *The road* winds *among the hills.* 2 to twine round and round: *The ivy* winds *around the tree.* ***n-*** a bend; twist; coil. [from Old English **windan** meaning "to wind; to circle around."] **—*n-* wind'er.**

wind off to unwind or reel off: *He* wound off *the cable.*

wind up 1 to bring to a close; put an end to. 2 to come to an end: *How did the discussion* wind up? 3 to make tense or excited. 4 of a baseball pitcher, to go through various swinging and kicking motions just before pitching the ball to the batter.

[3]**wind** (wīnd, wĭnd) ***vt-*** [**wind·ed** or **wound** (wound), **wind·ing**] to blow (a horn). [from [1]**wind** in a special sense but influenced in its first pronunciation by [2]**wind.**]

wind·age (wĭn'dĭj) ***n-*** effect of the wind in deflecting a missile; also, the extent of such deflection.

wind·bag (wĭnd'băg', wĭn'-) *Slang* ***n-*** person who talks much but says little.

wind·blown (wĭnd'blōn', wĭn'-) ***adj-*** 1 blown by the wind: *a scattering of* wind-blown *paper.* 2 of trees, twisted by the blowing of the wind.

wind·break (wĭnd'brāk, wĭn'-) ***n-*** a shelter or protection from the wind, such as a wall or row of trees.

wind·break·er (wĭnd'brā'kər, wĭn'-) ***n-*** 1 warm outer jacket that fits snug at the waist and around the wrists. 2 **Windbreaker** trademark name for such a jacket.

wind-bro·ken (wĭnd'brō'kən, wĭn'-) ***adj-*** of horses, having the heaves.

wind·burn (wĭnd'bûrn', wĭn'-) ***n-*** inflammation of the skin caused by exposure to wind. **—*adj-* wind'burned'.**

wind chill factor ***n-*** adjustment of the air temperature to estimate cooling effect on human skin of air temperature and wind speed combined.

wind·fall (wĭnd'fŏl', wĭn'-) ***n-*** 1 something blown down by the wind, such as fruit from a tree. 2 an unexpected piece of good fortune, especially unexpected money.

wind·flow·er (wĭnd'flou'ər, wĭn'-) ***n-*** anemone.

wind·ing (wīn'dĭng) ***adj-*** turning; curving; twisting: *a* winding *road.* ***n-*** 1 coil of wire wound on an electromagnet, armature of a generator or motor, etc. 2 single turn of such a coil. 3 method of arranging such coils.

winding sheet ***n-*** a sheet in which a dead body is wrapped; a shroud.

wind instrument ***n-*** musical instrument sounded by a current of air blown into it, such as a flute, saxophone, trumpet, clarinet, or oboe.

Windlass or winch

wind·jam·mer (wĭn'jăm'ər) *Informal* ***n-*** sailing vessel.

wind·lass (wĭnd'ləs) ***n-*** winch turned by a crank.

wind·mill (wĭnd'mĭl', wĭn'-) ***n-*** mill or machine operated by the force of the wind that acts to turn its large sails or vanes. Windmills are now used mostly for pumping water.

fight (or **tilt at**) **windmills** to fight an imaginary opponent or an imagined wrong, as Don Quixote attacked the windmills, believing that they were giants.

win·dow (wĭn'dō) ***n-*** 1 an opening in a wall of a building, side of an automobile, etc., usually supplied with glass, for admitting light. 2 the glass, with its frame, which fills such an opening. 3 opening in an envelope, usually covered with transparent paper, through which the address on an enclosure can be read. **—*adj-* win'dowed'.** ***adj-*** **win'dow·less.**

Windmill

window box ***n-*** long box for growing plants on a window ledge.

window dressing ***n-*** 1 decorative arrangement of merchandise in a show window, designed to attract customers. 2 something used to give a favorable, and often false, impression: *His folksy manner is* window dressing *for his sharp mind.* **—*n-* window dresser.**

win·dow·pane (wĭn'dō pān') ***n-*** sheet or panel of glass in a window.

win·dow-shop (wĭn'dō shŏp') ***vi-*** [**win·dow-shopped, win·dow-shop·ping**] to go looking at merchandise in store windows without buying. **—*n-* win'dow-shop'per.**

window sill ***n-*** shelf across the bottom of a window.

wind·pipe (wĭnd'pīp', wĭn'-) ***n-*** trachea.

wind·row (wĭn'drō') ***n-*** hay or grain raked into a row to dry.

wind scale ***n-*** Beaufort scale.

wind·shield (wĭnd'shēld', wĭn'-) ***n-*** window at the front of an automobile or other vehicle to protect its riders from wind, spray, dust, etc. *as **modifier**: a* windshield *wiper. Also Brit.* **wind'screen'** (-skrēn').

wind sleeve or **wind sock** ***n-*** a cone-shaped cloth tube, open at both ends and attached to the top of a pole, that shows the direction of the wind at an airfield.

Wind·sor (wĭn'zər) ***n-*** name adopted by the ruling family of England in 1917.

Windsor chair ***n-*** any chair having a solid wooden seat with sockets into which rounded wooden spindles or sticks are fixed to form the legs, back, arms, etc.

Windsor knot ***n-*** a broad knot used for tying a necktie.

wind·storm (wĭnd'stôrm', wĭn'stôrm', -stôrm') ***n-*** storm having high wind but little rain, snow, or hail.

wind·swept (wĭnd'swĕpt', wĭn'-) ***adj-*** marked by the occurrence of strong winds: *a* windswept *prairie.*

wind tunnel ***n-*** long, tubelike chamber in which aircraft, spacecraft, or models of them are subjected to winds of varying velocities in order to study their wind resistance and strains under flight conditions.

wind·up (wīnd′ŭp′) ***n-*** **1** the end; finish; conclusion: *the* windup *of a meeting*; the *windup of a tournament.* **2** in baseball, the various swinging and kicking motions a pitcher uses as he prepares to pitch to the batter. *as* ***modifier***: *a* windup *game*; *a* windup *speech.*

wind·ward (wĭnd′ wərd, wĭn′-) ***n-*** side facing or toward the wind: *We passed to the* windward *of the island.* ***adj-***: *the* windward *side.* ***adv-***: *They sailed* windward.

wind·y (wĭn′ dē) ***adj-*** **[wind·i·er, wind·i·est] 1** having much wind; breezy: *March is a* windy *month.* **2** exposed to the prevailing winds: *the* windy *side of a house.* **3** very talkative; wordy; noisy: *a* windy *speaker or speech.* **—*adv-*** **wind′ i·ly.** ***n-*** **wind′ i·ness.**

wine (wīn) ***n-*** **1** drink made of the fermented juice of grapes and having about 12 per cent of alcohol by volume. **2** similar drink made from other fruits or plants: *a good elderberry* wine; *dandelion* wine. **3** a deep-red color. ***adj-***: *a* wine *merchant*; wine *velvet.* ***vt-*** **[wined, win·ing]** to serve such a drink to. ***Hom-*** whine.
wine and dine to entertain lavishly.

wine·glass (wīn′ glăs′) ***n-*** a small glass, usually on a stem, for drinking wine.

wine·press (wīn′ prĕs′) ***n-*** machine for pressing the juice from grapes.

win·er·y (wī′ nə rē) ***n-*** [*pl.* **win·er·ies**] building or factory where wine is made.

wing (wĭng) ***n-*** **1** one of the pair of modified arms by which a bird or bat flies; also, one of the similar organs of an insect. **2** one of the main structures that supply lift in an airplane or helicopter; lifting airfoil. **3** part of a building projecting from the main structure: *the north* wing *of a house.* **4** in the Air Force, a unit next below an air division. **5** in military and naval operations, a force on the right or left of the center of a tactical grouping: *The general decided to advance his left* wing. **6** part or faction of a party, organization, nation, etc.; especially, a faction representing a political viewpoint. **7** in certain sports, a position that is to the right or left of center; also, a player in such a position. **8 wings** (1) the spaces on each side of a stage, behind the proscenium arch; also, scenery used at the sides of a stage. (2) badge showing that one is a military or airline pilot, or a member of a flying crew. ***vt-*** **1** to equip for, or as if for, flying: *to* wing *an arrow.* **2** to wound in the wing; also, to wound slightly: *to* wing *a bird with a rifle bullet.* ***vi-*** to fly; soar: *The hawk* winged *over the barnyard.* **—*adj-*** **wing′ less.** ***adj-*** **wing′ like′.**
on the wing in flight; flying: *flock of geese* on the wing. **take wing** to fly away; run away. **under (one's) wing** under (someone's) protection, teaching, or sponsorship.

wing·back (wĭng′ băk′) ***n-*** in football, a back on offense whose position is behind and slightly to the outside of an end.

wing case ***n-*** the hardened front wings of certain insects, which serve as a protective cover for other wings.

winged (wĭngd, *also* wĭng′ əd) ***adj-*** **1** having wings. **2** moving as if on wings; swift; rapid: *a* winged *message.*

wing·man (wĭng′ mən) ***n-*** [*pl.* **wing·men**] pilot who flies slightly to one side and to the rear of an airplane formation, and protects that side.

wing nut ***n-*** threaded nut having a flattened, upright head shaped like a pair of wings, which can be grasped between the thumb and forefinger for turning.

wing·o·ver (wĭng′ ō′ vər) ***n-*** flying maneuver in which an airplane banks as it climbs, turns entirely over at the top of the climb, and flies back in the opposite direction.

wing·span (wĭng′ spăn′) ***n-*** **1** distance from wing tip to wing tip of an airplane or glider. **2** wingspread.

wing·spread (wĭng′ sprĕd′) ***n-*** **1** distance from wing tip to wing tip of a bird, bat, or insect when its wings are outspread. **2** wingspan.

wing tip ***n-*** **1** the outer end of a wing of an airplane, bird, or the like. **2** upper front part of a shoe having a design with a point toward the back and a curved lobe on each side; also, a shoe with such a toe. **—*adj-*** **wing′ tipped′**: *a* wingtipped *shoe.*

wink (wĭngk) ***vi-*** **1** to close and open one eye quickly as a signal or hint. **2** to flash, blink, or twinkle: *The lights of a passing ship* winked. ***vt-***: *He* winked *his eyes.* ***n-*** **1** act of closing and opening an eye quickly as a hint or signal. **2** time taken in doing this; very short time; instant. **3** tiny gleam or sparkle: *the* wink *of lights.*
wink at to pretend not to see; overlook deliberately.

win·kle (wĭng′ kəl) ***n-*** any of several sea snails, some of which are used for food; periwinkle.

Win·ne·ba·go (wĭn′ ə bā′ gō) ***n-*** [*pl.* **Win·ne·ba·gos,** also **Win·ne·ba·go**] **1** one of a tribe of American Indians who formerly lived in eastern Wisconsin, south of Green Bay, where some still live. **2** the language of these Indians. ***adj-***: *a* Winnebago *farm.*

win·ner (wĭn′ ər) ***n-*** person or thing that wins.

win·ning (wĭn′ ĭng) ***adj-*** **1** in contests, successful; victorious: *the* winning *team.* **2** attractive; charming; persuasive: *a* winning *manner*; *a* winning *smile.* ***n-*** **winnings** something won or gained, especially money. **—*adv-*** **win′ ning·ly.**

win·now (wĭn′ ō) ***vt-*** **1** to blow or fan off the chaff and husks from (grain) by a stream of air. **2** to sift; separate: *to* winnow *good from bad.* **—*n-*** **win′ now·er.**

win·some (wĭn′ səm) ***adj-*** attractive; charming; winning: *a* winsome *girl*; *her* winsome *ways.* **—*adv-*** **win′ some·ly.** ***n-*** **win′ some·ness.**

win·ter (wĭn′ tər) ***n-*** **1** the coldest season of the year, between autumn and spring, and in the northern hemisphere usually from December 21 to March 21. **2** time of gloom or sorrow: *in the* winter *of one's life.* **3** a year of life: *a man of* seventy *winters.* ***vi-*** to spend the winter: *He* winters *in Florida.* ***vt-*** to keep and feed during the winter: *to* winter *cattle on silage. as* ***modifier***: *a* winter *sport*; winter *clothes.*

win·ter·green (wĭn′ tər grēn′) ***n-*** **1** low-growing, woody, evergreen plant with red berries, white flowers, and leaves that yield an aromatic oil. **2** the oil of this plant, used as a flavoring or in medicine. **3** flavoring made from this oil or from the bark of the black birch; also, the flavor itself. *as* ***modifier***: *a piece of* wintergreen *candy.*

win·ter·ize (wĭn′ tə rīz′) ***vt-*** **[win·ter·ized, win·ter·iz·ing]** to make ready for winter: *to* winterize *a car.*

win·ter·kill (wĭn′ tər kĭl′) ***vt-*** to kill (a plant) by exposure to winter cold. ***vi-*** of a plant, to die by exposure to winter cold.

win·ter·time (wĭn′ tər tīm′) ***n-*** time or season of winter. *as* ***modifier***: *a* wintertime *activity.*

winter wheat ***n-*** wheat that is planted in the fall for harvesting in early summer.

win·try (wĭn′ trē, -tə rē) ***adj-*** **[win·tri·er, win·tri·est] 1** of winter or like winter; cold, chilly, snowy, etc. **2** cold and unfriendly in manner or expression; lacking warmth: *a* wintry *smile.* Also **win′ ter·y.**

wipe (wīp) ***vt-*** **[wiped wip·ing] 1** to pass a cloth or some soft material over, in order to dry or cleanse: *to* wipe *the teacups*; *to* wipe *the windshield.* **2** to remove by rubbing: *to* wipe *tears from her cheeks*; *to* wipe *oil off the deck.* ***n-*** act of rubbing, drying, or cleansing: *to give the glasses a* wipe. **—*n-* wip′ er.**

wipe out to destroy completely; obliterate.

wire (wīər) ***n-*** **1** metal drawn out into a strand of any given thickness. **2** such a strand, or a cable of one or more strands, used for various purposes: *a length of baling* wire; *barbed* wire; *electric* wires. **3** a telegram. *as **modifier**: a* wire *netting*; wire *splice.* ***vt-*** **[wired, wir·ing] 1** to provide with metallic electrical conductors, usually insulated, for power or communication uses: *to* wire *a new house*; *to* wire *a television set.* **2** to bind with metal thread: *I'll* wire *these pieces together temporarily.* **3** to send a message to (someone) by telegraph: *He* wired *his parents.* **—*adj-* wire′ like′.**

in under the wire at the destination just in time. **pull wires** to use indirect influence to gain some end.

wire cutter ***n-*** any of various shears or pliers used for cutting wire. Also **wire cutters.**

wire-haired (wīər′ hârd′) ***adj-*** having hair that is stiff and coarse, like fine wire.

wire-haired terrier (wīər′ hârd′) ***n-*** fox terrier having stiff, wirelike hair. Also **wire′ hair′.**

wire·less (wīər′ ləs) *chiefly Brit.* ***n-*** **1** radio communication. **2** a radio receiver. *as **modifier**: by* wireless *telegraphy*; *a* wireless *set.*

wire·pho·to (wīər′ fō′ tō) ***n-*** [*pl.* **wire·pho·tos**] **1** method of sending or receiving photographs by telephonic electric signals. **2** photograph received by this method. **3 Wirephoto** a trademark name for this process.

wire·pull·er (wīər′ po͝ol′ ər) *Informal* ***n-*** person who uses means unknown to most others to achieve his aims, influence other persons, etc. **—*n-* wire′ pull′ ing.**

wire service ***n-*** any of several news-gathering organizations that provide articles to member newspapers over a teletype network.

wire·tap (wīər′ tăp′) ***vt-*** **[wire·tapped, wire·tap·ping]** to make a secret connection into (a telephone or other communication line) in order to listen to and record what passes over it. ***n-*** such a connection: *to install a* wiretap. **—*n-* wire′ tap′ per.**

wire·worm (wīər′ wûrm′) ***n-*** slender, hard-bodied larva of certain beetles, which eats the roots of plants.

wir·ing (wīər′ ĭng) ***n-*** system of electric wires and connections in a building, piece of equipment, appliance, etc. *as **modifier**: a* wiring *diagram.*

wir·y (wī′ rē) ***adj-*** **[wir·i·er, wir·i·est] 1** made of wire. **2** tough and bristly, like wire: *a tuft of* wiry *hair.* **3** lean but strong and sinewy: *a* wiry *horse*; *a* wiry *boxer.* **—*adv-* wir′ i·ly. *n-* wir′ i·ness.**

Wis. Wisconsin.

wis·dom (wĭz′ dəm) ***n-*** **1** good judgment and knowledge of what is right and true: *the* wisdom *of ancient philosophers.* **2** sympathetic knowledge of people, their needs and impulses, and the behavior to be expected of them under various conditions. **3** scholarly knowledge; learning.

wisdom tooth ***n-*** the last back tooth on either side of each human jaw, usually appearing when a person is fully grown.

[1]**wise** (wīz) ***adj-*** **[wis·er, wis·est] 1** having or showing knowledge and good judgment, especially about people: *a* wise *old man*; *a* wise *decision.* **2** having knowledge or information about; learned: *to be* wise *in the ways of lions.* **3** *Slang* bold in an offensive way; arrogant; fresh. [from Old English **wis.**] **—*adv-* wise′ ly.**

wise to *Informal* aware of; knowing of.

[2]**wise** (wīz) ***n-*** way, manner, or mode: *in no* wise; *in any* wise. [from Old English **wise** of the same meaning.]

-wise *suffix* (used to form adverbs) **1** in such a manner: *like*wise. **2** in such a position or direction: *slant*wise. ►The coining of new words having -WISE as a suffix, meaning "in regard to," is increasing: *Budget*wise (in regard to our budget), *we are doing well.* However, many careful writers and speakers consider this usage incorrect and unnecessary.

wise·a·cre (wīz′ ā′ kər) ***n-*** person who thinks he knows a great deal; smart aleck.

wise·crack (wīz′ krăk′) *Slang* ***n-*** clever or cute remark or answer, sometimes humorous but often arrogant or insulting. ***vi-*** to make such a remark. **—*n-* wise′ crack′ er.**

wish (wĭsh) ***vt-*** **1** to have as a desire, especially a desire that might not be fulfilled or could only be fulfilled by magic; will; want (usually takes a clause or infinitive as object): *I* wish *that I could be there. He* wishes *he were king. She* wished *to go. They* wish *an interview.* **2** to have as a hope: *I* wish *you the best.* Wish *me luck!* ***vi-***: *If you* wish *hard enough, you may get what you want.* ***n-*** **1** strong desire; longing; yearning: *His* wish *is for a quiet life.* **2** something desired or asked for, especially something that might be obtained only by magic: *Did you get your* wish? *Please state your* wishes. **—*n-* wish′ er.**

wish on (someone) to pass off on; palm off; foist.

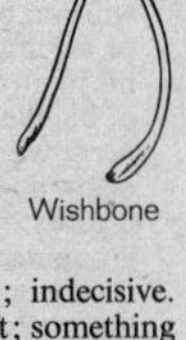
Wishbone

wish·bone (wĭsh′ bōn′) ***n-*** the forked bone in a fowl's breast, in front of the breastbone.

wish·ful (wĭsh′ fəl) ***adj-*** having or based on wishes; full of longing; desirous. **—*adv-* wish′ ful·ly. *n-* wish′ ful·ness.**

wishful thinking ***n-*** type of thinking by which a person assumes that what he would like to be true is true.

wish·y-wash·y (wĭsh′ ē wŏsh′ ē, -wŏsh′ ē) *Informal* ***adj-*** lacking in spirit and vigor; indecisive.

wisp (wĭsp) ***n-*** **1** small bundle or bunch; tuft; something thin and sometimes twisted: *a* wisp *of straw*; *a* wisp *of hair.* **2** a small or slight fragment or bit: *a* wisp *of smoke.* **3** something frail or slight: *a* wisp *of a girl.*

wisp·y (wĭs′ pē) ***adj-*** **[wisp·i·er, wisp·i·est]** like a wisp; thin; slight: *her* wispy *hair.*

wist (wĭst) *p.t. & p.p.* of [2]**wit.**

wis·ter·i·a (wĭs têr′ ē ə) ***n-*** any of several climbing and twining shrubs of North America and eastern Asia that bear drooping clusters of purple, blue, or white flowers. Also **wis·tar′ i·a** (târ′ ē ə).

wist·ful (wĭst′ fəl) ***adj-*** longing; wishful: *The child cast a* wistful *glance at the candy counter.* **—*adv-* wist′ ful·ly. *n-* wist′ ful·ness.**

Wisteria

[1]**wit** (wĭt) ***n-*** **1** ability to see and describe what is amusing or odd in a situation or idea. **2** person noted for this ability. **3** the clever or brilliant things such a person says or writes. **4** intelligence; wisdom: *He hasn't the* wit *to do it.* **5 wits** sanity. ***Hom-*** whit. [from Old English **witt.**]

at (one's) wit's end at the end of one's mental powers; at a loss. **have** or **keep (one's) wits about (one)** to remain alert or calm, especially in an emergency.

[2]**wit** (wĭt) *Archaic* ***vt- & vi-*** **[wist** (wĭst), **wit·ting]** to know. ***Hom-*** whit. [from Old English **witan.**]

to wit that is to say; namely.

witch (wĭch) ***n-*** **1** woman believed to have supernatural evil powers. **2** an ugly old woman; crone; hag. **3** person who believes in and practices the rites of what he thinks is the ancient pagan religion of Europe. ***vt-*** **1** to work an evil spell upon; bewitch. 2 *Informal* to search for or find (water, a well, etc.) with a divining rod. ***Hom-*** which.

witch·craft (wĭch′ krăft′) ***n-*** **1** craft or power of a witch; dealings with evil powers; sorcery. **2** the beliefs and rituals of persons who profess what they think is the ancient pagan religion of Europe.

witch doctor ***n-*** person in certain primitive tribes who claims to have the power to heal by witchcraft, counteract evil spells, etc.; medicine man.

witch·er·y (wĭch′ ə rē) ***n-*** [*pl.* **witch·er·ies**] **1** great charm; fascination: *There was* witchery *in the moonlight.* **2** witchcraft; magic; sorcery.

witches' Sabbath ***n-*** religious festival of witches, held at certain times during the year, including Halloween, and supposed to be presided over by Satan.

witch hazel ***n-*** **1** shrub with small yellow flowers which appear after the leaves have gone. **2** an extract from the bark and dried leaves of this shrub, used as a remedy for cuts, bruises, or soreness.

witch hunt ***n-*** an investigation of persons or organizations, ostensibly to expose subversion or disloyalty, but actually for someone's political advantage.

witch·ing (wĭch′ ĭng) ***adj-*** **1** of, relating to, or suitable for witchcraft or sorcery: *Midnight is regarded as the* witching *hour.* **2** bewitching.

with (wĭth, wĭth) ***prep-*** **1** in the company of; in the presence of: *Come* with *me to the barn.* **2** having; possessing: *I prefer the dress* with *the collar.* **3** on the side of: *Are you* with *me or against me?* **4** in spite of: *He still smiles,* with *all his troubles.* **5** against; in a situation that suggests opposition: *We argued* with *them.* **6** by means of; using: *to cure* with *drugs*; *to hear* with *one's ears.* **7** in the spirit of; in the condition of: *He said good-by* with *great sadness.* **8** at the same time as; during: *We rise* with *the sun every morning.* **9** in proportion to: *Many wines improve* with *age.* **10** as a result of; because of: *His hands froze* with *cold.* **11** from: *I hate to part* with *all this money.* **12** between oneself, and another: *pacts* with *foreign countries.* **13** in the care of: *He left the dog* with *his mother when he went away.* **14** in respect to; in regard to: *How are things* with *him?* **15** in the same group or mixture as: *Mix the salt* with *the spices.* **16** by: *a cup filled* with *milk.* **17** to or onto: *This wire is connected* with *the loudspeaker.* **18** because of: *I can do the job* with *his help.* **19** as well as: *He can sing* with *the best.* **20** in the opinion of: *It is all right* with *him.* **21** as a member of; in the service of: *He has been* with *us for years.* ***Hom-*** withe.

with·al (wĭth ȯl′, wĭth-) *Archaic* ***adv-*** in addition; as well; besides: *She had wealth, and beauty* withal.

with·draw (wĭth drȯ′, wĭth-) ***vt-*** [**with·drew, with·drawn, with·draw·ing**] **1** to draw back; pull away: *She* withdrew *her hand from the hot iron.* **2** to take back; retract: *to* withdraw *unkind words.* **3** to take away or out; remove: *to* withdraw *money from the bank.* ***vi-*** to go away; retreat: *The army* withdrew *under fire.*

with·draw·al (wĭth drȯ′ əl, wĭth-) ***n-*** **1** a removing: *a* withdrawal *from the room*; *a* withdrawal *of money from the bank.* **2** a taking back: *the* withdrawal *of a threat.*

with·drawn (wĭth drȯn′, wĭth-) ***adj-*** **1** removed; isolated: *a* withdrawn *mountain retreat.* **2** detached; unresponsive: *He has a* withdrawn *manner.*

withe (wĭth, wĭth, wĭth) ***n-*** tough, flexible twig for tying or binding; withy. ***Hom-*** with.

with·er (wĭth′ ər) ***vi-*** to dry out and shrivel: *In autumn the leaves* wither. *My skin* withers. ***vt-*** **1** to cause to dry out and shrivel. **2** to make (someone) feel uncomfortable or ashamed: *She* withered *him with a chilly glance.*

with·ers (wĭth′ ərz) ***n-*** *pl.* part of a horse's back between the shoulder blades.

with·hold (wĭth hōld′, wĭth-) ***vt-*** [**with·held, with·hold·ing**] **1** to keep back; refuse: *to* withhold *permission.* **2** to restrain; forbear: *to* withhold *angry words.*

withholding tax ***n-*** part of an employee's wages withheld by an employer and turned over to the government as partial or complete payment of the employee's income tax.

with·in (wĭth ĭn′, wĭth-) ***prep-*** **1** inside the limits of: *He promised to come* within *an hour. Their request seemed to be* within *reason.* **2** not beyond; not more than: *It will cost* within *ten dollars.* ***adv-*** **1** indoors; inside: *It is cold outside, but warm* within. **2** inwardly: *He seemed calm, but* within *he was all turmoil.*

without (wĭth out′, wĭth-) ***prep-*** **1** not having; lacking: *coffee* without *sugar*; *to travel* without *a passport.* **2** beyond: *It is true* without *any doubt.* **3** with neglect or avoidance of: *He walked by* without *speaking to us.* ***adv-*** on the outside; outdoors: *It was raining* without.

do without to get along although lacking: *to* do without *luxuries.*

with·stand (wĭth stănd′, wĭth-) ***vt-*** [**with·stood, with·stand·ing**] to oppose or resist successfully; endure.

with·y (wĭth′ ē) ***n-*** [*pl.* **with·ies**] withe.

wit·less (wĭt′ ləs) ***adj-*** **1** without good sense or sound judgment; foolish; stupid: *Her* witless *remarks hurt many people's feeling.* **2** lacking cleverness or humor. **—*adv-*** **wit′ less·ly.** ***n-*** **wit′ less·ness.**

wit·ness (wĭt′ nəs) ***n-*** **1** person who has first-hand knowledge of something. **2** person who tells in court under oath what he knows of a fact, event, or person. **3** person who is present at the signing of a legal document, and who also signs it as proof of this. **4** something that gives evidence or proof of a transaction, action, or event: *This receipt is* witness *that the bill was paid.* ***vt-*** **1** to see or observe in person: *to* witness *an accident*; *to* witness *the signing of a will.* **2** to sign (a document) to indicate knowledge of another person's having signed it: *to* witness *a will.* **3** to be or give proof or evidence of: *Her red face* witnessed *her embarrassment.*

bear witness to give or provide evidence or testimony about something: *She* bore witness *to his crimes.*

witness stand ***n-*** in a law court, a small platform, enclosure, etc., from which a witness gives evidence.

wit·ted (wĭt′ əd) ***adj-*** having or indicating a certain kind of mind or intelligence (used in compound words): *a sharp-*witted *man.*

wit·ti·cism (wĭt′ ə sĭz′ əm) ***n-*** witty remark or saying.

wit·ting·ly (wĭt′ ĭng lē) ***adv-*** with conscious knowledge; intentionally: *I would not* wittingly *offend him.*

wit·ty (wĭt′ ə) ***adj-*** [**wit·ti·er, wit·ti·est**] amusing in a sharp, clever way; full of or showing wit: *a* witty *man*; witty *tale.* **—*adv-*** **wit′ ti·ly.** ***n-*** **wit′ ti·ness.**

wive (wīv) *Archaic* ***vt- & vi-*** [**wived, wiv·ing**] to marry (a woman).

wi·vern (wī′ vərn) wyvern.

wives (wīvz) *pl.* of **wife.**

wiz·ard (wĭz′ ərd) ***n-*** **1** man who supposedly has magic powers; magician; sorcerer. **2** *Informal* person who is very clever at something: *He's a* wizard *at math.*

wiz·ard·ry (wĭz′ ər drē) ***n-*** [*pl.* **wiz·ard·ries**] **1** art, skill, or practices of a wizard; magic. **2** extraordinary skill.

---

fāte, făt, dâre, bärn, bē, bĕt, mêre; bīte, bĭt; nōte, hŏt, mȯre, dȯg; fŭn, fûr; to͞o, bo͝ok; oil; out; ta*r*; thin; then; hw for wh as in *wh*at; zh for s as in u*s*ual; ə for a, e, i, o, u, as in *a*go, lin*e*n, per*i*l, at*o*m, min*u*s

wiz·en (wĭz'ən) *vt-* to cause to become dried up or shriveled: *The sun had* wizened *her skin.* *vi-*: *The leather had* wizened *with age.*

W. long. west longitude.

WNW or **W.N.W.** west-northwest.

woad (wōd) *n-* **1** plant native to the Old World, with clusters of small, yellow flowers. **2** blue dye obtained from the leaves of this plant. It was used by the ancient Britons to color their faces and bodies.

wob·ble (wŏb'əl) *vi-* [**wob·bled, wob·bling**] **1** to move or sway unsteadily from side to side; rock; jiggle. **2** to be unsteady or indecisive; waver. *vt-* to cause to sway or rock. *n-* unsteady, swaying motion. **—*n-* wob'bler.**

wobble pump *n-* an auxiliary, hand-operated fuel pump used in a propeller-driven aircraft.

wob·bly (wŏb'lē) *adj-* [**wob·bli·er, wob·bli·est**] tending to shake or sway unsteadily; teetering; unsteady.

Wo·den (wō'dən) *n-* Odin.

woe (wō) *n-* **1** deep sorrow or grief. **2** cause of great sorrow or misfortune; affliction. ***interj-*** *Archaic* exclamation expressing great sorrow or distress.

woe is me *Archaic* how unhappy I am! alas!

woe·be·gone (wō'bĭ gŏn') *adj-* showing great grief or misery; wretched: *her* woebegone *appearance.*

woe·ful (wō'fəl) *adj-* **1** full of woe; sorrowful; mournful: *his* woeful *tale.* **2** distressing; lamentable: *their* woeful *ignorance.* **—*adv-* woe'ful·ly.** ***n-* woe'ful·ness.**

wok (wäk) *n-* Chinese cooking vessel that has a convex bottom.

woke (wōk) *p.t.* of [1]**wake.**

wold (wōld) *n-* uncultivated, treeless tract of land; a down or moor.

wolf (wo͝olf) *n-* [*pl.* **wolves** (wo͝olvz)] **1** any of various flesh-eating, wild animals related to and resembling the dog. Wolves sometimes travel in packs in winter, and are destructive to sheep and farm animals. **2** fierce, greedy, or destructive person. *vt-* to devour greedily and hurriedly: *Bob* wolfed *his food.* **—*adj-* wolf'like'.**

Timber wolf, about 5 1/2 ft. long

cry wolf to raise an alarm about imaginary or pretended danger. **keep the wolf from the door** to ward off extreme hunger, dire poverty, etc. **wolf in sheep's clothing** person who hides unfriendly intentions under the guise of friendliness.

wolf·hound (wo͝olf'hound') *n-* any of several breeds of large dogs formerly used for hunting wolves; especially the unusually large **Irish wolfhound,** and the slender, graceful **Russian wolfhound.**

wolf·ish (wo͝ol'fĭsh) *adj-* **1** typical of a wolf; fierce; savage: *his* wolfish *cruelty.* **2** greedy; voracious: *a* wolfish *appetite.* **—*adv-* wolf'ish·ly.** ***n-* wolf'ish·ness.**

wolf·ram (wo͝ol'frəm) *n-* tungsten.

wolf·ram·ite (wo͝ol'frə mīt') *n-* black or dark-brown mineral that is an important tungsten ore.

wol·ver·ine (wo͝ol'və rēn') *n-* ferocious, flesh-eating animal of northern forests, with a thick-set body and shaggy, blackish fur; glutton. Wolverines are noted for their cunning and greediness.

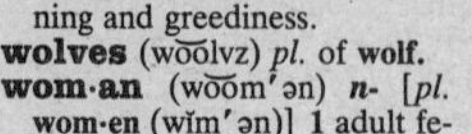

Wolverine, 2 1/2—3 ft. long

wolves (wo͝olvz) *pl.* of **wolf.**

wom·an (wo͝om'ən) *n-* [*pl.* **wom·en** (wĭm'ən)] **1** adult female human being. **2** female sex in general. **3** female servant or attendant. **—*adj* wom'an·like'.**

wom·an·hood (wo͝om'ən ho͝od') *n-* **1** condition of being a woman: *The little girl has grown to* womanhood. **2** women in general. **3** feelings or characteristics typical of women.

wom·an·ish (wo͝om'ən ĭsh) *adj-* considered typical of a woman, but not suitable for a man; unmanly. **wom'an·ish·ly.** ***n-* wom'an·ish·ness.**

wom·an·kind (wo͝om'ən kīnd') *n-* women in general.

wom·an·ly (wo͝om'ən lē) *adj-* typical of or appropriate to a woman; feminine. **—*n-* wom'an·li·ness.**

woman's rights *n-* [*pl.* **women's rights**] the rights of women to social, legal, and political equality with men.

woman suffrage *n-* the right of women to vote, established in the United States by the Nineteenth Amendment in 1920.

womb (wo͞om) *n-* **1** female organ in which the young of mammals develop before birth; uterus. **2** place in which something originates or begins to develop.

wom·bat (wŏm'băt') *n-* Australian pouched mammal that resembles a small bear.

Wombat, 2—4 ft. long

wo·men (wĭm'ən) *pl.* of **woman.**

wom·en·folk (wĭm'ĭn fōk)') *n- pl.* women in general; also, the women of a community, household, etc.

won (wŭn) *p.t. & p.p.* of **win.** ***Hom-*** one.

won·der (wŭn'dər) *n-* **1** feeling or state of mind produced by something amazing, curious, or awe-inspiring; astonishment. **2** thing, person, or event that causes such a feeling: *The Grand Canyon is one of the great natural* wonders *of the world.* *vi-* **1** to feel surprise or astonishment; be amazed: *The children* wondered *at the magician's tricks.* **2** to be curious or doubtful; speculate: *I* wonder *a lot about his candidacy.* *vt-* to be doubtful and curious about; want to know: *They* wondered *what was in the package.* **—*adv-* won'der·ing·ly:** *They looked* wonderingly *at the mile-deep canyon.*

do (or **work**) **wonders** to achieve or produce very good results. **no wonder** not surpsising.

won·der·ful (wŭn'dər fəl) *adj-* **1** causing wonder; astonishing; remarkable: *new and* wonderful *scientific discoveries.* **2** remarkably good; excellent. **—*adv-* won'der·ful·ly.** ***n-* won'der·ful·ness.**

won·der·land (wŭn'dər lănd', -lənd) *n-* **1** fantastic, imaginary land or place, as in a fairy tale. **2** scene or region that fills observers with wonder: *the* wonderland *of the Grand Canyon.*

won·der·ment (wŭn'dər mənt) *n-* feeling or state of wonder; amazement: *to stare in* wonderment.

won·drous (wŭn'drəs) *adj-* marvelous; astonishing. ***adv-*** *Archaic* remarkably; amazingly. **—*adv-* won'drous·ly.** ***n-* won'drous·ness.**

wont (wōnt, wônt, wŭnt) *n-* habit; custom: *It is her* wont. ***Homs-*** want, won't.

wont to accustomed to: *He is* wont to *take the bus to school.*

won't (wōnt, wŭnt) will not. ***Homs-*** want, wont.

wont·ed (wōn'təd, wôn'-, wŭn'-) *adj-* usual; customary: *a dancer's* wonted *grace.*

woo (wo͞o) *vt-* **1** to try to win the love of; seek in marriage; court. **2** to try to persuade or win over: *The politician* wooed *his audience with many promises.* **3** to seek to win or attain: *to* woo *fame and fortune.* *vi-* to go courting. **—*n-* woo'er.**

wood (wo͝od) *n-* **1** hard, fibrous material enclosed by bark and forming the stems and trunks of trees, shrubs, and some other plants. **2** this material, cut, often dried and specially treated, and used in building, for making furniture or other articles, as fuel, etc. **3** (often **woods**) thick growth of trees; forest; woodland: *The children were lost in the* wood. *The* woods *are full of game.* 4 golf club with a wooden head. *as* ***modifier***: *a* wood *carver*; *a* wood *merchant*; *a* wood *nymph.* ***Hom-*** would.

out of the woods safe after escaping from danger or overcoming difficulty.

wood alcohol ***n-*** methyl alcohol.

wood·bine (wŏŏd′ bīn′) ***n-*** any of several climbing vines, such as the Virginia creeper or a European plant related to the honeysuckle.

wood·block (wŏŏd′ blŏk′) ***n-*** **1** solid block of wood, especially one in which letters or designs are carved to produce an engraving. **2** a print, illustration, etc., made from this. *as* ***modifier***: *a* woodblock *engraving.*

wood·carv·ing (wŏŏd′ kär′ vĭng) ***n-*** **1** art or process of carving in wood. **2** a carving made in wood. ***—n-*** **wood′ carv′ er.**

wood·chuck (wŏŏd′ chŭk′) ***n-*** chunky, brown or grayish burrowing animal related to the squirrels and found in eastern North America; ground hog; marmot.

Woodchuck, 16 — 18 in. long

wood·cock (wŏŏd′ kŏk′) ***n-*** chunky, brown, short-legged game bird with a very long, pointed bill and a short, stubby tail.

wood·craft (wŏŏd′ krăft′) ***n-*** **1** skill and knowledge in anything pertaining to the woods, such as camping, hunting, forestry, etc. **2** skill in woodwork or in carving and making objects from wood.

wood·cut (wŏŏd′ kŭt′) ***n-*** **1** block of wood for printing designs or illustrations, in which the parts that will not print are cut away from the surface. **2** a print or illustration made from this. *as* ***modifier***: *a* woodcut *print.* See also *wood engraving.*

wood·cut·ter (wŏŏd′ kŭt′ ər) ***n-*** person who cuts wood or fells trees. ***—n-*** **wood′ cut′ ting.**

wood·ed (wŏŏd′ əd) ***adj-*** having many trees.

wood·en (wŏŏd′ ən) ***adj-*** **1** made of wood: *a* wooden *bucket.* **2** stiff; awkward: *the* wooden *gestures of a bad actor.* **3** lacking spirit or warmth; dull: *a* wooden *smile.* ***—adv-*** **wood′ en·ly.** ***n-*** **wood′ en·ness.**

wood engraving ***n-*** **1** block of wood for printing illustrations, in which an engraving of fine lines and tones is cut into the end grain with a graver. **2** illustration made from this. **3** the art of making such blocks or illustrations. See also *woodcut.* ***—n-*** **wood engraver.**

wood·en·head·ed (wŏŏd′ ən hĕd′ əd) ***adj-*** stupid.

wooden Indian ***n-*** **1** carved and painted wooden figure of an American Indian, formerly used as an advertisement in front of a store selling cigars, tobacco, etc. **2** *Informal* person who is dull, inarticulate, etc.

wood·en·ware (wŏŏd′ ən wâr′) ***n-*** dishes, spoons, and similar household articles made of wood.

wood·land (wŏŏd′ lənd, -lănd′) ***n-*** land covered with trees; forest. *as* ***modifier***: *a* woodland *brook.*

wood lot ***n-*** **1** piece of land having a stand of trees that are cut for firewood or other uses. **2** tree farm.

wood louse ***n-*** any of various small, flat, insectlike crustaceans, such as the sow bug, that are found under rocks, logs, tree bark, etc.

wood·man (wŏŏd′ mən) ***n-*** [*pl.* **wood·men**] **1** woodcutter. **2** woodsman.

wood nymph ***n-*** **1** in Greek or Roman mythology, a nymph who lives in the woods; dryad. **2** brown butterfly that has yellow markings and two round spots on each of its front wings.

wood·peck·er (wŏŏd′ pĕk′ ər) ***n-*** any of several birds with feet and tails adapted for climbing tree trunks. Their beaks can drill through the bark to get the insects and larvae on which they feed.

Woodpecker, about 8 in. long

wood·pile (wŏŏd′ pīl′) ***n-*** pile of wood, especially of cut logs to be used as firewood.

wood pulp ***n-*** wood that has been ground and specially treated to form a soft pulp, used especially in making paper.

wood pussy *Informal* ***n-*** skunk.

wood·rat (wŏŏd′ răt′) ***n-*** any of several rats that have soft fur and large ears and live in woods, fields, etc.; especially, the pack rat.

wood·shed (wŏŏd′ shĕd′) ***n-*** shed for storing cut wood, especially firewood.

woods·man (wŏŏdz′ mən) ***n-*** [*pl.* **woods·men**] man, such as a hunter, trapper, or lumberman, who is skilled in woodcraft and lives and works in the woods.

wood sorrel ***n-*** oxalis.

woods·y (wŏŏd′ zē) ***adj-*** [**woods·i·er, woods·i·est**] of, belonging to, or suggestive of woods or forests: *the* woodsy *odor of damp moss.* ***—n-*** **woods′ i·ness.**

wood tar ***n-*** tar produced by the distillation of wood, especially pine.

wood thrush ***n-*** North American thrush with a brown back, spotted breast, and a clear, melodious song.

wood turning ***n-*** skill or process of shaping wood on a lathe. ***—n-*** **wood turner.**

wood·wind (wŏŏd′ wĭnd′) ***n-*** **1** musical wind instrument, originally made of wood but now often of metal, such as the flute, clarinet, oboe, or bassoon. **2 woodwinds** the part of an orchestra that consists of these instruments. *as* ***modifier***: *a* woodwind *quartet.*

wood·work (wŏŏd′ wûrk′) ***n-*** parts or objects made from wood; especially, the interior wooden finishings of a house, such as doors, window frames, or cupboards.

wood·work·ing (wŏŏd′ wûr′ kĭng) ***n-*** art, skill, or process of making things from wood. *as* ***modifier***: *a set of* woodworking *tools.* ***—n-*** **wood′ work′ er.**

wood·y (wŏŏd′ ē) ***adj-*** [**wood·i·er, wood·i·est**] **1** having wood as a characteristic part or structure; consisting of or containing wood: *a* woody *plant.* **2** covered with trees; wooded. **3** resembling or suggesting wood: *the* woody *smell of a carpenter's shop.* ***—n-*** **wood′ i·ness.**

[1]**woof** (wŏŏf) ***n-*** **1** in weaving, the crosswise threads carried back and forth by the shuttle, and interwoven with the lengthwise threads of the warp. For picture, see *warp.* **2** texture of a fabric. [an altered form of **weave,** from Middle English **oof,** from Old English **owef,** from **o-** and **wefan** meaning "to weave."]

[2]**woof** (wŏŏf) ***n-*** low barking sound, such as that made by a dog. [from an imitation of the sound.]

woof·er (wŏŏf′ ər) ***n-*** radio or phonograph loudspeaker designed to reproduce sounds of low frequency with great accuracy.

wool (wŏŏl) ***n-*** **1** thick, springy, usually curly hair that forms the fleece of sheep and some other animals and is used to make yarn and textiles. **2** yarn or cloth made from this. **3** any dense, springy substance resembling

---

sheep's fleece, such as plant down, human hair, or metal fibers. *as **modifier**: a* wool *dress*; wool *thread.*

pull the wool over (someone's) eyes to deceive by pretense or trickery.

wool·en (wŏŏl′ən) ***adj-*** **1** made of wool. **2** of or having to do with wool or things made of wool: *the* woolen *trade.* ***n-*** **woolens** fabrics or garments made of wool.

wool·gath·er (wŏŏl′ găth′ər) ***vi-*** to indulge in idle dreaming. **—*n-* wool′gath′er·er.**

wool·ly (wŏŏl′ ē) ***adj-*** **[wool·li·er, wool·li·est] 1** consisting of or resembling wool: *a* woolly *fabric.* **2** covered with wool or a similar fuzzy material: *a* woolly *lamb*; *a* woolly *toy.* **3** not clear; confused; vague: *a* woolly *mind.* ***n-*** (usually **woollies**) clothing, especially underwear, made of wool. Also **wool′y. —*n-* wool′li·ness.**

wild and woolly resembling the early frontier life of western United States; rough and uncivilized.

woolly bear ***n-*** fuzzy, black-and-brown caterpillar of the tiger moth.

woo·zy (wōō′ zē, wŏŏz′ ē) *Informal* ***adj-*** **[woo·zi·er, woo·zi·est]** dazed and confused; dizzy; befuddled. **—*adv-* woo′zi·ly. *n-* woo′zi·ness.**

Worces·ter·shire sauce (wŏŏs′ tər shər) ***n-*** spicy sauce containing soy, vinegar, etc., originally made in Worcester, England, and used especially with meats.

word (wûrd) ***n-*** **1** a sound or a combination of sounds meaning a certain thing, feeling, idea, etc., and forming a grammatical part of speech. **2** written or printed representation of such a sound. **3** a brief expression; remark: *a* word *of warning.* **4** promise; guarantee. **5** news; information. **6** command; order: *the* word *to go ahead.* **7** password; slogan: *Let the* word *be: "On they come."* **8 words** (1) talk; conversation: *He is not given to* words. (2) language used in anger or reproach: *They had* words *yesterday.* **9 the Word** (1) Christ considered as the expression of the Divine Intelligence and as the mediator between God and men. (2) the Scriptures. ***vt-*** to say or write with words: *to* word *a message.*

be as good as (one's) words to keep (one's) word or promise. **break (one's) word** to fail to keep (one's) word or promise. **word of mouth** by speech, not by writing; orally. **eat (one's) words** to take back something (one) has said. **have a word with** to have a brief talk with. **have words with** to argue angrily with. **in a word** briefly; in short. **in so many words** precisely and plainly; exactly. **man of his word** person who keeps his word or promise. **take a person at his word** to take a person's words literally and deal with him accordingly. **take the words out of (one's) mouth** to say what (one) was just about to say (oneself). **word for word** entirely, and in the very words: *to repeat a message* word for word.

word·age (wûr′ dĭj) ***n-*** words, especially the number of words used in stating or writing something.

word·book (wûrd′bŏŏk′) ***n-*** **1** book in which words are listed and explained, such as a dictionary or vocabulary list. **2** the libretto of an opera.

word class *Grammar* ***n-*** category or group that includes words of the same kind or part of speech. Nouns constitute a word class.

word ending *Grammar* ***n-*** **1** an ending added to a word or stem to produce an inflected form; inflectional morpheme. Examples: "s" in "birds," "er" in "fairer," "ed" in "pushed," "s" in "George's," and the apostrophe (') in "the Jones' house." **2** suffix.

word·ing (wûr′ dĭng) ***n-*** way in which words are used to express something; choice of words.

word·less (wûrd′ ləs) ***adj-*** **1** not expressed by words: *a* wordless *message acted out in pantomime.* **2** speechless. **—*adv-* word′less·ly. *n-* word′less·ness.**

word of honor ***n-*** one's pledge or guarantee as an honorable person.

word order *Grammar* ***n-*** the order in which words follow one another in a phrase, clause, or sentence.

word pro·ces·sor (prŏs′ ĕs ər) ***n-*** partially computerized typewriter on which key strokes are recorded magnetically and modified in various ways before characters are typed on paper.

word·y (wûr′ dē) ***adj-*** **[word·i·er, word·i·est]** expressed in, or using, many or too many words: *a* wordy *speech*; *a* wordy *writer.* **—*adv-* word′i·ly. *n-* word′i·ness.**

wore (wôr) *p.t.* of **wear.**

work (wûrk) ***n-*** **1** physical or mental effort directed to some end or purpose; toil; labor: *He was too weak for hard* work. **2** occupation; business; trade: *What is his* work? **3** employment; job: *He is looking for* work. **4** task; undertaking: *This is* work *for ten people.* **5** something made by effort, especially by the effort of an artist or writer: *"Hamlet" is Shakespeare's best-known* work. **6** way of doing something; craftsmanship; workmanship: *painstaking* work; *careless* work. **7** materials, tools, etc., on which labor is being or is to be expended in the process of making something: *She took her* work *out on the porch.* **8 works** (1) (often takes singular verb) industrial plant; factory: *The iron* works *is shut down.* (2) structures connected with engineering projects, such as bridges, dams, or docks: *public* works. (3) the moving or operating parts of any machinery: *the* works *of a watch.* (4) deeds; accomplishments: *a man famous for his good* works. (5) *Informal* (often takes singular verb) a collection of things; the whole of anything; the lot: *He bought the* works. **9** *Physics* the effect of a force in displacing a mass, measured by the product of the force and the distance the mass is moved. *as **modifier**: his* work *clothes.* ***vi-*** **[worked** or **wrought** (wrôt), **work·ing] 1** to put forth physical or mental effort; labor; toil. **2** to be occupied in business; be employed: *He* works *in the steel mill.* **3** to operate or run properly; be operative or effective; function: *Will this machine* work? *His scheme* worked *very well.* **4** to ferment: *Cider* works *to produce vinegar.* **5** to admit of being manipulated, shaped, hammered, etc.: *This dough* works *easily.* **6** to move by reason of agitation or nervousness: *His features* worked *with emotion.* **7** to move slowly or with difficulty (often followed by "through," "loose," "out," etc.): *The rain* worked *through the roof. The nail* worked *loose.* ***vt-*** **1** to operate, manage, or set in motion: *to* work *a mine*; *to* work *a pump.* **2** to prepare for use; manipulate: *The farmers* worked *the soil.* **3** to win by labor; achieve gradually or with difficulty: *to* work *one's way.* **4** to bring into a specified condition by gradual effort: *She* worked *the stone into place.* **5** to perform; produce; cause: *This medicine* works *wonders for colds.* **6** to make or fashion; shape: *He* worked *the clay into a vase.* **7** to embroider: *She* worked *the linen with fine stitches.* **8** to exact labor from; cause to labor: *The farmer* worked *her horses hard.* **9** to carry on activity in; cover: *Two salesmen* work *this town.* **10** to solve: *to* work *a problem.* **11** to excite; rouse: *He* worked *himself into a frenzy.* **12** to manage; contrive; arrange (usually followed by "it"): *I think we can* work *the deal.* **13** to give motion to; move: *He* worked *the handle.*

at work 1 working. **2** at one's place of employment.

make short work of to complete or dispose of rapidly.

out of work without a job; unemployed.

work in (or **into**) to put in; also, to introduce, insert, or be inserted: *Spread the lotion and* work *it* in.

work off to get rid or dispel gradually or by effort.

work on (or **upon**) 1 to influence: *His music* works on *the mind of the listener.* 2 to try to persuade.
work out 1 to solve: *to* work out *a problem.* 2 to pay for with labor: *to* work out *one's board.* 3 to devise; form: *He* worked out *a plan to save money.* 4 to prove effective, satisfactory, suitable, etc.: *The new office boy did not* work out. *His plans* worked out *beautifully.* 5 to exhaust (a mine, vein, etc.) by working. 6 to effect by labor or exertion: *Each person* works out *his destiny.* 7 *Informal* to have an athletic workout.
work over 1 to do again; revise. 2 *Slang* to beat severely.
work up 1 to excite; stir up: *He* worked *himself* up *into a rage.* 2 to make progress by degrees: *to* work *oneself* up *in a profession.* 3 to develop.

work·a·ble (wûr′ kə bəl) ***adj-*** 1 such as can be put into operation or made to work; practicable: *a* workable *plan.* 2 such as can be worked, especially with the hands: *soft,* workable *clay.* **—*n-* work′a·bil′i·ty** or **work′a·ble·ness.**

work·a·day (wûr′ kə dā′) ***adj-*** 1 of, having to do with, or suited for daily or ordinary work: *one's* workaday *clothes.* 2 ordinary; commonplace: *plain,* workaday *language.*

work·bas·ket (wûrk′ băs′ kət) ***n-*** basket or similar container for holding articles used in sewing or mending.

work·bench (wûrk′ bĕnch′) ***n-*** table or bench at which work such as that of a mechanic or carpenter is done.

work·book (wûrk′ bo͝ok′) ***n-*** booklet or book based on a particular subject or course of study, and containing problems to be solved or questions to be answered, with space provided for this work.

work·day (wûrk′ dā′) ***n-*** 1 day on which work is generally done, as distinguished from a Sunday or holiday. 2 period of time spent in work on such a day: *a six-hour* workday.

work·er (wûr′ kər) ***n-*** 1 person who works: *a slow* worker. 2 person who works for a living, especially one who does manual labor. 3 in a colony of ants, bees, wasps, or termites, one of the members that performs the work of the colony and is incapable of producing offspring.

work·horse (wûrk′ hôrs′, -hôrs′) ***n-*** 1 horse used for heavy work, rather than for riding or racing. 2 person who works long and hard at arduous or difficult tasks.

work·house (wûrk′ hous′) ***n-*** 1 house of correction in which minor offenders are confined and put to work. 2 *chiefly Brit.* public institution where poor people are supported and given tasks to do; poorhouse.

work·ing (wûr′ kĭng) ***adj-*** 1 engaged in work or labor, especially to earn a living: *a* working *man.* 2 of, relating to, spent in, or used for work: *long* working *hours*; *a miner's* working *equipment.* 3 sufficient or good enough to operate, function, or suffice temporarily: *a* working *model of a machine*; *a* working *hypothesis.* ***n-*** 1 (often **workings**) way in which something works or functions. 2 (usually **workings**) digging operations for a mine, tunnel, archeological study, etc.

working capital ***n-*** 1 money, especially of a business or similar enterprise, that is not tied up in investments but is readily available for use. 2 in a business operation, assets on hand in excess of current liabilities.

work·ing·man (wûr′ kĭng măn′) ***n-*** [*pl.* **work·ing·men**] worker, especially a man who works with his hands; laborer. **—*n-* *fem.* work′ing·wom′an.**

work·man (wûrk′ mən) ***n-*** [*pl.* **work·men**] man who works at a trade or as a laborer; especially, a skilled artisan or craftsman.

work·man·like (wûrk′ mən līk′) ***adj-*** typical of a good workman; skilled: *a* workmanlike *repair job.*

work·man·ship (wûrk′ mən shĭp′) ***n-*** 1 work, skill, or technique of a workman or craftsman. 2 quality or distinctive finish of something made or done: *the fine* workmanship *of a piece of antique jewelry.*

work of art ***n-*** any skilled, original, or beautiful work produced by a fine artist or craftsman.

work·out (wûrk′ out′) ***n-*** 1 session of intensive training or exercise, usually in preparation for a contest, athletic event, etc. 2 test or trial to determine fitness, working order, etc.: *to give a car a* workout *before buying it.*

work·room (wûrk′ ro͞om′, -ro͝om′) ***n-*** room in which work is done.

work·shop (wûrk′ shŏp′) ***n-*** 1 room or building in which work, especially handwork, is done, often by a number of workers: *a potter's* workshop. 2 class or course of study intended to improve skills in certain kinds of work: *a* workshop *for writers.*

work·ta·ble (wûrk′ tā′ bəl) ***n-*** table at which work is done or where equipment, especially for sewing, is kept.

work·week (wûrk′ wēk′) ***n-*** amount of time within each week that is spent in working at one's employment.

world (wûrld) ***n-*** 1 the earth, together with all living things, signs of civilization, etc. 2 any planet or other heavenly body considered similar to the earth: *space travelers from another* world. 3 the entire universe. 4 definite part of the earth or division of civilization: *the New* World; *the Roman* world. 5 group or general category into which things, especially living things, are divided: *the plant* world. 6 people in general: *All the* world *is interested in space travel.* 7 any sphere of existence or area of interest or activity; also, distinctive group of people sharing the same interests or activities: *the* world *of dreams*; *the* world *of music*; *the* business *world.* 8 active or social life and its interests and pleasures, as distinguished from life devoted to spiritual things; also, the people devoted to such a life. 9 large amount; great deal: *to get a* world *of pleasure from reading.* *as* ***modifier***: *important* world *events.*
for all the world in every way; altogether. **out of this world** *Slang* extremely good; wonderful. **world without end** for all time; forever.

World Court ***n-*** 1 the International Court of Justice, the principal judicial organ of the United Nations, established in 1945. 2 (also **Permanent Court of International Justice**) international tribunal established under the League of Nations in 1921, and superseded by the International Court of Justice.

world·ling (wûrld′ lĭng) ***n-*** person concerned with worldly life and interests.

world·ly (wûrld′ lē) ***adj-*** [**world·li·er, world·li·est**] 1 of, having to do with, or devoted to the material pleasures and advantages of life, as distinguished from spiritual things; secular. 2 worldly-wise; sophisticated. **—*n-* world′li·ness.**

world·ly-mind·ed (wûrld′ lē mīn′ dəd) ***adj-*** devoted to worldly interests. **—*n-* world′ly-mind′ed·ness.**

world·ly-wise (wûrld′ lē wīz′) ***adj-*** wise in the ways of the world; sophisticated.

world power ***n-*** nation or government that has great power or influence throughout the world.

World Series or **world series** ***n-*** games played at the end of the baseball season between the winning teams in each of the major leagues, to determine the championship in U.S professional baseball for that year.

---

world war ***n-*** a war of very large proportions, involving the chief nations of the world and fought over an extensive area.

World War I ***n-*** the war from 1914 to 1918 in which nearly all the major nations were involved.

World War II ***n-*** the war from 1939 to 1945 in which most of the major nations were involved.

world-wea·ry (wûrld′ wêr′ ē) ***adj-*** bored, dissatisfied, and finding no pleasure in life, especially in its worldly aspects. ***—n-*** **world′-wear′i·ness.**

world-wide (wûrld′ wīd′) ***adj-*** **1** extending throughout the world: *a* world-wide *reputation.* **2** directed to the whole world: *a* world-wide *proclamation.*

worm (wûrm) ***n-*** **1** any of various animals without a backbone, having a long, soft, uncovered body. True worms belong to three groups: the flatworms, such as the tapeworm; the roundworms, such as the hookworm; and the annelids, such as the earthworm. **2** any animal resembling these, such as a grub or caterpillar. **3 worms** disease cause by any of various internal parasites such as the hookworm or tapeworm. **4** weak, insignificant, or contemptible person. **5** a slender, rotating machine part having threads. ***vt-*** **1** to cause to move or progress by crawling along or twisting in and out: *to* worm *oneself through a narrow opening*; *to* worm *one's way through a crowd.* **2** to get or put by slow, roundabout, sly, means: *to* worm *a secret from a friend.* **3** to rid (an animal) of internal parasitic worms. ***vi-*** to move by crawling, twisting, etc.: *to* worm *through a narrow tunnel.* ***—adj-*** **worm′like′.**

worm-eat·en (wûrm′ ē′ tən) ***adj-*** **1** eaten or tunneled into by worms. **2** decayed, dilapidated, or very shabby; also, out-of-date.

worm gear ***n-*** **1** worm wheel. **2** gear formed by a worm and a worm wheel.

Worm gear

worm·hole (wûrm′ hōl′) ***n-*** hole or narrow tunnel produced by the burrowing of a worm or worms.

worm wheel ***n-*** wheel having teeth that mesh with a short, rotating worm.

worm·wood (wûrm′ wŏŏd′) ***n-*** **1** any of various plants related to the daisy, having a strong, bitter smell and taste, and formerly used in the preparation of certain alcoholic liquors. **2** something bitter and vexing.

worm·y (wûr′ mē) ***adj-*** **[worm·i·er, worm·i·est] 1** full of, infested with, or damaged by worms: *a* wormy *apple*; wormy *rafters.* **2** resembling or typical of a worm or worms. ***—n-*** **worm′i·ness.**

worn (wôrn) *p.p.* of **wear.** ***adj-*** **1** showing signs of wear or long use: *a* worn, *tattered coat.* **2** showing the effects of continued stress, anxiety, etc.: *a* worn, *haggard face.*

worn-out (wôrn′ out′) ***adj-*** **1** useless, exhausted, or no longer capable of working because of long wear, use, or activity: *a* worn-out *pair of shoes*; worn-out *machinery; a* worn-out *athlete.* **2** not interesting or effective because of overuse; trite; hackneyed: *a* worn-out *phrase.*

wor·ried (wûr′ ēd) ***adj-*** feeling or showing signs of great concern: *a* worried *mother*; *a* worried *expression.*

wor·ri·some (wûr′ ĭ səm) ***adj-*** **1** causing worry or anxiety. **2** tending to worry or fret.

wor·ry (wûr′ ē) ***vi-*** **[wor·ried, wor·ry·ing]** to be anxious, troubled, or concerned. ***vt-*** **1** to cause (someone) to be anxious or concerned. **2** to bite, tear at, or shake with the teeth: *The puppy* worried *the bone.* ***n-*** [*pl.* **wor·ries**] **1** disturbance of mind; anxiety; care. **2** cause for anxiety or concern. ***—n-*** **wor′ri·er.**

worry along (or **through**) to do the best one can under the circumstances; manage somehow.

worse (wûrs) *compar.* of **bad, badly,** and **ill.** ***adj-*** **1** bad, disagreeable, undesirable etc., to a greater degree: *Today's weather is* worse *than yesterday's. The news couldn't be* worse. **2** less well in health; sicker: *The patient is* worse *today.* ***adv-***: *He played* worse *today.*

for the worse toward or into a less desirable or favorable condition: *The weather changed* for the worse. *The patient took a turn* for the worse. **worse off** in a less desirable or favorable condition or position.

wors·en (wûr′ sən) ***vi-*** to grow or become worse. ***vt-*** to make worse.

wor·ship (wûr′ shĭp) ***vt-*** **[wor·shiped** or **wor·shipped, wor·ship·ing** or **wor·ship·ping] 1** to honor or pay reverence to as divine; offer religious devotion to: *to* worship *God; to* worship *idols.* **2** to feel intense devotion toward; admire and adore; idolize: *He* worships *his older brother.* ***vi-*** to perform or take part in religious devotion: *We* worship *at the same church.* ***n-*** **1** act or expression of religious devotion: *to take part in divine* worship. **2** extreme devotion or admiration; adoration: *hero* worship. **3 Worship** *Brit.* title for a high official such as a judge or mayor, preceded by "your," "his," or "her." ***—n-*** **wor′ship·er** or **wor′ship·per.**

wor·ship·ful (wûr′ shĭp fəl) ***adj-*** **1** showing or feeling intense devotion or reverence: *to gaze with* worshipful *eyes.* **2** *Brit.* worthy of respect or honor (used as a formal title of respect): *your* worshipful *highness.* ***—adv-*** **wor′ship·ful·ly.**

worst (wûrst) *superl.* of **bad, badly,** and **ill.** ***adj-*** bad to the greatest degree; most unpleasant, undesirable, harmful, etc.: *the* worst *handwriting I've ever seen*; *the* worst *epidemic of measles in many years.* ***adv-***: *He does* worst *when he is tired.* ***n-*** thing, person, or circumstance that is bad, disagreeable, unfavorable, etc., to the greatest degree: *They've had to deal with the* worst *in sickness and poverty.* ***vt-*** to defeat; overcome; get the better of: *He* worsts *me in every game of checkers.* ***Hom-*** wurst.

at worst under the least favorable circumstances. **get** (or **have**) **the worst of it** be placed at the greatest disadvantage; undergo the severest defeat, humiliation, etc. **if worst comes to worst** if things turn out as badly as possible. **in the worst way** *Informal* very much.

wor·sted (wŏŏs′ təd, wûr′ stəd) ***n-*** **1** yarn made from long, closely twisted wool strands. **2** cloth made from this yarn. *as* ***modifier***: *a* worsted *suit.*

worth (wûrth) ***prep-*** **1** of a value equal to; priced or valued at: *a book* worth *five dollars.* **2** deserving of; meriting (often followed by the present participle used as a noun): *a man* worth *your attention*; *a story* worth *reading.* **3** having money or possessions equal to: *a rich man* worth *millions of dollars.* ***n-*** **1** quality that gives a person or thing value or merit; excellence: *a man of great* worth; *a gift of much* worth. **2** value as estimated or expressed in money: *What is the* worth *of these jewels?* **3** amount that is bought or sold at a certain price: *a dollar's* worth *of groceries.* **4** personal wealth; riches.

for all (one) is worth to the extent of (one's) powers or ability; to the utmost.

worth·less (wûrth′ ləs) ***adj-*** **1** having no value, merit, or excellence; worth nothing; useless: *a* worthless *collection of junk stored in the attic.* **2** lacking good qualities; good-for-nothing: *a* worthless *fellow.* ***—adv-*** **worth′less·ly.** ***n-*** **worth′less·ness.**

worth·while (wûrth′ hwīl′) ***adj-*** deserving the cost or effort expended: *a* worthwhile *charity*; worthwhile *work.*

wor·thy (wûr′ thē) ***adj-*** **[wor·thi·er, wor·thi·est] 1** having worth or excellence; meriting respect, admiration, support, etc.: *a* worthy *man*; *a* worthy *cause.* **2** deserving (of): *a deed* worthy *of praise.* ***n-*** [*pl.* **wor·thies**] important or distinguished person (now chiefly used sarcastically): *the town* worthies. —***adv-*** **wor′ thi·ly.** ***n-*** **wor′ thi·ness.**

wot (wŏt) *Archaic* form of [2]**wit** used with "I," "he," "she," or "it" in the present tense.

would (wŏŏd) ***auxiliary verb*** [*p.t.* of **will**] **1** was or were intending to: *She told us that she* would *return soon.* **2** was or were determined to: *They* would *play in the rain, no matter how cold it was.* **3** might be expected to: *You* would *do a thing like that.* **4** used to: *Every day last summer we* would *read a different book.* **5** used with polite requests: *Please,* would *you hand me that book?* **6** was or were certain to (used only in clauses expressing what might have been true): *He* would *have helped you if he had been there.* ***vt-*** *Archaic* to wish (takes only a clause as object): *Oh,* would *that it were true!* ***Hom-*** wood.

►For usage note see SHOULD.

would-be (wŏŏd′ bē′) ***adj-*** trying to be or become: *a* would-be *author.*

would·n't (wŏŏd′ ənt) would not.

wouldst (wŏŏdst) *Archaic* form of **would** used with "thou."

[1]**wound** (wōōnd) ***n-*** **1** physical injury in which skin or tissue is cut, pierced, or torn. **2** injury to the feelings or emotions. ***vt-*** **1** to injure so as to cut, pierce, or tear the skin or tissue. **2** to hurt emotionally; cause grief or pain to. [from Old English **wund** of the same meaning.]

[2]**wound** (wound) *p.t. & p.p.* of [2]**wind** and [3]**wind.**

wove (wōv) *p.t. & p.p.* of **weave.**

wo·ven (wō′ vən) *p.p.* of **weave.**

wow (wou) ***interj-*** *Slang* exclamation expressing great surprise, enthusiasm, pain, etc. ***n-*** of a sound-reproducing system, a distortion of sound marked by a rise and fall in pitch and caused by a phonograph or tape recording being played with variations in speed.

wrack (răk) ***n-*** seaweed or other floating plants cast ashore by the sea. ***Hom-*** rack.

wrack and ruin widespread and complete destruction.

wraith (rāth) ***n-*** **1** ghostly image of a person who is about to die or who has just died, supposedly appearing to another person. **2** any ghost or shadowy image.

wran·gle (răng′ gəl) ***vi-*** [**wran·gled, wran·gling**] to argue or quarrel noisily or violently. ***vt-*** **1** to obtain, persuade, etc., by persistent arguing. **2** in western United States, to herd cattle or horses. ***n-*** noisy or angry dispute. —***n-*** **wran′ gler.**

wrap (răp) ***vt-*** [**wrapped, wrap·ping**] **1** to enclose or enfold in an outer covering: *to* wrap *a baby in a blanket; to* wrap *a gift.* **2** to use to enclose or enfold; fold, roll, or wind: *She* wrapped *a blanket around the baby.* **3** to conceal: *Fog* wrapped *the mountain. His plans were* wrapped *in secrecy.* ***vi-*** to admit of being covered by folding, rolling, etc.: *These boxes* wrap *well.* ***n-*** **1** something, especially an article of clothing, put on as outer covering or protection. **2 wraps** outer garments used for warmth or protection. **3** something that conceals: *under the* wrap *of secrecy.* ***Hom-*** rap.

under wraps secret or hidden. **wrapped up in** deeply interested or absorbed in.

wrap up 1 to put on warm outer clothing. **2** *Informal* to bring to a conclusion: *That* wraps up *the job.*

wrap·a·round (răp′ ə round′) ***n-*** garment, such as a skirt or bathrobe, that has a wide overlap secured by a belt or fastening. *as* ***modifier:*** *a* wraparound *skirt.*

wrap·per (răp′ ər) ***n-*** **1** outer covering, usually of paper or similar material, enclosing a package, newspaper or magazine, etc. **2** person or thing that wraps packages or merchandise, especially in a store, factory, etc. **3** loose, comfortable garment worn by girls or women at home. **4** tobacco leaf of high quality used for the outer covering of a cigar.

wrap·ping (răp′ ĭng) ***n-*** **1** material, such as paper or plastic, used to wrap something. **2 wrappings** outer covering wrapped around something. *as* ***modifier:*** *a roll of* wrapping *paper.*

wrapt (răpt) *Archaic p.t.* of **wrap.** ***Hom-*** rapt.

wrap-up (răp′ ŭp′) *Informal* ***n-*** brief summary or report.

wrasse (răs) ***n-*** any of various small fish that are common in warm seas and are often very brightly colored.

wrath (răth) ***n-*** **1** intense or violent anger, especially toward an offender. **2** punishment or affliction.

wrath·ful (răth′ fəl) ***adj-*** full of wrath; intensely angry; furious: *the* wrathful *gods.* Also **wrath′ y [wrath·i·er, wrath·i·est].** —***adv-*** **wrath′ ful·ly.** ***n-*** **wrath′ ful·ness.**

wreak (rēk) ***vt-*** **1** to inflict (violence, vengeance, punishment, etc.): *The army* wreaked *havoc as it advanced.* **2** to give rein to; vent: *to* wreak *one's fury on a helpless victim.* ***Hom-*** reek.

wreath (rēth) ***n-*** **1** circle of intertwined or interwoven flowers, leaves, etc.: *Christmas* wreath. **2** circular band, wisp, etc., resembling this: *a* wreath *of clouds.*

Wreath

wreathe (rē*th*) ***vt-*** [**wreathed, wreath·ing**] **1** to weave or twist into a wreath: *Mary* wreathed *the flowers.* **2** to entwine; encircle: *Thick fog* wreathed *the ship.* **3** to hang or decorate with or as if with a wreath: *We* wreathed *the fireplace with Christmas greens.*

wreck (rĕk) ***vt-*** **1** to destroy or damage severely by violent impact or action: *The storm* wrecked *the ship. The crash* wrecked *the automobile.* **2** to ruin: *Poor habits can* wreck *one's health. Bad luck* wrecked *our plans.* **3** to tear down; dismantle: *to* wreck *an old building.* ***n-*** **1** remains of something destroyed or damaged, especially by violent action: *the* wreck *of an old ship.* **2** destruction or severe damage by collision or other violent action; also, an instance of this: *the* wreck *of a ship in a storm; a train* wreck. **3** person or thing in a ruined or broken-down condition. ***Hom-*** reck.

wreck·age (rĕk′ ĭj) ***n-*** **1** a wrecking or being wrecked; destruction: *the* wreckage *caused by the earthquake.* **2** remains of anything that has been wrecked.

wreck·er (rĕk′ ər) ***n-*** **1** person or thing that wrecks. **2** person or vehicle that clears away a wreck: *The* wrecker *towed the car off the road.* **3** person or device that tears down old buildings. **4** person or vessel employed to recover wrecked vessels or their cargoes.

House wren, about 5 in. long

wrecking bar ***n-*** slightly bent crowbar with a forked end, used in removing nails, prying crates open, etc.

wren (rĕn) ***n-*** any of various small, brownish birds with short wings and a short tail usually held erect, such as the **house wren,** which frequently builds its nest near dwellings.

fāte, făt, dâre, bärn; bē, bĕt, mêre; bīte, bĭt; nōte, hŏt, môre, dòg; fŭn, fûr; tōō, bŏŏk; oil; out; tar; thin; *th*en; hw for wh as in *wh*at; zh for s as in u*s*ual; ə for a, e, i, o, u, as in *a*go, lin*e*n, per*i*l, at*o*m, min*u*s

wrench (rĕnch) ***vt-*** **1** to twist and pull violently: *Bob* wrenched *off the lid of the jar.* **2** to injure by twisting or pulling; sprain: *Ellen* wrenched *her ankle.* **3** to force or drag as if by violent action: *to* wrench *oneself away from an interesting story.* ***n-*** **1** a violent pull or twist. **2** tool for holding or turning a bolt, nut, section of pipe, etc., usually having two jaws, one of which may be movable. **3** injury caused by a pulling or twisting motion; sprain. **4** sudden feeling of grief or pain; pang.

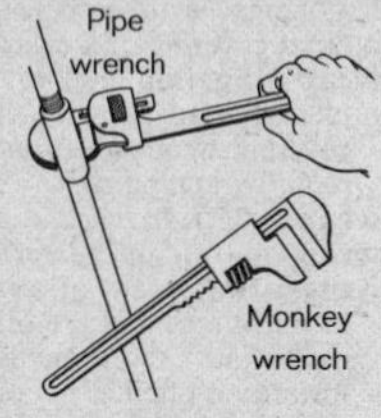

wrest (rĕst) ***vt-*** **1** to pull, twist, or take away by force: *He* wrested *the football from my arms.* **2** to obtain by making great efforts: *to* wrest *gold from the earth*; *to* wrest *the meaning from his essay.* ***Hom-*** rest.

wres·tle (rĕs′ əl) ***vi-*** **[wres·tled, wres·tling]** **1** to grapple with an opponent in an effort to force him to the ground. **2** to take part in a contest in which this is done. **3** to struggle, especially with something that is difficult to master: *to* wrestle *with an arithmetic problem*; *to* wrestle *with one's conscience.* ***vt-***: *He* wrestled *the bear to the ground.* ***n-*** **1** wrestling match. **2** hard struggle.

wres·tler (rĕs′ lər) ***n-*** person who wrestles, especially one who engages in wrestling matches.

wres·tling (rĕs′ lĭng) ***n-*** sport or act of grappling with and trying to force an opponent to the floor. *as* ***modifier***: *a* wrestling *match*; *the* wrestling *champion.*

wretch (rĕch) ***n-*** **1** unfortunate or miserable person. **2** hateful or contemptible person.

wretch·ed (rĕch′ əd) ***adj-*** **[wretch·ed·er, wretch·ed·est]** **1** full of woe or suffering; miserable; unhappy: *a* wretched *fellow.* **2** causing distress or misery; very bad: *in* wretched *health.* **3** far below acceptable standards; very poor or inadequate: *a* wretched *hovel*; wretched *work.* **—*adv-* wretch′ ed·ly.** ***n-*** **wretch′ ed·ness.**

wrig·gle (rĭg′ əl) ***vi-*** **[wrig·gled, wrig·gling]** **1** to move or progress with a twisting, side-to-side motion; squirm: *The worm* wriggled *along the ground. The children* wriggled *impatiently in their seats.* **2** to make one's way by shifty or tricky means: *to* wriggle *out of a difficulty.* ***vt-*** *She* wriggled *her toes. He* wriggled *his way out of it.* ***n-*** a squirming, twisting motion. **—*adj-* wrig′ gly.**

wrig·gler (rĭg′ lər) ***n-*** **1** person or thing that wriggles. **2** larva of the mosquito.

-wright *combining form* person who makes: *a play*wright; *a wheel*wright. [from Old English **wyhrta,** "worker."]

wring (rĭng) ***vt-*** **[wrang** (răng), **wrung** (rŭng), **wring·ing]** **1** to squeeze or twist (something) hard: *to* wring *wet clothes.* **2** to get by twisting or pressing; hence, to get by force or persuasion (often followed by "out"): *to* wring *a confession from someone.* **3** to cause pity or anguish in: *His sad plight* wrung *our hearts.* ***n-*** a twisting, squeezing movement. ***Hom-*** ring.

wring·er (rĭng′ ər) ***n-*** anything that wrings; especially, a device for pressing water from clothes after washing. ***Hom-*** ringer.

wrin·kle (rĭng′ kəl) ***n-*** ridge or fold on a surface; crease: *the* wrinkles *in skin*; *the* wrinkles *in a suit.* ***vt-*** **[wrin·kled, wrin·kling]** to form small creases in: *Rain* wrinkles *clothing.* ***vi-***: *This* wrinkles *easily.* **—*adj-* wrin′ kly.**

wrist (rĭst) ***n-*** joint connecting the hand and forearm.

wrist·band (rĭst′ bănd′) ***n-*** part of a sleeve that covers the wrist; also, a strap for a wrist watch.

wrist·bone (rĭst′ bōn′) ***n-*** any bone of the wrist; carpal.

wrist·let (rĭst′ lət) ***n-*** **1** leather or knitted band worn about the wrist. **2** ornamental bracelet.

wrist watch ***n-*** small watch fastened to a band or bracelet worn about the wrist.

writ (rĭt) *Archaic p.p. & p.t.* of **write.** ***n-*** in law, a written court order commanding a person to do or cease from doing something: *a* writ *of habeas corpus.*

write (rīt) ***vt-*** **[wrote, writ·ten, writ·ing]** **1** to trace or inscribe with a pencil, pen, or similar device: *She* wrote *her name in the sand.* **2** to make or create by such means: *to* write *a book*; *to* write *a will.* **3** to compose a letter to: *I* wrote *her last week.* **4** to say in a letter or other writing: *I* wrote *that I was fine. She* wrote *the truth.* ***vi-*** **1** to trace or inscribe letters, numbers, etc.: *to* write *with a pen.* **2** to be a writer or author: *to* write *for a living.* **3** to compose a letter, book, or other writing: *Please* write *soon. That author hasn't* written *in years.* **4** to be suited for tracing or inscribing: *The pen* writes *poorly.*

write down to put into writing.

write in **1** to write for tickets, information, etc. **2** to vote for (a person who is not listed on a ballot) by writing his name on the ballot.

write off **1** remove from an account: *to* write off *an expense.* **2** to regard as a loss or as not worth consideration: *I* wrote *him* off *after his rude outburst.*

write out **1** to put into writing. **2** to write in full.

write up to describe in detail by writing.

write-in (rīt′ ĭn′) ***n-*** vote cast for a candidate whose name is not on the ballot. *as* ***modifier***: *a* write-in *vote.*

write-off (rīt′ ȯf′, ŏf′) ***n-*** deduction from net income for depreciation, permitted for tax purposes.

writ·er (rī′ tər) ***n-*** **1** person who writes. **2** person whose occupation is writing; author.

write-up (rīt′ ŭp′) ***n-*** written description or account, usually a favorable one, in a magazine or newspaper.

writhe (rīth) ***vi-*** **[writhed, writh·ing]** to squirm or twist, as from acute pain or embarrassment: *to* writhe *in agony*; *to* writhe *at an insult.*

writ·ing (rī′ tĭng) ***n-*** **1** anything that is written, such as a letter, document, manuscript, or inscription. **2** handwriting; penmanship: *He couldn't make out her* writing. **3** manner of expressing oneself in writing; literary style: *His* writing *is crisp and concise.* **4** occupation of a writer or author: *He chose* writing *as a career.* **5** **writings** novels, plays, or other literary works: *the* writings *of Mark Twain.*

writ·ten (rĭt′ ən) *p.p.* of **write.** ***adj-*** **1** produced by writing. **2** clearly seen, as if displayed by writing: *Grief is* written *on his face.*

wrong (rȯng) ***adj-*** **1** not morally right or just; wicked; unlawful. **2** not according to fact; incorrect: *The answer is* wrong. **3** out of order; amiss: *The clock is* wrong. **4** not according to the rules: *the* wrong *way to handle a machine.* **5** unsuitable; inappropriate: *the* wrong *bolt*; *the* wrong *thing to say.* **6** not meant to be showing, arranged, or located in this way: *The glove is* wrong *side out. The tube is* wrong *end up.* ***n-*** **1** that which is contrary to moral right, fact, principles, etc.; evil; injury; crime: *to know right from* wrong. **2** an act of injustice; pain unjustly inflicted: *to suffer* wrongs. ***adv-*** in a wrong manner, direction, position, etc: *You've got it all* wrong. ***vt-*** to treat unjustly; harm; violate the rights of: *He* wronged *his neighbor by making an unjust accusation.* **—*adv-* wrong′ ly.** ***n-*** **wrong′ ness.**

go wrong **1** to turn out badly. **2** to go astray morally; turn out badly. **in the wrong** mistaken; guilty.

wrong·do·er (rȯng′ dōō′ ər) ***n-*** one who does wrong; especially, an offender against law. **—*n-* wrong′ do′ ing.**

wrong·ful (rông′ fəl) ***adj-*** **1** evil; unjust; injurious. **2** not legal; unlawful. ***—adv-*** **wrong′ ful·ly.** ***n-*** **wrong′ ful·ness.**

wrong·head·ed (rông′ hĕd′ əd) ***adj-*** obstinate in opinions; stubborn against persuasion or entreaty. ***—adv-*** **wrong′ head′ ed·ly.** ***n-*** **wrong′ head′ ed·ness.**

wrote (rōt) *p.p.* of **write.** ***Hom-*** rote.

wroth (rôth) *Archaic* ***adj-*** angry; indignant; wrathful.

wrought (rôt) *p.t. & p.p.* of **work** (now rarely used). ***adj-*** worked; fashioned; made: *beautifully* wrought *furniture.* **2** of metals, beaten into shape: *a candlestick of* wrought *iron; a* wrought *silver bracelet.*

wrought iron ***n-*** iron with low carbon content. It is tough but soft enough to be easily drawn out into wire and hammered into shape.

wrought-up (rôt′ ŭp′) ***adj-*** highly disturbed; agitated.

wrung (rŭng) *p.t. & p.p.* of **wring.** ***Hom-*** rung.

wry (rī) ***adj-*** **[wri·er** or **wry·er, wri·est** or **wry·est]** **1** twisted; contorted: *a* wry *face.* **2** ironical or bitter; cynical: *a* wry *remark.* ***—adv-*** **wry′ ly.** ***Hom-*** rye.

wry·neck (rī′ nĕk′) ***n-*** **1** bird related to the woodpeckers, which twists its head and neck in a peculiar way. **2** disease in which a contraction of the neck muscles causes the head to be twisted to one side. ***—adj-*** **wry′ necked′.**

WSW or **W.S.W.** west-southwest.

wt. weight.

wurst (wûrst, *also* wŏŏsht) ***n-*** sausage, especially a spicy German sausage.

W.Va. West Virginia.

Wyo. Wyoming.

wy·vern (wī′ vərn) ***n-*** on coats of arms, a two-legged winged dragon with a barbed and knotted tail. Also **wivern.**

X

X, x (ĕks) [*pl.* **X's, x's]** **1** the 24th letter of the English alphabet. **2** Roman numeral for ten. **3** sign used in multiplication. **4** symbol used to represent an unknown quantity, factor, etc. **5** mark used in diagrams, maps, and charts to point out something. **6** symbol used in letters and notes to indicate a kiss.

x-axis (ĕks′ ak′ səs) *Mathematics* ***n-*** the horizontal (or first) axis in a Cartesian co-ordinate system. For picture, see *abscissa.*

X chromosome See *sex chromosome.*

xe·bec (zē′ bĕk′) ***n-*** three-masted sailing ship with long overhanging bow and stern, formerly used by pirates.

xe·non (zē′ nŏn′) ***n-*** heavy, colorless, inert gaseous element that is present in the air in minute quantities. Symbol Xe, At. No. 54, At. Wt. 131.3.

xen·o·phobe (zĕn′ ə fōb′) ***n-*** person with xenophobia.

xen·o·pho·bi·a (zĕn′ ə fō′ bē ə) ***n-*** fear or hatred of foreigners or strangers.

xe·ro·phyte (zêr′ ə fīt′) ***n-*** any of various desert plants, such as the cactus, sagebrush, yucca, and agave, that store up water or give off very little to the air. ***—adj-*** **xe′ ro·phyt′ ic** (-fĭt′ ĭk).

Xmas (krĭs′ məs) Christmas.

X ray ***n-*** **1** electromagnetic radiation of high penetrating power and extremely short wavelength, ranging from about a hundredth of an angstrom to about 10 angstroms. X rays are produced by bombarding a substance with high-velocity electrons, and are used to photgoraph the interior of objects opaque to visible light. **2** instrument that produces such rays. **3** photograph made by such rays. *as* ***modifier*** **(X-ray):** *an* X-ray *examination.* ***vt-*** **(X-ray):** *The doctor* X-rayed *my chest.*

Xylophone

xy·lem (zī′ ləm) ***n-*** in botany, one of the inner, fleshy tissues that conduct water in most plants.

xy·lo·phone (zī′ lə fōn′) ***n-*** musical instrument made of strips of wood that give off different tones when struck with wooden hammers.

Y

Y, y (wī) [*pl.* **Y's, y's]** the 25th letter of the English alphabet.

Y symbol for yttrium.

[1]**-y** *suffix* (used to form adectives) **1** having; full of: *a dirty floor.* **2** inclined to; tending to: *a sleepy child*; *a rainy day.* **3** somewhat; rather: *a chilly morning*; *a salty cracker.* [from Middle English **-y** and **-ie.]**

[2]**-y** *suffix* (used to form nouns) quality or condition: *honesty*; *victory.* [from Middle English **-ie,** from Old English **-ig.]**

[3]**-y** *suffix* (used to form nouns) **1** small; tiny: *sonny.* **2** endearing or familar name or term: *Daddy*; *aunty.* [from Old French **-ie,** from Latin **-ia.]**

y. 1 yard. **2** year.

yacht (yŏt) ***n-*** any of various sailing or engine-driven vessels for pleasure cruises or racing. *as* ***modifier*:** *a* yacht *race.*

yacht·ing (yŏt′ ĭng) ***n-*** the sport or practice of sailing or racing in a yacht.

yachts·man (yŏts′ mən) ***n-*** [*pl.* **yachts·men]** person who owns or sails a yacht.

Ya·hoo (yä′ hōō′, yā-) ***n-*** in Swift's "Gulliver's Travels," any of the nasty creatures having the form and vices of man.

[1]**yak** (yăk) ***n-*** long-haired ox of Central Asia and Tibet, often domesticated and used as a beast of burden. [from Tibetan **ghyag.]**

Yak, about 6 ft. high at shoulder

[2]**yak** (yăk) *Slang* ***vi-*** **[yakked, yak·king]** **1** to chatter noisily or incessantly. **2** to laugh boisterously. [from an imitation of the sound used chiefly in comic strips.]

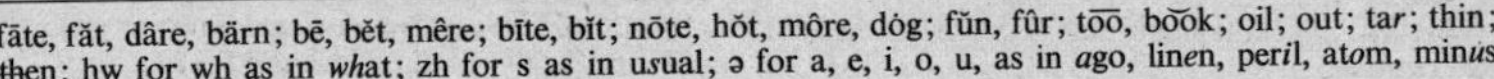

yam (yăm) ***n-*** **1** any of various climbing tropical plants with a fleshy, starchy, edible root; also, the root of any of these plants. **2** kind of sweet potato.

yank (yăngk) *Informal* ***vt-*** to pull with a sudden, quick movement; jerk: *to* yank *a coat from a hook.* ***vi-***: *He* yanked *at the rope.* ***n-***: *She gave the yarn a* yank.

Yank (yăngk) *Informal* ***n-*** Yankee.

Yan·kee (yăng′ kē) ***n-*** **1** person who is a native of the New England States. **2** native of the United States, especially of a northern State. **3** Union soldier in the Civil War.

Yankee Doodle ***n-*** humorous song popular during the American Revolution and still one of the national airs of the United States.

yap (yăp) ***n-*** **1** a sharp, shrill bark. **2** *Slang* the mouth. ***vi-*** **[yapped, yap·ping] 1** to bark sharply; yelp. **2** *Slang* to talk noisily or foolishly; jabber.

Ya·qui (yä′ kē) ***n-*** [*pl.* **Ya·quis,** also **Ya·qui**] **1** member of an Indian people of northern Mexico. **2** the language of these people. ***adj-***: *a* Yaqui *custom.*

[1]**yard** (yärd) ***n-*** **1** standard measure of length, equal to 3 feet or 36 inches. **2** one of the crosspieces on a ship's mast used to support sails. [from Old English **gerd** meaning "rod; measure."]

[2]**yard** (yärd) ***n-*** **1** enclosed or partially enclosed space adjoining a house, barn, school, or other building. **2** space, usually partly enclosed, used for some special work or occupation: *railway* yard; *lumber* yard; *navy* yard. *as* ***modifier***: *a* yard *boss.* [from Old English **geard.**]

yard·age (yär′ dĭj) ***n-*** amount as measured in yards: *the* yardage *gained by a football team.*

yard·arm (yärd′ ärm′) ***n-*** either side of a yard that supports a square sail.

yard goods ***n-*** *pl.* cloth that is sold by the yard.

yard·man (yärd′ mən) ***n-*** [*pl.* **yard·men**] man who works in a railroad or lumber yard.

yard·mas·ter (yärd′ măs′ tər) ***n-*** official in charge of a railroad yard.

yard·stick (yärd′ stĭk′) ***n-*** **1** flat stick a yard long, used for measuring. **2** any standard used for measuring or comparing: *Honesty is a* yardstick *of a man's worth.*

yar·mul·ke (yä′ məl kə) ***n-*** skullcap worn by Jewish men in the synagogue, and by some Orthodox Jews at all times.

yarn (yärn) ***n-*** **1** spun thread, especially a heavy woolen thread for knitting or crocheting. **2** *Informal* exaggerated tale or story: *a sailor's* yarns.

yar·row (yăr′ ō) ***n-*** strongly scented plant with clusters of small white flowers and finely divided leaves.

yaw (yȯ) ***vt-*** **1** of a ship, to turn unintentionally from a steady course; veer. **2** of an airplane or projectile, to swing to the right or left along a flight path. ***n-*** any of such, or similar, movements; also, the amount of such a movement.

yawl (yȯl) ***n-*** **1** sailboat with the mainmast well forward and a smaller mast far aft. For picture, see *sailboat.* **2** ship's small boat, usually rowed by four or six men.

yawn (yȯn, yŏn) ***vi-*** **1** to open the mouth wide with a deep breath because of sleepiness, fatigue, or boredom. **2** to be wide open; gape: *The chasm* yawned *below.* ***vt-*** to utter with a yawn: *He* yawned *his reply.* ***n-***: *The young boy's* yawns *told us he was growing very sleepy.* ***Hom-*** yon.

yaws (yȯz) ***n-*** *pl.* contagious skin disease of certain tropical regions.

y-axis (wī′ ăk′ səs) *Mathematics* ***n-*** the vertical (or second) axis in a Cartesian co-ordinate system. For picture, see *abscissa.*

Yb symbol for ytterbium.

Y chromosome See *sex chromosome.*

y·clept or **y·cleped** (ē klĕpt′) *Archaic* ***adj-*** called; named.

yd. yard.

[1]**ye** (yē) ***pron-*** old, poetic, or religious form of **you** (used always as a subject). [from Old English **gē.**]

[2]**ye** (thə, *also* yē) archaic spelling of **the.** [from the runic character þ for "th." Early printers misread the character as "y."]

yea (yā) ***adv-*** *Archaic* **1** yes. **2** indeed; truly. ***n-*** affirmative reply or vote: *The* yeas *outnumbered the nays.*

year (yêr) ***n-*** **1** length of time it takes the earth to revolve once around the sun, equal to 12 months, or 365 days, 5 hours, 48 minutes, and 46 seconds. **2** period of twelve consecutive months starting at any time: *within* a year. **3** period of time, usually less than a year, spent in some particular activity: *the school* year. **4 years** (1) age: *Mr. Jones is on in* years. (2) time; especially, a long time: *That happened* years *ago.*

year after year every year. **year by year** with each succeeding year; each year. **year in, year out** from one year to the next; always; continuously.

year·book (yêr′ bo͝ok′) ***n-*** **1** book published annually, giving information about the previous year. **2** school publication containing photographs of, and information about, a graduating class.

year·ling (yêr′ lĭng) ***n-*** animal between one and two years old. *as* ***modifier***: *a* yearling *colt.*

year·long (yêr′ lȯng′) ***adj-*** lasting or continuing for a full year: *a* yearlong *religious observance.*

year·ly (yêr′ lē) ***adj-*** **1** once a year or every year; annual: *a* yearly *vacation.* **2** for a year; annual: *a* yearly *salary.* ***adv-*** once a year; annually: *a celebration that occurs* yearly.

yearn (yûrn) ***vi-*** **1** to feel a deep desire or longing; pine: *to* yearn *for home.* **2** to be filled with pity or compassion; have sympathy: *to* yearn *for the oppressed.*

yearn·ing (yûr′ nĭng) ***n-*** deep, tender desire; longing: *a* yearning *for one's country.* **—*adv-*** **yearn′ ing·ly.**

yeast (yēst) ***n-*** any of various fungi that ferment sugars into ethyl alcohol and carbon dioxide. Yeast is used in making beer and wine and in raising bread.

yeast cake ***n-*** yeast mixed with starch and pressed into a small cake, used in brewing and baking.

yeast·y (yēs′ tē) ***adj-*** **[yeast·i·er, yeast·i·est] 1** of, resembling, or containing yeast. **2** frothy; foamy: *the* yeasty *scum on the waves.* **3** filled with change, growth, or ferment: *the* yeasty *years of his boyhood.*

yegg (yĕg) *Slang* ***n-*** burglar or safe cracker.

yell (yĕl) ***n-*** **1** a sharp, loud cry, as of pain, rage, or terror; shriek. **2** shout or cheer by a crowd, as at a school game. ***vi-***: *He* yelled *in pain.* ***vt-***: *I* yelled *a command.*

yel·low (yĕl′ ō) ***n-*** **1** the color of lemons, sunflowers, and buttercups. Yellow is between orange and green in the spectrum. **2** something, or a part of something, that has this color, especially the yolk of an egg. ***adj-*** **[yel·low·er, yel·low·est] 1** having this color: *a* yellow *sash.* **2** cowardly; dishonorable: *The boy has a* yellow *streak.* **3** concerned with scandal and other sensationalism rather than fact: *a* yellow *newspaper.* ***vt-***: *Time* yellowed *the pages.* ***vi-***: *The books* yellowed *with age.* **—*n-*** **yel′ low·ness.**

yel·low·bird (yĕl′ ō bûrd′) ***n-*** any of various yellow birds, such as the American goldfinch or yellow warbler.

yellow daisy ***n-*** the black-eyed Susan.

yellow fever ***n-*** acute virus disease of tropical regions, transmitted by the bite of an infected mosquito and marked by fever, chills, stomach pains, and jaundice.

yel·low·ham·mer (yĕl′ ō hăm′ ər) ***n-*** **1** the flicker, a woodpecker of North America. **2** European finch, the male of which has bright-yellow markings.

yel·low·ish (yĕl′ ō ĭsh) ***adj-*** somewhat yellow.

yellow jack ***n-*** **1** yellow fever. **2** yellow flag flown over a quarantined ship. **3** golden and silvery food fish of the Carribean Sea.

yellow jacket ***n-*** any of several small American wasps having bright yellow markings.

yellow pine ***n-*** **1** any of various American pines having a hard, yellowish wood; especially, a pine found in the South and valued as a source of turpentine. **2** the wood of any of these pines.

yel·low·throat (yĕl′ ō thrōt′) ***n-*** any of various American warblers.

yellow warbler ***n-*** small, bright-yellow warbler of the southern United States.

yelp (yĕlp) ***n-*** a sharp bark or cry, especially in pain: *the* yelp *of a hurt puppy.* ***vi-***: *The dog* yelped *when the cat bit it.*

[1]**yen** (yĕn) ***n-*** basic unit of money in Japan. [from Japanese, from Chinese **yüan** meaning "round; a dollar."]

[2]**yen** (yĕn) *Informal* ***n-*** deep desire or longing. [American word of uncertain origin.]

yeo·man (yō′ mən) ***n-*** [*pl.* **yeo·men**] **1** in the Navy and Coast Guard, a petty officer who does clerical duty. **2** in England, a small farmer who owns his own land. **3 Yeoman of the Guard** member of the bodyguard of the British royal family.

yeo·man·ry (yō′ mən rē) ***n-*** **1** yeomen of England collectively. **2** in Great Britain, formerly a volunteer cavalry force, now part of the territorial army.

yeoman's service ***n-*** exceptionally good or loyal service or support.

yes (yĕs) ***adv-*** **1** expression of affirmation, agreement, or assent; opposite of "no": *Are you coming?* Yes, *I am. Come here at once!* Yes, *sir.* Yes, *that's the man.* **2** more than that; even more: *It is very cold,* yes, *freezing.* ***n-*** [*pl.* **yes·es** or **yes·ses**] **1** reply in the affirmative: *Answer with a simple* "yes" *or* "*no.*" **2** affirmative vote or voter: *The* yeses *win the vote.*

ye·shi·vah (yə shē′ və) ***n-*** **1** seminary for the training of Orthodox rabbis. **2** Jewish parochial school. **3** school for Talmudic study. Also **ye·shi′ va.**

yes·man (yĕs′ măn′) *Informal* ***n-*** [*pl.* **yes·men**] person who agrees with every opinion or proposal of a superior without criticism; toady.

yester- *prefix* any time before the present day: yester*day*; yester*year*.

yes·ter·day (yĕs′ tər dē, -dā) ***n-*** **1** day before today: *He has been with us since* yesterday. **2** recent past: *the fashions of* yesterday. ***adv-*** **1** on the day before today: *We finished painting the house* yesterday. **2** recently: *Janey was in pigtails only* yesterday.

yes·ter·year (yĕs′ tər yêr′) ***n-*** **1** last year. **2** the recent past: *the heroes of* yesteryear.

yet (yĕt) ***adv-*** **1** up to this time; up to a particular time: *Nothing has happened* yet. **2** now; at the present time: *You can't leave* yet. **3** still; as before: *There is* yet *a faint chance.* **4** at some future time; eventually: *Henry may* yet *learn to ride a bicycle.* **5** in addition; besides: *There is much work* yet *to be done.* **6** after the long amount of time that has passed: *Haven't you finished* yet? ***conj-*** however; nevertheless: *She seems pleased,* yet *I can't be sure. I always try my best,* yet *he still finds something to complain about.*

as yet up to now.

yew (yo͞o) ***n-*** any of several evergreen trees or shrubs of Europe and Asia, with flat, needlelike leaves and red berries. **2** the hard, fine-grained wood of one of the yews, once used for archery bows. ***Homs-*** ewe, you.

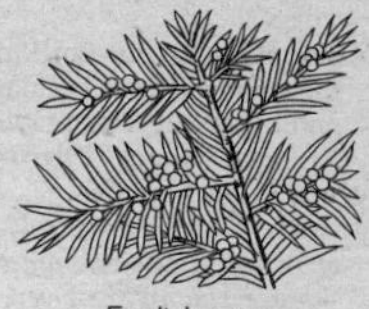
English yew

Yid·dish (yĭd′ ĭsh) ***n-*** Germanic language spoken by the Jews of eastern Europe and their descendants in many parts of the world. It is derived from the German spoken during the Middle Ages, and is usually written in Hebrew characters. ***adj-***: *the* Yiddish *theater.*

yield (yēld) ***vt-*** **1** to produce: *This land* yields *wheat.* **2** to concede; grant: *I* yield *the point.* **3** to surrender: *to* yield *territory.* **4** to give in return: *The money* yields *interest.* ***vi-*** **1** to assent; comply: *Her father* yielded *to her request.* **2** to give way under pressure; bend; collapse: *The door finally* yielded *to our pushing.* **3** to surrender: *We will not* yield *to the enemy.* ***n-*** **1** the return for labor expended or for money invested. **2** amount of a crop harvested per acre or other unit of farm land: *The bad weather resulted in a low* yield *of wheat.* **—*n-*** **yield′ er.**

yield·ing (yēl′ dĭng) ***adj-*** giving in easily; submissive: *a quiet,* yielding *man.* **—*adv-*** **yield′ ing·ly.**

yip (yĭp) ***n-*** sharp bark; yelp: *the happy* yips *of Tom's dog.* ***vi-*** **[yipped, yip·ping]**: *Tom's dog* yipped *at his approach.*

Y.M.C.A. Young Men's Christian Association.

Y.M.H.A. Young Men's Hebrew Association.

yo·del (yō′ dəl) ***n-*** musical call with quick changes from a natural voice to a falsetto, sung by Swiss and Austrian mountaineers. ***vi-*** to make such a call: *He* yodeled *as he walked down the road.* ***vt-***: *I* yodeled *a tune.* **—*n-*** **yo′ del·er** or **yo′ del·ler.**

yo·ga or **Yo·ga** (yō′ gə) ***n-*** in Hinduism, a mystic philosophy that teaches the practice of intense mental and physical exercises in order to achieve complete spiritual union with the universal soul.

yo·gi (yō′ gē) ***n-*** one who practices yoga.

yo·gurt or **yo·ghurt** (yō′ gərt) ***n-*** thick, low-calorie food made from fermented milk.

yoke (yōk) ***n-*** **1** wooden double collar for a pair of oxen or other draft animals. **2** two animals so coupled together: *a* yoke *of oxen.* **3** frame that fits over a person's shoulders, from the ends of which buckets can be hung. **4** part of a garment fitting over the shoulders or, sometimes, the hips. **5** slavery; bondage: *The people were under the* yoke *of a dictator.* **6** a tie; bond: *the* yoke *of friendship.* ***vt-*** **[yoked, yok·ing]** to join or link with, or as if with, a yoke: *to* yoke *oxen*; *to* yoke *opposites.* ***Hom-*** yolk.

yoke·fel·low (yōk′ fĕl′ ō) ***n-*** close friend; mate.

yo·kel (yō′ kəl) ***n-*** country fellow (used to show disfavor).

yolk (yōk) ***n-*** **1** the yellow part of an egg, especially a chicken egg, as distinct from the white part or albumen. **2** *Biology* the part of an animal egg, consisting chiefly

---

fāte, făt, dâre, bärn; bē, bĕt, mêre; bīte, bĭt; nōte, hŏt, môre, dȯg; fŭn, fûr; to͞o, bo͝ok; oil; out; t*ar*; thin; then; hw for wh as in *wh*at; zh for s as in u*s*ual; ə for a, e, i, o, u, as in *a*go, lin*e*n, per*i*l, at*o*m, min*u*s

of fats and proteins, that nourishes the developing embryo. 3 oily secretion found in sheep's wool. ***Hom-*** yoke.

Yom Kip·pur (yōm′kĭp′ər) ***n-*** the Day of Atonement, the chief religious holiday of the Jews, occurring in the fall and observed with prayer and fasting.

yon (yŏn) yonder. ***Hom-*** yawn.

yond (yŏnd) yonder.

yon·der (yŏn′dər) ***adj-*** **1** distant, but in sight: *the snow on* yonder *mountain.* **2** more distant; farther: *the* yonder *side of the river.* ***adv-*** over there: *Look* yonder.

yore (yôr) **of yore** in the distant past; of long ago: *in days* of yore. ***Homs-*** your, you're.

York (yȯrk, yôrk) ***n-*** royal house that ruled England from 1461 to 1485.

York·ist (yȯr′kĭst, yôr′-) ***n-*** member or follower of the House of York.

York·shire pudding (yȯrk′shər, yôrk′-) ***n-*** unsweetened batter baked in meat drippings.

Yorkshire terrier ***n-*** one of a breed of small, shaggy dogs, usually bluish gray, and originally from Yorkshire, England.

you (yōō) ***pron-*** (used as a singular or plural subject in the second person, but always taking a plural verb). **1** person or persons spoken to: *Are* you *happy?* **2** one; anyone; a person; people: *If* you *want to be sure of a seat,* you *should get tickets in advance.* ***Homs-*** ewe, yew.

you-all (yōō ȯl′, *also* yȯl) *Informal* ***pron-*** you (used in southern United States for speaking to two or more persons).

you'd (yōōd) **1** you had. **2** you would.

you'll (yōōl) you will; you shall. ***Hom-*** yule.

young (yŭng) ***adj-*** **[young·er, young·est] 1** in the early part of life or growth; not old. **2** having the qualities or appearance of youth; youthful: *How do you stay so* young? **3** vigorous; fresh: *a man of* young *ideas.* **4** immature; inexperienced: *Bob is* young *for his years.* ***n-*** [*pl.* **young**] offspring: *a tiger's* young.

the young young people. **with young** pregnant.

young·ber·ry (yŭng′bĕr′ē) ***n-*** [*pl.* **young·ber·ries**] sweet dark-red berry, a hybrid between a blackberry and a dewberry, grown in western and southern United States.

young blood ***n-*** **1** young people; youth. **2** youthful ideas, vigor, or enthusiasm.

young·ish (yŭng′ĭsh, -gĭsh) ***adj-*** rather young.

young·ling (yŭng′lĭng) ***n-*** young person, animal, or plant.

young·ster (yŭng′stər) ***n-*** young person; youth or child.

youn·ker (yŭng′kər) ***n-*** **1** formerly, a young gentleman or knight. **2** *Archaic* youngster.

your (yŏŏr, yôr *when stressed*; yər *when unstressed.*) ***determiner*** (possessive case of the pronoun "you," now usually called possessive adjective). **1** of or belonging to you: *This is* your *coat.* **2** coming from, or relating to, you: *I appreciate* your *kindness.* ***Homs-*** yore, you're.

you're (yŏŏr, yôr) you are. ***Homs-*** yore, your.

yours (yŏŏrz, yôrz) ***pron-*** (possessive pronoun) thing or things belonging to you: *Is this* yours? *That is no business of* yours.

your·self (yŏŏr′sĕlf′, yôr′-, yər-) ***pron-*** [*pl.* **your·selves** (-sĕlvz′)] **1** (reflexive form of **you**) your own self: *You are fooling* yourself. **2** your normal or true self: *You are not* yourself *when angry.* **3** intensive form of **you**: *You* yourself *should go to see him.*

yours truly formal phrase used before the signature in closing a letter. ***pron-*** *Informal* I or me.

youth (yōōth) ***n-*** [*pl.* **youths** (yōōths, yōōthz)] **1** a being young: *the energy of* youth. **2** period between childhood and maturity. **3** early stage in the growth or development of anything: *in our country's* youth. **4** young man. **5** young people: *the* youth *of a nation.*

youth·ful (yōōth′fəl) ***adj-*** **1** young; not old. **2** of or like a young person; fresh or vigorous: *his* youthful *spirit; the new,* youthful *styles.* ***—adv-*** **youth′ful·ly.** ***n-*** **youth′ful·ness.**

you've (yōōv) you have.

yowl (youl) ***n-*** long, loud, wailing sound: *the* yowl *of the bobcat.* ***vi-***: *The cat* yowled *all night on the backyard fence.*

Yo·yo (yō′yō′) ***n-*** trademark name for a toy, consisting of a grooved disk attached to one end of a string upon which it can be made to spin up and down.

Y.P.S.C.E. Young People's Society of Christian Endeavor.

yr. **1** year. **2** your.

yrs. **1** years. **2** yours.

yt·ter·bi·um (ĭ tûr′bē əm) ***n-*** a rare-earth element. Symbol Yb, At. No. 70, At. Wt. 173.04.

yt·tri·um (ĭ′trē əm) ***n-*** gray rare-earth metal element used in iron alloys. Symbol Y, At. No. 39, At. Wt. 88.905.

yuc·ca (yŭk′ə) ***n-*** **1** any of several plants of southwestern United States, Mexico, and Central America, with a tall stalk of white flowers and stiff, sharp, pointed leaves. **2** the flower of this plant.

Yucca

yule or **Yule** (yōōl) ***n-*** Christmas season; yuletide. ***Hom-*** you'll.

yule log ***n-*** huge log burned in a fireplace on Christmas Eve.

yule·tide or **Yule·tide** (yōōl′tīd′) ***n-*** Christmas season; yule.

yurt (yŏŏrt) ***n-*** round, portable tent of skins or felt stretched over a framework of branches, used by various nomadic peoples of central Asia.

Y.W.C.A. Young Women's Christian Association.

Y.W.H.A. Young Women's Hebrew Association.

Z

Z, z (zē) [*pl.* **Z's, z's**] the 26th letter of the English alphabet.

Zach·a·ri·ah (zăk′ə rī′ə) ***n-*** the father of St. John the Baptist. In the CCD Bible, **Zach′a·ri′a.**

za·ny (zā′nē) ***n-*** [*pl.* **za·nies**) in old comedies, a clown or acrobat who mimicked the principal actors; hence, a stupid person; fool. ***adj-*** **[za·ni·er, za·ni·est]** comical in a crazy, outlandish way; ludicrous: *the* zany *antics of a circus clown.*

Za·po·tec (zăp′ə tĕk′) ***n-*** [*pl.* **Za·po·tecs,** also **Za·po·tec**] **1** member of an Indian people of southern Mexico. **2** the language of these people. ***—adj-*** **Za′po·tec′an.**

zeal (zēl) ***n-*** eagerness; enthusiasm; earnestness: *patriotic* zeal; *his* zeal *for work.*

zeal·ot (zĕl′ ət) ***n-*** person of too great zeal; fanatic: *He is a* zealot *who can tolerate no religion but his own.*

Zebra, 4—5 ft. high at shoulder

zeal·ot·ry (zĕl′ ə trē) ***n-*** excessive zeal; fanaticism.

zeal·ous (zĕl′ əs) ***adj-*** eager; enthusiastic: *Nathan Hale was a* zealous *patriot.* **—*adv-*** **zeal′ ous·ly.** ***n-*** **zeal′ ous·ness.**

ze·bra (zē′ brə) ***n-*** wild African animal of the horse family, marked with black and white stripes.

ze·bu (zē′ byōō′, -bōō′) ***n-*** domesticated ox of Asia and East Africa, having a large hump on its shoulders.

Zebu

zed (zĕd) *Brit.* ***n-*** the letter Z or z.

Zen Buddhism (zĕn) ***n-*** form of Japanese Buddhism introduced in the 12th century from China, that seeks truth through introspection and intuition rather than through scripture. Also **Zen.**

ze·nith (zē′ nĭth) ***n-* 1** the point in the sky directly over a person. **2** greatest height; summit: *the* zenith *of success.*

Zeph·a·ni·ah (zĕf′ ə nī′ ə) ***n-*** book of the Old Testament bearing the name of its author, Zephaniah, a seventh-century B.C. prophet. In the CCD Bible, **Soph′ o·ni′ a** (sŏf′ ə-).

zeph·yr (zĕf′ ər) ***n-* 1** west wind. **2** soft, mild breeze: *A light* zephyr *rustled the leaves of the maples.* **3** fine, lightweight yarn or cloth.

zep·pe·lin or **Zep·pe·lin** (zĕp′ lən) ***n-*** type of huge, cigar-shaped, rigid airship, originally designed by Count Ferdinand von Zeppelin and launched in 1900; hence, any rigid airship; dirigible.

ze·ro (zêr′ ō) ***n-*** [*pl.* **ze·ros** or **ze·roes**] **1** *Mathematics* (1) the cardinal number of the empty set. (2) the number that is one less than 1. **2** figure that stands for naught (0): *There are three* zeros *in 1,000.* **3** point on a scale from which readings begin in either direction: *The temperature was five degrees below* zero. **4** nothing. **5** very low point: *Our hopes of getting a new car sank to* zero. *as* ***modifier***: *a* zero *point*; zero *weather*; *a* zero *grade.* ***vt-*** to fix a precise aiming point for; aim: *They* zeroed *their cannon on the church steeple.*

zero in 1 to correct the sights and aim of (a rifle, gun, etc.) by an exact matching of the point aimed at with the point struck. **2** to aim artillery with extreme accuracy.

zero gravity ***n-*** condition of an object, such as a spacecraft, in which the effect of gravity and other external forces cannot be detected by an observer within the object; weightlessness.

zero hour ***n-*** the time set for beginning a military attack; hence, the time set for beginning any important or serious action.

ze·ro-ze·ro (zêr′ ō zêr′ ō) ***adj-*** in aviation, having both ceiling and visibility zero.

zest (zĕst) ***n-* 1** enthusiasm; keen enjoyment; gusto: *a* zest *for life.* **2** exciting or pleasant element or flavor; relish; spice: *Your presence will add* zest *to the party.*

zest·ful (zĕst′ fəl) ***adj-*** full of zest or gusto: *a* zestful *love of life.* Also **zest′ y.** **—*adj-*** **zest′ ful·ly.** ***n-*** **zest′ ful·ness.**

Zeus (zōōs) ***n-*** in Greek mythology, the supreme deity; husband of Hera. He is identified with the Roman god Jupiter.

zib·el·ine (zĭb′ ə lēn′, -līn′) ***n-* 1** thick wool fabric with a nap of long, silky hairs. **2** sable fur.

zig·zag (zĭg′ zăg′) ***n-* 1** one of a series of sharp turns or angles alternating from one side to another; also, a series of such turns or angles. **2** something, such as a path or design, having such a pattern of turns or angles. ***adj-***: *a* zigzag *course.* ***adv-***: *The path climbs* zigzag. ***vt-*** [**zig·zagged, zig·zag·ging**]: *to* zigzag *lines.* ***vi-***: *Lightning* zigzagged *across the sky.*

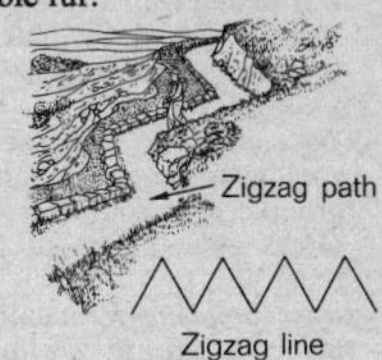

zinc (zĭngk) ***n-*** bluish-white metal element that is used as a protective coating for iron and steel, in alloys, and as a negative pole in batteries. Symbol Zn, At. No. 30, At. Wt. 65.37.

zinc ointment ***n-*** salve containing zinc oxide, used in treating skin disorders.

zinc oxide ***n-*** compound of zinc and oxygen (ZnO) in the form of a white, insoluble powder, used as a pigment and in ointments.

zinc white ***n-*** zinc oxide used as pigment in making white paint.

zing (zĭng) ***n-* 1** shrill whistling sound. **2** *Slang* vitality; vigor.

zin·ga·ro (tsĕng′ gä rō′) *Italian* ***n-*** [*pl.* **zin·ga·ri** (-rē)] gypsy. **—*n-*** *fem.* **zin′ ga·ra′** (-rä′).

zin·ni·a (zĭn′ ē ə) ***n-*** any of several annual garden plants related to the aster and daisy, with showy, colorful flowers.

Zi·on (zī′ ən) ***n-* 1** hill in Jerusalem, the site of the temple and royal house of David and his successors. **2** the chosen people. **3** heaven or the new Jerusalem. **4** the ideal nation envisaged by Judaism; utopia.

Zi·on·ism (zī′ ə nĭz′ əm) ***n-*** plan or movement to establish and promote a Jewish nation in Palestine.

Zi·o·nist (zī′ ə nĭst′) ***n-*** follower or supporter of Zionism. ***adj-***: *a* Zionist *rally.*

zip (zĭp) ***n-* 1** short hissing sound, such as that made by a moving bullet; whiz. **2** *Informal* energy; vim; vigor: *full of* zip. ***vi-*** [**zipped, zip·ping**] *Informal* to act or move with great speed: *to* zip *through homework.* ***vt-*** to fasten with a zipper.

Zip code ***n-*** any of the five-digit numbers assigned to postal zones under the U.S. Post Office plan for speeding and improving the delivery of mail.

zip gun ***n-*** homemade pistol consisting of a length of pipe attached to a handle, with a firing pin powered by a rubber band.

zip·per (zĭp′ ər) ***n-* 1** slide fastener consisting of two rows of tiny teeth that are interlocked or separated by a sliding tab. **2** any slide fastener. **—*adj-*** **zip′ pered:** *a* zippered *jacket.*

zip·py (zĭp′ ē) *Informal* ***adj-*** [**zip·pi·er, zip·pi·est**] full of energy; brisk.

zir·con (zûr′ kŏn′) ***n-* 1** mineral that is a silicate of zirconium and occurs in crystals of various colors. **2** the semiprecious gem made from a translucent variety of this mineral. *as* ***modifier***: *a* zircon *ring.*

zir·co·ni·um (zər kō′ nē əm) ***n-*** white metal element used as a structural material for nuclear reactors. Symbol Zr, At. No. 40, At. Wt. 91.22.

zith·er (zĭth′ ər, zĭth′-) ***n-*** musical instrument consisting of a shallow sounding box strung with 30 to 40 wire strings, played by plucking the strings with a pick.

Zither

Zn symbol for zinc.

-zoa *combining form* used in zoology to form the names of groups: *proto*zoa; *hydro*zoa. [from modern Latin, from Greek **zōia**, plural of **zōion** meaning "animal; living thing."]

-zoan *combining form* used in zoology to name one member of a group: *proto*zoan; *hydro*zoan. [from Greek **zōion.**]

zo·di·ac (zō′ dē ăk′) ***n-*** imaginary band across the sky along which the sun, moon, and principal planets seem to move around the earth. The zodiac is divided into twelve sections, called the **signs of the zodiac,** each named for a constellation within its area. These signs, which are now mainly used by astrologers for casting horoscopes, are Aquarius, Capricorn, Sagittarius, Scorpio, Libra, Virgo, Leo, Cancer, Gemini, Taurus, Aries, and Pisces.

zo·di·a·cal (zō′ dē ăk′ əl) ***adj-*** of or in the zodiac.

-zoic *combining form* subdivision of geological time: *Meso*zoic; *Ceno*zoic. [partly from **-zoa,** partly from Greek **zōē,** "life."]

zom·bi or **zom·bie** (zŏm′ bē) ***n-*** [*pl.* **zom·bis** or **zom·bies**] **1** corpse supposedly reanimated by supernatural power, but still dead. **2** cocktail made of several kinds of rum, liqueur, and fruit juice.

zon·al (zō′ nəl) ***adj-*** of or related to a zone: *a* zonal *law.*

zone (zōn) ***n-*** **1** any district, division, or section set off from another because of a special use or situation: *a time* zone; *hospital* zone; *postal* zone. **2** any of the five temperature belts into which the earth is divided (the two polar regions, the two temperate regions, and the tropics). ***vt-*** **[zoned, zon·ing] 1** to divide into specific districts or sections for some purpose: *They* zoned *the city into five voting districts.* **2** to assign or restrict (a district) to a particular purpose: *They* zoned *the East Side as a residential area.*

zoo (zo͞o) ***n-*** park in which living animals are kept for public exhibition; zoological garden.

zoo- *combining form* animal: *the study of* zoo*logy.* [from Greek **zōion.**]

zo·o·log·i·cal (zō′ ə lŏj′ ĭ kəl) ***adj-*** of or related to zoology or animal life: *Entomology is one of the* zoological *sciences.* ***—adv-*** **zo′ o·log′ i·cal·ly.**

zoological garden ***n-*** zoo.

zo·ol·o·gist (zō ŏl′ ə jĭst) ***n-*** person trained or skilled in the science of zoology and engaged in it as a profession.

zo·ol·o·gy (zō ŏl′ ə jē) ***n-*** **1** the scientific study of animal life. **2** the animal life of a region; fauna. *as* ***modifier***: *a* zoology *textbook.*

zoom (zo͞om) ***vi-*** **1** to make, or move with, a humming or buzzing sound: *The car* zoomed *past me.* **2** to take a sudden upward course in an airplane. ***vt-*** to cause (an airplane) to take a sudden upward course.

zoom lens ***n-*** in photography and television, a lens that permits continuous changes in focal length and image size without losing focus.

zo·o·phyte (zō′ ə fīt′) ***n-*** marine animal, such as a sea anenome or coral, that resembles a plant in appearance or manner of growth.

Zo·ro·as·tri·an (zôr′ ō ăs′ trē ən) ***n-*** disciple of Zoroaster or follower of Zoroastrianism. ***adj-***: *the* Zoroastrian *doctrines*.

Zo·ro·as·tri·an·ism (zôr′ ō ăs′ trē ə nĭz′ əm) ***n-*** the religious system founded by Zoroaster in Persia around 1000 B.C., based on the belief that there are two creative powers, good and evil, and that the good would triumph over evil in life after death.

Zou·ave (zo͞o äv′, zwäv) ***n-*** **1** member of certain French infantry regiments, originally made up of Algerians known for their bravery and colorful uniforms. **2** in the Civil War, a member of a Union volunteer regiment that imitated the dress of the French Zouaves.

zounds (zoundz) *Archaic* ***interj-*** mild oath, meaning "God's wounds."

Zr symbol for zirconium.

zuc·chi·ni (zo͞o kē′ nē) ***n-*** type of green summer squash, shaped like a cucumber.

Zu·lu (zo͞o′ lo͞o) ***n-*** [*pl.* **Zu·lus** or **Zu·lu**] **1** member of a south African Bantu people. **2** the language spoken by these people. ***adj-***: *Most* Zulu *villages are laid out in circles.*

Zu·ñi (zo͞o′ nyē; zo͞on′ ē) ***n-*** [*pl.* **Zu·ñis** or **Zu·ñi**] **1** one of a tribe of pueblo-dwelling Indians who are still living in New Mexico. **2** the language of these people. ***adj-***: *handsome* Zuñi *silver jewelry.*

zwie·back (zwī′ băk, swī′-, tsvē′-) ***n-*** kind of sweetened bread that is first sliced and then toasted after it has been baked.

zy·gote (zī′ gōt′) *Biology* ***n-*** cell formed by the union of two gametes.

zy·mase (zī′ mās′, -māz′) ***n-*** the enzyme in yeast that ferments sugars into alcohol and carbon dioxide.

Persons and Places in Mythology and Folklore

A

A·chil·les (ə kĭl′ēz) in the story of Troy, the foremost Greek hero of the Trojan War.

A·don·is (ə dŏn′əs) in Greek mythology, a beautiful youth beloved by Aphrodite.

Ae·ne·as (ə nē′əs) in classical legend, son of Venus and Priam, and hero of Virgil's poem, the **"Ae·ne′id"** (ə nē′ĭd).

Aes·cu·la·pi·us (ĕs′kə lā′pē əs) in Roman mythology, the god of medicine and healing. He is identified with the Greek **As·cle·pi·us** (ə sklē′pē əs).

Ag·a·mem·non (ăg′ə mĕm′nŏn) in Greek legend, a Greek king, brother of Menelaus, and leader of the Greeks in the Trojan War. On his return from Troy he was killed by his wife, Clytemnestra.

A·jax (ā′jăks′) a Greek hero in the Trojan War.

A·lad·din (ə lăd′ən) in the "Arabian Nights," a boy who by rubbing his magic lamp could summon a jinni to do his bidding.

A·li Ba·ba (ăl′ē bä′bə) in the "Arabian Nights," a poor woodcutter who became rich by outwitting a band of forty thieves.

Am·a·zon (ăm′ə zŏn′) in Greek legend, one of a group of female warriors who aided the Trojans in the Trojan War.

Am·mon (ăm′ən) ancient Egyptian god of life. Also **A′men.**

An·dro·cles (ăn′drə klēz′) in Roman legend, a slave whose life was spared by a lion from whose foot he had once drawn a thorn. Also **An′dro·clus′** (-kləs).

An·drom·a·che (ăn drŏm′ə kē) in the legend of Troy, the wife of Hector.

An·drom·e·da (ăn drŏm′ə də) in Greek mythology, the daughter of Cassiopeia. Andromeda was rescued from a sea monster by Perseus, who then married her.

An·tig·o·ne (ăn tĭg′ə nē) in Greek legend, a daughter of Oedipus. Antigone was sentenced to death by her uncle for illegally burying her brother.

Aph·ro·di·te (ăf rə dī′tē) in Greek mythology, the goddess of love and beauty, identified with the Roman Venus.

A·pol·lo (ə pŏl′ō) in Greek and Roman mythology, the god of music, poetry, prophecy, and medicine.

Ar·es (âr′ēz) in Greek mythology, the god of war. He is identified with the Roman Mars.

Ar·go·naut (är′gə nôt′) in Greek legend, any one of the men who sailed with Jason to find the Golden Fleece.

Ar·gus (är′gəs) in Greek mythology, a monster with a hundred eyes, who guarded the Golden Fleece.

Ar·i·ad·ne (ăr′ē ăd′nē) in Greek mythology, daughter of Minos, King of Crete. Ariadne gave Theseus a ball of thread to guide him out of the Labyrinth.

Ar·te·mis (är′tə məs) in Greek mythology, goddess of the moon and of the hunt, and twin sister of Apollo. She is identified with the Roman Diana.

Ar·thur (är′thər) legendary sixth-century king of the Britons; hero of the Round Table.

As·gard (ăs′gärd′) in Norse mythology, the home of the gods and the heros slain in battle.

As·tar·te (ə stär′tē) in Phoenician mythology, the goddess of love, identified with the Greek Aphrodite.

A·the·na (ə thē′nə) in Greek mythology, the goddess of wisdom and of women's arts and crafts, identified with the Roman Minerva. Also **A·the′ne** (-nē).

At·las (ăt′ləs) in Greek mythology, a Titan forced to bear the heavens on his shoulders.

Au·ro·ra (ô rôr′ə) Roman goddess of the dawn.

B

Bac·chus (băk′əs) in classical mythology, the god of wine, identified with the Greek Dionysus.

ban·shee (băn′shē′) in the folklore of Ireland and Scotland, a spirit whose wailing was believed to foretell death.

Bunyan, Paul See **Paul Bunyan.**

C

Cal·li·o·pe (kə lī′ə pē′) in Greek mythology, the Muse of eloquence and heroic poetry.

Ca·lyp·so (kə lĭp′sō) in Greek legend, a sea nymph who kept Ulysses on her island for seven years.

Cas·san·dra (kə săn′drə) in Greek legend, a daughter of King Priam of Troy. She was endowed with the gift of prophecy, but was never believed by anyone.

Cas·si·o·pe·ia (kăs′ē ō pē′ə) in Greek mythology, the mother of Andromeda.

Cas·tor and Pol·lux (kăs′tər ənd pŏl′əks) in Greek mythology, twin sons of Leda and Zeus.

cen·taur (sĕn′tôr′) in Greek mythology, a creature that is half man and half horse.

Cer·ber·us (sûr′bər əs) in classical mythology, the three-headed dog guarding the gates of Hades.

Ce·res (sĭr′ēz) in Roman mythology, the goddess of vegetation, identified with the Greek Demeter.

Char·on (kâr′ən) in Greek mythology, the boatman who ferried the souls of the dead over the river Styx to Hades.

Chi·ron (kī′rŏn′) in Greek mythology, a wise centaur, teacher of Achilles and other Greek heroes.

Cir·ce (sûr′sē) in the story of Ulysses, an enchantress who changed the companions of Ulysses into swine by means of a magic drink.

Cly·tem·nes·tra (klī′təm nĕs′trə) in Greek legend, the wife of Agamemnon. She killed her husband on his return from the Trojan War, and was later killed by her son, Orestes.

Cu·pid (kū′pĭd) in Roman mythology, the god of love and son of Venus. He is identified with the Greek Eros.

Cy·clops (sī′klŏps′) in the story of Ulysses, one of a group of one-eyed giants.

D

Daed·a·lus (dĕd′ə ləs) in Greek legend, a great creator and inventor who devised, among other things, the wings of Icarus.

Dam·o·cles (dăm′ə klēz) in Greek legend, a courtier who was made to sit at a banquet under a sword suspended by a single hair.

Daph·ne (dăf′nē) in Greek mythology, a nymph who escaped from Apollo by changing into a laurel tree.

De·me·ter (də mē′tər) in Greek mythology, the goddess of agriculture, fertility, and marriage. She is identified with the Roman Ceres.

Di·an·a (dī ăn′ə) in Roman mythology, the goddess of the moon and of the hunt. She is identified with the Greek Artemis.

Persons and Places in Mythology and Folklore

Di·do (dī'dō) in Roman legend, a queen who fell in love with Aeneas and stabbed herself to death when he left her.

Di·o·ny·sus (dī'ə nī'səs) in Greek mythology, a son of Zeus and god of wine and fertility. He is identified with the Roman Bacchus.

E

Ech·o (ĕk'ō) in Greek mythology, a nymph who, because of her love for Narcissus, pined away until only her voice remained.

Elaine of Astolat (ē lān' əv ăs'tə lät') in the story of King Arthur, a young girl who died of a broken heart when Lancelot ignored her love.

E·lec·tra (ĭ lĕk'trə) in Greek legend, a daughter of Agamemnon and Clytemnestra. Electra induced her brother, Orestes, to kill her mother for murdering her father.

Er·os (ĭr'ŏs', ĕr'ŏs') in Greek mythology, god of love and son of Aphrodite. He is identified with the Roman Cupid.

Eu·men·i·des (yŏŏ mĕn'ə dēz') in Greek mythology, the avenging Furies.

Eu·ryd·i·ce (yŏŏ rĭd'ə sē) wife of Orpheus.

F

Fates (fāts) in classical mythology, the three goddesses who controlled human destiny.

Frey·a (frā'ə) in Norse mythology, the goddess of love.

Fu·ries (fyŏŏr'ēz) in Greek and Roman mythology, the three goddesses who avenge crimes previously unpunished.

G

Gae·a (jē'ə) in Greek mythology, the wife of Uranus and mother of the Titans.

Gal·a·had (găl'ə hăd') in a later story of King Arthur, the noblest and purest knight of the Round Table, who was successful in his quest of the Holy Grail.

Gal·a·te·a (găl'ə tē'ə) in Greek mythology, an ivory statue of a maiden brought to life by Aphrodite after the sculptor, Pygmalion, had fallen in love with it.

Gan·y·mede (găn'ə mēd') in Greek mythology, a beautiful youth whom Zeus carried to Olympus to be his cupbearer.

Ga·wain (gə wān', gă'wən) in Arthurian legend, a knight of the Round Table, nephew of King Arthur.

gob·lin (gŏb'lĭn) in fable or myth, an evil or mischievous spirit having the form of an ugly, grotesque dwarf.

Golden Fleece in Greek legend, a fleece of gold guarded by a sleepless dragon. It was carried away by Jason and the Argonauts with the help of Medea.

Gor·gon (gôr'gən) in Greek mythology, any one of three sisters, of whom Medusa is best known, whose appearance was so terrifying that any person who looked at them was turned to stone.

Grail (grāl) in medieval legend, the cup used by Christ at the Last Supper. Also **Holy Grail.**

grif·fin or **grif·fon** (grĭf'ĭn) mythical monster with the head and wings of an eagle and the body of a lion.

Guin·e·vere (gwĭn'ə vĭr', -vər) in the story of King Arthur, wife of King Arthur. She fell in love with Lancelot.

H

Ha·des (hā'dēz) in Greek mythology, ruler of the world of the dead, and a brother of Zeus; Pluto; also, his realm.

Har·py (här'pĭ) in Greek mythology, one of several filthy, winged monsters who are part woman and part bird. **Har·pies.**

He·be (hē'bē) in Greek mythology, the goddess of youth and cupbearer to the gods.

Hec·a·te (hĕk'ə tē, *also* hĕk'ət) in Greek mythology, the goddess of the underworld. She was later associated with sorcery.

Hec·tor (hĕk'tər) in the story of Troy, a Trojan hero killed by Achilles. He was the son of Priam and Hecuba.

Hec·u·ba (hĕk'yə bə) in the story of Troy, the wife of Priam and mother of Hector, Paris, Cassandra, and others.

Hel·en of Troy (hĕl'ən əv troi') in Greek mythology, the beautiful wife of Menelaus, a Greek king. Her elopement with Paris caused the Trojan War.

He·li·os (hē'lē ŏs') in Greek mythology, the sun god who drove his chariot across the sky.

Hel·las (hĕl'əs) Greece.

Henry, John See **John Henry.**

He·ra (hĭr'ə) in Greek mythology, the queen of the gods, sister and wife of Zeus, and goddess of marriage. She is identified with the Roman Juno.

Her·a·cles (hĕr'ə klēz') Hercules.

Her·cu·les (hûr'kyə lēz') in Greek and Roman mythology, a son of Jupiter known for his great strength and for his performance of twelve gigantic tasks imposed on him by Juno.

Her·mes (hûr'mēz') in Greek mythology, the messenger of the gods. He is identified with the Roman Mercury.

He·ro (hĭr'ō) in Greek legend, a priestess of Aphrodite, whose lover, Leander, nightly swam the strait between Turkey and Greece to join her.

Hes·per·i·des (hĕs pĕr'ə dēz) in Greek mythology, the nymphs who guarded the golden apples of Hera.

Holy Grail See **Grail.**

Hy·dra (hī'drə) in Greek mythology, a nine-headed sea serpent that grew two heads for each one cut off, but was finally subdued by Hercules with a firebrand.

Hy·ge·ia (hī jē'ə) in Greek mythology, the goddess of health. She is the daughter of Aesculapius.

Hy·men (hī'mən) in Greek mythology, the god of marriage.

Hy·per·i·on (hī pĭr'ē ən) **1** in Greek mythology, the son of Uranus and the father of Helios. **2** in the story of Troy, Helios himself. **3** in later times, Apollo.

Hyp·nos (hĭp'nŏs') in Greek mythology, the god of sleep. He is identified with the Roman Somnus.

I

Ic·a·rus (ĭk'ə rəs) in Greek legend, the son of Daedalus, who escaped from Crete by flying with wings made by his father. He flew so near the sun that it melted the wax fastening his wings, and he fell into the sea and drowned.

Iph·i·ge·ni·a (ĭf'ə jə nī'ə) in Greek legend, the daughter of Agamemnon, who offered her as a sacrifice to Artemis. The goddess permitted her to live.

I·ris (ī'rĭs) in Greek mythology, the goddess of the rainbow, and in the story of Troy, the messenger of the gods.

I·seult (ē sŏŏlt') in the story of King Arthur, wife of King Mark of Cornwall. She was beloved by Tristram.

I·sis (ī'sĭs) in Egyptian mythology, the goddess of love and fertility. She was sometimes identified with Astarte.

Persons and Places in Mythology and Folklore

Ith·a·ca (ĭth'ə kə) an island of Greece, and in Greek mythology the home of Odysseus.

J

Ja·nus (jā'nəs) in Roman mythology, the god of portals, able to look into the past and future. He is usually represented with two heads.

Ja·son (jā'sən) in Greek legend, the hero who led the Argonauts in search of the Golden Fleece.

John Hen·ry (jŏn' hĕn'rĭ) in American folklore, a Negro railroad worker of unusually great strength.

Jove (jōv) Jupiter.

Ju·no (jo͞o'nō') in Roman mythology, the goddess of marriage, wife of Jupiter, and queen of the gods, identified with the Greek Hera.

Ju·pi·ter (jo͞o'pə tər) in Roman mythology, the ruler of gods and men, identified with the Greek Zeus; Jove.

L

Lab·y·rinth (lăb'ə rĭnth') in Greek mythology, a maze in Crete inhabited by the Minotaur.

Lan·ce·lot (lăns'ə lŏt') in Arthurian legend, the bravest and ablest knight of the Round Table.

Le·an·der (lē ăn'dər) in Greek legend, the lover of Hero.

Le·da (lē'də) in Greek mythology, the beloved of Zeus and mother of Helen of Troy and Castor and Pollux.

lep·re·chaun (lĕp'rə kôn') in Irish folklore, an elf, usually in the form of a little old man, who knows of hidden treasure.

Lo·ki (lō'kĭ) in Norse mythology, a God who took delight in wickedness and mischief.

M

Mars (märz) in Roman mythology, the god of war. He is identified with the Greek Ares.

Me·du·sa (mə do͞o'sə, mə dū'sə) in Greek mythology, one of the Gorgons killed by Perseus.

Mel·pom·e·ne (mĕl pŏm'ə nē) in Greek mythology, the Muse of tragedy.

Men·e·la·us (mĕn'ə lā'əs) in Greek legend, a king of Sparta, brother of Agamemnon and husband of Helen of Troy.

Mer·cu·ry (mûr'kyə rē) in Roman mythology, the messenger of the gods, who presided over commerce, skill of hand, or quickness of wit.

Mer·lin (mûr'lən) in medieval legends, especially those of King Arthur, a magician and prophet.

mer·maid (mûr'mād') imaginary creature with the head and upper body of a woman and the tail of a fish.

Mi·das (mī'dəs) in Greek legend, a king who had the power to turn anything he touched into gold.

Mi·ner·va (mĭ nûr'və) in Roman mythology, the goddess of wisdom who presided over useful and ornamental arts. She is identified with the Greek Athena.

Mi·nos (mī'nŏs') in Greek mythology, a king and lawgiver of Crete; a son of Zeus.

Min·o·taur (mĭn'ə tôr') in Greek mythology, a monster, half man and half bull, confined by Minos to the Labyrinth.

Mne·mos·y·ne (nə mŏs'ə nē) in Greek mythology, the goddess of memory and mother of the Muses.

Mo·dred (mō'drəd) in Arthurian legend, the treacherous nephew of King Arthur, who was killed in a battle with Arthur, but left Arthur with a mortal wound. Also spelled **Mor·dred** (môr'drəd).

Mor·gan le Fay (môr'gən lə fā') in Arthurian legend, the king's half sister, an enchantress.

Mor·phe·us (môr'fē əs) in Greek mythology, the god of dreams.

Muse (mūz) in Greek mythology, any one of the nine goddesses who presided over music, poetry, history, astronomy, etc.

Myr·mi·don (mûr'mə dŏn') in Greek legend, one of a band of warriors who followed Achilles in the Trojan War.

N

nai·ad (nā'ăd', nī'ăd') [*pl.* **nai·ads** or **nai·a·des** (-ə dēz)] in classical mythology, one of the nymphs supposed to live in fountains, rivers, lakes, etc.

Nem·e·sis (nĕm'ə sĭs) in Greek mythology, the goddess of justice or vengeance.

Nep·tune (nĕp'to͞on', nĕp'tūn') in Roman mythology, the god of the sea. He is identified with the Greek Poseidon.

Ne·re·id (nĭr'ē ĭd) in Greek mythology, one of the fifty sea nymphs, daughters of the sea god, **Ne·re·us** (nĭr'ē əs), who attended Poseidon.

Ni·ke (nī'kē) in Greek mythology, the goddess of victory, usually represented as a winged figure bearing a wreath and palm branch.

O

O·din (ō'dən) in Germanic mythology, the supreme god and the ruler of all the other gods.

O·dys·seus (ō dĭs'ē əs) Greek name for Ulysses.

Oed·i·pus (ē'də pəs, ĕd'ə pəs) in Greek legend, a king who unknowingly killed his father and married his mother.

O·lym·pus (ō lĭm'pəs) the highest mountain in Greece, and in Greek mythology, the home of the most important gods.

O·res·tes (ôr ĕs'tēz) in Greek legend, the son of Agamemnon and Clytemnestra. Orestes, induced by his sister Electra, killed his mother for murdering his father.

Or·phe·us (ôr'fē əs) in Greek legend, a musician whose music charmed even rocks and trees. When he descended into Hades to seek release of his wife, Eurydice, Pluto permitted him to lead her back provided he would not look at her on the way. He did look, however, and she was forced to return.

P

Pan (păn) in Greek mythology, a god of forests, flocks, and shepherds, shown as having the legs, hoofs, and horns of a goat. He is identified with the Roman Faunus.

Par·is (păr'ĭs, pâr'ĭs) in Greek mythology, the son of Priam and Hecuba, who carried Helen off to Troy, thereby causing the Trojan War.

Par·nas·sus (pär năs'əs) mountain in ancient Greece sacred to Apollo and the Muses.

Paul Bun·yan (pôl' bŭn'yən) in American folklore, a lumberjack hero, noted for his superhuman size and strength.

Peg·a·sus (pĕg'ə səs) in Greek mythology, a winged horse, the steed of the Muses.

Persons and Places in Mythology and Folklore

Per·ci·val (pûr′sə vəl) in Arthurian legend, a knight of the Round Table, who together with Sir Galahad succeeded in the search for the Holy Grail.

Per·seph·o·ne (pər sĕf′ə nē) in Greek mythology, a daughter of Zeus and Demeter, who was abducted by Pluto and became queen of the Underworld. She is identified with the Roman Proserpina.

Per·seus (pûr′sē əs, pûr′so͞os′) in Greek mythology, a son of Zeus and a mortal, who slew Medusa and saved Andromeda from a sea monster.

Phil·o·mel (fil′ə mĕl′) in Greek mythology, an Athenian princess who was changed into a nightingale.

Phoe·be (fē′bē) in Greek mythology, one of the names for Artemis.

phoe·nix (fē′niks) in ancient legend, a beautiful bird said to live over 500 years and then, after setting fire to itself, to arise, young and beautiful, from its own ashes.

Ple·ia·des (plē′ə dēz′) *pl.* [*sing.* **Ple·iad**] in Greek mythology, the seven daughters of Atlas who were transformed into a group of stars.

Plu·to (plo͞o′tō) in classical mythology, the god of the underworld.

Po·sei·don (pə sī′dən) in Greek mythology, the god of the sea. He is identified with the Roman Neptune.

Pri·am (prī′əm) in Greek legend, the king of Troy during the Trojan War, husband of Hecuba, and father of Paris, Hector, Cassandra, and many other children.

Pro·me·the·us (prə mē′thē əs) in Greek mythology, a Titan who stole fire from heaven and taught man how to use it. Zeus punished him with eternal torture.

Pro·ser·pi·na (prō sûr′pə nə) or **Pros·er·pine** (prŏs′ ər pin, prə sûr′pə nē) in Roman mythology, a daughter of Jupiter and Ceres, who was abducted by Pluto. She is identified with the Greek Persephone.

Pro·te·us (prō′tē əs) in Greek mythology, a sea god who had prophetic powers and could change his shape at will.

Psy·che (sī′kē) in classical mythology, a beautiful maiden beloved by Cupid. She is a symbol for the human soul.

Pyg·ma·li·on (pig māl′ē ən) in Greek legend, a sculptor of ancient Cyprus who fell in love with the statue he carved of Galatea.

R

Ra (rä) in Egyptian mythology, the god of the sun; the supreme diety. Also **Re** (rā).

Re·mus (rē′məs) in Roman legend, the twin brother of Romulus, by whom he was slain.

Rom·u·lus (rŏm′yə ləs) in Roman mythology, the son of Mars and founder of Rome, who together with his twin brother Remus was reared by a she-wolf.

Round Table **1** in medieval legend, a table at which King Arthur and his knights sat. **2** King Arthur and his knights.

S

Sat·urn (săt′ərn) Roman god of agriculture.

Sieg·fried (sēg′frēd, sig′frēd′) hero of several Germanic legends with many different versions, and a principal character in some of Richard Wagner's operas.

Som·nus (sŏm′nəs) in Roman mythology, the god of sleep, identified with the Greek Hypnos.

sphinx (sfingks) in Egyptian and Greek legend, a monster with a human head and a lion's body.

Styx (stiks) in Greek mythology, the principal river of Hades and Tartarus.

T

Tar·ta·rus (tär′tər əs) in Greek mythology, the deep abyss below Hades into which Zeus hurled the Titans who had rebelled against his authority.

The·seus (thē′sē əs) in Greek mythology, a king of Athens, famous for his defeat of the Minotaur in the Labyrinth.

The·tis (thē′tis) in Greek mythology, a Nereid and the mother of Achilles.

Thor (thôr) in Norse mythology, the god of war, thunder, and strength, for whom Thursday was named.

Ti·tan (tī′tən) in Greek mythology, a race of giant gods such as Atlas and Jupiter. They were the children of Gaea and Uranus.

Tris·tram (tris′trəm) knight of King Mark of Cornwall, who had a tragic love affair with Mark's wife, Iseult, after taking a magic love potion.

Troi·lus (troi′ləs) in Greek mythology, a son of Priam, slain by Achilles.

Tro·jan (trō′jən) one of the people of Troy.

Trojan horse in the story of Troy, a huge wooden horse filled with Greek soldiers and taken inside Troy's walls by the Trojans, who thought the gods had sent it to help them. Once inside the walls, the Greeks destroyed the city.

Trojan War the ten-year war between the Greeks and the Trojans, caused by the elopement of Helen, the wife of Menelaus, with Paris, a son of King Priam of Troy.

troll (trōl) in Scandinavian folklore, an ugly giant or, in later tales, an impish dwarf who was supposed to live in caves, hills, and such places.

U

U·lys·ses (ū lis′ēz) in Greek legend, king of Ithaca and a Greek leader in the Trojan War. Also called **Odysseus.**

u·ni·corn (ū′nə kôrn′) legendary animal somewhat resembling a horse, usually represented as having one long horn on its forehead, the hind legs of an antelope, and the tail of a lion.

U·ra·nus (yo͝or ā′nəs) in Greek mythology, the father of the Titans and the Cyclopes.

V

Val·hal·la (văl hăl′ə) in Norse mythology, the great hall of Odin, into which heroes slain in battle were brought by the Valkyries.

Val·ky·rie (văl kir′ē) in Norse mythology, one of Odin's warlike maidens who chose the fallen heroes from the battlefield and carried them to Valhalla.

vam·pire (văm′pī′ər) corpse that is superstitiously believed to rise from its grave at night and suck the blood of sleeping persons.

W

were·wolf (wir′wo͝olf′, wâr′wo͝olf′) in folklore, a person who can assume the form of a wolf at will for murderous acts.

Y

Y·mir (ē′mir) in Norse mythology, a wicked giant, whose body was used by the gods to make the earth.

Z

Zeus (zo͞os) in Greek mythology, the supreme deity; husband of Hera. He is identified with the Roman god Jupiter.

The Nations of the World

Name	*Capital*	*Location*
Afghanistan	Kabul	Southwest Asia
Albania	Tirana	Southeastern Europe
Algeria	Algiers	North Africa
Andorra	Andorra la Vella	Southwestern Europe
Angola	Luanda	Southwest Africa
Antigua-Barbuda	St. John's	Eastern Caribbean
Argentina	Buenos Aires	Southeastern South America
Australia	Canberra	South Pacific, southeast of Asia
Austria	Vienna	Central Europe
Bahamas	Nassau	South Atlantic Ocean
Bahrain	Manama	Persian Gulf
Bangladesh	Dacca	Southern Asia
Barbados	Bridgetown	Atlantic Ocean
Belgium	Brussels	Western Europe
Belize	Belmopan	Central America, East Coast
Benin	Porto-Novo	West Africa
Bhutan	Thimphu	Southern Asia
Bolivia	La Paz *and* Sucre	West Central South America
Botswana	Gaborone	Southern Africa
Bourkina Fasso	Ouagadougou	West Africa
Brazil	Brasilia	Central and Northeast South America
Brunei	Bandar Seri Begawan	Borneo Island, North Coast
Bulgaria	Sofia	Eastern Europe
Burma	Rangoon	Southeast Asia
Burundi	Bujumbura	Central Africa
Cameroon	Yaounde	West Africa
Canada	Ottawa	North America
Cape Verde	Praia	South Atlantic Ocean
Central African Republic	Bangui	Central Africa
Chad	N'Djamena	North Central Africa
Chile	Santiago	Western South America
China, People's Republic of (Mainland)	Beijing	Eastern Asia
China, Republic of (Taiwan)	Taipei	Eastern Asia, China Sea
Colombia	Bogota	Northwestern South America
Comoros	Moroni	3 islands between Madagascar and Africa
Congo, People's Republic of the	Brazzaville	Central Africa
Costa Rica	San José	Central America
Cuba	Havana	Caribbean Sea
Cyprus	Nicosia	Mediterranean Sea
Czechoslovakia	Prague	Central Europe
Denmark	Copenhagen	Northern Europe
Djibouti	Djibouti	East Africa
Dominica	Roseau	Eastern Caribbean Sea
Dominican Republic	Santo Domingo	Caribbean Sea
Ecuador	Quito	Northwest South America
Egypt (Arab Republic of Egypt)	Cairo	Northeast Africa

The Nations of the World *(continued)*

Name	*Capital*	*Location*
El Salvador	San Salvador	Central America
Equatorial Guinea	Malabo	Bioko Island off West African coast
Ethiopia	Addis Ababa	East Africa
Fiji	Suva	South Pacific Ocean
Finland	Helsinki	Northeast Europe
France	Paris	Western Europe
Gabon	Libreville	West Africa
Germany:		Northwest Central Europe
German Democratic Republic	East Berlin	(East Germany)
Federal Republic of Germany	Bonn	(West Germany)
Ghana	Accra	West Africa
Greece	Athens	Southeast Europe
Grenada	St. George's	Island in West Indies
Guatemala	Guatemala City	Central America
Guinea	Conakry	West Africa
Guinea-Bissau	Bissau	West Africa
Guyana	Georgetown	Northeast South America
Haiti	Port-au-Prince	Caribbean Sea
Honduras	Tegucigalpa	Central America
Hungary	Budapest	Central Europe
Iceland	Reykjavik	North Atlantic Ocean
India	New Delhi	Southern Asia
Indonesia	Jakarta	Malay Archipelago, Southeast Asia
Iran	Teheran	Southwest Asia
Iraq	Baghdad	Southwest Asia
Ireland	Dublin	Western Europe, Brtish Isles
Israel	Jerusalem	Southwest Asia
Italy	Rome	Southern Europe
Ivory Coast	Abidjan	West Africa
Jamaica	Kingston	Caribbean Sea
Japan	Tokyo	North Pacific Ocean
Jordan	Amman	Southwest Asia
Kampuchea, Democratic (Cambodia)	Phnom Penh	Southeast Asia
Kenya	Nairobi	East Africa
Kiribati	Tarawa	33 Micronesian islands in mid-Pacific Ocean
Korea, Democratic People's Republic of (North)	Pyongyang	Northeast Asia
Korea, Republic of (South)	Seoul	Northeast Asia
Kuwait	Kuwait	Southwest Asia
Laos	Vientiane	Southeast Asia
Lebanon	Beirut	Southwest Asia
Lesotho	Maseru	Southern Africa
Liberia	Monrovia	West Africa
Libya	Tripoli	North Africa
Liechtenstein	Vaduz	Alps
Luxembourg	Luxembourg	Northwest Central Europe

The Nations of the World *(continued)*

Name	*Capital*	*Location*
Madagascar	Antananarivo	Indian Ocean
Malawi	Lilongwe	East Africa
Malaysia	Kuala Lumpur	Southeast Asia
Maldives	Male	Indian Ocean
Mali	Bamako	West Africa
Malta	Valletta	Mediterranean Sea
Mauritania	Nouakchott	West Africa
Mauritius	Port Louis	Indian Ocean
Mexico	Mexico City	Southern North America
Monaco	Monaco Ville	Northwest Mediterranean coast
Mongolia	Ulaanbaatar	Central Asia
Morocco	Rabat	North Africa
Mozambique	Maputo	East Africa
Nauru	Yaren	Pacific Ocean
Nepal	Kathmandu	Southern Asia
Netherlands	Amsterdam	Northwest Europe
New Zealand	Wellington	South Pacific Ocean, east of Australia
Nicaragua	Managua	Central America
Niger	Niamey	Northwest Central Africa
Nigeria	Lagos	West Africa
Norway	Oslo	Northern Europe
Oman	Muscat	Southwest Asia
Pakistan	Islamabad	Southern Asia
Panama	Panama	Central America
Papua New Guinea	Port Moresby	South Pacific Ocean
Paraguay	Asunción	East Central South America
Peru	Lima	Western South America
Philippines	Quezon City	Pacific Ocean, Malay Archipelago
Poland	Warsaw	Eastern Europe
Portugal	Lisbon	Western Europe
Qatar	Doha	Southwest Asia
Romania	Bucharest	Eastern Europe
Rwanda	Kigali	Central Africa
Saint Kitts-Nevis	Basseterre	Eastern Caribbean Sea
Saint Lucia	Castries	Caribbean Sea
Saint Vincent and the Grenadines	Kingstown	Caribbean Sea
San Marino	San Marino	Central Italy
Sao Tome and Principe	Sao Tome	Gulf of Guinea
Saudi Arabia	Riyadh	Southwest Asia, Arabian Peninsula
Senegambia	Dakar	West Africa
Seychelles	Victoria	Indian Ocean
Sierra Leone	Freetown	Northwest Africa
Singapore	Singapore	Southeast Asia
Solomon Islands	Honiara	Pacific Ocean
Somalia	Mogadishu	East Africa
South Africa, Republic of	Pretoria *and* Capetown *and* Bloemfontein	South Africa
Spain	Madrid	Southwestern Europe

The Nations of the World *(concluded)*

Name	*Capital*	*Location*
Sri Lanka	Colombo	Indian Ocean
Sudan	Khartoum	East Africa
Suriname	Paramaribo	South America
Swaziland	Mbabane	Southern Africa
Sweden	Stockholm	Northern Europe
Switzerland	Bern	West Central Europe
Syria	Damascus	Middle East
Tanzania	Dar-es-Salaam	East Africa
Thailand	Bangkok	Southeast Asia
Togo	Lomé	West Africa
Tonga	Naku 'alofa	Pacific Ocean
Trinidad & Tobago	Port-of-Spain	Caribbean Sea
Tunisia	Tunis	North Africa
Turkey	Ankara	Asia and Europe
Tuvalu	Funafuti	9 islands in Pacific Ocean
Uganda	Kampala	Central Africa
Union of Soviet Socialist Republics:	Moscow	Europe and Asia
Byelorussian S.S.R.	Minsk	Western Russia
Ukrainian S.S.R.	Kiev	Southwestern Russia
United Arab Emirates	Abu Dhabi	Southwest Asia
United Kingdom of Great Britain and Northern Ireland	London	Western Europe, British Isles
United States of America	Washington	Central North America
Uruguay	Montevideo	Southeast South America
Vanuatu	Vila	Pacific Ocean
Vatican	Vatican	Southern Europe
Venezuela	Caracas	Northern South America
Vietnam, Socialist Republic of	Hanoi	Southeast Asia
Western Samoa	Apia	South Pacific Ocean
Yemen (Yemen Arab Republic)	Sanaa	Southwest Asia
Yemen, People's Democratic Republic of (South Yemen)	Aden	Southwest Asia
Yugoslavia	Belgrade	Central Europe
Zaire	Kinshasa	Central Africa
Zambia	Lusaka	Southern Africa
Zimbabwe	Salisbury	Southern Africa

The Presidents of the United States

Name	Term of Office	Party
1. George Washington	1789–1797	Federalist
2. John Adams	1797–1801	Federalist
3. Thomas Jefferson	1801–1809	Democratic-Republican†
4. James Madison	1809–1817	Democratic-Republican
5. James Monroe	1817–1825	Democratic-Republican
6. John Quincy Adams	1825–1829	Democratic-Republican
7. Andrew Jackson	1829–1837	Democrat
8. Martin Van Buren	1837–1841	Democrat
9. William Henry Harrison††	1841–1841	Whig†
10. John Tyler	1841–1845	Whig
11. James K. Polk	1845–1849	Democrat
12. Zachary Taylor††	1849–1850	Whig
13. Millard Fillmore	1850–1853	Whig
14. Franklin Pierce	1853–1857	Democrat
15. James Buchanan	1857–1861	Democrat
16. Abraham Lincoln††	1861–1865	Republican
17. Andrew Johnson	1865–1869	Republican
18. Ulysses S. Grant	1869–1877	Republican
19. Rutherford B. Hayes	1877–1881	Republican
20. James A. Garfield††	1881–1881	Republican
21. Chester A. Arthur	1881–1885	Republican
22. Grover Cleveland	1885–1889	Democrat
23. Benjamin Harrison	1889–1893	Republican
24. Grover Cleveland	1893–1897	Democrat
25. William McKinley††	1897–1901	Republican
26. Theodore Roosevelt	1901–1909	Republican
27. William Howard Taft	1909–1913	Republican
28. Woodrow Wilson	1913–1921	Democrat
29. Warren G. Harding††	1921–1923	Republican
30. Calvin Coolidge	1923–1929	Republican
31. Herbert C. Hoover	1929–1933	Republican
32. Franklin D. Roosevelt††	1933–1945	Democrat
33. Harry S. Truman	1945–1953	Democrat
34. Dwight D. Eisenhower	1953–1961	Republican
35. John F. Kennedy††	1961–1963	Democrat
36. Lyndon B. Johnson	1963–1969	Democrat
37. Richard M. Nixon	1969–1974	Republican
38. Gerald R. Ford	1974–1977	Republican
39. Jimmy (James Earl) Carter	1977–1981	Democrat
40. Ronald Reagan	1981–	Republican

† This party, founded by Thomas Jefferson and named by him Republican, was later called Democratic-Republican; it became the Democratic party in 1828. The modern Republican party was established in 1854; the Whig party opposed the Democrats from about 1834–1856.

†† Died in Office.

THE STATES OF THE UNITED STATES

Name	Postal Abbr.	Capital	Date Entered Union	Area (Sq. Mi.)	Nickname
Alabama	AL	Montgomery	1819	51,609	Yellowhammer State
Alaska	AK	Juneau	1959	586,412	The Last Frontier
Arizona	AZ	Phoenix	1912	113,909	Grand Canyon State
Arkansas	AR	Little Rock	1836	53,104	Land of Opportunity
California	CA	Sacramento	1850	158,693	Golden State
Colorado	CO	Denver	1876	104,247	Centennial State
Connecticut	CT	Hartford	1788	5,009	Nutmeg State
Delaware	DE	Dover	1787	2,057	First State
Florida	FL	Tallahassee	1845	58,560	Sunshine State
Georgia	GA	Atlanta	1788	58,876	Peach State
Hawaii	HI	Honolulu	1959	6,450	Aloha State
Idaho	ID	Boise	1890	83,557	Gem State
Illinois	IL	Springfield	1818	56,400	Prairie State
Indiana	IN	Indianapolis	1816	36,291	Hoosier State
Iowa	IA	Des Moines	1846	56,290	Hawkeye State
Kansas	KS	Topeka	1861	82,264	Sunflower State
Kentucky	KY	Frankfort	1792	40,395	Bluegrass State
Louisiana	LA	Baton Rouge	1812	48,523	Pelican State
Maine	ME	Augusta	1820	33,215	Pine Tree State
Maryland	MD	Annapolis	1788	10,577	Free State
Massachusetts	MA	Boston	1788	8,257	Bay State
Michigan	MI	Lansing	1837	58,216	Wolverine State
Minnesota	MN	St. Paul	1858	84,068	North Star State
Mississippi	MS	Jackson	1817	47,716	Magnolia State
Missouri	MO	Jefferson City	1821	69,686	Show-me State
Montana	MT	Helena	1889	147,138	Treasure State
Nebraska	NE	Lincoln	1867	77,227	Cornhusker State
Nevada	NV	Carson City	1864	110,540	Sagebrush State
New Hampshire	NH	Concord	1788	9,304	Granite State
New Jersey	NJ	Trenton	1787	7,836	Garden State
New Mexico	NM	Santa Fe	1912	121,666	Land of Enchantment
New York	NY	Albany	1788	49,576	Empire State
North Carolina	NC	Raleigh	1789	52,586	Tar Heel State
North Dakota	ND	Bismarck	1889	70,665	Sioux State
Ohio	OH	Columbus	1803	41,222	Buckeye State
Oklahoma	OK	Oklahoma City	1907	69,919	Sooner State
Oregon	OR	Salem	1859	96,981	Beaver State
Pennsylvania	PA	Harrisburg	1787	45,333	Keystone State
Rhode Island	RI	Providence	1790	1,214	The Ocean State
South Carolina	SC	Columbia	1788	31,055	Palmetto State
South Dakota	SD	Pierre	1889	77,047	Coyote State
Tennessee	TN	Nashville	1796	42,244	Volunteer State
Texas	TX	Austin	1845	267,338	Lone Star State
Utah	UT	Salt Lake City	1896	84,916	Beehive State
Vermont	VT	Montpelier	1791	9,609	Green Mountain State
Virginia	VA	Richmond	1788	40,817	The Old Dominion State
Washington	WA	Olympia	1889	68,192	Evergreen State
West Virginia	WV	Charleston	1863	24,181	Mountain State
Wisconsin	WI	Madison	1848	56,154	Badger State
Wyoming	WY	Cheyenne	1890	97,914	Equality State

Name	State Flower	State Bird	State Tree
Alabama	Camellia	Yellowhammer	Southern pine
Alaska	Forget-me-not	Willow ptarmigan	Sitka spruce
Arizona	Saguaro cactus	Cactus wren	Paloverde
Arkansas	Apple blossom	Mockingbird	Pine
California	Golden poppy	Valley quail	California redwood
Colorado	Columbine	Lark bunting	Colorado blue spruce
Connecticut	Mountain laurel	American robin	White oak
Delaware	Peach blossom	Blue Hen chicken	American holly
Florida	Orange blossom	Mockingbird	Sabal palmetto
Georgia	Cherokee rose	Brown thrasher	Live oak
Hawaii	Hibiscus	Nene (Hawaiian goose)	Kukui (Candlenut tree)
Idaho	Syringa	Mountain bluebird	White pine
Illinois	Violet	Cardinal	White oak
Indiana	Peony	Cardinal	Tulip tree
Iowa	Wild rose	Eastern goldfinch	Oak
Kansas	Sunflower	Western meadow lark	Cottonwood
Kentucky	Goldenrod	Kentucky cardinal	Coffeetree
Louisiana	Magnolia	Pelican	Bald cyprus
Maine	White pine cone and tassel	Chickadee	White pine tree
Maryland	Black-eyed susan	Baltimore oriole	White oak
Massachusetts	Mayflower	Chickadee	American elm
Michigan	Apple blossom	Robin	White pine
Minnesota	Showy lady slipper	Common loon	Red pine
Mississippi	Evergreen magnolia	Mockingbird	Magnolia
Missouri	Hawthorn	Bluebird	Dogwood
Montana	Bitterroot	Western meadow lark	Ponderosa pine
Nebraska	Goldenrod	Western meadow lark	Cottonwood
Nevada	Sagebrush	Mountain bluebird	Single-leaf pinon
New Hampshire	Purple lilac	Purple finch	White birch
New Jersey	Purple violet	Eastern goldfinch	Red oak
New Mexico	Yucca	Roadrunner	Pinon
New York	Rose	Bluebird	Sugar maple
North Carolina	Dogwood	Cardinal	Pine
North Dakota	Wild prairie rose	Western meadow lark	American elm
Ohio	Scarlet carnation	Cardinal	Buckeye
Oklahoma	Mistletoe	Scissor-tailed flycatcher	Redbud
Oregon	Oregon grape	Western meadow lark	Douglas fir
Pennsylvania	Mountain laurel	Ruffed grouse	Hemlock
Rhode Island	Violet (Unofficial)	Rhode Island Red	Red maple
South Carolina	Carolina yellow jessamine	Carolina wren	Palmetto tree
South Dakota	Pasqueflower	Ring-necked pheasant	Black Hills spruce
Tennessee	Iris	Mockingbird	Tulip poplar
Texas	Bluebonnet	Mockingbird	Pecan
Utah	Sego lily	Seagull	Blue spruce
Vermont	Red clover	Hermit thrush	Sugar maple
Virginia	Dogwood	Cardinal	Dogwood (Unofficial)
Washington	Rhododendron	Willow goldfinch	Western hemlock
West Virginia	Rhododendron	Cardinal	Sugar maple
Wisconsin	Wood violet	Robin	Sugar maple
Wyoming	Indian paintbrush	Meadow lark	Cottonwood

The Provinces and Territories of Canada

Name	Capital
Provinces	
Alberta (ăl bûr′tə)	Edmonton (ĕd′mən tən)
British Columbia (brĭt′ĭsh kə lŭm′bĭ ə)	Victoria (vĭk tôr′ĭ ə)
Manitoba (măn′ə tō′bə)	Winnipeg (wĭn′ə pĕg′)
New Brunswick (nū′ brŭns′wĭk)	Fredericton (frĕd ər ĭk tən)
Newfoundland (nū′fənd lănd′)	St. John's (sānt jŏnz′)
Nova Scotia (nō′və skō′shə)	Halifax (hăl′ə făks)
Ontario (ŏn târ′ĭ ō)	Toronto (tə rŏn′tō)
Prince Edward Island (prĭns ĕd′wərd ī′lənd)	Charlottetown (shär′lət toun)
Quebec (kwĭ bĕk′)	Quebec (kwĭ bĕk′)
Saskatchewan (săs kăch′ə wŏn)	Regina (rĭ jī′nə)
Territories	
Northwest Territories (nôrth′wĕst′ tĕr′ə tô′rĭz)	
Yukon (ū′kŏn)	Whitehorse (hwīt′hôrs′)

Sixty Indian Tribes of North America

Name	Original Home
Algonquin (ăl gŏng′kĭn *or* ăl gŏng′kwĭn)	Forest: Quebec
Apache (ə păch′ĭ)	Southwest: Arizona, New Mexico
Arapaho (ə răp′ə hō)	Plains: Colorado, Wyoming
Arikara (ə rĭk′ər ə)	Plains: North Dakota
Blackfeet (blăk′fēt)	Plains: Alberta, Saskatchewan, Montana
Caddo (kăd′ō)	Plains: Arkansas, Louisiana, Texas
Catawba (kə tô′bə)	Forest: North and South Carolina
Cayuse (kī ūs′)	Mountains: Oregon
Cherokee (chĕr′ə kĭ)	Forest: North and South Carolina, Georgia
Cheyenne (shī ăn′ *or* shī ĕn′)	Plains: North and South Dakota
Chickasaw (chĭk′ə sô)	Forest: Mississippi
Chinook (chə no͝ok′)	Northwest Coast: Washington, Oregon
Chippewa (chĭp′ə wä *or* chĭp′ə wā)	Forest: Minnesota, North Dakota, Ontario
Choctaw (chŏk′tô)	Forest: Mississippi, Alabama
Comanche (kə măn′chĭ)	Plains: Oklahoma, Texas
Cree (krē)	Forest: Manitoba, Saskatchewan
Creek (krēk)	Forest: Georgia, Alabama
Crow (krō)	Plains: Montana, Wyoming
Delaware (dĕl′ə wâr)	Forest: New Jersey, Pennsylvania, Delaware
Flathead (flăt′hĕd)	Plains: Montana
Gros Ventre (grō vän′trə)	Plains: North and South Dakota
Haida (hī′də)	Northwest Coast: British Columbia
Hopi (hō′pĭ)	Southwest: Arizona
Huron (hūr′ən)	Forest: Ontario
Illinois (ĭl′ə noi′ *or* ĭl′ə noiz′)	Forest: Illinois, Iowa, Missouri

Sixty Indian Tribes of North America *(continued)*

Name	*Original Home*
Iroquois (ĭr′ə kwoi)	Forest: New York, Quebec
Cayuga (kī ū′gə *or* kā ū′gə)	
Mohawk (mō′hôk)	
Oneida (ō nī′də)	
Onondaga (ŏn′ən dô′gə *or* ŏn′ən dä′gə)	
Seneca (sĕn′ə kə)	
Kiowa (kī′ə wä)	Plains: South Dakota
Leni-Lenape (lĕn′ĭ lĕn′ə pē′) Delaware Indians	
Mandan (măn′dăn)	Plains: North Dakota
Massachuset (măs′ə chōō′sĕt)	Forest: Massachusetts
Miami (mī ăm′ĭ)	Forest: Wisconsin, Michigan, Illinois, Indiana, Ohio
Micmac (mĭk′măk)	Forest: Nova Scotia, New Brunswick
Modoc (mō′dŏk)	Northwest Coast: California, Oregon
Mohican (mō hē′kən)	Forest: New York
Narragansett (năr′ə găn′sĭt)	Forest: Rhode Island
Natchez (năch′ĭz)	Forest: Mississippi
Navaho (năv′ə hō)	Southwest: New Mexico, Arizona
Nez Perce (nĕz′pûrs′)	Mountains: Idaho
Ojibwa (ō jĭb′wā)	Forests: Ontario, Wisconsin, Minnesota
Osage (o′sāj)	Plains: Missouri, Kansas
Pawnee (pô nē′)	Plains: Nebraska, Kansas
Paiute (pī ōōt′)	Plains: Nevada, Utah
Pequot (pē′kwŏt)	Forest: Connecticut
Potawatomi (pŏt′ə wŏt′ō mĭ)	Forest: Michigan, Illinois
Powhatan (pou′ə tăn′)	Forest: Virginia
Pueblo (pwĕb′lō)	Southwest: Arizona, New Mexico
Sac or Sauk (săk *or* sôk)	Forest: Illinois, Iowa, Missouri
Seminole (sĕm′ə nōl)	Forest: Alabama, Georgia
Shawnee (shô nē′)	Forest: Kentucky, Georgia, Ohio, Pennsylvania
Shoshoni (shō shō′nĭ)	Mountains: Idaho, Nevada, Utah, Montana
Sioux (sōō)	Plains: Wisconsin, Minnesota, North and South Dakota
Tuscarora (tŭs′kə rôr′ə)	Forest: North Carolina
Ute (ūt)	Mountains: Colorado, Utah, Arizona, New Mexico
Winnebago (wĭn′ə bā′gō)	Forest: Wisconsin
Zuñi (zōōn′yĭ)	Southwest: New Mexico

Domestic Weights and Measures

Long Measure

1 foot	12 inches
1 yard	3 feet
1 rod or pole	5½ yards
1 furlong	40 rods
1 statute mile	8 furlongs (1,760 yards, or 5,280 feet)
1 league	3 miles

Mariners' Measure

1 fathom	6 feet
1 cable length	100 fathoms, or about $\frac{1}{10}$ nautical mile
1 statute mile	5,280 feet
1 nautical mile	6,080.20 feet

Square Measure

1 square foot	144 square inches
1 square yard	9 square feet
1 square rod	30¼ square yards
1 acre	160 square rods or 43,560 square feet
1 square mile	640 acres
1 section	1 square mile

Cubic Measure

1 cubic foot	1,728 cubic inches
1 cubic yard	27 cubic feet
1 perch	24¾ cubic feet
1 cord	8 cord feet, or 128 cubic feet

(A pile 8′ long, 4′ wide, and 4′ high contains 1 cord.)

Dry Measure

1 pint	33.60 cubic inches
1 quart	2 pints
1 peck	8 quarts
1 bushel	4 pecks, or 2,150.42 cubic inches

Liquid Measure

1 fluid dram	.2256 cubic inch
1 fluid ounce	8 fluid drams
1 gill	4 fluid ounces
1 pint	16 fluid ounces or 4 gills
1 quart	2 pints
1 gallon	4 quarts
1 barrel	31½ gallons
1 hogshead	2 barrels

(A standard U.S. gallon, the unit of liquid measure, is the same as the English wine gallon, and contains 231 cubic inches. A gallon of water weighs about 8⅓ pounds. A barrel contains about 4⅕ cubic feet.)

Avoirdupois Weight

1 pound	16 ounces
1 short hundredweight	100 pounds
1 long hundredweight	112 pounds
1 ton	20 hundredweight
1 short ton	2,000 pounds, or 20 short hundredweight
1 long ton	2,240 pounds, or 20 long hundredweight

The Metric System Simplified

The following tables of the metric system of weights and measures have been simplified as much as possible by omitting such denominations as are not in practical, everyday use in the countries where the system is used.

Tables of the System

Length

The denominations in practical use are the millimeter (mm.), centimeter (cm.), and kilometer (km.).

10 millimeters	1 centimeter
100 centimeters	1 meter
1,000 meters	1 kilometer

Weight

The denominations in use are the milligram (mg.), gram (g.), kilogram (kg.), and ton (metric ton).

1,000 milligrams	1 gram
1,000 grams	1 kilogram
1,000 kilograms	1 metric ton

Capacity

The denominations in use are the cubic centimeter (c.c.) and liter (l.).

1,000 cubic centimeters	1 liter

Relation of capacity and weight to length: 1,000 cubic centimeters is, approximately, a liter; and a liter of water weighs one kilogram.

Approximate Equivalents

A meter (39.37 inches) is about a yard.

A kilogram (2.2 pounds) is about two pounds.

A liter (0.91 dry qt. and 1.06 liquid qts.) is about a quart.

A centimeter (0.39 inch) is about $\frac{4}{10}$ inch.

A metric ton (2204.6 pounds) is about a long ton.

A kilometer (0.62 mile, or 3280 feet) is about ⅝ mile.

A cubic centimeter is about a thimbleful.

A nickel weighs about five grams.

For postal purposes fifteen grams are considered the equivalent of one half ounce avoirdupois. At the mint a half dollar is considered to weigh 12.5 grams.

THE METRIC SYSTEM

Approximate Conversions to Metric Measures

	Symbol	*When You Know*	*Multiply by*	*To Find*	*Symbol*
Length	in	inches	2.54	centimeters	cm
	ft	feet	30	centimeters	cm
	yd	yards	0.9	meters	m
	mi	miles	1.6	kilometers	km
Area	in^2	square inches	6.5	square centimeters	cm^2
	ft^2	square feet	0.09	square meters	m^2
	yd^2	square yards	0.8	square meters	m^2
	mi^2	square miles	2.6	square kilometers	km^2
		acres	0.4	hectares	ha
Mass (weight)	oz	ounces	28	grams	g
	lb	pounds	0.45	kilograms	kg
		short tons (2000 lb)	0.9	tonnes	t
Volume	tsp	teaspoons	5	milliliters	ml
	Tbsp	tablespoons	15	milliliters	ml
	fl oz	fluid ounces	30	milliliters	ml
	c	cups	0.24	liters	l
	pt	pints	0.47	liters	l
	qt	quarts	0.95	liters	l
	gal	gallons	3.8	liters	l
	ft^3	cubic feet	0.03	cubic meters	m^3
	yd^3	cubic yards	0.76	cubic meters	m^3
Temperature	°F	Fahrenheit temperature	5/9 (after subtracting 32)	Celsius temperature	°C

Approximate Conversions from Metric Measures

	Symbol	*When You Know*	*Multiply by*	*To Find*	*Symbol*
Length	mm	millimeters	0.04	inches	in
	cm	centimeters	0.4	inches	in
	m	meters	3.3	feet	ft
	m	meters	1.1	yards	yd
	km	kilometers	0.6	miles	mi
Area	cm^2	square centimeters	0.16	square inches	in^2
	m^2	square meters	1.2	square yards	yd^2
	km^2	square kilometers	0.4	square miles	mi^2
	ha	hectares (10,000 m^2)	2.5	acres	
Mass (weight)	g	grams	0.035	ounces	oz
	kg	kilograms	2.2	pounds	lb
	t	tonnes (1000 kg)	1.1	short tons (2000 lb)	
Volume	ml	milliliters	0.03	fluid ounces	fl oz
	l	liters	2.1	pints	pt
	l	liters	1.06	quarts	qt
	l	liters	0.26	gallons	gal
	m^3	cubic meters	35	cubic feet	ft^3
	m^3	cubic meters	1.3	cubic yards	yd^3
Temperature	°C	Celcius temperature	9/5 (then add 32)	Fahrenheit temperature	°F

SIGNS AND SYMBOLS

COMMERCE AND FINANCE

$ dollar; dollars: $1; $5
¢ cent; cents: 1¢; 12¢
/ shilling; shillings: 1/6 is 1 shilling, 6 pence
£ pound (sterling); pound: £1; £5
@ at: gingham @ $1.50 a yard
% per cent

MATHEMATICS

+ plus: 3 + 2 = 5
− minus: 6 − 3 = 3
± plus or minus: 2 ± .1
× or · multiplied by: 6 × 2 = 12; 6 · 2 = 12
÷ divided by: 6 ÷ 2 = 3
> is greater than: 6 > 5
< is less than: 5 < 6
: is to: 6:3
: : as: 6:3 : : 8:4
∠ angle: ∠ABC
√‾ square root: $\sqrt{9} = \pm 3$
° degrees: 362°
′ minutes: 28°6′
″ seconds: 189° 32′ 58″
= equals: 3 + 2 = 5
≠ is not equal to: 3 + 2 ≠ 6
≥ or ≧ is greater than or equal to: $a \geq 4$
≤ or ≦ is less than or equal to: $b \leq 6$
≯ is not greater than: $x \ngtr 6$
≮ is not less than: $x \nless 7$
≈ or ≑ is approximately equal to: 2.01 ≈ 2
∟ right angle
⊥ is perpendicular to
∥ is parallel to
△ triangle

( ) or [ ] the enclosed quantities or elements are to be taken together
π pi
∞ infinity
)‾ or /‾ division sign: 23)‾27 ; 3/‾9

MISCELLANEOUS

© copyrighted
® registered trademark
& and: Smith & Co.
&c and the rest; and so forth; et cetera: peas, beans, &c
′ feet: a room 12′ by 8′
″ inches: paper 8½″ by 11″
× by: a room 12′ × 8′
number: a #4 screw
℅ care of: Mr. John Oaks, ℅ The Marks Hotel
♁ or ♂ male
♀ female

PUNCTUATION

, comma
; semicolon
: colon
. period
? question mark
! exclamation point
( ) parentheses
[ ] brackets
' apostrophe
— dash
- hyphen
“ ” opening and closing quotation marks
‘ ’ opening and closing single quotation marks

INTERNATIONAL SYMBOLS

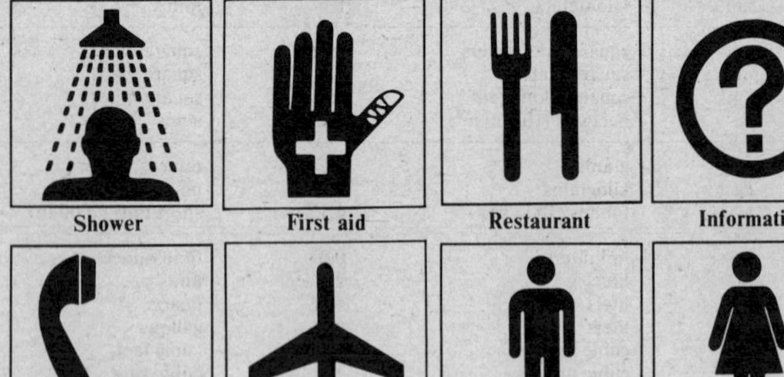

Shower | First aid | Restaurant | Information

Telephone | Air transportation | Toilets, men

Toilets, women

SKILLS PRACTICE PAGES

for the

NEW SCHOLASTIC DICTIONARY OF AMERICAN ENGLISH

The following skills pages provide practice in using the *New Scholastic Dictionary of American English.* The objective of the pages is to support and reinforce the instruction in dictionary form and function given in the You and Your Dictionary section at the beginning of the book.

The skills pages are divided into four topics: Finding Words, Pronouncing Words, Defining and Using Words, and Locating Information. There is a skills review page for each topic to consolidate individual skill achievement.

Two symbols consistently appear on the skills pages. The open-book symbol indicates a discussion exercise. These questions provide a framework for classroom dialogue and a means of acquainting the student with the skills of the page.

The pencil and paper symbol indicates a written exercise. Pencil and paper work will always follow oral exercises and will develop and expand the concepts begun in the open book section.

This page format provides the latitude for classroom adaptation. Some students may be able to pursue the open-book exercises independently. Other students may require teacher involvement to complete the pencil and paper exercises. The teacher can best adapt the page format to fit the needs of the individual classroom situation.

Contents

Alphabetical Order

It's easy to find words in a dictionary because all the words in any dictionary are listed or arranged in alphabetical order.

There is a separate section for each letter of the alphabet.

The more you know about alphabetical order and alphabetizing, the easier it is to use a dictionary.

1. Suppose you want to look up the word *manatee.* You open your dictionary to the section containing words beginning with the letter *o.* Tell whether you would have to go forward or back to find *manatee.*
2. Tell the correct alphabetical order for these six words: *fortress, forty, forte, fortune, forth, fortitude.* Which letter in each word did you have to look at to put these words in alphabetical order.
3. Tell which word in each pair comes first in correct alphabetical order:

   a. heater - heated
   b. numeral - numerable
   c. hide-out - hideous
   d. suggestive - suggestion

1. Write the following twelve words in correct alphabetical order on a piece of paper:

woven	motion	value	ominous	camel	gruesome
lemon	barter	equal	stirrup	total	peaceful

2. Write the following ten words in correct alphabetical order on a piece of paper. They all begin with *a,* so you must alphabetize them according to the *second* letter in each word.

average	assistant	automobile	activity	attitude
able	answer	armadillo	awkward	ample

3. Write the following ten words beginning with *fla* on a piece of paper in alphabetical order. Remember that since they all begin with the same three letters you will have to look at the *fourth* letter in each word to alphabetize them correctly.

flattery	flair	flaccid	flax	flabby
flange	flash	flapper	flag	flavor

Guide Words

This is the top of page 96 in your dictionary. The guide words for this page are **bridge** and **bring.** Note the large, heavy black type in which they are printed.

bridge **bring**

[2]**bridge** (brĭj) ***n-*** card game for four players. One of the most common types is **contract bridge.** [apparently from Russian **biritch,** an old card game.]
bridge·head (brĭj′ hĕd′) ***n-*** military position established on an enemy coast or riverbank in advance of the main attacking force.
bridge·work (brĭj′ wûrk′) ***n-*** **1** one or more dental bridges. **2** the building of bridges.

bright·en (brī′ tən) ***vi-*** to grow clearer or lighter: *The day brightens.* ***vt-*** to make more pleasant or cheerful: *Flowers brighten a room.*
bright-line spectrum ***n-*** spectrum given off by incandescent vapors, in which only particular wave lengths of light are emitted, appearing as bright lines on a dark background.

On this page you will find all the words that come between **bridge** and **bring** in alphabetical order.

1. Tell whether you would find the word *bride* on this page in your dictionary.
2. Tell whether you would find the word *brink* on this page in your dictionary.
3. Tell whether you would find the word *brief* on this page in your dictionary.
4. Tell whether you would find the word *brilliant* on this page in your dictionary.

1. Look for the word *grope* in your dictionary. Use the guide words to help you. Write on what page you found *grope.* Write the guide words for the page.
2. Find the word *odious* in you dictionary. Write on what page you found *odious.* Write the guide words for the page.
3. Now use the guide words to find *media.* Write on what page you found *media.* Write the guide words for the page.
4. Write the guide words on the page with the word *registrar.*
5. Write the guide words on the page with the word *livid.*
6. Write the guide words on the page with the word *dominion.*
7. Write the guide words on the page with the word *popular.*

Entry Words

All words listed alphabetically in your dictionary are called **entry words.** Each entry word shows you the correct spelling for that word and how the word is divided into syllables.

Clydes·dale (klīdz′ dāl′) ***n-*** big, strong work horse originally bred in the Clyde valley region of Scotland.

pas·tra·mi (pə strä′ mē) ***n-*** highly seasoned and smoked shoulder cut of beef. *as* ***modifier***: *a* pastrami *sandwich.*

1. Look at page 148 in your dictionary. Tell the first five entry words.
2. Tell which entry word on page 148 is an abbreviation.
3. Tell which entry words are made up of two separate words.
4. Tell the fourth entry word on page 629.
5. Tell the third entry word on page 428.
6. Tell what the abbreviation *Fe* stands for on page 282.

1. Turn to page 198 in your dictionary.
   - **a.** Write the sixth entry word on the page.
   - **b.** Write two hyphenated compound words found on this page.
   - **c.** Write nine entries found on this page that are made up of two separate words.
   - **d.** Write the entry that is made up of three separate words.
   - **e.** Write the entries that are abbreviations.
   - **f.** Write the entry that is a prefix.

2. Turn to page 305 in your dictionary.
   - **a.** Write the number of entry words on page 305.
   - **b.** Write the capitalized entry word.
   - **c.** Write how many syllables are in the word *formaldehyde.*
   - **d.** Write the entry word that is illustrated.
   - **e.** Write the entry word that is a hyphenated compound word.

Non-Entry Words—Inflected Forms

You will not be able to find certain forms of words you might want to look up in your dictionary listed as entry words. These words are called **inflected forms.** Only irregular inflected forms are shown in this dictionary.

1. Find the base word for each of the following inflected forms. Then tell why the inflected form either is or is not shown in brackets following the entry word.
   a. modified **b.** deprived **c.** planning **d.** defended **e.** grabbed **f.** climbing **g.** nodding **h.** defacing **i.** studied
2. Using your dictionary, tell the plural forms of the following nouns. Some words may have more than one plural. Remember: only irregular plurals are shown in this dictionary.
   a. alibi **b.** relish **c.** chrysalis **d.** key **e.** pony **f.** money **g.** rodeo **h.** torpedo **i.** zero **j.** buffalo **k.** caribou **l.** elk **m.** fungus **n.** calf

1. Write what the entry word would be for each of the following plurals.
   a. currants **b.** compasses **c.** dervishes **d.** reflexes **e.** wrenches **f.** kidneys **g.** bullies **h.** portfolios **i.** tomatoes
2. Write what the entry word would be for each of the following inflected forms. Underline the words you would find in brackets after the main entry word.
   a. slipped **b.** fried **c.** chasing **d.** wanted **e.** tamed **f.** stopping **g.** practiced **h.** notified **i.** stamping

You can add the endings *-er* and *-est* to most adjectives. All adjective forms are listed in brackets after the entry for the base word, **even if there are no spelling changes in the base word.**

1. Write the entry word for each underlined word below. Check your answers in your dictionary.
   a. He was a lot <u>angrier</u> than I thought he'd be.

b. They say this detergent will clean even the greasiest dishes.
c. This work is harder than I thought it would be.
d. She is the strongest girl in the room.
e. I need a larger notebook.
f. Jack is the nicest boy I know.
g. The fattest pig will win first prize at the fair.
h. One of my feet is bigger than the other one.

Run-on Entries

Some other words you will not find listed as entry words in your dictionary are base words to which suffixes such as *-ly*, *-ness*, or *-ion* have been added. These forms follow the base word entry in this dictionary.

1. Find and write the entry word for each of these non-entry words:
   a. hysterically d. clumsily g. immigration
   b. intently e. stubbornness h. suitability
   c. amazingly f. silliness i. dependability

2. Write the words below which are entry words.
   a. stack d. cash g. pan
   b. owe e. helper h. N.S.
   c. dog-like f. shrank i. naughtily
   After which entry words would you find the non-entry words from the exercise above?

3. Write the run-on entries for these words:
   a. interpretation e. scour i. disrespectful
   b. mendacious f. disloyal j. ape
   c. disreputable g. ragged k. muggy
   d. reckon h. stain l. violent

Spelling

Every entry word in your dictionary shows you the correct spelling for that word. When you want to be sure of the correct way to spell any word, look up the spelling by finding the word in the dictionary.

Some words may be spelled more than one way. Your dictionary will tell you this, too. Look up the words *ax* and *catalog.* Tell the other spellings for these two words. Find the word *tornado.* Tell the two ways the plural of the word *tornado* may be spelled.

One word in each pair of words below is spelled incorrectly. Look up the word in your dictionary. Write the correct spelling on a piece of paper.

lable label	defens defense	convertible convertable	greatful grateful
neice niece	career carreer	inevitable inevitible	irridescent iridescent
weird wierd	marraige marriage	inexhaustable inexhaustible	condense condence
aquaint acquaint	license lisence	computor computer	intefere interfere
pianoes pianos	spasial spatial	seargent sergeant	correspondent correspondant
cellar celler	tracter tractor	excelerate accelerate	commision commission

Review—Finding Words

1. Write these words in correct alphabetical order:

   prawn praise practice prattle
   prance prayer praline pragmatic

2. If your last name were an entry word in the dictionary, write the two words between which it would be found.
3. Write the guide words from the page where each of these words is found in this dictionary.

   seem semantic seismograph selection

4. Write which set of guide words is at the top of the dictionary page on which the word *hold* is found.

   holding—home **hobo—holder** **hook—horizontal**

5. Below are several entries from your dictionary. Use them to answer these questions:

ad·vise (əd vīz′, ăd-) ***vt-*** **[ad·vised, ad·vis·ing] 1** to give advice to: *He* advised *me to go.* **2** to notify: *He* advised *me of my promotion.* ***vi-*** to seek counsel; consult: *He* advised *with me about his trip.* ***—n-*** **ad·vis′er** or **ad·vi′sor.**

al·ve·o·lus (ăl vē′ə ləs) ***n-*** [*pl.* **al·ve·o·li** (-ə lī)] small hollow in the body, especially a tooth socket or one of the air sacs in the lungs.

can·ta·loupe or **can·ta·loup** (kăn′tə lōp′) ***n-*** melon with a hard, rough rind and sweet, juicy, orange-colored flesh.

Corp. 1 corporal. **2** corporation.

-ese *suffix* (used to form adjectives and nouns) **1** pertaining to the country or region of; also, an inhabitant of: *Japan*ese; *Senegal*ese; *Canton*ese. **2** language or jargon of: *Japan*ese; *Portugu*ese; *journal*ese.

grappling iron ***n-*** **1** tool with several hooks for clutching something. **2** grapnel.

odd (ŏd) ***adj-*** **[odd·er, odd·est] 1** unusual or strange; peculiar: *It is* odd *that he is so late. The* odd, *old man lives alone.* **2** without the rest of a pair or set: *an* odd *sock; an* odd *volume.* **3** plus a few more: *I've 40* odd *dollars in my pocket.* **4** extra: *The* odd *player can keep score or substitute.* **5** occasional: *at* odd *moments; an* odd *job.* **6** having a remainder of 1 after being divided by two: *1, 3, 17, and 239 are* odd *numbers.* ***—adv-*** **odd′ly.** ***n-*** **odd′ness.**

part-time (pärt′ tīm′) ***adj-*** **1** taking up only a part of one's possible working time: *a* part-time *job.* **2** working or serving as such during only a part of one's possible working time: *a* part-time *teacher.* ***—adv-***: *to work* part-time.

pre- *prefix* before: *a pre*historic *animal*; *a pre*paid *package.*

   a. Write the entry that is an abbreviation.
   b. Write the entry that is made up of two words.
   c. Write the entry that is a prefix.
   d. Write the entry that is a hyphenated compound word.
   e. Write the entry that may be spelled in two ways.

6. Write the plurals for each of the following words. If there is more than one way to form the plural, underline the form that is preferred. The preferred spelling is listed first.

   a. conch **c.** fox **e.** lackey **f.** attorney
   b. fish **d.** junco **f.** authority **h.** hippopotamus

Syllable Division and Accents

What is a syllable? Each syllable in a word contains one vowel sound. After each entry word the syllables are rewritten in parentheses to show you how to pronounce the word.

in·stru·men·tal (ĭn′ strə měn′ təl) **kil·o·gram** (kĭl′ ə grăm′) **pre·cip·i·ta·tion** (prĭ sĭp′ ə tā′ shən)

The syllable with the heavy accent mark is the one most strongly stressed in pronouncing the word. The syllable with the weak accent mark receives some emphasis or stress.

Find each word below in your dictionary. Pronounce it aloud showing which syllable is accented most heavily.

1. impulse
2. supplant
3. prevalent
4. condolence
5. integrate
6. pathologist
7. topography
8. retribution
9. rudimentary
10. superconductive
11. superlative
12. superstructure

1. Copy these words. Divide them into syllables for correct pronunciation.

a. cabin
b. stable
c. lesson
d. entire
e. create
f. faster
g. elbow
h. carton
i. rubble
j. sudden
k. handle
l. wasted

2. Copy these words. Divide them into syllables for correct pronunciation. Mark the accented syllable.

a. derrick
b. hazard
c. mahogany
d. panther
e. shadowy
f. unburden
g. conversion
h. grocery
i. nutrition
j. radial
k. without
l. humane

The Pronunciation Key — Short and Long Vowel Sounds

The correct pronunciation for each entry word in your dictionary is shown in parentheses after the entry word like this:

phi·lan·thro·pist (fə lăn′ thrə pĭst) **psy·chol·o·gy** (sī kŏl′ ə jē) **a·muse·ment** (ə myo͞oz′ mənt)

Match each pronunciation shown below in parentheses with the correct word.

1. ditch	**5.** cement	**9.** cane	**13.** come
2. judge	**6.** city	**10.** cute	**14.** crow
3. cell	**7.** seat	**11.** magic	**15.** use
4. hollow	**8.** hygiene	**12.** crime	**16.** copy

a. (krō)	**e.** (jŭj)	**i.** (krīm)	**m.** (kŏp′ ē)
b. (sĕl)	**f.** (kān)	**j.** (sĭt′ē)	**n.** (hī′ jēn)
c. (kŭm)	**g.** (dĭch)	**k.** (hŏl′ ō)	**o.** (sĭ mĕnt′)
d. (sēt)	**h.** (yo͞oz)	**l.** (kyo͞ot)	**p.** (măj′ ĭk)

1. Write the pronunciation respelling for each word below:

a. daunt	**d.** keyboard	**g.** pocket
b. event	**e.** madrigal	**h.** rascal
c. hayseed	**f.** optical	**i.** stall

2. Write the entry word that goes with the respelling?

a. lō′ kəl	local	locale
b. hāl	hall	hail
c. rīm	rim	rhyme

3. Write the pronunciation respellings of the words below.

a. bet	**d.** sat	**g.** lord
b. like	**e.** pool	**h.** he
c. lid	**f.** dun	**i.** cart

The Pronunciation Key — Special Vowel Sounds

Remember, all the symbols for all the vowel sounds are clearly shown in the pronunciation key on page 28A and at the bottom of every odd-numbered dictionary page. Use these keys to read the respellings.

Match each word below with its pronunciation as shown in parentheses.

1. full
2. scar
3. law
4. squirm
5. ruby
6. air
7. pool
8. ear
9. low
10. cross
11. pull
12. fool
13. square
14. score
15. world
16. all
17. germ
18. word

a. (â*r*)
b. (krȯs)
c. (fo͞ol)
d. (ê*r*)
e. (lȯ)
f. (fo͝ol)
g. (skô*r*)
h. (po͝ol)
i. (skwâ*r*)
j. (skär)
k. (skwû*r*m)
l. (po͞ol)
m. (lō)
n. (ro͞o′ bē)
o. (ȯl)
p. (wû*r*d)
q. (wû*r*ld)
r. (jû*r*m)

1. Write the respelling of the word *down.*

2. Write the letters that stand for the vowel sound of the word *down.*

3. Write the respelling of the word *ruby.*

4. Write the letters that stand for the first vowel sound of the word *ruby.*

5. Write the respelling of the word *pull.*

6. Write how the vowel sound of *pull* is different from the first vowel sound of *ruby.*

7. Write how we respell the vowel sound of the word *joy.*

8. Write how we respell the vowel sound of the word *cause.*

9. Write the words that have the same vowel sound as *dog.*
a. haul **b.** none **c.** stall **d.** modern

The Pronunciation Key — The Schwa

There is another vowel sound represented by a symbol shown in the pronunciation key. The symbol looks like this: ə. It is called a *schwa.* The *schwa* stands for the vowel sound heard in the unaccented syllables of words of two or more syllables.

Here are some examples from your dictionary. Tell in which syllable the *schwa* sound occurs.

a·go (ə gō′)	**per·il** (pĕr′ əl)	**fa·mous** (fā′ məs)
sen·ate (sĕn′ ət)	**trel·lis** (trĕl′ əs)	**moun·tain** (moun′ tən)
o·pen (ō′ pən)	**lem·on** (lĕm′ ən)	**tor·toise** (tôr′ təs, tôr′-)
mar·ket (mär′ kət)	**mi·nus** (mī′ nəs)	**pi·geon** (pĭj′ ən)

1. Write each word below on a piece of paper. Then look up the respelling of each word in your dictionary. Underline the letter or letters in each word that spell the *schwa* sound. Remember that the symbol for the *schwa* looks like this: ə.

a. sharpen	**e.** circus	**i.** terminal	**m.** considerate
b. bargain	**f.** luncheon	**j.** command	**n.** capital
c. period	**g.** porpoise	**k.** instant	**o.** pardon
d. metal	**h.** woman	**l.** marvelous	

2. Write the word for each respelling below:

a. ə pēl	**e.** ĕn ə mē	**i.** păr ət	**m.** păn də
b. bī sĭ kəl	**f.** fôr chən	**j.** băn ər	**n.** pə tā tō
c. kə nĕkt	**g.** jĕn rəl	**k.** nĭk əl	**o.** sĕn təns
d. dŭ bəl	**h.** hŭv ər	**l.** ôr dər	

3. Copy each word in the column on the left. Write the correct respelling for each word.

a. quiet	kwī ət	kwī ėt
b. maiden	mā dŏn	mād ən
c. rattle	răt əl	răt āl
d. appeal	ə pēl	ä pēl
e. porpoise	pôr pəs	pôr pīs

The Pronunciation Key — Consonant Sounds

If you look again at the pronunciation key on page 28A you will see that below the symbols for the vowel sounds are listed the symbols for consonant sounds.

1. Why does the letter *c* never appear in respelling? Tell what two letters spell the sounds of *c*.
2. Tell what two letters stand for the sound of *qu* at the beginning of a word.
3. Why does the letter *x* never appear in a respelling? Tell what three ways the sound of *x* is represented.

1. Copy the respellings. Circle the letters which spell the sound of *c*.

a. kôrt	**d.** prē sēd
b. pĕn sel	**e.** mākron
c. iskăp	**f.** fās

2. Copy the respellings. Circle the letter or letters which spell the sound of *q* at the beginning of *queen*.

a. kwĕst	**d.** plāt
b. kwī ĕt	**e.** kwāl
c. këlp	**f.** kwȯrt

3. Copy the respellings. Circle the letter or letters which spell the sound of the letter *x*.

a. tăksē	**d.** hĕks
b. ĕgzīl	**e.** ĕgzûrt
c. zēnŏn	**f.** zēbĕc

4. Write the words. Copy the correct pronunciation for each word.

a. that	(thăt)	(~~th~~ăt)
b. thing	(thĭng)	(~~th~~ĭng)
c. thought	(thȯt)	(~~th~~ȯt)
d. there	(thêr)	(~~th~~êr)
e. thank	(thăngk)	(~~th~~ăngk)

5. In which of these words does the letter *s* spell the sound represented by the consonant pronunciation symbol *zh*? Write them on a piece of paper. Look up the pronunciation of each word in the dictionary, if necessary.

assure	confusion
treasure	confession
exposure	expression
occasion	pleasure
permission	pressure
explosion	enclosure

6. Write each word below. Write the lower case letter of the correct pronunciation next to the word.

A. persuasion	**E.** torque	**I.** measure	**M.** wrath
B. exchange	**F.** quote	**J.** machine	**N.** where
C. examine	**G.** quarter	**K.** mirage	**O.** wither
D. equator	**H.** tax	**L.** method	**P.** whiskers

a. (mĕth´ əd)	**e.** (wĭth´ ər)	**i.** (tôrk)	**m.** (per swā´ zhən)
b. (ĕg zăm´ ən)	**f.** (mĕzh´ ər)	**j.** (tăks)	**n.** (mə räzh´)
c. (ĭ kwā´ tər)	**g.** (kwôr´tər)	**k.** (răth)	**o.** (hwĭs´ kərz)
d. (kwōt)	**h.** (ĕks chānj´)	**l.** (hwâr)	**p.** (mə shēn´)

7. In the pronunciation for *torque,* write the symbols that represent the sound the letters *que* spell.

8. In the pronunciation for *quarter,* write the two consonant symbols that represent the sounds the letters *qu* spell.

9. In the pronunciation for *tax,* write the two consonant symbols that represent the sounds the letter *x* spells.

10. In the pronunciation for *machine,* write the consonant symbol that represents the sound the letters *ch* spell.

11. In the pronunciation for *mirage,* write the consonant symbol that represents the sound the letter *g* spells.

12. Write the consonant symbol that spells the sound of the *c* in *cent.*

13. Write the consonant symbol that spells the sound of the *c* in *comic.*

14. Write the consonant symbols that spell the sound of the *x* in *flex.*

Variant Pronunciations

Many English words have more than one correct pronunciation. If you look up the words *aunt* and *advertisement* in your dictionary, you will find two pronunciations shown in the parentheses following the entry word.

Sometimes when a word has variant pronunciations the dictionary shows only a part of the second pronunciation—the part that is pronounced differently from the first pronunciation.

1. Look up the word *aunt.* Note its two respellings. Tell which way you say this word.
2. Look up the word *advertisement.* Note its two respellings. Tell which way you say the word.
3. Look at page 640. Two words have variant pronunciations. Tell which two they are.

1. Write the words in the left-hand column. Write the two variant pronunciations for each beside the word. Circle the variant pronunciation you use.

a. roof	hȯk	tə mä tō
b. creek	ro͝of	bȯt
c. hawk	no͞o	pə jă məz
d. room	bŏt	ro͞om
e. new	krĭk	kŏ fē
f. pa	tə mā tō	ro͞of
g. bought	pə jä məz	pȯ
h. pajamas	kȯ fē	hŏk
i. coffee	ro͝om	nyo͞o
j. tomato	pä	krēk

2. Use your dictionary to find out which of the following words have variant pronunciations. Write each word that has a variant pronunciation, and next to it write the pronunciation *you* use when you say the word.

due	application	pajamas	rodeo
duke	applicable	pimiento	radio
dude	complimentary	cauliflower	width
dune	complex	quarrel	with

Review — Pronouncing Words

1. Write the words below. Mark the stressed syllable in each pronunciation in the parentheses with an accent mark.

a•fraid — (ə frād)	gen•er•ous — (jĕn ər əs)
ba•con — (bā kən)	re•mem•ber — (rĭ mĕm bər)
con•nect — (kə nĕkt)	ap•point•ment — (ə point mənt)

2. Write the words below. Match each word with the vowel sound the letters *ai* spell in that word. Use the pronunciation key on odd-numbered pages.

A. pain	**a.** ə	**D.** plaid	**d.** â
B. fair	**b.** ă	**E.** fountain	**e.** ī
C. aisle	**c.** ā		

3. Write the words below. Match each word with the vowel sound the letters *ou* spell in that word. Use the pronunciation key on odd-numbered pages.

A. thought	**a.** ō	**D.** couple	**d.** ou
B. though	**b.** ȯ	**E.** court	**e.** o͞o
C. through	**c.** ô	**F.** drought	**f.** ŭ

4. Write the sentences below. Match each underlined word in the sentences with its correct pronunciation.

A. Which color do you like best?	**a.** (wâr)
B. I'm going to wear my witch costume.	**b.** (hwâr)
C. Please wipe off the table.	**c.** (wĭch)
D. Will you whip the cream for the cake?	**d.** (hwĭch)
E. I can only stay for a little while.	**e.** (wĭl)
F. I will never forgive you.	**f.** (hwīl)
G. What did you say?	**g.** (wīp)
H. This lamp takes a sixty watt bulb.	**h.** (hwĭp)
I. Where are you going?	**i.** (wŏt)
J. What are you going to wear?	**j.** (hwŏt)

5. In each word below one or more letters are underlined. Write the pronunciation symbol that represents the sound or sounds the underlined letter or letters spell. Use the dictionary to check your work.

a. fashion	**f.** hyperbola	**k.** parachute
b. alarm	**g.** scheme	**l.** sleuth
c. author	**h.** neophyte	**m.** cello
d. mourn	**i.** beige	**n.** worry
e. hysteria	**j.** accident	**o.** humus

Multiple Meanings and Parts of Speech

Each entry gives the definition or meaning of the word and tells you what part of speech the word is.

1. Tell which definition of *correspond* means to write a letter to someone.
2. Tell which definition of the word *comprehend* is used in the following sentence: definition number 1 or 2? *We couldn't answer the questions in our books because we couldn't comprehend what we had read.*

Look up the entries for *funnel, antenna, gondola,* and *trunk.*

1. Tell which entries have an illustration that shows more than one of the word's meanings.
2. Tell which definition of *gondola* is illustrated. Is it definition 1, 2, or 3?

1. Write what each of these abbreviations means.
   a. n- **e.** sing-
   b. vt- **f.** interj.
   c. adv- **g.** adj.
   d. conj- **h.** superl.
2. Write the abbreviation for:
   a. homophone **d.** plural
   b. et cetera **e.** Celsius
   c. feminine **f.** Spanish
3. Write the part of speech of the underlined word in each sentence below.
   a. The ball rolled down the hill.
   b. I bought a postage stamp.
   c. Is this the correct answer?
   d. The train stopped with a jolt.

More Parts of Speech

Look up the words *of* and *with* in your dictionary. The part-of-speech label for both words is **prep·**, meaning *preposition.* If you look up the words *but* or *though,* you will see the part-of-speech label **conj·,** which stands for *conjunction.* Words such as *he* and *they* are pronouns with the part-of-speech label **pron·.** The words *ah* and *ha* have the part-of-speech label **interj·,** standing for *interjection.*

1. Tell why there is a part-of-speech label after the entry word.
2. Find three words in your dictionary which can be used as more than one part-of-speech. Try looking at words beginning with "r;" with "pr;" with "l."

1. Find the word *gauge* in your dictionary. Then write the answers to the following questions:
   a. As what parts of speech can the word *gauge* be used?
   b. How many different meanings can *gauge* have when used as a noun?
   c. Is *gauge* used as a noun or as a verb in the sentence: *Jane looked at the other children and tried to gauge her chances of winning the race.*

2. Look up the word *shield* in your dictionary. Then write the answers to the following questions:
   a. As what parts of speech can the word *shield* be used?
   b. How many meanings are given for the word *shield* when used as a noun?
   c. Write the number of the meaning of *shield* shown in the illustration.
   d. Write the number of the meaning of *shield* used in this sentence: *The official used his umbrella as a shield from the hot sun.* Is *shield* used as a noun or as a verb in this sentence?

Homographs

Homographs are words that have the same spelling but have two completely different meanings and came into the English language from different sources. Each homograph in this dictionary is listed separately with a tiny raised number called a *superscript numeral* before the entry word.

1. Tell how the first homograph for *bat* came into English.
2. Tell what the Middle English word was from which the second homograph for *bat* came into the English language.
3. Two words in each column below are homographs. Look up each word in your dictionary and tell which words in each column are homographs.

A	B	C	D
back	face	land	seal
ball	file	lawn	season
bowl	fire	lean	seat

1. The underlined word in each sentence below is a homograph. Look up each word in this dictionary and write the superscript numeral of the homograph used in each sentence.
   a. *Went* is the past tense of *go.*
   b. I fell over the log.
   c. The bus driver asked the passengers to move to the rear so more people could get on the bus.
   d. When the weather is nice we can play in the yard.
2. Write the answers to the following questions. How many homographs are in your dictionary for the word *lead?*
   a. Which superscript numeral identifies the homograph pronounced (lēd)?
   b. Which superscript numeral identifies the homograph pronounced (lĕd)?
   c. Which homograph can only be used as a noun?
   d. Which homograph can be used as either a verb or as a noun?
   e. Which homograph means *to guide or show the way or go before?*

Prefixes and Suffixes

A **prefix** is a word part that may be put at the beginning of a base word to change the base word's meaning.

A **suffix** is a word part that may be added to the end of a base word to form a new word.

1. Tell what the base word is for the prefixed word *mismanage.*
2. Tell what word beginning with the prefix *dis-* would mean "the lack of comfort" or "the opposite of comfort".
3. Tell what the base word is for the suffixed word *sweetness.*

1. In each sentence below a word with the prefix *dis-* or *mis-* has been left out. Write the prefixed word that completes each sentence, using the italicized base word in the parentheses.
   - **a.** The teacher expressed her strong ______________ of the class's ______________. (lack of *approval;* opposite of *approval*) (wrong or bad *behavior*)
   - **b.** Being stuck in a traffic jam is a very ______________ experience. (the opposite of *agreeable*)
   - **c.** The votes had to be recounted because there had been a ____________. (wrong *count*)
   - **d.** I didn't bring enough money with me because I ____________ how much the trip would cost. (*calculated* wrongly)
2. In each sentence below a word with the suffix *-less* or *-ness* has been left out. Write the suffixed word that completes each sentence, using the italicized base word in the parentheses.
   - **a.** It was hard to get up this morning because I had a ____________ night. (without *sleep*)
   - **b.** He was ____________ after running up five flights of stairs. (lacking *breath*)
   - **c.** John doesn't like to meet new people because of his ____________ (condition or quality of being *shy*)

Combining Forms

A **combining form** is a type of word part. Combining forms usually come from Greek or Latin words and most often are combined with other Greek or Latin forms to produce new words. Combining forms have bracketed notes at the end of the entry explaining the meaning of the Greek or Latin root from which they come.

1. *-Cracy* is a combining form. In Greek, it means "government or rule by". If *demos* means "people", who rules in a democracy? Tell the definitions of these words:
   a. autocracy **c.** plutocracy
   b. aristocracy **d.** theocracy
2. *Auto-* means "self or by one's self". Tell the meanings of these words.
   a. automatic **c.** automobile
   b. autocrat **d.** autobiography

1. Write the meaning of these combining forms.
   a. *zoo-* **b.** *bio-* **c.** *geo-* **d.** *psycho-*
2. *-logy* means "the study of." Write the definitions of these words.
   a. zoology **c.** theology **e.** biology
   b. technology **d.** geology **f.** ecology
3. Write the meanings of the combining forms listed below.
   a. *di-* **c.** *multi-* **e.** *hydro-* **g.** *ortho-*
   b. *poly-* **d.** *astro-* **f.** *mega-* **h.** *stereo-*
4. Find a word in your dictionary which uses each of the combining forms above. Write the definition after the word.
5. Find the combining form *mono-* in your dictionary. Write the word beginning with *mono-* that means:
   a. long speech given by one person
   b. belief in one God
   c. eyeglass for one eye

Word History — Etymology

The bracketed note following a definition is the word history or *etymology.*

1. According to the word history for **etymology**, what did the Greek word *etymon* mean?
2. Tell which of these words has a word history as part of its entry.

   boysenberry   cranberry   loganberry   mulberry
3. Look up *hickory, sassafras,* and *tomato* in your dictionary.
   a. Tell which word originated from a Spanish word only.
   b. Tell which word originated from an Indian word only.
   c. Tell which word originated from both Indian and Spanish words.

1. Write the word that came from two Spanish words meaning "the lizard".

   iguana   salamander   alligator   crocodile
2. Write which of the following words came from the name of a city.

   cafeteria   delicatessen   frankfurter
3. Write which of the following words came from a person's name.

   boycott   corduroy   jumbo   travois
4. Write which of these words meant "fried flour" in its original language.

   flapjack   tortilla   pastry   chow mein
5. Write which of these words came from a French version of an American Indian word meaning "small stream".

   rivulet   brook   bayou   creek
6. Write the word which came from a Spanish form of a Mexican Indian word.

   bronco   coyote   mustang   wolf
7. Look up the words below in your dictionary and write the word history of each word:

   a. buckaroo   **d.** raccoon
   b. chipmunk   **e.** squash
   c. lariat   **f.** [2]guy

Homophones

Words that sound alike but are spelled differently and have different meanings are called *homophones.*

all (ȯl) ***determiner*** (traditionally called adjective or pronoun) **1** the whole of: *in* all *the world.* **2** each and every one of: *to* all *people.* **3** as much as possible: *with* all *speed.* **4** nothing but: *This is* all *work and no play.* **5** everyone: All *agreed.* ***n-*** **1** the whole number or quantity: *They asked* all *of us to the party.* **2** one's full resources, material or moral: *He would give* all *to win. They gave their* all. ***adv-*** wholly: *He's* all *wrong.* ***Hom-*** awl.

awl (ȯl) ***n-*** pointed tool for making small holes in leather or wood. ***Hom-*** all.

Note the abbreviation **Hom-** at the end of each of the entries, which calls your attention to the homophone for each word.

1. Tell the entry word in your dictionary that would have *too* and *two* listed as homophones?
2. Tell the entry word that would have *pare* and *pair* listed as homophones?
3. Identify and spell the homophones listed for each entry word below.

a. heart	**d.** slow	**g.** foul	**j.** read
b. ball	**e.** frank	**h.** rough	**k.** bore
c. file	**f.** style	**i.** time	**l.** flow

1. Write the words that have more than one homophone on a piece of paper. Copy the homophones given for the words you have written.

a. so	**e.** toe	**i.** low	**m.** new
b. one	**f.** wood	**j.** there	**n.** meat
c. ring	**g.** right	**k.** straight	**o.** sight
d. pair	**h.** pail	**l.** burrow	**p.** bury

2. Which words below have a homophone? Write the homophones.

gall	council	haul
rate	idol	post

Idioms

Expressions such as *rain cats and dogs* are called **idioms.** An idiom is a phrase or expression whose meaning cannot be understood simply by knowing the usual meanings of the words that make up the idiom. Idioms follow the body of the entry for the main word of the idiom.

1. Below is a little pep talk given by a coach to a team. The coach uses several idioms, which are underlined. Find the meaning of each idiom in your dictionary. Tell the entry word under which you found each idiom.

   The last time we played, the other team managed to get wind of our plans and beat it across the field. This time, if you carry out my orders to the letter, I know we can wipe out their winning streak once and for all.

1. Each sentence below contains an underlined idiom. Find each idiom in the dictionary and write its meaning on a piece of paper. Write the entry word under which you found each idiom.
   a. That Sue makes me so mad I'm fit to be tied. I guess I'm going to have to have it out with her.
   b. My parents are really going to raise the roof when I tell them I failed the math test.
   c. I don't know why you couldn't find your hairbrush; it was right under your nose.
   d. I just can't figure out this problem at all, and I've been working on it for half an hour. I'm ready to throw in the towel.
2. Which is an idiom for *successful*?

   uptight   on top   way out

3. Which idiom means *to be ruined*?

   toss up   flip out   go to pot

Usage Notes

The paragraph following the black pointer after an entry is called a **usage note.**

> **ain't** (ānt) **1** am not; are not. **2** have not; has not.
> ►Do not use AIN'T unless you are trying to show informality, or poor education, or folksiness: *The old gray mare, she* ain't *what she used to be.*

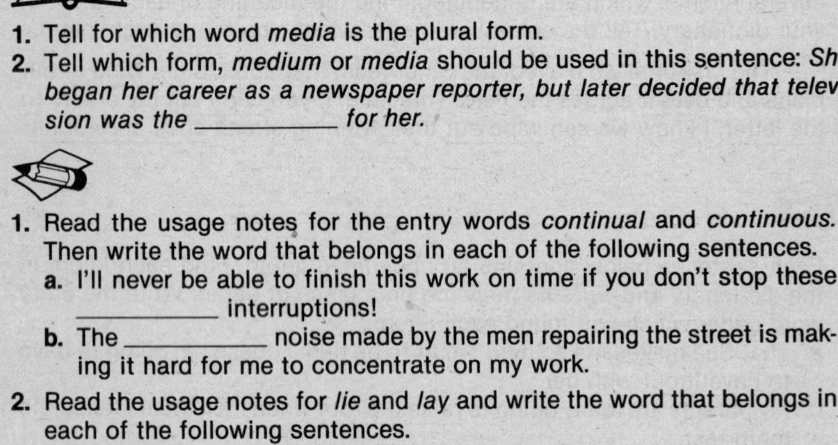

1. Tell for which word *media* is the plural form.
2. Tell which form, *medium* or *media* should be used in this sentence: *She began her career as a newspaper reporter, but later decided that television was the ________ for her.*

1. Read the usage notes for the entry words *continual* and *continuous.* Then write the word that belongs in each of the following sentences.
   a. I'll never be able to finish this work on time if you don't stop these ________ interruptions!
   b. The ________ noise made by the men repairing the street is making it hard for me to concentrate on my work.
2. Read the usage notes for *lie* and *lay* and write the word that belongs in each of the following sentences.
   a. I think I'll ________ down and take a nap.
   b. I'm so tired I'll probably fall asleep the minute I ________ my head on the pillow.
3. Read the usage notes for *farther* and *further.* Then write the word that should be used in each of the following sentences.
   a. I can't answer this question without ________ information.
   b. How much ________ is it to the motel?
4. Read the usage note for *already.* Then decide whether to use the word *already* to complete these sentences.
   a. We're ________ to get dressed to go out and play.
   b. We're ________ dressed to go out and play.

Review — Defining and Using Words

1. Look up the word *bridge* in your dictionary.
   a. On what page did you find the word *bridge?*
   b. What does the small superscript numeral before the entry for *bridge* tell you?
   c. Where did you find the other entry for *bridge?*
   d. How many homographs are there for *bridge?*
   e. What idiom is listed for the first homograph form of *bridge?* What is the meaning of this idiom?
   f. Which definition of the word *bridge* is illustrated? How many different types of bridges are shown in the illustration?

2. What are the homophones for *flew?* Fill in the missing word in each sentence with *flew, flu,* or *flue.*
   a. The fireplace kept belching smoke into the living room because the __________ was clogged.
   b. The past tense of the verb *fly* is __________.
   c. __________ is an illness caused by a virus.

3. Read the usage note for *only.* Add the word *only* to the sentence, *Amy can play the piano,* in two different ways, so that the new sentences formed will mean:

   Nobody but Amy can play the piano.
   Amy can't play any instrument but the piano.

4. Turn to page 542 in your dictionary. What combining form is listed as an entry on this page?
   a. What does this combining form mean?
   b. From what language did this combining form come?
   c. What word on page 542 made from this combining form means:
      1. a musical composition for eight performers
      2. a figure with eight sides and eight angles
      3. a sea animal with eight tentacles
      4. a person in his or her eighties

Entry Parts Practice

pre- *prefix* before: *a* pre*historic animal*; *a* pre*paid package.*

pré·cis (prā′ sē′) ***n-*** [*pl.* **pré·cis** (-sēz′)] brief summary giving the main points of a written work, speech, etc.

pre·judge (prē′ jŭj′) ***vt-*** [**pre·judged, pre·judg·ing**] to judge in advance or without waiting to learn all the facts of a case. ***—n-*** **pre′judg′ment** or **pre′judge′ment.**

pre·ma·ture (prē′mə cho͞or′, -tyo͞or′, -to͞or′) ***adj-*** happening or coming before the usual time; too early; untimely: *a* premature *arrival.* ***—adv-*** **pre′ma·ture′ly.**

pre·med·i·tate (prĭ mĕd′ ə tāt′) ***vt-*** [**pre·med·i·tat·ed, pre·med·i·tat·ing**] to think over and plan beforehand: *to* premeditate *a crime.* ***—n-*** **pre·med′i·ta′tion.**

prep. 1 preposition. 2 preparatory.

Pres. President.

pre·scribe (prĭ skrīb′) ***vt-*** [**pre·scribed, pre·scrib·ing**] **1** to order or advise (something) as a remedy or cure: *to* prescribe *medicine for a cough*; *to* prescribe *rest for an invalid.* **2** to order or direct, especially officially: *The law* prescribes *these procedures.* ***vi-*** **1** to write or give medical directions. **2** to give laws, rules, or directions.
►Should not be confused with PROSCRIBE.

[1]**pres·ent** (prĕz′ ənt) ***adj-*** **1** here in this place; there in that place; on hand; not absent: *The whole class is* present. *You are* present *in my thoughts.* **2** of concern now; at issue or under consideration now: *his* present *difficulties*; *the* present *quarrel.* ***n-*** **1** *Grammar* the present tense. **2 the present** the time passing now, as distinguished from the past and the future. **3 these presents** this legal or official document: *The diploma reads, "All men to whom* these presents *may come, Greetings."* [from Old French **present,** from Latin **praesens, praesentis** meaning "being in front of."]
at present just now; at this time.

[2]**pre·sent** (prĭ zĕnt′) ***vt-*** **1** to introduce: *The teacher* presented *the visitor to the class.* **2** to put before the public; show; exhibit: *to* present *a new French star*; *to* present *a gay appearance.* **3** to give as a gift. **4** to offer for consideration: *Taking a trip always* presents *the problem of what to do with the pets.* **5** to put (oneself) in another's presence: *He* presented *himself at my office.* **6** to deliver; submit: *to* present *a bill.* [from Old French **presenter,** from Latin **praesentare** meaning "to place before."]
present arms *Military* to salute by holding a rifle in front of one with the muzzle pointing upward.
present with to give, as a gift.

[3]**pres·ent** (prĕz′ ənt) ***n-*** a gift, especially one given on a birthday or holiday. [from [2]**present.**]

Note: The sample column above has been constructed for the purpose of this activity.

Review — Dictionary Entry Parts Practice

1. On the opposite page there is a sample portion of a dictionary column. Locate an example of each entry part listed below. Write the entry part exactly as it appears on the opposite page.
   a. entry word
   b. word history
   c. usage note
   d. pronunciation
   e. part of speech label
   f. guide word
   g. multiple meanings
   h. homographs with superscript numerals
   i. illustrative sentence
   j. variant pronunciations
   k. inflected forms—verb endings
   l. prefix

2. Use the sample on the opposite page to answer these questions. Write your answers.
   a. What idiom means "just now; at this time?"
   b. What entry word means "to think over and plan beforehand?"
   c. What is the first definition given for the abbreviation *prep.*?
   d. Which superscript numeral identifies the homograph of *present* that means "a gift?"
   e. What inflected forms are shown for the entry word *prescribe*?
   f. What run-on entry is shown for the word *premature*?
   g. What is the plural form of the entry word *precis*?

3. Use the following **made-up** information to construct a dictionary entry. Follow the style of the sample entries on the opposite page.
   a. The entry word is *wadwan.*
   b. Its pronunciation respelling is (wād´ wȯn).
   c. The word is a noun.
   d. Its definition is: *a shallow, freshwater pool*
   e. An illustrative sentence is: Even nonswimmers could get across the *wadwan* easily.
   f. The word comes from Old Pruscan, *waedenwater* meaning easily-crossed stream.
   g. The homophone for *wadwan* is *wadeone.*

Table of Contents

The Table of Contents can help you locate information in the dictionary. Whenever you are unsure of where to look, use the Table of Contents. It tells you where to find unusual spellings, the pronunciation key, a list of tables, and other reference sections.

1. Tell what information is in the section called Unusual Spellings of Sounds. If you were uncertain how to spell a word, how would this section help?
2. Suppose you found an abbreviation which you did not know. Look in the section called Abbreviations Used in Definitions. Tell how this section would help you to make the best use of the dictionary.
3. Tell what information is found in the tables at the back of the dictionary.

Use the Table of Contents to write answers to these questions:

1. On what page of your dictionary does the section listing the nations of the world begin?
2. In which section of your dictionary could you find the sign for number?
3. On what pages of this dictionary will you find the alphabetical listing of entry words?
4. In what section of your dictionary would you find an explanation of how the kind of English spoken in America developed?
5. On what page of your dictionary would you look to find out how many grams are in an ounce? How many grams **are** in an ounce?
6. What table would you use to find out which tree is the state tree of Texas? Which tree is it?
7. In what section of your dictionary would you look to find the sixteenth President of the United States? Who was he? When did he die?